Laura Lemay
Rodgers Cadenhead

SAMS
Teach Yourself
Java 2
in 21 Days

PROFESSIONAL REFERENCE EDITION
SECOND EDITION

SAMS

201 West 103rd St., Indianapolis, Indiana, 46290 USA

Sams Teach Yourself Java 2 in 21 Days, Professional Reference Edition, Second Edition

Copyright © 2001 by Sams Publishing

International Standard Book Number: 0-672-32061-4

Library of Congress Catalog Card Number: 00-109553

Printed in the United States of America

First Printing: April 2001

04   03   02   01   4   3   2   1

Trademarks

Warning and Disclaimer

ACQUISITIONS EDITOR
Mark Taber

DEVELOPMENT EDITOR
Scott D. Meyers

MANAGING EDITOR
Charlotte Clapp

PROJECT EDITOR
Leah Kirkpatrick

COPY EDITOR
Sean Medlock

INDEXER
Sheila Schroeder

PROOFREADER
Tony Reitz

TECHNICAL EDITOR
Dallas Releford

TEAM COORDINATOR
Amy Patton

MEDIA DEVELOPER
Dan Scherf

INTERIOR DESIGNER
Gary Adair

COVER DESIGNER
Aren Howell

Contents at a Glance

Contents

About the Authors

ROGERS CADENHEAD is a writer and Web publisher who has written 10 books on Internet-related topics, including *Sams Teach Yourself Java 2 in 24 Hours* and *Sams Teach Yourself Microsoft FrontPage 2000 in 24 Hours*, but not *Sams Teach Yourself to Tell Time in 10 Minutes*. He maintains this book's official Web site at `http://www.java21pro.com/`.

LAURA LEMAY is a technical writer and author. After spending six years writing software documentation for various computer companies in Silicon Valley, she decided that writing books would be much more fun. In her spare time, she collects computers, email addresses, interesting hair colors, and non-running motorcycles. She is also the perpetrator of *Sams Teach Yourself Web Publishing with HTML in a Week* and *Sams Teach Yourself Perl in 21 Days*.

Dedications

To my sons Max, Eli, and Sam, with all the love in the world. Thanks for reminding me on a daily basis about all the great things I forgot about when I got so old, like the joy of throwing stuff, knocking something over after you build it, running your toes through mud on the beach, and drawing funny faces on the inside of car windows.—Rogers

To Eric, for all the usual reasons (moral support, stupid questions, comfort in dark times, brewing big pots of coffee).—LL

Acknowledgments

From Rogers Cadenhead:

I thank Sams and the people there who contributed so much to the book, including Mark Taber, Scott Meyers, Leah Kirkpatrick, Dallas G. Releford, and Sean Medlock. Writing books is a great career when you have people like this making you look good. Finally, I thank my wife Mary Moewe and my sons, Max, Eli, and Sam.

From Laura Lemay:

To the folks on Sun's Java team, for all their hard work on Java, the language, and on the browser, and particularly to Jim Graham, who demonstrated Java and HotJava to me on very short notice in May 1995 and planted the idea for this book.

To everyone who bought my previous books and liked them: Buy this one, too.

Tell Us What You Think!

As the reader of this book, *you* are our most important critic and commentator. We value your opinion and want to know what we're doing right, what we could do better, what areas you'd like to see us publish in, and any other words of wisdom you're willing to pass our way.

You can email or write me directly to let me know what you did or didn't like about this book—as well as what we can do to make our books stronger.

Please note that I cannot help you with technical problems related to the topic of this book, and that due to the high volume of mail I receive, I might not be able to reply to every message.

When you write, please be sure to include this book's title and author as well as your name and phone or email address. I will carefully review your comments and share them with the author and editors who worked on the book.

Email: webdev@samspublishing.com

Mail: Mark Taber
              Associate Publisher
              Sams Publishing
              201 West 103rd Street
              Indianapolis, IN 46290 USA

Introduction

Some revolutions catch the world completely by surprise. The World Wide Web, the Linux operating system, and personal digital assistants rose to prominence unexpectedly and against conventional wisdom.

The remarkable success of the Java programming language, on the other hand, caught no one by surprise. Java has been the source of great expectations ever since Sun started incorporating it into Web browsers more than five years ago. A torrent of publicity welcomed the arrival of this new language. Anyone who passed within eyesight of a Web page, computer magazine, or newspaper business section knew about Java and how it was going to change the way software was developed.

Sun Microsystems cofounder Bill Joy didn't hedge his bets at all when describing the company's new language: "This represents the end result of nearly 15 years of trying to come up with a better programming language and environment for building simpler and more reliable software."

Since then, Java has lived up to a considerable amount of its hype. The language is becoming as much a part of software development as the beverage of the same name. One kind of java keeps programmers up nights, and the other kind enables programmers to rest easier after they develop software.

Java was originally considered a technology for enhancing Web sites, and it's still used for that purpose today. The AltaVista search engine reports that more than 13 million Web pages contain a Java program.

However, each new release of Java strengthens its capabilities as a general-purpose programming language for environments other than a Web browser. Java is used in desktop applications, Internet servers, middleware, personal digital assistants, embedded devices, and many other environments.

Now in its fourth major release—Java 2 version 1.3—this language is a full-featured competitor to other general-purpose development languages such as C++, Perl, Visual Basic, and Delphi.

You might be familiar with Java programming tools such as WebGain Visual Café, Borland JBuilder, and Sun Forté for Java. These programs will help you develop functional Java programs, but the best way to learn the full scope of the language is to work directly with it via Sun's Java Software Development Kit. This kit, which is available for free on the Web at `http://java.sun.com`, is a set of command-line tools for writing, compiling, and testing Java programs.

This is where *Sams Teach Yourself Java 2 in 21 Days, Professional Reference Edition* comes in. You'll be introduced to all aspects of Java software development, using the most current version of the language and the best available techniques. By the time you're done, you'll know why Java has become the most talked-about programming language of the past decade, and why it might be the most popular language of the *next* decade.

How This Book Is Organized

Sams Teach Yourself Java 2 in 21 Days covers the Java language and its class libraries in 21 days, organized into three separate weeks. Each week covers a different area of Java applet and application development.

This Professional Reference Edition also offers an extra week, covering advanced aspects of the Java language for programmers who want to enhance their skills.

In the first week you'll learn about the Java language itself:

- Day 1 is the basic introduction—what Java is, why to learn the language, and how to get the software needed to create Java programs. You'll also create your first Java application.
- On Day 2, you'll explore basic object-oriented programming concepts as they apply to Java.
- On Day 3, you'll start getting down to details with the basic Java building blocks—data types, variables, and expressions such as arithmetic and comparisons.
- Day 4 goes into detail about how to deal with objects in Java—how to create them, how to access their variables and call their methods, and how to compare and copy them. You'll also get your first glance at the Java class libraries.
- On Day 5, you'll learn more about Java with arrays, conditional statements, and loops.
- Day 6 fully explores the creation of classes—the basic building blocks of any Java program.
- Day 7 provides the basics of applets—how they differ from applications, how to create them, and how to use the Java Plug-in to run Java 2 applets in Netscape Navigator, Microsoft Internet Explorer, and other browsers.

Week 2 is dedicated primarily to graphical programming using Swing, which a set of classes introduced in Java 2 that enables you to offer a graphical user interface in your programs:

- Day 8 begins a four-day exploration of visual programming. You'll learn how to create a graphical user interface using Swing.
- Day 9 covers more than a dozen interface components that you can use in a Java program, including buttons, text fields, sliders, scrolling text areas, and icons.
- Day 10 covers how to make a user interface look good using layout managers, a set of classes that determine how components on an interface will be arranged.
- Day 11 concludes the coverage of Swing with event-handling classes, which enable a program to respond to mouse clicks and other user interactions.
- On Day 12, you'll learn about drawing shapes and characters on a user interface component, such as an applet window—including coverage of the new Java2D classes introduced in Java 2.
- On Day 13, you'll create multimedia programs that use shapes, graphics files, and animation sequences. You'll also get your first experience with multithreading, which is a way to get your programs to handle multiple tasks at the same time.
- Day 14 adds another layer of multimedia with Java's sound capabilities. You'll add sounds to applets and applications, and you'll work with JavaSound, an extensive new class library for playing, recording, and mixing sound.

Week 3 includes advanced topics such as JavaBeans and Java Database Connectivity:

- On Day 15, you'll learn more about interfaces and packages, which are useful for grouping classes and organizing a class hierarchy, as well as other advanced aspects of the core language itself.
- Day 16 covers exceptions—errors, warnings, and other abnormal conditions, generated either by the system or by you in your programs. You'll also learn about Java security.
- Day 17 covers input and output using streams, which are a set of classes that enable file access, network access, and other sophisticated data handling.
- Day 18 introduces object serialization, which is a way to make your objects exist even when no program is running. You save them to a storage medium such as a hard disk, read them into a program, and use them again as objects.
- On Day 19, you'll extend your knowledge of streams to write programs that communicate with the Internet, including socket programming and URL handling.
- Day 20 covers JavaBeans, a way to develop Java programs using the rapid application techniques that are so popular in tools such as Microsoft Visual Basic.
- Day 21 is an in-depth exploration of how data is handled in Java. You'll connect to databases using Java Database Connectivity (JDBC) and JDBC-ODBC, and then you'll learn about some sophisticated data structures such as vectors, stacks, and maps.

The bonus week, included only in this edition, covers the most advanced topics of Java 2:

- On Day 22, you'll get more experience with the tools of the Java 2 Software Development Kit, including an important one you haven't worked with before: `jdb`, the Java debugger.

- Day 23 describes how integrated development environments can be used for Java programming, reviewing two of the most popular in detail: WebGain Visual Café and Borland Jbuilder.

- Day 24 covers how to write Java applets using version 1.0 of the language, for programmers who want to reach the widest possible audience on the Web.

- Day 25 covers an element of Swing called the Accessibility classes, which enable you to create Java programs that work in conjunction with assistive technology such as screen readers and Braille terminals. They also make programs more usable for everyone running them.

- Day 26 is the first of two days spent on server-side programming in Java. You'll learn about Java servlets, which are applications that run on a Web server using the Tomcat API (a standard developed by Sun and the Apache Software Foundation).

- On Day 27, you'll work with JavaServer Pages, which enable you to incorporate Java servlets and the data they produce into Web documents.

- The last day of the bonus week covers the Java API for XML Processing. This is a new class library that enables Java programmers to work with XML, an emerging standard for the representation of data in a portable way.

About This Book

This book will teach you all about the Java language and how to use it to create applications for any computing environment, as well as applets that run in Web browsers. By the time you finish, you'll have a well-rounded knowledge of Java and the Java class libraries and will be able to develop your own programs for tasks such as data retrieval over the Internet, database connectivity, interactive gaming, and client-server programming.

In this book you'll learn by doing, creating several programs each day that demonstrate the topics being introduced. The source code for all of these programs is available on the book's official Web site at `http://www.java21pro.com`, along with other supplemental material such as answers to readers' questions.

Who Should Read This Book

This book teaches the Java language to three groups:

- Novices who are relatively new to programming
- People who have been introduced to Java 1.1 or 1.0
- Experienced developers in other languages such as Visual C++, Visual Basic, or Delphi

You'll learn how to develop applets, and you'll learn about the interactive Java programs that run as part of a Web page and applications, as well as programs that run anywhere else. When you finish this book, you'll be able to tackle any aspect of Java and dive into your own ambitious programming projects—on the Web or off.

If you're still reasonably new to programming, or if you've never written a program before, you might be wondering whether this is the right book to tackle. All the concepts in this book are illustrated with working programs, so you'll be able to work your way through each subject regardless of your experience level. If you understand what variables, loops, and functions are, you'll be able to benefit from this book.

You should read this book if any of the following rings true:

- You're a real whiz at HTML, you understand CGI programming in Perl, Visual Basic, or some other language, and you want to move on to the next level of Web page design.
- You had some BASIC or Pascal in school, you have a grasp of what programming is, and you've heard that Java is powerful, easy to learn, and cool.
- You've programmed C and C++ for a few years, you keep hearing accolades for Java, and you want to see whether it lives up to its hype.
- You've heard that Java is great for Web programming, and you want to see how well it can be used for other software development.

If you've never used object-oriented programming, which is the style of programming embodied by Java, you don't have to worry. This book assumes you have no background in object-oriented design, and you'll get a chance to learn this groundbreaking development strategy as you're learning Java.

If you're a complete beginner in programming, this book might move a little fast for you. Java is a good language to start with, though. If you take it slow and work through all the examples, you can still pick up Java and start creating your own programs.

How This Book Is Structured

This book is intended to be read and absorbed over the course of four weeks. Each week has seven chapters that present concepts related to the Java language and the creation of applets and applications.

Conventions

| A Note presents interesting and sometimes technical information related to the current topic. |

| A Tip offers advice or an easier way to do something. |

| A Caution advises you of potential problems and helps you steer clear of disaster. |

NEW TERM A new term is accompanied by a New Term icon, with the new term in *italics*.

Any text that you type or that should appear on your screen is presented in `monospace` type:

```
It will look like this
```

This font mimics the way text looks on your screen. Placeholders for variables and expressions appear in `monospace italic`.

Each lesson ends with some common questions and answers about that day's subject matter, a quiz to test your knowledge of the material, and exercises that you can try on your own. The solutions are on the book's official Web site at `http://www.java21pro.com/`.

WEEK 1

Java's Fundamental Concepts

- 21st Century Java
- Object-Oriented Programming
- The ABCs of Programming
- Working with Objects
- Lists, Logic, and Loops
- Creating Classes and Methods
- Writing Java Applets

1

2

3

4

5

6

7

DAY 1

21st Century Java

> *Big companies like IBM are embracing Java far more than most people realize. Half of IBM is busy recoding billions of lines of software to Java. The other half is working to make Java run well on all platforms, and great on all future platforms.*
>
> —PBS technology commentator *Robert X. Cringely*

In 1995, when Sun Microsystems first released the Java programming language, it was an inventive toy for the World Wide Web that had the potential to be much more.

The word "potential" is an unusual compliment, because it comes with an expiration date. Sooner or later, potential must be realized or new words such as "letdown," "waste," and "major disappointment to your mother and I" are used in its place.

Now in its fourth major release, Java appears to have lived up to the expectations that accompanied its arrival. More than two million people have learned the language and are using it in places such as NASA, IBM, Kaiser Permanente, ESPN, and New York's Museum of Modern Art. More than 1,700 books have been written about it, according to the most recent *JavaWorld Magazine* count.

First used to create simple programs on World Wide Web pages, Java can be found today in each of the following places and many more:

- Web servers
- Relational databases
- Mainframe computers
- Telephones
- Orbiting telescopes
- Personal digital assistants
- Credit card–sized "smartcards"

Over the next 21 days, you will write Java programs that reflect how the language is being used in the 21st century. In some cases, this is very different than how it was originally envisioned.

Although Java remains useful for Web developers trying to enliven sites, it extends far beyond the Web browser. Java is now a popular general-purpose programming language, and some surveys indicate that there are more professional Java programmers than C++ programmers.

As you develop your skills during the 21 one-day tutorials in *Sams Teach Yourself Java 2 in 21 Days, Second Edition*, you'll be in a good position to judge whether the language has lived up to years of hype.

You'll also become a Java programmer with a lot of potential.

Exploring Java 2

Whenever Sun releases a new version of Java, it makes a free development kit available over the Web to support that version. This book was created using the kit, which is called Java 2 Software Development Kit, Standard Edition, Version 1.3.

Although the authors of a book like this have no business poking fun at long-winded titles, Sun has given its main Java development tool a name that's longer than most celebrity marriages.

For the sake of a few trees, in this book the language will usually be referred to simply as Java and the kit as SDK 1.3. You might see the kit referred to elsewhere as Java Development Kit 1.3 or SDK 1.3.

If you work your way through the 21 days of this book, you'll become well-versed in Java's capabilities, including graphics, file input and output, user-interface design, event handling, JavaBeans, and database connectivity. You will write programs that run on Web pages and others that run on your personal computer, Web servers, and other computing environments.

Today's goals are reasonably modest. You'll learn about the following topics:

- What Java is like today and how it got there
- Why Java is worth learning
- Why Java is being chosen for software projects
- What you need to start writing Java programs
- How to create your first program

Java's Past, Present, and Future

Based on the enormous amount of press Java has received over the past several years and the huge number of books about Java, you might have an inflated impression of what Java is capable of.

Java is a programming language that's well suited to designing software that works in conjunction with the Internet. It's also an object-oriented programming language, making use of a methodology that is becoming increasingly useful in the world of software design. Additionally, it's a cross-platform language, which means its programs are designed to run without modification on Microsoft Windows, Apple Macintosh, Linux, Solaris, and other systems. Java extends beyond desktops to run on devices such as televisions, smart cards, and cellular phones.

Java is closer to programming languages such as C, C++, Python, Visual Basic, and Delphi than it is to a page-description language such as HTML, a Web scripting language such as JavaScript, or a data-description language such as XML.

Interactive Web Programming

Java first became popular because of its capability to run on World Wide Web pages. Netscape Navigator, Microsoft Internet Explorer, and other browsers can download a Java program included on a Web page and run it locally on the Web user's system.

These programs, which are called *applets*, appear on a Web page in a similar fashion to images. Unlike images, applets can be interactive—taking user input, responding to it, and presenting ever-changing content.

Applets can be used to create animation, charts, graphs, games, navigational menus, multimedia presentations, and other interactive effects.

Figure 1.1 shows an applet running in the Opera 3.61 Web browser. This applet, Every Icon, is an interactive work of art implemented as a Java program by John F. Simon, Jr., an artist and programmer who has taught at the School of Visual Arts in Manhattan. It has been shown at the 2000 Whitney Biennial art exhibition and purchased by the Guggenheim Museum and the San Francisco Museum of Modern Art.

FIGURE 1.1

A Java applet running on a Web page displayed in the Opera Web browser.

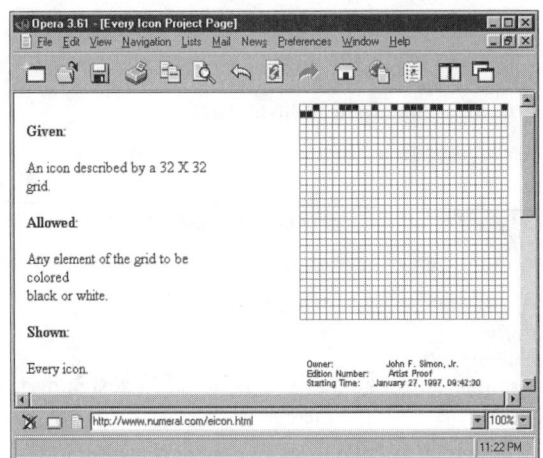

Note

The Every Icon applet is designed to display every possible icon that can be drawn using black or white squares in a simple 32-by-32 grid. Though the applet displays icons quickly, it takes more than 16 months on a Pentium-equipped computer to display all 4.29 billion variations possible on the top line of the grid alone. Displaying all variations on the top two lines would take around 16 billion years. You can find Every Icon and Simon's other art projects by visiting http://www.numeral.com.

Applets are downloaded over the World Wide Web just like HTML-formatted pages, graphics, and any other element of a Web site. On a Web browser that is equipped to handle Java, the applet will begin running when it finishes downloading.

Applets are written with the Java language, compiled into a form that can be run as a program, and placed on a Web server.

Most applets are written using Java 1.0 or Java 1.1, the first two versions of the language, because the leading browser developers have been slow to add built-in support for subsequent versions.

1

You can develop applets using Java 2, but the person viewing your applet must be using a browser that supports it. Sun has developed a free browser add-on called the Java Plug-in, and it can be downloaded to add current Java support to most popular browsers.

> **Note**
>
> You'll learn more about applets, browsers, and the Java Plug-in during Day 7, "Writing Java Applets."

Like Visual C++, Visual Basic, and Delphi, Java is a robust language that can be used to develop a wide range of software, supporting graphical user interfaces, networking, database connectivity, and other sophisticated functionality.

Java programs that don't run within a Web browser are called *applications*.

Java Grew from a Little Oak

The Java language was developed at Sun Microsystems in December 1990 as part of the Green project, a small research effort into consumer electronics. Researchers were working on a programming language for smart appliances of the future to talk to each other in the tradition of *The Jetsons* TV series—step one in realizing a society in which giant glass bubbles drop down over your body and dress you every morning.

To put its research into action, Green developed a prototype handheld device called the Star 7, a PalmPilot-like gadget that could communicate with others of its own kind.

The original idea was to develop the Star 7 operating system in C++, the hugely popular object-oriented programming language developed by Bjarne Stroustrup. However, Green project member James Gosling became fed up with how C++ was performing on the task, so he barricaded himself in his office and wrote a new language to better handle the Star 7.

The language was named Oak in honor of a tree Gosling could see out his office window. It was later renamed Java in honor of the lawyers who found out about another product called Oak and didn't want to go out on a limb.

Because Java was designed for embedded electronic devices instead of state-of-the-art PCs, it had to be small, efficient, and easily portable to a wide range of hardware devices. It also had to be reliable. People have learned to live with occasional system crashes and lockups in a 30MB software application. However, there aren't many people willing to debug an elevator while its programmers work out the kinks.

Although Java wasn't catching on as an appliance-development tool, just as things were looking grim for the Green project, the World Wide Web started to take off. Many of the things that made Java good for the Star 7 turned out to be good for the Web:

- Java is small—Programs load reasonably quickly on a Web page
- Java is secure—Safeguards protect against programs that cause damage, whether accidental or intentional
- Java is portable—Owners of Windows, Macintosh, Linux, and other operating systems can run the same program in their Web browsers without modification

In order to demonstrate Java's potential, in 1994 project members created HotJava, a Web browser that could run Java applets. The browser demonstrated two things about Java: what it offered the World Wide Web and what kind of program Java could create. Green programmers had used their new language to create the browser, rather than implementing it in C++.

Netscape became the first company to license the Java language in August 1995, incorporating a Java interpreter in its industry-leading Navigator Web browser. Microsoft followed by licensing Java for Internet Explorer, and millions of people could run interactive programs in their browsers for the first time.

Spurred by this huge audience of Web users, more than 300,000 people learned Java programming from 1995 to 1996. Sun added hundreds of employees to its Java effort, believing that the language was ideally suited for a wide variety of desktop, portable, and network computing platforms beyond the Web.

Versions of the Language

Sun has released four major versions of the Java language:

- Java 1.0—A small Web-centered version uniformly available in all popular Web browsers
- Java 1.1—A 1997 release with improvements to the user interface, completely rewritten event handling, and a component technology called JavaBeans
- Java 2 with SDK 1.2—A significantly expanded version released in 1998 with retooled graphical user interface features, database connectivity, and many other improvements
- Java 2 with SDK 1.3—A 2000 release that adds new core features such as improved multimedia, more accessibility, and faster compilation

A Java development kit has always been available at no cost from Sun's Java Web site at http://java.sun.com, and this availability is one of the factors behind the language's rapid growth. It is the first development tool that supports new versions of Java, often six months to a year before other Java development software.

In addition to Java's development kit, there are more than two dozen commercial development tools available for Java programmers. Some of the most popular:

- Symantec Visual Café
- Borland JBuilder
- IBM Visual Age for Java
- Sun Forte for Java

If you are going to use something other than SDK 1.3 to create Java programs as you read this book, you need to make sure that your development tool is up-to-date in its support for Java 2.

Note

> The programs in this book were tested with Java 2 SDK 1.3.0, the most current version of the kit available as the book went to press.

Java's Outlook

Anyone who can accurately predict the future of Java should be going after venture capital instead of writing a book. The technology firm Kleiner, Perkins, Caufield and Byers (KPCB) is investing $100 million in start-up companies on the basis of their future plans involving Java, and has already given millions to Active Software, Marimba, Viant, and a dozen other companies.

With the caveat that neither author of this book is pursuing venture capital, we predict a bright future for Java over the coming decade.

The new version of Java 2 incorporates the following key improvements:

- HotSpot—A new technology that runs Java programs more quickly and takes up less memory
- JavaSound—Greatly enhanced support for 8- and 16-bit playback and recording of WAV, AU, AIFF, and MIDI sound formats
- Swing—More than two dozen added features to components used in the graphical user interface of Java programs
- Performance—In addition to HotSpot, Sun has improved the speed and reliability of several aspects of the language: animation, database connectivity, networking, and multi-threaded programs, which can be used in animation, task scheduling, and other programs

You will work with these and other new features in the next three weeks.

Note | You can find out how to apply for KPCB's Java investment fund at the Web site `http://www.kpcb.com`. If your idea is funded and you become an overnight Internet millionaire, be aware that Macmillan USA does not forbid its authors from receiving a generous finder's fee.

Why to Choose Java

Java applets were a breakthrough in interactive content on the Web, and many top sites used them to deliver news, present information, and attract visitors. Today, ESPN.com uses Java applets for live events in its fantasy sports leagues, which have more than 100,000 subscribers.

Although there are still thousands of applets on the Web today, the most exciting Java-related developments are occurring elsewhere. Sun has extended the language far beyond its roots as an interesting Web technology.

A great example of this is Jini, Sun's Java-based technology for connecting computers and other devices together. The goal of Jini is effortless networking—connect two devices together and they instantly form a network, requiring no installation or configuration.

Jini, which ironically returns Java to the original goals of the Green project, is just one of the new areas where the language is being employed.

Regardless of where you find it running, Java's strengths remain its object-oriented nature, ease of learning, and platform neutrality.

Java Is Object-Oriented

If you're not yet familiar with object-oriented programming, you get plenty of chances to become so during the next week.

Object-oriented programming—also called *OOP*—is a way of conceptualizing a computer program as a set of separate objects that interact with each other. An object contains both information and the means of accessing and changing that information—an efficient way to create computer programs that can be improved easily and used later for other tasks.

Java inherits many of its object-oriented concepts from C++ and borrows concepts from other object-oriented languages as well. You learn more about this beginning on Day 2, "Object-Oriented Programming."

Java Is Easy to Learn

In part, Java was first created at the Green project in rejection of the complexity of C++. C++ is a language with numerous features that are powerful but easy to employ incorrectly.

Java was intended to be easier to write, compile, debug, and learn than other object-oriented languages. It was modeled strongly after C++ and takes much of its syntax from that language.

Note

> The similarity to C++ is so strong that most Java books, including previous editions of this one, make frequent comparisons between the features of the two languages. Today, it's more common for a Java programmer to learn this language either before or in place of C++. For this reason, you won't see many references to C++ in this book after today.

Despite Java's similarities to C++, the most complex and error-prone aspects of that language have been excluded from Java. You won't find pointers or pointer arithmetic because those features are easy to use incorrectly in a program and even harder to fix. Strings and arrays are objects in Java, as is everything else except a few simple data structures such as integers, floating-point numbers, and characters.

Additionally, memory management is handled automatically by Java rather than requiring the programmer to allocate and deallocate memory, and multiple inheritance is not supported.

Experienced C++ programmers will undoubtedly miss these features as they start to use Java, but everyone else will learn Java more quickly because of their absence.

Although Java is easier to learn than many other programming languages, a person with no programming experience at all will find Java challenging. It is more complicated than working in something such as HTML or JavaScript, but definitely something a beginner can accomplish.

Note

> Macmillan USA publishes another line of Java tutorials aimed directly at beginning programmers: *Sams Teach Yourself Java 2 in 24 Hours, Second Edition,* is written by Rogers Cadenhead, one of the coauthors of this book.

Java Is Platform Neutral

Because it was created to run on a wide variety of devices and computing platforms, Java was designed to be platform neutral, working the same no matter where it runs.

This was a huge departure in 1995, when Visual C++, Visual Basic, and other leading programming environments were designed almost exclusively to support Microsoft Windows 95 or Windows NT.

The original goal for Java programs to run without modification on all systems has not been realized. Java developers routinely test their programs on each environment they expect it to be run on, and sometimes are forced into cumbersome workarounds as a result. Even different versions of the same Web browser can require this kind of testing—Java game programmer Karl Hörnell calls it a "hopeless situation."

However, Java's platform-neutral design still makes it much easier to employ Java programs in a diverse range of different computing situations.

As with all high-level programming languages, Java programs are originally written as *source code*, a set of programming statements entered into a text editor and saved as a file.

When you compile a program written in most programming languages, the compiler translates your source file into *machine code*—instructions that are specific to the processor your computer is running. If you compile your code on a Windows system, the resulting program will run on other Windows systems but not on Macs, PalmPilots, and other machines. If you want to use the same program on another platform, you must transfer your source code to the new platform and recompile it to produce machine code specific to that system. In many cases, changes to the source will be required before it will compile on the new machine, because of differences in its processors and other factors.

Java programs are compiled into machine code for a *virtual machine*—a sort of computer-within-a-computer. This machine code is called *bytecode*, and the virtual machine interprets this code by converting it into a specific processor's machine code.

The virtual machine is more commonly known as the *Java interpreter*, and every environment that supports Java must have an interpreter tailored to its own operating system and processor.

Java also is platform neutral at the source level. Java programs are saved as text files before they are compiled, and these files can be created on any platform that supports Java. For example, you could write a Java program on a Windows 98 machine, upload it to a Linux machine over the Internet, and then compile it.

1

Java interpreters can be found in several places. For applets, the interpreter is either built into a Java-enabled browser or installed separately as a browser plug-in.

If you're used to the way other languages create platform-specific code, you might think the Java interpreter adds an unnecessary layer between your source file and the compiled machine code.

The interpreter does cause some significant performance issues—as a rule, Java bytecode executes more slowly than platform-specific machine code produced by a compiled language such as C or C++.

Sun, IBM, Symantec and other Java developers are addressing this with technology such as HotSpot, a new faster virtual machine included with Java 2, and compilers that turn bytecode into platform-specific machine code. Every new generation of processors also increases Java's sometimes laggard performance.

For some Java programs, speed might not be as much of an issue as portability and ease of development. The widespread deployment of Java in large business and government projects shows that the loss in speed is less of an issue than it was for early versions of the language.

Diving into Java Programming

Now that you've been introduced to Java as a spectator, it's time to put some of these concepts into play and create your first Java program.

Before you can get started, you must have SDK 1.3 or a fully compatible development environment on your system.

Selecting a Java Development Tool

If you're using a Microsoft Windows or Apple MacOS system, you probably have a Java interpreter installed that can run Java programs. Usually, this interpreter is part of a Web browser and only can run applets.

To develop Java programs, you need more than an interpreter. You also need a compiler and other tools that are used to create, run, and debug programs.

The programs in this book were tested with SDK 1.3, a set of command-line programs including a compiler, interpreter, appletviewer, file archiver, and several other programs.

A *command-line program* is one that must be run by typing a command at a prompt.

Note

On a Windows 95 or 98 system, you can get to a command-line prompt by clicking the Start button on the taskbar, choosing Programs, and then clicking MS-DOS Prompt.

Here's an example of a command you could type when using the development kit:

```
javac RetrieveMail.java
```

This command tells the `javac` program—the Java compiler included with Java 2 SDK 1.3—to read a source code file called `RetrieveMail.java` and turn it into one or more files of compiled bytecode.

People who are comfortable with MS-DOS, Linux, and other command-line environments will be at home using SDK 1.3. Everyone else will have to become accustomed to the lack of niceties such as a graphical environment and a mouse as they develop programs.

If you have another Java development tool and you're certain it is completely compatible with SDK 1.3, you can use it to create the sample programs in this book.

Caution

If you have any doubts regarding compatibility, or this book is your first experience with the Java language, you should use SDK 1.3. All the examples in the book were prepared using it.

Installing the Software Development Kit

SDK 1.3 is currently available for the following platforms:

- Windows 98
- Windows 95
- Windows 2000
- Windows NT

The kit requires a computer with a Pentium processor that is 166 MHz or faster, 32MB of memory, and 65MB of free disk space. Sun recommends at least 48MB of memory if you're going to work with Java 2 applets.

If you're using another platform, such as the Apple Macintosh, you can check to see whether it has an SDK 1.3–compliant environment by visiting Sun's site at `http://java.sun.com:80/cgi-bin/java-ports.cgi`.

You can download SDK 1.3 from Sun's Java Web site at http://java.sun.com.

The Web site's Products & APIs section offers links to the different Java development kits and related products from Sun. The product you should download is called Java 2 Software Development Kit, Standard Edition, version 1.3.

When you're looking for this product, you might find that the SDK has a third number after 1.3, such as SDK 1.3.1. To fix bugs and security problems, Sun periodically issues new releases of the SDK and numbers them with an extra period and digit after the main version number. Choose the most current version of SDK 1.3 that's offered, whether it's numbered 1.3.0, 1.3.1, 1.3.2, or higher.

Caution Take care not to download two similarly named products from Sun by mistake—the Java 2 Runtime Environment, Standard Edition, version 1.3 or the Java 2 Software Development Kit, Standard Edition, Source Release.

To go directly to the download page, the current address is http://java.sun.com/j2se/1.3.

To set up SDK 1.3, you must run an installation program that you have either downloaded from Sun or run from a CD.

Sun's Web site contains instructions for several ways to receive SDK 1.3's installation file. After choosing the version of the SDK that's designed for your operating system, you can download it as a single file that's around 25–30MB in size or download a bunch of smaller files. If you choose the latter option, follow Sun's documentation regarding how to combine them together before installing the kit.

After you have a single installation file—either by downloading it or combining a bunch of smaller files—you're ready to set up the development kit.

Windows Installation

Before installing SDK 1.3, you should make sure that no other Java development tools are installed on your system. Having more than one Java programming tool installed is likely to cause configuration problems when you use SDK 1.3.

Also, you should close all other Windows programs before installing SDK 1.3.

To set up the program on a Windows system, double-click the installation file or click Start, Run from the Windows taskbar to find and run the file.

The SDK Setup Wizard will guide you through the process of installing the software. If you accept Sun's terms and conditions for using the software, you'll be asked where to install the program, as shown in Figure 1.2.

FIGURE 1.2

Choose a destination location for SDK 1.3.

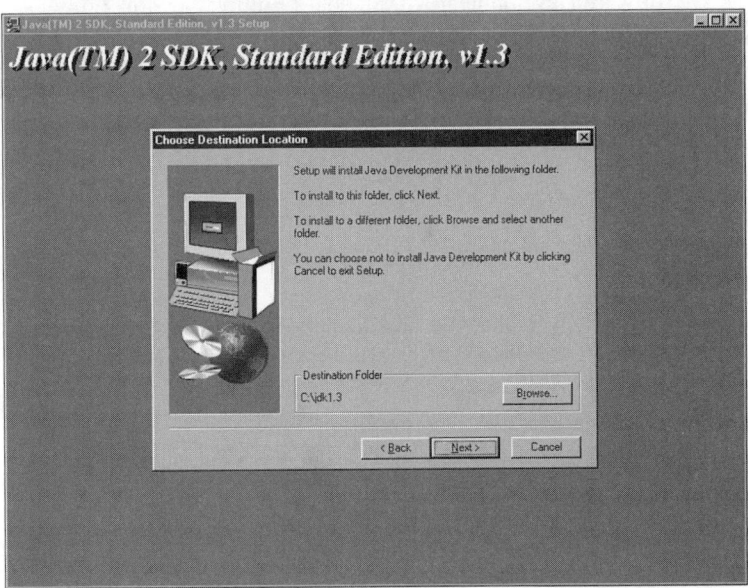

The Setup Wizard will suggest installing the program in a new jdk1.3 folder in the main hard drive on your system. Click the Next button to accept this choice, or Browse if you want to pick a different location.

Tip

Any configuration problems you might have with the SDK will be easier to fix if you install it in the folder recommended by the Setup Wizard.

The Setup Wizard will place a large number of programs and data files in the folder you have selected. Make a note of the folder, because you'll need to know it later when configuring how SDK 1.3 works on your system.

The next thing you'll be asked is what parts of the kit to install. This dialog box is shown in Figure 1.3.

FIGURE 1.3

Selecting components of SDK 1.3 to install.

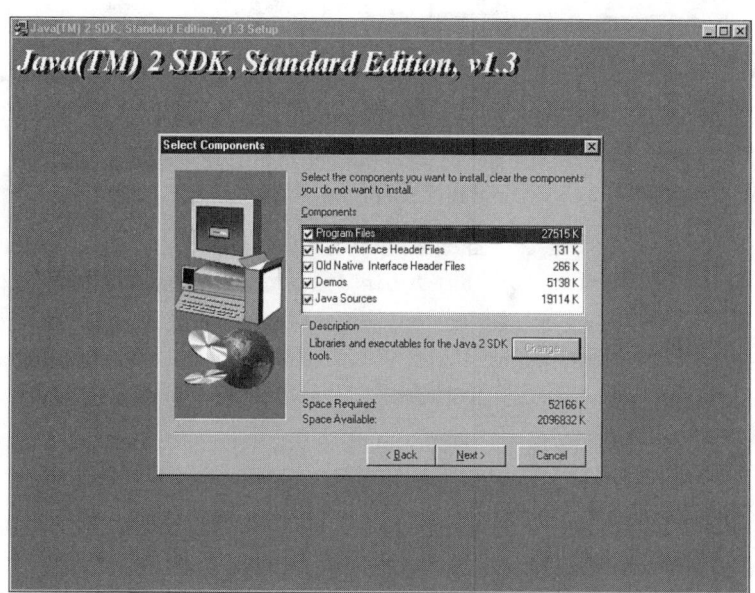

By default, the wizard will install all components of the SDK:

- Program Files—The executable programs needed to create, compile, and test your Java projects.

- Native Interface Header Files and Old Native Interface Header Files—Files used only by programmers who are combining Java code with programs written in other languages. You can omit these for the tutorials in this book.

- Demos—Java 2 programs, with versions you can run and source files you can examine to learn more about the language.

- Java Sources—The source code for the thousands of programs that make up the Java 2 class library.

If you accept the default installation, you need around 50–55MB of free hard disk space. You can save space by omitting everything but the program files, but the demo programs are nice to have around as you're experimenting with the language.

Neither the native header files nor Java source files are needed for any of the material in this book—both are primarily of interest to experienced Java programmers.

After you choose the components to install, click the Next button and the Setup Wizard will install the SDK 1.3 on your system.

Configuring the SDK

After the Setup Wizard installs SDK 1.3, you must adjust your computer's environment variables to include references to the SDK.

Experienced MS-DOS and command-line users can finish setting up the SDK by adjusting two settings, and then rebooting the computer:

- Edit the computer's PATH variable and add a reference to the SDK's bin folder (which is C:\jdk1.3\bin if you installed the SDK into the C:\jdk1.3 folder).
- Remove the CLASSPATH variable if you are not using it for some other Java-related programming. If you are, make sure that it contains a reference to the current folder—a period character ("." without the quotation marks).

These instructions might sound like gobbledygook to people who are used to a graphical, mouse-driven operating system such as Windows.

The following two sections cover how to set the PATH and CLASSPATH correctly on the different Windows systems supported by the SDK.

Users of other operating systems should follow the instructions provided by Sun on its SDK download page.

Windows 95 and 98 Configuration

To set your computer's PATH variable on a Windows 95 or 98 system, use the Windows Notepad text editor to open the AUTOEXEC.BAT file on your computer. It should be located in the root folder of the main hard drive on your computer (usually C:).

Scroll down to the bottom of AUTOEXEC.BAT and add a new line that has the following format:

```
PATH SDKFolder\bin;%PATH%
```

Replace SDKFolder with the name of the folder where you installed the SDK and add the rest without modification. For example, if you installed the SDK into C:\jdk1.3, the line should be the following:

```
PATH C:\jdk1.3\bin;%PATH%
```

After you make this change, keep AUTOEXEC.BAT open and look for any lines that begin with the text SET CLASSPATH=.

If you don't find any, you're done setting up the SDK. Save AUTOEXEC.BAT and reboot your computer.

If you find any CLASSPATH lines, add a new blank line at the bottom of AUTOEXEC.BAT and enter a line with the following format:

```
SET CLASSPATH=.;SDKFolder\lib\tools.jar;%CLASSPATH%
```

As you did with the PATH variable, replace *SDKFolder* with the folder where the SDK was installed. Save AUTOEXEC.BAT and reboot.

Windows NT and 2000 Configuration

To set any environment variables on a Windows NT or Windows 2000 system, choose Start, Control Panel, System, Environment from the taskbar. A dialog box will open where you can view the current values of environmental variables and make changes to them.

The PATH variable might be listed in System Variables or User Variables. PATH contains a list of folders separated by semicolons.

At the beginning of the PATH setting, insert the folder where you installed the SDK followed by the text \bin and a semicolon (";").

For example, if your PATH was c:\windows;c:\command and you installed the SDK into C:\jdk1.3, your new PATH should have the following value:

```
PATH c:\jdk1.3\bin;c:\windows;c:\windows\command
```

After making this change, look for a CLASSPATH variable. If you don't find it, you're done configuring the SDK. Click the Apply button to save your changes, and then reboot your computer.

If you do find CLASSPATH, place your cursor to the left of the existing CLASSPATH value and insert the SDK folder followed by the text \lib\tools.jar;.;.

For example, if you installed the SDK into C:\jdk1.3 and your CLASSPATH had the value c:\javaclasses, your CLASSPATH variable should have the following value:

```
c:\jdk1.3\lib\tools.jar;.;c:\javaclasses
```

After setting your CLASSPATH variable (if necessary), click the Apply button to make your changes permanent, and then reboot the computer.

Your First Java Program

Now that you have learned something about Java and installed development software, you're ready to start working with the language.

Before you do, you might want to take note of the most likely source of problems you'll run into—errors caused by a misconfigured SDK.

Appendix A, "Configuring the Software Development Kit," is a short tutorial for Windows users on how to use MS-DOS and correct errors in how the SDK is set up. See the appendix if you have problems compiling and running the first several examples from Day 1 and Day 2 on a Windows system—especially if you run into "bad command or filename" errors and "NoClassDefFound" errors.

| Tip | You also might want to read the appendix simply to learn a few MS-DOS commands. Windows users will be using the MS-DOS Prompt window throughout the book to compile and run Java programs. |

It's a programming tradition to make the first example in a book like this a short program that displays text. Usually the text is simply "Hello world," but this book will break from tradition a bit to display something a little longer—one of the most famous patently untrue predictions in U.S. history:

```
"The advancement of the arts, from year
to year, taxes our credulity, and seems
to presage the arrival of that period
when human improvement must end."
        Henry Ellsworth
        U.S. Commissioner of Patents
        1843 Annual Report of the Patent Office
```

The program that displays Ellsworth's quote will be an *application*, so you'll run it at a command line with the Java interpreter rather than loading it with a Web browser like an applet.

Although a Java program can be designed to be both an applet and an application, almost all programs you encounter will be one or the other.

Creating the Source File

Java programs begin as source code—a series of statements created using a text editor or word processor and saved as a text file. You can use any program you like to create these files, as long as it can save the file as plain unformatted text—a format that's also called ASCII text or DOS text.

Windows users can write Java programs with Notepad or Write, two editors that are included with the operating system. You also can use Microsoft Word, but must save files as text rather than in Word's proprietary format. UNIX and Linux users can author programs with emacs, pico, and vi; Macintosh users have SimpleText for Java source file creation.

The Software Development Kit does not include a text editor, but most other Java development tools include a built-in editor for creating source code files.

Writing the Program

Run your editor of choice and enter the Java program shown in Listing 1.1. Be careful that all the parentheses, braces, and quotation marks in the listing are entered correctly, and capitalize everything in the program exactly as shown. If your editor requires a filename before you start entering anything, use Ellsworth.java.

LISTING 1.1 Source Code of Ellsworth.java

```
 1: public class Ellsworth {
 2:     public static void main(String[] arguments) {
 3:         String line1 = "The advancement of the arts, from year\n";
 4:         String line2 = "to year, taxes our credulity, and seems\n";
 5:         String line3 = "to presage the arrival of that period\n";
 6:         String line4 = "when human improvement must end.";
 7:         String quote = line1 + line2 + line3 + line4;
 8:         String speaker = "Henry Ellsworth";
 9:         String title = "U.S. Commissioner of Patents";
10:         String from = "1843 Annual Report of the Patent Office";
11:         System.out.println('\u0022' + quote + '\u0022');
12:         System.out.println("\t" + speaker);
13:         System.out.println("\t" + title);
14:         System.out.println("\t" + from);
15:     }
16: }
```

The line numbers and colons along the left side of Listing 1.1 are not part of the program—they're included so that the authors of this book can refer to specific lines by number in each program. If you're ever unsure about the source code of a program in this book, you can compare it to a copy on the book's official World Wide Web site at the following address:

http://www.java21pro.com

After you finish typing in the program, save the file somewhere on your hard drive with the name Ellsworth.java.

Tip

> If you're a Windows user who is unfamiliar with MS-DOS, open the root folder on your main hard drive and create a new subfolder called J21work. Save Ellsworth.java and all other Java source files from this book into that folder to make it easier to find them within MS-DOS.

If you're using Windows, a text editor such as Notepad might add an extra .txt file extension to the filename of any Java source files you save (which turns a name like Ellsworth.java into Ellsworth.java.txt). To avoid this problem, place quotation marks around the filename when saving a source file. Figure 1.4 shows this technique being used to save the source file Ellsworth.java from Windows Notepad.

FIGURE 1.4

Saving a source file from Windows Notepad.

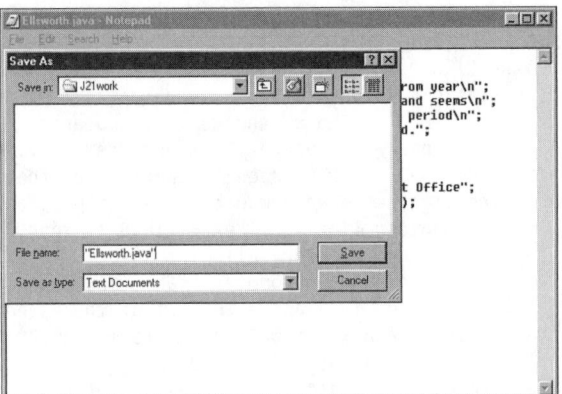

Tip

> A better solution is to use Windows Explorer to permanently associate .java files with the text editor you'll be using. This enables you to open a source file for editing by double-clicking the file in a Windows folder. To learn how to set this up, see Appendix B, "Using a Text Editor with the Software Development Kit."

Java source files must be saved with the extension .java.

Compiling and Running the Program Under Windows

Now you're ready to compile the source file. If you're using a development tool other than SDK 1.3, you should consult that software's documentation for details on how to compile Java programs.

With the SDK, you need to use the command-line tool javac, the Java compiler. The compiler reads a .java source file and creates one or more .class files that can be run by the Java virtual machine.

The compiler requires a command line. Windows users should open an MS-DOS Prompt window, then change folders to the one that contains Ellsworth.java.

If you saved the file into a newly created J21work folder inside the root folder on your main hard drive, the following MS-DOS command will open that folder:

```
cd \J21work
```

When you are in the correct folder, you can compile Ellsworth.java by entering the following at a command prompt:

```
javac Ellsworth.java
```

Figure 1.5 shows the MS-DOS commands used to switch to the \J21work folder and compile Ellsworth.java.

FIGURE 1.5

Compiling Java programs in an MS-DOS window.

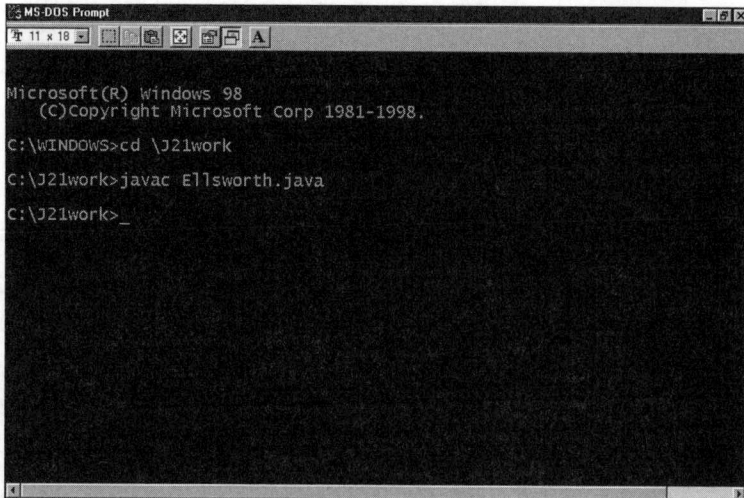

The SDK compiler does not display any message if the program compiles successfully. If there are problems, the compiler lets you know by displaying each error along with a line that triggered the error.

If the program compiled without any errors, a file called Ellsworth.class is created in the same folder that contains Ellsworth.java.

The class file contains the Java bytecode that will be executed by the Java interpreter. If you get any errors, go back to your original source file and make sure that you typed it exactly as it appears in Listing 1.1.

After you have a class file, you can run that file using a Java interpreter. The SDK's interpreter is called java, and it also is run from the command line.

Run the Ellsworth program by switching to the folder containing Ellsworth.class and entering the following:

java Ellsworth

You should see the Henry Ellsworth quotation displayed along with his name, job, and the place he wrote it.

Note

Make sure to leave off the .class extension when running a Java program with the java tool—entering java Ellsworth.class will result in a "NoClassDefFound" error. If you leave off the .class extension and still get this error, you probably need to adjust how the SDK is configured. Help for Windows users with this problem is provided in Appendix A.

Figure 1.6 shows the successful output of the Ellsworth application along with the commands used to get to that point.

FIGURE **1.6**

Compiling and running a Java application.

```
MS-DOS Prompt

Microsoft(R) Windows 98
      (C)Copyright Microsoft Corp 1981-1998.

C:\WINDOWS>cd \J21work

C:\J21work>javac Ellsworth.java

C:\J21work>java Ellsworth
"The advancement of the arts, from year
to year, taxes our credulity, and seems
to presage the arrival of that period
when human improvement must end."
       Henry Ellsworth
       U.S. Commissioner of Patents
       1843 Annual Report of the Patent Office

C:\J21work>_
```

You will begin learning about the syntax and structure of a Java program tomorrow—the purpose of today's tutorial is to compile and run a program successfully.

For now, it can be instructive to simply read source code such as Ellsworth.java and make an educated guess about what is happening in each line.

If the Ellsworth program were written in English instead of Java, the 16 lines could take the following form:

1. Create a Java class file called Ellsworth.

2. Begin the main part of the program.

3. Create a string called line1 and use it to hold the text "The advancement of the arts, from year" followed by a linefeed character ("\n").

4. Create a string called line2 and use it to hold "to year, taxes our credulity, and seems" followed by a linefeed.

5. Create the line3 string and use it to hold "to presage the arrival of that period" followed by a linefeed.

6. Create the line4 string and use it to hold "when human improvement must end."

7. Create the quote string and use it to hold the text contained in line1, line2, line3, and line4, in that order.

8. Create the speaker string and use it to hold "Henry Ellsworth".

9. Create the title string and use it to hold "U.S. Commissioner of Patents".

10. Create the from string and use it to hold "1843 Annual Report of the Patent Office".

11. Display a quotation mark (the Unicode character \u0022), the text contained in the quote string, and another quotation mark.

12. Display a tab character ("\t") followed by the contents of the speaker string.

13. Display a tab followed by the contents of title.

14. Display a tab followed by the contents of from.

15. End the main part of the program.

16. End the program.

Don't worry if you didn't guess right on the function of these lines—everything used in the Ellsworth program will be completely introduced this week.

Summary

Java is a different language today than it was in 1995.

This has a good side—a proven market for Java programmers exists at present and the skills are in huge demand. Five years ago you couldn't find "Java" in a classified ad outside of Silicon Valley, and even there the market consisted of Sun, Netscape, and only a few others.

This also has a bad side—Java is at least five times as large today as it was upon its first release, so there's much more to learn.

For this reason, today was the last day for Java to be described in the abstract. The next 20 days will be spent at the command line, creating Java applications and applets, running them with the interpreter or a Web browser, and exploring the fundamental concepts of the language.

Q&A

Q **The license for the SDK is only for 180 days. I thought the kit was free—don't you think you should have mentioned that rather predominately in your book?**

A Sun Microsystems has always made the SDK available for free, and it seems highly doubtful at this point that the company would change the policy. Although Sun has not made any official statements regarding the duration of the license, it appears to be a way to encourage developers to upgrade to new versions when they become available. Sun updates the SDK frequently, by issuing either a bug- and security-fix minor upgrade or a full upgrade such as the move to Java 2.

Q **Java 1.0 programs could be created with JDK 1.0. Java 1.1 programs could be created with JDK 1.1. Why is Java 2 using SDK 1.3? Shouldn't it be either Java 2 SDK 2 or Java 1.3 SDK 1.3?**

A Sun changed its naming scheme after Java 1.1 and JDK 1.1. The language was renamed Java 2 to capitalize on all the different products and technologies available in addition to the Software Development Kit. Although the Java Development Kit (JDK) was renamed as the Software Development Kit after JDK 1.1, it was numbered as version 1.2 instead of 2.

As a result of the changes, Java 1.2 is often used as a synonym for Java 2, JDK 2 is used when referring to SDK 1.2, and now JDK 1.3 is used in place of SDK 1.3. Sun, which received industry praise for the marketing savvy behind the choice of "Java" as a name for the language, has created a lot of confusion with this new numbering.

The current version of the language is called Java 2 and the current software development kit is Software Development Kit 1.3. The best way to figure out whether you're using the right version is to use SDK 1.3 or a tool that is fully compatible with SDK 1.3.

Quiz

Review today's material by taking this three-question quiz.

Questions

1. When Java was first introduced to the public, it was most useful in what computing environment?

   (a) Web servers

   (b) Web browsers

   (c) Personal digital assistants

2. What is the compiled form of a Java program called?

   (a) Machine code

   (b) Espresso

   (c) Bytecode

3. Why did James Gosling create the first version of the Java language?

   (a) He was frustrated with how C++ was performing on a project.

   (b) He was trying to save the Green project from being cancelled by Sun.

   (c) When you put C++ on a resume, personnel directors think it was your average in school.

Answers

1. b. Although Java could run on servers, the main source of interest in the language in 1995 was how it could run in a Web browser as part of a page.

2. c. The Java compiler turns a source code file into bytecode. A Java interpreter translates that bytecode into platform-specific machine code.

3. a. Gosling's inspiration was the difficulty in debugging a large-scale C++ project because of pointer errors, memory allocation problems, and similar issues.

Exercises

To extend your knowledge of the subjects covered today, try the following exercises:

- Take the linefeed characters out of the `Ellsworth` program, recompile the program, and run it to see how this changes the output.

- Visit Sun's Java applet showcase at `http://java.sun.com/applets` to see examples of Java programs running on the Web.

Where applicable, exercise solutions are offered on the book's Web site at `http://www.java21pro.com`.

WEEK 1

DAY 2

Object-Oriented Programming

The biggest challenge for a new Java programmer is learning object-oriented programming at the same time.

Although this might sound daunting if you are unfamiliar with this style of programming, think of it as a two-for-one discount for your brain. You will learn object-oriented programming by learning Java. There's no other way to make use of the language.

Object-oriented programming, also called *OOP*, is a way of building computer programs that mirrors how objects are assembled in the physical world.

By using this style of development, you will be able to create programs that are more reusable, reliable, and understandable.

To get to that point, you first must explore how Java embodies the principles of object-oriented programming. The following topics are covered:

- Organizing programs into elements called classes, and how these classes are used to create objects
- Defining a class by two aspects of its structure: how it should behave and what its attributes are
- Connecting classes to each other in a way that one class inherits functionality from another class
- Linking classes together through packages and interfaces

If you already are familiar with object-oriented programming, much of today's lesson will be a review for you. Even if you skim over the introductory material, you should create the sample program to get some experience developing, compiling, and running Java programs.

Thinking in Terms of Objects

There are many different ways to conceptualize a computer program. One way is to think of a program as a series of instructions carried out in sequence, and this is commonly called *procedural programming*. Most programmers start by learning a procedural language such as BASIC in its many versions or Pascal.

Procedural languages mimic the way a computer carries out instructions, so the programs you write are tailored to the computer's manner of doing things. One of the first things a procedural programmer must learn is how to break down a problem into a series of simple steps.

Object-oriented programming looks at a computer program from a different angle: focusing on the task you are using the computer for, rather than the way a computer handles tasks.

In object-oriented programming (OOP), a computer program is conceptualized as a set of objects that work together to accomplish a task. Each object is a separate part of the program, interacting with the other parts in specific, highly controlled ways.

For a real-life example of object-oriented design, consider a stereo system. Most systems are built by hooking together a bunch of different objects, which are more commonly called components:

- Speaker components play midrange and high-frequency sounds.
- Subwoofer components play low bass frequency sounds.

- Tuner components receive radio broadcast signals.
- CD player components read audio data from CDs.

These components are designed to interact with each other using standard input and output connectors. Even if you bought the speakers, subwoofer, tuner, and CD player from different companies, you can combine them to form a stereo system as long as they have standard connectors.

Object-oriented programming works under the same principle: You put together a program by combining newly created objects and existing objects in standard ways. Each object serves a specific role in the overall program.

New Term An *object* is a self-contained element of a computer program that represents a related group of features and is designed to accomplish specific tasks. Objects are also called *instances*.

Objects and Classes

Object-oriented programming is modeled on the observation that in the physical world, objects are made up of many kinds of smaller objects.

However, the capability to combine objects is only one aspect of object-oriented programming. Another important feature is the use of classes.

New Term A *class* is a template used to create an object. Every object created from the same class will have similar, if not identical, features.

Classes embody all features of a particular set of objects. When you write a program in an object-oriented language, you don't define individual objects. Instead, you define classes used to create those objects.

For example, you could create a Modem class that describes the features of all computer telephone modems. Some of those common features:

- They connect to a computer's serial port.
- They send and receive information.
- They dial phone numbers.

The Modem class serves as an abstract model for the concept of a modem. To actually have something concrete you can manipulate in a program, you must use the Modem class to create a Modem object. The process of creating an object from a class is called *instantiation*, and created objects are also called *instances*.

A Modem class can be used to create lots of different Modem objects in a program, and each of these objects could have different features:

- Some are internal modems and others are external modems.
- Some use the COM1 port and others use the COM2 port.
- Some have error control and others don't.

Even with these differences, two Modem objects still have enough in common to be recognizable as related objects. Figure 2.1 shows a Modem class and several objects created from that template.

FIGURE 2.1

The Modem *class and several* Modem *objects.*

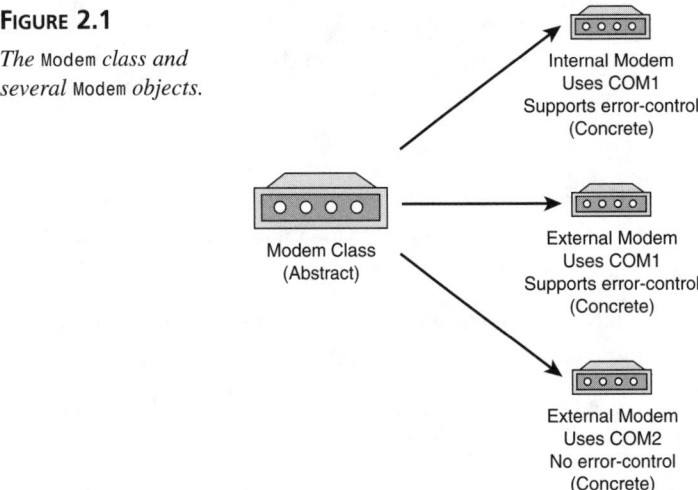

Internal Modem
Uses COM1
Supports error-control
(Concrete)

Modem Class
(Abstract)

External Modem
Uses COM1
Supports error-control
(Concrete)

External Modem
Uses COM2
No error-control
(Concrete)

Object Reuse

Using Java, you could create a class to represent all command buttons—those clickable boxes that show up on windows, dialog boxes, and other parts of a program's graphical user interface.

When the CommandButton class is developed, it could define these features:

- The text that identifies the button's purpose
- The size of the button
- Aspects of its appearance, such as whether it has a 3D shadow

The `CommandButton` class also could define how a button behaves:

- Whether the button needs a single click or a double-click to use
- Whether it should ignore mouse clicks entirely
- What it does when successfully clicked

After you define the `CommandButton` class, you can create instances of that button—in other words, `CommandButton` objects. The objects all take on the basic features of a click-able button as defined by the class, but each one could have a different appearance and slightly different behavior depending on what you need that object to do.

By creating a `CommandButton` class, you don't have to keep rewriting the code for each command button that you want to use in your programs. In addition, you can reuse the `CommandButton` class to create different kinds of buttons, as you need them, both in this program and in others.

Note

> One of Java's standard classes, `javax.swing.JButton`, encompasses all the functionality of this hypothetical `CommandButton` example and more. You get a chance to work with it during Day 8, "Working with Swing."

When you write a Java program, you design and construct a set of classes. When your program runs, objects are instantiated from those classes and used as needed. Your task as a Java programmer is to create the right set of classes to accomplish what your program needs to accomplish.

Fortunately, you don't have to start from scratch. The Java language includes hundreds of classes that implement most of the basic functionality you will need. These classes are called the Java 2 class library, and they are installed along with a development kit such as SDK 1.3.

When you're talking about using the Java language, you're actually talking about using this class library and some standard keywords and operators that are recognized by Java compilers.

The class library handles numerous tasks, such as mathematical functions, text handling, graphics, sound, user interaction, and networking. Working with these classes is no different than working with classes you create.

For complicated Java programs, you might create a whole set of new classes with defined interactions between them. These could be used to form your own class library for use in other programs.

Reuse is one of the fundamental benefits of object-oriented programming.

Attributes and Behavior

A Java class consists of two distinct types of information: attributes and behavior.

Both of these are present in `VolcanoRobot`, a project you will implement today as a class. This project, a computer simulation of a volcanic exploration vehicle, is patterned after the Dante II robot used by NASA's Telerobotics Research program to do research inside volcanic craters.

Attributes of a Class of Objects

Attributes are the data that differentiates one object from another. They can be used to determine the appearance, state, and other qualities of objects that belong to that class.

A volcanic exploration vehicle could have the following attributes:

- Status—`exploring, moving, returning home`
- Speed, in miles per hour
- Temperature, in Fahrenheit degrees

In a class, attributes are defined by variables—places to store information in a computer program. Instance variables are attributes that have values that differ from one object to another.

NEW TERM   An *instance variable* defines an attribute of one particular object. The object's class defines what kind of attribute it is, and each instance stores its own value for that attribute. Instance variables also are called *object variables*.

Each class attribute has a single corresponding variable; you change that attribute in an object by changing the value of the variable.

For example, the `VolcanoRobot` class could define a `speed` instance variable. This must be an instance variable because each robot travels at different speeds depending on the circumstances of the environment. The value of a robot's `speed` instance variable could be changed to make the robot move more quickly or slowly.

Instance variables can be given a value when an object is created and stay constant throughout the life of the object. They also can be given different values as the object is used in a running program.

For other variables, it makes more sense to have one value shared by all objects of that class. These attributes are called class variables.

NEW TERM   A *class variable* defines an attribute of an entire class. The variable applies to the class itself and to all of its instances, so only one value is stored no matter how many objects of that class have been created.

An example of a class variable for the VolcanoRobot class would be a variable that holds the current time. If an instance variable were created to hold the time, each object could have a different value for this variable, which could cause problems if the robots are supposed to perform tasks in conjunction with each other.

Using a class variable prevents this problem, because all objects of that class share the same value automatically. Each VolcanoRobot object would have access to that variable.

Behavior of a Class of Objects

2

Behavior refers to the things that a class of objects can do to themselves and other objects. Behavior can be used to change the attributes of an object, receive information from other objects, and send messages to other objects asking them to perform tasks.

A volcano robot could have the following behavior:

* Check current temperature
* Begin a survey
* Report its current location

Behavior for a class of objects is implemented using methods.

NEW TERM   *Methods* are groups of related statements in a class of objects that handle a task. They are used to accomplish specific tasks on their own objects and others, and are used in the way that functions and subroutines are used in other programming languages.

Objects communicate with each other using methods. A class or an object can call methods in another class or object for many reasons, including the following:

* To report a change to another object
* To tell the other object to change something about itself
* To ask another object to do something

For example, two volcano robots could use methods to report their locations to each other and avoid collisions, and one robot could tell another to stop so it could pass by.

Just as there are instance and class variables, there are also instance and class methods. *Instance methods*, which are so common they're usually just called *methods*, are used when you are working with an object of the class. If a method makes a change to an individual object, it must be an instance method. *Class methods* apply to a class itself.

Creating a Class

To see classes, objects, attributes, and behavior in action, you will develop a VolcanoRobot class, create objects from that class, and work with them in a running program.

 **Note**

The main purpose of this project is to explore object-oriented programming. You'll learn more about Java programming syntax during Day 3, "The ABCs of Java."

To begin creating a class, run the text editor you're using to create Java programs and open a new file. Enter the text of Listing 2.1 and save the file as VolcanoRobot.java in a folder you are using to work on programs from this book.

LISTING 2.1   The Full Text of VolcanoRobot.java

```
 1: class VolcanoRobot {
 2:     String status;
 3:     int speed;
 4:     float temperature;
 5:
 6:     void checkTemperature() {
 7:         if (temperature > 660) {
 8:             status = "returning home";
 9:             speed = 5;
10:         }
11:     }
12:
13:     void showAttributes() {
14:         System.out.println("Status: " + status);
15:         System.out.println("Speed: " + speed);
16:         System.out.println("Temperature: " + temperature);
17:     }
18: }
```

The class statement in Line 1 of Listing 2.1 defines and names the VolcanoRobot class. Everything contained between the bracket on Line 1 and the bracket on Line 18 is part of this class.

The VolcanoRobot class contains three instance variables and two instance methods.

The instance variables are defined in Lines 2–4:

```
String status;
int speed;
float temperature;
```

The variables are named status, speed, and temperature. Each will be used to store a different type of information:

- status holds a String object, a group of letters, numbers, punctuation, and other characters
- speed holds an int, an integer value
- temperature holds a float, a floating-point number

String objects are created from the String class, which is part of the Java class library and can be used in any Java program.

> **Tip**
>
> As you might have noticed from the use of String in this program, a class can use objects as instance variables.

The first instance method in the VolcanoRobot class is defined in Lines 6–11:

```
void checkTemperature() {
    if (temperature > 660) {
        status = "returning home";
        speed = 5;
    }
}
```

Methods are defined in a manner similar to a class. They begin with a statement that names the method, the kind of information the method produces, and other things.

The checkTemperature() method is contained within the brackets on Line 6 and Line 11 of Listing 2.1. This method can be called on a VolcanoRobot object to find out its temperature.

This method checks to see whether the object's temperature instance variable has a value greater than 660. If it does, two other instance variables are changed:

- The status is changed to the text "returning home", indicating that the temperature is too hot and the robot is heading back to its base.
- The speed is changed to 5. (Presumably, this is as fast as the robot can travel.)

The second instance method, showAttributes(), is defined in Lines 13–17:

```
void showAttributes() {
        System.out.println("Status: " + status);
        System.out.println("Speed: " + speed);
        System.out.println("Temperature: " + temperature);
}
```

This method uses System.out.println() to display the values of three instance variables along with some text explaining what each value represents.

Running the Program

If you compiled the VolcanoRobot class at this point, you couldn't actually use it to simulate the exploratory robots. The class you have created defines what a VolcanoRobot object would be like if it were used in a program. It doesn't, however, use one of these objects yet.

There are two ways to put this VolcanoRobot class to use:

- Create a separate Java program that uses this class.
- Add a special class method called main() to the VolcanoRobot class so that it can be run as an application, and then use VolcanoRobot objects in that method.

The latter is done for this exercise. Open VolcanoRobot.java again in your text editor and insert a blank line directly above the last line of the program (Line 18 in Listing 2.1).

In the space created by this blank line, insert the following class method:

```
public static void main(String[] arguments) {
    VolcanoRobot dante = new VolcanoRobot();
    dante.status = "exploring";
    dante.speed = 2;
    dante.temperature = 510;

    dante.showAttributes();
    System.out.println("Increasing speed to 3.");
    dante.speed = 3;
    dante.showAttributes();
    System.out.println("Changing temperature to 670.");
    dante.temperature = 670;
    dante.showAttributes();
    System.out.println("Checking the temperature.");
    dante.checkTemperature();
    dante.showAttributes();
}
```

With the main() method in place, the VolcanoRobot class can now be used as an application. Save the file as VolcanoRobot.java, and then do the following to compile the
program:

1. Go to a command line (in Windows 98 or 95, click Start, Programs, and then
   MS-DOS Prompt).

2. Open the folder where VolcanoRobot.java was saved.

3. Compile the program by typing **javac VolcanoRobot.java** at the command line.

Listing 2.2 shows the final VolcanoRobot.java source file.

Tip

If you encounter problems compiling or running any program in this book
with SDK 1.3, you can find a copy of the source file and other related files
on the book's official Web site at http://www.java21pro.com.

LISTING 2.2   The Final Text of VolcanoRobot.java

```
 1: class VolcanoRobot {
 2:     String status;
 3:     int speed;
 4:     float temperature;
 5:
 6:     void checkTemperature() {
 7:         if (temperature > 660) {
 8:             status = "returning home";
 9:             speed = 5;
10:         }
11:     }
12:
13:     void showAttributes() {
14:         System.out.println("Status: " + status);
15:         System.out.println("Speed: " + speed);
16:         System.out.println("Temperature: " + temperature);
17:     }
18:
19:     public static void main(String[] arguments) {
20:         VolcanoRobot dante = new VolcanoRobot();
21:         dante.status = "exploring";
22:         dante.speed = 2;
23:         dante.temperature = 510;
24:
25:         dante.showAttributes();
26:         System.out.println("Increasing speed to 3.");
27:         dante.speed = 3;
```

LISTING 2.2   continued

```
28:          dante.showAttributes();
29:          System.out.println("Changing temperature to 670.");
30:          dante.temperature = 670;
31:          dante.showAttributes();
32:          System.out.println("Checking the temperature.");
33:          dante.checkTemperature();
34:          dante.showAttributes();
35:      }
36: }
```

To run the VolcanoRobot application, open the folder containing the
VolcanoRobot.class file at a command line, then use the java command:

```
java VolcanoRobot
```

When you run the VolcanoRobot class, the output should be the following:

```
Status: exploring
Speed: 2
Temperature: 510.0
Increasing speed to 3.
Status: exploring
Speed: 3
Temperature: 510.0
Changing temperature to 670.
Status: exploring
Speed: 3
Temperature: 670.0
Checking the temperature.
Status: returning home
Speed: 5
Temperature: 670.0
```

Using Listing 2.2 as a guide, the following things take place in the main() class method:

- Line 19—The main() method is created and named. All main() methods take this
  format, and you'll learn more about them during Day 6, "Creating Classes and
  Methods." For now, the most important thing to note is the static keyword. This
  indicates that the method is a class method.

- Line 20, a new VolcanoRobot object is created using that class as a template. The
  object is given the name dante.

- Lines 21–23—Three instance variables of the dante object are given values:
  status is set to the text "exploring", speed is set to 2, and temperature is set
  to 510.

- Line 25—On this line and several that follow, the `showAttributes()` method of the `dante` object is called. This method displays the current values of the instance variables `status`, `speed`, and `temperature`.

- Line 26—On this line and others that follow, a `System.out.println()` statement is used to display the text within the parentheses.

- Line 27—The `speed` instance variable is set to the value 3.

- Line 30—The `temperature` instance variable is set to the value 670.

- Line 33—The `checkTemperature()` method of the `dante` object is called. This method checks to see whether the `temperature` instance variable is greater than 660. If it is, `status` and `speed` are assigned new values.

Organizing Classes and Class Behavior

An introduction to object-oriented programming in Java isn't complete without a first look at three concepts: inheritance, interfaces, and packages.

These three things all are mechanisms for organizing classes and class behavior. The Java class library uses these concepts, and the classes you create for your own programs also need them.

Inheritance

Inheritance is one of the most crucial concepts in object-oriented programming, and it has a direct effect on how you design and write your own Java classes.

 *Inheritance* is a mechanism that enables one class to inherit all the behavior and attributes of another class.

Through inheritance, a class immediately has all the functionality of an existing class. Because of this, the new class can be created by only indicating how it is different from an existing class.

With inheritance, all classes are arranged in a strict hierarchy—those you create and those from the Java class library and other libraries.

 A class that inherits from another class is called a *subclass*, and the class that gives the inheritance is called a *superclass*.

A class can have only one superclass, but each class can have an unlimited number of subclasses. Subclasses inherit all the attributes and behavior of their superclasses.

In practical terms, this means that if the superclass has behavior and attributes that your class needs, you don't have to redefine it or copy that code to have the same behavior and attributes. Your class automatically receives these things from its superclass, the superclass gets them from its superclass, and so on, all the way up the hierarchy. Your class becomes a combination of all the features of the classes above it in the hierarchy, as well as its own features.

The situation is pretty comparable to the way you inherited all kinds of things from your parents, such as height, hair color, love of ska music, and a reluctance to ask for directions. They inherited some of these things from their parents, who inherited from theirs, and backward through time to the Garden of Eden, Big Bang, or *insert personal cosmological belief here.*

Figure 2.2 shows the way a hierarchy of classes is arranged.

FIGURE 2.2

A class hierarchy.

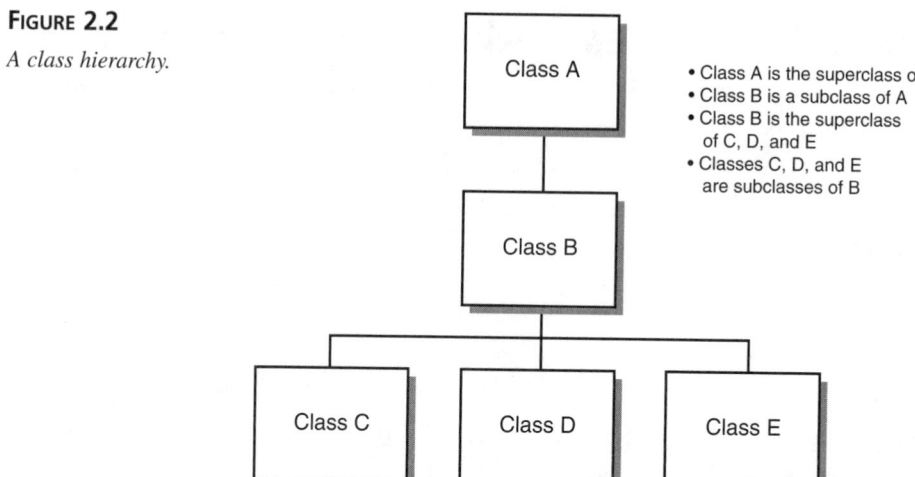

• Class A is the superclass of B
• Class B is a subclass of A
• Class B is the superclass of C, D, and E
• Classes C, D, and E are subclasses of B

At the top of the Java class hierarchy is the class `Object`—all classes inherit from this one superclass. `Object` is the most general class in the hierarchy, and it defines behavior inherited by all the classes in the Java class library. Each class further down the hierarchy becomes more tailored to a specific purpose. A class hierarchy defines abstract concepts at the top of the hierarchy. Those concepts become more concrete further down the line of subclasses.

Often when you create a new class in Java, you will want all the functionality of an existing class with some modifications of your own creation. For example, you might want a version of a `CommandButton` that makes a sound when clicked.

To receive all the `CommandButton` functionality without doing any work to re-create it, you can define your class as a subclass of `CommandButton`. Your class then would automatically inherit behavior and attributes defined in CommandButton, and behavior and attributes defined in the superclasses of CommandButton. All you have to worry about are the things that make your new class different from CommandButton itself. Subclassing is the mechanism for defining new classes as the differences between those classes and their superclass.

NEW TERM   *Subclassing* is the creation of a new class that inherits from an existing class. The only task in the subclass is to indicate the differences in behavior and attributes between it and the superclass.

2

If your class defines entirely new behavior and isn't a subclass of another class, you can inherit directly from the Object class. This allows it to fit neatly into the Java class hierarchy. In fact, if you create a class definition that doesn't indicate a superclass, Java assumes that the new class is inheriting directly from Object. The VolcanoRobot class you created inherited from the Object class.

Creating a Class Hierarchy

If you're creating a large set of classes, it makes sense for your classes to inherit from the existing class hierarchy and to make up a hierarchy themselves. Organizing your classes this way takes significant planning, but the advantages include the following:

- Functionality that is common to multiple classes can be put into a superclass, which enables it to be used repeatedly in all classes below it in the hierarchy.

- Changes to a superclass automatically are reflected in all its subclasses, their subclasses, and so on. There is no need to change or recompile any of the lower classes; they receive the new information through inheritance.

For example, imagine that you have created a Java class to implement all the features of a volcanic exploratory robot. (This shouldn't take much imagination.)

The VolcanoRobot class is completed, works successfully, and everything is copacetic. Now you want to create a Java class called MarsRobot.

These two kinds of robots have similar features—both are research robots that work in hostile environments and conduct research. Your first impulse might be to open up the VolcanoRobot.java source file and copy a lot of it into a new source file called MarsRobot.java.

A better plan is to figure out the common functionality of MarsRobot and VolcanoRobot and organize it into a more general class hierarchy. This might be a lot of work just for the classes VolcanoRobot and MarsRobot, but what if you also want to add MoonRobot, UnderseaRobot, and DesertRobot? Factoring common behavior into one or more reusable superclasses significantly reduces the overall amount of work that must be done.

To design a class hierarchy that might serve this purpose, start at the top with the class Object, the pinnacle of all Java classes. The most general class to which these robots belong might be called Robot. A robot, generally, could be defined as a self-controlled exploration device. In the Robot class, you define only the behavior that qualifies something to be a device, self-controlled, and designed for exploration.

There could be two classes below Robot: WalkingRobot and DrivingRobot. The obvious thing that differentiates these classes is that one travels by foot and the other by wheel. The behavior of walking robots might include bending over to pick something up, ducking, running, and the like. Driving robots would behave differently. Figure 2.3 shows what you have so far.

FIGURE 2.3

The basic Robot *hierarchy.*

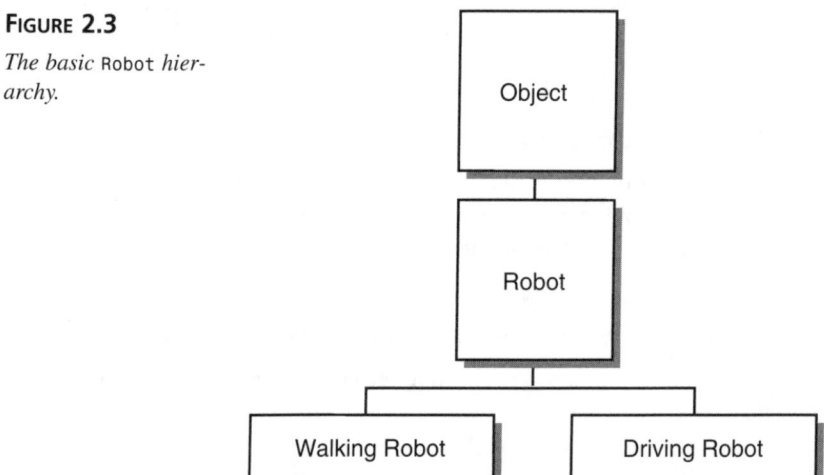

Now, the hierarchy can become even more specific. With WalkingRobot, you might have several classes: ScienceRobot, GuardRobot, SearchRobot, and so on. As an alternative, you could factor out still more functionality and have intermediate classes for TwoLegged and FourLegged robots, with different behaviors for each (see Figure 2.4).

Finally, the hierarchy is done, and you have a place for VolcanoRobot. It can be a subclass of ScienceRobot, which is a subclass of WalkingRobot, which is a subclass of Robot, which is a subclass of Object.

Where do qualities such as status, temperature, or speed come in? They come in at the place they fit into the class hierarchy most naturally. Because all robots have a need to keep track of the temperature of their environment, it makes sense to define temperature as an instance variable in Robot. All subclasses would have that instance variable as well. Remember that you need to define a behavior or attribute only once in the hierarchy, and it automatically is inherited by each subclass.

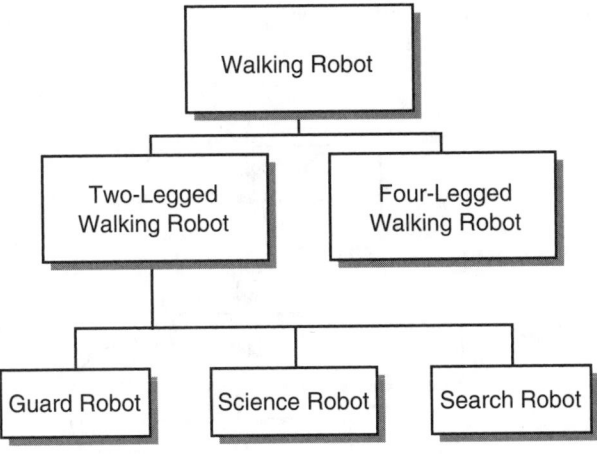

FIGURE 2.4

Two-legged and four-legged walking robots.

2

> **Note**
>
> Designing an effective class hierarchy involves a lot of planning and revision. As you attempt to put attributes and behavior into a hierarchy, you're likely to find reasons to move some classes to different spots in the hierarchy. The goal is to reduce the number of repetitive features that are needed.

Inheritance in Action

Inheritance in Java works much more simply than it does in the real world. There are no executors, judges, or courts of any kind required in Java.

When you create a new object, Java keeps track of each variable defined for that object and each variable defined for each superclass of the object. In this way, all the classes combine to form a template for the current object, and each object fills in the information appropriate to its situation.

Methods operate similarly: New objects have access to all method names of its class and superclass. This is determined dynamically when a method is used in a running program. If you call a method of a particular object, the Java interpreter first checks the object's class for that method. If the method isn't found, the interpreter looks for it in the superclass of that class, and so on, until the method definition is found. This is illustrated in Figure 2.5.

Things get complicated when a subclass defines a method that has the same name, return type, and arguments that a method defined in a superclass has. In this case, the method definition that is found first (starting at the bottom of the hierarchy and working upward) is the one that is used. Because of this, you can create a method in a subclass that prevents a method in a superclass from being used. To do this, you give the method with the same name, return type, and arguments as the method in the superclass. This procedure is called *overriding* (see Figure 2.6).

FIGURE 2.5

How methods are located in a class hierarchy.

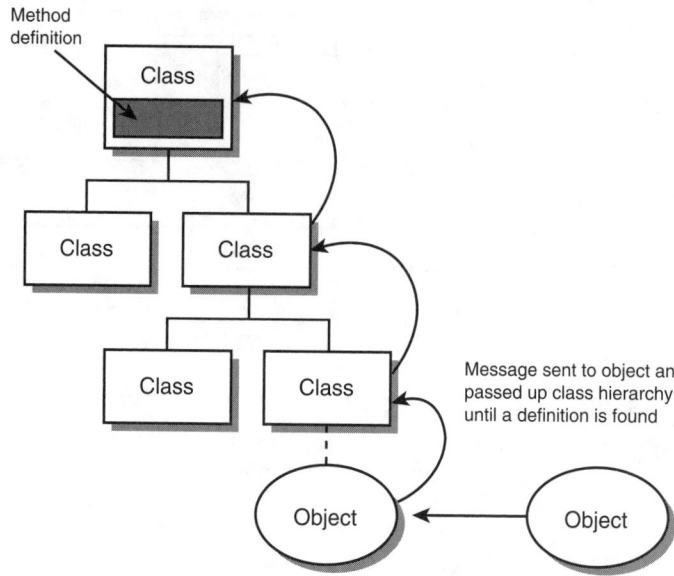

FIGURE 2.6

Overriding methods.

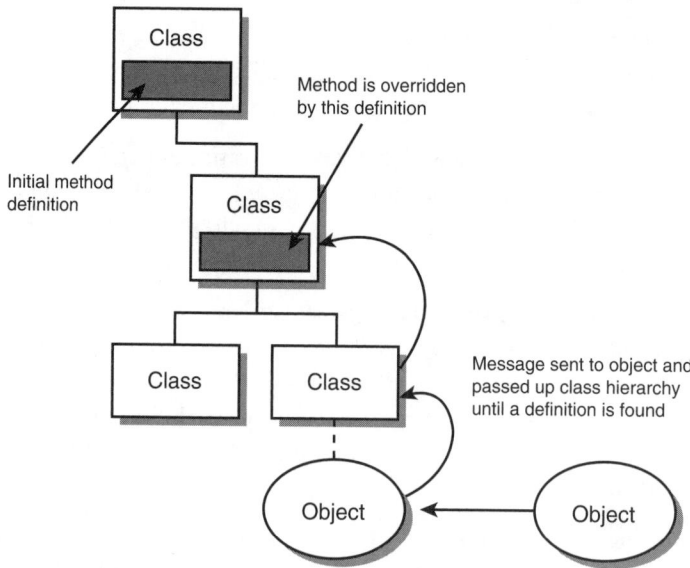

Single and Multiple Inheritance

Java's form of inheritance is called *single inheritance* because each Java class can have only one superclass (although any given superclass can have multiple subclasses).

In other object-oriented programming languages such as C++, classes can have more than one superclass, and they inherit combined variables and methods from all those superclasses. This is called *multiple inheritance*, and it provides the means to create classes that encompass just about any imaginable behavior. However, it significantly complicates class definitions and the code needed to produce them. Java makes inheritance simpler by allowing only single inheritance.

Interfaces

Single inheritance makes the relationship between classes and the functionality those classes implement easier to understand and to design. However, it also can be restrictive—especially when you have similar behavior that needs to be duplicated across different branches of a class hierarchy. Java solves the problem of shared behavior by using interfaces.

NEW TERM   An *interface* is a collection of methods that indicate a class has some behavior in addition to what it inherits from its superclasses. The methods included in an interface do not define this behavior—that task is left for the classes that implement the interface.

For example, the `Comparable` interface contains a method that compares two objects of the same class to see which one should appear first in a sorted list. Any class that implements this interface can determine the sorting order for objects of that class. This behavior would not be available to the class without the interface.

You learn more about interfaces during Day 15, "Packages, Interfaces, and Other Class Features."

Packages

Packages in Java are a way of grouping related classes and interfaces. Packages enable groups of classes to be available only if they are needed, and they eliminate potential conflicts between class names in different groups of classes.

For now, there are only a few things you need to know:

- *The class libraries in Java are contained in a package called* java. The classes in the java package are guaranteed to be available in any Java implementation and are the only classes guaranteed to be available across different implementations. The java package contains smaller packages that define specific subsets of the

Java language's functionality, such as standard features, file handling, multimedia, and many other things. Classes in other packages such as sun often are available only in specific implementations.

- *By default, your Java classes have access to only the classes in* `java.lang` *(basic language features).* To use classes from any other package, you have to refer to them explicitly by package name or import them in your source file.

- *To refer to a class within a package, you must normally use the full package name.* For example, because the `Color` class is contained in the `java.awt` package, you refer to it in your programs with the notation `java.awt.Color`.

Summary

If today was your first exposure to object-oriented programming, it probably seems theoretical and a bit overwhelming.

Don't be alarmed. You will be using object-oriented techniques for the rest of the book, and it will become familiar as you gain more experience using it.

At this point, you should have a basic understanding of classes, objects, attributes, and behavior. You also should be familiar with instance variables and methods. You'll be using these right away tomorrow.

The other aspects of object-oriented programming, such as inheritance and packages, will be covered in more detail on upcoming days.

To summarize today's material, here's a glossary of terms and concepts that were covered:

Class—A template for an object that contains variables to describe the object and methods to describe how the object behaves. Classes can inherit variables and methods from other classes.

Object—An instance of a class. Multiple objects that are instances of the same class have access to the same methods, but often have different values for their instance variables.

Instance—The same thing as an object. Each object is an instance of some class.

Method—A group of statements in a class that defines how the class's objects will behave. Methods are analogous to functions in other languages, but must always be located inside a class.

Class method—A method that operates on a class itself rather than on specific instances of a class.

Instance method—A method of an object that operates on that object by manipulating the values of its instance variables. Because instance methods are much more common than class methods, they often are just called methods.

Class variable—A variable that describes an attribute of a class instead of specific instances of the class.

Instance variable—A variable that describes an attribute of an instance of a class instead of the class itself.

Interface—A specification of abstract behavior that individual classes can then implement.

Package—A collection of classes and interfaces. Classes from packages other than java.lang must be explicitly imported or referred to by their full package and class name.

Subclass—A class further down the class hierarchy than another class, its superclass. Creating a new class that inherits from an existing one is often called subclassing. A class can have as many subclasses as necessary.

Superclass—A class further up the class hierarchy than another class, its subclass. A class only can have one superclass immediately above it, but that class also can have a superclass, and so on.

Q&A

Q **In effect, methods are functions that are defined inside classes. If they look like functions and act like functions, why aren't they called functions?**

A Some object-oriented programming languages do call them functions. (C++ calls them *member functions.*) Other object-oriented languages differentiate between functions inside and outside a body of a class or object, because in those languages the use of the separate terms is important to understanding how each function works. Because the difference is relevant in other languages, and because the term *method* is now in common use in object-oriented terminology, Java uses the term as well.

Q **What's the distinction between instance variables and methods and their counterparts, class variables and methods?**

A Almost everything you do in a Java program will involve instances (also called objects) rather than classes. However, some behavior and attributes make more sense if stored in the class itself rather than in the object. For example, the Math class in the java.lang package includes a class variable called PI that holds the approximate value of pi. This value does not change, so there's no reason different objects of that class would need their own individual copy of the `PI` variable. On the other hand, every `String` object contains a method called `length()` that reveals the number of characters in that `String`. This value can be different for each object of that class, so it must be an instance method.

Quiz

Review today's material by taking this three-question quiz.

Questions

1. What is another word for a class?

    (a) Object

    (b) Template

    (c) Instance

2. When you create a subclass, what must you define about that class?

    (a) It already is defined.

    (b) Things that are different from its superclass.

    (c) Everything about the class.

3. What does an instance method of a class represent?

    (a) The attributes of that class.

    (b) The behavior of that class.

    (c) The behavior of an object created from that class.

Answers

1. b. A class is an abstract template used to create objects that are similar to each other.

2. b. You define how the subclass is different from its superclass. The things that are similar are already defined for you because of inheritance. Answer a is technically correct, but if everything in the subclass is identical to the superclass, there's no reason to create the subclass at all.

3. c. Instance methods refer to a specific object's behavior. Class methods refer to the behavior of all objects belonging to that class.

Exercises

To extend your knowledge of the subjects covered today, try the following exercises:

- In the `main()` method of the `VolcanoRobot` class, create a second `VolcanoRobot` robot named `virgil`, set up its instance variables, and display them.

- Create an inheritance hierarchy for the pieces of a chess set. Decide where the instance variables `color`, `startingPosition`, `forwardMovement`, and `sideMovement` should be defined in the hierarchy.

Where applicable, exercise solutions are offered on the book's Web site at `http://www.java21pro.com`.

2

DAY **3**

The ABCs of Java

A Java program is made up of classes and objects, which in turn are made up of methods and variables. Methods are made up of statements and expressions, which are made up of operators.

At this point, you might be afraid that Java is like the Russian nesting dolls called *matryoshka*. Every one of those dolls seems to have a smaller doll inside it, which is as intricate and detailed as its larger companion.

This chapter clears away the big dolls to reveal the smallest elements of Java programming. You'll leave classes, objects, and methods alone for a day and examine the basic things you can do in a single line of Java code.

The following subjects are covered:

- Java statements and expressions
- Variables and data types
- Constants
- Comments
- Literals
- Arithmetic

- Comparisons
- Logical operators

 Because of Java's ties to C and C++, much of the material in this chapter will look familiar to programmers who are well versed in those languages.

Statements and Expressions

All tasks that you want to accomplish in a Java program can be broken down into a series of statements.

New Term A *statement* is a simple command written in a programming language that causes something to happen.

Statements represent a single action that is taken in a Java program. All of the following are simple Java statements:

```
int weight = 295;
```

```
System.out.println("Free the bound periodicals!");
```

```
song.duration = 230;
```

Some statements can convey a value, such as when you add two numbers together in a program or evaluate whether two variables are equal to each other. These kinds of statements are called expressions.

New Term An *expression* is a statement that results in a value being produced. The value can be stored for later use in the program, used immediately in another statement, or disregarded. The value produced by a statement is called its *return value*.

Some expressions produce a numerical return value, as in the example of adding two numbers together. Others produce a Boolean value—true or false—or can even produce a Java object. They are discussed later today.

Although many Java programs list one statement per line, this is a formatting decision that does not determine where one statement ends and another one begins. Each statement in Java is terminated with a semicolon character (;). A programmer can put more than one statement on a line and it will compile successfully, as in the following example:

```
dante.speed = 2; dante.temperature = 510;
```

Statements in Java are grouped using the opening curly brace ({) and closing curly brace (}). A group of statements organized between these characters is called a *block* or *block statement*, and you learn more about them during Day 5, "Lists, Logic, and Loops."

Variables and Data Types

In the `VolcanoRobot` application you created during Day 2, "Object-Oriented Programming," you used variables to keep track of information.

NEW TERM   *Variables* are a place where information can be stored while a program is running. The value can be changed at any point in the program—hence the name.

To create a variable, you must give it a name and identify what type of information it will store. You also can give a variable an initial value at the same time you create it.

There are three kinds of variables in Java: instance variables, class variables, and local variables.

Instance variables, as you learned yesterday, are used to define an object's attributes. *Class variables* define the attributes of an entire class of objects, and apply to all instances of it.

Local variables are used inside method definitions, or even smaller blocks of statements within a method. They can be used only while the method or block is being executed by the Java interpreter, and they cease to exist afterward.

Although all three kinds of variables are created in much the same way, class and instance variables are used in a different manner than local variables. You learn about local variables today and cover instance and class variables during Day 4, "Working with Objects."

> **Note**   Unlike other languages, Java does not have *global variables* (variables that can be used in all parts of a program). Instance and class variables are used to communicate information from one object to another, and these replace the need for global variables.

Creating Variables

Before you can use a variable in a Java program, you must create the variable by declaring its name and the type of information it will store. The type of information is listed first, followed by the name of the variable. The following are all examples of variable declarations:

```
int loanLength;
```

```
String message;
```

```
boolean gameOver;
```

 Note

You learn about variable types later today, but you might be familiar with the types used in this example. The `int` type represents integers, `boolean` is used for `true`/`false` values, and `String` is a special variable type used to store text.

Local variables can be declared at any place inside a method, just like any other Java statement, but they must be declared before they can be used. The normal place for variable declarations is immediately after the statement that names and identifies the method.

In the following example, three variables are declared at the top of a program's `main()` method:

```
public static void main(String[] arguments ) {
    int total;
    String reportTitle;
    boolean active;
}
```

If you are creating several variables of the same type, you can declare all of them in the same statement by separating the variable names with commas. The following statement creates three `String` variables named `street`, `city`, and `state`:

```
String street, city, state;
```

Variables can be assigned a value when they are created by using an equal sign (=) followed by the value. The following statements create new variables and give them initial values:

```
int zipCode = 02134;
```

```
int box = 350;
```

```
boolean pbs = true;
```

```
String name = "Zoom", city = "Boston", state = "MA";
```

As the last statement indicates, you can assign values to multiple variables of the same type by using commas to separate them.

Local variables must be given values before they are used in a program, or the program won't compile successfully. For this reason, it is good practice to give initial values to all local variables.

Instance and class variable definitions are given an initial value depending on the type of information they hold:

- Numeric variables   `0`
- Characters   `'\0'`
- Booleans   `false`
- Objects   `null`

Naming Variables

Variable names in Java must start with a letter, an underscore character (_), or a dollar sign ($). They cannot start with a number. After the first character, variable names can include any combination of letters or numbers.

> **Note**
> In addition, the Java language uses the Unicode character set, which includes the standard character set plus thousands of others to represent international alphabets. Accented characters and other symbols can be used in variable names as long as they have a Unicode character number.

When naming a variable and using it in a program, it's important to remember that Java is case sensitive—the capitalization of letters must be consistent. Because of this, a program can have a variable named X and another named x—and a `rose` is not a `Rose` is not a `ROSE`.

In programs in this book and elsewhere, Java variables are given meaningful names that include several words joined together. To make it easier to spot the words, the following rule of thumb is used:

- The first letter of the variable name is lowercase.
- Each successive word in the variable name begins with a capital letter.
- All other letters are lowercase.

The following variable declarations follow this rule of naming:

```
Button loadFile;

int areaCode;

boolean quitGame;
```

Variable Types

In addition to a name, a variable declaration must include the type of information being stored. The type can be any of the following:

- One of the basic data types
- The name of a class or interface
- An array

You learn how to declare and use array variables on Day 5. This lesson focuses on the other variable types.

Data Types

There are eight basic variable types for the storage of integers, floating-point numbers, characters, and Boolean values. These often are called *primitive types* because they are built-in parts of the Java language rather than being objects, which makes them more efficient to use. These data types have the same size and characteristics no matter what operating system and platform you're on, unlike some data types in other programming languages.

There are four data types that can be used to store integers. The one to use depends on the size of the integer, as indicated in Table 3.1.

TABLE 3.1 Integer Types

Type	Size	Values That Can Be Stored
byte	8 bits	−128 to 127
short	16 bits	−32,768 to 32,767
int	32 bits	−2,147,483,648 to 2,147,483,647
long	64 bits	−9,223,372,036,854,775,808 to 9,223,372,036,854,775,807

All these types are signed, which means that they can hold either positive or negative numbers. The type used for a variable depends on the range of values it might need to hold. None of these integer variables can reliably store a value that is too large or too small for its designated variable type, so you should take care when designating the type.

Another type of number that can be stored is a floating-point number, which has the type float or double. *Floating-point numbers* represent numbers with a decimal part. The float type should be sufficient for most uses because it can handle any number from 1.4E-45 to 3.4E+38. If not, the double type can be used for more precise numbers ranging from 4.9E-324 to 1.7E+308.

The char type is used for individual characters such as letters, numbers, punctuation, and other symbols.

The last of the eight basic data types is boolean. As you have learned, Boolean values hold either true or false in Java.

All these variable types are listed in lowercase, and you must use them as such in programs. There are classes with the same name as some of these data types but different capitalization—for example, Boolean and Char. These have different functionality in a Java program, so you can't use them interchangeably. You will see how these special classes are used tomorrow.

Class Types

In addition to the eight basic data types, a variable can have a class as its type, as in the following examples:

```
String lastName = "Hopper";

Color hair;

VolcanoRobot vr;
```

When a variable has a class as its type, the variable refers to an object of that class or one of its subclasses.

The last example in the preceding list, VolcanoRobot vr; creates a variable named vr that is reserved for a VolcanoRobot object, although the object itself might not exist yet. You'll learn tomorrow how to associate objects with variables.

Referring to a superclass as a variable type is useful when the variable might be one of several different subclasses. For example, consider a class hierarchy with a CommandButton superclass and three subclasses: RadioButton, CheckboxButton, and ClickButton. If you create a CommandButton variable called widget, it could be used to refer to a RadioButton, CheckboxButton, or ClickButton object.

Declaring a variable of type Object means that it can be associated with any kind of object.

Note

Java does not have anything comparable to the typedef statement from C and C++. To declare new types in Java, a new class is declared and variables can use that class as their type.

Assigning Values to Variables

After a variable has been declared, a value can be assigned to it with the assignment operator, an equal sign (=). The following are examples of assignment statements:

```
idCode = 8675309;

accountOverdrawn = false;
```

Constants

Variables are useful when you need to store information that can be changed as a program runs. If the value should never change during a program's runtime, you can use a special type of variable called a constant.

 A *constant*, which also is called a *constant variable*, is a variable with a value that never changes. This might seem like a misnomer, given the meaning of the word "variable."

Constants are useful in defining shared values for all methods of an object—in other words, for giving meaningful names to unchanging values that an entire object must have access to. In Java, you can create constants for all kids of variables: instance, class, and local.

> **Note**   Constant local variables were not possible in Java 1.0, but were added to the language for all subsequent versions. This becomes important if you're trying to create an applet that is fully compatible with Java 1.0, as you will learn during Day 7, "Writing Java Applets."

To declare a constant, use the `final` keyword before the variable declaration and include an initial value for that variable, as in the following:

```
final float PI = 3.141592;

final boolean DEBUG = false;

final int PENALTY = 25;
```

In the preceding statements, the names of the constants are capitalized: PI, DEBUG, and PENALTY. This isn't required, but it is a convention used by many Java programmers—Sun uses it in the Java class library. The capitalization makes it clear that you're using a constant.

Constants can be useful for naming various states of an object and then testing for those states. Suppose you have a program that takes directional input from the numeric keypad on the keyboard—push 8 to go up, 4 to go left, and so on. You can define those values as constant integers:

```
final int LEFT = 4;
final int RIGHT = 6;
final int UP = 8;
final int DOWN = 2;
```

Using constants often makes a program easier to understand. To illustrate this point, consider which of the following two statements is more informative of its function:

```
this.direction = 4;
```

```
this.direction = LEFT;
```

Comments

One of the most important ways to improve the readability of your program is to use comments.

NEW TERM *Comments* are information included in a program strictly for the benefit of humans trying to figure out what's going on in the program. The Java compiler ignores comments entirely when preparing a runnable version of a Java source file.

There are three different kinds of comments you can use in Java programs, and you can use each of them at your discretion.

The first way to add a comment to a program is to precede it with two slash characters (//). Everything from the slashes to the end of the line is considered a comment, as in the following statement:

```
int creditHours = 3; // set up credit hours for course
```

In this example, everything from the // to the end of the line is a comment and is disregarded by a Java compiler.

If you need to make a comment that takes up more than one line, you can begin it with the text /* and end it with the text */. Everything between these two delimiters is considered as a comment, as in the following:

```
/* This program occasionally deletes all files on
your hard drive and renders it completely unusable
when you spellcheck a document. */
```

The final type of comment is meant to be computer-readable as well as human-readable. If you begin a comment with the text /** (instead of /*) and end it with */, the comment is interpreted to be official documentation on how the class and its public methods work.

This kind of comment then can be read by utilities such as the javadoc tool included with the SDK. The javadoc program uses official comments to create a set of HTML documents that document the program, its class hierarchy, and its methods.

All the official documentation on Java's class library comes from javadoc-style comments. You can view current Java 2 documentation on the Web at the following page:

```
http://java.sun.com/j2se/1.3/docs
```

You also can download all this documentation for faster browsing on your own computer. The documents are more than 23MB in size and are available from the following page:

```
http://java.sun.com/j2se/1.3/docs.html
```

Literals

In addition to variables, you will also use a literal in a Java statement.

NEW TERM   A *literal* is any number, text, or other information that directly represents a value.

Literal is a programming term that essentially means that what you type is what you get. The following assignment statement uses a literal:

```
int year = 2000;
```

The literal is 2000, because it directly represents the integer value 2000. Numbers, characters, and strings all are examples of literals.

Although the meaning and usage of literals will seem intuitive most of the time, Java has some special types of literals that represent different kinds of numbers, characters, strings, and Boolean values.

Number Literals

Java has several integer literals. The number 4, for example, is an integer literal of the int variable type. It also can be assigned to byte and short variables because the number is small enough to fit into those integer types. An integer literal larger than an int can hold is automatically considered to be of the type long. You also can indicate that a literal should be a long integer by adding the letter L (L or l) to the number. For example, the following statement treats the value 4 as a long integer:

```
pennyTotal = pennyTotal + 4L;
```

To represent a negative number as a literal, prepend a minus sign (-) to the literal, as in -45.

If you need to use a literal integer with octal numbering, prepend a 0 to the number. For example, the octal number 777 would be the literal 0777. Hexadecimal integers are used as literals by prepending the number with 0x, as in 0x12 or 0xFF.

> **Note**
>
> Octal and hexadecimal numbering systems are convenient for many advanced programming uses, but unlikely to be needed by beginners. *Octal numbers* are a base-8 numbering system, which means they can only represent the values 0 through 7 as a single digit. The eighth number in octal is 10 (or 010 as a Java literal).
>
> Hexadecimal is a base-16 numbering system, and it can represent 16 numbers as a single digit. The letters A through F represent the last six digits, so the first 16 numbers are 0, 1, 2, 3, 4, 5, 6, 7, 8, 9, A, B, C, D, E, F.
>
> The octal and hexadecimal systems are better suited for certain tasks in programming than the normal decimal system is. If you have ever used HTML to set a Web page's background color, you might have used hexadecimal numbers.

Floating-point literals use a period character (.) for the decimal point, as you would expect. The following statement uses a literal to set up a `double` variable:

```
double myGPA = 2.25;
```

All floating-point literals are considered of the `double` variable type instead of `float`. To specify a literal of `float`, add the letter F (F or f) to the literal, as in the following example:

```
float piValue = 3.1415927F;
```

You can use exponents in floating-point literals by using the letter e or E followed by the exponent, which can be a negative number. The following statements use exponential notation:

```
double x = 12e22;
```

```
double y = 19E-95;
```

Boolean Literals

The Boolean values `true` and `false` also are literals. These are the only two values you can use when assigning a value to a `boolean` variable type or using a Boolean in a statement in other ways.

If you have used another language such as C, you might expect that a value of 1 is equivalent to `true` and `0` is equivalent to `false`. This isn't the case in Java—you must use the values `true` or `false` to represent Boolean values. The following statement sets a `boolean` variable:

```
boolean chosen = true;
```

Note that the literal `true` does not have quotation marks around it. If it did, the Java compiler would assume that it was a string of characters.

Character Literals

Character literals are expressed by a single character surrounded by single quotation marks, such as `'a'`, `'#'`, and `'3'`. You might be familiar with the ASCII character set, which includes 128 characters including letters, numerals, punctuation, and other characters useful in computing. Java supports thousands of additional characters through the 16-bit Unicode standard.

Some character literals represent characters that are not readily printable or accessible through a keyboard. Table 3.2 lists the special codes that can represent these special characters as well as characters from the Unicode character set. The letter *d* in the octal, hex, and Unicode escape codes represents a number or a hexadecimal digit (a-f or A–F).

TABLE 3.2   Character Escape Codes

Escape	Meaning
\n	New line
\t	Tab
\b	Backspace
\r	Carriage return
\f	Formfeed
\\	Backslash
\'	Single quotation mark
\"	Double quotation mark
\d	Octal
\xd	Hexadecimal
\ud	Unicode character

Note   C and C++ programmers should note that Java does not include character codes for \a (bell) or \v (vertical tab).

String Literals

The final literal that you can use in a Java program represents strings of characters. A string in Java is an object rather than being a basic data type, and strings are not stored in arrays as they are in languages such as C.

Because string objects are real objects in Java, methods are available to combine strings, modify strings, and determine whether two strings have the same value.

String literals consist of a series of characters inside double quotation marks, as in the following statements:

```
String quitMsg = "Are you sure you want to quit?";

String password = "swordfish";
```

Strings can include the character escape codes listed in Table 3.2 previously, as shown here:

```
String example = "Socrates asked, \"Hemlock is poison?\"";

System.out.println("Sincerely,\nMillard Fillmore\n");

String title = "Sams Teach Yourself Rebol While You Sleep\u2122"
```

In the last example here, the Unicode code sequence \u2122 produces a ™ symbol on systems that have been configured to support Unicode.

Caution

> Most users in English-speaking countries aren't likely to see Unicode characters when they run Java programs. Although Java supports the transmission of Unicode characters, the user's system also must support it for the characters to be displayed. Unicode support provides a way to encode its characters for systems that support the standard. Although Java 1.0 supported only the Latin subset of Unicode, Java 1.1 and subsequent versions support the display of any Unicode character that can be represented by a host font.
>
> For more information about Unicode, visit the Unicode Consortium Web site at http://www.unicode.org.

Although string literals are used in a manner similar to other literals in a program, they are handled differently behind the scenes.

When a string literal is used, Java stores that value as a String object. You don't have to explicitly create a new object, as you must do when working with other objects, so they are as easy to work with as basic data types. Strings are unusual in this respect—none of the basic types is stored as an object when used. You learn more about strings and the String class today and tomorrow.

Expressions and Operators

An *expression* is a statement that can convey a value. Some of the most common expressions are mathematical, such as in the following source code example:

```
int x = 3;
int y = x;
int z = x * y;
```

All three of these statements can be considered expressions—they convey values that can be assigned to variables. The first assigns the literal 3 to the variable x. The second assigns the value of the variable x to the variable y. The multiplication operator * is used to multiply the x and y integers, and the expression produces the result of the multiplication. This result is stored in the z integer.

An expression can be any combination of variables, literals, and operators. They also can be method calls, because methods can send back a value to the object or class that called the method.

The value conveyed by an expression is called a *return value*, as you have learned. This value can be assigned to a variable and used in many other ways in your Java programs.

Most of the expressions in Java use operators like *.

 *Operators* are special symbols used for mathematical functions, some types of assignment statements, and logical comparisons.

Arithmetic

There are five operators used to accomplish basic arithmetic in Java. These are shown in Table 3.3.

TABLE 3.3   Arithmetic Operators

Operator	Meaning	Example
+	Addition	3 + 4
-	Subtraction	5 - 7
*	Multiplication	5 * 5
/	Division	14 / 7
%	Modulus	20 % 7

Each operator takes two operands, one on either side of the operator. The subtraction operator also can be used to negate a single operand—which is equivalent to multiplying that operand by -1.

One thing to be mindful of when using division is the kind of numbers you're dealing with. If you store a division operation into an integer, the result will be truncated to the next lower whole number because the int data type can't handle floating-point numbers. As an example, the expression 31 / 9 results in 3 if stored as an integer.

Modulus division, which uses the % operator, produces the remainder of a division operation. Using 31 % 9 results in 4 because 31 divided by 9 leaves a remainder of 4.

Note that many arithmetic operations involving integers produce an int regardless of the original type of the operands. If you're working with other numbers, such as floating-point numbers or long integers, you should make sure that the operands have the same type you're trying to end up with.

Listing 3.1 is an example of simple arithmetic in Java.

LISTING 3.1 The Source File Weather.java

```
 1: class Weather {
 2:     public static void main(String[] arguments) {
 3:         float fah = 86;
 4:         System.out.println(fah + " degrees Fahrenheit is ...");
 5:         // To convert Fahrenheit into Celsius
 6:         // Begin by subtracting 32
 7:         fah = fah - 32;
 8:         // Divide the answer by 9
 9:         fah = fah / 9;
10:         // Multiply that answer by 5
11:         fah = fah * 5;
12:         System.out.println(fah + " degrees Celsius\n");
13:
14:         float cel = 33;
15:         System.out.println(cel + " degrees Celsius is ...");
16:         // To convert Celsius into Fahrenheit
17:         // Begin by multiplying it by 9
18:         cel = cel * 9;
19:         // Divide the answer by 5
20:         cel = cel / 5;
21:         // Add 32 to the answer
22:         cel = cel + 32;
23:         System.out.println(cel + " degrees Fahrenheit");
24:     }
25: }
```

If you run this Java application, it produces the following output:

```
86.0 degrees Fahrenheit is ...
30.0 degrees Celsius

33.0 degrees Celsius is ...
91.4 degrees Fahrenheit
```

In Lines 3–12 of this Java application, a temperature in Fahrenheit is converted to Celsius using the arithmetic operators:

- Line 3: The floating-point variable fah is created with a value of 86.
- Line 4: The current value of fah is displayed.
- Line 5: The first of several comments for the benefit of people trying to figure out what the program is doing. These comments are ignored by the Java compiler.
- Line 7: fah is set to its current value minus 32.
- Line 9: fah is set to its current value divided by 9.
- Line 11: fah is set to its current value multiplied by 5.
- Line 12: Now that fah has been converted to a Celsius value, fah is displayed again.

A similar thing happens in Lines 14–23, but in the reverse direction. A temperature in Celsius is converted to Fahrenheit.

This program also makes use of System.out.println() in several statements. The System.out.println() method is used in an application to display strings and other information to the standard output device, which usually is the screen.

System.out.println() takes a single argument within its parentheses: a string. To present more than one variable or literal as the argument to println(), you can use the + operator to combine these elements into a single string.

You learn more about this use of the + operator later today.

More About Assignment

Assigning a value to a variable is an expression, because it produces a value. Because of this feature, you can string assignment statements together the following way:

```
x = y = z = 7;
```

In this statement, all three variables end up with the value of 7.

The right side of an assignment expression always is calculated before the assignment takes place. This makes it possible to use an expression statement as in the following code example:

```
int x = 5;
x = x + 2;
```

In the expression x = x + 2, the first thing that happens is that x + 2 is calculated. The result of this calculation, 7, is then assigned to x.

Using an expression to change a variable's value is an extremely common task in programming. There are several operators used strictly in these cases.

Table 3.4 shows these assignment operators and the expressions they are functionally equivalent to.

TABLE 3.4   Assignment Operators

Expression	Meaning
x += y	x = x + y
x -= y	x = x - y
x *= y	x = x * y
x /= y	x = x / y

Caution

These shorthand assignment operators are functionally equivalent to the longer assignment statements for which they substitute. However, if either side of your assignment statement is part of a complex expression, there are cases where the operators are not equivalent. For example, if x equals 20 and y equals 5, the following two statements do not produce the same value:

```
x = x / y + 5;
```
```
x /= y + 5;
```

When in doubt, simplify an expression by using multiple assignment statements and don't use the shorthand operators.

Incrementing and Decrementing

Another common task is to add or subtract one from an integer variable. There are special operators for these expressions, which are called increment and decrement operations.

NEW TERM *Incrementing* a variable means to add 1 to its value, and *decrementing* a variable means to subtract 1 from its value.

The increment operator is ++ and the decrement operator is - -. These operators are placed immediately after or immediately before a variable name, as in the following code example:

```
int x = 7;
x = x++;
```

In this example, the statement x = x++ increments the x variable from 7 to 8.

These increment and decrement operators can be placed before or after a variable name, and this affects the value of expressions that involve these operators.

NEW TERM Increment and decrement operators are called *prefix* operators if listed before a variable name, and *postfix* operators if listed after a name.

In a simple expression such as standards - - ;, using a prefix or postfix operator produces the same result, making the operators interchangeable. When increment and decrement operations are part of a larger expression, however, the choice between prefix and postfix operators is important.

Consider the following two expressions:

```
int x, y, z;
x = 42;
y = x++;
z = ++x;
```

These two expressions yield very different results because of the difference between prefix and postfix operations. When you use postfix operators as in y=x++, y receives the value of x before it is incremented by one. When using prefix operators as in z = ++x, x is incremented by one before the value is assigned to z. The end result of this example is that y equals 42, z equals 44, and x equals 44.

If you're still having some trouble figuring this out, here's the example again with comments describing each step:

```
int x, y, z; // x, y, and z are all declared
x = 42;      // x is given the value of 42
y = x++;     // y is given x's value (42) before it is incremented
             // and x is then incremented to 43
z = ++x;     // x is incremented to 44, and z is given x's value
```

Caution

As with shorthand operators, increment and decrement operators can produce results you might not have expected when used in extremely complex expressions. The concept of "assigning x to y before x is incremented" isn't precisely right, because Java evaluates everything on the right side of an expression before assigning its value to the left side. Java stores some values before handling an expression in order to make postfix work the way it has been described in this section. When you're not getting the results you expect from a complex expression that includes prefix and postfix operators, try to break the expression into multiple statements to simplify it.

Comparisons

Java has several operators that are used when making comparisons between variables, variables and literals, or other types of information in a program.

These operators are used in expressions that return Boolean values of `true` or `false`, depending on whether the comparison being made is true or not. Table 3.5 shows the comparison operators.

TABLE 3.5   Comparison Operators

Operator	Meaning	Example
==	Equal	x == 3
!=	Not equal	x != 3
<	Less than	x < 3
>	Greater than	x > 3
<=	Less than or equal to	x <= 3
>=	Greater than or equal to	x >= 3

The following example shows a comparison operator in use:

```
boolean hip;
int age = 33;
hip = age < 25;
```

The expression `age < 25` produces a result of either `true` or `false`, depending on the value of the integer age. Because age is `33` in this example (which is not less than `25`), hip is given the Boolean value `false`.

Logical Operators

Expressions that result in Boolean values such as comparison operations can be combined to form more complex expressions. This is handled through logical operators. These operators are used for the logical combinations AND, OR, XOR, and logical NOT.

For AND combinations, the & or && logical operators are used. When two Boolean expressions are linked by the & or && operators, the combined expression returns a true value only if both Boolean expressions are true.

Consider this example, taken directly from the film *Harold & Maude*:

```
boolean unusual = (age < 21) & (girlfriendAge > 78);
```

This expression combines two comparison expressions: age < 21 and girlfriendAge > 78. If both of these expressions are true, the value true is assigned to the variable unusual. In any other circumstance, the value false is assigned to unusual.

The difference between & and && lies in how much work Java does on the combined expression. If & is used, the expressions on either side of the & are evaluated no matter what. If && is used and the left side of the && is false, the expression on the right side of the && never is evaluated.

For OR combinations, the | or || logical operators are used. These combined expressions return a true value if either Boolean expression is true.

Consider this *Harold & Maude*–inspired example:

```
boolean unusual = (grimThoughts > 10) || (girlfriendAge > 78);
```

This expression combines two comparison expressions: grimThoughts > 10 and girlfriendAge > 78. If either of these expressions is true, the value true is assigned to the variable unusual. Only if both of these expressions are false will the value false be assigned to unusual.

Note the use of || instead of |. Because of this usage, if grimThoughts > 10 is true, unusual is set to true and the second expression is never evaluated.

The XOR combination has one logical operator, ^. This results in a true value only if both Boolean expressions it combines have opposite values. If both are true or both are false, the ^ operator produces a false value.

The NOT combination uses the ! logical operator followed by a single expression. It reverses the value of a Boolean expression the same way that a minus symbol reverses the positive or negative sign on a number.

For example, if age < 30 returns a true value, !(age < 30) returns a false value.

These logical operators can seem completely illogical when encountered for the first time. You get plenty of chances to work with them in subsequent chapters, especially on Day 5.

Operator Precedence

When more than one operator is used in an expression, Java has an established precedence to determine the order in which operators are evaluated. In many cases, this precedence determines the overall value of the expression.

For example, consider the following expression:

```
y = 6 + 4 / 2;
```

The y variable receives the value 5 or the value 8, depending on which arithmetic operation is handled first. If the 6 + 4 expression comes first, y has the value of 5. Otherwise, y equals 8.

In general, the order from first to last is the following:

- Increment and decrement operations
- Arithmetic operations
- Comparisons
- Logical operations
- Assignment expressions

If two operations have the same precedence, the one on the left in the actual expression is handled before the one on the right. Table 3.6 shows the specific precedence of the various operators in Java. Operators farther up the table are evaluated first.

TABLE 3.6 Operator Precedence

Operator	Notes
. [] ()	Parentheses (()) are used to group expressions; period (.) is used for access to methods and variables within objects and classes (discussed tomorrow); square brackets ([]) are used for arrays. (This operator is discussed later in the week.)
++ -- ! ~ instanceof	The instanceof operator returns true or false based on whether the object is an instance of the named class or any of that class's subclasses (discussed tomorrow).
new (type)expression	The new operator is used for creating new instances of classes; () in this case is for casting a value to another type. (You learn about both of these tomorrow.)

TABLE 3.6   continued

Operator	Notes
* / %	Multiplication, division, modulus.
+ -	Addition, subtraction.
<< >> >>>	Bitwise left and right shift.
< > <= >=	Relational comparison tests.
== !=	Equality.
&	AND
^	XOR
|	OR
&&	Logical AND
||	Logical OR
? :	Shorthand for if...then...else (discussed on Day 5).
= += -= *= /= %= ^=	Various assignments.
&= |= <<= >>= >>>=	More assignments.

Returning to the expression y = 6 + 4 / 2, Table 3.6 shows that division is evaluated before addition, so the value of y will be 8.

To change the order in which expressions are evaluated, place parentheses around the expressions that should be evaluated first. You can nest one set of parentheses inside another to make sure that expressions evaluate in the desired order—the innermost parenthetic expression is evaluated first.

The following expression results in a value of 5:

y = (6 + 4) / 2

The value of 5 is the result because 6 + 4 is calculated before the result, 10, is divided by 2.

Parentheses also can be useful to improve the readability of an expression. If the precedence of an expression isn't immediately clear to you, adding parentheses to impose the desired precedence can make the statement easier to understand.

String Arithmetic

As stated earlier today, the + operator has a double life outside the world of mathematics. It can be used to concatenate two or more strings.

New Term   *Concatenate* means to link two things together. For reasons unknown, it is the verb of choice when describing the act of combining two strings—winning out over paste, glue, affix, combine, link, and conjoin.

In several examples, you have seen statements that look something like this:

```
String firstName = "Raymond";
System.out.println("Everybody loves " + firstName);
```

These two lines result in the following text being displayed:

```
Everybody loves Raymond
```

The + operator combines strings, other objects, and variables to form a single string. In the preceding example, the literal `Everybody loves` is concatenated to the value of the `String` object `firstName`.

Working with the concatenation operator is easy in Java because of the way it can handle any variable type and object value as if it were a string. If any part of a concatenation operation is a `String` or `String` literal, all elements of the operation will be treated as if they were strings:

```
System.out.println(4 + " score and " + 7 + " years ago.");
```

This produces the output text `4 score and 7 years ago.`, as if the integer literals 4 and 7 were strings.

There also is a shorthand += operator to add something to the end of a string. For example, consider the following expression:

```
myName += " Jr.";
```

This expression is equivalent to the following:

```
myName = myName + " Jr.";
```

In this example, it changes the value of `myName` (which might be something like `Efrem Zimbalist`) by adding `Jr.` at the end (`Efrem Zimbalist Jr.`).

Summary

Anyone who pops open a set of matryoska dolls has to be a bit disappointed to reach the smallest doll in the group. Ideally, advances in microengineering should enable Russian artisans to create ever-smaller and smaller dolls, until someone reaches the subatomic threshold and is declared the winner.

You have reached Java's smallest nesting doll today, but it shouldn't be a letdown. Using statements and expressions enables you to begin building effective methods, which make effective objects and classes possible.

Today you learned about creating variables and assigning values to them; using literals to represent numeric, character, and string values; and working with operators. Tomorrow you put these skills to use as you develop objects for Java programs.

To summarize today's material, Table 3.7 lists the operators you learned about. Be a doll and look them over carefully.

TABLE 3.7   Operator Summary

Operator	Meaning
+	Addition
-	Subtraction
*	Multiplication
/	Division
%	Modulus
<	Less than
>	Greater than
<=	Less than or equal to
>=	Greater than or equal to
==	Equal
!=	Not equal
&&	Logical AND
||	Logical OR
!	Logical NOT
&	AND
|	OR
^	XOR
=	Assignment
++	Increment
--	Decrement
+=	Add and assign
-=	Subtract and assign
*=	Multiply and assign
/=	Divide and assign
%=	Modulus and assign

Q&A

Q **What happens if you assign an integer value to a variable that is too large for that variable to hold?**

A Logically, you might think that the variable is converted to the next larger type, but this isn't what happens. Instead, an *overflow* occurs—a situation in which the number wraps around from one size extreme to the other. An example of overflow would be a `byte` variable that goes from 127 (acceptable value) to 128 (unacceptable). It would wrap around to the lowest acceptable value, which is –128, and start counting upward from there. Overflow isn't something you can readily deal with in a program, so you should be sure to give your variables plenty of living space in their chosen data type.

Q **Why does Java have all these shorthand operators for arithmetic and assignment? It's really hard to read that way.**

A Java's syntax is based on C++, which is based on C (more Russian nesting doll behavior). C is an expert language that values programming power over readability, and the shorthand operators are one of the legacies of that design priority. Using them in a program isn't required because effective substitutes are available, so you can avoid them in your own programming if you prefer.

Quiz

Review today's material by taking this three-question quiz.

Questions

1. Which of the following is a valid value for a `boolean` variable?

    (a) `"false"`

    (b) `false`

    (c) `10`

2. Which of these conventions is not used when naming variables in Java?

    (a) Each successive word after the first in the variable name begins with a capital letter.

    (b) The first letter of the variable name is lowercase.

    (c) All letters are capitalized.

3. Which of these data types holds numbers from -32,768 to 32,767?

   (a) `char`

   (b) `byte`

   (c) `short`

Answers

1. b. In Java, a `boolean` can only be `true` or `false`. If you put quotation marks around the value, it will be treated like a `String` rather than one of the two `boolean` values.

2. c. Constant names are capitalized to make them stand out from other variables.

3. c.

Exercises

To extend your knowledge of the subjects covered today, try the following exercises:

- Create a program that calculates how much a $14,000 investment would be worth if it increased in value by 40% during the first year, lost $1,500 in value the second year, and increased 12% in the third year.

- Write a program that displays two numbers and uses the `/` and `%` operators to display the result and remainder after they are divided. Use the `\t` character escape code to separate the result and remainder in your output.

Where applicable, exercise solutions are offered on the book's Web site at `http://www.java21pro.com`.

DAY 4

Working with Objects

When you do work in Java, you use objects to get the job done. As you learned two days ago, Java is a heavily object-oriented programming language.

Almost everything you can do using Java is accomplished with objects. You create objects, modify them, move them around, change their variables, call their methods, and combine them with other objects. You develop classes, create objects out of those classes, and use them with other classes and objects.

Today, you work extensively with objects. The following topics are covered:

- Creating objects (also called *instances*)
- Testing and modifying class and instance variables in those objects
- Calling an object's methods
- Converting objects and other types of data from one class to another

Creating New Objects

When you write a Java program, you define a set of classes. As you learned on Day 2, "Object-Oriented Programming," classes are templates that are used to create objects. These objects, which are also called instances, are self-contained elements of a program that contain related features and data. For the most part, you merely use the class to create instances and then work with those instances. In this section, therefore, you learn how to create a new object from any given class.

Remember strings from yesterday? You learned that using a *string literal* (a series of characters enclosed in double quotation marks) creates a new instance of the class `String` with the value of that string.

The `String` class is unusual in that respect. Although it's a class, there's an easy way to create instances of that class using a literal. To create instances of other classes, the `new` operator is used.

 Note
> What about the literals for numbers and characters—don't they create objects, too? Actually, they don't. The primitive data types for numbers and characters create numbers and characters, but for efficiency, they actually aren't objects. You can put object wrappers around them if you need to treat them like objects (which you learn to do on Day 6, "Creating Classes and Methods").

Using new

To create a new object, you use the `new` operator with the name of the class you want to create an instance of, followed by parentheses:

```
String name = new String();
URL address = new URL("http://www.prefect.com");
VolcanoRobot robbie = new VolcanoRobot();
```

The parentheses are important; don't leave them off. The parentheses can be empty, in which case the most simple, basic object is created, or the parentheses can contain arguments that determine the initial values of instance variables or other initial qualities of that object.

The following examples show objects being created with arguments:

```
Random seed = new Random(6068430714);

Point pt = new Point(0,0);
```

The number and type of arguments you can use inside the parentheses with `new` are defined by the class itself using a special method called a *constructor.* (You learn more about constructors later today.) If you try to create a new instance of a class with the wrong number or type of arguments (or if you give it no arguments and it needs some), you get an error when you try to compile your Java program.

Here's an example of creating different types of objects using different numbers and types of arguments: the StringTokenizer class, part of the java.util package, divides a string into a series of shorter strings called *tokens*.

A string is divided into tokens by using some kind of character or characters as a delimiter. For example, the text "02/20/67" could be divided into three tokens—02, 20, and 67—using the slash character ("/") as a delimiter.

Listing 4.1 is a Java program that creates StringTokenizer objects using new in two different ways and displays each token the objects contain.

LISTING 4.1   The Full Text of ShowTokens.java

```
 1: import java.util.StringTokenizer;
 2:
 3: class ShowTokens {
 4:
 5:     public static void main(String[] arguments) {
 6:         StringTokenizer st1, st2;
 7:
 8:         String quote1 = "VIZY 3 -1/16";
 9:         st1 = new StringTokenizer(quote1);
10:         System.out.println("Token 1: " + st1.nextToken());
11:         System.out.println("Token 2: " + st1.nextToken());
12:         System.out.println("Token 3: " + st1.nextToken());
13:
14:         String quote2 = "NPLI@9 27/32@3/32";
15:         st2 = new StringTokenizer(quote2, "@");
16:         System.out.println("\nToken 1: " + st2.nextToken());
17:         System.out.println("Token 2: " + st2.nextToken());
18:         System.out.println("Token 3: " + st2.nextToken());
19:     }
20: }
```

4

When you compile and run the program, the output should resemble the following:

```
Token 1: VIZY
Token 2: 3
Token 3: -1/16

Token 1: NPLI
Token 2: 9 27/32
Token 3: 3/32
```

In this example, two different StringTokenizer objects are created using different arguments to the constructor listed after new.

The first instance (line 9) uses new StringTokenizer() with one argument, a String object named quote1. This creates a StringTokenizer object that uses the default delimiters: black spaces, tab, newline, carriage return, or formfeed characters.

If any of these characters is contained in the string, it is used to divide the tokens. Because the quote1 string contains spaces, these are used as delimiters dividing each token. Lines 10–12 display the values of all three tokens: VIZY, 3, and -1/16.

The second StringTokenizer object in this example has two arguments when it is constructed in line 14: a String object named quote2 and an at-sign character ("@"). This second argument indicates that the "@" character should be used as the delimiter between tokens. The StringTokenizer object created in line 15 contains three tokens: NPLI, 9 27/32, and 3/32.

What new Does

Several things happen when you use the new operator: The new instance of the given class is created, memory is allocated for it, and a special method defined in the given class is called. This special method is called a constructor.

NEW TERM   *Constructors* are special methods for creating and initializing new instances of classes. Constructors initialize the new object and its variables, create any other objects that the object needs, and perform any other operations that the object needs to initialize itself.

Multiple constructor definitions in a class each can have a different number or type of arguments. When you use new, you can specify different arguments in the argument list, and the correct constructor for those arguments will be called. Multiple constructor definitions are what enabled the Random() class in the previous example to accomplish different things with the different uses of the new operator. When you create your own classes, you can define as many constructors as you need to implement the behavior of the class.

A Note on Memory Management

If you are familiar with other object-oriented programming languages, you might wonder whether the new statement has an opposite that destroys an object when it is no longer needed.

Memory management in Java is dynamic and automatic. When you create a new object, Java automatically allocates the right amount of memory for that object. You don't have to allocate any memory for objects explicitly. Java does it for you.

Because Java memory management is automatic, you do not need to deallocate the memory that object uses when you're done using the object. Under most circumstances, when you are finished with an object you have created, Java will be able to determine that the object no longer has any live references to it. (In other words, the object won't be assigned to any variables still in use or stored in any arrays.)

As a program runs, Java periodically looks for unused objects and reclaims the memory that those objects are using. This process is called *garbage collection*, and it's entirely automatic. You don't have to explicitly free the memory taken up by an object—you just have to make sure you're not still holding onto an object you want to get rid of.

Accessing and Setting Class and Instance Variables

At this point, you could create your own object with class and instance variables defined in it—but how do you work with those variables? Easy! Class and instance variables are used in largely the same manner as the local variables you learned about yesterday. You can use them in expressions, assign values to them in statements, and the like. You just refer to them slightly differently than you refer to regular variables in your code.

4

Getting Values

To get to the value of an instance variable, you use dot notation. With dot notation, an instance or class variable name has two parts: a reference to an object or class on the left side of the dot and a variable on the right side of the dot.

NEW TERM *Dot notation* is a way to refer to an object's instance variables and methods using a dot (.) operator.

For example, if you have an object assigned to the variable `myCustomer` and that object has a variable called `orderTotal`, you refer to that variable's value like this:

```
myCustomer.orderTotal;
```

This form of accessing variables is an expression (that is, it returns a value), and both sides of the dot also are expressions. That means you can nest instance variable access. If the `orderTotal` instance variable itself holds an object, and that object has its own instance variable called `layaway`, you could refer to it like this:

```
myCustomer.orderTotal.layaway;
```

Dot expressions are evaluated from left to right, so you start with `myCustomer`'s variable `orderTotal`, which points to another object with the variable `layaway`. You end up with the value of that `layaway` variable.

Changing Values

Assigning a value to that variable is equally easy—just tack on an assignment operator to the right side of the expression:

```
myCustomer.orderTotal.layaway = true;
```

This example sets the value of the layaway variable to true.

Listing 4.2 is an example of a program that tests and modifies the instance variables in a Point object. Point is part of the java.awt package and refers to a coordinate point with x and y values.

LISTING 4.2   The Full Text of SetPoints.java

```
 1: import java.awt.Point;
 2:
 3: class SetPoints {
 4:
 5: public static void main(String[] arguments) {
 6:     Point location = new Point(4, 13);
 7:
 8:     System.out.println("Starting location:");
 9:     System.out.println("X equals " + location.x);
10:     System.out.println("Y equals " + location.y);
11:
12:     System.out.println("\nMoving to (7, 6)");
13:     location.x = 7;
14:     location.y = 6;
15:
16:     System.out.println("\nEnding location:");
17:     System.out.println("X equals " + location.x);
18:     System.out.println("Y equals " + location.y);
19:     }
20: }
```

When you run this application, the output should be the following:

```
Starting location:
X equals 4
Y equals 13

Moving to (7, 6)

Ending location:
X equals 7
Y equals 6
```

In this example, you first create an instance of `Point` where x equals 4 and y equals 13 (line 6). Lines 9 and 10 display these individual values using dot notation. Lines 13 and 14 change the values of x to 7 and y to 6, respectively. Finally, lines 17 and 18 display the values of x and y again to show how they have changed.

Class Variables

Class variables, as you learned, are variables that are defined and stored in the class itself. Their values apply to the class and all its instances.

With instance variables, each new instance of the class gets a new copy of the instance variables that the class defines. Each instance then can change the values of those instance variables without affecting any other instances. With class variables, only one copy of that variable exists. Changing the value of that variable changes it for all instances of that class.

You define class variables by including the `static` keyword before the variable itself. For example, consider the following partial class definition:

```
class FamilyMember {
    static String surname = "Mendoza";
    String name;
    int age;
}
```

Instances of the class `FamilyMember` each have their own values for `name` and `age`. But the class variable `surname` has only one value for all family members: `"Mendoza"`. Change the value of `surname` and all instances of `FamilyMember` are affected.

 Note
> Calling these `static` variables refers to one of the meanings for the word *static*: fixed in one place. If a class has a `static` variable, every object of that class has the same value for that variable.

To access class variables, you use the same dot notation used with instance variables. To retrieve or change the value of the class variable, you can use either the instance or the name of the class on the left side of the dot. Both lines of output in this example display the same value:

```
FamilyMember dad = new FamilyMember();
System.out.println("Family's surname is: " + dad.surname);
System.out.println("Family's surname is: " + FamilyMember.surname);
```

Because you can use an instance to change the value of a class variable, it's easy to become confused about class variables and where their values are coming from—remember that the value of a class variable affects all its instances. For this reason, it's a good idea to use the name of the class when you refer to a class variable. It makes your code easier to read and makes strange results easier to debug.

Calling Methods

Calling a method in an object is similar to referring to its instance variables: Dot notation is used. The object whose method you're calling is on the left side of the dot, and the name of the method and its arguments are on the right side of the dot:

```
myCustomer.addToOrder(itemNumber, price, quantity);
```

Note that all methods must have parentheses after them, even if the method takes no arguments:

```
myCustomer.cancelAllOrders();
```

Listing 4.3 shows an example of calling some methods defined in the String class. Strings include methods for string tests and modification, similar to what you would expect in a string library in other languages.

LISTING 4.3   The Full Text of CheckString.java

```
 1: class CheckString {
 2:
 3:     public static void main(String[] arguments) {
 4:         String str = "Nobody ever went broke by buying IBM";
 5:         System.out.println("The string is: " + str);
 6:         System.out.println("Length of this string: "
 7:             + str.length());
 8:         System.out.println("The character at position 5: "
 9:             + str.charAt(5));
10:         System.out.println("The substring from 26 to 32: "
11:             + str.substring(26, 32));
12:         System.out.println("The index of the character v: "
13:             + str.indexOf('v'));
14:         System.out.println("The index of the beginning of the "
15:             + "substring \"IBM\": " + str.indexOf("IBM"));
16:         System.out.println("The string in upper case: "
17:             + str.toUpperCase());
18:     }
19: }
```

The following is displayed on your system's standard output device when you run the program:

```
The string is: Nobody ever went broke by buying IBM
Length of this string: 36
The character at position 5: y
The substring from 26 to 32: buying
The index of the character v: 8
The index of the beginning of the substring "IBM": 33
The string in upper case: NOBODY EVER WENT BROKE BY BUYING IBM
```

In line 4, you create a new instance of String by using a string literal. The remainder of the program simply calls different string methods to do different operations on that string:

- Line 5 prints the value of the string you created in line 4: "Nobody ever went broke by buying IBM".

- Line 7 calls the length() method in the new String object. This string has 36 characters.

- Line 9 calls the charAt() method, which returns the character at the given position in the string. Note that string positions start at position 0 rather than 1, so the character at position 5 is y.

- Line 11 calls the substring() method, which takes two integers indicating a range and returns the substring with those starting and ending points. The substring() method also can be called with only one argument, which returns the substring from that position to the end of the string.

- Line 13 calls the indexOf() method, which returns the position of the first instance of the given character (here, 'v'). Character literals are surrounded by single quotation marks—if double quotation marks surrounded the v in line 13, the literal would be considered a String.

- Line 15 shows a different use of the indexOf() method, which takes a string argument and returns the index of the beginning of that string.

- Line 17 uses the toUpperCase() method to return a copy of the string in all uppercase.

Nesting Method Calls

A method can return a reference to an object, a primitive data type, or no value at all. In the CheckString program, all the methods called on the String object str returned values that were displayed—for example, the charAt() method returned a character at a specified position in the string.

The value returned by a method also can be stored in a variable:

```
String label = "From";
String upper = label.toUpperCase();
```

In the preceding example, the `String` object `upper` contains the value returned by calling `label.toUpperCase()`—the text "From", an uppercase version of "From" .

If the method returns an object, you can call the methods of that object in the same statement. This makes it possible for you to nest methods as you would variables.

Earlier today, you saw an example of a method called with no arguments:

```
myCustomer.cancelAllOrders();
```

If the `cancelAllOrders()` method returns an object, you can call methods of that object in the same statement:

```
myCustomer.cancelAllOrders().talkToManager();
```

This statement calls the `talkToManager()` method, which is defined in the object returned by the `cancelAllOrders()` method of the `myCustomer` object.

You can combine nested method calls and instance variable references as well. In the next example, the `putOnLayaway()` method is defined in the object stored by the `orderTotal` instance variable, which itself is part of the `myCustomer` object:

```
myCustomer.orderTotal.putOnLayaway(itemNumber, price, quantity);
```

`System.out.println()`, the method you've been using in all program examples to display information, is an example of nesting variables and methods.

The `System` class, part of the `java.lang` package, describes behavior specific to the system on which Java is running. `System.out` is a class variable that contains an instance of the class `PrintStream`. This `PrintStream` object represents the standard output of the system, which is normally the screen, but can be redirected to a monitor or file. `PrintStream` objects have a `println()` method that sends a string to that output stream.

Class Methods

Class methods, like class variables, apply to the class as a whole and not to its instances. Class methods commonly are used for general utility methods that might not operate directly on an instance of that class but fit with that class conceptually. For example, the `String` class contains a class method called `valueOf()` that can take one of many different types of arguments (integers, Booleans, other objects, and so on). The `valueOf()` method then returns a new instance of `String` containing the string value of the argument. This method doesn't operate directly on an existing instance of `String`, but getting a string from another object or data type is definitely a String-like operation, and it makes sense to define it in the String class.

Class methods also can be useful for gathering general methods together in one place (the class). For example, the Math class, defined in the java.lang package, contains a large set of mathematical operations as class methods—there are no instances of the class Math, but you still can use its methods with numeric or Boolean arguments. For example, the class method Math.max() takes two arguments and returns the larger of the two. You don't need to create a new instance of Math—it can be called anywhere you need it, as in the following:

```
int maximumPrice = Math.max(firstPrice, secondPrice);
```

Dot notation is used to call a class method. As with class variables, you can use either an instance of the class or the class itself on the left side of the dot. However, for the same reasons noted in the discussion on class variables, using the name of the class makes your code easier to read. The last two lines in this example produce the same result—the string 5:

```
String s, s2;
s = "item";
s2 = s.valueOf(5);
s2 = String.valueOf(5);
```

References to Objects

As you work with objects, an important thing to understand is the use of references.

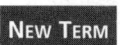 A *reference* is an address that indicates where an object's variables and methods are stored.

You aren't actually using objects when you assign an object to a variable or pass an object to a method as an argument. You aren't even using copies of the objects. Instead, you're using references to those objects.

To better illustrate the difference, Listing 4.4 shows how references work.

LISTING 4.4   The Full Text of ReferencesTest.java

```
1: import java.awt.Point;
2:
3: class ReferencesTest {
4:     public static void main(String[] arguments) {
5:         Point pt1, pt2;
6:         pt1 = new Point(100, 100);
```

LISTING 4.4   continued

```
 7:            pt2 = pt1;
 8:
 9:            pt1.x = 200;
10:            pt1.y = 200;
11:            System.out.println("Point1: " + pt1.x + ", " + pt1.y);
12:            System.out.println("Point2: " + pt2.x + ", " + pt2.y);
13:       }
14: }
```

The following is this program's output:

```
Point1: 200, 200
Point2: 200, 200
```

The following takes place in the first part of this program:

- Line 5   Two Point variables are created.
- Line 6   A new Point object is assigned to pt1.
- Line 7   The value of pt1 is assigned to pt2.

Lines 9–12 are the tricky part. The x and y variables of pt1 are both set to 200, and then all variables of pt1 and pt2 are displayed onscreen.

You might expect pt1 and pt2 to have different values. However, the output shows this is not the case. As you can see, the x and y variables of pt2 also were changed, even though nothing in the program explicitly changes them.

This happens because line 7 creates a reference from pt2 to pt1, instead of creating pt2 as a new object copied from pt1.

pt2 is a reference to the same object as pt1; this is shown in Figure 4.1. Either variable can be used to refer to the object or to change its variables.

If you wanted pt1 and pt2 to refer to separate objects, separate new Point() statements could be used on lines 6 and 7 to create separate objects, as shown in the following:

```
pt1 = new Point(100, 100);
pt2 = new Point(100, 100);
```

The use of references in Java becomes particularly important when arguments are passed to methods. You learn more about this later today.

Note   There are no explicit pointers or pointer arithmetic in Java as there are in C and C++. However, by using references and Java arrays, most pointer capabilities are duplicated without many of their drawbacks.

FIGURE 4.1

References to objects.

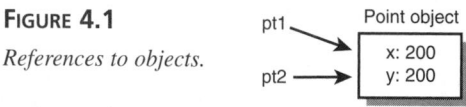

Casting and Converting Objects and Primitive Types

One thing you discover quickly about Java is how finicky it is about the information it will handle. Like Morris, the perpetually dissatisfied cat on the 9-Lives cat food commercials, Java expects things to be a certain way and won't put up with alternatives.

When you are sending arguments to methods or using variables in expressions, you must use variables of the right data types. If a method requires an `int`, the Java compiler responds with an error if you try to send a `float` value to the method. Likewise, if you're setting up one variable with the value of another, they must be of the same type.

Note

There is one area where Java's compiler is decidedly un-Morrislike: `Strings`. String handling in `println()` methods, assignment statements, and method arguments is simplified with the use of the concatenation operator (+). If any variable in a group of concatenated variables is a string, Java treats the whole thing as a `String`. This makes the following possible:

```
float gpa = 2.25F;
System.out.println("Honest, dad, my GPA is a " + (gpa+1.5));
```

Sometimes you'll have a value in your Java program that isn't the right type for what you need. It might be the wrong class, or the wrong data type—such as a `float` when you need an `int`.

You use casting to convert a value from one type to another.

NEW TERM   *Casting* is the process of producing a new value that has a different type than its source. The meaning is similar to acting, where a character on a TV show can be recast with another actor after a salary dispute or an unfortunate public lewdness arrest.

Although the concept of casting is reasonably simple, the usage is complicated by the fact that Java has both primitive types (such as `int`, `float`, and `boolean`), and object types (`String`, `Point`, `ZipFile`, and the like). There are three forms of casts and conversions to talk about in this section:

- Casting between primitive types, such as int to float or float to double
- Casting from an instance of a class to an instance of another class
- Casting primitive types to objects and then extracting primitive values from those objects

When discussing casting, it can be easier to think in terms of sources and destinations. The source is the variable being cast into another type. The destination is the result.

Casting Primitive Types

Casting between primitive types enables you to convert the value of one type to another primitive type. It most commonly occurs with the numeric types, and there's one primitive type that can never be used in a cast. Boolean values must be either true or false and cannot be used in a casting operation.

In many casts between primitive types, the destination can hold larger values than the source, so the value is converted easily. An example would be casting a byte into an int. Because a byte holds values from –128 to 127 and an int holds from –2100000 to 2100000, there's more than enough room to cast a byte to an int.

You can often automatically use a byte or a char as an int; you can use an int as a long, an int as a float, or anything as a double. In most cases, because the larger type provides more precision than the smaller, no loss of information occurs as a result. The exception is casting integers to floating-point values—casting an int or a long to a float, or a long to a double can cause some loss of precision.

 Note

> A character can be used as an int because each character has a corresponding numeric code that represents its position in the character set. If the variable i has the value 65, the cast (char)i produces the character value 'A'. The numeric code associated with a capital A is 65, according to the ASCII character set, and Java adopted this as part of its character support.

You must use an explicit cast to convert a value in a large type to a smaller type because converting that value might result in a loss of precision. Explicit casts take the following form:

(*typename*)*value*

In the preceding example, *typename* is the name of the data type you're converting to, such as short, int, or float. *value* is an expression that results in the value of the source type. For example, the value of x is divided by the value of y and the result is cast to an int in the following expression:

```
(int)(x / y);
```

Note that because the precedence of casting is higher than that of arithmetic, you have to use parentheses here—otherwise, the value of x would be cast to an int first and then divided by y, which could easily produce a different result.

Casting Objects

Instances of classes also can be cast to instances of other classes, with one restriction: The source and destination classes must be related by inheritance—one class must be a subclass of the other.

Analogous to converting a primitive value to a larger type, some objects might not need to be cast explicitly. In particular, because subclasses contain all the same information as their superclass, you can use an instance of a subclass anywhere a superclass is expected.

For example, consider a method that takes two arguments: one of type Object and another of type Window. You can pass an instance of any class for the Object argument because all Java classes are subclasses of Object. For the Window argument, you can pass in its subclasses such as Dialog, FileDialog, and Frame.

This is true anywhere in a program—not just inside method calls. If you had a variable defined as class Window, you could assign objects of that class or any of its subclasses to that variable without casting.

This is true in the reverse, and you can use a superclass when a subclass is expected. There is a catch, however: Because subclasses contain more behavior than their superclasses, there's a loss in precision involved. Those superclass objects might not have all the behavior needed to act in place of a subclass object. For example, if you have an operation that calls methods in objects of the class Integer, using an object of class Number won't include many methods specified in Integer. Errors occur if you try to call methods that the destination object doesn't have.

To use superclass objects where subclass objects are expected, you must cast them explicitly. You won't lose any information in the cast, but you gain all the methods and variables that the subclass defines. To cast an object to another class, you use the same operation that you used for primitive types:

```
(classname)object
```

In this case, *classname* is the name of the destination class and *object* is a reference to the source object. Note that casting creates a reference to the old object of the type *classname*; the old object continues to exist as it did before.

The following example casts an instance of the class VicePresident to an instance of the class Employee; VicePresident is a subclass of Employee with more information to define that the VicePresident has executive washroom privileges:

```
Employee emp = new Employee();
VicePresident veep = new VicePresident();
emp = veep; // no cast needed for upward use
veep = (VicePresident)emp; // must cast explicitly
```

Casting one object is necessary whenever you use Java2D graphics operations. You must cast a Graphics object to a Graphics2D object before you can draw onscreen. The following example uses a Graphics object called screen to create a new Graphics2D object called screen2D:

```
Graphics2D screen2D = (Graphics2D)screen;
```

Graphics2D is a subclass of Graphics, and both are in the java.awt package. You explore the subject fully during Day 12, "Color, Fonts, and Graphics."

In addition to casting objects to classes, you also can cast objects to interfaces—but only if that object's class or one of its superclasses actually implements the interface. Casting an object to an interface means that you can call one of that interface's methods even if that object's class does not actually implement that interface.

Converting Primitive Types to Objects and Vice Versa

One thing you can't do under any circumstance is cast from an object to a primitive data type, or vice versa. Primitive types and objects are very different things in Java and you can't automatically cast between the two or use them interchangeably.

As an alternative, the java.lang package includes classes that correspond to each primitive data type: Float, Boolean, Byte and so on. Most of these classes have the same name as the data type, except that the class names begin with a capital letter (Short instead of short, Double instead of double, and so on). Also, two classes have names that differ from the corresponding data type—Character is used for char variables and Integer for int variables.

Java treats the data types and their class versions very differently, and a program won't compile successfully if you use one when the other is expected.

Using the classes that correspond with each primitive type, you can create an object that holds the same value. The following statement creates an instance of the Integer class with the integer value 7801:

```
Integer dataCount = new Integer(7801);
```

After you have an object created in this manner, you can use it as you would any object (although you cannot change its value). When you want to use that value again as a primitive value, there are methods for that as well. For example, if you wanted to get an `int` value from a `dataCount` object, the following statement would be used:

```
int newCount = dataCount.intValue(); // returns 7801
```

A common translation you need in programs is converting a `String` to a numeric type, such as an integer. When you need an `int` as the result, this can be done by using the `parseInt()` class method of the `Integer` class. The `String` to convert is the only argument sent to the method, as in the following example:

```
String pennsylvania = "65000";
int penn = Integer.parseInt(pennsylvania);
```

The Java API documentation includes details on these classes. You can find these HTML pages in the Documentation section of Sun's Java Web site:

```
http://java.sun.com
```

Note

> The following classes can be used to work with objects instead of primitive data types: Boolean, Byte, Character, Double, Float, Integer, Long, Short, and Void.

4

Comparing Object Values and Classes

In addition to casting, there are three other common tasks you will perform often on objects:

- Comparing objects
- Finding out the class of any given object
- Testing to see whether an object is an instance of a given class

Comparing Objects

Yesterday you learned about operators for comparing values: equal, not equal, less than, and so on. Most of these operators work only on primitive types, not on objects. If you try to use other values as operands, the Java compiler produces errors.

The exceptions to this rule are the operators for equality: == (equal) and != (not equal). When used with objects, these operators don't do what you might first expect. Instead of checking whether one object has the same value as the other object, they determine whether both sides of the operator refer to the same object.

To compare instances of a class and have meaningful results, you must implement special methods in your class and call those methods.

A good example of this is the String class. It is possible to have two different String objects that contain the same values. If you used the == operator to compare these objects, however, they would be considered unequal. Although their contents match, they are not the same object.

To see whether two String objects have matching values, a method of the class called equals() is used. The method tests each character in the string and returns true if the two strings have the same values. Listing 4.5 illustrates this.

LISTING 4.5   The Full Text of EqualsTest.java

```
 1: class EqualsTest {
 2:     public static void main(String[] arguments) {
 3:         String str1, str2;
 4:         str1 = "Free the bound periodicals.";
 5:         str2 = str1;
 6:
 7:         System.out.println("String1: " + str1);
 8:         System.out.println("String2: " + str2);
 9:         System.out.println("Same object? " + (str1 == str2));
10:
11:         str2 = new String(str1);
12:
13:         System.out.println("String1: " + str1);
14:         System.out.println("String2: " + str2);
15:         System.out.println("Same object? " + (str1 == str2));
16:         System.out.println("Same value? " + str1.equals(str2));
17:     }
18: }
```

This program's output is as follows:

```
String1: Free the bound periodicals.
String2: Free the bound periodicals.
Same object? true
String1: Free the bound periodicals.
String2: Free the bound periodicals.
Same object? false
Same value? true
```

The first part of this program (lines 3–5) declares two variables (str1 and str2), assigns the literal `Free the bound periodicals.` to str1, and then assigns that value to str2. As you learned earlier, str1 and str2 now point to the same object, and the equality test at line 9 proves that.

In the second part of this program, you create a new String object with the same value as str1 and assign str2 to that new String object. Now you have two different string objects in str1 and str2, both with the same value. Testing them to see whether they're the same object by using the == operator (line 15) returns the expected answer (false— they are not the same object in memory). Testing them using the equals() method in line 16 also returns the expected answer (true—they have the same values).

Note

> Why can't you just use another literal when you change str2, rather than using new? String literals are optimized in Java—if you create a string using a literal and then use another literal with the same characters, Java knows enough to give you the first String object back. Both strings are the same objects—you have to go out of your way to create two separate objects.

4

Determining the Class of an Object

Want to find out what an object's class is? Here's the way to do it for an object assigned to the variable key:

```
String name = key.getClass().getName();
```

What does this do? The getClass() method is defined in the Object class, and therefore is available for all objects. The result of that method is a Class object (where Class is itself a class), which has a method called getName(). getName() returns a string representing the name of the class.

Another test that might be useful is the instanceof operator. instanceof has two operands: a reference to an object on the left and a class name on the right. The expression returns true or false based on whether the object is an instance of the named class or any of that class's subclasses:

```
"Texas" instanceof String // true
Point pt = new Point(10, 10);
pt instanceof String // false
```

The instanceof operator can also be used for interfaces; if an object implements an interface, the instanceof operator with that interface name on the right side returns true.

Summary

Now that you have spent two days exploring how object-oriented programming is implemented in Java, you're in a better position to decide how useful it can be in your own programming.

If you are a "glass is half empty" person, object-oriented programming is a level of abstraction that gets in the way of what you're trying to use a programming language for. You learn more about why OOP is thoroughly ingrained in Java in the coming chapters.

If you are a "glass is half full" person, object-oriented programming is worth using because of the benefits it offers: improved reliability, reusability, and maintenance.

Today you learned how to deal with objects: creating them, reading their values and changing them, and calling their methods. You also learned how to cast objects from one class to another, or from a data type to a class.

At this point, you possess the skills to handle most simple tasks in the Java language. All that remains are arrays, conditionals, and loops (which are covered tomorrow), and how to define and use classes on Day 6, "Creating Classes and Methods."

Q&A

Q I'm confused about the differences between objects and the primitive data types, such as `int` and `boolean`.

A The primitive types (`byte`, `short`, `int`, `long`, `float`, `double`, `boolean`, and `char`) represent the smallest things in the language. They are not objects, although in many ways they can be handled like objects: They can be assigned to variables and passed in and out of methods. Most of the operations that work exclusively on objects, however, will not work with primitive types.

Objects are instances of classes and, as such, are usually much more complex data types than simple numbers and characters, often containing numbers and characters as instance or class variables.

Q The `length()` and `charAt()` methods in Listing 4.3 don't appear to make sense. If `length()` says that a string is 36 characters long, shouldn't the characters be numbered from 1 to 36 when `charAt()` is used to display characters in the string?

A The two methods look at strings a little differently. The `length()` method counts the characters in the string, with the first character counting as 1, the second as 2, and so on. The string `"Charlie Brown"` has 13 characters. The `charAt()` method considers the first character in the string to be located at position number 0. This is the same numbering system used with array elements in Java. The string `Charlie Brown` has characters ranging from position 0—the letter `"C"`—to position 12—the letter `"n"`.

Q **No pointers in Java? If you don't have pointers, how are you supposed to do something like linked lists, where you have a pointer from one nose to another so you can traverse them?**

A It's untrue to say Java has no pointers at all—it has no explicit pointers. Object references are, effectively, pointers. To create something like a linked list, you would create a class called `Node`, which would have an instance variable also of type `Node`. To link together node objects, assign a node object to the instance variable of the object immediately before it in the list. Because object references are pointers, linked lists set up this way behave as you would expect them to.

Quiz

Review today's material by taking this three-question quiz.

Questions

1. What operator is used to call an object's constructor method and create a new object?

    (a) `+`

    (b) `new`

    (c) `instanceof`

2. What kind of methods apply to all objects of a class rather than an individual object?

    (a) Universal methods

    (b) Instance methods

    (c) Class methods

3. If you have a program with objects named `obj1` and `obj2`, what happens when you use the statement `obj2 = obj1`?

    (a) The instance variables in `obj2` are given the same values as `obj1`.

    (b) `obj2` and `obj1` are considered to be the same object.

    (c) Neither (a) nor (b).

4

Answers

1. b.

2. c.

3. b. The = operator does not copy values from one object to another. Instead, it makes both variables refer to the same objectc

Exercises

To extend your knowledge of the subjects covered today, try the following exercises:

- Create a program that turns a birthday in MM/DD/YYYY format (such as 4/23/2000) into three individual strings.

- Create a class with instance variables for `height`, `weight`, and `depth`, making each an integer. Create a Java application that uses your new class, sets each of these values in an object, and displays the values.

Where applicable, exercise solutions are offered on the book's Web site at `http://www.java21pro.com`.

DAY 5

Lists, Logic, and Loops

If you wrote a Java program with what you know so far, it would likely be a little dull. If you wrote a Java program with what you know so far, it would likely be a little dull. That last sentence isn't repeated twice because of an editorial mistake. It is a demonstration of how easy computers make it to repeat the same thing over and over. You learn today how to make part of a Java program repeat itself by using loops.

Additionally, you learn how to make a program decide whether to do something based on logic. (Perhaps a computer would decide it isn't logical to repeat the same sentence twice in a row in a book.)

You also learn how to organize groups of the same class or data type into lists called arrays.

First up on today's list is arrays. First up on today's list is arrays.

Arrays

At this point, you have dealt with only a few variables in each Java program. It's manageable to use individual variables to store information in some cases.

However, what if you had 20 items of related information to keep track of? You could create 20 different variables and set up their initial values, but that becomes progressively more cumbersome as you deal with larger amounts of information. What if there were 100 items, or even 1,000?

Arrays are a way to store a list of items that have the same primitive data type, the same class, or a common parent class. Each item on the list goes into its own slot, which is numbered, so you can access the information easily.

Arrays can contain any type of information that is stored in a variable, but once the array is created, you can use it for that information type only. For example, you can have an array of integers, an array of String objects, or an array of arrays, but you can't have an array that contains both String objects and integers.

Java implements arrays differently than some other languages do—as objects that can be treated just like other objects.

To create an array in Java, you must do the following:

1. Declare a variable to hold the array.

2. Create a new array object and assign it to the array variable.

3. Store information in that array.

Declaring Array Variables

The first step in array creation is to declare a variable that will hold the array. Array variables indicate the object or data type that the array will hold and the name of the array. To differentiate from regular variable declarations, a pair of empty brackets ([ ]) is added to the object or data type, or to the variable name.

The following statements are examples of array variable declarations:

```
String[] requests;
```

```
Point[] targets;
```

```
float[] donations;
```

You also can declare an array by putting the brackets after the variable name instead of the information type, as in the following statements:

```
String requests[];
```

```
Point targets[];
```

```
float donations[];
```

> The choice of which style to use is a matter of personal preference. The sample programs in this book place the brackets after the information type rather than the variable name.

Creating Array Objects

After you declare the array variable, the next step is to create an array object and assign it to that variable. To do this:

- Use the `new` operator
- Initialize the contents of the array directly

Because arrays are objects in Java, you can use the `new` operator to create a new instance of an array, as in the following statement:

```
String[] players = new String[10];
```

This statement creates a new array of strings with 10 slots that can contain `String` objects. When you create an array object by using `new`, you must indicate how many slots the array will hold. This statement does not put actual `String` objects in the slots—you must do that later.

Array objects can contain primitive types such as integers or Booleans, just as they can contain objects:

```
int[] temps = new int[99];
```

When you create an array object using `new`, all its slots automatically are given an initial value (0 for numeric arrays, `false` for Booleans, `'\0'` for character arrays, and `null` for objects).

> The Java keyword `null` refers to a `null` object (and can be used for any object reference). It is not equivalent to zero or the `'\0'` character as the `NULL` constant is in C.

5

You also can create and initialize an array at the same time by enclosing the elements of the array inside braces, separated by commas:

```
Point[] markup = { new Point(1,5), new Point(3,3), new Point(2,3) };
```

Each of the elements inside the braces must be the same type as the variable that holds the array. When you create an array with initial values in this manner, the array is the same size as the number of elements you have included within the braces. The preceding example creates an array of `Point` objects named `markup` that contains three elements.

Because `String` objects can be created and initialized without the `new` operator, you can do the same when creating an array of strings:

```
String[] titles = { "Mr.", "Mrs.", "Ms.", "Miss", "Dr." };
```

The preceding statement creates a five-element array of `String` objects named `titles`.

Accessing Array Elements

After you have an array with initial values, you can retrieve, change, and test the values in each slot of that array. The value in a slot is accessed with the array name followed by a subscript enclosed within square brackets. This name and subscript can be put into expressions, as in the following:

```
testScore[40] = 920;
```

The preceding statement sets the 40th element of the `testScore` array to a value of `920`. The `testScore` part of this expression is a variable holding an array object, although it also can be an expression that results in an array. The subscript expression specifies the slot to access within the array.

The first element of an array has a subscript of `0` rather than `1`, so an array with 12 elements has array slots that are accessed by using subscripts `0` through `11`.

All array subscripts are checked to make sure that they are inside the array's boundaries, as specified when the array was created. In Java, it is impossible to access or assign a value to an array slot outside the array's boundaries, which avoids problems that result from overrunning the bounds of an array in C-like languages. Note the following two statements:

```
float[] rating = new float[20];

rating[20] = 3.22F;
```

A program with the preceding two lines of code produces a compilation error when `rating[20]` is used. The error occurs because the `rating` array does not have a slot `20`—it has 20 slots that begin at `0` and end at `19`. The Java compiler would make note of this by displaying an `ArrayIndexOutOfBoundsException` error.

The Java interpreter produces an error if the array subscript is calculated when the program is running and the subscript ends up outside the array's boundaries. To be technically correct, the interpreter flags this error by generating an exception. You learn more about exceptions and how to use them on Day 16, "Error Handling and Security."

One way to keep from accidentally overrunning the end of an array in your programs is to use the `length` instance variable, which is part of all array objects, regardless of type. The `length` variable contains the number of elements in the array. The following statement displays the number of elements in the `rating` object:

```
System.out.println("Elements: " + rating.length);
```

Changing Array Elements

As you saw in the previous examples, you can assign a value to a specific slot in an array by putting an assignment statement after the array name and subscript, as in the following:

```
temperature[4] = 85;
```

```
day[0] = "Sunday";
```

```
manager[2] = manager[0];
```

An important thing to note is that an array of objects in Java is an array of references to those objects. When you assign a value to a slot in that kind of array, you are creating a reference to that object. When you move values around inside arrays, you are reassigning the reference rather than copying a value from one slot to another. Arrays of a primitive data type such as `int` or `float` do copy the values from one slot to another, as do elements of a `String` array, even though they are objects.

Arrays are reasonably simple to create and modify, but they provide an enormous amount of functionality for Java. Listing 5.1 shows a simple program that creates, initializes, and displays elements of three arrays.

5

LISTING 5.1   The Full Text of `HalfDollars.java`

```
 1: class HalfDollars {
 2:     public static void main(String[] arguments) {
 3:         int[] denver = { 15000006, 18810000, 20752110 };
 4:         int[] philadelphia = new int[denver.length];
 5:         int[] total = new int[denver.length];
 6:         int average;
 7:
 8:         philadelphia[0] = 15020000;
 9:         philadelphia[1] = 18708000;
10:         philadelphia[2] = 21348000;
11:
```

LISTING 5.1 continued

```
12:          total[0] = denver[0] + philadelphia[0];
13:          total[1] = denver[1] + philadelphia[1];
14:          total[2] = denver[2] + philadelphia[2];
15:          average = (total[0] + total[1] + total[2]) / 3;
16:
17:          System.out.println("1993 production: " + total[0]);
18:          System.out.println("1994 production: " + total[1]);
19:          System.out.println("1995 production: " + total[2]);
20:          System.out.println("Average production: "+ average);
21:      }
22:
```

The HalfDollars application uses three integer arrays to store production totals for U.S. half-dollar coins produced at the Denver and Philadelphia mints. The output of the program is as follows:

```
1993 production: 30020006
1994 production: 37518000
1995 production: 42100110
Average production: 36546038
```

The class that is created here, HalfDollars, has three instance variables that hold arrays of integers.

The first, which is named denver, is declared and initialized on line 3 to contain three integers: 15000006 in element 0, 18810000 in element 1, and 20752110 in element 2. These figures are the total half-dollar production at the Denver mint for three years.

The second and third instance variables, philadelphia and total, are declared in lines 4–5. The philadelphia array contains the production totals for the Philadelphia mint, and total is used to store the overall production totals.

No initial values are assigned to the slots of the philadelphia and total arrays in lines 4–5. For this reason, each element is given the default value for integers: 0.

The denver.length variable is used to give both of these arrays the same number of slots as the denver array—every array contains a length variable that you can use to keep track of the number of elements it contains.

The rest of the main() method of this application performs the following:

- Line 6 creates an integer variable called average.
- Lines 8–10 assign new values to the three elements of the philadelphia array: 15020000 in element 0, 18708000 in element 1, and 21348000 in element 2.

- Lines 12–14 assign new values to the elements of the `total` array. In line 12, `total` element `0` is given the sum of `denver` element `0` and `philadelphia` element `0`. Similar expressions are used in lines 13 and 14.

- Line 15 sets the value of the `average` variable to the average of the three `total` elements. Because `average` and the three `total` elements are integers, the average will be expressed as an integer rather than a floating-point number.

- Lines 17–20 display the values stored in the `total` array and the `average` variable, along with some explanatory text.

One last note to make about Listing 5.1 is that lines 12–14 and lines 17–19 are an inefficient way to use arrays in a program. These statements are almost identical, except for the subscripts that indicate which array element you are referring to. If the `HalfDollars` application was being used to track 100 years of production totals instead of three, your program would contain a lot of repetitive code.

Usually when dealing with arrays, you can use loops to cycle through an array's elements rather than dealing with each individually. This makes the code a lot shorter, and easier to read. When you learn about loops later today, you will see a rewrite of the current example.

Multidimensional Arrays

If you have used arrays in other languages, you might be expecting Java to support *multidimensional arrays*, which are arrays that contain more than one subscript and can store information in multiple dimensions.

A common use of a multidimensional array is to represent the data in an x,y grid of array elements.

Java does not support multidimensional arrays, but you can achieve the same functionality by declaring an array of arrays. Those arrays can also contain arrays, and so on, for as many dimensions as needed.

For example, consider a program that needs to accomplish the following tasks:

- Record an integer value each day for a year
- Organize those values by week

One way to organize this data is to create a 52-element array in which each element contains a 7-element array:

```
int[][] dayValue = new int[52][7];
```

This array of arrays contains a total of 365 integers, one for each day of the year. You could set the value for the first day of the 10th week with the following statement:

5

```
dayValue[10][1] = 14200;
```

You can use the `length` variable with these arrays as you would any other. The following statement contains a three-dimensional array of integers and displays the number of elements in each dimension:

```
int[][][] century = new int[100][52][7];
System.out.println("Elements in the first dimension: " + century.length);
System.out.println("Elements in the second dimension: " + century[0].length);
System.out.println("Elements in the third dimension: " + century[0][0].length);
```

Block Statements

Statements in Java are grouped into blocks. The beginning and ending of a block are noted with brace characters—an opening brace (`{`) for the beginning and a closing brace (`}`) for the ending.

You already have used blocks throughout the programs during the first five days. You've used them for both of the following:

- To contain the variables and methods in a class definition
- To define the statements that belong in a method

Blocks also are called *block statements* because an entire block can be used anywhere a single statement could be used (they're called *compound statements* in C and other languages). Each statement inside the block is then executed from top to bottom.

Blocks can be put inside other blocks, as you do when putting a method inside of a class definition.

An important thing to note about a block is that it creates a scope for the local variables that are created inside the block.

NEW TERM   *Scope* is the part of a program in which a variable exists and can be used. If you try to use a variable outside of its scope, an error will occur.

In Java, the scope of a variable is the block in which it was created. When you can declare and use local variables inside a block, those variables cease to exist after the block is finished executing. For example, the following `testBlock()` method contains a block:

```
void testBlock() {
    int x = 10;
    { // start of block
        int y = 40;
        y = y + x;
```

```
    } // end of block
}
```

There are two variables defined in this method: x and y. The scope of the y variable is the block it's in, and it can be used only within that block. An error would result if you tried to use the y variable in another part of the testBlock() method. The x variable was created inside the method but outside of the inner block, so it can be used anywhere in the method. You can modify the value of x anywhere within the method and this value will be retained.

Block statements usually are not used alone in a method definition, as they are in the preceding example. You use them throughout class and method definitions, as well as in the logic and looping structures you learn about next.

if Conditionals

One of the key aspects of programming is a program's capability to decide what it will do. This is handled through a special type of statement called a conditional.

NEW TERM   A *conditional* is a programming statement that is executed only if a specific condition is met.

The most basic conditional is the if keyword. The if conditional uses a Boolean expression to decide whether a statement should be executed. If the expression returns a true value, the statement is executed.

Here's a simple example that displays the message "You call that a haircut?" only on one condition: If the value of the age variable is greater than 39:

```
if (age > 39)
    System.out.println("You call that a haircut?");
```

If you want something else to happen in the case the if expression returns a false value, an optional else keyword can be used. The following example uses both if and else:

```
if (blindDateIsAttractive == true)
    restaurant = "Benihana's";
else
    restaurant = "Burritos-to-Go";
```

The if conditional executes different statements based on the result of a single Boolean test.

 **Note**

A difference between if conditionals in Java and those in C or C++ is that Java requires the test to return a Boolean value (true or false). In C, the test can return an integer.

Using `if`, you only can include a single statement as the code to execute if the test expression is true and another statement if the expression is false.

However, as you learned earlier today, a block can appear anywhere in Java that a single statement can. If you want to do more than just one thing as a result of an `if` statement, you can enclose those statements inside a block. Note the following snippet of code, which was used on Day 2, "Object-Oriented Programming":

```
if (temperature > 660) {
    status = "returning home";
    speed = 5;
}
```

The `if` statement in this example contains the test expression `temperature > 60`. If the `temperature` variable contains a value higher than `60`, the block statement is executed and two things occur:

- The status variable is given the value `returning home`.
- The `speed` variable is set to `5`.

All `if` and `else` statements use Boolean tests to determine whether statements will be executed. You can use a `boolean` variable itself for this test, as in the following:

```
if (outOfGas)
    status = "inactive";
```

The preceding example uses a `boolean` variable called `outOfGas`. It functions exactly like the following:

```
if (outOfGas == true)
    status = "inactive";
```

`switch` Conditionals

A common programming practice in any language is to test a variable against some value, and if it doesn't match, test it again against a different value, and so on. This process can become unwieldy if you're using only `if` statements, depending on how many different values you have to test. For example, you might end up with a set of `if` statements something like the following:

```
if (operation == '+')
    add(object1, object2);
else if (operation == '-')
    subtract(object1, object2);
else if (operation == '*')
    multiply(object1, object2);
```

```
else if (operation == '/')
    divide(object1, object2);
```

This use of `if` statements is called a nested `if` statement, because each `else` statement contains another `if` until all possible tests have been made.

A shorthand mechanism for nested `if` statements that you can use in some programming languages is to group tests and actions together in a single statement. In Java, you can group actions together with the `switch` statement, which behaves as it does in C. The following is an example of `switch` usage:

```
switch (grade) {
    case 'A':
        System.out.println("Great job!");
        break;
    case 'B':
        System.out.println("Good job!");
        break;
    case 'C':
        System.out.println("You can do better!");
        break;
    default:
        System.out.println("Consider cheating!");
}
```

The `switch` statement is built on a test; in the preceding example, the test is on the value of the `grade` variable, which holds a `char` value. The test variable, which can be any of the primitive types `byte`, `char`, `short`, or `int`, is compared in turn with each of the `case` values. If a match is found, the statement or statements after the test are executed.

If no match is found, the `default` statement or statements are executed. Providing a `default` statement is optional—if it is omitted and there is no match for any of the `case` statements, the `switch` statement completes without executing anything.

The Java implementation of `switch` is limited—tests and values can be only simple primitive types that are castable to `int`. You cannot use larger primitive types such as `long` or `float`, strings, or other objects within a `switch`, nor can you test for any relationship other than equality. These restrictions limit `switch` to the simplest cases. In contrast, nested `if` statements can work for any kind of test on any type.

The following is a revision of the nested `if` example shown previously. It has been rewritten as a `switch` statement:

```
switch (operation) {
    case '+':
        add(object1, object2);
        break;
```

5

```
case '*':
    subtract(object1, object2);
    break;
case '-':
    multiply(object1, object2);
    break;
case '/':
    divide(object1, object2);
    break;
}
```

There are two things to be aware of in this example: The first is that after each case, you can include a single result statement or more—you can include as many as you need. Unlike with `if`, you don't need to surround multiple statements with braces for it to work.

The second thing to note about this example is the `break` statement that is included with each `case` section. Without a `break` statement in a `case` section, after a match is made, the statements for that match and all the statements farther down the `switch` are executed until a `break` or the end of the switch is found. In some cases, this might be exactly what you want to do. However, in most cases, you should include the `break` to ensure that only the right code is executed. `break`, which you learn about in the section "Breaking Out of Loops," stops execution at the current point and jumps to the code outside of the next closing bracket (}).

One handy use of falling through without a `break` occurs when multiple values should execute the same statements. To accomplish this task, you can use multiple `case` lines with no result; the `switch` will execute the first statement that it finds. For example, in the following `switch` statement, the string x is an even number. is printed if x has the values of 2, 4, 6, or 8. All other values of x cause the string x is an odd number. to be printed.

```
switch (x) {
    case 2:
    case 4:
    case 6:
    case 8:
        System.out.println("x is an even number.");
        break;
    default: System.out.println("x is an odd number.");
}
```

In Listing 5.2, the `DayCounter` application takes two arguments, a month and a year, and displays the number of days in that month. A `switch` statement, `if` statements, and `else` statements are used.

LISTING 5.2   The Full Text of `DayCounter.java`

```
 1: class DayCounter {
 2:     public static void main(String[] arguments) {
 3:         int yearIn = 2001;
 4:         int monthIn = 2;
 5:         if (arguments.length > 0)
 6:             monthIn = Integer.parseInt(arguments[0]);
 7:         if (arguments.length > 1)
 8:             yearIn = Integer.parseInt(arguments[1]);
 9:         System.out.println(monthIn + "/" + yearIn + " has "
10:             + countDays(monthIn, yearIn) + " days.");
11:     }
12:
13:     static int countDays(int month, int year) {
14:         int count = -1;
15:         switch (month) {
16:             case 1:
17:             case 3:
18:             case 5:
19:             case 7:
20:             case 8:
21:             case 10:
22:             case 12:
23:                 count = 31;
24:                 break;
25:             case 4:
26:             case 6:
27:             case 9:
28:             case 11:
29:                 count = 30;
30:                 break;
31:             case 2:
32:                 if (year % 4 == 0)
33:                     count = 29;
34:                 else
35:                     count = 28;
36:                 if ((year % 100 == 0) & (year % 400 != 0))
37:                     count = 28;
38:         }
39:         return count;
40:     }
41: }
```

This application uses command-line arguments to specify the month and year to check. The first argument is the month, which should be expressed as a number from 1 to 12. The second argument is the year, which should be expressed a full four-digit year.

After compiling the program, type the following at a command line to see how many days were in February 2000:

```
java DayCounter 2 2000
```

The output will be the following:

```
2/2000 has 29 days.
```

If you run it without arguments, the default month of February 2001 will be used and the output will be the following:

```
2/2001 has 28 days.
```

The `DayCounter` application uses a `switch` statement to count the days in a month. This statement is part of the `countDays()` method in lines 13–40 of Listing 5.2.

The `countDays()` method has two `int` arguments: `month` and `year`. The number of days will be stored in the `count` variable, which is given an initial value of `-1` that will be replaced by the correct count later.

The `switch` statement that begins on line 15 uses `month` as its conditional value.

The number of days in a month is easy to determine for 11 months of the year. January, March, May, July, August, October, and December have 31 days. April, June, September, and November have 30 days.

The count for these 11 months is handled in lines 16–30 of Listing 5.2. Months are numbered from `1` (January) to `12` (December), as you would expect. When one of the `case` statements has the same value as `month`, every statement after that will be executed until `break` or the end of the `switch` statement is reached.

February is a little more complex, and is handled in lines 31–37 of the program. Every leap year has 29 days in February, whereas other years have 28. A leap year must meet either of the following conditions:

- The year must be evenly divisible by 4 and not evenly divisible by 100, or
- The year must be evenly divisible by 400.

As you learned on Day 3, "The ABCs of Java," the modulus operator `%` returns the remainder of a division operation. This is used with several `if-else` statements to determine how many days there are in February, depending on what year it is.

The `if-else` statement in lines 32–35 sets `count` to `29` when the year is evenly divisible by 4, and `28` otherwise.

The `if` statement in lines 36–37 uses the `&` operator to combine two conditional expressions: `year % 100 == 0` and `year & 400 != 0`. If both of these conditions are true, `count` is set to `28`.

The `countDays` method ends by returning the value of `count` in line 39.

When you run the `DayCounter` application, the `main()` method in lines 2–11 is executed.

In all Java applications, command-line arguments are stored in an array of `String` objects. This array is called `arguments` in `DayCounter`. The first command-line argument is stored in `argument[0]`, the second in `argument[1]`, and upwards until all arguments have been stored. If the application was run with no arguments, the array will be created with no elements.

Lines 3–4 create two `yearIn` and `monthIn`, two integer variables to store the year and month that should be checked. They are given the initial values of `2001` and `2`, respectively (February 2001).

The `if` statement in line 5 uses `arguments.length` to make sure the `arguments` array has at least one element. If it does, line 6 is executed.

Line 6 calls `parseInt()`, a class method of the `Integer` class, with `argument[0]` as an argument. This method takes a `String` object as an argument, and if the string could be a valid integer, it returns that value as an `int`. This converted value is stored in `monthIn`. A similar thing happens in line 7—`parseInt()` is called with `argument[1]`, and this is used to set `yearIn`.

The output of the program is displayed in lines 9–11. As part of the output, the `countDays()` method is called with `monthIn` and `yearIn`, and the value returned by this method is displayed.

for Loops

A `for` loop is used to repeat a statement until a condition is met. Although `for` loops frequently are used for simple iteration in which a statement is repeated a certain number of times, `for` loops can be used for just about any kind of loop.

The `for` loop in Java looks roughly like the following:

```
for (initialization; test; increment) {
    statement;
}
```

The start of the `for` loop has three parts:

- *initialization* is an expression that initializes the start of the loop. If you have a loop index, this expression might declare and initialize it, such as `int i = 0`. Variables that you declare in this part of the `for` loop are local to the loop itself; they cease to exist after the loop is finished executing. You can initialize more than one variable in this section by separating each expression with a comma. The statement `int i = 0, int j = 10` in this section would declare the variables i and j, and both would be local to the loop.

- *test* is the test that occurs before each pass of the loop. The test must be a Boolean expression or a function that returns a `boolean` value, such as `i < 10`. If the test is `true`, the loop executes. Once the test is `false`, the loop stops executing.

- *increment* is any expression or function call. Commonly, the increment is used to change the value of the loop index to bring the state of the loop closer to returning `false` and stopping the loop. The increment takes place after each pass of the loop. Similar to the *initialization* section, you can put more than one expression in this section by separating each expression with a comma.

The *statement* part of the `for` loop is the statement that is executed each time the loop iterates. As with `if`, you can include either a single statement or a block statement; the previous example used a block because that is more common. The following example is a `for` loop that sets all slots of a `String` array to the value `Mr.`:

```
String[] salutation = new String[10];
int i; // the loop index variable

for (i = 0; i < salutation.length; i++)
    salutation[i] = "Mr.";
```

In this example, the variable i serves as a loop index—it counts the number of times the loop has been executed. Before each trip through the loop, the index value is compared to `salutation.length`, the number of elements in the `salutation` array. When the index is equal to or greater than `salutation.length`, the loop is exited.

The final element of the `for` statement is i++. This causes the loop index to increment by 1 each time the loop is executed. Without this statement, the loop would never stop.

The statement inside the loop sets an element of the `salutation` array equal to `"Mr."`. The loop index is used to determine which element is modified.

Any part of the `for` loop can be an empty statement—that is, you can include a semicolon with no expression or statement and that part of the `for` loop will be ignored. Note that if you do use an empty statement in your `for` loop, you might have to initialize or increment any loop variables or loop indexes yourself elsewhere in the program.

You also can have an empty statement as the body of your `for` loop if everything you want to do is in the first line of that loop. For example, the following `for` loop finds the first prime number higher than `4,000`. (It calls a method called `notPrime()`, which returns a Boolean value, presumably to indicate when `i` is not prime.)

```
for (i = 4001; notPrime(i); i += 2)
;
```

A common mistake in `for` loops is to accidentally put a semicolon at the end of the line that includes the `for` statement:

```
for (i = 0; i < 10; i++);
    x = x * i; // this line is not inside the loop!
```

In this example, the first semicolon ends the loop without executing `x = x * i` as part of the loop. The `x = x * i` line will be executed only once because it is outside the `for` loop entirely. Be careful not to make this mistake in your Java programs.

To finish up `for` loops, the `HalfDollar` application will be rewritten using `for` loops to remove redundant code. The original example is long and repetitive and works only with an array that is three elements long. This version, shown in Listing 5.3, is shorter and more flexible (but it returns the same output).

LISTING 5.3   The Full Text of `HalfLoop.java`

```
 1: class HalfLoop {
 2:     public static void main(String[] arguments) {
 3:         int[] denver = { 15000006, 18810000, 20752110 };
 4:         int[] philadelphia = { 15020000, 18708000, 21348000 };
 5:         int[] total = new int[denver.length];
 6:         int sum = 0;
 7:
 8:         for (int i = 0; i < denver.length; i++) {
 9:             total[i] = denver[i] + philadelphia[i];
10:             System.out.println((i + 1993) + " production: "
11:                 + total[i]);
12:             sum += total[i];
13:         }
14:
15:         System.out.println("Average production: "
16:             + (sum / denver.length));
17:     }
18: }
```

The output of the program is as follows:

```
1993 production: 30020006
1994 production: 37518000
```

```
1995 production: 42100110
Average production: 36546038
```

Instead of going through the elements of the three arrays one by one, this example uses a
for loop. The following things take place in the loop, which is contained in lines 8–13 of
Listing 5.3:

- Line 8: The loop is created with an int variable called i as the index. The index
  will increment by 1 each pass through the loop, and stop when i is equal to or
  greater than denver.length, the total number of elements in the denver array.
- Lines 9–11: The value of one of the total elements is set using the loop index and
  then displayed with some text identifying the year.
- Line 12: The value of a total element is added to the sum variable, which will be
  used to calculate the average yearly production.

Using a more general-purpose loop to iterate over an array enables you to use the program with arrays of different sizes and still have it assign correct values to the elements
of the total array and display those values.

while and do Loops

The remaining types of loop are while and do. As with for loops, while and do loops
enable a block of Java code to be executed repeatedly until a specific condition is met.
Whether you use a for, while, or do loop is mostly a matter of your programming style.

while Loops

The while loop is used to repeat a statement as long as a particular condition is true.
The following is an example of a while loop:

```
while (i < 10) {
    x = x * i++; // the body of the loop
}
```

The condition that accompanies the while keyword is a Boolean expression—i < 10 in
the preceding example. If the expression returns true, the while loop executes the body
of the loop and then tests the condition again. This process repeats until the condition is
false. Although the preceding loop uses opening and closing braces to form a block
statement, the braces are not needed because the loop contains only one statement: x = x
* i++. Using the braces does not create any problems, though, and the braces will be
required if you add another statement inside the loop later on.

Listing 5.4 shows an example of a while loop that copies the elements of an array of
integers (in array1) to an array of floats (in array2), casting each element to a float

as it goes. The one catch is that if any of the elements in the first array is 1, the loop will immediately exit at that point.

LISTING 5.4   The Full Text of CopyArrayWhile.java

```
 1: class CopyArrayWhile {
 2:     public static void main(String[] arguments) {
 3:         int[] array1 = { 7, 4, 8, 1, 4, 1, 4 };
 4:         float[] array2 = new float[array1.length];
 5:
 6:         System.out.print("array1: [ ");
 7:         for (int i = 0; i < array1.length; i++) {
 8:             System.out.print(array1[i] + " ");
 9:         }
10:         System.out.println("]");
11:
12:         System.out.print("array2: [ ");
13:         int count = 0;
14:         while ( count < array1.length && array1[count] != 1) {
15:             array2[count] = (float) array1[count];
16:             System.out.print(array2[count++] + " ");
17:         }
18:         System.out.println("]");
19:     }
20: }
```

The output of the program is as follows:

```
array1: [ 7 4 8 1 4 1 4 ]
array2: [ 7.0 4.0 8.0 ]
```

Here's what's going on in the main() method:

- Lines 3–4 declare the arrays; array1 is an array of integers, which are initialized to some suitable numbers. array2 is an array of floating-point numbers that is the same length as array1 but doesn't have any initial values.

- Lines 6–10 are for output purposes; they simply iterate through array1 using a for loop to print out its values.

- Lines 13–17 are where the interesting stuff happens. This bunch of statements both assigns the values of array2 (converting the numbers to floating-point numbers along the array) and prints it out at the same time. You start with a count variable, which keeps track of the array index elements. The test in the while loop keeps track of the two conditions for existing the loop, where those two conditions are running out of elements in array1 or encountering a 1 in array1. (Remember, that was part of the original description of what this program does.)

5

- You can use the logical conditional `&&` to keep track of the test; remember that `&&` makes sure both conditions are `true` before the entire expression is `true`. If either one is `false`, the expression returns `false` and the loop exits.

The program's output shows that the first four elements in `array1` were copied to `array2`, but that there was a 1 in the middle that stopped the loop from going any further. Without the 1, `array2` should end up with all the same elements as `array1`.

If the `while` loop's test initially is `false` the first time it is tested (for example, if the first element in that first array is 1), the body of the `while` loop will never be executed. If you need to execute the loop at least once, you can do one of two things:

- Duplicate the body of the loop outside the `while` loop
- Use a do loop (which is described in the following section)

The do loop is considered the better solution of the two.

do...while Loops

The do loop is just like a `while` loop with one major difference: the place in the loop when the condition is tested. A `while` loop tests the condition before looping, so if the condition is `false` the first time it is tested, the body of the loop never will execute. A do loop executes the body of the loop at least once before testing the condition, so if the condition is `false` the first time it is tested, the body of the loop already will have executed once.

It's the difference between asking Dad to borrow the car and telling him later that you borrowed it. If Dad nixes the idea in the first case, you don't get to borrow it. If he nixes the idea in the second case, you already have borrowed it once.

The following example uses a do loop to keep doubling the value of a `long` integer until it is larger than 3 trillion:

```
long i = 1;
do {
    i *= 2;
    System.out.print(i + " ");
} while (i < 3000000000000L);
```

The body of the loop is executed once before the test condition, `i < 3000000000`, is evaluated; then, if the test evaluates as `true`, the loop runs again. If it is `false`, the loop exits. Keep in mind that the body of the loop executes at least once with do loops.

Breaking Out of Loops

In all of the loops, the loop ends when a tested condition is met. There might be times when something occurs during execution of a loop and you want to exit the loop early. For that you can use the `break` and `continue` keywords.

You already have seen `break` as part of the `switch` statement; `break` stops execution of the `switch` statement, and the program continues. The `break` keyword, when used with a loop, does the same thing—it immediately halts execution of the current loop. If you have nested loops within loops, execution picks up with the next outer loop. Otherwise, the program merely continues executing the next statement after the loop.

For example, recall the `while` loop that copied elements from an integer array into an array of floating-point numbers until the end of the array or a `1` was reached. You can test for that latter case inside the body of the `while` loop, and then use `break` to exit the loop:

```
int count = 0;
while (count < array1.length) {
    if (array1[count] == 1)
        break;
    array2[count] = (float) array2[count++];
}
```

The `continue` keyword starts the loop over at the next iteration. For `do` and `while` loops, this means that the execution of the block statement starts over again; with `for` loops, the increment expression is evaluated and then the block statement is executed. The `continue` keyword is useful when you want to make a special case out of elements within a loop. With the previous example of copying one array to another, you could test for whether the current element is equal to `1`, and use `continue` to restart the loop after every `1` so that the resulting array never will contain zero. Note that because you're skipping elements in the first array, you now have to keep track of two different array counters:

```
int count = 0;
int count2 = 0;
while (count++ <= array1.length) {
    if (array1[count] == 1)
        continue;

    array2[count2++] = (float)array1[count];
} >
```

Labeled Loops

Both `break` and `continue` can have an optional label that tells Java where to resume execution of the program. Without a label, `break` jumps outside the nearest loop to an enclosing loop or to the next statement outside the loop. The `continue` keyword restarts the loop it is enclosed within. Using `break` and `continue` with a label enables you to use `break` to go to a point outside a nested loop or to use `continue` to go to a loop outside the current loop.

To use a labeled loop, add the label before the initial part of the loop, with a colon between the label and the loop. Then, when you use `break` or `continue`, add the name of the label after the keyword itself, as in the following:

```
out:
    for (int i = 0; i <10; i++) {
        while (x < 50) {
            if (i * x++ > 400)
                break out;
            // inner loop here
        }
        // outer loop here
    }
```

In this snippet of code, the label `out` labels the outer loop. Then, inside both the `for` and `while` loops, when a particular condition is met, a `break` causes the execution to break out of both loops. Without the label `out`, the `break` statement would exit the inner loop and resume execution with the outer loop.

The Conditional Operator

An alternative to using the `if` and `else` keywords in a conditional statement is to use the conditional operator, sometimes called the *ternary operator*. The *conditional operator* is called a ternary operator because it has three operands.

The conditional operator is an expression, meaning that it returns a value—unlike the more general `if`, which can result in only a statement or block being executed. The conditional operator is most useful for short or simple conditionals and looks like the following line:

```
test ? trueresult : falseresult;
```

The `test` is an expression that returns `true` or `false`, just like the test in the `if` statement. If the `test` is `true`, the conditional operator returns the value of `trueresult`. If the `test` is `false`, the conditional operator returns the value of `falseresult`. For example, the following conditional tests the values of `myScore` and `yourScore`, returns the larger of the two as a value, and assigns that value to the variable `ourBestScore`:

```
int ourBestScore = myScore > yourScore ? myScore : yourScore;
```

This use of the conditional operator is equivalent to the following `if-else` code:

```
int ourBestScore;
if (myScore > yourScore)
    ourBestScore = myScore;
else
    ourBestScore = yourScore;
```

The conditional operator has a very low precedence—it usually is evaluated only after all its subexpressions are evaluated. The only operators lower in precedence are the assignment operators. For a refresher on operator precedence, refer to Table 3.7 in Day 3.

> **Caution**
>
> The ternary operator is of primary benefit to experienced programmers creating complex expressions. Its functionality is duplicated in simpler use of if-else statements, so there's no need to use this operator as you're beginning to learn the language. The main reason it's introduced in this book is because you'll encounter it in the source code of other Java programmers.

Summary

Now that you have been introduced to lists, loops, and logic, you can make a computer decide whether to repeatedly display the contents of an array.

You learned how to declare an array variable, assign an object to it, and access and change elements of the array. With the if and switch conditional statements, you can branch to different parts of a program based on a Boolean test. You learned about the for, while, and do loops, each enabling a portion of a program to be repeated until a given condition is met.

It bears repeating: You'll use all three of these features frequently in your Java programs.

You'll use all three of these features frequently in your Java programs.

5

Q&A

Q I declared a variable inside a block statement for an if. When the if was done, the definition of that variable vanished. Where did it go?

A In technical terms, block statements form a new *lexical scope*. What this means is that if you declare a variable inside a block, it's visible and usable only inside that block. When the block finishes executing, all the variables you declared go away.

It's a good idea to declare most of your variables in the outermost block in which they'll be needed—usually at the top of a block statement. The exception might be very simple variables, such as index counters in `for` loops, where declaring them in the first line of the `for` loop is an easy shortcut.

Q Why can't you use `switch` with strings?

A Strings are objects in Java, and `switch` works only for the primitive types `byte`, `char`, `short`, and `int`. To compare strings, you have to use nested `if` statements, which enable more general expression tests, including string comparison.

Quiz

Review today's material by taking this three-question quiz.

Questions

1. Which loop is used to execute the statements in the loop at least once before the conditional expression is evaluated?

   (a) `do-while`

   (b) `for`

   (c) `while`

2. Which operator returns the remainder of a division operation?

   (a) `/`

   (b) `%`

   (c) `?`

3. Which instance variable of an array is used to find out how big it is?

   (a) `size`

   (b) `length`

   (c) `MAX_VALUE`

Answers

1. a. In a `do-while` loop, the `while` conditional statement appears at the end of the loop. Even if it is initially false, the statements in the loop will be executed once.

2. b. The modulus operator ("`%`").

3. b.

Exercises

To extend your knowledge of the subjects covered today, try the following exercises:

- Using the `countDays()` method from the `DayCounter` application, create an application that displays every date in a given year in a single list from January 1 to December 31.

- Create a class that takes words for the first 10 numbers (`one` up to `ten`) and converts them into a single `long` integer. Use a `switch` statement for the conversion and command-line arguments for the words.

Where applicable, exercise solutions are offered on the book's Web site at `http://www.java21pro.com`.

5

DAY 6

Creating Classes and Methods

If you're coming to Java from another programming language, you might be struggling with the meaning of the term *class*. It seems synonymous to the term *program*, but you could be uncertain of the relationship between the two.

In Java, a program is made up of a main class and any other classes that are needed to support the main class. These support classes include any of those in Java's class library you might need (such as String, Math, and the like).

Today, the meaning of *class* will be clarified as you create classes and methods, which define the behavior of an object or class. You undertake each of the following:

- The parts of a class definition
- The creation and use of instance variables
- The creation and use of methods
- The main() method used in Java applications

- The creation of overloaded methods that share the same name but have different signatures and definitions
- The creation of constructor methods that are called when an object is created

Defining Classes

Because you have created classes during each of the previous days, you should be familiar with the basics of class definition at this point. A class is defined via the `class` keyword and the name of the class, as in the following example:

```
class Ticker {
    // body of the class
}
```

By default, classes inherit from the `Object` class. It's the superclass of all classes in the Java class hierarchy.

The `extends` keyword is used to indicate the superclass of a class. Look at the following subclass of `Ticker`:

```
class SportsTicker extends Ticker {
    // body of the class
}
```

Creating Instance and Class Variables

Whenever you create a class, you define behavior that makes the new class different from its superclass.

This behavior is defined by specifying the variables and methods of the new class. In this section, you work with three kinds of variables: class variables, instance variables, and local variables. The next section details methods.

Defining Instance Variables

On Day 3, "The ABCs of Java," you learned how to declare and initialize local variables, which are variables inside method definitions. Instance variables are declared and defined in almost the same way local variables are. The main difference is their location in the class definition. Variables are considered instance variables if they are declared outside a method definition and are not modified by the `static` keyword. By programming custom, most instance variables are defined right after the first line of the class definition. Listing 6.1 contains a simple class definition for the class `VolcanoRobot`, which inherits from its superclass, `ScienceRobot`.

LISTING 6.1 The Full Text of `VolcanoRobot.java`

```
1: class VolcanoRobot extends ScienceRobot {
2:
3:     String status;
4:     int speed;
5:     float temperature;
6:     int power;
7: }
```

This class definition contains four variables. Because these variables are not defined inside a method, they are instance variables. The variables are as follows:

- `status`—A string indicating the current activity of the robot (for example, `exploring` or `returning home`)
- `speed`—An integer that indicates the robot's current rate of travel
- `temperature`—A floating-point number that indicates the current temperature of the environment the robot is in
- `power`—An integer indicating the robot's current battery power

Class Variables

As you learned in previous lessons, class variables apply to a class as a whole, rather than being stored individually in objects of the class.

Class variables are good for communicating between different objects of the same class, or for keeping track of classwide information among a set of objects.

The `static` keyword is used in the class declaration to declare a class variable, as in the following:

```
static int sum;
static final int maxObjects = 10;
```

6

Creating Methods

As you learned on Day 4, "Working with Objects," methods define an object's behavior—anything that happens when the object is created and the various tasks the object can perform during its lifetime.

This section introduces method definition and how methods work. Tomorrow's lesson has more detail about advanced things you can do with methods.

Defining Methods

Method definitions have four basic parts:

- The name of the method
- A list of parameters
- The type of object or primitive type returned by the method
- The body of the method

The first two parts of the method definition form what's called the method's *signature*.

Note
> To keep things simpler today, two optional parts of the method definition have been left out: a modifier, such as public or private, and the throws keyword, which indicates the exceptions a method can throw. You learn about these parts of a method definition during Week 3, "Java's Advanced Features."

In other languages, the name of the method—which might be called a function, subroutine, or procedure—is enough to distinguish it from other methods in the program.

In Java, you can have several methods in the same class with the same name but differences in signatures. This practice is called *method overloading*, and you learn more about it tomorrow.

Here's what a basic method definition looks like:

```
returnType methodName(type1 arg1, type2 arg2, type3 arg3 ...) {
    // body of the method
}
```

The `returnType` is the primitive type or class of the value returned by the method. It can be one of the primitive types, a class name, or void if the method does not return a value at all.

Note that if this method returns an array object, the array brackets can either go after the `returnType` or after the parameter list. Because the former way is easier to read, it is used in this book's examples as in the following:

```
int[] makeRange(int lower, int upper) {
    // body of this method
}
```

The method's parameter list is a set of variable declarations, separated by commas, inside parentheses. These parameters become local variables in the body of the method, receiving their values when the method is called.

You can have statements, expressions, method calls on other objects, conditionals, loops, and so on inside the body of the method—everything you've learned about in the previous lessons.

Unless a method has been declared with void as its return type, the method returns some kind of value when it is completed. This value must be explicitly returned at some exit point inside the method, using the return keyword.

Listing 6.2 shows an example of a class that defines a makeRange() method. makeRange() takes two integers—a lower boundary and an upper boundary—and creates an array that contains all the integers between those two boundaries. The boundaries themselves are included in the array of integers.

LISTING 6.2   The Full Text of RangeClass.java

```
 1: class RangeClass {
 2:     int[] makeRange(int lower, int upper) {
 3:         int arr[] = new int[ (upper - lower) + 1 ];
 4:
 5:         for (int i = 0; i < arr.length; i++) {
 6:             arr[i] = lower++;
 7:         }
 8:         return arr;
 9:     }
10:
11:     public static void main(String[] arguments) {
12:         int theArray[];
13:         RangeClass theRange = new RangeClass();
14:
15:         theArray = theRange.makeRange(1, 10);
16:         System.out.print("The array: [ ");
17:         for (int i = 0; i < theArray.length; i++) {
18:             System.out.print(theArray[i] + " ");
19:         }
20:         System.out.println("]");
21:     }
22:
23: }
```

6

The output of the program is the following:

```
The array: [ 1 2 3 4 5 6 7 8 9 10 ]
```

The main() method in this class tests the makeRange() method by creating a range where the lower and upper boundaries of the range are 1 and 10, respectively, and then uses a for loop to print the new array's values in lines 5–7.

The `this` Keyword

In the body of a method definition, you might want to refer to the current object—the object the method was called on. This can be done to use that object's instance variables or to pass the current object as an argument to another method.

To refer to the current object in these cases, use the `this` keyword where you normally would refer to an object's name.

The `this` keyword refers to the current object, and you can use it anywhere a reference to an object might appear: in dot notation, as an argument to a method, as the return value for the current method, and so on. The following are some examples of using `this`:

```
t = this.x;          // the x instance variable for this object

this.resetData(this); // call the resetData method, defined in
                       // this class, and pass it the current
                       // object

return this;          // return the current object
```

In many cases, you might not need to explicitly use the `this` keyword because it will be assumed. For instance, you can refer to both instance variables and method calls defined in the current class simply by name because the `this` is implicit in those references. Therefore, you could write the first two examples as the following:

```
t = x;           // the x instance variable for this object

resetData(this); // call the resetData method, defined in this
                 // class
```

Note

> The viability of omitting the `this` keyword for instance variables depends on whether variables of the same name are declared in the local scope. You see more on this subject in the next section.

Because `this` is a reference to the current instance of a class, you should use it only inside the body of an instance method definition. Class methods, methods declared with the `static` keyword, cannot use `this`.

Variable Scope and Method Definitions

One of the things you must know in order to use a variable is its scope.

New Term   *Scope* is the part of a program in which a variable or other information can be used. When the part defining the scope has completed execution, the variable ceases to exist.

When you declare a variable in Java, that variable always has a limited scope. A variable with local scope, for example, can be used only inside the block in which it was defined. Instance variables have a scope that extends to the entire class, so they can be used by any of the instance methods within that class.

When you refer to a variable within a method definition, Java checks for a definition of that variable first in the current scope (which might be a block), next in each outer scope, and finally, in the current method definition. If the variable is not a local variable, Java then checks for a definition of that variable as an instance or class variable in the current class. If Java still does not find the variable definition, it searches each superclass in turn.

Because of the way Java checks for the scope of a given variable, it is possible for you to create a variable in a lower scope that hides (or replaces) the original value of that variable and introduces subtle and confusing bugs into your code.

For example, consider the following Java application:

```java
class ScopeTest {
    int test = 10;

    void printTest () {
        int test = 20;
        System.out.println("Test: " + test);
    }

    public static void main(String[] arguments) {
        ScopeTest st = new ScopeTest();
        st.printTest();
    }
}
```

In this class, you have two variables with the same name and definition. The first, an instance variable, has the name test and is initialized with the value 10. The second is a local variable with the same name, but with the value 20.

The local variable test within the printTest() method hides the instance variable test. When the printTest() method is called from within the main() method, it displays that test equals 20, even though there's a test instance variable that equals 10. You can avoid this problem by using this.test to refer to the instance variable and using just test to refer to the local variable, but a better solution is to avoid the duplication of variable names and definitions.

A more insidious example occurs when you redefine a variable in a subclass that already occurs in a superclass. This can create subtle bugs in your code; for example, you might call methods that are intended to change the value of an instance variable, but the wrong variable is changed. Another bug might occur when you cast an object from one class to

6

another; the value of your instance variable might mysteriously change because it was getting that value from the superclass instead of your class.

The best way to avoid this behavior is to be aware of the variables defined in all your class's superclasses. This awareness prevents you from duplicating a variable that's used higher in the class hierarchy.

Passing Arguments to Methods

When you call a method with object parameters, the objects you pass into the body of the method are passed by reference. Whatever you do to the objects inside the method affects the original objects. Keep in mind that such objects include arrays and all objects that are contained in arrays. When you pass an array into a method and modify its contents, the original array is affected. Primitive types, on the other hand, are passed by value.

Listing 6.3 demonstrates how this works.

LISTING 6.3   The PassByReference Class

```
 1: class PassByReference {
 2:     int onetoZero(int arg[]) {
 3:         int count = 0;
 4:
 5:         for (int i = 0; i < arg.length; i++) {
 6:             if (arg[i] == 1) {
 7:                 count++;
 8:                 arg[i] = 0;
 9:             }
10:         }
11:         return count;
12:     }
13:
14:     public static void main(String[] arguments) {
15:         int arr[] = { 1, 3, 4, 5, 1, 1, 7 };
16:         PassByReference test = new PassByReference();
17:         int numOnes;
18:
19:         System.out.print("Values of the array: [ ");
20:         for (int i = 0; i < arr.length; i++) {
21:             System.out.print(arr[i] + " ");
22:         }
23:         System.out.println("]");
24:
25:         numOnes = test.onetoZero(arr);
26:         System.out.println("Number of Ones = " + numOnes);
27:         System.out.print("New values of the array: [ ");
```

```
28:            for (int i = 0; i < arr.length; i++) {
29:                System.out.print(arr[i] + " ");
30:            }
31:            System.out.println("]");
32:        }
33: }
```

The following is this program's output:

```
Values of the array: [ 1 3 4 5 1 1 7 ]
Number of Ones = 3
New values of the array: [ 0 3 4 5 0 0 7 ]
```

Note the method definition for the onetoZero() method in lines 2–12, which takes a single array as an argument. The onetoZero() method does two things:

- It counts the number of 1s in the array and returns that value.

- For every 1 in the array, it substitutes a 0 in its place.

The main() method in the PassByReference class tests the use of the onetoZero() method. Go over the main() method line by line so that you can see what is going on and why the output shows what it does.

Lines 15–17 set up the initial variables for this example. The first one is an array of integers; the second one is an instance of the class PassByReference, which is stored in the variable test. The third is a simple integer to hold the number of 1s in the array.

Lines 19–23 print the initial values of the array; you can see the output of these lines in the first line of the output.

Line 25 is where the real work takes place; this is where you call the onetoZero() method defined in the object test and pass it the array stored in arr. This method returns the number of 1s in the array, which you then assign to the variable numOnes. It returns 3, as you would expect.

The last section of lines prints the array values. Because a reference to the array object is passed to the method, changing the array inside that method changes that array's original copy. Printing the values in lines 28–31 proves this—that last line of output shows that all the 1s in the array have been changed to 0s.

Class Methods

The relationship between class and instance variables is directly comparable to how class and instance methods work.

Class methods are available to any instance of the class itself and can be made available to other classes. In addition, unlike an instance method, a class does not require an instance of the class for its methods to be called.

For example, the Java class libraries include a class called Math. The Math class defines a set of math operations that you can use in any program or any of the various number types, as in the following:

```
double root = Math.sqrt(453.0);
```

```
System.out.print("The larger of x and y is " + Math.max(x, y));
```

To define class methods, use the static keyword in front of the method definition, just as you would use static in front of a class variable. For example, the class method max() used in the preceding example might have the following signature:

```
static int max(int arg1, int arg2) {
    // body of the method
}
```

Java supplies wrapper classes for each of the base types; for example, Java supplies Integer, Float, and Boolean classes. By using class methods defined in those classes, you can convert objects to primitive types and convert primitive types to objects.

For example, the parseInt() class method in the Integer class can be used with a string. The string is sent to the method as an argument, and this is used to calculate a return value to send back as an int.

The following statement shows how the parseInt() method can be used:

```
int count = Integer.parseInt("42");
```

In the preceding statement, the String value "42" is returned by parseInt() as an integer with a value of 42, and this is stored in the count variable.

The lack of a static keyword in front of a method name makes it an instance method. Instance methods operate in a particular object, rather than a class of objects. On Day 2, "Object-Oriented Programming," you created an instance method called checkTemperature() that checked the temperature in the robot's environment.

> **Tip**
>
> Most methods that operate on or affect a particular object should be defined as instance methods. Methods that provide some general capability, but do not directly affect an instance of the class, should be declared as class methods.

Creating Java Applications

Now that you know how to create classes, objects, class and instance variables, and class and instance methods, you can put it all together into a Java program.

Applications, to refresh your memory, are Java programs that run on their own. Applications are different from applets, which require a Java-enabled browser to view them. The projects you have created up to this point have been Java applications. You get a chance to dive into applets during Day 7, "Writing Java Applets." Applets require a bit more background to get them to interact with the browser, as well as draw and update with the graphics system.

A Java application consists of one or more classes and can be as large or as small as you want it to be. Although all the Java applications you've created up to this point do nothing but output some characters to the screen or to a window, you also can create Java applications that use windows, graphics, and user-interface elements, just as applets do.

The only thing you need in order to make a Java application run, however, is one class that serves as the starting point for the rest of your Java program.

The starting-point class for your application needs only one thing: a `main()` method. When the application is run, the `main()` method is the first thing that is called. None of this should be much of a surprise to you at this point; you've been creating Java applications with `main()` methods all along.

The signature for the `main()` method takes the following form:

```
public static void main(String[] arguments) {
    // body of method
}
```

Here's a rundown of the parts of the `main()` method:

- `public` means that this method is available to other classes and objects. The `main()` method must be declared `public`. You learn more about `public` and `private` methods during Week 3.

- `static` means that `main()` is a class method.

- `void` means that the `main()` method doesn't return a value.

- `main()` takes one parameter, which is an array of strings. This argument is used for program arguments, which you learn about in the next section.

The body of the `main()` method contains any code you need to start your application, such as the initialization of variables or the creation of class instances.

6

When Java executes the `main()` method, keep in mind that `main()` is a class method. An instance of the class that holds `main()` is not created automatically when your program runs. If you want to treat that class as an object, you have to create an instance of it in the `main()` method.

Helper Classes

Your Java application can have only one class, or in the case of most larger programs, it might be made up of several classes, where different instances of each class are created and used while the application is running. You can create as many classes as you want for your program.

 **Note**   If you're using the Java 2 SDK, the classes must be accessible from a folder that's listed in your CLASSPATH.

As long as Java can find the class, your program will use it when it runs. Note, however, that only the starting-point class needs a `main()` method. After it is called, the methods inside the various classes and objects used in your program take over. Although you can include `main()` methods in helper classes, they will be ignored when the program actually runs.

Java Applications and Command-Line Arguments

Because Java applications are standalone programs, it's useful to pass arguments or options to an application. You did this on Day 5, "Lists, Logic, and Loops," in the `DayCounter` project.

You can use arguments to determine how an application is going to run or to enable a generic application to operate on different kinds of input. You can use program arguments for many different purposes, such as to turn on debugging input or to indicate a filename to load.

Passing Arguments to Java Applications

How you pass arguments to a Java application varies based on the platform you're running Java on.

To pass arguments to a Java program on Windows or Solaris, the arguments should be appended to the command line when the program is run. For example:

```
java EchoArgs April 450 -10
```

In the preceding example, three arguments were passed to a program: April, 450, and -10. Note that a space separates each of the arguments.

To group arguments that include spaces, the arguments should be surrounded with quotation marks. For example, note the following command line:

```
java EchoArgs Wilhelm Niekro Hough "Tim Wakefield" 49
```

Putting quotation marks around Tim Wakefield causes that text to be treated as a single argument. The EchoArgs program would receive five arguments: Wilhelm, Niekro, Hough, Tim Wakefield, and 49. The quotation marks prevent the spaces from being used to separate one argument from another; they are not included as part of the argument when it is sent to the program and received using the main() method.

Caution

One thing the quotation marks are not used for is to identify strings. Every argument passed to an application is stored in an array of String objects, even if it has a numeric value (such as 450, -10, and 49 in the preceding examples).

Handling Arguments in Your Java Application

When an application is run with arguments, Java stores the arguments as an array of strings and passes the array to the application's main() method. Take another look at the signature for main():

```
public static void main(String[] arguments) {
    // body of method
}
```

Here, arguments is the name of the array of strings that contains the list of arguments. You can call this array anything you like.

Inside the main() method, you then can handle the arguments your program was given by iterating over the array of arguments and handling them in some manner. For example, Listing 6.4 is a simple Java program that takes any number of numeric arguments and returns the sum and the average of those arguments.

LISTING 6.4 The Full Text of SumAverage.java

```
1: class SumAverage {
2:     public static void main(String[] arguments) {
```

6

LISTING 6.4 continued

```
 3:          int sum = 0;
 4:
 5:          if (arguments.length > 0) {
 6:              for (int i = 0; i < arguments.length; i++) {
 7:                  sum += Integer.parseInt(arguments[i]);
 8:              }
 9:              System.out.println("Sum is: " + sum);
10:              System.out.println("Average is: " +
11:                  (float)sum / arguments.length);
12:          }
13:      }
14: }
```

The SumAverage application makes sure in line 5 that at least one argument was passed to the program. This is handled through length, the instance variable that contains the number of elements in the arguments array.

You must always do things like this when dealing with command-line arguments. Otherwise, your programs will crash with ArrayIndexOutOfBoundsException errors whenever the user supplies fewer command-line arguments than you were expecting.

If at least one argument was passed, the for loop in lines 6–8 iterates through all the strings stored in the arguments array.

Because all command-line arguments are passed to a Java application as String objects, you must convert them to numeric values before using them in any mathematical expressions. The parseInt() class method of the Integer class is used on line 6. It takes a String object as input and returns an int.

If you can run Java classes on your system with a command line, type the following:

```
java SumAverage 1 4 13
```

You should see the following output:

```
Sum is: 18
Average is: 6.0
```

 Note

> The array of arguments in Java is not analogous to argv in C and UNIX. In particular, arg[0] or arguments[0], the first element in the array of arguments, is the first command-line argument after the name of the class—not the name of the program, as it would be in C. Be careful of this as you write your Java programs.

Creating Methods with the Same Name, Different Arguments

When you work with Java's class library, you often encounter classes that have numerous methods with the same name.

Methods with the same name are differentiated from each other by two things:

- The number of arguments they take
- The data type or objects of each argument

These two things are part of a method's signature, and using several methods with the same name and different signatures is called *overloading*.

Method overloading can eliminate the need for entirely different methods that do essentially the same thing. Overloading also makes it possible for methods to behave differently based on the arguments they receive.

When you call a method in an object, Java matches the method name and arguments in order to choose which method definition to execute.

To create an overloaded method, you create different method definitions in a class, each with the same name but different argument lists. The difference can be the number, the type of arguments, or both. Java allows method overloading as long as each argument list is unique for the same method name.

Caution

> Java does not consider the return type when differentiating between overloaded methods. If you attempt to create two methods with the same signature and different return types, the class won't compile. In addition, the variable names that you choose for each argument to the method are irrelevant—all that matters are the number and the type of arguments.

6

The next project is creating an overloaded method. It begins with a simple class definition for a class called `MyRect`, which defines a rectangular shape with four instance variables to define the upper-left and lower-right corners of the rectangle, x1, y1, x2, and y2:

```
class MyRect {
    int x1 = 0;
    int y1 = 0;
    int x2 = 0;
    int y2 = 0;
}
```

When a new instance of the `MyRect` class is created, all its instance variables are initialized to 0.

A `buildRect()` instance method sets the variables to their correct values:

```
MyRect buildRect(int x1, int y1, int x2, int y2) {
    this.x1 = x1;
    this.y1 = y1;
    this.x2 = x2;
    this.y2 = y2;
    return this;
}
```

This method takes four integer arguments and returns a reference to the resulting `MyRect` object. Because the arguments have the same names as the instance variables, the keyword `this` is used inside the method when referring to the instance variables.

This method can be used to create rectangles—but what if you wanted to define a rectangle's dimensions in a different way? An alternative would be to use `Point` objects rather than individual coordinates because `Point` objects contain both an x and y value as instance variables.

You can overload `buildRect()` by creating a second version of the method with an argument list that takes two `Point` objects:

```
MyRect buildRect(Point topLeft, Point bottomRight) {
    x1 = topLeft.x;
    y1 = topLeft.y;
    x2 = bottomRight.x;
    y2 = bottomRight.y;
    return this;
}
```

For the preceding method to work, the `java.awt.Point` class must be imported so that the Java compiler can find it.

Another possible way to define the rectangle is to use a top corner, a height, and a width:

```
MyRect buildRect(Point topLeft, int w, int h) {
    x1 = topLeft.x;
    y1 = topLeft.y;
    x2 = (x1 + w);
    y2 = (y1 + h);
    return this;
}
```

To finish this example, a `printRect()` is created to display the rectangle's coordinates and a `main()` method tries everything out. Listing 6.5 shows the completed class definition.

LISTING 6.5   The Full Text of MyRect.java

```
 1: import java.awt.Point;
 2:
 3: class MyRect {
 4:     int x1 = 0;
 5:     int y1 = 0;
 6:     int x2 = 0;
 7:     int y2 = 0;
 8:
 9:     MyRect buildRect(int x1, int y1, int x2, int y2) {
10:         this.x1 = x1;
11:         this.y1 = y1;
12:         this.x2 = x2;
13:         this.y2 = y2;
14:         return this;
15:     }
16:
17:     MyRect buildRect(Point topLeft, Point bottomRight) {
18:         x1 = topLeft.x;
19:         y1 = topLeft.y;
20:         x2 = bottomRight.x;
21:         y2 = bottomRight.y;
22:         return this;
23:     }
24:
25:     MyRect buildRect(Point topLeft, int w, int h) {
26:         x1 = topLeft.x;
27:         y1 = topLeft.y;
28:         x2 = (x1 + w);
29:         y2 = (y1 + h);
30:         return this;
31:     }
32:
33:     void printRect(){
34:         System.out.print("MyRect: <" + x1 + ", " + y1);
35:         System.out.println(", " + x2 + ", " + y2 + ">");
36:     }
37:
38:     public static void main(String[] arguments) {
39:         MyRect rect = new MyRect();
40:
41:         System.out.println("Calling buildRect with coordinates 25,25,
             ➥50,50:");
42:         rect.buildRect(25, 25, 50, 50);
43:         rect.printRect();
44:         System.out.println("***");
45:
46:         System.out.println("Calling buildRect with points (10,10),
             ➥(20,20):");
```

6

LISTING 6.5   continued

```
47:          rect.buildRect(new Point(10,10), new Point(20,20));
48:          rect.printRect();
49:          System.out.println("***");
50:
51:          System.out.print("Calling buildRect with 1 point (10,10),");
52:          System.out.println(" width (50) and height (50):");
53:
54:          rect.buildRect(new Point(10,10), 50, 50);
55:          rect.printRect();
56:          System.out.println("***");
57:     }
58: }
```

The following is this program's output:

```
Calling buildRect with coordinates 25,25, 50,50:
MyRect: <25, 25, 50, 50>
***
Calling buildRect with points (10,10), (20,20):
MyRect: <10, 10, 20, 20>
***
Calling buildRect with 1 point (10,10), width (50) and height (50):
MyRect: <10, 10, 60, 60>
***
```

You can define as many versions of a method as you need to implement the behavior that is needed for that class.

When you have several methods that do similar things, using one method to call another is a shortcut technique to consider. For example, the buildRect() method in lines 17–23 can be replaced with the following, much shorter method:

```
MyRect buildRect(Point topLeft, Point bottomRight) {
    return buildRect(topLeft.x, topLeft.y,
        bottomRight.x, bottomRight.y);
}
```

The return statement in this method calls the buildRect() method in lines 9–15 with four integer arguments, producing the same result in fewer statements.

Constructor Methods

You also can define constructor methods in your class definition that are called automatically when objects of that class are created.

 A *constructor method* is a method that is called on an object when it is created—in other words, when it is constructed.

Unlike other methods, a constructor cannot be called directly. Java does three things when new is used to create an instance of a class:

- Allocates memory for the object
- Initializes that object's instance variables, either to initial values or to a default (0 for numbers, null for objects, false for Booleans, or '\0' for characters)
- Calls the constructor method of the class, which might be one of several methods

If a class doesn't have any constructor methods defined, an object still is created when the new operator is used in conjunction with the class. However, you might have to set its instance variables or call other methods that the object needs to initialize itself.

By defining constructor methods in your own classes, you can set initial values of instance variables, call methods based on those variables, call methods on other objects, and set the initial properties of an object. You also can overload constructor methods, as you can do with regular methods, to create an object that has specific properties based on the arguments you give to new.

Basic Constructors Methods

Constructors look a lot like regular methods, with three basic differences:

- They always have the same name as the class.
- They don't have a return type.
- They cannot return a value in the method by using the return statement.

For example, the following class uses a constructor method to initialize its instance variables based on arguments for new:

```
class VolcanoRobot {
    String status;
    int speed;
    int power;

    VolcanoRobot(String in1, int in2, int in3) {
        status = in1;
        speed = in2;
        power = in3;
    }
}
```

You could create an object of this class with the following statement:

```
VolcanoRobot vic = new VolcanoRobot("exploring", 5, 200);
```

The status instance variable would be set to exploring, speed to 5, and power to 200.

6

Calling Another Constructor Method

If you have a constructor method that duplicates some of the behavior of an existing constructor method, you can call the first constructor from inside the body of the second constructor. Java provides a special syntax for doing this. Use the following to call a constructor method defined in the current class:

```
this(arg1, arg2, arg3);
```

The use of `this` with a constructor method is similar to how `this` can be used to access a current object's variables. In the preceding statement, the arguments with `this()` are the arguments for the constructor method.

For example, consider a simple class that defines a circle using the (x,y) coordinate of its center and the length of its radius. The class, `MyCircle`, could have two constructors: one where the radius is defined, and one where the radius is set to a default value of 1:

```
class MyCircle {
    int x, y, radius;

    MyCircle(int xPoint, int yPoint, int radiusLength) {
        this.x = xPoint;
        this.y = yPoint;
        this.radius = radiusLength;
    }

    MyCircle(int xPoint, int yPoint) {
        this(xPoint, yPoint, 1);
    }
}
```

The second constructor in `MyCircle` takes only the x and y coordinates of the circle's center. Because no radius is defined, the default value of 1 is used. The first constructor is called with `xPoint`, `yPoint`, and the integer literal 1, all as arguments.

Overloading Constructors Methods

Like regular methods, constructor methods also can take varying numbers and types of parameters. This capability enables you to create an object with exactly the properties you want it to have, or lets the object calculate properties from different kinds of input.

For example, the `buildRect()` methods that you defined in the `MyRect` class earlier today would make excellent constructor methods because they are being used to initialize an object's instance variables to the appropriate values. So, instead of the original `buildRect()` method you had defined (which took four parameters for the coordinates of the corners), you could create a constructor.

Listing 6.6 shows a new class, MyRect2, that has the same functionality of the original MyRect, except that it uses overloaded constructor methods instead of overloaded buildRect() methods.

LISTING 6.6   The Full Text of MyRect2.java

```
 1: import java.awt.Point;
 2:
 3: class MyRect2 {
 4:     int x1 = 0;
 5:     int y1 = 0;
 6:     int x2 = 0;
 7:     int y2 = 0;
 8:
 9:     MyRect2(int x1, int y1, int x2, int y2) {
10:         this.x1 = x1;
11:         this.y1 = y1;
12:         this.x2 = x2;
13:         this.y2 = y2;
14:     }
15:
16:     MyRect2(Point topLeft, Point bottomRight) {
17:         x1 = topLeft.x;
18:         y1 = topLeft.y;
19:         x2 = bottomRight.x;
20:         y2 = bottomRight.y;
21:     }
22:
23:     MyRect2(Point topLeft, int w, int h) {
24:         x1 = topLeft.x;
25:         y1 = topLeft.y;
26:         x2 = (x1 + w);
27:         y2 = (y1 + h);
28:     }
29:
30:     void printRect() {
31:         System.out.print("MyRect: <" + x1 + ", " + y1);
32:         System.out.println(", " + x2 + ", " + y2 + ">");
33:     }
34:
35:     public static void main(String[] arguments) {
36:         MyRect2 rect;
37:
38:         System.out.println("Calling MyRect2 with coordinates 25,25 50,50:");
39:         rect = new MyRect2(25, 25, 50,50);
40:         rect.printRect();
41:         System.out.println("***");
42:
```

6

Listing 6.6   continued

```
43:        System.out.println("Calling MyRect2 with points (10,10), (20,20):");
44:        rect= new MyRect2(new Point(10,10), new Point(20,20));
45:        rect.printRect();
46:        System.out.println("***");
47:
48:        System.out.print("Calling MyRect2 with 1 point (10,10)");
49:        System.out.println(" width (50) and height (50):");
50:        rect = new MyRect2(new Point(10,10), 50, 50);
51:        rect.printRect();
52:        System.out.println("***");
53:
54:    }
55: }
```

Overriding Methods

When you call an object's method, Java looks for that method definition in the object's class. If it doesn't find one, it passes the method call up the class hierarchy until a method definition is found. Method inheritance enables you to define and use methods repeatedly in subclasses without having to duplicate the code.

However, there might be times when you want an object to respond to the same methods but have different behavior when that method is called. In that case, you can override the method. To override a method, define a method in a subclass with the same signature as a method in a superclass. Then, when the method is called, the subclass method is found and executed instead of the one in the superclass.

Creating Methods That Override Existing Methods

To override a method, all you have to do is create a method in your subclass that has the same signature (name, return type, and argument list) as a method defined by your class's superclass. Because Java executes the first method definition it finds that matches the signature, the new signature hides the original method definition.

Here's a simple example; Listing 6.7 contains two classes: `PrintClass`, which contains a method called `printMe()` that displays information about objects of that class, and `PrintSubClass`, a subclass that adds a z instance variable to the class.

Listing 6.7   The Full Text of `PrintClass.java`

```
1: class PrintClass {
2:     int x = 0;
```

```
 3:     int y = 1;
 4:
 5:     void printMe() {
 6:         System.out.println("x is " + x + ", y is " + y);
 7:         System.out.println("I am an instance of the class " +
 8:             this.getClass().getName());
 9:     }
10: }
11:
12: class PrintSubClass extends PrintClass {
13:     int z = 3;
14:
15:     public static void main(String[] arguments) {
16:         PrintSubClass obj = new PrintSubClass();
17:         obj.printMe();
18:     }
19: }
```

After compiling this file, run `PrintSubClass` with the Java interpreter to see the following output:

```
x is 0, y is 1
I am an instance of the class PrintSubClass
```

A `PrintSubClass` object was created and the `printMe()` method was called in the `main()` method of `PrintSubClass`. Because the `PrintSubClass` does not define this method, Java looks for it in the superclasses of `PrintSubClass`, starting with `PrintClass`. `PrintClass` has a `printMe()` method, so it is executed. Unfortunately, this method does not display the z instance variable, as you can see from the preceding output.

Note

There's an important feature of `PrintClass` to point out: It doesn't have a `main()` method. It doesn't need one; it isn't an application. `PrintClass` is simply a utility class for the `PrintSubClass` class, which is an application and therefore has a `main()` method. Only the class that you're actually executing with the Java interpreter with needs a `main()` method.

6

To correct the problem, you could override the `printMe()` method of `PrintClass` in `PrintSubClass`, adding a statement to display the z instance variable:

```
void printMe() {
    System.out.println("x is " + x + ", y is " + y +
        ", z is " + z);
    System.out.println("I am an instance of the class " +
        this.getClass().getName());
}
```

Calling the Original Method

Usually, there are two reasons why you want to override a method that a superclass already has implemented:

- To replace the definition of that original method completely
- To augment the original method with additional behavior

Overriding a method and giving the method a new definition hides the original method definition. There are times, however, when behavior should be added to the original definition instead of replacing it completely, particularly when behavior is duplicated in both the original method and the method that overrides it. By calling the original method in the body of the overriding method, you can add only what you need.

Use the super keyword to call the original method from inside a method definition. This keyword passes the method call up the hierarchy, as shown in the following:

```
void myMethod (String a, String b) {
    // do stuff here
    super.myMethod(a, b);
    // do more stuff here
}
```

The super keyword, somewhat like the this keyword, is a placeholder for the class's superclass. You can use it anywhere that you use this, but super refers to the superclass rather than the current object.

Overriding Constructors

Technically, constructor methods cannot be overridden. Because they always have the same name as the current class, new constructor methods are created instead of being inherited. This system is fine much of the time; when your class's constructor method is called, the constructor method with the same signature for all your superclasses is also called. Therefore, initialization can happen for all parts of a class that you inherit.

However, when you are defining constructor methods for your own class, you might want to change how your object is initialized, not only by initializing new variables added by your class, but also by changing the contents of variables that already are there. To do this, explicitly call the constructor methods of the superclass and subsequently change whatever variables need to be changed.

To call a regular method in a superclass, you use super.*methodname*(*arguments*). Because constructor methods don't have a method name to call, the following form is used:

```
super(arg1, arg2, ...);
```

Note that Java has a specific rule for the use of super(): It must be the very first statement in your constructor definition. If you don't call super() explicitly in your constructor, Java does it for you—using super() with no arguments. Because a call to a super() method must be the first statement, you can't do something like the following in your overriding constructor:

```
if (condition == true)
    super(1,2,3); // call one superclass constructor
else
    super(1,2); // call a different constructor
```

Similar to using this(...) in a constructor method, super(...) calls the constructor method for the immediate superclass (which might, in turn, call the constructor of its superclass, and so on). Note that a constructor with that signature has to exist in the superclass for the call to super() to work. The Java compiler checks this when you try to compile the source file.

You don't have to call the constructor in your superclass that has the same signature as the constructor in your class; you only have to call the constructor for the values you need initialized. In fact, you can create a class that has constructors with entirely different signatures from any of the superclass's constructors.

Listing 6.8 shows a class called NamedPoint, which extends the class Point from the java.awt package. The Point class has only one constructor, which takes an x and a y argument and returns a Point object. NamedPoint has an additional instance variable (a string for the name) and defines a constructor to initialize x, y, and the name.

LISTING 6.8 The NamedPoint Class

```
 1: import java.awt.Point;
 2:
 3: class NamedPoint extends Point {
 4:     String name;
 5:
 6:     NamedPoint(int x, int y, String name) {
 7:         super(x,y);
 8:         this.name = name;
 9:     }
10:
11:     public static void main(String[] arguments) {
12:         NamedPoint np = new NamedPoint(5, 5, "SmallPoint");
13:         System.out.println("x is " + np.x);
14:         System.out.println("y is " + np.y);
15:         System.out.println("Name is " + np.name);
16:     }
17: }
```

6

The output of the program is as follows:

```
x is 5
y is 5
Name is SmallPoint
```

The constructor method defined here for `NamedPoint` calls `Point`'s constructor method to initialize the instance variables of `Point` (x and y). Although you can just as easily initialize x and y yourself, you might not know what other things `Point` is doing to initialize itself. Therefore, it is always a good idea to pass constructor methods up the hierarchy to make sure everything is set up correctly.

Finalizer Methods

Finalizer methods are almost the opposite of constructor methods. A *constructor method* is used to initialize an object, and *finalizer methods* are called just before the object is collected for garbage and has its memory reclaimed.

The finalizer method is `finalize()`. The `Object` class defines a default finalizer method that does nothing. To create a finalizer method for your own classes, override the `finalize()` method using this signature:

```
protected void finalize() throws Throwable {
    super.finalize();
}
```

Note

> The `throws Throwable` part of this method definition refers to the errors that might occur when this method is called. Errors in Java are called *exceptions*; you learn more about them on Day 16, "Error Handling and Security." For now, all you need to do is include these keywords in the method definition.

Include any cleaning up that you want to do for that object inside the body of that `finalize()` method. You also can call `super.finalize()` to enable your class's superclasses to finalize the object, if necessary.

You can call the `finalize()` method yourself at any time—it's a method just like any other. However, calling `finalize()` does not trigger an object to be collected in the garbage. Only removing all references to an object causes it to be marked for deletion.

Finalizer methods are used best for optimizing the removal of an object—for example, by removing references to other objects. In most cases, you don't need to use `finalize()` at all.

Summary

After finishing today's lesson, you should have a pretty good idea of the relationship between classes in Java and programs you create using the language.

Everything you create in Java involves the use of a main class that interacts with other classes as needed. It's a different programming mindset than you might be used to with other languages.

Today you put together everything you have learned about creating Java classes. Each of the following topics was covered:

- Instance and class variables, which hold the attributes of a class and objects created from it.

- Instance and class methods, which define the behavior of a class. You learned how to define methods—including the parts of a method signature, how to return values from a method, how arguments are passed to methods, and how to use the `this` keyword to refer to the current object.

- The `main()` method of Java applications, and how to pass arguments to it from the command line.

- Overloaded methods, which reuse a method name by giving it different arguments.

- Constructor methods, which define the initial variables and other starting conditions of an object.

Tomorrow, you get some practical experience with subclassing as you create Java applets, programs that run as part of a World Wide Web page.

Q&A

Q In my class, I have an instance variable called `origin`. I also have a local variable called `origin` in a method, which, because of variable scope, gets hidden by the local variable. Is there any way to access the instance variable's value?

A The easiest way is to avoid giving your local variables the same names that your instance variables have. If you feel you must, you can use `this.origin` to refer to the instance variable and `origin` to refer to the local variable.

Q I created two methods with the following signatures:

```
int total(int arg1, int arg2, int arg3) {...}
float total(int arg1, int arg2, int arg3) {...}
```

The Java compiler complains when I try to compile the class with these method definitions, but their signatures are different. What have I done wrong?

6

A Method overloading in Java works only if the parameter lists are different—either in number or type of arguments. Return type is not relevant for method overloading. Think about it—if you had two methods with exactly the same parameter list, how would Java know which one to call?

Q **I wrote a program to take four arguments, but if I give it too few arguments, why does it crash with a runtime error?**

A Testing for the number and type of arguments your program expects is up to you in your Java program; Java won't do it for you. If your program requires four arguments, test that you have indeed been given four arguments, and return an error message if you haven't.

Quiz

Review today's material by taking this three-question quiz.

Questions

1. If a local variable has the same name as an instance variable, how can you refer to the instance variable in the scope of the local variable?

    (a) You can't; you should rename one of the variables.

    (b) Use the keyword `this` before the instance variable name.

    (c) Use the keyword `super` before the name.

2. Where are instance variables declared in a class?

    (a) Anywhere in the class

    (b) Outside of all methods in the class

    (c) After the class declaration and above the first method

3. How can you send an argument to a program that includes a space character?

    (a) Surround it with quotes

    (b) Separate the arguments with commas

    (c) Separate the arguments with period characters

Answers

1. b. Answer (a) is a good idea, though; variable name conflicts can be a source of subtle errors in your Java programs.

2. b. By custom, instance variables are declared right after the class declaration and before any methods. It's only necessary that they be outside of all methods, however.

3. a. The quotation marks will not be included in the argument when it is passed to the program.

Exercises

To extend your knowledge of the subjects covered today, try the following exercises:

- Modify the `VolcanoRobot` project from Day 2, "Object-Oriented Programming," so that it includes constructor methods.

- Create a class for four-dimensional points called `FourDPoint` that is a subclass of `Point` from the `java.awt` package.

Where applicable, exercise solutions are offered on the book's Web site at `http://www.java21pro.com`.

6

WEEK 1

DAY 7

Writing Java Applets

The first exposure of most people to the Java programming language was in late 1995, when Netscape Navigator began running *applets*—small Java programs that ran within a World Wide Web browser.

At the time, this was a revolutionary development for the Web—the first interactive content that could be delivered as part of a Web page. You can do similar things with Macromedia Flash, Microsoft ActiveX, and other technology today, but Java's still an effective language for Web-based programming.

Today, you start with the basics of applet programming:

- The differences between applets and applications
- How to create a simple applet
- How to put an applet onto a Web page
- How to send information from a Web page to an applet
- How to store an applet in an archive for faster download off a Web page
- How to create applets that are run by the Java Plug-in, a virtual machine that improves a Web browser's Java support

How Applets and Applications Are Different

The difference between Java applets and applications lies in how they are run.

Applications are run by using a Java interpreter to load the application's main class file. This normally is done from a command-line prompt using the java tool from the SDK, as you have done since Day 1, "21st Century Java," of this book.

Applets, on the other hand, are run on any browser that supports Java. At the present time, this includes current versions of Netscape Navigator, Microsoft Internet Explorer, Opera, and Sun's HotJava browser. Applets also can be tested by using the appletviewer tool included with the Java 2 Software Development Kit.

For an applet to run, it must be included on a Web page using HTML tags in the same way images and other elements are included. When a user with a Java-capable browser loads a Web page that includes an applet, the browser downloads the applet from a Web server and runs it on the Web user's own system. A separate Java interpreter is not needed—one is built into the browser. Like an application, a Java applet includes a class file and any other helper classes that are needed to run the applet. Java's standard class library is included automatically.

Because Java applets run inside a Java browser, some of the work of creating a user interface is already done for the applet programmer. There's an existing window for the applet to run in, a place to display graphics and receive information, and the browser's interface.

 **Note**

> It is possible for a single Java program to function as both an applet and an application. Although different procedures are used to create these types of programs, they do not conflict with each other. The features specific to applets would be ignored when the program runs as an application, and vice versa.

Applet Security Restrictions

Because Java applets are run on a Web user's system, there are some serious restrictions to what an applet is capable of doing. If these restrictions were not in place, a malicious Java programmer could easily write an applet that deletes user files, collects private information from the system, and commits other security breaches.

As a general rule, Java applets run under a "better safe than sorry" security model. Applets cannot do any of the following:

- They cannot read or write files on the user's file system.
- They cannot communicate with an Internet site other than the one that served the Web page that included the applet.
- They cannot run any programs on the reader's system.
- They cannot load programs stored on the user's system, such as executable programs and shared libraries.

All these rules are true for Java applets running under the browsers favored by most Web users today. Other Java-capable browsers and Java development tools might enable you to configure the level of security you want, permitting some file access to specific folders or network connections to selected Internet sites.

As an example, the `appletviewer` tool enables an access control list to be set for the folders to which an applet can read or write files. However, an applet developer can assume that most of the audience will be using a browser that implements the strictest security rules.

Java applications have none of the restrictions in place for applets. They can take full advantage of Java's capabilities.

Caution

Although Java's security model makes it extremely difficult for a malicious applet to do harm to a user's system, it will never be 100% secure. Search the Web for "hostile applets," and you'll find discussion of security issues in different versions of Java and how they have been addressed. You might even find examples of applets that cause problems for people using Java browsers. Java is more secure than other Web programming solutions such as ActiveX, but all browser users should acquaint themselves with the issue.

Choosing a Java Version

A Java programmer who writes applets must address this issue: For which Java version should I write?

At the time of this writing, Java 1.1 is the most up-to-date version of the language supported on the current versions of the Navigator, Internet Explorer, and Opera browsers, which comprise more than 90% of the applet-using world.

7

Note	Sun Microsystems offers a Web browser add-on called the Java Plug-in, which enables applet programmers to use Java 2 enhancements in their programs. You'll find out more about it later today.

Because of this split, applet programmers generally choose one of the following three options:

- Write an applet using only Java 1.0 features so that it will run on all Java-capable browsers.
- Write an applet using only Java 1.0 or 1.1 features so that it will run on Navigator 4.0 and higher, Internet Explorer 4 and higher, and Opera 3.6 and higher.
- Write an applet using all Java features and provide a way for users to download and install the Java Plug-in so that they can run the applet.

Java 2 has been designed so that in almost all circumstances, a program using only Java 1.0 features can compile and run successfully on a Java 1.0 interpreter or 1.0-capable browser. Likewise, an applet using Java 1.1 features can run on a browser supporting that language version.

If an applet uses any feature that was introduced with Java 2, the program won't run successfully on a browser that doesn't support that version of the language. The only test environment that always supports the most current version of Java is the latest `appletviewer` from the corresponding SDK.

This is a common source of errors for Java applet programmers. If you write a Java 2 applet and run it on a nonsupporting browser such as Microsoft Internet Explorer 4.0, you get security errors, class-not-found errors, and other problems that prevent it from running.

Note	In this book, Java 2 techniques are used for all programs, even applets. There's a wealth of information available in previous editions of this book for applet programmers who don't want to use Java 2, and Sun also offers full documentation for prior versions at `http://java.sun.com/infodocs`.

The security model described up to this point is the one introduced with Java 1.0. Java's current version includes a way for a Web user to trust an applet, so that applet can run without restriction on the user's system, just as an application can.

Java 2 enables very specific security controls to be put into place or removed from applets and applications. This is covered during Day 16, "Error Handling and Security."

Creating Applets

Most of the Java programs you've created up to this point have been Java applications—simple programs with a `main()` method that is used to create objects, set instance variables, and call other methods.

Applets do not have a `main()` method that automatically is called to begin the program. Instead, there are several methods that are called at different points in the execution of an applet. You learn about these methods today.

All applets are subclasses of either the `JApplet` class in the `javax.swing` package or its superclass, the `Applet` class in the `java.applet` package. The `JApplet` class is a better choice because it supports Swing, the windowing classes you'll be learning about during Week 2.

By inheriting from one of these classes, your applet has the following built-in behavior:

- It works as part of a Web browser and can respond to occurrences such as the browser page being reloaded
- It can present a graphical user interface and take input from users

Although an applet can make use of as many other classes as needed, the `JApplet` class is the main class that triggers the execution of the applet. The subclass of `JApplet` that you create takes the following form:

```
public class yourApplet extends javax.swing.JApplet {
    // Applet code here
}
```

All applets must be declared `public` because the `JApplet` class is a public class. This requirement is true only of your main `JApplet` class, and any helper classes can be public or private. More information on this kind of access control is described on Day 15, "Packages, Interfaces, and Other Class Features."

When a browser's built-in Java interpreter encounters a Java applet on a Web page, that applet's class is loaded along with any other helper classes it uses. The browser automatically creates an instance of the applet's class and calls methods of the `JApplet` class when specific events take place.

Different applets that use the same class use different instances, so you could place more than one copy of the same type of applet on a page, and each could behave differently.

7

Major Applet Activities

Instead of a `main()` method, applets have methods that are called when specific things occur as the applet runs.

An example of these methods is `paint()`, which is called whenever the applet's window needs to be displayed or redisplayed.

By default, these methods do nothing. For example, the `paint()` method that is inherited from `JApplet` is an empty method. For anything to be displayed on the applet window, the `paint()` method must be overridden with behavior to display text, graphics, and other things.

You learn here about `JApplet` class methods that should be overridden as the week progresses. The following sections describe five of the more important methods in an applet's execution: initialization, starting, stopping, destruction, and painting.

Initialization

Initialization occurs when the applet is loaded. *Initialization* might include creating the objects the applet needs, setting up an initial state, loading images or fonts, or setting parameters. To provide behavior for the initialization of an applet, you override the `init()` method as follows:

```
public void init() {
    // Code here
}
```

One useful thing to do when initializing an applet is to set the color of its background window. Colors are represented in Java by the `Color` class, part of the `java.awt` package. Call `setBackground(Color)` in an applet to make the background of the applet window the specified color.

The `Color` class has class variables that represent the most commonly used colors: `black`, `blue`, `cyan`, `darkGray`, `gray`, `green`, `lightGray`, `magenta`, `orange`, `pink`, `red`, `white`, and `yellow`. You can use one of these variables as the argument to the `setBackground()` method, as in the following example:

```
setBackground(Color.green);
```

If used in an applet's `init()` method, the preceding statement makes the entire applet window green.

You also can create your own `Color` objects using integer values for red, green, and blue as three arguments to the constructor:

```
Color avocado = new Color(102, 153, 102);
setBackground(avocado)
```

This code sets the background to avocado green.

Tip

> An applet window is a container—a component in a graphical user interface that can hold other components. You can use `setBackground()` on any container to establish its background color.

You'll learn more about using colors during Day 12, "Color, Fonts, and Graphics."

Starting

An applet is started after it is initialized. *Starting* also can occur if the applet was previously stopped. For example, an applet is stopped if the browser user follows a link to a different page, and it is started again when the user returns to the page containing the applet.

Starting can occur several times during an applet's life cycle, but initialization happens only once. To provide startup behavior for your applet, override the `start()` method as follows:

```
public void start() {
    // Code here
}
```

Functionality that you put in the `start()` method might include starting a thread to control the applet, sending the appropriate messages to helper objects, or in some way telling the applet to begin running.

Stopping

Stopping and starting go hand-in-hand. *Stopping* occurs when the user leaves the page that contains a currently running applet, or when an applet stops itself by calling `stop()` directly. By default, any threads the applet had started continue running even after the user leaves a page. By overriding `stop()`, you can suspend execution of these threads and restart them if the applet is viewed again. The following shows the form of a `stop()` method:

```
public void stop() {
    // Code here
}
```

7

Destruction

Destruction sounds more harsh than it is. The destroy() method enables the applet to clean up after itself just before it is freed from memory or the browser exits. You can use this method to kill any running threads or to release any other running objects. Generally, you won't want to override destroy() unless you have specific resources that need to be released, such as threads that the applet has created. To provide cleanup behavior for your applet, override the destroy() method as follows:

```
public void destroy() {
    // Code here
}
```

> **Note**
>
> You might be wondering how destroy() is different from finalize(), which was described on Day 6, "Creating Classes and Methods." The destroy() method applies only to applets; finalize() is a more general-purpose way for a single object of any type to clean up after itself.

Java has an automatic garbage collector that manages memory for you. The collector reclaims memory from resources after the program is done using them, so you don't normally have to use methods such as destroy().

Painting

Painting is how an applet displays something onscreen, be it text, a line, a colored background, or an image. Painting can occur many hundreds of times during an applet's life cycle: once after the applet is initialized, again if the browser window is brought out from behind another window onscreen, again if the browser window is moved to a different position onscreen, and so on. You must override the paint() method of your Applet subclass to display anything. The paint() method looks like the following: ().

```
public void paint(Graphics g) {
    // Code here
}
```

Note that unlike other methods described in this section, paint() takes an argument: an instance of the class Graphics. This object is created and passed to paint() by the browser, so you don't have to worry about it. However, you always must import the Graphics class (part of the java.awt package) into your applet code, usually through an import statement at the top of your Java source file, as in the following:

```
import java.awt.Graphics;
```

Tip

> If you are importing several classes from the same package, such as the Abstract Windowing Toolkit classes, you can use a wildcard character to load them all at the same time. For example, the statement `import java.awt.*;` makes every public class in the `java.awt` package available. The import statement does not include subclasses of the package, however, so the `import java.awt.*;` statement does not include the classes of the `java.awt.image` package.

The `paint()` method is called automatically by the environment that contains the applet—normally a Web browser—whenever the applet window must be redrawn.

There are times in an applet when you do something that requires the window to be repainted. For example, if you call `setBackground()` to change the applet's background to a new color, this won't be shown until the applet window is redrawn.

To request that the window be redrawn in an applet, call the applet's `repaint()` method without any arguments:

```
repaint();
```

The `Graphics` object passed to the applet's `paint()` method is required for all text and graphics you will draw in the applet window.

A `Graphics` object represents an area being drawn to; in this case, an applet window. You can use this object to draw text to the window and handle other simple graphical tasks. Many of the Java2D drawing and text-handling techniques you learn about next week are called on a subclass of `Graphics`, `Graphics2D`. To create a new `Graphics2D` object that you can use in an applet's `paint()` method, you must use casting, as in the following `paint()` method:

```
public void paint(Graphics screen) {
    Graphics2D screen2D = (Graphics2D)screen;
}
```

The `screen2D` object in this example was produced via casting. It is the `screen` object converted from the `Graphics` class into the `Graphics2D` class.

All Java2D graphics operations must be called on a `Graphics2D` object. `Graphics2D` is part of the `java.awt` package.

An Example Applet

The `Watch` applet displays the current date and time and updates it roughly once a second.

7

This project uses objects of several different classes:

- GregorianCalendar, a class in the java.util package that represents date/time values in the Gregorian calendar system, which is in use throughout the Western world
- Font, a java.awt class that represents the size, style and family of a display font
- Color and Graphics2D, two java.awt class described in the previous section

Listing 7.1 shows the source code for the applet.

LISTING 7.1   The Full Text of Watch.java

```
 1: import java.awt.*;
 2: import java.util.*;
 3:
 4: public class Watch extends javax.swing.JApplet {
 5:     private Color butterscotch = new Color(255, 204, 102);
 6:     private String lastTime = "";
 7:
 8:     public void init() {
 9:         setBackground(Color.black);
10:     }
11:
12:     public void paint(Graphics screen) {
13:         Graphics2D screen2D = (Graphics2D)screen;
14:         Font type = new Font("Monospaced", Font.BOLD, 20);
15:         screen2D.setFont(type);
16:         GregorianCalendar day = new GregorianCalendar();
17:         String time = day.getTime().toString();
18:         screen2D.setColor(Color.black);
19:         screen2D.drawString(lastTime, 5, 25);
20:         screen2D.setColor(butterscotch);
21:         screen2D.drawString(time, 5, 25);
22:         try {
23:             Thread.sleep(1000);
24:         } catch (InterruptedException e) {
25:             // do nothing
26:         }
27:         lastTime = time;
28:         repaint();
29:     }
30: }
```

After you have created this program, you can compile it but won't be able to try it out yet. The applet overrides the init() method in lines 8–10 to set the background color of the applet window to black.

The paint() method is where this applet's real work occurs. The Graphics object passed into the paint() method holds the graphics state, which keeps track of the current attributes of the drawing surface. The state includes details about the current font and color to use for any drawing operation, for example. By using casting in line 13, a Graphics2D object is created that contains all this information.

Lines 14–15 set up the font for this graphics state. The Font object is held in the type instance variable and set up as a bold, monospaced, 20-point font. The call to setFont() in line 15 establishes this font as the one that will be used for subsequent drawing operations in lines 19 and 21.

Lines 16–17 create a new GregorianCalendar object that holds the current date and time. The getTime() method of this object returns the date and time as a Date object, another class of the java.util package. Calling toString() on this object returns the date and time as a string you can display.

Lines 18–19 set the color for drawing operations to black and then calls drawString() to display the string lastTime in the applet window at the (x,y) position 5, 25. Because the background is black, nothing will appear—you'll see why this is done shortly.

Lines 20–21 set the color using a Color object called butterscotch, and then displays the string time using this color.

Lines 22–26 use a class method of the Thread class to make the program do nothing for 1,000 milliseconds (one second). Because the sleep() method will generate an InterruptedException error if anything occurs that should interrupt this delay, the call to sleep() must be enclosed in a try-catch block. (You'll work more with threads and exceptions on Day 13, "Threads and Animation.")

Line 27–28 make the lastTime variable refer to the same string as the time variable and then call repaint() to request that the applet window be redrawn.

Calling repaint() causes the applet's paint() method to be called again. When this occurs, lastTime is displayed in black text in line 19, overwriting the last time string that was displayed. This clears the screen so that the new value of time can be shown.

Caution

Calling repaint() within an applet's paint() method is not the ideal way to handle animation, as you'll see when you begin working with threads in Day 13. It's suitable here primarily because the applet is a simple one.

7

Note that the 0 point for x, y is at the top left of the applet's drawing surface, with positive y moving downward, so 50 is at the bottom of the applet. Figure 7.1 shows how the applet's bounding box and the string are drawn on the page.

FIGURE 7.1

Drawing the applet.

If you implement the right applet methods in your class (init(), start(), stop(), paint(), and so on), your applet just seamlessly works without needing an explicit jumping-off point.

Including an Applet on a Web Page

After you create the class or classes that compose your applet and compile them into class files, you must create a Web page to place the applet on.

Applets are placed on a page by using the <APPLET> tag, an HTML programming command that works like other HTML elements. There also are numerous Web-page development tools such as Claris Home Page and Macromedia Dreamweaver that can be used to add applets to a page without using HTML.

The purpose of <APPLET> is to place an applet on a Web page and control how it looks in relation to other parts of the page.

Java-capable browsers use the information contained in the tag to find and execute the applet's compiled class files. In this section, you learn how to put Java applets on a Web page and how to serve the executable Java files to the Web at large.

> The following section assumes that you have at least a passing understanding of writing HTML pages or know how to use a Web development tool to approximate HTML. If you need help in this area, one of the coauthors of this book, Laura Lemay, has written *Sams Teach Yourself Web Publishing with HTML 4 in 21 Days* with Denise Tyler.

The <APPLET> Tag

The <APPLET> tag is a special extension to HTML for including Java applets in Web pages; the tag is supported by all browsers that handle Java programs. Listing 7.2 shows a simple example of a Web page with an applet included.

LISTING 7.2   The Full Text of `Watch.html`

```
 1: <html>
 2: <head>
 3: <title>Watch Applet</title>
 4: </head>
 5: <body>
 6: <applet code="Watch.class" height="50" width="345">
 7: This program requires a Java-enabled browser.
 8: </applet>
 9: </body>
10: </html>
```

In Listing 7.2, the <APPLET> tag is contained in lines 6–8. In this example, the <APPLET> tag includes three attributes:

- CODE—Specifies the name of the applet's main class file
- WIDTH—Specifies the width of the applet window on the Web page
- HEIGHT—Specifies the height of the applet window

The class file indicated by the CODE attribute must be in the same folder as the Web page containing the applet, unless you use a CODEBASE attribute to specify a different folder. You learn how to do that later today.

WIDTH and HEIGHT are required attributes because the Web browser needs to know how much space to devote to the applet on the page. It's easy to draw to an area outside the applet window in a program, so you must be sure to provide a window large enough.

Text, images, and other Web page elements can be included between the <APPLET> and </APPLET> tags. These are displayed only on browsers that cannot handle Java programs, and including them is a good way to let people know they're missing out on a Java applet because their browser doesn't offer support for applets. If you don't specify anything between <APPLET> and </APPLET>, browsers that don't support Java display nothing in place of the applet.

Users who have Java browsers see the Watch applet on this page. Users who don't have Java see the alternate text that has been provided—This program requires a Java-enabled browser.

Testing the Result

After you have a main applet class file and an HTML file that uses the applet, you can load the HTML file into a Java-capable browser from your local disk. Using Netscape Navigator 4, local files can be loaded with the File, Open Page, Choose File command. In Internet Explorer, choose File, Open, Browse to find the right file on your system. The browser loads your Web page and the applet contained on it.

7

If you don't have a Java-capable browser, there should be a way to load applets included with your development environment. The SDK includes the `appletviewer` tool for testing your applets. Unlike a browser, `appletviewer` displays only the applets that are included on a Web page. It does not display the Web page itself.

Figure 7.2 shows the `Watch.html` page loaded in `appletviewer`.

FIGURE 7.2

The `Watch.html` *Web page in* `appletviewer`.

You should try to load this Web page with each of the browsers installed on your computer. If it works in `appletviewer` but does not work in others, the most likely cause is that you have tried to load it with a browser that doesn't support Java 2.

Putting Applets on the Web

After you have an applet that works successfully when you test it locally on your own system, you can make the applet available on the World Wide Web.

Java applets are presented by a Web server in the same way that HTML files, images, and other media are. You store the applet in a folder accessible to the Web server—often the same folder that contains the Web page that features the applet. The Web server should be configured to offer Java applets to browsers that support the language.

There are certain files you need to upload to a Web server:

- The HTML page containing the applet
- All `.class` files used by the applet that aren't part of Java's standard class library

If you know how to publish Web pages, image files, and other multimedia files, you don't have to learn any new skills to publish Java applets on your site.

More About the `<APPLET>` Tag

In its simplest form, the `<APPLET>` tag uses `CODE`, `WIDTH`, and `HEIGHT` attributes to create a space of the appropriate size, and then loads and runs the applet in that space. However, `<APPLET>` includes several other attributes that can help you better integrate an applet into a Web page's overall design.

Note   The attributes available for the `<APPLET>` tag are almost identical to those for the HTML `<IMG>` tag.

ALIGN

The `ALIGN` attribute defines how the applet will be aligned on a Web page in relation to other parts of the page. This attribute can have one of nine values:

- `ALIGN=LEFT` aligns the applet to the left of the text that follows the applet on the page.
- `ALIGN=RIGHT` aligns the applet to the right of the text that follows the applet on the page.
- `ALIGN=TEXTTOP` aligns the top of the applet with the top of the tallest text in the line.
- `ALIGN=TOP` aligns the applet with the topmost item in the line (which can be another applet, an image, or the top of the text).
- `ALIGN=ABSMIDDLE` aligns the middle of the applet with the middle of the largest item in the line.
- `ALIGN=MIDDLE` aligns the middle of the applet with the middle of the text's baseline.
- `ALIGN=BASELINE` aligns the bottom of the applet with the text's baseline. `ALIGN=BASELINE` is the same as `ALIGN=BOTTOM`, but `ALIGN=BASELINE` is a more descriptive name.
- `ALIGN=ABSBOTTOM` aligns the bottom of the applet with the lowest item in the line (which can be the text's baseline or another applet or image).

To end the formatting that is specified with the `ALIGN` attribute, you can use the HTML line break tag (`<BR>`) with the `CLEAR` attribute. This takes three values:

- `<BR CLEAR=LEFT>`—Continue displaying the rest of the Web page at the next clear left margin
- `<BR CLEAR=RIGHT>`—Continue displaying at the next clear right margin
- `<BR CLEAR=ALL>`—Continue displaying at the next clear left and right margin

Figure 7.3 shows the various alignment options, in which the smiley face in sunglasses is an applet.

7

FIGURE 7.3

Applet alignment options.

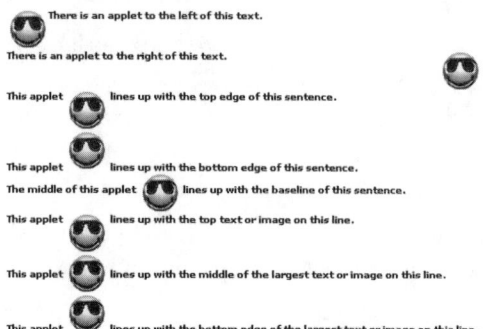

If you are using a Web development tool that enables you to place Java applets on a page, you should be able to set the ALIGN attribute by choosing LEFT, RIGHT, or one of the other values from within the program.

HSPACE and VSPACE

The HSPACE and VSPACE attributes are used to set the amount of space, in pixels, between an applet and its surrounding text. HSPACE controls the horizontal space to the left and right of the applet, and VSPACE controls the vertical space above and below the applet. For example, here's that sample snippet of HTML with vertical space of 50 and horizontal space of 10:

```
<APPLET CODE="ShowSmiley.class" WIDTH=45 HEIGHT=42
ALIGN=LEFT VSPACE=50 HSPACE=10>
Requires Java
</APPLET>
```

Figure 7.4 shows how this applet, which displays a smiley face on a white background, would be displayed with other elements of a Web page. The background of the page is a grid, and each grid is 10×10 pixels in size. You can use the grid to measure the amount of space between the applet and the text on the page.

FIGURE 7.4

Vertical and horizontal space.

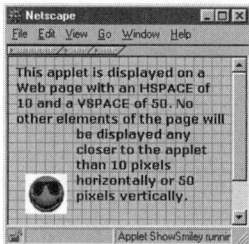

CODE and CODEBASE

The CODE and CODEBASE attributes, unlike other parts of the <APPLET> tag, are used to indicate where the applet's main class file and other files can be found. They are used by a Java-capable browser when it attempts to run an applet after downloading it from a Web server.

CODE indicates the filename of the applet's main class file. If CODE is used without an accompanying CODEBASE attribute, the class file will be loaded from the same place as the Web page containing the applet.

You must specify the .class file extension with the CODE attribute. The following is an example of an <APPLET> tag that loads an applet called Bix.class from the same folder as the Web page:

```
<APPLET CODE="Bix.class" HEIGHT=40 WIDTH=400>
</APPLET>
```

The CODEBASE attribute is used to cause the browser to look in a different folder for the applet and any other files it uses. CODEBASE indicates an alternative folder, or even an alternative World Wide Web site, from which to load the class and other files. The following loads a class called Bix.class from a folder called Torshire:

```
<APPLET CODE="Bix.class" CODEBASE="Torshire" HEIGHT=40 WIDTH=400>
</APPLET>
```

Here's an example where the Java class files are loaded from an entirely different Web site than the one containing the page:

```
<APPLET CODE="Bix.class" CODEBASE="http://www.prefect.com/javaclasses"
HEIGHT=40 WIDTH=400>
</APPLET>
```

The <OBJECT> Tag

The <APPLET> tag is an HTML extension introduced specifically to present Java programs on Web pages. Today there are other types of programs that can run interactively on a page, including ActiveX controls, NetRexx applets, and Python programs. In order to deal with all these program types without requiring a different tag for each, the <OBJECT> tag has been added to the HTML specification.

The <OBJECT> tag is used for all objects—interactive programs and other external elements—that can be presented as part of a Web page. It is supported by versions 4.0 and higher of Netscape Navigator and Microsoft Internet Explorer as well as appletviewer. Other browsers such as Opera do not support this new tag, so you might still be using <APPLET> in many cases.

7

The <OBJECT> tag takes the following form:

```
<OBJECT CODE="Bix.class" CODEBASE="http://www.prefect.com/javaclasses"
HEIGHT=40 WIDTH=400">
</OBJECT>
```

Switching from <APPLET> to <OBJECT> requires only that the <OBJECT> tag should be used in place of <APPLET>.

Otherwise, attributes remain the same, including CODEBASE, HEIGHT, WIDTH, and ALIGN. The <OBJECT> tag also can use optional <PARAM> tags, which are described later today.

Java Archives

The standard way of placing a Java applet on a Web page is to use <APPLET> or <OBJECT> to indicate the primary class file of the applet. A Java-enabled browser then downloads and runs the applet. Any other classes and any other files needed by the applet are downloaded from the Web server.

The problem with running applets in this way is that every single file an applet needs—be it another helper class, image, audio file, text file, or anything else—requires a separate connection from a Web browser to the server containing the file. Because a fair amount of time is needed just to make the connection itself, this can increase the amount of time it takes to download an applet and everything it needs to run.

The solution to this problem is a Java archive, or JAR file. A *Java archive* is a collection of Java classes and other files packaged into a single file. By using a Java archive, the browser makes only one connection to the server rather than several. By reducing the number of files the browser has to load from the server, you can download and run your applet more quickly. Java archives also can be compressed, making the overall file size smaller and therefore faster to download—although it will take some time on the browser side for the files to be decompressed before they can run.

Versions 4.0 and higher of the Navigator and Internet Explorer browsers include support for JAR files. To create these archives, the SDK includes a tool called jar that can pack files into Java archives as well as unpack them. JAR files can be compressed using the Zip format or packed without using compression. The following command packs all of a folder's class and GIF image files into a single Java archive called Animate.jar:

```
jar cf Animate.jar *.class *.gif
```

The argument cf specifies two command-line options that can be used when running the jar program. The c option indicates that a Java archive file should be created, and f indicates that the name of the archive file will follow as one of the next arguments.

You also can add specific files to a Java archive with a command such as the following:

```
jar cf AudioLoop.jar AudioLoop.class beep.au loop.au
```

This creates an `AudioLoop.jar` archive containing three files: `AudioLoop.class`, `loop.au`, and `beep.au`.

Run `jar` without any arguments to see a list of options that can be used with the program.

After you create a Java archive, the `ARCHIVE` attribute is used with the `<APPLET>` tag to show where the archive can be found. You can use Java archives with an applet with tags such as the following:

```
<applet code="AudioLoop.class" archive="AudioLoop.jar" width=45 height=42>
</applet>
```

This tag specifies that an archive called `AudioLoop.jar` contains files used by the applet. Browsers and browsing tools that support JAR files will look inside the archive for files that are needed as the applet runs.

 **Caution**

> Although a Java archive can contain class files, the `ARCHIVE` attribute does not remove the need for the `CODE` attribute. A browser still needs to know the name of the applet's main class file in order to load it.

Passing Parameters to Applets

With Java applications, you can pass parameters to the `main()` method by using arguments on the command line. You then can parse those arguments inside the body of your class, and the application acts accordingly based on the arguments it is given.

Applets, however, don't have a command line. Applets can get different input from the HTML file that contains the `<APPLET>` or `<OBJECT>` tag through the use of applet parameters. To set up and handle parameters in an applet, you need two things:

- A special parameter tag in the HTML file
- Code in your applet to parse those parameters

Applet parameters come in two parts: a name, which is simply a name you pick, and a value, which determines the value of that particular parameter. For example, you can indicate the color of text in an applet by using a parameter with the name `color` and the value `red`. You can determine an animation's speed using a parameter with the name `speed` and the value `5`.

7

In the HTML file that contains the embedded applet, you indicate each parameter using the <PARAM> tag, which has two attributes for the name and the value called (surprisingly enough) NAME and VALUE. The <PARAM> tag goes inside the opening and closing <APPLET> tags, as in the following:

```
<APPLET CODE="QueenMab.class" WIDTH=100 HEIGHT=100>
<PARAM NAME=font VALUE="TimesRoman">
<PARAM NAME=size VALUE="24">
A Java applet appears here.
</APPLET>
```

This particular example defines two parameters to the QueenMab applet: one named font with a value of TimesRoman, and one named size with a value of 24.

The usage of the <PARAM> tag is the same for applets that use the <OBJECT> tag instead of <APPLET>.

Parameters are passed to your applet when it is loaded. In the init() method for your applet, you can retrieve these parameters by using the getParameter() method. The getParameter() method takes one argument, a string representing the name of the parameter you're looking for, and returns a string containing the corresponding value of that parameter. (As with arguments in Java applications, all parameter values are returned as strings.) To get the value of the font parameter from the HTML file, you might have a line such as the following in your init() method:

```
String theFontName = getParameter("font");
```

Note

> The names of the parameters as specified in <PARAM> and the names of the parameters in getParameter() must match identically, including the same case. In other words, <PARAM NAME="eecummings"> is different from <PARAM NAME="EECummings">. If your parameters are not being properly passed to your applet, make sure the parameter cases match.

Note that if a parameter you expect has not been specified in the HTML file, getParameter() returns null. Most often, you will want to test for a null parameter and supply a reasonable default, as shown:

```
if (theFontName == null)
    theFontName = "Courier";
```

Keep in mind that getParameter() returns strings; if you want a parameter to be some other object or type, you have to convert it yourself. For example, consider the HTML file for the QueenMab applet. To parse the size parameter and assign it to an integer variable called theSize, you might use the following lines:

```
int theSize;
String s = getParameter("size");
if (s == null)
    theSize = 12;
else theSize = Integer.parseInt(s);
```

Listing 7.3 contains a modified version of the Watch applet that enables the background color to be specified as a parameter called background.

LISTING 7.3   The Full Text of NewWatch.java

```
 1: import java.awt.*;
 2: import java.util.*;
 3:
 4: public class NewWatch extends javax.swing.JApplet {
 5:     private Color butterscotch = new Color(255, 204, 102);
 6:     private String lastTime = "";
 7:     Color back;
 8:
 9: public void init() {
10:         String in = getParameter("background");
11:         back = Color.black;
12:         if (in != null) {
13:             try {
14:                 back = Color.decode(in);
15:             } catch (NumberFormatException e) {
16:                 showStatus("Bad parameter " + in);
17:             }
18:         }
19:         setBackground(back);
20:     }
21:
22:     public void paint(Graphics screen) {
23:         Graphics2D screen2D = (Graphics2D)screen;
24:         Font type = new Font("Monospaced", Font.BOLD, 20);
25:         screen2D.setFont(type);
26:         GregorianCalendar day = new GregorianCalendar();
27:         String time = day.getTime().toString();
28:         screen2D.setColor(back);
29:         screen2D.drawString(lastTime, 5, 25);
30:         screen2D.setColor(butterscotch);
31:         screen2D.drawString(time, 5, 25);
32:         try {
33:             Thread.sleep(1000);
34:         } catch (InterruptedException e) {
35:             // do nothing
36:         }
37:         lastTime = time;
38:         repaint();
39:     }
40: }
```

7

The NewWatch applet contains only a few minor changes outside of the init() method. A Color object is declared in line 7, and line 28 is changed so that it uses this object to set the current color instead of Color.black.

The init() method in lines 9–20 has been rewritten to work with a parameter called background. This parameter should be specified as a hexadecimal string—a pound character ("#") followed by three hexadecimal numbers that represent the red, green, and blue values of a color. Black is #000000, red is #FF0000, green is #00FF00, blue is #0000FF, white is #FFFFFF, and so on. If you are familiar with HTML, you have probably used hexadecimal strings like this before.

The Color class has a decode(String) class method that creates a Color object from a hexadecimal string. This occurs in line 14—the try-catch block handles the NumberFormatException error that occurs if in does not contain a valid hexadecimal string.

Line 19 sets the applet window to the color represented by the back object. To try this program, create the HTML document in Listing 7.4.

LISTING 7.4   The Full Text of NewWatch.html

```
 1: <html>
 2: <head>
 3: <title>Watch Applet</title>
 4: </head>
 5: <body bgcolor="#996633">
 6: <p>The current time:
 7: <applet code="NewWatch.class" height="50" width="345">
 8: <param name="background" value="#996633">
 9: This program requires a Java-enabled browser.
10: </applet>
11: </body>
12: </html>
```

Note the <APPLET> tag, which designates the class file for the applet and the appropriate width and height (345 and 50, respectively). Just below it (line 8) is the <PARAM> tag, which is used to pass the parameter to the applet. In this example, the NAME of the parameter is background, and the VALUE is the string #996633, which is a shade of brown. Line 5 sets the background color of the page using the same hexadecimal string.

Loading this HTML file in Opera produces the result shown in Figure 7.5.

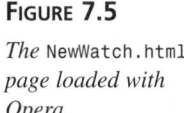

FIGURE 7.5

The NewWatch.html *page loaded with Opera.*

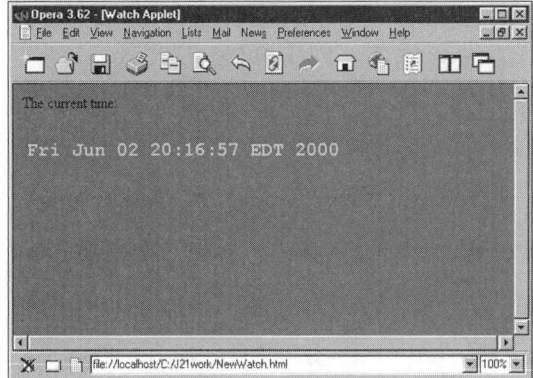

Because the applet window and Web page have the same background color, the edges of the applet are not visible in Figure 7.5. If no background parameter is specified in the HTML code loading the NewWatch applet, the default is black.

Developing Java 2 Applets

When you are planning a Java programming project that includes applets, one of the biggest decisions to make is what version of the language to employ in those applets.

Java 1.0, the first version, is supported in all Web browsers that can run applets. Netscape Navigator and Microsoft Internet Explorer have supported it for more than four years, and it's also offered in Opera and other browsers.

The most recent editions of these browsers also have added support for Java 1.1 in the past year, so you can now take advantage of the improved user interface, event handling, and other features while reaching a wide audience of browser users.

To support Java, browser developers have created their own Java interpreters and integrated them into the software. This has become progressively more difficult with each new version of Java, and it also adds to the size of the browser because the Java class library is more than five times as large today as it was in Java 1.1.

Sun offers the Java Plug-in, an interpreter that can run applets in Web browsers in place of the built-in interpreter. The Plug-in, which was originally called the Java Activator, supports the current version of Java 2, so it's available for applet programmers who want to use the most up-to-date techniques offered in the language.

7

Two things must happen for a Java applet to run using the Java Plug-in:

- The user must have installed the Plug-in.
- The page containing the applet must have HTML code that directs the Plug-in to run the applet.

The Java Plug-in is included with SDK 1.3, so you already should have a copy installed on your system. To download and install it separately, visit Sun's Java Web site at `http://java.sun.com/products/plugin` or visit the main page at `http://java.sun.com` and look in the Products & APIs section of the site.

Using the Plug-in on a Web Page

When you are relying on a browser's built-in Java interpreter, putting an applet on a Web page is simple. You use the `<APPLET>` or `<OBJECT>` tag to put the applet on a page, and use `<PARAM>` to send parameters that customize how the applet runs, as in the following example:

```
<applet code="NewWatch.class" height="50" width="345">
<param name="background" value="#996633">
This program requires a Java-enabled browser.
</applet>
```

Running an applet that uses the Java Plug-in is more complex. You must write HTML code that accounts for the different ways that Internet Explorer and Netscape Navigator handle plug-ins and embedded programs such as applets.

If you modified the preceding example so that it used the Plug-in to execute the applet, here's what the HTML code looks like:

```
<OBJECT classid="clsid:8AD9C840-044E-11D1-B3E9-00805F499D93" WIDTH ="345"
HEIGHT="50" codebase="http://java.sun.com/products/plugin/1.3/jinstall-13-
➥win32.cab#Version=1,3,0,0">
<PARAM NAME=CODE VALUE="NewWatch.class">
<PARAM NAME="type" VALUE="application/x-java-applet;version=1.3">
<PARAM NAME="scriptable" VALUE="false">
<PARAM NAME="background" VALUE="#996633">
<COMMENT>
<EMBED type="application/x-java-applet;version=1.3" CODE="NewWatch.class"
WIDTH="345" HEIGHT="50" background="#996633" scriptable=false
pluginspage="http://java.sun.com/products/plugin/1.3/plugin-install.html">
</COMMENT>
<NOEMBED>
This program requires a Java-enabled browser.
</NOEMBED>
</EMBED>
</OBJECT>
```

```
<!--
<APPLET CODE="NewWatch.class" WIDTH="345" HEIGHT="50">
<PARAM NAME="background" VALUE="#996633">
This program requires a Java-enabled browser.
</APPLET>
-->
```

As you can see, the HTML required by the Java Plug-in is more complex. Different tags are used to make the applet work on as wide a variety of browsers as possible.

Sun has created a Java application called HTMLConverter that converts an existing Web page so that all its applets are run by the Java Plug-in. After you have created a Web page that loads an applet using an <APPLET> tag, HTMLConverter will convert the Web page to use the Plug-in instead.

This program is available from the same page on the Java Web site as the Plug-in. At the time of this writing, the current version of HTMLConverter is offered as a ZIP archive. (Prior versions came with an installation program.)

After downloading the file, extract all the files within the ZIP archive into a folder using a program that handles the ZIP format and make sure that subfolders are created to hold all the files associated with HTMLConverter—your ZIP program should do this automatically. A new converter folder will be created.

If you extracted the files into c:\jdk1.3, the subfolder is c:\jdk1.3\converter. Add this folder to your system's CLASSPATH and reboot the system to make the change take effect.

Once HTMLConverter has been installed, run the program with the Java interpreter, using the name of the HTML document to convert as an argument. For example:

```
java HTMLConverter WatchApplet.html
```

The preceding command will convert all applets contained in WatchApplet.html to run the Java Plug-in.

Caution   The HTMLConverter application overwrites the existing HTML code on the page—if for some reason you also want the non-Plug-in version of the page, you should copy the HTML document and run HTMLConverter on that copy.

7

Running the Plug-in

The Java Plug-in works in conjunction with a browser like other browser plug-ins such as the Macromedia Flash player, Real streaming multimedia player, and PNG graphics viewers.

First, markup code is added to an HTML document to indicate that it contains a file requiring a plug-in. Other information is provided, such as the name of the plug-in and an address from which the plug-in can be downloaded.

When a user loads the document with a Web browser, the browser looks for the plug-in on the user's computer, and if it is found, opens the file with the plug-in.

If the plug-in is not found, a dialog box opens asking for permission to download and install the plug-in. Figure 7.6 shows what this dialog looks like in Internet Explorer 5. By default, Internet Explorer will not install a plug-in, ActiveX control, and other executable programs without the user's approval.

FIGURE 7.6

Deciding whether to install the Java Plug-in.

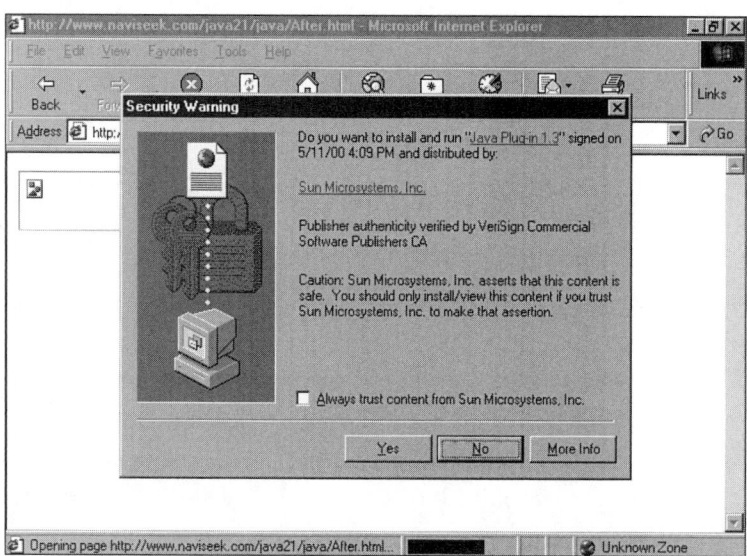

If the user decides to install the Plug-in, it will be downloaded and set up on the user's computer. This can be a time-consuming process—the Java Plug-in is more than 4.5MB at present and takes more than 30 minutes to download over a 28.8Kbps Internet connection.

Note

Because the Java Plug-in is so large, Sun recommends that it should be used only for intranets, large-scale corporate software, and other projects where the audience is well defined. Most applet programmers today whose work is open to all Web users employ Java 1.1 or 1.0 features only and do not require the Java Plug-in.

Once installation is complete, the Plug-in opens the file. All other files that require the plug-in will be run automatically, so that user will be able to use all Java 2 applets as if the browser had a built-in interpreter that supported them.

Summary

Although applets are no longer the focus of Java development, they are still the element of Java technology that reaches the most people. There are applets on thousands of World Wide Web sites—more than 13.6 million Web pages contain an applet, according to the AltaVista search engine at `http://www.altavista.com`.

Because they are executed and displayed within Web pages, applets can use the graphics, user interface, and event structure provided by the Web browser. This capability provides the applet programmer with a lot of functionality without a lot of extra toil.

Today you learned the basics of applet creation, including the following things:

- All applets are subclasses of the `java.applet.Applet` or `javax.swing.JApplet` class, which provide the behavior the program needs to run within a Web browser.
- Applets have five main methods that cover activities an applet performs as it runs: `init()`, `start()`, `stop()`, `destroy()`, and `paint()`. These methods are overridden to provide functionality in an applet.
- Applets are placed on Web pages using the `<APPLET>` or `<OBJECT>` tag in HTML, and the `<PARAM>` tag can be used to specify parameters that customize how the applet functions.
- To reduce the time it takes to download an applet from a Web server, you can use Java archive files.
- Applets can receive information from a Web page by using the `<PARAM>` tag in association with an applet. Inside the body of your applet, you can gain access to those parameters using the `getParameter()` method.
- If you want to use Java 2 features in your applets, you can create HTML documents that use the Java Plug-in rather than a browser's built-in interpreter.

7

Q&A

Q I have an applet that takes parameters and an HTML file that passes it those parameters, but when my applet runs, all I get are `null` values. What's going on here?

A Do the names of your parameters (in the `NAME` attribute) match exactly with the names you're testing for in `getParameter()`? They must be exact, including case, for the match to be made. Make sure also that your `<PARAM>` tags are inside the opening and closing `<APPLET>` tags and that you haven't misspelled anything.

Q Because applets don't have a command line or a standard output stream, how can I do simple debugging output like `System.out.println()` in an applet?

A Depending on your browser or other Java-enabled environment, you might have a console window where debugging output (the result of `System.out.println()`) appears, or it might be saved to a log file. (Netscape has a Java Console under the Options menu; Internet Explorer uses a Java log file that you must enable by choosing Options, Advanced.)

You can continue to print messages using `System.out.println()` in your applets—just remember to remove them after you're done, so that they don't confuse your actual users.

Q I've enabled Java logging on Internet Explorer 4.0. Now where the heck do I view the log?

A Unlike Netscape Navigator, which makes the Java output window available as a pull-down menu command, Microsoft Internet Explorer doesn't appear to have a built-in feature. Under Internet Explorer, you can find the log in the text file `java-log.txt` in your main `\WINDOWS\JAVA` folder (often `C:\WINDOWS\JAVA`).

Q The Watch applet compiles successfully and I can see the working program with appletviewer, but none of my browsers are able to show the applet. Do you have any idea what's wrong?

A The Watch applet is written using Java 2 techniques, so it won't run in a Web browser that doesn't support Java. At present, none of the major browser developers offer built-in support for this version of Java language. The Java Plug-in section of this chapter describes how support for Java 2 applets can be added to current browsers.

Questions

1. Which class should an applet inherit from if Swing features will be used in the program?

    (a) `java.applet.Applet`

    (b) `javax.swing.JApplet`

    (c) Either one

2. What method is called whenever an applet window is obscured and must be redrawn?

    (a) `start()`

    (b) `init()`

    (c) `paint()`

3. To reach the widest possible audience, what Java version should your applets employ?

    (a) Java 1.0

    (b) Java 1.1

    (c) Java 2

Answers

1. b. If you're going to use Swing's improved interface and event-handling capabilities, the applet must be a subclass of `JApplet`.

2. c. You also can request that the applet window be redisplayed by calling the applet's `repaint()` method.

3. The answer is a, although it's becoming a toss-up with answer b. More than 85% of the Web audience uses the current Navigator, Internet Explorer, or Opera browsers, which all support Java 1.1.

Exercises

To extend your knowledge of the subjects covered today, try the following exercises:

- Enhance the `NewWatch` applet so that you can set the color of the text with a parameter also.

- Create an applet that does the same thing as `Ellsworth.java` from Day 1, "21st Century Java."

Where applicable, exercise solutions are offered on the book's Web site at `http://www.java21pro.com`.

7

WEEK 2

Swing and Other Visual Java Programming

- Working with Swing
- Building a Swing Interface
- Arranging Components on a User Interface
- Responding to User Input
- Color, Fonts, and Graphics
- Threads and Animation
- Java Sound

DAY 8

Working with Swing

During the next four days, you will work with a set of classes called Swing that can implement a user-interface style called Metal. (Sounds like somebody at Sun Microsystems is either a music buff or a frustrated musician.)

Swing, which is part of the Java Foundation Classes library, provides a way to offer a graphical user interface in your Java programs and take user input with the keyboard, mouse, and other input devices.

The Swing library is an extension of the Abstract Windowing Toolkit, the package that offered limited graphical programming support in Java 1.0. Swing offers much-improved functionality over its predecessor—new components, expanded component features, better event handling, and a selectable look and feel.

Today you use Swing to create applications that feature a graphical user interface, using each of these components:

- Frames—windows that can include a title bar and menu bar, as well as maximize, minimize, and close buttons
- Containers—interface elements that can hold other components
- Buttons—clickable regions with text or graphics indicating their purpose

- Labels—text or graphics that provide information
- Text fields and text areas—windows that take keyboard input and allow text to be edited
- Drop-down lists—groups of related items that can be selected from drop-down menus or scrolling windows
- Check boxes and radio buttons—small windows or circles that can be selected or deselected

Creating an Application

The expression "look and feel" is used often when describing interface programming. As you might have guessed, it describes how a graphical user interface looks and feels to a user. Look and feel is something that becomes relevant in Java with the introduction of Swing.

This feature offers the most visually dramatic change from the Abstract Windowing Toolkit (AWT). Swing lets you create a Java program with an interface that uses the style of the native operating system, such as Windows or Solaris, or a new style that has been dubbed Metal, which is unique to Java.

Swing components, unlike their predecessors in previous versions of Java, are implemented entirely in Java. This makes them more compatible across different platforms than the AWT.

All elements of Swing are part of the `javax.swing` package, a standard part of the Java 2 class library. To use a Swing class, you must either use an `import` statement with that class or a catch-all statement such as the following:

```
import javax.swing.*;
```

 **Caution**

> The Swing package had several names before Sun settled on `javax.swing`. If you come across one of the older names in a program's source code—`com.sun.java.swing` or `java.awt.swing`—changing the package name might be all that's required to update the code for Java 2.

Two other packages that are used with graphical user interface programming are `java.awt`, the Abstract Windowing Toolkit, and `java.awt.event`, event-handling classes that handle user input.

When you use a Swing component, you work with objects of that component's class. You create the component by calling its constructor method and then calling methods of the component as needed for proper setup.

All Swing components are subclasses of the abstract class JComponent, which includes methods to set the size of a component, change the background color, define the font used for any displayed text, and set up *tooltips*—explanatory text that appears when a user hovers over the component for a few seconds.

> **Caution**
>
> Swing classes inherit from many of the same superclasses as the Abstract Windowing Toolkit, so it is possible to use Swing and AWT components together in the same interface. However, in some cases the two types of components will not be rendered correctly in a container. To avoid these problems, it's best to use Swing components unless you are writing an applet limited to Java 1.0 or 1.1 functionality—there's a Swing version of every AWT component.

Before components can be displayed in a user interface, they must be added to a *container*, a component that can hold other components. Swing containers, which can often be placed in other containers, are subclasses of java.awt.Container, a class in the Abstract Windowing Toolkit. This class includes methods to add and remove components from a container, arrange components using an object called a layout manager, and set up empty insets around the inside edges of a container.

Creating an Interface

The first step in creating a Swing application is to create a class that represents the graphical user interface. An object of this class will serve as a container, the component that holds all other components to be displayed.

In many projects, the main interface object will be either a simple window (the JWindow class) or a more specialized window called a frame (the JFrame class).

A window is a container that can be displayed on a user's desktop. It does not have a title bar; maximize, minimize and close buttons; or other features you see on most windows that open in a graphical user interface operating system. Windows that are enhanced with title bars, window management buttons, and other features are called frames.

In a graphical environment such as Windows or MacOS, users expect to have the ability to move, resize, and close the windows of programs that they run. The main place a window turns up is when programs are loading—there is sometimes a "title screen" with the program's name, logo, and other information.

One way to create a graphical Swing application is to make the interface a subclass of JFrame, as in the following class declaration:

```
public class Lookup extends JFrame {
    // ...
}
```

This leaves only a few things to do in the constructor method of the class:

- Call a constructor method of the superclass to handle any of its setup procedures.
- Set the size of the frame's window, in pixels.
- Decide what to do if a user closes the window.
- Display the frame.

The JFrame class has two constructors: JFrame() and JFrame(String). One sets the frame's title bar to the specified text, whereas the other leaves this empty. You can also set the title by calling the frame's setTitle(String) method.

The size of a frame can be established by calling the setSize(int, int) with the width and height as arguments. The size of a frame is indicated in pixels, so if you called setSize(600, 600), the frame would take up almost all of a screen at 800×600 resolution once it is displayed.

 Note

> You also can call the method setSize(Dimension) to set up a frame's size. Dimension, a class in the java.awt package, represents the width and height of a user interface component. Calling the Dimension(int, int) constructor will create a Dimension object representing the width and height specified as arguments.

Frames are invisible when they are created. You can make them visible by calling the frame's show() method with no arguments or setVisible(boolean) with the literal true as an argument.

If you want a frame to be displayed when it is created, call one of these methods in the constructor method. You also can leave the frame invisible, requiring any class that uses the frame to make it visible by calling show() or setVisible(true). (There are also methods of hiding a frame—call either hide() method or setVisible(false).)

When a frame is displayed, the default behavior is for it to be positioned in the upper left corner of the computer's desktop. You can specify a different location by calling the setBounds(*int, int, int, int*) method. The first two arguments to this method are the (x,y) position of the frame's upper left corner on the desktop, and the last two arguments set the width and height of the frame.

The following class represents a 400×100 frame with "Edit Payroll" in the title bar:

```
public class Payroll extends javax.swing.JFrame {
    public Payroll() {
        super("Edit Payroll");
        setSize(300, 100);
        show();
    }
}
```

Every frame has maximize, minimize, and close buttons on the title bar at the user's control—the same controls present in the interface of other software running on your system. In Java, the normal behavior when a frame is closed is for the application to keep running.

To change this, you must call a frame's setDefaultCloseOperation() method with one of four JFrame class variables as an argument:

- EXIT_ON_CLOSE—Exit the program when the frame is closed.
- DISPOSE_ON_CLOSE—Close the frame, dispose of the frame object, and keep running the application.
- DO_NOTHING_ON_CLOSE—Keep the frame open and continue running.
- HIDE_ON_CLOSE—Close the frame and continue running.

To prevent a user from closing a frame at all, add the following statement to the frame's constructor method:

```
setDefaultCloseOperation(JFrame.DO_NOTHING_ON_CLOSE);
```

If you are creating a frame to serve as an application's main user interface, the expected behavior is probably EXIT_ON_CLOSE, which shuts down the application along with the frame.

Developing a Framework

Listing 8.1 contains a simple application that displays a frame 300×100 pixels in size. This class can serve as a framework—pun unavoidable—for any applications you create that use a graphical user interface.

LISTING 8.1   The Full Text of `SimpleFrame.java`

```java
 1: import javax.swing.JFrame;
 2:
 3: public class SimpleFrame extends JFrame {
 4:     public SimpleFrame() {
 5:         super("Frame Title");
 6:         setSize(300, 100);
 7:         setDefaultCloseOperation(JFrame.EXIT_ON_CLOSE);
 8:         setVisible(true);
 9:     }
10:
11:     public static void main(String[] arguments) {
12:         SimpleFrame sf = new SimpleFrame();
13:     }
14:
15: }
```

When you compile and run the application, you should see the frame displayed in Figure 8.1.

FIGURE 8.1

Displaying a frame.

The `SimpleFrame` application isn't much to look at—this graphical user interface contains no components a user can actually interface with, aside from the standard maximize, minimize, and close ("X") buttons on the title bar shown in Figure 8.1. You will add components later today.

A `SimpleFrame` object is created in the `main()` method in lines 11–13. If you had not displayed the frame when it was constructed, you could call `sf.setVisible(true)` in the `main()` method to display the frame represented by `sf`.

The work involved in creating the frame's user interface takes place in the `SimpleFrame()` constructor method. If you were adding components to this frame, they could be created and added to the frame within this constructor.

Creating a window using `JWindow` is very similar to working with frames in Swing. The only things you can't do involve features that simple windows don't support—titles, closing a window, and so on.

Listing 8.2 contains an application that creates and opens a window, displays the first 10,000 integers in the command-line window, and then closes the window.

8

LISTING 8.2   The Full Text of `SimpleWindow.java`

```
 1: import javax.swing.JWindow;
 2:
 3: public class SimpleWindow extends JWindow {
 4:     public SimpleWindow() {
 5:         super();
 6:         setBounds(250, 225, 300, 150);
 7: }
 8:
 9:     public static void main(String[] arguments) {
10:         SimpleWindow sw = new SimpleWindow();
11:         sw.setVisible(true);
12:         for (int i = 0; i < 10000; i++)
13:             System.out.print(i + " ");
14:         sw.setVisible(false);
15:         System.exit(0);
16:     }
17:
18: }
```

Figure 8.2 shows this application running with the `SimpleWindow` container visible over the Java command-line window in Windows.

FIGURE 8.2

Displaying a window.

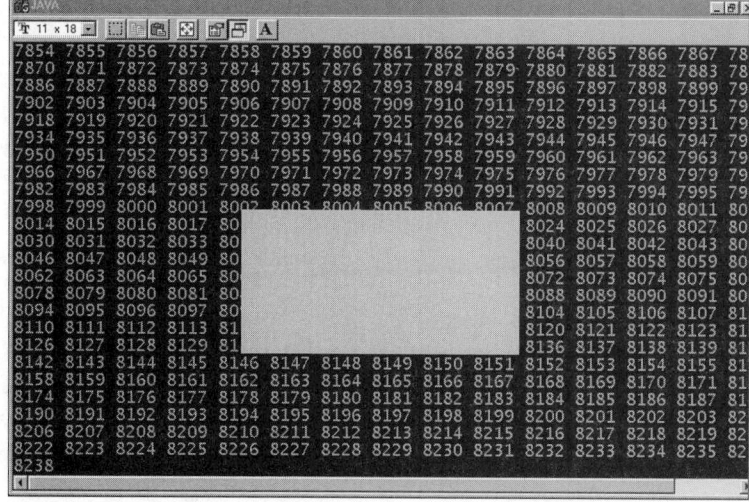

Because of the call to `setBounds(250, 225, 300, 150)` in line 6 of Listing 8.2, the window is 300×150 in size and displayed with its upper left corner at the (x,y) position 250, 225.

The `for` loop in lines 12–13 is included simply to take up a little time. There are better ways to make time pass in a Java program, as you will see in Day 13, "Threads and Animation."

Closing a Window

Prior to the introduction of the `setDefaultCloseOperation()` method in Java 2, the only way to close a graphical application after a user closed a window was to explicitly deal with the occurrence.

To do this, the window must be monitored to see if the user has done anything to close it, such as clicking a title bar close button. If so, a program can respond by exiting the program, closing the window, keeping it open, or something else appropriate to the situation.

Monitoring for user interaction requires the use of event-handling classes—features that you explore in great detail on Day 11, "Responding to User Input." The term *event-handling* in Java describes objects that wait for something to occur—such as a button-click or typing text into a field—and then call methods in response to that occurrence.

All of Java's event-handling classes belong to the `java.awt.event` package.

 Note

> Though this technique isn't necessary in Java 2, it is introduced here because you will see it in many existing Swing applications. It also provides a first look at how Java handles user input in a Swing interface.

To monitor a window in a user interface, your program must do three things:

- Create an object that will monitor the state of the window.
- Implement an interface in the object that handles each way the window can change.
- Associate the window with your user interface.

A window can be monitored by any object that implements the `WindowListener` interface. As you learned on Day 2, "Object-Oriented Programming," an interface is a set of methods that indicate a class supports more behavior than it has inherited from its superclasses.

In this example, a class that implements the `WindowListener` interface has behavior to keep track of what a user is doing to a window.

To implement an interface, a class must include all the methods in that interface. Classes that support `WindowListener` must have the following seven methods:

- `windowActivated()`—The window associated with this object is becoming the active window, which means that it will be able to receive keyboard input.

- `windowDeactivated()`—The window is about to become inactive, which means that it won't be able to receive keyboard input.

- `windowClosed()`—The window has been closed.

- `windowClosing()`—The window is being closed.

- `windowOpened()`—The window has been made visible.

- `windowIconified()`—The window has been minimized.

- `windowDeiconified()`—The window has been maximized.

As you can see, each method has something to do with how a user interacts with the window.

Another class in the `java.awt.event` package, `WindowAdapter`, implements this interface with seven empty methods that do nothing. By creating a subclass of `WindowAdapter`, you can override methods pertaining to the user-interaction events that you want to deal with, as shown in Listing 8.3.

LISTING 8.3   The Full Text of `ExitWindow.java`

```
1: import java.awt.event.*;
2:
3: public class ExitWindow extends WindowAdapter {
4:     public void windowClosing(WindowEvent e) {
5:         System.exit(0);
6:     }
7: }
```

The ExitWindow class inherits from `WindowAdapter`, which implements the `WindowListener` interface. As a result, `ExitWindow` objects can be used to monitor frames.

An `ExitWindow` object has only one job: Wait to see if a window is being closed, an event that causes `windowClosing()` method to be called automatically.

Line 5 of Listing 8.3 calls a class method of `java.lang.System`, `exit()`, which shuts down the currently running application. The integer argument to `exit()` should be 0 if the program ended normally or any other value if it ended because of an error of some kind.

Once you have created an object that can monitor a window, you associate it with that window by calling the component's `addWindowListener()` method, as in the following example:

```
JFrame main = new JFrame("Main Menu");
ExitWindow exit = new ExitWindow();
main.addWindowListener(exit);
```

This example associates the `ExitWindow` object with a frame called `main`.

You can use this `ExitWindow` class with the primary window of any application, provided that the program should shut down and do nothing else after the user closes the window.

Listing 8.4 contains the `SimpleFrame` application rewritten to use this technique.

LISTING 8.4   The Full Text of `ExitFrame.java`

```
 1: import javax.swing.JFrame;
 2:
 3: public class ExitFrame extends JFrame {
 4:     public ExitFrame() {
 5:         super("Frame Title");
 6:         setSize(300, 100);
 7:         ExitWindow exit = new ExitWindow();
 8:         addWindowListener(exit);
 9:         setVisible(true);
10:     }
11:
12:     public static void main(String[] arguments) {
13:         ExitFrame sf = new ExitFrame();
14:     }
15:
16: }
```

This application must have access to `ExitWindow.class` in order to compile and run successfully. The easiest way to do this is to compile both programs in the same folder.

Creating a Component

Creating a graphical user interface is a great way to get experience working with objects in Java because each aspect of the interface is represented by its own class.

You have already worked with the containers JFrame and JWindow and the event-handling class WindowAdapter. Yesterday, you used another container, JApplet.

To use an interface component in Java, you create an object of that component's class. One of the simplest to employ is JButton, the class that embodies clickable buttons.

In most programs, buttons trigger an action—click Install to begin installing software, click a Smiley button to begin a new game of Minesweeper, click the Minimize button to prevent your boss from seeing Minesweeper running, and so on.

A Swing button can feature a text label, a graphical icon, or a combination of both.

Constructor methods you can use include

- JButton(*String*)—Creates a button labeled with the specified text.
- JButton(*Icon*)—Creates a button that displays the specified icon.
- JButton(*String*, *Icon*)—Creates a button with the specified text and icon.

The following statements create three buttons:

```
JButton play = new JButton("Play");
JButton stop = new JButton("Stop");
JButton rewind = new JButton("Rewind");
```

Adding Components to a Container

Before you can display a user interface component, such as a button in a Java program, you must add it to a container and display that container.

To add a component to a simple container, you call the container's add(*Component*) method with the component as the argument (all user interface components in Swing inherit from java.awt.Component).

The simplest Swing container is the panel (the JPanel class). The following example creates a button and adds it to a panel:

```
JButton quit = new JButton("Quit");
JPanel panel = new JPanel();
panel.add(quit);
```

Most other Swing containers, including frames, windows, applets, and dialog boxes, do not allow components to be added in this manner.

These containers are broken down into *panes*, sort of containers-within-containers. Ordinarily, components are added to the container's *content pane*.

You can add components to a container's content pane using the following steps:

1. Create a panel.

2. Add components to the panel using its add(*Component*) method.

3. Call setContentPane(*Container*) with the panel as an argument.

The program in Listing 8.5 uses the application framework created earlier in this chapter, but adds a button to the frame's content pane.

LISTING 8.5   The Full Text of Buttons.java

```
 1: import javax.swing.*;
 2:
 3: public class Buttons extends JFrame {
 4:     JButton abort = new JButton("Abort");
 5:     JButton retry = new JButton("Retry");
 6:     JButton fail = new JButton("Fail");
 7:
 8:     public Buttons() {
 9:         super("Buttons");
10:         setSize(80, 140);
11:         setDefaultCloseOperation(JFrame.EXIT_ON_CLOSE);
12:         JPanel pane = new JPanel();
13:         pane.add(abort);
14:         pane.add(retry);
15:         pane.add(fail);
16:         setContentPane(pane);
17: }
18:
19:     public static void main(String[] arguments) {
20:         Buttons rb = new Buttons();
21:         rb.show();
22:     }
23: }
```

When you run the application, a small frame will open that contains three buttons (see Figure 8.3).

FIGURE 8.3

The Buttons *application.*

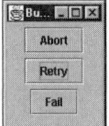

8

The Buttons class has three instance variables: the abort, retry, and fail JButton objects.

In lines 12–15, a new JPanel object is created and the three buttons are added to the panel by calling its add() method. When the panel is complete, the frame's setContentPane() method is called in line 16 with the panel as an argument, making it the frame's content pane.

 Note

> If you click the buttons, absolutely nothing will happen. Doing something in response to a button click is covered in Day 11.

Adding Components to an Applet

Another kind of container you can work with in Swing is the applet window. Because applets are already part of a graphical user interface in a Web browser, they don't require as much initial setup as the windows you create for applications. The window is already open when the applet begins running, and the dimensions are determined by HTML tags on the Web document that contains the applet.

A Swing applet is divided, separating the content pane from other panes. You must add components to the content pane rather than the applet itself.

 Note

> This is a departure from how Java 1.0 and Java 1.1 applets are used as containers. Those applets are subclasses of java.applet.Applet, and you add components directly to the applet using the add() method. They are not subdivided into panes.

Listing 8.6 contains the Buttons application rewritten as an applet.

LISTING 8.6   The Full Text of ButtonApplet.java

```
1: import javax.swing.*;
2:
3: public class ButtonApplet extends JApplet {
4:     JButton abort = new JButton("Abort");
5:     JButton retry = new JButton("Retry");
6:     JButton fail = new JButton("Fail");
7:
8:     public void init() {
9:         JPanel pane = new JPanel();
```

LISTING 8.6   continued

```
10:         pane.add(abort);
11:         pane.add(retry);
12:         pane.add(fail);
13:         setContentPane(pane);
14:    }
15: }
```

The following HTML can be used on a Web document to load the applet shown in
Figure 8.4:

```
<applet code="ButtonApplet.class" width="80" height="140">
</applet>
```

FIGURE 8.4

The ButtonApplet
applet loaded by
appletviewer.

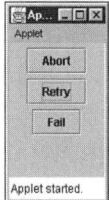

Working with Components

Swing offers more than two dozen different user interface components in addition to the
buttons and containers you have used thus far. You will work with many of these components for the rest of the day and on Day 9, "Building a Swing Interface."

All Swing components share a common superclass, javax.swing.JComponent, and
inherit several methods you will find useful in your own programs.

The setEnabled(*boolean*) method enables a component if the argument is true and disables it if the argument is false. Components are enabled by default, and they must be
enabled in order to receive user input. Many disabled components will change in appearance to indicate that they are not presently usable—for instance, a disabled JButton will
have light gray borders and gray text. If you want to check whether a component is
enabled, you can call the isEnabled() method, which returns a boolean value.

The setVisible(*boolean*) method works for all components the way it does for containers. Use true to display a component and false to hide it. There's also a boolean
isVisible() method.

The setSize(*int, int*) resizes the component to the width and height specified as arguments, and setSize(*Dimension*) uses a Dimension object to do the same thing. For most components, you do not need to set a size—the default is usually acceptable. To find out the size of a component, call its getSize() method, which returns a Dimension object with the dimensions in height and width instance variables.

As you will see, similar Swing components also have other methods in common, such as setText() and getText() for text components, and setValue() and getValue() for components that store a numeric value.

Image Icons

Earlier today, you created button components that were labeled with text. Swing also supports the use of ImageIcon objects on buttons and other components in which a label can be provided. *Icons* are small graphics, usually in GIF format, that can be placed on a button, label, or other user interface element to identify it. Current operating systems have icons everywhere—garbage cans and recycling bins for deleting files, folder icons for storing files, mailbox icons for email programs, and hundreds of others.

An ImageIcon object can be created by specifying a graphic's filename as the only argument to the constructor. The following example loads an icon from the file zap.gif and creates a JButton with the icon as its label:

```
ImageIcon zap = new ImageIcon("zap.gif");
JButton button = new JButton(zap);
JPanel pane = new JPanel();
pane.add(button);
setContentPane(pane);
```

Listing 8.7 contains a Java application that uses the same ImageIcon to create 24 buttons, add them to a panel, and then designate the panel as a frame's content pane.

LISTING 8.7   The Full Text of Icons.java

```
 1: import javax.swing.*;
 2:
 3: public class Icons extends JFrame {
 4:     JButton[] buttons = new JButton[24];
 5:
 6:     public Icons() {
 7:         super("Icons");
 8:         setSize(335, 318);
 9:         setDefaultCloseOperation(JFrame.EXIT_ON_CLOSE);
10:         JPanel pane = new JPanel();
11:         ImageIcon icon = new ImageIcon("3dman.gif");
12:         for (int i = 0; i < 24; i++) {
```

LISTING 8.7   continued

```
13:               buttons[i] = new JButton(icon);
14:               pane.add(buttons[i]);
15:          }
16:          setContentPane(pane);
17:          show();
18:     }
19:
20:     public static void main(String[] arguments) {
21:          Icons ike = new Icons();
22:     }
23: }
```

Figure 8.5 shows the result.

FIGURE 8.5

An interface contain-ing buttons labeled with icons.

The icon graphic referred to in line 12 can be found on this book's official Web site at
http://www.java21pro.com in the page for Day 8, "Working with Swing," under the
filename 3dman.gif.

> The 3D moviegoer icon is from Jeffrey Zeldman's Pardon My Icons! collec-
> tion, which includes hundreds of icons you can use in your own projects. If
> you're looking for icons to experiment with in Swing applications, you can
> find Pardon My Icons at the following address:
>
> http://www.zeldman.com/icon.html

Labels

A label is a user component that contains informative text, an icon, or both. Labels,
which are created from the JLabel class, are often used to identify the purpose of other
components on an interface. They cannot be directly edited by a user.

8

To create a label, you can use the following constructors:

- JLabel(*String*)—A label with the specified text
- JLabel(*String*, *int*)—A label with the specified text and alignment
- JLabel(*String*, *Icon*, *int*)—A label with the specified text, icon, and alignment

The alignment of a label determines how its text or icon are aligned in relation to the area taken up by the window. Three class variables of the SwingConstants interface are used to specify alignment: LEFT, CENTER, or RIGHT.

The contents of a label can be set with the setText(*String*) or setIcon(*Icon*) methods. You also can retrieve these things with getText() and getIcon() methods.

The following statements create three labels with left, center, and right alignment, respectively:

```
JLabel tinker = new JLabel("Tinker", SwingConstants.LEFT);
JLabel evers = new JLabel("Evers");
JLabel chance = new JLabel("Chance", SwingContestants.RIGHT);
```

No alignment is specified in the constructor for the evers label, so it is given the default, which is centered alignment.

Text Fields

A *text field* is an area on an interface where a user can enter and modify text with a keyboard. Text fields, which are represented by the JTextField class, can handle one line of input. A similar component, text areas, can handle multiple lines.

Constructor methods include the following:

- JTextField()—An empty text field
- JTextField(*int*)—A text field with the specified width
- JTextField(*String*, *int*)—A text field with the specified text and width

A text field's width attribute only has relevance if the interface is organized in a manner that does not resize components. You get more experience with this when you work with layout managers on Day 10, "Arranging Components on a User Interface."

The following statements create an empty text field that has enough space for roughly 30 characters and a text field of the same size with the starting text "Puddin N. Tane":

```
JTextField name = new JTextField(30);
JTextField name = new JTextField("Puddin N. Tane", 30);
```

Text fields and text areas both inherit from the superclass `JTextComponent` and share many common methods.

The `setEditable(boolean)` method determines whether a text component can be edited (an argument of `true`) or not (`false`). There's also an `isEditable()` method that returns a corresponding `boolean` value.

The `setText(String)` method changes the text to the specified string, and the `getText()` method returns the component's current text as a string. Another method retrieves only the text that a user has highlighted in the `getSelectedText()` component.

Also, a specialized subclass of text fields, called *password fields*, are used to hide the characters a user is typing into the field.

This class, `JPasswordField`, has the same constructor methods as its parent class.

Once you have created a password field, call its `setEchoChar(char)` method to obscure input with the specified character.

 Note   The `TextField` class in the Abstract Windowing Toolkit supports obscured text with the `setEchoCharacter(char)` method. This method is not support-ed in the `JTextField` class—improvements in Java's security necessitated the creation of a new class for obscured text.

The following statements create a password field and set its echo character to #:

```
JPasswordField codePhrase = new JPasswordField(20);
codePhrase.setEchoChar('#');
```

Text Areas

Text areas, editable text fields that can handle more than one line of input, are imple-mented with the `JTextArea` class.

`JTextArea` includes the following constructor methods:

- `JTextArea(int, int)`—A text area with the specified number of rows and columns
- `JTextArea(String, int, int)`—A text area with the specified text, rows, and columns

8

You can use the getText(), getSelectedText(), and setText(*String*) methods with text areas as you would text fields. Also, an append(*String*) method adds the specified text at the end of the current text and an insert(*String*, *int*) method inserts the specified text at the indicated position.

The setLineWrap(*boolean*) method determines whether text will wrap to the next line when it reaches the far edge of the component. Call setLineWrap(true) to cause line wrapping to occur.

The setWrapStyleWord(*boolean*) method determines what wraps to the next line—either the current word (an argument of true) or the current character (false).

The next project you will create, the Form application in Listing 8.8, uses several Swing components to collect user input: a text field, a password field, and a text area. Labels also are used to indicate the purpose of each text component.

LISTING 8.8   The Full Text of Form.java

```
1: import javax.swing.*;
2:
3: public class Form extends javax.swing.JFrame {
4:     JTextField username = new JTextField(15);
5:     JPasswordField password = new JPasswordField(15);
6:     JTextArea comments = new JTextArea(4, 15);
7:
8:     public Form() {
9:         super("Feedback Form");
10:        setSize(260, 160);
11:        setDefaultCloseOperation(EXIT_ON_CLOSE);
12:
13:        JPanel pane = new JPanel();
14:        JLabel usernameLabel = new JLabel("Username: ");
15:        JLabel passwordLabel = new JLabel("Password: ");
16:        JLabel commentsLabel = new JLabel("Comments:");
17:        comments.setLineWrap(true);
18:        comments.setWrapStyleWord(true);
19:        pane.add(usernameLabel);
20:        pane.add(username);
21:        pane.add(passwordLabel);
22:        pane.add(password);
23:        pane.add(commentsLabel);
24:        pane.add(comments);
25:        setContentPane(pane);
26:
27:        show();
28:     }
29:
```

LISTING 8.8   continued

```
30:     public static void main(String[] arguments) {
31:         Form input = new Form();
32:     }
33: }
```

Figure 8.6 shows the result.

FIGURE 8.6

The Form *application.*

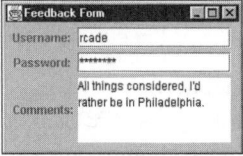

Scrolling Panes

Text areas in Swing do not include horizontal or vertical scroll bars, and there's no way to add them using this component alone. That's a difference between Swing text areas and their counterparts in the Abstract Windowing Toolkit.

The reason for the change is that Swing introduces a new container that can be used to hold any component that can be scrolled: JScrollPane.

A scrolling pane is associated with a component in the pane's constructor method. You can use either of the following:

- JScrollPane(*Component*)—A scrolling pane that contains the specified component
- JScrollPane(*Component*, *int*, *int*)—A scrolling pane with the specified component, vertical scrollbar configuration, and horizontal scrollbar configuration

Scrollbars are configured using class variables of the ScrollPaneConstants interface. You can use each of the following for vertical scrollbars:

- VERTICAL_SCROLLBAR_ALWAYS
- VERTICAL_SCROLLBAR_AS_NEEDED
- VERTICAL_SCROLLBAR_NEVER

There also are three similarly named variables for horizontal scrollbars.

After you create a scrolling pane containing a component, the pane should be added to containers in place of that component.

The following example creates a text area with a vertical scrollbar and no horizontal scrollbar, and then adds it to a content pane:

```
JPanel pane = new JPanel();
JTextArea letter = new JTextArea(5, 15);
JScrollPane scroll = new JScrollPane(letter,
    ScrollPaneConstants.VERTICAL_SCROLLBAR_ALWAYS,
    ScrollPaneConstants.HORIZONTAL_SCROLLBAR_NEVER);
pane.add(scroll);
setContentPane(pane);
```

Scrollbars

Scrollbars are components that enable a value to be selected by sliding a box between two arrows. Several components have built-in scrollbar functionality, including text areas and scrolling lists.

Scrollbars are normally created by specifying the minimum and maximum values that can be set using the component.

You can use the following constructor methods:

- JScrollBar(*int*)—A scrollbar with the specified orientation
- JScrollBar(*int*, *int*, *int*, *int*, *int*)—A scrollbar with the specified orientation, starting value, scroll box size, minimum value, and maximum value

The orientation is indicated by the JScrollBar class variables HORIZONTAL and VERTICAL.

You also can use JScrollbar(*int*, *int*, *int*, *int*, *int*), a third constructor with five integer arguments. The arguments for this method are in order here:

- Orientation is either JScrollBar.HORIZONTAL or JScrollBar.VERTICAL.
- The initial value of the scrollbar, which should be equal to or between the minimum and maximum values of the bar.
- The overall width or height of the box used to change the scrollbar's value. This can be equal to 0 when using the default size.
- The minimum value of the scrollbar.
- The maximum value.

The following statement creates a vertical scrollbar with a minimum value of 10, a maximum value of 50, and an initial value of 33.

```
JScrollBar bar = new JScrollBar(JScrollBar.HORIZONTAL,
    33, 0, 10, 50);
```

Check Boxes and Radio Buttons

The next two components you learn about are different only in appearance. Check boxes and radio buttons are both components that have only two possible values: selected or not selected. Both also can be grouped together so that only one component in a group can be selected at any time.

Check boxes (the JCheckBox class) are labeled or unlabeled boxes that contain a check mark when they are selected and nothing otherwise. Radio buttons (the JRadioButton class) are circles that contain a dot when selected and are also empty otherwise.

These components are typically used to make a simple yes-no or on-off kind of choice in a program. Both classes have several useful methods inherited from their common super-classes:

- setSelected(*boolean*)—Selects the component if the argument is true and deselects it otherwise.
- isSelected()—Returns a boolean indicating whether the component is currently selected.

The following constructors are available for the JCheckBox class:

- JCheckBox(*String*)—A check box with the specified text label
- JCheckBox(*String*, *boolean*)—A check box with the specified text label that is selected if the second argument is true
- JCheckBox(*Icon*)—A check box with the specified icon label
- JCheckBox(*Icon*, *boolean*)—A check box with the specified icon label that is selected if the second argument is true
- JCheckBox(*String*, *Icon*)—A check box with the specified text label and icon label
- JCheckBox(*String*, *Icon*, *boolean*)—A check box with the specified text label and icon label that is selected if the third argument is true

The JRadioButton class has constructors with the same arguments and functionality.

Check boxes and radio buttons are normally *nonexclusive*, meaning that if you have five check boxes in a container, all five can be checked or unchecked at the same time. To make them exclusive, you must organize related components into groups.

To organize several check boxes into a group, allowing only one to be selected at a time, create a ButtonGroup class object, as demonstrated in the following statement:

```
ButtonGroup choice = new ButtonGroup();
```

8

The ButtonGroup object keeps track of all check boxes or radio buttons in its group. Call the group's add(*Component*) method to add the specified component to the group.

The following example creates a group and two radio buttons that belong to it:

```
ButtonGroup betterDarrin = new ButtonGroup();
JRadioButton r1 = new JRadioButton ("Dick York", true);
betterDarrin.add(r1);
JRadioButton r2 = new JRadioButton ("Dick Sargent", false);
betterDarrin.add(r2);
```

The betterDarrin object is used to group together the r1 and r2 radio buttons. The r1 object, which has the label "Dick York", is selected. Only one member of the group can be selected at a time—if one component is selected, the ButtonGroup object will make sure that all others in the group are deselected.

Listing 8.9 contains an application with four radio buttons in a group.

LISTING 8.9   The Full Text of ChooseTeam.java

```
 1: import javax.swing.*;
 2:
 3: public class ChooseTeam extends JFrame {
 4:     JRadioButton[] teams = new JRadioButton[4];
 5:
 6:     public ChooseTeam() {
 7:         super("Choose Team");
 8:         setSize(140, 190);
 9:         setDefaultCloseOperation(JFrame.EXIT_ON_CLOSE);
10:         teams[0] = new JRadioButton("Colorado");
11:         teams[1] = new JRadioButton("Dallas", true);
12:         teams[2] = new JRadioButton("New Jersey");
13:         teams[3] = new JRadioButton("Philadelphia");
14:         JPanel pane = new JPanel();
15:         ButtonGroup group = new ButtonGroup();
16:         for (int i = 0; i < teams.length; i++) {
17:             group.add(teams[i]);
18:             pane.add(teams[i]);
19:         }
20:         setContentPane(pane);
21:         show();
22:     }
23:
24:     public static void main(String[] arguments) {
25:         ChooseTeam ct = new ChooseTeam();
26:     }
27: }
```

Figure 8.7 shows the application running. The four JRadioButton objects are stored in an array, and in the for loop in lines 16–19 each element is first added to a button group, and then added to a panel. After the loop ends, the panel is used for the application's content pane.

FIGURE 8.7

The ChooseTeam *application.*

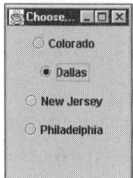

Drop-Down Lists and Combo Boxes

The Swing class JComboBox can be used to create two kinds of user interface components: drop-down lists and combo boxes.

Drop-down lists, also called *choice lists*, are components that enable a single item to be picked from a list. The list can be configured to appear only when a user clicks on the component, taking up less space in a graphical user interface.

Combo boxes are drop-down lists with an extra feature: a text field that also can be used to provide a response.

The following steps show how a drop-down list can be created:

1. The JComboBox() constructor is used with no arguments.
2. The combo box's addItem(*Object*) method adds items to the list.

In a drop-down list, users will only be able to select one of the items in the list. If the component's setEditable() method is called with true as an argument, it becomes a combo box rather than a drop-down list.

In a combo box, the user can enter text into the field instead of using the drop-down list to pick an item. This combination gives combo boxes their name.

The JComboBox class has several methods that can be used to control a drop-down list or combo box:

- The getItemAt(*int*) method returns the text of the list item at the index position specified by the integer argument. As with arrays, the first item of a choice list is at index position 0, the second at position 1, and so on.
- The getItemCount() method returns the number of items in the list.

- The `getSelectedIndex()` method returns the index position of the currently select-ed item in the list.

- The `getSelectedItem()` method returns the text of the currently selected item.

- The `setSelectedIndex(int)` method selects the item at the indicated index posi-tion.

- The `setSelectedIndex(Object)` method selects the specified object in the list.

- The `setMaximumRowCount(int)` method sets the number of rows in the combo box that are displayed at one time.

The `Expiration` application in Listing 8.10 contains an application that uses combo boxes to enter an expiration date, something you might use on an interface that conducts a credit-card transaction.

LISTING 8.10   The Full Text of `ChooseTeam.java`

```
 1: import javax.swing.*;
 2:
 3: public class Expiration extends JFrame {
 4:     JComboBox monthBox = new JComboBox();
 5:     JComboBox yearBox = new JComboBox();
 6:
 7:     public Expiration() {
 8:         super("Expiration Date");
 9:         setSize(220, 90);
10:         setDefaultCloseOperation(JFrame.EXIT_ON_CLOSE);
11:         JPanel pane = new JPanel();
12:         JLabel exp = new JLabel("Expiration Date:");
13:         pane.add(exp);
14:         for (int i = 1; i < 13; i++)
15:             monthBox.addItem("" + i);
16:         for (int i = 2000; i < 2010; i++)
17:             yearBox.addItem("" + i);
18:         pane.add(monthBox);
19:         pane.add(yearBox);
20:         setContentPane(pane);
21:         show();
22:     }
23:
24:     public static void main(String[] arguments) {
25:         Expiration ct = new Expiration();
26:     }
27: }
```

Figure 8.8 shows the application after a date has been selected.

FIGURE 8.8.

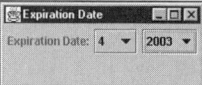

The Expiration *application.*

Summary

Today, you began working with Swing, the package of classes that enables you to offer a graphical user interface in your Java programs.

You used more than a dozen classes today, creating interface components such as buttons, labels, and text fields. You put each of these into containers, components that include panels, frames, windows, and applets.

Programming of this kind can be complex, and Swing represents the largest package of classes that a new Java programmer must deal with in learning the language.

However, as you have experienced with components such as text areas and text fields, Sun Microsystems has designed Swing so that components have many superclasses in common. This makes it easier to extend your knowledge into new components and containers, as well as the other aspects of Swing programming you will explore over the next three days.

Q&A

Q Can an application be created without Swing?

A Certainly. Swing is just an expansion of the Abstract Windowing Toolkit, and you can continue to use the AWT for applications with Java 2. However, event handling is different between the AWT and Swing, and there are many things in Swing that have no counterpart in the windowing toolkit. With Swing, you can use many more components and control them in more sophisticated ways.

Q Is there a way to change the font of text that appears on a button and other components?

A The JComponent class includes a setFont(Font) method that can be used to set the font for text displayed on that component. You will work with Font objects, color, and more graphics in Day 12, "Color, Fonts, and Graphics."

Q How can I find out what components are available in Swing and how to use them?

A This is the first of two days spent introducing user interface components, so you will learn more about them tomorrow. If you have Web access, you can find out what classes are in the Swing package by visiting Sun's online documentation for Java at the Web address http://java.sun.com/j2se/1.3/docs/api/.

Questions

1. Which of the following user interface components is not a container?

   (a) `JScrollPane`

   (b) `JScrollBar`

   (c) `JWindow`

2. Which container does not require the use of a content pane when adding components to it?

   (a) `JPanel`

   (b) `JApplet`

   (c) `JFrame`

3. If you use `setSize()` on an application's main frame or window, where will it appear on your desktop?

   (a) At the center of the desktop

   (b) At the same spot the last application appeared

   (c) At the upper left corner of the desktop

Answers

1. b.

2. a. `JPanel` is one of the simple containers that is not subdivided into panes, so you can call its `add(Component)` method to add components directly to the panel.

3. c. You can call `setBounds()` instead of `setSize()` to choose where a frame will appear.

Exercises

To extend your knowledge of the subjects covered today, try the following exercises:

- Create an application with a frame that includes all of the VCR controls as individual components: play, stop/eject, rewind, fast-forward, and pause. Choose a size for the window that enables all the components to be displayed on a single row.

- Create a frame that opens a smaller frame with fields asking for a username and password.

Where applicable, exercise solutions are offered on the book's Web site at `http://www.java21pro.com`.

WEEK 2

DAY 9

Building a Swing Interface

With the popularity of Apple MacOS and Microsoft Windows, most computer users expect software to feature a graphical user interface and things they can control with a mouse. These software amenities are user friendly but programmer unfriendly in many languages. Writing windowing software can be one of the more challenging tasks for a novice developer.

Java 2 has simplified the process with Swing, a set of classes for the creation and usage of graphical user interfaces.

Swing, an extension of the Abstract Windowing Toolkit introduced in Java 1.0, offers the following features:

- Common user interface components such as buttons, scrollbars, lists, and sliders
- Containers—interface components that can be used to hold other components
- Adjustable look and feel—the ability to change the style of an entire interface to resemble Windows, MacOS, or other distinctive designs

Swing Features

Most of the components and containers you learned about yesterday were Swing versions of classes that were part of the Abstract Windowing Toolkit, the original Java package for graphical user interface programming.

Swing offers many features that are completely new, including a definable look and feel, keyboard mnemonics, ToolTips, and standard dialog boxes.

Setting the Look and Feel

One of the more unusual features in Swing is the ability to define the look and feel of components—the way that the buttons, labels, and other elements of a graphical user interface are rendered onscreen.

Management of look and feel is handled by a user interface manager class in the `javax.swing` package, `UIManager`. The choices for look and feel vary depending on the Java development environment you're using. The following are available with Java 2 on a Windows platform:

- A Windows look and feel
- A Motif X Window system look and feel
- Metal, Swing's new cross-platform, look and feel

The `UIManager` class has a `setLookAndFeel(LookAndFeel)` method that is used to choose a program's look and feel. To get a `LookAndFeel` object that you can use with `setLookAndFeel()`, use one of the following `UIManager` methods:

- `getCrossPlatformLookAndFeelClassName()`—This method returns a `LookAndFeel` object representing Java's cross-platform Metal look and feel.
- `getSystemLookAndFeelClassName()`—This method returns a `LookAndFeel` object representing your system's look and feel.

The `setLookAndFeel()` method throws an `UnsupportedLookAndFeelException` if it can't set the look and feel.

The following statements can be used in any program to designate Metal as the look and feel:

```
try {
    UIManager.setLookAndFeel(
        UIManager.getCrossPlatformLookAndFeelClassName());
    } catch (Exception e) {
        System.err.println("Can't set look and feel: " + e);
}
```

To select your system's look and feel, use getSystemLookAndFeelClassName(), which is inside the setLookAndFeel() method call in the preceding example. This produces different results on different operating systems. A Windows user would get that platform's look and feel by using getSystemLookAndFeelClassName(). A UNIX user would get the Motif look and feel.

Standard Dialog Boxes

The JOptionPane class offers several methods that can be used to create standard dialog boxes: small windows that ask a question, warn a user, or provide a brief, important message. Figure 9.1 shows a dialog box with the Metal look and feel.

9

FIGURE 9.1

A standard dialog box.

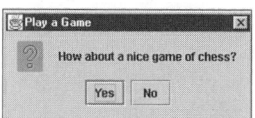

You have doubtlessly seen dialog boxes of this kind. When your system crashes, a dialog box appears and breaks the bad news. When you delete files, a dialog box might pop up to make sure that you really want to do that. These windows are an effective way to communicate with a user without the overhead of creating a new class to represent the window, adding components to it, and writing event-handling methods to take input. All these things are handled automatically when one of the standard dialog boxes offered by JOptionPane is used.

The four standard dialog boxes are as follows:

- ConfirmDialog—Asks a question, with buttons for Yes, No, and Cancel responses.
- InputDialog—Prompts for text input.
- MessageDialog—Displays a message.
- OptionDialog—Comprises all three of the other dialog box types.

Each of these dialog boxes has its own method in the JOptionPane class.

Confirm Dialog Boxes

The easiest way to create a Yes/No/Cancel dialog box is with the showConfirmDialog(*Component*, *Object*) method call. The *Component* argument specifies the container that should be considered to be the parent of the dialog box, and this information is used to determine where on the screen the dialog window should be displayed. If null is used instead of a container, or if the container is not a Frame object, the dialog box will be centered onscreen.

The second argument, *Object*, can be a string, a component, or an Icon object. If it's a string, that text will be displayed in the dialog box. If it's a component or an icon, that object will be displayed in place of a text message.

This method returns one of three possible integer values, each a class variable of JOptionPane: YES_OPTION, NO_OPTION, and CANCEL_OPTION.

The following example uses a confirm dialog box with a text message and stores the response in the `response` variable:

```
int response;
response = JOptionPane.showConfirmDialog(null,
    "Should I delete all of your irreplaceable personal files");
```

Another method offers more options for the confirm dialog:
showConfirmDialog(*Component, Object, String, int, int*). The first two arguments are the same as those in other showConfirmDialog() methods. The last three arguments are the following:

- A string that will be displayed in the dialog box's title bar.
- An integer that indicates which option buttons will be shown. It should be equal to the class variables YES_NO_CANCEL_OPTION or YES_NO_OPTION.
- An integer that describes the kind of dialog box it is, using the class variables ERROR_MESSAGE, INFORMATION_MESSAGE, PLAIN_MESSAGE, QUESTION_MESSAGE, or WARNING_MESSAGE. This argument is used to determine which icon to draw in the dialog box along with the message.

For example:

```
int response = JOptionPane.showConfirmDialog(null,
    "Error reading file. Want to try again?",
    "File Input Error",
    JOptionPane.YES_NO_OPTION,
    JOptionPane.ERROR_MESSAGE);
```

Figure 9.2 shows the resulting dialog box with the Windows look and feel.

FIGURE 9.2

A confirm dialog box.

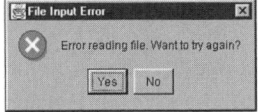

Input Dialog Boxes

An input dialog box asks a question and uses a text field to store the response. Figure 9.3 shows an example with the Motif look and feel.

FIGURE 9.3

An input dialog box.

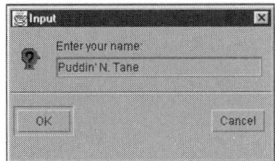

The easiest way to create an input dialog is with a call to the showInputDialog(*Component*, *Object*) method. The arguments are the parent component and the string, component, or icon to display in the box.

The input dialog method call returns a string that represents the user's response. The following statement creates the input dialog box shown in Figure 9.3:

```
String response = JOptionPane.showInputDialog(null,
    "Enter your name:");
```

You also can create an input dialog box with the showInputDialog(*Component*, *Object*, *String*, *int*) method. The first two arguments are the same as the shorter method call, and the last two are the following:

- The title to display in the dialog box title bar
- One of five class variables describing the type of dialog box: ERROR_MESSAGE, INFORMATION_MESSAGE, PLAIN_MESSAGE, QUESTION_MESSAGE, or WARNING_MESSAGE

The following statement uses this method to create an input dialog box:

```
String response = JOptionPane.showInputDialog(null,
    "What is your ZIP code?",
    "Enter ZIP Code",
    JOptionPane.QUESTION_MESSAGE);
```

Message Dialog Boxes

A message dialog box is a simple window that displays information. Figure 9.4 shows an example with the Metal look and feel.

FIGURE 9.4

A message dialog box.

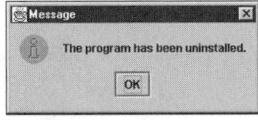

A message dialog box can be created with a call to the showMessageDialog(*Component*, *Object*) method. As with other dialog boxes, the arguments are the parent component and the string, component, or icon to display.

Unlike the other dialog boxes, message dialog boxes do not return any kind of response value. The following statement creates the message dialog shown in Figure 9.4:

```
JOptionPane.showMessageDialog(null,
    "The program has been uninstalled.");
```

You also can create a message input dialog box with the showMessageDialog(*Component*, *Object*, *String*, *int*) method. The use is identical to the showInputDialog() method, with the same arguments, except that showMessageDialog() does not return a value.

The following statement creates a message dialog box using this method:

```
JOptionPane.showMessageDialog(null,
    "An asteroid has destroyed the Earth.",
    "Asteroid Destruction Alert",
    JOptionPane.WARNING_MESSAGE);
```

Option Dialog Boxes

The most complex of the dialog boxes is the option dialog box, which combines the features of all the other dialogs. It can be created with the showOptionDialog(*Component*, *Object*, *String*, *int*, *int*, *Icon*, *Object[]*, *Object*) method.

The arguments to this method are as follows:

- The parent component of the dialog.
- The text, icon, or component to display.
- A string to display in the title bar.
- The type of box, using the class variables YES_NO_OPTION or YES_NO_CANCEL_OPTION, or the literal 0 if other buttons will be used instead.
- The icon to display, using the class variables ERROR_MESSAGE, INFORMATION_MES-SAGE, PLAIN_MESSAGE, QUESTION_MESSAGE, or WARNING_MESSAGE, or the literal 0 if none of these should be used.
- An Icon object to display instead of one of the icons in the preceding argument.
- An array of objects holding the components or other objects that represent the choices in the dialog box, if YES_NO_OPTION and YES_NO_CANCEL_OPTION are not being used.
- The object representing the default selection if YES_NO_OPTION and YES_NO_CANCEL option are not being used.

The last two arguments enable you to create a wide range of choices for the dialog box. You can create an array of buttons, labels, text fields, or even a mixture of different components as an object array. These components are displayed using the flow layout manager—there's no way to specify a different manager within the dialog.

The following example creates an option dialog box that uses an array of JButton objects for the options in the box and the gender[2] element as the default selection:

```
JButton[] gender = new JButton[3];
gender[0] = new JButton("Male");
gender[1] = new JButton("Female");
gender[2] = new JButton("None of Your Business");
int response = JOptionPane.showOptionDialog(null,
    "What is your gender?",
    "Gender",
    0,
    JOptionPane.INFORMATION_MESSAGE,
    null,
    gender,
    gender[2]);
```

Figure 9.5 shows the resulting dialog box with the Motif look and feel.

FIGURE 9.5

An option dialog box.

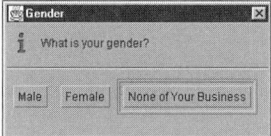

An Example: The Info Application

The next project shows a series of dialog boxes in a working program. The Info application uses dialogs to get information from the user, which is then placed into text fields on the application's main window.

Enter Listing 9.1 and compile the result.

LISTING 9.1   The Full Text of Info.java

```
 1: import java.awt.GridLayout;
 2: import java.awt.event.*;
 3: import javax.swing.*;
 4:
 5: public class Info extends JFrame {
 6:     private JLabel titleLabel = new JLabel("Title: ",
 7:         SwingConstants.RIGHT);
 8:     private JTextField title;
 9:     private JLabel addressLabel = new JLabel("Address: ",
10:         SwingConstants.RIGHT);
11:     private JTextField address;
12:     private JLabel typeLabel = new JLabel("Type: ",
13:         SwingConstants.RIGHT);
```

LISTING **9.1**   continued

```
14:    private JTextField type;
15:
16:    public Info() {
17:        super("Site Information");
18:        setDefaultCloseOperation(JFrame.EXIT_ON_CLOSE);
19:        // Site name
20:        String response1 = JOptionPane.showInputDialog(null,
21:            "Enter the site title:");
22:        title = new JTextField(response1, 20);
23:
24:        // Site address
25:        String response2 = JOptionPane.showInputDialog(null,
26:            "Enter the site address:");
27:        address = new JTextField(response2, 20);
28:
29:        // Site type
30:        String[] choices = { "Personal", "Commercial", "Unknown" };
31:        int response3 = JOptionPane.showOptionDialog(null,
32:            "What type of site is it?",
33:            "Site Type",
34:            0,
35:            JOptionPane.QUESTION_MESSAGE,
36:            null,
37:            choices,
38:            choices[0]);
39:        type = new JTextField(choices[response3], 20);
40:
41:        JPanel pane = new JPanel();
42:        pane.setLayout(new GridLayout(3, 2));
43:        pane.add(titleLabel);
44:        pane.add(title);
45:        pane.add(addressLabel);
46:        pane.add(address);
47:        pane.add(typeLabel);
48:        pane.add(type);
49:
50:        setContentPane(pane);
51:    }
52:
53:    public static void main(String[] arguments) {
54:        try {
55:            UIManager.setLookAndFeel(
56:                UIManager.getSystemLookAndFeelClassName());
57:        } catch (Exception e) {
58:            System.err.println("Couldn't use the system "
59:                + "look and feel: " + e);
60:        }
61:
```

```
62:          JFrame frame = new Info();
63:          frame.pack();
64:          frame.setVisible(true);
65:     }
66: }
```

Figure 9.6 shows the first of the three dialog boxes that appears when this application is run. After you fill in the fields in each dialog, you will see the application's main window, which is displayed in Figure 9.7 with the Windows look and feel. Three text fields have values supplied by dialog boxes.

FIGURE 9.6

The site address input dialog box.

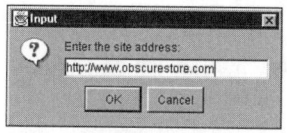

FIGURE 9.7

The main window of the Info application.

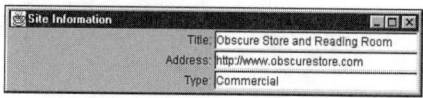

Much of this application is boilerplate code that can be used with any Swing application. The following lines relate to the dialog boxes:

- Lines 19–22—An input dialog asks the user to enter a site title. This title is used in the constructor for a JTextField object, which puts the title in the text field.

- Lines 24–27—A similar input dialog asks for a site address, which is used in the constructor for another JTextField object. Figure 9.7 shows this option dialog box.

- Line 30—An array of String objects called choices is created, and three elements are given values.

- Lines 31–38—An option dialog box asks for the site type. The choices array is the seventh argument, which sets up three buttons on the dialog with the strings in the array: Personal, Commercial, and Unknown. The last argument, choices[0], designates the first array element as the default selection in the dialog.

- Line 39—The response to the option dialog, an integer identifying the array element that was selected, is stored in a JTextField component called type.

Sliders

Sliders, which are implemented in Swing with the `JSlider` class, enable a number to be set by sliding a control within the range of a minimum and maximum value. In many cases, a slider can be used for numeric input instead of a text field, and it has the advantage of restricting input to a range of acceptable values.

Figure 9.8 shows an example of a `JSlider` component.

FIGURE 9.8

A `JSlider` component.

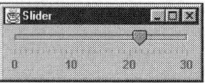

Sliders are horizontal by default. The orientation can be explicitly set using two class variables of the `SwingConstants` class: `HORIZONTAL` or `VERTICAL`.

You can use the following constructor methods:

- `JSlider(int, int)`—A slider with the specified minimum value and maximum value
- `JSlider(int, int, int)`—A slider with the specified minimum value, maximum value, and starting value
- `JSlider(int, int, int, int)`—A slider with the specified orientation, minimum value, maximum value, and starting value

Slider components have an optional label that can be used to indicate the minimum value, maximum value, and two different sets of tick marks ranging between the values.

The elements of this label are established by calling several methods of `JSlider`:

- `setMajorTickSpacing(int)`—Separates major tick marks by the specified distance. The distance is not in pixels, but in values between the minimum and maximum values represented by the slider.
- `setMinorTickSpacing(int)`—Separates minor tick marks by the specified distance. Minor ticks are displayed as half the height of major ticks.
- `setPaintTicks(boolean)`—Determines whether the tick marks should be displayed (a `true` argument) or not (a `false` argument).
- `setPaintLabels(boolean)`—Determines whether the numeric label of the slider should be displayed (`true`) or not (`false`).

These methods should be called on the slider before it is added to a container.

Listing 9.2 contains the `Slider.java` source code; the application is shown in Figure 9.8.

LISTING 9.2   The Full Text of `Slider.java`

```
 1: import java.awt.event.*;
 2: import javax.swing.*;
 3:
 4: public class Slider extends JFrame {
 5:
 6:     public Slider() {
 7:         super("Slider");
 8:         setDefaultCloseOperation(JFrame.EXIT_ON_CLOSE);
 9:         JSlider pickNum = new JSlider(JSlider.HORIZONTAL, 0, 30, 5);
10:         pickNum.setMajorTickSpacing(10);
11:         pickNum.setMinorTickSpacing(1);
12:         pickNum.setPaintTicks(true);
13:         pickNum.setPaintLabels(true);
14:         JPanel pane = new JPanel();
15:         pane.add(pickNum);
16:
17:         setContentPane(pane);
18:     }
19:
20:     public static void main(String[] args) {
21:         Slider frame = new Slider();
22:         frame.pack();
23:         frame.setVisible(true);
24:     }
25: }
```

9

Lines 9–17 contain the code that's used to create a `JSlider` component, set up its tick marks to be displayed, and add the component to a container. The rest of the program is a basic framework for an application that consists of a main `JFrame` container with no menus.

Scroll Panes

In versions of Java prior to 1.2, some components (such as text areas) had a built-in scrollbar. The bar could be used when the text in the component took up more space than the component could display. Scrollbars could be used in either the vertical or horizontal direction to scroll through the text.

One of the most common examples of scrolling is in a Web browser, where a scrollbar can be used on any page that is bigger than the browser's display area.

Swing changes the rules for scrollbars to the following:

- For a component to be able to scroll, it must be added to a JScrollPane container.
- This JScrollPane container is added to a container in place of the scrollable component.

Scroll panes can be created using the ScrollPane(*Object*) constructor, where *Object* represents the component that can be scrolled.

The following example creates a text area in a scroll pane and adds it to a container called mainPane:

```
textBox = new JTextArea(7, 30);
JScrollPane scroller = new JScrollPane(textBox);
mainPane.add(scroller);
```

As you're working with scroll panes, it can often be useful to indicate the size you would like it to occupy on the interface. This is done by calling the setPreferredSize(*Dimension*) method of the scroll pane before it is added to a container. The Dimension object represents the width and height of the preferred size represented in pixels.

The following code builds on the previous example by setting the preferred size of the scroller object:

```
Dimension pref = new Dimension(350, 100);
scroller.setPreferredSize(pref);
```

This should be handled before the scroller object is added to a container.

By default, a scroll pane does not display scrollbars unless they are needed. If the component inside the pane is no larger than the pane itself, the bars won't appear. In the case of components such as text areas, where the component size might increase as the program is used, the bars automatically appear when they're needed and disappear when they are not.

To override this behavior, you can set a policy when the JScrollBar component is created by using several ScrollPaneConstants class variables:

- HORIZONTAL_SCROLLBAR_ALWAYS
- HORIZONTAL_SCROLLBAR_AS_NEEDED
- HORIZONTAL_SCROLLBAR_NEVER
- VERTICAL_SCROLLBAR_ALWAYS
- VERTICAL_SCROLLBAR_AS_NEEDED
- VERTICAL_SCROLLBAR_NEVER

These class variables are used with the `ScrollPane(Object, int, int)` constructor, which specifies the component in the pane, the vertical scrollbar policy, and the horizontal scrollbar policy.

Toolbars

A *toolbar*, created in Swing with the `JToolBar` class, is a container that groups several components into a row or column. These components are most often buttons.

If you have used software such as Microsoft Word, Netscape Navigator, or Lotus WordPro, you are probably familiar with the concept of toolbars. In these programs and many others, the most commonly used program options are grouped together as a series of buttons. You can click these buttons as an alternative to using pull-down menus or shortcut keys.

Toolbars are horizontal by default, but the orientation is explicitly set with the `HORIZONTAL` or `VERTICAL` class variables of the `SwingConstants` interface.

Constructor methods include the following:

- `JToolBar()`—Creates a new toolbar.
- `JToolBar(int)`—Creates a new toolbar with the specified orientation.

Once you have created a toolbar, you can add components to it by using the toolbar's `add(Object)` method, where `Object` represents the component to place on the toolbar.

Many programs that use toolbars enable the user to move the bars. These are called *dockable toolbars* because you can dock them along an edge of the screen, similar to docking a boat to a pier. Swing toolbars can also be docked into a new window, separate from the original.

A dockable `JToolBar` component must be laid out using the `BorderLayout` manager. As you might recall, a border layout divides a container into five areas: north, south, east, west, and center. Each of the directional components takes up whatever space it needs, and the rest is allocated to the center.

The toolbar should be placed in one of the directional areas of the border layout. The only other area of the layout that can be filled is the center.

Figure 9.9 shows a dockable toolbar occupying the north area of a border layout. A text area has been placed in the center.

9

FIGURE 9.9

*A dockable toolbar
and a text area.*

Listing 9.3 contains the source code used to produce this application.

LISTING 9.3   The Full Text of `ToolBar.java`

```
 1: import java.awt.*;
 2: import java.awt.event.*;
 3: import javax.swing.*;
 4:
 5: public class ToolBar extends JFrame {
 6:
 7:     public ToolBar() {
 8:         super("ToolBar");
 9:         setDefaultCloseOperation(JFrame.EXIT_ON_CLOSE);
10:         ImageIcon image1 = new ImageIcon("button1.gif");
11:         JButton button1 = new JButton(image1);
12:         ImageIcon image2 = new ImageIcon("button2.gif");
13:         JButton button2 = new JButton(image2);
14:         ImageIcon image3 = new ImageIcon("button3.gif");
15:         JButton button3 = new JButton(image3);
16:         JToolBar bar = new JToolBar();
17:         bar.add(button1);
18:         bar.add(button2);
19:         bar.add(button3);
20:         JTextArea edit = new JTextArea(8,40);
21:         JScrollPane scroll = new JScrollPane(edit);
22:         JPanel pane = new JPanel();
23:         BorderLayout bord = new BorderLayout();
24:         pane.setLayout(bord);
25:         pane.add("North", bar);
26:         pane.add("Center", scroll);
27:
28:         setContentPane(pane);
29:     }
30:
31:     public static void main(String[] arguments) {
32:         ToolBar frame = new ToolBar();
33:         frame.pack();
34:         frame.setVisible(true);
35:     }
36: }
```

This application uses three images to represent the graphics on the buttons: `button1.gif`, `button2.gif`, and `button3.gif`. You can find these on the book's CD-ROM or the book's official World Wide Web site at `http://www.java21pro.com`. You also can use graphics from your own system, although they must be in GIF format and reasonably small.

The toolbar in this application can be grabbed by its handle—the area immediately to the left of the exclamation button in Figure 9.9. If you drag it within the window, you can dock it along different edges of the application window. When you release the toolbar, the application is rearranged using the border layout manager. You also can drag the toolbar out of the application window entirely.

Although toolbars are most commonly used with graphical buttons, they can contain textual buttons, combo boxes, and other components.

Progress Bars

If you have ever installed computer software, you're familiar with *progress bars*. These components are commonly used with long tasks to show the user how much time is left before it is complete.

Progress bars are implemented in Swing through the `JProgressBar` class. A sample Java program that makes use of this component is shown in Figure 9.10.

FIGURE 9.10

A progress bar in a frame.

Progress bars are used to track the progress of a task that can be represented numerically. They are created by specifying a minimum and a maximum value that represent the points at which the task is beginning and ending.

A software installation that consists of 335 different files is an example. The number of files transferred can be used to monitor the progress of the task. The minimum value is 0 and the maximum value 335.

Constructor methods include the following:

- `JProgressBar()`—Creates a new progress bar.
- `JProgressBar(int, int)`—Creates a new progress bar with the specified minimum value and maximum value.
- `JProgressBar(int, int, int)`—Creates a new progress bar with the specified orientation, minimum value, and maximum value.

The orientation of a progress bar can be established with the `SwingConstants.VERTICAL` and `SwingConstants.HORIZONTAL` class variables. Progress bars are horizontal by default.

The minimum and maximum values can also be set up by calling the progress bar's `setMinimum(int)` and `setMaximum(int)` values with the indicated values.

To update a progress bar, you call its `setValue(int)` method with a value indicating how far along the task is at that moment. This value should be somewhere between the minimum and maximum values established for the bar. The following example tells the `install` progress bar in the previous example of a software installation how many files have been uploaded thus far:

```
int filesDone = getNumberOfFiles();
install.setValue(filesDone);
```

In this example, the `getNumberOfFiles()` method represents some code that would be used to keep track of how many files have been copied so far during the installation. When this value is passed to the progress bar by the `setValue()` method, the bar is immediately updated to represent the percentage of the task that has been completed.

Progress bars often include a text label in addition to the graphic of an empty box filling up. This label displays the percentage of the task that has become completed, and you can set it up for a bar by calling the `setStringPainted(boolean)` method with a value of `true`. A `false` argument turns this label off.

Listing 9.4 contains `Progress`, the application shown at the beginning of this section in Figure 9.10.

LISTING 9.4   The Full Text of `Progress.java`

```
 1: import java.awt.*;
 2: import java.awt.event.*;
 3: import javax.swing.*;
 4:
 5: public class Progress extends JFrame {
 6:
 7:     JProgressBar current;
 8:     JTextArea out;
 9:     JButton find;
10:     Thread runner;
11:     int num = 0;
12:
13:     public Progress() {
14:         super("Progress");
15:
```

```
16:        setDefaultCloseOperation(JFrame.EXIT_ON_CLOSE);
17:        JPanel pane = new JPanel();
18:        pane.setLayout(new FlowLayout());
19:        current = new JProgressBar(0, 2000);
20:        current.setValue(0);
21:        current.setStringPainted(true);
22:        pane.add(current);
23:        setContentPane(pane);
24:    }
25:
26:
27:    public void iterate() {
28:        while (num < 2000) {
29:            current.setValue(num);
30:            try {
31:                Thread.sleep(1000);
32:            } catch (InterruptedException e) { }
33:            num += 95;
34:        }
35:    }
36:
37:    public static void main(String[] arguments) {
38:        Progress frame = new Progress();
39:        frame.pack();
40:        frame.setVisible(true);
41:        frame.iterate();
42:    }
43: }
```

The `Progress` application uses a progress bar to track the value of the num variable. The progress bar is created in line 19 with a minimum value of 0 and a maximum value of 2000.

The `iterate()` method in lines 27–35 loops while num is less than 2000 and increases num by 95 each iteration. The progress bar's `setValue()` method is called in line 29 of the loop with num as an argument, causing the bar to use that value when charting progress.

Using a progress bar is a way to make the program more user friendly when a computer program is going to be busy for more than a few seconds. Software users like progress bars because they indicate how much more time something's going to take, and this information can be a deciding factor in whether to wait at the computer, launch an expedition for something to drink, or take advantage of the company's lax policy in regard to personal long-distance calls. (If the task is especially time-consuming, a progress bar is essential—artists who create 3D computer scenes have become accustomed to tasks that take 12 hours or more to complete.)

Progress bars also provide another essential piece of information: proof that the program is still running and has not crashed.

Summary

You now know how to paint a user interface onto a Java application window using the components of the Swing package. The same techniques could be applied to applets, a container similar in many ways to a frame.

Swing includes classes for many of the buttons, bars, lists, and fields you would expect to see on a program, along with more advanced components such as sliders, dialog boxes, and progress bars. Interface components are implemented by creating an instance of their class and adding it to a container—such as a frame or an applet window—using the container's add() method.

Today you developed components and added them to a program. During the next two days, you learn more about two things that are needed to make a graphical interface usable: how to arrange components together to form a whole interface and receive input from a user through these components.

Q&A

Q Can an application be created without Swing?

A Certainly. Swing is just an expansion on the Abstract Windowing Toolkit, and if you are developing an applet for Java 1.0, you could only use AWT classes to design your interface and receive input from a user. Whether you should create an application without Swing is another issue. There's no comparison between Swing's capabilities and those offered by the AWT. With Swing, you can use many more components and control them in more sophisticated ways.

Questions

1. What is the default look and feel in a Java application?

    (a) Motif

    (b) Windows

    (c) Metal

2. Which user interface component is commonplace in software installation programs?

   (a) Sliders

   (b) Progress bars

   (c) Dialog boxes

3. Which Java class library includes a class for clickable buttons?

   (a) Abstract Windowing Toolkit

   (b) Swing

   (c) Both

9

Answers

1. c. If you want to use a look and feel other than Metal, you must explicitly establish that look and feel using a method of the `javax.swing.UIManager` class.

2. b. Progress bars are useful when used to display the progress of a file-copying or file-extracting activity.

3. c. Swing duplicates all the simple user interface components that are included in the Abstract Windowing Toolkit.

Exercises

To extend your knowledge of the subjects covered today, try the following exercises:

- Create an option dialog that can be used to set the title of the frame that loaded the dialog.

- Create a modified version of the `Progress` application that also displays the value of the `num` variable in a text field.

Where applicable, exercise solutions are offered on the book's Web site at `http://www.java21pro.com`.

DAY 10

Arranging Components on a User Interface

If designing a graphical user interface were comparable to painting, you could currently produce only one kind of art: abstract expressionism. You can put components onto an interface, but you don't have much control over where they go.

In order to impose some kind of form on an interface in Java, you must use a set of classes called *layout managers*.

Today you learn how to use five layout managers to arrange components into an interface. You'll take advantage of the flexibility of Swing, which was designed to be presentable on the many different platforms that support the language.

You also learn how to put several different layout managers to work on the same interface when one arrangement doesn't quite suit what you have in mind for a program.

We will start with the basic layout managers.

Basic Interface Layout

As you learned yesterday, a graphical user interface designed with Swing is a very fluid thing. Resizing a window can wreak havoc on your interface, as components move to places on a container that you might not have intended.

This fluidity is by necessity. Java is implemented on many different platforms, and there are subtle differences in the way each platform displays things such as buttons, scrollbars, and so on.

With programming languages such as Microsoft Visual Basic, a component's location on a window is precisely defined by its x,y coordinates. Some Java development tools allow similar control over an interface through the use of their own windowing classes.

When using Swing, a programmer gains more control over the layout of an interface by using layout managers.

Laying Out an Interface

A layout manager determines how components will be arranged when they are added to a container.

The default layout manager for panels is the `FlowLayout` class. This class lets components flow from left to right in the order that they are added to a container. When there's no more room, a new row of components begins immediately below the first, and the left-to-right order continues.

Java includes the `FlowLayout`, `GridLayout`, `BorderLayout`, `CardLayout`, and `GridBagLayout` layout managers. To create a layout manager for a container, an instance of the container is created using a statement such as the following:

```
FlowLayout flo = new FlowLayout();
```

After you create a layout manager, you make it the layout manager for a container by using the container's `setLayout()` method. The layout manager must be established before any components are added to the container. If no layout manager is specified, its default layout will be used—`FlowLayout` for panels and `BorderLayout` for frames, windows, and applets.

The following statements represent the starting point for an applet that creates a layout manager and uses `setLayout()` so that it controls the arrangement of all the components that will be added to the applet window:

```
public class Starter extends javax.swing.JApplet {
    FlowLayout lm = new FlowLayout();

    public void init() {
        JPanel pane = new JPanel();
        pane.setLayout(lm);
        setContentPane(pane);
    }
}
```

After the layout manager is set, you can start adding components to the container that it manages. For some of the layout managers such as FlowLayout, the order in which components are added is significant. You learn more in today's subsequent sections as you work with each of the managers.

Flow Layout

The FlowLayout class is the simplest of the layout managers. It lays out components in a manner similar to the way words are laid out on a page—from left to right until there's no more room, and then on to the next row.

By default, the components on each row will be centered when you use the FlowLayout() constructor with no arguments. If you want the components to be aligned along the left or right edge of the container, the FlowLayout.LEFT or FlowLayout.RIGHT class variable should be the constructor's only argument, as in the following statement:

```
FlowLayout righty = new FlowLayout(FlowLayout.RIGHT);
```

The FlowLayout.CENTER class variable is used to specify centered components.

The application in Listing 10.1 displays six buttons arranged by the flow layout manager. Because the FlowLayout.LEFT class variable was used in the FlowLayout() constructor, the components are lined up along the left side of the application window.

LISTING 10.1 The Full Text of Alphabet.java

```
 1: import java.awt.*;
 2: import java.awt.event.*;
 3: import javax.swing.*;
 4:
 5: class Alphabet extends JFrame {
 6:     JButton a = new JButton("Alibi");
 7:     JButton b = new JButton("Burglar");
 8:     JButton c = new JButton("Corpse");
 9:     JButton d = new JButton("Deadbeat");
10:     JButton e = new JButton("Evidence");
```

LISTING 10.1   continued

```
11:        JButton f = new JButton("Fugitive");
12:
13:        Alphabet() {
14:            super("Alphabet");
15:            setSize(360, 120);
16:            JPanel pane = new JPanel();
17:            FlowLayout lm = new FlowLayout(FlowLayout.LEFT);
18:            pane.setLayout(lm);
19:            pane.add(a);
20:            pane.add(b);
21:            pane.add(c);
22:            pane.add(d);
23:            pane.add(e);
24:            pane.add(f);
25:            setContentPane(pane);
26:        }
27:
28:        public static void main(String[] arguments) {
29:            JFrame frame = new Alphabet();
30:            ExitWindow exit = new ExitWindow();
31:            frame.addWindowListener(exit);
32:            frame.show();
33:        }
34: }
35:
36: class ExitWindow extends WindowAdapter {
37:     public void windowClosing(WindowEvent e) {
38:         System.exit(0);
39:     }
40: }
```

Figure 10.1 shows the application running.

FIGURE 10.1

Six buttons arranged in flow layout.

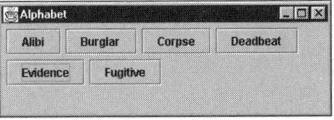

In the Alphabet application, the flow layout manager puts a gap of three pixels between each component on a row and three pixels between each row. You also can change the horizontal and vertical gap between components with some extra arguments to the FlowLayout() constructor.

The `FlowLayout(int, int, int)` constructor takes the following three arguments, in order:

- The alignment, which must be `FlowLayout.CENTER`, `FlowLayout.LEFT`, or `FlowLayout.RIGHT`
- The horizontal gap between components, in pixels
- The vertical gap, in pixels

The following constructor creates a flow layout manager with centered components, a horizontal gap of 30 pixels, and a vertical gap of 10:

```
FlowLayout flo = new FlowLayout(FlowLayout.CENTER, 30, 10);
```

Grid Layout

The grid layout manager arranges components into a grid of rows and columns. Components are added first to the top row of the grid, beginning with the leftmost grid cell and continuing to the right. When all the cells in the top row are full, the next component is added to the leftmost cell in the second row of the grid—if there is a second row—and so on.

Grid layouts are created with the `GridLayout` class. Two arguments are sent to the `GridLayout` constructor—the number of rows in the grid and the number of columns. The following statement creates a grid layout manager with 10 rows and 3 columns:

```
GridLayout gr = new GridLayout(10, 3);
```

As with flow layout, you can specify a vertical and horizontal gap between components with two extra arguments. The following statement creates a grid layout with 10 rows and 3 columns, a horizontal gap of 5 pixels, and a vertical gap of 8 pixels:

```
GridLayout gr2 = new GridLayout(10, 3, 5, 8);
```

The default gap between components under grid layout is 0 pixels in both vertical and horizontal directions.

Listing 10.2 contains an application that creates a grid with 3 rows, 3 columns, and a 10-pixel gap between components in both the vertical and horizontal directions.

LISTING 10.2   The Full Text of `Bunch.java`

```
1: import java.awt.*;
2: import java.awt.event.*;
3: import javax.swing.*;
4:
```

LISTING 10.2   continued

```
 5: class Bunch extends JFrame {
 6:     JButton marcia = new JButton("Marcia");
 7:     JButton carol = new JButton("Carol");
 8:     JButton greg = new JButton("Greg");
 9:     JButton jan = new JButton("Jan");
10:     JButton alice = new JButton("Alice");
11:     JButton peter = new JButton("Peter");
12:     JButton cindy = new JButton("Cindy");
13:     JButton mike = new JButton("Mike");
14:     JButton bobby = new JButton("Bobby");
15:
16:     Bunch() {
17:         super("Bunch");
18:         setSize(260, 260);
19:         JPanel pane = new JPanel();
20:         GridLayout family = new GridLayout(3, 3, 10, 10);
21:         pane.setLayout(family);
22:         pane.add(marcia);
23:         pane.add(carol);
24:         pane.add(greg);
25:         pane.add(jan);
26:         pane.add(alice);
27:         pane.add(peter);
28:         pane.add(cindy);
29:         pane.add(mike);
30:         pane.add(bobby);
31:         setContentPane(pane);
32:     }
33:
34:     public static void main(String[] arguments) {
35:         JFrame frame = new Bunch();
36:         ExitWindow exit = new ExitWindow();
37:         frame.addWindowListener(exit);
38:         frame.show();
39:     }
40: }
```

Figure 10.2 shows this application.

FIGURE 10.2

Nine buttons arranged in 3×3 grid layout.

One thing to note about the buttons in Figure 10.2 is that they expanded to fill the space available to them in each cell. This is an important difference between grid layout and some of the other layout managers.

Border Layout

Border layouts, which are created by using the BorderLayout class, divide a container into five sections: north, south, east, west, and center. The five areas of Figure 10.3 show how these sections are arranged.

FIGURE 10.3

Component arrangement under border layout.

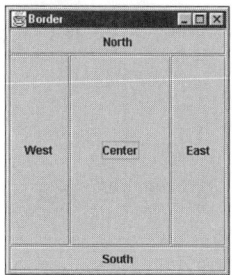

Under border layout, the components in the four compass points will take up as much space as they need—the center gets whatever space is left over. Ordinarily, this will result in an arrangement with a large central component and four thin components around it.

A border layout is created with either the BorderLayout() or BorderLayout(*int, int*) constructors. The first constructor creates a border layout with no gap between any of the components. The second constructor specifies the horizontal gap and vertical gap, respectively.

After you create a border layout and set it up as a container's layout manager, components are added using a call to the add() method that's different from what you have seen previously:

add(*String, Component*)

The first argument is a string indicating which part of the border layout to assign the component to. There are five possible values: "North", "South", "East", "West", or "Center".

The second argument to this method is the component that should be added to the container.

The following statement adds a button called `quitButton` to the north portion of a border layout:

```
add("North", quitButton);
```

Listing 10.3 contains the application used to produce Figure 10.3.

LISTING 10.3   The Full Text of `Border.java`

```
 1: import java.awt.*;
 2: import java.awt.event.*;
 3: import javax.swing.*;
 4:
 5: class Border extends JFrame {
 6:     JButton north = new JButton("North");
 7:     JButton south = new JButton("South");
 8:     JButton east = new JButton("East");
 9:     JButton west = new JButton("West");
10:     JButton center = new JButton("Center");
11:
12:     Border() {
13:         super("Border");
14:         setSize(240, 280);
15:         JPanel pane = new JPanel();
16:         pane.setLayout(new BorderLayout());
17:         pane.add("North", north);
18:         pane.add("South", south);
19:         pane.add("East", east);
20:         pane.add("West", west);
21:         pane.add("Center", center);
22:         setContentPane(pane);
23:     }
24:
25:     public static void main(String[] arguments) {
26:         JFrame frame = new Border();
27:         ExitWindow exit = new ExitWindow();
28:         frame.addWindowListener(exit);
29:         frame.show();
30:     }
31: }
```

Mixing Layout Managers

At this point, you might be wondering how Java's layout managers will work with the kind of graphical user interface you want to design. Choosing a layout manager is an experience akin to Goldilocks checking out the home of the three bears and finding it lacking: "This one is too square! This one is too disorganized! This one is too strange!"

To find the layout that is just right, you often have to combine more than one manager on the same interface.

This is done by adding containers to a main container such as a frame or an applet window, and giving each of these smaller containers their own layout managers.

The container to use for these smaller containers is the panel, which is created from the `JPanel` class. *Panels* are containers that are used to group components together. There are two things to keep in mind when working with panels:

- The panel is filled with components before it is put into a larger container.
- The panel has its own layout manager.

Panels are created with a simple call to the constructor of the `JPanel` class, as shown in the following example:

```
JPanel pane = new JPanel();
```

The layout method is set for a panel by calling the `setLayout()` method on that panel.

The following statements create a layout manager and apply it to a `JPanel` object called pane:

```
BorderLayout bo = new BorderLayout();
pane.setLayout(bo);
```

Components are added to a panel by calling the panel's `add()` method, which works the same for panels as it does for other containers, such as applets.

The following statement adds a text area called `dialogue` to a `Panel` object called pane:

```
pane.add(dialogue);
```

You'll see several examples of panel use in the rest of today's example programs.

Card Layout

Card layouts differ from the other layouts because they hide some components from view. A *card layout* is a group of containers or components that are displayed one at a time, in the same way that a blackjack dealer reveals one card at a time from a deck. Each container in the group is called a *card*.

If you have used software such as HyperCard on the Macintosh or a tabbed dialog box such as the System Properties portion of the Windows 98 Control Panel, you have worked with a program that uses card layout.

The most common way to use a card layout is to use a panel for each card. Components are added to the panels first, and then the panels are added to the container that is set to use card layout.

A card layout is created from the `CardLayout` class with a simple constructor call:

```
CardLayout cc = new CardLayout();
```

The `setLayout()` method is used to make this the layout manager for the container, as in the following statement:

```
setLayout(cc);
```

After you set a container to use the card layout manager, you must use a slightly different `add()` method call to add cards to the layout.

The method to use is `add(String, Container)`. The second argument specifies the container or component that is the card. If it is a container, all components must have been added to it before the card is added.

The first argument to the `add()` method is a string that represents the name of the card. This can be anything you want to call the card. You might want to number the cards in some way and use the number in the name, as in `"Card 1"`, `"Card 2"`, `"Card 3"`, and so on.

The following statement adds a panel called `options` to a container and gives this card the name `"Options Card"`:

```
add("Options Card", options);
```

After you have added a card to the main container for a program, such as an applet window, you can use the `show()` method of your card layout manager to display a card. The `show()` method takes two arguments:

- The container that all the cards have been added to
- The name that was given to the card

The following statement calls the `show()` method of a card layout manager called `cc`:

```
cc.show(this, "Fact Card");
```

The `this` keyword refers to the object that this statement is appearing in, and `"Fact Card"` is the name of the card to reveal. When a card is shown, the previously displayed card will be obscured. Only one card in a card layout can be viewed at a time.

If the container that holds each of the cards is a content pane, the first argument to the `show()` method should be the content pane rather than the object that the pane is a part of.

Grid Bag Layout

The last of the layout managers available through Java is grid bag layout, which is an extension of the grid layout manager. A grid bag layout differs from grid layout in the following ways:

- A component can take up more than one cell in the grid.
- The proportions between different rows and columns do not have to be equal.
- Components inside grid cells can be arranged in different ways.

To create a grid bag layout, you use the GridBagLayout class and a helper class called GridBagConstraints. GridBagLayout is the layout manager, and GridBagConstraints is used to define the properties of each component to be placed into the cell—its placement, dimensions, alignment, and so on. The relationship between the grid bag, the constraints, and each component defines the overall layout.

In its most general form, creating a grid bag layout involves the following steps:

1. Creating a GridBagLayout object and defining it as the current layout manager, as you would for any other layout manager.
2. Creating a new instance of GridBagConstraints.
3. Setting up the constraints for a component.
4. Telling the layout manager about the component and its constraints.
5. Adding the component to the container.

The following example adds a single button to a container implementing grid bag layout. (Don't worry about the various values for the constraints; they are covered later in this section.)

```
// set up layout
GridBagLayout gridbag = new GridBagLayout();
GridBagConstraints constraints = new GridBagConstraints();
getContentPane().setLayout(gridbag);

// define constraints for the button
JButton btn = new JButton("Save");
constraints.gridx = 0;
constraints.gridy = 0;
constraints.gridwidth = 1;
constraints.gridheight = 1;
constraints.weightx = 30;
constraints.weighty = 30;
constraints.fill = GridBagConstraints.NONE;
constraints.anchor = GridBagConstraints.CENTER;
```

10

```
// attach constraints to layout, add button
gridbag.setConstraints(btn, constraints);
getContentPane().add(b);
```

As you can see from this example, you have to set all the constraints for every component you want to add to the panel. Given the numerous constraints, it helps to have a plan and to deal with each kind of constraint one at a time.

Designing the Grid

The first place to start in the grid bag layout is on paper. Sketching out your user interface design beforehand—before you even write a single line of code—will help enormously in the long run with trying to figure out where everything goes. Put your editor aside for a second, pick up a piece of paper and a pencil, and build the grid.

Figure 10.4 shows the panel layout you'll be building for this project's application. Figure 10.5 shows the same layout with a grid imposed on top of it. Your layout will have a grid similar to this one, with rows and columns forming individual cells.

FIGURE 10.4

A grid bag layout.

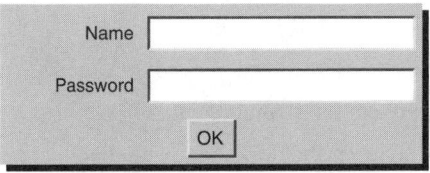

FIGURE 10.5

The grid bag layout from Figure 10.4, with grid imposed.

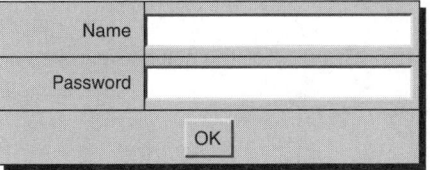

As you draw your grid, keep in mind that each component must have its own cell. You cannot put more than one component into the same cell. The reverse is not true, however; one component can span multiple cells in the x or y directions (as in the OK button in the bottom row, which spans two columns). In Figure 10.5, note that the labels and text fields have their own grids and that the button spans two column cells.

Label the cells with their x and y coordinates while you're still working on paper; this helps you later. They aren't pixel coordinates; rather, they're cell coordinates. The top-left cell is 0,0. The next cell to the right of it in the top row is 1,0. The cell to the right of that one is 2,0. Moving to the next row, the leftmost cell is 1,0, the next cell in the row is 1,1, and so on. Label your cells on the paper with these numbers; you'll need them later when you do the code for this example. Figure 10.6 shows the numbers for each of the cells in this example.

FIGURE 10.6

The grid bag layout from Figure 10.5, with cell coordinates.

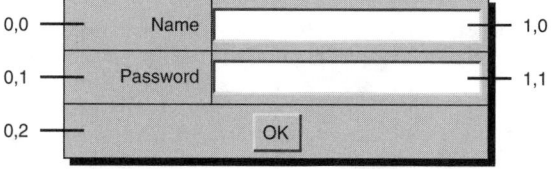

Creating the Grid

Now go back to Java and start implementing the layout you've just drawn on paper. Initially, you're going to focus exclusively on the layout—getting the grid and the proportions right. For that, it might be easier to use buttons as placeholders for the actual elements in the layout. They're easy to create, and they clearly define the space that a component will take up in the layout manager—or managers—that are in use. When everything is set up correctly, the buttons can be replaced with the right elements.

To cut down on the amount of typing you have to do to set up all those constraints, you can start by defining a helper method that takes several values and sets the constraints for those values. The buildConstraints() method takes seven arguments: a GridBagConstraints object and six integers representing the GridBagConstraints instance variables gridx, gridy, gridwidth, gridheight, weightx, and weighty. You'll learn later what these actually do; for now, here's the code to the helper method that you'll use later in this example:

```
void buildConstraints(GridBagConstraints gbc, int gx, int gy,
    int gw, int gh, int wx, int wy) {

    gbc.gridx = gx;
    gbc.gridy = gy;
    gbc.gridwidth = gw;
    gbc.gridheight = gh;
    gbc.weightx = wx;
    gbc.weighty = wy;
}
```

Now move on to the application's constructor method, where all the layout actually occurs. Here's the basic method definition, where you'll define the GridBagLayout to be the initial layout manager and create a constraints object (an instance of GridBagConstraints):

```
public NamePass() {
    super("Username and Password");
    setSize(290, 110);
```

```
        GridBagLayout gridbag = new GridBagLayout();
        GridBagConstraints constraints = new GridBagConstraints();
        JPanel pane = new JPanel();
        pane.setLayout(gridbag);

        setContentPane(pane);
        constraints.fill = GridBagConstraints.BOTH;
}
```

One more small note of explanation: The last line, which sets the value of con-
straints.fill, will be removed (and explained) later. It's there so that the components
will fill the entire cell in which they're contained, which helps you see what's going on.
Add it for now; you'll get a clearer idea of what it's for later.

Now add the button placeholders to the layout. (Remember that you're focusing on basic
grid organization at the moment, so you'll use buttons as placeholders for the actual user
interface elements you'll add later.) Start with a single button so that you can get a feel
for setting its constraints. This code will go into the constructor method just after the
setLayout line:

```
// Name label
 buildConstraints(constraints, 0, 0, 1, 1, 100, 100);
 JButton label1 = new JButton("Name:");
 gridbag.setConstraints(label1, constraints);
 add(label1);
```

These four lines set up the constraints for an object, create a new button, attach the constraints to the button, and then add it to the panel. Note that constraints for a component
are stored in the GridBagConstraints object, so the component doesn't even have to
exist to set up its constraints.

Now you can get down to details: Just what are the values for the constraints that you've
plugged into the helper method buildConstraints()?

The first two integer arguments are the gridx and gridy values of the constraints. They
are the cell coordinates of the cell containing this component. Remember how you wrote
these components down on paper in step one? With the cells neatly numbered on paper,
all you have to do is plug in the right values. Note that if you have a component that
spans multiple cells, the cell coordinates are those of the cell in the top-left corner.

This button is in the top-left corner, so its gridx and gridy (the first two arguments to
buildConstraints()) are 0 and 0, respectively.

The second two integer arguments are the gridwidth and gridheight. They are not the
pixel widths and heights of the cells; rather, they are the number of cells this component
spans: gridwidth for the columns and gridheight for the rows. Here this component
spans only one cell, so the values for both are 1.

The last two integer arguments are for `weightx` and `weighty`. They are used to set up the proportions of the rows and columns—that is, how wide or deep they will be. Weights can become very confusing, so for now, set both values to `100`. Weights are dealt with in step three.

After the constraints have been built, you can attach them to an object using the `setConstraints()` method. `setConstraints()`, which is a method defined in `GridBagLayout`, takes two arguments: the component (here a button) and the constraints for that component. Finally, you can add the button to the panel.

After you've set and assigned the constraints to one component, you can reuse that `GridBagConstraints` object to set up the constraints for the next object. You, therefore, duplicate these four lines for each component in the grid, with different values for the `buildConstraints()` method. To save space, the `buildConstraints()` methods will only be shown for the last four cells.

The second cell to add is the one to hold the text box for the name. The cell coordinates for this one are 1,0 (second column, first row); it too spans only one cell, and the weights (for now) are both `100`:

```
buildConstraints(constraints, 1, 0, 1, 1, 100, 100);
```

The next two components, which will be a label and a text field, are nearly identical to the previous two; the only difference is in their cell coordinates. The password label is at 0,1 (first column, second row), and the password text field is at 1,1 (second column, second row):

```
buildConstraints(constraints, 0, 1, 1, 1, 100, 100);
buildConstraints(constraints, 1, 1, 1, 1, 100, 100);
```

Finally, you need the OK button, which is a component that spans two cells in the bottom row of the panel. Here the cell coordinates are the left and topmost cell, where the span starts (0,2). Here, unlike the previous components, you'll set `gridwidth` and `gridheight` to be something other than 1 because this cell spans multiple columns. The `gridweight` is 2 (it spans two cells) and the `gridheight` is 1 (it spans only one row):

```
buildConstraints(constraints, 0, 2, 2, 1, 100, 100);
```

You've set the placement constraints for all the components that will be added to the grid layout. You also need to assign each component's constraints to the layout manager and then add each component to the panel. Figure 10.7 shows the result at this point. Note that you're not concerned about exact proportions here, or about making sure everything lines up. What you should keep track of at this point is making sure that the grid is working, that you have the right number of rows and columns, that the spans are correct, and that nothing strange is going on (cells in the wrong place, cells overlapping, that kind of thing).

10

FIGURE **10.7**

Grid bag layout, first pass.

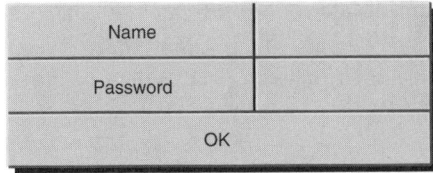

Determining the Proportions

The next step is to determine the proportions of the rows and columns in relation to other rows and columns. For example, in this case you'll want the labels (name and password) to take up less space than the text boxes. You might want the OK button at the bottom to be only half the height of the two text boxes above it. You arrange the proportions of the cells within your layout using the `weightx` and `weighty` constraints.

The easiest way to think of `weightx` and `weighty` is that their values are either percentages of the total width and height of the panel, or 0 if the weight or height has been set by some other cell. The values of `weightx` and `weighty` for all your components, therefore, should add up to 100.

Note

Actually, the `weightx` and `weighty` values are not percentages; they're simply proportions—they can have any value whatsoever. When the proportions are calculated, all the values in a direction are added up so that each individual value is in proportion to that total. To make this process easier to understand: Look at the weights as percentages and make sure that they add up to 100; that way, you can be sure everything is coming out right.

Which cells get values and which cells get 0? Cells that span multiple rows or columns should always be 0 in the direction they span. Beyond that, deciding is simply a question of picking a cell to have a value, and then all the other cells in that row or columns should be 0.

Look at the five calls to `buildConstraints()` made in the preceding step:

```
buildConstraints(constraints, 0, 0, 1, 1, 100, 100); //name
buildConstraints(constraints, 1, 0, 1, 1, 100, 100); //name text
buildConstraints(constraints, 0, 1, 1, 1, 100, 100); //password
buildConstraints(constraints, 1, 1, 1, 1, 100, 100); //password text
buildConstraints(constraints, 0, 2, 2, 1, 100, 100); //OK button
```

You'll be changing those last two arguments in each call to `buildConstraints` to be either a value or 0. Start with the x direction (the proportions of the columns), which is the second-to-last argument in the preceding list.

If you look back to Figure 10.5 (the picture of the panel with the grid imposed), note that the second column is much larger than the first. If you were going to pick theoretical percentages for those columns, you might say that the first is 10% and the second is 90%. (This is a guess; that's all you need to do as well.) With these two guesses, you can assign them to cells. You don't want to assign any values to the cell with the OK button because that cell spans both columns, and percentages there wouldn't work. Add them to the first two cells, the name label and the name text field:

```
buildConstraints(constraints, 0, 0, 1, 1, 10, 100); //name
buildConstraints(constraints, 1, 0, 1, 1, 90, 100); //name text
```

What about the values of the remaining two cells, the password label and text field? Because the proportions of the columns have already been set up by the name label and field, you don't have to reset them here. Give both of these cells as well as the one for the OK box 0 values:

```
buildConstraints(constraints, 0, 1, 1, 1, 0, 100); //password
buildConstraints(constraints, 1, 1, 1, 1, 0, 100); //password text
buildConstraints(constraints, 0, 2, 2, 1, 0, 100); //OK button
```

Note here that a 0 value does not mean that the cell has 0 width. These values are proportions, not pixel values. A 0 simply means that the proportion has been set somewhere else; all 0 says is "stretch it to fit."

Now that the totals of all the weightx constraints are 100, you can move on to the weighty arguments. Here you have three rows. Glancing over the grid you drew, it looks like the button has about 20% and the text fields have the rest (40% each). As with the x values, you have to set the value of only one cell per row (the two labels and the button), with all the other cells having a weightx of 0.

Here are the final five calls to buildConstraints() with the weights in place:

```
buildConstraints(constraints, 0, 0, 1, 1, 10, 40); //name
buildConstraints(constraints, 1, 0, 1, 1, 90, 0); //name text
buildConstraints(constraints, 0, 1, 1, 1, 0, 40); //password
buildConstraints(constraints, 1, 1, 1, 1, 0, 0); //password text
buildConstraints(constraints, 0, 2, 2, 1, 0, 20); //OK button
```

Figure 10.8 shows the result with the correct proportions.

FIGURE 10.8

Grid bag layout, second pass.

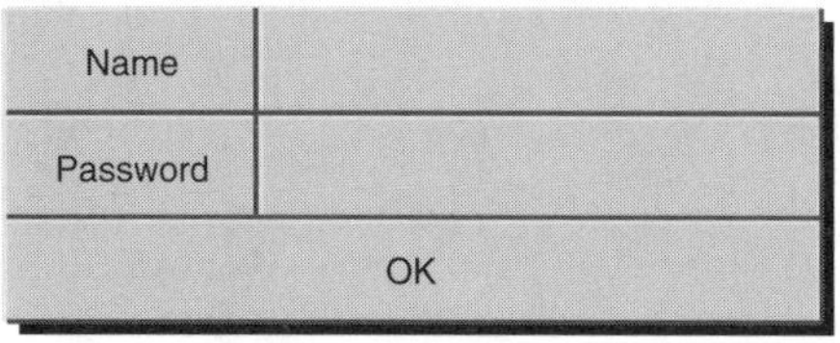

At this step, the goal is to try to come up with some basic proportions for how the rows and cells will be spaced on the screen. You can make some elementary estimates based on how big you expect the various components to be, but chances are you're going to use a lot of trial and error in this part of the process.

Adding and Arranging the Components

With the layout and the proportions in place, you can now replace the button placeholders with actual labels and text fields. Because you set up everything already, it should all work perfectly, right? Well, almost. Figure 10.9 shows what you get if you use the same constraints as before and replace the buttons with actual components.

FIGURE 10.9

Grid bag layout, almost there.

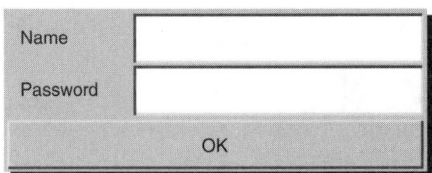

This layout is close, but it's weird. The text boxes are too tall, and the OK button stretches across the width of the cell.

What's missing are the constraints that arrange the components inside the cell. There are two of them: `fill` and `anchor`.

The `fill` constraint determines—for components that can stretch in either direction—in which direction to stretch (such as text boxes and buttons). `fill` can have one of four values, defined as class variables in the `GridBagConstraints` class:

- `GridBagConstraints.BOTH`, which stretches the component to fill the cell in both directions

- `GridBagConstraints.NONE`, which causes the component to be displayed in its smallest size

- `GridBagConstraints.HORIZONTAL`, which stretches the component in the horizontal direction

- `GridBagConstraints.VERTICAL`, which stretches the component in the vertical direction

Note Keep in mind that this layout is dynamic. You're not going to set up the actual pixel dimensions of any components; rather, you're telling these elements in which direction they can grow given a panel that can be of any size.

By default, the `fill` constraint for all components is `NONE`. Why are the text fields and labels filling the cells if this is the case? If you remember way back to the start of the code for this example, this line was added to the `init()` method:

```
constraints.fill = GridBagConstraints.BOTH;
```

Now you know what it does. For the final version of this application, you'll want to remove that line and add `fill` values for each independent component.

The second constraint that affects how a component appears in the cell is `anchor`. This constraint applies only to components that aren't filling the whole cell, and it tells Java where inside the cell to place the component. The possible values for the anchor constraint are `GridBagConstraints.CENTER`, which aligns the component both vertically and horizontally inside the cell, or one of eight direction values:

GridBagConstraints.NORTH	GridBagConstraints.SOUTH
GridBagConstraints.NORTHEAST	GridBagConstraints.SOUTHWEST
GridBagConstraints.EAST	GridBagConstraints.WEST
GridBagConstraints.SOUTHEAST	GridBagConstraints.NORTHWEST

The default value of anchor is `GridBagConstraints.CENTER`.

You set these constraints the same way you did all the other ones: by changing instance variables in the `GridBagConstraints` object. Here you can change the definition of `buildConstraints()` to take two more arguments (they're integers), or you could just set them in the body of the `init()` method. The latter is used on this project.

Be careful with defaults. Keep in mind that because you're reusing the same `GridBagConstraints` object for each component, you might have some values left over when you're done with one component. On the other hand, if a `fill` or `anchor` from one object is the same as the one before it, you don't have to reset that object.

For this example, three changes are going to be made to the `fill` and `anchor` values of the components:

- The labels will have no `fill` and will be aligned `EAST` (so they hug the right side of the cell).

- The text fields will be filled horizontally (so they start one line high, but stretch to the width of the cell).

- The button will have no `fill` and will be center-aligned.

This is reflected in the full code at the end of this section.

Making Adjustments

As you work with your own programs and grid bag layouts, you'll notice that the resulting layout often requires some tinkering. You might need to play with various values of the constraints to get an interface to come out right. There's nothing wrong with that—the goal of following the previous steps is to get things fairly close to the final positions, not to come out with a perfect layout every time.

Listing 10.4 shows the complete code for the layout you've been building up in this section. If you had trouble following the discussion up to this point, you might find it useful to go through this code line by line to make sure that you understand the various parts.

LISTING 10.4   The full Text of `NamePass.java`

```
 1: import java.awt.*;
 2: import javax.swing.*;
 3: import java.awt.event.*;
 4:
 5: public class NamePass extends JFrame {
 6:
 7:     void buildConstraints(GridBagConstraints gbc, int gx, int gy,
 8:         int gw, int gh, int wx, int wy) {
 9:
10:         gbc.gridx = gx;
11:         gbc.gridy = gy;
12:         gbc.gridwidth = gw;
13:         gbc.gridheight = gh;
14:         gbc.weightx = wx;
15:         gbc.weighty = wy;
16:     }
17:
18:     public NamePass() {
19:         super("Username and Password");
20:         setSize(290, 110);
21:         GridBagLayout gridbag = new GridBagLayout();
22:         GridBagConstraints constraints = new GridBagConstraints();
23:         JPanel pane = new JPanel();
24:         pane.setLayout(gridbag);
25:
26:         // Name label
27:         buildConstraints(constraints, 0, 0, 1, 1, 10, 40);
28:         constraints.fill = GridBagConstraints.NONE;
29:         constraints.anchor = GridBagConstraints.EAST;
```

```
30:        JLabel label1 = new JLabel("Name:", JLabel.LEFT);
31:        gridbag.setConstraints(label1, constraints);
32:        pane.add(label1);
33:
34:        // Name text field
35:        buildConstraints(constraints, 1, 0, 1, 1, 90, 0);
36:        constraints.fill = GridBagConstraints.HORIZONTAL;
37:        JTextField tfname = new JTextField();
38:        gridbag.setConstraints(tfname, constraints);
39:        pane.add(tfname);
40:
41:        // password label
42:        buildConstraints(constraints, 0, 1, 1, 1, 0, 40);
43:        constraints.fill = GridBagConstraints.NONE;
44:        constraints.anchor = GridBagConstraints.EAST;
45:        JLabel label2 = new JLabel("Password:", JLabel.LEFT);
46:        gridbag.setConstraints(label2, constraints);
47:        pane.add(label2);
48:
49:        // password text field
50:        buildConstraints(constraints, 1, 1, 1, 1, 0, 0);
51:        constraints.fill = GridBagConstraints.HORIZONTAL;
52:        JPasswordField tfpass = new JPasswordField();
53:        tfpass.setEchoChar('*');
54:        gridbag.setConstraints(tfpass, constraints);
55:        pane.add(tfpass);
56:
57:        // OK Button
58:        buildConstraints(constraints, 0, 2, 2, 1, 0, 20);
59:        constraints.fill = GridBagConstraints.NONE;
60:        constraints.anchor = GridBagConstraints.CENTER;
61:        JButton okb = new JButton("OK");
62:        gridbag.setConstraints(okb, constraints);
63:        pane.add(okb);
64:
65:        // Content Pane
66:        setContentPane(pane);
67:    }
68:
69:    public static void main(String[] arguments) {
70:        NamePass frame = new NamePass();
71:        ExitWindow exit = new ExitWindow();
72:        frame.addWindowListener(exit);
73:        frame.show();
74:    }
75: }
76:
77: class ExitWindow extends WindowAdapter {
78:    public void windowClosing(WindowEvent e) {
79:        System.exit(0);
80:    }
81: }
```

10

Cell Padding and Insets

Before you finish up with grid bag layouts, two more constraints deserve mentioning: ipadx and ipady. These two constraints control the *padding* (the extra space around an individual component). By default, no components have extra space around them (which is easiest to see in components that fill their cells).

ipadx adds space to either side of the component, and ipady adds it above and below.

The horizontal and vertical gaps that appear when you create a new layout manager (or use ipadx and ipady in grid bag layouts), are used to determine the amount of space between components in a panel. *Insets*, however, are used to determine the amount of space around the panel itself. The Insets class includes values for the top, bottom, left, and right insets, which are then used when the panel itself is drawn.

Insets determine the amount of space between the edges of a panel and that panel's components.

To include an inset for your layout, you override the insets() method for Java 1.02, or the getInsets() method for Java 2. These methods do the same thing.

Inside the insets() or getInsets() method, create a new Insets object, where the constructor to the Insets class takes four integer values representing the insets on the top, left, bottom, and right of the panel. The insets() method should then return that Insets object. Here's some code to add insets for a grid layout: 10 to the top and bottom and 30 to the left and right. Figure 10.10 shows the inset.

FIGURE 10.10

A panel with insets of 10 pixels on the top and bottom and 30 pixels to the left and right.

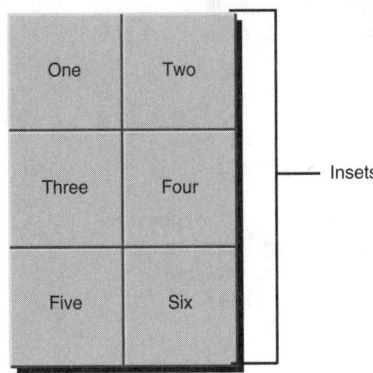

```
public Insets insets() {
    return new Insets(10, 30, 10, 30);
}
```

Summary

Abstract expressionism only goes so far, as you have seen today. Layout managers require some adjustment for people who are used to more precise control over the place that components appear on an interface.

You now know how to use the five different layout managers and panels. As you work with Swing and the Abstract Windowing Toolkit, you'll find that it can approximate any kind of interface through the use of nested containers and different layout managers.

Once you master the development of a user interface in Java, your programs can offer something that most other visual programming languages can't: an interface that works on multiple platforms without modification.

To borrow an oft-repeated phrase: I don't know if it's art, but I like it.

10

Q&A

Q **I really dislike working with layout managers; they're either too simplistic or too complicated (the grid bag layout, for example). Even with a whole lot of tinkering, I can never get my applets to look like I want them to. All I want to do is define the sizes of my components and put them at an x,y position on the screen. Can I do this?**

A It's possible, but very problematic. Java was designed in such a way that a program's graphical user interface could run equally well on different platforms and with different screen resolutions, fonts, screen sizes, and the like. Relying on pixel coordinates can cause a program that looks good on one platform to be unusable on others, where components overlap each other, are cut off by the edge of a container, and other layout disasters. Layout managers, by dynamically placing elements on the screen, get around these problems. Although there might be some differences between the end result on different platforms, the differences are less likely to be catastrophic.

Still not convinced? Use a null layout manager and the reshape() method to make a component a specific size and place it at a particular position:

```
setLayout(null);
Button myButton = new Button("OK");
myButton.reshape(10, 10, 30, 15);
```

You can find out more about reshape() in the Component class.

Q **I was exploring Java classes and I saw this subpackage called peer. References to the peer classes are also sprinkled throughout the Java API documentation. What do peers do?**

A *Peers* are responsible for the platform-specific parts of Java. For example, when you create a Java Swing window, you have an instance of the Window class that provides generic window behavior, and then you have an instance of a class implementing WindowPeer that creates the very specific window for that platform—a motif window under X Window, a Macintosh-style window under the Macintosh, or a Windows 98 window under Windows 98. These peer classes also handle communication between the window system and the Java window itself. By separating the generic component behavior (Java classes) from the actual system implementation and appearance (the peer classes), you can focus on providing behavior in your Java application and let the Java implementation deal with the platform-specific details.

Questions

1. What is the default layout manager for a panel in Java?

    (a) None

    (b) BorderLayout

    (c) FlowLayout

2. Which layout manager requires a compass direction or the word "Center" when adding a component to a container?

    (a) BorderLayout

    (b) MapLayout

    (c) FlowLayout

3. If you want a grid layout in which a component can take up more than one cell of the grid, which layout should you use?

    (a) GridLayout

    (b) GridBagLayout

    (c) None; it isn't possible to do that.

Answers

1. c.

2. a.

3. b.

Exercises

To extend your knowledge of the subjects covered today, try the following exercises:

- Create a user interface that displays a calendar for a single month, including headings for the seven days of the week and a title of the month across the top.

- Create an interface that incorporates more than one layout manager.

Where applicable, exercise solutions are offered on the book's Web site at
`http://www.java21pro.com`.

10

DAY 11

Responding to User Input

In order to turn a working Java interface into a working Java program, you must make the interface receptive to user events.

Swing handles events with a set of interfaces called *event listeners*. You create a listener object and associate it with the user interface component being listened to.

Today you learn how to add listeners of all kinds to your Swing programs, including those that handle action events, mouse events, and other interaction.

When you're done, you'll celebrate the event by completing a full Java application using the Swing set of classes.

Event Listeners

If a class wants to respond to a user event under the Java 2 event-handling system, it must implement the interface that deals with the events. These interfaces are called *event listeners*.

Each listener handles a specific kind of event, and a class can implement as many of them as needed.

NEW TERM The event listeners in Java include each of the following interfaces:

- `ActionListener` —*Action events*, which are generated by a user taking an action on a component, such as a click on a button
- `AdjustmentListener`—*Adjustment events*, which are generated when a component is adjusted, such as when a scrollbar is moved
- `FocusListener`—*Keyboard focus events*, which are generated when a component such as a text field gains or loses the focus
- `ItemListener`—*Item events*, which are generated when an item such as a check box is changed
- `KeyListener`—*Keyboard events*, which occur when a user enters text on the keyboard
- `MouseListener`—*Mouse events*, which are generated by mouse clicks, a mouse entering a component's area, and a mouse leaving a component's area
- `MouseMotionListener`—*Mouse movement events*, which track all movement by a mouse over a component
- `WindowListener`—*Window events*, which are generated by a window (such as the main application window) being maximized, minimized, moved, or closed

The following class is declared so that it can handle both action and text events:

```
public class Suspense extends JFrame implements ActionListener,
    TextListener {
    // ...
}
```

The `java.awt.event` package contains all the basic event listeners as well as the objects that represent specific events. In order to use these classes in your programs, you can import them individually or use a statement such as the following:

```
import java.awt.event.*;
```

Setting Up Components

When you make a class an event listener, you have set up a specific type of event to be heard by that class. This will never happen if you don't follow up with a second step: A matching listener must be added to the component. That listener generates the events when the component is used.

After a component is created, you can call one of the following methods on the component to associate a listener with it:

- `addActionListener()`—`JButton`, `JCheckBox`, `JComboBox`, `JTextField`, and `JRadioButton` components
- `addAdjustmentListener()`—`JScrollBar` components
- `addFocusListener()`—All Swing components
- `addItemListener()`—`JButton`, `JCheckBox`, `JComboBox`, and `JRadioButton` components
- `addKeyListener()`—All Swing components
- `addMouseListener()`—All Swing components
- `addMouseMotionListener()`—All Swing components
- `addWindowListener()`—All `JWindow` and `JFrame` components

> **Caution**
>
> Modifying a component after adding it to a container is an easy mistake to make in a Java program. You must add listeners to a component and handle any other configuration before it is added to any containers; otherwise these settings are disregarded when the program is run.

11

The following example creates a `JButton` object and associates an action event listener with it:

```
JButton zap = new JButton("Zap");
zap.addActionListener(this);
```

All the different add methods take one argument: the object that is listening for events of that kind. Using `this` indicates that the current class is the event listener. You could specify a different object, as long as its class implements the right listener interface.

Event-Handling Methods

When you associate an interface with a class, the class must handle all the methods contained in the interface.

In the case of event listeners, each of the methods is called automatically by the windowing system when the corresponding user event takes place.

The `ActionListener` interface has only one method: `actionPerformed()`. All classes that implement `ActionListener` must have a method with a structure similar to the following:

```
public void actionPerformed(ActionEvent evt) {
    // handle event here
}
```

If only one component in your program's graphical user interface has a listener for action events, this `actionPerformed()` method can be used to respond to an event generated by that component.

If more than one component has an action event listener, you must use the method to figure out which component was used and act accordingly in your program.

In the `actionPerformed()` method, you might have noticed that an `ActionEvent` object is sent as an argument when the method is called. This object can be used to discover details about the component that generated the event.

`ActionEvent` and all other event objects are part of the `java.awt.event` package, and they are subclasses of the `EventObject` class.

Every event-handling method is sent an event object of some kind. The object's `getSource()` method can be used to determine the component that sent the event, as in the following example:

```
public void actionPerformed(ActionEvent evt) {
    Object src = evt.getSource();
}
```

The object returned by the `getSource()` method can be compared to components by using the `==` operator. The following statements can be used inside the preceding `actionPerformed()` example:

```
if (src == quitButton)
    quitProgram();
else if (src == sortRecords)
    sortRecords();
```

This example calls the `quitProgram()` method if the `quitButton` object generated the event; it calls the `sortRecords()` method if the `sortRecords` button generated the event.

Many event-handling methods call a different method for each kind of event or component. This makes the event-handling method easier to read. In addition, if there is more than one event-handling method in a class, each one can call the same methods to get work done.

Using the `instanceof` keyword inside an event-handling method is another useful technique for checking what kind of component generated the event. The following example can be used in a program with one button and one text field, each of which generates an action event:

```
public void actionPerformed(ActionEvent evt) {
    Object src = evt.getSource();
    if (src instanceof JTextField)
        calculateScore();
    else if (src instanceof JButton)
        quitProgram();
}
```

The program in Listing 11.1 uses the application framework to create a JFrame and add components to it. The program itself sports two JButton components, which are used to change the text on the frame's title bar.

LISTING 11.1   The Full Text of ChangeTitle.java

```
 1: import java.awt.event.*;
 2: import javax.swing.*;
 3: import java.awt.*;
 4:
 5: public class ChangeTitle extends JFrame implements ActionListener {
 6:     JButton b1 = new JButton("Rosencrantz");
 7:     JButton b2 = new JButton("Guildenstern");
 8:
 9:     public ChangeTitle() {
10:         super("Title Bar");
11:
12:         b1.addActionListener(this);
13:         b2.addActionListener(this);
14:         JPanel pane = new JPanel();
15:         pane.add(b1);
16:         pane.add(b2);
17:
18:         setContentPane(pane);
19:     }
20:
21:     public static void main(String[] arguments) {
22:         JFrame frame = new ChangeTitle();
23:
24:         ExitWindow exit = new ExitWindow();
25:         frame.addWindowListener(exit);
26:
27:         frame.pack();
28:         frame.setVisible(true);
29:     }
30:
31:     public void actionPerformed(ActionEvent evt) {
32:         Object source = evt.getSource();
33:         if (source == b1)
34:             setTitle("Rosencrantz");
35:         else if (source == b2)
36:             setTitle("Guildenstern");
```

11

LISTING **11.1**   continued

```
37:            repaint();
38:        }
39: }
40:
41: class ExitWindow extends WindowAdapter {
42:     public void windowClosing(WindowEvent e) {
43:         System.exit(0);
44:     }
45: }
```

After you run this application with the Java interpreter, the program's interface should resemble Figure 11.1.

FIGURE **11.1**

The ChangeTitle
application.

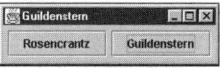

Only 11 lines were needed to respond to action events in this application:

- Line 1 imports the java.awt.event package.

- Lines 12 and 13 add action listeners to both JButton objects.

- Lines 31–38 respond to action events that occur from the two JButton objects. The evt object's getSource() method determines the source of the event. If it is equal to the b1 button, the title of the frame is set to Rosencrantz; if it is equal to b2, the title is set to Guildenstern. A call to repaint() is needed so that the frame is redrawn after any title change that might have occurred in the method.

Working with Methods

The following sections detail the structure of each event-handling method and the methods that can be used within them.

In addition to the methods described, the getSource() method can be used on any event object to determine which object generated the event.

Action Events

Action events occur when a user completes an action using one of the following components: JButton, JCheckBox, JComboBox, JTextField, or JRadioButton.

A class must implement the `ActionListener` interface in order to handle these events. In addition, the `addActionListener()` method must be called on each component that should generate an action event—unless you want to ignore that component's action events.

The `actionPerformed(Action Event)` method is the only method of the `ActionListener` interface. It takes the following form:

```
public void actionPerformed(ActionEvent evt) {
   // ...
}
```

In addition to the `getSource()` method, you can use the `getActionCommand()` method on the `ActionEvent` object to discover more information about the event's source.

The action command, by default, is the text associated with the component, such as the label on a `JButton`. You also can set a different action command for a component by calling its `setActionCommand(String)` method. The string argument should be the action command's desired text.

For example, the following statements create a `JButton` and a `JTextField` and give both of them the action command `"Sort Files"`:

```
JButton sort = new JButton("Sort");
JTextField name = new JTextField();
sort.setActionCommand("Sort Files");
name.setActionCommand("Sort Files");
```

11

Note

Action commands become exceptionally useful when you're writing a program in which more than one component should cause the same thing to happen. A program with a Quit button and a Quit option on a pull-down menu is an example of this. By giving both components the same action command, you can handle them with the same code in an event-handling method.

Adjustment Events

Adjustment events occur when a `JScrollBar` component is moved by using the arrows on the bar or on the box, or by clicking anywhere on the bar. To handle these events, a class must implement the `AdjustmentListener` interface.

The adjustmentValueChanged(*AdjustmentEvent*) method is the only method in the AdjustmentListener interface. It takes the following form:

```
public void adjustmentValueChanged(AdjustmentEvent evt) {
    // ...
}
```

To see what the current value of the JScrollBar is within this event-handling method, the getValue() method can be called on the AdjustmentEvent object. This method returns an integer representing the scrollbar's value.

You can also determine the way the user moved the scrollbar by using the AdjustmentEvent object's getAdjustmentType() method. This returns one of five values, each of which is a class variable of the Adjustment class:

- UNIT_INCREMENT—A value increase of 1, which can be caused by clicking a scrollbar arrow or using a cursor key
- UNIT_DECREMENT—A value decrease of 1
- BLOCK_INCREMENT—A larger value increase, caused by clicking the scrollbar in the area between the box and the arrow
- BLOCK_DECREMENT—A larger value decrease
- TRACK—A value change caused by moving the box

The program in Listing 11.2 illustrates the use of the AdjustmentListener interface. A scrollbar and an uneditable text field are added to a frame, and messages are displayed in the field whenever the scrollbar is moved.

LISTING 11.2   The Full Text of WellAdjusted.java

```
 1: import java.awt.event.*;
 2: import javax.swing.*;
 3: import java.awt.*;
 4:
 5: public class WellAdjusted extends JFrame implements AdjustmentListener {
 6:     JTextField value = new JTextField("50", 30);
 7:     JScrollBar bar = new JScrollBar(SwingConstants.HORIZONTAL,
 8:         50, 10, 0, 100);
 9:
10:     public WellAdjusted() {
11:         super("Well Adjusted");
12:         setSize(350, 100);
13:         bar.addAdjustmentListener(this);
14:         value.setHorizontalAlignment(SwingConstants.CENTER);
15:         value.setEditable(false);
16:         JPanel pane = new JPanel();
17:         pane.setLayout(new BorderLayout());
```

```
18:              pane.add(value, "Center");
19:              pane.add(bar, "South");
20:              setContentPane(pane);
21:      }
22:
23:      public static void main(String[] arguments) {
24:          JFrame frame = new WellAdjusted();
25:
26:          ExitWindow exit = new ExitWindow();
27:          frame.addWindowListener(exit);
28:
29:          frame.show();
30:      }
31:
32:      public void adjustmentValueChanged(AdjustmentEvent evt) {
33:          Object source = evt.getSource();
34:          if (source == bar) {
35:              int newValue = bar.getValue();
36:              value.setText("" + newValue);
37:          }
38:          repaint();
39:      }
40: }
```

11

Compiling this class requires ExitWindow.class, the subclass of WindowAdapter you have been using, to close applications after the main window closes. If you are creating all of today's programs in the same folder, you should already have ExitWindow.class in that folder.

Figure 11.2 shows a screen capture of the application after you run it with the Java interpreter.

FIGURE 11.2

The output of the WellAdjusted *application.*

Tip

NEW TERM   You might be wondering why there's an empty set of quotation marks in the call to setText() in line 36 of this program. The empty quotation is called a null *string*, and it is concatenated to the newValue integer to turn the argument into a string. As you might recall, if a string and nonstring are concatenated, Java always treats the result as a string. The null string is a shortcut when you want to display something that isn't already a string.

Focus Events

Focus events occur when any component gains or loses input focus on a graphical user interface. *Focus* describes the component that is currently active for keyboard input. If one of the fields has the focus (in a user interface with several editable text fields), a cursor will blink in the field. Any text entered goes into this component.

Focus applies to all components that can receive input. In a JButton object, a dotted outline appears on the button that has the focus.

To handle a focus event, a class must implement the FocusListener interface. There are two methods in the interface: focusGained(*FocusEvent*) and focusLost(*FocusEvent*). They take the following forms:

```
public void focusGained(FocusEvent evt) {
    // ...
}

public void focusLost(FocusEvent evt) {
    // ...
}
```

To determine which object gained or lost the focus, the getSource() method can be called on the FocusEvent object sent as an argument to the focusGained() and focusLost() methods.

Item Events

Item events occur when an item is selected or deselected on any of the following components: JButton, JCheckBox, JComboBox, or JRadioButton. A class must implement the ItemListener interface in order to handle these events.

itemStateChanged(*ItemEvent*) is the only method in the ItemListener interface. It takes the following form:

```
void itemStateChanged(ItemEvent evt) {
    // ...
}
```

To determine in which item the event occurred, the getItem() method can be called on the ItemEvent object.

You also can determine whether the item was selected or deselected by using the getStateChange() method. This method returns an integer that will equal either the class variable ItemEvent.DESELECTED or ItemEvent.SELECTED.

The use of item events is illustrated in Listing 11.3. The SelectItem application displays the choice from a combo box in a text field.

LISTING **11.3**   The Full Text of `SelectItem.java`

```
1: import java.awt.event.*;
2: import javax.swing.*;
3: import java.awt.*;
4:
5: public class SelectItem extends JFrame implements ItemListener {
6:     BorderLayout bord = new BorderLayout();
7:     JTextField result = new JTextField(27);
8:     JComboBox pick = new JComboBox();
9:
10:     public SelectItem() {
11:         super("Select Item");
12:
13:         pick.addItemListener(this);
14:         pick.addItem("Navigator");
15:         pick.addItem("Internet Explorer");
16:         pick.addItem("Opera");
17:         pick.setEditable(false);
18:         result.setHorizontalAlignment(SwingConstants.CENTER);
19:         result.setEditable(false);
20:         JPanel pane = new JPanel();
21:         pane.setLayout(bord);
22:         pane.add(result, "South");
23:         pane.add(pick, "Center");
24:
25:         setContentPane(pane);
26:     }
27:
28:     public static void main(String[] arguments) {
29:         JFrame frame = new SelectItem();
30:
31:         ExitWindow exit = new ExitWindow();
32:         frame.addWindowListener(exit);
33:
34:         frame.pack();
35:         frame.setVisible(true);
36:     }
37:
38:     public void itemStateChanged(ItemEvent evt) {
39:         Object source = evt.getSource();
40:         if (source == pick) {
41:             Object newPick = evt.getItem();
42:             result.setText(newPick.toString() + " is the selection.");
43:         }
44:         repaint();
45:     }
46: }
```

11

Figure 11.3 shows this application with the Opera item as the current selection in the combo box. The object's toString() method is used to retrieve the object's text returned by getItem().

FIGURE 11.3

The output of the
SelectItem
application.

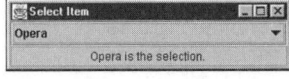

Key Events

Key events occur when a key is pressed on the keyboard. Any component can generate these events, and a class must implement the KeyListener interface to support them.

There are three methods in the KeyListener interface; keyPressed(*KeyEvent*), keyReleased(*KeyEvent*), and keyTyped(*KeyEvent*). They take the following forms:

```
public void keyPressed(KeyEvent evt) {
    // ...
}

public void keyReleased(KeyEvent evt) {
    // ...
}

public void keyTyped(KeyEvent evt) {
    // ...
}
```

KeyEvent's getKeyChar() method returns the character of the key associated with the event. If there is no Unicode character that can be represented by the key, getKeyChar() returns a character value equal to the class variable KeyEvent.CHAR_UNDEFINED.

Mouse Events

Mouse events are generated by several different types of user interaction:

- A mouse click
- A mouse entering a component's area
- A mouse leaving a component's area

Any component can generate these events, which are implemented by a class through the MouseListener interface. This interface has five methods:

```
mouseClicked(MouseEvent)

mouseEntered(MouseEvent)

mouseExited(MouseEvent)

mousePressed(MouseEvent)

mouseReleased(MouseEvent)
```

Each takes the same basic form as `mouseReleased (MouseEvent)`:

```
public void mouseReleased(MouseEvent evt) {
    // ...
}
```

The following methods can be used on `MouseEvent` objects:

- `getClickCount()`—Returns the number of times the mouse was clicked as an integer.
- `getPoint()`—Returns the x,y coordinates within the component where the mouse was clicked as a `Point` object.
- `getX()`—Returns the x position.
- `getY()`—Returns the y position.

Mouse Motion Events

Mouse motion events occur when a mouse is moved over a component. As with other mouse events, any component can generate mouse motion events. A class must implement the `MouseMotionListener` interface in order to support them.

There are two methods in the `MouseMotionListener` interface: `mouseDragged (MouseEvent)` and `mouseMoved(MouseEvent)`. They take the following forms:

```
public void mouseDragged(MouseEvent evt) {
    // ...
}

public void mouseMoved(MouseEvent evt) {
    // ...
}
```

Unlike the other event listener interfaces you have dealt with up to this point, `MouseMotionListener` does not have its own event type. Instead, `MouseEvent` objects are used.

Because of this, you can call the same methods you would for mouse events: `getClick()`, `getPoint()`, `getX()`, and `getY()`.

11

Window Events

Window events occur when a user opens or closes a window object such as a `JFrame` or a `JWindow`. Any component can generate these events, and a class must implement the `WindowListener` interface in order to support them.

There are seven methods in the `WindowListener` interface:

```
windowActivated(WindowEvent)

windowClosed(WindowEvent)

windowClosing(WindowEvent)

windowDeactivated(WindowEvent)

windowDeiconified(WindowEvent)

windowIconified(WindowEvent)

windowOpened(WindowEvent)
```

They all take the same form as the `windowOpened()` method:

```
public void windowOpened(WindowEvent evt) {
    // ...
}
```

The `windowClosing()` and `windowClosed()` methods are similar, but one is called as the window is closing and the other is called after it is closed. In fact, you can take action in a `windowClosing()` method to stop the window from being closed.

There's also an adapter class that implements the `WindowListener` interface called `WindowAdapter`. Throughout the past four days, this class has been subclassed to exit an application when its main window is closed.

An Example: An RGB-to-HSB Converter

As an opportunity to put the past several days' material to more use, the following application demonstrates layout creation, nested panels, interface creation, and event handling.

Figure 11.4 shows the SwingColorTest application, which enables a user to pick colors based on the sRGB or HSB color spaces—systems that describe colors based on their red, green, and blue content or hue, saturation, and brightness values, respectively.

The SwingColorTest application has three main parts: a colored box on the left side and two groups of text fields on the right. The first group indicates RGB values; the second group, HSB. If you change any of the values in any of the text boxes, the colored box is updated to the new color, as are the values in the other group of text boxes.

FIGURE 11.4

*The SwingColorTest
application.*

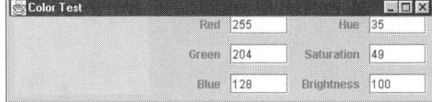

This application uses three classes:

- `SwingColorTest`, which inherits from `JFrame` and is the main class for the application itself.

- `SwingColorControls`, which inherits from `JPanel`. You create this class to represent a group of three text fields and to handle actions from them. Two instances of this class, one for the sRGB values and one for the HSB ones, are created and added to the application.

The code for this application is shown at the end of this section.

Designing the Layout

The first step in a Swing project is to worry about the layout first and the functionality second. When dealing with the layout, you should start with the outermost panel first and work inward.

Making a sketch of your user-interface design can help you figure out how to organize the panels inside your application to best take advantage of layout and space. Paper designs are helpful even when you're not using grid bag layouts, but doubly so when you are. (You'll be using a simple grid layout for this application.)

Figure 11.5 shows the `SwingColorTest` application with a grid drawn over it so that you can get an idea of how the panels and embedded panels work.

FIGURE 11.5

`SwingColorTest` *panels and components.*

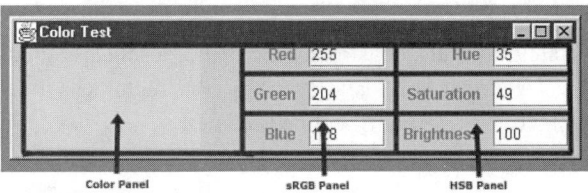

Start with the outermost panel—a `JFrame` component. This frame has three parts: the color box on the left, the RGB text fields in the middle, and the HSB fields on the right.

Because the outermost panel is the frame itself, the `SwingColorTest` class will inherit from `JFrame`. You also import the Swing, AWT, and event-handling classes here. (Note that because you use so many of them in this program, importing the entire package is easiest.)

```
import java.awt.*;
import java.awt.event.*;
import javax.swing.*;

public class SwingColorTest extends JFrame {
    // ...
}
```

This frame has three main elements to keep track of: the color box and the two subpanels. Each of the subpanels refers to different things, but they're extremely similar in how they look and the information they contain. Rather than duplicate a lot of code in this class, you can take this opportunity to create another class strictly for the subpanels, use instances of that class in the frame, and communicate between everything using methods. The new class called SwingColorControls will be defined in a bit.

For now, however, you know you need to keep a handle on all three parts of the application, so you can update them when they change. Create three instance variables: one of type JPanel for the color box and the other two of type SwingColorControls for the control panels:

```
SwingColorControls RGBcontrols, HSBcontrols;
JPanel swatch;
```

Now you can move onto the frame's constructor method, where all the basic initialization and layout of the application take place in the following steps:

1. Set up the class and create the layout for the big parts of the panel. Although a flow layout would work, creating a grid layout with one row and three columns is a better idea.

2. Create and initialize the three components of this application: a panel for the color box and two subpanels for the text fields.

3. Add these components to the application.

The first statement in the constructor method of a subclass should be a call to a constructor of the superclass. The JFrame(*String*) constructor sets the text of the frame's title bar to the indicated String. It will be used here:

```
super("Color Test");
```

Next, a panel is created and its layout is set to a grid layout;

```
JPanel pane = new JPanel();
pane.setLayout(new GridLayout(1, 3, 5, 15));
```

This panel, pane, will be set up completely and then used to create the frame's content pane—the portion of the frame that can contain other components.

The first component that will be added to `pane` is the color box, `swatch`: It is created as a `JPanel` and given the background color black:

```
swatch = new JPanel();
swatch.setBackground(Color.black);
```

You need also to create two instances of the currently nonexistent `SwingColorControls` panels here. Because you haven't created the class yet, you don't know what the constructors to that class will look like. In that case, put in some placeholder constructors here; you can fill in the details later.

```
RGBcontrols = new SwingColorControls(...);
HSBcontrols = new SwingColorControls(...);
```

Once all the components have been created, they are added to the panel, which is then used to set up the frame's content pane:

```
pane.add(swatch);
pane.add(RGBcontrols);
pane.add(HSBcontrols);
setContentPane(pane);
```

Because this application's main class is a user interface component, you can override the `getInsets()` method of the class to establish new inset values:

```
public Insets getInsets() {
    return new Insets(10, 10, 10, 10);
}
```

This gives the application frame 10 points of empty space along all outer edges. At this point your class should contain three instance variables, a constructor method, incomplete constructors for `RGBControls` and `HSBControls`, and a `getInsets()` method. Move on to creating the subpanel layout in the `SwingColorControls` class, which will enable you to fill in the incomplete constructors and finish up the layout.

Defining the Subpanels

The `SwingColorControls` class will have behavior for laying out and handling the subpanels that represent the RGB and HSB values for a color. `SwingColorControls` inherits from `JPanel`, a simple component that can contain other components:

```
class SwingColorControls extends JPanel {
    // ...
}
```

The `SwingColorControls` class needs a number of instance variables so that information from the panel can get back to the application. The first of these instance variables is a hook back up to the class that contains this panel. Because the outer application class controls the updating of each panel, this panel needs a way to tell the application that something has changed. To call a method in that application, you need a reference to the object; instance variable number one is a reference to an instance of the class SwingColorTest:

```
SwingColorTest frame;
```

If you figure that the `frame` class is updating everything, that class will be interested in the individual text fields in this subpanel. You create instance variables for these text fields:

```
JTextField[] tfield = new JTextField[3];
```

Now you can move on to the constructor method for this class. You establish the layout for the subpanel, create the text fields, and add them to the panel's content pane inside the constructor.

The goal here is to make the `SwingColorControls` class generic enough so that you can use it for both the panel of RGB fields and the panel of HSB fields. These two panels differ in only one respect: the labels for the text—that's three values to get before you can create the object. You can pass these three values in through the constructors in `SwingColorTest`. You also need one more: the reference to the enclosing application, which you can get from the constructor as well.

You now have two arguments to the basic constructor for the `ColorControls` class—a reference to the parent class and a `String` array containing the text field labels. Here's the signature for the constructor:

```
SwingColorControls(SwingColorTest parent, String[] label) {
    // ..
}
```

Start this constructor by first setting the value of `parent` to the `frame` instance variable:

```
frame = parent;
```

Next, create the layout for this panel. You can also use a grid layout for these subpanels, as you did for the application frame, but this time the grid will have three rows (one for each of the text field and label pairs) and two columns (one for the labels and one for the fields). Also, define a 10-point gap between the components in the grid:

```
setLayout(new GridLayout(3, 2, 10, 10));
```

Now you can create and add the components to the panel. First create a `for` loop named i that can iterate three times:

```
for (int i = 0; i < 3; i++) {
    // ...
}
```

Inside this loop, each text field and label will be created and added to a container. First, a text field will be initialized to the string "0" and assigned to the appropriate instance variable:

```
tfield[i] = new JTextField("0");
```

Next, the text field and a label are added to the panel using the String array sent to the SwingColorControls constructor as the text for the labels:

```
add(new JLabel(label[i], JLabel.RIGHT));
add(tfield[i]);
```

This completes the constructor for the subpanel class SwingColorControls, but you will also override getInsets() here to tinker with the panel's layout. Add the inset here as you did in the SwingColorTest class:

```
public Insets getInsets() {
        return new Insets(10, 10, 0, 0);
}
```

Now that a SwingColorControls class has been completed, you can fix the placeholder constructors in SwingColorTest for the subpanel.

The constructor for SwingColorControls that you just created now has two arguments: the SwingColorTest object and an array of strings containing three labels. Replace the RGBcontrols and HSBcontrols placeholder constructors in SwingColorTest so that the array labels are created and used in calls to the SwingColorTest constructor:

```
String[] rgbLabels = { "Red", "Green", "Blue" };
RGBcontrols = new SwingColorControls(this, rgbLabels);
String[] hsbLabels = { "Hue", "Saturation", "Brightness" };
HSBcontrols = new SwingColorControls(this, hsbLabels);
```

The this keyword is used to pass the SwingColorTest object to these constructors.

Note

> The number 0 (actually, the string "0") is used for the initial values of all the text fields in this example. For the color black, both the RGB and the HSB values are 0, which is why this assumption can be made. If you want to initialize the application to some other color, you might want to rewrite the SwingColorControls class to use initializer values as well as to initialize labels.

Converting Between sRGB and HSB

At this point, the SwingColorTest application will compile successfully, and you can take a look at the layout. It's common to do this in a programming project, resolving all issues with the interface before spending any time writing code to make the interface function.

This application's main purpose is to convert between sRGB and HSB values, and vice versa. When the value in a text field is changed, the color box updates to the new color, and the value of the fields in the opposite subpanel changes to reflect the new color.

The SwingColorTest class will be made responsible for actually doing the updating when a user has changed a value. A new method will be added to handle this: update().

This update() method takes a single argument: the SwingColorControls instance that contains the changed value. (You will get this argument from event-handling methods in the SwingColorControls object.)

> **Note**
>
> Won't this update() method interfere with the system's update() method? No. Remember, methods can have the same name, but different signatures and definitions. Because this update() has a single argument of type ColorControls, it doesn't interfere with the other version of update().

The update() method is responsible for updating all the panels in the application. To know which panel to update, you need to know which panel changed. You can find out by testing to see whether the argument you got passed from the panel is the same as the subpanels you have stored in the RGBcontrols and HSBcontrols instance variables:

```
void update(SwingColorControls control) {

    if (control == RGBcontrols) {
        // RGB has changed, update HSB
    } else {
        // HSB has changed, update RGB
    }
}
```

This test is the heart of the update() method. Start with the first case—a number has been changed in the RGB text fields. Now, based on these new sRGB values, you have to generate a new Color object and update the values on the HSB panel. You can create a few local variables to hold some basic values in order to reduce the amount of typing you have to do. In particular, the values of the text fields are strings whose values you can get to using the getText() method defined in the JTextField objects of the SwingColorControls object. Because most of the time you'll want to deal with these values as integers in this method, you can get these string values, convert them to integers, and store them in an array of integers, called value. Here's the code to take care of this job:

```
int[] value = new int[3];
for (int i = 0; i < 3; i++) {
    value[i] = Integer.parseInt(control.tfield[i].getText());
    if ((value[i] < 0) || (value[i] > 255)) {
        value[i] = 0;
        control.tfield[i].setText("" + value[i]);
    }
}
```

Each of the values collected from the JTextField objects is checked to see if it is less than 0 or greater than 255 (sRGB and HSB values are represented as integers from 0 to 255). If the value is out of the acceptable range, the text field is set back to its initial value, "0".

While you're defining local variables, you also need one for the new Color object:

```
Color c;
```

Now assume that one of the text fields in the RGB side of the application has changed and add the code to the if part of the update() method. You need to create a new Color object and update the HSB side of the panel. The first part is easy. Given the three sRGB values, you can create a new Color object using these values as arguments to the constructor:

```
c = new Color(value[0], value[1], value[2]);
```

Now you convert the sRGB values to HSB. Standard algorithms can convert an sRGB-based color to an HSB color, but you don't have to look them up. The Color class has a class method called RGBtoHSB() you can use. This method does the work for you—most of it, at least. The RGBtoHSB() method poses two problems, however:

- The RGBtoHSB() method returns an array of the three HSB values, so you have to extract these values from the array.

- The HSB values are measured in floating-point values from 0.0 to 1.0. I prefer to think of HSB values as integers, where the hue is a degree value around a color wheel (0 through 360), and saturation and brightness are percentages from 0 to 100.

Neither of these problems is insurmountable; you just have to add some extra lines of code. Start by calling RGBtoHSB() with the new RGB values you have. The return type of that method is an array of floats, so you create a local variable (HSB) to store the results of the RBGtoHSB() method. (Note that you also need to create and pass in an empty float array as the fourth argument to RGBtoHSB().)

```
float[] HSB = Color.RGBtoHSB(value[0], value[1], value[2],
    (new float[3]));
```

11

Now convert these floating-point values that range from `0.0` to `1.0` to values that range from `0` and `100` (for the saturation and brightness) and `0` to `360` (for the hue) by multiplying the appropriate numbers and reassigning the value back to the array:

```
HSB[0] *= 360;
HSB[1] *= 100;
HSB[2] *= 100;
```

Now you have the numbers you want. The last part of the update puts these values back into the text fields. Of course, these values are still floating-point numbers, so you have to cast them to `ints` before turning them into strings and storing them:

```
for (int i = 0; i < 3; i++) {
    HSBcontrols.tfield[i].setText(String.valueOf((int)HSB[i]));
```

The next part of the application is the part that updates the sRGB values when a text field on the HSB side has changed. This is the `else` in the big `if-else` that defines this method and determines what to update, given a change.

Generating sRGB values from HSB values is actually easier than doing the process the other way around. A class method in the `Color` class, `getHSBColor ()`, creates a new `Color` object from three HSB values. After you have a `Color` object, you can easily pull the RGB values out of there. The catch, of course, is that `getHSBColor` takes three floating-point arguments, and the values you have are integer values. In the call to `getHSBColor`, you'll have to cast the integer values from the text fields to `floats` and divide them by the proper conversion factor. The result of `getHSBColor` is a `Color` object. Therefore you can simply assign the object to the c local variable so that you can use it again later:

```
c = Color.getHSBColor((float)value[0] / 360,
    (float)value[1] / 100, (float)value[2] / 100);
```

With the `Color` object all set, updating the RGB values involves extracting these values from that `Color` object. The `getRed()`, `getGreen()`, and `getBlue()` methods, defined in the `Color` class, will do just that job:

```
RGBcontrols.tfield[0].setText(String.valueOf(c.getRed()));
RGBcontrols.tfield[1].setText(String.valueOf(c.getGreen()));
RGBcontrols.tfield[2].setText(String.valueOf(c.getBlue()));
```

Finally, regardless of whether the sRGB or HSB value has changed, you need to update the color box on the left to reflect the new color. Because you have a new `Color` object stored in the variable c, you can use the `setBackground` method to change the color. Also note that `setBackground` doesn't automatically repaint the screen, so fire off a `repaint()` as well:

```
swatch.setBackground(c);
swatch.repaint();
```

Handling User Events

Three classes are created for this project: SwingColorTest, SwingColorControls, and ExitWindow. SwingColorTest contains the application window and the main() method that is used to set up the window. SwingColorControls, a helper class, is a panel that holds three labels and three text fields used to choose a color. ExitWindow is the helper class used to close down the application when its main window is closed.

All the user input in this program takes place on the color controls—the text fields are used to define sRGB or HSB values.

Because of this, all the event-handling behaviors are added to the SwingColorControls class.

The first thing to do is make the SwingColorControls class handle two kinds of events: action events and focus events. The extends clause should be added to the class declaration statement so that the ActionListener and FocusListener interfaces are implemented. It is shown here:

```
class SwingColorControls extends JPanel
    implements ActionListener, FocusListener {
```

Action and focus listeners must next be added to the three text fields in the class, which are referenced using the tfield array. These listeners must be added after the text fields are created but before they are added to a container. The following statements can be used in a for loop called i that iterates through the tfield array:

```
tfield[i].addFocusListener(this);
tfield[i].addActionListener(this);
```

Finally, you must add all the methods that are defined in the three interfaces this class implements: actionPerformed(ActionEvent), focusLost(FocusEvent), and focusGained(FocusEvent).

The color controls enter a numeric value for a color, and this causes the color to be drawn on a panel. It also causes the other color controls to be updated to reflect the color change.

There are two ways a user can finalize a new color choice—by pressing Enter inside a text field, which generates an action event, or by leaving the field to edit a different field, which generates a focus event.

The following statements compose the actionPerformed() and focusLost() methods that should be added to the class:

```
public void actionPerformed(ActionEvent evt) {
    if (evt.getSource() instanceof JTextField)
        frame.update(this);
}
```

11

```
public void focusLost(FocusEvent evt) {
    frame.update(this);
}
```

One of these, `focusGained()`, doesn't need to be handled. Because of this, an empty method definition should be added:

```
public void focusGained(FocusEvent evt) { }
```

The event-handling methods added to `SwingColorControls` call a method in its parent class, `update(SwingColorControls)`.

This method doesn't contain any event-handling behavior—it updates the color swatch and all the color controls to reflect a color change.

Listing 11.4 contains the application, including the `SwingColorTest`, `SwingColorControls`, and `ExitWindow` classes.

LISTING 11.4   The Full Text of `SwingColorTest.java`

```
 1: import java.awt.*;
 2: import java.awt.event.*;
 3: import javax.swing.*;
 4:
 5: public class SwingColorTest extends JFrame {
 6:     SwingColorControls RGBcontrols, HSBcontrols;
 7:     JPanel swatch;
 8:
 9:     public SwingColorTest() {
10:         super("Color Test");
11:
12:         JPanel pane = new JPanel();
13:         pane.setLayout(new GridLayout(1, 3, 5, 15));
14:         swatch = new JPanel();
15:         swatch.setBackground(Color.black);
16:         String[] rgbLabels = { "Red", "Green", "Blue" };
17:         RGBcontrols = new SwingColorControls(this, rgbLabels);
18:         String[] hsbLabels = { "Hue", "Saturation", "Brightness" };
19:         HSBcontrols = new SwingColorControls(this, hsbLabels);
20:         pane.add(swatch);
21:         pane.add(RGBcontrols);
22:         pane.add(HSBcontrols);
23:
24:         setContentPane(pane);
25:     }
26:
27:     public static void main(String[] arguments) {
28:         JFrame frame = new SwingColorTest();
29:
30:         ExitWindow exit = new ExitWindow();
```

```
31:            frame.addWindowListener(exit);
32:
33:            frame.pack();
34:            frame.setVisible(true);
35:        }
36:
37:        public Insets getInsets() {
38:            return new Insets(10, 10, 10, 10);
39:        }
40:
41:        void update(SwingColorControls control) {
42:            Color c;
43:            // get string values from text fields, convert to ints
44:            int[] value = new int[3];
45:            for (int i = 0; i < 3; i++) {
46:                value[i] = Integer.parseInt(control.tfield[i].getText());
47:                if ((value[i] < 0) || (value[i] > 255)) {
48:                    value[i] = 0;
49:                    control.tfield[i].setText("" + value[i]);
50:                }
51:            }
52:            if (control == RGBcontrols) {
53:                // RGB has changed, update HSB
54:                c = new Color(value[0], value[1], value[2]);
55:
56:                // convert RGB values to HSB values
57:                float[] HSB = Color.RGBtoHSB(value[0], value[1], value[2],
58:                    (new float[3]));
59:                HSB[0] *= 360;
60:                HSB[1] *= 100;
61:                HSB[2] *= 100;
62:
63:                // reset HSB fields
64:                for (int i = 0; i < 3; i++) {
65:                    HSBcontrols.tfield[i].setText(String.valueOf((int)HSB[i]));
66:                }
67:            } else {
68:                // HSB has changed, update RGB
69:                c = Color.getHSBColor((float)value[0] / 360,
70:                    (float)value[1] / 100, (float)value[2] / 100);
71:
72:                // reset RGB fields
73:                RGBcontrols.tfield[0].setText(String.valueOf(c.getRed()));
74:                RGBcontrols.tfield[1].setText(String.valueOf(c.getGreen()));
75:                RGBcontrols.tfield[2].setText(String.valueOf(c.getBlue()));
76:            }
77:
78:            // update swatch
79:            swatch.setBackground(c);
80:            swatch.repaint();
81:        }
```

11

LISTING 11.4   continued

```
 82: }
 83:
 84: class SwingColorControls extends JPanel
 85:     implements ActionListener, FocusListener {
 86:
 87:     SwingColorTest frame;
 88:     JTextField[] tfield = new JTextField[3];
 89:
 90:     SwingColorControls(SwingColorTest parent, String[] label) {
 91:
 92:         frame = parent;
 93:         setLayout(new GridLayout(3, 2, 10, 10));
 94:         for (int i = 0; i < 3; i++) {
 95:             tfield[i] = new JTextField("0");
 96:             tfield[i].addFocusListener(this);
 97:             tfield[i].addActionListener(this);
 98:             add(new JLabel(label[i], JLabel.RIGHT));
 99:             add(tfield[i]);
100:         }
101:     }
102:
103:     public Insets getInsets() {
104:         return new Insets(10, 10, 0, 0);
105:     }
106:
107:     public void actionPerformed(ActionEvent evt) {
108:         if (evt.getSource() instanceof JTextField)
109:             frame.update(this);
110:     }
111:
112:     public void focusLost(FocusEvent evt) {
113:         frame.update(this);
114:     }
115:
116:     public void focusGained(FocusEvent evt) { }
117:
118: }
119:
120: class ExitWindow extends WindowAdapter {
121:     public void windowClosing(WindowEvent e) {
122:         System.exit(0);
123:     }
124: }
```

Summary

Internally, the event-handling system used with Swing is much more sound, and more easily extended to handle new types of user interaction.

Externally, the new system should also make more sense from a programming standpoint. Event handling is added to a program through the same steps:

- A listener interface is added to the class that will contain the event-handling methods.

- A listener is added to each component that will generate the events to handle.

- The methods are added, each with an `EventObject` class as the only argument to the method.

- Methods of that `EventObject` class, such as `getSource()`, are used to learn which component generated the event and what kind of event it was.

Once you know these steps, you can work with each of the different listener interfaces and event classes. You also can learn about new listeners as they are added to Swing with new components.

Q&A

Q Can a program's event-handling behavior be put into its own class instead of including it with the code that creates the interface?

A It can, and many programmers will tell you that it's a good way to design your programs. Separating interface design from your event-handling code enables the two to be developed separately—the `SwingColorTest` application today shows the alternative approach. This makes it easier to maintain the project; related behavior is grouped and isolated from unrelated behavior.

Questions

1. If you use `this` in a method call such as `addActionListener(this)`, what object is being registered as a listener?

    (a) An adapter class

    (b) The current class

    (c) No class

11

2. What is the benefit of subclassing an adapter class such as WindowAdapter (which implements the WindowListener interface)?

   (a) You inherit all the behavior of that class.

   (b) The subclass automatically becomes a listener.

   (c) You don't need to implement any WindowListener methods you won't be using.

3. What kind of event is generated when you press Tab to leave a text field?

   (a) FocusEvent

   (b) WindowEvent

   (c) ActionEvent

Answers

1. b. The current class must implement the correct listener interface and the required methods.

2. c. Because most listener interfaces contain more methods than you will need, using an adapter class as a superclass saves the hassle of implementing empty methods just to implement the interface.

3. a. A user interface component loses focus when the user stops editing that component and moves to a different part of the interface.

Exercises

To extend your knowledge of the subjects covered today, try the following exercises:

- Create an application that uses FocusListener to make sure that a text field's value is multiplied by -1 and redisplayed any time a user changes it to a negative value.

- Create a simple calculator that adds the contents of two text fields whenever a button is clicked and displays the result as a label.

Where applicable, exercise solutions are offered on the book's Web site at http://www.java21pro.com.

DAY 12

Color, Fonts, and Graphics

Today you work with Java classes that support graphical features in your programs—color, fonts, and images.

To use graphical features in your programs, you utilize classes of the `java.awt` and `javax.swing` packages, which deliver most of Java's visual pizzazz. With these classes you'll draw text and shapes like circles and polygons in an applet. You learn how to use different fonts and colors for the shapes you draw.

Because of the strong support for graphics in the Java class library, you can achieve complex visual effects in relatively few statements. Java2D, a set of classes introduced with Java 2, offers some eye-catching features:

- Anti-aliased objects
- Gradient fill patterns
- Drawing lines of different widths

Graphics Classes

Most of the basic drawing operations are methods defined in the Graphics class, which is part of the java.awt package. Objects of this class represent an environment in which something can be drawn, whether it's an applet window, a section in a graphical user interface, or a printer.

One way to think of an applet is as a canvas for graphical operations. During Day 8, "Putting Interactive Programs on the Web," you used the drawString() method to draw text onto an applet. The text's font and color were chosen prior to drawing the characters, the same way an artist would choose a color and a brush before painting.

Text isn't the only thing you can draw using the Graphics class. You can draw lines, ovals, circles, arcs, rectangles, and other polygons.

In an applet, you don't have to create a Graphics object in order to draw something—as you might recall, one of the paint() method's parameters is a Graphics object. This object represents the applet window and its methods are used to draw onto the applet.

The Graphics class is part of the java.awt package, so all applets that draw something must use the import statement to make Graphics available in the program.

Creating a Drawing Surface

Before you can start using the Graphics class, you need something to draw on.

One component that's suitable for this purpose is JPanel in the javax.swing package. This class represents panels in a graphical user interface that can be empty or contain other components.

The following example creates a frame and a panel, and adds the panel to the frame window:

```
JFrame main = new JFrame("Main Menu");
JPanel pane = new JPanel();
main.getContentPane().add(pane);
```

The frame's getContentPane() method returns an object representing the portion of the frame that can contain other components. That object's add() method is called to add the panel to the frame.

Like many other user interface components in Java, JPanel objects have a paintComponent(Graphics) method that is called automatically whenever the component should be redisplayed. The purpose is identical to the paint(Graphics) method in all applets.

By creating a subclass of JPanel, you can override this paintComponent() method and put all of your graphical operations in this method.

Casting a Graphics2D Object

Drawing operations are called on either a Graphics object or a Graphics2D object.

Choosing which class to use depends on whether you'll be using the Java2D graphics features introduced in Java 2. All Java2D graphics operations must be called on a Graphics2D object. Graphics2D is part of the java.awt package.

A Graphics or Graphics2D object represents an area being drawn to—such as an applet window or a frame window. For Java2D, this object must be used to create a new Graphics2D object, as in the following paintComponent() method:

```
public void paintComponent(Graphics comp) {
    Graphics2D comp2D = (Graphics2D)comp;
}
```

The comp2D object in this example was produced via casting.

Creating an Application

Listing 12.1 contains an application that brings all this together and draws the word "Florida" on a panel using the drawString() method to display text.

LISTING 12.1   The Starting Text of Map.java

```
 1: import java.awt.*;
 2: import java.awt.event.*;
 3: import javax.swing.*;
 4:
 5: public class Map extends JFrame {
 6:     public Map() {
 7:         super("Map");
 8:         setSize(350, 350);
 9:         ExitWindow exit = new ExitWindow();
10:         MapPane map = new MapPane();
11:         getContentPane().add(map);
12:         addWindowListener(exit);
13:     }
14:
15:     public static void main(String[] arguments) {
16:         Map frame = new Map();
17:         frame.show();
18:     }
19:
20: }
```

12

LISTING 12.1   continued

```
21:
22: class MapPane extends JPanel {
23:     public void paintComponent(Graphics comp) {
24:         Graphics2D comp2D = (Graphics2D)comp;
25:         comp2D.drawString("Florida", 185, 75);
26:     }
27: }
28:
29: class ExitWindow extends WindowAdapter {
30:     public void windowClosing(WindowEvent e) {
31:         System.exit(0);
32:     }
33: }
```

This application uses the comp2D object's drawString() method to draw the string "Florida" at the coordinates 185,75 (see Figure 12.1).

FIGURE 12.1

Drawing text in an application.

All the basic drawing commands you learn about today will be Graphics methods that are called within a component's paintComponent() method. This is an ideal place for all drawing operations because paintComponent() is automatically called anytime the component needs to be redisplayed. If another program's window overlaps the component, and it needs to be redrawn, putting all the drawing operations in paintComponent() makes sure that no part of the drawing is left out.

Tip

> All the drawing operations you use today can be employed in an applet's paint() method. Applets are windows that can contain objects and have many things in common with panels.

Continue to add to the Map application with each of the drawing methods covered in this section.

The Graphics Coordinate System

As in drawString(), all the drawing methods have arguments that indicate x,y coordinates. Some take more than one set of coordinates, such as a line, which has an x,y coordinate to identify its starting point and another x,y coordinate for its endpoint.

Java's coordinate system uses pixels as its unit of measure. The origin coordinate 0,0 is in the upper-left corner of the Applet window. The value of x coordinates increases to the right of 0,0, and y coordinates increase in a downward direction. This differs from other drawing systems in which the 0,0 origin is at the lower left and y values increase in an upward direction.

All pixel values are integers—you can't use decimal numbers to display something between integer values.

Figure 12.2 depicts Java's graphical coordinate system visually with the origin at 0,0. Two of the points of a rectangle are at 20,20 and 60,60.

FIGURE 12.2

The Java graphics coordinate system.

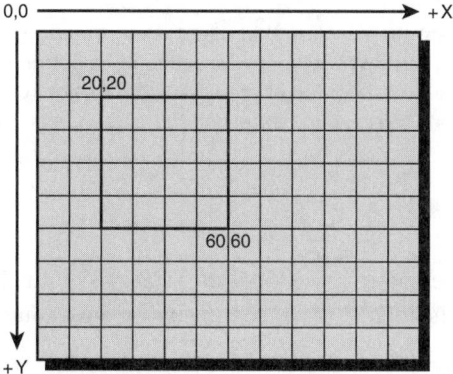

12

Drawing and Filling

Two kinds of drawing methods are available for many of the shapes you can draw onto a component: draw methods, which draw an outline of the object, and fill methods, which fill in the object with the current color. In each type of method, the outline of the object also is drawn with the current color.

Note

> You can also draw bitmap graphics files, such as GIF and JPG files, by using the `Image` class. You learn about this tomorrow.

Lines

The `drawLine()` method is used to draw a line between two points. The method takes four arguments: the x and y coordinates of the starting point and the x and y coordinates of the ending point, as follows:

```
drawLine(x1, y1, x2, y2);
```

This method draws a line from the point (x1, y1) to the point (x2, y2). The width of the line is fixed at 1 pixel.

Add the following statement to the `Map` application's `paintComponent()` method:

```
comp2D..drawLine(185, 80, 222, 80);
```

This draws a line from 185,80 to 222,80—an underline under the text "Florida".

 Note

> To prevent the whiplash that might result from repeatedly bouncing between this text and your Java source code editor, the final version of `Map.java` is listed in full at the end of this section. Until then, you can follow along with the text and enter the full Java code at one time.

Rectangles

There are `Graphics` methods for two kinds of rectangles: normal rectangles and those with rounded corners (similar to the edges of keys on most computer keyboards).

You can draw both types of rectangles in outline form or filled with the current color.

To draw a normal rectangle, use the `drawRect()` method for outlines and the `fillRect()` method for filled shapes.

Both of these methods take four arguments:

- The x and y coordinates of the rectangle's top-left corner
- The width of the rectangle
- The height of the rectangle

Add the following statement to the Map application:

```
comp2D.drawRect(2, 2, 335, 320);
```

This adds a rectangle outline just inside the outer edges of the application frame. If the `fillRect()` method had been used instead, a solid rectangle would have filled most of the application's frame and overwritten the underlined text `Florida`.

Rectangles with rounded corners require the `drawRoundRect()` and `fillRoundRect()` methods. They take the same first four arguments that regular rectangles take, with two arguments added at the end.

These last two arguments define the width and height of the area where corners are rounded. The bigger the area, the more round the corners. You can even make a rectangle look like a circle or an oval by making these arguments large enough.

Figure 12.3 shows several examples of rectangles with rounded corners. One rectangle has a width of 30 and a height of 10 for each rounded corner. Another has a width of 20 and a height of 20, and it looks more like a circle than a rectangle.

FIGURE 12.3

Rectangles with rounded corners.

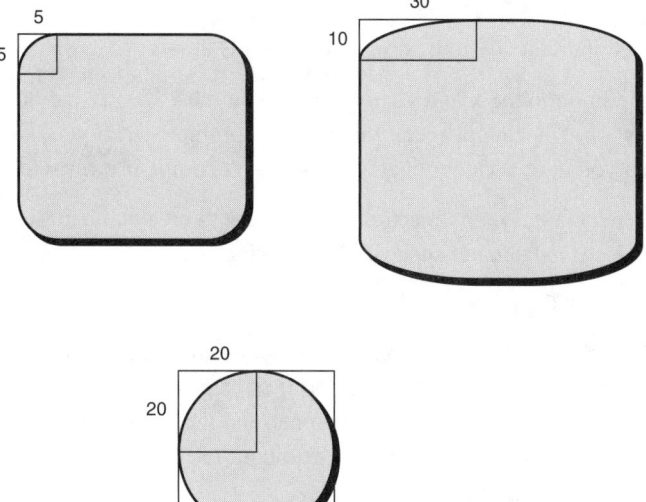

12

Add the following statement to the Map application's `paintComponent()` method:

```
comp2D.drawRoundRect(182, 61, 43, 24, 10, 8);
```

This draws a rounded rectangle at the coordinates 182,61 with a width of 43 pixels and a height of 24. The rectangular area of each rounded corner is 10 pixels wide and 8 tall. The result is shown in Figure 12.4, a close-up of a portion of the application.

FIGURE 12.4

*Adding a rounded
rectangle to the
application.*

Polygons

Polygons can be drawn with the `drawPolygon()` and `fillPolygon()` methods.

To draw a polygon, you need x,y coordinates for each point on the polygon. Polygons can be thought of as a series of lines that are connected to each other—one line is drawn from starting point to end point, that end point is used to start a new line, and so on.

You can specify these coordinates two ways:

- As a pair of integer arrays, one holding all the x coordinates and one holding all the y coordinates
- As a `Polygon` object that is created using an integer array of x coordinates and an integer array of y coordinates

The second method listed previously is more flexible because it enables points to be added individually to a polygon before it is drawn.

In addition to the x and y coordinates, you must specify the number of points in the polygon. You cannot specify more x,y coordinates than you have points, or more points than you have x,y coordinates set up for. A compiler error will result in either case.

To create a `Polygon` object, the first step is to create an empty polygon with a `new Polygon()` statement such as the following:

```
Polygon poly = new Polygon();
```

As an alternative, you can create a polygon from a set of points using integer arrays. This requires a call to the `Polygon(int[], int[], int)` constructor, which specifies the array of x points, array of y points, and the number of total points. The following example shows the use of this constructor:

```
int x[] = { 10, 20, 30, 40, 50 };
int y[] = { 15, 25, 35, 45, 55 };
int points = x.length;
Polygon poly = new Polygon(x, y, points);
```

After a `Polygon` object has been created, you can add points to it using the object's `addPoint()` method. This takes x,y coordinates as arguments and adds the point to the polygon. The following is an example:

```
poly.addPoint(60, 65);
```

When you have a `Polygon` object that has all the points it needs, you can draw it with the `drawPolygon()` or `fillPolygon()` methods. These take only one argument—the `Polygon` object, as shown here:

```
comp2D.drawPolygon(poly);
```

If you use `drawPolygon()` under Java 1.0, you can close off the polygon by making its last x,y coordinate the same as its first. Otherwise, the polygon will be open on one side.

The `fillPolygon()` method automatically closes off the polygon without requiring matching points.

> **Caution**
>
> The behavior of `drawPolygon()` changed after version 1.0 of Java. In version 2, `drawPolygon()` automatically closes off a polygon the same way `fillPolygon()` does. If you want to create an open-edged polygon with those versions of the language, you can use the `drawPolyline()` method. It works just like `drawPolygon()` worked under Java 1.0.

Add the following statements to the `paintComponent()` method of the Map application to see polygons in action:

```
int x[] = { 10, 234, 253, 261, 333, 326, 295, 259, 205, 211,
    195, 191, 120, 94, 81, 12, 10 };
int y[] = { 12, 15, 25, 71, 209, 278, 310, 274, 188, 171, 174,
    118, 56, 68, 49, 37, 12 };
int pts = x.length;
Polygon poly = new Polygon(x, y, pts);
comp2D.drawPolygon(poly);
```

Figure 12.5 shows what the Map application looks like with the polygon added to everything else already being drawn.

12

FIGURE 12.5

Adding a polygon to the application.

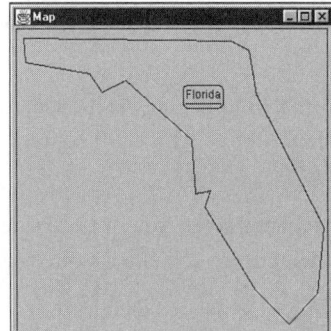

Ovals

The drawOval() and fillOval() methods are used to draw circles and ovals.

These methods take four arguments:

- The oval's x and y coordinates
- The oval's width and height, which are the same size on circles

Because an oval doesn't have any corners, you might be wondering what the x,y coordinate refers to. Ovals are handled in the same fashion as the corners of rounded rectangles. The x,y coordinate is at the upper-left corner of the area in which the oval is drawn, and will be to the left and above the actual oval itself.

Return to the Map application and add the following statements:

```
comp2D.fillOval(235,140,15,15);
comp2D.fillOval(225,130,15,15);
comp2D.fillOval(245,130,15,15);
```

These are fill methods rather than draw methods, so they create three black circles connected together at a spot in the center of the map of Florida.

Arcs

Of all the drawing operations, arcs are the most complex to construct. An arc is part of an oval, and is implemented in Java as an oval that is partially drawn.

Arcs are drawn with the drawArc() and fillArc() methods, which take six arguments:

- The oval's x,y coordinates
- The oval's width and height
- The angle at which to start the arc
- The number of degrees traveled by the arc

The first four arguments are the same as those for an oval and function in the same manner.

The arc's starting angle ranges from 0 to 359 degrees in a counterclockwise direction. On a circular oval, 0 degrees is the same as the 3 o'clock, 90 degrees is 12 o'clock, 180 degrees is 9 o'clock, and 270 degrees is 6 o'clock.

The number of degrees traveled by an arc ranges from 0 to 359 degrees in a counterclockwise direction, and 0 to –359 degrees in a clockwise direction.

Figure 12.6 shows how the last two arguments are calculated.

FIGURE 12.6

Measuring an arc.

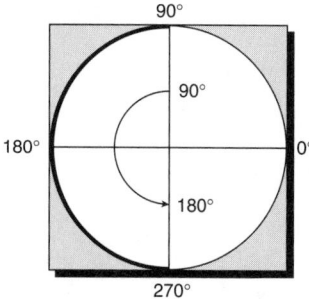

Filled arcs are drawn as if they were sections of a pie; instead of joining the two end-points, both endpoints are joined to the center of the arc's oval.

The following is an example of a drawArc() method call:

```
comp2D.drawArc(20, 25, 315, 150, 5, -190);
```

This statement draws an arc of an oval with the coordinates 20,25, a width of 315 pixels, and a height of 150 pixels. The arc begins at the 5-degree mark and travels 190 degrees in a clockwise direction. The arc is shown in an applet in Figure 12.7.

FIGURE 12.7

An arc.

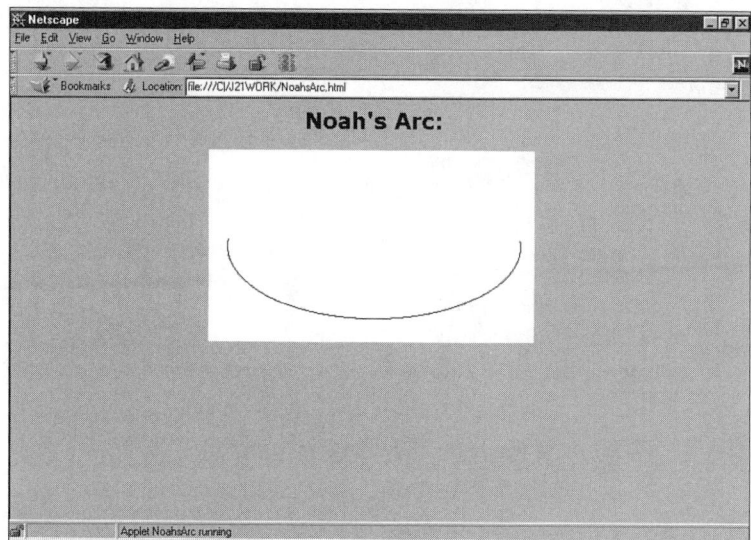

12

To iron out the last wrinkle in the Map application, a bunch of little arcs with four arguments that do not change will be drawn:

- Each arc's oval will have a width and height of 10 pixels, making the ovals circular.
- Each arc will begin at 0 degrees and head clockwise for 180 degrees, making them half circles.

The arc's x,y coordinates will change, and two `for` loops will cycle through a range of x and y values.

Add the following statements to the Map application's `paintComponent()` method:

```
for (int ax = 50; ax < 150; ax += 10)
    for (int ay = 120; ay < 320 ; ay += 10)
        comp2D.drawArc(ax, ay, 10, 10, 0, -180);
```

Putting one `for` loop inside another might appear confusing. Here are the first six x,y coordinates that are created by the loop:

50,120

50,130

50,140

50,150

50,160

50,170

As you can see, the x coordinate—specified by `ax`—does not change. It won't change until the entire ay loop has run its course. When that happens, ax increases by 10 and the ay loop runs again in full.

Compile the Map application to see what effect these loops produce by drawing a bunch of small half circles. Listing 12.2 shows the full, final source code for `Map.java`, including all the drawing statements that have been covered during this section.

LISTING 12.2   The Full, Final Text of `Map.java`

```
1: import java.awt.*;
2: import java.awt.event.*;
3: import javax.swing.*;
4:
5: public class Map extends JFrame {
```

```
 6:     public Map() {
 7:         super("Map");
 8:         setSize(350, 350);
 9:         ExitWindow exit = new ExitWindow();
10:         MapPane map = new MapPane();
11:         getContentPane().add(map);
12:         addWindowListener(exit);
13:     }
14:
15:     public static void main(String[] arguments) {
16:         Map frame = new Map();
17:         frame.show();
18:     }
19:
20: }
21:
22: class MapPane extends JPanel {
23:     public void paintComponent(Graphics comp) {
24:         Graphics2D comp2D = (Graphics2D)comp;
25:         comp2D.drawString("Florida", 185, 75);
26:         comp2D.drawLine(185, 80, 222, 80);
27:         comp2D.drawRect(2, 2, 335, 320);
28:         comp2D.drawRoundRect(182, 61, 43, 24, 10, 8);
29:         int x[] = { 10, 234, 253, 261, 333, 326, 295, 259, 205, 211,
30:             195, 191, 120, 94, 81, 12, 10 };
31:         int y[] = { 12, 15, 25, 71, 209, 278, 310, 274, 188, 171, 174,
32:             118, 56, 68, 49, 37, 12 };
33:         int pts = x.length;
34:         Polygon poly = new Polygon(x, y, pts);
35:         comp2D.drawPolygon(poly);
36:         comp2D.fillOval(235,140,15,15);
37:         comp2D.fillOval(225,130,15,15);
38:         comp2D.fillOval(245,130,15,15);
39:         for (int ax = 50; ax < 150; ax += 10)
40:             for (int ay = 120; ay < 320 ; ay += 10)
41:                 comp2D.drawArc(ax, ay, 10, 10, 0, -180);
42:     }
43: }
44:
45: class ExitWindow extends WindowAdapter {
46:     public void windowClosing(WindowEvent e) {
47:         System.exit(0);
48:     }
49: }
```

12

Figure 12.8 shows the Map application that has been painted with Java's basic drawing methods.

FIGURE 12.8

The Map *application.*

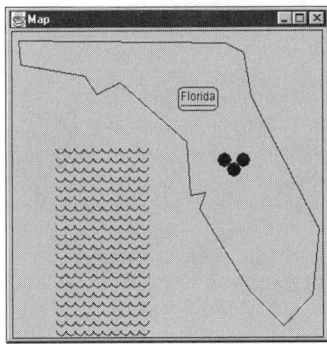

Although no cartographer would fear for his job security at this display of mapmaking, the application combines a sampling of most drawing features that are available through the Graphics class. A program like this could be expanded using Font and Color objects, and the drawing operations could be rearranged to improve the final product.

Copying and Clearing

The Graphics class also includes some cut-and-paste functionality:

- The copyArea() method, which copies a rectangular region of a window onto another region of the window
- The clearRect() method, which clears a rectangular region of a window

The copyArea() method takes six arguments:

- The x,y coordinates of the rectangular region to copy
- The width and the height of that region
- The horizontal and vertical distance, in pixels, to move away from the region before displaying a copy of it

The following statement copies a 100×100 pixel region to an area 50 pixels to the right and 25 pixels down, using a Graphics object called screen:

```
screen.copyArea(0, 0, 100, 100, 50, 25);
```

The clearRect() method takes the same four arguments as the drawRect() and fillRect() methods, and it fills the rectangular region with the current background color of a window. You learn how to set the background color later today.

If you want to clear an entire window, you can determine the window's size via the getSize() method. This returns a Dimension object, which has width and height variables; they represent the window's dimensions.

You can get to the actual values for width and height by using the `width` and `height` instance variables, as in the following statement:

```
screen.clearRect(0, 0, getSize().width, getSize().height);
```

Note

The `getsize()` method had a different name in Java 1.0: `size()`. Both methods return the same thing.

Text and Fonts

`java.awt.Font` class objects are used in order to use the `drawString()` method with different fonts. `Font` objects represent the name, style, and point size of a font. Another class, `FontMetrics`, provides methods to determine the size of the characters being displayed with a specified font, which can be used for things like formatting and centering text.

Creating Font Objects

A `Font` object is created by sending three arguments to its constructor:

- The font's name
- The font's style
- The font's point size

The name of the font can be a specific font name such as Arial or Garamond Old Style, and it will be used if the font is present on the system on which the Java program is running.

There also are names that can be used to select Java's built-in fonts: TimesRoman, Helvetica, Courier, Dialog, and DialogInput.

Caution

For Java 2, the font names TimesRoman, Helvetica, and Courier should be replaced with serif, sanserif, and monospaced, respectively. These generic names specify the style of the font without naming a specific font family used to represent it. This is a better choice because some font families might not be present on all implementations of Java, so the best choice for the selected font style (such as serif) can be used.

12

Three Font styles can be selected by using the constants Font.PLAIN, Font.BOLD, and Font.ITALIC. These constants are integers, and you can add them to combine effects.

The last argument of the Font() constructor is the point size of the font.

The following statement creates a 24-point Dialog font that is bold and italicized.

```
Font f = new Font("Dialog", Font.BOLD + Font.ITALIC, 24);
```

Drawing Characters and Strings

To set the current font, the Graphics class' setFont() method is used with a Font object. The following statement uses a Font object named ft:

```
screen.setFont(ft);
```

Text can be displayed in a window using the drawString() methods. This method uses the currently selected font; it uses the default if no font has been selected. A new current font can be set at any time using setFont().

The following paintComponent() method creates a new Font object, sets the current font to that object, and draws the string "I'm very font of you." at the coordinates 10,100.

```
public void paintComponent(Graphics comp) {
    Graphics2D comp2D = (Graphics2D)comp;
    Font f = new Font("TimesRoman", Font.PLAIN, 72);
    comp2D.setFont(f);
    comp2D.drawString("I'm very font of you.", 10, 100);
}
```

The last two arguments to the drawString() method are x and y coordinates. The x value is the start of the leftmost edge of the text, and y is the baseline for the entire string.

Finding Information About a Font

The FontMetrics class can be used for detailed information about the current font, such as the width or height of characters it can display.

To use this class' methods, a FontMetrics object must be created using the getFontMetrics() method. The method takes a single argument: a Font object.

Table 12.1 shows some of the information you can find using font metrics. All these methods should be called on a FontMetrics object.

TABLE 12.1   Font Metrics Methods

Method Name	Action
stringWidth(String)	Given a string, returns the full width of that string in pixels
charWidth(char)	Given a character, returns the width of that character
getHeight()	Returns the total height of the font

Listing 12.3 shows how the Font and FontMetrics classes can be used. The SoLong applet displays a string at the center of the applet window, using FontMetrics to measure the string's width using the current font.

LISTING 12.3   The Full Text of SoLong.java

```
 1: import java.awt.*;
 2:
 3: public class SoLong extends javax.swing.JApplet {
 4:
 5:     public void paint(Graphics screen) {
 6:         Graphics screen2D = (Graphics2D)screen;
 7:         Font f = new Font("monospaced", Font.BOLD, 18);
 8:         FontMetrics fm = getFontMetrics(f);
 9:         screen2D.setFont(f);
10:         String s = "So long, and thanks for all the fish.";
11:         int x = (getSize().width - fm.stringWidth(s)) / 2;
12:         int y = getSize().height / 2;
13:         screen2D.drawString(s, x, y);
14:     }
15: }
```

12

Listing 12.4 contains an HTML document that loads two copies of the SoLong applet with different sized windows.

LISTING 12.4   The Full Text of SoLong.html

```
1: <div align="Center">
2: <p>
3: <applet code="SoLong.class" height="150" width="425">
4: </applet>
5: <p>
6: <applet code="SoLong.class" height="150" width="550">
7: </applet>
8: </div>
```

Figure 12.9 shows two copies of the SoLong applet on a Web page, each with windows of different sizes.

FIGURE **12.9**

Two copies of the
SoLong *applet.*

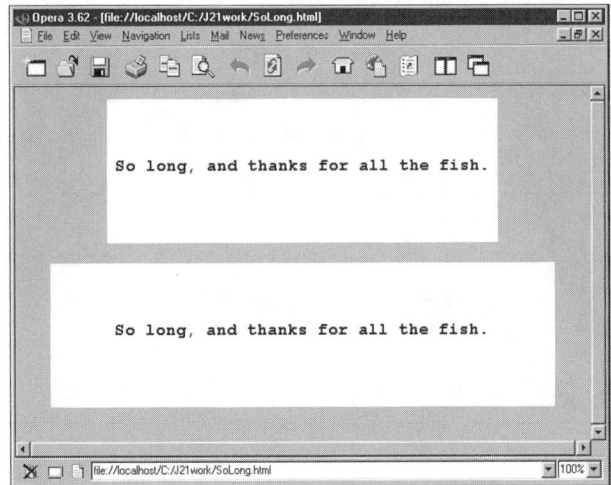

So long, and thanks for all the fish.

So long, and thanks for all the fish.

The getSize() method in lines 11 and 12 should be replaced with size() if you're writing a Java 1.0 applet. Determining the applet window's size within the applet is preferable to defining an exact size because it's more adaptable. You can change the applet's HTML code on the Web page without changing the program, and it will still work successfully.

Color

The Color and ColorSpace classes of the java.awt package can be used to make your applets and applications more colorful. With these classes you can set the current color for use in drawing operations, as well as the background color of an applet and other windows. You also can translate a color from one color-description system into another.

By default, Java uses colors according to a color-description system called sRGB. In this system, a color is described by the amount of red, green, and blue it contains—that's what the R, G, and B stand for. Each of the three components can be represented as an integer between 0 and 255. Black is 0,0,0—the complete absence of any red, green, or blue. White is 255,255,255—the maximum amount of all three. You also can represent sRGB values using three floating-point numbers ranging from 0 to 1.0. Java can represent millions of colors between the two extremes using sRGB.

A color-description system is called a *color space*, and sRGB is only one such space. There is also CMYK, a system used by printers that describes colors by the amount of cyan, magenta, yellow, and black they contain. Java 1.2 supports the use of any color space desired, as long as a ColorSpace object is used that defines the description system. You also can convert from any color space to sRGB, and vice versa.

Java's internal representation of colors using sRGB is just one color space that's being used in a program. An output device such as a monitor or printer also has its own color space.

When you display or print something of a designated color, the output device might not support the designated color. In this circumstance, a different color will be substituted or a *dithering* pattern will be used to approximate the unavailable color. This happens frequently on the World Wide Web, when an unavailable color is replaced by a dithering pattern of two or more colors that approximate the missing color.

The practical reality of color management is that the color you designated with sRGB will not be available on all output devices. If you need more precise control of the color, you can use ColorSpace and other classes in the java.awt.color package introduced in Java 2.

For most programs, the built-in use of sRGB to define colors will be sufficient.

Using Color Objects

To set the current drawing color, either a Color object must be created that represents it, or you must use one of the standard colors available from the Color class.

There are two ways to call the Color constructor method to create a color:

- Using three integers that represent the sRGB value of the desired color
- Using three floating-point numbers that represent the desired sRGB value

You can specify a color's sRGB value using either three int or float values. The following statements show examples of each:

```
Color c1 = new Color(0.807F,1F,0F);

Color c2 = new Color(255,204,102);
```

The c1 object describes a neon green color and c2 is butterscotch.

Note

It's easy to confuse floating-point literals like 0F and 1F with hexadecimal numbers, which were discussed on Day 3, "The ABCs of Java." Colors are often expressed in hexadecimal, such as when a background color is set up for a Web page using the HTML <BODY> tag. None of the Java classes and methods you work with take hexadecimal arguments, so when you see a literal such as 1F or 0F, you're dealing with floating-point numbers.

12

Testing and Setting the Current Colors

The current color for drawing is designated by using the `Graphics` class's `setColor()` method. This method must be called on the `Graphics` or `Graphics2D` object that represents the area you're drawing to.

One way to set the color is to use one of the standard colors available as class variables in the `Color` class.

These colors use the following `Color` variables (with sRGB values indicated within parentheses):

black (0,0,0)	magenta (255,0,255)
blue (0,0,255)	orange (255,200,0)
cyan (0,255,255)	pink (255,175,175)
darkGray (64,64,64)	red (255,0,0)
gray (128,128,128)	white (255,255,255)
green (0,255,0)	yellow (255,255,0)
lightGray (192,192,192)	

The following statement sets the current color for the `comp2D` object using one of the standard class variables:

```
comp2D.setColor(Color.pink);
```

If you have created a `Color` object, it can be set in a similar fashion:

```
Color brush = new Color(255,204,102);
comp2D.setColor(brush);
```

After you set the current color, all drawing operations will occur in that color.

You can set the background color for a component such as an applet window or frame by calling the component's `setBackground()` and `setForeground()` methods.

The `setBackground()` method sets the component's background color. It takes a single argument, a `Color` object:

```
setBackground(Color.white);
```

There is also a `setForeground()` method that is called on user-interface components instead of `Graphics` objects. It works the same as `setColor()`, but changes the color of an interface component such as a button or a window.

You can use `setForeground()` in the `init()` method to set the color for drawing operations. This color is used until another color is chosen with either `setForeground()` or `setColor()`.

If you want to find out what the current color is, you can use the `getColor()` method on a `Graphics` object, or the `getForeground()` or `getBackground()` methods of the component.

The following statement sets the current color of `comp2D`—a `Graphics2D` object—to the same color as an component's background:

```
comp2D.setColor(getBackground());
```

Advanced Graphics Operations Using Java2D

One of the enhancements offered with Java 2 is Java2D, a set of classes for offering high-quality 2D graphics, images, and text in your programs. The Java2D classes extend the capabilities of existing `java.awt` classes that handle graphics, such as those you have learned about today. They don't replace the existing classes though—you can continue to use the other classes and programs that implement them.

Java2D features include the following:

- Special fill patterns such as gradients and patterns
- Strokes that define the width and style of a drawing stroke
- Anti-aliasing to smooth edges of drawn objects

User and Device Coordinate Spaces

One of the concepts introduced with Java2D is the difference between an output device's coordinate space and the coordinate space you refer to when drawing an object.

NEW TERM   *Coordinate space* is any 2D area that can be described using x,y coordinates.

For all drawing operations up to this point and all operations prior to Java 2, the only coordinate space used was the device coordinate space. You specified the x,y coordinates of an output surface such as an applet window, and those coordinates were used to draw lines, text, and other elements.

Java2D requires a second coordinate space that you refer to when creating an object and actually drawing it. This is called the *user coordinate space*.

Before any 2D drawing has occurred in a program, the device space and user space have the 0,0 coordinate in the same place—the upper-left corner of the drawing area.

12

The user space's 0,0 coordinate can move as a result of the 2D drawing operations being conducted. The x and y axes even can shift because of a 2D rotation. You learn more about the two different coordinate systems as you work with Java2D.

Specifying the Rendering Attributes

The next step in 2D drawing is to specify how a drawn object will be rendered. Drawings that are not 2D can only select one attribute: color. 2D offers a wide range of attributes for designating color, including line width, fill patterns, transparency, and many other features.

2D Colors

Colors are specified using the setColor() method, which works the same as the Graphics method of the same name. The following is an example:

```
comp2D.setColor(Color.black);
```

Caution

Although some of the 2D methods work the same as their non-2D counter-parts, they must be called on a Graphics2D object in order to use Java2D's capabilities.

Fill Patterns

Fill patterns control how a drawn object will be filled in. With Java2D, you can use a solid color, gradient fill, texture, or a pattern of your own devising.

A fill pattern is defined by using the setPaint() method of Graphics2D with a Paint object as its only argument. Any class that can be a fill pattern, including GradientPaint, TexturePaint, and Color, can implement the Paint interface. The third might surprise you, but using a Color object with setPaint() is the same thing as filling using a solid color as the pattern.

 A *gradient fill* is a gradual shift from one color at one coordinate point to another color at a different coordinate point. The shift can occur once between the points, which is called an *acyclic gradient*, or it can happen repeatedly, which is a *cyclic gradient*.

Figure 12.10 shows examples of acyclic and cyclic gradients between white and a darker color. The arrows indicate the points that the colors shift between.

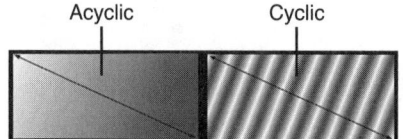

FIGURE 12.10

Acyclic and cyclic gradient shifts.

The coordinate points in a gradient do not refer directly to points on the Graphics2D object being drawn onto. Instead, they refer to user space and can even be outside the object being filled with a gradient.

Figure 12.11 illustrates this. Both rectangles on the applet are filled using the same GradientPaint object as a guide. One way to think of a gradient pattern is as a piece of clothing fabric that has been spread out over a flat surface. The shapes being filled with a gradient are the dress patterns cut from the fabric, and more than one pattern can be cut from the same piece of cloth.

FIGURE 12.11

Two rectangles using the same GradientPaint.

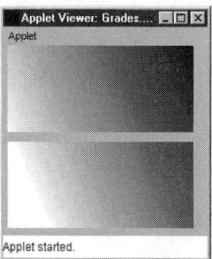

A call to the GradientPaint constructor method takes the following format:

```
GradientPaint(x1, y1, color1, x2, y2, color2);
```

The point x1,y1 is where the color represented by color1 begins, and x2,y2 is where the shift ends at color2.

If you want to use a cyclic gradient shift, an extra argument is added at the end:

```
GradientPaint(x1, y1, color1, x2, y2, color2, true);
```

The last argument is a Boolean value that is true for a cyclic shift. A false argument can be used for acyclic shifts, or you can leave this argument off entirely—acyclic shifts are the default behavior.

After you have created a GradientPaint object, you set it as the current paint attribute by using the setPaint() method. The following statements create and select a gradient:

```
GradientPaint pat = new GradientPaint(0f,0f,Color.white,
    100f,45f,Color.blue);
comp2D.setPaint(pat);
```

12

All subsequent drawing operations to the comp2D object will use this fill pattern until another one is chosen.

Setting a Drawing Stroke

As you have learned, the lines drawn in all non-2D graphics operations are 1 pixel wide. Java2D adds the capability to vary the width of the drawing line by using the setStroke() method with a BasicStroke.

A simple BasicStroke constructor takes three arguments:

- A float value representing the line width, with 1.0 as the norm
- An int value determining the style of cap decoration drawn at the end of a line
- An int value determining the style of juncture between two line segments

NEW TERM   The endcap- and juncture-style arguments use BasicStroke class variables. *Endcap* styles apply to the end of lines that do not connect to other lines. *Juncture* styles apply to the ends of lines that join other lines.

Possible endcap styles are CAP_BUTT for no endpoints, CAP_ROUND for circles around each endpoint, and CAP_SQUARE for squares. Figure 12.12 shows each endcap style. As you can see, the only visible difference between the CAP_BUTT and CAP_SQUARE styles is that CAP_SQUARE is longer because of the added square endcap.

FIGURE 12.12

Endpoint cap styles.

CAP_BUTT   CAP_ROUND   CAP_SQUARE

Possible juncture styles include JOIN_MITER, which joins segments by extending their outer edges, JOIN_ROUND, which rounds off a corner between two segments, and JOIN_BEVEL, which joins segments with a straight line. Figure 12.13 shows examples of each juncture style.

FIGURE 12.13

Endpoint juncture styles.

JOIN_MITER   JOIN_ROUND   JOIN_BEVEL

The following statements create a BasicStroke object and make it the current stroke:

```
BasicStroke pen = BasicStroke(2.0f,
    BasicStroke.CAP_BUTT,
    BasicStroke.JOIN_ROUND);
comp2D.setStroke(pen);
```

The stroke has a width of 2 pixels, plain endpoints, and rounded segment corners.

Creating Objects to Draw

After you have created a `Graphics2D` object and specified the rendering attributes, the final two steps are to create the object and draw it.

Drawn objects in Java2D are created by defining them as geometric shapes using the `java.awt.geom` package classes. You can draw each of the things created earlier today, including lines, rectangles, ellipses, arcs, and polygons.

The `Graphics2D` class does not have different methods for each of the shapes you can draw. Instead, you define the shape and use it as an argument to `draw()` or `fill()` methods.

Lines

Lines are created using the `Line2D.Float` class. This class takes four arguments: the x,y coordinates of one endpoint followed by the x,y coordinates of the other. Here's an example:

```
Line2D.Float ln = new Line2D.Float(60F,5F,13F,28F);
```

This statement creates a line between 60,5 and 13,28. Note that an `F` is used with the literals sent as arguments—otherwise, the Java compiler would assume that they are integers.

Rectangles

Rectangles are created by using the `Rectangle2D.Float` or `Rectangle2D.Double` classes. The difference between the two is that one takes `float` arguments and the other takes `double` arguments.

`Rectangle2D.Float` takes four arguments: x coordinate, y coordinate, width, and height. The following is an example:

```
Rectangle2D.Float rc = new Rectangle2D.Float(10F,13F,40F,20F);
```

This creates a rectangle at 10,13 that is 40 pixels wide and 20 pixels tall.

Ellipses

NEW TERM   Oval objects are called *ellipses* in Java2D, and they can be created with the `Ellipse2D.Float` class. It takes four arguments: x coordinate, y coordinate, width, and height.

The following statement creates an ellipse at 113,25 with a width of 22 pixels and a height of 40 pixels:

```
Ellipse2D.Float ee = new Ellipse2D.Float(113,25,22,40);
```

Arcs

Arcs are created with the `Arc2D.Float` class. They are created in a similar fashion to the non-2D counterpart, but there's an extra feature: You can define how the arc is closed.

`Arc2D.Float` takes seven arguments. The first four apply to the ellipse that the arc is a part of: x coordinate, y coordinate, width, and height. The last three arguments are the starting degree of the arc, the number of degrees it travels, and an integer describing how it is closed.

The number of degrees traveled by the arc is specified in a counterclockwise direction by using positive numbers. This is the opposite of the way a non-2D arc is handled.

The last argument uses one of three class variables: `Arc2D.OPEN` for an unclosed arc, `Arc2D.CHORD` to connect the arc's endpoints with a straight line, and `Arc2D.PIE` to connect the arc to the center of the ellipses like a pie slice. Figure 12.14 shows each of these styles.

FIGURE 12.14

Arc closure styles.

Arc2D.OPEN   Arc2D.CHORD   Arc2D.PIE

Note

The `Arc2D.OPEN` close style does not apply to filled arcs. A filled arc that has `Arc2D.OPEN` as its style will be closed using the same style as `Arc2D.CHORD`.

The following statement creates an `Arc2D.Float` object:

```
Arc2D.Float = new Arc2D.Float(27,22,42,30,33,90,Arc2D.PIE);
```

This creates an arc for an oval at 27,22 that is 42 pixels wide and 30 pixels tall. The arc begins at 33 degrees, extends 90 degrees in a clockwise direction, and will be closed like a pie slice.

Polygons

Polygons are created in Java2D by defining each movement from one point on the polygon to another. A polygon can be formed out of straight lines, quadratic curves, and bezier curves.

The movements to create a polygon are defined as a `GeneralPath` object, which also is part of the `java.awt.geom` package.

A `GeneralPath` object can be created without any arguments, as shown here:

```
GeneralPath polly = new GeneralPath();
```

The `moveTo()` method of `GeneralPath` is used to create the first point on the polygon. The following statement would be used if you wanted to start `polly` at the coordinates 5,0:

```
polly.moveTo(5f, 0f);
```

After creating the first point, the `lineTo()` method is used to create lines that end at a new point. This method takes two arguments: the x and y coordinates of the new point.

The following statements add three lines to the `polly` object:

```
polly.lineTo(205f, 0f);
polly.lineTo(205f, 90f);
polly.lineTo(5f, 90f);
```

The `lineTo()` and `moveTo()` methods require `float` arguments to specify coordinate points.

If you want to close a polygon, the `closePath()` method is used without any arguments, as shown here:

```
polly.closePath();
```

This method closes a polygon by connecting the current point with the point specified by the most recent `moveTo()` method. You can close a polygon without this method by using a `lineTo()` method that connects to the original point.

Once you have created an open or closed polygon, you can draw it like any other shape using the `draw()` and `fill()` methods. The `polly` object is a rectangle with points at 5,0, 205,0, 205,90, and 5,90.

Drawing Objects

After you have defined the rendering attributes, such as color and line width, and have created the object to be drawn, you're ready to draw something in all its 2D glory.

All drawn objects use the same `Graphics2D` class's methods: `draw()` for outlines and `fill()` for filled objects. These take an object as their only argument.

Strings in Java2D are drawn using the `drawString()` method. This takes three arguments: the `String` object to draw and its x,y coordinates. As with all coordinates in Java2D, floating-point numbers must be specified instead of integers.

12

A 2D Drawing Example

Earlier today you created a map of Florida using the drawing methods that are available through the Graphics class. The next project you create is a revised version of that map, which uses 2D drawing techniques and implements the program as an applet.

Listing 12.5 contains the Map2D applet. It's a longer program than many in this book because 2D requires more statements to accomplish a drawing operation.

LISTING **12.5**   The Full Text of `Map2D.java`

```
 1: import java.awt.*;
 2: import java.awt.geom.*;
 3:
 4: public class Map2D extends javax.swing.JApplet {
 5:     public void paint(Graphics screen) {
 6:         Graphics2D screen2D = (Graphics2D)screen;
 7:         setBackground(Color.blue);
 8:         // Draw waves
 9:         screen2D.setColor(Color.white);
10:         BasicStroke pen = new BasicStroke(2F,
11:             BasicStroke.CAP_BUTT, BasicStroke.JOIN_ROUND);
12:         screen2D.setStroke(pen);
13:         for (int ax = 10; ax < 340; ax += 10)
14:             for (int ay = 30; ay < 340 ; ay += 10) {
15:                 Arc2D.Float wave = new Arc2D.Float(ax, ay,
16:                     10, 10, 0, -180, Arc2D.OPEN);
17:                 screen2D.draw(wave);
18:             }
19:         // Draw Florida
20:         GradientPaint gp = new GradientPaint(0F,0F,Color.green,
21:             50F,50F,Color.orange,true);
22:         screen2D.setPaint(gp);
23:         GeneralPath fl = new GeneralPath();
24:         fl.moveTo(10F,12F);
25:         fl.lineTo(234F,15F);
26:         fl.lineTo(253F,25F);
27:         fl.lineTo(261F,71F);
28:         fl.lineTo(344F,209F);
29:         fl.lineTo(336F,278F);
30:         fl.lineTo(295F,310F);
31:         fl.lineTo(259F,274F);
32:         fl.lineTo(205F,188F);
33:         fl.lineTo(211F,171F);
34:         fl.lineTo(195F,174F);
35:         fl.lineTo(191F,118F);
36:         fl.lineTo(120F,56F);
37:         fl.lineTo(94F,68F);
38:         fl.lineTo(81F,49F);
```

```
39:            fl.lineTo(12F,37F);
40:            fl.closePath();
41:            screen2D.fill(fl);
42:            // Draw ovals
43:            screen2D.setColor(Color.black);
44:            BasicStroke pen2 = new BasicStroke();
45:            screen2D.setStroke(pen2);
46:            Ellipse2D.Float e1 = new Ellipse2D.Float(235,140,15,15);
47:            Ellipse2D.Float e2 = new Ellipse2D.Float(225,130,15,15);
48:            Ellipse2D.Float e3 = new Ellipse2D.Float(245,130,15,15);
49:            screen2D.fill(e1);
50:            screen2D.fill(e2);
51:            screen2D.fill(e3);
52:        }
53: }
```

In order to view the applet, you need to create a short HTML page that contains it, using Listing 12.6. Because it uses Java 2 classes and methods, the applet can only be viewed with `appletviewer` or a browser that supports this version of the language (unless you rewrite the HTML so the applet is loaded by the Java Plug-in).

LISTING 12.6   The Full Text of `Map2D.html`

```
1: <applet code="Map2D.class" height="370" width="350">
2: </applet>
```

Some observations about the Map2D applet:

- Line 2 imports the classes in the `java.awt.geom` package. This statement is required because `import java.awt.*;` in Line 1 only handles classes, not packages, available under `java.awt`.

- Line 6 creates the `screen2D` object that is used for all 2D drawing operations. It's a cast of the `Graphics` object that represents the Applet window.

- Lines 10–12 create a `BasicStroke` object that represents a line width of 2 pixels and then makes this the current stroke with the `setStroke()` method of `Graphics2D`.

- Lines 13–17 use two nested `for` loops to create waves out of individual arcs. This same technique was used for the Map application, but there are more arcs covering the applet window in Map2D.

- Lines 20 and 21 create a gradient fill pattern from the color green at 0,0 to orange at 50,50. The last argument to the constructor, `true`, causes the fill pattern to repeat itself as many times as needed to fill an object.

12

- Line 22 sets the current gradient fill pattern using the setPaint() method and the gp object that was just created.
- Lines 23–41 create the polygon shaped like the state of Florida and draw it. This polygon will be filled with green-to-orange strips because of the currently selected fill pattern.
- Line 43 sets the current color to black. This replaces the gradient fill pattern for the next drawing operation because colors are also fill patterns.
- Line 44 creates a new BasicStroke() object with no arguments, which defaults to a 1-pixel wide line width.
- Line 45 sets the current line width to the new BasicStroke object pen2.
- Lines 46–51 create three ellipses at 235,140, 225,130, and 245,130. Each is 15 pixels wide and 15 pixels tall, making them circles.

Figure 12.15 shows the output of the Map2D applet in appletviewer.

FIGURE 12.15

The Map2D *applet.*

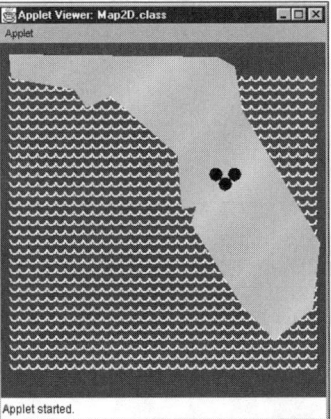

Summary

You now have some tools to improve the looks of a Java program. You can draw with lines, rectangles, ellipses, polygons, fonts, colors, and patterns onto a frame, an applet window, and other components using non-2D and 2D classes.

Non-2D drawing operations require the use of methods in the Graphics class, with arguments that describe the object being drawn.

Java2D uses the same two methods for each drawing operation—draw() and fill(). Different objects are created using classes of the java.awt.geom package, and these are used as arguments for the drawing methods of Graphics2D.

You get more chances to work with multimedia in Java in Day 13, "Threads and Animation." Those art lessons include animation, sound, and the display of image files.

Q&A

Q **I want to draw a line of text with a boldface word in the middle. I understand that I need two Font objects—one for the regular font and one for the bold— and that I'll need to reset the current font in between. The problem is that drawString() requires an x and a y position for the start of each string, and I can't find anything that refers to "current point." How can I figure out where to start the boldface word?**

A Java's text display capabilities are fairly primitive. Java has no concept of the current point, so you have to figure out yourself where the end of one string was in order to begin the next string. The stringWidth() methods can help you with this problem, both to find out the width of the string you just drew and to add the space after it.

Q **I am confused by what the lowercase "f" is referring to in source code today. It is added to coordinates, as in the polly method polly.moveTo(5f, 0f). Why is the "f" used for these coordinates and not others, and why is a capital "F" used elsewhere, such as the fl method fl.moveTo(10F, 12F)?**

A The F and f indicate that a number is a floating-point number rather than an integer, and they can be used interchangeably. If you don't use one of them, the Java compiler will assume that the number is an int value. Many methods and constructors in Java require floating-point arguments but can handle integers because an integer can be converted to floating-point without changing its value. For this reason, constructors like Arc2D.Float() can use arguments such as 10 and 180 instead of 10F and 180F.

Questions

1. What object is required before you can draw something in Java?
    (a) Graphics or Graphics2D
    (b) WindowListener
    (c) JFrame

12

2. Which of the following three fonts should not be used in a Java 2 program?

    (a) `serif`

    (b) `Courier`

    (c) monospaced

3. What does `getSize().width` refer to?

    (a) The width of the applet's window

    (b) The width of the frame's window

    (c) The width of any graphical user interface component in Java

Answers

1. a.

2. b. Choosing specific font names, as opposed to font descriptors like `serif` and `monospaced`, limits the flexibility of Java in selecting which font to use on a specific platform.

3. c. You can call `getSize().width` and `getSize().height` on any component in Java.

Exercises

To extend your knowledge of the subjects covered today, try the following exercises:

- Create an applet that draws a circle with its radius, x,y position, and color all determined by parameters.

- Create a version of `Map2D` that runs as an application instead of an applet.

Where applicable, exercise solutions are offered on the book's Web site at `http://www.java21pro.com`.

WEEK 2

DAY 13

Threads and Animation

When Java was introduced in 1995, hundreds of programmers put it to use creating animated applets. There was no other way at the time to offer animation on a Web page—animated GIF files were not supported in browsers and Shockwave, Flash, and ActiveX were not yet available—so Java was a great way to create dynamic content for visitors to your site.

Though a lot has changed since then, Java remains one of the easiest ways to create animated content (especially for complex effects) on and off the World Wide Web.

Animation in Java is accomplished by using the Abstract Windowing Toolkit, Swing, and the Thread class in the java.lang package.

Today, you learn how the various parts of Java work together to create moving figures and dynamically updated applications and applets. You explore the following topics:

- How Java animations work—The paint() method in applets and paintComponent() in applications and how to override these methods.

- Threads—How to put animation in its own thread, a task that runs separately from other parts of your programs.

- Using bitmapped images such as GIF, JPEG, and PNG files—Loading them into a program, tracking when they have loaded, and displaying them.

Creating Animation in Java

On previous days, you have drawn graphics and text by using either the `paint()` method in applets or the `paintComponent()` method in applications. These methods are used to draw something on a component whenever a program's interface needs to be redrawn. You can call a component's `repaint()` method to request that it be redrawn.

In most of the programs you have written thus far, these paint methods always draw the same thing—yesterday's `Map 2D` applet always draws Florida in the same way when the applet window is repainted.

When creating animation, you can draw the component in its paint method, as usual. Instead of creating content that never changes, provide a way for the paint method to draw different things each time it is called.

For example, the following `paint()` method draws the string `"Look to the cookie!"` in an applet window:

```
public void paint(Graphics screen) {
    Graphics2D screen2D = (Graphics2D)screen;
    screen2D.drawString("Look to the Cookie!", 15, 50);
}
```

The last two arguments to the `Graphics2D` object's `drawString()` method are (x,y) coordinates that determine where the string is drawn in the applet window. The following example is rewritten to use variables for these arguments:

```
public void paint(Graphics screen) {
    Graphics2D screen2D = (Graphics2D)screen;
    screen2D.drawString("Look to the Cookie!", xPosition, yPosition);
}
```

The string's drawn location depends on the value of the `xPosition` and `yPosition` variables. You can use this paint method to create animation by finding a way to dynamically change the values in these variables and then redrawing the applet window.

This technique can be used for all the animation you create, whether you are drawing text, graphics, image files, or a combination of all three.

Painting and Repainting

As you have learned, a component's paint method automatically is called when its display area must be redrawn. This occurs when the component is first loaded on an interface as well as whenever the component is obscured by something else—such as a dialog box—and then revealed again.

You can ask Java's windowing system to repaint a component by calling its `repaint()` method.

Note

The polite language is used here for a reason—`repaint()` is a request rather than a command. The Java windowing system receives this request and processes it as soon as possible, but if `repaint()` requests stack up faster than Java can handle them, some might be skipped. In most cases, the delay between the call to `repaint()` and the actual window redisplay is negligible.

In an animation program, the following two steps are often repeated:

1. The program makes a change that would affect what a component's paint method draws.

2. The component's `repaint()` method is called.

Step 1 does not usually take place in the component's paint method—if you think of animation as a series of individual frames, `paint()` or `paintComponent()` only handles the current frame.

Caution

Although you can call the `paint()` method yourself, you should make all requests to draw the display area using calls to `repaint()`. The `repaint()` method is easier to use—it doesn't require a `Graphics` object as an argument—unlike `paint()`—and it takes care of all the behavior needed to update the display area. You'll see this later today when you call `repaint()` to create an animated sequence.

Animating a Component

13

Several news- and technology-related Web sites use Java applets to present a scrolling window of current headlines.

The next project you create, the `Headlines` application, will display an animated panel component with several headlines that move from the bottom of the panel upwards.

The following class definition for `HeadlinePanel` creates a string array of news headlines and an integer variable:

```
class HeadlinePanel extends JPanel {
    String[] headlines = {
        "Grandmother of Eight Makes Hole in One",
        "Police Begin Campaign to Run Down Jaywalkers",
        "Dr. Ruth to Talk About Sex with Newspaper Editors",
        "Enraged Cow Injures Farmer with Axe "
    };
    int y = 76;
}
```

> **Note**
>
> These headlines from real newspapers were compiled by Ciarán P. McCarthy of the Salesian English Language Centre in Celbridge, Ireland. You can see the full list on his Web site at http://indigo.ie/~sdblang/personal/papers/headlines.htm.

To draw something on a component such as this panel, override its `paintComponent(Graphics)` method, which is analogous to the `paint(Graphics)` method of an applet.

The following method draws every element of the `headlines` array in the component:

```
public void paintComponent(Graphics comp) {
    Graphics2D comp2D = (Graphics2D)comp;
    Font type = new Font("monospaced", Font.BOLD, 14);
    comp2D.setFont(type);
    comp2D.setColor(getBackground());
    comp2D.fillRect(0, 0, getSize().width, getSize().height);
    comp2D.setColor(Color.black);
    for (int i = 0; i < headlines.length; i++)
        comp2D.drawString(headlines[i], 5, y + (20 * i));
}
```

This paint method uses the panel's y instance variable to determine where the headlines are drawn. This variable has the initial value 76, so when the panel is first displayed, the headlines are drawn at the following locations:

- "Grandmother of Eight Makes Hole in One" at (5, 76)
- "Police Begin Campaign to Run Down Jaywalkers" at (5, 96)
- "Dr. Ruth to Talk About Sex with Newspaper Editors" at (5, 116)
- "Enraged Cow Injures Farmer with Axe " at (5, 136)

At this point, you have created a panel with a paint method that is capable of drawing news headlines at different locations. All that remains is to provide a means to change the location of the headlines and to call `repaint()`:

```
void scroll() {
    while (true) {
        y = y - 1;
        if (y < -75)
            y = 76;
        repaint();
        try {
            Thread.sleep(250);
        } catch (InterruptedException e) { }
    }
}
```

The `while (true)` statement in the `scroll()` method causes an *infinite loop*, a loop that never ends. In the loop, the value of the y variable is lowered by 1 and the panel is redrawn. If y is less than -75, it is restored to its initial value, 76.

The `try-catch` block contains a call to `Thread.sleep()`, a class method that causes Java to pause for the specified number of milliseconds. This method is a convenient way to slow down an animated program.

Note

> The call to `sleep()` is enclosed within a `try-catch` block because the `sleep()` method will generate a type of error called an `InterruptedException` if something happens in the Java interpreter that interrupts the method. You learn more about exceptions on Day 16, "Error Handling and Security."

You can add the `HeadlinePanel` component to any application or applet window and call its `scroll()` method to begin the animation. Listing 13.1 contains a simple `Headlines` application that incorporates the panel.

13

LISTING 13.1 The Full Text of `Headlines.java`

```
1: import java.awt.*;
2: import javax.swing.*;
3: import java.util.*;
4:
5: public class Headlines extends JFrame {
6:     HeadlinePanel news = new HeadlinePanel();
7:
8:     public Headlines() {
9:         super("Headlines");
```

LISTING 13.1   continued

```
10:            setSize(420, 100);
11:            setDefaultCloseOperation(JFrame.EXIT_ON_CLOSE);
12:            JPanel pane = new JPanel();
13:            pane.setLayout(new GridLayout(1, 1, 15, 15));
14:            pane.add(news);
15:            setContentPane(pane);
16:            show();
17:            news.scroll();
18:        }
19:
20:        public static void main(String[] arguments) {
21:            Headlines head = new Headlines();
22:        }
23: }
24:
25: class HeadlinePanel extends JPanel {
26:        String[] headlines = {
27:            "Grandmother of Eight Makes Hole in One",
28:            "Police Begin Campaign to Run Down Jaywalkers",
29:            "Dr. Ruth to Talk About Sex with Newspaper Editors",
30:            "Enraged Cow Injures Farmer with Axe "
31:        };
32:        int y = 76;
33:
34:        void scroll() {
35:            while (true) {
36:                y = y - 1;
37:                if (y < -75)
38:                    y = 76;
39:                repaint();
40:                try {
41:                    Thread.sleep(250);
42:                } catch (InterruptedException e) { }
43:            }
44:        }
45:
46:        public void paintComponent(Graphics comp) {
47:            Graphics2D comp2D = (Graphics2D)comp;
48:            Font type = new Font("monospaced", Font.BOLD, 14);
49:            comp2D.setFont(type);
50:            comp2D.setColor(getBackground());
51:            comp2D.fillRect(0, 0, getSize().width, getSize().height);
52:            comp2D.setColor(Color.black);
53:            for (int i = 0; i < headlines.length; i++)
54:                comp2D.drawString(headlines[i], 5, y + (20 * i));
55:        }
56:
57: }
```

Using the `HeadlinePanel` component in another program is fairly straightforward—the panel itself handles everything but starting the animation.

Note that the panel draws headlines to negative coordinates from (5, -1) to (5, -75). Java will draw text and images even if their (x,y) coordinates are outside of a component, displaying only the portion that falls in the component's visible area. The `Headlines` application uses this to make headlines scroll off the top edge of the frame (and also to scroll up from the bottom edge).

Figure 13.1 shows the application running.

FIGURE 13.1

The `Headlines` *application.*

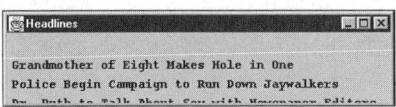

After the `scroll()` method is called, the infinite loop in that method causes the animation to continue until the application is exited when the frame is closed.

Controlling Animation Through Threads

One of the things to consider in animation programming is how system resources are being used. Moving a lot of graphics around can take up a lot of processor time, especially if you're doing complex things like transforming the graphics or detecting collisions between two moving things.

If you include a sophisticated animated component on a user interface, you might find that the elements of the interface respond slowly—drop-down lists take a second or more to appear, button clicks are recognized slowly, and so on.

Animation, like the other processor-hogging things in a Java program, can be run separately from the rest of a program using a feature of the Java language called threads.

NEW TERM *Threads* are parts of a program that are set up to run on their own while the rest of the program does something else. This also is called *multitasking* because the program can handle more than one task simultaneously.

Threads are ideal for anything that takes up a lot of processing time and runs continuously, such as the repeated drawing operations in the `Headlines` application that drew headlines in an infinite loop.

By putting the workload of the animation into a thread, you free up the rest of the program to handle other things. You also make handling the program easier for the runtime environment because all the intensive work is isolated into its own thread.

13

Writing a Threaded Program

Threads are implemented in Java with the Thread class in the java.lang package. You have already used one of its class methods, sleep(), to pause execution of a program.

One way to make use of threads is to put all the time-consuming behavior into its own class. In the Headlines application, the work involved in the animation is confined to the HeadlinePanel class, so this is already well suited to the use of threads.

To modify a class so that it uses threads, the class must implement the Runnable interface in the java.lang package. To do this, add the keyword implements to the class declaration followed by the name of the interface, as in the following example:

```
public class Cartoon extends JPanel implements Runnable {
    public void run() {
        // ...
    }
}
```

When a class implements an interface, it must include all methods of that interface. The Runnable interface contains only one method, run(), so it's included in the preceding example. You will see how to use this method in a moment.

The first step in creating a thread is to create a reference to an object of the Thread class:

```
Thread runner;
```

This statement creates a reference to a thread, but no Thread object has been assigned to it yet. Threads are created by calling the constructor Thread(*Object*) with the threaded object as an argument. You could create a threaded Cartoon object with the following statement:

```
Cartoon toon = new Cartoon();
Thread toonThread = new Thread(toon);
```

Three good places to create threads are the constructor method for an application, the constructor for a component (such as a panel), or the start() method of an applet.

A thread is begun by calling its start() method, as in the following statement:

```
toonThread.start();
```

Caution   Applets and threads both have start() methods, which can make things confusing when you are creating an applet that uses threads. The two methods are different and have no connection to each other.

The following statements can be used in a threaded object's class definition to start the thread:

```
Thread runner;
if (runner == null) {
    runner = new Thread(this);
    runner.start();
}
```

The `this` keyword used in the `Thread()` constructor refers to the object in which these statements are contained. The `runner` variable has a value of `null` before any object is assigned to it, so the `if` statement is used to make sure that the thread is not started more than once.

To run a thread, its `start()` method is called, as in this statement from the preceding example:

```
runner.start();
```

Calling a thread's `start()` method causes another method to be called—the `run()` method that must be present in the threaded object.

The `run()` method is the heart of a threaded class. In an animated program, it can be used to make changes that would affect what is drawn in a paint method. (Looking back at the `Headlines` application, the `scroll()` method would require few changes to be suitable as a `run()` method.)

By adding `implements Runnable`, creating a `Thread` object associated with the applet, and using the applet's `start()`, `stop()`, and `run()` methods, an applet becomes a threaded program.

A Threaded Clock Application

Threaded programming requires a lot of interaction between different objects, so it should become clearer when you see it in action.

Listing 13.2 contains an application that displays the current time on a panel component. The animation required to update the panel runs in its own thread.

13

LISTING 13.2   The Full Text of `DigitalClock.java`

```
1: import java.awt.*;
2: import javax.swing.*;
3: import java.util.*;
4:
5: public class DigitalClock extends JFrame {
6:     WatchPanel watch = new WatchPanel();
```

LISTING **13.2**   continued

```
 7:
 8:     public DigitalClock() {
 9:         super("Digital Clock");
10:         setSize(345, 60);
11:         setDefaultCloseOperation(JFrame.EXIT_ON_CLOSE);
12:         JPanel pane = new JPanel();
13:         pane.setLayout(new GridLayout(1, 1, 15, 15));
14:         pane.add(watch);
15:         setContentPane(pane);
16:         show();
17:     }
18:
19:     public static void main(String[] arguments) {
20:         DigitalClock clock = new DigitalClock();
21:     }
22: }
23:
24: class WatchPanel extends JPanel implements Runnable {
25:     Thread runner;
26:
27:     WatchPanel() {
28:         if (runner == null) {
29:             runner = new Thread(this);
30:             runner.start();
31:         }
32:     }
33:
34:     public void run() {
35:         while (true) {
36:             repaint();
37:             try {
38:                 Thread.sleep(1000);
39:             } catch (InterruptedException e) { }
40:         }
41:     }
42:
43:     public void paintComponent(Graphics comp) {
44:         Graphics2D comp2D = (Graphics2D)comp;
45:         Font type = new Font("Serif", Font.BOLD, 24);
46:         comp2D.setFont(type);
47:         comp2D.setColor(getBackground());
48:         comp2D.fillRect(0, 0, getSize().width, getSize().height);
49:         GregorianCalendar day = new GregorianCalendar();
50:         String time = day.getTime().toString();
51:         comp2D.setColor(Color.black);
52:         comp2D.drawString(time, 5, 25);
53:     }
54: }
```

The `DigitalClock` application is shown in Figure 13.2.

FIGURE 13.2

The `DigitalClock`
application.

Mon Jun 19 11:12:07 EDT 2000

If you didn't use threads in the `DigitalClock` application, the endless `while()` loop in lines 35–40 would run in the default Java system thread, which also is responsible for painting the screen, dealing with user input such as mouse clicks, and keeping everything internally up-to-date. A loop like this can easily monopolize the main system thread, slowing down things such as screen repainting to a crawl.

The `DigitalClock` application displays a frame that contains a single interface component, a panel object called `WatchPanel`. In lines 49–50, the `paintComponent()` method displays the current time by creating a `GregorianCalendar` object, calling the `getTime()` method of that object, and displaying it as a string.

Every time the panel is redrawn, it shows the current time. You don't have to make any changes outside of the paint method for this to happen—the `day` object created in line 49 represents the time at the moment of the object's creation.

For this reason, only one task needs to take place outside the paint method for animation to occur: Something must cause the component to be redrawn frequently. The `run()` method in lines 34–41 takes care of this. It will be called automatically when a thread associated with a `WatchPanel` object is started.

The `WatchPanel()` constructor in lines 27–32 creates and starts a `WatchPanel` thread by calling the thread's `start()` method. This thread will run concurrently with the rest of the application.

Stopping a Thread

Stopping a thread is a little more complicated than starting one. The `Thread` class includes a `stop()` method that can be called to stop a thread, but it has been deprecated in Java 2 because it creates instabilities in Java's runtime environment and can introduce hard-to-detect errors into a program.

One way to stop a thread is to make a loop in the thread's `run()` method end if a variable changes in value, as in the following example:

```
public void run() {
    while (okToRun == true) {
        // ...
    }
}
```

13

The okToRun variable could be an instance variable of the thread's class, and if it is changed to false, the loop inside the run() method will end.

Another thing you can do to stop a thread is to only loop in the run() method while the currently running thread has a variable that references it.

In previous examples, a Thread object called runner has been used to hold the current thread.

A class method, Thread.currentThread(), can be called in a thread to return a reference to the current thread.

The following run() method loops as long as runner and currentThread() refer to the same object:

```
public void run() {
    Thread thisThread = Thread.currentThread();
    while (runner == thisThread) {
        // ...
    }
}
```

If you use a loop like this, you can stop the thread anywhere in the class with the following statement:

```
runner = null;
```

This technique is demonstrated in the Checkers application in Listing 13.3, a program that draws a moving checker on a panel that is animated in its own thread. This thread is started and stopped using buttons on the application's interface.

LISTING 13.3   The Full Text of Checkers.java

```
 1: import java.awt.*;
 2: import java.awt.event.*;
 3: import javax.swing.*;
 4:
 5: public class Checkers extends JFrame implements ActionListener {
 6:     CheckersPanel checkers = new CheckersPanel();
 7:     JButton startButton = new JButton("Start");
 8:     JButton stopButton = new JButton("Stop");
 9:
10:     public Checkers() {
11:         super("Checkers");
12:         setSize(210, 170);
13:         setDefaultCloseOperation(JFrame.EXIT_ON_CLOSE);
14:         JPanel pane = new JPanel();
15:         BorderLayout border = new BorderLayout();
16:         pane.setLayout(border);
```

```
17:          pane.add(checkers, "Center");
18:
19:          JPanel buttonPanel = new JPanel();
20:          startButton.addActionListener(this);
21:          buttonPanel.add(startButton);
22:          stopButton.addActionListener(this);
23:          stopButton.setEnabled(false);
24:          buttonPanel.add(stopButton);
25:
26:          pane.add(buttonPanel, "South");
27:          setContentPane(pane);
28:          show();
29:      }
30:
31:      public void actionPerformed(ActionEvent evt) {
32:          if (evt.getSource() == startButton) {
33:              checkers.playAnimation();
34:              startButton.setEnabled(false);
35:              stopButton.setEnabled(true);
36:          } else {
37:              checkers.stopAnimation();
38:              startButton.setEnabled(true);
39:              stopButton.setEnabled(false);
40:          }
41:      }
42:
43:      public static void main(String[] arguments) {
44:          Checkers ck = new Checkers();
45:      }
46:
47: }
48:
49: class CheckersPanel extends JPanel implements Runnable {
50:      private Thread runner;
51:      int xPos = 5;
52:      int xMove = 4;
53:
54:      void playAnimation() {
55:          if (runner == null); {
56:              runner = new Thread(this);
57:              runner.start();
58:          }
59:      }
60:
61:      void stopAnimation() {
62:          if (runner != null); {
63:              runner = null;
64:          }
65:      }
66:
67:      public void run() {
```

13

LISTING **13.3**   continued

```
68:          Thread thisThread = Thread.currentThread();
69:          while (runner == thisThread) {
70:              xPos += xMove;
71:              if ((xPos > 105) | (xPos < 5))
72:                  xMove *= -1;
73:              repaint();
74:              try {
75:                  Thread.sleep(100);
76:              } catch (InterruptedException e) { }
77:          }
78:      }
79:
80:      public void paintComponent(Graphics comp) {
81:          Graphics2D comp2D = (Graphics2D)comp;
82:          comp2D.setColor(Color.black);
83:          comp2D.fillRect(0, 0, 100, 100);
84:          comp2D.setColor(Color.white);
85:          comp2D.fillRect(100, 0, 100, 100);
86:          comp2D.setColor(Color.red);
87:          comp2D.fillOval(xPos, 5, 90, 90);
88:      }
89: }
```

Most of the code in the Checkers application uses techniques that have already been introduced today or during previous days this week. This program demonstrates one way to produce animation using the shapes that can be drawn using Java2D techniques—in a CheckersPanel object, a black square and white square are drawn underneath a red circle representing a checkers piece.

The position of the red checkers piece depends on the value of a CheckersPanel instance variable, xPos. This variable changes in value inside the panel's run() method.

The Checkers class itself is a frame that represents the application's main interface. Two components are added to the frame's content pane: a CheckersPanel component and another panel called buttonPanel. The second panel contains two buttons, startButton and stopButton.

When the application runs (see Figure 13.3), the checker is drawn over the board but is not moving. The animation can be started and stopped by clicking the Start and Stop buttons.

FIGURE **13.3**

The Checkers *applica-
tion.*

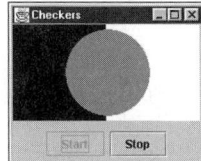

The changes to xPos that make the animation move occur in the run() method in lines 67–78. This method contains a while loop that continues as long as runner and thisThread refer to the same thread.

The checkers panel has two methods to start and stop its thread: playAnimation() in lines 54–59 and stopAnimation() in lines 61–65. These methods could easily be reused in any threaded object to start and stop the thread.

Retrieving and Using Images

Basic image handling in Java is conducted through the Image class, which is part of the java.awt package. Image objects can represent graphics in three file formats: GIF, JPEG, and PNG.

You cannot create Image objects directly. Applets have several methods for loading image files using its filename or a URL, an address indicating where the graphics file is available on the Internet. Applications can use class methods of the Toolkit class, part of the java.awt package, to work with images.

After you have an Image object, you can display it in a component using methods of the Graphics or Graphics2D classes.

Getting Images

To associate a graphics file with an Image object in an application, you can call the createImage() method of the Toolkit class.

Toolkit is a behind-the-scenes class used to support the presentation and maintenance of a graphical user interface in Java. You cannot create Toolkit objects, but you can get one by calling the class method getDefaultToolkit().

The Toolkit class can load images using the following methods:

- getImage(*String*)—Creates an Image object from the graphics file with the specified name, which can be a filename (such as fillmore.jpg) or a reference to a
folder and filename (such as c:\whigs\fillmore.jpg).

13

- getImage(*URL*)—Creates an Image object from the graphics file at the Internet address specified by the URL object.

Working with URL objects is covered in Day 19, "Communicating Across the Internet."

The following statements create an Image object associated with the file fillmore.jpg:

```
Toolkit kit = Toolkit.getDefaultToolkit();
back = kit.getImage("fillmore.jpg");
```

The JApplet class includes two methods to load images:

- getImage(*URL*)—Creates an Image object from the graphics file at the specified URL.
- getImage(*URL*, *String*)—Creates an Image object at an Internet address that combines the specified URL and filename reference.

By calling getCodeBase() in an applet, you can get a URL object that represents the folder where the applet's class file is stored. If you use this as the first argument to getImage(*URL*, *String*) and store the graphics file in the same folder, you can use the filename as the second argument.

For example, if you have an applet stored at http://www.naviseek.com/java21/java called Fillmore.class and a file called fillmore.jpg in the same folder, you can use the following statement to create an Image object associated with that graphics file:

```
Image millard = getImage(getCodeBase(), "fillmore.jpg");
```

Another applet method, getDocumentBase(), returns a URL associated with the Web page that loaded the applet.

By using getCodeBase() or getDocumentBase() when loading an image in an applet, you make it possible for the applet to work even if you move it (and the associated Web page) to another Web server.

 Note

> If you use a Java archive to present your applet, you can include image files and other data files in the archive. These files will be extracted from the archive automatically with any class files in the .JAR file.

Drawing Images

After you have loaded an image into an Image object, you can display it in a paint() or paintComponent() using the drawImage() method of the Graphics2D class.

To display an image, call the drawImage() method with four arguments:

- The Image object to display
- The x coordinate
- The y coordinate
- The keyword this

If a graphics file is stored in the img object, the following paintComponent() method can be used to display it in a user interface component:

```
public void paintComponent(Graphics comp) {
    Graphics2D comp2D = (Graphics2D)comp;
    comp2D.drawImage(img, 0, 0, this);
}
```

The (x,y) coordinates used with drawImage() are comparable to using (x,y) coordinates to display text or graphics such as polygons, circles, and rectangles. The point represents the upper-left corner of the image.

When you are determining the (x,y) coordinate at which to display something in a component, it's often useful to know the dimensions of the component. Use getSize().height and getSize().width to find out the height and width, respectively.

Caution

When using getHeight() and getWidth(), take care not to call these methods before the component has been created and displayed. If you call them in the component's constructor method, you won't get the values you might have been expecting.

A Note About Image Observers

The last argument of the drawImage() method is the keyword this. As you might recall, this can be used inside an object to refer to itself.

The this keyword is used in drawImage() to identify that the applet can keep track of an image as it is downloaded from the World Wide Web. Image loading is tracked through the ImageObserver interface. Classes that implement this interface, such as JApplet, can track the progress of an image. This would be useful to create a program that displays a message such as "Loading images…" while its graphics files are being loaded.

The existing support for ImageObserver should be sufficient for simple uses of images in applets, so the this keyword is used as an argument to drawImage().

13

Creating Animation Using Images

After you have graphics files loaded into `Image` objects, animating them requires the same techniques you used to move around text, circles, and other graphics. The biggest difference is that you have to devise a way to display the right images in the right places.

The best way to show how to animate images is to work through an example. The next project, one of the longest you will undertake, is an application that draws a cartoon penguin walking across a backdrop of ice blocks and stone barriers.

Pixel Pete Takes a Walk

The `Pete` application features an animated penguin called Pixel Pete, a character in a Java game applet called Iceblox that was written by Karl Hörnell. Hörnell, who publishes his games on the Web at `http://www.javaonthebrain.com`, is one of the most accomplished Java game programmers, winning awards from Gamelan and selling programs to Disney and other companies for their own Web sites.

 Tip

> Hörnell publishes the source code, graphics files, and development notes for most of his Java applets on his Web site, so it's a great place for an aspiring game programmer to visit.

For this example, you use seven different graphics files of Pixel Pete and his arctic environment. The animation you create in the `Pete` application will show Pete walking across a panel from left to right, stopping to blink a few times and wave, then walking to the right until he has gone beyond the edge of the panel. The animation loops continuously, so Pete will dutifully continue marching through the application's interface until you close the program down.

Collecting Your Images

The `Pete` animation uses a large graphics file containing Pete's environment and six smaller files representing the different movements that Pete can accomplish. All these files are in `GIF` format, which is well suited for small graphics with large amounts of solid color. You also could use `PNG` graphics for this purpose, if you have graphics software that supports the creation of these files.

The six versions of Pete are shown in Figure 13.4, and the environment is shown in Figure 13.5.

FIGURE **13.4**

The six images for Pete's trip across a panel (enlarged).

FIGURE **13.5**

The environment that Pete travels across.

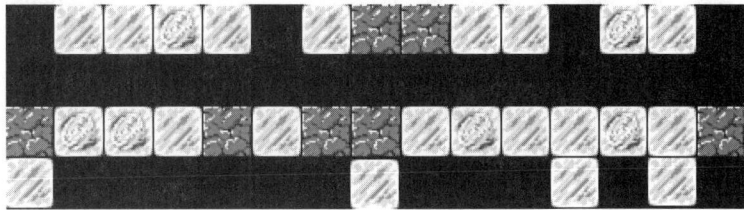

You must have these graphic files on your system in order to create this project. The files are available from the book's Web site at http://www.java21pro.com. Open the Day 13 page and download the following graphics to the same folder where you will compile the Pete application: backdrop.gif, blink.gif, right1.gif, right2.gif, right3.gif, stop.gif, and wave.gif.

Organizing and Loading the Images

The basic idea in the Pete application is to take the series of images and display them one at a time to create the appearance of movement. The penguin will move from left to right across the area that is free of ice blocks and stone barriers as shown in Figure 13.5.

One way to create an animation from graphics files is to store each image in an array of Image objects and use an integer to keep track of which array element to display.

The Pete application will be organized as a simple frame to hold the application and a PetePanel component in which the animation takes place. The panel will run in its own thread, and is designed so that you can plug it into applets and other graphical user interface programs.

The following instance variables, which will be placed in the PetePanel class, hold the images and an integer to track the image to display:

```
Thread runner;
Image petePics[] = new Image[6];
Image back;
int current = 0;
```

A Thread variable called runner is also declared, though it is not assigned to an object yet. This variable will hold a reference to the thread that animates the program.

13

Because Pete will be drawn in different positions in the panel, the current (x,y) coordinates are also instance variables:

```
int x = -10;
int y = 30;
```

The initial coordinates of (-10, 30) put Pete near the left edge of the component but do not display any part of him (Pete is 30 pixels wide). A common trick of animation programming is to put things "off-screen" as described and move them into the visible area.

The constructor method for PetePanel will create Image objects for all seven graphics files and start the panel's thread:

```
PetePanel() {
    super();
    setBackground(Color.black);
    String peteSrc[] = { "right1.gif", "right2.gif",
        "right3.gif", "stop.gif", "blink.gif",
        "wave.gif" };
    Toolkit kit = Toolkit.getDefaultToolkit();
    for (int i=0; i < petePics.length; i++) {
        petePics[i] = kit.getImage(peteSrc[i]);
    }
    back = kit.getImage("backdrop.gif");
    if (runner == null) {
        runner = new Thread(this);
        runner.start();
    }
}
```

The panel is a subclass of JPanel, like the other panels you have worked with today, and the first two statements call its superclass and set the panel's background color to black.

The filenames for the graphics files are stored in a String array, making it possible to use a for loop to iterate through that array and create Image objects for the petePicks array.

The Toolkit object created in the constructor is used in the for loop. By calling its getImage(String) method, you can fill the petePics array with the six graphics files of Pete. The backdrop.gif image is loaded individually into its own Image object, back.

The last thing that must be initialized in the constructor is to create the runner thread by calling its constructor with this as an argument. Using this makes the current object—in other words, the PetePanel object—the running thread.

Calling the start() method of this thread causes the panel's run() method to be called. You will create this in the next section.

Animating the Images

With the images loaded, the next step in the application is to begin animating the elements. Because this is a threaded applet, the run() method will be used for this purpose.

Pete takes five successive actions in the program:

- Walks in from the left edge of the panel
- Stops near the middle and blinks three times
- Waves four times
- Walks off the right edge of the panel
- Takes a short rest off-panel, and then repeats the process from the beginning

The run() method of PetePanel will call methods for each of the actions that Pete can accomplish:

```
public void run() {
    while (true) {
        walk(-10, 275);
        look();
        blink(3);
        wave(4);
        walk(x, getSize().width + 10);
        pause(1500);
    }
}
```

The names of these methods tell you what Pete is doing at each step in the animation. The arguments to the walk() method specify the starting and ending x coordinate of Pete's walk, the argument to blink() specifies the number of times Pete blinks, and the wave() argument specifies how often he waves.

The call to getSize() returns a Dimension object with two instance variables, width and height. By adding 10 to width in the second call to the walk() method, the ending coordinate of Pete's walk is set to 10 pixels beyond the right edge of the panel.

The pause() method causes Pete to do nothing for a designated amount of time. Pete will not be visible at the time this takes place, so it's a way to pause before Pete starts his animated journey again.

Each of Pete's activities is contained in its own method. This makes it possible to reuse some of the actions—such as the two calls to walk()—and to rearrange the order of things if desired. You also could expand Pete's repertoire of movements by adding new methods and calling them within the run() method.

13

The first method created is walk(), which takes two integers as arguments: start and end. These determine the x coordinate where Pete begins and ends running. By using arguments, you make the method reusable. Here's the starting code for the method body:

```
void walk(int start, int end) {
  // to do
}
```

There are three images that represent Pete walking: petePics[0], petePics[1], and petePics[2].

To make it appear that Pete is walking across the window, these images are displayed in succession. At the same time, the x coordinate of the image increases, so each image is drawn a little further to the right than its predecessor. A for loop cycles between the start and end values and increases the x coordinate.

The current integer keeps track of the current image to display, so it is changed during each pass through the for loop.

A call to repaint() causes the image tracked by current to display (as you will see when the panel's paintComponent() method is created).

The last thing to do in the walk() method is to pause inside the for loop before each walking image is replaced by a new one.

Several of Pete's movement methods require a pause of some kind, so it will be added as another method:

```
public void pause(int time) {
    try {
        Thread.sleep(time);
    } catch (InterruptedException e) { }
}
```

After the call to pause() is added, the walk() method consists of the following:

```
public void walk(int start, int end) {
    int showpic = 0;
    for (int i = start; i < end; i += 5) {
        x = i;
        // swap images
        current = showpic;
        repaint();
        pause(150);
        showpic++;
        if (showpic > 2)
            showpic = 0;
    }
}
```

The last part of the for() statement increments the loop by 5 pixels each time, which kicks the images that distance to the right with each update. This choice, like the 150-millisecond pause in the pause() method call, was reached through trial and error to determine what looks best when the animation sequence runs.

You have seen that the walk() method stores the value of the current frame in the current variable before calling repaint(). The paintComponent() method of the panel will do the actual work of displaying this image, as shown here:

```java
public void paintComponent(Graphics comp) {
    Graphics2D comp2D = (Graphics2D)comp;
    if (back != null)
        comp2D.drawImage(back, 0, 0, this);
    comp2D.setColor(Color.black);
    comp2D.fillRect(0, 30, 450, 30);
    if (petePics[current] != null)
        comp2D.drawImage(petePics[current], x, y, this);
}
```

Three things are drawn in this method:

1. The background image, back.

2. A black rectangle 450 pixels wide and 30 pixels high, with its upper left-hand corner at (0, 30).

3. The current Pete image, petePics[current].

These things are drawn from back to front, creating a composite image. The black rectangle is used to wipe out the last image of Pete, which otherwise would still appear on the panel. Before drawing either of the Image objects, the paint method makes sure that they exist by testing to confirm they do not equal null.

Note

In early versions of Java, drawing several different things in a paint method caused graphics to flicker. A common solution to this problem was to draw everything to a different Image object that was not visible, and then draw only that Image in the paint component. This technique is called buffering, and Java 2 supports it automatically within paintComponent() and paint().

13

Pete's second activity is to turn and look directly at the user, which is handled in the look() method:

```java
public void look() {
    current = 3;
    repaint();
    pause(1000);
}
```

By setting current to 3 and calling repaint(), petePics[3] is displayed.

Pete's next activity is to blink, an animation that requires a flip-flop between two images—petePics[4] and petePics[3]:

```
public void blink(int numtimes) {
    for (int i = numtimes; i > 0; i--) {
        current = 4;
        repaint();
        pause(200);
        current = 3;
        repaint();
        pause(1000);
    }
}
```

The for loop uses the numtimes argument to determine how many times to display the two images, making it easy to vary the number of times Pete blinks.

The last new activity for Pete is to wave:

```
public void wave(int numtimes) {
    for (int i = numtimes; i > 0; i--) {
        current = 3;
        repaint();
        pause(600);
        current = 5;
        repaint();
        pause(1100);
    }
}
```

This method has code that's almost identical to the blink() method. It requires a flip-flop between two images, petePics[3] and petePics[5].

Finishing the Application

At this point, you have a PetePanel component that can be added to a container such as a frame or an applet window.

The Pete application creates a frame and adds only one component, PetePanel. Listing 13.4 shows the complete source code for the project.

LISTING 13.4   The Full Text of Pete.java

```
1: import java.awt.*;
2: import javax.swing.*;
3: import java.util.*;
4:
5: public class Pete extends JFrame {
```

```
 6:     PetePanel pete = new PetePanel();
 7:
 8:     public Pete() {
 9:         super("Pixel Pete");
10:         setSize(452, 146);
11:         setDefaultCloseOperation(JFrame.EXIT_ON_CLOSE);
12:         JPanel pane = new JPanel();
13:         pane.setLayout(new GridLayout(1, 1, 15, 15));
14:         pane.add(pete);
15:         setContentPane(pane);
16:         show();
17:     }
18:
19:     public static void main(String[] arguments) {
20:         Pete penguin = new Pete();
21:     }
22: }
23:
24: class PetePanel extends JPanel implements Runnable {
25:     Thread runner;
26:     Image petePics[] = new Image[6];
27:     Image back;
28:     int current = 0;
29:     int x = -10;
30:     int y = 30;
31:
32:     PetePanel() {
33:         super();
34:         setBackground(Color.black);
35:         String peteSrc[] = { "right1.gif", "right2.gif",
36:             "right3.gif", "stop.gif", "blink.gif",
37:         "wave.gif" };
38:         Toolkit kit = Toolkit.getDefaultToolkit();
39:         for (int i=0; i < petePics.length; i++) {
40:             petePics[i] = kit.getImage(peteSrc[i]);
41:         }
42:         back = kit.getImage("backdrop.gif");
43:         if (runner == null) {
44:             runner = new Thread(this);
45:             runner.start();
46:         }
47:     }
48:
49:     public void paintComponent(Graphics comp) {
50:         Graphics2D comp2D = (Graphics2D)comp;
51:         if (back != null)
52:             comp2D.drawImage(back, 0, 0, this);
53:         comp2D.setColor(Color.black);
54:         comp2D.fillRect(0, 30, 450, 30);
55:         if (petePics[current] != null)
56:             comp2D.drawImage(petePics[current], x, y, this);
```

13

LISTING **13.4**   continued

```
57:     }
58:
59:     public void run() {
60:         while (true) {
61:             walk(-10, 275);
62:             look();
63:             blink(3);
64:             wave(4);
65:             walk(x, getSize().width + 10);
66:             pause(1500);
67:         }
68:     }
69:
70:     public void walk(int start, int end) {
71:         int showpic = 0;
72:         for (int i = start; i < end; i += 5) {
73:             x = i;
74:             // swap images
75:             current = showpic;
76:             repaint();
77:             pause(150);
78:             showpic++;
79:             if (showpic > 2)
80:                 showpic = 0;
81:         }
82:     }
83:
84:     public void blink(int numtimes) {
85:         for (int i = numtimes; i > 0; i--) {
86:             current = 4;
87:             repaint();
88:             pause(200);
89:             current = 3;
90:             repaint();
91:             pause(1000);
92:         }
93:     }
94:
95:     public void wave(int numtimes) {
96:         for (int i = numtimes; i > 0; i--) {
97:             current = 3;
98:             repaint();
99:             pause(600);
100:             current = 5;
101:             repaint();
102:             pause(1100);
103:         }
104:     }
105:
```

```
106:    public void look() {
107:        current = 3;
108:        repaint();
109:        pause(1000);
110:    }
111:
112:    public void pause(int time) {
113:        try {
114:            Thread.sleep(time);
115:        } catch (InterruptedException e) { }
116:    }
117: }
```

Figure 13.6 shows the application running.

FIGURE 13.6

The Pete *application.*

Tracking Image Loading

When the Pete application runs, you might notice an odd effect the first time Pete heads across the panel—he disappears for a moment before he changes from one image to another. This is most noticeable when he stops to look at the user, wave, and blink. On all subsequent trips, Pete displays normally without this glitch.

This disappearing act occurs because of how Java loads images when a method like getImage() is called. Contrary to what you might expect, the call to getImage() returns before the image has actually been loaded. Instead, a thread is begun that will load the image, and the program goes on to other tasks.

If you try to draw an Image object before it has been loaded, a blank image will be drawn. This is what happens whenever Pete disappears—the application tries to draw an image that has not yet been loaded.

You can track whether images have finished loading by using a class in the java.awt package, MediaTracker. A MediaTracker object is created by specifying the component where the image will eventually be drawn.

Inside the PetePanel class, you can create a MediaTracker object associated with the panel as follows:

```
MediaTracker track = new MediaTracker(this);
```

13

To begin tracking an image, call the MediaTracker object's addImage(*Image*, *int*) method. The first argument is the image to track. The second is an index number of your choosing which should be unique to this image.

After you have added an image to the track object, you cause a program (or better, a thread) to wait until it is done loading by calling the tracker's waitForID(*int*) with the index number of the image.

A MediaTracker object can keep track of multiple images. To wait for all of them to finish loading, call the tracker's waitForAll() method.

Both of these images must be enclosed in the same try-catch block that was used earlier today for calls to Thread.sleep().

The following PetePanel() constructor has been modified to wait for all images to load before creating the thread and beginning the animation:

```
PetePanel() {
    super();
    setBackground(Color.black);
    String peteSrc[] = { "right1.gif", "right2.gif",
        "right3.gif", "stop.gif", "blink.gif",
        "wave.gif" };
    MediaTracker track = new MediaTracker(this);
    Toolkit kit = Toolkit.getDefaultToolkit();
    for (int i=0; i < petePics.length; i++) {
        petePics[i] = kit.getImage(peteSrc[i]);
        track.addImage(petePics[i], i);
    }
    back = kit.getImage("backdrop.gif");
    track.addImage(back, petePics.length);
    try {
        track.waitForAll();
    } catch (InterruptedException e) { }
    if (runner == null) {
        runner = new Thread(this);
        runner.start();
    }
}
```

Summary

Animation remains one of the more entertaining things you can undertake with Java though it no longer is one of the main selling features. Animation can be used to convey information, attract attention, and play games.

Today, you learned how to create components that feature animation by writing paint methods that are able to change each time they are called.

Because animation can be a processor-hogging resource, you learned how to put it in a thread that executes separately from the rest of a program.

Java 2 takes care of many animation tasks automatically that required special programming in past versions of the language. One of these is buffering, the technique that enables several things to be drawn in a component without flickering problems.

Tomorrow, you continue the trip through Java's multimedia classes by learning how to add sound to your programs.

Q&A

Q I compiled and ran the `Pete` application. Something weird is going on; the animation starts in the middle and drops frames. It's as if only some of the images have loaded when the applet is run.

A That's precisely what's going on. Because image loading doesn't actually load the image right away, your program might be merrily animating blank screens while the images are still being loaded. Depending on how long it takes those images to load, your program might appear to start in the middle, to drop frames, or to not work at all.

There are three possible solutions to this problem. The first is to have the animation loop (that is, start over from the beginning when it stops). Eventually, the images will load and the animation will work correctly. The second solution, and not a very good one, is to sleep for a while before starting the animation, to pause while the images load. The third, and best solution, is to use image observers to make sure that no part of the animation plays before its images have loaded. Check out the documentation for the ImageObserver interface for details.

Q My applet and graphics files are stored in the same folder as the Web page that displays the applet. Should I use `getCodeBase()` or `getDocumentBase()` when creating images in the applet?

A The difference between `getDocumentBase()` and `getCodeBase()` only matters when an applet's Java class is stored in a different folder than the Web page that contains the applet. For the project you're describing, you can use either method call and get the same result.

13

Questions

1. If a class implements the `Runnable` interface, what methods must the class contain?

    (a) `start()`, `stop()`, and `run()`

    (b) `actionPerformed()`

    (c) `run()`

2. After creating a Thread object, how do you get the thread to begin executing?

    (a) Call the thread's `start()` method

    (b) Do nothing

    (c) Call the thread's `run()` method

3. When a `paint()` or `paintComponent()` method draws something over a background picture, what order will they be drawn in?

    (a) Doesn't matter

    (b) Draw the background first

    (c) Draw the background last

Answers

1. c. The `Runnable` interface is used for objects that can run in their own threads.

2. a. Calling `start()` causes the `run()` method of the threaded object to be called.

3. b. You should draw text, graphics, and images from the back forward.

Exercises

To extend your knowledge of the subjects covered today, try the following exercises:

- Create an applet that displays the Pete animation exactly like the `Pete` application does.

- Create a traffic light animation using circle and rectangle shapes that shift from green to yellow to red like a real light.

Where applicable, exercise solutions are offered on the book's Web site at `http://www.java21pro.com`.

DAY 14

JavaSound

Over the past six days, you have taken a sight-seeing tour of the Java language. All the different ways in which a program can be visually interesting—the user interface, graphics, images, and animation—involve the classes of the Swing and Abstract Windowing Toolkit packages.

To finish the week, you will focus on another one of the senses—hearing. Java 2 supports sound using some applet methods that have been available since the introduction of the language and an extensive new class library called JavaSound.

Today you make Java programs audible in two different ways.

First, you use methods of the `Applet` class, the superclass of all Java applets. You can use these methods to retrieve and play sound files in programs using a large number of formats, including `WAV`, `AU`, and `MIDI`.

Next, you begin working with JavaSound, several packages that enable the playback, recording, and manipulation of sound.

Retrieving and Using Sounds

Java supports the playback of sound files through the `Applet` class, and you can play a sound one time only or as a repeating sound loop.

Prior to Java 2, the language could handle only one audio format: 8KHz mono `AU` with mu-law encoding (named for the Greek letter "μ", or mu). If you wanted to use something that was in a format such as `WAV`, you had to translate it to mu-law `AU`, often at a loss of quality.

Java 2 adds much fuller support for audio. You can load and play digitized sound files in the following formats: `AIFF`, `AU`, and `WAV`. Three `MIDI`-based song file formats also are supported: Type 0 `MIDI`, Type 1 `MIDI`, and `RMF`. The greatly improved sound support can handle 8- or 16-bit audio data in mono or stereo, and the sample rates can range from 8KHz to 48KHz.

The simplest way to retrieve and play a sound is through the `play()` method of the `Applet` class. The `play()` method, like the `getImage()` method, takes one of two forms:

- `play()` with one argument—An `URL` object—loads and plays the audio clip stored at that URL.
- `play()` with two arguments—A base URL and a folder pathname—loads and plays that audio file. The first argument often will be a call to `getDocumentBase()` or `getCodeBase()`, as you have seen with `getImage()`.

The following statement retrieves and plays the sound `zap.au`, which is stored in the same place as the applet:

```
play(getCodeBase(), "zap.au");
```

The `play()` method retrieves and plays the given sound as soon as possible after it is called. If the sound file can't be found, the only indication you'll receive of a problem is the silence. No error message will be displayed.

To play a sound repeatedly, start and stop the sound, or play it repeatedly as a loop, you must load it into an `AudioClip` object by using the applet's `getAudioClip` method. `AudioClip` is part of the `java.applet` package, so it must be imported to be used in a program.

The `getAudioClip()` method takes one or two arguments in the same fashion as the `play()` method. The first (or only) argument is a `URL` argument identifying the sound file, and the second is a folder path reference.

The following statement loads a sound file into the `clip` object:

```
AudioClip clip = getAudioClip(getCodeBase(),
    "audio/marimba.wav");
```

In this example, the filename includes a folder reference, so the file `marimba.wav` will be loaded from the subfolder `audio`.

The `getAudioClip()` method can be called only within an applet. As of Java 2, applications can load sound files by using `newAudioClip()`, a class method of the `java.awt.Applet` class. Here's the previous example rewritten for use in an application:

```
AudioClip clip = Applet.newAudioClip("audio/marimba.wav");
```

After you have created an `AudioClip` object, you can call the `play()` (plays the sound), `stop()` (halts playback), and `loop()`(plays repeatedly) methods.

If the `getAudioClip()` or `newAudioClip()` methods can't find the sound file indicated by their arguments, the value of the `AudioClip` object will be `null`. Trying to play a `null` object results in an error, so test for this condition before using an `AudioClip` object.

More than one sound can play simultaneously—they will be mixed together during playback.

When using a sound loop in an applet, note that it won't stop automatically when the applet's running thread is stopped. If a Web user moves to another page, the sound continues playing, which isn't likely to win you any friends among the Web-surfing public.

You can fix this problem by using the `stop()` method on the looping sound at the same time the applet's thread is being stopped.

Listing 14.1 is an applet that plays two sounds: a looping sound named `train.wav` and another sound called `whistle.wav` that plays every 5 seconds.

LISTING 14.1   The Full Text of `Looper.java`

```
1: import java.awt.*;
2: import java.applet.AudioClip;
3:
4: public class Looper extends javax.swing.JApplet implements Runnable {
5:     AudioClip bgSound;
6:     AudioClip beep;
7:     Thread runner;
8:
9:     public void init() {
10:         bgSound = getAudioClip(getCodeBase(),"train.wav");
11:         beep = getAudioClip(getCodeBase(), "whistle.wav");
12:     }
13:
```

14

LISTING 14.1   continued

```
14:     public void start() {
15:         if (runner == null) {
16:             runner = new Thread(this);
17:             runner.start();
18:         }
19:     }
20:
21:     public void stop() {
22:         if (runner != null) {
23:             if (bgSound != null)
24:                 bgSound.stop();
25:             runner = null;
26:         }
27:     }
28:
29:     public void run() {
30:         if (bgSound != null)
31:             bgSound.loop();
32:         Thread thisThread = Thread.currentThread();
33:         while (runner == thisThread) {
34:             try {
35:                 Thread.sleep(9000);
36:                 if (beep != null)
37:                     beep.play();
38:             } catch (InterruptedException e) { }
39:         }
40:     }
41:
42:     public void paint(Graphics screen) {
43:         Graphics2D screen2D = (Graphics2D)screen;
44:         screen2D.drawString("Playing Sounds ...", 10, 10);
45:     }
46: }
```

To test `Looper`, create a Web page with an applet window of any height and width. The audio files `train.wav` and `whistle.wav` can be copied from the book's Web site (http://www.java21pro.com) into the `\J21work` folder on your system. When you run the applet, the only visual output is a single string, but you should hear two sounds playing as the applet runs.

The `init()` method in lines 9–12 loads the two sound files. No attempt is made in this method to make sure that the files were actually loaded—if they cannot be found, the `bgsound` and `beep` variables would equal `null`. Testing for `null` values in these variables will occur elsewhere before the sound files are used, such as in lines 30 and 36, when the `loop()` and `play()` methods are used on the `AudioClip` objects.

Lines 23–24 turn off the looping sound if the thread is also stopped.

JavaSound

The new version of Java includes several packages that greatly expand the sound playback and creation capabilities of the language.

JavaSound, which was offered separately prior to Java 2 version 1.3, has become an official part of the Java class library as the following packages:

- `javax.sound.midi`—Classes for playing, recording, and synthesizing sound files in `MIDI` format.
- `javax.sound.sampled`—Classes for playing, recording, and mixing recorded audio files.

The JavaSound library supports all the audio formats available for playback in applets and applications: `AIFF`, `AU`, `MIDI`, and `WAV`. It also supports `RMF`, a standard for Rich Media Format music files.

MIDI Files

The `javax.sound.midi` package offers extensive support for `MIDI` music files. `MIDI`, which stands for Musical Instrument Digital Interface, is a format for storing sound as a series of notes and effects to be produced by computer synthesized instruments.

Unlike sampled files representing actual sound recorded and digitized for computer presentation, such as `WAV` and `AU`, `MIDI` is closer to a musical score for a synthesizer than a realized recording. `MIDI` files are stored instructions that tell `MIDI` sequencers how to reproduce sound, which synthesized instruments to use, and other aspects of presentation. The sound of a `MIDI` file depends on the quality and variety of the instruments available on the computer or output device.

`MIDI` files are generally much smaller than recorded audio, and they're not suited to representing voices and some other types of sound. However, because of compactness and effects-capability, `MIDI` is used in many different ways—such as computer game background music, Muzak-style versions of pop songs, or the preliminary presentations of classical composition for composers and students.

`MIDI` files are played back by using a sequencer, which can be a hardware device or software program, to play a data structure called a sequence. A sequence is made up of one or more tracks each containing a series of time-coded `MIDI` note and effect instructions called `MIDI` events.

Each of these elements of MIDI presentation is represented by an interface or class in the `javax.sound.midi` package: the `Sequencer` interface and the `Sequence`, `Track`, and `MidiEvent` classes.

14

There also is a MidiSystem class that provides access to the MIDI playback and storage resources on a computer system.

Playing a MIDI File

To play a MIDI file using JavaSound, you must create a Sequencer object based on the MIDI handling capability of a particular system.

The MidiSystem class method getSequencer() returns a Sequencer object that represents a system's default sequencer:

```
Sequencer midi = MidiSystem.getSequencer();
```

This class method generates an exception—an object indicating an error—if the sequencer is unavailable for any reason. A MidiUnavailableException is generated in this circumstance.

You worked with exceptions briefly yesterday, enclosing calls to Thread.sleep() in try-catch blocks because that method generates InterruptedException errors if the method is interrupted.

You can handle the exception generated by getSequencer() with the following code:

```
try {
    Sequencer.midi = MidiSystem.getSequencer();
    // additional code to play a MIDI sequence ...
} catch (MidiUnavailableException exc) {
    System.out.println("Error: " + exc.getMessage());
}
```

In this example, if a sequencer is available when getSequencer() is called, the program continues to the next statement inside the try block. If the sequencer can't be accessed because of a MidiUnavailableException, the program executes the catch block, displaying an error message.

Several methods and constructors involved in playing a MIDI file generate exceptions. Rather than enclosing each one in its own try-catch block, it can be easier to handle all possible errors by using Exception, the superclass of all exceptions, in the catch statement:

```
try {
    Sequencer.midi = MidiSystem.getSequencer();
    // additional code to play a MIDI sequence ...
} catch (Exception exc) {
    System.out.println("Error: " + exc.getMessage());
}
```

This example doesn't just handle `MidiUnavailableException` problems in the `catch` block. When you add additional statements to load and play a MIDI sequence inside the `try` block, any exceptions generated by those statements will cause the `catch` block to be executed. Exceptions are covered fully on Day 16, "Error Handling and Security."

After you have created a `Sequencer` object that can play MIDI files, you call another class method of `MidiSystem` to retrieve a MIDI sequence from a data source:

- `getSequence(File)`—Loads a sequence from the specified file.
- `getSequence(URL)`—Loads a sequence from the specified Internet address.
- `getSequence(InputStream)`—Loads a sequence from the specified data input stream, which can come from a file, input device, or another program.

To load a `MIDI` sequence from a file, you must first create a `File` object using its filename or a reference to its filename and the folder where it can be found.

If the file is in the same folder as your Java program, you can create it using the `File(String)` constructor with that name. The following statement creates a `File` object for a `MIDI` file called `nevermind.mid`:

```
File sound = new File("nevermind.mid");
```

You can also use relative file references that include subfolders:

```
File sound = new File("tunes/nevermind.mid");
```

The `File` constructor generates a `NullPointerException` if the argument to the constructor has a `null` value.

After you have a `File` object associated with a `MIDI` file, you can call `getSequence(File)` to create a sequence:

```
File sound = new File("aboutagirl.mid");
Sequence seq = MidiSystem.getSequence(sound);
```

If all goes well, the `getSequence()` class method will return a `Sequence` object. If not, two kinds of errors can be generated by the method: `InvalidMidiDataException` if the system can't handle the MIDI data (or it isn't MIDI data at all), and `IOException` if file input was interrupted or failed for some reason.

At this point, if your program has not been derailed by an error, you have a `MIDI` sequencer and a sequence to play. You are ready to play the file—you don't have to deal with tracks or `MIDI` events just to play back an entire `MIDI` file.

14

Playing a sequence involves the following steps:

- Call the sequencer's open() method so the device prepares to play something.
- Call the sequencer's start() method to begin playing the sequence.
- Wait for the sequence to finish playing (or for a user to stop playback in some manner).
- Call the sequencer's close() method to free the device for other things.

The only one of these methods that generates an exception is open(), which produces a MidiUnavailableException if the sequencer can't be readied for playback.

Calling close() stops a sequencer, even if it is currently playing one or more sequences. You can use the sequencer method isRunning(), which returns a boolean value, to check whether it is still playing (or recording) MIDI sequences.

The following example uses this method on a sequencer object called playback that has a sequence loaded:

```
playback.open();
playback.start();
while (playback.isRunning()) {
    try {
        Thread.sleep(1000);
    } catch (InterruptedException e) { }
}
playback.close();
```

The while loop prevents the sequencer from being closed until the sequence has completed playback. The call to Thread.sleep() inside the loop slows it down so that isRunning() is only checked once per second (1000 milliseconds)—otherwise, the program will use a lot of resources by calling isRunning() numerous times per second.

The PlayMidi application in Listing 14.2 plays a MIDI sequence from a file on your system. The application displays a frame that contains a user interface component called MidiPanel, and this panel runs in its own thread and plays the file.

LISTING 14.2   The Full Text of PlayMidi.java

```
1: import javax.swing.*;
2: import javax.sound.midi.*;
3: import java.awt.GridLayout;
4: import java.io.File;
5:
6: public class PlayMidi extends JFrame {
7:
8:     PlayMidi(String song) {
```

```
 9:            super("Play MIDI Files");
10:            setSize(180, 100);
11:            setDefaultCloseOperation(JFrame.EXIT_ON_CLOSE);
12:            MidiPanel midi = new MidiPanel(song);
13:            JPanel pane = new JPanel();
14:            pane.add(midi);
15:            setContentPane(pane);
16:            show();
17:        }
18:
19:        public static void main(String[] arguments) {
20:            if (arguments.length != 1) {
21:                System.out.println("Usage: java PlayMidi filename");
22:            } else {
23:                PlayMidi pm = new PlayMidi(arguments[0]);
24:            }
25:        }
26: }
27:
28: class MidiPanel extends JPanel implements Runnable {
29:        Thread runner;
30:        JProgressBar progress = new JProgressBar();
31:        Sequence currentSound;
32:        Sequencer player;
33:        String songFile;
34:
35:        MidiPanel(String song) {
36:            super();
37:            songFile = song;
38:            JLabel label = new JLabel("Playing file ...");
39:            setLayout(new GridLayout(2, 1));
40:            add(label);
41:            add(progress);
42:            if (runner == null) {
43:                runner = new Thread(this);
44:                runner.start();
45:            }
46:        }
47:
48:        public void run() {
49:            try {
50:                File file = new File(songFile);
51:                currentSound = MidiSystem.getSequence(file);
52:                player = MidiSystem.getSequencer();
53:                player.open();
54:                player.setSequence(currentSound);
55:                progress.setMinimum(0);
56:                progress.setMaximum((int)player.getMicrosecondLength());
57:                player.start();
58:                while (player.isRunning()) {
59:                    progress.setValue((int)player.getMicrosecondPosition());
```

14

LISTING 14.2   continued

```
60:                    try {
61:                        Thread.sleep(1000);
62:                    } catch (InterruptedException e) { }
63:                }
64:                progress.setValue((int)player.getMicrosecondPosition());
65:                player.close();
66:            } catch (Exception ex) {
67:                System.out.println(ex.toString());
68:            }
69:        }
70: }
```

You must specify the name of a MIDI file as a command-line argument when running this application. If you don't have any MIDI files, one is available from the book's Web site—visit http://www.java21pro.com and open the Day 14 page.

 Tip

> Hundreds of MIDI archives are on the World Wide Web. To find some of the most popular archives, visit the search engine Google at http://www.google.com and search for the term MIDI files. Google displays sites in the order of their visitation frequency, so you should be able to find a few great MIDI resources quickly.

The following command runs the application with a MIDI file called betsy.mid (the 19th century folk song "Sweet Betsy from Pike," available from the book's Web site):

```
java PlayMidi betsy.mid
```

Figure 14.1 shows the application in mid-playback.

FIGURE 14.1

The PlayMidi *application playing a MIDI file.*

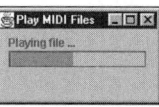

The application includes a progress bar that displays how much of the sequence has been played. This is handled using the JProgressBar user interface component and two sequencer methods:

- getMicrosecondLength()—The total length of the currently loaded sequence, expressed in microseconds as a long value

- getMicrosecondPosition()—The microsecond that represents the current position in the sequence, also a long value

A microsecond is equal to one-millionth of a second, so you can use these methods to get an astonishingly precise measurement of MIDI playback progress.

The progress bar is created as an instance variable of MidiPanel in line 30. Though you can create a progress bar with a minimum and maximum, there's no way to know the length of a sequence until it has been loaded.

The progress bar's minimum is set to 0 in line 55 and to the sequence's microsecond length in line 56.

Caution	The progress bar's setMinimum() and setMaximum() methods require integer arguments, so this application converts the microsecond values from long to int. Because of this loss of precision, the progress bar won't work correctly for files longer than 2.14 billion microseconds (around 35.6 minutes).

The run() method in lines 48–69 of Listing 14.2 loads the system sequencer and a MIDI file into a sequence, and plays the sequence. The while loop in lines 58–63 uses the sequencer's isRunning() method to wait until the file finishes playing before doing anything else. This loop also updates the progress bar by calling its setValue() method with the current microsecond position of the sequence.

After the file finishes playback and the while loop terminates, the microsecond position of the sequence is reported as 0, which is used in line 64 to set the progress bar back to its minimum value.

Manipulating Sound Files

Up to this point, you have used JavaSound to recreate functionality that's already available in the audio methods of the Applet class, which can play MIDI files in addition to the other supported formats.

JavaSound's strength as an alternative becomes apparent when you manipulate the sound files you are working with. You can change many aspects of the presentation and recording of audio using the JavaSound packages.

One way to change a MIDI file during playback is to alter its tempo, the speed at which the file is played.

To do this on an existing Sequencer object, call its setTempoFactor(float) method.

14

Tempo is represented as a float value from 0.0 upwards. Every MIDI sequence has its own established tempo, which is represented by the value 1.0. A tempo of 0.5 is half as fast, 2.0 twice as fast, and so on.

To retrieve the current tempo, call getTempoFactor(), which returns a float value.

The next project you create, MidiApplet, uses the same technique to load and play a MIDI file as the PlayMidi application—a panel is displayed that plays a MIDI file in its own thread. The MIDI file is loaded using a File object and played using a sequencer's open(), start(), and close() methods.

One difference in this project is that the MIDI file can be played over and over again, rather than just once.

Because this is an applet rather than an application, the MIDI file to play will be specified as a parameter. Listing 14.3 contains an example of an HTML document that can be used to load the applet.

LISTING 14.3   The Full Text of MidiApplet.html

```
1: <applet code="MidiApplet.class" height="100" width="250">
2: <param name="file" value="camptown.mid">
3: </applet>
```

The MIDI file used in this example, a MIDI version of "Camptown Races," is available from the book's Web site at http://www.java21pro.com on the Day 14 page. You can, of course, substitute any other MIDI file.

The MidiApplet project has three user interface components you can use to control how the file is played: Play and Stop buttons and a drop-down list for the selection of a tempo.

Figure 14.2 shows what the program looks like when loaded by appletviewer.

FIGURE 14.2

The MidiApplet *program playing "Camptown Races."*

Because applets will continue playing sound in a Web browser even after a user loads a different page, there must be a way to stop playback.

If you are running audio in its own thread, you can stop the audio by using the same thread-stopping techniques introduced for animation yesterday—run the thread in a Thread object, loop while that object and Thread.currentThread() represent the same object, and set runner to null when you are ready to stop the thread.

Listing 14.4 contains the MidiApplet project. The length of this program is primarily because of the creation of the graphical user interface and the event-handling methods to receive input from the user. The JavaSound-related aspects of the program will be introduced after you have created the applet.

LISTING 14.4   The Full Text of MidiApplet.java

```
 1: import javax.swing.*;
 2: import java.awt.event.*;
 3: import javax.sound.midi.*;
 4: import java.awt.GridLayout;
 5: import java.io.File;
 6:
 7: public class MidiApplet extends javax.swing.JApplet {
 8:     public void init() {
 9:         JPanel pane = new JPanel();
10:         MidiPlayer midi = new MidiPlayer(getParameter("file"));
11:         pane.add(midi);
12:         setContentPane(pane);
13:     }
14: }
15:
16: class MidiPlayer extends JPanel implements Runnable, ActionListener {
17:
18:     Thread runner;
19:     JButton play = new JButton("Play");
20:     JButton stop = new JButton("Stop");
21:     JLabel message = new JLabel();
22:     JComboBox tempoBox = new JComboBox();
23:     float tempo = 1.0F;
24:     Sequence currentSound;
25:     Sequencer player;
26:     String songFile;
27:
28:     MidiPlayer(String song) {
29:         super();
30:         songFile = song;
31:         play.addActionListener(this);
32:         stop.setEnabled(false);
33:         stop.addActionListener(this);
34:         for (float i = 0.25F; i < 7F; i += 0.25F)
35:             tempoBox.addItem("" + i);
36:         tempoBox.setSelectedItem("1.0");
```

14

LISTING 14.4 continued

```
37:             tempoBox.setEnabled(false);
38:             tempoBox.addActionListener(this);
39:             setLayout(new GridLayout(2, 1));
40:             add(message);
41:             JPanel buttons = new JPanel();
42:             JLabel tempoLabel = new JLabel("Tempo: ");
43:             buttons.add(play);
44:             buttons.add(stop);
45:             buttons.add(tempoLabel);
46:             buttons.add(tempoBox);
47:             add(buttons);
48:             if (songFile == null) {
49:                 play.setEnabled(false);
50:             }
51:         }
52:
53:         public void actionPerformed(ActionEvent evt) {
54:             if (evt.getSource() instanceof JButton) {
55:                 if (evt.getSource() == play)
56:                     play();
57:                 else
58:                     stop();
59:             } else {
60:                 String item = (String)tempoBox.getSelectedItem();
61:                 try {
62:                     tempo = Float.parseFloat(item);
63:                     player.setTempoFactor(tempo);
64:                     message.setText("Playing " + songFile + " at "
65:                         + tempo + " tempo");
66:                 } catch (NumberFormatException ex) {
67:                     message.setText(ex.toString());
68:                 }
69:             }
70:         }
71:
72:         void play() {
73:             if (runner == null) {
74:                 runner = new Thread(this);
75:                 runner.start();
76:                 play.setEnabled(false);
77:                 stop.setEnabled(true);
78:                 tempoBox.setEnabled(true);
79:             }
80:         }
81:
82:         void stop() {
83:             if (runner != null) {
84:                 runner = null;
85:                 stop.setEnabled(false);
```

```
 86:                    play.setEnabled(true);
 87:                    tempoBox.setEnabled(false);
 88:             }
 89:     }
 90:
 91:     public void run() {
 92:         try {
 93:             File song = new File(songFile);
 94:             currentSound = MidiSystem.getSequence(song);
 95:             player = MidiSystem.getSequencer();
 96:         } catch (Exception ex) {
 97:             message.setText(ex.toString());
 98:         }
 99:         Thread thisThread = Thread.currentThread();
100:         while (runner == thisThread) {
101:             try {
102:                 player.open();
103:                 player.setSequence(currentSound);
104:                 player.setTempoFactor(tempo);
105:                 player.start();
106:                 message.setText("Playing " + songFile + " at "
107:                     + tempo + " tempo");
108:                 while (player.isRunning() && runner != null) {
109:                     try {
110:                         Thread.sleep(1000);
111:                     } catch (InterruptedException e) { }
112:                 }
113:                 message.setText("");
114:                 player.close();
115:             } catch (Exception ex) {
116:                 message.setText(ex.toString());
117:                 break;
118:             }
119:         }
120:     }
121: }
```

Run MidiApplet by loading it on an HTML document using appletviewer or a Web browser that's equipped with the most up-to-date Java 2 plug-in. Internet Explorer 5 and Netscape Navigator 4 cannot run this applet without the plug-in because they do not fully support Java 2.

The tempo of the MIDI file is controlled by a drop-down list component called tempoBox. This component is created with a range of floating-point values from 0.25 to 6.75 in lines 34–35. The list's addItem(*Object*) method cannot be used with float values, so they are combined with an empty string—quote marks without any text inside—in line 36. This causes the combined argument to be sent to addItem() as a String object.

14

Though the tempo can be set using `tempoBox`, it is stored in its own instance variable, `tempo`. This variable is initialized in line 23 with a value of 1.0, the sequence's default playback speed.

If the drop-down list from which a user selects a value has an `ActionListener` associated with it, the listener's `actionPerformed` method will be called.

The `actionPerformed()` method in lines 53–70 handles all three kinds of possible user input:

- Clicking the Play button causes the `play()` method to be called.
- Clicking the Stop button causes the `stop()` method to be called.
- Choosing a new value from the drop-down list causes that value to become the new tempo.

Because all the items in `tempoBox` are stored as strings, you must convert them into floating-point values before you can use them to set the tempo.

This can be done by calling the class method `Float.parseFloat()`, which is comparable to the method `Integer.parseInt()` that has been used several times to work with integers during the past two weeks.

Like the other parse method, `parseFloat()` generates a `NumberFormatException` error if the string cannot be converted to a `float` value.

 Note

> When `tempoBox` was created, the only items added to it are strings that convert successfully to floating-point values, so there's no way a `NumberFormatException` can result from using this component to set the tempo. However, Java still requires that the exception be dealt with in a `try-catch` block.

Line 63 calls the sequencer's `setTempoFactor()` method with the tempo selected by the user. This takes effect immediately, so you can modify the tempo of a song to sometimes maniacal results.

After the sequencer and sequence have been created in the `run()` method, the `while` loop in lines 100–119 keeps playing the song until the `Thread` object `runner` has been set to `null`.

Another while loop, which is nested inside this one, makes sure that the sequencer is not closed while the song is playing. This loop in lines 108–112 is a little different from the one used in the PlayMidi application. Instead of looping while player.isRunning() returns the value true, it requires two conditions to be met:

```
while (player.isRunning() && runner != null) {
    // statements in loop
}
```

The and operator && causes the while loop to continue only if both expressions are true. If you did not test for the value of runner here, the thread would continue playing the MIDI file until the song ends, rather than stopping when runner has been set to null, which should signal the end of the thread.

The MidiApplet program does not stop the thread when the user goes to a different Web page.

Because MidiPanel has a stop() method that stops the thread, you can halt MIDI playback when the page is no longer being viewed in two steps:

1. Create an instance variable in MidiApplet for the user-interface component MidiPanel.
2. Override the applet's stop() method and use it to call the panel's stop() method.

Summary

During the past two days, you have worked with the dynamic multimedia features of the Java language.

One of the strengths of the Java class library is how complex programming tasks such as user interface programming and sound playback are encapsulated within easy-to-create and workable classes. You can play a MIDI file that can be manipulated in real time using only a few objects and class methods, in spite of the extremely complex behind-the-scenes development work.

Today, you played sound in programs using simple and more sophisticated techniques.

If you are only trying to play an audio file, working with getAudioClip() and newAudioClip() methods in the Applet class is probably sufficient.

If you want to do more complex things with the audio, such as changing its tempo and making other dynamic modifications, JavaSound packages such as javax.sound.midi can be used.

14

During the third week of the book, you will explore many of the advanced features of the Java language, including exception handling, file and data input and output, Java database connectivity, and JavaBeans.

Q&A

Q The method `getSequence(InputStream)` is mentioned in this chapter. What is an input stream, and how are they used with sound files?

A Input streams are objects that retrieve data as it is being sent from another source. The source can be a wide range of things capable of producing data—files, serial ports, servers, or even objects in the same program. You work with streams extensively on Day 17, "Handling Data Through Java Streams."

Q What other things are possible in JavaSound, in addition to what's presented here?

A JavaSound is a set of packages that rival Swing in complexity, and many of the classes involve sophisticated stream- and exception-handling techniques that will be covered next week. You can learn more about JavaSound and the things you can accomplish with the library on Sun's Web site at `http://java.sun.com/products/java-media/sound/`. Sun offers a Java application called the Java Sound Demo that collects some of the most impressive features of JavaSound: playback, recording, `MIDI` synthesis, and programmable `MIDI` instruments.

Questions

1. Which `Applet` class method can be used to create an `AudioClip` object in an application?

   (a) `newAudioClip()`

   (b) `getAudioClip()`

   (c) `getSequence()`

2. What class represents the `MIDI` resources that are available on a specific computer system?

   (a) `Sequencer`

   (b) `MIDISystem`

   (c) `MIDIEvent`

3. How many microseconds does it take to cook a 3-minute egg?

    (a) 180,000

    (b) 180,000,000

    (c) 180,000,000,000

Answers

1. a. It's a misnomer for this method to be included in the `Applet` class, but that's a quirk of Java 1.0 that remains in Java 2.0.

2. b. The `MIDISystem` class is used to create objects that represent sequencers, synthesizers, and other devices that handle `MIDI` audio.

3. b. One million microseconds are in a second, so 180 million microseconds is equal to 180 seconds.

Exercises

To extend your knowledge of the subjects covered today, try the following exercises:

- Create an application that uses `newAudioClip()` to play a sound file.
- Convert the `MidiApplet` project so that you can specify more than one `MIDI` file as parameters on a Web page and play each one in succession.

Where applicable, exercise solutions are offered on the book's Web site at `http://www.java21pro.com`.

14

WEEK 3

Java's Advanced Features

- Packages, Interfaces, and Other Class Features
- Error Handling and Security
- Handling Data Through Java Streams
- Object Serialization and Reflection
- Communicating Across the Internet
- Working with JavaBeans
- Java Database Connectivity and Data Structures

15

16

17

18

19

20

21

WEEK 3

DAY 15

Packages, Interfaces, and Other Class Features

The third week of this course extends what you already know. You could quit at this point and develop functional programs, but you would be missing some of the advanced features that express the real strengths of the language.

Today, you extend your knowledge of classes and how they interact with other classes in a Java program. The following subjects will be covered:

- Controlling access to methods and variables from outside a class
- Finalizing classes, methods, and variables so that their values or definitions cannot be subclasses or cannot be overridden
- Creating abstract classes and methods for factoring common behavior into superclasses
- Grouping classes into packages
- Using interfaces to bridge gaps in a class hierarchy

Modifiers

The techniques for programming you learn today involve different strategies and ways of thinking about how a class is organized. But the one thing all these techniques have in common is that they all use special modifier keywords in the Java language.

In Week 1, you learned how to define classes, methods, and variables in Java. Modifiers are keywords that you add to those definitions to change their meaning.

The Java language has a wide variety of modifiers, including

- Modifiers for controlling access to a class, method, or variable: `public`, `protected`, and `private`
- The `static` modifier, for creating class methods and variables
- The `final` modifier, for finalizing the implementations of classes, methods, and variables
- The `abstract` modifier, for creating abstract classes and methods
- The `synchronized` and `volatile` modifiers, which are used for threads

To use a modifier, you include its keyword in the definition of the class, method, or variable that is being modified. The modifier precedes the rest of the statement, as in the following examples:

```
public class MyApplet extends java.applet.Applet { ... }

private boolean offline;

static final double weeks = 9.5;

protected static final int MEANING_OF_LIFE = 42;

public static void main(String[] arguments) {
    ...
}
```

If you're using more than one modifier in a statement, you can place them in any order, as long as all modifiers precede the element they are modifying. Make sure to avoid treating a method's return type—such as `void`—as if it were one of the modifiers.

Modifiers are optional—which you should realize, after using very few of them in the preceding two weeks. You can come up with many good reasons to use them, though, as you'll see.

Access Control for Methods and Variables

The modifiers that you will use the most often in your programs are the ones that control access to methods and variables: `public`, `private`, and `protected`. These modifiers determine which variables and methods of a class are visible to other classes.

By using access control, you control how your class will be used by other classes. Some variables and methods in a class will be of use only within the class itself, and they should be hidden from other classes that might interact with the class. This process is called encapsulation: An object controls what the outside world can know about it and how the outside world can interact with it.

NEW TERM *Encapsulation* is the process of preventing the variables of a class from being read or modified by other classes. The only way to use these variables is by calling methods of the class, if they are available.

The Java language provides four levels of access control: `public`, `private`, `protected`, and a default level that is specified by using no modifier.

Default Access

For most of the examples in this book, you have not specified any kind of access control. Variables and methods were declared with statements such as the following:

```
String singer = "Phil Harris";
boolean digThatCrazyBeat() {
    return true;
}
```

A variable or method that is declared without any access control modifier is available to any other class in the same package. Previously, you saw how classes in the Java class library are organized into packages. The `java.awt` package is one of them—a set of related classes for behavior related to Java's Abstract Windowing Toolkit.

Any variable declared without a modifier can be read or changed by any other class in the same package. Any method declared the same way can be called by any other class in the same package. No other classes can access these elements in any way.

This level of access control doesn't control much access. When you start thinking more about how your class will be used by other classes, you'll be using one of the three modifiers more often than accepting the default control.

Note   The preceding discussion raises the question about what package your own classes have been in up to this point. As you'll see later today, you can make your class a member of a package by using the package declaration. If you don't use this approach, the class is put into a package with all other classes that don't belong to any other packages.

Private Access

To completely hide a method or variable from being used by any other classes, you use the private modifier. The only place these methods or variables can be seen is from within their own class.

A private instance variable, for example, can be used by methods in its own class but not by objects of any other class. In the same vein, private methods can be called by other methods in their own class but by no others. This restriction also affects inheritance: Neither private variables nor private methods are inherited by subclasses.

Private variables are extremely useful in two circumstances:

- When other classes have no reason to use that variable
- When another class could wreak havoc by changing the variable in an inappropriate way

For example, consider a Java class called Bingo that generates bingo numbers for an Internet gambling site. A variable in that class called winRatio could control the number of winners and losers that are generated. As you can imagine, this variable has a big impact on the bottom line at the site. If the variable were changed by other classes, the performance of Bingo would change greatly. To guard against this scenario, you can declare the winRatio variable as private.

The following class uses private access control:

```
class Writer {
    private boolean writersBlock = true;
    private String mood;
    private int income = 0;

    private void getIdea(Inspiration in) {
        // ...
    }

    Manuscript createManuscript(int numDays, long numPages) {
        // ...
    }
}
```

In this code example, the internal data to the class `Writer` (the variables `writersBlock`, `mood`, and `income` and the method `getIdea()`) is all private. The only method accessible from outside the `Writer` class is the `createManuscript()` method. `createManuscript()` is the only task other objects can ask the `Writer` object to perform. `Editor` and `Publisher` objects might prefer a more direct means of extracting a `Manuscript` object from the `Writer`, but they don't have the access to do so.

Using the `private` modifier is the main way that an object encapsulates itself. You can't limit the ways in which a class is used without using `private` in many places to hide variables and methods. Another class is free to change the variables inside a class and call its methods in any way desired if you don't control access.

Public Access

In some cases, you might want a method or variable in a class to be completely available to any other class that wants to use it. Think of the class variable `black` from the `Color` class. This variable is used when a class wants to use the color black, so `black` should have no access control at all.

Class variables often are declared to be `public`. An example would be a set of variables in a `Football` class that represent the number of points used in scoring. The `TOUCHDOWN` variable could equal 7, the `FIELDGOAL` variable could equal 3, and so on. These variables would need to be public so that other classes could use them in statements such as the following:

```
if (position < 0) {
    System.out.println("Touchdown!");
    score = score + Football.TOUCHDOWN;
}
```

The `public` modifier makes a method or variable completely available to all classes. You have used it in every application you have written so far, with a statement such as the following:

```
public static void main(String[] arguments) {
    // ...
}
```

The `main()` method of an application has to be public. Otherwise, it could not be called by the `java` interpreter to run the class.

Because of class inheritance, all public methods and variables of a class are inherited by its subclasses.

Protected Access

The third level of access control is to limit a method and variable to use by the following two groups:

- Subclasses of a class
- Other classes in the same package

You do so by using the `protected` modifier, as in the following statement:

```
protected boolean outOfData = true;
```

 Note

> You might be wondering how these two groups are different. After all, aren't subclasses part of the same package as their superclass? Not always. An example is the `Applet` class. It is a subclass of `java.awt.Panel` but is actually in its own package, `java.applet`. Protected access differs from default access this way; protected variables are available to subclasses, even if they aren't in the same package.

This level of access control is useful if you want to make it easier for a subclass to implement itself. Your class might use a method or variable to help the class do its job. Because a subclass inherits much of the same behavior and attributes, it might have the same job to do. Protected access gives the subclass a chance to use the helper method or variable, while preventing a nonrelated class from trying to use it.

Consider the example of a class called `AudioPlayer` that plays a digital audio file. `AudioPlayer` has a method called `openSpeaker()`, which is an internal method that interacts with the hardware to prepare the speaker for playing. `openSpeaker()` isn't important to anyone outside the `AudioPlayer` class, so at first glance you might want to make it `private`. A snippet of `AudioPlayer` might look something like this:

```
class AudioPlayer {

    private boolean openSpeaker(Speaker sp) {
        // implementation details
    }
}
```

This code works fine if `AudioPlayer` isn't going to be subclassed. But what if you were going to create a class called `StreamingAudioPlayer` that is a subclass of `AudioPlayer`? That class would want access to the `openSpeaker()` method so that it can override it and provide streaming audio-specific speaker initialization. You still don't want the method generally available to random objects (and so it shouldn't be `public`), but you want the subclass to have access to it.

Comparing Levels of Access Control

The differences between the various protection types can become very confusing, particularly in the case of `protected` methods and variables. Table 15.1, which summarizes exactly what is allowed where, helps clarify the differences from the least restrictive (`public`) to the most restrictive (`private`) forms of protection.

TABLE 15.1 The Different Levels of Access Control

Visibility	public	protected	default	private
From the same class	yes	yes	yes	yes
From any class in the same package	yes	yes	yes	no
From any class outside the package	yes	no	no	no
From a subclass in the same package	yes	yes	yes	no
From a subclass outside the same package	yes	yes	no	no

Access Control and Inheritance

One last issue regarding access control for methods involves subclasses. When you create a subclass and override a method, you must consider the access control in place on the original method.

You might recall that applet methods such as `init()` and `paint()` must be `public` in your own applets.

As a general rule, you cannot override a method in Java and make the new method more controlled than the original. You can, however, make it more public. The following rules for inherited methods are enforced:

- Methods declared `public` in a superclass must also be `public` in all subclasses. (For this reason, most of the applet methods are `public`.)
- Methods declared `protected` in a superclass must either be `protected` or `public` in subclasses; they cannot be `private`.
- Methods declared without access control (no modifier was used) can be declared more private in subclasses.

Methods declared `private` are not inherited at all, so the rules don't apply.

Accessor Methods

In many cases, you may have an instance variable in a class that has strict rules for the values it can contain. An example would be a `zipCode` variable. A ZIP Code in the United States must be a number that is five-digits long.

To prevent an external class from setting the zipCode variable incorrectly, you can declare it private with a statement such as the following:

```
private int zipCode;
```

However, what if other classes must be able to set the zipCode variable for the class to be useful? In that circumstance, you can give other classes access to a private variable by using an accessor method inside the same class as zipCode.

Accessor methods get their name because they provide access to something that otherwise would be off-limits. By using a method to provide access to a private variable, you can control how that variable is used. In the ZIP Code example, the class could prevent anyone else from setting zipCode to an incorrect value.

Often, separate accessor methods to read and write a variable are available. Reading methods have a name beginning with get, and writing methods have a name beginning with set, as in setZipCode(*int*) and getZipCode(*int*).

 Note

> This convention is becoming more standard with each version of Java. You might recall how the size() method of the Dimension class has been changed to getSize() as of Java 2. You might want to use the same naming convention for your own accessor methods, as a means of making the class more understandable.

Using methods to access instance variables is a frequently used technique in object-oriented programming. This approach makes classes more reusable because it guards against a variable being used improperly.

Static Variables and Methods

A modifier you already have used in programs is static, which was introduced during Day 6, "Creating Classes and Methods." The static modifier is used to create class methods and variables, as in the following example:

```
public class Circle {
    public static float pi = 3.14159265F;

    public float area(float r) {
        return  pi * r * r;
    }
}
```

Class variables and methods can be accessed using the class name followed by a dot and the name of the variable or method, as in `Color.black` or `Circle.pi`. You also can use the name of an object of the class, but for class variables and methods, using the class name is better. This approach makes clearer what kind of variable or method you're working with; instance variables and methods can never be referred to by class name.

The following statements use class variables and methods:

```
float circumference = 2 * Circle.pi * getRadius();
float randomNumber = Math.random();
```

 Tip   For the same reason that holds true for instance variables, class variables can benefit from being private and limiting their use to accessor methods only.

Listing 15.1 shows a class called `CountInstances` that uses class and instance variables to keep track of how many instances of that class have been created.

LISTING 15.1   The Full Text of `CountInstances.java`

```
 1: public class CountInstances {
 2:     private static int numInstances = 0;
 3:
 4:     protected static int getNumInstances() {
 5:         return numInstances;
 6:     }
 7:
 8:     private static void addInstance() {
 9:         numInstances++;
10:     }
11:
12:     CountInstances() {
13:         CountInstances.addInstance();
14:     }
15:
16:     public static void main(String[] arguments) {
17:         System.out.println("Starting with " +
18:             CountInstances.getNumInstances() + " instances");
19:         for (int  i = 0; i < 10; ++i)
20:             new CountInstances();
21:         System.out.println("Created " +
22:             CountInstances.getNumInstances() + " instances");
23:     }
24: }
```

The output of this program is as follows:

```
Started with 0 instances
Created 10 instances
```

This example has a number of features. In line 2, you declare a `private` class variable to hold the number of instances (called `numInstances`). It is a class variable (declared `static`) because the number of instances is relevant to the class as a whole, not to any one instance. And it's private so that it follows the same rules as instance variables' accessor methods.

Note the initialization of `numInstances` in that same line. Just as an instance variable is initialized when its instance is created, a class variable is initialized when its class is created. This class initialization happens essentially before anything else can happen to that class, or its instances, so the class in the example will work as planned.

In lines 4–6, you create a `get` method for that private instance variable to get its value (`getNumInstances()`). This method is also declared as a class method because it applies directly to the class variable. The `getNumInstances()` method is declared `protected`, as opposed to `public`, because only this class and perhaps subclasses will be interested in that value; other random classes are therefore restricted from seeing it.

Note that you don't have an accessor method to set the value. The reason is that the value of the variable should be incremented only when a new instance is created; it should not be set to any random value. Instead of creating an accessor method, therefore, you create a special private method called `addInstance()` in lines 8–10 that increments the value of `numInstances` by 1.

Lines 12–14 create the constructor method for this class. Remember, constructors are called when a new object is created, which makes this the most logical place to call `addInstance()` and to increment the variable.

Finally, the `main()` method indicates that you can run this as a Java application and test all the other methods. In the `main()` method, you create 10 instances of the `CountInstances` class, reporting after you're done the value of the `numInstances` class variable (which, predictably, prints `10`).

Final Classes, Methods, and Variables

The `final` modifier is used with classes, methods, and variables to indicate that they will not be changed. It has different meanings for each thing that can be made final, as follows:

- A `final` class cannot be subclassed.
- A `final` method cannot be overridden by any subclasses.
- A `final` variable cannot change in value.

Variables

You got a chance to work with final variables during Day 6. They are often called constant variables (or just constants) because they do not change in value at any time.

With variables, the `final` modifier often is used with `static` to make the constant a class variable. If the value never changes, you don't have much reason to give each object in the same class its own copy of the value. They all can use the class variable with the same functionality.

The following statements are examples of declaring constants:

```
public static final int TOUCHDOWN = 7;
static final TITLE = "Captain";
```

As of Java 2, any kind of variable can be a final variable: class, instance, or local variables. A local variable could not be final in Java 1.0, but that was changed as part of the addition of inner classes to the language.

Methods

Final methods are those that can never be overridden by a subclass. You declare them using the `final` modifier in the class declaration, as in the following example:

```
public final void getSignature() {
    // ...
}
```

The most common reason to declare a method `final` is to make the class run more efficiently. Normally, when a Java runtime environment such as the `java` interpreter runs a method, it checks the current class to find the method first, checks its superclass second, and onward up the class hierarchy until the method is found. This process sacrifices some speed in the name of flexibility and ease of development.

If a method is `final`, the Java compiler can put the executable bytecode of the method directly into any program that calls the method. After all, the method won't ever change because of a subclass that overrides it.

When you are first developing a class, you won't have much reason to use `final`. However, if you need to make the class execute more quickly, you can change a few methods into `final` methods to speed up the process. Doing so removes the possibility of the method being overridden in a subclass later on, so consider this change carefully before continuing.

The Java class library declares many of the commonly used methods `final` so that they can be executed more quickly when utilized in programs that call them.

 **Note** Private methods are final without being declared that way because they can't be overridden in a subclass under any circumstance.

Classes

You finalize classes by using the `final` modifier in the declaration for the class, as in the following:

```
public final class ChatServer {
    // ....
}
```

A final class cannot be subclassed by another class. As with final methods, this process introduces some speed benefits to the Java language at the expense of flexibility.

If you're wondering what you're losing by using final classes, you must not have tried to subclass something in the Java class library yet. Many of the popular classes are final, such as `java.lang.String`, `java.lang.Math`, and `java.net.InetAddress`. If you want to create a class that behaves like strings but with some new changes, you can't subclass `String` and define only the behavior that is different. You have to start from scratch.

All methods in a final class automatically are final themselves, so you don't have to use a modifier in their declarations.

Because classes that can bequeath their behavior and attributes to subclasses are much more useful, you should strongly consider whether the benefit of using `final` on one of your classes is outweighed by the cost.

Abstract Classes and Methods

In a class hierarchy, the higher the class, the more abstract its definition. A class at the top of a hierarchy of other classes can define only the behavior and attributes that are common to all the classes. More specific behavior and attributes are going to fall somewhere lower down the hierarchy.

When you are factoring out common behavior and attributes during the process of defining a hierarchy of classes, you might sometimes find yourself with a class that doesn't ever need to be instantiated directly. Instead, such a class serves as a place to hold common behavior and attributes shared by their subclasses.

These classes are called abstract classes, and they are created using the `abstract` modifier. The following is an example:

```
public abstract class Palette {
    // ...
}
```

An example of an abstract class is `java.awt.Component`, the superclass of all Abstract Windowing Toolkit components. All components inherit from this class, so it contains methods and variables useful to each of them. However, there's no such thing as a generic component that can be added to an interface, so you would never need to create a `Component` object in a program.

Abstract classes can contain anything a normal class can, including constructor methods, because their subclasses might need to inherit the methods. Abstract classes also can contain abstract methods, which are method signatures with no implementation. These methods are implemented in subclasses of the abstract class. Abstract methods are declared with the `abstract` modifier. You cannot declare an abstract method in a nonabstract class. If an abstract class has nothing but abstract methods, you're better off using an interface, as you'll see later today.

Packages

Using packages, as mentioned previously, is a way of organizing groups of classes. A package contains any number of classes that are related in purpose, in scope, or by inheritance.

If your programs are small and use a limited number of classes, you might find that you don't need to explore packages at all. But the more Java programming you create, the more classes you'll find you have. And although those classes might be individually well designed, reusable, encapsulated, and with specific interfaces to other classes, you might find the need for a bigger organizational entity that enables you to group your packages.

Packages are useful for several broad reasons:

- Packages enable you to organize your classes into units. Just as you have folders or directories on your hard disk to organize your files and applications, packages enable you to organize your classes into groups so that you use only what you need for each program.

- Packages reduce problems with conflicts in names. As the number of Java classes grows, so does the likelihood that you'll use the same class name as someone else, opening up the possibility of naming clashes and errors if you try to integrate groups of classes into a single program. Packages enable you to "hide" classes so that conflicts can be avoided.

- Packages enable you to protect classes, variables, and methods in larger ways than on a class-by-class basis, as you learned today. You'll learn more about protections with packages later.

- Packages can be used to identify your classes. For example, if you implement a set of classes to perform some task, you could name a package of those classes with a unique identifier that identifies you or your organization.

Although a package is most typically a collection of classes, packages can also contain other packages, forming yet another level of organization somewhat analogous to the inheritance hierarchy. Each "level" usually represents a smaller, more specific grouping of classes. The Java class library itself is organized along these lines. The top level is called java; the next level includes names such as io, net, util, and awt. The last of them has an even lower level, which includes the package image.

Note

> By convention, the first level of the hierarchy specifies the globally unique name to identify the author or owner of those packages. For example, Sun Microsystems's classes, which are not part of the standard Java environment, all begin with the prefix sun. Classes that Netscape includes with its implementation are contained in the netscape package. The standard package, java, is an exception to this rule because it is so fundamental and because it might someday be implemented by multiple companies.

Using Packages

You've been using packages all along in this book. Every time you use the import command, and every time you refer to a class by its full package name (java.awt.Color, for example), you use packages.

To use a class contained in a package, you can use one of three mechanisms:

- If the class you want to use is in the package java.lang (for example, System or Date), you can simply use the class name to refer to that class. The java.lang classes are automatically available to you in all your programs.

- If the class you want to use is in some other package, you can refer to that class by its full name, including any package names (for example, java.awt.Font).

- For classes that you use frequently from other packages, you can import individual classes or a whole package of classes. After a class or a package has been imported, you can refer to that class by its class name.

If you don't declare that your class belongs to a package, it is put into an unnamed default package. You can refer to that class simply by its class name from anywhere in your code.

Full Package and Class Names

To refer to a class in some other package, you can use its full name: the class name preceded by any package names. You do not have to import the class or the package to use it this way:

```
java.awt.Font f = new java.awt.Font()
```

For classes that you use only once or twice in your program, using the full name makes sense. If, however, you use that class multiple times, or if the package name is really long with lots of subpackages, you should import that class instead to save yourself some typing.

The `import` Declaration

To import classes from a package, use the `import` declaration, as you've used throughout the examples in this book. You can either import an individual class, like this:

```
import java.util.Vector;
```

Or you can import an entire package of classes, using an asterisk (*) to replace the individual class names, like this:

```
import java.awt.*;
```

Note

> Actually, to be technically correct, this declaration doesn't import all the classes in a package; it imports only the classes that have been declared `public`, and even then imports only those classes that the code itself refers to. You'll learn more about this topic in the section titled "Packages and Class Access Control."

Note that the asterisk (*) in this example is not like the one you might use at a command prompt to specify the contents of a folder or to indicate multiple files. For example, if you ask to list the contents of the directory `classes/java/awt/*`, that list includes all the `.class` files and subdirectories, such as `image` and `peer`. Writing `import java.awt.*` imports all the public classes in that package but does not import subpackages such as `image` and `peer`. To import all the classes in a complex package hierarchy, you must explicitly import each level of the hierarchy by hand. Also, you cannot indicate partial class names (for example, L* to import all the classes that begin with L). The only options when using an import declaration are to load all the classes in a package or just a single class.

The import declarations in your class definition go at the top of the file, before any class definitions (but after the package declaration, as you'll see in the next section).

So, should you take the time to import classes individually or just import them as a group? The answer depends on how specific you want to be. Importing a group of classes does not slow down your program or make it any larger; only the classes you actually use in your code are loaded as they are needed. But importing a package does make it a little more confusing for readers of your code to figure out where your classes are coming from. Using individual import declaration or importing packages is mostly a question of your own coding style.

 Note

> If you're coming to Java from C or C++, you might expect the import declaration to work like #include, which results in a very large program by including source code from another file. This isn't the case; import indicates only where the Java compiler can find a class. It doesn't do anything to expand the size of a class.

Name Conflicts

After you have imported a class or a package of classes, you can usually refer to a class name simply by its name, without the package identifier. In one case, you might have to be more explicit: when you have multiple classes with the same name from different packages.

Here's an example. Assume that you import the classes from two packages:

```
import com.naviseek.web.*;
import com.prefect.http.*;
```

Inside the com.naviseek.web package is a class called FTP. Unfortunately, inside the com.prefect.http package, you also find a class called FTP that has an entirely different meaning and implementation. You might wonder whose version of FTP is used if you refer to the FTP class in your own program like this:

```
FTP out = new FTP();
```

The answer is neither; the Java compiler will not compile your program because of the naming conflict. In this case, despite the fact that you imported both classes, you still have to refer to the appropriate FTP class by full package name, as follows:

```
com.prefect.http.FTP out = new
    com.prefect.http.FTP();
```

15

A Note About CLASSPATH and Where Classes Are Located

For Java to be able to use a class, it has to be able to find that class on the file system. Otherwise, you get an error that the class does not exist. Java uses two elements to find classes: the package name itself and the directories listed in your CLASSPATH variable (if you're on a Windows or Solaris system).

First, the package names: Package names map to directory names on the file system, so the class com.naviseek.Mapplet is actually found in the naviseek directory, which in turn is inside the com directory (com\naviseek\Mapplet.class, in other words).

Java looks for those directories, in turn, inside the directories listed in your CLASSPATH variable, if one is provided in your configuration. If you remember back to Day 1, "21st Century Java," when you installed the SDK, you might have used a CLASSPATH variable to point to the various places where your Java classes live. If no CLASSPATH is provided, the SDK looks only in the current folder for classes.

When Java looks for a class you've referenced in your source, it looks for the package and class name in each of those directories and returns an error if it can't find the class file. Most class not found errors result because of misconfigured CLASSPATH variables.

Creating Your Own Packages

Creating a package for some of your classes in Java is not much more complicated than creating a class. You must follow three basic steps, as outlined next.

Picking a Package Name

The first step is to decide on a name. The name you choose for your package depends on how you will be using those classes. Perhaps you will name your package after you or perhaps after the part of the Java system you're working on (such as graphics or messaging). If you intend to distribute your package to the Net at large or as part of a commercial product, you should use a package name that uniquely identifies the author.

A convention for naming packages recommended by Sun is to use your Internet domain name with the elements reversed. If your Internet domain name is naviseek.com, your package name might be com.naviseek. You might want to lengthen the name with something that describes the classes in the package, such as com.naviseek.canasta.

Note   Sun has not followed this recommendation with two of its own Java pack-
             ages—java, the package that comprises the Java class library, and javax,
             classes that extend the library.

The idea is to make sure your package name is unique. Although packages can hide conflicting class names, the protection stops there. You cannot make sure your package
won't conflict with someone else's package if you both use the same package name.

By convention, package names tend to begin with a lowercase letter to distinguish them
from class names. Thus, for example, in the full name of the built-in String class,
java.lang.String, you can more easily separate the package name from the class name
visually. This convention helps reduce name conflicts.

Creating the Folder Structure

Step two in creating packages is to create a folder structure on your hard drive that
matches the package name. If your package has just one name (myPackage), you must
create a folder for that one name only. If the package name has several parts, you have to
create folders within folders. For the package name com.naviseek.canasta, for example, you need to create a com folder, a naviseek folder inside com, and a canasta folder
inside naviseek. Your classes and source files can then go inside the canasta directory.

Adding a Class to a Package

The final step to putting your class inside packages is to add a statement to the class file
above any import declarations that are being used. The package declaration is used
along with the name of the package, as in the following:

```
package com.naviseek.canasta;
```

The single package declaration, if any, must be the first line of code in your source file,
after any comments or blank lines and before any import declarations.

After you start using packages, you should make sure that all your classes belong to
some package to reduce the chance of confusion about where your classes belong.

Packages and Class Access Control

Previously, you learned about access control modifiers for methods and variables. You
also can control access to classes, as you might have noticed when the public modifier
was used in some class declarations on past projects.

15

Classes have the default access control if no modifier is specified, which means that the class is available to all other classes in the same package but is not visible or available outside that package—not even to subpackages. It cannot be imported or referred to by name; classes with package protection are hidden inside the package in which they are contained.

Package protection comes about when you define a class as you have throughout this book, like this:

```
class TheHiddenClass extends AnotherHiddenClass {
    // ...
}
```

To allow a class to be visible and importable outside your package, you can give it public protection by adding the `public` modifier to its definition:

```
public class TheVisibleClass {
    // ...
}
```

Classes declared as `public` can be imported by other classes outside the package.

Note that when you use an `import` statement with an asterisk, you import only the public classes inside that package. Hidden classes remain hidden and can be used only by the other classes in that package.

Why would you want to hide a class inside a package? For the same reason you want to hide variables and methods inside a class: so that you can have utility classes and behavior that are useful only to your implementation, or so that you can limit the interface of your program to minimize the effect of larger changes. As you design your classes, you should take the whole package into consideration and decide which classes you want to declare `public` and which you want to be hidden.

Think of protections not as hiding classes entirely, but more as checking the permissions of a given class to use other classes, variables, and methods.

Creating a good package consists of defining a small, clean set of public classes and methods for other classes to use, and then implementing them by using any number of hidden support classes. You'll see another use for hidden classes later today.

Interfaces

Interfaces, like abstract classes and methods, provide templates of behavior that other classes are expected to implement. Interfaces, however, provide far more functionality to Java and to class and object design than do simple abstract classes and methods.

The Problem of Single Inheritance

After some deeper thought or more complex design experience, however, you might discover that the pure simplicity of the class hierarchy is restrictive, particularly when you have some behavior that needs to be used by classes in different branches of the same tree.

Look at an example that will make the problems clearer. Assume that you have a biological hierarchy with `Animal` at the top, and the classes `Mammal` and `Bird` underneath. Things that define a mammal include bearing live young and having fur. Behavior or features of birds include having a beak and laying eggs. So far, so good, right? So, how do you go about creating a class for the platypus, which has fur and a beak, and lays eggs? You would need to combine behavior from two classes to form the `Platypus` class. And, because classes can have only one immediate superclass in Java, this sort of problem simply cannot be solved elegantly.

Other OOP languages include the concept of multiple inheritance, which solves this problem. With multiple inheritance, a class can inherit from more than one superclass and get behavior and attributes from all its superclasses at once. A problem with multiple inheritance is that it makes a programming language far more complex to learn, to use, and to implement. Questions of method invocation and how the class hierarchy is organized become far more complicated with multiple inheritance, and more open to confusion and ambiguity. And because one of the goals for Java was that it be simple, multiple inheritance was rejected in favor of the simpler single inheritance.

So, how do you solve the problem of needing common behavior that doesn't fit into the strict class hierarchy? Java has another hierarchy altogether separate from the main class hierarchy, a hierarchy of mixable behavior classes. Then, when you create a new class, that class has only one primary superclass, but it can pick and choose different common behaviors from the other hierarchy. This other hierarchy is the interface hierarchy. A Java interface is a collection of abstract behavior that can be mixed into any class to add to that class's behavior that is not supplied by its superclasses. Specifically, a Java interface contains nothing but abstract method definitions and constants—no instance variables and no method implementations.

Interfaces are implemented and used throughout the Java class library whenever a behavior is expected to be implemented by a number of disparate classes. You'll use one of the interfaces in the Java class hierarchy, `java.lang.Comparable`, later today.

Interfaces and Classes

Classes and interfaces, despite their different definitions, have a great deal in common. Interfaces, like classes, are declared in source files and are compiled using the Java

15

compiler into .class files. And, in most cases, anywhere you can use a class (as a data type for a variable, as the result of a cast, and so on), you can also use an interface.

Almost everywhere that this book has a class name in any of its examples or discussions, you can substitute an interface name. Java programmers often say "class" when they actually mean "class or interface." Interfaces complement and extend the power of classes, and the two can be treated almost the same. One of the few differences between them is that an interface cannot be instantiated: new can create only an instance of a class.

Implementing and Using Interfaces

You can do two things with interfaces: use them in your own classes and define your own. For now, start with the former.

To use an interface, you include the implements keyword as part of your class definition:

```
public class AnimatedSign extends javax.swing.JApplet
    implements Runnable {
    //...
}
```

In this example, javax.swing.JApplet is the superclass, but the Runnable interface extends the behavior that it implements.

Because interfaces provide nothing but abstract method definitions, you then have to implement those methods in your own classes, using the same method signatures from the interface. Note that after you include an interface, you have to implement all the methods in that interface; you can't pick and choose the methods you need. By implementing an interface, you're telling users of your class that you support all of that interface.

After your class implements an interface, subclasses of your class inherit those new methods (and can override or overload them) just as if your superclass had actually defined them. If your class inherits from a superclass that implements a given interface, you don't have to include the implements keyword in your own class definition.

Examine one simple example now—creating the new class Orange. Suppose that you already have a good implementation of the class Fruit and an interface, Fruitlike, that represents what a Fruit is expected to be able to do. You want an orange to be a fruit, but you also want it to be a spherical object that can be tossed, rotated, and so on. Here's how to express it all. (Don't worry about the definitions of these interfaces for now; you'll learn more about them later today.)

```
interface  Fruitlike {
    void   decay();
    void   squish();
```

```
    // ...
}

class  Fruit implements Fruitlike {
    private Color myColor;
    private int daysTilIRot;
    // ...
}

interface  Spherelike {
    void  toss();
    void  rotate();
    // ...
}

class  Orange extends Fruit implements Spherelike {
    // toss()ing may squish() me (unique to me)
}
```

Note that the class Orange doesn't have to say implements Fruitlike because, by extending Fruit, it already has! One of the nice things about this structure is that you can change your mind about what class Orange extends (if a really great Sphere class is suddenly implemented, for example), yet class Orange still understands the same two interfaces:

```
class  Sphere implements Spherelike {    // extends Object
    private float  radius;
    // ...
}

class  Orange extends Sphere implements Fruitlike {
    // ... users of Orange never need know about the change!
}
```

Implementing Multiple Interfaces

Unlike with the singly inherited class hierarchy, you can include as many interfaces as you need in your own classes, and your class will implement the combined behavior of all the included interfaces. To include multiple interfaces in a class, just separate their names with commas:

```
public class AnimatedSign extends javax.swing.JApplet
    implements Runnable, Observable {

    // ...
}
```

Note that complications might arise from implementing multiple interfaces. What happens if two different interfaces both define the same method? You can solve this problem in three ways:

15

- If the methods in each of the interfaces have identical signatures, you implement one method in your class and that definition satisfies both interfaces.

- If the methods have different parameter lists, it is a simple case of method overloading; you implement both method signatures, and each definition satisfies its respective interface definition.

- If the methods have the same parameter lists but differ in return type, you cannot create a method that satisfies both. (Remember that method overloading is triggered by parameter lists, not by return type.) In this case, trying to compile a class that implements both interfaces produces a compiler error. Running across this problem suggests that your interfaces have some design flaws that you might need to reexamine.

Other Uses of Interfaces

Remember that almost everywhere that you can use a class, you can use an interface instead. So, for example, you can declare a variable to be of an interface type:

```
Runnable aRunnableObject = new MyAnimationClass()
```

When a variable is declared to be of an interface type, it simply means that any object the variable refers to is expected to have implemented that interface; that is, it is expected to understand all the methods that interface specifies. It assumes that a promise made between the designer of the interface and its eventual implementors has been kept. In this case, because aRunnableObject contains an object of the type Runnable, the assumption is that you can call aRunnableObject.run().

The important point to realize here is that although aRunnableObject is expected to be able to have the run() method, you could write this code long before any classes that qualify are actually implemented (or even created!). In traditional object-oriented programming, you are forced to create a class with "stub" implementations (empty methods, or methods that print silly messages) to get the same effect. You can also cast objects to an interface, just as you can cast objects to other classes. So, for example, go back to that definition of the Orange class, which implemented both the Fruitlike interface (through its superclass, Fruit) and the Spherelike interface. Here you can cast instances of Orange to both classes and interfaces:

```
Orange anOrange = new Orange();
Fruit aFruit = (Fruit)anOrange;
Fruitlike aFruitlike = (Fruitlike)anOrange;
Spherelike aSpherelike = (Spherelike)anOrange;


aFruit.decay(); // fruits decay
```

```
aFruitlike.squish(); // and squish

aFruitlike.toss(); // things that are fruitlike do not toss
aSpherelike.toss(); // but things that are spherelike do

anOrange.decay(); // oranges can do it all
anOrange.squish();
anOrange.toss();
anOrange.rotate();
```

Declarations and casts are used in this example to restrict an orange's behavior to acting more like a mere fruit or sphere.

Finally, note that although interfaces are usually used to mix in behavior to other classes (method signatures), interfaces can also be used to mix in generally useful constants. So, for example, if an interface defines a set of constants, and then multiple classes use those constants, the values of those constants could be globally changed without having to modify multiple classes. This is yet another example of a case in which the use of interfaces to separate design from implementation can make your code more general and more easily maintainable.

Creating and Extending Interfaces

After you use interfaces for a while, the next step is to define your own interfaces. Interfaces look a lot like classes; they are declared in much the same way and can be arranged into a hierarchy. However, you must follow certain rules for declaring interfaces.

New Interfaces

To create a new interface, you declare it like this:

```
interface Growable {
    // ...
}
```

This declaration is, effectively, the same as a class definition, with the word `interface` replacing the word `class`. Inside the interface definition, you have methods and constants. The method definitions inside the interface are `public` and `abstract` methods; you can either declare them explicitly as such, or they are turned into `public` and `abstract` methods if you do not include those modifiers. You cannot declare a method inside an interface to be either `private` or `protected`. So, for example, here's a `Growable` interface with one method explicitly declared `public` and `abstract` (`growIt()`) and one implicitly declared as such (`growItBigger()`):

15

```
public interface Growable {
    public abstract void growIt(); // explicitly public and abstract
    void growItBigger(); // effectively public and abstract
}
```

Note that, as with abstract methods in classes, methods inside interfaces do not have bodies. Remember, an interface is pure design; no implementation is involved.

In addition to methods, interfaces can also have variables, but those variables must be declared `public`, `static`, and `final` (making them constant). As with methods, you can explicitly define a variable to be `public`, `static`, and `final`, or it is implicitly defined as such if you don't use those modifiers. Here's that same `Growable` definition with two new variables:

```
public interface Growable {
    public static final int increment = 10;
    long maxnum = 1000000; // becomes public static and final

    public abstract void growIt(); //explicitly public and abstract
    void growItBigger(); // effectively public and abstract
}
```

Interfaces must have either public or package protection, just like classes. Note, however, that interfaces without the `public` modifier do not automatically convert their methods to `public` and `abstract` nor their constants to `public`. A non-`public` interface also has non-public methods and constants that can be used only by classes and other interfaces in the same package.

Interfaces, like classes, can belong to a package. Interfaces can also import other interfaces and classes from other packages, just as classes can.

Methods Inside Interfaces

Here's one trick to note about methods inside interfaces: Those methods are supposed to be abstract and apply to any kind of class, but how can you define parameters to those methods? You don't know what class will be using them! The answer lies in the fact that you use an interface name anywhere a class name can be used, as you learned earlier. By defining your method parameters to be interface types, you can create generic parameters that apply to any class that might use this interface.

So, for example, consider the interface `Fruitlike`, which defines methods (with no arguments) for `decay()` and `squish()`. You might also have a method for `germinateSeeds()`, which has one argument: the fruit itself. Of what type is that argument going to be? It can't be simply `Fruit` because you may have a class that's `Fruitlike` (that is, one that implements the `Fruitlike` interface) without actually being a fruit. The solution is to declare the argument as simply `Fruitlike` in the interface:

```
public interface Fruitlike {
    public abstract germinate(Fruitlike self) {
        // ...
    }
}
```

Then, in an actual implementation for this method in a class, you can take the generic `Fruitlike` argument and cast it to the appropriate object:

```
public class Orange extends Fruit {

    public germinate(Fruitlike self) {
        Orange theOrange = (Orange)self;
        // ...
    }
}
```

Extending Interfaces

As you can do with classes, you can organize interfaces into a hierarchy. When one interface inherits from another interface, that "subinterface" acquires all the method definitions and constants that its "superinterface" declared. To extend an interface, you use the extends keyword just as you do in a class definition:

```
interface Fruitlike extends Foodlike {
    // ...
}
```

Note that, unlike classes, the interface hierarchy has no equivalent of the `Object` class; this hierarchy is not rooted at any one point. Interfaces can either exist entirely on their own or inherit from another interface.

Note also that, unlike the class hierarchy, the inheritance hierarchy is multiply inherited. So, for example, a single interface can extend as many classes as it needs to (separated by commas in the extends part of the definition), and the new interface will contain a combination of all its parent's methods and constants. Here's an interface definition for an interface called `BusyInterface` that inherits from a whole lot of other interfaces:

```
public interface BusyInterface extends Runnable, Growable, Fruitlike,
    Observable {

    // ...
}
```

In multiply inherited interfaces, the rules for managing method name conflicts are the same as for classes that use multiple interfaces; methods that differ only in return type result in a compiler error.

Creating an Online Storefront

To explore all the topics covered up to this point today, the Storefront application uses packages, access control, interfaces, and encapsulation. This application manages the items in an online storefront, handling two main tasks:

- Calculating the sale price of each item depending on how much of it is presently in stock
- Sorting items according to sale price

The Storefront application consists of two classes, Storefront and Item. These classes will be organized as a new package called com.prefect.ecommerce, so the first task is to define a directory structure on your system where this package's classes will be stored.

SDK 1.3 and other Java development tools look for packages in the folders listed in the system's CLASSPATH. The package name is also taken into account, so if c:\jdk1.3 is in your CLASSPATH, Storefront.class and Item.class could be stored in c:\jdk1.3\com\prefect\ecommerce.

One way to manage your own packages is to create a new folder that will contain packages, and then add a reference to this folder when setting your CLASSPATH.

Tip

On a Windows 95 or 98 system, CLASSPATH can be set at a command line or by editing AUTOEXEC.BAT in the system's root folder. For help setting your CLASSPATH, read Appendix A, "Configuring the Software Development Kit."

After you have created a folder where this package's files will be stored, create Item.java from Listing 15.2.

LISTING 15.2 The Full Text of Item.java

```
1: package com.prefect.ecommerce;
2:
3: import java.util.*;
4:
5: public class Item implements Comparable {
6:     private String id;
7:     private String name;
8:     private double retail;
9:     private int quantity;
10:     private double price;
11:
```

15

LISTING 15.2   continued

```
12:      Item(String idIn, String nameIn, String retailIn, String quanIn) {
13:          id = idIn;
14:          name = nameIn;
15:          retail = Double.parseDouble(retailIn);
16:          quantity = Integer.parseInt(quanIn);
17:
18:          if (quantity > 400)
19:              price = retail * .5D;
20:          else if (quantity > 200)
21:              price = retail * .6D;
22:          else
23:              price = retail * .7D;
24:          price = Math.floor( price * 100 + .5 ) / 100;
25:      }
26:
27:      public int compareTo(Object obj) {
28:          Item temp = (Item)obj;
29:          if (this.price < temp.price)
30:              return 1;
31:          else if (this.price > temp.price)
32:              return -1;
33:          return 0;
34:      }
35:
36:      public String getId() {
37:          return id;
38:      }
39:
40:      public String getName() {
41:          return name;
42:      }
43:
44:      public double getRetail() {
45:          return retail;
46:      }
47:
48:      public int getQuantity() {
49:          return quantity;
50:      }
51:
52:      public double getPrice() {
53:          return price;
54:      }
55: }
```

The Item class is a support class that represents a product sold by an online store. There are private instance variables for the product ID code, name, how many are in stock (quantity), and the retail and sale prices.

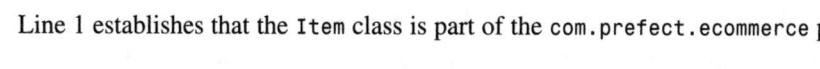

Because all the instance variables of this class are private, no other class can set or retrieve their values. Simple accessor methods are created in lines 36–54 of Listing 15.2 to provide a way for other programs to retrieve these values. Each method begins with get followed by the capitalized name of the variable, which is standard in the Java class library. For example, getPrice() returns a double containing the value of price. No methods are provided for setting any of these instance variables—that will be handled in the constructor method for this class.

Line 1 establishes that the Item class is part of the com.prefect.ecommerce package.

> **Note**
>
> Prefect.com is the personal domain of this book's co-author, so this project follows Sun's package-naming convention by beginning with a top-level domain (com), following it with the developer's domain name (prefect), and then by a name that describes the purpose of the package (ecommerce).

The Item class implements the Comparable interface (line 5), which makes it easy to sort objects of a class. This interface has only one method, compareTo(*Object*), which returns an integer.

The compareTo() method compares two objects of a class: the current object and another object passed as an argument to the method. The value returned by the method defines the natural sorting order for objects of this class:

- If the current object should be sorted above the other object, return -1.
- If the current object should be sorted below the other object, return 1.
- If the two objects are equal, return 0.

You determine in the compareTo() method which of an object's instance variables to consider when sorting. Lines 27–34 override the compareTo() method for the Item class, sorting on the basis of the price variable. Items are sorted by price from highest to lowest.

After you have implemented the Comparable interface for an object, there are two class methods that can be called to sort an array, linked list, or other collection of those objects. You will see this when Storefront.class is created.

The Item() constructor in lines 12–25 takes four String objects as arguments and uses them to set up the id, name, retail, and quantity instance variables. The last two must be converted from strings to numeric values using the Double.parseDouble() and Integer.parseInt() class methods, respectively.

The value of the price instance variable depends on how much of that item is presently in stock:

- If there are more than 400 in stock, price is 50 percent of retail (lines 18–19).

- If there are between 201 and 400, price is 60 percent of retail (lines 20–21).

- For everything else, price is 70 percent of retail (lines 22–23).

Line 24 rounds off price so that it contains two or fewer decimal points, turning a price such as $6.92999999999999 to $6.99. The Math.floor() method rounds off decimal numbers to the next lowest mathematical integer, returning them as a double values.

After you have compiled Item.class, you're ready to create a class that represents a storefront of these products. Create Storefront.java from Listing 15.3.

LISTING 15.3   The Full Text of Storefront.java

```
 1: package com.prefect.ecommerce;
 2:
 3: import java.util.*;
 4:
 5: public class Storefront {
 6:     private LinkedList catalog = new LinkedList();
 7:
 8:     public void addItem(String id, String name, String price,
 9:         String quant) {
10:
11:         Item it = new Item(id, name, price, quant);
12:         catalog.add(it);
13:     }
14:
15:     public Item getItem(int i) {
16:         return (Item)catalog.get(i);
17:     }
18:
19:     public int getSize() {
20:         return catalog.size();
21:     }
22:
23:     public void sort() {
24:         Collections.sort(catalog);
25:     }
26: }
```

The Storefront.class is used to manage a collection of products in an online store. Each product is an Item object, and they are stored together in a LinkedList instance variable named catalog (line 6).

15

The addItem() method in lines 8–13 creates a new Item object based on four arguments sent to the method: the ID, name, price, and quantity in stock of the item. After the item is created, it is added to the catalog linked list by calling its add() method with the Item object as an argument.

The getItem() and getSize() methods provide an interface to the information stored in the private catalog variable. The getSize() method in lines 19–21 calls the catalog.size() method, which returns the number of objects contained in catalog.

Because objects in a linked list are numbered like arrays and other data structures, you can retrieve them using an index number. The getItem() method in lines 15–17 calls catalog.get() with an index number as an argument, returning the object stored at that location in the linked list.

The sort() method in lines 23–25 is where you benefit from the implementation of the Comparable interface in the Item class. The class method Collections.sort() will sort a linked list and other data structures based on the natural sort order of the objects they contain, calling the object's compareTo() method to determine this order.

After you have created the Storefront class, you're ready to develop a program that actually makes use of the com.prefect.ecommerce package. Open the folder on your system where you've been creating the programs of this book (such as \J21work) and create GiftShop.java from Listing 15.4.

LISTING 15.4 The Full Text of Giftshop.java

```
 1: import com.prefect.ecommerce.*;
 2:
 3: public class GiftShop {
 4:     public static void main(String[] arguments) {
 5:         Storefront store = new Storefront();
 6:         store.addItem("C01", "MUG", "9.99", "150");
 7:         store.addItem("C02", "LG MUG", "12.99", "82");
 8:         store.addItem("C03", "MOUSEPAD", "10.49", "800");
 9:         store.addItem("D01", "T SHIRT", "16.99", "90");
10:         store.sort();
11:
12:         for (int i = 0; i < store.getSize(); i++) {
13:             Item show = (Item)store.getItem(i);
14:             System.out.println("\nItem ID: " + show.getId() +
15:                 "\nName: " + show.getName() +
16:                 "\nRetail Price: $" + show.getRetail() +
17:                 "\nPrice: $" + show.getPrice() +
18:                 "\nQuantity: " + show.getQuantity());
19:         }
20:     }
21: }
```

The GiftShop class demonstrates each part of the public interface that the Storefront and Item classes make available. You can do each of the following:

- Create an online store
- Add items to it
- Sort the items by sale price
- Loop through a list of items to display information about each one

Note If you have created the Item.class and Storefront.class files in the same folder as Giftshop.java, you might not be able to compile the program because the Java compiler expects to find those files in their package folder. Move those files to the com\prefect\ecommerce folder and compile Giftshop.java in another folder, such as \J21work.

The output of this program is the following:

```
Item ID: D01
Name: T SHIRT
Retail Price: $16.99
Price: $11.89
Quantity: 90

Item ID: C02
Name: LG MUG
Retail Price: $12.99
Price: $9.09
Quantity: 82

Item ID: C01
Name: MUG
Retail Price: $9.99
Price: $6.99
Quantity: 150

Item ID: C03
Name: MOUSEPAD
Retail Price: $10.49
Price: $5.25
Quantity: 800
```

Many of the implementation details of these classes are hidden from GiftShop and other classes that would make use of the package.

For instance, the programmer who developed GiftShop doesn't need to know that

Storefront uses a linked list to hold all the store's product data. If the developer of Storefront decided later to use a different data structure, as long as getSize() and getItem() returned the expected values, GiftShop would continue to work correctly.

Inner Classes

The classes you have worked with thus far are all members of a package, either because you specified a package name with the package declaration or because the default package was used. Classes that belong to a package are known as *top-level* classes. When Java was introduced, they were the only classes supported by the language.

Beginning with Java 1.1, you could define a class inside a class, as if it were a method or a variable. These types of classes are called *inner* classes. Listing 15.5 contains the Inner applet, which uses an inner class called BlueButton to represent clickable buttons that have a default background color of blue.

LISTING 15.5   The Full Text of Inner.java

```
 1: import java.awt.*;
 2: import javax.swing.*;
 3:
 4: public class Inner extends javax.swing.JApplet {
 5:     JButton b1 = new JButton("One");
 6:     BlueButton b2 = new BlueButton("Two");
 7:
 8:     public void init() {
 9:         Container pane = getContentPane();
10:         pane.setLayout(new FlowLayout());
11:         pane.add(b1);
12:         pane.add(b2);
13:     }
14:
15:     class BlueButton extends JButton {
16:         BlueButton(String label) {
17:             super(label);
18:             this.setBackground(Color.blue);
19:         }
20:     }
21: }
```

Figure 15.1 was produced on appletviewer using the following HTML tag:

```
<applet code="Inner.class" width="200" height="100">
</applet>
```

FIGURE 15.1

The Inner *applet.*

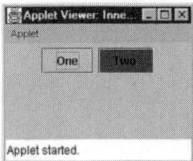

In this example, the BlueButton class isn't any different from a helper class that is included in the same source file as a program's main class file. The only difference is that the helper is defined inside the class file, which has several advantages:

- Inner classes are invisible to all other classes, which means that you don't have to worry about name conflicts between it and other classes.

- Inner classes can have access to variables and methods within the scope of a top-level class that they would not have as a separate class.

In many cases, an inner class is a short class file that exists only for a limited purpose. In the Inner applet, because BlueButton doesn't contain a lot of complex behavior and attributes, it is well suited for implementation as an inner class.

The name of an inner class is associated with the name of the class in which it is contained, and it is assigned automatically when the program is compiled. In the example of the BlueButton class, it is given the name Inner$BlueButton.class by the SDK.

 **Caution**

When you're using inner classes, you must be more careful to include all .class files when making a program available. Each inner class has its own class file, and these class files must be included along with any top-level classes. If you publish the Inner applet on the World Wide Web, for example, you must publish both the Inner.class and Inner$BlueButton.class files together.

Inner classes, although seemingly a minor enhancement, actually represent a significant modification to the language.

Rules governing the scope of an inner class closely match those governing variables. An inner class's name is not visible outside its scope, except in a fully qualified name, which helps in structuring classes within a package. The code for an inner class can use simple names from enclosing scopes, including class and member variables of enclosing classes, as well as local variables of enclosing blocks.

15

In addition, you can define a top-level class as a static member of another top-level class. Unlike an inner class, a top-level class cannot directly use the instance variables of any other class. The ability to nest classes in this way allows any top-level class to provide a package-style organization for a logically related group of secondary top-level classes.

Summary

Today, you learned how to encapsulate an object by using access control modifiers for its variables and methods. You also learned how to use other modifiers such as `static`, `final`, and `abstract` in the development of Java classes and class hierarchies.

To further the effort of developing a set of classes and using them, you learned how classes can be grouped into packages. These groupings better organize your programs and enable the sharing of classes with the many other Java programmers who are making their code publicly available.

Finally, you learned how to implement interfaces and inner classes, two structures that are helpful when designing a class hierarchy.

Q&A

Q Won't using accessor methods everywhere slow down my Java code?

A Not always. As Java compilers improve and can create more optimizations, they will be able to make accessor methods fast automatically, but if you're concerned about speed, you can always declare accessor methods to be `final`, and they'll be comparable in speed to direct instance variable accesses under most circumstances.

Q Based on what I've learned, `private abstract` methods and `final abstract` methods or classes don't seem to make sense. Are they legal?

A Nope, they're compile-time errors, as you have guessed. To be useful, `abstract` methods must be overridden, and `abstract` classes must be subclassed, but neither of those two operations would be legal if they were also `private` or `final`.

Questions

1. What packages are automatically imported into your Java classes?

   (a) None

   (b) The classes stored in the folders of your `CLASSPATH`

   (c) The classes in the `java.lang` package

2. According to the convention for naming packages, what should be the first part of the name of a package you create?

    (a) Your name followed by a period

    (b) Your top-level Internet domain followed by a period

    (c) The text `java` followed by a period

3. If you create a subclass and override a `public` method, what access modifiers can you use with that method?

    (a) `public` only

    (b) `public` or `protected`

    (c) `public`, `protected`, or default access

Answers

1. c. All other packages must be imported if you want to use short class names such as `LinkedList` instead of full package and class names such as `java.util.LinkedList`.

2. b. This convention assumes that all Java package developers will own an Internet domain or have access to one so that the package can be made available for download.

3. a. All `public` methods must remain `public` in subclasses.

Exercises

To extend your knowledge of the subjects covered today, try the following exercises:

- Create a modified version of the `Storefront` project that includes a `noDiscount` variable for each item. When this variable is `true`, sell the item at the retail price.

- Create a `ZipCode` class that uses access control to ensure that its `zipCode` instance variable always has a five-digit value.

Where applicable, exercise solutions are offered on the book's Web site at `http://www.java21pro.com`.

DAY 16

Error Handling and Security

Programmers in any language endeavor to write bug-free programs, programs that never crash, programs that can handle any situation with grace and that can recover from unusual situations without causing the user any undue stress. Good intentions aside, programs like this don't exist.

In real programs, errors occur either because the programmer didn't anticipate every situation the code would get into (or didn't have the time to test the program enough), or because of situations out of the programmer's control—bad data from users, corrupt files that don't have the right data in them, network connections that don't connect, hardware devices that don't respond, sun spots, gremlins, whatever.

In Java, these sorts of strange events that might cause a program to fail are called *exceptions*. Java defines a number of language features that deal with exceptions, including the following:

- How to handle them in your code and recover gracefully from potential problems

- How to tell Java and your methods' users that you're expecting a potential exception
- How to create an exception if you detect one
- How your code is limited, yet made more robust by exceptions

In addition to exceptions, you learn the system being established for Java 2 that enables applets to do things in a program that normally would cause security exceptions.

Exceptions, the Old and Confusing Way

Handling error conditions with most programming languages requires much more work than handling a program that is running properly. It can require a very confusing structure of statements, similar in functionality to Java's if...else and switch blocks, to deal with errors that might occur.

As an example, consider the following statements, which show the structure of how a file might be loaded from disk. Loading a file is something that can be problematic because of a number of different circumstances—disk errors, file-not-found errors, and the like. If the program must have the data from the file in order to operate properly, it must deal with any of these circumstances before continuing.

Here's the structure of one possible solution:

```
int status = loadTextfile();
if (status != 1) {
    // something unusual happened, describe it
    switch (status) {
        case 2:
            // file not found
            break;
        case 3:
            // disk error
            break;
        case 4:
            // file corrupted
            break;
        default:
            // other error
    }
} else {
    // file loaded OK, continue with program
}
```

This code tries to load a file with a method call to loadTextfile(), which has been defined elsewhere in the program. This method returns an integer that indicates whether the file loaded properly (`status == 1`) or an error occurred (`status` equals anything other than 1).

Depending on the error that occurs, the program uses a `switch` statement to try to work around it. The end result is an elaborate block of code in which the most common circumstance—a successful file load—can be lost amid the error-handling code. This is just to handle one possible error. If other errors might take place later in the program, you might end up with more nested `if...else` and `switch-case` blocks.

16

Error management can become a major problem after you start creating larger systems. Different programmers use different special values for handling errors, and might not document them well, if at all. You might inconsistently use errors in your own programs. Code to manage these kinds of errors can often obscure the program's original intent, making that code difficult to read and maintain. Finally, if you try dealing with errors in this way, there's no easy way for the compiler to check for consistency the way it can check to make sure you called a method with the right arguments.

Although the previous example uses Java syntax, you don't have to deal with errors that way in your programs. The language introduces a better way to deal with exceptional circumstances in a program: through the use of a group of classes called exceptions.

Exceptions include errors that could be fatal to your program, but also include other unusual situations. By managing exceptions, you can manage errors and possibly work around them.

Through a combination of special language features, consistency checking at compile time, and a set of extensible exception classes, errors and other unusual conditions in Java programs can be much more easily managed.

Given these features, you can now add a whole new dimension to the behavior and design of your classes, of your class hierarchy, and of your overall system. Your class and interface definitions describe how your program is supposed to behave given the best circumstances. By integrating exception handling into your program design, you can consistently describe how the program will behave when circumstances are not quite as good, and allow people who use your classes to know what to expect in those cases.

Java Exceptions

At this point in the book, it's likely that you've run into at least one Java exception—perhaps you mistyped a method name or made a mistake in your code that caused a problem. Maybe you tried to run a Java applet written using version 2 of the language in a browser that doesn't support it yet, and saw a `Security Exception` message on the browser's status line.

Chances are, a program quit and spewed a bunch of mysterious errors to the screen. Those errors are exceptions. When your program quits, it's because an exception was *thrown*. Exceptions can be thrown by the system, thrown by classes you use, or intentionally thrown in your own programs.

The term *thrown* is fitting because exceptions also can be caught. Catching an exception involves dealing with the exceptional circumstance so that your program doesn't crash—you learn more about this later. *An exception was thrown* is the proper Java terminology for *an error happened*.

The heart of the Java exception system is the exception itself. Exceptions in Java are actual objects—instances of classes that inherit from the class Throwable. An instance of a Throwable class is created when an exception is thrown.

Throwable has two subclasses: Error and Exception. Instances of Error are internal errors in the Java runtime environment (the virtual machine). These errors are rare and usually fatal; there's not much you can do about them (either to catch them or to throw them yourself), but they exist so that Java can use them if it needs to.

The class Exception is more interesting. Subclasses of Exception fall into two general groups:

- Runtime exceptions (subclasses of the class RuntimeException) such as ArrayIndexOutofBounds, SecurityException, and NullPointerException
- Other exceptions such as EOFException and MalformedURLException

Runtime exceptions usually occur because of code that isn't very robust. An ArrayIndexOutofBounds exception, for example, should never be thrown if you're properly checking to make sure your code stays within the bounds of an array. NullPointerException exceptions won't happen unless you try to use a variable before it has been set up to hold an object.

 **Caution**

> If your program is causing runtime exceptions under any circumstances whatsoever, you should fix those problems before you even begin dealing with exception management.

The final group of exceptions is the most interesting because these are the exceptions that indicate something very strange and out of control is happening. EOFExceptions, for example, happen when you're reading from a file and the file ends before you expect it to. A `MalformedURLException` happens when an URL isn't in the right format (perhaps your user typed it wrong). This group includes exceptions that you create to signal unusual cases that might occur in your own programs.

Exceptions are arranged in a hierarchy just as other classes are, where the `Exception` superclasses are more general errors and subclasses are more specific errors. This organization becomes more important to you as you deal with exceptions in your own code.

Most of the exception classes are part of the `java.lang` package (including `Throwable`, `Exception`, and `RuntimeException`). Many of the other packages define other exceptions, and those exceptions are used throughout the class library. For example, the `java.io` package defines a general exception class called `IOException`, which is subclassed not only in the `java.io` package for input and output exceptions (`EOFException` and `FileNotFoundException`), but also in the `java.net` classes for networking exceptions such as `MalformedURLException`.

Managing Exceptions

Now that you know what an exception is, how do you deal with one in your own code? In many cases, the Java compiler enforces exception management when you try to use methods that use exceptions; you need to deal with those exceptions in your own code or it simply won't compile. In this section, you learn about consistency checking and how to use the `try`, `catch`, and `finally` language keywords to deal with exceptions that might occur.

Exception Consistency Checking

The more you work with the Java class libraries, the more likely it is that you'll run into a compiler error (an exception!) similar to this one:

```
XMLParser.java:32: Exception java.lang.InterruptedException
must be caught or it must be declared in the throws clause
of this method.
```

What on earth does that mean? In Java, a method can indicate the kinds of errors it might possibly throw. For example, methods that read from files might potentially throw `IOException` errors, so those methods are declared with a special modifier that indicates potential errors. When you use those methods in your own Java programs, you have to protect your code against those exceptions. This rule is enforced by the compiler itself, in the same way the compiler checks to make sure that you're using methods with the right number of arguments and that all your variable types match the thing you're assigning to them.

16

Why is this check in place? It makes your programs less likely to crash with fatal errors because you know, up front, the kind of exceptions that can be thrown by the methods a program uses. You no longer have to carefully read the documentation or the code of an object you're going to use to ensure that you've dealt with all the potential problems—Java does the checking for you. On the other side, if you define your methods so that they indicate the exceptions they can throw, Java can tell your objects' users to handle those errors.

Protecting Code and Catching Exceptions

Assume that you've been happily coding and you ran into that exception message during a test compile. According to the message, you have to either catch the error or declare that your method throws it. Deal with the first case: catching potential exceptions.

You do two things to catch an exception:

- You protect the code that contains the method that might throw an exception inside a `try` block.
- You deal with an exception inside a `catch` block.

What `try` and `catch` effectively mean is, "Try this bit of code that might cause an exception. If it executes okay, go on with the program. If the code doesn't execute, catch the exception and deal with it."

You've seen `try` and `catch` before, when you first dealt with threads. On Day 13, "Threads and Animation," you used code to pause between each frame in an animation sequence:

```
try {
    Thread.sleep(1000);
} catch (InterruptedException e) { }
```

Although this example uses `try` and `catch`, it's not a very good use of it. Here's what's happening in these statements: The `Thread.sleep()` class method could potentially throw an exception of type `InterruptedException`, which signifies that the thread has been interrupted for some reason.

To handle this exception, the call to `sleep()` is placed inside a `try` block and an associated `catch` block has been set up. This `catch` block receives any `InterruptedException` objects that are thrown within the `try` block.

The reason this isn't a good example of exception handling is that there isn't anything inside the `catch` clause—in other words, you'll catch the exception if it happens, but then you'll do nothing to respond to its occurrence. In all but the simplest cases (such as this one, where the exception really doesn't matter), you need something inside the catch block that does something to clean up after the exception happens.

The part of the catch clause inside the parentheses is similar to a method definition's argument list. It contains the class of exception to be caught and a variable name (e is commonly used). You can refer to that exception object inside the catch block.

One common use for this object is to call its getMessage() method. This method is present in all exceptions, and it displays a detailed error message describing what happened.

16

The following example is a revised version of the try...catch statement used on Day 9:

```
try {
    Thread.sleep(1000);
} catch (InterruptedException e) {
    System.out.println("Error: " + e.getMessage());
}
```

For another example, revisit the subject of file handling in Java. If you have a program that reads from a file, it's likely to use one of the input/output stream classes you'll learn about on Day 17, "Handling Data Through Java Streams." The basic idea is that you open a connection to a file and use the read() method to get data from that file. This can cause several exceptions, such as a disk error or an attempt to read more data than the file contains. In either of these cases, the read() method would throw an IOException, which would either cause the program to stop executing if you didn't catch the exception or cause the program to crash.

By putting your read() method inside a try block, you can deal gracefully with that error inside a catch block. You could clean up after the error and return to some safe state, patch things up enough for the program to proceed, or if all else fails, save as much of the current program's state as possible and exit.

The following example tries to read from a file and catches exceptions if they happen:

```
try {
    while (numBytes <= mybuffer.length) {
        myInputStream.read(myBuffer);
        numBytes++;
    }
} catch (IOException e) {
    System.out.println("Oops! IO Exception -- only read " + numBytes);
    // other cleanup code
}
```

Here, the "other cleanup code" can be anything you want it to be; you can go on with the program using the partial information you got from the file, or perhaps you want to display a dialog box enabling the user to select a different file.

The examples you have seen thus far catch a specific type of exception. Because exception classes are organized into a hierarchy and you can use a subclass anywhere a superclass is expected, you can catch groups of exceptions within the same `catch` statement.

As an example, there are several different types of `IOException` exceptions, such as `EOFException` and `FileNotFoundException`. By catching `IOException`, you also catch instances of any `IOException` subclass.

What if you do want to catch very different kinds of exceptions, even if they aren't related by inheritance? You can use multiple `catch` blocks for a single `try`, like this:

```
try {
    // code that might generate exceptions
} catch (IOException e) {
    // handle IO exceptions
} catch (ClassNotFoundException e) {
    // handle class not found exceptions
} catch (InterruptedException e) {
    // handle interrupted exceptions
}
```

In a multiple `catch` block, the first `catch` block that matches will be executed and the rest ignored.

 **Caution**
> You can run into unexpected problems by using an `Exception` superclass in a `catch` block followed by one or more of its subclasses in their own `catch` blocks. For example, the input-output exception `IOException` is the superclass of the end-of-file exception `EOFException`. If you put an `IOException` block above an `EOFException` block, the subclass will never catch any exceptions.

The `finally` Clause

Suppose that there is some action in your code that you absolutely must do, no matter what happens, whether an exception is thrown or not. This is usually to free some external resource after acquiring it, to close a file after opening it, or something similar. Although you could put that action both inside a `catch` block and outside it, that would be duplicating the same code in two different places. Instead, put one copy of that code inside a special optional part of the `try...catch` block called `finally`. The following example shows how a `try...catch...finally` block is structured:

```
try {
    readTextfile();
} catch (IOException e) {
```

```
    // deal with IO errors
} finally {
    closeTextfile();
}
```

The `finally` statement is actually useful outside exceptions; you can also use it to execute cleanup code after a `return`, a `break`, or a `continue` inside loops. For the latter cases, you can use a `try` statement with a `finally` but without a `catch` statement.

Listing 16.1 shows how a `finally` statement can be used inside a method.

16

LISTING 16.1 The Full Text of `HexRead.java`

```
 1: class HexRead {
 2:     String[] input = { "000A110D1D260219 ",
 3:         "78700F1318141E0C ",
 4:         "6A197D45B0FFFFFF " };
 5:
 6:     public static void main(String[] arguments) {
 7:         HexRead hex = new HexRead();
 8:         for (int i = 0; i < hex.input.length; i++)
 9:             hex.readLine(hex.input[i]);
10:     }
11:
12:     void readLine(String code) {
13:         try {
14:             for (int j = 0; j + 1 < code.length(); j += 2) {
15:                 String sub = code.substring(j, j+2);
16:                 int num = Integer.parseInt(sub, 16);
17:                 if (num == 255)
18:                     return;
19:                 System.out.print(num + " ");
20:             }
21:         } finally {
22:             System.out.println("**");
23:         }
24:         return;
25:     }
26: }
```

The output of this program is as follows:

```
0 10 17 13 29 38 2 25 **
120 112 15 19 24 20 30 12 **
106 25 125 69 176 **
```

The `HexRead` application reads sequences of two-digit hexadecimal numbers and displays their decimal values. There are three sequences to read:

- 000A110D1D260219

- 78700F1318141E0C

- 6A197D45B0FFFFFF

As you learned on Day 3, "The ABCs of Java," hexadecimal is a base-16 numbering system where the single-digit numbers range from 00 (decimal 0) to 0F (decimal 15) and double-digit numbers range from 10 (decimal 16) to FF (decimal 255).

Line 15 of the program reads two characters from code, the string that was sent to the readLine() method, by calling the string's substring(*int*, *int*) method.

Note

> In the substring() method of the String class, you select a substring in a somewhat counterintuitive way. The first argument specifies the index of the first character to include in the substring, but the second argument does not specify the last character. Instead, the second argument indicates the index of the last character plus 1. A call to substring(2, 5) for a string would return the characters from index position 2 to index position 4.

The two-character substring contains a hexadecimal number stored as a String. The Integer class method parseInt can be used with a second argument to convert this number into an integer. Use 16 as the argument for a hexadecimal (base 16) conversion, 8 for an octal (base 8) conversion, and so on.

In the HexRead application, the hexadecimal FF is used to fill out the end of a sequence and should not be displayed as a decimal value. This is accomplished by using a try-finally block in lines 13–23 of Listing 16.1.

The try...finally block causes an unusual thing to happen when the return statement is encountered at line 18. You would expect return to cause the readLine() method to be exited immediately.

Because it is within a try...finally block, the statement within the finally block is executed no matter how the try block is exited. The text "**" is displayed at the end of a line of decimal values.

Declaring Methods That Might Throw Exceptions

In previous examples, you learned how to deal with methods (by protecting code and catching any exceptions that occur) that might throw exceptions. The Java compiler

16

checks to make sure that you've somehow dealt with a method's exceptions—but how did it know which exceptions to tell you about in the first place?

The answer is that the original method indicated in its signature contains the exceptions that it might possibly throw. You can use this mechanism in your own methods—in fact, it's good style to do so to make sure your classes' other users are alerted to the errors your methods may come across.

To indicate that a method may possibly throw an exception, you use a special clause in the method definition called `throws`.

The `throws` Clause

To indicate that some code in your method's body may throw an exception, simply add the `throws` keyword after the signature for the method (before the opening brace) with the name or names of the exception that your method throws:

```
public boolean myMethod(int x, int y) throws AnException {
    // ...
}
```

If your method may throw multiple kinds of exceptions, you can put them all in the `throws` clause, separated by commas:

```
public boolean myOtherMethod(int x, int y)
    throws AnException, AnotherException, AThirdException {
        // ...
}
```

Note that, as with `catch`, you can use a superclass of an exceptions group to indicate that your method may throw any subclass of that exception:

```
public void YetAnotherMethod() throws IOException {
    // ...
}
```

Keep in mind that adding a `throws` method to your method definition simply means that the method might throw an exception if something goes wrong, not that it actually will. The `throws` clause simply provides extra information to your method definition about potential exceptions and allows Java to make sure that your method is being used correctly by other people.

Think of a method's overall description as a contract between the designer of that method (or class) and the caller of the method. (You can be on either side of that contract, of course.) Usually the description indicates the types of a method's arguments, what it returns, and the general semantics of what it normally does. By using `throws`, you also add information about the abnormal things the method can do. This new part of the contract helps separate and make explicit all the places where exceptional conditions should be handled in your program, and that makes large-scale design easier.

Which Exceptions Should You Throw?

After you decide to declare that your method might throw an exception, you must decide which exceptions it might throw (and actually throw them or call a method that will throw them—you'll learn about throwing your own exceptions in the next section). In many instances, this is apparent from the operation of the method itself. Perhaps you're creating and throwing your own exceptions, in which case, you'll know exactly which exceptions to throw.

You don't really have to list all the possible exceptions that your method could throw; some exceptions are handled by the runtime itself and are so common (not common per se, but ubiquitous) that you don't have to deal with them. In particular, exceptions of either class `Error` or `RuntimeException` (or any of their subclasses) do not have to be listed in your `throws` clause. They get special treatment because they can occur anywhere within a Java program and are usually conditions that you, as the programmer, did not directly cause. One good example is `OutOfMemoryError`, which can happen anywhere, at any time, and for any number of reasons. These two kinds of exceptions are called *implicit exceptions*, and you don't have to worry about them.

Implicit exceptions are exceptions that are `RuntimeException` and `Error` subclasses. Implicit exceptions are usually thrown by the Java runtime itself. You do not have to declare that your method throws them.

 Note

> You can, of course, choose to list these errors and runtime exceptions in your `throws` clause if you like, but your method's callers will not be forced to handle them; only non-runtime exceptions must be handled.

All other exceptions are called *explicit exceptions* and are potential candidates for a `throws` clause in your method.

Passing On Exceptions

In addition to declaring methods that throw exceptions, there's one other instance in which your method definition may include a `throws` clause. In this case, you want to use a method that throws an exception, but you don't want to catch or deal with that exception. In many cases, it might make more sense for the method that calls your method to deal with that exception rather than for you to deal with it. There's nothing wrong with this; it's a fairly common occurrence that you won't actually deal with an exception, but will pass it back to the method that calls yours. At any rate, it's a better idea to pass on exceptions to calling methods than to catch them and ignore them.

Rather than using the `try` and `catch` clauses in your method's body, you can declare your method with a `throws` clause such that it, too, might possibly throw the appropriate exception. It's then the responsibility of the method that calls your method to deal with that exception. This is the other case that satisfies the Java compiler that you have done something with a given method. Here's another way of implementing an example that reads characters from a stream:

```
public void readFile(String filename) throws IOException {
    // open the file, initialize the stream here
    while (numBytes <= myBuffer.length) {
        myInputStream.read(myBuffer);
    numBytes;++
}
```

This example is similar to an example used previously today; remember that the `read()` method was declared to throw an `IOException`, so you had to use `try` and `catch` to use it. After you declare your method to throw an exception, however, you can use other methods that also throw those exceptions inside the body of this method, without needing to protect the code or catch the exception.

> **Note**
>
> You can, of course, deal with other exceptions using `try` and `catch` in the body of your method in addition to passing on the exceptions you listed in the `throws` clause. You also can both deal with the exception in some way and then rethrow it so that your method's calling method has to deal with it anyhow. You learn how to throw methods in the next section.

throws and Inheritance

If your method definition overrides a method in a superclass that includes a `throws` clause, there are special rules for how your overridden method deals with `throws`. Unlike other parts of the method signature that must mimic those of the method it is overriding, your new method does not require the same set of exceptions listed in the `throws` clause.

Because there's a possibility that your new method might deal better with exceptions rather than just throwing them, your method can potentially throw fewer types of exceptions. It could even throw no exceptions at all. That means that you can have the following two class definitions and things will work just fine:

```
public class RadioPlay {
    public void startPlaying() throws SoundException {
        // ...
    }
}
public class StereoPlay extends RadioPlay {
    public void startPlaying() {
        // ...
    }
}
```

The converse of this rule is not true: A subclass method cannot throw more exceptions (either exceptions of different types or more general exception classes) than its superclass method.

Creating and Throwing Your Own Exceptions

There are two sides to every exception: the side that throws the exception and the side that catches it. An exception can be tossed around a number of times to a number of methods before it's caught, but eventually it will be caught and dealt with.

Who does the actual throwing? Where do exceptions come from? Many exceptions are thrown by the Java runtime or by methods inside the Java classes themselves. You can also throw any of the standard exceptions that the Java class libraries define, or you can create and throw your own exceptions. This section describes all these things.

Throwing Exceptions

Declaring that your method throws an exception is useful only to your method's users and to the Java compiler, which checks to make sure that all your exceptions are being dealt with—but the declaration itself doesn't do anything to actually throw that exception should it occur; you have to do that yourself in the body of the method.

Remember that exceptions are all instances of some exception class, of which there are many defined in the standard Java class library. You need to create a new instance of an exception class to throw an exception. After you have that instance, use the throw statement to throw it. The simplest way to throw an exception is like this:

```
NotInServiceException() nis = new NotInServiceException();
throw nis;
```

Note

You can throw only objects that are subclasses of Throwable. This is different from C++'s exceptions, which enable you to throw objects of any type.

Depending on the exception class you're using, the exception also may have arguments to its constructor that you can use. The most common of these is a string argument, which enables you to describe the actual problem in greater detail (which can be very useful for debugging purposes). Here's an example:

```
NotInServiceException() nis = new
    NotInServiceException("Exception: Database Not in Service");
throw nis;
```

After an exception is thrown, the method exits immediately, without executing any other code (other than the code inside `finally`, if that block exists) and without returning a value. If the calling method does not have a `try` or `catch` surrounding the call to your method, the program might very well exit based on the exception you threw.

Creating Your Own Exceptions

Although there are a fair number of exceptions in the Java class library that you can use in your own methods, you might need to create your own exceptions to handle different kinds of errors your programs run into. Fortunately, creating new exceptions is easy.

Your new exception should inherit from some other exception in the Java hierarchy. All user-created exceptions should be part of the `Exception` hierarchy rather than the `Error` hierarchy, which is reserved for errors involving the Java virtual machine. Look for an exception that's close to the one you're creating; for example, an exception for a bad file format would logically be an `IOException`. If you can't find a closely related exception for your new exception, consider inheriting from `Exception`, which forms the "top" of the exception hierarchy for explicit exceptions. (Remember that implicit exceptions, which include subclasses of `Error` and `RuntimeException`, inherit from `Throwable`.)

Exception classes typically have two constructors: The first takes no arguments and the second takes a single string as an argument. In the latter case, you should call `super()` in that constructor to make sure that the string is applied to the right place in the exception.

Beyond those three rules, exception classes look just like other classes. You can put them in their own source files and compile them just as you would other classes:

```
public class SunSpotException extends Exception {
    public SunSpotException() {}
    public SunSpotException(String msg) {
        super(msg);
    }
}
```

Combining `throws`, `try`, and `throw`

What if you want to combine all the approaches shown so far? You'd like to handle incoming exceptions yourself in your method, but also you'd like to pass the exception up to your caller. Simply using `try` and `catch` doesn't pass on the exception, and simply adding a `throws` clause doesn't give you a chance to deal with the exception. If you want to both manage the exception and pass it on to the caller, use all three mechanisms: the `throws` clause, the `try` statement, and a `throw` statement to explicitly rethrow the exception.

```
public void responsibleExceptionalMethod() throws IOException {
    MessageReader mr = new MessageReader();

    try {
        mr.loadHeader();
    } catch (IOException e) {
        // do something to handle the
        // IO exception
        throw e; // rethrow the exception
    }
}
```

This works because exception handlers can be nested. You handle the exception by doing something responsible with it, but decide that it is too important to not give an exception handler that might be in your caller a chance to handle it as well. Exceptions float all the way up the chain of method callers this way (usually not being handled by most of them) until, at last, the system itself handles any uncaught exceptions by aborting your program and printing an error message. This is not such a bad idea in a standalone program, but it can cause the browser to crash in an applet. Most browsers protect themselves from this disaster by catching all exceptions themselves whenever they run an applet, but you can never tell. If it's possible for you to catch an exception and do something intelligent with it, you should.

When and When Not to Use Exceptions

Because throwing, catching, and declaring exceptions are related concepts and can be very confusing, here's a quick summary of when to do what.

When to Use Exceptions

You can do one of three things if your method calls another method that has a `throws` clause:

- Deal with the exception by using `try` and `catch` statements
- Pass the exception up the calling chain by adding your own `throws` clause to your method definition
- Perform both of the preceding methods by catching the exception using `catch` and then explicitly rethrowing it using `throw`

In cases where a method throws more than one exception, you can handle each of those exceptions differently. For example, you might catch some of those exceptions while allowing others to pass up the calling chain.

If your method throws its own exceptions, you should declare that it throws those methods using the `throws` statement. If your method overrides a superclass method that has a `throws` statement, you can throw the same types of exceptions or subclasses of those exceptions; you cannot throw any different types of exceptions.

Finally, if your method has been declared with a `throws` clause, don't forget to actually throw the exception in the body of your method using the `throw` statement.

16

When Not to Use Exceptions

There are several cases in which you should not use exceptions, even though they might seem appropriate at the time.

First, you should not use exceptions if the exception is something that you expect and could avoid easily with a simple expression. For example, although you can rely on an `ArrayIndexOutofBounds` exception to indicate when you've gone past the end of the array, it's easy to use the array's `length` variable to prevent you from going out of bounds.

In addition, if your users will enter data that must be an integer, testing to make sure that the data is an integer is a much better idea than throwing an exception and dealing with it somewhere else.

Exceptions take up a lot of processing time for your Java program. A simple test or series of tests will run much faster than exception handling and make your program more efficient. Exceptions should be used only for truly exceptional cases that are out of your control.

It's also easy to get carried away with exceptions and to try to make sure that all your methods have been declared to throw all the possible exceptions that they can possibly throw. This makes your code more complex in general; in addition, if other people will be using your code, they'll have to deal with handling all the exceptions that your methods might throw.

You're making more work for everyone involved when you get carried away with exceptions. Declaring a method to throw either few or lots of exceptions is a trade-off; the more exceptions your method can throw, the more complex that method is to use. Declare only the exceptions that have a reasonably fair chance of happening and that make sense for the overall design of your classes.

Bad Style Using Exceptions

When you first start using exceptions, it might be appealing to work around the compiler errors that result when you use a method that declared a throws statement. Although it is legal to add an empty catch clause or to add a throws statement to your own method (and there are appropriate reasons for doing both these things), intentionally dropping exceptions without dealing with them subverts the checks that the Java compiler does for you.

The Java exception system was designed so that if an error can occur, you're warned about it. Ignoring those warnings and working around them makes it possible for fatal errors to occur in your program—errors that you could have avoided with a few lines of code. Even worse, adding throws statements to your methods to avoid exceptions means that the users of your methods (objects further up in the calling chain) will have to deal with them. You've just made your methods more difficult to use.

Compiler errors regarding exceptions are there to remind you to reflect on these issues. Take the time to deal with the exceptions that might affect your code. This extra care will richly reward you as you reuse your classes in later projects and in larger and larger programs. Of course, the Java class library has been written with exactly this degree of care, and that's one of the reasons it's robust enough to be used in constructing all your Java projects.

Using Digital Signatures to Identify Applets

One of the fundamental assumptions of Java's applet security strategy is that you can't trust anyone on the World Wide Web. Such thinking might sound cynical, but what it means in practice is this: Java security assumes that someone might try to write malicious applets, so it prevents anything malicious from being attempted. As a result, any language feature that has potential for abuse has been blocked from use in applets. The prohibited features include the following:

- Reading files from the system on which the applet is running
- Writing files to the system on which the applet is running
- Getting information about a file on the system
- Deleting a file on the system
- Making a network connection to any machine other than the one that delivered the Web page containing the applet
- Displaying a window that does not include the standard "Java applet window" warning

Java 2 makes it possible for applets to do everything that a Java application can do—but only if they come from a trusted applet provider and are digitally signed to verify their authenticity. A digital signature is an encrypted file or files that accompany a program indicating exactly from whom the file(s) came. The document that represents this digital signature is called a *certificate*.

In order to establish trust, an applet provider must verify its identity using a group called a *certificate authority*. Ideally, these groups are not affiliated with the applet developer in any way, and they should have an established reputation as a reliable company. At present, the following companies are offering certificate authentication services in some form:

- VeriSign—The first and most widely established certificate authority, offering both Microsoft- and Netscape-specific authorization. `http://www.verisign.com`
- Thawte Certification—A newer authority for Microsoft, Netscape, and test certificates. `http://www.thawte.com`

Other companies offer certification for clients in specific geographic areas. Netscape lists the certificate authorities it works with at the following Web address:

`https://certs.netscape.com`

Users, armed with the knowledge of who produced a program, can decide whether that group or individual should be trusted. People who are familiar with ActiveX controls will recognize this system—it's similar to how ActiveX programs are made available on World Wide Web pages.

> **Note**
>
> The general security model described here is the official one created by Sun for use in its own HotJava browser and any browsers that fully support Java 2. Netscape and Microsoft have introduced their own security models for use in their browsers, so an applet must implement a different system for each browser in which it should run. Fortunately, the systems are similar, so mastering one makes it much easier to learn the others.

You also can establish levels of security other than complete trust (an applet can do anything) or no trust (an applet can't do anything that might be damaging). Java 2 enables this with a set of classes called *permissions*.

For now, all applets will be fully restricted unless the developer takes steps to digitally sign the applet and a user goes through the process of establishing that the developer is trustworthy.

A Digital Signature Example

You might find understanding the applet-trusting process easier if you use these three fictional entities: an applet developer called Fishhead Software, a Java industry group called J-Signer, and a Web user named Gilbert.

Fishhead Software offers a game applet on its Web site that saves high scores and other information on the user's hard drive. This capability isn't normally possible with an applet—disk access is a definite no-no. For the game to be playable, Fishhead must digitally sign the applet and enable users to establish Fishhead as a trusted programmer.

This process has five steps:

1. Fishhead Software uses `keytool`, a tool that comes with the SDK, to create two encrypted files called *a public key* and *a private key*. Together, these keys are an electronic ID card that fully identifies the company. Fishhead makes sure that its private key is hidden from anyone else. It can—and should—make its public key available to anyone as a partial form of ID.

2. Fishhead Software needs an entity that can verify who it is. It sends its public key and a descriptive file about Fishhead Software to an independent group that Java users are likely to trust—J-Signer.

3. J-Signer checks out Fishhead Software to see that it's a legitimate group with the same public key that was sent to J-Signer. When Fishhead passes muster, J-Signer creates a new encrypted file called a certificate. It is sent back to Fishhead.

4. Fishhead creates a Java archive file that contains its game applet and all related files. With a public key, private key, and a certificate, Fishhead Software can now use the `jar` tool to digitally sign the archive file.

5. Fishhead puts the signed archive on the Web site along with a way to download its public key.

Following this process is all that Fishhead Software needs to do to make the applet available to anyone who trusts the company enough to run it over the Web. One of the people who decides to trust Fishhead is a Web user named Gilbert, who has a Java 2–enabled browser.

His process is simpler:

1. Gilbert realizes that he can't run Fishhead's new game applet without establishing the company as a trustworthy programmer. He downloads Fishhead's public key.

2. Deciding that Fishhead is an organization he can trust, Gilbert uses another SDK security tool, `jarsigner`, in conjunction with Fishhead's public key to add the company to his system's list of trusted programmers.

Now Gilbert can play Fishhead's game applet to his heart's content. Depending on how the security permissions are established within the applet, it could possibly read and write files and open other network connections, as well as other insecure things. This means that malicious or unintentionally damaging code can be executed on Gilbert's system, but this is also true of any software that he could install and run on his computer. The advantage of a digital signature is that the programmers are clearly identified. Ask yourself how many virus writers would distribute their work under any kind of system that provided a trail of digital crumbs leading straight to their house.

One aspect of the new Java security model you might be unclear about is why you have a public key and a private key. If they can be used together to identify someone, how can the public key alone be used as an ID for Fishhead?

A public key and a private key are a matched set. Because they fully identify Fishhead Software, that entity is the only one that has access to both keys. Otherwise, someone else could pretend to be Fishhead and no one could tell it was a fake. If Fishhead protects its private key, it protects its identity and reputation.

When J-Signer uses a public key to verify Fishhead's identity, its main function is to make sure that the public key really belongs to the company. Because public keys can be given to anyone, Fishhead can make its public key available on its Web site. As part of its certification process, J-Signer could download this public key and compare it to the one it received. The certifying group acts as a substitute of sorts for the private key, verifying that the public key is legitimate. The certificate that is issued is linked to the public key, which can be used only with Fishhead's private key.

Anyone can issue a certificate for a public key using the `keytool` program—Fishhead Software could even certify itself. However, doing so would make it much harder for users to trust the company than if a well-established, independent certification group were used.

Working together, the public key, private key, and certificate can create a reliable digital signature for a Java archive. Sun's Java documentation for `keytool`, `jarsigner`, permissions, and other new security features are available from the following Web address:

```
http://java.sun.com/j2se/1.3/docs/guide/security/
```

Browser-Specific Signatures

At the time of this writing, the only way to digitally sign an applet is to use the procedures set up by the developers at Netscape and Microsoft for their own Web browsers. You have to use their own tools and sign an applet using both procedures if you want to reach the users of both browsers.

Signing an applet for use on Microsoft Internet Explorer requires the following:

- A Microsoft Authenticode digital ID from a company that verifies your identity, such as VeriSign or Thawte.
- Internet Explorer 4.0 or higher.
- The following tools from the Microsoft Java Software Development Kit: `cabarc.exe`, `chktrust.exe`, `signcode.exe`, and the `.DLL` files `javasign.dll` and `signer.dll`. This kit is available for download from Microsoft at `http://www.microsoft.com/java/download.htm`.

Signing an applet for Netscape Navigator browsers requires the following:

- A Netscape Object Signing software publishing digital ID, which can be acquired from one of the companies listed at the Web page with the address `https://certs.netscape.com`.
- The Netscape Signing Tool, which is available from the Web page with the address `http://developer.netscape.com/software/signedobj/jarpack.html`. The Signing Tool has a feature for using a test certificate before you have acquired a digital ID.

 Note

> Documentation for the use of these tools is available from the places at Microsoft and Netscape where they were downloaded from the Web. In addition, Daniel Griscom of Suitable Systems has compiled an excellent Java code signing resource at the following Web address:
>
> `http://www.suitable.com/Doc_CodeSigning.shtml`

Security Policies

Prior to Java 2, there was a built-in assumption that all applications should be completely trusted and allowed to use all features of the language.

To make it easier to create applications that are more limited, applications now are held to the same security scrutiny as applets.

In general practice, this will not change how applications are written or run—those you have created during this book should not have encountered any security exceptions as they ran on your system. This occurs because the security policy set up during the SDK installation is the most liberal possible, allowing all the features available to applications.

The security policy is stored in a file called `java.policy`. This file can be found in the `jre\lib\security\` subfolder of the main SDK installation folder. This file can be edited with any text editor, although you shouldn't alter it unless you're well versed in how it is established. You also can use a graphical policy-editing tool included with the SDK called `policytool`.

An overview of the security features implemented in Java 2 is available from Sun at the following Web page:

```
http://java.sun.com/j2se/1.3/docs/guide/security/spec/security-
spec.doc.html
```

16

Summary

Today you learned about how exceptions aid your program's design and robustness. Exceptions give you a way of managing potential errors in your programs and of alerting your programs' users that potential errors can occur. By using `try`, `catch`, and `finally`, you can protect code that might result in exceptions, catch and handle those exceptions if they occur, and execute code whether an exception was generated or not.

Handling exceptions is only half of the equation; the other half is generating and throwing exceptions yourself. Today you learned about the `throws` clause, which tells your method's users that the method might throw an exception. `throws` can also be used to pass on an exception from a method call in the body of your method.

In addition to the information given by the `throws` clause, you learned how to actually create and throw your own methods by defining new exception classes and by throwing instances of any exception classes using `throw`.

You also learned the basics of how Java 2's security model are being implemented, and how the different browser developers are offering a way to bypass the normal applet security with digital signatures.

Q&A

Q I'm still not sure I understand the differences between exceptions, errors, and runtime exceptions. Is there another way of looking at them?

A Errors are caused by dynamic linking or virtual machine problems, and are thus too low-level for most programs to care about—or be able to handle even if they did care about them. Runtime exceptions are generated by the normal execution of Java code, and although they occasionally reflect a condition you will want to handle explicitly, more often they reflect a coding mistake made by the programmer, and thus simply need to print an error to help flag that mistake. Exceptions that are non-runtime exceptions (IOException exceptions, for example) are conditions that, because of their nature, should be explicitly handled by any robust and well thought-out code. The Java class library has been written using only a few of these, but those few are extremely important to using the system safely and correctly. The compiler helps you handle these exceptions properly via its throws clause checks and restrictions.

Q **Is there any way to get around the strict restrictions placed on methods by the throws clause?**

A Yes. Suppose that you have thought long and hard and have decided that you need to circumvent this restriction. This is almost never the case because the right solution is to go back and redesign your methods to reflect the exceptions that you need to throw. Imagine, however, that for some reason a system class has you in a straitjacket. Your first solution is to subclass RuntimeException to make up a new, exempt exception of your own. Now you can throw it to your heart's content because the throws clause that was annoying you does not need to include this new exception. If you need a lot of such exceptions, an elegant approach is to mix in some novel exception interfaces to your new Runtime classes. You're free to choose whatever subset of these new interfaces you want to catch (none of the normal Runtime exceptions need be caught), while any leftover Runtime exceptions are allowed to go through that otherwise annoying standard method in the library.

Questions

1. What keyword is used to jump out of a try block and into a finally block?

    (a) catch

    (b) return

    (c) while

2. What class should be the superclass of any exceptions you create in Java?

    (a) Throwable

    (b) Error

    (c) Exception

3. If you want to digitally sign an applet you created, which of the following must you get from a trusted source rather than creating it yourself?

    (a) A public key

    (b) A private key

    (c) A certificate

Answers

1. b.

2. c. `Throwable` and `Error` are of use primarily by Java. The kinds of errors you'll want to note in your programs belong in the `Exception` hierarchy.

3. c. The certificate must be issued by a group that verifies your identity and is trusted by the audience that will use your applet.

16

Exercises

To extend your knowledge of the subjects covered today, try the following exercises:

- Create a modified version of the HexRead application that pauses for 10 seconds whenever a decimal value of 25 is read.

- Creat an application that takes a command-line argument and determines if it is an integer or not, using the `Integer.parseInt()` method described on Day 6. This method throws a `NumberFormatException`.

Where applicable, exercise solutions are offered on the book's Web site at `http://www.java21pro.com`.

Handling Data Through Java Streams

Many of the programs you create with Java will need to interact with some kind of data source. There are countless ways in which information can be stored on a computer, including files on a hard drive or CD-ROM, pages on a Web site, and even the computer's memory itself.

You might expect there to be a different technique to handle each of the different storage devices. Fortunately, that isn't the case.

In Java, information can be stored and retrieved using a communications system called streams, which are implemented in the `java.io` package.

Today, you learn how to create input streams to read information and output streams to store information. You'll work with each of the following:

- Byte streams, which are used to handle bytes, integers, and other simple data types

- Character streams, which handle text files and other text sources

You can deal with all data the same way once you know how to work with an input stream, whether it's coming from a disk, the Internet, or even another program. The converse is true for output streams.

Streams are a powerful mechanism for handling data, but you don't pay for that power with classes that are difficult to implement.

Introduction to Streams

All data in Java is written and read using streams. Streams, like the bodies of water that share the same name, carry something from one place to another.

NEW TERM A *stream* is a path traveled by data in a program. An *input stream* sends data from a source into a program, and an *output stream* sends data out of a program to a destination.

You deal with two different types of streams today: byte streams and character streams. *Byte streams* carry integers with values that range from 0 to 255. A diverse assortment of data can be expressed in byte format, including numerical data, executable programs, Internet communications, and bytecode—the class files that are run by a Java virtual machine.

In fact, every kind of data imaginable can be expressed using either individual bytes or a series of bytes combined with each other.

NEW TERM *Character streams* are a specialized type of byte stream that handles only textual data. They're distinguished from byte streams because Java's character set supports Unicode, a standard that includes many more characters than could be expressed easily using bytes.

Any kind of data that involves text should use character streams, including text files, Web pages, and other common types of text.

Using a Stream

Whether you're using a byte stream or a character stream, the procedure for using either in Java is largely the same. Before you start working with the specifics of the `java.io` classes, it's useful to walk through the process of creating and using streams.

For an input stream, the first step is to create an object that is associated with the data source. For example, if the source is a file on your hard drive, a `FileInputStream` object could be associated with this file.

After you have a stream object, you can read information from that stream by using one of the object's methods. `FileInputStream` includes a `read()` method that returns a byte read from the file.

When you're done reading information from the stream, you call the `close()` method to indicate that you're done using the stream.

For an output stream, you begin by creating an object that's associated with the data's destination. One such object can be created from the `BufferedWriter` class, which represents an efficient way to create text files.

The `write()` method is the simplest way to send information to the output stream's destination. For instance, a `BufferedWriter` `write()` method can send individual characters to an output stream.

As you do with input streams, the `close()` method is called on an output stream when you have no more information to send.

Filtering a Stream

The simplest way to use a stream is to create it and then call its methods to send or receive data, depending on whether it's an output stream or an input stream.

Many of the classes you work with today achieve more sophisticated results by associating a filter with a stream before reading or writing any data.

NEW TERM   A *filter* is a type of stream that modifies the way an existing stream is handled. Think of a beaver dam on a mountain stream. The dam regulates the flow of water from the points upstream to the points downstream. The dam is a type of filter—remove it, and the water would flow in a much less-controlled fashion.

The procedure for using a filter on a stream is basically as follows:

- Create a stream associated with a data source or a data destination.
- Associate a filter with that stream.
- Read or write data from the filter rather than the original stream.

The methods you call on a filter are the same as the methods you would call on a stream: There are `read()` and `write()` methods, just as there would be on an unfiltered stream.

You can even associate a filter with another filter, so the following path for information is possible: an input stream associated with a text file, which is filtered through a Spanish-to-English translation filter, which is then filtered through a no-profanity filter, and is finally sent to its destination—a human being who wants to read it.

If this is still confusing in the abstract, you get plenty of opportunity to see it in practice in the following sections.

17

Byte Streams

All byte streams are either a subclass of InputStream or OutputStream. These classes are abstract, so you cannot create a stream by creating objects of these classes directly. Instead, you create streams through one of their subclasses, such as the following:

- FileInputStream and FileOutputStream—Byte streams stored in files on disk, CD-ROM, or other storage devices.
- DataInputStream and DataOutputStream—A filtered byte stream from which data such as integers and floating-point numbers can be read.

InputStream is the superclass of all input streams.

File Streams

The byte streams you work with most are likely to be file streams, which are used to exchange data with files on your disk drives, CD-ROMs, or other storage devices you can refer to by using a folder path and filename.

You can send bytes to a file output stream and receive bytes from a file input stream.

File Input Streams

A file input stream can be created with the FileInputStream(*String*) constructor. The *String* argument should be the name of the file. You can include a path reference with the filename, which enables the file to be in a different folder than the class loading it. The following statement creates a file input stream from the file scores.dat:

```
FileInputStream fis = new FileInputStream("scores.dat");
```

After you create a file input stream, you can read bytes from the stream by calling its read() method. This method returns an integer containing the next byte in the stream. If the method returns a –1, which is not a possible byte value, this signifies that the end of the file stream has been reached.

To read more than one byte of data from the stream, call its read(*byte[ ]*, *int*, *int*) method. The arguments to this method are as follows:

- A byte array where the data will be stored
- The element inside the array where the data's first byte should be stored
- The number of bytes to read

Unlike the other read() method, this does not return data from the stream. Instead, it returns an integer that represents the number of bytes read or –1 if no bytes were read before the end of the stream was reached.

The following statements use a `while` loop to read the data in a `FileInputStream` object called `df`:

```
int newByte = 0;
while (newByte != -1) {
    newByte = df.read();
    System.out.print(newByte + " ");
}
```

This loop reads the entire file referenced by `df` one byte at a time and displays each byte followed by a space character. It also will display a –1 when the end of the file has been reached—you could guard against this easily with an `if` statement.

The `ReadBytes` application in Listing 17.1 uses a similar technique to read a file input stream. The input stream's `close()` method is used to close the stream after the last byte in the file is read. This must be done to free system resources associated with the open file.

17

LISTING 17.1   The Full Text of `ReadBytes.java`

```
 1: import java.io.*;
 2:
 3: public class ReadBytes {
 4:     public static void main(String[] arguments) {
 5:         try {
 6:             FileInputStream file = new
 7:                 FileInputStream("class.dat");
 8:             boolean eof = false;
 9:             int count = 0;
10:             while (!eof) {
11:                 int input = file.read();
12:                 System.out.print(input + " ");
13:                 if (input == -1)
14:                     eof = true;
15:                 else
16:                     count++;
17:             }
18:             file.close();
19:             System.out.println("\nBytes read: " + count);
20:         } catch (IOException e) {
21:             System.out.println("Error -- " + e.toString());
22:         }
23:     }
24: }
```

If you run this program, you'll get the following error message:

```
Error -- java.io.FileNotFoundException: class.dat (The system
cannot find the file specified).
```

This error message looks like the kind of exceptions generated by the compiler, but it's actually coming from the catch block in lines 20–22 of the ReadBytes application. The exception is being thrown by lines 6–7 because the class.dat file cannot be found.

You need a file of bytes in which to read. This can be any file—a suitable choice is the program's class file, which contains the bytecode instructions executed by the Java virtual machine. Create this file by making a copy of ReadBytes.class and renaming the copy class.dat. Don't rename ReadBytes.class itself, or you won't be able to run the program.

> **Tip**
>
> Windows 95 and Windows NT users can use the MS-DOS prompt to create class.dat. Go to the folder that contains ReadBytes.class and use the following DOS command:
>
> copy ReadBytes.class class.dat
>
> UNIX users can type the following at a command line:
>
> cp ReadBytes.class.dat

When you run the program, each byte in class.dat will be displayed, followed by a count of the total number of bytes. If you used ReadBytes.class to create class.dat, the last several lines of output should resemble the following:

```
101 109 46 111 117 116 46 112 114 105 110 116 108 110 40 34 92 110 66 121 116
101 115 32 114 101 97 100 58 32 34 32 43 32 99 111 117 110 116 41 59 13 10 32
32 32 32 32 32 32 32 125 32 99 97 116 99 104 32 40 73 79 69 120 99 101 112 116
105 111 110 32 101 41 32 123 13 10 32 32 32 32 32 32 32 32 32 32 32 32 83 121
115 116 101 109 46 111 117 116 46 112 114 105 110 116 108 110 40 34 69 114 114
111 114 32 45 45 32 34 32 43 32 101 46 116 111 83 116 114 105 110 103 40 41 41
59 13 10 32 32 32 32 32 32 32 125 13 10 32 32 32 32 125 13 10 125 13 10 -1
Bytes read: 717
```

The number of bytes displayed on each line of output depends on the column width that text can occupy on your system. The bytes shown depend on the file used to create class.dat.

File Output Streams

A file output stream can be created with the FileOutputStream(String) constructor. The usage is the same as the FileInputStream(String) constructor, so you can specify a path along with a filename.

You have to be careful when specifying the file to which to write an output stream. If it's the same as an existing file, the original will be wiped out when you start writing data to the stream.

You can create a file output stream that appends data after the end of an existing file with the FileOutputStream(*String*, *boolean*) constructor. The string specifies the file and the Boolean argument should equal true to append data instead of overwriting any existing data.

The file output stream's write(*int*) method is used to write bytes to the stream. After the last byte has been written to the file, the stream's close() method closes the stream.

To write more than one byte, the write(*byte[]*, *int*, *int*) method can be used. This works in a manner similar to the read(*byte[]*, *int*, *int*) method described previously. The arguments to this method are the byte array containing the bytes to output, the starting point in the array, and the number of bytes to write.

The WriteBytes application in Listing 17.2 writes an integer array to a file output stream.

17

LISTING 17.2 The Full Text of WriteBytes.java

```
 1: import java.io.*;
 2:
 3: public class WriteBytes {
 4:     public static void main(String[] arguments) {
 5:         int[] data = { 71, 73, 70, 56, 57, 97, 15, 0, 15, 0,
 6:             128, 0, 0, 255, 255, 255, 0, 0, 0, 44, 0, 0, 0,
 7:             0, 15, 0, 15, 0, 0, 2, 33, 132, 127, 161, 200,
 8:             185, 205, 84, 128, 241, 81, 35, 175, 155, 26,
 9:             228, 254, 105, 33, 102, 121, 165, 201, 145, 169,
10:             154, 142, 172, 116, 162, 240, 90, 197, 5, 0, 59 };
11:         try {
12:             FileOutputStream file = new
13:                 FileOutputStream("pic.gif");
14:             for (int i = 0; i < data.length; i++)
15:                 file.write(data[i]);
16:             file.close();
17:         } catch (IOException e) {
18:             System.out.println("Error -- " + e.toString());
19:         }
20:     }
21: }
```

The following things are taking place in this program:

- Lines 5–10   An integer array called data is created with 66 elements.
- Lines 12 and 13   A file output stream is created with the filename pic.gif in the same folder as the WriteBytes.class file.

- Lines 14 and 15   A for loop is used to cycle through the data array and write each element to the file stream.
- Line 16   The file output stream is closed.

After you run this program, you can display the pic.gif file in any Web browser or graphics editing tool. It's a small image file in the GIF format, as shown in Figure 17.1.

Figure 17.1

The pic.gif *file (enlarged).*

Filtering a Stream

NEW TERM   *Filtered streams* are streams that modify the information sent through an existing stream. They are created using one of the subclasses FilterInputStream or FilterOutputStream.

These classes do not handle any filtering operations themselves. Instead, they have subclasses such as BufferInputStream and DataOutputStream that handle specific types of filtering.

Byte Filters

Information is delivered more quickly if it can be sent in large chunks, even if those chunks are received faster than they can be handled.

As an example of this, consider which of the following book-reading techniques is faster:

- A friend loans you a book in its entirety and you read it.
- A friend loans you a book one page at a time, and doesn't give you a new page until you finish the previous one.

Obviously, the first technique is going to be faster and more efficient. The same benefits are true of buffered streams in Java.

NEW TERM A *buffer* is a storage place where data can be kept before it is needed by a program that reads or writes that data. By using a buffer, you can get data without always going back to the original source of the data.

Buffered Streams

A buffered input stream fills a buffer with data that hasn't been handled yet, and when a program needs this data, it looks to the buffer first before going to the original stream source. This is much more efficient—using a stream without a buffer is analogous to being given a book one page at a time. Any slowdowns from that stream will slow down efforts to use it.

Buffered byte streams use the `BufferedInputStream` and `BufferedOutputStream` classes.

A buffered input stream is created using one of the following two constructors:

- `BufferedInputStream(InputStream)`—Creates a buffered input stream for the specified `InputStream` object.
- `BufferedInputStream(InputStream, int)`—Creates the specified `InputStream` buffered stream with a buffer of `int` size.

The simplest way to read data from a buffered input stream is to call its `read()` method with no arguments, which normally returns an integer from 0 to 255 representing the next byte in the stream. If the end of the stream has been reached and no byte is available, -1 is returned.

You also can use the `read(byte[], int, int)` method available for other input streams, which loads stream data into a byte array.

A buffered output stream is created using one of these two constructors:

- `BufferedOutputStream(OutputStream)`—Creates a buffered output stream for the specified `OutputStream` object.
- `BufferedOutputStream(OutputStream, int)`—Creates the specified `OutputStream` buffered stream with a buffer of `int` size.

The output stream's `write(int)` method can be used to send a single byte to the stream, and the `write(byte[], int, int)` method writes multiple bytes from the specified byte array. The arguments to this method are the byte array, array starting point, and number of bytes to write.

When data is directed to a buffered stream, it will not be output to its destination until the stream fills up or the buffered stream's `flush()` method is called.

17

Note
Although the `write()` method takes an integer as input, the value should be from 0 to 255. If you specify a number higher than 255, it will be stored as the remainder of the number divided by 256. You can test this when running the project created later in this section.

The next project, the `BufferDemo` application, writes a series of bytes to a buffered output stream associated with a text file. The first and last integer in the series are specified as two command-line arguments, as in the following statement:

```
java BufferDemo 7 64
```

After writing to the textfile, `BufferDemo` creates a buffered input stream from the file and reads the bytes back in. Listing 17.3 contains the source code.

LISTING 17.3   The Full Text of `BufferDemo.java`

```
 1: import java.io.*;
 2:
 3: public class BufferDemo {
 4:     public static void main(String[] arguments) {
 5:         int start = 0;
 6:         int finish = 255;
 7:         if (arguments.length > 1) {
 8:             start = Integer.parseInt(arguments[0]);
 9:             finish = Integer.parseInt(arguments[1]);
10:         } else if (arguments.length > 0)
11:             start = Integer.parseInt(arguments[0]);
12:         ArgStream as = new ArgStream(start, finish);
13:         System.out.println("\nWriting: ");
14:         boolean success = as.writeStream();
15:         System.out.println("\nReading: ");
16:         boolean readSuccess = as.readStream();
17:     }
18: }
19:
20: class ArgStream {
21:     int start = 0;
22:     int finish = 255;
23:
24:     ArgStream(int st, int fin) {
25:         start = st;
26:         finish = fin;
27:     }
28:
29:     boolean writeStream() {
30:         try {
```

```
31:              FileOutputStream file = new
32:                  FileOutputStream("numbers.dat");
33:              BufferedOutputStream buff = new
34:                  BufferedOutputStream(file);
35:              for (int out = start; out <= finish; out++) {
36:                  buff.write(out);
37:                  System.out.print(" " + out);
38:              }
39:              buff.close();
40:              return true;
41:          } catch (IOException e) {
42:              System.out.println("Exception: " + e.getMessage());
43:              return false;
44:          }
45:      }
46:
47:      boolean readStream() {
48:          try {
49:              FileInputStream file = new
50:                  FileInputStream("numbers.dat");
51:              BufferedInputStream buff = new
52:                  BufferedInputStream(file);
53:              int in = 0;
54:              do {
55:                  in = buff.read();
56:                  if (in != -1)
57:                      System.out.print(" " + in);
58:              } while (in != -1);
59:              buff.close();
60:              return true;
61:          } catch (IOException e) {
62:              System.out.println("Exception: " + e.getMessage());
63:              return false;
64:          }
65:      }
66: }
```

17

This program's output depends on the two arguments specified at the command line. If you use java BufferDemo 4 13, the following output is shown:

```
Writing:
 4 5 6 7 8 9 10 11 12 13
Reading:
 4 5 6 7 8 9 10 11 12 13
```

This application consists of two classes: BufferDemo and a helper class called ArgStream. BufferDemo gets the two arguments' values, if they are provided, and uses them in the ArgStream() constructor.

The writeStream() method of ArgStream is called in line 14 to write the series of bytes to a buffered output stream, and the readStream() method is called in line 16 to read those bytes back.

Even though they are moving data in two different directions, the writeStream() and readStream() methods are substantially the same. They take the following format:

- The filename, numbers.dat, is used to create a file input or output stream.
- The file stream is used to create a buffered input or output stream.
- The buffered stream's write() method is used to send data, or the read() method is used to receive data.
- The buffered stream is closed.

Because file streams and buffered streams throw IOException objects if an error occurs, all operations involving the streams are enclosed in a try...catch block for this exception.

 Tip

The boolean return values in writeStream() and readStream() indicate whether the stream operation was completed successfully. They aren't used in this program, but it's good practice to let callers of these methods know if something goes wrong.

Data Streams

If you need to work with data that isn't represented as bytes or characters, you can use data input and data output streams. These streams filter an existing byte stream so that each of the following primitive types can be read or written directly from the stream: boolean, byte, double, float, int, long, and short.

A data input stream is created with the DataInputStream(InputStream) constructor. The argument should be an existing input stream such as a buffered input stream or a file input stream.

Conversely, a data output stream requires the DataOutputStream(OutputStream) constructor, which indicates the associated output stream.

The following list indicates the read and write methods that apply to data input and output streams, respectively:

- readBoolean(), writeBoolean(boolean)
- readByte(), writeByte(integer)

- readDouble(), writeDouble(*double*)
- readFloat(), writeFloat(*float)*
- readInt(), writeInt(*int*)
- readLong(), writeLong(*long*)
- readShort(), writeShort(*int*)

Each of the input methods returns the primitive data type indicated by the name of the method. For example, the readFloat() method returns a float value.

There also are readUnsignedByte() and readUnsignedShort() methods that read in unsigned byte and short values. These are not data types supported by Java, so they are returned as int values.

17

> **Note**
>
> Unsigned bytes have values ranging from 0 to 255. This differs from Java's byte variable type, which ranges from –128 to 127. Along the same line, an unsigned short value ranges from 0 to 65,535, instead of the –32,768 to 32,767 range supported by Java's short type.

A data input stream's different read methods do not all return a value that can be used as an indicator that the end of the stream has been reached.

As an alternative, you can wait for an EOFException (end-of-file exception) to be thrown when a read method reaches the end of a stream. The loop that reads the data can be enclosed in a try block, and the associated catch statement should only handle EOFException objects. You can call close() on the stream and take care of other cleanup tasks inside the catch block.

This is demonstrated in the next project. Listings 17.4 and 17.5 contain two programs that use data streams. The WritePrimes application writes the first 400 prime numbers as integers to a file called 400primes.dat. The ReadPrimes application reads the integers from this file and displays them.

LISTING 17.4 The Full Text of WritePrimes.java

```
1: import java.io.*;
2:
3: class WritePrimes {
4:     public static void main(String[] arguments) {
5:         int[] primes = new int[400];
6:         int numPrimes = 0;
```

LISTING 17.4   continued

```
 7:            // candidate: the number that might be prime
 8:            int candidate = 2;
 9:            while (numPrimes < 400) {
10:                if (isPrime(candidate)) {
11:                    primes[numPrimes] = candidate;
12:                    numPrimes++;
13:                }
14:                candidate++;
15:            }
16:
17:            try {
18:                // Write output to disk
19:                FileOutputStream file = new
20:                    FileOutputStream("400primes.dat");
21:                BufferedOutputStream buff = new
22:                    BufferedOutputStream(file);
23:                DataOutputStream data = new
24:                    DataOutputStream(buff);
25:
26:                for (int i = 0; i < 400; i++)
27:                    data.writeInt(primes[i]);
28:                data.close();
29:            } catch (IOException e) {
30:                System.out.println("Error -- " + e.toString());
31:            }
32:        }
33:
34:        public static boolean isPrime(int checkNumber) {
35:            double root = Math.sqrt(checkNumber);
36:            for (int i = 2; i <= root; i++) {
37:                if (checkNumber % i == 0)
38:                    return false;
39:            }
40:            return true;
41:        }
42: }
```

LISTING 17.5   The Full Text of ReadPrimes.java

```
1: import java.io.*;
2:
3: class ReadPrimes {
4:     public static void main(String[] arguments) {
5:         try {
6:             FileInputStream file = new
7:                 FileInputStream("400primes.dat");
8:             BufferedInputStream buff = new
```

```
 9:                        BufferedInputStream(file);
10:                DataInputStream data = new
11:                        DataInputStream(buff);
12:
13:        try {
14:            while (true) {
15:                int in = data.readInt();
16:                System.out.print(in + " ");
17:            }
18:        } catch (EOFException eof) {
19:            buff.close();
20:        }
21:    } catch (IOException e) {
22:        System.out.println("Error -- " + e.toString());
23:    }
24:  }
25: }
```

17

Most of the WritePrimes application is taken up with logic to find the first 400 prime numbers. After you have an integer array containing the first 400 primes, it is written to a data output stream in lines 17–31.

This application is an example of using more than one filter on a stream. The stream is developed in a three-step process:

- A file output stream that is associated with a file called 400primes.dat is created.
- A new buffered output stream is associated with the file stream.
- A new data output stream is associated with the buffered stream.

The writeInt() method of the data stream is used to write the primes to the file.

The ReadPrimes application is simpler because it doesn't need to do anything regarding prime numbers—it just reads integers out of a file using a data input stream.

Lines 6–11 of ReadPrimes are nearly identical to statements in the WritePrimes application, except that input classes are used instead of output classes.

The try...catch block that handles EOFException objects is in lines 13–20. The work of loading the data takes place inside the try block.

The while(true) statement creates an endless loop. This isn't a problem—an EOFException will automatically occur when the end of the stream is encountered at some point as the data stream is being read. The readInt() method in line 15 reads integers from the stream.

The last several output lines of the ReadPrimes application should resemble the following:

2137 2141 2143 2153 2161 2179 2203 2207 2213 2221 2237 2239 2243 22
51 2267 2269 2273 2281 2287 2293 2297 2309 2311 2333 2339 2341 2347
 2351 2357 2371 2377 2381 2383 2389 2393 2399 2411 2417 2423 2437 2
441 2447 2459 2467 2473 2477 2503 2521 2531 2539 2543 2549 2551 255
7 2579 2591 2593 2609 2617 2621 2633 2647 2657 2659 2663 2671 2677
2683 2687 2689 2693 2699 2707 2711 2713 2719 2729 2731 2741

Character Streams

After you know how to handle byte streams, you have most of the skills needed to handle character streams as well. Character streams are used to work with any text that is represented by the ASCII character set or Unicode, an international character set that includes ASCII.

Examples of files that you can work with through a character stream are plain text files, HTML documents, and Java source files.

The classes used to read and write these streams are all subclasses of `Reader` and `Writer`. These should be used for all text input instead of dealing directly with byte streams.

Note

> The techniques for handling character streams were greatly improved after Java 1.0 with the introduction of the `Reader` and `Writer` classes and their subclasses; they enable Unicode character support and better handling of text. A Java applet that's 1.0-ready can read characters by using the byte stream classes described previously.

Reading Text Files

`FileReader` is the main class used when reading character streams from a file. This class inherits from `InputStreamReader`, which reads a byte stream and converts the bytes into integer values that represent Unicode characters.

A character input stream is associated with a file using the `FileReader(String)` constructor. The string indicates the file, and it can contain path folder references in addition to a filename.

The following statement creates a new `FileReader` called `look` and associates it with a text file called `index.html`:

```
FileReader look = new FileReader("index.html");
```

After you have a file reader, you can call the following methods on it to read characters from the file:

- `read()` returns the next character on the stream as an integer.
- `read(char[], int, int)` reads characters into the specified character array with the indicated starting point and number of characters read.

The second method works like similar methods for the byte input stream classes. Instead of returning the next character, it returns either the number of characters that were read or -1 if no characters were read before the end of the stream was reached.

The following method loads a text file using the `FileReader` object `text` and displays its characters:

```
FileReader text = new
    FileReader("readme.txt");
int inByte;
do {
    inByte = text.read();
    if (inByte != -1)
        System.out.print( (char)inByte );
} while (inByte != -1);
System.out.println("");
text.close();
```

17

Because a character stream's `read()` method returns an integer, you must cast this to a character before displaying it, or storing it in an array, or using it to form a string. Every character has a numeric code that represents its position in the Unicode character set. The integer read off the stream is this numeric code.

If you want to read a line of text at a time instead of reading a file character by character, you can use the `BufferedReader` class in conjunction with a `FileReader`.

The `BufferedReader` class reads a character input stream and buffers it for better efficiency. You must have an existing `Reader` object of some kind to create a buffered version. The following constructors can be used to create a `BufferedReader`:

- `BufferedReader(Reader)`—Creates a buffered character stream associated with the specified `Reader` object, such as `FileReader`.
- `BufferedReader(Reader, int)`—Creates a buffered character stream associated with the specified `Reader` and with a buffer of `int` size.

A buffered character stream can be read using the `read()` and `read(char[], int, int)` methods described for `FileReader`. You can read a line of text using the `readLine()` method.

The `readLine()` method returns a `String` object containing the next line of text on the stream, not including the character or characters that represent the end of a line. If the end of the stream is reached, the value of the string returned will be equal to `null`.

An end-of-line is indicated by any of the following:

- A newline character (`'\n'`)
- A carriage return character (`'\r'`)
- A carriage return followed by a newline

The project contained in Listing 17.6 is a Java application that reads its own source file through a buffered character stream.

LISTING **17.6** The Full Text of ReadSource.java

```
 1: import java.io.*;
 2:
 3: public class ReadSource {
 4:     public static void main(String[] arguments) {
 5:         try {
 6:             FileReader file = new
 7:                 FileReader("ReadSource.java");
 8:             BufferedReader buff = new
 9:                 BufferedReader(file);
10:             boolean eof = false;
11:             while (!eof) {
12:                 String line = buff.readLine();
13:                 if (line == null)
14:                     eof = true;
15:                 else
16:                     System.out.println(line);
17:             }
18:             buff.close();
19:         } catch (IOException e) {
20:             System.out.println("Error -- " + e.toString());
21:         }
22:     }
23: }
```

Much of this program is comparable to projects created earlier today, as illustrated:

- Lines 6 and 7—An input source is created—the FileReader object associated with the file ReadSource.java.
- Lines 8 and 9—A buffering filter is associated with that input source—the BufferedReader object buff.
- Lines 11–17—A readLine() method is used inside a while loop to read the text file one line at a time. The loop ends when the method returns the value null.

The ReadSource application's output is the text file ReadSource.java.

Writing Text Files

The `FileWriter` class is used to write a character stream to a file. It's a subclass of `OutputStreamWriter`, which has behavior to convert Unicode character codes to bytes.

There are two `FileWriter` constructors: `FileWriter(String)` and `FileWriter(String, boolean)`. The string indicates the name of the file that the character stream will be directed into, which can include a folder path. The optional Boolean argument should equal `true` if the file is to be appended to an existing text file. As with other stream-writing classes, you must take care not to accidentally overwrite an existing file when you're appending data.

Three methods of `FileWriter` can be used to write data to a stream:

- `write(int)`—Write a character.
- `write(char[], int, int)`—Write characters from the specified character array with the indicated starting point and number of characters written.
- `write(String, int, int)`—Write characters from the specified string with the indicated starting point and number of characters written.

The following example writes a character stream to a file using the `FileWriter` class and the `write(int)` method:

```
FileWriter letters = new FileWriter("alphabet.txt");
for (int i = 65; i < 91; i++)
    letters.write( (char)i );
letters.close();
```

The `close()` method is used to close the stream after all characters have been sent to the destination file. The following is the `alphabet.txt` file produced by this code:

```
ABCDEFGHIJKLMNOPQRSTUVWXYZ
```

The `BufferedWriter` class can be used to write a buffered character stream. This class's objects are created with the `BufferedWriter(Writer)` or `BufferedWriter(Writer, int)` constructors. The `Writer` argument can be any of the character output stream classes, such as `FileWriter`. The optional second argument is an integer indicating the size of the buffer to use.

`BufferedWriter` has the same three output methods as `FileWriter`: `write(int)`, `write(char[], int, int)`, and `write(String, int, int)`.

Another useful output method is `newLine()`, which sends the preferred end-of-line character (or characters) for the platform being used to run the program.

| Tip | The different end-of-line markers can create conversion hassles when transferring files from one operating system to another, such as when a Windows 95 user uploads a file to a Web server that's running the Linux operating system. Using newLine() instead of a literal (such as '\n') makes your program more user-friendly across different platforms. |

The close() method is called to close the buffered character stream and make sure that all buffered data is sent to the stream's destination.

Files and Filename Filters

In all of the examples thus far, a string has been used to refer to the file that's involved in a stream operation. This often is sufficient for a program that uses files and streams, but if you want to copy files, rename files, or handle other tasks, a File object can be used.

File, which also is part of the java.io package, represents a file or folder reference. The following File constructors can be used:

- File(*String*)—Creates a File object with the specified folder—no filename is indicated, so this refers only to a file folder.

- File(*String*, *String*)—Creates a File object with the specified folder path and the specified name.

- File(*File*, *String*)—Creates a File object with its path represented by the specified *File* and its name indicated by the specified *String*.

You can call several useful methods on a File object.

The exists() method returns a Boolean value indicating whether the file exists under the name and folder path established when the File object was created. If the file exists, you can use the length() method to return a long integer indicating the size of the file in bytes.

The renameTo(*File*) method renames the file to the name specified by the *File* argument. A Boolean value is returned, indicating whether the operation was successful.

The delete() or deleteOnExit() method should be called to delete a file or a folder. The delete() method attempts an immediate deletion (returning a Boolean value indicating whether it worked). The deleteOnExit() method waits to attempt deletion until the rest of the program has finished running. This method does not return a value—you couldn't do anything with the information—and the program must finish at some point for it to work.

The `mkdir()` method can be used to create the folder specified by the `File` object it is called on. It returns a Boolean value indicating success or failure. There is no comparable method to remove folders because `delete()` can be used on folders as well as files.

As with any file-handling operations, these methods must be handled with care to avoid deleting the wrong files and folders or wiping out data. There's no method available to undelete a file or folder.

Each of the methods will throw a `SecurityException` if the program does not have the security to perform the file operation in question, so these need to be dealt with through a `try...catch` block or a `throws` clause in a method declaration.

The program in Listing 17.7 converts all the text in a file to uppercase characters. The file is pulled in using a buffered input stream, and one character is read at a time. After the character is converted to uppercase, it is sent to a temporary file using a buffered output stream. `File` objects are used instead of strings to indicate the files involved, which makes it possible to rename and delete files as needed.

17

LISTING 17.7   The Full Text of `AllCapsDemo.java`

```
 1: import java.io.*;
 2:
 3: public class AllCapsDemo {
 4:     public static void main(String[] arguments) {
 5:         AllCaps cap = new AllCaps(arguments[0]);
 6:         cap.convert();
 7:     }
 8: }
 9:
10: class AllCaps {
11:     String sourceName;
12:
13:     AllCaps(String sourceArg) {
14:         sourceName = sourceArg;
15:     }
16:
17:     void convert() {
18:         try {
19:             // Create file objects
20:             File source = new File(sourceName);
21:             File temp = new File("cap" + sourceName + ".tmp");
22:
23:             // Create input stream
24:             FileReader fr = new
25:                 FileReader(source);
26:             BufferedReader in = new
```

LISTING 17.7   continued

```
27:                    BufferedReader(fr);
28:
29:             // Create output stream
30:             FileWriter fw = new
31:                 FileWriter(temp);
32:             BufferedWriter out = new
33:                 BufferedWriter(fw);
34:
35:             boolean eof = false;
36:             int inChar = 0;
37:             do {
38:                 inChar = in.read();
39:                 if (inChar != -1) {
40:                     char outChar = Character.toUpperCase( (char)inChar );
41:                     out.write(outChar);
42:                 } else
43:                     eof = true;
44:             } while (!eof);
45:             in.close();
46:             out.close();
47:
48:             boolean deleted = source.delete();
49:             if (deleted)
50:                 temp.renameTo(source);
51:         } catch (IOException e) {
52:             System.out.println("Error -- " + e.toString());
53:         } catch (SecurityException se) {
54:             System.out.println("Error -- " + se.toString());
55:         }
56:     }
57: }
```

After you compile the program, you need a text file that can be converted to all capital letters. One option is to make a copy of AllCapsDemo.java and give it a name like TempFile.java.

The name of the file to convert is specified at the command line when running AllCapsDemo, as in the following example:

```
java AllCapsDemo TempFile.java
```

This program does not produce any output. Load the converted file into a text editor to see the result of the application.

Summary

You learned how to work with streams today in two different directions: pulling data into a program over an input stream and sending data out of a program using an output stream.

You used byte streams for many types of nontextual data and character streams to handle text. Filters were associated with streams to alter the way information was delivered through a stream, or to alter the information itself.

Today's lesson covers most `java.io` package classes, but there are other types of streams you might want to explore. Piped streams are useful when communicating data between different threads, and byte array streams can connect programs to a computer's memory.

Because the stream classes in Java are so closely coordinated, you already possess most of the knowledge you need to use these other types of streams. The constructors, read methods, and write methods are largely identical.

17

Streams are a powerful way to extend the functionality of your Java programs because they offer a connection to any kind of data you might want to work with.

Tomorrow you see how streams reach the largest data source imaginable: the Internet.

Q&A

Q A C program that I use creates a file of integers and other data. Can I read this using a Java program?

A You can, but one thing you have to consider is whether your C program represents integers in the same manner that a Java program represents them. As you might recall, all data can be represented as an individual byte or a series of bytes. An integer is represented in Java using four bytes that are arranged in what is called big-endian order. You can determine the integer value by combining the bytes from left-to-right. A C program implemented on an Intel PC is likely to represent integers in little-endian order, which means the bytes must be arranged from right-to-left to determine the result. You might have to learn about advanced techniques, such as bit shifting, to use a data file created with a programming language other than Java.

Q The `FileWriter` class has a `write(int)` method that's used to send a character to a file. Shouldn't this be `write(char)`?

A The `char` and `int` data types are interchangeable in many ways—you can use an `int` in a method that expects a `char`, and vice versa. This is possible because each character is represented by a numeric code that is an integer value. When you call the `write()` method with an `int`, it outputs the character associated with that integer value. When calling the `write()` method, you can cast an `int` value to a `char` to ensure that it's being used as you intended.

Questions

1. What happens when you create a `FileOutputStream` using a reference to an existing file?

    (a) An exception is thrown.

    (b) The data you write to the stream is appended to the existing file.

    (c) The existing file is replaced with the data you write to the stream.

2. What two primitive types are interchangeable when you're working with streams?

    (a) `byte` and `boolean`

    (b) `char` and `int`

    (c) `byte` and `char`

3. In Java, what is the maximum value of a `byte` variable and the maximum value of an unsigned byte in a stream?

    (a) Both are `255`

    (b) Both are `127`

    (c) `127` for a `byte` variable and `255` for an unsigned byte

Answers

1. c. That's one of the things to look out for when using output streams—you can easily wipe out existing files.

2. b. Because a `char` is represented internally by Java as an integer value, you can often use the two interchangeably in method calls and other statements.

3. c. The `byte` primitive data type has values ranging from `-128` to `127`, whereas an unsigned byte can range from `0` to `255`.

Exercises

To extend your knowledge of the subjects covered today, try the following exercises:

- Write a modified version of the `HexRead` program from Day 16, "Error Handling and Security," that reads two-digit hexadecimal sequences from a text file and displays their decimal equivalents.

- Write a program that reads a file to determine the number of bytes it contains, and then overwrites all those bytes with zeroes (0). (For obvious reasons, don't test this program on any file you intend to keep—the data in the file will be wiped out.)

Where applicable, exercise solutions are offered on the book's Web site at
`http://www.java21pro.com`.

17

DAY 18

Object Serialization and Reflection

An essential concept of object-oriented programming is the way it represents data. In an object-oriented language such as Java, an object represents two things:

- Behavior—The things an object can do.
- Attributes—The data that differentiates the object from other objects.

Combining behavior and attributes is a departure from many other programming languages. A program has typically been defined as a set of instructions that manipulate data. The data itself is a separate thing, as in the example of word-processing software. Most word processors are considered programs that are used to create and edit textual documents.

Object-oriented programming and other techniques are blurring the line between program and data. Current word processors such as Microsoft Word and Lotus WordPro might include programming instructions that affect how the document is formatted, edited, and displayed. These instructions are saved with a document, along with the text and formatting codes that compose the document's data.

Along the same lines, an object in a language such as Java encapsulates both instructions (behavior) and data (attributes).

Today you discover three ways that a Java program can take advantage of this representation:

- Object serialization—The capability to read and write an object using streams.
- Reflection—The capability of one object to learn details about another object.
- Remote method invocation—The capability to query another object to investigate its features and call its methods.

Object Serialization

Java handles access to external data via the use of a class of objects called streams. A *stream* is an object that carries data from one place to another. Some streams carry information from a source into a Java program. Others go the opposite direction and take data from a program to a destination.

A stream that reads a Web page's data into an array in a Java program is an example of the former. A stream that writes a `String` array to a disk file is an example of the latter.

Two types of streams were introduced during Day 17, "Handling Data Through Java Streams."

- *Byte streams*, which read and write a series of integer values ranging from `0` to `255`
- *Character streams*, which read and write textual data

These streams separate the data from the Java class that works with it. To use the data at a later time, you must read it in through a stream and convert it into a form the class can use, such as a series of variables or objects.

A third type of stream, *object streams*, makes it possible for data to be represented as part of an object rather than something external to it.

Object streams, like byte and character streams, are part of the `java.io` package. Working with them requires many of the same techniques you used during Day 17.

For an object to be saved to a destination such as a disk file, it must be converted to serial form.

> **Note**
>
> Serial data is sent one element at a time, like a line of cars on an assembly line. You might be familiar with the *serial port* on a computer, which is used to send information as a series of bits one after the other. Another way to send data is in *parallel*, where more than one element is transferred simultaneously.

An object indicates that it can be used with streams by implementing the `Serializable` interface. This interface, which is part of the `java.io` package, differs from other interfaces you have worked with—it does not contain any methods that must be included in the classes that implement it. The sole purpose of `Serializable` is to indicate that objects of that class can be stored and retrieved in serial form.

Objects can be serialized to disk on a single machine or can be serialized across a network such as the Internet, even in a case where different operating systems are involved. You can create an object on a Windows machine, serialize it to a UNIX machine, and load it back into the original Windows machine without introducing any errors. Java transparently works with the different formats for saving data on these systems when objects are serialized.

A programming concept involved in object serialization is *persistence*—the capability of an object to exist and function outside the program that created it.

Normally, an object that is not serialized is not persistent. When the program that uses the object stops running, the object ceases to exist.

Serialization enables object persistence because the stored object continues to serve a purpose even when no Java program is running. The stored object contains information that can be restored in a program so that it can resume functioning.

When an object is saved to a stream in serial form, all objects to which it contains references are saved also. This makes it easier to work with serialization; you can create one object stream that takes care of numerous objects at the same time.

You also can exclude some of an object's variables from serialization, which might be necessary to save disk space or prevent information that presents a security risk from being saved. As you see later today, this requires the use of the `transient` modifier.

18

Object Output Streams

An object is written to a stream via the ObjectOutputStream class.

An object output stream is created with the ObjectOutputStream(*OutputStream*) constructor. The argument to this constructor can be either of the following:

- An output stream representing the destination where the object should be stored in serial form
- A filter that is associated with the output stream leading to the destination

As with other streams, you can chain more than one filter between the output stream and the object output stream.

The following code creates an output stream and an associated object output stream:

```
FileOutputStream disk = new FileOutputStream(
    "SavedObject.dat");
ObjectOutputStream obj = new ObjectOutputStream(disk);
```

The object output stream created in this example is called obj. Methods of the obj class can be used to write serializable objects and other information to a file called SavedObject.dat.

After you have created an object output stream, you can write an object to it by calling the stream's writeObject(*Object*) method.

The following statement calls this method on disk, the stream created in the previous example:

```
disk.writeObject(userData);
```

This statement writes an object called userData to the disk object output stream. The class represented by userData must be serializable in order for it to work.

An object output stream also can be used to write other types of information with the following methods:

- write(*int*)—Write the specified integer to the stream.
- write(*byte[ ]*)—Write the specified byte array.
- write(*byte[ ]*, *int*, *int*)—Write a subset of the specified byte array. The second argument specifies the first array element to write and the last argument represents the number of subsequent elements to write.
- writeBoolean(*boolean*)—Write the specified boolean.
- writeByte(*int*)—Write the specified integer as a byte value.

- `writeBytes(String)`—Write the specified string as a series of bytes.
- `writeChar(int)`—Write the specified character.
- `writeChars(String)`—Write the specified string as a series of characters.
- `writeDouble(double)`—Write the specified `double`.
- `writeFloat(float)`—Write the specified `float`.
- `writeInt(int)`—Write the specified `int`.
- `writeLong(long)`—Write the specified `long`.
- `writeShort(short)`—Write the specified `short`.

The `ObjectOutputStream` constructor and all methods that write data to an object output stream throw `IOException` objects. These must be accounted for using a `try...catch` block or a `throws` clause.

Listing 18.1 contains a Java application that consists of two classes: `ObjectToDisk` and `Message`. The `Message` class represents a message that one person could send to another, perhaps as electronic mail or a short note in a private chat. This class has `from` and `to` objects that store the names of the sender and recipient, a `now` object that holds a `Date` value representing the time it was sent, and a `text` array of `String` objects that holds the message itself. There also is an `int` called `lineCount` that keeps track of the number of lines in the message.

When designing a program that transmits and receives electronic messages, it makes sense to use some kind of stream to save these messages to disk. The information that constitutes the message must be saved in some form as it is transmitted from one place to another; it also might need to be saved until the recipient is able to read it.

Messages can be preserved by saving each message element separately to a byte or character stream. In the example of the `Message` class, the `from` and `to` objects could be written to a stream as strings and the `text` object could be written as an array of strings. The `now` object is a little trickier because there isn't a way to write a `Date` object to a character stream. However, it could be converted into a series of integer values representing each part of a date: hour, minute, second, and so on. Those could be written to the stream.

Using an object output stream makes it possible to save `Message` objects without first translating them into another form.

The `ObjectToDisk` class in Listing 18.1 creates a `Message` object, sets up values for its variables, and saves it to a file called `Message.obj` via an object output stream.

18

LISTING 18.1   The Full Text of `ObjectToDisk.java`

```
 1: import java.io.*;
 2: import java.util.*;
 3:
 4: public class ObjectToDisk {
 5:     public static void main(String[] arguments) {
 6:         Message mess = new Message();
 7:         String author = "Sam Wainwright, London";
 8:         String recipient = "George Bailey, Bedford Falls";
 9:         String[] letter = { "Mr. Gower cabled you need cash. Stop.",
10:             "My office instructed to advance you up to twenty-five",
11:             "thousand dollars. Stop. Hee-haw and Merry Christmas." };
12:         Date now = new Date();
13:         mess.writeMessage(author, recipient, now, letter);
14:         try {
15:             FileOutputStream fo = new FileOutputStream(
16:                 "Message.obj");
17:             ObjectOutputStream oo = new ObjectOutputStream(fo);
18:             oo.writeObject(mess);
19:             oo.close();
20:             System.out.println("Object created successfully.");
21:         } catch (IOException e) {
22:             System.out.println("Error -- " + e.toString());
23:         }
24:     }
25: }
26:
27: class Message implements Serializable {
28:     int lineCount;
29:     String from, to;
30:     Date when;
31:     String[] text;
32:
33:     void writeMessage(String inFrom,
34:         String inTo,
35:         Date inWhen,
36:         String[] inText) {
37:
38:         text = new String[inText.length];
39:         for (int i = 0; i < inText.length; i++)
40:             text[i] = inText[i];
41:         lineCount = inText.length;
42:         to = inTo;
43:         from = inFrom;
44:         when = inWhen;
45:     }
46: }
```

You should see the following output after you compile and run the `ObjectToDisk` application:

`Object created successfully.`

Object Input Streams

An object is read from a stream using the `ObjectInputStream` class. As with other streams, working with an object input stream is very similar to working with an object output stream. The primary difference is the change in the data's direction.

An object input stream is created with the `ObjectInputStream(InputStream)` constructor. Two exceptions are thrown by this constructor: `IOException` and `StreamCorruptionException`. `IOException`, common to stream classes, occurs whenever any kind of input/output error occurs during the data transfer. `StreamCorruptionException` is specific to object streams, and it indicates that the data in the stream is not a serialized object.

An object input stream can be constructed from an input stream or a filtered stream.

The following code creates an input stream and an object input stream to go along with it:

```
try {
    FileInputStream disk = new FileInputStream(
        "SavedObject.dat");
    ObjectInputStream obj = new ObjectInputStream(disk);
} catch (IOException ie) {
    System.out.println("IO error -- " + ie.toString());
} catch (StreamCorruptionException se) {
    System.out.println("Error - data not an object.");
}
```

This object input stream is set up to read from an object that is stored in a file called `SavedObject.dat`. If the file does not exist or cannot be read from disk for some reason, an `IOException` is thrown. If the file isn't a serialized object, a thrown `StreamCorruptionException` indicates this problem.

An object can be read from an object input stream by using the `readObject()` method, which returns an `Object`. This object can be immediately cast into the class it belongs to, as in the following example:

`WorkData dd = (WorkData)disk.readObject();`

This statement reads an object from the `disk` object stream and casts it into an object of the class `WorkData`. In addition to `IOException`, this method throws `OptionalDataException` and `ClassNotFoundException` errors.

18

`OptionalDataException` indicates that the stream contains data other than serialized object data, which makes it impossible to read an object from the stream.

`ClassNotFoundException` occurs when the object retrieved from the stream belongs to a class that could not be found. When objects are serialized, the class itself is not saved to the stream. Instead, the name of the class is saved to the stream and the class is loaded by the Java interpreter when the object is loaded from a stream.

Other types of information can be read from an object input stream with the following methods:

- `read()`—Read the next byte from the stream, which is returned as an `int`.
- `read(byte[], int, int)`—Read bytes into the specified byte array. The second argument specifies the first array element where a byte should be stored. The last argument represents the number of subsequent elements to read and store in the array.
- `readBoolean()`—Read a `boolean` value from the stream.
- `readByte()`—Read a `byte` value from the stream.
- `readChar()`—Read a `char` value from the stream.
- `readDouble()`—Read a `double` value from the stream.
- `readFloat()`—Read a `float` value from the stream.
- `readInt()`—Read an `int` value from the stream.
- `readLine()`—Read a `String` from the stream.
- `readLong()`—Read a `long` value from the stream.
- `readShort()`—Read a `short` value from the stream.
- `readUnsignedByte()`—Read an unsigned byte value and return it as an `int`.
- `readUnsignedShort()`—Read an unsigned short value and return it as an `int`.

Each of these methods throws an `IOException` if an input/output error occurs as the stream is being read.

When an object is created by reading an object stream, it is created entirely from the variable and object information stored in that stream. No constructor method is called to create variables and set them up with initial values.

Listing 18.2 contains a Java application that reads an object from a stream and displays its variables to standard output. The `ObjectFromDisk` application loads the object that was serialized to the file `message.obj`.

This class must be run from the same folder that contains the file `message.obj`. In addition, the `Message` class must be either in the same folder or in a folder that is accessible from the `CLASSPATH` folders on your system.

LISTING 18.2 The Full Text of `ObjectFromDisk.java`

```
 1: import java.io.*;
 2: import java.util.*;
 3:
 4: public class ObjectFromDisk {
 5:     public static void main(String[] arguments) {
 6:         try {
 7:             FileInputStream fi = new FileInputStream(
 8:                 "message.obj");
 9:             ObjectInputStream oi = new ObjectInputStream(fi);
10:             Message mess = (Message) oi.readObject();
11:             System.out.println("Message:\n");
12:             System.out.println("From: " + mess.from);
13:             System.out.println("To: " + mess.to);
14:             System.out.println("Date: " + mess.when + "\n");
15:             for (int i = 0; i < mess.lineCount; i++)
16:                 System.out.println(mess.text[i]);
17:             oi.close();
18:         } catch (Exception e) {
19:             System.out.println("Error -- " + e.toString());
20:         }
21:     }
22: }
```

18

The output of this program is as follows:

```
Message:

From: Sam Wainwright, London
To: George Bailey, Bedford Falls
Date: Thu Jun 22 15:09:01 EDT 2000

Mr. Gower cabled you need cash. Stop.
My office instructed to advance you up to twenty-five
thousand dollars. Stop. Hee-haw and Merry Christmas.
```

Transient Variables

When creating an object that can be serialized, one design consideration is whether all the object's instance variables should be saved.

In some cases, an instance variable must be created from scratch each time the object is restored. A good example is an object referring to a file or input stream. Such an object must be created anew when it is part of a serialized object loaded from an object stream, so it doesn't make sense to save this information when serializing the object.

It's a good idea to exclude from serialization a variable that contains sensitive information. If an object stores the password needed to gain access to a resource, that password is more at risk if serialized into a file. The password also might be detected if it is part of an object that was restored over a stream that exists on a network.

A third reason not to serialize a variable is to save space on the storage file that holds the object. If its values can be established without serialization, you might want to omit the variable from the process.

To prevent an instance variable from being included in serialization, the `transient` modifier is used.

This modifier is included in the statement that creates the variable, preceding the class or data type of the variable. The following statement creates a transient variable called `limit`:

```
public transient int limit = 55;
```

Inspecting Classes and Methods with Reflection

On Day 4, "Working with Objects," you learned how to create `Class` objects that represent the class to which an object belongs. Every object in Java inherits the `getClass()` method, which identifies the class or interface of that object. The following statement creates a `Class` object named `keyclass` from an object referred to by the variable `key`:

```
Class keyClass = key.getClass();
```

By calling the `getName()` method of a `Class` object, you can find out the name of the class:

```
String keyName = keyClass.getName();
```

These features are part of Java's support for reflection, a technique that enables one Java class—such as a program you write—to learn details about any other class.

Through reflection, a Java program can load a class it knows nothing about, find the variables, methods, and constructors of that class, and work with them.

Inspecting and Creating Classes

The `Class` class, which is part of the `java.lang` package, is used to learn about and create classes, interfaces, and even primitive types.

In addition to using getClass(), you can create Class objects by appending .class to the name of a class, interface, array, or primitive type, as in the following examples:

```
Class keyClass = KeyClass.class;
Class thr = Throwable.class;
Class floater = float.class;
Class floatArray = float[].class;
```

You also can create Class objects by using the forName() class method with a single argument: a string containing the name of an existing class. The following statement creates a Class object representing a JLabel, one of the classes of the javax.swing package:

```
Class lab = Class.forName("javax.swing.JLabel");
```

The forName() method throws a ClassNotFoundException if the specified class cannot be found, so you must call forName() within a try-catch block or handle it in some other manner.

To retrieve a string containing the name of a class represented by a Class object, call getName() on that object. For classes and interfaces, this name will include the name of the class and a reference to the package to which it belongs. For primitive types, the name will correspond to the type's name (such as int, float, or double).

Class objects that represent arrays are handled a little differently when getName() is called on them. The name begins with one left bracket character ([) for each dimension of the array—float[] would begin with [, int[][] with [[, KeyClass[][][] with [[[, and so on.

If the array is of a primitive type, the next part of the name is a single character representing the type, as shown in Table 18.1.

TABLE 18.1 Type Identification for Primitive Types

Character	Primitive Type
B	byte
C	char
D	double
F	float
I	int
J	long
S	short
Z	boolean

18

For arrays of objects, the brackets are followed by an L and the name of the class. For example, if you called getName() on a String[][] array, the result would be [[Ljava.lang.String.

You also can use the Class class to create new objects. Call the newInstance() method on a Class object to create the object and cast it to the correct class. For example, if you have a Class object named thr that represents the Throwable interface, you can create a new object as follows:

```
Throwable thr2 = (Throwable)thr.newInstance();
```

The newInstance() method throws several kinds of exceptions:

- IllegalAccessException: You do not have access to the class, either because it is not public or because it belongs to a different package.

- IllegalAccessException: You cannot create a new object because the class is abstract.

- SecurityViolation: You do not have permission to create an object of this class.

When newInstance() is called and no exceptions are thrown, the new object is created by calling the constructor of the corresponding class with no arguments.

Note

You cannot use this technique to create a new object that requires arguments to its constructor method. Instead, you must use a newInstance() method of the Constructor class, as you see later today.

Working with Each Part of a Class

Although Class is part of the java.lang package, the primary support for reflection is the java.lang.reflect package, which includes the following classes:

- Field—Manage and find information about class and instance variables

- Method—Manage class and instance methods

- Constructor—Manage constructors, the special methods for creating new instances of classes

- Array—Manage arrays

- Modifier—Decode modifier information about classes, variables, and methods (which were described on Day 15, "Packages, Interfaces, and Other Class Features")

Each of these reflection classes has methods for working with an element of a class.

A Method object holds information about a single method in a class. To find out about all methods contained in a class, create a Class object for that class and call getDeclaredMethods() on that object. An array of Method[] objects will be returned that represents all methods in the class that were not inherited from a superclass. If no methods meet that description, the length of the array will be 0.

The Method class has several useful instance methods:

- getParameterTypes()—This method returns an array of Class objects representing each argument contained in the method signature.

- getReturnType()—This method returns a Class object representing the return type of the method, whether it's a class or primitive type.

- getModifiers()—This method returns an int value that represents the modifiers that apply to the method, such as whether it is public, private, and the like.

Because the getParameterTypes() and getReturnType() methods return Class objects, you can use getName() on each object to find out more about it.

The easiest way to use the int returned by getModifiers() is to call the Modifier class method toString() with that integer as an argument. For example, if you have a Method object named current, you can display its modifiers with the following code:

```
int mods = current.getModifiers();
System.out.println(Modifier.toString(mods));
```

18

The Constructor class has some of the same methods as the Method class, including getModifiers() and getName(). One method that's missing is getReturnType(), as you might expect—constructors do not contain return types.

To retrieve all constructors associated with a Class object, call getConstructors() on that object. An array of Constructor objects will be returned.

To retrieve a specific constructor, first create an array of Class objects that represents every argument sent to the constructor. When this is done, call getConstructors() with that Class array as an argument.

For example, if there is a KeyClass(String, int) constructor, you can create a Constructor object to represent this with the following statements:

```
Class kc = KeyClass.class;
Class[] cons = new Class[2];
cons[0] = String.class;
cons[1] = int.class;
Constructor c = kc.getConstructor(cons);
```

The getConstructor(*Class[]*) method throws a NoSuchMethodException if there isn't a constructor with arguments that match the Class[] array.

After you have a Constructor object, you can call its newInstance(*Object[]*) method to create a new instance using that constructor.

Inspecting a Class

To bring all this material together, Listing 18.3 is a short Java application named SeeMethods that uses reflection to inspect the methods in a class.

LISTING **18.3**   The Full Text of SeeMethods.java

```
 1: import java.lang.reflect.*;
 2:
 3: public class SeeMethods {
 4:     public static void main(String[] arguments)  {
 5:         Class inspect;
 6:         try {
 7:             if (arguments.length > 0)
 8:                 inspect = Class.forName(arguments[0]);
 9:             else
10:                 inspect = Class.forName("SeeMethods");
11:             Method[] methods = inspect.getDeclaredMethods();
12:             for (int i = 0; i < methods.length; i++) {
13:                 Method methVal = methods[i];
14:                 Class returnVal = methVal.getReturnType();
15:                 int mods = methVal.getModifiers();
16:                 String modVal = Modifier.toString(mods);
17:                 Class[] paramVal = methVal.getParameterTypes();
18:                 StringBuffer params = new StringBuffer();
19:                 for (int j = 0; j < paramVal.length; j++) {
20:                     if (j > 0)
21:                         params.append(", ");
22:                     params.append(paramVal[j].getName());
23:                 }
24:                 System.out.println("Method: " + methVal.getName() + "()");
25:                 System.out.println("Modifiers: " + modVal);
26:                 System.out.println("Return Type: " + returnVal.getName());
27:                 System.out.println("Parameters: " + params + "\n");
28:             }
29:         } catch (ClassNotFoundException c) {
30:             System.out.println(c.toString());
31:         }
32:     }
33: }
```

The SeeMethods application displays information about the public methods in the class
you specify at the command line (or SeeMethods itself, if you don't specify a class). To
try the program, enter the following at a command line:

```
java SeeMethods java.util.Random
```

If you run the application on the java.util.Random class, the program's output is the
following:

```
Method: next()
Modifiers: protected synchronized
Return Type: int
Parameters: int

Method: nextDouble()
Modifiers: public
Return Type: double
Parameters:

Method: nextInt()
Modifiers: public
Return Type: int
Parameters: int

Method: nextInt()
Modifiers: public
Return Type: int
Parameters:

Method: setSeed()
Modifiers: public synchronized
Return Type: void
Parameters: long

Method: nextBytes()
Modifiers: public
Return Type: void
Parameters: [B

Method: nextLong()
Modifiers: public
Return Type: long
Parameters:

Method: nextBoolean()
Modifiers: public
Return Type: boolean
Parameters:
```

18

```
Method: nextFloat()
Modifiers: public
Return Type: float
Parameters:

Method: nextGaussian()
Modifiers: public synchronized
Return Type: double
Parameters:
```

By using reflection, the SeeMethods application can learn every method of a class.

A Class object is created in lines 7–10 of the application. If a class name was specified as a command-line argument when SeeMethods was run, the Class.forName() method is called with that argument. Otherwise, SeeMethods is used as the argument.

After the Class object is created, its getDeclaredMethods() method is used in line 11 to find all the methods contained in the class (with the exception of methods inherited from a superclass). These methods are stored as an array of Method objects.

The for loop in lines 12–28 cycles through each method in the class, storing its return type, modifiers, and arguments and then displaying them.

Displaying the return type is straightforward: Each method's getReturnType() method is stored as a Class object in line 14, and that object's name is displayed in line 26.

When a method's getModifiers() method is called in line 15, an integer is returned that represents all modifiers used with the method. The class method Modifier.toString() takes this integer as an argument and returns the names of all modifiers associated with it.

Lines 19–23 loop through the array of Class objects that represents the arguments associated with a method. The name of each argument is added to a StringBuffer object named params in line 22.

Reflection is most commonly used by tools such as class browsers and debuggers as a way to learn more about the class of objects being browsed or debugged. It also is needed with JavaBeans, where the capability for one object to query another object about what it can do (and then ask it to do something) is useful when building larger applications. You learn more about JavaBeans during Day 20, "Working with JavaBeans."

Reflection is an advanced feature that you might not be readily using in your programs. It becomes most useful when you're working on object serialization, JavaBeans, and other programs that need runtime access to Java classes.

Remote Method Invocation

Remote method invocation (RMI) creates Java applications that can talk to other Java applications over a network. To be more specific, RMI allows an application to call methods and access variables inside another application, which might be running in a different Java environment or different operating system altogether, and to pass objects back and forth over a network connection. RMI is a more sophisticated mechanism for communicating between distributed Java objects than a simple socket connection is; the mechanisms and protocols by which you communicate between objects are defined and standardized. You can talk to another Java program by using RMI without having to know beforehand what protocol to speak to or how to speak it.

> **Note**
>
> Another form of communicating between objects is called RPC (*remote procedure calls*), where you can call methods or execute procedures in other programs over a network connection. Although RPC and RMI have a lot in common, the major difference is that RPC sends only procedure calls over the wire, with the arguments either passed along or described in such a way that they can be reconstructed at the other end. RMI actually passes whole objects back and forth over the Internet, and is therefore better suited for a fully object-oriented distributed object model.

18

Although the concept of RMI might bring up visions of objects all over the world merrily communicating with each other, RMI is most commonly used in a more traditional client/server situation: A single server application receives connections and requests from a number of clients. RMI is simply the mechanism by which the client and server communicate.

RMI Architecture

The goals for RMI were to integrate a distributed object model into Java without disrupting the language or the existing object model, and to make interacting with a remote object as easy as interacting with a local one. A programmer should be able to do the following:

- Use remote objects in precisely the same ways as local objects (assign them to variables, pass them as arguments to methods, and so on).
- Call methods in remote objects the same way that local calls are accomplished.

In addition, RMI includes more sophisticated mechanisms for calling methods on remote objects to pass whole objects or parts of objects either by reference or by value; it also includes additional exceptions for handling network errors that might occur while a remote operation is occurring.

RMI has several layers in order to accomplish all these goals, and a single method call crosses many of these layers to get where it's going (see Figure 18.1). There are actually three layers:

FIGURE 18.1

RMI layers.

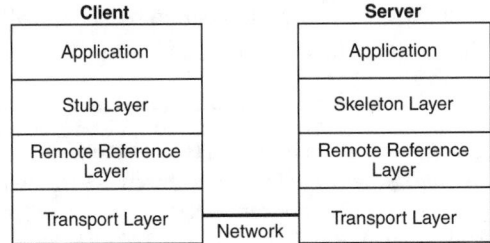

- The Stub and Skeleton Layers on the client and server, respectively. These layers behave as surrogate objects on each side, hiding the remoteness of the method call from the actual implementation classes. For example, in your client application you can call remote methods in precisely the same way that you call local methods; the stub object is a local surrogate for the remote object.

- The Remote Reference Layer, which handles packaging of a method call and its parameters and return values for transport over the network.

- The Transport Layer, which is the actual network connection from one system to another.

Having three layers for RMI allows each layer to be independently controlled or implemented. Stubs and skeletons allow the client and server classes to behave as if the objects they were dealing with were local, and to use exactly the same Java language features to access those objects. The Remote Reference Layer separates the remote object processing into its own layer, which can then be optimized or reimplemented independently of the applications that depend on it. Finally, the Network Transport Layer is used independently of the other two so that you can use different kinds of socket connections for RMI (TCP, UDP, or TCP with some other protocol, such as SSL).

When a client application makes a remote method call, the call passes to the stub and then onto the Remote Reference Layer, which packages the arguments if necessary. That layer then passes the call via the Network Layer to the server, where the Remote Reference Layer on the server side unpackages the arguments and passes them to the skeleton and then to the server implementation. The return values for the method call then take the reverse trip back to the client side.

The packaging and passing of method arguments is one of the more interesting aspects of RMI because objects have to be converted into something that can be passed over the network by using serialization. As long as an object can be serialized, RMI can use it as a method parameter or a return value.

Remote Java objects used as method parameters or return values are passed by reference, just as they would be locally. Other objects, however, are copied. Note that this behavior affects how you write your Java programs when they use remote method calls—you cannot, for example, pass an array as an argument to a remote method, have the remote object change that array, and expect the local copy to be modified. This is not how local objects behave, where all objects are passed as references.

Creating RMI Applications

To create an application that uses RMI, you use the classes and interfaces defined by the java.rmi packages, which include the following:

- java.rmi.server—For server-side classes
- java.rmi.registry—Which contains the classes for locating and registering RMI servers on a local system
- java.rmi.dgc—For garbage collection of distributed objects

The java.rmi package itself contains the general RMI interfaces, classes, and exceptions.

To implement an RMI-based client/server application, you first define an interface that contains all the methods your remote object will support. The methods in that interface must all include a throws RemoteException statement, which handles potential network problems that might prevent the client and server from communicating.

Listing 18.4 contains a simple interface that can be used with a remote object.

LISTING 18.4   The Full Text of PiRemote.java

```
1: package com.prefect.pi;
2:
3: import java.rmi.*;
4:
5: interface PiRemote extends Remote {
6:     double getPi() throws RemoteException;
7: }
```

18

An RMI interface like this must be part of a package for it to be accessible from a remote client program.

 **Caution**

> Using a package name causes the Java compiler and interpreter to be pickier about where a program's Java and class files are located. A package's root folder should be a folder in your system's CLASSPATH, and each part of a package name is used to create a subfolder. If the folder C:\jdk1.3 is on your system, the PiRemote.java file could be saved in a folder called C:\jdk1.3\com\prefect\pi. If you don't have a folder matching the package name, you should create it.

This interface doesn't do anything, requiring a class to implement it. For now, you can compile it by entering the following command from the folder where PiRemote is located:

```
javac PiRemote.java
```

The next step is to implement the remote interface in a server-side application, which usually extends the UnicastRemoteObject class. You implement the methods in the remote interface inside that class, and you also create and install a security manager for that server (to prevent random clients from connecting and making unauthorized method calls). You can, of course, configure the security manager to allow or disallow various operations. The Java class library includes a class called RMISecurityManager, which can be used for this purpose.

In the server application, you also register the remote application, which binds it to a host and port.

Listing 18.5 contains a Java server application that implements the PiRemote interface:

LISTING 18.5   The Full Text of Pi.java

```
1: package com.prefect.pi;
2:
3: import java.net.*;
4: import java.rmi.*;
5: import java.rmi.registry.*;
6: import java.rmi.server.*;
7:
8: public class Pi extends UnicastRemoteObject
```

```
 9:      implements PiRemote {
10:
11:      public double getPi() throws RemoteException {
12:          return Math.PI;
13:      }
14:
15:      public Pi() throws RemoteException {
16:      }
17:
18:      public static void main(String[] arguments) {
19:          System.setSecurityManager(new
20:              RMISecurityManager());
21:          try {
22:              Pi p = new Pi();
23:              Naming.bind("//Default:1010/Pi", p);
24:          } catch (Exception e) {
25:              System.out.println("Error -- " +
26:                  e.toString());
27:                  e.printStackTrace();
28:          }
29:      }
30: }
```

In the call to the bind() method in line 23, the text Default:1010 identifies the machine name and port for the RMI registry. If you were running this application from a Web server of some kind, the name Default would be replaced with a URL. The name Default should be changed to your machine's real name. On a Windows 95, 98, or 2000 system, you can find your system's name by selecting Settings, Control Panel, Network. Click the Identification tag to see the machine name, which is located in the Computer Name field.

On the client side, you implement a simple application that uses the remote interface and calls methods in that interface. A Naming class (in java.rmi) allows the client to transparently connect to the server. Listing 18.6 contains OutputPi.java.

LISTING 18.6   The Full Text of OutputPi.java

```
1: package com.prefect.pi;
2:
3: import java.rmi.*;
4: import java.rmi.registry.*;
5:
6: public class OutputPi {
7:     public static void main(String[] arguments) {
8:         System.setSecurityManager(
9:             new RMISecurityManager());
```

LISTING 18.6   continued

```
10:        try {
11:            PiRemote pr =
12:                (PiRemote)Naming.lookup(
13:                    "//Default:1010/Pi");
14:            for (int i = 0; i < 10; i++)
15:                System.out.println("Pi = " + pr.getPi());
16:        } catch (Exception e) {
17:            System.out.println("Error -- " + e.toString());
18:            e.printStackTrace();
19:        }
20:    }
21: }
```

At this point, you can compile these programs using the standard Java compiler. Before you can use these programs, you must use the `rmic` command-line program to generate the Stub and Skeleton Layers so that RMI can actually work between the two sides of the process.

To create the stubs and skeletons files for the current project, go to the folder that contains the file `Pi.class` and enter the following command:

`rmic com.prefect.pi.Pi`

Two files are created: `Pi_Stub.class` and `Pi_Skel.class`.

Finally, the `rmiregistry` program connects the server application to the network itself and binds it to a port so that remote connections can be made.

The `rmiregistry` program does not work correctly if the `Pi_Stub.class` and `Pi_Skel.class` files are located on your system's `CLASSPATH`. This is because the program assumes you don't need remote implementations of these files if they can be found locally.

The easiest way to avoid this problem is to run `rmiregistry` after temporarily disabling your `CLASSPATH`. This can be done on a Windows 95 or 98 system by opening a new MS-DOS window and entering the following command:

`set CLASSPATH=`

Because the client and server applications use port 1010, you should start the `rmiregistry` program with the following command:

`start rmiregistry 1010`

After starting the RMI registry, you should run the server program Pi. Because this application is part of a package, you must include its full package name when running the application with the Java interpreter.

You also must indicate where all the class files associated with the application can be found, including Pi_Stub.class and Pi_Skel.class. This is done by setting the java.rmi.server.codebase property.

If the application's class files were stored at http://www.naviseek.com/java21/java/, the following command could be used to run the application from the same folder that contains Pi.class:

```
java -Djava.rmi.server.codebase=http://www.naviseek.com/java21/
➡java/ com.prefect.pi.Pi
```

The last step is to run the client program OutputPi. Switch to the folder that contains OutputPi.class and enter the following:

```
java com.prefect.pi.OutputPi
```

This program produces the following output:

```
Pi = 3.141592653589793
Pi = 3.141592653589793
Pi = 3.141592653589793
Pi = 3.141592653589793
Pi = 3.141592653589793
Pi = 3.141592653589793
Pi = 3.141592653589793
Pi = 3.141592653589793
Pi = 3.141592653589793
Pi = 3.141592653589793
```

18

RMI and Security

RMI generates security errors when you attempt to run the Pi and OutputPi programs on some systems.

If you get AccessControlException error messages associated with calls to the Naming.bind() and Naming.lookup() methods, your system needs to be configured so that these RMI calls can execute successfully.

One way to do this is to set up a simple file that contains the most lax security policy possible for Java and use this file to set the java.security.policy property when you run Pi and OutputPi.

Listing 18.7 contains a text file that can be used for this purpose. Create this file using a text editor and save it as policy.txt in the same folder as OutputPi.class and Pi.class.

LISTING **18.7**   The Full Text of `policy.txt`

```
1: grant {
2:     permission java.security.AllPermission;
3:     // Allow everything for now
4: };
```

Security policy files of this kind are used to grant and deny access to system resources. In this example, all permissions are granted, which prevents the `AccessControlException` error from occurring as you run the RMI client and server programs.

The `-Djava.security.policy=policy.txt` option can be used with the Java interpreter. The following examples show how this can be done:

```
java –Djava.rmi.server.codebase=http://www.naviseek.com/java21/
➥java/ -Djava.security.policy=policy.txt com.prefect.pi.Pi
```

```
java -Djava.security.policy=policy.txt com.prefect.pi.OutputPi
```

Summary

Although Java has always been a network-centric language, with applets running on Web browsers since version 1.0, the topics covered today show how the language is extending in two directions.

Object serialization shows how objects created with Java have a lifespan beyond that of a Java program itself. You can create objects in a program that are saved to a storage device such as a hard drive and re-created later, long after the original program has ceased to run.

RMI shows how Java's method calls have a reach beyond that of a single machine. By using RMI's techniques and command-line tools, you can create Java programs that can work with other programs no matter where they're located, whether in another room or another continent.

Although both of these features can be used to create sophisticated networked applications, object serialization is suitable for many other tasks. You might see a need for it in some of the first programs that you create; persistence is an effective way to save elements of a program for later use.

Q&A

Q **Are object streams associated with the `Writer` and `Reader` classes that are used to work with character streams?**

A The `ObjectInputStream` and `ObjectOutputStream` classes are independent of the byte stream and character stream superclasses in the `java.io` package, although they function similarly to many of the byte classes.

There shouldn't be a need to use `Writer` or `Reader` classes in conjunction with object streams because you can accomplish the same things via the object stream classes and their superclasses (`InputStream` and `OutputStream`).

Q **Are `private` variables and objects saved when they are part of an object that's being serialized?**

A They are saved. As you might recall from today's discussion, no constructor methods are called when an object is loaded into a program using serialization. Because of this, all variables and objects that are not declared `transient` are saved to prevent the object from losing something that might be necessary to its function.

Saving `private` variables and objects might present a security risk in some cases, especially when the variable is being used to store a password or some other sensitive data. Using `transient` prevents a variable or object from being serialized.

18

Questions

1. What is returned when you call `getName()` on a `Class` object that represents a `String[]` array?

    (a) `java.lang.String`

    (b) `[Ljava.lang.String`

    (c) `[java.lang.String`

2. What is persistence?

    (a) The ability of an object to exist after the program that created it has stopped running.

    (b) An important concept of object serialization.

    (c) The ability to work through 18 days of a programming book and still be determined enough to answer these end-of-chapter questions.

3. What `Class` method is used to create a new `Class` object using a string containing the name of a class?

   (a) `newInstance()`

   (b) `forName()`

   (c) `getName()`

Answers

1. b. The bracket indicates the depth of the array, the `L` indicates that it is an array of objects, and the class name that follows is self-explanatory.

2. a, b, or c.

3. b. If the class is not found, a `ClassNotFoundException` will be thrown.

Exercises

To extend your knowledge of the subjects covered today, try the following exercises:

- Use reflection to write a Java program that takes a class name as a command-line argument and checks whether it is an application—all applications have a `main()` method with `public static` as modifiers, `void` as a return type, and `String[]` as the only argument.

- Write a program that creates a new object using `Class` objects and the `newInstance()` method that serializes the object to disk.

Where applicable, exercise solutions are offered on the book's Web site at `http://www.java21pro.com`.

WEEK 3

DAY 19

Communicating Across the Internet

One of the more remarkable things about Java is how Internet-aware the language is. As you might recall from Day 1, "21st Century Java," Java was developed initially as a language that would control a network of interactive consumer devices. Connecting machines together was one of the main purposes of the language when it was designed, and that remains true today.

The java.net package makes it possible to communicate over a network with your Java programs. The package provides cross-platform abstractions for simple networking operations, including connecting and retrieving files by using common Web protocols and creating basic UNIX-like sockets.

Used in conjunction with input and output streams, reading and writing files over the network becomes almost as easy as reading or writing files on disk.

Today you will write Java programs that are Net-aware and learn why it's harder to use networking in applets than applications. You will create a program that can load a document over the World Wide Web, a program that mimics a popular Internet service, and a client/server network program.

Networking in Java

 *Networking* is the capability of different computers to make connections with each other and to exchange information.

In Java, networking involves classes in the `java.net` package, which offers support for many different kinds of networking operations, including connecting and retrieving files by HTTP and FTP, as well as working at a lower level with basic UNIX-like sockets.

The easiest way to use Java's network capabilities is to create applications because they aren't subject to the same default security policies as applets. Applets cannot connect to any networked machine other than the one that hosts the server they were loaded from. Even with this restriction, you can accomplish a great deal and take advantage of the Web to read and process information over the Web.

This section describes three simple ways you can communicate with systems on the Net:

- Loading a Web page and any other resource with a URL from an applet
- Using the socket classes, `Socket` and `ServerSocket`, which open standard socket connections to hosts and read to and write from those connections
- Calling `getInputStream()`, a method that opens a connection to a URL and can extract data from that connection

Creating Links Inside Applets

Because applets run inside Web browsers, it's often useful to direct the browser to load a new Web document.

Before you can load anything, you must create a new instance of the class `URL` that represents the address of the resource you want to load. *URL* is an acronym for *uniform resource locator*, and it refers to the unique address of any document or other resource that is accessible on the Internet.

`URL` is part of the `java.net` package, so you must import the package or refer to the class by its full name in your programs.

To create a new `URL` object, use one of four constructors:

- `URL(String)` creates a URL object from a full Web address such as `http://www.java21pro.com` or `ftp://ftp.netscape.com`.
- `URL(URL, String)` creates an `URL` object with a base address provided by the specified `URL` and a relative path provided by the `String`. When specifying the address, you can call `getDocumentBase()` for the URL of the page containing your applet or `getCodeBase()` for the URL of the applet's class file. The relative path will be tacked onto the base address.

- URL(*String*, *String*, *int*, *String*) creates a new URL object from a protocol (such as "http", or "ftp"), host name (such as "www.naviseek.com" or "ftp.netcom.com"), port number (80 for HTTP), and a filename or path name.

- URL(*String*, *String*, *String*) is the same as the previous constructor minus the port number.

When you use the URL(*String*) constructor, you must deal with MalformedURLException objects. One way is by placing it in a try-catch block as shown in the following:

```
try {
    URL load = new URL("http://www.mcp.com");
} catch (MalformedURLException e) {
    System.out.println("Bad URL");
}
```

After you have a URL object, you pass it to the browser by calling the showDocument() method of the AppletContext class in your applet. AppletContext is an interface that represents the environment in which an applet runs—the Web browser, the page it is contained in, and the other applets on the same page.

Call getAppletContext() in your applet to get an AppletContext object to work with, and then call showDocument(*URL*) on that object:

```
getAppletContext().showDocument(load);
```

The browser that contains the Java applet with this code will then load and display the document at that URL.

Listing 19.1 contains two classes: WebMenu and a helper class called WebButton. The WebMenu applet displays three buttons that contain links to Web sites, as shown in Figure 19.1. Clicking the buttons causes the document to be loaded from the locations to which those buttons refer.

19

FIGURE 19.1

The WebMenu *applet.*

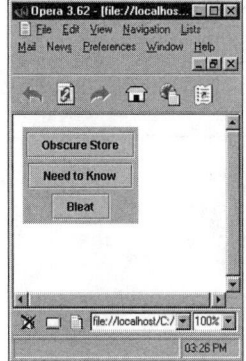

LISTING 19.1   The Full Text of `WebMenu.java`

```
 1: import java.net.*;
 2: import java.awt.event.*;
 3: import javax.swing.*;
 4:
 5: public class WebMenu extends JApplet implements ActionListener {
 6:     WebButton[] choices = new WebButton[3];
 7:
 8:     public void init() {
 9:         choices[0] = new WebButton("Obscure Store",
10:             "http://www.obscurestore.com/");
11:         choices[1] = new WebButton("Need to Know",
12:             "http://www.ntk.net/");
13:         choices[2] = new WebButton("Bleat",
14:             "http://www.lileks.com/bleats");
15:         FlowLayout flo = new FlowLayout();
16:         getContentPane().setLayout(flo);
17:         for (int i = 0; i < choices.length; i++) {
18:             choices[i].addActionListener(this);
19:             getContentPane().add(choices[i]);
20:         }
21:     }
22:
23:     public void actionPerformed(ActionEvent evt) {
24:         WebButton clicked = (WebButton)evt.getSource();
25:         try {
26:             URL load = new URL(clicked.address);
27:             getAppletContext().showDocument(load);
28:         } catch (MalformedURLException e) {
29:             showStatus("Bad URL:" + clicked.address);
30:         }
31:     }
32: }
33:
34: class WebButton extends JButton {
35:     String address;
36:
37:     WebButton(String iLabel, String iAddress) {
38:         super(iLabel);
39:         address = iAddress;
40:     }
41: }
```

This applet can be tested using the following HTML on a Web page:

```
<applet code="WebMenu.class" height="100" width="125">
</applet>
```

Note

This applet must be run from a Web browser rather than `appletviewer` for the buttons to load new pages. Because it uses event-handling techniques introduced after Java 1.0, you should use a current version of Opera, Netscape Navigator, or Microsoft Internet Explorer to run the applet.

Two classes make up this project: `WebMenu`, which implements the applet, and `WebButton`, a user-interface component that extends the `JButton` class to add an instance variable that holds a Web address.

This applet creates three `WebButton` instances (lines 9–14) and stores them in an array. Each button is assigned a name, which is used as a label, and a Web address, which is stored as a `String` rather than a `URL`. After each button is set up, an `ActionListener` is attached to it.

Because of these listeners, the `actionPerformed()` method in lines 23–31 is called when a button is pressed. This method determines which button was clicked, and then uses the `address` variable of that button to construct a new `URL` object. After you have a `URL` object, the call to `showDocument()` in line 27 tells the browser to load that Web page in the current window.

Tip

You can also load a URL in a new browser window or a specific frame. For a new window, call `showDocument(URL, String)`, using `"_blank"` as the second argument. For a frame, use its name as the second argument.

19

Because the Web page information is stored in the applet, you must recompile the class file every time you add, remove, or modify an address. A better way to implement this program would be to store the Web page names and URLs as parameters in an HTML document, which was described in Day 7, "Writing Java Applets."

Opening Web Connections

As you have seen when working with applets, it is easy to load a Web page or anything else with a URL. If the file you want to grab is stored on the Web and can be accessed by using the more common URL forms (HTTP, FTP, and so on), your Java program can use the URL class to get it.

For security reasons, applets by default can connect only to the same host from which they originally loaded. That means if you have your applets stored on a system called `www.naviseek.com`, the only machine your applet can open a connection to will be that same host—and that same hostname. If the file that the applet wants to retrieve is on that same system, using URL connections is the easiest way to get it.

This restriction will change how you write and test applets that load files through their URLs. Because you haven't been dealing with network connections, you've been able to do all your testing on the local disk simply by opening the HTML files in a browser or with the `appletviewer` tool. You cannot do this with applets that open network connections. For those applets to work correctly, you must do one of two things:

- Run your browser on the same machine on which your Web server is running. If you don't have access to your Web server, you can often install and run a Web server on your local machine.

- Upload your class and HTML files to your Web server each time you want to test them. You then run the applet off the uploaded Web page instead of running it locally.

You'll know when you're not doing things correctly in regard to making sure your applet and the connection it's opening are on the same server. If you try to load an applet or a file from a different server, you get a security exception, along with a lot of other error messages printed to your screen or to the Java console. Because of this, you might want to work with applications when you're connecting to the Internet and using its resources.

Opening a Stream over the Net

As you learned during Day 17, "Handling Data Through Java Streams," there are several ways you can pull information through a stream into your Java programs. The classes and methods you choose depend on what form the information is in and what you want to do with it.

One of the resources you can reach from your Java programs is a text document on the World Wide Web, whether it's an HTML file or some other kind of plain text document.

You can use a four-step process to load a text document off the Web and read it line by line:

1. Create a URL object that represents the resource's World Wide Web address.
2. Create a `URLConnection` object that can load that URL and make a connection to the site hosting it.
3. Use the `getInputStream()` method of that `URLConnection` object, create an `InputStreamReader` that can read a stream of data from the URL.
4. Using that input stream reader, create a `BufferedReader` object that can efficiently read characters from an input stream.

There's a lot of interaction going on between Point A—the Web document—and Point B—your Java program. The URL is used to set up a URL connection, which is used to set up an input stream reader, which is used to set up a buffered input stream reader. The need to catch any exceptions that occur along the way adds more complexity to the process.

This is a confusing process, so it's useful to step through a program that implements it. The GetFile application in Listing 19.2 uses the four-step technique to open a connection to a Web site and read an HTML document from it. When the document is fully loaded, it is displayed in a text area.

LISTING 19.2   The Full Text of GetFile.java

```
 1: import javax.swing.*;
 2: import java.awt.*;
 3: import java.awt.event.*;
 4: import java.net.*;
 5: import java.io.*;
 6:
 7: public class GetFile {
 8:     public static void main(String[] arguments) {
 9:         if (arguments.length == 1) {
10:             PageFrame page = new PageFrame(arguments[0]);
11:             page.show();
12:         } else
13:             System.out.println("Usage: java GetFile url");
14:     }
15: }
16:
17: class PageFrame extends JFrame {
18:     JTextArea box = new JTextArea("Getting data ...");
19:     URL page;
20:
21:     public PageFrame(String address) {
22:         super(address);
23:         setSize(600, 300);
24:         JScrollPane pane = new JScrollPane(box);
25:         getContentPane().add(pane);
26:         WindowListener l = new WindowAdapter() {
27:             public void windowClosing(WindowEvent evt) {
28:                 System.exit(0);
29:             }
30:         };
31:         addWindowListener(l);
32:
33:         try {
34:             page = new URL(address);
35:             getData(page);
```

19

LISTING 19.2   continued

```
36:            } catch (MalformedURLException e) {
37:                System.out.println("Bad URL: " + address);
38:            }
39:        }
40:
41:    void getData(URL url) {
42:        URLConnection conn = null;
43:        InputStreamReader in;
44:        BufferedReader data;
45:        String line;
46:        StringBuffer buf = new StringBuffer();
47:        try {
48:            conn = this.page.openConnection();
49:            conn.connect();
50:            box.setText("Connection opened ...");
51:
52:            in = new InputStreamReader(conn.getInputStream());
53:            data = new BufferedReader(in);
54:
55:            box.setText("Reading data ...");
56:            while ((line = data.readLine()) != null)
57:                buf.append(line + "\n");
58:
59:            box.setText(buf.toString());
60:        } catch (IOException e) {
61:            System.out.println("IO Error:" + e.getMessage());
62:        }
63:    }
64:
65: }
```

To run the `GetFile` application, specify a URL as the only command-line argument. For example:

```
java GetFile http://tycho.usno.navy.mil/cgi-bin/timer.pl
```

Any URL can be chosen—try `http://www.mcp.com` for Macmillan USA's Web site or `http://random.yahoo.com/bin/ryl` for a random link from the Yahoo! directory. The preceding example loads a page from the U.S. Naval Observatory's official timekeeping site, as shown in Figure 19.2.

Two-thirds of Listing 19.2 is devoted to running the application, creating the user interface, and creating a valid `URL` object. The only thing that's new in this project is the `getData()` method in lines 41–63, which loads data from the resource at a URL and displays it in a text area.

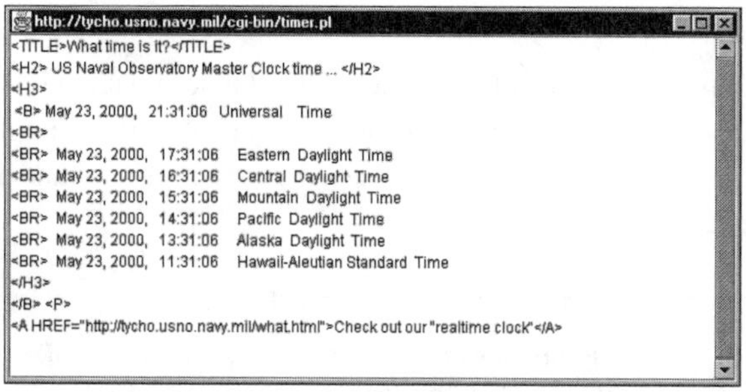

FIGURE 19.2

The GetFile
application.

First, three objects are initialized: a URLConnection, InputStreamReader, and BufferedReader. These will be used together to pull the data from the Internet to the Java application. In addition, two objects are created to actually hold the data when it arrives—a String and a StringBuffer.

Lines 48–49 open a URL connection, which is necessary to get an input stream from that connection.

Line 52 uses the URL connection's getInputStream() method to create a new input stream reader.

Line 53 uses that input stream reader to create a new buffered input stream reader—a BufferedReader object called data.

After you have this buffered reader, you can use its readLine() method to read a line of text from the input stream. The buffered reader puts characters in a buffer as they arrive, and pulls them out of the buffer when requested.

The while loop in lines 56–57 reads the Web document line by line, appending each line to the StringBuffer object that was created to hold the page's text. A string buffer is used instead of a string because you can't modify a string at runtime in this manner.

After all the data has been read, line 59 converts the string buffer into a string with the toString() method and then puts that result in the program's text area by calling the component's append(String) method.

One thing to note about this example is that the part of the code that opened a network connection, read from the file, and created a string is surrounded by a try and catch statement. If any errors occur while you're trying to read or process the file, these statements enable you to recover from them without the entire program crashing. (In this case, the program exits with an error because there's little else to be done if the application can't read the file.) The try and catch give you the ability to handle and recover from errors.

Sockets

For networking applications beyond what the URL and URLconnection classes offer (for example, for other protocols or for more general networking applications), Java provides the Socket and ServerSocket classes as an abstraction of standard TCP socket programming techniques.

Note

> Java also provides facilities for using datagram (UDP) sockets, which are not covered here. See the Java documentation for the java.net package if you're interested in working with datagrams.

The Socket class provides a client-side socket interface similar to standard UNIX sockets. Create a new instance of Socket to open a connection (where *hostName* is the host to connect to and *portNum* is the port number):

```
Socket connection = new Socket(hostName, portNum);
```

After you create a socket, you should set its timeout value, which determines how long the application will wait for data to arrive. This is handled by calling the socket's setSoTimeOut(*int*) method with the number of milliseconds to wait as the only argument:

```
connection.setSoTimeOut(50000);
```

By using this method, any efforts to read data from the socket represented by connection will only wait for 50,000 milliseconds (50 seconds). If the timeout is reached, an InterruptedIOException will be thrown, which gives you an opportunity in a try-catch block to either close the socket or try to read from it again.

If you don't set a timeout in a program that uses sockets, it might hang indefinitely waiting for data.

Tip

> This problem is usually avoided by putting network operations in their own thread and running them separately from the rest of the program, a technique used with animation on Day 13, "Threads and Animation."

After the socket is open, you can use input and output streams to read and write from that socket:

```
BufferedInputStream bis = new
    BufferedInputStream(connection.getInputStream());
DataInputStream in = new DataInputStream(bis);

BufferedOutputStream bos = new
    BufferedOutputStream(connection.getOutputStream());
DataOutputStream out= new DataOutputStream(bos);
```

Because you really don't need names for all these objects—they are only used to create a stream or stream reader—an efficient shortcut is to combine several statements, as in this example using a `Socket` object named `sock`:

```
DataInputStream in = new DataInputStream(
    new BufferedInputStream(
    sock.getInputStream()));
```

In this statement, the call to `sock.getInputStream()` returns an input stream associated with that socket. This stream is used to create a `BufferedInputStream`, and the buffered input stream is used to create a `DataInputStream`. The only variables you are left with are `sock` and `in`, which would still be needed as you receive data from the connection and close it afterward. The intermediate objects—a `BufferedInputStream` and an `InputStream`—are needed only once.

After you're done with a socket, don't forget to close it by calling the `close()` method. This also closes all the input and output streams you might have set up for that socket. For example:

```
connection.close();
```

Socket programming can be used for a large number of services that are delivered using TCP/IP networking, including telnet, SMTP (incoming mail), NNTP (Usenet news), and finger.

The last of these, finger, is a protocol for asking a system about one of its users. By setting up a finger server, a system administrator enables an Internet-connected machine to answer requests for user information. Users can provide more information about themselves by creating `.plan` files, which are sent back to anyone who uses finger to find out more about them.

Although it has fallen into disuse in recent years because of security concerns, before the World Wide Web was introduced, finger was the most popular way that Internet users published facts about themselves and their activities. You could use finger on a friend's account at another college to see if that person was online and read the most current `.plan` file.

19

Note

> Today, there's still one community that spreads personal messages by finger
> rather than Web site or mailing list—the game-programming community.
> The GameFinger Web site, which acts as a gateway between the Web and
> finger, has links to hundreds of these throwbacks at http://finger.plan-
> etquake.com/.

As an exercise in socket programming, the Finger application is a rudimentary finger
client (see Listing 19.3).

LISTING 19.3   The Full Text of Finger.java

```
 1: import java.io.*;
 2: import java.net.*;
 3: import java.util.*;
 4:
 5: public class Finger {
 6:     public static void main(String[] arguments) {
 7:         String user;
 8:         String host;
 9:         if ((arguments.length == 1) && (arguments[0].indexOf("@") > -1)) {
10:             StringTokenizer split = new StringTokenizer(arguments[0],
11:                 "@");
12:             user = split.nextToken();
13:             host = split.nextToken();
14:         } else {
15:             System.out.println("Usage: java Finger user@host");
16:             return;
17:         }
18:         try {
19:             Socket digit = new Socket(host, 79);
20:             digit.setSoTimeout(20000);
21:             PrintStream out = new PrintStream(digit.getOutputStream());
22:             out.print(user + "\015\012");
23:             BufferedReader in = new BufferedReader(
24:                 new InputStreamReader(digit.getInputStream()));
25:             boolean eof = false;
26:             while (!eof) {
27:                 String line = in.readLine();
28:                 if (line != null)
29:                     System.out.println(line);
30:                 else
31:                     eof = true;
32:             }
33:             digit.close();
34:         } catch (IOException e) {
35:             System.out.println("IO Error:" + e.getMessage());
```

```
36:         }
37:     }
38: }
```

When making a finger request, you specify a username followed by an at sign ("@") and a host name, the same format as an email address. One real-life example is romero@ionstorm.com, the finger address of Quake and Daikatana designer John Romero. You can request his .plan file by running the Finger application as follows:

```
java Finger romero@ionstorm.com
```

If romero has an account on the ionstorm.com finger server, the output of this program will be his .plan file and perhaps other information. The server also will let you know if a user can't be found.

The GameFinger site includes addresses for other game designers who provide .plan updates, including Kenn Hoekstra (khoekstra@ravensoft.com), Markus Mäki (markus@remedy.fi), Chris Hargrove (chrish@finger.3drealms.com), and Chris Norden (cnorden@ionstorm.com).

The Finger application uses the StringTokenizer class to convert an address in *user@host* format into two String objects: user and host (lines 10–13).

The following socket activities are taking place:

- Lines 19–20: A new Socket is created using the host name and port 79, the port that is traditionally reserved for finger services, and a timeout of 20 seconds is set.
- Line 21: The socket is used to get an OutputStream, which feeds into a new PrintStream object.
- Line 22: The finger protocol requires that the username be sent through the socket, followed by a carriage return ('\015') and linefeed ('\012'). This is handled by calling the print() method of the new PrintStream.
- Lines 23–24: After the username has been sent, an input stream must be created on the socket to receive input from the finger server. A BufferedReader stream, in, is created by combining several stream-creation expressions together. This stream is well suited for finger input because it can read a line of text at a time.
- Lines 26–32: The program loops as lines are read from the buffered reader. The end of output from the server causes in.readLine() to return null, ending the loop.

The same techniques used to communicate with a finger server through a socket can be used to connect to other popular Internet services. You could turn it into a telnet or Web reading client with a port change in line 19 and little other modification.

19

Socket Servers

Server-side sockets work similarly to client sockets, with the exception of the `accept()` method. A server socket listens on a TCP port for a connection from a client; when a client connects to that port, the `accept()` method accepts a connection from that client. By using both client and server sockets, you can create applications that communicate with each other over the network.

Create a new instance of `ServerSocket` with the port number in order to create a server socket and bind it to a port:

```
ServerSocket servo = new ServerSocket(8888);
```

Use the `accept()` method to listen on that port (and to accept a connection from any clients if one is made):

```
servo.accept();
```

After the socket connection is made, you can use input and output streams to read from and write to the client.

In the next section, you implement a simple socket-based application.

To extend the behavior of the socket classes—for example, to allow network connections to work across a firewall or a proxy—you can use the abstract class `SocketImpl` and the interface `SocketImplFactory` to create a new transport-layer socket implementation. This design fits with the original goal of Java's socket classes: to allow those classes to be portable to other systems with different transport mechanisms. The problem with this mechanism is that although it works for simple cases, it prevents you from adding other protocols on top of TCP (for example, to implement an encryption mechanism such as SSL) and from having multiple socket implementations per Java runtime.

For these reasons, sockets were extended after Java 1.0 so that the `Socket` and `ServerSocket` classes are not final and extendable. You can create subclasses of these classes that use either the default socket implementation or one of your own making. This allows much more flexible network capabilities.

To finish up the discussion on networking in Java, here's an example of a Java program that uses the `Socket` classes to implement a simple network-based server application, `TriviaServer`.

The TriviaServer application presents a trivia quiz with multiple choice answers. It works like this:

1. The server program waits for a client to connect.

2. When a client connects, the server sends a question to the client and waits for a response.

3. When the client sends an answer, the server notifies the client whether it is correct or incorrect. If it is incorrect, the correct answer is provided.

4. The server then asks the client whether the quiz should continue. If any response other than N or n is received, the process repeats.

Designing a Server Application

It's usually a good idea to perform a brief preliminary design before you start churning out code. With that in mind, take a look at what is required of the TriviaServer and a client.

On the server side, you need a program that monitors a particular port on the host machine for client connections. Port 4413 was chosen arbitrarily for this project, but it could be any number from 1024 to 65535.

Note

The Internet Assigned Numbers Authority controls the usage of ports 0 to 1023, but claims are staked to the higher ports on a more informal basis. When choosing port numbers for your own client/server applications, it's a good idea to do research on what ports are currently being used by others. Search the Web for references to the port you want to use and plug the terms "Registered Port Numbers" and "Well-Known Port Numbers" into search engines to find lists of in-use ports. A good guide to port usage is available on the Web at http://www.sockets.com/services.htm.

19

When a client is detected, the server picks a random question and sends it to the client over the specified port. This begins an exchange of information between the server and client, with the server doing almost all of the work.

The client's only responsibility in this client/server project is to establish a connection to the server, display messages received from the server, take input from a user, and send that input to the server.

Although you could develop a simple client for a project like this, you also can use any telnet application to act as the client, as long as it can connect to a port you designate. Windows includes a command-line application called telnet you can use for this purpose.

Implementing the Server

The heart of the instance variables defined in the TriviaServer class follow:

```
private static final int WAIT_FOR_CLIENT = 0;
private static final int WAIT_FOR_ANSWER = 1;
private static final int WAIT_FOR_CONFIRM = 2;
private String[] questions;
private String[] answers;
private Socket sock;
private int numQuestions;
private int num = 0;
private int state = WAIT_FOR_CLIENT;
private Random rand = new Random();
```

The WAIT_FOR_CLIENT, WAIT_FOR_ANSWER, and WAIT_FOR_CONFIRM variables are all constants that define different states that the server can be in; you see these constants in action in a moment. The questions and answers variables are string arrays used to store the questions and corresponding answers. The sock instance variable keeps up with the server-socket connection. numQuestions is used to store the total number of questions, whereas num is the number of the current question being asked. The state variable holds the current state of the server as defined by the three state constants (WAIT_FOR_CLIENT, WAIT_FOR_ANSWER, and WAIT_FOR_CONFIRM). Finally, the rand variable is used to pick questions at random.

The TriviaServer constructor doesn't do much except create a Socket rather than a DatagramSocket:

```
public TriviaServer() {
    super("TriviaServer");
    try {
        sock = new ServerSocket(4413);
        System.out.println("TriviaServer up and running ...");
    } catch (IOException e) {
        System.err.println("Error: couldn't create socket.");
        System.exit(1);
    }
}
```

Most of the action takes place in the run() method:

```
public void run() {
    Socket client = null;
```

```
// Initialize the question and answer data
if (!loadData()) {
    System.err.println("Error: couldn't initialize Q&A data.");
    return;
}

// Look for clients and ask trivia questions
while (true) {
    // Wait for a client
    if (sock == null)
        return;
    try {
        client = sock.accept();
    } catch (IOException e) {
        System.err.println("Error: couldn't connect to client.");
        System.exit(1);
    }

    // Process questions and answers
    try {
        InputStreamReader isr = new InputStreamReader(
            client.getInputStream());
        BufferedReader is = new BufferedReader(isr);
        PrintWriter os = new PrintWriter(new
            BufferedOutputStream(client.getOutputStream()), false);
        String outLine;
        // Output server request
        outLine = processInput(null);
        os.println(outLine);
        os.flush();

        // Process and output user input
        while (true) {
            String inLine = is.readLine();
            if (inLine.length() > 0)
                outLine = processInput(inLine);
            else
                outLine = processInput("");
            os.println(outLine);
            os.flush();
            if (outLine.equals("Bye."))
                break;
        }

        // Clean up
        os.close();
        is.close();
        client.close();
    } catch (Exception e) {
        System.err.println("Error: " + e);
        e.printStackTrace();
```

19

```
            }
        }
    }
```

The `run()` method first initializes the questions and answers by calling `loadData()`, which you learn about in a moment. An infinite `while` loop that waits for a client connection is then entered.

When a client connects, the appropriate input and output streams are created and the communication is handled via the `processInput()` method. This method continually processes client responses and handles asking new questions until the client user decides not to receive any more questions. The server acknowledges this by sending the string `"Bye."` and closing the streams and client socket.

The `processInput()`method keeps up with the server state and manages the logic of the question/answer process:

```
String processInput(String inStr) {
    String outStr = null;

    switch (state) {
        case WAIT_FOR_CLIENT:
            // Ask a question
            outStr = questions[num];
            state = WAIT_FOR_ANSWER;
            break;
        case WAIT_FOR_ANSWER:
            // Check the answer
            if (inStr.equalsIgnoreCase(answers[num]))
                outStr="\015\012That's correct! Want another (y/n)?";
            else
              outStr="\015\012Wrong, the correct answer is " + answers[num] +
                    ". Want another (y/n)?";
            state = WAIT_FOR_CONFIRM;
            break;
        case WAIT_FOR_CONFIRM:
            // See if they want another question
            if (!inStr.equalsIgnoreCase("N")) {
                num = Math.abs(rand.nextInt()) % questions.length;
                outStr = questions[num];
                state = WAIT_FOR_ANSWER;
            } else {
                outStr = "Bye.";
                state = WAIT_FOR_CLIENT;
            }
            break;
    }
    return outStr;
}
```

The first thing to note about the processInput() method is the outStr local variable. This string's value is sent back to the client in the run method when processInput returns, so keep an eye on how processInput uses outStr to convey information to the client.

In TriviaServer, the state WAIT_FOR_CLIENT represents the server when it is idle and waiting for a client connection. Understand that each case statement in processInput() represents the server leaving the given state. For example, the WAIT_FOR_CLIENT case statement is entered when the server has just left the WAIT_FOR_CLIENT state—a client has just connected to the server. When this occurs, the server sets the output string to the current question and sets the state to WAIT_FOR_ANSWER.

If the server is leaving the WAIT_FOR_ANSWER state, the client has responded with an answer. processInput() checks the client's answer against the correct answer and sets the output string accordingly. It then sets the state to WAIT_FOR_CONFIRM.

The WAIT_FOR_CONFIRM state represents the server waiting for a confirmation answer from the client. In processInput(), the WAIT_FOR_CONFIRM case statement indicates that the server is leaving the state because the client has returned a confirmation (yes or no). If the client gave any answer other than N or n, processInput picks a new question and sets the state back to WAIT_FOR_ANSWER. Otherwise, the server tells the client "Bye." and returns the state to WAIT_FOR_CLIENT to await a new client connection.

The questions and answers in Trivia are stored in a text file called qna.txt, which is organized into a list of questions and answers in alternating question, answer, question, answer sequence. To mark the end of a question or answer, a pound sign ("#") is used. A listing for the first two questions and answers in the qna.txt file follows:

```
Which one of the Smothers Brothers did Bill Cosby once punch out?
(a) Dick
(b) Tommy
(c) both#
b#

What's the nickname of Dallas Cowboys fullback Daryl Johnston?
(a) caribou
(b) moose
(c) elk#
b#
```

19

Tip

> You can create your own questions and answers for this trivia quiz by following the format above, or download a full qna.txt file from the book's Web site—visit http://www.java21pro.com and go to the Day 19 page.

The `loadData()` method handles the work of reading the questions and answers from the text file and storing them in separate string arrays, as shown here:

```java
private boolean loadData() {
    try {
        File inFile = new File("qna.txt");
        FileInputStream inStream = new FileInputStream(inFile);
        byte[] data = new byte[(int)inFile.length()];

        // Read questions and answers into a byte array
        if (inStream.read(data) <= 0) {
            System.err.println("Error: couldn't read q&a.");
            return false;
        }

        // See how many question/answer pairs there are
        for (int i = 0; i < data.length; i++)
            if (data[i] == (byte)'#')
                numQuestions++;
        numQuestions /= 2;
        questions = new String[numQuestions];
        answers = new String[numQuestions];

        // Parse questions and answers into String arrays
        int start = 0, index = 0;
        boolean isQuestion = true;
        for (int i = 0; i < data.length; i++)
            if (data[i] == (byte)'#') {
                if (isQuestion) {
                    questions[index] = new String(data, start,
                        i - start);
                    isQuestion = false;
                } else {
                    answers[index] = new String(data, start,
                        i - start);
                    isQuestion = true;
                    index++;
                }
                start = i + 3;
            }
    } catch (FileNotFoundException e) {
        System.err.println("Exception: couldn't find the Q&A file.");
        return false;
    } catch (IOException e) {
        System.err.println("Exception: couldn't read the Q&A file.");
        return false;
    }
    return true;
}
```

The loadData() method uses two arrays and fills them with alternating strings from the qna.txt file: first a question, and then an answer, alternating until the end of the file is reached.

The only remaining method in TriviaServer is main(), which simply creates the server object and gets it started with a call to the start method:

```
public static void main(String[] arguments) {
    TriviaServer server = new TriviaServer();
    server.start();
}
```

Listing 19.4 contains the full source code for the server application.

LISTING 19.4 The Full Text of TriviaServer.java

```
 1: import java.io.*;
 2: import java.net.*;
 3: import java.util.Random;
 4:
 5: public class TriviaServer extends Thread {
 6:     private static final int WAIT_FOR_CLIENT = 0;
 7:     private static final int WAIT_FOR_ANSWER = 1;
 8:     private static final int WAIT_FOR_CONFIRM = 2;
 9:     private String[] questions;
10:     private String[] answers;
11:     private ServerSocket sock;
12:     private int numQuestions;
13:     private int num = 0;
14:     private int state = WAIT_FOR_CLIENT;
15:     private Random rand = new Random();
16:
17:     public TriviaServer() {
18:         super("TriviaServer");
19:         try {
20:             sock = new ServerSocket(4413);
21:             System.out.println("TriviaServer up and running ...");
22:         } catch (IOException e) {
23:             System.err.println("Error: couldn't create socket.");
24:             System.exit(1);
25:         }
26:     }
27:
28:     public static void main(String[] arguments) {
29:         TriviaServer server = new TriviaServer();
30:         server.start();
31:     }
32:
33:     public void run() {
34:         Socket client = null;
```

19

LISTING 19.4   continued

```
35:
36:        // Initialize the question and answer data
37:        if (!loadData()) {
38:            System.err.println("Error: couldn't initialize Q&A data.");
39:            return;
40:        }
41:
42:        // Look for clients and ask trivia questions
43:        while (true) {
44:            // Wait for a client
45:            if (sock == null)
46:                return;
47:            try {
48:                client = sock.accept();
49:            } catch (IOException e) {
50:                System.err.println("Error: couldn't connect to client.");
51:                System.exit(1);
52:            }
53:
54:            // Process questions and answers
55:            try {
56:                InputStreamReader isr = new InputStreamReader(
57:                    client.getInputStream());
58:                BufferedReader is = new BufferedReader(isr);
59:                PrintWriter os = new PrintWriter(new
60:                    BufferedOutputStream(client.getOutputStream()), false);
61:                String outLine;
62:
63:                // Output server request
64:                outLine = processInput(null);
65:                os.println(outLine);
66:                os.flush();
67:
68:                // Process and output user input
69:                while (true) {
70:                    String inLine = is.readLine();
71:                    if (inLine.length() > 0)
72:                        outLine = processInput(inLine);
73:                    else
74:                        outLine = processInput("");
75:                    os.println(outLine);
76:                    os.flush();
77:                    if (outLine.equals("Bye."))
78:                        break;
79:                }
80:
81:                // Clean up
82:                os.close();
83:                is.close();
```

```
 84:                    client.close();
 85:                } catch (Exception e) {
 86:                    System.err.println("Error: " + e);
 87:                    e.printStackTrace();
 88:                }
 89:            }
 90:        }
 91:
 92:    private boolean loadData() {
 93:        try {
 94:            File inFile = new File("qna.txt");
 95:            FileInputStream inStream = new FileInputStream(inFile);
 96:            byte[] data = new byte[(int)inFile.length()];
 97:
 98:            // Read questions and answers into a byte array
 99:            if (inStream.read(data) <= 0) {
100:                System.err.println("Error: couldn't read q&a.");
101:                return false;
102:            }
103:
104:            // See how many question/answer pairs there are
105:            for (int i = 0; i < data.length; i++)
106:                if (data[i] == (byte)'#')
107:                    numQuestions++;
108:            numQuestions /= 2;
109:            questions = new String[numQuestions];
110:            answers = new String[numQuestions];
111:
112:            // Parse questions and answers into String arrays
113:            int start = 0, index = 0;
114:            boolean isQuestion = true;
115:            for (int i = 0; i < data.length; i++)
116:                if (data[i] == (byte)'#') {
117:                    if (isQuestion) {
118:                        questions[index] = new String(data, start,
119:                            i - start);
120:                        isQuestion = false;
121:                    } else {
122:                        answers[index] = new String(data, start,
123:                            i - start);
124:                        isQuestion = true;
125:                        index++;
126:                    }
127:                    start = i + 3;
128:                }
129:        } catch (FileNotFoundException e) {
130:            System.err.println("Exception: couldn't find the Q&A file.");
131:            return false;
132:        } catch (IOException e) {
133:            System.err.println("Exception: couldn't read the Q&A file.");
134:            return false;
```

19

LISTING 19.4   continued

```
135:            }
136:        return true;
137:    }
138:
139:    String processInput(String inStr) {
140:        String outStr = null;
141:
142:        switch (state) {
143:            case WAIT_FOR_CLIENT:
144:                // Ask a question
145:                outStr = questions[num];
146:                state = WAIT_FOR_ANSWER;
147:                break;
148:
149:            case WAIT_FOR_ANSWER:
150:                // Check the answer
151:                if (inStr.equalsIgnoreCase(answers[num]))
152:                    outStr="\015\012That's correct! Want another (y/n)?";
153:                else
154:                    outStr="\015\012Wrong, the correct answer is "
155:                        + answers[num] +". Want another (y/n)?";
156:                state = WAIT_FOR_CONFIRM;
157:                break;
158:
159:            case WAIT_FOR_CONFIRM:
160:                // See if they want another question
161:                if (!inStr.equalsIgnoreCase("N")) {
162:                    num = Math.abs(rand.nextInt()) % questions.length;
163:                    outStr = questions[num];
164:                    state = WAIT_FOR_ANSWER;
165:                } else {
166:                    outStr = "Bye.";
167:                    state = WAIT_FOR_CLIENT;
168:                }
169:                break;
170:        }
171:        return outStr;
172:    }
173: }
```

Testing the Server

The TriviaServer application must be running in order for a client to be able to connect to it. To get things started, you must first run the server:

```
java TriviaServer
```

The server will display only one line of output if it is running successfully:

```
TriviaServer up and running ...
```

With the server running, you can connect to it using a telnet program such as the one that's included with Windows.

To run `telnet` on Windows, click Start, Run to open the Run dialog, and then type **telnet** in the Open text field and press Enter. A telnet window will open.

To make a telnet connection using this program, choose the menu command Connect, Remote System. A Connect dialog box will open, as shown in Figure 19.3. Enter **localhost** in the Host Name field, 4413 in the Port field, and leave the default value—vt100—in the TermType field.

FIGURE 19.3

Making a telnet *connection.*

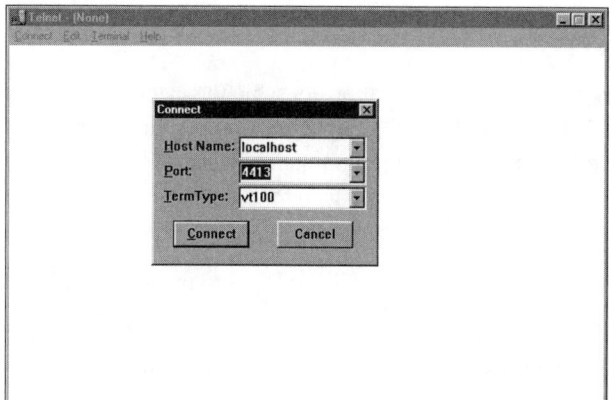

19

The host name `localhost` represents your own machine—the system running the application. You can use it to test server applications before deploying them permanently on the Internet.

Depending on how Internet connections have been configured on your system, you might need to log on to the Internet before a successful socket connection can be made between a telnet client and the `TriviaServer` application.

If the server was on another computer connected to the Internet, you would specify that computer's host name or IP address instead of `localhost`.

Figure 19.4 shows a Windows `telnet` session connected to the `TriviaServer` application.

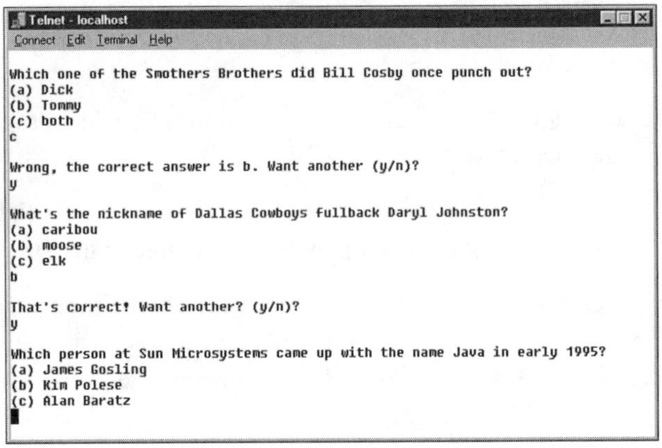

FIGURE 19.4

A client's view of the TriviaServer *connection.*

```
Telnet - localhost
Connect  Edit  Terminal  Help

Which one of the Smothers Brothers did Bill Cosby once punch out?
(a) Dick
(b) Tommy
(c) both
c

Wrong, the correct answer is b. Want another (y/n)?
y

What's the nickname of Dallas Cowboys fullback Daryl Johnston?
(a) caribou
(b) moose
(c) elk
b

That's correct! Want another? (y/n)?
y

Which person at Sun Microsystems came up with the name Java in early 1995?
(a) James Gosling
(b) Kim Polese
(c) Alan Baratz
```

Summary

Networking has many applications of which your programs can make use. You might not have realized it, but the GetFile project was a rudimentary Web browser. It brought a Web page's text into a Java program and displayed it. Of course, the HTML parsing is what turns a bunch of markup tags into a real Web page. Sun wrote an entire Web browser in Java—HotJava.

Today you learned how to use URLs, URL connections, and input streams in conjunction to pull data from the World Wide Web into your program.

You created a socket application that implements the basics of the finger protocol, a method for retrieving user information on the Internet.

You also learned how client and server programs are written in Java and how a server program makes connections to clients and exchanges information with them.

Q&A

Q How can I mimic an HTML form submission in a Java applet?

A Currently, applets make it difficult to do this. The best (and easiest way) is to use GET notation to get the browser to submit the form contents for you.

HTML forms can be submitted two ways: either by using the GET request or by using POST. If you use GET, your form information is encoded in the URL itself, something like this:

```
http://www.blah.com/cgi-bin/myscript?foo=1&bar=2&name=Laura
```

Because the form input is encoded in the URL, you can write a Java applet to mimic a form, get input from the user, and then construct a new URL object with the form data included on the end. Then just pass that URL to the browser by using `getAppletContext()` and `showDocument()`, and the browser will submit the form results itself. For simple forms, this is all you need.

Q **How can I do POST form submissions?**

A You have to mimic what a browser does to send forms using POST. Create a URL object for the form-submission address such as `http://www.prefect.com/cgi/mail2rogers.cgi`, and then call this object's `openConnection()` method to create a `URLConnection` object. Call the connection's `setDoOutput()` method to indicate that you will be sending data to this URL, and then send the connection a series of name-value pairs that hold the data, separated by ampersand characters (`"&"`).

For instance, the `mail2rogers.cgi` form is a CGI program that sends mail to Rogers Cadenhead, the coauthor of this book. It transmits `name`, `subject`, `email`, `comments`, `who`, `rcode`, and `scode` data. If you have created a `PrintWriter` stream called `pw` that is connected to this CGI program, you can post information to it using the following statement:

```
pw.print("name=YourName&subject=Your+Book&email=you@yourdomain.com&"
    + "comments=Your+POST+example+works.+I+owe+you+$1,000&"
    + "who=preadm&rcode=21javaproscode=%2Fmailsent.html");
```

Questions

1. What network action is not permitted in an applet under the default security level for Java?

    (a) Loading a graphic from the server that hosts the applet

    (b) Loading a graphic from a different server

    (c) Loading a Web page from a different server in the browser containing the applet

2. In the finger protocol, which program makes a request for information about a user?

    (a) The client

    (b) The server

    (c) Both can make that request

19

3. Which method is preferred for loading the data from a Web page into your Java application?

    (a) Creating a `Socket` and an input stream from that socket

    (b) Creating a `URL` and a `URLConnection` from that object

    (c) Loading the page using the applet method `showDocument()`

Answers

1. b. Applets cannot make network connections to any machine other than the one from which they were served.

2. a. The client requests information and the server sends something back in response. This is traditionally how client/server applications function, although some programs can act as both client and server.

3. b. Sockets are good for low-level connections, such as when you are implementing a new protocol. For existing protocols such as HTTP, there are classes that are better suited to that protocol—`URL` and `URLConnection`, in this case.

Exercises

To extend your knowledge of the subjects covered today, try the following exercises:

- Modify the `WebMenu` program so that it generates 10 URLs that begin with `http://www.`, end with `.com`, and contain three random letters or numbers in between (such as `http://www.mcp.com`, `http://www.cbs.com`, and `http://www.eod.com`). Use these URLs in 10 `WebButton` objects on an applet.

- Write a program that takes finger requests, looks for a `.plan` file matching the username requested, and sends it if found. Send a "user not found" message otherwise.

Where applicable, exercise solutions are offered on the book's Web site at `http://www.java21pro.com`.

DAY **20**

Working with JavaBeans

As you have learned, one of the primary advantages of object-oriented programming is the capability to reuse an object in different programs. If you have created a spellchecker object that works great with your word-processing program, you should be able to use the same object with an email program also.

Sun has extended this principle with the introduction of JavaBeans. A *JavaBean*, also called a *bean*, is a software object that interacts with other objects according to a strict set of guidelines—the JavaBeans Specification. By following these guidelines, the bean can most easily be used with other objects. After you know how to work with one JavaBean according to these rules, you know how to work with them all.

Another advantage of JavaBeans occurs when you're using a programming tool that has been developed with beans in mind. These environments, including Sun's own free JavaBeans Development Kit, make it possible to develop Java programs quickly by using existing beans and establishing the relationships between them.

Today, you'll explore the following subjects:

- Creating reusable software objects in Java
- How JavaBeans relates to the Java class library
- The JavaBeans API
- JavaBeans development tools
- The JavaBeans Development Kit
- Working with JavaBeans
- Creating an applet with JavaBeans

Reusable Software Components

A growing trend in the field of software development is the use of *reusable components*—elements of a program that can be used with more than one software package.

 A *software component* is a piece of software isolated into a discrete, easily reusable structure.

If you develop parts of a program so that they are completely self-contained, it should be possible for these components to be assembled into programs with much greater development efficiency. This notion of reusing carefully packaged software was borrowed, to some extent, from the assembly-line approach that became so popular in the United States during the Industrial Revolution. This idea, as applied to software, is to build small, reusable components once and then reuse them as much as possible, thereby streamlining the entire development process.

Perhaps the greatest difficulty that component software has had to face is the wide range of disparate microprocessors and operating systems in use today. There have been several reasonable attempts at component software, but they've always been limited to a specific operating system. Microsoft's VBX and OCX component architectures have had great success in the Intel PC world, but they've done little to bridge the gap between PCs and other operating systems.

 Microsoft's ActiveX technology, which is based on its OCX technology, aims to provide an all-purpose component technology that's compatible across a wide range of platforms. However, considering the dependency of ActiveX on 32-bit Windows code, it remains to be seen how Microsoft will solve the platform-dependency issue.

Some existing component technologies also suffer from having been developed in a particular programming language or for a particular development environment. Just as platform-dependency cripples components at runtime, limiting component development to a particular programming language or development environment cripples components at the development end. Software developers want to decide for themselves which language is the most appropriate for a particular task. Likewise, they want to select the development environment that best fits their needs, rather than being forced to use an environment based on a component technology. Therefore, any realistic long-term component technology must deal with both platform-dependency and language-dependency.

Java has been a major factor in making platform-independent software development a reality, and it offers software component development through JavaBeans.

JavaBeans is an architecture- and platform-independent set of classes for creating and using Java software components. It takes advantage of the portable Java platform to provide a component software solution.

The Goal of JavaBeans

JavaBeans was designed to be compact because components will often be used in distributed environments where entire components are transferred across a low-bandwidth Internet connection. The second part of this goal relates to the ease with which the components are built and used. It's not such a stretch to imagine components that are easy to use, but creating a component architecture that makes it easy to build components is a different issue altogether.

The second major goal of JavaBeans is to be fully portable. As a result, developers will not need to worry about including platform-specific libraries with their Java applets.

The existing Java architecture already offers a wide range of benefits that are easily applied to components. One of the more important (but rarely mentioned) features of Java is its built-in class discovery mechanism, which allows objects to interact with each other dynamically. This results in a system where objects can be integrated with each other, independent of their respective origins or development histories. The class discovery mechanism is not just a neat Java feature; it is a necessary requirement in any component architecture.

20

NEW TERM Another example of JavaBeans inheriting existing Java functionality is *persistence*, which is the capability of an object to store and retrieve its internal state. Persistence is handled automatically in JavaBeans by using the serialization mechanism already present in Java. *Serialization* is the process of storing or retrieving information through a standard protocol. Alternatively, developers can create customized persistence solutions whenever necessary.

Although support for distributed computing is not a core element of the JavaBeans architecture, it is provided. JavaBeans component developers can select the distributed computing approach that best fits their needs. Sun provides a distributed computing solution in its Remote Method Invocation (RMI) technology, but JavaBeans developers are in no way handcuffed to this solution. Other options include CORBA (Common Object Request Broker Architecture) and Microsoft's DCOM (Distributed Component Object Model), among others.

Distributed computing has been cleanly abstracted from JavaBeans to keep things tight while still giving a wide range of options to developers who require distributed support. JavaBeans's final design goal deals with design-time issues and how developers build applications by using JavaBeans components.

The JavaBeans architecture includes support for specifying design-time properties and editing mechanisms to better facilitate visual editing of JavaBeans components. The result is that developers will be able to use visual tools to assemble and modify JavaBeans components in a seamless fashion, much the way existing PC visual tools work with components such as VBX or OCX controls. In this way, component developers specify the way in which the components are to be used and manipulated in a development environment.

How JavaBeans Relates to Java

Although Java's object-oriented nature provides a means for objects to work in conjunction with each other, there are a few rules or standards governing how object interactions are conducted. These rules are needed for a robust component software solution, and they are provided through JavaBeans.

JavaBeans specifies a rich set of mechanisms for interaction between objects, along with common actions that most objects will need to support, such as persistence and event handling. It also provides the framework by which this component communication can take place. Even more important is the fact that JavaBeans components can be easily tweaked via a standard set of well-defined properties.

JavaBeans components aren't limited to user-interface objects such as buttons, however. You can just as easily develop nonvisual JavaBeans components that perform some background function in concert with other components. In this way, JavaBeans merges the power of visual Java applets with nonvisual Java applications under a consistent component framework.

Note

> **NEW TERM** A *nonvisual component* is any component that doesn't have a visible output. If you think of components in terms of Swing components such as buttons and menus, this might seem a little strange. However, keep in mind that a component is simply a tightly packaged program and doesn't need to be visual. A good example is a timer component, which fires timing events at specified intervals and is nonvisual. Timer components are very popular in other component development environments, such as Microsoft Visual Basic.

With visual tools, you can use a variety of JavaBeans components together without necessarily writing any code. JavaBeans components expose their own interfaces visually, providing a means to edit their properties without programming. Furthermore, by using a visual editor, you can drop a JavaBeans component directly into an application without writing any code. This is an entirely new level of flexibility and reusability that was impossible in Java alone.

The JavaBeans API

JavaBeans is ultimately a programming interface, meaning that all its features are implemented as extensions to the standard Java class library. All the functionality provided by JavaBeans is actually implemented in the JavaBeans API, a suite of smaller APIs devoted to specific functions (services). The following is a list of the main component services in the JavaBeans API that are necessary for all the features you're been learning about today:

- Graphical user interface merging
- Persistence
- Event handling
- Introspection
- Application builder support

If you understand these services and how they work, you'll have much more insight into exactly what type of technology JavaBeans is. These services are implemented as smaller APIs contained within the larger JavaBeans API.

The user-interface–merging APIs enable a component to merge its elements with a container. Most containers have menus and toolbars that display any special features provided by the component. The interface-merging APIs allow the component to add features to the container document's menu and toolbar. These APIs also define the mechanism that facilitates interface layout between components and their containers.

20

The persistent APIs specify the mechanism by which components can be stored and retrieved within the context of a containing document. By default, components inherit the automatic serialization mechanism provided by Java. Developers are also free to design more elaborate persistence solutions based on the specific needs of their components.

The event-handling APIs specify an event-driven architecture that defines how components interact with each other. Java already includes a powerful event-handling model, which serves as the basis for the event-handling component APIs. These APIs are critical in giving components the freedom to interact with each other in a consistent fashion.

The introspection APIs define the techniques by which components make their internal structure readily available at design time. These APIs allow development tools to query a component for its internal state, including the interfaces, methods, and member variables of which the component is composed.

These APIs are divided into two distinct sections, based on the level at which they are being used. For example, the low-level introspection APIs give development tools direct access to component internals, which is a function you wouldn't necessarily want in the hands of component users. This brings us to the high-level APIs, which use the low-level APIs to determine which parts of a component are exported for user modification. Although development tools will undoubtedly use both APIs, they will use the high-level APIs only when providing component information to the user.

The application builder support APIs provide the overhead necessary for editing and manipulating components at design time. These APIs are used largely by visual development tools to visually lay out and edit components while constructing an application. The section of a component that provides visual editing capabilities is specifically designed to be physically separate from the component itself. This is because standalone runtime components should be as compact as possible. In a purely runtime environment, components are transferred with only the necessary runtime component. Developers who want to use only the design-time portion of the component can do so.

The JavaBeans specifications are available at the Java Web site at
`http://java.sun.com/j2se/1.3/docs/guide/beans/`.

Development Tools

The best way to understand JavaBeans is to work with them in a programming environment that supports bean development.

Bean programming requires an environment with a fairly sophisticated graphical user interface because much of the development work is done visually. In an integrated development environment such as Symantec Visual Café, you can establish a relationship between two beans in an interface by dragging a line between them with your mouse.

The tools in the Software Development Kit are almost exclusively used from the command line without a graphical interface. Because of this, you need a different programming tool to develop JavaBeans when using the SDK tools. Most of the commercially available Java development tools support JavaBeans, including Visual Café, Metrowerks CodeWarrior Professional, IBM VisualAge for Java, and Borland JBuilder.

> **Caution**
>
> If you're shopping for a Java integrated development environment that supports JavaBeans, an important thing to note is whether it supports Java 1.1, Java 2 SDK 1.2, or the current edition, Java 2 SDK 1.3.

If you don't have a development tool that supports JavaBeans programming, you can use the free JavaBeans Development Kit from Sun.

JavaBeans Development Kit

Sun's JavaBeans Development Kit, also called the BDK, is a free tool that can be used if no other bean-enabled programming environment is available.

If this sounds like damning the BDK with faint praise, it is. Sun makes the following recommendation on its Java Web site: "The BDK is not intended for use by application developers, nor is it intended to be a full-fledged application development environment. Instead, application developers should consider the various Java application development environments supporting JavaBeans."

When the BDK was released, it served a similar purpose to the original Java Development Kit: enabling programmers to work with a new technology when no other alternative was available. With the arrival of numerous JavaBeans-capable programming tools, Sun has not focused its efforts on extending the functionality of the BDK and improving its performance. The BDK is now useful primarily as an introduction to JavaBeans development, and that's what it will be used for today.

20

The BDK is available for Windows and Solaris. It was developed using the Java language, so there also is a platform-independent version that you can use on other Java-enabled operating systems. It currently can be downloaded from

```
http://java.sun.com/beans/software/bdk_download.html
```

> **Caution**
>
> If this page is not available, visit the main page at Sun's Java site at `http://java.sun.com`. The JavaBeans Development Kit and other programming tools are available in the "Products & APIs" section of the site.

The BDK is 2.4MB in size, requiring up to 20 minutes to download on a 28,800-baud Internet connection. While you're waiting for the file transfer to finish, be sure to read the installation instructions and last-minute notes on the BDK download page. You might need to make changes to your system's CLASSPATH setting for the BDK to function properly.

The BDK is transferred as a single executable file that must be run to install the software.

> **Caution**
>
> At the time of this writing, on a Windows system, the BDK installation program recommends `\Program Files\bdk1.1` as the place to install the program. Some Java tools have trouble with the space in the folder name, so you might want to choose a different folder, such as `\bdk1.1` or `\jdk1.3\bdk1.1`.

During the installation, you will select the Java virtual machine that the BDK will use. Choose the Java interpreter that you've been using to run Java 2 programs as you worked through the lessons in this book.

The following things are included in the BDK:

- The BeanBox—a JavaBean container that can be used to manipulate sample beans and work with those of your own creation.
- More than a dozen sample beans, including a Juggler bean that displays a juggling animation, a Molecule bean that displays a 3D molecule, and OrangeButton, a user interface component.
- The complete Java source code of the BeanBox.
- Makefiles—configuration scripts that can be used to re-create the BDK.
- A tutorial about JavaBeans and the BeanBox from Sun.

Working with JavaBeans

As you work with JavaBeans in a development environment such as the BDK, you'll quickly discover how different they are from Java classes that weren't designed to be beans.

JavaBeans differ from other classes in a fairly major way: They can interact with a development environment, running inside it as if a user were running them. The development environment also can interact directly with the JavaBean, calling its methods and setting up values for its variables.

If you have installed the BDK, you can use it in the following sections to work with existing JavaBeans and create a new one. If not, you'll still learn more about how JavaBeans are used in conjunction with a development environment.

Bean Containers

The AWT (Abstract Windowing Toolkit) and Swing use *containers*—user interface components that hold other components.

JavaBeans development takes place within a bean container. The BDK includes the BeanBox, a rudimentary container that can be used to do the following:

- Save a bean
- Load a saved bean
- Drop beans into a window where they can be laid out
- Move and resize beans
- Edit a bean's properties
- Configure a bean
- Associate a bean that generates an event with an event handler
- Associate the properties of different beans with each other
- Convert a bean into an applet
- Add new beans from a Java archive (jar files)

To run the BeanBox application, go to the folder where the BDK was installed and open the beanbox subfolder. This subfolder contains two batch-command files that can be used to run the BeanBox: run.bat for Windows systems, and run.sh for Solaris systems.

These batch files load the BeanBox application using the Java interpreter you selected during BDK installation, which is probably the Java 2 interpreter. Four windows will open, as shown in Figure 20.1.

20

FIGURE 20.1

The windows that make up the BeanBox application.

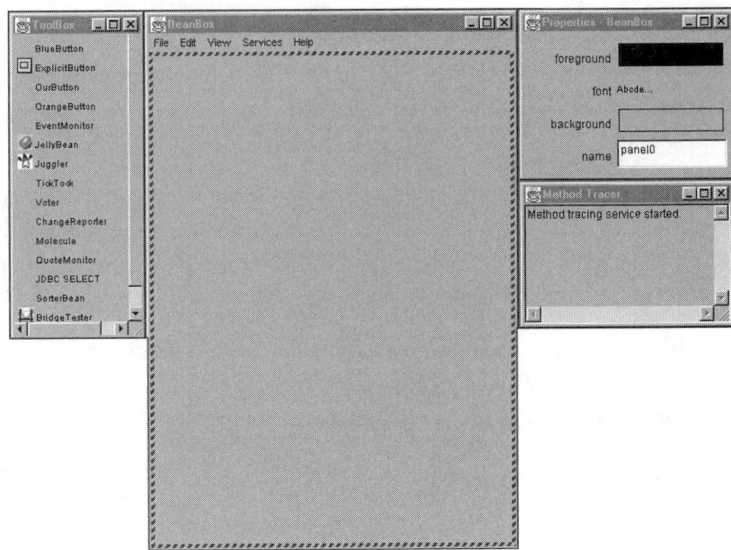

The largest window is the BeanBox composition window, which arranges beans and creates their associations with each other.

The other two windows along the top are the Toolbox window (on the left), which lists several JavaBeans that can be selected for placement in the composition window, and a Properties window (on the right), which is used to configure the bean. The fourth window in the lower-right corner is the Method Tracer window, which provides more information on how components are interacting in the BeanBox.

Most of the work will be done within the composition window, which is comparable to the main window of a drawing program such as Adobe Illustrator. All beans are placed, rearranged, lined up, and selected for editing within this window.

Placing a Bean

The first step in placing a bean in the BeanBox is to select it in the Toolbox window. When you do this, your cursor will switch to a cross-hairs symbol. With the cross hairs, you can click anywhere in the main composition window to place the selected type of bean in it. When you place a bean, it's best to choose someplace near the middle of the composition window. You can use the Edit, Cut and Edit, Paste menu commands to move the bean if needed. You also can move a bean by placing your cursor over the edge of the bean until the cursor becomes a set of compass-direction arrows, dragging the bean to a new location, and releasing the mouse.

Try this out by clicking the Juggler label in the Toolbox window and then clicking somewhere in the middle of the main composition window. An animation of a juggling bicuspid will appear in the main window (see Figure 20.2). You'll probably recognize the juggler—rather than a tooth, he's Duke, the official mascot of the Java language. Appropriately enough, the objects he's tossing around are giant beans.

FIGURE 20.2

Duke juggles some giant beans in the main BeanBox window.

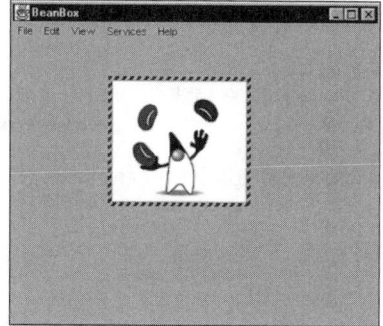

In Figure 20.2, the striped line around the Juggler bean indicates that it is currently selected for editing. You can select the BeanBox window itself by clicking anywhere other than the Juggler bean, and you can select the Juggler bean again by clicking it. You can edit, copy, cut, and paste a bean only if it has been selected for editing.

Adjusting a Bean's Properties

When a bean has been selected in the main composition window of the BeanBox, its editable properties, if any, are displayed in the Properties window. This window for the current project is shown in Figure 20.3.

FIGURE 20.3

Editable properties of a bean, shown in the Properties window.

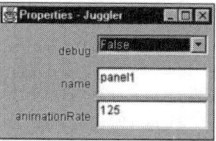

20

As shown in Figure 20.3, the Juggler bean has three editable properties: debug, animationRate, and name.

Changes to a JavaBean's properties will be reflected in the bean. If you give the Juggler bean's animationRate property a higher integer value, there'll be a longer pause between each frame of the animation. If you decrease the property, the animation will speed up.

After you change the `animationRate` property, the bean will change accordingly after you skip to a different property by either pressing the Tab key or clicking a different property's value. Try entering extreme values such as 1 and 1000 for the animation speed to see the response in the Juggler bean itself.

A JavaBean's editable properties can be established by public methods within the bean itself. Each property that can be set has a `set()` method whose full name matches the name of the property in the Properties window of the BeanBox. Likewise, each property whose value can be read has a corresponding `get()` method. A JavaBeans development environment such as the BeanBox uses reflection to find these methods, and then makes it possible for you to work with the properties at design time or as a program is running.

For example, the `animationRate` property of the Juggler bean could have two methods like the following:

```
public int getAnimationRate(){
    return animRate;
}

public void setAnimationRate(int newRate) {
    animRate = newRate;
}
```

In these two methods, `animRate` is a private variable that determines the pause between frames of the juggling animation.

By using the prefixes `set` and `get` for these method names, the Juggler bean developer indicates that the `animationRate` property can be altered from within a JavaBean development environment such as the BeanBox.

The BeanBox, like all bean development tools that follow the standards established by Sun, calls the public `get()` methods of the bean to determine which properties to include in the Properties window. When one of the properties is changed, a `set()` method is called with the changed value as an argument.

The developer of a bean can override this behavior by providing a `BeanInfo` class that indicates the methods, properties, events, and other things that should be accessible from a bean development environment.

Tip

Keeping a variable private and using `get()` and `set()` methods to read and change it is a good principle in all object-oriented programming, even when you're not trying to develop a JavaBean. This practice is called *encapsulation*, and it is used to control how an object can be accessed by other objects. The more encapsulated an object is, the harder it becomes for other objects to use it incorrectly.

Creating Interactions Between Beans

Another purpose of the BeanBox is to establish interactions between different beans.

To see how this works, first place two ExplicitButton beans anywhere in the main composition window of the BeanBox. If they overlap with the Juggler bean or with each other, move the beans farther away from each other.

To move a bean, first click it so that a striped line appears around it in the BeanBox window. Then, place your cursor above the lower edge of the bean until the cursor changes to a four-sided arrow. After this happens, drag the bean to a new location. Figure 20.4 shows two buttons along the bottom edge of the Juggler bean.

FIGURE 20.4

Two ExplicitButton beans and a Juggler bean in the main BeanBox window.

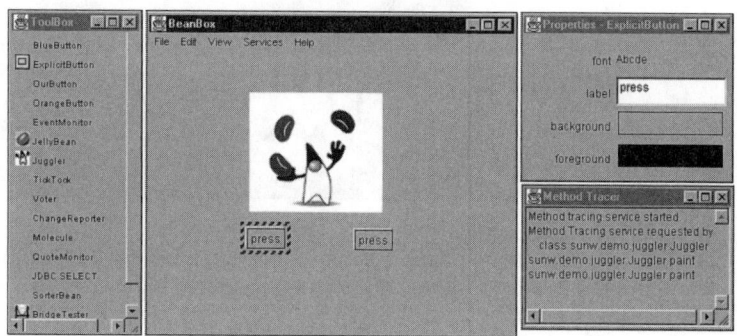

ExplicitButton beans are similar to the JButton components that you have used in graphical user interfaces. They have a background color, a foreground color, and a text label with configurable fonts.

After placing the buttons, give one the label "Stop!" and change its background color to red. Give the other the label "Go!" and change its background color to green.

To change a button's label, click the button in the BeanBox, and then edit the label textfield in the Properties window. To change the background color, click the panel next to the label Background in the Properties window. A new Color Editor dialog will open that enables you to select a color by entering numeric values for red, green, and blue or by using a list box. The changes that you make will be reflected instantly in the bean.

At this point, the purpose of these buttons should be fairly obvious: One will stop the animation, and the other will start it. For these things to take place, you must establish a relationship between the buttons and the Juggler bean.

20

The first step is to select the bean that is causing something to take place. In the current example, that bean would be either of the ExplicitButton beans. Clicking one of these should cause something to happen to the Juggler bean.

After selecting the bean, choose the menu command Edit, Events, button push, actionPerformed. A red line will connect the button and the cursor, as shown in Figure 20.5.

FIGURE 20.5

Establishing an event association between two beans.

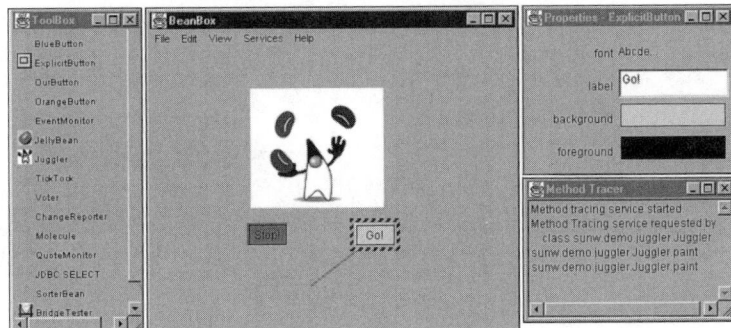

This red line should connect the ExplicitButton bean with the Juggler bean. Drag the line to the Juggler bean, and then click it to establish the association between the two beans.

When this association has been established, you'll see an EventTargetDialog window that lists different methods in the target bean, as shown in Figure 20.6. The method that is chosen will be called automatically when the specified ExplicitButton bean fires an actionPerformed event. (This event occurs when the button is clicked or the Enter key is pressed while the button has the input focus on the interface.)

FIGURE 20.6

Choosing a method to call in the EventTargetDialog window.

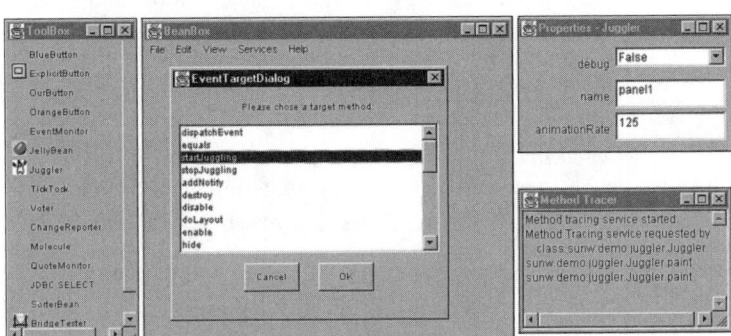

The Juggler bean contains two methods that are used to either stop or start the juggling animation. These are called `stopJuggling()` and `startJuggling()`, respectively. By separating behavior like this into its own method, the Juggler developer enables these methods to be useful in an interaction between different beans. Organizing a bean's methods in this way, offering as many different interactions as necessary, is one of the biggest tasks in JavaBeans development.

The Stop! button should be associated with the Juggler bean's `stopJuggling()` method, and the Go! button should be associated with `startJuggling()`.

By establishing this interaction between three JavaBeans, you have created a simple, functional Java program that can display, start, and stop an animation.

Creating a JavaBeans Program

After you have placed one or more JavaBeans on a shared interface, set up their properties, and established interactions between them, you have created a Java program.

To save a project in the BeanBox, use the File, Save menu command. This enables you to save the following information to a file:

- The beans as they are currently configured
- The arrangement of the beans
- The size of the window the beans occupy
- The interactions between the beans

This does not save the project as a Java program that you can run outside of the BeanBox. To save a project in a form that you can run, use the File, MakeApplet command. This command requires two things: the name to give the applet's main class file, and the name of the `jar` archive that will hold all files needed to run the applet, including class files and other data.

After you specify these items, an applet will be created with a sample HTML page that loads it. The HTML file will be placed in the same folder that contains the applet's `jar` archive. You can load this page by using appletviewer or any Web browser that supports Java 2.

These applets are distributed using `jar` archives for the applet itself and any beans in it. Listing 20.1 contains the applet tag generated by BeanBox for the applet, which was named JugglingFool.

20

LISTING 20.1   The Applet Tag Generated by BeanBox

```
 1: <html>
 2: <head>
 3: <title>Test page for JugglingFool as an APPLET</Title>
 4: </head>
 5: <body>
 6: <h1>Test for JugglingFool as an APPLET</h1>
 7: This is an example of the use of the generated
 8: JugglingFool applet.  Notice the Applet tag requires several
 9: archives, one per JAR used in building the Applet
10: <p>
11: <applet
12:     archive="./JugglingFool.jar,./support.jar
13:          ,./buttons.jar
14:          ,./juggler.jar
15:     "
16:     code="JugglingFool"
17:     width=382
18:     height=513
19: >
20: Trouble instantiating applet JugglingFool!!
21: </applet>
```

Figure 20.7 shows the Juggler animation applet running in the appletviewer tool.

FIGURE 20.7

*A JavaBeans applet
running in
appletviewer.*

The size of the applet's window will be determined by the size of the main composition window in the BeanBox. To resize the window, select it by clicking outside all JavaBeans inside the window and then resize it as you would a bean.

Working with Other JavaBeans

Developing software by using prepackaged components like this is a form of *rapid application development*. Unlike many of the terms you have learned in this book, rapid application development, also called RAD, is self-explanatory jargon. It's often used to quickly create a working version of software for demonstration or prototype purposes.

A common example of RAD is using Microsoft Visual Basic to create a prototype of a Visual C++ program. One of the strengths of Visual Basic is its speedy graphical user interface design, which makes it a more effective solution for prototyping than the more complex Visual C++.

JavaBeans make RAD development more commonplace in Java software development. A programmer can swiftly cobble together a working program by using existing JavaBeans components.

Hundreds of JavaBeans are available from Sun and other developers, including those at the following sites:

- The JavaBeans resource directory of the Java Applet Ratings Service: `http://www.jars.com/jars_resources_javabeans.html`
- *JavaWorld* Magazine's Developer Tools Guide: `http://www.javaworld.com/javaworld/tools/`
- Sun's JavaBeans home page: `http://java.sun.com/beans`

Beans are packaged into `jar` archives. If you have downloaded a bean and would like it to show up in the Toolbox window of the BeanBox, save the bean's `jar` archive in BDK's `jars` folder. This folder can be found in the folder where the BDK was installed on your system—if you installed the BDK in `c:\bdk1.1`, the `jar` file for beans you would like to use should be saved in `c:\bdk1.1\jars`.

Summary

When combined with an integrated development environment that supports them, JavaBeans enable rapid application development of Java programs.

Today, you learned about the underlying principles of reusable software components and how these principles are realized in Java. Putting these ideas into practice, you saw how Sun's JavaBeans Development Kit (BDK) can be used to work with existing beans, establish relationships between them, and create full Java programs.

Although you should seek a more capable development tool than the BDK for developing your own programs with JavaBeans, you can use the BDK to evaluate the applicability of beans to your own programming tasks.

You also should use the JavaBeans resources on the World Wide Web. Many of the beans that are available over the Web already accomplish tasks you'll try to handle in your own programs. By using beans, you can reduce the number of things you must create from scratch.

20

Q&A

Q **Will the JavaBeans Development Kit be upgraded into a fully featured bean programming tool?**

A At the time of this writing, Sun continues to state that the BDK is intended for testing beans and providing a reference version of how beans should be used inside development environments. It appears that professional programming tools, such as Visual Café and others, are going to remain the best choice for JavaBeans development.

Q **In the Juggler example, the `animationRate` property has a different capitalization in the `setAnimationRate()` and `getAnimationRate()` methods. What accounts for this difference?**

A The capitalization is different because of the following naming conventions for Java programs: All variables and method names begin with a lowercase letter, and all words but the first in a variable name begin with a single uppercase letter.

Questions

1. If you develop a bean that has a `getWindowHeight()` method that returns an integer and a `setWindowHeight(int)` method, what property will show up in a bean development environment?

    (a) `WindowHeight`

    (b) windowHeight

    (c) Nothing unless you also set up something in a `BeanInfo` file

2. When can you modify a bean's properties?

    (a) At design time

    (b) At runtime

    (c) Both

3. How do you change the size of an applet created using the BDK?

    (a) Edit the HTML generated by the BDK after you create the applet.

    (b) Edit a property of the BeanBox.

    (c) Resize the BeanBox before creating the applet.

Answers

1. b. Although you can also use a `BeanInfo` file to exclude `windowHeight` from showing up as a property in a bean development environment.

2. c. As you have seen with the Juggler example, beans will even run as they are being designed.

3. c. Although answer a is also true because you can edit the HTML directly, and modify the `HEIGHT` and `WEIGHT` attributes of the `APPLET` tag.

Exercises

To extend your knowledge of the subjects covered today, try the following exercises:

- Download a bean from the Java Applet Ratings Service and make use of it in the BeanBox.

- Add a TickTock bean—a bean that causes something to happen at set intervals—to the Juggler project. Experiment with the bean and see whether you can make it restart the juggling bean every 30 seconds.

Where applicable, exercise solutions are offered on the book's Web site at `http://www.java21pro.com`.

20

DAY 21

Java Database Connectivity and Data Structures

Almost all Java programs deal with data in some way. You have used primitive types, objects, arrays, and linked lists to represent data up to this point, but as you develop more sophisticated programs, those might not be the best choices.

Today, you will finish the three-week trip into Java programming by working with data in more sophisticated ways.

You begin by exploring Java Database Connectivity (JDBC), a class library that connects Java programs to relational databases developed by Microsoft, Sybase, Oracle, Informix, and other sources. By using a driver as a bridge to the database source, you can store and retrieve data directly from Java.

Next, you will look at how data is represented internally in Java, working with new data structures that complement arrays and linked lists.

Today's lesson looks at data structures and database connectivity, and you are introduced to the following subjects:

- Using JDBC drivers to work with different relational databases
- Accessing a database with Structured Query Language (SQL)
- Moving through the records that result from an SQL database operation
- Setting up a JDBC data source
- Working with stacks, bit sets, hash tables, and other data structures
- Creating classes that implement the `Iterator` interface

By the end of today's lesson, you'll have a much larger arsenal of solutions when you are working with data in your programs.

Java Database Connectivity

Java Database Connectivity (JDBC) is a set of classes that can be used to develop client/server database applications using Java. Client/server software connects a user of information with a provider of that information, and it's one of the most commonplace forms of programming. You use it every time you surf the Web: A client program called a Web browser requests Web pages, image files, and other documents using a Uniform Resource Locator or URL. Different server programs provide the requested information, if it can be found, for the client.

One of the biggest obstacles faced by database programmers is the wide variety of database formats in use, each with its own proprietary method of accessing data. To simplify using relational database programs, a standard language called SQL (Structured Query Language) has been introduced. This language supplants the need to learn different database-querying languages for each database format.

In database programming, a request for records in a database is called a *query*. Using SQL, you can send complex queries to a database and get the records you're looking for in any order you specify.

Consider the example of a database programmer at a student loan company who has been asked to prepare a report on the most delinquent loan recipients. The programmer could use SQL to query a database for all records in which the last payment was more than 180 days ago and the amount due is more than $0.00. SQL also can be used to control the order in which records are returned, so the programmer can get the records in the order of Social Security number, recipient name, amount owed, or another field in the loan database.

All this is possible with SQL, and the programmer hasn't used any of the proprietary languages associated with popular database formats.

Note

> SQL is strongly supported by many database formats, so in theory you should be able to use the same SQL commands for each database tool that supports the language. However, you still might need to learn some idiosyncrasies of a specific database format when accessing it through SQL.

SQL is the industry-standard approach to accessing relational databases. JDBC supports SQL, enabling developers to use a wide range of database formats without knowing the specifics of the underlying database. It also enables the use of database queries that are specific to a database format.

The JDBC class library's approach to accessing databases with SQL is comparable to existing database development techniques, so interacting with an SQL database by using JDBC isn't much different than it is by using traditional database tools. Java programmers who already have some database experience can hit the ground running with JDBC. The JDBC API has already been widely endorsed by industry leaders, including some development-tool vendors who have announced future support for JDBC in their development products.

The JDBC library includes classes for each of the tasks that are commonly associated with database usage:

- Making a connection to a database
- Creating a statement using SQL
- Executing that SQL query in the database
- Viewing the resulting records

These JDBC classes are all part of the `java.sql` package in Java 2.

Database Drivers

Java programs that use JDBC classes can follow the familiar programming model of issuing SQL statements and processing the resulting data. The format of the database and the platform it was prepared on don't matter.

This platform- and database-independence is made possible in a Java program by a driver manager. The classes of the JDBC class library are largely dependent on driver managers, which keep track of the drivers required to access database records. You'll need a different driver for each database format that's used in a program, and sometimes might need several different drivers for different versions of the same format.

21

JDBC database drivers can be either written entirely in Java or implemented using native methods to bridge Java applications to existing database access libraries.

JDBC also includes a driver that bridges JDBC and another database connectivity standard, called ODBC.

The JDBC-ODBC Bridge

ODBC, Microsoft's common interface for accessing SQL databases, is managed on a Windows system by the ODBC Data Source Administrator. This is run from the Control Panel on a Windows system by clicking the Start button and then Settings, Control Panel, ODBC Data Sources. The administrator adds ODBC drivers, configures drivers to work with specific database files, and logs SQL use. Figure 21.1 shows the ODBC Data Source Administrator on a Windows system.

FIGURE 21.1

The ODBC Data Source Administrator on a Windows system.

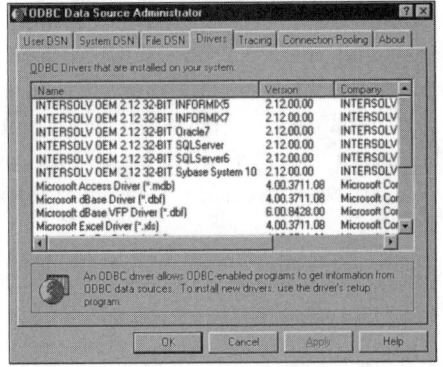

In Figure 21.1, the Drivers tabbed dialog box lists all the ODBC drivers that are present on the system. Some of the drivers are specific to a database company's format, including the Microsoft Access Driver. Other drivers work with a server that is centered around SQL itself, including the INTERSOLV SQLServer driver.

The JDBC-ODBC bridge allows JDBC drivers to be used as ODBC drivers by converting JDBC method calls into ODBC function calls.

Using the JDBC-ODBC bridge requires three things:

- The JDBC-ODBC bridge driver included with Java 2:
  `sun.jdbc.odbc.JdbcOdbcDriver`
- An ODBC driver
- An ODBC data source that has been associated with the driver using software such as the ODBC Data Source Administrator

ODBC data sources can be set up from within some database programs. For example, when a new database file is created in Lotus Approach, users have the option of associating it with an ODBC driver.

All ODBC data sources must be given a short descriptive name. This name will be used inside Java programs when a connection is made to the database that the source refers to.

On a Windows system, after an ODBC driver is selected and the database is created, they will show up in the ODBC Data Source Administrator. Figure 21.2 shows an example of this for a data source named World Energy.

FIGURE 21.2

A listing of data sources in the ODBC Data Sources Administrator.

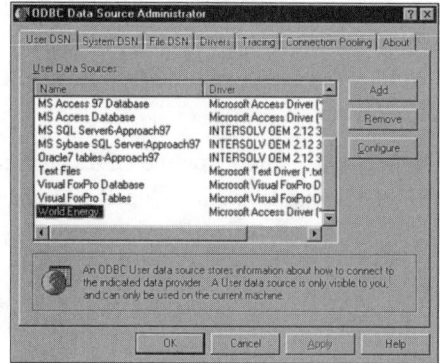

The data source World Energy is associated with a Microsoft Access driver, according to Figure 21.2.

Note

Microsoft Access includes ODBC drivers that can be used to connect to an Access database file. Most Windows database programs will include one or more ODBC drivers that correspond to the format.

Connecting to an ODBC Data Source

Your first project today is a Java application that uses a JDBC-ODBC bridge to connect to a Microsoft Access file.

21

The Access file for this project is `world20.mdb`, a database of world energy statistics published by the U.S. Energy Information Administration. The Coal table in this database includes these fields:

- `Country`
- `Year`
- `Anthracite Production`

The database used in this project is included on this book's official Web site at `http://www.java21pro.com`.

To use this database, you must have an ODBC driver on your system that supports Microsoft Access files. Using the ODBC Data Source Administrator (or a similar program if you're on a non-Windows system), you must create a new ODBC data source that is associated with `world20.mdb`.

Other setup work might be needed depending on the ODBC drivers that are present on your system, if any. Consult the documentation included with the ODBC driver.

 **Caution**

This aspect of JDBC-ODBC bridge programming often can be more difficult than using the JDBC class library in a program. You might need to install an ODBC driver and learn more about its use before you try to create a JDBC-ODBC application.

After you have downloaded `world20.mdb` to your computer or found another database that's compatible with the ODBC drivers on your system, the final step in getting the file ready for JDBC-ODBC is to create a data source associated with it. Unlike other input-output classes in Java, JDBC doesn't use a filename to identify a data file and use its contents. Instead, a tool such as the ODBC Data Source Administrator is used to name the ODBC source and indicate the file folder where it can be found.

In the ODBC Data Source Administrator, click the User DSN tab to see a list of data sources that are currently available. To add a new one associated with `world20.mdb` (or your own database), click the Add button, choose an ODBC driver, and then click the Finish button.

A Setup window will open that you can use to provide a name, short description, and other information about the database. Click the Select button to find and choose the database file.

Figure 21.3 shows the Setup window used to set up `world20.mdb` as a data source in the ODBC Data Sources Administrator.

FIGURE 21.3

The driver Setup window.

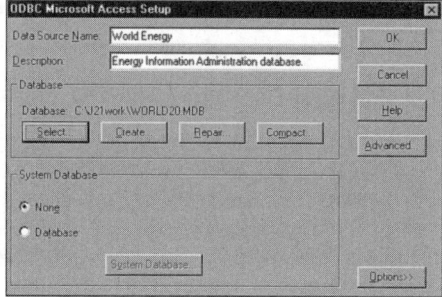

After a database has been associated with an ODBC data source, working with it in a Java program is relatively easy if you are conversant with SQL.

The first task in a JDBC program is to load the driver (or drivers) that will be used to connect to a data source. A driver is loaded with the `Class.forName(String)` method. `Class`, part of the `java.lang` package, can be used to load classes into the Java interpreter. The `forName(String)` method loads the class named by the specified string. A `ClassNotFoundException` may be thrown by this method.

All programs that use an ODBC data source will use `sun.jdbc.odbc.JdbcOdbcDriver`, the JDBC-ODBC bridge driver that is included with Java 2. Loading this class into a Java interpreter requires the following statement:

```
Class.forName("sun.jdbc.odbc.JdbcOdbcDriver");
```

After the driver has been loaded, you can establish a connection to the data source by using the `DriverManager` class in the `java.sql` package.

The `getConnection(String, String, String)` method of `DriverManager` can be used to set up the connection. It returns a reference to a `Connection` object representing an active data connection.

The three arguments of this method are as follows:

- A name identifying the data source and the type of database connectivity used to reach it
- A username
- A password

The last two items are needed only if the data source is secured with a username and a password. If not, these arguments can be null strings (`""`).

21

The name of the data source is preceded by the text `jdbc:odbc:` when using the JDBC-ODBC bridge, which indicates the type of database connectivity in use.

The following statement could be used to connect to a data source called `Payroll` with a username of `Doc` and a password of `Notnow`:

```
Connection payday = DriverManager.getConnection(
    "jdbc:odbc:Payroll", "Doc", "Notnow");
```

The `getConnection()` method and all others called on a data source will throw `SQLException` errors if something goes wrong as the data source is being used. SQL has its own error messages, and they will be passed along as part of `SQLException` objects.

An SQL statement is represented in Java by a `Statement` object. `Statement` is an interface, so it can't be instantiated directly. However, it is returned by the `createStatement()` method of a `Connection` object, as in the following example:

```
Statement lookSee = payday.CreateStatement();
```

After you have a `Statement` object, you can use it to conduct an SQL query by calling the object's `executeQuery(String)` method. The `String` argument should be an SQL query that follows the syntax of that language. Although you need to learn SQL to do any extensive work with it, a lot of the language is easy to pick up from any examples you can find.

The following is an example of an SQL query that could be used on the Coal table of the `world20.mdb` database:

```
SELECT Country, Year, Anthracite Production FROM Coal
    WHERE (Country Is Not Null) ORDER BY Year
```

This SQL query retrieves several fields for each record in the database where the `Country` field is not equal to null. The records that are returned are sorted according to their `Country` field, so Afghanistan would precede Burkina Faso.

If the SQL query has been phrased correctly, the `executeQuery()` method will return a `ResultSet` object holding all the records that have been retrieved from the data source.

When a `ResultSet` is returned from `executeQuery()`, it is positioned at the first record that has been retrieved. The following methods of `ResultSet` can be used to pull information out of the current record:

- `getDate(String)`—Returns the `Date` value stored in the specified field name.
- `getDouble(String)`—Returns the `double` value stored in the specified field name.
- `getFloat(String)`—Returns the `float` value stored in the specified field name.

- getInt(*String*)—Returns the int value stored in the specified field name.
- getLong(*String*)—Returns the long value stored in the specified field name.
- getString(*String*)—Returns the String stored in the specified field name.

These are just the simplest methods that are available in the ResultSet interface. The methods you should use depend on the form that the field data took when the database was created, although methods such as getString() and getInt() can be more flexible in the information they retrieve from a record.

You also can use an integer as the argument to any of these methods, such as getString(5), instead of a string. The integer indicates which field to retrieve (1 for the first field, 2 for the second field, and so on).

An SQLException will be thrown if a database error occurs as you try to retrieve information from a result set. You can call this exception's getSQLState() and getErrorCode() methods to learn more about the error.

After you have pulled the information you need from a record, you can move to the next record by calling the next() method of the ResultSet object. This method returns a false Boolean value when it tries to move past the end of a result set.

You also can move through the records in a result set with these other methods:

- afterLast()—Moves to a place immediately after the last record in the set.
- beforeFirst()—Moves to a place immediately before the first record in the set.
- first()—Moves to the first record in the set.
- last()—Moves to the last record in the set.
- previous()—Moves to the previous record in the set.

With the exception of afterLast() and beforeFirst(), these methods return a false Boolean value if no record is available at that position in the set.

When you're done using a connection to a data source, you can close it by calling the connection's close() method with no arguments.

Listing 21.1 contains the CoalTotals application, which uses the JDBC-ODBC bridge and an SQL statement to retrieve some records from a database of favorite Web sites. Four fields are retrieved from each record indicated by the SQL statement: FIPS, Country, Year, and Anthracite Production. The result set is sorted according to the Year field, and these fields are displayed to standard output.

21

LISTING **21.1**   The Full Text of `CoalTotals.java`

```
 1: import java.sql.*;
 2:
 3: public class CoalTotals {
 4:     public static void main(String[] arguments) {
 5:         String data = "jdbc:odbc:World Energy";
 6:         try {
 7:             Class.forName("sun.jdbc.odbc.JdbcOdbcDriver");
 8:             Connection conn = DriverManager.getConnection(
 9:                 data, "", "");
10:             Statement st = conn.createStatement();
11:             ResultSet rec = st.executeQuery(
12:                 "SELECT * " +
13:                 "FROM Coal " +
14:                 "WHERE " +
15:                 "(Country='" + arguments[0] + "') " +
16:                 "ORDER BY Year");
17:             System.out.println("FIPS\tCOUNTRY\tYEAR\t" +
18:                 "ANTHRACITE PRODUCTION");
19:             while(rec.next()) {
20:                 System.out.println(rec.getString(1) +  "\t"
21:                     + rec.getString(2) + "\t"
22:                     + rec.getString(3) + "\t"
23:                     + rec.getString(4));
24:             }
25:             st.close();
26:         } catch (SQLException s) {
27:             System.out.println("SQL Error: " + s.toString() + " "
28:                 + s.getErrorCode() + " " + s.getSQLState());
29:         } catch (Exception e) {
30:             System.out.println("Error: " + e.toString()
31:                 + e.getMessage());
32:         }
33:     }
34: }
```

This program must be run with a single argument specifying the `Country` field in the database form which to pull records. If the application were run with an argument of `Poland`, the output from the sample database would be the following:

```
FIPS   COUNTRY   YEAR   ANTHRACITE PRODUCTION
PL     Poland    1990   0.0
PL     Poland    1991   0.0
PL     Poland    1992   0.0
PL     Poland    1993   174.165194805424
PL     Poland    1994   242.50849909616
PL     Poland    1995   304.237935229728
PL     Poland    1996   308.64718066784
```

```
PL    Poland   1997   319.67029426312
PL    Poland   1998   319.67029426312
```

Try running the program with other countries that produce anthracite, such as France, Swaziland, and New Zealand. For any country that has a space in the name, remember to put quotation marks around it when running the program.

JDBC Drivers

Creating a Java program that uses a JDBC driver is substantially similar to creating one that uses the JDBC-ODBC bridge.

The first step is to acquire and install a JDBC driver. Sun does not include a JDBC driver with Java 2, but more than a dozen companies now sell them or package them with commercial products, including Informix, Oracle, Symantec, IBM, and Sybase. A list of JDBC drivers that are currently available can be found on Sun's JDBC site at `http://java.sun.com/products/jdbc/jdbc.drivers.html`.

Some of these drivers are available to download for evaluation. You can use one of them, NetDirect's JDataConnect Server, for today's next project. The JDataConnect Server is currently available for trial download from `http://www.j-netdirect.com/`.

The steps for setting up a data source for JDBC are the same as with JDBC-ODBC:

- Create the database.
- Associate the database with a JDBC driver.
- Establish a data source, which may include selecting a database format, database server, username, and password.

NetDirect's JDataConnect Server uses the ODBC Data Source Administrator to create a new data source associated with a database.

Listing 21.2 is a Java application that uses the JDataConnect JDBC driver to access a database file called `People.mdb`. This database is a Microsoft Access file with contact information for U.S. presidents.

LISTING 21.2   The Full Text of `Presidents.java`

```
1: import java.sql.*;
2:
3: public class Presidents {
4:     public static void main(String[] arguments) {
6:         String data = "jdbc:JDataConnect://localhost:1150/Presidents";
7:         try {
8:             Class.forName("JData2_0.sql.$Driver");
```

21

LISTING 21.2   continued

```
09:                Connection conn = DriverManager.getConnection(
10:                    data, "", "");
11:                Statement st = conn.createStatement();
12:                ResultSet rec = st.executeQuery(
13:                    "SELECT NAME, ADDRESS1, ADDRESS2, PHONE, E-MAIL " +
14:                    "FROM People.mdb Contacts " +
15:                    "ORDER BY NAME");
16:                while(rec.next()) {
17:                    System.out.println(rec.getString("NAME") +  "\n"
18:                        + rec.getString("ADDRESS1") + "\n"
19:                        + rec.getString("ADDRESS2") + "\n"
20:                        + rec.getString("PHONE") + "\n"
21:                        + rec.getString("E-MAIL") + "\n");
22:                }
23:                st.close();
24:            } catch (Exception e) {
25:                System.out.println("Error -- " + e.toString());
26:            }
27:        }
28: }
```

Before this program will run successfully, the JDataConnect Server must be started. The reference to localhost:1150 in line 6 refers to this server—localhost is a substitute for the name of your own machine, and 1150 is the default port number on which the JDataConnect server runs.

The JDataConnect Server can be used to connect remotely to servers on the Internet, so localhost could be replaced with an Internet address, such as db.naviseek.com:1150, if a JDataConnect Server is running at that location and port.

Line 6 creates the database address that will be used when creating a Connection object representing the connection to the Presidents data source. This address includes more information than the one used with the JDBC-ODBC bridge driver, as shown:

jdbc:JDataConnect://localhost:1150/Presidents

Line 8 of the Presidents application loads the JDBC driver included with JDataConnect Server:

JData2_0.sql.$Driver

Configuration information for the data source and driver will be provided by the company that developed the JDBC driver. The database address can vary widely from one JDBC driver implementation to another, although there should always be a reference to a server, a database format, and the name of the data source.

If the `People.mdb` database exists and the JDBC driver has been set up correctly, the output of the `Presidents` application should be similar to the following (depending on the records in the database):

```
Gerald Ford
Box 927
Rancho Mirage, CA 92270
(734) 741-2218
library@fordlib.nara.gov

Jimmy Carter
Carter Presidential Center
1 Copenhill, Atlanta, GA 30307
(404) 727-7611
carterweb@emory.edu

Ronald Reagan
11000 Wilshire Blvd.
Los Angeles, CA 90024
library@reagan.nara.gov

George Bush
Box 79798
Houston, TX 77279
(409) 260-9552


Bill Clinton
White House, 1600 Pennsylvania Ave.
Washington, DC 20500
(202) 456-1414
president@whitehouse.gov
```

Data Structures

Many Java programs that you create will rely on some means of storing and manipulating data within a class. Up to this point, you have used two structures for storing and retrieving data: arrays and linked lists. If you don't understand the full range of programming options in terms of data structures, you'll find yourself trying to use arrays and lists when other options would be more efficient or easier to implement.

A solid understanding of data structures and when to use them will be applicable throughout your Java programming efforts.

Outside of primitive data types, arrays are the simplest data structures supported by Java. An array is simply a series of data elements of the same primitive type or objects of any class. It's treated as a single entity, just as a primitive data type is, but contains multiple

21

elements that can be accessed independently. Arrays are useful whenever you need to store and access related information.

The glaring limitation of arrays is that they can't change in size to accommodate more or fewer elements. That means you can't add new elements to an array that's already full. Because linked lists and vectors do not have this limitation, these objects can be used as an alternative.

The Java class library provides a set of data structures in the java.util package that give you more flexibility in approaching the organization and manipulation of data.

 **Note**
Unlike the data structures provided by the java.util package, arrays are considered such a core component of Java that they are implemented in the language itself. Therefore, you can use arrays in Java without importing any packages.

Java Data Structures

The data structures provided by the java.util package are very powerful and perform a wide range of functions. These data structures consist of the Iterator interface, the Map interface, and classes such as the following:

- BitSet
- Vector
- Stack
- Hashtable

Each of these data structures provides a way to store and retrieve information in a well-defined manner. The Iterator interface isn't itself a data structure, but it defines a means to retrieve successive elements from a data structure. For example, Iterator defines a method called next() that gets the next element in a data structure that contains multiple elements.

 Note
Iterator is an expanded and improved version of the Enumeration interface that was added in Java 2. Although Enumeration is still supported, Iterator has simpler method names and support for removing items.

The `BitSet` class implements a group of bits, or flags, that can be set and cleared individually. This class is very useful when you need to keep up with a set of Boolean values; you just assign a bit to each value and set or clear it as appropriate.

NEW TERM A *flag* is a Boolean value that represents one of a group of on/off type states in a program.

The `Vector` class is similar to a traditional Java array, except that it can grow as necessary to accommodate new elements. Like an array, elements of a `Vector` object can be accessed via an index into the vector. The nice thing about using the `Vector` class is that you don't have to worry about setting it to a specific size upon creation; it shrinks and grows automatically when necessary.

The `Stack` class implements a last-in-first-out stack of elements. You can think of a stack literally as a vertical stack of objects; when you add a new element, it's stacked on top of the others. When you pull an element off the stack, it comes off the top. In other words, the last element you added to the stack is the first one to come back off. That element is removed from the stack completely, unlike a structure such as an array, where the elements are always available.

The `Dictionary` class is an abstract class that defines a data structure for mapping keys to values. This is useful when you want to access data through a particular key rather than an integer index. Because the `Dictionary` class is abstract, it provides only the framework for a key-mapped data structure rather than a specific implementation.

NEW TERM A *key* is an identifier used to reference, or look up, a value in a data structure.

An actual implementation of a key-mapped data structure is provided by the `Hashtable` class, which organizes data based on some user-defined key structure. For example, in an address list hash table, you could store and sort data based on a key such as ZIP Code rather than on a person's name. The specific meaning of keys in a hash table is totally dependent on how the table is used and the data it contains.

The next section looks at the data structures provided by the `java.util` package in more detail to show how they work.

Iterator

The `Iterator` interface provides a standard means of iterating through a list of elements in a defined sequence, which is a common task for many data structures. Even though you can't use the interface outside a particular data structure, understanding how the `Iterator` interface works will help you understand other Java data structures.

21

With that in mind, take a look at the methods defined by the `Iterator` interface:

```
public boolean hasNext();

public Object next();

public void remove();
```

The `hasNext()` method determines whether the structure contains any more elements. You will typically call this method to see whether you can continue iterating through a structure. An example of this is calling `hasNext()` in the conditional clause of a `while` loop that is iterating through a list.

The `next()` method retrieves the next element in a structure. If there are no more elements, `next()` will throw a `NoSuchElementException` exception. To avoid generating this exception, use `hasNext()` in conjunction with `next()` to make sure there is another element to retrieve.

The following is a `while` loop that uses these two methods to iterate through a data structure object called `users` that implements the `Iterator` interface:

```
while (users.hasNext()) {
    Object ob = users.next();
    System.out.println(ob);
}
```

This sample code displays the contents of each list item by using the `hasNext()` and `next()` methods.

 Note

Because `Iterator` is an interface, you'll never use it directly as a data structure. Rather, you'll use the methods defined by `Iterator` within the context of other data structures. The significance of this architecture is that it provides a consistent interface for many of the standard data structures, which makes them easier to learn and use.

Bit Sets

The `BitSet` class is useful whenever you need to represent a group of Boolean flags. The nice thing about using the `BitSet` class is that you can use individual bits to store Boolean values without the mess of extracting bit values by using bitwise operations. You simply refer to each bit using an index. Another nice feature is that it automatically grows to represent the number of bits required by a program. Figure 21.4 shows the logical organization of a bit set data structure.

FIGURE 21.4

The logical organization of a bit set data structure.

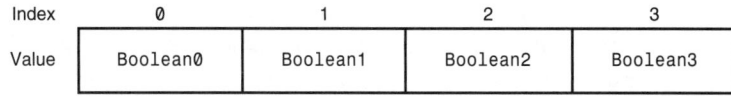

For example, you can use `BitSet` as an object with a number of attributes that can easily be modeled by Boolean values. Because the individual bits in a bit set are accessed via an index, you can define each attribute as a constant index value:

```
class SomeBits {
    public static final int READABLE = 0;
    public static final int WRITEABLE = 1;
    public static final int STREAMABLE = 2;
    public static final int FLEXIBLE = 3;
}
```

Notice that the attributes are assigned increasing values, beginning with `0`. You can use these values to get and set the appropriate bits in a bit set. But first, you need to create a `BitSet` object:

```
BitSet bits = new BitSet();
```

This constructor creates a bit set with no specified size. You can also create a bit set with a specific size:

```
BitSet bits = new BitSet(4);
```

This creates a bit set containing four Boolean bit fields. Regardless of the constructor used, all bits in new bit sets are initially set to `false`. After you have a bit set created, you can easily set and clear the bits by using the `set` and `clear` methods along with the bit constants you defined:

```
bits.set(SomeBits.WRITEABLE);
bits.set(SomeBits.STREAMABLE);
bits.set(SomeBits.FLEXIBLE);
bits.clear(SomeBits.WRITEABLE);
```

In this code, the `WRITEABLE`, `STREAMABLE`, and `FLEXIBLE` attributes are set and then the `WRITEABLE` bit is cleared. Notice that the fully qualified name is used for each attribute because the attributes are declared as static in the `SomeBits` class.

You can get the value of individual bits in a bit set by using the `get` method:

```
boolean canIWrite = bits.get(SomeBits.WRITEABLE);
```

You can find out how many bits are being represented by a bit set by using the `size` method:

```
int numBits = bits.size();
```

21

The BitSet class also provides other methods for performing comparisons and bitwise operations on bit sets such as AND, OR, and XOR. All these methods take a BitSet object as their only argument.

Vectors

The Vector class implements an expandable array of objects. Because the Vector class is responsible for expanding as necessary to support more elements, it has to decide when and how much to grow as new elements are added. You can easily control this aspect of vectors upon creation.

Before getting into that, take a look at how to create a basic vector:

```
Vector v = new Vector();
```

This constructor creates a default vector containing no elements. Actually, all vectors are empty upon creation. One of the attributes that determines how a vector sizes itself is its initial capacity, or the number of elements it allocates memory for by default.

NEW TERM The *size* of a vector is the number of elements currently stored in it.

NEW TERM The *capacity* of a vector is the amount of memory allocated to hold elements, and is always greater than or equal to the size.

The following code shows how to create a vector with a specified capacity:

```
Vector v = new Vector(25);
```

This vector will allocate enough memory to support 25 elements. Once 25 elements have been added, however, the vector must decide how to expand to accept more elements. You can specify the value by which a vector grows using another Vector constructor:

```
Vector v = new Vector(25, 5);
```

This vector has an initial size of 25 elements, and will expand in increments of 5 elements when more than 25 elements are added to it. That means the vector will jump to 30 elements in size, and then 35, and so on. A smaller growth value results in greater memory management efficiency at the cost of more execution overhead because more memory allocations are taking place. A larger growth value results in fewer memory allocations, but sometimes memory might be wasted if you don't use all the extra space created.

You can't just use square brackets ([ ]) to access the elements in a vector, as you can in an array. You must use methods defined in the Vector class. Use the add() method to add an element to a vector, as in the following example:

```
v.add("Watson");
v.add("Palmer");
v.add("Nicklaus");
```

This code shows how to add some strings to a vector. To retrieve the last string added to the vector, you can use the lastElement() method:

```
String s = (String)v.lastElement();
```

Notice that you have to cast the return value of lastElement() because the Vector class is designed to work with the Object class. Although lastElement() certainly has its usefulness, you will probably find more value in the get() method, which enables you to retrieve a vector element using an index.

The following is an example of the get() method:

```
String s1 = (String)v.get(0);
String s2 = (String)v.get(2);
```

Because vectors are zero-based, the first call to get() retrieves the "Watson" string and the second call retrieves the "Palmer" string. Just as you can retrieve an element at a particular index, you can also add and remove elements at an index by using the add() and remove() methods:

```
v.add(1, "Hogan");
v.add(0, "Jones");
v.remove(3);
```

The first call to add() inserts an element at index 1, between the "Watson" and "Palmer" strings. The "Palmer" and "Nicklaus" strings are moved up an element in the vector to accommodate the inserted "Hogan" string. The second call to add() inserts an element at index 0, which is the beginning of the vector. All existing elements are moved up one space in the vector to accommodate the inserted "Jones" string. At this point, the contents of the vector look like this:

- "Jones"
- "Watson"
- "Hogan"
- "Palmer"
- "Nicklaus"

21

The call to remove() removes the element at index 3, which is the "Palmer" string. The resulting vector consists of the following strings:

- "Jones"
- "Watson"
- "Hogan"
- "Nicklaus"

You can use the set() method to change a specific element:

```
v.set(1, "Woods");
```

This method replaces the "Watson" string with the "Woods" string, resulting in the following vector:

- "Jones"
- "Woods"
- "Hogan"
- "Nicklaus"

If you want to clear out the vector completely, you can remove all the elements with the clear() method:

```
v.clear();
```

The Vector class also provides some methods for working with elements without using indexes. These methods actually search through the vector for a particular element. The first of these methods is the contains() method, which simply checks if an element is in the vector:

```
boolean isThere = v.contains("O'Meara");
```

Another method that works in this manner is the indexOf() method, which finds the index of an element based on the element itself:

```
int i = v.indexOf("Nicklaus");
```

The indexOf() method returns the index of the element in question if it is in the vector, or -1 if not. The removeElement() method works similarly, removing an element based on the element itself rather than on an index:

```
v.removeElement("Woods");
```

If you're interested in working sequentially with all the elements in a vector, you can use the iterator() method, which returns a list of the elements you can iterate through:

```
Iterator it = v.iterator();
```

As you learned earlier today, you can use an iterator to step through elements sequentially. In this example, you can work with the it list using the methods defined by the Iterator interface.

At some point you might want to work with the size of a vector. Fortunately, the Vector class provides a few methods for determining and manipulating a vector's size. First, the size method determines the number of elements in the vector:

```
int size = v.size();
```

If you want to explicitly set the size of the vector, you can use the setSize() method:

```
v.setSize(10);
```

The setSize() method expands or truncates the vector to the size specified. If the vector is expanded, null elements are inserted as the newly added elements. If the vector is truncated, any elements at indexes beyond the specified size are discarded.

Recall that vectors have two different attributes relating to size: size and capacity. The size is the number of elements in the vector, and the capacity is the amount of memory allocated to hold all the elements. The capacity is always greater than or equal to the size. You can force the capacity to exactly match the size by using the trimToSize() method:

```
v.trimToSize();
```

You can also check to see what the capacity is by using the capacity() method:

```
int capacity = v.capacity();
```

Stacks

Stacks are a classic data structure used to model information that is accessed in a specific order. The Stack class in Java is implemented as a last-in-first-out (LIFO) stack, which means that the last item added to the stack is the first one to be removed. Figure 21.5 shows the logical organization of a stack.

21

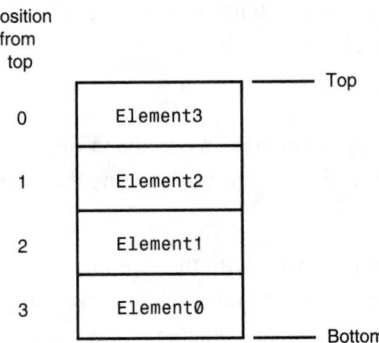

FIGURE 21.5

The logical organization of a stack data structure.

Position from top

0	Element3	— Top
1	Element2	
2	Element1	
3	Element0	— Bottom

You might wonder why the numbers of the elements don't match their positions from the top of the stack. Keep in mind that elements are added to the top, so Element0, which is on the bottom, was the first element added to the stack. Likewise, Element3, which is on top, was the last element added. Also, because Element3 is at the top of the stack, it will be the first to be removed.

The Stack class defines only one constructor, which is a default constructor that creates an empty stack. You use this constructor to create a stack like this:

```
Stack s = new Stack();
```

You add new elements to a stack by using the push() method, which pushes an element onto the top of the stack:

```
s.push("One");
s.push("Two");
s.push("Three");
s.push("Four");
s.push("Five");
s.push("Six");
```

This code pushes six strings onto the stack, with the last string ("Six") remaining on top. You pop elements back off the stack by using the pop() method:

```
String s1 = (String)s.pop();
String s2 = (String)s.pop();
```

This code pops the last two strings off the stack, leaving the first four strings. This code results in the s1 variable containing the "Six" string and the s2 variable containing the "Five" string.

If you want to get the top element on the stack without actually popping it off the stack, you can use the peek() method:

```
String s3 = (String)s.peek();
```

This call to peek() returns the "Four" string but leaves the string on the stack. You can search for an element on the stack by using the search() method:

```
int i = s.search("Two");
```

The search() method returns the distance from the top of the stack of the element if it is found, or -1 if not. In this case, the "Two" string is the third element from the top, so the search() method returns 2 (zero-based).

Note

> As in all Java data structures that deal with indexes or lists, the Stack class reports element position in a zero-based fashion. This means that the top element in a stack has a location of 0, and the fourth element down has a location of 3.

The only other method defined in the Stack class is empty, which determines whether a stack is empty:

```
boolean isEmpty = s.empty();
```

Although the Stack class isn't quite as useful as the Vector class, it provides the functionality for a very common and established data structure.

Map

The Map interface defines a framework for implementing a basic key-mapped data structure. You can put the key-mapped approach to work by using the Hashtable class, which implements the Map interface, or by creating your own class that uses the interface. You'll learn about the Hashtable class in the next section.

The Map interface defines a means of storing and retrieving information based on a key. This is similar in some ways to the Vector class, in which elements are accessed through an index, which is a specific type of key. However, keys in the Map interface can be just about anything. You can create your own classes to use as the keys for accessing and manipulating data in a dictionary. Figure 21.6 shows how keys map to data in a dictionary.

The Map interface declares a variety of methods for working with the data stored in a dictionary. Implementing classes will have to implement all of those methods to actually be useful. The put and get methods are used to put objects in the dictionary and get them back. Assuming look is a class that implements the Map interface, the following code shows how to use the put method to add elements:

21

```
look.put("small", new Rectangle(0, 0, 5, 5));
look.put("medium", new Rectangle(0, 0, 15, 15));
look.put("large", new Rectangle(0, 0, 25, 25));
```

FIGURE 21.6

*The logical organiza-
tion of a key-mapped
data structure.*

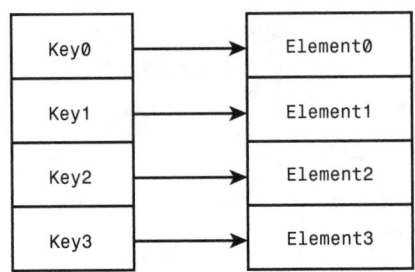

This code adds three rectangles to the dictionary, using strings as the keys. To get an
element, use the get method and specify the appropriate key:

```
Rectangle r = (Rectangle)look.get("medium");
```

You also can remove an element with a key by using the remove() method:

```
look.remove("large");
```

You can find out how many elements are in the structure by using the size() method,
much as you did with the Vector class:

```
int size = look.size();
```

You also can check whether the structure is empty by using the isEmpty() method:

```
boolean isEmpty = look.isEmpty();I~data structures;dictionaries>
```

Hash Tables

The Hashtable class is derived from Dictionary, implements the Map interface, and provides a complete implementation of a key-mapped data structure. Hash tables enable you
to store data based on some type of key and have an efficiency defined by the load factor
of the table. The *load factor* is a number between 0.0 and 1.0 that determines how and
when the hash table allocates space for more elements.

Like vectors, hash tables have a capacity, or the amount of allocated memory. Hash
tables allocate memory by comparing the current size of the table with the product of the
capacity and the load factor. If the size of the hash table exceeds this product, the table
increases its capacity by rehashing itself.

Load factors that are closer to 1.0 result in more efficient use of memory at the expense of a longer lookup time for each element. Similarly, load factors closer to 0.0 result in more efficient lookups but also tend to be more wasteful with memory. Determining the load factor for your own hash tables is dependent on how you use each hash table and whether your priority is performance or memory efficiency.

You can create hash tables in any one of three ways. The first constructor creates a default hash table:

```
Hashtable hash = new Hashtable();
```

The second constructor creates a hash table with the specified initial capacity:

```
Hashtable hash = new Hashtable(20);
```

Finally, the third constructor creates a hash table with the specified initial capacity and load factor:

```
Hashtable hash = new Hashtable(20, 0.75F);
```

All the abstract methods defined in Map are implemented in the Hashtable class. In addition, the Hashtable class implements a few others that perform functions specific to supporting hash tables. One of these is the clear() method, which clears a hash table of all its keys and elements:

```
hash.clear();
```

The contains() method checks whether an object is stored in the hash table. This method searches for an object value in the hash table rather than searching for a key. The following code shows how to use the contains() method:

```
boolean isThere = hash.contains(new Rectangle(0, 0, 5, 5));
```

Similar to contains(), the containsKey() method searches a hash table, but is based on a key rather than a value:

```
boolean isThere = hash.containsKey("Small");
```

As mentioned earlier, a hash table will rehash itself when it determines that it must increase its capacity. You can force a rehash yourself by calling the rehash() method:

```
hash.rehash();
```

The practical use of a hash table is actually in representing data that is too time-consuming to search or reference by value. In other words, hash tables often come in handy when you're working with complex data and it's much more efficient to access the data by using a key rather than comparing the data objects themselves.

21

Furthermore, hash tables typically compute a key for elements, which is called a hash code. For example, a string can have an integer hash code computed for it that uniquely represents the string. When a bunch of strings are stored in a hash table, the table can access the strings by using integer hash codes as opposed to using the contents of the strings themselves. This results in much more efficient searching and retrieving capabilities.

NEW TERM   A *hash code* is a computed key that uniquely identifies each element in a hash table.

This technique of computing and using hash codes for object storage and reference is exploited heavily throughout the Java system. The parent of all classes, `Object`, defines a `hashCode()` method that is overridden in most standard Java classes. Any class that defines a `hashCode()` method can be efficiently stored and accessed in a hash table. A class that wants to be hashed must also implement the `equals()` method, which defines a way of telling whether two objects are equal. The `equals()` method usually just performs a straight comparison of all the member variables defined in a class.

Hash tables are an extremely powerful data structure that should probably be integrated into some of your programs that manipulate large amounts of data. The fact that hash tables are so widely supported in the Java class library via the `Object` class should give you a clue as to their importance in Java programming.

Summary

In today's lesson, you learned about working with existing data stored in popular database formats such as Microsoft Access, MySQL, and xBase. Using either Java Database Connectivity (JDBC) or a combination of JDBC and ODBC, you can incorporate existing data storage solutions into your Java programs.

You also learned several ways to work with data that doesn't exist yet, by using some of the data structures that are more sophisticated than arrays and linked lists.

These standard data structures provide a range of options that cover many practical programming scenarios.

In the bonus week to this book, you have an opportunity to work with additional aspects of the language, such as Swing accessibility, JavaServer Pages, servlets, and the Java debugger.

This book has an official Web site at `http://www.java21pro.com`. It features answers to frequently asked questions, all the book's source code, error corrections, and supplementary material.

Q&A

Q Can the JDBC-ODBC bridge driver be used in an applet?

A The default security in place for applets does not allow the JDBC-ODBC bridge to be used because the ODBC side of the bridge driver employs native code rather than Java. Native code can't be held to the security restrictions in place for Java, so there's no way to ensure that this code is secure.

JDBC drivers that are implemented entirely in Java can be used in applets, and they have the advantage of requiring no configuration on the client computer.

Q What is the importance of using a hash table?

A Calculating a hash code for a complex piece of data is important because you can lessen the overhead involved in searching for the data. The hash code enables you to home in on a particular point in a large set of data before you begin the arduous task of searching based on the data itself. This can greatly improve performance.

Q How are linked lists different from vectors in the storage of individual elements?

A Vectors manage the memory requirements of all elements by allocating a certain amount of memory upon creation. When a vector is required to grow, it will allocate enough memory to hold the existing data and the new data and will then copy everything to it. Even if a vector holds only references to objects, it must still manage the memory that holds the references. Linked lists don't manage any of the memory for the elements contained in the list, except for references to the start and end elements.

Questions

1. What does a `Statement` object represent in a database program?

    (a) A connection to a database

    (b) A database query written in Structured Query Language

    (c) A data source

2. What kind of driver is not included with Java 2 SDK 1.3?

    (a) A JDBC driver

    (b) A JDBC-ODBC driver

    (c) Both

21

3. Which of the following data structures cannot grow in size after it is created?

   (a) Vectors

   (b) Arrays

   (c) Linked lists

Answers

1. b. The class, part of the `java.sql` package, represents an SQL statement.

2. a. Many relational database programs include a JDBC driver, but one is not shipped with the SDK at this writing.

3. b.

Exercises

To extend your knowledge of the subjects covered today, try the following exercises:

- Modify the `CoalTotals` application to pull fields from the Country Oil Totals table instead of the Coal table.

- Create an application that uses a vector to issue new license plate tags and reject requests for tags that are already taken.

Where applicable, exercise solutions are offered on the book's Web site at `http://www.java21pro.com`.

BONUS WEEK

Expanding Your Java Knowledge

- The Software Development Kit
- Java Programming Environments
- Writing Java 1.0 Applets
- Accessibility
- Writing Java Servlets
- Using JavaServer Pages
- Reading XML Files

22

23

24

25

26

27

28

DAY 22

The Software Development Kit

The Software Development Kit (SDK) is used throughout this book to create, compile, and run Java programs.

The tools that make up the SDK contain numerous features that many programmers don't explore at all, and some of the tools themselves might be new to you.

This appendix covers features of the SDK you can use to create more reliable, better-tested, and faster-running Java programs.

The following topics will be covered:

- Running Java applications with the interpreter
- Compiling programs with the compiler
- Running Java applets with the `appletviewer`
- Creating documentation with the documentation tool
- Finding bugs in your program and learning more about its performance with the debugger
- Setting system properties with the interpreter and `appletviewer`

An Overview of the SDK

Although there are several dozen software packages that you can use to create Java programs, the most widely used is the Software Development Kit (SDK) from Sun Microsystems. The SDK is the set of command-line tools that are used to develop software with the Java language.

There are two main reasons for the popularity of the SDK:

- It's free. You can download a copy at no cost from Sun's official Java World Wide Web site at http://java.sun.com.
- It's first. Whenever Sun releases a new version of the language, the first tools that support this version are in the SDK.

The SDK uses the command line—also called the MS-DOS prompt on Windows 95, 98, and Me systems and the console on Windows NT and 2000 systems. Commands are entered using the keyboard, as in the following example:

```
javac VideoBook.java
```

This command compiles a Java program called VideoBook.java using the SDK compiler. There are two elements to the command: the name of the SDK compiler, javac, followed by the name of the program to compile, VideoBook.java. A space character separates the two elements.

Each SDK command follows the same format: the name of the tool to use, followed by one or more elements indicating what the tool should do. These elements are called *arguments*.

The following illustrates the use of command-line arguments:

```
java VideoBook add VHS "Bad Influence"
```

This command tells the Java interpreter to run a class file called VideoBook with three command-line arguments: the strings add, VHS, and Bad Influence.

Note

> You might think there are four command-line arguments because of the space between the words Bad and Influence. The quotation marks around "Bad Influence" cause it to be considered one command-line argument rather than two. This makes it possible to include a space character in an argument.

Some arguments used with the SDK modify how a tool will function. These arguments are preceded by a hyphen character and are called *options*.

The following command shows the use of an option:

```
java -version
```

22

This command tells the Java interpreter to display its version number rather than trying to run a class file. It's a good way to find out whether the SDK is correctly configured to run Java programs on your system. Here's an example of the output run on a system equipped with SDK 1.3.0:

```
java version "1.3.0"
Java(TM) 2 Runtime Environment, Standard Edition (build1.3.0)
Java HotSpot(TM) Client VM (build 1.3.0, mixed mode)
```

In some instances, you can combine options with other arguments. If you compile a Java class that uses deprecated methods, you can see more information on these methods by compiling the class with a -deprecation option, as in the following:

```
javac -deprecation OldVideoBook.java
```

The `java` Interpreter

`java`, the Java interpreter, is used to run Java applications from the command line. It takes as an argument the name of a class file to run, as in the following example:

```
java BidMonitor
```

Although Java class files end with the `.class` extension, this extension is not specified when using the interpreter.

The class loaded by the Java interpreter must contain a `main()` method that takes the following form:

```
public static void main(String[] arguments) {
    // Method here
}
```

Some simple Java programs might use only one class—the one containing the `main()` method. In other cases, the interpreter automatically loads any other classes that are needed.

The Java interpreter runs bytecode—the compiled instructions that are executed by a Java virtual machine. After a Java program is in bytecode form as a `.class` file, it can be run by different interpreters without modification. If you have compiled a Java 2 program, it should be compatible with any interpreter that fully supports Java 2.

Note

> Interestingly enough, Java is no longer the only language that you can use to create Java bytecode. NetRexx, JPython, and several other languages will compile into `.class` files of executable bytecode through the use of compilers specific to those languages. A list of these languages is currently available from the Web page at http://grunge.cs.tu-berlin.de/~tolk/vmlanguages.html.

There are two different ways to specify the class file that should be run by the Java interpreter. If the class is not part of any package, you can run it by specifying the name of the class, as in the preceding `java BidMonitor` example and all the examples in prior chapters of this book. If the class is part of a package, you must specify the class by using its full package and class name.

For example, consider a `SellItem` class that is part of the `com.prefect.auction` package. To run this application, the following command would be used:

```
java com.prefect.auction.SellItem
```

Each element of the package name corresponds to its own subfolder The Java interpreter will look for the `SellItem.class` file in several different places:

- The `com\prefect\auction` subfolder of the folder where the `java` command was entered. (If the command was made from the `C:\J21work` folder, for example, the `SellItem.class` file could be run successfully if it was in the `C:\J21work\com\prefect\auction` folder.)
- The `com\prefect\auction` subfolder of any folder in your `CLASSPATH` setting.

If you're creating your own packages, an easy way to manage them is to add a folder to your `CLASSPATH` that's the root folder for any packages you create, such as `C:\javapackages` or something similar. After creating subfolders that correspond to the name of a package, place the package's class files in the correct subfolder.

The javac Compiler

`javac`, the Java compiler, converts Java source code into one or more class files of bytecode that can be run by a Java interpreter.

Java source code is stored in a file with the `.java` file extension. This file can be created with any text editor or word processor that can save a document without any special formatting codes. The terminology varies depending on the text-editing software being used, but these files are often called plain text, ASCII text, DOS text, or something similar.

A Java source code file can contain more than one class, but only one of the classes can be declared to be public. A class can contain no public classes at all if desired, although this isn't possible with applets because of the rules of inheritance.

If a source code file contains a class that has been declared to be public, the name of the file must match the name of that class. For example, the source code for a public class called BuyItem must be stored in a file called BuyItem.java.

To compile a file, the javac tool is run with the name of the file as an argument, as in the following:

```
javac BidMonitor.java
```

You can compile more than one source file by including each separate filename as a command-line argument, such as this command:

```
javac BidMonitor.java SellItem.java
```

You also can use wildcard characters such as * and ?. Use the following command to compile all .java files in a folder:

```
javac *.java
```

When you compile one or more Java source code files, a separate .class file will be created for each Java class that compiles successfully.

> **Caution**
>
> An easy mistake to make when you're putting a Java applet on the Web is to forget some of the .class files that make up the applet. You can combine several files into a single archive using the jar tool, which you learned about on Day 7, "Writing Java Applets." jar enables all files associated with an applet to be grouped together into a single file.

One of the javac tool's options is -deprecation, which you can use to find out more about the deprecated methods being employed in a Java program. Normally, the compiler will issue a single warning if it finds any deprecated methods in a program. The -deprecation option causes the compiler to list each method that has been deprecated, as in the following command:

```
javac -deprecation SellItem.java
```

If you're more concerned with the speed of a Java program than the size of its class files, you can compile its source code with the -O option. This creates class files that have been optimized for faster performance. Methods that are static, final, or private might be compiled *inline*, a technique that makes the class file larger but causes the methods to be executed more quickly.

Normally, the Java compiler doesn't provide a lot of information. In fact, if all the source code compiles successfully and no deprecated methods are employed, you won't see any output from the compiler at all. No news is good news in this case.

If you'd like to see more information on what the `javac` tool is doing as it compiles source code, use the `-verbose` option. The more verbose compiler will describe the time it takes to complete different functions, the classes that are being loaded, and the overall time required.

The `appletviewer` Browser

`appletviewer`, the Java applet viewer, is used to run Java programs that require a Web browser and are presented as part of an HTML document.

`appletviewer` takes an HTML document as a command-line argument, as in the following example:

```
appletviewer NewAuctions.html
```

When an HTML document is loaded by `appletviewer`, every applet on that document will begin running in its own window. The size of these windows depends on the `HEIGHT` and `WIDTH` attributes that were set in the applet's HTML tag.

Unlike a Web browser, `appletviewer` cannot be used to view the HTML document itself. If you want to see how the applet is laid out in relation to the other contents of the document, you must use a Java-capable Web browser such as Netscape Navigator or Microsoft Internet Explorer.

Note   At the time of this writing, neither Navigator nor Internet Explorer offers built-in support for Java 2 applets. The Java Plug-in from Sun can be used to run a Java 2 applet with either browser, as long as the HTML document containing the applet has been designed to work with the Plug-in. You can download it from Sun's Web site at http://java.sun.com/products/plugin/. SDK's `appletviewer` is the only tool that runs Java 2 applets on HTML documents that aren't configured to use the Plug-in.

Using `appletviewer` is reasonably straightforward, but you may not be familiar with some of the menu options that are available as the viewer runs an applet. Figure 22.1 shows the options on the `appletviewer` tool's Applet pull-down menu.

Figure 22.1

The Applet pull-down menu of appletviewer.

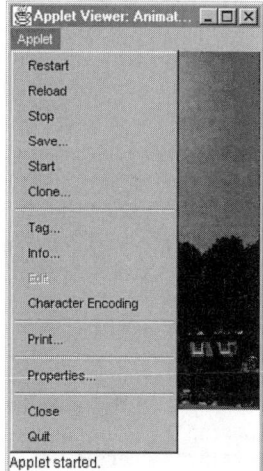

The following menu options are available:

- The Restart and Reload options are used to restart the execution of the applet. The difference between these two options is that Restart does not unload the applet before restarting it, whereas Reload does. The Reload option is equivalent to closing the applet viewer and opening it up again on the same Web page.

- The Start and Stop options are used to directly call the start() and stop() methods of the applet.

- The Clone option creates a second copy of the same applet running in its own window.

- The Tag option displays the program's <APPLET> tag, along with the HTML for any <PARAM> tags that configure the applet.

Another option on the Applet pull-down menu is Info, which calls the getAppletInfo() and getParameterInfo() methods of the applet. A programmer can implement these methods to provide more information about the applet and the parameters that it can handle. The getAppletInfo() method should return a string that describes the applet. The getParameterInfo() method should return an array of string arrays that specify the name, type, and description of each parameter.

Listing 22.1 contains an applet that demonstrates the use of these methods.

LISTING 22.1 The Full Text of `AppInfo.java`

```
 1: import java.awt.Graphics;
 2:
 3: public class AppInfo extends java.applet.Applet {
 4:     String name, date;
 5:     int version;
 6:
 7:     public String getAppletInfo() {
 8:         String response = "This applet demonstrates the "
 9:             + "use of the Applet's Info feature.";
10:         return response;
11:     }
12:
13:     public String[][] getParameterInfo() {
14:         String[] p1 = { "Name", "String", "Programmer's name" };
15:         String[] p2 = { "Date", "String", "Today's date" };
16:         String[] p3 = { "Version", "int", "Version number" };
17:         String[][] response = { p1, p2, p3 };
18:         return response;
19:     }
20:
21:     public void init() {
22:         name = getParameter("Name");
23:         date = getParameter("Date");
24:         String versText = getParameter("Version");
25:         if (versText != null)
26:             version = Integer.parseInt(versText);
28:     }
29:
30:     public void paint(Graphics screen) {
31:         screen.drawString("Name: " + name, 5, 50);
32:         screen.drawString("Date: " + date, 5, 100);
33:         screen.drawString("Version: " + version, 5, 150);
34:     }
35: }
```

The main function of this applet is to display the value of three parameters: Name, Date, and Version. The getAppletInfo() method returns the following string:

```
This applet demonstrates the use of the Applet's Info feature.
```

The getParameterInfo() method is a bit more complicated if you haven't worked with multidimensional arrays. The following things are taking place:

- Line 13 defines the return type of the method as a two-dimensional array of String objects.

22

- Line 14 creates an array of `String` objects with three elements: `"Name"`, `"String"`, and `"Programmer's Name"`. These elements describe one of the parameters that can be defined for the `AppInfo` applet. They describe the name of the parameter (`Name` in this case), the type of data that the parameter should hold (a string), and a description of the parameter (`"Programmer's Name"`). The three-element array is stored in the `p1` object.

- Lines 15–16 define two more `String` arrays for the `Date` and `Version` parameters.

- Line 17 uses the `response` object to store an array that contains three string arrays: `p1`, `p2`, and `p3`.

- Line 18 uses the `response` object as the method's return value.

Listing 22.2 contains a Web page that can be used to load the `AppInfo` applet.

LISTING 22.2   The Full Text of `AppInfo.html`

```
1: <applet code="AppInfo.class" height=200 width=170>
2: <param name="Name" value="Rogers Cadenhead">
3: <param name="Date" value="04/07/00">
4: <param name="Version" value="2">
5: </applet>
```

Figure 22.2 shows the applet running with the applet viewer, and Figure 22.3 is a screen capture of the dialog box that opens when the viewer's Info menu option is selected.

FIGURE 22.2

The `AppInfo` *applet running in* `appletviewer`.

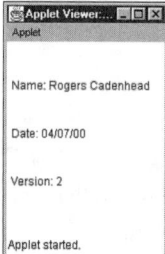

These features require a browser that makes this information available to users. The `appletviewer` handles this through the Info menu option, but browsers such as Internet Explorer do not offer anything like it at this time.

FIGURE 22.3

The Info dialog box of the AppInfo *applet.*

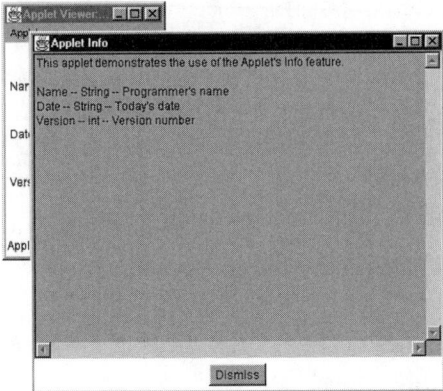

The javadoc Documentation Tool

javadoc, the Java documentation creator, takes a .java source code file or package name as input and generates detailed documentation in HTML format.

For javadoc to create full documentation for a program, a special type of comment statement must be used in the program's source code. Tutorial programs in this book use //, /*, and */ in source code to create *comments*—information for people who are trying to make sense of the program.

Java also has a more structured type of comment that can be read by the javadoc tool. This comment is used to describe program elements such as classes, variables, objects, and methods. It takes the following format:

```
/** A descriptive sentence or paragraph.
 * @tag1 Description of this tag.
 * @tag2 Description of this tag.
 */
```

A Java documentation comment should be placed immediately above the program element it is documenting and should succinctly explain what the program element is. For example, if the comment precedes a class statement, it should describe the purpose of the class.

In addition to the descriptive text, different items can be used to further document the program element. These items, called *tags,* are preceded by an @ sign and are followed by a space and a descriptive sentence or paragraph.

Listing 22.3 contains a thoroughly documented version of the `AppInfo` applet called `AppInfo2`. The following tags are used in this program:

- `@author`—The program's author. This tag can be used only when documenting a class, and it will be ignored unless the `-author` option is used when `javadoc` is run.

- `@version text`—The program's version number. This also is restricted to class documentation, and it requires the `-version` option when you're running `javadoc` or the tag will be ignored.

- `@return text`—The variable or object returned by the method being documented.

- `@serial text`—A description of the data type and possible values for a variable or object that can be serialized. More information about serialization is available during Day 18, "Object Serialization and Reflection."

LISTING 22.3   The Full Text of `AppInfo2.java`

```
 1: import java.awt.Graphics;
 2:
 3: /** This class creates displays the values of three parameters:
 4:  * Name, Date and Version.
 5:  * @author <a href="http://www.java21pro.com">
      ➥Rogers Cadenhead</a>
 6:  * @version 2.0
 7:  */
 8: public class AppInfo2 extends java.applet.Applet {
 9:     /**
10:      * @serial The programmer's name.
11:      */
12:     String name;
13:     /**
14:      * @serial The current date.
15:      */
16:     String date;
17:     /**
18:      * @serial The program's version number.
19:      */
20:     int version;
21:
22:     /**
23:      * This method describes the applet for any browsing tool that
24:      * request information out the program.
25:      * @return A String describing the applet.
26:      */
27:     public String getAppletInfo() {
28:         String response = "This applet demonstrates the "
```

LISTING 22.3   continued

```
29:                + "use of the Applet's Info feature.";
30:         return response;
31:     }
32:
33:     /**
34:      * This method describes the parameters that the applet can take
35:      * for any browsing tool that requests this information.
36:      * @return An array of String[] objects for each parameter.
37:      */
38:     public String[][] getParameterInfo() {
39:         String[] p1 = { "Name", "String", "Programmer's name" };
40:         String[] p2 = { "Date", "String", "Today's date" };
41:         String[] p3 = { "Version", "int", "Version number" };
42:         String[][] response = { p1, p2, p3 };
43:         return response;
44:     }
45:
46:     /**
47:      * This method is called when the applet is first initialized.
48:      */
49:     public void init() {
50:         name = getParameter("Name");
51:         date = getParameter("Date");
52:         String versText = getParameter("Version");
53:         if (versText != null)
54:             version = Integer.parseInt(versText);
55:     }
56:
57:     /**
58:      * This method is called when the applet's display window is
59:      * being repainted.
60:      */
61:     public void paint(Graphics screen) {
62:         screen.drawString("Name: " + name, 5, 50);
63:         screen.drawString("Date: " + date, 5, 100);
64:         screen.drawString("Version: " + version, 5, 150);
65:     }
66: }
```

The following command would be used to create HTML documentation from the source code file AppInfo2.java:

```
javadoc -author -version AppInfo2.java
```

The Java documentation tool will create several different Web pages in the same folder as AppInfo2.java. These pages will document the program in the same manner as Sun's official documentation for the Java language.

Tip

> To see the official documentation for Java 2, SDK 1.3, and the Java class libraries, visit http://java.sun.com/products/JDK/1.3/docs/.

22

To see the documentation that javadoc has created for AppInfo2, load the newly created Web page index.html on your Web browser. Figure 22.4 shows this page loaded with Internet Explorer.

FIGURE 22.4

Java documentation for the AppInfo2 program.

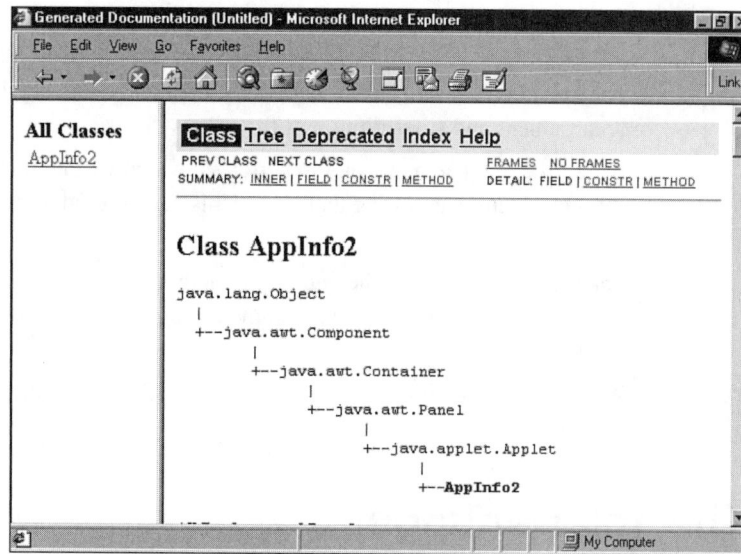

The javadoc tool produces extensively hyperlinked Web pages. Navigate through the pages to see where the information in your documentation comments and tags shows up.

If you're familiar with HTML programming, you can use HTML tags such as <A>, <TT>, and <B> within your documentation comments. Line 5 of the AppInfo2 program uses an <A> tag to turn the text "Rogers Cadenhead" into a hyperlink to this book's Web site.

The javadoc tool also can be used to document an entire package by specifying the package name as a command-line argument. HTML files will be created for each .java file in the package, along with an HTML file indexing the package.

If you would like the Java documentation to be produced in a different folder than the default, use the -d option followed by a space and the folder name.

The following command creates Java documentation for `AppInfo2` in a folder called
`C:\JavaDocs\`:

```
javadoc -author -version -d C:\JavaDocs\ AppInfo2.java
```

The following list details the other tags you can use in Java documentation comments:

- `@deprecated` *text*—A note that this class, method, object, or variable has been deprecated. This causes the `javac` compiler to issue a deprecation warning when the feature is used in a program that's being compiled.

- `@exception` *class description*—Used with methods that throw exceptions, this tag documents the exception's class name and its description.

- `@param` *name description*—Used with methods, this tag documents the name of an argument and a description of the values the argument can hold.

- `@see` *class*—The name of another class, which will be turned into a hyperlink to the Java documentation of that class. This can be used without restriction in comments.

- `@see` *class#method*—The name of a method of another class, which will be used for a hyperlink directly to the documentation of that method. This is usable without restriction.

- `@since` *text*—A note describing when a method or feature was added to its class library.

The `jdb` Debugger

`jdb`, the Java debugger, is a sophisticated tool that helps you find and fix bugs in Java programs. You can also use it to better understand what is taking place behind the scenes in the Java interpreter as a program is running. It has a large number of features, including some that might be beyond the expertise of a Java programmer who is new to the language.

You don't need to use the debugger to debug Java programs. This is fairly obvious, especially if you've been creating your own Java programs as you read this book. After the Java compiler generates an error, the most common response is to load the source code into an editor, find the line cited in the error message, and try to spot the problem. This dreaded compile-curse-find-fix cycle is repeated until the program compiles without complaint.

After using this debugging method for a while, you might think that the debugger isn't necessary to the programming process because it's such a complicated tool to master.

22

This reasoning makes sense when you're fixing problems that cause compiler errors. Many of these problems are simple things such as a misplaced semicolon, unmatched { and } brackets, or the use of the wrong type of data as a method argument. However, when you start looking for logic errors—more subtle bugs that don't stop the program from compiling and running—a debugger is an invaluable tool.

The Java debugger has two features that are extremely useful when you're searching for a bug that can't be found by other means: single-step execution and breakpoints. *Single-step execution* pauses a Java program after every line of code is executed. *Breakpoints* are points where execution of the program will pause. Using the Java debugger, these breakpoints can be triggered by specific lines of code, method calls, or caught exceptions.

The Java debugger works by running a program using a version of the Java interpreter that it has complete control over.

Before you use the Java debugger, you should compile the program with the -g option, which causes extra information to be included in the class file. This information greatly aids in debugging. Also, you shouldn't use the -O option because its optimization techniques might produce a class file that does not directly correspond with the program's source code.

Debugging Applications

If you're debugging an application, the jdb tool can be run with a Java class as an argument. This is shown in the following:

```
jdb WriteBytes
```

This example runs the debugger with WriteBytes.class, an application that's available from the book's Web site at http://www.java21pro.com. Visit the site and select the Appendix C page, and then save the files WriteBytes.class and WriteBytes.java in the same folder that you run the debugger from.

The WriteBytes application writes a series of bytes to disk to produce the file pic.gif.

The debugger loads this program but does not begin running it, displaying the following output:

```
Initializing jdb...
>
```

The debugger is controlled by typing commands at the > prompt.

To set a breakpoint in a program, the `stop in` or `stop at` commands are used. The `stop in` command sets a breakpoint at the first line of a specific method in a class. You specify the class and method name as an argument to the command, as in the following example:

```
stop in SellItem.SetPrice
```

This command sets a breakpoint at the first line of the `SetPrice` method. Note that no arguments or parentheses are needed after the method name.

The `stop at` command sets a breakpoint at a specific line number within a class. You specify the class and number as an argument to the command, as in the following example:

```
stop at WriteBytes:14
```

If you're trying this with the `WriteBytes` class, you'll see the following output after entering this command:

```
breakpoint set at WriteBytes:14
```

You can set as many breakpoints as desired within a class. To see the breakpoints that are currently set, use the `clear` command without any arguments. The `clear` command lists all current breakpoints by line number rather than method name, even if they were set using the `stop in` command.

By using `clear` with a class name and line number as an argument, you can remove a breakpoint. If the hypothetical `SellItem.SetPrice` method was located at line 215 of `SellItem`, you could clear this breakpoint with the following command:

```
clear SellItem:215
```

Within the debugger, you can begin executing a program with the `run` command. The following output shows what the debugger displays after you begin running the `WriteBytes` class:

```
run WriteBytes
running...
main[1]
Breakpoint hit: WriteBytes.main(WriteBytes:14)
```

After you have reached a breakpoint in the `WriteBytes` class, experiment with the following commands:

- `list`—At the point where execution stopped, this displays the source code of the line and several lines around it. This requires access to the `.java` file of the class where the breakpoint has been hit, so you must have `WriteBytes.java` in either the current folder or one of the folders in your `CLASSPATH`.

- `locals`—Lists the values for local variables that are currently in use or will soon be defined.
- `print` *text*—Displays the value of the variable, object, or array element specified by *text*.
- `step`—Executes the next line and stops again.
- `cont`—Continues running the program at the point it was halted.
- `!!`—Repeats the previous debugger command.

After trying out these commands within the application, you can resume running the program by clearing the breakpoint and using the `cont` command. Use the `exit` command to end the debugging session.

The `WriteBytes` application creates a file called `pic.gif`. You can verify that this file ran successfully by loading it with a Web browser or image editing software. You'll see a small letter *J* in black and white.

After you have finished debugging a program, you should remember to recompile it without the `-g` option.

Debugging Applets

You can't debug an applet by loading it using the `jdb` tool. Instead, use the `-debug` option of the `appletviewer`, as in the following example:

```
appletviewer -debug AppInfo.html
```

This will load the Java debugger, and when you use a command such as `run`, the `appletviewer` will begin running also. Try out this example to see how these tools interact with each other.

Before you use the `run` command to execute the applet, set a breakpoint in the program at the first line of the `getAppletInfo` method. Use the following command:

```
stop in AppInfo.getAppletInfo
```

After you begin running the applet, the breakpoint won't be hit until you cause the `getAppletInfo()` method to be called. This is accomplished by selecting Applet, Info from the `appletviewer`'s menu.

Advanced Debugging Commands

With the features you have learned about so far, you can use the debugger to stop execution of a program and learn more about what's taking place. This might be sufficient for many of your debugging tasks, but the debugger also offers many other commands. These include the following:

- up—Moves up the stack frame so that you can use `locals` and `print` to examine the program at the point before the current method was called.
- down—Moves down the stack frame to examine the program after the method call.

In a Java program, often there are places where a chain of methods is called. One method calls another method, which calls another method, and so on. At each point where a method is being called, Java keeps track of all the objects and variables within that scope by grouping them together. This grouping is called a *stack*, as if you were stacking these objects like a deck of cards. The various stacks in existence as a program runs are called the *stack frame*.

By using up and down along with commands such as `locals`, you can better understand how the code that calls a method interacts with that method.

You can also use the following commands within a debugging session:

- classes—Lists the classes currently loaded into memory.
- methods—Lists the methods of a class.
- memory—Lists the total memory and the amount that isn't currently in use.
- threads—Lists the threads that are executing.

The `threads` command numbers all the threads, which enables you to use the `suspend` command followed by that number to pause the thread, as in `suspend 1`. You can resume a thread by using the `resume` command followed by its number.

Another convenient way to set a breakpoint in a Java program is to use the `catch text` command, which pauses execution when the `Exception` class named by `text` is caught.

You can also cause an exception to be ignored by using the `ignore text` command with the `Exception` class named by `text`.

Using System Properties

One obscure feature of the SDK is that the command-line option `-D` can modify the performance of the Java class library.

If you have used other programming languages prior to learning Java, you might be familiar with environment variables, which provide information about the operating system in which a program is running. An example is the `CLASSPATH` setting, which indicates the folders in which the Java interpreter should look for a class file.

Because different operating systems have different names for their environment variables, they cannot be read directly by a Java program. Instead, Java includes a number of different system properties that are available on any platform with a Java implementation.

Some properties are used only to get information. The following system properties are among those that should be available on any Java implementation:

- `java.version` — The version number of the Java interpreter.
- `java.vendor` — A string identifying the vendor associated with the Java interpreter.
- `os.name` — The operating system in use.
- `os.version` — The version number of that operating system.

Other properties can affect how the Java class library performs when being used inside a Java program. An example of this is the `java2d.font.usePlatformFont` property. If this property has a value of `true`, a Java program will use the Java 1.1 style of font rendering rather than the system used in subsequent versions of the language. This property became useful with a beta version of Java 2 that had some bugs in how the `appletviewer` tool handled fonts.

A property can be set at the command line by using the `-D` option followed by the property name, an equal sign, and the new value of the property, as in this command:

```
java -Djava2d.font.usePlatformFont=true Auctioneer
```

The use of the system property in this example will cause the `Auctioneer` application to use 1.1-style fonts.

You also can create your own properties and read them using the `getProperty()` method of the `System` class, which is part of the `java.lang` package.

Listing 22.4 contains the source code of a simple program that displays the value of a user-created property.

LISTING 22.4   The Full Text of `ItemProp.java`

```
1: class ItemProp {
2:     public static void main(String[] arguments) {
3:         String n = System.getProperty("item.name");
4:         System.out.println("The item is named " + n);
5:     }
6: }
```

If this program is run without setting the item.name property on the command line, the output is the following:

```
The item is named null
```

The item.name property can be set using the -D option, as in this command:

```
java -Ditem.name="Microsoft Bob" ItemProp
```

The output is the following:

```
The item is named Microsoft Bob
```

The -D option is used with the Java interpreter. To use it with the appletviewer as well, all you have to do differently is precede the -D with -J. The following command shows how this can be done:

```
appletviewer -J-Djava2d.font.usePlatformFont=true AuctionSite.html
```

This example causes appletviewer to use Java 1.1-style fonts with all applets on the Web page AuctionSite.html.

Summary

Today you explored several features of the SDK that are increasingly helpful as you develop more experience with Java:

- Using the Java debugger with applets and applications
- Creating an optimized version of a compiled class
- Writing applet methods that provide information to a browser upon request
- Using the Java documentation creation tool to fully describe a class, its methods, and other aspects of the program

These SDK features weren't required during the first 21 days of this book because of the relative simplicity of the tutorial programs. Although it can be complicated to develop a Swing application or to work with threads and streams for the first time, your biggest challenge is to integrate concepts like these into more sophisticated Java programs.

Tools such as javadoc and the debugger really come into their own on complex projects.

When a bug occurs because of how two classes interact with each other, or similar subtle logic errors creep into your code, a debugger is the best way to identify and repair the problems.

As you create an entire library of classes, javadoc can easily document these classes and show how they are interrelated.

Q&A

Q **The official Java documentation is filled with long paragraphs that describe classes and methods. How can these be produced using javadoc?**

A In the Java documentation creator, there's no limit to the length of a description. Although they're often as brief as a sentence or two, they can be longer if necessary. End the description with a period, immediately followed by a new line with a tag of some kind or the end of the comment.

Q **Do I have to document everything in my Java classes if I'm planning to use the javadoc tool?**

A The Java documentation creator will work fine no matter how many or how few comments you use. Deciding which elements of the program need to be documented is up to you. You probably should describe the class and all methods, variables, and objects that aren't hidden from other classes.

The javadoc tool will display a warning each time a serializable object or variable is defined in a program without a corresponding Java documentation comment.

Questions

1. How many public classes can be contained in a single Java source file?

    (a) Only one public class

    (b) Either zero or one public class

    (c) As many public classes as you like

2. After you hit a breakpoint in the Java debugger, what command will list the source code of lines around that breakpoint?

    (a) locals

    (b) list

    (c) cont

3. What command-line option is used to set a property when running a Java application?

    (a) -D

    (b) -G

    (c) -CLASSPATH

Answers

1. b. If you include a public class, it must be the only public class in the file.

2. b. The `list` command.

3. a. The `-D` option is followed by the name of the property, an equals sign ("="), and the value of the property, as in `-Ditem.font=Courier`.

Exercises

To extend your knowledge of the subjects covered today, try the following exercises:

- Create an application that counts the number of lines in a text file, but only displays each line of the file if a property called `display.verbose` is set to true.

- Add `javadoc` style comments to one of the exercise projects you created for a preceding chapter, then use `javadoc` to produce documentation for that project.

BONUS WEEK

DAY 23

Java Programming Environments

Although the Java 2 Software Development Kit can be used to write, compile, and debug Java programs, it's extremely primitive compared to some of the commercial development software that's available for Java programmers.

Often you can develop Java programs more quickly and efficiently by using a suite of tools called an integrated development environment, also known as an IDE.

An IDE is software for computer programming that combines several development tools into a single package—such as a program source code editor, compiler, interpreter, debugger, and other tools.

Today, you'll take a detailed look at two of the most popular IDEs for Java programming:

- Borland JBuilder 4
- WebGain VisualCafé 4.1

Java IDEs

All of the tools in the Software Development Kit are used at the command line (the MS-DOS prompt on Windows systems). You run one of these tools by typing the name of the program followed by one or more arguments that control how it runs.

One of the main benefits of using an IDE is that you can create, compile, and test Java programs without ever using the command line.

An IDE combines the tools you need to handle these tasks in a graphical environment such as Microsoft Windows or Apple MacOS. The tools complement each other as you go through the process of creating programs.

Most professional IDEs use drag-and-drop, cut-and-paste, multiple windows, and other graphical features. If these features work well, designing a program should be faster and more efficient than using a more rudimentary tool, such as the Software Development Kit. Programs also should be easier to debug.

Many IDEs embody the principle of rapid application development, also known as RAD, in their approach to programming. RAD is a strategy to speed up program development by using tools such as a graphical user interface designer. Product advertisements that promise the capability to "create Java programs without writing a line of code" are referring to a RAD feature.

Most Java programming environments use RAD tools primarily in the design of a user interface, and use Java code to handle user events. For example, in Borland JBuilder 4, you can place a clickable button onto a frame and immediately open an `actionPerformed()` method to handle action events generated by that button. The IDE takes care of implementing the event-handling interface and setting up listeners.

More than 50 Java development environments have been released over the past five years. Today you'll be introduced to two of them that are popular with Java programmers and well-supported by their developers.

Choosing Development Software

As you evaluate IDEs in terms of your own programming tasks, any issues related to the Java language can make a difference in your choice. Ask yourself these questions:

- Is graphical interface design important in your programs?
- How important is it for your programs to run on more than one type of computer system, instead of being specific to a Microsoft Windows machine, an Apple Macintosh, or another system?

- Have you used IDE tools before?
- Will you be using other programming languages in addition to Java?

Graphical Interface Design Tools

With the continued popularity of Microsoft Windows and Apple MacOS, most computer users today expect to use windowing systems and a graphical environment to operate their machines. They expect software to support mouse input and offer common features such as resizable windows and cut-and-paste. These expectations make user interface design important to consider when you're developing a program.

In the same vein, interface design is important to consider when you're selecting an IDE. The available Java IDEs take different approaches to interface design and the other features that should be available as you design an interface. Many interface development tools can automatically create Java code that handles user events. Visual Basic programmers will be familiar with this feature because that language's IDE enables quick interface design and programming.

Most of the interface builders function similarly to drawing programs. User interface elements are arranged in a palette and can be dropped directly onto a workspace. Most of the components come from the Swing and Abstract Windowing Toolkit packages in Java. The developer of the IDE may also include a few new components. The Standard Edition of WebGain VisualCafé includes 10 new multimedia Abstract Windowing Toolkit components that play sounds, display images, or play animated sequences such as a fireworks show.

Writing Fully Portable Java Programs

One feature to look for as you evaluate the different IDEs is adherence to Java's promise of platform independence. Some of the development tools are no different than using the Software Development Kit—they produce programs that are fully usable in all Java implementations. Many of these IDEs, including the two you'll explore today, can be configured to use SDK 1.3 tools such as the compiler and interpreter behind the scenes.

Almost all IDEs are designed to help you write portable, platform-independent programs. A notable exception is Visual J++, an integrated development tool for Java programmers that has been discontinued. This IDE offered features that were specific to Microsoft Windows systems and couldn't be handled by other platforms. If a program developed with J++ used any Windows-specific features, it wouldn't be "100% pure Java" and might not work on all systems with a Java interpreter.

23

Although platform-independent programs are an important part of Java, most IDEs aren't completely independent themselves, even when written using Java. These development tools are available only for specific platforms, primarily because they use native code, which consists of parts of Java programs that are written using other languages such as C++ or C.

Experience Using Other IDEs

As you look over the sales pitches for IDEs, one thing that doesn't get enough attention is that many of these tools require you to have a lot of skill and experience to use them successfully. It can be difficult for an IDE to improve your performance as a programmer if you can't figure out how that IDE works.

IDEs often are the most complicated software you'll use. Because so much functionality has to be crammed into a single program, IDEs may include multiple-document windows, tabbed toolbars, numerous configuration options, and other complicated features.

Novice programmers can become frustrated with the complexity of many IDEs, especially if they're still learning how to use a new programming language. For this reason, the IDE you choose should be suited to your experience level as a programmer and IDE user.

Using an IDE for More Than One Language

If you're using more than one language as you develop software, another thing to consider about your IDE is whether you can use it with multiple languages. MetroWerks CodeWarrior is one of the best examples of a development environment suited to multi-language programmers. It supports Java, C, and C++ development on Macintosh, Windows, Linux, and even Sony Playstation systems.

One advantage to using an IDE that works with multiple languages is that you don't have to learn a different IDE for each language. (Of course, no IDE is easy to learn the first time around.) Another plus to using a multilanguage tool is that you can write Java statements and non-Java native methods with the same tool.

Evaluating an IDE

An IDE should make you a better programmer and make it easier or more enjoyable for you to develop programs. As you evaluate the products described today, you can determine which of the features of a specific IDE you might need. Of course, you can always use the Software Development Kit and enhance it by using custom interface builders, your preferred word processor, and other software.

 **Caution**   If you download trial copies of several different IDEs, as in this chapter, you might run into difficulties because of how each IDE configures your system. Many Java development tools use environment variables such as CLASSPATH and PATH, which could be set up incorrectly if another IDE has already configured them. Before installing a test version of an IDE, you should uninstall any other Java IDEs that are present on your system.

23

Borland JBuilder

Since its founding in 1983, the Borland company in Scottsville, California, has produced some of the most popular tools for C, C++, Pascal, and assembly language programming. One of these tools is Borland Delphi, an object-oriented extension of Pascal that can be used for rapid application development of Microsoft Windows software.

In 1997, Borland introduced JBuilder, an IDE for Java programming. This software, which is in its fourth release, can be used to create Java programs in several Windows, Linux, and Solaris environments.

JBuilder fully supports Java 2 SDK 1.3, so it can be used to create, compile, and run the tutorial programs in this book. If you're trying to create something using a prior version of the Java language, JBuilder also can be configured to use a previous version of the SDK instead.

You can use JBuilder 4 on Windows 98, NT, and 2000, as well as Linux distributions such as Red Hat 6.2, Mandrake 6, and SuSE Linux 6.3 (or subsequent versions of those distributions). The programs you create with JBuilder can be used on any system that supports Java.

Like many programming tools, JBuilder is offered in several different versions:

- JBuilder 4 Foundation, an introductory version retailing for $49.95.
- JBuilder 4 Professional, a $999 version that adds data storage and retrieval features.
- JBuilder 4 Enterprise, a $2,999 expanded version offering extensive support for Java development.

Each version of JBuilder 4 has the same user interface and core features.

The Foundation edition supports all of the standard Java class libraries, including all of the classes you've used during the preceding 22 days. You can create a graphical user interface using components from Swing or the Abstract Windowing Toolkit, and you can use preexisting JavaBeans.

The Professional edition offers tools that make it easier to develop Java programs that store and retrieve data. You can connect to a database using JDBC or ODBC, make SQL queries to retrieve data, and work with all of the major database servers on the market. There's also support for Remote Method Invocation, JavaBeans development, and servlets.

Note

> Java servlets are applications that are run by a Web server in the manner of CGI programs, PHP, and other tools for generating Web content interactively. Several development tools can be used to create, test, and deploy servlets. You will learn more during Day 26, "Writing Java Servlets."

The Archive Builder tool included in JBuilder Professional makes it easier to deploy Java applets on the Web. After you finish creating and testing an applet, Archive Builder packages all class files and other resources needed by the applet into a single Java archive (JAR) file.

There's also support for creating a single JAR file that contains everything you need to run a Java application at a command line.

Tip

> If you are planning on using a version of JBuilder to develop Java programs that you make available to others, the Professional edition makes this task much simpler. By handling it automatically, you reduce the possibility for errors such as omitting a class file or putting a class in the wrong folder.

The Enterprise edition offers support for some of the most sophisticated technology available to Java programmers:

- Enterprise JavaBeans, components employed in client/server computing
- Extensible Markup Language (XML), a popular standard for representing different kinds of data in a self-documenting, easy to use format
- JavaServer Pages, a Web technology used to embed Java source code in Web documents that is interpreted by a Web server
- Common Object Request Broker Architecture (CORBA), a standard for objects written in different languages to communicate with each other in a client/server environment

Exploring JBuilder

Although JBuilder Foundation leaves out a lot of useful features offered in the expanded versions of the software, it should be sufficient as you learn the Java language and use the packages that compose Java 2.

The Foundation version also offers a user interface designer, project management, and a built-in help system that documents JBuilder and Java 2.

JBuilder 4 Foundation is available for purchase online from Borland's eStore at `http://shop.borland.com`. At the time of this writing, you can also download a free trial version from Borland's Web site at `http://www.borland.com/jbuilder/`.

Figure 23.1 shows JBuilder being used to edit a Java program.

23

FIGURE 23.1

Editing Java programs in JBuilder 4 Foundation.

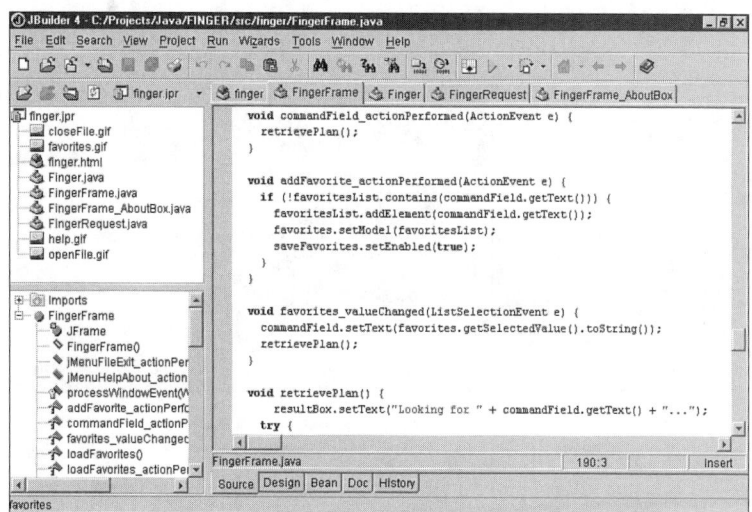

In Figure 23.1, the source code of a Java class called `FingerFrame` is being edited. JBuilder's source editor offers several features that make it easier to write programs.

When you're editing source code, JBuilder uses different colors for comments, arguments to methods, and Java keywords such as `void`, `if`, and `true`.

JBuilder also offers an easy way to find matching curly brackets ({}) in a program. If you put your cursor to the left of a bracket and press Alt+[, the cursor will move to the corresponding bracket.

As you're typing statements in the source code editor, sometimes JBuilder will display a pop-up dialog box with documentation related to what you're typing.

This feature, part of a help system called CodeInsight, appears in JBuilder 4 Foundation when you enter an object's name (or class name) and follow it with a period. JBuilder recognizes that you're about to type in the name of an object's variable or method, and it pops open a dialog box with the relevant documentation.

Figure 23.2 shows a CodeInsight dialog box.

Current line

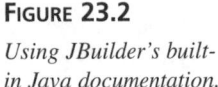

FIGURE 23.2

Using JBuilder's built-in Java documentation.

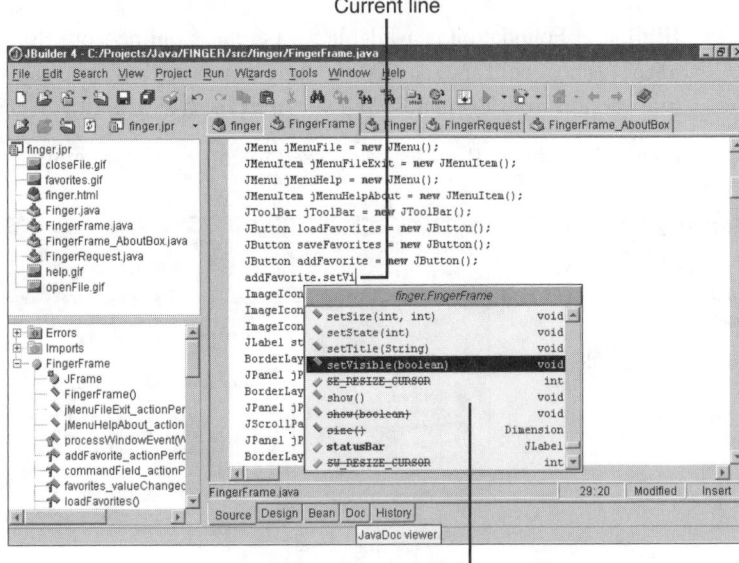

CodeInsight dialog box

As a programmer types in the text `addFavorite.setVi`, JBuilder recognizes that this is the start of a method call to a `JButton` object named `addFavorite`. In response, a list of `JButton` methods is displayed in the CodeInsight dialog box, along with the arguments each method takes. One of the method calls is highlighted—`setVisible(boolean)`. By pressing Enter, a programmer can add the highlighted method call to the source code without typing it in.

JBuilder offers CodeInsight documentation for classes, errors, expressions, and other aspects of the Java language—although some of these features require the Professional or Enterprise versions. You can use JBuilder strictly to write source code in an editor like this, taking advantage of its project management features and menu commands to compile and run Java programs.

The real strength of the IDE is the User Interface Designer, which makes it possible to create an interface and handle user events visually. Figure 23.3 shows JBuilder as a user interface is being developed.

FIGURE 23.3.

Designing a user interface with JBuilder.

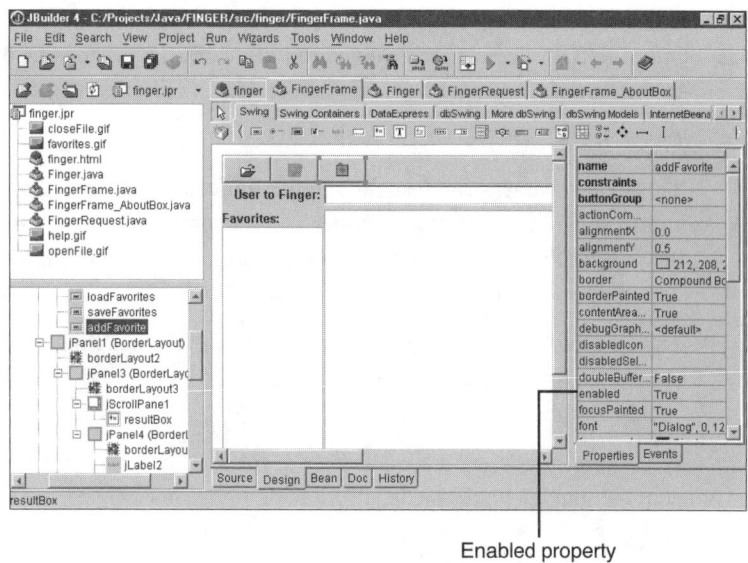

Enabled property

23

To design a user interface, you choose Swing or Abstract Windowing Toolkit components from a toolbar, and then you click the place on a container where the component should be located.

You can do all of the following tasks without writing any Java code:

- Change the layout manager of a container.
- Add components to a container.
- Rearrange components.
- Define a component's text label or default text value.
- Change a component's size, colors, and font.
- Enable and disable a component.

As you're designing an interface, JBuilder adds Java statements to your program that implement your design. The development environment can use the same components, layout managers, and event-handling classes you've learned about during the preceding three weeks.

For example, in Figure 23.3, a button called addFavorite has been selected for editing, causing all of its properties to be displayed in a window next to the interface designer. One of these properties, enabled, indicates whether the button can receive user input. It has a value of True in Figure 23.3, which means it can be clicked.

To change this property, a programmer double-clicks the word True. A list box appears in which the value can be changed to False. JBuilder then adds the following statement to the part of the program where the addFavorite button is set up:

```
addFavorite.setEnabled(false);
```

This Java statement can be edited in the source code editor. If you change the method call to setEnabled(true), JBuilder will recognize this change the next time you work in the interface designer. You don't lose any flexibility by designing an interface visually as opposed to creating it in the source code editor.

The JBuilder interface designer also supports event-handling. You can double-click a component in the user interface to open up the source code editor and begin creating an event-handling method.

For example, let's say a programmer decides to add event-handling to a JButton component by double-clicking it. The following things occur:

- The class is modified so it supports action events.
- The button is registered as an ActionListener.
- A new empty actionPerformed(ActionEvent) method is added to the class.
- The source code editor is opened in the middle of the new method.

You don't have to worry about registering listeners or implementing any event-handling interfaces—JBuilder takes care of these tasks automatically.

When you compile and run a Java program in JBuilder, the Java 2 interpreter and compiler are used behind the scenes. Any errors that occur are displayed in a tabbed window, as shown in Figure 23.4.

The error window in Figure 23.4 displays a single error:

```
"FingerFrame.java": Error #: 300 : method retrievePlane() not found
in class finger.FingerFrame at line 180, column 5
```

If this message is clicked, JBuilder opens the source code editor on line 180—the place where the Java compiler halted with an error.

JBuilder also supports breakpoints, step commands, and other debugging techniques, although the Foundation edition includes only a small fraction of these features compared to other versions.

Like most IDEs, JBuilder can be daunting for a new programmer to use. Even in the slimmed-down Foundation edition, JBuilder's interface includes more than 300 menu commands, toolbar buttons, and tabbed windows.

FIGURE 23.4.

*Debugging a Java pro-
gram in JBuilder.*

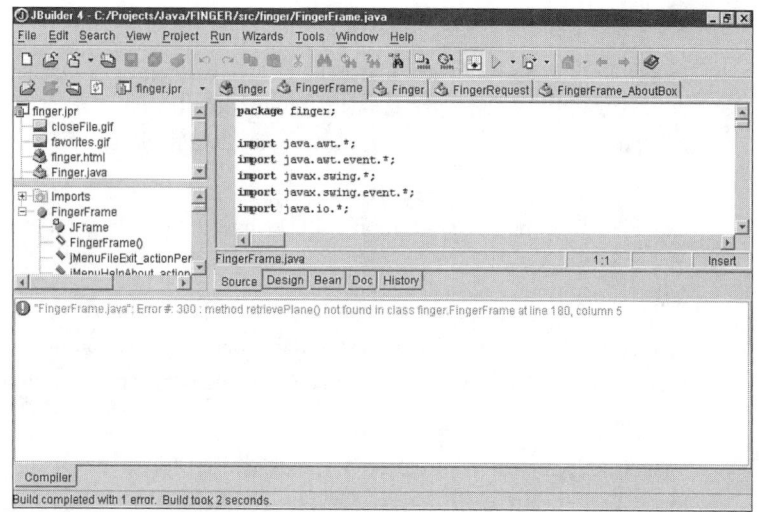

One of the more difficult aspects of JBuilder is laying out components using the user interface designer. Placing components and containers can be a confusing process. Sometimes a component will disappear when a new component is placed in the same area.

When you can't see a component in the interface designer, the only way you can edit it is by using the structure pane, which is a window that lists containers and the components that they contain. Using drag-and-drop to move components is supported within the user interface designer, but not in the structure pane. This makes it cumbersome to move components that have been laid out incorrectly—you have to select the component, cut it to the clipboard, select the new location, and then paste it back again.

Once you become comfortable with using workarounds like this in JBuilder, the software can speed up your Java programming projects. Using this development environment, you can create and debug Java programs appreciably faster than you can with the SDK, especially with programs that have a graphical user interface.

The Windows version of JBuilder 4 Foundation was evaluated in preparation for this chapter, and its performance was impressive. SunSoft Java Workshop and other early Java development environments were sluggish on a Windows system, but that's not the case with JBuilder.

Overall, the quality of JBuilder 4 is comparable to some of the best Microsoft development environments, such as Visual C++ and Visual Basic. The Professional edition is better suited to full-time programming and other sizeable tasks than the Foundation edition, but both are worth a serious look as you evaluate development environments for Java.

WebGain VisualCafé

In 1995, Symantec released Café, the first IDE for Java programming. This product, based heavily on Symantec C++, included tools from the Java 1.0 software development kit and its own compiler, interface designer, and debugger.

Subsequent releases of the software were renamed VisualCafé, highlighting the product's capabilities in the areas of graphical user interface design and rapid application development.

In March 2000, Symantec sold its Internet tools division to investors, who spun it off as a new company called WebGain. The main focus of WebGain is the continued development of VisualCafé, which continues to be one of the most popular development environments for Java.

VisualCafé, currently in release 4.1, can be used for Java development on Windows systems. There are three different versions available:

- VisualCafé Standard Edition, which retails for $99, is an introductory version.
- VisualCafé Expert Edition is an expanded $799 version that adds database access and the capability to compile Java programs into .EXE files.
- VisualCafé Enterprise Edition, which retails for $2,995, is a complete version that supports Enterprise JavaBean development and servlet programming.

Version 4.1 of the VisualCafé Standard Edition supports the standard Java class libraries and has a built-in, just-in-time compiler that supports Java 2 SDK 1.2. The Expert and Enterprise editions of the software can be configured with other SDK compilers, enabling full support for SDK 1.3.

 **Caution**

The packaging for VisualCafé 4.1 Standard Edition indicates that it supports SDK 1.3, but there doesn't appear to be a way to configure the software to use the SDK 1.3 compiler.

The Expert Edition adds database support and the creation of executable Windows programs and dynamic link libraries (DLLs). You can use JDBC and SQL to connect to a database and retrieve data, and it includes SQL beans to simplify data access.

In addition to the Windows features, the Expert Edition can package Java programs as a single JAR file, making it easy to deploy your software.

The Enterprise Edition adds the following features:

- The capability to create, debug, and run Java servlets, which are programs that run interactively on a Web server.
- Support for the creation and use of Enterprise JavaBeans, which are used in sophisticated client/server environments such as e-commerce and financial transactions.
- Integration with the WebLogic Application Server.

Exploring VisualCafé

VisualCafé Standard Edition, like most introductory versions of IDEs, is stripped down to the core features: creating, compiling, and running programs. The Standard Edition supports all of the classes in the Java 2 class library, including the Swing and Abstract Windowing Toolkit packages.

In keeping with its name, the software supports the visual design of a graphical user interface, and it also offers project management and context-sensitive help for both VisualCafé and Java 2.

WebGain sells the Standard Edition from its Web site at `http://www.webgain.com/Purchase/`, and this version includes a 300-page user's guide. You can also download it for free from the site at `http://www.webgain.com/download/`.

The VisualCafé interface is shown in Figure 23.5.

Text field

FIGURE 23.5.

Editing Java programs in WebGain Visual Café 4.1.

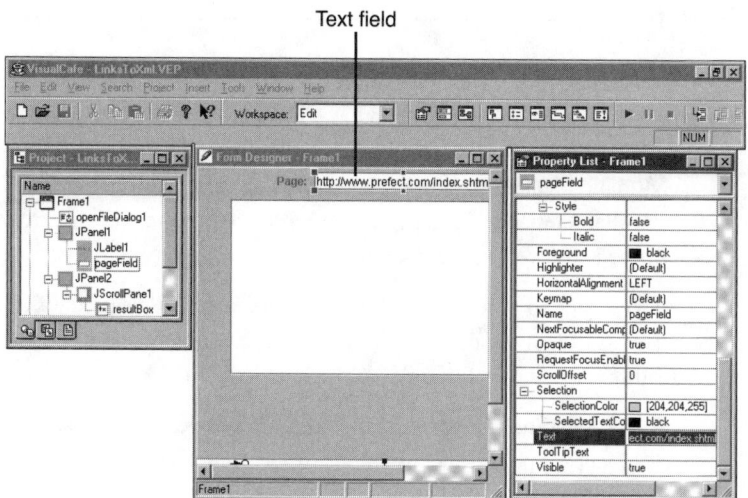

In Figure 23.5, a text field component on a frame is being edited in the software's Form Designer. The properties of the component, such as its name, foreground color, and default text, are displayed in the Property List window.

You can edit these properties by double-clicking the values next to their names. VisualCafé displays a text box, a list box, or some other method of making a change.

When you edit a user interface component in this manner, VisualCafé changes the source code of the program accordingly. For example, the component shown in Figure 23.5 is named pageField. If you used VisualCafé to set the component's ToolTipText property to "Name of the Web Page" and then examined the program's source code, you would find the following statement:

```
pageField.setToolTipText("Name of the Web Page");
```

Changes made in the Form Designer are reflected in the source code editor automatically. And vice versa—changes made to the source will show up in the Form Designer.

Caution

> If you modify the source code created by the Form Designer, you must use the same programming techniques as VisualCafé. Every graphical user interface created in this environment includes a warning in the source code: "To modify the code, only use code syntax that matches what Visual Cafe can generate, or Visual Cafe may be unable to back your Java file into its visual environment."

The source code editor in VisualCafé has several features that make it more usable than a generic text editor such as Windows Notepad. The elements of a Java program—comments, keywords, class names, method calls, and literals—have differently colored text. This can make it easier to spot errors. For example, if you begin a multiline comment with the "/*" characters and forget to end it with "*/", the rest of the program below that point will be displayed in green text.

As you type in a method call, package name, or other parts of a Java statement, VisualCafé will display a help menu if it can determine what you're trying to do. This feature is shown in Figure 23.6.

As an object method is being called on the current line, VisualCafé lists the methods that the object supports. The arguments of each method are displayed.

This feature is similar to CodeInsight, part of the context-sensitive help system in JBuilder 4 Foundation. Both IDEs offer many of the same features, organized in different ways.

FIGURE 23.6.

Using VisualCafé's built-in Java documentation.

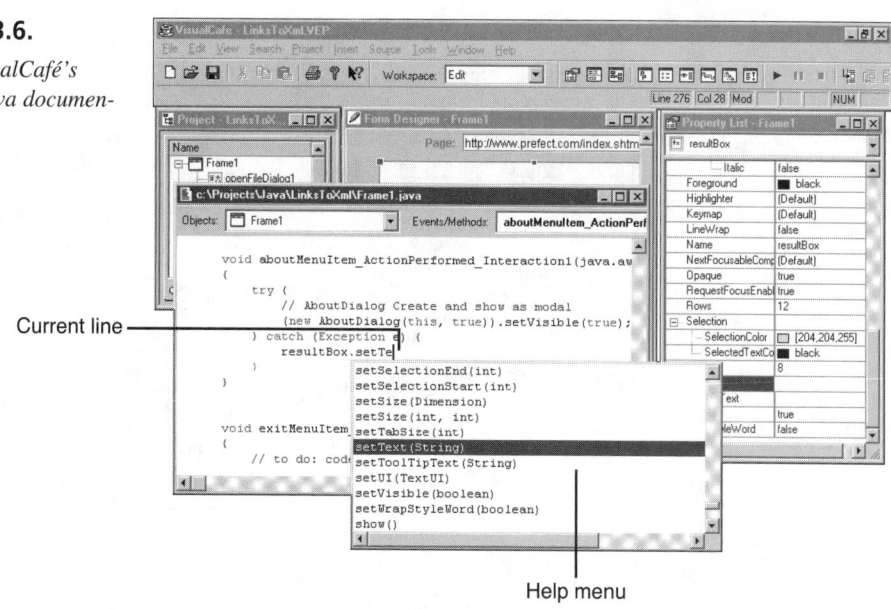

Current line

Help menu

To support event-handling in VisualCafé, you double-click the component that will generate an event and then choose an event-handling method. The source code editor opens with your cursor in the middle of the newly added method. You don't have to associate listeners with the component or implement any interfaces—this is taken care of automatically.

As you're creating a program's graphical user interface, it can be easy to place a component in the wrong container. If you're unclear about the placement of components, you can use the Project window to see where everything has been placed.

The Project window, which is shown in Figure 23.7, lists all classes in the project and the components they contain, if the class has a user interface.

In Figure 23.7, one of the components that is listed in the Project window is resultBox, a Swing text area. As you may recall from Day 8, "Working with Swing," a text area must be placed within a scroll pane in order to support scrolling. The Project window shows that resultBox has been added to a component called JScrollPane1, which in turn has been added to a component called JPanel2.

One of the advantages of VisualCafé over JBuilder is that drag-and-drop is supported in the Project window. If a component isn't in the right container, you can move it to the correct location easily.

FIGURE 23.7.

Viewing how a graphical user interface is organized.

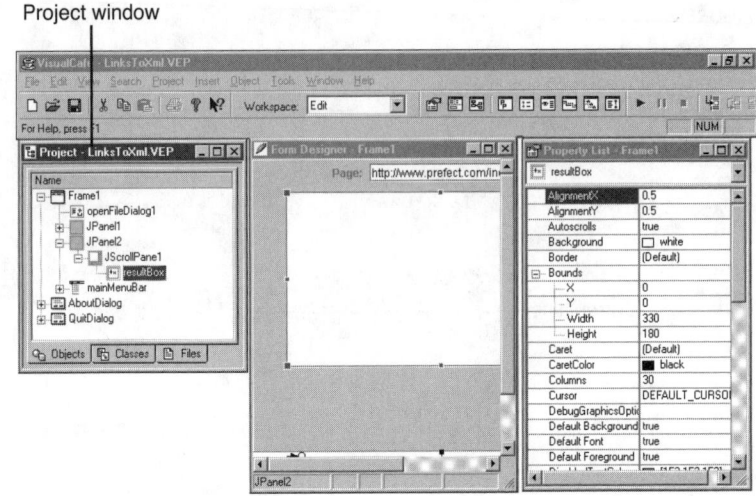

WebGain VisualCafé is a complex IDE, which makes it less than ideal for a complete beginner who is learning the Java language.

The software's capabilities are comparable to those of JBuilder, but it's slightly slower at tasks such as opening and closing menus, compiling a program, and running it.

The VisualCafé Standard Edition is suitable for simple Java projects such as the ones you've tackled up to this point in the book. As you venture into more sophisticated programming projects or put your Java skills to work on a job, it makes sense to upgrade to the Professional Edition. The capability to create Windows executable programs (in other words, .EXE files) isn't offered in any version of JBuilder 4, and that's one of VisualCafé's strongest selling points.

In its Standard and Professional editions, VisualCafé doesn't offer support for as many new Java-related technologies as JBuilder. Two of the biggest omissions are features for XML data and JavaServer Pages.

WebGain VisualCafé is an impressive development environment that carries its age well. Thousands of programmers have contributed to the quality of the software with bug reports, feature suggestions, and informal user group discussions on Usenet and the Web.

This software is likely to receive strong support from its developers in the future because WebGain's founders believed strongly enough in it to build a company around it.

Summary

An integrated development environment (IDE) can greatly increase your productivity as a Java programmer. To reach that point, you have to master some new skills:

- Organizing the classes and other files that make up a Java project.
- Configuring an IDE to work with the right compiler and other tools.
- Designing a graphical user interface visually, using a mouse in a point-and-click environment.
- Learning how to use all the toolbars, tabbed windows, menu commands, and other features of the IDE interface.

23

The two Java development environments that were evaluated today, Borland JBuilder and WebGain VisualCafé, have been popular among developers for the past several years. Neither of these tools is recommended for complete beginners because of their complexity, but they're both strong choices for programmers who want to move beyond the command-line tools in the Java 2 Software Development Kit.

Q&A

Q What happened to SunSoft Java WorkShop?

A Sun Microsystems released two versions of the Java WorkShop IDE from 1996 to 1998. Version 1.0 had a simple Web-like interface and was intended to be easier for new Java programmers, but it performed sluggishly on Windows systems and was never widely adopted. Version 2.0 adopted an interface similar to VisualCafé and other IDEs, but Sun discontinued the product because of slow sales.

Q None of the projects I'm working on requires a graphical user interface. Will I benefit from using an IDE?

A You would benefit from using Borland JBuilder or VisualCafé because both have robust source code editors with built-in help features that save a lot of time. Unless you have a photographic memory, from time to time you'll be consulting Java's class library documentation when you can't remember the name and arguments of a method, the name of a package, and similar details. The editors in both of these IDEs try to figure out what you're typing and display a window that will help jog your memory.

Another feature in both programs that saves time is the error window. When your program generates an error message, you can click on that message to open the source code editor at the statement associated with the error. This is a dramatic improvement over handling errors displayed at the command line by the Java interpreter and compiler.

Quiz

Review today's material by taking this three-question quiz.

Questions

1. What do the initials *RAD* stand for?

   a. Read Access Database

   b. Rapid Application Development

   c. Reliable Application Development

2. Which IDE supports multilanguage development?

   a. Borland JBuilder

   b. VisualCafé

   c. MetroWerks CodeWarrior

3. What are Java programs that run on a Web server called?

   a. Servlets

   b. Service applications

   c. CGI scripts

Answers

1. b. Rapid Application Development, the capability to design a program quickly using a visual user interface designer and related tools.

2. c. MetroWerks CodeWarrior supports Java, C, and C++ programming at the same time. This makes it easy to write a Java program that includes native C++ code.

3. a. Servlets.

Exercises

To extend your knowledge of the subjects covered today, try the following exercises:

- Download the trial version of Borland JBuilder 4 Foundation and use it to re-create the ChangeTitle application from Day 11, "Responding to User Input."

- Do the same with the free version of WebGain VisualCafé 4.1 Standard Edition.

Where applicable, exercise solutions are offered on the book's Web site at `http://www.java21pro.com`.

DAY 24

Writing Java 1.0 Applets

When Java was introduced in 1995, it was quickly added to the two most popular Web browsers, Netscape Navigator and Microsoft Internet Explorer. Browser developers included their own built-in Java interpreters to load and run applets embedded in Web pages.

This was the main way that most people were introduced to Java, and it was a big reason for the language's success. There was no other interactive content on the Web at the time, and several hundred thousand people learned Java in the first two years of its existence with an eye toward developing applets.

Unfortunately, Java 1.0 is the only version of the language to be fully supported as a built-in feature of Web browsers today. This leaves many programmers stuck in a time warp where their applets are concerned, using 1.0 techniques to reach the largest possible audience of Java users.

Today you'll learn how to write applets that are fully compatible with Java 1.0, covering these topics:

- Creating applets
- Drawing text and shapes in an applet window
- Designing a graphical user interface for an applet

- Laying out components on an applet
- Handling user events in an applet

Java 1.0 Programming

Normally, when a new version of a programming language comes out, all prior versions quickly fall into disuse among developers. Technology moves into new areas quickly, and there's always strong incentive to stay current, incorporate new techniques, and take advantage of improvements.

Today's Java language is 10 times as large as Java 1.0 was in 1995, measured by the number of classes and interfaces contained in each. The original version of Java was simple in scope, containing less than 170 classes, and it was hard to predict how it would perform on different platforms. It was also slow, especially if your program created a lot of objects.

These deficiencies created a lot of work for programmers who were using Java, and you might expect the first version of the language to be entirely forgotten today. This isn't the case because Java 1.0 is the only version of the language that's fully supported by Microsoft Internet Explorer and Netscape Navigator, which are used by more than 90 percent of the people on the Web.

> **Tip**
>
> The Sun Web site offers complete documentation for the Java 1.0 class library at http://java.sun.com/products/jdk/1.0.2/api/.

Creating an Applet

Java 1.0 applets are subclasses of the Applet class, which is part of the java.applet package. They have most of the same behavior as Swing applets. The life cycle of an applet occurs in the following four public methods:

- The init() method is called when the applet is first loaded for any initialization that needs to take place.
- The start() method is called after init() and each time the Web page containing the applet is revisited.
- The stop() method is called just before the Web page containing the applet is replaced with another page.
- The destroy() method is called right before the Web browser displaying the applet is closed.

Applets also have the same methods for retrieving parameters (getParameter(*String*)), loading an image using a URL (getImage(*URL*) and getImage(*URL*, *String*)), and finding out the applet's CodeBase and DocumentBase folders (getCodeBase() and getDocumentBase()).

The most significant difference between Java 1.0 and Swing is how an applet functions as a container for user interface components. Java 1.0 doesn't support content panes—you add components directly to a container by calling one of the container's add() methods.

For example, Java 1.0 includes a Button component that can be created with a statement such as the following:

```
Button exit = new Button("Exit Program");
```

You could add this button to an applet by calling its add() method with the button as an argument:

```
add(exit);
```

The layout manager for an applet window is established using classes in the java.awt package, which is part of the Abstract Windowing Toolkit. The BorderLayout, CardLayout, FlowLayout, GridLayout, and GridBagLayout classes are available to arrange components.

The default layout manager for an applet is flow layout. To choose something else, call the applet's setLayout() method with a different layout manager as an argument. The following statements create a BorderLayout object and make it an applet's layout manager:

```
BorderLayout border = new BorderLayout();
setLayout(border);
```

Note

> Layout managers work the same way in Java 1.0 and Swing, with one notable exception. When you're adding a component to a container managed with BorderLayout in Java 1.0, you call the container's add(*String*, *Component*) method with the component's position ("North", "South", "East", "West", or "Center") as the first argument. This order is reversed in Swing.

In Java 1.0, you determine the size of an applet or any other component by calling its size() method (rather than the getSize() method used for the same purpose in Swing).

A `Dimension` object is returned with two integer variables, `height` and `width`, that represent the applet's current dimensions.

To display text, an image, or some animation in an applet, you override the `paint(Graphics)` method. The `Graphics` object represents the applet's display area, and this object supports some of the same string, image, and polygon drawing methods you learned about on Day 12, "Color, Fonts, and Graphics."

Listing 24.1 contains a Java 1.0 applet that draws a plus sign at a spot roughly in the center of the applet window.

LISTING 24.1   The Full Text of `CrossHair.java`

```
 1: import java.awt.*;
 2:
 3: public class CrossHair extends java.applet.Applet {
 4:     String mark = "+";
 5:
 6:     public void paint(Graphics screen) {
 7:         Dimension appletWindow = size();
 8:         int height = appletWindow.height;
 9:         int width = appletWindow.width;
10:         screen.drawString(mark, width/2, height/2);
11:     }
12: }
```

You can compile this applet's class file using the SDK 1.3 compiler. When you do, you'll see the following message:

```
Note: CrossHair.java users or overrides a deprecated API.
Note: Recompile with -deprecation for details.
```

Although this looks like an error message, the Java compiler has successfully compiled the file into `CrossHair.class`. The "deprecated API" warning is something you'll see often when compiling Java 1.0 applets with the SDK 1.3 compiler. It means that one or more of the methods in your program has been replaced with a better method.

To see more information about a deprecation warning, compile with the `-deprecation` command-line option:

```
java -deprecation CrossHair.java
```

The Java compiler will display the line (or lines) that employ deprecated methods.

In Listing 24.1, line 7 triggers this warning message by calling the applet's `size()` method. After Java 1.0, Sun introduced a `getSize()` method that does the same thing.

You should ignore deprecation warnings when you're writing Java 1.0 applets. The preferred methods such as `getSize()` were introduced after 1.0, and they may not be supported by the built-in Java interpreter included with Internet Explorer and Netscape Navigator.

Listing 24.2 contains the HTML code for a Web document that contains the `CrossHair` applet.

LISTING 24.2 The Full Text of `CrossHair.html`

```
1: <applet code="CrossHair.class" width="200" height="130">
2: </applet>
```

You can run this applet in any Web browser or the appletviewer tool (shown in Figure 24.1). If you run it with appletviewer, you can resize the dimensions of the applet window and see how the crosshair is repositioned at the center each time.

FIGURE 24.1

The CrossHair *applet running in appletviewer.*

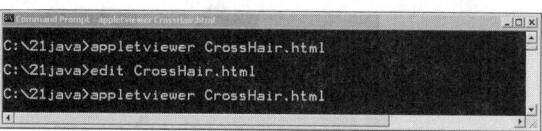

Drawing Inside an Applet

Inside an applet's `paint()` method, Java 1.0 only supports one class for drawing things: `Graphics`, which is part of the `java.awt` package.

The `Graphics` class represents an environment in which graphics and text can be drawn. In an applet, a `Graphics` object represents the applet window, and there are methods in the class for all of the shapes you can draw in Java 1.0. Any of these shapes, other than a line, can be drawn as an outline or filled in with a solid color.

Methods for drawing shapes begin with either the word `draw` or `fill`, followed by the name of the shape being drawn. The `draw-` methods are used to draw an outline of a shape, while `fill-` methods draw a solid shape instead.

24

Strings, Lines, and Rectangles

Strings are drawn exactly the same way as they are in Swing. Call the drawString(`String`, `x`, `y)` method, specifying the string and the (x,y) coordinates where it should be displayed.

To draw a line, call the drawLine(`int`, `int`, `int`, `int`) method. The first two arguments are the (x,y) coordinates of one point, and the last two arguments are the (x,y) coordinates of the other.

Java 1.0 doesn't support variable line width—all lines are one pixel wide. Call either drawRect(`int`, `int`, `int`, `int`) or fillRect(`int`, `int`, `int`, `int`) with four arguments: the (x,y) coordinates of the rectangle's upper-left corner and its width and height.

Every drawing operation must be done with a single color, which you can choose by calling the setColor(`Color`) method. The `Color` class has 13 class variables you can use: black, blue, cyan, darkGray, gray, green, lightGray, magenta, orange, pink, red, white, and yellow. You also can create a `Color` object by calling the `Color`(`int`, `int`, `int`) constructor with three arguments: the amount of red, green, and blue in the color, which are expressed as integers from 0 to 255.

Ovals

The drawOval() and fillOval() methods are used to draw circles and ellipses. You specify the location and size of an oval by describing an invisible rectangle-shaped boundary around it. The oval is drawn so that its outermost edges touch this invisible boundary.

To draw an oval, you specify four arguments to the drawOval() and fillOval() methods:

- The x coordinate of the boundary
- The y coordinate of the boundary
- The width of the boundary
- The height of the boundary

If the height and width of the boundary have the same value, the oval is a circle. Otherwise, it's an ellipse.

Listing 24.3 contains a Java applet that draws a grid with lines that are 20 pixels apart, and then draws a circle with a boundary at (20, 20) that's 160 pixels wide and 160 pixels tall.

LISTING 24.3 The Full Text of `Oval.java`

```
 1: import java.awt.*;
 2:
 3: public class Oval extends java.applet.Applet {
 4:     public void paint(Graphics screen) {
 5:         setBackground(Color.white);
 6:         screen.setColor(Color.black);
 7:         for (int i = 0; i <= 200; i += 20) {
 8:             screen.drawLine(0, i, 200, i);
 9:             screen.drawLine(i, 0, i, 200);
10:         }
11:         screen.setColor(Color.red);
12:         screen.fillOval(30, 30, 160, 160);
13:     }
14: }
```

Listing 24.4 contains the HTML code for a Web page that displays the applet.

LISTING 24.4 The Full Text of `Oval.html`

```
1: <applet code="Oval.class" height="205" width="205">
2: </applet>
```

Figure 24.2 displays two applets on a Web page in Internet Explorer 5. The applet on the left is the `Oval` applet, and the one on the right shows the same applet with one change: a rectangle is drawn at the same place as the oval's boundary.

FIGURE 24.2

The `Oval` applet and a modified version running in Internet Explorer 5.

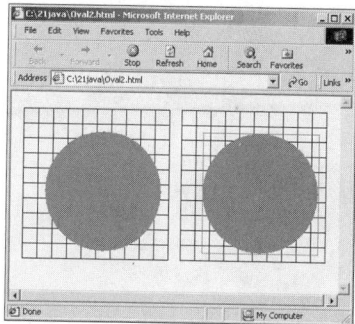

Arcs

Arcs are drawn like ovals, except that two extra arguments are used to specify the starting and ending point of the arc, represented as degrees on a circle.

The drawArc() and fillArc() methods take six integer arguments, in this order:

- The x coordinate of the boundary of the arc
- The y coordinate of the boundary
- The width of the boundary
- The height of the boundary
- The starting point of the arc, in degrees
- The number of degrees the arc travels, counterclockwise

Polygons

The first step in drawing a polygon is to create a Polygon object that represents the object. This class, which is part of the java.awt package, has integer variables to hold each set of (x,y) points in the polygon.

One way to create a polygon is by starting with an empty polygon and adding points to it one at a time. Call the Polygon() constructor to create the empty polygon, and then call its addPoint(*int*, *int*) method to add each point as an (x,y) coordinate.

After you've created the polygon, draw it by calling the drawPolygon(*Polygon*) or fillPolygon(*Polygon*) methods on a Graphics object.

Listing 24.5 contains a Java 1.0 version of the Map2D project from Day 12.

LISTING 24.5   The Full Text of Map.java

```
 1: import java.awt.*;
 2:
 3: public class Map extends java.applet.Applet {
 4:     public void paint(Graphics screen) {
 5:         setBackground(Color.blue);
 6:         // Draw waves
 7:         screen.setColor(Color.white);
 8:         for (int ax = 10; ax < 340; ax += 10)
 9:             for (int ay = 30; ay < 340 ; ay += 10) {
10:                 screen.drawArc(ax, ay, 10, 10, 0, -180);
11:             }
12:         // Draw Florida
13:         screen.setColor(Color.green);
14:         Polygon fl = new Polygon();
15:         fl.addPoint(10, 12);
16:         fl.addPoint(234, 15);
17:         fl.addPoint(253, 25);
18:         fl.addPoint(261, 71);
19:         fl.addPoint(344, 209);
20:         fl.addPoint(336, 278);
```

LISTING 24.5   continued

```
21:        fl.addPoint(295, 310);
22:        fl.addPoint(259, 274);
23:        fl.addPoint(205, 188);
24:        fl.addPoint(211, 171);
25:        fl.addPoint(195, 174);
26:        fl.addPoint(191, 118);
27:        fl.addPoint(120, 56);
28:        fl.addPoint(94, 68);
29:        fl.addPoint(81, 49);
30:        fl.addPoint(12, 37);
31:        screen.fillPolygon(fl);
32:        // Draw ovals
33:        screen.setColor(Color.black);
34:        screen.fillOval(235, 140, 15, 15);
35:        screen.fillOval(225, 130, 15, 15);
36:        screen.fillOval(245, 130, 15, 15);
37:    }
38: }
```

The Map applet doesn't support Swing drawing features such as gradient paint and variable pen size. Listing 24.6 contains the HTML code for a Web page that can display the applet, and you can see it running in Figure 24.3.

LISTING 24.6   The Full Text of Map.html

```
1: <applet code="Map.class" height="370" width="350">
2: </applet>
```

FIGURE 24.3

The Map applet running in appletviewer.

Creating a Graphical User Interface

The Abstract Windowing Toolkit is used to implement a graphical user interface in Java 1.0. The toolkit's interface classes are contained in the java.awt package.

Every user interface component in the Abstract Windowing Toolkit was re-created as a Swing class, and some of them work the same way. You can create Java 1.0 components using the following classes: `Button`, `Canvas`, `Checkbox`, `Choice`, `Label`, `List`, `Scrollbar`, `TextArea`, and `TextField`. There also are several additional classes for creating menus and menu commands: `CheckboxMenuItem`, `Menu`, `MenuBar`, and `MenuItem`.

To design a user interface, you create components and add them to a container: `Applet`, `Frame`, `Panel`, or `Window`. There are also two special-purpose containers that have their own built-in components: `Dialog` and `FileDialog`.

Before adding any components to a container, you can define how they'll be laid out by calling the container's `setLayout(LayoutManager)` method. There are five layout managers you can use—`BorderLayout`, `CardLayout`, `FlowLayout`, `GridLayout`, and `GridBagLayout`—and each one works in the same manner as its Swing counterpart.

Creating Buttons and Text Components

Four components in the Abstract Windowing Toolkit are used to display text or receive simple input from the user: buttons, labels, text fields, and text areas.

The following constructors can be used to create these components:

- `Button(String)`: Create a clickable button with the specified string as a label.
- `Label(String)`: Create text with the specified string. Labels are often used to identify another component's purpose or provide help on how to use a graphical interface.
- `TextField(int)`: Create a single-line text input field with the specified number of characters the field can display.
- `TextArea(int, int)`: Create a multiline text input box. The first argument specifies the number of lines the box can display. The second argument specifies the number of characters it can display on one line.

You can change the text for these components as a program is running. To set the text for a label, text field, or text area, call the component's `setText(String)` method with the text as the argument. To do the same for a button, call its `setLabel(String)` method. There are also methods for retrieving the current text of these components: `getText()` for labels, text fields, and text areas, and `getLabel()` for buttons.

You can enable or disable a component's capability to receive input. By default, all components can receive input. To change this, call the component's `enable(Boolean)` method with an argument of `false`. To change it back, call the `enable()` method without any arguments.

Text fields also support a feature that hides the text that a user is entering into the field. This is useful when you need a field to collect confidential information such as a password. To set it up, call the component's setEchoCharacter(*char*) method with the obscuring character as the argument. For example, the following statements create a text field that uses asterisks to hide the actual input:

```
TextField password = new TextField(20);
password.setEchoCharacter('*');
```

Creating Multi-Item Components and Scrollbars

There are three components in the Abstract Windowing Toolkit that enable a user to choose one or more items from a list: Choice, CheckBox, and List.

The Choice component is a pop-up menu that allows the user to pick one item. To create this component, call the Choice() constructor with no arguments, and then call the component's addItem() method to add each item. The following statements create a choice list with three items:

```
Choice title = new Choice();
title.addItem("Mr.");
title.addItem("Mrs.");
title.addItem("Ms.");
```

To find out which item a user has selected from a Choice component, call its getSelectedItem() method, which returns a string containing the text of the item.

A List component is a pull-down list that can display multiple items at the same time and accept more than one item as input.

To create a List component, call the List(*int*, *Boolean*) constructor. The first argument specifies the number of items to display at one time. The second argument determines whether more than one item can be picked:

```
List party = new List(5, false);
party.addItem("Democrat");
party.addItem("Green");
party.addItem("Libertarian");
party.addItem("Reform");
party.addItem("Republican");
```

If only one item can be selected from a list, you can call its getSelectedItem() method to find out which item was selected—a string is returned.

If more than one item can be selected, call the getSelectedItems() method, which returns a String array containing each selected item.

The Checkbox component enables the user to select one of two options. This can be used for yes/no, on/off, or true/false questions, and check boxes can be grouped together so that only one box can be selected at a time.

24

To create a single Checkbox, call the Checkbox(*String*) constructor. The string specified as an argument enables you to give the box a label that explains its purpose.

If the check box is to be selected by default, call the component's setState(*Boolean*) method with true as the argument. The following statement creates a Checkbox:

```
Checkbox florida = new Checkbox("Florida resident");
```

The CheckboxGroup class is used to group several check boxes together so that only one box can be selected at a time. Call the CheckboxGroup() constructor with no arguments, and then call the group's add(*Checkbox*) method to add a check box to the group.

Once you've added all the check boxes to the group, add the group to a container rather than adding the check boxes individually.

To find out which check box in a group has been selected, call the group's getCurrent() method. A Checkbox is returned that represents the selected box, or null if no box has been selected.

Use the Scrollbar component to select a numeric value by moving a scrollbar, which can be either horizontal or vertical. The scrollbar can be moved from a minimum value to a maximum one, limiting input to a specified range.

To create this, call the Scrollbar(*int*, *int*, *int*, *int*, *int*) constructor. The five arguments are integers that represent the following:

- The orientation of the scrollbar, defined by using the class variables Scrollbar.HORIZONTAL or Scrollbar.VERTICAL
- The starting value of the scrollbar
- The amount of the scrollbar represented by the *bubble*, which is the box that can be moved around as an alternative to scrolling
- The minimum value of the scrollbar
- The maximum value of the scrollbar

The following statement creates a horizontal scrollbar that can range in value from 1 to 100 and has a starting value of 10:

```
Scrollbar percentage = new Scrollbar(Scrollbar.HORIZONTAL,
    10, 15, 1, 100);
```

Drawing in an Interface

The Canvas class represents an area on an interface where something can be drawn or displayed. It's similar to a panel, except that a canvas cannot serve as a container.

To use this class, you create a subclass of Canvas that overrides its paint(*Graphics*) method. This method serves the same purpose as an applet's paint() method—you use it to draw any of the images or shapes you want to display within the component's area.

Listing 24.7 contains Plot, a Java applet that has a graphical user interface containing canvas and label components.

LISTING 24.7   The Full Text of Plot.java

```
 1: import java.awt.*;
 2:
 3: public class Plot extends java.applet.Applet {
 4:     Label statLabel = new Label("Current Statistics:");
 5:     Graph stats = new Graph();
 6:
 7:     public void init() {
 8:         BorderLayout border = new BorderLayout();
 9:         setLayout(border);
10:         add("North", statLabel);
11:         add("Center", stats);
12:     }
13: }
14:
15: class Graph extends java.awt.Canvas {
16:     int[] point = { 1, 10, 3, 5, 8, 7, 2, 2, 5, 9 };
17:
18:     public void paint(Graphics screen) {
19:         for (int i = 0; i < 10; i++) {
20:             Color blueHue = new Color(0, 0, 255 - (i*20));
21:             screen.setColor(blueHue);
22:             screen.fillRect(20, i * 20, point[i] * 20, 17);
23:         }
24:     }
25: }
```

24

Listing 24.8 contains HTML code you can use to display the Plot applet on a Web page. This applet displays 10 bars in a graph, representing the numbers from 1 to 10. Each bar is a different shade of blue, which is handled in lines 20-21 of the program. Figure 24.4 shows the applet running in Internet Explorer 5.

LISTING 24.8   The Full Text of Plot.html

```
1: <applet code="Plot.class" width="260" height="240">
2: </applet>
```

FIGURE 24.4

The Plot *applet running in Internet Explorer 5.*

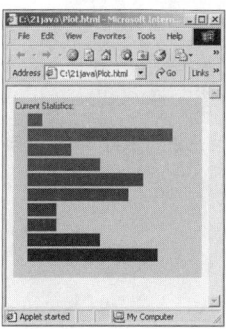

The Plot applet draws rectangles inside a canvas. You can also display image files, which are represented in Java 1.0 by Image, a class in the java.awt package.

To draw an image in an applet, it must be stored on the same Web server as the applet. One way to handle this is to keep the image in the same folder as the applet's class files.

Before you can display an image, you must load it into the applet. Call the applet's getImage(*URL*, *String*) method with two arguments: a call to applet's getCodeBase() method and the filename of the graphic. An Image object will be returned that contains the graphic.

> **Note**
>
> The getCodeBase() method returns a URL object that represents the address of the applet on the Web. This is the most flexible way to load images for a file because it lets you move the applet and all of its files to a new Web server without changing the program.

Once you have an image loaded, you can display it inside the paint() method of the canvas component. To display an image, call the drawImage(*Image*, *int*, *int*, *ImageObserver*) method of the Graphics class. The four arguments to this method represent the following:

- The image to display
- The x and y coordinates where the upper-left corner of the image should be positioned
- The object that should be notified when the image is done loading

The last argument refers to ImageObserver, an interface in the java.awt.image package of Java 1.0. This is used when you need to know precisely when an image has been loaded by a Java program. If you don't need this knowledge, the keyword `this` can be used as an argument. The `this` keyword refers to the current object—in this example, the canvas that contains the image.

Listing 24.9 contains an applet that displays a graphics file.

LISTING 24.9   The Full Text of `Picture.java`

```
1: import java.awt.*;
2:
3: public class Picture extends java.applet.Applet {
4:     Image searchImage;
5:
6:     public void init() {
7:         searchImage = getImage(getCodeBase(), "faulkner.jpg");
8:     }
9:
10:     public void paint(Graphics screen) {
11:         screen.drawImage(searchImage, 0, 0, this);
12:     }
13: }
```

24

Java 1.0 supports the display of graphics files in the GIF and JPEG formats. These files usually have filenames that end with `.gif`, `.jpg`, or `.jpeg`. You can use any image to test the `Picture` applet as long as you change Line 7 to reflect the filename of your image.

The image file referred to in Listing 24.9, `faulkner.jpg`, is a portrait of the novelist William Faulkner from Creative Americans, a collection of Carl Van Vechten photographs archived by the Library of Congress. You can download it from the book's Web site at `http://www.java21pro.com`. The image file can be found on the site's Day 24 page.

Listing 24.10 contains the HTML for a Web page that contains the `Picture` applet, and it's shown in Figure 24.5.

LISTING 24.10   The Full Text of `Picture.html`

```
1: <applet code="Picture.class" width="277" height="386">
2: </applet>
```

Note

There are more than 1,300 photographs taken by the Carl Van Vechten from 1932 to 1964 available online at the American Memory Web site, published by the Library of Congress. To see more of his work, visit `http://memory.loc.gov/ammem/vvhome.html`.

FIGURE 24.5

The Picture *applet running in applet-viewer.*

Handling User Events

Java 1.0 doesn't use any of the event-handling techniques you've employed in the current version of the language. Instead of implementing event-handling interfaces and adding listeners to components, you receive user events through inherited methods available in an applet and all other Abstract Windowing Toolkit components.

The following methods are inherited from the Component class by all user-interface components:

- action(*Event, Object*)—A method that's called when the component generates an action event.

- gotFocus(*Event, Object*) and lostFocus(*Event, Object*)—Methods that are called when the component receives or loses the input focus.

- keyDown(*Event, int*) and keyUp(*Event, int*)—Methods that are called when a key is pressed or released.

- mouseDown(*Event, int, int*) and mouseUp(*Event, int, int*)—A method that's called when a mouse button is clicked or released.

- mouseEnter(*Event, int, int*) and mouseExit(*Event, int, int*)—Methods that are called when a mouse first moves over a component or first moves off of it.

- mouseDrag(*Event, int, int*)—A method that's called when a mouse moves over a component with a button pressed.

- mouseMove(*Event, int, int*)—A method that's called when a mouse moves over a component without any buttons pressed.

All of these methods return a Boolean value. User events in Java 1.0 originate in the component that generated the event and can be sent to the container that holds the component.

When you override an event-handling method and you fully handle user events in that method, return a Boolean value of `true`. Otherwise, return `false` to send it to the container for additional handling.

An applet can be used to receive all events generated by the components that it contains. To do this, use the `Event` object sent as an argument to each of these methods. The `Event` class, part of the `java.awt` package, includes an instance variable called `target` that represents the component that generated the event.

The `keyDown()` and `keyUp()` methods include an `int` argument that holds the integer value of the character that is associated with the event.

The mouse event-handling methods include two integers as arguments. They represent the (x,y) position of the mouse when the event occurred. (0,0) is the upper-left corner of the component, which uses the same coordinate system employed for drawing graphics and text.

Listing 24.11 contains an applet that overrides several event-handling methods to collect input from a user. The `Draw` applet displays a picture from a graphics file and enables the user to doodle on the picture by clicking or dragging the mouse. An Erase button is provided to clear all of the doodling the user has added to the picture.

LISTING 24.11 The Full Text of `Draw.java`

```
 1: import java.awt.*;
 2:
 3: public class Draw extends java.applet.Applet {
 4:     Button erase = new Button("Erase");
 5:     DrawPanel canvas;
 6:
 7:     public void init() {
 8:         canvas = new DrawPanel(getImage(getCodeBase(), "faulkner.jpg"));
 9:         BorderLayout bord = new BorderLayout();
10:         setLayout(bord);
11:         add(canvas, "Center");
12:         Panel commandPanel = new Panel();
13:         commandPanel.add(erase);
14:         add(commandPanel, "South");
15:     }
16:
17:     public boolean action(Event evt, Object obj) {
18:         if (evt.target == erase) {
19:             canvas.numPoints = -1;
20:             canvas.repaint();
21:         }
```

LISTING 24.11 continued

```
22:           return true;
23:       }
24: }
25:
26: class DrawPanel extends Panel {
27:       Image picture;
28:       int[] drawX = new int[1000];
29:       int[] drawY = new int[1000];
30:       int numPoints = -1;
31:
32:       DrawPanel(Image inputImage) {
33:           picture = inputImage;
34:       }
35:
36:       public void paint(Graphics screen) {
37:           screen.drawImage(picture, 0, 0, this);
38:           screen.setColor(Color.black);
39:           for (int i = 0; i <= numPoints; i++) {
40:               screen.fillOval(drawX[i]-3, drawY[i]-3, 6, 6);
41:           }
42:       }
43:
44:       public void update(Graphics screen) {
45:           paint(screen);
46:       }
47:
48:       public boolean mouseDown(Event evt, int x, int y) {
49:           if (numPoints < 1000) {
50:               numPoints++;
51:               drawX[numPoints] = x;
52:               drawY[numPoints] = y;
53:           }
54:           repaint();
55:           return true;
56:       }
57:
58:       public boolean mouseDrag(Event evt, int x, int y) {
59:           mouseDown(evt, x, y);
60:           return true;
61:       }
62: }
```

Listing 24.12 contains the HTML code for a Web page that displays this applet, which is shown in Figure 24.6.

LISTING 24.12   The Full Text of `Draw.html`

```
1: <applet code="Draw.class" width="277" height="386">
2: </applet>
```

FIGURE 24.6

The Draw *applet running in Internet Explorer 5.*

The `Draw` applet is written to use `faulkner.jpg`, which is the same image displayed by the `Picture` applet. You can substitute any graphics file in GIF or JPEG format, as long as you change Line 8 of Listing 24.11 and store the file in the same folder as the applet's class files.

The program consists of an applet class and `DrawPanel`, a subclass of `Panel` that contains the picture and behavior for drawing on it with a mouse.

The `DrawPanel` class includes four instance variables:

- `picture`, an `Image` object containing the graphics file that's displayed in the panel.
- `numPoints`, an integer keeping track of the number of points that have been drawn on the image.
- `drawX`, an array of integers containing the x coordinate of each point.
- `drawY`, an array of integers containing the y coordinate of each point.

All graphics are drawn in the panel's `paint()` method, just as they are for any component in a user interface. The picture is drawn every time this method is called, followed by each point that has been doodled on the picture.

The `update()` method on lines 44-46 demonstrates a common technique in Java 1.0 for eliminating flickering in an applet. This method is inherited from `Applet`, and its normal function is to erase everything in the applet window each time it's repainted. The method is overridden so that it calls the paint() method without erasing anything, and the graphics in the applet won't flicker each time a new point is drawn.

The mouseDown() method in lines 48-56 handles all user events that occur when a mouse is clicked on the panel. The (x,y) coordinate of the click is added to the drawX and drawY arrays, numPoints is incremented by 1, and the repaint() method is called so the new point will be displayed after it's drawn.

> **Caution**
>
> Calling repaint() does *not* guarantee that paint() will be called by the Java interpreter running the applet. Instead, calling repaint() is a request for the applet to be repainted, and there are times when some requests are ignored. This usually happens when the interpreter can't repaint something as fast as requests are coming in, which occurs more often in Java 1.0 than in subsequent versions of the language.

The mouseDown() event-handling method can only handle mouse clicks. If a user clicks the mouse and drags it to a new location, the mouseDown() method is called only once—at the (x,y) location of the click.

The mouseDrag() method in lines 58-61 handles mouse drags. Because it's called each time the mouse is moved with the button held down, you can use it to capture each (x,y) position of the mouse as it's dragged from one place to another.

There's more event-handling behavior in the Draw class, which represents the applet window. The applet contains three things: a DrawPanel object, a button called erase, and a panel that contains the button.

The erase button generates an action event when it's clicked, and this is handled in lines 17-23. This method makes sure that the component that generated the event is the erase button. If it is, the DrawPanel object's numPoints variable is set to –1, which wipes out all points doodled on the panel. The panel's repaint() method is then called so it will be redrawn without any of the points.

Summary

Anyone who's learning Java 1.0 after learning a more current version of the language will be surprised by its simplicity. It's possible to become conversant in all of the classes and interfaces in the Java 1.0 class library—there are fewer than 170—but even the most experienced programmer would find it difficult to do the same in Java 2.

The lack of complexity in Java 1.0 is shown by the lack of options for graphical user interface design. Most programmers who are using Java 1.0 for applets use their own interface components and those created by other programmers because there are gaps in the language.

When you're launching a serious applet programming project using Java 1.0, the best place to start is to look for user interface components and other classes designed by others that could be useful in your own project. Two valuable resources on the Web are the Java Applet Ratings Service at `http://www.jars.com` and JavaWorld Magazine at `http://www.javaworld.com`.

Q&A

Q My Java applet works fine in Internet Explorer but crashes in Navigator. Shouldn't it work in both browsers under Java's "write-once, run-anywhere" principle?

A One of the facts of life for Java 1.0 programmers is that Web browsers implement the Java language differently in their built-in interpreters. There are bugs, user interface inconsistencies, and other issues that you can only resolve by testing in as wide a range of browsers and versions as possible.

One tactic adopted by some applet programmers is to test first in versions 3 and 4 of Netscape Navigator. This is because the Java interpreter in those browsers is the most likely to have trouble running an applet successfully.

One thing you can never rely on in Java 1.0 is testing the applet solely in the appletviewer. It runs applets much better than any browser interpreter, because it supports Java fully and doesn't contain any of the major bugs or inconsistencies you encounter when running Java in a browser.

Quiz

Review today's material by taking this three-question quiz.

Questions

1. What method can you use in Java 1.0 to find out the size of an applet window?

    a. `getSize()`

    b. `size()`

    c. `width()`

2. Should deprecated methods be used in your Java 1.0 applets?

    a. No, because they've been replaced by better techniques.

    b. Yes, because there's no other choice in Java 1.0.

    c. It doesn't matter—you can't use them at all.

3. Which component can you use to select three items from a list of 12?

    a. `List`

    b. `Choice`

    c. `TextArea`

Answers

1. b. The `size()` method is used in Java 1.0. This method was renamed `getSize()` for subsequent versions of the language.

2. b. Deprecation warnings apply to people using subsequent versions of the language. A programmer who's trying to use nothing but Java 1.0 in an applet has no choice but to use deprecated methods, despite the warning.

3. a. The `List` component can be configured to allow multiple items to be selected.

Exercises

To extend your knowledge of the subjects covered today, try the following exercises:

- Write a Java 1.0 applet with a graphical user interface that collects the name, address, city, state, and ZIP code from a user. Limit the states to five states in an area, such as "FL", "GA", "AL", "SC", and "NC".

- Convert the Expiration applet from Day 7, "Writing Java Applets," to Java 1.0.

Where applicable, exercise solutions are offered on the book's Web site at `http://www.java21pro.com`.

DAY 25

Accessibility

Of all the enhancements introduced with Java 2, the improvements to the user interface are the most extensive. The introduction of Swing, Java 2D, and related class libraries enable more sophisticated interaction between a user and a Java program.

One of the most dramatic changes involves how Java programs work for people who need assistive technology in order to interact with their computers. The Accessibility classes included as a standard part of Java 2 make it possible for Java programs to work in conjunction with products such as Braille terminals, screen readers, and speech recognition systems. These classes also offer features that benefit everyone who uses a Swing-developed interface in a Java program.

The following topics will be covered today:

- Using keyboard shortcut keys in a program
- Setting up ToolTip text to document what an interface component is used for
- Associating a label with the component it describes
- Describing a component's name and purpose
- Implementing the `Accessible` interface

Making Programs More Accessible

The Java Accessibility classes enable Java programs to be controlled with a range of input devices other than a mouse and keyboard:

- Screen readers that use a speech synthesizer to read the contents of a screen aloud.
- Screen magnifiers that enlarge elements of a monitor's display area up to 16 times regular size.
- Software keyboards that use speech recognition and word prediction features for people who can't type on a keyboard.

In order for these devices to function, software either must work directly with them (such as a Web browser designed specifically for visually impaired users) or must include features that are compatible with assistive technology.

A Java program that uses the Accessibility classes doesn't require assistive devices in order to function. Instead, the program has additional capabilities for those who need them. These capabilities allow computing in environments away from the desktop, which is becoming more important because Java is being included in embedded devices such as personal information managers and kiosks.

One of the examples on Sun's Accessibility home page is a dashboard computer on a car. Accessibility could be used to check email via voice input and output. If you've ever watched someone apply makeup or eat a four-course meal while driving, you should understand the need for alternative-input devices.

 Note

> The Accessibility home page is currently available at http://java.sun.com/ products/jfc/accessibility/doc/. In addition to documentation on the Accessibility classes and a list of frequently asked questions, the site describes the company's overall approach to the technology and provides a set of Accessibility utilities you can run.

The Accessibility classes are part of the Java Foundation Class library, so you work with Swing as you develop accessible programs. One of the Swing features included in Java's approach to accessibility is pluggable look-and-feel. This was covered during Day 9, "Building a Swing Interface."

Pluggable look-and-feel changes the appearance of a Java interface without requiring any changes to the program. Although this was used for cosmetic purposes on Day 9, when you changed the appearance of interface components to achieve a Windows or Metal look-and-feel, this can be extended to support assistive technology. For example, an interface's entire appearance and functionality would require changes in order to adapt to a screen reader.

The Accessibility Classes

Java Accessibility is offered in three distinct areas:

- The `javax.accessibility` package
- Methods in Swing classes that provide accessible features
- A set of Accessibility utilities that can be used by assistive technology providers

The `javax.accessibility` package is used to define the way a Java interface component communicates with an assistive device. Swing components already implement this functionality, so you don't have to work directly with the Accessibility classes when you're working with the standard user-interface components. When you're creating new user-interface components, you'll be working with this package to make the components accessible.

The main class in the `javax.accessibility` package is the `Accessible` interface. A user-interface component must implement `Accessible` in order to be compatible with assistive devices.

This interface has one method, `getAccessibleContext()`, which returns an `AccessibleContext` object.

The `AccessibleContext` class describes the necessary information that an accessible object provides to other classes. This includes the object's name, a description of its purpose, the role it plays in an interface, and its current state.

Accessing a Swing Component

Figure 25.1 shows a Java application with a combo box that's used to select a profession from a list of six choices.

FIGURE 25.1

The Combo application.

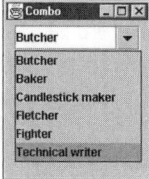

25

This application uses the Swing component `JComboBox`, so it contains some built-in support for accessibility. One thing you can do is toggle the pop-up state of the box. If it has popped up, the list of six choices is visible, as shown in Figure 25.1. If it hasn't popped up, only the current selection is visible.

Listing 25.1 contains the Combo application.

LISTING 25.1   The Full Text of *Combo.java*

```
 1: import java.awt.*;
 2: import javax.swing.*;
 3: import java.awt.event.*;
 4: import javax.accessibility.*;
 5:
 6: public class Combo extends JFrame {
 7:     JComboBox job = new JComboBox();
 8:
 9:     public Combo() {
10:         super("Combo");
11:         setSize(160, 190);
12:         setDefaultCloseOperation(JFrame.EXIT_ON_CLOSE);
13:         Container pane = getContentPane();
14:         FlowLayout flo = new FlowLayout();
15:         job.addItem("Butcher");
16:         job.addItem("Baker");
17:         job.addItem("Candlestick maker");
18:         job.addItem("Fletcher");
19:         job.addItem("Fighter");
20:         job.addItem("Technical writer");
21:         job.setEditable(true);
22:         AccessibleContext ac = job.getAccessibleContext();
23:         ac.setAccessibleDescription(
24:            "Select a profession from a combo box.");
25:         ac.setAccessibleName("Profession");
26:         pane.setLayout(flo);
27:         pane.add(job);
28:         setContentPane(pane);
29:         setVisible(true);
30:         ComboSpy spy = new ComboSpy(job);
31:     }
32:
33:     public static void main(String[] arguments) {
34:         Combo app = new Combo();
35:     }
36: }
```

All `JComboBox` objects provide information to the Accessibility classes regarding the role and actions that the object can take. An accessible object also can provide a name and a description. These two things can't be provided by default for all combo boxes because they depend on the purpose of the component.

You can provide a textual description of a Swing component via a two-step process:

1. Get the `AccessibleContext` object associated with the component by calling the component's `getAccessibleContext()` method.

2. Call that object's `setAccessibleDescription()>(String)` method. The string argument should be the component's text description.

For example, the following example sets the description of a `JButton` object:

```
JButton quit = new JButton("Quit");
quit.getAccessibleContext().setAccessibleDescription(
    "When you click this button, the program terminates.");
```

The `setAccessibleName()>(String)` method works the same way `setAccessibleDescription(String)` works. It can be used to give a name to the component that succinctly describes its purpose. Quit Button is an appropriate name for the `quit` object in the previous example. The next example sets the name for a text field called `nm` to `"Name Field"`:

```
JTextField nm = new JTextField();
nm.getAccessibleContext().setAccessibleName("Name Field");
```

In order to support assistive devices, an accessible name should be established for any component that isn't already labeled with a string. A `JButton` component usually has a text label that describes the button, and this is used as its name unless `setAccessibleName()` gives it a different one.

Along the same lines, a description should be set up for any component that doesn't have a ToolTip associated with it. *ToolTips* appear on top of a component when the mouse hovers over it for a moment. You'll learn more about them in the next section.

The accessible name and the description of the combo box in the Combo application are set in lines 22-25 of Listing 25.1.

Line 30 of the application contains the following statement:

```
ComboSpy spy = new ComboSpy(job);
```

This creates a new `ComboSpy` object. Listing 25.2 contains this class's source code. The class spies on the Combo application, using different `AccessibleContext` methods to discover more about the application's combo box, and actually manipulates the combo box.

25

LISTING 25.2   The Full Text of `ComboSpy.java`

```
 1: import java.awt.*;
 2: import javax.swing.*;
 3: import javax.accessibility.*;
 4:
 5: public class ComboSpy implements Runnable {
 6:     Thread runner;
 7:     JComboBox profession;
 8:
 9:     ComboSpy(JComboBox pro) {
10:         profession = pro;
11:         if (runner == null) {
12:             runner = new Thread(this);
13:             runner.start();
14:         }
15:     }
16:
17:     public void run() {
18:         AccessibleContext ac =
19:             profession.getAccessibleContext();
20:         System.out.println("\nName: " +
21:             ac.getAccessibleName());
22:         System.out.println("Description: " +
23:             ac.getAccessibleDescription());
24:         System.out.println("Role: " +
25:             ac.getAccessibleRole());
26:         while (runner != null) {
27:             try {
28:                 Thread.sleep(3000);
29:             } catch (InterruptedException e) { }
30:             AccessibleAction aa =
31:                 ac.getAccessibleAction();
32:             int count = aa.getAccessibleActionCount();
33:             for (int i = 0; i < count; i++)
34:                 System.out.println("ActionDescription: " +
35:                     aa.getAccessibleActionDescription(i));
36:             try {
37:                 aa.doAccessibleAction(0);
38:             } catch (IllegalComponentStateException e) { }
39:         }
40:     }
41: }
```

To test the `Combo` application, compile `ComboSpy` and type the following at a command line:

```
java Combo
```

The ComboSpy class implements the Runnable interface and runs in its own thread, separate from the Combo class.

In lines 18-19, ComboSpy creates an AccessibleContext object associated with profession, an object that refers to the Combo application's combo box. This AccessibleContext object contains all of the accessible information about the component.

The name and description of the combo box are available as strings returned by the getAccessibleName() and getAccessibleDescription() methods of the AccessibleContext class.

Swing combo boxes also support the AccessibleAction interface, which is used to determine the actions that can take place when the combo box is manipulated.

Lines 30-31 create an AccessibleAction object associated with the combo box.

Before you can find out which actions are associated with an Accessible component, you must use the getAccessibleActionCount() method to find out how many actions there are. This method returns that value as an integer, as shown in line 32.

The getAccessibleActionDescription(*int*) method determines the textual description of each action that can be taken. Lines 33-35 loop through the combo box's possible actions and display each description.

Up to this point in the program, all communication has been one-way: Information about the combo box has been received by the ComboSpy class.

You also can use Accessibility features to control a user-interface component. Every user-interface component that supports accessible actions can be manipulated via the doAccessibleAction(*int*) method. The integer argument represents the action that should be performed.

Line 37 uses doAccessibleAction() to perform the first action that the combo box can perform. A try-catch block is used to catch an IllegalComponentStateException, which occurs if an accessible action is performed on a component that is no longer visible.

When you run the Combo application, the ComboSpy class displays output that should be similar to the following:

```
Name: Profession
Description: Select a profession from a combo box.
Role: Combo box
ActionDescription: togglePopup
ActionDescription: togglePopup
```

25

```
ActionDescription: togglePopup
ActionDescription: togglePopup
ActionDescription: togglePopup
ActionDescription: togglePopup
```

The last line of the output is repeated each time `ComboSpy` causes the combo box's `togglePopup` action to be performed.

By calling the `togglePopup` action repeatedly, the `ComboSpy` class causes the combo box list to appear and disappear on its own. If you know any Java programmers who aren't familiar with Accessibility yet, this technique is a good way to make them believe in ghosts.

 **Note**

> This technique has use beyond the realm of the supernatural as well. It can create programs that test a graphical user interface by simulating its use and selecting all available options.

Many Swing components have standard features that are used by an `Accessible` class to discover more information about the component.

You've already made a component more accessible if you've done any of the following:

- Used the `super(String)` method in a window or frame class to put text in the component's title bar.
- Placed text on a button or label.
- Employed other features that make a component's purpose more self-explanatory.

Using Accessibility Features

Accessibility support is built into `JButton`, `JLabel`, `JFrame`, and all other Swing components, so a lot of the work of supporting assistive devices is done automatically.

There are other things you can do to make your programs more accessible, both to users with various abilities and others who are trying to make sense of a user interface with the standard mouse and keyboard. These include the following:

- Use ToolTips (text that appears over a component whenever a mouse hovers over it for a moment).
- Use keyboard mnemonics (shortcut keys that can be pressed to simulate a mouse-click on a component).

- Whenever a label is used to describe another component, use the component's setLabelFor(*object*) method to indicate this relationship.

- If a component is identified by an ImageIcon object rather than a textual label, use the component's setDescription() method to provide an assistive text description.

Another thing you can do is use containers to group components that logically belong with each other. If three buttons are used to start, stop, and pause an animation applet, for instance, you can associate them with each other by placing them within the same JPanel container.

Keyboard Mnemonics

A *keyboard mnemonic*, also called a *key accelerator* or *shortcut key*, is a keyboard sequence that can be used to control a user-interface component.

Keyboard mnemonics simulate mouse actions, and the method varies depending on the platform being used. On a computer running Windows 95, 98, or Me, you use a keyboard mnemonic by holding down the Alt key in combination with another key.

Keyboard mnemonics are set by calling the setMnemonic(*char*) method on the component that the mnemonic can control. The *char* argument is the key that should be used as part of the mnemonic. The following example creates a JButton object and associates the character 'i' with the button:

```
JButton infoButton = new JButton("Information");
infoButton.setMnemonic('i');
```

Pressing Alt+I causes the infoButton component to be clicked.

When a keyboard mnemonic has been set for a component that has a textual label, the key should be one of the characters on that label whenever possible. This causes the selected character to be underlined on the label.

Figure 25.2 shows several command buttons that have keyboard mnemonics associated with them.

ToolTips

Another way to make a program more user-friendly is to associate ToolTips with components on an interface.

A ToolTip describes the component's purpose. When you're learning to use a program for the first time, ToolTips are an excellent learning resource.

25

FIGURE 25.2

Several command buttons with underlined keyboard mnemonics.

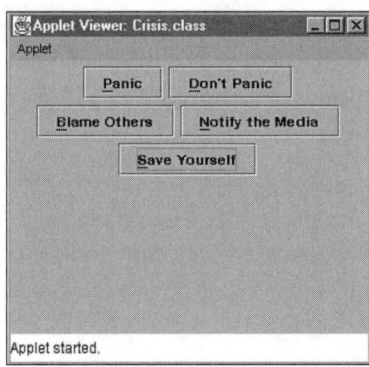

Call the `setToolTipText(String)` method of the component to set up a ToolTip for a component. The string should be a concise description of the component's purpose.

The following example creates a `JScrollBar` component and associates a ToolTip with it:

```
JScrollBar speed = new JScrollBar();
speed.setToolTipText("Move to set animation speed");
```

The ToolTip's text can only be one line long, so you cannot use the newline character (`'\n'`) to break the text over multiple lines.

If a keyboard mnemonic has been established for a component that has a ToolTip, the mnemonic is displayed along with the tip.

Figure 25.3 shows several command buttons that have keyboard mnemonics associated with them.

FIGURE 25.3

A ToolTip for a command button.

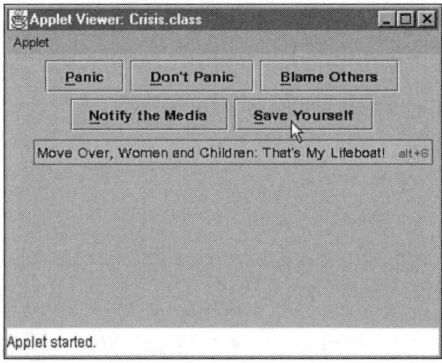

Associating Labels with Components

Some components in a user interface have fairly obvious uses. For example, a clickable button labeled Quit Program is used to quit a program.

Others are less obvious, such as a JTextField or JTextArea component. These usually require a text or image label that identifies the purpose of the text input component.

The setLabelFor(Object) method makes the relationship between a label and component known to assistive devices. This method is called on the component that's being labeled. The single Object argument should be the component that serves as its label.

When you use the setLabelFor() method to establish this relationship, a keyboard mnemonic for the label works on the component it identifies.

The following example creates a labeled text field:

```
JTextField name = new JTextField(20);
JLabel nameLabel = new JLabel("Enter Your Name:");
nameLabel.setMnemonic('n');
name.setLabelFor(nameLabel);
```

An Accessible Application: PageData

25

Today's last project is PageData, a Java application that supports several of the Accessibility features that you've learned about today. This application enables you to enter a Web page address and discover information about that document and the Web server that provided it. Although this is a fairly extensive program, most of it uses Swing and Java networking features that were introduced during the second and third weeks. One new concept introduced in this application is the getHeaderField(String) method of the java.net.URLConnection class. This method retrieves information from the Web server that's sending information through the URLConnection object. HTTP protocol, which determines how a server communicates with other programs, includes a number of items that describe the server, the document it's serving, and other related information. Each of these items is called a *header*, just as a printed document's header can be used to describe the document.

An example of an HTTP header is Server, which is used to identify the software used to run the Web server. This information can be requested using a call to getHeaderField("Server"). The following example requests this information from an URLConnection object called pipe and stores it in a string called serv:

```
String serv = pipe.getHeaderField("Server");
```

If the server has been configured to provide this information, it's returned as a string. Otherwise, the return value is null.

The PageData program is made accessible to assistive technology in several ways:

- The super() method gives the application's main frame the title Page Data.
- Each button is labeled with text that identifies its purpose.
- Labels are associated with text fields using the setLabelFor() method.
- ToolTips and keyboard mnemonics are associated with each command button.

Listing 25.3 contains the full source code for this project.

LISTING 25.3   The Full Text of PageData.java

```
 1: import java.awt.*;
 2: import java.awt.event.*;
 3: import java.net.*;
 4: import java.io.*;
 5: import javax.swing.*;
 6:
 7: public class PageData extends JFrame implements ActionListener,
 8:     Runnable {
 9:
10:     Thread runner;
11:     String[] headers = { "Content-Length", "Content-Type",
12:         "Date", "Public", "Expires", "Last-Modified",
13:         "Server" };
14:
15:     URL page;
16:     JTextField url;
17:     JLabel[] headerLabel = new JLabel[7];
18:     JTextField[] header = new JTextField[7];
19:     JButton readPage, clearPage, quitLoading;
20:     JLabel status;
21:
22:     public PageData() {
23:         super("Page Data");
24:         setDefaultCloseOperation(JFrame.EXIT_ON_CLOSE);
25:         JPanel pane = new JPanel();
26:         pane.setLayout(new GridLayout(10, 1));
27:
28:         JPanel first = new JPanel();
29:         first.setLayout(new FlowLayout(FlowLayout.RIGHT));
30:         JLabel urlLabel = new JLabel("URL:");
31:         url = new JTextField(22);
32:         urlLabel.setLabelFor(url);
33:         first.add(urlLabel);
```

LISTING 25.3   continued

```
34:            first.add(url);
35:            pane.add(first);
36:
37:            JPanel second = new JPanel();
38:            second.setLayout(new FlowLayout());
39:            readPage = new JButton("Read Page");
40:            clearPage = new JButton("Clear Fields");
41:            quitLoading = new JButton("Quit Loading");
42:            readPage.setMnemonic('r');
43:            clearPage.setMnemonic('c');
44:            quitLoading.setMnemonic('q');
45:            readPage.setToolTipText("Begin Loading the Web Page");
46:            clearPage.setToolTipText("Clear All Header Fields Below");
47:            quitLoading.setToolTipText("Quit Trying to Load the Web Page");
48:            readPage.setEnabled(true);
49:            clearPage.setEnabled(false);
50:            quitLoading.setEnabled(false);
51:            readPage.addActionListener(this);
52:            clearPage.addActionListener(this);
53:            quitLoading.addActionListener(this);
54:            second.add(readPage);
55:            second.add(clearPage);
56:            second.add(quitLoading);
57:            pane.add(second);
58:
59:            JPanel[] row = new JPanel[7];
60:            for (int i = 0; i < 7; i++) {
61:                row[i] = new JPanel();
62:                row[i].setLayout(new FlowLayout(FlowLayout.RIGHT));
63:                headerLabel[i] = new JLabel(headers[i]+":");
64:                header[i] = new JTextField(22);
65:                headerLabel[i].setLabelFor(header[i]);
66:                row[i].add(headerLabel[i]);
67:                row[i].add(header[i]);
68:                pane.add(row[i]);
69:            }
70:
71:            JPanel last = new JPanel();
72:            last.setLayout(new FlowLayout(FlowLayout.LEFT));
73:            status = new JLabel("Enter a URL address to check.");
74:            last.add(status);
75:            pane.add(last);
76:
77:            setContentPane(pane);
78:        }
79:
80:    public void actionPerformed(ActionEvent evt) {
81:        Object source = evt.getSource();
82:        if (source == readPage) {
83:            try {
```

25

LISTING 25.3   continued

```
84:                     page = new URL(url.getText());
85:                     if (runner == null) {
86:                         runner = new Thread(this);
87:                         runner.start();
88:                     }
89:                     quitLoading.setEnabled(true);
90:                     readPage.setEnabled(false);
91:                 }
92:                 catch (MalformedURLException e) {
93:                     status.setText("Bad URL: " + page);
94:                 }
95:             } else if (source == clearPage) {
96:                 for (int i = 0; i < 7; i++)
97:                     header[i].setText("");
98:                 quitLoading.setEnabled(false);
99:                 readPage.setEnabled(true);
100:                clearPage.setEnabled(false);
101:            } else if (source == quitLoading) {
102:                runner = null;
103:                url.setText("");
104:                quitLoading.setEnabled(false);
105:                readPage.setEnabled(true);
106:                clearPage.setEnabled(false);
107:            }
108:        }
109:
110:    public void run() {
111:        URLConnection conn = null;
112:        try {
113:            conn = this.page.openConnection();
114:            conn.connect();
115:            status.setText("Connection opened ...");
116:            for (int i = 0; i < 7; i++)
117:                header[i].setText(conn.getHeaderField(headers[i]));
118:            quitLoading.setEnabled(false);
119:            clearPage.setEnabled(true);
120:            status.setText("Done");
121:            runner = null;
122:        }
123:        catch (IOException e) {
124:            status.setText("IO Error:" + e.getMessage());
125:        }
126:    }
127:
128:    public static void main(String[] arguments) {
129:        PageData frame = new PageData();
130:        frame.pack();
131:        frame.setVisible(true);
132:    }
133: }
```

The PageData application requires an active Internet connection, so you should log onto your service provider before running it with the Java interpreter.

The ToolTips, selective enabled components, and other features should make using this program easy to learn. If the Web address you've entered isn't being loaded, you should use the Quit Loading button to stop attempting to connect. The program is doggedly persistent and won't give up unless you tell it to.

Figure 25.4 shows the PageData application after it has been used to load information about a Web page. A ToolTip associated with the Clear Fields button is visible because the mouse cursor was directly over the button for several seconds.

FIGURE 25.4

A ToolTip for a command button.

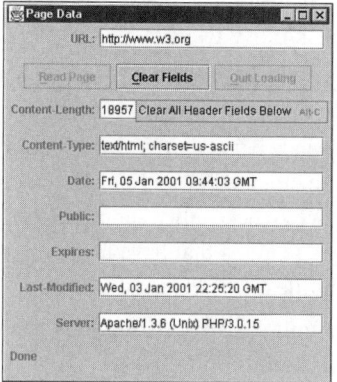

Summary

During the last 15 years, the standard for computer interfaces has progressed from type-and-read to point-and-click. The all-text environment of an operating system such as MS-DOS has been replaced with windowing platforms from Microsoft, Apple, Be, and other companies.

This change has been of great benefit to most computer users, who find today's software easier to learn and use because of the ubiquitous graphical user interface. (Some of us holdouts have an Amish-like love for the era when DOS, CP/M, UNIX, and the like were king, but we're definitely in the minority.)

The push to adopt windowing environments has created a greater challenge for developers who want their programs to be useful for the widest possible audience. As Sun states on its Accessibility home page, there are more than 40 million people with various disabilities in the United States alone.

25

Swing and the Accessibility classes make Java 2 the most accessible version of the language. By using ToolTips, keyboard mnemonics, textual components, and the classes of the `javax.accessibility` package, you can make Java programs that work with assistive technologies such as screen readers, Braille terminals, and voice-driven input and output systems.

These features have benefits for everyone who uses your programs because they make the user interface easier to learn and use.

Q&A

Q **What's the difference between Sun's Accessibility classes and those offered by Microsoft in its Active Accessibility technology?**

A Although Microsoft participated in early planning for Sun's Accessibility classes, the company elected to implement its own accessibility solution before the release of Java 2. The primary difference between the two is compatibility. Sun's Accessibility features are implemented entirely in Java and can work with any platform that supports Java. Active Accessibility supports only the Win32 platform and provides hooks into Windows features that have no analogue on other operating systems, such as online Help files.

Q **How can I find out more about assistive technology devices and pluggable look-and-feel that supports Accessibility?**

A At the time of this writing, Sun is actively maintaining an Accessibility home page at `http://java.sun.com/products/jfc/accessibility/doc/`. In addition to supporting the classes and features described today, this page describes advances in assistive computing technology as a whole.

Quiz

Review today's material by taking this three-question quiz.

Questions

1. What's displayed when you hover your mouse over a Swing component for a few seconds?

   a. The component's label.

   b. The component's `ToolTip`.

   c. The component's name.

2. When a Java program supports Accessibility, which of the following statements is true?

   a. The program requires assistive technology such as a screen reader.

   b. The program offers additional support for assistive technology.

   c. The program is unusable by assistive technology.

3. How do you indicate that one component is used as a label for another component?

   a. Call the label component's `setLabelFor(Component)` method.

   b. Put both components in the same container.

   c. Set up a keyboard mnemonic for the label component.

Answers

1. b. The text of the ToolTip will be displayed, if one has been defined for the component.

2. b. By supporting Accessibility, a Java programmer makes a program more useful to someone who's trying to run it through assistive technology.

3. a. Call `setLabelFor(Component)` with the component being labeled as an argument.

Exercises

To extend your knowledge of the subjects covered today, try the following exercises:

- Add ToolTips and keyboard mnemonics to one of the programs created during a prior day in the book.

- Write a Swing application that collects a user's name and address and saves it to a file. Use Accessibility features to make sure the application can be used entirely without a mouse.

Where applicable, exercise solutions are offered on this book's Web site at `http://www.java21pro.com`.

BONUS WEEK

DAY 26

Writing Java Servlets

As Java has matured, it has moved beyond applets that run on a Web page and applications that run on your computer. Servlets, which are applications run by a server connected to the World Wide Web, are among the most popular avenues for Java development today.

Servlets employ Java on the Web without the prohibitive security restrictions that are in place for applets. They run on a server rather than on the users' computers, so they can use all the features of the language. They're used to create Web applications—programs that collect information and present it as pages on the World Wide Web.

Today, you'll learn about the following topics:

- How servlets differ from applications and applets
- How servlets are run by a Web server
- How to use Sun's servlet class library
- How to run servlets as part of the Apache Web server and other servers
- How to receive data from a Web page form

- How to store and retrieve cookies

- How to use servlets to generate Web content dynamically

Using Web Servlets

Although servlets were designed for use with different kinds of Internet servers, Sun and other servlet developers are focusing on how to employ servlets on the World Wide Web.

Java servlets are run by a Web server that has an interpreter that supports the Java Servlet specification. This interpreter, which is often called a *servlet engine*, is optimized to run servlets with a minimum of the Web server's resources.

Java servlets serve the same purpose as programs that are implemented using the Common Gateway Interface, which is a protocol for writing software that sends and receives information through a Web server. CGI programming has been supported on the Web for most of its existence. Most CGI programs, which are also called CGI *scripts*, have been written using languages such as Perl, Python, C, and C++.

You've doubtlessly used hundreds of CGI programs as you browsed the Web. CGI is used for these purposes:

- Collecting data from a form on a Web page.

- Receiving information from fields in a URL.

- Running programs on the computer that runs the Web server.

- Storing and retrieving configuration information for each user of a Web page—a feature more commonly known as "browser cookies."

- Sending data back to a Web user in the form of an HTML document, a GIF file, or another common format.

Java servlets can do all these things, and they also support some behavior that's extremely difficult to implement using most CGI scripting languages.

Servlets offer full support for sessions, which are a way to keep track of how a Web user navigates the different parts of a Web site, opening and closing pages over a period of time. They also can communicate directly with a Web server using a standard interface. As long as the server supports Java servlets, it can exchange information with those programs.

Java servlets have the same portability advantages as the language itself. Although Sun's official implementation of servlets was created with the designers of the Apache Web server, other server developers also have introduced tools to support Java servlets, including IBM WebSphere Application Server, BEA WebLogic, and the Microsoft Internet Information Server.

Servlets also run efficiently in memory. If 10 people are using the same CGI script simultaneously, a Web server will have 10 copies of that script loaded into memory. If 10 people are using a Java servlet, however, only one copy of the servlet will be loaded, and this servlet will spawn threads to handle each user.

Supporting Servlets

Java servlets are supported by Sun Microsystems through Tomcat, which was developed by Sun Microsystems and the Apache Software Foundation, the group that oversees the Apache Web server. Tomcat combines Java servlets and a related technology called JavaServer Pages, which you'll learn about tomorrow.

Tomcat includes two Java class libraries, `javax.servlet` and `javax.servlet.http`, and software that adds servlet functionality to Apache Web server. There's also a standalone servlet interpreter that you can use to test servlets before deploying them on the Web.

You can find out more about Tomcat from two Web sites:

- Sun's Java servlet site at `http://java.sun.com/products/servlet/`
- Apache's Tomcat site at `http://jakarta.apache.org/tomcat/`

Before you can use servlets, you must have a Web server that offers support for these programs. If you have an Apache Web server and are conversant in how to extend its functionality, you can add Tomcat support to the server. Your current Web server or Web application server may already include support for servlets.

26

If you don't have a server but you'd like to begin developing servlets, there are several companies that offer commercial Web hosting with Java servlet support. These companies have already installed Tomcat and configured it to work with their servers, so all you have to worry about is creating and compiling servlets using the classes of the `javax.servlet` and `javax.servlet.http` packages.

The Open Directory Project lists more than a dozen companies that offer built-in servlet hosting. Visit `http://www.dmoz.org` and search for "servlet hosting."

> **Note**
>
> Motivational Marketing Associates offers Java servlet hosting on an Apache Web server and was used throughout the preparation of today's lesson. You can find out more about its commercial hosting services by visiting `http://www.mmaweb.com/`.

Because servlets are supported by several different Web servers, the installation process for servers is not documented today.

To compile servlets on your computer, you must install the two Java servlet packages, `javax.servlet` and `javax.servlet.http`. These packages aren't part of the standard Java class library included with Java 2 SDK 1.3. At the time of this writing, the last full release of these packages is Tomcat version 3.2.1. To download it, visit the Java Servlet site at `http://java.sun.com/products/servlet/` and click the Download link.

Tip

> You also may be able to go directly to `http://java.sun.com/products/servlet/download.html` to download the servlet packages, although from time to time Sun moves pages around on its Java site.

These packages are currently available as ZIP archive files, which you must open using WinZIP or similar software. When you're extracting these files to your computer, choose the option to use the existing folder names in the archive.

Tomcat version 3.2.1 includes all of the class files in the two packages, Javadoc documentation for the classes, and a JAR file that also contains all of the classes. This Java archive is named `servlet.jar`, and it will be installed into a `lib` subfolder. Add this file to your computer's `CLASSPATH`.

Developing Servlets

Java servlets are created and compiled just like any other Java application. You can compile them with the Java compiler included with SDK 1.3, as long as the compiler can find the `javax.servlet` and `javax.servlet.http` packages.

To create a servlet, you subclass the `HttpServlet` class, which is part of the `javax.servlet` package. This class includes methods that represent the life cycle of a servlet and methods that receive information from the Web server running the servlet.

The `init(ServletConfig)` method is called automatically when a Web server first brings a servlet online to handle a user's request. As mentioned earlier, one Java servlet can handle multiple requests from different Web users. The `init()` method is called only once, when a servlet comes online. If a servlet is already online when another request to use the servlet is received, the `init()` method won't be called again.

The `init()` method has one argument—`ServletConfig`, an interface in the `javax.servlet` package that contains methods to find out more about the environment that a servlet is running in.

The destroy() method is called when a Web server takes a servlet offline. Like the init() method, this is called only once, when all users have finished receiving information from the servlet. If this doesn't take place in a specified amount of time, destroy() will be called automatically, which prevents a servlet from being hung up while it waits for information to be exchanged with a user.

One of the main tasks of a servlet is to collect information from a Web user and present something back in response. You can collect information from a user by using a *form*, which is a group of text boxes, radio buttons, text areas, buttons, and other input fields on a Web page.

Figure 26.1 shows a Web form on a page loaded with Microsoft Internet Explorer 5.

FIGURE 26.1

Collecting information with a Web form.

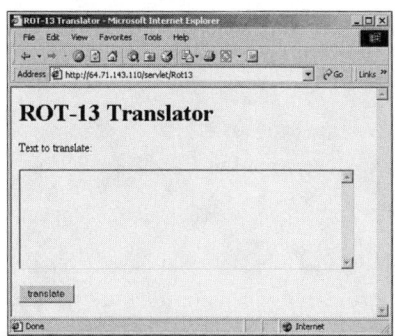

The form displayed in Figure 26.1 contains two fields: a text area and a clickable button labeled "translate". The HyperText Markup Language (HTML) tags used to display this page are the following:

```
<html>
<body>
<head><title>ROT-13 Translator</title></head>
<h1>ROT-13 Translator</h1>
<p>Text to translate:
<form action="Rot13" method="POST">
<textarea name="text" ROWS=8 COLS=55>
</textarea>
<p><input type="submit" value="translate">
</form>
</body>
</html>
```

The form is contained within the <form> and </form> HTML tags. Each field on the form is represented by its own tags: <textarea> and </textarea> for the text area and <input> for the "translate" button. The text area is given a name, text.

26

Tip

Web servlets require you to have a basic familiarity with HTML because the only user interface for a servlet is a Web page running in a browser. Two books that are good for learning HTML are *Sams Teach Yourself HTML in 24 Hours* by Dick Oliver and *Sams Teach Yourself Web Publishing with HTML 4 in 21 Days, Second Edition* by Denise Tyler and Laura Lemay (one of the authors of this book).

Each field on a form stores information that can be transmitted to a Web server and then sent to a Java servlet. Web browsers communicate with servers by using hypertext transfer protocol (HTTP). Form data can be sent to a server using two kinds of HTTP requests: GET and POST.

When a Web page calls a server using GET or POST, the name of the program that will handle the request must be specified as a Web address, also called a uniform resource locator (URL).

A GET request affixes all data on a form to the end of a URL, as in this example:

```
http://www.java21pro.com/servlets/beep?number=5551220&repeat=no
```

A POST request includes form data as a header that is sent separately from the URL. This is generally preferred, and it's required when confidential information is being collected on the form.

Java servlets handle both of these requests through methods inherited from the HttpServlet class: doGet(*HttpServletRequest*, *HttpServletResponse*) and doPost(*HttpServletRequest*, *HttpServletResponse*). These methods throw two kinds of exceptions: ServletException, which is part of the javax.servlet package, and IOException, an exception in the standard java.io package that involves input and output streams.

These methods function identically within Java, so a common technique in Java servlet programming is to use one method to call the other, as in the following:

```
public void doGet(HttpServletRequest request,
    HttpServletResponse response) throws ServletException, IOException {

    doPost(request, response);
}
```

The doGet() and doPost() methods have two arguments: an HttpServletRequest object and an HttpServletResponse object. These objects belong to classes in the javax.servlet.http package. A servlet receives information about how it was run by calling methods of the HttpServletRequest class. For example, when a Web form is submitted to a servlet, each field on the form is stored as a string by the `HttpServletRequest` class.

You can retrieve these fields in a servlet by calling the `getParameter(String)` method with the name of the field as an argument. This method returns `null` if no field of that name exists.

A servlet communicates with the user by sending back an HTML document, an image file, or another type of information supported by a Web browser. It sends this information by calling the methods of the `HttpServletResponse` class.

The first thing you must do when preparing a response is define the kind of content the servlet is sending to a browser. Call the `setContentType(String)` method with the content type as an argument.

The most common form for a response is HTML, which is set by calling `setContentType("text/html")`. You can also send a response as text (`"text/plain"`), graphics files (`"image/gif"`, `"image/jpeg"`), and application-specific formats such as `"application/msword"`.

To send data to a browser, you create a servlet output stream associated with the browser and then call the `println(String)` method on that stream. Servlet output streams are represented by the `ServletOutputStream` class, which is part of the `javax.servlet` package. You can get one of these streams by calling the `getOutputStream()` method of the `HttpServletResponse` class.

The following example creates a servlet output stream from an `HttpServletResponse` object called `response` and then sends a short Web page to that stream:

```
ServletOutputStream out = response.getOutputStream();
out.println("<html>");
out.println("<body>");
out.println("<h1>Hello World!</h1>");
out.println("</body>");
out.println("</html>");
```

Listing 26.1 contains a Java servlet that receives data from the form displayed in Figure 26.1.

LISTING 26.1   The Full Text of `Rot13.java`

```
1: import java.io.*;
2:
3: import javax.servlet.*;
4: import javax.servlet.http.*;
5:
```

26

LISTING 26.1 continued

```
6: public class Rot13 extends HttpServlet {
7:
8:     public void doPost(HttpServletRequest req, HttpServletResponse res)
9:         throws ServletException, IOException {
10:
11:         String text = req.getParameter("text");
12:         String translation = translate(text);
13:         res.setContentType("text/html");
14:         ServletOutputStream out = res.getOutputStream();
15:         out.println("<html>");
16:         out.println("<body>");
17:         out.println("<head><title>ROT-13 Translator</title></head>");
18:         out.println("<h1>ROT-13 Translator</h1>");
19:         out.println("<p>Text to translate:");
20:         out.println("<form action=\"Rot13\" method=\"POST\">");
21:         out.println("<textarea name=\"text\" ROWS=8 COLS=55>");
22:         out.println(translation);
23:         out.println("</textarea>");
24:         out.println("<p><input type=\"submit\" value=\"translate\">");
25:         out.println("</form>");
26:         out.println("</body>");
27:         out.println("</html>");
28:     }
29:
30:     public void doGet(HttpServletRequest req, HttpServletResponse res)
31:         throws ServletException, IOException {
32:
33:         doPost(req, res);
34:     }
35:
36:     String translate(String input) {
37:         StringBuffer output = new StringBuffer();
38:         if (input != null) {
39:             for (int i = 0; i < input.length(); i++) {
40:                 char inChar = input.charAt(i);
41:                 if ((inChar >= 'A') & (inChar <= 'Z')) {
42:                     inChar += 13;
43:                     if (inChar > 'Z')
44:                         inChar -= 26;
45:                 }
46:                 if ((inChar >= 'a') & (inChar <= 'z')) {
47:                     inChar += 13;
48:                     if (inChar > 'z')
49:                         inChar -= 26;
50:                 }
51:                 output.append(inChar);
52:             }
53:         }
```

LISTING 26.1 continued

```
54:        return output.toString();
55:    }
56: }
```

After saving the servlet, compile it with the Java compiler.

The `Rot13` servlet receives text from a Web form, translates it using ROT-13, and then displays the result in a new Web form. ROT-13 is a simple method of encrypting text through letter substitution. Each letter of the alphabet is replaced with the letter that's 13 places away: A becomes N, N becomes A, B becomes O, O becomes B, C becomes P, P becomes C, and so on.

Since the ROT-13 encryption scheme is easy to decode, it isn't used when it's important to keep information secret. Instead, it's used casually on Internet discussion forums such as Usenet newsgroups. For example, if someone on a movie newsgroup wants to share a "spoiler" that reveals a plot detail about an upcoming movie, she can encode it in ROT-13 to prevent people from reading it accidentally.

Note

> Want to know the big secret from the 1973 film *Soylent Green*? Decode this ROT-13 text: Fbba gurl'yy or oerrqvat hf yvxr pnggyr! Lbh're tbg gb jnea rirelbar naq gryy gurz! Fblyrag terra vf znqr bs crbcyr! Lbh're tbg gb gryy gurz! Fblyrag terra vf crbcyr!

To make the ROT-13 servlet available, you must publish its class files in a folder on your Web server that has been designated for Java servlets. On an Apache server equipped with Tomcat, servlets are often put in a `WEB-INF/classes` subfolder of your main Web folder. (For instance, if `/htdocs` is the root folder of your Web site, servlets would be in `/htdocs/WEB-INF/classes`.)

You run a servlet by typing its URL, such as `http://www.cadenhead.org/servlet/Rot13`, into a Web browser's address bar. Replace the first part of the URL with the name or IP address of your own Web server.

Tip

> You can try out a working ROT-13 servlet on the book's Web site—visit `http://www.java21pro.com` and open the Day 26 page.

26

Using Cookies

Many Web sites can be customized to keep track of information about you and the features you want the site to display. This customization is possible because of a Web browser feature called *cookies*. These are small files containing information that a Web site wants to remember about a user, such as his username, the number of times he's visited, and the like. The files are stored on the user's computer, and a Web site can only read cookies on the user's system that the site has created.

Because of privacy considerations, most Web browsers can be configured to reject all cookies or ask permission first before allowing a site to create a cookie. The default behavior for most browsers is to accept all cookies.

With servlets, you can easily create and retrieve cookies as a user runs your program. Cookies are supported by the `Cookie` class in the `javax.servlet.http` package.

To create a cookie, call the `Cookie(String, String)` constructor. The first argument is the name you want to give the cookie, and the second is the cookie's value.

One use for cookies is to count the number of times someone has loaded a servlet. The following statement creates a cookie named visits and gives it the initial value of 1:

```
Cookie visitCookie = new Cookie("visits", "1");
```

When you create a cookie, you must decide how long it should remain valid on a user's computer. Cookies can be valid for an hour, a day, a year, or any time in-between. When a cookie is no longer valid, the Web browser will delete it automatically.

Call a cookie's `setMaxAge(int)` method to set up the amount of time the cookie will remain valid, in seconds. If you use a negative value as an argument, the cookie will only remain valid while the user's Web browser is open. If you use 0 as a value, the cookie will not be stored on a user's computer.

> **Note**
>
> The purpose of creating a cookie with a maximum age of 0 is to tell the Web browser to delete the cookie if it already has one.

Cookies are sent to a user's computer along with the data that's displayed by the Web browser. To send a cookie, call the `addCookie(Cookie)` method of an `HttpServletResponse` object.

You can add more than one cookie to a response. When cookies are stored on a user's computer, they're associated with the URL of the Web page or program that created the cookie. You can associate several different cookies with the same URL.

When a Web browser requests a URL, the browser checks if it has any cookies associated with that URL. If it does, they're sent along with the request.

In a servlet, call the getCookies() method of an HttpServletRequest object to receive an array of Cookie objects. You can call each cookie's getName() and getValue() methods to find out about that cookie and do something with the data.

Listing 26.2 contains SetColor, a servlet that enables a user to select the background color of the page that the servlet displays. The color is stored as a cookie called color, and the servlet requests the cookie from a Web browser every time the servlet is loaded.

LISTING 26.2 The Full Text of SetColor.java

```
 1: import java.io.*;
 2:
 3: import javax.servlet.*;
 4: import javax.servlet.http.*;
 5:
 6: public class SetColor extends HttpServlet {
 7:
 8:     public void doPost(HttpServletRequest req, HttpServletResponse res)
 9: throws ServletException, IOException {
10:
11:         String pageColor;
12:         String colorParameter = req.getParameter("color");
13:         if (colorParameter != null) {
14:             Cookie colorCookie = new Cookie("color", colorParameter);
15:             colorCookie.setMaxAge(31536000);
16:             res.addCookie(colorCookie);
17:             pageColor = colorParameter;
18:         } else {
19:             pageColor = retrieveColor(req.getCookies());
20:         }
21:         ServletOutputStream out = res.getOutputStream();
22:         res.setContentType("text/html");
23:         out.println("<html>");
24:         out.println("<body bgcolor=\"" + pageColor + "\">");
25:         out.println("<head><title>The U.S. Constitution</title></head>");
26:         out.println("<h1>The U.S. Constitution</h1>");
27:         displayFile("constitution.html", out);
28:         out.println("<h5>Choose a new color</h5>");
29:         out.println("<form action=\"SetColor\" method=\"POST\">");
30:         out.println("<input type=\"text\" name=\"color\" value=\"" +
31:             pageColor + "\" SIZE=40>");
32:         out.println("<p><input type=\"submit\" value=\"Change Color\">");
33:         out.println("</form>");
34:         out.println("</body>");
```

26

LISTING 26.2   continued

```
35:             out.println("</html>");
36:         }
37:
38:     public void doGet(HttpServletRequest req, HttpServletResponse res)
39:         throws ServletException, IOException {
40:
41:         doPost(req, res);
42:     }
43:
44:     String retrieveColor(Cookie[] cookies) {
45:         String inColor = "#FFFFFF";
46:         for (int i = 0; i < cookies.length; i++) {
47:             String cookieName = cookies[i].getName();
48:             if (cookieName.equals("color")) {
49:                 inColor = cookies[i].getValue();
50:             }
51:         }
52:         return inColor;
53:     }
54:
55:     void displayFile(String pageName, ServletOutputStream out) {
56:         try {
57:             ServletContext servletContext = getServletContext();
58:         String filename = servletContext.getRealPath(pageName);
59:             FileReader file = new FileReader(filename);
60:             BufferedReader buff = new BufferedReader(file);
61:             boolean eof = false;
62:             while (!eof) {
63:                 String line = buff.readLine();
64:                 if (line == null)
65:                     eof = true;
66:                 else
67:                     out.println(line);
68:             }
69:             buff.close();
70:         } catch (IOException e) {
71:             log("Error -- " + e.toString());
72:         }
73:     }
74: }
```

The SetColor servlet displays the contents of an HTML file along with the rest of the page. This example uses constitution.html, a copy of the U.S. Constitution in HTML format. You can download this file from the book's Web site at http://www.java21pro.com (open the Day 26 page). You also can use any other HTML file by changing lines 25-27 of the program.

After you compile the servlet and put it on your Web server in the servlets folder, you can run it by loading the servlet's URL into a browser, such as `http://www.cadenhead.org/servlet/SetColor`.

Figure 26.2 shows the bottom of the page displayed by the servlet.

FIGURE 26.2

A Web page generated by the SetColor *servlet.*

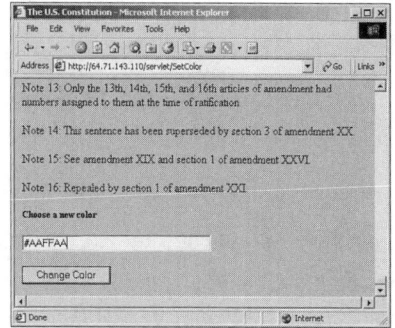

To change the page's background color, type a new value into the "Choose a new color" text field and click the Change Color button.

Colors are expressed as a # sign followed by three two-digit hexadecimal numbers (in Figure 26.2, the numbers are AA, FF, and AA). These numbers represent the amount of red, green, and blue the color contains, ranging from a minimum of 00 to a maximum of FF. If you aren't familiar with hexadecimal colors, you can try these out while testing the servlet:

- #FF0000: Bright red
- #00FF00: Bright green
- #0000FF: Bright blue
- #FFAAAA: Light red
- #AAFFAA: Light green
- #AAAAFF: Light blue
- #FFCC66: Butterscotch

26

Summary

The main purpose of the classes in the `javax.servlet` and `javax.servlet.http` packages is to exchange information with a Web server. Java servlets are an alternative to the Common Gateway Interface, which is the most popular way that programming languages are used to retrieve and present data on the Web. Because servlets can use all features of the Java language with the exception of a graphical user interface, you can use them to create sophisticated Web applications.

Servlets are being used today to run e-commerce storefronts, take orders from users, connect to a database of products, and collect billing information when a purchase is made. They're also used to run discussion boards, content-management systems, and many other types of dynamically generated Web sites.

Tomorrow, you'll learn about the other half of Tomcat: JavaServer Pages.

Q&A

Q Is there a way to make a Java applet communicate with a servlet?

A If you want the applet to continue running after it contacts the servlet, the servlet must be on the same machine as the Web page that contains the applet. For security reasons, applets cannot make a network connection to any machine other than the one that hosts the applet.

If you want an applet to load a servlet in the Web browser, you can call the applet's `getAppletContext()` method to get an `AppletContext` object, and then call that object's `showDocument(URL)` method with the servlet's URL as the argument.

Quiz

Review today's material by taking this three-question quiz.

Questions

1. If a servlet is run at the same time by five different Web users, how many times is the servlet's `init()` method called?

   a. 5

   b. 1

   c. 0-1

2. What technology is *not* included as part of Tomcat?

   a. Java servlets

   b. JavaServer Pages

   c. Java API for XML Processing

3. When data is submitted from a form on a Web page and it shows up in the browser's address bar as part of a URL, what kind of request is being used?

   a. A GET request

   b. A POST request

   c. A HEAD request

Answers

1. c. The init() method is called when the Web server first loads the servlet. This may have taken place before all five of these users requested the servlet, so it could call init() one time or not at all.

2. c. The Java API for XML Processing.

3. a. A GET request encodes fields from a form into a URL and then submits that URL to a Web browser as a request.

Exercises

To extend your knowledge of the subjects covered today, try the following exercises:

- Create a modified version of the SetColor servlet that lets you choose a different color for the text on the page also.

- Create a servlet that stores the contents of data entered in a form into a file.

Where applicable, exercise solutions are offered on the book's Web site at http://www.java21pro.com.

26

DAY **27**

Using JavaServer Pages

Java servlets make it easy to generate HTML text dynamically, producing pages that change in response to user input and data. However, servlets make it hard to generate HTML text that never changes, because it's cumbersome and tedious to use Java statements to output HTML.

Servlets also require the services of a Java programmer whenever the HTML needs to be changed. The servlet must be edited, recompiled, and deployed on the Web, and very few organizations are comfortable handing that task to a non-programmer.

The solution to this problem is JavaServer Pages, which create documents that mix static HTML with the output of servlets and elements of the Java language, such as expressions and Java statements.

Today you'll learn about the following topics:

- How Web servers support JavaServer Pages
- How to create a JavaServer Page
- How to use servlet variables on a page
- How to include a Java expression on a page

- How to use Java statements on a page
- How to declare Java variables on a page
- How to call a servlet on a page

JavaServer Pages

As you may recall from yesterday, JavaServer Pages are part of the Tomcat specification from Sun Microsystems and the Apache Software Foundation. JavaServer Pages are a compliment to servlets, rather than a replacement. They make it easy to separate two kinds of Web content:

- Static content—The portions of a Web page that don't change, such as an online store's description of each product.
- Dynamic content—The portions of a Web page that are generated by a servlet, such as the store's pricing and availability data for each product, which can change as items sell out.

When you only use servlets on a project, it becomes extremely difficult to make minor changes such as correcting a typo in text, rewording a paragraph, or altering some HTML tags to change how the page is presented. Any kind of change requires the servlet to be edited, compiled, tested, and redeployed on the Web server.

With JavaServer Pages, you can put the static content of a Web page in an HTML document and call servlets from within that content. You also can use other parts of the Java language on a page, such as expressions, if-then blocks, and variables. A Web server that supports the Tomcat specification knows how to read these pages and execute the Java code they contain, generating an HTML document as if you wrote a servlet to handle the whole task. In actuality, JavaServer Pages do use servlets for everything.

You create a JavaServer Page as you would an HTML document—in a text editor or Web publishing program such as Microsoft FrontPage 2002 or Macromedia Dreamweaver. When you save the page, use the .jsp file extension to indicate that it's a JavaServer Page instead of an HTML document. Then the page can be published on a Web server like an HTML document (although the server must support Tomcat).

When a user requests the JavaServer Page for the first time, the Web server compiles a new servlet that presents the page. This servlet combines everything that has been put into the page:

- Text marked up with HTML
- Calls to Java servlets

- Java expressions and statements
- Special JavaServer Pages variables

Writing a JavaServer Page

A JavaServer Page consists of three kinds of elements, each with its own special markup tag that's similar to HTML:

- Scriptlets—Java statements executed when the page is loaded. Each of these statements is surrounded by <% and %> tags.
- Expressions—Java expressions that are evaluated, producing output that's displayed on the page. These are surrounded by <%= and %> tags.
- Declarations—Statements to create instance variables and handle other setup tasks required in the presentation of the page. These are surrounded by <%! and %> tags.

Using Expressions

Listing 27.1 contains a JavaServer Page that includes one expression, a call to the `java.util.Date()` constructor. This constructor produces a string containing the current time and date. Enter this file with any text editor that can save files as plain text. (The editor you've been using to create Java source code will work for this purpose as well.)

LISTING 27.1   The Full Text of `time.jsp`

```
 1: <html>
 2: <head>
 3: <title>Clock</title>
 4: </head>
 5: <body>
 6: <h1 align="Center">
 7: <%= new java.util.Date() %>
 8: </h1>
 9: </body>
10: </html>
```

27

After saving the file, upload it to your Web server in a folder where other Web pages are stored. Unlike Java servlets, which must be in a folder that has been designated for servlets, JavaServer Pages can be placed in any folder that's accessible on the Web.

When you load the page's URL for the first time, the Web server will compile the JavaServer Page into a servlet. This causes the page to load slowly, but it won't happen again because the server keeps this servlet around for all subsequent requests.

The output of `time.jsp` is shown in Figure 27.1.

FIGURE 27.1

Using an expression in a JavaServer Page.

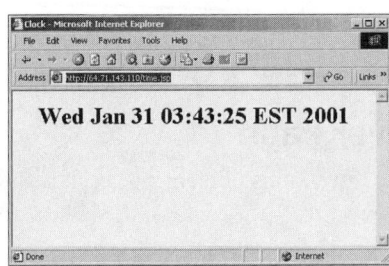

When a JavaServer Page includes an expression, it's evaluated to produce a value and displayed on the page. If the expression produces different values each time it's run, as time.jsp does, this will be reflected in the page when it's loaded in a Web browser.

There are several servlet variables you can refer to in expressions and other elements of a JavaServer Page:

- application—The servlet context used to communicate with the Web server
- config—The servlet configuration object used to see how the servlet was initialized
- out—The servlet output stream
- request—The HTTP servlet request
- response—The HTTP servlet response
- session—The current HTTP session

Each of these variables refers to an object you worked with yesterday, and you can call the same methods from within a JavaServer Page that were available in a servlet.

The next page you'll create, environment.jsp, shows how the request variable can be used on a page. This variable represents an object of the HttpServletRequest class, and you can call the object's getHeader(*String*) method to retrieve HTTP headers that describe the request in more detail. See Listing 27.2.

LISTING 27.2   The Full Text of environment.jsp

```
1: <html>
2: <head>
3: <title>Environment Variables</title>
4: </head>
5: <body>
6: <ul>
7: <li>Accept: <%= request.getHeader("Accept") %>
```

LISTING 27.2 continued

```
 8: <li>Accept-Encoding: <%= request.getHeader("Accept-Encoding") %>
 9: <li>Connection: <%= request.getHeader("Connection") %>
10: <li>Content-Length: <%= request.getHeader("Content-Length") %>
11: <li>Content-Type: <%= request.getHeader("Content-Type") %>
12: <li>Cookie: <%= request.getHeader("Cookie") %>
13: <li>Host: <%= request.getHeader("Host") %>
14: <li>Referer: <%= request.getHeader("Referer") %>
15: <li>User-Agent: <%= request.getHeader("User-Agent") %>
16: </ul>
17: </body>
18: </html>
```

In lines 7-15 of the `environment.jsp` page, each line contains a call to `getHeader()` that retrieves a different HTTP request header. An example of the output is shown in Figure 27.2. The values reported for each header depend on your Web server and the Web browser you're using, so you won't see the same values for User-Agent, Referer, and other headers.

FIGURE 27.2

Using servlet variables on a JavaServer Page.

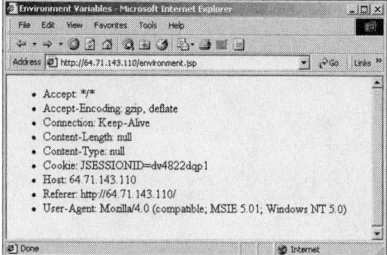

Using Scriptlets

You can also use Java statements in your JavaServer Page—calling methods, assigning values to variables, creating conditional statements, and so on. These statements begin with the `<%` tag and end with the `%>` tag. More than one statement can be enclosed within these tags.

Statements that appear inside a JavaServer Page are called *scriptlets*. You can use any of the servlet variables that were available for expressions.

Listing 27.3 contains `shopforbooks.jsp`, a Web page that displays a list of books, with hyperlinks to each book's page at an online bookstore.

27

LISTING 27.3   The Full Text of `shopforbooks.jsp`

```
 1: <html>
 2: <head>
 3: <title>Shop for Books</title>
 4: </head>
 5: <body>
 6: <h2 align="Left">Favorite Books</h2>
 7: <%
 8: String[] bookTitle = { "Catch-22", "Something Happened",
 9:     "Good as Gold" };
10: String[] isbn = { "0684833395", "0684841215", "0684839741" };
11: String amazonLink = "http://www.amazon.com/exec/obidos/ASIN/";
12: String bnLink = "http://shop.bn.com/booksearch/isbnInquiry.asp?isbn=";
13:
14: String store = request.getParameter("store");
15: if (store == null) {
16:     store = "Amazon";
17: }
18: for (int i = 0; i < bookTitle.length; i++) {
19:     if (store.equals("Amazon"))
20:         out.println("<li><a href=\"" + amazonLink + isbn[i] + "\">" +
21:             bookTitle[i] + "</a>");
22:     else
23:         out.println("<li><a href=\"" + bnLink + isbn[i] + "\">" +
24:             bookTitle[i] + "</a>");
25: }
26: %>
27: <p>Preferred Bookstore:
28: <form action="shopforbooks.jsp" method="POST">
29: <p><input type="radio" value="Amazon" <%= (store.equals("Amazon")) ? "
➥checked" : "") %>
30: name="store"> Amazon.Com
31: <p><input type="radio" value="BN" <%= (store.equals("BN")) ? " checked"
➥: "") %>
32: name="store"> Barnes & Noble
33: <p><input type="submit" value="Change Store">
34: </form>
35: </body>
36: </html>
```

This JavaServer Page includes a form at the bottom of the page that lets users pick which bookstore they like to use for online shopping.

In line 28, the form is being submitted to the URL of the JavaServer Page. Because pages are actually servlets, they can also receive form data that's sent by POST or GET.

This page uses the store field to hold "Amazon" if Amazon.com is the preferred store, and "BN" if Barnes & Noble is the preferred store.

One thing to note as you test the server page is how the radio buttons on the form always match the store you've chosen. This occurs because of expressions that appear on lines 29 and 31. Here's one of those expressions:

```
<%= (store.equals("Amazon") ? " checked" : "") %>
```

This expression uses the ternary operator with the conditional `store.equals("Amazon")`. If this condition is true, the word `"checked"` is the value of the expression. Otherwise, an empty string (`""`) is the value.

The value of expressions is displayed as part of the JavaServer Page. Figure 27.3 shows what this page looks like in a Web browser.

FIGURE 27.3

Displaying dynamic content using scriptlets.

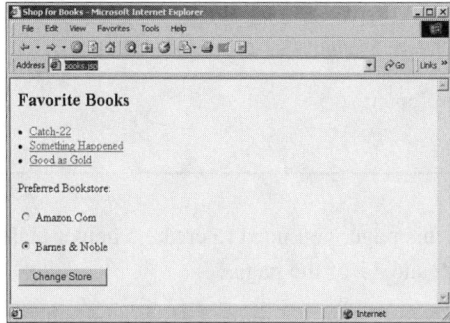

Using Declarations

The last element you can insert into a JavaServer Page is a declaration, which is a statement that sets up a variable or method that will be defined in the page when it's compiled into a servlet. This feature is primarily used in conjunction with expressions and servlets.

Declarations are surrounded by `<%!` and `%>` tags, as in the following example:

```
<!% boolean noCookie = true %>
<!% String userName = "New user" %>
```

These declarations create two instance variables: `noCookie` and `userName`. When the JavaServer Page is compiled into a servlet, these variables will be part of the definition of that class.

Listing 27.4 contains a JavaServer Page that uses a declaration to present a counter.

27

LISTING 27.4   The Full Text of `counter.jsp`

```
 1: <html>
 2: <head>
 3: <title>Counter Example</title>
 4: </head>
 5: <body>
 6: <h1>JSP Stats</h1>
 7: <%! Counter visits; %>
 8: <%! int count; %>
 9:
10: <%
11: visits = new Counter(application.getRealPath("counter.dat"));
12: count = visits.getCount() + 1;
13: %>
14:
15: <p>This page has been loaded <%= count %> times.
16:
17: <% visits.setCount(count); %>
18: </body>
19: </html>
```

Before you can try out this page, you need to create a helper class that's called by statements in lines 7, 11, 12, and 17 of the page.

The `Counter` class in Listing 27.5 represents a Web counter that tallies up each hit to a page.

LISTING 27.5   The Full Text of `Counter.java`

```
 1: import java.io.*;
 2: import java.util.*;
 3:
 4: public class Counter {
 5:     private int count;
 6:     private String filepath;
 7:
 8:     public Counter(String inFilepath) {
 9:         count = 0;
10:         filepath = inFilepath;
12:     }
13:
14:     public int getCount() {
15:         try {
16:             File countFile = new File(filepath);
17:             FileReader file = new FileReader(countFile);
18:             BufferedReader buff = new BufferedReader(file);
19:             String current = buff.readLine();
```

LISTING 27.5   continued

```
20:                count = Integer.parseInt(current);
21:                buff.close();
22:            } catch (IOException e) {
23:                // do nothing
24:            } catch (NumberFormatException nfe) {
25:                // do nothing
26:            }
27:            return count;
28:        }
29:
30:        public void setCount(int newCount) {
31:            count = newCount;
32:            try {
33:                File countFile = new File(filepath);
34:                FileWriter file = new FileWriter(countFile);
35:                BufferedWriter buff = new BufferedWriter(file);
36:                String output = "" + newCount;
37:                buff.write(output, 0, output.length());
38:                buff.close();
39:            } catch (IOException e) {
40:                // do nothing
41:            }
42:        }
43: }
```

After you compile this class successfully, store it in the same folder on your Web server as the Java servlets you created yesterday. The Counter class isn't a servlet, but Tomcat looks in that folder for classes that are referenced on a JavaServer Page.

The Counter class loads an integer value from a file stored on the Web server called counter.dat. The getCount() method retrieves the current value of the counter, and the setCount(*int*) method sets the current value. After the value is set, it's saved to the file so that the counter continues to increment upwards.

Figure 27.4 shows counter.jsp being loaded simultaneously in two Web browser windows, illustrating that the same counter file is used by both pages.

27

FIGURE 27.4

Using servlets to count visits to a Web page.

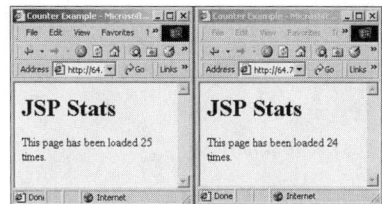

Creating a Web Application

By combining Java classes, servlets, and JavaServer Pages, you can create interactive Web applications—sites that dynamically generate content in response to user input in a sophisticated, cohesive way.

Every time you shop on an e-commerce site, such as Amazon.com, or use an online reference, such as the Internet Movie Database (IMDB), you're running a Web application.

To see how several different aspects of Java technology can work together on the Web, you'll create Guestbook, a Web application that enables visitors to leave a message for the creator of a site.

The Guestbook project is made up of three things:

- guestbook.jsp, a JavaServer Page that displays guestbook entries from a text file on a Web server and provides a form where the visitor can add an entry.

- guestbookpost.jsp, a JavaServer Page that saves a new guestbook entry to the text file.

- Guestbook.java, a class that is used to filter out some characters before they're saved in the guestbook.

The JavaServer Pages in this project make heavy use of scriptlets and expressions. Listing 27.6 contains the source code for guestbook.jsp.

LISTING 27.6   The Full Text of guestbook.jsp

```
 1: <%@ page import="java.util.*,java.io.*" %>
 2: <html>
 3: <head>
 4: <title>Visitors Who Signed our Guestbook</title>
 5: </head>
 6: <body>
 7: <h3>Visitors Who Signed our Guestbook</h3>
 8: <%
 9: String id = request.getParameter("id");
10: boolean noSignatures = true;
11: try {
12:     String filename = application.getRealPath(id + ".gbf");
13:     FileReader file = new FileReader(filename);
14:     BufferedReader buff = new BufferedReader(file);
15:     boolean eof = false;
16:     while (!eof) {
17:         String entry = buff.readLine();
18:         if (entry == null)
19:             eof = true;
```

LISTING 27.6   continued

```
20:          else {
21:              StringTokenizer entryData = new StringTokenizer(entry, "^");
22:              String name = (String) entryData.nextElement();
23:              String email = (String) entryData.nextElement();
24:              String url = (String) entryData.nextElement();
25:              String entryDate = (String) entryData.nextElement();
26:              String ip = (String) entryData.nextElement();
27:              String comments = (String) entryData.nextElement();
28:              out.print("<p>From: " + name);
29:              if (!email.equals("None"))
30:                  out.println(" <" + email + "><br>");
31:              else
32:                  out.println("<br>");
33:              if (!url.equals("None"))
34:                  out.println("Home Page: <a href=\"" + url + "\">" + url +
    ➥"</a><br>");
35:              out.println("Date: " + entryDate + "<br>");
36:              out.println("IP: " + ip);
37:              out.println("<blockquote>");
38:              out.println("<p>" + comments);
39:              out.println("</blockquote>");
40:              noSignatures = false;
41:          }
42:      }
43:      buff.close();
44: } catch (IOException e) {
45:      out.println("<p>This guestbook could not be read because of an error.");
46:      log("Guestbook Error: " + e.toString());
47: }
48: if (noSignatures)
49:      out.println("<p>No one has signed our guestbook yet.");
50: %>
51: <h3>Sign Our Guestbook</h3>
52: <form method="POST" action="guestbookpost.jsp">
53:   <table border="0" cellpadding="5" cellspacing="0" width="100%">
54:     <tr>
55:       <td width="15%" valign="top" align="right">Your Name:</td>
56:       <td width="50%"><input type="text" name="name" size="40"></td>
57:     </tr>
58:     <tr>
59:       <td width="15%" valign="top" align="right">Your E-mail Address:</td>
60:       <td width="50%"><input type="text" name="email" size="40"></td>
61:     </tr>
62:     <tr>
63:       <td width="15%" valign="top" align="right">Your Home Page:</td>
64:       <td width="50%"><input type="text" name="url" size="40"></td>
65:     </tr>
66:     <tr>
67:       <td width="15%" valign="top" align="right">Your Comments:</td>
```

27

LISTING 27.6   continued

```
68:        <td width="50%"><textarea rows="6" name="comments" cols="40">
➥</textarea></td>
69:     </tr>
70:   </table>
71:   <p align="center"><input type="submit" value="Submit" name="B1">
72:   <input type="reset" value="Reset" name="Reset"></p>
73: <input type="hidden" name="id" value="<%= id %>">
74: </form>
75: </body>
76: </html>
```

After you save this page, store it in any folder on your Tomcat-equipped Web server where pages can be stored. You can test this out even before anything else in the project is done, as long as you have an empty guestbook file.

To create this file, save an empty text file on your system and give it the name `cinema.gbf`. Store it on the Web in the same folder as `guestbook.jsp`.

When you load this JavaServer Page, you must include a parameter that specifies the ID of the guestbook to load, as in this URL:

```
http://www.java21pro.com/guestbook.jsp?id=cinema
```

The server name and folder depends on where you have published `guestbook.jsp`.

Figure 27.5 shows what your guestbook should look like when your JavaServer Page compiles successfully and tries to display the contents of the `cinema.gbf` file.

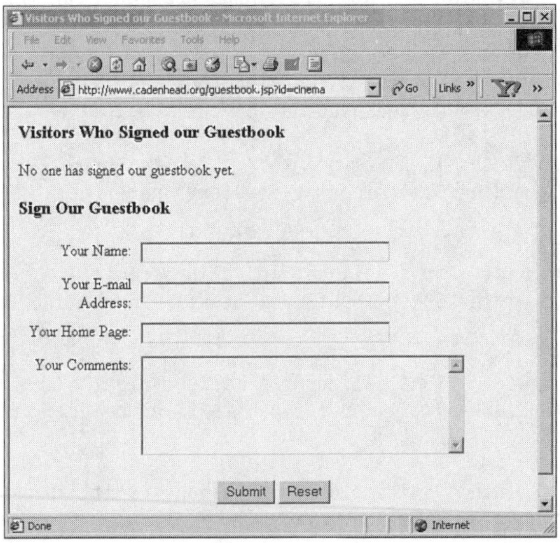

FIGURE 27.5

Testing the
`guestbook.jsp`
page.

The guestbook file stores each guestbook entry on its own line, with a caret (^) separating each field in the entry. The visitor can provide his name, e-mail address, home page address, and a comment. Two other things are saved for each entry: the date and time it was written and the IP address of the visitor.

The following text is an example of a guestbook file that contains two entries:

```
John Smith^jsmith@prefect.com^http://www.tvguide.com^Thu Feb 22
➥01:19:27 EST 2001^65.80.105.19^Your Web site is great.
D. James^deejay@naviseek.com^http://www.imdb.com^ Thu Feb
➥22 01:19:53 EST 2001^165.40.10.18^Thanks for the information.
```

The next JavaServer Page to create is guestbookpost.jsp, which updates the guestbook with new entries submitted by visitors. (See Listing 27.7.)

LISTING 27.7 The Full Text of guestbookpost.jsp

```
 1: <%@ page import="java.util.*,java.io.*" %>
 2: <html>
 3: <head>
 4: <title>Thank You For Signing Our Guestbook</title>
 5: </head>
 6: <body>
 7: <h3>Thank You For Signing Our Guestbook</h3>
 8: <%
 9: String id = request.getParameter("id");
10: String[] entryFields = { "name", "email", "url", "comments" };
11: String[] entry = new String[4];
12: for (int i = 0; i < entryFields.length; i++) {
13:     entry[i] = Guestbook.filterString(request.getParameter(entryFields[i]));
14: }
15: Date now = new Date();
16: String entryDate = now.toString();
17: String ip = request.getRemoteAddr();
18: %>
19:
20: <p>Your entry looks like this:
21: <p>From: <%= entry[0] %><%= (!entry[1].equals("None") ? "<"+entry[1]+">" :
➥"") %><br>
22: <% if (!entry[2].equals("None")) { %>
23: Home Page: <a href="<%= entry[2] %>"><%= entry[2] %></a><br>
24: <% } %>
25: Date: <%= entryDate %><br>
26: IP: <%= ip %>
27: <blockquote>
28: <p><%= entry[3] %>
29: </blockquote>
30:
31: <%
```

27

LISTING 27.7   continued

```
32: try {
33:     boolean append = true;
34:     String filename = application.getRealPath(id + ".gbf");
35:     FileWriter fw = new FileWriter(filename, append);
36:     BufferedWriter fileOut = new BufferedWriter(fw);
37:     String newEntry = entry[0] + "^" + entry[1] + "^" + entry[2] + "^"
38:         + entryDate + "^" + ip + "^" + entry[3];
39:     fileOut.write(newEntry, 0, newEntry.length());
40:     fileOut.newLine();
41:     fileOut.close();
42: } catch (IOException e) {
43:     out.println("<p>This guestbook could not be updated because of an
➡error.");
44:     log("Guestbook Error: " + e.toString());
45: }
46: %>
47:
48: <p><a href="guestbook.jsp?id=<%= id %>">View the Guestbook</a>
49: </body>
50:
51: </html>
```

The guestbookpost.jsp JavaServer Page collects data from a Web form, removes characters from the data that can't be put in the guestbook, and stores the result in a text file.

Each guestbook has its own file, with a name that begins with the ID parameter of the book and ends with the .gbf file extension. If the guestbook has an ID of cinema, the filename is cinema.gbf.

Like the other JavaServer Pages included in this Web application, guestbookpost.jsp can be stored in any folder on your Web server where HTML documents are kept. For this project, store the page in the same folder as guestbook.jsp and cinema.gbf.

Before you can try out the Guestbook application, you must create a Java class that will be used to filter some unwanted text out of guestbook entries before they're posted. There are three characters that cannot be included in the guestbook because of the way entries are stored in a file:

- The caret (^)
- Return characters, which have the integer value of 13 in Java
- Linefeed characters, which have the integer value of 10

To remove these characters before they're saved in a guestbook, a helper class called `Guestbook` will be created. This class has a static method called `filterString(String)` that removes those three characters from a string.

Listing 27.8 contains the source code for this class.

LISTING 27.8   The Full Text of `Guestbook.java`

```
 1: public class Guestbook {
 2:     public static String filterString(String input) {
 3:         input = replaceText(input, '^', ' ');
 4:         input = replaceText(input, (char)13, ' ');
 5:         input = replaceText(input, (char)10, ' ');
 6:         return input;
 7:     }
 8:
 9:     private static String replaceText(String inString, char oldChar,
10:         char newChar) {
11:
12:         while (inString.indexOf(oldChar) != -1) {
13:             int oldPosition = inString.indexOf(oldChar);
14:             StringBuffer data = new StringBuffer(inString);
15:             data.setCharAt(oldPosition, newChar);
16:             inString = data.toString();
17:         }
18:         return inString;
19:     }
20: }
```

The `replaceText()` method on lines 9-19 of Listing 27.8 does most of the work in the class. It takes three arguments:

- A string that might contain unwanted characters.
- A character that should be removed.
- A character that should be added in its place.

When you compile the `Guestbook` class, put it on your Web server in the same place where servlets are stored. On an Apache Web Server equipped with Tomcat, the folder is probably `/WEB-INF/classes` or `/htdocs/WEB-INF/classes`.

To test the `guestbookpost.jsp` server page, open up the page that displays guestbook entries using an `ID` parameter of `cinema` again, as in this example:

`http://www.java21pro.com/guestbook.jsp?id=cinema`

When you add an entry to the guestbook and click the Submit button, you should see a page resembling Figure 27.6.

27

FIGURE 27.6

Adding an entry to a guestbook.

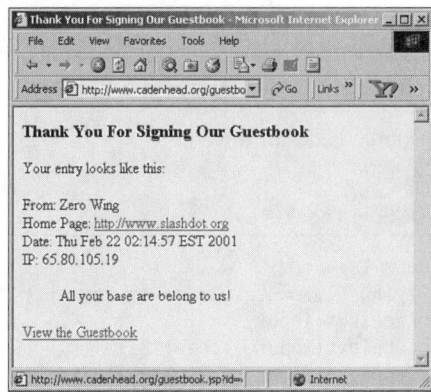

Go ahead and add a few guestbook entries to see how they're displayed in the guestbook. Figure 27.7 shows the finished product: a guestbook you can use on your own Web sites.

FIGURE 27.7

Using the guestbook Web application.

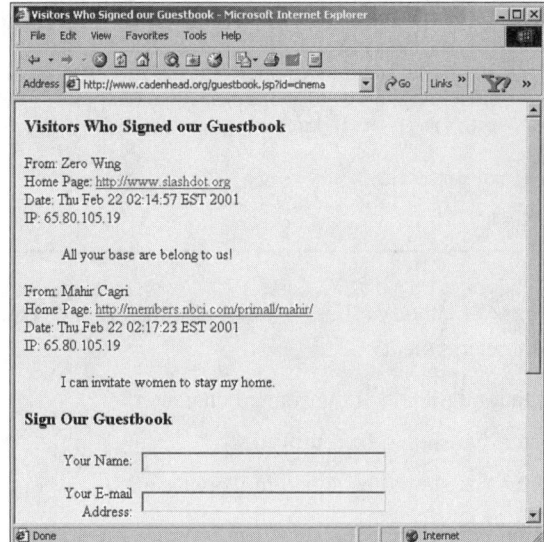

Summary

At this point, you now have three different ways to use the Java language on the World Wide Web: applets, servlets, and JavaServer Pages.

Assuming that you have a Web server that supports Tomcat, JavaServer Pages are the easiest way to put Java to work on your own Web sites. By using expressions, statements, and declarations, you can write Java programs on server pages without ever needing to compile a program, lay it out on a Web page, design an interface, or publish class files.

JavaServer Pages are an effective way to separate static content on Web pages from the dynamic content generated by servlets for those pages. This technique makes it easier to modify the text and presentation of a Web page without requiring changes to the servlet and other classes the page uses.

Q&A

Q Why do servlets and JavaServer Pages require the `getRealPath()` method to determine where a file is located on the Web server? Can't you store the file in the same folder as a servlet and use the filename without referring to a path?

A Tomcat doesn't support relative filenames inside servlets or JavaServer Pages. You must know the exact location of a file on the Web server in order to read or write data in the file. Since this information isn't always available to you in a live Web hosting environment, the `ServletContext` interface includes the `getRealPath()` method. This method asks the Web server for the full pathname of a file. One of the biggest advantages of using Tomcat over Common Gateway Interface scripts is that you can communicate directly with the server.

In the `counter.jsp` example earlier today, the `counter.dat` file was created in the same folder where `counter.jsp` is stored. Tomcat doesn't store files in the same folder as servlets.

Q I'm writing a Java Web application that uses the Java API for XML Processing. How can I make those classes available on a JavaServer Page?

A First, you have to install the classes of the Java API for XML Processing on your Web server. They should be stored in a subfolder of the main folder where servlets are published. For example, if that folder is `/htdocs/WEB-INF/classes`, the `javax.xml.parsers` package should be in `/htdocs/WEB-INF/classes/javax/xml/parsers`.

After installing all of the packages on your server, you can import them into your page with statements such as the following:

```
<%@ page import="javax.xml.parsers.*" %>
```

27

Quiz

Review today's material by taking this three-question quiz.

Questions

1. If you see a `request` variable on a JavaServer Page, what class in `javax.servlets.http` is it referring to?

    a. `HttpServletResponse`

    b. `HttpServletRequest`

    c. `ServletContext`

2. Which tools do you need on your computer to create a JavaServer Page?

    a. A Java interpreter and compiler

    b. A Java interpreter, compiler, and appletviewer

    c. None of the above

3. Which of the JavaServer Pages elements uses the `<%=` and `%>` tags?

    a. Declarations

    b. Expressions

    c. Statements

Answers

1. b. `HttpServletRequest`
2. c. All you need is a text editor. When you publish the page, Tomcat will compile it into a servlet and then run the program.
3. b. The expression inside the tags will be evaluated and its value will be displayed on the page at the expression's location.

Exercises

To extend your knowledge of the subjects covered today, try the following exercises:

- Create a version of yesterday's `SetColor` servlet that uses JavaServer Pages instead of a servlet.
- Write a JavaServer Page that displays one greeting for Internet Explorer users and another greeting for everyone else.

Where applicable, exercise solutions are offered on the book's Web site at `http://www.java21pro.com`.

BONUS WEEK

DAY **28**

Reading XML Files

One of the main selling points of Java is that it produces programs that can run on different operating systems without modification. This portability is a big convenience in today's computing environment, where Windows, Linux, MacOS, and a half-dozen other operating systems are in wide use and many people work with multiple systems.

About 18 months after Java was introduced, a portable standard for data was introduced: XML, which stands for Extensible Markup Language. XML makes data completely portable. It can be read and written by different software on different operating systems without compatibility problems.

Today, you'll explore XML and learn about the following features of this markup language:

- How to represent data as XML
- Why XML is a useful way to store data
- How to use XML to create a new data format
- How to document the elements of your new format
- How to read XML data using Java

Using XML

XML is a format for storing and organizing data that's independent of any software program that works with the data. Data that's compliant with XML is easier to reuse for several reasons.

First, the data is structured in a standard way, making it possible for software programs to read and write the data as long as they support XML. If you create an XML file that represents your company's employee database, there are several dozen XML parsers that can read the file and make sense of its contents.

This is true no matter what kind of information you collect about each employee. If your database contains only the employee's name, ID number, and current salary, XML parsers can read it. If it contains 25 different items, including birthday, blood type, and hair color, parsers can read that too.

Second, the data is self-documenting, making it easier for people to understand the purpose of a file just by looking at it in a text editor. Anyone who opens your XML employee database should be able to figure out the structure and content of each employee record without any assistance from you.

This is evident in Listing 28.1, which contains an XML file.

LISTING 28.1   The Full Text of `collection.librml`

```
 1: <?xml version="1.0"?>
 2: <!DOCTYPE Library SYSTEM "librml.dtd">
 3: <Library>
 4:    <Book>
 5:        <Author>Joseph Heller</Author>
 6:        <Title>Catch-22</Title>
 7:        <PublicationDate edition="Trade" isbn="0684833395">09/1996
➥</PublicationDate>
 8:        <Publisher>Simon and Schuster</Publisher>
 9:        <Subject>Fiction</Subject>
10:        <Review>heller-catch22.html</Review>
11:    </Book>
12:    <Book>
13:        <Author>Kurt Vonnegut</Author>
14:        <Title>Slaughterhouse-Five</Title>
15:        <PublicationDate edition="Paperback" isbn="0440180295">12/1991
➥</PublicationDate>
16:        <Publisher>Dell</Publisher>
17:        <Subject>Fiction</Subject>
18:    </Book>
19: </Library>
```

Enter this text using a word processor or text editor and save it as plain text under the name `collection.librml`. (You can also download a copy of it from the book's Web site at `http://www.java21pro.com` on the Day 28 page.)

Can you tell what the data represents? Although the `?xml` and `!DOCTYPE` tags at the top may be indecipherable, the rest is clearly a book database of some kind.

The `?xml` tag in the first line of the file has an attribute called `version` that has a value of 1.0. All XML files must begin with an `?xml` tag like this.

Data in XML is surrounded by tag elements that describe the data. Start tags begin with a < character followed by the name of the tag and a > character. End tags begin with the `</` characters followed by a name and a > character. In Listing 28.1, for example, `<Book>` on line 12 is a start tag and `</Book>` on line 18 is an end tag. Everything within those tags is considered to be the value of that element.

Tags can be nested within other tags, creating a hierarchy of XML data that establishes relationships within that data. In Listing 28.1, everything in lines 13-17 is related—each tag defines something about the same book.

XML also supports tag elements that are defined by a single tag rather than a pair of tags. These tags begin with a < character followed by the name of the tag and the `/>` characters. For example, the book database could include a `<outOfPrint/>` tag that indicates a book isn't presently available for sale.

Tag elements also can include attributes, which are made up of extra data that supplements the rest of the data associated with the tag. Attributes are defined within a start tag element. The name of an attribute is followed by an equal sign and text within quotation marks. In line 7 of Listing 28.1, the `PublicationDate` tag includes two attributes: `edition`, which has a value of `"Trade"`, and `isbn`, which has a value of `"0684833395"`.

XML encourages the creation of data that's understandable and usable even if the user doesn't have the program that created it and cannot find any documentation that describes it.

By insisting upon well-formed markup, XML simplifies the task of writing programs that work with the data.

One of the major motivations behind the development of XML in 1996 was the inconsistency of HTML. It's a wildly popular way to organize data for presentation to users, but Web browsers have always been designed to allow for inconsistent use of HTML tags. Web page designers can break numerous rules of valid HTML, as it's defined by the World Wide Web Consortium, and their work still loads normally into a browser such as Netscape Navigator. Millions of people are putting content on the Web without paying

28

any heed to valid HTML at all. They test their content to make sure that it's viewable in Web browsers, but they don't worry whether it's structured according to all of the rules of HTML.

> **Note**
>
> The World Wide Web Consortium, founded by Web inventor Tim Berners-Lee, is the group that developed HTML and maintains the standard version of the language. You can find out more from the consortium Web site at http://www.w3.org. If you'd like to validate a Web page to see whether it follows all the rules of standard HTML, visit http://validator.w3.org.

There's strong demand on the World Wide Web for software that collects data from Web pages and interacts with services offered over the Internet, such as e-commerce shopping agents that collect price and availability data from online stores, enabling customers to do price comparisons. The developers of services like this quickly run into the inconsistency in how HTML is used to organize Web content. Even if you can write software that puzzles through the markup tags on a page to extract information, any changes to the site's design can stop your program from working correctly.

Designing an XML Dialect

Although XML is described as a language and is compared to HTML, it's actually much larger in scope than that. XML is a markup language that defines how to define a markup language.

That's an odd distinction to make, and it sounds like the kind of thing you'd encounter in a philosophy textbook. This concept is important to understand, though, because it explains how XML can be used to define data as varied as health care claims, genealogical records, newspaper articles, and molecules.

The "X" in XML stands for Extensible, and it refers to organizing data for your own purposes. Data that's organized using the rules of XML can represent anything you like:

- A programmer at a telemarketing company can use XML to store data on each outgoing call, saving the time of the call, the number, the operator who made the call, and the result.
- A hobbyist can use XML to keep track of the annoying telemarketing calls she receives, noting the time of the call, the company, and the product being peddled.
- A programmer at a government agency can use XML to track complaints about telemarketers, saving the name of the marketing firm and the number of complaints.

Each of these examples uses XML to define a new language that suits a specific purpose. Although you could call them XML languages, they're more commonly described as XML dialects or XML document types.

When a new XML dialect is created, the formal way to document it is to create a document type definition (DTD). This determines the rules that the data must follow to be considered well-formed in that dialect.

Listing 28.2 contains the DTD for the book database listed earlier.

LISTING 28.2   The Full Text of `librml.dtd`

```
1: <!ELEMENT Library (Book?)+ >
2: <!ELEMENT Book (Author?, Title, PublicationDate?, Publisher?, Subject?,
➥Review?)* >
3: <!ELEMENT Author (#PCDATA)>
4: <!ELEMENT Title (#PCDATA)>
5: <!ELEMENT PublicationDate (#PCDATA)>
6: <!ATTLIST PublicationDate edition CDATA "" isbn CDATA "">
7: <!ELEMENT Publisher (#PCDATA)>
8: <!ELEMENT Subject (#PCDATA)>
9: <!ELEMENT Review (#PCDATA)>
```

In Listing 28.1, the XML file contained the following line:

```
<!DOCTYPE Library SYSTEM "librml.dtd">
```

The `!DOCTYPE` tag is used to identify the DTD that applies to the data. When a DTD is present, many XML tools can read XML created for that DTD and determine if the data follows all the rules correctly. If it doesn't, it will be rejected with a reference to the line that caused the error. This process is called *validating the XML*.

One thing you'll run into as you work with XML is data that has been structured as XML but wasn't defined using a DTD. This data can be parsed (presuming it's well-formed), so you can read it into a program and do something with it, but you can't check its validity to make sure it's organized correctly according to the rules of its dialect.

Tip

> To get an idea of what kind of XML dialects have been created, visit the Schema.Net Web site at http://www.schema.net. It includes a directory of XML dialects covering science, commerce, multimedia, the Internet, and many other subjects.

28

Processing XML with Java

Sun Microsystems has announced plans to support XML as a standard part of the Java class library, but this hasn't taken place yet at the time of this writing.

Sun supports XML through the Java Application Programming Interface for XML Processing, a set of Java classes for reading, writing, and manipulating XML data currently in version 1.1. To find out more about these classes and download them from Sun's Web site, visit `http://java.sun.com/xml/`.

At present, the Java API for XML Processing is available as three class libraries that are packaged in JAR files: `crimson.jar`, `jaxp.jar`, and `xalan.jar`. There also are sample XML files, example programs, and Web pages documenting the classes in the API.

Follow the instructions for downloading and installing the API, making sure to modify your system's CLASSPATH setting to include references to any JAR files that it includes. The interpreter and compiler require the CLASSPATH to include references to the XML Processing API's JAR files.

The Java API for XML Processing includes nine packages:

- `javax.xml.parsers`
- `javax.xml.transform`
- `javax.xml.transform.dom`
- `javax.xml.transform.sax`
- `javax.xml.transform.stream`
- `org.w3c.dom`
- `org.xml.sax`
- `org.xml.sax.ent`
- `org.xml.sax.helpers`

The `javax.xml.parsers` package is the entry point to all the other packages. You can use the classes of this package to parse and validate XML data using two different techniques: the Simple API for XML (SAX) and the Document Object Model (DOM).

Before getting too bogged down in any more TLAs (three-letter acronyms), let's look at how to use SAX with the `javax.xml.parsers` package and see XML parsing in action.

Reading an XML File

As you learned on Day 17, "Handling Data Through Java Streams," in order to read a file from disk in Java, you must set up a series of stream or reader objects that work in conjunction with each other. For instance, to read a buffered stream of bytes from a file, a

`File` object is used to create a `FileInputStream` object, which is then used to create a `BufferedInputStream`.

Parsing an XML file using SAX and the `javax.xml.parsers` package requires the same kind of relationship between classes. First, you create a `SAXParserFactory` object by calling the class method `SAXParserFactory.newInstance()`, as in this statement:

```
SAXParserFactory factory = SAXParserFactory.newInstance();
```

The purpose of a SAX parser factory is to create a SAX parser according to your specifications. One specification is whether or not the SAX parser should validate XML with a DTD. To support validation, call the parser factory's `setValidating(Boolean)` method with an argument of `true`:

```
factory.setValidating(true);
```

After you've set up the factory to produce the parser you want, call the factory's `newSaxParser()` method to create a `SAXParser` object:

```
SAXParser sax = factory.newSAXParser();
```

This method generates a `ParserConfigurationException` if the factory cannot create a parser that meets your specifications, so you must deal with it in a `try-catch` block or a `throws` statement in the method where `newSAXParser()` is called.

The SAX parser can read XML data from files, input streams, and other sources. To read from a file, the parser's `parse(File, DefaultHandler)` method is called. This method throws two kinds of exceptions: `IOException` if an error occurs as the file is being read; and `SAXException` if the SAX parser runs into some kind of problem parsing data.

`SAXException` is a class in the `org.xml.sax` package, one of three packages created by the XML industry group XML.Org that's included in the Java API for XML Processing. This exception is the superclass of all SAX exceptions, and you can call the exception object's `getMessage()` method in a `catch` block to display more information about the specific problem that triggered the exception.

The second argument to the `parse()` method is an object of the class `DefaultHandler`, part of the `org.xml.sax.helpers` package. The `DefaultHandler` class is a do-nothing class that implements four interfaces of the `org.xml.sax` package: `ContentHandler`, `DTDHandler`, `EntityResolver`, and `ErrorHandler`. These four interfaces are implemented by classes that want to be notified of specific events that occur as the `parse()` method reads XML data.

28

To implement all of these interfaces, the DefaultHandler class includes the following methods:

- startDocument()—The parser has reached the beginning of XML data.
- endDocument()—The parser has reached the end of XML data.
- startElement(*String*, *String*, *String*, *Attributes*)—The parser has read a start tag element.
- characters(*char[]*, *int*, *int*)—The parser has read character data located between a start tag and an end tag.
- endElement(*String*, *String*, *String*)—The parser has read an end tag element.

Each of these methods throws SAXException exceptions.

In order to do something with XML data that's being parsed, you create a subclass of DefaultHandler that overrides the methods you want to deal with.

Counting XML Tags

Listing 28.3 contains CountTag, a Java application that counts the number of times a starting tag element appears in an XML file. You specify the filename and tag as command-line arguments, so it can work with any XML file you'd like to inspect.

LISTING 28.3   The Full Text of CountTag.java

```
 1: import javax.xml.parsers.*;
 2: import org.xml.sax.*;
 3: import org.xml.sax.helpers.*;
 4: import java.io.*;
 5:
 6: public class CountTag extends DefaultHandler {
 7:
 8:     public static void main(String[] arguments) {
 9:         if (arguments.length > 1) {
10:             CountTag ct = new CountTag(arguments[0], arguments[1]);
11:         } else {
12:             System.out.println("Usage: java CountTag filename tagName");
13:         }
14:     }
15:
16:     CountTag(String xmlFile, String tagName) {
17:         File input = new File(xmlFile);
18:         SAXParserFactory factory = SAXParserFactory.newInstance();
19:         factory.setValidating(false);
20:         try {
```

LISTING 28.3   continued

```
21:                    SAXParser sax = factory.newSAXParser();
22:                    CountTagHandler cth = new CountTagHandler(tagName);
23:                    sax.parse(input, cth);
24:                    System.out.println("The " + cth.tag + " tag appears "
25:                        + cth.count + " times.");
26:                } catch (ParserConfigurationException pce) {
27:                    System.out.println("Could not create that parser.");
28:                    System.out.println(pce.getMessage());
29:                } catch (SAXException se) {
30:                    System.out.println("Problem with the SAX parser.");
31:                    System.out.println(se.getMessage());
32:                } catch (IOException ioe) {
33:                    System.out.println("Error reading file.");
34:                    System.out.println(ioe.getMessage());
35:                }
36:        }
37: }
38:
39: class CountTagHandler extends DefaultHandler {
40:     String tag;
41:     int count = 0;
42:
43:     CountTagHandler(String tagName) {
44:         super();
45:         tag = tagName;
46:     }
47:
48:     public void startElement(String uri, String localName,
49:         String qName, Attributes attributes) {
50:
51:         if (localName.equals(tag))
52:             count++;
53:     }
54: }
```

Two classes are defined in Listing 28.3: CountTag, which creates a SAX parser and tells it to parse a File object, and CountTagHandler, which counts tags.

This application includes a helper class, CountTagHandler, which is a subclass of DefaultHandler. To count the number of times a start tag appears in an XML file, the startElement(*String, String, String, Attributes*) method is overridden.

When a SAX parser calls startElement(), the arguments to the method provide information about the tag:

- The first argument is the tag's Uniform Resource Indicator (URI).
- The second argument is the tag's qualified name.

28

- The third argument is the tag's local name.
- The fourth argument is an `Attributes` object that contains information about the attributes associated with a tag.

A tag's URI and qualified name refer to XML namespaces, which currently aren't supported in the Java API for XML Processing. Namespaces make it possible to identify XML tags and attributes in a way that's globally unique across the Internet, preventing two different tags from being accessible using the same URI and qualified name.

The only name that the `CountTagHandler` class looks for is the local name of a tag. In an XML file that doesn't use namespaces, the local name is the text that falls between the < and > characters on the tag.

If `CountTag.class` is in the same folder as `collection.librml`, you can run it with the following command:

```
java CountTag collection.librml Book
```

The output of this application should be the following:

```
The Book tag appears 2 times.
```

The `CountTag` application uses a non-validating parser, so you can try it with any XML file stored on your system. If you'd like to test it with a longer file, the Day 28 page of this book's Web site at `http://www.java21pro.com` includes the file `history.opml`.

 Note   Outliner Processor Markup Language (OPML) is an XML dialect created by UserLand Software to represent information that's stored as an outline. You can find out more about this dialect at `http://www.opml.org`.

Reading XML Data

As you work with a subclass of `DefaultHandler`, you can keep track of start tags by overriding the `startElement()` method. When a parser detects a start tag, you don't know anything about the data that follows the tag. If you're trying to extract data from an XML file, you must override a few more methods inherited from `DefaultHandler`.

Retrieving data from an XML tag is a three-step process:

1. Override the `startElement()` method to find out when a new start tag is parsed.
2. Override the `characters()` method to find out what a tag contains.
3. Override the `endElement()` method to find out when an end tag is reached.

A parser calls the characters(*char[]*, *int*, *int*) method when a tag contains character data—in other words, text. The first argument is an array of characters that holds the
data.

You don't use this entire character array, however. The data within the tag is contained in
a portion of the array. The second argument to characters() indicates the first element
of the array to read data from, and the third argument indicates the number of characters
to read.

The following character() method uses character data to create a String object and
then displays it:

```
public void characters(char[] text, int first, int length) {
    String data = new String(text, first, length);
    System.out.println(data);
}
```

A parser calls the endElement(*String*, *String*, *String*) method when an end tag is
reached. The three arguments to this method are the same as the first three arguments of
the startElement() method—the URI, qualified name, and local name of the tag.

The SAX parser doesn't consider </ or > to be a part of a tag's name. If the parser reads
an end tag called </Source>, it will call the endElement() method with Source as its
third argument.

The last two methods you may want to override in a DefaultHandler subclass are
startDocument() and endDocument(), which don't have any arguments.

Validating XML Data

Today's last project is ReadLibrary, a Java application that reads the XML file created
with the dialect introduced earlier today—the book database format used in the file
collection.librml and defined in the file librml.dtd.

Because a DTD is available for this dialect, the SAX parser you create with a
SAXParserFactory object should be validating. This is accomplished by calling the factory's setValidating(*Boolean*) method with an argument of true.

Caution   Support for validating parsers is still in early development as of version 1.1
of the Java API for XML Processing. The SAX parser you use in this project
may not validate, but that won't stop the application from running successfully and producing the desired output.

28

The ReadLibrary project is organized in much the same way as the last project—there's a main application class called ReadLibrary.class, a helper called LibraryHandler.class, and a helper class called Book.class.

The ReadLibrary class loads a file specified by a command-line argument, creates a SAX parser, and tells it to parse the file.

The LibraryHandler class, a subclass of DefaultHandler, contains the methods that keep track of what the parser is doing and take actions at different steps of the XML-parsing process.

When you're reading XML data using SAX, the characters() method needs to know the last start tag read by the parser. Otherwise, there's no way to find out which tag contains the data. To keep track of this, the LibraryHandler class has an instance variable called currentActivity that stores the current parsing activity as an integer value.

The integer value assigned to currentActivity will be one of seven class variables, which are set up in the following statements:

```
static int READING_TITLE = 1;
static int READING_AUTHOR = 2;
static int READING_PUBLISHER = 3;
static int READING_PUBLICATION_DATE = 4;
static int READING_SUBJECT = 5;
static int READING_REVIEW = 6;
static int READING_NOTHING = 0;
```

Using class variables for integer values makes the class easier for a programmer to understand and minimizes the chance that incorrect values will be used in a statement.

The LibraryHandler class also has a variable called libraryBook that's an instance of the Book class. Here are the statements that make up that class:

```
class Book {
    String title;
    String author;
    String publisher;
    String publicationDate;
    String edition;
    String isbn;
    String subject;
    String review;
}
```

The Book class is used to hold the different elements of each library book as they're read from an XML file.

Inside the `startElement()` method, a tag's local name is stored in the `localName` variable. The following statement is used in the method:

```
if (localName.equals("Title"))
    currentActivity = READING_TITLE;
```

This statement sets the `currentActivity` variable to the value of the class variable `READING_TITLE` when the SAX parser encounters the `<Title>` tag.

When character data has been received in the `characters()` method, the `currentActivity` variable is used to figure out which tag contains the data. The following statements appear in the method:

```
String value = new String(ch, start, length);
if (currentActivity == READING_TITLE)
    libraryBook.title = value;
```

The first statement creates a string called `value` that contains the character data within the tag. If the parser currently is reading the title tag, `value` is assigned to the `libraryBook` object's `title` variable.

The last thing that you must set up in the `LibraryHandler` class is displaying the information about each book when all of its XML data has been parsed. This takes place in the `endElement()` method, which stores each ending tag's local name in a variable called `localName`. When `localName` is equal to `"Book"`, the parser has reached the `</BOOK>` tag in the XML file. This tag signifies that no more information about the current book has been defined.

The following statement appears in the method:

```
if (localName.equals("Book"))
System.out.println("\nTitle: " + libraryBook.title);
```

Listing 28.4 contains the full source code of the `ReadLibrary` application.

LISTING 28.4   The Full Text of `ReadLibrary.java`

```
 1: import javax.xml.parsers.*;
 2: import org.xml.sax.*;
 3: import org.xml.sax.helpers.*;
 4: import java.io.*;
 5:
 6: public class ReadLibrary extends DefaultHandler {
 7:
 8:     public static void main(String[] arguments) {
 9:         if (arguments.length > 0) {
10:             ReadLibrary read = new ReadLibrary(arguments[0]);
11:         } else {
```

28

LISTING 28.4   continued

```
12:                    System.out.println("Usage: java ReadLibrary filename");
13:            }
14:        }
15:
16:    ReadLibrary(String libFile) {
17:        File input = new File(libFile);
18:        SAXParserFactory factory = SAXParserFactory.newInstance();
19:        factory.setValidating(true);
20:        try {
21:            SAXParser sax = factory.newSAXParser();
22:            sax.parse(input, new LibraryHandler() );
23:        } catch (ParserConfigurationException pce) {
24:            System.out.println("Could not create that parser.");
25:            System.out.println(pce.getMessage());
26:        } catch (SAXException se) {
27:            System.out.println("Problem with the SAX parser.");
28:            System.out.println(se.getMessage());
29:        } catch (IOException ioe) {
30:            System.out.println("Error reading file.");
31:            System.out.println(ioe.getMessage());
32:        }
33:    }
34: }
35:
36: class LibraryHandler extends DefaultHandler {
37:    static int READING_TITLE = 1;
38:    static int READING_AUTHOR = 2;
39:    static int READING_PUBLISHER = 3;
40:    static int READING_PUBLICATION_DATE = 4;
41:    static int READING_SUBJECT = 5;
42:    static int READING_REVIEW = 6;
43:    static int READING_NOTHING = 0;
44:    int currentActivity = READING_NOTHING;
45:    Book libraryBook = new Book();
46:
47:    LibraryHandler() {
48:        super();
49:    }
50:
51:    public void startElement(String uri, String localName,
52:        String qName, Attributes attributes) {
53:
54:        if (localName.equals("Title"))
55:            currentActivity = READING_TITLE;
56:        else if (localName.equals("Author"))
57:            currentActivity = READING_AUTHOR;
58:        else if (localName.equals("Publisher"))
59:            currentActivity = READING_PUBLISHER;
```

LISTING 28.4   continued

```
 60:            else if (localName.equals("PublicationDate"))
 61:                currentActivity = READING_PUBLICATION_DATE;
 62:            else if (localName.equals("Subject"))
 63:                currentActivity = READING_SUBJECT;
 64:            else if (localName.equals("Review"))
 65:                currentActivity = READING_REVIEW;
 66:
 67:            if (currentActivity == READING_PUBLICATION_DATE) {
 68:                libraryBook.isbn = attributes.getValue("isbn");
 69:                libraryBook.edition = attributes.getValue("edition");
 70:            }
 71:        }
 72:
 73:    public void characters(char[] ch, int start, int length) {
 74:        String value = new String(ch, start, length);
 75:        if (currentActivity == READING_TITLE)
 76:            libraryBook.title = value;
 77:        if (currentActivity == READING_AUTHOR)
 78:            libraryBook.author = value;
 79:        if (currentActivity == READING_PUBLISHER)
 80:            libraryBook.publisher = value;
 81:        if (currentActivity == READING_PUBLICATION_DATE)
 82:            libraryBook.publicationDate = value;
 83:        if (currentActivity == READING_SUBJECT)
 84:            libraryBook.subject = value;
 85:        if (currentActivity == READING_REVIEW)
 86:            libraryBook.review = value;
 87:    }
 88:
 89:    public void endElement(String uri, String localName, String qName) {
 90:        if (localName.equals("Book")) {
 91:            System.out.println("\nTitle: " + libraryBook.title);
 92:            System.out.println("Author: " + libraryBook.author);
 93:            System.out.println("Publisher: " + libraryBook.publisher);
 94:            System.out.println("Publication Date: "
 95:                + libraryBook.publicationDate);
 96:            System.out.println("Edition: " + libraryBook.edition);
 97:            System.out.println("ISBN: " + libraryBook.isbn);
 98:            System.out.println("Review: " + libraryBook.review);
 99:            libraryBook = new Book();
100:        }
101:    }
102: }
103:
104: class Book {
105:     String title;
106:     String author;
```

28

LISTING 28.4   continued

```
107:        String publisher;
108:        String publicationDate;
109:        String edition;
110:        String isbn;
111:        String subject;
112:        String review;
113: }
```

The ReadLibrary application reads an XML file that uses the library book dialect shown in Listings 28.1 and 28.2. To read the collection.librml file with the application, type the following at a command line:

```
java ReadLibrary collection.librml
```

The program will display the following output:

```
Title: Catch-22
Author: Joseph Heller
Publisher: Simon and Schuster
Publication Date: 09/1996
Edition: Trade
ISBN: 0684833395
Review: heller-catch22.html

Title: Slaughterhouse-Five
Author: Kurt Vonnegut
Publisher: Dell
Publication Date: 12/1991
Edition: Paperback
ISBN: 0440180295
Review: null
```

Summary

In many ways, XML is the data equivalent of the Java language. It liberates data from the software used to create it and the operating system that the software ran on, just as Java can liberate software from a particular operating system.

Today, you learned the basics of XML and how to use the Java API for XML Processing to retrieve data from an XML file. Writing XML data in Java doesn't require this API. You can create XML files simply by writing strings to a file, an output stream, or another medium.

One of the biggest advantages to representing data using XML is that you'll always be able to get that data back. If you decide to move the data into a relational database, a MySQL database, or some other form, you can retrieve the information easily.

You also can transform XML into other forms (such as HTML) with a variety of technologies, both in Java and through tools developed in other languages.

Q&A

Q Why is Extensible Markup Language called XML instead of EML?

A None of the founders of the language appears to have documented the reason for choosing XML as the acronym. The general consensus in the XML community is that it was chosen because it "sounds cooler" than EML. Before you snicker at that distinction, Sun Microsystems used the same criteria when it chose the name Java for its programming language, turning down more technical-sounding alternatives such as DNA and WRL.

Also, it's possible that the founders of XML were trying to avoid confusion with an earlier programming language called EML (Extended Machine Language).

Quiz

Review today's material by taking this three-question quiz.

Questions

1. When all the start element tags, end element tags, and other markup is applied consistently in a document, what adjective best describes that document?

   a. Validating

   b. Parsable

   c. Well-formed

2. What class in the `javax.xml.parsers` package is used to create SAX parsers?

   a. `SAXParserFactory`

   b. `SAXParser`

   c. `DefaultHandler`

3. Which of the following would be an acceptable end element tag in XML?

   a. `</Category>`

   b. `<Category/>`

   c. `<Category>`

28

Answers

1. c. In order for data to be considered XML, it must be well-formed.

2. a. The SAXParserFactory class is used to create a SAX parser according to your specifications.

3. a. Every end element tag must be a name surrounded by the characters </ and >. (<Category/> would be acceptable only as an element tag that doesn't surround any data.)

Exercises

To extend your knowledge of the subjects covered today, try the following exercises:

- Create an XML file that holds the trivia questions and answers used in the TriviaServer project from Day 19, "Communicating Across the Internet."

- Create a modified version of TriviaServer that loads trivia questions and answers from that XML file.

Where applicable, exercise solutions are offered on the book's Web site at http://www.java21pro.com.

Appendixes

A

B

APPENDIX **A**

Configuring the Software Development Kit

Java 2 Software Development Kit 1.3 (SDK 1.3) is a set of command-line utilities that are used to create, compile, and run Java programs.

This appendix covers two things that can throw new Java users for a loop:

- How to use the command line.
- How to fix any SDK configuration errors that might occur.

If you haven't installed the SDK yet, you should do so before reading this appendix. That topic is covered during Day 1, "21st Century Java."

The following material is primarily focused on Windows because different Windows operating systems can handle the SDK differently.

Using a Command-Line Interface

The Java Software Development Kit requires you to use the command line to compile Java programs, run them, and handle other tasks. The command line is a way to operate your computer entirely by typing commands at your keyboard, rather than using your mouse.

Very few programs designed for today's Windows users require the command line. To use a command line on a Windows system, you need to do the following:

- In Windows 95 or 98, click the Start button, choose Programs, and then click MS-DOS Prompt (see Figure A.1).

- In Windows NT, click the Start button, choose Programs, and then click Command Prompt.

- In Windows 2000, click the Start button, choose Programs, choose Accessories, and then click Command Prompt (see Figure A.2).

- In Windows Me, click the Start button, choose Programs, choose Accessories, and then click MS-DOS Prompt.

FIGURE A.1

Finding a command line from the Windows 95 or 98 taskbar.

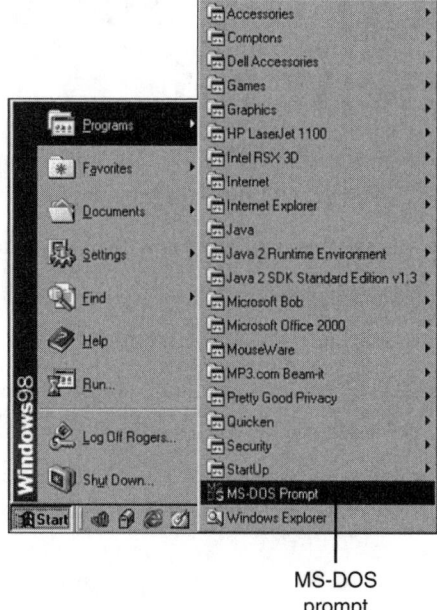

MS-DOS
prompt

FIGURE A.2

Finding a command line from the Windows 2000 taskbar.

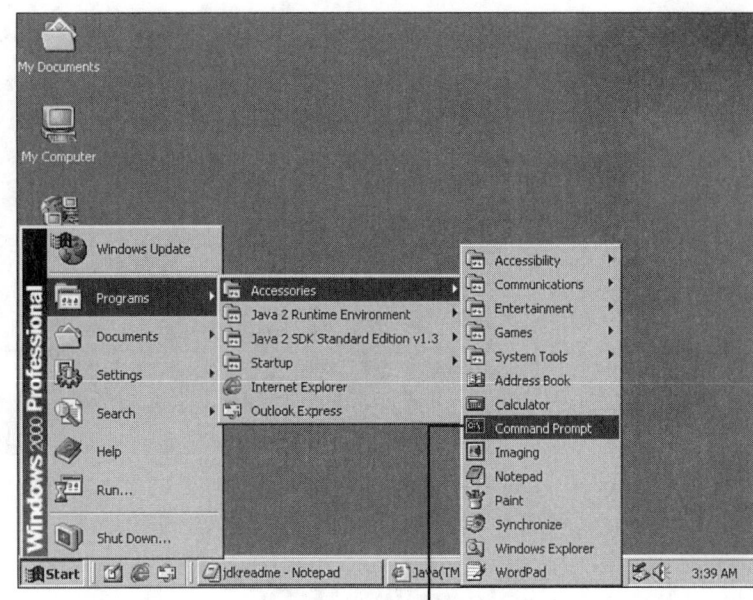

Command Prompt

The command line in Windows uses MS-DOS, the Microsoft operating system that preceded Windows. MS-DOS supports all the same basic functions as Windows—copying, moving, and deleting files and folders, running programs, scanning and repairing a hard drive, formatting a floppy disk, and so on.

Figure A.3 shows what the MS-DOS window looks like when it first opens.

In the MS-DOS window, a cursor will blink on the command line when MS-DOS is ready for you to type in a new command. In Figure A.3, `C:\WINDOWS>` is the command line.

Because MS-DOS can be used to delete files and even format your hard drive, you should learn something about this operating system before experimenting with its commands. One DOS book to consider is *Using MS-DOS 6.22, Second Edition*, published by Que.

However, you only need to know a few things about MS-DOS to use the Software Development Kit: how to create a folder, how to open a folder, and how to run a program.

Figure A.3

Using an MS-DOS window.

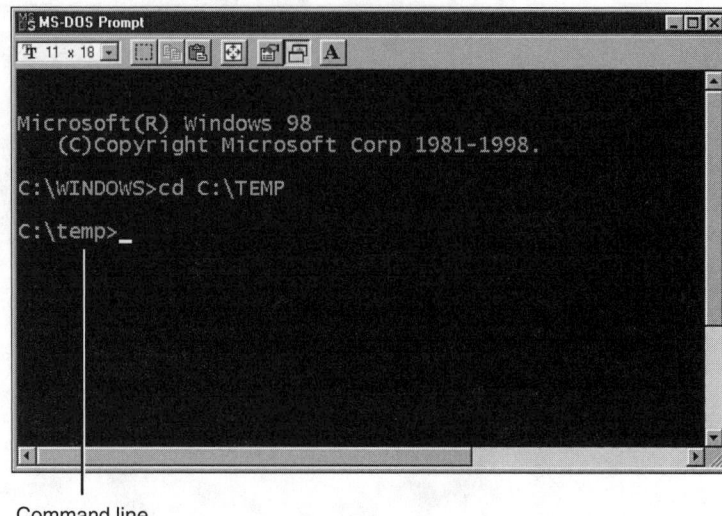

Command line

Opening Folders in MS-DOS

When you're using MS-DOS on a Windows system, you'll have access to all of the folders you normally use in Windows. For example, if you have a Windows folder on your C: hard drive, the same folder is accessible as C:\Windows from an MS-DOS Prompt.

To open a folder in MS-DOS, type the command CD followed by the name of the folder and press Enter, such as in the following example:

CD C:\TEMP

When you enter this command, the TEMP folder on your system's C: drive will be opened (if it exists). After you open a folder, your command line will be updated with the name of that folder, as shown in Figure A.4.

You also can use the CD command in other ways:

- CD \—Opens the root folder on the current hard drive.
- CD *subfoldername*—Opens a subfolder matching the name you've used in place of *subfoldername*, if that subfolder exists.
- CD ..—Opens the folder that contains the current folder. For example, if you're in C:\Windows\Cookies and you use the CD .. command, C:\Windows will be opened.

FIGURE A.4

Opening a folder at a command line.

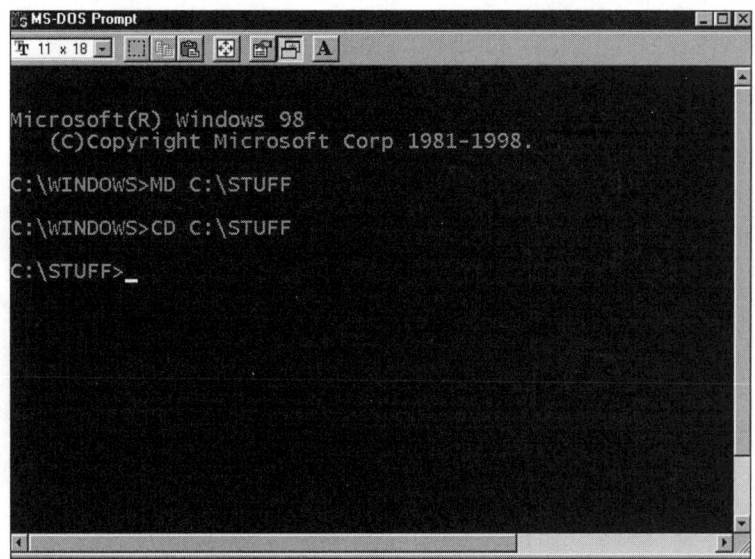

One of the suggestions in Day 1, "21st Century Java," is to create a folder called J21work so you have a place to edit, compile, and run the Java programs covered in each hour. If you've already done this, you can switch to that folder by using the following commands:

- CD \
- CD J21work

If you haven't created that folder yet, you can accomplish this task within MS-DOS.

Note

The CD command stands for "change directory." A directory is the same thing as a file folder. In the next section you'll work with MD, which stands for "make directory."

Creating Folders in MS-DOS

To create a folder from a command line, type the MD command followed by the name of the folder, as in the following example:

MD C:\STUFF

Then press Enter. The STUFF folder will be created in the root folder of the system's C: drive. To open a newly created folder, use the CD command followed by that folder's name, as shown in Figure A.5.

FIGURE A.5

Creating a new folder at a command line.

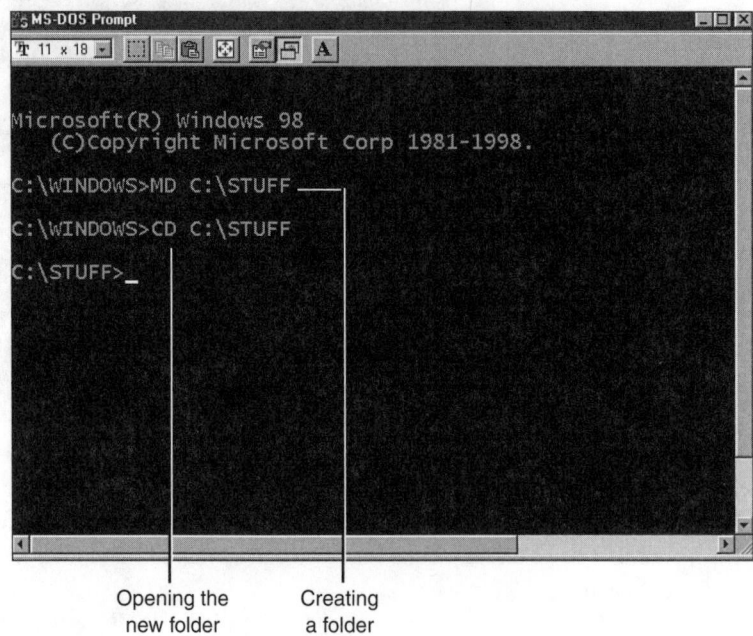

Opening the   Creating
new folder   a folder

This book recommends creating a J21work folder where you can do all your Java-related work. If you haven't already done this within Windows, you can do it from a command line:

1. Change to the root folder (using the CD \ command).
2. Type the MD J21work command and press Enter.

After you've created the J21work folder, you can go to it at any time from a command line by using the CD \J21work command.

The last thing you need to learn about MS-DOS so you can use the Software Development Kit is how to run programs.

Running Programs in MS-DOS

The simplest way to run a program at a command line is to type its name and press Enter. For example, type DIR and press Enter to see a list of files and subfolders in the current folder.

Also, you can run a program by typing its name followed by a space and some options that control how the program runs. These options are called *arguments.*

To see an example of this, change to the root folder (using CD \) and type DIR J21work. You'll see a list of files and subfolders contained in the J21work folder, if it contains any.

After you've installed the Software Development Kit, you should run the Java interpreter to make sure it works. Type the following command at a command line:

```
java -version
```

In this example, java is the name of the Java interpreter program and -version is an argument that tells the interpreter to display its version number.

You can see an example of this in Figure A.6, but your version number might be a little different depending on your version of the SDK.

Running a program

FIGURE A.6

Running the Java interpreter at a command line.

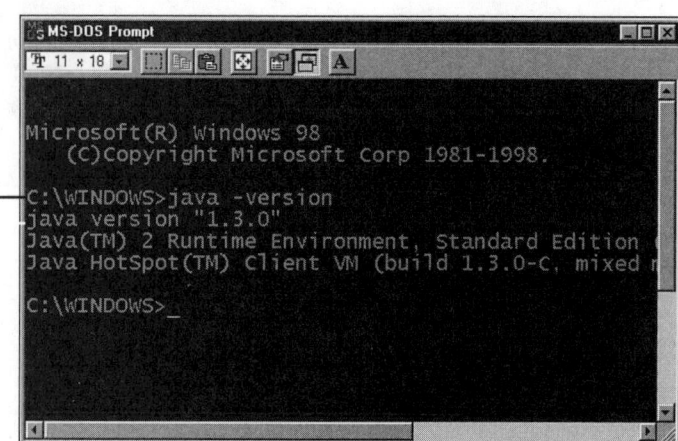

If java -version works and you see a version number, it should begin with 1.3 because you're using SDK 1.3. Sun sometimes tacks on a third number, such as 1.3.0 or 1.3.1, when it releases a minor upgrade to fix bugs or address a security issue. As long as the version number begins with 1.3, you're using the correct version of the Software Development Kit.

If you see an incorrect version number or an error message after running java -version, you need to make some changes to how the Software Development Kit is configured on your system.

> **Note**   In Windows 95, 98, and Me, the most common error message when you're
> running `java -version` is "Bad command or file name." This indicates that
> your system couldn't find the Java interpreter. In Windows NT and 2000, the
> same error is noted with the message "'java' is not recognized as an internal
> or external command."

Configuring the Software Development Kit

When you're writing and compiling Java programs for the first time, the most likely
source of problems isn't typos, syntax errors, or other programming mistakes. Most
errors result from a misconfigured Software Development Kit.

If you type `java -version` at a command line and get a "Bad command or file name"
error or something similar, it indicates that MS-DOS can't find the folder with `java.exe`,
the Java interpreter.

You can correct these errors by editing the `Path` environment variable, which contains a
list of folders. When you run a program at a command line without specifying the folder
it's in, Windows will look for the program in every folder listed in `Path`.

The procedure for editing your `Path` variable is different depending on the Windows
operating system you're using. The next section covers Windows 95, 98, and Me,
followed by a section covering Windows NT and 2000.

Setting Up the `Path` Variable in Windows 95, 98, and Me

On a Windows 95, 98, or Me system, the value of the `Path` variable is set in a file called
`AUTOEXEC.BAT`, which can be found in the root folder of your system's main hard drive.
This file is used by MS-DOS to configure how the operating system functions. Some
programs also use it for configuration purposes, such as the SDK and some anti-virus
programs.

`AUTOEXEC.BAT` is a text file you can edit with Windows Notepad. Start Notepad by clicking Start, Programs, Accessories, Notepad from the Windows taskbar. The Notepad text
editor will open. Choose File, Open from Notepad's menu bar and open the file
`\AUTOEXEC.BAT`. (The slash in front of the filename causes Notepad to look for it in the
root folder.)

When you open the file, you'll see a series of MS-DOS commands, each on its own line
(see Figure A.7).

FIGURE A.7

Editing the AUTOEXEC.BAT file with Notepad.

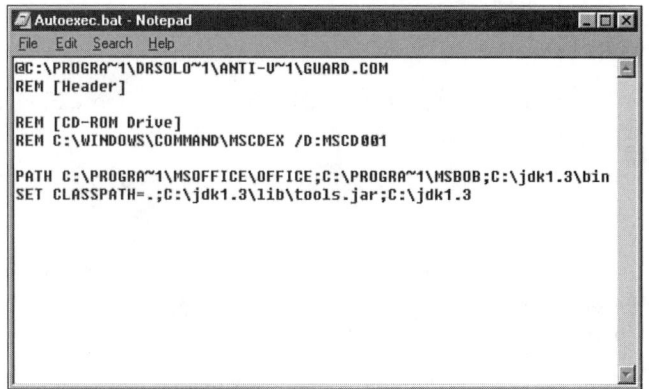

The only commands you need to look for are those that begin with PATH, SET PATH=, or SET CLASSPATH=.

If the PATH command appears, it will be followed by a space and the value that should be assigned to the Path variable: a series of folder names separated by semicolons.

In the PATH command shown in Figure A.7, the Path variable contains three folders:

- C:\PROGRA~1\MSOFFICE\OFFICE
- C:\PROGRA~1\MSBOB
- C:\jdk1.3\bin

You also may see SET PATH= followed by a list of folder names separated by folders. This functions the same way as the PATH command—the folders will be assigned to the Path variable.

You can see what your system's Path variable has been set to by typing the following command at a command line:

PATH

To set up the Software Development Kit correctly, the folder that contains the Java interpreter must be included in the PATH command in AUTOEXEC.BAT. The interpreter has the filename java.exe. If you installed SDK 1.3 in the C:\jdk1.3 folder on your system, java.exe is located in C:\jdk1.3\bin.

If you can't remember where you installed the SDK, you can look for `java.exe` by searching your system:

- In Windows 95 and 98, click the Start button, choose Find, and click Files or Folders.
- In Windows Me, click the Start button, choose Search, and click For Files or Folders.

You might find several copies of `java.exe` in different folders, including some that are completely unrelated to the SDK. To see which one is correct, open an MS-DOS window and do the following for each copy you find:

1. Use the `CD` command to open a folder that contains `java.exe`.
2. Run the command `java -version` in that folder.

When you know the correct folder, create a blank line at the bottom of the `AUTOEXEC.BAT` file and add the following:

`PATH rightfoldername;%PATH%`

For example, if `c:\javajdk\bin` is the correct folder, the following line should be added at the bottom of `AUTOEXEC.BAT`:

`PATH c:\javajdk\bin;%PATH%`

The `%PATH%` text keeps you from wiping out any other `PATH` commands in `AUTOEXEC.BAT`.

After making changes to `AUTOEXEC.BAT`, save the file and reboot your computer. After the reboot, try the `java -version` command again.

If it displays the right SDK version, your system can find the Java interpreter correctly and might not need any other adjustments.

Setting Up the `Path` Variable in Windows NT and 2000

On a Windows NT or 2000 system, the `Path` environment variable is edited using the System Properties dialog box. To open this dialog box, right-click the My Computer icon on your desktop and click the Properties command, as shown in Figure A.8.

 Tip

Another way to open the System Properties dialog box is to click the Start button, choose Settings, and then click the Control Panel command. The Control Panel folder will open, displaying icons for more than two dozen programs you can run to configure the system. Double-click the System icon to open the System Properties dialog box.

FIGURE A.8

Opening the System Properties dialog box.

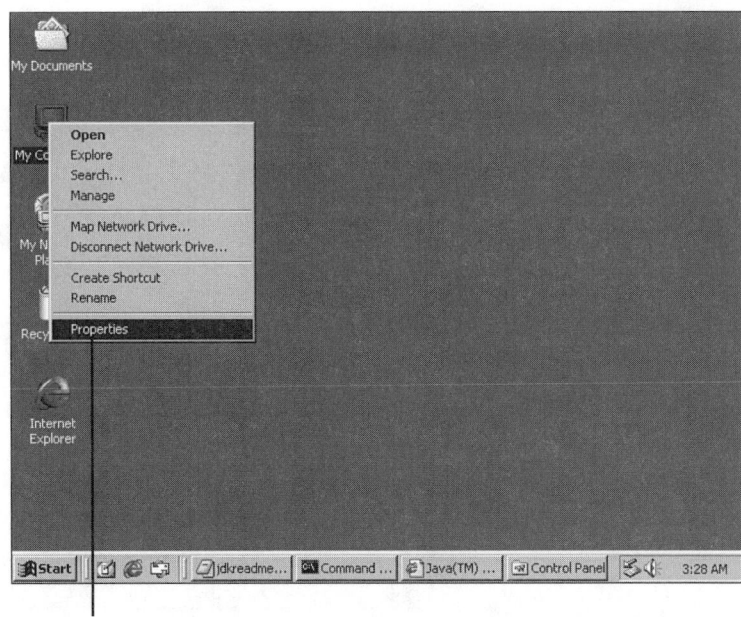

Properties

The System Properties dialog box includes several tabs that you can use to view different windows. To edit your system's environment variables, open the Environment Variables dialog box by clicking the Advanced tab and then clicking the Environment Variables button, as shown in Figure A.9.

The variables listed in the Environment Variables dialog box are used to configure your operating system and some programs on your system, such as the SDK. If your system already has a Path variable set up, which is likely, it will be listed under the System variables heading.

Scroll through the list of variables to find the Path variable item. (Windows isn't case sensitive in regard to these variables, so PATH and Path refer to the same thing.) To edit this variable, click its name on the list and then click the Edit button, as shown in Figure A.10. An Edit System Variable dialog box will open.

Note

If you don't find the Path variable in the list, you can create one by clicking the New button instead of the Edit button.

Advanced tab

FIGURE A.9

*Opening the
Environment Variables
dialog box.*

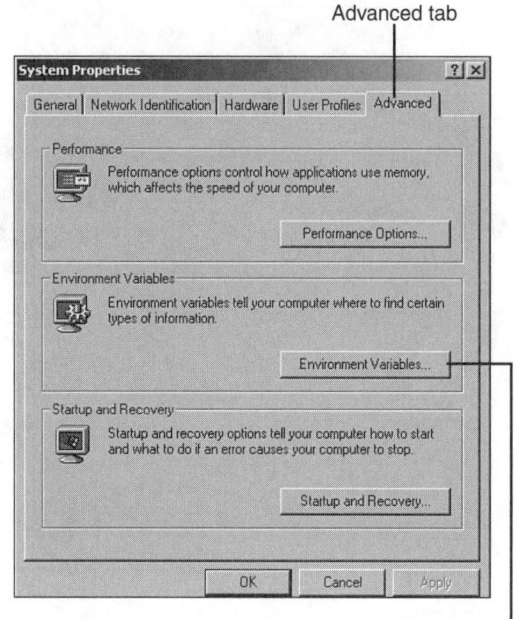

Environment Variables
button

FIGURE A.10

*Editing the PATH envi-
ronment variable.*

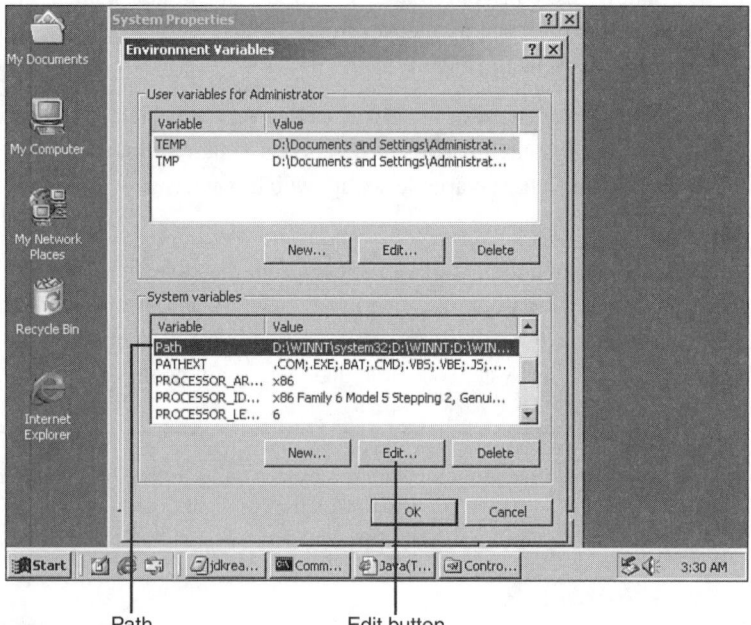

Path   Edit button

The Edit System Variable dialog box contains two text fields: Variable Name, which should be `Path`, and Variable Value, which lists one or more folders on your system.

Here's an example of what a `Path` environment variable might contain:

`C:\PROGRA~1\MSOFFICE\OFFICE;C:\PROGRA~1\MSBOB;C:\javadev`

In the preceding example, the `Path` variable includes three folders:

- `C:\PROGRA~1\MSOFFICE\OFFICE`
- `C:\PROGRA~1\MSBOB`
- `C:\javadev`

To set up the Software Development Kit correctly, you must include the folder that contains the Java interpreter in the `Path` variable. The interpreter has the filename `java.exe`. If you installed SDK 1.3 in the `C:\jdk1.3` folder on your system, `java.exe` is probably in `C:\jdk1.3\bin`.

If you can't remember where you installed the SDK, you can look for `java.exe` by searching your system:

- In Windows NT, click the Start button, choose Find, and click Files or Folders.
- In Windows 2000, click the Start button, choose Search, and click For Files or Folders.

You might find several copies of `java.exe` in different folders, including some that are completely unrelated to the SDK. To see which one is correct, open an MS-DOS window and do the following for each copy you find:

1. Use the `CD` command to open a folder that contains `java.exe`.
2. Run the command `java -version` in that folder.

When you know the correct folder, return to the Edit System Variable dialog box and place your cursor at the end of the Variable Value text field. Add this folder to your `Path` variable in one of two ways:

- If there are other folders in your `Path` variable, add a semicolon followed by the folder that contains `java.exe`.
- If there are no folders in your `Path` variable, enter the folder that contains `java.exe` in the Variable Value field without any semicolons.

For example, if your `Path` isn't empty and `D:\jdk1.3\bin` is the correct folder, `;D:\jdk1.3\bin` should be added to the end of the `Path` variable, as shown in Figure A.11.

FIGURE A.11

Adding a folder to your Path *variable.*

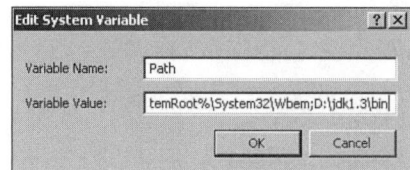

After making changes to your Path variable, click the OK button to exit the Edit Environment Variable dialog box, click OK to exit the Environment Variables dialog box, and then click OK to exit the System Properties dialog box. This saves your change to the Path variable so that all MS-DOS windows you open from now on will include the folder containing java.exe. (If you've left an MS-DOS window open while reconfiguring the Path variable, close it—the value of Path in that window will not be updated to reflect the change you've made.)

Open a new MS-DOS window and try running the java -version command again. If it displays the right SDK version, your system can find the Java interpreter correctly and might not need any other adjustments.

Setting Up the CLASSPATH Variable

When you compile a Java program with the Software Development Kit, you type a command such as the following at a command line:

```
javac VolcanoRobot.java
```

The VolcanoRobot.java argument refers to a program created during Day 2, "Object-Oriented Programming."

If you compile a program successfully, you won't see any output. If you've compiled VolcanoRobot.java, try to run the program with the following command:

```
java VolcanoRobot
```

Note

You can also download VolcanoRobot.class, the compiled version of VolcanoRobot.java, from the book's Web site. Visit http://www.java21pro.com and open the Day 2 page to find links to all files from that chapter.

If your programs compile and run successfully, the Software Development Kit has been configured correctly. You don't need to make any more changes.

If you see a Class not found error or a NoClassDef error whenever you try to run a program, you need to adjust another environment variable on your system, CLASSPATH.

The purpose of CLASSPATH is to help the Java compiler find the Java class library and other class files that it needs. A CLASSPATH can contain folders (such as c:\jdk1.3) and files (c:\jdk1.3\lib\tools.jar). It also can contain a period (.), which is another way to refer to the current folder in MS-DOS.

Here's an example of a CLASSPATH value:

```
.;c:\jdk1.3\lib\tools.jar;c:\jdk1.3
```

In this example, there are three things in the CLASSPATH, separated by semicolons:

- .
- c:\jdk1.3\lib\tools.jar
- c:\jdk1.3

To see what CLASSPATH has been set to, type the following at a command line:

```
ECHO %CLASSPATH%
```

If your CLASSPATH doesn't contain anything, you'll see the text Echo is ON. Otherwise, you'll see a list of folders and files separated by semicolons.

If your CLASSPATH contains a reference to any folder, it must contain two things for the SDK to work:

- A reference to the current folder—in other words, a period.
- A reference to the folder that contains SDK 1.3's version of tools.jar.

Editing your CLASSPATH requires the same procedure that you used to set up the Path variable. Read the section corresponding to your version of Windows.

Setting Up CLASSPATH in Windows 95, 98, and Me

In Windows 95, 98, and Me, the CLASSPATH variable is set up in the AUTOEXEC.BAT file.

When you run Notepad and open \AUTOEXEC.BAT, you'll see a series of MS-DOS commands like those shown in Figure A.12.

The SET CLASSPATH= command is followed by a series of folders and filenames separated by semicolons.

If your CLASSPATH includes folders or files that you know are no longer on your computer, you should remove the references to them on the SET CLASSPATH= line in AUTOEXEC.BAT. Make sure to remove any extra semicolons also.

Figure A.12

*Editing the
AUTOEXEC.BAT file
with Notepad.*

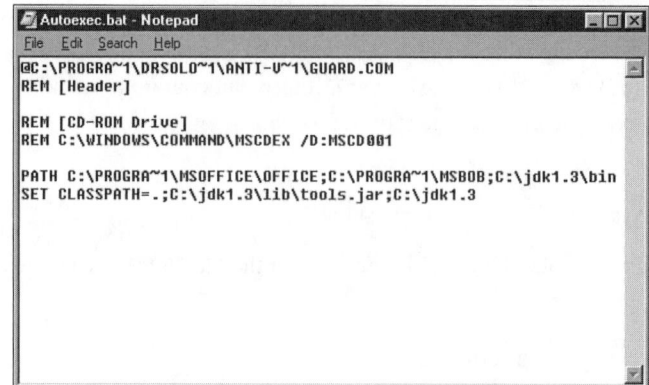

To set up the Software Development Kit correctly, you must include the file containing
the Java class library in the SET CLASSPATH= command. The interpreter has the filename
tools.jar. If you installed the SDK in the C:\jdk1.3 folder on your system, tools.jar
is probably in the C:\jdk1.3\lib folder.

If you can't remember where you installed the SDK, you can look for tools.jar by
searching your system:

- In Windows 95 or 98, click Start, Find, Files or Folders.
- In Windows Me, click Start, Search, For Files or Folders.

If you find several copies, you should be able to find the correct one by opening an MS-
DOS window and using this method:

1. Use CD to open the folder that contains the Java interpreter (java.exe).
2. Enter the CD .. command.
3. Enter the CD lib command.

The lib folder normally contains the correct copy of tools.jar.

When you know the correct location, create a blank line at the bottom of the
AUTOEXEC.BAT file and add the following:

```
SET CLASSPATH=%CLASSPATH%;.;rightlocation
```

For example, if tools.jar file is in the c:\javajdk\lib folder, the following line should
be added at the bottom of AUTOEXEC.BAT:

```
SET CLASSPATH=%CLASSPATH%;.;c:\javajdk\lib\tools.jar
```

As you might expect, the %CLASSPATH% text keeps you from removing any other
CLASSPATH commands in AUTOEXEC.BAT.

After making changes to AUTOEXEC.BAT, save the file and reboot your computer. Then try to compile one of the programs from the first several days of the book. You should be able to compile and run them without any SDK-related problems.

Tip

> If you're still having problems with the Software Development Kit, this book has a Web site with a version of this appendix and a way to contact the author. The site is available at http://www.java21pro.com.

Setting Up CLASSPATH in Windows NT and 2000

In Windows NT and 2000, you edit the CLASSPATH variable by using the Environment Variables dialog box, which is also used to modify the Path variable:

1. On the desktop, right-click the My Computer icon and then click Properties. The System Properties dialog box will open.

2. Click the Advanced tab and then click the Environment Variables button. An Environment Variables dialog box will open.

Look for CLASSPATH in the System variables list. If you find it, click it and then click the Edit button, as shown in Figure A.13.

FIGURE A.13

Editing the CLASSPATH environment variable.

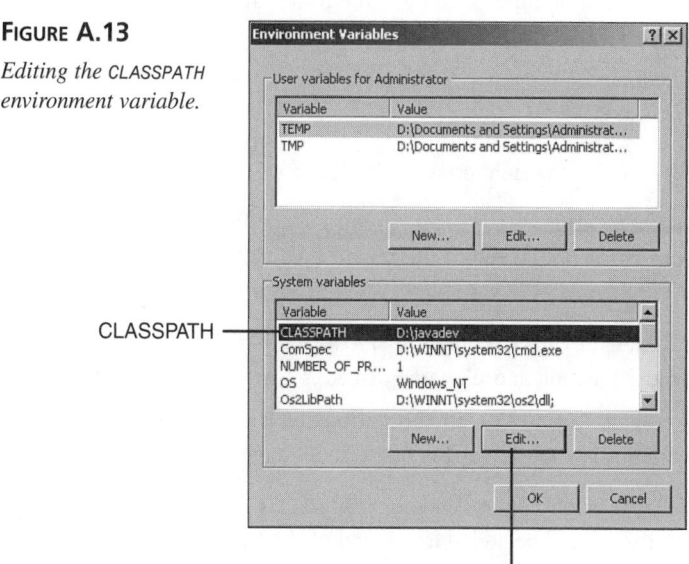

CLASSPATH

Edit button

Note If you don't find the CLASSPATH variable in the list, you can create one by clicking the New button instead of the Edit button.

If your CLASSPATH variable includes folders or files that you know are no longer on your computer, you should remove the references to them in the Variable Value text field. Make sure to remove any extra semicolons also.

To set up the Software Development Kit correctly, you must include the file containing the Java class library in the CLASSPATH variable. The interpreter has the filename tools.jar. If you installed the SDK in the C:\jdk1.3 folder on your system, tools.jar is probably in the folder C:\jdk1.3\lib.

If you can't remember where you installed the SDK, you can look for tools.jar by searching your system:

- In Windows NT, click the Start button, choose Find, and click Files or Folders.
- In Windows 2000, click the Start button, choose Search, and click For Files or Folders.

If there are several copies, you should be able to find the correct one using this method:

1. Open an MS-DOS window and use CD to open the folder that contains the Java interpreter (java.exe).
2. Enter the CD .. command.
3. Enter the CD lib command.

The lib folder normally contains the right copy of tools.jar.

When you know the correct location of tools.jar, return to the Edit System Variable dialog box and place your cursor at the end of the Variable Value text field. Add the reference to tools.jar to your CLASSPATH variable in one of two ways:

- If there are other folders or files in your CLASSPATH, add a period and a semicolon, followed by the folder location and filename of tools.jar.
- If there's nothing in your CLASSPATH, enter a period and a semicolon, followed by the folder location and filename of tools.jar without any semicolons.

For example, if your CLASSPATH isn't empty and D:\jdk1.3\lib\tools.jar is correct, ;D:\jdk1.3\lib\tools.jar should be added to the end of the CLASSPATH variable, as shown in Figure A.14.

FIGURE A.14

Adding a file to your CLASSPATH *variable.*

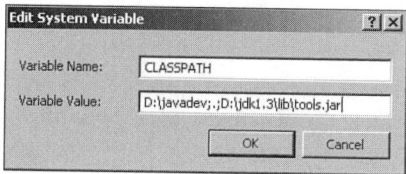

After making changes to your CLASSPATH variable, click the OK button to exit the Edit Environment Variable dialog box, click OK to exit the Environment Variables dialog box, and then click OK to exit the System Properties dialog box. This saves your change.

Open a new MS-DOS window and try compiling one of the programs from the first several days of this book. You should be able to compile and run them without any SDK-related problems.

> **Tip**
>
> If you're still having problems with the Software Development Kit, this book has a Web site, http://www.java21pro.com, with a version of this appendix and a way to contact the author.

Unix Configuration

To configure the SDK on a Solaris system, add the java/bin or JDK/bin directory to your execution path. You can usually do this by adding a line like the following to your .profile, .cshrc, or .login file:

```
set path= (~/java/bin/ $path)
```

This line assumes that you've installed the SDK into the directory java in your home directory. An installation elsewhere will require a change to the directory added to your execution path.

These changes won't take effect until you log out and back in again, or until you use the source command with the name of the file you changed. If you altered the .login file, the source command would be as follows:

```
source ~/.login
```

Fixing Class Not Found Errors on Other Platforms

To correct any Class not found errors on Solaris systems, the best thing to do is to make sure that the CLASSPATH environment variable isn't being set automatically at login.

To see whether CLASSPATH is being set, enter the following at a command line:

`echo $CLASSPATH`

If a CLASSPATH value has been set, you can unset it by entering the following command:

`unsetenv CLASSPATH`

To make this change permanent, remove the command that sets up CLASSPATH from your .profile, .cshrc, or .login file.

These changes won't take effect until you log out and back in again, or until you use the source command with the name of the file you changed. If you altered the .login file, the source command would be as follows:

`source ~/.login`

Appendix B

Using a Text Editor with the Software Development Kit

Unlike Java development tools such as Visual Café and Borland JBuilder, Java 2 Software Development Kit 1.3 (SDK 1.3) doesn't come with a text editor for creating source files.

In this appendix, you'll learn how to select an editor for use with the SDK and how to configure your system to work with that editor. Like the preceding material on SDK configuration, this is primarily aimed at Windows users.

Choosing a Text Editor

For an editor or word processor to work with the SDK, it must be able to save text files with no formatting.

This feature has different names in different editors. When you save a document or set the properties for a document, look for one of the following format options:

- Plain text
- ASCII text
- DOS text
- Text-only

If you're using Windows, there are several editors included with the operating system.

Windows Notepad (available from the Start button at Programs, Accessories, Notepad) is a no-frills text editor that only works with plain-text files. It can handle only one document at a time.

Windows WordPad (available from the Start button at Programs, Accessories, WordPad) is a step above Notepad. It can handle more than one document at a time and can handle both plain-text and Microsoft Word formats. It also remembers the last several documents it has worked on and makes them available from the File pull-down menu.

DOS Edit, which can be run from an MS-DOS prompt with the `edit` command, is another simple editor that handles plain-text documents. It will seem crude to a Windows user who isn't familiar with MS-DOS, but it and some other text editors do have one feature that Notepad and WordPad lack: They show you the number of the line you're currently editing. Numbering begins with 1 at the topmost line in the file and increases as you move downward.

Figure B.1 shows DOS Edit. The line number is indicated in the lower-right corner of the program window.

Seeing the line number helps in Java programming because many Java compilers indicate the line number at which an error has occurred. Take a look at the following error generated by the SDK compiler:

```
Palindrome.java:2: Class Font not found in type declaration.
```

The number 2 after the name of the Java source file indicates the line that triggered the compiler error. With a text editor that supports numbering, you can go directly to that line and start looking for the error.

Usually there are better ways to debug a program with a commercial Java programming package, but SDK users must search for compiler-generated errors using the line number indicated by the `javac` tool. Because of this, it's best to use a text editor that supports numbering.

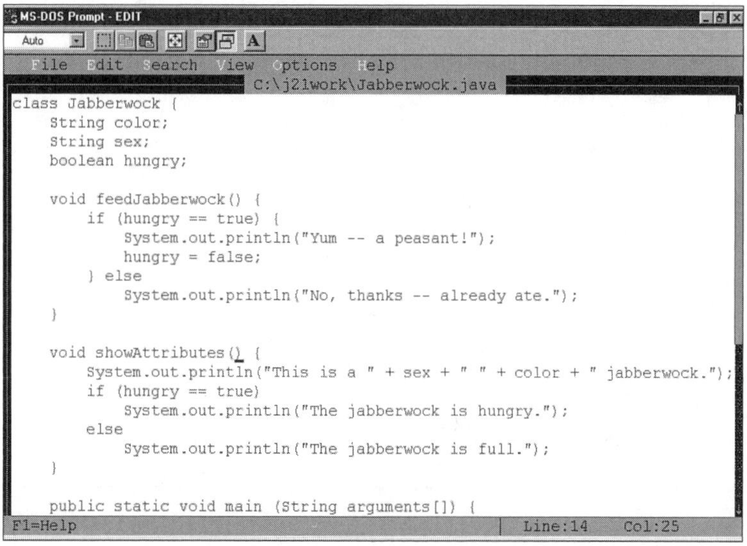
MS-DOS Prompt - EDIT
Auto
File Edit Search View Options Help
C:\j21work\Jabberwock.java
class Jabberwock {
String color;
String sex;
boolean hungry;
void feedJabberwock() {
if (hungry == true) {
System.out.println("Yum -- a peasant!");
hungry = false;
} else
System.out.println("No, thanks -- already ate.");
}
void showAttributes() {
System.out.println("This is a " + sex + " " + color + " jabberwock.");
if (hungry == true)
System.out.println("The jabberwock is hungry.");
else
System.out.println("The jabberwock is full.");
}
public static void main (String arguments[]) {
F1=Help
Line:14 Col:25

FIGURE B.1

A Java source file loaded in DOS Edit.

Creating a File Association in Windows

After a text editor has been selected, Windows users should associate that editor with the `.java` file extension. This makes it possible to open a `.java` source file by double-clicking its name in a folder. It also prevents editors such as Windows Notepad from incorrectly adding the `.txt` file extension to `.java` source files.

Using a Batch File

One way to create a file association in Windows is to edit the Windows Registry, which is the database that keeps track of how programs on your computer are configured.

You can make changes to the Registry by using RegEdit, which loads all current registry settings and lets you examine them in an environment similar to Windows Explorer. RegEdit can be configured using a batch file—a list of commands indicating how the registry should be altered.

To create a file, start Windows Notepad by clicking the Start button, Programs, Accessories, Notepad. In the Notepad editing window, enter the code in Listing B.1, leaving off the number and colon at the beginning of each line.

LISTING B.1   The Full Text of java.reg

```
 1: REGEDIT4
 2:
 3: [HKEY_CLASSES_ROOT\.java]
 4: @="java"
 5:
 6: [HKEY_CLASSES_ROOT\java]
 7: @="Java source file"
 8: "EditFlags"=hex:00,00,01,00
 9:
10: [HKEY_CLASSES_ROOT\java\shell]
11:
12: [HKEY_CLASSES_ROOT\java\shell\open]
13: @=""
14:
15: [HKEY_CLASSES_ROOT\java\shell\open\command]
16: @="C:\\WINDOWS\\NOTEPAD.EXE %1"
```

Tip   You also can download this file from the book's official Web site. Go to
http://www.java21pro.com and open the Appendix B page.

Line 16 of Listing B.1 assumes that the C:\Windows folder is your main Windows folder
and you want to use Notepad to create Java programs. You should change this line if
either of these isn't true.

If you want to use Wordpad as your editor, replace Line 16 with the following:

```
@="C:\\WINDOWS\\WRITE.EXE %1"
```

If you want to use DOS Edit instead, replace Line 16 with this:

```
@="C:\\WINDOWS\\COMMAND\\EDIT.COM %1"
```

When you're done, save the file as java.reg. This file contains a series of statements
that set values in the Windows Registry. To put it into effect, double-click it. You'll be
asked to confirm that the settings should be added to the registry.

The RegEdit program will execute all of the statements in java.reg, associating the editor you've chosen with .java files.

To make sure that this has worked, open a folder that contains one of the Java source
code files you've created for a tutorial in this book. Double-click a file that ends with the
.java file extension. The editor should open with that Java source file in the main editing window.

If this works, you don't need to do anything else to configure a text editor for Java programming.

Creating an Association Manually

Another way to associate .java files with your preferred text editor is to do it manually within Windows.

To set up a file association manually, first you must have a file to work on. Open a folder in Windows and create a new text document by selecting File, New, Text Document from the folder's menu bar (see Figure B.2).

FIGURE B.2

Creating a new text document in a Windows folder.

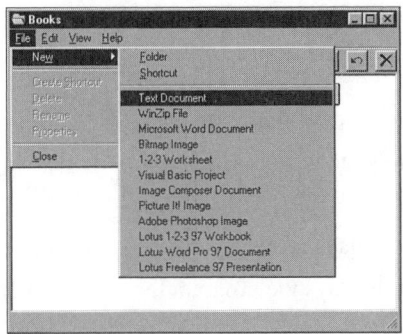

A new text document called New Text Document.txt is created, and you have a chance to rename it. Change the name to Anything.java and confirm this new name when Windows asks whether you really want to change the file extension.

Double-click Anything.java. If your system doesn't associate the .java file extension with any program, you'll see an Open With window. You can use this to associate the .java file extension with your chosen editor. Skip to "Creating a New Association" later in this appendix.

If anything else happens, you must delete the existing .java association before you can create a new one.

Deleting an Existing File Association

If your system already has something associated with the .java file extension, you can remove this association from any Windows folder. Select View, Options from a folder's menu bar to open an Options window with three tabs. Select the File Types tab (see Figure B.3).

FIGURE B.3

The File Types tab.

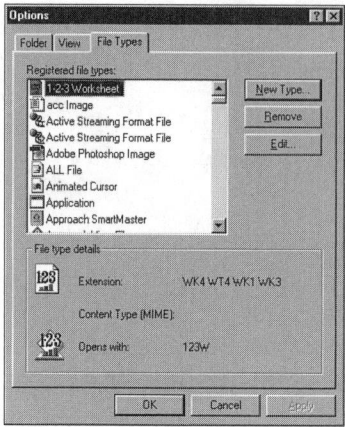

The Registered File Types list box in this window shows all the file extensions that are associated with programs on your system. Highlight a file type in the list box to see two other fields that provide information about it:

- The Extensions field displays all file extensions that work with this file type.
- The Opens With field displays the program that's used to open this file type.

The file type 1-2-3 Worksheets in Figure B.3 has four file extensions: WK4, WT4, WK1, and WK3. Any file with these extensions can be opened with the 123W program (which is the Lotus 1-2-3 spreadsheet application).

Scroll through the Registered File Types list until you find one that includes JAVA in its Extension field. The most likely place to find it is under a heading such as "Java files" or "Java programs," but that might not be the case on your system.

When you find the right file type, you must delete the existing association so that you can replace it with a new one. Select Remove to delete the existing association, and click Yes to confirm that you want to remove it. After you do this, you can create a new association for the .java file extension.

Creating a New Association

When you double-click a file that has no known association for its file extension, an Open With window opens. This is shown in Figure B.4.

FIGURE B.4

Associating a file extension with a program.

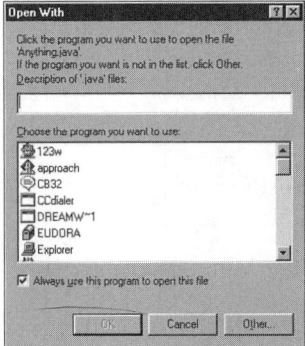

Use the following steps to create a .java file association:

- In the Description of .java Files text box, enter `Java source file` or something similar.
- In the Choose the Program You Want to Use list box, find the text editor or word processor you want to use with Java source files. If you don't find it, click the Other button and find the program manually. If you're using DOS Edit, on most systems it can be found in the `\Windows\Command` folder with the filename `edit` or `edit.exe`.
- Make sure that the Always Use This Program to Open This File option is checked.

When you click OK to confirm these settings, your chosen editor opens the `Anything.java` file and any other files that have the `.java` file extension.

Associating an Icon with a File Type

After you've associated `.java` files with your chosen editor, an icon is assigned to all `.java` files on your system by default.

If you want to change this icon, select View, Options, File Types from a folder's menu bar to see the File Types dialog box. Scroll through the registered file types to find the one associated with the JAVA file extension.

When this file type is highlighted, select Edit to open the Edit File Type window, which is shown in Figure B.5.

FIGURE B.5

The Edit File Type window.

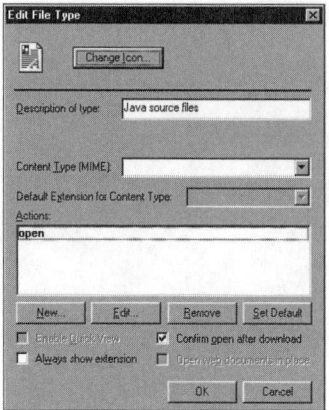

Select Change Icon from the Edit File Type window and choose a different icon to display for all .java files. If you like one of the icons displayed in the Current Icon window, highlight that icon and click OK to make the change. If you would like to look at other icons, select Browse to look inside files on your system to see the icons they contain. You can open any icon file, Windows program, or .DLL file to see the icons it contains. They're displayed in the Current Icon window after you select a file.

Once you've found an icon you like, highlight it and click OK to select it.

INDEX

Symbols

2D graphics, 298, 301
  arcs, 307-309
    drawing, 306, 322
    filling, 307
  coordinate spaces, 317-318
  coordinate system, 301
  copy/paste functions, 310-311
  ellipses, 321
  Graphics2D objects, 171, 299
  lines
    drawing, 302, 321
  Map2D applet, 323-326
  ovals, 306
  polygons, 304, 322-323

  rectangles
    drawing, 302, 321
    filling, 303
    rounded corders, 303
  rendering attributes, 318-320
& (ampersand), AND operators, 78
* (asterisk), 171, 395
[ ] (brackets), 108, 114
^ (caret), 78, 681
!! command (jdb), 589
/**...*/ comment notation, 68
/*...*/ comment notation, 67
// comment notation, 67
{ } (curly braces), 61
= (equal sign), 77
  assignment operator, 62, 66
  equality operator (==), 102

! (exclamation point), NOT operator, 78
> (greater than), 77
>= (greater than or equal to), 77
!= (inequality operator), 77, 102
< (less than), 77
<= (less than or equal to), 77
- (minus signs), 69, 76
. (period), 89, 721
| (pipe character), 78
+ (plus sign)
  concatenation operator (+), 81
  increment operator (++), 76
; (semicolon), 60

A

Q-R

Sun Microsystems, Inc.
Binary Code License Agreement

READ THE TERMS OF THIS AGREEMENT AND ANY PROVIDED SUPPLEMEN-
TAL LICENSE TERMS (COLLECTIVELY "AGREEMENT") CAREFULLY BEFORE
OPENING THE SOFTWARE MEDIA PACKAGE. BY OPENING THE SOFTWARE
MEDIA PACKAGE, YOU AGREE TO THE TERMS OF THIS AGREEMENT. IF YOU
ARE ACCESSING THE SOFTWARE ELECTRONICALLY, INDICATE YOUR
ACCEPTANCE OF THESE TERMS BY SELECTING THE "ACCEPT" BUTTON AT
THE END OF THIS AGREEMENT. IF YOU DO NOT AGREE TO ALL THESE
TERMS, PROMPTLY RETURN THE UNUSED SOFTWARE TO YOUR PLACE OF
PURCHASE FOR A REFUND OR, IF THE SOFTWARE IS ACCESSED ELECTRONI-
CALLY, SELECT THE "DECLINE" BUTTON AT THE END OF THIS AGREEMENT.

1. **License to Use**. Sun grants you a non-exclusive and non-transferable license for
   the internal use only of the accompanying software and documentation and any
   error corrections provided by Sun (collectively "Software"), by the number of users
   and the class of computer hardware for which the corresponding fee has been paid.

2. **Restrictions**. Software is confidential and copyrighted. Title to Software and all
   associated intellectual property rights is retained by Sun and/or its licensors.
   Except as specifically authorized in any Supplemental License Terms, you may not
   make copies of Software, other than a single copy of Software for archival purposes. Unless enforcement is prohibited by applicable law, you may not modify,
   decompile, or reverse engineer Software. You acknowledge that Software is not
   designed, licensed, or intended for use in the design, construction, operation or
   maintenance of any nuclear facility. Sun disclaims any express or implied warranty
   of fitness for such uses. No right, title or interest in or to any trademark, service
   mark, logo, or trade name of Sun or its licensors is granted under this Agreement.

3. **Limited Warranty**. Sun warrants to you that for a period of ninety (90) days from
   the date of purchase, as evidenced by a copy of the receipt, the media on which
   Software is furnished (if any) will be free of defects in materials and workmanship
   under normal use. Except for the foregoing, Software is provided "AS IS". Your
   exclusive remedy and Sun's entire liability under this limited warranty will be at
   Sun's option to replace Software media or refund the fee paid for Software.

4. **Disclaimer of Warranty**. UNLESS SPECIFIED IN THIS AGREEMENT, ALL
   EXPRESS OR IMPLIED CONDITIONS, REPRESENTATIONS AND WAR-
   RANTIES, INCLUDING ANY IMPLIED WARRANTY OF MERCHANTABILI-
   TY, FITNESS FOR A PARTICULAR PURPOSE OR NON-INFRINGEMENT
   ARE DISCLAIMED, EXCEPT TO THE EXTENT THAT THESE DIS-
   CLAIMERS ARE HELD TO BE LEGALLY INVALID.

5. **Limitation of Liability**. TO THE EXTENT NOT PROHIBITED BY LAW, IN NO EVENT WILL SUN OR ITS LICENSORS BE LIABLE FOR ANY LOST REVENUE, PROFIT OR DATA, OR FOR SPECIAL, INDIRECT, CONSEQUENTIAL, INCIDENTAL OR PUNITIVE DAMAGES, HOWEVER CAUSED REGARDLESS OF THE THEORY OF LIABILITY, ARISING OUT OF OR RELATED TO THE USE OF OR INABILITY TO USE SOFTWARE, EVEN IF SUN HAS BEEN ADVISED OF THE POSSIBILITY OF SUCH DAMAGES. In no event will Sun's liability to you, whether in contract, tort (including negligence), or otherwise, exceed the amount paid by you for Software under this Agreement. The foregoing limitations will apply even if the above stated warranty fails of its essential purpose.

6. **Termination**. This Agreement is effective until terminated. You may terminate this Agreement at any time by destroying all copies of Software. This Agreement will terminate immediately without notice from Sun if you fail to comply with any provision of this Agreement. Upon Termination, you must destroy all copies of Software.

7. **Export Regulations**. All Software and technical data delivered under this Agreement are subject to US export control laws and may be subject to export or import regulations in other countries. You agree to comply strictly with all such laws and regulations and acknowledge that you have the responsibility to obtain such licenses to export, re-export, or import as may be required after delivery to you.

8. **U.S. Government Restricted Rights**. If Software is being acquired by or on behalf of the U.S. Government or by a U.S. Government prime contractor or subcontractor (at any tier), then the Government's rights in Software and accompanying documentation will be only as set forth in this Agreement; this is in accordance with 48 CFR 227.7201 through 227.7202-4 (for Department of Defense (DOD) acquisitions) and with 48 CFR 2.101 and 12.212 (for non-DOD acquisitions).

9. **Governing Law**. Any action related to this Agreement will be governed by California law and controlling U.S. federal law. No choice of law rules of any jurisdiction will apply.

10. **Severability**. If any provision of this Agreement is held to be unenforceable, this Agreement will remain in effect with the provision omitted, unless omission would frustrate the intent of the parties, in which case this Agreement will immediately terminate.

11. **Integration**. This Agreement is the entire agreement between you and Sun relating to its subject matter. It supersedes all prior or contemporaneous oral or written communications, proposals, representations and warranties and prevails over any conflicting or additional terms of any quote, order, acknowledgment, or other communication between the parties relating to its subject matter during the term of this Agreement. No modification of this Agreement will be binding, unless in writing and signed by an authorized representative of each party.

For inquiries, please contact: Sun Microsystems, Inc. 901 San Antonio Road, Palo Alto, California 94303

JAVA™ 2 SOFTWARE DEVELOPMENT KIT STANDARD EDITION VERSION 1.3 SUPPLEMENTAL LICENSE TERMS

These supplemental license terms ("Supplemental Terms") add to or modify the terms of the Binary Code License Agreement (collectively, the "Agreement"). Capitalized terms not defined in these Supplemental Terms shall have the same meanings ascribed to them in the Agreement. These Supplemental Terms shall supersede any inconsistent or conflicting terms in the Agreement, or in any license contained within the Software.

1. **Internal Use and Development License Grant**. Subject to the terms and conditions of this Agreement, including, but not limited to, Section 2 (Redistributables) and Section 4 (Java Technology Restrictions) of these Supplemental Terms, Sun grants you a non-exclusive, non-transferable, limited license to reproduce the Software for internal use only for the sole purpose of development of your Java™applet and application ("Program"), provided that you do not redistribute the Software in whole or in part, either separately or included with any Program.

2. **Redistributables**. In addition to the license granted in Paragraph 1above, Sun grants you a nonexclusive, non-. transferable, limited license to reproduce and distribute, only as part of your separate copy of JAVA™ 2 RUNTIME ENVIRONMENT STANDARD EDITION VERSION 1.3 software, those files specifically identified as redistributable in the JAVA™ 2 RUNTIME ENVIRONMENT STANDARD EDITION VERSION 1.3 "README" file (the "Redistributables") provided that: (a) you distribute the Redistributables complete and unmodified (unless otherwise specified in the applicable README file), and only bundled as part of the JavaTM applets and applications that you develop (the "Programs:); (b) you do not distribute additional software intended to supersede any component(s) of the Redistributables; (c) you do not remove or alter any proprietary legends or notices contained in or on the Redistributables; (d) you only distribute the Redistributables

pursuant to a license agreement that protects Sun's interests consistent with the terms contained in the Agreement, and (e) you agree to defend and indemnify Sun and its licensors from and against any damages, costs, liabilities, settlement amounts and/or expenses (including attorneys' fees) incurred in connection with any claim, lawsuit or action by any third party that arises or results from the use or distribution of any and all Programs and/or Software.

3. **Separate Distribution License Required**. You understand and agree that you must first obtain a separate license from Sun prior to reproducing or modifying any portion of the Software other than as provided with respect to Redistributables in Paragraph 2 above.

4. **Java Technology Restrictions**. You may not modify the Java Platform Interface ("JPI", identified as classes contained within the "java" package or any subpackages of the "java" package), by creating additional classes within the JPI or otherwise causing the addition to or modification of the classes in the JPI. In the event that you create an additional class and associated API(s) which (i) extends the functionality of a Java environment, and (ii) is exposed to third party software developers for the purpose of developing additional software which invokes such additional API, you must promptly publish broadly an accurate specification for such API for free use by all developers. You may not create, or authorize your licensees to create additional classes, interfaces, or subpackages that are in any way identified as "java", "javax", "sun" or similar convention as specified by Sun in any class file naming convention. Refer to the appropriate version of the Java Runtime Environment binary code license (currently located at http://www.java.sun.com/jdk/index.html) for the availability of runtime code which may be distributed with Java applets and applications.

5. **Trademarks and Logos**. You acknowledge and agree as between you and Sun that Sun owns the Java trademark and all Java.related trademarks, service marks, logos and other brand designations including the Coffee Cup logo and Duke logo ("Java Marks"), and you agree to comply with the Sun Trademark and Logo Usage Requirements currently located at http://www.sun.com/policies/trademarks. Any use you make of the Java Marks inures to Sun's benefit.

6. **Source Code**. Software may contain source code that is provided solely for reference purposes pursuant to the terms of this Agreement.

7. **Termination**. Sun may terminate this Agreement immediately should any Software become, or in Sun's opinion be likely to become, the subject of a claim of infringement of a patent, trade secret, copyright or other intellectual property right.

JAVA™ DEVELOPMENT TOOLS FORTE™ FOR JAVA™, RELEASE 2.0, COMMUNITY EDITION SUPPLEMENTAL LICENSE TERMS

These supplemental license terms ("Supplemental Terms") add to or modify the terms of the Binary Code License Agreement (collectively, the "Agreement"). Capitalized terms not defined in these Supplemental Terms shall have the same meanings ascribed to them in the Agreement. These Supplemental Terms shall supersede any inconsistent or conflicting terms in the Agreement, or in any license contained within the Software.

1. **Software Internal Use and Development License Grant**. Subject to the terms and conditions of this Agreement, including, but not limited to Section 3 (Java(TM) Technology Restrictions) of these Supplemental Terms, Sun grants you a non-exclusive, non-transferable, limited license to reproduce internally and use internally the binary form of the Software complete and unmodified for the sole purpose of designing, developing and testing your [Java applets and] applications intended to run on the Java platform ("Programs").

2. **License to Distribute Redistributables**. In addition to the license granted in Section 1 (Redistributables Internal Use and Development License Grant) of these Supplemental Terms, subject to the terms and conditions of this Agreement, including but not limited to Section 3 (Java Technology Restrictions) of these Supplemental Terms, Sun grants you a non-exclusive, non-transferable, limited license to reproduce and distribute those files specifically identified as redistributable in the Software "README" file ("Redistributables") provided that: (i) you distribute the Redistributables complete and unmodified (unless otherwise specified in the applicable README file), and only bundled as part of your Programs, (ii) you do not distribute additional software intended to supersede any component(s) of the Redistributables, (iii) you do not remove or alter any proprietary legends or notices contained in or on the Redistributables, (iv) for a particular version of the Java platform, any executable output generated by a compiler that is contained in the Software must (a) only be compiled from source code that conforms to the corresponding version of the OEM Java Language Specification; (b) be in the class file format defined by the corresponding version of the OEM Java Virtual Machine Specification; and (c) execute properly on a reference runtime, as specified by Sun, associated with such version of the Java platform, (v) you only distribute the Redistributables pursuant to a license agreement that protects Sun's interests consistent with the terms contained in the Agreement, and (vi) you agree to defend and indemnify Sun and its licensors from and against any damages, costs, liabilities,

settlement amounts and/or expenses (including attorneys' fees) incurred in connection with any claim, lawsuit or action by any third party that arises or results from the use or distribution of any and all Programs and/or Software.

3. **Java Technology Restrictions**. You may not modify the Java Platform Interface ("JPI", identified as classes contained within the "java" package or any subpackages of the "java" package), by creating additional classes within the JPI or otherwise causing the addition to or modification of the classes in the JPI. In the event that you create an additional class and associated API(s) which (i) extends the functionality of the Java platform, and (ii) is exposed to third party software developers for the purpose of developing additional software which invokes such additional API, you must promptly publish broadly an accurate specification for such API for free use by all developers. You may not create, or authorize your licensees to create, additional classes, interfaces, or subpackages that are in any way identified as "java", "javax", "sun" or similar convention as specified by Sun in any naming convention designation.

4. **Java Runtime Availability**. Refer to the appropriate version of the Java Runtime Environment binary code license (currently located at http://www.java.sun.com/jdk/index.html) for the availability of runtime code which may be distributed with Java applets and applications.

5. **Trademarks and Logos**. You acknowledge and agree as between you and Sun that Sun owns the SUN, SOLARIS, JAVA, JINI, FORTE, STAROFFICE, STARPORTAL and iPLANET trademarks and all SUN, SOLARIS, JAVA, JINI, FORTE, STAROFFICE, STARPORTAL and iPLANET.related trademarks, service marks, logos and other brand designations ("Sun Marks"), and you agree to comply with the Sun Trademark and Logo Usage Requirements currently located at http://www.sun.com/policies/trademarks. Any use you make of the Sun Marks inures to Sun's benefit.

6. **Source Code**. Software may contain source code that is provided solely for reference purposes pursuant to the terms of this Agreement. Source code may not be redistributed unless expressly provided for in this Agreement.

7. **Termination for Infringement**. Either party may terminate this Agreement immediately should any Software become, or in either party's opinion be likely to become, the subject of a claim of infringement of any intellectual property right.

For inquiries please contact: Sun Microsystems, Inc. 901 San Antonio Road, Palo Alto, California 94303

Other Related Titles

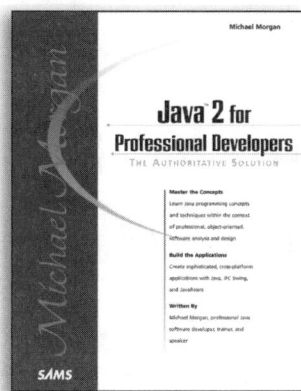

Java 2 for Professional Developers
Mike Morgan
0-672-31697-8
$34.99 USA/$52.95 CAN

Pure Java 2
Kenneth Litwak, Ph.D.
0-672-31654-4
$24.99 USA/$29.95 CAN

Java Thread Programming
Paul Hyde
0-672-31585-8
$34.99 USA/$52.95 CAN

The Official VisiBroker for Java Handbook
Michael McCaffery and Bill Scott
0-672-31451-7
$39.99 USA/$59.95 CAN

Java 2 Platform Unleashed
Jamie Jaworski
0-672-31631-5
$49.99 USA/$74.95 CAN

Building Java Enterprise Systems with J2EE
Paul J. Perrone and Venkata Chaganti
0-672-31795-8
$55.99 USA/$89.95 CAN

JavaBeans Unleashed
Donald Doherty, Rick Leinecker, et al.
0-672-31424-X
$49.99 USA/$74.95 CAN

XML Unleashed
Michael Morrison
0-672-31514-9
$49.99 USA/$74.95 CAN

COM/DCOM Unleashed
Randy Abernethy
0-672-31352-9
$39.99 USA/$59.95 CAN

Sams Teach Yourself CORBA in 14 Days
Jeremy Rosenberger
0-672-31208-5
$29.99 USA/$44.95 CAN

Pure JSP-Java Server Pages
James Goodwill
0-672-13902-0
$34.99 USA/$52.95 CAN

Developing Java Servlets
James Goodwill
0-672-31600-5
$29.99 USA/$44.95 CAN

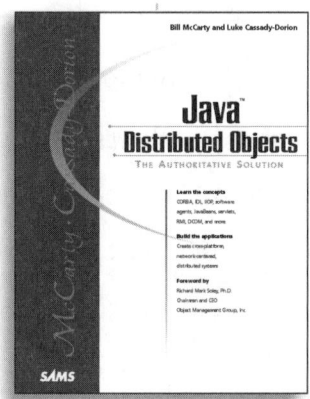

Java Distributed Objects
Bill McCarty and Luke Cassady-Dorion
0-672-31537-8
$49.99 USA/$71.95 CAN

SAMS

www.samspublishing.com

All prices are subject to change.

Hey, you've got enough worries.

Don't let IT training be one of them.

Get on the fast track to IT training at InformIT,
your total Information Technology training network.

■ Hundreds of timely articles on dozens of topics ■ Discounts on IT books
from all our publishing partners, including Sams Publishing ■ Free, unabridged
books from the InformIT Free Library ■ "Expert Q&A"—our live, online chat
with IT experts ■ Faster, easier certification and training from our Web- or
classroom-based training programs ■ Current IT news ■ Software downloads
■ Career-enhancing resources

Windows 95, 98, Me, Windows NT 4.0, or Windows 2000 Installation Instructions

1. Insert the disc into your CD-ROM drive.

2. From the Windows desktop, double-click the My Computer icon.

3. Double-click the icon representing your CD-ROM drive.

4. Double-click the icon titled START.EXE to run the installation program.

5. Follow the onscreen prompts to finish the installation.

Note If you have the AutoPlay feature enabled, the START.EXE program starts automatically whenever you insert the disc into your CD-ROM drive.

Linux and Unix Installation Instructions

These installation instructions assume that you have a passing familiarity with Unix commands and the basic setup of your machine. As Unix has many flavors, only generic commands are used. If you have any problems with the commands, please consult the appropriate manual page or your system administrator.

1. Insert CD-ROM in CD drive.

2. If you have a volume manager, mounting of the CD-ROM will be automatic. If you don't have a volume manager, you can mount the CD-ROM by typing `mount -tiso9660/dev/cdrom/mnt/cdrom`.

Note `/mnt/cdrom` is just a mount point, but it must exist when you issue the mount command. You may also use any empty directory for a mount point if you don't want to use `/mnt/cdrom`.

3. Open the readme.txt file for descriptions and installation instructions.

What's on the CD-ROM

The companion CD-ROM contains Sun Microsystem's Java™ 2 Software Development Kit Standard Edition version 1.3 for Windows, Solaris SPARC/x86, and Linux (Intel x86), Forte for Java, release 2.0, Community Edition, plus the source code from the book.

License Information

Use of this software is subject to the Sun Microsystems, Inc. Binary Code License Agreement contained on page 785 of the accompanying book. Read this agreement carefully. By opening this package, you are agreeing to be bound by the terms and conditions of this agreement.

By opening this package, you are also agreeing to be bound by the following agreement:

You may not copy or redistribute the entire CD-ROM as a whole. Copying and redistribution of individual software programs on the CD-ROM is governed by terms set by individual copyright holders.

The installer and code from the author(s) are copyrighted by the publisher and the author(s). Individual programs and other items on the CD-ROM are copyrighted or are under GNU license by their various authors or other copyright holders.

This software is sold as-is without warranty of any kind, either expressed or implied, including but not limited to the implied warranties of merchantability and fitness for a particular purpose. Neither the publisher nor its dealers or distributors assumes any liability for any alleged or actual damages arising from the use of this program. (Some states do not allow for the exclusion of implied warranties, so the exclusion may not apply to you.)

NOTE: This CD-ROM uses long and mixed-case filenames requiring the use of a protected-mode CD-ROM Driver.

W9-BAA-635

BRIEF CONTENTS

Focus on
ADULT HEALTH
Medical-Surgical Nursing

Linda Honan Pellico, RN, PhD, CNS-BC
Associate Professor
Yale University School of Nursing
New Haven, Connecticut

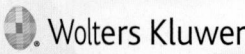

Wolters Kluwer | Lippincott Williams & Wilkins
Health

Philadelphia • Baltimore • New York • London
Buenos Aires • Hong Kong • Sydney • Tokyo

Acquisitions Editor: Julie Stegman
Product Manager: Helen Kogut
Editorial Assistant: Jacalyn Clay
Design Coordinator: Joan Wendt
Illustration Coordinator: Brett MacNaughton
Manufacturing Coordinator: Karin Duffield
Prepress Vendor: Aptara, Inc.

9 8 7 6 5

Printed in China

Library of Congress Cataloging-in-Publication Data

Focus on adult health : medical-surgical nursing / [edited by] Linda Honan Pellico.—1st ed.
  p. ; cm.
Includes index.
ISBN 978-1-58255-877-6 (alk. paper)
I. Pellico, Linda Honan.
[DNLM: 1. Perioperative Nursing–methods.   2. Nursing Care–methods.
3. Nursing Process. WY 161]
617′.0231—dc23

2011041570

Care has been taken to confirm the accuracy of the information presented and to describe generally accepted practices. However, the author(s), editors, and publisher are not responsible for errors or omissions or for any consequences from application of the information in this book and make no warranty, expressed or implied, with respect to the currency, completeness, or accuracy of the contents of the publication. Application of this information in a particular situation remains the professional responsibility of the practitioner; the clinical treatments described and recommended may not be considered absolute and universal recommendations.

The author(s), editors, and publisher have exerted every effort to ensure that drug selection and dosage set forth in this text are in accordance with the current recommendations and practice at the time of publication. However, in view of ongoing research, changes in government regulations, and the constant flow of information relating to drug therapy and drug reactions, the reader is urged to check the package insert for each drug for any change in indications and dosage and for added warnings and precautions. This is particularly important when the recommended agent is a new or infrequently employed drug.

Some drugs and medical devices presented in this publication have Food and Drug Administration (FDA) clearance for limited use in restricted research settings. It is the responsibility of the health care provider to ascertain the FDA status of each drug or device planned for use in his or her clinical practice.

LWW.com

To Mary and Timothy Honan, who have given me more love and support than any child could hope for; to John, Ryan, and Katie who have made my life complete; to all those who tolerated my many absences over the past two years; and to the graduate entry students at Yale University School of Nursing who have honed my skills as a nurse and educator for nearly a quarter of a century. I am in your debt.

To Mary and Timothy Hallett, who have given me more love and support than any child could hope for; to John, Ryan, and Katie who have made my life complete; to all those who tolerated my many absences over the past two years; and to the graduate entry students at Yale University School of Nursing who have honed my skills as a nurse and educator for nearly a quarter of a century. I am in your debt.

Laura Kierol Andrews, PhD, APRN, ACNP-BC
Assistant Professor
Yale University School of Nursing
New Haven, Connecticut
And
Senior Acute Care Nurse Practitioner
Critical Care Medicine
Hospital of Central Connecticut at New Britain General
New Britain, Connecticut
Chapter 10, Nursing Management: Patients With Chest and Lower Respiratory Tract Disorders

Donna M. Avanecean, APRN, CNRN
Nurse Practitioner
Hartford Hospital
Hartford, Connecticut
Chapter 43, Neurologic Function

Lisa M. Barbarotta, RN, MSN, AOCNS, APRN-BC
Nurse Practitioner
Hematology-Oncology Service
Smilow Cancer Hospital at Yale-New Haven
New Haven, Connecticut
Chapter 6, Cancer Care
Chapter 19, Nursing Assessment: Hematologic Function
Chapter 20, Nursing Management: Patient With Hematologic Disorders

Mary E. Bartlett, RN, MSN, FNP-BC, AAHIVS
Family Nurse Practitioner and HIV Specialist
Fair Haven Community Health Center
And
Clinical Instructor
Yale University School of Nursing
New Haven, Connecticut
Chapter 36, Nursing Assessment: Immune Function
Chapter 37, Nursing Management: Patients With Immunodeficiency, HIV Infection, and AIDS

Cynthia Bautista, RN, PhD, CNRN
Neuroscience Clinical Nurse Specialist
Yale-New Haven Hospital
New Haven, Connecticut
Chapter 46, Nursing Management: Patients With Neurologic Disorders

Dawn K. Beland, RN, MSN, CCRN, CS, CNRN
Stroke Center Coordinator
Hartford Hospital
Hartford, Connecticut
Chapter 43, Nursing Assessment: Neurologic Function

Carolynn Spera Bruno, PhDc, APRN, CNS, FNP-BC
Lecturer, Adult-Gerontological, Family, and Women's Health NP Specialty
Yale University School of Nursing
New Haven, Connecticut
Chapter 49, Nursing Management: Patients With Eye and Vision Disorders
Chapter 50, Nursing Management: Patients With Hearing and Balance Disorders

Stephanie L. Calcasola, RN, MSN, BC
Director of Quality and Medical Management
Division of Healthcare Quality
Baystate Medical Center
Springfield, Massachusetts
Chapter 15, Nursing Management: Patients With Complications From Heart Disease

Patricia Dale Cork, RN, BSN, MS
Assistant Director
Riverside School of Professional Nursing and Riverside School of Practical Nursing
Newport News, Virginia
Chapter 30, Nursing Management: Diabetes Mellitus

Sally R. Dalton, RN, MSN
Assistant Professor
Fairfield University
And
Veteran's Administration Nursing Academy Faculty
Veteran's Hospital
West Haven, Connecticut
Chapter 53, Nursing Management: Patients With Burn Injury

Sharon Druce, RN, MSN, NE-BC, CCRN
Nurse Manager Progressive Care and Stroke Unit
Mission Hospital
Mission Viejo, California
Chapter 56, Nursing Management: Emergencies and Disasters

Linda S. Dune, RN, PhD, CCRN, CNL,
  Dipl ABT
Assistant Professor, Coordinator Second Degree
  Program
University of Houston—Victoria
Sugar Land, Texas
  Chapter 7, Pain Management
  Chapter 48, Nursing Assessment: Sensorineural
    Function

Christa Palancia Esposito, MS, BSN, CNM
Certified Nurse Midwife
Women's Obstetrics and Gynecology
Trumbull, Connecticut
  Chapter 35, Nursing Management: Patients With
    Sexually Transmitted Infections

Geriann B. Gallagher, DNP, APRN,
  MAOM, Lic.Ac
Orthopedic Nurse Practitioner, Acupuncturist
Connecticut Orthopedic Associates
Bloomfield, Connecticut
  And
Clinical Instructor
Yale University School of Nursing
New Haven, Connecticut
  Chapter 40, Nursing Assessment: Musculoskeletal
    Function
  Chapter 41, Nursing Management: Patients With
    Musculoskeletal Disorders

Priscilla K. Gazarian, RN, PhD
Assistant Professor
Simmons College
Boston, Massachusetts
  Chapter 17, Nursing Management: Patients With
    Arrhythmias and Conduction Problems

Nicole C. Gora, RN, MSN, FNP
Adjunct Clinical Faculty
Yale University
New Haven, Connecticut
  And
Nurse Practitioner
MinuteClinic
Hamden, Connecticut
  And
Nurse Practitioner
MedNow
Stratford, Connecticut
  Chapter 38, Nursing Management: Patients With
    Allergic Disorders

Kelly S. Grimshaw, RN, MSN, APRN, CCRN, CCTN
Service Line Educator, Transplant
Yale New Haven Hospital
New Haven, Connecticut
  And
Member, Board of Directors
Medecins Sans Frontieres—USA
New York, New York
  Chapter 1, The Nurse's Role in Adult Health Nursing
  Chapter 55, Nursing Management: Critical Care

Margaret Campbell Haggerty, APRN, AE-C
Pulmonary Nurse Practitioner
Director, Pulmonary Rehabilitation
Norwalk Hospital
Norwalk, Connecticut
  And
Assistant Clinical Professor
Yale University School of Nursing
New Haven, Connecticut
  Chapter 11, Nursing Management: Patients With Chronic
    Obstructive Pulmonary Disease and Asthma

Rose A. Harding, RN, MSN
Instructor
JoAnne Gay Dishman Department of Nursing
Lamar University
Beaumont, Texas
  Chapter 21, Nursing Assessment: Digestive,
    Gastrointestinal, and Metabolic Function

Lianne F. Herbruck, RN, MSN, CNM
Frances Payne Bolton School of Nursing
Hamilton College
Case Western Reserve University
Chagrin Falls, Ohio
  Chapter 32, Nursing Assessment: Female and Male
    Reproductive Function

Aaron C. Huston, MSN, ACNP
Nurse Practitioner—Trauma Surgery and Critical Care
Tacoma Trauma Trust
Tacoma, Washington
  Chapter 54, Nursing Management: Shock and
    Multisystem Failure

Tara Jennings, MSN, ANP-BC
Adjunct Faculty
Simmons College
  And
Nurse Practitioner
Department of Neurology
Massachusetts General Hospital
Boston, Massachusetts
  Chapter 45, Nursing Management: Patients With
    Neurologic Trauma

Julia Merrill Jones, RN, MSN, AOCNP, CMS
Cancer Care Network Quality Manager
UAB Comprehensive Cancer Center
University of Alabama at Birmingham
Birmingham, Alabama
Chapter 33, Nursing Management: Patients
With Female Reproductive and Breast Disorders

Jill Keller, MSN, FNP-BC, OCN
Nurse Practitioner—Oncology
Bridgeport Hospital
Bridgeport, Connecticut
Chapter 44, Nursing Management: Patients With
Headache and Oncologic Disorders

Zachary R. Krom, RN, MSN, CCRN
Service Line Educator—Adult Surgery
Yale-New Haven Hospital
New Haven, Connecticut
Chapter 22, Nursing Management: Patients With Oral
and Esophageal Disorders

Michelle J. Lajiness, BSN, MS, FNP-BC
Nurse Practitioner—Urology
Beaumont Hospital Royal Oak
Royal Oak, Michigan
Chapter 26, Nursing Assessment: Renal and Urinary
Tract Function
Chapter 28, Nursing Management: Patients With
Urinary Disorders

James Mark Lazenby, RN, APRN, PhD
Assistant Professor of Nursing
Divinity Core Faculty
Council on Middle East Studies
Yale University School of Nursing
And
Advanced Oncology Certified Nurse Practitioner
Smilow Cancer Hospital at Yale New Haven
New Haven, Connecticut
Chapter 3, Chronic Illness and End-of-Life Care

Sylvia M. Lempit, MSN, APRN-BC
Clinical Transplant Nurse Coordinator
Yale New Haven Transplant Center
Department of Surgery
Yale New Haven Hospital
New Haven, Connecticut
Chapter 25, Nursing Management: Patients
With Hepatic and Biliary Disorders

Andrea Rothman Mann, RN, MSN, CNE
Instructor and Third Level Chair
Aria Health School of Nursing
Philadelphia, Pennsylvania
Chapter 13, Nursing Management: Patients With
Hypertension
Chapter 27, Nursing Management: Patients With
Renal Disorders

Philip R. Martinez, Jr., MSN, APRN-BC, CCRN-CMC
Clinical Faculty/Lecturer
Yale University School of Nursing
New Haven, Connecticut
And
Advanced Practice Registered Nurse
Middlesex Hospital/Critical Care
Middletown, Connecticut
Chapter 4, Fluid and Electrolyte and Acid–Base Imbalances
Chapter 24, Nursing Management: Patients With
Intestinal and Rectal Disorders

Jeanine L. May, MSN, MPH, APRN, ACNP-BC
Project Director, PULSE Trial
Yale University School of Nursing
And
Nurse Practitioner
Yale Health Center
New Haven, Connecticut
Chapter 16, Nursing Management: Patients With Structural,
Inflammatory, and Infectious Cardiac Disorders

Ruth McCorkle, RN, PhD, FAAN
Florence Wald Professor of Nursing
Yale University
School of Nursing
New Haven, Connecticut
Chapter 3, Chronic Illness and End-of-Life Care

Karin V. Nyström, MSN, APRN
Clinical Coordinator
Department of Neurology
Yale-New Haven Hospital
New Haven, Connecticut
Chapter 47, Nursing Management: Patients With
Cerebrovascular Disorders

Janet A. Parkosewich, RN, DNSc, FAHA
Nurse Researcher
Yale-New Haven Hospital
New Haven, Connecticut
Chapter 12, Nursing Assessment: Cardiovascular and
Circulatory Function

Havovi D. Patel, MD, MS
Associate Professor
Department of Nursing
Oakwood University
Huntsville, Alabama
  Chapter 29, Nursing Assessment: Endocrine Function

Mary G. Pierson, MSN, APRN, ACNS-BC
Clinical Manager, Cardiothoracic and Vascular Surgery
Yale-New Haven Hospital
New Haven, Connecticut
  Chapter 14, Nursing Management: Patients With
    Coronary Vascular Disorders

Linda Alessie Podolak, RN, DNP, ACNS-BC, CNE
Lecturer
Yale University School of Nursing
New Haven, Connecticut
  And
Associate Director
Bridgeport Hospital School of Nursing
Bridgeport, Connecticut
  Chapter 39, Nursing Management: Patients With
    Rheumatic Disorders

Vanessa Pomarico-Denino, MSN, FNP-BC, APRN
Nurse Practitioner
Medical Associates of North Haven, LLC
North Haven, Connecticut
  Chapter 33, Nursing Management: Patients With Female
    Reproductive and Breast Disorders

Jancee Pust-Marcone, RN, MS, CCRN
Nurse Manager—SICU at Bridgeport Hospital
Adjunct Instructor
Bridgeport Hospital School of Nursing
Bridgeport, Connecticut
  Chapter 9, Nursing Management: Patients With
    Upper Respiratory Tract Disorders
  Chapter 23, Nursing Management: Patients With Gastric
    and Duodenal Disorders

Susanne A. Quallich, ANP-BC, NP-C, CUNP
Andrology Nurse Practitioner
Division of Sexual and Reproductive Health
Department of Urology
University of Michigan
Ann Arbor, Michigan
  Chapter 26, Nursing Assessment: Renal and Urinary
    Tract Function
  Chapter 28, Nursing Management: Patients With
    Urinary Disorders
  Chapter 32, Nursing Assessment: Female and Male
    Reproductive Function
  Chapter 34, Nursing Management: Patients With
    Male Reproductive Disorders

Susan Seiboldt, RN, MSN, CNE
Assistant Professor of Nursing
Carl Sandburg College
Galesburg, Illinois
  Unit Case Studies and Related Answers
  NCLEX-Style Review Questions, Chapters 18, 36, 43,
    47, 52

Mary Sieggreen, MSN, NP, APRN-BC, CVN
Nurse Practitioner, Vascular Surgery
Harper Hospital, Detroit Medical Center
Detroit, Michigan
  Chapter 18, Nursing Management: Patients With
    Vascular Disorders and Problems of Peripheral
    Circulation

Elaine Siow, RN, MSN, ACNP-BC
Doctoral Student
University of Pennsylvania, School of Nursing
Philadelphia, Pennsylvania
  Chapter 31, Nursing Management: Patients With
    Endocrine Disorders

Patina S. Walton-Geer, MS, NP-C, RN-BC,
  CWCN, CFCN
Advanced Practice Registered Nurse
United States Public Health Service Commissioned Corps.
Edgefield, South Carolina
  And
Wound, Ostomy, Continence, and Foot Care
Nurse Clinician
AnMed Health Medical Center
Anderson, South Carolina
  Chapter 51, Nursing Assessment: Integumentary
    Function
  Chapter 52, Nursing Management: Patients With
    Dermatologic Problems

Carol Ann Wetmore, RN, MSN, ACM
Owner/Partner
Seniors Helping Seniors
Fairfield, Connecticut
  And
Clinical Faculty and Lecturer
University of Connecticut
Mansfield, Connecticut
  Chapter 2, Health Education and Health Promotion

Ena M. Williams, RN, MSM, MBA
Nursing Director, Perioperative Services
Yale-New Haven Hospital
New Haven, Connecticut
  Chapter 5, Perioperative Nursing

Joyce Brasfield Adams, EdS
Instructor
Hinds Community College
Jackson, Mississippi

Hannah M. Anderson, MSN, RN-BC
Associate Professor and Nursing Program Coordinator
Thomas Nelson Community College
Hampton, Virginia

Sheri L. Banovic, RN, MSN, FNP-BC
Associate Professor and Nursing Program Coordinator
Lewis and Clark Community College
Godfrey, Illinois

Wanda G. Barlow, RN, MSN, FNP
Nursing Instructor
Winston-Salem State University
Winston-Salem, North Carolina

Joyce Basham, MN, CNS
Nursing Instructor
Midlands Technical College
Columbia, South Carolina

Mary Bergmann, RN, MSN
Professor
San Antonio College
San Antonio, Texas

Roberta Bernardini, MSN, BSN
Professor
Tidewater Community College
Portsmouth, Virginia

Sabrina T. Beroz, RN, MSN
Professor
Montgomery College
Takoma Park, Maryland

Sophia Beydoun, RN, MSN
Nursing Faculty
Henry Ford Community College
Dearborn, Michigan

Deborah A. Beyer, RN, MSN
Assistant Professor
Miami University
Hamilton, Ohio

Carol Blakeman, MSN, BSN, AA
Professor
College of Central Florida
Ocala, Florida

Jill E. Bobb, RN, BSN
Full-Time Faculty
Edison State Community College
Piqua, Ohio

Cynthia A. Bowman, MSN, RNC, CNE
Nursing Instructor
Penn State
Altoona, Pennsylvania

Victoria Brioso-Ang, RN, MSN, CNE
Associate Professor
Sentara College of Health Sciences
Chespeake, Virginia

Angie Brindowski, RN, MSN, BSN
Clinical Assistant Professor
Carroll University
Waukesha, Wisconsin

Michele Bunning, RN, MSN
Associate Professor
Good Samaritan College of Nursing & Health Science
Cincinnati, Ohio

Darlene M. Cantu, RNC, MSN
Assistant Professor
San Antonio College
San Antonio, Texas

Cecelia Carew, RN (BC), MA, CNE, CCRN, CPAN, CEN, LNC
Associate Professor
Department of Nursing
Bronx Community College
Bronx, New York

Kristine Carey, RN, MSN
Nursing Faculty
Normandale Community College
Bloomington, Minnesota

Mary Rose Chasler, RN, MSN
Associate Professor of Nursing
Jamestown Community College
Jamestown, New York

Maria J. Colón, RN, MSN
Faculty Professor
Interamerican University of Puerto Rico—Metropolitan
    Campus
San Juan, Puerto Rico

Ruth S. Conner, RN, PhD(c), FNP-BC
Instructor
Medical University of South Carolina
Charleston, South Carolina

Patricia Dale Cork, RN, BSN, MS
Assistant Director
Riverside School of Professional Nursing and Riverside
    School of Practical Nursing
Newport News, Virginia

Theresa Delahoyde, RN, EdD
Dean of Nursing and Associate Professor of Nursing
BryanLGH College of Health Sciences
Lincoln, Nebraska

Fernande E. Deno, RN, MSN
Instructor
Anoka Ramsey Community College
Coon Rapids, Minnesota

Larinda Dixon, RN, EdD, MS
Professor of Nursing
College of DuPage
Matteson, Illinois

Sarah J. Doty, MSN, BSN, BSW
Instructor and Student Health
Southeast Missouri Hospital College of Nursing
    and Health Sciences
Cape Girardeau, Missouri

Linda K. Dunaway, RN, MSN, SANE
Professor
Maysville Community and Technical College
Maysville, Kentucky

Carrin Dvorak, RN, MSN, CNE
Assistant Professor of Nursing
Cuyahoga Community College
Cleveland, Ohio

Stacey Estridge, RN, MN
Nursing Faculty
Midlands Technical College
Columbia, South Carolina

Patricia Ferrell, RN, BSN
Nursing Instructor
San Jacinto College North
Houston, Texas

Julie A. Fisher, PhD, MSN, BSN, RNC
Professor of Nursing
Wesley College
Dover, Delaware

Rebecca Flynn, MSN, ARNP, CPNP
Assistant Professor of Nursing
Mercy College of Health Sciences
Des Moines, Iowa

Kristi France, RN, BSN, MS
National Director of Product Development–Nursing &
    Allied Health
Lincoln Educational Services
West Orange, New Jersey

Connie P. Gazmen, RN, MS, OCN
Instructor and Program Director of Adult Health Clinical
    Nurse Specialist Program
School of Nursing and Dental Hygiene
University of Hawaii at Manoa
Honolulu, Hawaii

Christy Gee, RN, MSN, FNP-BC
Doctoral Student
South College
Asheville, North Carolina

Gwendolyn Greene, RN, MSN/ED, BSN
Nursing Instructor
Midlands Technical College
Columbia, South Carolina

Karla Hall, RN, MSN
Assistant Professor
Mercy College of Health Sciences
Des Moines, Iowa

Janet R. Hamilton, RN, MSN
Allied Health Department Chair
    And
Assistant Professor
Lamar State College
Port Arthur, Texas

Janice Hancock, RN, MS, BS
Faculty
North Hennepin Community College
Brooklyn Park, Minnesota

Carol Ann Hanna, RN, PhD, BC
Faculty
Delaware County Community College
Media, Pennsylvania

Elaine C. Hannigan, RN, MSN
Continuing Lecturer
Purdue University
West Lafayette, Indiana

Lisa Harding, RN, MSN, CEN
Associate Professor
Bakersfield College
Bakersfield, California

Celia G. Hay, RN, PhD
Chair of Nursing Department
LaGrange College
LaGrange, Georgia

Lori Hendrickx, RN, EdD, CCRN
Associate Professor
South Dakota State University
College of Nursing
Brookings, South Dakota

Barbara A. Hoglund, RN, EdD, MSN, FNP-BC
Associate Professor of Nursing
Bethel University
St. Paul, Minnesota

Nina J. Hollifield, RN, MS
Assistant Professor
College of Southern Idaho
Twin Falls, Ohio

Barbie Hoover, RN, MSN
Instructor
School of Health Sciences
School of Nursing
Pennsylvania College of Technology
Williamsport, Pennsylvania

Laura J. Hope, RN, MSN, CDE
Nursing Faculty
Florence-Darlington Technical College
Florence, South Carolina

Catherine Howell, RN, MSN
Professor of Nursing Education
San Diego City College
San Diego, California

Claudette Jacobs, DNP, MS, BSN, RN-BC
Instructor of Nursing
Howard Community College
Columbia, Maryland

Uletha M. Jones, MSN, CCRN
Nursing Faculty
Pensacola State College
Pensacola, Florida

Melanie M. Jorgenson, RN, BSN
Nursing Instructor
North Seattle Community College
Seattle, Washington

Penny Kessler, RN, MN
Clinical Assistant Professor
School of Nursing
University of Minnesota
Minneapolis, Minnesota

Jonni K. Pielin Kircher, RN, MSN, CSN
Assistant Professor of Nursing
Westmoreland County Community College
Youngwood, Pennsylvania

Andrea Knesek, RN, MSN, BC (DNPc)
Nursing Faculty
Macomb Community College
Clinton Township, Michigan

Stephen D. Krau, RN, PhD, CNE
Associate Professor
School of Nursing
Vanderbilt University Medical Center
Nashville, Tennessee

Donna Kubesh, RN, PhD, MS
Associate Professor
Luther College
Decorah, Iowa

Karen Kulhanek, RN, MEd, BSN
Nursing Professor
Kellogg Community College
Battle Creek, Michigan

Marjorie J. Kurt, RN, MSN
Clinical Professor
Indiana University
School of Nursing
Indianapolis, Indiana

Jill J. Lambert, RN, MSN, GNP/CNS
Associate Professor
Charity School of Nursing
Delgado Community College
New Orleans, Louisiana

Marci L. Langenkamp, RN (AD), MS, BSN
Assistant Professor of Nursing
Edison Community College
Piqua, Ohio

Ronnette C. Langhorne, RN, MS
Assistant Professor
Thomas Nelson Community College
Hampton, Virginia

Heidi Loucks, RN, MS, CNE
Nurse Educator
Casper College
Casper, Wyoming

Lynn Lowery, RN, MSN, FCN, CCHC, CDE
Associate Professor
Charity School of Nursing
Delgado Community College
New Orleans, Louisiana

Jennifer Lunny, RN, MSN
Assistant Professor of Nursing
Broward College
Coconut Creek, Florida

Elisa Mangosing-Lemmon, RN, MSN, BSN, CMSRN
Nursing Instructor
Riverside School of Health Careers
School of Professional Nursing
Newport News, Virginia

Patricia Ann Martin, RN, MSN, FNP-BC, CNE
Associate Professor
West Kentucky Community and Technical College
Paducah, Kentucky

Ellen McAcoy, RN, MA, CNE
Associate Professor
Hillsborough Community College
Tampa, Florida

Connie McFadden, RN, MSN, CNE
Assistant Professor
The Christ College of Nursing and Health Sciences
Cincinnati, Ohio

Barbara McGraw, RN, MSN, CNE
Nursing Instructor and Curriculum Coordinator
Central Community College
Grand Island, Nebraska

Anthony McGuire, RN, PhD, CCRN, ACNP-BC
Nursing School Lecturer
California State—Long Beach
Long Beach, California
Delete this entry and add

Mary Elizabeth McKenna-Dailey, APRN-BC
Professor and Nurse Education/Family Nurse Practitioner
North Shore Community College
Danvers, Massachusetts

Heather M. McKnight, RN, MSN
Assistant Professor
Texarkana College
Texarkana, Texas

Kathleen McNeese, RN, MN, CNS
Tenured Faculty
Glendale Community College
Glendale, California

Cynthia Moore, RN, MSN, PLNC
Nursing Faculty
Minnesota State Community and Technical College
Detroit Lakes, Minnesota

Cindy Neely, RN, MSN
Campus Clinical Lab Coordinator and Professor of Nursing
Oklahoma City Community College
Oklahoma City, Oklahoma

Susan E. Nelson, RN, MSN, WCC, CLNC
Regional Nursing Department Chair
Ivy Tech Community College
Anderson, Indiana

Kathy Newton, RN, MSN, BSN
Nurse Educator
Kellogg Community College
Battle Creek, Michigan

Lynn Noell, RN, MSN
Associate Professor
Department of Nursing Education
Joliet Junior College
Joliet, Illinois

Karen Noss, RN, MSN, OCN
Associate Professor
Luzerne County Community College
Nanticoke, Pennsylvania

Annette Oberhaus, RN, MSN
Clinical Teaching Assistant
Northwest State Community College
Archbold, Ohio

Catherine J. Pagel, RN, MSN
Assistant Professor of Nursing
Mercy College of Health Sciences
Des Moines, Iowa

Karen Parker
Professor and Clinical Coordinator
Lorain County Community College
Elyria, Ohio

Michelle M. Pelter, RN, PhD
Assistant Professor
Orvis School of Nursing
University of Nevada
Reno, Nevada

Sherily Pereia, RNA, PhD, MSN
Instructor
Medical Sciences Campus and School of Nursing
University of Puerto Rico
San Juan, Puerto Rico

Norma Jean Peters, MSN
Nursing Instructor
Madison College–Reedsburg
Reedsburg, Wisconsin

Vicki Plagenz, RN, MSN
Assistant Professor
Montana State University Northern
Lewistown, Montana

Julia R. Popp, RN, MSN
Professor of Nursing
Owens Community College
Toldeo, Ohio

Dale Powis, RN, MSN
Professor
Community College of Rhode Island
Warwick, Rhode Island

Kathleen Puri, RN, MSN
Associate Professor
Chattanooga State Community College
Chattanooga, Tennessee

Loretta G. Quigley, RN, MS
Associate Dean
St. Joseph's College of Nursing
Syracuse, New York

Sharon Rappold, RN, MSN, BC
Instructor
Wharton County Junior College
Wharton, Texas

Lucille Rayford, MSN
Adjunct Faculty
California State University—Dominguez Hill
Carson, California

Emily Reece, RN, PhD, MSN
Nursing Professor
El Centro College
Dallas, Texas

Gwendolyn E. Richardson, RN, ACNS-BC
Instructor of Nursing
Midlands Technical College
Columbia, South Carolina

Tami Rogers, DVM, MSN, CNE
Lead Nursing Professor, Adult Health
Keiser University
Orlando, Florida

Martha Kathryn Findley Roper, RN, MSN
Nursing Instructor
Wallace State Community College
Hanceville, Alabama

Kathleen S. Rose, RN, MSN, BSN
Associate Professor of Nursing
Coordinator for LPN and Paramedic to RN
    Transition Programs
Chattanooga State Community College
Chattanooga, Tennessee

Kristin E. Sandau, RN, PhD
Associate Professor of Nursing and Staff RN at
    United Hospital
Department of Nursing
Bethel University
St. Paul, Minnesota

Kathy Sheats, RN, MSN
Associate Professor
University of the Virgin Islands
Kingshill, United States Virgin Islands

Leslee H. Shepard, RN, EdD, MSN, CMSRN
Assistant Professor of Nursing
Winston-Salem State University
Winston-Salem, North Carolina

Margaret Sherer, RN, MS, CEN, CNE
Nursing Faculty
Portland Community College
Portland, Oregon

Mandy M. Sheriff, RN, MSN
Instructor
Western Illinois University
School of Nursing
Macomb, Illinois

Karin Sherill, RN, MSN, CNE
Faculty Nursing Educator and Simulation Coordinator
Maricopa Nursing at Mesa Community College
Mesa, Arizona

Louise A. Shirk, MSN
Instructor, Medical-Surgical Nursing
Midlands Technical College
Columbia, South Carolina

Michelle Sink, RN, MSN
Professor of Nursing
Florida State College at Jacksonville
Jacksonville, Florida

Julie Skrabel, RN, MSN
Assistant Professor
Bryan LGH College of Health Sciences
Lincoln, Nebraska

June R. Soto, RN, MEd, APRN
Assistant Professor of Nursing
Borough of Manhattan Community College
New York, New York

Denise Spohler, RN, MSN
Professor of Nursing
Owens Community College
Toledo, Ohio

Nancy Steffen, RN, MSN
Nursing Instructor
Century College
White Bear, Minnesota

Elizabeth Zion Stratton, RN, MS
Assistant Professor of Nursing
Monroe Community College
Rochester, New York

Stephanie B. Turner, RN, EdD, MSN
Nursing Instructor
Wallace State Community College
Hanceville, Alabama

Timothy J. Voytilla, MSN, ARNP
Nursing Program Director
Keiser University–Tampa Campus
Tampa, Florida

Gerry Walker, RN, MSN, DHEd
Nursing Program Chair and Assistant Professor of Nursing
Park University
Parkville, Missouri

Terri L. Walker, RN, MSN
Assistant Nursing Program Director and Team Leader
   NPIV
Oklahoma City Community College
Oklahoma City, Oklahoma

Kathleen Warner, RN, MSN
Assistant Professor of Nursing
Viterbo University
La Crosse, Wisconsin

Cynthia L. Williams, RN, MS, CMSRN
Professor of Nursing
Oklahoma City Community College
Oklahoma City, Oklahoma

Cheryl Winter, RN, MSN, FNP-BC
Associate Professor of Nursing
Erma Byrd Higher Education Center
Bluefield State College
Beaver, West Virginia

Christine Wood, RN, MSN
Nursing Professor
Des Moines Area Community College
Ankeny, Iowa

Mary E. Wright, RN, MSN, BSN, PHN
Professor of Nursing Medical Surgical
Mount San Jacinto College
Menifee, California and
MiraCosta College
Oceanside, California

Regina L. Wright
Assistant Clinical Professor
Drexel University
Philadelphia, Pennsylvania

Jamie Zwicky, RN, MSN-Ed
Faculty
Bryant and Stratton College
Waukesha, Wisconsin

I have researched the experience of becoming a nurse and have discovered what you already know—that learning nursing is more difficult than you anticipated. I have also taught educators of nursing and can tell you that they too discover that teaching basic nursing is more difficult than anticipated. Thus, the idea for this book was to meet the needs of both students and teachers. I began this journey with a thoughtful analysis of what core content, values, and skills should form the foundation of medical–surgical nursing, and that is how this book was built. No, this book will not provide all answers to questions related to internal medical and surgical care; rather it focuses on what is essential. That said, it is not a cursory viewpoint but one that will give depth and breadth to essential content. You, the reader, will be the judge of our success.

Additionally, I wanted expert clinicians to write this book. Nurses who continue to live in the real world of clinical practice and have strong opinions about essential nursing knowing have informed this book with their wisdom.

I also know that often seeing the weight and thickness of medical–surgical texts scares you to the point that you never crack the binding. Thus, we have aimed to distill the essential and place the rest online. As an example, although we rigorously researched current references, we have placed them online for you, if needed, rather than add to the pages in this text. I am hoping for cracked binding, dog-eared pages, multicolored highlights, and notes in the margins of this book. They will stand as evidence of our success.

FEATURES

We have designed some special features to help engage you, the reader, and assist you in your understanding of the content and the nurse's role in caring for patients.

GUIDELINES FOR NURSING CARE provide steps and rationales for important procedures.

Focused Assessment boxes summarize important assessment criteria and significant findings related to a particular disorder.

Risk Factors provide a bulleted list of risk factors for a particular disorder, drawing attention to factors that can impair health.

Patient Education summarizes patient teaching, home care, and discharge planning.

Health Promotion reviews important points the nurse should discuss with the patient to prevent common health problems from developing.

Gerontologic Considerations highlight information that pertains specifically to the care of older adults who comprise the fastest-growing segment of our population.

Laboratory and Diagnostic Tests tables list common lab tests for particular disorders along with normal values, critical values, and nursing implications.

Nursing Research: Bridging the Gap to Evidence-Based Practice demonstrates the nursing implications of important research.

Focus on Pathophysiology highlights and describes important pathophysiologic processes.

Nutrition Alert highlights nutritional considerations for particular disorders.

NURSING ALERTS offer brief tips or highlight red-flag warnings for clinical practice.

DRUG ALERTS highlight key nursing considerations and drug safety information.

PEDAGOGICAL FEATURES

The following features will help you focus your attention on important content and relate it to the challenges of nursing and patient care.

UNIT CASE STUDY Each unit opens with a short case study and related questions to help prepare you for the content to be presented and to engage your critical thinking skills. Answers to the unit case studies appear at the end of the book so that you can instantly check your knowledge of the subject.

Learning Objectives appear at the beginning of each chapter to help guide and focus you on the important content in the chapter.

Critical Thinking Exercises appear at the end of each chapter and use situation-based questions to aid you in applying the knowledge you have gained.

NCLEX-Style Review Questions test your comprehension and application of the content. Answers to these review questions are available on the Instructor's Resource DVD-ROM and the Instructor's Resources on thePoint.

🖰 **References and Selected Readings** can be found on thePoint⁎ in addition to a large array of resources that will aid your comprehension and expand your knowledge of the subject matter.

GLOSSARY appears at the end of the book to assist you in understanding key terminology.

COMPREHENSIVE LEARNING PACKAGE

A carefully designed ancillary package is available to students who purchase the book and to faculty who adopt the book to further facilitate teaching and learning. A wide variety of multimedia tools are readily available and are just a click away on the Web site that accompanies the text. Visit http://thepoint.lww.com/Pellico1e.

Resources for Students

Find the following resources on thePoint⁎

- E-book
- NCLEX-Style Student Review Questions
- Animations
- Video clips
- Audio glossary
- Journal articles
- Learning objectives
- Breath sounds
- Internet resources
- References from the book
- Plan of Nursing Care for selected chapters
- And more!

Additional print resources are also available for students.

STUDY GUIDE FOR FOCUS ON ADULT HEALTH: MEDICAL-SURGICAL NURSING. Available at bookstores and lww.com, this study guide presents a variety of exercises to reinforce content and enhance learning.

HANDBOOK FOR FOCUS ON ADULT HEALTH: MEDICAL-SURGICAL NURSING. Available at bookstores and lww.com, this clinical reference presents need-to-know information on commonly encountered disorders in an easy-to-use alphabetized format.

FOCUS ON ADULT HEALTH'S HANDBOOK OF LABORATORY & DIAGNOSTIC TESTS. Available at bookstores and lww.com, this full-color handbook includes a review of specimen collection procedures followed by an alphabetical list of tests. Tests include important information about reference values and abnormal values as well as associated nursing implications, interfering factors, and essential nursing considerations before, during, and after the test.

Resources for Instructors

Instructor resources are available on an Instructor's Resource DVD-ROM and online at http://thepoint.lww.com/Pellico1e.

In addition to all of the student assets, instructor resources include the following items:

- Test Generator Questions
- PowerPoint Presentations
- Image Bank
- Pre-lecture Quizzes
- Guided Lecture Notes
- Topics for Discussion and Suggested Answers
- Assignments and Suggested Answers
- Case Studies and Suggested Answers
- Syllabus
- E-book
- Answers to NCLEX-Style Chapter Review Questions from the book
- QSEN Competency KSAs Mapped to *Focus on Adult Health: Medical-Surgical Nursing*

For 2 years, I have barraged four friends with endless e-mails, phone calls, and visits, and I must thank them for their willingness to go on this seemingly endless journey with me. They include Walter Zawalich, my GEPN soul mate who always came through with answers to my pathophysiology questions; Lisa B. Meland, my pharmacology guru who answered questions from standard dosages to interactions, and everything in between; and, finally, my anatomy sages William Stewart and Shanta Kapadia for all their support. To Megan Klim Duttera, this project's developmental editor who cajoled me, pushed me, and thankfully edited artfully my often tangential thought processes. Finally, my thanks to all the clinician colleagues who wrote chapters about their day-to-day practice so that this book is grounded in the real world of clinical.

CONTENTS

Basics of Adult Health Nursing

A 70-YEAR-OLD patient diagnosed with hypertension is being seen in the health clinic. When gathering information on the patient, the nurse notes a definite problem with medication compliance. The patient states, "I just forget to take the medication. It's no big deal!" His current BP is 170/90. His history notes that he has had previous TIAs and a stroke. He also has visual and hearing deficits.

➡ What areas of health education would be important to emphasize for this patient?
➡ Discuss variables that could effect this patient's medication compliance.
➡ What teaching strategies could be incorporated into the plan of care for this 70-year-old patient?

The Nurse's Role in Adult Health Nursing

KELLY S. GRIMSHAW

Learning Objectives

After reading this chapter, you will be able to:

1. Define nursing.
2. Understand nursing's role in the health care industry and society.
3. Describe the practitioner, leadership, and research roles of nurses.
4. Describe nursing care delivery models.
5. Describe factors causing significant changes in the health care delivery system and their impact on the health care field and the nursing profession.

THE NURSING PROFESSION AND THE HEALTH CARE INDUSTRY

To obtain a foundation for examining the role of the nurse and delivery of nursing care, it is necessary to understand the nursing profession, health care consumers, and the health care delivery system, including their interactions and the forces acting upon them.

Nursing Defined

Since Florence Nightingale wrote in 1859 that the goal of nursing was "to put the patient in the best condition for nature to act upon him," nursing leaders have described nursing as both an art and a science. Over time, the definition of nursing has evolved. In the 20th century, Virginia Henderson (1966) defined nursing as the profession that "[assists] the individual, sick or well, in the performance of those activities contributing to health or its recovery (or to peaceful death) that he would perform unaided if he had the necessary strength, will, or knowledge." More recently, in its Social Policy Statement (American Nurses Association [ANA], 2003), the American Nurses Association (ANA) defined nursing as the diagnosis and treatment of human responses to health and illness. These definitions have developed as the role of nursing has developed, and they will continue to do so.

The Health Care Industry

Since Philadelphia Hospital first opened its doors with the aid of private donations in 1753, health care in the United States has grown into an industry consuming 15.2% of our gross domestic product spending (World Health Organization [WHO], 2008). The health care industry is comprised of public and private organizations and individuals who provide preventative, diagnostic, and therapeutic services (Business Dictionary, 2009). It also includes research and development groups, professional associations and societies, medical equipment and pharmaceutical manufacturers, regulatory bodies, and health insurance companies. These groups encompass all goods and services designed to maintain and promote health for individuals and populations.

Nursing's Role in the Health Care Industry

The U.S. Department of Labor (2008) estimates that 145 million adults comprise the American workforce. Of these, more than 3.1 million (HRSA, 2010) are nurses, who comprise the largest professional group in the health care industry. Each individual nurse is placed in the unique position of standing with the patient and the patient's family at the center of the health care industry. Clinical nurses are at the bedside to act as a care provider and liaison to other health care workers in an effort to provide and coordinate this care (Fig. 1-1).

General Professional Nursing

Each individual nurse has the responsibility to carry out his or her role as described in the Social Policy Statement (ANA, 2003), and to comply with the Code for Nurses (ANA, 1985) and the Nurse Practice Act of the state in which she or he practices. The ANA, in the Nursing's Social Policy Statement

(2003, p. 6), defines nursing as "the protection, promotion, and optimization of health and abilities, prevention of illness and injury, alleviation of suffering through the diagnosis and treatment of human response, and advocacy in the care of individuals, families, communities, and populations." This definition supports the claim that nurses must be actively involved in the decision-making process regarding ethical concerns surrounding health care and human responses.

The Code of Ethics (Box 1-1), established by the ANA, consists of ethical standards, each with its own interpretive statements. The interpretive statements provide guidance to address and resolve ethical dilemmas by incorporating universal moral principles (ANA's Code of Ethics Project Task Force, 2001). The code is an ideal framework for nurses to use in ethical decision making.

The role of nurses is specified by individual state boards of nursing and is termed *scope of practice*. Scope of practice is used to delineate actions that are legally permitted

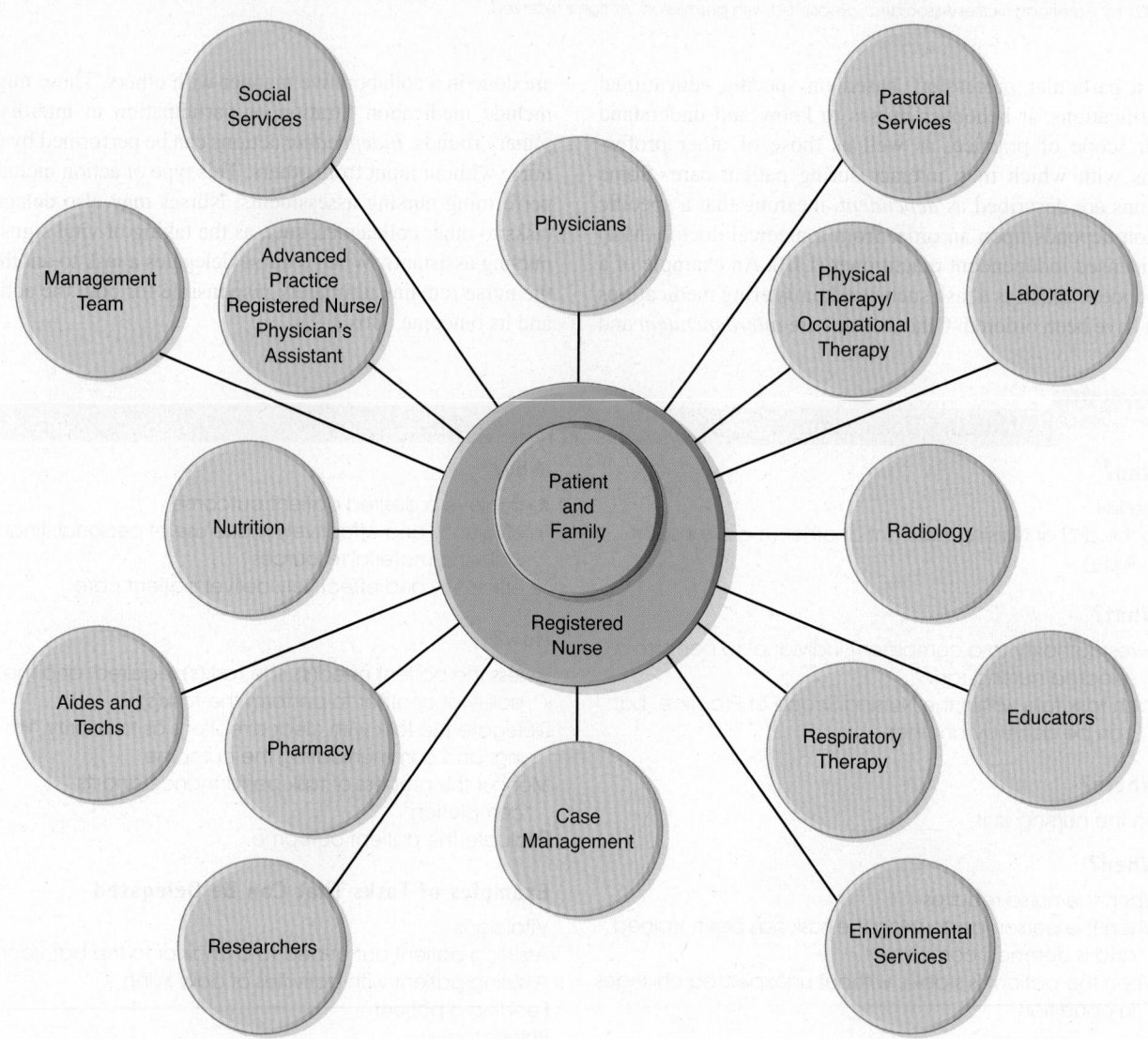

FIGURE 1-1 The Team Player.

BOX 1–1

American Nurses Association Code of Ethics for Nurses

1. The nurse, in all professional relationships, practices with compassion and respect for the inherent dignity, worth, and uniqueness of every individual, unrestricted by considerations of social or economic status, personal attributes, or the nature of health problems.
2. The nurse's primary commitment is to the patient, whether an individual, family, group, or community.
3. The nurse promotes, advocates for, and strives to protect the health, safety, and rights of the patient.
4. The nurse is responsible and accountable for individual nursing practice and determines the appropriate delegation of tasks consistent with the nurse's obligation to provide optimum patient care.
5. The nurse owes the same duties to self as to others, including the responsibility to preserve integrity and safety, to maintain competence, and to continue personal and professional growth.
6. The nurse participates in establishing, maintaining, and improving health care environments and conditions of employment conducive to the provision of quality health care and consistent with the values of the profession through individual and collective action.
7. The nurse participates in the advancement of the profession through contributions to practice, education, administration, and knowledge development.
8. The nurse collaborates with other health professionals and the public in promoting community, national, and international efforts to meet health needs.
9. The profession of nursing, as represented by associations and their members, is responsible for articulating nursing values, for maintaining the integrity of the profession and its practice, and for shaping social policy.

for a particular profession, based on specific educational qualifications. It behooves nurses to know and understand their scope of practice, as well as those of other professions with which they interact during patient care. Some actions are described as *dependent*, meaning that a specific action depends upon an order from a medical doctor (MD) or licensed independent practitioner (LIP). An example of a dependent action is a task such as administering medications that have been ordered. Other actions are *interdependent* and are done in a collaborative manner with others. These might include medication titration or participation in interdisciplinary rounds. *Independent* actions can be performed by the nurse without input from others. This type of action includes performing nursing assessments. Nurses may also delegate tasks to other colleagues, such as the taking of vital signs to nursing assistants. When a nurse delegates a task to another, the nurse remains ultimately responsible for both the action and its outcome (Box 1-2).

BOX 1–2

Nursing Delegation

Who?
The RN
To the LPN or Nursing Assistant or other (e.g., Transport Aide)

What?
Gives authority to a competent individual to perform a selected nursing task
Each task falls within the Nursing Scope of Practice, but can be done by another

Where?
On the nursing unit

When?
When the nurse requires
When the person performing the task has been trained and is deemed competent
When the patient is stable, without unexpected changes in condition

Why?
To achieve a desired patient outcome
To efficiently and effectively make use of personal, financial, and material resources
To efficiently and effectively deliver patient care

How?
Assess the patient need(s), the task(s) required, and the ability of another to perform the task(s)
Delegate the task with clear directions as to priority, timing, and communicating the outcome
Monitor the process of task performance and its completion
Evaluate the patient outcome

Examples of Tasks That Can Be Delegated
Vital signs
Assisting patient out of bed to a chair or to the bathroom
Assisting patient with activities of daily living
Feeding a patient
Phlebotomy

Expanded Nursing Roles

The explosions of knowledge and technology, and changing societal demographics, have provided nursing with unique challenges and opportunities. General nursing has become specialized, with many nurses focusing their practice on a particular population or category of illness. Professional nursing has also adapted with expanded roles to meet evolving health needs and expectations.

Advanced Practitioner Role

The advanced practitioner role, developed in the 1960s, was designed with a direct clinical focus, to help fill gaps in the health care delivery system by providing care to those in geographically and socially underserved areas. These mid-level practitioners, educated and regulated by state boards of nursing, are present in all specialties. They include, among others, nurse practitioners (NPs), certified nurse–midwives (CNMs), and certified registered nurse anesthetists (CRNA). These and similar advanced practice roles have helped distribute health care services at a decreased cost. The advanced practice role has also provided the nurse with an avenue of personal and professional development. With advanced practice roles has come a continuing effort by professional nursing organizations to yet again define nursing. While no single definition for advanced practice has been agreed upon, the ANA (1995) states that advanced practice nursing extends the scope of nursing through autonomous practice, increased use of nursing knowledge, and contributions to nursing research. Nurses who function in these roles provide direct care to patients through independent practice, practice within a health care agency, or collaboration with a physician. More specifically, advanced practice nurses hold a master's degree in nursing and are credentialed by the American Nurses Credentialing Center (ANCC) or by a specialty's national certification body, such as the Council on Certification for Nurse Anesthetists. They have the ability to diagnose disease, order, perform, and interpret diagnostic tests and prescribe medications.

The American Association of Colleges of Nursing (AACN) has taken the position that, by 2015, the doctoral level of education will become the entry level for advanced clinical practice (American Association of Colleges of Nursing [AACN], 2004). These programs include a focus on clinical care, leadership, and application of research or evidenced-based care.

Leadership Roles

Nursing has many avenues of practice, and the leadership role is inherent in all of them. Leadership is essentially the art of providing vision, knowledge, and inspiration, and leading change toward a common goal, which in nursing is quality patient care. Leadership involves those actions that all nurses execute when they assume responsibility for the actions of others directed toward determining and achieving patient care goals. Many staff nurses now work in settings in which they are held accountable for the nursing care delivered by unlicensed assistive personnel (UAPs), who work under their direct supervision. Beyond the role of direct caregiver, managers and educators also serve in leadership roles.

Nurse executives are charged with developing a vision or strategy of a particular institution and ensuring that the processes required to reach this vision are in place. An example of this may be setting the goal of achieving Magnet status within the Magnet Recognition Program®, in which a hospital is accredited by the ANCC for meeting certain criteria that attract and retain high-functioning nursing staff in order to obtain improved patient outcomes. Nurse Managers are charged with applying the Magnet strategy on the unit level, and they act as translators of strategy into actual practice. This may mean scheduling staff to facilitate participation in educational programs or in an institutional activity outside normal job limits, such as community health fairs. Other areas of focus include team coordination, financial responsibilities, policy implementation, staff development, and monitoring of quality of care.

Nurse educators can have a number of different advanced degrees, such as the clinical nurse specialist (CNS). Clinical nurse specialists have both the educational background and the clinical expertise to serve the patient, staff, and organization in applying the strategy of the institution on a front-line level. Their focus includes disease management and the application of evidence-based practice. Nurse educators may work within a specific unit of an institution, be community-based, or work in an academic setting, teaching and training nursing students.

Nurse Researchers

Like other disciplines, nursing strives for scholarship, to obtain new information and advance the art and science of the profession. This would not be possible without nurse researchers. Researchers are prepared at the doctoral level, obtaining degrees such as a doctor of philosophy (PhD) or doctor of nursing science (DNSc), in order to work in academic or research-intensive settings. The goal of nurse researchers is to establish the effectiveness of nursing interventions and nursing care and to further evidence-based practice. Evidence is researched and evaluated to formulate guidelines to be used in clinical practice. This evidence is in turn evaluated by the nurse in clinical practice, who is often in the best position to participate in data collection and facilitate the study through communication with the patient, family, and other health care professionals. The nurse directly involved in patient care is also ideally suited to identify nursing problems and important issues that can serve as a basis for research.

THE PATIENT: CONSUMER OF NURSING AND HEALTH CARE

The central figure in health care services is the patient. The term *patient* is derived from a Latin verb meaning "to suffer." It has traditionally been used to describe those who are

recipients of care. Patients' needs vary, depending on their roles (as a member of a family, as a member of a particular community), associated circumstances, and past experiences, as well as the problem or problems for which they sought health care. Among the nurse's important functions in health care delivery is obtaining an understanding of the patient's situation and identifying his or her immediate needs, in order to address them.

Certain needs are basic to all people. Noted psychologist Abraham H. Maslow (1954) developed a theory describing basic human needs and how these needs build upon one another to achieve physical, social, and spiritual health and well-being. This model is now known as Maslow's *hierarchy of needs* (Fig. 1-2). Maslow ranked human needs as physiologic needs, safety and security, sense of belonging and affection, esteem and self-respect, and self-actualization. This last level—self actualization—refers to fulfilling ones individual potential, and includes the desire to know and understand, as well as aesthetics. Once a basic or essential need is met, people usually experience a need on another next level. Depending on an individual's certain situation (e.g., minor vs. major illness or injury), he or she may move among levels. Lower-level needs always remain, but a person's ability to pursue higher-level needs generally indicates movement toward improved health and well-being. This hierarchy provides a useful framework that can be applied to the patient when assessing strengths, limitations, and needs as a consumer of nursing and health care.

The patient who seeks care for a health issue is also an individual person, a member of a family, and a citizen of the community. The ultimate goal of care is to return the patient to the various roles he or she holds in life. Many patients, as consumers of health care, have become more knowledgeable about health care options and are assuming a collaborative approach with the nurse and the health care system.

Consumers of nursing and health care are as varied as their numbers are large. There are countless differences in demographics, personalities, and abilities that must be understood, so that the patient can participate in his or her own health care decisions. A basic tenet of nursing is to determine the consumers' needs and wants, in order to guide them through their health care experience.

HEALTH, WELLNESS, AND HEALTH PROMOTION

The health care system of the United States, which traditionally has been disease-oriented, is placing increasing emphasis on health and health promotion. Many nurses who would formerly have been involved in the care of acutely ill patients are engaged in health promotion and illness prevention.

Health

How health is perceived depends on how health is defined. The World Health Organization (WHO), in the preamble to its constitution, defines health as a "state of complete physical, mental, and social well-being and not merely the absence of disease and infirmity" (WHO, 1948). Although this definition of health does not allow for any variation in degrees of wellness or illness, the concept of a health–illness continuum allows for a greater range in describing a person's health status. By viewing health and illness on a continuum, it is possible to consider a person as being neither completely healthy nor completely ill. Instead, a person's state of health is ever-changing and has the potential to range from high-level wellness to extremely poor health and imminent death. Use of the health–illness continuum makes it possible to view a person as simultaneously possessing degrees of both health and illness.

The limitations of the WHO definition of health are clear in relation to chronic illness and disability. Chronically ill people do not meet the standards of health as established by the WHO definition. However, when viewed from the perspective of the health–illness continuum, people with a chronic illness or disability may be viewed as having the potential to attain a high level of wellness, if they are successful in meeting their health potential within the limits of their chronic illness or disability.

Wellness

Wellness has been defined as being equivalent to health. However, the term *wellness* implies a proactive process toward a goal of physical, psychological, and spiritual well-being in which people of any age and in various stages of health are willing to "work hard" (Kiefer, 2008). Pender conceptualized five dimensions of wellness: (1) self-responsibility, (2) nutritional awareness, (3) physical fitness, (4) stress management, and (5) sensitivity to the effects

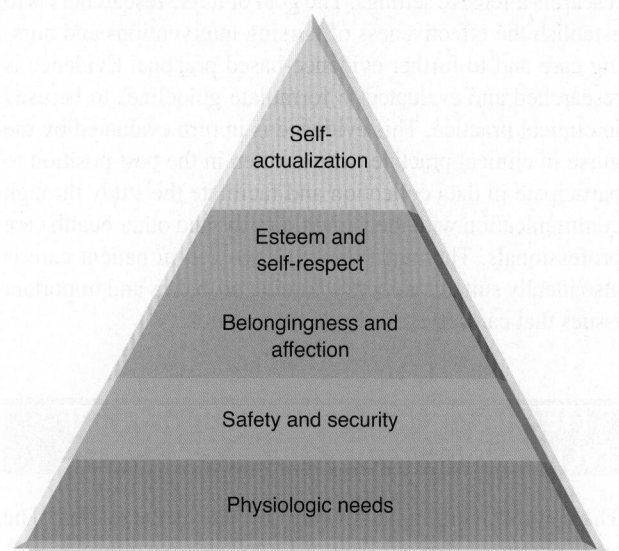

Self-actualization

Esteem and self-respect

Belongingness and affection

Safety and security

Physiologic needs

FIGURE 1-2 Maslow's hierarchy of needs.

of the environment on wellness (Pender, 1982). With this in mind, it is the goal of health care providers to promote positive changes that are directed toward health and well-being. Wellness has a subjective aspect, and the nurse must understand the importance of recognizing and responding to patient individuality and diversity in health care.

Health Promotion

Today, increasing emphasis is placed on health, health promotion, wellness, and self-care. Health is seen as resulting from a lifestyle oriented toward wellness. The result has been the evolution of a wide range of health promotion strategies, including screening, genetic testing, lifetime health monitoring, environmental and mental health programs, risk reduction, and nutrition and health education.

A growing interest in self-care skills is evidenced by the large number of health-related publications, Internet sites, conferences, and workshops designed for the lay public. These programs are designed to promote self-care education, often emphasizing health promotion and disease prevention. As people become increasingly knowledgeable about their health, they often take more interest in and responsibility for their health and well-being.

Special efforts need to be made by health care professionals to determine which organizations, websites, and other venues are providing peer-reviewed and up-to-date information, to ensure people's ability to obtain accurate information concerning health-promoting behaviors. Health-related information and sources of health promotion, whether received from health care professionals, through self-help groups, or from publications, is intended to reach and motivate members of various cultural and socioeconomic groups about lifestyle and health practices.

MODELS OF NURSING CARE

Nursing has evolved from the hospital or home care of the individual during illness to caring for individuals, communities, and populations across the health care continuum in an ever-growing number of ambulatory and inpatient settings. Shortened hospital stays, combined with economic constraints, an aging population, and a greater number of individuals with chronic disease, have necessitated changes in models of nursing care to those best suited to a particular population or setting. Nursing models, such as team nursing, in which nursing staff performed different functions such as medication administration or dressing changes, and primary nursing, in which one nurse provided all assessments and assistance for an individual throughout his or her healthcare visit, have changed.

Patient- and Family-Centered Care

The current paradigm of patient- and family-centered care is defined by the Institute for Family-Centered Care (2009, p. 1)

as a model in which the patient and family are cared for by an interdisciplinary group of health care professionals, with the active participation of the patient and family and their collaboration in informed decision making:

> In their efforts to improve health care quality and safety, hospital leaders today increasingly realize the importance of including a perspective too long missing from the health care equation: the perspective of patients and families. The experience of care, as perceived by the patient and family, is a key factor in health care quality and safety. Bringing the perspectives of patients and families directly into the planning, delivery, and evaluation of health care, and thereby improving its quality and safety, is what patient- and family-centered care is all about. Studies increasingly show that when health care administrators, providers, and patients and families work in partnership, the quality and safety of health care rise, costs decrease, and provider and patient satisfaction increase.

This model appears adaptable to the many facilities through which a person may move during the period of care.

Collaborative Practice

The patient- and family-centered model is a collaborative model and should be a primary goal for nursing. The nursing profession recognizes that it does not practice in a vacuum, and acknowledges the need for participation by the patient and family. With the greater focus on patient safety and improved outcomes at a lower cost, nursing continues to recognize the importance of interaction and communication with other professionals, support staff, and patients and their families in an effort known as *collaborative practice*. Nurses, physicians, and ancillary health personnel perform their particular functions but share in the responsibility of making clinical decisions. The importance of interdisciplinary rounding and collaborative decision making cannot be underestimated in terms of its ability to provide improved patient care while fostering team cohesion. This is a venture that promotes shared participation, responsibility, and accountability in a health care environment that is striving to meet the complex health care needs of the public.

INFLUENCES ON HEALTH CARE DELIVERY

Scientific and technological advances throughout the 20th and into the 21st century have led to social, political, and economic changes. These profound changes have forced the health care industry in general, and nursing practice in particular, to adapt.

Population Demographics

First among the many significant shifts are changes in population demographics, including an increase in the number of

people comprising the general population. The 2008 U.S. Bureau of Census (2008) estimated that 307,212,000 live in the United States. Population growth is attributed in part to improved public health services and improved nutrition. The 20th century witnessed a mass migration from rural to urban areas, with the majority of the population now living in urban areas.

Immigration

The United States also has an increasingly culturally diverse population, as growing numbers of people from different national backgrounds enter the country. Some projections indicate that, by 2050, one in five Americans will be an immigrant; and changes will occur in the balance of racial and ethnic minority groups, with Hispanics constituting 29% of the population and non-Hispanic white people becoming a minority (47%). It is projected that the elderly population in the United States will double in size (Passel & Cohn, 2008).

As the cultural composition of the population changes, it is increasingly important to address cultural considerations in the delivery of health care. Patients from diverse socio-cultural groups not only bring various health care beliefs, values, and practices to the health care setting, but they also have a variety of risk factors for some disease conditions and unique reactions to treatment. These factors significantly affect an individual's responses to health care problems or illnesses, to caregivers, and to the care itself. Unless these factors are understood and respected by health care providers, the care delivered may be ineffective, and health care outcomes may be negatively affected. A goal should be set to encourage and foster the education of ethnic minority groups in health care professions. If achieved, one day a balance will be struck between the health care professional staff and the actual population it serves.

Acknowledging and adapting to the cultural needs of patients and significant others are important components of nursing care. In addition, facilitating access to cultur-ally appropriate health care is critical if nursing care is to be holistic. Culturally competent nursing care is a dynamic process that requires comprehensive knowledge of culture-specific information and an awareness of and sensitivity to the effect that culture has on the care situation. Exploring one's own cultural beliefs and how they might conflict with the beliefs of the patient being cared for is a first step toward becoming culturally competent. Specific areas to be consid-ered when providing care include the amount of space and distance needed to feel comfortable, eye contact, attitudes related to time, the use of touch, observance of civil and reli-gious holidays, and the cultural meanings associated with food.

Because the nurse–patient interaction is the focal point of nursing, nurses should consider their own cultural orienta-tion when conducting assessments of patients and patients' families and friends. The guidelines in Box 1-3 may prove useful to nurses wishing to provide culturally appropriate

---

BOX 1-3

Culturally Appropriate Care

- Know your own cultural attitudes, values, beliefs, and practices.
- Regardless of good intentions, everyone has cultural "baggage" that ultimately results in ethnocentrism.
- Maintain a broad, open attitude. Expect the unex-pected. Enjoy surprises.
- Avoid seeing all people as alike; that is, avoid cultural stereotypes, such as "all Chinese like rice" or "all Ital-ians eat spaghetti."
- Try to understand the reasons for any behavior by dis-cussing commonalities and differences.
- If a patient has said or done something that you do not understand, ask for clarification. Be a good lis-tener. Most patients will respond positively to ques-tions that arise from a genuine concern for and inter-est in them.
- If at all possible, speak the patient's language (even simple greetings and social courtesies are appreci-ated). Avoid feigning an accent or using words that are ordinarily not part of your vocabulary.
- Be yourself. There is no right or wrong way to learn about cultural diversity.

---

care. Box 1-4 provides suggestions on overcoming language barriers.

Aging Population

The increase in lifespan experienced in the United States over the last century has resulted in a tripling of the number of elderly citizens, most of whom are women. The elderly population in the United States has increased significantly, and will continue to grow in future years. The American Geriatrics Society Foundation for Health in Aging (2009) states that, by 2030, one out of every five people living in America will be over the age of 65. In addition, people 85 years of age and older constitute one of the fastest-growing segments of the population. The health care needs of older adults are often chronic in nature, with intermit-tent exacerbations or acute episodes. This makes their care more complex and demands significant human, material, and financial investment by the health care industry.

Changing Patterns of Disease

The past century has seen a dramatic shift in disease pat-terns, which is generally considered to be a move from the predominance of infectious disease to that of chronic illness. Public health measures, such as sanitation and vaccinations, have saved countless lives. That said, infectious diseases such as rhinovirus (the common cold) and influenza remain, and the incidence of tuberculosis and HIV infection con-tinues to rise. Methicillin-resistant *Staphylococcus aureus* (MRSA) and vancomycin-resistant *Enterococcus* (VRE) are

BOX 1-4 Overcoming Language Barriers

- Greet the patient using the last or complete name. Avoid being too casual or familiar. Point to yourself and say your name. Smile.
- Proceed in an unhurried manner. Pay attention to any effort by the patient or family to communicate.
- Speak in a low, moderate voice. Avoid talking loudly. Remember that there is a tendency to raise the volume and pitch of your voice when the listener appears not to understand. The listener may perceive that you are shouting and/or angry.
- Organize your thoughts. Repeat and summarize frequently. Use audiovisual aids when feasible.
- Use short, simple sentence structure and speak in the active voice.
- Use simple words, such as "pain" rather than "discomfort." Avoid medical jargon, idioms, and slang. Avoid using contractions, such as *don't, can't, won't.*
- Use nouns repeatedly instead of pronouns. *Example*: Do not say: "He has been taking his medicine, hasn't he?" Do say: "Does Juan take medicine?"
- Pantomime words (use gestures) and simple actions while verbalizing them.
- Give instructions in the proper sequence. *Example*: Do not say: "Before you rinse the bottle, sterilize it." Do say: "First, wash the bottle. Second, rinse the bottle."
- Discuss one topic at a time, and avoid giving too much information in a single conversation. Avoid using conjunctions. *Example*: Do not say: "Are you cold and in pain?" Do say (while pantomiming/ gesturing): "Are you cold?" "Are you in pain?"
- Talk directly to the patient, rather than to the person who accompanied him or her.
- Validate whether the person understands by having him or her repeat instructions, demonstrate the procedure, or act out the meaning.
- Use any words you know in the person's language. This indicates that you are aware of and respect the patient's primary means of communicating.
- Try a third language. Many Indo-Chinese speak French. Europeans often know three or four languages. Try Latin words or phrases, if you are familiar with the language.
- Be aware of culturally based gender and age differences and diverse socioeconomic, educational, and tribal/ regional differences when choosing an interpreter.
- Obtain phrase books from a library or bookstore, make or purchase flash cards, contact hospitals for a list of interpreters, and use both formal and informal networking to locate a suitable interpreter. Although they are costly, some telecommunication companies provide translation services.

only two of many current and evolving antibiotic-resistant organisms complicating treatment of infectious disease.

Despite the ongoing battle with infectious disease, advances in medical knowledge have presented many diagnostic and treatment avenues previously unavailable. This has led to the cure or effective management of illness over a long period of time and contributed to increasing lifespan. Heart disease, once uniformly disabling or fatal, is managed with medications, radiological procedures, and surgeries. These advancements, however, are a double-edged sword, as the art and science of medicine and nursing enable a population subset to live but be unable to cope or function independently. Nursing, which has always encouraged patients to take control of their conditions, plays a prominent role in the current focus on the management of chronic illness and disability.

Two disorders on the rise in the United States are obesity and diabetes, and one is linked to the other. With lifestyle changes and easy access to food, obesity has become commonplace, and more than 30% of adults and 16% of children are now classified as obese (Centers for Disease Control and Prevention [CDC], 2009) This condition is a leading cause of secondary illness, ranging from asthma to cancer and diabetes.

The Centers for Disease Control and Prevention (CDC) (2006) estimates that 16.8 million people in the United States have been diagnosed with diabetes, which is triple the number diagnosed in 1980. Both the elderly and those who are significantly overweight account for a large part of this population. Diabetes leads to increased morbidity, mortality, and cost for the individual and the health care system alike.

Advances in Technology

Advances in technology have occurred with greater frequency during the past several decades than in all other periods of civilization. Sophisticated devices have revolutionized how disease is prevented, how patients are diagnosed and treated, and even how communication to and about patients is conducted. Advanced technology has provided access to faster, less invasive, and less painful testing and procedures. In fact, many tests and procedures that once required a hospital stay are routinely performed on an outpatient basis. A disorder that once may have required an operation for diagnosis can many times be diagnosed via computed tomography (CT) or magnetic resonance imaging (MRI). Computers are also significantly changing workflow, as medical records become completely electronic, resulting in improved communication among caregivers, efficient documentation, and ease of medical investigation and research.

Public Safety

The U.S. health care system is based on public trust. This translates into people's confidence that the care they will

receive in a hospital or other health care setting will meet legal and social standards. Thus, this large and diverse system is charged with the protection and maintenance of these standards when providing a safe work environment for employees and a healing environment for clients and patients.

Regulatory Bodies

To ensure that minimal standards are maintained, governing and oversight bodies regulate the health care system. Agencies involved in oversight include those in the following discussion.

Occupational Health and Safety Administration

Under the Occupational Safety and Health Act of 1970, employers are responsible for providing a safe and healthy workplace for their employees. The role of the Occupational Safety and Health Administration (OSHA) is to promote the safety and health of working people by setting and enforcing standards; providing training, outreach, and education; establishing partnerships; and encouraging continual process improvement in workplace safety and health.

The Joint Commission

The Joint Commission is a private, nonprofit organization whose mission is to "continuously improve the safety and quality of care provided to the public through the provision of health care accreditation and related services that support performance improvement in health care organizations" (Joint Commission, 2009). At present, the Joint Commission accredits approximately 88% of the nation's hospitals (Joint Commission, 2009).

Centers for Medicare and Medicaid Services

The Centers for Medicare and Medicaid Services (CMS) is the federal agency that manages Medicare, which is the health insurance program for people over 65 years of age, people with certain disabilities under age 65, and those with end-stage renal disease (ESRD). The CMS also manages Medicaid, which is a state-administered program for low-income individuals and families who fit into an eligibility group recognized by federal and state law. In addition, the CMS manages the children's health insurance program (CHIP), which provides coverage for millions of uninsured children. The CMS exists to ensure effective up-to-date health care coverage and to promote quality care for beneficiaries.

Department of Public Health

Each state has its own Department of Public Health (DPH), with its own mission. They all are generally charged with the protection of the health and well-being of the state's population and environment. The State Board of Nursing falls within this department and serves to regulate the practice of nursing and the licensing of individual nurses.

Professional Societies and Associations

Associations and societies have a specific focus. They help ensure basic standards, as well as promote and recognize advanced knowledge and expertise.

The ANA is the only full-service professional organization representing the nation's more than 3.1 million registered nurses (RNs) through its 54 constituent member associations. The ANA advances the nursing profession by fostering high standards of nursing practice, promoting the rights of nurses in the workplace, projecting a positive and realistic view of nursing, and lobbying Congress and regulatory agencies on health care issues affecting nurses and the public.

Hospitals and Institutions

In the 1980s, hospitals and other health care agencies implemented programs designed to measure the quality of care they provided. These programs, known as *quality assurance* (QA) or *quality improvement* (QI), were required to be in place for reimbursement for services and for accreditation by the Joint Commission on Accreditation of Healthcare Organizations (JCAHO; now known simply as the Joint Commission). They sought to establish and maintain accountability to society on the part of the health professions by meeting minimal criteria for the quality, appropriateness, and cost of health services.

In the early 1990s, *continuous quality improvement* (CQI) was identified as a more effective mechanism for improving the quality of health care. Unlike QA, which focuses on individual incidents or errors and minimal expectations, CQI focuses on the processes used to provide care, with the aim of improving quality by assessing and improving those interrelated processes that most affect patient care outcomes and patient satisfaction. Continuous quality improvement involves analyzing, understanding, and improving clinical, financial, and operational processes. Problems that occur as more than isolated events are subject to examination, and all issues that may affect patient outcome are studied. Nurses directly involved in the delivery of care are engaged in analyzing data and refining the processes used in CQI. Their knowledge of the processes and conditions that affect patient care is critical in designing changes to improve the quality of the care provided and ensuring that this care meets or exceeds Joint Commission standards.

Individual Employees

Every individual accepts responsibility for his or her position. For nurses, this entails:

- Maintaining licensure
- Maintaining health requirements, such as annual tuberculosis screening
- Maintaining annual competencies, such as those established by corporate compliance

- Participating in continuing education and certification activities
- Participating in hospital committee and quality review activities
- Providing safe and current care to patients and families.

Economics

The belief that comprehensive, quality health care should be provided for all citizens prompted government concern about rising health care costs and wide variations in charges among providers. In 1983, the United States Congress passed the most significant health legislation since the Medicare program was enacted in 1965. The federal government was no longer able to afford to reimburse hospitals for patient care that was delivered without any defined limits on costs. Therefore, it approved a *prospective payment system* for hospital inpatient services. Based on diagnosis-related groups (DRGs), prospective payment sets the rates of reimbursement for hospital services for Medicare patients. Hospitals receive payment at a fixed rate for patients with diagnoses that fall into a specific DRG. A fixed payment has been predetermined for more than 470 possible diagnostic categories, covering the majority of medical diagnoses of patients admitted to the hospital. Hospitals receive the same payment for every patient with a given diagnosis, or who falls within a given DRG. If the cost of the patient's care is lower than the payment, the hospital makes a profit; if the cost is higher, the hospital incurs a loss. As a result, hospitals are placing greater emphasis on reducing costs, monitoring utilization of services, and limiting length of patient stay.

There is also the renewed focus on overhauling the nation's health care system in an effort to control its ever-increasing cost. At this writing, attempts at health care reform are under way although the results and effects remain far from certain. Any future changes will most likely prove to have profound effects on regulatory agencies, health care organizations, individual practitioners, and patients.

Nurses in hospitals now care for patients who are older and sicker and require more nursing services. Nurses in the community are caring for patients who have been discharged earlier and need high-technology acute care services as well as long-term care. The importance of effective discharge planning, along with utilization review and quality improvement, cannot be overstated. Nurses in acute care settings must work with other health care team members to maintain quality care while facing pressures to discharge patients earlier and decrease costs.

Chapter Review

Critical Thinking Exercises

1. The roles of nurses continue to develop and change. What avenues of continued education are available to the new nurse in order to adapt to these changing roles?
2. What responsibilities do individual nurses have regarding their participation in monitoring and evaluating patient safety and the quality of care they provide?
3. What other influences on the health care delivery system are not necessarily discussed in this chapter?

NCLEX-Style Review Questions

1. Under the Occupational Safety and Health Act (OSHA) of 1970, employers are responsible for providing a safe and healthy workplace for their employees. Which of the following would be inconsistent with the role of OSHA?
   A. Financial assistance
   B. Outreach
   C. Education
   D. Establishing partnerships
2. Nursing has evolved from the hospital or home care of the individual during illness to caring for individuals, communities, and populations across the health care continuum. Which of the following necessitated changes in models of nursing care?
   A. Less individuals with chronic disease
   B. Increased aging population
   C. Less inpatient settings
   D. Lengthened hospital stays
3. Which of the following entities are charged with the protection of health and well-being of the state's population and environment?
   A. Joint Commission
   B. Occupational Health and Safety Administration
   C. Department of Public Health
   D. Centers of Medicare and Medicaid Services
4. Based on DRGs, prospective payment sets the rates of reimbursement for hospital services for Medicare patients. Which of the following is an accurate statement regarding the use of DRGs?
   A. If the cost of the patient's care is lower than the payment, the hospital takes a loss.
   B. If the cost of the patient's care is higher than the payment, the hospital takes a loss.
   C. Hospitals receive various payments for every patient with a given diagnosis.
   D. If the cost of the patient's care is higher than the payment, the hospital makes a profit.

(continued on page 12)

Chapter Review (*continued*)

5. Nurses should consider their own cultural orientation when interacting with patients. Which of the following is a technique that can be used to overcome a language barrier when interacting with a patient?

A. Talk loudly so that the patient will understand.

B. Give the patient a substantial amount of information.

C. Give instructions in proper sequence.

D. Talk directly to the person that accompanied the patient.

Try these additional resources to enhance your learning and understanding of this chapter:

• thePoint online resource available at **http://thepoint.lww.com/Pellico1e**

• *Handbook for Focus on Adult Health: Medical-Surgical Nursing*

• *Study Guide for Focus on Adult Health: Medical-Surgical Nursing*

References and Selected Readings

References and selected readings associated with this chapter can be found on the website that accompanies the book. Visit http://thepoint.lww.com/Pellico1e to access the references and other additional resources associated with this chapter.

Health Education and Health Promotion

CAROL ANN WETMORE

Learning Objectives

After reading this chapter, you will be able to:

1. Describe the purposes and significance of health education.

2. Describe the concept of adherence to a therapeutic regimen.

3. Identify variables influencing a person's adherence to a therapeutic regimen.

4. Describe strategies that facilitate adults' learning abilities.

5. Describe the relationship of health education to the nursing process.

6. Develop a teaching plan for a patient.

7. Define health promotion and discuss the role of the nurse related to it.

Teaching, as a function of nursing, is included in all state nurse practice acts and in the *Standards of Clinical Nursing Practice* of the American Nurses Association (American Nurses Association [ANA], 2004). **Health education** is an independent function of nursing practice and is a primary nursing responsibility. All nursing care is directed toward promoting, maintaining, and restoring health; preventing illness; and helping people adapt to the residual effects of illness. Many of these nursing activities are accomplished through health education or patient teaching. Nurses who serve as teachers are challenged to focus on the educational needs of communities, as well as on specific patient and family educational needs. Health education is important to nursing care because it affects the abilities of people and families to perform important self-care activities.

Every contact an individual nurse has with a health care consumer, whether or not that person is ill, should be considered an opportunity for health teaching. Although people have a right to decide whether or not to learn, nurses have the responsibility to present information that motivates people to recognize the need to learn. Therefore, nurses must use opportunities in all health care settings to promote **wellness**. Educational environments may include homes, hospitals, community health centers, schools, places of business, service agencies, shelters, and consumer action or support groups.

HEALTH EDUCATION

Trends in Health Education

Much of the core of health education today is focused on increasing patient involvement and accountability for individual care and treatment plans. Health education programs are often designed as patient safety initiatives and are geared toward encouraging increased communication between patients and care providers. In March 2002, The Joint Commission, together with the Centers for Medicare and Medicaid Services, launched SPEAK UP, a national campaign to urge patients to take a role in preventing health care errors by becoming active, involved, and informed participants on the health care team. The Agency for Healthcare Research and Quality (AHRQ) has developed the resource *Questions Are*

the Answer: Getting Patients Involved in Their Healthcare. This program provides the message to patients that "clinicians, the government, and many other groups are working hard to improve health care quality, but it's a team effort. You can improve your care and the care of your loved ones by taking an active role in your health care. Ask questions. Understand your condition. Evaluate your options" (http://www.ahrq.gov/questionsaretheanswer/). Patients are being encouraged to play an active role in the care and information they receive. Likewise, the Partnership for Clear Health Communication at the National Patient Safety Foundation has developed the *Ask Me 3* program. *Ask Me 3* promotes three simple but essential questions that patients should ask their providers in every health care interaction:

What is my main problem?
What do I need to do?
Why is it important for me to do this?

Purpose of Health Education

The goal of patient and family education is to improve patient outcomes. For purposes of this discussion, family shall be considered to be the person(s) who play a significant role in the patient's life. This may include person(s) not legally related to the patient. Effective health education lays a solid foundation for individual and community wellness. Teaching is an integral tool that all nurses use to assist patients and families in developing effective health behaviors and in altering lifestyle patterns that predispose people to health risks.

People with chronic illnesses and disabilities are among those most in need of health education. As the lifespan of the population increases, the number of people with such illnesses also increases. People with chronic illness need health care information to participate actively in and assume responsibility for much of their own care. Health education can help favorably change a patient's behavior, increase the ability to cope with and manage health, and improve understanding of the options, risks, and benefits of care, treatment, and services. It can also prevent crisis situations and reduce the potential for rehospitalization resulting from inadequate information about self-care. The goal of health education is to teach people to live life to its healthiest—that is, to strive toward achieving their maximum health potential.

In addition to the public's right to and desire for health education, patient education is also a strategy for promoting self-care at home and in the community, reducing health care costs by preventing illness, avoiding expensive medical treatments, decreasing lengths of hospital stays, and facilitating earlier discharge.

Adherence to the Therapeutic Regimen

One of the goals of patient education is to encourage people to adhere to their **therapeutic regimen**. **Adherence** to treatment usually requires that a person make one or more lifestyle changes to carry out specific activities that promote and maintain health. Common examples of behaviors facilitating health include taking prescribed medications, maintaining a healthy diet, increasing daily activities and exercise, self-monitoring for signs and symptoms of illness, practicing specific hygiene measures, seeking recommended health evaluations and screenings, and performing other therapeutic and preventive measures.

Many people do not adhere to their prescribed regimens; rates of adherence are generally low, especially when the regimens are complex or of long duration. Nonadherence to prescribed therapy has been the subject of many studies; a wide range of variables appears to influence the degree of adherence, including the following:

• Inadequate cognitive, psychomotor, or language skills
• Personal values, beliefs, misconceptions, and attitudes coupled with their associated anxiety, depression, and/or fear
• Distrust if loss of control occurs in the decision-making process
• Difficulty in adopting recommended changes
• Insufficient social support or outright sabotage by that support
• Poor self-concept or self-efficacy

Nurses' success with promoting adherence can be improved by creating a collaborative relationship that addresses patient's priorities, circumstances, and goals. Nurses become colleagues, offering guidance and support.

Health Literacy and Willingness to Learn

Before initiating a teaching–learning program, it is important to assess the person's physical and emotional readiness to learn, as well as his or her ability to learn what is being taught. This information then becomes the basis for establishing goals that can motivate the person. Involving learners in establishing mutually acceptable goals serves the purpose of encouraging active involvement in the learning process and shared responsibility for learning.

The strongest predictor of a patient's health status is the health literacy skills he or she possesses. Literacy means more than reading level, "it requires a complex group of reading, listening, analytical, and decision-making skills, and the ability to apply these skills to health situations" (National Network of Libraries of Medicine [NNLM], 2010). Consider the complexity of medication regimens (dosing, timing, calculations), informed consent, technology (peak flow meters, glucose monitoring devises, etc.), and the nurse can gain insight into the impact of health literacy on patients' well-being. People with low literacy have less knowledge about their health problems, are less likely to seek help early in the course of a disease, have less knowledge of self-care instructions, are at higher risk

BOX 2-1

Gerontologic Considerations

Elderly people frequently have one or more chronic illnesses that are managed with numerous medications and complicated by periodic acute episodes. Elderly people may also have other problems that affect adherence to therapeutic regimens, such as increased sensitivity to medications and their side effects, difficulty in adjusting to change and stress, financial constraints, forgetfulness, inadequate support systems, lifetime habits of self-treatment with over-the-counter medications, visual and hearing impairments, and mobility limitations. An important predictor of patient adherence to a therapeutic regime is concordance of the patient and physicians' perception of their health.

Changes in cognition with age may include slowed mental functioning; decreased short-term memory, abstract thinking, and concentration; and slowed reaction time. These changes are often accentuated by the health problems that cause the elderly person to seek health care in the first place. Effective teaching strategies include a slow-paced presentation of small amounts of material at a time; frequent repetition of information; and the use of reinforcement techniques, such as audiovisual and written materials and repeated practice sessions. Distracting stimuli should be minimized as much as possible in the teaching environment.

Sensory changes associated with aging also affect teaching and learning. Teaching strategies to accommodate decreased visual acuity include large-print and easy-to-read materials printed on nonglare paper. To maximize hearing, teachers must speak distinctly with a normal or lowered pitch, facing the person so that speech reading can occur as needed. Visual cues often help to reinforce verbal teaching.

Family members should be involved in teaching sessions when possible. They provide another source for reinforcement of material and can help the elderly person recall instructions later. Family members can also provide valuable assessment information about the person's living situation and related learning needs.

When nurses, families, and other involved health care professionals work collaboratively to facilitate the elderly person's learning, chances of success are maximized. Successful learning for the elderly should result in improved self-care management skills, enhanced self-esteem, confidence, and a willingness to learn in the future. Above all, health care professionals must work together to provide continuous, coordinated care; otherwise, the efforts of one health care professional may be negated by those of another.

---

for hospitalization, and lack the skills needed to negotiate the health care system. As many as 90 million people in the United States have difficulty understanding and using health information (Nielsen-Bohlman, Panzer, & Kindig, 2004), and vulnerable populations related to health literacy include the elderly (two-thirds of U.S. adults age 60 and over have inadequate or marginal literacy skills); minority and immigrant populations; those from low income households, and those with chronic disease (NNLM, 2010). Box 2-1 discusses gerontologic considerations. Recent findings suggest the need to reduce the reading level required by print materials to reflect fifth- or sixth-grade competencies (Bennett, Chen, Soroui, et al., 2009; Walker, Pepa, & Gerard, 2010). The nurse assesses the educational level of patients with the understanding that grade level attained does not always equal with health literacy. The Rapid Estimate of Adult Literacy in Medicine—Short Form (REALM-SF) is a 7-item word recognition test to provide clinicians with a valid quick assessment of patient health literacy (Box 2-2). The REALM-SF has been validated and field tested in diverse research setting, and has excellent agreement with the 66-item REALM instrument in terms of grade-level assignments. All materials presented to patients should be easy to read and in plain language. The Patient Education boxes presented throughout this textbook are written with the patient as the audience and provide easy-to-understand instructions.

NURSING PROCESS

Patient Teaching

The steps of the nursing process—assessment, diagnosis, planning, implementation, and evaluation—are used when constructing a teaching plan to meet people's teaching and learning needs (Box 2-3). An example of an individualized plan of nursing care is available online at http://thePoint.lww.com/Pellico1e.

Assessment

Assessment in the teaching–learning process is directed toward the systematic collection of data about the person's learning needs and style and readiness to learn, as well as the family's learning needs. Box 2-4 on page 18 discusses the Stages of Change model in relation to teaching and behavior change.

Learning Readiness

One of the most significant factors influencing learning is a person's **learning readiness.** This is a crucial step in the assessment process. If patients are not ready to learn, change, or alter their behavior, education can be fruitless. For adults, readiness is based on culture, attitude, personal values, physical and emotional status, and past experiences in learning. Experiential readiness to learn refers to past experiences that may influence a person's ability to learn.

(continued on page 16)

BOX 2-2 Rapid Estimate of Adult Literacy in Medicine—Short Form (REALM-SF)

REALM-SF Form

Patient name _____ Date of birth _____ Reading level _____
Date _____ Examiner _____ Grade completed _____

Menopause ☐
Antibiotics ☐
Exercise ☐
Jaundice ☐
Rectal ☐
Anemia ☐
Behavior ☐

Instructions for Administering the REALM-SF

1. Give the patient a laminated copy of the REALM-SF form and score answers on an unlaminated copy that is attached to a clipboard. Hold the clipboard at an angle so that the patient is not distracted by your scoring. Say:

   "I want to hear you read as many words as you can from this list. Begin with the first word and read aloud. When you come to a word you cannot read, do the best you can or say, 'blank' and go onto the next word."

2. If the patient takes more than 5 seconds on a word, say "blank" and point to the next word, if necessary, to move the patient along. If the patient begins to miss every word, have him or her pronounce only known words.

3. Count as an error any word not attempted or mispronounced. Score by marking a plus (+) after each correct word, a check (✓) after each mispronounced word, and a minus (−) after words not attempted. Count as correct any self-corrected word.

4. Count the number of correct words for each list and record the numbers in the "SCORE" box. Total the numbers and match the total score with its grade equivalent in the table below.

Scores and Grade Equivalents for the REALM-SF

Score	Grade range
0	Third grade and below; will not be able to read most low-literacy materials; will need repeated oral instructions, materials composed primarily of illustrations, or audio or video tapes.
1–3	Fourth to sixth grade; will need low-literacy materials, may not be able to read prescription labels.
4–6	Seventh to eighth grade; will struggle with most patient education materials; will not be offended by low-literacy materials.
7	High school; will be able to read most patient education materials.

Available at http://www.ahrq.gov/populations/sahlsatool.htm

Previous educational experiences and life experiences in general are significant determinants of a person's approach to learning. People with little or no formal education may not be able to understand the instructional materials presented. People who have had difficulty learning in the past may be hesitant to try again. Many behaviors required for reaching maximum health potential require knowledge, physical skills, and positive attitudes. In their absence, learning may be very difficult and very slow. For example, a person who does not understand the basics of normal nutrition may not be able to understand the restrictions of a specific diet. A person who does not view the desired learning as personally meaningful may reject teaching efforts. A person who is not future-oriented may be unable to appreciate many aspects of preventive health teaching. Experiential readiness is closely related to emotional readiness, because motivation tends to be stimulated by an appreciation for the need to learn and by those learning tasks that are familiar, interesting, and meaningful.

A practical way of assessing the patient's learning readiness is to ask how they view their health-related problem and what actions do they see that can be taken. Other questions that might be asked are "What changes would you like to make now?" and "Are there any problems that prevent you from learning right now?" The wording of such questions can make significant difference in the success a patient experiences with your interventions. For instance, patients asked "Is there something else you want to address?" rather than "Is there anything else you want to address?" will ask more questions and report that their unmet concerns were better addressed (Heritage, 2007). It is important for the nurse to view patients as individuals when providing information that meets their needs and understand that they have different desires for information about their disease and treatments. This will influence the way their health is managed long term (Duggan & Bates, 2008).

Detecting Communication Issues

Lack of communication skills is one of the most significant barriers to patient education. This can include both a patient's reading and computer skills. Patients who struggle with written material may appear disinterested in learning rather than admitting that they may not understand. Watch

BOX 2-3   A Guide to Patient Education

Assessment

1. Assess the person's readiness for health education.
   A. What are the person's health beliefs and behaviors?
   B. What physical and psychosocial adaptations does the person need to make?
   C. Is the learner ready to learn?
   D. Is the person able to learn these behaviors?
   E. What additional information about the person is needed?
   F. Are there any variables (e.g., hearing or visual impairment, cognitive issues, and literacy issues) that will affect the choice of teaching strategy or approach?
   G. What are the person's expectations?
   H. What does the person want to learn?
2. Organize, analyze, synthesize, and summarize the collected data.

Planning and Goals

1. Specify the learning goals established by teacher and learner together.
2. Identify teaching strategies appropriate for goal attainment.
3. Establish expected outcomes.
4. Develop the written teaching plan.
   A. Include diagnoses, goals, teaching strategies, and expected outcomes.
   B. Put the information to be taught in logical sequence.
   C. Write down the key points.
   D. Select appropriate teaching aids.
   E. Keep the plan current and flexible to meet the person's changing learning needs.
5. Involve the learner, family or significant others, nursing team members, and other health care team members in all aspects of planning.

Implementation

1. Put the teaching plan into action.
2. Use language the person can understand.
3. Use appropriate teaching aids and provide Internet resources if appropriate.
4. Use the same equipment that the person will use after discharge.
5. Encourage the person to participate actively in learning.
6. Record the learner's responses to the teaching actions.
7. Provide feedback.

Evaluation

1. Collect objective data.
   a. Observe the person.
   b. Ask questions to determine whether the person understands.
   c. Use rating scales, checklists, anecdotal notes, and written tests when appropriate.
2. Compare the person's behavioral responses with the expected outcomes. Determine the extent to which the goals were achieved.
3. Include the person, family or significant others, nursing team members, and other health care team members in the evaluation.
4. Identify alterations that need to be made in the teaching plan.
5. Make referrals to appropriate sources or agencies for reinforcement of learning after discharge.
6. Continue all steps of the teaching process: assessment, diagnosis, planning, implementation, and evaluation.

---

a patient's eyes while he is "reading"; the eyes should move left to right as he examines a document. Using computerized resources to support learning with inexperienced users requires careful assessment and planning. Computer-based education will work best and make the most efficient use of time when it is matched to the skill level of the patient.

Another communication barrier can be the nurse's lack of awareness of the specific mores of the patient's culture. A cultural assessment will allow the nurse to adapt information and delivery to a patient's cultural beliefs and preferences (Box 2-5). An individual's culture can affect her viewpoint in many ways, such as the meaning of a diagnosis, the expectation of reporting symptoms, how much information is desired, how death and dying will be managed, gender roles, family participation, and decision

making. Culturally specific nonverbal norms also play an important role in how to present information. Eye contact, personal space, touching, and gender roles can be very specific (Cutilli, 2006). A balance is necessary; it is important to avoid overemphasizing cultural-specific beliefs so as not to reinforce stereotypes.

Language barriers, once identified, must be addressed. Hospitals accredited by the Joint Commission are required to "respect patients' right to and need for effective communication, including the provision of interpreter and translation services when needed." While this is a struggle for many organizations, it is critical for successful patient and family education. Interpreters must be competent and trained as medical interpreters. Using family members or even untrained support staff as interpreters raises quality,

(continued on page 18)

BOX 2-4
Stages of Change

An approach to health teaching is the use of the transtheoretical model, which considers decisional balance (weighing the pro's and con's of the proposed behavioral change), self-efficacy (confidence in one's ability to change), and the relationship between stage of change and behavior (Prochasca et al., 1994; Prochaska, 1999, 2008). The model considers educational interventions that are not "one size fits all" but rather individualized interventions based upon patients' current stage of readiness to learn or motivational readiness. The transtheoretical model- based measures have been developed for smoking, alcohol use, sun exposure, and exercise, to name a few. The nurse considers the patient's current stage when planning educational needs. These stages are: precontemplation (the patient is not considering any change in behavior in the next 6 months), contemplation (the patients has serious consideration of change, but it is sometime in the future), preparation (the patient has taken initial behavioral

steps toward change and intends to make changes in the next 30 days), action (concrete activities that lead to the desired change have been made for less than 6 months), and maintenance (active efforts to sustain the changes made for more than 6 months). The model is not linear but expects that patients will move between stages until successful behavioral changes are established. By definition, precontemplators would be expected to disagree with suggestions that a change in behavior is needed, and would not be expected to exert effort toward making changes in the "problem" behavior. At this stage, nurses would offer suggestions and material for patients to consider the need for behavior change and encourage them to consider behavioral changes in the future. On the other hand, individuals in the action stage would be expected to endorse the need for change and engage in specific behaviors that would lead to change in the "problem" behavior. Engagement in educational activities would be expected at this stage.

---

ethical, and possible legal issues. Family members, including children, may incorporate bias into their interpretations and should be used as a resource of last resort. Box 2-6 discusses using an interpreter effectively.

Diagnosis

Diagnoses related to health education may include:

- Effective therapeutic regimen management
- Ineffective therapeutic regimen management
- Ineffective family therapeutic regimen management

BOX 2-5
Cultural Assessment Components to Consider When Formulating a Teaching Plan

When formulating a teaching plan, consider the patient's beliefs about:
- Body size, shape, boundaries, and functions
- Beauty and strength
- Value of the mind or brain
- Nature and function of blood
- Diet and nutrition
- Communication
- Gender
- Family and social support
- Physical health and illness
- Mental health and illness
- Age-related changes
- Pain
- Medicine, herbs, and talismans
- Spirituality or religion

- Health-seeking behaviors
- Ineffective health maintenance
- Readiness for enhanced management of therapeutic regimen
- Deficient knowledge
- Readiness for enhanced knowledge

Planning

Once assessment data are collected, the planning component of the teaching–learning process is established in accordance with the steps of the nursing process:

1. Specify the immediate, intermediate, and long-term goals of learning.
2. Identify specific teaching strategies appropriate for attaining goals.
3. Specify the expected outcomes.
4. Document the goals, teaching strategies, and expected outcomes of the teaching plan.

Developing the plan and goals of teaching should be a joint effort by the nurse and the patient and family members. Consideration must be given to the urgency of the patient's learning needs; the most critical needs should receive the highest priority.

After the learning priorities have been established, it is important to identify the immediate and long-term goals and the teaching strategies appropriate for attaining those goals. Teaching is most effective when the objectives of both the patient and nurse are in agreement (Simmons & Baker, 2009). Learning begins with the establishment of goals that are appropriate to the situation and realistic in

BOX 2-6

Using an Interpreter Effectively

- Arrange the seating in a triangle (if possible) or some configuration so that you are looking directly at the client. A sign language interpreter will ideally sit beside and slightly behind you to ensure that the patient can see both you and the interpreter. In Sign Language, using facial expressions, mouthing, gestures, and body language are integral parts of communicating. These actions help give meaning to what is being signed, much like vocal tones and inflections give meaning to spoken words.
- Use a warm tone of voice and body language that will communicate to the patient/family your interest and concern.
- The interpreter should be viewed as a neutral party. You should maintain eye contact with the patient and address the patient in the second person, as if the interpreter were not even there. For example, you should ask "Where do you feel the pain?", rather than "Ask her where she feels the pain."
- Speak slowly and clearly. Make sure that you keep your statements or questions short and pause frequently to allow for the interpretation to occur. Use a normal volume of voice. An interview or session when an interpreter is involved will take longer. You must be sensitive to the fact that there may not be words in the target language that match English words, so the interpreter may need to explain what is said in a different way.

- Keep in mind that interpreters are trained to interpret everything that is said either word for word or phrase for phrase. Therefore, do not say anything that you do not want the client to hear.
- Expect (and do not be offended!) that the interpreter will interrupt when necessary for clarification.
- Use a simple style of speech, and try to avoid jargon or technical and medical terms. Sometimes no word in the target language coincides with the English word. Be prepared to repeat yourself using different words and simpler communication.
- You must make every effort to ensure that the client understands what is being said. It is often appropriate for you to summarize their comments frequently throughout the interview and ask the client to explain back to you what they have understood. The patient should be constantly encouraged to ask questions, to comment on what they are hearing, and to tell you if they are unclear.
- Although it is preferable to have the interpreter present during a physical examination, ask the patient whether he or she has any objections to the interpreter being present.
- When using an interpreter for a patient with a mental health issue, particularly with psychosis, work with the interpreter so that he or she is aware that it is possible that the patient will say things that do not make immediate sense.

Available at http://www.calgaryhealthregion.ca/programs/diversity/int_and_trans_services/working_eff_interpreter.pdf

terms of the patient's ability and desire to achieve them. Involving the patient and family in establishing goals and in planning teaching strategies promotes their cooperation in implementing the teaching plan.

Expected outcomes of teaching strategies can be stated in terms of behaviors of patients, families, or both. Outcomes should be realistic and measurable, and the critical time periods for attaining them should also be identified. The desired outcomes and the critical time periods serve as a basis for evaluating the effectiveness of the teaching strategies.

During the planning phase, the nurse must consider the sequence in which the subject matter is presented in each of the teaching strategies. Critical information (e.g., survival skills for a patient with diabetes) and material that the person or family identifies to be of particular importance will be high priority. An outline is often helpful for arranging the subject matter and for ensuring that all necessary information is included. In addition, appropriate teaching aids to be used in implementing teaching strategies are prepared or selected at this time.

The Learning Environment

Although learning can take place without teachers, most people who are attempting to learn new or altered health

behaviors benefit from the services of nurses. The interpersonal interaction between the person and the nurse who is attempting to meet the person's learning needs may be formal or informal, depending on the method and techniques of teaching.

Learning may be optimized by minimizing factors that interfere with the learning process. For example, the room temperature, lighting, noise levels, and other environmental conditions should be appropriate to the learning situation.

Timing

The time selected for teaching should be suited to the needs of the individual person. Scheduling a teaching session at a time of day when a patient is fatigued, uncomfortable, or anxious about a pending diagnostic or therapeutic procedure, or when visitors are present, is not conducive to learning. However, if the family is to participate in providing care, the sessions should be scheduled when family members are present, so that they can learn any necessary skills or techniques.

Teaching Techniques

Teaching techniques and methods enhance learning if they are appropriate to the patient's needs (Table 2-1). Numerous

(continued on page 20)

TABLE
2-1 Teaching People With Disabilities

Type of Disability	Teaching Strategy
Physical, emotional, or cognitive disability	Adapt information to accommodate the person's cognitive, perceptual, and behavioral disabilities. Give clear written and oral information. Highlight significant information for easy reference. Avoid medical terminology.
Hearing impairment	Use slow, directed, deliberate speech. Use sign language or interpreter services if appropriate. Position yourself so that the person can see your mouth if speech reading. Use telecommunication devices (TTY or TDD) for the hearing impaired. Use written materials and visual aids, such as models and diagrams. Use captioned videos, films, and computer-generated materials. Teach on the side of the "good ear" if unilateral deafness is present.
Visual impairment	Use optical devices such as a magnifying lens. Use proper lighting and proper contrast of colors on materials and equipment. Use large-print materials. Use Braille materials if appropriate. Convert information to auditory and tactile formats. Obtain audiotapes and talking books. Explain noises associated with procedures, equipment, and treatments. Arrange materials in clockwise pattern.
Learning disabilities *Input disability*	If visual perceptual disorder: • Explain information verbally, repeat, and reinforce frequently. • Use audiotapes. • Encourage learner to verbalize information received. If auditory perceptual disorder: • Speak slowly with as few words as possible, repeat, and reinforce frequently. • Use direct eye contact to focus person on task. • Use demonstration and return demonstration such as modeling, role playing, and hands-on experiences. • Use visual tools, written materials, and computers.
Output disability	Use all senses as appropriate. Use written, audiotape, and computer information. Review information and give time to interact and ask questions. Use hand gestures and motions.
Developmental disability	Base information and teaching on developmental stage, not chronologic age. Use nonverbal cues, gestures, signing, and symbols as needed. Use simple explanations and concrete examples with repetition. Encourage active participation. Demonstrate information and have the person perform return demonstrations.

techniques are available, including lectures, group teaching, and demonstrations, all of which can be enhanced with specially prepared teaching materials.

In general patients remember information in approximately the following ratios:

- 10% of what they read
- 25% of what they hear
- 45% of what they see
- 65% of what they hear and see
- 70% of what they say and write
- 90% of what they say as they perform a task (Bateman, Kramer, & Glassman, 1999)

The lecture or explanation method of teaching is commonly used but should always be accompanied by discussion. Discussion is important because it affords learners opportunities to express their feelings and concerns, to ask questions, and to receive clarification. Group teaching is appropriate for some people because it allows them not only to receive needed information but also to feel secure as members of a group. People with similar problems or learning needs have the opportunity to identify with each other and gain moral support and encouragement. Patients with lower education levels obtain significantly increased knowledge when education is provided in a group setting (Neilson & Ryg, 2008). Group visits allow interactions in a more

natural setting, and conversations between patients help them feel less isolated and possibly less threatened. Also, if group teaching is used, assessment and follow-up are imperative to ensure that each person has gained sufficient knowledge and skills. Demonstration and practice are essential ingredients of a teaching program, especially when teaching skills. It is best to demonstrate the skill and then give the learner ample opportunity for practice. When special equipment is involved, such as syringes, colostomy bags, dialysis equipment, dressings, or suction apparatus, it is important to teach with the same equipment that will be used in the home setting. Learning to perform a skill with one kind of equipment and then having to change to a different kind may lead to confusion, frustration, and mistakes.

Patients who have the opportunity to give providers written information about needs, emotional concerns, and functional status in advance were less anxious or showed improvement in functional status (Kinnersley, 2008). Other steps or tools that can improve success include collaborative agendas or goal setting, in which the patient and the nurse build the agenda together regarding items for discussion. Patients should be engaged to help prioritize items for best time management. A communication/demonstration technique known as *ask–tell–ask–close the loop* can help improve communication and patient understanding:

- *Ask* permission to give information about a topic of importance to the patient
- *Tell*: Explanations and written materials are most effective when given in response to the patient's expressed agenda and tailored to his ability to understand.
- *Ask* for understanding, and provide additional information or clarification as necessary
- *Close the loop*: Ask the patient to restate the information as the patient understands it.

Teaching aids used to enhance learning include books, pamphlets, pictures, films, slides, audio and video tapes, models, programmed instruction, CD-ROMs, and computer-assisted learning modules. These are made available as needed for home, clinic, or hospital use, and they allow review and reinforcement of content and enhanced visual and auditory learning. Such teaching aids are invaluable when used appropriately and can save a significant amount of personnel time and related cost. However, all such aids should be reviewed before use to ensure that they meet the patient's learning needs. Developing tools as part of a multidisciplinary group has also been shown to yield benefits. The participants of groups working together to develop tools—taking into consideration literacy levels, behavioral theories, and role modeling—showed that significant knowledge was gained by participation, which led to enriched professional development (Stonecypher, 2009).

Reinforcement and follow-up are important because learning takes time. Allowing ample time to learn, then reinforcing what is learned, are important teaching strategies; a single teaching session is rarely adequate. Follow-up sessions are imperative to promote the learner's confidence in his or her abilities and to plan for additional teaching sessions. For hospitalized patients who may not be able to transfer what they have learned in the hospital to the home setting, follow-up after discharge is essential to ensure that they have realized the full benefits of a teaching program.

The entire planning phase of the teaching–learning process concludes with the documentation of the teaching plan. This teaching plan communicates information to all members of the nursing and health care team. Documentation enhances the continuity of care for the patient and communication among caregivers. Documentation should include:

- The learner, instructor and interpreter (if used)
- The patient's need assessment
- Learning objectives and goals
- Information and skills taught
- Teaching methods used
- Teaching materials provided or used
- Patient and family response to teaching
- Evaluation of what the patient learned
- Further learning needs
- Revised goals (if necessary)

Implementation

In the implementation phase of the teaching–learning process, the patient, the family, and other members of the nursing and health care team carry out the activities outlined in the teaching plan. The nurse coordinates these activities.

Flexibility during the implementation phase of the teaching–learning process and ongoing assessment of patient responses to the teaching strategies support modification of the teaching plan as necessary. Creativity in promoting and sustaining the patient's motivation to learn is essential. New learning needs that may arise after discharge from the hospital or after home care visits have ended should also be taken into account.

Feedback about progress also motivates learning. Such feedback should be presented in the form of positive reinforcement when the learner is successful, and in the form of constructive suggestions for improvement when he or she is unsuccessful.

The implementation phase ends when the teaching strategies have been completed and when the patient's responses to the actions have been recorded. This record serves as the basis for evaluating how well the defined goals and expected outcomes have been achieved.

Evaluation

Evaluation of the teaching–learning process determines how effectively the patient has responded to teaching and

(*continued on page 22*)

to what extent the goals have been achieved. An evaluation must be made to determine what was effective and what needs to be changed or reinforced. It cannot be assumed that patients have learned just because teaching has occurred; learning does not automatically follow teaching. An important part of the evaluation phase addresses the question, "What can be done to improve teaching and enhance learning?" Answers to this question direct the changes to be made in the teaching plan.

A variety of measurement techniques can be used to identify changes in patient behavior as evidence that learning has taken place. These techniques include directly observing the behavior; using rating scales, checklists, or anecdotal notes to document the behavior; and indirectly measuring results using oral questioning and written tests. All direct measurements should be supplemented with indirect measurements whenever possible. Using more than one measuring technique enhances the reliability of the resulting data and decreases the potential for error from a measurement strategy.

In many situations, measurement of actual behavior is the most accurate and appropriate technique. Nurses often perform comparative analyses using patient admission data as the baseline: selected data points observed when nursing care is given and self-care is initiated are compared with the patient's baseline data. In other cases, indirect measurement may be used. Some examples of indirect measurement are patient satisfaction surveys, attitude surveys, and instruments that evaluate specific health status variables.

However, measurement is only the beginning of evaluation, which must be followed by data interpretation and value judgments about learning and teaching. These aspects of evaluation should be conducted periodically throughout the teaching–learning program, at its conclusion, and at varying periods after the teaching has ended.

Evaluation of learning after hospitalization is highly desirable, because the analysis of teaching outcomes must extend into home care. With shortened lengths of hospital stay and with short-stay and same-day surgical procedures, follow-up evaluation in the home is especially important. Coordination of efforts and sharing of information between hospital- and community-based nursing personnel facilitate post discharge teaching and home care evaluation.

Evaluation is not the final step in the teaching–learning process, but the beginning of the iterative process of a new patient assessment. The information gathered during evaluation should be used to redirect teaching actions, with the goal of improving the patient's responses and outcomes.

HEALTH PROMOTION

Health teaching and **health promotion** are linked by a common goal—to encourage people to achieve as high a level of wellness as possible, so that they can live maximally healthy lives and avoid preventable illnesses. Patients are the primary managers of their health conditions. Nurses are in an ideal position to provide the kind of support that patients need to manage their conditions. Health promotion has become a cornerstone in health policy because of the need to control costs and reduce unnecessary sickness and death.

Health goals for the nation were also established in the publication *Healthy People 2000 and 2010*. The priorities from this initiative were identified as health promotion, health protection, and the use of preventive services. *Healthy People 2020* builds on past achievements, reaffirms the overarching goals from the past decade, and adds more: promoting quality of life, healthy development, and healthy behaviors across life stages, and creating social and physical environments that promote good health.

Definition

Health promotion is defined as the process of enabling people to increase control over their health and its determinants, thereby improving their health (World Health Organization [WHO], 2009). The purpose of health promotion is to focus on the person's potential for wellness and to encourage appropriate alterations in personal habits, lifestyle, and environment in ways that reduce risks and enhance health and well-being. Health promotion is an active process; that is, it is not something that can be prescribed or dictated. It is up to each person to decide whether to make changes to promote a higher level of wellness. Only the individual can make these choices.

The concepts of health, wellness, health promotion, and disease prevention have been a topic of extensive discussion in the lay literature and news media, as well as in professional journals. As a result, public demand for health information has increased, and health care professionals and agencies have responded by providing this information. As employers strive to reduce costs associated with absenteeism, health insurance, hospitalization, disability, excessive turnover of personnel, and premature death, the workplace has become an important site for health promotion programs. The concept of health promotion has evolved because of a changing definition of health and an awareness that wellness exists at many levels of functioning. Health is viewed as a dynamic, ever-changing condition that enables people to function at an optimal potential at any given time. The ideal health status is one in which people are successful in achieving their full potential, regardless of any limitations they might have.

Wellness, as a reflection of health, involves a conscious and deliberate attempt to maximize one's health. Wellness does not just happen; it requires planning and conscious commitment, and is the result of adopting lifestyle behaviors for the purpose of attaining one's highest potential for well-being. Wellness is not the same for every person. The person with a chronic illness or disability may still be able to achieve a desirable level of wellness. The key to wellness

is to function at the highest potential within the limitations over which there is no control.

Self-Responsibility

Taking responsibility for oneself is the key to successful health promotion. The concept of **self-responsibility** is based on the understanding that the individual controls his or her life. Each person alone must make the choices that determine how healthy his or her lifestyle is. As more people recognize that lifestyle and behavior significantly affect health, they may assume responsibility for avoiding high-risk behaviors such as smoking, alcohol and drug abuse, overeating, driving while intoxicated, risky sexual practices, and other unhealthy habits. They may also assume responsibility for adopting routines that have been found to have a positive influence on health, such as engaging in regular exercise, wearing seat belts, and eating a healthy diet.

A variety of different techniques have been used to encourage people to accept responsibility for their health,

ranging from extensive educational programs to reward systems. No one technique has been found to be superior to any other. Instead, self-responsibility for health promotion is very individualized and depends on a person's desires and inner motivations. Health promotion programs are important tools for encouraging people to assume responsibility for their health and to develop behaviors that improve health.

Health Promotion Throughout the Lifespan

Health promotion is a concept and a process that extends throughout the lifespan. Studies have shown that the health of a child can be affected either positively or negatively by the health practices of the mother during the prenatal period. Therefore, health promotion starts before birth and extends through childhood, adolescence, adulthood, and old age. Health promotion includes health screening. Table 2–2 presents' recommendations for periodic health examinations and screenings by gender and age.

TABLE
2-2 Routine Health Screening for Adults

Type of Screening	Suggested Time Frame
Routine health examination	Yearly
Blood chemistry profile	Baseline at age 20, then as mutually determined by patient and clinician
Complete blood count	Baseline at age 20, then as mutually determined by patient and clinician
Lipid profile	Baseline at age 20, then as mutually determined by patient and clinician
Hemoccult screening	Yearly after age 50
Electrocardiogram	Baseline at age 40, then as mutually determined by patient and clinician
Blood pressure	Yearly, then as mutually determined by patient and clinician
Tuberculosis skin test	Every 2 years or as mutually determined by patient and clinician
Chest x-ray film	For positive PPD results
Skin examination	Yearly or as mutually determined by patient and clinician
Vision screening	Every 2–3 years
Glaucoma	Baseline at age 40, then every 2–3 years until age 70, then yearly
Dental screening	Every 6 months
Hearing screening	As needed
Health risk appraisal	As needed
Nutritional screening	As mutually determined by patient and clinician
Digital rectal examination	Yearly
Colonoscopy	Every 3–5 years after age 50 or as mutually determined by patient and clinician
Females	
Breast self-examination	Monthly
Mammogram	Yearly for women over 40, or earlier or more often if indicated
Clinical breast examination	Yearly
Gynecologic examination	Yearly
Pap test	Yearly
Bone density screening	Based on identification of primary and secondary risk factors (prior to onset of menopause, if indicated)
Males	
Prostate examination	Yearly
Prostate-specific antigen	Every 1–2 years after age 50
Testicular examination	Monthly
Adult Immunizations	
Hepatitis B (if not received as a child)	Series of three doses (now, 1 month later, then 5 months after the second date)
Influenza vaccine	Yearly

Note: Any of these screenings may be performed more frequently if deemed necessary by the patient or recommended by the health care provider.

Young and Middle-Aged Adults

Young and middle-aged adults represent an age group that not only expresses an interest in health and health promotion but also responds enthusiastically to suggestions that show how lifestyle practices can improve health. Adults are frequently motivated to change their lifestyles in ways that are believed to enhance their health and wellness. Many adults who wish to improve their health turn to health promotion programs to help them make the desired changes in their lifestyles. Many have responded to programs that focus on topics such as general wellness, smoking avoidance or cessation, exercise, physical conditioning, weight control, conflict resolution, and stress management. Because of the nationwide emphasis on health during the reproductive years, young adults actively seek programs that address prenatal health, parenting, family planning, and women's health issues.

Programs that provide health screening, such as those that screen for cancer, high cholesterol, hypertension, diabetes, abdominal aneurysm, and visual and hearing impairments, are quite popular with young and middle-aged adults. Programs that involve health promotion for people with specific chronic illnesses, such as cancer, diabetes, heart disease, and pulmonary disease, are also popular. It is becoming more evident that chronic disease and disability do not preclude health and wellness; rather, positive health attitudes and practices can promote optimal health for people who must live with the limitations imposed by their chronic illnesses and disabilities.

Health promotion programs can be offered almost anywhere in the community. Common sites include the workplace, local clinics, elementary and high schools, community colleges, recreation centers, churches, and even private homes. Health fairs are frequently held in civic centers and shopping malls. The outreach idea for health promotion programs has served to meet the needs of many adults who otherwise would not avail themselves of opportunities to strive toward a healthier lifestyle.

Workplace programs usually include employee health screening and counseling, physical fitness, nutritional awareness, work safety, and stress management and stress reduction. In addition, efforts are made to promote a safe and healthy work environment. Many large businesses provide exercise facilities for their employees and offer their health promotion programs to retirees. If employers can show cost-containment benefits from such programs, their dollars will be considered well spent, and more businesses will provide health promotion programs as a benefit of employment.

Older Adults

Health promotion is as important for the elderly as it is for other adults and children. Although their chronic illnesses and disabilities cannot be eliminated, these adults can benefit from activities that help them maintain independence and achieve an optimal level of health. The elderly often describe cognitive health as "staying sharp or being in the right mind," as well as living to an advanced age, having good physical health, having a positive mental outlook, being alert, having a good memory, and being socially involved (Wilcox & Sharley, 2009). Focus groups of older adults believe that physical activity can protect cognitive health. Research suggests the need for improved communication around health promotion information and, in particular, the need for culturally suitable, language-appropriate material, and consistent media coverage (Friedman et al., 2009). Health promotion materials could include information about healthy actions, nutritional information based on ethnicity and a healthy diet, as well as the frequency, duration, and intensity of physical activity and their affect on health.

Nursing Implications

By virtue of nurses' expertise in health and health care and our long-established credibility with consumers, nurses play a vital role in health promotion. In many instances, nurses have initiated health promotion and health screening programs or have participated with other health care personnel in developing and providing wellness services in a variety of settings. As health care professionals, nurses have a responsibility to promote activities that foster well-being, self-actualization, and personal fulfillment. Every interaction with consumers of health care must be viewed as an opportunity to promote positive health attitudes and behaviors. Health Promotion boxes throughout this textbook provide readers with health promotion information that nurses can apply in their patient care.

Chapter Review

Critical Thinking Exercises

1. A nurse is designing a patient teaching plan for a 57-year-old woman with a history of gastrointestinal problems. This woman has been diagnosed with osteoporosis, and her physician has recommended that she begin taking alendronate sodium (Fosamax). Describe the health promotion strategies you would develop for this patient. Determine what variables may influence her willingness to follow the recommended therapy.

2. A home health nurse is instructing a 55-year-old man with cardiovascular disease about healthy eating habits.

He has recently been widowed, and his service animal (seeing-eye dog) of 15 years died last month. What physiologic and psychosocial variables would be relevant to understanding this patient's needs? How would a teaching plan be constructed to promote adequate nutrition? How would you modify the teaching plan, knowing that the patient is visually impaired?

3. A 72-year-old man is informed by an advanced practice nurse about a health fair being held at the local community center across the street from his home. He declines to attend, saying, "I am too old, and it is too late to be concerned about health promotion. The damage to my body has already been done." What resources would you use to identify evidence of the effectiveness of health promotion activities for the elderly? Discuss the strength of the evidence. Identify the criteria used to evaluate the strength of the evidence. What information would you then include in a discussion with the patient about promoting health in the elderly?

NCLEX-Style Review Questions

1. A nurse is providing discharge teaching for an elderly patient who is fully dressed, watching television, and waiting for family. The nurse sits in a chair facing the patient and shows the patient a handout. The patient squints while reading and periodically looks at the television. The nurse is about to review the information and determine the patient's understanding of the material when the family enters the room. The nurse determines the need for further education due to learning barriers. Which barriers affected the patient's ability to comprehend the information? Select all that apply.
   A. Patient is watching television.
   B. The patient is elderly.
   C. The patient squints while reading.
   D. The family entered the room while teaching.
   E. The patient is fully dressed.

2. The nurse is to provide discharge teaching to a patient with newly diagnosed coronary artery disease. In what order should the following steps be prioritized and completed?
   A. Implement teaching plan.
   B. Collect and analyze data regarding the patient's knowledge of coronary artery disease.
   C. Form education nursing diagnoses.
   D. Reassess patient's knowledge as needed.
   E. Develop teaching plan.
   F. Identify learning needs.
   G. Update and change plan.

3. The nurse is discussing postoperative discharge instructions with an Asian American patient. The patient looks at the floor, smiles, and then nods his head. The nurse interprets this behavior as which of the following?
   A. Acceptance of the instructions
   B. Understanding of the material
   C. A reflection of cultural values
   D. The patient's ability to follow through on the instructions

4. When constructing a teaching plan, steps of the nursing process are utilized. In which step are teaching strategies identified?
   A. Assessment
   B. Planning
   C. Implementation
   D. Evaluation

5. Which of the following is an accurate statement with regards to adult learner readiness?
   A. Learning readiness is based solely on past life experiences.
   B. Physical skills play little role in learner readiness.
   C. Experimental readiness is not related to emotional readiness.
   D. It is based on culture, attitude, and personal values.

Try these additional resources to enhance your learning and understanding of this chapter:
• thePoint online resource available at http://thepoint.lww.com/Pellico1e
• Handbook for Focus on Adult Health: Medical-Surgical Nursing
• Study Guide for Focus on Adult Health: Medical-Surgical Nursing

References and Selected Readings

References and selected readings associated with this chapter can be found on the website that accompanies the book. Visit http://thepoint.lww.com/Pellico1e to access the references and other additional resources associated with this chapter.

RUTH McCORKLE
JAMES MARK LAZENBY

Chronic Illness and End-of-Life Care

Learning Objectives

After reading this chapter, you will be able to:

1. Define "chronic illness."

2. Identify factors related to the increasing incidence of chronic diseases.

3. Describe characteristics of chronic illness and its impact on patients.

4. Describe implications of caring for patients with chronic illnesses for nursing practice.

5. Define and compare palliative and hospice care.

6. Describe the principles and components of hospice care.

7. Identify barriers to improving care at the end of life.

8. Identify and describe eight tasks that are essential for nurses to manage patients at the end of life.

9. Apply skills for communicating with terminally ill patients and their families.

Chronic diseases account for seven of the ten leading causes of death in the United States, including the four most frequently occurring diseases (heart disease, stroke, cancer, and diabetes) that result from preventable causes (tobacco use, improper diet and physical inactivity, and alcohol use). Chronic illnesses affect people of all ages and ethnic, cultural, and racial groups, although some illnesses occur more frequently in some groups than in others (Centers for Disease Control and Prevention [CDC], 2009a). Although chronic disease occurs in all socioeconomic groups, people who have low incomes and disadvantaged backgrounds are more likely to report poor health. Factors such as poverty and inadequate health insurance decrease the likelihood that people with chronic illness receive health care and health screening measures, such as mammography, cholesterol testing, and routine checkups (U.S. Department of Health and Human Services [USDHHS], 2005).

Many people with chronic illnesses function independently with only minor inconvenience to their everyday lives; others require frequent and close monitoring or placement in long-term care facilities. Certain illnesses require advanced technology for survival, as in the late stages of amyotrophic lateral sclerosis or end-stage renal disease, or intensive care for periods of weeks or months. People with diseases such as these have been described as chronically critically and progressively ill. Some chronic illnesses have little effect on quality of life, but others have a considerable effect because they can result in progressive decline. The nurse recognizes that many patients admitted to acute care institutions have preexisting chronic diseases that must continue to be managed in concert with their acute illnesses.

OVERVIEW OF CHRONICITY

Although each chronic disease has its own specific physiologic characteristics, chronic diseases do share common features. Many chronic diseases, for example, have pain and fatigue as associated symptoms. Some degree of physical decline is usually present in severe or advanced chronic illness, limiting the patient's participation in many activities. Many chronic diseases require therapeutic regimens to keep them under control. Unlike the term "acute," which implies a curable and relatively short disease course, the term "chronic" describes a long disease course and illnesses

that may be incurable. This often makes managing chronic illnesses difficult for those who must live with them (Larsen & Lubkin, 2008).

People who develop chronic illnesses may react with shock, disbelief, depression, anger, resentment, or a number of other emotions. How people react to and cope with chronic illness is usually similar to how they react to other events in their lives, depending, in part, on their understanding of the illness and their perceptions of its potential impact on their own and their family's lives. Adjustment to chronic illness is affected by various factors:

- Suddenness, extent, and duration of lifestyle changes necessitated by the illness
- Family and individual resources for dealing with stress
- Stages of individual/family life cycle
- Previous experience with illness and crises
- Underlying personality characteristics
- Unresolved anger or grief from the past

Psychological, emotional, and cognitive reactions to chronic illnesses are likely to occur at the onset of the illness and to recur if symptoms worsen or recur after a period of remission. Symptoms associated with chronic illnesses are often unpredictable and may be perceived as crisis events by patients and their families, who must contend with both the uncertainty of chronic illness and the changes it brings to their lives. These possible effects can guide nursing assessment and interventions for the patient who has a chronic illness.

Definition of Chronic Illnesses

Chronic illnesses are often defined as medical illnesses or health problems with associated symptoms or disabilities that require long-term management (3 months or longer). Chronic illness refers to diseases that are caused by nonreversible pathology; are characterized by a slow, progressive decline in normal physiological function; are permanent, with cure unlikely; and require long-term surveillance, leaving residual disability (Larsen & Lubkin, 2008). The specific condition may be a result of illness, genetic factors, or injury; it may be a consequence of illnesses or unhealthy behaviors that began during childhood and young adulthood. Management of chronic illnesses includes learning to live with symptoms and coming to terms with identity changes resulting from having a chronic condition. It also consists of carrying out the lifestyle changes and regimens designed to control symptoms and to prevent complications. Although some people assume what might be called a "sick role" identity, most people with chronic illness do not consider themselves to be sick or ill, and try to live as normal a life as possible. Only when complications develop or symptoms interfere with activities of daily living (ADLs) do most people with chronic illnesses think of themselves as being sick or disabled (Larsen & Lubkin, 2008).

Prevalence and Causes of Chronic Illnesses

Chronic illnesses occur in people of every age group, socioeconomic level, and culture. In the United States, in 2005, an estimated 133 million people—one out of every two adults—were living with at least one chronic illness (Table 3-1; Ogden, Carroll, McDowell et al., 2007). As the incidence of chronic illnesses increases, the costs associated with these illnesses (i.e., hospital costs, equipment, medications, supportive services) also increase. Expenditures for health care for people with chronic illnesses exceed billions of dollars every year, and are associated with 75% of the $2 trillion health care costs each year in the United States (CDC, 2009a).

Although some chronic health illnesses cause little or no inconvenience, others are severe enough to cause major activity limitations. When people with activity limitations are unable to meet their needs for health care and personal services, they may be unable to carry out their therapeutic regimens or have their prescriptions filled on time, may miss appointments and office visits with their health care providers, and may be unable to carry out their ADLs.

Chronic disease is a global issue that affects both rich and poor nations. With the advent and distribution of highly active antiretroviral therapies and other treatments for communicable diseases, and, thus, longer lifespans, the incidence of chronic illness is increasing in developing countries of the Global South, even while they try to cope with new and emerging infectious diseases. In developed Western countries of the Global North, chronic illnesses have become the major cause of health-related problems. Causes of the increasing number of people with chronic illnesses include the following:

- A decrease in mortality from infectious diseases, such as smallpox, diphtheria, and other serious illnesses

TABLE
3-1 Percentage of Adults With Chronic Diseases in United States

Chronic Diseases	Adults With the Disease (%)
Arthritis	27.5
Asthma	8.3
Cardiovascular disease	
Hypercholesterolemia	37.5
Hypertension	27.5
Heart attack (Myocardial infarction)	4.2
Angina or coronary artery disease	4.1
Stroke	2.6
Diabetes	8.1
Physical, emotional, or psychological problems that causes limitations in activities	18.8

Adapted from Centers for Disease Control and Prevention, 2009b.

- Longer lifespans because of advances in technology and pharmacology, improved nutrition, safer working conditions, and greater access (for some people) to health care
- Improved screening and diagnostic procedures, enabling early detection and treatment of diseases
- Prompt and aggressive management of acute illnesses, such as myocardial infarction and AIDS-related infections
- The tendency to develop chronic illnesses with advancing age
- Lifestyle factors, such as smoking, chronic stress, and sedentary lifestyle, which increase the risk for chronic health problems such as respiratory disease, hypertension, cardiovascular disease, and obesity

Consequences of unhealthy lifestyles include an alarming increase in the incidence of diabetes, hypertension, obesity, and cardiac and chronic respiratory disorders. Physiologic changes in the body often occur before the appearance of symptoms of chronic disease. Therefore, the goal of emphasizing healthy lifestyles early in life is to improve overall health status and slow the development of such disorders.

Characteristics of Chronic Illnesses

Sometimes it is difficult for people who are disease-free to understand the often profound effect of chronic illness on the lives of patients and their families. It is easy for health professionals to focus on the illness itself while overlooking the person who has the disorder. In all illnesses, but even more so with chronic illnesses, the illness cannot be separated from the person. People with chronic illness must contend with it daily. To relate to what people must cope with or to plan effective interventions, nurses must understand what it means to have a chronic illness. Characteristics of chronic illness include the following:

- Managing chronic illness involves more than managing medical problems. Associated psychological and social problems must also be addressed, because living for long periods with illness symptoms and disability can threaten identity, bring about role changes, alter body image, and disrupt lifestyles. These changes require continuous adaptation and accommodation, depending on age and situation in life. Each decline in functional ability requires physical, emotional, and social adaptation for patients and their families.
- Chronic illnesses usually involve many different phases over the course of a person's lifetime. There can be acute periods, stable and unstable periods, flare-ups, and remissions. Each phase brings its own set of physical, psychological, and social problems, and each requires its own regimens and types of management. Table 3-2 describes the phases in the trajectory model of chronic illness.
- Keeping chronic illnesses under control requires persistent adherence to therapeutic regimens. Failing to adhere to a treatment plan or to do so consistently increases the risks

of developing complications and accelerating the disease process. However, the realities of daily life, including the impact of culture, values, and socioeconomic factors, affect the degree to which people adhere to a treatment regimen. Managing a chronic illness takes time, requires knowledge and planning, and can be uncomfortable and inconvenient. It is not unusual for patients to stop taking medications or alter dosages because of side effects that are more disturbing or disruptive than symptoms of the illness, or to cut back on regimens they consider overly time-consuming, fatiguing, or costly.

- One chronic disease can lead to the development of other chronic illnesses. Diabetes, for example, can eventually lead to neurologic and vascular changes that may result in visual, cardiac, and kidney disease and erectile dysfunction (CDC, 2009a). The presence of a chronic illness also contributes to a higher risk of morbidity and mortality in patients admitted to the intensive care unit with acute health illnesses.
- Chronic illness affects the entire family. Family life can be dramatically altered as a result of role reversals, unfilled roles, loss of income, time required to manage the illness, decreases in family socialization activities, and the costs of treatment. Stress and caretaker fatigue are common with severe chronic illnesses, and the entire family rather than just the patient may need care. However, some families are able to master the treatment regimen and changes that accompany chronic illness, as well as make the treatment regimen a routine part of life. Furthermore, they are able to keep the chronic illness from becoming the focal point of family life.
- The day-to-day management of illness is largely the responsibility of people with chronic disorders and their families. As a result, the home, rather than the hospital, is the center of care in chronic illnesses. Hospitals, clinics, physicians' offices, nursing homes, nursing centers, and community agencies (home care services, social services, and disease-specific associations and societies) are considered adjuncts or backup services to daily home management.
- The management of chronic illnesses is a process of discovery. People can be taught how to manage their illnesses. However, each person must discover how his or her own body reacts under varying circumstances—for example, what it is like to be hypoglycemic, what activities are likely to bring on angina, and how these or other illnesses can best be prevented and managed.
- Managing chronic illnesses must be a collaborative process that involves many different health care professionals working together with patients and their families to provide the full range of services that are often needed for management at home. The medical, social, and psychological aspects of chronic health problems are often complex, especially in severe illnesses.
- The management of chronic illnesses is expensive. Many of the expenses incurred by an individual patient (e.g., costs

TABLE
3-2 Phases in the Trajectory Model of Chronic Illness

Phase	Description	Focus of Nursing Care
Pre-trajectory	Genetic factors or lifestyle behaviors that place a person or community at risk for a chronic condition	Refer for genetic testing and counseling if indicated; provide education about prevention of modifiable risk factors and behaviors
Trajectory onset	Appearance or onset of noticeable symptoms associated with a chronic disorder; includes period of diagnostic workup and announcement of diagnosis; may be accompanied by uncertainty as patient awaits a diagnosis and begins to discover and cope with implications of diagnosis	Provide explanations of diagnostic tests and procedures and reinforce information and explanations given by primary health care provider; provide emotional support to patient and family
Stable	Illness course and symptoms are under control as symptoms, resulting disability and everyday life activities are being managed within limitations of illness; illness management centered in the home	Reinforce positive behaviors and offer ongoing monitoring; provide education about health promotion and encourage participation in health-promoting activities and health screening
Unstable	Characterized by an exacerbation of illness symptoms, development of complications, or reactivation of an illness in remission Period of inability to keep symptoms under control or reactivation of illness; difficulty in carrying out everyday life activities May require more diagnostic testing and trial of new treatment regimens or adjustment of current regimen, with care usually taking place at home	Provide guidance and support; reinforce previous teaching
Acute	Severe and unrelieved symptoms or the development of illness complications necessitating hospitalization, bed rest, or interruption of the person's usual activities to bring illness course under control	Provide direct care and emotional support to the patient and family members
Crisis	Critical or life-threatening situation requiring emergency treatment or care and suspension of everyday life activities until the crisis has passed	Provide direct care, collaborate with other health care team members to stabilize patient's condition
Comeback	Gradual recovery after an acute period and learning to live with or to overcome disabilities and return to an acceptable way of life within the limitations imposed by the chronic condition or disability; involves physical healing, limitations stretching through rehabilitative procedures, psychosocial coming-to-terms, and biographical reengagement with adjustments in everyday life activities	Assist in coordination of care; rehabilitative focus may require care from other health care providers; provide positive reinforcement for goals identified and accomplished
Downward	Illness course characterized by rapid or gradual worsening of a condition; physical decline accompanied by increasing disability or difficulty in controlling symptoms; requires biographical adjustment and alterations in everyday life activities with each major downward step	Provide home care and other community-based care to help patient and family adjust to changes and come to terms with these changes; assist patient and family to integrate new treatment and management strategies; encourage identification of end-of-life preferences and planning
Dying	Final days or weeks before death; characterized by gradual or rapid shutting down of body processes, biographical disengagement and closure, and relinquishment of everyday life interests and activities	Provide direct and supportive care to patients and their families through hospice programs

Adapted from Corbin, J.M. (1998). The Corbin and Stauss Chronic Illness Trajectory Model: An update. *Scholarly Inquiry for Nursing Practice, 12*(1), 33–41.

for hospital stays, diagnostic tests, equipment, medications, and supportive services) may be covered by health insurance and by federal and state agencies. However, the cost increases affect society as a whole as insurance premiums increase to cover these costs. Cost increases at the government level decrease resources that might benefit society. In addition, many out-of-pocket expenses are not reimbursed. Many people with chronic disorders, including the elderly and people who are working, are uninsured, or underinsured, may be unable to afford the high costs of care often associated with chronic illnesses. Absence from work because of chronic disorders may jeopardize job security and income.

- Chronic illnesses raise difficult ethical issues for patients, health care professionals, and society. Problematic questions include how to establish cost controls, how to allocate scarce resources (e.g., organs for transplantation), and what constitutes quality of life and when life support should be withdrawn.
- Living with chronic illness means living with uncertainty. Although health care providers may be aware of the usual progression of a chronic disease such as Parkinson's disease, no one can predict with certainty a person's illness course because of individual variation. Even when a patient is in remission or symptom-free, he or she often fears that the illness will reappear.

Implications of Managing Chronic Illnesses

Chronic illnesses have implications for everyday living and management for people and their families as well as for society at large. Most importantly, individual efforts should be directed at preventing chronic illnesses, because many chronic illnesses or disorders are linked to unhealthy lifestyles or behaviors such as smoking, inactivity, and overeating. Therefore, changes in lifestyle can prevent some chronic disorders, or at least delay onset until a later age. Because most people resist change, bringing about alterations in people's lifestyles is a major challenge for nurses today.

Once a chronic condition has occurred, the focus shifts to managing symptoms, avoiding complications (e.g., eye complications in a person with diabetes), and avoiding the development of other acute illnesses (e.g., pneumonia in a person with chronic obstructive lung disease). Quality of life, often overlooked by health professionals in their approach to people with chronic illnesses, is also important. Health-promoting behaviors, such as exercise, are essential to quality of life, even in people who have chronic illnesses, because regular exercise helps to maintain functional status.

Although coworkers, extended family, and health care professionals are affected by chronic illnesses, the problems of living with chronic illnesses are most acutely experienced by patients and their immediate families. They experience the greatest impact, with lifestyle changes that directly affect quality of life. Nurses provide direct care, especially during acute episodes, but they also provide the teaching and secure the resources and other supports that enable people to integrate their illness into their lives and to have an acceptable quality of life despite the illness. To understand what nursing care is needed, it is important to recognize and appreciate the issues that people with chronic illness and their families contend with and manage, often on a daily basis. The challenges of living with chronic illnesses include the need to accomplish the following:

- Alleviate and manage symptoms
- Psychologically adjust to and physically accommodate disabilities

- Prevent and manage crises and complications
- Carry out regimens as prescribed
- Validate individual self-worth and family functioning
- Manage threats to identity
- Normalize personal and family life as much as possible
- Live with altered time, social isolation, and loneliness
- Establish the networks of support and resources that can enhance quality of life
- Return to a satisfactory way of life after an acute debilitating episode (e.g., another myocardial infarction or stroke) or reactivation of a chronic condition
- Die with dignity and comfort

Many people with chronic illness must face an additional challenge: the need to deal with more than one chronic illness at a time. The symptoms or treatment of a second chronic condition may aggravate the first chronic condition. Patients need to be able to deal with their various chronic illnesses separately, as well as in combination. Some Medicare beneficiaries have five or more chronic illnesses, see an average of 13 physicians per year, and fill an average of 50 prescriptions per year (Anderson, 2005). Furthermore, the effects of increasing longevity among Americans are likely to increase health care costs in the future.

Even more challenging for many people with chronic illness is the need to hire and oversee caregivers who come into their homes to assist with ADLs and instrumental activities of daily living (IADLs). ADLs and IADLs are the activities that let an individual live independently in a community such as preparing meals, shopping, telephone use, and taking medications correctly. It is difficult for many people to be in a position of hiring, supervising, and sometimes firing people who may provide them with intimate physical care. The need to balance the role of recipient of care and oversight of the person providing care may lead to blurring of role boundaries.

The challenges of living with and managing a chronic illness are well known, and people with chronic illnesses often report receiving inadequate care, information, services, and counseling. This provides an opportunity for nurses to assume a more active role in addressing many of the issues experienced, coordinating care, and serving as an advocate for patients who need additional assistance to manage their illness while maintaining a quality of life that is acceptable to them.

Phases of Chronic Illnesses

Chronic illnesses can pass through different phases, as described in Table 3-2. However, this course may be too uncertain to predict with any degree of accuracy. The course of an illness can be thought of as a trajectory that can be managed or shaped over time, to some extent, through proper illness management strategies. It is important to keep in mind that not all phases occur in all patients; some phases do not occur at all, and some phases may recur. Each phase is characterized by different medical and psychosocial issues. For example, the needs of a patient with a stroke

who is a good candidate for rehabilitation are very different from those of a patient with terminal cancer. By thinking in terms of phases and individual patients within a phase, nurses can target their care more specifically to each person. Not every chronic condition is necessarily life-threatening, and not every patient passes through each possible phase of a chronic condition in the same order.

Using the trajectory model enables the nurse to put the present situation into the context of what might have happened to the patient in the past—that is, the life factors and understandings that might have contributed to the present state of the illness. In this way, the nurse can more readily address the underlying issues and problems.

NURSING CARE OF PATIENTS WITH CHRONIC ILLNESSES

Nursing care of patients with chronic illnesses is varied and occurs in a variety of settings. Care may be direct or supportive. *Direct care* may be provided in the clinic or health provider's office, the hospital, or the patient's home, depending on the status of the illness. Examples of direct care include assessing the patient's physical status, providing wound care, managing and overseeing medication regimens, and performing other technical tasks. The availability of this type of nursing care may allow the patient to remain at home and return to a more normal life after an acute episode of illness. *Supportive care* may include ongoing monitoring, teaching, counseling, serving as an advocate for the patient, making referrals, and case-managing. Giving supportive care is just as important as giving technical care. For example, through ongoing monitoring, either in the home or in a clinic, a nurse might detect early signs of impending complications and make a referral (i.e., contact the provider or consult the medical protocol in a clinic) for medical evaluation, thereby preventing a lengthy and costly hospitalization.

Working with people with chronic illness requires not just dealing with the medical aspects of their disorders, but also working with the whole person—physically, emotionally, and socially. This holistic approach to care requires nurses to draw on their knowledge and skills, including knowledge from the social sciences and psychology in particular. Although quality of life is usually affected by chronic illness, especially if the illness is severe, patients' perceptions of what constitutes quality of life often drive their management behaviors or affect how they view advice about health care. Nurses and other health care professionals need to recognize this, even though it may be difficult to see patients make unwise choices and decisions about lifestyles and disease management. People have the right to receive care without fearing ridicule or refusal of treatment, even if their behaviors (e.g., smoking, substance abuse, overeating, and failure to follow health care providers' recommendations) may have contributed to their chronic disorder.

Skills for Communicating With the Chronically Ill

Nurses need to develop skill and comfort in assessing patients' and families' responses to chronic illness and planning interventions that will support their values and choices throughout the continuum of care. Patients and families need ongoing assistance: Telling a patient something once is not teaching, and hearing the patient's words is not the same as active listening. Throughout the course of illness, patients and their families encounter complicated treatment decisions, bad news about disease progression, and recurring emotional responses. In addition to the time of initial diagnosis, lack of response to the treatment course, decisions to continue or withdraw particular interventions, and decisions about hospice care are examples of critical points on the treatment continuum that demand patience, empathy, and honesty from nurses. Discussing sensitive issues such as progressive illness, hopes for survival, and fears associated with death is never easy. However, the art of therapeutic communication can be learned and, like other skills, must be practiced to gain expertise. Similar to other skills, communication should be practiced in a "safe" setting, such as a classroom or clinical skills laboratory with other students or clinicians.

Although communication with each patient and family should be tailored to their particular level of understanding and values concerning disclosure, general guidelines for nurses include the following:

- Deliver and interpret the technical information necessary for making decisions without hiding behind medical terminology.
- Realize that the best time for the patient to talk may be when it is least convenient for you.
- Being fully present during any opportunity for communication is often the most helpful form of communication.
- Allow the patient and family to set the agenda regarding the depth of the conversation.
- Realize that beginning the conversation requires additional opportunities to continue the conversation.

When Patients and Families Receive Bad News

Communicating about a life-threatening diagnosis or about disease progression is best accomplished by the interdisciplinary team in any setting: a physician, nurse, and social worker should be present whenever possible to provide information, facilitate discussion, and address concerns. Most importantly, the presence of the team conveys caring and respect for the patient and family. If the patient wishes to have family present for the discussion, arrangements should be made to have the discussion at a time that is best for everyone. A quiet area with a minimum of disturbances should be used. All clinicians present should turn off beepers, cell

phones, and other communication devices for the duration of the meeting and should allow sufficient time for the patient and family to absorb and respond to the news. Finally, the space in which the meeting takes place should be conducive to seating all participants at eye level.

After the initial discussion of a life-threatening illness or progression of a disease, the patient and family have many questions and may need to be reminded of factual information. Coping with news about a serious diagnosis or poor prognosis is an ongoing process. The nurse should be sensitive to these ongoing needs and may need to repeat previously provided information or simply be present while the patient and family react emotionally. Seriously ill patients and their families need time and support to cope with the changes brought about by changes in the patient's condition and the prospect of impending death. The nurse who is able to sit comfortably with another's suffering, time and time again, without judgment and without the need to solve the patient's and family's problems, provides an intervention that is a gift beyond measure.

THE CHANGING TRAJECTORY OF CHRONIC ILLNESS TO END-OF-LIFE CARE

As individuals become progressively ill, their health shifts between stable and unstable and acute and crisis events. During these periods of health status changes, patients will use increased health care services to regain their balance and recover. There are peaks and valleys to these patterns, and eventually patients reach a point from which they do not rebound, and they become progressively ill, decline, and die. It is during these periods of times when chronically ill patients come in contact with members of the health care team who should evaluate them for palliative and supportive services to enhance their care and improve and sustain their quality of living.

Providing end-of-life care for someone chronically ill is very different from providing it to someone who may have died suddenly from an accident, trauma, disaster, or homicide. When a death is sudden, there is tremendous shock and disbelief by the person's survivors that the person has died. The shock is compounded if the death was thought to be preventable, or if it resulted from a reckless act of irresponsibility, such as from a drunken driving accident. When a person has a chronic disease that progresses with a known trajectory, it gives the patient and family members opportunities to plan and participate in decisions about treatment choices and resources to use to facilitate their quality of life individually and as a family.

Sociocultural Context

Although each person experiences terminal illness uniquely, that illness is also shaped substantially by the social and cultural contexts in which it occurs. In the United States, life-threatening illness, life-sustaining treatment decisions, dying, and death occur in a social environment in which illness is largely considered a foe and battles are either lost or won (Benoliel, 1993). A care–cure dichotomy emerged early on in modern medicine, in which health care providers may view cure as the ultimate goal and care as second best, and only acceptable when cure is no longer possible. In this model of health care, alleviating suffering is not as valued as curing disease, and patients who cannot be cured feel distanced from the health care team, concluding that, when treatment has failed, they too have failed. Patients and families who have internalized the socially constructed meaning of care as second-best to cure may fear that any shift from curative goals in the direction of comfort-focused care will result in no care or lower-quality care, and that the clinicians on whom they have come to rely will abandon them if they withdraw from the battle for cure.

The reduction of patients to their diseases is exemplified in the frequently relayed message in late-stage illness that "nothing more can be done." This all-too-frequently used statement communicates the belief of many clinicians that there is nothing of value to offer patients who are beyond cure. In a care-focused perspective, mind, body, and spirit are inextricable, and treating the body without attending to the mind and spirit is considered inadequate to evoke true healing. The idea of healing as care, along with and beyond cure, implies that healing can take place throughout life and outside the boundaries of contemporary medicine. In this expanded definition, there continue to be opportunities for physical, spiritual, emotional, and social healing, even as body systems begin to fail at the end of life.

Clinicians' attitudes toward the terminally ill and dying remain the greatest barrier to improving care at the end of life. Kübler-Ross illuminated the concerns of the seriously ill and dying in her seminal work, *On Death and Dying*, published in 1969. At that time, it was common for patients to be kept uninformed about life-threatening diagnoses, particularly cancer, and for physicians and nurses to avoid open discussion of death and dying with their patients. Kübler-Ross taught the health care community that having open discussion about life-and-death issues did not harm patients, and that the patients in fact welcomed such openness. She was openly critical of what she called "a new but depersonalized science in the service of prolonging life rather than diminishing human suffering" (Kübler-Ross, 1969). She taught the health care community that healing could not take place in a conspiracy of silence, and that as clinicians break the silence and enter the patient's world, they too can be enriched by being partners with their patients. Her work revealed that, given adequate time and some help in working through the process, patients could reach a stage of acceptance in which they were neither angry nor depressed about their fate.

Clinicians' reluctance to discuss disease and death openly with patients stems from their own anxieties about death, as

well as misconceptions about what and how much patients want to know about their illnesses. In a seminal study of care of the dying in hospital settings, sociologists Glaser and Strauss (1965) identified that health care professionals in hospital settings avoided direct communication about dying in hopes that the patient would discover it on his or her own. They identified four "awareness contexts" that described awareness of the patient's status by providers, patients, and family members. These contexts included *closed awareness*, in which the patient is unaware of his or her terminal state; *suspected awareness*, in which the patient suspects what others know and attempts to find out details about his or her condition; *mutual pretense*, in which the patient, family, and providers are aware that the patient is dying but all pretend otherwise; and *open awareness*, in which the patient, family, and providers are aware that the patient is dying and openly acknowledge that reality (Glaser & Strauss, 1965). The two major reasons they identified that clinicians avoided direct communication with patients about the seriousness of their illness were (1) patients already knew the truth or would ask if they wanted to know, or (2) patients would subsequently lose all hope, give up, or be psychologically harmed by disclosure. Glaser and Strauss' findings were published decades ago, yet their observations remain valid today. Although a growing number of health care providers are becoming comfortable with assessing patients' and families' information needs and disclosing honest information about the seriousness of illness, many still avoid the topic of death in hope that the patient will ask or find out on his or her own. Despite progress on many health care fronts, those who work with dying patients have identified the persistence of a "conspiracy of silence" about dying.

The Importance of Palliative Care in Chronic Illness

As patients decline and treatments become complex, there has been an international recognition of the need to help patients transition from a cure orientation to one of care.

Palliative care and hospice care have been recognized as important bridges between a medical bias in the direction of cure-oriented treatment and the needs of the terminally ill patients and their families for comprehensive care in the final years, months, or weeks of life. This bridge has been built by experts in the field who advocate that palliative care needs to be extended throughout the course of illness from the time when the patient is first diagnosed and not limited to end-of-life care. The goal is a seamless integration of palliative care into the medical diagnosis and treatment of major chronic diseases (Ferris et al., 2009).

Palliative care encompasses a wide range of therapeutic interventions that aim to prevent and relieve suffering caused by multiple issues that patients and family caregivers face at any stage during an acute or chronic illness. In providing palliative care to the whole person, health care providers attend

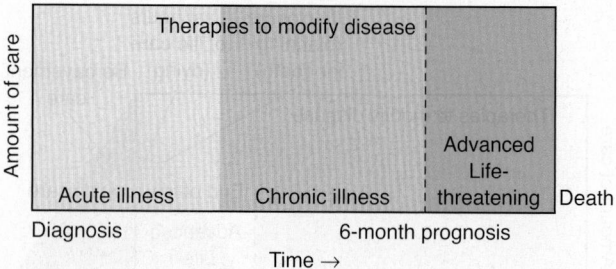

FIGURE 3-1 Model of cancer care in which only therapies directed at the disease are considered as part of standard care. From Irwin, S. A., & von Guntun, C. F. (2010). The role of palliative care in cancer care transitions. In J. C. Holland, W. S. Bretibart, P. B. Jacobsen, M. S. Lederberg, M. J. Loscalzo, & R. McCorkle (Eds.). *Psycho-Oncology* (2nd ed., pp. 277–283). New York: Oxford University Press. By permission of Oxford University Press, Inc.

to all domains of the human experience of illness that may be involved: physical, psychological, social, and spiritual. A number of models of care have described the difference in these approaches to treatment. An exclusively "cure-oriented" approach to chronic illness care can be conceptualized in Figure 3-1; here, the treatment is compartmentalized by the type of illness and disease events. In Figure 3-2, the treatment of a disease diminishes over time as it becomes less effective. In Figure 3-3, palliative care is instituted when the patient with a chronic illness is not responding to the previous treatments and additional symptom management efforts are needed. Figure 3-4 illustrates how palliative care can begin at diagnosis and become integrated throughout the entire course of the chronic illness trajectory for the patient and family caregiver. Ideally, palliative care should precede the time when the provider recognizes that hospice care is needed. When palliative care coexists with disease-oriented treatment, patients and their families benefit from the more comprehensive management of the illness experience.

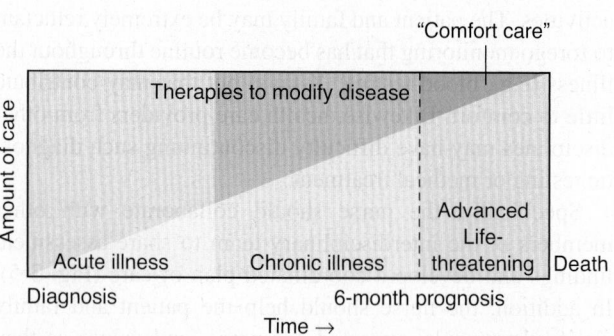

FIGURE 3-2 Model of cancer care in which antidisease treatment diminishes over time as it becomes less and less effective. From Irwin, S. A., & von Guntun, C. F. (2010). The role of palliative care in cancer care transitions. In J. C. Holland, W. S. Bretibart, P. B. Jacobsen, M. S. Lederberg, M. J. Loscalzo, & R. McCorkle (Eds.). *Psycho-Oncology* (2nd ed., pp. 277–283). New York: Oxford University Press. By permission of Oxford University Press, Inc.

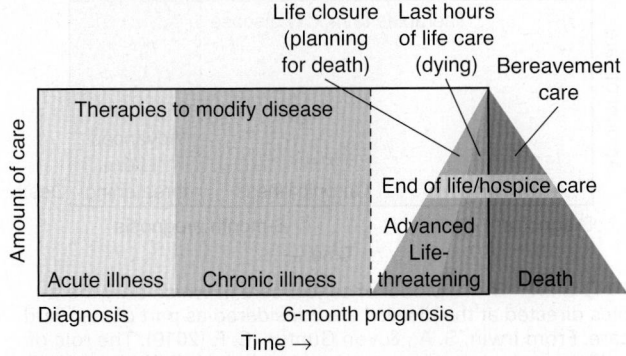

FIGURE 3-3 Model of cancer care in which palliative care begins after efforts directed at the disease end. From Irwin, S. A., & von Guntun, C. F. (2010). The role of palliative care in cancer care transitions. In J. C. Holland, W. S. Bretibart, P. B. Jacobsen, M. S. Lederberg, M. J. Loscalzo, & R. McCorkle (Eds.). *Psycho-Oncology* (2nd ed., pp. 277–283). New York: Oxford University Press. By permission of Oxford University Press, Inc.

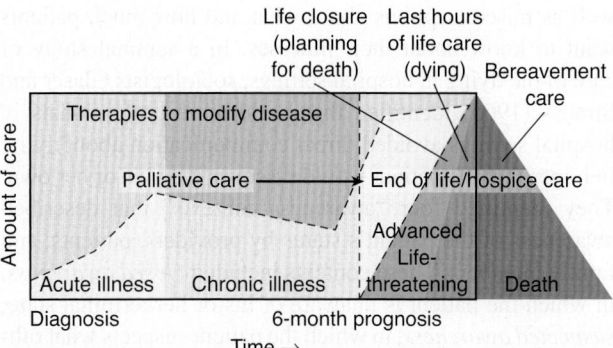

FIGURE 3-4 Model of cancer care in which palliative care begins at diagnosis and is integrated throughout the course of treatment. From Irwin, S. A., & von Guntun, C. F. (2010). The role of palliative care in cancer care transitions. In J. C. Holland, W. S. Bretibart, P. B. Jacobsen, M. S. Lederberg, M. J. Loscalzo, & R. McCorkle (Eds.). *Psycho-Oncology* (2nd ed., pp. 277–283). New York: Oxford University Press. By permission of Oxford University Press, Inc.

Goal Setting in Palliative Care

As treatment goals begin to shift in the direction of comfort care over aggressive disease-focused treatment, symptom relief and patient-and-family-defined quality of life assume greater prominence in treatment decision making. Patients, families, and health care providers may all be accustomed to an almost automatic tendency to pursue exhaustive diagnostic testing to locate and treat the source of patients' illnesses or symptoms. Each decision to withdraw treatment or discontinue diagnostic testing is an extremely emotional one for the patient and family. They may fear that the support from health care providers on whom they have come to rely will be withdrawn along with the treatment.

Throughout the course of the illness, and especially as the patient's functional status and symptoms indicate approaching death, the provider should help the patient and family weigh the benefits of continued diagnostic testing and disease-focused medical treatment against the burdens of those activities. The patient and family may be extremely reluctant to forego monitoring that has become routine throughout the illness (e.g., blood testing, X-rays) but that may contribute little to comfort. Likewise, health care providers from other disciplines may have difficulty discontinuing such diagnostic testing or medical treatment.

Specifically, the nurse should collaborate with other members of the interdisciplinary team to share assessment findings and develop a coordinated plan of care (Fig. 3-5). In addition, the nurse should help the patient and family clarify their goals, expected outcomes, and values as they consider treatment options (Box 3-1). The nurse should work with interdisciplinary colleagues to ensure that the patient and family are referred for continuing psychosocial support, symptom management, and assistance with other care-related challenges (e.g., arrangements for home care or hospice support, referrals for financial assistance).

Hospice Care in the United States

The broadening of the concept of palliative care actually followed the development of the hospice movement in the United States. Hospice care is in fact palliative care. The difference is that hospice care is associated with the end of the patient's life, and although it focuses on quality of life, hospice care by necessity usually includes realistic emotional, social, spiritual, and financial preparation for death. The hospice movement in the United States is based on the belief that meaningful living is achievable during terminal illness and that it is best supported in the home, free from technologic interventions that prolong physiologic dying.

BOX 3-1

Assessing The Patient and Family Perspective: Goal Setting in Palliative Care

Patient and Family

- **Awareness of diagnosis, illness stage, and prognosis:** "Tell me your understanding of your illness right now.
- **Values:** "Tell me what is most important to you as you are thinking about the treatment options available to you/your loved one."
- **Preferences:** "You've said that being comfortable and pain-free is most important to you right now. Where would you like to receive care (home, hospital, long-term care facility, doctor's office), and how can I help?"
- **Expected/desired outcomes:** "What are your hopes and expectations for this (diagnostic test (e.g., CT scan) or treatment)?"
- **Benefits and burdens:** "Is there a point at which you would say that the testing or treatment is outweighed by the burdens it is causing you (e.g., getting from home to the hospital, pain, nausea, fatigue, interference with other important activities)?"

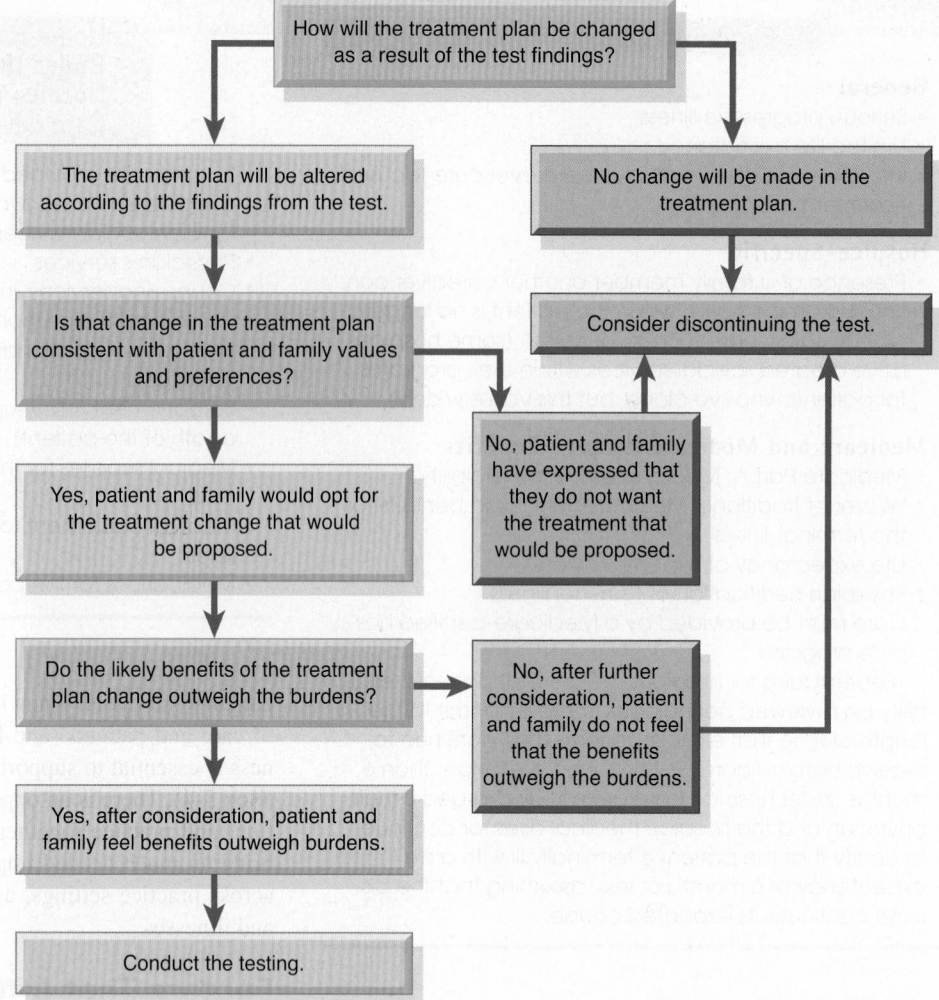

FIGURE 3-5 An algorithm for decision making about diagnostic testing at the end of life.

The landmark Study to Understand Prognoses and Preferences for Outcomes and Risks of Treatments (SUPPORT Principal Investigators, 1995) documented troubling deficiencies in the care of the dying in hospital settings:

- Many patients received unwanted care at the end of life.
- Clinicians were not aware of patient preferences for life-sustaining treatment, even when preferences were documented in the clinical record.
- Pain was often poorly controlled at the end of life.
- Efforts to enhance communication were ineffective.

Despite more than 40 years of existence in the United States, hospice remains an option for end-of-life care that has not been fully integrated into mainstream health care. Although hospice care is available to people with any life-limiting condition, it has primarily been used by patients with advanced cancer, in which the disease staging and trajectory lend themselves to more reliable prediction about the timing of a person's dying. Many reasons have been suggested to explain the reluctance of providers to refer patients to hospice and the reluctance of patients to accept this form

of care. These include the difficulties in making a terminal prognosis and advances in "curative" treatment options in late-stage illness, as well as the values and attitudes of health care providers. The result is that patients who could benefit from the comprehensive, interdisciplinary support offered by hospice programs frequently do not enter hospice care until their final days (or hours) of life.

After hospice care was recognized as a distinct program of services under Medicare in the early 1980s, organizations providing hospice care were able to receive Medicare reimbursement if they could demonstrate that the hospice program met the Medicare "conditions of participation." State Medical Assistance (Medicaid) also provides coverage for hospice care, as do most commercial insurers. Federal reimbursement for hospice care ushered in a new era in hospice, in which program standards developed and published by the federal government codified what had formerly been a grassroots, loosely organized, and somewhat undefined ideal for care at the end of life. In many aspects, Medicare standards have come to largely define hospice philosophy and services.

BOX 3-2
Eligibility Criteria for Hospice Care

General
- Serious, progressive illness
- Limited life expectancy
- Informed choice of palliative care over cure-focused treatment

Hospice-Specific
- Presence of a family member or other caregiver continuously in the home when the patient is no longer able to safely care for him- or herself (some hospices have created special services within their programs for patients who live alone, but this varies widely)

Medicare and Medicaid Hospice Benefits
- Medicare Part A; Medical Assistance eligibility
- Waiver of traditional Medicare/Medicaid benefits for the terminal illness
- Life expectancy of 6 months or less
- Physician certification of terminal illness
- Care must be provided by a Medicare-certified hospice program

    Federal rules for hospices require that patients' eligibility be reviewed periodically. There is no limit to the length of time that eligible patients may continue to receive hospice care. Patients who live longer than 6 months under hospice care are not discharged if their physician and the hospice medical director continue to certify that the patient is terminally ill with a life expectancy of 6 months or less, assuming that the disease continues its expected course.

BOX 3-3
Home Hospice Services Covered Under the Medicare/Medicaid Hospice Benefit Routine Home Care Level

- Nursing care provided by or under the supervision of a registered nurse, available 24 hours a day
- Medical social services
- Physician's services
- Counseling services, including dietary counseling
- Home health aide/homemaker
- Physical/occupational/speech therapists
- Volunteers
- Bereavement follow-up (for up to 13 months after the death of the patient)
- Medical supplies for the palliation of the terminal illness
- Medical equipment for the palliation of the terminal illness
- Medications for the palliation of the terminal illness

In most programs, the Medicare definitions for patient eligibility are used to guide all enrollment decisions. According to Medicare, the patient who wishes to use his or her Medicare Hospice Benefit must be certified by a physician as terminally ill, with a life expectancy of 6 months or less if the disease follows its natural course (Box 3-2). Thus, hospice has come to be defined as care provided to terminally ill persons and their families in the last 6 months of the patient's life. Most hospice care is provided at the "routine home care" level and includes the services depicted in Box 3-3. Because of additional Medicare rules concerning completion of all cure-focused medical treatment before the Medicare Hospice Benefit may be accessed, many patients delay enrollment in hospice programs until very close to the end of life.

NURSING CARE OF TERMINALLY ILL PATIENTS

Nurses can have a significant and lasting effect on the way in which patients live until they die, the manner in which the death occurs, and the enduring memories of that death for the patient's survivors. Knowledge about end-of-life principles of care and patients' and families' unique responses to illness is essential to supporting their unique values and goals (Box 3-4). There is an opportunity to bring research, education, and practice together to change the culture of dying, bringing much needed improvement to care that is relevant across practice settings, age groups, cultural backgrounds, and illnesses.

Factors That Influence Dying

Many factors can directly or indirectly affect how a person dies and what happens to one's body and one's survivors after death. It is useful for nurses to think of these factors as those that cannot be changed by one's actions and those that can be influenced in some fashion.

Unalterable Factors

Unalterable factors are those that are constant, including the age, gender, and personality of the dying person. Cultural attitudes toward death and dying also cannot be influenced, but must be taken into account in providing care. Other factors that need to be assessed, and that may affect a person's dying or bereavement, are previous experiences with illness and death, the type of disease of the dying person and its expected course, and the actual cause of death for the bereaved. Death by suicide or from neglected care will affect the family's recovery and grief process negatively compared to a death that is expected, with opportunities for the family to bring closure to their relationships and participate in maintaining the dying person's comfort. Certain diseases are associated with a trajectory or expected course of dying. Some patients will die very suddenly, and others will have ample time to participate in decisions surrounding their care.

BOX 3-4
Nursing Research

Bridging the Gap to Evidence-Based Practice

Substantial empirical work has been done over the last two decades describing essential training for nurses in providing quality end-of-life care. The most well-recognized program, the End-of-Life Nursing Education Consortium (ELNEC), is a national educational initiative led by Drs. Ferrell and Grant to improve end-of-life care in the United States. The project provides undergraduate and graduate nursing faculty, continuing education providers, staff development educators, and specialty nurses in pediatrics, oncology, critical care, and geriatrics, in end-of-life care so they can teach this essential information to nursing students and practicing nurses in educational and clinical settings. The project, which began in February 2000, was initially funded by a major grant from the Robert Wood Johnson Foundation (RWJF). The curriculum is revised annually on the basis of participant recommendations and new advances in the field. ELNEC trainings are held multiple times each year in locations across the country. To date, over 5,000 nurses representing all 50 states and over 40 countries have received ELNEC training and are sharing this new expertise in educational and clinical settings. The ELNEC program is designed in eight modules, with cultural aspects of care integrated into each:

1. Palliative Care in End-of-Life Care
2. Pain Management
3. Symptom Management
4. Communication
5. Ethical Decision Making in End-of-Life Care
6. Final Hours of Life
7. Loss Grief and Bereavement
8. Achieving Quality Care at End of Life

Ferrell, Virani, Grant, et al. 2005; Ferrell, Virani, & Malloy, 2005; Malloy, Paice, Virani, et al. 2008.

The nurse needs to understand the natural course of diseases and the changes that can be expected from treatment regimens. The survivors of people who die suddenly or take their own lives have more emotional and physical problems than do survivors of people with long-term illnesses.

Changeable Factors

Changeable factors are those that can be influenced by nurses. These factors need ongoing reassessment because they *are* subject to change. These factors include the dying person's previous and current relationship with health care providers, the medical management of the illness, treatment effects, the projected prognosis, the meaning the dying person invests in the experience, and the resources available for support, including the primary caregiver's health and willingness to provide care. The overwhelming majority of patients repeatedly report they prefer to die at home, and if these factors are

assessed and the patient's goals are taken into account, dying at home is possible for those patients and families who work together to accomplish the patient's wishes.

Critical Time Periods of Terminal Care

There are three critical time periods during terminal care: Before death, the death event, and bereavement. In each period, guiding principles can direct nursing care for people who are dying and for their survivors. Although a dying person and the survivors progress sequentially through the three time periods of terminal care, unfortunately the same nurse does not care for the patient and family throughout all three phases; therefore, it is essential there is consensus about the critical aspects of care, so that continuity can be provided to the patient and family.

Predeath Period

Quint-Benoliel (1967), in her landmark study of the nurse and the dying patient, determined that progressively ill patients need the opportunity for three kinds of experiences that are difficult to achieve in today's society. They need to (1) know what is happening to them and be able to talk about its reality with someone who will listen, (2) be allowed to experience the pain of "feeling bad" instead of having to hide their feelings to protect other people from the pain of their own feelings, and (3) participate in the decisions affecting how they will live their final days and how they will die (Quint, 1967). The primary responsibility of the nurse during the predeath period is to establish a relationship with the dying person. Through this relationship, the nurse should share information with the dying person about what is happening to him or her, as well as the available choices for care. It is important to establish this relationship while the dying person feels well enough to converse with the nurse about his or her goals and wishes as death approaches. It is primarily a time of assessment, not action, in which the nurse gathers data on how the person and family are coping with what is happening to them and how the options available fit within the person's lifestyle and goals for the future. Documentation regarding the person's disease state, responses to treatment, personal goals, and changes in family interactions is essential so that consistent care can be provided over time. As symptoms occur or change, the nurse elicits the meaning of the experience and helps the patient be informed about alternatives in treatment. Specific interventions are planned and evaluated after discussing alternatives available, their effects, and long-term consequences with the patient.

The Death Event

Many people have misconceptions about how people die and whether dying patients are aware of what is happening to them. Most health care providers have seen people die only in institutional settings and when advanced medical

technology was used to sustain life. The majority of health providers have not had an opportunity to witness a person dying without medical intervention and in the natural setting of home or another place of preference. Gradually, as the patient becomes more socially and physically dependent on others for assistance, the dying person and the family need increased supervision by providers. The primary purpose in being present as death becomes imminent is to anticipate problems, such as distressing symptoms or family disruptions, before they interfere with the dying person's wishes. The best of plans, well made over a period of months or weeks of preparation, can easily be unintentionally undermined by any member of the health care team or family. Distressing symptoms that warrant hospitalization can generally be prevented if the nurse and provider are working closely together, and the family has the resources for maintaining the person in the home. Some patients may prefer to be institutionalized because they do not want to be a burden on their family.

If possible, the nurse is present when the patient dies or arranges to be called shortly thereafter, to assist with the preparation of the body and to support the family. If the patient dies in the hospital, the family needs ample time in private to be with the body. The nurse assists the family with answering questions, making telephone calls, and expressing grief. The nurse may assist with helping to clean the patient's room after the death. Some families may want these tasks done for them, and others have a need to do them themselves. Nothing should be removed without the family's permission. Once the death event is over, most nurses need an opportunity to debrief with someone they trust about the experience. It is important for nurses to develop a support network of their own to share their feelings and validate their care with others.

Bereavement

The third critical time period is the time after the death. Most members of the family may need several opportunities to relive the events surrounding the death, and the nurse is in a unique position to listen, having been a part of the experience. Often family and friends do not want to hear the events over and over from each other and frequently send messages that the grieving person should get on with living. Part of the support given in reliving the death experience involves reinforcing the family's sense that they did a good job supporting the dead person's wishes and communicating to them that everything was done that could be done. The length of time a nurse sees a family for bereavement varies. Usually, at least 3 months are needed to assist making decisions and disposing of the dead person's belongings and to assess the family's coping with the loss. Family members need encouragement not to act impulsively and to think through the consequences of their decisions. The nurse helps the family to discuss options available and to talk not only about the major loss associated with the death but also the

consequential losses. If a family member needs additional help, the nurse can make a referral to a mental health provider, support group, or primary care provider.

Communicating With the Terminally Ill

To develop a level of comfort and expertise in communicating with seriously and terminally ill patients and their families, nurses and other clinicians should first consider their own experiences with and values concerning illness and death. Reflection, reading, and talking with family members, friends, and colleagues can help nurses examine beliefs about death and dying. Talking with people from different cultural backgrounds can help nurses view personally held beliefs through a different lens and can help nurses become sensitive to death-related beliefs and practices in other cultures. Discussion with nursing and non-nursing colleagues can also be useful; it may reveal the values shared by many health care professionals and identify diversity in the values of patients in their care. Values clarification and personal death awareness exercises can provide a starting point for self-discovery and discussion.

Ethical Decision Making in End-of-Life Care

Nurses are responsible for educating patients about the possibilities and probabilities inherent in their illness and their life with the illness, and for supporting them as they conduct life review, values clarification, treatment decision making, and end-of-life closure. The only way to do this effectively is to try to appreciate and understand the illness from the patient's perspective. It is also important that patients have had an opportunity to identify their preferences for how decisions are made at the end-of-life through legal documents recognized on a federal and state level (Box 3-5).

At the same time, nurses should be both culturally aware and sensitive in their approaches to communication with patients and families about death. Attitudes toward open disclosure about terminal illness vary widely among different cultures, and direct communication with patients about such matters may be viewed as harmful. To provide effective patient- and family-centered care at the end of life, nurses must be willing to set aside their own assumptions and attitudes so that they can discover what type and amount of disclosure is most meaningful to each patient and family within their unique belief systems.

Providing Culturally Sensitive Care at the End of Life

Although death, grief, and mourning are universally accepted aspects of living, one's values, expectations, and practices during serious illness, as death approaches, and after death are culturally bound and expressed. Health care providers

BOX 3-5 Methods of Stating End-of-Life Preferences

Advance directives: Written documents that allow the individual of sound mind to document preferences regarding end-of-life care that should be followed when the signer is terminally ill and unable to verbally communicate his or her wishes. The documents are generally completed in advance of serious illness, but may be completed after a diagnosis of serious illness if the signer is still of sound mind. The most common types are the durable power of attorney for health care and the living will.

Durable power of attorney for health care: A legal document through which the signer appoints and authorizes another individual to make medical decisions on his or her behalf when he or she is no longer able to speak for him- or herself. This is also known as a health care power of attorney or a proxy directive.

Living will: A type of advance directive in which the individual documents treatment preferences. It provides instructions for care in the event that the signer is terminally ill and not able to communicate his or her wishes directly and often is accompanied by a durable power of attorney for health care. This is also known as a medical directive or treatment directive.

Information about the advance care planning and state-specific advance directive documents and instructions are available from the website of Caring Connections (http://caringinfo.org). The legality of these documents may vary across states and within institutions, and it is important that people have someone they have spoken to and trust who can advocate for individual preferences if needed.

may share very similar values concerning end-of-life care or may find that they are inadequately prepared to assess for and implement care plans that support culturally diverse perspectives. Historical mistrust of the health care system and unequal access to even basic medical care may underlie the beliefs and attitudes among ethnically diverse populations. In addition, lack of education or knowledge about end-of-life care treatment options and language barriers influence decisions among many socioeconomically disadvantaged groups.

Much of the formal structure concerning health care decisions in the United States is rooted in the Western notions of autonomy, truth telling, and the acceptability of withdrawing or withholding life-prolonging medical treatment at the end of life. In many cultures, however, interdependence is valued over autonomy, leading to communication styles that favor relinquishment of decision making to family members or to perceived authority figures, such as physicians. In addition, there is variation in preference regarding the use of life-prolonging medical treatments such as cardiopulmonary resuscitation and artificially provided nutrition and hydration at the end of life; some groups are less likely to agree with withholding or withdrawing such life supports from the patient with a terminal illness.

The nurse's role is to assess the values, preferences, and practices of every patient, regardless of ethnicity, socioeconomic status, or background. The nurse can share knowledge about a patient's and family's cultural beliefs and practices with the health care team and facilitate the adaptation of the care plan to accommodate these practices. For example, a nurse may find that a male patient prefers to have his eldest son make all of his care decisions. Institutional practices and laws governing informed consent are also rooted in the Western notion of autonomous decision making and informed consent. If a patient wishes to defer decisions to his son, the nurse can work with the team to negotiate informed consent, respecting the patient's right not to participate in decision making and honoring his family's cultural practices.

The nurse should assess and document the patient's and family's specific beliefs, preferences, and practices regarding end-of-life care, preparation for death, and after-death rituals. The nurse must use judgment and discretion about the timing and setting for eliciting this information. Some patients may wish to have a family member speak for them or may be unable to provide information because of advanced illness. The nurse should give the patient and family a context for the discussion, such as, "It is very important to us to provide care that addresses your needs and the needs of your family. We want to honor and support your wishes, and want you to feel free to tell us how we are doing, and what we could do to better meet your needs. I'd like to ask you some questions; what you tell me will help me to understand and support what is most important to you at this time. You don't need to answer anything that makes you uncomfortable. Is it all right to ask some questions?" The assessment of end-of-life beliefs, preferences, and practices probably should be carried out in short segments over a period of time (for example, across multiple days of an inpatient hospital stay or in conjunction with multiple patient visits to an outpatient setting). The discomfort of novice nurses with asking questions and discussing this type of sensitive content can be reduced by prior practice in a classroom or clinical skills laboratory, observation of interviews conducted by experienced nurses, and partnering with experienced nurses during the first few assessments.

Symptom Management

Many patients suffer unnecessarily when they do not receive adequate attention for the symptoms accompanying serious illness. Careful evaluation of the patient should include not only the physical problems but also the psychological, social, and spiritual dimensions of the patient's and family's experience of serious illness. This approach contributes to a more comprehensive understanding of how the patient's and family's life has been affected by illness and leads to nursing care that addresses the needs in every dimension.

Clinical depression should not be accepted as an inevitable consequence of dying, nor should it be confused with sadness and anticipatory grieving, which are normal reactions to the losses associated with impending death. Emotional and spiritual support and control of disturbing physical symptoms are appropriate interventions for situational depression associated with terminal illness. Cancer patients with advanced disease are especially vulnerable to delirium, depression, suicidal ideation, and severe anxiety. Higher levels of debilitation predict higher levels of pain and depressive symptoms, and the presence of pain increases the likelihood of developing major psychiatric complications of illness. Patients and their families must be given space and time to experience sadness and to grieve, but patients should not have to endure untreated depression at the end of their lives. An effective combined approach to clinical depression includes relief of physical symptoms, attention to emotional and spiritual distress, and pharmacologic intervention with psychostimulants, selective serotonin reuptake inhibitors, and tricyclic antidepressants.

Patients approaching the end of life experience many of the same symptoms, regardless of their underlying disease processes. Symptoms in terminal illness may be caused by the disease, either directly (e.g., dyspnea due to chronic obstructive lung disease) or indirectly (e.g., nausea and vomiting related to pressure in the gastric area); by the treatment for the disease; or by a coexisting disorder that is unrelated to the disease. Some of the most challenging symptoms that occur as death approaches include management of pain, feeding and hydration, changes in consciousness delirium, dyspnea, and secretions (Emanuel, Ferris, von Gunten et al., 2010). Chapter 7 presents assessment principles for pain that include identifying the effect of the pain on the patient's life, the importance of believing the patient's report of the pain and its effect, and the importance of systematic assessment of pain. Similarly, symptoms such as dyspnea, nausea, weakness, and anxiety should also be carefully and systematically assessed and managed. Questions that guide the assessment of symptoms are listed in Box 3-6.

The patient's goals should guide symptom management. Medical interventions may be aimed at treating the underlying causes of the symptoms or reducing the impact of symptoms. For example, a medical intervention such as thoracentesis (an invasive procedure in which fluid is drained from the pleural space) may be performed to temporarily relieve dyspnea in a patient with pleural effusion secondary to lung cancer. Pharmacologic and nonpharmacologic methods for symptom management may be used in combination with medical interventions to modify the physiologic causes of symptoms. In addition, pharmacologic management with low-dose oral morphine is very effective in relieving dyspnea, and guided relaxation may reduce the anxiety associated with the sensation of breathlessness. As is true with pain, the principles of pharmacologic symptom management are use of the smallest dose of the medication to achieve the

---

BOX 3-6

Assessing Symptoms Associated With Terminal Illness

- How is this symptom affecting the patient's life?
- What is the meaning of the symptom to the patient? To the family?
- How does the symptom affect physical functioning, mobility, comfort, sleep, nutritional status, elimination, activity level, and relationships with others?
- What makes the symptom better?
- What makes it worse?
- Is it worse at any particular time of the day?
- What are the patient's expectations and goals for managing the symptom? The family's?
- How is the patient coping with the symptom?
- What is the economic effect of the symptom and its management?

Adapted from Jacox, A., Carr, D.B., & Payne, R. (1994). *Management of cancer pain*. Rockville, MD: AHCPR.

---

desired effect, avoidance of polypharmacy, anticipation and management of medical side effects, and creation of a therapeutic regimen that is acceptable to the patient based on his or her goals for maximizing quality of life.

The patient's goals take precedence over the clinicians' goals to relieve all symptoms at all costs. Although clinicians may believe that symptoms must be completely relieved whenever possible, the patient might choose instead to decrease symptoms to a tolerable level rather than to relieve them completely if the side effects of medications are unacceptable to him or her. This often allows the patient to have greater independence, mobility, and alertness, and to devote attention to issues he or she considers of higher priority and greater importance.

Anticipating and planning interventions for symptoms that have not yet occurred is a cornerstone of end-of-life care. Both patients and family members cope more effectively with new symptoms and exacerbations of existing symptoms when they know what to expect and how to manage it. Hospice programs typically provide "emergency kits" containing ready-to-administer doses of a variety of medications that are useful to treat symptoms in advanced illness. For example, a kit might contain small doses of oral morphine liquid for pain or shortness of breath, a benzodiazepine for restlessness, and an acetaminophen suppository for fever. Family members can be instructed to administer a prescribed dose from the emergency kit, often avoiding prolonged suffering for the patient as well as rehospitalization for symptom management.

Pain Management

Numerous studies have shown that patients with advanced illness, particularly cancer, experience considerable pain. Pain is a significant symptom for many cancer patients

throughout their treatment and disease course; it results from both the disease and the modalities used to treat it. Pain and suffering are among the most feared consequences of cancer. Poorly managed pain affects the psychological, emotional, social, and financial well-being of patients.

Patients who are taking an established regimen of analgesics should continue to receive those medications as they approach the end of life. Inability to communicate pain should not be equated with the absence of pain. Although most pain can be managed effectively using the oral route, as the end of life nears, patients may be less able to swallow oral medications due to somnolence or nausea. Patients who have been receiving opioids should continue to receive equianalgesic doses via rectal or sublingual routes. Concentrated morphine solution can be very effectively delivered by the sublingual route, because the small liquid volume is well tolerated even if swallowing is not possible. As long as the patient continues to receive opioids, a regimen to combat constipation must be implemented. If the patient cannot swallow laxatives or stool softeners, rectal suppositories or enemas may be necessary.

The nurse should teach the family about continuation of comfort measures as the patient approaches the end of life, how to administer analgesics via alternative routes, and how to assess for pain when the patient cannot verbally report pain intensity. Because the analgesics administered orally or rectally are short-acting, typically scheduled as frequently as every 3 to 4 hours around the clock, there is always a strong possibility that a patient approaching the end of life will die in close proximity to the time of analgesic administration. If the patient is at home, family members administering analgesics should be prepared for this possibility. They need reassurance that they did not "cause" the death of the patient by administering a dose of analgesic medication.

Nutrition and Hydration at the End of Life

Anorexia and cachexia are common problems in the seriously ill. The profound changes in the patient's appearance and the concomitant lack of interest in the socially important rituals of mealtime are particularly disturbing to families. The approach to the problem varies depending on the patient's stage of illness, level of disability associated with the illness, and desires. The anorexia–cachexia syndrome is characterized by disturbances in carbohydrate, protein, and fat metabolism; endocrine dysfunction; and anemia. The syndrome results in severe asthenia (loss of energy).

Although causes of anorexia may be controlled for a period of time, progressive anorexia is an expected and natural part of the dying process. Anorexia may be related to or exacerbated by situational variables (e.g., the ability to have meals with the family versus eating alone in the "sick room"), progression of the disease, treatment for the disease, or psychological distress. The patient and family should be instructed in strategies to manage the variables associated with anorexia (Table 3-3).

A number of pharmacologic agents are commonly used to stimulate appetite in anorectic patients. Commonly used medications for appetite stimulation include dexamethasone (Decadron), megestrol acetate (Megace), and dronabinol (Marinol). Although several of these agents may result in temporary weight gain, their use is not associated with an increase in lean body mass in the terminally ill patient. Dexamethasone initially increases appetite and may provide short-term weight gain in some patients. However, therapy may need to be discontinued in patients with a longer life expectancy, because after 3 to 4 weeks, corticosteroids interfere with the synthesis of muscle protein.

Megestrol acetate produces temporary weight gain of primarily fatty tissue, with little effect on protein balance. Because of the time required to see any effect from this agent, therapy should not be initiated if life expectancy is less than 30 days.

Dronabinol is a psychoactive compound found in cannabis that may be helpful in reducing nausea and vomiting, appetite loss, pain, and anxiety, thereby improving food and fluid intake in some patients. However, dronabinol is not as effective as the other agents for appetite stimulation in most patients.

Cachexia

Cachexia refers to severe muscle wasting and weight loss associated with illness. Although anorexia may exacerbate cachexia, it is not the primary cause. Cachexia is associated with changes in metabolism that include hypertriglyceridemia, lipolysis, and accelerated protein turnover, leading to depletion of fat and protein stores. However, the pathophysiology of cachexia in terminal illness is not well understood. In terminal illness, the severity of tissue wasting is greater than would be expected from reduced food intake alone, and typically increasing appetite or food intake does not reverse cachexia in the terminally ill.

Anorexia and cachexia differ from starvation (simple food deprivation) in several important ways. Appetite is lost early in the process, the body becomes catabolic in a dysfunctional way, and supplementation by gastric feeding (tube feeding) or parenteral nutrition in advanced disease does not replenish lean body mass that has been lost. At one time, it was believed that cancer patients with rapidly growing tumors developed cachexia because the tumor created an excessive nutritional demand and diverted nutrients from the rest of the body. Research links cytokines produced by the body in response to a tumor to a complex inflammatory-immune response present in patients whose tumors have metastasized, leading to anorexia, weight loss, and altered metabolism.

Artificial Nutrition and Hydration

Along with breathing, eating and drinking are essential to survival throughout life. Near the end of life, the body's nutritional needs change, and the desire for food and fluid may diminish. People may no longer be able to use, eliminate,

TABLE
3-3 Measures for Managing Anorexia

Nursing Interventions	Patient and Family Teaching Tips
Initiate measures to ensure adequate dietary intake without adding stress to the patient at mealtimes.	Reduce the focus on "balanced" meals; offer the same food as often as the patient desires it.
Assess the impact of medications (e.g., chemotherapy, antiretrovirals) or other therapies (radiation therapy, dialysis) that are being used to treat the underlying illness.	Increase the nutritional value of meals. For example, add dry milk powder to milk, and use this fortified milk to prepare cream soups, milkshakes, and gravies.
Administer and monitor effects of prescribed treatment for nausea, vomiting, and delayed gastric emptying.	
Encourage patient to eat when effects of medications have subsided.	Allow and encourage the patient to eat when hungry, regardless of usual meal times.
Assess and modify environment to eliminate unpleasant odors and other factors that cause nausea, vomiting, and anorexia.	Eliminate or reduce noxious cooking odors, pet odors, or other odors that may precipitate nausea, vomiting, or anorexia.
Remove items that may reduce appetite (soiled tissues, bedpans, emesis basins, clutter).	Keep patient's environment clean, uncluttered, and comfortable.
Assess and manage anxiety and depression to the extent possible.	Make mealtime a shared experience away from the "sick" room whenever possible.
	Reduce stress at mealtimes.
	Avoid confrontations about the amount of food consumed.
	Reduce or eliminate routine weighing of the patient.
Position to enhance gastric emptying.	Encourage patient to eat in a sitting position; elevate the head of the patient's bed.
	Plan meals (food selection and portion size) that the patient desires.
Assess for constipation and/or intestinal obstruction.	Provide small frequent meals if they are easier for patient to eat.
	Ensure that patient and family understand that prevention of constipation is essential, even when the patient's intake is minimal.
Prevent and manage constipation on an ongoing basis, even when the patient's intake is minimal.	Encourage adequate fluid intake, dietary fiber, and use of bowel program to prevent constipation.
Provide frequent mouth care, particularly following nourishment.	Assist the patient to rinse after every meal. Avoid mouthwashes that contain alcohol or glycerine, which dry mucous membranes.
Ensure that dentures fit properly.	Weight loss may cause dentures to loosen and cause irritation. Remove them to inspect the gums and to provide oral care.
Administer and monitor effects of topical and systemic treatment for oropharyngeal pain.	The patient's comfort may be enhanced if medications for pain relief given on an as-needed basis for breakthrough pain are administered before mealtimes.

or store nutrients and fluids adequately. For patients with progressive illness, food preparation and mealtimes often become battlegrounds in which well-meaning family members argue, plead, and cajole to encourage ill people to eat. It is not unusual for seriously ill patients to lose their appetites entirely, to develop strong aversions for foods they have enjoyed in the past, or to crave a particular food to the exclusion of all other foods.

Although nutritional supplementation may be an important part of the treatment plan in early or chronic illness, unintended weight loss and dehydration are expected sequelae of progressive illness. As illness progresses, patients, families, and clinicians may believe that, without artificial nutrition and hydration, terminally ill patients will "starve," causing profound suffering and hastened death. However, starvation should not be viewed as the failure to implant tubes for nutritional supplementation or hydration of terminally ill patients with irreversible progression of disease. Studies have demonstrated that terminally ill patients who were hydrated had neither improved biochemical parameters nor improved states of consciousness. Similarly, survival was not increased when terminally ill patients with advanced dementia received enteral feeding. Furthermore, in patients who are close to death, there are beneficial effects to withholding or withdrawing artificial nutrition and hydration, such as decreased urine output and incontinence, decreased gastric fluids and emesis, decreased pulmonary secretions and respiratory distress, decreased edema, and decreased discomfort from pressure associated with accumulated fluids in the tissues (Emanuel, Ferris, von Gunten et al., 2010).

As the patient approaches the end of life, the family and health care providers should offer the patient what he or she prefers and can most easily tolerate. The nurse should instruct the family how to separate feeding from caring, demonstrating love, and sharing by being with the loved one in other ways. Preoccupation with appetite, feeding, and weight loss diverts energy and time that the patient and family could use in other meaningful activities. The following are tips to promote nutrition for terminally ill patients:

• Offer small portions of favorite foods.
• Do not be overly concerned about a "balanced" diet.
• Cool foods may be better tolerated than hot foods.
• Offer cheese, eggs, peanut butter, mild fish, chicken, or turkey. Meat (especially beef) may taste bitter and unpleasant.
• Add milkshakes, powdered instant drinks, or other liquid supplements.
• Add dry milk powder to milkshakes and cream soups to increase protein and calorie content.
• Place nutritious foods at the bedside (fruit juices, milkshakes in insulated drink containers with straws).
• Schedule meals when family members can be present to provide company and stimulation.
• Avoid arguments at mealtime.
• Help the patient to maintain a schedule of oral care. Rinse the mouth after each meal or snack. Avoid mouthwashes that contain alcohol. Use a soft toothbrush. Treat oral ulcers or lesions. Make sure dentures fit well.
• Treat pain and other symptoms.
• Offer ice chips made from frozen fruit juices.
• Allow the patient to refuse foods and fluids.

Changes in Consciousness and Delirium

Many patients remain alert, arousable, and able to communicate until very close to death. Others sleep for long intervals and awaken only intermittently, with eventual somnolence until death. Delirium refers to concurrent disturbances in level of consciousness, psychomotor behavior, memory, thinking, attention, and sleep–wake cycle. In some patients, a period of agitated delirium precedes death, sometimes causing families to be hopeful that suddenly active patients may be getting better. Confusion may be related to underlying, treatable conditions such as medication side effects or interactions, pain or discomfort, hypoxia or dyspnea, or a full bladder or impacted stool. In patients with cancer, confusion may be secondary to brain metastases. Delirium may also be related to metabolic changes, infection, and organ failure.

Patients with delirium may become hypoactive or hyperactive, restless, irritable, and fearful. Sleep deprivation and hallucinations may occur. If treatment of the underlying factors contributing to these symptoms brings no relief, a combination of pharmacologic intervention with neuroleptics or benzodiazepines may be effective in decreasing distressing symptoms. Haloperidol (Haldol) may reduce hallucinations and agitation. Benzodiazepines (e.g., lorazepam [Ativan])

can reduce anxiety but do not clear the sensorium and may contribute to worsening cognitive impairment if used alone.

Nursing interventions are aimed at identifying the underlying causes of delirium, acknowledging the family's distress over its occurrence, reassuring family members about what is normal, teaching family members how to interact with and ensure safety for the patient with delirium, and monitoring the effects of medications used to treat severe agitation, paranoia, and fear. Confusion may mask the patient's unmet needs and fears about dying. Spiritual intervention, music therapy, gentle massage, and therapeutic touch may provide some relief. Reduction of environmental stimuli, avoidance of harsh lighting or very dim lighting (which may produce disturbing shadows), presence of familiar faces, and gentle reorientation and reassurance are also helpful.

Dyspnea

Dyspnea is an uncomfortable awareness of breathing or breathlessness that is common in patients approaching the end of life. Dyspnea is a highly subjective symptom that often is not associated with visible signs of distress, such as tachypnea, diaphoresis, or cyanosis. Patients with primary lung tumors, lung metastases, pleural effusion, or restrictive lung disease may experience significant dyspnea. Although the underlying cause of the dyspnea can be identified and treated in some cases, the burdens of additional diagnostic evaluation and treatment aimed at the physiologic problem may outweigh the benefits. The treatment of dyspnea varies depending on the patient's general physical condition and imminence of death. For example, a blood transfusion may provide temporary symptom relief for a patient with anemia earlier in the disease process; however, as the patient approaches the end of life, the benefits are typically short-lived or absent. As with assessment and management of pain, reports of dyspnea by patients must be believed. As is true for physical pain, what dyspnea means to an individual patient may increase his or her suffering. For example, the patient may interpret increasing dyspnea as a sign that death is approaching. For some patients, sensations of breathlessness may invoke frightening images of drowning or suffocation, and the resulting cycle of fear and anxiety may increase the sensation of breathlessness. Therefore, the nurse should conduct a careful assessment of the psychosocial and spiritual components of the dyspnea. Physical assessment parameters include:

• Symptom intensity, distress, and interference with activities (scale of 0 to 10)
• Auscultation of lung sounds
• Assessment of fluid balance
• Measurement of dependent edema (circumference of lower extremities)
• Measurement of abdominal girth
• Temperature
• Skin color
• Sputum quantity and character
• Cough

To determine the intensity of dyspnea and its interference with daily activities, the patient can be asked to report the severity of the dyspnea using a scale of 0 to 10, where 0 is no dyspnea and 10 is the worst imaginable dyspnea. The patient's baseline measurement before treatment and subsequent measurements taken during exacerbation of the symptom, periodically during treatment, and whenever the treatment plan changes provide ongoing objective evidence for the efficacy of the treatment plan. In addition, physical assessment findings may assist in locating the source of the dyspnea and selecting nursing interventions to relieve the symptom. The components of the assessment change as the patient's condition changes. Like other symptoms at the end of life, dyspnea can be managed effectively in the absence of assessment and diagnostic data (i.e., arterial blood gases) that are standard when a patient's illness or symptom is reversible.

Nursing management of dyspnea at the end of life is directed toward administering medical treatment for the underlying pathology, monitoring the patient's response to treatment, helping the patient and family manage anxiety (which exacerbates dyspnea), altering the perception of the symptom, and conserving energy (Box 3-7). Pharmacologic intervention is aimed at modifying lung physiology and improving performance, as well as in altering the perception of the symptom. Bronchodilators and corticosteroids are examples of medications used to treat underlying obstructive pathology, thereby improving overall lung function. Low doses of opioids are very effective in relieving dyspnea, although the mechanism of relief is not entirely clear. Although dyspnea in terminal illness is typically not associated with diminished blood oxygen saturation, low-flow oxygen often provides psychological comfort to both patients and families, particularly in the home setting.

As previously mentioned, dyspnea may be exacerbated by anxiety, and anxiety may trigger episodes of dyspnea, setting off a respiratory crisis in which the patient and family may panic. For patients receiving care at home, patient and family instruction should include anticipation and management of crisis situations and a clearly communicated emergency plan. The patient and family should be instructed about medication administration, condition changes that should be reported to the provider and nurse, and strategies for coping with diminished reserves and increasing symptomatology as the disease progresses. The patient and family need reassurance that the symptom can be effectively managed at home without the need for activation of the emergency medical services or hospitalization, and that a nurse will be available at all times via telephone or to make a visit.

Secretions

If family members have been prepared for the time of death, they are less likely to panic and are better able to be with their loved ones in a meaningful way. Noisy, gurgling breathing or moaning is generally most distressing to family members. In most cases, the sounds of breathing at the end of life are

---

BOX 3-7 **Palliative Nursing Interventions for Dyspnea**

Decrease Anxiety
- Administer prescribed anxiolytic medications as indicated for anxiety or panic associated with dyspnea.
- Assist with relaxation techniques, guided imagery.
- Provide the patient with a means to call for assistance (call bell/light within reach in a hospital or long-term care facility; handheld bell or other device for home).

Treat Underlying Pathology
- Administer prescribed bronchodilators and corticosteroids (obstructive pathology).
- Administer blood products, erythropoietin as prescribed (typically not beneficial in advanced disease).
- Administer prescribed diuretics and monitor fluid balance.

Alter Perception of Breathlessness
- Administer prescribed oxygen therapy via nasal cannula, if tolerated; masks may not be well tolerated.
- Administer prescribed low-dose opioids via oral route (morphine sulfate is used most commonly).
- Provide air movement in the patient's environment with a portable fan.

Reduce Respiratory Demand
- Teach the patient and family to implement energy conservation measures.
- Place needed equipment, supplies, and nourishment within reach.
- For home or hospice care, offer a bedside commode, electric bed (with head that elevates).

---

related to oropharyngeal relaxation and diminished awareness. Family members may have difficulty believing that the patient is not in pain or that the patient's breathing could not be improved by suctioning secretions. Patient positioning and family reassurance are the most helpful responses to these symptoms.

When death is imminent, patients may become increasingly somnolent and unable to clear sputum or oral secretions, which may lead to further impairment of breathing from pooled or dried and crusted secretions. The sound ("terminal bubbling") and appearance of the secretions are often more distressing to family members than is the presence of the secretions to the patient. Family distress over the changes in the patient's condition may be eased by supportive nursing care. Continuation of comfort-focused interventions and reassurance that the patient is not in any distress can do much to ease family concerns. Gentle mouth care with a moistened swab or very soft toothbrush helps maintain the integrity of the patient's mucous membranes. In addition, gentle oral suctioning, positioning to

TABLE 3-4 Pharmacologic Management of Excess Oral/Respiratory Secretions When Death Is Imminent

Medication	Dose
Atropine sulfate drops 1%	1 or 2 drops 1% PO/sublingual q4–6h p.r.n. or around the clock (ATC) up to 12 drops/d
Atropine injection	0.4–0.6 mg IV/SC/IM q4–6h p.r.n. or ATC (if PO therapy is ineffective)
Glycopyrrolate (Robinul)	1–2 mg PO/rectal/sublingual TID p.r.n. or ATC (maximum dose 6 mg/d)
Hyoscyamine (Levsin)	0.125–0.25 mg PO/sublingual q4–6h p.r.n. or ATC (maximum dose 1.5 mg/d)
Scopolamine (Transderm Scop)	1–3 patches q3d (maximum dose 3 patches every 72 h)

Reprinted with permission from ExcelleRx, Inc. (2008). *Hospice pharmacia pharmaceutical care tool kit* (9th ed.). Philadelphia: Author.

enhance drainage of secretions, and sublingual or transdermal administration of anticholinergic drugs reduces the production of secretions and provides comfort to the patient and support to the family (Table 3-4). Deeper suctioning may cause significant discomfort to the dying patient and is rarely of any benefit, because secretions reaccumulate rapidly.

Palliative Sedation at the End of Life

Effective control of symptoms can be achieved under most conditions, but some patients may experience distressing, intractable symptoms. Although **palliative sedation** remains controversial, it is offered in some settings to patients who are close to death or who have symptoms that do not respond to conventional pharmacologic and nonpharmacologic approaches, resulting in unrelieved suffering. Palliative sedation is distinguished from **euthanasia** or physician-assisted suicide in that the intent of palliative sedation is to relieve symptoms, not to hasten death. Palliative sedation is most commonly used when the patient exhibits intractable pain, dyspnea, seizures, or delirium, and it is generally considered appropriate in only the most difficult situations. Before implementing palliative sedation, the health care team should assess for the presence of underlying and treatable causes of suffering, such as depression or spiritual pain. Finally, the patient and family should be fully informed about the use of this treatment and alternatives.

Palliative sedation is accomplished through infusion of a benzodiazepine or barbiturate in doses adequate to induce sleep and eliminate physical signs of discomfort (McWilliams, Keeley, & Waterhouse, 2010; Quill & Byock, 2000). Nurses act as collaborating members of the interdisciplinary health care team, providing emotional

support to patients and families, facilitating clarification of values and preferences, and providing comfort-focused physical care. Once sedation has been induced, the nurse should continue to comfort the patient, monitor the physiologic effects of the sedation, support the family during the final hours or days of their loved one's life, and ensure communication within the health care team and between the team and family.

NURSING CARE OF PATIENTS AND FAMILIES IN THE FINAL HOURS OF LIFE

Providing care to patients who are close to death and being present at the time of death can be one of the most rewarding experiences a nurse can have. Patients and their families are understandably fearful of the unknown, and the approach of death may prompt new concerns or cause previous fears or issues to resurface. Family members who have always had difficulty communicating or who are part of families in which there are old resentments and hurts may experience heightened difficulty as their loved ones near death. In contrast, the time at the end of life can also afford opportunities to resolve old hurts and learn new ways of being a family. Regardless of the setting, skilled practitioners can make the dying patient comfortable, make space for their loved ones to remain present when they wish, and can give family members the opportunity to experience growth and healing. Likewise, regardless of setting, the patient and family may be less apprehensive near the time of death if they know what to expect and how to respond.

Expected Physiologic Changes

As death approaches and organ systems begin to fail, observable, expected changes in the body take place. Nursing care measures aimed at patient comfort should be continued: pain medications (administered rectally or sublingually), turning, mouth care, eye care, positioning to facilitate draining of secretions, and measures to protect the skin from urine or feces (if the patient is incontinent) should be continued. The nurse should consult with the provider about discontinuing measures that no longer contribute to patient comfort, such as drawing blood, administering tube feedings, suctioning (in most cases), and invasive monitoring. The nurse should prepare the family for the normal, expected changes that accompany the period immediately preceding death. Although the exact time of death cannot be predicted, it is often possible to identify when the patient is very close to death. Hospice programs frequently provide written information for families so they know what to expect and what to do as death nears (Box 3-8).

Although every death is unique, it is often possible for experienced clinicians to assess that the patient is "actively"

BOX 3-8

Signs of Approaching Death

The person will show less interest in eating and drinking. For many patients, refusal of food is an indication that they are ready to die. Fluid intake may be limited to that which will keep the mouth from feeling too dry.

- What you can do: Offer, but do not force, fluids and medication. Sometimes, pain or other symptoms that have required medication in the past may no longer be present. For most patients, pain medications will still be needed, and can be provided by concentrated oral solutions placed under the tongue or by rectal suppository.

Urinary output may decrease in amount and frequency.

- What you can do: No response is needed unless the patient expresses a desire to urinate and cannot. Call the hospice nurse for advice if you are not sure.

As the body weakens, the patient will sleep more and begin to detach from the environment. He or she may refuse your attempts to provide comfort.

- What you can do: Allow your loved one to sleep. You may wish to sit with him or her, play soft music, or hold hands. Your loved one's withdrawal is normal and is not a rejection of your love.

Mental confusion may become apparent, as less oxygen is available to supply the brain. The patient may report strange dreams or visions.

- What you can do: As he or she awakens from sleep, remind him or her of the day and time, where he or she is, and who is present. This is best done in a casual, conversational way.

Vision and hearing may become somewhat impaired, and speech may be difficult to understand.

- What you can do: Speak clearly but no more loudly than necessary. Keep the room as light as the patient wishes, even at night. Carry on all conversations as if they can be heard, because hearing may be the last of the senses to cease functioning.
- Many patients are able to talk until minutes before death and are reassured by the exchange of a few words with a loved one.

Secretions may collect in the back of the throat and rattle or gurgle as the patient breathes though the mouth. He or she may try to cough, and his or her mouth may become dry and encrusted with secretions.

- What you can do: If the patient is trying to cough up secretions and is experiencing choking or vomiting, call the hospice nurse for assistance.
- Secretions may drain from the mouth if you place the patient on his or her side and provide support with pillows.
- Cleansing the mouth with moistened mouth swabs will help to relieve the dryness that occurs with mouth breathing.
- Offer water in small amounts to keep the mouth moist. A straw with one finger placed over the end can be used to transfer sips of water to the patient's mouth.

Breathing may become irregular with periods of no breathing (apnea). The patient may be working very hard to breathe and may make a moaning sound with each breath. As the time of death nears, the breathing remains irregular and may become more shallow and mechanical.

- What you can do: Raising the head of the bed may help the patient to breathe more easily. The moaning sound does not mean that the patient is in pain or other distress; it is the sound of air passing over very relaxed vocal cords.

As the oxygen supply to the brain decreases, the patient may become restless. It is not unusual for the patient to pull at the bed linens, to have visual hallucinations, or even to try to get out of bed at this point.

- What you can do: Reassure the patient in a calm voice that you are there. Prevent him or her from falling out of bed. Soft music or a back rub may be soothing.

The patient may feel hot one moment and cold the next as the body loses its ability to control its temperature. As circulation slows, the arms and legs may become cool and bluish. The underside of the body may darken. It may be difficult to feel a pulse at the wrist.

- What you can do: Provide and remove blankets as needed. Avoid using electric blankets, which may cause burns because the patient cannot tell you if he or she is too warm.
- Sponge the patient's head with a cool cloth if this provides comfort.

Loss of bladder and bowel control may occur around the time of death.

- What you can do: Protect the mattress with waterproof padding and change the padding as needed to keep the patient comfortable.

As people approach death, many times they report seeing gardens, libraries, or family or friends who have died. They may ask you to pack their bags and find tickets or a passport. Sometimes they may become insistent and attempt to do these chores themselves. They may try getting out of bed (even if they have been confined to bed for a long time) so that they can "leave."

- What you can do: Reassure the patient that it is all right; he or she can "go" without getting out of bed. Stay close, share stories, and be present.

Used with permission from the Family Home Hospice of the Visiting Nurse Association of Greater Philadelphia.

or imminently dying and to prepare the family in the final days or hours leading to death. As death nears, the patient may withdraw, sleep for longer intervals, or become somnolent. Family members should be encouraged to be with the patient, to speak and reassure the patient of their presence, to stroke or touch the patient, or to lie alongside the patient (even in the hospital or long-term care facility) if the family members are comfortable with this degree of closeness and can do so without causing discomfort to the patient.

The family may have gone to great lengths to ensure that their loved one will not die alone. However, despite the best intentions and efforts of the family and clinicians, the patient may die at a time when no one is present. In any setting, it is unrealistic for family members to be at the patient's bedside 24 hours a day, and it is not unusual for a patient to die when family members have stepped away from the bedside just briefly. Experienced hospice clinicians have observed and reported that some patients appear to "wait" until family members are away from the bedside to die, perhaps to spare their loved ones the pain of being present at the time of death. Nurses can reassure family members throughout the death vigil by being present intermittently or continuously, modeling behaviors (such as touching and speaking to the patient), providing encouragement in relation to family caregiving, providing reassurance about normal physiologic changes, and encouraging family rest breaks. If a patient dies while family members are away from the bedside, they may express feelings of guilt and profound grief and may need emotional support.

After-Death Care

The time of death is generally preceded by a period of gradual diminishment of bodily functions in which increasing intervals between respirations, a weakened and irregular pulse, diminishing blood pressure, and skin color changes or mottling may occur. For patients who have received adequate management of symptoms and for families who have received adequate preparation and support, the actual time of death is commonly peaceful and occurs without struggle. Nurses may or may not be present at the time of a patient's death. In many states, nurses may be authorized to make the pronouncement of death and sign the death certificate. The determination of death is made through a physical examination that includes auscultation for the absence of breathing and heart sounds. Home care or hospice programs in which nurses make the time-of-death visit and pronouncement of death have policies and procedures to guide the nurse's actions during this visit. Immediately on cessation of vital functions, the body begins to change. It becomes dusky or bluish, waxen-appearing, and cool; blood darkens and pools in dependent areas of the body (e.g., the back and sacrum if the body is in a supine position); and urine and stool may be evacuated.

Immediately after death, family members should be allowed and encouraged to spend time with the deceased.

Normal responses of family members at the time of death vary widely and range from quiet expressions of grief to overt expressions that include wailing and prostration. The family's desire for privacy during their time with the deceased should be honored. Family members may wish to independently manage or assist with care of the body after death. If the death occurs in a long-term care facility, nurses follow the facility's procedure for preparation of the body and transportation to the facility's morgue. However, the needs of families to remain with the deceased, to wait until other family members arrive before the body is moved, and to perform after-death rituals should be honored. When an expected death occurs in the home setting, the funeral director often transports the body directly to the funeral home or mortuary.

Loss, Grief, and Bereavement

A wide range of feelings and behaviors are normal, adaptive, and healthy reactions to the loss of a loved one. **Grief** refers to the personal feelings that accompany an anticipated or actual loss. **Mourning** refers to individual, family, group, and cultural expressions of grief and associated behaviors. **Bereavement** refers to the period of time during which mourning takes place. Both grief reactions and mourning behaviors change over time as people learn to live with the loss. Although the pain of the loss may be tempered by the passage of time, loss is an ongoing developmental process, and time may never heal the bereaved individual completely. That is, the bereaved do not get over a loss entirely, nor do they return to who they were before the loss. Rather, they develop a new sense of who they are and where they fit in a world that has changed dramatically and permanently without their loved one and that relationship.

Anticipatory Grief and Mourning

Denial, sadness, anger, fear, and anxiety are normal grief reactions in people with life-threatening illness and those close to them. Kübler-Ross (1969) described five common emotional reactions to dying that are applicable to the experience of any loss: denial, anger, bargaining, depression, and acceptance. Kübler-Ross cautioned that not every patient or family member experiences every stage; many patients never reach a stage of acceptance, and patients and families fluctuate on a sometimes daily basis in their emotional responses. Individual and family coping with the anticipation of death is complicated by the varied and conflicting trajectories that grief and mourning may assume in families. For example, although the patient may be experiencing sadness while contemplating role changes that have been brought about by the illness, the patient's spouse or partner may be expressing or suppressing feelings of anger about the current changes in role and impending loss of the relationship. Others in the family may be engaged in denial (e.g., "Dad will get better; he just needs to eat more"), fear

("Who will take care of us?" or "Will I get sick too?"), or profound sadness and withdrawal. Although each of these behaviors is normal, tension may arise when one or more family members perceive that others are less caring, too emotional, or too detached.

The nurse should assess the characteristics of the family system and intervene in a manner that supports and enhances the cohesion of the family unit. The nurse can encourage family members to talk about their feelings and help them understand what is happening to them in the broader context of anticipatory grief and mourning. Acknowledging and expressing feelings, continuing to interact with the patient in meaningful ways, and planning for the time of death and bereavement are adaptive family behaviors. Professional support provided by grief counselors and social workers, whether in the community, at a local hospital, in the long-term care facility, or associated with a hospice program, can help both the patient and the family sort out and acknowledge feelings and make the end of life as meaningful as possible.

Grief and Mourning After Death

When a loved one dies, the family members enter a new phase of grief and mourning as they begin to accept the loss, feel the pain of permanent separation, and prepare to live a life without the deceased. Even if the loved one died after a long illness, preparatory grief experienced during the terminal illness does not preclude the grief and mourning that follow the death. With a death after a long or difficult illness, family members may experience conflicting feelings of relief that the loved one's suffering has ended, compounded by guilt and grief related to unresolved issues or the circumstances of death. Grief work may be especially difficult if a patient's death was painful, prolonged, accompanied by unwanted interventions, or unattended. Families who had no preparation or support during the period of imminence and death may have a more difficult time finding a place for the painful memories.

Although some family members may experience prolonged or complicated mourning, most grief reactions fall within a "normal" range. The feelings are often profound, but bereaved people eventually reconcile the loss and find a way to reengage with their lives. Grief and mourning are affected by several factors, including individual characteristics, coping skills, and experiences with illness and death; the nature of the relationship to the deceased; factors surrounding the illness and the death; family dynamics; social support; and cultural expectations and norms. Uncomplicated grief and mourning are characterized by emotional feelings of sadness, anger, guilt, and numbness; physical sensations such as hollowness in the stomach and tightness in the chest, weakness, and lack of energy; cognitions that include preoccupation with the loss and a sense of the deceased as still present; and behaviors such as crying, visiting places that

are reminders of the deceased, social withdrawal, and restless overactivity.

After-death rituals, including preparation of the body, funeral practices, and burial rituals, are socially and culturally significant ways in which family members begin to accept the reality and finality of death. Preplanning of funerals is becoming increasingly common, and hospice professionals in particular help the family make plans for death, often involving the patient, who may wish to play an active role. Preplanning of the funeral relieves the family of the burden of making decisions in the intensely emotional period after a death.

In general, the period of mourning is an adaptive response to loss during which mourners come to accept the loss as real and permanent, acknowledge and experience the painful emotions that accompany the loss, experience life without the deceased, overcome impediments to adjustment, and find a new way of living in a world without the loved one. Particularly, immediately after the death, mourners begin to recognize the reality and permanence of the loss by talking about the deceased and telling and retelling the story of the illness and death. Societal norms in the United States are frequently at odds with the normal grieving processes of people; time excused from work obligations is typically measured in days, and mourners are often expected to get over the loss quickly and get on with life.

In reality, the work of grief and mourning takes time, and avoiding grief work after the death often leads to long-term adjustment difficulties. Mourning for a loss involves the "undoing" of psychosocial ties that bind mourners to the deceased, personal adaptation to the loss, and learning to live in the world without the deceased. In his classic work, Worden (1991) described four tasks of mourning:

- Acceptance of the reality of the loss
- Working through the pain of grief
- Adjusting to the environment in which the deceased is gone
- Emotional "relocation" of the deceased to move on with life

Although many people complete the work of mourning with the informal support of families and friends, many find that talking with others who have had a similar experience, such as in formal support groups, normalizes the feelings and experiences and provides a framework for learning new skills to cope with the loss and create a new life. Hospitals, hospices, religious organizations, and other community organizations often sponsor bereavement support groups. Groups for parents who have lost a child, children who have lost a parent, widows, widowers, and gay men and lesbians who have lost a life partner are some examples of specialized support groups available in many communities.

Complicated Grief and Mourning

Complicated grief and mourning are characterized by prolonged feelings of sadness and feelings of general worthlessness or hopelessness that persist long after the death, prolonged symptoms that interfere with activities of daily living (anorexia, insomnia, fatigue, panic), or self-destructive behaviors such as alcohol or substance abuse and suicidal ideation or attempts. Complicated grief and mourning require a referral for a psychiatric assessment and evaluation to determine if pharmacologic and additional psychological interventions are needed.

COPING WITH DEATH AND DYING: PROFESSIONAL CAREGIVER ISSUES

Whether practicing in the trauma center, intensive care unit or other acute care setting, home care, hospice, long-term care, or the many locations where patients and their families receive ambulatory services, the nurse is closely involved with complex and emotionally laden issues surrounding loss of life. To be most effective and satisfied with the care he or she provides, the nurse should attend to his or her own emotional responses to the losses witnessed every day. Like family members, nurses need opportunities to grieve and express sorrow at the losses experienced and the sadness associated with a person dying before fulfilling one's dreams, leaving children prematurely, or completing one's commitments. Well before the nurse exhibits symptoms of stress or burnout, he or she should acknowledge the difficulty of coping with others' pain on a daily basis and put healthy practices in place that guard against emotional exhaustion. In hospice settings, where death, grief, and loss are expected outcomes of patient care, interdisciplinary colleagues rely on each other for support, using meeting time to express frustration, sadness, anger, and other emotions; to learn coping skills from each other; and to speak about how they were affected by the lives of those patients who have died since the last meeting. In many settings, staff members organize or attend memorial services to support families and other caregivers, who find comfort in joining each other to remember and celebrate the lives of patients. Finally, healthy personal habits, including diet, exercise, stress reduction activities (e.g., dance, yoga, tai chi, meditation), and sleep, help guard against the detrimental effects of stress.

SUMMARY

Chronic illnesses, those that last longer than 3 months, may be caused by injury or disease. Some of these diseases may be the result of genetic factors, while others may be the result of unhealthy lifestyles and behaviors earlier in life. Chronic illness is not merely a disease that has a nonreversible pathology; it is also the slow, progressive decline in normal function that brings with it disability and the need for long-term surveillance. Given its prevalence, nurses encounter people who have been living with the symptoms or disabilities that accompany chronic illness. When they do, nurses will encounter people who are living with uncertainty. Chronic illness waxes and wanes, and with these modulations come a different set of health care regimens and types of management, often placing variable demands on family caregivers. Nurses need to be aware of the phases of the trajectory model of chronic illness, and they need to tailor the care they give to the care demanded, depending on the phase.

As people with chronic illness move in and out of the different phases of the trajectory model of care, and treatments become more complex, focus shifts from cure to care. There has been an international movement to recognize the need to help patients and families transition from cure to care. The goal of this movement is a seamless integration of palliative care into treatment from the beginning—at the time of diagnosis. Palliative care, encompassing a wide range of therapeutic interventions, seeks to prevent and relieve suffering. Because suffering has many and varied sources, nurses who provide palliative care should attend to the whole patient—that is, to the physical, psychological, social, and spiritual domains of human experience. As patients move into the downward phase of chronic illness, they need hospice or hospice-like care. Hospice care includes palliative care, but unlike palliative care, hospice care is associated with the patient's end of life: it helps patients and families prepare for death—emotionally, socially, spiritually, and financially. Nurses who provide end-of-life care have eight tasks: (1) They provide pain and symptom management. (2) With an ease that comes from expertise, they communicate effectively with dying patients and their families. (3) They educate patients and families about end-of-life decision making and (4) help other professional caregivers to develop a coordinated plan of care that coheres with the wishes of patients and families. (5) They provide care to patients who are close to death, and (6) often, are present at death. (7) After death, they attend to families' loss, grief, and bereavement. (8) Finally, they achieve quality of care at the end of life by providing culturally sensitive care throughout the entire hospice-care experience.

Providing nursing care for patients and families who live with chronic illness is nursing at its fullest and deepest, for from the onset of disease to the end of life, care of the chronically ill centers on the whole person.

Chapter Review

Critical Thinking Exercises

1. A 55-year-old married mother of three adult children has been referred for hospice care. During your initial visit to the patient's home, you assess that she is experiencing severe pain in her ribs and pelvis (she reports a score of 8 on a 0–10 pain intensity scale). In addition, she reports that she is unable to sleep. Her provider has prescribed morphine for her pain, but you assess that she has used very few doses of the morphine. Her husband tells you privately that he has discouraged her use of the medicine because it has made her very sleepy and nauseated in the past. The interdisciplinary team is meeting to discuss the patient's treatment plan. What additional assessment data are needed to determine the wishes and expectations of the patient as well as the husband? What are the team's options for intervention? What are the pros and cons of each option?

2. A 28-year-old woman with two children younger than 3 years of age has recently been diagnosed with type 1 diabetes. She is very active in her community and church, and states that she cannot fit learning about diabetes, treatments, or blood glucose testing into her busy life. Identify approaches you would use to establish a plan of care with her. Link your teaching to the trajectory onset phase of chronic illness. How would your teaching plan change in the acute and crisis stages of chronic illness?

3. After having a seizure at her law office, a 34-year-old woman, a wife and mother of a 3-year-old son, was diagnosed 2 months ago with an aggressive form of brain cancer. The tumor's growth progresses rapidly. As a result, she experiences uncontrolled seizures, and her cognitive abilities decline. The neuro-oncologist has prognosticated death within a few months. What is one of the primary responsibilities of the nurse in this period of the patient's and family's life? What should the nurse document in the nursing assessment? How should the nurse respond to the patient and family when symptoms, such as seizure and cognitive decline, occur and intensify?

NCLEX-Style Review Questions

1. When educating patients about chronic diseases, such as diabetes, which of the following should the nurse include in the rationale for effective management of the disease? Select all that apply.
   A. An unmanaged chronic disease may lead to the development of other chronic illnesses.
   B. When a patient is admitted to the ICU with a comorbid chronic disease, that patient faces a greater risk of morbidity and mortality.

C. Although chronic disease affects the entire family system, management of the disease is the patient's sole responsibility.
   D. By managing a chronic disorder early in the disease process, the patient may be able to save him- or herself the high costs associated with the sequelae of unmanaged disease.

2. A patient is nearing death from metastatic cancer and is receiving hospice care in the home. The home care nurse visits. The patient's family caregiver states that the patient has not eaten well for the last several days and rarely wishes to drink, only sucking on ice now and then. The caregiver thinks that it is cruel to let the dying patient starve to death, or die from dehydration. What would the nurse's best response be?
   A. "I think it is cruel, too. If this were my mother, I would not let her die like that."
   B. "Tell me why you feel that way?"
   C. "It's okay, because this may hasten death and relieve suffering."
   D. "This is what happens when people die."

3. The sounds of breathing, including terminal bubbling, at the time of death may be distressing for families to hear. When the nurse hears these sounds, she should do which of the following? Select all that apply.
   A. Reposition the patient in an attempt to move secretions out of the oropharynx.
   B. Educate the family about what they are hearing and that the sound does not mean that the patient is in any distress.
   C. Suction the patient deeply and often to rid the oropharynx of the build-up of secretions.
   D. Suggest to the provider that now is the time for an anticholinergic drug (such as glycopyrrolate).

4. Chronic illnesses are characterized by which of the following? Select all that apply.
   A. A nonreversible pathology
   B. A slow, progressive decline in normal physiological function
   C. A decreasing prevalence nationally and internationally
   D. Necessitating long-term surveillance

5. A dying patient has sudden onset of confusion, waxing and waning consciousness, and loss of orientation, thinking she is at home when she is in the hospital. The nurse recognizes this as _____ and knows that the most appropriate pharmacologic treatment for it includes _____.
   A. Dementia, donepezil
   B. Delirium, lorazepam
   C. Delirium, haloperidol
   D. Dementia, haloperidol

Try these additional resources to enhance your learning and understanding of this chapter:
- thePoint online resource available at **http://thepoint.lww.com/Pellico1e**
- *Handbook for Focus on Adult Health: Medical-Surgical Nursing*
- *Study Guide for Focus on Adult Health: Medical-Surgical Nursing*

References and Selected Readings

References and selected readings associated with this chapter can be found on the website that accompanies the book. Visit http://thepoint.lww.com/Pellico1e to access the references and other additional resources associated with this chapter.

Concepts and Challenges in Patient Management

A 45-YEAR-OLD patient has recently been diagnosed with brain cancer. She will be undergoing surgery, followed by chemotherapy. She is very anxious and has fears about her overall prognosis.

➡ What psychosocial aspects may be affected by this diagnosis?
➡ Explain postoperative risks that may occur following surgery.
➡ Discuss the special needs of a patient undergoing chemotherapy.

PHILIP R. MARTINEZ, JR.
LINDA HONAN PELLICO

Fluid and Electrolyte and Acid—Base Imbalances

Learning Objectives

After reading this chapter, you will be able to:

1. Differentiate between osmosis, diffusion, filtration, and active transport.

2. Describe the role of the kidneys, lungs, and endocrine glands in regulating the body's fluid composition and volume.

3. Identify the effects of aging on fluid and electrolyte regulation.

4. Plan effective care of patients with the following imbalances: hypovolemia, hypervolemia, hyponatremia, hypernatremia, hypokalemia, and hyperkalemia.

5. Describe the cause, clinical manifestations, management, and nursing interventions for the following imbalances: hypocalcemia, hypercalcemia, hypomagnesemia, hypermagnesemia, hypophosphatemia, hyperphosphatemia, hypochloremia, and hyperchloremia.

6. Explain the roles of the lungs, kidneys, and chemical buffers in maintaining acid–base balance.

7. Compare metabolic acidosis and alkalosis with regard to causes, clinical manifestations, diagnosis, and management.

Fluid and electrolyte balance is a dynamic process that is crucial for life and **homeostasis.** Potential and actual disorders of fluid and electrolyte balance occur in every setting, with every disorder, and with a variety of changes that affect healthy people as well as those who are ill. The blood's acid–base balance is precisely controlled, and because deviations from the normal pH range of 7.35 to 7.45 can cause severe effects in body function, the nurse needs to competently interpret arterial blood gases (ABGs).

FUNDAMENTAL CONCEPTS

AMOUNT AND COMPOSITION OF BODY FLUIDS

Approximately 60% of the weight of a typical adult consists of fluid (water and electrolytes). Factors that influence the amount of body fluid are age, gender, and body fat. In general, younger people have a higher percentage of body fluid than do older people, and men have proportionately more body fluid than do women. People who are obese have less fluid than those who are thin, because fat cells contain little water.

Body fluid is located in two fluid compartments: the intracellular space (ICS, fluid in the cells) and the extracellular space (ECS, fluid outside the cells). Approximately two-thirds of body fluid is intracellular fluid (ICF) and is located primarily in the skeletal muscle mass. Approximately one third is in the extracellular fluid (ECF).

The ECF compartment is further divided into the intravascular, interstitial, and transcellular fluid spaces. The intravascular space (IVS; the fluid within the blood vessels) contains plasma. Plasma is water, along with molecules, electrolytes, and proteins, minus blood cells and platelets. Approximately 3.5 L of the average 6 L of blood volume is made up of plasma, which has a straw-colored appearance. The remaining 2.5 L is made up of erythrocytes (red blood cells [RBC]), leukocytes (white blood cells [WBC]), and thrombocytes (platelets). The interstitial space contains the fluid between the cells, tissues, organs, blood vessels, and totals about 10 L in an adult. Lymph fluid is an interstitial fluid. The transcellular space is the smallest division of the ECF compartment and contains approximately 1 L. Examples of transcellular fluids are cerebrospinal, pericardial, synovial, intraocular, and pleural fluids; sweat; and digestive secretions. Figure 4-1 demonstrates the composition of body compartments.

8. Compare respiratory acidosis and alkalosis with regard to causes, clinical manifestations, diagnosis, and management.

9. Interpret arterial blood gas measurements.

10. Describe measures used for preventing complications of IV therapy.

Body fluid normally shifts between the two major compartments or spaces (ICS and ECS) in an effort to transport gases, nutrients, and wastes while maintaining overall bodily function. Loss of fluid from the body can disrupt this equilibrium. Sometimes fluid is not lost from the body but is unavailable for use by either the ICF or ECF. Loss of ECF into a space that does not contribute to equilibrium between the ICF and the ECF is referred to as an *interstitial fluid shift*, or *third-spacing*.

⚡ NURSING ALERT
Early evidence of third-space fluid shifting is a decrease in urine output despite adequate fluid intake. Urine output decreases because fluid shifts out of the intravascular space; the kidneys then receive less blood and attempt to compensate by decreasing urine output. Other signs and symptoms of third spacing that indicate an intravascular fluid volume deficit (FVD) include increased heart rate, decreased blood pressure, decreased central venous pressure, edema, increased body weight, and imbalances in fluid intake and output (I&O). Third-space shifts occur in ascites, burns, peritonitis, bowel obstruction, and massive bleeding into a joint or body cavity.

Electrolytes in body fluids are active chemicals (cations that carry positive charges and anions that carry negative charges). The major cations in body fluid are sodium, potassium (K^+), calcium, magnesium, and hydrogen ions. The major anions are chloride, bicarbonate, phosphate, sulfate, and proteinate ions.

These chemicals unite in varying combinations. Therefore, electrolyte concentration in the body is expressed in terms of milliequivalents (mEq) per liter, a measure of chemical activity, rather than in terms of milligrams (mg), a unit of weight. More specifically, a milliequivalent is defined as being equivalent to the electrochemical activity of 1 mg of hydrogen. In a solution, cations and anions are equal in milliequivalents per liter.

Although all body fluid contains equal amounts of cations and anions, the electrolyte concentrations in the ICF are markedly different from those in the ECF, as reflected in Table 4-1. Sodium ions, which are positively charged, far outnumber the other cations in the ECF. Because sodium

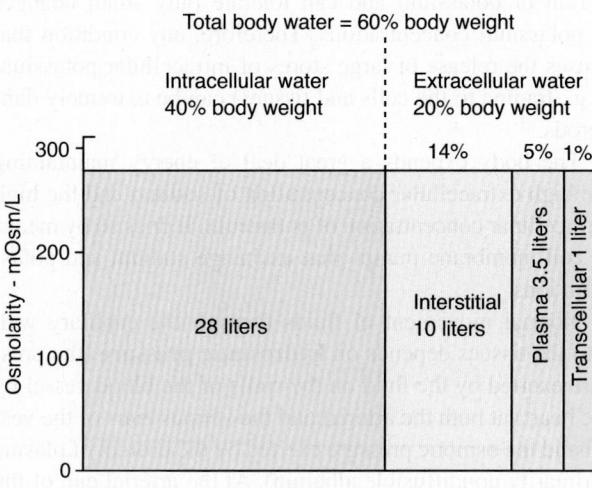

FIGURE 4-1 Approximate size of body compartments in a 70 kg man. From Porth, C.M., & Matfin, G. (2009). Pathophysiology: Concepts of altered health status (8th ed.). Philadelphia: Lippincott Williams & Wilkins.

TABLE
4-1 Approximate Major Electrolyte Content in Body Fluid

Electrolytes	mEq/L
Extracellular Fluid (Plasma)	
Cations	
Sodium (Na)	142
Potassium (K)	5
Calcium (Ca^{++})	5
Magnesium (Mg^{++})	2
Total cations	154
Anions	
Chloride (Cl$^-$)	103
Bicarbonate (HCO$_3^-$)	26
Phosphate (HPO$_4^-$)	2
Sulfate (SO$_4^-$)	1
Organic acids	5
Proteinate	17
Total anions	154
Intracellular Fluid	
Cations	
Potassium (K$^+$)	150
Magnesium (Mg^{++})	40
Sodium (Na$^+$)	10
Total cations	200
Anions	
Phosphates and sulfates	150
Bicarbonate (HCO$_3^-$)	10
Proteinate	40
Total anions	200

concentration affects the overall concentration of the ECF, sodium is important in regulating the volume of body fluid. Approximately 90% of the serum osmolality (discussed later) is determined by the serum sodium level. Retention of sodium is associated with fluid retention, and conversely excessive loss of sodium is usually associated with decreased volume of body fluid.

As shown in Table 4-1, the major electrolytes in the ICF are potassium and phosphate. The ECF has a low concentration of potassium and can tolerate only small changes in potassium concentrations. Therefore, any condition that causes the release of large stores of intracellular potassium (e.g., trauma to the cells and tissues) can be extremely dangerous.

The body expends a great deal of energy maintaining the high extracellular concentration of sodium and the high intracellular concentration of potassium. It does so by means of cell membrane pumps that exchange sodium and potassium ions.

Normal movement of fluids through the capillary wall into the tissues depends on **hydrostatic pressure** (the pressure exerted by the fluid on the walls of the blood vessel by the heart) at both the arterial and the venous ends of the vessel and the osmotic pressure exerted by the protein of plasma (primarily nondiffusible albumin). At the arterial end of the capillary, fluids are filtered through its wall by a hydrostatic

pressure that exceeds the oncotic pressure exerted by plasma protein; thus, water and electrolytes leave the bloodstream to feed the interstitial and intracellular spaces. At the venous end of the capillaries, the oncotic pressure (exerted primarily by albumin) is greater than hydrostatic pressure in the venous end of the capillary, thus fluids reenter the capillary. The direction of fluid movement depends on the differences in these two opposing forces (hydrostatic vs. osmotic pressure). Any fluid left in the interstitial space can be returned to the bloodstream via the lymphatics.

In addition to electrolytes, the ECF transports other substances, such as enzymes and hormones. It also carries blood components, such as RBCs, WBCs, and platelets, throughout the body.

REGULATION OF BODY FLUID COMPARTMENTS

Osmosis and Osmolality

When two different solutions are separated by a membrane that is impermeable to the dissolved substances, fluid shifts through the membrane from the region of low solute concentration to the region of high solute concentration until the solutions are of equal concentration. The movement of water caused by a concentration gradient is known as **osmosis** (Fig. 4-2A). The magnitude of this force depends on the number of particles dissolved in the solutions, not on their weights. The number of dissolved particles contained in a unit of fluid determines the osmolality of a solution, which influences the movement of fluid between the fluid compartments. **Tonicity** is the ability of all the solutes to cause an osmotic driving force that promotes water movement from one compartment to another (Porth, 2011). IV solutions are termed isotonic, hypotonic, or hypertonic. If a solution is isotonic (e.g., 0.9% sodium chloride), it has the same effective osmolality as body fluids (close to 285 milliosmolal [mOsm]). Sodium, mannitol, glucose, and sorbitol are all effective osmoles (capable of affecting water movement; see later discussion of IV solutions).

> **NURSING ALERT**
> It is important to understand osmotic diuresis, which is an increase in urine output caused by the excretion of substances such as glucose, mannitol, or contrast agents in the urine, which exert an osmotic pull on water. For example, because glucose is an osmotic agent (capable of affecting water movement), when glucose is present or "spilled" in the urine, it will bring water with it, causing polyuria and FVD.

Diffusion

Diffusion is the natural tendency of a substance to move from an area of higher concentration to one of lower concentration

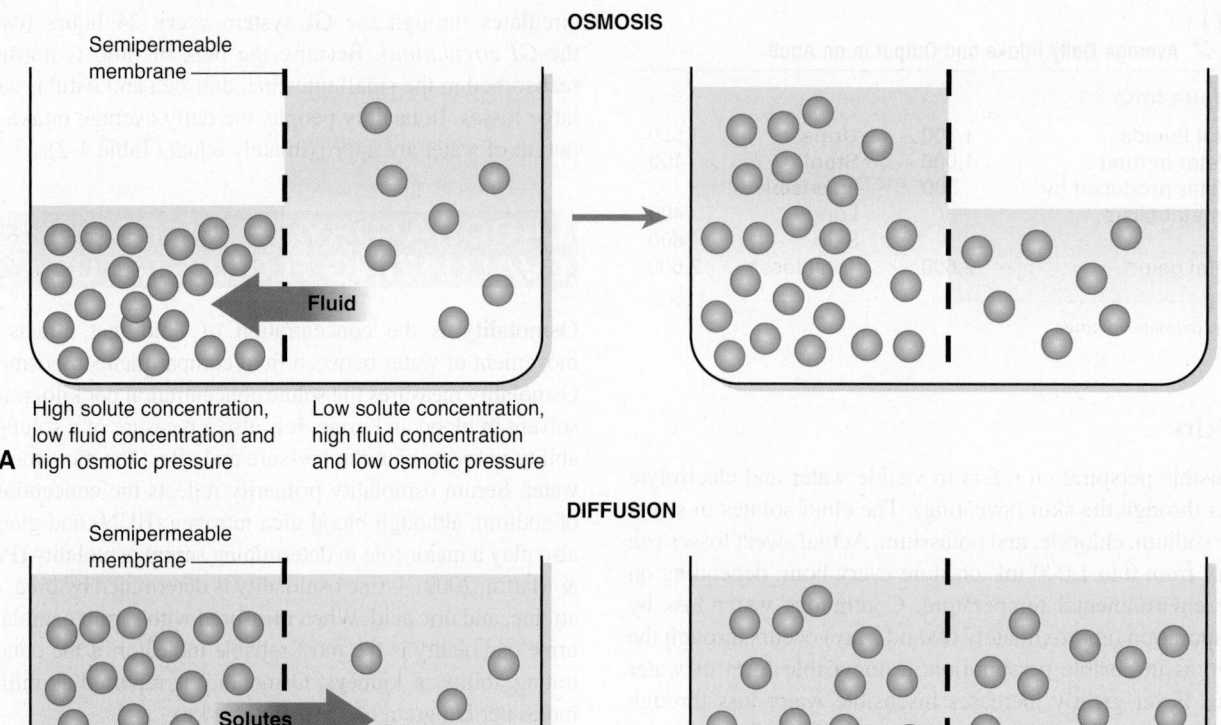

FIGURE 4-2 **(A)** Osmosis: Movement of fluid from an area of lower solute concentration to an area of higher solute concentration with eventual equalization of the solute concentrations. **(B)** Diffusion: Movement of solutes from an area of greater concentration to an area of lesser concentration, leading ultimately to equalization of the solute concentrations.

(see Fig. 4-2B). Examples of diffusion are the exchange of oxygen and carbon dioxide between the pulmonary capillaries and alveoli.

Filtration

Hydrostatic pressure in the capillaries tends to filter fluid out of the intravascular compartment into the interstitial fluid. Movement of water and solutes occurs from an area of high hydrostatic pressure to an area of low hydrostatic pressure. Filtration allows the kidneys to filter 180 L of plasma per day.

Sodium–Potassium Pump

As previously stated, the sodium concentration is greater in the ECF than in the ICF, and because of this, sodium tends to enter the cell by diffusion. This tendency is offset by the sodium–potassium pump, which is located in the cell membrane and actively moves sodium from the cell into the ECF. Conversely, the high intracellular potassium concentration is

maintained by pumping potassium into the cell. By definition, **active transport** implies that energy must be expended for the movement to occur against a concentration gradient.

ROUTES OF GAINS AND LOSSES

Water and electrolytes are gained in various ways. A healthy person gains fluids by drinking and eating. Fluids may be provided by the parenteral route (IV or subcutaneously) or by means of an enteral feeding tube in the stomach or intestine.

Kidneys

The usual daily urine volume in the adult is 1.5 L. A general rule is that the output is approximately .5 to 1 mL of urine per kilogram of body weight per hour (.5 to 1 mL/kg/h) in all age groups.

TABLE
4-2 Average Daily Intake and Output in an Adult

Intake (mL)			
Oral liquids	1,300	Urine	1,500
Water in food	1,000	Stool	100
Water produced by	300	Insensible	
metabolism		Lungs	400
		Skin	600
Total gain*	2,600	Total loss*	2,600

*Approximate volumes.

Skin

Sensible perspiration refers to visible water and electrolyte loss through the skin (sweating). The chief solutes in sweat are sodium, chloride, and potassium. Actual sweat losses can vary from 0 to 1,000 mL or more every hour, depending on the environmental temperature. Continuous water loss by evaporation (approximately 600 mL/day) occurs through the skin as insensible perspiration, a nonvisible form of water loss. Fever greatly increases insensible water loss through the lungs and the skin, as does loss of the natural skin barrier (e.g., through major burns).

Lungs

The lungs normally eliminate water vapor (insensible loss) at a rate of approximately 400 mL every day. The loss is much greater with increased respiratory rate or depth, or in a dry climate.

Gastrointestinal Tract

The usual loss through the gastrointestinal (GI) tract is only 100 mL daily, even though approximately 8 L of fluid circulates through the GI system every 24 hours (called the *GI circulation*). Because the bulk of fluid is normally reabsorbed in the small intestine, diarrhea and fistulas cause large losses. In healthy people, the daily average intake and output of water are approximately equal (Table 4-2).

LABORATORY TESTS FOR EVALUATING FLUID STATUS

Osmolality is the concentration of fluid that affects the movement of water between fluid compartments by osmosis. Osmolality measures the solute concentration per kilogram of solvent in blood and urine. It is also a measure of a solution's ability to create osmotic pressure and affect the movement of water. Serum osmolality primarily reflects the concentration of sodium, although blood urea nitrogen (BUN) and glucose also play a major role in determining serum osmolality (Porth & Matfin, 2009). Urine osmolality is determined by urea, creatinine, and uric acid. When measured with serum osmolality, urine osmolality is the most reliable indicator of the concentrating ability of kidneys. Osmolality is reported as milliosmoles per kilogram of water (mOsm/kg).

Osmolarity, another term that describes the concentration of solutions, is measured in milliosmoles per liter (mOsm/L). The term *osmolality* is used more often in clinical practice. Normal serum osmolality is 275 to 300 mOsm/kg, and normal urine osmolality is 250 to 900 mOsm/kg.

Factors that increase and decrease serum and urine osmolality are identified in Table 4-3. Serum osmolality may be measured directly through laboratory tests or estimated at the bedside by doubling the serum sodium level or by using the following formula:

Plasma osmolality (mOsm/kg) = 2 [serum sodium]
+ Glucose/18 + BUN/2.8

TABLE
4-3 Factors Affecting Serum and Urine Osmolality

Fluid	Factors Increasing Osmolality	Factors Decreasing Osmolality
Serum (275–300 mOsm/kg water)	• Severe dehydration • Free water loss • Diabetes insipidus • Hypernatremia • Hyperglycemia • Stroke or head injury • Renal tubular necrosis • Consumption of methanol or ethylene glycol (antifreeze)	• Fluid volume excess • Syndrome of inappropriate antidiuretic hormone (SIADH) • Renal failure • Diuretic use • Adrenal insufficiency • Hyponatremia • Overhydration • Paraneoplastic syndrome associated with lung cancer
Urine (250–900 mOsm/kg water)	• Fluid volume deficit • SIADH • Congestive heart failure • Acidosis	• Fluid volume excess • Diabetes insipidus • Hyponatremia • Aldosteronism • Pyelonephritis

The calculated value usually is within 10 mOsm of the measured osmolality.

Urine specific gravity measures the kidneys' ability to excrete or conserve water. The specific gravity of urine is compared to the weight of distilled water, which has a specific gravity of 1.000. The normal range of urine specific gravity is 1.010 to 1.025. Urine specific gravity can be measured at the bedside by placing a calibrated hydrometer or urinometer in a cylinder of approximately 20 mL of urine. Specific gravity can also be assessed with a refractometer or dipstick with a reagent for this purpose. Specific gravity varies inversely with urine volume; normally, the larger the volume of urine, the lower the specific gravity. Specific gravity is a less reliable indicator of concentration than urine osmolality; increased glucose or protein in urine can cause a falsely elevated specific gravity. Factors that increase or decrease urine osmolality are the same as those for urine specific gravity.

BUN is made up of urea, which is an end product of the metabolism of protein (from both muscle and dietary intake) by the liver. The normal BUN is 10 to 20 mg/dL (3.6 to 7.2 µmol/L). The BUN level varies with urine output. Factors that increase BUN include decreased renal function, GI bleeding, dehydration, increased protein intake, fever, and sepsis. Those that decrease BUN include end-stage liver disease, a low-protein diet, starvation, and any condition that results in expanded fluid volume (e.g., pregnancy).

Creatinine is the end product of muscle metabolism. It is a better indicator of renal function than BUN because it does not vary with protein intake and metabolic state. The normal serum creatinine is approximately 0.7 to 1.4 mg/dL (62 to 124 µmol/L); however, its concentration depends on lean body mass and varies from person to person. Serum creatinine levels increase when renal function decreases.

Hematocrit measures the volume percentage of RBC (erythrocytes) in whole blood and normally ranges from 42% to 52% for males and 35% to 47% for females. Conditions that increase the hematocrit value are dehydration and polycythemia, and those that decrease hematocrit are over-hydration and anemia.

Urine sodium values change with sodium intake and the status of fluid volume: as sodium intake increases, excretion increases; as the circulating fluid volume decreases, sodium is conserved. Normal urine sodium levels range from 75 to 200 mEq/24 h (75 to 200 mmol/24 h). A random specimen usually contains more than 40 mEq/L of sodium. Urine sodium levels are used to assess volume status and are useful in the diagnosis of hyponatremia and acute renal failure.

HOMEOSTATIC MECHANISMS

The body is equipped with remarkable homeostatic mechanisms to keep the composition and volume of body fluid within narrow limits of normal. Organs involved in homeo-stasis include the kidneys, lungs, heart, adrenal glands, parathyroid glands, and pituitary gland.

Kidney Functions

Vital to the regulation of fluid and electrolyte balance, the kidneys normally filter 170 L of plasma every day in the adult, while excreting only 1.5 L of urine. They act both autonomously and in response to bloodborne messengers, such as aldosterone and antidiuretic hormone (ADH) (Porth & Matfin, 2009). Major functions of the kidneys in maintaining normal fluid balance include the following:

- Regulation of ECF volume and osmolality by selective retention and excretion of body fluids
- Regulation of electrolyte levels in the ECF by selective retention of needed substances and excretion of unneeded substances
- Regulation of pH of the ECF by retention of hydrogen ions and/or bicarbonate (HCO_3)
- Excretion of metabolic wastes and toxic substances

Given these functions, it is readily apparent that renal failure results in multiple fluid and electrolyte abnormalities. Renal function declines with advanced age, as do muscle mass and daily exogenous creatinine production. Therefore, high-normal and minimally elevated serum creatinine values may indicate substantially reduced renal function in the elderly.

Heart and Blood Vessel Functions

The pumping action of the heart circulates blood through the kidneys under sufficient pressure to allow for urine formation. Failure of this pumping action interferes with renal perfusion and thus with water and electrolyte regulation.

Lung Functions

The lungs are also vital in maintaining homeostasis. Through exhalation, the lungs remove approximately 400 mL of water daily in the normal adult. Abnormal conditions, such as hyperpnea (abnormally deep respiration) or continuous coughing, increase this loss; mechanical ventilation with excessive moisture decreases it. The lungs also play a major role in maintaining acid–base balance. Normal aging results in decreased respiratory function, causing increased difficulty in pH regulation in older adults with major illness or trauma.

Pituitary Functions

The hypothalamus manufactures ADH, which is stored in the posterior pituitary gland and released as needed. ADH is sometimes called the *water-conserving hormone* because it causes the body to retain water. Functions of ADH include maintaining the osmotic pressure of the cells by controlling the retention or excretion of water by the kidneys and by regulating blood volume (Fig. 4-3).

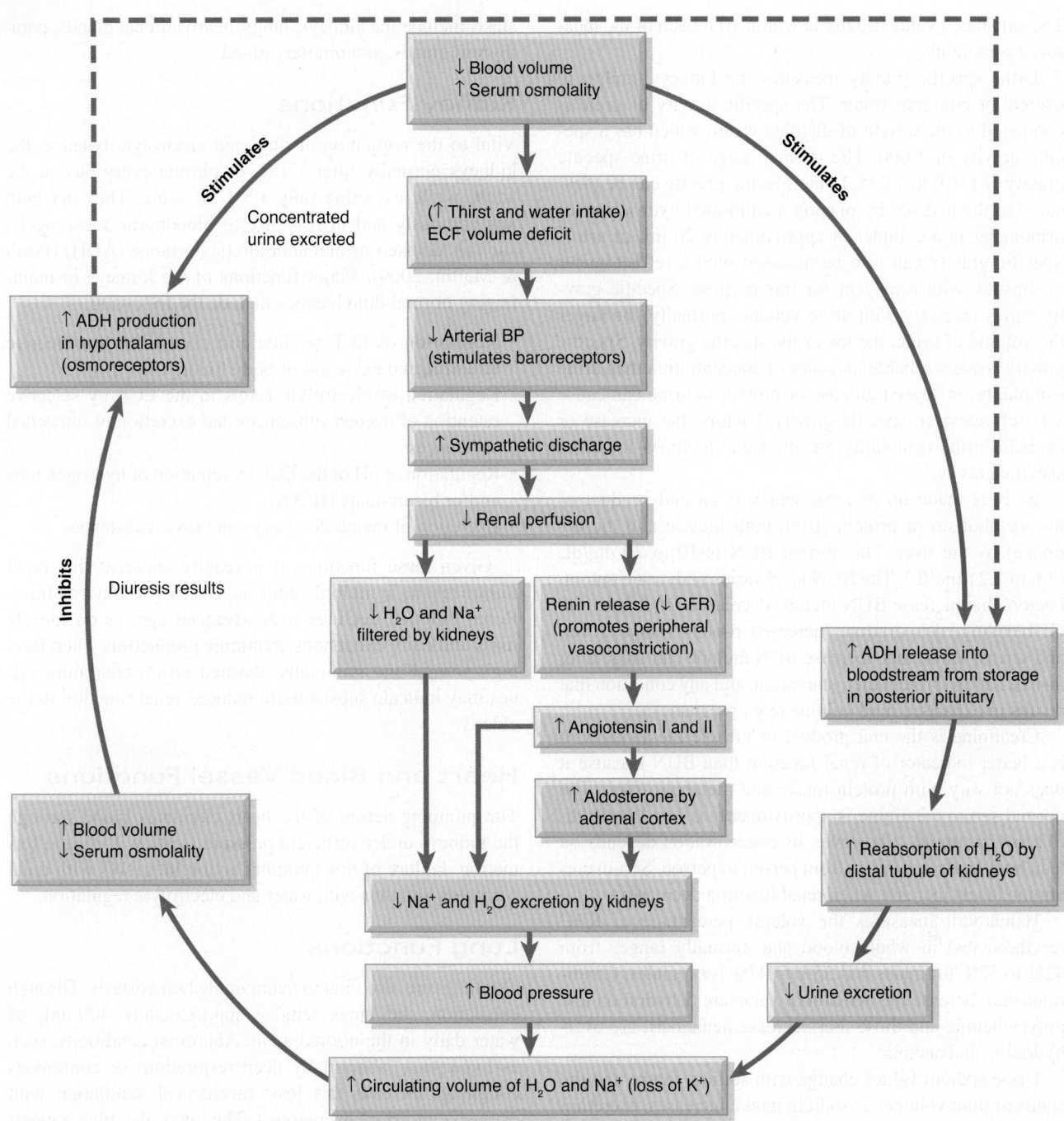

FIGURE 4-3 Fluid regulation cycle.

Adrenal Functions

Aldosterone, a mineralocorticoid secreted by the zona glomerulosa (outer zone) of the adrenal cortex, has a profound effect on fluid balance. Increased secretion of aldosterone causes sodium retention (and thus water retention) and potassium loss. Conversely, decreased secretion of aldosterone causes sodium and water loss and potassium retention.

Cortisol, another adrenocortical hormone, has only a fraction of the mineralocorticoid potency of aldosterone.

However, when secreted in large quantities (or administered as corticosteroid therapy), it can also produce sodium and fluid retention.

Parathyroid Functions

The parathyroid glands, embedded in the thyroid gland, regulate calcium and phosphate balance by means of parathyroid hormone (PTH). PTH influences bone resorption (movement of calcium out of bone to the blood), calcium

absorption from the intestines, and calcium reabsorption from the renal tubules.

Other Mechanisms

Changes in the volume of the interstitial compartment within the ECF can occur without affecting body function. However, the vascular compartment cannot tolerate change as readily and must be carefully maintained to ensure that tissues receive adequate nutrients.

Baroreceptors

The baroreceptors are small nerve receptors that detect changes in pressure within blood vessels and transmit this information to the central nervous system (CNS). They are responsible for monitoring the circulating volume, and they regulate sympathetic and parasympathetic neural activity as well as endocrine activities. They are categorized as either low-pressure or high-pressure baroreceptors. Low-pressure baroreceptors are in the cardiac atria, particularly the left atrium. High-pressure baroreceptors are nerve endings in the aortic arch and the carotid sinus, as well as in the afferent arteriole of the juxtaglomerular apparatus of the nephron.

As arterial pressure decreases, baroreceptors transmit fewer impulses from the carotid sinuses and the aortic arch to the vasomotor center. A decrease in impulses stimulates the sympathetic nervous system and inhibits the parasympathetic nervous system. The outcome is an increase in cardiac rate, conduction, and contractility, and an increase in circulating blood volume. Sympathetic stimulation constricts renal arterioles; this increases the release of aldosterone, decreases glomerular filtration, and increases sodium and water reabsorption and potassium loss (discussed below). Conversely, if high-pressure baroreceptors are stimulated, the outcome is a lowered heart rate and lowered blood vessel resistance.

Renin–Angiotensin–Aldosterone System

Renin is an enzyme that converts angiotensinogen, an inactive substance formed by the liver, into angiotensin I (Porth & Matfin, 2009). Renin is released by the juxtaglomerular cells of the kidneys in response to decreased renal perfusion. Angiotensin-converting enzyme (ACE) converts angiotensin I (AI) to angiotensin II (AII). AII, with its vasoconstrictor properties, increases arterial perfusion pressure and also stimulates thirst. When the sympathetic nervous system is stimulated, aldosterone is released in response to an increased release of renin. Aldosterone is a volume regulator and is also released as serum potassium increases, serum sodium decreases, or adrenocorticotropic hormone (ACTH) increases. The net effect of aldosterone is to increase the reabsorption of sodium, which increases water reabsorption thus increasing plasma volume.

Antidiuretic Hormone and Thirst

ADH and the thirst mechanism play important roles in maintaining sodium concentration and oral intake of fluids. Oral intake is controlled by the thirst center, located in the hypothalamus (Porth & Matfin, 2009). As serum concentration or osmolality increases or blood volume decreases, neurons in the hypothalamus are stimulated by intracellular dehydration; thirst then occurs, and the person increases his or her intake of oral fluids. An increase in osmolality of only 1% to 2% is sufficient to stimulate thirst. Water excretion is controlled by ADH, aldosterone, and baroreceptors, as mentioned previously. The presence or absence of ADH is the most significant factor in determining whether the urine that is excreted is concentrated or dilute.

Osmoreceptors

Located on the surface of the hypothalamus, osmoreceptors sense changes in sodium concentration. As the serum osmolality increases, the neurons become dehydrated and quickly generate action potentials resulting in increased release of ADH from the posterior pituitary. The ADH then travels in the blood to the kidneys, where it alters permeability to water, causing increased reabsorption of water and decreased urine output. The retained water dilutes the ECF and returns its concentration to normal. Restoration of normal serum osmolality provides feedback to the osmoreceptors to inhibit further ADH release (see Fig. 4-3).

Release of Atrial Natriuretic Peptide

Atrial natriuretic peptide (ANP), also called *atrial natriuretic factor*, is synthesized, stored, and released by muscle cells of the atria of the heart in response to several factors. These factors include increased atrial pressure, angiotensin II stimulation, endothelin (a powerful vasoconstrictor of vascular smooth muscle peptide released from damaged endothelial cells in the kidneys or other tissues), and sympathetic stimulation (Porth & Matfin, 2009). In addition, any condition that results in volume expansion (e.g., pregnancy), hypoxia, or increased cardiac filling pressures (e.g., high sodium intake, heart failure, chronic renal failure, atrial tachycardia, or use of vasoconstrictor agents such as epinephrine) increases the release of ANP. The action of ANP is the direct opposite of the renin–angiotensin–aldosterone system; ANP decreases blood pressure and volume (Fig. 4-4). The ANP measured in plasma is normally 20 to 77 pg/mL (20 to 77 ng/L). This level increases in paroxysmal atrial tachycardia, hyperthyroidism, subarachnoid hemorrhage, and small cell lung cancer. In congestive heart failure and cirrhosis with ascites, ANP is elevated but not sufficiently to prevent fluid volume excess. Brain natriuretic peptide (BNP) that is stored primarily in ventricular myocardium and released when ventricular diastolic pressure rises, has actions similar to ANP. Normal BNP levels are less than 100 pg/mL. In edematous states, there is abnormal resistance to the action of ANP and BNP (Braunwald & Loscalzo, 2008).

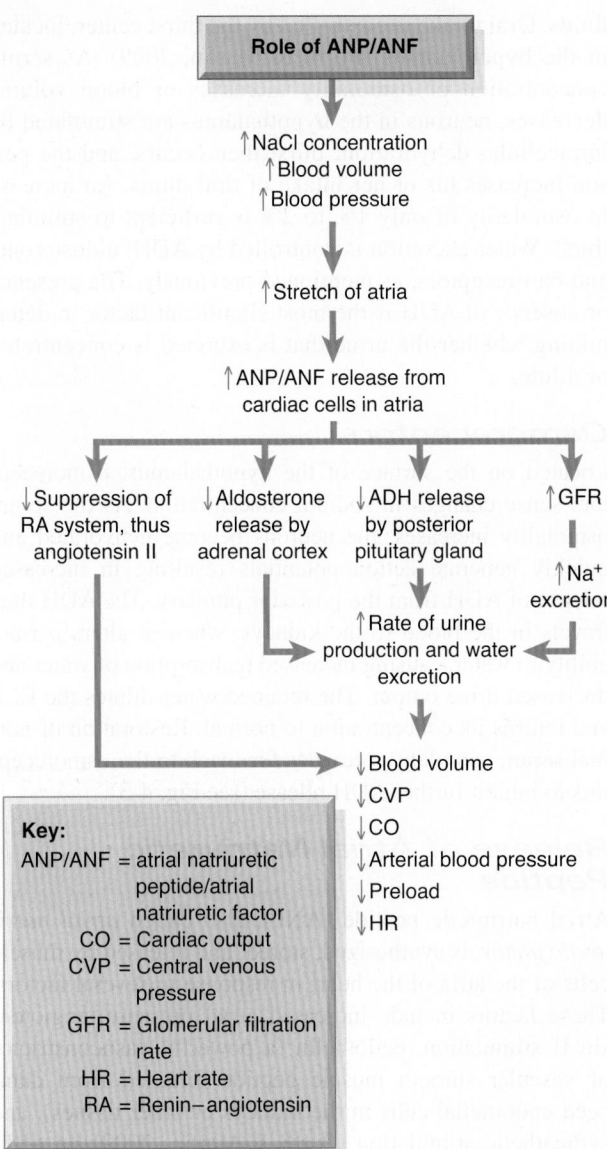

Role of ANP/ANF

↑NaCl concentration
↑Blood volume
↑Blood pressure

↓

↑Stretch of atria

↓

↑ANP/ANF release from cardiac cells in atria

↓Suppression of RA system, thus angiotensin II

↓Aldosterone release by adrenal cortex

↓ADH release by posterior pituitary gland

↑GFR

↑Na⁺ excretion

↑Rate of urine production and water excretion

↓Blood volume
↓CVP
↓CO
↓Arterial blood pressure
↓Preload
↓HR

Key:
ANP/ANF = atrial natriuretic peptide/atrial natriuretic factor
CO = Cardiac output
CVP = Central venous pressure
GFR = Glomerular filtration rate
HR = Heart rate
RA = Renin–angiotensin

FIGURE 4-4 Role of atrial natriuretic peptide (ANP) in maintenance of fluid balance.

Gerontologic Considerations

Normal physiologic changes of aging, including reduced cardiac, renal, and respiratory function and reserve, and alterations in the ratio of body fluids to muscle mass, may alter the responses of elderly people to fluid and electrolyte changes and acid–base disturbances. In addition, the frequent use of medications in the older adult can affect renal and cardiac function and fluid balance, thereby increasing the likelihood of fluid and electrolyte disturbances. Routine procedures, such as the vigorous administration of laxatives before colon X-ray studies, may produce a serious FVD, necessitating the use of IV fluids to prevent hypotension and other effects of hypovolemia.

Alterations in fluid and electrolyte balance that may produce minor changes in young and middle-aged adults have the potential to produce profound changes in older adults, accompanied by a rapid onset of signs and symptoms. In elderly patients, the clinical manifestations of fluid and electrolyte disturbances may be subtle or atypical. For example, fluid deficit may cause confusion or cognitive impairment in the elderly person, whereas in the young or middle-aged person the first sign commonly is increased thirst. Rapid infusion of an excessive volume of IV fluids may produce fluid overload and cardiac failure in the elderly patient. These reactions are likely to occur more quickly and with the administration of smaller volumes of fluid than in healthy young and middle-aged adults because of the decreased cardiac reserve and reduced renal function that accompany aging. Dehydration in the elderly is common as a result of decreased reserve capacity of the kidney from the aging process, disease, and use of medications.

Increased sensitivity to fluid and electrolyte changes in elderly patients requires careful assessment, with attention to intake and output of fluids from all sources and to changes in daily weight; careful monitoring of side effects and interactions of medications; and prompt reporting and management of disturbances.

FLUID VOLUME DISTURBANCES

Appendix A summarizes the major fluid and electrolyte imbalances that are described in this chapter.

HYPOVOLEMIA

FVD, or hypovolemia, occurs when loss of ECF volume exceeds the intake of fluid. It occurs when water and electrolytes are lost in the same proportion as they exist in normal body fluids, so that the ratio of serum electrolytes to water remains the same. FVD should not be confused with the term *dehydration*, which refers to loss of water alone, with increased serum sodium levels. FVD may occur alone or in combination with other imbalances. Unless other imbalances are present concurrently, serum electrolyte concentrations remain essentially unchanged.

Pathophysiology

FVD results from loss of body fluids and occurs more rapidly when coupled with decreased fluid intake. FVD can develop from inadequate intake alone if the decreased intake is prolonged. Causes of FVD include abnormal fluid losses, such as those resulting from vomiting, diarrhea, GI suctioning, and sweating, and decreased intake, as in nausea or inability to gain access to fluids.

Additional risk factors include diabetes insipidus, adrenal insufficiency, osmotic diuresis, hemorrhage, and coma. Third-space fluid shifts, or the movement of fluid from the

vascular system to other body spaces (e.g., with edema formation in burns, ascites with liver dysfunction), also cause FVD.

Clinical Manifestations and Assessment

FVD can develop rapidly and can be mild, moderate, or severe, depending on the degree of fluid loss. Important signs include acute weight loss; decreased skin turgor; oliguria (urinary output <400 mL/Day); concentrated urine with a high specific gravity; postural hypotension (a 15 mm Hg decrease in systolic pressure or a 10 mm Hg decrease in diastolic pressure with position change); a weak, rapid heart rate; flattened neck veins; decreased central venous pressure; cool, clammy skin related to peripheral vasoconstriction; a smaller tongue with additional longitudinal furrows; dry oral mucous membranes; delayed capillary refill; altered sensorium; and thirst. Diagnostic testing includes BUN and its relation to serum creatinine concentration. A volume-depleted patient has a BUN elevated out of proportion to the serum creatinine (ratio >20:1). The BUN can also be elevated because of decreased renal perfusion and function. The cause of abnormal laboratory findings may be determined through the health history and physical findings.

The hematocrit level is greater than normal in dehydration because the RBC become suspended in a decreased plasma volume, which is also known as *hemoconcentration.*

Serum electrolyte changes may also exist. Potassium and sodium levels can be reduced (hypokalemia, hyponatremia) or elevated (hyperkalemia, hypernatremia):

- Hypokalemia occurs with GI and renal losses.
- Hyperkalemia occurs with adrenal insufficiency.
- Hyponatremia occurs with increased thirst and ADH release.
- Hypernatremia results from increased insensible losses and diabetes insipidus.

Urine specific gravity is increased in relation to the kidneys' attempt to conserve water and decreased with diabetes insipidus. Urine osmolality is greater than 450 mOsm/kg because the kidneys try to compensate by conserving water.

Medical Management

When planning the correction of fluid loss for the patient with FVD, the health care provider considers the usual maintenance requirements of the patient and other factors (e.g., fever) that can influence fluid needs. If the deficit is not severe, the oral route is preferred, provided the patient can drink. However, if fluid losses are acute or severe, the IV route is required. Isotonic electrolyte solutions (e.g., lactated Ringer's solution, 0.9% sodium chloride) are frequently used to treat the hypotensive patient with FVD because they expand plasma volume. ICS is essentially sodium free, thus

for every liter of 0.9% sodium chloride administered, 1,000 mL will remain in the ECS, of which approximately 250 mL will remain in the IVS, re-expanding the plasma volume. Because this solution can expand the IVS, patients must be assessed for signs and symptoms of fluid volume excess (discussed shortly). As soon as the patient becomes normotensive (normalization of their blood pressure), a hypotonic electrolyte solution (e.g., 0.45% sodium chloride) is often used to provide both electrolytes and water for renal excretion of metabolic wastes. These and additional fluids are discussed later in the chapter.

Accurate and frequent assessments of I&O, weight, vital signs, central venous pressure, level of consciousness, breath sounds, and skin color should be performed to determine when therapy should be slowed to avoid volume overload. The rate of fluid administration is based on the severity of loss and the patient's hemodynamic response to volume replacement.

If the patient with severe FVD is not excreting enough urine and is therefore oliguric, the health care provider needs to determine whether the depressed renal function is caused by reduced renal blood flow secondary to FVD (prerenal azotemia or increased nitrogen levels in the blood) or, more seriously, by acute tubular necrosis from prolonged FVD. The test used in this situation is referred to as a *fluid challenge test.* During a fluid challenge test, volumes of fluid are administered at specific rates and intervals while the patient's hemodynamic response to this treatment is monitored (i.e., vital signs, breath sounds, sensorium, central venous pressure, pulmonary capillary wedge pressure values, and urine output).

An example of a typical fluid challenge involves administering 100 to 200 mL of normal saline solution over 15 minutes. The goal is to provide fluids rapidly enough to attain adequate tissue perfusion without compromising the cardiovascular system. The response by a patient with FVD but normal renal function is increased urine output and an increase in blood pressure and central venous pressure.

Shock can occur when the volume of fluid lost exceeds 25% of the intravascular volume, or when fluid loss is rapid. Shock and its causes and treatment are discussed in detail in Chapters 20 and 54.

Nursing Management

Assessing Fluid Status

To assess for FVD, the nurse monitors and measures fluid I&O at least every 8 hours, and sometimes hourly. As FVD develops, body fluid losses exceed fluid intake. This loss may be in the form of excessive urination (polyuria), diarrhea, vomiting, and so on. Later, after FVD fully develops, the kidneys attempt to conserve needed body fluids, leading to a urine output of less than 30 mL/h in an adult. Urine in this instance is concentrated and represents a healthy renal response. Daily body weights are monitored; an acute

loss of 0.5 kg (1 lb) represents a fluid loss of approximately 500 mL. (One liter of fluid weighs approximately 1 kg, or 2.2 lb.)

Vital signs are closely monitored. The nurse observes for a weak, rapid pulse and postural hypotension (i.e., a decrease in systolic pressure exceeding 15 mm Hg when the patient moves from a lying to a sitting position).

Skin and tongue turgor is monitored on a regular basis. In a healthy person, pinched skin immediately returns to its normal position when released. This elastic property, referred to as *turgor,* is partially dependent on interstitial fluid volume. In a person with FVD, the skin flattens more slowly after the pinch is released. In a person with severe FVD, the skin may remain elevated for many seconds. Skin turgor is best measured by pinching the skin over the sternum, inner aspects of the thighs, or forehead.

> ! **NURSING ALERT**
> Skin turgor is a less valid assessment in the elderly patient because the skin has lost some of its elasticity due to the decreased number of papillae and collagen fibers; therefore, other assessment measures (e.g., slowness in filling of veins of the hands and feet) become more useful in detecting FVD. In elderly patients, skin turgor is best tested over the forehead or the sternum, because alterations in skin elasticity are less marked in these areas.

Tongue turgor is not affected by age. In a normal person, the tongue has one longitudinal furrow. In the person with FVD, there are additional longitudinal furrows, and the tongue is smaller because of fluid loss. The degree of oral mucous membrane moisture is also assessed; a dry mouth may indicate either FVD or mouth breathing.

Urine concentration is monitored by measuring the urine specific gravity. In a volume-depleted patient, the urine specific gravity should be greater than 1.020, indicating healthy renal conservation of fluid.

Mental function is eventually affected in severe FVD as a result of decreasing cerebral perfusion. Decreased peripheral perfusion can result in cold extremities. In patients with relatively normal cardiopulmonary function, a low central venous pressure is indicative of hypovolemia. Patients with acute cardiopulmonary decompensation require more extensive hemodynamic monitoring of pressures in both sides of the heart to determine if hypovolemia exists.

Preventing Fluid Volume Deficit

To prevent FVD, the nurse identifies patients at risk and takes measures to minimize fluid losses. For example, if the patient has diarrhea, diarrhea control measures should be implemented and replacement fluids administered. These measures may include administering antidiarrheal medications and small volumes of oral fluids at frequent intervals.

Correcting Fluid Volume Deficit

When administering oral fluids, consideration is given to the patient's likes and dislikes. The type of fluid the patient has lost is also considered, and attempts are made to select fluids most likely to replace the lost electrolytes. If the patient is reluctant to drink because of oral discomfort, the nurse assists with frequent mouth care and provides nonirritating fluids. If nausea is present, antiemetics may be ordered and administered before oral fluid replacement is initiated.

If the patient cannot eat and drink, fluid may need to be administered by an alternative route (enteral or parenteral) until adequate circulating blood volume and renal perfusion are achieved. Isotonic fluids are prescribed to increase ECF volume.

> ! **NURSING ALERT**
> When fluid balance is critical, all routes of gain and all routes of loss must be recorded and all volumes compared. Organs of fluid loss include the kidneys, skin, lungs, and GI tract.

HYPERVOLEMIA

Fluid volume excess (FVE), or hypervolemia, refers to an isotonic expansion of the ECF caused by the abnormal retention of water and sodium in approximately the same proportions in which they normally exist in the ECF. It is always secondary to an increase in the total body sodium content, which, in turn, leads to an increase in total body water. Because there is isotonic retention of body substances, the serum sodium concentration remains essentially normal.

Pathophysiology

FVE may be related to simple fluid overload or diminished function of the homeostatic mechanisms responsible for regulating fluid balance. Contributing factors can include heart failure, renal failure, and cirrhosis of the liver. Another contributing factor is consumption of excessive amounts of table or other sodium salts. Excessive administration of sodium-containing fluids in a patient with impaired regulatory mechanisms may predispose him or her to a serious FVE as well.

Clinical Manifestations and Assessment

Clinical manifestations of FVE stem from expansion of the ECF and include edema, distended neck veins, and crackles (abnormal lung sounds) in lung fields. Other manifestations include tachycardia; increased blood pressure, pulse pressure, and central venous pressure; increased weight; increased urine output; shortness of breath, and/or wheezing.

Laboratory data useful in diagnosing FVE include BUN and hematocrit levels. In FVE, both of these values may be decreased because of plasma dilution, termed *hemodilution.*

Other causes of abnormalities in these values include low protein intake and anemia. Azotemia (increased nitrogen levels in the blood) can also occur with FVE when urea and creatinine are not excreted due to decreased perfusion by the kidneys and decreased excretion of wastes. In chronic renal failure, both serum osmolality and the sodium level are decreased due to excessive retention of water (inability of the kidneys to excrete the normal 1.5 L per day). The urine sodium level is increased if the kidneys are attempting to excrete excess volume. Chest X-rays may reveal pulmonary congestion. Hypervolemia occurs when aldosterone is chronically stimulated (i.e., cirrhosis, heart failure, and nephrotic syndrome). Therefore, the urine sodium level does not increase in these conditions.

Medical Management

Management of FVE is directed at the causes. If the fluid excess is related to excessive administration of sodium-containing fluids, discontinuing the infusion may be all that is needed. Symptomatic treatment consists of administering diuretics and restricting fluids and sodium.

Pharmacologic Therapy

Diuretics are prescribed when dietary restriction of sodium alone is insufficient to reduce fluid excess, which inhibits the reabsorption of sodium and water by the kidneys. The choice of diuretic is based on the severity of the hypervolemic state, the degree of impairment of renal function, and the potency of the diuretic. Thiazide diuretics block sodium reabsorption in the distal tubule, where only 5% to 10% of filtered sodium is reabsorbed. Loop diuretics, such as furosemide (Lasix), or bumetanide (Bumex), can cause a greater loss of both sodium and water because they block sodium reabsorption in the ascending limb of the loop of Henle, where 20% to 30% of filtered sodium is normally reabsorbed. Generally, thiazide diuretics, such as hydrochlorothiazide (HydroDIURIL) or metolazone (Mykrox, Zaroxolyn), are prescribed for mild to moderate hypervolemia and loop diuretics for severe hypervolemia.

Electrolyte imbalances may result from the effect of the diuretic. Hypokalemia can occur with all diuretics except those that work in the last distal tubule of the nephrons (e.g., spironolactone). Potassium supplements can be prescribed to avoid this complication. Hyperkalemia can occur with diuretics that work in the last distal tubule, especially in patients with decreased renal function.

Hemodialysis

If renal function is so severely impaired that pharmacologic agents cannot act efficiently, other modalities are considered to remove sodium and fluid from the body. Hemodialysis or peritoneal dialysis may be used to remove nitrogenous wastes and control potassium and acid–base balance, and to remove sodium and fluid. Continuous renal replacement therapy may also be required. See Chapter 27 for discussion of these treatment modalities.

Nutritional Therapy

Treatment of FVE usually involves dietary restriction of sodium. An average daily diet not restricted in sodium contains 6 to 15 g of salt, whereas low-sodium diets can range from a mild restriction to as little as 250 mg of sodium per day, depending on the patient's needs. A mild sodium-restricted diet allows only light salting of food (about half the usual amount) in cooking and at the table, and no addition of salt to commercially prepared foods that are already seasoned. Of course, foods high in sodium must be avoided. It is the sodium salt, sodium chloride, rather than sodium itself that contributes to edema. Therefore, patients are instructed to read food labels carefully to determine salt content.

Because about half of ingested sodium is in the form of seasoning, seasoning substitutes can play a major role in decreasing sodium intake. Lemon juice, onions, and garlic are excellent substitute flavorings, although some patients prefer salt substitutes. Most salt substitutes contain potassium and must therefore be used cautiously by patients taking potassium-sparing diuretics (e.g., spironolactone, triamterene, amiloride). They should not be used at all in conditions associated with potassium retention, such as advanced renal disease. Salt substitutes containing ammonium chloride can be harmful to patients with liver damage.

In some communities, the drinking water may contain too much sodium for a sodium-restricted diet. Depending on its source, water may contain as little as 1 mg or more than 1,500 mg per quart. Patients may need to use distilled water if the local water supply is very high in sodium. Bottled water can have a sodium content from 0 to 1,200 mg/L; therefore, if sodium is restricted, the label must be carefully examined for sodium content before purchasing and drinking bottled water. Also, patients on sodium-restricted diets should be cautioned to avoid water softeners that add sodium to water in exchange for other ions, such as calcium.

Nursing Management

Assessing the Patient

To assess for FVE, the nurse measures I&O at regular intervals to identify excessive fluid retention. The patient is weighed daily, and acute weight gain is noted. An acute weight gain of 2.2 lb (1 kg) is equivalent to a gain of approximately 1 L of fluid. The nurse also needs to assess breath sounds at regular intervals in at-risk patients, particularly if parenteral fluids are being administered. The nurse monitors the degree of edema in the most dependent parts of the body, such as the feet and ankles in ambulatory patients and the sacral region in patients confined to bed. The degree of pitting edema is assessed, and the extent of peripheral edema is monitored by measuring the circumference of the extremity with a tape marked in millimeters. In general, edema is associated with a minimum of 2.5 L of fluid in the interstitial space, and pitting edema is associated with a gain of 4.5 L (LeBlond, Brown, & DeGowin, 2008).

Preventing Fluid Volume Excess

Specific interventions vary somewhat with the underlying condition and the degree of FVE. However, most patients require sodium-restricted diets in some form, and adherence to the prescribed diet is encouraged. Patients are instructed to avoid over-the-counter medications without first checking with a health care provider, because these substances may contain sodium. If fluid retention persists despite adherence to a prescribed diet, hidden sources of sodium, such as the water supply or use of water softeners, should be considered.

Correcting Fluid Volume Excess

It is important to detect FVE before the condition becomes critical. Interventions include restricting sodium intake, monitoring parenteral fluid therapy, and administering appropriate medications.

Sodium and fluid restriction should be instituted as indicated. Because most patients with FVE require diuretics, the patient's response to these agents is monitored. The rate of parenteral fluids and the patient's response to these fluids are also closely monitored. If dyspnea or orthopnea is present, the patient is placed in a semi-Fowler's position to promote lung expansion. The patient is turned and positioned at regular intervals and skin is assessed at regular intervals because edematous tissue is fragile and more prone to skin breakdown than normal tissue. Because conditions predisposing to FVE are likely to be chronic, patients are taught to monitor their response to therapy by monitoring their fluid I&O and documenting daily body weight changes.

Teaching Patients About Edema

Because edema is a common manifestation of FVE, patients need to recognize its symptoms and understand its importance. Edema can occur as a result of increased capillary fluid pressure, decreased capillary oncotic pressure, or increased interstitial oncotic pressure, causing expansion of the interstitial fluid compartment (Porth & Matfin, 2009). Edema can be localized (e.g., in the ankle, as in rheumatoid arthritis) or generalized (as in cardiac and renal failure). Severe generalized edema is called *anasarca*.

Edema occurs when there is a change in the capillary membrane, increasing the formation of interstitial fluid or decreasing the removal of interstitial fluid. Sodium retention is a frequent cause of the increased ECF volume. Burns and infection are examples of conditions associated with increased interstitial fluid volume. Obstruction to lymphatic outflow, decreased plasma albumin levels, or a decrease in plasma oncotic pressure contributes to increased interstitial fluid volume. The kidneys retain sodium and water when decreased ECF volume occurs as a result of decreased cardiac output from heart failure. A thorough medication history is necessary to identify any medications that could cause edema, such as nonsteroidal anti-inflammatory drugs (NSAIDs), estrogens, corticosteroids, and antihypertensive agents.

Ascites is a form of edema in which fluid accumulates in the peritoneal cavity; it results from nephrotic syndrome, cirrhosis, and some malignant tumors. The patient commonly reports shortness of breath and a sense of pressure because of pressure on the diaphragm.

Edema usually affects dependent areas. It can be seen in the ankles, sacrum, scrotum, or the periorbital region of the face. Pitting edema is so named because a pit forms after a finger is pressed into edematous tissue. In pulmonary edema, the amount of fluid in the pulmonary interstitium and the alveoli increases. Manifestations include shortness of breath, increased respiratory rate, diaphoresis, and crackles and wheezing on auscultation of the lungs. Decreased hematocrit resulting from hemodilution, and decreased serum sodium and osmolality from retention of fluid may occur with edema. The goal of treatment is to preserve or restore the circulating intravascular fluid volume. In addition to treating the cause, other treatments may include diuretic therapy, restriction of fluids and sodium, elevation of the extremities, application of elastic compression stockings, paracentesis, dialysis, and continuous renal replacement therapy in cases of renal failure or life-threatening fluid volume overload.

ELECTROLYTE IMBALANCES

Disturbances in electrolyte balances are common in clinical practice and must be corrected for the patient's health and safety.

SODIUM IMBALANCES

Sodium is the most abundant electrolyte in the ECF; its concentration ranges from 135 to 145 mEq/L (135 to 145 mmol/L). Consequently, sodium is the primary determinant of ECF osmolality. Sodium plays a major role in controlling water distribution throughout the body because it does not easily cross the cell membrane and because of its abundance and high concentration in the body. Sodium also functions in establishing the electrochemical state necessary for muscle contraction and the transmission of nerve impulses. Sodium is regulated by ADH, thirst, and the renin–angiotensin–aldosterone system. A loss or gain of sodium is usually accompanied by a loss or gain of water.

The two most common sodium imbalances are sodium deficit and sodium excess.

HYPONATREMIA (SODIUM DEFICIT)

Hyponatremia refers to a serum sodium level that is below normal (<135 mEq/L [135 mmol/L]).

Pathophysiology

Plasma sodium concentration represents the ratio of total body sodium to total body water. A decrease in this ratio can

occur because of salt loss that is greater than water loss (e.g., diarrhea, diuretics, NG tube suctioning), or there is an excess of water relative to total body sodium (e.g., congestive heart failure, cirrhosis of the liver, excessive water intake without salt, syndrome of inappropriate secretion of antidiuretic hormone [SIADH]). Therefore, a hyponatremic state can be superimposed on an existing FVD or FVE.

Sodium may be lost by way of vomiting, diarrhea, fistulas, or sweating, or it may be lost as the result of the use of diuretics, particularly in combination with a low-salt diet. A deficiency of aldosterone, as occurs in adrenal insufficiency, also predisposes to sodium deficiency.

In dilutional hyponatremia (water intoxication), the patient's serum sodium level is diluted by an increase in the ratio of water to sodium. Dilutional hyponatremia, therefore, results from an increased ECF volume and a normal or increased total body sodium. Predisposing conditions for this type of hyponatremia include cirrhotic ascites; SIADH; hyperglycemia, which causes increased water to be drawn into the IVS; and increased water intake through the administration of electrolyte-poor parenteral fluids, the use of tap-water enemas, or the irrigation of nasogastric tubes with water instead of normal saline solution. Water may be gained abnormally by the excessive parenteral administration of hypotonic solutions such as dextrose and water solutions, particularly during periods of stress. It may also be gained by compulsive water drinking (psychogenic polydipsia).

The basic physiologic disturbances in SIADH are excessive ADH activity, with water retention and dilutional hyponatremia, and inappropriate urinary excretion of sodium in the presence of hyponatremia. SIADH can be the result of either sustained secretion of ADH by the hypothalamus or production of an ADH-like substance from a tumor (aberrant ADH production). Conditions associated with SIADH include oat-cell lung tumors, head injuries, endocrine and pulmonary disorders, physical or psychological stress, and a variety of medications (e.g., vincristine, phenothiazines, tricyclic antidepressants, and thiazide diuretics). SIADH is discussed in more detail in Chapter 31.

Clinical Manifestations and Assessment

Clinical manifestations of hyponatremia depend on the cause, magnitude, and speed with which the deficit occurs. Patients can present with FVD, as euvolemic (SIADH), or with FVE. With true salt loss, poor skin turgor, dry mucosa, headache, decreased saliva production, orthostatic fall in blood pressure, nausea, and abdominal cramping occur. With water gain in excess of sodium, clinical manifestations are associated with FVE, such as edema, crackles, ascites, and JVD. Symptoms are primarily neurological. They are related to osmotic water shift as water from the relatively dilute ECF is pulled into the cell, leading to increased ICF volume, specifically brain cell swelling or cerebral edema

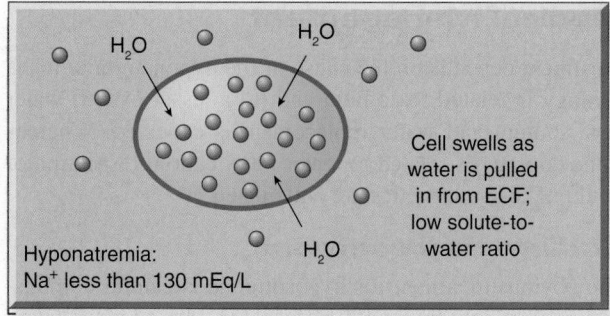
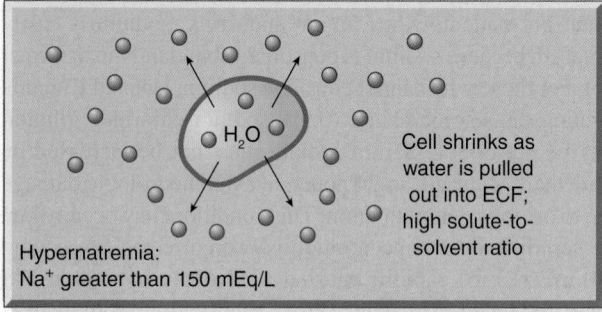

FIGURE 4-5 Effect of extracellular sodium level on cell size.

(Fig. 4-5). The skull limits the brain's ability to expand, which results in increased ICP, the precursor to brain damage. Neurologic changes include altered mental status, headache, lethargy, seizures, and a progressively decreased level of consciousness eventuating in coma. When the serum sodium level decreases to less than 115 mEq/L (115 mmol/L), signs of increasing intracranial pressure, such as lethargy, confusion, muscle twitching, focal weakness, hemiparesis, papilledema, and seizures, may occur. In general, patients with an acute decrease in serum sodium levels have more cerebral edema and higher mortality rates than do those with more slowly developing hyponatremia. Acute decreases in sodium, developing in less than 48 hours, may be associated with brain herniation and compression of midbrain structures.

Regardless of the cause of hyponatremia, the serum sodium level is less than 135 mEq/L; in SIADH it may be as low as 100 mEq/L (100 mmol/L) or even less. Serum osmolality is also decreased, except in azotemia or ingestion of toxins. When hyponatremia is due primarily to sodium loss, the urinary sodium content is less than 20 mEq/L (20 mmol/L), suggesting increased proximal reabsorption of sodium secondary to ECF volume depletion, and the specific gravity is low (1.002 to 1.004). However, when hyponatremia is due to SIADH, the urinary sodium content is greater than 20 mEq/L, and the urine specific gravity is usually greater than 1.012. Although the patient with SIADH retains water abnormally and therefore gains body weight, there is no peripheral edema; instead, fluid accumulates inside the cells.

Medical Management

Treatment depends on the cause of the hyponatremia. If the etiology is related to sodium and (to a lesser extent) water loss, sodium and water replacement is expected. Whereas if the etiology is related to water intoxication, restriction of fluid intake and diuretics are anticipated.

Sodium Replacement

The obvious treatment for hyponatremia is careful administration of sodium by mouth, nasogastric tube, or a parenteral route. For patients who can eat and drink, sodium is easily replaced, because sodium is consumed abundantly in a normal diet. For those who cannot consume sodium, lactated Ringer's solution or isotonic saline (0.9% sodium chloride) solution may be prescribed. Serum sodium must not be increased by more than 12 mEq/L in 24 hours, to avoid neurologic damage due to osmotic demyelination. This condition may occur when the serum sodium concentration is overcorrected (exceeding 140 mEq/L) too rapidly, causing a relatively hypotonic ICS compared to the ECS. This causes water to flow from the ICS to the ECS, causing cell volume collapse. Osmotic demyelination presents as flaccid paralysis, dysarthria (speech that is slurred, slow, and difficult to produce), dysphagia (difficulty in swallowing), and quadriparesis. The usual daily sodium requirement in adults is approximately 100 mEq, provided no abnormal losses occur. Selected water and electrolyte solutions are described later in the chapter.

In SIADH, the administration of hypertonic saline solution alone cannot change the plasma sodium concentration. Excess sodium would be excreted rapidly in a highly concentrated urine. With the addition of the diuretic furosemide (Lasix), urine is not concentrated, and isotonic urine is excreted to effect a change in water balance. In patients with SIADH, in whom water restriction is difficult, lithium or demeclocycline can antagonize the osmotic effect of ADH on the medullary collecting tubule.

Water Restriction

In a patient with normal or excess fluid volume, hyponatremia is treated by restricting fluid to a total of 800 mL in 24 hours. This is far safer than sodium administration and is usually effective. However, if neurologic symptoms are present, it may be necessary to administer small volumes of a hypertonic sodium solution, such as 3% sodium chloride. Incorrect use of these fluids is extremely dangerous, because 1 L of 3% sodium chloride solution contains 513 mEq of sodium with a osmolality of 1,026. If edema exists alone, sodium is restricted; if edema and hyponatremia occur together, both sodium and water are restricted.

Nursing Management

The nurse needs to identify patients at risk for hyponatremia, so that they can be monitored. Early detection and treatment of this disorder are necessary to prevent serious consequences. For patients at risk, the nurse monitors fluid I&O as well as daily body weight. It is also necessary to note abnormal losses of sodium or gains of water, as well as GI manifestations such as anorexia, nausea, vomiting, and abdominal cramping. The nurse must be particularly alert for CNS changes, such as lethargy, confusion, muscle twitching, and seizures. In general, more severe neurologic signs are associated with very low sodium levels that have fallen rapidly because of fluid overloading. Serum sodium is monitored very closely in patients who are at risk for hyponatremia; when indicated, urine sodium and specific gravity are also monitored.

Hyponatremia is a frequently overlooked cause of confusion in elderly patients, who have an increased risk for hyponatremia because of changes in renal function and subsequent decreased ability to excrete excessive water loads. Administration of medications causing sodium loss or water retention is a predisposing factor.

Correcting Hyponatremia

For a patient who is experiencing abnormal losses of sodium and can consume a general diet, the nurse encourages foods and fluids with a high sodium content. For example, broth made with one beef cube contains approximately 900 mg of sodium; 8 oz of tomato juice contains approximately 700 mg of sodium. The nurse also needs to be familiar with the sodium content of parenteral fluids (see later discussion and Table 4-6 on pages 91 and 92).

For the patient taking lithium, the nurse observes for lithium toxicity, particularly when sodium is lost by an abnormal route. In such instances, supplemental salt and fluid are administered. Because diuretics promote sodium loss, the patient taking lithium is instructed not to use diuretics without close medical supervision. For all patients on lithium therapy, adequate salt intake should be ensured.

Excess water supplements are avoided in patients receiving isotonic or hypotonic enteral feedings, particularly if abnormal sodium loss occurs or water is being abnormally retained (as in SIADH). Actual fluid needs are determined by evaluating fluid I&O, urine specific gravity, and serum sodium levels.

HYPERNATREMIA (SODIUM EXCESS)

Hypernatremia is a higher-than-normal serum sodium level (exceeding 145 mEq/L [145 mmol/L]).

Pathophysiology

Hypernatremia can be caused by a gain of sodium in excess of water or by a loss of water in excess of sodium. It can occur in the euvolemic patient or those with FVD or FVE. With a water loss, the patient loses more water than sodium; as a result, the serum sodium concentration increases and the increased concentration pulls fluid out of the cell. This is both an extracellular and an intracellular FVD. In sodium excess, the patient ingests or retains more sodium than water.

A common cause of hypernatremia is fluid deprivation in unconscious patients who cannot perceive, respond to, or

communicate their thirst (Porth & Matfin, 2009). Most often affected are very old, very young, and cognitively impaired patients. Administration of hypertonic enteral feedings without adequate water supplements leads to hypernatremia, as does watery diarrhea and greatly increased insensible water loss (e.g., hyperventilation, denuding effects of burns).

Diabetes insipidus, a deficiency of ADH from the posterior pituitary gland, leads to hypernatremia if the patient does not experience, or cannot respond to thirst, or if fluids are excessively restricted. Neurogenic or nephrogenic causes of diabetes insipidus should be considered in the assessment (refer to Chapter 31).

IV administration of hypertonic saline, hypertonic feeding preparations, or excessive use of sodium bicarbonate can also cause hypernatremia.

Clinical Manifestations and Assessment

The clinical manifestations of hypernatremia are primarily neurologic and are the consequence of increased plasma osmolality caused by an increase in plasma sodium concentration. Water moves out of the ICS into the ECS, resulting in cellular dehydration (see Fig. 4-5). Clinically, these changes may be manifested by restlessness and weakness in moderate hypernatremia and by disorientation, delusions, and hallucinations in severe hypernatremia. Dehydration (resulting in hypernatremia) is often overlooked as the primary reason for behavioral changes in elderly patients. If hypernatremia is severe, permanent brain damage can occur (especially in children). Brain damage is apparently due to subarachnoid hemorrhages that result from brain contraction. A primary characteristic of hypernatremia is thirst. Thirst is such a strong defender of serum sodium levels in healthy people that hypernatremia never occurs unless the person is unconscious or does not have access to water. However, ill people may have an impaired thirst mechanism. Other signs include a dry, swollen tongue and sticky mucous membranes. Flushed skin, peripheral and pulmonary edema, postural hypotension, and increased muscle tone and deep tendon reflexes are additional signs and symptoms of hypernatremia. Body temperature may increase mildly, but it returns to normal after the hypernatremia is corrected. In hypernatremia, the serum sodium level exceeds 145 mEq/L (145 mmol/L), and the serum osmolality exceeds 300 mOsm/kg (300 mmol/L). The urine specific gravity and urine osmolality are increased as the kidneys attempt to conserve water (provided the water loss is from a route other than the kidneys).

Medical Management

Treatment of hypernatremia consists of a gradual lowering of the serum sodium level by the infusion of a hypotonic electrolyte solution or an isotonic nonsaline solution (e.g., dextrose 5% in water [D₅W]). D₅W is indicated when water needs to be replaced without sodium. Many clinicians consider a hypotonic sodium solution to be safer than D₅W

because it allows a gradual reduction in the serum sodium level, thereby decreasing the risk of cerebral edema. It is the solution of choice in severe hyperglycemia with hypernatremia. A rapid reduction in the serum sodium level temporarily decreases the plasma osmolality below that of the fluid in the brain tissue, causing dangerous cerebral edema. Diuretics also may be prescribed to treat the sodium gain.

There is no consensus about the exact rate at which serum sodium levels should be reduced. As a general rule, the serum sodium level is reduced at a rate no faster than 0.5 to 1 mEq/L per hour to allow sufficient time for readjustment through diffusion across fluid compartments. Desmopressin acetate (DDAVP), a synthetic antidiuretic hormone, may be prescribed to treat diabetes insipidus if it is the cause of hypernatremia (Porth & Matfin, 2009).

Nursing Management

As in hyponatremia, fluid losses and gains are carefully monitored in patients who are at risk for hypernatremia. The nurse should assess for abnormal losses of water or low water intake and for large gains of sodium, as might occur with ingestion of over-the-counter medications that have a high sodium content (e.g., Alka-Seltzer). In addition, the nurse obtains a medication history, because some prescription medications have a high sodium content. The nurse also notes the patient's thirst or elevated body temperature and evaluates it in relation to other clinical signs. The nurse monitors for changes in behavior, such as restlessness, disorientation, and lethargy.

Preventing Hypernatremia

The nurse attempts to prevent hypernatremia by offering fluids at regular intervals, particularly in debilitated or unconscious patients who are unable to perceive or respond to thirst. If fluid intake remains inadequate, the nurse consults with the provider to plan an alternative route for intake, either by enteral feedings or by the parenteral route. If enteral feedings are used, sufficient water should be administered to keep the serum sodium and BUN within normal limits. As a rule, the higher the osmolality of the enteral feeding, the greater the need for water supplementation.

For patients with diabetes insipidus, adequate water intake must be ensured. If the patient is alert and has an intact thirst mechanism, merely providing access to water may be sufficient. If the patient has a decreased level of consciousness or other disability interfering with adequate fluid intake, parenteral fluid replacement may be prescribed. This therapy can be anticipated in patients with neurologic disorders, particularly in the early postoperative period.

POTASSIUM IMBALANCES

Potassium is the major intracellular electrolyte; in fact, 98% of the body's potassium is inside the cells. The remaining 2% is in the ECF, and it is this 2% that is important in

neuromuscular function. The normal serum potassium concentration ranges from 3.5 to 5.0 mEq/L (3.5 to 5 mmol/L), and even minor variations are significant.

To maintain potassium balance, the renal system must function, because 80% of the potassium excreted daily leaves the body by way of the kidneys; the other 20% is lost through the bowel. Intestinal fluid may contain as much as 30 mEq/L of potassium. However, the kidneys are the primary regulators of potassium balance; they accomplish this by adjusting the amount of potassium that is excreted in the urine. Aldosterone also increases the excretion of potassium by the kidney. Because the kidneys do not conserve potassium as well as they conserve sodium, potassium may still be lost in urine in the presence of a potassium deficit. Potassium imbalances are commonly associated with a variety of diseases, injuries, medications (diuretics, laxatives, antibiotics), and special treatments, such as parenteral nutrition and chemotherapy.

(HYPOKALEMIA) POTASSIUM DEFICIT

Hypokalemia (below-normal serum potassium concentration) usually indicates an actual deficit in total potassium stores. However, it may occur in patients with normal potassium stores, such as when alkalosis is present, since it causes a temporary shift of serum potassium into the cells (see later discussion).

Pathophysiology

Hypokalemia (<3.5 mEq/L) is a common imbalance. It is associated with conditions that cause an increased output of K^+ (diuretics, diarrhea, vomiting, gastric suction, recent ileostomy, intestinal drains, villous adenoma [a tumor of the intestinal tract characterized by excretion of potassium-rich mucus]); decreased intake (NPO, anorexia, vomiting, alcoholism, fasting diets); or redistribution of K^+ (metabolic alkalosis).

The nurse considers clinical conditions that cause increased loss. Approximately 5 to 10 mEq/L K^+ are found in upper GI fluid, whereas 30 to 100 mEq/L is lost with diarrhea. Thus, relatively large amounts of potassium are lost in intestinal fluids.

Potassium-losing diuretics, such as the thiazides, can induce hypokalemia, particularly when administered in large doses to patients with inadequate potassium intake. Other medications that can lead to hypokalemia include corticosteroids, sodium penicillin, carbenicillin, and amphotericin B.

Increased loss is also seen with hyperaldosteronism, which causes a reabsorption of sodium and renal excretion of K^+. Primary hyperaldosteronism is seen in patients with adrenal adenomas. Secondary hyperaldosteronism occurs in disorders that activate the renin–angiotensin–aldosterone system to maintain serum sodium concentrations such as cirrhosis, nephrotic syndrome, or heart failure.

Decreased intake occurs in patients who are unable or unwilling to eat a normal diet. This may occur in debilitated elderly people, patients with alcoholism, and patients with anorexia nervosa. In addition to poor intake, people with bulimia frequently suffer increased potassium loss through self-induced vomiting and laxative and diuretic abuse.

Redistribution is associated with alterations in acid–base balance or certain medications, such as insulin. In general, a hypokalemia is associated with an alkalosis and, in turn, an alkalosis can cause hypokalemia. The mechanism involves shifts of hydrogen and potassium ions between the ICS and the ECF. For example, hydrogen ions move out of the cells in alkalotic states to help correct the high pH, and potassium ions move in to maintain an electrically neutral state (see later discussion of acid–base balance).

Because insulin promotes the entry of potassium into skeletal muscle and hepatic cells, patients with persistent insulin hypersecretion may experience hypokalemia, which is often the case in patients receiving high-carbohydrate parenteral fluids (as in parenteral nutrition). The nurse anticipates that patients requiring IV insulin are at risk for hypokalemia.

Finally, a magnesium depletion can cause a renal potassium loss and must be corrected or urine loss of potassium will continue.

Clinical Manifestations and Assessment

Potassium deficiency can result in widespread derangements in physiologic function. Severe hypokalemia can cause death through cardiac or respiratory arrest. Clinical signs rarely develop before the serum potassium level has decreased to less than 3 mEq/L (3 mmol/L) unless the rate of decline has been rapid. Manifestations of hypokalemia include fatigue, anorexia, nausea, vomiting, muscle weakness, leg cramps, decreased bowel motility, paresthesias (numbness and tingling), arrhythmias, and increased sensitivity to digitalis.

If prolonged, hypokalemia can lead to an inability of the kidneys to concentrate urine, causing dilute urine (resulting in polyuria, nocturia) and excessive thirst. Potassium depletion depresses the release of insulin and results in glucose intolerance. Decreased muscle strength and tendon reflexes can be found on physical assessment.

In hypokalemia, the serum potassium concentration is less than the lower limit of normal. Electrocardiographic (ECG) changes can include flat T waves or inverted T waves or both, suggesting ischemia, and depressed ST segments (Fig. 4-6). An elevated U wave is specific to hypokalemia. Hypokalemia increases sensitivity to digitalis, predisposing the patient to digitalis toxicity at lower digitalis levels.

Medical Management

If hypokalemia cannot be prevented by conventional measures, such as increased intake in the daily diet, it is treated with oral or IV replacement therapy. Potassium loss must

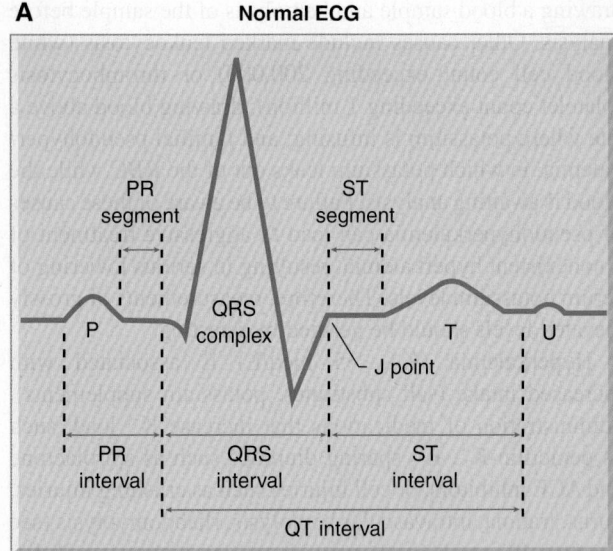

Normal ECG

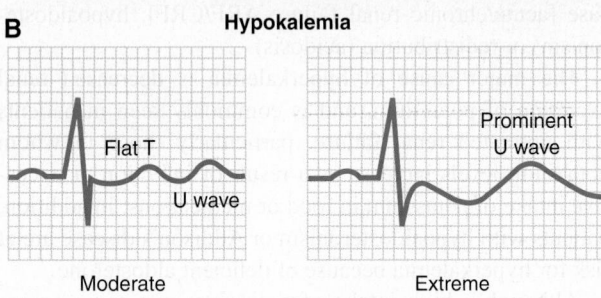

Hypokalemia

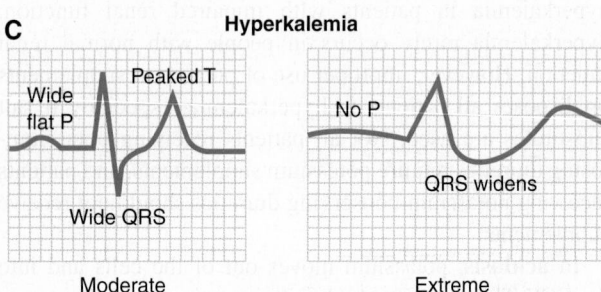

Hyperkalemia

FIGURE 4-6 Effect of potassium on the electrocardio-gram (ECG). **(A)** Normal tracing. **(B)** Hypokalemia: Serum potassium level below normal. *Left,* flattening of the T wave and the appearance of a U wave. *Right,* further flattening with prominent U wave. **(C)** Hyperkalemia: Serum potassium level above normal. *Left,* moderate elevation with wide, flat P wave, wide QRS complex, and peaked T wave. *Right,* ECG changes seen with extreme potassium elevation: widening of QRS complex and absence of P wave.

be corrected daily; administration of 40 to 80 mEq/day of potassium is adequate in the adult if there are no abnormal losses of potassium.

For patients who are at risk for hypokalemia, a diet containing sufficient potassium should be provided. Dietary intake of potassium in the average adult is 50 to 100 mEq/day. Foods high in potassium include most fruits and vegetables, legumes, whole grains, milk, and meat.

If dietary intake is inadequate for any reason, the provider may prescribe oral or IV potassium supplements. Many salt substitutes contain 50 to 60 mEq of potassium per teaspoon and may be sufficient to prevent hypokalemia.

If oral administration of potassium is not feasible, the IV route is indicated. The IV route is mandatory for patients with severe hypokalemia (e.g., serum level of <2 mEq/L). Although potassium chloride is usually used to correct potassium deficits, potassium acetate or potassium phosphate may be prescribed.

Nursing Management

Because hypokalemia can be life-threatening, the nurse needs to monitor for its early presence in patients who are at risk. Fatigue, anorexia, muscle weakness, decreased bowel motility, paresthesias, and arrhythmias are signals that warrant assessing the serum potassium concentration. When available, the ECG may provide useful information. For example, patients receiving digitalis who are at risk for potassium deficiency should be monitored closely for signs of digitalis toxicity, because hypokalemia potentiates the action of digitalis.

Preventing Hypokalemia

Measures are taken to prevent hypokalemia when possible. Prevention may involve encouraging the patient at risk to eat foods rich in potassium (when the diet allows). Sources of potassium include fruit and fruit juices (bananas, melon, citrus fruit), fresh and frozen vegetables, fresh meats, milk, and processed foods. If the hypokalemia is caused by abuse of laxatives or diuretics, patient education may help alleviate the problem.

Correcting Hypokalemia

Great care should be exercised when administering potassium, particularly in older adults, who have lower lean body mass and total body potassium levels and therefore lower potassium requirements. In addition, because of the physiologic loss of renal function with advancing years, potassium may be retained more readily in older than in younger people.

> ! **NURSING ALERT**
> *Oral potassium supplements can produce small-bowel lesions; therefore, the patient must be assessed for and cautioned about abdominal distention, pain, or GI bleeding.*

Potassium should be administered only after adequate urine flow has been established. A decrease in urine volume to less than 20 mL/h for 2 consecutive hours is an indication to stop the potassium infusion until the situation is evaluated. Potassium is primarily excreted by the kidneys; therefore, when oliguria occurs, potassium administration can cause the serum potassium concentration to rise dangerously. Each health care facility has its own standard of care for the

administration of potassium, which should be consulted; however, the maximum concentration of potassium that should be administered on a medical-surgical unit through a peripheral IV line is 20 mEq/100 mL and the rate no faster than 10 to 20 mEq/h. Concentrations of potassium greater than 20 mEq/100 mL should be administered through a central IV catheter using an infusion pump with the patient monitored by ECG. Caution must be used when selecting the correct premixed solution of IV fluid containing potassium chloride as the concentrations range from 10 to 40 mEq/100 mL. IV bags of 1000 mL of fluid containing potassium are also available with 20 to 40 mEq/L. IV pumps should always be used with potassium administration. Rapid infusion can cause sudden hyperkalemia and cardiac arrest.

!**NURSING ALERT**
Potassium is never administered by IV push or intramuscularly to avoid replacing potassium too quickly. IV potassium must be administered using an infusion pump.

Renal function should be monitored through BUN and creatinine levels and urine output if the patient is receiving potassium replacements, and the provider should be notified of changes in renal function to prevent complications.

!**NURSING ALERT**
Potassium supplements are extremely dangerous for patients who have impaired renal function and thus decreased ability to excrete potassium. Even more dangerous is the IV administration of potassium to such patients, because serum levels can rise very quickly. Aged (stored) blood should not be administered to patients with impaired renal function, because the serum potassium concentration of stored blood increases as the storage time increases, a result of red blood cell deterioration. It is possible to exceed the renal tolerance of any patient with rapid IV potassium administration, as well as when large amounts of oral potassium supplements are ingested.

HYPERKALEMIA (POTASSIUM EXCESS)

Hyperkalemia (greater-than-normal serum potassium concentration) seldom occurs in patients with normal renal function.

Pathophysiology

Like hypokalemia, hyperkalemia is often caused by iatrogenic (treatment-induced) causes. Although hyperkalemia is less common than hypokalemia, it is usually more dangerous, because cardiac arrest is more frequently associated with high serum potassium levels.

Pseudohyperkalemia (a variation of hyperkalemia) has a number of causes. The most common causes are the use of a tight tourniquet around an exercising extremity while drawing a blood sample and hemolysis of the sample before analysis. Other causes include marked leukocytosis (white blood cell count exceeding 200,000) or thrombocytosis (platelet count exceeding 1 million); drawing blood above a site where potassium is infusing; and familial pseudohyperkalemia, in which potassium leaks out of the RBC while the blood is awaiting analysis. Failure to be aware of these causes of pseudohyperkalemia can lead to aggressive treatment of a nonexistent hyperkalemia, resulting in serious lowering of serum potassium levels. Therefore, measurements of grossly elevated levels should be verified by retesting.

Hyperkalemia (K^+ >5 meq/L) is associated with increased intake (salt substitutes, potassium supplements), administration of medications that increase K^+ load, such as penicillin-K^+, K^+ sparing diuretics such as spirolactone and ACE inhibitors, or cell injuries such as crushing injuries, burns, trauma, intravascular hemolysis, rhabdomyolysis (see Chapter 42) or chemotherapy, decreased output (renal disease [acute/chronic renal failure ARF/CRF], hypoaldosteronism) or redistribution (acidosis).

The major cause of hyperkalemia is decreased renal excretion of potassium, and is commonly seen in patients with untreated renal failure, particularly those in whom potassium levels increase as a result of infection or excessive intake of potassium in food or medications. In addition, patients with hypoaldosteronism or Addison's disease are at risk for hyperkalemia because of deficient aldosterone.

Although a high intake of potassium can cause severe hyperkalemia in patients with impaired renal function, hyperkalemia rarely occurs in people with normal renal function. However, improper use of potassium supplements predisposes all patients to hyperkalemia, especially if salt substitutes are used. Not all patients receiving potassium-losing diuretics require potassium supplements, and patients receiving potassium-conserving diuretics should not receive supplements.

In **acidosis**, potassium moves out of the cells and into the ECF. This occurs as hydrogen ions enter the cells, a process that buffers the pH of the ECF (see later discussion). An elevated ECF potassium level should be anticipated when extensive tissue trauma has occurred, as in burns, crushing injuries, or severe infections. Similarly, it can occur with lysis of malignant cells after chemotherapy.

Clinical Manifestations and Assessment

The most important consequence of hyperkalemia is its effect on the myocardium. Cardiac effects of elevated serum potassium are usually not significant when the level is less than 7 mEq/L (7 mmol/L), but they are almost always present when the level is 8 mEq/L (8 mmol/L) or greater. As the plasma potassium level rises, disturbances in cardiac conduction occur. The earliest changes, often occurring at a serum potassium level greater than 6 mEq/L (6 mmol/L),

are peaked, narrow T waves; ST-segment depression; and a shortened QT interval. If the serum potassium level continues to increase, the PR interval becomes prolonged and is followed by disappearance of the P waves. Finally, there is decomposition and prolongation of the QRS complex (see Fig. 4-6). Ventricular arrhythmias and cardiac arrest may occur at any point in this progression. Severe hyperkalemia causes skeletal muscle weakness and even paralysis, related to a depolarization block in muscle. Similarly, ventricular conduction is slowed. Although hyperkalemia has marked effects on the peripheral nervous system, it has little effect on the CNS. Rapidly ascending muscular weakness leading to flaccid quadriplegia has been reported in patients with very high serum potassium levels. Paralysis of respiratory and speech muscles can also occur. In addition, GI manifestations, such as nausea, intermittent intestinal colic, and diarrhea, may occur in hyperkalemic patients. Serum potassium levels and ECG changes are crucial to the diagnosis of hyperkalemia, as discussed previously. ABG analysis may reveal metabolic acidosis; in many cases, hyperkalemia occurs with acidosis, owing to shifts of hydrogen and potassium ions between the ICS and the ECF. For example, hydrogen ions move into the cells in acidotic states to help correct the low serum pH, and potassium ions move out of the cells in exchange causing a hyperkalemia.

Medical Management

In nonacute situations, restriction of dietary potassium and potassium-containing medications may suffice. For example, eliminating the use of potassium-containing salt substitutes in a patient who is taking a potassium-conserving diuretic may be all that is needed to deal with mild hyperkalemia.

Prevention of serious hyperkalemia by the administration, either orally or by retention enema, of cation exchange resins (e.g., Kayexalate) may be necessary in patients with renal impairment. Cation exchange resins were once used as the primary agent for physical removal of potassium in the body; they act by binding potassium within the bowel and excreting it within the stool. However, research now suggests that cation exchange resins actually increase the risk of bowel ischemia, and no study to date has clearly stated that cation exchange resins do in fact lower the potassium levels. Therefore this practice has begun to fall out of favor among health care providers (Sterns, Rojas, Bernstein et al., 2010).

Emergency Pharmacologic Therapy

If serum potassium levels are dangerously elevated, it may be necessary to administer IV calcium gluconate. Within minutes after administration, calcium antagonizes the action of hyperkalemia on the heart. Infusion of calcium does not reduce the serum potassium concentration, but it immediately antagonizes the adverse cardiac conduction abnormalities. Calcium chloride and calcium gluconate are not interchangeable: calcium gluconate contains 4.5 mEq of calcium, and calcium chloride contains 13.6 mEq of calcium; therefore, caution must be used.

Monitoring the blood pressure is essential to detect hypotension, which may result from the rapid IV administration of calcium gluconate. The ECG should be continuously monitored during administration; the appearance of bradycardia is an indication to stop the infusion. The myocardial-protective effects of calcium are transient, lasting about 30 minutes. Extra caution is required if the patient has been "digitalized" (i.e., has received accelerated dosages of a digitalis-based cardiac glycoside to reach a desired serum digitalis level rapidly), because parenteral administration of calcium sensitizes the heart to digitalis and may precipitate digitalis toxicity.

IV administration of sodium bicarbonate may be necessary to alkalinize the plasma and cause a temporary shift of potassium into the cells. Also, sodium bicarbonate furnishes sodium to antagonize the cardiac effects of potassium. Effects of this therapy begin within 30 to 60 minutes and may persist for hours; however, they are temporary.

IV administration of regular insulin and a hypertonic dextrose solution causes a temporary shift of potassium into the cells. Glucose and insulin therapy has an onset of action within 30 minutes and lasts for several hours. Loop diuretics, such as furosemide (Lasix), increase excretion of water by inhibiting sodium, potassium, and chloride reabsorption in the ascending loop of Henle and distal renal tubule.

Beta-2 agonists, such as albuterol (Proventil, Ventolin), can be effective in decreasing potassium; however, large doses are needed to elicit potassium shifting into the cells. The nurse is aware that beta-2 agonists may cause tachycardia and observes cardiac response to treatment, and the provider may consider other options in the patient with ischemic cardiac disease. Administration of these medications is a stopgap measure that only temporarily protects the patient from hyperkalemia. If the hyperkalemic condition is not transient, actual removal of potassium from the body is required; this may be accomplished by using peritoneal dialysis, hemodialysis, or other forms of renal replacement therapy.

Nursing Management

Patients at risk for potassium excess (e.g., those with renal failure) should be identified, so that they can be monitored closely for signs of hyperkalemia. The nurse observes for signs of muscle weakness and arrhythmias. The presence of paresthesias and GI symptoms, such as nausea and intestinal colic, are noted.

Because measurements of elevated serum potassium levels may be erroneous, highly abnormal levels should always be verified by repeating the test. To avoid false reports of hyperkalemia, prolonged use of a tourniquet while drawing the blood sample is avoided, and the patient is cautioned not

to exercise the extremity immediately before the blood sample is obtained. The blood sample is delivered to the laboratory as soon as possible, because hemolysis of the sample results in a falsely elevated serum potassium level.

Preventing Hyperkalemia

Measures are taken to prevent hyperkalemia in patients at risk, when possible, by encouraging the patient to adhere to the prescribed potassium restriction. Potassium-rich foods to be avoided include many fruits and vegetables, legumes, whole-grain breads, meat, milk, eggs, coffee, tea, and cocoa. Conversely, foods with minimal potassium content include butter, margarine, cranberry juice or sauce, ginger ale, gumdrops or jellybeans, hard candy, root beer, sugar, and honey.

Correcting Hyperkalemia

As previously stated, it is possible to exceed the tolerance for potassium in any person if it is administered rapidly by the IV route. Therefore, great care should be taken to administer and monitor potassium solutions closely, paying attention to the solution's concentration and rate of administration. When potassium is added to parenteral solutions, the potassium is mixed with the fluid by inverting the bottle several times. Potassium chloride should never be added to a hanging bottle, because the potassium might be administered as a bolus (potassium chloride is heavy and settles to the bottom of the container).

It is important to caution patients to use salt substitutes sparingly if they are taking other supplementary forms of potassium or potassium-conserving diuretics. Also, potassium-conserving diuretics, such as spironolactone (Aldactone), triamterene (Dyrenium), and amiloride (Midamor); potassium supplements; and salt substitutes should not be administered to patients with renal dysfunction. Most salt substitutes contain approximately 50 to 60 mEq of potassium per teaspoon.

CALCIUM IMBALANCES

More than 99% of the body's calcium is located in the skeletal system, where it provides strength and stability to the skeletal system and serves as a source for extracellular calcium (Porth, 2011). Approximately 0.1% to 0.2% of calcium (8.5 to 10.5 mg/dL) circulates in the serum, 40% is bound to plasma proteins (mostly albumin), 10% is complexed or chelated with substances such as phosphorus and sulfate, and approximately 50% is ionized or free to leave the blood stream and participate in cellular function (Porth, 2011). Calcium plays a major role in transmitting nerve impulses and helps regulate muscle contraction and relaxation, including cardiac muscle; thus, it is important for cardiac conduction, neuromuscular activity, and blood coagulation. Calcium is also instrumental in activating enzymes that stimulate many essential chemical reactions in the body. Because many factors affect calcium regulation, both hypocalcemia and hypercalcemia are relatively common disturbances.

Calcium is absorbed from foods (milk and milk products) in the presence of normal gastric acidity and vitamin D. Calcium is excreted in feces and urine. The serum calcium level is controlled by PTH and calcitonin. As ionized or free serum calcium decreases, the parathyroid glands secrete PTH. This, in turn, increases calcium absorption from the GI tract (mediated by an increase in renal vitamin D synthesis), increases calcium reabsorption from the renal tubule, and releases calcium from the bone. The subsequent increase in calcium ion concentration suppresses PTH secretion. When calcium increases excessively, the thyroid gland secretes calcitonin, the antagonist of PTH. It briefly inhibits calcium reabsorption from bone, encourages calcium salt deposits in the bone matrix, and decreases the serum calcium concentration. Additionally, blood phosphate (most phosphorus is present as phosphate) levels have a reciprocal relationship with calcium levels. Increases in blood phosphate result in a fall in free calcium concentrations. PTH secretion is stimulated, and this reduces renal excretion of calcium and increases renal phosphate excretion. These adaptations prevent the potentially damaging effects of calcium phosphate crystal deposition that can form in soft tissues when the normal calcium phosphorus ratio is disturbed.

⚡ NURSING ALERT

In conditions such as renal failure, the kidneys are unable to excrete excess phosphate, nor are they able to activate vitamin D, which decreases the ability to absorb calcium. This excess phosphate binds with free calcium, forming an insoluble compound that can be deposited in the heart, lungs, eyes, kidneys, skin, and soft tissues. The subsequent fall in serum calcium increases PTH secretion, which dissolves more calcium from the bone to attempt to maintain a normal serum calcium level. The net effect is the development of hyperparathyroidism and a variety of symptoms (renal osteodystrophy, bone pain, fractures, and bleeding) (see Chapters 27 and 31).

HYPOCALCEMIA (CALCIUM DEFICIT)

Hypocalcemia (lower-than-normal serum concentration of calcium), or less than 8.5 mg/dL and an ionized calcium of less than 4.6 mg/dL, occurs in a variety of clinical situations (Fischbach & Dunning, 2009).

Pathophysiology

Factors associated with hypocalcemia include inadequate calcium intake, increased calcium loss, malabsorption of calcium, decreases in serum protein levels, and increased binding of calcium. Inadequate intake is associated with chronic alcoholism and malnutrition. Increased calcium loss is associated with pancreatic insufficiency and acute pancreatitis. Inflammation of the pancreas causes the breakdown of proteins and lipids. It is thought that calcium ions combine with the fatty acids released by lipolysis, forming soaps. As

a result of this process, hypocalcemia occurs and is common in pancreatitis. It has also been suggested that hypocalcemia might be related to excessive secretion of glucagon from the inflamed pancreas, which results in increased secretion of calcitonin (a hormone that lowers serum calcium). Inadequate secretion of PTH by the parathyroid gland results in hypocalcemia and can be related to hypoparathyroidism or other parathyroid gland disorders, use of certain drugs, surgery of the thyroid gland with inadvertent removal of the parathyroids, radiation injury to the thyroid, and radical neck dissection. This is likely to occur in the first 24 to 48 hours postoperatively.

Medications predisposing to hypocalcemia include aluminum-containing antacids, aminoglycosides, anticonvulsants (phenytoin and phenobarbital), corticosteroids, mithramycin, phosphates, isoniazid, and loop diuretics. Malabsorption of calcium may be seen in severe diarrhea, laxative abuse, decreased exposure to sunlight or conditions that impair vitamin D, high phosphorus level in the intestines, reduced gastric acidity, and renal failure. Additionally, hypoalbuminemia, alkalosis, and massive blood transfusion are associated with hypocalcemia. Recall that approximately 40% of calcium is bound to albumin; thus, a decrease in serum albumin will result in a decrease in total serum calcium, but it does not affect the concentration of the ionized form of calcium that is essential for body function (Fischbach & Dunning, 2009). When the arterial pH increases (alkalosis), more calcium becomes bound to protein. As a result, the ionized portion decreases, thus symptoms of hypocalcemia may occur with alkalosis. Transient hypocalcemia can occur with massive administration of citrated blood (adults who experience massive hemorrhage and shock), because citrate (which is used in blood transfusions to prevent clotting in blood) can combine with ionized calcium and temporarily remove it from the circulation.

Clinical Manifestations and Assessment

If ionized calcium level is normal despite low total calcium levels, patients are generally asymptomatic, whereas large changes in ionized calcium levels leads to a variety of symptoms associated with neuromuscular hyperactivity and cardiovascular effects detailed below. Tetany (the most characteristic manifestation of hypocalcemia) and convulsions are seen when the total calcium level is less than 4.4 mg/dL, and/or the ionized calcium is less than 2.0 mg/dL (Fischbach & Dunning, 2009). *Tetany* refers to the entire symptom complex induced by increased neural excitability. These symptoms are caused by spontaneous discharges of both sensory and motor fibers in peripheral nerves. Sensations of tingling may occur in the tips of the fingers, around the mouth, and, less commonly, in the feet. Spasms of the muscles of the extremities and face may occur. Pain may develop as a result of these spasms.

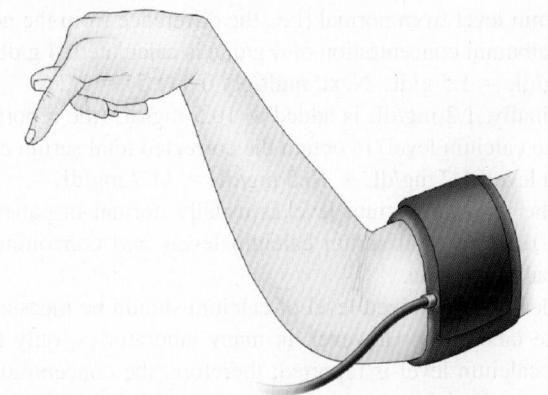

FIGURE 4-7 Trousseau's sign. Ischemia-induced carpal spasm can occur with hypocalcemia or hypomagnesemia. Occluding the brachial artery with a blood pressure cuff for 3 minutes can produce carpal spasm that mimics the spasm that occurs with hypocalcemia or hypomagnesemia.

Trousseau's sign (Fig. 4-7) can be elicited by inflating a blood pressure cuff on the upper arm to about 20 mm Hg above systolic pressure; within 2 to 5 minutes, carpal spasm (an adducted thumb, flexed wrist and metacarpophalangeal joints, extended interphalangeal joints with fingers together) will occur as ischemia of the ulnar nerve develops. *Chvostek's sign* consists of twitching of muscles supplied by the facial nerve when the nerve is tapped about 2 cm anterior to the earlobe, just below the zygomatic arch.

Seizures occur because hypocalcemia causes irritability of the CNS as well as of the peripheral nerves. Other changes associated with hypocalcemia include mental changes, such as depression, impaired memory, confusion, delirium, and even hallucinations. A prolonged QT interval is seen on the ECG due to prolongation of the ST segment, which predisposes patients to a form of ventricular tachycardia called *torsades de pointes* (see Chapter 17). Respiratory effects with decreasing calcium include dyspnea and laryngospasm (stridor). Signs and symptoms of chronic hypocalcemia include hyperactive bowel sounds, dry and brittle hair and nails, and abnormal clotting. When evaluating serum calcium levels, variables such as the serum albumin level and the arterial pH must be considered. Because abnormalities in serum albumin levels may affect interpretation of the serum calcium level, it may be necessary to calculate the corrected serum calcium if the serum albumin level is abnormal. For every decrease in serum albumin of 1 g/dL below 4 g/dL, the total serum calcium level is underestimated by approximately 0.8 mg/dL. The following is a quick method to calculate the corrected serum calcium level:

Corrected calcium = measured calcium
+ 0.8 (4.0 − measured serum albumin)

An example of the calculations needed to obtain the corrected total serum calcium level is as follows: A patient's reported serum albumin level is 2.5 g/dL; the reported serum calcium level is 10.5 mg/dL. First, the decrease in serum

albumin level from normal (i.e., the difference from the normal albumin concentration of 4 g/dL) is calculated: 4 g/dL − 2.5 g/dL = 1.5 g/dL. Next, multiply 0.8 (1.5) = 1.2

Finally, 1.2 mg/dL is added to 10.5 mg/dL (the reported serum calcium level) to obtain the corrected total serum calcium level: 1.2 mg/dL + 10.5 mg/dL = 11.7 mg/dL

The ionized calcium level is usually normal in patients with reduced total serum calcium levels and concomitant hypoalbuminemia.

Ideally, the ionized level of calcium should be measured in the laboratory. However, in many laboratories, only the total calcium level is reported; therefore, the concentration of the ionized fraction must be estimated by simultaneous measurement of the serum albumin level. Additionally, PTH levels and magnesium and phosphorus levels need to be assessed to identify possible causes of decreased calcium.

Medical Management

Acute symptomatic hypocalcemia is life-threatening and requires prompt treatment with IV administration of calcium. Although calcium chloride produces a significantly higher ionized calcium level than does calcium gluconate, it is not used as often because it is more irritating and can cause sloughing of tissue if it infiltrates. Administering IV calcium too rapidly can cause cardiac arrest, preceded by bradycardia. IV administration of calcium is particularly dangerous in patients receiving digitalis-derived medications, because calcium ions exert an effect similar to that of digitalis and can cause digitalis toxicity, with adverse cardiac effects. Therefore, calcium should be diluted in D_5W and administered via a slow IV infusion using a volumetric infusion pump. The IV site must be observed often for any evidence of infiltration because of the risk of extravasation and resultant cellulitis or necrosis. A 0.9% sodium chloride solution should not be used with calcium because it increases renal calcium loss. Solutions containing phosphates or bicarbonate should not be used with calcium because they cause precipitation when calcium is added. The nurse must clarify with the provider which calcium salt to administer, because calcium gluconate yields 4.5 mEq of calcium, and calcium chloride provides 13.6 mEq of calcium. Because calcium can cause postural hypotension, the patient is kept in bed during IV replacement, and blood pressure is monitored.

Vitamin D therapy may be instituted to increase calcium absorption from the GI tract. Aluminum hydroxide, calcium acetate, or calcium carbonate antacids may be prescribed to decrease elevated phosphorus levels before treating hypocalcemia in the patient with chronic renal failure. Increasing the dietary intake of calcium to at least 1,000 to 1,500 mg/day in the adult is recommended; calcium-containing foods include milk products; green, leafy vegetables; canned salmon; sardines; and fresh oysters. Hypomagnesemia can also cause tetany; if the tetany does not respond to IV calcium, then a low magnesium level is considered as a possible cause.

Nursing Management

It is important to observe for hypocalcemia in patients at risk. Seizure precautions are initiated if hypocalcemia is severe. The status of the airway is closely monitored, because laryngeal stridor can occur. A tracheotomy tray should be kept at the bedside, and a manual resuscitation bag nearby, in case of laryngospasm in patients with audible stridor. Safety precautions are taken, as indicated, if confusion is present. Because of the cardiac complications, ECG monitoring should be instituted to detect changes in heart rate and rhythm, especially if the patient is receiving digoxin.

People who have a high risk for osteoporosis are instructed about the need for adequate dietary calcium intake; it is important to teach the patient which foods are rich in calcium. The nurse must also advise the patient to consider calcium supplements if sufficient calcium is not consumed in the diet. Such supplements should be taken in divided doses with meals. In addition, the value of regular weight-bearing exercise in decreasing bone loss should be emphasized, as well as the effect of medications on calcium balance. For example, alcohol and caffeine in high doses inhibit calcium absorption, and moderate cigarette smoking increases urinary calcium excretion. Additional teaching includes discussion of bisphosphonate medications to reduce the rate of bone loss. Teaching also includes strategies to reduce the risk of falls. The patient is also cautioned to avoid the overuse of laxatives and antacids that contain phosphorus, because their use decreases calcium absorption.

HYPERCALCEMIA (CALCIUM EXCESS)

Hypercalcemia (excess of calcium in the plasma) is a dangerous imbalance. Hypercalcemic crisis (an acute increase in calcium level) has an extremely high mortality rate if not corrected promptly, often related to cardiac arrest (Porth & Matfin, 2009).

Pathophysiology

Ninety percent of hypercalcemia cases are related to either malignancy or hyperparathyroidism (Skugor, 2010). Considered an oncological emergency, hypercalcemia occurs in 10% to 20% of patients with advanced cancer (Yahalom, 2008). It is associated with increased osteoclast activity resulting in bone demineralization and/or tumor-produced factors that affect bone resorption and/or tubular calcium reabsorption. Tumor cells can secrete PTH-related protein, resulting in increased serum calcium. The excessive PTH secretion associated with hyperparathyroidism causes increased release of calcium from the bones and increased intestinal and renal absorption of calcium. Calcifications of soft tissue occur when the calcium–phosphorus product (serum calcium × serum phosphorus) exceeds 70 mg/dL.

Bone mineral is lost during immobilization, and sometimes this causes elevation of total (and especially ionized)

calcium in the bloodstream. Symptomatic hypercalcemia from immobilization is rare; when it does occur, it is virtually limited to people with high calcium turnover rates (e.g., adolescents during a growth spurt). Most cases of hypercalcemia secondary to immobility occur after severe or multiple fractures or spinal cord injury.

Thiazide diuretics can cause a slight elevation in serum calcium levels because they potentiate the action of PTH on the kidneys, reducing urinary calcium excretion. A rare condition, called *milk-alkali syndrome* has occurred in patients with peptic ulcer treated previously for a prolonged period with milk and alkaline antacids, particularly calcium carbonate. Vitamin A and D intoxication, as well as the use of lithium, can cause calcium excess.

Clinical Manifestations and Assessment

As a rule, the symptoms of hypercalcemia are proportional to the degree of elevation of the serum calcium level. Hypercalcemia reduces neuromuscular excitability because it suppresses activity at the myoneural junction. Symptoms such as muscle weakness, incoordination, anorexia, and constipation may be caused by decreased tone in smooth and striated muscle. Cardiovascular effects include hypertension and a shortened QT interval, which can cause increased sensitivity to digitalis and deposition of calcium in heart valves, myocardium, or coronary arteries (Skugor, 2010). Cardiac standstill can occur when the serum calcium level is about 18 mg/dL (4.5 mmol/L).

Anorexia, nausea, vomiting, and constipation are common symptoms of hypercalcemia. Abdominal and bone pain may also be present. Abdominal distention and paralytic ileus may complicate severe hypercalcemic crisis. Excessive urination due to disturbed renal tubular function produced by hypercalcemia may occur. In fact, nephrogenic diabetes insipidus is seen in 20% of patients with this disorder (Skugor, 2010). Severe thirst secondary to the polyuria caused by the high solute (calcium) load is expected. Although uncommon, patients with chronic hypercalcemia may develop symptoms similar to those of peptic ulcer because hypercalcemia increases the secretion of acid and pepsin by the stomach.

Confusion, impaired memory, slurred speech, lethargy, acute psychotic behavior, or coma may occur. The more severe symptoms tend to appear when the serum calcium level is approximately 16 mg/dL (4 mmol/L) or higher. However, some patients become profoundly disturbed with serum calcium levels of only 12 mg/dL (3 mmol/L). These symptoms resolve as serum calcium levels return to normal after treatment.

Hypercalcemic crisis refers to an acute rise in the serum calcium level to 17 mg/dL (4.3 mmol/L) or higher. Severe thirst and polyuria are often present. Other findings may include muscle weakness, intractable nausea, abdominal cramps, obstipation (very severe constipation) or diarrhea, peptic ulcer symptoms, and bone pain. Lethargy, confusion,

and coma may also occur. This condition is very dangerous and may result in cardiac arrest. The mnemonic "bones (bone pain), stones (kidney), groans (pain) and psychic moans (anxiety, psychiatric symptoms)" may be helpful to recall the cascade of symptoms associated with hypercalcemia. The serum calcium level is greater than 10.2 mg/dL (2.6 mmol/L). The double-antibody PTH test may be used to differentiate between primary hyperparathyroidism and malignancy as a cause of hypercalcemia: PTH levels are increased in primary or secondary hyperparathyroidism and suppressed in malignancy. X-rays may reveal the presence of osteoporosis if the patient has hypercalcemia secondary to a malignancy or bone cavitation. A 24-hour urine calcium collection may be ordered; hypercalciuria is defined as calcium excretion of greater than 400 mg/day.

Medical Management

Therapeutic aims in hypercalcemia include decreasing the serum calcium level and reversing the process causing hypercalcemia. Treating the underlying cause (e.g., chemotherapy for a malignancy, partial parathyroidectomy for hyperparathyroidism) is essential.

General measures include administering fluids to dilute serum calcium and promote its excretion by the kidneys, mobilizing the patient, and restricting intake of fluids and medications that contain calcium. IV administration of 0.9% sodium chloride solution is expected since it temporarily dilutes the serum calcium level and increases urinary calcium excretion by inhibiting tubular reabsorption of calcium. Furosemide (Lasix) is often used in conjunction with administration of a saline solution; in addition to causing diuresis, furosemide increases calcium excretion and is useful in preventing fluid volume excess associated with saline administration.

Calcitonin can be used to lower the serum calcium level and is particularly useful for patients with heart disease or renal failure who cannot tolerate large sodium loads. Calcitonin reduces bone resorption, increases the depositing of calcium and phosphorus in the bones, and increases urinary excretion of calcium and phosphate. Although several forms are available, calcitonin derived from salmon is commonly used. Skin testing for allergy to salmon calcitonin is necessary before the hormone is administered. Systemic allergic reactions are possible because this hormone is a protein; resistance to the medication may develop later because of antibody formation. Calcitonin is administered by intramuscular injection rather than subcutaneously, because patients with hypercalcemia have poor perfusion of subcutaneous tissue.

For patients with cancer, treatment is directed at controlling the condition by surgery, chemotherapy, or radiation therapy. Corticosteroids may be used to decrease bone turnover and tubular reabsorption for patients with sarcoidosis, myelomas, lymphomas, and leukemias; patients with solid tumors are less responsive. The bisphosphonates inhibit osteoclast activity and may be used to lower serum calcium

levels. Mithramycin, a cytotoxic antibiotic, inhibits bone resorption and thus lowers the serum calcium level. This agent must be used cautiously because it has significant side effects, including thrombocytopenia, nephrotoxicity, rebound hypercalcemia when discontinued, and hepatotoxicity. Inorganic phosphate salts can be administered orally or by nasogastric tube (in the form of Phospho-Soda or Neutra-Phos), rectally (as retention enemas), or intravenously. IV phosphate therapy is used with extreme caution in the treatment of hypercalcemia, because it can cause severe tissue calcification, hypotension, tetany, and acute renal failure. Typically, IV phosphate is reserved for hypercalcemia that is unresponsive to other agents. Finally, hemodialysis or peritoneal dialysis with low calcium levels in dialysis fluid may be considered since both treatments are effective for removing calcium from circulation. Additionally, dialysis may be considered for patients with renal insufficiency and congestive heart failure in which saline infusion is not suitable (Skugor, 2010).

Nursing Management

It is important to monitor for hypercalcemia in patients who are at risk. Interventions such as increasing patient mobility and encouraging fluids can help prevent hypercalcemia, or at least minimize its severity. Fluids containing sodium should be administered unless contraindicated because sodium favors calcium excretion. Patients are encouraged to drink 3 to 4 quarts of fluid daily. Adequate fiber should be provided in the diet to offset the tendency for constipation. Safety precautions are implemented, as necessary, when mental symptoms of hypercalcemia are present. The patient and family are informed that these mental changes are reversible with treatment. Increased calcium potentiates the effects of digitalis; therefore, the patient is assessed for signs and symptoms of digitalis toxicity. Because ECG changes (premature ventricular contractions, paroxysmal atrial tachycardia, and heart block) can occur, the cardiac rate and rhythm are monitored for any abnormalities.

MAGNESIUM IMBALANCES

Magnesium is the most abundant intracellular cation after potassium. It acts as an activator for many intracellular enzyme systems and plays a role in both carbohydrate and protein metabolism. The normal serum magnesium level is 1.3 to 2.3 mEq/L (1.8 to 3.0 mg/dL; 0.8 to 1.2 mmol/L). Approximately one-third of serum magnesium is bound to protein; the remaining two thirds exists as free cations—the active component (Mg^{++}). Magnesium balance is important in neuromuscular function. Because magnesium acts directly on the myoneural junction, variations in the serum concentration of magnesium affect neuromuscular irritability and contractility. Magnesium produces its sedative effect at the neuromuscular junction, probably by inhibiting the release of the neurotransmitter acetylcholine.

Magnesium exerts effects on the cardiovascular system, acting peripherally to produce vasodilation. Magnesium is thought to have a direct effect on peripheral arteries and arterioles, which results in a decreased total peripheral resistance. IV magnesium may also be helpful in patients with acute asthma by potentially improving both bronchodilation and airflow. Magnesium is predominantly found in bone and soft tissues. It is primarily eliminated by the kidneys.

HYPOMAGNESEMIA (MAGNESIUM DEFICIT)

Hypomagnesemia refers to a below-normal serum magnesium concentration (1.3 to 2.3 mEq/L; 1.8 to 3.0 mg/dL; 0.8 to 1.2 mmol/L). Magnesium is similar to calcium in two aspects: (1) it is the ionized fraction of magnesium that is primarily involved in neuromuscular activity and other physiologic processes, and (2) magnesium levels should be evaluated in combination with albumin levels. Low serum albumin levels decrease total magnesium.

Pathophysiology

Hypomagnesemia is a common yet often overlooked imbalance in acutely and critically ill patients. It may occur with withdrawal from alcohol and administration of tube feedings or parenteral nutrition.

An important route of magnesium loss is the GI tract. Loss of magnesium from the GI tract may occur with nasogastric suction, diarrhea, or fistulas. Because fluid from the lower GI tract has a higher concentration of magnesium (10 to 14 mEq/L) than fluid from the upper tract (1 to 2 mEq/L), losses from diarrhea and intestinal fistulas are more likely to induce magnesium deficit than are those from gastric suction. Although magnesium losses are relatively small in nasogastric suction, hypomagnesemia will occur if losses are prolonged and magnesium is not replaced through IV infusion. Because the distal small bowel is the major site of magnesium absorption, any disruption in small-bowel function, as in intestinal resection or inflammatory bowel disease, can lead to hypomagnesemia.

Alcoholism is currently the most common cause of symptomatic hypomagnesemia in the United States. Hypomagnesemia is particularly troublesome during treatment of alcohol withdrawal. Therefore, the serum magnesium level should be routinely measured in patients undergoing withdrawal from alcohol. The serum magnesium level may be normal on admission but may decrease as a result of metabolic changes, such as the intracellular shift of magnesium associated with IV glucose administration.

During nutritional replacement, the major cellular electrolytes move from the serum to newly synthesized cells. Patients on enteral or parenteral feedings should have magnesium levels routinely measured as serious hypomagnesemia can occur

with magnesium-deficient formulas, especially in those who have undergone a period of starvation. Other causes of hypomagnesemia include the administration of aminoglycosides, cyclosporine, cisplatin, diuretics, digitalis, and amphotericin, and the rapid administration of citrated blood, especially to patients with renal or hepatic disease. Magnesium deficiency often occurs in diabetic ketoacidosis, secondary to increased renal excretion during osmotic diuresis and shifting of magnesium into the cells with insulin therapy. Other contributing causes are sepsis, burns, and hypothermia.

Clinical Manifestations and Assessment

Clinical manifestations of hypomagnesemia are largely confined to the neuromuscular system. Some of the effects are due directly to the low serum magnesium level; others are due to secondary changes in potassium and calcium metabolism. Symptoms do not usually occur until the serum magnesium level has dropped to less than 1 mEq/L (0.5 mmol/L).

Among the neuromuscular changes are hyperexcitability with muscle weakness, tremors, and *athetoid movements* (slow, involuntary twisting and writhing). Others include tetany, generalized tonic–clonic or focal seizures, laryngeal stridor, and positive Chvostek's and Trousseau's signs (see earlier discussion), which occur, in part, because of accompanying hypocalcemia.

Hypomagnesemia may be accompanied by marked alterations in mood. Apathy, depression, apprehension, and extreme agitation have been noted, as well as ataxia, dizziness, insomnia, and confusion. At times, delirium, auditory or visual hallucinations, and frank psychoses may occur.

On laboratory analysis, the serum magnesium level is less than 1.3 mEq/L or 1.8 mg/dL (0.75 mmol/L). Hypomagnesemia is frequently associated with hypokalemia and hypocalcemia. About 25% of magnesium is protein-bound, principally to albumin. A decreased serum albumin level can, therefore, reduce the measured total magnesium concentration. ECG evaluations reflect magnesium, calcium, and potassium deficiencies, tachyarrhythmias, prolonged PR and QT intervals, widening QRS, ST-segment depression, flattened T waves, and a prominent U wave. Torsades de pointes is associated with a low magnesium level. Premature ventricular contractions, paroxysmal atrial tachycardia, and heart block may also occur. Digitalis toxicity is associated with low serum magnesium levels. This is important, because patients receiving digoxin are also likely to be receiving diuretic therapy, predisposing them to renal loss of magnesium. Urine magnesium levels may be helpful in identifying causes of magnesium depletion and are measured after a loading dose of magnesium sulfate is administered.

Medical Management

Mild magnesium deficiency can be corrected by diet alone. Principal dietary sources of magnesium, which is a compo-

nent of chlorophyll, are green leafy vegetables, nuts, seeds, legumes, whole grains, and seafood. Magnesium is also plentiful in peanut butter and cocoa.

If necessary, magnesium salts can be administered orally in an oxide or gluconate form to replace continuous excessive losses. Diarrhea is a common complication of excessive ingestion of magnesium. Patients receiving parenteral nutrition require magnesium in the IV solution to prevent hypomagnesemia. Magnesium sulfate must be administered intravenously by an infusion pump typically at a rate of 1 to 2 grams over an hour. A bolus dose of magnesium sulfate given too rapidly can produce alterations in cardiac conduction leading to heart block or asystole. Vital signs must be assessed frequently during magnesium administration to detect changes in cardiac rate or rhythm, hypotension, and respiratory distress. Monitoring urine output is essential before, during, and after magnesium administration; the provider is notified if urine volume decreases to less than 100 mL over 4 hours (Lippincott, 2010). Calcium gluconate must be readily available to treat hypocalcemic tetany or hypermagnesemia.

Overt symptoms of hypomagnesemia are treated with parenteral administration of magnesium. Magnesium sulfate is the most commonly used magnesium salt. Serial measurements of serum magnesium levels can be used to regulate the dosage.

Nursing Management

The nurse should be aware of patients who are at risk for hypomagnesemia and observe them for its signs and symptoms. Patients receiving digitalis are monitored closely because a deficit of magnesium can predispose them to digitalis toxicity. If hypomagnesemia is severe, seizure precautions are implemented. Other safety precautions are instituted, as indicated, if confusion is observed.

Because difficulty in swallowing (dysphagia) may occur in magnesium-depleted patients, a nursing swallowing evaluation should be performed before oral medications or foods are offered. Dysphagia is probably related to the athetoid or *choreiform* (rapid, involuntary, and irregular jerking) movements associated with magnesium deficit. To determine neuromuscular irritability, the nurse needs to assess and grade deep tendon reflexes (refer to Chapter 43).

Teaching plays a major role in treating magnesium deficit, particularly that resulting from abuse of diuretic or laxative medications. In such cases, the nurse instructs the patient about the need to consume magnesium-rich foods. For patients experiencing hypomagnesemia from abuse of alcohol, the nurse provides teaching, counseling, support, and possible referral to alcohol abstinence programs or other professional help.

HYPERMAGNESEMIA (MAGNESIUM EXCESS)

Hypermagnesemia is a rare electrolyte abnormality because the kidneys are efficient in excreting magnesium. A serum

magnesium level can appear falsely elevated if blood specimens are allowed to hemolyze or are drawn from an extremity with a tourniquet that was applied too tightly or for too long a period of time prior to blood draw.

Pathophysiology

By far the most common cause of hypermagnesemia is renal failure. In fact, most patients with advanced renal failure have at least a slight elevation in serum magnesium levels. This condition is aggravated when such patients receive magnesium to control seizures or inadvertently take one of the many commercial antacids that contain magnesium salts.

Hypermagnesemia can occur in a patient with untreated diabetic ketoacidosis when catabolism causes the release of cellular magnesium that cannot be excreted because of profound fluid volume depletion and resulting oliguria. An excess of magnesium can also result from excessive magnesium administered to treat hypertension of pregnancy or to treat low hypomagnesemia. Increased serum magnesium levels can also occur in adrenocortical insufficiency, Addison's disease, or hypothermia. Excessive use of antacids (e.g., Maalox, Riopan, Mylanta); laxatives (Milk of Magnesia); and medications that decrease GI motility, including opioids and anticholinergics, can also increase serum magnesium levels. Decreased elimination of magnesium or its increased absorption due to intestinal hypomotility from any cause can contribute to hypermagnesemia. Lithium intoxication can also cause an increase in serum magnesium levels.

Clinical Manifestations and Assessment

Acute elevation of the serum magnesium level depresses the CNS as well as the peripheral neuromuscular junction. At mildly increased levels, there is a tendency for lowered blood pressure because of peripheral vasodilation. Nausea, vomiting, weakness, soft tissue calcifications, facial flushing, and sensations of warmth may also occur. At higher magnesium concentrations, lethargy, difficulty speaking (dysarthria), and drowsiness can occur. Deep tendon reflexes are lost, and muscle weakness and paralysis may develop. The respiratory center is depressed when serum magnesium levels exceed 10 mEq/L (5 mmol/L). Coma, atrioventricular heart block, and cardiac arrest can occur when the serum magnesium level is greatly elevated and not treated. High levels of magnesium also result in platelet clumping and delayed thrombin formation. On laboratory analysis, the serum magnesium level is greater than 2.5 mEq/L or 3.0 mg/dL (1.25 mmol/L). Increased potassium and calcium are present concurrently. ECG findings may include a prolonged PR interval, tall T waves, a widened QRS, and a prolonged QT interval, as well as an atrioventricular block.

Medical Management

Hypermagnesemia can be prevented by avoiding the administration of magnesium to patients with renal failure and by carefully monitoring seriously ill patients who are receiving magnesium salts. In patients with severe hypermagnesemia, all parenteral and oral magnesium salts are discontinued. In emergencies, such as respiratory depression or defective cardiac conduction, ventilatory support and IV calcium gluconate are indicated. In addition, hemodialysis with a magnesium-free dialysate can reduce the serum magnesium to a safe level within hours. Administration of loop diuretics (Lasix) and sodium chloride or lactated Ringer's IV solution enhances magnesium excretion in patients with adequate renal function. IV calcium gluconate antagonizes the cardiovascular and neuromuscular effects of magnesium.

Nursing Management

Patients at risk for hypermagnesemia are identified and assessed. The nurse monitors the vital signs, noting hypotension and shallow respirations, or ECG abnormalities. The nurse also observes for decreased deep tendon reflexes and changes in the level of consciousness. Medications that contain magnesium are not administered to patients with renal failure or compromised renal function, and patients with renal failure are cautioned to check with their health care providers before taking over-the-counter medications. Caution is essential when preparing and administering magnesium-containing fluids parenterally, because available parenteral magnesium solutions (e.g., 2 mL ampules, 50 mL vials) differ in concentration.

PHOSPHORUS IMBALANCES

Phosphorus is a critical constituent of all the body's tissues. It is essential to the function of muscle and RBC, the formation of adenosine triphosphate (ATP) and of 2,3-diphosphoglycerate, which facilitates release of oxygen from hemoglobin, and the maintenance of acid–base balance, as well as to the nervous system and the intermediary metabolism of carbohydrate, protein, and fat. It provides structural support to bones and teeth in the form of phosphate. Phosphorus is the primary anion of the ICF. About 85% of phosphorus is located in bones and teeth, 14% in soft tissue, and less than 1% in the ECF. The normal serum phosphorus level is 2.5 to 4.5 mg/dL (0.8 to 1.45 mmol/L).

HYPOPHOSPHATEMIA (PHOSPHORUS DEFICIT)

Pathophysiology

Hypophosphatemia is a below-normal serum concentration of inorganic phosphorus; it may occur under a variety of circumstances in which total body phosphorus stores are

normal. Conversely, phosphorus deficiency is an abnormally low content of phosphorus in lean tissues that may exist in the absence of hypophosphatemia. It can be caused by an intracellular shift of potassium from serum into cells, by increased urinary excretion of potassium, or by decreased intestinal absorption of potassium.

Hypophosphatemia may occur during the administration of calories to patients with severe protein–calorie malnutrition. It is most likely to occur with overzealous intake or administration of simple carbohydrates. This syndrome can be induced in anyone with severe protein–calorie malnutrition, such as patients with anorexia nervosa or alcoholism, or elderly debilitated patients who are unable to eat. Approximately 50% of patients hospitalized due to chronic alcoholism have hypophosphatemia.

Marked hypophosphatemia may develop in malnourished patients who receive parenteral nutrition if the phosphorus loss is not adequately corrected. Other causes of hypophosphatemia include pain, heat stroke, prolonged intense hyperventilation, alcohol withdrawal, poor dietary intake, diabetic ketoacidosis, hepatic encephalopathy, and major thermal burns. Low magnesium levels, low potassium levels, and hyperparathyroidism related to increased urinary losses of phosphorus contribute to hypophosphatemia. Loss of phosphorus through the kidneys also occurs with acute volume expansion, osmotic diuresis, use of carbonic anhydrase inhibitors (acetazolamide [Diamox]), and some malignancies. Respiratory alkalosis can cause a decrease in phosphorus because of an intracellular shift of phosphorus, which often stimulates intracellular glycolysis.

Excess phosphorus binding by antacids containing magnesium, calcium, or albumin may decrease the phosphorus available from the diet to an amount lower than required to maintain serum phosphorus balance. The degree of hypophosphatemia depends on the amount of phosphorus in the diet compared to the dose of antacid. Phosphate loss can occur with chronic diarrhea or through severe potassium restriction. Vitamin D regulates intestinal ion absorption; therefore, a deficiency of vitamin D may cause decreased calcium and phosphate (phosphorus) levels, which may lead to osteomalacia (softened, brittle bones).

Clinical Manifestations and Assessment

A wide range of neurologic symptoms, such as irritability, fatigue, apprehension, weakness, numbness, paresthesias, dysarthria, dysphagia, diplopia, confusion, seizures, and coma, may occur. Low levels of diphosphoglycerate may reduce the delivery of oxygen to peripheral tissues, resulting in tissue anoxia. Hypoxia then leads to an increase in respiratory rate and respiratory alkalosis, causing phosphorus to move into the cells and potentiating hypophosphatemia. Hemolytic anemia may lead to pale skin and conjunctivae. It is thought that hypophosphatemia may predispose a person to infection due to a decrease in granulocyte function.

Muscle damage may develop as the ATP level in the muscle tissue declines. Clinical manifestations are muscle weakness, which may be subtle or profound and may affect any muscle group, muscle pain, and at times acute rhabdomyolysis (disintegration of striated muscle). Weakness of respiratory muscles may greatly impair ventilation. Hypophosphatemia also may predispose a person to insulin resistance and thus hyperglycemia. Chronic loss of phosphorus can cause bruising and bleeding from platelet dysfunction.

On laboratory analysis, the serum phosphorus level is less than 2.5 mg/dL (0.80 mmol/L) in adults. When reviewing laboratory results, the nurse should keep in mind that glucose or insulin administration causes a slight decrease in the serum phosphorus level. If hypophosphatemia is associated with hyperparathyroidism, the serum PTH levels are increased. Likewise, if etiology of hypophosphatemia is related to increased osteoblastic activity serum alkaline, phosphatase is increased. X-rays may show skeletal changes of osteomalacia or rickets.

Medical Management

Prevention of hypophosphatemia is the goal. In patients at risk for hypophosphatemia, serum phosphate levels should be closely monitored and correction initiated before deficits become severe. Adequate amounts of phosphorus should be added to parenteral solutions, and attention should be paid to the phosphorus levels in enteral feeding solutions.

Severe hypophosphatemia is dangerous and requires prompt attention. Aggressive IV phosphorus correction is usually limited to the patient whose serum phosphorus levels decrease to less than 1 mg/dL (0.3 mmol/L) and whose GI tract is not functioning. Possible dangers of IV administration of phosphorus include tetany from hypocalcemia and calcifications in tissues (blood vessels, heart, lung, kidney, eyes) from hyperphosphatemia. IV preparations of phosphorus are available as sodium or potassium phosphate. The rate of phosphorus administration should not exceed 10 mEq/h, and the site should be carefully monitored because tissue sloughing and necrosis can occur with infiltration. In less acute situations, oral phosphorus replacement is usually adequate.

Nursing Management

The nurse identifies patients who are at risk for hypophosphatemia and monitors them. Because malnourished patients receiving parenteral nutrition are at risk when calories are introduced too aggressively, preventive measures involve gradually introducing the solution to avoid rapid shifts of phosphorus into the cells.

For patients with documented hypophosphatemia, careful attention is given to preventing infection, because hypophosphatemia may alter the granulocytes. In patients requiring correction of phosphorus losses, the nurse frequently monitors serum phosphorus levels and documents and reports

early signs of hypophosphatemia (apprehension, confusion, change in level of consciousness). If the patient experiences mild hypophosphatemia, foods such as milk and milk products, organ meats, nuts, fish, poultry, and whole grains should be encouraged. With moderate hypophosphatemia, supplements such as Neutra-Phos capsules (250 mg phosphorus/capsule) or Fleet's Phospho-Soda (815 mg phosphorus/5 mL) may be prescribed.

HYPERPHOSPHATEMIA (PHOSPHORUS EXCESS)

Hyperphosphatemia is a serum phosphorus level that exceeds normal. Various conditions can lead to this imbalance, but the most common is renal failure. Other causes include increased intake, decreased output, or a shift from the intracellular to extracellular space. Other causes include chemotherapy for neoplastic disease, hypoparathyroidism, metabolic or respiratory acidosis, diabetic ketoacidosis, acute hemolysis, high phosphate intake, profound muscle necrosis, and increased phosphorus absorption. The primary complication of increased phosphorus is metastatic calcification (soft tissue, joints, and arteries), which occurs when the calcium–magnesium product (calcium × magnesium) exceeds 70 mg/dL.

Clinical Manifestations and Assessment

An increased serum phosphorus level causes few symptoms. Symptoms that do occur usually result from decreased calcium levels and soft tissue calcifications. The most important short-term consequence is tetany. Because of the reciprocal relationship between phosphorus and calcium, a high serum phosphate level tends to cause a low serum calcium concentration. Tetany can result, causing tingling sensations in the fingertips and around the mouth. Anorexia, nausea, vomiting, bone and joint pain, muscle weakness, hyperreflexia, and tachycardia may occur.

The major long-term consequence is soft tissue calcification, which occurs mainly in patients with a reduced glomerular filtration rate. High serum levels of inorganic phosphorus promote precipitation of calcium phosphate in nonosseous sites, decreasing urine output, impairing vision, and producing palpitations.

On laboratory analysis, the serum phosphorus level exceeds 4.5 mg/dL (1.5 mmol/L) in adults. Serum phosphorus levels are normally higher in children, presumably because of the high rate of skeletal growth. The serum calcium level is useful also for diagnosing the primary disorder and assessing the effects of treatments. X-ray studies may show skeletal changes with abnormal bone development. PTH levels are decreased in hypoparathyroidism. BUN and creatinine levels are used to assess renal function. Renal ultrasonography may be indicated as part of the diagnostic assessment for renal failure; bone studies and coronary calcification studies also provide information about the chronicity and prognosis of renal failure.

Medical Management

When possible, treatment is directed at the underlying disorder. For example, hyperphosphatemia may be related to volume depletion or respiratory or metabolic acidosis. In renal failure, elevated PTH production contributes to a high phosphorus level and bone disease. Measures to decrease the serum phosphate level in these patients include vitamin D preparations, such as calcitriol, which is available in both oral (Rocaltrol) and parenteral (Calcijex, paricalcitol [Zemplar]) forms. IV administration of calcitriol does not increase the serum calcium unless its dose is excessive, thus permitting more aggressive treatment of hyperphosphatemia with calcium-binding antacids (calcium carbonate or calcium citrate), phosphate-binding gels or antacids, restriction of dietary phosphate, forced diuresis with a loop diuretic, volume repletion with saline, and dialysis. Surgery may be indicated for removal of large calcium-phosphorus deposits.

Nursing Management

The nurse monitors patients at risk for hyperphosphatemia. If a low-phosphorus diet is prescribed, the patient is instructed to avoid phosphorus-rich foods such as hard cheese, cream, nuts, meats, whole-grain cereals, dried fruits, dried vegetables, kidneys, sardines, sweetbreads, and foods made with milk. When appropriate, the nurse instructs the patient to avoid phosphate-containing substances such as laxatives and enemas. The nurse also teaches the patient to recognize the signs of impending hypocalcemia and to monitor for changes in urine output.

CHLORIDE IMBALANCES

Chloride, the major anion of the ECF, is found more in interstitial and lymph fluid compartments than in blood. Chloride is also contained in gastric and pancreatic juices, sweat, bile, and saliva. The choroid plexus, where cerebrospinal fluid forms in the brain, depends on sodium and chloride to attract water to form the fluid portion of the cerebrospinal fluid. Sodium and chloride in water make up the composition of the ECF and assist in determining osmotic pressure. The serum level of chloride reflects a change in dilution or concentration of the ECF and does so in direct proportion to the sodium concentration. Serum osmolality parallels chloride levels as well. The normal serum chloride level is 97 to 107 mEq/L (97 to 107 mmol/L). Inside the cell, the chloride level is 4 mEq/L.

Plasma bicarbonate has an inverse relationship with chloride. For example, the carbonic anhydrase reaction in RBCs generates both hydrogen and bicarbonate from metabolically produced CO_2. Hydrogen facilitates the dissociation of oxygen

from hemoglobin. The intracellular accumulation of bicarbonate is prevented by its movement out of the cell into the plasma. To maintain electrical neutrality, chloride enters the RBC, a response referred to as the *chloride shift*. It is important to note that when the level of one of these three electrolytes (sodium, bicarbonate, or chloride) is disturbed, the other two are also affected. Chloride is important not only in maintaining acid–base balance, but it also mediates the hyperpolarizing effect of many neurotransmitters on the membrane potential. Chloride is primarily obtained from the diet as table salt.

HYPOCHLOREMIA (CHLORIDE DEFICIT)

Chloride control depends on the intake of chloride and the excretion and reabsorption of its ions in the kidneys. Chloride is produced in the stomach, where it combines with hydrogen to form hydrochloric acid. A small amount of chloride is lost in the feces. GI tube drainage and severe vomiting and diarrhea, laxatives, ileostomy, and fistulas are risk factors for hypochloremia. Administration of chloride-deficient formulas, low sodium intake, decreased serum sodium levels, metabolic alkalosis, prolonged therapy with IV dextrose (water intoxication), diuretic therapy, burns, and fever may also cause hypochloremia. As chloride decreases (usually because of volume depletion), sodium and bicarbonate ions are retained by the kidney to balance the loss. Bicarbonate accumulates in the ECF, which raises the pH and leads to hypochloremic metabolic alkalosis.

Clinical Manifestations and Assessment

Because hypochloremia rarely occurs in the absence of other abnormalities, signs and symptoms of hypochloremia are associated with hyponatremia, hypokalemia, and metabolic alkalosis. Metabolic alkalosis is a disorder that results in a high pH and a high serum bicarbonate level as a result of excess alkali intake or loss of hydrogen ions. With compensation, the partial pressure of carbon dioxide in arterial blood (PaCO$_2$) increases to 50 mm Hg. Hyperexcitability of muscles, tetany, hyperactive deep tendon reflexes, weakness, twitching, and muscle cramps may result. Hypokalemia can cause hypochloremia, resulting in cardiac arrhythmias. In addition, because low chloride levels parallel low sodium levels, a water excess may occur. Hyponatremia can cause seizures and coma.

In addition to the chloride level, sodium and potassium levels are also evaluated, because these electrolytes are lost along with chloride. Arterial blood gas analysis identifies the acid–base imbalance, which is usually metabolic alkalosis. The urine chloride level, which is also measured, decreases in hypochloremia.

Medical Management

Treatment involves correcting the cause of hypochloremia and the contributing electrolyte and acid–base imbalances.

Normal saline (0.9% sodium chloride) or half-strength saline (0.45% sodium chloride) solution is administered by IV to replace the chloride. The provider may reevaluate whether the patient receiving a diuretic (loop, osmotic, or thiazide) should discontinue the medications or change to another diuretic.

Foods high in chloride are provided; these include tomato juice, bananas, dates, eggs, cheese, milk, salty broth, canned vegetables, and processed meats. A patient who drinks free water (water without electrolytes) or bottled water excretes large amounts of chloride; therefore, the patient is instructed to avoid this kind of water. Ammonium chloride, an acidifying agent, may be prescribed to treat metabolic alkalosis; the dosage depends on the patient's weight and serum chloride level. This agent is metabolized by the liver, and its effects last for about 3 days. Its use should be avoided in patients with impaired liver or renal function.

Nursing Management

The nurse monitors the patient's I&O, ABG values, and serum electrolyte levels, as well as level of consciousness and muscle strength and movement. Changes are reported to the provider promptly. Vital signs are monitored, and respiratory assessment is carried out frequently. The nurse teaches the patient about foods with high chloride content.

HYPERCHLOREMIA (CHLORIDE EXCESS)

Hyperchloremia exists when the serum level of chloride exceeds 107 mEq/L (107 mmol/L).

Pathophysiology

Because chloride has an affinity for sodium and an inverse relationship with bicarbonate, hyperchloremia is related to hypernatremia, bicarbonate loss, and metabolic acidosis. Hyperchloremic metabolic acidosis is also known as *normal anion gap acidosis* (see later discussion). It is usually caused by the loss of bicarbonate ions via the kidney or the GI tract with a corresponding increase in chloride ions. Chloride ions in the form of acidifying salts accumulate and acidosis occurs with a decrease in bicarbonate ions. Hyperchloremia results from increased intake either by mouth or by hypertonic IV fluid administration. It can also result from decreased chloride loss as in hyperparathyroidism, hyperaldosteronism, and renal failure.

Clinical Manifestations and Assessment

The signs and symptoms of hyperchloremia are the same as those of metabolic acidosis, hypervolemia, and hypernatremia. Tachypnea; weakness; lethargy; deep, rapid respirations; diminished cognitive ability; and hypertension occur. If untreated, hyperchloremia can lead to a decrease in cardiac output, arrhythmias, and coma. A high chloride level is

often accompanied by a high sodium level and fluid retention. Laboratory analysis reveals the serum chloride level is 108 mEq/L (108 mmol/L) or greater, the serum sodium level is greater than 145 mEq/L (145 mmol/L), the serum pH is less than 7.35, and the serum bicarbonate level is less than 22 mEq/L (22 mmol/L).

Medical Management

Correcting the underlying cause of hyperchloremia and restoring electrolyte, fluid, and acid–base balance are essential. Hypotonic IV solutions may be given to restore balance. Lactated Ringer's solution may be prescribed to convert lactate to bicarbonate in the liver, which increases the base bicarbonate level and corrects the acidosis. IV sodium bicarbonate may be administered to increase bicarbonate levels, which leads to the renal excretion of chloride ions as bicarbonate and chloride compete for combination with sodium. Diuretics may be administered to eliminate chloride as well. Sodium, chloride, and fluids are restricted.

Nursing Management

Monitoring vital signs, ABG values, and the patient's I&O status is important to assess the patient's status and the effectiveness of treatment. Assessment findings related to respiratory, neurologic, and cardiac systems are documented, and changes discussed with the provider. The nurse teaches the patient about the diet that should be followed to manage hyperchloremia and maintain adequate hydration.

ACID–BASE DISTURBANCES

Acid–base disturbances are commonly encountered in clinical practice. Identification of the specific acid–base imbalance is important in identifying the underlying cause of the disorder and determining appropriate treatment.

Plasma pH is an indicator of hydrogen ion (H^+) concentration. Homeostatic mechanisms keep pH within a normal range (7.35 to 7.45). These mechanisms consist of buffer systems, the kidneys, and the lungs. The H^+ concentration is extremely important: The greater the concentration, the more acidic the solution and the lower the pH; the lower the H^+ concentration, the more alkaline the solution and the higher the pH. The process causing an acidemia (condition when the blood is acid) is termed either metabolic or respiratory acidosis, whereas the process causing an alkalemia (condition when the blood is alkaline) is either metabolic or respiratory alkalosis. Blood pH must be kept within narrow limits because a pH outside the range of 6.8 or 7.8 is incompatible with life.

Buffer systems prevent major changes in the pH of body fluids by removing or releasing H^+; they can act quickly to prevent excessive changes in H^+ concentration. Hydrogen ions are buffered by both intracellular and extracellular buffers. The body's major extracellular buffer system is the bicarbonate–carbonic acid buffer system, which is assessed when arterial blood gases are measured. The sources for bicarbonate (HCO_3^-) are the intestinal lumen, the pancreas, kidney, and to a lesser extent, diet. The kidneys role is to reabsorb filtered bicarbonate (Seifter, 2007), and make new bicarbonate. The bicarbonate ion acts as a H^+ ion acceptor, and is responsible for buffering 90% of the hydrogen ions in blood. Normally, there are 20 parts of bicarbonate (HCO_3^-) to one part of carbonic acid (H_2CO_3). If this ratio is altered, the pH will change. It is the ratio of HCO_3^- to H_2CO_3 that is important in maintaining pH, not absolute values. Carbon dioxide (CO_2) is regulated by the lungs and, when dissolved in water, becomes carbonic acid ($CO_2 + H_2O = H_2CO_3$). Therefore, when CO_2 is increased, the carbonic acid content is also increased, and vice versa. If either bicarbonate or carbonic acid is increased or decreased so that the 20:1 ratio is no longer maintained, an acid–base imbalance will result. Less important buffer systems in the ECF include the inorganic phosphates and the plasma proteins. Intracellular buffers include proteins, organic and inorganic phosphates and, in RBC, hemoglobin.

The kidneys regulate the bicarbonate level in the ECF; they can regenerate bicarbonate ions as well as reabsorb them from the renal tubular cells. In respiratory acidosis, the kidneys respond to the increased CO_2 (carbonic acid) and decreased pH by excreting hydrogen ions and conserving bicarbonate ions to help restore balance. Whereas in respiratory alkalosis, the kidneys response to the decreased CO_2 (carbonic acid) and increased pH is to retain hydrogen ions and excrete bicarbonate ions to help restore balance. However, the renal compensation for imbalances described above is relatively slow (a matter of hours or days).

The lungs, under the control of the pons and the medulla, regulate the CO_2 and thus the carbonic acid content of the ECF. They do so by adjusting ventilation in response to the amount of CO_2 in the blood. A rise in the partial pressure of CO_2 in arterial blood ($PaCO_2$) is a powerful stimulant to respiration. Of course, the partial pressure of oxygen in arterial blood (PaO_2) also influences respiration. However, its effect is not as marked as that produced by the $PaCO_2$.

In metabolic acidosis, the respiratory rate increases, causing greater elimination of CO_2 (to reduce the acid load). Whereas, in metabolic alkalosis, the respiratory rate decreases, causing CO_2 to be retained (to increase the acid load). Both mechanisms are an attempt to return the pH to normal, and the respiratory response is instantaneous.

To review, a normal pH is 7.35 to 7.45 and is associated with three conditions: (1) a normal level of acid and base; (2) an abnormal process in which too many bases are produced (alkalosis), and the body counteracts this base load by allowing more acids to accumulate (20 base to 1 acid ratio maintained); (3) an abnormal process in which too many acids are produced, and the body counteracts by allowing more base to accumulate (20 base to 1 acid ratio maintained). The second and third conditions are considered compensation and will be discussed later in the chapter. If the pH is greater than

7.45, an alkalemia (blood is excessively alkaline) exists. If the pH is less than 7.35, an acidemia (blood is excessively acid) exist.

BASE BICARBONATE IMBALANCES

ACUTE AND CHRONIC METABOLIC ACIDOSIS (BASE BICARBONATE DEFICIT)

Metabolic acidosis is a clinical disturbance characterized by a low pH (increased H^+ concentration) and a low plasma bicarbonate concentration (<22 mEq/l). It can be produced by a gain of hydrogen ions or a loss of bicarbonate, and is divided clinically into two forms according to the values of the serum anion gap: high anion gap acidosis and normal anion gap acidosis. The anion gap reflects unmeasured anions (phosphates, sulfates, and proteins) in plasma. Recall cations are positively charged ions (Na^+, K^+, H^+) and anions are negatively charged ions (HCO_3^-, Cl^-). Under normal conditions the cation to anion ratio is not equal; that is, the Na^+ and K^+ levels are greater than the number of HCO_3^- and Cl^-. In actuality, the ECF is, under normal circumstances, electroneutral, and the sum of cations does equal the sum of anions. However, since not all anions are measured, there is a gap. The anion gap can be calculated by either one of the following equations:

$$(Na^+ + K^+) - (HCO_3^- + Cl^-)$$

or

$$Na^+ - (HCO_3^- + Cl^-)$$

Potassium is often omitted from the equation because of its low level in the plasma; therefore, the second equation is used more often than the first.

The normal value for an anion gap is about 8 to 12 mEq/L (8 to 12 mmol/L) without potassium in the equation. If potassium is included in the equation, the normal value for the anion gap is 12 to 16 mEq/L (12 to 16 mmol/L). Thus, unmeasured anions in the serum (the gap) are normally less than 16 mEq/L. An anion gap greater than 16 mEq/L (16 mmol/L) is termed a *high anion gap metabolic acidosis* and results from excessive accumulation of fixed acid. High anion gap occurs in the ketoacidosis of uncontrolled diabetes or starvation, lactic acidosis, the late phase of salicylate poisoning, uremia, and methanol or ethylene glycol toxicity. In each of these situations the excess hydrogen is buffered by HCO_3^-, causing the bicarbonate concentration to fall. This is the reason for the high anion gap.

Normal anion gap acidosis results from the direct loss of bicarbonate, and can occur in diarrhea, lower intestinal fistulas, ureterostomies, diuretic therapy, early renal insufficiency, excessive administration of chloride (recall .9% NaCl contains 154 mEq of Cl^- per liter) and the administration of parenteral nutrition without bicarbonate or bicarbonate-producing solutes (e.g., lactate). Pancreatic drains are also associated with the direct loss of bicarbonate. In these situations, the direct loss of HCO_3^- is associated with an increase in plasma chloride and the anion gap remains normal. This condition is also referred to as *hyperchloremic acidosis*.

Clinical Manifestations and Assessment

Signs and symptoms of metabolic acidosis vary with the severity of the acidosis. They may include headache, lethargy, confusion, sluggishness, increased respiratory rate and depth, nausea, and vomiting. Peripheral vasodilation and decreased cardiac output occur when the pH drops to less than 7. Additional physical assessment findings include decreased blood pressure, cold and clammy skin, arrhythmias, and shock. Chronic metabolic acidosis is usually seen with chronic renal failure. The bicarbonate and pH decrease slowly, and the patient is asymptomatic until the bicarbonate is approximately 15 mEq/L or less.

Arterial blood gas measurements reveal a low bicarbonate level (<22 mEq/L) and a low pH (<7.35). Hyperkalemia may accompany metabolic acidosis as a result of the shift of potassium out of the cells. Later, as the acidosis is corrected, potassium moves back into the cells and hypokalemia may occur. Hyperventilation decreases the CO_2 level as a compensatory action. As stated previously, calculation of the anion gap is helpful in determining the cause of metabolic acidosis. An ECG detects arrhythmias caused by the associated increased serum potassium.

Medical and Nursing Management

Treatment is directed at correcting the underlying metabolic defect. When the problem results from excessive intake of chloride, treatment is aimed at eliminating the source of the chloride. When necessary, bicarbonate is administered if the pH is less than 7.1 and the serum bicarbonate level is less than 10 mEq/L. Although hyperkalemia occurs with acidosis, hypokalemia may occur with reversal of the acidosis and subsequent movement of potassium back into the cells. Therefore, the serum potassium level is monitored closely, and hypokalemia is corrected as acidosis is reversed.

In chronic metabolic acidosis, low serum calcium levels are treated before the chronic metabolic acidosis is treated, to avoid tetany resulting from an increase in pH and subsequent decrease in ionized calcium. Alkalizing agents may be administered if the serum bicarbonate level is less than 12 mEq/L. Treatment modalities may also include hemodialysis or peritoneal dialysis.

ACUTE AND CHRONIC METABOLIC ALKALOSIS (BASE BICARBONATE EXCESS)

Metabolic alkalosis is a clinical disturbance characterized by a high pH (decreased H^+ concentration) and a high plasma

bicarbonate concentration. It can be produced by a gain of bicarbonate or a loss of H^+.

Pathophysiology

A common cause of metabolic alkalosis is related to volume depletion from vomiting or gastric suction, with loss of hydrogen and chloride ions. The disorder also occurs in pyloric stenosis, in which only gastric fluid is lost. Gastric fluid has an acid pH (usually 1 to 3), and loss of this highly acidic fluid increases the alkalinity of body fluids. Other situations predisposing to metabolic alkalosis include those associated with loss of potassium, such as diuretic therapy that promotes excretion of potassium (e.g., thiazides, furosemide), and excessive adrenocorticoid hormones (as in hyperaldosteronism and Cushing's syndrome).

Hypokalemia produces alkalosis in two ways: (1) the kidneys conserve potassium, and therefore H^+ excretion increases; and (2) cellular potassium moves out of the cells into the ECF in an attempt to maintain near-normal serum levels (as potassium ions leave the cells, hydrogen ions must enter to maintain electroneutrality). A helpful cue to recall the association of a decreased K^+ to alkalosis is "al-K^+-low-sis" (Diepenbrock, 2008).

Excessive alkali ingestion from antacids containing bicarbonate or from use of sodium bicarbonate during cardiopulmonary resuscitation can also cause metabolic alkalosis.

Chronic metabolic alkalosis can occur with long-term diuretic therapy (thiazides or furosemide), villous adenoma (GI polyp), external drainage of gastric fluids, significant potassium depletion, cystic fibrosis, and the chronic ingestion of milk and calcium carbonate.

Clinical Manifestations and Assessment

Alkalosis is primarily manifested by symptoms related to decreased calcium ionization, such as tingling of the fingers and toes, dizziness, and hypertonic muscles. The ionized fraction of serum calcium decreases in alkalosis as more calcium combines with serum proteins. Because it is the ionized fraction of calcium that influences neuromuscular activity, symptoms of hypocalcemia are often the predominant symptoms of alkalosis. Respirations are depressed as a compensatory action by the lungs. Atrial tachycardia may occur. As the pH increases to greater than 7.6 and hypokalemia develops, ventricular disturbances may occur. Decreased motility and paralytic ileus may also occur.

Symptoms of chronic metabolic alkalosis are the same as for acute metabolic alkalosis, and as potassium decreases, frequent premature ventricular contractions or U waves are seen on the ECG.

Evaluation of ABG reveals a pH greater than 7.45 and a serum bicarbonate concentration greater than 26 mEq/L. The $PaCO_2$ increases as the lungs attempt to compensate for the excess bicarbonate by retaining CO_2. This hypoventilation is more pronounced in semiconscious, unconscious, or debilitated patients than in alert patients. The former may develop marked hypoxemia as a result of hypoventilation. Hypokalemia and hypocalcemia are expected.

Medical and Nursing Management

Treatment of metabolic alkalosis is aimed at correcting the underlying acid–base disorder. Because of volume depletion from GI loss, the patient's fluid I&O must be monitored carefully.

Sufficient chloride must be supplied for the kidney to absorb sodium with chloride (allowing the excretion of excess bicarbonate). Treatment also includes restoring normal fluid volume by administering sodium chloride fluids (because continued volume depletion serves to maintain the alkalosis). In patients with hypokalemia, potassium is administered as KCl to replace both K^+ and Cl^- losses. Carbonic anhydrase inhibitors are useful in treating metabolic alkalosis in patients who cannot tolerate rapid volume expansion (e.g., patients with heart failure).

CARBONIC ACID IMBALANCES

ACUTE AND CHRONIC RESPIRATORY ACIDOSIS (CARBONIC ACID EXCESS)

Respiratory acidosis is a clinical disorder in which the pH is less than 7.35 and the $PaCO_2$ is greater than 45 mm Hg. It may be either acute or chronic.

Pathophysiology

Respiratory acidosis is always due to inadequate excretion of CO_2 with inadequate ventilation, resulting in elevated plasma CO_2 concentrations and, consequently, increased levels of carbonic acid. Any condition that causes hypoventilation is associated with an elevated $PaCO_2$, and usually a decrease in PaO_2. Acute respiratory acidosis occurs in emergency situations, such as aspiration of a foreign object, atelectasis, diaphragmatic paralysis, overdose of sedatives, sleep apnea syndrome, administration of high-flow oxygen to a patient with chronic hypercapnia (excessive CO_2 in the blood), severe pneumonia, and acute respiratory distress syndrome. Respiratory acidosis can also occur in diseases that impair respiratory muscles, such as muscular dystrophy, myasthenia gravis, and Guillain-Barré syndrome.

Mechanical ventilation may be associated with hypercapnia if the rate of effective alveolar ventilation is inadequate (respiratory rate or tidal volume too low).

Additionally, some disorders, such as pulmonary edema and pneumothorax, may initially cause hyperventilation but as respiratory fatigue develops, the CO_2 level will rise and acidosis will develop. Therefore, the nurse cannot assume that a clinical condition will cause a predicted disturbance.

Rather, the nurse considers whether the respiratory center is capable of continuing to exhale the respiratory acid.

Clinical Manifestations and Assessment

Clinical signs in acute and chronic respiratory acidosis vary. Sudden hypercapnia (elevated $PaCO_2$) can cause increased pulse and respiratory rate, mental cloudiness, dull headache, or weakness. An elevated $PaCO_2$ causes cerebrovascular vasodilation and increased cerebral blood flow, particularly when it is greater than 60 mm Hg. Ventricular fibrillation may be the first sign of respiratory acidosis in anesthetized patients.

If respiratory acidosis is severe, intracranial pressure may increase, resulting in papilledema and dilated conjunctival blood vessels. Hyperkalemia may result as the hydrogen concentration overwhelms the compensatory mechanisms and H^+ moves into cells, causing a shift of potassium out of the cell.

Chronic respiratory acidosis occurs with pulmonary diseases such as chronic emphysema and bronchitis, obstructive sleep apnea, and obesity. As long as the $PaCO_2$ does not exceed the body's ability to compensate, the patient will be asymptomatic. However, if the $PaCO_2$ increases rapidly, cerebral vasodilation will increase the intracranial pressure, and cyanosis and tachypnea will develop. Patients with chronic obstructive pulmonary disease (COPD) who gradually accumulate CO_2 over a prolonged period (days to months) may not develop symptoms of hypercapnia because compensatory renal changes have had time to occur.

Arterial blood gas analysis reveals a pH lower than 7.35, a $PaCO_2$ greater than 45 mm Hg, and a variation in the bicarbonate level, depending on the duration of the acute respiratory acidosis. When compensation (renal retention of bicarbonate) has fully occurred, the arterial pH may be within the lower limits of normal. Depending on the cause of respiratory acidosis, other diagnostic measures would include monitoring of serum electrolyte levels, chest X-ray for determining any respiratory disease, and a drug screen if an overdose is suspected. An ECG to identify any cardiac arrhythmias may be indicated.

Medical and Nursing Management

Treatment is directed at treating the cause of the hypoventilation; exact measures vary with the cause of inadequate ventilation. Pharmacologic agents are used as indicated. For example, bronchodilators help reduce bronchial spasm, antibiotics are used for respiratory infections, and thrombolytics or anticoagulants are used for pulmonary emboli.

Pulmonary hygiene measures are initiated, when necessary, to clear the respiratory tract of mucus and purulent drainage. Adequate hydration (2 to 3 L/day) is indicated to keep the mucous membranes moist and thereby facilitate the removal of secretions as long as not contraindicated by car-

diac, liver, or renal disease. Supplemental oxygen is administered as necessary.

NURSING ALERT
If the $PaCO_2$ is chronically higher than 50 mm Hg, the respiratory center becomes relatively insensitive to CO_2 as a respiratory stimulant, leaving hypoxemia as the major drive for respiration. Oxygen administration may remove the stimulus of hypoxemia, and the patient develops "carbon dioxide narcosis" unless the situation is quickly reversed. Therefore, oxygen is administered with caution.

Mechanical ventilation may be required to improve pulmonary ventilation. Inappropriate mechanical ventilation (e.g., increased dead space, insufficient rate or volume settings, high fraction of inspired oxygen [FiO_2] with excessive CO_2 production) must be corrected with appropriate ventilator setting changes. Proper patient positioning in a semi-Fowler's position facilitates expansion of the chest wall.

ACUTE AND CHRONIC RESPIRATORY ALKALOSIS (CARBONIC ACID DEFICIT)

Respiratory alkalosis is a clinical condition in which the arterial pH is greater than 7.45 and the $PaCO_2$ is less than 35 mm Hg. As with respiratory acidosis, acute and chronic conditions can occur.

Pathophysiology

Respiratory alkalosis is always caused by hyperventilation, which causes excessive "blowing off" of CO_2 and, hence, a decrease in the plasma carbonic acid concentration. Causes of respiratory alkalosis can include extreme anxiety, hypoxemia, the early phase of salicylate intoxication (since the medulla is directly stimulated by the drug and the respiratory rate increases), high fever, gram-negative bacteremia, or inappropriate ventilator settings that do not match the patient's requirements.

Chronic respiratory alkalosis results from chronic hypocapnia, and decreased serum bicarbonate levels are the consequence. Chronic hepatic insufficiency and cerebral tumors are predisposing factors.

Clinical Manifestations and Assessment

Clinical signs consist of lightheadedness due to vasoconstriction and decreased cerebral blood flow, inability to concentrate, numbness and tingling from decreased calcium ionization, tinnitus, and sometimes loss of consciousness. Cardiac effects of respiratory alkalosis include tachycardia and ventricular and atrial arrhythmias.

Analysis of ABG reveals an elevated pH (>7.45) as a result of a low $PaCO_2$ (<35 mm Hg) and a normal bicarbonate level. (The kidneys cannot alter the bicarbonate

level quickly.) In the compensated state, the kidneys have had sufficient time to lower the bicarbonate level to a near-normal level. Evaluation of serum electrolytes is indicated to identify any decrease in potassium as hydrogen is pulled out of the cells in exchange for potassium; decreased calcium, as in severe alkalosis calcium becomes bound to protein. As a result, the ionized portion decreases, thus symptoms of carpopedal spasms and tetany occur. A toxicology screen should be performed to rule out salicylate intoxication.

Patients with chronic respiratory alkalosis are usually asymptomatic, and the diagnostic evaluation and plan of care are the same as for acute respiratory alkalosis.

Medical and Nursing Management

Treatment depends on the underlying cause of respiratory alkalosis. If the cause is anxiety, the patient is instructed to breathe more slowly to allow CO_2 to accumulate or to breathe into a closed system (such as a paper bag). A sedative may be required to relieve hyperventilation in very anxious patients. Treatment of other causes of respiratory alkalosis is directed at correcting the underlying problem.

MIXED ACID–BASE DISORDERS

Patients can simultaneously experience two or more independent acid–base disorders. A normal pH in the presence of changes in the $PaCO_2$ and plasma HCO_3^- concentration immediately suggests a mixed disorder. The only mixed disorder that cannot occur is a mixed respiratory acidosis and alkalosis, because it is impossible to have alveolar hypoventilation and hyperventilation at the same time. An example of a mixed disorder is the simultaneous occurrence of metabolic acidosis and respiratory acidosis during respiratory and cardiac arrest.

Compensation

Generally, the pulmonary and renal systems compensate for each other to return the pH to normal. In a single acid–base disorder, the system not causing the problem will try to compensate by returning the ratio of bicarbonate to carbonic acid to the normal 20:1. The lungs compensate for metabolic disturbances by changing CO_2 excretion. The kidneys compensate for respiratory disturbances by altering bicarbonate retention and H^+ secretion.

In respiratory acidosis, excess hydrogen is excreted in the urine in exchange for bicarbonate ions. In respiratory alkalosis, the renal excretion of bicarbonate increases, and hydrogen ions are retained. In metabolic acidosis, the compensatory mechanisms increase the ventilation rate, whereas in metabolic alkalosis, the respiratory system compensates by decreasing ventilation to conserve CO_2 and increase the $PaCO_2$. Because the lungs respond to acid–base disorders

TABLE **4-4** Acid–Base Disturbances and Compensation

Disorder	Initial Event	Compensation
Respiratory acidosis	↓ pH, ↑ or normal HCO_3^-, ↑ $PaCO_2$	↑ Renal acid excretion and ↑ serum HCO_3^-
Respiratory alkalosis	↑ pH, ↓ or normal HCO_3^-, ↓ $PaCO_2$	↓ Renal acid excretion and ↓ serum HCO_3^-
Metabolic acidosis	↓ pH, ↓ HCO_3^-, ↓ or normal $PaCO_2$	Hyperventilation with resulting ↓ $PaCO_2$
Metabolic alkalosis	↑ pH, ↑ HCO_3^-, ↑ or normal $PaCO_2$	Hypoventilation with resulting ↑ $PaCO_2$

within minutes, compensation for metabolic imbalances occurs faster than does compensation for respiratory imbalances. Table 4-4 summarizes compensation effects.

Blood Gas Analysis

Blood gas analysis is often used to identify the specific acid–base disturbance and the degree of compensation that has occurred (see Box 4-1 and Box 4-2 on page 90). The analysis is usually based on an arterial blood sample, but if an arterial sample cannot be obtained, a mixed venous sample may be used. Results of ABG analysis provide information about alveolar ventilation, oxygenation, and acid–base balance. The health history, physical examination, previous blood gas results, and serum electrolytes should always be part of the assessment used to determine the cause of the acid–base disorder (Porth, 2011). Before obtaining an ABG from the radial artery, the nurse assesses patency of the ulnar artery by performing the Allen test (refer to Chapter 12). Treatment of the underlying condition usually corrects most acid–base disorders. Table 4-5 compares normal ranges of venous and ABG values.

PARENTERAL FLUID THERAPY

When no other route of administration is available, fluids are administered intravenously in hospitals, outpatient diagnostic and surgical settings, clinics, and homes to replace fluids, administer medications, and provide nutrients. Typical indications for giving a fluid bolus include hypotension, low urine output, and inadequate cardiac output for tissue needs (Magder, 2010).

PURPOSE

The choice of an IV solution depends on the purpose of its administration. Generally, IV fluids are administered to achieve one or more of the following goals:

- To provide water, electrolytes, and nutrients to meet daily requirements

BOX 4-1   Assessing Arterial Blood Gases

The following steps are recommended to evaluate arterial blood gas (ABG) values. They are based on the assumption that the average values are:

pH = 7.4
$PaCO_2$ = 40 mm Hg
HCO_3^- = 24 mEq/L

1. *First, note the pH.* It can be high, low, or normal, as follows:
   pH > 7.4 (alkalosis)
   pH < 7.4 (acidosis)
   pH = 7.4 (normal)
   A normal pH may indicate perfectly normal blood gases, *or* it may be an indication of a *compensated* imbalance. A compensated imbalance is one in which the body has been able to correct the pH by either respiratory or metabolic changes (depending on the primary problem). For example, a patient with primary metabolic acidosis starts out with a low bicarbonate level but a normal CO_2 level. Soon afterward, the lungs try to compensate for the imbalance by exhaling large amounts of CO_2 (hyperventilation). As another example, a patient with primary respiratory acidosis starts out with a high CO_2 level; soon afterward, the kidneys attempt to compensate by retaining bicarbonate. If the compensatory mechanism is able to restore the bicarbonate to carbonic acid ratio back to 20:1, full compensation (and thus normal pH) will be achieved.
2. The next step is to determine the primary cause of the disturbance. This is done by evaluating the $PaCO_2$ and HCO_3^- in relation to the pH.

Example: pH > 7.4 (alkalosis)
a. If the $PaCO_2$ is <40 mm Hg, the primary disturbance is respiratory alkalosis. (This situation occurs when a patient hyperventilates and "blows off" too much CO_2. Recall that CO_2 dissolved in water becomes carbonic acid, the acid side of the "carbonic acid–bicarbonate buffer system.")
b. If the HCO_3^- is >24 mEq/L, the primary disturbance is metabolic alkalosis. (This situation occurs when

the body gains too much bicarbonate, an alkaline substance. Bicarbonate is the basic or alkaline side of the "carbonic acid–bicarbonate buffer system.")

Example: pH < 7.4 (acidosis)
a. If the $PaCO_2$ is >40 mm Hg, the primary disturbance is respiratory acidosis. (This situation occurs when a patient hypoventilates and thus retains too much CO_2, an acidic substance.)
b. If the HCO_3^- is <24 mEq/L, the primary disturbance is metabolic acidosis. (This situation occurs when the body's bicarbonate level drops, either because of direct bicarbonate loss or because of gains of acids such as lactic acid or ketones.)

3. The next step involves determining if compensation has begun. This is done by looking at the value other than the primary disorder. If it is moving in the same direction as the primary value, compensation is under way. Consider the following gases:

pH	$PaCO_2$	HCO_3^-
(1) 7.2	60 mm Hg	24 mEq/L
(2) 7.4	60 mm Hg	37 mEq/L

The first set (1) indicates acute respiratory acidosis without compensation (the $PaCO_2$ is high, the HCO_3^- is normal). The second set (2) indicates chronic respiratory acidosis. Note that compensation has taken place; that is, the HCO_3^- has elevated to an appropriate level to balance the high $PaCO_2$ and produce a normal pH.

4. Two distinct acid–base disturbances may occur simultaneously. These can be identified when the pH does not explain one of the changes.

Example: Metabolic and respiratory acidosis

A. pH	7.2 decreased acid
B. $PaCO_2$	52 increased acid
C. HCO_3	13 decreased acid

This is an example of metabolic and respiratory acidosis.

TABLE 4-5 Normal Values for Arterial and Mixed Venous Blood

Parameter	Arterial Blood	Mixed Venous Blood
pH	7.35–7.45	7.33–7.41
$PaCO_2$	35–45 mm Hg	41–51 mm Hg
PaO_2*	80–100 mm Hg	35–40 mm Hg
HCO_3^-	22–26 mEq/L	22–26 mEq/L
Base excess/deficit	± 2 mEq/L	± 2 mEq/L
Oxygen saturation	>94%	75%

*At altitudes of 3,000 feet and higher, the values for oxygen are decreased.

- To replace water and correct electrolyte deficits
- To administer medications and blood products

IV solutions contain dextrose or electrolytes mixed in various proportions with water. Pure, electrolyte-free water can never be administered IV because it rapidly enters RBC and causes them to rupture.

TYPES OF IV SOLUTIONS

Crystalloid solutions are often categorized as **isotonic**, **hypotonic**, or **hypertonic**, according to whether their total

Nursing Research

Bridging the Gap to Evidence-Based Practice

Online Tutorials for Arterial Blood Gas Analysis

Schneiderman, J., & Corbridge, S. (2009). Demonstrating the effectiveness of an online, computer-based learning module for ABG analysis. *Clinical Nurse Specialist, 23*(3), 151–155.

Purpose

The purpose of this study was to identify whether it was possible to use computer-based learning to teach registered nurses arterial blood gas (ABG) analysis.

Design

Malcolm Knowles' adult learning theory states that an individual learns when motivated to learn while feeling the "need to know" the information. The learner's experiences and the applicability are also important factors.

Furthermore, the *Sensory Stimulation Theory* realized that the majority of learning was accomplished through seeing; therefore, stimulation of the senses is quite important in retaining knowledge.

The authors use a pre-/post-test model to assess the registered nurses' ability to learn appropriate techniques to interpret ABGs. They utilized a computer-based learning module. The test consisted of seven clinical scenarios, each with multiple choice questions. Identical tests were given to subjects before and after the module.

Findings

The subjects mean pretest score was 4.62, while the mean posttest score was 5.72, revealing a statistically significant increase in scores after the learning module ($p < 0.001$). There was no difference in scores between associate- and bachelor degree-level nurses. Finally, there was no difference in scores between intensive care unit nurses and floor staff nurses, suggesting that a computer-based module would service all nursing staff.

Nursing Implications

This study concluded that an online computer-based learning module is capable of increasing the nurse's knowledge of ABG interpretation. The results were identical in the intensive care unit and on the hospital wards. This learning module can be utilized as both an educational model and as a learning tool for experienced nurses to further knowledge, and may be broadened to provide other practices and procedures to nursing staff. Future studies should identify whether online computer-based learning modules are as successful with topics other than ABG analysis.

---

osmolality is the same as, less than, or greater than that of blood (see earlier discussion of osmolality). Crystalloid fluids generally contain three basic components: water, electrolytes, and sugar (Kaplan & Kellum, 2010).

Electrolyte solutions are considered isotonic if the total electrolyte content (anions + cations) is approximately 310 mEq/L, hypotonic if the total electrolyte content is less than 250 mEq/L, and hypertonic if the total electrolyte content is greater than 375 mEq/L. The nurse must also consider a solution's osmolality, keeping in mind that the osmolality of plasma is approximately 300 mOsm/L (300 mmol/L). For example, a 10% dextrose solution has an osmolality of approximately 505 mOsm/L.

When administering parenteral fluids, the nurse monitors the patient's response to the fluids, considering the fluid volume, the content of the fluid, and the patient's clinical status. Some fluids may actually initiate an inflammatory process within the body, especially when overused in patients with hemorrhage shock (Rhee, 2010). Refer to Table 4-6 for various IV solutions.

NURSING ALERT

When administering fluids to patients with cardiovascular disease, the nurse assesses for signs of circulatory overload (e.g., cough, dyspnea, puffy eyelids, dependent edema, weight gain in 24 hours). The lungs are auscultated for crackles.

Extreme care is taken when administering highly hypertonic sodium fluids (e.g., 3% or 5% sodium chloride), because these fluids can be lethal if infused carelessly.

Isotonic Fluids

Isotonic fluids have a total osmolality close to that of the ECF and do not cause RBC to shrink or swell. The composition of these fluids may or may not approximate that of the ECF. Isotonic fluids expand the ECF volume. One liter of isotonic fluid expands the ECF by 1 L; however, it expands the plasma by only 0.25 L because it is a crystalloid fluid and diffuses quickly into the ECF compartment. In patients hospitalized for shock, as much as 20 mL/kg of isotonic fluid boluses may be initially required to maintain renal perfusion. However, since these fluids expand the intravascular space, patients with hypertension and heart failure should be carefully monitored for signs of fluid overload.

D_5W

A solution of D_5W has a serum osmolality of 252 mOsm/L. Once administered, the glucose is rapidly metabolized, and this initially isotonic solution then disperses as a hypotonic fluid, one-third extracellular and two-thirds intracellular. It is essential to consider this action of D_5W, especially if the patient is at risk for increased intracranial pressure. During fluid resuscitation, this solution should not be used, because

T A B L E
4-6 Selected Water and Electrolyte Solutions

Solution	Comments
Isotonic Solutions 0.9% NaCl (isotonic, also called normal saline [NS]) Na^+ 154 mEq/L Cl^- 154 mEq/L (308 mOsm/L) Also available with varying concentrations of dextrose (the most frequently used is a 5% dextrose concentration)	• An isotonic solution that expands the ECF (ECF) volume, used in hypovolemic states, resuscitative efforts, shock, diabetic ketoacidosis, metabolic alkalosis, hypercalcemia, mild Na^+ deficit • Supplies an excess of Na^+ and Cl^-; can cause fluid volume excess and hyperchloremic acidosis if used in excessive volumes, particularly in patients with compromised renal function, heart failure, or edema • Not desirable as a routine maintenance solution, as it provides only Na^+ and Cl^- (and these are provided in excessive amounts) • When mixed with 5% dextrose, the resulting solution becomes hypertonic in relation to plasma and, in addition to the above described electrolytes, provides 170 cal/L • Only solution that may be administered with blood products
Lactated Ringer's solution Na^+ 130 mEq/L K^+ 4 mEq/L Ca^{++} 3 mEq/L Cl^- 109 mEq/L Lactate (metabolized to bicarbonate) 28 mEq/L (274 mOsm/L) Also available with varying concentrations of dextrose (the most common is 5% dextrose)	• An isotonic solution that contains multiple electrolytes in roughly the same concentration as found in plasma (note that solution is lacking in Mg^{++}): provides 9 cal/L • Used in the treatment of hypovolemia, burns, fluid lost as bile or diarrhea, and for acute blood loss replacement • Lactate is rapidly metabolized into HCO_3^- in the body. Lactated Ringer's solution should not be used in lactic acidosis because the ability to convert lactate into HCO_3^- is impaired in this disorder. • Not to be given with a pH > 7.5 because bicarbonate is formed as lactate breaks down, causing alkalosis • Should not be used in renal failure because it contains potassium and can cause hyperkalemia • Similar to plasma
5% dextrose in water (D_5W) No electrolytes 50 g of dextrose	• An isotonic solution that supplies 170 cal/L and free water to aid in renal excretion of solutes • Used in treatment of hypernatremia, fluid loss, and dehydration • Should not be used in excessive volumes in the early postoperative period (when antidiuretic hormone secretion is increased due to stress reaction) • Should not be used solely in treatment of fluid volume deficit, because it dilutes plasma electrolyte concentrations • Contraindicated in head injury because it may cause increased intracranial pressure • Should not be used for fluid resuscitation because it can cause hyperglycemia • Should be used with caution in patients with renal or cardiac disease because of risk of fluid overload • Electrolyte-free solutions may cause peripheral circulatory collapse, anuria in patients with sodium deficiency, and increased body fluid loss. • Converts to hypotonic solution as dextrose is metabolized by body. Over time, D_5W without NaCl can cause water intoxication (ICF volume excess [FVE]) because the solution is hypotonic.
Hypotonic Solutions 0.45% NaCl (half-strength saline) Na^+ 77 mEq/L Cl^- 77 mEq/L (154 mOsm/L) Also available with varying concentrations of dextrose (the most common is a 5% concentration)	• Provides Na^+, Cl^-, and free water • Free water is desirable to aid the kidneys in elimination of solute. • Lacking in electrolytes other than Na^+ and Cl^- • When mixed with 5% dextrose, the solution becomes slightly hypertonic to plasma and in addition to the above-described electrolytes provides 170 cal/L. • Used to treat hypertonic dehydration, Na^+ and Cl^- depletion, and gastric fluid loss • Not indicated for third-space fluid shifts or increased intracranial pressure • Administer cautiously, because it can cause fluid shifts from vascular system into cells, resulting in cardiovascular collapse and increased intracranial pressure.
Hypertonic Solutions 3% NaCl (hypertonic saline) Na^+ 513 mEq/L Cl^- 513 mEq/L (1026 mOsm/L)	• Used to increase ECF volume, decrease cellular swelling • Highly hypertonic solution used only in critical situations to treat hyponatremia • Must be administered slowly and cautiously, because it can cause intravascular volume overload and pulmonary edema • Supplies no calories • Assists in removing ICF excess

(continued on page 92)

TABLE
4-6 Selected Water and Electrolyte Solutions (continued)

Solution	Comments
5% NaCL (hypertonic solution) Na$^+$ 855 mEq/L Cl$^-$ 855 mEq/L (1710 mOsm/L)	• Highly hypertonic solution used to treat symptomatic hyponatremia • Administered slowly and cautiously, because it can cause intravascular volume overload and pulmonary edema • Supplies no calories
Colloid Solutions Dextran in NS or 5% D$_5$W Available in low-molecular-weight (Dextran 40) and high-molecular-weight (Dextran 70) forms	• Colloid solution used as volume/plasma expander for intravascular part of ECF • Affects clotting by coating platelets and decreasing ability to clot • Remains in circulatory system up to 24 hours • Used to treat hypovolemia in early shock to increase pulse pressure, cardiac output, and arterial blood pressure • Improves microcirculation by decreasing red blood cell aggregation • Contraindicated in hemorrhage, thrombocytopenia, renal disease, and severe dehydration • Not a substitute for blood or blood products

of its limited ability to expand the intravascular volume. Therefore, D$_5$W is used mainly to supply water and to correct an increased serum osmolality. About 1 L of D$_5$W provides fewer than 200 kcal and is a minor source of the body's daily caloric requirements.

Normal Saline Solution

Normal saline (0.9% sodium chloride) solution has a total osmolality of 308 mOsm/L. Because the osmolality is entirely contributed by electrolytes, the solution remains within the ECF. For this reason, normal saline solution is often used to correct an extracellular volume deficit. Normal saline contains only sodium and chloride and does not actually simulate the ECF. It is used with administration of blood transfusions and to replace large sodium losses, as in burn injuries. It is not used for heart failure, pulmonary edema, renal impairment, or sodium retention. Normal saline does not supply calories. Historically, in patients with trauma or penetrating injury, initial treatment consisted of large amounts of isotonic saline administration to maintain a systolic blood pressure greater than 90. Recently, data have suggested maintaining a slightly hypotensive state until hemostasis has been achieved; therefore, the rapid administration of 0.9% normal saline is not ordered as often as it had been (Roppolo, Wigginton, & Pepe, 2010). Hemorrhage can also begin a process of coagulopathy, acidosis, and hypothermia within the body, necessitating a decision for light versus aggressive parenteral fluid administration (Kor & Gajic, 2010).

Other Isotonic Solutions

Several other solutions contain ions in addition to sodium and chloride and are somewhat similar to the ECF in composition. Lactated Ringer's solution contains potassium and calcium in addition to sodium and chloride and can be used to correct dehydration and sodium depletion or to replace GI losses. Lactated Ringer's solution contains bicarbonate precursors as well. Lactated Ringer's is typically not used in patients with severe acidosis or in advanced liver disease, which can affect lactate metabolism.

Hypotonic Fluids

One purpose of hypotonic solutions is to replace cellular fluid. Another is to provide free water for excretion of body wastes. At times, hypotonic sodium solutions are used to treat hypernatremia and other hyperosmolar conditions. Half-strength saline (0.45% sodium chloride) solution, with an osmolality of 154 mOsm/L, is frequently used. Multiple-electrolyte solutions are also available. Excessive infusions of hypotonic solutions can lead to intravascular fluid depletion by causing a fluid shift from blood vessels to cells, resulting in decreased blood pressure, cellular edema, and cell damage. These solutions exert less osmotic pressure than the ECF.

Hypertonic Fluids

When normal saline solution or lactated Ringer's solution contains 5% dextrose, the total osmolality exceeds that of the ECF. However, the dextrose is quickly metabolized, and only the isotonic solution remains. Therefore, any effect on the intracellular compartment is temporary.

Higher concentrations of dextrose, such as 50% dextrose in water, are administered to help meet caloric requirements. These solutions are strongly hypertonic and must be administered into central veins, so that they can be diluted by rapid blood flow.

Saline solutions are also available in osmolar concentrations greater than that of the ECF. These solutions draw water from the ICF to the ECF and cause cells to shrink. If administered rapidly or in large quantity, they may cause an extracellular volume excess and precipitate circulatory

overload. As a result, these solutions must be administered cautiously and usually only when the serum osmolality has decreased to dangerously low levels. Hypertonic solutions exert an osmotic pressure greater than that of the ECF.

⚡ **NURSING ALERT**
Highly hypertonic sodium solutions (3% and 5% sodium chloride) should be administered only in intensive care settings under close observation, because only small volumes are needed to elevate the serum sodium concentration. These fluids are administered slowly and in small volumes, and the patient is monitored closely for fluid overload. The purpose is to relieve acute manifestations of cerebral edema and to prevent neurologic complications, rather than to specifically correct the sodium concentration. Along with the sodium solution, the patient may receive a loop diuretic to prevent ECF volume overload and to increase water excretion.

Other IV Substances

When the patient's GI tract is unable to tolerate food, nutritional requirements are often met using the IV route. Parenteral solutions may include high concentrations of glucose, protein, or fat to meet nutritional requirements (see Chapter 22). The parenteral route may also be used to administer colloids, plasma expanders, and blood products including packed RBC, fresh frozen plasma, and platelets.

Many medications are also delivered by the IV route, either by infusion or directly into the vein. Because IV medications enter the circulation rapidly, administration by this route is potentially very hazardous. While all medications may produce reactions IV medications are especially dangerous due to the rapid introduction and absorption within the bloodstream. Astute nursing includes knowledge of the administration rates and recommended dilutions for any medication given.

NURSING MANAGEMENT OF THE PATIENT RECEIVING IV THERAPY

The ability to perform venipuncture to gain access to the venous system for administering fluids and medication is an expected nursing skill in many settings. This responsibility includes selecting the appropriate venipuncture site and type of cannula and being proficient in the technique of vein entry. This skill should be mastered by all bedside nurses, and it is up to each individual nurse to seek out the opportunity to learn and practice venipuncture.

Preparing to Administer IV Therapy

Before performing venipuncture, the nurse performs hand hygiene, applies gloves, and informs the patient about the procedure. Next, the nurse selects the most appropriate insertion site and type of cannula for a particular patient. Factors influencing these choices include the type of solution to be administered, the expected duration of IV therapy, the patient's general condition, and the availability of veins. The skill of the person initiating the infusion is also an important consideration. Some institutions have organized specialized "IV therapy" teams who assist in IV placement and management.

Choosing an IV Site

Veins of the extremities are designated as peripheral locations and are ordinarily the only sites used by nurses. Because they are relatively safe and easy to enter, arm veins are most commonly used (Fig. 4-8). The metacarpal, cephalic, basilic, and median veins and their branches are recommended sites because of their size and ease of access. More distal sites should be used first, with more proximal sites used subsequently. Leg veins should rarely, if ever, be used because of the high risk of thromboembolism. Additional sites to avoid include veins distal to a previous IV infiltration or phlebitic area, sclerosed or thrombosed veins, an arm with an arteriovenous shunt or fistula, and an arm affected by edema, infection, blood clot, or skin breakdown.

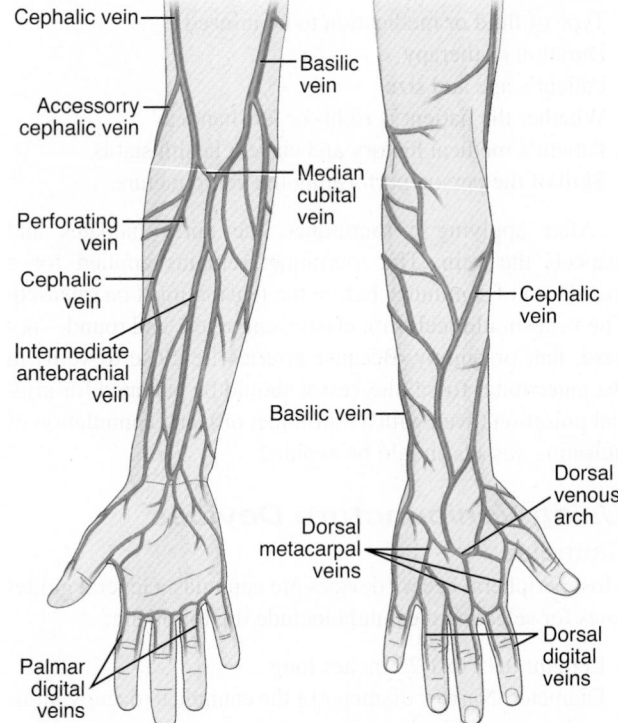

FIGURE 4-8 Site selection for peripheral cannulation of veins: anterior (palmar) veins at *left,* posterior (dorsal) veins at *right.* Adapted from Agur, A. M. R., Lee, M. J., & Boileau Grant, M. J. (1999). *Grant's atlas of anatomy* (10th ed.). Philadelphia: Lippincott Williams & Wilkins.

Central veins commonly used by physicians and trained health providers include the subclavian and internal jugular veins. It is possible to gain access to (or cannulate) these larger vessels even when peripheral sites have collapsed, and they allow for the administration of hyperosmolar solutions and vasoconstrictive drugs. However, the potential hazards are much greater and include inadvertent entry into an artery or the pleural space, as well as a higher risk of infection.

Ideally, both arms and hands are carefully inspected before a specific venipuncture site that does not interfere with mobility is chosen. For this reason, the antecubital fossa is avoided, except as a last resort. The most distal site of the arm or hand is generally used first, so that subsequent IV access sites can be moved progressively upward. The following factors should be considered when selecting a site for venipuncture:

- Condition of the vein
- Type of fluid or medication to be infused
- Duration of therapy
- Patient's age and size
- Whether the patient is right- or left-handed
- Patient's medical history and current health status
- Skill of the person performing the venipuncture

After applying a tourniquet, the nurse palpates and inspects the vein. The tourniquet remains applied for a maximum of 3 minutes before the tension must be released. The vein should feel firm, elastic, engorged, and round—not hard, flat, or bumpy. Because arteries lie close to veins in the antecubital fossa, the vessel should be palpated for arterial pulsation (even with a tourniquet on), and cannulation of pulsating vessels should be avoided.

Using Venipuncture Devices
Cannulas
Most peripheral access devices are cannulas. General guidelines for selecting a cannula include the following:

- Length: 0.75 to 1.25 inches long
- Diameter: Narrow diameter of the cannula to occupy minimal space within the vein
- Gauge: 20 to 22 gauge for most IV fluids; a larger gauge for caustic or viscous solutions; 14 to 18 gauge for blood administration and for trauma patients and those undergoing surgery

Cannulas have an obturator inside a tube that is later removed. "Catheter" and "cannula" are terms that are used interchangeably. The main types of cannula devices available are those referred to as winged infusion sets (butterfly) with a steel needle or as over-the-needle catheters with wings; indwelling plastic cannulas that are inserted over a steel needle; and indwelling plastic cannulas that are inserted through a steel needle. Scalp vein or butterfly needles are short steel needles with plastic wing handles. These are easy to insert, but because they are small and nonpliable, infiltration occurs easily. The use of these needles should be limited to obtaining blood specimens and not for IV medications because they increase the risk of vein injury and infiltration.

Plastic cannulas inserted through a hollow needle are usually called *intracatheters*. They are available in long lengths and are well suited for placement in central locations. Because insertion requires threading the cannula through the vein for a relatively long distance, these can be difficult to insert. The most commonly used infusion device is the over-the-needle catheter. A hollow metal stylet is preinserted into the catheter and extends through the distal tip of the catheter to allow puncture of the vessel, in an effort to guide the catheter as the venipuncture is performed. The vein is punctured and a flashback of blood appears in the closed chamber behind the catheter hub. Once the flashback has occurred, the catheter is threaded through the stylet into the vein and the stylet is then removed. All institutions should carry safety over-the-needle catheter designs with retracting stylets to protect health care workers from needlestick injuries.

Many types of cannulas are available for IV therapy. Some of the variations in these cannulas include the thickness of the cannula wall (affects rate of flow), the sharpness of the insertion needles (determines needle insertion technique), the softening properties of the cannula (influences the length of time the cannula can remain in place), safety features (minimizes risk of needlestick injuries and bloodborne exposure), and the number of lumens (determines the number of solutions that can be infused simultaneously).

Needleless IV Delivery Systems
The federal Needlestick Safety and Prevention Act, which was signed into law in November 2000, requires needleless systems in an effort to decrease needlestick injuries and exposure to HIV, hepatitis, and other bloodborne pathogens. These systems have built-in protection against needlestick injuries and provide a safe means of using and disposing of an IV administration set (which consists of tubing, an area for inserting the tubing into the container of IV fluid, and an adapter for connecting the tubing to the needle). Numerous companies produce needleless components. IV line connectors allow the simultaneous infusion of IV medications and other intermittent medications (known as a *piggyback delivery*) without the use of needles. Technology is advancing and moving away from use of the traditional stylet. Many examples of these devices are on the market. Each institution must evaluate

products to determine its own needs based on Occupational Safety and Health Administration (OSHA) guidelines and the institution's policies and procedures.

Peripherally Inserted Central Catheter or Peripheral-Midline Catheter Access Lines

Patients who need moderate- to long-term parenteral therapy often receive a peripherally inserted central catheter (PICC or PIC line) or a peripheral-midline catheter. These catheters are also used for patients with limited peripheral access who require IV antibiotics, blood, vasopressors, or parenteral nutrition. For these devices to be used, the median cephalic, basilic, and cephalic veins must be patent and undamaged. Insertion of these catheters are typically performed by specialized nurses who are trained in the use of them, as well as in the use of ultrasonography (which is used to visualize the vein to be cannulized).

If these veins are damaged, then central venous access via the subclavian or internal jugular vein, or surgical placement of an implanted port or a vascular access device, must be considered as an alternative. Table 4-7 compares peripherally inserted central and peripheral-midline catheters.

The provider prescribes the line and the solution to be infused. Insertion of either catheter requires sterile technique. The size of the catheter lumen chosen is based on the type of solution, the patient's body size, and the vein to be used. The patient's consent is obtained before use of these catheters. Use of the dominant arm is recommended as the site for inserting the cannula into the superior vena cava to ensure adequate arm movement, which encourages blood flow and reduces the risk of dependent edema or emboli formation. Contraindications to arm choice include prior mastectomy, pacemaker placement, hemiparesis, and dialysis shunt. Review each institutions policy regarding PICC lines for further contraindications.

Teaching the Patient

Except in emergency situations, a patient should be prepared in advance for an IV infusion. The venipuncture, the expected length of infusion, and activity restrictions are explained. Then, the patient should have an opportunity to ask questions and express concerns. For example, some patients believe that they will die if small bubbles in the tubing enter their veins. After acknowledging this fear, the nurse can explain that usually only relatively large volumes of air administered rapidly are dangerous.

Preparing the IV Site

Before preparing the skin, the nurse should ask the patient whether he or she is allergic to latex or iodine, products commonly used in preparing for IV therapy. Excessive hair at the selected site may be removed by clipping to increase the visibility of the veins and to facilitate insertion of the cannula and adherence of dressings to the IV insertion site. Shaving should not be performed due to increased risk of infection.

Because infection can be a major complication of IV therapy, the IV device, the fluid, the container, and the tubing must be sterile. The insertion site is scrubbed with a sterile pad soaked in 10% povidone–iodine (Betadine) or chlorhexidine gluconate solution for 30 seconds, working in a circular motion from the center of the area to the periphery and allowing the area to air dry for approximately 2 minutes. The site should not be wiped with 70% alcohol, because the alcohol negates the effect of the disinfecting solution. (Alcohol pledgets are used for 30 seconds instead, only if the patient is allergic to iodine.) The nurse must perform hand hygiene and put on gloves. Gloves (nonsterile, disposable) must be worn during the venipuncture procedure because of the likelihood of coming into contact with the patient's blood.

Performing Venipuncture

IV therapy initiation is a specialized nursing skill. Institutional policies and procedures determine whether all nurses must be certified to perform venipuncture. A nurse certified in IV therapy or an IV team can be consulted to assist with initiating IV therapy. Refer to each institution's guidelines on venipuncture for specific policies regarding this skill.

Understanding Factors Affecting Flow

The flow of an IV infusion is governed by the same principles that govern fluid movement in general. Flow is directly proportional to the height on the infusion. Raising the infusion bag may improve sluggish flow. The clamp on IV tubing regulates the flow by changing the tubing diameter. In addition, the flow is faster through large-gauge rather than small-gauge cannulas. Issues such as length of IV tubing and viscosity of the fluid being infused may also affect the flow rate.

Monitoring Flow

Because so many factors influence gravity flow, a solution does not necessarily continue to run at the speed originally set. Therefore, the nurse monitors IV infusions frequently to make sure that the fluid is flowing at the intended rate. The IV container should be marked with tape to indicate at a glance whether the correct amount has infused. The flow rate is calculated when the solution is originally started and then monitored at least hourly. To calculate the flow rate, the nurse determines the number of drops delivered per milliliter; this varies with equipment and is usually printed on the administration set packaging. In an effort to decrease the amount of medication errors, it has become standard for all intermittent IV infusions to be given with an electronic infusion device.

A variety of electronic infusion devices are available to assist in IV fluid delivery. These devices allow more accurate administration of fluids and medications than is possible

TABLE
4-7 Comparison of Peripherally Inserted Central and Peripheral-Midline Catheters

	Peripherally Inserted Central Catheter	Peripheral-Midline Catheter
Indications	Parenteral nutrition; IV fluid replacement; administration of chemotherapy agents, analgesics, and antibiotics; removal of blood specimens	Parenteral nutrition; IV fluid replacement; administration of analgesics and antibiotics (no solution or medications with a pH <5 or >9 or osmolarity >500 mOsm/L); removal of blood specimens
Features	Single- and double-lumen catheters available 40–60 cm long; gauge variable (16–24 gauge)	Single- and double-lumen catheters available (16–24 gauge) 7.5–20 cm in length. Can increase two gauges in size as it softens
Material	Radiopaque, polymer (polyurethane), Silastic materials. Flexible.	Silicone, polyurethane, and their derivatives; available impregnated with heparin to ↓ thrombogenicity (radiopaque or clear, with radiopaque strip)
Insertion sites	Venipuncture performed in the antecubital fossa, above or below it into the basilic, cephalic, or axillary veins of the dominant arm. The median basilic is the ideal insertion site.	Venipuncture performed 1½ inches above or below the antecubital fossa through the cephalic, basilic, or median cubital vein.
Catheter placement	The tip of the catheter lies in the superior vena cava. The catheter is placed via the basilic or cephalic vein at the antecubital fossa.	Between the antecubital area and the head of the clavicle (tip in axilla region). The tip terminates in the proximal portion of the extremity below axilla and proximal to central veins and is advanced 3–10 inches.
Insertion method	Through-the-needle technique, with or without a guide wire, breakaway needle with introducer or cannula with introducer (peel-away sheath). (A peripherally inserted central catheter can also be used as a midline catheter.)	No separate guide wire or introducer is needed. Stiff catheter is passed using the catheter advancement tab.
	Insertion can be accomplished at the bedside using sterile technique. Arm to be used should be positioned in abduction to 90-degree angle. Consent is required.	Insertion can be accomplished at the bedside using sterile technique. Arm to be used should be positioned in abduction to 45-degree angle. Consent is required.
	Catheter may stay in place for up to 12 months or as long as required without complications.	Catheter may stay in place for 2–4 weeks.
Potential complications	Malposition, pneumothorax, hemothorax, hydrothorax, arrhythmias, nerve or tendon damage, respiratory distress, catheter embolism, thrombophlebitis, or catheter occlusion. Compared with centrally placed catheters, venipuncture in the antecubital space reduces risk of insertion complications.	Thrombosis, phlebitis, air embolism, infection, vascular perforation, bleeding, catheter transection, occlusion
Contraindications	Dermatitis, cellulitis, burns, high fluid volume infusions, rapid bolus injections, hemodialysis, and venous thrombosis. No clamping of this catheter or splinting of the arm permitted. No blood pressure or tourniquets to be used on extremity where peripherally inserted central catheter is inserted.	Dermatitis, cellulitis, burns, high fluid volume infusions, rapid bolus injection, hemodialysis, and venous thrombosis. No blood pressure or tourniquet to be used on extremity where midline catheter is placed.
Catheter maintenance	Sterile dressing changes according to agency policy and procedures. Generally, dressing is changed every 2–3 days or when wet, soiled, or nonocclusive. Line is flushed every shift with 3 mL normal saline followed by heparin 3 mL (100 U/mL) per lumen. The nurse follows institutional policy for flushing catheter.	Sterile dressing changes according to policy and procedures. Generally, dressing is changed every 2–3 days or when wet, soiled, or nonocclusive. Line is flushed after each infusion or every shift with 5–10 mL normal saline followed by 1 mL of heparin (100 U/mL). Catheter must be anchored securely to prevent its dislodgment. The nurse follows institutional policy for flushing catheter.

	Peripherally Inserted Central Catheter	Peripheral-Midline Catheter
Postplacement	Chest X-ray needed to confirm placement of catheter tip.	Chest X-ray to assess placement may be obtained if unable to flush catheter, if no free flow blood return, if difficulty with catheter advancement, or if guide wire is difficult to remove or bent on removal.
Assessment	Daily measurement of arm circumference (4 inches above insertion site) and length of exposed catheter	Daily measurement of arm circumference (4 inches above insertion site) and length of exposed catheter
Removal	Catheter should be removed when no longer indicated for use, if contaminated, or if complications occur. Arm is abducted during removal. Patient should be in a dorsal recumbent position with head of bed flat and should perform the Valsalva maneuver while catheter is withdrawn. Pressure is applied on removal with a sterile dressing and antiseptic ointment to site. Dressing is changed every 24 hours until epithelialization occurs.	Catheter should be removed when no longer indicated for use, if contaminated, or if complications occur. Arm is abducted during removal. Pressure is applied on removal with a sterile dressing and antiseptic ointment to site. Dressing is changed every 24 hours until epithelialization occurs.
Advantages	Reduces cost and avoids repeated venipunctures compared with centrally placed catheters. Decreases incidence of catheter-related infections.	Reduces cost and avoids repeated venipunctures compared with centrally placed catheters. Decreases incidence of catheter-related infections.

with routine gravity-flow setups. A pump is a positive-pressure device that uses pressure to infuse fluid at a pressure of 10 psi; newer models use a pressure of 5 psi. The pressure exerted by the pump overrides vascular resistance (increased tubing length, low height of the IV container).

Volumetric pumps calculate the volume delivered by measuring the volume in a reservoir that is part of the set and is calibrated in milliliters per hour (mL/h). A controller is an infusion assist device that relies on gravity for infusion; the volume is calibrated in drops (gtt) per minute. A controller uses a drop sensor to monitor the flow. Factors essential for the safe use of pumps include alarms to signify the presence of air in the IV line or an occlusion. The standard for the accurate delivery of fluid or medication via an electronic IV infusion pump is plus or minus 5%. The manufacturer's directions must be read carefully before use of any infusion pump or controller because there are many variations in available models. Use of these devices does not eliminate the need for the nurse to monitor the infusion and the patient frequently; however, it does limit the amount of bedside drug calculations and medication administration errors.

Flushing of a vascular device is performed to ensure patency and to prevent the mixing of incompatible medications or solutions. This procedure should be carried out at established intervals, according to hospital policy and procedure, especially for intermittently used catheters. Most manufacturers and researchers suggest the use of saline for flushing. The volume of the flush solution should be at least twice the volume capacity of the catheter. The catheter should be clamped before the syringe is completely empty and withdrawn to prevent reflux of blood into the lumen, which could cause catheter clotting and infiltration.

Discontinuing an Infusion

The removal of an IV catheter is associated with two possible dangers: bleeding and catheter embolism. To prevent excessive bleeding, a dry, sterile pressure dressing should be held over the site as the catheter is removed. Firm pressure is applied until hemostasis occurs.

If a plastic IV catheter is severed, the patient is at risk for catheter embolism. To detect this complication when the catheter is removed, the nurse compares the expected length of the catheter with its actual length. Plastic catheters should be withdrawn carefully and their length measured to make certain that no fragment has broken off in the vein.

Great care must be exercised when using scissors around the dressing site. If the catheter clearly has been severed, the nurse can attempt to occlude the vein above the site by applying a tourniquet to prevent the catheter from entering the central circulation (until surgical removal is possible). However, as always, it is better to prevent a potentially fatal problem than to deal with it after it has occurred. Fortunately, catheter embolism can be prevented easily by following simple rules:

- Avoid using scissors near the catheter.
- Avoid withdrawing the catheter through the insertion needle.

- Follow the manufacturer's guidelines carefully (e.g., cover the needle point with the bevel shield to prevent severance of the catheter).

Managing Systemic Complications

IV therapy predisposes the patient to numerous hazards, including both local and systemic complications. Systemic complications occur less frequently but are usually more serious than are local complications. They include circulatory overload, air embolism, febrile reaction, and infection.

Overloading the circulatory system with excessive IV fluids causes increased blood pressure and central venous pressure. Signs and symptoms of fluid overload include moist crackles on auscultation of the lungs, edema, weight gain, dyspnea, and respirations that are shallow and have an increased rate. Possible causes include rapid infusion of an IV solution or hepatic, cardiac, or renal disease. The risk of fluid overload and subsequent pulmonary edema is especially increased in elderly patients with cardiac disease; this is referred to as *circulatory overload.*

The treatment for circulatory overload is decreasing the IV rate, monitoring vital signs frequently, assessing breath sounds, and placing the patient in a high Fowler's position. The provider is contacted immediately. This complication can be avoided by using an infusion pump for infusions and by carefully monitoring all infusions. Complications of circulatory overload include heart failure and pulmonary edema.

The risk of air embolism is rare but ever-present. It is most often associated with cannulation of central veins. Manifestations of air embolism include dyspnea and cyanosis; hypotension; weak, rapid pulse; loss of consciousness; and chest, shoulder, and low back pain. Treatment calls for immediately clamping the cannula and replacing a leaking or open infusion system, placing the patient on the left side in the Trendelenburg position, assessing vital signs and breath sounds, and administering oxygen. Air embolism can be prevented by using a Luer-Lock adapter on all lines, filling all tubing completely with solution, and using an air detection alarm on an IV pump. Complications of air embolism include shock and death. The amount of air necessary to induce death in humans is not known; however, the rate of entry is probably as important as the actual volume of air.

Pyrogenic substances in either the infusion solution or the IV administration set can induce a febrile reaction and septicemia. Signs and symptoms include an abrupt temperature elevation shortly after the infusion is started, backache, headache, increased pulse and respiratory rate, nausea and vomiting, diarrhea, chills and shaking, and general malaise. In severe septicemia, vascular collapse and septic shock may occur. Causes of septicemia include contamination of the IV product or a break in aseptic technique, especially in immunocompromised patients. Treatment is symptomatic and includes culturing of the IV cannula, tubing, or solution if it is suspect, and establishing a new IV site for medication

or fluid administration. See Chapter 54 for a discussion of septic shock.

Infection ranges in severity from local involvement of the insertion site to systemic dissemination of organisms through the bloodstream, as in septicemia. Measures to prevent infection are essential at the time the IV line is inserted and throughout the entire infusion. Prevention includes the following:

- Careful hand hygiene before every contact with any part of the infusion system or the patient
- Examining the IV containers for cracks, leaks, or cloudiness; these findings may indicate a contaminated solution
- Using strict aseptic technique
- Firmly anchoring the IV cannula to prevent to-and-fro motion
- Inspecting the IV site daily and replacing a soiled or wet dressing with a dry sterile dressing (antimicrobial agents that should be used for site care may include 2% tincture of iodine, 10% povidone–iodine, alcohol, or chlorhexidine gluconate, used alone or in combination per the institution's policy)
- Disinfecting injection/access ports with antimicrobial solution before use
- Removing the IV cannula at the first sign of local inflammation, contamination, or complication
- Replacing the peripheral IV cannula every 72 hours, or as indicated
- Replacing the IV cannula inserted during emergency conditions (with questionable asepsis) as soon as possible
- Using a 0.2-μm air-eliminating and bacteria/particulate retentive filter with non–lipid-containing solutions that require filtration. The filter can be added to the proximal or distal end of the administration set. If added to the proximal end between the fluid container and the tubing spike, the filter ensures sterility and particulate removal from the infusate container and prevents inadvertent infusion of air. If added to the distal end of the administration set, it filters air particles and contaminants introduced from add-on devices, secondary administration sets, or interruptions to the primary system.
- Replacing the solution bag and administration set in accordance with agency policy and procedure
- Infusing or discarding medication or solution within 24 hours of its addition to an administration set
- Changing primary and secondary continuous administration sets every 96 hours, or immediately if contamination is suspected (Gillies, Wallen, Morrison et al., 2008)
- Changing primary administration sets containing lipid based solutions every 24 hours, or immediately if contamination is suspected (Gillies, Wallen, Morrison et al., 2008)

Managing Local Complications

Local complications of IV therapy include infiltration and extravasation, phlebitis, thrombophlebitis, hematoma, and clotting of the needle.

Infiltration is the unintentional administration of a non-vesicant solution or medication into surrounding tissue. This can occur when the IV cannula dislodges or perforates the wall of the vein. Infiltration is characterized by edema around the insertion site, leakage of IV fluid from the insertion site, discomfort and coolness in the area of infiltration, and a significant decrease in the flow rate. When the solution is particularly irritating, sloughing of tissue may result. Close monitoring of the insertion site is necessary to detect infiltration before it becomes severe.

Infiltration is usually easily recognized if the insertion area is larger than the same site of the opposite extremity; however, it is not always so obvious. A common misconception is that a backflow of blood into the tubing proves that the catheter is properly placed within the vein. However, if the catheter tip has pierced the wall of the vessel, IV fluid will seep into tissues as well as flow into the vein. Although blood return occurs, infiltration has occurred as well. A more reliable means of confirming infiltration is to apply a tourniquet above (or proximal to) the infusion site and tighten it enough to restrict venous flow. If the infusion continues to drip despite the venous obstruction, infiltration is present.

As soon as the nurse notes infiltration, the infusion should be stopped, the IV discontinued, and a sterile dressing applied to the site after careful inspection to determine the extent of infiltration. The infiltration of any amount of blood product, irritant, or vesicant is considered the most severe.

The IV infusion should be started in a new site or proximal to the infiltration if the same extremity must be used again. A warm compress may be applied to the site if small volumes of noncaustic solutions have infiltrated over a long period, or if the solution was isotonic with a normal pH; the affected extremity should be elevated to promote the absorption of fluid. If the infiltration is recent and the solution was hypertonic or had an increased pH, a cold compress may be applied to the area. Infiltration can be detected and treated early by inspecting the site every hour for redness, pain, edema coolness at the site, and IV fluid leaking from the IV site. Using the appropriate size and type of cannula for the vein prevents this complication.

Extravasation is similar to infiltration, with an inadvertent administration of vesicant or irritant solution or medication into the surrounding tissue. Medications such as dopamine, calcium preparations, and chemotherapeutic agents can cause pain, burning, and redness at the site. Blistering, inflammation, and necrosis of tissues can occur. The extent of tissue damage is determined by the concentration of the medication, the quantity that extravasated, the location of the infusion site, the tissue response, and the duration of the process of extravasation.

The infusion must be stopped and the provider notified promptly. The agency's protocol to treat extravasation is initiated; the protocol may specify specific treatments, including antidotes specific to the medication that extravasated, and may indicate whether the IV line should remain in place or be removed before treatment. The protocol often specifies infiltration of the infusion site with an antidote prescribed after assessment by the provider, removal of the cannula, and application of warm compresses to sites of extravasation from vinca alkaloids or cold compresses to sites of extravasation from alkylating and antibiotic vesicants (Weinstein, 2007). The affected extremity should not be used for further cannula placement. Thorough neurovascular assessments of the affected extremity must be performed frequently.

Reviewing the institution's IV policy and procedures and incompatibility charts and checking with the pharmacist before administering any IV medication, whether given peripherally or centrally, is a prudent way to determine incompatibilities and vesicant potential to prevent extravasation. Careful, frequent monitoring of the IV site, avoiding insertion of IV devices in areas of flexion, securing the IV line, and using the smallest catheter possible that accommodates the vein help minimize the incidence and severity of this complication. In addition, when vesicant medication is administered by IV push, it should be given through a side port of an infusing IV solution to dilute the medication and decrease the severity of tissue damage if extravasation occurs.

Signs of phlebitis and infiltration may be assessed using a scale such as the Infusion Nurses Society (INS) infiltration scale (Hawes, 2007). The scale ranges from 0, or no edema, to 4, which includes pitting edema, moderate to severe pain at the site, or circulatory impairment. Extravasation should always be rated as a grade 4 on the infiltration scale.

Phlebitis is defined as inflammation of a vein, which can be categorized as chemical, mechanical, or bacterial; however, two or more of these types of irritation often occur simultaneously. Chemical phlebitis can be caused by an irritating medication or solution (increased pH or high osmolality of a solution), rapid infusion rates, and medication incompatibilities. Mechanical phlebitis results from long periods of cannulation, catheters in flexed areas, catheter gauges larger than the vein lumen, and poorly secured catheters. Bacterial phlebitis can develop from poor hand hygiene, lack of aseptic technique, failure to check all equipment before use, and failure to recognize early signs and symptoms of phlebitis. Other factors include poor venipuncture technique, catheter in place for a prolonged period, and failure to adequately secure the catheter. Phlebitis is characterized by a reddened, warm area around the insertion site or along the path of the vein, pain or tenderness at the site or along the vein, and swelling. The incidence of phlebitis increases with the length of time the IV line is in place, the composition of the fluid or medication infused (especially its pH and tonicity), the size and site of the cannula inserted, ineffective filtration, inadequate anchoring of the line, and the introduction of microorganisms at the time of insertion. Treatment consists of discontinuing the IV and restarting it in another site, and applying a warm, moist compress to the affected site. Phlebitis can be prevented by using aseptic

technique during insertion, using the appropriate-size cannula or needle for the vein, considering the composition of fluids and medications when selecting a site, observing the site hourly for any complications, anchoring the cannula or needle well, and changing the IV site according to agency policy and procedures.

Thrombophlebitis refers to the presence of a clot plus inflammation in the vein. It is evidenced by localized pain, redness, warmth, and swelling around the insertion site or along the path of the vein, immobility of the extremity because of discomfort and swelling, sluggish flow rate, fever, malaise, and leukocytosis.

Treatment includes discontinuing the IV infusion; applying a cold compress first, to decrease the flow of blood and increase platelet aggregation, followed by a warm compress; elevating the extremity; and restarting the line in the opposite extremity. If the patient has signs and symptoms of thrombophlebitis, the IV line should not be flushed (although flushing may be indicated in the absence of phlebitis to ensure cannula patency and to prevent mixing of incompatible medications and solutions). The catheter must be removed promptly. In some circumstances, the catheter tip may be sent to the laboratory for culture, and it should be removed and placed in a sterile container prior to sending to the lab. Thrombophlebitis can be prevented by avoiding trauma to the vein at the time the IV is inserted, observing the site every hour, and checking medication additives for compatibility.

Hematoma results when blood leaks into tissues surrounding the IV insertion site. Leakage can result if the opposite vein wall is perforated during venipuncture, the needle slips out of the vein, or insufficient pressure is applied to the site after removal of the needle or cannula. The signs of a hematoma include ecchymosis, immediate swelling at the site, and leakage of blood at the insertion site.

Treatment includes removing the needle or cannula and applying light pressure with a sterile, dry dressing; applying ice for 24 hours to the site to avoid extension of the hematoma; elevating the extremity; assessing the extremity for any circulatory, neurologic, or motor dysfunction; and restarting the line in the other extremity if indicated. A hematoma can be prevented by carefully inserting the needle and by using diligent care with patients who have a bleeding disorder, are taking anticoagulant medication, or have advanced liver disease.

Blood clots may form in the IV line as a result of kinked IV tubing, a very slow infusion rate, an empty IV bag, or failure to flush the IV line after intermittent medication or solution administrations. The signs are decreased flow rate and blood backflow into the IV tubing. If blood clots in the IV line, the infusion must be discontinued and restarted in another site with a new cannula and administration set. The tubing should not be irrigated or milked. Neither the infusion rate nor the solution container should be raised, and the clot should not be aspirated from the tubing. Clotting of the needle or cannula may be prevented by not allowing the IV solution bag to run dry, taping the tubing to prevent kinking and maintain patency, maintaining an adequate flow rate, and flushing the line after intermittent medication or other solution administration. In some cases, a specially trained nurse or physician may inject a thrombolytic agent.

Chapter Review

Critical Thinking Exercises

1. A 28-year-old man with a history of diabetes mellitus has an open fracture of the tibia as the result of a motorcycle crash. In the emergency department, his temperature is 103°F. His laboratory test results are as follows: blood glucose, 450 mg/dL; BUN, 35 mg/dL; sodium, 140 mEq/L; potassium, 4.1 mEq/L; pH, 7.1; PCO_2, 10 mm Hg; and HCO_3^-, 12 mEq/L. His urine ketones are 3+. What fluid and electrolyte or acid–base disorders is the patient experiencing? What IV fluids would you anticipate being prescribed? Give the rationale for their use. What treatments would address the patient's fluid and electrolyte or acid–base disorders?

2. A 30-year-old woman comes to the emergency department with nausea, confusion, dehydration, and oliguria. Her mother reports that she has been depressed after losing her job as a bank executive. An empty bottle of aspirin was found in her bathroom sink. Her laboratory values are as follows: pH, 7.35; $PaCO_2$, 16 mm Hg; PaO_2, 98 mm Hg; and HCO_3^-, 15 mEq/L. What acid–base disorder does this patient have? What treatments and relevant nursing actions related to the underlying disorder and its treatment should the nurse anticipate?

3. A 58-year-old woman is vomiting bright red blood. She is hypotensive. Her pulse rate is 108 bpm, and her pulse is weak and thready. Her ABG results are as follows: pH, 7.34; $PaCO_2$, 35 mm Hg; PaO_2, 69 mm Hg; and HCO_3^-, 20 mEq/L. Her hemoglobin is 4 g/dL. How do you interpret the patient's blood gas values? What treatment would you anticipate?

NCLEX-Style Review Questions

1. A nurse is analyzing her patient's ABG values. Which of the following is inconsistent with the diagnosis of respiratory acidosis?
   A. pH 7.3
   B. pCO_2 48
   C. Hyperventilation
   D. Hypoventilation

2. A patient diagnosed with SIADH. Which of the following disturbances should the nurse be aware of related to this diagnosis?
   A. Excess water loss
   B. Dilutional hyponatremia
   C. Serum sodium level of 148 mg/dL
   D. Decreased urine osmolality

3. A nurse working on a trauma unit is initiating IV fluids for a patient. Normal saline is used for which of the following patient problems?

A. Renal impairment
B. Pulmonary edema
C. Burns
D. Heart failure

4. When entering a patient's room, the nurse notices blood clots in the IV line. What is the most appropriate nursing intervention at this time?
   A. Milk the tubing.
   B Discontinue the infusion.
   C. Irrigate the tubing and catheter.
   D. Aspirate clot from tubing.

5. The nurse would expect which of the following to occur on the ECG reading when serum potassium levels rise to greater than 6 mEq/L?
   A. Peaked, widened T waves
   B. ST-segment elevation
   C. Lengthen QT interval
   D. ST-segment depression

Try these additional resources to enhance your learning and understanding of this chapter:
- the Point online resource available at **http://thepoint.lww.com/Pellico1e**
- *Handbook for Focus on Adult Health: Medical-Surgical Nursing*
- *Study Guide for Focus on Adult Health: Medical-Surgical Nursing*

References and Selected Readings

References and selected readings associated with this chapter can be found on the website that accompanies the book. Visit http://thepoint.lww.com/Pellico1e to access the references and other additional resources associated with this chapter.

ENA M. WILLIAMS
LINDA HONAN PELLICO

Perioperative Nursing

Learning Objectives

After reading this chapter, you will be able to:

1. Define the three phases of perioperative nursing

2. Describe a comprehensive preoperative assessment to identify surgical risk factors.

3. Identify legal and ethical considerations related to informed consent.

4. Describe the immediate preoperative preparation, and intraoperative and postoperative management of the surgical patient.

5. Identify the nurse's role in patient safety and regulatory compliance in the perioperative setting.

6. Describe the principles of surgical asepsis.

7. Identify adverse effects of surgery and anesthesia.

8. Describe types of anesthetic approaches and the implications for nursing care in the perioperative setting.

9. Describe perioperative nursing measures that decrease the risk for complications.

Surgery, whether elective or emergent, is a stressful, complex event. The special field known as **perioperative** and perianesthesia nursing includes a wide variety of nursing functions associated with the patient's surgical experience during the perioperative period.

INTRODUCTION

Phases

Perioperative and perianesthesia nursing addresses the nursing roles relevant to the three phases of the surgical experience: preoperative, intraoperative, and postoperative. Each phase begins and ends at a particular point in the sequence of events that constitutes the surgical experience, and each includes a wide range of activities the nurse performs using the nursing process and based on the standards of practice (American Society of Perianesthesia Nurses, 2008). Box 5-1 represents nursing activities characteristic of the three perioperative phases of care.

Surgical Settings

Today, as a result of advances in surgical techniques and instrumentation, as well as in **anesthesia**, the number of surgeries, imaging studies, and diagnostic tests performed outside of hospitals is growing rapidly. These procedures are primarily moving to **ambulatory surgery** centers (ASC), which provide outpatient surgical services not requiring an overnight stay, independent diagnostic and testing facilities, and health providers' offices. Innovation in medical technology and surgical techniques, along with preferences of multiple players in the health care system, has driven the migration of care to nonhospital settings. Less invasive surgical techniques and advances in anesthesia have made it possible for more procedures to be performed in outpatient settings, where recovery time is limited. As a result, today, many patients arrive at the hospital on the morning of surgery and go home after recovering from the anesthesia in the postanesthesia care unit (PACU). Often, surgical patients who require hospital stays are trauma patients, acutely ill patients, and/or patients undergoing major surgery.

BOX 5-1
Examples of Nursing Activities in the Perioperative Phases of Care

Preoperative Phase
Preadmission Testing

1. Initiates initial preoperative assessment
2. Initiates teaching appropriate to patient's needs
3. Involves family in interview
4. Verifies completion of preoperative testing
5. Verifies understanding of surgeon-specific preoperative orders (e.g., bowel preparation, preoperative shower)
6. Assesses patient's need for postoperative transportation and care

Admission to Surgical Center or Unit

1. Completes preoperative assessment
2. Assesses patient's status, including nutritional status and baseline level of pain
3. Assesses for risks for postoperative complications
4. Reports unexpected findings or any deviations from normal
5. Verifies that operative consent and all appropriate documents have been signed
6. Coordinates patient teaching with other nursing staff and reinforces previous teaching
7. Explains phases in perioperative period and expectations. Answers patient's and family's questions
8. Develops a plan of care
9. Removes and secures prosthesis, dentures, glasses, jewelry
10. Ensures interpreter is present if patient requires
11. Encourages patient to void immediately preop
12. Establishes IV line
13. Administers medications if prescribed, reminds patient not to get OOB after premedicated
14. Takes measures to ensure patient's comfort
15. Provides psychological support
16. Communicates patient's emotional status to other appropriate members of the health care team

Intraoperative Phase
Maintenance of Safety

1. Maintains aseptic, controlled environment
2. Effectively manages human resources, equipment, and supplies for individualized patient care
3. Transfers patient to operating room bed or table
4. Positions the patient:
   a. Functional alignment and secures patient to operating room table
   b. Initiates pressure ulcer reduction and skin injury processes
   c. Exposure of surgical site
5. Applies grounding device to patient

6. Ensures that the sponge, needle, and instrument counts are correct
7. Ensures that the final verification (time out) is conducted and documented
8. Completes intraoperative documentation
9. Maintains an environment to support patients' body temperature as per procedural protocol

Psychological Support (Before Induction and When Patient Is Conscious)

1. Provides emotional support to patient
2. Stands near or touches patient during procedures and induction
3. Continues to assess patient's emotional status

Postoperative Phase
Transfer of Patient to Postanesthesia Care Unit

1. Communicates intraoperative information:
   a. Identifies patient by name
   b. States type of surgery performed
   c. Identifies type of anesthetic used
   d. Reports patient's response to surgical procedure and anesthesia
   e. Describes intraoperative factors (e.g., insertion of drains or catheters; administration of blood, analgesic agents, or other medications during surgery; occurrence of unexpected events)
   f. Describes physical limitations
   g. Reports patient's preoperative level of consciousness
   h. Communicates necessary equipment needs
   i. Communicates presence of family and/or significant others

Postoperative Assessment Recovery Area

1. Determines patient's immediate response to surgical intervention
2. Monitors patient's physiologic status
3. Assesses patient's pain level and administers appropriate pain relief measures
4. Maintains patient's safety (airway, circulation, prevention of injury)
5. Administers medications, fluid, and blood component therapy, if prescribed
6. Provides oral fluids if prescribed for ambulatory surgery patient
7. Assesses patient's readiness for transfer to in-hospital unit or for discharge home based on institutional policy

(continued on page 104)

BOX 5-1

Examples of Nursing Activities in the Perioperative Phases of Care (continued)

Surgical Unit

1. Continues close monitoring of patient's physical and psychological response to surgical intervention
2. Assesses patient's pain level and administers appropriate pain relief measures
3. Provides teaching to patient during immediate recovery period
4. Assists patient in recovery and preparation for discharge home
5. Determines patient's psychological status
6. Assists with discharge planning

Home or Clinic

1. Provides follow-up care during office or clinic visit or by telephone contact
2. Reinforces previous teaching and answers patient's and family's questions about surgery and follow-up care
3. Assesses patient's response to surgery and anesthesia and their effects on body image and function
4. Determines family's perception of surgery and its outcome

Although each setting (ambulatory, outpatient, or inpatient) offers its own unique advantages for the delivery of patient care, they all require comprehensive preoperative nursing assessment and nursing interventions, and a sound knowledge of all aspects of perioperative and perianesthesia nursing.

Surgical Classifications

Surgery may be performed for various reasons. A surgical procedure may be diagnostic (e.g., biopsy, exploratory laparotomy), curative (e.g., excision of a tumor or an inflamed appendix), or reparative (e.g., multiple wound repair). It may be reconstructive or cosmetic (e.g., mammoplasty or a face-lift) or palliative (e.g., to relieve pain or correct a problem—for instance, a gastrostomy tube may be inserted to compensate for the inability to swallow food). Surgery may also be classified according to the degree of urgency involved (Table 5-1).

Emergency Surgery

Emergency surgeries are unplanned and occur with little time for preparation of the patient or the perioperative team. The unpredictable nature of trauma and emergency surgery poses unique challenges to the nurse throughout the perioperative period. All of the factors that affect patients preparing to undergo surgery apply to these patients, usually in a very condensed time frame. The only preoperative assessment may take place at the same time as resuscitation in the emergency department. For the unconscious patient, informed consent and essential information, such as pertinent past medical history and allergies, need to be obtained from a family member, if one is available. A quick visual survey of the patient is essential to identify all sites of injury if the emergency surgery is due to trauma. The patient, who may have undergone a very frightening experience, may need extra support, including an explanation of the surgery.

TABLE
5-1 Categories of Surgery Based on Urgency

Classification	Indications for Surgery	Examples
I. Emergent—Patient requires immediate attention; disorder may be life-threatening	Without delay	Severe bleeding Bladder or intestinal obstruction Fractured skull Gunshot or stab wounds Extensive burns
II. Urgent—Patient requires prompt attention	Within 24–30 hours	Acute gallbladder infection Kidney or ureteral stones
III. Required—Patient needs to have surgery	Plan within a few weeks or months	Prostatic hyperplasia without bladder obstruction Thyroid disorders Cataracts
IV. Elective—Patient should have surgery	Failure to have surgery not catastrophic	Repair of scars Simple hernia Vaginal repair
V. Optional—Decision rests with patient	Personal preference	Cosmetic surgery

Special Populations

Patients Who Are Elderly

Advances in nutrition, public health, education, and social services have produced a major change in human longevity in industrialized societies, and elderly patients now account for more than a third of all hospital care days in the United States. In addition, almost one-third of all surgical patients are 65 years of age or older, and an even larger fraction is anticipated in the next two decades (Rooke, 2009). Although the decision to operate lies within the purview of the physician, perioperative nurses should be aware of its implications. Surgical intervention should be tailored to the patient's symptoms, overall functional and health status, and predicted benefit of the intervention. Important factors that need to be evaluated are (1) disease course versus life expectancy, (2) state of independence, (3) personal motivation, and (4) surgical risk factors versus nonoperative management (Rothrock, 2011).

Preoperative pain assessment and teaching are important in the elderly patient. The older person undergoing surgery may have a combination of chronic illnesses and health issues in addition to the specific one for which surgery is indicated. Elderly people frequently do not report symptoms, perhaps because they fear a serious illness may be diagnosed or because they accept such symptoms as part of the aging process. Subtle clues alert the nurse to underlying problems.

Health care staff must remember that the hazards of surgery for the aged are proportional to the number and severity of coexisting health problems and the nature and duration of the operative procedure. The underlying principle that guides the preoperative assessment, surgical care, and postoperative care is that the aged patient has less physiologic reserve (the ability of an organ to return to normal after a disturbance in its equilibrium) than does a younger patient. Refer to Table 5-2 for the implications of aging on operative course. The nurse plans interventions based upon the patient's medical history, clinical presentation, and knowledge of the physiological impact of aging. For example, arthritis is common in older people and may affect mobility, making it difficult for the patient to turn from one side to the other or ambulate without discomfort. The elderly patient has less subcutaneous fat, poor skin turgor, and tissue fragility. Aging-related changes in the musculoskeletal system accentuate bony prominences and decrease range of motion. These changes, along with limitations imposed by chronic pain, make positioning one of the most important considerations for this population of surgical patients. Protective measures include adequate padding for tender areas, moving the patient slowly, and protecting bony prominences

---

TABLE
5-2 **GERONTOLOGICAL CONSIDERATIONS** / Age-Related Changes and Impact on Operative Course

Structural or Functional Change	Impact
Increased incidence of coexisting disease	Elderly patients face higher risks from anesthesia and surgery than do younger adult patients.
Aging heart and blood vessels	Decreased ability to respond to stress
Reduced cardiac output and limited cardiac reserve	Increased vulnerability to changes in circulating volume and blood oxygen levels. In addition, excessive or rapid administration of IV solutions can cause pulmonary edema.
Decreased ability to compensate for hypoxia	Increased risk of cerebral ischemia, thrombosis, embolism, infarction, and anoxia
Decrease in the percentage of lean body tissue and a steady increase in fatty tissue (from 20 to 90 years of age).	Anesthetic agents that have an affinity for fatty tissue concentrate in body fat and the brain. The elderly patient needs fewer and smaller amounts of anesthetic agents to produce anesthesia, and eliminates the anesthetic agent over a longer period of time, compared with a younger patient.
If malnourished or has low plasma protein levels (hypoalbuminemia)	With decreased plasma proteins, more of the anesthetic agent remains free or unbound, and the result is more potent action.
Reduced liver size and potential for reduced renal function	Decreases the rate at which the liver can inactivate many anesthetic agents, and decreased kidney function slows the elimination of waste products and anesthetics
Impaired ability to increase metabolic rate and impaired thermoregulatory mechanisms	Increased susceptibility to hypothermia
Bone loss (25% in women, 12% in men)	Increased risk of musculoskeletal problems post operatively
Loss of collagen and muscle, thinning, sagging skin	Increased risk of skin complications
Impaired vision or hearing and reduced tactile sensitivity	Increased potential for communication issues, increased risk of skin complications
Increased tooth loss and periodontal disease, increased incidence of dental devices (dentures, partial plates, crowns)	Increased risk of airway occlusion due to dental device dislodgement

from prolonged pressure. Precautions are taken when moving an elderly person because of the fragility of skin, and a lightweight cotton blanket is an appropriate cover when an elderly patient is moved to and from the operating room (OR) because of temperature sensitivity.

Additionally, many elderly people have experienced personal illnesses and the possibly life-threatening illnesses of friends and family. Such experiences may result in fears about the surgery and about the future. Providing an opportunity to express these fears enables the patient to gain some peace of mind.

Because the elderly patient may face greater risks during the perioperative period, the following factors are critical: (1) skillful preoperative assessment and treatment, (2) skillful anesthesia and surgery, and (3) meticulous and competent postoperative and postanesthesia management. In addition, the nurse should incorporate pain management information and pain communication skills when teaching the elderly patient how to obtain greater postoperative pain relief.

Patients Who Are Obese

Like age, obesity increases the risk and severity of complications associated with surgery. During surgery, fatty tissues are especially susceptible to infection. In addition, obesity increases technical and mechanical problems related to surgery. Therefore, dehiscence (wound separation) and wound infections are more common. Moreover, the obese patient may be more difficult to care for because of the added weight. The patient tends to have shallow respirations when supine, which increases the risk of hypoventilation and postoperative pulmonary complications. It has been estimated that for each 30 pounds of excess weight, about 25 additional miles of blood vessels are needed, and this places increased demands on the heart. Thus, nursing management includes careful assessment of the cardiopulmonary status of obese patients and thorough wound assessments.

Patients With Disabilities

Special considerations for patients with mental or physical disabilities include the need for appropriate assistive devices, modifications in preoperative teaching, and additional assistance with and attention to positioning or transferring. Assistive devices include hearing aids, eyeglasses, braces, prostheses, and other devices. People who are hearing-impaired may need a sign interpreter or some alternative communication system perioperatively. If the patient relies on signing or speech (lip) reading, and his or her eyeglasses or contact lenses are removed or the health care staff wears surgical masks, an alternative method of communication will be needed. These needs must be identified during the preoperative evaluation and clearly communicated to the appropriate personnel. Specific strategies for accommodating the patient's needs must be identified in advance. Ensuring the security of assistive devices is important, because these devices are expensive and can be easily misplaced.

Most patients are directed to move from the stretcher to the OR table and back again. In addition to being unable to see or hear instructions, the patient with a disability may be unable to move without special devices or a great deal of assistance. The patient with a disability that affects body position (e.g., cerebral palsy, post-polio syndrome, and other neuromuscular disorders) may need special positioning during surgery to prevent pain and injury. Moreover, these patients may be unable to sense whether their extremities are positioned incorrectly.

Patients with respiratory problems related to a disability (e.g., multiple sclerosis, muscular dystrophy) may experience pulmonary difficulties unless the problems are made known to the anesthesiologist or anesthetist and adjustments are made. These factors need to be clearly identified in the preoperative period and communicated to the appropriate personnel.

PREOPERATIVE NURSING

The **preoperative phase** begins when the decision to proceed with surgical intervention is made, and ends with the transfer of the patient onto the OR table. The scope of nursing activities during this time involves establishing a baseline evaluation of the patient before surgery by carrying out a preoperative interview (which includes a physical and emotional assessment, previous anesthetic and medical history, and identification of known allergies or genetics issues that may affect the surgical outcome), ensuring that necessary tests have been or will be performed during the preadmission testing (PAT) visit, arranging appropriate consultations, and providing education about recovery from anesthesia and postoperative care.

Informed Consent

The surgical experience, except in extreme emergencies, begins after a patient has consented to a recommended surgical procedure. Voluntary and written **informed consent** from the patient is necessary before nonemergent surgery can be performed. The Department of Health and Human Services, Centers for Medicare and Medicaid Services (CMS), believes that a patient or his or her representative (as allowed under state law) has the right to make informed decisions regarding his or her care. The guidelines further indicate that, for the surgical patient, a properly executed informed consent form for the operation must be in the patient's chart before surgery, except in emergencies. The primary purpose of the informed consent process for surgical services is to ensure that the patient, or the patient's representative, is provided information necessary to enable him or her to evaluate the proposed surgery before agreeing to it (DiGiulio, 2008). A written consent protects the patient from unsanctioned surgery and protects the surgeon from claims of an unauthorized

operation. It is normally the responsibility of the performing surgeon to obtain the informed surgical consent, which should consist of the following four basic elements:

- The physician documents that the patient or surrogate has capacity to make a medical decision.
- The surgeon discloses to the patient details regarding the diagnosis and treatment options sufficiently for the patient to make an informed choice.
- The patient demonstrates understanding of the disclosed information.
- The patient freely authorizes a specific treatment plan without undue influence (Hall, Angelos, Dunn, et al., 2010).

Informed consent is necessary in the following circumstances:

- Invasive procedures, such as a surgical incision, a biopsy, a cystoscopy, or paracentesis
- Procedures requiring sedation and/or anesthesia
- A nonsurgical procedure, such as an arteriography, that carries more than slight risk to the patient
- Procedures involving radiation

If the patient has doubts and has not had the opportunity to investigate alternative treatments, a second opinion may be requested. No patient should be urged or coerced to give informed consent. Refusing to undergo a surgical procedure is a person's legal right and privilege.

The consent process can be improved by providing audiovisual materials to supplement discussion, by ensuring that the wording of the consent form is understandable, and by using other strategies and resources as needed to help the patient understand its content. It is required to have the consent available in multiple languages or have a trained medical interpreter available for non–English speaking patients. In many cases, it is required to have alternative forms of communication (e.g., Braille, large print, sign interpreter) for the elderly and disabled.

Preoperative Health Assessment

Before any surgical treatment is initiated, a health history is obtained, a physical examination is performed during which vital signs are noted, and a database is established for future comparisons. Preoperative blood tests, X-rays, and other diagnostic tests are obtained.

The goal in the preoperative period is for the patient to have as many positive health factors as possible. Many risk factors may lead to complications (Box 5-2). Every attempt is made to stabilize those conditions that otherwise hinder recovery.

Nutritional and Fluid Status

Optimal nutrition is an essential factor in promoting healing and resisting infection and other surgical complications. Assessment of a patient's nutritional status identifies factors that can affect the patient's surgical course, such as obesity,

---

BOX 5-2 | **Risk Factors for Surgical Complications**

- Hypovolemia
- Dehydration or electrolyte imbalance
- Nutritional deficits
- Extremes of age (very young, very old)
- Extremes of weight (emaciation, obesity)
- Infection and sepsis
- Toxic conditions
- Immunologic abnormalities
- Pulmonary disease:
  - Obstructive disease
  - Restrictive disorder
  - Respiratory infection
- Renal or urinary tract disease:
  - Decreased renal function
  - Urinary tract infection
  - Obstruction
- Pregnancy (because of diminished maternal physiologic reserve)
- Cardiovascular disease:
  - Coronary artery disease or previous myocardial infarction
  - Cardiac failure
  - Arrhythmias
  - Hypertension
  - Prosthetic heart valve
  - Thromboembolism
  - Hemorrhagic disorders
- Cerebrovascular disease
- Endocrine dysfunction:
  - Diabetes mellitus
  - Adrenal disorders
  - Thyroid malfunction
- Hepatic disease:
  - Cirrhosis
  - Hepatitis
- Preexisting mental or physical disability

---

undernutrition, weight loss, malnutrition, deficiencies in specific nutrients, metabolic abnormalities, and the effects of medications on nutrition. Nutritional needs may be determined by measurement of body mass index (BMI) and waist circumference (U.S. Department of Health and Human Services, 2008). A BMI of 18.5 to 24.9 is normal; less than 18.5 is underweight, greater than 25 is overweight, and greater than 30 is obese. A waist circumference measurement of greater than 40 inches in men and 35 inches in women is associated with increased cardiac risk.

If possible, any nutritional deficiency, such as malnutrition, should be corrected before surgery to provide adequate protein for tissue repair. The nutrients needed for wound healing are summarized in Table 5-3. Dehydration, hypovolemia, and electrolyte imbalances can also lead to significant problems in patients with comorbid medical conditions

TABLE
5-3 Nutrients Important for Wound Healing

Nutrient	Rationale for Increased Need
Protein	To allow collagen deposition and wound healing to occur; clotting factor production; white blood cell (WBC) production and migration; cell-mediated phagocytosis; fibroblast proliferation; granulation tissue formation, neovascularization
Arginine (amino acid)	To provide necessary substrate for collagen synthesis and nitric oxide (crucial for wound healing) at wound site
	To increase wound strength and collagen deposition
	To stimulate T-cell response
	Associated with a variety of essential reactions of intermediary metabolism
Carbohydrates and fats	Primary source of energy in the body and consequently in the wound healing process
	To meet the demand for increased essential fatty acids needed for cellular function after an injury
	To spare protein
	Fibroblast proliferation is sensitive to glucose deficiencies.
Water	To maintain homeostasis
Vitamin C	Important for capillary formation, tissue synthesis, and wound healing through collagen formation
	Needed for antibody formation, WBC production; deficiency is associated with abnormal scar tissue formation
Vitamin B complex	Indirect role in wound healing through their influence on host resistance
Vitamin E	An antioxidant responsible for normal fat metabolism and collagen synthesis
Vitamin A	Increases inflammatory response in wounds, reduces anti-inflammatory effects of corticosteroids on wound healing, is; essential for epidermal proliferation, reepithelialization, and epithelium maintenance
Vitamin K	Important for normal blood clotting
	Impaired intestinal synthesis associated with the use of antibiotics
Magnesium	Essential cofactor for many enzymes that are involved in the process of protein synthesis and wound repair
Copper	Responsible for collagen cross-linking and erythropoiesis
Zinc	A cofactor for collagen formation, also metabolizes protein, liberates vitamin A from storage in the liver, interacts with platelets in blood clotting, and assists in immune function

Sources: Williams, J., & Barbul, A. (2003). Nutrition and wound healing. *Surgical clinics of North America 83*(3), 571–596; Posthauer, M., & Thomas, D. (2008). *Wound care essentials: Practice principles.* Philadelphia: Lippincott Williams & Wilkins; and Brown, K., & Phillips, T. (2010). Nutrition and wound healing, *Clinics in Dermatology, 28*(4), 432–439.

or in patients who are elderly. The severity of fluid and electrolyte imbalances is often difficult to determine. Mild volume deficits may be treated during surgery; however, additional time may be needed to correct pronounced fluid and electrolyte deficits to promote the best possible preoperative condition.

Drug or Alcohol Use

People who abuse drugs or alcohol frequently deny or attempt to hide it. In such situations, the nurse who is obtaining the patient's health history needs to ask frank questions with patience, care, and a nonjudgmental attitude. Because acutely intoxicated people are susceptible to injury, surgery is postponed if possible. If emergency surgery is required, local, spinal, or regional block anesthesia is used for minor surgery. Otherwise, to prevent vomiting and potential aspiration, a nasogastric tube is inserted before general anesthesia is administered.

The person with a history of chronic alcoholism often suffers from malnutrition and other systemic problems that increase surgical risk. Alcohol withdrawal syndrome or delirium tremens may be anticipated between 48 and 72 hours after alcohol withdrawal and is associated with a significant mortality rate when it occurs postoperatively.

Respiratory Status

The goal for surgical patients is optimal respiratory function. Because adequate ventilation is potentially compromised during all phases of surgical treatment, surgery is usually postponed if the patient has a respiratory infection. Patients with underlying respiratory disease (e.g., asthma, chronic obstructive pulmonary disease) are assessed carefully for current threats to their pulmonary status. Patients should be evaluated for conditions such as respiratory infection and neuromuscular diseases, such as Parkinson's disease, which may affect respiratory function.

The use of tobacco is an important risk factor but one that usually cannot be influenced. Even among smokers who have not developed chronic lung disease, smoking is associated with significant changes in lung function. While

cessation for 2 days prior to surgery is recommended, a prospective study by Warner (1984) revealed that smoking cessation for up to 8 weeks was necessary to reduce the rate of postoperative pulmonary complications. However, the ideal duration of cessation of smoking before surgery remains unclear. What it known is that, within 12 hours of quitting smoking, a decrease in carbon monoxide levels is seen, as well as improved oxygen delivery (Sweitzer & Smetana, 2009).

Cardiovascular Status

The goal in preparing any patient for surgery is to ensure a well-functioning cardiovascular system to meet the oxygen, fluid, and nutritional needs of the perioperative period. If the patient has uncontrolled hypertension, surgery may be postponed until the blood pressure is stabilized. At times, surgical treatment can be modified to meet the cardiac tolerance of the patient. For example, in a patient with obstruction of the descending colon and coronary artery disease, a temporary simple colostomy may be performed rather than a more extensive colon resection that would require a prolonged period of anesthesia.

Hepatic and Renal Function

The presurgical goal is optimal function of the liver and urinary systems, so that medications, anesthetic agents, body wastes, and toxins are adequately processed and removed from the body.

The liver is important in the biotransformation of anesthetic compounds. Therefore, any disorder of the liver has an effect on how anesthetic agents are metabolized. The limited ability of a failing liver increases the perioperative risks and presents significant challenges. Increased morbidity and mortality is associated with varying degrees of liver insufficiency; thus, it is important to quantify and grade preoperative liver dysfunction using various serum liver function tests (Kaufman & Roccaforte, 2009). Because the kidneys are involved in excreting anesthetic medications and their metabolites, and because acid–base status and metabolism are also important considerations in anesthesia administration, surgery is contraindicated if a patient has acute nephritis, acute renal insufficiency with oliguria or anuria, or other acute renal problems. The exception is surgery that is performed as a life-saving measure or that is necessary to improve urinary function, as in the case of an obstructive uropathy.

Endocrine Function

Diabetes is the most common endocrinopathy, and has acute and chronic disease manifestations. Because of this and other factors, patients with diabetes are more likely to require surgery. The majority of patients with diabetes develop disease in more than one body system, thus a thorough assessment of major organ disease (cardiac, renal, peripheral vascular) must be identified and managed carefully during the perioperative period. The patient with diabetes who is undergoing surgery

is at risk for hypoglycemia and hyperglycemia. Hypoglycemia may develop during anesthesia or postoperatively from inadequate carbohydrates or excessive administration of insulin. Hyperglycemia, which can increase the risk for surgical wound infection, and fluid and electrolyte loss, may result from the stress of surgery because it triggers increased release of catecholamines. Surgical patients with type 1 diabetes are also at risk for developing ketoacidosis. Recent studies have sparked a trend toward tighter perioperative glucose control. Management of patients with diabetes is aimed at preventing extremes of hyperglycemia and hypoglycemia; however, at present, research is less clear as to how "tight" glucose control should be and optimal target glucose level. Refer to Chapter 30 for details on management of patients with diabetes.

Patients who have received corticosteroids are at risk of adrenal insufficiency. Therefore, the use of corticosteroids for any purpose during the preceding year must be reported to the anesthesiologist, anesthetist (usually a nurse anesthetist), and surgeon. The patient is monitored for signs of adrenal insufficiency, which frequently presents with hyponatremia, hypoglycemia, hyperkalemia, and complaints of weakness and fatigue.

Patients with uncontrolled thyroid disorders are at risk for thyrotoxicosis (with hyperthyroid disorders) or respiratory failure (with hypothyroid disorders). Therefore, the patient is assessed for a history of these disorders.

Immune Function

The nurse determines the presence of allergies. It is especially important to identify and document any sensitivity to medications and past adverse reactions to these agents. The nurse asks the patient to identify any substances that precipitated previous allergic reactions, including medications, blood transfusions, contrast agents, latex, and food products, and to describe the signs and symptoms produced by these substances. A sample latex allergy screening questionnaire is shown in Figure 5-1.

Immunosuppression is common with corticosteroid therapy, renal transplantation, radiation therapy, chemotherapy, and disorders affecting the immune system, such as AIDS and leukemia. The mildest symptoms or slightest temperature elevation must be investigated. Because patients who are immunosuppressed are highly susceptible to infection, great care is taken to ensure strict asepsis.

Medication Use

A medication history is obtained from each patient because of the possible effects of medications on the patient's perioperative course, including the possibility of drug interactions. Any medication the patient is using or has used in the past is documented, including the frequency with which the medication is used. Potent medications have an effect on physiologic functions; interactions of such medications with anesthetic agents can cause serious problems, such as arterial hypotension and circulatory collapse.

Ask the patient the following questions. Check "Yes" or "No" in the box.	YES	NO
1. Has a doctor ever told you that you are allergic to latex?		
2. Do you have on-the-job exposure to latex?		
3. Were you born with problems involving your spinal cord?		
4. Have you ever had allergies, asthma, hay fever, eczema, or problems with rashes?		
5. Have you ever had respiratory distress, rapid heart rate, or swelling?		
6. Have you ever had swelling, itching, hives, or other symptoms after contact with a balloon?		
7. Have you ever had swelling, itching, hives, or other symptoms after a dental examination or procedure?		
8. Have you ever had swelling, itching, hives, or other symptoms following a vaginal or rectal examination or after contact with a diaphragm or condom?		
9. Have you ever had swelling, itching, hives, or other symptoms during or within 1 hour after wearing rubber gloves?		
10. Have you ever had a rash on your hands that lasted longer than 1 week?		
11. Have you ever had swelling, itching, hives, runny nose, eye irritation, wheezing, or asthma after contact with any latex or rubber product?		
12. Have you ever had swelling, itching, hives, or other symptoms after being examined by someone wearing rubber or latex gloves?		
13. Are you allergic to bananas, avocados, kiwi, or chestnuts?		
14. Have you ever had an unexplained anaphylactic episode?		

Preop RN Signature: _____

Patient Name: _____

Procedure: _____

Scheduled Date / Time : _____

Surgeon: _____

FIGURE 5-1 Example of a latex allergy assessment form. Courtesy of Inova Fairfax Hospital, Falls Church, Virginia.

The potential effects of prior medication therapy are evaluated by the anesthesiologist or certified registered nurse anesthetist (CRNA), who considers the length of time the patient has used the medication, the physical condition of the patient, and the nature of the proposed surgery. Medications that cause particular concern are listed in Table 5-4.

In addition, many patients take self-prescribed or over-the-counter (OTC) medications. Aspirin is a common OTC medication that inhibits platelet aggregation; therefore, it is prudent to stop aspirin at least 7 to 10 days before surgery if possible, especially for surgeries in which excess bleeding would cause significant complications, such as brain or spinal cord surgeries. Because of the effects of aspirin or other OTC medications and possible interactions with prescribed medications and anesthetic agents, it is important to ask a patient about their use. The information is noted in the patient's chart and conveyed to the anesthesiologist, CRNA, and surgeon.

The use of herbal medications is widespread among patients; because of their potential effects on coagulation and potentially lethal interactions with other medications, the nurse must ask surgical patients specifically about the use of these agents, document their use, and inform the surgical team and anesthesiologist or CRNA. Decisions should be made by the surgical team about the discontinuation of herbal medications prior to surgery. Currently, there are no studies demonstrating specific adverse interactions between herbals and anesthetic drugs; however, some have been implicated related to pharmacokinetic and pharmacodynamic interactions (Rosow & Levine, 2009).

Psychosocial Factors

All patients have some type of emotional reaction before any surgical procedure, be it obvious or hidden, normal or abnormal. For example, preoperative anxiety may be an anticipatory response to an experience the patient views as a threat to his or her customary role in life, body integrity, or life itself. Psychological distress directly influences body functioning. In addition to providing anticipatory guidance about what the patient will experience during the operative procedure, the nurse provides opportunities for the patient to ask questions, so that concerns can be addressed.

Most patients who are about to undergo surgery have fears, including fear of the unknown, of death, of anesthesia, of pain, or of cancer. Concerns about loss of work time, loss of job, increased responsibilities or burden on family members, and the threat of permanent incapacity further contribute to the emotional strain created by the prospect of surgery. Less obvious concerns may occur because of previous experiences with the health care system and people the patient has known with the same condition.

People express fear in different ways. For example, some patients may repeatedly ask many questions, even though answers were given previously. Others may withdraw, deliberately avoiding communication, perhaps by reading, watching television, or talking about trivialities. Assessing the patient's readiness to learn and determining the best approach to maximize comprehension provides the basis for preoperative patient education. Consequently, the nurse must be empathetic, listen well, and provide information that helps alleviate concerns.

An important outcome of the psychosocial assessment is the determination of the extent and role of the patient's support network. The value and reliability of all available support systems are assessed. Other information, such as usual level of functioning and typical daily activities, may assist in the patient's care and rehabilitation plans.

TABLE
5-4 Examples of Medications with the Potential to Affect the Surgical Experience

Agent (Generic and Trade Example)	Effect of Interaction with Anesthetics
Corticosteroids Prednisone (Deltasone)	Cardiovascular collapse can occur if discontinued suddenly. Therefore, a bolus of corticosteroid may be administered intravenously immediately before and after surgery.
Diuretics Hydrochlorothiazide (HydroDIURIL)	During anesthesia, may cause excessive respiratory depression resulting from an associated electrolyte imbalance
Phenothiazines Chlorpromazine (Thorazine)	May increase the hypotensive action of anesthetics
Tranquilizers Diazepam (Valium)	May cause anxiety, tension, and even seizures if withdrawn suddenly
Insulin	Interaction between anesthetics and insulin must be considered when a patient with diabetes is undergoing surgery. IV insulin may need to be administered to keep the blood glucose within the normal range.
Antibiotics Erythromycin (Ery-Tab)	When combined with a curariform muscle relaxant, nerve transmission is interrupted and apnea from respiratory paralysis may result.
Anticoagulants Warfarin (Coumadin)	Can increase the risk of bleeding during the intraoperative and postoperative periods; should be discontinued in anticipation of elective surgery. The surgeon will determine how long before the elective surgery the patient should stop taking an anticoagulant, depending on the type of planned procedure and the medical condition of the patient.
Antiseizure Medications	IV administration of medication may be needed to keep the patient seizure-free in the intraoperative and postoperative periods.
Monoamine Oxidase (MAO) Inhibitors Phenelzine sulfate (Nardil)	May increase the hypotensive action of anesthetics
Thyroid Hormone Levothyroxine sodium (Levothroid)	IV administration may be needed during the postoperative period to maintain thyroid levels.

Spiritual and Cultural Beliefs

Spiritual beliefs play an important role in how people cope with fear and anxiety. Regardless of the patient's religious affiliation, spiritual beliefs can be as therapeutic as medication. Every attempt must be made to help the patient obtain the spiritual support that he or she requests. Faith has great sustaining power. Therefore, the beliefs of each patient should be respected and supported. Additionally, the nurse communicates and documents if the patient declines blood transfusions for religious reasons (Jehovah's Witnesses), as this information needs to be clearly identified in the preoperative period. Some nurses avoid the subject of a clergy visit lest the suggestion alarm the patient. Asking whether the patient's spiritual advisor knows about the impending surgery is a caring, nonthreatening approach.

Showing respect for a patient's cultural values and beliefs facilitates rapport and trust. Some areas of assessment include identifying the ethnic group to which the patient relates and the customs and beliefs the patient holds about illness and health care providers. For example, patients from some cultural groups are unaccustomed to expressing feelings openly. Nurses need to consider this pattern of communication when assessing pain. Nurses should familiarize themselves with these cultural similarities and differences and, recently, the Joint Commission has developed standards of cultural competency for health care workers.

Perhaps the most valuable skill at the nurse's disposal is listening carefully to the patient, especially when obtaining the history. Invaluable information and insights may be gained through effective communication and interviewing skills. An unhurried, understanding, and caring nurse promotes confidence on the part of the patient.

Presence of Genetic Disorders

In the preoperative period, attention needs to be paid to patients with various genetic disorders (listed below) since surgical outcomes may be altered related to complications with anesthesia.

- Malignant hyperthermia (MH) (discussed later in the chapter)
- Central core disease (CCD), is a genetic disorder that presents in the neonatal period or infancy with muscle weakness and hypotonia and mild facial weakness. This condition increases the risk of developing MH.
- Duchenne muscular dystrophy and Becker dystrophy are two types of muscular dystrophies associated with risk of developing MH.

- Hyperkalemic periodic paralysis is a genetic disorder that causes episodes of extreme muscle weakness and occasionally hyperkalemia. It is also associated with MH.
- King-Denborough syndrome, a rare genetic disorder associated with musculoskeletal abnormalities, is associated with MH.

Preoperative Nursing Management

Providing Preoperative Teaching

Nurses have long recognized the value of preoperative instruction (Rothrock, 2011). Each patient is taught as an individual, with consideration for any unique concerns or learning needs. Preoperative teaching is initiated as soon as possible, includes different modalities (verbal, written, electronic, return demonstration), and should be tailored to the needs of the patient. It should start in the surgeon's office or at the time of PAT, continued until the patient arrives in the OR and extends to discharge.

Timing and Technique

It is best to begin teaching early, when the patient and family may be less anxious and can make adjustments or prepare for the postoperative period more effectively. The ideal timing for preoperative teaching is not on the day of surgery but during the preadmission visit, when diagnostic tests are performed. At this time, the nurse or resource person answers questions and provides important patient teaching. During this visit, the patient can meet and ask questions of the perioperative nurse and health care team members, view audiovisual resources, receive written materials, and be given the telephone number to call as questions arise closer to the date of surgery. Many institutions provide access to websites where patients can view and review written instructions, communicate electronically, and ask questions with caregivers.

Teaching should go beyond descriptions of the procedure and should include explanations of the sensations the patient will experience. For example, telling the patient only that preoperative medication will cause relaxation before the operation is not as effective as also noting that the medication may result in lightheadedness and drowsiness. Knowing what to expect will help the patient anticipate these reactions and thus attain a higher degree of relaxation than might otherwise be expected. Knowing ahead of time about the possible need for a ventilator, drainage tubes, or other types of equipment helps decrease anxiety in the postoperative period. In addition, preoperative teaching includes instruction in the breathing and leg exercises used to prevent postoperative complications such as pneumonia and deep vein thrombosis (DVT). These exercises may be performed in the hospital or at home. The nurse should guide the patient through the experience and allow ample time for questions. For some patients, overly detailed descriptions increase anxiety; the nurse should be sensitive to this and provide less detail.

Deep Breathing, Coughing, and Incentive Spirometry

One goal of preoperative nursing care is to teach the patient how to promote optimal lung expansion and consequent blood oxygenation after anesthesia. The patient assumes a sitting position to enhance lung expansion. The nurse then demonstrates how to take a deep, slow breath and how to exhale slowly. After practicing deep breathing several times, the patient is instructed to breathe deeply, exhale through the mouth, take a short breath, and cough deeply (see Box 5-3). The nurse also demonstrates how to use an incentive spirometer, a device that provides measurement and feedback related to breathing effectiveness. In addition to enhancing respiration, these exercises may help the patient relax.

If a thoracic or abdominal incision is anticipated, the nurse demonstrates how to splint the incision to minimize pressure and control pain. The patient should put the palms of both hands together, interlacing the fingers snugly. Placing the hands across the incisional site acts as an effective splint when coughing. In addition, the patient is informed that medications are available to relieve pain and should be taken regularly for pain relief, so that effective deep breathing and coughing exercises can be performed. The goal in promoting coughing is to mobilize secretions, so that they can be removed. Deep breathing before coughing stimulates the cough reflex. If the patient does not cough effectively, atelectasis (collapse of the alveoli), pneumonia, or other lung complications may occur.

Promoting Mobility

The goals of promoting mobility postoperatively are to improve circulation, prevent venous stasis, and promote optimal respiratory function. The nurse explains the rationale for frequent position changes after surgery and then shows the patient how to turn from side to side and how to assume the lateral position without causing pain or disrupting IV lines, drainage tubes, or other equipment. The nurse uses proper body mechanics when turning the patient, and instructs the patient to do the same. Whenever the patient is positioned, his or her body needs to be properly aligned.

Additionally, some patients require instruction about special positions that are required after surgery (e.g., abduction or elevation of an extremity). The importance of maintaining as much mobility as possible despite restrictions is discussed. Reviewing the process before surgery is helpful, because the patient may be too uncomfortable or drowsy after surgery to absorb new information.

Exercise of the extremities includes extension and flexion of the knee and hip joints (similar to bicycle riding while lying on the side). The foot is rotated as though tracing the largest possible circle with the great toe (see Box 5-3). The elbow and shoulder are also put through their range of motion. At first, the patient is assisted and reminded to perform these exercises. Later, the patient is encouraged to

BOX 5-3 **Patient Education**

Preoperative Instructions to Prevent Postoperative Complications

Diaphragmatic Breathing

Diaphragmatic breathing refers to a flattening of the dome of the diaphragm during inspiration, with resultant enlargement of the upper abdomen as air rushes in. During expiration, the abdominal muscles contract.

1. Practice in the same position you would assume in bed after surgery: a semi-Fowler's position, propped in bed with the back and shoulders well supported with pillows.
2. With your hands in a loose-first position, allow the hands to rest lightly on the front of the lower ribs, with your fingertips against lower chest to feel the movement.

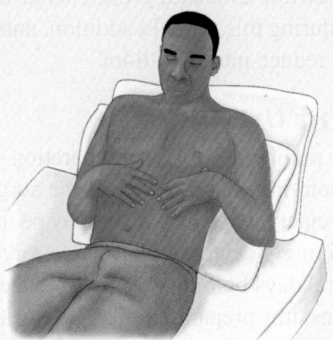
Diaphragmatic breathing

3. Breathe out gently and fully as the ribs sink down and inward toward midline.
4. Then take a deep breath through your nose and mouth, letting the abdomen rise as the lungs fill with air.
5. Hold this breath for a count of five.
6. Exhale and let out *all* the air through your nose and mouth.
7. Repeat this exercise 15 times with a short rest after each group of five.
8. Practice this twice a day preoperatively.

Coughing

1. Lean forward slightly from a sitting position in bed, interlace your fingers together, and place your hands across the incisional site to act as a splintlike support when coughing.

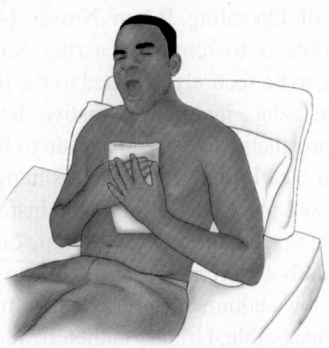
Splinting of chest when coughing

2. Breathe with the diaphragm as described under "Diaphragmatic Breathing."
3. With your mouth slightly open, breathe in fully.
4. "Hack" out sharply for three short breaths.
5. Then, keeping your mouth open, take in a quick deep breath and immediately give a strong cough once or twice. This helps clear secretions from your chest. It may cause some discomfort but will not harm your incision.

Leg Exercises

1. Lie in a semi-Fowler's position and perform the following simple exercises to improve circulation.
2. Bend your knee and raise your foot—hold it a few seconds, then extend the leg and lower it to the bed.

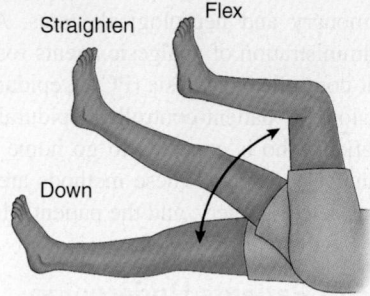
Leg exercises

3. Do this five times with one leg, then repeat with the other leg.
4. Then trace circles with the feet by bending them down, in toward each other, up, and then out.
5. Repeat these movements five times.

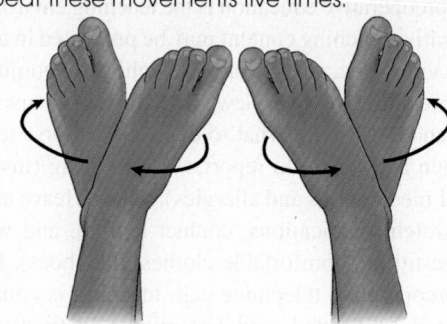
Foot exercises

Turning to the Side

1. Turn on your side with the uppermost leg flexed most and supported on a pillow.
2. Grasp the side rail as an aid to maneuver to the side.
3. Practice diaphragmatic breathing and coughing while on your side.

Getting Out of Bed

1. Turn on your side.
2. Push yourself up with one hand as you swing your legs out of bed.

do them independently. Muscle tone is maintained so that ambulation will be easier.

Pain Management

The nurse is guided by the recommendations of the Joint Commission that the "hospital uses methods to assess pain that are consistent with the patient's age, conditions, and ability to understand" (www.jc.org, 2010). A pain assessment should include differentiation between acute and chronic pain. A pain intensity scale should be introduced and explained to the patient to promote more effective postoperative pain management.

Once a patient answers yes to whether he or she has pain or not, the nurse should perform a comprehensive pain assessment and an appropriate pain assessment scale selected (see Chapter 7 for these).

Patients are informed that medications will be administered to relieve pain and maintain comfort without compromising the cardiopulmonary and neurological status. Anticipated methods of administration of analgesic agents for inpatients include patient-controlled analgesia (PCA), epidural catheter bolus or infusion, or patient-controlled epidural analgesia (PCEA). A patient who is expected to go home will likely receive oral analgesic agents. These methods are discussed with the patient before surgery, and the patient's interest and willingness to use them are assessed.

Instruction for Patients Undergoing Ambulatory Surgery

Preoperative education for the same-day or ambulatory surgical patient comprises all the material presented above as well as collaborative planning with the patient and family for discharge and follow-up home care. The major difference in outpatient preoperative education is the teaching environment.

Preoperative teaching content may be presented in a group class, on a videotape, at PAT, or by telephone in conjunction with the preoperative interview. In addition to answering questions and describing what to expect, the nurse tells the patient when and where to report, what to bring (insurance card, list of medications and allergies), what to leave at home (jewelry, watch, medications, contact lenses), and what to wear (loose-fitting, comfortable clothes; flat shoes). During the final preoperative telephone call, teaching is completed or reinforced as needed, and last-minute instructions are given. The patient is reminded not to eat or drink as directed.

Managing Nutrition and Fluids

The major purpose of withholding food and fluid before surgery is to prevent aspiration. Until recently, fluid and food were restricted preoperatively overnight and often longer. However, the American Society of Anesthesiologists reviewed this practice and has made new recommendations for people undergoing elective surgery who are otherwise healthy.

Specific recommendations depend on the age of the patient and the type of food eaten. For example, adults may be advised to fast for 8 hours after eating fatty food and

4 hours after ingesting milk products. Many healthy patients are allowed clear fluids up to 2 to 3 hours prior to surgery, especially if undergoing minor and very short procedures (White & Eng, 2009).

Preparing the Bowel

Enemas are not commonly prescribed preoperatively unless the patient is undergoing abdominal or pelvic surgery. In this case, a cleansing enema or laxative may be prescribed the evening before surgery and may be repeated the morning of surgery. The goals of this preparation are to allow satisfactory visualization of the surgical site and to prevent trauma to the intestine or contamination of the peritoneum by feces. Unless the condition of the patient presents some contraindication, the toilet or bedside commode, rather than the bedpan, is used for evacuating the enema if the patient is hospitalized during this time. In addition, antibiotics may be prescribed to reduce intestinal flora.

Preparing the Skin

The goal of preoperative skin preparation is to decrease bacteria without injuring the skin. If the surgery is not performed as an emergency, the patient may be instructed to use a soap containing a detergent-germicide to cleanse the skin area for several days before surgery to reduce the number of skin organisms; this preparation may be carried out at home.

Generally, hair is not removed preoperatively unless the hair at or around the incision site is likely to interfere with the operation. If hair must be removed, electric clippers are used for safe hair removal immediately before the operation.

Providing Immediate Preoperative Care

The patient changes into a hospital gown that is tied loosely and opens in the back. The patient with long hair may braid it, remove hairpins, and cover the head completely with a disposable paper cap.

The mouth is inspected, and dentures or plates are removed. If left in the mouth, these items could easily fall to the back of the throat during induction of anesthesia and cause respiratory obstruction.

Jewelry is not worn to the OR; wedding rings and jewelry of body piercings should be removed to prevent injury (Association of Operating Room Nurses [AORN], 2010). If a patient objects to removing a ring, some institutions allow the ring to be securely fastened to the finger with tape. All articles of value, including assistive devices, dentures, glasses, and prosthetic devices, are given to family members or are labeled clearly with the patient's name and stored in a safe and secure place according to the institution's policy.

All patients (except those with urologic disorders) should void immediately before going to the OR to promote continence during low abdominal surgery and to make abdominal organs more accessible. Urinary catheterization is performed in the OR as necessary.

Maintaining the Preoperative Record

Preoperative checklists contain critical elements that must be checked and verified preoperatively (Rothrock, 2011). The nurse completes the preoperative assessment and plan of care, as well as the portion of the universal protocol/safety checklist that focuses on patient identification, correct documents, and patient understanding of the surgical procedure. The World Health Organization has developed a safety checklist as a guide for institutions to modify and use to support the safety of patients (Fig. 5-2). The surgical site may be marked during this phase as well and is documented also by the admitting nurse. The completed chart (with the preoperative checklist and verification form) accompanies the patient to the OR with the most recent history and physical (within the past 30 days), anesthetic assessment, and surgical consent form attached, along with all laboratory reports and nurses' records. Any unusual last-minute observations that may have a bearing on anesthesia or surgery are noted prominently at the front of the chart. Many institutions document these preoperative requirements electronically. To support this process, institutions are required to ensure that a standard hand-off process is in place to communicate critical and pertinent information to the next caregiver.

Administering Preanesthetic Medication

The use of preanesthetic medication is a minimal dose with ambulatory or outpatient surgery. If prescribed, it is usually administered in the preoperative holding area. If a preanesthetic medication is administered, the patient is kept in bed with the side rails raised, because the medication can cause

Before induction of anaesthesia	Before skin incision	Before patient leaves operating room
(with at least nurse and anaesthetist)	(with nurse, anaesthetist and surgeon)	(with nurse, anaesthetist and surgeon)
Has the patient confirmed his/her identity, site, procedure, and consent? ☐ Yes **Is the site marked?** ☐ Yes ☐ Not applicable **Is the anaesthesia machine and medication check complete?** ☐ Yes **Is the pulse oximeter on the patient and functioning?** ☐ Yes **Does the patient have a:** **Known allergy?** ☐ No ☐ Yes **Difficult airway or aspiration risk?** ☐ No ☐ Yes, and equipment/assistance available **Risk of >500ml blood loss (7ml/kg in children)?** ☐ No ☐ Yes, and two IVs/central access and fluids planned	☐ **Confirm all team members have introduced themselves by name and role.** ☐ **Confirm the patient's name, procedure, and where the incision will be made.** **Has antibiotic prophylaxis been given within the last 60 minutes?** ☐ Yes ☐ Not applicable **Anticipated Critical Events** **To Surgeon:** ☐ What are the critical or non-routine steps? ☐ How long will the case take? ☐ What is the anticipated blood loss? **To Anaesthetist:** ☐ Are there any patient-specific concerns? **To Nursing Team:** ☐ Has sterility (including indicator results) been confirmed? ☐ Are there equipment issues or any concerns? **Is essential imaging displayed?** ☐ Yes ☐ Not applicable	**Nurse Verbally Confirms:** ☐ The name of the procedure ☐ Completion of instrument, sponge and needle counts ☐ Specimen labeling (read specimen labels aloud, including patient name) ☐ Whether there are any equipment problems to be addressed **To Surgeon, Anaesthetist and Nurse:** ☐ What are the key concerns for recovery and management of this patient?

This checklist is not intended to be comprehensive. Additons and modifcations to fit local practice are encouraged.

FIGURE 5-2 Surgical safety checklist. Based on the WHO Surgical Safety Checklist, http://whqlibdoc.who.int/publications/2009/9789241598590_eng_checklist.pdf. © World Health Organization (WHO), 2011. All rights reserved.

lightheadedness or drowsiness. During this time, the nurse observes the patient for any untoward reaction to the medications. The immediate surroundings are kept quiet to promote relaxation.

Often, surgery is delayed or OR schedules are changed, and it becomes impossible to request that a medication be given at a specific time. In these situations, the preoperative medication is prescribed "on call to OR." The nurse can have the medication ready to administer as soon as a call is received from the OR staff. It usually takes 15 to 20 minutes to prepare the patient for the OR. If the nurse gives the medication before attending to the other details of preoperative preparation, the patient will have at least partial benefit from the preoperative medication and will have a smoother anesthetic and operative course.

⚡ NURSING ALERT

Protecting patients from injury is one of the major roles of the perioperative nurse. Specific nursing interventions to decrease the risk of falling are to elevate the side rails after the premedication is administered and reminding the patient that out of bed (OOB) activity is not permitted due to potential medication side effects such as dizziness.

Transporting the Patient to the Presurgical Area

The patient is transferred to the holding area or presurgical suite in a bed or on a stretcher about 30 to 60 minutes before the anesthetic is to be given. The stretcher should be as comfortable as possible, with a sufficient number of blankets to prevent chilling in an air-conditioned room. A small head pillow is usually provided.

The patient is taken to the preoperative holding area, greeted by name, and positioned comfortably on the stretcher or bed. The surrounding area should be kept quiet if the preoperative medication is to have maximal effect. Unpleasant sounds or conversation should be avoided, because a sedated patient who overhears might misinterpret them. Patients may go directly to the operating room and bypass the holding area, and in many institutions patients also walk to the OR.

Patient safety in the preoperative area is a priority. Use of a process to verify patient identification, the surgical procedure, and the surgical site is imperative to maximize patient safety. This process should be performed at the time of admission in the presurgical unit and during all hand-offs from caregiver to caregiver. This allows for prompt intervention if any discrepancies are identified.

Attending to Family Needs

Most hospitals and ambulatory surgery centers have a waiting room where family members and significant others can wait while the patient is undergoing surgery. This room may be equipped with comfortable chairs, television, telephones, and facilities for light refreshment. Volunteers may remain with the family, offer them coffee, and keep them informed of the patient's progress. After surgery, the surgeon may meet the family in the waiting room and discuss the outcome.

The family and significant others should never judge the seriousness of an operation by the length of time the patient is in the OR. A patient may be in surgery much longer than the actual operating time for several reasons:

- Patients are routinely transported well in advance of the actual operating time.
- The anesthesiologist or anesthetist often makes additional preparations that may take 30 to 60 minutes.
- The surgeon may take longer than expected with the preceding case, which delays the start of the next surgical procedure.

After surgery, the patient is taken to the PACU to ensure safe emergence from anesthesia. Family members and significant others waiting to see the patient after surgery should be informed that the patient may have certain equipment or devices (e.g., IV lines, indwelling urinary catheter, nasogastric tube, oxygen lines, monitoring equipment, blood transfusion lines) in place when he or she returns from surgery. Many hospitals now adopt the model of patient- and family-centered care and allow visitations in the PACU for short periods after the patient is stabilized and made comfortable. In ambulatory surgery and pediatric settings, family members are brought early in the recovery process and are integral to the preparation for discharge. When the patient returns to the room, the nurse provides explanations regarding the frequent postoperative observations that will be made. However, it is the responsibility of the surgeon, not the nurse, to relay the surgical findings and the prognosis, even when the findings are favorable.

INTRAOPERATIVE NURSING

The **intraoperative phase** begins when the patient is transferred onto the OR table and ends with admission to the PACU. In this phase, the scope of nursing activities includes providing for the patient's safety, maintaining an aseptic environment, ensuring proper function of equipment, providing the surgeon with specific instruments and supplies for the surgical field, completing appropriate documentation, providing emotional support during induction of general anesthesia, assisting in positioning the patient on the OR table using appropriate principles of body alignment, or acting as scrub nurse, circulating nurse, or registered nurse first assistant (RNFA).

The intraoperative experience has undergone many changes that make it safer and less disturbing to patients. However, even with these advances, anesthesia and surgery place the patient at risk for several complications or adverse events. Consciousness or full awareness, mobility, protective biologic functions, and personal control are totally or partially relinquished by the patient when entering the OR.

Staff from the departments of anesthesia, nursing, and surgery work collaboratively to implement professional standards of care, to control iatrogenic (adverse condition in a patient resulting from treatment) and individual risks, to prevent complications, and to promote high-quality patient outcomes.

The Surgical Team

The surgical team includes the **circulating nurse** (also known as the **circulator**), scrub person (scrub role), RNFA, surgeon, **anesthesiologist**, and **anesthetist**. Table 5-5 summarizes the roles of each member. Every member of the surgical team verifies the patient's name, procedure, and surgical site using objective documentation and data before beginning the surgery, as mandated by the Joint Commission. This is referred to as the "time out" or final pause and must be performed prior to incision, preferably with the patient involved; if patient's surgical site was marked, it should be visible.

The Surgical Environment

The surgical environment is known for its stark appearance and cool temperature. The surgical suite is behind double doors, and access is limited to authorized personnel. To provide the best possible conditions for surgery, the OR is situated in a location that is central to all supporting services (e.g., pathology, X-ray, laboratory). The OR has special air filtration devices to screen out contaminating particles, dust, and pollutants.

Maintaining the Environment

External precautions, include adhering to principles of surgical asepsis, and strict control of the OR environment is required, including traffic pattern restrictions. Policies governing this environment address such issues as the health of the staff; the cleanliness of the rooms; the sterility of equipment and surfaces; processes for scrubbing, gowning, and gloving; and OR attire.

TABLE
5-5 The Surgical Team

Team Member	Responsibilities
Circulating Nurse (preferably an RN; in some states required to be an RN)	Checking and managing the OR conditions (ensuring cleanliness, proper temperature, humidity, lighting, safe function of equipment, and the availability of supplies and materials) Continually assessing the patient for signs of injury and implementing appropriate interventions Verifying consent and ensuring documentation is correct Coordinating the team Monitoring aseptic practices to avoid breaks in technique while coordinating the movement of related personnel (medical, X-ray, and laboratory) Implementing fire safety precautions and accounting for all surgical counts in collaboration with scrub person Ensuring that the second verification of the surgical procedure and site takes place and is documented Specimen management
Scrub person	Performing a surgical hand scrub Setting up the sterile tables Preparing sutures, ligatures, and special equipment (e.g., laparoscope) Anticipating the instruments and supplies that will be required, such as sponges, drains, and other equipment As the surgical incision is closed, counting all needles, sponges, and instruments with the nurse to be sure they are accounted for and not retained as a foreign body in the patient
Registered nurse first assistant (RNFA)	Handling tissue Providing exposure at the operative field Suturing Maintaining hemostasis
Surgeon (he or she is a licensed physician, osteopath, oral surgeon, or podiatrist who is specially trained and qualified)	Performing the surgical procedure Heading the surgical team
Anesthesiologist (a physician specifically trained in the art and science of anesthesiology) and anesthetist (a qualified health care professional who administers anesthetics; most are certified registered nurse anesthetists [CRNAs])	Assessing the patient before surgery Selecting the anesthesia and administering it Intubating the patient if necessary Managing any technical problems related to the administration of the anesthetic agent Supervising the patient's condition throughout the surgical procedure

Primary National Patient Safety Goals for 2011

- Improve the accuracy of patient identification
- Improve effectiveness of communication among caregivers
- Improve safety of using medications
- Improve safety of using infusion pumps
- Reduce the risk of health care–associated infections
- Accurately and completely reconcile medications across continuum of care
- Reduce the risk of surgical fires
- Prevent wrong site surgery–universal protocol

From http:www.jointcomission.org/PatientSafety/NationalPatient SafetyGoals.

Preventing Surgical Fire

Most of the Joint Commission's 2010 National Patient Safety Goals pertain to the perioperative areas (Box 5-4). One that has direct relevance to the OR is the reduction of the risk of surgical fires. Fires in the OR are as much a danger as they were 100 years ago due to the increased use of potential sources of ignition, such as the electrocautery units, lasers, and fiberoptic lights used in an environment rich in flammable sources (Ehrenwerth & Seifert, 2009). Surgical drapes provide an opportunity for oxygen to concentrate; a stray spark could more easily ignite a fire. This occurs most commonly in ambulatory surgery settings (Joint Commission, 2010). To further improve safety, electrical hazards, emergency exit clearances, and storage of equipment and anesthetic gases are monitored periodically by official agencies, such as the state department of health and the Joint Commission. All operating room personnel must be familiar with and educated about fire prevention and how to respond in the event that a fire should occur in the operating room.

Donning Proper Attire

To help decrease microbes, the surgical area is divided into three zones: the **unrestricted zone**, where street clothes are allowed; the **semirestricted zone**, where attire consists of scrub clothes and caps; and the **restricted zone**, where scrub clothes, shoe covers, caps, and masks are worn. The surgeons and other surgical team members wear additional sterile clothing and protective devices during the operation.

The Association of Perioperative Registered Nurses, formerly known as the Association of Operating Room Nurses (still abbreviated as AORN), recommends specific practices for personnel wearing surgical attire to promote a high level of cleanliness in a particular practice setting (AORN, 2010). OR attire includes close-fitting cotton dresses, pantsuits, jumpsuits, and gowns. Knitted cuffs on sleeves and pant legs prevent organisms shed from the perineum, legs, and arms from being released into the immediate surroundings. Shirts

and waist drawstrings should be tucked inside the pants to prevent accidental contact with sterile areas and to contain skin shedding. Wet or soiled garments should be changed.

Masks are worn at all times in the restricted zone of the OR. High-filtration masks decrease the risk of postoperative wound infection by containing and filtering microorganisms from the oropharynx and nasopharynx. Masks should fit tightly, should cover the nose and mouth completely, and should not interfere with breathing, speech, or vision. Masks must be adjusted to prevent venting from the sides. Disposable masks have a filtration efficiency exceeding 95%. Masks are changed between patients and should not be worn outside the surgical department. The mask must be either on or off; it must not be allowed to hang around the neck.

Headgear should completely cover the hair (head and neckline, including beard), so that single strands of hair, bobby pins, clips, and particles of dandruff or dust do not fall on the sterile field.

Shoes should be comfortable and supportive. Shoe covers are worn when it is reasonably anticipated that spills or splashes will occur. If worn, the covers should be changed whenever they become wet, torn, or soiled (Rothrock, 2011).

Barriers such as scrub attire and masks do not entirely protect the patient from microorganisms. Upper respiratory tract infections, sore throats, and skin infections in staff and patients are sources of pathogens and must be reported.

Because artificial fingernails harbor microorganisms and can cause nosocomial infections, a ban on artificial nails by OR personnel is supported by the Centers for Disease Control and Prevention (CDC), AORN, and the Association of Professionals in Infection Control. Short, natural fingernails are encouraged.

Using Environmental Controls

In addition to the protocols described previously, surgical asepsis requires meticulous cleaning and maintenance of the OR environment. Floors and horizontal surfaces are cleaned frequently with detergent, soap, and water or a detergent germicide. Sterilizing equipment is inspected regularly to ensure optimal operation and performance.

All equipment that comes into direct contact with the patient must be sterile. Sterilized linens, drapes, and solutions are used. Instruments are cleaned and sterilized in a unit near the OR. Individually wrapped sterile items are used when additional individual items are needed.

Airborne bacteria are a concern. To decrease the amount of bacteria in the air, standard OR ventilation provides 15 air exchanges per hour, at least three of which are fresh air (CDC, 2010). A temperature of 20° to 24°C (68° to 73°F), humidity between 30% and 60%, and positive pressure relative to adjacent areas are maintained. Staff members shed skin scales, resulting in about 1,000 bacteria-carrying particles (or colony-forming units [CFUs]) per cubic foot per minute. With the standard air exchanges, air counts

of bacteria are reduced to 50 to 150 CFUs per cubic foot per minute. Systems with high-efficiency particulate air (HEPA) filters are needed to remove particles larger than 0.3 μm (Rothrock, 2011). Unnecessary personnel and physical movement may be restricted to minimize bacteria in the air and achieve an OR infection rate no greater than 3% to 5% in clean, infection-prone surgery.

Some ORs have laminar airflow units. These units provide 400 to 500 air exchanges per hour (CDC, 2010). The goal for a laminar airflow–equipped OR is an infection rate of less than 1%. An OR equipped with this unit is frequently used for total joint replacement or organ transplant surgery. Constant surveillance and conscientious technique in carrying out aseptic practices are necessary to reduce the risk of contamination and infection.

Health Hazards Associated with the Surgical Environment

Safety issues in the OR include exposure to blood and body fluids, and exposure to latex and adhesive substances, radiation, and toxic agents and laser plumes. Internal monitoring of the OR includes the analysis of surface swipe samples and air samples for infectious and toxic agents. In addition, policies and procedures for minimizing exposure to body fluids and reducing the dangers associated with lasers and radiation have been established.

An additional hazard is the unintentional leaving of an object in a person during a surgical procedure. The risk that foreign objects may be left in a person increases in the following situations: when the procedure is performed on an emergency basis, when there is an unplanned change in the procedure, and when the patient has a high BMI. Many complications can occur from the retention of an object, and the patient is subjected to the risk of an additional surgical procedure.

Exposure to Blood and Body Fluids

OR attire has changed dramatically since the advent of HIV/AIDS. Double-gloving is routine in trauma and other types of surgery where sharp bone fragments are present. Goggles, or a wrap-around face shield, are worn to protect against splashing when the surgical wound is irrigated or when bone drilling is performed. In hospitals where numerous total joint procedures are performed, a complete bubble mask may be used. This mask provides full-barrier protection from bone fragments and splashes. Ventilation is accomplished through an accompanying hood with a separate air-filtration system.

Latex Allergy

The AORN has recommended standards of care for the patient with latex allergy (AORN, 2010). These recommendations include early identification of patients with latex allergies, preparation of a latex allergy supply cart, and maintenance of latex allergy precautions throughout the perioperative period. Because of the increased number of patients with latex allergies, many latex-free products are now available. For safety, manufacturers and hospital material managers need to take

responsibility for identifying the latex content in items used by patients and health care personnel. Additional discussion of latex allergy can be found in Chapter 38.

Laser Risks

The AORN has recommended practices for laser safety. While lasers are in use, warning signs must be clearly posted to alert personnel. Safety precautions are implemented to reduce the possibility of exposing the eyes and skin to laser beams, to prevent inhalation of the laser plume (smoke and particulate matter), and to protect the patient and personnel from fire and electrical hazards. Several types of lasers are available for clinical use; perioperative personnel should be familiar with the unique features, specific operation, and safety measures for each type of laser used in the practice setting.

Nurses and other intraoperative personnel working with lasers must have a thorough eye examination before participating in procedures involving lasers. All personnel wear special protective goggles, specific to the type of laser used in the procedure (ANSI, 2007).

Whether protection is needed to avoid the laser plume and the effects of its inhalation is controversial. Smoke evacuators are used in some procedures to remove the laser plume from the operative field. In recent years, this technology has been used to protect the surgical team from the potential hazards associated with the generalized smoke plume generated by standard electrocautery units.

The Surgical Experience

During the surgical procedure, the patient will need sedation, anesthesia, or some combination of these. In addition, strict surgical asepsis is maintained.

Anesthesia and Sedation

Anesthesia today is very safe, and although anesthesia-related morbidity and mortality is difficult to quantify, more recent studies estimate anesthesia-related death rate in the United States to be less than 1 per 10,000 anesthetics (Posner & Domino, 2009). When the patient arrives in the OR, the anesthesiologist or anesthetist reassesses the patient's physical condition immediately prior to initiating anesthesia. For the patient, the anesthesia experience consists of having an IV line inserted, if it was not inserted earlier; receiving a sedating agent prior to induction with an anesthetic agent; losing consciousness; being intubated, if indicated; and then receiving a combination of anesthetic agents. Typically, the experience is a smooth one, and the patient has no recall of the events. The main types of anesthesia are general anesthesia, regional anesthesia, moderate sedation, monitored anesthesia care, and local anesthesia.

During surgery, the anesthesiologist or anesthetist monitors the patient's blood pressure, pulse, and respirations as well as the electrocardiogram (ECG), blood oxygen saturation level, tidal volume, blood gas levels, blood pH, alveolar gas concentrations, and body temperature. Monitoring by

electroencephalography (measure of brain waves) is sometimes required. Levels of anesthetics in the body can also be determined; a mass spectrometer can provide instant readouts of critical concentration levels on display terminals. This information helps personnel assess the patient's ability to breathe unassisted or the need for mechanical assistance if ventilation is poor and the patient is not breathing well independently. Even with the availability of automatic monitoring equipment, the anesthesiologists and or nurse must remain in close contact with the patient to immediately observe any significant physiological changes.

General Anesthesia

Anesthesia is a state of narcosis (severe central nervous system [CNS] depression produced by pharmacologic agents), analgesia, relaxation, and reflex loss. Patients under general anesthesia are not arousable, not even to painful stimuli. They lose the ability to maintain ventilatory function and require assistance in maintaining a patent airway. Cardiovascular function may be impaired as well.

! NURSING ALERT
In 2004, the Joint Commission issued an alert regarding the phenomenon of patients being partially awake while under general anesthesia (referred to as anesthesia awareness). Patients at greatest risk of anesthesia awareness are cardiac, obstetric, and major trauma patients. The entire surgical team must be aware of this phenomenon and help prevent or manage it.

General anesthesia consists of four stages, each associated with specific clinical manifestations (Box 5-5) (Rothrock, 2011).

Anesthetic agents used in general anesthesia are inhaled or administered by IV (Fig. 5-3). Anesthetics produce anesthesia because they are delivered to the brain at a high partial pressure that enables them to cross the blood–brain barrier. Relatively large amounts of anesthetic must be administered during induction and the early maintenance phases because the anesthetic is recirculated and deposited in body tissues. As these sites become saturated, smaller amounts of the anesthetic agent are required to maintain anesthesia because equilibrium or near equilibrium has been achieved between brain, blood, and other tissues.

Any condition that diminishes peripheral blood flow, such as vasoconstriction or shock, may reduce the amount of anesthetic required. Conversely, when peripheral blood flow is unusually high, as in a muscularly active or apprehensive patient, induction is slower, and greater quantities of anesthetic are required because the brain receives a smaller quantity of anesthetic.

Inhaled Administration

Inhalation anesthetics are commonly used for the provision of general **anesthesia**. With the addition of a volatile (readily vaporized) anesthetic to inspired oxygen, a state of unconsciousness and amnesia can be established. When combined with additional medications (e.g., opioids and benzodiazepines), further sedation/

BOX 5-5 | **Stages of General Anesthesia**

- *Stage I: Beginning anesthesia.* As the patient breathes in the anesthetic mixture, warmth, dizziness, and a feeling of detachment may be experienced. The patient may have a ringing, roaring, or buzzing in the ears and, although still conscious, may sense an inability to move the extremities easily. During this stage, noises are exaggerated; even low voices or minor sounds seem loud and unreal. For this reason, unnecessary noises and motions are avoided when anesthesia begins.
- *Stage II: Excitement.* The excitement stage, characterized variously by struggling, shouting, talking, singing, laughing, or crying, is often avoided if the anesthetic is administered smoothly and quickly. Because of the possibility of uncontrolled movements of the patient during this stage, the anesthesiologist or anesthetist must always be assisted by someone ready to help restrain the patient. The patient should not be touched except for purposes of restraint, but restraints should not be applied over the operative site.
- *Stage III: Surgical anesthesia.* Surgical anesthesia is reached by continued administration of the anesthetic vapor or gas. The patient is unconscious and lies quietly on the table. With proper administration of

the anesthetic, this stage may be maintained for hours in one of several planes, ranging from light (1) to deep (4), depending on the depth of anesthesia needed.
- *Stage IV: Medullary depression.* This stage is reached when too much anesthesia has been administered. Cyanosis develops and, without prompt intervention, death rapidly follows. If this stage develops, the anesthetic is discontinued immediately and respiratory and circulatory support is initiated to prevent death. Stimulants, although rarely used, may be administered; narcotic antagonists can be used if the overdosage is due to opioids.

When opioid agents (narcotics) and neuromuscular blockers (relaxants) are administered, several of the stages are absent. During smooth administration of an anesthetic, there is no sharp division between stages I, II, and III, and there is no stage IV. The patient passes gradually from one stage to another, and it is through close observation of the signs exhibited by the patient that an anesthesiologist or anesthetist controls the situation. The responses of the pupils, the blood pressure, and the respiratory and cardiac rates are among the most reliable guides to the patient's condition.

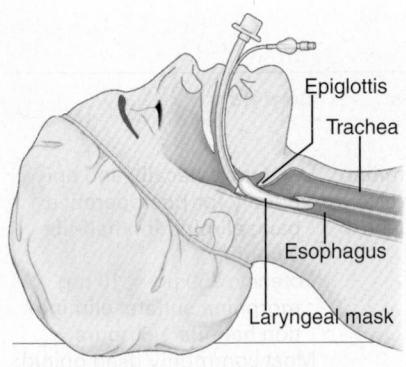
A. Laryngeal Mask Airway (LMA)

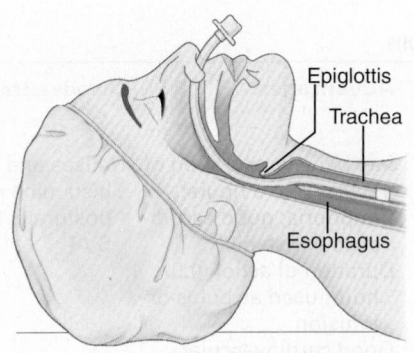
B. Intranasal intubation

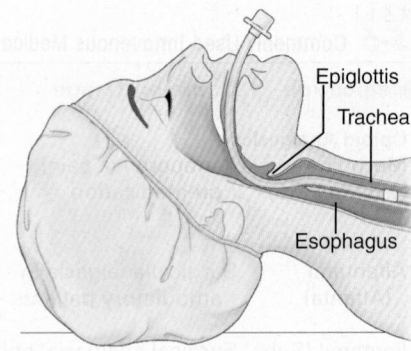
C. Oral intubation

FIGURE 5-3 Anesthetic delivery methods: **(A)** laryngeal mask airway (LMA), **(B)** nasal endotracheal catheter (in position with cuff inflated), and **(C)** oral endotracheal intubation (tube is in position with cuff inflated).

hypnosis, and amnesia is established. They are considered easy to administer, inexpensive, and reliable in terms of ability to monitor their effects with both clinical signs and end-tidal concentrations (Ebert & Schmid, 2009). Additionally, they are important in situations where there is a lack of venous access and anticipated airway difficulty.

INTRAVENOUS ADMINISTRATION. General anesthesia can be produced by the IV administration of various substances, such as barbiturates, benzodiazepines, nonbarbiturate hypnotics, dissociative agents, and opioid agents. Table 5-6 lists commonly used IV anesthetic and analgesic agents, including IV medications used as muscle relaxants in the intraoperative period. These medications may be administered to induce (initiate) or maintain anesthesia. Although they are often used in combination with inhalation anesthetics, they may be used alone. They may also be used to produce moderate sedation.

An advantage of IV anesthesia is that the onset of anesthesia is pleasant; there is none of the buzzing, roaring, or dizziness known to follow administration of an inhalation anesthetic. For this reason, induction of anesthesia usually begins with an IV agent and is often preferred by patients who have experienced various methods. The duration of action is brief, and the patient awakens with little nausea or vomiting.

The IV anesthetic agents are nonexplosive, require little equipment, and are easy to administer. The low incidence of postoperative nausea and vomiting makes the method useful in eye surgery because in this setting vomiting would increase intraocular pressure and endanger vision in the operated eye. IV anesthesia is useful for short procedures but is used less often for the longer procedures of abdominal surgery. It is not indicated for children, who have small veins, or for those who require intubation because of their susceptibility to respiratory obstruction.

A disadvantage of an IV anesthetic such as thiopental (Pentothal) is its powerful respiratory depressant effect. It must be administered by a skilled anesthesiologist or anesthetist and only when some method of oxygen administration is

immediately available in case of difficulty. Sneezing, coughing, and laryngospasm are sometimes noted with its use.

IV neuromuscular blockers (muscle relaxants) block the transmission of nerve impulses at the neuromuscular junction of skeletal muscles. Muscle relaxants are used to relax muscles in abdominal and thoracic surgery, relax eye muscles in certain types of eye surgery, facilitate endotracheal intubation, treat laryngospasm, and assist in mechanical ventilation.

Local Anesthesia
Local anesthesia is used to block nerves in the peripheral and central nervous systems. Local anesthesia provides anesthesia and analgesia by blocking the transmission of pain sensation along nerve fibers. The degree of blockage depends on both drug concentration and volume (Liu & Lin, 2009). Local anesthesia can be used alone or in conjunction with other types of anesthesia. It is usually administered by the surgeon to specific area of the body by topical application or local infiltration. In most cases, the patient will be monitored by a nurse. To ensure safety and quality of care, the AORN has developed recommended practices for nurses who monitor patients receiving local anesthesia (AORN, 2010). The nurse should also monitor the quantity of medication administered since toxic reactions are dose related (Marek & Bochnlein, 2007).

REGIONAL ANESTHESIA. Regional anesthesia is a form of local anesthesia in which an anesthetic agent is injected around nerves, so that the area supplied by these nerves is anesthetized. The most common techniques are spinal, epidural, and peripheral nerve blocks. Regional anesthesia is an attractive anesthetic option for many types of operative procedures and can provide excellent postoperative pain management in selected patients (Townsend Jr., Beauchamp, Evers et al., 2008). The effect depends on the type of nerve involved. A local anesthetic blocks motor nerves least readily and sympathetic nerves most readily. An anesthetic cannot be regarded as having worn off until all three systems (motor, sensory, and autonomic) are no longer affected.

TABLE
5-6 **Commonly Used Intravenous Medications**

Medication	Common Usage	Advantages	Disadvantages	Comments
Opioid Analgesics				
Morphine sulfate (MS)	Perioperative pain; premedication	Inexpensive; duration of action 4 to 5 hours; euphoria; good cardiovascular stability	Nausea and vomiting; histamine release; postural ↓ BP and ↓ SVR	Used intrathecally and epidurally for postoperative pain; elimination half-life 3 hours
Alfentanil (Alfenta)	Surgical analgesia in ambulatory patients	Duration of action 0.5 hour; used as bolus or infusion		Potency: 750 µg = 10 mg morphine sulfate; elimination half-life 1.6 hours
Fentanyl (Sublimaze)	Surgical analgesia: epidural infusion for postoperative analgesia; add to SAB	Good cardiovascular stability; duration of action 0.5 hour		Most commonly used opioid; potency: 100 µg = 10 mg morphine sulfate; elimination half-life 3.6 hours
Remifentanil (Ultiva)	IV infusion for surgical analgesia; small boluses for brief, intense pain	Easily titratable; metabolized by blood and tissue esterases; very short duration; good cardiovascular stability	New; expensive; requires mixing; may cause muscle rigidity	Potency: 25 µg = 10 mg morphine sulfate; 20 to 30 times potency of alfentanil; elimination half-life 3 to 10 min
Sufentanil (Sufenta)	Surgical analgesia	Good cardiovascular stability; duration of action 0.5 hour; prolonged analgesia	Prolonged respiratory depression	Potency: 15 µg = 10 mg morphine sulfate; elimination half-life 2.7 hours
Nondepolarizing Muscle Relaxants—Intermediate Onset and Duration				
Rocuronium (Zemuron)	Intubation; maintenance of relaxation	Rapid onset (dose-dependent); elimination via kidney and liver	Vagolytic; may ↑ HR	Duration similar to atracurium and vecuronium
Vecuronium (Norcuron)	Intubation; maintenance of relaxation	No significant cardiovascular or cumulative effects; no histamine release	Requires mixing	Mostly eliminated in bile, some in urine
Intravenous Anesthetics				
Etomidate (Amidate)	Induction	Good cardiovascular stability; fast, smooth induction and recovery	May cause pain with injection and myotonic movements	
Diazepam (Valium, Dizac)	Amnesia; hypnotic; preoperative medication	Good sedation	Prolonged duration	Residual effects for 20 to 90 hr; increased effect with alcohol
Ketamine (Ketalar)	Induction, occasional maintenance (IV or IM)	Short acting; patient maintains airway; good in small children and burn patients	Large doses may cause hallucinations and respiratory depression	Need darkened, quiet room for recovery; often used in trauma cases
Midazolam (Versed)	Hypnotic; anxiolytic; sedation; often used as adjunct to induction	Excellent amnesia; water-soluble (no pain with IV injection); short-acting	Slower induction than thiopental	Often used for amnesia with insertion of invasive monitors or regional anesthesia
Propofol (Diprivan)	Induction and maintenance; sedation with regional anesthesia or MAC	Rapid onset; awakening in 4 to 8 min	May cause pain when injected	Short elimination half-life (34–64 min)
Sodium methohexital (Brevital)	Induction	Ultrashort-acting barbiturate	May cause hiccups	Can be given rectally
Thiopental sodium (Pentothal)	Induction	Induction	May cause laryngospasm; can be given rectally	Large doses may cause apnea and cardiovascular depression

BP, blood pressure; HR, heart rate; IM, intramuscular; IV, IV; MAC, monitored anesthesia care; PO, oral; SAB, subarachnoid block; SVR, stroke volume ratio.

From Rothrock, J. C. (2011). Commonly used anesthetic drugs. In J.C. Rothrock (ed.), *Alexander's care of the patient in surgery* (13th ed.; Table 4–2, pp. 112–113). St. Louis: Mosby.

The patient receiving regional anesthesia is awake and aware of his or her surroundings unless medications are given to produce mild sedation or to relieve anxiety. The nurse must avoid careless conversation, unnecessary noise, and unpleasant odors; these may be noticed by the patient in the OR and may contribute to a negative response to the surgical experience. A quiet environment is therapeutic. The diagnosis must not be stated aloud if the patient is not to know it at this time.

SPINAL ANESTHESIA. Spinal anesthesia is an extensive conduction nerve block that is produced when a local anesthetic is introduced into the subarachnoid space at the lumbar level, usually between L4 and L5 (Fig. 5-4). It produces anesthesia of the lower extremities, perineum, and lower abdomen. For the lumbar puncture procedure, the patient usually lies on the side in a knee-to-chest position. Sterile technique is used as a spinal puncture is made and the medication is injected through the needle. As soon as the injection has been made, the patient is positioned on his or her back. If a relatively high level of block is sought, the head and shoulders are lowered.

A few minutes after induction of a spinal anesthetic, anesthesia and paralysis affect the toes and perineum and then gradually the legs and abdomen. If the anesthetic reaches the upper thoracic and cervical spinal cord in high concentrations, a temporary partial or complete respiratory paralysis results. Paralysis of the respiratory muscles is managed by mechanical ventilation until the effects of the anesthetic on the cranial and thoracic nerves have worn off.

Nausea, vomiting, and pain may occur during surgery when spinal anesthesia is used. As a rule, these reactions result from manipulation of various structures, particularly those within the abdominal cavity. The simultaneous IV administration of a weak solution of thiopental and inhalation of nitrous oxide may prevent such reactions.

Headache may be an after-effect of spinal anesthesia. Several factors are related to the incidence of headache: the size of the spinal needle used, the leakage of fluid from the subarachnoid space through the puncture site, and the patient's hydration status. Measures that increase cerebrospinal pressure are helpful in relieving headache. These include maintaining a quiet environment, keeping the patient lying flat, and keeping the patient well hydrated.

In continuous spinal anesthesia, the tip of a plastic catheter remains in the subarachnoid space during the surgical procedure, so that more anesthetic may be injected as needed. This technique allows greater control of the dosage, but there is greater potential for postanesthetic headache because of the large-gauge needle used.

EPIDURAL ANESTHESIA. Epidural anesthesia, a commonly used conduction block, is achieved by injecting a local anesthetic into the epidural space that surrounds the dura mater of the spinal cord (refer to Fig. 5-4). In contrast, spinal anesthesia involves injection through the dura mater into the subarachnoid space surrounding the spinal cord. Epidural anesthesia blocks sensory, motor, and autonomic functions; it differs from spinal anesthesia by the site of the injection

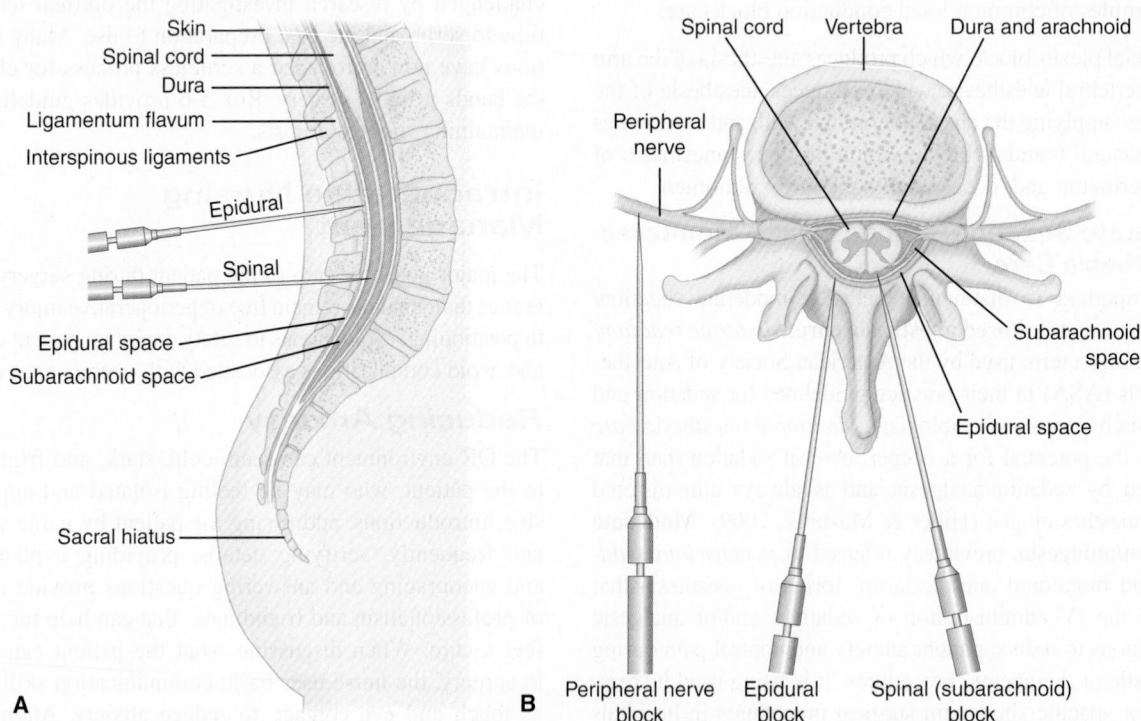

FIGURE 5-4 **(A)** Injection sites for spinal and epidural anesthesia. **(B)** Cross-section of injection sites for peripheral nerve, epidural, and spinal blocks.

and the amount of anesthetic agent used. Epidural doses are much higher because the epidural anesthetic does not make direct contact with the spinal cord or nerve roots

Epidural anesthetics, if placed correctly, can cause less hypotension and less hemodynamic changes. However, since the needle used for epidural anesthesia is much larger (17 to 18 gauge) than that used in spinal anesthesia (22 to 24 gauge), the severity of the headache with inadvertent puncture of the dura is much greater. Another disadvantage is the greater technical challenge of introducing the anesthetic into the epidural rather than the subarachnoid space. If inadvertent puncture of the dura occurs during epidural anesthesia and the anesthetic travels toward the head, high spinal anesthesia can result; this can produce severe hypotension and respiratory depression and arrest. Treatment of these complications includes airway support, IV fluids, and use of vasopressors.

Peripheral Nerve Blocks. Blockade of the brachial plexus (arm), lumbar plexus, and specific peripheral nerves is an effective means of providing surgical anesthesia and postoperative analgesia for many surgical procedures involving the upper and lower extremities. The advantages of peripheral nerve block (PNB) is reduced physiological stress in comparison to spinal or epidural anesthesia, avoidance of airway manipulation and the potential complications associated with endotracheal intubation, and avoidance of potential side effects associated with general anesthesia. All patients undergoing PNB should receive a full perioperative evaluation under the assumption that general anesthesia could be used if the block is inadequate (Sherwood, Williams, & Prough, 2009).

Examples of common local conduction blocks are:

- Brachial plexus block, which produces anesthesia of the arm
- Paravertebral anesthesia, which produces anesthesia of the nerves supplying the chest, abdominal wall, and extremities
- Transsacral (caudal) block, which produces anesthesia of the perineum and, occasionally, the lower abdomen

Moderate Sedation/Analgesia and Monitored Anesthesia Care

It is important to distinguish between moderate sedation/analgesia and **monitored anesthesia care**. *Moderate sedation/analgesia* is a term used by the American Society of Anesthesiologists (ASA) in their practice guidelines for sedation and analgesia by nonanesthesiologists. *Monitored anesthesia care* implies the potential for a deeper level of sedation than that provided by sedation/analgesia and is always administered by an anesthesiologist (Hiller & Mazurek, 2009). **Moderate sedation/analgesia**, previously referred to as *conscious sedation*, and monitored anesthesia are forms of anesthesia that involve the IV administration of sedatives and/or analgesic medications to reduce patient anxiety and control pain during diagnostic or therapeutic procedures. It is being used increasingly for specific short-term surgical procedures in hospitals and ambulatory care centers (Rothrock, 2011). The goal is to depress a patient's level of consciousness to a moderate level to enable surgical, diagnostic, or therapeutic procedures to be

performed while ensuring the patient's comfort during and cooperation with the procedures. Moderate sedation and monitored analgesia allow the patient to maintain a patent airway, retain protective airway reflexes, respond to verbal and physical stimuli and recover more rapidly post procedure.

Moderate sedation can be administered by an anesthesiologist, anesthetist, or other specially trained and credentialed physician or nurse. The patient receiving moderate sedation is never left alone and is closely monitored by a physician or nurse who is knowledgeable and skilled in detecting arrhythmias, administering oxygen, and performing resuscitation. The continual assessment of the patient's vital signs, level of consciousness, and cardiac and respiratory function is an essential component of moderate sedation. Pulse oximetry, ECG monitor, and frequent measurement of vital signs are used to monitor the patient. The regulations for use and administration of moderate sedation differ from state to state, and its administration is addressed by standards issued by the Joint Commission and by institutional policies and nursing specialty organizations, including the AORN (2010).

Surgical Asepsis

Surgical asepsis prevents the contamination of surgical wounds. The patient's natural skin flora or a previously existing infection may cause postoperative wound infection. Rigorous adherence to the principles of surgical asepsis by OR personnel is basic to preventing surgical site infections.

Traditionally, the surgeon, surgical assistants, and nurses prepared themselves by scrubbing their hands and arms with antiseptic soap and water, but this traditional practice is being challenged by research investigating the optimal length of time to scrub and the best preparation to use. Many institutions have now introduced a scrubless process for cleaning the hands prior to surgery. Box 5-6 provides guidelines for maintaining surgical asepsis.

Intraoperative Nursing Management

The major goals for care of the patient during surgery are to reduce their anxiety, remain free of perioperative injury related to positioning, avoid threats to safety, maintain patient dignity, and avoid complications associated with operative events.

Reducing Anxiety

The OR environment can seem cold, stark, and frightening to the patient, who may be feeling isolated and apprehensive. Introductions, addressing the patient by name warmly and frequently, verifying details, providing explanations, and encouraging and answering questions provide a sense of professionalism and friendliness that can help the patient feel secure. When discussing what the patient can expect in surgery, the nurse uses basic communication skills, such as touch and eye contact, to reduce anxiety. Attention to physical comfort (warm blankets, position changes) helps the patient feel more comfortable. Telling the patient who else will be present in the OR, how long the procedure is

BOX 5-6 Basic Guidelines for Maintaining Surgical Asepsis

All practitioners involved in the intraoperative phase have a responsibility to provide and maintain a safe environment. Adherence to aseptic practice is part of this responsibility. The basic principles of aseptic technique follow:

- All materials in contact with the surgical wound or used within the sterile field must be sterile. Sterile surfaces or articles may touch other sterile surfaces or articles and remain sterile; contact with unsterile objects at any point renders a sterile area contaminated.
- Gowns of the surgical team are considered sterile in front from the chest to the level of the sterile field. The sleeves are also considered sterile from 2 inches above the elbow to the stockinette cuff.
- Sterile drapes are used to create a sterile field. Only the top surface of a draped table is considered sterile. During draping of a table or patient, the sterile drape is held well above the surface to be covered and is positioned from front to back.
- Items are dispensed to a sterile field by methods that preserve the sterility of the items and the integrity of the sterile field. After a sterile package is opened, the edges are considered unsterile. Sterile supplies, includ-

ing solutions, are delivered to a sterile field or handed to a scrubbed person in such a way that the sterility of the object or fluid remains intact.

- The movements of the surgical team are from sterile to sterile areas and from unsterile to unsterile areas. Scrubbed persons and sterile items contact only sterile areas; circulating nurses and unsterile items contact only unsterile areas.
- Movement around a sterile field must not cause contamination of the field. Sterile areas must be kept in view during movement around the area. At least a 1-foot distance from the sterile field must be maintained to prevent inadvertent contamination.
- Whenever a sterile barrier is breached, the area must be considered contaminated. A tear or puncture of the drape permitting access to an unsterile surface underneath renders the area unsterile. Such a drape must be replaced.
- Every sterile field is constantly monitored and maintained. Items of doubtful sterility are considered unsterile. Sterile fields are prepared as close as possible to the time of use.

---

expected to take, and other details helps the patient prepare for the experience and gain a sense of control.

Preventing Intraoperative Positioning Injury

The patient's position on the operating table depends on the surgical procedure to be performed as well as on the patient's physical condition (Fig. 5-5). The potential for transient discomfort or permanent injury is present, because many positions are awkward. Hyperextending joints, compressing arteries, or pressing on nerves and bony prominences usually results in discomfort simply because the position must be sustained for a long period of time (Rothrock, 2011). Factors to consider include the following:

- The patient should be in as comfortable a position as possible, whether conscious or unconscious.
- The operative field must be adequately exposed.
- An awkward position, undue pressure on a body part, or use of stirrups or traction should not obstruct the vascular supply.
- Respiration should not be impeded by pressure of arms on the chest or by a gown that constricts the neck or chest.
- Nerves must be protected from undue pressure. Improper positioning of the arms, hands, legs, or feet can cause serious injury or paralysis. Shoulder braces must be well padded to prevent irreparable nerve injury, especially when the Trendelenburg position (head down) is necessary. The complication of compartment syndrome is associated with intraoperative positioning (Denholm, 2009; Singisetti, 2009). Refer to Chapter 42 for information related to clinical manifestations of compartment syndrome.

- Precautions for patient safety must be observed, particularly with thin, elderly, or obese patients and those with a physical deformity.
- The patient may need light restraint before induction in case of excitement.

The usual position for surgery, called the dorsal recumbent position, is flat on the back. One arm is positioned at the side of the table, with the hand placed palm down; the other is carefully positioned on an arm board to facilitate IV infusion of fluids, blood, or medications. This position is used for most abdominal surgeries except for surgery of the gallbladder or pelvis (see Fig. 5-5a).

The Trendelenburg position usually is used for surgery on the lower abdomen and pelvis to obtain good exposure by displacing the intestines into the upper abdomen. In this position, the head and upper body are lowered. The patient is held in position by padded shoulder braces (see Fig. 5-5b).

The lithotomy position is used for nearly all perineal, rectal, and vaginal surgical procedures (see Fig. 5-5c). The patient is positioned on the back with the legs and thighs flexed. The position is maintained by placing the feet in stirrups.

The Sims' or lateral position is used for renal surgery. The patient is placed on the nonoperative side with an air pillow 12.5 to 15 cm (5 to 6 inches) thick under the loin, or on a table with a kidney or back lift (see Fig. 5-5d).

Other procedures, such as neurosurgery or abdominothoracic surgery, may require unique positioning and supplemental apparatus, depending on the operative approach.

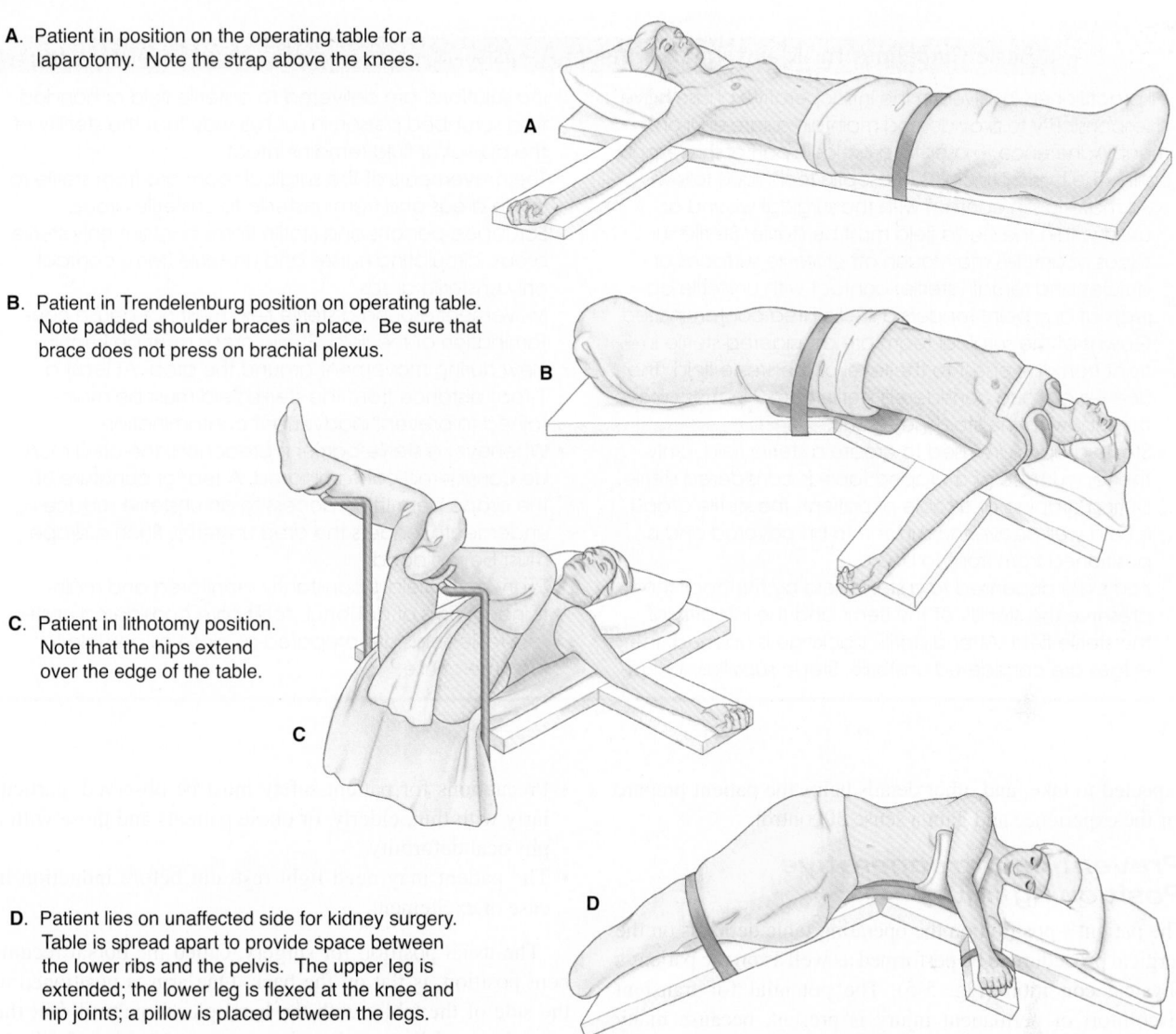

A. Patient in position on the operating table for a laparotomy. Note the strap above the knees.

B. Patient in Trendelenburg position on operating table. Note padded shoulder braces in place. Be sure that brace does not press on brachial plexus.

C. Patient in lithotomy position. Note that the hips extend over the edge of the table.

D. Patient lies on unaffected side for kidney surgery. Table is spread apart to provide space between the lower ribs and the pelvis. The upper leg is extended; the lower leg is flexed at the knee and hip joints; a pillow is placed between the legs.

FIGURE 5-5 Positions on the operating table. Captions call attention to safety and comfort features. All surgical patients wear caps to cover the hair completely.

Protecting the Patient From Injury

A variety of activities are used to address the diverse patient safety issues that arise in the OR. The nurse protects the patient from injury by providing a safe environment. Verifying information, checking the chart for completeness, and maintaining surgical asepsis and an optimal environment are critical nursing responsibilities. Verifying that all required documentation is completed is one of the first functions of the intraoperative nurse. The patient is identified, and the planned surgical procedure, correct surgical site, and type of anesthesia are verified. It is important to review the patient's record for the following:

- Correct informed surgical consent, with patient's signature
- Completed records for health history and physical examination
- Results of diagnostic studies
- Allergies (including latex)

In addition to checking that all necessary patient data are complete, the perioperative nurse obtains the necessary equipment specific to the procedure. The need for nonroutine medications, blood components, instruments, and other equipment and supplies is assessed, and the readiness of the room, completeness of physical setup, and completeness of instrument, suture, and dressing setups are determined. Any aspects of the OR environment that may negatively affect the patient are identified. These include physical features, such as room temperature and humidity; electrical hazards; potential contaminants (dust, blood, and discharge on floor or surfaces, uncovered hair, faulty attire of personnel, jewelry worn by personnel); and unnecessary traffic. The circulating nurse also sets up and maintains suction equipment in working order, sets up invasive monitoring equipment, assists with insertion of vascular access and monitoring devices (arterial, Swan-Ganz, central venous pressure, IV

Risk Factors for Retained Surgical Sponges

- Emergency surgery
- Unplanned changes in procedure
- Patient with higher body mass index
- Multiple surgeons involved in same operation
- Multiple procedures performed on same patient
- Multiple operating room nurses/staff members involved in the surgery
- Case duration covers multiple nursing "shifts"

From Chen et al., 2010.

lines), and initiates appropriate physical comfort measures for the patient.

Preventing physical injury includes using safety straps and side rails and not leaving the sedated patient unattended. Transferring the patient from the stretcher to the OR table requires safe transferring practices. Other safety measures include properly positioning the grounding pad under the patient to prevent electrical burns and shock, removing excess antiseptic solution from the patient's skin, and promptly and completely draping exposed areas after the sterile field has been created to decrease the risk for hypothermia.

Nursing measures to prevent "never events" in surgery such as prevention of retained foreign objects, wrong site surgery, and pressure ulcers cannot be overemphasized. The Joint Commission and the AORN have developed guidelines that should be implemented in each facility to avoid these from occurring. There are also technological devices that can support the safe counting of surgical instruments and supplies to prevent retention of foreign objects. It is estimated that retained foreign bodies (RFB) range from one case per 8,000 to 18,000 operations, or 1 case or more per year for a typical large hospital, or approximately 1,500 per year in large hospitals in the United States (Chen, Shapiro, Angood et al., 2010). The risk of RFB increases during certain surgical conditions (Box 5-7).

Nursing measures to prevent injury from excessive blood loss include blood conservation using equipment such as a cell-saver (a device for recirculating the patient's own blood cells) and administration of blood products. Few patients undergoing an elective procedure require blood transfusion, but those undergoing higher-risk procedures (such as orthopedic or cardiac surgeries) may require an intraoperative transfusion. The circulating nurse anticipates this need, checks that blood has been cross-matched and held in reserve, and is prepared to support the anesthesiologist with administration when needed.

Serving as Patient Advocate

Because the patient undergoing general anesthesia or moderate sedation experiences temporary sensory/perceptual alteration or loss, he or she has an increased need for protection and advocacy. Patient advocacy in the OR entails maintaining the patient's physical and emotional comfort, privacy, rights, and dignity. Patients, whether conscious or unconscious, should not be subjected to excess noise, inappropriate conversation, or, most of all, derogatory comments. As surprising as this sounds, banter in the OR occasionally includes jokes about the patient's physical appearance, job, personal history, and so forth. Cases have been reported in which seemingly deeply anesthetized patients recalled the entire surgical experience, including disparaging personal remarks made by OR personnel. As an advocate, the nurse never engages in this conversation and discourages others from doing so. Other advocacy activities include minimizing the clinical, dehumanizing aspects of being a surgical patient by making sure the patient is treated as a person, respecting cultural and spiritual values, providing physical privacy, and maintaining confidentiality.

Monitoring and Managing Potential Complications

It is the responsibility of the surgeon and the anesthesiologist or anesthetist to monitor and manage complications. The intraoperative nurse also plays an important role. Being alert to and reporting changes in vital signs and symptoms of nausea and vomiting, anaphylaxis, hypoxia, hypothermia, malignant hyperthermia, or disseminated intravascular coagulation (DIC) and assisting with their management are important nursing functions. Each of these complications will be discussed shortly. It is the responsibility of all members of the health care team to maintain asepsis.

Nausea and Vomiting

Nausea and vomiting, or regurgitation, may affect patients during the intraoperative period. If gagging occurs, the patient is turned to the side, the head of the table is lowered, and a basin is provided to collect the vomitus. Suction is used to remove saliva and vomited gastric contents. The advent of new anesthetics has reduced the incidence; however, there is no single way to prevent nausea and vomiting. An interdisciplinary approach involving the surgeon, anesthesiologist or anesthetist, and nurse is best.

In some cases, the anesthesiologist or anesthetist administers antiemetics preoperatively or intraoperatively to counteract possible aspiration. If the patient aspirates vomitus, an asthma-like attack with severe bronchial spasms and wheezing is triggered. Pneumonitis and pulmonary edema can subsequently develop, leading to extreme hypoxia. Increasing medical attention is being paid to silent regurgitation of gastric contents (not related to preoperative fasting times), which occurs more frequently than previously realized. The volume and acidity of the aspirate determine the extent of damage to the lungs. Patients may be given Bicitra, a clear, nonparticulate antacid to increase gastric fluid pH or a histamine-2 (H_2) receptor antagonist such as cimetidine (Tagamet), ranitidine (Zantac), or famotidine (Pepcid) to decrease gastric acid production (Rothrock, 2011).

Anaphylaxis

Anaphylaxis is an acute life-threatening allergic reaction to a specific antigen or hapten (a small molecule that can cause an immune response when bound to a protein) resulting in urticaria (hives), pruritus (itching), or angioedema (swelling is beneath the skin rather than on the surface), and quickly deteriorating to vascular collapse, shock, and respiratory distress. Any time the patient comes into contact with a foreign substance, there is the potential for an anaphylactic reaction. Because medications are the most common cause of anaphylaxis, intraoperative nurses must be aware of the type and method of anesthesia used as well as the specific agents. An anaphylactic reaction can occur in response to many medications, latex, or other substances.

Hypoxia and Other Respiratory Complications

Inadequate ventilation, occlusion of the airway, inadvertent intubation of the esophagus, and hypoxia are significant potential complications associated with general anesthesia. Many factors can contribute to inadequate ventilation. Respiratory depression caused by anesthetic agents, aspiration of respiratory tract secretions or vomitus, and the patient's position on the operating table can compromise the exchange of gases. Anatomic variation can make the trachea difficult to visualize and result in the artificial airway's being inserted into the esophagus rather than into the trachea. In addition to these dangers, asphyxia caused by foreign bodies in the mouth, spasm of the vocal cords, relaxation of the tongue, or aspiration of vomitus, saliva, or blood can occur. Brain damage from hypoxia occurs within minutes; therefore, vigilant monitoring of the patient's oxygenation status is a primary function of the anesthesiologist or anesthetist and the circulating nurse. Peripheral perfusion is checked frequently, and pulse oximetry values are monitored continuously.

Hypothermia

During anesthesia, the patient's temperature may fall. This condition is called *hypothermia* and is indicated by a core body temperature that is lower than normal (36.6°C [98.0°F] or less). Inadvertent hypothermia may occur as a result of a low temperature in the OR, infusion of cold fluids, inhalation of cold gases, open body wounds or cavities, decreased muscle activity, advanced age, or the pharmaceutical agents used (e.g., vasodilators, phenothiazines, general anesthetics). Hypothermia may also be intentionally induced in selected surgical procedures (e.g., cardiac surgeries requiring cardiopulmonary bypass) to reduce the patient's metabolic rate and energy demands.

Preventing unintentional hypothermia is a major objective. If hypothermia occurs, the goal of intervention is to minimize or reverse the physiologic process. If hypothermia is intentional, the goal is safe return to normal body temperature. Environmental temperature in the OR can temporarily be set at 25° to 26.6°C (78° to 80°F). IV and irrigating fluids are warmed to 37°C (98.6°F). Wet gowns and drapes are removed promptly and replaced with dry materials, because wet linens promote heat loss. Whatever methods are used to rewarm the patient, warming must be accomplished gradually, not rapidly. Conscientious monitoring of core temperature, urinary output, ECG, blood pressure, arterial blood gas (ABG) levels, and serum electrolyte levels is required.

NURSING ALERT

Shivering is associated with hypothermia. The nurse is aware that shivering can increase oxygen demand by 300% to 400%, thus supplemental oxygen should be administered, and oxygen saturation monitoring should be continuous.

Malignant Hyperthermia

Malignant hyperthermia is a rare inherited muscle disorder that is chemically induced by anesthetic agents (Rothrock, 2011), occurring in approximately 1 in 100,000 (Brandom, 2009). At one time, mortality rates exceeded 80%. Since the introduction of dantrolene sodium in 1979, the development of genetics testing, and early detection and treatment with specific protocols, fatalities have been reduced to approximately 10% (Noble, 2007). Identification of patients at risk for MH is imperative. Susceptible people include those with strong and bulky muscles, familial genetic mutations as described earlier, first-degree relatives of persons who have been diagnosed or suspected of MH, and an unexplained death of a family member during surgery that was accompanied by a febrile response.

During anesthesia, potent agents such as inhalation anesthetics (halothane, enflurane) and muscle relaxants (succinylcholine) may trigger the symptoms of MH (refer to Table 5-5 for list of anesthetic agents). Stress and some medications, such as sympathomimetics (epinephrine), theophylline, aminophylline, anticholinergics (atropine), and cardiac glycosides (digitalis), can induce or intensify such a reaction. The pathophysiology is related to a hypermetabolic condition in skeletal muscle cells that involves altered mechanisms of calcium function at the cellular level. This disruption of calcium causes clinical symptoms of hypermetabolism, which in turn increases muscle contraction (rigidity). The sustained muscle contraction causes hyperthermia (fever may exceed 110°F) and subsequent damage to the CNS.

The skeletal muscle cells, when depleted of the source of cellular energy (adenosine triphosphate [ATP]), break down and release the muscle cell contents, including myoglobin (a protein released from muscle when injury occurs), creatine phosphokinase (CPK), and potassium into the systemic circulation. The resulting hyperkalemia has a dramatic effect on the heart, causing ventricular arrhythmias. The muscle pigment myoglobin has an affinity for the kidneys, resulting in potential for renal failure (refer to Chapter 42, Box 42-7 for details). If untreated, cardiac arrest, kidney failure, blood coagulation problems, internal hemorrhage, brain injury, liver failure, and death can result.

The initial symptoms of MH are related to cardiovascular and musculoskeletal activity. Tachycardia (heart rate >150 bpm) is often the earliest sign. In addition to the tachycardia, sympathetic nervous stimulation leads to ventricular arrhythmia, hypotension, decreased cardiac output, oliguria, and, later, cardiac arrest. With the abnormal transport of calcium,

rigidity or tetanus-like movements occur, often in the jaw. The rise in temperature is actually a late sign that develops rapidly; body temperature can increase 1° to 2°C (2° to 4°F) every 5 minutes (Rothrock, 2011). The core body temperature can reach or exceed 42°C (104°F) in a very short time and must be properly monitored and recorded during surgery. Recent research reveals that the order of clinical signs of patients with MH (from highest to lowest percentage) is: hypercarbia (92.2%), sinus tachycardia (72.9%), rapidly increasing temperature (64.7%), elevated temperature (52.2%), generalized muscular rigidity (40.8%), tachypnea (27.1%), masseter spasm (26.7%), sweating (17.6%), cola-colored urine (13.7%), cyanosis (9.4%), skin mottling (6.3%), ventricular tachycardia (3.5%), excessive bleeding (2.7%), and ventricular fibrillation (2.4%) (Larach, Gronert, Allen et al., 2010). The entire health team is alert for the presence of any of the aforementioned signs.

Recognizing symptoms early and discontinuing anesthesia promptly are imperative. The immediate response is the discontinuation of the triggering agent and hyperventilation of the patient with 100% oxygen and immediate administration of at least 2.5 mg/kg of dantrolene sodium intravenously (Brandom, 2009). Additional incremental doses may be required until the signs of MH are controlled. Because dantrolene is available in 20 mg multidose vials that must be reconstituted with 50 mL of sterile water only, it is expected that at least two nurses will be reconstituting the drug during the crisis. If the patient is hyperthermic, active cooling is initiated with iced saline administration, lavage of the stomach, bladder, rectum, and open body cavities if appropriate with iced saline, use of a hypothermia blanket, and use of ice packs. Monitoring of the patient's temperature to assess treatment efficacy and avoidance of hypothermia is essential. Antiarrhythmic medications, such as procainamide, are expected for management of ventricular arrhythmias; IV glucose and insulin, as well as calcium chloride, infusion is anticipated for the hyperkalemia. Sodium bicarbonate may be administered to treat the metabolic acidosis based upon ABG analysis. Additionally, diuretics may be administered to assist with the clearance of filtered myoglobin into the urine; hourly urine output and color of urine are closely observed (Nobel, 2007).

Goals of treatment are to decrease metabolism, reverse metabolic and respiratory acidosis, correct arrhythmias, decrease body temperature, provide oxygen and nutrition to tissues, and correct electrolyte imbalance. The Malignant Hyperthermia Association of the United States (MHAUS) publishes a treatment protocol that should be posted in the OR and be readily available on a MH cart. Although MH is uncommon, all providers must identify patients at risk, recognize the signs and symptoms, have the appropriate medication and equipment available, and be knowledgeable about the protocol to follow. This preparation may be life-saving for the patient.

Disseminated Intravascular Coagulation
DIC is a dynamic systemic disorder that results in widespread hemorrhage and microthrombosis with ischemia. It can be a side effect of MH or a precursor to the development

of MH. The mortality rate can exceed 80%, and clinical manifestations may be bleeding from mucous membranes, venipuncture sites, and the GI and urinary tracts. Bleeding can range from minimal occult internal bleeding to profuse hemorrhage from all orifices. It is important that all providers are alert for the subtle cues of developing DIC. Refer to Chapter 33 for complete details of DIC.

POSTOPERATIVE NURSING

The **postoperative phase** begins with the admission of the patient to the PACU and ends with a follow-up evaluation in the clinical setting or home. The scope of nursing care covers a wide range of activities including maintaining the patient's airway, monitoring vital signs, assessing the effects of the anesthetic agents, assessing the patient for complications, and providing comfort and pain relief. Nursing activities also focus on promoting the patient's recovery and initiating the teaching, follow-up care, and referrals essential for recovery and rehabilitation after discharge.

Nursing Management During Postanesthesia Care

Postanesthesia care in some hospitals and ambulatory surgical centers is divided into two phases. In **phase I PACU**, which is the immediate recovery phase, intensive nursing care is provided. In **phase II PACU**, the patient is prepared for self-care or care in the hospital, an extended care setting, or discharge. Recliners rather than stretchers or beds are standard in many phase II units. Patients may remain in a PACU unit for as long as 4 to 6 hours, depending on the type of surgery and any preexisting conditions. In facilities without separate phases, the patient remains in the PACU and may be discharged home directly from this unit (American Society of PeriAnesthesia Nurses [ASPAN], 2010).

The nursing management objectives for the patient in the PACU are to provide care until the patient has recovered from the effects of anesthesia (e.g., until resumption of motor and sensory functions), is oriented or returns to baseline cognition, has stable vital signs, and shows no evidence of hemorrhage or other complications. All PACU nurses have special skills, including strong assessment skills. The PACU nurse provides frequent (every 15 minutes) monitoring of the patient's pulse, ECG, respiratory rate, blood pressure, and pulse oximeter value (blood oxygen level). In some cases, the end-tidal carbon dioxide ($ETCO_2$) level is monitored as well. The patient's airway may become obstructed because of the latent effects of recent anesthesia, and the PACU nurse must be prepared to assist in reintubation and in handling other emergencies that may occur. Nurses in PACUs must also possess excellent patient teaching skills.

Admitting the Patient to the PACU
Transferring the postoperative patient from the OR to the PACU is the responsibility of the anesthesiologist or

anesthetist. During transport from the OR to the PACU, the anesthesia provider remains at the head of the stretcher (to maintain the airway), and a surgical team member remains at the opposite end. Transporting the patient involves special consideration of the incision site, potential vascular changes, and exposure. The surgical incision is considered every time the postoperative patient is moved; many wounds are closed under considerable tension, and every effort is made to prevent further strain on the incision. The patient is positioned so that he or she is not lying on and obstructing drains or drainage tubes. Serious orthostatic hypotension may occur when a patient is moved too quickly from one position to another (e.g., from a lithotomy position to a horizontal position or from a lateral to a supine position), so the patient must be moved slowly and carefully. As soon as the patient is placed on the stretcher or bed, the soiled gown is removed and replaced with a dry gown. The patient is covered with lightweight blankets and warmed. Three side rails may be raised to prevent falls.

Assessing the Patient

Frequent, skilled assessments of the blood oxygen saturation level, pulse rate and regularity, depth and nature of respirations, skin color, level of consciousness, and ability to respond to commands are the cornerstones of nursing care in the PACU. The nurse performs a baseline assessment, then checks the surgical site for drainage or hemorrhage and makes sure that all drainage tubes and monitoring lines are connected and functioning. The nurse checks any IV fluids or medications currently infusing and verifies dosage and rate.

After the initial assessment, the patient's vital signs and general physical status are assessed at least every 15 minutes. Patency of the airway and respiratory function are always evaluated first, followed by assessment of cardiovascular function, the condition of the surgical site, and function of the CNS. Any surgical procedure has the potential for injury due to disrupted neurovascular integrity resulting from prolonged awkward positioning in the OR, manipulation of tissues, inadvertent severing of nerves, or tight bandages. Any orthopedic surgery or surgery involving the extremities carries a risk of peripheral nerve damage. Vascular surgeries, such as replacing sections of diseased peripheral arteries or inserting an arteriovenous graft, put the patient at risk for thrombus formation at the surgical site and subsequent ischemia of tissues distal to the thrombus. Assessment of *circulation, sensation, and mobility* (CSM) includes having the patient move the hand or foot distal to the surgical site through a full range of motion, assessing all surfaces for intact sensation, and assessing peripheral pulses (Rothrock, 2011). The nurse must be aware of any pertinent information from the patient's history that may be significant (e.g., patient is deaf or hard of hearing, has a history of seizures, has diabetes, is allergic to certain medications or to latex).

Maintaining a Patent Airway

The primary objective in the immediate postoperative period is to maintain pulmonary ventilation and thus prevent hypoxemia (reduced oxygen in the blood) and hypercapnia (excess carbon dioxide in the blood). Both can occur if the airway is obstructed and ventilation is reduced (hypoventilation). Besides checking the physician's orders for and administering supplemental oxygen, the nurse assesses respiratory rate and depth, ease of respirations, oxygen saturation, and breath sounds.

Patients who have experienced prolonged anesthesia usually are unconscious, with all muscles relaxed. This relaxation extends to the muscles of the pharynx. When the patient lies on his or her back, the lower jaw and the tongue fall backward and the air passages become obstructed (Fig. 5-6). This is called *hypopharyngeal obstruction*. Signs of occlusion include choking; noisy and irregular respirations; decreased oxygen saturation; and within minutes, a blue, dusky color (cyanosis) of the skin. Because movement of the thorax and the diaphragm does not necessarily indicate that the patient is breathing, the nurse needs to place the palm of her hand at the patient's nose and mouth to feel the exhaled breath.

The anesthesiologist or anesthetist may leave a hard rubber or plastic airway in the patient's mouth or naris to maintain a patent airway. Such a device should not be removed until signs such as gagging indicate that reflex action is returning. Alternatively, the patient may enter the PACU with an endotracheal tube still in place and may require continued mechanical ventilation. The nurse assists in initiating the use of the ventilator and in the weaning and extubation processes. Some patients, particularly those who have had extensive or lengthy surgical procedures, may be transferred from the OR directly to the intensive care unit (ICU) or from the PACU to the ICU while still intubated and receiving mechanical ventilation.

Respiratory difficulty can also result from excessive secretion of mucus or aspiration of vomitus. Placing the patient on his or her side in the recovery position will allow the fluid to escape from the mouth. The head of the bed is elevated 15 to 30 degrees unless contraindicated, and the patient is closely monitored to maintain the airway as well as to minimize the risk of aspiration. If vomiting occurs, the patient is turned to the side to prevent aspiration, and the vomitus is collected in the emesis basin. Mucus or vomitus obstructing the pharynx or the trachea is suctioned with a pharyngeal suction tip or a nasal catheter introduced into the nasopharynx or oropharynx. Caution is necessary in suctioning the throat of a patient who has had a tonsillectomy or other oral or laryngeal surgery because of risk of bleeding and discomfort.

Maintaining Cardiovascular Stability

To monitor cardiovascular stability, the nurse assesses the patient's mental status; vital signs; cardiac rhythm; skin temperature, color, and moisture; and urine output. Central venous pressure, pulmonary artery pressure, and arterial lines are monitored if the patient's condition requires such assessment. The nurse also assesses the patency of all IV

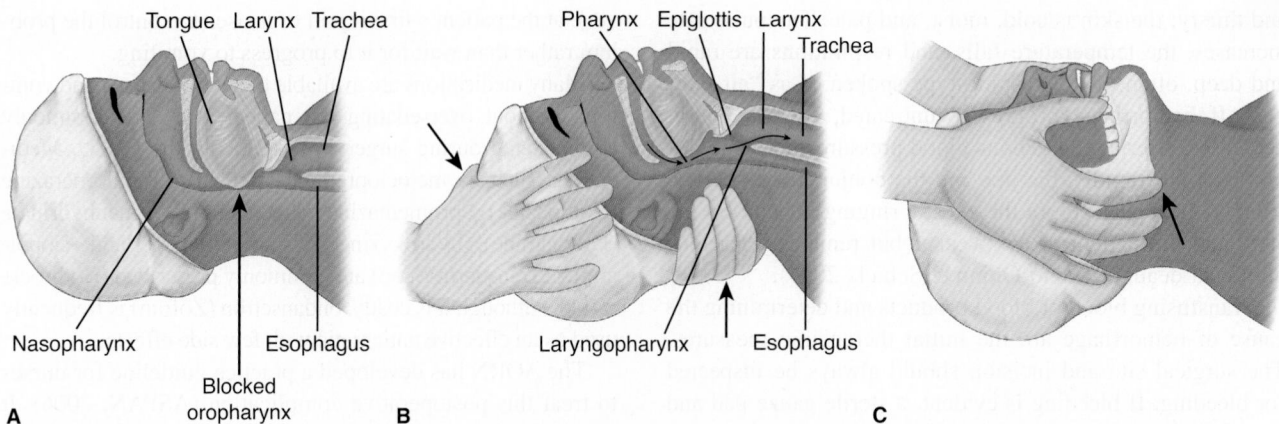

FIGURE 5-6 (**A**) A hypopharyngeal obstruction occurs when neck flexion permits the chin to drop toward the chest; obstruction almost always occurs when the head is in the midposition. (**B**) Tilting the head back to stretch the anterior neck structure lifts the base of the tongue off the posterior pharyngeal wall. The direction of the arrows indicates the pressure of the hands. (**C**) Opening the mouth is necessary to correct valve-like obstruction of the nasal passage during expiration, which occurs in about 30% of unconscious patients. Open the patient's mouth (separate lips and teeth) and move the lower jaw forward, so that the lower teeth are in front of the upper teeth. To regain backward tilt of the neck, lift with both hands at the ascending rami of the mandible.

lines. The primary cardiovascular complications seen in the PACU include hypotension and shock, hemorrhage, hypertension, and arrhythmias.

Hypotension and Shock

Hypotension can result from blood loss, hypoventilation, position changes, pooling of blood in the extremities, or side effects of medications and anesthetics. The most common cause is loss of circulating volume through blood and plasma loss. If the amount of blood loss exceeds 500 mL (especially if the loss is rapid), replacement is usually indicated.

Fluid loss is a significant potential problem for surgical patients, owing to their preoperative NPO status, evaporation of fluid intraoperatively, and significant shifting of sodium-rich fluid from the intravascular space to the extracellular space because of inflammatory process, trauma, or infection. The loss of fluid from the blood stream sequesters in the tissues or "third spaces," which may be noted by the presence of edema. It is important for the nurse to understand that, although the patient may clinically present with edema (often associated with fluid volume excess), a hypovolemia exists intravascularly that can progress to shock if fluids are not managed adequately. In addition, the nurse considers fluid loss related to evaporation in the OR. For example, it is estimated that, with surgery involving an open abdomen, insensible fluid losses can reach 500 to 1,000 mL/hour (Kuo & Klingensmith, 2008). The nurse considers fluid loss from the nasogastric tube, urinary output, drains, estimated blood loss, and evaporation when evaluating the patient's fluid volume status.

Shock, one of the most serious postoperative complications, can result from hypovolemia and decreased intravascular volume. The types of shock are classified as hypovolemic, cardiogenic, neurogenic, anaphylactic, and septic. See Chapter 54 for more information on shock.

Hemorrhage

Hemorrhage is an uncommon yet serious complication of surgery that can result in death. It can present insidiously or emergently at any time in the immediate postoperative period or up to several days after surgery (Table 5-7). When blood loss is extreme, the patient is apprehensive, restless,

TABLE
5-7 Classifications of Hemorrhage

Classification	Defining Characteristic
Time Frame	
Primary	Hemorrhage occurs at the time of surgery.
Intermediary	Hemorrhage occurs during the first few hours after surgery when the rise of blood pressure to its normal level dislodges insecure clots from untied vessels.
Secondary	Hemorrhage may occur some time after surgery if a suture slips because a blood vessel was not securely tied, became infected, or was eroded by a drainage tube.
Type of Vessel	
Capillary	Hemorrhage is characterized by a slow, general ooze.
Venous	Darkly colored blood bubbles out quickly.
Arterial	Blood is bright red and appears in spurts with each heartbeat.
Visibility	
Evident	Hemorrhage is on the surface and can be seen.
Concealed	Hemorrhage is in a body cavity and cannot be seen.

and thirsty; the skin is cold, moist, and pale. The pulse rate increases, the temperature falls, and respirations are rapid and deep, often of the gasping type spoken of as "air hunger." If hemorrhage progresses untreated, cardiac output decreases, arterial and venous blood pressure and hemoglobin level fall rapidly, the lips and the conjunctivae become pale, spots appear before the eyes, a ringing is heard in the ears, and the patient grows weaker but remains conscious until near death (Defazio-Quinn & Schick, 2004).

Transfusing blood or blood products and determining the cause of hemorrhage are the initial therapeutic measures. The surgical site and incision should always be inspected for bleeding. If bleeding is evident, a sterile gauze pad and a pressure dressing are applied, and the site of the bleeding is elevated to heart level if possible. The patient is placed in the shock position (flat on back; legs elevated at a 20-degree angle; knees kept straight). If hemorrhage is suspected but cannot be visualized, the patient may be taken back to the OR for emergency exploration of the surgical site.

In addition, the nurse should be aware of any special considerations related to blood loss replacement. Certain patients may decline blood transfusions for religious or cultural reasons and may identify this request on their advance directives or living will.

Hypertension and Arrhythmias

Hypertension is common in the immediate postoperative period secondary to sympathetic nervous system stimulation from pain, hypoxia, or bladder distention. Arrhythmias are associated with electrolyte imbalance, altered respiratory function, pain, hypothermia, stress, and anesthetic agents. Both hypertension and arrhythmias are managed by treating the underlying causes.

Relieving Pain and Anxiety

IV opioid analgesics are administered judiciously and often in the PACU. IV opioids provide immediate pain relief and are short-acting, thus minimizing the potential for drug interactions or prolonged respiratory depression while anesthetics are still active in the patient's system. The PACU nurse monitors the patient's physiologic status, manages pain, and provides psychological support in an effort to relieve the patient's fears and concerns. The nurse checks the medical record for special needs and concerns of the patient. When the patient's condition permits, a close member of the family may visit in the PACU. This often decreases the family's anxiety and makes the patient feel more secure.

Controlling Nausea and Vomiting

Postoperative and postdischarge nausea and vomiting (PONV/PDNV) is one of the most commonly occurring postoperative complications, frequently resulting in prolonged postoperative stay, unanticipated admission, and increased health care costs. Health care providers have yet to reach consensus regarding an evidence-based multidisciplinary, multimodel treatment approach to PONV/PDNV. The nurse should inter-

vene at the patient's first report of nausea to control the problem rather than wait for it to progress to vomiting.

Many medications are available to control nausea and vomiting without oversedating the patient; they are commonly administered during surgery, as well as in the PACU. Medications such as metoclopramide (Reglan), prochlorperazine (Compazine), promethazine (Phenergan), dimenhydrinate (Dramamine), hydroxyzine (Vistaril, Atarax), and scopolamine (Transderm-Scop) are commonly prescribed (Rothrock, 2011). Although it is costly, ondansetron (Zofran) is frequently used as an effective antiemetic with few side effects.

The AORN has developed a practice guideline for nurses to treat this postoperative complication (ASPAN, 2006). It includes the identification of risk factors and recommended treatments, which can range from no prophylaxis treatment to several antiemetic combinations for patients at higher risk (http://www.aspan.org/Portals/6/docs/ClinicalPractice/Guidelines/ASPAN_ClinicalGuideline_PONV_PDNV.pdf).

Preparing for Discharge from the PACU

A patient remains in the PACU until fully recovered from the anesthetic agent. Indicators of recovery include stable blood pressure, adequate respiratory function, adequate oxygen saturation level compared with baseline, and spontaneous movement or movement on command. Ordinarily, the following measures are used to determine the patient's readiness for discharge from the PACU (ASPAN, 2010):

- Stable vital signs
- Orientation to person, place, events, and time
- Uncompromised pulmonary function
- Pulse oximetry readings indicating adequate blood oxygen saturation
- Urine output at least 30 mL/hour
- Nausea and vomiting absent or under control
- Minimal pain

Many hospitals use a scoring system (e.g., Aldrete score) to determine the patient's general condition and readiness for transfer from the PACU. Throughout the recovery period, the patient's physical signs are observed and evaluated by means of a scoring system based on a set of objective criteria (Aldrete & Wright, 1992) that includes level of consciousness, activity, respiration, and blood pressure. The patient is assessed at regular intervals (e.g., every 15 minutes), and a total score is calculated and recorded on the assessment record. Patients remain in the PACU until their condition improves or they can be safely transferred to an ICU or surgical unit, or discharged (depending on their preoperative baseline score).

The patient is discharged from the phase I PACU by the anesthesiologist or anesthetist to the critical care unit, the medical-surgical unit, the phase II PACU, or home with a responsible family member. In some hospitals and ambulatory care centers, patients are discharged to a phase II PACU, where they are prepared for discharge.

Nursing Management of Direct Discharge Home

To ensure patient safety and recovery, expert patient teaching and discharge planning are necessary when a patient undergoes same-day or ambulatory surgery. Because anesthetics cloud memory for concurrent events, verbal and written instructions should be given to both the patient and the adult who will be accompanying the patient home. Alternative formats (e.g., large print, Braille) of instructions or use of a sign interpreter may be required to ensure patient and family understanding. A translator may be required if the patient and family members do not understand English.

The patient and caregiver (e.g., family member or friend) are informed about expected outcomes and immediate, anticipated postoperative changes. Written instructions about wound care, activity and dietary recommendations, medications, and follow-up visits to the same-day surgery unit or the surgeon are provided. The patient's caregiver at home is provided with verbal and written instructions about what to look for and about the actions to take if complications occur. Prescriptions are given to the patient. The nurse's or surgeon's telephone number is provided, and the patient and caregiver are encouraged to call with questions and to schedule follow-up appointments.

Although recovery time varies depending on the type and extent of surgery and the patient's overall condition, instructions usually advise limited activity for 24 to 48 hours. During this time, the patient should not drive a vehicle, drink alcoholic beverages, or perform tasks that require energy or skill. Fluids may be consumed as desired, and smaller-than-normal amounts may be eaten at mealtime. Patients are cautioned not to make important decisions at this time, because the medications, anesthesia, and surgery may affect their decision-making ability.

Nursing Management of the Hospitalized Postoperative Patient

Given the complexities of patient care treatment and management, multisystem disease, and workplace demands, it is important that the traditional "nurse-to-nurse patient" report now be a comprehensive, thorough, and sophisticated account of patient information focusing on patient safety (Amato-Vealey, Barba, & Vealey, 2008). Hand-off communication must also allow opportunity for questions to be answered. The *SBAR* is an increasingly popular approach to the standardization of relaying of this crucial information. SBAR is a mnemonic for: situation (What is happening at the present time?), background (What are the circumstances leading up to this situation?), assessment (What do I think the problem is?), and recommendation (What should we do to correct the problem?) (Institute for Healthcare Improvement [IHI], 2010). Whatever approach is used in each institution, it is essential that the method is used by all staff members during all hand-offs across all phases of surgical patient care.

Receiving the Patient in the Clinical Unit

The patient's room is readied by assembling the necessary equipment and supplies: IV pole, drainage receptacle holder, suction equipment, oxygen, emesis basin, tissues, disposable pads, blankets, and postoperative documentation forms. When the call comes to the unit about the patient's transfer from the PACU, the need for any additional items is communicated. The PACU nurse reports data about the patient to the receiving nurse. The report includes relevant demographic data, medical diagnosis, procedure performed, comorbid conditions, allergies, unexpected intraoperative events, estimated blood loss, types and amounts of fluids received, medications administered for pain, types of IV fluids or medications infused, whether the patient has voided, and information that the patient and family have received about the patient's condition. Usually, the surgeon speaks to the family after surgery and relates the general condition of the patient. The receiving nurse reviews the postoperative orders, admits the patient to the unit, performs an initial assessment, and attends to the patient's immediate needs.

Providing Care for the First 24 Hours After Surgery

During the first 24 hours after surgery, nursing care of the hospitalized patient on the general medical-surgical unit involves continuing to help the patient recover from the effects of anesthesia, frequently assessing the patient's physiologic status, monitoring for complications, managing pain, and implementing measures designed to achieve the long-range goals of independence with self-care, successful management of the therapeutic regimen, discharge to home, and full recovery. In the initial hours after admission to the clinical unit, adequate ventilation, hemodynamic stability, incisional pain, surgical site integrity, nausea and vomiting, neurologic status, and spontaneous voiding are primary concerns. The pulse rate, blood pressure, and respiration rate are recorded at least every 15 minutes for the first hour and every 30 minutes for the next 2 hours. Thereafter, they are measured less frequently if they remain stable. The temperature is monitored every 4 hours for the first 24 hours.

Patients usually begin to return to their usual state of health several hours after surgery or after waking up the next morning. Although pain may still be intense, many patients feel more alert, less nauseous, and less anxious. They have begun their breathing and leg exercises, and many will have dangled their legs over the edge of the bed, stood, and ambulated a few feet or been assisted out of bed to the chair at least once. Many will have tolerated a light meal and had IV fluids discontinued. The focus of care shifts from intense physiologic management and symptomatic relief of the adverse effects of anesthesia to regaining independence with self-care and preparing for discharge (all discussed in the following nursing process section).

NURSING PROCESS

The Hospitalized Patient Recovering From Surgery

Assessment

Assessment of the hospitalized postoperative patient includes monitoring vital signs and completing a review of the systems, and observing for potential postoperative complications on arrival of the patient to the clinical unit and at regular intervals thereafter.

Respiratory status is important, because pulmonary complications are among the most frequent and serious problems encountered by the surgical patient. The nurse observes for airway patency, watching for laryngeal edema, which is often heralded by inspiratory stridor. The quality of respirations, including depth, rate, and sound, are assessed regularly. Chest auscultation verifies that breath sounds are normal (or abnormal) bilaterally, and the findings are documented as a baseline for later comparisons. Often, because of the effects of analgesic and anesthetic medications, respirations are slow. Shallow and rapid respirations may be caused by pain, constricting dressings, gastric dilation, abdominal distention, or obesity. Noisy breathing may be due to obstruction by secretions or the tongue.

The nurse assesses the patient's pain level using a verbal or visual analogue scale and assesses the characteristics of the pain. The patient's appearance, pulse, respirations, blood pressure, skin color (adequate or cyanotic), and skin temperature (cold and clammy, warm and moist, or warm and dry) are clues to cardiovascular function. When the patient arrives in the clinical unit, the surgical site is observed for bleeding, type and integrity of dressings, and functioning of all tubes and drains.

The nurse also assesses the patient's mental status and level of consciousness, speech, and orientation, and compares them with the preoperative baseline. Although a change in mental status or postoperative restlessness may be related to anxiety, pain, or medications, it may also be a symptom of oxygen deficit, hypoglycemia, or hemorrhage. These serious causes must be investigated and excluded before other causes are pursued.

General discomfort resulting from lying in one position on the operating table, the surgeon's handling of tissues, the body's reaction to anesthesia, and anxiety are also common causes of restlessness. These discomforts may be relieved by administering the prescribed analgesics, changing the patient's position frequently, and assessing and alleviating the cause of anxiety. Drainage-soaked bandages may cause discomfort. The nurse reinforces or changes the dressing completely, as prescribed by the provider, which may make the patient more comfortable. The bladder is assessed for distention, because urinary retention can also cause restlessness.

Diagnosis

Major nursing diagnoses may include the following:

- Risk for ineffective airway clearance related to depressed respiratory function, pain, and bed rest
- Acute pain related to surgical incision
- Decreased cardiac output related to shock or hemorrhage
- Risk for activity intolerance related to generalized weakness secondary to surgery
- Impaired skin integrity related to surgical incision and drains
- Ineffective thermoregulation related to surgical environment and anesthetic agents
- Risk for imbalanced nutrition, less than body requirements related to decreased intake and increased need for nutrients secondary to surgery
- Risk for constipation related to effects of medications, surgery, dietary change, and immobility
- Impaired urinary elimination related to urinary retention
- Risk for injury related to surgical procedure/positioning or anesthetic agents
- Anxiety related to surgical procedure
- Risk for ineffective self-health management of therapeutic regimen related to wound care, dietary restrictions, activity recommendations, medications, follow-up care, or signs and symptoms of complications

Planning

The major goals for the patient include optimal respiratory function, relief of pain, optimal cardiovascular function, increased activity tolerance, unimpaired wound healing, maintenance of body temperature, and maintenance of nutritional balance. Further goals include resumption of usual pattern of bowel and bladder elimination, identification of any perioperative positioning injury, acquisition of sufficient knowledge to manage self-care after discharge, and absence of complications.

Nursing Interventions

Promoting Respiratory Function

Increasing age, smoking, COPD, long duration of surgery, and incisional site (chest and upper abdomen), as well as comorbidities, such as heart failure, arrhythmias, diabetes mellitus, and patients with swallowing disorders, are associated with an increased risk for postoperative pulmonary complications. Respiratory depressive effects of opioid medications, decreased lung expansion secondary to pain, operative position that may have limited maximum respiratory function, impaired mucociliary clearance of secretions, and decreased mobility combine to put the patient at risk for common respiratory complications, particularly atelectasis (alveolar collapse; incomplete expansion of the alveoli), pneumonia, and hypoxemia (Rothrock, 2011). Atelectasis remains a risk for the patient who is not moving well or ambulating, or who is not performing deep breathing or

coughing out retained secretions, or who is not using an incentive spirometer. Signs and symptoms include decreased breath sounds over the affected area, crackles, and cough. Pneumonia is characterized by chills and fever, tachycardia, and tachypnea. Cough may or may not be present and may or may not be productive. Risk factors for postoperative pneumonia are patients with COPD, impaired cough, and acute bronchitis or lower airway infections.

The types of hypoxemia that can affect postoperative patients are subacute and episodic. Subacute hypoxemia is a constant low level of oxygen saturation, although breathing appears normal. Episodic hypoxemia develops suddenly, and the patient may be at risk for cerebral dysfunction, myocardial ischemia, and cardiac arrest. Risk for hypoxemia is present in patients who have undergone major surgery (particularly thoracic or abdominal), are obese, or have pre-existing pulmonary problems. Hypoxemia can be detected by pulse oximetry, which measures blood oxygen saturation. Factors that may affect the accuracy of pulse oximetry readings include cold extremities, tremors, atrial fibrillation, and acrylic nails. Current research reveals that nail polish does not demonstrate altered pulse oximetry readings in mechanically ventilated patients to a clinically relevant extent, nor in healthy hypoxic subjects (Hinkelbein & Genzwuerker, 2008; Yamamoto, Yamamoto, Yamamoto et al., 2008).

Preventive measures and timely recognition of signs and symptoms help avert pulmonary complications. Strategies to prevent respiratory complications include use of an incentive spirometer and deep-breathing exercises, and sitting in an upright position that is unrestricted, thus allowing for maximum pulmonary expansion. Mobilization of patients is an important nursing intervention that will assist in maximizing lung expansion and improving circulation, thus facilitating gas exchange while additionally decreasing the risk of DVT (Perme & Chandrashekar, 2009). Crackles indicate static pulmonary secretions that need to be mobilized by coughing retained secretions and deep-breathing exercises. When a mucus plug obstructs one of the bronchi entirely, the pulmonary tissue beyond the plug collapses, and massive atelectasis results. Thus, coughing is also encouraged to dislodge mucus plugs. It is important to consider that coughing is a forced expiratory maneuver, thus the nurse should encourage the patient to use the incentive spirometer or take deep breaths after coughing to re-expand alveoli. A common recommendation for use of the incentive spirometer is 10 deep breaths every hour while awake.

To clear secretions and prevent pneumonia, the nurse encourages the patient to turn frequently (every 2 hours) and take deep breaths hourly. These pulmonary exercises should begin as soon as the patient arrives on the clinical unit and continue until the patient is discharged. Even if he or she is not fully awake from anesthesia, the patient can be asked to take several deep breaths. This helps expel residual anesthetic agents, mobilize secretions, and prevent alveolar collapse (atelectasis). Careful splinting of abdominal or thoracic incision sites helps the patient overcome the fear that the exertion of coughing might open the incision. Analgesic agents are administered to permit more effective coughing, and oxygen is administered as prescribed to prevent or relieve hypoxia. To encourage lung expansion, the patient is encouraged to yawn or take sustained maximal inspirations to create a negative intrathoracic pressure and expand lung volume to total capacity.

⚠ NURSING ALERT

Coughing is contraindicated in patients who have head injuries or who have undergone intracranial surgery (because of the risk for increasing intracranial pressure), as well as in patients who have undergone eye surgery (because of the risk for increasing intraocular pressure) or plastic surgery (because of the risk for increasing tension on delicate tissues).

Relieving Pain

Most patients experience some pain after a surgical procedure. Many factors (motivational, affective, cognitive, and emotional) influence the pain experience. The degree and severity of postoperative pain and the patient's tolerance for pain depend on the incision site, the nature of the surgical procedure, the extent of surgical trauma, the type of anesthetic agent, and how the agent was administered. The Agency for Healthcare Research and Policy reports that the most reliable indicator of the existence and intensity of pain is the patient's self-report. It is therefore important to complete a thorough preoperative pain evaluation and develop pain goals for the surgical patient. This preparation, which includes information such as what to expect, how the pain will be managed, how to report, and reassurance, can contribute to reducing anxiety and possibly the level of postoperative pain experienced. Refer to Chapter 7 for details on patient-controlled analgesia (PCA) and epidural infusions.

INTRAPLEURAL ANESTHESIA. Intrapleural anesthesia involves the administration of local anesthetic by a catheter between the parietal and visceral pleura. It provides sensory anesthesia without affecting motor function to the intercostal muscles. This anesthesia allows more effective coughing and deep breathing in conditions such as cholecystectomy, renal surgery, and rib fractures, in which pain in the thoracic region would interfere with these exercises. Intrapleural anesthesia has fewer adverse effects than do systemic opioids and is associated with a lowered incidence of nausea, vomiting, and pruritus when compared with opioid analgesia (Richman, Liu, Courpas et al., 2006). However, results from multiple studies in selected trauma patients reveal improved pain relief and reduction in pulmonary complications with thoracic epidural infusion compared to systemic opioids or intrapleural catheters (Fishman, Ballantyne, & Rathmell, 2010).

(continued on page 136)

OTHER PAIN RELIEF MEASURES. For pain that is difficult to control, a subcutaneous pain management system may be used. This is a silicone catheter that is inserted at the site of the affected area. The catheter is attached to a pump that delivers a continuous amount of local anesthetic at a specific amount determined and prescribed by the provider.

Complete absence of pain in the area of the surgical incision may not occur for a few weeks, depending on the site and nature of the surgery, but the intensity of postoperative pain gradually subsides on subsequent days. However, pain control continues to be an important concern for the patient and the nurse. Effective pain management allows the patient to participate in care, perform deep-breathing and leg exercises, and tolerate activity. Poor pain control contributes to postoperative complications and increased length of stay. The nurse continues to assess the pain level, the effectiveness of analgesic agents, and factors that influence pain tolerance (e.g., energy level, stress level, cultural background, meaning of pain to the patient). The nurse explains that taking an analgesic agent before the pain becomes intense is more effective, and offers medication to the patient at intervals rather than waiting for the patient to request it.

Nonpharmacologic pain relief measures, such as imagery, music, relaxation, massage, application of heat or cold (if prescribed), and distraction, are discussed in Chapter 7.

Promoting Cardiac Output

If signs and symptoms of shock or hemorrhage occur, treatment and nursing care are implemented as described in the discussion of care in the PACU.

Although most patients do not hemorrhage or go into shock, changes in circulating volume, the stress of surgery, and the effects of medications and preoperative preparations all affect cardiovascular function. IV fluid replacement is standard for up to 24 hours after surgery or until the patient is stable and tolerating oral fluids. Close monitoring is indicated to detect and correct conditions such as fluid volume deficit, altered tissue perfusion, and decreased cardiac output, all of which can increase the patient's discomfort, place him or her at risk of complications, and prolong the hospital stay. Some patients are at risk of fluid volume excess secondary to existing cardiovascular or renal disease, advanced age, or the release of adrenocorticotropic hormone and antidiuretic hormone as a result of the stress of surgery (O'Brien & Dickinson, 2009). Consequently, fluid replacement must be carefully managed, and intake and output records must be accurate.

Nursing management includes assessing the patency of the IV lines and ensuring that the correct fluids are administered at the prescribed rate. Intake and output, including emesis and output from wound drainage systems, are recorded separately and totaled to determine fluid balance. If the patient has an indwelling urinary catheter, hourly outputs are monitored, and rates of less than 30 mL/hour

are reported; if the patient is voiding, an output of less than 240 mL per 8-hour shift is reported. Electrolyte levels and hemoglobin and hematocrit levels are monitored. Decreased hemoglobin and hematocrit levels can indicate blood loss or dilution of circulating volume by IV fluids. Recall that the fluid changes associated with surgery cause fluid extravasation into the tissues. This "third spaced" fluid usually returns to the intravascular space by postop day (POD) 2 or 3. At this time period, the nurse assesses for evidence of fluid volume excess. If hemodilution is contributing to the decreased hemoglobin and hematocrit levels, the nurse expects that, as the stress response abates and fluids are mobilized and excreted, the hemoglobin and hematocrit will rise.

Venous stasis from dehydration, immobility, and pressure on leg veins during surgery put the patient at risk for DVT. Leg exercises and frequent position changes are initiated early in the postoperative period to stimulate circulation. Patients should avoid positions that compromise venous return, such as raising the bed's knee gatch, placing a pillow under the knees, sitting for long periods, and dangling the legs with pressure at the back of the knees. Venous return is promoted by elastic compression stockings, sequential compression devices (SCDs), and early ambulation. Early ambulation has a significant effect on recovery and the prevention of complications and can begin, in many instances, on the evening of surgery. Postoperative activity orders are checked before the patient is assisted in getting out of bed. Sitting up at the edge of the bed for a few minutes may be all that the patient who has undergone a major surgical procedure can tolerate at first.

Encouraging Activity

Most surgical patients are encouraged to be out of bed as soon as possible. Early ambulation reduces the incidence of postoperative complications, such as atelectasis, hypostatic pneumonia, GI discomfort, and circulatory problems. Ambulation improves ventilation and reduces the stasis of bronchial secretions in the lungs. It also reduces postoperative abdominal distention by increasing GI tract and abdominal wall tone and stimulating peristalsis. Early ambulation prevents stasis of blood by increasing the rate of circulation in the extremities; as a result, thrombophlebitis or phlebothrombosis occurs less frequently. Pain is often decreased when early ambulation is possible, and the hospital stay is shorter and less costly, a further advantage to the patient and the hospital.

Despite the advantages of early ambulation, patients may be reluctant to get out of bed on the evening of surgery. Reminding them of the importance of early mobility in preventing complications may help patients overcome their fears. When a patient gets out of bed for the first time, orthostatic hypotension, also called postural hypotension, is a concern. Orthostatic hypotension is an abnormal drop in blood pressure that occurs as the patient changes from a supine to a standing position. It is common after

surgery because of changes in circulating blood volume and bed rest. Signs and symptoms include an increase in heart rate with either a 15 mm Hg decrease in systolic pressure or a 10 mm Hg decrease in diastolic pressure with position change. Patients often also complain of weakness, dizziness, leg buckling, visual blurring. Older adults are at increased risk for orthostatic hypotension secondary to age-related changes in vascular tone. Refer to Chapter 12 for details on assessing for orthostatic hypotension.

To assist the postoperative patient in getting out of bed for the first time after surgery, the nurse:

- Helps the patient move gradually from the lying position to the sitting position by raising the head of the bed, and encourages the patient to splint the incision when applicable. It may be easier for postoperative patients with abdominal incisions to roll on their side first with the head of the bed elevated. Once on his side, the nurse has the patient move his feet off the side of the bed and push off his elbow into a sitting position.
- Positions the patient completely upright (sitting) and turned, so that both legs are hanging over the edge of the bed. The nurse allows the patient to sit for a few minutes and assesses for dizziness and vital sign changes if indicated. If patient is asymptomatic, the nurse asks the patient to push down with his arms on the mattress and stand up.
- Helps the patient stand beside the bed

After becoming accustomed to the upright position, the patient may start to walk. The nurse should be at the patient's side to give physical support and encouragement. Care must be taken not to tire the patient; the extent of the first few periods of ambulation varies with the type of surgical procedure and the patient's physical condition and age.

Whether or not the patient can ambulate early in the postoperative period, bed exercises are encouraged to improve circulation. Unless contraindicated by the operative event, bed exercises consist of the following:

- Arm exercises (full range of motion, with specific attention to abduction and external rotation of the shoulder)
- Hand and finger exercises
- Foot exercises to prevent DVT, foot drop, and toe deformities, and to aid in maintaining good circulation
- Leg flexion and leg-lifting exercises to prepare the patient for ambulation
- Abdominal and gluteal contraction exercises

Hampered by pain, dressings, IV lines, or drains, many patients cannot engage in activity without assistance. Prolonged inactivity may lead to pressure ulcers, DVT, atelectasis, constipation, anorexia, and malaise. Helping the patient increase his or her activity level on the first postoperative day is an important nursing function. One way to increase the patient's activity is to have the patient perform as much routine hygiene care as possible. Setting up the patient to bathe with a bedside wash basin or, if possible, assisting the

patient to the bathroom to sit in a chair at the sink not only gets the patient moving but helps restore a sense of self-control and prepares the patient for discharge.

To be safely discharged to home, patients need to be able to ambulate a functional distance (e.g., length of the house or apartment), get in and out of bed unassisted, and be independent with toileting. Patients can be asked to perform as much as they can and then to call for assistance. The patient and the nurse can collaborate on a schedule for progressive activity that includes ambulating in the room and hallway and sitting out of bed in the chair. Assessing the patient's vital signs and oxygen saturation before, during, and after a scheduled activity helps the nurse and patient determine the rate of progression. By providing physical support, the nurse maintains the patient's safety; by communicating a positive attitude about the patient's ability to perform the activity, the nurse promotes the patient's confidence. The nurse should make sure the patient continues to perform bed exercises, wears pneumatic compression or thigh-high elastic compression stockings when in bed, and rests as needed. If the patient has had orthopedic surgery of the lower extremities or will require a mobility aid (i.e., walker, crutches) at home, a physical therapist may be involved the first time the patient gets out of bed to teach him or her to ambulate safely or to use the mobility aid correctly. If patients are required to climb steps at home, their ability to do so must be assessed before discharge.

Promoting Wound Healing

Ongoing assessment of the surgical site involves inspection for approximation of wound edges, integrity of sutures or staples, redness, discoloration, warmth, swelling, unusual tenderness, or drainage. The area around the wound should also be inspected for a reaction to tape or trauma from tight bandages.

PRINCIPLES OF WOUND HEALING. With shorter hospital stays, much of the healing takes place at home, and both the hospital and home care nurse should be informed about the principles of wound healing. Surgical wound healing occurs in three phases: inflammatory, proliferative, and maturation (Table 5-8). Wounds also heal by different mechanisms, depending on the condition of the wound. These mechanisms are first-, second-, and third-intention wound healing (Fig. 5-7) (Rothrock, 2011).

FIRST-INTENTION HEALING. Wounds made aseptically with a minimum of tissue destruction that are properly closed heal with little tissue reaction by first intention (primary union). When wounds heal by **first-intention healing**, granulation tissue is not visible and scar formation is minimal. Postoperatively, many of these wounds are covered with a dry sterile dressing. If a cyanoacrylate tissue adhesive (LiquiBand) was used to close the incision without sutures, a dressing is contraindicated.

SECOND-INTENTION HEALING. **Second-intention healing** (granulation) occurs in infected wounds (abscess) or in wounds in

(continued on page 138)

TABLE
5-8 Phases of Wound Healing

Phase	Duration	Events
Inflammatory (also called lag or exudative phase)	1–4 days	Blood clot forms Wound becomes edematous Debris of damaged tissue and blood clot are phagocytosed
Proliferative (also called fibroblastic or connective tissue phase)	5–20 days	Collagen produced Granulation tissue forms Wound tensile strength increases
Maturation (also called differentiation, resorptive, remodeling, or plateau phase)	21 days to months or even years	Fibroblasts leave wound Tensile strength increases Collagen fibers reorganize and tighten to reduce scar size

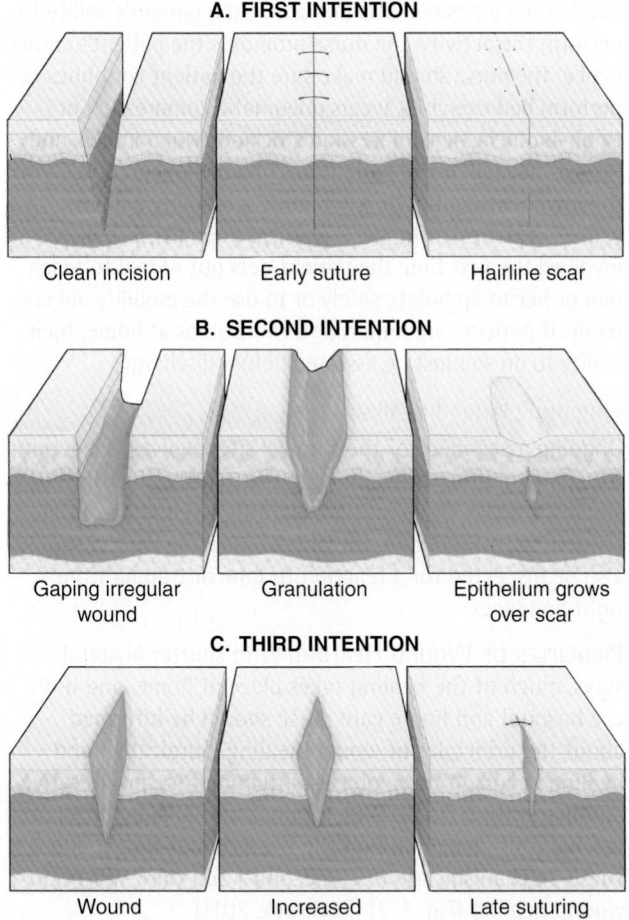

A. FIRST INTENTION

Clean incision   Early suture   Hairline scar

B. SECOND INTENTION

Gaping irregular wound   Granulation   Epithelium grows over scar

C. THIRD INTENTION

Wound   Increased granulation   Late suturing with wide scar

FIGURE 5-7 Types of wound healing: first-intention healing, second-intention healing, and third-intention healing.

which the edges have not been approximated. When an abscess is incised, it collapses partly, but the dead and dying cells forming its walls are still being released into the cavity. For this reason, drainage tubes or gauze packing is inserted into the abscess pocket to allow drainage to escape easily. Gradually, the necrotic material disintegrates and escapes, and the abscess cavity fills with a red, soft, sensitive tissue

that bleeds easily. This tissue is composed of minute, thin-walled capillaries and buds that later form connective tissue. These buds, called *granulations*, enlarge until they fill the area left by the destroyed tissue. Healing is complete when skin cells (epithelium) grow over these granulations. This method of repair is called *healing by granulation*, and it takes place whenever pus is formed or when loss of tissue has occurred for any reason. When the postoperative wound is to be allowed to heal by secondary intention, it is usually packed with saline-moistened sterile dressings and covered with a dry sterile dressing.

THIRD-INTENTION HEALING. **Third-intention healing** (secondary suture) is used for deep wounds that either have not been sutured early or break down and are resutured later, thus bringing together two apposing granulation surfaces. This results in a deeper and wider scar. These wounds are also packed postoperatively with moist gauze and covered with a dry sterile dressing.

As a wound heals, many factors, such as adequate nutrition, cleanliness, rest, and position, determine how quickly healing occurs. Specific nursing assessments and interventions that address these factors and help promote wound healing are presented in Table 5-9. Management of surgical drains and dressings is discussed in more detail below.

MANAGING DRAINS. Wound drains are tubes that exit the peri-incisional area, either into a portable wound suction device (closed) or into the dressings (open). The principle involved is to allow the escape of blood and serous fluids that could otherwise serve as a culture medium for bacteria. In portable wound suction, the use of gentle, constant suction enhances drainage of these fluids and collapses the skin flaps against the underlying tissue, thus removing "dead space." Types of wound drains include the Penrose, Hemovac, and Jackson-Pratt drains (Fig. 5-8). Output from wound drainage systems and all new drainage is recorded. The amount of bloody drainage on the surgical dressing is assessed frequently. Spots of drainage on the dressings are outlined with a pen, and the date and time of the outline

(continued on page 140)

TABLE
5-9 Factors Affecting Wound Healing

Factors	Rationale	Nursing Interventions
Age of patient	The older the patient, the less resilient the tissues.	Handle all tissues gently.
Handling of tissues	Rough handling causes injury and delayed healing.	Handle tissues carefully and evenly.
Hemorrhage	Accumulation of blood creates dead spaces as well as dead cells that must be removed. The area becomes a growth medium for organisms.	Monitor vital signs. Observe incision site for evidence of bleeding and infection.
Hypovolemia	Insufficient blood volume leads to vasoconstriction and reduced oxygen and nutrients available for wound healing.	Monitor for volume deficit (circulatory impairment). Correct by fluid replacement as prescribed.
Patient overactivity	Prevents approximation of wound edges. Resting favors healing.	Use measures to keep wound edges approximated: taping, bandaging, splints. Encourage rest.
Immunosuppressed state	Patient is more vulnerable to bacterial and viral invasion; defense mechanisms are impaired.	Provide maximum protection to prevent infection. Restrict visitors with colds; institute mandatory hand hygiene by all staff.
Local factors		
Edema	Reduces blood supply by exerting increased interstitial pressure on vessels	Elevate part; apply cool compresses.
Inadequate dressing technique		Follow guidelines for proper dressing technique.
Too small	Permits bacterial invasion and contamination	
Too tight	Reduces blood supply carrying nutrients and oxygen	
Nutritional deficits	Protein–calorie depletion may occur. Insulin secretion may be inhibited, causing blood glucose to rise.	Correct deficits; this may require parenteral nutritional therapy. Monitor blood glucose levels. Administer vitamin supplements as prescribed.
Foreign bodies	Foreign bodies retard healing.	Keep wounds free of dressing threads and talcum powder from gloves.
Oxygen deficit (tissue oxygenation insufficient)	Insufficient oxygen may be due to inadequate lung and cardiovascular function as well as localized vasoconstriction.	Encourage deep breathing, turning, controlled coughing, and supplemental oxygen as prescribed.
Drainage accumulation	Accumulated secretions hamper healing process.	Monitor closed drainage systems for proper functioning. Institute measures to remove accumulated secretions.
Medications		
Corticosteroids	May mask presence of infection by impairing normal inflammatory response	Be aware of action and effect of medications patient is receiving.
Anticoagulants	May cause hemorrhage	
Broad-spectrum and specific antibiotics	Effective if administered immediately before surgery for specific pathology or bacterial contamination. If administered after wound is closed, ineffective because of intravascular coagulation.	
Systemic disorders		
Hemorrhagic shock Acidosis Hypoxia Renal failure Hepatic disease Sepsis	These depress cell functions that directly affect wound healing.	Be familiar with the nature of the specific disorder. Administer prescribed treatment. Cultures may be indicated to determine appropriate antibiotic.
Wound stressors		
Vomiting Valsalva maneuver Heavy coughing Straining	Produce tension on wounds, particularly of the torso.	Encourage frequent turning and ambulation and administer antiemetic medications as prescribed. Assist patient in splinting incision.

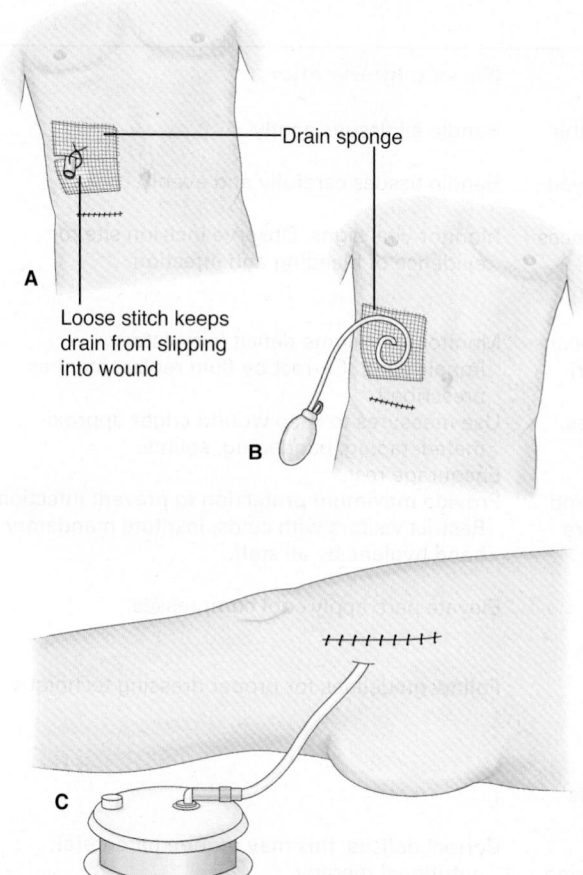

FIGURE 5-8 Types of surgical drains: (**A**) Penrose, (**B**) Jackson-Pratt, (**C**) Hemovac.

are recorded on the dressing, so that increased drainage can be easily seen. A certain amount of bloody drainage in a wound drainage system or on the dressing is expected, but excessive amounts should be reported to the surgeon. Increasing amounts of fresh blood on the dressing should be reported immediately. Some wounds are irrigated heavily before closure in the OR, and open drains exiting the wound may be embedded in the dressings. These wounds may drain large amounts of blood-tinged fluid that saturate the dressing. The dressing can be reinforced with sterile gauze bandages; the time at which they were reinforced should be documented. If drainage continues, the surgeon should be notified, so that the dressing can be changed. Multiple similar drains are numbered or otherwise labeled (e.g., left lower quadrant, left upper quadrant), so that output measurements can be reliably and consistently recorded.

CHANGING THE DRESSING. Although the first postoperative dressing is usually changed by a member of the surgical team, subsequent dressing changes in the immediate postoperative period are usually performed by the nurse. A dressing is applied to a wound for one or more of the following reasons: (1) to provide a proper environment for

wound healing; (2) to absorb drainage; (3) to splint or immobilize the wound; (4) to protect the wound and new epithelial tissue from mechanical injury; (5) to protect the wound from bacterial contamination and from soiling by feces, vomitus, and urine; (6) to promote hemostasis, as in a pressure dressing; and (7) to provide mental and physical comfort for the patient.

The patient is told that the dressing is to be changed and that changing the dressing is a simple procedure associated with little discomfort. The dressing change is performed at a suitable time (e.g., not at mealtimes or when visitors are present). Privacy is provided, and the patient is not unduly exposed. The nurse should avoid referring to the incision as a scar, because the term may have negative connotations for the patient. Assurance is given that the incision will shrink as it heals and that the redness will fade.

The nurse carries out hand hygiene before and after the dressing change and wears disposable gloves for the dressing change itself. The tape or adhesive portion of the dressing is removed by pulling it parallel with the skin surface and in the direction of hair growth, rather than at right angles. Nonirritating solvents aid in removing adhesive painlessly and quickly. The old dressing is removed and then deposited in a container designated for disposal of biomedical waste. In accordance with standard precautions, dressings are never touched by ungloved hands because of the danger of transmitting pathogenic organisms.

Currently, there is a lack of lack of evidence regarding the influence of sterile or aseptic versus clean gloves in clinical care, therefore the nurse will perform dressing changes depending upon institutional policy (Charrier, Serafini, Chiono et al., 2010; Flores, 2008).

If the patient is sensitive to adhesive tape, the dressing may be held in place with hypoallergenic tape. Many tapes are porous to permit ventilation and prevent skin maceration. The correct way to apply tape is to place the tape at the center of the dressing and then press the tape down on both sides, applying tension evenly, away from the midline. The incorrect way to apply tape—to fix one end of the tape to the skin and to pull it tight over the dressing—often wrinkles and pulls the skin in the process. The resulting continuous and forceful traction produces a shearing effect, causing the epidermal layer to slip sideways and become separated from the deeper dermal layers. Some wounds become edematous after having been dressed, causing considerable tension on the tape. If the tape is not flexible, the stretching bandage will also cause a shear injury to the skin. This can result in denuded areas or large blisters and should be avoided. An elastic adhesive bandage (Elastoplast, Microfoam-3M) may be used to hold dressings in place over mobile areas, such as the neck or the extremities, or where pressure is required.

While changing the dressing, the nurse has an opportunity to teach the patient how to care for the incision and change the dressings at home. The nurse observes for indicators of the patient's readiness to learn, such as looking at

the incision, expressing interest, or assisting in the dressing change.

Maintaining Normal Body Temperature

The patient is still at risk for MH and hypothermia in the postoperative period. Efforts are made to identify MH and to treat it early and promptly.

Patients who have been anesthetized are susceptible to chills and drafts. Attention to hypothermia management, begun in the intraoperative period, extends into the postoperative period to prevent significant nitrogen loss and catabolism. Signs of hypothermia are reported to physician member of the surgical team. The room is maintained at a comfortable temperature, and blankets are provided to prevent chilling. Treatment includes oxygen administration, adequate hydration, and proper nutrition. The patient is also monitored for cardiac arrhythmias. The risk of hypothermia is greater in the elderly and in patients who were in the cool OR environment for a prolonged period.

Managing GI Function and Resuming Nutrition

GI discomfort (nausea, vomiting, hiccups) and resumption of oral intake are issues for both the patient and the nurse. Nausea and vomiting are common after anesthesia (Rothrock, 2011). They are more common in women, in obese people (fat cells act as reservoirs for the anesthetic), in patients prone to motion sickness, and in patients who have undergone lengthy surgical procedures. Other causes of postoperative vomiting include an accumulation of fluid in the stomach, inflation of the stomach, and the ingestion of food and fluid before peristalsis resumes.

If vomiting is likely because of the nature of surgery, a nasogastric tube is inserted preoperatively and remains in place throughout the surgery and the immediate postoperative period. A nasogastric tube also may be inserted before surgery if postoperative distention is anticipated. In addition, a nasogastric tube may be inserted if a patient who has food in the stomach requires emergency surgery.

Hiccups, produced by intermittent spasms of the diaphragm secondary to irritation of the phrenic nerve, can occur after surgery. The irritation may be direct, such as from stimulation of the nerve by a distended stomach, subdiaphragmatic abscess, or abdominal distention; indirect, such as from toxemia or uremia that stimulates the nerve; or reflexive, such as irritation from a drainage tube or obstruction of the intestines. Usually, these occurrences are mild, transitory attacks that cease spontaneously. If hiccups persist, they may produce considerable distress and serious effects such as vomiting, exhaustion, and wound dehiscence. The provider may prescribe phenothiazine medications (e.g., Thorazine) for intractable hiccups (Moretti & Torre, 2010).

Once nausea and vomiting have subsided and the patient is fully awake and alert, and the nurse documents resumption of bowel sounds; the sooner the patient can tolerate a usual diet, the more quickly normal GI function will resume.

Taking food by mouth stimulates digestive juices and promotes gastric function and intestinal peristalsis. The return to normal dietary intake should proceed at a pace set by the patient. Of course, the nature of the surgery and the type of anesthesia directly affect the rate at which normal gastric activity resumes. Liquids are typically the first substances desired and tolerated by the patient after surgery. Water, juice, and tea may be given in increasing amounts. Cool fluids are tolerated more easily than are those that are ice cold or hot. Soft foods (gelatin, custard, milk, and creamed soups) are added gradually after clear fluids have been tolerated. As soon as the patient tolerates soft foods well, solid food may be given.

Assessment and management of GI function are important after surgery because the GI tract is subject to uncomfortable or potentially life-threatening complications. Any postoperative patient may suffer from abdominal distention, resulting from the accumulation of gas in the intestinal tract. Manipulation of the abdominal organs during surgery may produce a loss of normal peristalsis for 24 to 48 hours, depending on the type and extent of surgery. Even though nothing is given by mouth, swallowed air and GI secretions enter the stomach and intestines; if not propelled by peristalsis, they collect in the intestines, producing distention and causing the patient to complain of fullness or pain in the abdomen. Most often, the gas collects in the colon. Abdominal distention is further increased by immobility, anesthetic agents, and the use of opioid medications.

After major abdominal surgery, distention may be avoided by having the patient turn frequently, exercise, and ambulate as early as possible. This also alleviates distention produced by swallowing air, which is common in anxious patients. A nasogastric tube inserted before surgery may remain in place until full peristaltic activity (indicated by the passage of flatus) has resumed. The nurse can determine when peristaltic bowel sounds return by listening to the abdomen with a stethoscope. Bowel sounds are documented, so that diet progression can occur.

Paralytic ileus and intestinal obstruction are potential postoperative complications that occur more frequently in patients undergoing intestinal or abdominal surgery.

Promoting Bowel Function

Constipation is common after surgery and can range from a minor to a serious complication. Decreased mobility, decreased oral intake, and opioid analgesics contribute to difficulty having a bowel movement. In addition, irritation and trauma to the bowel during surgery may inhibit intestinal movement for several days. The combined effect of early ambulation, improved dietary intake, and a stool softener (if prescribed) promotes bowel elimination. Until the patient reports return of normal bowel function, the nurse should assess the abdomen for distention and the presence and frequency of bowel sounds. If the abdomen is not distended and bowel sounds are normal, and if the patient

(continued on page 142)

does not have a bowel movement by the second or third postoperative day, the provider should be notified so that a laxative can be given that evening.

Managing Voiding

Urinary retention after surgery can occur for various reasons. Anesthetics, anticholinergic agents, and opioids interfere with the perception of bladder fullness and the urge to void and inhibit the ability to initiate voiding and completely empty the bladder. Abdominal, pelvic, and hip surgery may increase the likelihood of retention secondary to pain. In addition, some patients find it difficult to use the bedpan or urinal in the recumbent position.

Bladder distention and the urge to void should be assessed at the time of the patient's arrival on the unit and frequently thereafter. The patient is expected to void within 8 hours after surgery (this includes time spent in the PACU). If the patient has an urge to void and cannot, or if the bladder is distended and no urge is felt or the patient cannot void, a portable ultrasound device (bladder scan) should be performed to assess degree of distention and possible need for urinary catheterization. All methods to encourage the patient to void should be tried (e.g., letting water run, applying heat to the perineum). The bedpan should be warm; a cold bedpan causes discomfort and automatic tightening of muscles (including the urethral sphincter). If the patient cannot void on a bedpan, it may be possible to use a commode rather than resorting to catheterization. Male patients are often permitted to sit up or stand beside the bed to use the urinal, but safeguards should be taken to prevent the patient from falling or fainting due to loss of coordination from medications or orthostatic hypotension. If the patient cannot void in the specified time frame, and bladder scan verifies distention, the patient is catheterized and the catheter is removed after the bladder has emptied. Straight intermittent catheterization is preferred over indwelling catheterization, because the risk of infection is increased with an indwelling catheter.

Even if the patient voids, the bladder may not necessarily be empty. The nurse notes the amount of urine voided and uses the bladder scan to assess residual volume. If more than 100 mL of residual urine is seen on the bladder scanner, it is considered diagnostic of urinary retention. If a bladder scan is not available in your institution, the nurse can palpate the suprapubic area for distention or tenderness after the patient urinates to assess for residual urine. Intermittent catheterization may be prescribed every 4 to 6 hours until the patient can void spontaneously and the postvoid residual is less than 100 mL.

Maintaining a Safe Environment

During the immediate postoperative period, the patient recovering from anesthesia should have three side rails up, and the bed should be in the low position. The nurse assesses the patient's level of consciousness and orientation and determines whether the patient needs his or her eyeglasses or hearing aid, because impaired vision, inability to hear postoperative instructions, or inability to communicate verbally places the patient at risk for injury. All objects the patient may need should be within reach, especially the call light. Any immediate postoperative orders concerning special positioning, equipment, or interventions should be implemented as soon as possible. The patient is instructed to ask for assistance with any activity. Although restraints are occasionally necessary for the disoriented patient, they should be avoided if at all possible. Agency policy on the use of restraints must be consulted and followed.

Providing Emotional Support to the Patient and Family

Although patients and families are undoubtedly relieved that surgery is over, anxiety levels may remain high in the immediate postoperative period. Many factors contribute to this anxiety: pain, being in an unfamiliar environment, inability to control one's circumstances or care for oneself, fear of the long-term effects of surgery, fear of complications, fatigue, spiritual distress, altered role responsibilities, ineffective coping, and altered body image are all potential reactions to the surgical experience. The nurse helps the patient and family work through their anxieties by providing reassurance and information and by spending time listening to and addressing their concerns. The nurse describes hospital routines and what to expect in the ensuing hours and days until discharge, and explains the purpose of nursing assessments and interventions. Informing patients when they will be able to drink fluids or eat, when they will be getting out of bed, and when tubes and drains will be removed helps them gain a sense of control and participation in recovery, and engages them in the plan of care. Acknowledging family members' concerns and accepting and encouraging their participation in the patient's care assists them in feeling that they are helping their loved one. The nurse can modify the environment to enhance rest and relaxation by providing privacy, reducing noise, adjusting lighting, providing enough seating for family members, and encouraging a supportive atmosphere.

Managing Potential Complications

The RN must be alert for the development of additional postoperative complications that include:

CARDIAC COMPLICATIONS. A postoperative cardiac complication is a myocardial ischemia/infarction (MI). The mortality rate for surgical patients who experience a MI after noncardiac surgery is 15% to 25%. (Kuo & Klingensmith, 2008). The nurse is aware that in the postoperative patient, clinical presentation is often subtle. Perioperative MIs are frequently silent or may present with dyspnea, hypotension, or atypical pain. If suspected, the nurse alerts the surgical team, obtains vital signs, oxygen saturation, and performs a cardiac, peripheral vascular, and pulmonary assessment and electrocardiogram.

As a result of excessive IV fluid administration intraoperatively, the nurse is alert for the development of congestive

heart failure (CHF), which can present in the immediate postoperative period, or on POD 2 to 3 when fluid shifting causes increased intravascular volume. Daily weights are an important parameter for judging fluid balance. In addition, the nurse observes for jugular vein distention, rales, dyspnea, wheezing, cough, and fatigue. Refer to Chapters 14 and 15 for details of care of the MI and CHF patient.

DEEP VEIN THROMBOSIS AND PULMONARY EMBOLISM. DVT and other complications, such as pulmonary embolism (PE), are serious potential complications of surgery (Box 5-8). The stress response that is initiated by surgery inhibits the fibrinolytic system, resulting in blood hypercoagulability. Dehydration, low cardiac output, blood pooling in the extremities, and bed rest add to the risk of thrombosis formation. Although all postoperative patients are at some risk, factors such as a history of thrombosis, malignancy, trauma, obesity, indwelling venous catheters, and hormone (e.g., estrogen) use increase the risk. The first symptom of DVT may be a pain or cramp in the calf. Initial pain and tenderness may be followed by a painful swelling of the entire leg, often accompanied by a fever, chills, and diaphoresis.

Prophylactic treatment for postoperative patients at risk is common practice, until the patient is ambulatory. External pneumatic compression and thigh-high elastic compression stockings can be used alone or in combination with low-dose heparin. The benefits of early ambulation and hourly leg exercises in preventing DVT cannot be overemphasized, and these activities are recommended for all patients, regardless of their risk. It is important to avoid the use of blanket rolls, pillow rolls, or any form of elevation that can constrict vessels under the knees. Even prolonged "dangling" (having the patient sit on the edge of the bed with legs hanging over the side) can be dangerous and is not recommended in susceptible patients because pressure under the knees can impede circulation. Adequate hydration is also encouraged; the patient can be offered juices and water throughout the day to avoid dehydration.

PE from DVT is a postoperative risk for patients owing to immobility, venous stasis, venous trauma, and hypercoagulability. Clinically, symptoms of a PE includes sudden onset of shortness of breath, tachypnea, tachycardia, low-grade temperature, chest pain (pleuritic in nature), and apprehension. Patients who have had major orthopedic surgery of a lower extremity, including hip or knee arthroplasty and hip fracture surgeries, as well as major trauma patients, are at high risk for PE. Some form of prophylactic therapy is expected in high-risk patients to reduce the risk of DVT and PE. Refer to Chapter 10 for more details on PE.

HEMATOMA. At times, concealed bleeding occurs beneath the skin at the surgical site. This hemorrhage usually stops spontaneously but results in clot (hematoma) formation within the wound. If the clot is small, it will be absorbed and need not be treated. If the clot is large, the wound usually bulges somewhat, and healing will be delayed unless the clot is removed. After several sutures are removed by a member of the surgical team, the clot is evacuated and the wound is packed lightly with gauze. Healing occurs usually by granulation, or a secondary closure may be performed.

INFECTION (WOUND SEPSIS). The creation of a surgical wound disrupts the integrity of the skin and its protective function. Exposure of deep body tissues to pathogens in the environment places the patient at risk for infection of the surgical site, a potentially life-threatening complication. Surgical site infection increases hospital length of stay, costs of care, risk for further complications, and readmission to a hospital.

Multiple factors place the patient at risk for wound infection. One risk factor relates to the type of wound. Surgical wounds are classified according to the degree of contamination. Table 5-10 defines the terms used to describe surgical wounds and gives the expected rate of wound infection per category. Other risk factors include both patient-related factors and those associated with the surgical procedure. Factors related to the surgical procedure include the method of preoperative skin preparation, surgical attire of the team, method of sterile draping, duration of surgery, antimicrobial prophylaxis, aseptic technique, factors related to surgical technique, drains or foreign material, OR ventilation, length of procedure, and exogenous microorganisms. Efforts to prevent wound infection are directed at reducing these risks. Current guidelines to prevent surgical site infections suggest that an appropriate prophylactic antibiotic that is based on current recommendation be administered within 1 hour before surgical incision (2 hours are allowed for the administration of vancomycin and fluoroquinolones) and discontinuation of prophylactic antibiotics within 24 hours after surgery, owing to the link between the development of resistant organisms to excessive use of antibiotics. Discontinuation of the antibiotic is extended to

(continued on page 144)

BOX 5-8

Risk Factors for Postoperative Deep Vein Thrombosis

- Orthopedic patients having hip surgery, knee reconstruction, and other lower extremity surgery
- Urologic patients having transurethral prostatectomy and older patients having urologic surgery
- General surgical patients older than 40 years of age, those who are obese, those with a malignancy, those who have had prior DVT or PE, and those undergoing extensive, complicated surgical procedures
- Gynecologic (and obstetric) patients older than 40 years of age with added risk factors (varicose veins, previous venous thrombosis, infection, malignancy, obesity)
- Neurosurgical patients, similar to other surgical high-risk groups (in patients with stroke, for instance, the risk of DVT in the paralyzed leg is as high as 75%)

TABLE
5-10 Wound Classification and Associated Surgical Site Infection Risk

Surgical Category	Determinants of Category	Expected Risk of Postsurgical Infection (%)
Clean	Nontraumatic site Uninfected site No inflammation No break in aseptic technique No entry into respiratory, alimentary, genitourinary, or oropharyngeal tracts	1–3
Clean-contaminated	Entry into respiratory, alimentary, genitourinary or oropharyngeal tracts without unusual contamination Appendectomy Minor break in aseptic technique Mechanical drainage	3–7
Contaminated	Open, newly experienced traumatic wounds Gross spillage from GI tract Major break in aseptic technique Entry into genitourinary or biliary tract when urine or bile is infected	7–16
Dirty	Traumatic wound with delayed repair, devitalized tissue, foreign bodies, or fecal contamination Acute inflammation and purulent drainage encountered during procedure	16–29

within 48 hours for cardiothoracic procedures for adult patients (Yokoe, Mermel, Anderson et al., 2008).

Wound infection may not be evident until at least POD 5. Most patients are discharged before that time, and more than half of wound infections are diagnosed after discharge, highlighting the importance of patient education regarding wound care. Risk factors for wound sepsis include wound contamination, foreign body, faulty suturing technique, devitalized tissue, hematoma, debilitation, dehydration, malnutrition, anemia, advanced age, extreme obesity, shock, length of preoperative hospitalization, duration of surgical procedure, and associated disorders (e.g., diabetes mellitus, immunosuppression). Signs and symptoms of wound infection include increased pulse rate and temperature; an elevated white blood cell count; wound swelling, warmth, tenderness, or discharge; and incisional pain. Local signs may be absent if the infection is deep. *Staphylococcus aureus* accounts for many postoperative wound infections. Other infections may result from *Escherichia coli, Proteus vulgaris, Aerobacter aerogenes, Pseudomonas aeruginosa*, and other organisms. Although they are rare, beta-hemolytic streptococcal or clostridial infections can be rapid and deadly. If wound infection due to beta-hemolytic streptococcus or clostridium occurs, strict infection control practices are needed to prevent the spread of infection to others. Intensive medical and nursing care is essential if the patient is to survive.

When a wound infection is diagnosed in a surgical incision, the surgeon may remove one or more sutures or staples and, using aseptic precautions, separate the wound edges with a pair of blunt scissors or a hemostat. Once the incision is opened, a drain is inserted. If the infection is deep, an incision and drainage procedure may be necessary. Antimicrobial therapy and a wound care regimen are also initiated.

WOUND DEHISCENCE AND EVISCERATION. Wound **dehiscence** (disruption of surgical incision or wound) and **evisceration** (protrusion of wound contents) are serious surgical complications (Fig. 5-9). Dehiscence and evisceration are especially

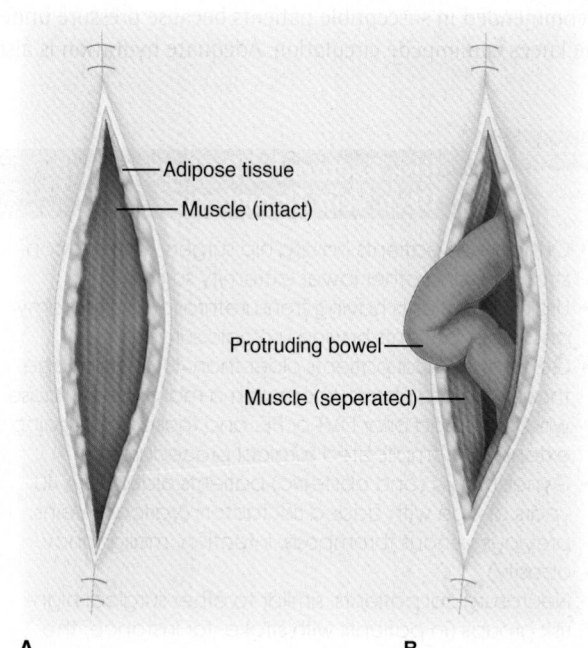

Adipose tissue

Muscle (intact)

Protruding bowel

Muscle (seperated)

A   B

FIGURE 5-9 (**A**) Wound dehiscence; (**B**) wound evisceration.

BOX 5-9   Patient Education

Wound Care Instructions

Until Sutures Are Removed

1. Keep the wound dry and clean:
   - If there is no dressing, ask your nurse or provider if you can bathe or shower.
   - If a dressing or splint is in place, do not remove it unless it is wet or soiled.
   - If wet or soiled, change dressing yourself if you have been taught to do so; otherwise, call your nurse or provider for guidance.
   - If you have been taught, instruction might be as follows:
     - Cleanse area *gently* with sterile normal saline once or twice daily.
     - Cover with a sterile Telfa pad or gauze square large enough to cover wound.
     - Apply hypoallergenic tape (Dermicel or paper). Adhesive is not recommended because it is difficult to remove without possible injury to the incisional site.

2. Immediately report any of these signs of infection:
   - Increasing redness, swelling, tenderness, pain, or increased warmth around wound.
   - Red streaks in skin near wound
   - Pus or discharge, foul odor
   - Chills or temperature higher than 37.7°C (100°F)

3. If soreness or pain causes discomfort, apply a dry cool pack (containing ice or cold water) or take prescribed acetaminophen tablets (2) every 4-6 hours. Avoid using aspirin without direction or instruction because bleeding can occur with its use.

4. Swelling after surgery is common. To help reduce swelling, elevate the affected part to the level of the heart:
   - Hand or arm:
     - Sleep: Elevate arm on pillow at side
     - Sitting: Place arm on pillow on adjacent table
     - Standing: Rest affected hand on opposite shoulder; support elbow with unaffected hand
   - Leg or foot:
     - Sitting: Place a pillow on a facing chair; provide support underneath the knee
     - Lying: Place a pillow under affected leg

After Sutures Are Removed

Although the wound appears to be healed when sutures are removed, it is still tender and will continue to heal and strengthen for several weeks.

1. Follow recommendations of physician or nurse regarding extent of activity.
2. Keep suture line clean; do not rub vigorously; pat dry. Wound edges may look red and may be slightly raised. This is normal.
3. If the site continues to be red, thick, and painful to pressure after 8 weeks, consult the health care provider. (This may be due to excessive collagen formation and should be checked.)

---

serious when they involve abdominal incisions or wounds. These complications result from sutures giving way, from infection, or, more frequently, from marked distention or strenuous cough. They may also occur because of increasing age, poor nutritional status (hypoproteinemia), steroid use, or pulmonary or cardiovascular disease in patients undergoing abdominal surgery.

When the wound edges separate slowly, the intestines may protrude gradually or not at all, and the earliest sign may be a gush of bloody (serosanguineous) peritoneal fluid from the wound. When a wound ruptures suddenly, coils of intestine may push out of the abdomen. The patient may report that "something gave way." The evisceration causes pain and may be associated with vomiting.

An abdominal binder, properly applied, is an excellent prophylactic measure against an evisceration and often is used along with the primary dressing, especially in patients with weak or pendulous abdominal walls or when rupture of a wound has occurred. If evisceration occurs, the nurse aseptically covers the abdominal contents with moist saline dressings to prevent drying of the bowel, notifies the surgical team immediately and assesses the patient's vital signs, including oxygen saturation. The patient remains in bed and knees are bent to reduce abdominal muscle tension. The patient should be NPO and an IV established for fluid management. After the patient returns from surgery, review splinting of the abdomen and anticipate the use of an abdominal binder.

Providing Discharge Teaching

Patients have always required detailed discharge instructions to become proficient in special self-care needs after surgery; however, dramatically reduced hospital lengths of stay during the past decade have greatly increased the amount of information needed while reducing the amount of time in which to provide it. Box 5-9 provides patient education about wound care.

Evaluation

Expected patient outcomes may include the following:

1. Maintains optimal respiratory function:
   a. Performs deep-breathing exercises
   b. Displays clear breath sounds
   c. Uses incentive spirometer as prescribed
   d. Splints incisional site when coughing to reduce pain
2. Indicates that pain is decreased in intensity
3. Increases activity as prescribed:
   a. Alternates periods of rest and activity
   b. Progressively increases ambulation
   c. Resumes normal activities within prescribed time frame
   d. Performs activities related to self-care
4. Wound heals without complication
5. Maintains body temperature within normal limits
6. Resumes oral intake:
   a. Reports absence of nausea and vomiting
   b. Eats at least 75% of usual diet
   c. Is free of abdominal distress and gas pains
   d. Exhibits normal bowel sounds
7. Reports resumption of usual bowel elimination pattern
8. Resumes usual voiding pattern
9. Is free of injury
10. Exhibits decreased anxiety
11. Acquires knowledge and skills necessary to manage therapeutic regimen
12. Experiences no complications

Gerontologic Considerations

Elderly patients recover more slowly, have longer hospital stays, and are at greater risk for the development of postoperative complications. Some of the major threats to recovery include pneumonia, decline in functional ability, exacerbation of comorbid conditions, pressure ulcers, decreased oral intake, GI disturbance, and falls. Expert nursing care can help the older adult avoid these complications or minimize their effects.

Postoperative delirium, characterized by confusion, perceptual and cognitive deficits, altered attention levels, disturbed sleep patterns, and impaired psychomotor skills, is a significant problem for older adults. Causes of delirium are multifactorial (refer to Box 5-10 for causes of delirium). Skilled and frequent assessment of mental status and of all physiologic factors influencing mental status helps the nurse plan care, because delirium may be the initial or only early indicator of infection, fluid and electrolyte imbalance, or deterioration of respiratory or hemodynamic status in the elderly patient.

Recognizing postoperative delirium and identifying and treating its underlying cause are the goals of care. Postoperative delirium is sometimes mistaken for preexisting dementia or is attributed to age. In addition to monitoring and managing identifiable causes, the nurse implements support-

ive interventions. Keeping the patient in a well-lit room and close to the nurses' station can help with sensory deprivation. At the same time, distracting and unfamiliar noises should be minimized. Because pain can contribute to postoperative delirium, adequate pain control is essential. The nurse collaborates with the physician or geriatric nurse specialist and the patient to achieve pain relief without oversedation.

The patient is reoriented as often as necessary, and staff should introduce themselves each time they come in contact with the patient. Engaging the patient in conversation and care activities and placing a clock and calendar nearby may improve cognitive function. Physical activity should not be neglected while the patient is confused, because physical deterioration can worsen delirium and place the patient at increased risk for other complications. Restraints should be avoided, because they can also worsen confusion. If possible, a family member or staff member is asked to stay with the patient instead. Antianxiety medication may be administered during episodes of acute confusion, but they should be discontinued as soon as possible to avoid side effects.

Other problems confronting the elderly postoperative patient, such as pneumonia, altered bowel function, DVT, weakness, and functional decline, often can be prevented by early and progressive ambulation. Ambulation means walking, not just getting out of bed and sitting in a chair.

BOX 5-10 Causes of Postoperative Delirium

- Acid–base disturbances
- Age greater than 80 years
- Fluid and electrolyte imbalance
- Dehydration
- History of dementia-like symptoms
- Hypoxia
- Hypercarbia
- Infection (urinary tract, wound, respiratory)
- Medications (anticholinergics, benzodiazepines, central nervous system depressants)
- Unrelieved pain
- Blood loss
- Decreased cardiac output
- Cerebral hypoxia
- Heart failure
- Acute myocardial infarction
- Hypothermia or hyperthermia
- Unfamiliar surroundings and sensory deprivation
- Emergent surgery
- Alcohol withdrawal
- Urinary retention
- Fecal impaction
- Polypharmacy
- Presence of multiple diseases
- Sensory impairments
- High stress or anxiety levels

Prolonged sitting positions that promote venous stasis in the lower extremities should be avoided. Assistance with ambulation may be required to keep the patient from bumping into objects and falling. A physical therapy referral may be indicated to promote safe, regular exercise for the older adult.

Urinary incontinence can be prevented by providing easy access to the call bell and the commode and by prompting voiding. Early ambulation and familiarity with the room help the patient to become self-sufficient sooner.

Optimal nutritional status is important for wound healing, return of normal bowel function, and fluid and electrolyte balance. The nurse and patient can consult with the dietitian to plan appealing, high-protein meals that provide sufficient fiber, calories, and vitamins. Nutritional supplements, such as Ensure or Sustacal, may be recommended. Multivitamins, iron, and vitamin C supplements aid in tissue healing, formation of new red blood cells, and overall nutritional status and are commonly prescribed postoperatively.

In addition to monitoring and managing physiologic recovery of the older adult, the nurse identifies and addresses psychosocial needs. The older adult may require much encouragement and support to resume activities, and the pace may be slow. Sensory deficits may require frequent repetition of instructions, and decreased physiologic reserve may necessitate frequent rest periods. The older adult may require extensive discharge planning to coordinate both professional and family care providers, and the nurse, social worker, or nurse case manager may institute the plan for continuing care.

Chapter Review

Critical Thinking Exercises

1. An 80-year-old patient with Parkinson's disease is scheduled for surgery to replace a fractured hip. Identify the considerations and associated responsibilities of the OR nurse for safe intraoperative care of this patient.
2. A patient develops a temperature of 38°C (100°F) and becomes tachycardic halfway through an abdominal surgery. Five minutes later, the patient's temperature is 42°C (104°F). Describe the protocol you would follow and the medication you would administer for this condition.
3. A male patient is scheduled for major surgery and asks how long before the surgery he will be without food and fluids. What resources would you use to identify the current fasting guidelines? What is the evidence base for the patient's being NPO after midnight as opposed to a 2 hour fast before surgery? Identify the criteria used to evaluate the strength of the evidence for this practice.

NCLEX-Style Review Questions

1. A 70-year-old elderly patient is admitted to the preoperative unit for a liver resection that is scheduled for 6 hours of surgery. What is one of the basic principles that should guide the preoperative nurse's assessment?
   A. Elderly patients do not experience as much preoperative anxiety as younger patients.
   B. The elderly patient has less physiological reserve than the younger patient.
   C. Elderly patients experience less pain.
   D. Preoperative pain assessment and teaching should occur following the procedure as the elderly patient may not retain the information.

2. A nurse is caring for a postoperative patient who had spinal anesthesia. The patient complains of headache. Which of the following actions should the nurse take?
   A. Lower the head of the patient's bed.
   B. Keep the patient lying flat, maintain a quiet environment, and keep the patient hydrated.
   C. Encourage the patient to lay on his right side.
   D. Do nothing, as this is a normal response to the spinal anesthesia.

3. Which of the following describes the postoperative phase?
   A. Starting with admission of the patient to the OR
   B. Starting with the admission of the patient to the PACU and ending when the patient is discharged to the unit or home
   C. Starting with the admission of the patient to the PACU and ending with follow-up evaluation in the clinical setting or home
   D. Starting with admission to the PACU

4. A nurse is caring for a postoperative patient on POD 2. The patient had a large upper abdominal incision. While assessing the patient at the beginning of her shift, the nurse noted decreased breath sounds, crackles, and a mild cough. What is the patient most likely experiencing?
   A. Atelectasis
   B. Pneumonia
   C. Acute bronchitis
   D. Hypoxemia

5. Surgical wound healing occurs in:
   A. Two phases: inflammatory and maturation
   B. Three phases: inflammatory, proliferative, and maturation
   C. First-, second-, and third-intention wound healing
   D. First and proliferative phase

Try these additional resources to enhance your learning and understanding of this chapter:
- thePoint online resource available at **http://thepoint.lww.com/Pellico1e**
- *Handbook for Focus on Adult Health: Medical-Surgical Nursing*
- *Study Guide for Focus on Adult Health: Medical-Surgical Nursing*

References and Selected Readings

References and selected readings associated with this chapter can be found on the website that accompanies the book. Visit http://thepoint.lww.com/Pellico1e to access the references and other additional resources associated with this chapter.

LISA M. BARBAROTTA

Cancer Care

Learning Objectives

After reading this chapter, you will be able to:

1. Compare the structure and function of the normal cell and the cancer cell.

2. Differentiate between benign and malignant tumors.

3. Identify agents and factors that have been found to be carcinogenic.

4. Describe the significance of health education and preventive care in decreasing the incidence of cancer.

5. Differentiate among the purposes of surgical procedures used in cancer treatment, diagnosis, prophylaxis, and palliation.

6. Describe the roles of surgery, radiation therapy, chemotherapy, biotherapy, other therapies in treating cancer.

7. Describe the special nursing needs of patients receiving chemotherapy.

8. Describe common nursing diagnoses and collaborative problems of patients with cancer.

(continued on page 150)

Cancer is not a single disease with a single cause; rather, it is a group of distinct diseases with different causes, manifestations, treatments, and prognoses. Cancer nursing practice encompasses all age groups and nursing specialties and is carried out in a variety of health care settings, including the home, community, acute care institutions, rehabilitation centers, and hospice. The scope, responsibilities, and goals of cancer nursing, also called **oncology** nursing, are as diverse and complex as those of any nursing specialty. Cancer nurses must be prepared to support patients and families through a wide range of physical, emotional, social, cultural, and spiritual experiences.

EPIDEMIOLOGY OF CANCER

Although cancer affects people of all ages, most cancers occur in people older than 65 years of age. Overall, the incidence of cancer is higher in men than in women and higher in industrialized nations.

More than 1.5 million Americans are diagnosed with cancer each year (Fig. 6-1). More than 560,000 Americans die from a **malignant** process each year. The leading causes of cancer death in the United States, in order of frequency, are lung, prostate, and colorectal cancer in men and lung, breast, and colorectal cancer in women. Notable trends in the United States include stabilization of the incidence rates for all cancer sites in men and women since 1999 and a continued decline in death rates since 1991. Despite this progress in decreased death rates, improved survival, and stable incidence, cancer still accounts for more deaths than heart disease in people under 85 years old (Jemal, Siegel, Ward et al., 2009).

Relative 5-year survival rates for African Americans compared to Caucasians are lower for cancer of every site. In the United States, cancer mortality in African Americans is higher than in any other racial group. This finding is related to the higher incidence and later stage of diagnosis among African Americans. The increased cancer morbidity and mortality in this group are largely a result of a combination of factors including: differences in exposure to risk factors, economics, education, and access to health care, rather than racial characteristics alone (Jemal et al., 2009).

9. Describe the concept of hospice in providing care for patients with advanced cancer.

10. Discuss the role of the nurse in assessment and management of common oncologic emergencies.

PATHOPHYSIOLOGY

Cancer can be characterized by the presence of the following:

- A series of cellular and genetic changes that cause a loss of normal cell regulation; this is the hallmark of malignancy
- Abnormal cell proliferation or growth
- Unchecked local growth and invasion of surrounding tissue
- The ability to metastasize to distant organs

Characteristics of Malignant Cells

The primary difference between malignant (cancerous) and benign cells is that malignant cells have abnormal regulation of growth. Cancer cells continue to grow, even at the expense of their host. They demonstrate uncontrolled cell growth that follows no physiologic demand.

Benign and malignant growths are classified and named by tissue of origin. Benign and malignant cells differ in many cellular growth

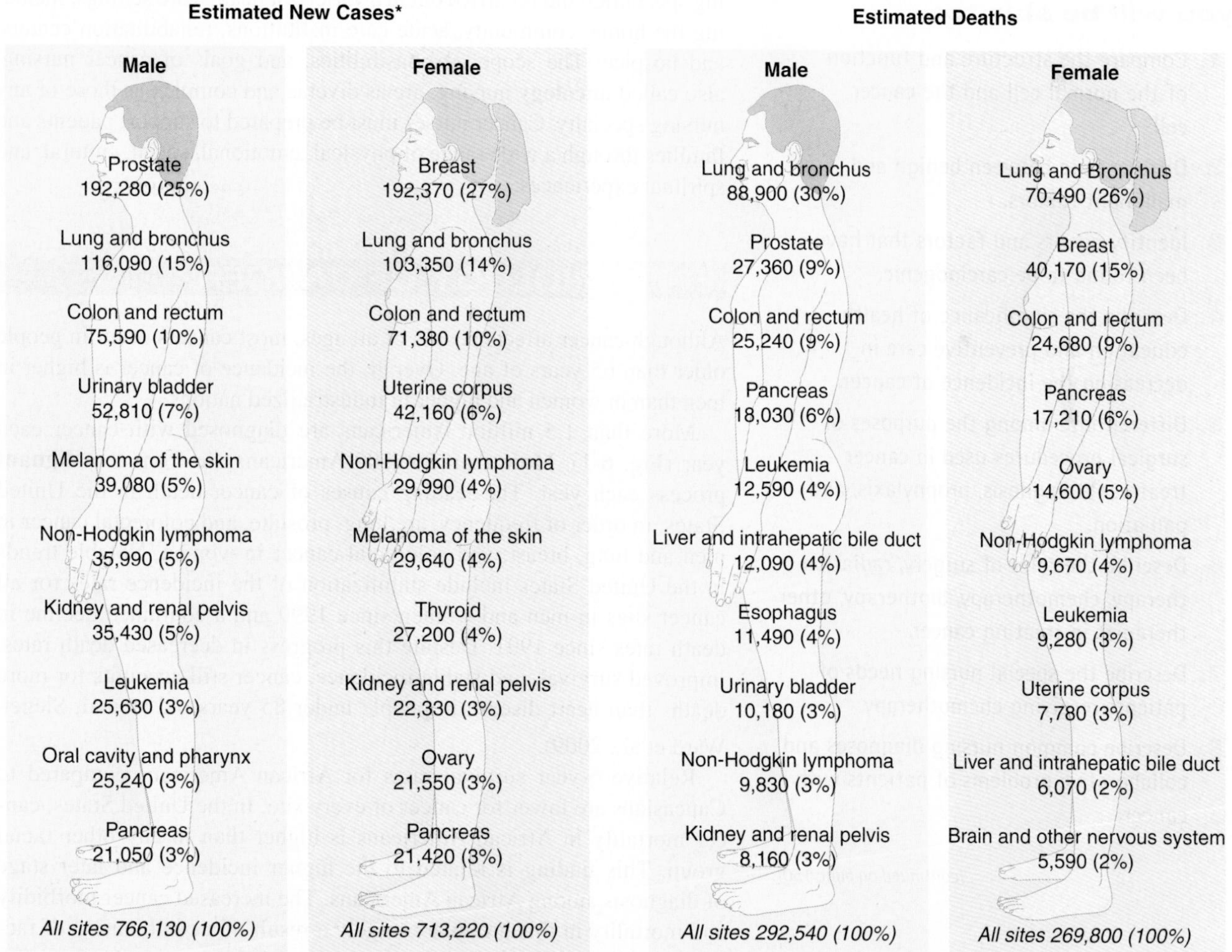

Estimated New Cases*

Male

Prostate
192,280 (25%)

Lung and bronchus
116,090 (15%)

Colon and rectum
75,590 (10%)

Urinary bladder
52,810 (7%)

Melanoma of the skin
39,080 (5%)

Non-Hodgkin lymphoma
35,990 (5%)

Kidney and renal pelvis
35,430 (5%)

Leukemia
25,630 (3%)

Oral cavity and pharynx
25,240 (3%)

Pancreas
21,050 (3%)

All sites 766,130 (100%)

Female

Breast
192,370 (27%)

Lung and bronchus
103,350 (14%)

Colon and rectum
71,380 (10%)

Uterine corpus
42,160 (6%)

Non-Hodgkin lymphoma
29,990 (4%)

Melanoma of the skin
29,640 (4%)

Thyroid
27,200 (4%)

Kidney and renal pelvis
22,330 (3%)

Ovary
21,550 (3%)

Pancreas
21,420 (3%)

All sites 713,220 (100%)

Estimated Deaths

Male

Lung and bronchus
88,900 (30%)

Prostate
27,360 (9%)

Colon and rectum
25,240 (9%)

Pancreas
18,030 (6%)

Leukemia
12,590 (4%)

Liver and intrahepatic bile duct
12,090 (4%)

Esophagus
11,490 (4%)

Urinary bladder
10,180 (3%)

Non-Hodgkin lymphoma
9,830 (3%)

Kidney and renal pelvis
8,160 (3%)

All sites 292,540 (100%)

Female

Lung and Bronchus
70,490 (26%)

Breast
40,170 (15%)

Colon and rectum
24,680 (9%)

Pancreas
17,210 (6%)

Ovary
14,600 (5%)

Non-Hodgkin lymphoma
9,670 (4%)

Leukemia
9,280 (3%)

Uterine corpus
7,780 (3%)

Liver and intrahepatic bile duct
6,070 (2%)

Brain and other nervous system
5,590 (2%)

All sites 269,800 (100%)

FIGURE 6-1 Ten leading types of cancer and cancer deaths by gender determined on the basis of estimated new cancer cases and deaths in the United States in 2008. *Excludes basal and squamous cell skin cancers and in situ carcinomas except urinary bladder. Estimates rounded to the nearest 10. Adapted from Jemal, A., Siegel, R., Ward, E., et al. (2009). Cancer Statistics, 2008. *CA: A Cancer Journal for Clinicians*, 59, 225–249.

TABLE
6-1 Characteristics of Benign and Malignant Neoplasms

Characteristics	Benign Neoplasms	Malignant Neoplasms
Cell characteristics	Well-differentiated cells that resemble cells in the tissue of origin	Cells are undifferentiated, with anaplasia and atypical structure that often bear little resemblance to cells in the tissue of origin
Mode of growth	Grows by expansion without invading the surrounding tissues; usually encapsulated	Grows by invasion, sending out processes that infiltrate the surrounding tissues
Rate of growth	Usually progressive and slow; may come to a standstill or regress	Variable and depends on level of differentiation; the more undifferentiated the cells, the more rapid the rate of growth
Metastasis	Does not spread by metastasis	Gains access to the blood and lymph channels to metastasize to other areas of the body

From Porth, C. M., & Matfin (2009). *Pathophysiology: Concepts of altered health states* (8th ed.). Philadelphia: Lippincott Williams & Wilkins.

characteristics, including the method and rate of growth, ability to metastasize or spread, general effects, destruction of tissue, and ability to cause death. These differences are summarized in Table 6-1.

Despite their individual differences, all cancer cells share some common cellular characteristics in relation to the cell membrane, special proteins, the nuclei, chromosomal abnormalities, and the rate of mitosis and growth. Characteristics of cancer cells include:

- Pleomorphism: Cells vary in size and shape
- Polymorphism: Nucleus is enlarged and variable in shape
- Chromosomal mutations including translocations, deletions, amplification, and aneuploidy (abnormal number of chromosomes)
- Production of surface enzymes that aid in invasion and metastasis
- Loss of antigens that label the cell as "self"
- Production of new tumor-associated antigens that label the cell as "non-self"
- Increased rate of anaerobic metabolism
- Loss of contact inhibition, which normally halts cell division once cells are in contact with one another
- Defect in cell recognition and adhesion (cancer cells do not recognize and adhere to each other as normal cells do)
- Loss of control of proliferation
- Increased mitotic index: Tumors have a larger number of cells that are in mitosis
- Abnormal lifespan: Cancer cells tend to live longer than do normal cells

Malignant Process

Cancer cells are genetically unstable and prone to mutations, including chromosomal rearrangements, duplications, and deletions. Cancer is a disease process that begins when one abnormal cell is transformed by a genetic mutation of the cellular DNA. This abnormal cell forms a clone and begins to proliferate abnormally, ignoring growth-regulating signals in the environment surrounding the cell. This is known as the *monoclonal origin of cancer*. While initially the malignant cells in a tumor may look alike, over time, the differences among individual cells increases as a result of ongoing random mutations during tumor progression.

All cells, both healthy and malignant, proliferate by way of the cell cycle (see Fig. 6-2). The cell cycle time is the time required for one cell to divide and reproduce two identical daughter cells. The cell cycle of any cell has four distinct phases, each with a vital underlying function:

1. G_1 phase: RNA and protein synthesis occur
2. S phase: DNA synthesis occurs
3. G_2 phase: Premitotic phase; DNA synthesis is complete, mitotic spindle forms
4. Mitosis: Cell division occurs

The G_0 phase, the resting or dormant phase of cells, can occur after mitosis and during the G_1 phase. In the G_0 phase there are cells that are not actively dividing but have the potential to enter into the cell cycle. Mitosis (cell division) occurs more frequently in malignant cells than in normal cells. As the cells grow and divide, more glucose and oxygen are needed. If glucose and oxygen are unavailable, malignant cells use anaerobic metabolic channels to produce energy, which makes the cells less dependent on the availability of a constant oxygen supply.

Oncogenes

Cellular oncogenes, which exist in all mammalian systems, are responsible for the vital cellular functions of growth and differentiation. Cellular proto-oncogenes act as an "on switch" for cellular growth. When proto-oncogenes are mutated, cell growth and differentiation are stimulated.

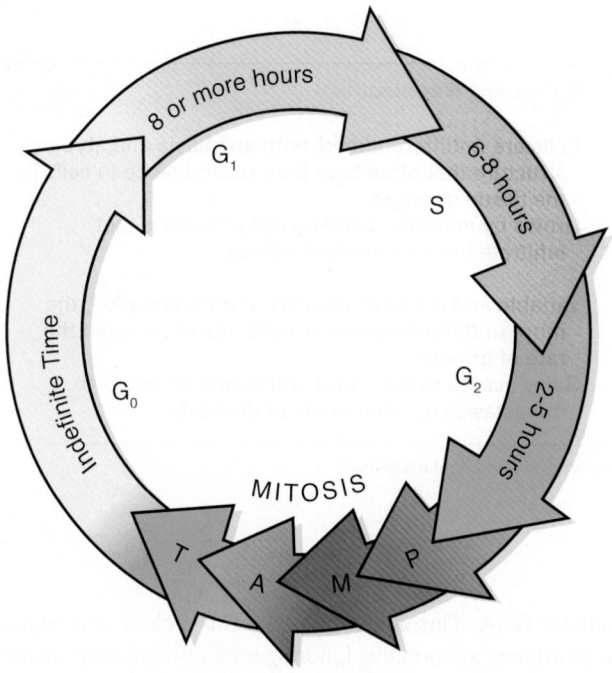

FIGURE 6-2 Phases of the cell cycle extend over the interval between the midpoint of mitosis and the subsequent end point in mitosis in a daughter cell. G_1 is the postmitotic phase during which ribonucleic acid (RNA) and protein syntheses are increased and cell growth occurs. G_0 is the resting, or dormant, phase of the cell cycle. In the S phase, nucleic acids are synthesized and chromosomes are replicated in preparation for cell mitosis. During G_2, RNA and protein synthesis occur as in G_1. P, prophase; M, metaphase; A, anaphase; T, telophase. Redrawn from Porth, C. M. (2002). *Pathophysiology: Concepts of altered health states* (6th ed.). Philadelphia: Lippincott Williams & Wilkins.

Just as proto-oncogenes "turn on" cellular growth, tumor suppressor genes "turn off," or regulate, unneeded cellular proliferation. When tumor suppressor genes become mutated, rearranged, or amplified, or lose their regulatory capabilities, malignant cells are allowed to reproduce. The p53 gene *(TP53)* is a tumor suppressor gene that is frequently mutated in many human cancers. This gene determines whether cells will live or die after their DNA is damaged. **Apoptosis** is the innate cellular process of programmed cell death. Alterations in *TP53* may decrease apoptotic signals, thus decreasing the body's ability to kill mutated cells, giving rise to a survival advantage for mutant cell populations. Mutant *TP53* is associated with a poor prognosis and may be used to determine response to treatment.

Carcinogenesis

Carcinogenesis is the process by which cancer arises. Previously referred to as the "two-hit" theory, carcinogenesis is now understood to be a multistep process involving initiation, promotion, progression, and metastasis. During *initiation,* initiators (carcinogens), such as chemicals, physical factors, and biologic agents, escape normal enzymatic mechanisms and alter the genetic structure of the cellular DNA. Normally, these alterations are reversed by DNA repair mechanisms, or

the abnormal changes stimulate apoptosis. Occasionally, cells escape these protective mechanisms, and permanent genetic mutations occur. These mutations usually are not significant to cells unless they are further exposed to carcinogens.

During *promotion,* repeated exposure to promoting agents (co-carcinogens) results in one of the following changes: reversible damage to the growth mechanism of the cell, or, irreversible damage to the growth mechanism, resulting in cancer cell transformation.

During *progression,* the cellular changes formed during initiation and promotion exhibit increased malignant behavior. The cancer cells continue to divide, and the tumor increases in size, causing increased bulk, pressure, and secretion of enzymes resulting in local spread and invasion into surrounding tissues. During progression, the tumor forms blood vessels to provide access to oxygen and nutrients. This process is referred to as *neovascularization* or *angiogenesis.*

Metastasis

Metastasis is the dissemination or spread of malignant cells from the primary tumor to distant sites by direct spread of tumor cells to body cavities or through lymphatic and blood circulation. The most common sites of metastasis include the bones, lungs, liver, and central nervous system (CNS). The site of metastasis is influenced by the availability of a blood supply, cell receptors and genes that may direct the malignant cell to travel to specific sites, and the presence of growth factors essential for metastatic growth that may only be elicited in selected organs.

Lymphatic Spread

The transport of tumor cells through the lymphatic circulation is the most common mechanism of metastasis. Tumor emboli enter the lymph channels by way of the interstitial fluid, which communicates with lymphatic circulation. Malignant cells also may penetrate lymphatic vessels by invasion. After entering the lymphatic circulation, malignant cells either lodge in the lymph nodes or pass between the lymphatic and venous circulations. Tumors arising in areas of the body with rapid and extensive lymphatic circulation are at high risk for metastasis through lymphatic channels. Breast tumors frequently metastasize in this manner through axillary, clavicular, and thoracic lymph channels.

Hematogenous Spread

Hematogenous spread is the dissemination of malignant cells via the bloodstream, and is directly related to the vascularity of the tumor. Malignant cells are able to travel through the bloodstream, attach to endothelium and attract fibrin, platelets, and clotting factors to seal themselves from immune system surveillance. The endothelium retracts, allowing the malignant cells to enter the basement membrane and secrete lysosomal enzymes. These enzymes destroy surrounding body tissues and thereby allow implantation.

Angiogenesis

Angiogenesis is the process by which a new blood supply is formed. Once a tumor reaches a size of 2 mm^3, this

blood supply is necessary for continued growth. The newly formed blood vessels provide nutrition and oxygen to the tumor and also provide a route for metastasis. The process of angiogenesis is mediated by the release of growth factors and enzymes such as vascular endothelial growth factor (VEGF). These proteins rapidly stimulate formation of new blood vessels. Therapies that target VEGF or its receptors are being used to treat many cancers effectively.

Etiology

Categories of agents or factors implicated in carcinogenesis include viruses and bacteria, physical agents, chemical agents, genetic or familial factors, dietary factors, and hormonal agents.

Viruses and Bacteria

Viruses are thought to incorporate themselves into the genetic structure of cells, thus altering future generations of that cell population—perhaps leading to cancer. The example most commonly seen in practice is the human papilloma virus (HPV), which accounts for almost 100% of cervical cancer cases and 80% to 90% of anal cancers (Saslow, Castle, Cox et al., 2007). Infection with HPV-16 also increases the risk of developing oral squamous cell cancers (Cohan, Popat, Kaplan et al., 2009).

Physical Agents

Physical factors associated with carcinogenesis include exposure to sunlight or radiation. Exposure to ionizing radiation can occur with repeated diagnostic X-ray procedures or with radiation therapy used to treat disease. Fortunately, improved X-ray equipment appropriately minimizes the risk of extensive radiation exposure to healthy tissue. Radiation therapy used in disease treatment and exposure to radioactive materials at nuclear weapon manufacturing sites or nuclear power plants are associated with a higher incidence of leukemias, multiple myeloma, and cancers of the lung, bone, breast, thyroid, and other tissues. Background radiation from the natural decay processes that produce radon has also been associated with lung cancer.

Chemical Agents

About 75% of all cancers are thought to be related to the environment. Tobacco remains the single largest preventable cause of disease and early death, and accounts for at least 30% of all cancer deaths (Cokkinides, Bandi, McMahon et al., 2009). Smoking is strongly associated with cancers of the lung, head and neck, esophagus, pancreas, cervix, and bladder. Tobacco may also act synergistically with other substances, such as alcohol, asbestos, uranium, and viruses, to promote cancer development.

Many chemical substances found in the workplace have proved to be carcinogens or co-carcinogens. The extensive list of suspected chemical substances continues to grow and includes aromatic amines and aniline dyes; pesticides and formaldehydes; arsenic, soot, and tars; asbestos; benzene; betel nut and lime; cadmium; chromium compounds; nickel and zinc ores; wood dust; beryllium compounds; and polyvinyl chloride.

Genetics and Familial Factors

Observations over time have shown that cancers cluster in some families. This may be due to genetics, shared environments, cultural or lifestyle factors, or chance alone. Genetic factors play a role in cancer cell development. Abnormal chromosomal patterns and cancer have been associated with extra chromosomes, too few chromosomes, or translocated chromosomes. Specific cancers with underlying genetic abnormalities include Burkitt's lymphoma, chronic myelogenous leukemia, meningiomas (tumors that develop from the meninges, the membrane surrounding the brain and spinal cord), acute leukemias (cancer of the blood or bone marrow usually affecting white blood cells [WBCs]), retinoblastomas (cancer in the cells of the retina), Wilms' tumor (malignant tumor of the kidney) and skin cancers, including malignant melanoma.

Approximately 5% of cancers in adults display a familial predisposition. The hallmarks of families with a hereditary cancer syndrome include multiple primary tumors in the same organ, multiple primary tumors in different organs, bilateral primary tumors in paired organs, younger than usual age at cancer diagnosis, two or more first-degree relatives with the same or related tumor type, and two or more first-degree relatives with rare tumor types (Lindor, McMaster, Lindor et al., 2008). Cancers associated with familial inheritance include retinoblastomas, nephroblastomas (kidney tumor), pheochromocytomas (adrenal medulla tumor), malignant neurofibromatosis (tumors of nerve tissue), and breast, ovarian, colorectal, stomach, prostate, and lung cancers.

In the 1990s, the BRCA1 and BRCA2 genes were identified and linked to breast and ovarian cancer syndrome. Mutations in BRCA1 are associated with a 40% to 80% increased risk of breast cancer and a 40% risk of ovarian cancer by 70 years of age (Mahoney, Bevers, Linos et al., 2008).

Dietary Factors

Second to tobacco, weight control, dietary choices, and levels of physical activity are the most important modifiable determinants of cancer risk. Evidence suggests that one-third of cancer deaths that occur in the United States each year can be attributed to poor diet and lack of physical activity, including obesity (Kushi, Byers, Doyle et al., 2006).

Dietary substances that appear to increase the risk of cancer include fats, alcohol, salt-cured or smoked meats, and nitrate- and nitrite-containing foods. A high-caloric dietary intake is also associated with an increased cancer risk. Obesity has been associated with endometrial cancer and breast cancer (Mahoney et al., 2008).

Consumption of high-fiber foods (such as fruits, vegetables, and whole-grain cereals) and cruciferous vegetables (such as cabbage, broccoli, cauliflower, brussel sprouts, and kohlrabi) appears to decrease the risk of cancer.

Hormonal Agents

Tumor growth may be promoted by disturbances in hormonal balance, either by the body's own (endogenous) hormone production or by administration of exogenous hormones. Cancers of the breast, prostate, and uterus are thought to depend on endogenous hormonal levels for growth. Diethylstilbestrol (DES) has long been recognized as a cause of vaginal carcinomas. Oral contraceptives and prolonged estrogen replacement therapy are associated with an increased incidence of hepatocellular, endometrial, and breast cancers, but they decrease the risk of ovarian cancer (IARC, 2007).

Hormonal changes with reproduction are also associated with cancer incidence. Increased numbers of pregnancies and increased length of time lactating are associated with a decreased incidence of breast, endometrial, and ovarian cancers.

Role of the Immune System

In humans, malignant cells can develop at any time in the life span. However, some evidence indicates that the immune system can detect the development of malignant cells and destroy them before cell growth becomes uncontrolled. When the immune system fails to identify and stop the growth of malignant cells, clinical cancer develops.

Patients who are immunoincompetent have been shown to have an increased incidence of cancer. Organ transplant recipients who receive immunosuppressive therapy to prevent organ rejection have an increased incidence of lymphoma, Kaposi's sarcoma, squamous cell cancer of the skin, and cervical and anogenital cancers. Patients with immunodeficiency diseases, such as AIDS, have an increased incidence of Kaposi's sarcoma, lymphoma, and rectal and head and neck cancers.

Some patients who have received alkylating chemotherapeutic agents to treat Hodgkin's lymphoma have an increased incidence of secondary malignancies. Autoimmune diseases, such as rheumatoid arthritis and Sjögren syndrome, are associated with increased cancer development. Finally, age-related changes, such as declining organ function, increased incidence of chronic diseases, and diminished immunocompetence, may contribute to an increased incidence of cancer in older people.

Normal Immune Responses

An intact immune system has the ability to combat cancer cells in several ways. Usually, the immune system recognizes as foreign certain antigens on the cell membranes of many cancer cells. These antigens, known as *tumor-associated antigens* (also called *tumor cell antigens*), are capable of stimulating both cellular and humoral immune responses.

Along with the macrophages, T lymphocytes, the soldiers of the cellular immune response, are responsible for recognizing tumor-associated antigens. When T lymphocytes recognize tumor antigens, other T lymphocytes that are toxic to the tumor cells are stimulated. These lymphocytes proliferate and are released into the circulation. In addition to possessing cytotoxic (cell-killing) properties, T lymphocytes can stimulate other components of the immune system to rid the body of malignant cells.

Immune System Failure

How is it, then, that malignant cells can survive and proliferate despite the elaborate immune system defense mechanisms? Several theories suggest how tumor cells can evade an apparently intact immune system. If the body fails to recognize the malignant cell as different from "self" (i.e., as non-self or foreign), the immune response may not be stimulated. When tumors do not possess tumor-associated antigens that label them as foreign, the immune response is not alerted. The failure of the immune system to respond promptly to the malignant cells allows the tumor to grow too large to be managed by normal immune mechanisms.

PREVENTION

Nurses and physicians have traditionally been involved with tertiary prevention; that is, prevention of disease progression, as well as the care, treatment, and rehabilitation of patients after cancer diagnosis. However, in recent years, the American Cancer Society, the National Cancer Institute, clinicians, and researchers have placed greater emphasis on primary and secondary prevention of cancer. Primary prevention is concerned with reducing the risks of cancer in healthy people. Secondary prevention involves detection and screening to achieve early diagnosis and prompt intervention to halt the cancer process.

Primary Prevention

By acquiring the knowledge and skills necessary to educate the community about cancer risk, nurses in all settings play a key role in cancer prevention. One way to reduce the risk of cancer is to help patients avoid known carcinogens. Another way involves encouraging patients to make dietary and various lifestyle changes that epidemiologic and laboratory studies show influence the risk for cancer. Nurses can use their teaching and counseling skills to encourage patients to participate in cancer prevention programs and to adopt healthy lifestyles. Several clinical trials have been conducted to identify medications that may help reduce the incidence of certain types of cancer. For example, a number of studies have demonstrated that daily use of the medication tamoxifen can significantly reduce a woman's life-time risk of developing breast cancer in selected populations (Chen, 2008).

Secondary Prevention

Nurses must be aware of factors such as race, cultural influences, access to care, provider–patient relationship, level of education, income, and age, which influence the knowledge, attitudes, and beliefs people have about cancer. These factors also may affect the health-promoting behaviors people practice.

Public awareness about health-promoting behaviors can be provided in a variety of ways, including health education and health maintenance programs. Although primary prevention programs may focus on the hazards of tobacco use or the importance of nutrition, secondary prevention programs focus on early detection. Nurses and physicians must encourage people to comply with detection efforts as suggested by the American Cancer Society (Table 6-2). Many

TABLE 6-2 American Cancer Society Recommendations for Early Detection of Cancer in Asymptomatic, Average Risk People

Site	Gender	Age (y)	Evaluation	Frequency
Breast	F	20–39	Clinical breast examination (CBE)	Every 3 years
			Self breast examination (SBE)	Every month
		≥40	CBE	Every year
			SBE	Every month
			Mammogram	Every year
			MRI	
		Women with a strong family history of breast or ovarian cancer and women treated for Hodgkin's lymphoma		
Colon/rectum	F/M	≥50	Fecal occult blood test *or*	Every year
			Fecal immunochemistry test *and*	Every year
			Flexible sigmoidoscopy *or*	Every 5 years
			Colonoscopy *or*	Every 10 years
			Double-contrast barium enema *or*	Every 5 years
			CT colonography (virtual colonoscopy)	Every 5 years
Prostate	M	≥50 45 if at high risk: African American men Men with ≥1 first-degree relatives diagnosed with prostate cancer at a young age	Prostate-specific antigen and digital rectal examination	No evidence based guidelines exist; the patients' individual risks should be assessed and subsequent testing should be based on overall risk. Patients who are African American or have a family history of prostate cancer before age 65 may be at increased risk and may require testing starting at age 45 years. Screening tests include PSA and digital rectal exam.
Cervix	F	≥21 or within 3 years after starting to have vaginal intercourse	Papanicolaou (Pap) test*	Every year if regular Pap; every 2 years if liquid Pap test
			Pelvic examination	Every year
Cancer-related checkups	M/F	≥20–39	Examination for cancers of the thyroid, testicles, ovaries, lymph nodes, oral cavity, and skin, as well as counseling about health practices and risk factors	Every 3 years
		40+	Same as for 20–39	Every year

*At or after age 30, in women who have had three or more consecutive normal examinations, the Pap test may be performed every 2–3 years at the discretion of the physician; human papillomavirus (HPV) test should be included at that time. Women ≥70 years with three or more consecutive negative Pap smears in the last 10 years may choose to stop screening.

Adapted from American Cancer Society (2010). American Cancer Society Guidelines for early detection of cancer. Available at: http://www.cancer.org/healthy/findcancerearly/cancerscreeningguidelines/american-cancer-society-guidelines-for-the-early-detection-of-cancer.

organizations conduct cancer-screening events that focus on cancers with the highest incidence rates or those that have improved survival rates if diagnosed early, such as breast or prostate cancers. These events offer education and examinations such as mammograms, digital rectal examinations, and prostate-specific antigen (PSA) blood tests for minimal or no cost. These programs are often targeted to people who lack access to health care or cannot afford to participate on their own. In developing these programs, nurses must use strategies that are culturally sensitive to foster participation. One example of a creative intervention targeted to high-risk populations is the Barbershop Initiative™ launched by The Prostate Net. The program involved training local barbers from minority communities to function as lay health educators to motivate their customers to participate in prostate cancer screening (The Prostate Net, 2008).

DIAGNOSIS

A cancer diagnosis is based on an assessment of physiologic and functional changes and results of the diagnostic evaluation.

Diagnostic Evaluation

The diagnostic evaluation is guided by information obtained through a complete history and physical examination. Knowledge of suspicious symptoms and of the behavior of particular types of cancer assists in determining which diagnostic tests are most appropriate. Patients with suspected cancer undergo extensive testing to (1) determine the presence of tumor and its extent, (2) identify possible spread (metastasis) of disease or invasion of other body tissues, (3) evaluate the function of involved and uninvolved body systems and organs, and (4) obtain tissue and cells for analysis to assist in the evaluation of tumor type, stage, and grade.

Patients undergoing extensive testing are usually fearful of the procedures and anxious about the possible test results. The nurse can help relieve the patient's fear and anxiety by explaining the tests to be performed, the sensations likely to be experienced, and the patient's role in the test procedures. The nurse encourages the patient and family to voice their fears about the test results, supports the patient and family throughout the test period, and reinforces and clarifies information conveyed by the primary care provider.

Tumor Staging and Grading

A complete diagnostic evaluation includes identifying the stage and grade of the tumor. This is accomplished before treatment begins to provide baseline data for evaluating outcomes of therapy and to maintain a systematic and consistent approach to ongoing diagnosis and treatment. Treatment options and prognosis are based on stage and grade of disease.

Staging

Staging determines the size of the tumor and the extent of disease. Several systems exist for classifying the disease

BOX 6-1	TNM Classification System

T	The extent of the primary tumor
N	The absence or presence and extent of regional lymph node metastasis
M	The absence or presence of distant metastasis

The use of numerical subsets of the TNM components indicates the progressive extent of the malignant disease.

Primary Tumor (T)

Tx	Primary tumor cannot be assessed
T0	No evidence of primary tumor
Tis	Carcinoma in situ
T1,T2,T3,T4	Increasing size and/or local extent of the primary tumor

Regional Lymph Nodes (N)

Nx	Regional lymph nodes cannot be assessed
N0	No regional lymph node metastasis
N1,N2,N3	Increasing involvement of regional lymph nodes

Distant Metastasis (M)

Mx	Distant metastasis cannot be assessed
M0	No distant metastasis
M	Distant metastasis

From Green, F., et al. (Eds.). (2002). *AJCC cancer staging manual* (6th ed.). New York: Springer-Verlag.

stage. The TNM system is frequently used for many solid tumor types. In this system, "T" refers to the extent of the primary tumor, "N" refers to lymph node involvement, and "M" refers to the extent of metastasis (Box 6-1). A variety of other staging systems are used to describe the extent of cancers (such as CNS cancers, hematologic cancers, and malignant melanoma) that are not well described by the TNM system. Staging systems also provide a convenient shorthand notation that condenses lengthy descriptions into manageable terms for comparisons of treatments and prognoses.

Grading

Grading refers to the classification of the tumor cells. Grading systems seek to define the type of tissue from which the tumor originated and the degree to which the tumor cells retain the functional and histologic characteristics of the tissue of origin. Samples of cells to be used to establish the grade of a tumor may be obtained through cytology (examination of cells from tissue scrapings, body fluids, secretions, or washings), biopsy, or surgical excision.

This information helps the health care team predict the behavior and prognosis of various tumors. The tumor is assigned a numeric value ranging from I to IV (Box 6-2). Grade I tumors, also known as *well-differentiated tumors*, closely resemble the tissue of origin in structure and function.

From Polovich, M., Whitford, J. M., & Olsen, M. (2009). *Chemotherapy & biotherapy guidelines and recommendations for practice* (3rd ed.). Pittsburgh: Oncology Nursing Society.

BOX 6-2 Grading

GX   Grade cannot be assessed
G1   Well-differentiated (resembles tissue of origin)
G2   Moderately differentiated
G3   Poorly differentiated (little resemblance to tissue of origin)
G4   Undifferentiated (unable to tell tissue of origin)

Tumors that do not clearly resemble the tissue of origin in structure or function are described as *poorly differentiated* or *undifferentiated* and are assigned grade IV. These tumors tend to be more aggressive and less responsive to treatment than are well-differentiated tumors.

MANAGEMENT

The range of possible treatment goals may include complete eradication of malignant disease (**cure**), prolonged survival and containment of cancer cell growth (**control**), or relief of symptoms associated with the disease (**palliation**).

A number of factors are considered when determining a treatment plan, including the tumor type, stage, grade; functional or **performance status** of the patient; comorbidities; and organ function. After tumor type, performance status is the most important factor to consider when determining appropriate treatment (Polovich, Whitford, & Olsen, 2009). Performance status is used to quantify cancer patients' general well-being and ability to perform daily activities. Multiple modalities are commonly used in cancer treatment. A variety of approaches, including surgery, radiation therapy, chemotherapy, and targeted therapies, may be used at various times throughout treatment. Understanding the principles of each treatment modality and how they interrelate is important in understanding the rationale and goals of treatment.

The health care team, the patient, and the patient's family must have a clear understanding of the treatment options and goals. Open communication and support are vital as the patient and family periodically reassess treatment plans and goals when complications of therapy develop or disease progresses.

Surgery

Surgery is used for a variety of different reasons and at different times during the cancer trajectory. Surgery may be the primary method of treatment, or it may be prophylactic, palliative, or reconstructive. Diagnostic surgery is the definitive method of identifying the cellular characteristics that influence all treatment decisions.

Diagnostic Surgery

Diagnostic surgery, such as a **biopsy**, must be performed to obtain a tissue sample for analysis of cells suspected to be malignant. In most instances, the biopsy is taken from the actual tumor, but in some situations, it is necessary to biopsy lymph nodes near the suspicious tumor. Many cancers metastasize from the primary site to other areas of the body through the lymphatic circulation. Knowing whether adjacent lymph nodes contain tumor cells helps providers plan for systemic therapies instead of or in addition to surgery, to combat tumor cells that have gone beyond the primary tumor site.

Surgery As Primary Treatment

When surgery is the primary approach in treating cancer, the goal is to remove the entire tumor or as much as is feasible (a procedure sometimes called *debulking*) and any involved surrounding tissue, including regional lymph nodes.

Two common surgical approaches used for treating primary tumors are local and wide excisions.

- A *local excision* is warranted when the mass is small. It includes removal of the mass and a small margin of normal tissue that is easily accessible.
- *Wide* or *radical excisions* (*en bloc dissections*) include removal of the primary tumor, lymph nodes, adjacent involved structures, and surrounding tissues that may be at high risk for tumor spread. This surgical method can result in disfigurement and altered functioning. However, wide excisions are considered if the tumor can be removed completely and the chances of cure or control are good.

Prophylactic Surgery

Prophylactic surgery involves removing nonvital tissues or organs that are likely to develop cancer. Several factors are considered when providers and patients discuss possible prophylactic surgery; these include family history and genetic predisposition, presence or absence of symptoms, potential risks and benefits, ability to detect cancer at an early stage, and the patient's acceptance of the postoperative outcome.

Colectomy (surgical resection of the colon), mastectomy (removal of breast), and oophorectomy (removal of ovary[ies]) are examples of prophylactic surgeries. Recent developments in the ability to identify genetic markers indicative of a predisposition to develop some types of cancer may play a role in decisions concerning prophylactic surgeries. Several factors are considered when deciding to proceed with a prophylactic mastectomy, including a strong family history of breast cancer; positive *BRCA1* or *BRCA2* findings; an abnormal physical finding on breast examination, such as progressive nodularity and cystic disease; a proven history of breast cancer in the opposite breast; abnormal mammography findings; and abnormal biopsy results.

Because the long-term physiologic and psychological effects are unknown, prophylactic surgery is offered selectively to patients and discussed thoroughly with patients and families. Preoperative teaching and counseling, as well as long-term follow-up, are provided.

⚡ NURSING ALERT
Although only 5% to 6% of breast cancers are related to genetic mutations, two genes have been specifically identified with the majority of inherited breast cancers. BRCA-1 and BRCA-2 are clinical markers associated with the hereditary development of breast and ovarian cancer. Carriers of BRCA-1 (normally a tumor suppression gene) mutation have an 85% risk for developing breast cancer and a 45% risk for developing ovarian cancer by age 85 (Fischbach & Dunning, 2009). BRCA-2 is also a tumor suppressor gene; mutations in this gene are associated with breast cancer, particularly invasive ductal carcinomas, as well as cancers of the ovary, colon, prostate, pancreas, gallbladder, bile duct, stomach, and melanoma in some affected individuals (Brunicardi, Anderson, Billiar et al., 2010).

Palliative Surgery

When cure is not possible, the goals of treatment are to make the patient as comfortable as possible and to improve quality of life as defined by the patient. Palliative surgery is performed in an attempt to relieve complications of cancer, such as ulcerations, obstructions, hemorrhage, pain, and malignant effusions. Honest and informative communication with the patient and family about the risks, benefits, and goals of surgery is essential.

Nursing Management in Cancer Surgery

A multidisciplinary approach to patient care is essential during and after any type of surgery. The effects of surgery on the patient's body image, self-esteem, and functional abilities are addressed. If necessary, a plan for postoperative rehabilitation is made before the surgery is performed.

Patients undergoing surgery for cancer require general perioperative nursing care, as described in Chapter 5, along with specific care related to age, organ impairment, nutritional deficits, disorders of coagulation, and altered immunity that may increase the risk of postoperative complications. Combining other treatment methods, such as radiation and chemotherapy, with surgery also contributes to postoperative complications, such as infection, impaired wound healing, altered pulmonary or renal function, and the development of venous thromboembolism (VTE), also known as deep vein thrombosis (DVT). Some cancer types result in an increase in circulating procoagulants, which can significantly increase the risk for DVT.

⚡ NURSING ALERT
Approximately 50% of patients with DVT are asymptomatic. The nurse should inquire about an ache or pain in the calf, aggravated by standing or walking. In addition, it is important to assess for asymmetry of the limbs, as slight swelling may be noted as well as erythema and warmth of the involved extremity. Venous distention in the affected limb that persists despite elevation of the extremity may be noted. Patients may also present with low-grade fever and tachycardia.

The nurse must complete a thorough preoperative assessment for factors that may affect the patient undergoing the surgical procedure and target interventions to minimize the risk of complications.

Patients who are undergoing surgery for the diagnosis or treatment of cancer are often anxious about the surgical procedure, possible findings, postoperative limitations, changes in normal body functions, and prognosis. The patient and family require time, support, and assistance to deal with the possible changes and outcomes resulting from the surgery.

The nurse provides education and emotional support by assessing the needs of the patient and family and by discussing their fears and coping mechanisms with them. The nurse encourages the patient and family to take an active role in decision-making when possible. If the patient or family asks about the results of diagnostic testing and surgical procedures, the nurse's response is guided by the information the primary care provider has previously conveyed to the patient and family. The patient and family may also ask the nurse to explain and clarify information that the provider initially provided, but that they did not grasp because they were anxious at the time. It is important that the nurse communicate frequently with providers and other members of the health care team to be certain that the information provided is consistent.

After surgery, the nurse assesses the patient's responses to the surgery and monitors the patient for possible complications, such as infection, bleeding, thrombophlebitis, wound dehiscence, fluid and electrolyte imbalance, and organ dysfunction. The nurse also provides for the patient's comfort. Postoperative teaching addresses wound care, activity, nutrition, and medication information.

Plans for discharge, follow-up and home care, and treatment are initiated as early as possible to ensure continuity of care from hospital to home or from a cancer referral center to the patient's local hospital and health care provider. Patients and families are also encouraged to use community resources, such as the American Cancer Society, for support and information.

Radiation Therapy

In **radiation therapy**, ionizing radiation is used to interrupt cellular growth. More than half of patients with cancer receive a form of radiation therapy at some point during treatment. Radiation may be used to cure the cancer, as in Hodgkin's lymphoma, testicular seminomas, thyroid carcinomas, localized cancers of the head and neck, and cancers of the uterine cervix. Radiation therapy may also be used to control malignant disease when a tumor cannot be removed surgically or when local nodal metastasis is present, or it can be used prophylactically to prevent leukemic infiltration to the brain or spinal cord.

Palliative radiation therapy is used to relieve the symptoms of metastatic disease, especially when the cancer has

spread to brain, bone, or soft tissue, or to treat oncologic emergencies, such as superior vena cava syndrome (SVCS) or spinal cord compression.

Two types of ionizing radiation—electromagnetic rays (X-rays and gamma rays) and particles (electrons [beta particles], protons, neutrons, and alpha particles)—can lead to tissue disruption. Radiation disrupts malignant cell proliferation through the alteration in DNA structure. Ionizing radiation breaks the strands of the DNA helix, leading to cell death. Ionizing radiation can also ionize constituents of body fluids, especially water, leading to the formation of free radicals and irreversibly damaging DNA. If the DNA is incapable of repair, the cell may die immediately, or it may initiate apoptosis (Witt, 2005).

Cells are most vulnerable to the disruptive effects of radiation during DNA synthesis and mitosis. Therefore, those body tissues that undergo frequent cell division are most sensitive to radiation therapy. These tissues include bone marrow, lymphatic tissue, epithelium of the GI tract, hair cells, and gonads. Slower-growing tissues and tissues at rest are relatively radioresistant (less sensitive to the effects of radiation). Such tissues include muscle, cartilage, and connective tissues.

A radiosensitive tumor is one that can be destroyed by a dose of radiation that still allows for cell regeneration in the normal tissue. Tumors that are well oxygenated also appear to be more sensitive to radiation. In theory, therefore, radiation therapy may be enhanced if more oxygen can be delivered to tumors. In addition, if the radiation is delivered when most tumor cells are cycling through the cell cycle, the number of cancer cells destroyed (cell kill) is maximal (Witt, 2005). Certain chemicals, including chemotherapy agents, act as radiosensitizers and sensitize more hypoxic (oxygen-poor) tumors to the effects of radiation therapy.

Radiation Delivery

Radiation is delivered to tumor sites by external or internal means.

External Radiation

If external radiation therapy is used, one of several delivery methods may be chosen, depending on the depth of the tumor. Kilovoltage therapy devices deliver the maximal radiation dose to superficial lesions, such as lesions of the skin and breast, whereas linear accelerators and betatron machines produce higher-energy X-rays and deliver their dosage to deeper structures with less harm to the skin and less scattering of radiation within the body tissues.

Internal Radiation

Internal radiation implantation, or **brachytherapy**, delivers a high dose of radiation to a localized area. The specific radioisotope for implantation is selected on the basis of its half-life, which is the time it takes for half of its radioactivity to decay. This internal radiation can be implanted by means of needles, seeds, beads, or catheters into body cavities (e.g.,

vagina, abdomen, pleura) or interstitial compartments (e.g., breast). With internal radiation therapy, the farther the target tissue is from the radiation source, the lower the dosage. This spares the noncancerous tissue from the radiation dose and toxicity. Brachytherapy may also be administered orally, as with the isotope iodine-131, which is used to treat thyroid carcinomas.

INTRACAVITARY RADIATION. Intracavitary radioisotopes are frequently used to treat gynecologic cancers. In these malignancies, the radioisotopes are inserted into applicators specially positioned in the cervix and vagina, after the position is verified by X-ray. These radioisotopes remain in place for a prescribed time period and then are removed. The patient is maintained on bed rest and log-rolled to prevent displacement of the intracavitary delivery device. The head of the bed must not be elevated greater than 15 degrees due to the risk of perforating the uterus with the appliance. An indwelling urinary catheter is inserted to ensure that the bladder remains empty. This minimizes the exposure of the bladder to radiation. Low-residue diets and antidiarrheal agents, such as diphenoxylate (Lomotil), are provided to prevent bowel movements during therapy to prevent displacement of the radioisotopes. Pain management is also a priority for these patients, as the presence of the appliance can be painful. Patient-controlled analgesia is a common method used for pain management in this population.

SAFETY. Because patients receiving internal radiation emit radiation while the implant is in place, contacts with the health care team are guided by principles of *time, distance,* and *shielding* to minimize exposure of personnel to radiation. As the amount of *time* with the patient increases, the nurses' exposure to radiation increases. The goal of nursing care for this population is to deliver safe, efficient care that meets the patients' needs in the shortest amount of time; in general, no more than 30 minutes per 8-hour shift (Swearingen, 2006). The *principle of distance* means that the closer you are to the patient, the greater the radiation exposure. When not providing direct care (e.g., when talking with the patient), stand 6 feet from the patient to minimize exposure. Organize activities outside the room when possible; examples include meal and medication preparation. *Shielding* refers to the use of a lead shield to buffer the exposure to radiation. Often, the rooms that patients stay in may be lead-lined, or portable lead shields or aprons may be available to minimize exposure.

Other safety precautions used in caring for a patient receiving brachytherapy include assigning the patient to a private room, posting appropriate notices about radiation safety precautions, having staff members wear dosimeter badges, ensuring that pregnant staff members are not assigned to the patient's care, prohibiting visits by children or pregnant visitors, limiting visits from others to 30 minutes daily, and seeing that visitors maintain a 6-foot distance from the radiation source.

Nurses must be prepared to respond to a radiation emergency. If the radiation implant becomes dislodged, the nurses' first priority is to ensure the safety of the patient. Metal forceps and a lead-lined container should be available in the room. The nurse can use the forceps to pick up the radiation source and place the source into the lead-lined container. Once the source is contained, the radiation safety officer should be contacted immediately. The patient, nurse, and room will then be monitored for radioactivity using a Geiger counter. The staff exposed should also go to their Occupational Health department for an evaluation. Nurses should refer to their institution's radiation safety committee's guidelines for specific measures.

Radiation Dosage

The radiation dosage is dependent on the sensitivity of the target tissues to radiation and on the tumor size. The lethal tumor dose is defined as the dose that will eradicate 95% of the tumor yet preserve normal tissue. With external radiation, the total radiation dose is delivered over several weeks to allow healthy tissue to repair and to achieve greater cell kill by exposing more cells to the radiation as they begin active cell division. Repeated radiation treatments over time (fractionated doses) also allow for the periphery of the tumor to be reoxygenated repeatedly, because tumors shrink from the outside inward. This increases the radiosensitivity of the tumor, thereby increasing tumor cell death (Witt, 2005).

Toxicity

Toxicity of radiation therapy is localized to the region being irradiated. Toxicity may be increased if concomitant chemotherapy is administered. Acute local reactions occur when normal cells in the treatment area are also destroyed and cellular death exceeds cellular regeneration. Altered skin integrity is a common effect and can include **alopecia** (hair loss), erythema, and shedding of skin (desquamation). Re-epithelialization occurs after treatments have been completed.

Alterations in oral mucosa secondary to radiation therapy include **stomatitis**, **xerostomia** (dryness of the mouth), change and loss of taste, and decreased salivation. The entire GI mucosa may be involved and esophageal irritation with chest pain and dysphagia may result. Anorexia, nausea, vomiting, and diarrhea may occur if the stomach or colon is in the irradiated field. Symptoms subside and GI re-epithelialization occurs after treatments have been completed.

Bone marrow cells proliferate rapidly, and if sites containing bone marrow (e.g., the iliac crest, sternum) are included in the radiation field, anemia, leukopenia (decreased WBCs), and **thrombocytopenia** (a decrease in platelets) may result. The patient is then at increased risk for infection and bleeding until blood cell counts return to normal. Chronic anemia may occur commonly due to the cumulative effects of radiation and may be evidenced by shortness of breath, dizziness, fatigue, decreased oxygen saturation, and decreased activity tolerance (Hinkel, Li, & Sherman, 2010).

Certain systemic side effects are also commonly experienced by patients receiving radiation therapy. These manifestations, which are generalized, include fatigue, malaise, and anorexia. These symptoms may be secondary to substances released when tumor cells break down. The effects are temporary, but may take weeks to subside following the cessation of treatment.

Late effects of radiation therapy may also occur in various body tissues. These effects are chronic, usually produce fibrotic changes secondary to a decreased vascular supply, and are irreversible. These late effects can be most severe when they involve vital organs such as the lungs, heart, CNS, and bladder. Toxicities may intensify when radiation is combined with other treatment modalities.

Nursing Management in Radiation Therapy
Providing Patient Education

Patients receiving radiation therapy, and their families, often have questions and concerns about its safety. To answer questions and allay fears about the effects of radiation on the tumor and on the patient's normal tissues and organs, the nurse explains the procedure for delivering radiation and describes the equipment, the duration of the procedure (often minutes only), the possible need for immobilizing the patient during the procedure, and the sensory experience, including the absence of pain, during the procedure.

If a radioactive implant is used, the nurse informs the patient and family about the restrictions placed on visitors and health care personnel and other radiation precautions. The patient also should understand his or her own role before, during, and after the procedure. Patients with seed implants may be able to return home because the radiation exposure to others is minimal. Information about any precautions, if needed, is provided to the patient and family members to ensure safety. See Chapter 33 and 34 for further discussion of radiation treatment for gynecologic cancers and prostatic cancer respectively.

Protecting Skin and Oral Mucosa

The nurse regularly assesses the patient's skin, oral mucosa, nutritional status, and general feeling of well-being. The nurse must educate the patient on early identification of symptoms and self-care guidelines.

The skin in the radiation field must be protected from irritation, and the patient is instructed to avoid using ointments, lotions, or powders on the treated area. The patient is instructed to gently cleanse the skin with a mild soap using fingertips instead of a washcloth and gently pat the area dry. If temporary skin markings were applied to facilitate external radiation treatments, warn the patient not to remove the markings. Emollients such as Aquaphor® may be used as directed by the radiation oncologist to soothe and moisturize irritated skin. However, even approved emollients should not be used up to 4 hours before the

BOX 6-3 **Patient Education**

Mouth Care for Patients Receiving Head and Neck Radiation Therapy

- Use a bland mouth rinse (such as salt water or baking soda and water) often. Gently swish and gargle with this before and after meals and at bedtime. You may use it more often as needed to soothe a dry or sore mouth. To make the mouth rinse: Mix 1 teaspoon of baking soda with 16 ounces of water; or 1 teaspoon of table salt with 16 ounces of water.
- Use fluoride preparations daily as instructed by your dentist. Brush your teeth using a soft bristled toothbrush 3 to 4 times a day. Floss your teeth daily.
- Dentures should be left out if they are irritating to the gums or are poorly fitting.
- Avoid alcoholic beverages, tobacco, highly spiced foods, and commercial mouthwashes containing alcohol.
- Once you begin to experience pain or sensitivity in your mouth, avoid foods and drinks that are too hot, or too cold. Room temperature is best. Avoid carbonated drinks such as soda or sparkling water.
- Avoid acidic fruits and juices like tomato, orange, lemon, grapefruit, and pineapple. Avoid rough, crunchy foods such as pretzels, nuts, and chips.
- Inspect your mouth daily and report any changes to your nurse or doctor.
- For a dry mouth, drink 8 ounces of water or other noncaffeinated beverage every 2 to 3 hours. Keep a cool mist humidifier running, especially at night.
- Moisturize lips frequently with water-based moisturizer.

BOX 6-4 **Investigational Antineoplastic Therapies and Clinical Trials**

Evaluation of the effectiveness and toxic potential of promising new modalities for preventing, diagnosing, and treating cancer is accomplished through clinical trials. Before new chemotherapy agents are approved for clinical use, they are subjected to rigorous and lengthy evaluations to identify beneficial effects, adverse effects, and safety.

- *Phase I* clinical trials determine optimal dosing, scheduling, toxicity, and pharmacokinetics.
- *Phase II* trials determine effectiveness with specific tumor types and further define toxicities. Participants in these early trials are most often those who have not responded to standard forms of treatment. Because phase I and II trials may be viewed as last-chance efforts, patients and families are fully informed about the experimental nature of the trial therapies. Although it is hoped that investigational therapy will effectively treat the disease, the purpose of early-phase trials is to gather information concerning maximal tolerated doses, adverse effects, and effects of the antineoplastic agents on tumor growth.
- *Phase III* clinical trials establish the effectiveness of new medications or procedures as compared with conventional approaches. Nurses may assist in the recruitment, consent, and education processes for patients who participate. In many cases, nurses are instrumental in monitoring adherence, assisting patients to adhere to the parameters of the trial, and documenting data describing patients' responses. The physical and emotional needs of patients in clinical trials are addressed in much the same way as those of patients who receive standard forms of cancer treatment.
- *Phase IV* testing further investigates medications in terms of new uses, dosing schedule, and toxicities.

treatment time. Lotions and emollients may amplify the effects of the radiation on the skin. Electric razors should be used for shaving. Patients should be instructed to avoid constrictive clothing that may irritate skin. Loose, cotton clothing is usually most comfortable. Other instructions include avoiding sun exposure, heating lamps, heating pads, and ice packs to the area being treated—these are all potential sources of thermal injury.

Gentle oral hygiene is essential to remove debris, prevent irritation, and promote healing (see Box 6-3 for detailed instructions). If systemic symptoms, such as weakness and fatigue, occur, the patient may need assistance with activities of daily living and personal hygiene (see Nursing Process later in the chapter). In addition, the nurse offers reassurance by explaining that these symptoms are a result of the treatment and do not represent deterioration or progression of the disease.

Chemotherapy

In **chemotherapy**, antineoplastic agents are used in an attempt to destroy tumor cells by interfering with cellular functions, including replication. Chemotherapy is used primarily to treat systemic disease rather than localized lesions that are amenable to surgery or radiation. Chemotherapy may be combined with surgery, radiation therapy, or both, to reduce tumor size preoperatively (neoadjuvant), to destroy any remaining tumor cells postoperatively (adjuvant), or to treat hematologic malignancies such as lymphoma and leukemia. The goals of chemotherapy (cure, control, palliation) define the medications to be used and the aggressiveness of the treatment plan. Chemotherapy may also be delivered in the setting of a clinical trial (see Box 6-4).

Cell Kill and the Cell Cycle

Each time a tumor is exposed to a chemotherapeutic agent, a percentage of tumor cells (20% to 99%, depending on dosage) are destroyed. Repeated doses of chemotherapy are necessary over a prolonged period to achieve regression

of the tumor. Eradication of 100% of the tumor is almost impossible. Instead, the goal of treatment is eradication of enough of the tumor so that the remaining tumor cells can be destroyed by the body's immune system.

Actively dividing cells within a tumor are the most sensitive to chemotherapeutic agents. Nondividing cells capable of future proliferation (cells in the G_0 phase, see Fig. 6-2) are the least sensitive to antineoplastic medications and consequently are potentially dangerous. However, the nondividing cells must also be destroyed to eradicate a cancer. As dividing cells are killed by chemotherapy, nondividing cells are recruited into the cell cycle to divide, in order to replace the dying cells. Repeated cycles of chemotherapy must be used to kill these newly dividing cells.

Chemotherapy drugs are often given in combination (referred to as a *protocol* or *regimen*). The goal of combination chemotherapy is to overcome drug resistance and take advantage of the synergistic effects of some drugs while minimizing toxicity. Considerations for combination chemotherapy include the use of drugs with different mechanisms of action and different side effect profiles.

Classification of Chemotherapeutic Agents

Chemotherapeutic agents may be classified by their relationship to the cell cycle. Certain chemotherapeutic agents that are specific to certain phases of the cell cycle are termed *cell cycle–specific agents*. These agents destroy cells that are actively reproducing by means of the cell cycle; most affect cells in the S phase by interfering with DNA and RNA synthesis. Other agents, such as the vinca or plant alkaloids, are specific to the M phase, where they halt mitotic spindle formation. Chemotherapeutic agents that act independently of the cell cycle phases are termed *cell cycle–nonspecific agents*. These agents usually have a prolonged effect on cells, leading to cellular damage or death. Many treatment plans combine cell cycle–specific and cell cycle–nonspecific agents to increase the number of vulnerable tumor cells killed during a treatment period (Polovich, Whitford, & Olsen, 2009).

Chemotherapeutic agents are also classified by chemical group, each with a different mechanism of action. These include the alkylating agents, nitrosoureas, antimetabolites, antitumor antibiotics, plant alkaloids, hormonal agents, and miscellaneous agents. The classification, mechanism of action, common drugs, and common side effects of selected antineoplastic agents are listed in Table 6-3.

Administration of Chemotherapeutic Agents

Chemotherapeutic agents may be administered in the hospital, clinic, or home setting by a variety of routes including topical, oral, IV, intramuscular, subcutaneous, arterial, intracavitary, and intrathecal routes. Intrathecal chemotherapy is the administration of medication into the cerebrospinal fluid. This can be accomplished through a lumbar puncture or

through the placement of an intraventricular catheter with the tip lying in the fourth ventricle of the brain. This route is used to treat or prevent CNS metastasis. The route of administration usually depends on the type of agent; the required dose; and the type, location, and extent of tumor being treated. Guidelines for the administration of chemotherapy have been developed by the Oncology Nursing Society (ONS) (Polovich, Whitford, & Olsen, 2009). The use of oral agents to treat cancer is increasing. Patient education and consistent monitoring of patient adherence is essential to maximize safety if chemotherapy is administered in the home.

Dosage

Dosage of antineoplastic agents is based primarily on the patient's total body surface area, previous response to chemotherapy or radiation therapy, function of major organ systems, and performance status.

> **⚠ N U R S I N G   A L E R T**
>
> *Because of the high potential for error related to chemotherapy dosing, the standard expectation is that two nurses verify the chemotherapy doses to ensure accuracy. The Mosteller Equation for calculation of body surface area is the most commonly used formula in the United States: square root of (height in cm × weight in kg) ÷ 3600*
>
> $$\sqrt{\frac{height\,(cm) \times weight\,(kg)}{3600}}$$

Infusion-Related Events

Nurses administering chemotherapy must carefully assess the patient for infusion-related events such as hypersensitivity and extravasation. Specific assessments vary based on the medication being administered (see Table 6-3). Hypersensitivity reactions (HSRs) occur in 5% to 15% of patients receiving chemotherapy and biotherapy agents. The risk of hypersensitivity varies based on the type of agent being administered. Prompt recognition of the symptoms of hypersensitivity reactions and quick intervention are critical roles of oncology nurses who administer these agents. Common symptoms observed in patients experiencing hypersensitivity reactions range from flushing, rash, and anxiety to bronchospasm and hemodynamic collapse. Nursing response to HSRs includes stopping the infusion as soon as symptoms are observed; monitoring vital signs; maintaining a patent airway; administering oxygen as needed; maintaining a patent IV with running normal saline; administering emergency medications such as antihistamines, epinephrine, and corticosteroids as ordered; and providing emotional support to the patient. In most cases, the treatment can be safely resumed after the resolution of symptoms by infusing the agent at a slower rate (Van Gerpen, 2009; Polovich, Whitford, & Olsen, 2009).

EXTRAVASATION. Special care must be taken whenever IV vesicant agents are administered. **Vesicants** are agents

TABLE
6-3 Selected Antineoplastic Agents

Drug Class and Examples	Mechanism of Action	Cell Cycle Specificity	Most Common Side Effects
Alkylating Agents Busulfan, carboplatin, chlorambucil, cisplatin, cyclophosphamide, dacarbazine, ifosfamide, melphalan, nitrogen mustard, oxaliplatin, thiotepa	Alter DNA structure by misreading DNA code, initiating breaks in the DNA molecule, cross-linking DNA strands	Cell cycle–nonspecific	Bone marrow suppression, nausea, vomiting, cystitis (cyclophosphamide, ifosfamide), stomatitis, alopecia, gonadal suppression, renal toxicity (cisplatin)
Nitrosoureas Carmustine (BCNU), lomustine (CCNU), semustine (methyl CCNU), streptozocin	Similar to the alkylating agents; cross the blood–brain barrier	Cell cycle–nonspecific	Delayed and cumulative myelosuppression, especially thrombocytopenia; nausea, vomiting
Topoisomerase I Inhibitors Irinotecan, topotecan	Induce breaks in the DNA strand by binding to enzyme topoisomerase I, preventing cells from dividing	Cell cycle–specific (S phase)	Bone marrow suppression, diarrhea, nausea, vomiting, hepatotoxicity
Antimetabolites 5-Azacytadine, capecitabine (Xeloda), cytarabine, fludarabine, 5-fluorouracil (5-FU), floxuridine, gemcitabine, hydroxyurea, Leustatin, 6-mercaptopurine, methotrexate, pentostatin, 6-thioguanine	Interfere with the biosynthesis of metabolites or nucleic acids necessary for RNA and DNA synthesis	Cell cycle–specific (S phase)	Nausea, vomiting, diarrhea, bone marrow suppression, stomatitis, renal toxicity (methotrexate), hepatotoxicity
Antitumor Antibiotics Bleomycin, dactinomycin, daunorubicin, doxorubicin (Adriamycin), idarubicin, mitomycin, mitoxantrone, plicamycin	Interfere with DNA synthesis by binding DNA; prevent RNA synthesis	Cell cycle–nonspecific	Bone marrow suppression, nausea, vomiting, alopecia, anorexia, cardiac toxicity (doxorubicin, daunorubicin, idarubicin, mitoxantrone)
Mitotic Spindle Poisons *Plant alkaloids:* etoposide, teniposide, vinblastine, vincristine (VCR), vindesine, vinorelbine *Taxanes:* paclitaxel, docetaxel	Arrest metaphase by inhibiting mitotic tubular formation (spindle); inhibit DNA and protein synthesis Arrest metaphase by inhibiting tubulin depolymerization	Cell cycle–specific (M phase) Cell cycle–specific (M phase)	Bone marrow suppression (mild with VCR), neuropathies (VCR), stomatitis Bradycardia, hypersensitivity reactions, bone marrow suppression, alopecia, neuropathies
Hormonal Agents Androgens and antiandrogens, estrogens and antiestrogens, progestins and antiprogestins, aromatase inhibitors, luteinizing hormone–releasing hormone analogues, steroids	Bind to hormone receptor sites that alter cellular growth; block binding of estrogens to receptor sites (antiestrogens); inhibit RNA synthesis; suppress aromatase of P450 system, which decreases estrogen level	Cell cycle–nonspecific	Hypercalcemia, increased appetite, masculinization, feminization, sodium and fluid retention, nausea, vomiting, hot flashes, vaginal dryness
Miscellaneous Agents Asparaginase, procarbazine	Unknown or too complex to categorize	Varies	Anorexia, nausea, vomiting, bone marrow suppression, hepatotoxicity, anaphylaxis, hypotension, altered glucose metabolism

that, if deposited into the subcutaneous tissue (**extravasation**), cause tissue ulceration and necrosis, and damage to underlying tendons, nerves, and blood vessels. Although the complete mechanism of tissue destruction is unclear, it is known that the pH of many antineoplastic drugs is responsible for the severe inflammatory reaction as well as the ability of some of these drugs (e.g., anthracyclines) to bind to tissue DNA. Sloughing and ulceration of the tissue may be so severe that skin grafting may be necessary. The full extent of tissue damage may take several weeks to become apparent. Some examples of medications classified as vesicants include dacarbazine, doxorubicin (Adriamycin), nitrogen mustard, mitomycin, vincristine, and vinorelbine.

Only specially trained providers should administer vesicants. Careful selection of peripheral veins, skilled venipuncture, and careful administration of medications are essential.

NURSING ALERT
Indications of extravasation during administration of vesicant agents include:
- *Absence of blood return from the IV catheter*
- *Resistance to flow of IV fluid*
- *Swelling, pain, or redness at the site, or if using a central venous access device, pain in the upper arm, upper back, chest, neck, or jaw*

If any one of the above signs is present, extravasation should be suspected. The medication administration should be stopped immediately. The nurse should attempt to aspirate any residual drug from the IV line. If an antidote is indicated, the nurse should administer it immediately. Selection of the neutralizing solution or antidote depends on the extravasated agent. Examples of neutralizing solutions include sodium thiosulfate, hyaluronidase, and sodium bicarbonate. Ice is applied to the site (unless the extravasated vesicant is a vinca alkaloid), and the patient is educated to avoid further trauma to the site (including heat, constrictive clothing, sunlight) and to report changes in the skin integrity and appearance of the extravasation site to the provider immediately. Recommendations and guidelines for managing vesicant extravasation have been issued by individual medication manufacturers, pharmacies, and the ONS, and they differ for each medication.

If frequent, prolonged administration of antineoplastic vesicants is anticipated, central venous access devices may be inserted to promote safety during medication administration and reduce problems with access to the circulatory system (Figs. 6-3 and 6-4). Complications associated with their use include infection and thrombosis.

Protecting Caregivers
Nurses involved in handling chemotherapeutic agents may be exposed to low doses of the agents by direct contact, inhalation, or ingestion. Urinalyses of personnel repeatedly exposed to cytotoxic agents have demonstrated the presence of these agents. Although long-term studies of nurses who handle chemotherapeutic agents have not been conducted,

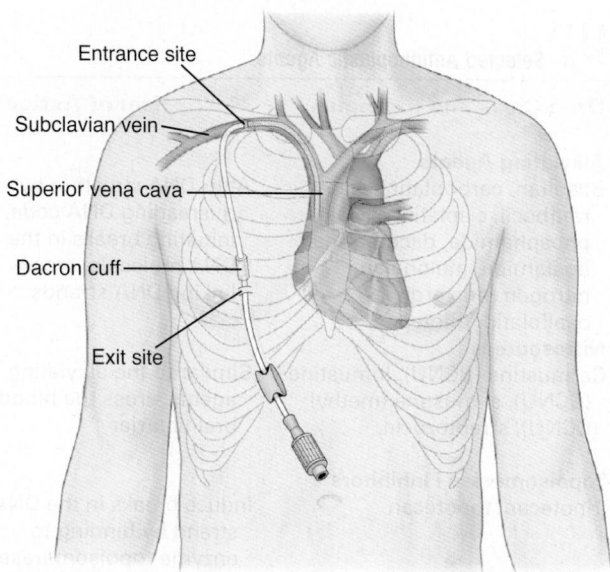

FIGURE 6-3 Right atrial catheter. The right atrial catheter is inserted into the subclavian vein and advanced until its tip lies in the superior vena cava just above the right atrium. The proximal end is then tunneled from the entry site through the subcutaneous tissue of the chest wall and brought out through an exit site on the chest. The Dacron cuff anchors the catheter in place and serves as a barrier to infection.

chemotherapeutic agents are associated with secondary formation of cancers and chromosomal abnormalities. In addition, nausea, vomiting, dizziness, alopecia, and nasal mucosal ulcerations have been reported in health care personnel who have handled chemotherapeutic agents (Polovich, Whitford, & Olsen, 2009). In an effort to minimize the exposure of health care workers to hazardous substances, the Occupational Safety and Health Administration, ONS, hospitals, and other health care agencies have developed specific precautions for health care providers involved in the preparation and administration of chemotherapy (Box 6-5).

Toxicity
Cells with rapid growth rates (e.g., epithelium, bone marrow, hair follicles, sperm) are most susceptible to the effects of chemotherapy.

GI System
Nausea and vomiting are the most common side effects of chemotherapy and may persist for as long as 24 to 48 hours after its administration. Delayed nausea and vomiting may persist for up to 1 week after chemotherapy. The vomiting centers in the brain are stimulated by the following mechanisms:

- Activation of the receptors found in the chemoreceptor trigger zone (CTZ) of the medulla by serotonin, substance P, and other neurotransmitters such as dopamine
- Stimulation of peripheral autonomic pathways (GI tract and pharynx)
- Stimulation of the vestibular pathways (inner ear imbalances, labyrinth input)

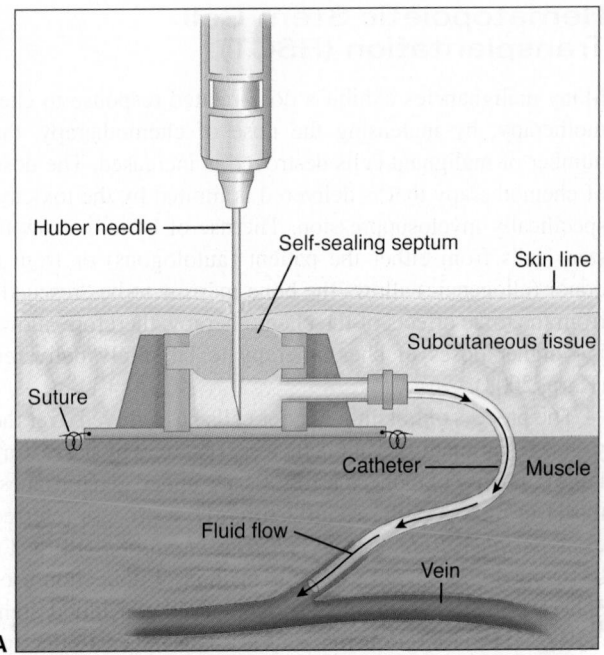

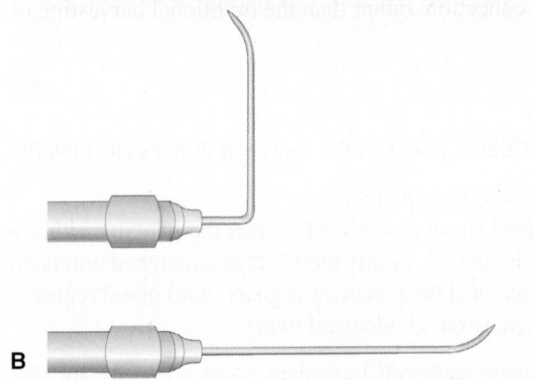

FIGURE 6-4 Implanted vascular access device. (**A**) A schematic diagram of an implanted vascular access device used for administration of medications, fluids, blood products, and nutrition. The self-sealing septum permits repeated puncture by Huber needles without damage or leakage. (**B**) Two Huber needles used to enter the implanted vascular port. The 90-degree needle is used to access the port.

- Cognitive stimulation (CNS disease, anticipatory nausea, and vomiting)
- A combination of these factors

Medications that can decrease nausea and vomiting include serotonin antagonists, such as ondansetron, granisetron, dolasetron, and palonosetron, which block serotonin receptors of the GI tract and CTZ, and dopaminergic blockers, such as metoclopramide (Reglan), which block dopamine receptors of the CTZ. Newer agents include neurokinin-1 receptor antagonists (e.g., aprepitant [Emend]), which block the activity of substance P (Lohr, 2008; Tipton, McDaniel, & Barbour et al., 2007). Nausea and vomiting involve multiple pathways; therefore, corticosteroids, phenothiazines, sedatives, and antihistamines are helpful, especially when used in combination with serotonin blockers to

---

BOX 6-5

Safety in Administering Chemotherapy

Safety recommendations from the Occupational Safety and Health Administration (OSHA), Oncology Nursing Society (ONS), hospitals, and other health care agencies for the preparation and handling of antineoplastic agents include:

- Use a biologic safety cabinet for the preparation of all chemotherapy agents.
- Wear gloves that have been tested with chemotherapeutic agents when handling antineoplastic drugs and the excretions of patients who received chemotherapy.
- Wear disposable, nonabsorbent long-sleeved gowns with cuffs when preparing and administering chemotherapy agents.
- Use Luer-Lok fittings on all IV tubing used to deliver chemotherapy.
- Dispose of all equipment used in chemotherapy preparation and administration in appropriate, leakproof, puncture-proof containers.
- Dispose of all chemotherapy wastes as hazardous materials.

When followed, these precautions greatly minimize the risk of exposure to chemotherapy agents.

---

provide improved antiemetic protection. Delayed nausea and vomiting that occur longer than 48 to 72 hours after chemotherapy are troublesome for some patients. To minimize discomfort, antiemetic medications may be necessary for the first week at home after chemotherapy.

Hematopoietic System

Most chemotherapeutic agents cause **myelosuppression** (depression of bone marrow function), resulting in decreased production of blood cells. Myelosuppression decreases the number of WBCs (leukopenia), red blood cells (RBCs) (anemia), and platelets (thrombocytopenia) and increases the risk of infection and bleeding. Depression of these cells is a common reason for decreasing the dose of the chemotherapeutic agents. Monitoring blood cell counts frequently is essential, because it allows strategies to be implemented to protect patients from infection and injury.

Other agents, called colony-stimulating factors (granulocyte colony-stimulating factor [G-CSF], granulocyte-macrophage colony-stimulating factor [GM-CSF], and erythropoietin [EPO]), can be administered after chemotherapy. G-CSF and GM-CSF stimulate the bone marrow to produce WBCs, including neutrophils, at an accelerated rate, thus decreasing the duration of **neutropenia**. The G-CSFs decrease the episodes of infection and reduce the need for antibiotics, allowing for timelier cycling of chemotherapy with less need for dose reductions.

Erythropoietin stimulating agents (ESAs) stimulate RBC production, thus decreasing the symptoms of chronic anemia

and reducing the need for blood transfusions (Savona & Silver, 2008). Recent evidence has demonstrated that the use of ESAs in certain malignancies, including head and neck, non-small cell lung, lymphoid, cervical, and breast cancers, has resulted in decreased survival rates. Based on this data, the use of ESAs is not recommended in those diseases when the goal is cure. Other studies have demonstrated an increase in cardiac events, including cerebrovascular events and myocardial infarction, when hemoglobin (Hgb) targets of greater than 12 mg/dL were used. Specific guidelines are now available to improve the safety of ESA administration, including holding ESAs for Hgb levels greater than 10 mg/dL, assessing the Hgb and Hct prior to each ESA dose, and discontinuing ESA use in patients who do not achieve a significant benefit within the first 8 weeks of administration (Arbuckle, Griffit, Iacovelli et al., 2008; Savona & Silver, 2008).

Reproductive System

Ovarian and testicular function can be affected by chemotherapeutic agents, resulting in possible sterility. Abnormal ovulation, early menopause, or permanent sterility may occur. In men, temporary or permanent azoospermia (absence of spermatozoa) may develop. Reproductive cells may be damaged during treatment, resulting in chromosomal abnormalities in offspring. Banking of sperm is recommended for males of reproductive age before treatments are initiated. Sperm banking requires daily sperm collections for 2 to 3 days in order to collect a sufficient sample. Women should be counseled regarding options for fertility preservation prior to initiating treatment. Embryo cryopreservation is the most well established method for fertility preservation. Oocyte cryopreservation and cryopreservation of ovarian tissue are considered investigational (Lee, Schover, Partridge, et al., 2006). Fertility preservation options for women require more time (2 to 6 weeks) and may result in treatment delays, which may impact overall outcomes (Polovich, Whitford, & Olsen, 2009).

Prior to initiating treatment, patients and their partners need to be informed about potential changes in reproductive and sexual function resulting from chemotherapy. They are advised to use reliable methods of birth control while receiving chemotherapy, and not to assume that sterility has resulted.

Nursing Management in Chemotherapy

Nurses play an important role in assessing and managing many of the problems experienced by patients undergoing chemotherapy. Chemotherapeutic agents have systemic effects on normal cells as well as malignant ones, which means that these problems are often widespread, affecting many body systems. Nurses must recognize the potential side effects specific to the drug or drug(s) that the patient is receiving and target assessments based on expected side effects. Common side effects seen with chemotherapy include myelosuppression, alopecia, nausea and vomiting, anorexia, and fatigue. The nursing care specific to these side effects is discussed in the nursing process section.

Hematopoietic Stem Cell Transplantation (HSCT)

Many malignancies exhibit a dose-related response to chemotherapy; by increasing the dose of chemotherapy, the number of malignant cells destroyed is increased. The dose of chemotherapy that is delivered is limited by the toxicity, specifically myelosuppression. The use of bone marrow or stem cells from either the patient (autologous) or from a donor (allogeneic) allows the bone marrow to be "rescued" from the toxic effects of the chemotherapy, therefore allowing higher doses of chemotherapy to be safely delivered (Karp, 2008).

The process of obtaining donor cells has evolved over the years. Traditionally, donor cells were obtained by harvesting large amounts of bone marrow tissue under general anesthesia in the operating room. Currently, a process referred to as *peripheral blood stem cell transplantation* (PBSCT), has gained widespread use. This method of collection uses apheresis methods to collect donor peripheral blood stem cells (PBSCs) for reinfusion. This is a safe and cost-effective means of collection, rather than the traditional harvesting of marrow.

Types

Types of PBSCT based on the source of donor cells include:

- Autologous (from patient)
- Allogeneic (from a donor other than the patient); either a related donor (i.e., family member) or a matched unrelated donor (national bone marrow registry, cord blood registry)
- Syngeneic (from an identical twin)

Allogeneic stem cell transplant, used primarily for disease of the bone marrow, depends on the availability of a human leukocyte antigen–matched donor. An advantage of allogeneic PBSCT is that the transplanted cells should be immunologically intolerant of a patient's malignancy. The donor's healthy immune system is able to recognize the patient's malignancy as foreign and kill any remaining tumor cells. This is referred to as the **graft-versus-tumor effect**. Allogeneic PBSCT may involve either myeloablative (high-dose) or nonmyeloablative (reduced-intensity) chemotherapy. In myeloablative allogeneic PBSCT, the recipient must undergo high doses of chemotherapy and possibly total body irradiation to destroy all existing bone marrow and malignant disease. The harvested donor marrow or PBSCs are infused intravenously, similar to a blood transfusion, into the recipients. The infused cells travel to the bone marrow, where the cells mature and proliferate. When the new bone marrow becomes functional, producing RBCs, WBCs, and platelets, engraftment is considered complete (2 to 4 weeks).

In nonmyeloablative allogeneic PBSCT, the chemotherapy doses are lower and are aimed at suppressing the recipient's immune system to allow engraftment of donor bone marrow or PBSCs. The lower doses of chemotherapy create less organ

toxicity and thus can be offered to older patients or those with underlying organ dysfunction, for whom high-dose chemotherapy would be prohibitive. Once the transplanted donor cells begin to grow and reproduce, a process referred to as engraftment, a graft-versus-disease effect results in which the donor's healthy immune system keeps the patient's cancer cells from growing (Storb, 2009).

Before engraftment, patients are at high risk for infection, sepsis, and bleeding. Side effects of the high-dose chemotherapy and total body irradiation can be acute and chronic. Acute side effects include alopecia, hemorrhagic cystitis (inflammation of the bladder), nausea, vomiting, diarrhea, and severe stomatitis. Chronic side effects include sterility, pulmonary dysfunction, cardiac dysfunction, and liver disease.

To prevent **graft-versus-host disease (GVHD)**, patients receive immunosuppressant drugs, such as cyclosporine (Neoral), tacrolimus (FK 506, Prograf), or sirolimus (Rappamune). In allogeneic transplant recipients, GVHD occurs when the T lymphocytes proliferating from the transplanted donor marrow or PBSCs become activated and mount an immune response against the recipient's tissues (skin, GI tract, liver). T lymphocytes respond in this manner because they view the recipient's tissue as "foreign," immunologically different from what they recognize as "self" in the donor. GVHD may occur acutely (within the first 100 days) or chronically (after 100 days).

The first 100 days after allogeneic HSCT are crucial for patients; the immune system and blood-making capacity (hematopoiesis) must recover sufficiently to prevent infection and hemorrhage. Most acute side effects, such as nausea, vomiting, and mucositis (inflammation and ulceration of the mucous membranes lining the digestive tract), also resolve in the initial 100 days after transplantation. In addition to acute GVHD, patients are also at risk for hepatic venous occlusive disease (VOD) or hepatic sinusoidal obstruction syndrome, a vascular injury to the liver caused by high-dose chemotherapy, in the first 30 days following transplant. VOD can lead to acute liver failure and death (Krimmel & Williams, 2008) and presents as hepatomegaly (enlarged liver), elevated bilirubin levels, ascites, and weight gain in the absence of other causes.

Autologous HSCT is considered for patients with disease of the bone marrow who do not have a suitable donor for allogeneic HSCT and for patients who have healthy bone marrow but require myeloablative doses of chemotherapy to cure an aggressive malignancy. Stem cells are collected from the patient and preserved for reinfusion; if necessary, they are treated to kill any malignant cells within the marrow. The patient is then treated with myeloablative chemotherapy and, possibly, total body irradiation to eradicate any remaining tumor. Stem cells are then reinfused. Until engraftment occurs in the bone marrow, there is a high risk of infection, sepsis, and bleeding. Acute and chronic toxicities from chemotherapy and radiation therapy may be severe. The risk of VOD is also present after autologous transplantation. No immunosuppressant medications are necessary after autologous bone marrow transplant because the patient does not receive foreign tissue. A disadvantage of autologous transplantation is the risk that viable tumor cells may remain in the bone marrow despite high-dose chemotherapy.

Syngeneic transplants use an identical twin as the donor. Syngeneic transplants result in less incidence of GVHD and graft rejection; however, there is also less graft-versus-tumor effect to fight the malignancy. For this reason, even when an identical twin is available for marrow donation, another matched sibling or even an unrelated donor may be the most suitable option to combat an aggressive malignancy.

Nursing Management in Stem Cell Transplantation

Providing Care During Treatment

Skilled nursing care is required during the conditioning phase of transplant when high-dose chemotherapy with or without total body irradiation are administered. The acute toxicities of nausea, vomiting, diarrhea, mucositis, and hemorrhagic cystitis require close monitoring and constant attention by the nurse.

Nursing management during the bone marrow or stem cell infusions consists of monitoring the patient's vital signs and blood oxygen saturation; assessing for adverse effects, such as fever, chills, shortness of breath, chest pain, cutaneous reactions (hives), nausea, vomiting, hypotension or hypertension, tachycardia, anxiety, and taste changes; and providing ongoing support and patient teaching.

Throughout the period of bone marrow aplasia (inability to create new cells) until engraftment of the new marrow occurs, the patient is at high risk for death from sepsis and bleeding. The patient requires support with blood products and hematopoietic growth factors. Potential infections may be bacterial, viral, fungal, or protozoan in origin. Renal complications may arise from the nephrotoxic chemotherapy agents used in the conditioning regimen or those used to treat infection (amphotericin B, aminoglycosides). Tumor lysis syndrome (Box 6-6) and acute tubular necrosis are also risks after conditioning therapy.

GVHD requires skillful nursing assessment to detect early effects on the skin, liver, and GI tract, including red maculopapular rash commonly found on the palms of the hands and soles of the feet, elevated liver function tests (LFTs), weight gain, jaundice, right upper quadrant pain, diffuse abdominal pain, early satiety, and diarrhea. Diarrhea resulting from GVHD may be of large volume; therefore, all stools must be measured and monitored for the presence of blood. VOD resulting from the conditioning regimens used in HSCT can result in fluid retention, jaundice, abdominal pain, ascites, tender and enlarged liver, and encephalopathy. Pulmonary complications, such as pulmonary edema, interstitial pneumonia, and other pneumonias, often complicate the recovery after transplant.

Focus on Pathophysiology: Tumor Lysis Syndrome

Malignant cells contain higher intracellular levels of potassium, phosphorous, and nucleic acids than do healthy cells. As the malignant cells are killed by chemotherapy, biotherapy, or corticosteroids, the intracellular contents are released into the bloodstream, leading to hyperkalemia, hyperphosphatemia, and hyperuricemia. The elevation in phosphorous results in an inverse decline in calcium levels. The crystallization of phosphates and uric acid salts in the kidneys can result in acute kidney injury, evidenced by an increase in serum creatinine and acidemia. The treatment plan includes aggressive hydration, urinary alkalinization, administration of medications that block uric acid accumulation (such as Allopurinol) and medications that break uric acid down into a soluble substance that can be excreted through the urine (Rasburicase®) and control of electrolyte disturbances (Porth, 2007). Nursing considerations include strict monitoring of urine output and intake, monitoring of weight changes, and assessment of signs and symptoms of electrolyte disturbances.

Providing Posttransplantation Care

Ongoing nursing assessment in follow-up visits is essential to detect late effects of therapy after HSCT, which occur 100 days or more after the procedure. Late effects include infections (e.g., varicella zoster infection), restrictive pulmonary abnormalities, and recurrent pneumonias. Sterility often results. Chronic GVHD involves the skin, liver, intestine, esophagus, eyes, lungs, joints, and oral and vaginal mucosa. Cataracts may also develop after total body irradiation.

Psychosocial assessments by nursing staff must be ongoing. In addition to the stressors affecting patients at each phase of the transplantation experience, marrow donors and family members also have psychosocial needs that must be addressed.

Targeted Therapies

Recent advances in the fields of molecular biology, biochemistry, immunology, and genetics have led to an improved understanding of cancer development. Traditional therapies such as chemotherapy and radiation are nonspecific, affecting all rapidly dividing cells. As a result, both healthy and malignant cells are subject to harmful systemic effects of treatment. **Targeted therapies** seek to minimize the negative effects on healthy tissues by disrupting specific cancer cell functions, such as malignant transformation, communication pathways, processes for growth and metastasis, as well as genetic coding.

Mechanisms of action of targeted therapies include stimulation or augmentation of immune responses through the use of **biologic response modifiers** (BRMs), targeting of cancer cell growth factors and proteins, promotion of apoptosis (programmed cell death), and genetic manipulation through gene therapy (Polovich, Whitford, & Olsen, 2009). Tables 6-4 and 6-5 provide examples of targeted therapies and BRMs.

Nursing Management in Biologic Response Modifier Therapy

Patients receiving BRM therapy have many of the same needs as cancer patients undergoing other treatment approaches. The nurse should be familiar with each agent given and its potential effects. Adverse effects, including flu-like symptoms such as fever, chills, myalgia, nausea, and vomiting, as seen with interferon (IFN) therapy, may not be life-threatening. However, the nurse must be aware of the impact of these side effects on the patient's quality of life. Other life-threatening adverse effects (e.g., capillary leak syndrome, pulmonary edema, hypotension) may occur with interleukin-2 (IL-2) therapy. The nurse must work closely with providers to assess and manage potential toxicities of BRM therapy. The specific nursing care required will depend on the agent being administered.

The nurse teaches patients self-care and assists in providing for continuing care. Some BRMs, such as IFN, EPO, and G-CSF, can be administered by the patient or family members at home. As needed, the nurse teaches the patient and family how to administer these agents through subcutaneous injections. The nurse also provides instructions about side effects and helps the patient and family identify strategies to manage many of the common side effects of BRM therapy, such as fatigue, anorexia, and flu-like symptoms.

Referral for home care may be indicated to monitor the patient's responses to treatment and to continue to reinforce patient and family teaching. During home visits, the nurse assesses the patient's and family members' technique in administering medications. The nurse collaborates with providers, third-party payers, and pharmaceutical companies to help the patient obtain reimbursement for home administration of BRM therapies. The nurse also reminds the patient about the importance of keeping follow-up appointments with providers and assesses the patient's need for changes in care.

NURSING PROCESS

The Patient With Cancer

Nurses play a critical role in monitoring for changes over time, identifying problems and alterations in quality of life, and collaborating with patients, families, and members of the multidisciplinary team to optimize patient care. The nursing approach to the most common problems in patients with cancer will be discussed here. A plan of nursing care

(continued on page 170)

TABLE
6-4 Selected Food and Drug Administration–Approved Therapeutic Monoclonal Antibodies

Monoclonal Antibody	Indication	Target	Selected Side Effects
Alemtuzumab (Campath)	Chronic lymphocytic leukemia	Marker on cell membrane of lymphocytes, monocytes, and macrophages	Allergic/anaphylactic reactions; fever; chills; rash; hives; itching; decreased WBC, platelet, and RBC counts
Bevacizumab (Avastin)	Metastatic colorectal cancer	Vascular endothelial growth factor	Arterial and venous thrombosis, hypertension, hemorrhage, GI perforation, proteinuria, congestive heart failure
Cetuximab (Erbitux)	Metastatic colorectal cancer	Epidermal growth factor	Allergic/anaphylactic reactions, fever, chills, rash, hives, itching, acne-like rash, lung inflammation, kidney failure, diarrhea, nausea, abdominal pain, vomiting
Gemtuzumab ozogamicin (Mylotarg)	Acute leukemia	Marker on cell membrane of leukemic cells	Allergic/anaphylactic reactions; fever; chills; weakness; headache; tachycardia; hemorrhage; local skin reaction; rash; stomatitis; decreased platelet, WBC, and RBC counts; increased liver function tests
Ibritumomab-tiuxetan (Zevalin "B" lymphocytes)	Non-Hodgkin lymphoma	Marker on cell membrane of lymphocytes	Decreased platelets, WBC, and RBC counts; weakness; fever; chills
Rituximab (Rituxan "B" lymphocytes)	Non-Hodgkin lymphoma	Marker on cell membrane of lymphocytes	Allergic/anaphylactic reactions, fever, chills, back pain, night sweats, infection
Tositumomab (Bexxar "B" lymphocytes)	Non-Hodgkin lymphoma	Marker on cell membrane of lymphocytes	Allergic/anaphylactic reactions, fever chills, rash, hives, itching, anemia, thrombocytopenia, decreased WBC count
Trastuzumab (Herceptin)	Breast cancer	Growth factor protein on cell membrane	Allergic/anaphylactic reactions, hypotension, fever, chills, heart failure

TABLE
6-5 Selected Side Effects of Food and Drug Administration-Approved Biologic Response Modifiers

Agent Cytokines	Selected Side Effects
Interferon alfa	Flu-like symptoms (fever, chills, weakness, muscle and joint pain, headaches); fatigue; anorexia; mental status changes; depression; irritability; insomnia; rash; pruritus; irritation at the injection site; decreased WBC, RBC, and platelet counts; abnormal liver function values
Interleukin-2	Flu-like symptoms (fever, chills, weakness, muscle and joint pain, headaches); fatigue, anorexia, nausea, vomiting, diarrhea, capillary leak syndrome, edema and fluid retention, hypotension, tachycardia, skin rash, erythema, desquamation
Filgrastim (granulocyte growth factor)	Bone pain, malaise, fever, fatigue, headache, skin rash
Sargramostim (granulocyte-macrophage growth factor)	Allergic/anaphylactic reaction with first dose, bone pain, fever, fatigue, headache, weakness, chills, skin rash, infection
Epoetin alfa (erythrocyte growth factor)	Fever, fatigue, weakness, diarrhea, dizziness, edema, shortness of breath
Oprelvekin (platelet growth factor)	Edema, fever, headache, rash, chills, bone pain, fatigue, nausea, vomiting, abdominal pain, constipation, rhinitis, cough, arrhythmia, skin discoloration, bleeding

for a patient with cancer is available online at http://thePoint.lww.com/Pellico1e.

Assessment

Individuals with cancer may experience a range of side effects with varying severity depending on the cancer type, tumor stage, and treatment modalities being used. Assessment of common problems is presented with related interventions below.

Diagnosis

Appropriate nursing diagnoses of the patient with cancer may include:

- Impaired oral mucous membranes
- Impaired skin integrity
- Nausea
- Pain, acute
- Pain, chronic
- Imbalanced nutrition: Less than body requirements
- Fatigue
- Activity intolerance
- Risk for infection
- Risk for bleeding
- Disturbed body image

Based on the assessment data, potential complications include the following:

- Infection and sepsis
- Hemorrhage
- Superior vena cava syndrome (SVCS)
- Spinal cord compression
- Hypercalcemia
- Pericardial effusion
- Disseminated intravascular coagulation (DIC)
- Syndrome of inappropriate secretion of antidiuretic hormone (SIADH)
- Tumor lysis syndrome

See the section on oncologic emergencies for more information.

Planning

The major goals for the patient may include management of stomatitis, maintenance of tissue integrity, maintenance of nutrition, relief of pain, relief of fatigue, improved body image, effective progression through the grieving process, and absence of complications.

Nursing Interventions

Preventing/Minimizing Fatigue

To make an accurate assessment, the nurse must distinguish between acute fatigue, which occurs after an energy-demanding experience, and chronic fatigue, which is often overwhelming, excessive, and not responsive to rest. Acute fatigue serves a protective function, whereas chronic fatigue does not. Chronic fatigue seriously affects quality of life. Fatigue is the most commonly reported side effect in patients who receive chemotherapy and radiation therapy. Fatigue is a subjective symptom that must be assessed in a systematic way, similarly to pain, relying on the patient's self-report. The nurse should ask the patient to describe the severity of the fatigue. The patient can use a scale of 0–10, with 0 being no fatigue and 10 being severe fatigue, or patients can simply state none, mild, moderate, or severe (Piper, Borneman, Chih-Yi Sun et al., 2008). The nurse should also assess the onset of fatigue, as well as aggravating and alleviating factors, including physiologic and psychological stressors that can contribute to fatigue, such as pain, nausea, dyspnea, constipation, fear, and anxiety. The nurse assesses for feelings of weariness, weakness, lack of energy, inability to carry out necessary and valued daily functions, lack of motivation, and inability to concentrate. The patient may become less verbal and may appear pale, with relaxed facial musculature. The nurse helps the patient and family understand that fatigue is an expected side effect of cancer and cancer treatment. Fatigue may be exacerbated by the stress of coping with cancer. It does not always signify that the cancer is advancing or that the treatment is failing.

Nursing strategies are implemented to minimize fatigue or help the patient cope with existing fatigue. Educational interventions, including providing anticipatory guidance that fatigue is an expected side effect of cancer treatment, have been shown to reduce the severity of cancer-related fatigue (Barsevick, Newhall, & Brown, 2008). Helping the patient identify sources of fatigue aids in selecting appropriate and individualized interventions.

Ways to conserve energy are developed to help the patient plan daily activities. Alternating periods of rest and activity are beneficial. Strong evidence exists to support that regular exercise may decrease fatigue and facilitate coping, whereas lack of physical activity and "too much rest" can actually contribute to deconditioning and associated fatigue (Barsevick, Newhall, & Brown, 2008). The nurse also assists in educating the patient on sleep hygiene, including: do not stay in bed if you are not sleeping; go to bed only when sleepy and at the same time every night; use the bed only for sleep and sexual activity; avoid daytime napping or if needed, limit naps to 30 minutes; and avoid caffeine, nicotine, and alcohol after noon; and use a relaxing routine within 2 hours of going to bed, such as a warm bath or shower, reading, or listening to music (Berger, 2009; Page, Berger, & Johnson, 2006).

The patient is encouraged to maintain as normal a lifestyle as possible by continuing with activities that he or she values and enjoys. Prioritizing necessary and valued activities can help the patient plan for each day. The patient and family are encouraged to plan to reallocate responsibilities, such as attending to child-care, cleaning, and preparing

meals. Patients who are employed full-time may need to reduce the number of hours worked each day or week. The nurse helps the patient and family cope with these changing roles and responsibilities. The nurse also addresses factors that contribute to fatigue, such as pain, nausea, and depression, and implements pharmacologic and nonpharmacologic strategies to manage these symptoms. The nurse provides nutrition counseling to patients who are not eating enough calories or protein. Small, frequent meals require less energy for digestion. The nurse monitors the patient for deficiencies in serum hemoglobin and hematocrit and administers blood products or ESAs as prescribed. In addition, the nurse monitors the patient for alterations in oxygenation and electrolyte balances. Physical therapy and assistive devices are beneficial for patients with impaired mobility. A number of studies are being conducted to evaluate the use of psychostimulants, such as methylphenidate and modafinil, for the treatment of fatigue; however, more data are needed before these interventions can be safely implemented (Breitbart & Alici, 2008).

Monitoring and Managing Infection and Sepsis

MONITORING FOR INFECTION. For patients in all stages of cancer, the nurse assesses risk factors for infection and observes for clinical signs and symptoms, as infection is the leading cause of death in cancer patients. The nurse monitors laboratory studies to detect early changes in WBC counts. Common sites of infection, such as the oropharynx, skin, perianal area, urinary tract, GI tract, and respiratory tract, are assessed frequently. The typical signs of infection (swelling, redness, drainage, and pain) may not occur in immunosuppressed patients because of a diminished local inflammatory response. Fever or localized tenderness may be the only sign of infection. The nurse also monitors the patient for sepsis, particularly if invasive catheters or venous access devices are in place.

WBC function is often impaired in patients with cancer. There are 2 types of WBCs: granulocytes (neutrophils, eosinophils, basophils) and agranulocytes (lymphocytes, monocytes, macrophages). The neutrophils, totaling 60% to 70% of the body's total WBCs, play a major role in combating infection by engulfing and destroying microorganisms in a process called phagocytosis. Both the total WBC count and the number of neutrophils are important in determining the patient's ability to fight infection. A decrease in circulating WBCs is referred to as *leukopenia. Granulocytopenia* or *neutropenia* is a decrease in neutrophils.

A differential WBC count identifies the relative numbers of WBCs and permits tabulation of the absolute neutrophil count (ANC). The ANC includes the number of polymorphonuclear neutrophils (mature neutrophils, reported as "polys," PMNs, or "segs") and immature forms of neutrophils (reported as bands, metamyelocytes, and "stabs"). The ANC is calculated by the following formula:

Total WBC × [%segs +%bands]

For example, if the total WBC count is 6,000 cells/mm³, with segmented neutrophils 25% and bands 25%, the ANC is 3,000 cells/mm³. That is 6,000 × [.25 +.25] = 6,000 ×.5 = 3,000.

Neutropenia, an abnormally low ANC, is associated with an increased risk for infection. The risk for infection rises as the ANC decreases and persists. An ANC of less than 500 cells/mm³ reflects a severe risk of infection. **Nadir** is the lowest ANC after myelosuppressive chemotherapy or radiation therapy. Therapies that suppress bone marrow function are called *myelosuppressive*. Therapies that severely suppress bone marrow function are called *myeloablative*. The nadir is reached, on average, 7–10 days following chemotherapy treatment and takes an additional 7–14 days to recover. The patient is at increased risk for infection throughout the duration of neutropenia.

Gram-positive bacteria (*Streptococcus* and *Staphylococcus* species) and gram-negative organisms (*Escherichia coli, Klebsiella pneumoniae*, and *Pseudomonas aeruginosa*) are the most frequently isolated causes of infection. Fungal organisms, such as *Candida albicans*, also contribute to the incidence of serious infection. Viral infections in immunocompromised patients are caused most commonly by herpes viruses and respiratory viruses.

NURSING ALERT
Normal WBC levels in adults is 4.5 to 10.5 × 10³ cells/mm³ or 4,500 to 10,500 cells/mm³. For African American adults, normal levels are 3,200 to 10,000 cells/mm³. A WBC level (count) of <500 or >30,000 are critical values (Fischbach & Dunning, 2009).

MANAGING PATIENTS WITH FEBRILE NEUTROPENIA. A fever in a patient with neutropenia is considered an emergency due to the high mortality rate associated with sepsis in neutropenic patients. Hospitalized patients who are neutropenic and become febrile are assessed immediately for infection. Cultures of blood, sputum, urine, stool, catheter, or wounds, are obtained. In addition, a chest X-ray is often included to assess for pulmonary infections. If a patient is at home and develops neutropenic fever, he is instructed to notify his health care provider and seek medical attention immediately.

NURSING ALERT
Fever is often the only sign of infection in immunocompromised patients. Although fever may be related to a variety of noninfectious conditions, including the underlying cancer, any temperature of 38.0°C (100.4°F) or higher is reported and addressed promptly.

Empiric antibiotics are initiated to treat infections immediately after cultures are obtained. The term *empiric*

(continued on page 172)

antibiotics refer to the use of broad-spectrum antibiotics used to treat infection before a definitive organism is identified. Often, Gram stains are ordered along with cultures to assist providers in identifying the most appropriate antibiotic. Empiric antibiotics have been employed due to the high incidence of mortality associated with untreated infection in neutropenic patients. Broad-spectrum antibiotic coverage or empiric therapy most often includes a combination of medications to defend the body against the major pathogenic organisms (both gram-positive and gram-negative). It is important for the nurse to administer these medications promptly, immediately after cultures are obtained, according to the prescribed schedule, to achieve adequate blood levels of the medications.

MINIMIZING THE RISK OF INFECTION IN NEUTROPENIC PATIENTS. Strict asepsis is essential when handling IV lines, catheters, and other invasive equipment. Exposure of the patient to others with active infections and to crowds is avoided. Patients with profound immunosuppression, such as HSCT recipients, may need to be placed in a protective environment, where the air is filtered. To reduce the risk of food-borne illnesses, patients are educated to avoid soft cheeses, raw meat or fish, and deli meats and eat only fruits and vegetables that can be washed well, eliminating soft fruits such as berries. Hand hygiene and appropriate general hygiene are critical to reduce exposure to potentially harmful bacteria and to eliminate environmental contaminants. Invasive procedures, such as injections, vaginal or rectal examinations, rectal temperatures, and surgery, are avoided. The patient is encouraged to cough and to perform deep-breathing exercises frequently to prevent atelectasis and other respiratory problems. Prophylactic antimicrobial therapy may be used for patients who are expected to be profoundly immunosuppressed and at risk for certain infections, such as patients undergoing autologous or allogeneic stem cell transplant and patients with lymphoma. The nurse teaches the patient and family to recognize signs and symptoms of infection to report, perform effective hand hygiene, use antipyretics, maintain skin integrity, and administer hematopoietic growth factors when indicated.

Monitoring and Managing Bleeding and Hemorrhage

The nurse assesses the patient with cancer for factors that may contribute to bleeding. Bleeding may result from a reduction in the quantity or quality of platelets, a decrease in clotting factors, or from DIC. Treatment related factors include bone marrow suppression from radiation, chemotherapy, and other medications that interfere with coagulation and platelet functioning, such as aspirin and other nonsteroidal anti-inflammatory medications, dipyridamole (Persantine), heparin, or warfarin (Coumadin).

Thrombocytopenia often results from bone marrow depression after certain types of chemotherapy and radiation therapy. Tumor infiltration of the bone marrow can also impair the normal production of platelets. In some cases, platelet destruction is associated with an enlarged spleen (hypersplenism) and abnormal antibody function, which occur with leukemia and lymphoma.

Platelets are essential for normal blood clotting and coagulation (hemostasis). Thrombocytopenia, a decrease in the circulating platelet count, is the most common cause of bleeding in patients with cancer and is usually defined as a platelet count of less than 100,000/mm^3 (0.1 × 10^{12}/L). When the platelet count decreases to between 20,000 and 50,000/mm^3 (0.02 to 0.05 × 10^{12}/L), the risk of bleeding increases. Platelet counts lower than 20,000/mm^3 (0.02 × 10^{12}/L) are associated with an increased risk for spontaneous bleeding. For the majority of patients, a platelet threshold of 10,000/mm^3 should be maintained. In patients requiring minor procedures (e.g., vascular access device placement), febrile patients, patients with necrotic tumors, bladder tumors, or highly vascular tumors who are at increased risk for bleeding, the transfusion threshold should be maintained at 20,000/mm^3 or higher. Patients who require major surgery should have a platelet count of 50,000/mm^3 or more (Brant, Damron, Friend et al., 2006).

In addition to monitoring laboratory values, the nurse continues to assess the patient for bleeding. Common bleeding sites include skin (ecchymosis [bruising], petechiae) and mucous membranes (bleeding with mouth care, epistaxis [nose bleeds]); the intestinal, urinary, and respiratory tracts; and the brain. Gross hemorrhage, as well as blood in the stools (melena), urine (hematuria), sputum (hemoptysis), or vomitus (hematemesis); oozing at injection sites; and changes in mental status, are monitored and reported promptly.

The nurse takes steps to prevent trauma and minimize the risk of bleeding by encouraging the patient to use a soft toothbrush or a sponge toothette and an electric razor. In addition, the nurse avoids unnecessary invasive procedures (e.g., rectal temperatures, intramuscular injections, catheterization), and helps the patient and family identify and remove environmental hazards that may lead to falls or other trauma. Soft foods, increased fluid intake, and stool softeners, if prescribed, may be indicated to reduce trauma to the GI tract. The joints and extremities are handled and moved gently to minimize the risk of spontaneous bleeding. Following venipuncture, pressure must be applied for 3 to 5 minutes.

The nurse administers platelet transfusions as ordered and monitors for signs of transfusion reaction including fever, chills, urticaria, and shortness of breath. In limited circumstances, the nurse may administer IL-11, which has been approved by the U.S. Food and Drug Administration (FDA) to prevent severe thrombocytopenia and to reduce the need for platelet transfusions after myelosuppressive chemotherapy in patients with nonmyeloid malignancies (Polovich, Whitford, & Olsen, 2009). In some instances, the nurse teaches the patient or family members to administer IL-11 in the home.

When a hospitalized patient experiences bleeding, the nurse monitors blood pressure and pulse and respiratory rates every 15 to 30 minutes. Serum hemoglobin and hematocrit

are monitored carefully for changes indicating blood loss. The nurse tests all urine, stool, and emesis for occult blood. Neurologic assessments are performed to detect changes in orientation and behavior. Headaches reported by the patient, or abnormal neurologic findings must be reported to the provider immediately, as even subtle signs may indicate an intracranial hemorrhage. The nurse administers fluids and blood products as prescribed to replace any losses.

! NURSING ALERT

One unit of platelets is approximately 50 to 70 mL; in general, four to eight units are pooled for a platelet transfusion and infused according to patient's tolerance. The platelet transfusion is anticipated to increase the platelet count 5000 to 10,000/μL per unit (Fauci, Kasper, Longo et al., 2008).

Assessing and Managing Stomatitis

Mucositis is a common side effect of radiation and some types of chemotherapy that may lead to inflammation and ulceration of any portion of the GI tract from the oral cavity throughout the alimentary canal. One form of mucositis, stomatitis, is an inflammatory response of the oral tissues that is characterized by mild redness (erythema) and edema or, if severe, by painful ulcerations, bleeding, and secondary infection. Stomatitis commonly develops 5 to 14 days after patients receive myelosuppressive chemotherapeutic agents and often coincides with the WBC nadir. As many as 40% of patients receiving chemotherapy experience some degree of stomatitis during treatment. Patients receiving dose-intensive chemotherapy (considerably higher doses than conventional dosing), such as those undergoing HCST, are at increased risk for stomatitis. Stomatitis may also occur after radiation treatments to the head and neck.

As a result of normal everyday wear and tear, the epithelial cells that line the oral cavity undergo rapid turnover and slough off routinely. Until recently, stomatitis was thought to occur because chemotherapy and radiation interfered with this process. Recent molecular studies have improved understanding of the processes involved. Both chemotherapy and radiation generate chemical substances that lead to microvascular injury and connective tissue damage, followed by epithelial damage (Sonis, 2007). This initiates the inflammatory process, leading to further tissue damage. The end result is ulceration and impaired oral tissues. The normal flora of the oral cavity invades these ulcerations, resulting in additional damage. Poor oral hygiene, existing dental disease, use of other medications that dry mucous membranes, advanced age, smoking, previous cancer treatment, diminished renal function, and impaired nutritional status all contribute to morbidity associated with stomatitis. Radiation-induced xerostomia (dry mouth) associated with decreased function of the salivary glands may contribute to stomatitis in patients who have received radiation to the head and neck.

Myelosuppression (bone marrow depression), resulting from underlying disease or its treatment, predisposes the patient to oral bleeding and infection. Severe pain associated with ulcerated oral tissues can significantly interfere with nutritional intake, speech, and a willingness to maintain oral hygiene. Severe stomatitis may cause or prolong hospitalizations. In addition, stomatitis may lead to interruptions in chemotherapy and radiation administration or decreases in the intended dosing until the inflammation subsides. Further, it may significantly reduce the patient's quality of life.

Nurses must perform routine oral assessments in patients at risk for developing stomatitis and in patients with established stomatitis. Standardized oral assessment guides exist to facilitate objective descriptions of the oral mucosa (Jaroneski, 2006). The assessment should include the color and moisture of the lips and oral mucosa; presence of ulcerations; presence of edema of the lips, buccal mucosa, or tongue; and quantity and quality of saliva. The nurse also assesses the level of pain that the patient experiences secondary to stomatitis, alterations in the patient's ability to talk or sleep, and nutritional intake.

Although multiple studies on stomatitis have been published, the optimal prevention and treatment approaches have not been identified. Future studies will focus on addressing the cascade of inflammatory events and release of chemical substances that leads to the cellular and tissue destruction underlying stomatitis. At this time, most clinicians agree that routine, good oral hygiene, including brushing, flossing, and rinsing, is necessary to minimize the risk of oral complications associated with cancer therapies. Soft-bristled toothbrushes and nonabrasive toothpaste prevent or reduce trauma to the oral mucosa. Oral swabs with sponge-like applicators may be used in place of a toothbrush for painful oral tissues. Flossing may be performed unless it causes pain or bleeding. Oral rinses with saline solution or tap water after meals and at bedtime may be necessary for patients who cannot tolerate toothbrushing. Products that irritate oral tissues or impair healing, such as alcohol-based mouth rinses, are avoided. Foods that are difficult to chew or are hot or spicy are avoided to minimize further trauma. The patient's lips are lubricated to keep them from becoming dry and cracked. Topical anti-inflammatory and anesthetic agents may be prescribed to promote healing and minimize discomfort. Products that coat or protect oral mucosa are used to promote comfort and prevent further trauma. Patients who experience severe pain and discomfort with stomatitis require systemic analgesics.

Adequate fluid and food intake is encouraged. In some instances, parenteral hydration and nutrition are necessary. Topical or systemic antifungal and antibiotic medications are prescribed to treat local or systemic infections.

Palifermin (Kepivance), a synthetic form of human keratinocyte growth factor, is an IV medication approved in 2005 by the FDA for treatment of mucositis in patients with

(*continued on page 174*)

hematologic malignancies who are undergoing high-dose chemotherapy or total body radiation prior to HCST. Palifermin appears to promote more rapid replacement of cells in the mouth and GI tract, decreasing the incidence and duration of severe mucositis (Harris, Eilers, Harriman et al., 2008; Polovich, Whitford, & Olsen, 2009). It has not yet been tested in other patients with cancer. Careful timing of administration and monitoring are essential for maximum effectiveness and to detect adverse effects.

Caring for Patients With Nausea and Vomiting

Nausea is an unpleasant sensation experienced in the back of the throat, epigastrium, or stomach that may result in vomiting. Nausea is one of the most feared side effects of cancer treatment. The potential causes of nausea are numerous, and nurses should not assume that nausea is due to chemotherapy; all potential causes must be considered. Causes of nausea include primary or metastatic tumor involving the CNS; gastroparesis (slowed gastric emptying); obstruction in the GI tract; infection; hypercalcemia; renal or hepatic dysfunction; hyponatremia; side effects of medications including chemotherapy, morphine, antibiotics. Risk factors for treatment-induced nausea include younger age, female sex, and a history of treatment-induced nausea and vomiting.

Nausea is a subjective phenomenon analogous to pain. Nausea is best assessed by eliciting the patient's self-report. The following components should be assessed: timing of nausea in relation to treatment, perceived meaning of nausea to the patient, onset, frequency, associated symptoms, precipitating and alleviating factors, and previous experiences with nausea. Physical assessment should include signs of sweating, tachycardia, dizziness, pallor, excessive salivation, weakness, gastric distention, abdominal tenderness, and evaluation of bowel sounds. Laboratory values including electrolytes and renal function should be monitored.

The prevention of chemotherapy-induced nausea and vomiting is a priority. The use of combinations including corticosteroids and serotonin receptor antagonists, as discussed earlier, are the mainstays of prevention. Patients with anxiety related to their chemotherapy treatment may benefit from benzodiazepines, such as lorazepam, 1 hour prior to treatment to minimize anticipatory nausea. For nausea and vomiting unrelated to chemotherapy, medications including serotonin receptor antagonists (e.g., ondansetron), dopamine receptor antagonists (e.g., metoclopramide), phenothiazines (e.g., prochlorperazine), corticosteroids (e.g., dexamethasone), and cannabinoids (e.g., dronabinol) can be used. Antiemetics should be administered around the clock, with breakthrough doses as needed. Nonpharmacologic interventions that have proven to be effective in decreasing nausea include relaxation, guided imagery, acupressure, acupuncture, deep breathing, and eliminating odors. Patients should be instructed to avoid reclining within the first 30 minutes after eating. Dietary interventions include eating small, frequent meals and eating bland, chilled foods.

Maintaining Skin Integrity

The nurse assesses the patient with cancer for any skin problems. Maintaining integrity of skin and tissue poses a problem for patients with cancer because of the effects of chemotherapy, radiation therapy, surgery, and invasive procedures carried out for diagnosis and therapy. As part of the assessment, the nurse identifies which of these predisposing factors is present and assesses the patient for other risk factors, including nutritional deficits, bowel and bladder incontinence, immobility, immunosuppression, multiple skin folds, and changes related to aging. The nurse notes the presence of skin lesions, ulcers, rashes, or ulcerations secondary to the tumor or the effects of treatment.

Some of the most frequently encountered disturbances of tissue integrity, in addition to stomatitis, include skin and tissue reactions to radiation therapy, alopecia, and metastatic skin lesions. Patients with skin and tissue reactions to radiation therapy require careful skin care to prevent further skin irritation, drying, and damage. The skin over the affected area is handled gently; avoiding rubbing and use of hot or cold water, soaps, powders, lotions, and cosmetics. Patients may avoid tissue injury by wearing loose-fitting, cotton clothes and avoiding clothes that constrict, irritate, or rub the affected area. If blistering occurs, care is taken not to disrupt the blisters, thus reducing the risk of introducing bacteria. Moisture- and vapor-permeable dressings, such as hydrocolloids and hydrogels, are helpful in promoting healing and reducing pain. Aseptic wound care is indicated to minimize the risk for infection and sepsis. Topical antibiotics, such as 1% silver sulfadiazine cream (Silvadene), may be prescribed for use on areas of moist desquamation (painful, red, moist skin).

MANAGING MALIGNANT SKIN LESIONS. Skin lesions may occur with local extension of the tumor or embolization of the tumor into the epithelium and its surrounding lymph and blood vessels. Secondary growth of cancer cells into the skin may result in redness (erythematous areas), or it may progress to wounds involving tissue necrosis and infection. The most extensive lesions tend to disintegrate and are purulent and malodorous. In addition, these lesions are a source of considerable pain and discomfort. Although this type of lesion is most often associated with breast cancer and head and neck cancers, it can also occur with lymphoma, leukemia, melanoma, and cancers of the lung, uterus, kidney, colon, and bladder. The development of severe skin lesions is usually associated with a poor prognosis for extended survival.

Ulcerating skin lesions usually indicate widely disseminated disease that is unlikely to be eradicated. Managing these lesions becomes a nursing priority. Nursing care includes carefully assessing and cleansing the skin, reducing superficial bacteria, controlling bleeding, reducing odor, protecting the skin from further trauma, and relieving pain. The patient and family require assistance and guidance to care for these skin lesions at home. Referral for home care is indicated.

HELPING PATIENTS COPE WITH ALOPECIA. The nurse notes the presence of alopecia (hair loss), which is another form of tissue disruption common in patients with cancer who receive radiation therapy or chemotherapy. In addition, the nurse assesses the psychological impact of this side effect on the patient and family.

The temporary or permanent thinning or complete loss of hair is a potential adverse effect of various radiation therapies and chemotherapeutic agents. The extent of alopecia depends on the type, dose, and duration of therapy. These treatments cause alopecia by damaging stem cells and hair follicles. As a result, the hair is brittle and may fall out or break off at the surface of the scalp. Loss of other body hair is less frequent. Hair loss usually begins 2 to 3 weeks after the initiation of treatment; regrowth begins within 8 weeks after the last treatment and may take up to 6 months for complete regrowth. Some patients who undergo radiation to the head may sustain permanent hair loss. Many health care providers view hair loss as a minor problem when compared with the potentially life-threatening consequences of cancer. However, for many patients, hair loss is a major assault on body image, resulting in depression, anxiety, anger, rejection, and isolation. To patients and families, hair loss can serve as a constant reminder of the challenges cancer places on coping abilities, interpersonal relationships, and sexuality.

The nurse provides information about alopecia and supports the patient and family in coping with changes in body image. The patient is encouraged to acquire a wig or hairpiece before hair loss occurs, so that the replacement matches the patient's own hair. Use of attractive scarves and hats may make the patient feel less conspicuous. The nurse can refer the patient to supportive programs, such as "Look Good, Feel Better," offered by the American Cancer Society. Knowledge that hair usually begins to regrow after therapy is completed may comfort some patients, although patients must be prepared that the color and texture of the new hair may be different.

Improving Nutritional Status

Assessment of the patient's nutritional status is an important nursing role. Impaired nutritional status may contribute to disease progression, decreased survival, immune incompetence, increased incidence of infection, delayed tissue repair, diminished functional ability, decreased capacity to continue antineoplastic therapy, increased length of hospital stay, and impaired psychosocial functioning. Altered nutritional status, weight loss, and cachexia (muscle wasting, emaciation) are complex states and may be secondary to decreased protein and caloric intake, metabolic or mechanical effects of the cancer, systemic disease, side effects of the treatment, or the patient's emotional status.

The nursing assessment of nutritional status includes monitoring the patient's weight and caloric intake consistently. Other information obtained by assessment includes diet history, any episodes of anorexia, changes in appetite,

situations and foods that aggravate or relieve anorexia, and medication history. Difficulty in chewing or swallowing is identified, and the presence of nausea, vomiting, or diarrhea is noted. The patient should also be asked about the ability to prepare and obtain food to assist in identifying the need for additional resources.

Clinical and laboratory data useful in assessing nutritional status include anthropometric measurements (triceps skin fold and middle-upper arm circumference), serum protein levels (albumin, prealbumin, and transferrin), serum electrolytes, lymphocyte count, hemoglobin levels, hematocrit, urinary creatinine levels, and serum iron levels.

> **! NURSING ALERT**
>
> A normal Serum albumin is 3.5 to 5.2 g/dL or 35 to 52 g/L, and gives the clinician a quick assessment of protein stores. In a seminal study by Seltzer et al. (1979), a sixfold increase in mortality was seen with an albumin level of less than 35 g/L, while additional studies associate serum albumin levels of less than 30 g/L with significant morbidity and mortality regardless of patient age and diagnosis (Agarwall, Acevedo, Leighton et al., 1988; Gibbs, Cull, Henderson et al., 1999). However, since albumin is degraded over 14 to 21 days, it is not a good measure for assessing recent nutritional deficits. Prealbumin has a half-life of 2 days and therefore is a better measure of response to dietary treatments. The normal reference range for prealbumin in males is 19 to 37 mg/dL, and in females, 17 to 31 mg/dL.

UNDERSTANDING CANCER-RELATED CAUSES OF MALNUTRITION. Most patients with cancer experience some weight loss during their illness. Anorexia, malabsorption, and cachexia are examples of nutritional problems that commonly occur in patients with cancer; special attention is needed to prevent weight loss and promote nutrition.

ANOREXIA. Anorexia is defined as an involuntary loss of appetite. Anorexia has been noted in up to one-half of newly diagnosed patients with cancer (Adams, Cunningham, Caruso et al., 2007). Among the many causes of anorexia in patients with cancer is alterations in taste, manifested by increased salty, sour, and metallic taste sensations, and altered responses to sweet and bitter flavors. These changes lead to decreased appetite, decreased nutritional intake, and protein–calorie malnutrition. Taste alterations may result from mineral (e.g., zinc) deficiencies, increases in circulating amino acids and cellular metabolites, or the administration of chemotherapeutic agents. Patients undergoing radiation therapy to the head and neck may experience "mouth blindness," (MacCarthy-Leventhalm, 1959) which is a severe impairment of taste. Alterations in the sense of smell also alter taste; this is a common experience of patients with head and neck cancers.

Anorexia may occur because people feel full after eating only a small amount of food. This is referred to as *early satiety.* This sense of fullness occurs secondary to a decrease in

(*continued on page 176*)

digestive enzymes, abnormalities in the metabolism of glucose and triglycerides, and prolonged stimulation of gastric volume receptors, which convey the feeling of being full. Psychological distress (e.g., fear, pain, depression, and isolation) throughout illness may also have a negative impact on appetite. Patients may develop an aversion to food because of nausea and vomiting after treatment.

CACHEXIA. Cachexia is common in patients with cancer, especially in advanced disease, affecting as many as 50% of patients with cancer. Cancer cachexia is related to inadequate nutritional intake along with increasing metabolic demand, increased energy expenditure due to anaerobic metabolism of the tumor, impaired glucose metabolism, competition of the tumor cells for nutrients, altered lipid metabolism, and a suppressed appetite. In addition, cachexia in cancer may be related to a cytokine-induced inflammatory response that results in anorexia and loss of muscle mass. Cachexia is characterized by loss of body weight, adipose tissue, visceral protein, and skeletal muscle. Patients with cachexia complain of loss of appetite, early satiety, and fatigue. As a result of protein losses, they often have anemia and peripheral edema. Cachexia can lead to an increased incidence of adverse events, decreased response to treatment, and increased mortality (Reid, McKenna, Fitzsimons et al., 2009).

PROMOTING NUTRITION. Whenever possible, every effort is used to maintain adequate nutrition through the oral route. Food should be prepared in ways that make it appealing. Unpleasant smells are avoided. Family members are included in the plan of care to encourage adequate food intake. The patient's preferences, as well as physiologic and metabolic requirements, are considered when selecting foods. Small, frequent meals are provided, with supplements between meals. Patients often tolerate larger amounts of food earlier in the day rather than later, so meals can be planned accordingly. To avoid early satiety, the patient should avoid drinking fluids while eating. Oral hygiene before mealtime often makes meals more pleasant. It is important to assess and manage pain, nausea, and other symptoms that may interfere with nutrition. Medications, such as corticosteroids or progestational agents such as megestrol acetate, have been used successfully as appetite stimulants. Prokinetic agents such as metoclopramide are used to increase gastric emptying in patients with early satiety and delayed gastric emptying.

If adequate nutrition cannot be maintained by oral intake, nutritional support via the enteral route may be necessary. Short-term nutritional supplementation may be provided through a nasogastric tube. However, if nutritional support is needed for longer than several weeks, a gastrostomy or jejunostomy tube may be inserted. The patient and family are taught to administer enteral nutrition in the home.

If malabsorption is a problem, enzyme and vitamin replacement may be instituted. Additional strategies include

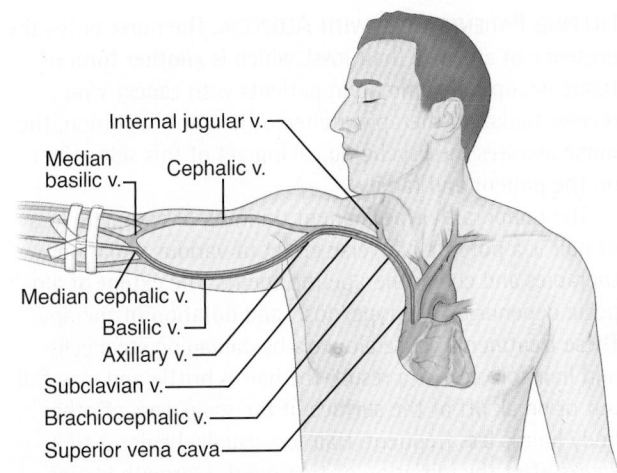

FIGURE 6-5 A peripherally inserted central catheter (PICC) is advanced through the cephalic or basilic vein to the axillary, subclavian, or brachiocephalic vein or the superior vena cava.

changing the feeding schedule, using simple diets, and relieving diarrhea. If malabsorption is severe, parenteral nutrition may be necessary. Parenteral nutrition can be administered in several ways: by a long-term venous access device (e.g., right atrial catheter), by an implanted venous port, or by a peripherally inserted central catheter (PICC) (Fig. 6-5). The nurse teaches the patient and family to care for venous access devices and to administer parenteral nutrition when appropriate. Home care nurses may assist with or supervise parenteral nutrition administration in the home.

Interventions to reduce cachexia usually do not prolong survival or improve nutritional status significantly. Further study is needed to assess the effects of nutritional intervention on disease status and the patient's quality of life. Before invasive nutritional strategies are instituted, the nurse should assess the patient carefully and discuss options with the patient and family.

Relieving Pain

The nurse assesses the patient with cancer for the source and site of pain. In cancer, pain and discomfort may be related to underlying disease, pressure exerted by the tumor, diagnostic procedures, or the cancer treatment itself. As in any other situation involving pain, cancer pain is affected by both physical and psychosocial influences. A comprehensive pain assessment is completed including onset, duration, location, quality or characteristics, quantity, aggravating and alleviating factors, associated symptoms and the treatments that the patient has used to relieve pain.

The nurse also assesses those factors that increase the patient's perception of pain, such as fear and apprehension, fatigue, anger, and social isolation. Pain assessment scales (see Chapter 7) are useful for assessing the patient's pain before pain-relieving interventions are instituted and for evaluating the effectiveness of these interventions.

Pain occurs in approximately 50% of patients with all stages of disease and 75% of patients with advanced disease (Goudas, Bloch, Gialeli-Goudas et al., 2005). In fact, 85% of advanced cancer patients complain of more than one pain source (Dobratz, 2009). Although the pain may be acute, it is more frequently characterized as chronic. As in other situations involving pain, the experience of cancer pain is influenced by both physical and psychosocial factors.

Cancer can cause pain in various ways. Pain may be associated with various cancer treatments. Acute pain is linked with trauma from surgery. Occasionally, chronic pain syndromes, such as postsurgical neuropathies (pain related to nerve tissue injury), occur. Some chemotherapeutic agents cause tissue necrosis, peripheral neuropathies, and stomatitis—all potential sources of pain—whereas radiation therapy can cause pain secondary to skin or organ inflammation.

For many patients, pain is a signal that the tumor is growing and that death is approaching. As patients anticipate the pain and their anxiety increases, pain perception heightens, producing fear and further pain. Chronic cancer pain, then, can be best described as a cycle progressing from pain to anxiety to fear and back to pain.

Pain tolerance, the point past which pain can no longer be tolerated, varies among people. Pain tolerance is decreased by fatigue, anxiety, fear of death, anger, powerlessness, social isolation, changes in role identity, loss of independence, and past experiences. Adequate rest and sleep, diversion, mood elevation, empathy, and medications such as antidepressants, antianxiety agents, and analgesics enhance tolerance to pain.

Inadequate pain management is most often the result of misconceptions and insufficient knowledge about pain assessment and pharmacologic interventions on the part of patients, families, and health care providers. Successful management of cancer pain is based on thorough and objective pain assessment that examines physical, psychosocial, environmental, and spiritual factors. A multidisciplinary team approach is essential to determine optimal management of the patient's pain.

The World Health Organization advocates a three-step approach to treat cancer pain (Fig. 6-6). Analgesics are administered based on the patient's level of pain. Nonopioid analgesics (e.g., acetaminophen) are used for mild pain; weak opioid analgesics (e.g., codeine) are used for moderate pain; and strong opioid analgesics (e.g., morphine) are used for severe pain. If the pain escalates, the dose of the analgesic medication is increased until the pain is controlled. Adjuvant medications are also administered to enhance the effectiveness of analgesics and to manage other symptoms that may contribute to the pain experience. Examples of adjuvant medications include antiemetics, antidepressants, anxiolytics, antiseizure agents, stimulants, local anesthetics, radiopharmaceuticals (radioactive agents that may be used to treat painful bone tumors), and corticosteroids. A cancer

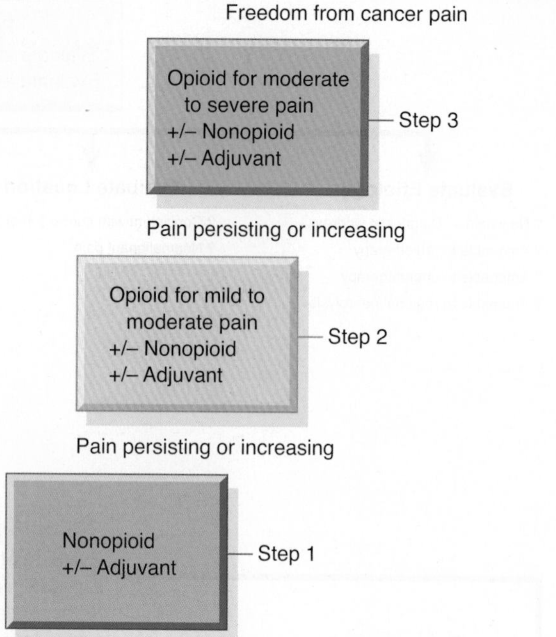

FIGURE 6-6 Adapted from the World Health Organization three-step ladder approach to relieving cancer pain. Various opioid (narcotic) and nonopioid medications may be combined with other medications to control pain.

pain algorithm, developed as a set of analgesic guiding principles, is given in Figure 6-7.

Preventing and reducing pain help to decrease anxiety and break the pain cycle. This can be accomplished best by administering analgesics on a regularly scheduled basis as prescribed (the preventive, preferred approach to pain management), with additional analgesics administered for breakthrough pain as needed and as prescribed.

Various pharmacologic and nonpharmacologic options are available for managing cancer pain. No reasonable approaches, even those that may be invasive, should be overlooked because of a poor or terminal prognosis. The nurse helps the patient and family take an active role in managing pain. The nurse provides education and support to correct fears and misconceptions about opioid use. Inadequate pain control leads to suffering, anxiety, fear, immobility, isolation, and depression. The goal, regardless of the patient's disease status, is to maximize quality of life and optimize functional ability by adequately managing pain.

Improving Body Image

The nurse identifies potential threats to the patient's body image and assesses the patient's ability to cope with the many assaults to body image he or she experiences throughout the course of disease and treatment. Entry into the health care system is often accompanied by depersonalization. Threats to self-concept are enormous as the patient faces the realization of illness, disfigurement, possible

(*continued on page 179*)

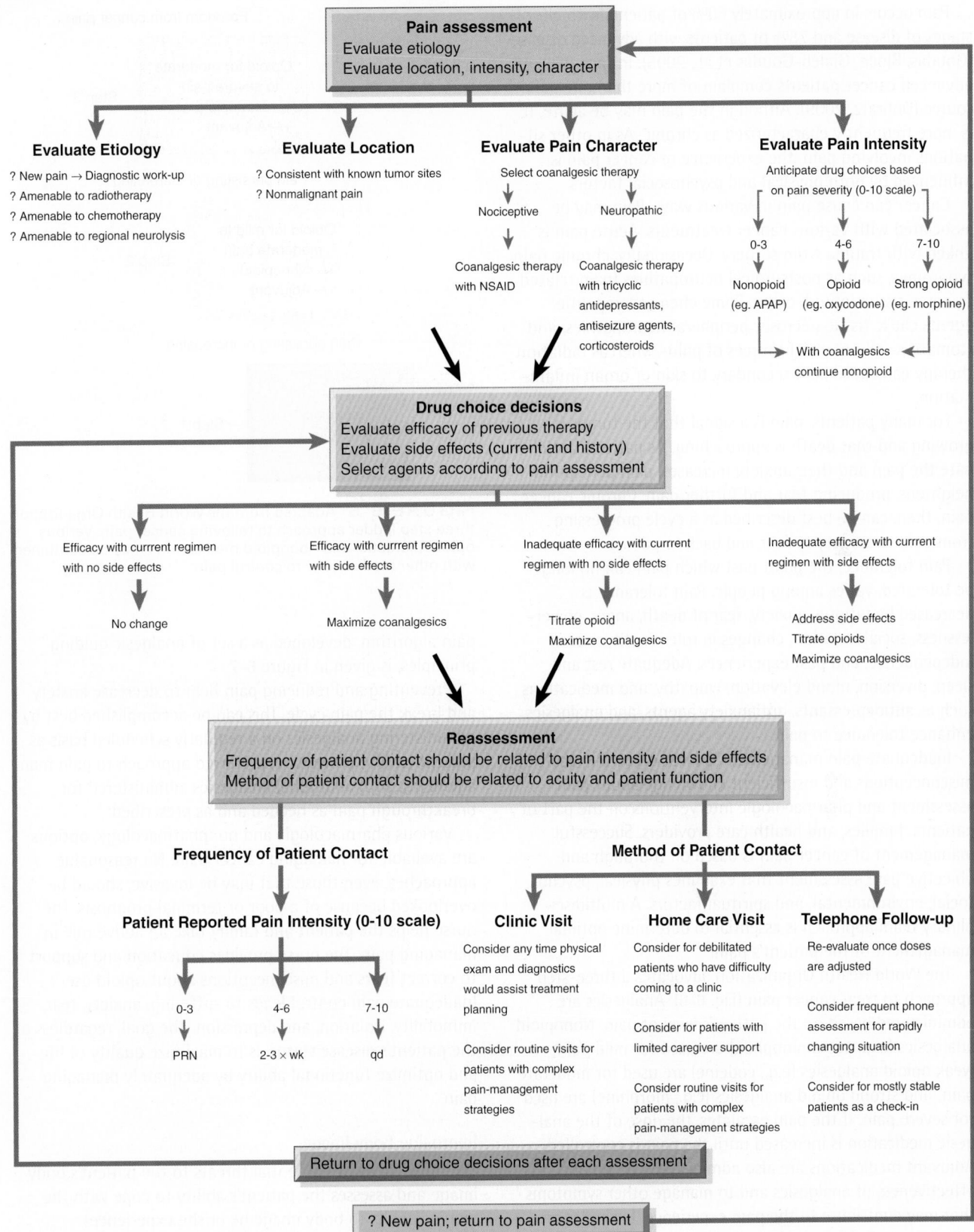

Pain assessment
Evaluate etiology
Evaluate location, intensity, character

Evaluate Etiology

? New pain → Diagnostic work-up
? Amenable to radiotherapy
? Amenable to chemotherapy
? Amenable to regional neurolysis

Evaluate Location

? Consistent with known tumor sites
? Nonmalignant pain

Evaluate Pain Character

Select coanalgesic therapy

Nociceptive | Neuropathic

Coanalgesic therapy with NSAID | Coanalgesic therapy with tricyclic antidepressants, antiseizure agents, corticosteroids

Evaluate Pain Intensity

Anticipate drug choices based on pain severity (0-10 scale)

0-3 | 4-6 | 7-10

Nonopioid (eg. APAP) | Opioid (eg. oxycodone) | Strong opioid (eg. morphine)

With coanalgesics continue nonopioid

Drug choice decisions
Evaluate efficacy of previous therapy
Evaluate side effects (current and history)
Select agents according to pain assessment

Efficacy with currrent regimen with no side effects | Efficacy with currrent regimen with side effects | Inadequate efficacy with currrent regimen with no side effects | Inadequate efficacy with currrent regimen with side effects

No change | Maximize coanalgesics | Titrate opioid Maximize coanalgesics | Address side effects Titrate opioids Maximize coanalgesics

Reassessment
Frequency of patient contact should be related to pain intensity and side effects
Method of patient contact should be related to acuity and patient function

Frequency of Patient Contact

Patient Reported Pain Intensity (0-10 scale)

0-3 | 4-6 | 7-10

PRN | 2-3 × wk | qd

Method of Patient Contact

Clinic Visit

Consider any time physical exam and diagnostics would assist treatment planning

Consider routine visits for patients with complex pain-management strategies

Home Care Visit

Consider for debilitated patients who have difficulty coming to a clinic

Consider for patients with limited caregiver support

Consider routine visits for patients with complex pain-management strategies

Telephone Follow-up

Re-evaluate once doses are adjusted

Consider frequent phone assessment for rapidly changing situation

Consider for mostly stable patients as a check-in

Return to drug choice decisions after each assessment

? New pain; return to pain assessment

FIGURE 6-7 The cancer pain algorithm (highest-level view) is a decision-tree model for pain treatment that was developed as an interpretation of the AHCPR Guideline for Cancer Pain, 1994. Reproduced with permission from DuPen, A. R., DuPen, S., Hansberry, J., et al. (2000). An educational implementation of a cancer pain algorithm for ambulatory care. *Pain Management Nursing, 1* (4), 118.

disability, and death. To accommodate treatments or because of the disease, many patients with cancer are forced to alter their lifestyles. Priorities and values change when body image is threatened. Disfiguring surgery, hair loss, cachexia, skin changes, altered communication patterns, and sexual dysfunction are some of the devastating results of cancer and its treatment that threaten the patients' self-esteem and body image.

A positive approach is essential when caring for patients with altered body image. To help the patient retain control and positive self-esteem, it is important to encourage independence and continued participation in self-care and decision-making. The patient is assisted to assume those tasks and participate in those activities that are personally of most value. Any negative feelings that the patient has or threats to body image should be identified and discussed. The nurse serves as a listener and counselor to both the patient and the family. Referral to a support group can provide the patient with additional assistance in coping with the changes resulting from cancer or its treatment. In many cases, cosmetologists can provide ideas about hair or wig styling, makeup, and the use of scarves and turbans to help with body image concerns.

Patients who experience alterations in sexuality and sexual function are encouraged to discuss concerns openly with the health care team and with their partners. Alternative forms of sexual expression are explored with patients and their partners to promote positive self-worth and acceptance. Nurses who identify serious physiologic, psychological, or communication difficulties related to sexuality or sexual function are in a key position to help patients and partners seek further counseling if necessary.

Teaching Patients Self-Care

Many patients with cancer return home from acute-care facilities to receive treatment in the home or outpatient area. The shift from the acute-care setting also shifts the responsibility for care to the patient and family. As a result, family members and friends must assume increased involvement in patient care, which requires teaching that enables them to provide quality care. Teaching initially focuses on providing information needed by the patient and family to address the most immediate care needs likely to be encountered at home.

Side effects of treatments and changes in the patient's status that should be reported are reviewed verbally and reinforced with written information. Strategies to deal with side effects of treatment are discussed with the patient and family. Other learning needs are identified based on the priorities conveyed by the patient and family, as well as on the complexity of care provided in the home.

Technological advances allow home administration of chemotherapy, parenteral nutrition, blood products, parenteral antibiotics, and parenteral analgesics, as well as management of symptoms and care of vascular access devices. Although home care nurses provide care and support for patients receiving this advanced technical care, patients and families need instruction and ongoing support that allow them to feel comfortable and proficient in managing these treatments at home. Follow-up visits and telephone calls from the nurse are often reassuring and increase the patient's and family's comfort in dealing with complex and new aspects of care. Continued contact facilitates evaluation of the patient's progress and assessment of the ongoing needs of the patient and family.

Continuing Care

Referral for home care is often indicated for patients with cancer. The responsibilities of the home care nurse include assessing the home environment, suggesting modifications in the home or in care to help the patient and family address the patient's physical needs, providing physical care, and assessing the psychological and emotional impact of the illness on the patient and family.

Assessing changes in the patient's physical status and reporting relevant changes to the provider helps ensure that appropriate and timely modifications in therapy are made. The home care nurse also assesses the adequacy of pain management and the effectiveness of other strategies to prevent or manage the side effects of treatment modalities.

It is necessary to assess the patient's and family's understanding of the treatment plan and management strategies and to reinforce previous teaching. The nurse often facilitates coordination of patient care by maintaining close communication with all involved health care providers. The nurse may make referrals and coordinate available community resources (e.g., local office of the American Cancer Society, home aides, church groups, parish nurses, support groups) to assist patients and caregivers.

Evaluation

Nurses play an important role in evaluating the expected outcomes for patients with cancer. To maximize beneficial outcomes and intervene with potential complications, evaluation of the patient's and family's needs are assessed because cancer affects not only the patient but also the family members. In addition, with the shift away from inpatient care, many families are caring for patients at home and should be considered members of the health care team. The nurse can refer the patient and family to a variety of support groups sponsored by the American Cancer Society or available community resources. The nurse also collaborates with a variety of providers (e.g., physical, occupational, enterostomal therapists, nutritionists, pharmacists, psychologists, and clergy or spiritual advisors) to help identify appropriate interventions that support the goal of regaining the highest level of function and independence possible for the patient.

(continued on page 180)

Expected patient outcomes may include the following:

1. Maintains integrity of oral mucous membranes
2. Maintains adequate tissue integrity
3. Maintains adequate nutritional status
4. Achieves relief of pain and discomfort
5. Demonstrates increased activity tolerance and decreased fatigue
6. Exhibits improved body image and self-esteem
7. Progresses through the grieving process
8. Experiences no complications, such as infection, or sepsis, and no episodes of bleeding or hemorrhage

GERONTOLOGIC CONSIDERATIONS

As a result of an increased life expectancy and an increased risk of cancer with age, nurses are providing cancer-related care for growing numbers of elderly patients. More than 58% of all cancers occur in people older than 65 years of age, and about two-thirds of all cancer deaths occur in people 65 years of age and older. Nursing care of this population addresses special needs, including physical, psychosocial, and financial concerns.

Oncology nurses working with the elderly population must understand the normal physiologic changes that occur with aging. These changes include decreased skin elasticity; decreased skeletal mass, structure, and strength; decreased organ function and structure; impaired immune system mechanisms; alterations in neurologic and sensory functions; and altered drug absorption, distribution, metabolism, and elimination. These changes ultimately influence the ability of elderly patients to tolerate cancer treatment. In addition, many elderly patients have other chronic diseases and associated treatments that may limit tolerance to cancer treatments.

Potential chemotherapy-related toxicities, such as renal impairment, myelosuppression, fatigue, and cardiomyopathy, may increase as a result of declining organ function and diminished physiologic reserves. The recovery of normal tissues after radiation therapy may be delayed, and older patients may experience more severe adverse effects, such as mucositis, nausea and vomiting, and myelosuppression. Because of decreased tissue healing capacity and declining pulmonary and cardiovascular functioning, older patients are slower to recover from surgery. Elderly patients are also at increased risk for complications such as atelectasis, pneumonia, and wound infections.

Access to cancer care for elderly patients may be limited by discriminatory or fatalistic attitudes of health care providers, caregivers, and patients themselves. Issues such as the gradual loss of supportive resources, declining health or loss of a spouse, and unavailability of relatives or friends may result in limited access to care and unmet needs for assistance with activities of daily living. In addition, the economic impact of health care may be difficult for those living on fixed incomes.

Nurses must be aware of the special needs of the aging population. Cancer prevention, detection, and screening efforts are directed toward the elderly, as well as toward the younger population. Nurses carefully monitor elderly patients receiving cancer treatments for signs and symptoms of adverse effects. In addition, elderly patients are instructed to report all symptoms to their provider. It is not uncommon for elderly patients to delay reporting symptoms, attributing them to "old age." Many elderly people do not want to report illness for fear of losing their independence or financial security. Sensory losses (e.g., hearing and visual losses) and memory deficits are considered when planning patient education because they may affect the patient's ability to process and retain information. In such cases, the nurse acts as a patient advocate, encouraging independence and identifying resources for support when indicated.

END-OF-LIFE CONSIDERATIONS

The needs of patients with terminal illnesses are best met by a comprehensive multidisciplinary program that focuses on quality of life, palliation of symptoms, and provision of psychosocial and spiritual support for patients and families when cure and control of the disease are no longer possible. The concept of hospice, which originated in Great Britain, best addresses these needs. Most important, the focus of care is on the family, not just the patient. Hospice care can be provided in several settings: free-standing, hospital-based, and community or home-based settings.

Hospice care is often delivered through coordination of services provided by hospitals and the community. Although physicians, social workers, clergy, dietitians, pharmacists, physical therapists, and volunteers are involved in patient care, nurses are most often the coordinators of all hospice activities. It is essential that home care and hospice nurses possess advanced skills in assessing and managing pain, nutrition, dyspnea, bowel dysfunction, and skin impairments.

In addition, hospice programs facilitate clear communication among family members and health care providers. Most patients and families are informed of the prognosis and are encouraged to participate in decisions regarding pursuing or terminating cancer treatment. Through collaboration with other support disciplines, the nurse helps the patient and family cope with changes in role identity, family structure, grief, and loss. Hospice nurses are actively involved in bereavement counseling. In many instances, family support for survivors continues for approximately 1 year.

ONCOLOGIC EMERGENCIES

For information about these emergencies and related nursing care, see Table 6-6.

TABLE
6-6 Oncologic Emergencies: Manifestations and Management

Emergency	Diagnostic Approaches and Clinical Manifestations	Medical & Nursing Management

Superior Vena Cava Syndrome (SVCS)
Compression or invasion of the superior vena cava by tumor, enlarged lymph nodes, or intraluminal thrombus that obstructs venous circulation, or drainage of the head, neck, arms, and thorax. Compression of the SVC restricts venous return, decreasing cardiac output. Typically SVCS is associated with bronchogenic cancer but can be associated with other cancers such as lymphoma. Internal occlusion can precipitate SVCS if a central vein catheter becomes occluded. If untreated, SVCS may lead to cerebral anoxia (because not enough oxygen reaches the brain), laryngeal edema, bronchial obstruction, and death (Kuzin, 2006).
	Diagnostic
	Diagnosis is confirmed by
	• Clinical findings
	• Chest X-ray
	• Thoracic computed tomography (CT) scan
	• Thoracic magnetic resonance imaging (MRI)
	Intraluminal thrombosis may be identified by venogram.
	Biopsy to obtain tissue diagnosis to determine cause is important in initiating treatment.
	Clinical
	Gradually or suddenly impaired venous drainage giving rise to:
	• Progressive dyspnea, cough, hoarseness, chest pain, and facial swelling, cyanosis, plethora (redness) of the face, complaints of difficulty buttoning shirt collars
	• Engorged and distended jugular, temporal, and arm veins
	• Dilated thoracic vessels causing prominent venous patterns on the chest wall
	Blood pressure that is elevated in the upper extremities and low in the lower extremities
	Tachycardia
	Late signs: Increased intracranial pressure, associated visual disturbances, headache, dizziness, syncope and altered mental status, irritability, lethargy (Colen, 2008)
		Medical
		• The goal is control or cure of the underlying malignancy or cause by:
		  • Radiation therapy to shrink tumor size, relieving symptoms
		  • Chemotherapy for chemosensitive cancers (e.g., lymphoma, small cell lung cancer) or when the mediastinum has been irradiated to maximum tolerance
		  • Anticoagulant or thrombolytic therapy for intraluminal thrombosis
		  • Stent placement to restore blood flow
		• Supportive measures such as oxygen therapy, corticosteroids, diuretics, and anxiolytics
		Nursing
		• Identify patients at risk for SVCS.
		• Monitor and report clinical manifestations of SVCS.
		• Monitor cardiopulmonary and neurologic status.
		• Facilitate breathing by positioning the patient properly. Assist the patient to maintain an upright position (elevated 45 degrees). This helps to promote comfort and reduce anxiety and reduce intracranial pressure
		• Remove rings and restrictive clothing.
		Monitor the patient's fluid volume status: Assess weights and I/Os regularly.
		Ensure that the patient avoids the Valsalva maneuver, which may worsen symptoms, by providing cough suppressants and stool softeners as needed.

Spinal Cord Compression Occurs when a malignant disease or a pathologically collapsed vertebrae compresses or displaces the thecal sac that contains the spinal cord, leading to neurologic impairment. The prognosis depends on the severity and rapidity of onset. Presenting signs and symptoms depend on the location of compression. About 60% of compressions occur at the thoracic level, 30% in the lumbosacral level, and 10% in the cervical region (Abrahm, 2004). Metastatic cancers (breast, lung, kidney, prostate, myeloma, lymphoma) and related bone erosion are associated with spinal cord compression (Flounders, 2003a).	*Diagnostic* • MRI, myelogram, spinal cord X-rays, bone scans, and CT scan *Clinical* Percussion tenderness at the level of compression • Abnormal reflexes • Sensory and motor abnormalities • Local or radicular back or neck pain along the dermatomal areas innervated by the affected nerve root (Flounders, 2003) (e.g., thoracic radicular pain extends in a band around the chest or abdomen) • Pain exacerbated by movement, supine recumbent position, coughing, sneezing, or the Valsalva maneuver • Neurologic dysfunction, and related motor and sensory deficits (numbness, tingling, feelings of coldness in the affected area, inability to detect vibration, loss of positional sense)	*Medical* • Radiation therapy to reduce tumor size to halt progression Corticosteroid therapy to decrease inflammation and swelling at the compression site • Surgery if symptoms progress despite radiation therapy or if vertebral fracture leads to additional nerve damage; surgery is also an option when the tumor is not radiosensitive or is located in an area that was previously irradiated (Flounders, 2003a). • Chemotherapy as adjuvant to radiation therapy for patients with lymphoma or small cell lung cancer • *Note:* Despite treatment, patients with poor neurologic function before treatment are less likely to regain complete motor and sensory function; patients who develop complete paralysis usually do not regain all neurologic function (Abrahm, 2004). Pain management is a priority.

(continued on page 182)

TABLE
6-6 Oncologic Emergencies: Manifestations and Management (continued)

Emergency	Diagnostic Approaches and Clinical Manifestations	Medical & Nursing Management
	• Motor loss ranging from subtle weakness to flaccid paralysis • Bladder and/or bowel dysfunction depending on level of compression (above S2, overflow incontinence; from S3 to S5, flaccid sphincter tone and bowel incontinence).	**Nursing** • Perform ongoing assessment of neurologic function to identify existing and progressing dysfunction. • Control pain with pharmacologic and nonpharmacologic measures. • Prevent complications of immobility resulting from pain and decreased function (e.g., skin breakdown, urinary stasis, thrombophlebitis, decreased clearance of pulmonary secretions). • Maintain muscle tone by assisting with range-of-motion exercises in collaboration with physical and occupational therapists. • Institute intermittent urinary catheterization and bowel training programs for patients with bladder or bowel dysfunction. Maintain safety by assisting the patient with ADLs and ambulation.
Hypercalcemia In patients with cancer, hypercalcemia is a potentially life-threatening metabolic abnormality resulting when the calcium released from the bones exceeds the kidneys ability to excrete or the bones can reabsorb. It may be the result of: • Bone destruction by tumor cells and subsequent release of calcium • Production of prostaglandins and osteoclast-activating factors, which stimulate bone breakdown and calcium release (Shuey, 2004) • Tumors that produce parathyroid-like substances that promote calcium release (Kaplan, 2006)	**Diagnostic** Serum calcium level exceeding 11 mg/dL (2.74 mmol/L) **Clinical** Early signs: Fatigue, weakness, lethargy, irritability, cognitive changes, personality changes, confusion, decreased level of responsiveness, hyporeflexia, nausea, vomiting, constipation, anorexia, polyuria (excessive urination), polydipsia (excessive thirst), nocturia, dehydration. Late signs: ataxia, stupor, seizures, coma, arrythmias, ileus, renal failure, heart block, cardiac arrest (Kaplan, 2006).	**Medical** See Chapters 4 and 31. **Nursing** • Identify patients at risk for hypercalcemia and assess for signs and symptoms of hypercalcemia. • Educate patient and family on prevention including hydration and ambulation. • Teach at-risk patients to recognize and report signs and symptoms of hypercalcemia promptly. • Ensure that patients consume (PO or IV) a total of 3–4 liters of fluid daily unless contraindicated by existing renal or cardiac disease. Monitor I/O. • Explain the use of dietary and pharmacologic interventions such as stool softeners and laxatives for constipation. Discuss antiemetic therapy if nausea and vomiting occur. • Advise patients to maintain nutritional intake without restricting normal calcium intake. • Implement safety measures including fall and seizure precautions (Kaplan, 2006) • Promote mobilization by assisting with ambulation, providing active resistive exercises for patients on bedrest and emphasize the importance of mobility in preventing demineralization and breakdown of bones (Shuey & Brant, 2004).

Emergency	Diagnostic Approaches and Clinical Manifestations	Medical & Nursing Management

Pericardial Effusion and Cardiac Tamponade

Cardiac tamponade is an accumulation of fluid in the pericardial space. The fluid compresses the heart and thereby impedes expansion of the ventricles, limiting cardiac filling during diastole. As ventricular volume and cardiac output fall, the heart pump fails, and circulatory collapse develops.

With gradual onset, fluid accumulates slowly, and the outer layer of the pericardial space stretches to compensate for rising pressure. Large amounts of fluid accumulate before symptoms of heart failure occur. With rapid onset, pressures rise too quickly for the pericardial space to compensate.

Malignancies, particularly from adjacent thoracic tumors (lung, breast cancer, lymphoma), and side effects of cancer treatment are the most common causes of cardiac tamponade. Radiation therapy of 4,000 cGy or more to the mediastinal area has also been implicated in pericardial fibrosis, pericarditis, and resultant cardiac tamponade. Untreated pericardial effusion and cardiac tamponade lead to circulatory collapse and cardiac arrest (Story, 2006).

Diagnostic
- Electrocardiography (ECG)
- In small effusion, chest X-rays show small amounts of fluid in the pericardium; in large effusions, X-ray films disclose "water-bottle" heart (obliteration of vessel contour and cardiac chambers)
- CT scans help diagnose pleural effusions and evaluate effect of treatment

Clinical
- Fatigue, dyspnea, orthopnea, nonproductive cough, dull or diffuse chest pain.
Neck vein distention during inspiration (Kussmaul's sign)
- Pulsus paradoxus (systolic blood pressure decrease exceeding 10 mm Hg during inspiration; pulse gets stronger on expiration)
- Distant heart sounds, rubs and gallops, cardiac dullness
- Compensatory tachycardia (heart beats faster to compensate for decreased cardiac output)
- Increased venous and vascular pressures
- Narrow pulse pressure (the difference between systolic and diastolic blood pressure).
- Shortness of breath and tachypnea
- Weakness, chest pain, orthopnea, anxiety, diaphoresis, lethargy, and altered consciousness from decreased cerebral perfusion (Story, 2006, Ezzone, 2006).

Medical
- Pericardiocentesis (the aspiration or withdrawal of pericardial fluid by a large-bore needle inserted into the pericardial space). In malignant effusions, pericardiocentesis provides only temporary relief; fluid usually reaccumulates. Windows or openings in the pericardium can be created surgically as a palliative measure to drain fluid into the pleural space. Catheters may also be placed in the pericardial space and sclerosing agents (such as doxycycline, talc, bleomycin) are injected to prevent fluid from reaccumulating (Keefe, 2000).
- Radiation therapy; antineoplastic agents. In mild effusions, prednisone and diuretic medications may be used.

Nursing
- Monitor vital signs, oxygen saturation, cardiac and respiratory exam frequently.
- Assess for pulsus paradoxus.
- Monitor ECG tracings.
- Assess heart and lung sounds, neck vein filling, level of consciousness, respiratory status, and skin color and temperature.
- Monitor and record intake and output.
- Review laboratory findings (e.g., arterial blood gas and electrolyte levels).
- Elevate the head of the patient's bed to ease breathing.
- Minimize patient's physical activity to reduce oxygen requirements; administer supplemental oxygen as prescribed.
- Provide frequent oral hygiene.
- Reposition and encourage the patient to cough, used pursed lip breathing, and take deep breaths.
Maintain oxygen saturation >92%.
Administer analgesics and anxiolytics as ordered.
Assist patients with relaxation techniques.

Disseminated Intravascular Coagulation (DIC, also called consumption coagulopathy)

Complex disorder of coagulation and fibrinolysis (destruction of clots), which results in thrombosis and bleeding. DIC is most commonly associated with hematologic cancers (leukemia); cancer of prostate, GI (GI) tract, and lungs; chemotherapy (methotrexate, prednisone, L-asparaginase, vincristine, and 6-mercaptopurine); and disease processes such as sepsis, hepatic failure, and anaphylaxis.

Diagnostic
- Prolonged prothrombin time (PT or protime)
Prolonged INR
- Prolonged partial thromboplastin time (PTT)
- Prolonged thrombin time (TT)
- Decreased fibrinogen level
- Decreased platelet level
- Decrease in clotting factors
- Decreased hemoglobin
- Decreased hematocrit
- Elevated fibrin split products (or fibrin degradation products)
Elevated D-dimer test
- Positive protamine sulfate precipitation test (thrombin activation test) (Krimmel, 2003)

Medical
The underlying cause of DIC must be treated.
- Chemotherapy, biologic response modifier therapy, radiation therapy, or surgery is used to treat the underlying cancer.
- Antibiotic therapy is used for sepsis.
- Anticoagulants, such as heparin or antithrombin III, decrease the stimulation of the coagulation pathways. Anticoagulants must be used with caution in patients who have experienced or are at risk for bleeding.

(continued on page 184)

Emergency	Diagnostic Approaches and Clinical Manifestations	Medical & Nursing Management
Blood clots form when normal coagulation mechanisms are triggered. Once activated, the clotting cascade continues to consume clotting factors and platelets faster than the body can replace them, which can result in bleeding. Clots are deposited in the microvasculature, placing the patient at great risk for impaired circulation, tissue hypoxia, and necrosis. In addition, fibrinolysis occurs, breaking down clots and increasing the circulating levels of anticoagulant substances, thereby placing the patient at risk for hemorrhage (Ezzone, 2006).	**Clinical** *Chronic DIC:* Characterized by diffuse thrombosis or subacute bleeding (Ezzone, 2006). Few or no observable symptoms or easy bruising, prolonged bleeding from venipuncture and injection sites, bleeding of the gums, and slow GI bleeding *Acute DIC:* life-threatening hemorrhage and infarction; clinical symptoms of this syndrome are varied and depend on the organ system involved in thrombus and infarction or bleeding episodes. Bleeding can occur anywhere.	• Transfusion of fresh-frozen plasma or cryoprecipitates (which contain clotting factors and fibrinogen), packed RBCs, and platelets may be used as replacement therapy to prevent or control bleeding. • Although controversial, antifibrinolytic agents such as aminocaproic acid (Amicar), which is associated with increased thrombus formation, may be used. **Nursing** • Monitor vital signs. • Measure and document intake and output. • Assess skin color and temperature; lung, heart, and bowel sounds; level of consciousness, headache, visual disturbances, chest pain, decreased urine output, and abdominal tenderness. • Inspect all body orifices, tube insertion sites, incisions, and bodily excretions for bleeding. • Review laboratory test results. • Minimize physical activity to decrease injury risks and oxygen requirements. • Prevent bleeding; apply pressure to all venipuncture sites, and avoid nonessential invasive procedures; avoid the use of tourniquets; provide electric rather than straight-edged razors; avoid tape on the skin and advise gentle but adequate oral hygiene with use of a soft toothbrush or toothette. • Assist the patient to turn, cough, and take deep breaths every 2 hours. • Reorient the patient, if needed; maintain a safe environment; and provide appropriate patient education and supportive measures.
Syndrome of Inappropriate Secretion of Antidiuretic Hormone (SIADH) SIADH is a result of the failure in the negative feedback mechanism that normally regulates the release of antidiuretic hormone (ADH). Some malignancies, such as small cell lung cancer, inappropriately release antidiuretic hormone (ADH). The excessive release of ADH produced by tumor cells or by the abnormal stimulation of the hypothalamic–pituitary network, leads to uncontrolled water reabsorption. Most of the reabsorbed water resides in the intracellular (vs. intravascular) space, causing intracellular edema, hyponatremia, and increased excretion of urinary sodium (Clancey, 2006). The most common cause of SIADH is cancer, especially small cell cancer of the lung.	**Diagnostic** • Decreased serum sodium level Decreased serum osmolality • Increased urine osmolality • Increased urinary sodium level Increased urine specific gravity • Decreased blood urea nitrogen (BUN), creatinine, and serum albumin levels secondary to dilution • Abnormal water load test results **Clinical** *Mild SIADH:* serum sodium 125–134 mEq/L Signs and symptoms include: increased thirst, anorexia, nausea, fatigue, weakness, headache (Clancey, 2006) *Moderate SIADH:* Serum sodium levels <115–124 mEq/L (120 mmol/L) *Signs and symptoms include:* personality changes, irritability, nausea, anorexia, vomiting, weight gain, oliguria, fatigue, muscular pain (myalgia), headache, lethargy, and confusion (Langfeldt & Cooley, 2003).	**Medical** The underlying cause of SIADH must be treated in order to effectively treat SIADH. Discontinue the offending medication. Fluid intake limited to 500–1,000 mL/day to increase the serum sodium level. If water restriction alone is not effective in correcting or controlling serum sodium levels, demeclocycline is often prescribed to inhibit ADH secretion and promote water excretion. If neurologic symptoms are severe, parenteral sodium replacement and diuretic therapy are indicated. Electrolyte levels are monitored carefully to detect secondary magnesium, potassium, and calcium imbalances. After the symptoms of SIADH are controlled, the underlying cancer is treated. If water excess continues despite treatment, pharmacologic intervention (urea and furosemide) may be indicated (Flounders, 2003a; Casciato, 2004).

Emergency	Diagnostic Approaches and Clinical Manifestations	Medical & Nursing Management

Medications, including antineo-plastics—vincristine, vinblastine, cisplatin, and cyclophospha-mide—and morphine also stimulate ADH secretion

Severe SIADH: Serum sodium levels <115 mEq/L Signs & symptoms include: seizure, abnormal reflexes, delirium, ataxia, papilledema, coma, and death.

Number and severity of symptoms depends on the rate of onset; the faster the onset of SIADH, the more symptomatic the patient may be (Clancey, 2006).

Signs and symptoms of fluid volume overload, including edema are rare.

Hypertonic (3%) saline may be administered for a short time (1–3 hours) in an intensive care setting with frequent (q2h) serum sodium levels (Keenan, 2005).

The goal is to increase the serum sodium level slowly. Increasing the serum sodium level too quickly can cause intracellular dehydration, which may result in serious neurologic impairment.

Nursing

Early identification of at risk patients is essential to promote early intervention.

- Maintain intake and output measurements; assess urine specific gravity.
- Assess level of consciousness, lung and heart sounds, vital signs, daily weight; also assess for nausea, vomiting, anorexia, edema, fatigue, and lethargy.
- Monitor laboratory test results, including serum electrolyte levels, osmolality, and BUN, creatinine, and urinary sodium levels.
- Minimize the patient's activity; provide appropriate oral hygiene; maintain environmental safety; and restrict fluid intake if necessary.

Maintain safety: implement fall and seizure precautions for sodium levels <120 mEq/L.

Medical

Prevention, early detection, and prompt management are critical in decreasing morbidity and mortality.

- To prevent renal failure and restore electrolyte balance, aggressive hydration is initiated 48 hours before the initiation of cytotoxic therapy to increase urine volume and eliminate uric acid and electrolytes. Hydration and alkalization should be continued through the at-risk period.

Urine is alkalinized by adding sodium bicarbonate to IV fluid to maintain a urine pH of ≥7; this prevents renal failure secondary to uric acid precipitation in the kidneys by increasing the solubility of uric acid.

- Following aggressive hydration, diuretic therapy may be used to increase electrolyte excretion (potassium, uric acid).
- Allopurinol therapy should be started prior to the initiation of chemotherapy to inhibit the conversion of nucleic acids to uric acid (Cope, 2004).

Rasburicase therapy may be initiated as prophylaxis or treatment of hyperuricemia. Rasburicase converts uric acid into allantoin, which is a substance that is soluble in urine.

Tumor Lysis Syndrome (TLS)

TLS is a rapidly developing oncologic emergency that results from the rapid release of intracellular contents as a result of radiation- or chemotherapy-induced cell destruction of large or rapidly growing cancers such as leukemia. lymphoma, and small cell lung cancer (Colen, 2008). Cancer cells have an abnormally high amount of potassium, phosphate, and nucleic acids. The release of these intracellular contents from the tumor cells leads to electrolyte imbalances—hyperkalemia, hypocalcemia, hyperphosphatemia, and hyperuricemia—because the kidneys can no longer excrete large volumes of the released intracellular metabolites. These metabolic abnormalities may result in life-threatening arrhythmias, seizures, and renal failure.

Diagnostic

Electrolyte imbalances identified by laboratory test results (Coiffier et al., 2008) including:

Uric acid >6 mg/dL
Phosphorus >4.5 mg/dL
Potassium >5.5 mEq/L
Calcium <8.5 mg/dL

Clinical

Clinical manifestations depend on the extent of metabolic abnormalities.

- Neurologic: fatigue, weakness, memory loss, altered mental status, muscle cramps, irritability, paresthesias (numbness and tingling), tetany seizures
- Cardiac: hypotension, peaked T waves, flattened P waves, widened QRS waves, ST depression, dysrhythmias, cardiac arrest
- GI: anorexia, nausea, vomiting, abdominal cramps, diarrhea
- Renal: flank pain, oliguria, anuria, renal failure, hematuria, acidic urine pH

(continued on page 186)

TABLE
6-6 Oncologic Emergencies: Manifestations and Management (continued)

Emergency	Diagnostic Approaches and Clinical Manifestations	Medical & Nursing Management
		• Administration of a cation-exchange resin, such as sodium polystyrene sulfonate (Kayexalate) to treat hyperkalemia by binding and eliminating potassium through the bowel. (Refer to Chapter 4 for treatment of hyperkalemia.) • Administration of hypertonic dextrose and regular insulin temporarily shifts potassium into cells and lowers serum potassium levels. • Administration of phosphate-binding gels, such as aluminum hydroxide, to treat hyperphosphatemia by promoting phosphate excretion in the feces. • Hemodialysis when patients have persistently elevated electrolytes with worsening renal function, or patients with symptomatic electrolyte imbalances or fluid volume overload from TLS management (Coiffier et al., 2008). **Nursing** • Identify at-risk patients. • Institute essential preventive measures as described above. • Assess patient for signs and symptoms of electrolyte imbalances. • Assess urine pH to confirm alkalization. Urine pH should be between 7 and 8.5 to facilitate excretion of phosphate and uric acid. • Monitor serum electrolyte and uric acid levels • Assess for evidence of fluid volume overload secondary to aggressive hydration by monitoring I/O and daily weights. • Instruct patients to report symptoms indicating electrolyte disturbances.

Chapter Review

Critical Thinking Exercises

1. Your patient has been receiving high doses of chemotherapy to treat leukemia. She reports that she wants to stop the chemotherapy because of the oral ulcerations and pain that have developed since she started on the chemotherapy. What would your response be to her? What evidence-based nursing interventions would you implement to relieve the ulcers and her pain? What is the evidence for the interventions you identified? How strong is that evidence, and what criteria did you use to assess the strength of that evidence?

2. A 74-year-old patient with prostate cancer and metastasis to the bone is to begin a continuous subcutaneous infusion of analgesia through an ambulatory infusion pump to relieve his severe pain. The patient's wife is afraid that he will become addicted, and his adult children state that his pain remains unrelieved. As a home care nurse, what assessments would be of highest priority to you during your initial visit to this patient? What nursing interventions and teaching would be indicated in this situation? How would you modify your interventions if the patient is receiving fentanyl by transdermal patch and still reporting severe pain?

3. Your 68-year-old patient with lung cancer has been admitted for emergent radiation therapy for the diagnosis of SVCS. Describe the underlying pathology that can lead to the signs and symptoms of SVCS. What patient monitoring will be essential during this patient's course of care? Describe the medical and nursing management strategies that will be used for this patient.

NCLEX-Style Review Questions

1. In assessing the neutropenic patient's understanding of discharge education, which statement indicates the need for further education?
   A. "I should stay away from crowds and people who are sick."
   B. "I should wash my hands carefully after using the bathroom and before eating meals."
   C. "If I have a fever or chills, I should take acetaminophen immediately and recheck my temperature an hour later."
   D. "My WBC count should recover about 14 days after my treatment is completed."

2. You are the nurse caring for a patient receiving brachytherapy for cervical cancer. Which of the following statements regarding the nursing care of this patient is false?
   A. The patient must be maintained on bedrest.
   B. The head of the bed must be elevated more than 30 degrees to decrease the risk of aspiration.
   C. Pain management is a priority.
   D. The patient will have an indwelling urinary catheter.

3. You are caring for a patient receiving external beam radiation therapy for head and neck cancer. The patient reports moderate pain to the tongue and buccal mucosa that is interfering with his ability to eat, sleep, and speak. Which of the following interventions would not be recommended for this patient?
   A. Take pain medication 30 minutes before meals.
   B. Avoid acidic, spicy, and sharp foods such as chips.
   C. Keep dentures out when not eating to promote healing.
   D. Rinse the oral mucosa regularly with an alcohol-based solution.

4. You have been asked to create a public health intervention that targets teenagers at risk for skin cancer secondary to sun and tanning bed exposure. Which of the following is an example of primary prevention?
   A. Establishing a van that travels to high schools to perform skin assessments
   B. Establishing a clinic based in the school nurses office that performs screening exams for skin cancer
   C. Developing an educational intervention to teach skin self-assessment
   D. Developing a television commercial, to be aired on the music television network, educating teens on the risks of sun exposure

5. You are caring for a patient with newly diagnosed leukemia who is receiving chemotherapy for the first time. Twenty-four hours after the first dose of chemotherapy, the patient experiences decreased urine output, an abnormal heart rate, and lethargy. Which of the following laboratory results would help support your suspicion for tumor lysis syndrome?
   A. Serum calcium 13.0 mg/dL, potassium 3.5 mEq/L, magnesium 2.0 mg/dL
   B. Potassium 2.0 mEq/L, phosphorous 3.0 mg/dL, calcium 6.0 mg/dL
   C. Uric acid 4.0 mg/dL, creatinine 3.0
   D. Uric acid 10.0 mg/dL, potassium 4.5 mEq/L, phosphorous 5.0 mg/dL

Try these additional resources to enhance your learning and understanding of this chapter:
- thePoint online resource available at **http://thepoint.lww.com/Pellico1e**
- *Handbook for Focus on Adult Health: Medical-Surgical Nursing*
- *Study Guide for Focus on Adult Health: Medical-Surgical Nursing*

References and Selected Readings

References and selected readings associated with this chapter can be found on the website that accompanies the book. Visit http://thepoint.lww.com/Pellico1e to access the references and other additional resources associated with this chapter.

LINDA S. DUNE

Pain Management

Learning Objectives

After reading this chapter, you will be able to:

1. Compare characteristics of acute pain, chronic (persistent) pain, and cancer pain.

2. Describe the effects of acute and chronic pain.

3. Describe the pathophysiology of pain.

4. Describe factors that can alter the response to pain.

5. Demonstrate appropriate use of pain measurement instruments.

6. Explain the nursing role in multidisciplinary pain management.

7. Identify nonpharmacologic pain relief interventions for selected groups of patients.

8. Develop a plan to prevent and treat the adverse effects of analgesic agents.

9. Use the nursing process as a framework for the care of patients with pain.

Pain has been defined as an unpleasant sensory and emotional experience associated with actual or potential tissue damage (Merskey & Bogduk, 1994). It is the most common reason for seeking health care (Todd, Ducharme, Choiniere et al., 2007). It is associated with many disorders, diagnostic tests, and treatments. It disables, distresses more people than any single disease, varies widely in intensity, and spares no age group. Because nurses spend more time with patients in pain than other health care providers, nurses need to understand the pathophysiology of pain, the physiologic and psychological consequences of acute and chronic (persistent) pain, and the methods used to treat pain. Nurses encounter patients in pain in a variety of settings, including acute care, outpatient, and long-term care settings, as well as in the home. Therefore, they must have the knowledge and skills to assess pain, implement pain relief strategies, and evaluate the effectiveness of these strategies, regardless of setting.

PAIN: THE FIFTH VITAL SIGN

Pain assessment is referred to as "the fifth vital sign" to emphasize its significance in data collection and to increase the awareness among health care professionals of the importance of the relationship between pain and health. Assessment of pain should be as automatic as taking a patient's temperature, blood pressure, pulse, and respirations. Documentation of pain assessment is now as prominent as documentation of the "traditional" vital signs. Pain assessment and management are also mandated by the Joint Commission (2009).

The role of primary health care providers is to assess and relieve pain by administering medications and other treatments. Nurses collaborate with other health care professionals while administering most pain relief interventions, evaluating their effectiveness, and serving as patient advocates when the intervention is ineffective. In addition, nurses serve as educators to patients and families, teaching them to manage the pain relief regimen themselves when appropriate.

The definition of pain forwarded by the International Association for the Study of Pain identified at the beginning of this chapter encompasses the multidimensional nature of pain. An early broad definition of pain by McCaffery is, "whatever the person says it is, existing whenever the experiencing person says it does" (McCaffery & Pasero, 1999, p. 5). This

Pain Care Bill of Rights

Although not always required by law, these are the rights you should expect, and if necessary demand, for your pain care.

As a person with pain, you have the right to:

- Have your report of pain taken seriously and be treated with dignity and respect by doctors, nurses, pharmacists, and other health care professionals.
- Have your pain thoroughly assessed and promptly treated.
- Be informed by your health care provider about what may be causing the pain, possible treatments, and the benefits, risks, and cost of each.
- Participate actively in decisions about how to manage your pain.
- Have your pain reassessed regularly and your treatment adjusted if your pain has not been eased.
- Be referred to a pain specialist if your pain persists.
- Get clear and prompt answers to your questions, take time to make decisions, and refuse a particular type of treatment if you choose.

Courtesy of the American Pain Foundation, 201 N. Charles Street, Suite 710, Baltimore, Maryland, 21201, *www.painfoundation.org*

definition emphasizes the highly subjective nature of pain and pain management. Patients are the best authority on the existence of pain. Therefore, validation of the existence of pain is based on the patient's report that it exists.

Although it is important to believe patients who report pain, it is equally important to be alert to patients who deny pain in situations where pain would be expected. A nurse who suspects pain in a patient who denies it should explore with the patient the reason for suspecting pain, such as discussing the fact that the disorder or procedure is painful for most people or pointing out that the patient grimaces when moving or avoids movement. It may also be helpful to explore why the patient may be denying pain. Some people deny pain because they fear the treatment that may result if they report or admit pain. Others deny pain for fear of becoming addicted to **opioids** (previously referred to as narcotics) if these medications are prescribed. The American Pain Foundation developed the Pain Care Bill of Rights, which addresses the importance of pain management (Box 7-1).

TYPES OF PAIN

Pain is categorized according to its duration, location, and etiology. Three basic categories of pain are generally recognized: acute pain, chronic (persistent, nonmalignant) pain, and cancer-related pain.

Acute Pain

Usually of recent onset and commonly associated with a specific injury, acute pain indicates that damage or injury has occurred. Pain is significant in that it draws attention to a threat and teaches people to avoid similar potentially painful situations. Thus, pain is both a sensation and a warning signal. If no lasting damage occurs and no systemic disease exists, acute pain usually decreases as healing occurs. Acute pain can be an isolated one time incident or recur at regular intervals, such as menstrual cramping, or sporadically, as with angina or migraine headaches.

Chronic Pain

Chronic pain is constant or intermittent pain that persists beyond the expected healing time. It is associated with a variety of degenerative or traumatic conditions such as arthritis and intervertebral disk herniations, but often a specific cause or injury for the chronic pain may not be found. It may have a poorly defined onset, and it is often difficult to treat because the cause or origin may be unclear. Although acute pain may be a useful signal that something is wrong, chronic or persistent pain may become a patient's primary disorder. Medical-surgical nurses care for patients with chronic pain when these patients are admitted to the hospital for management or develop other new etiologies.

Cancer-Related Pain

Pain associated with cancer may be acute or chronic. Pain resulting from cancer is so ubiquitous that when cancer patients are asked about the most feared consequences of cancer, pain is reported most frequently (Bruera & Kim, 2003; Tavoli, Montazeri, Roshan et al., 2008). Pain in patients with cancer can be directly associated with the cancer (e.g., bony infiltration with tumor cells or nerve compression), a result of cancer treatment (e.g., surgery or radiation), or unrelated to the cancer (e.g., trauma). However, most pain associated with cancer is a direct result of tumor involvement. Cancer-related pain is discussed in Chapter 6.

EFFECTS OF PAIN

Regardless of its nature, pattern, or cause, pain that is inadequately treated has harmful effects beyond the suffering it causes.

Effects of Acute Pain

Unrelieved acute pain can affect the pulmonary, cardiovascular, GI, endocrine, and immune systems. The stress response (neuroendocrine response to stress) that occurs with trauma also occurs with severe pain. The widespread endocrine, immunologic, and inflammatory changes that occur with stress can have significant negative effects. This is particularly harmful in patients whose health is already compromised by age, illness, or injury.

BOX 7-2	Physiologic Response to Acute Pain
Endocrine and metabolic response	Activation of sympathetic nervous system and an increase in glucagon secretion, which causes hyperglycemia, increased lipolysis (fat breakdown), accelerated protein breakdown, and nitrogen loss. The stress response presents as hypertension, tachycardia, arrhythmias, myocardial ischemia, protein catabolism, immune system suppression, and impaired renal excretory function.
Pulmonary function	Decreased phrenic nerve activity and diaphragmatic dysfunction manifested as a decrease in functional residual capacity and a decrease in tidal volume.
GI motility	Decrease in gastric motility, especially in the colon. The stomach and small intestines recovers within 12 to 24 hours after abdominal surgery; however, the colon is inhibited for at least 48 to 72 hours.
Cardiovascular	Increased sympathetic tone, which causes an increase in heart rate and blood pressure, and a redistribution of blood to and within various organs. The redistribution predisposes patients to myocardial ischemia in the presence of coronary artery disease and may induce arrhythmias
Immune system	Decrease in responsiveness to antigens, delayed hypersensitivity, natural killer cell activity, and antibody response.

Adapted from Peeters-Asdourian, C., & Akhouri, V. (2004). Acute pain management in the adult. In C. Warfield & Z. Bajwa (Eds.), *Principles and practices of pain management* (2nd ed.). New York: McGraw-Hill.

The stress response generally consists of increased metabolic rate and cardiac output, impaired insulin response, increased production of cortisol, and increased retention of fluids. Box 7-2 discusses the physiological impact of acute pain. The stress response may increase the risk of physiologic disorders (e.g., myocardial infarction, pulmonary infection, thromboembolism, prolonged paralytic ileus). Patients with severe pain and associated stress may be unable to take deep breaths and may experience increased fatigue and decreased mobility. Although these effects may be tolerated by young, healthy people, they may hamper recovery in elderly, debilitated, or critically ill people. Effective pain relief may result in faster recovery and improved outcomes.

Effects of Chronic Pain

Like acute pain, chronic pain also has adverse effects. Suppression of the immune function associated with chronic pain may promote tumor growth. In addition, chronic pain often results in anger, depression, fatigue, and disability. Patients may be unable to continue the activities and interpersonal relationships they engaged in before the pain began, with resultant impact on their quality of life. Disabilities may range from curtailing participation in physical activities to being unable to take care of personal needs, such as dressing or eating. Regardless of how patients cope with persistent pain, disability can result if the pain persists for an extended period.

Nurses should understand the effects of chronic pain on patients and families and should be knowledgeable about pain relief strategies and appropriate resources to assist effectively with pain management. Although health care providers may express concern about the large quantities of opioid medications required to control progressive chronic pain, failure to administer adequate pain relief may be unsafe because of the consequences of unrelieved pain.

PATHOPHYSIOLOGY OF PAIN

The processing of noxious stimuli and the resulting perception of pain involve the peripheral and central nervous systems. Various nerve mechanisms and structures are involved in the transmission of pain to and from the brain, including nociceptors, or pain receptors, and chemical mediators. **Nociceptors** are free nerve endings found in the skin. These receptors are preferentially sensitive to intense, potentially damaging mechanical, thermal, or chemical stimuli. Although the skin contains the highest density of nociceptors, they are also found in joints, skeletal muscle, fascia, tendons, and cornea, and have the potential to respond to painful stimuli. When stimulated, nociceptors send signals to local blood vessels, mast cells, hair follicles, and sweat glands, often resulting in clinical findings associated with pain, such as vasomotor, autonomic, and visceral effects.

The large internal organs (viscera) have a low density of nociceptors that respond only to painful stimuli (Fauci, Braunwald, Kasper et al., 2008). Typically, pain originating in these organs results from intense stimulation of multipurpose receptors that respond to inflammation, stretching, ischemia, dilation, and spasm of the internal organs. An intense response in these fibers can cause severe pain.

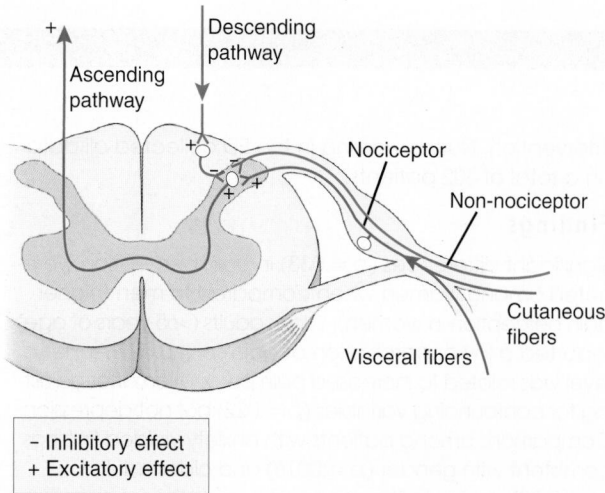

- Inhibitory effect
+ Excitatory effect

FIGURE 7-1 A schematic representation of aspects of nociceptive system.

Peripheral Nervous System Response

A number of **algogenic** (pain-causing) substances that enhance the sensitivity of nociceptors are released into the extracellular tissue as a result of tissue damage. Histamine, bradykinin, acetylcholine, serotonin, and substance P are chemicals that increase the transmission of pain. **Prostaglandins** are chemical substances that are believed to increase the sensitivity of pain receptors by enhancing the pain-provoking effect of bradykinin. It is interesting to note that aspirin and other nonsteroidal anti-inflammatory drugs (NSAIDs) block the enzyme needed for prostaglandin synthesis, resulting in pain control. At the peripheral nervous system level, two main types of fibers are involved in **nociception** (the neurologic transmission of pain impulses). The larger myelinated A delta fibers transmit the initial pain sensation rapidly, at a rate of 10 to 30 m/sec, to the brain (acute pain, or "fast pain"). This type of pain is frequently associated with mechanical or thermal stimuli. The smaller unmyelinated C fibers transmit impulses at a rate of .5 to 2.5 m/sec. This is called "second pain" or "slow-wave pain" due to delayed onset and longer duration. It has dull, aching, or burning qualities, which last longer than the initial fast pain. Chronic pain is believed to be associated with C-fiber stimulation.

If there is repeated C-fiber stimulation, there is a heightened response in spinal cord neurons, causing the person to perceive more pain. For this reason, it is important to treat patients with analgesic agents when they first feel pain. Patients require less medication and experience more effective pain relief if analgesia is administered before they become sensitized to the pain.

Central Nervous System Response

For pain to be consciously perceived, neurons in the ascending system must be activated. Activation occurs as a result of input from the nociceptors. After tissue injury occurs, nociception continues, and relays the impulses to the dorsal horn of the spinal cord. Upon entering the spinal cord at the dorsal horn, the pain impulse crosses the spinal cord and passes upward to the brain by the anterolateral pathway to the thalamus. The pain signals are then transmitted to other areas of the brain and sensory cortex where the conscious experience or perception of pain occurs. Figure 7-1 illustrates pain transmission.

Chemicals that reduce or inhibit the transmission or perception of pain include **endorphins**, **enkephalins**, and **dynorphins** (Porth, 2009). These chemical, morphine-like neurotransmitters are endogenous (produced by the body) and reduce nociceptive transmission.

Just as the ascending system relays signal up to the brain for interpretation, the descending control system is considered inhibitory. It is always somewhat active, and it prevents continuous transmission of painful stimuli, partly through the action of the endorphins. Cognitive processes may stimulate endorphin production in the descending control system. The effectiveness of this system is illustrated by the effects of distraction. The distractions of visitors or a favorite television show may increase activity in the descending control system. Therefore, patients who have visitors or who are engaged in a television program may not report pain, because activation of the descending control system results in less noxious or painful information being transmitted to consciousness. Additionally, tactile stimulation can modulate pain through a complex process of tactile information transmitted by large and small fibers throughout the central nervous system (Porth, 2009).

The neuromatrix theory of pain provides a conceptual framework to examine chronic pain. It proposes in response to injury, inflammation, disease, or chronic stress, the body–self neuromatrix which activates perceptual, homeostatic, and behavioral responses. Endocrine, autonomic, immune, and opioid systems contribute to this interactive cognitive interpretation of pain (Melzack, 2001). Thus, pain occurs in response to a widely distributed neural network in the brain, rather than only to the sensory input of injury, inflammation, or pathology.

FACTORS INFLUENCING PAIN RESPONSE

Several factors, including past experiences with pain, anxiety, culture, age, gender, genetics, and expectations about pain relief, influence a person's experience of pain. These factors may increase or decrease perception of pain, increase or decrease tolerance for pain, and affect responses to pain.

Past Experience

The way a person responds to pain is a result of many separate painful events during a lifetime. The more experience

BOX 7-3

Nursing Research

Bridging the Gap to Evidence-Based Practice

Pain Perception of Patients With Anxiety or Depression

Oktay, C., Eken, C., Ozbek, K. et. al. (2008). Pain perception of patients predisposed to anxiety and depressive disorders in emergency department. *Pain Management Nursing, 9*(4): 150–153.

Purpose

Pain is one of the most common reasons for patients' visits to the emergency department (ED). To manage pain effectively, assessment must include all aspects of the multidimensional phenomenon of pain. This study sought to investigate the relationship between the psychologic status of the patient and perception of pain in the ED. The researchers also analyzed other factors that influence the patient's perception of pain.

Design

This randomized prospective study included a convenience sample of ED patients to receive an intramuscular injection of diclofenac sodium in the lateral gluteus maximus muscle. A Visual Analogue Scale was used to measure pain intensity and the Hospital Anxiety and Depression Scale was completed by patients before intervention. Nurses working in the ED collected all data on a total of 302 patients.

Findings

Significant differences ($p = .033$) in pain perception were noted among women when compared to men (higher pain perception in women). Older adults (>65 years of age) reported a lower perception of pain ($p = 0.02$). Anxiety level was related to increased pain perception after adjusting for confounding variables ($p = .022$) but not depression. Comparisons among patients with anxiety yielded findings consistent with gender ($p = .0016$) and older adults ($p = 0.32$), similar to the reported perception of pain.

Nursing Implications

The results of this study suggest that anxiety levels of patients in ED might increase pain perception of patients. Since effective pain management should improve patient satisfaction and shorten the length of stay in the ED, anxiety levels of patients should be considered when assessing patients. Further studies are needed to identify psychological factors contributing to pain perception, so that effective antianxiety interventions can be incorporated into ED pain management protocols.

---

a person has had with pain, the more frightening the subsequent painful events may be. The person may be less able to tolerate pain, and pain may be more likely to occur if the person has received inadequate pain relief in the past. Therefore, the nurse must be aware of the patient's past experiences with pain. If pain is relieved promptly and adequately, the person may be less fearful of future pain and better able to tolerate it.

Anxiety and Depression

Although it is commonly believed that anxiety increases pain, this is not necessarily true (Box 7-3). However, anxiety that is associated with pain may increase the patient's perception of pain. For example, the patient who was treated 2 years ago for breast cancer and who now has hip pain may fear that the pain indicates metastasis. In this case, the patient's anxiety may result in increased pain. However, anxiety that is unrelated to the pain (e.g., anxiety about who is taking care of the pets while the patient is in the hospital) may distract the patient and may actually decrease the perception of pain.

Just as anxiety is associated with pain because of concerns and fears about an underlying disease, depression is associated with chronic pain and unrelieved cancer pain. In cases of chronic pain, the incidence of depression is increased (Samwel, Kraaimaat, Crul et al., 2009), and often is associated with major life changes caused by the limiting effects of persistent pain.

Culture

Beliefs about pain and how to respond to it differ from one culture to the next. Early in childhood, people learn from those around them what responses to pain are acceptable or unacceptable. For example, a child may learn that a sports injury is not expected to hurt as much as a comparable injury caused by a motor vehicle crash. The child also learns what stimuli are expected to be painful and what behavioral responses are acceptable.

Cultural factors must be taken into account to manage pain effectively. Factors that help explain differences in a cultural group include age, gender, education level, and income. In addition, the degree to which patients identify with a culture influences the extent to which they will adopt new health behaviors or rely on traditional health beliefs and practices. A wide range of behaviors may be seen in response to pain ranging from moaning and complaining about pain, and describing pain as "unbearable," to behaving in a quiet, stoic manner rather than expressing the pain verbally. The nurse must respond to the person's perception of pain and not to the person's behavior, because the

BOX 7-4 Common Concerns and Misconceptions About Pain and Analgesia

Misconception	Evidence
Chronic pain patients have a higher tolerance to pain.	Chronic pain patients have a decreased tolerance to pain, associated with decreased endorphins, the effect of neurotransmitters, and physiological responses. In patients with chronic pain, signals for pain and muscle spasm continue to be transmitted by the nervous system.
Chronic pain is due to psychological disturbance.	When unable to find a physiological reason for pain, providers often attribute chronic pain to a psychological issue and, in addition, have demonstrated more positive responses to patients when pathology is found.
Chronic pain is caused by stress, and if the stress is relieved, pain abates.	No evidence exists that stress causes pain.
Patients will exaggerate their pain in order to receive increased compensation payments.	No evidence exists that patients report increased pain when seeking compensation or litigation.
Patients in chronic pain demonstrate manipulative behavior.	It is rare for chronic pain patients to misrepresent their symptoms. Rather, some patients may seek out a variety of providers to obtain relief.
Depression causes chronic pain.	There is a corollary between chronic pain and depression; however, it is more likely that the stress of managing the chronic pain leads to depression.
People get addicted to pain medicine easily	Research suggests a negligible risk of addiction when prescribed opioids for pain. Misconceptions are related to a lack of knowledge of tolerance, physical dependence, and addiction.
Patients are often noncompliant and to blame for their physical symptoms.	Evidence shows that chronic pain patients are generally compliant and, if not, the reasons are attributed to treatment side effects or lack of treatment response.

From Shaw, S., & Lee, A. (2009). Student nurses' misconceptions of adults with chronic nonmalignant pain. *American Society for Pain Management Nursing, 11*(1), 2–14.

behavior may differ from the nurse's cultural expectations. The nurse who recognizes cultural differences has insight into the impact of pain on the patient, and is more accurate in assessing pain and in planning appropriate treatments to relieve pain.

The main issues to consider when caring for patients of a different culture are

- What does the illness mean to the patient?
- Are there culturally based stigmas related to this illness or pain?
- What is the role of the family in health care decisions?
- Are traditional pain-relief remedies used?
- What is the role of stoicism in the patient's culture?
- Are there culturally determined ways of expressing and communicating pain?
- Does the patient have any fears about the pain?
- Has the patient seen or does the patient want to see a traditional healer?

The nurse should avoid stereotyping the patient by culture, and should provide individualized care rather than assuming that a patient of a specific culture will exhibit

more or less pain. In addition to avoiding stereotyping, health care providers should individualize the amount of medications or therapy according to the information provided by the patient. The nurse should recognize that stereotypes exist and become sensitive to how they negatively affect care. A study of nursing students revealed that when dealing with patients with chronic nonmalignant pain, many misconceptions, defined as inaccurate knowledge and inadequate attitudes exist (Box 7-4; Shaw & Lee, 2009). The study suggests that opportunities to examine students' attitudes and knowledge be explicitly explored in order to meet the needs of this population. In addition, patients must be instructed about how and what to communicate about their pain.

Age

Age has long been the focus of research on pain perception and pain tolerance, with inconsistent findings (Gagliese, 2009). For example, although some researchers have found that older adults require a higher intensity of noxious stimuli than do younger adults before they report pain, others have found no differences in responses of younger and

TABLE
7-1  **GERONTOLOGIC CONSIDERATIONS** / for Pain Management

Physiologic Changes Influencing Pain Response	Pain Management Interventions
• Higher incidence of chronic illnesses • Increased use of prescription and OTC medications • Sensitivity to medications and increased risk for drug toxicity • Changes in medication absorption and metabolism due to decreased liver, renal, and GI functions • Altered distribution of medications due to changes in body weight, protein stores, and distribution of body fluid. • Slowed metabolism of medications • Higher blood levels of medications • Susceptibility to depression of both the nervous and the respiratory systems • Decreased binding of meperidine by plasma proteins, with possible result of twice the levels found in younger patients	• Obtain a careful medication history to identify potential drug interactions • Administer analgesic agents, keeping a balance between minimal side effects and effective pain relief. • Possible need for slightly smaller initial dose of analgesic medication than prescribed for younger patients • May need prolonged dosing interval for subsequent doses • May not administer meperidine because its active neurotoxic metabolite, normeperidine, is more likely to accumulate and cause central nervous system excitation and seizures • May need to refer to clinical practice guidelines for managing persistent pain (Ickowicz, 2009) • Frequent assessments and evaluation of patient responses to pain interventions

older adults. Experts in the field of pain management have concluded that if pain perception is diminished in elderly people, it is most likely secondary to a disease process (e.g., diabetes) rather than to aging (Ickowicz, 2009). More research is needed in the area of aging and its effects on pain perception to understand what the elderly are experiencing. Unrelieved pain contributes to the problems of depression, social relationships, activities of daily living, and symptom management in older adults (Carmaciu, Iliffe, Khariacha et al., 2007).

Older adults deal with pain according to their lifestyle, personality, and cultural background, as do younger adults. Many elderly people are fearful of addiction and, as a result, do not report that they are in pain or ask for medication to relieve pain. Others fail to seek care because they fear that the pain may indicate serious illness or that pain relief will be associated with a loss of independence. Nurses are aware that confusion in the elderly may be a result of untreated and unrelieved pain. In some cases, postoperative confusion clears once the pain is relieved. Judgments about pain and the adequacy of treatment should be based on the patient's report of pain and pain relief rather than on age. Table 7-1 provides gerontological considerations related to pain management.

Gender

Researchers have compared pain intensity, pain unpleasantness, and pain-related emotions (depression, anxiety, frustration, fear, and anger) in men and women who were asked to rate their experiences with chronic pain. Once again, inconsistent results related to gender were found in regard to pain levels and response to pain. However, two important

considerations supported by research that the nurse contemplates when caring for patients in a medical surgical unit are that: (1) Men and women are thought to be socialized to respond differently and to differ in their expectations about pain (Bernardes, Keogh, & Lima, 2007), and (2) the pharmacokinetics and pharmacodynamics of opioids differ in men and women and have been attributed to genetic differences that may influence enzymes responsible for their metabolism (Toomey, 2008). Thus, the highly individualized nature of pain indicates that a "one size fits all" treatment plan for pain is ineffective and potentially harmful.

THE NURSE'S ASSESSMENT OF PAIN

The highly subjective nature of pain means that pain assessment and management present challenges for all clinicians. The report of pain is a social transaction; that is, the assessment and management of pain will require the establishment of rapport and trust with the person in pain. In assessing a patient with pain, the nurse reviews the patient's description of the pain and other factors that may influence pain (e.g., previous experience, anxiety, age), as well as the patient's response to pain relief strategies. Documentation of the pain level as rated on a pain scale becomes part of the patient's medical record, as does the record of the pain relief obtained from interventions.

Pain assessment includes determining what level of pain relief the acutely ill patient believes is needed to recover quickly or improve function, or what level of relief the chronically or terminally ill patient requires to maintain

comfort. Part of a thorough pain assessment is understanding the patient's expectations and misconceptions about pain, which may include the notion that pain is a normal experience, that pain builds character, that pain medication side effects are worse than the pain, and the fear of becoming addicted to narcotics. People who understand that pain relief not only contributes to comfort but also hastens recovery are more likely to request or self-administer treatment appropriately (see Box 7-4).

Characteristics of Pain

The factors to consider in a complete pain assessment are the intensity, timing, location, quality, and personal meaning of pain; aggravating and alleviating factors; and pain behaviors. Pain assessment begins by careful patient observation, noting overall posture and presence or absence of overt pain behaviors. In addition, it is essential to ask the patient to describe the specifics of the pain. The words used to describe the pain may point toward the cause. For example, the classic description of chest pain that results from a myocardial infarction includes pressure or squeezing on the chest. A detailed history should follow the initial description of pain.

Intensity

The intensity of pain ranges from none to mild discomfort to excruciating. There is no correlation between reported intensity and the stimulus that produced it. The reported intensity is influenced by the person's **pain threshold** and **pain tolerance**. Pain threshold is the smallest stimulus for which a person reports pain, and pain tolerance is the maximum amount of pain a person can tolerate. To understand variations, the nurse can ask about the present pain intensity, as well as the least and the worst pain intensity. Various scales and surveys are helpful to patients trying to describe pain intensity; see the later discussion of Instruments for Assessing the Perception of Pain on pages 196–198.

Timing

Sometimes the cause of pain can be determined when its temporal aspects are known. Therefore, the nurse inquires about the onset, duration, relationship between time and intensity (e.g., at what time is the pain worst), and changes in rhythmic patterns. The patient is asked if the pain began suddenly or increased gradually. Sudden pain that rapidly reaches maximum intensity is indicative of tissue rupture, thus immediate assessment and intervention is necessary. Pain from ischemia gradually increases and becomes intense over a longer time. The chronic (or persistent) pain of arthritis illustrates the usefulness of determining the relationship between time and intensity because people with arthritis usually report that pain is worse in the morning.

Location

The location of pain is best determined by having the patient point to the area of the body involved. Some general assessment forms include drawings of human figures, on which the patient is asked to shade in the area involved. This is especially helpful if the pain radiates (**referred pain**). The shaded figures are helpful in determining the effectiveness of treatment or change in the location of pain over time.

Quality

The nurse asks the patient to describe the pain without offering clues. For example, the nurse asks the patient to describe what the pain feels like. The nurse must give the patient sufficient time to describe the pain, and then record all words in the answer. If the patient cannot describe the quality of the pain, the nurse can suggest words such as burning, aching, throbbing, or stabbing. It is important to document the exact words used by the patient to describe the pain and which words were suggested by the nurse conducting the assessment.

Personal Meaning

Pain means different things to different people; as a result, patients experience pain differently. The meaning of the pain experience helps the clinician understand how the patient is affected and assists in planning treatment. It is important to ask how the pain impacts the person's daily life. Some people with pain can continue to work or study, whereas others may be disabled by their pain, which may affect family finances. For some patients, the recurrence of pain may mean worsening of disease, such as the spread of cancer.

Aggravating and Alleviating Factors

The nurse asks the patient what, if anything, makes the pain worse and what makes it better, and asks specifically about the relationship between activity and pain. This helps detect factors associated with pain. For example, in a patient with advanced metastatic cancer, pain with coughing may signal spinal cord compression. The nurse also ascertains whether environmental factors influence pain, because they may easily be modified. Making the room warmer may aid in patient relaxation, which may decrease the person's pain. Finally, the nurse asks the patient whether the pain is influenced by or affects the quality of sleep or anxiety. Both can significantly influence pain intensity and the quality of life.

Knowledge of alleviating factors assists the nurse in developing a treatment plan. Therefore, it is important to ask about the patient's use of medications (prescribed and over-the-counter [OTC]), including amount and frequency. In addition, the nurse asks if herbal remedies, nonpharmacologic interventions, or alternative therapies have been used with success. This information assists the nurse in determining teaching needs.

Pain Behaviors

When experiencing pain, people express pain through many different behaviors. These nonverbal and behavioral expressions of pain are not consistent or reliable indicators

of the quality or intensity of pain, and they should not be used to determine the presence of or the severity of pain experienced. A patient may grimace, cry, rub the affected area, guard the affected area, or immobilize it. Others may moan, groan, grunt, or sigh. Not all patients exhibit the same behaviors, and different meanings may be associated with the same behavior.

Sometimes, in nonverbal patients, pain behaviors are used as a proxy to assess pain. It is unwise to make judgments and formulate treatment plans based on behaviors that may or may not indicate pain. In unconscious patients, pain should be assumed to be present and treated. All patients have a right to adequate pain management.

Physiologic responses to pain, such as tachycardia, hypertension, tachypnea, pallor, diaphoresis, mydriasis (pupillary dilatation), hypervigilance, and increased muscle tone, are related to stimulation of the autonomic nervous system. These responses are short-lived as the body adapts to the stress. These physiologic signs could be the result of a change in the patient's condition, such as the onset of hypovolemia. Use of physiologic signs to indicate pain is unreliable. Although it is important to observe for any and all pain behaviors, the absence of these behaviors does not indicate an absence of pain.

Instruments for Assessing the Perception of Pain

Only the patient can accurately describe and assess the individual pain experience. Therefore, a number of pain assessment tools have been developed to assist in the assessment of the patient's perception of pain. Such tools may be used to document the need for intervention, to evaluate the effectiveness of the intervention, and to identify the need for alternative or additional interventions if the initial intervention is ineffective in relieving the pain. For a pain assessment tool to be useful, it must require little effort on the part of the patient, be easy to understand and use, be easily scored, and be sensitive to small changes in the characteristic being measured. Figure 7-2 shows a pain assessment pathway that can be used at the time of assessment to direct clinical decisions for pain management.

Visual Analogue Scales

Visual analogue scales (VAS) are useful in assessing the intensity of pain (Fig. 7-3, p. 198). One version of the scale includes a horizontal 10 cm line, with anchors (ends) indicating the extremes of pain. The patient is asked to place a mark indicating where the current pain lies on the line. The left anchor usually represents "none" or "no pain," whereas the right anchor usually represents "severe" or "worst possible pain." To score the results, a ruler is placed along the line, and the distance the patient marked from the left or low end is measured and reported in millimeters or centimeters.

Some patients (e.g., children, elderly patients, visually or cognitively impaired patients) may find it difficult to use an unmarked VAS. In those circumstances, ordinal scales, such as a simple descriptive pain intensity scale or a 0-to-10 numeric pain intensity scale, may be used.

Faces Pain Scale–Revised

The revised faces pain scale uses six facial expressions that range from contented to obvious distress (Fig. 7-4, p. 198). The patient is asked to point to the face that most closely resembles the experienced pain intensity.

Guidelines for Using Pain Assessment Scales

Using a written scale to assess pain may not be possible if a person is seriously ill, is in severe pain, or has just returned from surgery. In these cases, the nurse can ask the patient, "On a scale of 0 to 10, 0 being no pain and 10 being pain as bad as it can be, how bad is your pain now?" For patients who have difficulty with a 0 to 10 scale, a 0 to 5 scale may be tried. Whichever scale is used, it should be used consistently. Most patients usually can respond without difficulty. Ideally, the nurse teaches the patient how to use the pain scale before the pain occurs (e.g., before surgery). The patient's numerical rating is documented and used to assess the effectiveness of pain relief interventions.

If a particular patient does not speak English or cannot clearly communicate information needed to manage pain, an interpreter, translator, or family member familiar with the person's method of communication should be consulted and a method established for pain assessment. Often, a chart can be constructed with English words on one side and the foreign language on the other. The patient can then point to the corresponding word to tell the nurse about the pain.

When people with pain are cared for at home by family caregivers or home care nurses, a pain scale may help assess the effectiveness of the interventions if the scale is used before and after the interventions are implemented. Scales that address the location and pattern of pain may be useful in identifying new sources or sites of pain in chronically or terminally ill patients and in monitoring changes in the patient's level of pain. For example, a home care nurse who sees a patient only at intervals may benefit from consulting the patient's or family's written record of pain scores to evaluate how effective the pain management strategies have been over time.

On occasion, a person will deny having pain when most people in similar circumstances would report significant pain. For example, it is not uncommon for a patient recovering from a total joint replacement to deny feeling "pain," but on further questioning will readily admit to having a "terrible ache, but I wouldn't call it pain." From then on, when evaluating this person's pain, the nurse would use the patient's words rather than the word "pain."

Guidelines for Assessing Pain in Patients With Disabilities

Alternative forms of communication may be necessary for people with sensory impairments or other disabilities.

- For people who are blind and who know how to read Braille, pain assessment instruments can be obtained in Braille. In addition, computer software is available that allows written documents to be scanned and converted into

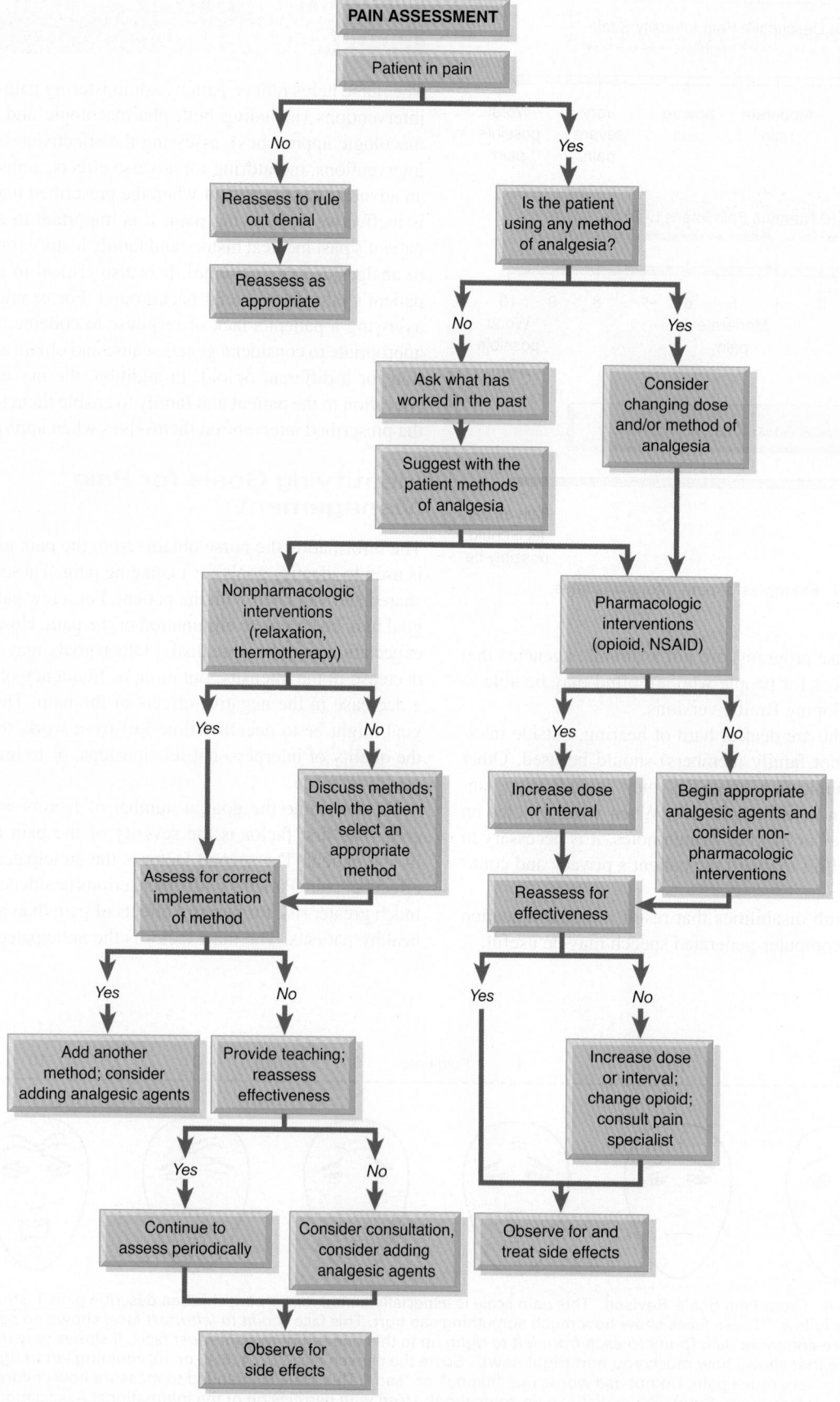

FIGURE 7-2 Pain assessment pathway.

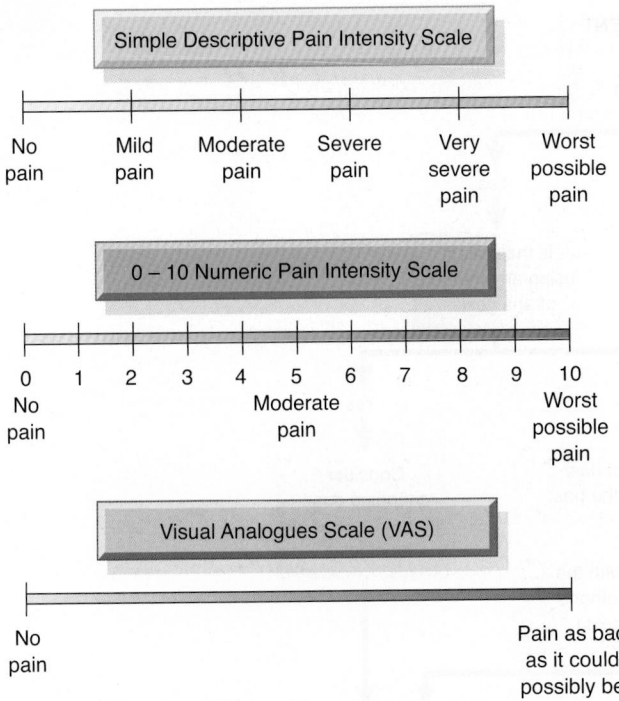

FIGURE 7-3 Examples of pain intensity scales.

Braille. If these programs are not available, agencies that provide services for people who are blind may be able to assist in developing Braille versions.

• For people who are deaf or hard of hearing, outside interpreters (i.e., not family members) should be used. Other useful communication strategies may include sign language, written notes, or pictures. When writing notes on a "magic slate" or making written notes, it is necessary to make every effort to guard the patient's privacy and confidentiality.

• For people with disabilities that result in communication impairment, computer-generated speech may be useful.

THE NURSE'S ROLE IN PAIN MANAGEMENT

The nurse helps relieve pain by administering pain-relieving interventions (including both pharmacologic and nonpharmacologic approaches), assessing the effectiveness of those interventions, monitoring for adverse effects, and serving as an advocate for the patient when the prescribed intervention is ineffective in relieving pain. It is important to assess the patient's past medical history and family history for response to analgesics (e.g., codeine). It is also critical to assess the patient's ethnic and racial background. For example, when assessing a patient's lack of response to codeine, it may be appropriate to consider a genetic cause and obtain a prescription for a different opioid. In addition, the nurse provides education to the patient and family to enable them to manage the prescribed intervention themselves when appropriate.

Identifying Goals for Pain Management

The information the nurse obtains from the pain assessment is used to identify goals for managing pain. These goals are shared and validated with the patient. For a few patients, the goal may be complete elimination of the pain. However, this expectation may be unrealistic. Other goals may include a decrease in the intensity, duration, or frequency of pain and a decrease in the negative effects of the pain. Therefore, a goal might be to decrease time lost from work, to increase the quality of interpersonal relationships, or to improve the quality of sleep.

To determine the goal, a number of factors are considered. The first factor is the severity of the pain as judged by the patient. The second factor is the anticipated harmful effects of pain. Patients with other serious health issues are at much greater risk for harmful effects of pain than are young, healthy patients. The third factor is the anticipated duration

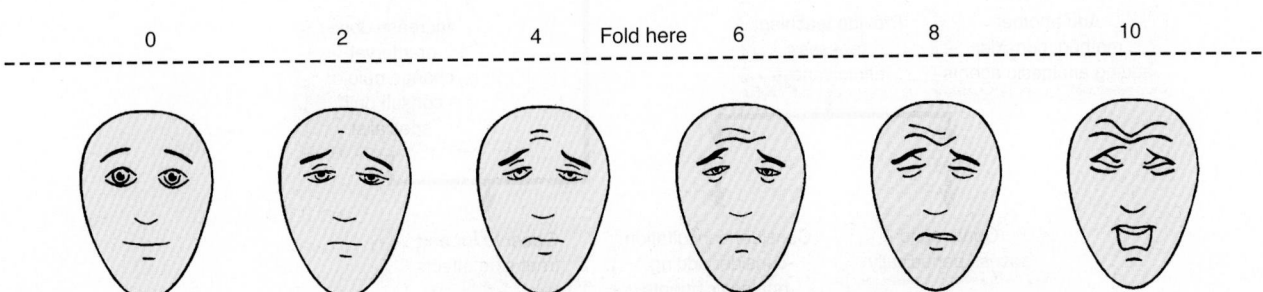

FIGURE 7-4 Faces Pain Scale–Revised. This pain scale is especially suited for helping children describe pain. Instructions for using this scale follow: "These faces show how much something can hurt. This face (*point to left-most face*) shows *no pain*. The faces show more and more pain (*point to each from left to right*) up to this one (*point to right-most face*). It shows *very much pain*. Point to the face that shows how much you hurt (right now)." Score the chosen face 0, 2, 4, 6, 8, or 10, counting left to right, so 0 = no pain and 10 = very much pain. Do not use words like "happy" or "sad." This scale is intended to measure how children feel inside, not how their face looks. From *The pediatric pain sourcebook*. Used with permission of the International Association for the Study of Pain and the Pain Research Unit, Sydney Children's Hospital, Randwick NSW 2031, Australia.

of the pain. In patients with pain from a disease such as cancer, the pain may be prolonged, possibly for the remainder of the patient's life. Therefore, interventions will be needed for some time and should not detract from the patient's quality of life. In the acute stages of illness, the patient may be unable to participate actively in relief measures, but when sufficient mental and physical energy is present, the patient may learn self-management techniques to relieve the pain. Therefore, as the patient progresses through the stages of recovery, increased patient use of self-management pain relief measures may be a goal.

Patients who receive palliative care for pain when they are conscious should continue to receive pain treatment when they cannot communicate. It should be assumed that the pain persists even if the patient is unconscious. Family members often can be taught what unique behaviors to look for to assess for pain: a furrowed brow, stiffening of a part of the body, or moaning.

Providing Patient Education

Patient education is extremely important, since the patient or family may be responsible for managing the pain at home and preventing or managing side effects. Teaching about pain and strategies to relieve it may reduce the threat of the pain and, thus, the pain itself, in the absence of other relief measures and may enhance the effectiveness of the pain relief measures used.

The nurse also provides information by explaining how pain can be controlled. For example, the patient should be informed that pain should be reported in the early stages. When the patient waits too long to report pain, **sensitization** may occur, and the pain may become so intense that it is difficult to relieve. Sensitization results from a heightened nervous system response after exposure to a noxious (pain) stimulus. This results in an increased and prolonged pain experience. When health care providers assess and treat pain before it becomes severe, sensitization is diminished or avoided, and less medication is needed.

Providing Physical Care

Patients in pain may be unable to participate in the usual activities of daily living or to perform usual self-care and may need assistance to carry out these activities. Patients are usually more comfortable when physical and self-care needs have been met and efforts have been made to ensure as comfortable a position as possible. A fresh gown and change of bed linens, along with efforts to make the person feel refreshed (e.g., brushing teeth, combing hair), often increase the level of comfort and improve the effectiveness of the pain relief measures (Taylor, 2011).

In acute, long-term, and home settings, the nurse who provides physical care to patients also has the opportunity to perform complete assessments and to identify problems that may contribute to the patient's discomfort and pain.

Appropriate and gentle physical touch during care may be reassuring and comforting. If topical treatments such as fentanyl (an opioid analgesic) patches or IV or intraspinal catheters are used, the skin around the patch or catheter should be assessed for integrity during physical care.

Managing Anxiety Related to Pain

Anxiety may affect the patient's response to pain. A patient who anticipates pain may become increasingly anxious. Anticipatory guidance about the nature of the impending painful experience and the ways to reduce pain often decreases anxiety. The nurse is aware that, often, people who experience pain use previously learned strategies; therefore, it is important to teach the patient about measures to relieve pain. This nursing action may lessen the threat of pain and give the patient a sense of control. The patient's anxiety may be reduced by explanations that point out the degree of pain relief that can be expected from each measure. For example, a patient who is informed that an intervention may not eliminate pain completely is less likely to become anxious when a certain amount of pain persists. A positive nurse–patient relationship characterized by trust is essential. Acknowledging to the patient, "I know that you have pain," often has positive impact on the patient's psychological state. Occasionally, patients who fear that no one believes their pain feel relieved to know that the nurse believes that the pain exists.

A patient who is anxious about pain may be less tolerant of the pain, which in turn may increase anxiety levels. To prevent the pain and anxiety from escalating, the anxiety-producing cycle must be interrupted. Pain relief measures should be used before pain becomes severe. It is important to explain to all patients that pain relief or control is more successful if such measures begin before the pain becomes unbearable.

PAIN MANAGEMENT STRATEGIES

Reducing pain to a "tolerable" level was once considered the goal of pain management. However, even patients who have described pain relief as adequate often report disturbed sleep and marked distress because of pain. In view of the harmful effects of pain and inadequate pain management, the goal of tolerable pain has been replaced by the goal of relieving pain. Pain management strategies include both pharmacologic and nonpharmacologic approaches. These approaches are selected on the basis of the requirements and goals of particular patients. Appropriate analgesic medications are used as prescribed. They are not considered a last resort to be used only when other pain relief measures fail. As previously discussed, any intervention is most successful if it is initiated before pain sensitization occurs, and the greatest success is usually achieved if several interventions are applied simultaneously.

Pharmacologic Interventions

Pharmacologic management of pain is accomplished in collaboration and communication with health care providers, patients, and, often, families. A physician or nurse practitioner prescribes specific medications for pain or may insert an IV line for administration of analgesic medications. Alternatively, an anesthesiologist or nurse anesthetist may insert an epidural catheter for administration of such analgesic agents. However, it is the nurse who maintains the analgesia, assesses its effectiveness, and reports whether the intervention is ineffective or produces side effects.

There are three general categories of analgesic agents: opioids, NSAIDs, and local anesthetics. These agents work by different mechanisms. Other adjunctive agents, such as antidepressant and antiseizure medications, may also be used.

Opioid Analgesic Agents

The goal of administering opioids is to relieve pain and improve quality of life; therefore, the route of administration, dose, and frequency of administration are determined on an individual basis. Factors that are considered in determining the route, dose, and frequency of medication include the characteristics of the pain (e.g., its expected duration and severity), the overall status of the patient, the patient's response to analgesic medications, and the patient's report of pain. Opioids can be administered by various routes—oral, IV, subcutaneous, intraspinal, intranasal, rectal, and transdermal. Although the oral route is usually preferred for opioid administration, oral opioids must be given frequently enough and in large enough doses to be effective. Opioid analgesic agents given orally may provide a more consistent serum level than those given intramuscularly.

If the patient is expected to require opioid analgesic agents at home, the clinician should consider the ability of the patient and family to administer opioids as prescribed at the planning stages and should take steps to ensure that the required medications will be available to the patient. Many pharmacies, especially those in smaller rural areas or inner cities, may be reluctant to stock large amounts of opioids. Therefore, arrangements for obtaining these prescription medications must be made ahead of time.

Side Effects

With the administration of opioids by any route, side effects must be considered and anticipated. Clinicians who take steps to minimize the side effects increase the likelihood that the patient will receive adequate pain relief without interrupting therapy to treat the effects.

RESPIRATORY DEPRESSION AND SEDATION. Respiratory depression is the most serious adverse effect of opioid analgesic agents administered by intravenously, subcutaneously, or by an epidural route. However, it is relatively rare because doses administered through these routes are small, and tolerance to respiratory depressant effects increases if the dose is increased slowly. The risk of respiratory depression increases with age and with the concomitant use of other opioids or other CNS depressants. The risk of respiratory depression also increases when the epidural catheter is placed in the thoracic area and when the intra-abdominal or intrathoracic pressure is increased.

A patient who receives opioids by any route must be assessed frequently for changes in respiratory status. Specific notable changes are shallow respirations and decreasing respiratory rate. Despite the risks associated with their use, IV and epidural opioids are considered safe, with the risks related to epidural administration no greater than those related to IV or other systemic routes of administration. Sedation, which may occur with any method of opioid administration, is likely to occur when opioid doses are increased. However, patients often develop tolerance quickly, so that in a short time they are no longer sedated by the dose that initially caused sedation. Increasing the time between doses or reducing the dose temporarily, as prescribed, usually prevents deep sedation from occurring. Patients at risk for sedation must be monitored closely for changes in respiratory status. Patients are also at risk for problems associated with sedation and immobility. The nurse must initiate strategies to prevent problems such as skin breakdown.

NAUSEA AND VOMITING. Nausea and vomiting frequently occur with opioid use. Usually these effects occur some hours after the initial injection. Patients, especially postoperative patients, may not think to tell the nurse that they are nauseated, particularly if the nausea is mild. However, a patient receiving opioids should be assessed for nausea and vomiting, which may be triggered by a position change and may be prevented by having the patient change positions slowly. Adequate hydration and the administration of antiemetic agents may also decrease the incidence of nausea. Opioid-induced nausea and vomiting often subside within a few days.

CONSTIPATION. Constipation, a common side effect of opioid use, may become so severe that the patient is forced to choose between relief of pain and relief of constipation. This situation can occur in patients after surgery and in patients receiving large doses of opioids to treat cancer-related pain. Preventing constipation must be a high priority in all patients receiving opioids, and an effective bowel program is needed. Whenever a patient receives opioids, a bowel regimen should begin at the same time. Tolerance to this side effect does not occur; rather, constipation persists even with long-term use of opioids.

Several strategies may help prevent and treat opioid-related constipation. Mild laxatives and a high intake of fluid and fiber may be effective in managing mild constipation. Unless contraindicated, a mild laxative and a stool softener should be administered on a regular schedule. However, continued severe constipation often requires the use of a stimulating cathartic agent, such as senna derivatives (Senokot™) or bisacodyl (Dulcolax™).

PRURITUS AND URINARY RETENTION. When asked about drug allergies, patients with previous hospital experience (especially for surgery) may report that they are "allergic" to morphine. This report should be thoroughly investigated. Commonly, this allergy is described as itching only. Pruritus (itching) is a frequent side effect of opioids administered by any route, but it is not an allergic reaction. It can be relieved by administering prescribed antihistamines. Epidurally administered opioids may also cause urinary retention. The patient should be monitored and may require urinary catheterization. Small doses of naloxone may be prescribed to relieve these problems in patients who are receiving epidural opioids for the relief of acute postoperative pain.

Inadequate Pain Relief

One factor commonly associated with ineffective pain relief is an inadequate dose of opioids. This is most likely to occur when the caregiver underestimates the patient's pain or fails to consider differences in absorption and action after a change in the route of administration (Box 7-5). Consequently, the patient receives doses that are too small to be effective and, possibly, too infrequent to relieve pain. For example, if opioid delivery is changed from the IV route to the oral route, the oral dose must be approximately three times greater than that given parenterally to provide relief. Because of differences in absorption of orally administered opioids among individuals, patients must be assessed carefully to ensure that the pain is relieved.

Table 7-2 lists opioids and dosages that are equivalent to morphine; Table 7-3 is an equianalgesic table that providers may use when changing routes of administration (e.g., from IV to oral medications in preparation for patient discharge). These tables serve only as a guide; the doses listed are not necessarily the most appropriate doses for all patients. However, the tables do give clinicians some idea of equivalency.

After administering the first dose of an opioid, the nurse should perform a complete pain assessment to determine the efficacy of that dose. The time, date, patient's pain rating (scale of 0 to 10), analgesic agent, other pain relief measures, side effects, and patient activity are recorded. If the pain has not decreased in 30 minutes (sooner if an IV route is used) and the patient is reasonably alert and has a satisfactory respiratory status, blood pressure, and pulse rate, then some change in analgesia is indicated. In general, no recalculation needs to be done when changing from one brand of an agent to another brand of the same medication, with the exception of extended-release oral morphine. Although extended-release agents come in the same dosage form and contain the same drug, they are not considered therapeutically equivalent because they use different release mechanisms. Patients who need to change brands should be monitored carefully both for overdose and for inadequate pain relief.

Because of the fear of promoting addiction or causing respiratory depression, health care providers tend to prescribe and administer inadequate dosages of opioid agents to treat acute pain or persistent pain, particularly in termi-

---

Inadequate Pain Management

Situation

When taking over the care of ethnic minority patients at the change of shift from a particular colleague, you usually find these patients to be in a great deal of pain. Your nonsystematic observations have led you to conclude that these patients receive only a small portion of the analgesia prescribed for them. You have heard a nurse colleague state a belief that people of certain ethnic groups have "no pain tolerance" and are "just looking for drugs."

Dilemma

Racial biases are difficult to deal with and change. To confront this nurse may not alter the behavior but will certainly disrupt the working relationships on the unit. It would be easier to look the other way. On the other hand, you believe that the nurse is giving inadequate and unethical care to selected patients and placing them at greater risk for postoperative complications.

Discussion

- What information would you need to collect before acting?
- From whom could you seek counsel?
- Are the two aspects of the dilemma equally important?

---

nally ill patients. However, even prolonged administration of opioid agents is associated with an extremely low incidence of addiction (less than 1%). Genetic factors play a role in the varied responses to NSAIDs and opioids seen in patients. There appears to be a higher incidence of poor drug metabolism among Caucasians and Asian Americans compared with African Americans. The most **extensively** studied genetic variation related to pain in humans is in the metabolism of codeine. Drug metabolism involves genetically controlled enzyme activity for absorption, distribution, inactivation, and excretion. In studies of both experimental and clinical pain, multiple polymorphisms (DNA proteins with variant alleles) result both in poor metabolism and poor analgesic efficacy, leading to changes in drug absorption, distribution, and elimination (Miaskowski, 2009).

! NURSING ALERT

Conversion tables available for the transdermal systems should be used only to establish the initial dose of the transdermal fentanyl or buprenorphine when patients switch from oral morphine to the transdermal route of delivery (and not vice versa). If these tables are inappropriately used to determine the dosages of oral morphine for patients who have been receiving transdermal fentanyl or buprenorphine, many patients will not achieve satisfactory analgesia and will require an increase in their opioid dose to treat breakthrough pain.

TABLE
7-2 Selected Opioid Analgesic Agents Commonly Used for Moderate and Severe Pain in Adults

| Name | Starting Dose (milligrams) | | Comments | Precautions and Contraindications |
	Moderate Pain	Severe Pain		
Morphine	—	30–60 (oral) 10 parenteral)	Agonist at specific opioid receptors in the CNS to produce analgesia, euphoria, and sedation.	Use with caution, especially in elderly patients, very ill patients, and those with respiratory impairment. Major risks include respiratory depression, apnea, circulatory depression, and respiratory arrest, shock, and cardiac arrest. Obtain history of hypersensitivity to opioids. Monitor patient closely. If prescribed in correct dose, oral preparations (MS Contin™) are effective in treating moderate and severe pain.
Codeine	15–30 (oral)	60 (oral) up to 360/ 24 hr	Agonist at specific opioid receptors in the CNS to produce analgesia, euphoria, and sedation. Is also an antitussive. 10% of people lack the enzyme needed to make codeine active. Codeine may cause more nausea and constipation per unit of analgesia than other mu agonist opioids.	Many preparations of codeine and the other opioids in this table are combinations with nonopioid analgesics. Caution must be used in patients with impaired ventilation, bronchial asthma, increased intracranial pressure, or impaired liver function and in elderly and very ill patients.
Oxycodone (OxyContin™)	5 (oral)	10–20 (oral)	Agonist at specific opioid receptors in the CNS to produce analgesia, euphoria, and sedation.	Caution must be used in patients with impaired ventilation, bronchial asthma, increased intracranial pressure, or impaired liver function and in elderly and very ill patients.
Meperidine (Demerol™)	50 (oral)	300 (oral) 75 (parenteral)	Agonist at specific opioid receptors in the CNS to produce analgesia, euphoria, and sedation. Shorter acting than morphine. Meperidine is biotransformed to normeperidine, a toxic metabolite.	Normeperidine, a toxic metabolic of meperidine, accumulates with repetitive dosing, causing CNS excitation. High risk for seizures. Should be avoided in patients with impaired renal function who are receiving MAO inhibitors. Is irritating to tissues with repeated intramuscular injections. Chronic use should be avoided. Should not be used for more than 1 or 2 days.
Propoxyphene (Darvon™)	65–130 (oral)	—	Weak analgesic; acts as an agonist at specific opioid receptors in the CNS to produce analgesia, euphoria, and sedation. Many preparations include nonopioid analgesics; biotransformed to potentially toxic metabolite (norpropoxyphene).	Accumulation of propoxyphene and toxic metabolites occurs with repetitive dosing. Overdose is complicated by seizures. Propoxyphene is not recommended for older adults or patients with renal impairment.
Hydrocodone (Vicodin™)	5–10 (oral)	—	—	Most preparations are combined with nonopioid analgesics.
Tramadol (Ultram™)	50–100 (oral)	—	Unique mechanism; analgesia results from the synergy of two mechanisms. Maximum dose is 400 mg/day.	Most common side effects are dizziness, nausea, constipation, and somnolence. Lowers seizure threshold.

CNS, central nervous system; MAO, monoamine oxidase.
Adapted from American Pain Society. (2008). *Principles of analgesic use in the treatment of acute pain and chronic cancer pain* (6th ed.). Skokie, IL; and Karch, A. M. (2008). *Focus on nursing pharmacology.*
Philadelphia: Lippincott Williams & Wilkins.

TABLE
7-3 National Cancer Institute (2009): Approximate Dose Equivalents for Opioid Analgesics

Drug	Oral Dose (mg)	Parenteral Dose[b]
Morphine[c]	30	10 mg
Codeine[d]	200	100 mg
Fentanyl[e,f]	NA	100 μg
Hydrocodone (Vicodin)	30–45	NA
Hydromorphone (Dilaudid)[c]	8	2 mg
Levorphanol (Levo-Dromoran)	4	2 mg
Methadone[g,h]	The conversion ratio of methadone is variable. Please refer to the Opioid Types section and Opioid switching section.	
Oxycodone (OxyContin)[d]	20–30	10–15 mg
Oxymorphone (Opana, Opana ER, and Opana IV[c])	10	1 mg

IV = IV; NA = not available.

[a]Published tables vary in the suggested doses that are equianalgesic to morphine. Many of these doses are based on clinical consensus rather than well-controlled trials. Clinical response is the criterion that must be applied for each patient; titration to clinical response is necessary. Because there is not complete cross-tolerance among these drugs, it is usually necessary to use a lower-than-equianalgesic dose when changing drugs and retitrate according to response.

[b]Parenteral dosing includes IV and subcutaneous administration. Onset and duration may vary slightly between these routes; however, doses remain approximately equal. The intramuscular route is not recommended because of variability in uptake of the drug and painful injection.

[c]Caution: For morphine, hydromorphone, and oxymorphone, rectal administration is an alternate route for patients unable to take oral medications. Equianalgesic doses may differ from oral to parenteral doses because of pharmacokinetic differences. Note: A short-acting opioid should normally be used for initial therapy of moderate-to-severe pain.

[d]Caution: Doses of aspirin and acetaminophen in combination opioid/NSAID preparations must be adjusted to the patient's body weight.

[e]Transdermal fentanyl is an alternative. Transdermal fentanyl dosage is not calculated as equianalgesic to a single morphine dosage but is calculated based on a 24-hour opioid dose. See package insert for dosing calculations. Transdermal fentanyl should not be used in opioid-naïve patients.

[f]Transmucosal and buccal fentanyl are also available and indicated for breakthrough pain, although they are not bioequivalent. Titration of either should be conducted gradually; neither should be used in opioid-naïve patients.

[g]Caution: Methadone is much more potent than indicated in older published literature. On average, it is ten times more potent than morphine. However, its potency relative to morphine is not linear. When morphine at lower doses (e.g., 30–60 mg/d orally) is switched to methadone, the potency may be 3 to 5 times; when switched from high doses (e.g., >300 mg/d orally), the potency may be 12 times or even higher.

[h]Caution: The oral to IV dose ratio of methadone is not well established. The IV route is very seldom used, except in cancer centers with pain service familiar with parenteral methadone. IV use of methadone in combination with chlorobutanol is associated with QTc wave prolongation. Subcutaneous administration may cause irritation.

From American Cancer Society. Pain Management Pocket Tool, Accessible at http://www.cancer.org/docroot/PRO/content/PRO_1_1_Pain_Management_Pocket_Tool.asp

Source: http://www.cancer.gov/cancertopics/pdq/supportivecare/pain/HealthProfessional/Table 3

⚠ NURSING ALERT

If the conversion table or equation is used incorrectly to calculate a morphine dose, there is a risk of overdose. If a patient requires a change from transdermal fentanyl or buprenorphine back to oral or IV morphine (as in the case of surgery), the patch should be removed and IV morphine administered on an as-needed basis. Before a new patch is applied, the patient should be carefully checked for any older, forgotten patches, which should be removed and discarded. Patches should be replaced every 72 hours.

Opioid Use With Selected Conditions and Medication

A number of factors may influence the safety and effectiveness of opioid administration. Opioid analgesic agents are primarily metabolized by the liver and excreted by the kidney. Therefore, metabolism and excretion of analgesic medications are impaired in patients with liver or kidney disease, increasing the risk of cumulative or toxic effects. In addition, normeperidine, a metabolite of meperidine, may rapidly or unexpectedly accumulate to toxic levels. This is more likely to occur in patients with impaired kidney function, and may result in seizures in susceptible patients. Many institutions no longer stock meperidine because of the risks associated with the metabolite normeperidine and because most providers do not prescribe a high enough dose for it to be effective.

Patients with untreated hypothyroidism are more susceptible to the analgesic effects and side effects of opioids. In contrast, patients with hyperthyroidism may require larger doses for pain relief. Patients with a decreased respiratory reserve from disease or aging may be more susceptible to the depressant effects of opioids and must be carefully monitored for respiratory depression.

Patients who are dehydrated are at increased risk for the hypotensive effects of opioids. Patients who become hypotensive after the administration of an opioid should be kept recumbent and rehydrated unless fluids are contraindicated. Patients who are dehydrated are also more likely to

experience nausea and vomiting with opioid use. Rehydration usually relieves these symptoms.

Patients receiving certain other medications, such as monoamine oxidase inhibitors, phenothiazines, or tricyclic antidepressants, may have an exaggerated response to the depressant effects of opioids. Patients taking these medications should receive small doses of opioids and must be monitored closely. Continued pain in these patients indicates that a therapeutic level of the analgesic has not been achieved. Patients must be monitored for sedation even if an analgesic effect has not been obtained.

Tolerance and Addiction

There is no maximum safe dosage of opioids, nor is there any easily identifiable therapeutic serum level. Both the maximal safe dosage and the therapeutic serum level are relative and individual.

TOLERANCE. Tolerance (the need for increasing doses of opioids to achieve the same therapeutic effect) develops in almost all patients taking opioids for extended periods. Patients requiring opioids over a long term, especially cancer patients, need increasing dosages to relieve pain, although after the first few weeks of therapy, the progressively increasing dosages will no longer be required and the patient can be placed on maintenance dosages. Patients who become tolerant to the analgesic effects of large doses of morphine may obtain pain relief by changing to a different opioid. Symptoms of physical dependence may occur when the opioids are discontinued; dependence often occurs with opioid tolerance and does not indicate an addiction. It is an expected physiologic response that will occur in all people exposed to continuous opioid administration (Trescot, Helm, Hansen et al., 2008).

> **! NURSING ALERT**
> *Although patients may need increasing levels of opioids, they are not addicted. Physical tolerance usually occurs in the absence of addiction. Tolerance to opioids is common and becomes a problem primarily in terms of delivering or administering the medication. On the other hand, addiction is rare and should not be the primary concern of nurses caring for patients in pain.*

ADDICTION. Addiction is a behavioral pattern of substance use characterized by a compulsion to take the substance (drug or alcohol) primarily to experience its psychic effects. Fear that patients will become addicted or dependent on opioids has contributed to inadequate treatment of pain. This fear is commonly expressed by health care providers as well as patients, and results from lack of knowledge about the low risk of addiction.

Addiction after therapeutic opioid administration is so negligible that it should not be a consideration when car-

ing for patients in pain. Therefore, patients and health care providers should be discouraged from withholding opioid analgesics because of concerns about addiction.

Currently, over 20 million people in the United States are dealing with substance abuse disorders; thus, it is likely that nurses in acute care will encounter patients with a history of addiction seeking care for acute or chronic pain (Substance Abuse and Mental Health Services Administration, 2010). When caring for people with a known history of addiction, nurses should consider that each individual person has the right to be treated for pain. No formula has been established for the treatment of pain with opioids in patients with a history of addiction; however, the use of NSAIDs is suggested as a starting point, and if opioids are necessary, the use of long-acting agents are suggested, with collaboration of a multidisciplinary team (Morgan and White, 2009). If prescribed, the opioids should be tapered slowly to prevent withdrawal symptoms (Trescot et al., 2008). The use of complementary therapies is also suggested and is described later in the chapter.

> **! NURSING ALERT**
> *Patients admitted to the hospital suffering from an acute illness who have a history of substance abuse and are currently on methadone maintenance treatment (MMT) should have their methadone dose continued or an equivalent opioid given to prevent craving. The patient's methadone treatment facility should also be consulted. Opioids are prescribed without consideration of the methadone, and doses may need to be higher than those prescribed to patients who have never received opioid drugs. (Pillet & Eschiti, 2008)*

NSAIDs

NSAIDs are thought to decrease pain by inhibiting cyclooxygenase (COX), the enzyme involved in the production of prostaglandin (which is believed to increase the sensitivity of pain receptors) from traumatized or inflamed tissues. There are two types of COX: COX-1 and COX-2.

COX-1 mediates prostaglandin formation involved in the maintenance of physiologic functions, such as platelet aggregation, which prevents ischemia and promotes mucosal integrity. Inhibition of COX-1 results in gastric ulceration, bleeding, and renal damage.

COX-2 mediates prostaglandin formation that results in symptoms of pain, inflammation, and fever. Therefore, inhibition of COX-2 is desirable. Celecoxib (Celebrex™) is an example of a COX-2 inhibitor. There is evidence of increased cardiovascular risk associated with COX-2 inhibitors. Ibuprofen (Advil™, Motrin™), another NSAID, blocks both COX-1 and COX-2. It is effective in relieving mild to moderate pain and has a low incidence of adverse effects. Aspirin, the oldest NSAID, also blocks COX-1 as well as COX-2; however,

because it causes frequent and severe side effects, aspirin is infrequently used to treat significant acute or persistent pain.

NSAIDs are very helpful in treating arthritic diseases and may be especially powerful in treating cancer-related bone pain. They have been effectively combined with opioids to treat postoperative and other severe pain. The use of NSAIDs in combination with opioids relieves pain more effectively than the use of opioids alone. In such cases, patients may obtain pain relief with decreased doses of opioids and with fewer side effects. A regimen of a fixed-dose, time-contingent NSAID (e.g., every 4 hours) and a separately administered fluctuating dose of opioid may be effective in managing moderate to severe cancer pain. In more severe pain, the opioid dose is also fixed, with an additional fluctuating dose as needed for **breakthrough pain** (a sudden increase in pain despite the administration of pain-relieving medications). Most patients tolerate NSAIDs well. However, those with impaired kidney function may require a smaller dose and must be monitored closely for side effects. Patients taking NSAIDs bruise easily because the agents have some anticoagulant effect. Furthermore, NSAIDs may displace other medications, such as warfarin (Coumadin™), from serum proteins and increase their effects. High doses or prolonged use can irritate the stomach and in some cases result in GI bleeding as well. For this reason, monitoring for GI bleeding is indicated, and gastroprotective agents should be prescribed to prevent this complication (Goldstein, Howard, Walton et al., 2006).

Local Anesthetic Agents

Local anesthetics work by blocking nerve conduction when applied directly to the nerve fibers. They can be applied directly to the site of injury (e.g., a topical anesthetic spray for sunburn) or directly to nerve fibers by injection or at the time of surgery. They can also be administered through an epidural catheter (see later discussion of Intraspinal and Epidural Administration).

Local anesthetic agents have been successful in reducing the pain associated with thoracic or upper abdominal surgery when injected by the surgeon intercostally. Local anesthetic agents are rapidly absorbed into the bloodstream, resulting in decreased availability at the surgical or injury site and an increased anesthetic level in the blood, increasing the risk of toxicity. Therefore, a vasoconstrictive agent (e.g., epinephrine or phenylephrine) is added to the anesthetic agent to decrease its systemic absorption and maintain its concentration at the surgical or injury site.

A topical anesthetic agent known as *eutectic mixture* (emulsion of local anesthetics), or EMLA cream, has been effective in preventing the pain associated with invasive procedures such as lumbar puncture or the insertion of IV lines. To be effective, EMLA must be applied to the site 60 to 90 minutes before the procedure.

A lidocaine 5% patch acts locally by targeting damaged nerves responsible for discharging pain impulses and is approved for limited use. The lidocaine 5% patch provides suf-ficient medication for anesthetic effect but not enough to cause total sensory block in the area of application, so it has a wide margin of safety. The recommended dose is one to three patches at a time applied over the affected area for 12 hours daily.

Antidepressant and Antiseizure Medications

Pain of neurologic origin (e.g., causalgia [intense burning pain and sensitivity to the slightest vibration or touch]), tumor impingement on a nerve, postherpetic neuralgia) is difficult to treat and in general is not responsive to opioid therapy. If these pain syndromes are accompanied by dysesthesia (burning or cutting pain), they may be responsive to tricyclic antidepressants or antiseizure agents. When indicated, tricyclic antidepressant agents, such as amitriptyline (Elavil™) or imipramine (Tofranil™), are prescribed in doses considerably smaller than those generally used for depression. Patients need to know that a therapeutic effect may not occur until they have taken the medication for 3 weeks. Antiseizure medications such as phenytoin (Dilantin™) or carbamazepine (Tegretol™) also are used in doses lower than those prescribed for seizure disorders. Because a variety of medications can be tried, nurses should be familiar with the possible side effects and should teach patients and families how to recognize these effects.

Approaches to Using Analgesic Agents

The nurse obtains the patient's medication history (e.g., current, usual, or recent use of prescription or OTC medications or herbal agents), along with a history of health disorders and allergies. Certain medications or conditions may affect the analgesic medication's effectiveness or its metabolism and excretion. Table 7-4 lists adverse interactions of herbal substances or foods with analgesics. Before administering analgesic agents, the nurse should assess the patient's pain status, including the intensity of current pain, changes in pain intensity after the previous dose of medication, and side effects of the medication. Medications are most effective when the dose and interval between doses are individualized to meet the needs of a particular patient. The only safe and effective way to administer analgesic medications is by asking the patient to rate the pain and by observing the response to medications.

Balanced Analgesia

Pharmacologic interventions are most effective when a multimodal, or balanced, analgesia approach is used. **Balanced analgesia** refers to the use of more than one form of analgesia concurrently to obtain more pain relief with fewer side effects. Using two or three types of agents simultaneously can maximize pain relief while minimizing the potentially toxic effects of any one agent. When one agent is used alone, it usually must be used in a higher dose to be effective. In other words, although it might require 15 mg morphine to relieve a certain pain, it may take only 8 mg morphine plus 30 mg ketorolac (an NSAID) to relieve the same pain.

TABLE
7-4 Adverse Interactions of Herbal Substances or Food With Analgesics

Analgesic	Herb, Supplement, or Food	Potential Interaction
NSAID	Bilberry fruit (*Vaccinium myrtillus*)	Potential for increased bleeding if taken with anticoagulants and other antiplatelet drugs; use cautiously if taking medicinal quantities
	Chondroitin	Do not take with anticoagulants; may potentiate bleeding
	German or Hungarian chamomile (*Matricaria recutita*)	Anticoagulants may potentiate effect; use cautiously together
	Dong quai (*Angelica sinensis*)	May increase bleeding time if used with warfarin and other anticoagulant drugs
	Fenugreek (*Trigonella foenum-graecum*)	May potentiate effects of anticoagulants
	Feverfew (*Tanacetum parthenium*)	May increase bleeding; use cautiously with anticoagulants
	Garlic (*Allium sativum*)	May increase bleeding; use cautiously with anticoagulants
	Ginger (*Zingiber officinale*)	May increase bleeding; use cautiously with anticoagulants
	Melatonin (N-acetyl-5-methoxytryptamine)	NSAIDs and antidepressants may deplete melatonin
	Pau D'arco (*Tabebuia impetiginosa, T. ipe*)	May potentiate effects of anticoagulants; avoid concurrent use
	Red clover (*Trifolium pratense*)	May increase bleeding; use cautiously with anticoagulants and antiplatelet agents
	Turmeric (*Curcuma longa*)	Avoid using large doses with anticoagulants and NSAIDs; possible additive effect for bleeding
	Willow (*Salix* spp.)	Use cautiously with NSAIDs; may increase likelihood of GI irritation and bleeding due to tannins.
Ibuprofen	St. John's Wort (*Hypericum perforatum*)	Mean residence time of ibuprofen may be reduced with concurrent use of St. John's Wort.
Acetaminophen	Watercress	May inhibit the oxidative pathway of acetaminophen metabolism.
Aspirin	Ginkgo (*Ginkgo biloba*)	May increase bleeding tendencies; patients taking aspirin should avoid concurrent use of ginkgo biloba
	Dan shen (*Salvia miltiorrhiza*)	Avoid concurrent use with sedatives, warfarin, and aspirin
Opioids (sedatives)	Kava-kava (*Piper methysticum*)	May potentiate action of alcohol, tranquilizers (barbiturates), and antidepressants
	Sarsaparilla (*Smilax* spp.)	May increase elimination of sedatives
	Valerian (*Valeriana officinalis*)	May intensify effects of sedatives
Alfentanil, fentanyl, sufentanil	Grapefruit	Inhibits CYP3A4 and P-glycoprotein; if used in combination with drugs that are metabolized through 3A4 or via P-glycoprotein may increase in concentration leading to potential adverse effects.
	St. John's Wort (*Hypericum perforatum*)	May increase or decrease cyclic P-450 activity; may affect medications that are metabolized by this pathway

From *Drug interactions facts™: Herbal supplements and food.* (2008). St. Louis: Wolters Kluwer Health/Facts and Comparisons; and Kuhn, M., & Winston, D. (2008). *Herbal therapy & supplements: A scientific and traditional approach.* Philadelphia: Wolters Kluwer Health/Lippincott Williams & Wilkins.

Preventive Approach

With the preventive approach, analgesic agents are administered at set intervals, so that the medication acts before the pain becomes severe and before the serum opioid level decreases to a subtherapeutic level. For example, a patient takes prescribed morphine or a prescribed NSAID (e.g., ibuprofen) every 4 hours rather than waiting until the pain is severe. If the pain is likely to occur around the clock or for a substantial portion of a 24-hour period, a regular around-the-clock schedule of administering analgesia may be indicated. Even if the analgesic is prescribed *pro re nata* (PRN), or "as needed," it can be administered on a preventive basis before

the patient is in severe pain, as long as the prescribed interval between doses is observed. The preventive approach reduces the peaks and troughs in the serum level and provides more pain relief with fewer adverse effects.

Smaller doses of medication are needed with the preventive approach because the pain does not escalate to a level of severe intensity. Therefore, a preventive approach may result in the administration of less medication over a 24-hour period, helping prevent tolerance to analgesic agents and decreasing the severity of side effects (e.g., sedation, constipation). Better pain control can be achieved with a preventive approach, reducing the amount of time patients are in pain.

In using the preventive approach, the nurse assesses the patient for sedation before administering the next dose. It is not safe to medicate the patient with opioids repeatedly if the patient is sedated or not in pain.

Individualized Dosage

Providers may have prescribed opioids with orders that allow the nurse to determine doses of medication to be administered and the intervals between doses based on the nurse's assessment of the patient.

The dosage and the interval between doses should be based on the patient's requirements, rather than on an inflexible standard or routine. As noted earlier, metabolism and absorption of medications is highly variable. Therefore, a certain dose of an opioid medication given at specified intervals may be effective for one patient but ineffective for another.

As in the preventive approach discussed above, the nurse does not wait for the patient to complain of pain and then administer analgesia. To receive pain relief from an opioid analgesic, the serum level of that opioid must be maintained at a minimum therapeutic level (Fig. 7-5). The lower the serum opioid level, the more difficult it is to achieve the therapeutic level with the next dose. Using an individualized method, the only way to ensure significant periods of analgesia is to give doses large enough to produce periodic sedation.

Routes of Administration

The route selected for administration of an analgesic agent (Table 7-5) depends on the condition of the individual patient and the desired effect of the medication. Analgesic agents can be administered by parenteral, oral, rectal, transdermal (skin patch), transmucosal, intraspinal, or epidural routes. Each method of administration has advantages and disadvantages. The route chosen should be based on patient need. Box 7-6 discusses the safe use of transdermal fentanyl administration.

Patient-Controlled Analgesia

Used to manage postoperative pain as well as persistent pain in hospitals or home settings, **patient-controlled analgesia** (PCA) allows patients to control the administration of their own medication within predetermined safety limits.

The PCA pump permits the patient to self-administer a predetermined amount of medication safely, and to administer extra medication (bolus doses) with episodes of increased pain or painful activities. A PCA pump is electronically controlled by a timing device. A patient experiencing pain can administer small amounts of medication directly into the IV, subcutaneous, or epidural catheter by pressing a button. The pump then delivers a preset amount of medication.

The PCA pump also can be programmed to deliver a constant, background infusion of medication (or basal rate) and still allow the patient to administer additional bolus doses as needed. The timer can be programmed to prevent additional doses from being administered until a specified time period has elapsed (lock-out time) and until the first dose has had time to exert its maximal effect. Even if the patient pushes

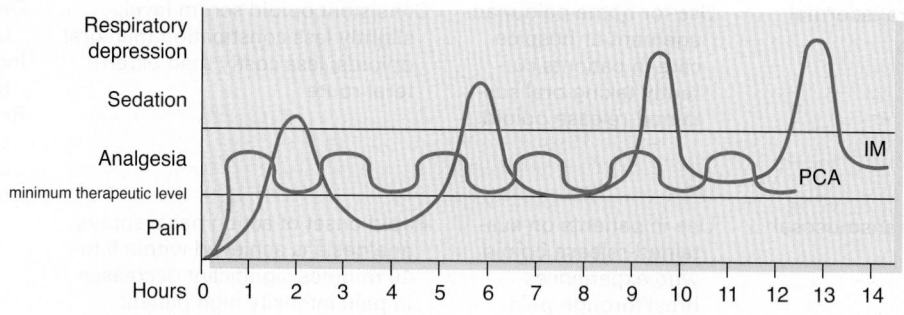

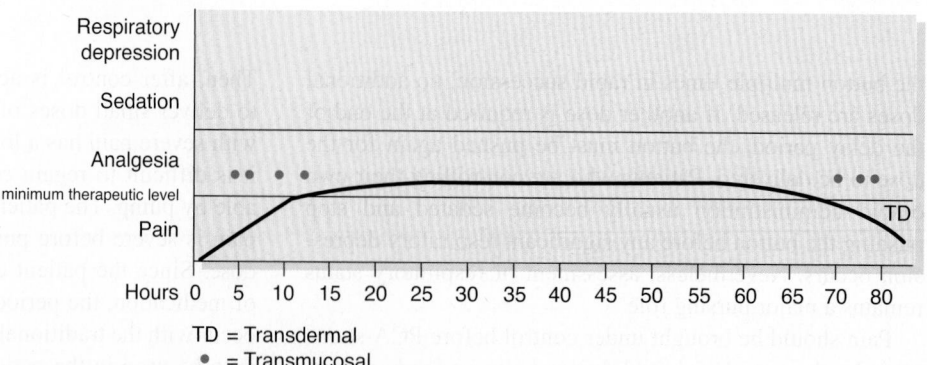

FIGURE 7-5 Relationship of mode of delivery of analgesia to serum analgesic level. **Top:** Intramuscular (IM) and IV patient-controlled analgesia (PCA). **Bottom:** Transdermal (TD) and transmucosal (•) delivery.

TD = Transdermal
• = Transmucosal

TABLE
7-5 Administration Routes for Analgesics

Route	Patient Factors	Advantages	Disadvantages
IV	Can be used if patient has had nothing by mouth. Side effects are nausea, vomiting.	Rapid, reliable effect, more comfortable; may be administered by push or slow push (e.g., over a 5 to 10 minute period); may be by continuous infusion with a pump. Continuous infusion provides a steady level of analgesia over 24 hour period.	Short duration; careful calculation of dosage needed. Possible respiratory depression
Intramuscular	Can be used if patient has had nothing by mouth. Side effects are nausea, vomiting.		Slower entry into bloodstream; slow metabolism. Absorption depends on site selected and amount of body fat.
Subcutaneous	Use if patient is in severe pain or had limited IV sites Used for home pain management	Effective, convenient	Limited to small volume that can be administered at one time into the subcutaneous tissue
Oral	Preferred over parenteral administration if patient can take medication by mouth	Easy, noninvasive, not painful. Severe pain can be relieved with oral opioids if dose is high enough. Gradual dose increase provides additional pain relief without producing respiratory depression or sedation	Increased doses needed as the disease progresses; tolerance may develop to the medication. Change from parenteral to oral route requires equianalgesic dosing to avoid withdrawal reaction and recurrence of pain
Rectal	Use if patient is unable to take medications by any other route. Side effects include bleeding problems.	Prolonged duration of action	Onset of action unclear; delayed absorption compared with other routes of administration
Transdermal	Use for home pain management or hospice care in patients currently taking oral sustained-release opioid.	Consistent opioid serum level; slightly less constipation than oral opioids; less costly than parenteral route	Delay in effect while the dermal layer is saturated. Increased absorption in febrile patients. Require short-acting opioids for breakthrough pain; more expensive than sustained-release opioids
Transmucosal	Use in patients on sustained-release opioid who experiences breakthrough pain.	Rapid onset of action nasal sprays analgesia is achieved within 5 to 10 minutes significant decreases in pain intensity high patient satisfaction.	

the button multiple times in rapid succession, no additional doses are released. If another dose is required at the end of the delay period, the button must be pushed again for the dose to be delivered. Patients who are controlling their own opioid administration usually become sedated and stop pushing the button before any significant respiratory depression occurs. Nevertheless, assessment of respiratory status remains a major nursing role.

Pain should be brought under control before PCA starts, often by the use of an initial, larger *bolus* or *loading dose*.

Then, after control is achieved, the pump is programmed to deliver small doses of medication at a time. If a patient with severe pain has a low serum level of opioid analgesic, it is difficult to regain control with the small doses available by pump. The patient is instructed not to wait until the pain is severe before pushing the button to obtain a bolus dose. Since the patient can maintain a near-constant level of medication, the periods of severe pain and sedation that occur with the traditional PRN regimen are avoided. If PCA is to be used in the patient's home, the patient and family

Safe Use of Transdermal Fentanyl

The U.S. Food and Drug Administration issued a public health advisory in 2009 about the use of fentanyl skin patches, and warned patients and health care providers about the need for the patches to be used as intended. The advisory also included precautions about safe storage and disposal of fentanyl skin patches:

- Fentanyl skin patches are very strong opioids and should always be prescribed at the lowest dose needed for pain relief. They should be used only for patients with chronic pain that is not well controlled with shorter-acting opioids.
- Patients should be cautioned that a sudden and possibly dangerous rise in the level of fentanyl in their blood can occur with use of alcohol or other medications that affect brain function; an increase in body temperature or exposure to heat; or use of other medicines that affect the metabolism of fentanyl.
- Patients should be informed about signs and symptoms of fentanyl overdose (i.e., shallow or difficult breathing; fatigue, extreme sleepiness, or sedation; inability to think, talk, or walk normally; and feeling faint, dizzy, or confused).

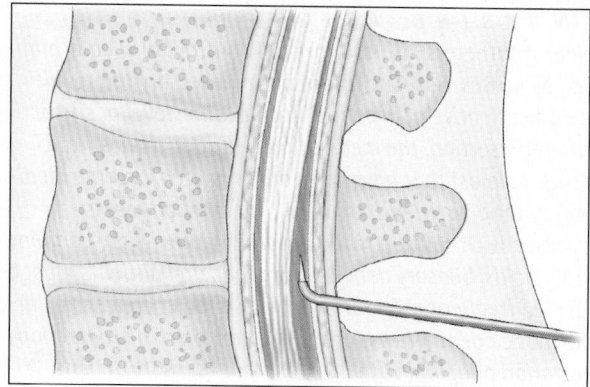

A

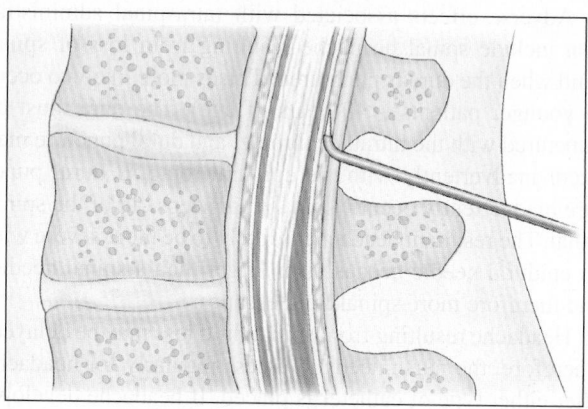

B

FIGURE 7-6 Placement of intraspinal catheters for administration of analgesic medications: (**A**) intrathecal route; (**B**) epidural route.

are taught about the operation of the pump, as well as about the side effects of the medication and strategies to manage them.

NURSING ALERT

Family members are cautioned not to push the button for a patient, especially if the patient is asleep, because this overrides some of the safety features of the PCA system.

Intraspinal and Epidural Administration

Infusion of opioids or local anesthetic agents into the subarachnoid space (intrathecal space, or spinal canal) or epidural space has been used for effective control of pain in postoperative patients and those with chronic pain unrelieved by other methods. A catheter is inserted into the subarachnoid or epidural space at the thoracic or lumbar level for administration of opioid or anesthetic agents (Fig. 7-6). With intrathecal administration, medication infuses directly into the subarachnoid space and cerebrospinal fluid, which surrounds the spinal cord. With epidural administration, medication is deposited in the dura of the spinal canal and diffuses into the subarachnoid space. It is believed that pain relief from intraspinal administration of opioids is based on the existence of opioid receptors in the spinal cord.

A single-dose extended-release epidural morphine (DepoDur™) may also be administered into the epidural space at the lumbar level immediately prior to surgery. Although supplemental analgesic agents may be needed, patients who have received DepoDur tend to report less intense pain and greater satisfaction with pain relief (Gambling, Hughes, & Manvelian, 2009).

An epidural anesthetic agent can be administered continuously in low doses, intermittently on a schedule, or on demand as the patient requires it, and it is often combined with the epidural administration of opioids. Surgical patients treated with this combination experience fewer complications after surgery (Ferguson, Malhotra, Venkatraman et al., 2009).

For patients who have persistent, severe pain that fails to respond to other treatments, or who obtain pain relief only with the risk of serious side effects, medication administered by a long-term intrathecal or epidural catheter may be effective. After the physician tunnels the catheter through the subcutaneous tissue and places the inlet (or port) under the skin, the medication is injected through the skin into the inlet and catheter, which delivers the medication directly into the epidural space.

! *NURSING ALERT*

Epidural catheters inserted for pain control are usually managed by nurses. Baseline information necessary to provide safe and effective pain control includes the level or site of catheter insertion, the medications (e.g., local anesthetic agents, opioids) that have been administered, and the medications anticipated in the future. The infusion rate is increased with caution when anesthetic agents are combined with opioids. Sensory deficits can occur, and patients must be assessed frequently. An infusion with a lower concentration of anesthetic agent allows for administration of a greater concentration of opioid with a lower risk of sensory deficits.

Adverse effects associated with intraspinal administration include spinal headache resulting from loss of spinal fluid when the dura is punctured. This is more likely to occur in younger patients (<40 years of age). The dura must be punctured with the intrathecal route, and dural puncture may occur inadvertently with the epidural route. If dural puncture inadvertently occurs, spinal fluid seeps out of the spinal canal. The resultant headache is likely to be more severe with an epidural needle because it is larger than a spinal needle, and therefore more spinal fluid escapes.

Headache resulting from spinal fluid loss may be delayed. Therefore, the nurse needs to assess regularly for headache after either type of catheter is placed. If headache develops, the patient should remain flat in bed and should be given large amounts of fluids (provided the medical condition allows), and the physician should be notified. An epidural blood patch may be performed to reduce leakage of spinal fluid.

Respiratory depression generally peaks 6 to 12 hours after epidural opioids are administered, but it can occur earlier or up to 24 hours after the first injection. Depending on the lipophilicity (affinity for body fat) of the opioid injected, the time frame for respiratory depression can be short or long. Morphine is hydrophilic (it has an affinity to water), and the time for peak effect is longer than that of fentanyl, which is lipophilic. The nurse must assess and record respiratory status and sedation levels using a sedation scale according to agency policy. The health care provider will need to be notified if the patient has a sedation scale of less than three (3) on the Pasero Opioid-Induced Sedation Scale (POSS) and a respiratory rate of less than eight breaths per minute (Nisbet & Mooney-Cotter, 2009). The POSS evaluates the patient's level of consciousness since sedation precedes respiratory depression (Box 7-7). The patient should be easily aroused if slightly drowsy, and should be able to remain awake during conversation. Opioid antagonist agents such as naloxone must be available for IV use if respiratory depression occurs.

Cardiovascular effects (hypotension and decreased heart rate) may result from relaxation of the vasculature in the lower extremities. Therefore, the nurse should assess frequently for decreases in blood pressure, pulse rate, and urine output.

BOX 7-7

Pasero Opioid–Induced Sedation Scale (POSS)

S = Sleep, easy to arouse
Acceptable; no action necessary; may increase opioid dose if needed

1 = Awake and alert
Acceptable; no action necessary; may increase opioid dose if needed

2 = Slightly drowsy, easily aroused
Acceptable; no action necessary; may increase opioid dose if needed

3 = Frequently drowsy, arousable, drifts off to sleep during conversation
Unacceptable; monitor respiratory status and sedation level closely until sedation level is stable at less than 3 and respiratory status is satisfactory; decrease opioid dose 25% to 50%[1] or notify prescriber[2] or anesthesiologist for orders; consider administering a non-sedating, opioid-sparing nonopioid, such as acetaminophen or a NSAID, if not contraindicated.

4 = Somnolent, minimal or no response to verbal and physical stimulation
Unacceptable; stop opioid; consider administering naloxone[3,4]; notify prescriber[2] or anesthesiologist; monitor respiratory status and sedation level closely until sedation level is stable at less than 3 and respiratory status is satisfactory.

---

*Appropriate action is given in italics at each level of sedation.
[1]Opioid analgesic orders or a hospital protocol should include the expectation that a nurse will decrease the opioid dose if a patient is excessively sedated.
[2]For example, the physician, nurse practitioner, advanced practice nurse, or physician assistant responsible for the pain management prescription.
[3]Mix 0.4 mg of naloxone and 10 mL of normal saline in syringe and administer this dilute solution very slowly (0.5 mL over 2 minutes) while observing the patient's response (titrate to effect) (Source for naloxone administration: Pasero, Portenoy, McCaffery M. Opioid analgesics, in *Pain: Clinical Manual* (ed 2). St. Louis, MO, Mosby 1999, p. 267; American Pain Society (APS). *Principles of Analgesic Use in The Treatment of Acute Pain and Chronic Cancer Pain* (ed 5), Glenview, IL, APS, 2003.)
[4]Hospital protocols should include the expectation that a nurse will administer naloxone to any patient suspected of having life-threatening opioid-induced sedation and respiratory depression.
Pasero Opioid-Induced Sedation Scale (POSS). Copyright 1994, Chris Pasero. Used with permission.*

Urinary retention and pruritus may develop, and the health care provider may prescribe small doses of naloxone to combat these effects. The nurse administers doses that are small enough to reverse the side effects of the opioids without reversing the analgesic effects. Diphenhydramine may also be used to relieve opioid-related pruritus.

Precautions must be taken to avoid infection at the catheter site and catheter displacement. Only medications without preservatives should be administered into the subarachnoid or epidural space because of the potential neurotoxic effects of preservatives.

Placebo Effect

A **placebo effect** occurs when a person responds to the medication or other treatment because of an expectation that the treatment will work rather than because it actually does so. The American Society for Pain Management Nurses contends that placebos (tablets or injections with no active ingredients) should not be used to assess or manage pain in any patient, regardless of age or diagnosis (Arnstein, et al., 2010). Furthermore, the group recommends that all health care institutions have policies in place prohibiting the use of placebos for this purpose. Educational programs should be conducted to educate nurses and other health care providers about effective pain management, and ethics committees should assist in developing and disseminating these policies.

Nonpharmacologic Interventions

Analgesic medication is the most powerful tool for pain relief that is available, but it is not the only one. Nonpharmacologic nursing interventions can assist in pain relief, usually with low risk to the patient. Although such measures are not a substitute for medication, they may be all that is necessary or appropriate to relieve episodes of pain lasting only seconds or minutes. In instances of severe pain that lasts for hours or days, combining nonpharmacologic interventions with medications may be the most effective way to relieve pain.

Cutaneous Stimulation and Massage

Massage, which is generalized cutaneous stimulation of the body, often concentrates on the back and shoulders. A massage does not specifically stimulate the nonpain receptors in the same receptor field as the pain receptors, but it may have an impact through the descending control system (see previous discussion). Massage also promotes comfort because it produces muscle relaxation and might reduce anxiety (Wilkinson, Barnes, & Storey, 2008).

Thermal Therapies

Ice and heat therapies may be effective pain relief strategies in some circumstances; however, their effectiveness and mechanisms of action need further study. Proponents believe that ice and heat stimulate the nonpain receptors in the same receptor field as the injury. Both ice and heat therapy must be applied carefully and monitored closely to avoid injuring the skin. Neither therapy should be applied to areas with impaired circulation or used in patients with impaired sensation.

For greatest effect, ice should be placed on the injury site immediately after injury or surgery. Ice therapy after joint surgery can significantly reduce the amount of analgesic medication required. Ice therapy may also relieve pain if applied later. Care must be taken to assess the skin before treatment and to protect the skin from direct application of the ice. Ice should be applied to an area for no longer than

15 to 20 minutes at a time, and should be avoided in patients with compromised circulation (Porth, 2009). Prolonged applications of ice may result in frostbite or nerve injury.

Application of heat increases blood flow to an area and contributes to pain reduction by speeding healing. Both dry and moist heat may provide some analgesia, but their mechanisms of action are not well understood.

NURSING ALERT

Heat should not be applied to a painful area that is the site of acute, untreated infection (e.g., mastitis, tooth abscess) because it may cause increased pain with increased blood flow to the site.

Transcutaneous Electrical Nerve Stimulation

Transcutaneous electrical nerve stimulation (TENS) uses a battery-operated unit with electrodes applied to the skin to produce a tingling, vibrating, or buzzing sensation in the area of pain. It has been used in both acute and chronic pain relief, and is thought to decrease pain by stimulating the nonpain receptors in the same area as the fibers that transmit the pain. This mechanism is consistent with the gate control theory of pain, which proposes that the perception of pain can be inhibited by activation of nerves that do not transmit pain signals, thus interrupting the nociceptors signals. This theory explains the effectiveness of cutaneous stimulation when applied in the same area as an injury. For example, when TENS is used in a postoperative patient, the electrodes are placed around the surgical wound. Other possible explanations for the effectiveness of TENS are the differential stimulation of large A fibers and release of endorphins and enkephalins (Robertson, Ward, Low et al., 2006).

Distraction

Distraction helps relieve both acute and chronic pain (Zeidan, 2010). Distraction, which involves focusing the patient's attention on something other than the pain, may be the mechanism responsible for other effective cognitive techniques. Distraction is thought to reduce the perception of pain by stimulating the descending control system, resulting in fewer painful stimuli being transmitted to the brain. The effectiveness of distraction depends on the patient's ability to receive and create sensory input other than pain. Distraction techniques may range from simple activities, such as watching television or listening to music, to highly complex physical and mental exercises. Pain relief generally increases in direct proportion to the patient's active participation, the number of sensory modalities used, and interest in the stimuli. Therefore, the stimulation of sight, sound, and touch is likely to be more effective in reducing pain than is the stimulation of a single sense.

Visits from family and friends are effective in relieving pain. Watching an action-packed movie on a large screen

with "surround sound" through headphones may be effective (provided the patient finds it acceptable). Others may benefit from games and activities (e.g., chess, crossword puzzles) that require concentration. Not all patients obtain pain relief with distraction, especially those in severe pain. Severe pain may prevent patients from concentrating well enough to participate in complex physical or mental activities.

Relaxation Techniques

Skeletal muscle relaxation is believed to reduce pain by relaxing tense muscles that contribute to the pain. A simple relaxation technique consists of abdominal breathing at a slow, rhythmic rate. The patient may close both eyes and breathe slowly and comfortably. A constant rhythm can be maintained by counting silently and slowly with each inhalation ("in, two, three") and exhalation ("out, two, three"). When teaching this technique, the nurse may count out loud with the patient at first. Slow, rhythmic breathing may also be used as a distraction technique. Relaxation techniques, as well as other noninvasive pain relief measures, may require practice before the patient becomes skilled in using them. Patients who already know a relaxation technique may need to be reminded to use it to reduce or prevent increased pain. Almost all people with persistent pain can benefit from some method of relaxation. Regular relaxation periods may help combat the fatigue and muscle tension that occur with and increase chronic pain.

Guided Imagery

Guided imagery is using one's imagination in a special way to achieve a specific positive effect. Guided imagery for relaxation and pain relief may consist of combining slow, rhythmic breathing with a mental image of relaxation and comfort. The nurse instructs the patient to close the eyes and breathe slowly in and out. With each slowly exhaled breath, the patient imagines muscle tension and discomfort being breathed out, carrying away pain and tension and leaving behind a relaxed and comfortable body. With each inhaled breath, the patient imagines healing energy flowing to the area of discomfort.

If guided imagery is to be effective, it requires a considerable amount of time to explain the technique and time for the patient to practice it. Usually, the patient is asked to practice guided imagery for approximately 5 minutes, three times per day. Several days of practice may be needed before the intensity of pain is reduced. Many patients begin to experience the relaxing effects of guided imagery the first time they try it. Pain relief can continue for hours after the imagery is used. Patients should be informed that guided imagery may work only for some people. Guided imagery should be used only in combination with all other forms of treatment that have demonstrated effectiveness.

Hypnosis

Hypnosis, which has been effective in relieving pain or decreasing the amount of analgesic agents required in patients with acute and chronic pain, may promote pain relief in particularly difficult situations (e.g., burns). The mechanism by which hypnosis acts is unclear. Its effectiveness depends on the hypnotic susceptibility of the individual (Carli, Huber, & Santarcangelo, 2008). In some cases, hypnosis may be effective in the first session, with effectiveness increasing in additional sessions. In other cases, hypnosis does not work at all. Usually, hypnosis must be induced by specially skilled people (a psychologist or a nurse with specialized training in hypnosis). Some patients may learn to perform self-hypnosis.

Music Therapy

Music therapy is an inexpensive and effective therapy for the reduction of pain and anxiety in some patient populations. Research has shown that it significantly decreases postoperative pain and cumulative opioid consumption (Ebneshahidi & Mohseni, 2008). Music therapy was found to decrease pain in persons with coronary heart disease (Bradt & Dileo, 2009) and in those with osteoarthritis. More research needs to be done to determine the mechanism by which music exerts its positive effect on pain relief.

Alternative Therapies

Although currently there is limited scientific evidence to support the efficacy of alternative therapies, patients may find any one of them helpful. Most alternative therapies have yet to be established as effective by the standards used to evaluate the effectiveness of medical and nursing interventions. The National Institutes of Health has established the National Council for Complementary and Alternative Medicine (CAM) to examine the effectiveness of complementary and alternative therapies (National Center for Complementary and Alternative Medicine, 2011). The new field of integrative medicine allows for a combination of mainstream medicine and alternative therapies that enhance effectiveness and safety for patients seeking CAM therapies for pain and other disorders.

When caring for patients who are using or considering using untested therapies, it is imperative for the nurse not to diminish the patient's hope. This must be weighed against the nurse's responsibility to protect the patient from costly and potentially harmful and dangerous therapies that the patient is not in a position to evaluate scientifically. The nurse encourages the patient to assess the effectiveness of the therapy, continually using standard pain assessment techniques. All use of alternative and complementary therapies needs to be discussed with the patient's health care provider.

Neurological and Neurosurgical Approaches to Pain Management

In some situations, especially with long-term and severe intractable pain, usual pharmacologic and nonpharmacologic methods of pain relief are ineffective. In those situations, neurologic and neurosurgical approaches to pain

management may be considered. Intractable pain refers to pain that cannot be relieved satisfactorily by the usual approaches, including medications. Such pain often is the result of malignancy (especially of the cervix, bladder, prostate, and lower bowel), but it may occur in other conditions, such as postherpetic neuralgia, trigeminal neuralgia, spinal cord arachnoiditis, and uncontrollable ischemia and other forms of tissue destruction.

Neurologic and neurosurgical methods available for pain relief include: (1) stimulation procedures (intermittent electrical stimulation of a tract or center to inhibit the transmission of pain impulses), (2) administration of intraspinal opioids (see previous discussion), and (3) interruption of the tracts conducting the pain impulse from the periphery to cerebral integration centers. Stimulation of nerves with minute amounts of electricity is used if other pharmacologic and nonpharmacologic treatments fail to provide adequate relief. These treatments are reversible. If they need to be discontinued, the nervous system continues to function. However, methods that involve interruption of the tracts are destructive or ablative procedures. They are used only after other methods of pain relief have failed, because their effects are permanent.

Stimulation Procedures

Electrical stimulation, or neuromodulation, is a method of suppressing pain by applying controlled low-voltage electrical pulses to the different parts of the nervous system. Electrical stimulation is thought to relieve pain by blocking painful stimuli. This pain-modulating technique is administered by many modes. TENS (discussed earlier) and dorsal spinal cord stimulation are the most common types of electrical stimulation used. There are also brain-stimulating techniques in which electrodes are implanted in the periventricular area of the posterior third ventricle, allowing the patient to stimulate this area to produce analgesia.

Spinal cord stimulation is a technique used for the relief of persistent, intractable pain, ischemic pain, and pain from angina. A surgically implanted device allows the patient to apply pulsed electrical stimulation to the dorsal aspect of the spinal cord to block pain impulses (the largest accumulation of afferent fibers is found in the dorsal column of the spinal cord; Kunnumpurath, 2009). The dorsal column stimulation unit consists of a radiofrequency stimulation transmitter, a transmitter antenna, a radiofrequency receiver, and a stimulation electrode. The battery-powered transmitter and antenna are worn externally; the receiver and electrode are implanted. A laminectomy is performed above the highest level of pain input, and the electrode is placed in the epidural space over the posterior column of the spinal cord. The placement of the stimulating systems varies. A subcutaneous pocket is created over the clavicular area or at some other site for placement of the receiver. The two are connected through a subcutaneous tunnel. Careful

patient selection is necessary, and not all patients receive total pain relief.

Deep brain stimulation is performed in patients with special pain problems if there is no response to the usual techniques of pain control. Under local anesthesia, electrodes are introduced through a burr hole in the skull and inserted into a selected site in the brain, depending on the location or type of pain. After the effectiveness of stimulation is confirmed, the implanted electrode is connected to a radiofrequency device or pulse-generator system operated by external telemetry. It is used in patients with neuropathic pain that may be caused by damage or injury from a stroke, chronic cluster headaches, brain or spinal cord injuries, or phantom limb pain.

Interruption of Pain Pathways

Pain-conducting fibers can be interrupted at any point from their origin to the cerebral cortex. Some part of the nervous system is destroyed, resulting in varying amounts of neurologic deficit and incapacity. In time, pain usually returns as a result of either regeneration of axonal fibers or the development of alternative pain pathways. Destructive procedures used to interrupt the transmission of pain include cordotomy and rhizotomy. These procedures are offered if it is thought that the patient is near the end of life and the procedure will result in an improved quality of life (Kanapolat, 2009). Often these procedures can provide pain relief for the duration of the patient's life. The use of other methods to interrupt pain transmission is decreasing because intraspinal therapies and newer pain management treatments are available.

EVALUATING PAIN MANAGEMENT STRATEGIES

An important aspect of caring for patients in pain is reassessing the pain after the intervention has been implemented. The measure's effectiveness is based on the patient's assessment of pain, as reflected in pain assessment tools. If the intervention was ineffective, the nurse should consider other measures. If these are ineffective, pain relief goals need to be reassessed in collaboration with the physician. The nurse serves as the patient's advocate in obtaining additional pain relief.

After interventions have had a chance to work, the nurse asks the patient to rate the intensity of pain. The nurse repeats this assessment at appropriate intervals after the intervention and compares the result with the previous rating. These assessments indicate the effectiveness of the pain relief measures and provide a basis for continuing or modifying the plan of care. A plan of nursing care for a patient with pain is available online at http://thePoint.lww.com/Pellico1e. Expected patient outcomes are given in Box 7-8.

BOX 7-8

Expected Patient Outcomes for the Patient With Pain

Relief of pain, evidenced when the patient:
- Rates pain at a lower intensity (on a scale of 0 to 10) after intervention.
- Rates pain at a lower intensity for longer periods.

Correct administration of prescribed analgesic medications, evidenced when the patient or family:
- States correct dose of medication.
- Administers correct dose using correct procedure.
- Identifies side effects of medication.
- Describes actions taken to prevent or correct side effects.

Use of nonpharmacologic pain strategies as recommended, evidenced when the patient:
- Reports practice of nonpharmacologic strategies.
- Describes expected outcomes of nonpharmacologic strategies.

Minimal effects of pain and minimal side effects of interventions, evidenced when the patient:
- Participates in activities important to recovery (e.g., drinking fluids, coughing, ambulating).
- Participates in activities important to self and to family (e.g., family activities, interpersonal relationships, parenting, social interaction, recreation, work).
- Reports adequate sleep and absence of fatigue and constipation.

Chapter Review

Critical Thinking Exercises

1. A 35-year-old man who is a recovering heroin addict is admitted to the hospital for an emergency appendectomy. During surgery, the appendix ruptures, and the patient remains hospitalized for several days for IV antibiotics. He tells the nurse that he has been "clean" for the past 3 months. He complains of pain (7 on a 0 to 10 scale) and refuses to use the patient-controlled analgesia that is prescribed for him. He states, "I don't want to get hooked again." Describe how you would address pain relief in this patient, and give the rationale for your actions. Who would you consult to help with this patient's pain management?

2. A 48-year-old woman has severe chronic pain associated with cancer metastasis to the bone. She is reluctant to take opioids because she wants to remain alert to enjoy being around her family. Furthermore, she is concerned about having opioids around the house because of the presence of young children in the home. Identify pharmacologic alternatives and nonpharmacologic interventions that might be appropriate. Identify the evidence base and the strength of the evidence for the use of the nonpharmacologic interventions.

NCLEX-Style Review Questions

1. The nurse is managing an epidural catheter for a patient diagnosed with cancer. The patient has developed a spinal headache. Which of the following interventions should be completed at this time?
   A. Increase the dosage of anesthetic.
   B. Place in semi-Fowler's position.
   C. Continue to monitor the patient.
   D. Initiate administration of prescribed fluids.

2. The nurse is caring for an 80-year-old woman following right hip surgery. When administering pain medication to this patient, it is important to remember which of the following?
   A. Elderly patients have a faster metabolism than their younger counterparts.
   B. Elderly patients have an increased risk for drug toxicity.
   C. Elderly patients have a lower incidence of chronic illness.
   D. Elderly patients infrequently use OTC medications.

3. Mr. Hogan has a pancreatic tumor and history of alcoholism. He has morphine 2 mg subcutaneously every 3 to 4 hours for treatment of pain associated with the tumor. After 2 days of receiving this dose every 4 hours, he tells the nurse that he needs the medication more frequently to control the pain. In responding to Mr. Hogan's request, which decision by the nurse reflects an understanding of his situation?
   A. Mr. Hogan is becoming addicted to the morphine, and he should be administered the medication less frequently than every 4 hours.
   B. A tolerance to the morphine is developing, and Mr. Hogan should receive the drug every 3 hours.
   C. Administering the morphine every 3 hours will increase Mr. Hogan's physical dependence on the drug.
   D. Physical dependence should be avoided at all costs, and the drug should continue to be administered every 4 hours.

4. A patient who had abdominal surgery 5 days ago complains of sharp, throbbing abdominal pain that ranks 8 on a scale of 1 (no pain) to 10 (worst pain). His pain rating has averaged at a 3/10 for the first 5 days

postoperatively on epidural administration of hydromorphone. However, his narcotic administration via his epidural catheter was discontinued earlier this morning. Which of the following would be the nurse's first action?

A. Obtain an order to restart the epidural narcotic administration.

B. Assess the patient to rule out possible complications secondary to surgery.

C. Check the patient's chart to determine what additional pain medications can be administered.

D. Explain to the patient that his pain should not be this severe 5 days postoperatively.

5. Which precaution or issue should the nurse stress when teaching the preoperative patient about correct use of the PCA device?

A. Push the button when you feel the pain beginning rather than waiting until the pain is at its worst.

B. Push the button every 15 minutes whether you feel pain at that time or not.

C. Instruct your family or visitors to press the button for you when you are sleeping.

D. Try to go as long as you possibly can before you press the button.

Try these additional resources to enhance your learning and understanding of this chapter:

- thePoint online resource available at **http://thepoint.lww.com/Pellico1e**
- *Handbook for Focus on Adult Health: Medical-Surgical Nursing*
- *Study Guide for Focus on Adult Health: Medical-Surgical Nursing*

References and Selected Readings

References and selected readings associated with this chapter can be found on the website that accompanies the book. Visit http://thepoint.lww.com/Pellico1e to access the references and other additional resources associated with this chapter.

Problems Related to Gas Exchange and Respiratory Function

A 43-YEAR-OLD patient diagnosed with laryngeal cancer will undergo a total laryngectomy. He is very anxious about how he will deal with his care at home. How can the nurse address his fears?

➡ Discuss potential complications that may arise following a total laryngectomy.
➡ Discuss areas to be included in teaching the patient self-care.
➡ Discuss area support groups for laryngectomy patients.

Nursing Assessment: Respiratory Function

LINDA HONAN PELLICO

Disorders of the respiratory system are commonly encountered by nurses in every setting from the community to the intensive care unit. Expert assessment skills must be developed and used when caring for patients with acute and chronic respiratory problems. In addition, an understanding of respiratory function and the significance of abnormal diagnostic test results is essential.

ANATOMIC AND PHYSIOLOGIC OVERVIEW

The respiratory system is composed of the upper and lower respiratory tracts, blood vessels, thoracic cage (spine, ribs, and sternum) and respiratory muscles, chiefly the diaphragm (Fig. 8-1). Respiration requires concert of **ventilation** (movement of air from the atmosphere to the alveoli [the functional unit of the lung]), **diffusion** (exchange of oxygen [O_2] and carbon dioxide [CO_2] at the alveolar–capillary membrane), and perfusion (blood flow). In addition, innervations of the respiratory system are controlled by the neurological system (medulla, pons, spinal nerves) and chemical regulation.

Anatomy of the Upper Respiratory Tract

Upper airway structures consist of the nose, sinuses and nasal passages, pharynx, tonsils and adenoids, and larynx, which warm, humidify, and filter atmospheric air.

Nose

The anterior nares (nostrils) are the external openings of the nasal cavities. The internal portion of the nose is divided into two by a narrow vertical divider, the *septum*, which is richly supplied with sensory nerves and blood vessels. Each nasal cavity is divided into three passageways by the projection of the turbinates (also called conchae), which are highly sensitive. The middle meatus (passageway), which lies under the middle turbinate, contains the ostia (openings) of three of paranasal sinuses (discussed below) that drain into this area. Prolonged obstruction of the ostia (as with a nasoendotracheal tube) is associated with sinusitis (Wolfson, 2010). The nasal cavities are lined with highly vascular ciliated mucous membranes

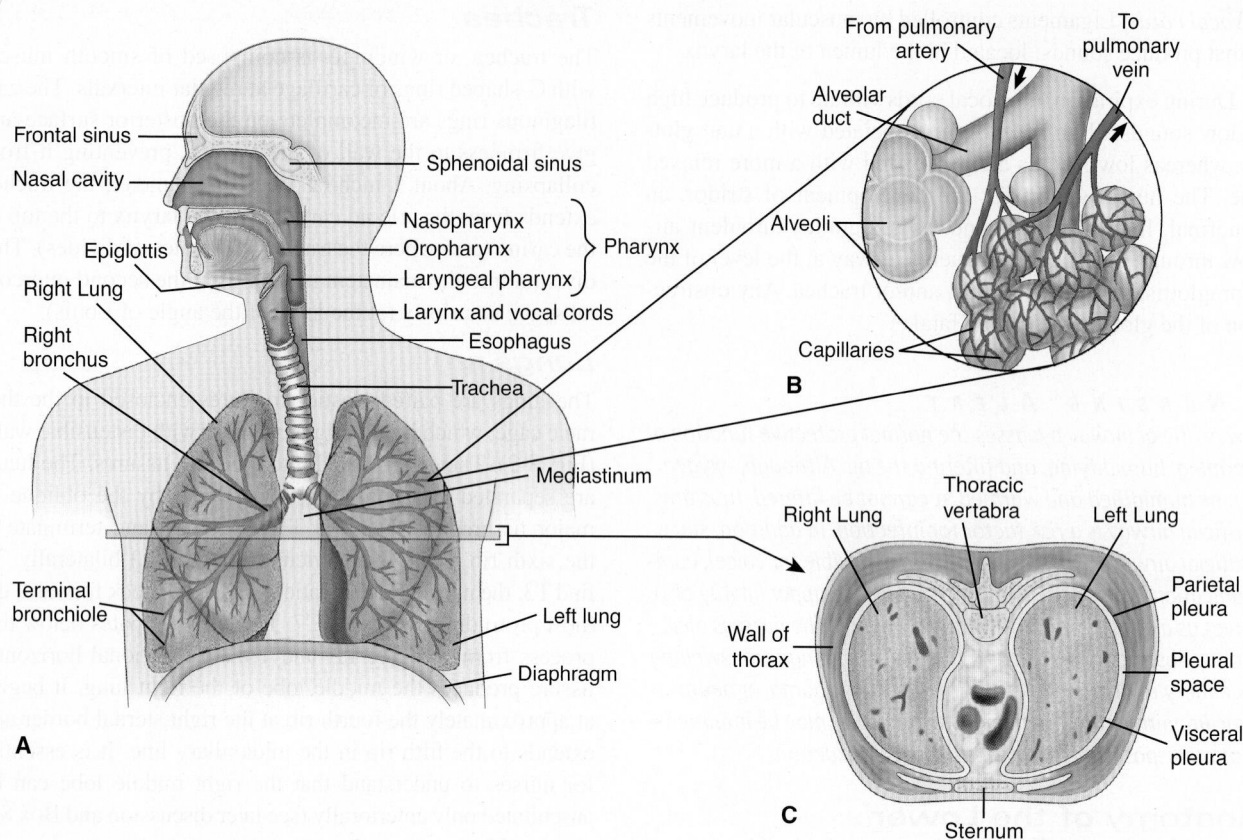

FIGURE 8-1 The respiratory system. **(A)** Upper respiratory structures and the structures of the thorax. **(B)** Alveoli. **(C)** A horizontal cross-section of the lungs.

(nasal mucosa). Mucus, secreted continuously by goblet cells, covers the surface of the nasal mucosa and is moved back to the nasopharynx by the action of the **cilia** (fine hairs).

Paranasal Sinuses

The paranasal sinuses include four pairs of bony cavities or air spaces that drain into the nasal cavity and lighten the weight of the skull. Named by their location: frontal (above the eyebrows), ethmoidal (between the eyes and behind the nose), sphenoidal (behind the ethmoid sinuses), and maxillary (located on the cheeks below the eyes), they serve as a resonating chamber in speech and are a common site of infection.

Pharynx, Tonsils, and Adenoids

The pharynx, or throat, is a tube like structure that connects the nasal and oral cavities to the larynx and is a passageway for the respiratory and digestive tracts. It is divided into three regions: nasal, oral, and laryngeal. The nasopharynx is located posterior to the nose and above the soft palate. The adenoids, or pharyngeal tonsils, are located in the roof of the nasopharynx. Air entering reaches the nasopharynx, where it contacts sensitive nerves. Some of these nerves detect odors; others provoke sneezing to expel irritating dust. The eustachian tubes are also located here, they connect the middle ear to the nasopharynx and function to drain mucus and equalize

pressures. The oropharynx houses the faucial, or palatine, tonsils. The tonsils, the adenoids, and other lymphoid tissue encircle the throat. These structures are important links in the chain of lymph nodes guarding the body from invasion by organisms entering the nose and the throat. The laryngopharynx extends from the hyoid bone to the cricoid cartilage.

Larynx

The larynx, or voice organ, connects the pharynx and the trachea. The major function of the larynx is vocalization. It also protects the lower airway from foreign substances and facilitates coughing. It is frequently referred to as the voice box and consists of the following:

- *Epiglottis*: A valve flap of cartilage (lid-like structure) that covers the entrance to the larynx during swallowing; it is essential to prevent aspiration (inhalation of food or fluid into the lungs).
- *Glottis*: The opening between the vocal cords in the larynx
- *Thyroid cartilage*: The largest of the cartilage structures; it can be felt anteriorly as the "Adam's apple"
- *Cricoid cartilage*: The only complete cartilaginous ring in the larynx (located below the thyroid cartilage)
- *Arytenoid cartilages*: Used in vocal cord movement with the thyroid cartilage

- *Vocal cords*: Ligaments controlled by muscular movements that produce sounds; located in the lumen of the larynx

During expiration, the vocal cords vibrate to produce high or low sounds. High sounds are associated with a taut glottis, whereas low sounds are associated with a more relaxed one. The nurse is alert for the development of stridor, an abnormal, high-pitched sound, as it signifies turbulent airflow through a partially obstructed airway at the level of the supraglottis, glottis, subglottis, and/or trachea. Any obstruction of the glottis area can be fatal.

☀ N U R S I N G   A L E R T

Any artificial airway bypasses the normal protective function of warming, humidifying, and filtering the air. Although, oxygen can be humidified and warmed, it cannot be filtered, thus any artificial airway is a risk factor for infection. In addition, since artificial airways bypass the larynx (responsible for voice), communication is a priority nursing concern. The upper airway also serves as a conduit for air to reach the lungs. The nurse is alert for any obstruction—such as a foreign body, tongue, or swelling secondary to allergic reaction, infection, or trauma, or neurologic impairment in which nerves or muscles may be impaired—that predisposes the patient to airway obstruction.

Anatomy of the Lower Respiratory Tract

The lower respiratory tract consists of the trachea, right and left mainstem bronchi, secondary bronchi, bronchioles, and lungs, and can be further subdivided into the conducting airways and the acinus, where the respiratory bronchioles and alveoli (functional unit of the lung) are located.

Trachea

The trachea, or windpipe, is composed of smooth muscle with C-shaped rings of cartilage at regular intervals. The cartilaginous rings are incomplete on the posterior surface and give firmness to the wall of the trachea, preventing it from collapsing. About 1 inch (2.5 cm) in diameter, the trachea extends from the cricoid cartilage of the larynx to the top of the carina (area where the trachea bifurcates or divides). This division into the mainstem bronchi is at the second intercostal space anteriorly (at the level of the angle of Louis).

Lungs

The lungs are paired elastic structures enclosed in the thoracic cage, which is an airtight chamber with distensible walls (Fig. 8-2). They are divided into lobes by fissures. The lungs are separated into upper and lower lobes by the oblique or major fissures that begin at T3 posteriorly and terminate at the sixth rib in the midclavicular line (MCL) bilaterally. To find T3, the nurse asks the patient to flex the neck forward; the most protruding process is C7. The nurse palpates below this process from here T1, T2, and T3. An additional horizontal fissure produces the middle lobe of the right lung. It begins at approximately the fourth rib at the right sternal border and extends to the fifth rib in the midaxillary line. It is essential for nurses to understand that the right middle lobe can be auscultated only anteriorly (see later discussion and Box 8-7 on page 234).

Bronchi and Bronchioles

The bronchi begin at the carina. The right main bronchus, which provides air to the right lung, is wider, shorter (about 2.5 cm. long), and more vertical in direction than the left main bronchus, which supplies the left lung. Because of the

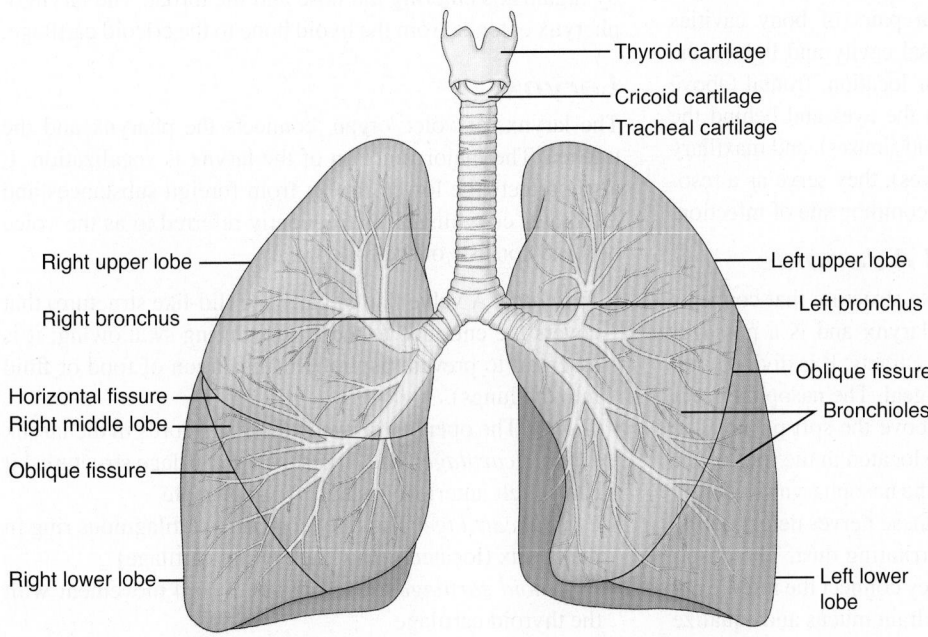

Thyroid cartilage
Cricoid cartilage
Tracheal cartilage

Right upper lobe
Right bronchus

Horizontal fissure
Right middle lobe
Oblique fissure

Right lower lobe

Left upper lobe
Left bronchus
Oblique fissure
Bronchioles

Left lower lobe

F I G U R E 8 - 2 Anterior view of the lungs. The lungs consist of five lobes. The right lung has three lobes (upper, middle, lower); the left has two (upper and lower). The lobes are further subdivided by fissures. The bronchial tree, another lung structure, inflates with air to fill the lobes.

anatomical structure, aspiration of material tends to occur in the right lung. The mainstem bronchi divide into five lobar bronchi (three in the right lung and two in the left lung, to correspond with each respective lobe of the lung), which enter the lung at the hilum (a fissure or opening) along with blood vessels, nerves, and lymphatics. The lobar bronchi branch into segmental bronchi (ten on the right and eight on the left). They are the structures identified when choosing the most effective postural drainage position for a given patient. The segmental bronchi further subdivide until they branch into bronchioles. Bronchioles have no cartilage in their walls, thus patency depends entirely on the elastic recoil of the surrounding smooth muscle and on the alveolar pressure. The terminal bronchioles then become respiratory bronchioles that have actual alveolar sacs imbedded in their walls, so that gas exchange can occur. Up until this point, the exchange of oxygen and carbon dioxide has not occurred, thus it is termed *anatomical dead space* and is calculated to be 150 mL.

Most of the conducting airways produce mucus, have serous glands that secrete a watery substance containing antibacterial enzymes, and have surfaces covered with cilia. These cilia create a constant whipping motion that propels mucus and foreign substances away from the lungs toward the larynx, where the patient coughs out the substances.

Alveoli

The lung is made up of about 300 million alveoli (see Fig. 8-1), which are arranged in clusters of 15 to 20. There are three types of alveolar cells. Type I alveolar cells are epithelial cells that form the alveolar walls. Type II alveolar cells are metabolically active. These cells secrete surfactant, a phospholipid that decreases the surface tension in the alveoli and prevents their collapse. Stimulus for surfactant production is thought to be related to maximum deep inspiration sustained for a few seconds or sighing, in which a person's normal tidal volume (normal breath of approximately 500 mL) is increased one to two times normal. Type III alveolar cell macrophages are large phagocytic cells that ingest foreign matter (e.g., mucus, bacteria) and act as an important defense mechanism.

Pleura

The lungs and wall of the thorax are lined with a serous membrane called the pleura. The visceral pleura covers the lungs; the parietal pleura lines the thorax. Only the parietal pleura has fibers for pain transmission. The intrapleural space which lies between these two layers contains a small amount of pleural fluid (5 to 15 mL) that serves to provide a frictionless surface between the two pleura in response to changes in respiration. The intrapleural space is negative with the average resting interpleural pressure −4 cm H_2O and remains so during inspiration and expiration. Refer to Table 8-1 for pleural pressures.

Mediastinum

The mediastinum is in the middle of the thorax, between the pleural sacs. It contains the great vessels of the heart, the

T A B L E
8-1 Pressures: Atmospheric, Intrapulmonary and Intrapleural

Pressure	At Rest	Inspiratory	Expiratory
Atmospheric*	760	760	760
Intrapulmonary	760	757	763
Intrapleural	756	750	756

Atmospheric pressure remains constant at 760 mm Hg. For air to enter the lungs, the pressure within the airways and alveoli (intrapulmonary pressure) must become less than atmospheric so that the air can be pulled in. This is accomplished in inspiration because of the action of the diaphragm and the external intercostal muscles. At expiration, the intrapulmonary pressure is now higher than atmospheric pressure and air escapes from the lungs. The intrapleural pressure (pressure within the pleural cavity) fluctuates with inspiration and expiration but always remain negative.

heart, esophagus, trachea, thoracic duct, thymus, and lymph nodes, as well as the vagus, cardiac, and phrenic nerves.

Lobes

Each lung is divided into lobes. The left lung consists of an upper and lower lobe, whereas the right lung has an upper, middle, and lower lobe (see Fig. 8-2). The upper lobes of the lungs rise 1 inch above the inner one-third of the clavicle, thus there is always a risk of a pneumothorax (air in the pleural space) when inserting venous catheters in the neck. The base of each lung (when in a neutral position) is at the sixth rib in the MCL, the eighth rib in the midaxillary line (MAL), and the tenth rib posteriorly at rest. With inspiration, the lungs can descend to the eighth rib in the MCL, tenth rib in the MAL, and twelfth rib at the vertebral border.

Thoracic Cage

The 12 ribs, costal cartilages (cartilages that connect the sternum and the ends of the ribs; termed the *costochondral junction*), manubrium, sternum, xiphoid process, and vertebral column provide the structure that support and protect the lung. The notch on the top of the manubrium may be referred to as the *suprasternal notch, sternal notch*, or *jugular notch*. Seven ribs and their costal cartilages articulate directly to the body of the sternum, ribs 8 to 10 attach to cartilage of the seventh rib, and rib 11 ends anterolaterally and the twelfth rib ends laterally. Posteriorly, each rib attaches to a vertebra. An important landmark for nurses to use when counting ribs is the angle of Louis, which is where the manubrium (top of sternum, approximately 4 cm long) and the body of the sternum meet at the second rib. This area is also termed the manubriosternal junction and can be palpable as a transverse ridge in most patients. The second costal cartilages articulates with the sternum here (angle of Louis), the intercostal space (ICS) below the angle is the second ICS.

It is important to recognize that any disorder to the bony structure of the thorax affects the ability of the lungs to function. The costal angle (lower parts of the anterior rib cage near the xiphoid process) normally is about 90 degrees.

Respiratory Muscles

Ventilation requires movement of the walls of the thoracic cage and of its floor, the *diaphragm.* The diaphragm is a dome-shaped muscle that, when contracted (during inspiration), pulls the lungs in a downward and forward direction, the abdomen appears to enlarge because the abdominal contents are being compressed by the diaphragm. With inspiration, the diaphragmatic pull elongates the chest cavity, and the external intercostal muscles (located between and along the lower borders of the ribs) contract to raise the ribs, which expands the anteroposterior diameter. The effect of these movements is to decrease the intrapulmonary pressure (pressure within the lung) to less than atmospheric pressure, which causes air to rush into the lung (see Table 8-1). With expiration, the diaphragm and intercostals recoil, which increases the intrapulmonary pressure over atmospheric pressure, so that gases are expelled from the lung. While inspiration is an active process, expiration is passive. In respiratory diseases, such as chronic obstructive pulmonary disease (COPD), the act of breathing becomes work requiring energy.

Additional accessory muscles of inspiration, including the scalene (elevates the first two ribs), sternocleidomastoid (raise the sternum), and the alae nasi (faring of nostrils), may be called upon to assist with inspiration when exercising, while the abdominal and internal intercostals muscles may be used to increase expiration.

☀ NURSING ALERT

The diaphragm is innervated by the phrenic nerve, which exits the spinal column at the level of C3–C5. Any fracture at or above this will cause respiratory paralysis.

Neuroanatomy Related to Respiration

The rhythm of breathing is controlled by the medulla oblongata and pons. In addition, central chemoreceptors located in the medulla respond to changes in PCO_2 and pH levels the cerebrospinal fluid, and alter the depth and then the rate of ventilation to correct an imbalance. Additionally, peripheral chemoreceptors are located in the aortic arch and the carotid arteries that respond first to changes in PaO_2 (<60 to 65 mm Hg), then to $PaCO_2$ and pH by altering the depth and rate of respiration (Ault & Stock, 2009). These chemoreceptors no longer respond to $PaCO_2$ or pH in patients with COPD because of the persistently high levels of $PaCO_2$ that exist with this disorder, thus the primary drive to breathe comes from a low oxygen level rather than a high carbon dioxide level. If oxygen is administered at a high enough rate to raise the PaO_2 to normal, there is a risk of obliterating the hypoxic drive, thus low-flow oxygen is administered to a patient with COPD, while the nurse carefully assesses for complications.

A final reflex to consider is the Hering–Breuer reflex that prevents overinflation of the lung. It is activated by stretch receptors located within the smooth muscle of large and small airways that inhibit further inspiration. Tidal volumes of 800 to 1,500 mL are generally required to elicit this reflex in conscious, normally breathing adults (Levitzky, 2007).

Function of the Respiratory System

The cells of the body require oxygen. Certain vital tissues, such as the brain and the heart, cannot survive for long without a continuous supply. However, as a result of oxidation in the body tissues, carbon dioxide is produced and must be removed from the cells to prevent the buildup of acid waste products. The respiratory system performs this life-sustaining function of gas exchange.

Respiration

The process of **respiration** requires gas exchange both in the lungs, termed *external or pulmonary respiration,* and ultimately in the tissues, termed *internal or cellular respiration.* External respiration requires three processes: 1) *ventilation,* the act of breathing inspiration and expiration); 2) *perfusion,* blood flow to the alveoli, so that gases can be exchanged; and 3) *diffusion,* movement of gases from a higher area of concentration to a lower area across the alveolar–capillary membrane. Systemic veins carry venous blood richer in CO_2 and poorer in O_2 than the systemic arteries to the pulmonary circulation. The oxygen concentration in blood within the capillaries of the lungs is lower than in the alveoli. Because of this concentration gradient, oxygen diffuses from the alveoli to the blood. Carbon dioxide, which has a higher concentration in the blood than in the alveoli, diffuses from the blood into the alveoli. The end result is oxygen-rich blood leaving the pulmonary veins (the only veins other than the umbilical vein to carry oxygenated blood) to systemic circulation. Internal respiration refers to the process by which oxygen is supplied to, and carbon dioxide is removed from the body cells by way of the circulating blood. Cells are in close contact with capillaries, the thin walls of which permit easy passage or exchange of oxygen and carbon dioxide. Oxygen diffuses from the capillaries through the capillary walls to the interstitial fluid. At this point, it diffuses through the membrane of tissue cells, where it is used by mitochondria for cellular respiration. The movement of carbon dioxide occurs by diffusion in the opposite direction—from cell to blood. These processes are critical for survival.

Ventilation

During inspiration, air flows from the environment into the trachea, bronchi, bronchioles, and alveoli. During expiration, alveolar gas travels the same route in reverse.

Physical factors that govern air flow in and out of the lungs are collectively referred to as the *mechanics of ventilation* and include air pressure variances, resistance to air flow (the narrower the airway, the greater the resistance to flow), and lung compliance (the dispensability of the lung, or how well the lung stretches).

Causes of Increased Airway Resistance

Common phenomena that may alter bronchial diameter, which affects airway resistance, include the following:

- Contraction of bronchial smooth muscle—as in asthma
- Thickening of bronchial mucosa—as in chronic bronchitis
- Obstruction of the airway—by mucus, a tumor, or a foreign body
- Loss of lung elasticity—as in emphysema, which is characterized by connective tissue encircling the airways, thereby keeping them open during both inspiration and expiration

Airway Resistance

Resistance is determined chiefly by the radius or size of the airway through which the air is flowing. Any process that changes the bronchial diameter or width affects airway resistance and alters the rate of air flow for a given pressure gradient during respiration (Box 8-1). With increased resistance, greater-than-normal respiratory effort is required to achieve normal levels of ventilation.

Compliance

Compliance is a measure of the elasticity, expandability, and distensibility of the lungs and thoracic structures. Consider

an elastic band: When it is stretched, it easily returns to its normal shape; so too should the lungs. Factors that determine lung compliance are the surface tension of the alveoli (normally low with the presence of surfactant) and the connective tissue (i.e., collagen and elastin) of the lungs.

Compliance is normal (1.0 L/cm H_2O) if the lungs and thorax easily stretch and distend when pressure is applied. High or increased compliance occurs if the lungs have lost their elasticity (cannot return to normal state) and the thorax is overdistended (i.e., in emphysema). Low or decreased compliance occurs if the lungs and thorax are "stiff" (difficult to stretch). Conditions associated with decreased compliance include pneumothorax, hemothorax, pleural effusion, pulmonary edema, atelectasis, pulmonary fibrosis, and acute respiratory distress syndrome (ARDS), all of which are discussed in later chapters in this unit.

Lung Volumes and Capacities

Lung function, which reflects the mechanics of ventilation, is viewed in terms of lung volumes and lung capacities. These terms are described in Table 8-2 on page 224 and illustrated in Figure 8-3 below. Three common measurements that the medical surgical nurse should understand are tidal volume, minute ventilation, and vital capacity. The volume of each breath is referred to as the *tidal volume* and can be measured by a bedside spirometer. If the patient is breathing through an endotracheal tube or tracheostomy, the spirometer is directly attached to it, and the exhaled volume is obtained from the reading on the gauge. In other patients, the spirometer is attached to a face mask or a mouthpiece positioned so that it is airtight, and the exhaled volume is measured.

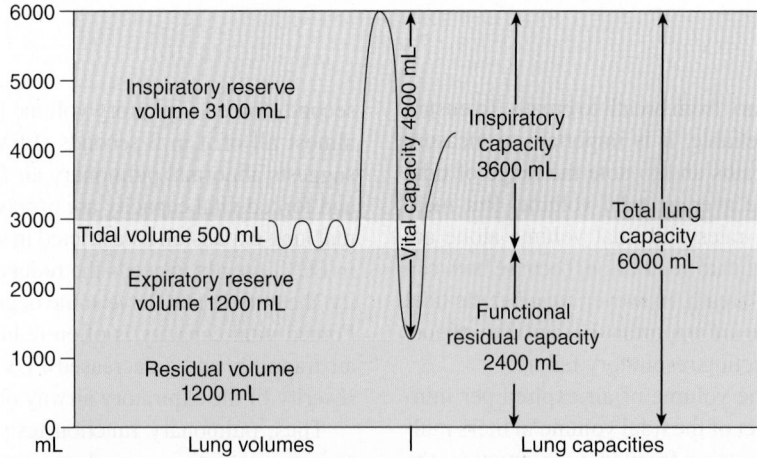

FIGURE 8-3 Tracings of respiratory volumes (*left*) and lung capacities (*right*) as they would appear if made using a spirometer. The tidal volume (*yellow*) represents the amount of air inhaled and exhaled during normal breathing; the inspiratory reserve volume (*pink*), the maximal amount of air in excess of the tidal volume that can be forcefully inhaled; the maximal expiratory reserve (*blue*), the maximal amount of air that can be exhaled in excess of tidal volume; and the residual volume (*green*), the air that continues to remain in the lung after maximal expiratory effort. The inspiratory capacity represents the sum of inspiratory reserve volume and the tidal volume; the functional residual capacity, the sum of the maximal expiratory reserve and the residual volumes; and the total lung capacity, the sum of all volumes. From Porth, C. M., & Matfin, G. (2009). *Pathophysiology: Concepts of altered health states* (8th ed.). Philadelphia: Lippincott Williams & Wilkins.

TABLE
8-2 Lung Volumes and Lung Capacities

Term	Symbol	Description	Normal Value*	Significance
Lung Volumes				
Tidal volume	VT or TV	The volume of air inhaled and exhaled with each breath	500 mL or 5–10 mL/kg	The tidal volume may not vary, even with severe disease.
Inspiratory reserve volume	IRV	The maximum volume of air that can be inhaled after a normal inhalation	3,000 mL	
Expiratory reserve volume	ERV	The maximum volume of air that can be exhaled forcibly after a normal exhalation	1,100 mL	Expiratory reserve volume is decreased with restrictive conditions, such as obesity, ascites, pregnancy.
Residual volume	RV	The volume of air remaining in the lungs after a maximum exhalation	1,200 mL	Residual volume may be increased with obstructive disease.
Lung Capacities				
Vital capacity	VC	The maximum volume of air exhaled from the point of maximum inspiration VC = TV + IRV + ERV	4,600 mL	A decrease in vital capacity may be found in neuromuscular disease, generalized fatigue, atelectasis, pulmonary edema, and COPD.
Inspiratory capacity	IC	The maximum volume of air inhaled after normal expiration IC = TV + IRV	3,500 mL	A decrease in inspiratory capacity may indicate restrictive disease; may also be decreased in obesity
Functional residual capacity	FRC	The volume of air remaining in the lungs after a normal expiration FRV = ERV + RV	2,300 mL	Functional residual capacity may be increased with COPD and decreased in ARDS.
Total lung capacity	TLC	The volume of air in the lungs after a maximum inspiration TLC = TV + IRV + ERV + RV	5,800 mL	Total lung capacity may be decreased with restrictive disease (atelectasis, pneumonia) and increased in COPD.

*Values for healthy men; women are 20%–25% less.
ARDS, acute respiratory distress syndrome; COPD, chronic obstructed pulmonary disease.

The tidal volume may vary from breath to breath. To ensure that the measurement is reliable, it is important to measure the volumes of several breaths and to note the range of tidal volumes, together with the average tidal volume. But measurements like respiratory rates and tidal volume alone are unreliable indicators of adequate ventilation, because both can vary widely from breath to breath. However, together the tidal volume and respiratory rate are important because the minute ventilation is useful in detecting respiratory failure.

Minute ventilation is the volume of air expired per minute. It is equal to the product of the tidal volume in liters multiplied by the respiratory rate or frequency. In practice, the minute ventilation is not calculated but is measured directly using a spirometer. Minute ventilation may be decreased by a variety of conditions that result in hypoventilation. When the minute ventilation falls, alveolar ventilation in the lungs also decreases, and the $PaCO_2$ increases.

Forced vital capacity requires having the patient take in a maximal breath and exhale fully and forcefully. Most patients can exhale at least 80% of their vital capacity in 1

second (forced expiratory volume in 1 second, or FEV_1) and almost all of it in 3 seconds (FEV_3). A reduction in FEV_1 suggests abnormal pulmonary air flow. If the patient's FEV_1 and forced vital capacity are proportionately reduced, maximal lung expansion is restricted in some way. If the reduction in FEV_1 greatly exceeds the reduction in forced vital capacity, the patient may have some degree of airway obstruction. Forced vital capacity is often reduced in COPD because of air trapping, and a decreased FEV is a valuable clue to the severity of the expiratory airway obstruction.

Thus, pulmonary function tests (PFTs) can aid in diagnosing restrictive or obstructive pulmonary disorders. Restrictive disorders are ones that make the lungs stiff; they decrease the total volume of air the lungs can hold. This is typically due to a decrease in the elasticity of the lungs or the inability of the chest wall to expand during inhalation. Examples of restrictive lung diseases are asbestosis, sarcoidosis, and pulmonary fibrosis. Obstructive disorders cause a narrowing or blockage in exhaled airflow and are commonly associated with COPD (discussed in Chapter 10).

Diffusion and Perfusion

Diffusion is the process by which oxygen and carbon dioxide are exchanged at the air–blood interface. The alveolar–capillary membrane is ideal for diffusion because of its thinness and large surface area. In the normal, healthy adult, oxygen and carbon dioxide travel across the alveolar–capillary membrane without difficulty as a result of differences in gas concentrations in the alveoli and capillaries.

Pulmonary perfusion is the actual blood flow through the pulmonary circulation. The blood is pumped into the lungs by the right ventricle through the pulmonary artery. The pulmonary artery divides into the right and left branches to supply both lungs. These two branches divide further to supply all parts of each lung. Normally, about 2% of the blood pumped by the right ventricle does not perfuse the alveolar capillaries. This "shunted" blood drains into the left side of the heart without participating in alveolar gas exchange.

The pulmonary circulation is considered a low-pressure system because the systolic blood pressure in the pulmonary artery is 20 to 30 mm Hg and the diastolic pressure is 5 to 15 mm Hg. Because of these low pressures, the pulmonary vasculature normally can vary its capacity to accommodate the blood flow it receives. However, when a person is in an upright position, the pulmonary artery pressure is not great enough to supply blood to the apex of the lung against the force of gravity. Thus, when a person is upright, the lung may be considered to be divided into three sections: an upper part with poor blood supply, a lower part with maximal blood supply, and a section between the two with an intermediate supply of blood. When a person lying down turns to one side, more blood passes to the dependent lung. Thus, the nurse should consider that the dependent lung, regardless of position, is better perfused.

Perfusion is also influenced by alveolar pressure. The pulmonary capillaries are sandwiched between adjacent alveoli. If the alveolar pressure is sufficiently high, the capillaries are squeezed. Depending on the pressure, some capillaries completely collapse, whereas others narrow.

Pulmonary artery pressure, gravity, and alveolar pressure determine the patterns of perfusion. In lung disease, these factors vary, and the perfusion of the lung may become very abnormal.

Ventilation and Perfusion Balance and Imbalance

Ventilation is the flow of gas in and out of the lungs (normally at a rate of 4 L/min), and perfusion is the filling of the pulmonary capillaries with blood (normally at a rate of 5 L/min). Thus, the alveolar (ventilation) to capillary (perfusion) ratio is 4:5 or 0.8. Adequate gas exchange depends on an adequate ventilation–perfusion ($\dot{V}/\dot{Q}$) ratio.

$\dot{V}/\dot{Q}$ imbalance occurs as a result of inadequate ventilation, inadequate perfusion, or both. There are four possible $\dot{V}/\dot{Q}$ states in the lung: normal $\dot{V}/\dot{Q}$ ratio, low $\dot{V}/\dot{Q}$ ratio (shunt), high $\dot{V}/\dot{Q}$ ratio (dead space), and absence of ventilation and perfusion (silent unit) (Box 8-2).

Shunting is the term used to describe conditions in which ventilation is impaired and perfusion is adequate. Normal shunting is about 2%; severe **hypoxia** results when the amount of shunting exceeds 20%. This can occur secondary to airway obstruction from a variety of causes (mucus plug, atelectasis, infective process, tumor), where blood is bypassing the alveoli without gas exchange. Adequate ventilation but impaired perfusion (as in pulmonary emboli, which is a blood clot in pulmonary vessels) is termed *increased dead space*. In this situation, the alveolus has inadequate perfusion, and gas exchange does not occur. Both conditions result in **hypoxia** (low levels of cellular oxygen). Supplemental oxygen is of use in conditions causing an increase in dead space, as long as the impaired perfusion is not massive; supplemental oxygen may not improve **hypoxemia** in shunting, however, as the oxygen does not come in contact with alveoli (areas of diffusion).

Gas Exchange

The air we breathe is a gaseous mixture consisting mainly of nitrogen (78.62%) and oxygen (20.84%), with traces of carbon dioxide (0.04%), water vapor (0.05%), helium, and argon.

Oxygen and carbon dioxide are transported simultaneously, dissolved in blood, or combined with some of the elements of blood. Oxygen is carried in the blood in two forms: first, as physically dissolved oxygen in the plasma, and second, in combination with the hemoglobin of the red blood cells. Each 100 mL of normal arterial blood carries 0.3 mL of oxygen physically dissolved in the plasma and 20 mL of oxygen in combination with hemoglobin. Thus, much more oxygen is normally transported combined with hemoglobin (~97%) than is physically dissolved in the blood (<3%). Hemoglobin is essential to supply sufficient oxygen to meet tissue demands (Levitzky, 2007). Figure 8-4 demonstrates differences in O_2 and CO_2 in venous, arterial, alveolus, and atmosphere.

NURSING ALERT
Hemoglobin rapidly combines reversibly with oxygen (half-time of 0.01 second or less); that is, it allows oxygen to be released quickly to the tissues to satisfy metabolic needs. Some hemoglobin exists in forms such as methemoglobin (commonly seen in drug reaction) or is combined with carbon monoxide (as in smoke inhalation), in which case the hemoglobin cannot bind oxygen, resulting in tissue hypoxia and lactic acidosis. Thus, the nurse is aware that oxygen delivery to tissues is dependent upon hemoglobin, oxygen content, and cardiac output. While a healthy heart can generally increase cardiac output to compensate for diseased lungs or a low hemoglobin level, a diseased heart may be unable to. It is important for the nurse to consider that a combination of poor oxygenation, low hemoglobin level, and low cardiac output may be rapidly fatal (Grogan & Pronovost, 2004; Fritz, 2008).

BOX 8-2 **Understanding Ventilation and Perfusion**

Normal Ventilation and Perfusion

When ventilation and perfusion ($\dot{V}/\dot{Q}$) are matched, unoxygenated blood from the venous system returns to the right side of the heart through the pulmonary arteries to the lung, carrying carbon dioxide (CO_2). The arteries branch into alveolar capillaries. Gas exchange takes place in the alveolar capillaries. Normal ventilation is 4 liters/min, and perfusion is normally at a rate of 5 liters/min. Thus, the alveolar (ventilation) to capillary (perfusion) ratio is 4:5 or 0.8.

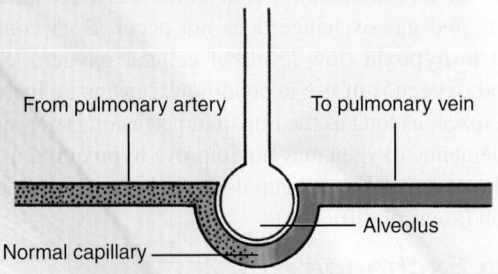

Ventilation and Perfusion Mismatch

Conditions that may produce a $\dot{V}/\dot{Q}$ mismatch include the following.

1. Shunting (reduced ventilation to a lung unit) causes unoxygenated blood to move from the right side of the heart to the left side and into systemic circulation; it may result from obstruction of the distal airways, such as with pneumonia, atelectasis, tumor, or a mucus plug. When the $\dot{V}/\dot{Q}$ ratio is low, pulmonary circulation is adequate, but not enough oxygen (O_2) is available to the alveoli for normal diffusion. To illustrate, assume the ventilation is now 2 L/min versus a perfusion of 5 L/min. The ratio is now 2:5 or reduced to 0.4. A portion of the blood flowing through the pulmonary vessels doesn't become oxygenated.

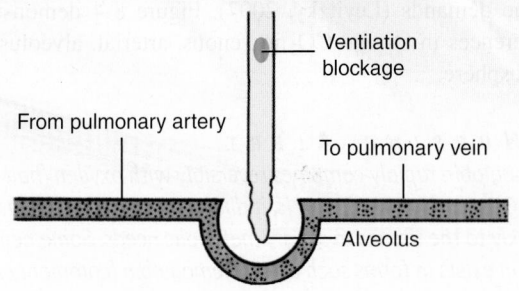

2. Dead-space ventilation (reduced perfusion to a lung unit) occurs when alveoli do not have adequate blood supply for gas exchange to occur, such as with pulmonary emboli (PE) and pulmonary infarction. When the $\dot{V}/\dot{Q}$ ratio is high, as shown here, ventilation is normal, but alveolar perfusion is reduced or absent. Note the narrowed capillary, indicating poor perfusion. This commonly occurs from a perfusion defect, such as PE, or a disorder that decreases cardiac output (cardiogenic shock). In this situation, assume the ventilation is normal at 4 L/min but perfusion is reduced to 3 L/min; thus, the ratio is 4:3 or increased to 1.3.

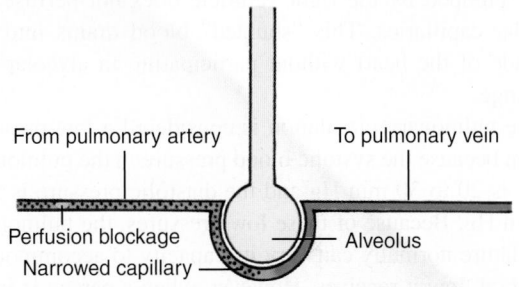

3. A silent unit (a combination of shunting and dead-space ventilation) occurs when little or no ventilation and perfusion are present, such as in acute respiratory distress syndrome.

The silent unit indicates an absence of ventilation and perfusion to the lung area.

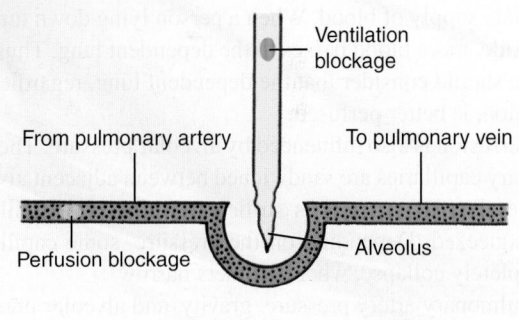

Key to the figures: Blue = blood with CO_2; Red = blood rich in O_2; Purple = blood with CO_2 and O_2.
Adapted from *Hemodynamic monitoring made incredibly visual*. (2011). Philadelphia: Lippincott Williams & Wilkins.

Gerontologic Considerations

A gradual decline in respiratory function begins in early to middle adulthood and affects the structure and function of the respiratory system. With aging (≥ 40 years), changes occur in the alveoli that reduce the surface area available for the exchange of oxygen and carbon dioxide. At approximately 50 years of age, the alveoli begin to lose elasticity. A decrease in vital capacity occurs with loss of chest wall mobility, which restricts the tidal flow of air. The amount of respiratory dead space increases with age. These changes result in a decreased diffusion capacity for oxygen with increasing age, producing lower oxygen levels in the arterial circulation. Gerontologic changes in the respiratory system are summarized in Table 8-3.

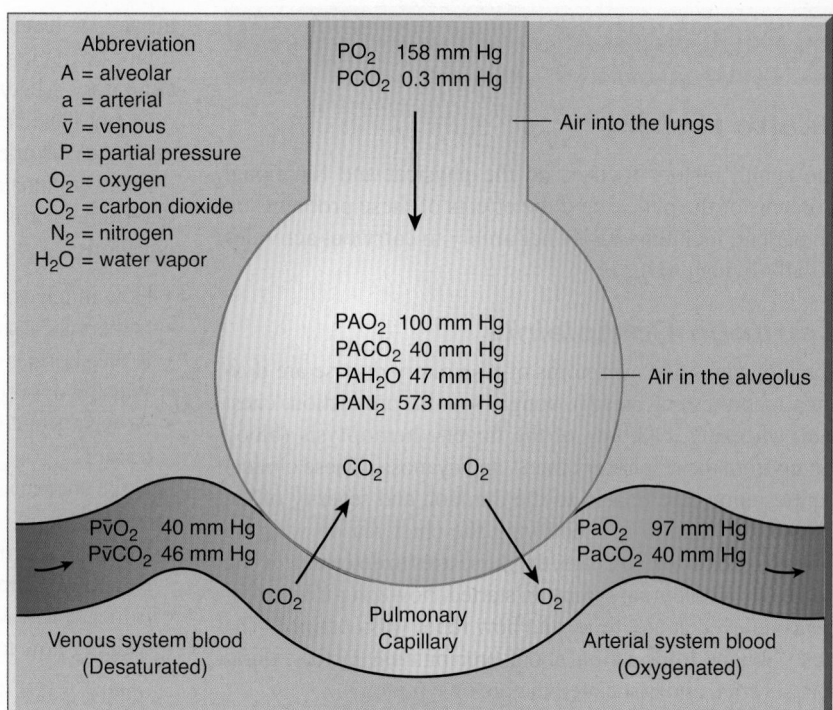

Abbreviation
A = alveolar
a = arterial
v̄ = venous
P = partial pressure
O_2 = oxygen
CO_2 = carbon dioxide
N_2 = nitrogen
H_2O = water vapor

PO_2 158 mm Hg
PCO_2 0.3 mm Hg

— Air into the lungs

PAO_2 100 mm Hg
$PACO_2$ 40 mm Hg
PAH_2O 47 mm Hg
PAN_2 573 mm Hg

— Air in the alveolus

CO_2 O_2

$P\bar{v}O_2$ 40 mm Hg
$P\bar{v}CO_2$ 46 mm Hg

CO_2

PaO_2 97 mm Hg
$PaCO_2$ 40 mm Hg

O_2

Venous system blood
(Desaturated)

Pulmonary
Capillary

Arterial system blood
(Oxygenated)

FIGURE 8-4 Changes occur in the partial pressure of gases during respiration. These values vary as a result of the exchange of oxygen and carbon dioxide, and the changes that occur in their partial pressures as venous blood flows through the lungs.

TABLE
8-3 Age-Related Changes in the Respiratory System

Component	Structural Changes	Functional Changes	History and Physical Findings
Defense mechanisms (respiratory and nonrespiratory)	↓ Number of cilia and ↓ mucus ↓ Cough and gag reflex Loss of surface area of the capillary membrane Lack of a uniform or consistent ventilation and/or blood flow	↓ Protection against foreign particles ↓ Protection against aspiration ↓ Antibody response to antigens ↓ Response to hypoxia and hypercapnia (chemoreceptors)	↓ Cough reflex and mucus ↑ Infection rate History of respiratory infections, COPD, pneumonia. Risk factors: smoking, environmental exposure, TB exposure
Lung	↓ Size of airway ↑ Diameter of alveolar ducts ↑ Collagen of alveolar walls ↑ Thickness of alveolar membranes ↓ Elasticity of alveolar sacs	↑ Airway resistance ↑ Pulmonary compliance ↓ Expiratory flow rate ↓ Oxygen diffusion capacity ↑ Dead space Premature closure of airways ↑ Air trapping ↓ Expiratory flow rates Ventilation–perfusion mismatch ↓ Exercise capacity ↑ Anteroposterior (AP) diameter	Unchanged total lung capacity (TLC) ↑ Residual volume (RV) ↓ Inspiratory reserve volume (IRV) ↓ Expiratory reserve volume (ERV) ↓ Forced vital capacity (FVC) and vital capacity (VC) ↑ Functional residual capacity (FRC) ↓ PaO_2 ↑ CO_2
Chest wall and muscles	Calcification of intercostal cartilages Arthritis of costovertebral joints ↓ Continuity of diaphragm Osteoporotic changes ↓ Muscle mass Muscle atrophy	↑ Rigidity and stiffness of thoracic cage ↓ Respiratory muscle strength ↑ Work of breathing ↓ Capacity for exercise ↓ Peripheral chemosensitivity ↑ Risk for inspiratory muscle fatigue	Kyphosis, barrel chest Skeletal changes ↑ AP diameter Shortness of breath ↑ Abdominal and diaphragmatic breathing ↓ Maximum expiratory flow rates

↑, increased; ↓, decreased

ASSESSMENT OF THE RESPIRATORY SYSTEM

Health History

The health history focuses on the physical and functional problems of the patient and the effects of these problems on the patient, including his or her ability to carry out activities of daily living (ADLs).

Common Complaints

Common signs and symptoms of respiratory disease are **dyspnea** (shortness of breath), cough, sputum production, chest pain, wheezing, clubbing of the fingers, **hemoptysis** (blood spit up from the respiratory tract), and cyanosis. These clinical manifestations are related to the duration and severity of the disease. In addition to identifying the chief reason why the patient is seeking health care, the nurse tries to determine when the health problem or symptom started, how long it lasted, if it was relieved at any time, and how relief was obtained. The nurse obtains information about precipitating factors, duration, severity, and associated factors or symptoms.

Dyspnea

As defined by the American Thoracic society, dyspnea is "a subjective experience of breathing discomfort that consists of qualitatively distinct sensations that vary in intensity" (American Thoracic Society, 1999). Dyspnea (difficult or labored breathing, breathlessness, shortness of breath) is a symptom common in many pulmonary (94% of patients with chronic lung disease, 90% of lung cancer patients) and cardiac disorders (50% heart disease) (Galbraith, Fagan, Perkins et al., 2010). It may also be associated with neurologic or neuromuscular disorders (i.e., myasthenia gravis, Guillain-Barré syndrome, muscular dystrophy), renal (failure, acidosis), hepatic (ascites), endocrine (hyperthyroidism), and hematologic (anemia, hemoglobinopathy) diseases that affect respiratory function. Dyspnea can also occur after physical exercise in people without disease (Porth & Matfin, 2009). It is also a symptom at the end of life, associated with anxiety, depression, and fear in patients and helplessness in caregivers (Gysels & Higginson, 2009). If the patient is experiencing severe dyspnea, the nurse may need to modify or abbreviate the questions asked and the timing of the health history to avoid increasing the patient's breathlessness and anxiety.

CLINICAL SIGNIFICANCE. In general, acute diseases of the lungs produce a more severe grade of dyspnea than do chronic diseases. Sudden dyspnea in a healthy person may indicate pneumothorax (air in the pleural space), acute respiratory obstruction, or ARDS. In immobilized patients, sudden dyspnea may denote pulmonary embolism (PE). **Orthopnea** (inability to breathe unless sitting or standing) may be found in patients with heart disease and occasionally in patients with COPD; dyspnea with an expiratory **wheeze** occurs with COPD. Noisy breathing may result from a narrowing of the

airway or localized obstruction of a major bronchus by a tumor or foreign body. The presence of both inspiratory and expiratory wheezing usually signifies asthma if the patient does not have heart failure. Since dyspnea can occur with a variety of disorders, a thorough health history is essential.

The circumstance that produces the dyspnea must be determined; it is important to ask the patient the following questions:

- How much exertion triggers shortness of breath?
- Is there an associated cough?
- Is the shortness of breath related to other symptoms?
- Was the onset of shortness of breath sudden or gradual?
- At what time of day or night does the shortness of breath occur?
- Is the shortness of breath worse when the patient is flat in bed?
- Does the shortness of breath occur at rest? With exercise? Running? Climbing stairs?
- Is the shortness of breath worse while walking? If so, when walking how far? How fast?

Other issues that are important in the assessment of dyspnea include the following: the patient's rating of the intensity of breathlessness, the effort required to breathe, and the severity of the breathlessness or dyspnea. Patients use a variety of terms and phrases to describe breathlessness, such as "can't get enough air," "hard to breath," "feeling tight," and the nurse needs to clarify what terms are most familiar to the patient and what these terms mean (Schwartzstein & Adams, 2010). Several scales are available to assess the severity of dyspnea, including visual analog scales similar to pain scales, where one side denotes no dyspnea and the extreme is maximal dyspnea. These scales that can be used to assess changes in the severity of dyspnea over time (Porth & Matfin, 2009; Schwartzstein & Adams, 2010). Box 8-3 illustrates one such scale.

RELIEF MEASURES. The management of dyspnea is aimed at identifying and correcting its cause. Relief of the symptom sometimes is achieved by placing the patient at rest with the head elevated (high Fowler's position), encouraging the patient to lean forward with arms and upper body supported on a table (orthopneic position), and using pursed-lip breathing (that is, breathing in through the mouth and exhaling slowly through pursed lips to facilitate exhalation of air). Using a handheld fan (blowing air across the nose and mouth) has demonstrated success in reducing the sensation of breathlessness (Galbraith et al., 2010), and, in some cases, administering oxygen may help (Box 8-4). Strategies that enable patients with chronic or persistent dyspnea to decrease or prevent breathlessness and to cope with it can lead to improved quality of life (Duncan, Bott, Thompson et al., 2009). Medical and nursing intervention may include use of opioids, oxygen administration in patients with hypoxemia (low oxygen saturation), benzodiazepines (anti-anxiety agents), and breathlessness rehabilitation techniques

Grading Dyspnea

To assess **dyspnea** as objectively as possible, ask your patient to briefly describe how various activities affect his breathing. Then document his response using this grading system:

- *Grade 0*: Not troubled by breathlessness except with strenuous exercise
- *Grade 1*: Troubled by shortness of breath when hurrying on a level path or walking up a slight hill
- *Grade 2*: Walks more slowly on a level path because of breathlessness than do people of the same age or has to stop to breathe when walking on a level path at his own pace
- *Grade 3*: Stops to breathe after walking about 100 yards (91 m) on a level path
- *Grade 4*: Too breathless to leave the house or breathless when dressing or undressing.

for cancer-related dyspnea (Ben-Aharon, Gafter-Gvili, Paul et al., 2008). See Chapter 11 for interventions for COPD.

Cough

Although cough is a reflex that protects the lungs from the accumulation of secretions or the inhalation of foreign bodies, it can also be a symptom of a number of disorders of the pulmonary system, or it can be suppressed in other disorders. It is the most common reason for seeking heath care in the United States (Chung & Widdicombe, 2010).

Involuntary coughing can be initiated by a variety of nerve receptors in the oropharynx, larynx, and tracheobronchial tree that can be stimulated by irritation (airborne irritants such as smoke, smog, perfume, powders, dust), excess secretions, or a foreign body. These signals are transmitted to the vagus nerve to the cough center (medulla).

A persistent and frequent cough can be exhausting and have significant impact on the patient's lifestyle and sense of well-being. Coughs can be significant enough to cause incontinence, vomiting, rib fractures, pain, and syncope. They may indicate serious pulmonary disease, but it may be caused by a variety of other problems, including cardiac disease, medications (e.g., amiodarone, angiotensin-converting enzyme [ACE] inhibitors), smoking, postnasal drip, and gastroesophageal reflux disease (Chung & Widdicombe, 2010).

It is important to consider that the cough reflex may be impaired by weakness or paralysis of the respiratory or abdominal muscles. Risk factors include prolonged inactivity, surgery, the presence of a nasogastric tube (may prevent closure of the glottis), or depressed function of the medullary centers in the brain (e.g., anesthesia, drugs that depress the cough center, brain disorders) predisposing the patient to pulmonary problems (Porth & Matfin, 2009).

CLINICAL SIGNIFICANCE. To help determine the cause of the cough, the nurse describes the characteristics of the cough. A dry, irritative cough is a feature of an upper respiratory tract infection of viral origin, or a side effect of ACE inhibitor therapy. Laryngotracheitis causes an irritative, high-pitched

Nursing Research

Bridging the Gap to Evidence-Based Practice

Does the Use of a Handheld Fan Improve Chronic Dyspnea?

Galbraith, S., Fagan, P., Perkins, P., Lynch, A., & Booth, S. (2010). *Journal of Pain Symptom Management*, May 39(5):831–838.

Purpose

Dyspnea, or the sensation of breathlessness, is a disabling distressing symptom common in advanced disease. Facial cooling has been shown to reduce the sensation of breathlessness when induced in volunteers but has not been formally investigated in dyspnea associated with disease. The purpose of this study was to explore whether a handheld fan reduces the sensation of breathlessness in patients with advanced disease.

Design

Fifty participants with advanced disease were randomized to use a handheld fan for 5 minutes directed to their face or leg first and then crossed over to the other treatment. The primary outcome measure was a decrease of greater than 1 cm in breathlessness recorded on a 10 cm visual analog scale (VAS).

Findings

There was a significant difference in the VAS scores between the two treatments, with a reduction in breathlessness when the fan was directed to the face ($P = 0.003$).

Nursing Implications

The findings of this study support the hypothesis that a handheld fan directed to the face reduces the sensation of breathlessness. The fan was acceptable to participants: it is inexpensive, portable, enhances self-efficacy, and is available internationally. It should be recommended as part of a palliative management strategy for reducing breathlessness associated with advanced disease.

cough. Tracheal lesions produce a brassy cough. Pertussis has a characteristic long, strident inspiratory noise (a whoop) before the cough. A hacking cough may be suggestive of pneumonia. A severe or changing cough may indicate bronchogenic carcinoma. Pleuritic chest pain that accompanies coughing may indicate pleural or chest wall (musculoskeletal) involvement.

The time of coughing is also noted. Coughing at night may herald the onset of left-sided heart failure or bronchial asthma. A cough in the morning with sputum production may indicate bronchitis. A cough that worsens when the patient is supine suggests postnasal drip (sinusitis) or reflux (spill-over of gastric contents into the larynx). Coughing after food intake may indicate aspiration of material into the tracheobronchial tree. A cough of recent onset is usually from a viral or upper respiratory tract infection. Duration is also a factor; a cough is considered acute if present for less than 3 weeks, persistent if between 3 to 8 weeks, and chronic if greater than 8 weeks.

RELIEF MEASURES. Treatment depends on the cause of the cough. Treatment may include cautious use of cough suppressants because they may relieve the cough, but do not address the cause of the cough. Other treatments are antihistamines, decongestants, or nasal corticosteroids if the etiology of the cough is postnasal drip; or H_2-blockers or proton-pump inhibitors when cough is associated with GERD. If the cough is a result of irritation, smoking cessation strategies are indicated. Drinking warm beverages may relieve cough caused by throat irritation.

Sputum Production

A patient who coughs long enough almost invariably produces sputum. Sputum production is the reaction of the lungs to any constantly recurring irritant. It also may be associated with a nasal discharge. It is estimated that a person produces approximately 10 mL of colorless sputum per day that is unnoticed and swallowed, thus any complaint of sputum is investigated. To help quantify the amount of sputum production, patients are asked to describe the volume of sputum production in terms of teaspoon (~5 mL) to cupful (~240 mL); however, this is difficult to calculate because patients may swallow sputum. A productive cough is considered more than 30 mL/day of sputum (Chung, Widdicombe, & Boushey, 2008).

CLINICAL SIGNIFICANCE. The nature of the sputum is indicative of the causal condition. A profuse amount of purulent sputum (thick and yellow, green) is a common sign of bacterial infection, lung abscess, bronchiectasis, or bronchopleural fistula communicating with an empyema (pus in the pleural space) (Leblond, Brown, & DeGowin, 2009). A small amount of purulent sputum is associated with acute bronchitis, pneumonia during resolution, small tuberculous cavities, or lung abscess. Sputum that looks like currant jelly is associated with *Klebsiella pneumoniae* or *Streptococcus pneumoniae*. Purulent rust-colored sputum suggests *pneumococcal pneumonia*. Thin, mucoid sputum frequently

results from viral bronchitis. A gradual increase of sputum over time may indicate the presence of chronic bronchitis or bronchiectasis, which can produce a daily volume from 200 to 500 mL (Leblond et al., 2009). Pink-tinged mucoid sputum suggests a lung tumor. Profuse, frothy, white or pink material, often welling up into the throat, may indicate pulmonary edema. Foul-smelling sputum and bad breath point to the presence of a lung abscess, bronchiectasis, or an infection caused by anaerobic organisms. A musty odor may indicate pseudomonas infection (Siela, 2008).

RELIEF MEASURES. If the sputum is too thick for the patient to expectorate, it is necessary to decrease its viscosity by increasing its water content through adequate hydration (drinking water) and inhalation of aerosolized solutions, which may be delivered by any type of nebulizer.

Smoking is contraindicated with excessive sputum production because it interferes with ciliary action, increases bronchial secretions, causes inflammation and hyperplasia of the mucous membranes, and reduces production of surfactant. When a person stops smoking, sputum volume decreases and resistance to bronchial infections increases.

The patient's appetite may decrease because of the odor of the sputum or the taste it leaves in the mouth. The nurse encourages adequate oral hygiene and wise selection of food, measures that stimulate the appetite. Citrus juices at the beginning of the meal may increase palatability, because these juices cleanse the palate of the sputum taste.

Hemoptysis

Hemoptysis is a symptom of both pulmonary and cardiac disorders. The onset of hemoptysis is usually sudden, and it may be intermittent or continuous. Signs, which vary from blood-stained sputum to a large sudden hemorrhage, always merit investigation. Frank bloody sputum may indicate a pulmonary emboli, bronchogenic carcinoma, or erosion of a bronchial artery by cavitary tuberculosis, whereas blood-stained sputum (streaks of blood) may indicate inflammation in the nose, nasopharynx, gums, larynx, or bronchi, or airway trauma from severe coughing (Lippincott, 2008). The amount of blood produced is not always proportional to the seriousness of the cause.

> ! **NURSING ALERT**
> *Blood from the lung is usually bright red, frothy, and mixed with sputum. Initial symptoms include a tickling sensation in the throat, a salty taste, a burning or bubbling sensation in the chest, and perhaps chest pain, in which case the patient tends to splint the bleeding side. The term* hemoptysis *is reserved for the coughing up of blood arising from a pulmonary hemorrhage. This blood has an alkaline pH (>7.0). If the hemorrhage is in the stomach, the blood is vomited (hematemesis) rather than coughed up. Blood that has been in contact with gastric juice is sometimes so dark that it is referred to as "coffee grounds." This blood has an acid pH (<7.0).*

Chest Pain

Chest pain or discomfort may be associated with pulmonary or cardiac disease. Chest pain associated with pulmonary conditions may be sharp, stabbing, and intermittent, or it may be dull, aching, and persistent. The pain usually is felt on the side where the pathologic process is located, but it may be referred elsewhere—for example, to the neck, back, or abdomen.

CLINICAL SIGNIFICANCE. Chest pain may occur with pneumonia, PE with lung infarction, and pleurisy. It also may be a late symptom of bronchogenic carcinoma. In carcinoma, the pain may be dull and persistent because the cancer has invaded the chest wall, mediastinum, or spine.

Lung disease does not always cause thoracic pain, because the lungs and the visceral pleura lack sensory nerves and are insensitive to pain stimuli. However, the parietal pleura has a rich supply of sensory nerves that are stimulated by inflammation and stretching of the membrane. Pleuritic pain from irritation of the parietal pleura is sharp and seems to "catch" on inspiration; patients often describe it as "like the stabbing of a knife." The nurse assesses the quality, intensity, and radiation of pain, and identifies and explores precipitating factors and their relationship to the patient's position. In addition, it is important to assess the relationship of pain to the inspiratory and expiratory phases of respiration.

RELIEF MEASURES. Analgesic medications may be effective in relieving chest pain, but care must be taken not to depress the respiratory center or a productive cough, if present. Nonsteroidal anti-inflammatory drugs (NSAIDs) achieve this goal and therefore are used for pleuritic pain. A regional anesthetic block may be performed to relieve extreme pain. Patients may be more comfortable when they lie on the affected side, because this splints the chest wall, limits expansion and contraction of the lung, and reduces the friction between the injured or diseased pleura on that side. Pain associated with cough may be reduced manually by splinting the rib cage.

Wheezing

Wheezing is often the major finding in a patient with bronchoconstriction or airway narrowing. It is heard with or without a stethoscope, depending on its location. Wheezing is a high-pitched, musical sound heard mainly on expiration.

Wheezing is associated with a variety of clinical conditions other than asthma. The nurse needs to assess for all possible etiologies (discussed later in this chapter). Oral or inhalant bronchodilator medications reverse wheezing in most instances.

Past and Family History

The nurse also assesses for risk factors and genetics factors that may contribute to the patient's lung condition (Box 8-5 and Box 8-6).

Social History

The nurse inquires about current or past smoking and calculates pack/year history. This is calculated by the number of packs smoked per day times the years the patient has smoked. Thus, 1 pack per day times 20 years equals a 20 pack/year history. Note that after 20 years of smoking, pathophysiologic changes in the lungs develop and progress proportionally to smoking intensity and duration (Burns, 2009).

The impact of signs and symptoms on the patient's ability to perform ADLs and to participate in usual work and family activities is assessed. Questions related to sleep–rest patterns should include asking about nocturnal dyspnea (waking up with shortness of breath [SOB]), orthopnea, and quantifying the number of pillows used at night. In addition, psychosocial factors that may affect the patient are explored. These factors include anxiety, role changes, family relationships, financial problems, employment status, and the strategies the patient uses to cope with them. It is also important to ask questions concerning immunizations, medications, exposure to environmental hazards, use of oxygen, hospitalizations, and past medical and surgical history.

Many respiratory diseases are chronic and progressively debilitating and disabling. Therefore, ongoing assessment of the patient's physical abilities, psychosocial supports, and quality of life is needed to plan appropriate interventions. It is important that the patient with a respiratory disorder understand the condition and be familiar with necessary self-care interventions. The nurse evaluates these factors over time and provides education as needed.

BOX 8-5

Risk Factors for Respiratory Disease

- Smoking (the single most important contributor to lung disease)
- Exposure to secondhand smoke
- Personal or family history of lung disease
- Genetic make-up
- Allergens and environmental pollutants
- Recreational and occupational exposure

BOX 8-6

Risk Factors for Hypoventilation

- Limited neurologic impulses transmitted from the brain to the respiratory muscles, as in spinal cord trauma, cerebrovascular accidents, tumors, myasthenia gravis, Guillain-Barré syndrome, polio, and drug overdose
- Depressed respiratory centers in the medulla, as with anesthesia, sedation, and drug overdose
- Limited thoracic movement (kyphoscoliosis), limited lung movement (pleural effusion, pneumothorax), or reduced functional lung tissue (chronic pulmonary diseases, severe pulmonary edema)

Physical Assessment

Complete respiratory assessment includes assessment of the integument and upper and lower respiratory structures. The nurse also observes the work of breathing (e.g., nasal flaring, mouth breathing, use of accessory muscles, splinting, etc.).

Assessment of the Integumentary System

Respiratory conditions may have skin and nail manifestations.

Inspection of Color

Cyanosis, a bluish coloring of the skin, is a very late indicator of hypoxia. The presence or absence of cyanosis is determined by the amount of unoxygenated hemoglobin in the blood. Cyanosis appears when there is at least 5 g/dL of unoxygenated hemoglobin (normal hemoglobin is ~15 g/dL). Thus, a full one-third of the hemoglobin is deoxygenated before cyanosis is observed. Additionally, a patient with anemia rarely manifests cyanosis, and a patient with polycythemia may appear cyanotic even if adequately oxygenated. Thus, cyanosis is *not* a reliable sign of hypoxia.

Assessment of cyanosis is affected by room lighting, the patient's skin color, and the distance of the blood vessels from the surface of the skin. Central cyanosis (tongue and lips), often associated with clubbing of the fingers and toes, indicates inadequate oxygenation of blood, whereas peripheral cyanosis (nailbeds) results from vasoconstriction or diminished peripheral blood flow in the distal extremities from a variety of causes and does not necessarily indicate a central systemic problem. Additionally, the two may coexist. In people of color, the nurse assesses for central cyanosis by examining for dull, dark color in the buccal mucosa (inside of the cheek) and hard palate (roof of the mouth).

Inspection for Clubbing of the Fingers

Clubbing of the fingers is found in patients with chronic hypoxic conditions, chronic lung and pleural infections, or malignancies of the lung and pleural. It is also associated with cyanotic congenital heart disease, infective endocarditis, and cirrhosis (Chesnutt & Prendergast, 2010). It is painless, usually bilateral and may be reversed if the causative factor is removed (Leblond et al., 2009).This finding may be manifested initially as sponginess of the nail bed and loss of the nail bed angle, resulting in a bulbous enlargement of the distal segments of the fingers and toes (see Chapter 51, Box 51-4).

Assessment of Upper Respiratory Structures

For a routine examination of the upper airway, only a simple light source, such as a penlight, is necessary.

Inspection and Palpation of Nose and Sinuses

The nurse inspects the external nose for lesions, asymmetry, or inflammation, and then asks the patient to tilt the head

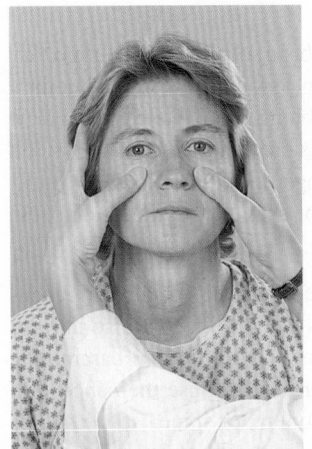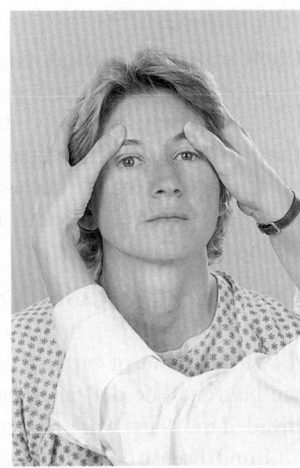

FIGURE 8-5 Technique for palpating the frontal sinuses at left and the maxillary sinuses at right.

backward. Gently pushing the tip of the nose upward, the nurse examines the internal structures of the nose, inspecting the mucosa and septum for color, swelling, exudate, or bleeding. The nasal mucosa is normally redder than the oral mucosa. It may appear swollen and hyperemic if the patient has a common cold, but in allergic rhinitis, the mucosa appears pale and swollen. Most people have a slight degree of septal deviation, but actual displacement of the cartilage into either the right or left side of the nose may produce nasal obstruction. Such deviation usually causes no symptoms. Observation of nasal flaring and mouth breathing suggests respiratory distress. Next, the nurse may palpate the frontal and maxillary sinuses for tenderness, which suggests inflammation. Using the thumbs, gentle pressure is applied in an upward fashion at the supraorbital ridges (frontal sinuses) and in the cheek area adjacent to the nose (maxillary sinuses) (Fig. 8-5).

Inspection of Pharynx and Mouth

The mouth and pharynx is assessed by asking the patient to open the mouth wide and take a deep breath. Usually, this flattens the posterior tongue and briefly allows a full view of the anterior and posterior pillars, tonsils, uvula, and posterior pharynx (Fig. 8-6). These structures are inspected for color, symmetry, and evidence of exudate, ulceration, or enlargement. If a tongue blade is needed to depress the tongue to visualize the pharynx, it is pressed firmly beyond the midpoint of the tongue to avoid a gagging response.

Palpation of the Trachea

The position and mobility of the trachea are noted by placing the thumb and index finger of one hand on either side of the trachea just above the sternal notch. The trachea is highly sensitive, and palpating too firmly may trigger a coughing or gagging response. The trachea is normally in the midline as it enters the thoracic inlet behind the sternum, but it may be deviated by masses in the neck or mediastinum. The

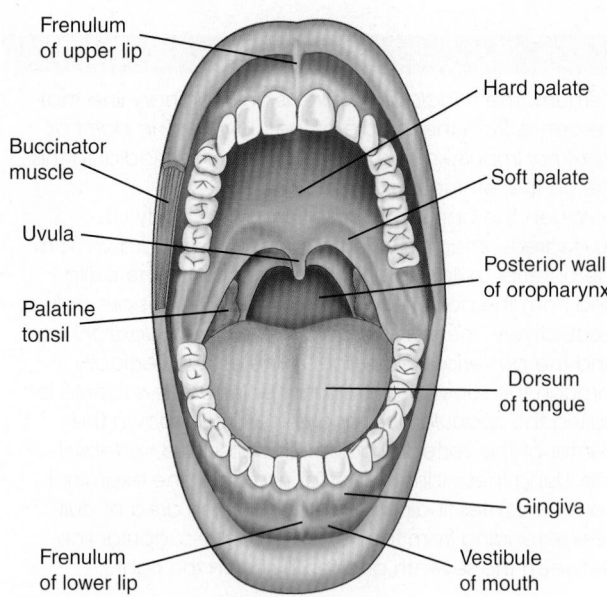

Frenulum of upper lip

Hard palate

Buccinator muscle

Soft palate

Uvula

Posterior wall of oropharynx

Palatine tonsil

Dorsum of tongue

Gingiva

Frenulum of lower lip

Vestibule of mouth

FIGURE 8-6 The pharynx and other oral structures—pillars, tonsils, uvula, hard and soft palates, posterior pharynx, and tongue—are easily seen when the mouth is open.

trachea may deviate away from a life-threatening tension pneumothorax, and toward an atelectasis or fibrosis of the lung (Leblond et al., 2009).

Physical Assessment of the Lower Respiratory Structures and Breathing

Lower respiratory assessment consists of four areas: inspection, palpation, percussion, and auscultation. The patient should be positioned upright, if possible, to assess the posterior thorax and lungs, and supine to assess the anterior chest and lung with chest exposed.

Thoracic Inspection

The nurse observes the skin over the thorax for color and turgor and for evidence of loss of subcutaneous tissue (19%–60% of patients with COPD are classified as malnourished) (Kane, 2008). In recording or reporting the findings, anatomic landmarks are used as points of reference (Box 8-7). Normally, there is symmetry in chest movement. It is important to note asymmetry, if present. In thin people, it is quite normal to note a slight retraction of the intercostal spaces during quiet breathing. Bulging of the intercostal spaces during expiration implies obstruction of expiratory airflow, as in emphysema. Marked retraction on inspiration, particularly if asymmetric, implies blockage of a branch of the respiratory tree. Asymmetric bulging of the intercostal spaces, on one side or the other, is created by an increase in pressure within the hemithorax. This may be a result of air trapped under pressure within the pleural cavity, where it is not normally

present (pneumothorax), or the pressure of fluid within the pleural space (pleural effusion).

CHEST CONFIGURATION. Normally, the ratio of the anteroposterior diameter to the lateral diameter is 1:2. However, four main deformities of the chest are associated with respiratory disease that alter this relationship: barrel chest, funnel chest (pectus excavatum), pigeon chest (pectus carinatum), and kyphoscoliosis.

Barrel chest occurs as a result of lung hyperinflation, as in emphysema. There is an increase in the anteroposterior diameter of the thorax, so that it approximates a 1:1 ratio. In a patient with emphysema, note the costal angle will also be greater than 90 degrees.

Funnel chest is a common developmental deformity where there is a depression in the lower portion of the sternum, so that the sternum appears "bowl-like," and the ratio may be less than 1:2. It may be symmetrical or asymmetrical to the midline of the sternum. Refer to a pediatric resource for further details. Most patients are asymptomatic but may have decreased tidal volume and decreased thoracic volume with aging; thus, medical surgical nurses should thoroughly assess these patients' pulmonary function and encourage the use of the incentive spirometer (IS) (Jaroszewski, Notrica, McMahon et al., 2010).

Pectus carinatum is also a congenital structural abnormality of the sternum, in which it is displaced anteriorly, increasing the anteroposterior diameter. For some patients, this deformity is associated with a rigid chest wall, in which the anteroposterior (AP) diameter is almost fixed in full inspiration. In these patients, respiratory efforts are less efficient, and use of IS should be encouraged.

A *kyphoscoliosis* is characterized by elevation of the scapula and a corresponding S-shaped spine. This deformity limits lung expansion within the thorax. It may occur with osteoporosis and other skeletal disorders that affect the thorax.

Additionally, the nurse notes the presence of paradoxical chest movements known as a *flail chest*, which occurs with multiple ipsilateral (same side) rib fractures. In this condition, asymmetrical chest movements are observed; during inspiration, the unstable chest wall collapses inward, then bulges outward with expiration. It is associated with respiratory distress and crepitus (see later discussion).

BREATHING PATTERNS AND RESPIRATORY RATES. Observing the rate and depth of respiration is a simple but important aspect of assessment. The normal adult who is resting comfortably takes 12 to 18 breaths per minute. Except for occasional sighs, respirations are regular in depth and rhythm. This normal pattern is described as *eupnea*.

Certain patterns of respiration are characteristic of specific disease states. Normal inspiration versus expiration is 1:2; that is, inspiration is half as long as expiration. Respiratory rhythms and their deviation from normal are important observations that the nurse reports and documents. The rates and depths of various patterns of respiration are presented in Table 8-4.

BOX 8-7 **Locating Thoracic Landmarks**

With respect to the thorax, location is defined both horizontally and vertically. With respect to the lungs, location is defined by lobe.

Horizontal Reference Points

Horizontally, thoracic locations are identified according to their proximity to the rib or the intercostal space under the examiner's fingers. On the anterior surface, identification of a specific rib is facilitated by first locating the angle of Louis. This is where the manubrium joins the body of the sternum in the midline. The second rib joins the sternum at this prominent landmark.

Other ribs may be identified by counting down from the second rib. The intercostal spaces are referred to in terms of the rib immediately above the intercostal space; for example, the fifth intercostal space is directly below the fifth rib.

Locating ribs on the posterior surface of the thorax is more difficult. The first step is to identify the spinous process. This is accomplished by finding the seventh cervical vertebra (*vertebra prominens*), which is the most prominent spinous process. When the neck is slightly flexed, the seventh cervical spinous process stands out. Other vertebrae are then identified by counting downward.

Vertical Reference Points

Several imaginary lines are used as vertical referents or landmarks to identify the location of thoracic findings. The *midsternal line* passes through the center of the sternum. The *midclavicular line* is an imaginary line that descends from the middle of the clavicle. The *point of maximal impulse* of the heart normally lies medial to this line on the left thorax.

When the arm is abducted from the body at 90 degrees, imaginary vertical lines may be drawn from the anterior axillary fold, from the middle of the axilla, and from the posterior axillary fold. These lines are called, respectively, the *anterior axillary line*, the *midaxillary line*, and the *posterior axillary line*. A line drawn vertically through the superior and inferior poles of the scapula is called the *scapular line*, and a line drawn down the center of the vertebral column is called the *vertebral line*. Using these landmarks, for example, the examiner communicates findings by referring to an area of dullness extending from the vertebral to the scapular line between the seventh and tenth ribs on the right.

Lobes of the Lungs

The lobes of the lung may be mapped on the surface of the chest wall in the following manner. The fissure that divide the right and left lung into upper and lower lobes posteriorly is termed the oblique fissure. It begins at T3 (spinous process) and obliquely to sixth rib in the midclavicular line (MCL) bilaterally. The right lung is further divided anteriorly by the horizontal fissure, which runs close to the fourth rib at the sternal border (SB) to the fifth rib in the midaxillary line (MAL). There is no presentation of the right middle lobe on the posterior surface of the chest.

Anterior thorax

Clavicle
Suprasternal notch
First rib
First intercostal space
Angle of Louis
Manubrium
Xyphoid process
Costal angle
Costal margin
Midclavicular Lines

Posterior thorax

C7
T1
Scapula
Spinous process
T12
Midscapular lines

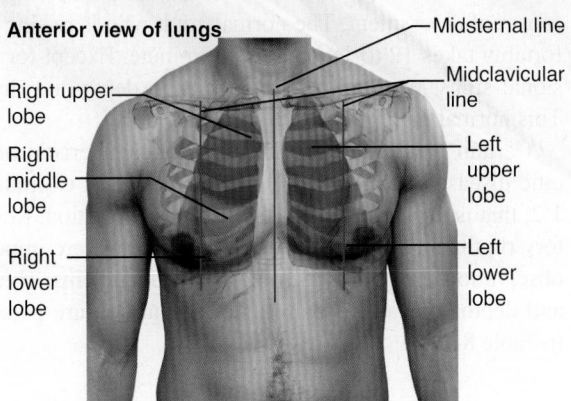

Anterior view of lungs

Midsternal line
Midclavicular line
Right upper lobe
Right middle lobe
Right lower lobe
Left upper lobe
Left lower lobe

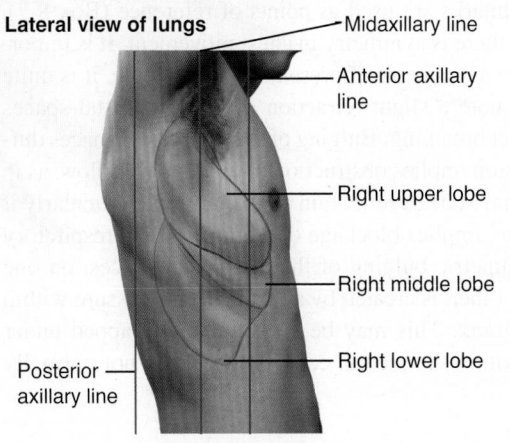

Lateral view of lungs

Midaxillary line
Anterior axillary line
Right upper lobe
Right middle lobe
Right lower lobe
Posterior axillary line

TABLE
8-4 Rates and Depths of Respiration

	Definition
Eupnea	Normal, breathing at 12–18 breaths/min

Bradypnea	Slower than normal rate (<10 breaths/min), with normal depth and regular rhythm; associated with increased intracranial pressure, brain injury, CNS depressants, and drug overdose

Tachypnea	Rapid, shallow breathing >24 breaths/min; commonly seen in patients with a number of causes including metabolic acidosis, septicemia, severe pain, and rib fracture

Hypoventilation	Shallow, irregular breathing; associated with decreased medullary respiratory center drive, weakness of the respiratory muscles from a variety of neurological disorders

Hyperventilation	Increased rate and depth of breathing (called *Kussmaul's respiration* if caused by diabetic ketoacidosis); associated with severe acidosis of diabetic or renal origin and hypoxemia

Apnea	Period of cessation of breathing. Time duration varies; apnea may occur briefly during other breathing disorders, such as with sleep apnea. Life-threatening if sustained.

Cheyne-Stokes	Regular cycle in which the rate and depth of breathing increase, then decrease until apnea (usually about 20 seconds) occurs. It may be seen during the sleep of normal children and the aged, also associated with heart failure and damage to the respiratory center (drug-induced, tumor, trauma).

Biot's respiration	Periods of normal breathing (3–4 breaths) followed by a varying period of apnea (usually 10–60 seconds). Uncommon, but associated with some central nervous system disorders, meningitis.

NURSING ALERT

One should not rely only on visual inspection of the rate and depth of a patient's respiratory excursions to determine the adequacy of ventilation. Respiratory excursions may appear normal or exaggerated due to an increased work of breathing, but the patient may actually be moving only enough air to ventilate the dead space. If there is any question regarding adequacy of ventilation, auscultation or pulse oximetry (or both) should be used for additional assessment of respiratory status.

Thoracic Palpation

The nurse palpates the thorax for tenderness, masses, lesions, respiratory excursion, vocal fremitus, and crepitus.

RESPIRATORY EXCURSION. Respiratory excursion is an estimation of thoracic range and expansion, and may disclose significant information about thoracic movement during breathing. The patient is instructed to inhale deeply while the movement of the nurse's thumbs (placed along the

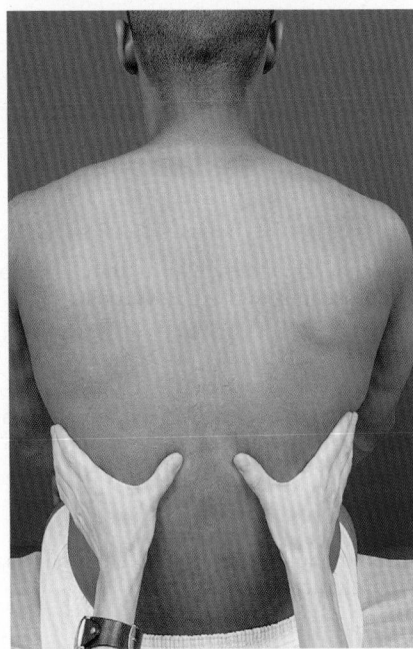

FIGURE 8-7 Method for assessing posterior respiratory excursion. Place both hands posteriorly at the level of T9 or T10. Slide hands medially to pinch a small amount of skin between your thumbs. Observe for symmetry as the patient exhales fully following a deep inspiration.

costal margin on the anterior chest wall) during inspiration and expiration is observed. This movement is normally symmetric.

Posterior assessment is performed by placing the thumbs adjacent to the spinal column at the level of the tenth rib (Fig. 8-7). The hands lightly grasp the lateral rib cage. Sliding the

thumbs medially about 2.5 cm (1 inch) raises a small skinfold between the thumbs. The patient is instructed to take a full inspiration and to exhale fully. The nurse observes for normal flattening of the skinfold and feels the symmetric movement of the thorax.

Asymmetric excursion may be due to a problem in the underlying chest wall, pleura, or lung; causes include pain (fractured ribs, trauma, splinting secondary to pleurisy or incisional pain), fibrosis, consolidation (lobar pneumonia), pleural effusion, or unilateral bronchial obstruction (Bickley & Szilagyi, 2009; LeBlond et al., 2009). Equal but diminished expansion is seen in neurological disease and emphysema.

TACTILE FREMITUS. The detection of palpable sound vibration transmitted to the chest wall as the patient speaks is called *tactile fremitus*. Normal fremitus is widely varied. It is influenced by thickness of the chest wall, especially if that thickness is muscular; increase in subcutaneous tissue associated with obesity; and pitch (lower-pitched sounds travel better and produce greater vibration of the chest wall). Fremitus is most pronounced in the second ICS lateral to the sternum and medial to the scapula, the level of the bronchus. Therefore, it is most palpable in the upper thorax, anteriorly and posteriorly.

The patient is asked to repeat "ninety-nine" or "one, two, three," or "eee, eee, eee" as the nurse's hands move down the patient's thorax comparing vibrations from similar areas (Fig. 8-8). The vibrations are detected with the palmar surfaces of the fingers and hands, or the ulnar aspect of the extended hands, on the thorax. Bony areas are not tested.

Air does not conduct sound well, but a solid substance such as a tumor, or fluid that increases the density of the lung, such as occurs in pneumonia, does. Therefore, an increase in

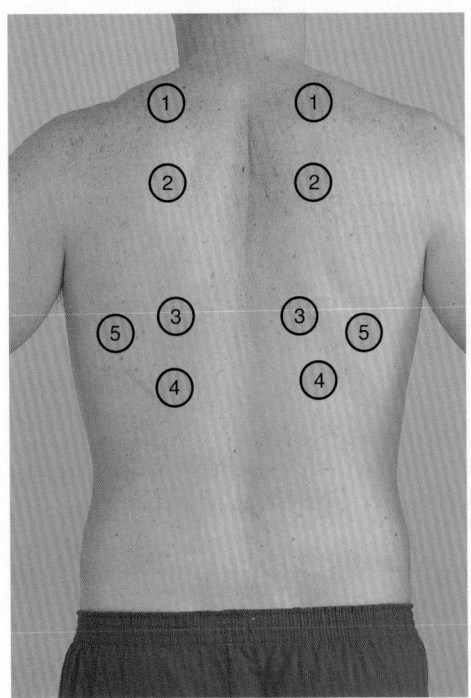

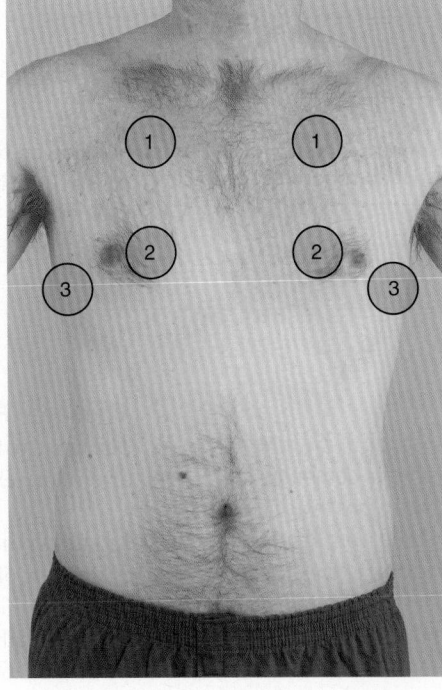

FIGURE 8-8 The palpation sequence for tactile fremitus.

solid tissue of the normally air-filled lung enhances fremitus, and an increase in air of the lung impedes sound. Patients with emphysema, which results in trapping of air, exhibit almost no tactile fremitus. A patient with consolidation of a lobe of the lung from pneumonia has increased tactile fremitus over that lobe. Air in the pleural space does not conduct sound; thus, a pneumothorax will have absent fremitus (Bickley & Szilagyi, 2009). In the case of pleural effusion, decreased fremitus is noted at the effusion; however, the lung above the effusion may reveal increased fremitus as the fluid has increased the density of the lung.

CREPITUS. Crepitus or subcutaneous emphysema is air bubbles present in the subcutaneous tissues or underlying muscle; upon palpation, the sensation of bubbles under the fingers can be felt and occasionally crackling can be heard. Crepitus is not painful. The gas bubbles move with palpation. It is associated with pneumothorax, trauma (e.g., fractured rib piercing the lung), surgical wounds, or gas gangrene.

Thoracic Percussion

Percussion sets the chest wall and underlying structures in motion, producing audible and tactile vibrations. It helps to determine whether underlying tissues are filled with air, fluid, or solid material, and is used to estimate diaphragmatic excursion. If possible, the patient is positioned in a sitting position with the head flexed forward and the arms crossed on the lap, which exposes more lung area for assessment by separating the scapulae widely. The nurse maintains a position to the side of the patient in order to comfortably and firmly hyperextend the middle finger of the nondominant hand (pleximeter finger) in the ICSs, being careful to avoid contact with any other finger on the chest wall as sound will be dampened. Bony structures (scapulae or ribs) are not percussed. While the middle finger is positioned firmly against the chest wall in the ICS, the middle finger of the opposite hand strikes the pleximeter finger in a quick and sharp manner. The striking finger aims for the distal interphalangeal joint (below the nail and above the distal joint). The term to describe the sound heard over a normal lung is resonant. Dullness is normally heard over bone, thus if this sound is noted over lung tissue, it is associated with consolidation, such as from pneumonia or a tumor. Hyperresonant sounds, which are louder and lower-pitched sounds, are associated with COPD or pneumothorax. It takes practice to develop comfort striking the finger with a quick, sharp but relaxed wrist motion and training to distinguish dullness, resonance, and hyperresonance (Bickley & Szilagyi, 2009). The sound will penetrate only 5 to 7 cm, thus any density below this depth will not be discovered. The nurse proceeds down the posterior thorax, percussing symmetric areas at intervals of 5 to 6 cm (2 to 2.5 inches) (Fig 8-9). Dullness over the lung occurs when air-filled lung tissue is replaced by fluid or solid tissue.

DIAPHRAGMATIC EXCURSION. The normal resonance of the lung stops at the diaphragm. The position of the diaphragm is different during inspiration and expiration. Initially, the nurse

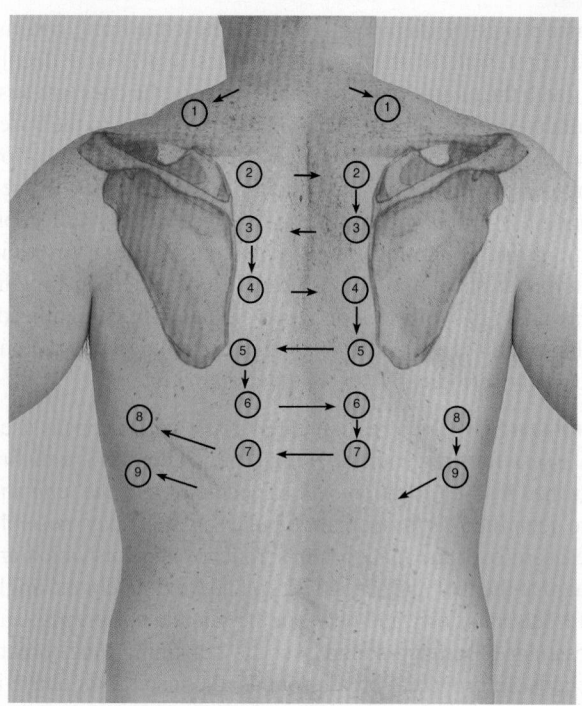

FIGURE 8-9 Percussion of the posterior thorax. With the patient in a sitting position, symmetric areas of the lungs are percussed at 5 cm intervals. This progression starts at the apex of each lung and concludes with percussion of each lateral chest wall.

determines the change from resonance (normal lung) to dullness (structures below the diaphragm) during normal breathing. Posteriorly, the lung normally ends at the tenth ICS with quiet respiration, and the diaphragm is generally two interspaces below this level. The point on the midscapular line at which the percussion changes from resonance to dullness is marked with a pen. An additional area medially or laterally to this area should be assessed to confirm the change to dullness. The patient is then instructed to inhale fully and hold it while the nurse again percusses downward from the marked area to the new level of dullness of the diaphragm. With deep inspiration, the diaphragm descends. This point is also marked. The distance between the two markings indicates the range of motion of the diaphragm. Maximal excursion of the diaphragm may be up to 7.5 cm in deep respiration (normally 5–6 cm) (Sayeed & Darling, 2007), with the right side of the diaphragm approximately 2 cm (0.75 inches) higher than the left because of the position of the liver. Decreased diaphragmatic excursion may occur with pleural effusion, a paralyzed hemidiaphragm, and emphysema.

Thoracic Auscultation

Auscultation is useful in assessing the flow of air through the bronchial tree and in evaluating the presence of fluid or solid obstruction in the lung. The nurse auscultates for normal breath sounds, adventitious sounds, and voice sounds.

Examination includes auscultation of the anterior, posterior, and lateral thorax and is performed as follows. The

nurse places the diaphragm of the stethoscope firmly against the chest wall as the patient breathes slowly and deeply through the mouth. Corresponding areas of the chest are auscultated in a systematic fashion from the apices to the bases and along midaxillary lines. The sequence of auscultation and the positioning of the patient are similar to those used for percussion. It often is necessary to listen to two full inspirations and expirations at each anatomic location for valid interpretation of the sound heard. Repeated deep breaths may result in symptoms of hyperventilation (e.g., lightheadedness); this is avoided by having the patient rest and breathe normally periodically during the examination.

BREATH SOUNDS. The diaphragm of the stethoscope is used to assess for lung sounds. Normal breath sounds are distinguished by their location over a specific area of the lung and are identified as bronchial (tubular), which may possibly be heard over the manubrium; bronchovesicular, which are heard at the first and second ICS, at approximately the angle of Louis anteriorly and between the scapula posteriorly; and vesicular (dominant sound over the remaining lung) breath sounds. In bronchial breath sounds, the inspiration phase is shorter than expiration; in bronchovesicular sounds, inspiration and expiration phases are equal; and with vesicular sounds, inspiration is longer than expiration.

The location, quality, and intensity of breath sounds are determined during auscultation. As the nurse moves down the chest wall, the sounds decrease. When airflow is decreased by fluid (pleural effusion) or tissue (obesity), breath sounds may be diminished or absent. For example, the breath sounds of the patient with emphysema are faint or often completely inaudible. Bronchial and bronchovesicular sounds that are audible anywhere except over the main bronchus in the lungs signify pathology, usually indicating consolidation in the lung (e.g., pneumonia). This finding requires further evaluation.

ADVENTITIOUS SOUNDS. An abnormal condition that affects the bronchial tree and alveoli may produce adventitious (additional or abnormal) sounds that are superimposed over usual breath sounds. Adventitious sounds are divided into two categories: discrete, noncontinuous sounds (**crackles**), and continuous musical sounds (wheezes) (Table 8-5). The duration of the sound is the important distinction to make in identifying the sound as noncontinuous or continuous.

Crackles (formerly referred to as *rales*) are discrete, noncontinuous sounds that result from delayed reopening of deflated airways. Crackles may or may not be cleared by coughing. They reflect underlying inflammation or congestion and are often present in such conditions as pneumonia, bronchitis, heart failure, bronchiectasis, and pulmonary fibrosis. Crackles are usually heard on inspiration, but they may also be heard on expiration.

Pleural friction rubs are specific examples of crackles. Friction rubs result from inflammation of the pleural surfaces that induces a crackling, grating sound usually heard in inspiration and expiration. The sound can be enhanced by applying pressure to the chest wall with the diaphragm of the stethoscope.

Wheezes are associated with bronchial wall oscillation and changes in airway diameter. Usually heard on expiration, wheezes may be heard on inspiration, or both phases. They are commonly heard in patients with asthma, chronic bronchitis, or bronchiectasis. *Stridor*, a high-pitched, harsh inspiratory wheeze associated with partial obstruction of the larynx or trachea, demands immediate attention (Bickley & Szilagyi, 2009).

VOICE SOUNDS. The sound heard through the stethoscope as the patient speaks is known as *vocal resonance*. The vibrations produced in the larynx are transmitted to the chest wall as they pass through the bronchi and alveolar tissue. During the process, the sounds are diminished in intensity and altered so that syllables are not distinguishable. Voice sounds are usually assessed by having the patient repeat "ninety-nine" or "eee" while the nurse listens with the stethoscope in corresponding areas of the chest, from the apices to the bases.

Bronchophony describes vocal resonance that is more intense and clearer than normal. *Egophony* describes voice sounds that are distorted. It is best appreciated by having the patient repeat the letter E. The distortion produced by consolidation transforms the sound into a clearly heard "A" rather than "E." Bronchophony and egophony have precisely the same significance as bronchial breathing with an increase in tactile fremitus. When an abnormality is detected, it should be evident using more than one assessment method. A change in tactile fremitus is more subtle and can be missed, but bronchial breathing and bronchophony can be noted loudly and clearly.

Whispered pectoriloquy is a very subtle finding, which is heard only in the presence of rather dense consolidation of the lungs. Transmission of the high-frequency components of sound is so enhanced by the consolidated tissue that even whispered words are heard, a circumstance not noted in normal physiology. The significance is the same as that of bronchophony (Bickley & Szilagyi, 2009).

The physical findings for the most common respiratory diseases are summarized in Table 8-6.

Diagnostic Evaluation

A wide range of diagnostic studies, described on the following pages, may be performed to aid in diagnosing or monitoring patients with a variety of respiratory conditions.

Pulmonary Function Tests

PFTs are routinely used in patients with chronic respiratory disorders. They are performed to assess respiratory function and to determine the extent of dysfunction. PFTs are useful in screening patients for major surgery, monitoring the course of a patient with an established respiratory disease, and assessing the response to therapy. They are useful as screening tests in potentially hazardous industries, such as coal mining and those that involve exposure to asbestos and other noxious fumes, dusts, or gases.

TABLE
8-5 Abnormal (Adventitious) Breath Sounds

Breath Sound	Description	Etiology
Crackles		
Crackles in general	Soft, high-pitched, discontinuous popping sounds that occur during inspiration; sounds like several hair rubbing together between the thumb and index finger	Secondary to fluid in the airways or alveoli or to opening of collapsed alveoli; When present in patients without lung disease, rales are specific for heart failure.
Coarse crackles	Discontinuous popping sounds heard in early inspiration; harsh, louder, lower-pitched moist sound originating in the large bronchi	Associated with obstructive pulmonary disease, asthma
Fine crackles	Discontinuous popping sounds heard in late inspiration; originates in the alveoli	Associated with interstitial pneumonia, restrictive pulmonary disease (e.g., fibrosis), congestive heart failure (CHF). In CHF, crackles may be heard widely over both lung fields (typically beginning at the bases) and may be accompanied by expiratory wheezing (cardiac asthma). Fine crackles in early inspiration are associated with bronchitis or pneumonia.
Wheezes		
Wheezes in general	Usually heard on expiration, but may be heard on inspiration or both phases	Associated with turbulent airflow and small airway vibration in which there is partial obstruction
Sonorous wheezes (rhonchi)	Deep, low-pitched rumbling sounds heard primarily during expiration; caused by air moving through narrowed tracheobronchial passages	Secretions within the larger airways that clear or change significantly after an effective cough.
Sibilant wheezes	Continuous, musical, high-pitched, whistle-like sounds heard during inspiration and expiration caused by air passing through narrowed or partially obstructed airways; may clear with coughing	Bronchospasm, asthma, and buildup of secretions
Friction rubs		
Pleural friction rub	Harsh, crackling sound, like two pieces of leather being rubbed together. Heard during inspiration alone or during both inspiration and expiration. May subside when patient holds breath. Coughing will not clear sound. Auscultate in the region where patient complains of pleuritic pain	Secondary to inflammation and loss of lubricating pleural fluid

TABLE
8-6 Assessment Findings in Common Respiratory Disorders

Disorder	Tactile Fremitus	Percussion	Auscultation
Consolidation (e.g., pneumonia)	Increased	Dull	Bronchial breath sounds, crackles, bronchophony, egophony, whispered pectoriloquy
Bronchitis	Normal	Resonant	Normal to decreased breath sounds, wheezes
Emphysema	Decreased	Hyperresonant	Decreased intensity of breath sounds, usually with prolonged expiration
Asthma (severe attack)	Normal to decreased	Resonant to hyperresonant	Wheezes
Pulmonary edema	Normal	Resonant	Crackles at lung bases, possibly wheezes
Pleural effusion	Absent	Dull to flat	Decreased to absent breath sounds, bronchial breath sounds and bronchophony, egophony, and whispered pectoriloquy above the effusion over the area of compressed lung
Pneumothorax	Decreased	Hyperresonant	Absent breath sounds
Atelectasis	Absent	Flat	Decreased to absent breath sounds

PFTs generally are performed by a technician using a spirometer that has a volume-collecting device attached to a recorder that demonstrates volume and time simultaneously. A number of tests are carried out, because no single measurement provides a complete picture of pulmonary function.

PFT results are interpreted on the basis of the degree of deviation from normal, taking into consideration the patient's height, weight, age, and gender. Because there is a wide range of normal values, PFTs may not detect early localized changes.

Patients with respiratory disorders may be taught how to measure their peak flow rate (which reflects maximal expiratory flow) at home using a spirometer to monitor progress of therapy, assess effect of alteration of medications, and use as a guide for when to notify the health care provider.

Arterial Blood Gas Studies

Measurements of blood pH and of arterial oxygen and carbon dioxide tensions are obtained when managing patients with respiratory problems and adjusting oxygen therapy as needed. The arterial oxygen tension (PaO_2) indicates the degree of oxygenation of the blood, and the arterial carbon dioxide tension ($PaCO_2$) indicates the adequacy of alveolar ventilation (that is, how effectively CO_2 is exhaled from the body). Arterial blood gas (ABG) studies aid in assessing the ability of the lungs to provide adequate oxygen and remove carbon dioxide and the ability of the kidneys to reabsorb or excrete bicarbonate ions to maintain normal body pH. ABG levels are obtained through an arterial puncture at the radial, brachial, or femoral artery, or through an indwelling arterial catheter. Before obtaining an ABG from the radial artery, it is necessary to test the patency of the ulnar artery by performing the Allen test (refer to Chapter 12 for details).

Pulse Oximetry

Pulse oximetry is a noninvasive method of continuously monitoring the oxygen saturation of hemoglobin (SaO_2). When oxygen saturation is measured with pulse oximetry, it is referred to as SpO_2. Although pulse oximetry does not replace ABG measurement, it is an effective tool to monitor for subtle or sudden changes in oxygen saturation.

A probe or sensor is attached to a well-perfused fingertip (Fig. 8-10), forehead, earlobe, or bridge of the nose. The sensor detects changes in oxygen saturation levels by monitoring light signals generated by the oximeter and reflected by blood pulsing through the tissue at the probe. Normal SpO_2 values are 95% to 100%. Values of less than 90% implies inadequate oxygenation, and further evaluation is needed (Gomella & Haist, 2007). SpO_2 values obtained by pulse oximetry are unreliable in cardiac arrest and shock, if dyes (i.e., methylene blue) or vasoconstrictor medications have been used, or if the patient has severe anemia or a high carbon monoxide level (smoke inhalation and carbon monoxide poisoning). Furthermore, they are not reliable detectors of hypoventilation if the patient is receiving supplemental oxygen.

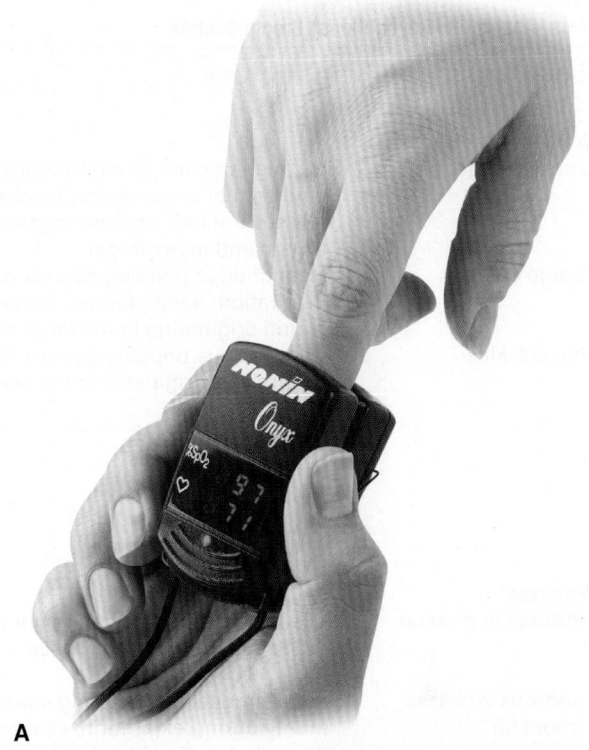

A

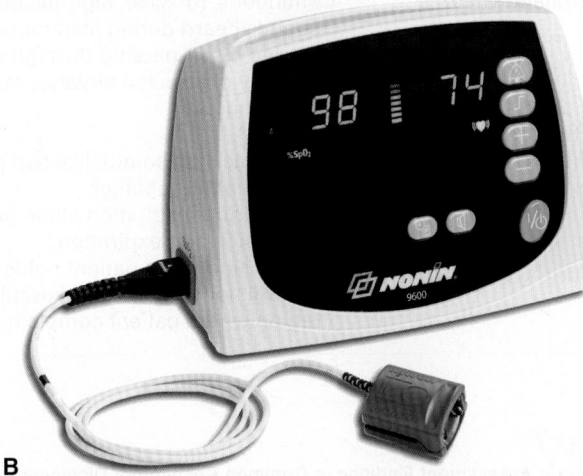

B

FIGURE 8-10 Measuring blood oxygenation with pulse oximetry reduces the need for invasive procedures, such as drawing blood for analysis of oxygen levels. **(A)** Self-contained digital fingertip pulse oximeter, which incorporates the sensor and display into one unit. **(B)** Table top model with sensor attached. Memory permits tracking heart rate and oxygen saturation over time.

Sputum Studies

Sputum is obtained for analysis to identify pathogenic organisms and to determine whether malignant cells are present. It also may be used to assess for hypersensitivity states (in which there is an increase in eosinophils). In general, sputum cultures are used in diagnosis, for drug sensitivity testing, and to guide treatment.

Expectoration is the usual method for collecting a sputum specimen. The patient is instructed to clear the nose and throat and rinse the mouth to decrease contamination of the sputum. After taking a few deep breaths, the patient coughs forcefully on exhalation (rather than spits), using the diaphragm, and expectorates into a sterile container. An early morning specimen is best for collection; 1 to 3 mL is generally a sufficient amount (Fischbach & Dunning, 2008).

If the sputum cannot be raised spontaneously, respiratory therapy personnel may assist the patient in obtaining an "aerosol-induced" specimen with an ultrasonic nebulizer until a strong cough reflex is initiated. The specimen is labeled as being aerosol induced. Other methods of collecting sputum specimens include endotracheal aspiration, bronchoscopic removal, bronchial brushing, and transtracheal aspiration.

NURSING ALERT

A sputum specimen is delivered to the laboratory within 2 hours by the patient or nurse. Allowing the specimen to stand for several hours in a warm room results in the overgrowth of contaminant organisms and may make it difficult to identify the pathogenic organisms (especially Mycobacterium tuberculosis).

Imaging Studies

Imaging studies, including X-rays, computed tomography (CT), magnetic resonance imaging (MRI), contrast studies, and radioisotope diagnostic scans may be part of any diagnostic workup, ranging from a determination of the extent of infection in sinusitis to tumor growth in cancer.

Chest X-Ray

Normal pulmonary tissue is radiolucent; therefore, densities produced by fluid, tumors, foreign bodies, and other pathologic conditions can be detected by X-ray examination. The routine chest X-ray consists of two views—the posteroanterior projection and the lateral projection. Chest X-rays are usually taken after full inspiration (a deep breath), because the lungs are best visualized when they are well aerated. Also, the diaphragm is at its lowest level and the largest expanse of lung is visible.

Computed Tomography

CT is an imaging method in which the lungs are scanned in successive layers by a narrow-beam X-ray. The images produced provide a cross-sectional view of the chest. CT can distinguish fine tissue density, and may be used to define pulmonary nodules and small tumors adjacent to pleural surfaces that are not visible on routine chest X-rays, and to demonstrate mediastinal abnormalities and hilar adenopathy, which are difficult to visualize with other techniques. Contrast agents are useful when evaluating the mediastinum and its contents. Computed tomography pulmonary angiography (CTPA), which is the injection of contrast media directly into

a vein or artery via a needle and/or catheter, has become the standard imaging technique for diagnosing PE (Kim & Bartholomew, 2010).

Magnetic Resonance Imaging

MRI is similar to CT except that magnetic fields and radiofrequency signals are used instead of a narrow-beam X-ray. MRI yields a much more detailed diagnostic image than CT. MRI is used to characterize pulmonary nodules, to help stage bronchogenic carcinoma (assessment of chest wall invasion), and to evaluate inflammatory activity in interstitial lung disease, acute PE, and chronic thrombolytic pulmonary hypertension.

Fluoroscopic Studies

Fluoroscopy is used to assist with invasive procedures, such as a chest needle biopsy or transbronchial biopsy, that are performed to identify lesions. It also may be used to study the movement of the chest wall, mediastinum, heart, and diaphragm; to detect diaphragm paralysis; and to locate lung masses.

Pulmonary Angiography

Pulmonary angiography is used to investigate thromboembolic disease of the lungs, such as pulmonary emboli, and congenital abnormalities of the pulmonary vascular tree. It involves the rapid injection of a radiopaque agent into the vasculature of the lungs for radiographic study of the pulmonary vessels. It is an invasive procedure that involves injecting a radiopaque agent into a vein in one or both arms (simultaneously) or into the femoral vein, with a needle or catheter. The agent also can be injected into a catheter that has been inserted into the main pulmonary artery or its branches or into the great veins proximal to the pulmonary artery. It is associated with respiratory failure (0.4%), renal failure (0.3%), and hemorrhage, myocardial perforation or rupture, ventricular arrhythmias and conduction defects, hematoma formation, infection, adverse reaction to the contrast medium, cardiac valve damage, and right-sided heart failure (Hargett, 2008; Lippincott, 2007). Due to introduction of CTPA, it is used infrequently.

Radioisotope Diagnostic Procedures (Lung Scans)

Several types of lung scans—V/Q scan, gallium scan, and positron emission tomography (PET)—are used to assess normal lung functioning, pulmonary vascular supply, and gas exchange.

A V/Q lung scan is performed by injecting a radioactive agent into a peripheral vein and then obtaining a scan of the chest to detect radiation. The isotope particles pass through the right side of the heart and are distributed into the lungs in proportion to the regional blood flow, making it possible to trace and measure blood perfusion through the lung. This procedure is used clinically to measure the integrity of the pulmonary vessels relative to blood flow and to evaluate blood flow abnormalities, as seen in pulmonary emboli. The

imaging time is 20 to 40 minutes, during which the patient lies under the camera with a mask fitted over the nose and mouth. This is followed by the ventilation component of the scan. The patient takes a deep breath of a mixture of oxygen and radioactive gas, which diffuses throughout the lungs. A scan is performed to detect ventilation abnormalities in patients who have regional differences in ventilation. Ventilation without perfusion is seen with pulmonary emboli.

A gallium scan is a radioisotope lung scan used to detect inflammatory conditions, abscesses, adhesions, and the presence, location, and size of tumors. It is used to stage bronchogenic cancer and document tumor regression after chemotherapy or radiation. Gallium is injected intravenously, and scans are taken at intervals (e.g., 6, 24, and 48 hours) to evaluate gallium uptake by the pulmonary tissues.

PET is a radioisotope study with advanced diagnostic capabilities that is used to evaluate lung nodules for malignancy. PET can detect and display metabolic changes in tissue, distinguish normal tissue from diseased tissue (such as in cancer), differentiate viable from dead or dying tissue, show regional blood flow, and determine the distribution and fate of medications in the body. PET is more accurate in detecting malignancies than CT and has equivalent accuracy in detecting malignant nodules when compared with invasive procedures such as thoracoscopy (pleural cavity is examined with an endoscope).

Endoscopic Procedures
Bronchoscopy

Bronchoscopy is the direct inspection and examination of the larynx, trachea, and bronchi for diagnosis of infectious, inflammatory, and malignant disease of the chest through a flexible or rigid fiberoptic bronchoscope (Fig. 8-11).

Therapeutic bronchoscopy is used to (1) remove foreign bodies from the tracheobronchial tree, (2) perform difficult endotracheal intubations, (3) remove secretions obstructing the tracheobronchial tree when the patient cannot clear them, (4) treat postoperative atelectasis, and (5) destroy and excise lesions, (6) place endobronchial radiation therapy (brachytherapy) and laser therapy of obstructive airway lesions, (7) stent obstructing endobronchial lesions and (8) dilate stenotic airways.

Possible complications of bronchoscopy include a reaction to the local anesthetic, infection, aspiration, bronchospasm, **hypoxemia** (low blood oxygen level), pneumothorax, bleeding, and perforation.

Before the procedure, a signed consent form is obtained from the patient. Food and fluids are withheld for 8 hours before the test to reduce the risk of aspiration when the cough reflex is blocked by anesthesia. The nurse explains the procedure to the patient to reduce fear and decrease anxiety and administers preoperative medications if required.

The patient must remove dentures and other oral prostheses. The examination is usually performed under local

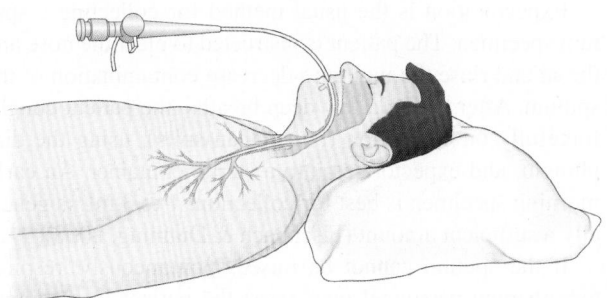
Fiberoptic bronchoscopy

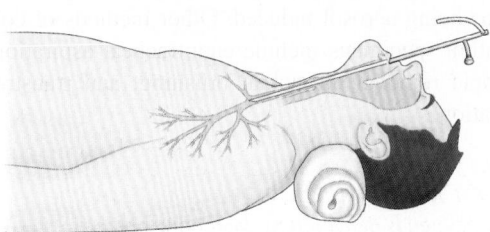
Rigid bronchoscopy

FIGURE 8-11 Endoscopic bronchoscopy permits visualization of bronchial structures. The bronchoscope is advanced into bronchial structures orally. Bronchoscopy permits the clinician not only to diagnose but also to treat various lung problems.

anesthesia or moderate sedation. A topical anesthetic such as lidocaine (Xylocaine) may be sprayed on the pharynx or dropped on the epiglottis and vocal cords and into the trachea to suppress the cough reflex and minimize discomfort. Sedatives or opioids are administered intravenously as prescribed to provide moderate sedation. Resuscitative and suctioning equipment should be available (Wilson, 2007).

After the procedure, it is important that the patient takes nothing by mouth until the cough reflex returns, because the preoperative sedation and local anesthesia impair the protective laryngeal reflex and swallowing for several hours. The patient is instructed to spit out saliva rather than swallow it until the gag reflex returns. Once the patient demonstrates a cough reflex, the nurse may offer ice chips and eventually fluids. The nurse also monitors the patient's respiratory status and observes for hypoxia, hypotension, tachycardia, arrhythmias, hemoptysis, and dyspnea. Any abnormality is reported promptly. The patient is not discharged from the recovery area until adequate cough reflex and respiratory status are present. The nurse instructs the patient and family caregivers to report any shortness of breath or bleeding immediately.

NURSING ALERT
Anesthesia can temporarily impair the pharyngeal reflex (ninth, tenth, CN), which is responsible for the gag reflex and swallowing; to prevent aspiration, before refeeding the patient, the nurse must reassess return of this reflex (refer to Chapter 43 for details on assessment).

BOX 8-8

GUIDELINES FOR NURSING CARE

Assisting the Patient Undergoing Thoracentesis

Equipment

- Thoracentesis tray
- Sterile gloves
- Germicide solution
- Local anesthetic
- Sterile collection bottles

Implementation

ACTIONS	RATIONALE
1. Ascertain in advance that a chest X-ray and ultrasound (if available) has been ordered and completed and the consent form has been signed. The nurse also anticipates that coagulation studies are evaluated and any coagulopathy corrected before the procedure.	1. Posteroanterior and lateral decubitus chest X-ray films are obtained before the procedure and ultrasound if available to determine optimal site for thoracentesis (Seijo, 2008). When thoracentesis is performed under ultrasound guidance, it has a lower rate of complications than when it is performed without ultrasound guidance, including a decrease in post procedure pneumothorax from 18% to 3% (Seijo, 2008). If fluid is loculated (isolated in a pocket of pleural fluid), ultrasound scans are performed to help select the best site for needle aspiration. Correction of coagulopathy may be necessary to decrease the bleeding risk with this procedure.
2. Assess the patient for allergy to the local anesthetic to be used.	2. If the patient is allergic to the initially prescribed anesthetic, assessment findings provide an opportunity to use a safer anesthetic.
3. Administer sedation if prescribed.	3. Sedation enables the patient to cooperate with the procedure and promotes relaxation
4. Inform the patient about the nature of the procedure and: a. The importance of remaining immobile b. Pressure sensations to be experienced c. That minimal discomfort is anticipated after the procedure	4. An explanation helps to orient the patient to the procedure, provides anticipatory guidance, and provides an opportunity to ask questions and verbalize anxiety.
5. Position the patient comfortably with adequate supports. If possible, place the patient upright or in one of the following positions: a. Sitting on the edge of the bed with the feet supported and arms and head on a padded over-the-bed table b. Straddling a chair with arms and head resting on the back of the chair c. Lying on the unaffected side with the head of the bed elevated 30 to 45 degrees if unable to assume a sitting position	5. The upright position facilitates the removal of fluid that usually localizes at the base of the thorax. A position of comfort helps the patient to relax.
6. Support and reassure the patient during the procedure: a. Prepare the patient for the cold sensation of skin germicide solution and for a pressure sensation from infiltration of local anesthetic agent. b. Encourage the patient to refrain from coughing.	6. Sudden and unexpected movement, such as coughing, by the patient can traumatize the visceral pleura and lung.

(continued on page 244)

BOX 8-8 GUIDELINES FOR NURSING CARE (continued)

ACTIONS	RATIONALE
7. Expose the entire chest. The site for aspiration is visualized by chest X-ray and percussion. If fluid is in the pleural cavity, the thoracentesis site is determined by the chest X-ray, ultrasound scanning, and physical findings, with attention to the site of maximal dullness on percussion.	**7.** If air is in the pleural cavity, the thoracentesis site is usually in the second or third intercostal space in the midclavicular line because air rises in the thorax.
8. The procedure is performed under aseptic conditions. After the skin is cleansed, the provider uses a small-caliber needle to inject a local anesthetic slowly into the intercostal space.	**8.** An intradermal wheal is raised slowly; rapid injection causes pain. The parietal pleura is very sensitive and should be well infiltrated with anesthetic before the physician passes the thoracentesis needle through it.
9. The provider advances the thoracentesis needle with the syringe attached. When the pleural space is reached, suction may be applied with the syringe: **a.** A 20 mL syringe with a three-way stopcock is attached to the needle (one end of the adapter is attached to the needle and the other to the tubing leading to a receptacle that receives the fluid being aspirated). **b.** If a considerable quantity of fluid is removed, the needle is held in place on the chest wall with a small hemostat. **c.** The nurse should anticipate that no more than 1–1½ liter will be removed from the chest.	**9.** Use of thoracentesis needle allows proper insertion: **a.** When a large quantity of fluid is withdrawn, a three-way stopcock serves to keep air from entering the pleural cavity. **b.** The hemostat steadies the needle on the chest wall. Sudden pleuritic chest pain or shoulder pain may indicate that the needle point is irritating the visceral or the diaphragmatic pleura. **c.** To prevent reexpansion pulmonary edema.
10. After the needle is withdrawn, pressure is applied over the puncture site and a small, airtight, sterile dressing is fixed in place.	**10.** Pressure helps to stop bleeding, and the airtight dressing protects the site and prevents air from entering the pleural cavity.
11. Advise the patient that he or she will be on bed rest and a chest X-ray will be obtained after thoracentesis.	**11.** A chest X-ray verifies that there is no pneumothorax.
12. Record the total amount of fluid withdrawn from the procedure and document the nature of the fluid, its color, and its viscosity. If indicated, prepare samples of fluid for laboratory evaluation. A specimen container with formalin may be needed for a pleural biopsy.	**12.** The fluid may be clear, serous, bloody, purulent, etc.
13. Monitor the patient at intervals for increasing respiratory rate; increased dyspnea, asymmetry in respiratory movement; faintness; vertigo; tightness in chest; uncontrollable cough; blood-tinged, frothy mucus; a rapid pulse; and signs of hypoxemia.	**13.** Pneumothorax, tension pneumothorax, subcutaneous emphysema, and pyrogenic infection are complications of a thoracentesis. Pulmonary edema or cardiac distress can occur after a sudden shift in mediastinal contents when large amounts of fluid are aspirated.

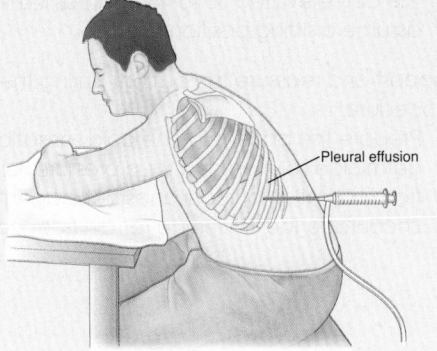

Pleural effusion

Thoracentesis

A thoracentesis (aspiration of fluid or air from the pleural space) is performed on patients with various clinical problems. As a diagnostic or therapeutic procedure, thoracentesis may be used for removal of fluid and air from the pleural cavity, aspiration of pleural fluid for analysis, pleural biopsy, or instillation of medication into the pleural space. Care of the patient undergoing thoracentesis is discussed in Box 8-8 on pages 243–244. A needle biopsy of the pleura may be performed at the same time. Studies of pleural fluid include Gram stain culture and sensitivity, acid-fast staining and culture, differential cell count, cytology, pH, specific gravity, total protein, and lactic dehydrogenase.

Chapter Review

Critical Thinking Exercises

1. A man with a long history of smoking (60 pack/years) is scheduled for surgery to remove a nonfunctioning kidney. In preparation for surgery, he is scheduled for PFTs, which he refuses to have because he says his breathing has nothing to do with his kidney problem or his scheduled kidney surgery. How would you respond to his statement? What impact does his 60 pack/year history of cigarette smoking have on your preoperative, intraoperative, and postoperative assessment?

2. When obtaining a health history from a 55-year-old patient who is seeking health care because of a persistent cough and extreme fatigue, you note that she is able to speak only in short sentences before having to stop to catch her breath. What specific information about signs and symptoms would you obtain during the health history? How would you modify your physical examination based on your observations? What initial laboratory tests would you anticipate will be ordered for this patient?

NCLEX-Style Review Questions

1. Before an ABG is drawn from the patient's radial artery, what test should be performed?
   A. Doppler flow test
   B. Allen test
   C. Babinski's test
   D. A/B Index

2. Mr. Border, age 62, has a chronic cough with thick sputum. He undergoes a bronchoscopy for diagnostic purposes. Following the bronchoscopy, which action by the nurse is most appropriate?
   A. Encourage fluid intake to promote elimination of contrast media.
   B. Monitor hemoglobin and hematocrit to evaluate blood loss.
   C. Check vital signs every 15 minutes for 4 hours.
   D. Keep NPO until the gag reflex returns.

3. A patient is admitted to the ICU after falling from a roof and sustaining fractures of the first three ribs on the right side. The patient is dyspneic, and crepitus (subcutaneous emphysema) can be palpated. Auscultation reveals decreased breath sounds on the right. The chest X-ray reveals a pneumothorax. Upon percussion, what does the nurse expect to hear?
   A. Dullness on the right
   B. Resonance on the right
   C. Tympany on the right
   D. Hyper-resonance on the right

4. The finding of normal breath sounds on the right chest and diminished, distant breath sounds on the left chest of a newly intubated patient is probably due to which of the following?
   A. A left pneumothorax
   B. A right hemothorax
   C. Intubation of the right mainstem bronchus
   D. A malfunctioning mechanical ventilator

5. A patient presents to the emergency room with pulmonary edema. The nurse expects to hear what adventitious sound?
   A. Decreased breath sounds
   B. Inspiratory and expiratory wheezing
   C. Crackles
   D. Friction rub

Try these additional resources to enhance your learning and understanding of this chapter:
- thePoint online resource available at **http://thepoint.lww.com/Pellico1e**
- *Handbook for Focus on Adult Health: Medical-Surgical Nursing*
- *Study Guide for Focus on Adult Health: Medical-Surgical Nursing*

References and Selected Readings

References and selected readings associated with this chapter can be found on the website that accompanies the book. Visit http://thepoint.lww.com/Pellico1e to access the references and other additional resources associated with this chapter.

JANCEE PUST-MARCONE

Nursing Management: Patients With Upper Respiratory Tract Disorders

Learning Objectives

After reading this chapter, you will be able to:

1. Compare and contrast the upper respiratory tract infections with regard to cause, incidence, clinical manifestations, management, and the significance of preventive health care.

2. Use the nursing process as a framework for care of patients with upper airway infection.

3. Describe the nursing management of the patient with obstructive sleep apnea.

4. Describe the nursing management for patients receiving continuous positive-pressure (CPAP) or bi-level (BiPAP) breathing.

5. Describe nursing management of the patient with epistaxis.

6. Describe nursing management of patients undergoing laryngectomy.

7. Describe the nursing care for a patient with an endotracheal tube or a tracheostomy.

8. Demonstrate the procedure of tracheal suctioning.

Many upper airway disorders are relatively minor, and their effects are limited to mild and temporary discomfort for the patient. Others may be acute, severe, and life-threatening, and may require permanent alterations in breathing and speaking. The nurse must have expert assessment skills, an understanding of the wide variety of disorders that may affect the upper airway, and an awareness of the impact of these alterations on patients.

UPPER AIRWAY INFECTIONS

Upper airway infections, also known as upper respiratory tract infections (URIs), are the most common cause of illness and affect most people on occasion. There are many causative organisms, and people are susceptible throughout life.

Some infections are acute, with symptoms that last several days; others are chronic, with symptoms that last a long time or recur. Patients with these conditions seldom require hospitalization. URIs affect the nasal cavity, ethmoidal air cells, and frontal, maxillary, and sphenoid sinuses, as well as the larynx and trachea. About 90% of upper respiratory disorders stem from a viral infection of the upper respiratory passages and subsequent mucous membrane inflammation.

RHINITIS

Rhinitis is a group of disorders characterized by inflammation and irritation of the mucous membranes of the nose. It may be acute or chronic, nonallergic or allergic (see Chapter 38 for information about allergic rhinitis).

Viral rhinitis is the most frequent viral infection in the general population and is referred to as the "common cold."

Pathophysiology

Nonallergic rhinitis may be caused by a variety of factors, including environmental factors such as changes in temperature or humidity, odors, or foods; infection; age; systemic disease; drugs (e.g., cocaine), over-the-counter (OTC) and prescribed nasal decongestants; and the presence of a foreign body.

The most common cause of nonallergic rhinitis is the common cold. Colds are believed to be caused by as many as 200 different viruses.

TABLE
9-1 Causes of Rhinitis

Category	Causes
Allergic	Seasonal (pollens)
	Perennial (dust / mold)
Vasomotor	Idiopathic
	Abuse of nasal decongestants (rhinitis medicamentosa)
	Drugs (reserpine, prazosin, cocaine abuse)
	Psychological stimulation (anger, sexual arousal)
	Irritants (smoke, air pollution, exhaust fumes, cocaine)
Mechanical	Tumor
	Deviated septum
	Crusting
	Hypertrophied turbinates
	Foreign body
	Cerebrospinal fluid leak
Chronic inflammatory	Polyps (in cystic fibrosis)
	Sarcoidosis
	Wegener's granulomatosis
	Midline granuloma
Infectious	Acute viral infection
	Acute or chronic sinusitis
	Rare nasal infections (syphilis, tuberculosis)
Hormonal	Pregnancy
	Hypothyroidism
	Use of oral contraceptives
	Hypothyroidism

Adapted from Carr, M. M. Differential diagnosis of rhinitis. Accessed July 31, 2009, from icarus.med.utoronto.ca/carr/manual/ddxrhinitis.html.

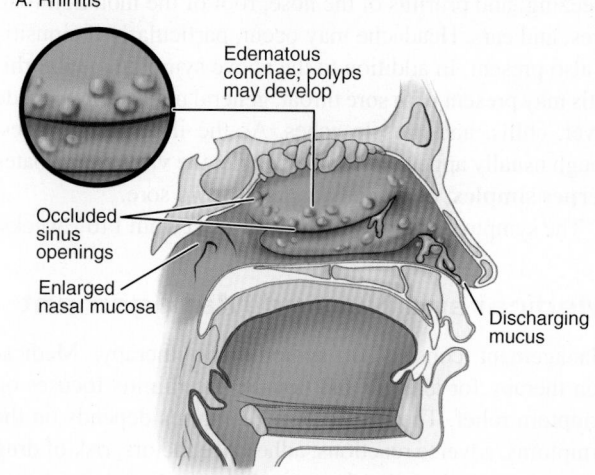

A. Rhinitis

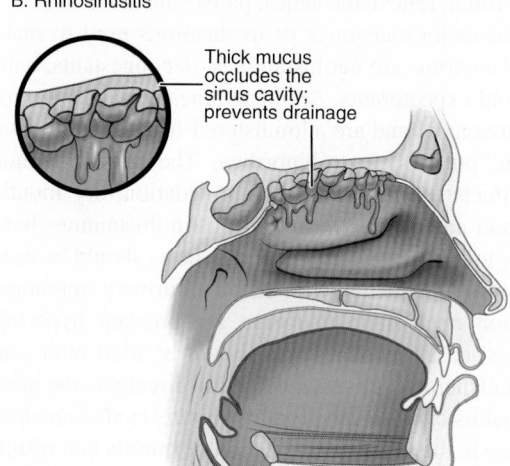

B. Rhinosinusitis

FIGURE 9-1 Pathophysiologic processes in rhinitis and rhinosinusitis. Although pathophysiologic processes are similar in rhinitis and sinusitis, they affect different structures. In rhinitis **(A)**, the mucous membranes lining the nasal passages become inflamed, congested, and edematous. The swollen nasal conchae block the sinus openings, and mucus is discharged from the nostrils. Rhinosinusitis **(B)** is also marked by inflammation and congestion, with thickened mucous secretions filling the sinus cavities and occluding the openings.

Rhinoviruses are the most likely causative organisms, and are believed to cause more than 40% of colds. Other viruses implicated in the common cold include coronaviruses, adenovirus, respiratory syncytial virus (RSV), influenza virus, and parainfluenza virus. Each virus may have multiple strains. Because of this diversity, development of a vaccine is almost impossible. Immunity after recovery is variable and depends on many factors, including a person's natural host resistance and the specific virus that caused the cold. Drug-induced rhinitis is associated with use of antihypertensive agents, oral contraceptives, and chronic use of nasal decongestants. Other causes of rhinitis are identified in Table 9-1. Figure 9-1 shows the pathologic processes involved in rhinitis and sinusitis.

Risk Factors

Colds are highly contagious because virus is shed for about 2 days before the symptoms appear and during the first part of the symptomatic phase. Adults in the United States average two to three colds each year (American Lung Association, 2009). Adult women are more susceptible than adult men. Viral rhinitis can occur at any time of the year, but three time periods account for the epidemics in the United States: in September, just after the opening of school; in late January; and toward the end of April. Cold temperatures and exposure to cold, rainy weather do not increase the incidence or severity of the common cold.

Clinical Manifestations and Assessment

The signs and symptoms of nonallergic rhinitis include **rhinorrhea** (excessive nasal drainage, runny nose); nasal congestion; nasal discharge (purulent with bacterial rhinitis);

sneezing; and pruritus of the nose, roof of the mouth, throat, eyes, and ears. Headache may occur, particularly if sinusitis is also present. In addition to the above symptoms, viral rhinitis may present with sore throat, general malaise, low-grade fever, chills, and muscle aches. As the illness progresses, cough usually appears. In some people, the virus exacerbates **herpes simplex**, commonly called a "cold sore."

The symptoms of viral rhinitis may last from 1 to 2 weeks.

Medical and Nursing Management

Management consists of symptomatic therapy. Medication therapy for allergic and nonallergic rhinitis focuses on symptom relief. The choice of medications depends on the symptoms, adverse reactions, adherence factors, risk of drug interactions, and cost to the patient. Acetaminophen or nonsteroidal anti-inflammatory agents (NSAIDs), such as aspirin or ibuprofen, relieve the aches, pains, and fever.

The four major categories of medications used to manage cold symptoms are antihistamines, decongestants, antitussives, and expectorants. Antihistamines remain the most common treatment and are administered for sneezing, nasal congestion, pruritus, and rhinorrhea. The most common adverse effects of antihistamines are sedation, dry mouth, and GI upset and cardiac arrhythmias. Antihistamines have been show to aggravate certain conditions as should be used with caution in patients with asthma, urinary retention, hypertension, open-angle glaucoma, and prostatic hypertrophy. Topical nasal decongestants should be used with caution. Topical therapy delivers medication directly to the nasal mucosa, but its overuse can produce *rhinitis medicamentosa* (an increase in the severity or duration of rhinitis that results from prolonged use of decongestant nasal spray) or rebound rhinitis. Oral decongestant agents may be used for congestive nasal obstruction. Use of saline nasal spray can act as a mild decongestant and can liquefy mucus to prevent crusting. Expectorants are available without a prescription and are used to promote removal of secretions. Several antiviral medications are available by prescription. Antimicrobial agents (antibiotics) should not be used, because they do not affect the virus or reduce the incidence of bacterial complications, and they have been implicated in development of organisms resistant to therapy.

Herbal medicines (e.g., echinacea, zinc lozenges, zinc nasal spray) are frequently used to treat the common cold; however, evidence regarding their effectiveness in shortening the symptomatic phase is questionable (Wu, Zhang, Qiu et al., 2007). The inhalation of stream or heated, humidified air has been a mainstay of home remedies for common cold sufferers, but the value of this therapy has not been demonstrated.

If symptoms suggest a bacterial infection, an antimicrobial agent will be used. Other treatment measures include adequate fluid intake, adequate rest, prevent chilling, and warm saltwater gargles to soothe the sore throat. Patients with nasal septal deformities or nasal polyps may be referred to an ear, nose, and throat (ENT) specialist.

RHINOSINUSITIS

Rhinosinusitis, formerly called *sinusitis*, is an inflammatory process involving the paranasal sinuses and nasal cavity (Chan & Kuhn, 2009). The clinical practice guideline for adult rhinosinusitis released by the American Academy of Otolaryngology – Head and Neck Surgery Foundation recommends use of the term rhinosinusitis because sinusitis is almost always accompanied by inflammation of the nasal mucosa (Rosenfeld, Andes, Bhattachaaryya et al., 2007). Rhinosinusitis affects 1 in 7 Americans, about 31 million people in the United States, and accounts for billions of dollars in direct health care costs (Rosenfeld et al., 2007). Uncomplicated rhinosinusitis does not extend beyond the paranasal sinuses and nasal cavity. Rhinosinusitis is classified by duration of symptoms as acute (less than 4 weeks), subacute (4 to 12 weeks), and chronic (more than 12 weeks) with or without acute exacerbations (Chan & Kuhn, 2009). Rhinosinusitis can be further classified as an **acute bacterial rhinosinusitis** (ABRS) or **acute viral rhinosinusitis** (AVRS) (Chan & Kuhn, 2009). Recurrent acute rhinosinusitis is characterized by four or more acute episodes of ABRS per year without symptoms of rhinosinusitis between episodes (Rosenfeld et al., 2007). Chronic rhinosinusitis (CRS) affects 14% to 16% of the U.S. population. It occurs more often in women than men and accounts for almost 20 million office visits annually. In about 29% to 36% of patients, CRS is accompanied by nasal polyps.

Pathophysiology

Acute rhinosinusitis usually follows a viral URI or cold, such as an unresolved viral or bacterial infection, or an exacerbation of allergic rhinitis. Nasal congestion, caused by inflammation, edema, and transudation of fluid secondary to URI, leads to obstruction of the sinus cavities (see Fig. 9-1). This provides an excellent medium for bacterial growth.

CRS occurs with episodes of prolonged inflammation and with repeated or inadequate treatment of acute infections. Irreversible damage to the mucosa may occur, and symptoms last for longer than 3 months.

Bacterial organisms account for more than 60% of the cases of acute rhinosinusitis. *Streptococcus pneumoniae, Haemophilus influenzae,* and less commonly *Staphylococcus aureus* and *Moraxella catarrhalis* (Tierney, McPhee, & Papadakis, 2007) are implicated. Other organisms that are occasionally isolated include *Chlamydia pneumoniae, Streptococcus pyogenes,* viruses, and fungi (*Aspergillus fumigatus*). Immunodeficiency should be considered in patients with CRS or acute recurrent rhinosinusitis. Acute fulminant/invasive sinusitis is a life-threatening illness and is commonly attributed to *Aspergillus*.

Risk Factors

Some people are more prone to rhinosinusitis because exposure to environmental hazards such as paint, sawdust, and chemicals may result in chronic inflammation of the nasal passages. If sinus drainage is obstructed by a deviated septum or by hypertrophied turbinates, spurs, or nasal polyps or tumors, sinus infection may persist as a smoldering (persistent) secondary infection or progress to an acute suppurative process (causing purulent discharge). Other conditions that can block the normal flow of sinus secretions include abnormal structures of the nose, enlarged adenoids, diving and swimming, tooth infection, trauma to the nose, tumors, and the pressure of foreign objects. Immunocompromised patients are at increased risk for development of fungal sinusitis. Fungal sinusitis in immunocompromised patients can be divided into three categories: (1) fungus ball, (2) chronic erosive (noninvasive) sinusitis, and (3) allergic fungal sinusitis. *A. fumigatus* is the most common organism associated with fungal sinusitis. The fungus ball is usually a brown or greenish-black material with the consistency of peanut butter or cottage cheese.

Clinical Manifestations and Assessment

Symptoms of ABRS include purulent nasal drainage accompanied by nasal obstruction or a combination of facial pain, pressure, or a sense of fullness (referred to collectively as facial pain-pressure-fullness), or both (Rosenfeld et al., 2007). The facial pain-pressure-fullness may involve the anterior face or the periorbital region. The patient may also report cloudy or colored nasal discharge, congestion, blockage, or stuffiness, as well as a localized or diffuse headache. The occurrence of symptoms for 10 days or more after the initial onset of upper respiratory symptoms indicates ABRS.

The symptoms of AVRS are similar to those of ABRS with the exceptions of the duration of symptoms. Symptoms of AVRS occur for less than 10 days after the onset of upper respiratory symptoms and do not worsen (Rosenfeld et al., 2007).

Clinical manifestations of CRS are similar to ABRS and include mucopurulent drainage, nasal obstruction, cough, chronic hoarseness, chronic headaches in the periorbital area, facial pain or pressure, and **hyposmia** (decreased sense of smell) (Chan & Kuhn, 2009). As a result of chronic nasal congestion, the patient is usually required to breathe through the mouth. Snoring, sore throat, and, in some situations, adenoidal hypertrophy may also occur. These symptoms are generally most pronounced on awakening in the morning.

To diagnose the rhinosinusitis, a careful history and physical examination are performed. It is essential to obtain any history of comorbid conditions, including asthma, and history of tobacco use. A history of fever, fatigue, previous episodes and treatments, and previous response to therapies is also obtained.

The head and neck, particularly the nose, ears, teeth, sinuses, pharynx, and chest, are examined. The physical assessment includes examination of the external nose for evidence of anatomical abnormality. Nasal mucous membranes are assessed for erythema, pallor, atrophy, edema, crusting, discharge, polyps, erosions, and septal perforations or deviations. There may be tenderness to palpation over the infected sinus area.

Diagnostic imaging (X-ray, computed tomography [CT], magnetic resonance imaging [MRI]) is not recommended for the diagnosis of acute rhinosinusitis if the patient meets clinical diagnostic criteria (Rosenfeld et al., 2007). Diagnostic testing may be required to rule out other local or systemic disorders, such as tumor, fistula, and allergy for the patient with CRS. Nasal endoscopy may be indicated to rule out underlying diseases, tumors, and sinus mycetomas (fungus balls).

Medical and Nursing Management

Treatment of acute and CRS depends on the cause. The goals of treatment of acute rhinosinusitis are to treat the infection, shrink the nasal mucosa, and relieve pain.

General measures include adequate hydration, steam inhalation for 20 to 30 minutes three times per day if possible, saline irrigation (Harvey, Hannan, Badia et al., 2007), and saline nose drops. Patients are instructed to sleep with the head of the bed elevated and to avoid exposure to cigarette smoke and fumes. Patients are cautioned to avoid caffeine and alcohol, which can lead to dehydration.

Treatment of acute and CRS typically involves nasal saline lavage and decongestants. Decongestants or nasal saline spray can improve patency of the ostiomeatal unit (area where the frontal and maxillary sinuses normally drain into the nasal cavity), and improve drainage of the sinuses. Topical decongestants are used only in adults and should not be used for longer than 3 or 4 days. Oral decongestants must be used cautiously in patients with hypertension. OTC antihistamines and prescription antihistamines are used if an allergic component is suspected. Heated mist and saline irrigation also may be effective for opening blocked passages. If the patient continues to have symptoms after 7 to 10 days, the sinuses may need to be irrigated.

Observation without the use of antibiotics is an option for some patients with uncomplicated ABRS (mild pain, temperature of less than 38.3°C [101°F]). Follow-up is essential. Studies suggest that most patients will improve spontaneously, and antibiotics should be reserved for those with prolonged symptoms (Sharp, Denman, Puumala et al., 2007). When ABRS is confirmed, antibiotic therapy is prescribed. Prescribed medications may be required for a period of 3 to 4 weeks for CRS and recurrent acute rhinosinusitis.

For patients with concomitant asthma, leukotriene inhibitors (which block the binding of *leukotrienes*, which are inflammatory mediators) may be used. If allergies are a

possible cause of CRS, oral antihistamines or nasal corticosteroids may be prescribed. The use of intranasal inhalations has been associated with a significant improvement of symptoms of CRS and a reduction in nasal bacteria (Harvey et al., 2007). Intranasal corticosteroids have been shown to produce complete or marked improvement in acute symptoms of rhinosinusitis, but they are not recommended for routine treatment (Rosenfeld et al., 2007).

If standard medical therapy fails to treat CRS and symptoms persist, endoscopic sinus surgery (ESS) may be indicated to correct structural deformities that obstruct the ostia (openings) of the sinuses (Chester, 2009). Patients undergoing ESS report a reduction of symptoms including headache, nasal obstruction, fatigue, body pains, and hyposmia (Chester, 2009). Excising and cauterizing nasal polyps, correcting a deviated septum, incising and draining the sinuses, aerating the sinuses, and removing tumors are some of the specific procedures performed. If sinusitis is caused by a fungal infection, surgery is required to excise the fungus ball and necrotic tissue and drain the sinuses. Antimicrobial agents are administered before and after surgery. Some patients with severe chronic sinusitis obtain relief only by moving to a dry climate.

Complications

If untreated, acute rhinosinusitis may lead to severe complications. Local complications include osteomyelitis and mucocele (cyst of the paranasal sinuses). Osteomyelitis requires prolonged antibiotic therapy and at times removal of necrotic bone. Intracranial complications are rare but include cavernous sinus thrombosis, meningitis, brain abscess, ischemic brain infarction, and severe orbital cellulites (Tierney et al., 2007). Complications of CRS, although uncommon, include severe orbital cellulitis, subperiosteal abscess, cavernous sinus thrombosis, meningitis, encephalitis, and ischemic infarction. CRS can also lead to intracranial infection.

PHARYNGITIS

Acute **pharyngitis** is a sudden inflammation of the pharynx involving the back portion of the tongue, soft palate, and tonsils. Chronic pharyngitis is a persistent inflammation of the pharynx.

Pathophysiology

Most cases of acute pharyngitis are caused by viral infection. Responsible viruses include the adenovirus, influenza virus, Epstein-Barr virus, and herpes simplex virus. Bacterial organisms account for the remainder of the cases. Ten percent of adults with pharyngitis have group A beta-hemolytic streptococcus (GABHS), which is commonly referred to as group A streptococcus (GAS) or streptococcal pharyngitis. Other bacterial organisms found in acute pharyngitis include *Mycoplasma pneumoniae*, *Neisseria gonorrhoeae*, and *H. influenzae* type B.

Risk Factors

Acute pharyngitis is more common in patients less than 25 years of age (usually between 5 and 15 years). Chronic pharyngitis is common in adults who work or live in dusty surroundings, use their voice to excess, suffer from chronic cough, or habitually use alcohol and tobacco.

Clinical Manifestations and Assessment

The signs and symptoms of acute pharyngitis include a fiery-red pharyngeal membrane and tonsils, lymphoid follicles that are swollen and flecked with white-purple exudate, enlarged and tender cervical lymph nodes, and no cough (Fig. 9-2). Creamy exudates may be present in the tonsillar pillars. A fever greater than 100.4°F (38°C), malaise, and sore throat also may be present. Patients with GAS pharyngitis may exhibit vomiting, anorexia, and a scarlatina-form rash with urticaria known as *scarlet fever*.

Patients with chronic pharyngitis complain of a constant sense of irritation or fullness in the throat, mucus that collects in the throat and can be expelled by coughing, and difficulty swallowing. A sore throat that is worse with swallowing in the absence of pharyngitis suggests the possibility of thyroiditis and should be referred for evaluation.

Accurate diagnosis of pharyngitis is essential to determine the causative organism and to initiate treatment early. Rapid strep test (RSAT) and strep culture (sometimes referred to as STCX) require proper collection technique because improper collection reduces the accuracy of the test.

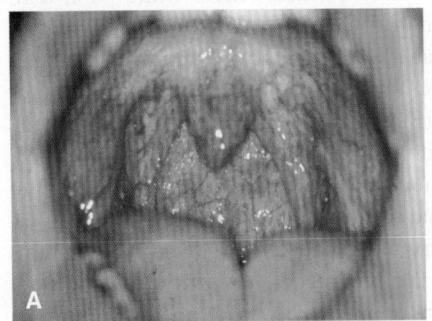 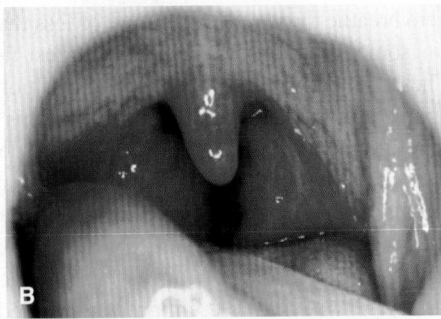

FIGURE 9-2 Pharyngitis, inflammation without exudate. **(A)** Redness and vascularity of the pillars and uvula are mild to moderate. **(B)** Redness is diffuse and intense. Each patient would probably complain of a sore throat. From Bickley, L. S., & Szilagyi, P. G. (2007). *Bates' guide to physical examination and history taking* (9th ed.). Philadelphia: Lippincott Williams & Wilkins.

Medical and Nursing Management

Viral pharyngitis is treated with supportive measures. Antibiotics will have no effect on the organism.

If a bacterial cause is suggested or demonstrated, penicillin is usually the treatment of choice in the treatment of acute pharyngitis. Nasal congestion may be relieved by short-term use of nasal sprays or medications containing ephedrine sulfate or phenylephrine hydrochloride. For a patient with a history of allergy, one of the antihistamine decongestant medications, is prescribed orally every 4 to 6 hours. Aspirin or acetaminophen is recommended for its anti-inflammatory and analgesic properties.

Treatment of chronic pharyngitis is based on relieving symptoms, avoiding exposure to irritants, and correcting any upper respiratory, pulmonary, or cardiac condition that might cause a chronic cough. For adults with chronic pharyngitis, tonsillectomy is an effective option.

Complications

Uncomplicated viral infections usually subside promptly, within 3 to 10 days after the onset. However, pharyngitis caused by more virulent bacteria, such as GAS, is a more severe illness. If left untreated, the complications can be severe and life-threatening. Complications include rhinosinusitis, otitis media, peritonsillar abscess, mastoiditis, and cervical adenitis. In rare cases, the infection may lead to bacteremia, pneumonia, meningitis, rheumatic fever, or glomerulonephritis. Acute poststreptococcal glomerulonephritis (APSGN) is a complication that follows roughly 10 days after the onset of streptococcal infection and results in temporary kidney failure. APSGN is characterized by the rapid onset of gross hematuria, edema (leading to respiratory distress and pulmonary edema), and hypertension, and is usually preceded by an episode of GAS pharyngitis or pyoderma (skin infection with pustules) (Ahn & Ingulli, 2008). Prognosis is not good for the elderly patient with other risk factors for kidney disease (Rodriguez-Iturbe & Musser, 2008).

LARYNGITIS

Laryngitis is inflammation of the larynx.

Pathophysiology

Laryngitis often occurs as a result of voice abuse or exposure to dust, chemicals, smoke, and other pollutants, or as part of a URI. It also may be caused by infection involving the vocal cords. Laryngitis is also associated with gastroesophageal reflux.

Laryngitis is very often caused by the same pathogens that cause the common cold and pharyngitis; a virus. Laryngitis is often associated with allergic rhinitis or pharyngitis. The onset of infection may be associated with exposure to sudden temperature changes, dietary deficiencies, malnutrition, or an immunosuppressed state. Viral laryngitis is common in the winter and is easily transmitted to others.

Clinical Manifestations and Assessment

Signs of acute laryngitis include hoarseness or **aphonia** (complete loss of voice) and severe cough. Other signs of acute laryngitis include sudden onset aggravated by cold dry wind. The throat feels worse in the morning and improves when the patient is indoors in a warmer climate. At times, the patient presents with a dry cough and a dry, sore throat that worsens in the evening hours. If allergies are present, the uvula will be visibly edematous. Many patients also complain of a "tickle" in the throat that is made worse by cold air or cold liquids. Chronic laryngitis is marked by persistent hoarseness.

Medical and Nursing Management

Management of acute or chronic laryngitis includes resting the voice, avoiding irritants (including smoking), resting, and inhaling cool steam or an aerosol. The majority of patients recover with conservative treatment; however, laryngitis tends to be more severe in elderly patients and may be complicated by pneumonia.

If laryngitis is part of a more extensive respiratory infection caused by a bacterial organism, or if it is severe, appropriate antibacterial therapy is instituted. For chronic laryngitis, the use of topical corticosteroids may be given by inhalation. These preparations have few systemic or long-lasting effects and may reduce local inflammatory reactions. Treatment for reflux laryngitis typically involves use of proton pump inhibitors given once daily.

NURSING PROCESS

The Patient With Upper Airway Infection

Assessment

A health history may reveal signs and symptoms of headache, sore throat, pain around the eyes and on either side of the nose, difficulty in swallowing, cough, hoarseness, fever, stuffiness, and generalized discomfort and fatigue. Determining when the symptoms began, what precipitated them, what (if anything) relieves them, and what aggravates them is part of the assessment. Inspection may reveal swelling, lesions, or asymmetry of the nose, as well as bleeding or discharge. The nurse inspects the nasal mucosa for abnormal findings such as increased redness, swelling, exudate, and nasal polyps, which may develop in chronic rhinitis. The mucosa of the nasal turbinates may also be swollen (boggy) and pale, bluish-gray. The nurse palpates the frontal and maxillary sinuses for tenderness, which suggests inflammation, and then inspects the throat by having the patient

open the mouth wide and take a deep breath. The tonsils and pharynx are inspected for abnormal findings such as redness, asymmetry, or evidence of drainage, ulceration, or enlargement. The nurse also palpates the trachea to determine the midline position in the neck and to detect any masses or deformities. The neck lymph nodes are palpated for enlargement and tenderness.

Diagnosis

Appropriate nursing diagnoses may include:

- Ineffective airway clearance related to excessive mucus production secondary to retained secretions and inflammation
- Acute pain related to upper airway irritation secondary to an infection
- Impaired verbal communication related to physiologic changes and upper airway irritation secondary to infection, swelling, hoarseness, or loss of speech.
- Deficient fluid volume related to decreased fluid intake and increased fluid loss secondary to diaphoresis associated with a fever
- Deficient knowledge regarding prevention of URIs, treatment regimen, surgical procedure, or postoperative care

Planning

The major goals for the patient may include maintenance of a patent airway, relief of pain, maintenance of effective means of communication, normal hydration, knowledge of how to prevent upper airway infections, and absence of complications.

Nursing Interventions

Maintaining a Patent Airway

An accumulation of secretions can block the airway in patients with URI. As a result, changes in the respiratory pattern occur, and the work of breathing increases to compensate for the blockage. The nurse can implement several measures to loosen thick secretions or to keep the secretions moist, so that they can be easily expectorated. Increasing fluid intake helps thin the mucus. Use of room vaporizers or steam inhalation also loosens secretions and reduces inflammation of the mucous membranes. To enhance drainage from the sinuses, the nurse instructs the patient about the best position to assume; this depends on the location of the infection or inflammation.

Promoting Comfort

URIs usually produces localized discomfort. The nurse encourages the patient to take analgesics as prescribed. Other helpful measures include topical anesthetic agents for symptomatic relief of herpes simplex blisters and sore throats, hot packs to relieve the congestion of rhinosinusitis and promote drainage, and warm-water gargles or

irrigations to relieve the pain of a sore throat. The benefits of this treatment depend on the degree of heat that is applied. The nurse encourages rest to relieve the generalized discomfort and fever that accompany many upper URIs.

Promoting Communication

URIs may result in hoarseness or loss of speech. The nurse instructs the patient to refrain from speaking as much as possible. Additional strain on the vocal cords may delay full return of the voice. The nurse encourages the patient and family to use alternative forms of communication, such as a memo pad.

Encouraging Fluid Intake

In URIs, the work of breathing and the respiratory rate increase as inflammation and secretions develop. This may increase insensible fluid loss. Fever further increases the metabolic rate, diaphoresis, and fluid loss. Sore throat, malaise, and fever may interfere with a patient's willingness to eat and drink. The nurse provides a list of easily ingested foods to increase caloric intake during the acute phase of illness. These include soups, pudding, yogurt, cottage cheese, high-protein drinks, and popsicles. The nurse encourages the patient to drink 2 to 3 L of fluid per day during the acute stage of airway infection, unless contraindicated, to thin the secretions and promote drainage. Liquids (hot or cold) may be soothing, depending on the disorder. In severe situations, IV fluids may be needed.

Preventing Infection

Prevention of most URIs is difficult because of the many potential causes. But because most URIs are transmitted by hand-to-hand contact, the nurse teaches the patient and family techniques to minimize the spread of infection to others, including frequent handwashing. The nurse advises the patient to avoid exposure to people who are at risk for serious illness including elderly adults, immunosuppressed people, and those with chronic health problems. The nurse may advise elderly patients and those at increased risk from a respiratory infection to consider an annual influenza and pneumococcal vaccine as recommended by the primary care provider (PCP). A follow-up appointment with the PCP may be indicated for patients with compromised health status to ensure that the respiratory infection has resolved.

Monitoring and Managing Potential Complications

Because most patients with URIs are managed at home, patients and their families must be instructed to monitor for signs and symptoms and to seek immediate medical care if the patient's condition does not improve or if the patient's physical status appears to be worsening. Symptoms that require further attention include persistent or high fever, increasing shortness of breath, confusion, and increasing weakness and malaise. Potential complications include sepsis, meningitis or brain abscess, and peritonsillar abscess, otitis media, or rhinosinusitis.

Sepsis and meningitis may occur in patients with compromised immune status or in those with an overwhelming bacterial infection. The nurse explains to the patient that fever, severe headache, and **nuchal rigidity** (stiffness of the neck/inability to bend the neck) are signs of potential complications. The patient with sepsis requires expert care to treat the infection, stabilize vital signs, and prevent or treat septicemia and shock. Deterioration of the patient's condition necessitates intensive care measures (e.g., hemodynamic monitoring and administration of vasoactive medications, IV fluids, nutritional support, corticosteroids) to monitor the patient's status and to support the patient's vital signs. High doses of antibiotics may be administered to treat the causative organism. The nurse's role is to monitor the patient's vital signs, hemodynamic status, and laboratory values; administer needed treatment; alleviate the patient's physical discomfort; and provide explanations, teaching, and emotional support to the patient and family. Refer to Chapter 54 for management of septic shock.

The patient and family are instructed about the signs and symptoms of otitis media and rhinosinusitis (periorbital edema, severe facial pain on palpation) and about the importance of follow-up with the PCP to ensure adequate evaluation and treatment of these conditions.

Potential for airway compromise is possible in severe pharyngitis. Symptoms that require provider referral include dyspnea, drooling, inability to swallow, and inability to fully open the mouth. The skin should be examined for possible rash, because acute pharyngitis may precede some other communicable diseases (e.g., rubella). For the patient with laryngitis, the signs and symptoms that require contacting the health care provider include loss of voice with sore throat that makes swallowing saliva difficult, hemoptysis, and noisy respirations.

Evaluation

Expected outcomes include:

1. Maintains a patent airway by managing secretions:
   a. Reports decreased congestion.
   b. Assumes best position to facilitate drainage of secretions.
   c. Uses self-care measures appropriately and consistently to manage secretions during the acute phase of illness.
2. Reports relief of pain and discomfort using pain intensity scale:
   a. Uses comfort measures: Analgesics, hot packs, gargles, rest.
   b. Demonstrates adequate oral hygiene.
   c. Free of pain in ears, sinuses, and throat.
3. Demonstrates ability to communicate needs, wants, level of comfort.
4. Maintains adequate fluid and nutrition intake.

5. Utilizes strategies to prevent upper airway infections:
   a. Demonstrates hand hygiene technique.
   b. Identifies the value of the influenza and pneumococcal vaccines.
6. Absence of complications:
   a. No signs of sepsis: Fever, hypotension, deterioration of cognitive status
   b. Vital signs and hemodynamic status normal
   c. No evidence of neurologic involvement
   d. No signs of development of brain abscess
   e. Resolution of URI without development of otitis media or rhinosinusitis

OBSTRUCTION AND TRAUMA OF THE UPPER RESPIRATORY AIRWAY

OBSTRUCTION DURING SLEEP

Obstructive sleep apnea syndrome (OSA) is a disorder characterized by recurrent episodes of upper airway obstruction and a reduction in ventilation. It is defined as cessation of breathing (**apnea**) during sleep, usually caused by repetitive upper airway obstruction. It interferes with the person's ability to obtain adequate rest and ultimately can affect memory, learning, and decision making. As many as 18 million Americans suffer from sleep apnea (Patil, Schneider, Schwartz et al., 2007).

Various definitions of OSA—also referred to as obstructive sleep apnea/hypopnea syndrome (OSAHS) or upper respiratory resistance syndrome (UARS)—exist, leading to overestimation of the prevalence of this syndrome.

Pathophysiology

OSA is a disorder characterized of recurrent episodes of upper airway obstruction, causing a reduction in ventilation followed by frequent arousals and periodic oxyhemoglobin desaturations during sleep (Patil et al., 2007). OSA is defined as the presence of at least five obstructive events (apneas and hypopneas [slow or shallow breathing]) per hour during sleep (Basner, 2007). Repetitive apneic events result in hypoxia and hypercapnia, which trigger a sympathetic response (increased heart rate and decreased tone and contractility of smooth muscle). An obstruction may be caused by mechanical factors such as a reduced diameter of the upper airway or dynamic changes in the upper airway during sleep.

Patients with OSA have a higher prevalence of hypertension and an increased risk of myocardial infarction, stroke, and death (Basner, 2007). In patients with underlying cardiovascular disease, the nocturnal **hypoxemia** may predispose to arrhythmias. Patients who have a diagnosis of heart failure and who have untreated OSA are at increased risk of

death (Wang, Parker, Newton et al., 2007). OSA can also increase insulin resistance and other metabolic changes that can increase the risk of vascular disease (McArdle, Hillman, Beilin et al., 2007). OSA is more prevalent in people with coronary artery disease, congestive heart failure, metabolic syndrome, and type 2 diabetes, suggesting that screening for OSA is indicated in patients with these pathologies (Patil et al., 2007).

Risk Factors

Sleep apnea is more prevalent in men, especially those who are older and overweight. The major risk factor for OSA is obesity around the neck that narrows and compresses the upper airway. The elderly have a higher prevalence of OSA (Strohl, 2007). Other associated factors include alteration in the upper airway, such as structural changes (e.g., tonsillar hypertrophy, abnormal posterior positioning of one or both jaws, excessive fat deposits in the lateral walls of the pharynx, and craniofacial structural abnormalities) that contribute to the collapsibility of the airway and increase the risk of sleep apnea.

Clinical Manifestations and Assessment

OSA is characterized by frequent and loud snoring with breathing cessation for 10 seconds or longer, for at least five episodes per hour, followed by awakening abruptly with a loud snort as the blood oxygen level drops. Classic signs and symptoms of OSA are presented in Box 9-1. Symptoms typically progress with increases in weight, aging, and during the transition to menopause (Patil et al., 2007).

Several screening tools/questionnaires are available to assess the frequency and severity of symptoms (Berry, 2008). The diagnosis of sleep apnea is based on clinical symptoms plus polysomnographic findings (sleep study).

BOX 9-1   **Focused Assessment**

Obstructive Sleep Apnea (OSA)

Be alert for the following signs and symptoms:
- Excessive daytime sleepiness
- Frequent nocturnal awakening
- Insomnia
- Loud snoring
- Morning headaches
- Intellectual deterioration
- Personality changes, irritability
- Impotence
- Systemic hypertension
- Arrhythmias
- Pulmonary hypertension, cor pulmonale
- Polycythemia
- Enuresis

This overnight sleep study measures multiple physiologic signals related to sleep (electroencephalogram [EEG], electrocardiogram [ECG], and airflow), measuring oxyhemoglobin saturation, brain activity, eye movement, thoracic muscle activity, body position, respiratory rate, heart rate, cardiac arrhythmias, chest impedance, and airflow (Patil et al., 2007; Berry, 2008).

Medical Management

Treatments are varied but include weight loss and avoidance of alcohol and hypnotic medications initially (Tierney et al., 2007). Weight loss reduces the number of apneas and hypopneas per hour of total sleep time as measured by the apnea-hypopnea index (AHI) (Berry, 2008; Patil et al., 2007). Oral appliances designed to reposition the mandible or tongue may be useful in select patients. These devices are not very beneficial in the elderly patient, as full dentition is required (Weaver & Chasens, 2007).

Noninvasive Positive-Pressure Ventilation

In more severe cases of OSA involving hypoxemia with severe carbon dioxide retention (hypercapnia), the treatment includes continuous positive airway pressure (CPAP) or bilevel positive airway pressure (BiPAP) therapy with supplemental oxygen via nasal cannula. Patients are considered candidates for noninvasive ventilation if they have acute or chronic respiratory failure, acute pulmonary edema, chronic obstructive pulmonary disease (COPD), chronic heart failure, or OSA. The device also may be used at home to improve tissue oxygenation and to rest the respiratory muscles while the patient sleeps at night.

CPAP provides positive pressure to the airways throughout the respiratory cycle preventing collapse (Basner, 2007). An air pressure source (special fan) generates the air flow, generally ranging from 20 to 60 L/min (Basner, 2007). It is used with a leak-proof mask to keep alveoli open, thereby preventing respiratory failure. CPAP is the most effective treatment for OSA because the positive pressure acts as a splint, keeping the upper airway and trachea open during sleep. To use CPAP, the patient must be breathing independently.

BiPAP ventilation offers independent control of inspiratory and expiratory pressures while providing pressure-support ventilation. It delivers two levels of positive airway pressure provided via a nasal or oral mask, nasal pillow, or mouthpiece with a tight seal and a portable ventilator. Each inspiration can be initiated either by the patient or by the machine (programmed backup rate). The backup rate ensures that the patient will receive a set number of breaths per minute. BiPAP is most often used for patients who require ventilatory assistance at night, such as those with severe COPD or sleep apnea. Tolerance is variable; BiPAP usually is most successful with highly motivated patients.

BOX 9-2

Nursing Research

Bridging the Gap to Evidence-Based Practice

Determining Whether to Use Continuous Positive Airway Pressure

Ayow, T.M., Paquet, F., Dallaire, J., Purden, M., & Champagne, K.A. (2009). Factors influencing the use and nonuse of continuous positive airway pressure therapy: A comparative case study. *Rehabilitation Nursing, 34*(6), 230–236.

Purpose

Continuous positive airway pressure (CPAP) is the treatment of choice for patients with obstructive sleep apnea (OSA). The rate of compliance of CPAP therapy among adults with OSA is not optimal despite the proven efficacy of this treatment modality. There is evidence that psychosocial and physical factors are contributory to this data.

Design

The authors conducted a comprehensive literature review of the qualitative evidence of the psychological variables associated with CPAP use. Hypochondriacal, claustrophobic and depressive personality traits have been associated with nonadherence with CPAP therapy. Patient psychological variables such as personal health value, health locus of control, and self-efficacy could be predictive of success of CPAP use. Physical problems, such as age and gender, may also be predictive of nonuse. In this study, the authors recruited a purposive sample of eight patients from a sleep disorder clinic at a tertiary health center—four users of CPAP and four nonusers. Inclusion criteria for patients were (1) adult diagnosis with OSA, (2) prescription for CPAP therapy, and (3) ability to speak and read English. Interviews were conducted using a qualitative descriptive design, with recording to prevent transcription errors.

Findings

Using a comparative approach in this case study, several perceived physical, psychological, and social factors were identified that facilitated and impeded CPAP use. Factors influencing use of CPAP included physical benefits of more energy, improved fitness, weight loss,

and reduction of comorbidities such as gastroesophageal reflux disease (GERD) and diabetes. Factors influencing nonuse were physical discomfort of the mask. Psychological factors for CPAP use centered on feelings around the ease of device use, consideration for sleep partner, and not worrying about daytime sleepiness affecting work. Nonusers related feeling "like a monster" with the device strapped to their face, and not being able to sleep with device on as it seems to be intrusive. Social comparison (the relating of features of one's self to others) and stigmas are two important issues found in this study to be influential on patients' decisions to use or abandon CPAP therapy. Social comparison is a means for individuals to reduce uncertainty and validate their attitudes, and is described as directional. *Downward comparison* is thought to compare self to others that are worse off and is a method of self-enhancement. *Upward comparison* is looking at others as being better off and aspiring to be more like them (i.e., those persons without OSA). The stigma of a diagnosis of OSA and CPAP therapy may also subject patients to negative comparison, ridicule, and rejection. This study has shown that the way patients feel about themselves and are viewed by others is very important and influences how they will successfully manage or abandon CPAP treatment for OSA.

Nursing Implications

Strategies for assessment and management of physical, psychological, and social factors of patients with OSA can impact the patients' success or failure at CPAP therapy. When teaching patients about OSA and CPAP, it is important to include people close to the patient, to help create an accepting social environment and to minimize stigma. Providing for open communication about feelings regarding the device and its effect on body image are important. In addition, support groups have been shown to be successful in providing practical advice and information about adaptations in incorporating CPAP into a healthy lifestyle and perseverance with treatment.

Problems with CPAP or BiPAP therapy are common. Commonly reported adverse effects of CPAP include skin irritations, pain, rash, or breakdown at the mask contact points (usually the bridge of the nose). Dryness or irritation of the nasal and pharyngeal membranes, nasal congestion, and eye irritation from leakage from the mask are also reported (Basner, 2007). Proper fitting of the mask should allow for therapy to continue. Although these treatments are effective in managing OSA, patient compliance with treatment continues to be a major concern (Lin, Prasad, Pan

et al., 2007). Nursing research on the factors (physical, psychological, and social) influencing the use and nonuse of continuous positive airway pressure therapy is described in Box 9-2.

Surgical Management

Surgical procedures (e.g., tonsillectomy or **uvulopalato-pharyngoplasty** [termed UPPP, the surgical resection of pharyngeal soft tissue and uvula]) may be performed to correct the obstruction, should the airway be in jeopardy or the

patient has been unsuccessful with CPAP therapy. Effective in about 40% of patients, it is more effective in eliminating snoring than in eliminating apnea (Li, 2009). Nasal septoplasty may be performed for anatomic nasal septal deformities. Tracheostomy relieves upper airway obstruction but has many adverse effects, including speech difficulties and increased risk of infections. These procedures, as well as other maxillofacial surgeries, are reserved for patients with life-threatening arrhythmias or severe disabilities who have not responded to conventional therapy (Tierney et al., 2007).

Pharmacologic Therapy

Although medications are not generally recommended for OSA, modafinil (Provigil) has been shown to reduce daytime sleepiness (Valentino & Foldvary-Schaefer, 2007). Protriptyline (Triptil) given at bedtime may increase the respiratory drive and improve upper airway muscle tone. Patients must understand that these medications are not a substitute for CPAP or BiPAP therapy. Administration of low-flow nasal oxygen at night can help relieve hypoxemia in some patients but has little effect on the frequency or severity of apnea. Further study on the effectiveness of pharmacologic therapy is needed.

Nursing Management

The patient with OSA may not recognize the potential consequences of the disorder. The nurse explains the disorder and relates symptoms (daytime sleepiness, morning headaches, heartburn, insomnia, snoring) to the underlying disorder. The nurse also instructs the patient and family about treatments, including weight loss, avoiding alcohol and sedative medications, and the correct and safe use of prescribed therapies, CPAP, BiPAP, and oxygen therapy.

EPISTAXIS (NOSEBLEED)

Epistaxis, a hemorrhage from the nose, is caused by the rupture of tiny, distended vessels in the mucous membrane of any area of the nose. Most commonly, the site is the anterior septum, where three major blood vessels enter the nasal cavity. Several risk factors may be associated with epistaxis and are described in Box 9-3.

Medical Management

Management of epistaxis depends on its cause and the location of the bleeding site. Initial treatment includes applying direct pressure. The patient sits upright with the head tilted forward to prevent swallowing and aspiration of blood and is directed to pinch the soft outer portion of the nose against the midline septum for 5 or 10 minutes continuously. If this measure is unsuccessful, the nose must be examined using good illumination and suction to determine the site of bleeding. Cotton applicators soaked in a vasoconstricting solution (i.e., epinephrine, ephedrine, cocaine) may be inserted into the nose to reduce the blood flow. Visible bleeding sites may

---

> **BOX 9-3** | **Risk Factors for Epistaxis**
>
> - Local infections (vestibulitis, rhinitis, sinusitis)
> - Systemic infections (scarlet fever, malaria)
> - Drying of nasal mucous membranes
> - Nasal inhalation of illicit drugs (e.g., cocaine)
> - Trauma (digital trauma as in picking the nose; blunt trauma; fracture; forceful nose blowing)
> - Arteriosclerosis
> - Hypertension
> - Tumor (sinus or nasopharynx)
> - Thrombocytopenia
> - Use of aspirin
> - Liver disease
> - Osler-Weber-Rendu (hereditary hemorrhagic telangiectasia)

---

be cauterized with silver nitrate or electrocautery (high-frequency electrical current). A supplemental patch of Surgicel or Gelfoam may be used (Tierney et al., 2007). If the origin of the bleeding cannot be identified, the nose may be packed with gauze impregnated with petrolatum jelly or antibiotic ointment. The packing may remain in place for 48 hours or up to 5 or 6 days if necessary to control bleeding. Antibiotics may be prescribed because of the risk of iatrogenic sinusitis and toxic shock syndrome.

Nursing Management

The nurse monitors the patient's vital signs, assists in the control of bleeding, and provides tissues and an emesis basin to allow the patient to expectorate any excess blood. The nurse continuously assesses the patient's airway and breathing, as well as vital signs. On rare occasions, a patient with significant hemorrhage requires IV infusions of crystalloid solutions (normal saline) as well as cardiac and pulse oximetry monitoring.

Once the bleeding is controlled, the nurse instructs the patient to avoid vigorous exercise for several days and to avoid hot or spicy foods and tobacco, as they may cause vasodilation and an increased risk of rebleeding. Discharge teaching includes reviewing ways to prevent epistaxis: avoiding forceful nose blowing, straining, high altitudes, and nasal trauma. Adequate humidification may prevent drying of the nasal passages. The nurse instructs the patient how to apply direct pressure to the nose in case of a recurrent nosebleed. If recurrent bleeding cannot be stopped, the patient is instructed to seek additional medical attention.

NASAL OBSTRUCTION

The passage of air through the nostrils is frequently obstructed by a deviation of the nasal septum, hypertrophy of the turbinate bones, or the presence of nasal polyps. Chronic nasal congestion forces the patient to breathe through the

mouth, producing dryness of the oral mucosa and problems including persistent dry, cracked lips. Patients with chronic nasal congestion often suffer from sleep deprivation due to difficulty maintaining an adequate airway while lying flat and during sleep.

Medical Management

The treatment of nasal obstruction requires the removal of the obstruction, followed by measures to treat chronic infection. Measures to reduce or alleviate nasal obstruction include nonsurgical as well as surgical techniques. Commonly used medications include nasal corticosteroids. Treatment with nasal corticosteroids for 1 to 3 months is beneficial in treatment of small polyps, avoiding surgical intervention. Additional medications may include antibiotics for the treatment of underlying infection or antihistamines for management of allergies. Hypertrophied turbinates may be treated by applying an astringent agent to shrink them. A more aggressive approach in treating nasal obstruction caused by turbinate hypertrophy involves surgical reduction of the hypertrophy, a procedure known as functional rhinoplasty.

Nursing Management

Most of these surgical procedures are performed on an outpatient basis. Postoperatively, the nurse elevates the head of the bed to promote drainage and to alleviate discomfort from edema. Frequent oral hygiene is encouraged to overcome dryness caused by breathing through the mouth. Before discharge, the patient is instructed to avoid blowing the nose with force during the postoperative recovery period. The patient is also instructed about the signs and symptoms of bleeding and infection and when to contact the provider.

FRACTURES OF THE NOSE

Nasal fracture is the most common fracture in the body. Fractures of the nose usually result from a direct assault. Nasal fractures may affect the ascending process of the maxilla and the septum. The torn mucous membrane results in a nosebleed. In a series of complications, the patient could ultimately experience a hematoma, infection, abscess, and a vascular/septic necrosis. However, as a rule, serious consequences usually do not occur.

Clinical Manifestations and Assessment

The signs and symptoms of a nasal fracture are pain, bleeding from the nose externally and internally into the pharynx, swelling of the soft tissues adjacent to the nose, periorbital ecchymosis, nasal obstruction, and deformity. The patient's nose may have an asymmetric appearance that may not be obvious until the edema subsides.

The nose is examined internally to rule out the possibility that the injury may be complicated by a fracture of the nasal septum and a submucosal septal hematoma. Intranasal examination is performed to rule out septal hematoma (Tierney et al., 2007). Clear fluid draining from either nostril suggests a fracture of the cribriform plate with leakage of cerebrospinal fluid (CSF). Because CSF contains glucose, it can readily be differentiated from nasal mucus by means of a dipstick. Refer to Chapter 45 for details of CSF leaks.

> **NURSING ALERT**
>
> *If CSF is suspected, the patient is instructed not to cough or blow the nose. If the patient has to sneeze, do so with an open mouth; the head of bed should be elevated and nothing should be inserted into the nares. The primary concern of CSF rhinorrhea (leakage of CSF via the nares) is the complication of meningitis.*

Careful inspection or palpation discloses any deviations of the bone or disruptions of the nasal cartilages. An X-ray may reveal displacement of the fractured bones and may help rule out extension of the fracture into the skull.

Medical Management

Any bleeding is controlled with the use of packing. For the patient who has sustained traumatic force to break the nose or any facial bone, the possibility of a cervical spine fracture must be considered. If suspected, stabilize the cervical spine and log roll patient if turning is required. Uncomplicated nasal fractures may be treated initially with analgesic agents, use of ice to reduce swelling, and ENT follow-up.

Treatment of nasal fractures is aimed at restoring nasal function and returning the aesthetic appearance of the nose to baseline. Reduction of the fracture is performed as soon as possible. If edema is too severe to reduce the fraction immediately, it is performed within 3 to 7 days. Fractures that heal but are misaligned may require surgical intervention, such as rhinoplasty, to reshape the external appearance of the nose. In patients who develop a septal hematoma, the provider will drain the hematoma through a small incision. Antibiotic coverage is expected after septal hematoma evacuation. A septal hematoma that is not drained can lead to permanent deformity of the nose.

Nursing Management

Immediately after the fracture, the nurse applies ice and encourages the patient to keep the head elevated. The nurse instructs the patient to apply ice packs to the nose for 20 minutes, four times each day, to decrease swelling. The packing inserted to stop the bleeding may be uncomfortable and unpleasant, and obstruction of the nasal passages by the packing forces the patient to breathe through the mouth. This in turn causes the oral mucous membranes to become dry. Mouth rinses help to moisten the mucous membranes and to reduce the odor and taste of dried blood in the oropharynx and nasopharynx. Use

of analgesic agents, such as acetaminophen, or of NSAIDs, such as ibuprofen or naproxen, is encouraged. The nurse reminds the patient to avoid sports activities, especially contact sports, for 6 weeks.

LARYNGEAL OBSTRUCTION

Obstruction of the larynx caused by edema is a serious, often fatal, condition. The larynx contains a narrow space between the vocal cords (glottis), through which air must pass. Swelling of the laryngeal mucous membranes may close off the opening tightly, leading to life-threatening hypoxia or suffocation.

Pathophysiology

Edema of the glottis occurs rarely in patients with acute laryngitis, occasionally in patients with urticaria, and more frequently in patients with severe inflammation of the throat, as in scarlet fever. It is an occasional but usually preventable cause of death in severe anaphylaxis (angioedema). Hereditary angioedema (HAE) is also characterized by episodes of life-threatening laryngeal edema. Laryngeal edema in people with HAE can occur at any age, although young adults are at greatest risk.

Risk Factors

Risk factors for laryngeal obstruction are provided in Box 9-4. Foreign bodies frequently are aspirated into the pharynx, the larynx, or the trachea.

Clinical Manifestations and Assessment

The foreign objects obstruct the air passages and cause difficulty in breathing, hoarseness, and stridor, which may lead to asphyxia; and later, they may be drawn farther down, entering the bronchi or a bronchial branch and causing symptoms of irritation, such as a croupy cough, expectoration of blood or mucus, or labored breathing. The patient may demonstrate lowered oxygen saturation; however, normal oxygen

---

BOX 9-4	**Risk Factors for Laryngeal Obstruction**

- History of allergies that may result in anaphylaxis
- Inhalation/ingestion of foreign body (balloon fragments, chewing gum, drug packets)
- Heavy alcohol consumption or tobacco use (causing a tumor)
- Family history of airway problems (suggests angio-edema)
- Use of ACE inhibitors
- Recent throat pain or fever (suggests infectious process)
- History of surgery or previous tracheostomy (suggests possible subglottic stenosis)

---

saturation should not be interpreted as a sign that the obstruction is not significant. Use of accessory muscles to maximize airflow may occur and is often manifested by retractions in the neck or abdomen during inspirations. Patients who demonstrate these symptoms may need ventilatory support (i.e., mechanical ventilation or positive-pressure ventilation).

A thorough history can be very useful to the health care team in diagnosing and treating the patient with a laryngeal obstruction. The nurse obtains a history from the patient or family about alcohol or tobacco consumption, current medications, family history of airway problems, recent infections, pain or fever, dental pain or poor dentition, and any previous surgeries or trauma. Emergency measures to secure the patient's airway should not be delayed to obtain a history or perform tests. The patient's clinical presentation and X-ray findings confirm the diagnosis of laryngeal obstruction.

Medical and Nursing Management

Medical management is based on the initial evaluation of the patient and the need to ensure a patent airway. If the airway is obstructed by a foreign body and signs of asphyxia are apparent, immediate treatment is necessary. Frequently, if the foreign body has lodged in the pharynx and can be visualized, the finger can dislodge it. If the obstruction is in the larynx or the trachea, the clinician or other rescuer tries the subdiaphragmatic abdominal thrust (Heimlich) maneuver. If all efforts are unsuccessful, an immediate tracheotomy is necessary. If the obstruction is caused by edema resulting from an allergic reaction, treatment may include administration of subcutaneous epinephrine and a corticosteroid (see Chapter 38). Continuous pulse oximetry is essential. Box 9-5 describes nursing management of an upper airway obstruction.

CANCER OF THE LARYNX

Cancer of the larynx is a malignant tumor in and around the larynx (voice box). Squamous cell carcinoma is the most common form of cancer of the larynx (95%). Approximately 55% of patients with laryngeal cancer present with involved lymph nodes at time of diagnosis (DeVita, Hellman, & Rosenberg, 2008).

Carcinogens associated with laryngeal cancer include tobacco (smoke, smokeless) and alcohol and their combined effects. Occupational or environmental exposure to asbestos, wood dust, coal dust, steel dust, cement dust, tar products, leather, formaldehyde, and iron compounds and fumes have also been implicated. Other contributing factors include straining the voice, chronic laryngitis, nutritional deficiencies (riboflavin), family predisposition, and a weakened immune system.

Metastatic disease from the true vocal cords is very rare, because they are devoid of lymph nodes. The prognosis for

BOX 9-5   Management of Upper Airway Obstruction

Adequate ventilation is dependent on free movement of air through the upper and lower airways. Maintaining a patent (open) airway is achieved through meticulous airway management, whether in an emergency situation, such as airway obstruction, or in long-term management, as in caring for a patient with an endotracheal or a tracheostomy tube. The patient with an altered level of consciousness from any cause is at risk for upper airway obstruction because of loss of the protective reflexes (cough and swallowing) and loss of the tone of the pharyngeal muscles, which causes the tongue to fall back and block the airway.

The nurse makes rapid observations to assess for signs and symptoms of upper airway obstruction; assessing the patient's level of consciousness (LOC), inspecting the chest for movement and use or retraction of accessory muscles, noting skin color and any obvious signs of deformity or obstruction of the airway (trauma, food, teeth, vomitus). The nurse should palpate the trachea for midline location and look for any specific areas of tenderness, fracture, or subcutaneous emphysema (crepitus). Auscultation is performed to assess for audible air movement, stridor (inspiratory crowing sound), or wheezing (high-pitched musical sound) that may be present over the lower trachea and bilaterally in all lobes. As soon as an upper airway obstruction is identified, the nurse takes the following emergency measures:

Clearing the Airway

- Hyperextend the patient's neck by placing one hand on the forehead and placing the fingers of the other hand underneath the jaw and lifting upward and forward. This action pulls the tongue away from the back of the pharynx. Note that this position is used **only** if cervical spine is free of injury.

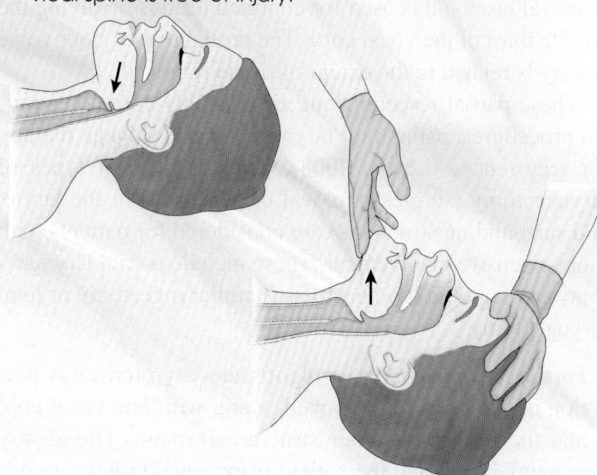

Assess the patient by observing the chest and listening and feeling for the movement of air.

- Use a cross-finger technique to open the mouth and observe for obvious obstructions, such as secretions, blood clots, or food particles.
- If no passage of air is detected, apply five quick sharp

abdominal thrusts just below the xiphoid process to expel the obstruction. Repeat this procedure until the obstruction is expelled.

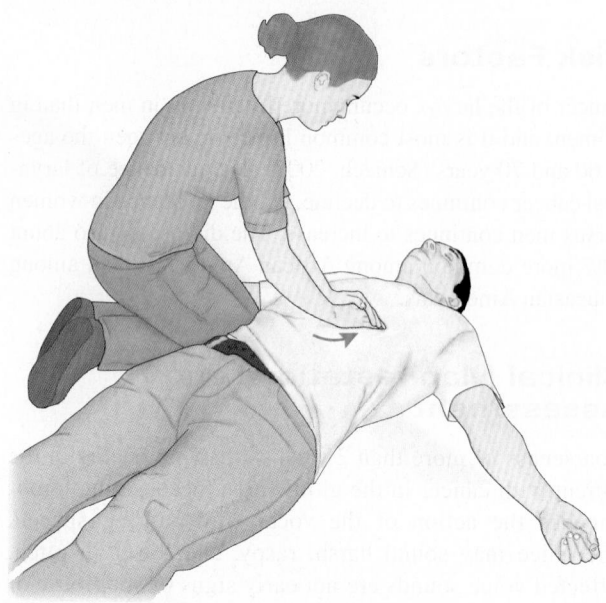

- After the obstruction is expelled, roll the patient as a unit onto the side for recovery.
- When the obstruction is relieved, if the patient can breathe spontaneously but not cough, swallow, or gag, insert an oral or nasopharyngeal airway.

Bag and Mask Resuscitation

- Use a resuscitation bag and mask if assisted ventilation is required.
- Apply the mask to the patient's face and create a seal by pressing the thumb of the nondominant hand on the bridge of the nose and the index finger on the chin. Using the rest of the fingers on that hand, pull on the chin and the angle of the mandible to maintain the head in extension. Use the dominant hand to inflate the lungs by squeezing the bag to its full volume.

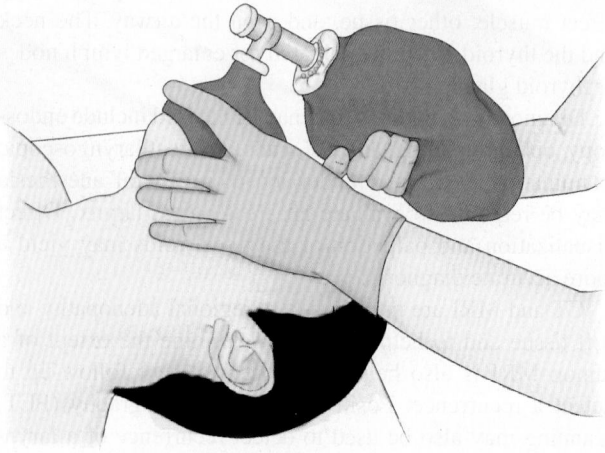

patients who have small laryngeal cancers without evidence of spread to the lymph nodes is about 75% to 95%. Recurrence occurs usually within the first 2 to 3 years after diagnosis. The presence of disease after 5 years is very often secondary to a new primary malignancy.

Risk Factors

Cancer of the larynx occurs more frequently in men than in women, and it is most common in people between the ages of 60 and 70 years (Schiech, 2007). The incidence of laryngeal cancer continues to decline, but the incidence in women versus men continues to increase. The disease is also about 50% more common among African Americans than among Caucasian Americans.

Clinical Manifestations and Assessment

Hoarseness of more than 2 weeks' duration occurs in the patient with cancer in the glottic area, because the tumor impedes the action of the vocal cords during speech. The voice may sound harsh, raspy, and lower in pitch. Affected voice sounds are not early signs of subglottic or supraglottic cancer. The patient may complain of a persistent cough or sore throat and pain and burning in the throat, especially when consuming hot liquids or citrus juices. A lump may be felt in the neck. Later symptoms include **dysphagia**, dyspnea (difficulty breathing), unilateral nasal obstruction or discharge, persistent hoarseness, persistent ulceration, and foul breath. Cervical lymph adenopathy, unintentional weight loss, a general debilitated state, and pain radiating to the ear may occur with metastasis.

An initial assessment includes a complete history and physical examination of the head and neck. An indirect laryngoscopy, using a flexible endoscope, is initially performed by the otolaryngologist to visually evaluate the pharynx, larynx, and possible tumor. Mobility of the vocal cords is assessed; if normal movement is limited, the growth may affect muscle, other tissue, and even the airway. The neck and the thyroid gland are palpated for enlarged lymph nodes or thyroid gland.

Diagnostic procedures that may be utilized include endoscopy, optical imaging, and CT scans. A direct laryngoscopic examination performed under local or general anesthesia may be required to evaluate all areas of the larynx. Direct visualization and palpation of the vocal folds may yield a more accurate diagnosis.

CT and MRI are used to assess regional adenopathy and soft tissue and to help stage and determine the extent of a tumor. MRI is also helpful in post-treatment follow-up to detect a recurrence. Positron emission tomography (PET) scanning may also be used to detect recurrence of a laryngeal tumor after treatment.

Medical Management

The goals of treatment of laryngeal cancer include cure, preservation of safe, effective swallowing, preservation of useful voice, and avoidance of permanent tracheostomy (Tierney et al., 2007). Treatment options include surgery, radiation therapy, and chemotherapy. The prognosis depends on a variety of factors: tumor stage, the patient's gender and age, and pathologic features of the tumor, including the grade and depth of infiltration. The treatment plan also depends on whether this is an initial diagnosis or a recurrence.

Surgery and radiation therapy are both effective methods in the early stages of cancer of the larynx. Chemotherapy traditionally has been used for recurrence or metastatic disease. It has also been used more recently in conjunction with radiation therapy, to avoid a total laryngectomy, or preoperatively, to shrink a tumor before surgery.

Surgical Management

Surgical management depends largely on the stage of the disease. Complete removal of the larynx (total **laryngectomy**) can provide the desired cure, but it also leaves the patient with significant loss of the natural voice and the need to breathe through a stoma created in the lower neck. The stoma is a permanent opening into the trachea. Several different procedures are available that can offer voice-sparing results while achieving a positive cure rate for the patient who has an early laryngeal carcinoma. These procedures include vocal cord stripping and cordectomy. Vocal cord stripping involves removal of the mucosa of the edge of the cord using an operating microscope. It is used to treat dysplasia, hyperkeratosis, and leukoplakia and is often the curative treatment for this classification of lesions. A cordectomy is an excision of the vocal cord (cordectomy) performed via transoral laser and is used for confined lesions involving the middle third of the vocal cord. The probability of poor voice quality is related to the extent of tissue removed.

These partial resections are increasingly common surgical procedures, using total laryngectomy as salvage therapy for recurrences (Lewis, 2008). Several different types of laryngectomy (surgical removal of part or all of the larynx and surrounding structures) are considered for patients with more extensive involvement. These include partial laryngectomy, supraglottic laryngectomy, hemilaryngectomy or total laryngectomy.

- *Partial laryngectomy* (laryngofissure–thyrotomy): A portion of the larynx is removed, along with one vocal cord and the tumor; all other structures remain. The airway remains intact, and the patient is expected to have no difficulty swallowing. The voice quality may change, or the patient may sound hoarse. It is associated with a high cure rate.
- *Supraglottic laryngectomy*: A voice-sparing operation; the hyoid bone, glottis, and false cords are removed. The true vocal cords, cricoid cartilage, and trachea remain intact.

A tracheostomy is left in place until the glottic airway is established. Postoperative irradiation may be indicated. The quality of the voice may change.

- *Hemilaryngectomy*: The thyroid cartilage of the larynx is split in the midline of the neck, and the portion of the vocal cord (one true cord and one false cord) is removed with the tumor. Some change may occur in the voice quality. The voice may be rough, raspy, and hoarse and have limited projection. The airway and swallowing remain intact.
- *Total laryngectomy*: A complete removal of the larynx, including the hyoid bone, epiglottis, cricoid cartilage, and two or three rings of the trachea. The tongue, pharyngeal walls, and trachea are preserved. This procedure is performed for advanced laryngeal cancer. Results in permanent loss of the voice and a change in the airway.

Surgery for laryngeal cancer is more difficult when the lesion involves the midline structures or both vocal cords. With or without neck dissection, a total laryngectomy requires a permanent tracheal stoma (Fig. 9-3) because the larynx that provides the protective sphincter is no longer present. The tracheal stoma prevents the aspiration of food and fluid into the lower respiratory tract. The patient will have no voice but will have normal swallowing. A total laryngectomy changes the manner in which airflow is used for breathing and speaking, as depicted in Figure 9-4. Patients who have this procedure require alternatives to normal speech.

Complications that may occur include a salivary leak, wound infection from the development of a pharyngocutaneous fistula, stomal stenosis, and dysphagia secondary to pharyngeal and cervical esophageal stricture. Advances in surgical techniques for treating laryngeal cancer may minimize the cosmetic and functional deficits previously seen with total laryngectomy. Some microlaryngeal surgery can be performed endoscopically. Many patients who have undergone a total laryngectomy report a good quality of life overall (Woodard, Oplatek, & Petruzzelli, 2007).

Radiation Therapy

The goal of radiation therapy is to eradicate the cancer and preserve the function of the larynx. The decision to use radiation therapy is based on several factors, including the staging of the tumor and the patient's overall health status, lifestyle (including occupation), and personal preference. Early-stage vocal cord tumors are initially treated with irradiation. One of the benefits of radiation therapy is that patients retain a near-normal voice. A few develop chondritis (inflammation of the cartilage) or stenosis; a small number may later require laryngectomy. Radiation therapy may also be used preoperatively to reduce the tumor size. Radiation therapy is combined with surgery in advanced laryngeal cancer as adjunctive therapy to surgery or chemotherapy and as a palliative measure.

Advances in research and treatment of these tumors with surgery, chemotherapy, and radiation therapy have improved

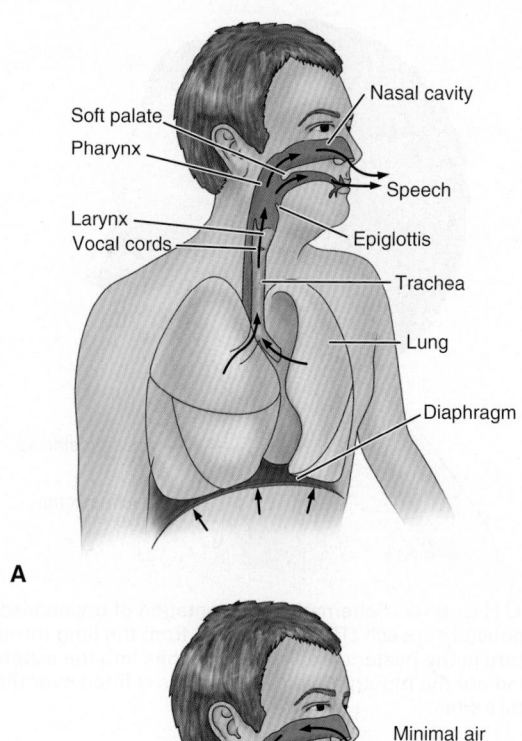

A

B

FIGURE 9-3 Total laryngectomy produces a change in airflow for breathing and speaking. **(A)** Normal airflow. **(B)** Airflow after total laryngectomy.

outcomes and decreased the incidence of post-treatment morbidities (DeVita et al., 2008). Complications from radiation therapy are a result of external radiation to the head and neck area, which may also include the parotid gland, which is responsible for mucus production. Symptoms may include acute mucositis, ulceration of the mucous membranes, pain, **xerostomia** (dry mouth), and loss of taste, dysphasia, fatigue, and skin reactions. Complications occurring late may include laryngeal necrosis, edema, and fibrosis.

Speech Therapy

The patient who undergoes a laryngectomy faces potentially complex and frustrating communication problems. These are related to alterations in communication methods, perceived

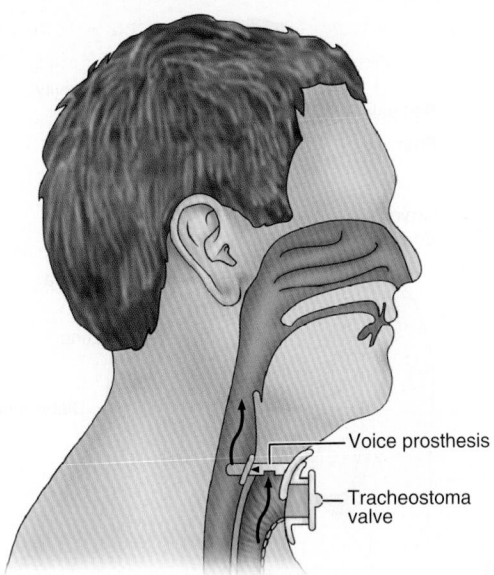

FIGURE 9-4 Schematic representation of tracheoesophageal puncture speech (TEP). Air travels from the lung through a puncture in the posterior wall of the trachea into the esophagus and out the mouth. A voice prosthesis is fitted over the puncture site.

voice quality, and perceptions of quality of life related to communication, disfigurement, and socialization. To minimize anxiety and frustration for the patient and family, the loss or alteration of speech is discussed with the patient and family before surgery, and the speech therapist conducts a preoperative evaluation. The nurse discusses with the patient and family those methods of communication that will be available in the immediate postoperative period. These include writing, lip speaking, and communication or word boards. A system of communication is established with the patient, family, nurse, and physician, and is implemented consistently after surgery.

In addition, a long-term postoperative communication plan for **alaryngeal communication** is developed. The three most common techniques of alaryngeal communication are esophageal speech, artificial larynx (electrolarynx), and tracheoesophageal puncture.

With esophageal speech, patients compress air into the esophagus and expel it, setting off a vibration of the pharyngeal esophageal segment. The technique can be taught once the patient begins oral feedings after surgery. The patient learns to belch and use this action to transform simple explosions of air from the esophagus to sound for speech purposes. The speech therapist continues to work with the patient to make speech intelligible. The success rate is low.

With the electrolarynx, a battery-powered apparatus projects sound into the oral cavity. When the mouth forms words (articulation), the sounds from the electrolarynx become audible words. The voice that is produced sounds mechanical, and some words may be difficult to understand. The advantage

is that the patient is able to communicate with relative ease while working to become proficient at either esophageal or tracheoesophageal puncture speech.

With tracheoesophageal puncture, a valve is placed in the tracheal stoma to divert air into the esophagus and out the mouth. Once the puncture is surgically created and has healed, a voice prosthesis (Blom-Singer) is fitted over the puncture site. A speech therapist teaches the patient how to produce sounds. Moving the tongue and lips to form the sound into words produces speech. To prevent airway obstruction, the prosthesis is removed and cleaned when mucus builds up (see Fig. 9-4). It most resembles normal speech and is easily learned.

The success of these various approaches to preserve or restore speech varies. In one study that evaluated the effectiveness of these methods, the electrolarynx was used more often than the other methods of speaking, and tracheoesophageal speech was preferred over esophageal speech (DeVita et al., 2008).

Nursing Management

Teaching the Patient Preoperatively

The nurse reinforces information related to diagnosis and treatment options given to the patient and family by the physician and clarifies any misconceptions. Informational materials (written and audiovisual) about the surgery are given to the patient and family for review and reinforcement. If a complete laryngectomy is planned, the patient must understand that the natural voice will be lost, but that special training can provide a means for communicating. The patient needs to know that temporarily communication will be possible by writing, or by using a special communication board. The patient's ability to sing, laugh, and whistle will be lost.

The nurse reviews equipment and treatments for postoperative care with the patient and family, teaches important coughing and deep-breathing exercises, and assists the patient to perform return demonstrations. The nurse clarifies the patient's role in the postoperative and rehabilitation periods.

Reducing Anxiety and Depression

Patients undergoing surgery for laryngeal cancer may have many fears. These fears may relate to the diagnosis of cancer and the possibility of permanent loss of the voice and disfigurement. The nurse provides the patient and family with opportunities to ask questions, verbalize feelings, and discuss perceptions. The nurse should address any questions and misconceptions the patient and family have. During the preoperative or postoperative period, a visit from someone who has had a laryngectomy may reassure the patient that people are available to assist with rehabilitation.

In the immediate postoperative period, the nurse spends time with the patient, focusing on building trust and reducing the patient's anxiety. Clear instructions and explanations are

given to the patient and family in a calm, reassuring manner before and during each contact with the patient. The nurse seeks to learn from the patient what activities promote feelings of comfort and assists the patient in such activities (e.g., listening to music, reading). Relaxation techniques, such as guided imagery and meditation, are often helpful.

Maintaining a Patent Airway

The nurse promotes a patent airway by positioning the patient in the semi-Fowler's or Fowler's position after recovery from anesthesia. This position decreases surgical edema and promotes lung expansion. Observing the patient for restlessness, labored breathing, apprehension, and increased pulse rate helps to identify possible respiratory or circulatory problems. The nurse assesses the patient's lung sounds and reports changes that may indicate impending complications. Medications that depress respiration, particularly opioids, should be used cautiously. Adequate use of analgesic medications is essential for pain relief, as postoperative pain can result in shallow breathing and an ineffective cough. The nurse encourages the patient to turn, cough, and take deep breaths. If needed, suctioning may be performed to remove secretions, but the nurse must avoid disruption of suture lines. The nurse also encourages and assists the patient with early ambulation to prevent atelectasis, pneumonia, and deep vein thrombosis. Pulse oximetry is used to monitor the patient's oxygen saturation level.

If a total laryngectomy was performed, a laryngectomy tube may not be used; in others, it is used temporarily; and in many, it is used permanently. The laryngectomy tube, which is shorter than a tracheostomy tube but has a larger diameter, is the patient's only airway. The care of this tube is the same as for a tracheostomy tube (see discussion later in the chapter). If a tracheostomy tube without an inner cannula is used, humidification and suctioning of this tube is essential to prevent formation of mucous plugs.

Frequently, the patient coughs up large amounts of mucus through this opening. Because air passes directly into the trachea without being warmed and moistened by the upper respiratory mucosa, the tracheobronchial tree compensates by secreting excessive amounts of mucus. The patient will have frequent coughing episodes and may develop a brassy-sounding, mucus-producing cough. The nurse reassures the patient that these problems will diminish in time, as the tracheobronchial mucosa adapts to the altered physiology.

After the patient coughs, the tracheostomy opening must be wiped clean and clear of mucus. A simple gauze dressing, washcloth, or even paper towel (because of its size and absorbency) worn below the tracheostomy may serve as a barrier to protect the clothing from the copious mucus that the patient may initially expel.

One of the most important factors in decreasing cough, mucus production, and crusting around the stoma is adequate humidification of the environment. Mechanical humidifiers and aerosol generators (nebulizers) increase the humidity and are important for the patient's comfort. The laryngectomy tube may be removed when the stoma is well healed, within 3 to 6 weeks after surgery. The nurse teaches the patient how to clean and change the tube and remove secretions.

Wound drains, inserted during surgery, may be in place to assist in removal of fluid and air from the surgical site. Suction also may be used, but cautiously, to avoid trauma to the surgical site and incision. The nurse observes, measures, and records drainage. When drainage is less than 30 mL/day for 2 consecutive days, a member of the surgical team usually removes the drains.

Promoting Alternative Communication Methods

Establishing an effective means of communication is the primary goal in the rehabilitation of the laryngectomy patient. To understand and anticipate the patient's postoperative needs, the nurse works with the patient, speech therapist, and family to encourage use of alternative communication methods. These means of communication are established preoperatively and must be used consistently by all personnel who come in contact with the patient. The patient is unable to use an intercom system. A call bell or hand bell must be placed within easy reach of the patient. A reusable writing board often is used for communication, so the nurse documents which hand the patient uses for writing so that the opposite arm can be used for IV infusions. To ensure the patient's privacy, the nurse discards any old notes used for communication. If the patient cannot write, a picture-word-phrase board or hand signals can be used. Writing everything or communicating through gestures can be very time-consuming and frustrating. The patient must be given adequate time to communicate his or her needs. The patient may become impatient and angry when not understood.

Promoting Adequate Nutrition and Hydration

Postoperatively, the patient may not be permitted to eat or drink for several days. Alternative sources of nutrition and hydration include IV fluids, enteral feedings through a naso-gastric or gastrostomy tube, and parenteral nutrition.

When the patient is ready to start oral feedings, a speech therapist or radiologist may conduct a swallow study to evaluate the patient's risk for aspiration. Once the patient is cleared for oral feedings, the nurse explains that thick liquids will be used first, because they are easy to swallow. Different swallowing maneuvers are attempted with various food consistencies. Once the patient is cleared for food intake, the nurse stays with the patient during initial oral feedings and keeps a suction setup at the bedside for needed suctioning. The nurse observes the patient for any difficulty swallowing, particularly when eating resumes, and reports its occurrence to the provider.

The nurse instructs the patient to avoid sweet foods, which increase salivation and suppress the appetite. Solid foods are introduced as tolerated. The patient is instructed to rinse the mouth with warm water or mouthwash after oral feedings and to brush the teeth frequently.

Because taste and smell are so closely related, taste sensations are altered for a while after surgery because inhaled air passes directly into the trachea, bypassing the nose and the olfactory end organs. Over time the patient usually accommodates to this change and olfactory sensation adapts, often with return of interest in eating. The patient's weight and laboratory data are monitored to ensure that nutritional and fluid intake are adequate. Skin turgor and vital signs are assessed for signs of decreased fluid volume.

Promoting Positive Body Image and Self-Esteem

Disfiguring surgery and an altered communication pattern are a threat to a patient's body image and self-esteem. The reaction of family members and friends is a major concern for the patient. The nurse encourages the patient to express feelings about the changes brought about by surgery, particularly feelings related to fear, anger, depression, and isolation. Encouraging use of previous effective coping strategies may be helpful. Referral to a support group, such as the International Association of Laryngectomees [IAL]) and I Can Cope (the American Cancer Society), may help the patient and family deal with the changes in their lives. In addition to its work through support groups, the IAL encourages an exchange of ideas and methods for teaching and learning alaryngeal methods of communication.

Promoting Self-Care

A positive approach is important when caring for the patient and includes promotion of self-care activities. The patient and family should begin participating in self-care activities as soon as possible. The nurse assesses the patient's readiness for decision making and encourages the patient to participate actively in performing care. The nurse needs to support the patient and the family, especially when explaining the tubes, dressings, and drains that are in place postoperatively.

Monitoring and Managing Potential Complications

The potential complications after laryngectomy include respiratory distress and hypoxia, hemorrhage, infection, wound breakdown, aspiration, and tracheostomal stenosis.

Respiratory Distress and Hypoxia

The nurse monitors the patient for signs and symptoms of respiratory distress and hypoxia, particularly restlessness, irritation, agitation, confusion, tachypnea, use of accessory muscles, and decreased oxygen saturation on pulse oximetry (SpO_2). Any change in respiratory status requires immediate intervention. Hypoxia may cause restlessness and an initial rise in blood pressure; this is followed by hypotension and

somnolence. Cyanosis is a late sign of hypoxia. Obstruction needs to be ruled out immediately by suctioning and by having the patient cough and breathe deeply. Hypoxia and airway obstruction, if not immediately treated, are life-threatening.

Other nursing measures include repositioning of the patient to ensure an open airway and administering oxygen as prescribed and used with caution in patients with chronic obstructive pulmonary disease. The nurse should always be prepared for possible intubation and mechanical ventilation. The nurse must be knowledgeable about the hospital's emergency code protocols and skilled in use of emergency equipment. The nurse must remain with the patient at all times during respiratory distress. The emergency call bell and telephone should be used to initiate a code, call for further assistance, and summon the provider immediately if nursing measures do not improve the patient's respiratory status.

! **NURSING ALERT**
After a total laryngectomy, if the patient suffers a respiratory arrest, the nurse is aware that the naso/oro pharynx are now distinct from the tracheal bronchial tree, thus intubation must be managed via a laryngectomy tube, mouth to neck breathing, and oxygen delivery to the stoma.

Hemorrhage

Bleeding from the drains at the surgical site or with tracheal suctioning may signal the occurrence of hemorrhage. The nurse promptly notifies the surgeon of any active bleeding from the surgical site, drains, and trachea. Rupture of the carotid artery is especially dangerous. Should this occur, the nurse must apply direct pressure over the artery, summon assistance, and provide emotional support to the patient until the vessel is ligated. The nurse monitors vital signs for increased pulse rate, decreased blood pressure, rapid deep respirations, restlessness, and delayed capillary refill. Cold, clammy, pale skin may indicate active bleeding. IV fluids and blood components may be administered and other measures implemented to prevent or treat hemorrhagic shock.

Infection

The nurse monitors the patient for signs of postoperative infection. These include an increase in temperature and pulse, a change in the type of wound drainage, and increased areas of redness or tenderness at the surgical site. Other signs include purulent drainage, odor, and increased wound drainage. The nurse monitors the patient's white blood cell (WBC) count. An elevation in WBCs may indicate the body's effort to combat infection. In elderly patients, infection can be present without an increase in the patient's WBC count. WBCs will be suppressed in the patient with decreased immune function (e.g., patients with HIV infection, those receiving chemotherapy or radiation therapy); this predisposes the patient to a severe infection and sepsis. Antimicrobial (antibiotic) medications must be administered as scheduled. All suspicious

drainage is cultured, and the patient may be placed in isolation as indicated. The nurse reports any significant change in the patient's status to the surgeon.

Wound Breakdown

Wound breakdown caused by infection, poor wound healing, development of a fistula, radiation therapy, or tumor growth can create a life-threatening emergency. The carotid artery, which is close to the stoma, may rupture from erosion if the wound does not heal properly. The nurse observes the stoma area for wound breakdown, hematoma, and bleeding and reports this to the surgeon. If wound breakdown occurs, the patient must be monitored carefully and identified as being at high risk for carotid hemorrhage.

Aspiration

The patient who has undergone a laryngectomy is at risk for aspiration and aspiration pneumonia due to depressed cough, the sedating effects of anesthetic and analgesic medications, alteration in the airway, impaired swallowing, and the administration of tube feedings. The nurse assesses for the presence of nausea and administers antiemetic medications, as prescribed. The nurse keeps a suction set-up available in the hospital and instructs the family to do so at home, for use if needed. Patients receiving tube feedings are positioned with the head of the bed at 30 degrees or higher during feedings and for 30 to 45 minutes after tube feedings. For patients with a nasogastric or gastrostomy tube, the placement of the tube and residual gastric volume must be checked before each feeding. High residual volumes indicate delayed gastric emptying and can lead to reflux and aspiration. Risks for aspiration include a low level of consciousness, heavy sedation, low head-of-bed elevation, and vomiting. Gastric residual volumes significantly associated with aspiration include two or more residual volumes of 200 mL or greater, one or more volumes of 250 mL or greater, and two or more volumes of 250 mL or greater (Ackley, Ladwig, Swan et al., 2008; Metheny, 2008). Current research evidence suggests feedings should be held if gastric residuals are greater than 200mL on two separate occasions (Ackley et al., 2008). Residual volumes from the small bowel are usually less than 10 mL; however, limited research is available to suggest a volume that suggests aspiration risk. If intestinal residual volumes are similar to gastric residual volumes, the nurse should be suspicious for dislocation of the distal portion of the intestinal tube upward into the stomach. (Metheny, 2008). Refer to Chapter 22 for details of gastric and intestinal feedings.

Tracheostomal Stenosis

Tracheostomal stenosis is an abnormal narrowing of the trachea or the tracheostomy stoma. Infection at the stoma site, excessive traction on the tracheostomy tube by the connecting tubing, and persistent high tracheostomy cuff pressure are risk factors for tracheostomal stenosis. Cuff pressures should be below 25 cm H_2O (18 mm Hg) (Buehner & Bodenham, 2009). The incidence of this condition varies widely and is often pre-

ventable. The nurse assesses the patient's stoma for signs and symptoms of infection and immediately reports any evidence of this to the provider. Tracheostomy care is performed routinely. The nurse assesses the connecting tubing (e.g., ventilation tubing) and secures the tubing to avoid excessive traction on the patient's tracheostomy. The nurse ensures that, for the patient who is breathing independently (without ventilator), the tracheostomy cuff is deflated (for a patient with a cuffed tube).

> **NURSING ALERT**
> *An inflated tracheostomy cuff will not prevent aspiration. The decision to administer medications or food in a patient with a tracheostomy should be made as a team, which should include a formal swallowing evaluation and consideration of the patient's medical and psychological status (Batty, 2009; Brown et al., 2011).*

Teaching Patients Self-Care

In preparing the patient to go home, the nurse assesses the patient's readiness to learn and the level of knowledge about self-care management. The patient will need to learn a variety of self-care behaviors, including tracheostomy and stoma care (described later in the chapter), wound care, and oral hygiene. The nurse also instructs the patient about the need for adequate dietary intake, safe hygiene, and recreational activities.

Special precautions are needed in the shower to prevent water from entering the stoma. Wearing a loose-fitting plastic bib over the tracheostomy or simply holding a hand over the opening is effective. Swimming is not recommended because a person with a laryngectomy can drown without submerging his or her face. Hair sprays, loose hair, and powder should not get near the stoma, because they can block or irritate the trachea and possibly cause infection.

The nurse teaches the patient and caregiver the signs and symptoms of infection and identifies indications that require contacting the physician after discharge. The nurse teaches the patient and family to wash their hands before and after caring for the tracheostomy, to use tissue to remove mucous, and to dispose of soiled dressings and equipment properly. If the patient's surgery included cervical lymph node dissection, the nurse teaches the patient exercises for strengthening the shoulder and neck muscles.

Recreation and exercise are important for the patient's well-being and quality of life, and all but very strenuous exercise can be enjoyed safely. Avoidance of strenuous exercise and fatigue is important because the patient will have more difficulty speaking when tired, which can be discouraging. Additional safety points to address include the need for the patient to wear or carry medical identification—such as a bracelet or card—to alert medical personnel to the special requirements for resuscitation should this need arise. If resuscitation is needed, direct mouth-to-stoma ventilation should be performed. For home emergency situations, prerecorded emergency messages for police, the fire department, or other rescue services can be kept near the phone to be used quickly.

The nurse instructs and encourages the patient to perform oral care on a regular basis to prevent halitosis and infection. If the patient is receiving radiation therapy, synthetic saliva may be required because of decreased saliva production. The nurse instructs the patient to drink water or sugar-free liquids throughout the day and to use a humidifier at home. Brushing the teeth or dentures and rinsing the mouth several times a day will assist in maintaining proper oral hygiene.

It is important that the person who has had a laryngectomy have regular physical examinations and seek advice concerning any problems related to recovery and rehabilitation. The patient is also reminded to participate in health promotion activities and health screening, and about the importance of keeping scheduled appointments with the physician, speech therapist, and other health care providers.

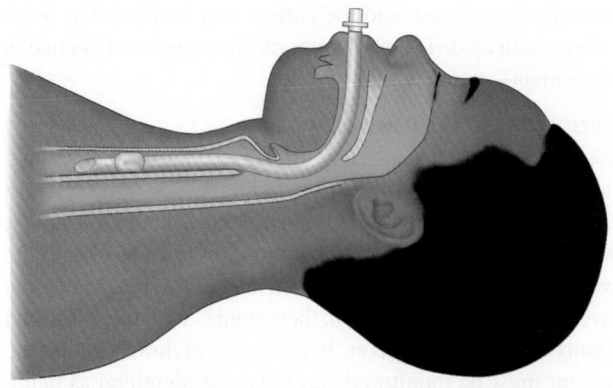

FIGURE 9-5 Endotracheal tube in place. The tube has been inserted using the oral route. The cuff has been inflated to maintain the tube's position and to minimize the risk of aspiration.

ARTIFICIAL AIRWAYS

The patient with an airway disorder such as a laryngeal obstruction or cancer may require the use of a temporary, or in some cases, a permanent artificial airway. Two types of artificial airways that may be used include an endotracheal tube (ETT) or a tracheostomy tube. General recommendations are to favor a tracheostomy tube rather than ETT if the patients will be intubated for 21 days of greater, and to favor the ETT over a tracheostomy if support will be required for 10 days or less (Apezteguia, Ríos, & Pezzola, 2005).

To provide for adequate ventilation, mechanical ventilation may be required to provide for adequate oxygenation.

ETT and tracheostomy tubes have several disadvantages. The tubes cause discomfort, the cough reflex is depressed because closure of the glottis is hindered, and secretions tend to become thicker because the warming and humidifying effect of the upper respiratory tract has been bypassed. The swallowing reflexes are depressed because of prolonged disuse and the mechanical trauma produced by the endotracheal or tracheostomy tube, thus increasing the risk of aspiration. In addition, ulceration and stricture of the larynx or trachea may develop. Of great concern to the patient is the inability to talk and to communicate needs.

ENDOTRACHEAL INTUBATION

Endotracheal intubation is a temporary means of providing an airway for patients who cannot maintain an adequate airway on their own (e.g., comatose patients, patients with upper airway obstruction), for patients needing mechanical ventilation, and for suctioning secretions from the pulmonary tree.

NURSING ALERT

For any patient with an artificial airway, a self-inflating bag-valve mask device or Ambu bag must be at the bedside, as well as suction catheters and suctions source.

Endotracheal intubation involves passing an ETT through the mouth or nose into the trachea (Fig. 9-5) with the aid of a laryngoscope by specifically trained personnel. It is the method of choice in emergency care. Once the tube is inserted, a cuff is inflated to prevent air from leaking around the outer part of the tube, to minimize the possibility of subsequent aspiration, and to prevent movement of the tube.

The nurse should be aware that complications could occur from pressure exerted by the cuff on the wall of the trachea. Low cuff pressure can increase the risk for aspiration pneumonia. High cuff pressure can cause tracheal bleeding, ischemia, and pressure necrosis. Routine deflation of the cuff is not recommended because of the increased risk for aspiration and hypoxia. The cuff must be deflated before the ETT is removed. Tracheobronchial secretions are suctioned through the tube (see description in tracheostomy section). Warmed, humidified oxygen should always be introduced through the tube, whether the patient is breathing spontaneously or is receiving ventilatory support. Endotracheal intubation should be used until a time when it is prudent to consider a tracheostomy to decrease oropharyngeal irritation and trauma to the tracheal lining, to reduce the incidence of vocal cord paralysis (secondary to laryngeal nerve damage), and to decrease the work of breathing.

Unintentional or premature removal of the tube is a potentially life-threatening complication of endotracheal intubation that is a frequent problem in intensive care units and occurs mainly during nursing care or by the patient.

TRACHEOSTOMY

A **tracheotomy** is a surgical procedure in which an opening is made into the trachea. The indwelling tube inserted into the trachea is called a **tracheostomy tube**. A tracheostomy may be either temporary or permanent.

A tracheostomy is used to bypass an upper airway obstruction, to allow removal of tracheobronchial secretions,

to permit the long-term use of mechanical ventilation, to prevent aspiration of oral or gastric secretions in the unconscious or paralyzed patient (by closing off the trachea from the esophagus), and to replace an endotracheal tube. Many disease processes and emergency conditions make a tracheostomy necessary, including total laryngectomy.

Procedure

A surgical opening is made between the second and third tracheal rings. After the trachea is exposed, an obturator guides insertion of the cuffed tracheostomy tube by creating a pathway for the tracheostomy tube. It is removed immediately after the tracheostomy tube is in place. The obturator should be available in the room in case of accidental dislodgement of the tracheostomy tube. The cuff is inflated to occlude the space between the tracheal walls and the tube, to permit effective mechanical ventilation and to decrease the risk of aspiration. The tracheostomy tube is held in place by tapes fastened around the patient's neck. Usually a square of sterile gauze is placed between the tube and the skin to absorb drainage and reduce the risk for infection.

Tube Types

Types of tracheostomy tubes include (Fig. 9-6):

- *Cuffed tracheostomy tube*: This is required when placing a patient on a ventilator because the balloon prevents air from being diverted out to the upper airway (Fig. 9-6A).

- *Fenestrated tube*: This tube allows some air flow up to the larynx, which allows for vocalization (Fig. 9-6B).
- *Uncuffed (cuffless) tube*: This tube does not permit ventilator management, but will allow talking if the airway is not edematous and the patient covers or "buttons" the end of the tube. This allows air to flow from the nose and mouth past the larynx and vocalization (Fig. 9-6C).

⚠ NURSING ALERT

In an emergency, the nurse understanding that if an Ambu bag or ventilator was used on a cuffless tube, that air will follow the path of least resistance (out the nose and mouth), rather than into the lungs. Therefore, any patient who has a cuffless tracheostomy must have the exact size tracheostomy tube at the bedside with a cuff. In an emergency, the provider will change the cuffless tube to a cuffed tube, inflate the balloon, allowing for ventilation with an Ambu bag or ventilator.

Complications

Complications may occur early or late in the course of tracheostomy tube management. Early complications include bleeding, pneumothorax, air embolism, aspiration, subcutaneous or mediastinal emphysema, recurrent laryngeal nerve damage, and posterior tracheal wall penetration. Long-term

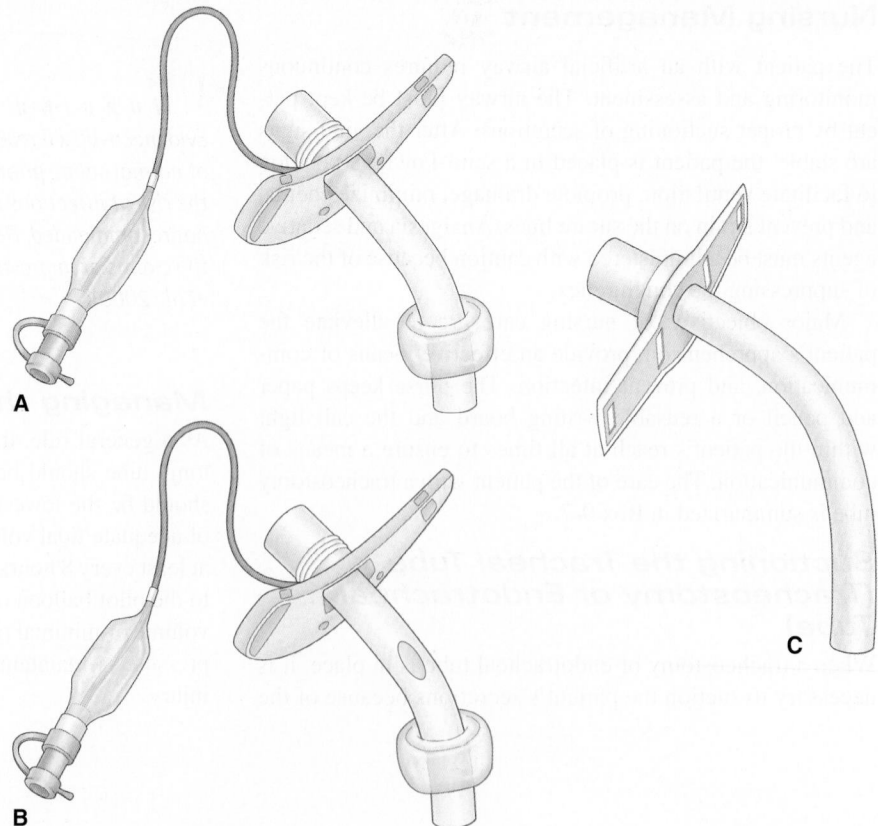

FIGURE 9-6 Tracheostomy tubes. **(A)** Cuffed tracheostomy tube; used for patients on mechanical ventilation. **(B)** Cuffed fenestrated tube; allows the patient to talk. **(C)** Uncuffed tracheostomy tube; not used for adult patients on mechanical ventilation; often used for permanent tracheostomy patients who are not ventilator dependent.

BOX 9-6

Preventing Complications Associated With Endotracheal and Tracheostomy Tubes

- Administer adequate warmed humidity.
- Maintain cuff pressure at appropriate level.
- Suction as needed per assessment findings.
- Maintain skin integrity. Change tape and dressing as needed or per protocol.
- Auscultate lung sounds.
- Monitor for signs and symptoms of infection, including temperature and white blood cell count.
- Administer prescribed oxygen and monitor oxygen saturation.
- Monitor for cyanosis.
- Maintain adequate hydration of the patient.
- Use sterile technique when suctioning and performing tracheostomy care.

complications include airway obstruction from accumulation of secretions or protrusion of the cuff over the opening of the tube, infection, rupture of the innominate artery, dysphagia, tracheoesophageal fistula, tracheal dilation, and tracheal ischemia and necrosis. Tracheal stenosis may develop after the tube is removed. Box 9-6 provides information about preventing complications.

Nursing Management

The patient with an artificial airway requires continuous monitoring and assessment. The airway must be kept patent by proper suctioning of secretions. After the vital signs are stable, the patient is placed in a semi-Fowler's position to facilitate ventilation, promote drainage, minimize edema, and prevent strain on the suture lines. Analgesia and sedative agents must be administered with caution because of the risk of suppressing the cough reflex.

Major objectives of nursing care are to alleviate the patient's apprehension, provide an effective means of communication, and prevent infection. The nurse keeps paper and pencil or a reusable writing board and the call light within the patient's reach at all times to ensure a means of communication. The care of the patient with a tracheostomy tube is summarized in Box 9-7.

Suctioning the Tracheal Tube (Tracheostomy or Endotracheal Tube)

When a tracheostomy or endotracheal tube is in place, it is necessary to suction the patient's secretions because of the decreased effectiveness of the cough mechanism. Tracheal suctioning is performed when adventitious breath sounds are detected or whenever secretions are obviously present. Unnecessary suctioning can initiate bronchospasm and cause mechanical trauma to the tracheal mucosa.

All equipment that comes into direct contact with the patient's lower airway must be sterile to prevent pulmonary and systemic infections. The procedure for suctioning a tracheostomy is presented in Box 9-8 on page 270. Recent research analysis suggests using minimally invasive endotracheal suctioning, in which the suction catheter is inserted to the length of the ETT or tracheostomy tube only. The suction catheter is inserted to the carina and then retracted 1 to 2 cm before suctioning is performed; an alternative option is to measure the length of the suction catheter estimated by measuring an identical ETT (Pedersen, Rosendahl-Nielsen, Hjermind et al., 2009, p. 24). However deep suctioning may be necessary in patients with large amounts of secretions in the lower airways, since minimally invasive suctioning removes secretions from central airways only. Deep suctioning may lead to episodes of bradycardia. As research studies data are analyzed, best practice related to suctioning practices will be established.

In mechanically ventilated patients, an in-line suction catheter may be used to allow rapid suction when needed and to minimize cross-contamination by airborne pathogens. An in-line suction device allows the patient to be suctioned without being disconnected from the ventilator circuit.

NURSING ALERT

Evidenced-based research reveals that the routine instillation of normal saline prior to endotracheal suctioning increases the risk of infections and patient discomfort, and is therefore not recommended. Research indicates no evidence to support the claims of improving secretion clearance (Pedersen et al., 2009).

Managing the Cuff

As a general rule, the cuff on an endotracheal or tracheostomy tube should be inflated. The pressure within the cuff should be the lowest possible pressure that allows delivery of adequate tidal volumes. Cuff pressure must be monitored at least every 8 hours by attaching a handheld pressure gauge to the pilot balloon of the tube or by using the minimal leak volume or minimal occlusion volume technique. Usually the pressure is maintained at less than 25 cm H_2O to prevent injury.

BOX 9-7

GUIDELINES FOR NURSING CARE

Providing Care for a Patient With a Tracheostomy Tube

Equipment

- Sterile gloves
- Hydrogen peroxide
- Normal saline solution or sterile water
- Cotton-tipped applicators
- Dressing and twill tape

Implementation

ACTIONS	RATIONALE
1. Gather the needed equipment.	1. Everything needed to care for a tracheostomy should be readily on hand for the most effective care.
2. Provide patient and family instruction on the key points for tracheostomy care, inspect the tracheostomy dressing for moisture or drainage.	2. The tracheostomy dressing is changed as needed to keep the skin clean and dry. To prevent potential breakdown, moist or soiled dressings should not remain on the skin.
3. Perform hand hygiene.	3. Hand hygiene reduces bacteria on hands.
4. Explain procedure to patient and family.	4. A patient with a tracheostomy is apprehensive and requires ongoing assurance and support.
5. Put on clean gloves; remove and discard the soiled dressing in a biohazard container. Discard gloves.	5. Observing body substance isolation reduces cross-contamination from soiled dressings. Having necessary supplies and equipment readily available allows the procedure to be completed efficiently.
6. Prepare sterile supplies, including hydrogen peroxide, normal saline solution or sterile water, cotton-tipped applicators, dressing, and tape.	6. Sterile equipment minimizes transmission of surface flora to the sterile respiratory tract.
7. Put on sterile gloves. (Some physicians approve clean technique for long-term tracheostomy patients in the home.)	7. Clean technique may be used in the home because of decreased exposure to potential pathogens.
8. Cleanse the wound and the plate of the tracheostomy tube with sterile cotton-tipped applicators moistened with hydrogen peroxide. Rinse with sterile saline solution.	8. Hydrogen peroxide is effective in loosening crusted secretions. Rinsing prevents skin residue.
9. Soak inner cannula in peroxide or sterile saline; rinse with saline solution; inspect to be sure all dried secretions have been removed. Dry and reinsert inner cannula or replace with a new disposable inner cannula.	9. Soaking loosens and removes secretions from the inner lumen of the tracheostomy tube. Retained secretions could harbor bacteria, leading to infection. Some plastic tracheostomy tubes may be damaged by using peroxide.
10. Place clean twill tape in position to secure the tracheostomy tube by inserting one end of the tape through the side opening of the outer cannula. Take the tape around the back of the patient's neck and thread it through the opposite opening of the outer cannula. Bring both ends around, so that they meet on one side of the neck. Tighten the tape until only two fingers can be comfortably inserted under it. Secure with a knot. For a new tracheostomy, two people should assist with tape changes. Remove soiled twill tape after the new tape is in place.	10. This taping technique provides a double thickness of tape around the neck, which is needed because the tracheostomy tube can be dislodged by movement or by a forceful cough if left unsecured. Therefore, changing ties should always be a two-person task. A dislodged tracheostomy tube is difficult to reinsert, and respiratory distress may occur. Dislodgement of a new tracheostomy is a medical emergency.

(continued on page 270)

BOX 9-7

GUIDELINES FOR NURSING CARE (continued)

ACTIONS	RATIONALE
11. Remove old tapes and discard in a waste container after the new tape is in place.	11. Tapes with old secretions may harbor bacteria.
12. Although some long-term tracheostomies with healed stomas may not require a dressing, other tracheostomies do. Use a sterile tracheostomy dressing, fitting it securely under the twill tapes and flange of tracheostomy tube, so that the incision is covered, as shown below.	12. Healed tracheostomies with minimal secretions do not need a dressing. Dressings that will shred are not used around a tracheostomy because of the risk that pieces of material, lint, or thread may get into the tube, and eventually into the trachea, causing obstruction or abscess formation.
13. Dispose of all used equipment in waste receptacle, remove and discard gloves, and perform hand hygiene.	13. Disposing of all used equipment, cleaning agents, and gloves prevents the spread of contaminants/bacteria. Performing hand hygiene prevents the spread of infection.

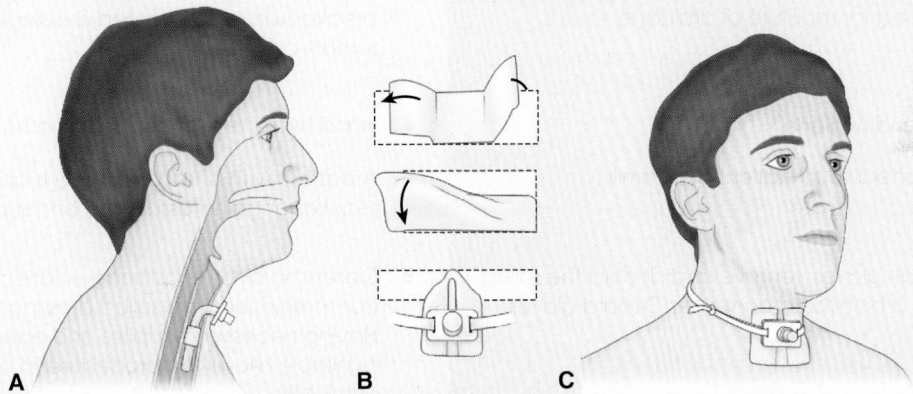

A   B   C

(A) The cuff of the tracheostomy tube fits smoothly and snugly in the trachea in a way that romotes circulation but seals off the escape of secretions and air surrounding the tube. **(B)** For a dressing change, a specially designed drain sponge or a 4 × 4-inch gauze pad may be folded (cutting would promote shredding, placing the patient at risk for aspiration) around the tracheostomy tube and **(C)** stabilized by slipping the neck tape ties through the neck plate slots of the tracheostomy tube. The ties may be fastened to the side of the neck to eliminate the discomfort of lying on the knot.

BOX 9-8

GUIDELINES FOR NURSING CARE

Performing Tracheal Suction

Equipment

- Suction catheters
- Gloves (sterile and nonsterile), gown, mask, and goggles
- Basin for sterile normal saline solution for irrigation
- Manual resuscitation bag with supplemental oxygen
- Suction source

Implementation

ACTIONS	RATIONALE
1. Explain the procedure to the patient before beginning and offer reassurance during suctioning. Unless contraindicated, elevate the head of the patient's bed.	1. Patients are apprehensive and require ongoing assurance and support. Elevation of bed maximizes diaphragmatic excursion.

ACTIONS (continued)

2. Perform hand hygiene. Put on nonsterile gloves, goggles, gown, and mask.

3. Secure the end of the suction tubing to the suction device. Place the open end within reach in preparation for connecting to the suction catheter. Turn on suction source (pressure should not exceed 150 mm Hg).

4. To perform open-suction technique:
   Open suction catheter kit on a clean surface, using the inside of the wrapping as a sterile field. Suction catheter should be less than half of the internal lumen of the endotracheal tube or tracheostomy.

   Set up a sterile solution container. Fill basin with approximately 100 mL of sterile normal saline or water. Be careful not to touch the inside of the container. Don sterile gloves.
   Pick up suction catheter; avoid touching nonsterile surfaces. With the nondominant hand, pick up the connecting tubing. Secure the suction catheter to the suction tubing.

   Check equipment for proper functioning by suctioning a small amount of sterile saline solution from the container.
   To perform closed-suction technique:
   Connect the suction tubing to the closed system suction port, according to the manufacturer's guidelines. The sterile suction catheter is in a clear plastic sleeve (see illustration). This system allows the patient to remain connected to the ventilator during suctioning.

RATIONALE (continued)

2. Hand hygiene reduces transmission of microorganisms and body secretions; donning PPE follows standard precautions.

3. High vacuum pressures are associated with mucosal injury.

4. If the catheter is too small, it will not adequately remove secretions, and if it is too large, it will obstruct airflow around the catheter during insertion. To calculate the catheter size needed, note the interior diameter (id) of the tracheostomy tube, divide by two, and then multiply by three to obtain the French size. For example, a size 8 tracheostomy tube would accommodate a 12-French suction catheter (Roberts & Hedges, 2010).

   This maintains sterility and follows standard precautions.

   This maintains catheter security. The dominant hand should not come in contact with the connecting tubing. Wrapping the sterile catheter around the sterile dominant hand helps to prevent inadvertent contamination of the catheter.
   Ensures equipment function.

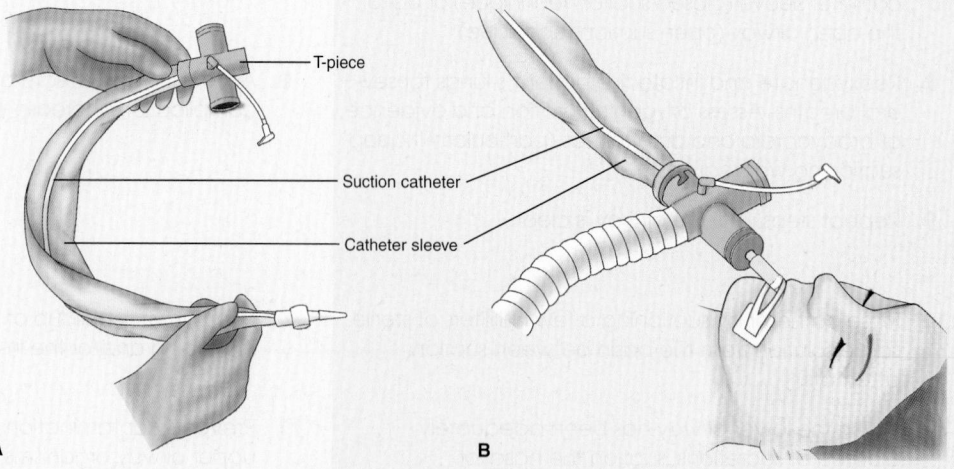

Closed airway suction system. **(A)** Closed tracheal suction system. **(B)** Closed system connected by a T-piece to the endotracheal tube and ventilator.

(continued on page 272

BOX 9-8

GUIDELINES FOR NURSING CARE (continued)

ACTIONS	RATIONALE

5. Follow institution guidelines related to hyperoxygenating the patient's lungs before suctioning. In general for the non–ventilator-dependent patient, humidified oxygen via a trach mask is placed over the tracheostomy for several deep breaths before suctioning, or if on a ventilator, pre-oxygenate the patient with 100% oxygen for at least 30 seconds prior to and after suctioning.
 	
    Press the suction hyperoxygenation button on the ventilator with the nondominant hand.
OR
    Increase the baseline faction of inspired oxygen (FIO_2) level on the mechanical ventilator. Disconnect the ventilator or gas delivery tubing from the end of the endotracheal or tracheostomy tube, attach the manual resuscitation bag (MRB) to the tube with the nondominant hand, and administer five to six breaths.
	5. Routine use of hyperinflation is not recommended due to the risk of barotraumas (damage to the lung from rapid or excessive pressure changes) from large volumes, high peak pressures and patient discomfort. Hyperoxygenation with 100% oxygen is used to prevent a decrease in arterial oxygen levels during the suctioning procedures.
	
	Attach a PEEP valve to the MRB for patients on more than 5 cm H_2O PEEP (refer to Chapter 55). Verify 100% oxygen delivery capabilities of MRB.

6. With the suction off, gently and quickly insert the catheter with the dominant hand into the artificial airway to the extent of the tracheostomy or ETT (not to pass beyond the tip of the tubes), which can be measured. Other researchers suggest passing the catheter to the carina (strong cough reflex or where resistance is felt), then pull back 1 to 2 cm before suctioning is performed; this is termed *minimally invasive suctioning*. Deeper suctioning may be necessary in patients with large amounts of secretions in the lower airways, since minimally invasive suctioning removes secretions from central airways only.	6. Suction should be applied only as needed to remove secretions and for as short a time as possible to minimize decreases in arterial oxygen levels.
7. Place the nondominant thumb over the control vent of the suction catheter and apply continuous or intermittent suction. Rotate the catheter 360 degrees between the dominant thumb and forefinger as you withdraw the catheter for ≤10 seconds in the sterile catheter sleeve (closed suction technique) or out of the open airway (open suction technique).	7. Tracheal damage from suctioning is similar with intermittent or continuous suction. Decreases in arterial oxygen levels during suctioning can be kept to a minimum with brief suction periods.
8. Reoxygenate and inflate the patient's lungs for several breaths. Assess oxygen saturation and evidence of bradycardia and arrhythmias (particularly if deep suctioning was required).	8. Arterial oxygen desaturation and cardiopulmonary complications increase with each successive pass.
9. Repeat steps until the airway is clear.	
10. Rinse catheter by suctioning a few milliliters of sterile saline solution from the basin between suction attempts.	10. Removes the buildup of secretions in the connecting tubing and/or the in-line suction catheter.
11. When the lower airway has been adequately cleared of secretions, suction the nasal or oropharyngeal cavity.	11. Prevents contamination of the lower airways with upper airway organisms.

ACTIONS (continued)

12. Rinse suction tubing.

13. Discard catheter, gloves, and basin appropriately. If using the open-suction technique, wrap the catheter around the dominant hand. Pull glove off inside out. Catheter remains in the glove. Pull other glove off in the same manner. Discard both gloves, and turn off suction device.

14. Perform hand hygiene.

RATIONALE (continued)

13. Reduces transmission of microorganisms. Solutions and catheters that come in direct contact with the lower airways during suctioning must be kept sterile to decrease the risk of nosocomial pneumonia.

Chapter Review

Critical Thinking Exercises

1. A 55-year-old woman is brought to the emergency department by her husband, who tells you that her nose has been bleeding for more than 3 hours. The patient reports that she takes one aspirin a day (325 mg), has a history of atrial fibrillation, and takes medication for hypertension. What immediate action would you take to care for this patient? What are the risk factors for epistaxis in this patient? What medical treatment would you anticipate for her? What nursing measures would you provide for this patient? How would you modify your discharge instructions if the patient lived alone? What strategies would you recommend to the patient and her husband to stop a nosebleed if it occurs again at home? What is the evidence for your recommendations? How will you determine the strength of the evidence on which your recommendations are based?

2. You are caring for a 78-year-old patient on a medical-surgical nursing unit. He has recently been diagnosed with cancer of the larynx and is scheduled for a total laryngectomy in the morning. What patient education is needed before this patient's surgery? Discuss nursing management of the patient's airway in the immediate postoperative period. What critical elements would you include in teaching the patient how to care for his tracheostomy? What community resources would you provide or arrange for this patient once he is discharged? What modifications in teaching and care would be necessary if this man had one-sided weakness secondary to an earlier stroke?

3. A 65-year-old man is referred for home care after a total laryngectomy performed to treat cancer of the larynx. As the home health nurse, you are responsible for providing continued patient education regarding tracheostomy care and gastric tube feedings. The overall plan is for the patient to begin oral feedings; however, both the patient and his wife believe that he is not ready to begin to eat. What are your priorities in terms of assessment of this patient? What are your recommendations to the patient regarding fear, anxiety, communication, and nutrition? What additional medical and support services will the patient need to assist him in his recovery? How would your care differ if this patient lived alone?

NCLEX-Style Review Questions

1. The nurse is providing preoperative teaching for the patient who is to undergo a total laryngectomy. Which nursing intervention is most important?
   A. Having the patient restrict food and fluids
   B. Teaching the care required for the tracheostomy tube
   C. Assessing the patient's ability to read and write
   D. Demonstrating cough and deep breathing exercises

2. A patient who has just had a total laryngectomy for cancer is being discharged. Which statement indicates the patient needs further teaching on care of the tracheostomy?
   A. "I must avoid getting any objects in the stoma."
   B. "I can take a shower when I get home."
   C. "I can learn to speak with an electric larynx."
   D. "I need to clean around the stoma everyday."

3. Which statement indicates further teaching is required for the patient diagnosed with obstructive sleep apnea (OSA)?
   A. "The CPAP machine will help me be more awake during the day."

B. "If I exercise and lose weight, I may not need to use CPAP."

C. "I will use the CPAP machine only when I really need to sleep well."

D. "The CPAP helps to keep my airway open when I sleep."

4. The nurse would assess the patient with acute pharyngitis for what signs and symptoms that indicate a complication of GAS pharyngitis?

A. Pain and spasm of the lower leg muscles

B. Gross hematuria, edema, and hypertension

C. Reduced visual fields, blurred vision

D. Insomnia, heartburn, and abdominal distension

5. A patient will be going home with a tracheal stoma. What information would be important to include in the discharge teaching for this patient?

A. Water sports are permitted.

B. Wear a medical identification bracelet.

C. Mouth-to-mouth ventilation should be performed in an emergency.

D. Fifteen minutes of strenuous exercise will improve overall strength.

Try these additional resources to enhance your learning and understanding of this chapter:

- thePoint online resource available at **http://thepoint.lww.com/Pellico1e**
- *Handbook for Focus on Adult Health: Medical-Surgical Nursing*
- *Study Guide for Focus on Adult Health: Medical-Surgical Nursing*

References and Selected Readings

References and selected readings associated with this chapter can be found on the website that accompanies the book. Visit http://thepoint.lww.com/Pellico1e to access the references and other additional resources associated with this chapter.

LAURA KIEROL ANDREWS

Nursing Management: Patients With Chest and Lower Respiratory Tract Disorders

Learning Objectives

After reading this chapter, you will be able to:

1. Identify patients at risk for atelectasis and describe nursing interventions related to its prevention and management.

2. Compare the various pulmonary infections with regard to causes, clinical manifestations, nursing management, complications, and prevention.

3. Use the nursing process as a framework for care of the patient with pneumonia.

4. Describe the nursing management for patients receiving oxygen therapy, mini-nebulizer therapy, incentive spirometry, chest physiotherapy, and breathing retraining.

5. Relate pleurisy, pleural effusion, and empyema to pulmonary infection.

6. Relate the therapeutic management techniques of acute respiratory distress syndrome (ARDS) to the underlying pathophysiology of the syndrome.

7. Describe risk factors and measures appropriate for prevention and management of pulmonary embolism (PE).

8. Describe risk factors for the development of occupational lung disease.

(continued on page 276)

It is common for patients in medical and surgical areas to have lower respiratory tract conditions. The care of these patients requires judicious assessment and management skills, as these conditions are often serious and life-threatening and have a significant impact on activities of daily living and quality of life.

ATELECTASIS

Atelectasis is the collapse of alveoli, leading to the loss of lung volume. It is classified by its cause (absorptive, obstructive, or compressive), and can affect subsegmental, segmental, lobar, or whole lung areas. The diagnosis of atelectasis is based on both clinical and radiologic findings.

Pathophysiology

Absorptive atelectasis occurs by surfactant inactivation or when less than normal levels of inhaled nitrogen (*nitrogen wash-out*) are present in the alveoli. The most common condition that causes an inactivation of surfactant is acute respiratory distress syndrome (ARDS), in which pulmonary edema fluid dilutes and/or reduces surfactant production. The loss of surfactant causes a reduction in alveoli surface tension and leads to their collapse. Nitrogen wash-out is a condition that occurs when high levels of inhaled oxygen (FiO_2 >60%) lessens the amount of nitrogen gas needed to stent open alveoli. Additionally, the use of some general anesthetics can cause an absorptive atelectasis.

Compressive atelectasis occurs as a result of external forces compressing pleural and/or lung tissues. Common causes of this type of atelectasis are pleural effusions, lung tumors, pneumothoraces (air in the pleural space), hemothoraces (blood in the pleural space), and abdominal distention.

Obstructive atelectasis occurs when there is a mechanical obstruction of airways (secretions, airway tumors, foreign bodies) or from low-tidal-volume breathing (which results in hypoventilation of alveoli then absorption of alveolar gases), causing lung tissue collapse (Fig. 10-1).

Each type of atelectasis can cause a mismatching of lung ventilation in relation to perfusion that results in deoxygenated blood reaching systemic circulation and lowering oxygen supply to tissues. The most common

cause of atelectasis is the obstruction of airways by secretions, mucus, foreign bodies, bronchial tumors, and oxygen toxicity.

Risk Factors

Postoperative patients, especially those who undergo abdominal and/or thoracic procedures, are at risk to develop atelectasis due to anesthetic- and/or narcotic-induced hypoventilation, incisional pain, abdominal distention, and immobility, all of which impair the ability to breathe deeply (expand lung volume) and cough (expel secretions). Additional risk factors for developing atelectasis include chronic lung disease, morbid obesity, tobacco use, anesthesia time greater than 4 hours, prior cerebrovascular accident (CVA), lung cancer, pleural effusions, and nasogastric tube placement.

Clinical Manifestations and Assessment

Signs and symptoms include dyspnea, cough, leukocytosis, and sputum production. Fever is often cited as a clinical sign of atelectasis, but there is no correlation between the severity of atelectasis on chest radiology and the presence of fever. Physical examination findings relate to the severity of collapse. For a small atelectatic area, findings include crackles, decreased breath sounds, and decreased tactile fremitus over the affected lung area(s). For a large atelectatic area, findings include tracheal deviation toward the atelectatic area, decreased fremitus, bronchial breath sounds, egophony (secondary to lobar or lung collapse), and asymmetry of the chest (LeBlond, Brown, & DeGowin, 2009).

If obstruction by an airway tumor or foreign body is the cause, wheezing and stridor can occur. Patients with acute atelectasis or atelectasis involving large areas, such as segments, lobes, or whole lung areas, can develop significant respiratory distress manifested by dyspnea, tachycardia, tachypnea, anxiety, restlessness, pleural pain, and hypoxemia. They may also have paroxysmal breathing, retractions, and use of accessory muscles. Chronic atelectasis has manifestations similar to those of acute atelectasis, and chronic patients are at risk of developing a postobstructive pneumonia.

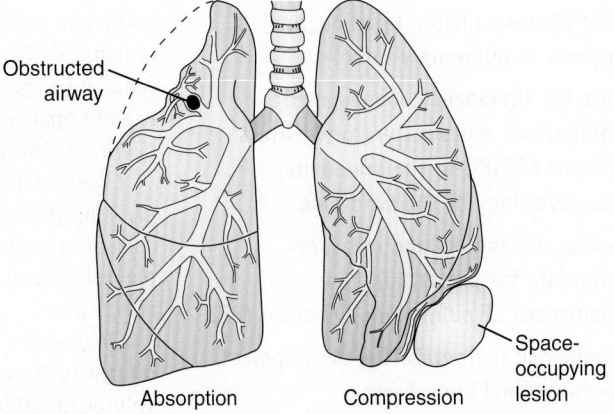

FIGURE 10-1 Atelectasis caused by airway obstruction and absorption of air from the involved lung area (*left*) and by compression of the lung tissue (*right*). From Porth , C.M., & Matfin, G. (2009). *Pathophysiology: Concepts of altered health states* (8th ed., p. 708). Philadelphia: Lippincott Williams & Wilkins.

Atelectasis is diagnosed by radiologic studies such as chest X-ray or computed tomography (CT) scanning. Radiologic findings of atelectasis may reveal opacity or patchy infiltrates underlying the affected tissue. Larger areas of collapse can reveal shifting of the heart border, hilar vessels, and hemidiaphragm toward the affected sections.

Chest X-rays can detect pleural effusions and hemo- or pneumothoraces. CT scanning of the chest is used to evaluate lung nodules and masses, and assess the size of effusions or pneumothoraces. Hypoxemia can be detected by arterial blood gas (ABG) analysis, which shows a decreased PaO_2 and oxygen saturation. Noninvasive pulse oximetry (POX) can be used to detect hypoxemia (SpO_2 <90%), but ABGs are the gold standard.

Medical and Nursing Management

The prevention of atelectasis is the primary management goal in at-risk patients (Box 10-1). Patients need to be educated and perform maneuvers that can improve ventilation and remove secretions. Immobile patients should be turned frequently, and all patients should be ambulated as soon as possible to improve lung expansion and mobilization of secretions. Lung volume expansion maneuvers, such as controlled deep breathing, coughing exercises, and use of incentive spirometry, should be initiated early in the postoperative period. Patients who have asthma, chronic obstructive pulmonary disease (COPD), lung cancer, and thoracic or abdominal surgeries are at very high risk for developing atelectasis. These patients require additional interventions to prevent atelectasis. The use of aerosolized (nebulized) bronchodilators and or mucolytics, followed by chest physiotherapy (chest percussion and postural drainage), may be instituted.

BOX 10-1 **Health Promotion**

Preventing Atelectasis

- Change patient's position frequently, especially from supine to upright position, to promote ventilation and prevent secretions from accumulating.
- Encourage early mobilization from bed to chair, followed by early ambulation.
- Encourage appropriate deep breathing and coughing to mobilize secretions and prevent them from accumulating.
- Teach/reinforce appropriate technique for incentive spirometry.
- Administer prescribed opioids and sedatives judiciously to prevent respiratory depression.
- Perform postural drainage and chest percussion, if indicated.
- Institute suctioning to remove tracheobronchial secretions, if indicated.

BOX 10-2 **Patient Education**

Using an Incentive Spirometer

The inhalation of air, in a slow and controlled manner, helps inflate the lungs. The marker within the spirometer will measure the depth of each breath.
- Assume an upright position if possible (sitting or semi-Fowler's).
- Breathe using your diaphragm.
- Place mouthpiece firmly in the mouth, to breathe in deeply and slowly, holding each breath in for 3 to 4 seconds and exhaling slowly.
- Repeat 6 to 10 times per session.
- Use spirometer every hour while awake (keep it within reach).
- Try coughing, with splinting of incision, after each use.

Incentive Spirometry

Incentive spirometry (IS) is a method of deep breathing that provides visual feedback to encourage the patient to inhale slowly and deeply, via a handheld spirometer. This prevents or reduces atelectasis by stimulating alveolar cells to secrete surfactant which decreases the surface tension in the alveoli, and improves inspiratory muscle performance. The use of IS is discussed in Box 10-2.

> ⚡ **N U R S I N G   A L E R T**
> *Surfactant, which decreases the surface tension in the alveoli, thus reducing their risk of collapse, needs to be continuously replaced. One stimulus for replacement is maximum deep inhalation that is sustained for a few seconds. Adults sigh or deep breath at one and a half to two times their normal tidal volume (~500 mL) six to eight times every hour. Any etiology that results in monotonous hypoventilation will lead to atelectasis. IS encourages the patient to sigh or deep breath. The three balls typically are graduated to 1.5 L. Coughing is a forced expiratory maneuver that can "squeeze" alveoli. If coughing is needed to expel secretions, the nurse should follow the coughing maneuvers with the use of IS to re-expand the alveoli and encourage surfactant replacement.*

Nebulizer Therapy

Nebulizer therapy dispenses aerosolized medications to a patient's lungs via hand-held or face mask devices. The medication is injected with a flow of compressed air or oxygen, producing a visible mist that the patient inhales. The patient breaths through the mouth, taking slow, deep breaths, and then holds the breath for a few seconds. The patient is encouraged to cough during the treatment, which assists in increasing intrathoracic pressure and promoting secretion expectoration. Antibiotics, bronchodilators, and mucolytic medications can be nebulized.

Chest Physiotherapy

Chest physiotherapy (CPT), with or without nebulizer medications, can also be used to prevent or treat atelectasis, bronchial obstructions, and pneumonias. CPT includes **postural drainage**, **chest percussion**, and vibration and breathing retraining. The goals of CPT are to remove bronchial secretions, improve ventilation, and increase the efficiency of the respiratory muscles. In addition, teaching the patient effective coughing technique is an important part of CPT.

Postural drainage uses specific positions that allow gravity to aid in the removal of pulmonary secretions. Patients who lie supine will have secretions accumulate in the posterior lung sections, whereas upright patients will pool secretions in their lower lobes. By changing positions (Fig. 10-2), secretions can drain from the affected bronchioles into the bronchi and trachea and then be removed by coughing or suctioning. Postural drainage is usually performed two to four times daily, prior to meals (to prevent nausea, vomiting, or aspiration) and at bedtime. Prescribed nebulizer therapy should be given prior to postural drainage to dilate the bronchioles, reduce bronchospasm, and thin secretions. The patient is instructed to remain in each position for 10 to 15 minutes, inhaling slowly through the nose and exhaling slowly through pursed lips. If the patient cannot tolerate a position, the nurse modifies it for comfort. When changing positions, the nurse instructs the patient to deep breath and cough out secretions, or the nurse may have to suction the patient if he is unable to cough.

Chest percussion and vibration can be used in each position to loosen secretions (Fig. 10-3). Percussion is performed by the nurse or respiratory therapist by rapidly "clapping" their cupped hands over the affected lung lobe. This is done for 1 to 2 minutes in each postural area. Vibration is performed, either manually or with a mechanical device. The nurse places his or her hands over the affected area and rapidly contracts the arms and shoulders while the patient exhales. This maneuver is done for 5 to 10 breaths over each lung area.

Other Treatments

If the cause of atelectasis is bronchial obstruction from secretions, the secretions must be removed by forceful coughing or suctioning to allow air to reenter that portion of the lung. Mucolytic agents such as acetylcysteine (Mucomyst) or dornase alfa (Pulmozyme) can be added to loosen and thin tenacious mucus. If intensive pulmonary toilet maneuvers and nebulizers fail to remove the obstructive mucus, a bronchoscopy can be preformed. A bronchoscopy can also be used to remove foreign bodies from airways. Patients with airways tumors may also undergo biopsy for diagnostic purposes, cryotherapy (cold therapy), or laser therapy via bronchoscopy. Additional therapies for these patients include airway stents or radiation and chemotherapy.

If the cause of atelectasis is compression of lung tissue, the goal is to decrease or remove the compression. Large pleural effusions that collapse lung tissue can be removed by **thoracentesis** (removal of fluid by needle aspiration) or chest tube insertion (thoracostomy). A **hemothorax** or **pneumothorax** usually is treated by chest tube insertion to drain the blood or air that is collapsing the lung. No matter what the cause of atelectasis, in patients with significant hypoxemia, intubation and mechanical ventilation with **positive end-expiratory pressure (PEEP)** may be necessary to provide adequate ventilation and oxygenation.

Complications

Mild atelectasis can usually be managed with lung expansion maneuvers, CPT, and mobilization of patient, but in some cases patients can develop severe hypoxia, respiratory distress, or pneumonia. Mortality is highest in patients who require intubation and mechanical intubation, especially for more than 48 hours. Complications can also occur from treatments used to treat atelectasis, such as bronchoscopy, thoracentesis, and thoracostomy, all of which place the patient at risk for infection, bleeding, and pneumothorax.

RESPIRATORY INFECTIONS

PNEUMONIA

Pneumonia is the infection of the lower respiratory track caused by a variety of microorganisms including, bacteria, viruses, fungi, protozoa, and parasites. Pneumonia is common and is associated with considerable mortality and morbidity (Mandell, Wunderlink, Anzueto et al., 2007). It is the most common infectious cause of death and the eighth leading cause of death in the United States (Centers for Disease Control and Prevention [CDC], 2006).

Classifications

Pneumonia may be classified in a wide variety of ways, including by its microbiologic cause, host condition, and host setting. Currently, the most common classifications for pneumonia are community-acquired pneumonia (CAP), hospital-acquired (**nosocomial**) pneumonia (HAP), ventilator-associated pneumonia (VAP), health care–associated pneumonia (HCAP), and pneumonia in an immunocompromised patient (Anand & Kollef, 2009).

Community-Acquired Pneumonia

CAP occurs either in the community-dwelling person or within the first 48 hours after hospitalization or institutionalization. Most cases of CAP occur in the winter and early spring months, and prevalence rates are higher in men and in African Americans. Each year approximately 20% of CAP patients require hospitalization; these patients have a mortality rate of 3.7% to 16% (Brown, Jones, Jephson et al., 2009; Ho, Cheng, & Chu, 2009; Renaud, Santin, Coma et al., 2009).

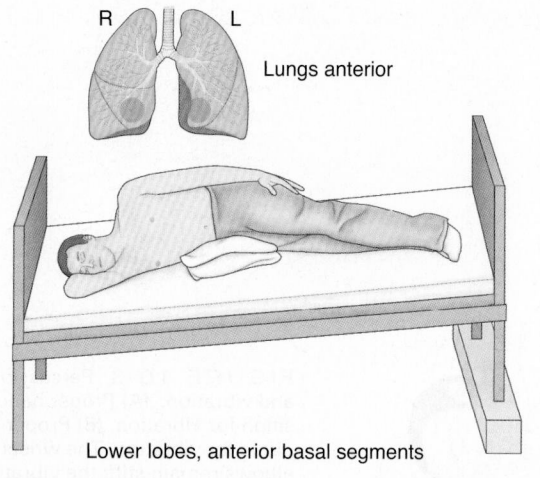

Lower lobes, anterior basal segments

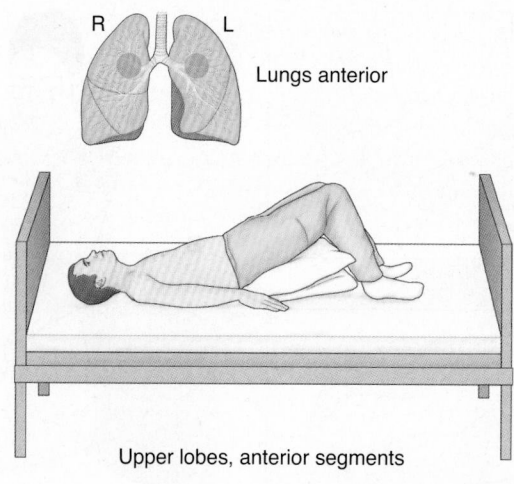

Upper lobes, anterior segments

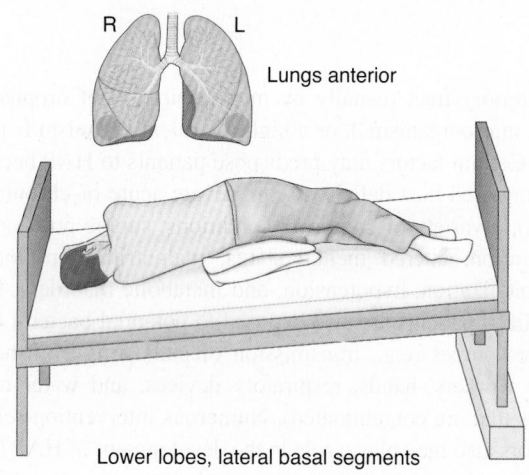

Lower lobes, lateral basal segments

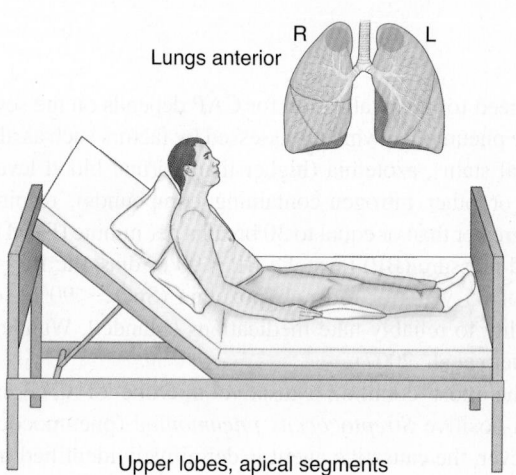

Upper lobes, apical segments

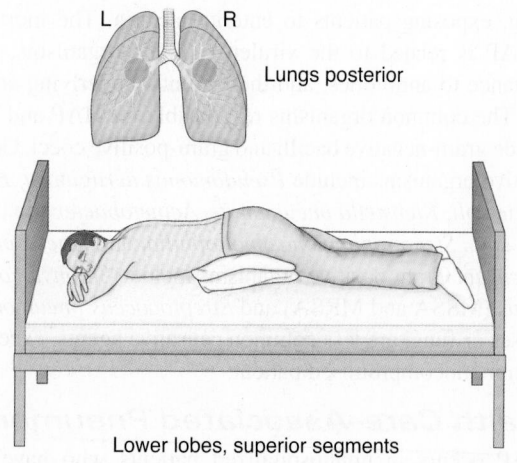

Lower lobes, superior segments

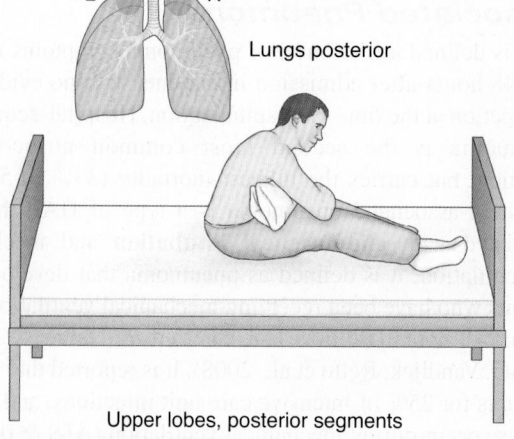

Upper lobes, posterior segments

FIGURE 10-2 Positions used in lung drainage.

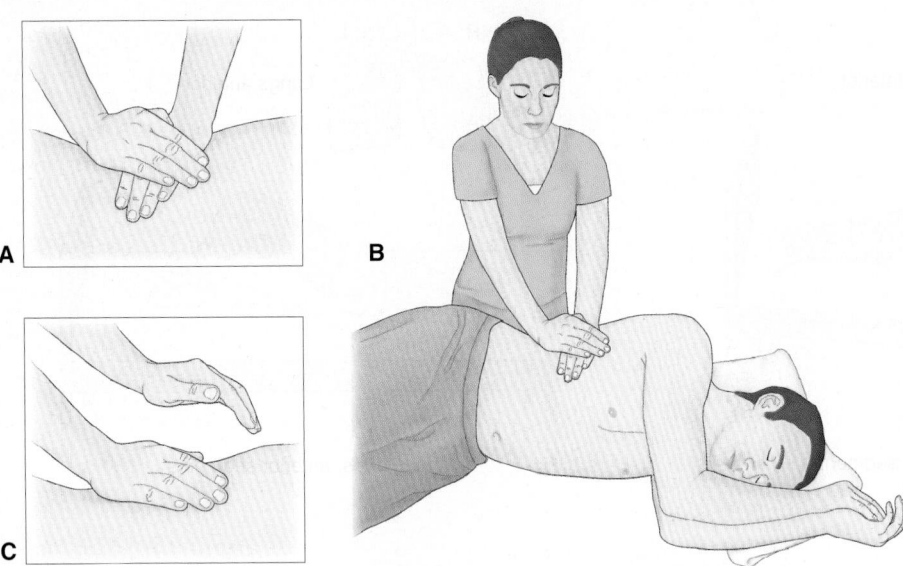

FIGURE 10-3 Percussion and vibration. **(A)** Proper hand position for vibration. **(B)** Proper technique for vibration. The wrists and elbows remain stiff; the vibrating motion is produced by the shoulder muscles. **(C)** Proper hand position for percussion.

The need for hospitalization for CAP depends on the severity of the pneumonia, which is assessed by factors such as altered mental status, azotemia (higher than normal blood levels of urea or other nitrogen-containing compounds), respiratory rate greater than or equal to 30 breaths per minute (BPM), low blood pressure (BP) (systolic BP <90 or diastolic BP <60), age of 65 years or older, hypoxemia (SpO_2 <90%), or an inability to reliably take medications (Mandell, Wunderlink, Anzueto et al., 2007).

The most common causative microbe of CAP is the gram-positive *Streptococcus pneumoniae* (pneumococcus); however, the causative agent is definitively identified in less than 30% of CAP cases. Other causative agents are *Haemophilus influenza, Staphylococcus aureus, Legionella* spp., and *viruses*.

Hospital-Acquired and Ventilator-Associated Pneumonia

HAP is defined as the onset of pneumonia symptoms more than 48 hours after admission in patients with no evidence of infection at the time of hospitalization. Hospital-acquired pneumonia is the second most common nosocomial infection, but carries the highest mortality (33% to 50%). Ventilator-associated pneumonia is a type of HAP that is associated with **endotracheal intubation** and mechanical ventilation; it is defined as pneumonia that develops in patients who have been receiving mechanical ventilation for at least 48 hours (Dellit, Chan, Skerrett, & Nathens, 2008; Labeau, Vandijck, Rello et al., 2008). It is reported that HAP accounts for 25% of intensive care unit infections, and 90% of these occur during mechanical ventilation (ATS & IDSA, 2005). VAP carries a mortality rate of 24% to 76% (Dellit et al., 2008; Kollef, Morrow, Baughman et al., 2008).

HAP occurs when at least one of three conditions exists: host defenses are impaired, microorganisms reach the lower respiratory tract (usually by microaspiration of oropharyngeal microorganisms), or a highly virulent organism is present. Certain factors may predispose patients to HAP because of impaired host defenses (e.g., severe acute or chronic illness), a variety of comorbid conditions, supine positioning, aspiration, altered mental status, malnutrition, prolonged hospitalization, hypotension, and metabolic disorders. Hospitalized patients are also exposed to potential bacteria from other sources (e.g., transmission of pathogens from health care workers' hands, respiratory devices, and water reservoirs that are contaminated). Numerous intervention-related factors also may play a role in the development of HAP (e.g., therapeutic agents that cause central nervous system (CNS) depression with hypoventilation, endotracheal intubation, or inappropriate use of antibiotics). Alterations in the gastric pH due to illness and medications can disrupt the stomach lining, exposing patients to enteric bacteria. The mortality of HAP is related to the virulence of the organisms, their resistance to antibiotics, and the patient's underlying condition. The common organisms responsible for HAP and VAP include gram-negative bacilli and gram-positive cocci. Gram-negative organisms include *Pseudomonas aeruginosa, Escherichia coli, Klebsiella pneumoniae, Acinetobacter* spp., *Serratia* spp., *Stenotrophomonas maltophilia,* and *Haemophilus influenzae*. Gram-positive organisms include *Staphylococcus aureus* (MSSA and MRSA) and *Streptococcus pneumoniae*. Viruses or fungi are less common causative agents, except in the immunocompromised patient.

Health Care–Associated Pneumonia

HCAP occurs in nonhospitalized patients who have had extensive health care contact, as defined as one of the following: resident of a nursing home or other type of long-term care facility, acute care hospitalization for 2 or more days within the last 90 days, intravenous antibiotic therapy,

wound care, or chemotherapy, or attended a hospital or hemodialysis clinic within the last 30 days (Seymann et al., 2009). Causative microorganisms are similar to those listed for HAP and VAP.

Pneumonia in the Immunocompromised Host

Pneumonia in immunocompromised hosts includes *Pneumocystis* pneumonia (PCP), fungal pneumonias, and *Mycobacterium tuberculosis*. Pneumonia in the immunocompromised host occurs with use of corticosteroids or other immunosuppressive agents, chemotherapy, nutritional depletion, use of broad-spectrum antimicrobial agents, acquired immune deficiency syndrome (AIDS), genetic immune disorders, and long-term life-support technology (mechanical ventilation). In addition, increasing numbers of patients with impaired defenses develop HAP from gram-negative bacilli (Huang, Morris, Limper et al., 2006).

Pneumonia in immunocompromised hosts may be caused by the organisms also observed in CAP or HAP. PCP is rarely observed in immunocompetent hosts and is often an initial AIDS-defining complication. Whether patients are immunocompromised or immunocompetent, the clinical presentation of pneumonia is similar, but PCP has a subtle onset, with progressive dyspnea, fever, and a nonproductive cough. Refer to Chapter 37 for more information about PCP and HIV.

Pathophysiology

Pneumonia can arise from several vectors: from normal flora present in patients whose resistance has been altered; from aspiration of flora present in the nasopharynx or oropharynx; the inhalation of airborne microorganisms from other persons (sneezing, coughing, or talking); from contaminated water sources or respiratory equipment; or from blood-borne organisms that enter the pulmonary circulation and become trapped in the pulmonary capillary beds.

Normal host defenses (cough, ciliary clearance, and alveolar macrophages) and intact upper airway defense mechanisms usually prevent potentially infectious particles from reaching the sterile lower respiratory tract.

Once the microorganisms reach the lower airways and alveoli, their presence activates an inflammatory response that begins with the migration of white blood cells (mainly neutrophils), plasma fluid, and immune complexes into the alveoli, filling the normally air-filled spaces with exudative liquids and cellular debris. This causes alveolar edema and lung tissue consolidation. Additional damage can occur when some microorganisms release toxins that further damage respiratory cells. Alveolar and bronchial tissues become swollen and infiltrated with white blood cells, causing **consolidation** of lung tissue that can be seen on X-ray. The damage caused by toxins and inflammatory mediators and immune complexes interferes with the diffusion of oxygen and carbon dioxide, leading to clinical manifestations of the pneumonia. A mismatch between ventilation and perfusion occurs in the affected area of the lung, and poorly oxygenated blood returns from the pulmonary vasculature to the heart, resulting in arterial hypoxemia.

Risk Factors

Risk factors are summarized in Box 10-3. Patients with comorbid diseases such as COPD, heart failure, diabetes, and chronic liver or kidney disease have higher mortality rates than do those without comorbid diseases.

BOX 10-3 **Risk Factors for Pneumonia**

Community-Acquired Pneumonia (CAP)
- Smoking
- Alcohol abuse
- Preexisting hypoxemia
- Acidosis
- Toxic inhalations
- Pulmonary edema
- Altered mental status (e.g., seizure, CVA)
- Renal disease with uremia
- Malnutrition
- Immunosuppressive therapies
- Bronchial obstructions
- Age older than 65 years
- Intravenous drug abuse
- Cystic fibrosis
- Bronchiectasis
- Chronic obstructive pulmonary disease
- Previous episodes of pneumonia

Hospital-Acquired Pneumonia (HAP) and Ventilator-Associated Pneumonia (VAP)
- Debilitation
- Malnutrition
- Altered mental status
- Previous exposure to antibiotics (within the last 90 days)
- Hospital stays of 5 days or longer
- High rates of antibiotic resistance (hospital or unit-specific)
- Immunosuppressive therapies or diseases
- Prolonged (>48 hours) intubation or a tracheostomy

Health Care-Acquired Pneumonia (HCAP)
- Hospitalization for 2 or more days in the last 3 months
- Chronic dialysis within the last month
- Home wound care
- Home IV therapy
- Resident of a skilled nursing or extended-care facility
- Family member with drug-resistant microorganism

Clinical Manifestations and Assessment

Pneumonia varies in its signs and symptoms depending on the causal organism and the presence of underlying disease; however, it is not possible to diagnose a specific type of pneumonia by clinical manifestations alone. The classic clinical manifestations of pneumonia are fever, cough (productive or nonproductive), dyspnea, and leukocytosis. Patients can also present with rigors (shaking chills), pleuritic chest pain, tachypnea, use of accessory muscles, tachycardia, fatigue, and anorexia. Some patients initially exhibit an upper respiratory tract infection (nasal congestion, sore throat), and the onset of symptoms of pneumonia is gradual and nonspecific. The predominant symptoms may then be headache, low-grade fever, pleuritic pain, myalgia, rash, and pharyngitis.

Physical examinations findings may reveal bronchial breath sounds over consolidated lung areas, crackles, increased tactile fremitus (vocal vibration detected on palpation), percussion dullness, egophony, and whispered pectoriloquy (whispered sounds are easily auscultated through the chest wall). These changes occur because sound is transmitted better through solid or dense tissue (consolidation) than through normal air-filled tissue. **Purulent** sputum or slight changes in respiratory symptoms may be the only sign of pneumonia in patients with COPD. It may be difficult to determine whether an increase in symptoms is an exacerbation or an infectious process.

The diagnosis of pneumonia is made by history (particularly of a recent respiratory tract infection), physical examination, chest X-ray, blood culture (bloodstream invasion, called *bacteremia*, occurs frequently), sputum examination (Gram stain and culture), and rapid bacterial antigen testing of urine or oropharyngeal swabs.

The sputum sample is obtained by having patients do the following: (1) rinse the mouth with water to minimize contamination by normal oral flora, (2) breathe deeply several times, (3) cough deeply, and (4) expectorate the raised sputum into a sterile container. The best time to collect the sputum culture is in the morning because the sputum is more concentrated and less likely to be contaminated with saliva and nasopharyngeal secretions (Daniels, 2010). More invasive procedures may be used to collect sputum specimens (nasotracheal or orotracheal suctioning or bronchoscopy).

Chest X-ray findings associated with pneumonia vary depending upon microbial causes, but a new pulmonary infiltrate or consolidation is often seen within 48 hours of onset of symptoms. Infiltrates can involve segments, lobes, or be multilobar.

Medical and Nursing Management

Pharmacologic Therapy

The treatment of pneumonia includes administration of the appropriate antibiotic. The choice of antibiotic is determined by the classification of pneumonia (i.e., CAP vs.

TABLE
10-1 Empiric Antibiotic Therapy for Hospital-Acquired, Ventilator-Associated, or Health Care–Acquired Pneumonia

Type	Drugs
Early onset (<5 days), with no risk factors for multiple-drug resistant pathogens	Ampicillin-sulbactam OR Ceftriaxone OR Levofloxacin, moxifloxacin, or ciprofloxacin OR ertapenem
Late onset (≥5 days) or risk factors for multidrug resistant pathogens	Cefepime or ceftazidime OR Imipenem or meropenem OR Piperacillin-tazobactam AND Ciprofloxacin or levofloxacin OR amikacin, gentamicin or tobramycin AND Linezolid or vancomycin (MRSA)

ATS/IDS 2005, pp. 401–402.

HAP), results of Gram stains, culture sensitivities, antigen testing, and patient's comorbid conditions. Initial treatment for CAP is empiric unless sputum culture and sensitivity results are available. Empiric therapy for non-CAP is usually initiated with a broad-spectrum IV antibiotic and may be monotherapy or combination therapy. The choice of antibiotics is based on assessment of risk of multidrug resistance pathogens (MDR) and early versus late onset of HAP or VAP symptoms (Table 10-1). Once the microbacterial cultures and sensitivities are available, therapy should be narrowed to avoid emergence of drug-resistant pathogens. Box 10-4 depicts the risk factors for developing MDR pathogens.

Prompt administration of antibiotics in patients is a key treatment measure. If specific pathogens responsible for the pneumonia are identified, more specific, less broad-spectrum agents should be used. The recommended duration of treatment for CAP is a minimum of 5 days. Patients should be afebrile for at least 2 days before antibiotics are discontinued. Patients with nosocomial pneumonias are

---

BOX 10-4 **Risk Factors for the Development of Multidrug-Resistant Pathogens**

- Antibiotic use in preceding 90 days
- Current hospitalization 5 days or longer
- Immunocompromised (by disease or therapies)
- Increased frequency of drug resistance in the community or hospital unit
- Presence of risk factors for HCAP

treated for 7 to 10 days, as long as the patient is showing signs of clinical improvement. Emerging data are demonstrating that shorter durations of antibiotic use are producing good clinical responses and fewer emergences of MDR pathogens (Siegel et al., 2006).

Antibiotics are ineffective in viral pneumonia, and their use may be associated with adverse effects (superinfections, MDR pathogens). Patients who develop pneumonia, who are at risk for influenza can be treated with antiviral agents. The recent pandemic of H_1N_1 (swine flu) prompted the antiviral treatment of patients at high risk for seasonal influenza complications, such as pneumonia, and patients suspected of having influenza (CDC, 2009c).

Oxygen Inhalation Therapy

Oxygen inhalation therapy is the administration of oxygen at a concentration greater that that found in the environmental atmosphere. At sea level, the concentration of oxygen in room air is 21%. The goal of using oxygen therapy is to prevent or correct tissue hypoxia, which is decreased oxygen supply to the tissues (Box 10-5). Hypoxia is often confused with hypoxemia. Hypoxemia is a decrease in the arterial oxygen content or arterial oxygen tension (partial pressure of oxygen, PaO_2) and is measured by ABG or POX. Hypoxemia is defined as a PaO_2 level of less than 60 mm Hb and/or a POX level of less than 90%. When administering oxygen to a patient, a nurse must keep in mind that oxygen transport to the tissues is dependent not only on the arterial oxygen content, but also cardiac output, hemoglobin concentration, and metabolic requirements.

Indications for Oxygen Therapy

The use of oxygen to *treat* patients with hypoxia is based on clinical indicators such as subjective information (dyspnea, chest pain), ABG analysis, POX, and physical examination findings. A change in respiratory rate or pattern (bradypnea, tachypnea, Cheyne-Stokes breathing), change in mental status (agitation, anxiety, disorientation, confusion, lethargy, coma), change in BP, change in heart rate (bradycardia or tachycardia), development of arrhythmias, cyanosis (late sign), diaphoresis, or cool extremities are signs of hypoxia. The development of these signs and symptoms depends on how suddenly the hypoxia develops. Acute onset tends to show signs of neurologic and cardiovascular impairment, while with chronic onset, patients complain of fatigue, drowsiness, dyspnea on exertion, and inattentiveness.

The administration of oxygen to *prevent* hypoxemia in high-risk patients who do not have clinical indicators of hypoxia is common in hospitals. High-risk patients are those who are at risk of rapidly developing hypoxemia, or who will not tolerate even mild hypoxemia. Patients with pneumonia, PE, suspected myocardial injury or infarction, and head trauma or injury are just a few examples.

Methods of Oxygen Administration

Oxygen is dispensed from a cylinder or a piped-in system, and a flow meter regulates the flow of oxygen in liters per minute. When oxygen is used at high flow rates (> 6 L/min), it should be moistened by passing it through a humidification system to prevent it from drying the mucous membranes of the respiratory tract. A variety of oxygen delivery systems

---

BOX 10-5   Types of Hypoxia

Hypoxia can occur from either severe pulmonary disease (inadequate oxygen supply) or from extrapulmonary disease (inadequate oxygen delivery) affecting gas exchange at the cellular level. The four general types of hypoxia are hypoxemic hypoxia, circulatory hypoxia, anemic hypoxia, and histotoxic hypoxia.

Hypoxemic Hypoxia
Hypoxemic hypoxia is a decreased oxygen level in the blood resulting in decreased oxygen diffusion into the tissues. It may be caused by hypoventilation, high altitudes, ventilation–perfusion mismatch (as in pulmonary embolism), shunts in which the alveoli are collapsed and cannot provide oxygen to the blood (commonly caused by atelectasis), and pulmonary diffusion defects. It is corrected by increasing alveolar ventilation or providing supplemental oxygen.

Circulatory Hypoxia
Circulatory hypoxia results from inadequate capillary circulation. It may be caused by decreased cardiac

output, local vascular obstruction, low-flow states such as shock, or cardiac arrest. Although tissue partial pressure of oxygen (PO_2) is reduced, arterial oxygen (PaO_2) remains normal. Circulatory hypoxia is corrected by identifying and treating the underlying cause.

Anemic Hypoxia
Anemic hypoxia is a result of decreased effective hemoglobin concentration, which causes a decrease in the oxygen-carrying capacity of the blood. It is rarely accompanied by hypoxemia. Carbon monoxide poisoning, because it reduces the oxygen-carrying capacity of hemoglobin, produces similar effects but is not strictly anemic hypoxia because hemoglobin levels may be normal.

Histotoxic Hypoxia
Histotoxic hypoxia occurs when a toxic substance, such as cyanide, interferes with the ability of tissues to use available oxygen.

TABLE
10-2 Oxygen Administration Devices

Device	Suggested Flow Rate (L/min)	O$_2$ Percentage Setting	Advantages	Disadvantages
Low-Flow Systems				
Cannula	1–2	23–30	Lightweight, comfortable, inexpensive, continuous use with meals and activity	Nasal mucosal drying, variable FiO$_2$
	3–5	30–40		
	6	42		
Oropharyngeal catheter	1–6	23–42	Inexpensive, does not require a tracheostomy	Nasal mucosa irritation; catheter should be changed frequently to alternate nostril
Mask, simple	6–8	40–60	Simple to use, inexpensive	Poor fitting, variable FiO$_2$, must remove to eat
Mask, partial rebreather	8–11	50–75	Moderate O$_2$ concentration	Warm, poorly fitting, must remove to eat
Mask, non-rebreather	12	80–100	High O$_2$ concentration	Poorly fitting
High-Flow Systems				
Transtracheal catheter	¼–4	60–100	More comfortable, concealed by clothing, less oxygen liters per minute needed than nasal cannula	Requires frequent and regular cleaning, requires surgical intervention
Mask, Venturi	4–6	24, 26, 28	Provides low levels of supplemental O$_2$	Must remove to eat
	6–8	30, 35, 40	Precise FiO$_2$, additional humidity available	
Mask, aerosol	8–10	30–100	Good humidity, accurate FiO$_2$	Uncomfortable for some
Tracheostomy collar	8–10	30–100	Good humidity, comfortable, fairly accurate FiO$_2$	
Face tent	8–10	30–100	Good humidity, fairly accurate FiO$_2$	Bulky and cumbersome
Oxygen-Conserving Devices				
Pulse dose (or demand)	10–40 mL/ breath		Deliver O$_2$ only on inspiration, conserve 50% to 75% of O$_2$ used	Must carefully evaluate function individually

are available (Table 10-2). Each system and oxygen flow rate is designed to provide a specific **fraction of inspired oxygen** (FiO$_2$) or percentage of oxygen. The appropriate form of oxygen therapy is best determined by ABG levels, which indicate the patient's oxygenation status.

Oxygen delivery systems are classified as low-flow or high-flow delivery systems. Low-flow systems contribute partially to the inspired gas the patient breathes, which means that the patient breathes some room air along with the oxygen. These systems do not provide a constant or known concentration of inspired oxygen. The amount of inspired oxygen changes as the patient's breathing changes. Examples of low-flow systems include nasal cannula, simple mask, partial-rebreather, and non-rebreather masks. In contrast, high-flow systems provide the total amount of inspired air. A specific percentage of oxygen is delivered independent of the patient's breathing. High-flow systems are indicated

for patients who require a constant and precise amount of oxygen. Examples of such systems include transtracheal catheters, Venturi masks, aerosol masks, tracheostomy collars, and face tents.

A nasal cannula is used when the patient requires a low to medium concentration of oxygen for which precise accuracy is not essential. This method is relatively simple and allows the patient to move about in bed, talk, cough, and eat without interrupting oxygen flow. Flow rates in excess of 6 to 8 L/min may lead to swallowing of air or may cause irritation and drying of the nasal and pharyngeal mucosa. When oxygen is administered via cannula, the percentage of oxygen reaching the lungs varies with the depth and rate of respirations, particularly if the nasal mucosa is swollen or if the patient is a mouth breather.

Oxygen masks come in several forms (Fig. 10-4). Each is used for different purposes. *Simple masks* are used to

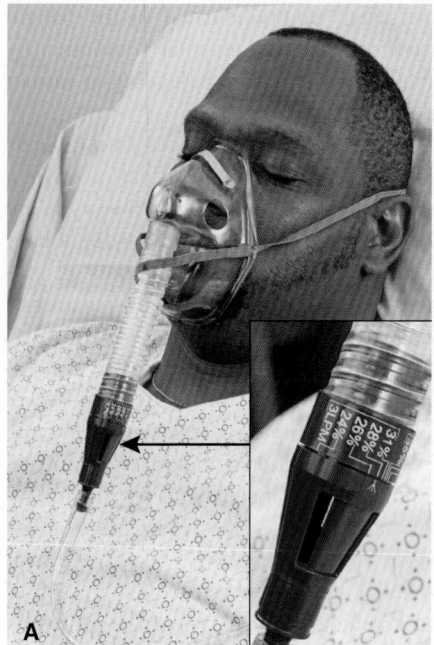
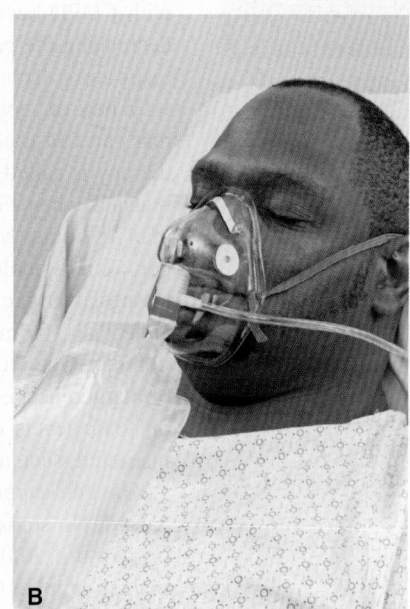
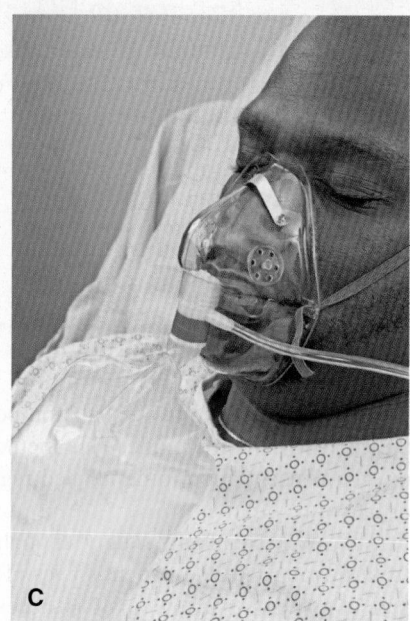

FIGURE 10-4 Types of oxygen masks used to deliver varying concentrations of oxygen. (A) Venturi mask. (B) Nonrebreather. (C) Partial rebreather.

administer low to moderate concentrations of oxygen. The body of the mask itself gathers and stores oxygen between breaths. The patient exhales directly through openings or ports in the body of the mask. If oxygen flow ceases, the patient can draw air in through these openings around the mask edges. Although widely used, these masks cannot be used for controlled oxygen concentrations and must be adjusted for proper fit. They should not press too tightly against the skin, because this can cause a sense of claustrophobia, as well as skin breakdown; adjustable elastic bands are provided to ensure comfort and security.

Partial-rebreathing masks have a reservoir bag that *must remain inflated during both inspiration and expiration.* The nurse adjusts the oxygen flow to ensure that the bag does not collapse during inhalation. A high concentration of oxygen can be delivered, because both the mask and the bag serve as reservoirs for oxygen. Oxygen enters the mask through small-bore tubing that connects at the junction of the mask and bag. As the patient inhales, gas is drawn from the mask, from the bag, and potentially from room air through the exhalation ports. As the patient exhales, the first third of the exhalation fills the reservoir bag. This is mainly dead space and does not participate in gas exchange in the lungs. Therefore, it has a high oxygen concentration. The remainder of the exhaled gas is vented through the exhalation ports. The actual percentage of oxygen delivered is influenced by the patient's ventilatory pattern.

Non-rebreathing masks are similar in design to partial-rebreathing masks except that they have additional valves. A one-way valve located between the reservoir bag and the base of the mask allows gas from the reservoir bag to enter the mask on inhalation, but prevents gas in the mask from flowing back into the reservoir bag during exhalation. One-way valves located at the exhalation ports prevent room air from entering the mask during inhalation. They also allow the patient's exhaled gases to exit the mask on exhalation. As with the partial-rebreathing mask, *it is important to adjust the oxygen flow so that the reservoir bag does not completely collapse on inspiration.* In theory, if the non-rebreathing mask fits the patient snugly, and both side exhalation ports have one-way valves, it is possible for the patient to receive 100% oxygen, making the non-rebreathing mask a high-flow oxygen system. However, because it is difficult to get an exact fit from the mask on every patient, and some non-rebreathing masks have only one one-way exhalation valve, it is almost impossible to ensure 100% oxygen delivery, thus making it a low-flow oxygen system.

The *Venturi mask* is the most reliable and accurate method for delivering precise concentrations of oxygen through non-invasive means. The mask is constructed in a way that allows a constant flow of room air blended with a fixed flow of oxygen. It is used primarily for patients with COPD because it can accurately provide appropriate levels of supplemental oxygen, thus avoiding the risk of suppressing the hypoxic drive (refer to Chapter 11 for further details).

The Venturi mask uses the Bernoulli principle of air entrainment (trapping the air like a vacuum), which provides a high air flow with controlled oxygen enrichment. For each liter of oxygen that passes through a jet orifice, a fixed proportion of room air is entrained. A precise volume of oxygen can be delivered by varying the size of the jet orifice and adjusting the flow of oxygen. Excess gas leaves

Approximate FiO₂ of Nasal Cannula Flow Rates

Each liter (L) of flow is approximately an addition of 4% FiO_2
- 1 L/min = 24% FiO_2
- 2 L/min = 28% FiO_2
- 3 L/min = 32% FiO_2
- 4 L/min = 36% FiO_2
- 5 L/min = 40% FiO_2
- 6 L/min = 44% FiO_2

(Diepenbrock, 2008)

the mask through the two exhalation ports, carrying with it the exhaled carbon dioxide. This method allows a constant oxygen concentration to be inhaled regardless of the depth or rate of respiration.

The mask should fit snugly enough to prevent oxygen from flowing into the patient's eyes. The nurse checks the patient's skin for irritation. It is necessary to remove the mask so that the patient can eat, drink, and take medications, at which time supplemental oxygen is provided through a nasal cannula.

The nurse must understand how to convert percentage of oxygen with a mask to liters per minute for a nasal cannula (Box 10-6).

The *transtracheal oxygen catheter* is inserted directly into the trachea and is indicated for patients with chronic oxygen therapy needs. These catheters are more comfortable, less dependent on breathing patterns, and less obvious than other oxygen delivery methods. Because no oxygen is lost into the surrounding environment, the patient achieves adequate oxygenation at lower rates, making this method less expensive and more efficient.

Other oxygen devices include *aerosol masks, tracheostomy collars,* and *face tents,* all of which are used with aerosol devices (nebulizers) that can be adjusted for oxygen concentrations from 27% to 100% (0.27 to 1.00). If the gas mixture flow falls below patient demand, room air is pulled in, diluting the concentration. The aerosol mist must be available for the patient during the entire inspiratory phase.

Hyperbaric oxygen therapy is the administration of oxygen at pressures greater than 1 atmosphere. As a result, the amount of oxygen dissolved in plasma is increased, which increases oxygen levels in the tissues. During therapy, the patient is placed in a small (single patient use) or large (multiple patient use) cylindrical chamber. Hyperbaric oxygen therapy is used to treat conditions such as air embolism, carbon monoxide poisoning, gangrene, tissue necrosis, and hemorrhage. Potential side effects include ear trauma, CNS disorders, and oxygen toxicity.

Complications

Oxygen, like other medications, should be administered with caution and a careful assessment of patient response. A high

concentration of oxygen is contraindicated in the patient with COPD because it may worsen alveolar ventilation by decreasing the patient's ventilatory drive, leading to further respiratory decompensation.

When oxygen is metabolized, it produces free radicals that can cause cellular damage. This side effect of oxygen therapy is called *oxygen toxicity.* Toxic levels of oxygen are reached when FiO_2 levels are greater than 60% for longer than 48 hours (Marino, 2007). Signs and symptoms of oxygen toxicity include chest pain, paresthesias, dyspnea, restlessness, fatigue, malaise, progressive respiratory distress, atelectasis, pulmonary infiltrates, and fibrosis. The prevention of oxygen toxicity is achieved by using the lowest level of oxygen needed clinically. If a patient remains hypoxemic on toxic levels of oxygen, additional measures should be instituted, such as intubation and mechanical ventilation.

Oxygen supports combustion; therefore, its use is a fire hazard. No smoking or open flames should be allowed near oxygen use. Additionally, the risk of cross-contamination of oxygen supplies (mask, tubing, cannulas) should be addressed and equipment changed per infection control policy.

Supportive Care

Supportive care for pneumonia includes hydration to combat insensible fluid losses from fever and tachypnea. Antipyretics may be used to treat headache, aches, and fever. Warm, moist inhalations are helpful in relieving bronchial irritation.

Additional therapies must be considered for the hospitalized pneumonia patient. Nutritional assessment and support, deep vein thrombosis prophylaxis, nebulized bronchodilators or mucolytics, and comfort care measures should be individualized for each patient.

Gerontologic Considerations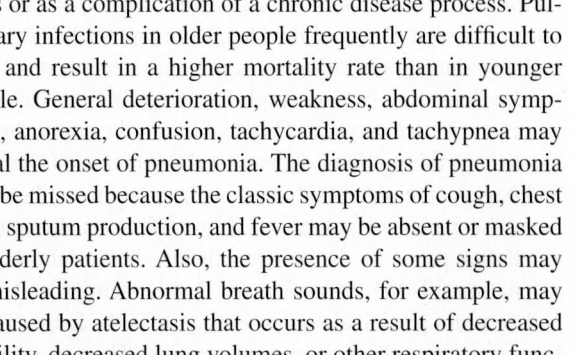

Pneumonia in elderly patients may occur as a primary diagnosis or as a complication of a chronic disease process. Pulmonary infections in older people frequently are difficult to treat and result in a higher mortality rate than in younger people. General deterioration, weakness, abdominal symptoms, anorexia, confusion, tachycardia, and tachypnea may signal the onset of pneumonia. The diagnosis of pneumonia may be missed because the classic symptoms of cough, chest pain, sputum production, and fever may be absent or masked in elderly patients. Also, the presence of some signs may be misleading. Abnormal breath sounds, for example, may be caused by atelectasis that occurs as a result of decreased mobility, decreased lung volumes, or other respiratory function changes. It may be necessary to obtain chest X-rays to differentiate chronic heart failure, which is often seen in the elderly, from pneumonia as the cause of clinical signs and symptoms.

Supportive treatment includes hydration (with caution and with frequent assessment because of the risk of fluid overload in the elderly), supplemental oxygen therapy, and

assistance with deep breathing, coughing, frequent position changes, and early ambulation. All of these are particularly important in the care of elderly patients with pneumonia. To reduce or prevent serious complications of pneumonia in the elderly, vaccination against pneumococcal and influenza infections is recommended.

Prevention

Pneumococcal disease is more prevalent (three- to fivefold higher) in African American adults as compared with Caucasians. Pneumococcal vaccination has been demonstrated to prevent pneumonia in otherwise healthy populations by 50% (Vila-Corcoles, 2007). The vaccine provides specific prevention against pneumococcal pneumonia and other infections caused by *S. pneumoniae* (otitis media, other upper respiratory tract infections). Vaccines should be avoided during the first trimester of pregnancy (Kroger, Atkinson, Marcuse et al., 2006).

To reduce or prevent serious complications of CAP in high-risk groups, vaccination against pneumococcal infection is advised for persons 2 to 64 years of age with chronic illnesses and for everyone 65 years or older. If vaccine was given prior to age 65, it should be repeated once after 5 years (CDC, 2010).

NURSING PROCESS

The Patient With Pneumonia

Assessment

Nursing assessment is critical in detecting pneumonia. Patients with fever, chills, dyspnea, and cough should alert the nurse to the possibility of pneumonia. Respiratory assessment further identifies the clinical manifestations of pneumonia: pleuritic-type pain, fatigue, tachypnea, use of accessory muscles for breathing, tachycardia, coughing, and purulent sputum. The nurse monitors the patient for the following:

- Changes in temperature and pulse
- Amount, odor, and color of secretions
- Frequency and severity of cough
- Degree of tachypnea or shortness of breath
- Pulse oximetry
- Changes in physical assessment findings (primarily assessed by inspecting and auscultating the chest)
- Changes in the chest X-ray findings

In addition, it is important to assess patients, especially elderly patients, for unusual behavior, altered mental status, dehydration, excessive fatigue, and concomitant heart failure.

Diagnosis

Appropriate nursing diagnoses may include:

- Ineffective airway clearance related to copious tracheobronchial secretions
- Impaired gas exchange
- Activity intolerance related to impaired respiratory function
- Risk for deficient fluid volume related to fever, a rapid respiratory rate, and sepsis
- Imbalanced nutrition: less than body requirements
- Deficient knowledge about the treatment regimen and preventive health measures

Collaborative problems or potential complications that may occur include the following:

- Continuing symptoms after initiation of therapy
- Shock
- Respiratory failure
- Atelectasis
- Pleural effusion
- Confusion
- Superinfection

Planning

The major goals may include improved airway patency, rest to conserve energy, maintenance of proper fluid volume, maintenance of adequate nutrition, an understanding of the treatment protocol and preventive measures, and absence of complications.

Nursing Interventions

Improving Airway Patency

Removing secretions is important, because retained secretions interfere with gas exchange and may slow recovery. The nurse encourages hydration (2 to 3 L/day), because adequate hydration thins and loosens pulmonary secretions. Hydration must be achieved more slowly and with careful monitoring in patients with preexisting conditions, such as heart failure. Humidification may be used to loosen secretions and improve ventilation. A high-humidity face mask (using either compressed air or oxygen) delivers warm, humidified air to the tracheobronchial tree and helps to liquefy secretion. Coughing can be initiated either voluntarily or by reflex. Lung expansion maneuvers, such as deep breathing with an incentive spirometer, may induce a cough. A directed cough may be necessary to improve airway patency. The nurse encourages the patient to perform an effective, directed cough, which includes correct positioning, a deep inspiratory maneuver, glottic closure, contraction of the expiratory muscles against the closed glottis, sudden glottic opening, and an explosive expiration.

(continued on page 288)

In general, the dependent lung is associated with improved perfusion. If the goal is to match ventilation with perfusion, the "good lung down" is a position that will facilitate this. However, any position for a prolonged period of time is associated with stagnation of secretions and pressure on the dependent lung, increasing the risk of atelectasis in the dependent lung. Therefore, the nurse turns the patient at regular intervals. The nurse is aware that when the affected lung is positioned dependently, the oxygen saturation should be assessed to note the impact of this position on oxygen level. Additionally, the nurse is aware that in the case of unilateral (one lung) pulmonary hemorrhage or pulmonary abscess "good lung down" is contraindicated to prevent blood or infected material from draining into the good lung (Marklew, 2006). Recent research reveals that the standard schedule of turning every 2 hours is insufficient in some critically ill patients to maintain oxygenation and prevent HCA pneumonia (Rauen, Chulay, Bridges et al., 2008) and more frequent turning should be considered.

CPT is important in loosening and mobilizing secretions. Indications for CPT include sputum retention not responsive to spontaneous or directed cough, a history of pulmonary problems previously treated with CPT, continued evidence of retained secretions (decreased or abnormal breath sounds, change in vital signs), abnormal chest X-ray findings consistent with atelectasis or infiltrates, and deterioration in oxygenation.

The nurse may consult the respiratory therapy department for volume-expansion protocols and secretion-management protocols that help direct the respiratory care of the patient and match the patient's needs with appropriate treatment schedules.

After each position change, the nurse encourages the patient to breathe deeply and cough. If the patient is too weak to cough effectively, the nurse may need to remove the mucus by nasotracheal suctioning. It may take time for secretions to mobilize and move into the central airways for expectoration. Therefore, it is important for the nurse to monitor the patient for cough and sputum production after the completion of CPT.

The nurse also administers and titrates oxygen therapy as prescribed or via protocols. The effectiveness of oxygen therapy is monitored by improvement in clinical signs and symptoms, patient comfort, and adequate oxygenation values as measured by POX or ABG analysis.

Promoting Rest and Conserving Energy

The nurse encourages the debilitated patient to rest and avoid overexertion and possible exacerbation of symptoms. The patient should assume a comfortable position to promote rest and breathing (e.g., semi-Fowler's position) and should change positions frequently to enhance secretion clearance and ventilation and perfusion in the lungs. It is important to instruct outpatients not to overexert themselves and to engage in only moderate activity during the initial phases of treatment.

Promoting Fluid Intake

The respiratory rate of patients with pneumonia increases because of the increased workload imposed by labored breathing and fever. An increased respiratory rate leads to an increase in insensible fluid loss during exhalation and can lead to dehydration. Therefore, it is important to encourage increased fluid intake (at least 2 L/day), unless contraindicated.

Maintaining Nutrition

Many patients with shortness of breath and fatigue have a decreased appetite and consume only fluids. Fluids with electrolytes and protein-supplementation drinks can be prescribed to patients. In addition, IV fluids and nutrients may be administered if necessary.

Promoting Patients' Knowledge

The patient and family are instructed about the cause of pneumonia, management of symptoms of pneumonia, signs and symptoms that should be reported to the health care provider or nurse, and the need for follow-up. The patient also needs information about factors (both patient risk factors and external factors) that may have contributed to development of pneumonia and strategies to promote recovery and prevent recurrence. If the patient is hospitalized, he or she is instructed about the purpose and importance of management strategies that have been implemented and about the importance of adhering to them during and after the hospital stay. Explanations should be given in simple and clear language that the patient can understand. If possible, written instructions and information should be provided, with alternative formats available for patients with hearing or vision loss, if necessary. Because of the severity of symptoms, the patient may require that instructions and explanations be repeated several times.

Monitoring and Managing Potential Complications

CONTINUING SYMPTOMS AFTER INITIATION OF THERAPY. The patient is observed for response to antibiotic therapy; patients usually begin to respond to treatment within 24 to 48 hours after antibiotic therapy is initiated. If the patient started taking antibiotics before evaluation by culture and sensitivity of the causative organisms, antibiotics may need to be changed once the results are available. The patient is monitored for changes in physical status (deterioration of condition or resolution of symptoms) and for persistent or recurrent fever, which may be a result of medication allergy (signaled possibly by a rash); medication resistance or slow response (greater than 48 hours) of the susceptible organism to therapy; superinfection; pleural effusion; or pneumonia caused by an unusual organism, such as *P. jiroveci* or *Aspergillus fumigatus*. Failure of the pneumonia to resolve

or persistence of symptoms despite changes on the chest X-ray raises the suspicion of other underlying disorders, such as lung cancer. As previously described, lung cancers may invade or compress airways, causing an obstructive atelectasis that may lead to pneumonia.

In addition to monitoring for continuing symptoms of pneumonia, the nurse also monitors for other complications, such as shock and multisystem failure and atelectasis, which may develop during the first few days of antibiotic treatment.

SHOCK AND RESPIRATORY FAILURE. Severe complications of pneumonia include severe sepsis and septic shock and respiratory failure. These complications are encountered primarily in patients who have received either nonspecific, inadequate, or delayed treatment in combination with particularly virulent pathogens. These complications are also encountered when the infecting organism is resistant to therapy, when a comorbid disease complicates the pneumonia, or when the patient is immunocompromised.

Severe sepsis is defined as a systemic inflammatory response related to an infection such as pneumonia, with dysfunction or failure of one or more organs (e.g., renal insufficiency, ARDS, or disseminated intravascular coagulation). *Septic shock* occurs when severe sepsis is accompanied by hypotension that is refractory to the infusion of IV fluids. Severe sepsis and septic shock can lead to multiorgan dysfunction and carries a high mortality rate.

If the patient is seriously ill, aggressive therapy may include hemodynamic and ventilator support to combat peripheral vascular collapse, maintain arterial blood pressure, and provide adequate oxygenation. A vasopressor agent may be administered by continuous IV infusion and at a rate adjusted in accordance with the blood pressure response. Corticosteroids may be administered parenterally to combat shock and toxicity in patients who are extremely ill with pneumonia and at apparent risk for death from the infection, or who have adrenal insufficiency. Patients may require endotracheal intubation and mechanical ventilation. Heart failure, cardiac arrhythmias, pericarditis, and myocarditis also are complications of pneumonia that may lead to shock.

The nurse assesses for signs and symptoms of shock and respiratory failure by evaluating the patient's vital signs, POX values, and hemodynamic monitoring parameters. The nurse reports signs of deteriorating patient status and assists in administering IV fluids and medications prescribed to combat shock. Intubation and mechanical ventilation may be required if respiratory failure occurs.

ATELECTASIS AND PLEURAL EFFUSION. Atelectasis (from obstruction of a bronchus or small airways by accumulated secretions) may occur at any stage of acute pneumonia. Parapneumonic **pleural effusions** occur in at least 40% of bacterial pneumonias. A parapneumonic effusion is any pleural effusion associated with bacterial pneumonia, lung

abscess, or bronchiectasis. After the pleural effusion is detected on a chest X-ray or CT scan, a thoracentesis may be performed to remove the fluid. The fluid is sent to the laboratory for analysis. There are three stages of parapneumonic pleural effusions based on pathogenesis: uncomplicated, complicated, and empyema. An **empyema** occurs when thick, purulent fluid accumulates within the **pleural space**, often with fibrin development and a loculated (walled-off) area where the infection is located (see later discussion). A chest tube may be inserted to treat pleural infection by establishing proper drainage of the empyema. Sterilization of the empyema cavity requires 4 to 6 weeks of antibiotics, but sometimes surgical management is required.

The patient is assessed for atelectasis, and preventive measures are initiated to prevent its development. If pleural effusion develops and thoracentesis is performed to remove fluid, the nurse assists in the procedure and explains it to the patient. After thoracentesis, the nurse monitors the patient for pneumothorax or recurrence of pleural effusion. If a chest tube needs to be inserted, the nurse monitors the patient's respiratory status and assesses functioning of the chest drainage system (see later discussion).

SUPERINFECTION. Superinfections may occur with the administration of any antibiotic, but are more common with the use of high-dose, broad-spectrum, and multiple antibiotics. Superinfections are the overgrowth of endogenous flora. Common superinfections are oral yeast (thrush) and vaginal candidiasis, and *Clostridium difficile* colitis (pseudomembranous colitis). The patient is monitored for manifestations of superinfection (i.e., white coating of tongue or oral mucosa, vaginal discharge, and diarrhea). These signs are reported, and the nurse assists in implementing therapy to treat superinfection.

CONFUSION. A patient with pneumonia is assessed for confusion and other more subtle changes in cognitive status. Confusion and changes in cognitive status resulting from pneumonia are poor prognostic signs. Confusion may be related to hypoxemia, fever, dehydration, sleep deprivation, or developing sepsis. The patient's underlying comorbid conditions may also play a part in the development of confusion. Addressing the underlying factors and ensuring patient safety are important nursing interventions.

Promoting Health

The nurse encourages the patient to stop smoking. Smoking inhibits tracheobronchial ciliary action, which is the first line of defense of the lower respiratory tract. Smoking also irritates the mucous cells of the bronchi and inhibits the function of alveolar macrophage (scavenger) cells. The patient is instructed to avoid stress, fatigue, sudden changes in temperature, and excessive alcohol intake, all of which lower resistance to pneumonia. The nurse reviews with the patient the principles of adequate nutrition and rest, because one episode of pneumonia may

(continued on page 290)

make a patient susceptible to recurring respiratory tract infections.

Evaluation

Expected patient outcomes may include the following:

1. Demonstrates improved airway patency, as evidenced by adequate oxygenation by POX or ABG analysis, normal temperature, normal breath sounds, and effective coughing
2. Rests and conserves energy by limiting activities and remaining in bed while symptomatic and then slowly increasing activities
3. Maintains adequate hydration, as evidenced by an adequate fluid intake and urine output and normal skin turgor
4. Consumes adequate dietary intake, as evidenced by maintenance or increase in body weight without excess fluid gain
5. States explanation for management strategies
6. Complies with management strategies
7. Exhibits no complications:

   - Exhibits acceptable vital signs, POX, and ABG measurements
   - Reports productive cough that diminishes over time
   - Has absence of signs or symptoms of shock, respiratory failure, or pleural effusion
   - Remains oriented and aware of surroundings
   - Maintains or increases weight
   - Complies with treatment protocol and prevention strategies

PULMONARY TUBERCULOSIS

Tuberculosis (TB) is an infectious disease that primarily affects the lung parenchyma. The primary infectious agent, *M. tuberculosis,* is an acid-fast aerobic bacilli that grows slowly and is sensitive to heat and ultraviolet light. It is a resistant bacterium that can persist in calcified and necrotic lesions and remain able to reinitiate growth.

TB is a worldwide public health problem, and mortality and morbidity rates continue to rise. *M. tuberculosis* infects an estimated one-third of the world's population and remains the leading cause of death from infectious disease in the world. TB is closely associated with poverty, malnutrition, overcrowding, substandard housing, and inadequate health care (American Thoracic Society, Centers for Disease Control and Prevention, Infectious Disease Society of America [ATS, CDC, & IDSA], 2003; CDC, 2009a).

Pathophysiology

TB spreads from person to person by airborne transmission. An infected person releases droplet nuclei (usually particles 1 to 5 μm in diameter) through talking, coughing, sneezing, laughing, or singing. Larger droplets settle; smaller droplets remain suspended in the air and are inhaled. Several factors determine the transmission of *M. tuberculosis* and include characteristics of the source case, exposed person, and the exposure; and the virulence of the *M. tuberculosis* strain (ATS, CDC, & IDSA, 2005). Box 10-7 depicts risk factors.

TB begins when a susceptible person inhales mycobacteria and the bacteria are transmitted through the airways to the alveoli, where macrophages ingest the bacilli. If the bacilli escape the antimicrobial activities of the macrophages, an

---

BOX 10-7 **Risk Factors for Tuberculosis (TB)**

- Being born in foreign countries with high prevalence of TB
- Being medically underserved and/or with low income. Populations include:
  - Homeless
  - Impoverished
  - Minorities, particularly children under age of 15 years and young adults between 15 and 44 years
  - Those living in overcrowded, substandard housing
- Being a resident or employee of correction centers, homeless shelters, long-term care facilities
- Being a health care worker caring for high-risk patients
- Being a health care worker performing high-risk activities:
  - Administration of aerosolized medications
  - Sputum induction procedures, including suctioning and coughing procedures
  - Bronchoscopy
  - Intubations

- Unprotected exposure to TB patients
- Advanced age
- Traveling abroad to work endemic areas (Southeastern Asia, Africa, Latin America, Caribbean)
- Infants and children exposed to high-risk patients
- Substance abuse (IV/injection drug users and alcoholics)
- Immunocompromise:
  - Human immunodeficiency virus (HIV) infections
  - Malignancies: Head, neck, lung, hematologic
  - Long-term corticosteroid use
  - Immunosuppressive drug therapies
  - Organ transplantation
- Comorbidities:
  - Malnutrition
  - Diabetes
  - Silicosis
  - Chronic kidney disease
  - Gastric or intestinal bypass surgery

infection begins. This stage, called *primary TB*, usually is clinically silent and is due to the chronic inflammatory response that the bacterium provokes. The bacilli may be transported via the lymph system and bloodstream to other parts of the body (kidneys, bones, cerebral cortex) and other areas of the lungs (upper lobes). The spreading of TB via lymphatics and blood is called *miliary TB*. The body's immune system responds by initiating an inflammatory reaction. Phagocytes (neutrophils and macrophages) engulf many of the bacteria, and TB-specific lymphocytes destroy the bacilli along with normal tissue. This tissue reaction results in the accumulation of exudate in the alveoli, causing bronchopneumonia. The initial infection usually occurs 2 to 10 weeks after exposure.

Granulomas, new tissue masses of live and dead bacilli, are surrounded by macrophages, which form a protective wall. They are then transformed to a fibrous tissue mass, the central portion of which is called a Ghon tubercle. The material (bacteria and macrophages) becomes necrotic, forming a cheesy mass. This mass may become calcified and form a collagenous scar. At this point, the bacteria become dormant, and there is no further progression of active disease.

After initial exposure and infection, active disease may develop because of a compromised or inadequate immune system response. Active disease also may occur with reinfection and activation of dormant bacteria. In this case, the Ghon tubercle ulcerates, releasing the cheesy material into the bronchi. The bacteria then become airborne, resulting in further spread of the disease. The ulcerated tubercle heals and forms scar tissue. This causes the infected lung to become more inflamed, resulting in further development of bronchopneumonia and tubercle formation.

Unless the process is arrested, it spreads slowly downward to the hilum of the lungs and later extends to adjacent lobes. The process may be prolonged and is characterized by long remissions when the disease is arrested, followed by periods of renewed activity. Approximately 10% of people who are initially infected develop active disease. Some people develop reactivation TB. This type of TB results from a breakdown of the host defenses. It most commonly occurs in the lungs, usually in the apical (upper) or posterior segments of the upper lobes or the superior segments of the lower lobes.

Clinical Manifestations and Assessment

The signs and symptoms of pulmonary TB are insidious. Most patients have a low-grade fever, cough, night sweats, fatigue, and weight loss. The cough is initially nonproductive, but progresses to be mucopurulent. Dyspnea, chest pain, and **hemoptysis** (bloody sputum) occur as the disease progresses. Both the systemic and the pulmonary symptoms are chronic and may have been present for weeks to months. Elderly patients usually present with less pronounced symptoms than do younger patients. Extrapulmonary disease occurs in up to 16% of cases in the United States. In patients with AIDS, extrapulmonary disease is more prevalent and is manifested by neurologic deficits, bone pain, meningitis symptoms (stiff neck, headache, fever, confusion, and seizures), and urinary tract symptoms (dysuria).

A complete history, physical examination, tuberculin skin test, chest X-ray, AFB smear, and sputum culture are used to diagnose TB. If the patient is infected with TB, the chest X-ray usually reveals lesions in the upper lobes, and the AFB smear contains mycobacteria.

Tuberculin Skin Test

The Mantoux test is used to determine whether a person has been infected with the TB bacillus. The Mantoux test is a standardized procedure and should be performed only by those trained in its administration and reading (Fig. 10-5). Tubercle bacillus extract (tuberculin), purified protein derivative (PPD), is injected into the intradermal layer of the inner aspect of the forearm, approximately 4 inches below the elbow. Intermediate-strength PPD, in a tuberculin syringe with a .5-inch 26- or 27-gauge needle, is used. The needle, with the bevel facing up, is inserted beneath the skin. Then, 0.1 mL of PPD is injected, creating an elevation in the skin, a *wheal* or *bleb*. The site, antigen name, strength, lot number, date, and time of the test are recorded. The test result is read 48 to 72 hours after injection. Tests read after 72 hours tend to underestimate the true size of **induration** (hardening).

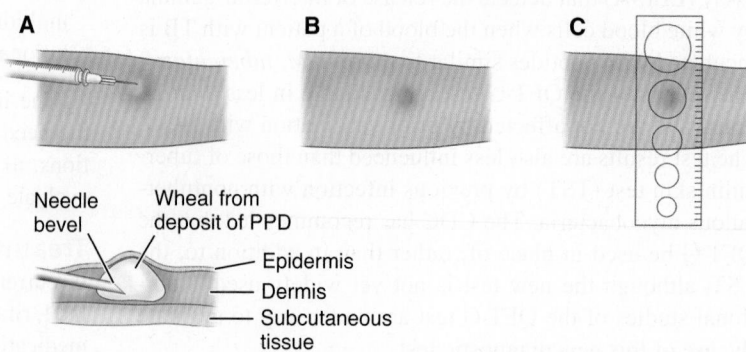

FIGURE 10-5 The Mantoux test for tuberculosis. **(A)** Correct technique for inserting the needle involves depositing the purified protein derivative (PPD) subcutaneously with the needle bevel facing upward. **(B)** The reaction to the Mantoux test usually consists of a *wheal*, a hive-like, firm welt. **(C)** To determine the extent of the reaction, the wheal is measured using a commercially prepared gauge. Interpretation of the Mantoux test is discussed on page 292.

A reaction occurs when an induration at the injection site is present. After the area is inspected for induration, it is lightly palpated across the injection site, from the area of normal skin to the margins of the induration. The diameter of the induration (not erythema) is measured in millimeters at its widest part, and the size of the induration is documented. Erythema without induration is not considered significant. The size of the induration determines the significance of the reaction. A reaction of 0 to 4 mm is considered not significant; a reaction of 5 mm or greater may be significant in people who are considered to be at risk. An induration of 10 mm or greater is usually considered significant in people who have normal or mildly impaired immunity. A significant reaction indicates past exposure to *M. tuberculosis* or vaccination with Bacille Calmette-Guérin (BCG) vaccine. The BCG vaccine is used in Europe and Latin America but not routinely in the United States.

A reaction of 5 mm or greater is defined as positive in patients who are HIV-positive or have HIV risk factors and are of unknown HIV status; in those who are close contacts of someone with active TB; and in those who have chest X-ray results consistent with TB. HIV-positive patients are at risk for developing cutaneous anergy from impaired cellular immunity and may have a false-negative reaction to PPD skin testing. These patients may undergo Mantoux-method skin testing with mumps and candida antigens to assess for anergy. A positive test result is an induration of 5 mm or greater, meaning the patient has relatively intact cell-mediated immunity and can mount a reaction to PPD testing.

A significant (positive) reaction does not necessarily mean that active disease is present in the body. More than 90% of people who are tuberculin-significant reactors do not develop clinical TB. However, all significant reactors are candidates for active TB. A nonsignificant (negative) skin test does not exclude TB infection or disease, because patients who are immunosuppressed cannot develop an immune response that is adequate to produce a positive skin test.

QuantiFERON-TB Gold (QFT-G) Test

In 2005, the U.S. Food and Drug Administration approved a new test for the detection of TB. The QuantiFERON-TB Gold (QFT-G) test is an enzyme-linked immunosorbent assay (ELISA) that detects the release of interferon-gamma by white blood cells when the blood of a patient with TB is incubated with peptides similar to those in *M. tuberculosis*. The results of the QFT-G test are available in less than 24 hours and are not affected by prior vaccination with BCG. The test results are also less influenced than those of tuberculin skin test (TST) by previous infection with nontuberculous mycobacteria. The CDC has recommended that the QFT-G be used in place of, rather than in addition to, the TST, although the new test is not yet widely used. Additional studies of the QFT-G test are under way to evaluate the use of this new diagnostic test.

Classification

Data from the history, physical examination, TB test, chest X-ray, and microbiologic studies are used to classify TB into one of five classes. A classification scheme provides public health officials with a systematic way to monitor epidemiology and treatment of the disease (ATS & CDC, 2000):

- Class 0: No exposure; no infection
- Class 1: Exposure; no evidence of infection
- Class 2: Latent infection; no disease (e.g., positive PPD reaction but no clinical evidence of active TB)
- Class 3: Disease; clinically active
- Class 4: Disease; not clinically active
- Class 5: Suspected disease; diagnosis pending

Gerontologic Considerations

TB may have atypical manifestations in elderly patients, whose symptoms may include unusual behavior and altered mental status, fever, anorexia, and weight loss. In many elderly patients, the tuberculin skin test produces no reaction (loss of immunologic memory) or delayed reactivity for up to 1 week (recall phenomenon). A second skin test is performed in 1 to 2 weeks.

Medical and Nursing Management

Pharmacologic Therapy

Pulmonary TB is treated primarily with antituberculosis agents, as either active disease treatment or prophylactic treatment for persons exposed and at risk for developing the disease. A prolonged treatment duration is necessary to ensure eradication of the organisms and to prevent relapse. The continuing (since the 1950s) and increasing resistance of *M. tuberculosis* to TB medications is a worldwide concern and challenge in TB therapy. Several types of drug resistance must be considered when planning effective therapy:

- *Primary drug resistance*: Resistance to one of the first-line antituberculosis agents in people who have not had previous treatment
- *Secondary or acquired drug resistance*: Resistance to one or more antituberculosis agents in patients undergoing therapy
- *Multidrug resistance*: Resistance to two agents, isoniazid (INH) and rifampin. The populations at greatest risk for multidrug resistance are those who are HIV-positive, institutionalized, or homeless.

The increasing prevalence of drug resistance points out the need to begin TB treatment with four or more medications, to ensure completion of therapy, and to develop and evaluate new anti-TB medications.

Treatment Regimens

In current TB therapy, four first-line medications are used INH, rifampin, pyrazinamide, and ethambutol. Combination medications, such as INH and rifampin (Rifamate) or INH,

pyrazinamide, and rifampin (Rifater), and other medications administered twice a week (e.g., rifapentine) are available to help improve patient adherence. Capreomycin, ethionamide, para-aminosalicylate sodium, and cycloserine are second-line medications. Additional potentially effective medications include other aminoglycosides, quinolones, rifabutin, clofazimine, and combinations of medications (ATS, CDC, & IDSA, 2003).

Recommended treatment guidelines for newly diagnosed cases of active pulmonary TB have two parts: an initial treatment phase and a continuation phase. The initial phase consists of multiple medications (INH, rifampin, pyrazinamide, and ethambutol) and multiple dosing regimen choices of these four medications. This initial intensive treatment regimen is administered for 8 weeks and has 4 dosing options that range from daily to 2 or 5 times per week. The continuation phase of treatment, which includes INH and rifampin or INH and rifapentine, lasts for an additional 18 or 31 weeks. The 18-week period is used for the large majority of patients. The 31-week period is recommended for patients with cavitary pulmonary TB whose sputum culture after the initial 2 months of treatment is positive; those whose initial phase of treatment did not include pyrazinamide (PZA); and those being treated once weekly with INH and rifapentine whose sputum culture is positive at the end of the initial phase of treatment. People are generally considered noninfectious after 2 to 3 weeks of continuous medication therapy. Vitamin B (pyridoxine) is usually administered with INH to prevent INH-associated peripheral neuropathy. The total number of doses taken, not simply the duration of treatment, more accurately determines whether a course of therapy has been completed (ATS, CDC, & IDSA, 2003). INH also may be used as a prophylactic (preventive) measure for people who are at risk for significant disease, including:

- Household family members of patients with active disease
- Patients with HIV infection who have a PPD test reaction with 5 mm of induration or greater
- Patients with fibrotic lesions suggestive of old TB detected on a chest X-ray and a PPD reaction with 5 mm of induration or greater
- Patients whose current PPD test results show a change from former test results, suggesting recent exposure to TB and possible infection (skin test converters)
- Users of IV/injection drugs who have PPD test results with 10 mm of induration or greater
- Patients with high-risk comorbid conditions and a PPD result with 10 mm of induration or greater

Other candidates for preventive INH therapy are those 35 years or younger who have PPD test results with 10 mm of induration or more and one of the following criteria:

- Foreign-born individuals from countries with a high prevalence of TB
- High-risk, medically underserved populations
- Institutionalized patients

Prophylactic INH treatment involves taking daily doses for 6 to 12 months. Liver enzymes, blood urea nitrogen (BUN), and creatinine levels are monitored monthly to detect changes in liver and kidney function. Sputum culture results are monitored for AFB to evaluate the effectiveness of treatment and the patient's adherence to the treatment regimen.

Side Effects of Medication Therapy

It is important to assess medication side effects, because they are often a reason why patients fail to adhere to the prescribed medication regimen. Efforts are made to reduce the side effects and to motivate the patient to take the medications as prescribed.

The nurse instructs the patient to take the medication either on an empty stomach or at least 1 hour before meals, because food interferes with medication absorption (although taking medications on an empty stomach frequently results in gastrointestinal upset). Patients taking INH should avoid foods that contain tyramine and histamine (tuna, aged cheese, red wine, soy sauce, yeast extracts), because eating them while taking INH may result in headache, flushing, hypotension, lightheadedness, palpitations, and diaphoresis.

In addition, rifampin can increase the metabolism of certain other medications, making them less effective. These medications include beta-blockers, oral anticoagulants such as warfarin, digoxin, quinidine, corticosteroids, oral hypoglycemic agents, oral contraceptives, theophylline, and verapamil. This issue should be discussed with the prescriber and pharmacist, so that medication dosages can be adjusted accordingly. The nurse informs the patient that rifampin may discolor contact lenses and that the patient may want to wear eyeglasses during treatment. The nurse monitors for other side effects of anti-TB medications, including hepatitis, neurologic changes (hearing loss, neuritis), and rash. Renal and hepatic function tests as well as sputum AFB results are monitored closely. The nurse carefully monitors vital signs and observes for spikes in temperature or changes in the patient's clinical status. Changes in the patient's respiratory status are reported to the primary health care provider. The nurse instructs the patient about the risk of drug resistance if the medication regimen is not strictly and continuously followed.

The strict adherence to complex medication regimens is an important area of education of the TB patient. Drugs must be taken exactly as prescribed, and noncompliance can lead to continued infection and drug resistance. Directly observed therapy (DOT) can be implemented to ensure that patients are compliant with medications regimens. In DOT, a trained health care provider administers each dose of anti-TB medication. DOT can be prescribed by a health care provider such as a physician, nurse practitioner, or a local board of health.

Patient Teaching

The care of TB patients involves education related to halting the spread of the infection and its complex drug regimens. Patients should be instructed to cover their mouth and nose

when they cough or sneeze, dispose of facial tissues in plastic bags, and wear a mask when in public until sputum samples are documented as free of AFB.

Patients in hospital settings will be placed on airborne precautions, including staying in a negative-pressure room that vents air to the outside, and staff must wear fitted filtration masks (N95 or high-efficiency particulate air respirators) when in the room. Patients must also wear surgical masks when outside of the negative-pressure rooms.

Malnutrition may be a consequence of the patient's lifestyle, lack of knowledge about adequate nutrition and its role in health maintenance, lack of resources, fatigue, or lack of appetite because of coughing and mucus production and medication side effects. To counter the effects of these factors, the nurse collaborates with the dietitian, provider, social worker, family, and patient to identify strategies to ensure an adequate nutritional intake and the availability of nutritious food. Identifying facilities (e.g., shelters, soup kitchens, Meals on Wheels) that provide meals in the patient's neighborhood may increase the likelihood that the patient with limited resources and energy will have access to a more nutritious intake. High-calorie nutritional supplements may be suggested as a strategy for increasing dietary intake using food products normally found in the home. Purchasing food supplements may be beyond the patient's budget, but dietitians can help develop recipes to increase caloric intake despite minimal resources.

PULMONARY EDEMA

Pulmonary edema is defined as abnormal accumulation of fluid in the lung tissue, the alveolar space, or both. Acute pulmonary edema, often called "flash" pulmonary edema is a severe, life-threatening condition. Classification of pulmonary edema is based on its causative origin: cardiogenic, or noncardiogenic. Noncardiogenic pulmonary edema include ARDS, neurologic, re-expansion, and negative pressure pulmonary edema. ARDS will be discussed later in this chapter, and cardiogenic pulmonary edema is discussed in Chapter 15.

Pathophysiology

In each type of pulmonary edema, capillary fluid leaks or is forced by high capillary hydrostatic pressure into alveolar spaces. The edematous alveoli are unable to participate in gas exchange, causing intrapulmonary shunting of blood and hypoxemia. The pathophysiology of cardiogenic pulmonary edema is discussed in Chapter 15. The most common form of noncardiogenic pulmonary is ARDS, in which a precipitating injury (direct or indirect) to the lung triggers a systemic inflammatory response that causes pulmonary capillaries to leak fluid into the alveoli. Neurologic pulmonary edema can occur after head or brain injury, as the result of the Cushing's reflex (increased sympathetic

stimulation to the heart to increase mean arterial pressure and therefore blood flow to ischemic brain areas). Re-expansion pulmonary edema may result from a rapid reinflation of the lung after removal of air from a pneumothorax or evacuation of fluid from a large pleural effusion. This rapid negative pressure change within the lungs causes capillary fluid to be pulled into the alveolar spaces. This is similar to negative-pressure pulmonary edema, in which an obstruction in the trachea or large bronchi causes a person to attempt to forcefully inhale against a closed glottis or airway. This pulls fluid into the alveolar spaces. Common causes of this type of edema are choking, angioedema, and manual strangulation.

Clinical Manifestations and Assessment

Increasing respiratory distress, characterized by dyspnea, air hunger, and hypoxemia is present. Patients are usually very anxious and often agitated. As the fluid leaks into the alveoli and mixes with air, a foam or froth is formed (more common in cardiogenic edema). The patient coughs up (or the nurse suctions out) these foamy, frothy, and often blood-tinged or pink secretions. The patient experiences acute respiratory distress and may become confused or stuporous.

Auscultation reveals crackles in the lung bases (especially in the dependent lung areas) that rapidly progress toward the apices of the lungs. These crackles are caused by the movement of air through the alveolar fluid. The chest X-ray reveals increased interstitial markings, with or without cardiomegaly. The patient may have tachycardia. Pulse oximetry values begin to fall, and ABG analysis demonstrates worsening hypoxemia.

Medical Management

Management focuses on correcting the underlying disorder. If the pulmonary edema is cardiac in origin, then improvement in left ventricular function is the goal (see Chapter 15). Oxygen is administered to correct the hypoxemia; in some circumstances, intubation and mechanical ventilation are necessary. Noncardiogenic pulmonary edema treatment is aimed at treating the underlying cause of the **acute lung injury** (i.e., infection), removing obstructions causing negative-pressure edema and providing supportive care such as oxygen, mechanical ventilation, and judicious IV fluids.

Nursing Management

Nursing management includes assisting with administration of oxygen and intubation and mechanical ventilation if respiratory failure occurs. The nurse also administers medications (e.g., morphine, vasodilators, inotropic medications, and pre- and afterload agents) as prescribed, and monitors the patient's responses.

PLEURAL CONDITIONS

Pleural conditions are disorders that involve the membranes covering the lungs (visceral pleura) and the surface of the chest wall (parietal pleura) or disorders affecting the pleural space. The most common pleural conditions are pleurisy, pleural effusions, and empyemas.

PLEURISY

Pathophysiology

Pleurisy (pleuritis) refers to inflammation of both layers of the pleurae (parietal and visceral). Pleurisy may develop in conjunction with pneumonia or an upper respiratory tract infection, TB, or collagen disease; after trauma to the chest, pulmonary infarction, or PE; in patients with primary or metastatic cancer; and after **thoracotomy**. The parietal pleura has nerve endings; the visceral pleura does not. When the inflamed pleural membranes rub together during respiration (intensified on inspiration), the result is severe, sharp, knife-like pain.

Clinical Manifestations and Assessment

The key characteristic of pleuritic pain is its relationship to respiratory movement: Taking a deep breath, coughing, or sneezing worsens the pain. Pleuritic pain is limited in distribution rather than diffuse; it usually occurs only on one side. The pain may become minimal or absent when the breath is held, leading to rapid shallow breathing. It may be localized or radiate to the shoulder or abdomen. Later, as pleural fluid accumulates, the pain decreases.

Medical and Nursing Management

The objectives of treatment are to discover the underlying condition causing the pleurisy and to relieve the pain. As the underlying disease (e.g., pneumonia, infection) is treated, the pleuritic inflammation usually resolves. At the same time, it is necessary to monitor for signs and symptoms of pleural effusion, such as shortness of breath, pain, assumption of a position that decreases pain, and decreased chest wall excursion.

Prescribed analgesics and topical applications of heat or cold provide symptomatic relief. Nonsteroidal anti-inflammatory agents (NSAIDs) may provide pain relief while allowing the patient to take deep breaths and cough more effectively. If the pain is severe, a narcotic or an intercostal nerve block may be required.

PLEURAL EFFUSION AND EMPYEMA

Pleural effusion, a collection of fluid in the pleural space, is rarely a primary disease process but usually occurs secondary to other diseases (Fig. 10-6). Normally, the pleural space

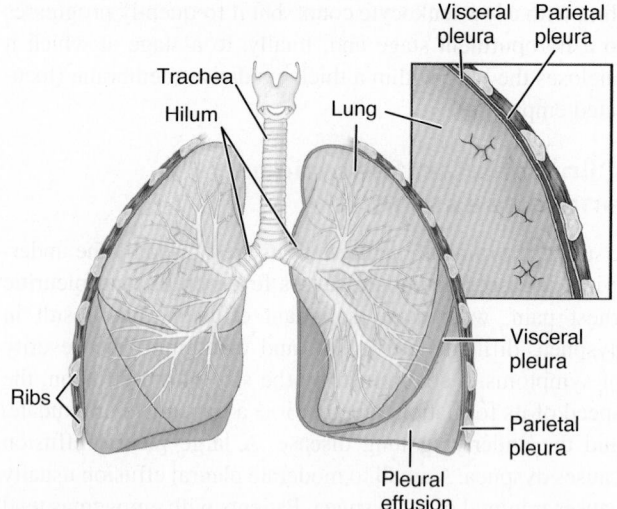

FIGURE 10-6 In pleural effusion, an abnormal volume of fluid collects in the pleural space, causing pain and shortness of breath. Pleural effusion is usually secondary to other disease processes.

contains a small amount of fluid (20 to 25 cc), which acts as a lubricant that allows the pleural surfaces to move without friction. Pleural effusion may be a complication of heart failure, TB, pneumonia, pulmonary infections (particularly viral infections), nephrotic syndrome, connective tissue disease, pulmonary embolus, and neoplastic tumors. The most common malignancies associated with a pleural effusion are bronchogenic carcinoma and breast cancer. An empyema is an accumulation of thick, purulent fluid (pus) within the pleural space and is a type of pleural effusion.

Pathophysiology

In certain disorders, fluid may accumulate in the pleural space to a point at which it becomes clinically evident. This almost always has pathologic significance. A pleural effusion can be composed of a relatively clear fluid, or it can be bloody or purulent. An effusion of clear fluid may be a transudate or an exudate. A transudate (filtrate of plasma that moves across intact capillary walls) occurs when factors influencing the formation and reabsorption of pleural fluid are altered, usually by imbalances in hydrostatic or oncotic pressures. The finding of a transudative effusion generally implies that the pleural membranes are not diseased. A transudative effusion most commonly results from heart failure. An exudate (extravasation of fluid into tissues or a cavity) usually results from inflammation by bacterial products or tumors involving the pleural surfaces. Empyemas are exudative pleural effusions by definition.

Most empyemas occur as complications of bacterial pneumonia or lung abscess. They also result from penetrating chest trauma, hematogenous infection of the pleural space, nonbacterial infections, and iatrogenic causes (after thoracic surgery or thoracentesis). At first, the pleural fluid is

thin, with a low leukocyte count, but it frequently progresses to a fibropurulent stage and, finally, to a stage at which it encloses the lung within a thick exudative membrane (loculated empyema).

Clinical Manifestations and Assessment

Usually, the clinical manifestations are caused by the underlying disease. Pneumonia causes fever, chills, and pleuritic chest pain, whereas a malignant effusion may result in dyspnea, difficulty lying flat, and coughing. The severity of symptoms is determined by the size of the effusion, the speed of its formation, whether it is a transudate or exudate, and the underlying lung disease. A large pleural effusion causes dyspnea. A small to moderate pleural effusion usually causes minimal or no dyspnea. Patients with empyemas tend to be acutely ill, with more severe inflammatory symptoms (fever, chills, pain, cough, dyspnea).

Assessment of the area of the pleural effusion reveals decreased or absent breath sounds, decreased fremitus, and a dull, flat sound on percussion. In the case of an extremely large or rapidly accumulating pleural effusion, the assessment reveals a patient in acute respiratory distress. The patient may have tracheal deviation away from the affected side, hypoxemia (SpO_2 <90%), hypotension, and tachycardia.

Physical examination, chest X-ray, chest CT, ultrasound, and thoracentesis confirm the presence of fluid. In some instances, a lateral decubitus X-ray is obtained. For this X-ray, the patient lies on the unaffected side in a side-lying position. A pleural effusion can be diagnosed because this position allows for the "layering out" of the fluid, and an air–fluid line is visible.

Pleural fluid is analyzed by bacterial culture, Gram stain, AFB stain (for TB), red and white blood cell counts, chemistry studies (glucose, amylase, lactic dehydrogenase, protein), cytologic analysis for malignant cells, and pH. A pleural biopsy also may be performed as a diagnostic tool.

Medical Management

The objectives of treatment are to discover the underlying cause of the pleural effusion; to prevent reaccumulation of fluid; and to relieve discomfort, dyspnea, and respiratory compromise. Specific treatment is directed at the underlying cause (e.g., heart failure, pneumonia, cirrhosis). If the pleural fluid is an exudate, more extensive diagnostic procedures are performed to determine the cause. Treatment for the primary cause is then instituted.

Thoracentesis is performed to remove fluid, to obtain a specimen for analysis, and to relieve dyspnea and respiratory compromise. Thoracentesis may be performed under ultrasound guidance or blindly. Depending on the size of the pleural effusion, the patient may be treated by removing the fluid during the thoracentesis procedure or by inserting a chest tube connected to a water-seal drainage system or suction to evacuate the pleural space and re-expand the lung.

However, if the underlying cause is a malignancy, the effusion tends to recur within a few days or weeks. Repeated thoracenteses result in pain, depletion of protein and electrolytes, and sometimes pneumothorax. Once the pleural space is adequately drained, a chemical pleurodesis may be performed to obliterate the pleural space and prevent reaccumulation of fluid. Pleurodesis may be performed using either a thoracoscopic approach or a chest tube. A chemically irritating agent (e.g., talc, bleomycin, doxycycline,) is instilled into the pleural space. With the chest tube approach, after the agent is instilled, the chest tube is clamped for 60 to 90 minutes and the patient is assisted to assume various positions to promote uniform distribution of the agent and to maximize its contact with the pleural surfaces. The tube is unclamped as prescribed, and chest drainage may be continued several days longer to prevent reaccumulation of fluid and to promote the formation of adhesions between the visceral and parietal pleurae.

Other treatments for malignant pleural effusions include surgical pleurectomy and decortication. Pleuracotomy involves the insertion of a small catheter attached to a drainage bottle for outpatient management (Pleurx catheter [Denver Biomedical]), or implantation of a pleuroperitoneal shunt. A pleuroperitoneal shunt consists of two catheters connected by a pump chamber containing two one-way valves. Fluid moves from the pleural space to the pump chamber and then to the peritoneal cavity. The patient manually pumps on the reservoir daily to move fluid from the pleural space to the peritoneal space. Decortication is the surgical removal of fibrous tissue in the pleural space; this procedure is called a *pleural peel*.

Nursing Management

The nurse's role in the care of patients with a pleural effusion or empyema includes implementing the medical regimen. The nurse prepares and positions the patient for thoracentesis and offers support throughout the procedure. The nurse is responsible for making sure the thoracentesis fluid amount is recorded and sent for appropriate laboratory testing. If a chest tube drainage and water-seal system is used, the nurse is responsible for monitoring the system's function and recording the amount of drainage at prescribed intervals. Nursing care related to the underlying cause of the pleural effusion is specific to the underlying condition.

If a chest tube is inserted for pleurodesis, pain management is a priority. Premedication for the procedure with a narcotic analgesic and antianxiety drug should be considered. Patients require frequent turning and movement to facilitate adequate spreading of the pleurodesic over the pleural surface. Treatment of pleurisy pain is similar to the care of patients with chest tubes because the patient has considerable pain on inspiration. The nurse offers suggestions to enhance

comfort, such as turning frequently onto the affected side to splint the chest wall and reduce the stretching of the pleurae. The nurse also teaches the patient to use the hands or a pillow to splint the rib cage while coughing. Administration and assessment of the effects of narcotics or NSAIDs is necessary.

ACUTE RESPIRATORY FAILURE

Respiratory failure is a sudden and life-threatening deterioration of the gas exchange function of the lung. It exists when the exchange of oxygen for carbon dioxide in the lungs cannot keep up with the rate of oxygen consumption and carbon dioxide production by the cells of the body. Acute respiratory failure (ARF) is classified as hypoxemic (decrease in arterial oxygen tension [PaO_2] to <50 mm Hg on room air) and or hypercapnic (increase in arterial carbon dioxide tension [$PaCO_2$] to >50 mm Hg with an arterial pH of <7.35).

It is important to distinguish between ARF and chronic respiratory failure. Chronic respiratory failure is defined as deterioration in the gas exchange function of the lung that has developed insidiously or has persisted for a long period after an episode of ARF. The absence of acute symptoms and the presence of a chronic respiratory acidosis (elevated $PaCO_2$ and bicarbonate, and hypoxemia) suggest the chronicity of the respiratory failure. Two causes of chronic respiratory failure are COPD (discussed in Chapter 11) and neuromuscular diseases (discussed in Chapter 46). Patients with these disorders develop a tolerance to the gradually worsening hypoxemia and hypercapnia. However, patients with chronic respiratory failure can develop ARF. For example, a patient with COPD may develop an exacerbation or infection that causes additional deterioration of gas exchange. The principles of management of acute versus chronic respiratory failure are different; the following discussion is limited to ARF.

Pathophysiology

In ARF, the ventilation or perfusion mechanisms in the lung are impaired. Impaired respiratory system mechanisms leading to ARF include:

- *Alveolar hypoventilation*, which is the inability to deliver oxygen to the alveoli and remove CO_2 from the alveoli, may be due to a variety of causes including obesity, chest wall deformities, neuromuscular disorders, CNS depression, or COPD.
- *Diffusion abnormalities*, related to problems with gas transfer across the alveolar–capillary membrane, which may be due to increased resistance, increased thickness of the alveolar–capillary membrane, or any pathology that impacts the alveolar epithelium, the capillary endothelium, or the interstitial space between them.

- *Ventilation–perfusion mismatching*. Alveolar ventilation brings oxygen to the lung and removes the alveolar CO_2 (ventilation), while blood brings CO_2 to the alveoli and takes up the O_2 from the alveoli (perfusion). Thus, the O_2 and CO_2 levels are determined by the matching of ventilation with perfusion.
- *Shunting*, in which perfusion is adequate to the lung but ventilation is impaired, thus deoxygenated blood continues to the left side of the heart. (Conditions associated with this include right-to-left shunts with cardiac abnormalities such as septal defects, or pulmonary diseases such as pneumonia or pulmonary edema, in which the alveoli are affected and unable to be ventilated).
- *Increased physiologic dead space*, which describes situations in which ventilation of the lung is adequate but perfusion is impaired, as with pulmonary emboli. This mismatch also results in impaired gas exchange.

Common causes of ARF can be classified into four categories: decreased respiratory drive, dysfunction of the chest wall, dysfunction of the lung parenchyma, and other causes.

Decreased Respiratory Drive

Decreased respiratory drive may occur with severe brain injury, lesions of the brainstem (multiple sclerosis, tumor, or herniation), use of sedative medications, and metabolic disorders such as severe hypothyroidism. These disorders impair the response of chemoreceptors in the brain to normal respiratory stimulation.

Dysfunction of the Chest Wall

The impulses arise in the respiratory center and travel through nerves that extend from the brainstem down the spinal cord to receptors in the muscles of respiration. Any disease or disorder of the nerves, spinal cord, muscles, or neuromuscular junction involved in respiration seriously affects ventilation and may ultimately lead to ARF. These include musculoskeletal disorders (muscular dystrophy, polymyositis, chest wall trauma), neuromuscular junction disorders (myasthenia gravis, poliomyelitis), some peripheral nerve disorders, and spinal cord disorders (amyotrophic lateral sclerosis, Guillain-Barré syndrome, and cervical spinal cord injuries).

> **⚠ N U R S I N G   A L E R T**
> With cervical spinal injuries, the rigid cervical collar is left in place until the provider confirms stability of the C spine. The nurse is aware that motor innervations to the diaphragm is from the phrenic nerve at the C3–C5 level, thus any fracture in the area risks respiratory paralysis.

Dysfunction of Lung Parenchyma

Pleural effusion, hemothorax, pneumothorax, and airway obstruction are conditions that interfere with ventilation by preventing expansion of the lung. These conditions, which

may cause respiratory failure, usually are produced by an underlying lung disease, pleural disease, or trauma and injury. Other diseases and conditions of lung parenchyma that lead to ARF include pneumonia, status asthmaticus, atelectasis, PE, exacerbation of COPD, and pulmonary edema.

Other Causes

In the postoperative period, especially after major thoracic or abdominal surgery, inadequate ventilation and respiratory failure may occur because of several factors. During this period, for example, ARF may be caused by the effects of anesthetic agents, analgesics, and sedatives, which may depress respiration (as described earlier) or enhance the effects of opioids and lead to hypoventilation. Pain may interfere with deep breathing and coughing.

Clinical Manifestations and Assessment

Early signs are those associated with impaired oxygenation and may include restlessness, fatigue, headache, dyspnea, air hunger, mild tachycardia and tachypnea, and increased BP. As the hypoxia progresses, more obvious signs may be present, including confusion, lethargy, tachycardia, tachypnea, **central cyanosis**, diaphoresis, and finally respiratory arrest. Physical findings are those of acute respiratory distress, including use of accessory muscles, decreased breath sounds if the patient cannot adequately ventilate, and other findings related specifically to the underlying disease process and cause of ARF.

Medical Management

The objectives of treatment are to correct the underlying cause and to restore adequate gas exchange in the lungs. Supplemental oxygen administration is used to improve hypoxemia. If narcotics are thought to be the cause of hypoventilation, reversal agents, such as naloxone (for opiates) or flumazenil (for benzodiazepines) can be administered. Mechanical ventilation may be required to maintain adequate ventilation and oxygenation while the underlying cause is corrected.

Nursing Management

Nursing management of patients with ARF includes assisting with intubation and maintaining mechanical ventilation. Patients are usually managed in the ICU. The nurse assesses the patient's respiratory status by monitoring the level of responsiveness, ABG levels, POX, and vital signs. In addition, the nurse assesses the entire respiratory system and implements strategies (e.g., turning schedule, mouth care, skin care, range-of-motion exercises for the extremities) to prevent complications. The nurse also assesses the patient's understanding of the management strategies that are used and initiates some form of communication to enable the patient to express concerns and needs to the health care team.

Finally, the nurse addresses the problems that led to the ARF. As the patient's status improves, the nurse assesses the patient's knowledge of the underlying disorder and provides teaching as appropriate to address the disorder.

ACUTE RESPIRATORY DISTRESS SYNDROME

Acute respiratory distress syndrome (previously called adult respiratory distress syndrome) is a severe form of **acute lung injury** that affects over 200,000 persons each year. This clinical syndrome is characterized by a sudden and progressive pulmonary edema, increasing bilateral infiltrates on chest X-ray, hypoxemia refractory to supplemental oxygen, and reduced lung compliance. These signs occur in the absence of left-sided heart failure. Patients with ARDS usually require mechanical ventilation with a higher-than-normal airway pressure. Acute respiratory distress syndrome has been associated with a mortality rate as high as 50% to 60%. The major cause of death in ARDS is multisystem organ failure.

Pathophysiology

Acute respiratory distress syndrome occurs as a result of an inflammatory trigger that initiates the release of cellular and chemical mediators, causing diffuse epithelial cell injury to the alveolar capillary membrane. This leads to leakage of protein-rich fluid and blood cells into the alveolar interstitial spaces and alterations in the capillary bed.

Severe ventilation–perfusion mismatching occurs in ARDS. Alveoli collapse because of the inflammatory infiltrate, blood, fluid, and surfactant dysfunction. Small airways are narrowed because of interstitial fluid and bronchial obstruction. Lung compliance becomes markedly decreased (stiff lungs), and the result is a characteristic decrease in functional residual capacity (FRC) and severe hypoxemia. The blood returning to the lung for gas exchange is pumped through the nonventilated, nonfunctioning areas of the lung, causing shunting. This means that blood is interfacing with nonfunctioning alveoli, and gas exchange is markedly impaired, resulting in severe, refractory hypoxemia. Figure 10-7 shows the sequence of pathophysiologic events leading to ARDS.

Risk Factors

A wide range of factors are associated with the development of ARDS, including direct injury to the lungs (e.g., smoke inhalation, pulmonary contusion) or indirect insult to the lungs (e.g., septic shock, massive fluid resuscitation) (Box 10-8).

Clinical Manifestations and Assessment

Clinically, the acute phase of ARDS is marked by a rapid onset of severe dyspnea that usually occurs 12 to 48 hours

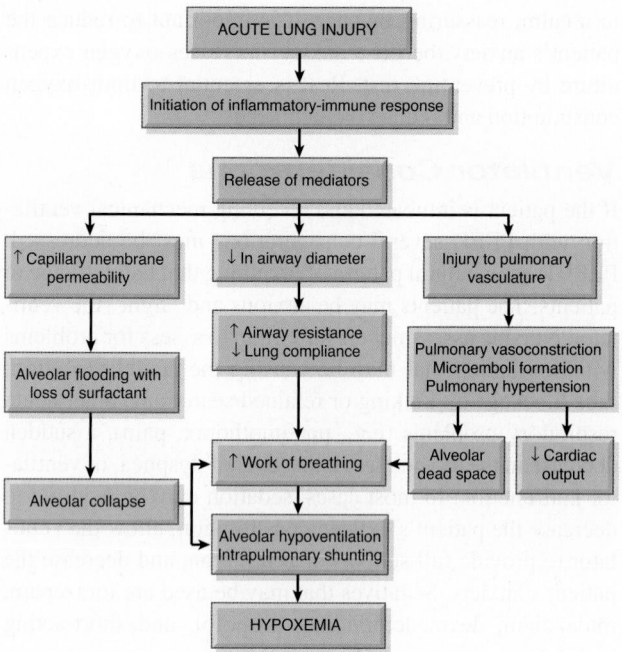

FIGURE 10-7 Pathogenesis of acute respiratory distress syndrome (ARDS).

after the initiating event. A characteristic feature is arterial hypoxemia that does not respond to supplemental oxygen. On chest X-ray, the findings are similar to those seen with cardiogenic pulmonary edema and appear as bilateral, patchy infiltrates that quickly worsen. On chest CT, bilateral, patchy infiltrates with consolidation are usually more pronounced in the dependent (posterior) lung areas. The acute lung injury then progresses to fibrosing alveolitis with persistent, severe hypoxemia. The patient also has increased alveolar dead space (ventilation to nonperfused alveoli) and decreased pulmonary compliance ("stiff lungs," which are difficult to ventilate). Clinically, the patient is thought to be in the recovery

---

BOX 10-8

Risk Factors for Acute Respiratory Distress Syndrome (ARDS)

- Aspiration
- Drug ingestion and overdose
- Hematologic disorders (e.g., disseminated intravascular coagulopathy, massive transfusions, cardiopulmonary bypass)
- Prolonged inhalation of high concentrations of oxygen
- Localized infection
- Metabolic disorders (pancreatitis, uremia)
- Shock
- Trauma
- Major surgery
- Fat or air embolism
- Systemic sepsis

---

phase if the hypoxemia gradually resolves, the chest X-ray improves, and the lungs become more compliant.

Intercostal retractions and crackles, as the fluid begins to leak into the alveolar interstitial space, are evident on physical examination. Arterial blood gases are analyzed to assess the severity of hypoxemia. A diagnosis of ARDS may be made based on the following criteria: a history of systemic or pulmonary risk factors, acute onset of respiratory distress, bilateral pulmonary infiltrates, clinical absence of left-sided heart failure, and a ratio of PaO_2 to fraction of inspired oxygen (FiO_2) of less than 200 mm Hg (severe refractory hypoxemia). The normal ratio of PaO_2 to FiO_2 is over 300 mm Hg.

Medical Management

The primary focus in the management of ARDS includes identification and treatment of the underlying causative condition. Aggressive, supportive care must be provided to compensate for the severe respiratory dysfunction. This supportive therapy almost always includes intubation and mechanical ventilation. In addition, circulatory support, adequate fluid volume, and nutritional support are important. Supplemental oxygen is used as the patient begins the initial spiral of hypoxemia. As the hypoxemia progresses, intubation and mechanical ventilation are instituted. The concentration of oxygen and ventilator settings and modes are determined by the patient's status. This is monitored by ABG analysis, POX, and bedside pulmonary compliance testing.

Positive End-Expiratory Pressure

PEEP is a critical part of the treatment of ARDS. Use of PEEP helps increase FRC and reverse alveolar collapse by keeping the alveoli open, resulting in improved arterial oxygenation and a reduction in the severity of the ventilation–perfusion imbalance. The use of PEEP can also allow for the use of lower, safer FiO_2 levels ($\leq 60\%$ FiO_2). The goal is a PaO_2 of greater than 60 mm Hg or an oxygen saturation level of greater than 90% at the lowest possible FiO_2. Evidence suggests that ARDS should be managed with a low tidal volume (6 cc/Kg of ideal body weight), pressure-limited approach (plateau pressure ≤ 30 mm Hg) with low or moderately high PEEP (ARDS Network, 2000; Grasso, Stripoli, Me Michele et al., 2007; Villar, Perez-Mendez, Lopez et al., 2007).

The use of positive-pressure ventilation (as opposed to normal negative-pressure breathing) increases intrathoracic pressure and causes a decrease in preload to the heart. This drop in preload can result in decreased cardiac output and hypotension. Systemic hypotension may also occur in ARDS as a result of hypovolemia secondary to leakage of fluid into the interstitial spaces. Hypovolemia must be carefully treated without causing further fluid overload. IV crystalloid solutions are administered, with careful monitoring of pulmonary status. Inotropic (e.g., dobutamine) or vasopressor agents (e.g., norepinephrine, dopamine) may be required.

Pulmonary artery pressure catheters may be used to monitor the patient's fluid status and the severe and progressive pulmonary hypertension sometimes observed in ARDS. Arterial catheterization is required, as patients with ARDS need frequent blood gas analysis. If suctioning of the patient is required while on PEEP, the nurse is aware that any break in the closed ventilator system causes the loss of PEEP, therefore respiratory therapy is consulted to add "in-line suctioning" as an alternative to traditional suctioning.

Pharmacologic Therapy

Numerous pharmacologic treatments are under investigation to stop the cascade of events leading to ARDS. These include human recombinant interleukin-1 receptor antagonist, neutrophil inhibitors, pulmonary-specific vasodilators, surfactant replacement therapy, antisepsis agents, antioxidant therapy, and corticosteroids administered late in the course of ARDS.

ARDS patients often require IV sedation and pain medication to combat anxiety and agitation from hypoxemia and intubation. In extreme cases, patients may require chemical paralysis with neuromuscular blockers in order to adequately ventilate and oxygenate them.

Nutritional Therapy

Adequate nutritional support is vital in the treatment of ARDS. Patients with ARDS require 15 to 20 kcal/kg/day to meet caloric requirements. Enteral feeding is the first consideration; however, parenteral nutrition also may be required (Martindale, McClave, Vanek et al., 2009).

Nursing Management

General Measures

A patient with ARDS is critically ill and requires close monitoring in the intensive care unit. Many different respiratory modalities can be used in this situation (oxygen administration, nebulizer therapy, chest physiotherapy, endotracheal intubation or tracheostomy, mechanical ventilation, suctioning, bronchoscopy). Frequent assessment of the patient's status is necessary to evaluate the effectiveness of treatment.

In addition to implementing the medical plan of care, the nurse considers other patient needs. Positioning is important. The nurse turns the patient frequently to improve ventilation and perfusion in the lungs and enhance secretion drainage. However, the nurse must closely monitor the patient for deterioration in oxygenation with changes in position. Oxygenation in patients with ARDS is sometimes improved in the prone position. This position may be evaluated for improvement in oxygenation and used in special circumstances. Devices and specialty beds are available to assist the nurse in placing the patient in a prone position (Mancebo et al., 2006).

The patient can be extremely anxious and agitated because of the increasing hypoxemia, dyspnea, and intubation. The nurse explains all procedures and provides care in a calm, reassuring manner. It is important to reduce the patient's anxiety, because anxiety increases oxygen expenditure by preventing rest. Rest is essential to limit oxygen consumption and reduce oxygen needs.

Ventilator Considerations

If the patient is intubated and receiving mechanical ventilation with PEEP, several considerations must be addressed. PEEP is an unnatural pattern of breathing that feels strange to patients. The patients may be anxious and "fight" the ventilator. Nursing assessment is important to assess for problems with ventilation that may be causing the anxiety reaction: tube blockage by kinking or retained secretions, other acute respiratory problems (e.g., pneumothorax, pain), a sudden decrease in the oxygen level, the level of dyspnea, or ventilator malfunction. In most cases, sedation may be required to decrease the patient's oxygen consumption, allow the ventilator to provide full support of ventilation, and decrease the patient's anxiety. Sedatives that may be used are lorazepam, midazolam, dexmedetomidine, propofol, and short-acting barbiturates.

If satisfactory oxygen levels cannot be maintained despite the use of sedatives, neuromuscular blocking agents, such as pancuronium, vecuronium, atracurium, or rocuronium, may be administered to paralyze the patient. These agents paralyze skeletal muscles, including respiratory muscles, leading to respiratory arrest if the patient is not intubated and on adequate ventilator settings. With paralysis, the patient appears to be unconscious, loses motor function, and cannot breathe, talk, or blink independently. However, the patient retains sensation and is awake and able to hear. Paralytic agents should only be used by personnel who are trained in airway and ventilator management. The nurse must reassure the patient that the paralysis is a result of the medication and is temporary. Paralysis should be used for the shortest possible time and never without adequate sedation and pain management.

Use of paralytic agents has many dangers and side effects. The nurse must be sure the patient does not become disconnected from the ventilator, because respiratory muscles are paralyzed and the patient will be apneic. Consequently, the nurse ensures that the patient is closely monitored, and all ventilator and patient alarms must be on at all times. Eye care is important as well, because the patient cannot blink, thus increasing the risk of corneal abrasions. Neuromuscular blockers predispose the patient to deep venous thrombi, muscle atrophy, and skin breakdown, therefore passive range of motion exercises and skin assessment are important nursing actions. The concurrent use of aminoglycosides and/or steroids increases the chance of chemically paralyzed patient developing *critical illness polyneuropathy*. This is a severe form of muscle atrophy and deconditioning that can occur within 24 hours; it requires intensive physical therapy to correct, increases patients' risks of developing complications, and prolongs hospital lengths of stay.

The patient may have discomfort or pain but cannot communicate these sensations. Signs of pain, such as tachycardia, diaphoresis, and hypertension, must be assessed for and treated. Analgesia **must** be administered concurrently with neuromuscular blocking agents. The nurse must anticipate the patient's needs regarding pain and comfort. The nurse checks the patient's position to ensure it is comfortable and in normal body alignment.

The nurse talks to, and not about, the patient while in the patient's presence. In addition, it is important for the nurse to describe the purpose and effects of the paralytic agents to the patient's family. If family members are unaware that these agents have been administered, they may become distressed by the change in the patient's status.

PULMONARY ARTERIAL HYPERTENSION

Pulmonary circulation is a low-pressure system intended to accommodate high blood flow from the right ventricle. The pulmonary vasculature is compliant and thin walled in order to facilitate gas exchange. The normal mean pulmonary pressure is 12 to 15 mm Hg, with the capacity to dilate and constrict as needed. Pulmonary arterial hypertension (PAH) exists when the mean pulmonary artery pressure exceeds 25 mm Hg at rest or 30 mm Hg with activities. Unlike systemic BP, these pressures cannot be measured indirectly; instead, they must be measured via right-sided heart catheterization with a pulmonary artery catheter. In the absence of these measurements, clinical recognition becomes the only indicator for the presence of pulmonary hypertension; however, PAH is a condition that is not clinically evident until late in its progression.

There are two types of PAH: idiopathic PAH (formerly known as primary) and secondary PAH due to a known cause. Idiopathic hypertension is a very uncommon disease. It occurs most often in women 20 to 40 years of age, either sporadically or in patients with a family history, and is usually fatal within 5 years of diagnosis. There are several possible causes, but the exact cause is unknown (McLaughlin et al., 2009; McPhee & Papadakis, 2009).

In contrast, secondary PAH due to a known cause is more common and results from existing cardiac (left ventricular failure, mitral stenosis) or pulmonary disease (emphysema, pulmonary fibrosis, or thromboembolism). The prognosis depends on the severity of the underlying disorder and the changes in the pulmonary vascular bed. A common cause of PAH is pulmonary artery constriction due to chronic hypoxemia and hypercapnia from COPD (Box 10-9) (McPhee & Papdakis, 2009).

Pathophysiology

Conditions such as collagen vascular disease, congenital heart disease, portal hypertension, and HIV infection

---

BOX 10-9

Causes of Pulmonary Arterial Hypertension

- Collagen vascular diseases
- Congenital systemic-to-pulmonary shunts
- Portal hypertension
- Altered immune mechanisms (HIV infection)
- Diseases associated with significant venous or capillary involvement
- Chronic thrombotic or embolic disease
- Pulmonary venous hypertension
- Pulmonary vasoconstriction due to hypoxemia
- Chronic obstructive pulmonary disease (COPD), interstitial lung disease, sleep-disordered breathing
- Miscellaneous causes: Sarcoidosis, histiocytosis, compression of pulmonary vessels

---

increase the risk for PAH in susceptible patients. The pulmonary vasculature is injured, which leads to endothelial and smooth muscle thickening and hypertrophy, leading to noncompliant and narrowed vessels. Normally, the pulmonary vascular bed can handle the blood volume delivered by the right ventricle. It has a low resistance to blood flow and compensates for increased blood volume by dilation of the vessels in the pulmonary circulation. However, if the pulmonary vascular bed is destroyed or obstructed, the ability to handle whatever flow or volume of blood it receives is impaired, and the increased blood flow then increases the pulmonary artery pressure. As the pulmonary arterial pressure increases, the pulmonary vascular resistance also increases. This increased workload affects right ventricular function. The myocardium ultimately cannot meet the increasing demands imposed on it, leading to right ventricular hypertrophy (enlargement and dilation) and failure.

Clinical Manifestations and Assessment

Dyspnea, the main symptom of both types of PAH, occurs at first with exertion and eventually at rest. Other signs and symptoms include chest pain, weakness, fatigue, syncope, occasional hemoptysis, and signs of right-sided heart failure (peripheral edema, ascites, distended neck veins, hepatomegaly, crackles, heart murmur, splitting of second heart sound).

Diagnosis of idiopathic PAH is made by exclusion of secondary causes such as COPD, PE, HIV, and cardiac disease. Several tests are used to determine whether there is a known cause for the pulmonary hypertension. Complete diagnostic evaluation includes a history, physical examination, chest X-ray, pulmonary function studies, electrocardiogram (ECG), echocardiogram, ventilation–perfusion scan, CT or magnetic resonance (MR) angiography, sleep studies, autoantibody tests (to identify diseases of collagen vascular

origin), HIV tests, liver function testing, hypercoagulation studies, and cardiac catheterization. Pulmonary function studies may be normal or show a slight decrease in vital capacity and lung compliance, with a mild decrease in the diffusing capacity. The PaO_2 also is decreased (hypoxemia). Complete blood count may show polycythemia (hematocrit of >54% in males or 51% in females). The electrocardiogram (ECG) reveals right atrial enlargement (and tall peaked P waves in inferior leads), right axis deviation, right ventricular hypertrophy (tall R waves in V_2 and tall R waves in V_5); and ST-segment depression, T-wave inversion, or both in V_{1-4}. An echocardiogram can assess the progression of the disease and rule out other conditions with similar signs and symptoms. A ventilation–perfusion scan or pulmonary CT or MR angiography detects defects in pulmonary vasculature, such as pulmonary emboli. Cardiac catheterization of the right side of the heart reveals elevated pulmonary arterial pressure and determines whether there is a vasoactive component to the pulmonary hypertension. Acute vasodilator testing can be performed with the right heart catheterization to determine if there is a reduction in mean pulmonary artery pressure when a short-acting vasodilator (adenosine, epoprostenol, or inhaled nitric oxide) is administered.

Medical Management

The goal of treatment is to manage the underlying condition related to PAH of known cause. Hypoxemia, at rest or during exertion, should be treated with supplemental oxygen. Appropriate oxygen therapy can reverse the vasoconstrictive effect and reduce the pulmonary hypertension. Pharmacologic agents such as diuretics, digoxin, anticoagulant therapy, and calcium-channel blockers (nifedipine, diltiazem) may be prescribed. Because calcium-channel blockers are effective in only a small percentage of patients, other treatment options, including prostacyclin, are often necessary (McLaughlin et al., 2009).

Vasodilating agents can be used to improve exercise tolerance and hemodynamic function, and extend survival. Epoprostenol is given by continuous infusion, treprostinil by subcutaneous injection, bosentan and sildenafil by mouth, and iloprost by inhalation. Current therapies are not curative, have considerable side effects, and are often quite expensive. Lung or heart–lung transplantation is reserved for patients who have advanced disease despite maximal medical therapy (McPhee & Papadakis, 2009).

Nursing Management

The major nursing goal is to identify patients at high risk for PAH, such as those with COPD, pulmonary emboli, congenital heart disease, and mitral valve disease. The nurse also must be alert for signs and symptoms of deterioration such as worsening dyspnea, hypoxemia, and right ventricular failure. Oxygen therapy is administered as ordered, and the patient and family are instructed about the use of home

oxygen supplementation. In patients treated with prostacyclin (i.e., epoprostenol or treprostinil), education about the need for central venous access (epoprostenol), or subcutaneous infusion (treprostinil) is discussed. In addition, the nurse reviews proper administration and dosing of the medication, usual side effects such as pain at the injection site, and potential severe side effects of hypotension, flushing of skin, bradycardia, and headache associated with IV administration. Emotional and psychosocial aspects of this disease must be addressed.

PULMONARY EMBOLISM

Pulmonary embolism (PE) refers to the obstruction of the pulmonary artery or one of its branches by a thrombus (or thrombi) that originates somewhere in the venous system or right side of the heart. Hospitalized patients are at a high risk for PE; it is estimated that more than 300,000 deaths are attributed to PE annually (Tapson, 2008). It is the third leading cause of death in hospitalized patients, often not diagnosed until autopsy. PE is a common disorder and often is associated with trauma, arrhythmia (atrial fibrillation), surgery (orthopedic, major abdominal, pelvic, gynecologic), pregnancy, heart failure, malignancies, age greater than 50 years, hypercoagulable states, and prolonged immobility. It also may occur in apparently healthy people. Risk factors for PE are identified in Box 10-10.

Pathophysiology

Most commonly, PE is due to a blood clot or thrombus. However, there are other types of emboli: air, fat, amniotic fluid, tumor cells, intravenously injected particulates, and

---

BOX 10-10 **Risk Factors for Thromboembolism**

- Acute medical illness (CVA, acute MI, heart failure, neuromuscular diseases)
- Major surgery (abdominal, orthopedic, gynecologic, urologic, neurosurgical, oncologic)
- Trauma (multisystem trauma, spinal cord injury or fracture, hip or pelvic fractures)
- Cancer (localized or metastatic) receiving chemotherapy or radiation therapy
- History of thromboembolism
- Obesity
- Immobility for more than 2 days
- Age older than 40 years
- Hypercoagulable conditions
- Prolonged mechanical ventilation
- Neuromuscular paralytic use
- Central venous catheters
- Severe sepsis
- Heparin-induced thrombocytopenia (HIT)

septic (from bacterial invasion of the thrombus). Although most thrombi originate in the deep veins of the legs, other sites include the pelvic veins and the right atrium of the heart. Venous thrombosis can result from slowing of blood flow (stasis) secondary to damage to the blood vessel wall (particularly the endothelial lining) or changes in the blood coagulation mechanism. In atrial fibrillation, blood stagnates in the fibrillating atria, and stagnant blood forms clots. These clots can travel into the pulmonary circulation.

When a thrombus completely or partially obstructs a pulmonary artery or its branches, the alveolar dead space is increased. Alveolar dead space is an area that is ventilated but receives little or no blood flow. Therefore, gas exchange is impaired or absent in this area. In addition, various vasoactive substances are released from the clot and surrounding area, and these cause regional blood vessels and bronchioles to constrict. The reflex bronchoconstriction and vasoconstriction causes impaired gas exchange and the loss of alveolar surfactant, which results in atelectasis and hypoxemia. The hemodynamic consequences are increased pulmonary vascular resistance and pulmonary artery pressures, which put a strain on the right ventricle. When the work requirements of the right ventricle exceed its capacity, right ventricular failure occurs, leading to a decrease in cardiac output followed by a decrease in systemic blood pressure and the development of shock.

Clinical Manifestations and Assessment

Symptoms depend on the size of the thrombus and the area of the pulmonary artery occluded by the thrombus. Acute onset of dyspnea is the most frequent symptom, followed by chest pain, cough, leg pain, hemoptysis, and palpitations. The most common signs found on physical assessment are tachypnea, crackles, tachycardia, and presence of an S_4 heart sound, split S_2, and cyanosis (hypoxemia). Deep venous thrombosis (DVT) is closely associated with development of PE. Typically, patients report sudden onset of pain and/or swelling and warmth of the proximal or distal extremity, skin discoloration, and superficial vein distention.

Shock can develop with massive PEs ("saddle" embolisms) or in patients with preexisting heart failure. Pronounced dyspnea, sudden substernal pain, rapid and weak pulse, hypotension, syncope, and sudden death can occur. Multiple small emboli can lodge in the terminal pulmonary arterioles, producing multiple small infarctions of the lungs. A pulmonary infarction causes ischemic necrosis of an area of the lung. The clinical picture may mimic that of bronchopneumonia or heart failure. In atypical instances, PE causes few signs and symptoms, whereas in other instances it mimics various other cardiopulmonary disorders.

Death from PE commonly occurs within hours of the onset of symptoms; therefore, early recognition and diagnosis are priorities. Because the symptoms of PE can vary from mild to severe, a diagnostic workup is performed to rule out

other diseases. The initial diagnostic workup includes chest X-ray, ECG, peripheral vascular studies (ultrasound, venogram), ABG analysis, d-dimer, and ventilation–perfusion ($\dot{V}/\dot{Q}$) scan.

The chest X-ray is most helpful in excluding other possible causes such as pneumonia, COPD, and pulmonary edema due to heart failure. Arterial blood gas analysis may show hypoxemia and hypocapnia (from tachypnea); however, ABG measurements may be normal even in the presence of PE. The classic ECG pattern associated with PE, although rare, is S_1, Q_3, T_3, meaning a deep S wave in lead I, a Q wave in lead III and an inverted T wave in lead III. More common ECG findings are sinus tachycardia, PR-interval depression, and nonspecific T-wave changes. Peripheral vascular studies used to diagnose a DVT may include impedance plethysmography, Doppler ultrasonography, or venography. If a DVT is present with the associated signs and symptoms of PE, the patient is treated for both. A ventilation and perfusion scan was once the second choice for diagnosis of a PE (with pulmonary angiogram [discussed below] considered the best diagnostic procedure). It is still used, especially in facilities that do not have access to a spiral CT scanner. The $\dot{V}/\dot{Q}$ scan is minimally invasive, involving the administration of a radioactive agent (both IV and inhaled). This scan evaluates different regions of the lung (upper, middle, lower) and allows comparisons of the percentage of ventilation and perfusion in each area. This test has a high sensitivity but can be more cumbersome than a CT scan and is not as accurate as a pulmonary angiogram. Patients who have an underlying lung disease, such as COPD or pneumonia, often have inconclusive $\dot{V}/\dot{Q}$ scan results; also patients who are mechanically ventilated cannot undergo this test.

Spiral or contrast angiogram CT scan has gained popularity for use in the diagnosis of PE. Limitations to the use of CT scanning are that patients must be cooperative and able to have IV contrast (no contrast allergies, normal renal function), and it is less sensitive than a pulmonary angiogram. Pulmonary angiography allows for the visualization of the pulmonary vasculature under fluoroscopy with IV contrast. It requires interventional radiologists to perform the test with specific equipment and personnel that may not be available in many hospitals, and in addition, the test is costly.

The D-dimer assay is becoming a more commonly used method for evaluating patients with possible PE. Emergency departments in particular have used this as a rapid, cost-effective test. D-dimer is a product of fibrin degradation and occurs as a result of fibrin lysis. D-dimer is used only to rule out a PE; as a negative result, it has a 95% predictive ability, meaning 95% of patients with PE have an elevated D-dimer.

Prevention

For patients at risk for PE, the most effective approach for prevention is to prevent DVT. Active leg exercises to avoid venous stasis, early ambulation, and use of elastic compression

TABLE
10-3 Recommended Deep Vein Thrombosis Prophylaxis

Risk Level	Recommended Prophylaxis
Low risk: Minor surgery + age <40 years and no additional DVT risk factors	Early mobilization
Moderate risk: Major surgery + age >40 years and no additional DVT risk factors	Unfractionated heparin: 5,000 units SC q12h (start 2 hours prior to surgery) or Low-molecular-weight heparin (Enoxaparin) 40 units SC daily or Dalteparin 5,000 units SC daily
High risk: Major surgery + Age >40yrs and/or other DVT risk factors	Mechanical aid (intermittent pneumatic compression or graded compression stockings AND Unfractionated heparin: 5,000 units SC q8h (start 2 hours prior to surgery) or Low-molecular-weight heparin (Enoxaparin) 40 units SC daily or Dalteparin 5,000 units SC daily

or intermittent pneumatic compression stockings are general preventive measures.

Prophylactic anticoagulation therapy is prescribed based on assessment of a patient's risk level. Table 10-3 illustrates the risk stratification and recommended prophylaxis. Anticoagulant therapy may be prescribed for patients who are older than 40 years of age, whose hemostasis is adequate, and who are undergoing major abdominal or thoracic surgery. Low doses of heparin may be administered before surgery to reduce the risk of postoperative DVT and PE. Heparin should be administered subcutaneously 2 hours before surgery and continued every 8 to 12 hours until the patient is discharged. Low-dose heparin is thought to enhance the activity of antithrombin III, a major plasma inhibitor of clotting factor X. This regimen is not recommended for patients with an active thrombotic process or for those undergoing major orthopedic surgery, open prostatectomy, or surgery on the eye or brain. Low-molecular-weight heparins (e.g., enoxaparin [Lovenox], dalteparin [Fragmin], fondaparinux [Arixtra]) are additional therapies. They have a longer half-life, enhanced subcutaneous absorption, a reduced incidence of thrombocytopenia, and reduced interaction with platelets, compared with unfractionated heparin (ACCP, 2008).

Sequential compression devices (SCDs) are often used to prevent venous stasis through compression and relaxation of the calf muscles, similar to the effect of muscle contraction. Sequential compression devices have been proved to effectively reduce the risk of DVT and have been shown to be an effective primary therapy for patients who are unable to receive anticoagulation therapy (American College of Chest Physicians [ACCP], 2008). Several types of SCDs, using foot, calf, and thigh-high compression as well as graduated, asymmetric, and circumferential compression, are available. There is little evidence favoring any particular type of compression. Graduated compression involves the sequential movement of air in the sleeve up the leg, followed by relaxation of the sleeve. The advantage of this therapy is the extended duration

of compression compared with standard inflation. Asymmetric compression involves inflating only the area on the back of the leg or foot. Circumferential compression involves even compression of the entire leg (ACCP, 2008).

Medical Management

Because PE is often a medical emergency, emergency management is of primary concern. After emergency measures have been initiated and the patient is stabilized, the treatment goal is to dissolve (lyse) the existing emboli and prevent new ones from forming. Treatment may include a variety of modalities:

- General measures to improve respiratory and vascular status
- Anticoagulation therapy
- Thrombolytic therapy
- Surgical intervention

Emergency Management

Massive PE is a life-threatening emergency. The immediate objective is to stabilize the cardiopulmonary system. A sudden increase in pulmonary resistance increases the work of the right ventricle, which can cause acute right-sided heart failure with cardiogenic shock. Emergency management consists of the following actions:

- Oxygen is administered immediately to relieve hypoxemia, respiratory distress, and central cyanosis.
- Intravenous infusion lines are inserted to establish routes for medications or fluids that will be needed.
- A perfusion scan, hemodynamic measurements, and ABG determinations are performed. spiral (helical) CT or pulmonary angiography may be performed.
- Hypotension is treated with IV fluid resuscitation, vasopressors (dopamine, norepinephrine) or inotropic support (dobutamine).
- The ECG is monitored continuously for arrhythmias and right ventricular failure, which may occur suddenly.

- Digitalis glycosides, IV diuretics, and antiarrhythmic agents are administered when appropriate.
- Blood is drawn for serum electrolytes, complete blood count, and coagulation studies (PT, international normalized ratio [INR], partial thromboplastin time [PTT], d-dimer).
- If clinical assessment and ABG analysis indicate the need, the patient is intubated and placed on a mechanical ventilator.
- If the patient has suffered massive embolism and is hypotensive, an indwelling urinary catheter is inserted to monitor urinary output.
- Small doses of IV morphine or sedatives are administered to relieve patient anxiety, to alleviate chest discomfort, to improve tolerance of the endotracheal tube, and to ease adaptation to the mechanical ventilator.
- IV thrombolytic agents (tissue plasminogen activator [Alteplase, Reteplase]) maybe used in patients who are hemodynamically unstable (hypotension, ECG strain patterns) to lyse the clot(s).
- Initiation of low-molecular weight heparins (SC route) or IV heparin should be considered.

Pharmacologic Therapy

Anticoagulation Therapy

Anticoagulant therapy (unfractionated or low-molecular-weight heparins) is traditionally the primary method for managing acute DVT and PE. Heparin is used to prevent recurrence of emboli but has no effect on emboli that are already present. Heparin is generally recommended for all patients who have been diagnosed with PE. Generally, a therapeutic heparin dose is administered as a one-time 80 units/kg bolus and a continuous IV infusion (18 units/kg/hr) is then started to maintain the PTT at 1.5 to 2.5 times the normal level (European Society of Cardiology, 2008). Enoxaparin, a low-molecular-weight heparin, is administered subcutaneously at 1 mg/kg every 12 hours. This should be reserved for hemodynamically stable patients in order to ensure that the drug is being absorbed into the vasculature. Enoxaparin has an advantage over heparin as its levels do not need to be monitored and IV access is not an issue (Marino, 2007).

Therapy may be changed to an oral regimen, such as warfarin, as soon as the patient is able to take oral medications. Heparin must be continued until the INR is within a therapeutic range, typically 2.0 to 3 (Kearon, Kahn, Agnelli, et al., 2008). Once the patient starts an oral regimen, it is important that he or she continue to take the same brand of warfarin, because the bioavailability may vary greatly among brands.

High doses of subcutaneous low-molecular-weight heparin or heparinoids may also be used to maintain a therapeutic PTT while oral anticoagulation therapy is being adjusted. Lepirudin (Refludan) and argatroban are alternatives for patients in whom heparin or heparinoids are contraindicated (e.g., patients with heparin-induced thrombocytopenia [HIT]). (Refer to Chapter 14 for more details on HIT.) These agents are direct thrombin inhibitors; therefore, they require

less frequent monitoring and dose adjustment. Both medications have contraindications and side effects that the nurse must be aware of before administration. Heparins, lepirudin, and argatroban are all contraindicated in patients with overt major bleeding and in patients who are hypersensitive to these agents or at high risk for bleeding (e.g., recent CVA), anomaly of vessels or organs, recent major surgery, recent puncture of large vessels, or organ biopsy). Major side effects are bleeding anywhere in the body and anaphylactic reaction resulting in shock or death. Other side effects include fever, abnormal liver function, and allergic skin reaction. Patients must continue to take some form of anticoagulation for at least 3 to 6 months after the embolic event.

Thrombolytic Therapy

Thrombolytic therapy (urokinase, streptokinase, alteplase, anistreplase, reteplase) also may be used in treating PE, particularly for patients who are severely compromised (e.g., those who are hypotensive, RV dysfunction, patent foramen ovale, large or saddle embolism, or have significant hypoxemia despite oxygen supplementation). Thrombolytic therapy dissolves the thrombi or emboli more quickly and restores more normal hemodynamic functioning of the pulmonary circulation, thereby reducing pulmonary hypertension and improving perfusion, oxygenation, and cardiac output. However, bleeding is a significant side effect. Absolute contraindications to thrombolytic therapy include history of hemorrhagic CVA, active intracranial neoplasm, recent brain or spinal surgery (<2 months), and internal bleeding within the last 6 months. Relative contraindications for thrombolytic therapy are bleeding tendency, uncontrolled hypertension (SBP >200 or DBP >100), nonhemorrhagic CVA within 2 months, surgery in the last 10 days, or thrombocytopenia of less than 100,000 platelet per mm^3.

Before thrombolytic therapy is started, INR, PTT, hematocrit, and platelet counts are obtained. Heparin is stopped prior to administration of a thrombolytic agent. During therapy, all but essential invasive procedures are avoided because of potential bleeding. If necessary, packed red cells, cryoprecipitate, or frozen plasma is administered to replace blood loss and reverse the bleeding tendency. After the thrombolytic infusion is completed (which varies in duration according to the agent used and the condition being treated), anticoagulant therapy is initiated.

Surgical Management

A surgical embolectomy is rarely performed but may be indicated if the patient has a massive PE, hemodynamic instability, and must have the clot removed to help reduce right-sided heart failure, or if there are contraindications to thrombolytic therapy. This invasive procedure involves removal of the actual clot and must be performed by a cardiovascular surgical team with the patient on cardiopulmonary bypass. The procedure has a high intraoperative mortality rate and has typical postoperative complications.

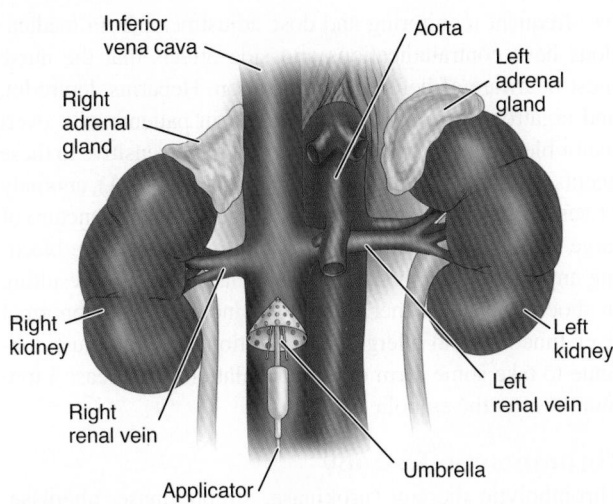

FIGURE 10-8 An umbrella filter is in place in the inferior vena cava to prevent pulmonary embolism. The filter (compressed within an applicator catheter) is inserted through an incision in the right internal jugular vein. The applicator is withdrawn when the filter fixes itself to the wall of the inferior vena cava after ejection from the applicator.

Venous catheter embolectomy via rheolytic (injection of pressured saline) or rotating blades can be used to break up clots in the pulmonary vasculature. These catheters are placed via the femoral vein, threaded through the right heart, and up to the clot. An inferior vena cava filter is usually inserted at the time of surgery to protect against a recurrence.

Inferior vena cava (IVC) filters are mesh-like devices used to trap thrombi from the pelvic and lower extremities to prevent them from traveling to the lungs. IVC filters (e.g., Greenfield filter) are inserted via the femoral or internal jugular vein (Fig. 10-8). This filter is advanced into the inferior vena cava, where it is opened. These types of filters are placed in patients who have contraindications to anticoagulation, experience significant bleeding while on anticoagulation, or have recurrent PE despite adequate treatment.

Nursing Management

Minimizing the Risk of Pulmonary Embolism

A key role of the nurse is to identify the patient at high risk for PE and to minimize the risk of PE in all patients. The nurse must have a high degree of suspicion for PE in all patients, but particularly in those with conditions predispose to a slowing of venous return.

Preventing Thrombus Formation

Preventing thrombus formation is a major nursing responsibility. The nurse encourages ambulation and active and passive leg exercises to prevent venous stasis in patients prescribed bed rest. The nurse instructs the patient to move the legs in a "pumping" exercise, so that the leg muscles can

help increase venous flow. The nurse also advises the patient not to sit or lie in bed for prolonged periods, not to cross the legs, and not to wear constrictive clothing. Legs should not be dangled or feet placed in a dependent position while the patient sits on the edge of the bed; instead, feet should rest on the floor or on a chair. In addition, IV catheters (for parenteral therapy or measurements of central venous pressure) should not be left in place for prolonged periods.

Assessing Potential for Pulmonary Embolism

All patients are evaluated for risk factors for thrombus formation and PE. The nurse does a careful assessment of the patient's health history, family history, and medication record. On a daily basis, the patient is asked about pain or discomfort in the extremities. In addition, the extremities are evaluated for unilateral leg warmth, redness, and inflammation.

Monitoring Thrombolytic Therapy

The nurse is responsible for monitoring thrombolytic and anticoagulant therapy. Thrombolytic therapy (streptokinase, urokinase, tissue plasminogen activator) causes lysis of deep vein thrombi and pulmonary emboli, which helps dissolve the clots. During thrombolytic infusion, while the patient remains on bed rest, vital signs are assessed every 15 minutes for 2 hours, then every 2 hours for 4 hours, and invasive procedures are avoided. PTT testing should be performed every 6 hours after thrombolytics are started.

> **❗ NURSING ALERT**
> *The activated PTT (APTT) is a more sensitive test than the PTT for the monitoring of heparin therapy. A normal APTT is 21 to 35 seconds. The goal of heparin therapy is to extend the APTT to 2 or 2.5 the normal level. The nurse is aware that when the APTT is over 70 seconds, the risk for spontaneously bleeding increases. Many institutions have protocols for increasing or decreasing the heparin dosage depending on the APTT. The nurse follows hospital protocol but anticipates that if the APTT is over 90 seconds to stop the anticoagulant for 1 hour and restart as mandated by protocol, typically at a lower rate per hour. In general, heparin infusion should be restarted (without a bolus) when PTT is less than 60 seconds. If no protocols are available, the nurse contacts the provider immediately with APTTs of greater than 90 seconds.*

The INR was developed as a consistent way of monitoring prothrombin times, which are used for monitoring Coumadin therapy. A normal INR is about 1. The goal of Coumadin therapy is to extend the INR to 2 to 3, depending on the reason the patient is anticoagulated. The higher the number, the longer the blood takes to clot. A patient with atrial fibrillation may have a goal INR of 2.5, whereas a patient with a mechanical heart valve may have a maximum goal of an INR of 3.5. Any INR over 3.6 is a critical value that necessitates notification of the patient's provider. With an elevated APTT

and/or INR, the nurse observes the patient for hematuria, hematemesis, melena, petechiae, unusual bruising, and any evidence of bleeding (hypotension, tachycardia, dyspnea, etc.) (Fischbach & Dunning, 2009).

Managing Pain

Chest pain, if present, is usually pleuritic rather than cardiac in origin. A semi-Fowler's position provides a more comfortable position for breathing. It is important to continue to turn patients frequently and reposition them to improve the **ventilation–perfusion ratio** in the lung. The nurse administers opioid analgesics as prescribed for severe pain.

Managing Oxygen Therapy

It is important to ensure that the patient understands the need for continuous oxygen therapy. The nurse assesses the patient frequently for signs of hypoxemia and monitors the POX values to evaluate the effectiveness of the oxygen therapy. Deep breathing and incentive spirometry are indicated for all patients to minimize or prevent atelectasis and improve ventilation. Nebulizer therapy or percussion and postural drainage may be used for management of secretions.

Relieving Anxiety

The nurse encourages the stabilized patient to talk about any fears or concerns related to this frightening episode, answers the patient's and family's questions concisely and accurately, explains the therapy, and describes how to recognize untoward effects early.

Monitoring for Complications

When caring for a patient who has had PE, the nurse must be alert for the potential complication of cardiogenic shock or right ventricular failure subsequent to the effect of PE on the cardiovascular system.

Providing Postoperative Care

The nurse measures the patient's pulmonary arterial pressure and urinary output. The nurse also assesses the insertion site of the arterial catheter for hematoma formation and infection. It is important to maintain the BP at a level that supports perfusion of vital organs. To prevent peripheral venous stasis and edema of the lower extremities, the nurse elevates the foot of the bed and encourages isometric exercises, use of elastic compression stockings, and walking when the patient is permitted out of bed. Sitting is discouraged, because hip flexion compresses the large veins in the legs.

OCCUPATIONAL LUNG DISEASES

Diseases of the lungs occur in numerous occupations as a result of exposure to several different types of agents. Examples include mineral dusts (asbestos, silica, coal), metal dusts, biological dusts (spores, mycelia, bird droppings),

manufactured fibers (glass or ceramic fibers), and toxic fumes (nitrogen dioxide, sulfur dioxide, chlorine, ammonia). One category of occupational lung disease that causes chronic fibrotic lung disease is pneumoconiosis, which is caused by the inhalation of inert, inorganic, or silicate dusts. The effects of inhaling these materials depend on the composition of the substance, its concentration, its ability to initiate an immune response, its irritating properties, the duration of exposure, and the individual's response or susceptibility to the irritant. The most common types of pneumoconiosis are coal worker's pneumoconiosis, silicosis, and **asbestosis**. Smoking may compound the problem and may increase the risk of lung cancers in people exposed to the mineral asbestos and other potential carcinogens. Many people with early pneumoconiosis are asymptomatic, but advanced disease often is accompanied by disability and premature death. Between 1996 and 2005, pneumoconiosis was cited as the cause of death of 9,646 people in the United States (CDC, 2008).

Silicosis is a chronic fibrotic pulmonary disease caused by inhalation of silica dust (silicon dioxide). Exposure to silica and silicates occurs in almost all mining, quarrying, and tunneling operations. Glass manufacturing, stone-cutting, manufacturing of abrasives and pottery, and foundry work are other occupations with exposure hazards. Finely ground silica, such as that found in soaps, polishes, and filters, is extremely dangerous (McPhee & Papadakis, 2009).

Asbestosis is a disease characterized by diffuse nodular interstitial fibrosis from the inhalation of asbestos dust. Current laws restrict the use of asbestos, but many industries used it in the past. Therefore, exposure occurred, and may still occur, in people in numerous occupations, including asbestos mining and manufacturing, shipbuilding, demolition of structures containing asbestos, and roofing. Materials such as shingles, cement, vinyl asbestos tile, fireproof paint and clothing, brake linings, and filters all contained asbestos at one time, and many of these materials are still in existence. Chronic exposure may also occur by washing clothes that have been in contact with asbestos. Additional diseases related to asbestos exposure include lung cancer, mesothelioma, and asbestos-related pleural effusion (McPhee & Papadakis, 2009).

Coal worker's pneumoconiosis ("black lung disease") includes a variety of respiratory diseases found in coal workers who have inhaled coal dust over the years. Coal miners are exposed to dusts that are mixtures of coal, kaolin, mica, and silica (McPhee & Papadakis, 2009).

Pathophysiology

The pathophysiology of each type of pneumoconioses begins with the inhalation and deposition of industrial dusts or particles in the lungs. In silicosis, the inhaled silica particles form nodular lesions throughout the lungs. With the passage of time and further exposure, the nodules enlarge

and coalesce. Dense masses form in the upper portion of the lungs, resulting in the loss of pulmonary volume. **Restrictive lung disease** (disease of the lungs that limits their ability to expand fully) and obstructive lung disease from secondary emphysema result. Cavities can form as a result of superimposed TB. Exposure of 15 to 20 years is usually required before the onset of the disease and shortness of breath occurs. Fibrotic destruction of pulmonary tissue can lead to emphysema, pulmonary hypertension, and cor pulmonale (right ventricular failure).

In asbestosis, inhaled asbestos fibers enter the alveoli, where they are surrounded by fibrous tissue. The fibrous tissue eventually obliterates the alveoli. Fibrous changes also affect the pleura, which thickens and develops plaque. The result of these physiologic changes is a restrictive lung disease, with a decrease in lung volume, diminished exchange of oxygen and carbon dioxide, and hypoxemia.

When coal dust is deposited in the alveoli and respiratory bronchioles, macrophages engulf the particles (by phagocytosis) and transport them to the terminal bronchioles, where they are removed by mucociliary action. In time, the clearance mechanisms cannot handle the excessive dust load, and the macrophages aggregate in the respiratory bronchioles and alveoli. Fibroblasts appear and a network of reticulin is laid down surrounding the dust-laden macrophages. The bronchioles and the alveoli become clogged with coal dust, dying macrophages, and fibroblasts. This leads to the formation of the coal macule, the primary lesion of the disorder. Macules appear as blackish dots on the lungs. Fibrotic lesions develop and, as the macules enlarge, the weakening bronchioles dilate, with subsequent development of localized emphysema. The disease begins in the upper lobes of the lungs but may progress to the lower lobes.

Clinical Manifestations and Assessment

Patients with acute silicosis present with dyspnea, fever, cough, and weight loss, and progression of the disease is rapid. Symptoms are more severe in patients whose disease is complicated by progressive massive fibrosis. More commonly, this disease is a chronic problem with a long latency period. In patients with asbestosis, the onset of the disease is insidious, and patients have progressive dyspnea, persistent, dry cough, mild to moderate chest pain, anorexia, weight loss, and malaise. Early physical findings include bibasilar fine, end-inspiratory crackles and, in more advanced cases, clubbing of the fingers. Patients with coal miner's disease usually present with a chronic cough and sputum production, similar to the signs encountered in chronic bronchitis. As the disease progresses, patients develop dyspnea and cough up large amounts of sputum with varying amounts of black fluid (melanoptysis), particularly if they are smokers.

As each of these diseases progress, worsening dyspnea and hypoxemia occurs. Eventually, patients develop respiratory failure and cor pulmonale. A high proportion of workers who have been exposed to asbestos dust, especially those who smoke or have a history of smoking, die of lung cancer. Malignant mesothelioma, a rare cancer of the pleura or peritoneum that is strongly associated with asbestos exposure, may also occur.

Medical Management

The medical treatment for these specific pneumoconioses is limited to supportive care, as the fibrotic process is irreversible. Oxygen therapy, diuretics, inhaled beta-adrenergic agonists, anticholinergics, and bronchodilator therapy can be used to maximize pulmonary and cardiac function and preserve activity tolerance. It is imperative that patients avoid any additional environmental exposures and stop smoking. There is a higher incidence of TB in patients with silicosis, therefore they should have a tuberculin skin test and chest radiograph. Preventing this disease is key, because there is no effective treatment. Instead, treatment focuses on early diagnosis and management of complications.

CHEST TUMORS

Tumors of the lung may be benign or malignant. A malignant chest tumor can be primary, arising within the lung, chest wall, or mediastinum, or it can be a metastasis from a primary tumor site elsewhere in the body. Metastatic lung tumors occur frequently because the bloodstream transports cancer cells from primary cancers elsewhere in the body to the lungs.

LUNG CANCER (BRONCHOGENIC CARCINOMA)

Lung cancer is the leading cancer killer among men and women in the United States. In 2005, 196,687 people in the United States were diagnosed with lung cancer. That same year, 159,217 people died of the disease. For men, the incidence of lung cancer has remained relatively constant, but in women there has been an increase in occurrences since 1991 (CDC, 2009b). In approximately 70% of patients with lung cancer, the disease has spread to regional lymphatics and other sites by the time of diagnosis. As a result, the long-term survival rate is low.

Pathophysiology

Eighty percent of lung cancer in women and 90% in men is caused by cigarette smoking, with the remainder being attributed to other carcinogens, including radon gas and occupational and environmental agents (Jemal, Thun, Ries et al., 2008).

Classification and Staging

For purposes of staging and treatment, most lung cancers are classified into one of two major categories: small cell lung

TABLE
10-4 Lung Cancer Types and Characteristics

Tumor Classification	Growth Rate	Clinical Manifestations	Treatment	Metastasis
Non-small cell lung cancer (NSCLC)				
Adenocarcinoma	Moderate	Dyspnea, pleuritic chest pain, pleural effusions, unexplained weight loss	Surgical resection, adjunctive chemotherapy	Early: Liver, brain, bones, kidneys, adrenals
Squamous cell	Slow	Cough, hemoptysis, pneumonia, atelectasis, chest pain (late sign), unexplained weight loss	Surgical resection, adjunctive chemotherapy	Late: Brain, liver, bones, adrenals
Large cell (undifferentiated)	Rapid	Chest wall pain, cough, sputum production, hemoptysis, pleural effusion, pneumonia, unexplained weight loss	Surgical resection	Early: Brain, liver, bones, adrenals
Small cell lung cancer (SCLC)				
Oat cell and intermediate cell type	Very Rapid	Cough, unexplained weight loss, dyspnea, airway obstruction, hilar mass on X-ray, pneumonia, paraneoplastic syndromes (SIADH, hypercalcemia, Cushing's, myopathies)	Chemotherapy, Radiation therapy	Early: Liver, bone, bone marrow, brain, adrenals

SIADH, syndrome of inappropriate antidiuretic hormone secretion.

cancer (25% of lung cancers) and non–small cell lung cancer (75% of lung cancers) (Table 10-4). In non–small cell lung carcinoma (NSCLC), the cell types include squamous cell carcinoma (20% to 30%), large cell carcinoma (10%), and adenocarcinoma (30% to 40%), including bronchoalveolar carcinoma. Most small cell carcinomas arise in the major bronchi and spread by infiltration along the bronchial wall.

In addition to classification according to cell type, lung cancers are staged. The stage of the tumor refers to the size of the tumor, its location, whether lymph nodes are involved, and whether the cancer has spread (Goldstraw, Crowley, Chansky et al., 2007). NSCLC is staged as I to IV. Stage I is the earliest stage and has the highest cure rates, whereas stage IV designates metastatic spread. Small cell lung cancers are classified as limited or extensive. Diagnostic tools and further information on staging are described in Chapter 6.

Risk Factors

Various factors have been associated with the development of lung cancer (Box 10-11). Other factors that have been associated with lung cancer include genetic predisposition and underlying respiratory diseases, such as COPD and TB.

Clinical Manifestations and Assessment

Often, lung cancer develops insidiously and is asymptomatic until late in its course. The signs and symptoms depend on

the location and size of the tumor, the degree of obstruction, and the existence of metastases to regional or distant sites. The most frequent symptom of lung cancer is cough or change in a chronic cough. The cough starts as a dry, persistent cough, without sputum production. When obstruction of airways occurs, the cough may become productive due to infection.

Dyspnea occurs in many patients. Hemoptysis or blood-tinged sputum may be expectorated. Chest or shoulder pain may indicate chest wall or pleural involvement by a tumor. Pain also is a late manifestation and may be related to metastasis to the bone.

In some patients, a recurring fever is an early symptom in response to a persistent infection in an area distal to the

BOX 10-11
Risk Factors Associated With Lung Cancer

- Tobacco smoking: Assess pack/year history (# of packs smoked per day x years of smoking)
- Passive smoking
- Second-hand smoke (closed areas; home, building, automobile)
- Environmental and occupational exposure (vehicle emissions, pollutants, urban areas, radon gas, arsenic, asbestos, chromates, coal fumes, radiation
- Family history (close relative with lung cancer)
- Low intake of fruits and vegetables

tumor. In fact, cancer of the lung should be suspected in people with repeated unresolved upper respiratory tract infections. If the tumor spreads to adjacent structures and regional lymph nodes, the patient may present with chest pain and tightness, hoarseness (involving the recurrent laryngeal nerve), dysphagia, head and neck edema, and symptoms of pleural or pericardial effusion. The most common sites of metastases are lymph nodes, bone, brain, contralateral lung, adrenal glands, and liver. Nonspecific symptoms of weakness, anorexia, and weight loss also may be present.

If pulmonary symptoms occur in smokers, cancer of the lung should always be considered. A chest X-ray is performed to search for pulmonary densities, pulmonary nodules, atelectasis, and infection. CT scans of the chest are used to identify small nodules not easily visualized on the chest X-ray and also to examine areas for lymphadenopathy.

Fiberoptic bronchoscopy provides a detailed study of the tracheobronchial tree and allows for brushings, washings, and biopsies of suspicious areas. For peripheral lesions not amenable to bronchoscopic biopsy, a transthoracic **fine-needle aspiration** may be performed under CT guidance to aspirate cells from a suspicious area. In some circumstances, an endoscopy with esophageal ultrasound may be used to obtain a transesophageal biopsy of enlarged subcarinal (below the carina) lymph nodes that are not easily accessible by other means.

A variety of scans may be used to assess for metastasis of the cancer. These may include bone scans, abdominal scans, positron emission tomography (PET) scans, and liver ultrasound. CT of the brain, magnetic resonance imaging (MRI), and other neurologic diagnostic procedures are used to detect CNS metastases. Mediastinoscopy or mediastinotomy may be used to obtain biopsy samples from lymph nodes in the mediastinum.

If surgery is a potential treatment, the patient is evaluated to determine whether the tumor is resectable and whether the patient can tolerate the physiologic impairment resulting from such surgery. Pulmonary function tests, ABG analysis, ventilation–perfusion scans, and exercise testing may all be used as part of the preoperative assessment.

Medical Management

The objective of management is to provide a cure, if possible. Treatment depends on the cell type, the stage of the disease, and the patient's physiologic status (particularly cardiac and pulmonary status). In general, treatment may involve surgery, radiation therapy, or chemotherapy—or a combination of these. Newer and more specific therapies to modulate the immune system (gene therapy, therapy with defined tumor antigens) are under study.

Surgical Management

Surgical resection is the preferred method of treating patients with localized non–small cell tumors, no evidence of metastatic spread, and adequate cardiopulmonary function. The cure rate of surgical resection depends on the type and stage of the cancer. Surgery is primarily used for NSCLCs, because small cell cancer of the lung grows rapidly and metastasizes early and extensively. Lesions of many patients with bronchogenic cancer are inoperable at the time of diagnosis.

Several different types of lung resection may be performed. The most common surgical procedure for a small, apparently curable tumor of the lung is lobectomy (removal of a lobe of the lung). In some cases, an entire lung may be removed (pneumonectomy).

Radiation Therapy

Radiation therapy (XRT) may offer cure in a small percentage of patients. It is useful in controlling neoplasms that cannot be surgically resected but are responsive to radiation. Irradiation also may be used to reduce the size of a tumor, to make an inoperable tumor operable, or to relieve the pressure of the tumor on vital structures. It can reduce symptoms of spinal cord metastasis and superior vena caval compression. Also, XRT is used to treat metastases to the brain. Radiation therapy may help relieve cough, chest pain, dyspnea, hemoptysis, and bone and liver pain. Relief of symptoms may last from a few weeks to many months and is important in improving the quality of the remaining period of life. Radiofrequency ablation and cryoablation are two types of nonsurgical therapies that have been used to treat lung tumors.

Chemotherapy

Chemotherapy is used to alter tumor growth patterns, to treat distant metastases or small cell cancer of the lung, and as an adjunct to surgery or radiation therapy. Chemotherapy may provide relief, especially of pain, but it does not usually cure the disease or prolong life to any great degree. Chemotherapy is also accompanied by side effects. It is valuable in reducing pressure symptoms of lung cancer and in treating brain, spinal cord, and pericardial metastases.

The choice of agent depends on the growth of the tumor cell and the specific phase of the cell cycle that the medication affects. In combination with surgery, chemotherapy may be administered before surgery (neoadjuvant therapy) or after surgery (adjuvant therapy). Combinations of two or more medications may be more beneficial than single-dose regimens.

Palliative Therapy

Palliative therapy may include radiation therapy or chemotherapy to shrink the tumor to provide pain relief, a variety of bronchoscopic interventions to open a narrowed bronchus or airway, and pain management and other comfort measures. Evaluation and referral for hospice care are important in planning for comfortable and dignified end-of-life care for the patient and family.

Treatment-Related Complications

A variety of complications may occur as a result of treatment for lung cancer. Surgical resection may result in respiratory failure, particularly if the cardiopulmonary system is compromised before surgery. Surgical complications and

prolonged mechanical ventilation are potential outcomes. Radiation therapy may result in diminished cardiopulmonary function and other complications, such as pulmonary fibrosis, pericarditis, myelitis, and cor pulmonale. Chemotherapy, particularly in combination with radiation therapy, can cause pneumonitis. Pulmonary and systemic toxicity is a potential side effect of chemotherapy.

Nursing Management

Nursing care of patients with lung cancer is similar to that for other patients with cancer and addresses the physiologic and psychological needs of the patient. The physiologic problems are primarily due to the respiratory manifestations of the disease. Nursing care includes strategies to ensure relief of pain and discomfort and to prevent complications.

Managing Symptoms

The nurse instructs the patient and family about the potential side effects of the specific treatment and strategies to manage them. Strategies for managing such symptoms as dyspnea, fatigue, nausea and vomiting, anorexia, and fatigue help the patient and family cope with therapeutic measures. See Chapter 6.

Relieving Breathing Problems

Airway clearance techniques are key to maintaining airway patency through the removal of excess secretions. This may be accomplished through deep-breathing exercises, CPT, directed cough, suctioning, and in some instances, bronchoscopy. Bronchodilator medications may be prescribed to promote bronchial dilation. As the tumor enlarges or spreads, it may compress a bronchus or involve a large area of lung tissue, resulting in an impaired breathing pattern and poor gas exchange. At some stage of the disease, supplemental oxygen will probably be necessary.

Nursing measures focus on decreasing dyspnea by encouraging the patient to assume positions that promote lung expansion and to perform breathing exercises for lung expansion and relaxation. Patient education about energy conservation and airway clearance techniques is also necessary. Many of the techniques used in pulmonary rehabilitation can be applied to patients with lung cancer. Depending on the severity of disease and the patient's wishes, a referral to a pulmonary rehabilitation program may be helpful in managing respiratory symptoms.

Providing Psychological Support

Another important part of the nursing care of patients with lung cancer is provision of psychological support and identification of potential resources for the patient and family. Refer to Chapter 6.

Gerontologic Considerations

At the time of diagnosis of lung cancer, most patients are older than 65 years of age and have stage III or IV disease (Jemal et al., 2008). Although age is not a significant prognostic factor for overall survival and response to treatment for either NSCLC or small cell lung cancer, older patients have specific needs. Depending on the comorbidities and functional status of elderly patients, chemotherapy agents, doses, and cycles may need to be adjusted to maintain quality of life. Issues that must be considered in the care of elderly patients with lung cancer include functional status, comorbid conditions, nutritional status, cognition, concomitant medications, and psychological and social support.

TUMORS OF THE MEDIASTINUM

Tumors of the mediastinum include neurogenic tumors, tumors of the thymus, lymphomas, germ cell tumors, cysts, and mesenchymal tumors. These tumors may be malignant or benign. They are usually described in relation to location: anterior, middle, or posterior masses or tumors.

Clinical Manifestations and Assessment

Nearly all symptoms of mediastinal tumors result from the pressure of the mass against important intrathoracic organs. Symptoms may include cough, wheezing, dyspnea, anterior chest or neck pain, bulging of the chest wall, heart palpitations, angina, other circulatory disturbances, central cyanosis, superior vena cava syndrome (i.e., swelling of the face, neck, and upper extremities), marked distention of the veins of the neck and the chest wall (evidence of the obstruction of large veins of the mediastinum by extravascular compression or intravascular invasion), and dysphagia and weight loss from pressure or invasion into the esophagus.

Most often, chest X-rays are used to diagnose mediastinal tumors and cysts. CT is the standard diagnostic test for assessment of the mediastinum and surrounding structures. MRI, as well as PET, may be used in some circumstances.

Medical and Nursing Management

If the tumor is malignant and has infiltrated the surrounding tissue and complete surgical removal is not feasible, radiation therapy, chemotherapy, or both are used.

Many mediastinal tumors are benign and operable. The location of the tumor (anterior, middle, or posterior compartment) in the mediastinum dictates the type of incision. The common incision used is a median sternotomy; however, a thoracotomy may be used, depending on the location of the tumor. Additional approaches include a bilateral anterior thoracotomy (clamshell incision) and video-assisted thoracoscopic surgery (VATS). The care is the same as for any patient undergoing thoracic surgery. Major complications include hemorrhage, injury to the phrenic or laryngeal nerve, and infection.

CHEST TRAUMA

Major chest trauma may occur alone or in combination with multiple other injuries. Chest trauma is classified as either blunt or penetrating. Blunt chest trauma results from rapid deceleration injury (e.g., motor vehicle accident [MVA], falls) or direct injury (abuse, crushing, and explosions). Penetrating trauma occurs when a foreign object penetrates the chest wall (stabbing, gunshot wounds, and shrapnel).

BLUNT TRAUMA AND PENETRATING TRAUMA

Blunt thoracic injures are responsible for approximately 13% of all trauma admissions (Sharma, Oswanski, Jolly et al., 2008; National Highway Traffic Safety Administration [NHTSA], 2009). It is often difficult to identify the extent of the damage because the symptoms may be occult and vague.

Pathophysiology

The most common causes of blunt chest trauma are MVAs (trauma from steering wheel, seat belt), falls, and bicycle crashes (trauma from handlebars) (O'Connor, Jufera, Kerns et al., 2009b). Mechanisms of blunt chest trauma include acceleration (moving object hitting the chest or patient being thrown into an object), deceleration (sudden decrease in rate of speed or velocity, such as a MVA), shearing (stretching forces to areas of the chest causing tears, ruptures, or dissections), and compression (direct blow to the chest, such as a crush injury or explosion) (Lotfipour, Kaku, Vaca et al., 2009). Injuries to the chest are often life-threatening and result in one or more of the following pathologic states:

• Hypoxemia from disruption of the airway; injury to the lung parenchyma, rib cage, and respiratory musculature; massive hemorrhage; collapsed lung; pulmonary contusion and pneumothorax
• Hypovolemia from massive fluid loss from the great vessels, cardiac rupture, or hemothorax
• Cardiac failure from cardiac tamponade, cardiac contusion, or increased intrathoracic pressure

These pathologic states frequently result in impaired ventilation and perfusion leading to ARF, hypovolemic shock, and death.

Gunshot and stab wounds are the most common causes of penetrating chest trauma. These wounds are classified according to their velocity. Stab wounds are generally considered low-velocity trauma because the weapon destroys a small area around the wound. The appearance of the external wound may be very deceptive, because pneumothorax, hemothorax, lung contusion, and cardiac tamponade, along with severe and continuing hemorrhage, can occur from any small wound, even one caused by a small-diameter instrument such as an ice pick.

Gunshot wounds may be classified as low-, medium-, or high-velocity. The factors that determine the velocity and resulting extent of damage include the distance from which the gun was fired, the caliber of the gun, and the construction and size of the bullet. A bullet can cause damage at the site of penetration and along its pathway, and a gunshot wound to the chest can produce a variety of pathophysiologic changes. The bullet may ricochet off bony structures and damage the chest organs and great vessels or can travel into the abdomen. If the diaphragm is involved in a gunshot wound or a stab wound, injury to the chest cavity must be considered.

Clinical Manifestations and Assessment

Time is critical in treating chest trauma. Therefore, it is essential to assess the patient immediately to determine the following:

• Time elapsed since injury occurred
• Mechanism of injury
• Level of responsiveness
• Specific injuries
• Estimated blood loss
• Recent drug or alcohol use
• Prehospital treatment

Initial assessment of thoracic injuries includes assessment for airway obstruction, **tension pneumothorax,** open pneumothorax, massive hemothorax, flail chest, and cardiac tamponade and rupture. These injuries are life-threatening and require immediate treatment. Secondary assessment includes assessment for simple pneumothorax, hemothorax, pulmonary contusion, traumatic aortic rupture, tracheobronchial disruption, sternal fracture, esophageal perforation, traumatic diaphragmatic injury, and penetrating wounds to the mediastinum. Although listed as secondary, these injuries may be life-threatening as well (Arthurs, Starnes, Sohn et al., 2009; Mizobuchi, Iwai, Kohno et al., 2009; Nan, Lu, Liu et al., 2009; O'Connor, Byrne, Scalea et al., 2009a; Recinos, Inaba, Dubose et al., 2009; Wilson, Ellsmere, Tallon et al., 2009).

The rapid assessment of thoracic injuries involves the use of the Advanced Trauma Life Support (ATLS) algorithm of "**A**irway, **B**reathing, **C**irculation, **D**isability (neurologic), and **E**xposure":

• *Airway*: Assessment includes noting the rate and depth of breathing and observing for abnormalities such as stridor, cyanosis, nasal flaring, use of accessory muscles, drooling, and overt trauma to the face, mouth, or neck.
• *Breathing*: The chest is assessed for symmetric movement, symmetry of breath sounds, open chest wounds, entrance or exit wounds, impaled objects, distended neck veins, and paradoxical chest wall motion. The thorax is palpated for tenderness and crepitus (subcutaneous emphysema), and the position of the trachea is also assessed. In addition, the

chest wall is assessed for bruising, petechiae, lacerations, and burns.

- *Circulation*: The vital signs and skin color are assessed for signs of shock.
- *Disability*: Assess the patient's level of consciousness and note if concurrent head or spinal cord injuries are present.
- *Exposure*: Assess for exposure injuries such as hypothermia or hyperthermia.

The initial diagnostic workup includes a chest X-ray, CT scan, complete blood count, clotting studies, type and cross-match, electrolytes, oxygen saturation, ABG analysis, and ECG. The patient is completely undressed to avoid missing additional injuries that may complicate care. Many patients with injuries involving the chest have associated head and abdominal injuries that require attention. Ongoing assessment is essential to monitor the patient's response to treatment and to detect early signs of clinical deterioration.

Medical Management

The medical management of penetrating and blunt chest trauma are similar. The objective of immediate management is to restore and maintain cardiopulmonary function. After an adequate airway is ensured and ventilation is established, examination for shock and intrathoracic and intra-abdominal injuries is necessary. There is a high risk for associated intra-abdominal injuries with stab wounds below the level of the fifth anterior intercostal space.

The diagnostic workup includes a chest X-ray, chemistry profile, ABG analysis, POX, and ECG. The patient's blood is typed and cross-matched in case blood transfusion is required. After the status of the peripheral pulses is assessed, a large-bore IV line is inserted. An indwelling catheter is inserted to monitor urinary output. A nasogastric tube is inserted and connected to low suction to prevent aspiration, minimize leakage of abdominal contents, and decompress the gastrointestinal tract.

Shock is treated simultaneously with colloid solutions, crystalloids, or blood, as indicated by the patient's condition. Diagnostic procedures are carried out as dictated by the needs of the patient (e.g., CT scans of chest or abdomen, flat plate X-ray of the abdomen, abdominal ultrasound to check for bleeding).

A chest tube is inserted into the pleural space in most patients with penetrating wounds of the chest to achieve rapid and continuing reexpansion of the lungs, especially in wounds above the fifth intercostals space (nipple line). The insertion of the chest tube frequently results in a complete evacuation of the blood and air. The chest tube also allows early recognition of continuing intrathoracic bleeding, which would make surgical exploration necessary. If the patient has a penetrating wound of the heart or great vessels, the esophagus, or the tracheobronchial tree, surgical intervention is required.

Patients with penetrating chest wound usually require exploratory surgery. In extreme cases, an emergency thoracotomy may be performed in the trauma room to access bleeding from large vessels such as the aorta, pulmonary artery, or heart (Ahmad, Ahmad, Hussain et al., 2009).

Chest Tubes

Chest tubes may be inserted to drain fluid or air from any of the three compartments of the thorax (the right and left pleural spaces and the mediastinum). The pleural space, located between the visceral and parietal pleura, normally contains 25 mL or less of fluid, which helps lubricate the visceral and parietal pleura. Surgical incision of the chest wall almost always causes some degree of pneumothorax (air accumulating in the pleural space) or hemothorax (buildup of serous fluid or blood in the pleural space). Air and fluid collect in the pleural space, restricting lung expansion and reducing gas exchange. Placement of a chest tube in the pleural space restores the normal negative intrathoracic pressure needed for lung re-expansion after surgery or trauma.

The mediastinal space is an extrapleural space that lies between the right and left thoracic cavities and contains the large blood vessels, heart, mainstem bronchus, and thymus gland. If fluid accumulates here, the heart can become compressed and stop beating, causing death. Mediastinal chest tubes can be inserted either anteriorly or posteriorly to the heart to drain blood after surgery.

Catheters

There are two types of chest tubes: small-bore and large-bore catheters. Small-bore catheters (7 to 12 Fr) have a one-way valve apparatus to prevent air from moving back into the patient (Fig. 10-9). They can be inserted through a small skin incision. Large-bore catheters, which range in size up to 40 Fr, are usually connected to a **chest drainage system** to collect any pleural fluid and monitor for air leaks. After the chest tube is positioned, it is sutured to the skin and connected to a drainage apparatus to remove the residual air and fluid from the pleural or mediastinal space. This results in the re-expansion of remaining lung tissue.

Chest Drainage Systems

Chest drainage systems have a suction source, a collection chamber for pleural drainage, and a mechanism to prevent air from re-entering the chest with inhalation. Various types of chest drainage systems are available for use in removal of air and fluid from the pleural space and re-expansion of the lungs. Chest drainage systems come with either wet (water seal) or dry suction control. In wet suction systems, the amount of suction is determined by the amount of water instilled in the suction chamber. Wet systems use a water seal to prevent air from moving back into the chest on inspiration. Dry systems use a one-way valve and may have a suction control dial in place of the water. Both systems can operate by gravity drainage, without a suction source (Fig. 10-9; Box 10-12, p. 315).

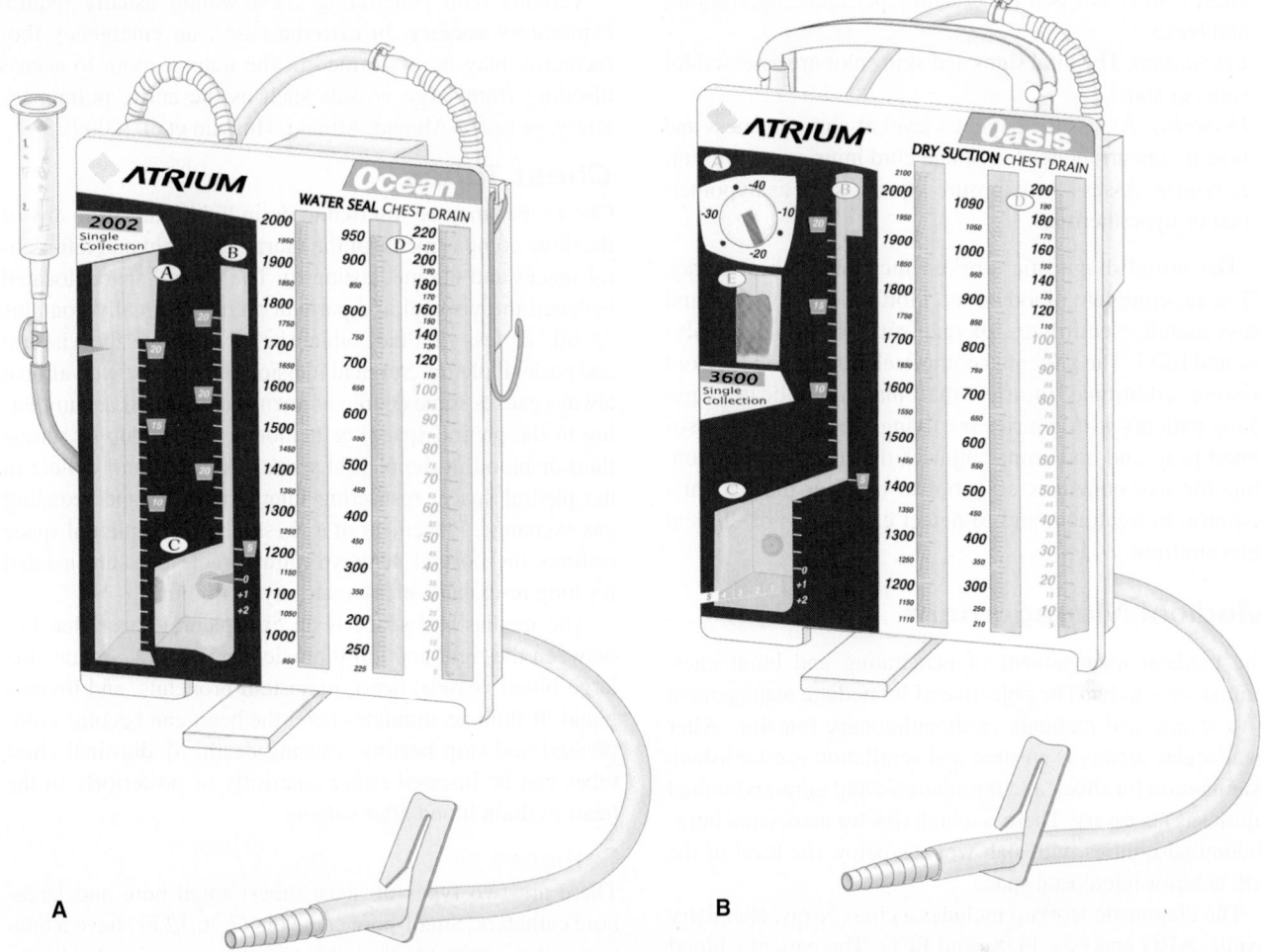

A

B

FIGURE 10-9 Chest drainage systems. **(A)** The Atrium Ocean is an example of a water seal chest drain system composed of a drainage chamber and water seal chamber. The suction control is determined by the height of the water column in that chamber (usually 20 cm). *A,* suction control chamber; *B,* water seal chamber; *C,* air leak zone; *D,* collection chamber. **(B)** The Atrium Oasis is an example of a dry suction water seal system that uses a mechanical regulator for vacuum control, a water seal chamber, and a drainage chamber. *A,* dry suction regulator; *B,* water seal chamber; *C,* air leak monitor; *D,* collection chamber; *E,* suction monitor bellows. Art redrawn with permission from Atrium Medical Corporation, Hudson, New Hampshire.

WATER SEAL SYSTEMS. The traditional water seal system (or wet suction) for chest drainage has three chambers: a collection chamber, a water seal chamber, and a wet suction control chamber. The collection chamber acts as a reservoir for fluid draining from the chest tube. It is graduated to permit easy measurement of drainage. Suction may be added to create negative pressure and promote drainage of fluid and removal of air. The suction control chamber regulates the amount of negative pressure applied to the chest. The amount of suction is determined by the water level. It is usually set at 20 cm H_2O; adding more fluid results in more suction. After the suction is turned on, bubbling appears in the suction chamber. A positive-pressure valve is located at the top of the suction chamber that automatically opens with increases in positive pressure within the system. Air is automatically released through a positive-pressure relief valve if the suction tubing is inadvertently clamped or kinked.

The water seal chamber has a one-way valve or water seal that prevents air from moving back into the chest when the patient inhales. There is an increase in the water level with inspiration and a return to the baseline level during exhalation; this is referred to as *tidaling*. If bubbling is present, either intermittent or continuous, an air leak is present within the system or the patient. The nurse must investigate the system for loose connections. Bubbling and tidaling do not occur when the tube is placed in the mediastinal space; however, fluid may pulsate with the patient's heartbeat. If the chest tube is connected to gravity drainage only, suction is not used. Two-chamber chest drainage systems (water seal

BOX 10-12

GUIDELINES FOR NURSING CARE

Managing Chest Drainage Systems

Equipment

- Chest drainage system
- Sterile water
- Marker
- Dressings
- Tape

ACTION	RATIONALE
1. If using a chest drainage system with a water seal, fill the water seal chamber with sterile water to the level specified by the manufacturer.	**1.** Water seal drainage allows air and fluid to escape into a drainage chamber. The water acts as a seal and keeps the air from being drawn back into the pleural space.
2. When using suction in chest drainage systems with a water seal, fill the suction control chamber with sterile water to the 20 cm level or as prescribed. In systems without a water seal, set the regulator dial at the appropriate suction level.	**2.** The water level regulator dial setting determines the degree of suction applied.

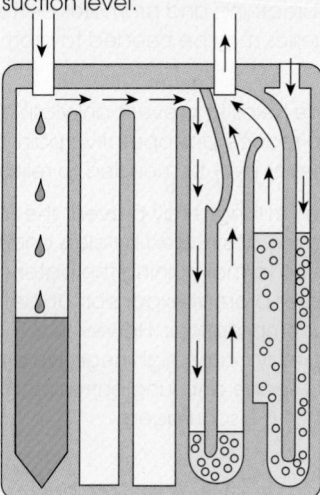

Pleur-Evac System.

ACTION	RATIONALE
3. Attach the drainage catheter exiting the thoracic cavity to the tubing coming from the collection chamber. Tape securely with adhesive tape.	**3.** In chest drainage units, the system is closed.
4. If suction is used, connect the suction control chamber tubing to the suction unit. If using a wet suction system, turn on the suction unit and increase pressure until slow but steady bubbling appears in the suction control chamber. If using a chest drainage system with a dry suction control chamber, turn the regulator dial to 20 cm H_2O.	**4.** With a wet suction system, the degree of suction is determined by the amount of water in the suction control chamber and is not dependent on the rate of bubbling or the pressure gauge setting on the suction unit. With a dry suction control chamber, the regulator dial replaces the water.
5. Mark the drainage from the collection chamber with tape on the outside of the drainage unit. Mark hourly/daily increments (date and time) at the drainage level.	**5.** This marking shows the amount of fluid loss and how fast fluid is collecting in the drainage chamber. It serves as a basis for determining the need for blood replacement, if the fluid is blood. Visibly bloody drainage will appear in the chamber in the immediate postoperative period but should gradually becomes serous. If the patient is bleeding as heavily as 100 mL every

(continued on page 316)

BOX 10-12

GUIDELINES FOR NURSING CARE (continued)

ACTION	RATIONALE
	15 minutes, check the drainage every few minutes. A reoperation or autotransfusion may be needed. Drainage of 200 mL/hr is usually associated with bleeding complications. The transfusion of blood collected in the drainage chamber must be reinfused within 4 to 6 hours. Usually, however, drainage decreases progressively in the first 24 hours.
6. Ensure that the drainage tubing does not kink, loop, or interfere with the patient's movements.	6. Kinking, looping, or pressure on the drainage tubing can produce back pressure, which may force fluid back into the pleural space or impede its drainage.
7. Encourage the patient to assume a comfortable position with good body alignment. With the lateral position, make sure that the patient's body does not compress the tubing. The patient should be turned and repositioned every 1.5 to 2 hours. Provide adequate analgesia.	7. Frequent position changes promote drainage, and good body alignment helps prevent postural deformities and contractures. Proper positioning also helps breathing and promotes better air exchange. Analgesics may be needed to promote comfort.
8. Assist the patient with range-of-motion exercises for the affected arm and shoulder several times daily. Provide adequate analgesia.	8. Exercise helps to prevent ankylosis of the shoulder and to reduce postoperative pain and discomfort. Analgesics may be needed to relieve pain.
9. If the drainage is bloody, gently drain the tubing in the direction of the drainage chamber. Gentle "milking" may be warranted if allowed according to institutional policy in cases of active bleeding to prevent obstruction in the tubing. If "gentle milking" is allowed, do not compress the tubing completely. In general the prevention of dependent loops, laying of the tubing horizontally across the bed that then drops vertically into the chest drainage system is sufficient for fluid drainage.	9. Gentle "milking" may prevent the tubing from becoming obstructed by clots and fibrin. Constant attention to maintaining the patency of the tube facilitates prompt expansion of the lung and minimizes complications. However compressing the tubing may cause high negative pressure in the pleural space and lung entrapment, thus routine "milking" is discouraged.
10. Make sure there is fluctuation ("tidaling") of the fluid level in the water seal chamber (in wet systems), or check the air leak indicator for leaks (in dry systems with a one-way valve). *Note:* Fluid fluctuations in the water seal chamber or air leak indicator area will stop when: • The lung has reexpanded • The tubing is obstructed by blood clots, fibrin, or kinks • A loop of tubing hangs below the rest of the tubing • Suction motor or wall suction is not working properly	10. Fluctuation of the water level in the water seal shows effective connection between the pleural cavity and the drainage chamber and indicates that the drainage system remains patent. Fluctuation is also a gauge of intrapleural pressure in systems with a water seal (wet and dry, but not with the one-way valve).
11. With a dry system, assess for the presence of the indicator (bellows or float device) when setting the regulator dial to the desired level of suction.	11. An air leak indicator shows changes in intrathoracic pressure in dry systems with a one-way valve. Bubbles will appear if a leak is present. The air leak indicator takes the place of fluid fluctuations in the water seal chamber. The indicator shows that the vacuum is adequate to maintain the desired level of suction.

ACTION (continued)	RATIONALE (continued)
12. Observe for air leaks in the drainage system; they are indicated by constant bubbling in the water seal chamber, or by the air leak indicator in dry systems with a one-way valve. Also assess the chest tube system for correctable external leaks. Notify the physician immediately of excessive bubbling in the water seal chamber not due to external leaks.	**12.** Leaking and trapping of air in the pleural space can result in tension pneumothorax.
13. When turning down the dry suction, depress the manual high-negativity vent, and assess for a rise in the water level of the water seal chamber.	**13.** A rise in the water level of the water seal chamber indicates high negative pressure in the system that could lead to increased intrathoracic pressure.
14. Observe and immediately report rapid and shallow breathing, cyanosis, pressure in the chest, subcutaneous emphysema, symptoms of hemorrhage, or significant changes in vital signs.	**14.** Many clinical conditions can cause these signs and symptoms, including tension pneumothorax, mediastinal shift, hemorrhage, severe incisional pain, pulmonary embolus, and cardiac tamponade. Surgical intervention may be necessary.
15. Encourage the patient to breathe deeply and cough at frequent intervals. Provide adequate analgesia. If needed, request an order for patient-controlled analgesia. Also teach the patient how to perform incentive spirometry.	**15.** Deep breathing and coughing help to raise the intrapleural pressure, which promotes drainage of accumulated fluid in the pleural space. Deep breathing and coughing also promote removal of secretions from the tracheobronchial tree, which in turn promotes lung expansion and prevents atelectasis (alveolar collapse).
16. If the patient is lying on a stretcher and must be transported to another area, place the drainage system below the chest level. If the tubing disconnects, cut off the contaminated tips of the chest tube and tubing, insert a sterile connector in the cut ends, and reattach to the drainage system. Do not clamp the chest tube during transport.	**16.** The drainage apparatus must be kept at a level lower than the patient's chest to prevent fluid from flowing backward into the pleural space. Clamping can result in a tension pneumothorax.
17. When assisting in the chest tube's removal, instruct the patient to perform a gentle Valsalva maneuver or to breathe quietly. The chest tube is then clamped and quickly removed. Simultaneously, a small bandage is applied and made airtight with petrolatum gauze covered by a 4 × 4-inch gauze pad and thoroughly covered and sealed with nonporous tape.	**17.** The chest tube is removed as directed when the lung is re-expanded (usually 24 hours to several days), depending on the cause of the pneumothorax. During tube removal, the chief priorities are preventing air from entering the pleural cavity as the tube is withdrawn and preventing infection.

chamber and collection chamber) are available for use with patients who need only gravity drainage.

The water level in the water seal chamber reflects the negative pressure present in the intrathoracic cavity. A rise in the water level of the water-seal chamber indicates negative pressure in the pleural or mediastinal space. Excessive negative pressure can cause trauma to tissue. Most chest drainage systems have an automatic means to prevent excessive negative pressure. By pressing and holding a manual high-negativity vent (usually located on the top of the chest drainage system) until the water level in the water seal chamber returns to the 2 cm mark, excessive negative pressure is avoided, thus preventing damage to tissue.

DRY SUCTION WATER SEAL SYSTEMS. Dry suction water seal systems, also referred to as dry suction, have a collection chamber for drainage, a water seal chamber, and a dry suction control chamber. The water seal chamber is filled with water to the 2 cm level. Bubbling in this area can indicate an air leak. The dry suction control chamber contains a regulator dial that conveniently regulates vacuum to the chest drain. Water is not needed for suction in these systems. Without the bubbling in the suction chamber, the machine is quieter. However, if the container is knocked over, the water seal may be lost.

Once the tube is connected to the suction source, the regulator dial allows the desired level of suction to be dialed in;

the suction is increased until an indicator appears. The indicator has the same function as the bubbling in the traditional water seal system; that is, it indicates that the vacuum is adequate to maintain the desired level of suction. Some drainage systems use a bellows (a chamber that can be expanded or contracted) or an orange-colored float device as an indicator of when the suction control regulator is set.

When the water in the water seal rises above the 2 cm level, intrathoracic pressure increases. Dry suction water seal systems have a manual high-negativity vent located on top of the drain. The manual high-negativity vent is pressed until the indicator appears (either a float device or bellows) and the water level in the water seal returns to the desired level, indicating that the intrathoracic pressure is decreased.

DRY SUCTION SYSTEMS WITH A ONE-WAY VALVE. A third type of chest drainage system is dry suction with a one-way mechanical valve. This system has a collection chamber, a one-way mechanical valve, and a dry suction control chamber. The valve permits air and fluid to leave the chest but prevents their movement back into the pleural space. This model lacks a water seal chamber and therefore can be set up quickly in emergency situations, and the dry control drain still works even if it is knocked over. This makes the dry suction systems useful for the patient who is ambulating or being transported. However, without the water seal chamber, there is no way to tell by inspection whether the pressure in the chest has changed, even though an air leak indicator is present so that the system can be checked. If an air leak is suspected, 30 mL of water is injected into the air leak indicator or the container is tipped so that fluid enters the air leak detection chamber. Bubbles will appear if a leak is present.

If the chest tube has been inserted to re-expand a lung after pneumothorax, or if very little fluid drainage is expected, a one-way valve (Heimlich valve) may be connected to the chest tube (Fig. 10-10). This valve may be attached to a collection bag or covered with a sterile dressing if no drainage is expected.

STERNAL AND RIB FRACTURES

Sternal fractures are most common in MVAs, caused by a direct blow to the sternum via the steering wheel. Rib fractures are the most common type of chest trauma, occurring in more than 62% of patients admitted with blunt chest injury (Sharma et al., 2008). Most rib fractures are benign and are treated conservatively. Fractures of the first three ribs are rare but can result in a high mortality rate because they are associated with laceration of the subclavian artery or vein. The fifth through ninth ribs are the most common sites of fractures. Fractures of the lower ribs are associated with injury to the spleen and liver, which may be lacerated by fragmented sections of the rib.

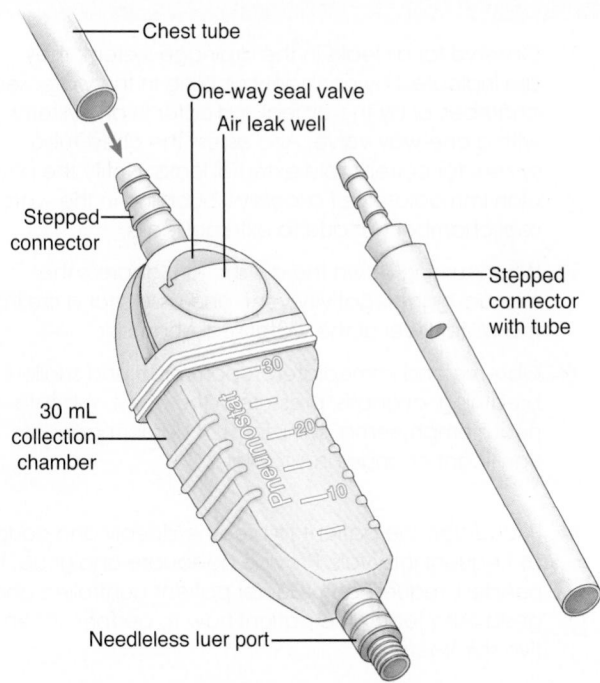

FIGURE 10-10 One-way (Heimlich) valve, a disposable, single-use chest drainage system with 30 mL collection volume. Used when minimal volume of chest drainage is expected.

Clinical Manifestations and Assessment

Patients with sternal fractures have anterior chest pain, overlying tenderness, ecchymosis, crepitus, swelling, and possible chest wall deformity. For patients with rib fractures, clinical manifestations are similar: severe pain, point tenderness, and muscle spasm over the area of the fracture that is aggravated by coughing, deep breathing, and movement. The area around the fracture may be bruised. To reduce the pain, the patient splints the chest by breathing in a shallow manner and avoids sighs, deep breaths, coughing, and movement. This reluctance to move or breathe deeply results in diminished ventilation, atelectasis (collapse of unaerated alveoli), pneumonitis, and hypoxemia. Respiratory insufficiency and failure can be the outcomes of such a cycle.

The patient must be closely evaluated for underlying cardiac or abdominal injuries. A crackling, grating sound in the thorax (subcutaneous crepitus) may be detected with auscultation or palpation. The diagnostic workup may include a chest X-ray, rib films of a specific area, ECG, continuous POX, and ABG analysis.

Medical and Nursing Management

Medical management is directed toward relieving pain, avoiding excessive activity, and treating any associated inju-

ries. Surgical fixation is rarely necessary unless fragments are grossly displaced and pose a potential for further injury.

The goals of treatment for rib fractures are to control pain and to detect and treat the injury. Narcotics are most often used to relieve pain and to allow deep breathing and coughing. Care must be taken to avoid oversedation and suppression of respiratory drive. Alternative strategies to relieve pain include an intercostal nerve block and ice over the fracture site. A chest binder may be used as supportive treatment to provide stability to the chest wall and may decrease pain. The patient is instructed to apply the binder snugly enough to provide support, but not to impair respiratory excursion. Usually the pain abates in 5 to 7 days, and discomfort can be relieved with epidural analgesia, patient-controlled analgesia, or nonopioid analgesia (NSAIDs). Most rib fractures heal in 3 to 6 weeks.

FLAIL CHEST

Flail chest is frequently a complication of blunt chest trauma from a steering wheel injury. It usually occurs when three or more adjacent ribs (multiple contiguous ribs) are fractured at two or more sites, resulting in free-floating rib segments. It may also result as a combination fracture of ribs and costal cartilages or sternum (Fig. 10-11). As a result, the chest wall loses stability, causing respiratory impairment and usually severe respiratory distress. Additionally, due to the force needed to break ribs or the sternum, an underlying pulmonary or cardiac contusion is often present.

Pathophysiology

During inspiration, as the chest expands, the detached part of the rib segment (flail segment) moves in a paradoxical manner (pendelluft movement) in that it is pulled inward during inspiration, reducing the amount of air that can be drawn into the lungs. On expiration, because the intrathoracic pressure exceeds atmospheric pressure, the flail segment bulges out-

ward, impairing the patient's ability to exhale. The mediastinum then shifts back to the affected side. This paradoxical action results in increased dead space, a reduction in alveolar ventilation, and decreased compliance. Retained airway secretions and atelectasis frequently accompany flail chest. The patient has hypoxemia, and if gas exchange is greatly compromised, respiratory acidosis develops as a result of carbon dioxide retention. Hypotension, inadequate tissue perfusion, and metabolic acidosis often follow as the paradoxical motion of the mediastinum decreases cardiac output.

Medical and Nursing Management

As with rib fracture, treatment of flail chest is usually supportive. Management includes providing ventilatory support, clearing secretions from the lungs, and controlling pain. Specific management depends on the degree of respiratory dysfunction. If only a small segment of the chest is involved, the objectives are to clear the airway through positioning, coughing, deep breathing, and suctioning to aid in the expansion of the lung, and to relieve pain by intercostal nerve blocks, high thoracic epidural blocks, or cautious use of IV opioids.

For mild to moderate flail chest injuries, the underlying pulmonary contusion is treated by monitoring fluid intake and appropriate fluid replacement while relieving chest pain. Pulmonary physiotherapy focusing on lung volume expansion includes deep breathing exercises, incentive spirometry, and nebulized bronchodilators and mucolytics.

For severe flail chest injuries, endotracheal intubation and mechanical ventilation are required to provide internal pneumatic stabilization of the flail chest and to correct abnormalities in gas exchange. This helps treat the underlying pulmonary contusion, serves to stabilize the thoracic cage to allow the fractures to heal, and improves alveolar ventilation and intrathoracic volume by decreasing the work of breathing. In rare circumstances, surgery may be required to more quickly stabilize the flail segment.

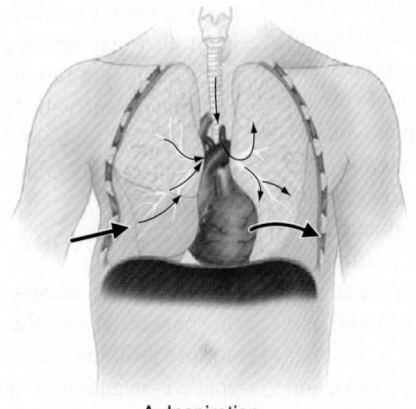 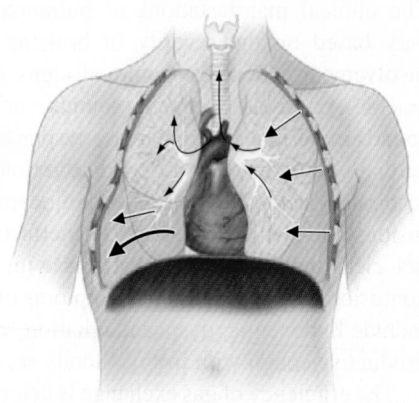

FIGURE 10-11 Flail chest is caused by a free-floating segment of rib cage resulting from multiple rib fractures. **(A)** Paradoxical movement on inspiration occurs when the flail rib segment is sucked inward and the mediastinal structures shift to the unaffected side. The amount of air drawn into the affected lung is reduced. **(B)** On expiration, the flail segment bulges outward, and the mediastinal structures shift back to the affected side.

A. Inspiration   B. Expiration

Regardless of the type of treatment, the patient is carefully monitored by serial chest X-rays, ABG analysis, POX, and bedside pulmonary function monitoring. Pain management is key to successful treatment. Patient-controlled analgesia, intercostal nerve blocks, epidural analgesia, and intrapleural administration of opioids may be used to relieve or manage thoracic pain.

PULMONARY CONTUSION

Pulmonary contusion is a common thoracic injury and is frequently associated with blunt trauma. It is defined as damage to the lung tissues resulting in hemorrhage and localized edema (i.e., bruised lung). Pulmonary contusion represents a spectrum of lung injury characterized by the development of infiltrates and various degrees of respiratory dysfunction and sometimes respiratory failure. A contusion is sustained in 30% to 70% of patients who experience blunt force trauma (O'Connor et al., 2009b). Pulmonary contusion may not be evident initially on examination but develops in the post-traumatic period; it may involve a small portion of one lung, a massive section of a lung, one entire lung, or both lungs.

Pathophysiology

The primary pathologic defect is an abnormal accumulation of fluid in the interstitial and intra-alveolar spaces. It is thought that injury to the lung parenchyma and its capillary network results in a leakage of serum protein and plasma. The leaking serum protein exerts an osmotic pressure that enhances loss of fluid from the capillaries. Blood, edema, and cellular debris (from cellular response to injury) enter the lung and accumulate in the bronchioles and alveoli, where they interfere with gas exchange. The patient has hypoxemia and carbon dioxide retention. Occasionally, a contused lung occurs on the other side of the point of body impact; this is called a *contrecoup contusion*.

Clinical Manifestations and Assessment

The clinical manifestations of pulmonary contusions can vary based on the severity of bruising and parenchymal involvement. The most common signs and symptoms are crackles, decreased breath sounds, or bronchial breath sounds in peripheral lung areas, dyspnea, tachypnea, tachycardia, chest pain, blood-tinged secretions, hypoxemia, and respiratory acidosis. Patients with moderate pulmonary contusions often have a constant, but ineffective cough and cannot clear their secretions. Patients with severe pulmonary contusion have the signs and symptoms of ARDS; these may include hypoxemia, dyspnea, agitation, combativeness, and productive cough with frothy, bloody secretions.

The efficiency of gas exchange is determined by POX and ABG measurements. Pulse oximetry is also used to measure oxygen saturation continuously. The initial chest X-ray may show no changes; changes may not appear for 1 or 2 days after the injury and appear as pulmonary infiltrates on chest X-ray.

Medical and Nursing Management

Treatment priorities include maintaining the airway, providing adequate oxygenation, and controlling pain. In mild pulmonary contusion, judicious hydration via IV fluids and oral intake is important to mobilize secretions. However, fluid intake must be closely monitored to avoid hypervolemia, which can worsen the contusion. Volume expansion techniques, postural drainage, physiotherapy including coughing, and endotracheal suctioning are used to remove the secretions. Pain is managed by intercostal nerve blocks or by opioids via patient-controlled analgesia or other methods. Supplemental oxygen is usually given by mask or cannula for hypoxemia (sats <90%).

In patients with moderate pulmonary contusions, bronchoscopy may be required to remove secretions. Intubation and mechanical ventilation with PEEP may also be necessary to maintain the pressure and keep the lungs inflated. In patients with severe contusion, who may develop respiratory failure, aggressive treatment with endotracheal intubation and ventilatory support, diuretics, and fluid restriction may be necessary.

Antimicrobial medications may be prescribed for the treatment of pulmonary infection. This is a common complication of pulmonary contusion because the fluid and blood that extravasates into the alveolar and interstitial spaces serve as an excellent culture medium.

CARDIAC TAMPONADE

Cardiac tamponade is compression of the heart resulting from fluid or blood within the pericardial sac. It usually is caused by blunt or penetrating trauma to the chest. A penetrating wound of the heart is associated with a high mortality rate. Cardiac tamponade also may follow diagnostic cardiac catheterization, angiographic procedures, and pacemaker insertion, which can produce perforations of the heart and great vessels. Pericardial effusion with fluid compressing the heart also may develop from metastases to the pericardium from malignant tumors of the breast, lung, or mediastinum and may occur with lymphomas and leukemias, renal failure, TB, and high-dose radiation to the chest. Cardiac tamponade is discussed in detail in Chapter 15.

PNEUMOTHORAX

Pneumothorax occurs when the parietal or visceral pleura are punctured and the pleural space is exposed to positive atmospheric pressure. Normally, the pressure in the pleural space is negative or subatmospheric; this negative pressure is required to maintain lung inflation. When either pleura is

Open pneumothorax

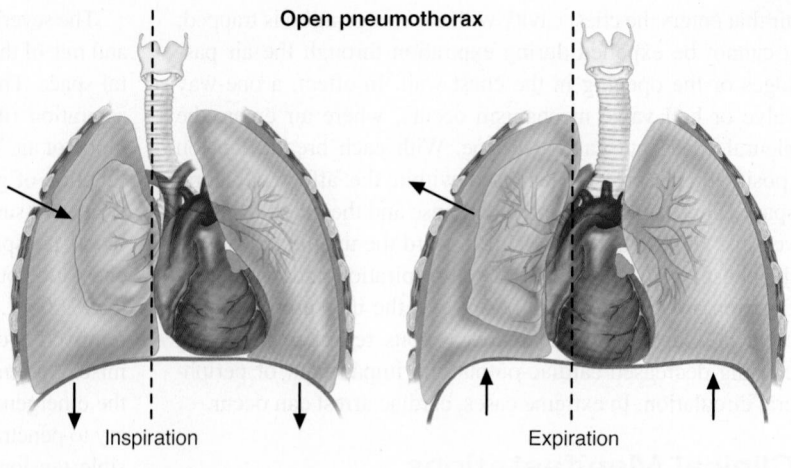

Inspiration   Expiration

Tension pneumothorax

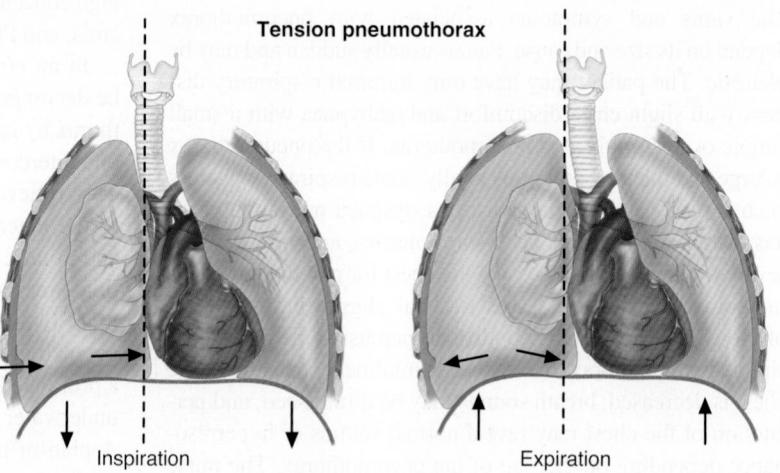

FIGURE 10-12 Open and tension pneumothorax.

Inspiration   Expiration

breached, air enters the pleural space, and the lung or a portion of it collapses.

Types of Pneumothorax

Types of pneumothorax include simple, traumatic, and tension pneumothorax (Fig. 10-12).

Simple Pneumothorax

A simple, or spontaneous, pneumothorax most commonly occurs as air enters the pleural space through the rupture of a bleb or a bronchopleural fistula. A spontaneous pneumothorax may occur in an apparently healthy person (most commonly in young men) in the absence of trauma due to rupture of an air-filled bleb, or blister, on the surface of the lung, allowing air from the airways to enter the pleural cavity. It may also be associated with bullous lung diseases such as emphysema or pulmonary fibrosis.

Traumatic Pneumothorax

A traumatic pneumothorax occurs when air escapes from a laceration in the lung itself and enters the pleural space, or enters the pleural space through a wound in the chest wall. It may result from blunt trauma, penetrating chest or abdomi-

nal trauma, or diaphragmatic tears. Traumatic pneumothorax may occur during invasive thoracic procedures (i.e., thoracentesis, **transbronchial** lung biopsy, insertion of a subclavian line) in which the pleura is inadvertently punctured, or with barotrauma from mechanical ventilation. A traumatic pneumothorax resulting from major trauma to the chest is often accompanied by a hemothorax (collection of blood in the pleural space resulting from torn intercostal vessels, lacerations of the great vessels, or lacerations of the lungs). Often both blood and air are found in the chest cavity (hemopneumothorax) after major trauma.

Open pneumothorax is one form of traumatic pneumothorax. It occurs when a wound in the chest wall is large enough to allow air to pass freely in and out of the thoracic cavity with each attempted respiration. Because the rush of air through the wound in the chest wall produces a sucking sound, such injuries are termed *sucking chest wounds*.

Tension Pneumothorax

A tension pneumothorax occurs when air is drawn into the pleural space from a lacerated lung or through a small opening or wound in the chest wall. It may be a complication of other types of pneumothorax. In contrast to open pneumothorax, the

air that enters the chest cavity with each inspiration is trapped; it cannot be expelled during expiration through the air passages or the opening in the chest wall. In effect, a one-way valve or ball valve mechanism occurs, where air enters the pleural space but cannot escape. With each breath, tension (positive pressure) is increased within the affected pleural space. This causes the lung to collapse and the heart, the great vessels, and the trachea to shift toward the unaffected side of the chest (mediastinal shift). Both respiration and circulatory function are compromised because of the increased intrathoracic pressure, which decreases venous return to the heart, causing decreased cardiac output and impairment of peripheral circulation. In extreme cases, cardiac arrest can occur.

Clinical Manifestations

The signs and symptoms associated with pneumothorax depend on its size and cause. Pain is usually sudden and may be pleuritic. The patient may have only minimal respiratory distress with slight chest discomfort and tachypnea with a small simple or uncomplicated pneumothorax. If the pneumothorax is large and the lung collapses totally, acute respiratory distress occurs. The patient is anxious, has dyspnea and air hunger, has increased use of the accessory muscles, and may develop severe hypoxemia. In assessing the chest for any type of pneumothorax, the nurse assesses tracheal alignment, expansion of the chest, and breath sounds, and percusses the chest. In a simple pneumothorax, the trachea is midline, expansion of the chest is decreased, breath sounds may be diminished, and percussion of the chest may reveal normal sounds or hyperresonance depending on the size of the pneumothorax. The nurse assesses the affected lung for crepitus or subcutaneous emphysema and notes the extent of it in the patient's record.

In a tension pneumothorax, the trachea may shift away from the affected side, chest expansion may be decreased or fixed in a hyperexpansion state, breath sounds are diminished or absent, and percussion to the affected side is hyperresonant. The clinical picture is one of air hunger, agitation, increasing hypoxemia, central cyanosis, hypotension, and tachycardia.

Medical and Nursing Management

Medical management of pneumothorax depends on its cause and severity. The goal of treatment is to evacuate the air or blood from the pleural space. A thoracostomy tube (chest tube) is used to evacuate any accumulated air or fluid. A small, simple pneumothorax is treated with a small chest tube (20 Fr, or 10–12 Fr pigtail catheter) inserted near the second intercostal space. Larger pneumothoraxes, especially if there is fluid or blood present, are managed with larger-sized tubes (32–36 Fr) that are placed in the fourth or fifth intercostal space at the midaxillary line. The tube is directed posteriorly to drain the fluid and air. Once the chest tube or tubes are inserted and suction is applied (usually to -20 mm Hg suction), effective decompression of the pleural cavity (drainage of blood or air) occurs.

The severity of open pneumothorax depends on the amount and rate of thoracic bleeding and the amount of air in the pleural space. The pleural cavity can be decompressed by needle aspiration (thoracentesis) or by chest tube drainage of the blood or air. The lung is then able to re-expand and resume the function of gas exchange. As a rule of thumb, the chest wall is opened surgically (thoracotomy) if more than 1,500 mL of blood is aspirated initially by thoracentesis (or is the initial chest tube output) or if chest tube output continues at greater than 200 mL/hour. The urgency with which the blood must be removed is determined by the degree of respiratory compromise. An emergency thoracotomy may also be performed in the emergency department if a cardiovascular injury secondary to penetrating trauma is suspected. The patient with a possible tension pneumothorax should immediately be given a high concentration of supplemental oxygen to treat the hypoxemia, and POX should be used to monitor oxygen saturation.

In an emergency situation, a tension pneumothorax can be decompressed or quickly converted to a simple pneumothorax by inserting a large-bore needle (14-gauge) at the second intercostal space, midclavicular line on the affected side. This relieves the pressure and vents the positive pressure to the external environment. A chest tube is then inserted and connected to suction to remove the remaining air and fluid, reestablish the negative pressure, and re-expand the lung. If the lung re-expands and air leakage from the lung parenchyma stops, further drainage may be unnecessary. If a prolonged air leak continues despite chest tube drainage to underwater seal, surgery may be necessary to close the leak. A plan of nursing care for the patient after thoracotomy is available online at http://thePoint.lww.com/Pellico1e.

SUBCUTANEOUS EMPHYSEMA

No matter what kind of chest trauma a patient has, when the lung or the air passages are injured, air may enter the tissue planes and pass for some distance under the skin (e.g., neck, chest). The tissues give a crackling sensation when palpated, and the subcutaneous air produces an alarming appearance as the face, neck, body, and scrotum become misshapen by subcutaneous air. Fortunately, subcutaneous emphysema is of itself usually not a serious complication. The subcutaneous air is spontaneously absorbed if the underlying air leak is treated or stops spontaneously. In severe cases, in which there is widespread subcutaneous emphysema, a tracheostomy is indicated if airway patency is threatened.

ASPIRATION

Aspiration of stomach contents into the lungs is a serious complication that can cause pneumonia and result in the clinical picture of tachycardia, dyspnea, hypoxemia, hypertension, hypotension, and finally death. It can occur when the protective airway reflexes are decreased or absent due to a variety of factors.

Risk Factors for Aspiration

- Altered level of consciousness (cerebrovascular accident, head trauma, intracranial mass/tumor, drug overdose, alcohol intoxication, seizures, oversedation)
- Neurological disorders (Parkinson's disease, myasthenia gravis, multiple sclerosis, amyotrophic lateral sclerosis)
- Dysphagia (esophageal stricture, diverticula or neoplasm, tracheoesophageal fistula, cardiac sphincter incompetence, achalasia)
- Disruption via mechanical instruments (endotracheal intubation, tracheostomy, naso-/orogastric tube (any size), bronchoscopy, laryngoscopy, upper GI endoscopy)
- Recumbent position
- Protracted vomiting
- Nasogastric feeding
- Gastric outlet obstruction

Pathophysiology

The primary factors responsible for death and complications after aspiration of gastric contents are the volume and character of the aspirated gastric contents. For example, a small, localized aspiration from regurgitation can cause pneumonia and acute respiratory distress; a massive aspiration is usually fatal. Factors that increase the risk of aspiration are discussed in Box 10-13.

A full stomach contains food particles. If these are aspirated, the problem then becomes one of mechanical blockage of the airways and secondary infection or chemical pneumonitis. During periods of fasting, the stomach contains acidic gastric juice, which, if aspirated, can be very destructive to the alveoli and capillaries. Fecal contamination (more likely seen in intestinal obstruction) increases the likelihood of death, because the endotoxins produced by intestinal organisms may be absorbed systemically, or the thick proteinaceous material found in the intestinal contents may obstruct the airway, leading to atelectasis and secondary bacterial invasion.

Aspiration pneumonitis may develop from aspiration of gastric contents, which can also cause a chemical burn of the tracheobronchial tree and pulmonary parenchyma. An ensuing inflammatory response occurs. This results in the destruction of alveolar–capillary endothelial cells, with a consequent outpouring of protein-rich fluids into the interstitial and intra-alveolar spaces. As a result, surfactant is lost, which in turn causes the airways to close and the alveoli to collapse. Finally, the impaired exchange of oxygen and carbon dioxide causes respiratory failure.

Aspiration pneumonia develops after inhalation of colonized oropharyngeal material. The pathologic process involves an acute inflammatory response to bacteria and bacterial products. Most commonly, the bacteriologic findings include gram-positive cocci, gram-negative rods, and occasionally anaerobic bacteria (Shariatzadeh, Huang, & Marrie, 2006).

Prevention

Prevention is the primary goal when caring for patients at risk for aspiration. Examples of risk factors for aspiration include decreased level of consciousness, supine positioning, presence of a nasogastric tube, tracheal intubation and mechanical ventilation, bolus or intermittent feeding delivery methods, and advanced age (Coffin, Klompas, Classen et al., 2008). Evidence confirms that one of the main preventive measures for aspiration is placing at-risk patients in a semirecumbent position (elevation of the head of the bed to a 30- to 45-degree angle) (McClave, Martindale, Vanek et al., 2009).

Compensating for Absent Reflexes

Aspiration may occur if the patient cannot adequately coordinate protective glottic, laryngeal, and cough reflexes. This hazard is increased if the patient has a distended abdomen, is supine, has the upper extremities immobilized by IV infusions or hand restraints, receives local anesthetics to the oropharyngeal or laryngeal area for diagnostic procedures, has been sedated, or has had long-term intubation.

When vomiting, people can normally protect their airway by sitting up or turning on the side and coordinating breathing, coughing, gag, and glottic reflexes. If these reflexes are active, an oral airway should not be inserted. If an airway is in place, it should be pulled out the moment the patient gags so as not to stimulate the pharyngeal gag reflex and promote vomiting and aspiration. Suctioning of oral secretions with a catheter should be performed with minimal pharyngeal stimulation.

Assessing Feeding Tube Placement

When a patient is intubated, aspiration may occur even with a nasogastric tube in place and may result in nosocomial pneumonia. Assessment of nasogastric tube placement is key to the prevention of aspiration. The best method for determining tube placement is via an X-ray taken immediately after an enteral feeding tube is placed, and prior to beginning feeds. Nurses should mark the place where the tube exits the nares or lips and note this in the patient's chart. This marking should be assessed whenever medication is administered via the tube or at least every 4 hours. Other methods of tube confirmation have been studied such as observation of the aspirate color, testing of its pH or glucose content, and auscultation over the stomach for an air bolus. None of these methods has been shown to accurately assess the placement of the tube (Bourgault, Ipe, Weaver et al., 2007).

Patients who receive continuous or timed-interval tube feedings must be positioned properly. Patients receiving continuous infusions are given small volumes under low pressure in an upright position, which helps prevent aspiration. Patients receiving tube feedings at timed intervals are maintained in an

upright or semi-recumbent position (elevation of the head of the bed to a 30- to 45-degree angle) during the feeding and for a minimum of 30 minutes afterward to allow the stomach to empty partially (McClave et al., 2009). Tube feedings must be given only when it is certain that the feeding tube is positioned correctly in the stomach. Many patients today receive enteral feeding directly into the small intestine through a small-bore flexible feeding tube or surgically implanted tube. Feedings are given slowly and are regulated by a feeding pump (refer to Chapter 22 for more details).

Chapter Review

Critical Thinking Exercises

1. You are caring for an 82-year-old woman who was recently transferred to the hospital from a nursing home with the diagnosis of presumed health care–associated pneumonia. She has a nasogastric feeding tube in place and is lethargic, dehydrated, and confused. What strategies would you initiate to prevent aspiration? What nursing care interventions would you use to assess for aspiration? What is the evidence base for the interventions that you consider? How will you evaluate the strength of the evidence? What suggestions might you have regarding appropriate devices for long-term enteral feeding in this patient once she is discharged back to the nursing home?

2. On a surgical unit, you are caring for a 42-year-old woman who underwent a total abdominal hysterectomy and bilateral salpingo-oophorectomy and has developed a postoperative DVT that resulted in a PE. She is a smoker and is taking multiple medications. She was stable when you started your shift, but she has become increasingly anxious with some shortness of breath in the past hour. What are potential risk factors you might observe or identify in this patient? What assessment strategies would you use to evaluate changes in her respiratory status? What decision process would you use to determine when the provider should be contacted?

3. You are caring for a patient who experienced blunt chest trauma in an MVA. A chest tube has been inserted to treat a simple pneumothorax and hemothorax. The chest drainage system has drained 400 mL of light red fluid during the first 6 hours after insertion. The patient has become increasingly short of breath during the past hour. What physical assessment skills and strategies would you use to determine potential changes in the patient's respiratory condition? What are potential causes of this increasing shortness of breath? What would you do to prepare for an emergency situation in this patient?

4. On a surgical unit, you are caring for a 62-year-old man who has undergone right upper lobectomy for lung cancer. The patient has COPD and has continued to smoke despite the diagnoses of COPD and lung cancer. What strategies would you use to prevent or minimize pulmonary complications in this patient? What are methods you might use to assess the patient's progress from a respiratory standpoint? What strategies would you consider to encourage the patient to stop smoking? What is the evidence base for the strategies that you consider? How will you evaluate the strength of the evidence?

NCLEX-Style Review Questions

1. The nurse is caring for a client diagnosed with ARDS. In evaluating the use of PEEP, the nurse would expect which of the following outcomes?
   A. Increased ventilation–perfusion mismatch
   B. Increased FRC
   C. Decreased intrathoracic pressure
   D. Decreased FRC

2. A nurse working on a general medical-surgical floor is discussing the clinical manifestations of PAH with a recent graduate. The nurse would be correct in explaining which of the following as the main symptom of PAH?
   A. Chest pain
   B. Fatigue
   C. Dyspnea
   D. Hemoptysis

3. A patient is receiving thrombolytic therapy for treatment of a PE. The nurse must monitor for which of the following side effects during therapy?
   A. Chest pain
   B. Rash
   C. Hyperthermia
   D. Bleeding

4. A nurse is caring for a patient diagnosed with lung cancer who has a chest tube. The chest tube has continuous bubbling in the water seal chamber. The nurse understands that this indicates which of the following?
   A. Tidaling
   B. The tube in the mediastinum
   C. The system is functioning properly.
   D. An air leak in the system

5. The nurse is assessing a patient with a blunt chest trauma due to a MVA. Which of the following findings would be indicative of a flail chest?
   A. Hypertension
   B. Metabolic alkalosis
   C. Paradoxical chest movement
   D. Respiratory alkalosis

Try these additional resources to enhance your learning and understanding of this chapter:
- thePoint online resource available at **http://thepoint.lww.com/Pellico1e**
- *Handbook for Focus on Adult Health: Medical-Surgical Nursing*
- *Study Guide for Focus on Adult Health: Medical-Surgical Nursing*

References and Selected Readings

References and selected readings associated with this chapter can be found on the website that accompanies the book. Visit http://thepoint.lww.com/Pellico1e to access the references and other additional resources associated with this chapter.

MARGARET CAMPBELL
HAGGERTY

Nursing Management: Patients With Chronic Obstructive Pulmonary Disease and Asthma

Learning Objectives

After reading this chapter, you will be able to:

1. Describe the pathophysiology of chronic obstructive pulmonary disease (COPD).

2. Discuss the major risk factors for developing COPD and interventions used to minimize or prevent these risk factors.

3. Describe nursing management of patients with COPD.

4. Develop a teaching plan for patients with COPD.

5. Describe the pathophysiology of asthma.

6. Discuss the medications used in asthma management.

7. Describe asthma self-management strategies.

Chronic obstructive pulmonary disease (COPD) and asthma are the most common chronic pulmonary disorders. Nurses working with patients with these chronic pulmonary diseases care for them across the spectrum of care, from outpatient and home care to emergency, inpatient and critical care, and finally in the hospice setting. Patients with COPD and asthma need care from nurses who not only have astute assessment and clinical management skills but who also understand how these disorders can affect quality of life. In addition, the nurse's knowledge of palliative and end-of-life care is important for affected patients. Patient and family teaching is an important nursing intervention to enhance self-management in patients with any chronic pulmonary disorder.

CHRONIC OBSTRUCTIVE PULMONARY DISEASE

COPD is a disease state characterized by chronic airflow limitation that is not fully reversible. The airflow limitation in COPD is usually progressive and is associated with an inflammatory response of the lungs (Global Initiative for Chronic Obstructive Lung Disease [GOLD], 2009).

An estimated 12 to 14 million Americans have the diagnosis of COPD (Centers for Disease Control and Prevention [CDC], 2008). The actual incidence of COPD is thought to be much higher, as many cases are undiagnosed. COPD is the fourth leading cause of death in the United States with nearly 130,000 deaths attributed to the disease, with more women than men dying from COPD. Additionally, COPD accounts for an annual cost estimated to be nearly $50 billion, including health care expenditures, mortality costs, lost work days and other indirect costs (American Lung Association, 2010).

Pathophysiology

The pathological changes that characterize COPD include an increase in mucus-producing cells, chronic inflammation in

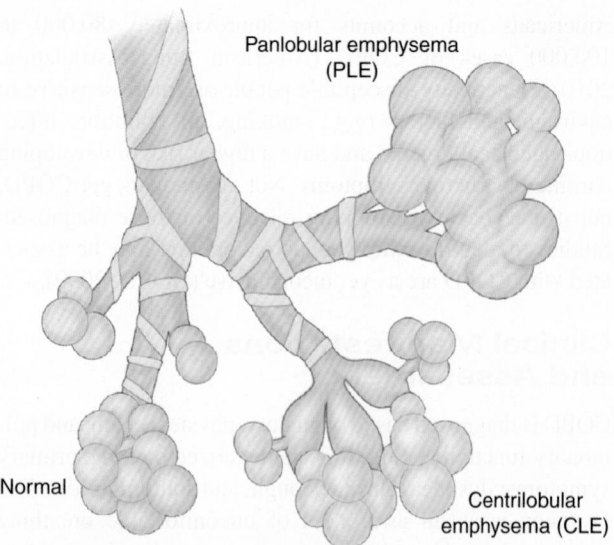

FIGURE 11-1 Changes in the alveolar structure in centrilobular and panlobular emphysema. In panlobular emphysema, the bronchioles, alveolar ducts, and alveoli are destroyed, and the airspaces within the lobule are enlarged. On centrilobular emphysema, the pathologic changes occur in the lobule, whereas the peripheral portions of the acinus are preserved.

different parts of the lung, and structural changes that result from a continuing cycle of destruction and repair. Many parts of the lung are affected, including the proximal and peripheral airways, lung parenchyma, and pulmonary vasculature. The inflammatory response found in COPD is thought to be an amplification of the normal inflammatory response. Oxidative stress and an excess of destructive cytokines in the lungs may amplify inflammation. A number of biomarkers are being studied for their relationship to disease activation and progression (Kim, Rogers, & Criner, 2008). Individuals may have predominantly emphysema, chronic bronchitis, or heightened airway responsiveness. Many people have a combination of these processes.

Emphysema

Emphysema describes an abnormal enlargement of the air spaces beyond the terminal bronchioles, with destruction of the walls of the alveoli. In emphysema, the alveolar and interstitial attachments are reduced and predisposed to collapse during exhalation. External airway compression and obstruction is caused by hyperinflation and air trapping. This results in "less room to breathe."

Emphysema is divided into two main types: panacinar or panlobular (hereditary form related to deficiency of alpha$_1$-antitrypsin, which causes uniform destruction of acinus [where alveoli are located]) and centrilobular (related to smoking, in which the alveolar ducts and bronchioles in the center of lobules of the upper lobes are primarily affected) (Fig. 11-1).

Chronic bronchitis

Chronic obstructive bronchitis is defined as the presence of cough and sputum production for at least 3 months in each of two consecutive years. In simple chronic bronchitis, pulmonary function remains normal. Chronic mucus hypersecretion causes lung function decline, exacerbations, and infections. Thickening of the epithelium, smooth muscle hypertrophy, and airway inflammation are implicated in remodeling of the airways (Fig. 11-2). This remodeling causes the airway lumen to be smaller (Kim et al., 2008).

Most patients will have elements of both emphysema and chronic bronchitis, and as both diseases have chronic airflow limitations that are not reversible, they are classified as COPD. In the later stages of COPD, gas exchange is often impaired. As the alveolar walls continue to break down, the pulmonary capillary bed is reduced in size. Resistance to pulmonary blood flow is increased, forcing the right ventricle to maintain an increasingly higher pressure in the pulmonary artery. Chronic hypoxemia (low oxygen) increases pulmonary artery pressures. Right-sided heart hypertrophy and failure (*cor pulmonale*) may result. Additionally, decreased carbon dioxide elimination results in increased carbon dioxide tension in arterial blood (hypercapnia) and leads to respiratory acidosis and chronic respiratory failure. In acute illness, worsening hypercapnia can lead to acute respiratory failure.

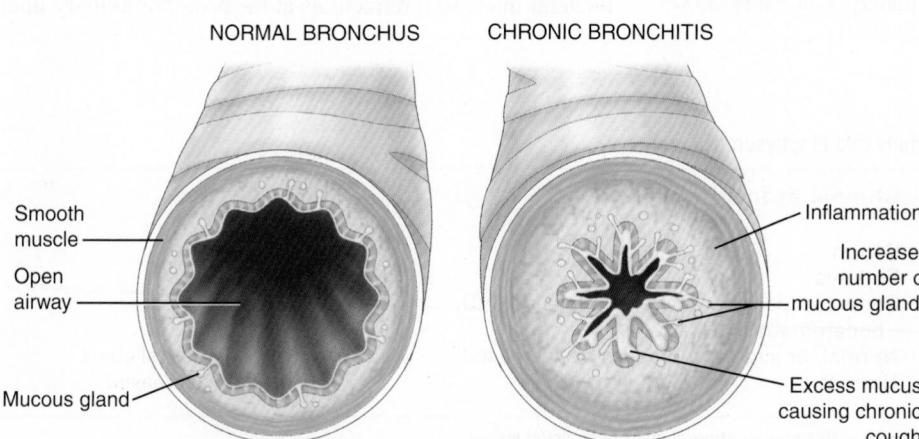

NORMAL BRONCHUS   CHRONIC BRONCHITIS

Smooth muscle
Open airway
Mucous gland

Inflammation
Increased number of mucous glands
Excess mucus causing chronic cough

FIGURE 11-2 Pathophysiology of chronic bronchitis as compared to a normal bronchus. The bronchus in chronic bronchitis is narrowed and has impaired air flow due to multiple mechanisms: inflammation, excess mucus production, and potential smooth muscle constriction (bronchospasm).

Risk Factors for Chronic Obstructive Pulmonary Disease

- Tobacco smoke (cigarette, pipe, cigar)
- Environmental tobacco smoke (second-hand smoke, fetal exposure due to smoking during pregnancy)
- Occupational dust and chemicals (organic dusts, inorganic dusts, chemical agents, fumes)
- Indoor and outdoor air pollution (biomass cooking in poorly ventilated areas, heating in poorly ventilated areas)
- Infection (history of severe respiratory infections, history of tuberculosis in those >40 years old)

Alveoli adjacent to the bronchioles may become damaged and fibrosed, resulting in altered function of the alveolar macrophages. The pathophysiological changes make the individual more susceptible to respiratory infection. A wide range of viral, bacterial, and mycoplasmal infections can produce acute episodes of bronchitis, a leading cause of exacerbations. (Kim et al., 2008). COPD is now considered a systemic disease and may affect skeletal muscle, cardiovascular, neurologic, psychiatric and endocrine system function (Stone & Nici, 2007).

Risk Factors

The risk factors for the development for COPD are outlined in Box 11-1. The most important risk factor is cigarette smoking. The effects of cigarette smoke are complex and lead to the development of COPD in approximately 15% to 20% of smokers. Many experts now think the incidence may be as high as 30% to 50% in smokers (Niewoehner, 2010). Tobacco smoke irritates the airways and, in susceptible individuals, results in mucus hypersecretion and airway inflammation.

A host risk factor for COPD, specifically emphysema, is deficiency of alpha$_1$-antitrypsin, an enzyme inhibitor that protects the lung parenchyma from injury. **Alpha$_1$-antitrypsin deficiency** affects approximately 1 in every 3,000

Americans and accounts for approximately 80,000 to 100,000 cases of COPD (American Lung Association, 2010). Genetically susceptible people are more sensitive to environmental factors (e.g., smoking, air pollution, infectious agents, allergens) and have a higher risk of developing chronic obstructive symptoms. Not all smokers get COPD, but it does occur in smoking relatives of those diagnosed. Studies to identify other genetic factors that may be associated with COPD are as yet inconclusive (GOLD, 2009).

Clinical Manifestations and Assessment

COPD is diagnosed based on history, physical exam, and pulmonary function testing. It is characterized by three primary symptoms: dyspnea, chronic cough, and sputum production. Dyspnea is as an awareness of uncomfortable breathing (or shortness of breath) that may vary in intensity. It often starts as mild and is only noticed with higher-level activities, such as stair climbing and playing sports. As the disease progresses, dyspnea may become severe and often interferes with the person's activities of daily living (ADLs). In more severe COPD, dyspnea can occur at rest. Chronic cough and sputum production often precede the development of airflow limitation by many years. In early-stage disease, the person may note an early morning cough productive of a small to moderate amount of white to clear sputum. During exacerbations increased sputum amount and viscosity may occur, and the sputum may change color. Table 11-1 differentiates emphysema and chronic bronchitis.

A positive history of progressive dyspnea and/or a productive cough in a cigarette smoker leads to a suspicion of COPD. Smoking history is usually expressed as *pack/years*: the number of packs per day smoked times the number of years smoked. A person who has smoked an average of 2 packs per day for 20 years has a smoking history of 40 pack/years. Physical examination findings may be near normal in those with beginning and sometimes moderate disease. Findings consistent with more advanced COPD may include signs of hyperinflation: an increased anterior to posterior diameter of the chest, referred to as "barrel chest"; bilateral intercostal retractions at the posterior axillary line;

TABLE
11-1 Comparison of Chronic Bronchitis and Emphysema*

Aspect	Chronic Bronchitis	Emphysema
Primary Symptom	Cough	Dyspnea
Sputum production	Copious	Scant
Cor pulmonale	Common (peripheral edema, elevated JVD, hepatomegaly)	Rare
Total lung capacity	Normal, or slightly increased or decreased	Increased; barrel chest
Elastic recoil	Normal	Markedly decreased

*It is understood that many patient's will present with a combination of symptoms listed above.

horizontal fixation of the ribs in the inspiratory position; and hyper-resonance to percussion, particularly in thin individuals. Breath sounds may be diminished; prolonged exhalation is usually heard throughout the chest; adventitious sounds (coarse crackles, also called *rhonchi* and wheezes) are often heard when the patient has increased secretions and bronchial hyper-reactivity, and during an exacerbation.

Pulmonary function studies are used to help confirm the diagnosis, determine disease severity, and monitor disease progression. **Spirometry** is used to evaluate airflow obstruction. Spirometry results are expressed as an absolute value and as a percentage of the predicted value using appropriate normal values for gender, race, age, weight, and height. With obstruction, the patient has difficulty exhaling or cannot forcibly exhale air from the lungs, thus reducing the forced expired volume in one second (**FEV$_1$**). Obstructive lung disease is defined as an FEV$_1$ of less than 80% and an FEV$_1$/FVC (forced expired volume in 1 second / forced vital capacity [maximal amount of air that can be expired after a maximum inhalation]) ratio of less than 70%.

Bronchodilator reversibility testing may be performed to rule out asthma and to guide initial treatment. Spirometry is first obtained; the patient is given an inhaled bronchodilator treatment according to a protocol, and spirometry is repeated. The patient demonstrates a degree of reversibility if the pulmonary function values improve significantly (>12%) after administration of the bronchodilator. Patients who demonstrate complete reversibility to normal values are usually diagnosed as having asthma. Patients who demonstrate some reversibility that does not reach normal values may be diagnosed with COPD with some reversible component or a combination of COPD and asthma. Patients who do not show a significant response to a bronchodilator test may still be given a trial of bronchodilator treatment to determine if it helps relieve symptoms. Additional tests of pulmonary function include total lung capacity (TLC) and diffusion capacity. These tests are used to diagnose coexisting restrictive disease (disorders that restrict lung expansion or decrease lung compliance [elasticity of the lungs]) and help predict the contribution of emphysema in the diagnosis.

Arterial blood gas (ABG) measurements may be obtained to assess baseline oxygenation and gas exchange and are especially important in advanced COPD. In addition, a chest X-ray may be obtained to establish the patient's baseline and to exclude alternative diagnoses. A chest X-ray is seldom diagnostic in COPD unless obvious bullous (large, air-filled "blisters") disease or severe hyperinflation is present. Chest X-rays are more commonly used in exacerbations to determine if the patient has an infiltrate or a concomitant lung mass. A computed tomography (CT) scan is not routinely obtained in the diagnosis of COPD, but a high-resolution CT scan may help in the differential diagnosis or to evaluate patients for surgical procedures, such as bullectomy or long volume reduction surgery. Screening for alpha$_1$-antitrypsin

deficiency is usually recommended for symptomatic patients younger than 45 years and for those with a strong family history of COPD.

Different methods are used to classify COPD by stages, depending on severity (Niewoehner, 2010). Staging is used to determine prognosis, guide therapy, and to develop research protocols. In mild disease, the patient may be asymptomatic. As lung function (FEV$_1$ and FEV$_1$/FVC) declines, symptoms start to appear. The more severe the decline in lung function, the more severe the COPD. When the FEV$_1$ is less than 50% predicted, COPD is classified as severe. Other factors that determine prognosis include history of cigarette smoking in terms of pack/years, continued cigarette smoking, passive smoking exposure, age, rate of decline of FEV$_1$, hypoxemia, pulmonary artery pressure, resting heart rate, weight loss, number of exacerbations, and reversibility of airflow obstruction. Staging severity serves as a guideline to treatment protocols, but variation occurs depending on the patient characteristics, comorbid conditions, and response to interventions.

Asthma, heart failure, bronchiectasis, tuberculosis, lung cancer, and bronchiolitis may coexist with COPD, and as many as 66% of patients have one comorbidity. Cardiac disease, peripheral atherosclerosis, stroke, diabetes mellitus, arthritis, malignancy, anxiety, and depression are additional common comorbid conditions (Viegi, Pistelli, Sherrill et al., 2007).

Medical Management

The goals of medical therapy are to stabilize, manage, and monitor the disease; reduce symptoms; reduce exacerbation risk and rate; promote maximal functional ability; prevent premature disability; assist the individual to adapt to handicap and limited prognosis as the disease progresses. The management of the patient depends on the severity of the COPD. In early-stage disease, clinical strategies are aimed at maximizing pulmonary function, keeping the patient active, preventing exacerbations, and engaging the patient in self-management. In progressive stages, more intensive therapies are added (Fig. 11-3).

Smoking Cessation

Smoking cessation slows the accelerated decline in lung function and the progression of COPD (GOLD, 2009). Factors associated with continued smoking vary among patients and may include the strength of the nicotine addiction, continued exposure to smoking-associated stimuli (at work or in social settings), stress, depression, and habit.

Because multiple factors are associated with continued smoking, successful cessation often requires multiple strategies. Health care providers should promote cessation by explaining the risks of smoking and personalizing the "at-risk" message to the patient. Encouraging the patient to set a definite "quit date" is associated with more successful

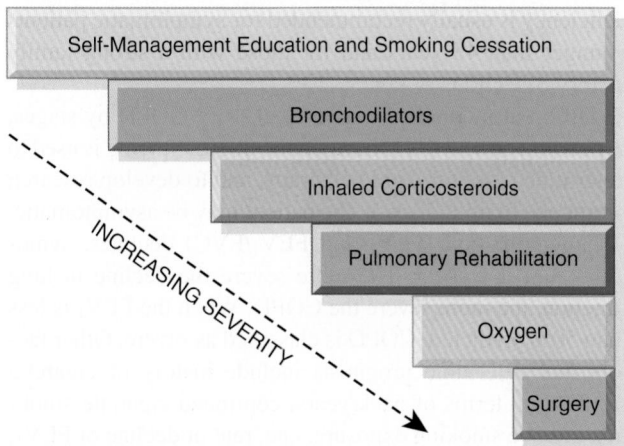

Self-Management Education and Smoking Cessation

Bronchodilators

Inhaled Corticosteroids

Pulmonary Rehabilitation

Oxygen

Surgery

FIGURE 11-3 Treatment options for COPD. Redrawn from *Breathing Better with a COPD Diagnosis,* U.S. Department of Health and Human Services, NIH Publication No. 07-5841.

smoking cessation. Brief counseling may work for many smokers; referral to a smoking cessation program may be helpful for those unable to quit on their own. Follow-up within a few days after the established quit date to review progress and to address any problems is associated with an increased rate of success. Continued reinforcement with telephone calls or clinic visits is also beneficial. Relapses should be analyzed, and the patient and health care provider should jointly identify possible solutions to prevent future backsliding.

Pharmacotherapy increases long-term smoking abstinence rates when used in conjunction with smoking cessation counseling. Nicotine replacement (gum, inhaler, nasal spray, transdermal patch, sublingual tablet, or lozenges) may be used as a single agent or in combination with other pharmacologic agents. Antidepressants such as bupropion SR (Zyban®, Wellbutrin®) and nortriptyline (Aventyl®) also have been shown to increase long-term quit rates. Bupropion is particularly useful in those concerned with weight gain during smoking abstinence as it may result in weight loss. Varenicline (Chantix®) reduces nicotine withdrawal symptoms and has been associated with increased quit rates (Anzueto & Martinez, 2007).

DRUG ALERT

Bupropion is contraindicated in patients with a history of seizures as it may lower the seizure threshold.

Pharmacologic Therapy

Pharmacological agents are an important part of the treatment of COPD and fall into several categories, including bronchodilators and corticosteroids, as well as other medications.

Bronchodilators and Corticosteroids

Bronchodilators relieve bronchospasm, reduce airway obstruction, and aid in secretion clearance. The most frequently used classes of bronchodilators include sympathomimetics (which "mimic" the sympathetic nervous system and thus causes bronchodilatation; also called beta adrenergic [both short- and long-acting]), anticholinergics, or a combination of the two agents. Methylxanthines (i.e., theophylline-like medications) are used less frequently than in the past but may still be useful in some patients. The currently available methylxanthines have a narrow therapeutic range and have serious side effects. They are often used as third-line agents when other bronchodilators don't completely control symptoms. Newer agents in this class are under investigation and may soon be available.

Bronchodilators are usually delivered by the inhaled route (**metered dose inhalers [MDIs],** dry powder inhalers [DPIs], or nebulizers, see below discussion). Oral forms of bronchodilators are infrequently given because of side effects. Long-acting sympathomimetics (also known as long-acting beta adrenergics or LABAs) and anticholinergic bronchodilators are considered maintenance medications and are usually administered on a regular basis. Short-acting sympathomimetics (also known as short-acting beta adrenergics or SABAs) are most often used on an as-needed basis to help with dyspnea and secretion clearance. SABAs may be used prophylactically before the patient participates in a dyspnea-producing activity, such as eating or walking.

Anticholinergics come in two main forms: short-acting ipratropium bromide given as 2 to 6 puffs by MDI four times a day, and the long-acting tiotropium, given by a dry powdered device once a day. Additionally, ipratropium is also available in combination with albuterol by metered dose inhaler and by nebulizer.

Inhaled and systemic corticosteroids (oral or IV) may also be used in COPD. Systemic steroids are usually reserved for acute exacerbations and for those with severe symptoms that do not respond adequately to bronchodilators. A short trial course of oral corticosteroids may be prescribed for stable patients to determine whether pulmonary function improves and symptoms decrease. Long-term treatment with oral corticosteroids is associated with an increased incidence of side effects, some of which are serious (hyperglycemia, osteoporosis). Inhaled corticosteroids are less likely to cause serious side effects and may be used alone by inhaler devices or in combination with LABAs. Patients should be instructed to rinse and gargle after using inhaled steroid preparations to decrease the risk of oral thrush.

Medication regimens used to manage the symptoms of COPD are based on disease and symptom severity. For mild COPD, a short-acting bronchodilator is usually prescribed for symptom relief. For moderate to severe COPD, a short-acting bronchodilator along with regular treatment with a LABA, a LABA/steroid combination, and/or an anticholinergic may be used. For severe or very severe COPD, medication therapy includes regular treatment with one or more bronchodilators, including a methylxanthine, and inhaled or systemic corticosteroids (GOLD, 2009). Table 11-2 summarizes commonly inhaled medications used to treat COPD.

TABLE
11-2 Common Inhaled Medications Used in COPD and Asthma

Medication Class	Generic Name *Trade name®*	COPD	Asthma
Short-acting beta adrenergic (SABA)	Albuterol sulfate HFA *ProAir®* *Proventil®* *Ventolin®* Levalbuterol HFA *Xopenex®* Pirbuterol *Maxair® (breath actuated)*	Used "as needed for quick relief" or on a timed basis; generally given as 2 puffs as needed or 4 times a day	Quick relief generally given as 2 puffs; may be monotherapy in mild, intermittent asthma
Anticholinergic (short-acting)	Ipratropium HFA *Atrovent®*	Used as a timed medication generally given as 2 to 6 puffs, 4 times a day	Not first-line therapy, used as a substitute for SABA
Anticholinergic (long-acting)	Tiotropium *Spiriva HandiHaler®*	First-line therapy for moderate to severe disease	Not usually recommended unless patient also has COPD
Anticholinergic/SABA combination	Ipratropium/albuterol *Combivent®*	May be used as first-line therapy or for quick relief; generally given as 2 puffs, 4 times a day	Not usually recommended unless patient also has COPD
Corticosteroids	Mometasone *Asmanex Twisthaler®* Fluticasone HFA *Flovent®* *(comes in 3 strengths)* Budesonide DPI *Pulmicort Flexhaler®* Beclomethasone *QVAR HFA®*	Generally used in later stages of COPD; patients need to rinse out their mouths to prevent oral thrush	Used as controller medications and is a mainstay of asthma management in persistent asthma; used with a spacer; patients need to rinse out their mouths to prevent oral thrush
Long-acting beta adrenergic (LABA)	Salmeterol DPI *Serevent®* Formoterol DPI *Foradil®*	Used in moderate to severe COPD, often in combination with corticosteroids	Used only in combination with inhaled corticosteroids (see drug alert)
LABA/Corticosteroid Combination	Fluticasone/salmeterol *Advair HFA®* *Advair Discus®* Budesonide/formoterol *Symbicort HFA®* Mometasone/formoterol (*Dulera®*)	Used in moderate to severe COPD; patients need to rinse out their mouths to prevent oral thrush	Used as controller medications in persistent asthma; patients need to rinse out their mouths to prevent oral thrush *Dulera®* approved 6/2010 for asthma

HFA, hydrofluoroalkane used as propellant; DPI, dry powder inhaler.

Medication Delivery Systems

An MDI is a pressurized device that contains an aerosolized suspension of medication. A measured amount of medication is released with each activation of the canister. Patients must be instructed on the correct use of inhalers. With correct technique, 15% to 20% of the dose of medication is inhaled into the lung. Proper technique is important to ensure adequate deposition into the airways. Common mistakes made by patients using MDIs include having difficulty coordinating actuation with inhalation, breathing in too quickly, and not breath-holding after inhalation. Box 11-2 provides education about proper technique.

 D R U G   A L E R T

Prior to 2010, MDIs contained chlorofluorocarbons (CFCs) as propellants. CFCs are no longer allowed in MDIs because of concern about their effect on the Earth's ozone layer. Newer MDIs use different propellants. Patients familiar with CFC propellants may note a difference in the way their inhaler sprays. The newer inhalers often have a "softer" spray and may taste differently. They also need to be primed and cleaned more often as the hole may occlude more easily. The nurse should instruct the patient to follow the package insert for inhaler cleaning and priming.

BOX 11-2 Patient Education

Using Inhalers

Inhaled medicine goes directly to the lungs. With perfect technique, you get about 15% to 20% of the medication in your lungs. *Good technique* is very important.

To use an inhaler:

- Remove the cap from mouthpiece of inhaler.
- Shake your inhaler for 5 to 6 seconds.
- Place the mouthpiece of the inhaler in your mouth, with your tongue and teeth out of the way.
- As you depress the inhaler take a deep breath with your mouth wide open. Inhale for 5 to 6 seconds if you can. *Slow is the way to go.* The more slowly you breathe in, the deeper the medicine gets.
- At the end of the deep breath, hold your breath for at least 3 to 10 seconds.
- Exhale through pursed lips.
- If more than one puff is prescribed, repeat the above steps.
- After your last puff, rinse your mouth with mouthwash or water to help prevent dryness. If you are using inhaled steroids, rinse, gargle and spit out the water or mouthwash.

- Rinse the mouthpiece thoroughly with warm water at least once a day. Let it air dry before assembling and storing it.

Other points to remember:

- Do not use your inhaler more often than your doctor recommends. An occasional extra puff or treatment of your quick-acting bronchodilator is fine. But, if you find yourself using your inhaler more frequently than usual, that may be a sign that you're getting ill and need to contact your health care provider. Other inhaled medicines, for example, those obtained without a prescription, should not be used unless approved by your health care provider. You can have serious side effects by mixing certain medications.

To determine how long your inhaler will last:

- Mark the date that you first started using a new inhaler.
- Note how many puffs the inhaler contains.
- Divide the total number of puffs in the inhaler by your daily dose. (For example: The inhaler contains 200 puffs. You use two puffs four times a day, totaling eight puffs per day. Two hundred divided by eight is 25. Your inhaler will last 25 days.)
- Refill your prescription for your inhaler several days before it is due to run out.

A **spacer** (holding chamber) may also be used for patients who have difficulty coordinating activation of the MDI with inspiration (Box 11-3). These are particularly useful for MDI steroids as less medication deposits in the oropharynx, thus decreasing inhaled steroid side effects. Spacers come in several designs, but all are attached to the MDI and have a mouthpiece on the opposite end. Once the canister is activated, the aerosol particles stay suspended in the chamber for several seconds, allowing the patient to inhale after actuating the inhaler. DPIs include the Discus (Advair®), the Aerolizer (Foradil®), the Handihaler (Spiriva®), and the Flexhaler (Pulmicort®). Specific package insert information is available on the use of these inhalers.

Nebulized medications (aerosolization of medication via a jet nebulizer and an air compressor) may also be effective in patients who cannot use an MDI properly or who prefer this method of administration. Several formulations of medications are available for nebulization: SABAs used alone or in combination with anticholinergics, one LABA (arfomoterol tartrate, Brovana®), and some corticosteroids. The patient needs to learn proper technique for administration by nebulizers. Disinfection of the medication cup needs to be performed on a regular basis to avoid bacterial growth and inhalation by the patient.

Other Medications

Influenza and pneumococcal vaccinations reduce the incidence of pneumonia, hospitalizations for cardiac conditions, and deaths in the general elderly population. As a preventive measure, patients should receive a yearly influenza vaccine. The Centers for Disease Control and Prevention (CDC) currently recommend pneumococcal vaccine for patients with COPD at the time of diagnosis and at age 65. A vaccine to protect against *Haemophilus influenza*, a common cause of COPD exacerbations, is currently in development.

BOX 11-3 Patient Education

Using Spacer Devices

Spacer devices are used with inhalers when:

- You have a hard time using your inhaler correctly.
- The taste of the propellant in the inhaler is disturbing.
- You are using inhaled steroids and have problems with yeast infections in your mouth.

To use an inhaler with a spacer:

- Take the cap off the inhaler and the spacer.
- Place the inhaler mouthpiece in the end of the spacer.
- Shake your inhaler for 5 to 6 seconds.
- Place the spacer mouthpiece in your mouth.
- Depress the inhaler into the spacer.
- Inhale slowly, over 5 to 6 seconds.
- Hold your breath for about 10 seconds.
- Repeat the steps for each puff of medication.

Other pharmacologic treatments that may be used in COPD include alpha$_1$-antitrypsin augmentation therapy for those with a diagnosed deficiency, antibiotic agents for acute infection, and mucolytic agents for help with secretion clearance. Cough suppressants are usually reserved for nighttime use when cough interferes with sleep. In very severe COPD, narcotics and other agents may be administered to relieve uncontrolled dyspnea (Mahler, Selecky, & Harrod, 2010).

Oxygen Therapy

Oxygen therapy may be administered during an acute exacerbation, as long-term continuous therapy for chronic hypoxemia, and during exercise and sleep for select patients. The goal of oxygen therapy is to maintain tissue oxygenation and decrease the work of the cardiopulmonary system. Oxygen is generally administered to acutely ill patients with COPD when their room air oxygen saturation is less than 90% or if they are showing signs of increased cardiopulmonary work (i.e., increased shortness of breath, tachypnea, tachycardia, or elevated blood pressure). Oxygen is administered to maintain an oxygen saturation of greater than or equal to 90%.

! NURSING ALERT

A small subset of patients with COPD and chronic hypercapnia (elevated $PaCO_2$ levels) may be at some risk for respiratory failure if they receive too high an oxygen concentration. Concern persists that such patients would lose their "drive to breathe" also called "hypoxic drive. Overconcern may lead to giving patients too little oxygen, resulting in hypoxemia. While hypercapnic patients are at increased risk for respiratory failure, the risk is related to the severity of their COPD. Adequate oxygenation is important in their management and should never be withheld.

Monitoring and assessment is key to caring for patients with COPD on supplemental oxygen. Pulse oximetry is helpful in assessing response to therapy. ABGs are needed to assess $PaCO_2$ levels. Adequate oxygenation of patients (keeping the oxygen saturation ≥90%) is important while monitoring for any possible complications of oxygen supplementation. Alternate delivery devices such as Venturi masks or ventilatory support (noninvasive by mask or by intubation) may be necessary during acute exacerbations to ensure adequate gas exchange (Beachey, 2009).

Long-term oxygen therapy (>15 hours per day) is associated with increased survival, improved quality of life, a modest reduction in pulmonary arterial pressure, and decreased dyspnea (British Medical Research Working Party Group [1980], Nocturnal Oxygen Therapy Trial Group [1981]). Long-term oxygen therapy is usually introduced in severe COPD. Indications generally include a PaO_2 of 55 mm Hg or less or an oxygen saturation of 88% or less. Evidence of tissue hypoxia and organ damage, such as pulmonary hypertension, secondary **polycythemia,** edema from right-sided heart failure, or impaired mental status, indicates a need for

long-term oxygen therapy. For patients with exercise-induced hypoxemia, oxygen supplementation during exercise may improve performance. Patients who are hypoxemic while awake are likely to be so during sleep. Therefore, nighttime oxygen therapy is recommended as well; the prescription for oxygen therapy is for continuous, 24-hour use. Intermittent oxygen therapy is indicated for patients who desaturate only during exercise or sleep. Oxygen may also be prescribed in patients who become hypoxemic in high-altitude situations (e.g., air travel and high-altitude environments). Specialized studies done in a pulmonary function lab can determine which patients may need oxygen during high altitude exposure.

Home oxygen is usually supplied by several different methods: by oxygen concentrators, compressed gas cylinders, liquid oxygen, or some combination of these. Newer concentrator/compressors allow appropriate patients to fill their own gas cylinders. Demand portable oxygen systems (liquid and gas systems) and small portable oxygen concentrators have allowed many patients to have more freedom and time away from their stationary systems. Patients need to be evaluated with the chosen system to ensure adequate oxygen saturation (Heuer & Scanlan, 2009).

! NURSING ALERT

Less than 10% of patients with COPD develop hypoventilation and CO_2 retention with oxygen therapy. If oxygen is administered at an FiO$_2$ of 24% to 28% (1 to 2 L/min), increases in oxygen saturation without CO_2 retention are seen (Leach, 2010). The Venturi mask allows for precise administration of supplemental oxygen (refer to Chapter 10) and should be titrated to maintain an oxygen saturation of 90% saturation or greater. Higher saturations risk exacerbating hypercapnia and respiratory acidosis. The nurse observes for changes in mental status, such as drowsiness or fatigue; assesses respiratory rate and lung sounds; and monitors pulse oximetry readings.

Surgical Treatments

Bullae are enlarged airspaces that do not contribute to ventilation but occupy space in the thorax. Bullae may compress areas of healthier lung and impair gas exchange. If they are limited in number, bullae may be surgically excised. A bullectomy (surgical excision of the bullae) may help reduce dyspnea and improve lung function. It can be performed thoracoscopically (with a video-assisted thoracoscope) or via a limited thoracotomy incision.

Lung volume reduction surgery (LVRS) is an option for a subset of patients with severe emphysema. Patients with predominately upper lobe disease benefit most. LVRS involves the removal of a portion of the diseased lung parenchyma. Successful LVRS results in reduced hyperinflation and improved elastic recoil and diaphragmatic mechanics. LVRS is not curative but may decrease dyspnea, improve lung function, and improve the patient's overall quality of life. Careful selection of patients for LVRS is essential to decrease morbidity and

mortality. The National Emphysema Treatment Trial found that the addition of LVRS to optimal medical management and rehabilitation led to overall improvement in exercise tolerance and survival in a subgroup of patients with predominantly upper lobe disease (National Emphysema Treatment Trial Research Group, 2003).

Lung transplantation is an alternative surgical treatment for end-stage COPD. It has been shown to improve quality of life and functional capacity in a select group of patients with COPD (GOLD, 2009). Single-lung transplantation may be considered for patients with end-stage emphysema who have an FEV_1 of less than 25% of predicted and who have complications such as pulmonary hypertension, marked hypoxemia, and hypercapnia. Specific criteria exist for referral for lung transplantation. Patients are prioritized based on the severity of their disease, age, and prognosis. Limited organ availability is a concern, and may limit transplantation as an option. Patients who have had a lung transplant need special care when hospitalized. Transplanted patients are on multiple medications to prevent organ rejection and are at markedly increased risk for infection. Coordinating care with the transplant center should be undertaken when patients require hospitalization.

Pulmonary Rehabilitation

Pulmonary rehabilitation for patients with COPD is well established and widely accepted as a means to alleviate symptoms and optimize functional status. It is now considered part of the recommended treatment for symptomatic COPD. The primary goals of rehabilitation are to reduce symptoms, improve quality of life, and increase participation in everyday activities (GOLD, 2009; Ries, Bauldoff, Carlin et al., 2007). Pulmonary rehabilitation services are multidisciplinary and include assessment, education, physical reconditioning, skills training, and psychological support. Patients are taught methods to alleviate symptoms through breathing exercises and by learning how to pace activities. Physical conditioning through endurance and strength training is an essential component of rehabilitation. Energy conservation skills are used to improve functional status and decrease dyspnea and fatigue. Nutritional counseling and medication education are other important components of rehabilitation.

The demonstrated benefits of pulmonary rehabilitation include improvement in symptoms and exercise tolerance, improved quality of life, and a reduction in hospitalizations. Selection of a program depends on the patient's physical, functional, and psychosocial status, insurance coverage, geographic location, and preference. Patients with moderate to severe lung disease may benefit most from pulmonary rehabilitation. Patients with very severe disease may also benefit.

Preventing and Managing Exacerbations and Complications

Exacerbations of COPD are defined as "events in the natural course of the disease characterized by a change in the patient's baseline dyspnea, cough, and/or sputum beyond day-to-day variability sufficient to warrant a change in management" (GOLD, 2009, p. 334). Exacerbations of COPD are associated with worsening prognosis and an accelerated decline in pulmonary function. Signs and symptoms may include increased dyspnea, increased sputum production and purulence, respiratory failure, changes in mental status, or worsening blood gas abnormalities. The primary causes of acute exacerbations include infection (bacterial and viral), heart failure, and response to pollutants and allergens. Severe exacerbations requiring hospitalization are associated with a 33% to 49% increase in mortality at 6 months and 2 years, respectively. Worsening respiratory failure from lung cancer, pulmonary embolus, and pneumothorax account for approximately 5% of severe exacerbations (Anzueto & Martinez, 2007).

Prevention of exacerbations is associated with preservation of pulmonary function and a decrease in hospitalizations. Some pharmacological agents—inhaled long-acting beta adrenergics (LABAs) combined with steroids (Advair™ Symbicort™) and the anticholinergic agent Spiriva™—have been associated with a prolonged time between exacerbations (Anzueto & Martinez, 2007; Niewoehner, 2010).

During an exacerbation, optimization of bronchodilator medications, inhaled or systemic corticosteroids, antibiotic agents, oxygen therapy, and intensive respiratory interventions may also be used. Early treatment with antibiotics in patients needing hospitalization for an acute exacerbation may result in improved outcomes.

Indications for hospitalization for an acute exacerbation of COPD include severe dyspnea that does not respond adequately to initial therapy, confusion or lethargy, respiratory muscle fatigue, paradoxical chest wall movement, peripheral edema, worsening or new onset of central cyanosis, persistent or worsening hypoxemia, and the need for noninvasive or invasive assisted mechanical ventilation (GOLD, 2009). The risk of death from an exacerbation of COPD is closely related to the development of respiratory acidosis, the presence of significant comorbidities, and the need for noninvasive or invasive positive-pressure ventilatory support.

Respiratory insufficiency and failure are major life-threatening complications of COPD. The acuity of the onset and the severity of respiratory failure depend on baseline pulmonary function, pulse oximetry or ABG values, comorbid conditions, and the severity of other complications of COPD. Respiratory insufficiency and failure may be chronic (with severe COPD) or acute (with a severe exacerbation or pneumonia in a patient with severe COPD). Acute respiratory insufficiency and failure may necessitate ventilatory support until the underlying cause, such as infection, can be treated. Management of the patient requiring ventilatory support is discussed in Chapter 55.

Other complications of COPD include pneumonia, atelectasis, pneumothorax, and pulmonary arterial hypertension (refer to Chapter 10). Pulmonary hypertension is more common in patients with hypoxemia and severe disease, and

is associated with decreased survival. The diagnosis of pulmonary hypertension associated with COPD is suspected in patients complaining of dyspnea and fatigue that appear to be disproportionate to pulmonary function abnormalities. Enlargement of the central pulmonary arteries on chest X-ray, echocardiography suggestive of right ventricular enlargement, and elevated plasma brain natriuretic peptide (BNP) may be present. Medical management of pulmonary hypertension associated with COPD includes stabilization of the underlying lung disease and administration of long-term supplemental oxygen and diuretics. During acute episodes, treatment may include positive-pressure ventilation (Girgis & Mathai, 2007).

NURSING ALERT
The hormone BNP is produced by the ventricles of the heart. Elevation of BNP occurs when ventricular volume expands and/or ventricular pressure increases. Thus, it is a marker of ventricular dysfunction. A normal BNP level is less 100 pg/mL or less than 100 ng/L (Fischbach & Dunning, 2009).

Nursing Management

In all settings, nurses play a key role in the care of the patient with COPD. A plan of nursing care for a patient with COPD is available online at http://thePoint.lww.com/Pellico1e.

Assessing the Patient

Assessment includes obtaining information about current symptoms, as well as previous disease manifestations. In addition to the questions obtained in a basic health history, key questions should focus around the main symptoms of patients with COPD: shortness of breath (dyspnea), cough, and sputum production (see discussion of clinical manifestations and assessment above). To assess progress of the disease, it is helpful to use a numerical scale based on 0 to 10 (with 0 being no shortness of breath and 10 being the worst) when quantifying dyspnea. For example, if the patient's usual rating of shortness of breath is a 4 and is now a 7, a significant change has occurred. A change in sputum color, quantity, or consistency is also significant. Additional symptoms of a change in condition may include increased fatigue and a decreased ability to perform one's usual activities.

Other assessment questions may include the presence of other medical problems (cardiovascular, diabetes, stroke, history of pneumonia, cancer), allergies, history of smoking in pack/years, current smoking, a history of past exacerbations and pulmonary hospitalizations including a history of intubations, a description of how the patient spends a usual day, sleep quality and amount, problems with mood (anxiety and/or depression), and what self-care measures the patient is currently using.

Physical examination should focus on observing the patient's breathing pattern and body position. Accessory muscle use, shoulder elevation, and the tripod position (leaning forward with the arms braced on the knees) are associated with increased respiratory distress. A change in respiratory rate is also a significant exam finding. A normal resting respiratory rate is 8 to16 breaths per minute (bpm) (a respiratory rate of 20 is considered the upper limit of normal by some sources). Many patients with COPD will have respiratory rates of 20 to 24 bpm at baseline. When the respiratory rate is greater than the patient's baseline, it may signal an acute problem. It is helpful to ask patients if they are aware of their increased respiratory rate. They may relate this to a recent exacerbation of symptoms. Assessment of breath sounds should include quality (good aeration or diminished), the presence of adventitious sounds (crackles or wheezes), and whether the adventitious sounds clear with cough. A review of laboratory data aids in the assessment of patients: pulmonary function tests, tests of oxygenation, and radiological studies.

Promoting Smoking Cessation

Although many patients believe that smoking cessation is futile, continued smoking increases the rate of lung function decline and disabling symptoms. Even brief counseling by nurses and other health professionals about the hazards of smoking can be beneficial. Hospitalized smokers may present a "teachable moment." Relating the cause of the hospitalization to smoking behavior personalizes the message to the patient. Administering and teaching patients about pharmacological agents that increase the likelihood of a successful quit attempt is an additional nursing intervention. Box 11-4 provides information aimed at helping smokers to quit.

Managing Chronic Dyspnea

Chronic dyspnea is one of the most common problems of patients with moderate to severe COPD. Acute dyspnea occurs during an exacerbation, with increased activity, from anxiety and panic, and because of acute coexisting medical conditions (e.g., anemia, heart failure, pneumonia). Chronic dyspnea is different from acute dyspnea in that the patient may exhibit no visible signs of distress. Analogous to pain, dyspnea occurs when the patient says it does and feels like the patient says it does.

The management of dyspnea focuses on assessing the underlying causes and administering therapies to reduce the symptom. Nursing management includes administering bronchodilators to increase airway patency, assisting acutely ill patients with ADLs to decrease the work of breathing, administering oxygen therapy when hypoxemia contributes to dyspnea, and teaching strategies for relieving increased shortness of breath and for limiting future episodes.

Ineffective breathing patterns and shortness of breath are partially due to the ineffective respiratory mechanics of the chest wall, lungs, and diaphragm; airway obstruction; the metabolic cost of breathing; and stress. Breathing retraining

---

BOX 11-4 **Patient Education**

Quitting Smoking

Cigarette smoking has long been known to damage the heart, lungs, and other organs of the body. Smoking is the single most preventable cause of premature death and disability. Quitting smoking increases your chance of living a longer, healthier life. Here are some tips for helping you quit:

* *Determine your readiness to quit: how motivated are you?*
   * Have you set a date to quit? A willingness to set a quit-date within 2 weeks indicates good motivation for quitting.
   * Can you list your reasons for wanting to quit? Examples include health, saving money, feeling control over your habits, smelling better, setting an example for others. Make your reasons for quitting personal.
   * What obstacles do you anticipate?
   * Have you prepared for quitting?
      * Did you throw away all smoking related materials: Cigarettes, ashtrays, lighters?
      * Did you make a plan for dealing with smoking urges?
* *Develop an action plan.*
   * For immediate urges to smoke: practice the "4 D's"
      * ***Delay:*** The urge to smoke will lessen in 3 minutes whether or not you have a cigarette.

   * ***Deep breathe:*** Take several deep breaths when the urge strikes to help take the edge off.
   * ***Drink water:*** It helps to clear out the nicotine faster.
   * ***Do something else:*** Distraction helps you ignore the urges to smoke.
   * Change your thinking: Remind yourself that you are choosing to become a nonsmoker and that it takes active work to do so.
   * Reward yourself for not smoking. Set aside the money you would have spent on cigarettes and buy yourself something as a reward.
* *Discuss the need for nicotine replacement or other medications.*

Many smokers are much more successful in quitting with the assistance of medications like Zyban™, Chantix™, and/or one of the nicotine replacement products (patch, gum, inhaler, nasal spray, or lozenge). Discuss this with your doctor or health care provider.

* *Don't give up if you have a slip or relapse.*

Many people need several tries at quitting before they are successful. Keep at it, and you will be successful.

* *Seek help if trying to quit on your own hasn't worked.*

Find a local stop-smoking program in your area. Your health care provider, local hospital, visiting nurse, or lung association may be able to recommend a local program.

Adapted from the Norwalk Hospital Patient Education Guidelines.

---

may help improve breathing patterns. Pursed-lip breathing helps slow exhalation and is thought to prevent the collapse of the small airways, effectively allowing more air to be exhaled and decreasing hyperinflation. A simple explanation to patients is that pursed lip breathing makes "more room to breathe." It may promote relaxation and allow patients to gain control of their breathing and reduce feelings of panic. Box 11-5 discussed managing an acute episode of chronic dyspnea.

An additional patient teaching strategy is to advise the use of a small handheld fan, letting the air flow onto the cheek. Patients frequently report that cool and moving air reduces their sensation of dyspnea. Relaxation techniques, such as progressive muscle relaxation, may also be useful (Mahler et al., 2010).

Diaphragmatic breathing has long been taught to patients with COPD. However, the technique is difficult to learn by most patients, and its benefits are limited. Patients with milder disease and those with voice or woodwind musical training may feel the technique to be beneficial. Those with more severe disease may find diaphragm breathing too difficult to do. Inspiratory muscle training (IMT) involves having the patient train against a resistive load. Several commercial devices are available. Training may be of benefit in some patients, but it is not currently recommended as standard care (Ries et al., 2010).

Limiting future episodes of shortness of breath includes exercise training to improve endurance, teaching patients how to pace their activities with their breathing, and helping patients anticipate dyspnea-producing activities and plan how they will keep their dyspnea at a manageable level. For example, if a patient is short of breath when climbing stairs, climbing more slowly and only during exhalation may help keep dyspnea at a manageable level. A simple teaching strategy is "pause-breathe in, exhale and climb one to two steps."

In very severe COPD, simple tasks may cause severe dyspnea that is not adequately responsive to medications and breathing techniques. The administration of opioids may be needed to keep dyspnea under control. Patients and families need to be taught how to use opioids effectively. Concerns over physical dependence, addiction, and respiratory depression need to be addressed, but opioids should not be withheld in very severe patients for whom palliative care is the goal. Noninvasive positive pressure ventilation (NPPV) has also been used for treating dyspnea in patients with severe COPD (Mahler et. al, 2010).

BOX 11-5 **Patient Education**

Managing an Acute Episode of Shortness of Breath

If you become short of breath from overexertion or anxiety, use this method to control your breathing and to help you avoid panic:

Step One: Position
Find the most comfortable position to help the air move in and out of your lungs. Try:
- Leaning forward with your back straight
- Leaning over a table with your arms resting on the table
- Placing pillows under your arms and keeping them supported and relaxed

Step Two: Breathing
Begin to control your breathing:
- Breathe out through pursed or slightly puckered lips.
- Breathe in through your mouth if you are very short of breath.
- It may help to puff your cheeks out as you breathe out.
- Breathe out longer and longer each breath until it starts to feel more comfortable.
- As your breathing gets more comfortable, breathe in through your nose and out through pursed lips.

Step Three: Relaxation
Once your breathing starts to slow down:
- Relax your neck and shoulders.
- Allow your arms to become limp.
- Close your eyes if that helps you to relax.

Additional Information
- When your breathing is in control, resume your previous activity but at a slower pace.
- It may help to use your quick-relief medication in addition to pursed-lip breathing.
- Breathe out for the hardest part of the exertion. (*Example:* While climbing stairs, breathe in while standing still; breathe out while climbing one or more steps. Pause again to breathe in; breathe out while you climb.)
- Practice *position, breathing, and relaxation* when you are not short of breath to help you avoid panic.
- *If your shortness of breath continues or gets worse, call your health care provider.*

Managing Impaired Gas Exchange

Patients with more severe disease and those experiencing an exacerbation are at increased risk for hypoxemia, oxygen desaturation, and hypercapnia. Nursing care includes monitoring the patient for hypoxemia by pulse oximetry and ABG measurements and administering supplemental oxygen. As mentioned under medical management, overconcern

about hypercapnia should never result in undertreating the patient. Adequate oxygenation (keeping the oxygen saturation $\geq 90\%$) is important to protect vital organ function.

Patients requiring oxygen therapy need to be taught the importance of adhering to the oxygen prescription. Patients often think they can tell by their symptoms when they need oxygen. The presence or absence of dyspnea is unreliable in detecting the need for supplemental oxygen. Many hypoxemic patients do not feel dyspnea. Additionally, many patients who are dyspneic do not have significant hypoxemia or oxygen desaturation.

The pulmonary arteries respond to hypoxemia by constricting, causing increased pulmonary pressure to occur. Pulmonary hypertension and right ventricular hypertrophy and failure may occur as a result of chronic, untreated hypoxemia. Additionally, chronic hypoxemia affects the function of other vital organs. Cognitive impairment is greater in hypoxemic patients. Long-term oxygen is the prescribed treatment. Teaching patients who need home oxygen should include an explanation of supplemental oxygen's effect on improved cardiac and cognitive function and improved prognosis. Additionally, the teaching plan should include the number of hours per day to wear oxygen, the dose of oxygen (usually give as number of liters per minute), and special instructions for using oxygen during sleep and exercise. Home care companies supplying oxygen to patients usually employ respiratory therapists and/or nurses. Home care professionals help patients use their oxygen more effectively, identify special equipment needs, troubleshoot equipment, and explore the use of oxygen for work and travel.

Managing Cough and Ineffective Airway Clearance

Patients with chronic bronchitis as part of their COPD and those experiencing an acute exacerbation may have increased sputum quantity and viscosity (Fig. 11-4). Additionally, many patients are too weak or fatigued to effectively clear secretions.

Diminishing the quantity and viscosity of sputum can help clear the airways and improve pulmonary ventilation and gas exchange. Pulmonary irritants should be eliminated or reduced, particularly cigarette smoking, second-hand smoke, aerosol cleaning and household products, and cooking that produces fumes. Nursing interventions include instruction in directed or controlled coughing (Box 11-6) and drinking enough fluid to prevent dehydration.

Some patients require more intense secretion clearance techniques. Chest physiotherapy with postural drainage and/or mechanical percussion and vibration, the use of positive expiratory pressure devices (PEP therapy), and suctioning may be needed for patients who are unable to effectively cough out sputum. Patients receiving one or more of these more intense techniques need to be monitored for their response to treatment. Very frail patients may experience

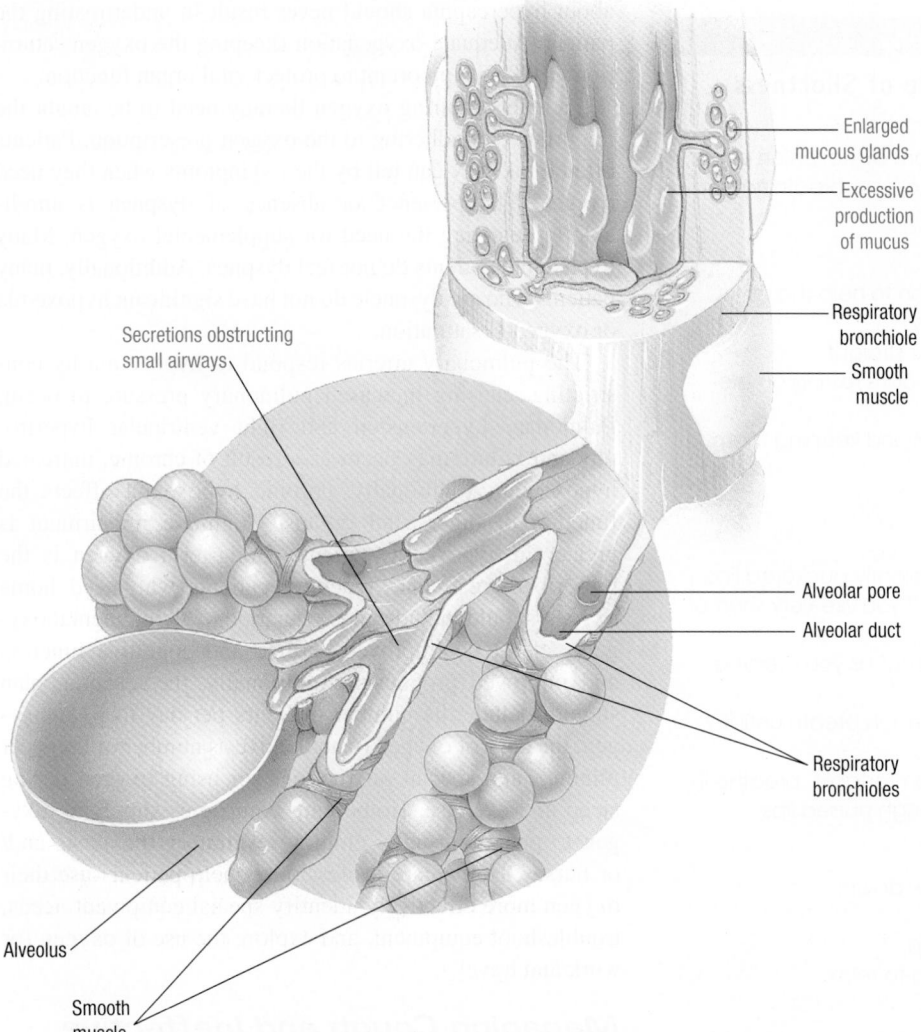

Enlarged
mucous glands

Excessive
production
of mucus

Respiratory
bronchiole

Smooth
muscle

Secretions obstructing
small airways

Alveolar pore

Alveolar duct

Respiratory
bronchioles

Alveolus

Smooth
muscle

FIGURE 11-4 Mucus
buildup in chronic bronchitis.
Courtesy of the Anatomical Chart
Company.

too much fatigue, pain or, dyspnea from such intensive treatment. Respiratory therapists are often consulted when these more intense forms of secretion clearance are needed.

Improving Exercise Tolerance

Patients with advanced COPD experience progressive activity and exercise intolerance and disability. Exacerbations and hospitalizations add to decreased activity, muscle weakness, and fatigue. Interventions used during acute exacerbations may weaken the patient further; for example, systemic corticosteroids are associated with myopathy (muscle weakness), particularly in the leg muscles.

Nursing interventions focus on therapies to help the patient recover from the effects of an acute exacerbation, maintain or regain independence in ambulation and performing ADLs, and improve stamina and strength. Early mobilization in patients experiencing an acute exacerbation, including those in intensive care, is associated with improvements in exercise tolerance and may help patients recover more quickly (see Box 11-7 for exercises that can be performed in a bed or a chair).

Interventions preparing the patient for discharge or when working with outpatients may include teaching alternating high-energy with low-energy activities throughout the day to better manage energy expenditure. The patient may benefit from exercise training to strengthen the muscles of the upper and lower extremities and to improve exercise tolerance and endurance. Use of walking aids may be recommended to improve activity levels, balance, and ambulation. Pulmonary rehabilitation staff, occupational therapists, and physical therapists can be consulted to assist patients with improving exercise tolerance and self-care.

Promoting Nutrition

Patients with COPD may have a number of issues related to nutrition. Some individuals become underweight and have difficulty consuming enough calories to meet their body's metabolic requirements. Others may be normal weight but have decreased muscle mass. Some may be overweight because of increased fat mass or increased fluid retention. Therapy is aimed at assessing the nutritional status of the patient, treating the underlying cause, and stabilizing weight and body composition.

Patient Education

Controlled Cough

An effective cough moves secretions (also called sputum, phlegm, or mucus) out of the smaller airways of lungs. An effective cough should use just enough effort to remove secretions, but not so much as to cause pain, coughing spasms, or exhaustion.

Coughing Technique

To perform a controlled cough:

- Sit up, leaning slightly forward, with your back straight and your head tilted down.
- Take two slow deep breaths and exhale through pursed lips.
- Take another deep breath in, hold your breath for 2 to 3 seconds.
- Open your mouth, so that your lips are slightly parted. Cough the air out of your lungs with little coughs: Cough, cough, cough from your stomach without breathing in.
- If coughing from the stomach is too hard, try: huff, huff, huffing the air out.
- Finish exhaling through pursed lips.

- Breathe in slowly through nose and exhale through pursed lips, 2 to 3 times. Then try clearing your throat or coughing the secretions out of your mouth.
- Repeat, if necessary.
- Check your sputum for color, quantity, and consistency.

If you don't cough out any sputum after two to three controlled coughs, wait 15 to 20 minutes and try again. Avoid continuous coughs to minimize your risk of injury or fatigue. Try using your inhaled bronchodilator before coughing to make it easier to get results.

Controlling Coughing Spasms

If you go into a coughing spasm:

- Take several short sniffs of air in through the nose to help cut down on the irritation.
- Avoid inhaling quickly through your mouth as it may make you cough more; breathe out through pursed lips and relax your shoulders.

It may take a few breaths to control the coughing spasm, so be patient and keep trying. Once you get the cough under control and after resting a few minutes, try the controlled cough.

Hospitalized patients may have difficulty eating because the act of eating may cause increased dyspnea. Oral nutritional supplements are useful for increasing body weight and respiratory function. Weight gain in underweight patients results in improved exercise capacity and quality of life. However, some patients negate the effectiveness of the supplements by using them as meal substitutes (Schols, 2009).

Nursing interventions include timing bronchodilator therapy before meals; assisting severely dyspneic patients during meal times to minimize energy spent eating; teaching patients to eat small, frequent meals to help them avoid becoming too full; encouraging the choice of calorie-rich foods; and providing patients with oral supplements. Additional interventions include referring patients to dieticians

---

Patient Education

Exercises To Do in Bed or in a Chair
Deep Breathing

- *Every hour* you are awake, take *ten slow, deep breaths.* Exhale through pursed lips.
- If you get tired after five breaths, rest a minute or two and do the second five.

Moving in Bed

Roll from side to side in the bed at least every hour. This helps your breathing, circulation, and skin.

Leg Work

- *Ankle pumps:* Flex your ankles and point your toes toward your head and then point your toes down.
- *Quad sets:* Tighten your knee and press it into the bed or chair for a count of 5.
- *Buttocks squeeze:* Squeeze your buttocks together for a count of 5.
- *Leg lifts:* Bend your knee and bring your leg up toward your chest. Lower your knee slowly back down on the

bed. You can also try lifting your leg up and down slowly with your knee in the straight position.

Arm Work

Raise your arms above your head as you breathe in and lower them back down to your sides as you breathe out.

Tips

- *Remember to breathe as you do the exercises.* Avoid holding your breath.
- Try doing five of each arm or leg exercise every 2 to 3 hours. Pretty soon you'll feel stronger and improve your stamina.
- *As soon as you can, get out of bed to a chair.* Get up several times a day for short periods to improve your stamina and avoid too much fatigue.
- *Take short walks.* Walk with your nurse if you feel unsure of your balance
- Wear your oxygen for activity if your provider prescribes it.

and encouraging progressive periods of exercise aimed at increasing muscle mass. Overweight patients may need the help of nutrition education by a dietician to help them lose weight safely. Exercise should be encouraged to help them increase muscle mass.

NURSING ALERT
Carbohydrates generate CO_2 production, thus may be limited in COPD patients; however, experts suggest that low-carbohydrate, high-lipid feeds (to reduce CO_2 generation) are rarely necessary (Leach, 2009, p. 37–38). Rather, body mass index (BMI) should be used to evaluate nutritional status. BMI should be maintained in the range between 20 and 25. If the BMI is less than 20, improved nutritional status is associated with respiratory muscle strength and prognosis. Weight reduction (if the BMI is >25) is associated with decreased dyspnea and improved functional status (Leach, 2009).

Managing Exacerbations and Complications

Prevention and early recognition of exacerbations of COPD are important self-care measures for patients to learn.

Infection

Patients should take precautions to prevent infection. Preventative measures include handwashing to minimize the transmission of infectious agents, avoiding or minimizing contact with sick individuals, and receiving immunizations against influenza and pneumococcal pneumonia. Patients should be taught to report signs of infection: increased dyspnea, fever, or change in sputum color, character, consistency, or amount. Any marked worsening of symptoms (chest tightness, dyspnea, and fatigue) also suggests infection and should be reported by patients to their health care provider. Viral infections may make patients more susceptible to more serious bacterial infections.

NURSING ALERT
High fevers of 102° F or greater accompanied by shaking chills are signs of a more serious infection, such as pneumonia. Patients should be instructed to go to the nearest emergency room as soon as possible.

Patients with more severe disease often have significant variation in daily symptoms and may have difficulty determining if they are becoming acutely ill. A change in normal routines, increased activity, family events, and increased stress and fatigue are some of the causes of "bad breathing days." A knowledge of the patient's past response to "bad breathing" days can help guide patient teaching.

Pneumothorax

Pneumothorax is a less common complication of COPD but can be life-threatening in patients who have minimal pulmonary reserve. Patients with severe emphysematous

changes can develop large bullae, which may rupture and cause a pneumothorax. Development of a pneumothorax may be spontaneous or related to an activity, such as severe coughing or large intrathoracic pressure changes. Signs and symptoms of a pneumothorax include sudden chest pain that is sharp and abrupt, a significant and sudden increase in severe shortness of breath, asymmetry of chest movement, unilateral retractions, bilateral differences in breath sounds, and/or oxygen desaturation. Pneumothorax in a patient with underlying lung disease is a medical emergency. Rapid-response teams or emergency services should be initiated. Refer to Chapter 10 for details on pneumothorax.

Respiratory Failure

Patients with severe and very severe COPD and those with hypercapnia are at increased risk for acute respiratory failure. Nursing interventions of hospitalized patients include frequent monitoring for signs and symptoms of impending respiratory failure, more intensive treatments aimed at clearing the airways, and frequent communication and coordination of care with other members of the health care team (e.g., internists, hospitalists, pulmonologists and respiratory therapists).

NURSING ALERT
The nurse should be alert for the following signs of impending respiratory failure and need for intensive care:
- *Severe dyspnea not responding to treatment*
- *Tachypnea alternating with bradypnea (slow respiratory rate <8 bpm) and apnea as fatigue ensues*
- *Hyperventilation that may deteriorate to rapid and shallow breathing*
- *Anxiety*
- *Change in mental status*
- *Worsening hypoxemia that is unresponsive to oxygen therapy*
- *Worsening hypercapnia*
- *Evidence of respiratory muscle fatigue: increased use of accessory muscles paroxysmal respiratory movement (inward movement of abdomen on inspiration) (Abousouan, 2009)*

Patients who show signs and symptoms of impending acute respiratory failure must be monitored more closely until transfer to an intensive care facility can be accomplished. Additional interventions include providing adequate oxygenation, administration of medications to maximize bronchodilatation, and keeping the patient awake until more intensive therapy can be initiated. NPPV may be initiated. Patients not responding to NPPV may require intubation and invasive ventilatory support. Chapter 55 covers these therapies in more detail. Patients transferred to a medical unit following an acute episode of respiratory failure require the same close monitoring to avoid another episode.

Enhancing Individual Coping Strategies

COPD and its progression promote a cycle of physical, social, and psychological consequences, all of which are interrelated. Depression may occur in as many as 30% to 50% of patients with significant disease (Emery, Huffman, & Busby, 2009). Nursing interventions include assessing patients for anxiety and depression, and promoting interventions to maximize physical functioning, psychological, and emotional stability, and social support. After the initial assessment of the patient, the nurse may provide referrals to psychiatric and social services, pulmonary rehabilitation, pastoral care, and home care.

❗ N U R S I N G   A L E R T

Anxiety may be a sign of worsening respiratory status and impending respiratory failure. Anxiety should not be attributed to psychological causes until the patient is assessed: vital signs, tests of oxygenation, mental status changes. Anxiolytics are generally contraindicated in patients with impending acute respiratory failure. Certain medications, particularly high-dose systemic corticosteroids, can also make patients feel extremely anxious and should be considered as a possible cause.

Any factor that interferes with normal breathing may induce anxiety, depression, and changes in behavior. Fatigue is a major symptom in many patients with COPD. Restricted activity, reversal of family roles due to loss of employment, the frustration of having to work to breathe, and the realization that the disease is prolonged and unrelenting may cause the patient to become angry, depressed, and demanding (Emery et al., 2009). Sexual function may be compromised, which also diminishes self-esteem. Nursing interventions include discussions with patients and families about the chronic nature of lung disease, support as roles change and spouses or significant others assume responsibilities once managed by the patient, and palliative and hospice care when patients near end-stage disease (Heffner & Curtis, 2009). Patients with severe anxiety and depression may need a referral to a mental health specialist. Many areas have support groups for patients with chronic lung disease; these are usually administered by local pulmonary rehabilitation programs or local chapters of the American Lung Association (ALA). Participation in support groups may help many patients discuss their common problems with professionals and patients with similar issues.

Enhancing Self-Care Strategies

Self-management strategies are aimed at involving the patient in the decision-making process and goal formation. It is important for patients to participate in setting and accepting realistic short-term and long-range goals. If COPD is mild or moderate, the goals may be to increase exercise tolerance and prevent further loss of pulmonary function. In severe disease, the goals are to preserve current pulmonary function, increase activity tolerance, and relieve symptoms as much as possible. In very severe disease, the goals may shift to relief of severe dyspnea and preparing for a peaceful death. As severity increases, goals and expectations may change.

Examples of patient goals compatible with the concept of self-care include learning to balance diminished exercise tolerance with the desire to maintain participation in important activities; recognizing the effect environmental factors have on breathing and dealing with respiratory irritants; preventing and recognizing the signs and symptoms of exacerbations and complications; learning how to handle an exacerbation and/or complication; managing a complex medical regimen that includes medication, exercise, oxygen, nutrition, and other medical conditions; and deciding on the course of treatment in very severe disease.

Interventions that help patients plan participation in favorite activities with less shortness of breath can be very helpful. For example, attendance at a special event, such as a wedding or graduation, may be very tiring for patients with more severe disease, yet they may still wish to participate. Strategies to minimize stress and shortness of breath may include using quick-relief medications prior to the event; planning to attend part of the event, such as only the ceremony or reception, to minimize fatigue; using an assistive device during the event; and maintaining prescribed medications, oxygen, and exercise program to maximize physical health. Helping patients delineate and decide on possible strategies may allow participation and enhance self-efficacy.

Many patients with COPD are sensitive to changes in air quality, fluctuations in temperature and humidity, and respiratory irritants in the environment. Nursing interventions include teaching patients to check local weather conditions and air alerts for extremes of temperature, humidity, and poor air quality. Teaching patients to create "transition zones" when they go from one extreme temperature to another can be useful. For example, during hot, humid weather, patients can be taught to turn the air-conditioning off in the car and crack the window to allow the outside air to gradually mix with the inside air. The more gradual transition to hotter, more humid air may make breathing easier for many patients.

Continuing Care

Nursing interventions include assessment for and referral to community resources when hospitalized patients are nearing discharge. Nurses caring for outpatients with COPD may also identify community care needs as patients become more disabled. Referral to an inpatient pulmonary rehabilitation program or extended care facility may be needed for patients who have had prolonged hospital stays and are severely disabled. Home care through a nursing agency may be appropriate for many patients. Home visits provide a more accurate assessment of the patient's daily life, physical and

psychological status, and adherence to the prescribed regimen. Home care visits by physical and occupational therapists may help the patient gain endurance and strength enough to attend an outpatient pulmonary rehabilitation program.

As patients become more severely ill, medical therapy may not adequately relieve symptoms. Discussions about prognosis and end of life are difficult for many patients, families, and professionals. Fears of suffering, a desire to stay alive as long as possible, and depression are some of the factors that may interfere with discussions about the end of life. Areas identified as being of major importance for patients with end-stage COPD include adequate symptom management (particularly avoiding severe, uncontrolled dyspnea); meeting psychological, emotional, and spiritual needs; and maintaining privacy and dignity. Assurances that patients and families will not be abandoned as the disease progresses and that every effort will be made to help the patient avoid suffering are important parts of caring (Heffner & Curtis, 2009).

Advanced care planning includes discussing patients' wishes should the need for more invasive procedures arise, such as intubation, acute and long-term mechanical ventilation, and feeding tube and tracheostomy tube placement. Nursing interventions include participation in these discussions with patients and families and providing support to them as they struggle with decision making. Chapter 3 presents a more thorough discussion of end-of-life care.

ASTHMA

Asthma is a common, complex disease of the airways characterized by recurring and variable symptoms, airflow obstruction, and bronchial hyper-responsiveness. Inflammation is the key underlying feature and leads to recurrent episodes of asthma symptoms: cough, chest tightness, wheeze, and dyspnea. The Expert Panel Guidelines, first produced in 1997 and updated in 2002 and 2007, provide evidence-based information to assist in the diagnosis and management of patients with asthma (Expert Panel 3 Report, 2007).

An estimated 16 million American adults have asthma. Additionally, asthma accounts for 11 million outpatient visits, 2 million emergency room visits, approximately 500,000 hospitalizations, and nearly 4,000 deaths per year. In adults, hospitalizations are more common in women and African Americans (Corbridge & Corbridge, 2010).

Asthma is largely reversible, either spontaneously or with treatment. Patients with asthma may experience symptom-free periods alternating with acute exacerbations that last from minutes to hours or days. Asthma is the most common chronic disease of childhood, but occurs for the first time at any age, including the elderly. Asthma may affect school and work attendance, occupational choices, physical activity, and general quality of life.

Pathophysiology

The underlying pathology in asthma is reversible and diffuse airway inflammation. Figures 11-5 and 11-6 depict the interaction between inflammation and clinical symptoms. Acute inflammation leads to airflow limitation and changes in the airways. Bronchoconstriction, the contraction of the smooth muscle of the airways, occurs in response to a variety of allergens and irritants. The airways become hyper-responsive (respond to stimuli in an exaggerated manner). Airway edema (swelling of the membranes that line the airways) becomes more progressive as asthma severity increases. Mucus hypersecretion and mucus plugs can occur. The airways of some asthmatics may undergo "remodeling," which includes persistent changes in airway structure, the development of sub-basement fibrosis, injury to the cells lining the airways, and hypertrophy of airway smooth muscle. Advanced changes in the airways lead to airway narrowing and potentially irreversible airflow limitation (Expert Panel 3 Report, 2007).

Many cells and cellular elements play a role in the inflammation of asthma. Mast cells, neutrophils, eosinophils, and lymphocytes are implicated. Mast cells, when activated, release several chemicals called *mediators*, which include histamine, bradykinin, prostaglandins, and leukotrienes. These mediators perpetuate the inflammatory response and cause increased blood flow, vasoconstriction, fluid leak into the airways, attraction of white blood cells to the area, and bronchoconstriction (Expert Panel 3 Report, 2007). Regulation of these chemicals is the aim of much of the current research regarding pharmacologic therapy for asthma.

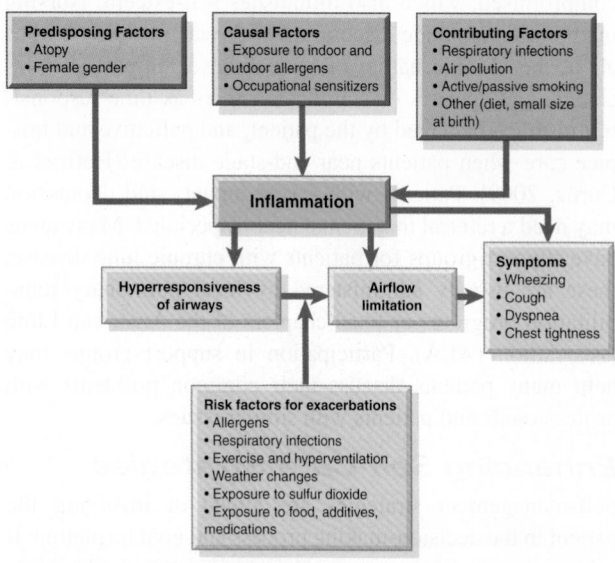

FIGURE 11-5 Pathophysiology of asthma. Adapted from material developed for the Global Initiative for Asthma (GINA). Available from: http://www.ginasthma.org.

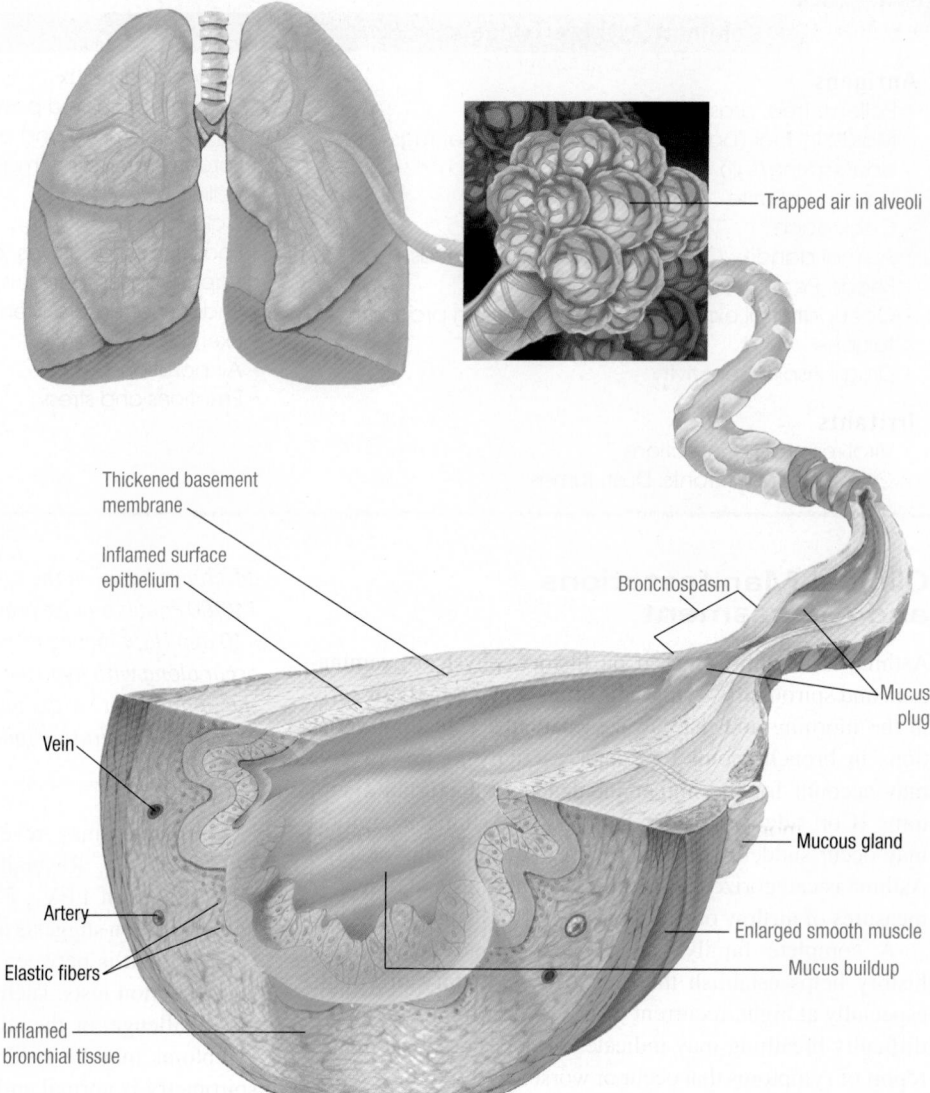

Trapped air in alveoli

Thickened basement membrane

Inflamed surface epithelium

Bronchospasm

Mucus plug

Vein

Mucous gland

Artery

Enlarged smooth muscle

Elastic fibers

Mucus buildup

Inflamed bronchial tissue

FIGURE 11-6 In asthma, inflammation and smooth-muscle spasms severely constrict the airways. Released histamine stimulates the mucous membranes to secrete excessive mucus, further narrowing the bronchial lumen. On inhalation, the narrowed bronchial lumen can still expand slightly, allowing air to reach the alveoli. On exhalation, increased intrathoracic pressure may close the bronchial lumen. Mucus fills the lung bases, inhibiting alveolar ventilation. Courtesy of the Anatomical Chart Company.

Risk Factors

Atopy, the genetic predisposition for the development of an IgE-mediated response to allergens, is the most common identifiable predisposing factor for asthma. Chronic exposure to airway allergens may sensitize IgE antibodies and the cells of the airway. Common allergens can be seasonal (grass, tree, and weed pollens) or perennial (e.g., mold, dust, roaches, animal dander). Atopy may also occur in the absence of asthma (Velsor-Friedrich & Janson-Bjerklie, 2008).

Innate immunity affecting the development of T cells, genetics, and environmental factors are thought to influence the development of asthma. The incidence of asthma is lower in children who are exposed to other children, spend more time outdoors, and have less exposure to antibiotics. Asthma has an inheritable component, but the exact relationship is not yet clear. Exposure to environmental factors, airborne allergens, and viral respiratory infections are associated with an increased incidence of asthma. Exposure to tobacco smoke, air pollution, and diet may be linked to the development of asthma and is the subject of ongoing research (Expert Panel 3 Report, 2007).

A variety of nonallergen triggers may also cause asthma symptoms and exacerbations. Box 11-8 lists the common asthma triggers. Most people with asthma are sensitive to a variety of triggers, both allergens and nonallergens. Asthma may vary in an individual person at different points in time. The dose and response to environmental exposures, activities engaged in, the particular asthma control measures used, the frequency of exacerbations, and other factors influence the disease course in a given individual.

BOX 11-8

Common Asthma Triggers

Antigens

- Pollens: Tree, grass, ragweed
- Molds: Indoor (basements, bathrooms, wet rugs) outdoor (spring/fall)
- House dust mite
- Cockroach
- Animal dander: Cats, dogs, guinea pigs, birds
- Foods: Peanut, strawberries, shellfish
- Occupational exposures: Animals, baking products, toluene
- Drugs: Aspirin sensitivity

Irritants

- Viral respiratory infections
- Occupational irritants: Dust, fumes

- Esophageal reflux
- Sinus infection and post nasal drip
- Cigarette smoke and odor: Primary and second-hand
- Forceful respiratory maneuvers: Hard laughing, crying, yelling
- Cold, dry air
- Foods, food additives, and preservatives
- Vapors, gases, aerosols
- Endocrine factors: Menses, pregnancy, thyroid disease
- Exercise
- Air pollution
- Emotions and stress

Clinical Manifestations and Assessment

Asthma is diagnosed based on history, physical examination, and spirometry. Symptoms often occur at night or early in the morning and may awaken patients. Circadian variations in bronchomotor tone and reactivity of the airways may account for the higher incidence of nocturnal symptoms (Corbridge & Corbridge, 2010). Asthma symptoms may occur suddenly or develop over several hours or days. Asthma is categorized according to symptoms and objective measures of airflow obstruction.

A complete family, environmental, and occupational history helps establish the diagnosis. A history of cough, especially at night, recurrent wheeze, chest tightness, and/or difficulty breathing may indicate the presence of asthma. A report of symptoms that occur or worsen with exercise, exposure to allergens, irritants, occupational irritants, weather changes, stress, menstrual cycles, or strong expression of emotions such as hard laughing or crying increases the suspicion. Cough, with or without mucus production may be the only symptom reported by some patients. Exercise-induced asthma is common and is defined as symptoms occurring during or soon after stopping exercise. Occupational asthma is worse on work days and improved on days off. Many patients develop chronic asthma after years of exposure to an occupational trigger and may have persistent asthma even when not working.

Physical examination findings may reveal generalized wheezing initially heard during expiration. In between asthma episodes, physical exam findings may be normal.

☀ NURSING ALERT

The occurrence of a severe, continuous reaction is referred to as status asthmaticus and is considered life-threatening. In more severe episodes, diaphoresis, wheezing upon inspiration, tachycardia, and a widened pulse pressure (PP;

difference between the systolic and diastolic pressure; e.g., 140/80 equals a pulse pressure of 60 mm Hg; normal PP is ~40 mm Hg; widened PP is >50 mm Hg; Lippincott, 2010) may occur along with hypoxemia. When airflow rates are very low, the "quiet chest" with minimal air movement may signal impending respiratory failure (Corbridge & Corbridge, 2010).

Spirometry may reveal an obstructive pattern (FEV_1/ FVC% <70%). Reversibility, defined as a 12% or 200 mL increase of FEV_1, FVC, or both, after bronchodilator administration suggests asthma. Spirometry may be normal if the patient is between asthma episodes. Special pulmonary function tests, such as methacholine challenge, exercise challenge, or the administration of cold air to induce symptoms may be used to diagnose asthma when simple spirometry is normal and asthma is suspected.

Other laboratory tests that are performed less often may include blood tests to detect elevated levels of eosinophils and immunoglobulin E, chest X-rays to exclude alternative diagnoses, and blood gas analysis when patients experience symptoms of a severe exacerbation. Other conditions that may cause asthma-like symptoms include vocal cord dysfunction, foreign body obstruction, congestive heart failure, pulmonary embolism, cough secondary to drugs (e.g., angiotensin-converting enzyme [ACE] inhibitors), benign or malignant tumors obstructing airways, eosinophilic pneumonia, and COPD. In addition to being part of the differential diagnosis, COPD and asthma can coexist (Corbridge & Corbridge, 2010; Expert Panel 3 Report, 2007).

Once asthma is diagnosed, an assessment of disease severity and control is made. Using the Expert Panel Guidelines, asthma is classified as intermittent, mild, moderate, or severe. Classification is based on impairment of pulmonary function, frequency of symptoms, and use of SABAs for symptom control, asthma's interference with normal activity, and nighttime awakenings with symptoms.

Medical Management

The goals of management are to prevent chronic and troublesome symptoms, maintain normal or near normal pulmonary function, maintain normal activity, prevent recurrent exacerbations, provide optimal pharmacotherapy, and to meet patients' and families expectations of care.

Ongoing Assessment and Monitoring

Once asthma is diagnosed and disease severity is determined, ongoing assessment and monitoring includes a determination of how well asthma is controlled and of how responsive it is to treatment. A determination of the patient's degree of risk for exacerbations is also useful. Monitoring adverse reactions from treatment may guide changes in treatment. Measures used to periodically assess established asthma include written or verbal reports of symptoms and symptom relief (asthma diaries), the frequency of the use of quick-relief medications, the individual's ability to participate in normal activities, the frequency of exacerbations, and monitoring of pulmonary function by periodic spirometry or home peak-flow monitoring.

Home peak-flow monitoring may be useful in some patients with asthma. A peak-flow meter is a small handheld device that measures the fastest flow the patient can generate after taking a deep breath in and blowing out as hard and fast as possible. Peak-flow monitoring is sometimes used to establish the diagnosis in symptomatic patients with normal spirometry, and to monitor disease in patients with more severe disease or a history of frequent exacerbations or in patients who have difficulty perceiving an asthma exacerbation until it becomes severe. Proper technique is essential to make peak-flow monitoring useful (Box 11-9). Once the baseline or personal best peak flow is determined, changes in peak flow can be used to determine the need to adjust medication protocols. Written asthma action plans based on fluctuations in peak flow and/or symptoms are useful for many patients.

Patient Education

Asthma is a chronic illness and requires life-long management by patients and clinicians to achieve the goals of therapy. The concept of partnership is one in which the clinician and patient work together to establish mutually agreed upon goals and treatments. Patients need to learn and manage multiple areas, such as the identification and management of triggers, monitoring for early warning signs of an acute episode, and taking prescribed medications correctly. Comorbid conditions, side effects, financial issues, living conditions, different beliefs about asthma, and other factors may influence the patient's adherence to the asthma management plan. Involving the patient in the decision-making process may increase adherence and positively affect outcomes. The research profile by Wilson and colleagues (2010) provide an excellent example of using partnership to affect positive results (Box 11-10).

BOX 11-9

Patient Education

Using a Peak Flow Meter

- Stand or sit up straight.
- Put the peak-flow marker at zero.
- Take a full, deep breath in.
- Place the meter in your mouth with your tongue and teeth out of the way, and seal your lips around the meter.
- Blow out as hard and fast as possible.
- Repeat the procedure two more times.
- Write down the highest reading.

Use your peak-flow meter at the same time of day for 2 weeks to establish your "personal best." Work with your health care provider, nurse, or asthma educator to help you use your peak-flow numbers to help you control your asthma better and help you decide when to call your provider or come to the emergency room.

Pharmacologic Therapy

The pharmacological management of asthma involves a stepwise approach (see Figure 11-7). Medication prescriptions are based on the severity and control of asthma symptoms.

Quick-Relief and Long-Acting Medications

Quick-relief medications are used for the immediate treatment of asthma symptoms; long-acting medications are used to achieve and maintain control of persistent asthma. The lowest dose of medications to achieve control is recommended. When patients are stable for 3 months, a decrease in medications may be tried (Expert Panel 3 Report, 2007). The major inhaled medications used for asthma are listed in Table 11-2 on page 331.

For patients with mild intermittent disease, a SABA administered by MDI may be all that is needed. Control of persistent asthma is accomplished primarily with regular use of anti-inflammatory medications. Inhaled corticosteroids are the treatment of choice. The dose of inhaled corticosteroids is adjusted based on patient symptoms and asthma control. A spacer should be used with inhaled corticosteroids; patients should gargle with water and spit it out after administration to prevent thrush, a troublesome complication associated with the use of inhaled corticosteroids. Inhaled corticosteroids may be used alone or in combination with LABAs.

 D R U G   A L E R T
A black box warning has been issued for LABAs (salbutamol and formoterol) for patients with asthma. One large clinical trial found an increase in asthma deaths and exacerbations in patients using a LABA. The current guidelines recommend using LABAs only in combination with inhaled corticosteroids. The daily dose of LABAs should not exceed 100 mcg of salmeterol and 24 mcg formoterol (Expert Panel 3 Report, 2007).

BOX 11-10 Nursing Research

Bridging the Gap to Evidence-Based Practice

What is the Effect of Shared Treatment Decision Making for Patients With Poorly Controlled Asthma?

Wilson, R., Strub, P., Buist, S., Knowles, S., Lavori, P., Lapidus, J., Volmer, W., & the Better Outcomes of Asthma Treatment Study Group. (2010). Shared treatment decision making improves adherence and outcomes in poorly controlled asthma. *American Journal of Respiratory and Critical Care Medicine, 18,* 566–577.

Purpose

The purpose of the study was to measure adherence to controller medications in patients with poorly controlled asthma utilizing one of two decision-making models compared to usual care. Nurses and nurse practitioners participated as care managers in the treatment arms of the study.

Design

The Better Outcomes of Asthma Treatment (BOAT) was a multicenter trial of 612 patients with poorly controlled asthma. Computerized records of overuse of rescue medication, recent emergency room visit, or hospitalization were used to identify patients with poorly controlled asthma. Patients were then randomized to usual care or to one of two experimental interventions: a shared decision making arm (SDM), in which the nonphysician clinician negotiated a treatment regimen that considered patient preferences and goals, and a treatment prescribed by the clinician that did not elicit the patient's goals or preferences. Both intervention arms provided face-to-face education and telephone follow-up. Nonphysician clinicians (care managers) included nurse practitioners, nurses, physician assistants, respiratory therapists, and pharmacists trained in asthma management.

Patients were followed for 2 years. Care was coordinated with the patient's physician. The Expert Panel 3 guidelines were followed. The use of controller medications was measured by using records of medication acquisition through pharmacy records. The Juniper Mini Asthma Quality of Life Scale was used to measure asthma-related quality of life. Health care utilization data was extracted from data bases from the involved study sites. Multivariable generalized linear regression analysis was used to measure the intervention effect on each outcome.

Findings

A total of 5,414 patients were found to be potentially eligible; 2,534 were able to be contacted and gave informed consent to be screened for inclusion. The final sample size was 612 (204 in each of the three groups). The mean age of the subjects was similar in each group (45.1–46.9). There were more women than men, but there was equal distribution in the groups. Subjects in the shared decision-making arm had a significantly better adherence to controller medications ($p = 0.03$) when compared with the usual care group and the arm of the study in which the clinician made the decisions. Additionally, they had significantly better clinical outcomes (asthma-related quality of life, health care use, rescue medication use, asthma control, and lung function) when compared with the usual-care group.

Nursing Implications

Nurses are key members of the health care team when caring for patients with chronic diseases such as asthma. The nurse is often the professional who teaches patients about their disease and its treatments. This study supports the concept of partnership discussed in the guidelines for asthma diagnosis and management: Allowing the patient to share in some of the decision-making helps to keep asthma in control.

Other Medications

Leukotriene modifiers (inhibitors), or antileukotrienes, are a class of medications that include montelukast (Singulair®), zafirlukast (Accolate®), and zileuton (Zyflo®). Leukotriene inhibitors act either by interfering with leukotriene synthesis or by blocking the receptors where leukotrienes exert their action. They may provide an alternative to inhaled corticosteroids for mild persistent asthma, or they may be added to a regimen of inhaled corticosteroids in more severe asthma to improve control. Careful monitoring of liver function is recommended for patients taking zileuton.

Cromolyn sodium and nedocromil stabilize mast cells. They are primarily used for mild persistent asthma as an alternative medication in patients not tolerating inhaled corticosteroids or as a preventive treatment for exercise asthma.

Omalizumab (anti-IgE) is used as an additional therapy for patients with severe, persistent asthma who have sensitivity to specific allergens (e.g., cats, dogs, and cockroaches). Omalizumab is administered intravenously. Because of the potential for serious allergic reactions during administration, careful monitoring and possible treatment for anaphylaxis is required.

Other occasionally useful medications include methylxanthines and anticholinergics. Methylxanthines, sustained-release theophylline medications, are mild to moderate bronchodilators. They are mainly used as an adjunct when long-term controllers fail to achieve relief of nighttime symptoms. Methylxanthines have a narrow therapeutic range, necessitating monitoring of the serum theophylline level. The anticholinergic ipratropium may be used as an alternative quick-relief medication when the patient cannot tolerate SABAs.

Oral corticosteroids are used to gain quick control of asthma and during acute exacerbations. Patients with severe persistent asthma that is not adequately controlled may need long-term oral corticosteroids.

Intermittent Asthma

Persistent Asthma: Daily Medication
Consult with asthma specialist if step 4 care or higher is required.
Consider consultation at step 3.

Step 1
Preferred:
SABA PRN

Step 2
Preferred:
Low-dose ICS
Alternative:
Cromolyn, LTRA, nedocromil, or theophylline

Step 3
Preferred:
Low-dose ICS + LABA
OR
Medium-dose ICS
Alternative:
Low-dose ICS + either LTRA, theophylline, or zileuton

Step 4
Preferred:
Medium-dose ICS + LABA
Alternative:
Medium-dose ICS + either LTRA, theophylline, or zileuton

Step 5
Preferred:
High-dose ICS + LABA
AND
Consider omalizumab for patients who have allergies

Step 6
Preferred:
High-dose ICS + LABA + oral corticosteroid
AND
Consider omalizumab for patients who have allergies

Step up if needed
(first, check adherence, environmental control, and comorbid conditions)
Assess control
Step down if possible
(and asthma is well controlled at least 3 months)

Each step: Patient education, environmental control, and management of comorbidities.
Steps 2–4: Consider subcutaneous allergen immunotherapy for patients who have allergic asthma (see notes).

Quick-Relief Medication for All Patients
- SABA as needed for symptoms. Intensity of treatment depends on severity of symptoms: up to 3 treatments at 20-minute intervals as needed. Short course of oral systemic corticosteroids may be needed.
- Use of SABA >2 days a week for symptom relief (not prevention of EIB) generally indicates inadequate control and the need to step up treatment.

Key: **Alphabetical order is used when more than one treatment option is listed within either preferred or alternative therapy.** EIB, exercise-induced bronchospasm; ICS, inhaled corticosteroid; LABA, inhaled long-acting beta$_2$-agonist; LTRA, leukotriene receptor antagonist; SABA, inhaled short-acting beta$_2$-agonist

Notes:

■ The stepwise approach is meant to assist, not replace, the clinical decision making required to meet individual patient needs.

■ If alternative treatment is used and response is inadequate, discontinue it and use the preferred treatment before stepping up.

■ Zileuton is a less desirable alternative due to limited studies as adjunctive therapy and the need to monitor liver function. Theophylline requires monitoring of serum concentration levels.

■ In step 6, before oral systemic corticosteroids are introduced, a trial of high-dose ICS + LABA + either LTRA, theophylline, or zileuton may be considered, although this approach has not been studied in clinical trials.

■ Steps 1, 2, and 3 preferred therapies are based on evidence A; step 3 alternative therapy is based on evidence A for LTRA, evidence B for theophylline, and evidence D for zileuton. Step 4 preferred therapy is based on evidence B, and alternative therapy is based on evidence B for LTRA and theophylline and evidence D for zileuton. Step 5 preferred therapy is based on evidence B. Step 6 preferred therapy is based on (EPR−2 1997) and evidence B for omalizumab.

■ Immunotherapy for steps 2–4 is based on evidence B for house-dust mites, animal danders, and pollens; evidence is weak or lacking for molds and cockroaches. Evidence is strongest for immunotherapy with single allergens. The role of allergy in asthma is greater in children than in adults.

■ Clinicians who administer immunotherapy or omalizumab should be prepared and equipped to identify and treat anaphylaxis that may occur.

FIGURE 11-7 Stepwise approach for managing asthma in youths 12 years of age and older and adults. Redrawn from Expert Panel 3 Report. (2007). *Guidelines for the diagnosis and management of asthma* (p. 343). NIH Publication Number 08–5846. National Asthma Education and Prevention Program. Summary Report. Bethesda, MD. U.S. Department of Health and Human Services, National Heart, Lung and Blood Institute.

Environmental Control and Management of Triggers and Comorbid Conditions

Reducing exposure to asthma triggers may reduce asthma symptoms, inflammation, and the need for higher doses of medications. Skin testing is useful in some patients to identify specific allergens and in patients who may be candidates for immunotherapy. Effective allergen and trigger avoidance may be complicated when the patient's asthma is triggered by multiple allergens and irritants. Ongoing education and prioritizing the contribution of specific triggers in individuals may be needed. When patients have many triggers, specific trigger management may need to be designed to stress the management of the most troublesome triggers first and manage less troublesome triggers later. For example, if a patient has a severe reaction to cockroach antigen and less of a reaction to dust mites, initial efforts should be directed at cockroach control.

✎ D R U G   A L E R T

Patients with persistent asthma, nasal polyps, and sensitivity to aspirin or nonsteroidal anti-inflammatory drugs (NSAIDs) need to avoid using aspirin and NSAIDs because of the risk of severe or even fatal reactions.

Comorbid conditions, particularly allergic bronchopulmonary aspergillosis (fungal infection), gastroesophageal reflux disease (GERD), obesity, obstructive sleep apnea, rhinitis, sinusitis, stress, and depression complicate asthma management. Adequately treating these conditions may improve the control of asthma.

Managing Complications and Exacerbations

An asthma exacerbation is an acute or subacute episode of worsening shortness of breath, cough, wheezing, and/or chest tightness. Asthma exacerbations are classified by the severity of symptoms, the response to treatment, and peak-flow measurements. The standard classifications are mild, moderate, severe, and life-threatening. Mild exacerbations are usually treated by the patient at home. Moderate exacerbations usually require an office visit or close contact with the patient's health care provider. Severe exacerbations usually result in an emergency room visit, followed by possible admission to the hospital. Very severe episodes require emergency room visits and probable admission to the hospital or intensive care.

⚡ N U R S I N G   A L E R T

Patients at high risk for asthma death need to seek medical care early during an exacerbation. Risk factors that place the patient at high risk include a history of a previous severe exacerbation requiring intensive care and/or intubation, two or more hospitalizations or more than three emergency room visits in the past year, using more than two canisters of a SABA per month, difficulty perceiving worsening asthma, low socioeconomic status/inner-city residence, illicit drug use, severe psychiatric illness, and major comorbid conditions.

Complications of asthma may include worsening disease, status asthmaticus, and respiratory failure. Airway obstruction, particularly during acute asthmatic episodes, often results in hypoxemia, requiring the administration of oxygen and the monitoring of pulse oximetry and ABGs. Antibiotics are rarely needed, but may be used for concomitant pneumonia or bacterial sinusitis.

Status asthmaticus is a severe asthma episode that is refractory to initial therapy. It is a medical emergency. Patients report rapid progressive chest tightness, wheezing, dry cough, and shortness of breath. Status asthmaticus may occur following a viral respiratory infection, exposure to a trigger, or following exercise in cold environment. Infection, anxiety, nebulizer abuse, nonadherence to controller medications, dehydration, increased adrenergic blockage, and nonspecific irritants may contribute to these episodes. It may also occur with little or no warning and can progress rapidly to severe obstruction.

Patients in status asthmaticus are monitored closely in the emergency room or intensive care unit. Oxygen, adequate hydration, frequent or continuous nebulization of SABAs, plus ipratropium, theophylline, and systemic corticosteroids are frequently used to manage status asthmaticus. Other treatments that may be tried include IV magnesium sulfate, inhaled heliox (a mixture of oxygen and helium), and inhaled leukotriene modifiers. These latter three treatments have not been well tested in patients with status asthmaticus. Intubation and mechanical ventilation may be needed when patients do not respond to initial treatment (Saadeh, 2010). Frequent communication and consultation with physicians, respiratory therapists, and rapid-response teams is important in any patient hospitalized for asthma. Discharge criteria include an FEV_1 or peak flow measurement of 70% predicted or better (good response) or a 50% to 70% of better predicted FEV_1 in some patients (moderate response), a sustained response to bronchodilator treatment, no or mild distress, and the absence of hypoxemia.

⚡ N U R S I N G   A L E R T

A quiet chest is worrisome; the nurse considers that airflow can be so limited that wheezing cannot be detected. Wheezing may begin to be audible with bronchodilator treatment, when the airways are dilated enough to detect a wheeze.

Nursing Management

Nursing care of patients with asthma depends upon the setting the nurse works in and on the severity of the patient's disease. Patients may be treated successfully as outpatients if asthma symptoms are relatively mild or may require hospitalization and intensive care if symptoms are acute and severe. Asthma episodes may be frightening to patients and families. Reassurance and a calm approach are important aspects of care.

Nursing assessment includes taking a history of the patient's symptoms, self-care measures used, sequence of the current asthma episode, and response to medication and

treatments used. A history of allergic reactions to medications, current prescription and nonprescription medications (including complementary and alternative medicine [CAM] therapy), recent exposure to allergens and triggers, previous hospitalizations, emergency room visits, intensive care unit admissions, intubations for asthma, and the patient's perception of asthma severity are additional elements to include in a nursing assessment. Physical exam is similar to that used with COPD. Peak flow measurements and pulse oximetry are additional assessment measures.

Nursing interventions for patients admitted for an asthma exacerbation include administering medications and treatments as prescribed, monitoring patients' response, preparing patients for discharge, and educating patients about treatment, medication administration, identification of and management of asthma triggers, prevention and treatment of future exacerbations, and medical follow-up.

The main focus of nursing management of patients in status asthmaticus is to actively assess the patient's airway and the response to treatment. Nursing care includes frequent monitoring of patients' vital signs, oxygen saturation, and cardiac rhythm until status asthmaticus is under control; assessing for signs of dehydration and managing fluid intake; administering systemic corticosteroids, bronchodilators, and other medications as ordered (often given as continuous therapy); assisting patients with daily activity to help them conserve energy; and providing a quiet environment that is free of respiratory irritants including flowers, perfumes, or odors of cleaning agents. The administration of heliox and magnesium sulfate are additional interventions that may be used and require close monitoring.

Patients being discharged from an emergency room or hospital may benefit from referral to an asthma clinic, asthma or pulmonary specialist, and/or visiting nurse agency. Home visits may be particularly useful for patients with recurrent exacerbations and emergency room visits. The home visit may give a more accurate picture of the individual's allergens and triggers.

Patient teaching is a critical component of the nursing care of patients with asthma. Complex treatment regimens including multiple and different types of inhalers, monitoring of asthma control, antiallergy therapy, therapy for comorbid conditions, identification of early warning signs, and recognition and avoidance of triggers are essential for long-term control. Patient education may include the nature of asthma as a chronic inflammatory disease; the definition of inflammation and bronchoconstriction; the purpose and action of each medication (quick-relief medications and controllers); triggers to avoid, and how to do so; proper inhalation technique; performance and recording of peak flow; implementation of an action plan designed with their health care provider; and recognition of the signs and symptom indicating the need for prompt medical assistance.

An assortment of excellent educational materials is available from the National Heart, Lung, and Blood Institute and other sources. The choice of educational materials used should be based on the patient's diagnosis, causative factors, educational and reading level, and cultural background. Select references and websites for professionals and patients are included at the end of this chapter.

Chapter Review

Critical Thinking Exercises

1. A 74-year-old man with severe COPD has been admitted with an acute exacerbation. He is extremely anxious and short of breath. He is unable to lie flat in bed and is on supplemental oxygen at 2 L/min. What tests or examinations might be appropriate to assess the severity of the patient's respiratory symptoms and his oxygenation status? What other nursing measures would you institute for this patient?

2. A 69-year-old woman with COPD reports that she has been using continuous oxygen for the past 5 years. She reports that she doesn't always use her oxygen as prescribed, only when "she feels she needs it." What should you teach her about oxygen?

3. As a nurse in an outpatient asthma clinic in a tertiary care medical center, you see a 35-year-old woman with asthma. When you inquire about symptom management and medication history, she reports that she uses an

inhaler a few times a day when her breathing gets "really bad." She notes wheeze and cough several times a day. The inhaler she has with her is albuterol. She wakes up 3 times a week with asthma symptoms. In her medical record, you note that use of a combination LABA/corticosteroid to be taken twice a day has been repeatedly prescribed for her, but she reports that she does not use it very often. Using Figure 11-7 from the Expert Panel guidelines, describe the assessment method you would use to evaluate her asthma symptoms and severity. Describe teaching techniques you might use to assess the patient's knowledge of her medications and provide education about the action of her controller and quick-relief medications, frequency of use, and correct administration. What methods would you use to monitor use of her medications and reinforce teaching?

4. As a nurse in your hospital's community outreach clinic, you are responsible for providing group education and

(continued on page 350)

Chapter Review (continued)

counseling to patients with newly diagnosed asthma. What areas would you address regarding triggers for asthma? How might you have patients assess or change their home and work environments? What resources might you suggest?

NCLEX-Style Review Questions

1. During morning rounds on a medical floor, the nurse assesses a patient admitted the previous evening with an exacerbation of COPD. The patient is complaining of increased dyspnea. He is sitting on the side of the bed with his arms braced against his knees. His respiratory rate was 20 on admission and is now 28. His breath sounds are diminished, with coarse crackles heard throughout. His oxygen saturation is 93% on 2 L/min of supplemental oxygen. The nurse would perform which of the following actions? Select all that apply.
   A. Administer albuterol using a spacer that has been ordered "as needed."
   B. Switch the patient's oxygen to a Venturi mask at 32%.
   C. Instruct the patient to begin pursed-lip breathing.
   D. Instruct the patient in controlled cough.

2. The following day, the patient's symptoms are improving. He is less short of breath and able to walk to the bathroom with minimal assistance. In preparing for discharge, a home oxygen assessment is ordered. The patient's room air oxygen saturation is 88% at rest and 86% with exertion. Oxygen administered by nasal cannula at 2 L/min raises the oxygen saturation to 94% at rest and 92% when walking. Home oxygen is ordered as 2 L/min 24 hours a day. What would the nurse include in patient teaching about home oxygen?
   A. Oxygen improves cardiac and cognitive function and improves prognosis.
   B. Oxygen only needs to be worn when the patient is short of breath.
   C. Oxygen improves cardiac and cognitive function but does not improve prognosis.
   D. Home oxygen is dangerous and will explode.

3. A 62-year-old woman is seen at the doctor's office for an initial evaluation of her symptoms of shortness of breath, cough, and sputum production. Her spirometry reveals an FEV_1 of 65% predicted. Her FVC is 90%. Her FEV_1/FVC is 60%. She has been given a diagnosis

of COPD. She reports a smoking history of 35 years. She now smokes 10 cigarettes a day. She has tried to quit several times and has been able to stay quit for 1 week a few years ago. She is concerned about weight gain if she quits smoking. The doctor gave her a prescription for bupropion and nicotine nasal spray. The nurse is asked to review an approach to smoking cessation. Which of the following approaches should be included in a teaching plan? Select all that apply.
   A. Bupropion and nicotine replacement can assist in the quitting process.
   B. Successful smoking cessation includes multiple approaches.
   C. Dealing with the habit of smoking is important to success.
   D. Quitting smoking once COPD is diagnosed has no effect on prognosis.

4. A hospital conducts an outpatient clinic for patients with asthma. The nurse working in the clinic is responsible for teaching patients about their medications. Which of the following statements is true about inhaled medications?
   A. All inhalers must be given with a spacer device.
   B. Inhaled corticosteroids are used on an as needed basis for quick relief.
   C. LABAs can be used as monotherapy to control asthma.
   D. LABAs and inhaled corticosteroids are used as controllers in the management of asthma.

5. A 45-year-old woman with a diagnosis of asthma comes to the emergency room with worsening symptoms of cough and wheeze. She has been using her albuterol inhaler every 3 hours for the past 2 days. She denies allergies to medications, foods, and the environment. She has no other major medical problems, and has never been a smoker. She is recovering from a viral respiratory infection. Her respiratory rate is 28; she is sitting upright on the stretcher. Her breath sounds are markedly diminished. Her room air oxygen saturation is 89%. Which of the following actions should the nurse take?
   A. Administer oxygen to keep her oxygen saturation ≥92%.
   B. Recommend discharge with follow-up to her primary care doctor.
   C. Administer inhaled corticosteroids.
   D. Review asthma triggers and early warning signs.

Try these additional resources to enhance your learning and understanding of this chapter:
- thePoint online resource available at **http://thepoint.lww.com/Pellico1e**
- *Handbook for Focus on Adult Health: Medical-Surgical Nursing*
- *Study Guide for Focus on Adult Health: Medical-Surgical Nursing*

References and Selected Readings

References and selected readings associated with this chapter can be found on the website that accompanies the book. Visit **http://thepoint.lww.com/Pellico1e** to access the references and other additional resources associated with this chapter.

Problems Related to Cardiovascular and Circulatory Function

THE NURSE is caring for an obese 60-year-old African American who smokes two packs of cigarettes a day. He is being seen in the cardiology clinic for evaluation and treatment of hypertension. His current blood pressure is 180/90. He has congestive heart failure and is currently nonadherent with his medication regimen and has not followed up with a doctor for 3 years.

➡ Discuss current and potential problems of the patient's nonadherence.

➡ What areas of teaching would be important to emphasize with this patient?

➡ Discuss target organs that may be affected by the patient's nonadherence with prescribed medications.

JANET A. PARKOSEWICH

Nursing Assessment: Cardiovascular and Circulatory Function

After reading this chapter, you will be able to:

1. Describe the relationship between the anatomic structures and physiologic function of the heart and peripheral circulation.

2. Discuss the significance of the health history and physical assessment to the diagnosis of cardiovascular disorders.

3. Discuss the clinical indications, patient preparation, and other related nursing implications for common tests and procedures used to assess cardiovascular and circulatory function.

4. Compare the various methods of hemodynamic monitoring (e.g., central venous pressure, pulmonary artery pressure, and arterial pressure monitoring) with regard to indications for use, potential complications, and nursing responsibilities.

Cardiovascular disease (CVD) refers to diseases involving the heart and blood vessels. CVD affects more than 80 million Americans and claims the life of 1 person every 37 seconds (American Heart Association [AHA], 2009). Given the prevalence of CVD, nurses practicing in most settings will be assessing and managing patients with one or more disorders associated with the heart or blood vessels. An understanding of the structure and function of the cardiovascular system in health and disease is essential to the development of cardiovascular assessment skills.

ANATOMIC AND PHYSIOLOGIC OVERVIEW

The unique function of the cardiovascular system is to circulate blood through a network of blood vessels (arteries, capillaries, and veins) via two interdependent circulatory systems called the *pulmonary circulatory system* (right heart) and *systemic circulatory system* (left heart) (Fig. 12-1). The *lymphatic system* complements the function of the circulatory system, by draining excessive interstitial fluid from the tissues and returning it into the bloodstream via the internal jugular and subclavian veins.

Anatomy and Physiology of the Vascular System

The vascular system is composed of blood vessels that circulate blood throughout the body and back to the heart. There are several types of blood vessels, including arteries, arterioles, capillaries, venules, and veins.

Arteries and Arterioles

Arteries are thick-walled structures that transport blood containing oxygen and nutrients from the heart to the tissues of the body. The aorta, the largest artery, has a diameter of approximately 25 mm (1 inch) in the average-sized adult. It has numerous branches that continue to divide into progressively smaller arteries, eventually reaching 4 mm in diameter. Once these vessels diminish to approximately 30 μm in diameter, they become *arterioles*, which are embedded within the tissues.

The walls of the arteries and arterioles are composed of the *intima*, a thin smooth endothelial cell layer; the *media*, the middle layer of smooth

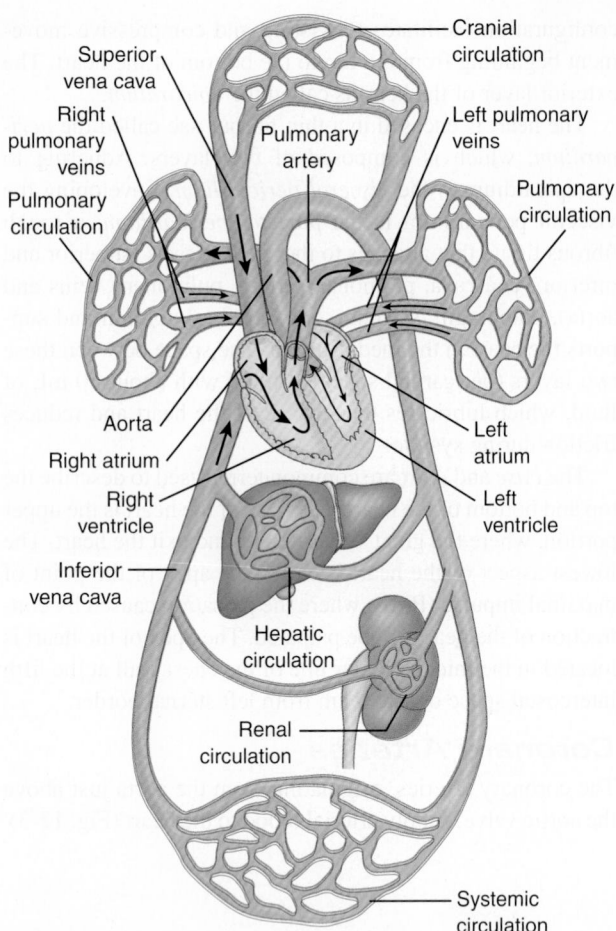

FIGURE 12-1 Pulmonary and systemic circulation. Oxygen-rich blood from the pulmonary circulation is pumped from the left heart into the aorta and the systemic arteries to the capillaries, where the exchange of nutrients and waste products takes place. The deoxygenated blood returns to the right heart by way of the systemic veins and is pumped into the pulmonary circulation. Arrows represent the direction of blood flow through the great vessels and chambers of the heart. The blue shading represents venous blood and the red shading represents arterial blood.

muscles and elastic fibers; and the *adventitia*, a protective layer of connective tissue that anchors these vessels to surrounding structures. The media is well-developed in the arteries, whereas in smaller arteries and arterioles there is much less elastic tissue.

Capillaries

Capillaries are narrow vessels (5 to 10 µm) formed by a single layer of endothelial cells that permit continuous movement of fluid and exchange of oxygen and nutrients to the cells and removal of carbon dioxide and other metabolic wastes. The amount of oxygen extracted differs by tissue type. For example, the heart has large metabolic requirements, extracting approximately 70% to 80% of the oxygen delivered, whereas other organs extract about 25%.

Capillary membrane permeability and hydrostatic and osmotic pressures are the primary controls for the amount

and direction of fluid filtering across the capillary membrane into the interstitium (space around the cells). Under normal conditions, capillary permeability remains constant. Hydrostatic pressure is generated by the blood pressure (BP), whereas osmotic pressure is created by plasma proteins (primarily albumin). The hydrostatic pressure, which is higher on the arterial side of the capillaries, tends to drive fluid out of the capillaries and into the interstitium. Interstitial fluid is reabsorbed into the capillaries on the venous side of the capillary bed, as the osmotic force predominates over hydrostatic pressure at this location. The excess interstitial fluid that is not reabsorbed into the venous end of the capillary enters the lymphatic system. These processes—filtration, reabsorption, and lymph formation—aid in maintaining tissue fluid volume and removing tissue waste and debris.

Tissue *edema*, an accumulation of excessive interstitial fluid, occurs for a variety of reasons including: abnormal conditions that obstruct lymph drainage, increased capillary membrane permeability, significantly elevated venous pressure, or decreased osmotic force generated by the plasma proteins.

Venules and Veins

The venous system has venules and veins, which are responsible for returning blood to the heart after cellular exchange of oxygen, nutrients, and metabolic waste products. The return of blood to the heart begins as capillaries merge to form thin-walled vessels called *venules* that merge to form larger vessels or veins. The veins contain approximately 75% of total blood volume. Compared with arteries, veins have three thin, less muscular layers. Thus, veins readily distend, permitting large volumes of blood to accumulate in these blood vessels under low pressure. Transport of venous blood back to the right heart is facilitated by the pumping action of the skeletal muscles and the presence of one-way valves, which prevent backward blood flow and enhance the pumping action of skeletal muscles.

Circulatory Needs of Tissues

The amount of arterial blood flow needed to meet the demand for oxygen and other substances is determined by the rate of tissue metabolism, the availability of oxygen, and the function of the tissues. The central nervous system, circulating hormones, and certain chemicals are primarily responsible for regulating blood flow. When metabolic requirements increase (e.g., due to physical activity, local heat application, fever, or infection) blood vessels dilate (vasodilatation) to increase blood flow to the tissues. Vasodilatation and resultant lowering of BP is caused by relaxation of the blood vessel smooth muscles. This develops when potent substances, such as nitric oxide, prostacyclin, histamine, bradykinin, and prostaglandin, enter the circulation.

Blood vessels constrict (vasoconstriction) to reduce blood flow when metabolic demands are low (e.g., due to rest, local cold application, and cooling of the body). Vasoconstriction is due to contraction of the smooth muscles of the arteries,

arterioles, and veins. This action causes narrowing of the lumen of the blood vessels and an elevation in BP. It is stimulated by the release of norepinephrine from the sympathetic nervous system, epinephrine from the adrenal medulla, and angiotensin II. Angiotensin II is the end result of a series of interactions beginning with renin (synthesized by the kidney) and angiotensinogen, a circulating serum protein produced by the liver, which forms angiotensin I. An enzyme (angiotensin-converting enzyme) secreted by the pulmonary vasculature converts angiotensin I into angiotensin II.

Anatomy and Physiology of the Heart

The heart is a hollow, muscular organ located in the center of the thorax, where it occupies the space between the lungs (mediastinum) and rests on the diaphragm. It weighs approximately 300 g (10.6 oz) and is about the size of a clenched fist, although size varies based on age, gender, body stature, physical condition, and presence of CVD.

The walls of the heart are made up of three layers (Fig. 12-2). The inner layer, or *endocardium*, consists of endothelial tissue and lines the inside of the heart and valves. The middle layer, or myocardium, forms an interconnected network of muscle fibers, which encircles the heart in a figure-of-eight pattern. During myocardial contraction, this configuration facilitates a twisting and compressive movement beginning from the top to the bottom of the heart. The exterior layer of the heart is called the *epicardium*.

The heart is encased in a thin fibrous sac called the *pericardium*, which is composed of two layers. Adhering to the epicardium is the *visceral pericardium*. Enveloping the visceral pericardium is the *parietal pericardium*, a tough fibrous tissue that attaches to the great vessels (superior and inferior vena cava, pulmonary artery, pulmonary veins and aorta), diaphragm, sternum, and vertebral column and supports the heart in the mediastinum. The space between these two layers (pericardial space) is filled with about 30 mL of fluid, which lubricates the surface of the heart and reduces friction during systole.

The *base* and *apex* are common terms used to describe the top and bottom of the heart. The base of the heart is the upper portion, where the great vessels enter and exit the heart. The lowest aspect of the heart is called the apex or the point of maximal impulse (PMI), where the pulsation caused by contraction of the heart can be palpated. The apex of the heart is located in the midclavicular line of the chest wall at the fifth intercostal space or 7 to 9 cm from left sternal border.

Coronary Arteries

The coronary arteries, originating from the aorta just above the aortic valve, supply arterial blood to the heart (Fig. 12-3).

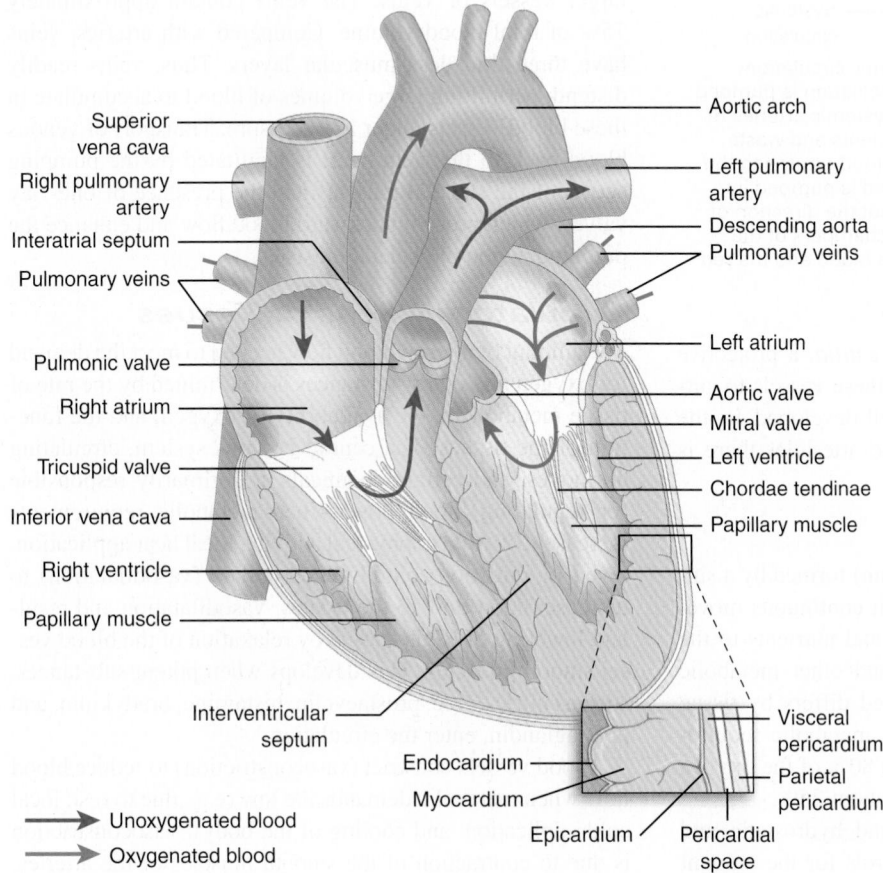

Superior vena cava
Right pulmonary artery
Interatrial septum
Pulmonary veins
Pulmonic valve
Right atrium
Tricuspid valve
Inferior vena cava
Right ventricle
Papillary muscle
Interventricular septum
Endocardium
Myocardium
Epicardium

Aortic arch
Left pulmonary artery
Descending aorta
Pulmonary veins
Left atrium
Aortic valve
Mitral valve
Left ventricle
Chordae tendinae
Papillary muscle
Visceral pericardium
Parietal pericardium
Pericardial space

→ Unoxygenated blood
→ Oxygenated blood

FIGURE 12-2 Anatomy of the heart. Arrows represent blood flow through the chambers of the heart.

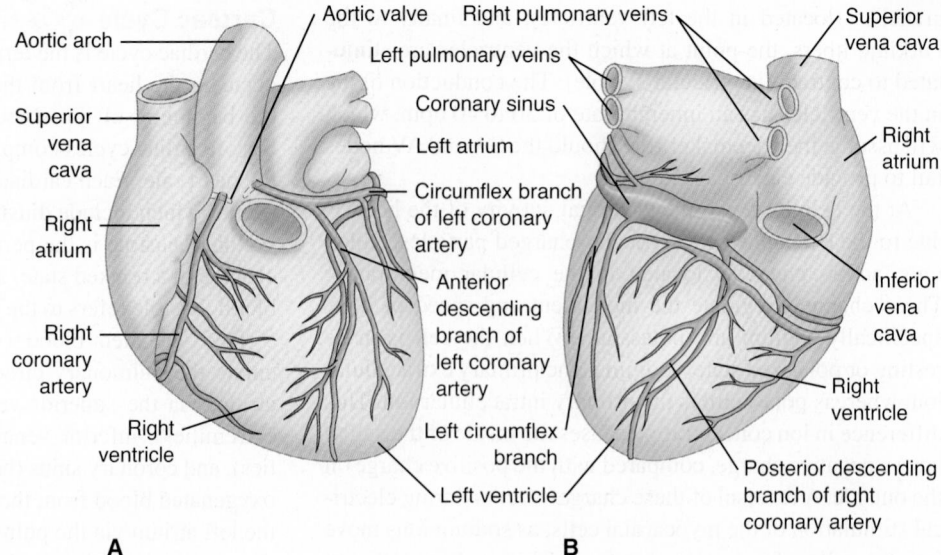

FIGURE 12-3 The coronary arteries supply the heart muscle with oxygenated blood, adjusting the flow according to metabolic needs. **(A)** Anterior view and **(B)** posterior view of the heart.

The coronary arteries, which feed the heart muscle, receive most of the blood during diastole, when the aortic valve closes. The left coronary, often referred to as the *left main coronary artery*, bifurcates into the left anterior descending artery that supplies the anterior wall of the heart and the *circumflex artery* that circles to the left side feeding the lateral wall of the heart.

The right side of the heart is supplied by the right coronary artery, which progresses around to the bottom or inferior wall of the left ventricle. The right coronary artery branches into the posterior descending artery, which supplies the posterior wall of the left ventricle. Superficial to the coronary arteries are the coronary veins. Venous blood from these veins returns to the heart primarily through the coronary sinus, which is located in posterior wall of the right atrium.

Heart Chambers, Valves, and Great Vessels

The right and left heart each have an upper chamber or atrium that collects blood and a larger lower pumping chamber, called a *ventricle* (see Fig. 12-2). Blood flows into the right atrium from the superior and inferior vena cava, passes through the tricuspid valve to the right ventricle. The right ventricle pumps the blood in need of oxygenation to the lungs via the pulmonary artery. The pulmonary artery is the only artery carrying deoxygenated blood. Oxygenated blood returns to the left atrium via the pulmonary veins. The left atrium contracts and blood flows through the mitral valve to the left ventricle. The left ventricle pumps the blood through the aortic valve into systemic circulation. Thus, two sets of valves are located within the right and left heart that provide one-way blood flow through these chambers. Valves separating the atria from the ventricles are termed *atrioventricular (AV) valves*, whereas valves located between the right and left ventricles and their respective great vessels (pulmonary artery and aorta) are called *semilunar valves*.

Cardiac Conduction System

The cardiac conduction system is composed of specialized cells that are capable of spontaneously initiating an electrical impulse (automaticity), responding to an electrical impulse (excitability), and propagating these impulses from one cell to another (conductivity) (Fig. 12-4). The **sinoatrial (SA) node**, the primary pacemaker of the heart, initiates electrical impulses at an inherent rate of 60 to 100 beats per minute (bpm). These impulses move across the atria via internodal pathways causing the atria to contract, then move onto the atrioventricular (AV) node. At the AV node, a slight delay occurs, which synchronizes atrial and ventricular activity and permits adequate time for the ventricles to fill. If the SA node fails in its pacemaker role, the AV node is capable of assuming this function by discharging electrical impulses at an inherent rate of 40 to 60 bpm. Impulses are then conducted to the ventricles via the bundle of His, to the right bundle branch (located in the right ventricle) and left bundle

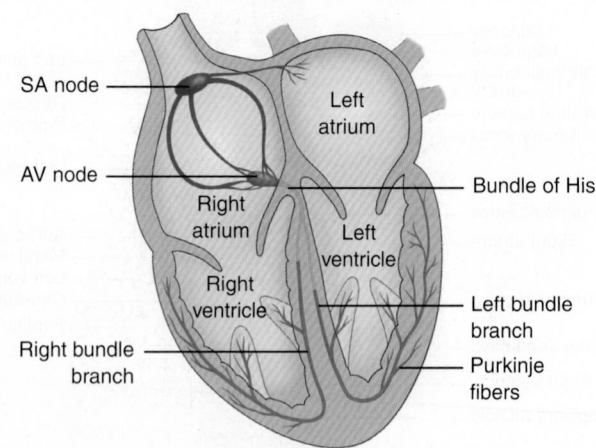

FIGURE 12-4 Cardiac conduction system. AV, atrioventricular; SA, sinoatrial.

branches (located in the left ventricle), and finally to the Purkinje fibers, the point at which the ventricles are stimulated to contract (ventricular systole). The conduction tissue in the ventricles has an inherent rate of 30 to 40 bpm, which will assume the pacemaker role should the SA and AV nodes fail to provide electrical impulses.

At the cellular level, the electrical activity of the heart is due to the exchange of electrically charged particles, called *ions*, across channels located in the cellular membranes. These channels regulate the movement and speed of ions, specifically sodium and potassium. When the cell is in its resting or polarized state, sodium is the primary extracellular ion, whereas potassium is the primary intracellular ion. This difference in ion concentration causes the inside of the cell to have a negative charge, compared with the positive charge on the outside. A reversal of these charges occurs during electrical stimulation of the myocardial cells, as sodium ions move into the cell and potassium ions exit. This exchange of ions characterizes the period known as **depolarization**, which is followed rapidly by the contraction of the stimulated myocardium. Once depolarization is complete, the exchange of ions reverts back to its polarized state. This period is known as **repolarization**. It is analogous to a rest period that allows the myocardial cells to prepare for the next depolarization and subsequent contraction.

Cardiac Hemodynamics

Cardiac hemodynamics describes the pumping forces or pressure required by the heart to maintain blood flow throughout the cardiovascular system. An important determinant of blood flow is the principle that fluid flows from a region of higher pressure to one of lower pressure. The pressures responsible for blood flow are generated during systole and diastole. Figure 12-5 identifies the pressures in the great vessels and heart chambers during systole and diastole.

Cardiac Cycle

The cardiac cycle is the term used to describe the events that occur in the heart from the beginning of one heart beat to the beginning of the subsequent one. Therefore, the number of cardiac cycles completed in a minute is dependent on the heart rate. Each cardiac cycle has three major sequential events, which include **diastole**, atrial **systole**, and ventricular systole. Diastole is the period in which the atria and ventricles are in a relaxed state, allowing the ventricles to fill with blood. Systole refers to the period of myocardial contraction.

Deoxygenated blood (venous blood) from the tissues enters the pulmonary circulation by flowing into the right atrium via the superior vena cava (head, neck, and upper extremities), inferior vena cava (trunk and lower extremities), and coronary sinus (heart). On the left side of the heart, oxygenated blood from the pulmonary circulation returns to the left atrium via the pulmonary veins. During diastole, the pressure in the ventricles is reduced, allowing the AV valves (tricuspid valve in the right heart and mitral valve in the left heart) to open. Blood flows freely from both atria into the ventricles. At the end of diastole, the atria contract (atrial systole), forcing the remaining blood into the ventricles. Atrial systole, better known as the "atrial kick," is an important event because it augments ventricular blood volume by 15% to 25%.

> **NURSING ALERT**
>
> *Loss of the atrial kick decreases cardiac output, leading to the development of symptoms in the patient such as dizziness, light headedness, syncope, decreased activity tolerance, and hypotension. Atrial fibrillation is an arrhythmia that is known to be associated with the loss of the atrial kick. Loss of coordinated atrial contraction into the ventricle will decrease the left ventricular preload and significantly lower cardiac output.*

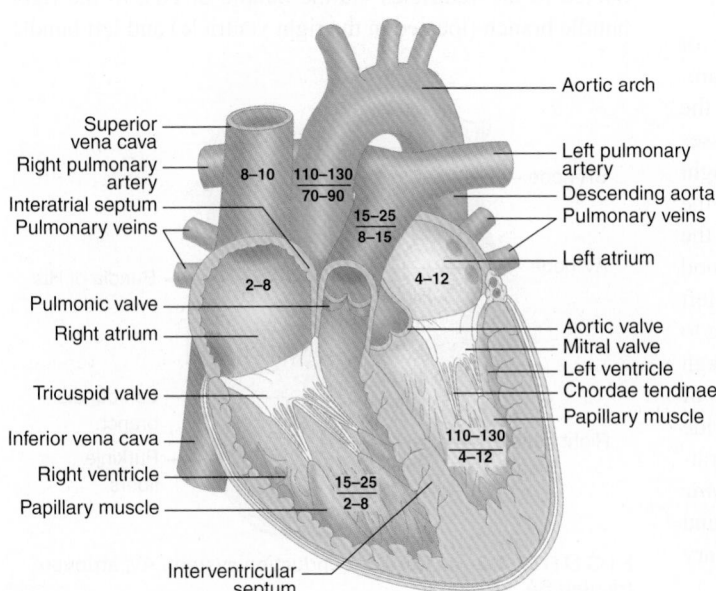

FIGURE 12-5 Great vessel and chamber pressures. Pressures are identified in mm Hg as mean pressure or systolic over diastolic pressure.

During ventricular systole, rising pressure in the ventricles closes the AV valves and forces the semilunar valves (pulmonic valve in the right heart and aortic valve in the left heart) to open. Additional structures attached to the AV valves (chordae tendineae and papillary muscles) keep the valve leaflets closed, thereby preventing regurgitation of blood into the atria. This function permits the one-way flow of blood from the right ventricle into the pulmonary artery and into the lungs for oxygenation (pulmonary circulation) and from the left ventricle into the aorta and out into the remainder of the body via the systemic circulation.

Cardiac Output

Cardiac output refers to the amount of blood pumped by each ventricle in liters per minute. In an adult at rest, the cardiac output is about 4 to 6 L/min, but varies greatly depending on the metabolic needs of the body.

Cardiac output is a function of the **stroke volume** and the heart rate. Stroke volume is the amount of blood ejected with each heartbeat. The average resting stroke volume is about 70 mL. Each time the heart beats only a fraction of the blood present in the ventricles is ejected, which is referred to as the **ejection fraction** (EF). The EF of the left ventricle (normally 50% to 70%) is commonly assessed because it is an important noninvasive measure of myocardial contractility: the EF is lower in conditions that depress myocardial contractility (e.g., myocardial infarction [MI] and heart failure [HF]).

EFFECT OF HEART RATE ON CARDIAC OUTPUT. Cardiac output meets the metabolic demands of the tissues, in part, by changes in heart rate. For example, the heart rate increases during periods of high oxygen demand, such as physical activity, and returns to baseline heart rate at rest. Changes in heart rate are accomplished by inhibition or stimulation of the SA node, through the parasympathetic and sympathetic divisions of the autonomic nervous system. The parasympathetic impulses, which travel to the SA node via the vagus nerve, slow the heart rate, whereas sympathetic innervations via beta$_1$ receptor sites increase heart rate.

Heart rate is also stimulated by an increased level of circulating catecholamines (secreted by the adrenal gland) and by excess thyroid hormone, which produces a catecholamine-like effect.

In addition, heart rate is affected by central nervous system and baroreceptor activity. **Baroreceptors**, located in the aortic arch and the right and left internal carotid arteries (at the point of bifurcation from the common carotid arteries), are sensitive to changes in BP. During elevations in BP (**hypertension**), these cells increase their rate of discharge, transmitting impulses to the medulla. This initiates parasympathetic activity and inhibits sympathetic response, lowering the heart rate and the BP. In contrast, low BP (hypotension) exerts less baroreceptor stimulation, decreasing the parasympathetic action on the SA node and allowing for enhanced sympathetic activity. The resultant vasoconstriction and increased heart rate elevate the BP.

EFFECT OF STROKE VOLUME ON CARDIAC OUTPUT. Stroke volume is a major determinant of cardiac output and is influenced by three interdependent factors: preload, afterload, and contractility.

Preload refers to the pressure generated in the ventricles at the end of diastole and the resultant stretching of the muscle fibers. A direct relationship exists between end-diastolic blood volume and the degree of stretch. As the volume of blood increases, the degree of stretch increases, resulting in stronger contraction and a greater stroke volume. This relationship, called the Frank-Starling (or Starling) law of the heart, is maintained until the physiologic limit of the muscle is reached.

Preload is decreased by a reduction in the volume of blood returning to the ventricles. Vasodilatation and loss of fluid volume from bleeding, diuresis, vomiting, or excessive diaphoresis reduce preload. Preload is increased by increasing the return of circulating blood volume to the ventricles. Controlling the loss of blood or body fluids and replacing fluids (i.e., blood transfusions and IV fluid administration) are examples of ways to increase preload.

Afterload, the amount of resistance to ejection of blood from the ventricle, is the second determinant of stroke volume. The right heart collects venous blood, which has a very low pressure and is met with little resistance as blood is ejected into the pulmonary vascular system, better known as **pulmonary vascular resistance**. On the other hand, the left heart requires significantly higher pressures to overcome resistance created by the arteries in the systemic circulation. This resistance is called **systemic vascular resistance**.

An inverse relationship exists between afterload and stroke volume. For example, afterload is increased by arterial vasoconstriction, which leads to decreased stroke volume. The opposite is true with arterial vasodilation, a situation that reduces afterload and improves stroke volume.

Contractility refers to the force generated by the contracting myocardium under any given condition. Contractility is enhanced by circulating catecholamines, sympathetic neuronal activity, and certain medications (e.g., digoxin [Lanoxin], IV dopamine [Intropin], or dobutamine [Dobutrex]). Increased contractility results in increased stroke volume. Contractility is depressed by hypoxemia, acidosis, and certain medications (e.g., beta-adrenergic blocking medications).

Anatomy and Physiology of the Lymphatic System

The lymphatic system and the cardiovascular system are closely linked. The lymphatic system is formed by lymph, lymph vessels, and lymph nodes. This system collects interstitial fluid, called lymph, and returns it to the cardiovascular system, thus helping to maintain preload. The lymphatic system plays an important role in the immune system, as well, by producing lymphocytes, which defend the body against disease.

Lymph is a clear fluid similar to plasma that contains plasma proteins, lymphocytes, and other factors. It is formed by the filtration of interstitial fluid into the lymph vessels. Lymph vessels are a complex network of thin-walled vessels that resemble veins with a few exceptions: lymph vessels have thinner walls, have more valves, and contain lymph nodes. Lymph readily filters into these vessels because they are very permeable and are not pressurized.

As lymph circulates through these vessels, it passes through one or more lymph nodes before it is returned to the venous blood via openings in the right or left subclavian vein. Lymph nodes, small bean-shaped structures, filter lymph and provide an environment for lymphocytes to perform their immune function after exposure to foreign antigens, such as bacteria or viruses. Lymph nodes are located in clusters primarily in the neck, axilla, and groin.

The lymphatic vessels converge into two main structures: the thoracic duct and the right lymphatic duct. The lymphatic vessels rely on one-way valves, arterial pulsations, and contraction of the lymphatic walls and adjacent skeletal muscle to propel lymph toward the venous drainage points in the subclavian veins.

Gerontologic Considerations

As people age, myocardial muscle mass shrinks (atrophy) and its walls thicken (hypertrophy). The aging process also results in decreased elasticity and widening of the aorta, calcification and stiffening of the blood vessels, thickening and increased rigidity of the cardiac valves, and increased connective tissue in the cardiac conduction system. These changes lead to decreased cardiac output and impaired blood flow to the tissues. As a result, the aging heart has limited ability to respond to increased demands for oxygen and nutrients caused by physical or emotional stress and disease states. These age-associated changes place the elderly at risk for the development of serious symptoms including fatigue, shortness of breath, angina, palpitations, leg pain, dizziness, or syncope. Age-related changes of the cardiovascular system are summarized in Table 12-1.

Gender Considerations

The heart of a woman is smaller and weighs less, compared with the heart of a man. Coronary arteries of the female heart are smaller, thus occlude from **atherosclerosis** more easily and make procedures such as cardiac catheterization and angioplasty technically more difficult, with a higher incidence of post-procedural complications. In addition, the resting heart rate, stroke volume, and EF of a woman's heart are higher than those of a man's heart. The first onset of coronary artery disease (CAD) in women is almost a decade later than their male counterparts. These gender differences in disease presentation are attributed to the premenopausal protection of circulating estrogen.

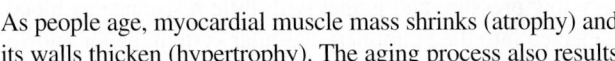

TABLE
12-1 **GERONTOLOGIC CONSIDERATIONS** / **Age-Related Changes in the Cardiovascular System**

Cardiovascular System Component	Structural Changes	Functional Changes	History and Physical Exam Findings
Ventricular myocardium	Loss of muscle mass Hypertrophy	Stiff, noncompliant ventricles Decrease in cardiac output	Fatigue, ↓ exercise tolerance HF or arrhythmia signs/ symptoms PMI palpated lateral to midclavicular line Auscultation reveals S₄
Valves	Calcification of AV valves	Turbulent blood flow across valves	Murmurs and thrills
Conduction system	Deposits of connective tissue	↓ SA node rate and ↓ speed of conduction	Bradycardia Heart block
Sympathetic nervous system	↓ response to beta-adrenergic stimulation	↓ HR and contractility response exercise ↑ time for HR to return to baseline	Fatigue and ↓ exercise tolerance
Aorta and arteries	Calcification and stiffening of the blood vessels ↓ Elasticity and widening of aorta	Left ventricular hypertrophy	Progressive ↑ systolic BP; ↑ diastolic BP Widening pulse pressure
Baroreceptor response	↓ Baroceptor sensitivity to episodes of hypertension and hypotension	Baroreceptors fail to regulate HR and vascular tone causing a slow response to postural changes	Postural hypotension, dizziness, or syncope when sitting or standing up

AV, atrioventricular; BP, blood pressure; HF, heart failure; HR, heart rate; PMI, point of maximal impulse; SA, sinoatrial; ↓, decreased; ↑, increased.

ASSESSMENT OF THE CARDIOVASCULAR SYSTEM

The frequency and extent of the nursing assessment of the cardiovascular system are based on several factors, including the severity of the patient's symptoms, the presence of risk factors, the practice setting, and the purpose of the assessment. Although the key components of the cardiovascular assessment remain the same, the assessment priorities vary according to the needs of the patient. For example, an emergency department nurse caring for a patient who is admitted with symptoms associated with acute coronary syndrome (ACS) performs a rapid and focused assessment because treatment of ACS is time-dependent.

Health History

Nurses practicing in settings where patients with CVD are seen must be expert at recognizing cardiac symptoms, as well as expediting timely and oftentimes lifesaving care. Likewise, patients must be able to recognize when they are experiencing these symptoms and know how to manage them. All too often, patients fail to appreciate the significance of new or worsening cardiac symptoms. This problem results in prolonged delays in seeking treatment. Major barriers to seeking prompt lifesaving care include lack of knowledge about personal risk and symptoms of heart disease, attributing symptoms to a benign source, denying symptom significance, and feeling embarrassed about having symptoms (Moser, Kimble, Alberts et al., 2007). Box 12-1 discusses the gender differences in knowledge, attitudes, and beliefs about heart disease and implications for providing evidence-based nursing care.

Common Complaints

Common CVD signs and symptoms, with related medical diagnoses in parentheses, are covered in the section below.

- Chest pain or discomfort (ACS that includes unstable angina and acute MI, arrhythmias, valvular heart disease)

BOX 12-1 | Nursing Research

Bridging the Gap to Evidence-Based Practice

Is There Any Evidence Suggesting That There Are Gender Differences in Knowledge, Attitudes, and Beliefs About Heart Disease?

Jensen, L. A. & Moser, D. K. (2008). Gender differences in knowledge, attitudes, and beliefs about heart disease. *Nursing Clinics of North America, 43*(1), 77–104.

Purpose
There is a prevailing assumption by health care professionals that women, compared with men, have less knowledge about heart disease. This assumption may be misleading, as the majority of surveys examining these concepts have included women only. The purpose of this paper was to review the literature on the differences between men and women regarding their knowledge, attitudes, and beliefs about heart disease.

Design
A computerized search was conducted using MEDLINE database, PsychINFO, Community of Science, and Cumulative Index of Nursing and Allied Health Literature (CINAHL) to identify studies published in the English language between 1990 and present. Thirty-one studies were identified, and 12 of these were surveys conducted with female subjects only. In addition, the reference lists from these studies were hand searched for other articles of interest not captured in the computerized search.

Findings
The methodological differences among all of these studies limit the generalizability of these findings. However, nurses will find that certain themes emerging from this review are translatable into clinical practice. For example, more men and women than ever before are aware that heart disease is the leading cause of death, but this fact remains underappreciated in both genders. In general, women continue to believe that heart disease is a man's health problem and believe that breast cancer is their greatest health concern. Both men and women had difficulty identifying cardiac risk factors, and those who were able to failed to personalize their risk. This finding was also evident in people who had a history of heart disease. In fact, people with known disease often did not recall being informed that they had risk factors for heart disease.

An additional disturbing finding was that the majority of people described severe chest pain as the predominate symptom of acute MI (AMI). There was little appreciation for non–chest pain symptoms heralding the onset of an AMI. Men and women who had experienced an AMI commonly attributed their symptoms to a benign source because their symptoms were not as expected, creating prolonged delays to seeking medical care.

Nursing Implications
Nurses must not make assumptions about their patients' heart disease knowledge, attitudes, and beliefs, particularly in patients at high risk for or with known heart disease. Patients who are unaware of their risk for heart disease are less likely to engage in primary prevention strategies and, in the setting of an AMI, will be unprepared to recognize symptoms and seek timely life-saving care. An important goal of the health assessment is to identify patients' knowledge deficits with regard to personal risk factors, lifestyle behaviors, symptom recognition, and health-seeking behavior, so a teaching plan can be tailored to meet their individual needs.

- Pain or discomfort in other areas of upper body, including one or both arms, back, neck, jaw, or stomach (ACS)
- Dizziness, syncope, or changes in level of consciousness (ACS, cardiogenic shock, cerebrovascular disorders, arrhythmias, hypotension, postural hypotension, vasovagal episode)
- **Intermittent claudication** or rest pain in lower extremities, especially at night [peripheral arterial disease (PAD)]
- Palpitations or tachycardia (ACS, caffeine or other stimulants, electrolyte imbalances, HF, stress, valvular heart disease, ventricular aneurysm)
- Peripheral edema (HF, PAD), weight gain (HF), or ascites and abdominal distension due to enlarged liver and spleen (HF)
- Shortness of breath or dyspnea, with or without chest pain (ACS, cardiogenic shock, HF, pulmonary edema, valvular heart disease)
- Unusual fatigue characterized by feeling more tired or fatigued than usual (early warning symptom of ACS, HF, valvular heart disease)

Chest Pain

Chest pain and chest discomfort are common symptoms caused by a number of cardiac and noncardiac problems. Table 12-2 identifies the characteristics of common causes of chest pain. To differentiate among these causes of pain, the nurse asks the patient to identify the quantity (0 = no pain to 10 = worst pain), location, and quality of pain. It is important to identify the events that precipitated symptom onset, the duration of the symptom, measures that aggravate or relieve the symptom, and associated signs and symptoms, such as diaphoresis or nausea. The nurse should keep the following points in mind when assessing patients with chest pain or discomfort:

- The severity and duration of chest pain or discomfort does not predict the seriousness of its cause. For example, a patient experiencing esophageal spasm may rate chest pain as a "10/10", whereas, a patient experiencing an acute MI may report only mild to moderate chest pressure.
- More than one cardiac condition may occur simultaneously. During an acute MI, patients may report chest pain from myocardial **ischemia** (inadequate oxygen supply to the tissues), shortness of breath from HF, and palpitations from arrhythmias. Both HF and arrhythmias are complications of acute MI.

Symptoms of Acute Coronary Syndrome

Nurses must take complaints of patients with cardiac symptoms seriously until the cause is determined. Because CAD is so prevalent, all patients reporting new or worsening cardiac symptoms, particularly those at risk for CAD or who have a history of CAD, should be evaluated initially for ACS. There are several distinct characteristics of ACS symptoms that need to be kept in mind during assessment:

- The majority of patients with ACS experience prodromal symptoms sometimes a month or more prior to developing this acute event. Prodromal symptoms include unusual fatigue, shortness of breath, sleep disturbances, anxiety, or fleeting chest discomfort (aching, pressure) that comes and goes. Because these symptoms are less severe than what is experienced during ACS, patients often attribute them to a benign problem, such as stress, and fail to seek medical care. Nurses should include a question regarding presence of prodromal symptoms when assessing patients with cardiac symptoms.
- Approximately 50% of men and women with ACS experience chest symptoms, whereas the remainder may develop a variety of symptoms such as upper back, shoulder, arm, or neck pain, epigastric burning, or shortness of breath. There are many misconceptions that men and women have about their cardiac risk factors and signs and symptoms of heart disease.
- During the onset of ACS, people experience a group of at least four or more symptoms that can include chest discomfort or pain; upper back, shoulder, arm, or neck pain; epigastric burning or indigestion; shortness of breath; unusual fatigue; and diaphoresis. The combination of symptoms can vary from person to person and are sometimes referred to as ACS symptom clusters (Ryan, DeVon, & Horne, 2007).
- Neuropathies in elderly patients and those with diabetes may prevent these patients from experiencing pain or discomfort associated with myocardial ischemia. Instead, they may report unusual fatigue or shortness of breath. In some patients, ACS may be asymptomatic, which is referred to as *silent ischemia.*
- A 12-lead electrocardiogram (ECG) and serum laboratory analysis of cardiac biomarkers are necessary to determine if the patient with ACS symptoms is experiencing unstable angina or acute MI.

Past History

Epidemiologic studies show that certain conditions or behaviors (i.e., risk factors) are associated with a greater incidence of CAD, cerebrovascular disease, and PAD (AHA, 2009). The nurse might ask some of the following questions:

- How is your health? Have you noticed any changes from last year? From 5 years ago?
- Do you have a cardiologist or primary health care provider? How often do you go for checkups?
- What are your risk factors for heart disease? What do you do to reduce these risk factors? Box 12-2 on page 365 lists risk factors for CVD and treatment goals.

Patients who lack understanding of their risk factors and diagnosis may be less motivated to make lifestyle changes or manage their cardiac disease effectively. On the other hand, patients who have this awareness and believe that they have the power to modify their risk factors may be more likely to

TABLE
12-2 Characteristics of Cardiac and Noncardiac Causes of Chest Pain

Location	Character	Duration	Precipitating Events and Aggravating Factors	Alleviating Factors
Angina pectoris Acute coronary syndrome (ACS) (unstable angina, myocardial infarction [MI]) Usual distribution of pain with myocardial ischemia Jaw Epigastrium Right side Back Less common sites of pain with myocardial ischemia	Angina: Uncomfortable pressure, squeezing, or fullness in substernal chest area Can radiate across chest to the medial aspect of one or both arms and hands, jaw, shoulders, upper back, or epigastrium Radiation to arms and hands, described as numbness, tingling, or aching	Angina: 5–15 min	Angina: Physical exertion, emotional upset, eating large meal, or exposure to extremes in temperature	Angina: Rest, nitroglycerin, oxygen
	ACS: Same as angina pectoris Pain or discomfort ranges from mild to severe Associated with shortness of breath, diaphoresis, palpitations, unusual fatigue, and nausea or vomiting	ACS: >15 min	ACS: Emotional upset or unusual physical exertion occurring within 24 hr of symptom onset Can occur at rest or while asleep	ACS: Morphine, reperfusion of coronary artery with thrombolytic agent or percutaneous coronary intervention
Pericarditis	Sharp, severe substernal or epigastric pain Can radiate to neck, arms, and back Associated symptoms include fever, malaise, dyspnea, cough, nausea, dizziness, and palpitations	Intermittent	Sudden onset Pain increases with inspiration, swallowing, coughing, and rotation of trunk	Sitting upright, analgesia, anti-inflammatory medications
Pulmonary disorders (pneumonia, pulmonary embolism)	Sharp, severe substernal or epigastric pain arising from inferior portion of pleura (referred to as pleuritic pain) Patient may be able to localize the pain	≥30 min	Follows an infectious or noninfectious process (MI, cardiac surgery, cancer, immune disorders, uremia) Pleuritic pain increases with inspiration, coughing, movement, and supine positioning Occurs in conjunction with community-acquired or nosocomial lung infections (pneumonia) or deep vein thrombosis (pulmonary embolism)	Treatment of underlying cause

(continued on page 364)

Location	Character	Duration	Precipitating Events and Aggravating Factors	Alleviating Factors
Esophageal disorders (hiatal hernia, reflux esophagitis or spasm)	Substernal pain described as sharp, burning, or heavy Often mimics angina Can radiate to neck, arm, or shoulders	5–60 min	Recumbency, cold liquids, exercise	Food or antacid
Anxiety and panic disorders	Pain described as stabbing to dull ache Associated with diaphoresis, palpitations, shortness of breath, tingling of hands or mouth, feeling of unreality, or fear of losing control	Peaks in 10 min	Can occur at any time including during sleep Can be associated with a specific trigger	Removal of stimulus, relaxation, medications to treat anxiety or underlying disorder
Musculoskeletal disorders (costochondritis)	Sharp or stabbing pain localized in anterior chest Most often unilateral Can radiate across chest to epigastrium or back	Hours to days	Most often follows respiratory tract infection with significant coughing, vigorous exercise, or posttrauma Some cases are idiopathic Exacerbated by deep inspiration, coughing, sneezing, and movement of upper torso or arms	Rest, ice, or heat Analgesic or anti-inflammatory medications
Dissecting aorta	Severe, persistent tearing pain in anterior chest / back Radiates to shoulders, epigastrium or abdomen Associated with sweating and tachycardia.	Sudden onset	Hypertension, blunt chest trauma, or cocaine use	Medical or surgical interventions

Risk Factors for Cardiovascular Diseases (CVD)

Nonmodifiable Risk Factors

- Older age
- Male gender
- Heredity, including race

Modifiable Risk Factors and Treatment Goals*

- Hyperlipidemia (LDL <100 mg/dL and preferably <70 mg/dL if CAD present; LDL <160 mg/dL if ≤1 risk factor or 130 mg/dL if ≤2 risk factors; HDL >40 mg/dL and triglycerides <150 mg/dL)
- Hypertension (<140/90 mm Hg; <130/80 if diabetes or chronic renal disease present)
- Cigarette smoking (complete cessation, no second-hand tobacco exposure)
- Diabetes mellitus (fasting serum glucose <110 mg/dL and hemoglobin A_{1c} <7%)
- Obesity and overweight (BMI 18.5 to 24.9 kg/m²; waist circumference: male ≤40 inches, female ≤35 inches)
- Physical inactivity (30–60 minutes moderate intensity aerobic activity 5 days or more)

*American Heart Association; recommended goals are given in parentheses.

engage in prevention measures. Once patients' risk factors are identified, the nurse determines if patients have a plan for making necessary lifestyle changes and if assistance is needed to support these changes.

Family History

The nurse inquires about a history of cardiac disease in the patient's family, including:

- A history of sudden death in family members of all ages with or without symptoms or known CAD
- A family member with a biochemical or neuromuscular condition (e.g., hemochromatosis [excessive iron retention in the body] or muscular dystrophy)
- DNA mutation or other genetic testing that was performed on any family member

Cardiovascular disorders associated with genetic abnormalities include familial hypercholesterolemia, hypertrophic cardiomyopathy, long QT syndrome, hereditary hemochromatosis, and elevated homocysteine levels.

Social History

Medications

Nurses collaborate with other health care providers to obtain a complete list of patient's medications including dose and frequency. Vitamins, herbals, and over-the-counter medications are included on this list. During this aspect of the health assessment, the nurse solicits answers to the following questions to ensure that patients are safely and effectively taking their mediations.

- Is the patient independent in taking medications?
- Are the medications taken as prescribed?
- Does the patient know what side effects to report to the prescriber?
- Does the patient understand why the medication regimen is important?
- Are doses ever forgotten or skipped, or does the patient ever decide to stop taking a medication?

An aspirin a day is a common nonprescription medication that improves patient outcomes after an acute MI. However, if patients are not aware of this benefit, they may be inclined to stop taking aspirin if they think it is a trivial medication. A careful medication history often uncovers common medication errors and causes for nonadherence to the medication regimen.

Nutrition and Metabolism

Dietary modifications, exercise, weight loss, and careful monitoring are important strategies for managing three major cardiovascular risk factors: hyperlipidemia, hypertension, and diabetes mellitus. Diets that are restricted in sodium, fat, cholesterol, and/or calories are commonly prescribed. The nurse obtains the following information:

- How often the patient self-monitors BP, blood glucose, and weight as appropriate to the medical diagnoses
- The patient's knowledge regarding target goals for each of the risk factors, and any problems achieving or maintaining these goals
- What the patient normally eats and drinks in a typical day, and any food preferences (including cultural or ethnic preferences)
- Eating habits (canned or commercially prepared foods versus fresh foods, restaurant cooking versus home cooking, assessing for high-sodium foods, dietary intake of fats)
- Who shops for groceries and prepares meals

Elimination

Typical bowel and bladder habits need to be identified. Nocturia (awakening at night to urinate) is common in patients with HF. Fluid collected in the dependent tissues (extremities) during the day redistributes into the circulatory system once the patient is recumbent at night. The increased circulatory volume is excreted by the kidneys (increased urine production).

When straining during defecation, the patient bears down (the Valsalva maneuver), which momentarily increases pressure on the baroreceptors. This triggers a vagal response, causing the heart rate to slow, which may lead to syncope in some patients. Straining during urination can produce the same response.

Because many cardiac medications can cause GI side effects or bleeding, the nurse asks about bloating, diarrhea,

constipation, stomach upset, heartburn, loss of appetite, nausea, and vomiting. Patients taking platelet-inhibiting medications such as aspirin and clopidogrel (Plavix); platelet aggregation inhibitors such as abciximab (ReoPro), eptifibatide (Integrilin), and tirofiban (Aggrastat); and anticoagulants such as low-molecular-weight heparin (i.e., dalteparin [Fragmin], enoxaparin [Lovenox]), heparin, or warfarin (Coumadin) are screened for bloody urine or stools.

Activity and Exercise

Changes in patients' activity tolerance may be gradual and go unnoticed. The nurse determines if there are recent changes by comparing the patient's current activity level with that performed in the past 6 to 12 months. New symptoms or a change in the usual symptoms during activity is a significant finding. Activity-induced angina or shortness of breath, may indicate CAD, which requires medical attention. Arterial insufficiency is suspected if the patient experiences intermittent claudication, described as a lower extremity muscular, cramping pain that occurs with activity and is relieved by rest. Angina and intermittent claudication occur when there is tissue ischemia or inadequate arterial blood supply, in the setting of increased demand (e.g., exercise, stress, or anemia). As the tissues are forced to function without adequate nutrients and oxygen, muscle metabolites and lactic acid are produced. Pain is experienced as the metabolites aggravate the nerve endings of the surrounding tissue. **Rest pain** is a persistent pain in the anterior portion of the foot at rest that can worsen at night and indicates significant arterial insufficiency and a critical state of ischemia.

Fatigue, associated with a low left ventricular EF (<40%) and certain medications (e.g., beta-adrenergic blocking agents), can result in activity intolerance. Patients with fatigue may benefit from having their medications adjusted and learning energy-conservation techniques.

Additional areas to explore include the presence of architectural barriers in the home (stairs, multilevel home), the patient's involvement in cardiac rehabilitation, and the patient's typical exercise pattern, including intensity, frequency, and duration.

Sleep and Rest

Clues to worsening cardiac disease, especially HF, can be revealed by sleep-related events. Determining where the patient sleeps or rests and any recent changes in sleep habits is important. Worsening HF is characterized by pulmonary congestion resulting in dyspnea at rest or when lying down. *Orthopnea* is the term used to indicate the need to sit upright or stand to avoid dyspnea. Thus, patients with worsening HF will report that they sleep upright in a chair instead of in bed; increase the number of pillows used; awaken from sleep with sudden onset of dyspnea, often associated with coughing and wheezing, called *paroxysmal nocturnal dyspnea* (PND); or awaken with angina (nocturnal angina). PND occurs at night and is caused by the reabsorption of fluid from dependent areas of the body (arms and legs) back into the circulatory system within hours of lying in bed. This sudden fluid shift increases preload and places too great a demand on the heart of patients with HF, causing sudden pulmonary congestion.

Cognition and Perception

Evaluating cognitive ability helps determine whether the patient has the capacity to manage safe and effective self-care independently. Is the patient's short-term memory intact? Is there any history of dementia? Is there evidence of depression or anxiety? Can the patient read? Can the patient read English? What is the patient's reading level? What is the patient's preferred learning style? What information does the patient perceive as important? Providing the patient with written information can be a valuable part of patient education, but only if the patient can read and comprehend the information.

Related assessments include possible hearing or visual impairments. If vision is impaired, patients with HF may not be able to weigh themselves independently or keep records of weight, BP, pulse, or other data requested by the health care team.

Self-Perception and Self-Concept

Self-perception and self-concept are related to the cognitive and emotional processes that people use to formulate their beliefs and feelings about themselves. It is important for the nurse to understand patients' beliefs and feelings about their health, as these concepts are key determinants of patients' adherence to new medical regimens and lifestyle changes (e.g., smoking cessation, weight reduction, exercise), which are necessary for effective self-management after an acute cardiac event (Lau-Walker, 2007; van der Wal, Jaarsma, Moser et al., 2007). Patients who have misperceptions about the health consequences of their cardiac illness are at risk for nonadherence to their treatment plan. Responses of patients to the following questions will guide the nurse in planning interventions to assure that patients are prepared to manage their illness and that adequate services are in place to support the patient's recovery and self-management needs.

- What is your cardiac problem, and what do you think has contributed to this problem?
- What consequences do you think this illness will have on your current lifestyle (leisure and physical activities, work, role in the family and social relationships)?
- How much of an influence do you think you have on controlling this illness?

Sexuality and Reproduction

A common problem for patients with cardiac diseases is a decrease in frequency of and satisfaction with sexual activity. These changes are associated with inadequate information, depression, and fear of having a cardiac event (e.g., AMI, sudden death) or development of bothersome symptoms (e.g., chest discomfort, shortness of breath, palpitations) (Mosack & Steinke, 2009). In men, impotence may develop as a side

effect of cardiac medications (e.g., beta-blockers); some men will stop taking their medication as a result. Other medications may be substituted, so patients should be encouraged to discuss this problem with their health care providers.

Patients and their partners may not have adequate information about the physical demands related to sexual activity and ways in which these demands can be modified. The physiologic demands are greatest during orgasm, reaching 5 or 6 metabolic equivalents (METs), which is equivalent to walking 3 to 4 miles per hour on a treadmill. The METs expended before and after orgasm are considerably less, at 3.7 METs. Sharing this information may make the patient and his or her partner more comfortable about resuming sexual activity.

A reproductive history is necessary for women of childbearing age, particularly those with seriously compromised cardiac function. These women may be advised by their health care providers not to become pregnant. The reproductive history includes information about previous pregnancies, plans for future pregnancies, oral contraceptive use (especially in women older than 35 years of age who smoke), menopausal status, and use of hormone therapy.

Coping and Stress Tolerance

Anxiety, depression, and stress are known to influence both the development of and recovery from CAD and HF. High levels of anxiety are associated with an increased incidence of CAD and in-hospital complications after MI. Patients with a diagnosis of an acute MI and depression have an increased risk of rehospitalizations and death, more frequent angina, more physical limitations, and poorer quality of life, compared with people without depression. Although the association between depression and CAD is not completely understood, it is postulated that both biologic factors (e.g., platelet abnormalities, inflammatory responses) and lifestyle factors contribute to the development of CAD. People who are depressed are known to be less motivated to adhere to the recommended lifestyle changes and medical regimens necessary to prevent future cardiac events. Patients with CVD should be assessed for depression by asking them if they are feeling sad or blue, if they have lost interest in things they usually enjoy, or have thoughts about death or suicide. Other indications of depression include feelings of worthlessness or guilt, problems falling asleep or staying asleep, having difficulty concentrating, restlessness, and recent changes in appetite or weight.

Stress initiates a variety of physiologic responses, including increased levels of catecholamines and cortisol, and has been strongly linked to cardiovascular events. Therefore, patients need to be assessed for sources of stress, previous coping styles and effectiveness, and perception of their current mood and coping ability. Consultation with a psychiatric advanced practice nurse, psychologist, psychiatrist, or social worker is indicated for anxious or depressed patients or those patients having difficulty coping with their cardiac illness.

Physical Assessment

During the physical assessment, the nurse is evaluating the cardiovascular system for any deviations from normal with regard to the following (examples of abnormalities are in parentheses):

- The heart as a pump (reduced pulse pressure, gallop sounds, murmurs, displaced PMI)
- Atrial and ventricular filling volumes and pressures (elevated jugular venous distension, peripheral edema, ascites, crackles, postural changes in BP)
- Cardiac output (reduced pulse pressure, hypotension, tachycardia, reduced urine output, or level of consciousness)
- Compensatory mechanisms (peripheral vasoconstriction, tachycardia)

Assessment of General Appearance and Cognition

The nurse notes signs of distress, which may include pain or discomfort, shortness of breath, or anxiety.

The patient's height and weight are measured to calculate body mass index (BMI) (weight in kilograms/square of the height in meters^2), as well as the waist circumference. These measures are used to determine if obesity (BMI >30 kg/M^2) and abdominal fat (males, waist >40 inches; and females, waist >35 inches) are placing the patient at risk for CAD.

To assess cognition, the nurse evaluates the patient's level of consciousness (alert, lethargic, stuporous, comatose) and mental status (oriented to person, place, time; coherence). Changes in level of consciousness and mental status may be attributed to inadequate perfusion of the brain from a compromised cardiac output or thromboembolic event (stroke).

Inspection and Palpation of the Skin

The signs and symptoms of an acute obstruction of arterial blood flow in the extremities are referred to as the six Ps, which are *p*ain, *p*allor, *p*ulselessness, *p*aresthesia, *p*oikilothermia (coldness), and *p*aralysis. Additional changes resulting from a chronically reduced oxygen and nutrient supply to the skin include hair loss, brittle nails, dry or scaling skin, atrophy, skin color changes, and ulcerations. Table 12-3 summarizes common skin findings in patients with CVD.

The nurse assesses capillary refill time, which indicates the adequacy of arterial perfusion to the extremities. To perform this test, the nurse compresses the nail bed briefly to occlude perfusion (nail bed blanches). Then, the nurse releases pressure and determines the time it takes to restore perfusion. Normally, reperfusion occurs within 2 seconds, as evidenced by the return of color to the nail bed. Prolonged capillary refill time indicates compromised arterial perfusion, a problem associated with cardiogenic shock and HF.

Peripheral edema, fluid accumulation in dependent areas of the body (feet, legs, and sacrum in the bedridden patient), is a common finding in patients with CVD. The nurse assesses the patient for pitting edema (a depression over an

TABLE
12-3 Common Skin Findings Associated With Cardiovascular Diseases

Findings	Associated Causes and Conditions
Clubbing of the fingers or toes (thickening of the skin under the fingers or toes)	Chronic hemoglobin desaturation most often due to congenital heart disease, advanced pulmonary diseases
Cool/cold skin and diaphoresis	Low cardiac output (e.g., cardiogenic shock, AMI) causing sympathetic nervous system stimulation with resultant vasoconstriction
Cold, pain, pallor of the fingertips or toes	Intermittent arteriolar vasoconstriction (Raynaud's disease). Skin may change in color from white, blue, and red accompanied by numbness, tingling, and burning pain.
Cyanosis, central (a bluish tinge observed in the lips, tongue, and buccal mucosa)	Serious cardiac disorders (pulmonary edema, cardiogenic shock, congenital heart disease) as venous blood passes through the pulmonary circulation without being oxygenated.
Cyanosis, peripheral (a bluish tinge, most often of the nails and extremities)	Peripheral vasoconstriction, allowing more time for the hemoglobin molecules to become desaturated. It can be caused by exposure to cold environment, anxiety, or ↓ cardiac output.
Ecchymosis or bruising (a purplish-blue color fading to green, yellow, or brown)	Blood leaking outside of the blood vessels. Excessive bruising is a risk for patients on anticoagulants or platelet-inhibiting medications.
Edema, lower extremities (collection of fluid in the interstitial spaces of the tissues)	HF and vascular problems (PAD, chronic venous insufficiency, DVT, thrombophlebitis)
Hematoma (localized collection of clotted blood in the tissue)	Bleeding after catheter removal/tissue injury in patients on anticoagulant/antithrombotic agents.
Pallor (↓ skin color in fingernails, lips, oral mucosa and lower extremities)	Anemia or ↓ arterial perfusion. Suspected PAD if feet develop pallor after elevating legs 60° from a supine position.
Rubor (A reddish-blue discoloration of the legs, seen within 20 seconds to 2 minutes after placing in a dependent position)	Filling of dilated capillaries with deoxygenated blood, indicative of PAD.
Ulcers, feet and ankles (Superficial, irregular ulcers at medial malleolus. Red to yellow granulation tissue)	Rupture of small skin capillaries from chronic venous insufficiency
(Painful, deep, round ulcers on feet or from exposure to pressure. Pale to black wound base).	Prolonged ischemia to tissues due to PAD. Can lead to gangrene.
Thinning of skin around a pacemaker or an implantable cardioverter defibrillator	Erosion of the device through the skin.
Xanthelasma (yellowish, raised plaques observed along nasal portion of eyelids)	Elevated cholesterol levels (hypercholesterolemia)

AMI, acute myocardial infarction; DVT, deep vein thrombosis; HF, heart failure; PAD, peripheral arterial disease.

area of pressure) by using the thumb to place firm pressure over the dorsum of each foot, behind each medial malleolus, over the shins or sacral area for 5 seconds. The depression created by this pressure is graded as absent or as present on a scale from slight (1+) to very marked (4+). Scales exist to measure the degree of pitting edema that rely on a clinician's judgment of depth of edema or time the indentation remains after release of pressure. It is important that clinicians use a consistent scale in order to ensure reliable clinical measurements and management.

Peripheral edema is observed in patients with HF and peripheral vascular diseases, such as deep vein thrombosis or chronic venous insufficiency.

Assessment of Blood Pressure

Systemic arterial BP is the pressure exerted on the walls of the arteries during ventricular systole and diastole. It is affected by factors such as cardiac output; distention of the arteries; and the volume, velocity, and viscosity of the blood.

The ideal BP is 120/80 mm Hg. A BP of 140/90 mm Hg or greater is defined as *hypertension*, whereas a BP of less than 90/60 mm Hg is called *hypotension*.

During the first encounter with a new patient, BP measurements should be obtained in both arms. There may be a 5 to 10 mm Hg difference in pressure between extremities. A BP difference greater than 10 mm Hg may be indicative of arterial obstruction or aortic dissection and requires further evaluation. See Chapter 13 for more information on BP.

Pulse Pressure

Pulse pressure is the difference between the systolic and the diastolic pressures, which normally is 30 to 40 mm Hg. It indicates how well the body is maintaining cardiac output.

! NURSING ALERT
A pulse pressure of less than 30 mm Hg signifies a serious reduction in cardiac output and requires further evaluation.

Postural Blood Pressure Changes

Postural (orthostatic) hypotension is a significant decrease in BP with a change in body position from supine to sitting/standing or from sitting to standing. It may be accompanied by dizziness, lightheadedness, or syncope.

The most common cause of postural hypotension in patients with CVD is due to a reduction in preload from over-diuresis, dehydration, or use of medications that cause vasodilatation (nitrates and antihypertensive agents). The following recommendations are important when assessing the patient for postural changes in BP:

- The patient is positioned supine for 10 minutes before obtaining the initial BP and heart rate.
- After obtaining supine measurements, the patient is positioned on the side of the bed with feet dangling, then, if appropriate, with the patient standing at the side of the bed.
- Wait 1 to 3 minutes after each position change before obtaining the BP and heart rate.
- Return the patient to a supine position if dizziness or lightheadedness is reported after the patient sits or stands.
- Record heart rate and BP in each position and any symptoms that accompany the postural change.

Normal postural responses that occur when a person moves from a lying to a sitting or standing position include (1) a heart rate increase of 5 to 20 bpm above the resting rate (to offset reduced stroke volume and maintain cardiac output); (2) 10 mm Hg or less decrease in systolic pressure, and (3) a slight increase of 5 mm Hg in diastolic pressure. An increase in heart rate with either a 15 mm Hg decrease in systolic pressure or a 10 mm Hg decrease in diastolic pressure are abnormal findings and require further evaluation to determine etiology.

Palpation of Arterial Pulses

The examination of arterial pulses involves assessment of the pulse rate, rhythm, and quality.

Pulse Rate

The normal pulse rate varies from a low of 50 bpm in healthy, athletic young adults to rates well in excess of 100 bpm after exercise or during times of excitement. Anxiety frequently raises the pulse rate during the physical examination. If the rate is higher than expected, the nurse should reassess the pulse at the end of the physical examination when the patient may be more relaxed.

Pulse Rhythm

The rhythm of the pulse is normally regular; although slight irregularities in rhythm can occur due to changes in vagal tone during the respiratory cycle (pulse rate accelerates with inspiration and slows with expiration). This phenomenon, called *sinus arrhythmia*, normally occurs in children and young adults.

During the initial cardiac examination, or if the pulse rhythm is irregular, the nurse assesses pulse rate for a *pulse deficit*, defined as the difference between the apical and the peripheral pulse rates. The pulse deficit is ascertained by simultaneously auscultating the apical pulse and palpating the radial pulse for one minute. The nurse should anticipate finding a pulse deficit in patients with arrhythmias, especially atrial fibrillation, atrial flutter, and ventricular arrhythmias. Some of the ventricular systoles generated by these arrhythmias may be much weaker than others, therefore, they are heard during auscultation, but do not produce a palpable pulse.

Pulse Quality

The pulse quality or amplitude is indicative of the BP in the artery and is used to assess peripheral arterial circulation. The right and left temporal, common carotid, brachial, radial, and lower extremity arteries are palpated, one side at a time and compared for symmetry in quality. Light palpation is essential as firm finger pressure can obliterate the temporal, dorsalis pedis, and posterior tibial arteries.

The quality of each of the pulses is reported by using descriptors (absent, diminished, normal, or bounding) or the following 0-to-4 scale:

   0: Pulse not palpable or absent
+1: Weak, thready pulse; difficult to palpate; obliterated with pressure
+2: Diminished pulse; cannot be obliterated
+3: Easy to palpate, full pulse; cannot be obliterated
+4: Strong, bounding pulse; may be abnormal

When documenting the pulse quality specify the artery location and scale range (e.g., "left radial +3/+4"). Other pulse scales exist; the nurse uses the institution's scale to ensure consistent clinical measurements and management.

Inspection of Jugular Venous Pulsations

Right-sided heart function can be estimated by observing the pulsations of the jugular veins of the neck, which reflects the central venous pressure (CVP) (right ventricular end-diastolic pressure). If internal jugular vein pulsations are difficult to visualize, the external jugular veins are used because they are more superficial and visible right above the clavicles, adjacent to the sternocleidomastoid muscles. In the supine position, the patient's external jugular veins are quite visible, but disappear as the head is elevated greater than 30 degrees.

Obvious distention of the veins with the patient's head elevated 45 to 90 degrees indicates an abnormal increase in the CVP. This occurs with right-sided HF, less commonly with obstruction of blood flow in the superior vena cava, and rarely with acute massive pulmonary embolism.

Inspection and Palpation of the Heart

The heart is examined by inspection, palpation, and auscultation of the precordium or anterior chest wall that covers the heart and lower thorax. A systematic approach is

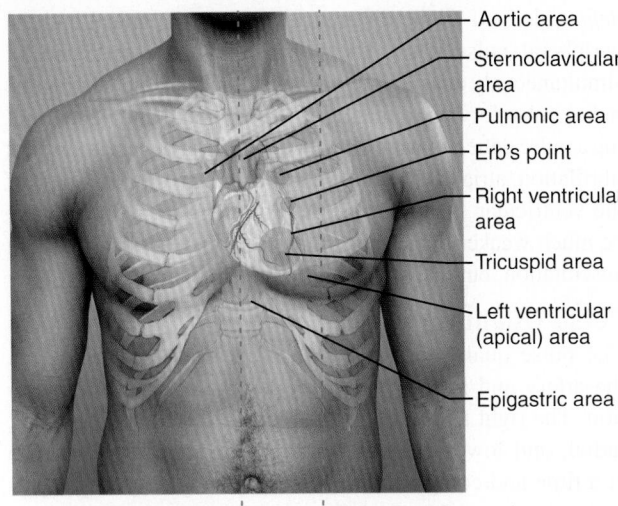

Midsternum   Midclavicular line

FIGURE 12-6 Areas of the precordium to be assessed when evaluating heart function.

used to examine the precordium in the following areas (see Fig. 12-6).

1. *Aortic area*: Second intercostal space to the right of the sternum. To determine the correct intercostal space, the nurse first finds the angle of Louis by locating the bony ridge, at the junction of the body of the sternum and the manubrium. From this angle, the second intercostal space is located by sliding one finger to the right of the sternum. Subsequent intercostal spaces are located from this reference point by palpating down the rib cage.

2. *Pulmonic area*: Second intercostal space, left sternal border

3. *Erb's point*: Third intercostal space, left sternal border

4. *Tricuspid area*: Fourth and fifth intercostal spaces, left sternal border

5. *Mitral (apical area)*: Left fifth intercostal space at the midclavicular line

6. *Epigastric area*: Below the xiphoid process

For most of the examination, the patient lies supine, with the head of the bed slightly elevated. A right-handed examiner stands at the right side of the patient, a left-handed examiner at the left side.

Each area of the precordium is inspected for abnormal pulsations. A subtle pulsation located over the apical area, called the **apical impulse** or point of maximal impulse (PMI), is a normal finding observed in young patients and adults who have thin chest walls. The nurse uses the palm of the hand to locate the apical impulse initially and the fingerpads to assess its size and quality. Palpation of the apical impulse may be facilitated by placing the patient in the left lateral position, as this position brings the heart into closer contact with the chest wall (see Fig. 12-7).

Normally, the apical impulse is palpable in only one intercostal space. Feeling the impulse in two or more adjacent intercostal spaces indicates left ventricular enlargement. A vibration or purring sensation felt over any of the precordial areas indicates abnormal, turbulent blood flow. It is best detected by using the palm of the hand. This vibration is called a *thrill*, which is associated with a loud murmur. Depending on the location of the thrill, it may be indicative of serious valvular heart disease or a defect (abnormal opening) in the septum of the atria or ventricles. Thrills that are palpated over blood vessels are associated with significant obstruction of a large artery, such as the carotid artery.

Auscultation of the Heart

A stethoscope is used to auscultate each of the locations, with the exception of the epigastric area, identified in Figure 12-6, to assess heart rate and rhythm, and to evaluate heart sounds. The apical area is auscultated for 1 minute to determine the apical pulse rate and the regularity of the heart beat.

Heart Sounds

NORMAL HEART SOUNDS. Normal heart sounds, referred to as S_1 and S_2, are produced by closure of the AV valves and the semilunar valves, respectively. The period between S_1 and S_2 corresponds with ventricular systole (Fig. 12-8). When the heart rate is within the normal range, diastole (period between S_2 and S_1) is twice as long as systole. However, as the heart rate increases, diastole shortens.

S_1—FIRST HEART SOUND. Tricuspid and mitral valve closure creates the first heart sound (S_1). The word "lub" is used to

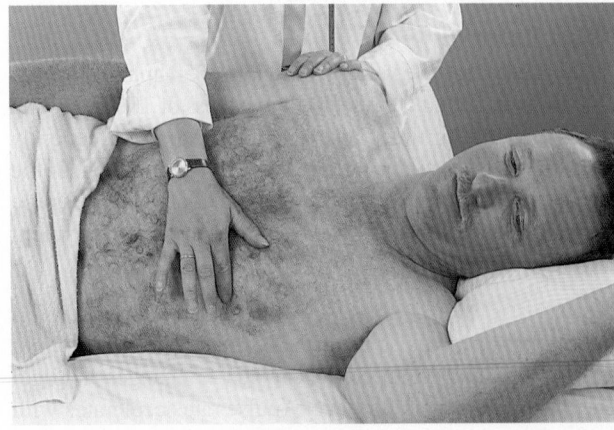

FIGURE 12-7 Locating and palpating the apical impulse, also called the point of maximal impulse (PMI), in the left lateral position. The apical pulse is normally located at the fifth intercostal space to the left of the sternum at the midclavicular line. The nurse locates the impulse with the palm of the hand and palpates with the fingerpads. © B. Proud.

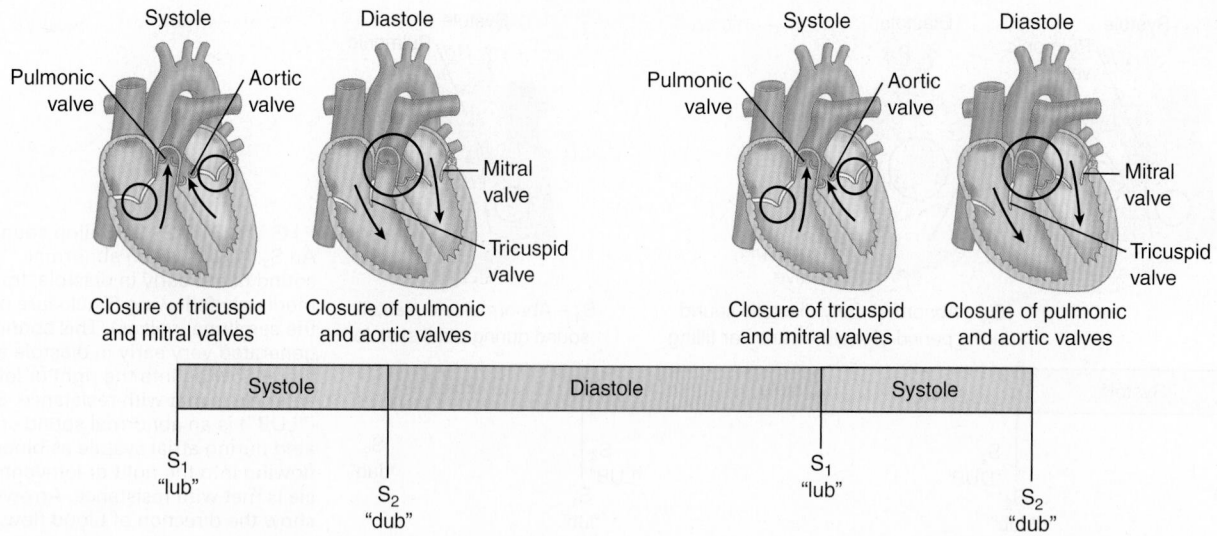

FIGURE 12-8 Normal heart sounds. The first heart sound (S_1) is produced by closure of the mitral and tricuspid valves ("lub"). The second heart sound (S_2) is produced by closure of the aortic and pulmonic valves ("dub"). Arrows represent the direction of blood flow during systole and diastole.

replicate its sound. S_1 is usually heard the loudest at the apical area. S_1 is easily identifiable and serves as the point of reference for the remainder of the cardiac cycle. If you are having difficulty determining S_1 from S_2, palpate the pulse, which will cue you into the S_1.

S_2—SECOND HEART SOUND. Closure of the pulmonic and aortic valves produces the second heart sound (S_2), commonly referred to as the "dub" sound. S_2 is heard the loudest over the aortic and pulmonic areas.

ABNORMAL HEART SOUNDS. Abnormal sounds develop during systole or diastole when structural or functional heart problems are present.

S_3—THIRD HEART SOUND. An S_3 is an abnormal sound heard early in diastole as blood flows from the atrium into a noncompliant ventricle. It is heard immediately after S_2. "Lub-dub-DUB" is used to imitate the abnormal sound of a beating heart when an S_3 (DUB) is present. It represents a normal finding in children and young adults, up to 35 or 40 years of age. In these cases it is called a *physiologic S_3* (Fig. 12-9). In adults, S_3 is a significant finding, suggesting HF. It is heard best by using the bell of the stethoscope with the patient in the left lateral position.

S_4—FOURTH HEART SOUND. S_4 occurs late in diastole (see Fig. 12-9). S_4, heard just before S_1, is generated during atrial contraction as blood forcefully enters a noncompliant ventricle. This resistance to blood flow is due to ventricular hypertrophy caused by hypertension, CAD, cardiomyopathies, aortic stenosis, and numerous other conditions. The mnemonic used to imitate this gallop sound is "LUB-lub-dub." S_4 (LUB) is auscultated using the bell of the stethoscope over the apical area with the patient in the left lateral position. There are times when both S_3 and S_4 are present, creating a quadruple rhythm, which sounds like "LUB lub-dub DUB." During a tachycardia, all four sounds combine into a loud sound, referred to as a *summation gallop*.

SNAPS AND CLICKS. Opening and closing of diseased valve leaflets create abnormal sounds, called snaps and clicks. Opening snaps are high-pitched diastolic sounds heard as stenotic AV valves are forced open. Systolic clicks, a brief high-pitched sound, are heard early in systole as ridged, calcified semilunar valves are forced open during ventricular contraction. These sounds are the loudest in the areas directly over the diseased valve.

MURMURS. These are a result of turbulent blood flow across rigid, calcified valves; leaky valves that allow backward blood flow (regurgitation); defects (abnormal openings) in the septum, aorta, or pulmonary artery; or abnormally high velocity of blood flow through a normal structure (e.g., with fever, pregnancy, hyperthyroidism). Murmurs are described by several characteristics (see Box 12-3) that are used to determine the cause and clinical significance.

FRICTION RUB. A harsh, grating sound that can be heard in both systole and diastole is called a friction rub. It is caused by abrasion of the inflamed pericardial surfaces from pericarditis. A pericardial friction rub can be heard best using the diaphragm of the stethoscope, with the patient sitting up and leaning forward.

Auscultative Procedure

During auscultation, the patient remains supine. Using the diaphragm of the stethoscope, the nurse auscultates the precordium to identify S_1 and S_2 and then listens for abnormal systolic or diastolic sounds. Repositioning the patient into the left lateral position may facilitate detection of S_3, S_4, and murmurs. The characteristics of abnormal findings are

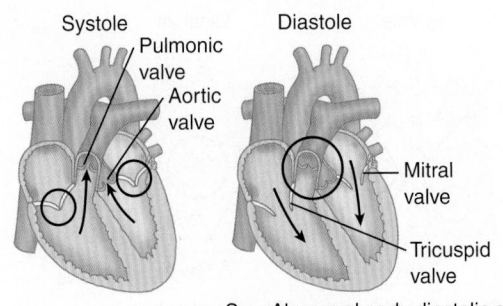

S₃ – Abnormal early diastolic sound
during period of rapid ventricular filling

S_3 – Abnormal early diastolic sound during period of rapid ventricular filling

S_4 – Abnormal late diastolic sound during atrial systole

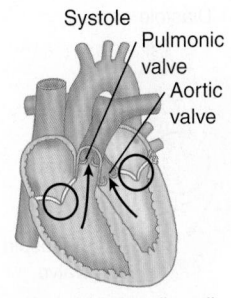

Systole	Diastole	Systole

S_1 "lub"

S_3 "DUB"

S_2 "dub"

S_4 "LUB"

S_1 "lub"

S_2 "dub"

FIGURE 12-9 Gallop sounds. An S_3 ("DUB") is an abnormal sound heard early in diastole, immediately following S_2 (closure of the semilunar valves). This sound is generated very early in diastole as blood flowing into the right or left ventricle is met with resistance. S_4 ("LUB") is an abnormal sound created during atrial systole as blood flowing into the right or left ventricle is met with resistance. Arrows show the direction of blood flow.

documented by identifying the location, timing, intensity, pitch, quality, and presence of radiation (see Box 12-3).

Evaluation of Other Systems

Lungs

The details of the respiratory assessment are described in Chapter 8. Abnormal findings exhibited by patients with CVD include the following:

- *Hemoptysis*: Pink, frothy sputum indicative of acute pulmonary edema.
- *Cough*: A dry, hacking cough from irritation of small airways from pulmonary congestion associated with HF.
- *Crackles*: Typically, first noted at the bases (due to the effect of gravity on fluid accumulation and decreased ventilation of basilar tissue). Crackles may progress to all portions of the lung fields as a result of worsening HF or atelectasis associated with bed rest, splinting from ischemic pain, or the effects of analgesics, sedatives, or anesthetic agents.
- *Wheezes*: Compression of the small airways by interstitial pulmonary edema may cause wheezing. Beta-adrenergic blocking agents (beta-blockers), such as propranolol (Inderal), may cause airway narrowing, especially in patients with underlying pulmonary disease.

Abdomen

The abdomen is assessed for distention and ascites, hepatojugular reflux, and pulsatile mass.

- *Abdominal distension*: A protuberant abdomen with bulging flanks indicates ascites. Ascites develops in the late stages of HF as abnormally high pressures in the right heart impede the return of venous blood. As a result, the liver and spleen become engorged with excessive venous blood (hepatosplenomegaly). As pressure in the portal system rises, fluid shifts from the vascular bed into the abdominal cavity. Ascitic fluid, found in the dependent or lowest points in the abdomen, will shift with position changes.
- *Hepatojugular reflux*: This test is performed when right ventricular or biventricular HF is suspected. The patient is positioned so that the jugular venous pulse is visible in the lower part of the neck. While observing the jugular venous pulse, firm pressure is applied over the right upper quadrant of the abdomen for 30 to 60 seconds. An increase of 1 cm or more in jugular venous pressure is indicative of a positive hepatojugular reflux. This positive test aids in confirming the diagnosis of HF.

- *Pulsatile mass*: The most important diagnostic indication of an abdominal aortic **aneurysm** (a localized dilation formed at a weak point in the arterial wall) is a pulsatile mass in the middle and upper abdomen. About 80% of aneurysms that are 5 cm or larger can be palpated. A systolic **bruit** (abnormal sound associated with turbulent blood flow in an artery) may be heard over the mass.

Gerontologic Considerations

Peripheral pulses of elderly patients are readily palpable because of decreased elasticity of the arteries and a loss of adjacent connective tissue. In older patients, symptoms of PAD may be more pronounced than in younger patients. Intermittent claudication may occur after walking only a few blocks or after walking up a slight incline. Prolonged pressure exerted on areas of the toes or feet further compromises arterial perfusion, which can lead to ulceration, infection, and gangrene.

Isolated systolic hypertension, associated with significant cardiovascular morbidity and mortality, is a common finding in the elderly. There is a higher risk for postural hypotension in the elderly, reflecting a decrease in the sensitivity of the postural reflexes and must be considered prior to prescribing new cardiovascular medications.

It may be difficult to palpate the PMI or detect audible heart sounds due to changes in the shape of the chest (e.g., chronic obstructive lung disease) and spinal deformities (e.g., kyphoscoliosis), which worsen with the aging process. When heart sounds are audible, an S_4 is detectable in most elderly patients, caused by a decrease in compliance of the left ventricle. The S_2 is usually split, meaning that the semilunar valves are not closing simultaneously. Murmurs are also audible in more than one-half of elderly patients due to sclerotic changes in the aortic valve. These murmurs are heard over the aortic valve during systole (systolic ejection murmur).

Diagnostic Evaluation

Diagnostic tests and procedures are used to confirm the data obtained by the history and physical assessment. Some tests are easy to interpret, but others must be interpreted by expert clinicians. All tests should be explained to the patient. Some necessitate special preparation before they are performed and special monitoring by the nurse after the procedure.

Laboratory Tests

Laboratory tests may be performed for the following reasons:

- To assist in identifying the cause of cardiovascular signs and symptoms
- To identify abnormalities in the blood that effect the prognosis of a patient with CVD
- To assess the degree of inflammation
- To screen for risk factors associated with CAD
- To determine baseline values before initiating therapeutic interventions

- To ensure that therapeutic levels of medications (e.g., antiarrhythmic agents and warfarin) are maintained
- To assess the effects of medications (e.g., the effects of diuretics on serum potassium levels)

Because different laboratories use various types of equipment and methods of measurements, normal test values may vary depending on the laboratory and the health care institution.

Cardiac Biomarker Analysis

Plasma levels of cardiac biomarkers are used to diagnose acute MI in conjunction with the history, physical examination, and ECG. These substances leak into the bloodstream after injured myocardial cells rupture their cell membranes. Biomarkers have a specific timeline for when they first rise, peak, and return to normal. This timeline helps the clinician decide which test to order, based on the timing of patient's symptom onset.

- *Creatine kinase (CK)/CK-MB*: CK is released from three types of damaged tissue (myocardium, skeletal muscle, brain). CK-MB is the cardiac-specific isoenzyme that rises within 4 to 8 hours after myocardial injury, peaks in 12 to 24 hours, and returns to normal within 3 to 4 days.
- *Myoglobin*: This heme protein transports oxygen. Its small molecular structure allows it to be rapidly released from damaged myocardial tissue and accounts for its early rise. Myoglobin is not used alone to diagnose MI, because elevations can also occur in patients with renal or musculoskeletal disease. However, negative results are helpful in ruling out acute MI. Myoglobin rises within 1 to 3 hours of tissue injury, peaks in 4 to 12 hours, and returns to normal in 24 hours.
- *Troponin T and I*: These heme proteins regulate the contractile function of the myocardium. After myocardial injury, these biomarkers rise early (within 3 to 4 hours), peak in 4 to 24 hours, and remain elevated for 1 to 3 weeks. These early and prolonged elevations make very early diagnosis of acute MI possible and allow for late diagnosis in patients who have delayed seeking care for several days after the onset of acute MI symptoms.

Blood Chemistry, Hematology, and Coagulation Studies

Table 12-4 provides information about common serum laboratory tests and the implications for patients with CVD.

LIPID PROFILE. The lipid profile helps evaluate a person's risk for developing atherosclerosis or to diagnose a specific lipoprotein abnormality. Cholesterol and triglycerides are transported in the blood by combining with protein molecules to form lipoproteins. The lipoproteins are referred to as low-density lipoproteins (LDL) and high-density lipoproteins (HDL). The risk of CAD increases as the ratio of LDL to HDL or the ratio of total cholesterol (LDL + HDL) to HDL increases. The blood specimen for the lipid profile should be obtained after a 12-hour fast.

Laboratory Test/Reference Range	Implications
Blood Chemistries Sodium (Na^+) 135–145 mEq/L	*Hyponatremia:* ↓ Na levels can be due to thiazide diuretics or from fluid excess, as seen in HF *Hypernatremia:* ↑ Na levels indicate fluid deficits and can result from ↓ water intake or hypovolemia.
Potassium (K^+) 3.5–5 mEq/L	*Hypokalemia:* ↓ K levels often due to use of K-excreting diuretics, which can cause ventricular tachycardia and fibrillation and predispose digitalis toxicity in patients taking digoxin. *Hyperkalemia:* ↑ K levels due to ↑ intake of foods high in K or overuse of K supplements; ↓ renal excretion of K; use of K-sparing diuretics (e.g., spironolactone); or use of angiotensin-converting enzyme inhibitors (ACE inhibitors). Can cause heart block, asystole, and ventricular arrhythmias.
Calcium (Ca^{++}) 8.5–10.2 mg/dL	Necessary for blood coagulability, neuromuscular activity, and automaticity of the sinoatrial and atrioventricular nodes. *Hypocalcemia:* ↓ calcium levels slow nodal function and impair myocardial contractility. Latter effect ↑ risk of HF. *Hypercalcemia:* ↑ Ca levels are associated with use of thiazide diuretics that ↓ renal excretion of Ca. Hypercalcemia potentiates digitalis toxicity, causes ↑ myocardial contractility, and ↑ risk of heart block and ventricular fibrillation.
Magnesium (Mg^{++}) 1.3–2.3 mEq/L	Needed to absorb Ca, maintain K stores, metabolize adenosine triphosphate, synthesize protein and carbohydrate, and maintain muscular contraction. *Hypomagnesemia:* ↓ Mg levels are due to enhanced renal excretion of Mg from diuretic or digitalis therapy. ↓ Mg levels predispose patients to atrial or ventricular tachycardias. *Hypermagnesemia:* ↑ magnesium levels are caused by use of cathartics or antacids containing Mg. ↑ Mg levels depress myocardial contractility and excitability heart block or asystole.
Blood urea nitrogen (BUN) 10–20 mg/dL Creatinine Males: 0.9–1.4 mg/dL Females: 0.8–1.3 mg/dl	End products of protein metabolism excreted by the kidneys. Renal impairment is detected by an ↑ in BUN and creatinine. A normal creatinine level and an ↑ BUN detect an intravascular fluid volume deficit, bleeding, or increased protein intake.
Glucose (fasting): 65–110 mg/dL	↑ Glucose levels result from stress as endogenous epinephrine is mobilized to convert of liver glycogen to glucose.
Glycosylated hemoglobin (HbA$_{1c}$) 2.2%–4.8%	Monitored in people with diabetes, as it reflects blood glucose levels over 2 to 3 months. Goal: hemoglobin A$_{1C}$ <7%.
Coagulation Studies Activated partial thromboplastin time (aPTT) 23–32 seconds	It is used to monitor patient's response to unfractionated heparin. Heparin dose is adjusted to maintain a therapeutic range of 1.5–2.5 times baseline values. aPTT is a more sensitive version of partial thromboplastin time (PTT) used to monitor heparin therapy.
Prothrombin time (PT) 12–15 seconds	Measures the activity of five factors in the blood clotting pathway (prothrombin, fibrinogen, factors V, VII, X). Used to monitor patients on warfarin therapy. Therapeutic range is 1.5–2 times normal.
International Normalized Ratio (INR)	Standardized method for monitoring prothrombin levels in patients receiving warfarin therapy. Therapeutic range 2–3.5, depending upon diagnosis.
Hematologic Studies Complete blood count (CBC)	Identifies the total number of white and red blood cells and platelets, and measures hemoglobin and hematocrit.
White blood cell count (WBC) 4,500–11,000/mm^3	WBC counts are monitored in immunocompromised patients (e.g., post heart transplant) or those at risk for infection (e.g., after invasive procedures or surgery).
Hematocrit Male: 40–50% Female: 38–47% Hemoglobin Male: 13.5–18 g/100 mL Female: 12–16 g/100 mL	Represents the percentage of red blood cells found in 100 mL of whole blood. The red blood cells contain hemoglobin, which transports oxygen to the cells. Low hemoglobin and hematocrit levels can cause more frequent angina episodes or acute MI in patients with cardiovascular diseases.
Platelets 150,000–400,000/mm^3	Initiate thrombus formation by clumping together at sites of vessel wall injury. Monitor for thrombocytopenia if aspirin, clopidogrel (Plavix), eptifibatide [Integrilin], or tirofiban [Aggrastat] is prescribed.

CHOLESTEROL LEVELS. Cholesterol is a lipid required for hormone synthesis and cell membrane formation. Cholesterol comes from the diet (animal products) and the liver, where cholesterol is synthesized. Elevated cholesterol levels increase the risk of atherosclerosis. Factors that contribute to variations in cholesterol levels include age, gender, diet, exercise patterns, genetics, menopause, tobacco use, and stress levels. Normal level is less than 200 mg/dL.

LDL is the primary transporter of cholesterol and triglycerides into the cell. One harmful effect of LDL is the deposition of these substances into the walls of arteries. Normal level is less than 160 mg/dL. Elevated LDL levels are associated with a greater incidence of CAD. In people with known CAD or diabetes, the LDL goal is less than 70 mg/dL.

HDL has a protective action by transporting cholesterol away from the arterial wall to the liver for excretion. Normal level for men is 35 to 70 mg/dL, for women, 35 to 85 mg/dL. Higher HDL levels are known to lower CAD risk, therefore, an HDL level over 40 mg/dL is desirable in patients with known CAD. Factors associated with lowering HDL levels are smoking, diabetes, obesity, and physical inactivity.

TRIGLYCERIDES. Triglycerides, composed of free fatty acids and glycerol, are stored in the adipose tissue and are a source of energy. Normal level is less than 150 mg/dL. Triglyceride levels increase after meals and are affected by stress. Diabetes, alcohol use, and obesity can elevate triglyceride levels. Triglyceride levels have a direct correlation with LDL and an inverse one with HDL.

BRAIN (B-TYPE) NATRIURETIC PEPTIDE. Brain (B-type) natriuretic peptide (BNP), secreted from the ventricles, is a neurohormone that responds to volume overload in the heart by acting as a diuretic and vasodilator. BNP levels are useful for the prompt diagnosis of HF. A BNP level of 100 to 300 pg/mL indicates HF is present, and increasingly higher values are correlated with greater severity of HF.

C-REACTIVE PROTEIN. C-Reactive protein (CRP) is protein produced by the liver in response to systemic inflammation. Inflammation is thought to play a role in the development and progression of atherosclerosis. High levels of CRP (3.0 mg/dL) are used as an adjunct to other tests to predict CAD risk.

HOMOCYSTEINE. Homocysteine, an amino acid, can damage the endothelial lining of arteries and promote thrombus formation. Elevated levels are linked to the development of atherosclerosis and an increased risk for CAD, stroke, and peripheral vascular disease. Elevated homocysteine levels are associated with genetic factors and a diet low in folic acid, vitamin B_6, and vitamin B_{12}. A 12-hour fast is necessary prior to obtaining the blood sample. Test results are interpreted as normal (5 to 15 µmol/L), moderate (16 to 30 µmol/L), intermediate (31 to 100 µmol/L), and severe (more than 100 µmol/L).

Electrocardiogram

The ECG is a graphic recording of the electrical activity of the heart. The ECG is obtained by placing disposable electrodes in standard positions on the skin of the chest wall and extremities. The standard 12-lead ECG records electrical impulses of the heart on special graph paper from 12 different reference points referred to as *leads*. It is used to diagnose arrhythmias, conduction abnormalities, enlarged heart chambers, and myocardial ischemia or infarction.

The ECG is continuously observed by placing the patient on a bedside (hardwire) monitor or **telemetry** (battery-operated transmitting device worn by the patient), both of which transmit to a central bank of monitors. The telemetry system is wireless and allows patients to be monitored while ambulating. Patients requiring ECG monitoring need to be informed of the purpose of the monitoring and cautioned that it does not detect symptoms such as dyspnea or chest pain. Therefore, patients need to be advised to report symptoms to the nurse whenever they occur. Continuous ECG monitoring is discussed in Chapter 17.

Stress Testing

Stress testing is used to evaluate the response of the cardiovascular system to increased demands for oxygen and nutrients. It is used to determine the (1) presence of atherosclerosis in the arteries of the heart and lower extremities, (2) functional capacity of the heart after an MI or heart surgery, and (3) effectiveness of the medical regimen.

Procedure

During an exercise stress test, the patient walks on a treadmill (most common), pedals a stationary bicycle, or uses an arm crank. Exercise intensity progresses according to established protocols in which the speed and grade of the treadmill are increased every few minutes. If the patient is unable to exercise, a pharmacologic stress test is performed by injecting a vasodilating agent (dipyridamole [Persantine] or adenosine [Adenocard]) to mimic the physiologic effects of exercise. The stress test may be combined with an echocardiogram or radionuclide imaging techniques to examine myocardial function during exercise and at rest.

Throughout the test, the patient is assessed for signs and symptoms of myocardial or leg ischemia (claudication) by monitoring the ECG, BP, physical appearance, perceived exertion, and symptoms, including chest pain, dyspnea, dizziness, leg cramping, and fatigue. The stress test is said to be "positive" if evidence of myocardial ischemia is detected by changes in the patient's ECG or claudication is validated by a decrease in ankle pressure. A positive stress test is an indication for additional testing.

Nursing Interventions

Patients are instructed to fast for 4 hours before the test, avoiding tobacco, caffeine, and other stimulants. Medications may be taken with sips of water. Clothes and rubber-soled shoes suitable for exercising should be worn. The nurse

describes the monitoring equipment, symptoms to report, and reviews the exercise protocol and the need for the patient to put forth his or her best efforts to complete the test. If vasodilating agents are used, patients are informed that they may have transient flushing or nausea. If the stress test is to be combined with imaging techniques, information related to these techniques is also reviewed. After the test, patients are monitored for 10 to 15 minutes or until stable, then patients may resume their usual activities.

Echocardiography

Traditional Echocardiography

Echocardiography, a noninvasive ultrasound test, is used to examine cardiac function.

PROCEDURE. A handheld transducer generates high-frequency sound waves through the chest wall into the heart and records the return signals for display on an oscilloscope and recording on a videotape. An ECG is recorded simultaneously to assist with interpreting the echocardiogram. Two-dimensional or cross-sectional echocardiography, an enhancement of this technique, creates a sophisticated, spatially correct image of the heart. Other techniques, such as Doppler and color flow imaging echocardiography, show the direction and velocity of the blood flow through the heart.

NURSING INTERVENTIONS. The nurse prepares the patient for the test by explaining that it is a painless procedure and that the transducer emits sound waves as it is moved across the surface of the chest wall. Gel applied to the skin helps transmit the sound waves. Periodically, the patient is asked to turn onto the left side or hold a breath. The test takes about 30 to 45 minutes.

Transesophageal Echocardiography

PROCEDURE. Transesophageal echocardiography (TEE) involves threading a small transducer through the mouth and into the esophagus. This technique provides clearer images than other ultrasound methods because ultrasound waves are passed through less dense tissue. It is an important diagnostic tool for determining if atrial or ventricular thrombi are present in patients with HF, valvular heart disease, and arrhythmias.

A topical anesthetic and moderate sedation are used during a TEE because of the discomfort associated with the positioning of the transducer. Once the patient is sedated, the transducer is inserted into the mouth and the patient is asked to swallow several times until it is positioned in the esophagus.

Complications are uncommon during TEE, but if they do occur they are serious. These complications are caused by sedation and impaired swallowing resulting from the topical anesthesia (respiratory depression and aspiration) and by insertion and manipulation of the transducer into the esophagus and stomach (vasovagal response or esophageal perforation). The patient must be assessed before TEE for a

history of dysphagia or radiation therapy to the chest, which increases the risk of complications.

NURSING INTERVENTIONS. Prior to the test, the nurse provides preprocedure education and ensures that patients have a clear understanding of what the test entails and why it is being performed. Patients are instructed to not eat or drink anything for 6 hours before the study; that an IV will be inserted to administer medications, including a sedative to keep the patient comfortable; and after the removal of dentures, a topical anesthetic agent is used to numb the throat. After the procedure, the nurse informs patients that they will remain in bed with head of bed elevation to 45 degrees, and will be offered something to drink as soon as they are recovered from the sedation and local anesthetic agent. Patients are reminded that a sore throat may be present for the next 24 hours. They are to report the presence of a persistent sore throat, shortness of breath, or difficulty swallowing. If the procedure is performed in an outpatient setting, patients must have someone transport them home.

The nurse follows the organization's moderate sedation policy. During the test, the nurse provides emotional support and monitors the patient's comfort level, level of consciousness, BP, ECG, respiration, and oxygen saturation (SpO$_2$). Liquids and food are withheld until patients are fully alert and the effect of the topical anesthetic agent is reversed, usually 2 hours. Once the patient begins taking liquids, the patient should be assessed for dysphagia (difficulty swallowing).

Radionuclide Imaging

Radionuclide imaging studies involve the use of radioisotopes to evaluate coronary artery perfusion noninvasively, to detect myocardial ischemia and infarction, and to assess left ventricular function. **Radioisotopes** are atoms in an unstable form. Thallium 201 (Tl^{201}) and technetium 99m (Tc^{99m}) are two radioisotopes used in cardiac nuclear medicine studies. As they decay, they give off small amounts of energy in the form of gamma rays. When they are injected into the bloodstream, the energy emitted can be detected by a gamma scintillation camera positioned over the body. Planar imaging, used with thallium, provides a one-dimensional view of the heart from three locations. Single photon emission computed tomography (SPECT) provides three-dimensional images. With SPECT, the patient is positioned supine with arms raised above the head, while the camera moves around the patient's chest in a 180- to 360-degree arc to identify the areas of decreased myocardial perfusion more precisely.

Myocardial Perfusion Imaging

The radioisotope Tl^{201}, better known as thallium, resembles potassium and readily crosses into the cells of healthy myocardium. It is taken up in smaller amounts by myocardial cells that are ischemic, but it does not cross into necrotic tissue (e.g., MI).

Thallium is used with exercise or pharmacologic stress testing to assess changes in myocardial perfusion at rest and

after exercise. At the end of the stress test, thallium is injected and images are taken immediately. Areas without thallium uptake indicate either MI or "stress-induced" myocardial ischemia. Resting images, taken 3 hours later, help differentiate infarction from ischemia. A previous MI is indicated if the defect (referred to as *lack of isotope uptake*) remains the same size during exercise and rest. Ischemic myocardium, on the other hand, recovers in a few hours. If perfusion is restored, thallium crosses into the myocardial cells, and the area of defect on the resting images is either smaller or completely reversed. A reversible defect constitutes a positive stress test. Further evaluation with cardiac catheterization is indicated to determine if percutaneous coronary intervention (PCI) or coronary artery bypass graft surgery is needed.

Tc^{99m} sestamibi (Cardiolite) is another radioisotope that is distributed to myocardial cells in proportion to its perfusion, making it an excellent tracer for assessing perfusion to the myocardium. Unlike thallium, resting images using Tc^{99m} sestamibi can be obtained before or after the exercise images, due to its short half-life and because it is injected before each scan. SPECT imaging, used with Tc^{99m} sestamibi, provides high-quality images.

The patient undergoing nuclear imaging techniques with stress testing should be prepared for the type of stressor to be used (exercise or drug) and the type of imaging technique (planar or SPECT). The patient may be concerned about receiving a radioactive substance and needs to be reassured that these tracers are safe—the radiation exposure is similar to that of other diagnostic X-ray studies. No postprocedure radiation precautions are necessary.

When providing teaching for a patient undergoing SPECT, the nurse instructs the patient that the arms will need to be positioned over the head for about 20 to 30 minutes. If the patient is physically unable to do this, thallium with planar imaging can be used.

Test of Ventricular Function and Wall Motion

Equilibrium radionuclide angiocardiography (ERNA), also known as multiple-gated acquisition (MUGA) scanning, is a noninvasive technique that uses a conventional scintillation camera interfaced with a computer to record images of the heart during several hundred heartbeats. The computer processes the data and allows for sequential images of the functioning heart. These images are analyzed to evaluate left ventricular function, wall motion, and EF. This scanning procedure can be used to assess for differences in left ventricular function during rest and exercise. The patient is reassured that there is no radiation danger and is instructed to remain motionless during the scan.

Cardiac Catheterization

This invasive diagnostic procedure uses fluoroscopy (an imaging technique that visualizes the heart on an X-ray screen) to guide catheter placement into the heart and to view

chambers and coronary arteries. This procedure is usually performed in the outpatient setting, unless the condition of the patient is serious enough to require hospitalization, such as HF or acute MI.

Cardiac catheterization is the gold standard for diagnosing CAD and quantifying the extent of coronary artery obstruction (reported as percentage of coronary artery obstruction). Cardiac catheterization is also used to diagnose pulmonary hypertension and valvular heart disease. Results of this procedure are used to determine if revascularization procedures (PCI or coronary artery bypass surgery) or valve replacement/repair are indicated.

Prior to the procedure, blood tests are performed to identify abnormalities that may complicate recovery. These tests include blood urea nitrogen, creatinine, complete blood cell count, electrolytes levels, and if the patient is on anticoagulants, prothrombin time (PT)/**International Normalized Ratio (INR)** (warfarin) or activated thromboplastin time (aPTT) (heparin).

During cardiac catheterization, the patient has an IV catheter in place for the administration of sedatives, fluids, heparin, and other medications. BP and multiple ECG leads are monitored to observe for hemodynamic instability and arrhythmias. In addition, an important role of the nurse is to prepare the patient and family for the cardiac catheterization. Box 12-4 outlines the information that should be reviewed prior to the procedure.

Procedure

RIGHT-HEART CATHETERIZATION. Right-heart catheterization is performed to evaluate pressures and oxygen saturations in the right heart chambers and the function of the tricuspid and pulmonary valves. It involves the passage of a catheter from an antecubital or femoral vein into the right

---

BOX 12-4 | **Patient Education**

Preparing for a Cardiac Catheterization

Goal: To assure adequate preparation for the procedure

- Express concerns or fears you have about the procedure.
- Fast, usually for 8 to 12 hours, before the procedure.
- Understand the procedure involves lying on a hard table for about an hour.
- Medications will be given to maintain comfort.
- It is normal to experience palpitations due to extra heartbeats that can occur as the catheter is advanced through the heart. Flushing and a sensation similar to the need to void may occur after injection of the contrast agent, which subsides in 1 minute or less.

atrium, right ventricle, and pulmonary artery. Complications, although rare, include arrhythmias, infection, and perforation of the septum or chamber wall.

LEFT-HEART CATHETERIZATION. Left-heart catheterization is performed to evaluate the patency of the coronary arteries and the function of the left ventricle and the mitral and aortic valves. It is performed by the insertion of a catheter into the brachial or femoral artery that is advanced into the aorta, left ventricle, and coronary arteries. Rare complications include arrhythmias, acute MI, perforation of the heart or great vessels, and systemic embolization.

ANGIOGRAPHY. Angiography involves the injection of a contrast agent into the vascular system to visualize the heart and blood vessels. *Coronary angiography* is produced through the injection of the contrast agent into the coronary arteries to determine patency. An *aortogram* is produced through the injection of the contrast agent to highlight the aorta and its major arteries.

Prior to the cardiac catheterization, the patient is assessed for previous reactions to contrast agents or allergies to iodine-containing substances (e.g., seafood), as some contrast agents contain iodine. If allergic reactions are of concern, antihistamines or methylprednisolone (Solu-Medrol) may be administered to the patient before angiography is performed.

Contrast agents can induce contrast-induced nephropathy, a form of acute renal failure in patients who have diabetes, HF, renal insufficiency or renal disease, hypotension, or dehydration. Preventive strategies under investigation in these high-risk patients include pre- and postprocedure IV hydration with saline or sodium bicarbonate, and the administration of the antioxidant acetylcysteine (Mucomyst) (Briguori, Airoldi, D'Andrea et al., 2007).

ARTERIAL HEMOSTASIS. Once the arterial catheter is removed, either manual pressure, mechanical compression devices, percutaneously deployed vascular closure devices, or external patches are used to achieve hemostasis. Major benefits of the vascular closure devices include immediate hemostasis and a shorter time on bed rest. Rare complications associated with these devices include bleeding around the closure device, infection, and arterial obstruction.

Nursing Interventions

After cardiac catheterization, the nurse:

- Assesses the catheter access site frequently for bleeding or hematoma formation.
- Assesses for arrhythmias using cardiac monitoring or by assessing the apical and peripheral pulses for a pulse deficit. A vagal response, causing bradycardia and hypotension, can be triggered by discomfort from manual pressure used to obtain hemostasis as the arterial or venous catheter

is removed. It is reversed by promptly elevating the lower extremities above heart level, infusing IV fluid, and administering IV atropine to treat the bradycardia, as prescribed.

- Maintains bed rest for 2 to 6 hours after the procedure until hemostasis of the involved blood vessels is achieved. Variations in time on bedrest is dependent on the size of the catheter used, catheter insertion site, anticoagulation status of the patient, and other patient variables (e.g., advanced age, obesity, bleeding disorder). If manual or mechanical pressure was used, bed rest is maintained for up to 6 hours with the affected leg straight and the head elevated to 30 degrees. For comfort, the patient may be turned from side to side with the affected extremity straight. If a percutaneous closure device or patch was deployed, the nurse reviews local nursing care standards and anticipates that the patient will have fewer activity restrictions. Analgesic medication is administered for discomfort.
- Instructs the patient to report chest pain and bleeding or sudden discomfort from the catheter insertion sites immediately.
- Assesses for contrast agent–induced renal failure by monitoring for an increase in creatinine levels. Oral and IV hydration is used to flush the contrast agent from the urinary tract; accurate intake and output are recorded.
- Ensures patient safety by instructing the patient to ask for help when getting out of bed the first time. The patient is assessed for bleeding from the catheter access site and for orthostatic hypotension.
- Provides patients with additional instructions at time of discharge (see Box 12-5).

Hemodynamic Monitoring

Hemodynamic monitoring continuously assesses the cardiovascular function of critically ill patients. It requires a special catheter and pressure monitoring system composed of a continuous flushing device to maintain catheter patency, a transducer to convert the pressure coming from the artery or heart chamber into an electrical signal, and a monitor, which displays the pressure waveform on a bedside oscilloscope.

Procedure

CENTRAL VENOUS PRESSURE MONITORING. CVP is measured by positioning a catheter in the vena cava (superior or inferior) or right atrium. It reflects right ventricle preload, because pressure in the vena cava, right atrium, and right ventricle are all equal at the end of diastole. Normal CVP is 2 to 8 mm Hg. A CVP of greater than 8 mm Hg indicates hypervolemia (excessive fluid circulating in the body) or right-sided HF. On the contrary, a CVP of less than 2 mm Hg indicates a reduction in preload or hypovolemia. Complications of CVP monitoring are infection, pneumothorax, and air embolism.

Patient Education

Self-Management After Cardiac Catheterization

Goal: To assure that patients have information they need to reduce the risk of postprocedure complications and to understand their treatment plan.

- For the next 24 hours, do not bend at the waist, strain, or lift heavy objects.
- Avoid tub baths, but shower as desired.
- Ask your provider about when you may resume your usual activities.
- Call your provider if you have any bleeding, swelling, new bruising, or pain from your procedure puncture site, or a temperature of 101.5°F (38.6°C) or more.
- Talk with your provider about getting assistance with lifestyle changes to reduce your risk for future heart problems. If test results show that you have coronary artery disease, ask your provider to refer you to a local cardiac rehabilitation program.
- Your provider may prescribe new medications. If you suspect that any of these are causing side effects, call your provider immediately. Do not stop taking any medications before talking to your doctor.

PULMONARY ARTERY PRESSURE MONITORING. Pulmonary artery (PA) pressure monitoring involves the use of a balloon-tipped catheter that is inserted through a large vein (subclavian, jugular, or femoral) and connected to the pressure monitoring system (see Fig. 12-10). The catheter is threaded through the right side of the heart into the PA. It is used in critically ill patients to measure the cardiac output and right atrial, PA systolic and diastolic, and pulmonary capillary wedge pressures (see Fig. 12-5, p. 358 for normal pressures).

The PA diastolic and pulmonary artery wedge pressures are used most often because they reflect left ventricular preload. These readings are possible because, at the end of diastole, when the ventricle is completely filled and the mitral valve is open, there is equalization of pressure within all left heart chambers and vessels (left ventricle and atrium, pulmonary veins and arteries). The PA diastolic and pulmonary artery wedge pressures are used to diagnose the etiology of shock and evaluate the response of the patient's cardiovascular system to medical interventions.

The pulmonary capillary wedge pressure is obtained by inflating the balloon tip that causes the catheter to float out into a smaller branch of the PA. This is an occlusive maneuver, therefore, the measurement must be taken immediately, the balloon deflated, and the waveform assessed to ensure that the catheter returned to its normal position in the PA.

Complications of PA pressure monitoring include infection, PA rupture, pulmonary thromboembolism, pulmonary infarction, arrhythmias, and air embolism.

INTRA-ARTERIAL BP MONITORING. Intra-arterial BP monitoring is used to obtain continuous systolic, diastolic, and mean arterial pressure (MAP) readings and blood samples. MAP is used to reflect the perfusion pressure to major organs. During one cardiac cycle, the heart spends two-thirds of the time in diastole, compared with systole. The formula for calculating MAP is: MAP = (2 × diastolic) + systolic/3. The cardiac monitor automatically makes the calculation, or if the BP is taken by cuff pressure, it can be manually calculated. Major organs require a MAP of 60 mmHg (normal range 70 to 110 mmHg).

The Allen test is used to assess for adequate perfusion of the hand via the ulnar artery prior to cannulating the radial artery for pressure monitoring. The Allen test is performed by compressing the radial and ulnar arteries simultaneously and asking the patient to make a fist, which causes the hand to blanch. After the patient opens the fist, the nurse releases the pressure on the ulnar artery while maintaining pressure on the radial artery. The patient's hand will turn pink if the ulnar artery is patent. If other arteries are selected for cannulation, a Doppler ultrasound is used to assess perfusion to the involved limb.

Complications associated with arterial monitoring include arterial obstruction with distal ischemia, hemorrhage, air embolism, arteriospasm, and infection.

Nursing Interventions

Nurses receive comprehensive training prior to using hemodynamic monitoring technologies. The following guidelines are used to ensure safe and effective care:

- The insertion site is prepared following local hospital policy, which includes clipping excessive hair, cleansing with an antiseptic solution, and using a local anesthetic.
- CVP and pulmonary artery catheters are used for infusing IV fluids and drugs, and drawing blood specimens.
- The nurse assures that the system is set up and maintained properly. The pressure monitoring system must be kept patent, free of air bubbles, and calibrated to atmospheric pressure (referred to as the zero reference point).
- Before the pressure measurements are obtained, the nurse positions the stopcock of the transducer at the phlebostatic axis. Figure 12-11 describes landmarks to use to locate the phlebostatic axis.
- The pressure monitoring system and catheter insertion site dressing are changed according to hospital policy. In general, the dressing is kept dry and air occlusive. Dressing changes are performed using sterile technique.
- CVP and pulmonary artery catheter placement is confirmed by chest X-ray.

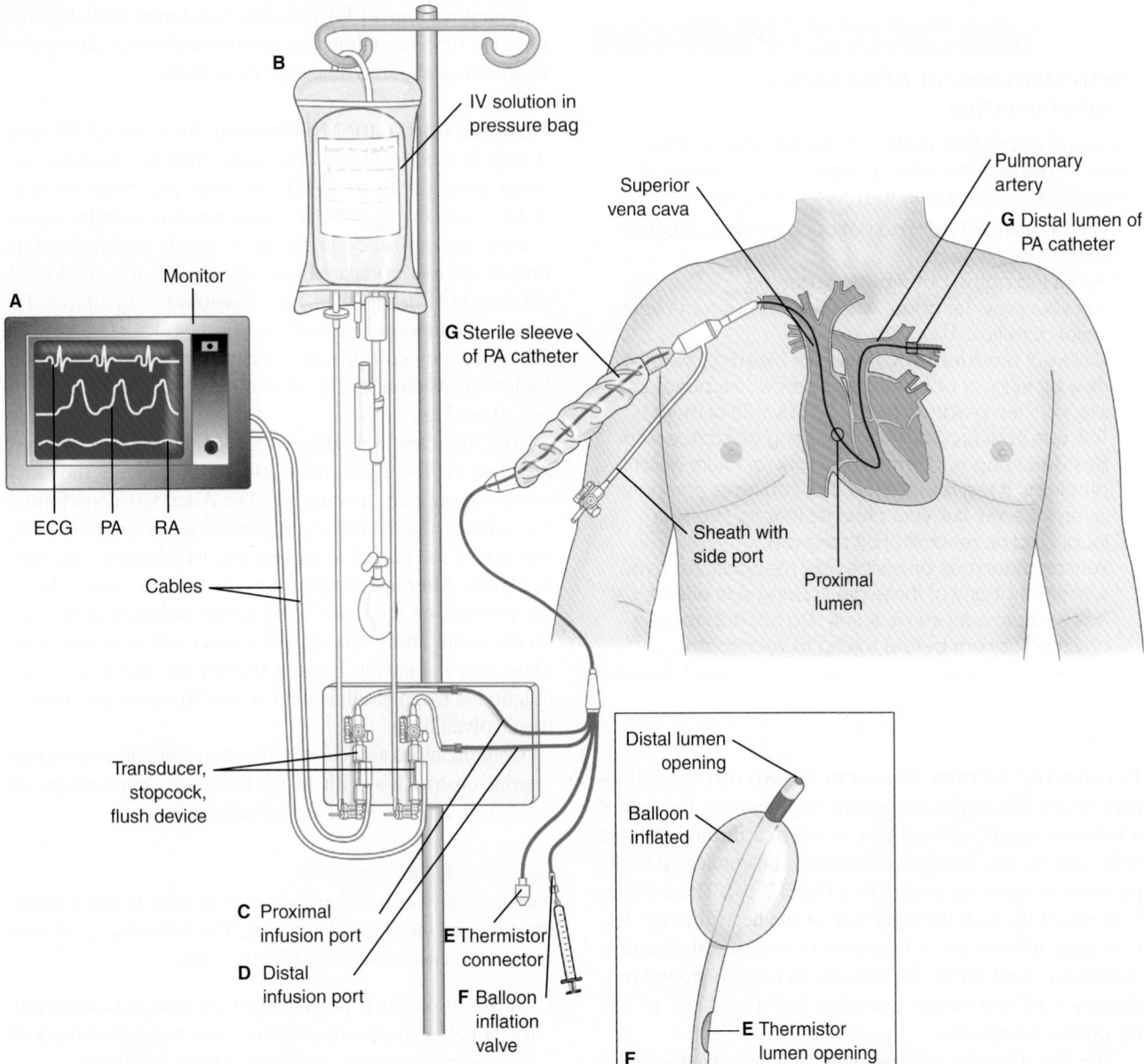

FIGURE 12-10 Pulmonary artery (PA) catheter and pressure monitoring systems. **(A)** Bedside monitor that connects with cables to **(B)** the pressure monitoring systems (includes IV solution in a pressure bag, IV tubing, and two transducers with stopcocks and flush devices). This system connects to **(C)** the proximal infusion port that opens in the right atria and is used to infuse fluids or medications and monitor central venous pressures and **(D)** the distal infusion port. This port opens in the PA and is used to monitor PA pressures. **(E)** The thermistor connector is attached to the bedside cardiac monitor to obtain cardiac output. **(F)** An air filled-syringe is attached to the balloon inflation valve during catheter insertion and measurement of PA wedge pressure. **(G)** PA catheter positioned in the PA. Note the sterile sleeve over the PA catheter. The PA catheter is threaded through the sheath until it reaches the desired position in the PA. The side port on the sheath is used to infuse medications or fluids. ECG, electrocardiogram; RA, right atrium.

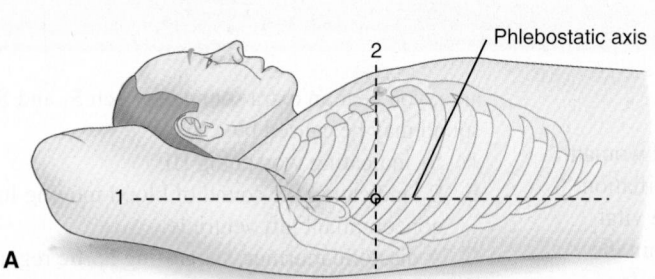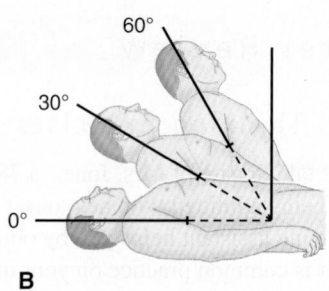

FIGURE 12-11 **(A)** The phlebostatic axis is the reference point for the atrium when the patient is in supine position. It is the intersection of two lines on the left chest wall.
(1) the midaxillary line drawn between the anterior and posterior surfaces of the chest and (2) the line drawn through the fourth intercostal space. Its location is identified with a skin marker. The stopcock of the transducer used in hemodynamic monitoring is "leveled" at this mark prior to obtaining pressure measurements. **(B)** Measurements can be taken with the head of the bed (HOB) elevated to 60 degrees. Note the phlebostatic axis changes as the HOB is elevated, so that the stopcock and the transducer must be repositioned after each position change.

- The nurse monitors the patient for complications associated with the various forms of hemodynamic monitoring and reports findings immediately.

Doppler Ultrasound Flow Studies

Doppler ultrasound studies are most often used to detect obstruction of blood flow to the extremities or head due to a thrombus and determine if atherosclerosis is present in the lower extremities in patients with intermittent claudication. This technology uses a handheld device, called a *transducer*, which sends and receives sound waves that "echo" or bounce off of blood cells. The transducer is placed in contact with the skin over the blood vessel being examined. Normally,

the transducer detects rhythmic changes in the sound waves that are generated as blood cells flow through patent blood vessels. Obstruction to blood flow is evidenced by no change in sound waves.

Standard Doppler ultrasound studies are combined with computer technology to provide additional information about blood flow. Duplex Doppler ultrasound provides a picture of the blood vessel and a graph describing the speed and direction of blood flow and color Doppler ultrasound produces colors to visualize these dimensions of blood flow.

When the nurse has difficulty finding a pulse, the continuous wave Doppler, a portable device, can be used. This device is used to hear, rather than feel the pulse. Box 12-6 describes how to use the continuous wave Doppler to evaluate pulses in the lower extremities.

The continuous wave Doppler is also used to obtain systolic BPs in the extremities to calculate the **ankle-brachial index (ABI)**. This ratio compares the ankle to arm systolic BPs and is an indicator of perfusion to the lower extremities. The ABI for each lower extremity is calculated by selecting the higher of the two ankle systolic pressures (obtained from both the posterior tibial and dorsalis pedis arteries) and dividing it by the higher of the right and left brachial systolic pressures. The ankle systolic pressure is normally the same or slightly higher than the brachial systolic pressure, resulting in an ABI of 1 to 1.1. As PAD progresses, the systolic BP in the ankle of the affected extremity decreases. An ABI of 0.8 to 0.99 indicates mild PAD, 0.5 to .79 moderate PAD (claudication present), and less than 0.5 severe PAD (pain at rest).

BOX 12-6

Evaluating Lower Extremity Pulse Using a Continuous Wave Doppler

The patient is placed in supine position with the head of the bed elevated to 20 to 30 degrees; the legs are externally rotated, to permit adequate access to the medial malleolus. Acoustic gel is applied to the skin to permit uniform transmission of the ultrasound wave (do not use electrocardiogram gel). The tip of the Doppler transducer is positioned at a 45- to 60-degree angle over the expected location of the artery and angled slowly to identify arterial blood flow. Avoid using excessive pressure, as diseased arteries can collapse if too much pressure is applied over the artery.

Chapter Review

Critical Thinking Exercises

1. You are taking care of Mrs. Jones, a 78-year-old woman, who is being admitted with new-onset atrial fibrillation. The nursing assistant helps you by obtaining the vital signs. It is common practice on your unit to obtain the BP and heart rate using an automated BP device. Is using this device the best method for obtaining the BP and heart rate in a patient with an irregular heart rhythm? What other methods might you use for assessing an accurate heart rate and BP in patients with irregular heart rhythms? Is assessing vital signs for patients with atrial fibrillation a role for a nursing assistant? How have the results of recent nursing research studies informed your answer to these questions?

2. As you are reviewing Mr. Robinson's medical record, you discover that in the last 4 months he has had three readmissions for HF. A thorough health history is needed to assess this patient's health perception and his self-care abilities before you are able to identify his specific problems and develop a nursing plan of care aimed at preventing future readmissions. Describe all the questions you think you will need to ask this patient during the health history. Which of these questions are priorities that must be answered? If the patient is unsure of the answers, what other sources of information might be available to you?

3. You are considering taking a position in an emergency department and plan to observe the triage nurse on the evening shift. You want to prepare for this experience by familiarizing yourself with the common types of patients who present with cardiovascular-related complaints. Name five common cardiovascular diseases and signs and symptoms associated with these disorders. What additional information do you need to consider when quickly assessing patients for a potentially life-threatening illness? Describe how you will focus your physical assessment on the cardiovascular system.

NCLEX-Style Review Questions

1. You are performing a cardiac examination of your patient who has HF. When auscultating over the apical area, you hear an extra sound between S_1 and S_2. This sound may be caused by:
   A. S_3, indicating worsening HF
   B. S_4, indicating the sound of blood moving into a noncompliant left ventricle
   C. A diastolic murmur, suggesting aortic regurgitation
   D. A systolic murmur, indicating a leaky mitral valve

2. After which of the following diagnostic tests will the patient need to remain on bedrest for 2 to 6 hours?
   A. Exercise stress test
   B. Cardiac catheterization
   C. Myocardial perfusion imaging
   D. Traditional echocardiography

3. Mr. Paulsen was just admitted after experiencing chest pain and shortness of breath. Blood tests were sent while he was in the emergency department, and you are evaluating the results. An elevation in which one of the following blood tests indicates that he is having an acute MI?
   A. Troponin
   B. Cholesterol
   C. Brain natriuretic peptide (BNP)
   D. C-reactive protein (CRP)

4. A 45-year-old black woman who has a history of diabetes, hypertension, and cigarette smoking walks into the emergency room with shortness of breath, indigestion, and diaphoresis. She should be evaluated immediately for:
   A. Community-acquired pneumonia
   B. Acute MI
   C. Pulmonary embolus
   D. Aortic dissection

5. Which of the following signs or symptoms are indications for performing an ankle-brachial index (ABI)?
   A. Irregular, superficial ulcer along the medial malleolus
   B. 4+ pitting edema to lower extremities
   C. Intermittent claudication
   D. Pulse deficit greater than 20 mm Hg

Try these additional resources to enhance your learning and understanding of this chapter:
- thePoint online resource available at **http://thepoint.lww.com/Pellico1e**
- *Handbook for Focus on Adult Health: Medical-Surgical Nursing*
- *Study Guide for Focus on Adult Health: Medical-Surgical Nursing*

References and Selected Readings

References and selected readings associated with this chapter can be found on the website that accompanies the book. Visit http://thepoint.lww.com/Pellico1e to access the references and other additional resources associated with this chapter.

Nursing Management: Patients With Hypertension

ANDREA ROTHMAN MANN

Learning Objectives

After reading this chapter, you will be able to:

1. Compare and contrast the continuum of normotension, prehypertension, hypertension, and hypertensive crisis.

2. Assess for risk factors for primary and secondary hypertension.

3. Correlate pathophysiology of hypertension to complications in target organs.

4. Identify nursing management of patients with prehypertension and hypertension including lifestyle changes and pharmacologic therapy.

5. Summarize management of the patient experiencing hypertensive crisis.

6. Incorporate current evidence when caring for the client with prehypertension and hypertension (including systolic hypertension).

Currently, 65 million adults in the United States and 1 billion individuals worldwide have hypertension (DeSimone, 2009; NIH, 2003; Porth & Matfin, 2009). It is the most common condition causing visits to a health care provider (Schlomann & Schmitke, 2007). Presently, control of hypertension is grossly undermanaged. Of individuals treated for hypertension, approximately 70% do not achieve adequate blood pressure (BP) control, which is well below the Healthy People 2010 goal of 50% (DeSimone, 2009). Goals for Healthy People 2020 are currently being established (healthypeople. gov). An additional 30% of individuals are unaware that they have hypertension, placing them at risk for complications. When undetected or untreated, end organ damage to the eye, heart, kidney, and brain results.

⚡ NURSING ALERT

Every 10 years, the U.S. Department of Health and Human Services (HHS) provides scientific insights and lessons from the decade, along with new knowledge from current data, trends, and innovations. Healthy People 2020 will reflect assessments of major risks to health and wellness, changing public priorities, and emerging issues related to national preparedness and prevention.

DEFINITION

The Joint National Committee on Prevention, Detection, Evaluation and Treatment of High BP (**JNC7**) of the National Institute of Health (2003) defines a BP of less than 120/80 mm Hg diastolic as normal, BP of 120 to 139/80 to 89 mm Hg as **prehypertension**, and a BP of 140/90 mm Hg or higher as hypertension. Hypertension is further classified as stage 1 or 2 depending on its severity (Table 13-1) (Porth & Matfin, 2009). Stage 1 hypertension occurs when the systolic pressure is 140 to 159 mm Hg or greater and/or the diastolic pressure is 90 to 99 mm Hg or greater. Stage 2 hypertension occurs when the diastolic pressure is 160 mm Hg or higher, or the diastolic pressure is 100 mm Hg or higher. If the systolic and diastolic pressures are in separate categories, the higher classification is used.

Classifying hypertension on a continuum as opposed to a single value promotes an understanding that elevation in BP from pre-hypertension through stages 1 and 2 is associated with increasing morbidity and mortality.

TABLE
13-1 Classification of Blood Pressure (BP) for Adults Age 18 and Older*

BP Classification*	Systolic BP (mm Hg)		Diastolic BP (mm Hg)
Normal	<120	and	<80
Prehypertension	120–139	or	or 80–89
Stage 1 hypertension	140–159	or	90–99
Stage 2 hypertension	≥160	or	≥100
Hypertensive Crisis	>180		>120

*Based on the average of two or more properly measured, seated readings taken on each of two or more office visits. From the Seventh Report of the Joint National Committee on Prevention, Detection, Evaluation, and Treatment of High BP. (2003). *Hypertension, 42*(6), 1206–1252; Horne & Gordon, 2009.

This health risk rises with elevations of either the systolic or diastolic pressure. Diagnosis of hypertension as defined by the JNC 7 is based on the average of two or more accurate BP measurements taken during two or more contacts with a health care provider.

PATHOPHYSIOLOGY

BP is the product of cardiac output multiplied by peripheral resistance. Cardiac output is the volume of blood being pumped by the heart per minute and is the product of the heart rate (HR) multiplied by the stroke volume (SV), which is the amount of blood pumped out from the ventricles per beat. Peripheral vascular resistance (PVR) is related to the diameter of the blood vessel and the viscosity of the blood. The thicker the blood or smaller the radius of the blood vessel, the higher the resistance. Conversely, the larger the diameter

of the vessel or thinner the blood, the lower the PVR (Porth & Matfin, 2009). For hypertension to develop, there must be a change in one or more factors affecting peripheral vascular resistance or cardiac output (Fig. 13-1). In addition, there must also be a problem with the body's control systems that monitor or regulate pressure. Management of hypertension aims to decrease peripheral resistance, blood volume, or the strength, force, and rate of myocardial contraction.

Of patients with hypertension, 95% have **primary hypertension**; that is, high BP from an unidentified cause (Porth & Matfin, 2009). This type of hypertension has also been called *essential* or *idiopathic* hypertension. The remaining 5% of this group have **secondary hypertension**, which is high BP secondary to an identified cause. These causes include narrowing of the renal arteries or renal artery stenosis, renal disease, hyperaldosteronism (mineralocorticoid hypertension), medications, pregnancy, and coarctation of the aorta (Porth & Matfin, 2009).

White-coat hypertension and *masked hypertension* are two additional types of hypertension not traditionally treated aggressively; however, there is currently emerging concern for complications (AHA, 2009). The patient with white-coat hypertension has normal ambulatory BP readings but elevated pressures (>140/90) in a health care office or clinic. Masked hypertension presents as normal pressure readings in provider settings but elevated BPs at home or work. About 1 in 7 individuals may fall into this latter category. Masked hypertension may be related to daily stressors at work, smoking or alcohol use, oral contraceptive use, and sedentary habits. The nurse should also suspect masked hypertension in men, those with diabetes, renal disease, and those with transiently elevated BPs (Papadopoulos & Makris, 2007). Those with masked hypertension have an increased prevalence of metabolic risk factors, left ventricular hypertrophy, and carotid plaque, demonstrating the impact of hypertension on organ function. When the at-risk individual is identified, the nurse advocates for the use

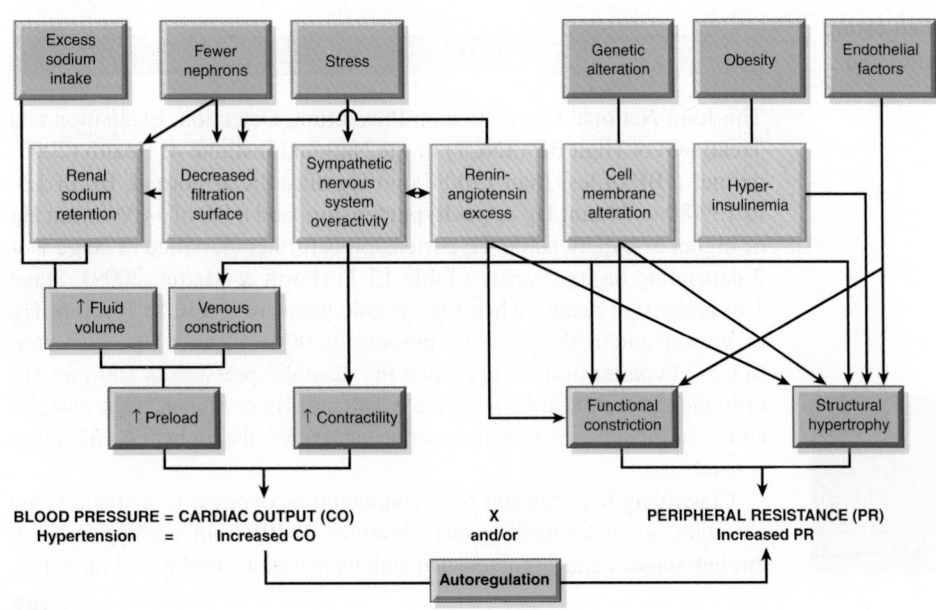

FIGURE 13-1 Factors involved in control of BP. Adapted from Kaplan, N. M., Lieberman, E., & Neal, W. (2006). *Kaplan's clinical hypertension* (9th ed.). Philadelphia: Lippincott Williams & Wilkins.

of home BP monitoring to confirm the diagnosis and monitor treatment. Engaging the patient in the process of self-care results in better outcomes.

RISK FACTORS

Although no precise cause can be identified for most cases of hypertension, it is understood that hypertension is a multifactorial condition. Hypertension increases with aging. Persons who are normotensive at age 44 years have a 90% lifetime risk for the development of hypertension. A rise in systolic pressure continues throughout life, while diastolic pressure rises until approximately 50 years old, tends to level off over the next decade, and may remain the same or fall later in life. Systolic hypertension is the most common form of hypertension and is a major risk factor for cardiovascular disease. Diastolic hypertension predominates before 50 years of age, either alone or in combination with systolic BP (SBP) elevation. Diastolic hypertension is a more potent cardiovascular risk factor than an elevated SBP until age 50; thereafter, SBP elevation is more important (NIH, 2003). As the "baby boomer" generation ages, the incidence of hypertension is expected to increase (Porth & Matfin, 2009). Hypertension is more common in younger men than women, until the time of menopause.

Obesity is one of the common risk factors for the development of hypertension. A rise in childhood obesity forewarns of increasing numbers of hypertensive adults (Aschenbrenner & Venable, 2009). Hypertension, a risk factor for atherosclerotic heart disease, often coexists with **dyslipidemia** (see Chapter 14), diabetes mellitus (see Chapter 30), and a sedentary lifestyle. Metabolic syndrome or syndrome X occurs when three of the following symptoms are present: BP elevation greater than 130/85, insulin resistance, dyslipidemia, and/or abdominal obesity. Metabolic syndrome places the patient at risk for cardiovascular disease and diabetes (American Heart Association, 2009). The risk for cardiovascular disease doubles with each increment of 20/10 mm Hg above 115/75 mm Hg.

The incidence of hypertension is higher among African Americans, who have an earlier onset, higher prevalence, and a greater rate of stage 2 hypertension, leading to higher incidences of nonfatal stroke, death from heart disease, and end-stage renal disease. This increases when the African American individual is male, overweight or obese, physically inactive, and is diabetic (Aschenbrenner & Venable, 2009).

Oral contraceptive use causes a small increase in systolic and diastolic BP, which, when accompanied by smoking and obesity, results in hypertension three times more than those without these risk factors. Cigarette smoking does not cause high BP; however, if a person with hypertension smokes, his or her risk of dying from heart disease or related disorders increases significantly (Aschenbrenner & Venable, 2009; Dochi, Sakata, Oishi et al., 2008).

Factors contributing to hypertension may include increased sympathetic nervous system activity and increased renal reabsorption of sodium, chloride, and water. Increased activity of the renin-angiotensin-aldosterone system, causing expansion of extracellular fluid volume and increased systemic vascular resistance, or dysfunction of the vascular endothelium contribute to hypertension. Resistance to insulin may be a common factor linking hypertension, type 2 diabetes mellitus, hypertriglyceridemia, obesity, and glucose intolerance.

GERONTOLOGIC CONSIDERATIONS

The prevalence of hypertension increases with aging; half of individuals aged 60 to 69 and 75% of individuals over 70 are affected (Firdaus, Sivaram, & Reynolds, 2008; Porth & Matfin, 2009). Aging causes structural and functional changes in the heart and blood vessels, including atherosclerosis and decreased elasticity of the major blood vessels. Because of increased wall stiffness, the arteries are less able to buffer the pressure created as blood is ejected from the left ventricle and unable to store the energy to exert diastolic pressure. Isolated systolic hypertension with widened pulse pressure is more common in older adults. This is associated with cardiovascular and cerebrovascular morbidity and mortality, as well as dementia (Pannarale, 2008; Porth & Matfin, 2009).

> **! NURSING ALERT**
> *Pulse pressure is the difference between the systolic and diastolic pressure; normally, it is approximately 40 mm Hg. As an example, 120/80 equals a pulse pressure of 40 mm Hg. A widened pulse pressure, over 50 mm Hg, is associated with increasing intracranial pressure, atherosclerosis, aortic insufficiency, and fever. It is detected with routine BP measurement.*

To reduce the cardiovascular and cerebrovascular risks, older adults should begin treatment with lifestyle modifications. If medications are needed to achieve the BP goal of less than 140/90 mm Hg, the starting dose should be half that used in younger patients and increased slowly. Many practitioners advocate for "start low and go slow" with medication regimens and the geriatric population. Compliance may be more difficult for the elderly when memory impairment exists or due to the expense of treatment plans. The nurse should ensure that the patient understands the regimen, and can see and read instructions, open the medication container, and get the prescription refilled. Family or caregivers should be included in the teaching program, so that they can assist with the regimen as necessary, can encourage adherence to the treatment plan, and know when and whom to call for questions or problems.

> **! NURSING ALERT**
> *The elderly are more sensitive to volume depletion caused by diuretics and to sympathetic inhibition caused by adrenergic antagonists. Teach patients to change positions slowly when moving from a lying or sitting position to a standing position, and to use supportive devices, such as hand rails and walkers, to prevent falls that could result from dizziness.*

BOX 13-1

GUIDELINES FOR NURSING CARE

Measuring BP

Assessment is based on the average of at least two readings. (If two readings differ by more than 5 mm Hg, additional readings are taken and an average reading is calculated from the results.)

Equipment

- Mercury sphygmomanometer, recently calibrated aneroid manometer, or validated electronic device
- Cuff
- Stethoscope

Implementation

NURSING ACTION	RATIONALE
1. Instruct the patient to: • Avoid smoking cigarettes or drinking caffeine for 30 minutes before BP is measured. • Sit quietly for 5 minutes before the measurement. • Sit comfortably with the forearm supported at heart level on a firm surface, with both feet on the ground; avoid talking while the measurement is being taken.	1. Listening carefully helps ensure an accurate measurement is taken.
2. Select the size of the cuff based upon the size of the patient. (The cuff size should have a bladder width of at least 40% of limb circumference and length at least 80% of limb circumference.) The average adult cuff is 12 to 14 cm wide and 30 cm long.	2. Using a cuff that is too small will give a higher BP measurement, and using a cuff that is too large results in a lower BP measurement compared to one taken with a properly sized cuff.
3. Wrap the cuff firmly around the arm. Center the cuff bladder directly over the brachial artery.	3. Required for accurate reading. If cuff is too loose, a falsely high reading occurs and vice versa.
4. Position the patient's arm at the level of the heart.	4. Positioning arm above heart level will give falsely low reading; below heart level reading will be falsely elevated.
5. Palpate the systolic pressure before auscultating.	5. This technique helps to detect the presence of an auscultatory gap more readily.
6. Ask the patient to sit quietly while the BP is measured.	6. BP can increase when the patient is engaged in conversation.
7. Tighten the thumbscrew of the pressure bulb and rapidly inflate the cuff 30 mm Hg above the palpated systolic pressure. Slowly loosen the thumbscrew to deflate the cuff of the sphygmomanometer, releasing the pressure at about 2 mm Hg per second. Listen carefully. Note the pressure at which repetitive sounds first appears. This is the systolic reading. Continue to listen to the Korotkoff sounds. Determine the pressure when the pulsations disappear completely, this is the diastolic reading.	7. Listening carefully ensures an accurate measurement.
8. Initially, record BP results of both arms and take subsequent measurements from the arm with the higher BP.	8. A difference of .10 to 15 mm Hg may indicate arterial obstruction on the side with the lower value.
9. Record the site where the BP was measured and the position of the patient (e.g., right arm).	9. This is especially important when assessing for orthostatic changes.
10. Inform the patient of his or her BP value and what it means. Emphasize the need for periodic reassessment, and encourage patients who measure BP at home to keep a written record of readings.	10. This engages patient in teaching process and correlation of diet, medication adherence with BP.

CLINICAL MANIFESTATIONS AND ASSESSMENT

Proper technique for assessment of BP is essential. The nurse should ensure proper BP measurement technique is being used (see Box 13-1) and that manometers used are calibrated. The nurse should select a cuff with a length of about 80% of the arm circumference and a width of about 40% of the arm circumference (Bickley & Szilagyi, 2009). To avoid under-measurement of the SBP with **auscultatory gap**, the nurse should inflate the cuff to palpate the brachial artery until the pulse is obliterated, deflate the cuff, add 30 mm Hg to the palpated pressure, and then measure the BP (Bickley, 2009).

! NURSING ALERT
Normally, the BP should vary by no more than 5 mm Hg between arms. If there is a difference, record both initially. Later, record the higher number. A difference of 10 mm Hg or more between the patient's arms may indicate thoracic outlet syndrome or arterial obstruction on the side with the lower value.

Because there are typically no symptoms of hypertension, physical examination may be unremarkable, other than elevated BP. The nurse should assess for signs and symptoms of target organ damage by asking about anginal pain; shortness of breath; alterations in speech, vision, or balance; epistaxis (nosebleeds); headaches; dizziness; or nocturia. Further assessment includes asking about personal, social, or financial factors, or unacceptable pharmaceutical side effects that may interfere with the patients' ability to adhere to the medication regimen.

Hypertension may be asymptomatic and remain so for many years; however, when signs and symptoms appear, vascular damage related to the organs served by the involved vessels has occurred. Coronary artery disease with angina or myocardial infarction is a common consequence of hypertension. Left ventricular hypertrophy occurs in response to the increased workload placed on the ventricle as it contracts against higher systemic pressure. When heart damage is extensive, heart failure follows; 90% of the time, hypertension precedes congestive heart failure (Aschenbrenner & Venable, 2009). Pathologic changes in the kidneys, indicated by microalbuminuria, increased blood urea nitrogen (BUN) and serum creatinine levels, and nocturia result. Cerebrovascular involvement may lead to stroke or transient ischemic attack, manifested by alterations in vision or speech, dizziness, weakness, a sudden fall, or hemiplegia. Occasionally, retinal changes such as hemorrhages, exudates (fluid accumulation), arteriolar narrowing, and cotton-wool spots (small infarctions) occur. In severe hypertension, papilledema (swelling of the optic disc) may be seen. A risk factor assessment, as advocated by JNC 7, is needed to classify and guide the treatment of hypertensive people at risk for cardiovascular damage. Risk factors and cardiovascular problems related to hypertension are presented in Box 13-2.

BOX 13-2   Risk Factors for Cardiovascular Problems in Hypertensive Patients

Major Risk Factors (in Addition to Hypertension)
- Smoking
- Dyslipidemia (elevated LDL (or total) cholesterol and/or low HDL cholesterol)*
- Diabetes mellitus*
- Impaired renal function (GFR <60 mL/min and/or microalbuminuria)
- Obesity (body mass index (BMI) ≥30 kg/m²)*
- Physical inactivity
- Age (>55 years for men, 65 years for women)
- Family history of cardiovascular disease (in female relative <65 years or male relative <55 years)

Target Organ Damage or Clinical Cardiovascular Disease
- Heart disease (left ventricular hypertrophy, angina or previous myocardial infarction, previous coronary revascularization, heart failure)
- Stroke (cerebrovascular accident, brain attack) or TIA
- Chronic kidney disease
- Peripheral arterial disease
- Retinopathy

*These risk factors plus hypertension, elevated triglyceride levels, and abdominal obesity are components of the metabolic syndrome. Adapted from Table 6 of the Seventh Report of the Joint National Committee on Prevention, Detection, Evaluation, and Treatment of High BP. (2003). *Hypertension, 42*(6), 1206–1252.

Routine laboratory tests include urinalysis, evaluation for microalbuminuria or proteinuria, blood chemistry (i.e., analysis of sodium, potassium, BUN and creatinine, fasting glucose, and total and high density lipoprotein [HDL] cholesterol levels), and a 12-lead electrocardiogram (ECG). Left ventricular hypertrophy can be assessed by echocardiography. Additional studies, such as creatinine clearance, renin level, urine tests, and 24-hour urine protein, may be performed.

MEDICAL AND NURSING MANAGEMENT

The treatment goal for individuals with hypertension and without complicating conditions is a BP of less than 140/90 mm Hg. The aim for individuals with prehypertension and no complicating conditions is to lower BP to normal. To prevent or delay progression to hypertension, JNC 7 urges health care providers to encourage people with BPs in the pre-hypertension category to begin lifestyle modifications, such as dietary changes and exercise (see below). JNC 7 recommends that people with stage 1 hypertension be treated with pharmacologic therapy and lifestyle changes. Health care providers should monitor these patients every month until their BP goal is reached, and every 3 to 6 months thereafter. People with stage 2 hypertension or

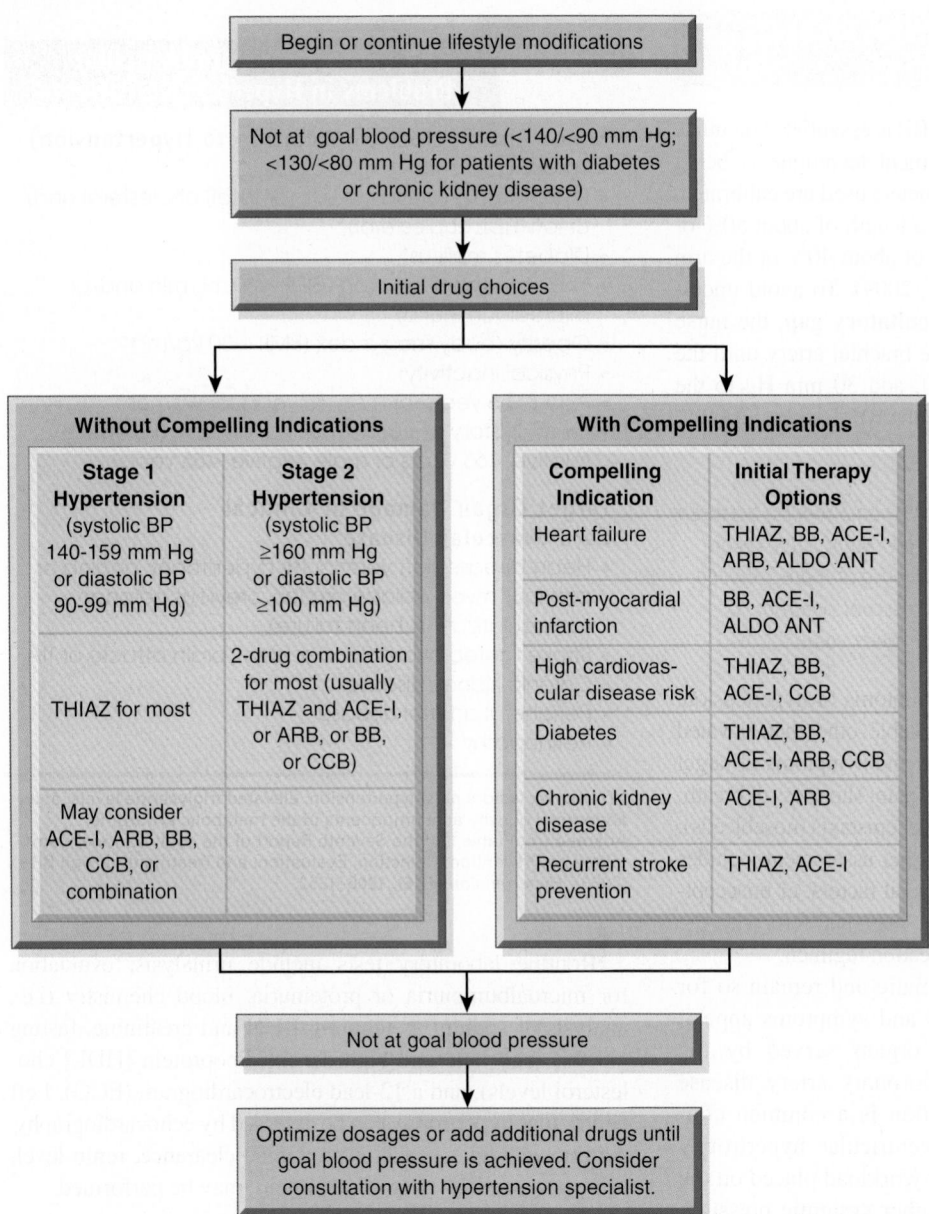

Begin or continue lifestyle modifications

Not at goal blood pressure (<140/<90 mm Hg; <130/<80 mm Hg for patients with diabetes or chronic kidney disease)

Initial drug choices

Without Compelling Indications

Stage 1 Hypertension (systolic BP 140-159 mm Hg or diastolic BP 90-99 mm Hg)	Stage 2 Hypertension (systolic BP ≥160 mm Hg or diastolic BP ≥100 mm Hg)
THIAZ for most	2-drug combination for most (usually THIAZ and ACE-I, or ARB, or BB, or CCB)
May consider ACE-I, ARB, BB, CCB, or combination	

With Compelling Indications

Compelling Indication	Initial Therapy Options
Heart failure	THIAZ, BB, ACE-I, ARB, ALDO ANT
Post-myocardial infarction	BB, ACE-I, ALDO ANT
High cardiovascular disease risk	THIAZ, BB, ACE-I, CCB
Diabetes	THIAZ, BB, ACE-I, ARB, CCB
Chronic kidney disease	ACE-I, ARB
Recurrent stroke prevention	THIAZ, ACE-I

Not at goal blood pressure

Optimize dosages or add additional drugs until goal blood pressure is achieved. Consider consultation with hypertension specialist.

FIGURE 13-2 Algorithm of hypertension treatment. Treatment begins with lifestyle modifications and continues with various medication regimens. ACEI, angiotensin converting enzyme inhibitor; ALDO ANT, aldosterone antagonist; ARB, angiotensin receptor blocker; BB, beta blocker; CCB, calcium channel blocker; THIAZ, thiazide diuretic. From the Seventh Report of the Joint National Committee on Prevention, Detection, Evaluation, and Treatment of High BP (JNC 7). Reference card available from the National, Heart, Lung, and Blood Institute (NHLBI), available at http://www.nhlbi.nih. gov.

with other complicating conditions need to be seen more frequently. For individuals with diabetes or chronic kidney disease, JNC 7 specifies a target pressure of less than 130/80 mm Hg.

The management of hypertension is summarized in the treatment algorithm issued by JNC 7 (Fig. 13-2). The clinician uses the treatment algorithm, risk factor assessment data, and the patient's BP category to choose treatment plans for the patient.

The nurse encourages self-management, which may include self BP monitoring, and education to initiate and maintain lifestyle changes. It is important to assess the patient's beliefs about hypertension (Box 13-3). Research indicates that patients with hypertension who receive self-management

education and are empowered to ask questions and voice concerns are less likely to be hospitalized, have fewer emergency department and unscheduled medical visits, and have fewer days off from work (DeSimone & Crowe, 2009; Schlomann & Schmitke, 2007).

The nurse should routinely ask whether patients take herbal supplements or over-the-counter (OTC) medications that may increase BP. These include caffeine and ephedra, which are stimulants; licorice, which has an aldosterone-like effect; and oral contraceptives, acetaminophen and NSAIDs, which may lead to fluid retention. In addition, certain agents have been touted as BP lowering agents such as coenzyme Q10, garlic, vitamin C, and L-arginine. Patients should be cautioned that nutritional supplements are not regulated in

BOX 13-3 Nursing Research

Bridging the Gap to Evidence-Based Practice

Importance of Assessing Patient's Beliefs About Hypertension

Schlomann, P. & Schmitke, J. (2007). Lay beliefs about hypertension: An interpretive synthesis of the qualitative research. *Journal of the American Academy of Nurse Practitioners, 19,* 358–367.

Purpose

The purpose was to explore lay beliefs about high BP and its treatment in order to develop a foundation for better partnering with patients.

Design

This was a meta-interpretation of 11 qualitative studies from 2000 through 2005. Populations studies included Hmong shamans (from Laos), African American, Latinos, rural poor, urban poor, and urban without economic designation. The researchers identified that there was a heavy emphasis on African American populations.

Findings

Lay beliefs about hypertension often were in opposition to those of health care professionals. Certain populations believed hypertension and high BP were different diseases and that hypertension was a curable response to stress that "tightens up the blood vessels and increases the heart rate." High BP or "high blood" was seen as a problem that is incurable and caused by foods, especially fatty food or pork, which cause the blood to become thick. Stress stemming from racism, interpersonal issues, and financial difficulties was seen as a cause of high BP. While some noted salt, fast food, or fatty food, or excessive food intake as causes by some of the study groups, sea salt was considered an intervention. Some participants saw no relationship between diet and BP; in fact, Hmong shamans do not have a word in their vocabulary for hypertension, nor was chronic illness a part of their culture. In each study, there were individuals who questioned the accuracy of a diagnosis of hypertension when a family history of hypertension did not exist. Other reasons the study group thought hypertension developed included blood traveling too fast to the brain due to a self-regulating response (in these cases, they felt medication was not necessary), or that the hypertension was a necessary adjustment for African Americans to a stressful life.

While professional literature describes hypertension as the "silent killer," many participants felt there were typically three to seven symptoms of hypertension including headaches (seen as not serious); change in heart rate or force (i.e., pounding heart beat); dizziness or faintness (which could be relieved with stress reducing activities); weakness, fatigue, or sluggishness; nosebleeds, irritability; a vague sense of unwellness; or ears popping. The notion of a disease without symptoms did not match the paradigm of disease in study participants. This set the professional up as the "expert" and "right" while lay beliefs were depicted as inferior and "wrong." Physicians cited failure of treatment as a failure in patient compliance, whereas participants deemed nonadherent perceived more side effects and fewer benefits from prescribed treatment. Some participants believed that treatment is time limited, works effectively for all racial/ethnic groups, and does not require adjustments.

Nursing Implications

Adherence to the medication increased when participants saw physicians who were described as "honest, "caring", "listening" or a "friend." Caring behaviors included sitting down, making eye contact, the tone of voice, and developing joint goal setting with reciprocal communication and clear education. Distrust of care providers was perceived as absence of caring behaviors and discrimination when nonadherent, especially when attempting to "correct the lay paradigm." Participants said that a provider who was "indirect or hard to follow" was not helpful. Some participants felt that doctors prefer to prescribe medications because they are not trained to teach about diet and lifestyle changes and focus on life-long therapy. Additionally, being told to reduce working to reduce stress and BP placed additional stressor on the individual. Nurses and nurse practitioners were not included in the comments except when BP measurements were taken, reflecting that participants may not view nurses as playing a significant role in hypertension management.

Nurses should regard the patient with respect and appreciate the patient's overall needs. Language such as "compliant" and "adherent" reinforces the unequal power structure and might be replaced by "mutual goal setting" and "planning," which empower the client. Correcting the lay perspective that hypertension has no symptoms may cause distrust; emphasizing that symptoms may or not be present at all times may prove more helpful in the long run. Counseling people they must make major life change and need medication for life is contradictory for some who posit that if lifestyle changes can decrease BP, lifelong medication should not be necessary. Focusing on the present rather than the future may be more effective in the long run. Nurses must play a role in educating patients, so that all populations do not overlook the nurse as an excellent resource for health care education.

TABLE
13-2 Lifestyle Modifications to Prevent and Manage Hypertension*

Modification	Recommendation	Goal of SBP[†] Reduction (Range)[‡]
Weight reduction	Maintain normal body weight (body mass index 18.5–24.9 kg/m²).	5–20 mm Hg/10 kg
Adopt DASH (Dietary Approaches to Stop Hypertension) eating plan	Consume a diet rich in fruits, vegetables, fiber, potassium and low-fat dairy products, and reduce animal protein, fat and saturated fat.	8–14 mm Hg
Dietary sodium reduction	Reduce dietary sodium intake to 2.4 g sodium or 6 g sodium chloride per day.	2–8 mm Hg
Physical activity	Engage in regular aerobic physical activity such as 30 minutes of brisk walking 3 to 5 days per week	4–9 mm Hg
Moderation of alcohol consumption	Limit consumption to no more than 2 drinks (e.g., 24 oz beer, 10 oz wine, or 3 oz 80-proof whiskey) per day in most men and to no more than 1 drink per day in women and lighter-weight people.	2–4 mm Hg

* For overall cardiovascular risk reduction, stop smoking.
[†]SBP, Systolic BP.
[‡]The effects of implementing these modifications are dose- and time-dependent and could be greater for some individuals.
From the Seventh Report of the Joint National Committee on Prevention, Detection, Evaluation, and Treatment of High BP. (2003). *Hypertension, 42*(6), 1206–1252.

the same manner as pharmaceuticals, and all products used should be reported to the health care provider (DeSimone & Crowe, 2009).

Lifestyle Changes

Table 13-2 summarizes recommended lifestyle modifications. Research findings demonstrate that smoking cessation, weight loss, reduced alcohol and sodium intake, and regular physical activity are effective lifestyle adaptations to reduce BP (Narkiewicz, 2006). The nurse should emphasize the concept of life-long BP control rather than cure.

Specific information regarding lifestyle changes should include the importance of achieving a waist circumference of less than 40 inches for a man and less than 35 inches for a woman and a body mass index (BMI) between 18.5 and 24.9 kg/m². For patients not meeting that goal, modification involves caloric restriction and increased physical activity. A weight loss of only 10 pounds may result in a 5 to 20 mm Hg reduction in SBP, offering tangible results to the patient. The nurse encourages the patient to formulate a plan for weight loss, consulting a dietician or using support groups if necessary. The bariatric patient may benefit from surgical intervention. A pedometer may assist the patient in increasing his physical activity (DeSimone & Crowe, 2009).

Adhering to the American Heart Associations' DASH approach (Dietary Approaches to Stop Hypertension) can decrease systolic BP by 8 to 14 mm Hg. The DASH approach includes increasing fruits, vegetables, whole grains, fiber, nuts, legumes, and low-fat dairy products while limiting animal proteins and fats, especially saturated fats (Table 13-3).

Specific information should be provided on reading labels for foods that contain less than 400 mg of sodium per serving and for reducing the intake of table salt to 1 teaspoon (2.4 g of sodium) daily (DeSimone & Crowe, 2009). Teach the patient that it takes 2 to 3 months for the taste buds to adapt to changes in salt intake to encourage perseverance (Dudek, 2008). The JNC 7 endorses the American Public Health Association resolution that food manufacturers and restaurants reduce sodium in the food supply by 50% over the next decade (Havas, Roccella, & Lenfant, 2004).

NURSING ALERT

Reducing table salt to about 1 teaspoon per day, or 2.4 grams of sodium, can reduce systolic BP by 2 to 8 mm Hg.

TABLE
13-3 The DASH (Dietary Approaches to Stop Hypertension) Diet

Food Group	Number of Servings Per Day
Grains and grain products	7 or 8
Vegetables	4 or 5
Fruits	4 or 5
Low-fat or fat-free dairy foods	2 or 3
Meat, fish, and poultry	2 or fewer
Nuts, seeds, and dry beans	4 or 5 weekly

The diet is based on 2,000 calories per day.
From www.nhlbi.nih.gov/health/public/heart/hbp/dash/index.htm

Limiting one's daily alcohol to 24 ounces of beer, 10 ounces of wine, or 3 ounces of whiskey for men, and half that for women is recommended (Woods & Moshang, 2005). Smoking cessation may reduce the systolic BP by 4 mm Hg and the diastolic BP by 3 mm Hg (DeSimone & Crowe, 2009).

Alternate Therapies

Evidence suggests that device-guided breathing can lower BP without adverse effects. Lower respiratory rates decrease sympathetic outflow, microvascular tone, and peripheral resistance, thereby lowering BP. The device consisting of a belt-type sensor and headphones. The sensor senses respirations and creates a personalized inhale–exhale melody that guides patients to breathe more slowly through prolonged exhalation. The RESPeRATE by InterCure, Inc. is approved by the U.S. Food and Drug Administration (FDA) and has been shown to lower BP by 14/8 mm Hg. As with all BP-lowering interventions, consistent use is key (DeSimone & Crowe, 2009). Complementary and alternative medicine therapies and mind–body interventions are potentially effective in reducing BP. Relaxation, meditation, guided imagery, hypnosis, and yoga are some examples of these therapies. While there is a lack of well-controlled studies, yoga has been shown to have beneficial effects on the cardiovascular system (DeSimone & Crowe, 2009).

Blood Pressure Monitoring

The nurse must ensure that follow-up is provided for any person identified as having an elevated BP level. Each person should be given a written record of his or her BP at the screening. The American Heart Association and the National Heart, Lung, and Blood Institute provide printed and electronic patient education materials (see reference resources web addresses). Reductions in BP are greater when self-management education includes a written action plan, self-monitoring, and regular review (DeSimone & Crowe, 2009).

Pharmacologic Therapy

The nurse collaborates with the patient to support adherence to the medication regimen because up to 50% of individuals prescribed antihypertensive medications do not continue for more than 1 year. The most effective therapy prescribed by the most careful clinician will control hypertension only if patients are motivated. Motivation improves when patients have positive experiences with and trust in the clinician. Empathy builds trust and is a potent motivator (Havas et al., 2004).

For patients with uncomplicated hypertension, the recommended initial medication is a thiazide diuretic. Thiazide diuretics are useful in the elderly and in patients with osteoporosis because they decrease bone breakdown and preserve bone integrity (Woods & Moshang, 2005). The provider begins with low doses of medication. If BP does not

fall to less than 140/90 mm Hg, the dose may be increased gradually or additional medications added. The advantage of adding a medication, rather than increasing the dose of the first medication, is that side effects may be avoided. Most patients requiring medication need two drugs for effective treatment because hypertension is cause by multiple factors.

For patients with documented diabetes, heart failure, or cardiovascular disease, an angiotensin-converting enzyme inhibitor (ACE inhibitor) or angiotensin receptor blocker (ARB) is recommended. These drugs protect and preserve renal function and protect the vascular endothelium (Salinitri, Berlie, & Desai, 2009). Beta blockers are additional first-line agents; these are recommended for patients with heart cardiovascular heart disease and heart failure. Cardioselective beta blockers are indicated for patients with pulmonary diseases such as asthma or chronic obstructive pulmonary disease. Calcium channel blockers, such as amlopidipine, exert their major effect on blood vessels and are recommended for treatment of hypertension, while medications that affect heart rate, such as diltiazem, are better suited to rhythm control (Woods & Moshang, 2005). Alpha$_2$ stimulating agents, alpha–beta blockers, and direct vasodilators are also used.

💊 DRUG ALERT

Use of NSAIDs with ACE inhibitors and ARBs may decrease their antihypertensive effects.

When the BP is less than 140/90 mm Hg for at least 1 year, gradual reduction of the types and doses of medication is indicated. To promote compliance, clinicians try to prescribe the simplest treatment schedule possible, ideally one pill once each day. Failure to titrate or combine medications, despite knowing the patient is not at goal BP, represents clinical inertia and must be overcome (DeSimone & Crowe, 2009; Gimpel, Schoj, & Rubinstein, 2006). This may be related to lack of awareness, failure to intensify treatment regimens, or patients' noncompliance with therapies. The nurse needs to emphasize and support both pharmacologic and nonpharmacologic strategies; contracting, goal setting, counseling, and referral to support groups are some of the strategies used. A patient may be diagnosed with resistant hypertension, which is a failure to reach goal BP in patients who adhere to full doses of an appropriate three-drug regimen that includes a diuretic. Table 13-4 describes the pharmacologic agents that are recommended for treatment of hypertension.

The nurse should include education when drug treatment for other risk factors is combined with antihypertensive therapy. For example, a statin to lower cholesterol is prescribed if the patient has a cardiac vascular disease risk or has target organ damage. Low-dose aspirin therapy is indicated once BP is controlled to limit cardiovascular complications (Feather, 2006; Woods & Moshang, 2005). There is evidence that depression is associated with poor adherence to medication regimens and

TABLE
13.4 Medication Therapy for Hypertension

Medication	Major Action	Considerations
Diuretics (Thiazide and Thiazide-Like, Loop, Potassium-Sparing)		
Hydrochlorothiazide and metazolone, furosemide, spironolactone	Decreases blood volume, renal blood flow, and cardiac output Natriuresis, negative sodium balance Directly affects vascular smooth muscle	Side effects: Dry mouth, thirst, nausea, weakness, drowsiness, postural hypotension Considerations: Monitor for signs of sodium, potassium, and magnesium imbalance.
Central Alpha₂-Agonists and Other Centrally Acting Drugs		
Clonidine, methyldopa	Impairs synthesis and reuptake of norepinephrine Displaces norepinephrine from storage sites Stimulates central alpha₂ adrenergic receptors	Side effects: Hypotension, postural hypotension, bradycardia, dizziness, drowsiness, dry mouth, depression, nasal congestion, rebound hypertension, impotence
Beta Blockers		
Atenolol, propranolol, metoprolol, nadolol, timolol	Blocks beta adrenergic receptors of sympathetic nervous system causing vasodilation, decreased cardiac output and heart rate	Side effects: Hypotension, bradycardia, congestive heart failure, fatigue, depression, weakness, impotence, rebound hypertension, hypoglycemia Contraindications: Asthma, COPD
Alpha₁ Blockers		
Doxazosin, prazosin hydrochloride, terazosin	Peripherally acting vasodilator	Side effects: Vomiting and diarrhea, urinary frequency, and tachycardia if not controlled with beta blocker, drowsiness
Combined Alpha and Beta Blockers		
Carvedilol, labetalol hydrochloride	Blocks alpha- and beta-adrenergic receptors; causes peripheral dilation and decreases peripheral vascular resistance	Side effects: Orthostatic hypotension, tachycardia or bradycardia Contraindications: Asthma and COPD
Vasodilators		
Fenoldopam mesylate	Stimulates dopamine and alpha₂-adrenergic receptors	Side effects: Headache, flushing, hypotension, sweating
Hydralazine	Decreases peripheral resistance; concurrently elevates cardiac output; acts directly on smooth muscle of blood vessels	Side effects: Headache, tachycardia, flushing, and dyspnea, lupus erythematosus–like syndrome
Minoxidil	Direct-acting arterial vasodilator	Side effects: Hirsutism, dizziness, headache, nausea, edema, tachycardia, profound hypotension, thiocyanate toxicity
Sodium nitroprusside	Peripheral vasodilation by relaxation of smooth muscle	Side effects: Hypotension, tachycardia, flushing, headache
Nitroglycerin USP	Arterial and venous vasodilator	
Angiotensin-Converting Enzyme (ACE) Inhibitors		
Captopril, enalaprilat/enalapril, fosinopril, lisinopril, quinapril, ramipril	Inhibits conversion of angiotensin I to angiotensin II; reduces peripheral resistance	Side effects: Hypotension, tachycardia, hyperkalemia, azotemia, angioedema (rare but life threatening) Contraindications: Pregnancy
Angiotensin II Receptor Blockers (ARBs)		
Candesartan irbesartan, losartan olmesartan, telmisartan, valsartan	Blocks the effects of angiotensin II at the receptor; reduces peripheral resistance	Side effects: Hypotension, hyperkalemia Contraindications: Pregnancy
Calcium Channel Blockers **Nondihydropyridines**		
Diltiazem, verapamil **Dihydropyridines**	Inhibits calcium ion influx; reduces cardiac afterload, workload	Side effects: Hypotension, Bradycardia, CHF dizziness, edema
Amlodipine, felodipine, isradipine, nifedipine		Considerations: Do not discontinue suddenly. Contraindications: Sick sinus syndrome, heart blocks

COPD, chronic obstructive pulmonary disease.

that posttraumatic stress disorder (PTSD) is associated with hypertension, thus directing the nurse to develop further psychosocial interventions and reinforce collaborative pharmacologic interventions (Kibler, Joshi, & Ma, 2008).

The nurse provides written information about the expected effects and side effects of antihypertensive medications, warning the patient not to abruptly stop medications because **rebound hypertension** may occur. Both female and male patients should be informed that certain medications, such as beta blockers, may cause sexual dysfunction or dissatisfaction and that other medications are available should this problem develop. As always, the patient should be encouraged to provide honest feedback to the health care provider to achieve optimum BP control. Patients should be cautioned to avoid OTC medications, especially nasal decongestants containing vasoconstrictors, which can further elevate BP.

Medication compliance increases when patients actively participate in self-care, including self-monitoring of BP, diet, and exercise—possibly because patients receive immediate feedback and have a greater sense of control. Evidence demonstrates that compliance further increases when the provider takes time in counseling, takes into account cultural perspectives on causes and treatment of hypertension, and avoids viewing the patient as responsible for treatment failures. An attitude of honesty, caring, listening, or friendliness was important for patients to return for clinic visits, as was giving direct and clear instructions (Schlomann & Schmitke, 2007).

COMPLICATIONS

Prolonged BP elevation damages blood vessels, particularly in target organs such as the heart, kidneys, brain, and eyes. The consequences of prolonged, uncontrolled hypertension are myocardial infarction, heart failure, left ventricular hypertrophy, renal failure, stroke, and impaired vision. An acute elevation in BP associated with end-organ damage is termed *hypertensive crisis*.

HYPERTENSIVE CRISES

Hypertensive crisis is defined by JNC 7 as a systolic BP of higher than 180 mm Hg or a diastolic BP of higher than 120 mm Hg. Approximately 1% to 2% of individuals with hypertension will have a hypertensive crisis at some point. Hypertensive crises occur in patients whose hypertension has been poorly controlled or in those who have discontinued their medications. These crises are more common in men, older adults, and African Americans (McCowan, 2009). Other causes of hypertensive crises include head injury, pheochromocytoma, food–drug interactions (such as tyramine combined with a monamine oxidase [MAO] inhibitors), eclampsia or preeclampsia, substance abuse (e.g., cocaine intoxication), and renal disease (Horne & Gordon, 2009).

Once the crisis has been managed, the nurse strategizes with the patient and provider to take control of his or her BP and prevent recurrence. JNC 7 describes two classes of hypertensive crisis that require immediate intervention: hypertensive emergency and hypertensive urgency (Varon, 2008).

A **hypertensive emergency** is a situation in which BP is higher than 180/120 mm Hg and must be lowered quickly to halt or prevent damage to the target organs (Horne & Gordon, 2009; Varon, 2008). Conditions associated with hypertensive emergency include hypertension of pregnancy, acute myocardial infarction (MI), dissecting aortic aneurysm, and intracranial hemorrhage. The therapeutic goals are reduction of the mean BP by up to 25% within the first hour of treatment, a further reduction to a goal pressure of about 160/100 mm Hg over a period of 2 to 6 hours, and then a more gradual reduction in pressure to the target goal over a period of days (Horne & Gordon, 2009; Varon, 2008). It is important not to become over-eager and lower the BP too quickly, thus reducing tissue perfusion and causing an MI or cerebrovascular accident (CVA). The exception is treatment of aortic dissection, in which the systolic pressure should be reduced to less than 100 mm Hg (Varon, 2008). This patient will most likely receive care in an intensive care unit with BP measured every 5 minutes while unstable. The nurse evaluates the patient for a precipitous drop in BP, which requires immediate action to restore BP to normal levels.

Hypertensive urgency describes a situation in which BP is severely elevated, but there is no evidence of impending or progressive target organ damage (Horne & Gordon, 2009; Varon, 2008). Elevated BPs associated with severe headache, epistaxis, or anxiety are classified as urgencies. The goal is to reduce BP to 160/110 over several hours to several days. This can be accomplished by keeping the patient in the emergency department for several hours, followed by outpatient management using oral medications.

Pharmacologic Management of Hypertensive Crises

The medications of choice in hypertensive emergencies are best managed with continuous IV infusion of a short-acting titratable antihypertensive agent. The nurse avoids the sublingual and IM routes as their absorption and dynamics are unpredictable. Medications may include labetalol, nicardipine or clevidipine hydrochloride, fenoldopam mesylate, enalaprilat, esmolol, hydralazine, or nitroglycerin or sodium nitroprusside, which have immediate, short-lived actions. Nitroprusside is no longer recommended as first-line treatment due to thiocyanate toxicity, erratic responses, and risk for severe hypotension (Horne & Gordon, 2009; Varon, 2008). For more information about these medications, see Table 13-4.

Oral doses of fast-acting agents such as beta-adrenergic blocking agents, ACE inhibitors, or alpha$_2$-agonists are recommended for the treatment of hypertensive urgencies (see Table 13-4).

DRUG ALERT

ACE inhibitors and ARBs block aldosterone and may cause hyperkalemia when used with potassium-sparing diuretics or salt substitutes that contain potassium. The nurse should monitor the potassium level.

The nurse follows-up with teaching about the hypertensive crisis and encourages the patient to take charge of managing hypertension.

Chapter Review

Critical Thinking Exercises

1. A 72-year-old man arrives in the emergency department with a laceration of his right forearm from a minor gardening injury, which will require suturing. The patient's BP on his left arm is 164/78. You tell the patient his BP and express concern that his systolic BP is high. He shrugs and tells you, "The top number is always elevated, but it's nothing to worry about." What teaching should the nurse provide, based on current evidence regarding untreated isolated systolic hypertension? What other information do you plan to gather from this patient? What plan of action might you initiate?

2. You are volunteering at a church-sponsored BP screening offered after Sunday services, in tandem with a fund-raising buffet breakfast. The pastor approaches you and notes that the breakfast buffet contains a variety of egg dishes, hash browns, sausage patties, bacon, and pastries. He asks you what effects, if any, this food may have on his parishioners' BPs. What effect might this type of diet have on the parishioners' BPs today? Discuss the evidence that supports specific dietary strategies aimed at preventing and treating hypertension and its complications. Include the DASH approach.

NCLEX-Style Review Questions

1. The nurse is reviewing the BPs of a patient admitted with cellulitis whose BP is 136/86. Which of the following should the nurse teach the patient about this BP reading?
   A. "Your BP is in the normal range, you don't need to worry."
   B. "This BP is considered pre-hypertension; consider cutting down on sodium and seeing your health care provider."
   C. "I will notify the provider of your BP, a BP of 136/86 indicates you have hypertension."
   D. "You are at risk for organ damage, this BP indicates hypertensive urgency."

2. During routine screening, the nurse notes a BP of 172/96. The patient states, "I feel fine—what's the big deal?" Which of the following indicates the best response by the nurse?
   A. "As long as you are feeling well, there is no need to worry."
   B. "Untreated high BP may result in kidney failure, heart attack, or stroke."
   C. "This BP elevation indicates you have not been compliant with your medication."
   D. "Have you had any unusual nosebleeds or headaches lately?"

3. A patient is admitted with angina and hypertensive crisis. On admission, the BP is 240/120. The nurse recognizes which of the following is consistent with current BP management strategies?
   A. In 2 hours, the target BP is 140/90.
   B. In 1 hour, the patient's target BP should be 180/90.
   C. Lowering the BP too quickly may lead to rebound hypertension.
   D. The nurse should anticipate using oral medications for hypertensive urgency.

4. The nurse is teaching a patient about BP self-monitoring. Which of the following should be included in the plan of care?
   A. You may sit or stand when taking your BP.
   B. Do not eat or drink for at least 2 hours before measuring your BP.
   C. Make sure the cuff is loose enough to avoid squeezing your arm too tightly.
   D. Keep your arm at heart level and avoid talking during BP measurement.

5. A nurse is completing medication teaching for a patient diagnosed with hypertension. Which of the following would be important to include in the plan to prevent rebound hypertension?
   A. Caution the use of OTC medications.
   B. Inform that beta blockers can cause sexual dysfunction.
   C. Avoid abruptly stopping the medication.
   D. Nasal decongestants should be avoided.

Try these additional resources to enhance your learning and understanding of this chapter:
- thePoint online resource available at **http://thepoint.lww.com/Pellico1e**
- *Handbook for Focus on Adult Health: Medical-Surgical Nursing*
- *Study Guide for Focus on Adult Health: Medical-Surgical Nursing*

References and Selected Readings

References and selected readings associated with this chapter can be found on the website that accompanies the book. Visit **http://thepoint.lww.com/Pellico1e** to access the references and other additional resources associated with this chapter.

Nursing Management: Patients With Coronary Vascular Disorders

MARY G. PIERSON

Learning Objectives

After reading this chapter, you will be able to:

1. Summarize the pathophysiology, risk factors, clinical manifestations, and treatment of coronary atherosclerosis.

2. Summarize the pathophysiology, clinical manifestations, and treatment of angina pectoris.

3. Describe percutaneous coronary interventional (PCI) and coronary artery revascularization procedures.

4. Explain the nursing care of a patient who has had a PCI procedure for treatment of coronary artery disease.

5. Describe the nursing care of a patient who has undergone cardiac surgery.

6. Summarize the pathophysiology, clinical manifestations, and treatment of myocardial infarction.

Cardiovascular disease (CVD) is the leading cause of death in the United States for men and women of all racial and ethnic groups (American Heart Association [AHA], 2008). Research related to the identification and treatment of CVD now includes all segments of the population affected by cardiac conditions, including women, children, and people of diverse racial and ethnic backgrounds.

Coronary artery disease (CAD) is the most prevalent type of CVD in adults. For this reason, it is important for nurses to become familiar with various manifestations of coronary artery conditions and methods for assessing, preventing, and treating these disorders medically and surgically.

CORONARY ATHEROSCLEROSIS

The most common cause of CVD in the United States is **atherosclerosis**, an abnormal accumulation of lipid, or fatty substances and fibrous tissue in the lining of arterial blood vessel walls. These substances create blockages and narrow the coronary vessels in a way that reduces blood flow to the myocardium. It is now known that atherosclerosis involves a repetitious inflammatory response to injury to the artery wall and subsequent alteration in the structural and biochemical properties of the arterial walls.

Pathophysiology

Atherosclerosis begins as fatty streaks of lipids that are deposited in the intima of the arterial wall. These lesions commonly begin early in life, perhaps even in childhood. Not all fatty streaks later develop into more advanced lesions. Genetics and environmental factors influence the progression of these lesions. The continued development of atherosclerosis involves an inflammatory response, which begins with injury to the vascular endothelium. The injury may be initiated by smoking, hypertension (HTN), and other factors. The presence of inflammation has multiple effects on the arterial wall, including the attraction of inflammatory cells (including macrophages or monocytes, white blood cells [WBCs]) (Baldellino, 2008). The macrophages infiltrate the injured vascular endothelium and ingest lipids, which turns them into what are called "foam cells." These foam cells are present in all stages of atherosclerotic plaque

formation (Porth & Matfin, 2009). Activated macrophages also release biochemical substances that can further damage the endothelium, attracting platelets and initiating clotting.

Smooth muscle cells within the vessel wall subsequently proliferate and form a fibrous cap over a center that is filled with lipid and inflammatory infiltrate. These deposits, called **atheromas** or plaques, protrude into the lumen of the vessel, narrowing it and obstructing blood flow (Fig. 14-1). If the fibrous cap of the plaque is thick and the lipid pool remains relatively stable, it can resist the stress from blood flow and vessel movement. If the cap is thin and inflammation is ongoing, the lipid core may grow, causing it to rupture, and this ruptured plaque is a focus for thrombus formation. The thrombus may then obstruct blood flow, leading to sudden cardiac death or an acute **myocardial infarction (MI)**, which is the death of a portion of the heart muscle. Thus, atherosclerosis can produce narrowing of the lumen of a blood vessel, sudden obstruction of a blood vessel due to plaque rupture, and weakening of a blood vessel, resulting in aneurysm formation or emboli formation because of direct damage to the endothelium.

The anatomic structure of the coronary arteries makes them particularly susceptible to the mechanisms of atherosclerosis. There are three major coronary arteries and they have multiple branches; atherosclerotic lesions most often form where the vessels branch (Fig. 14-2). Although heart disease is most often caused by atherosclerosis of the coronary arteries, other phenomena may also decrease blood flow to the heart. Examples include vasospasm (sudden constriction or narrowing) of a coronary artery, myocardial trauma from internal or external forces, structural disease, congenital anomalies, decreased oxygen supply (e.g., from acute blood loss, anemia, or low blood pressure), and increased oxygen demand (e.g., from rapid heart rate, thyrotoxicosis, or use of cocaine).

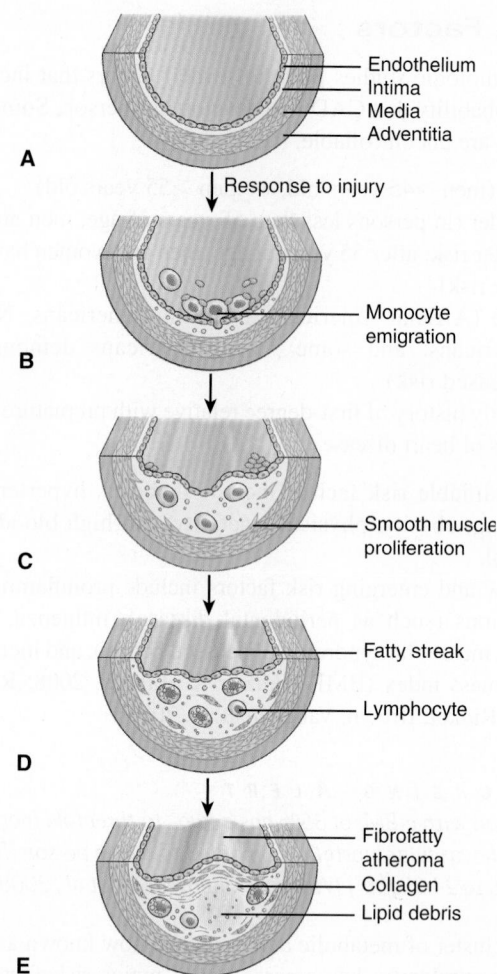

FIGURE 14-1 Atherosclerosis begins as monocytes and lipids enter the intima of an injured vessel (**A, B**). Smooth muscle cells proliferate within the vessel wall (**C**) contributing to the development of fatty accumulations and atheroma (**D**). As the plaque enlarges, the vessel narrows and blood flow decreases (**E**). The plaque may rupture and a thrombus might form, obstructing blood flow.

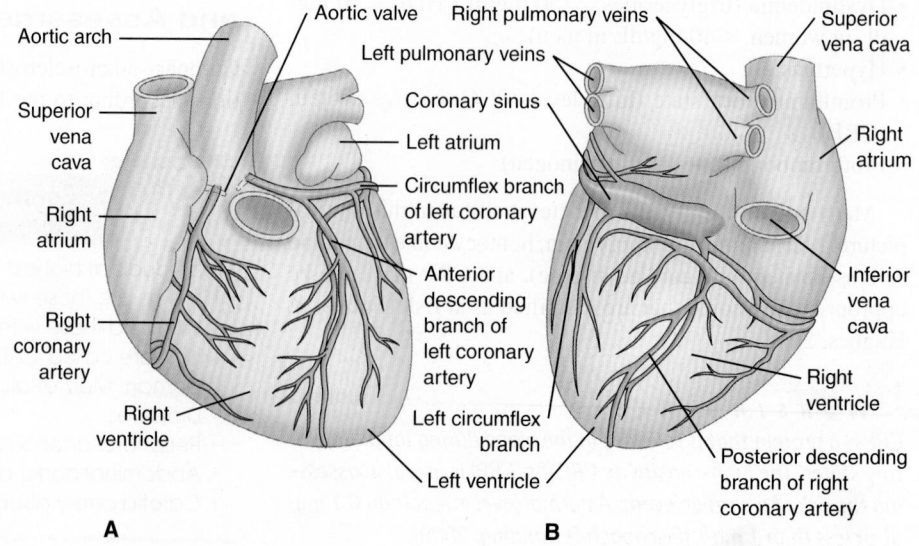

FIGURE 14-2 The coronary arteries supply the heart muscle with oxygenated blood, adjusting the flow according to metabolic needs. (**A**) Anterior view, and (**B**) posterior view of heart.

Risk Factors

Epidemiologic studies point to several factors that increase the probability that CAD will develop in a person. Some risk factors are uncontrollable, including:

- Age (men >45 years old, women >55 years old)
- Gender (in persons less than 55 years of age, men are at a greater risk; after 55 years of age, men and women have the same risk)
- Race (African Americans, Mexican Americans, Native Americans, and some Asian Americans demonstrate increased risk)
- Family history of first-degree relative with premature diagnosis of heart disease

Modifiable risk factors include diabetes, hypertension, smoking, obesity, physical inactivity, and high blood cholesterol.

New and emerging risk factors include proinflammatory conditions (such as periodontal disease), influenza, sleep apnea, metabolic syndrome (discussed below), and increased body mass index (BMI) (Frazier & Hughes, 2008; Ridker, 2003; Ridker, Brown, Vaughan et al., 2004).

! NURSING ALERT

A person with a BMI of 35% has a two- to threefold increase in cardiovascular mortality compared to a lean person (BMI of 18.5 to 24.9 kg/m². (Warziski, Choo, Novak et al., 2008).

A cluster of metabolic abnormalities now known as **metabolic syndrome** has emerged as a major risk factor for CAD (Fig. 14-3). A diagnosis of this syndrome includes three of the following conditions:

- Insulin resistance (fasting glucose >100 mg/dL or abnormal glucose tolerance test)
- Abdominal obesity (waist circumference >35 inches in women, >40 inches in men)
- Dyslipidemia (triglycerides >150 mg/dL; HDL <50 mg/dL in women, <40 mg/dL in men)
- Hypertension
- Proinflammatory state (high levels of C-reactive protein [CRP])
- Prothrombotic state (high fibrinogen)

Many people with type 2 diabetes mellitus fit this clinical picture. Measurement of lipoprotein, homocysteine (an amino acid associated with cardiac disease), and CRP may also be appropriate in people that are identified as at risk (Frazier & Hughes, 2008).

! NURSING ALERT

CRP is a protein that is released in the blood during inflammatory states. The high-sensitivity CRP (hs-CRP) is useful in assessing the risk of a cardiac event. A normal level is less than 0.1 mg/dL or less than 1 mg/L (Fischbach & Dunning, 2009).

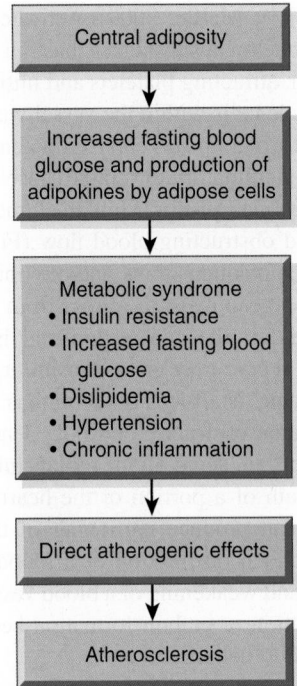

FIGURE 14-3 Pathophysiology of CVD in metabolic syndrome. Both central adiposity and the immune system play a role in the development of metabolic syndrome. Adipokines (such as leptin) and cytokines (such as tumor necrosis factor) are thought to contribute to the development of metabolic abnormalities. The eventual effect of these processes is the promotion of atherosclerosis.

Additionally, a risk equivalent is a condition that places patients at high risk for experiencing a cardiac event, such as a myocardial infarction. Having one or more of these conditions may place patients at the same risk of having a cardiac event as someone who has already experienced one (Grundy, Cleeman, Merz et al., 2004). Risk equivalents for cardiac events are detailed in Box 14-1.

Clinical Manifestations and Assessment

Coronary atherosclerosis produces symptoms and complications according to the location and degree of narrowing of

---

BOX 14-1

Coronary Artery Disease Risk Equivalents

Individuals at highest risk for a cardiac event within 10 years are those with existing coronary artery disease (CAD) and those with any of the following diseases, which are called CAD risk equivalents (Grundy, Cleeman, Merz et al., 2004):

- Diabetes
- Peripheral arterial disease
- Abdominal aortic aneurysm
- Carotid artery disease

the arterial lumen, thrombus formation, and obstruction of blood flow to the myocardium. This impediment to blood flow is usually progressive, causing an inadequate blood supply that deprives the cardiac muscle cells of oxygen needed for their survival. The condition is known as **ischemia**. **Angina pectoris** refers to chest pain that is brought about by myocardial ischemia. If the decrease in blood supply is significant enough, of long enough duration, or both, death of myocardial cells, or MI, may result. Over time, irreversibly damaged myocardium undergoes degeneration and is replaced by scar tissue, causing various degrees of myocardial dysfunction. Significant myocardial damage may result in persistently low cardiac output, and if the heart cannot support the body's needs for oxygenated blood, the result is heart failure. Myocardial hypoxia due to CAD may also lead to lethal cardiac rhythm disturbances that may result in sudden cardiac death.

NURSING ALERT

Classic signs and symptoms of myocardial ischemia include: acute onset of chest pain (often described as crushing pain, usually substernal but may be in other areas of the chest, jaw, back, or arms), shortness of breath (dyspnea [particularly in the elderly]), extreme fatigue, diaphoresis, and nausea and vomiting. The pain of an MI may be differentiated from angina by persistence of the pain despite rest and nitroglycerine. Women often complain of atypical chest pain and nonspecific signs and symptoms.

In the elderly, sometimes there are no symptoms ("silent" CAD), making recognition and diagnosis a clinical challenge. Elderly patients should be encouraged to recognize their chest pain–like symptom (e.g., weakness) as an indication that they should rest or take prescribed medications. Pharmacologic stress testing may be used to diagnose CAD in elderly patients because other conditions (e.g., peripheral vascular disease, arthritis, degenerative disk disease, physical disability, foot problems) may limit the patient's ability to exercise.

Prevention and Medical and Nursing Management

Controlling cholesterol and treating hyperlipidemia, and managing hypertension and diabetes mellitus are discussed here; additional medical and nursing management is discussed under angina.

Controlling Cholesterol Abnormalities

The association of a high blood cholesterol level with CAD is well established. The metabolism of fats is an important contributor to the development of CAD. Fats, which are insoluble in water, are encased in water-soluble lipoproteins that allow them to be transported within the circulatory system. The various lipoproteins are categorized by their protein content,

which is measured in density. The density increases when more protein is present. Four elements of fat metabolism—total cholesterol, LDL, HDL, and triglycerides—affect the development of heart disease. Cholesterol is processed by the GI tract into lipoprotein globules called *chylomicrons*. These are reprocessed by the liver as lipoproteins (Fig. 14-4). This is a physiologic process necessary for the formation of lipoprotein-based cell membranes and other important metabolic processes. When an excess of LDL is produced, LDL particles adhere to vulnerable points in the arterial endothelium. Here, macrophages ingest them, leading to the formation of foam cells and the beginning of plaque formation.

All adults 20 years of age or older should have a fasting lipid profile (total cholesterol, LDL, HDL, and triglyceride) performed at least once every 5 years and more often if the profile is abnormal. Patients younger than 20 years of age with known family history of hyperlipidemia and/or vascular disease should probably be tested earlier. Patients who have had an acute event (e.g., MI), a **percutaneous coronary intervention (PCI)**, or a **coronary artery bypass graft (CABG)** require assessment of the LDL cholesterol level within a few months of the event or procedure, because LDL levels may be low immediately after the acute event or procedure. Subsequently, lipids should be monitored every 6 weeks until the desired level is achieved and then every 4 to 6 months (Grundy et al., 2004).

LDL exerts a harmful effect on the coronary vasculature because the small LDL particles can be easily transported into the vessel lining. In contrast, HDL promotes the use of total cholesterol by transporting LDL to the liver, where it is biodegraded and then excreted. The level of HDL should exceed 40 mg/dL and should ideally be more than 60 mg/dL. A high HDL level is a strong negative risk factor for heart disease (i.e., it protects against disease).

The goal is to have low LDL values and high HDL values. The desired level of LDL depends on the patient:

- Less than 160 mg/dL for patients with one or no risk factors
- Less than 130 mg/dL for patients with two or more risk factors
- Less than 100 mg/dL for patients with CAD or at high risk for CAD.
- Less than 70 mg/dL is desirable for patients at very high risk for an acute coronary event (Hughes, 2009)

Serum cholesterol and LDL levels can often be controlled by diet and physical activity. Depending on the patient's LDL level and risk of CAD, medication to treat hyperlipidemia may also be prescribed. Medication should be used in conjunction with a heart-healthy diet and an exercise program. Refer to Table 14-1 for commonly prescribed medications affecting lipoprotein metabolism.

Treating Hyperlipidemia

Lipid-lowering medications can reduce CAD mortality in patients with elevated lipid levels and in at-risk patients with

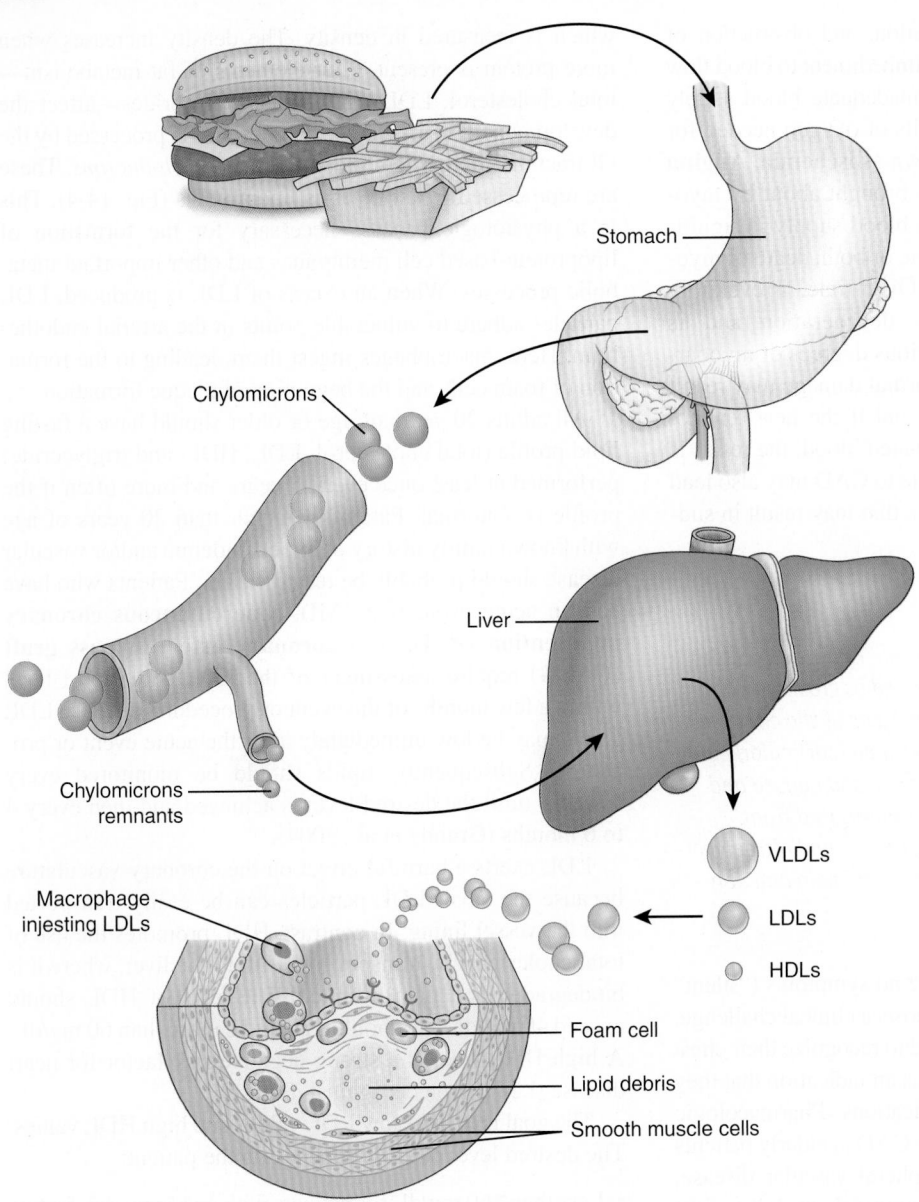

FIGURE 14-4 Lipoproteins and the development of atherosclerosis. As dietary cholesterol and saturated fat are processed by the GI tract, chylomicrons enter the blood. They are broken down into chylomicron remnants in the capillaries. The liver processes them into lipoproteins. When these are released into the circulation, excess low-density lipoproteins (LDLs) adhere to receptors on the intimal wall. Macrophages also ingest LDLs and transport them into the vessel wall, beginning the process of plaque formation. HDLs, high-density lipoproteins; VLDL, very-low-density lipoprotein.

normal lipid levels. Patients with elevated cholesterol levels should be monitored for adherence to the therapeutic plan, the effect of cholesterol-lowering medications, and the development of side effects. Lipid levels are obtained and adjustments made to the diet and medication every 6 weeks until the lipid goal or maximum dose is achieved and then every 6 months thereafter (Grundy et al., 2004). Lifestyle changes need to be incorporated into any treatment regime and include:

- Dietary measures include a heart-healthy diet (monitor and treat hyperlipidemia if dietary control is not enough).
- Increase physical activity (at least 30 minutes of moderate exercise daily or at least 10,000 steps a day) (Haffey, 2009; National Heart, Lung, and Blood Institute, 2005).

- Smoking cessation (people who stop smoking reduce their risk of heart disease 30% to 50% within the first year, and the risk continues to decline)
- Stress management
- Hypertension management
- Diabetes management

Managing Hypertension

The risk of CVD increases as blood pressure increases. Elevated blood pressure may result in increased stiffness of the vessel walls, leading to vessel injury and a resulting inflammatory response within the intima. Inflammatory mediators then lead to the release of growth-promoting factors that cause vessel hypertrophy and hyper-responsiveness. These changes

TABLE
14-1 Medications Affecting Lipoprotein Metabolism

Medication and Daily Dosage	Lipid/Lipoprotein Effects	Side Effects	Contraindications
HMG-CoA Reductase Inhibitors (statins) Lovastatin (Mevacor) Pravastatin (Pravachol) Simvastatin (Zocor) Fluvastatin (Lescol) Atorvastatin calcium (Lipitor) Rosuvastatin (Crestor)	LDL ↓ 18%–55% HDL ↑ 5%–15% TG ↓ 7%–30%	Myopathy, increased liver enzyme levels	Absolute: Active or chronic liver disease Relative: Concomitant use of certain drugs*
Nicotinic Acid Niacin (Niacor, Niaspan) Immediate-release nicotinic acid Extended-release nicotinic acid Sustained-release nicotinic acid	LDL ↓ 5%–25% HDL ↑ 15%–35% TG ↓ 20%–50%	Flushing, hyperglycemia, hyperuricemia (or gout), upper GI distress, hepatotoxicity	Absolute: Chronic liver disease, severe gout Relative: Diabetes, hyperuricemia, peptic ulcer disease
Fibric Acids Fenofibrate (TriCor) Clofibrate (Atromid-S)	LDL ↓ 5%–20% (may be increased in patients with high TG) HDL ↑ 10%–20% TG ↓ 20%–50%	Dyspepsia, gallstones, myopathy, unexplained non-CHD deaths	Absolute: Severe renal disease, severe hepatic disease
Bile Acid Sequestrants Cholestyramine (LoCholest, Questran, Prevalite) Colesevelam (WelChol) Colestipol HCl (Colestid)	LDL ↓ 15%–30% HDL ↑ 3%–5% TG no change or increase	GI distress, constipation, decreased absorption of other drugs	Absolute: dysbetalipo-proteinemia, TG >400 mg/dL Relative: TG >200 mg/dL

HMG-CoA, 3-hydroxy-3-methylglutaryl coenzyme A; LDL, low-density lipoprotein; HDL, high-density lipoprotein; TG, triglycerides; ↓ decrease, ↑ increase; CHD, coronary heart disease.
*Cyclosporine (Neoral, Sandimmune, SangCya); macrolide antibiotics (azithromycin [Zithromax], clarithromycin [Biaxin]; dirithromycin [Dynabac]; erythromycin [Aknemycin, E-mycin, Ery-Tab]); various antifungal agents and cytochrome P-450 inhibitors; fibrates; and niacin should be used with appropriate caution (Grundy, Cleeman, Merz et al., 2004).

result in acceleration and aggravation of atherosclerosis. Hypertension also increases the work of the left ventricle, which must pump harder to eject blood into the arteries. Over time, the increased workload causes the heart to enlarge and thicken, and may eventually lead to cardiac failure.

Early detection of high blood pressure and adherence to a therapeutic regimen can prevent the serious consequences associated with untreated elevated blood pressure. Hypertension is discussed in detail in Chapter 13.

Controlling Diabetes Mellitus

The relationship between diabetes mellitus and heart disease has been confirmed. For 50% to 75% of patients with diabetes, CVD is identified as the cause of death (Porth & Matfin, 2009). Hyperglycemia fosters dyslipidemia, increased platelet aggregation, and altered red blood cell function, which can lead to thrombus formation. Effective treatment with appropriate anti-hyperglycemic agents and diet has shown improvement in endothelial function and improved endothelial-dependent dilation (Lago & Nesto, 2009). Diabetes is considered equivalent to existing CAD as a risk factor for a

cardiac event within 10 years (Buse, Ginsberg, Bakris et al., 2007). Diabetes is discussed in detail in Chapter 30.

ANGINA PECTORIS

Angina pectoris is a clinical syndrome usually characterized by episodes or paroxysms of pain or pressure in the anterior chest. The cause is insufficient coronary blood flow (usually caused by atherosclerotic disease) resulting in a decreased oxygen supply when there is increased myocardial demand for oxygen in response to physical exertion or emotional stress. In other words, the need for oxygen exceeds the supply. The severity of angina is based on the precipitating activity and its effect on activities of daily living. Types of angina are listed in Box 14-2.

Pathophysiology

Angina is usually caused by atherosclerotic disease. Almost invariably, angina is associated with a significant obstruction of

Types of Angina

- *Stable angina*: Predictable and consistent pain that occurs on exertion and is relieved by rest
- *Unstable angina* (also called preinfarction angina or crescendo angina): Symptoms occur more frequently and last longer than in stable angina. The threshold for pain is lower, and pain may occur at rest.
- *Intractable or refractory angina*: Severe incapacitating chest pain
- *Variant angina* (also called **Prinzmetal's angina**): Pain at rest with reversible ST-segment elevation; thought to be caused by coronary artery vasospasm
- *Silent ischemia*: Objective evidence of ischemia (such as electrocardiogram changes with a stress test), but patient reports no symptoms

a major coronary artery. Normally, the myocardium extracts a large amount of oxygen from the coronary circulation to meet its continuous demands. When there is an increase in demand, flow through the coronary arteries needs to be increased. When there is blockage in a coronary artery, flow cannot be increased, and ischemia results. Because angina is a symptom of coronary atherosclerosis, the risk factors are the same.

Clinical Manifestations and Assessment

Ischemia of the heart muscle may produce pain or other symptoms, varying in severity from mild indigestion to a choking or heavy sensation in the upper chest that ranges from discomfort to agonizing pain accompanied by severe apprehension and a feeling of impending death. Typically, the pain or discomfort is poorly localized and may radiate to the neck, jaw, shoulders, and inner aspects of the upper arms, usually the left arm. The patient often feels tightness or a heavy, choking, or strangling sensation that has a viselike, insistent quality. The patient with diabetes mellitus may not have severe pain with angina because diabetic neuropathy can dull the perception of pain. A woman may have different symptoms than a man, because coronary disease in women tends to be more diffuse and affects long segments of the artery rather than discrete segments. Table 14-2 discusses anginal pain.

The nurse is alert for complaints of weakness or numbness in the arms, wrists, and hands, as well as shortness of breath, pallor, diaphoresis, anxiety, dizziness or lightheadedness, and nausea and vomiting that may accompany the pain (termed associated signs and symptoms). Angina may subside with rest or nitroglycerin. In many patients, anginal symptoms follow a stable, predictable pattern.

The diagnosis of angina begins with the patient's history related to the clinical manifestations of ischemia. A 12-lead electrocardiogram (ECG) and blood laboratory biomarker values help in making the diagnosis. The patient may undergo an exercise or pharmacologic stress test in which the heart is monitored by ECG, echocardiogram, or both. The patient may also be referred for a nuclear scan or invasive procedure (e.g., cardiac catheterization, coronary artery angiography).

Medical Management

The objectives of the medical management of CAD and angina are to decrease the oxygen demand of the myocardium and to increase the oxygen supply. Medically, these objectives are met through pharmacologic therapy and control of risk factors. Alternatively, reperfusion procedures may be used to restore the blood supply to the myocardium. These include PCI (percutaneous coronary intervention) procedures (e.g., **percutaneous transluminal coronary angioplasty [PTCA]**, intracoronary stents, and atherectomy), and CABG.

TABLE
14-2 Assessing Angina

Acronym	Factors About Pain That Need To Be Assessed	Assessment Questions
P	Position/Location	"Where is the pain? Can you point to it?"
	Provocation	"What were you doing when the pain began?"
Q	Quality	"How would you describe the pain?"
		"Is it like the pain you had before?"
	Quantity	"Has the pain been constant?"
R	Radiation	"Can you feel the pain anywhere else?"
	Relief	"Did anything make the pain better?"
S	Severity	"How would you rate the pain on a 0–10 scale, with 0 being no pain and 10 being the most amount of pain?" (or use visual analog scale or adjective rating scale)
	Symptoms	"Did you notice any other symptoms with the pain?" (such as nausea, vomiting, diaphoresis)
T	Timing	"How long ago did the pain start?"

From Jarvis, C. (2007). *Physical examination and health assessment* (7th ed.) St. Louis: Saunders.

Pharmacologic Therapy

Several types of drugs are used to treat coronary vascular disease:

- *Positive inotrope*: A medication that increases myocardial contractility (force of contraction)
- *Negative inotrope*: A medication that decreases myocardial contractility
- *Positive chronotrope*: A medication that increases heart rate
- *Negative chronotrope*: A medication that decreases heart rate

Nitrates

Nitrates remain the mainstay for treatment of coronary ischemia. A vasoactive agent (Nitroglycerin, Nitrostat, Nitrol, Nitro-Bid, Nitro-paste) is administered to reduce myocardial oxygen consumption, which decreases ischemia and relieves pain. Nitroglycerin dilates primarily the veins and, in higher doses, also the arteries. Dilation of the veins causes venous pooling of blood throughout the body. As a result, less blood returns to the heart, and filling pressure (preload) is reduced. If the patient is hypovolemic (does not have adequate circulating blood volume), the decrease in filling pressure can cause a significant decrease in cardiac output and blood pressure, thus it is important for the nurse to monitor the patient's response to nitrates. Nitrates also relax the systemic arteriolar bed and increase oxygen supply, bringing about a more favorable balance between supply and demand.

When nitroglycerin is administered sublingually (SL), the patient's response is assessed (relief of chest pain and effect on blood pressure and heart rate). If the chest pain is unchanged or is lessened but still present, nitroglycerin SL administration is repeated up to three doses. Each time, blood pressure, heart rate, and the ST segment (if the patient is on a monitor with ST-segment monitoring capability) are assessed. If the pain is significant and continues after these interventions, the patient is further evaluated for acute MI and further intervention is necessary.

DRUG ALERT

The nurse should always check the expiration dates on the bottle of nitroglycerin tablets.

Most patients with angina pectoris must self-administer nitroglycerin on an as-needed basis. A key nursing role in such cases is educating patients about the medication and how to take it (Box 14-3). SL nitroglycerin comes in tablet and spray forms.

Beta-Adrenergic Blocking Agents

Beta blockers such as metoprolol (Lopressor, Toprol) and atenolol (Tenormin) reduce myocardial oxygen consumption by blocking beta-adrenergic sympathetic stimulation to the heart. The result is a reduction in heart rate, slowed conduction of impulses through the conduction system, decreased blood pressure, and reduced myocardial **contractility** (negative chronotrope and negative inotrope) to balance the myocardial oxygen

---

BOX 14-3 — Patient Education

Self-Administration of Nitroglycerin

- Instruct the patient to make sure the mouth is moist, the tongue is still, and saliva is not swallowed until the nitroglycerin tablet dissolves. If the pain is severe, the patient can crush the tablet between the teeth to hasten sublingual absorption.
- Advise the patient to carry the medication at all times as a precaution. However, because nitroglycerin is very unstable, it should be carried securely in its original container (e.g., capped dark glass bottle); tablets should never be removed and stored in metal or plastic pillboxes.
- Explain that nitroglycerin is volatile and is inactivated by heat, moisture, air, light, and time. Instruct the patient to renew the nitroglycerin supply every 6 months.
- Inform the patient that the medication should be taken in anticipation of any activity that may produce pain. Because nitroglycerin increases tolerance for exercise and stress when taken prophylactically (i.e., before angina-producing activity, such as exercise, stair-climbing, or sexual intercourse), it is best taken before pain develops.
- Recommend that the patient note how long it takes for the nitroglycerin to relieve the discomfort. Advise the patient that if pain persists after taking three sublingual tablets at 5-minute intervals, emergency medical services should be called.
- Discuss possible side effects of nitroglycerin, including flushing, throbbing headache, hypotension, and tachycardia.
- Advise the patient to sit down for a few minutes when taking nitroglycerin to avoid hypotension and syncope.

---

needs (demands) and the amount of oxygen available (supply). This helps control chest pain and delays the onset of ischemia during work or exercise. Beta blockers reduce the incidence of recurrent angina, infarction, and cardiac mortality. Patients taking beta blockers are cautioned not to stop taking them abruptly, because angina may worsen and MI may develop.

Calcium Channel Blocking Agents

Calcium channel blockers (calcium ion antagonists such as Norvasc, Cardizem) have a variety of effects. These agents decrease sinoatrial node automaticity and atrioventricular node conduction, resulting in a slower heart rate and a decrease in the strength of the heart muscle contraction (negative inotropic and negative chronotropic effects). These effects decrease the workload of the heart. Calcium channel blockers also relax the blood vessels, causing a decrease in blood pressure and an increase in coronary artery perfusion. Calcium channel blockers increase myocardial oxygen supply by dilating the smooth muscle wall of the coronary arterioles; they decrease myocardial oxygen demand by reducing systemic arterial pressure and the workload of the

left ventricle. They may be prescribed to prevent and treat vasospasm (as in variant angina). The calcium channel blockers most commonly used are amlodipine (Norvasc) and diltiazem (Cardizem, Tiazac).

Antiplatelet and Anticoagulant Medications

Antiplatelet medications are administered to prevent platelet aggregation and subsequent thrombosis, which impedes blood flow. The patient receiving anticoagulation therapy should be monitored for signs and symptoms of external and internal bleeding, such as low blood pressure, increased heart rate, and decreased serum hemoglobin and hematocrit. The patient should be placed on bleeding precautions, which include:

- Applying pressure to the site of any needle puncture for a longer time than usual
- Avoiding intramuscular (IM) injections
- Avoiding tissue injury and bruising from trauma or use of constrictive devices (e.g., continuous use of an automatic blood pressure cuff)

Examples of antiplatelet and anticoagulant medications include aspirin, clopidogrel, heparin, and glycoprotein IIb, IIIa inhibitors.

Aspirin prevents platelet activation and reduces the incidence of MI and death in patients with CAD.

Clopidogrel (Plavix) or ticlopidine (Ticlid) is given to patients who are allergic to aspirin or is given in addition to aspirin in patients at high risk for MI. Unlike aspirin, these medications take a few days to achieve their antiplatelet effect. They also may cause GI upset.

IV unfractionated heparin (UFH) prevents the formation of new blood clots. Treating patients with unstable angina with heparin reduces the occurrence of MI. A decrease in platelet count or evidence of thrombosis may indicate a serious complication called *heparin-induced thrombocytopenia* (HIT), an antibody-mediated reaction to heparin that may result in thrombosis. Patients who have received heparin within the past 3 months and those who have been receiving UFH for 5 to 15 days are at high risk for HIT.

💊 D R U G   A L E R T

HIT is a complication of anticoagulation with UFH or low-molecular-weight heparin (LMWH). It is an immune-mediated disorder in which antibodies form against the heparin-platelet factor 4 complex. The antibody complex attaches to the platelet, causing its aggregation. The reticuloendothelial system destroys activated platelets, thus resulting in decreased platelet counts. Frequently, procoagulants are also generated, resulting in thrombosis. A complication of HIT is heparin-associated thrombocytopenia and thrombosis (HITT). In the presence of unexplained thrombocytopenia, or venous or arterial thrombosis associated with thrombocytopenia, HIT should be considered. Discontinuation of heparin as soon as diagnosis is suspected is warranted (Warkentin, Greinacher, Koster et al., 2008).

IV administration of glycoprotein *(GP) IIb/IIIa agents* (abciximab [ReoPro], tirofiban [Aggrastat], eptifibatide [Integrilin]) is indicated for hospitalized patients with unstable angina and as adjunct therapy for PCI. These agents prevent platelet aggregation by blocking the GPIIb/IIIa receptors on the platelets, preventing adhesion of fibrinogen and other factors that crosslink platelets to each other and thereby would normally allow platelets to form a thrombus (clot). As with heparin, bleeding is the major side effect, and bleeding precautions should be initiated.

Oxygen Administration

Oxygen therapy is usually initiated at the onset of chest pain in an attempt to increase the amount of oxygen delivered to the myocardium and to decrease pain. Blood oxygen saturation is monitored by pulse oximetry; the normal oxygen saturation (SpO_2) level is greater than 95%.

Percutaneous Coronary Interventions

PCIs to treat angina and CAD include PTCA and intracoronary stent implantation. The patient in whom an acute MI is suspected may be referred for an immediate PCI, in which case the occluded coronary artery is opened and reperfusion to the area that has been deprived of oxygen is reestablished. Superior outcomes have been reported with use of PCI compared to thrombolytics because PCI treats the underlying atherosclerotic lesion (Stenestrand, Lindback, & Wallentin, 2006). The duration of oxygen deprivation is directly related to the number of cells that die, therefore the time from the patient's arrival in the emergency department to the time PCI is performed is critical and should be less than 60 minutes (time is muscle!). This is frequently referred to as *door-to-balloon time*. A cardiac catheterization laboratory and staff must be available if an emergent PCI is to be performed within this short time.

⚡ N U R S I N G   A L E R T

It is imperative that an accurate assessment of a patient's peripheral vascular system is documented pre-procedure. This data will be used to evaluate postoperative vascular status. The assessment should include extremities color, sensation, temperature, capillary refill, and peripheral perfusion using the grading scale common to the nurse's institution. The affected extremity is assessed every 15 minutes for the first hour and then according to hospital protocol.

Percutaneous Transluminal Coronary Angioplasty

In PTCA, an invasive interventional procedure, a balloon-tipped catheter is used to open blocked coronary vessels and resolve ischemia. It is used in patients with angina and as an intervention for acute MI. Catheter-based interventions can also be used to open blocked CABGs (coronary artery

bypass grafts). The purpose of PTCA is to improve blood flow within a coronary artery by compressing and "cracking" the atheroma. The procedure is attempted when the cardiologist believes that PTCA can improve blood flow to the myocardium.

PTCA is carried out in the cardiac catheterization laboratory. Hollow catheters called *sheaths* are inserted, usually in the femoral artery, providing a conduit for other catheters. Catheters are then threaded through the femoral artery, up through the aorta, and into the coronary arteries. Angiography is performed using injected radiopaque contrast agents (commonly called *dye*) to identify the location and extent of the blockage. A balloon-tipped dilation catheter is passed through the sheath and positioned over the lesion. The physician determines the catheter position by examining markers on the balloon that can be seen with fluoroscopy. When the catheter is properly positioned, the balloon is inflated with high pressure for several seconds and then deflated. The pressure compresses and possibly "cracks" the atheroma (Fig. 14-5). The media and adventitia of the coronary artery are also stretched.

Several inflations and several balloon sizes may be required to achieve the goal, usually defined as an improvement in blood flow and a residual stenosis of less than 20%. Other measures of the success of a PTCA are an increase in the artery's lumen, a difference of less than 20 mm Hg in blood pressure from one side of the lesion to the other, and no clinically obvious arterial trauma. Because the blood supply to the coronary artery decreases while the balloon is inflated, the patient may complain of chest pain and the ECG may display significant ST-segment changes. Intracoronary stents are usually positioned in the intima of the vessel to maintain patency after the balloon is withdrawn. Refer to Table 14-3 for complications after PTCA.

Coronary Artery Stent

After PTCA, the area that has been treated may close off partially or completely, a process called *restenosis*. The intima of the coronary artery has been injured and responds by initiating an acute inflammatory process. This process may include release of mediators that lead to vasoconstriction, clotting, and scar tissue formation. A coronary artery stent is placed to overcome these risks. A **stent** is a metal mesh that provides structural support to a vessel at risk of acute closure. The stent is positioned over the angioplasty balloon. When the balloon is inflated, the mesh expands and presses against the vessel wall, holding the artery open. The balloon is withdrawn, but the stent is left permanently in place within the artery; eventually endothelium covers the stent, and it is incorporated into the vessel wall. Because of the risk of thrombus formation in the stent, the patient receives antiplatelet medications (examples are clopidogrel [Plavix] and aspirin). These medications are routinely continued for at least 3 to 6 months to decrease the risk of thrombus formation.

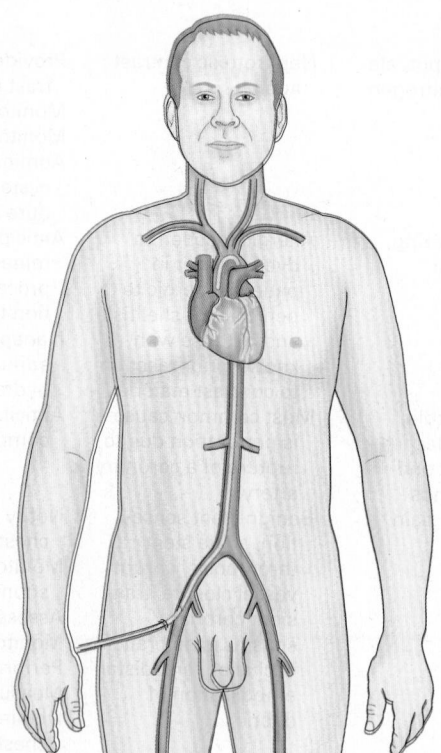

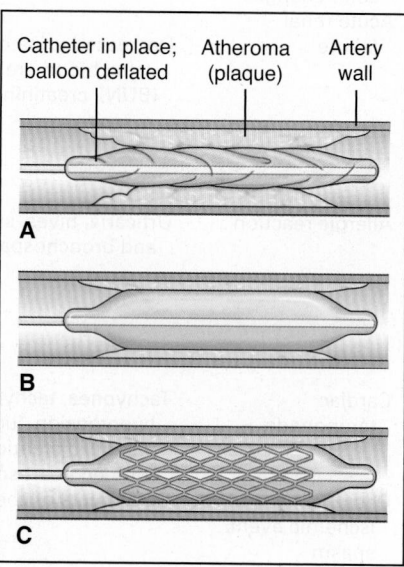

FIGURE 14-5 Percutaneous transluminal coronary angioplasty. **(A)** A balloon-tipped catheter is passed into the affected coronary artery and placed across the area of the atheroma (plaque). **(B)** The balloon is then rapidly inflated and deflated with controlled pressure. **(C)** A stent is placed to maintain patency of the artery, and the balloon is removed.

T A B L E
14-3 Complications After Percutaneous Transluminal Coronary Angioplasty (PTCA)

Complication	Signs and Symptoms	Possible Causes	Nursing Actions
Bleeding or hematoma	Expanding mass surrounding puncture site. Hard lump or bluish tinge at sheath insertion site	Anticoagulant therapy, coughing, vomiting, bending leg or hip, obesity, bladder distention, high blood pressure	Keep the patient on bedrest. Apply manual pressure at site of sheath insertion. Outline extent of hematoma with a marking pen. Monitor results of complete blood cell count. If bleeding does not stop, notify physician or nurse practitioner. Anticipate interruption of anticoagulant and antiplatelet therapies. Blood transfusion may be indicated.
Lost or weakened pulse distal to sheath insertion site	Extremity cool, cyanotic, pale, or painful	Arterial thrombus or embolus	Assessment of peripheral circulation by comparing bilateral pulses; note temperature, capillary refill, sensation, and movement, as well as color of the affected extremity. Notify physician or nurse practitioner. Anticipate surgery and anticoagulation or thrombolytic therapy.
Pseudoaneurysm and arteriovenous fistula; if they rupture, sudden massive swelling and severe pain will be seen.	A large painful pulsatile mass felt or bruit heard near sheath insertion site	Vessel trauma during procedure	Notify physician or nurse practitioner. Anticipate ultrasound-guided compression. If the pseudoaneurysm is small (<2 cm), it may be observed and monitored clinically. Assess circulation, sensation, and motility of involved extremity. Prepare patient for surgery to close fistula if indicated.
Retroperitoneal bleeding (blood collecting in the retroperitoneal space may not produce obvious swelling or skin color changes)	Back or flank pain Unexplained hypotension Tachycardia Restlessness and agitation Decreased hemoglobin/hematocrit	Arterial tear causing bleeding into flank area	Notify physician or nurse practitioner immediately. Stop any anticoagulation medication. Anticipate need for IV fluids and/or administration of blood.
Acute renal failure	Decreased urine output, elevated blood urea nitrogen (BUN), creatinine	Nephrotoxic contrast agent	Provide hydration to promote excretion of contrast material. Monitor urine output. Monitor BUN and creatinine. Administer renal protective agents (e.g., acetylcysteine [Mucomyst] before and after procedure as prescribed.
Allergic reaction	Urticaria, hives, sneezing, and bronchospasm	Allergic reaction to dye is higher in patients allergic to penicillin or shellfish and in those with known prior reaction to contrast material.	Anticipate administering prednisone, antihistamines, and H_2 blockers before the coronary procedure for patients with known prior reaction to contrast material or shellfish. If anaphylaxis occurs, the nurse anticipates administering epinephrine and IV saline for hydration.
Cardiac tamponade	Tachypnea, tachycardia, hypotension, jugular venous distention, and muffled heart sounds	Most common cause is perforation due to rupture of a coronary artery.	Anticipate a pericardiocentesis in patients with compromised hemodynamic status.
Chest pain/acute ischemic event/ spasm	Complaints of chest pain	Benign stent sensation, acute stent thrombosis, abrupt vessel closure, transient coronary spasms, side branch occlusion, and distal embolization of debris	Notify the provider when patient complains of chest pain. Monitor vital signs, O_2 sat, lung and cardiac sounds. Assess peripheral perfusion. Monitor electrocardiogram (ECG). Perform serial tests for cardiac markers. Measure troponin. Obtain a 12-lead ECG with any episodes of chest pain.

From Shoulders-Odom, B. (2008). Management of patients after percutaneous coronary interventions. *Critical Care Nurse, 28*, 26–40.

Complications that can occur during a PCI procedure include dissection, perforation, abrupt closure, or vasospasm of the coronary artery, acute MI, acute arrhythmias (e.g., ventricular tachycardia), and cardiac arrest. These may require emergency surgical treatment. Complications after the procedure may include abrupt closure of the coronary artery and vascular complications, such as bleeding at the insertion site, retroperitoneal bleeding, hematoma, pseudo-aneurysm, arteriovenous fistula, or arterial thrombosis and distal embolization, as well as acute renal failure.

⚠ NURSING ALERT
Severe renal failure is associated with post PCI procedural mortality (Osten, Ivanov, Eichhofer et al., 2008; Zouaoui, Ouldzein, Boudou et al., 2008). Patients admitted with chronic renal insufficiency are at a higher risk for renal failure and more adverse cardiac events (MACE) after PCI, therefore monitoring of urinary output and renal function tests are particularly critical in this patient population.

Post-Procedure Care

Patient care is similar to that for a cardiac catheterization. Many patients are admitted to the hospital the day of the PCI and discharged the next day (Kaluski, Alfano, Randhawa et al., 2008). When the PCI is performed emergently to relieve acute coronary syndrome (ACS), the patient will usually go to a critical care unit and stay in the hospital for a few days. During the PCI, patients receive IV heparin and are monitored closely for signs of bleeding. Patients may also receive a GPIIb/IIIa agent (e.g., eptifibatide [Integrilin]) for several hours following the PCI to prevent platelet aggregation and thrombus formation in the coronary artery. Hemostasis is achieved, and femoral sheaths may be removed at the end of the procedure by using a vascular closure device (e.g., Angio-Seal, VasoSeal) or a device that sutures the vessels. Hemostasis after sheath removal may also be achieved by direct manual pressure, a mechanical compression device (e.g., C-shaped clamp), or a pneumatic compression device (e.g., FemoStop).

The patient may return to the nursing unit with the large peripheral vascular access sheaths in place. The sheaths are then removed after blood studies (e.g., ACT [activated clotting time]) indicate that the heparin is no longer active and the clotting time is within an acceptable range. This usually takes a few hours, depending on the amount of heparin given during the procedure. The patient must remain in bed and keep the affected leg straight; the head of bed (HOB) is not elevated beyond 30 degrees, until the sheaths are removed and then for a few hours afterward to maintain hemostasis. Sheath removal and the application of pressure on the vessel insertion site may cause the heart rate to slow and the blood pressure to decrease (vasovagal response). An IV bolus of atropine is usually given to treat this response.

Some patients with unstable lesions and at high risk for abrupt vessel closure are restarted on heparin after sheath removal, or they receive an IV infusion of a GPIIb/IIIa inhibitor. These patients are monitored more closely and may recover more slowly.

After hemostasis is achieved, a pressure dressing is applied to the site. Patients resume self-care and ambulate unassisted within a few hours of the procedure. The duration of immobilization depends on the size of the sheath inserted, the amount of anticoagulant administered, the method of hemostasis, the patient's underlying condition, and the physician's preference. On the day after the procedure, the site is inspected and the dressing replaced with an adhesive bandage. The nurse teaches the patient to monitor the site for bleeding or development of a hard mass indicative of hematoma.

⚠ NURSING ALERT
Post PTCA, IV fluids may be administered to promote excretion of the contrast medium. The nurse is alert for signs of fluid volume excess that may include complaints of shortness of breath (SOB) at rest or with exertion, orthopnea, paroxysmal nocturnal dyspnea, cough, development or increased crackles in the lungs, S3 gallop, jugular vein distention (JVD), and pulsus alternans (characterized by alternating strong and weak peripheral pulses). Vital signs changes will vary depending on whether cardiac output is increased (hypertension) or reduced (hypotension).

Surgical Procedures: Coronary Artery Revascularization

Advances in diagnostics, medical management, and surgical and anesthesia techniques, as well as the care provided in critical care and surgical units, home care, and rehabilitation programs, have continued to make surgery a viable treatment option for patients with CAD. CABG has been done for about 35 years now, with techniques ever evolving and improving. CABG is a surgical procedure in which a blood vessel is grafted to the occluded coronary artery, so that blood can flow beyond the occlusion; it is also called a bypass graft.

Major indications for CABG include:

- Alleviation of angina that cannot be controlled with medication or PCI
- Treatment of left main coronary artery stenosis or multivessel CAD
- Prevention and treatment of MI, arrhythmias, or heart failure
- Treatment for complications from an unsuccessful PCI

The recommendation for CABG is determined by a number of factors, including the number of diseased coronary vessels, the degree of left ventricular dysfunction, the presence of other comorbidities, the patient's symptoms, and any

previous treatment. Historically, studies have shown that CABG may be the preferred treatment for high-risk patients, such as those with severe triple-vessel CAD, ventricular dysfunction, and diabetes; however, recent studies comparing clinical outcomes of CABG and PCI in patients with CAD fuel an ongoing debate (Dunlay, Rihal, Sundt et al., 2009; Lange & Hillis, 2009; Tarantini, Ramondo, Napodano et al., 2009).

For a patient to be considered for CABG, the coronary arteries to be bypassed must have approximately a 70% occlusion (60% if in the left main coronary artery). If significant blockage is not present, the flow through the artery will compete with the flow through the bypass, and circulation to the ischemic area of myocardium may not be improved. It is also necessary that the artery be patent beyond the area of blockage, or the flow through the bypass will be impeded.

A vessel commonly used for CABG is the greater saphenous vein, followed by the lesser saphenous vein (other veins may also be used) (Fig 14-6). The vein to be used is removed from its original location and grafted to the ascending aorta and to the coronary artery distal to the lesion. The saphenous veins are used in emergency CABG procedures because they can be obtained quickly by one surgeon while another performs the chest surgery. A common adverse effect of vein removal is edema in the extremity from which the vein was taken. The degree of edema varies and usually diminishes over time. Within 5 to 10 years, atherosclerotic changes often develop in saphenous vein grafts.

The right and left internal mammary arteries and occasionally the radial arteries are also used for CABG. Arterial grafts are preferred to venous grafts because they do not develop atherosclerotic changes as quickly and remain patent longer. The surgeon leaves the proximal end of the mammary artery intact and detaches the distal end of the artery from the chest wall. This end of the artery is then grafted to the coronary artery distal to the occlusion. The internal mammary arteries may not be long enough to use for multiple bypasses. Because of this, many CABG procedures are performed with a combination of venous and arterial grafts.

After CABG, as many as 41% to 87% of patients develop pleural effusions (fluid collection within the pleural space) in the immediate postoperative period, which is associated with a variety of etiologies including accumulation of pleural fluid because of congestive heart failure, surgical tissue trauma, hemorrhage from harvesting of the IMA, postoperative atelectasis and diaphragmatic dysfunction, or chylothorax (lymphatic fluid in the pleural space) because of unintended thoracic duct injury during the operative event (Heidecker & Sahn, 2006). Signs and symptoms vary based upon the etiology; however, the nurse is alert for dyspnea, cough, orthopnea (SOB when lying flat), splinting, dullness to percussion, decreased breath sounds, and decreased respiratory excursion on the affected side (for further details refer to Chapter 10).

Coronary Artery Bypass Graft Surgery

TRADITIONAL TECHNIQUE. The traditional CABG procedure is performed with the patient under general anesthesia. The surgeon makes a median sternotomy incision and connects the patient to the cardiopulmonary bypass (CPB) machine (discussed below). Next, a blood vessel from another part of the patient's body (e.g., saphenous vein, left internal mammary artery) is grafted distal to the coronary artery lesion, bypassing the obstruction (Fig. 14-7). CPB is

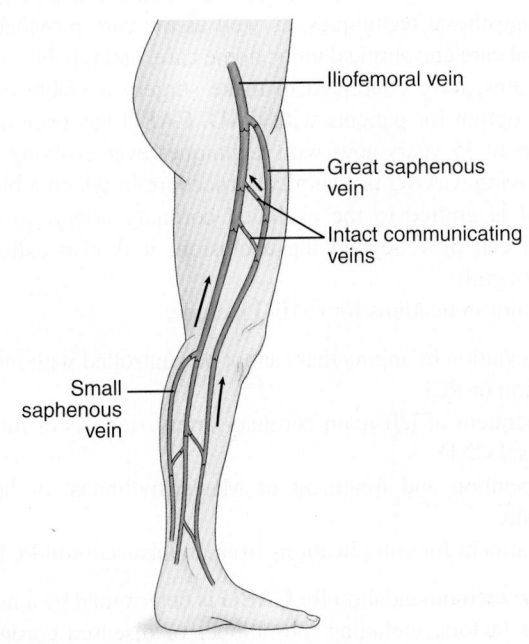

FIGURE 14-6 The greater and lesser saphenous veins are commonly used in bypass graft procedures.

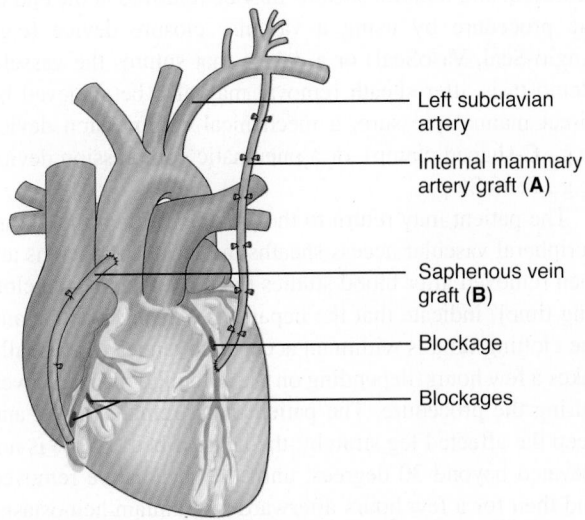

FIGURE 14-7 Coronary artery bypass grafts. One or more procedures may be performed using various veins and arteries. (A) Left internal mammary artery, used frequently because of its functional longevity. (B) Saphenous vein, also used as bypass graft.

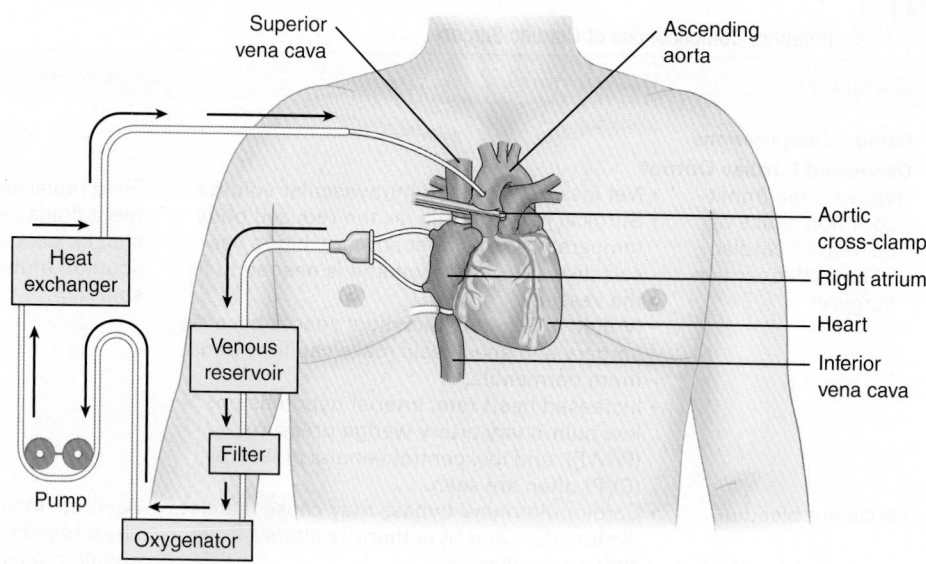

FIGURE 14-8 The cardiopulmonary bypass (CPB) system, in which cannulas are placed through the right atrium into the superior and inferior vena cavae to divert blood from the body and into the bypass system. The pump system creates a vacuum, pulling blood into the venous reservoir. The blood is cleared of air bubbles, clots, and particulates by the filter and then is passed through the oxygenator, releasing carbon dioxide and obtaining oxygen. Next, the blood is pulled to the pump and pushed out to the heat exchanger, where its temperature is regulated. The blood is then returned to the body via the ascending aorta.

then discontinued, chest tubes and epicardial pacing wires are placed, and the incision is closed. The patient then is admitted to a critical care unit and typically stays for about 24 hours before being transferred to the step-down unit.

Many cardiac surgical procedures are possible because of CPB (i.e., extracorporeal circulation) (Fig. 14-8). The procedure mechanically circulates and oxygenates blood for the body while bypassing the heart and lungs. CPB maintains perfusion to body organs and tissues and allows the surgeon to complete the anastomoses in a motionless, bloodless surgical field.

CPB is accomplished by placing a cannula in the right atrium, vena cava, or femoral vein to withdraw blood from the body. The cannula is connected to tubing filled with an isotonic crystalloid solution (usually 5% dextrose in lactated Ringer's solution). Venous blood removed from the body by the cannula is filtered, oxygenated, cooled, or warmed by the machine, and then returned to the body. The cannula used to return the oxygenated blood is usually inserted in the ascending aorta, or it may be inserted in the femoral artery. The heart is stopped by the injection of cardioplegia solution, which is high in potassium, into the coronary arteries. The patient receives heparin to prevent clotting and thrombus formation in the bypass circuit when blood comes in contact with the foreign surfaces of the tubing. At the end of the procedure, when the patient is disconnected from the bypass machine, protamine sulfate is administered to reverse the effects of heparin.

During the procedure, hypothermia is maintained, usually 28°C to 32°C (82.4°F to 89.6°F). The blood is cooled during CPB and returned to the body. The cooled blood slows the body's basal metabolic rate, thereby decreasing the demand for oxygen. Cooled blood usually has a higher

viscosity, but the crystalloid solution used to prime the bypass tubing dilutes the blood. When the surgical procedure is completed, the blood is rewarmed as it passes through the CPB circuit. Urine output, arterial blood gases (ABGs), electrolytes, and coagulation studies are monitored to assess the patient's status during CPB.

ALTERNATE TECHNIQUE. Another type of CABG procedure often done today is the "off pump" CABG or "OPCAB." The potential benefits of OPCAB include a decrease in the incidence of stroke and other neurologic complications, reduced blood usage, less renal failure, and fewer cardiac rhythm disturbances. Also done today is the "MIDCAB" or minimally invasive coronary artery bypass surgery. The MIDCAB is performed on a beating heart via a thoracotomy incision and is only suitable for single-vessel disease located in the anterior portions of the heart. Patients undergoing any type of CABG surgery will go to the intensive care unit for approximately 24 hours, then transfer to the step-down unit. The average overall hospital stay for CABG surgery is anticipated at 5 days.

Complications of Coronary Artery Bypass Graft

CABG may result in complications such as MI, arrhythmias, hemorrhage, and renal dysfunction. Table 14-4 presents an overview of the potential complications in the postoperative cardiac surgical patient. Although most patients improve symptomatically following surgery, CABG is not a cure for CAD, and angina, exercise intolerance, or other symptoms experienced before CABG may recur. Medications required before surgery may need to be continued. Lifestyle modifications recommended before surgery remain important to treat the underlying CAD and for the continued viability of the newly implanted grafts.

TABLE
14-4 Potential Complications of Cardiac Surgery

Complication	Description	Assessment and Management
Cardiac Complications		
Decreased Cardiac Output		
Hypovolemia (most common cause of decreased cardiac output after cardiac surgery)	• Net loss of blood and intravascular volume • Surgical hypothermia (as the reduced body temperature rises after surgery, blood vessels dilate and more volume is needed to fill the vessels). • IV fluid loss to the interstitial spaces because surgery and anesthesia make capillary beds more permeable. • Increased heart rate, arterial hypotension, low pulmonary artery wedge pressure (PAWP), and low central venous pressures (CVP) often are seen.	• Fluid replacement may be prescribed. Replacement fluids include: Colloid (albumin, hetastarch), packed red blood cells, or crystalloid solution (normal saline, lactated Ringer's solution).
Persistent bleeding	• Cardiopulmonary bypass may cause platelet dysfunction, and hypothermia alters clotting mechanisms. • Surgical trauma causing tissues and blood vessels to ooze bloody drainage • Intraoperative anticoagulant (heparin) therapy • Postoperative coagulopathy may also result from liver dysfunction and depletion of clotting components.	• Accurate measurement of wound bleeding and chest tube blood is essential. Bloody drainage should not exceed 200 mL/h for the first 4 to 6 hours. Drainage should decrease and stop within a few days, while progressing from sanguineous to serosanguineous and serous drainage. • Protamine sulfate may be administered to neutralize unfractionated heparin; vitamin K and blood products may be used to treat hematologic deficiencies. • If bleeding persists, the patient may return to the operating room.
Cardiac tamponade	• Fluid and clots accumulate in the pericardial sac, which compresses the heart, preventing blood from filling the ventricles. • Signs and symptoms include arterial hypotension, tachycardia, muffled heart sounds, decreasing urine output, and ↑ CVP. Additional signs and symptoms: arterial pressure waveform demonstrating a pulsus paradoxus (decrease of more than 10 mm Hg during inspiration) and decreased chest tube drainage (suggesting that the drainage is trapped or clotted in the mediastinum).	• The chest drainage system is checked to eliminate possible kinks or obstructions in the tubing. • Drainage system patency may be reestablished by milking the tubing (taking care not to strip the tubing, creating negative pressure within the chest, which may harm the surgical repair or trigger an arrhythmia). • Chest X-ray may show a widening mediastinum. • Emergency medical management is required; may include pericardiocentesis or return to surgery.
Fluid overload	• High PAWP, CVP, and pulmonary artery diastolic pressures, as well as crackles indicate fluid overload.	• Diuretics are prescribed and the rate of IV fluid administration is reduced. • Alternative treatments include continuous renal replacement therapy and dialysis.
Hypothermia	• Low body temperature leads to vasoconstriction, shivering, and arterial hypertension.	• Patient is rewarmed gradually after surgery, decreasing vasoconstriction.
Hypertension	• Results from postoperative vasoconstriction. It may stretch suture lines and cause postoperative bleeding. The condition may be transient.	• Vasodilators (nitroglycerin [Tridil], nitroprusside [Nipride, Nitropress]) may be used to treat hypertension. Administer cautiously to avoid hypotension.
Tachyarrhythmias	• Increased heart rate is common with perioperative volume changes. Uncontrolled atrial fibrillation commonly occurs during the first few days postoperatively.	• If a tachyarrhythmia is the primary problem, the heart rhythm is assessed and medications (e.g., adenosine [Adenocard, Adenoscan], amiodarone [Cordarone], digoxin [Lanoxin], diltiazem [Cardizem], esmolol [Brevibloc], lidocaine [Xylocaine], procainamide [Pronestyl]), may be prescribed. Patients may be prescribed antiarrhythmics before coronary artery bypass graft (CABG) to minimize the risk of postoperative tachyarrhythmias.

Complication	Description	Assessment and Management
		• Carotid massage may be performed by a physician to assist with diagnosing or treating the arrhythmia. • Cardioversion and defibrillation are alternatives for symptomatic tachyarrhythmias. • For patients who cannot attain normal sinus rhythm, an alternate goal may be to establish a stable rhythm that produces a sufficient cardiac output.
Bradycardias	• Decreased heart rate	• Many postoperative patients will have temporary pacer wires that can be attached to a pulse generator (pacemaker) to stimulate the heart to beat faster. Less commonly, atropine, epinephrine, or isoproterenol may be used to increase heart rate.
Cardiac failure	• Myocardial contractility may be decreased perioperatively.	• The nurse observes for and reports falling mean arterial pressure; rising PAWP, pulmonary artery diastolic pressure, and CVP; increasing tachycardia; restlessness and agitation; peripheral cyanosis; venous distention; labored respirations; and edema. • Medical management includes diuretics, digoxin, and IV inotropic agents.
MI (may occur intraoperatively or postoperatively)	• Portion of the cardiac muscle dies; therefore, contractility decreases. Impaired ventricular wall motion further decreases cardiac output. Symptoms may be masked by the postoperative surgical discomfort or the anesthesia–analgesia regimen.	• Careful assessment to determine the type of pain the patient is experiencing; myocardial infarction (MI) suspected if the mean blood pressure is low with normal preload. • Serial electrocardiograms (ECGs) and cardiac biomarkers assist in making the diagnosis (alterations may be due to the surgical intervention). Analgesics are prescribed in small amounts while the patient's blood pressure and respiratory rate are monitored (because vasodilation secondary to analgesics or decreasing pain may occur and compound the hypotension). • Activity progression depends on the patient's activity tolerance.

Pulmonary Complications

Impaired gas exchange	• During and after anesthesia, patients require mechanical assistance to breathe. • Potential exists for postoperative atelectasis. • Anesthetic agents stimulate production of mucus and chest incision pain may decrease the effectiveness of ventilation.	• Pulmonary complications are often detected during assessment of breath sounds, oxygen saturation levels, arterial blood gases, and when monitoring peak pressure and exhaled tidal volumes on the ventilator. • Extended periods of mechanical ventilation may be required while complications are treated.

Fluid Volume Complications

Hemorrhage	• Untoward and excessive bleeding may be life-threatening.	• Serial hemoglobin, hematocrit, and coagulation studies are performed to guide therapy. • Administration of fluids, colloids, and blood products: packed red blood cells, fresh frozen plasma, platelet concentrate. • Administration of aprotinin (Trasylol) perioperatively to reduce blood transfusion needs. • Administration of desmopressin acetate (DDAVP) to enhance platelet function.

Neurologic Complications

Neurologic changes; stroke	• Inability to follow simple command within 6 hours of recovery from anesthetic; different capabilities on right or left side of body	• Neurologically, most patients begin to recover from anesthesia in the operating room. • Patients who are elderly or who have renal or hepatic failure may take longer to recover. • Patient should be evaluated for stroke when neurologic changes are evident.

(continued on page 412)

TABLE
14-4 Potential Complications of Cardiac Surgery (continued)

Complication	Description	Assessment and Management
Renal Failure and Electrolyte Imbalance		
Renal failure	• Usually acute and resolves within 3 months, but may become chronic and require ongoing dialysis	• May respond to diuretics or may require continuous renal replacement therapy (CRRT) or dialysis
Acute tubular necrosis	• Often results from hypoperfusion of the kidneys or from injury to the renal tubules by nephrotoxic medications	• Fluids, electrolytes, BUN, and creatinine, and urine output are monitored frequently.
Electrolyte imbalance	• Postoperative imbalances in potassium, magnesium, sodium, calcium, and blood glucose are related to surgical losses, metabolic changes, and the administration of medications and IV fluids.	• Monitor electrolytes and basic metabolic studies frequently. • Implement treatment to correct electrolyte imbalance promptly (see Chart 14-13).
Other Complications		
Hepatic failure	• Most common in patients with cirrhosis, hepatitis, or prolonged right-sided heart failure	• Use of medications metabolized by the liver must be minimized. • Bilirubin, albumin, and amylase levels are monitored, and nutritional support must be provided.
Infection	• Surgery and anesthesia alter the patient's immune system. Many invasive devices are used to monitor and support the patient's recovery and may serve as a source of infection.	• The following must be monitored to detect signs of possible infection: body temperature, white blood cell (WBC) counts and differential counts, incision and puncture sites, cardiac output and systemic vascular resistance, urine (clarity, color, and odor), bilateral breath sounds, sputum (color, odor, amount), as well as nasogastric secretions. • Antibiotic therapy may be expanded or modified as necessary. • Invasive devices must be discontinued as soon as they are no longer required. Institutional protocols for maintaining and replacing invasive lines and devices must be followed to minimize the patient's risk for infection.

The patient may require interventions for more than one complication at a time. Collaboration among nurses, physicians, pharmacists, respiratory therapists, and dietitians is necessary to achieve the desired patient outcomes.

NURSING PROCESS

The Postoperative Cardiac Surgery Patient

Initial postoperative care focuses on achieving or maintaining hemodynamic stability and recovery from general anesthesia. Care will be provided in the PACU or intensive care unit, with the patient transferred to the step-down or progressive care unit usually within 24 hours. Care focuses on the monitoring of cardiopulmonary status, pain management, wound care, progressive activity, and nutrition. Education about medications and risk factor modification is emphasized. Discharge from the hospital may occur 3 to 5 days after CABG in patients without complications.

The immediate postoperative period for the patient who has undergone cardiac surgery presents many challenges to the health care team. Specific information about the surgical procedure and important factors about postoperative management are communicated by the surgical team and anesthesia personnel to the critical care nurse, who then assumes responsibility for the patient's care. A plan of nursing care for the patient after cardiac surgery is available online at http://thePoint.lww.com/Pellico1e.

Assessment

In the critical care environment, a complete assessment of all systems is performed hourly for at least 12 hours to determine the postoperative status of the patient compared with the preoperative baseline and to identify anticipated changes since surgery. The following parameters are assessed:

• *Neurologic status:* Level of responsiveness, pupil size and reaction to light, reflexes, facial symmetry, movement and strength of upper and lower extremities.

• *Cardiac/hemodynamic status:* Heart rate and rhythm, heart sounds, pacemaker status, arterial blood pressure, central venous pressure (CVP), pulmonary artery pressure, pulmonary artery wedge pressure (PAWP), waveforms from the invasive blood pressure lines, cardiac output or index, systemic and pulmonary vascular resistance,

pulmonary artery oxygen saturation (SvO$_2$), and bleeding (from mediastinal chest tubes). Refer to Chapter 55 for a detailed description of hemodynamic monitoring.

- *Respiratory status*: Chest movement, breath sounds, ventilator settings, respiratory rate, peak inspiratory pressure, arterial oxygen saturation (SaO$_2$), percutaneous oxygen saturation (SpO$_2$), end-tidal CO$_2$, ABGs
- *Peripheral vascular status*: Peripheral pulses; color of skin, nail beds, mucosa, lips, and earlobes; skin temperature; edema; condition of dressings and invasive lines
- *Renal function*: Urinary output; urine specific gravity and osmolality may be assessed, serum blood urea nitrogen (BUN) and creatinine

- *Fluid and electrolyte status*: Intake, output from all drainage tubes, all cardiac output parameters, mucous membranes, skin turgor, presence of edema, and analysis of laboratory values including electrolytes, calcium, and magnesium
- *Pain*: Nature, type, location, and duration (incisional pain must be differentiated from anginal pain); apprehension; response to analgesics

Assessment also includes observing all equipment and tubes to determine whether they are functioning properly (Fig. 14-9).

As the patient regains consciousness and progresses through the postoperative period, the nurse also assesses indicators of psychological and emotional status. The patient

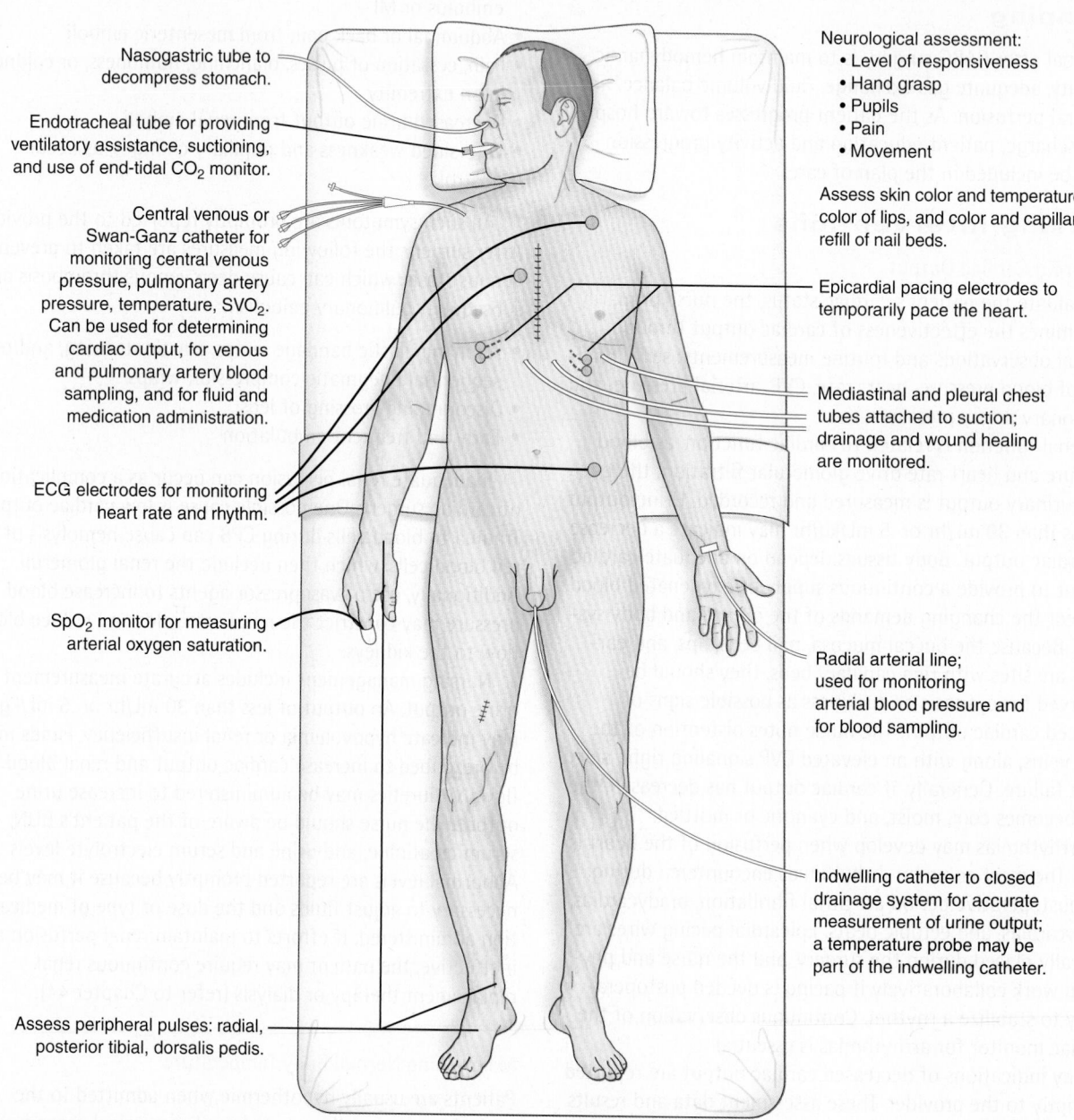

Nasogastric tube to decompress stomach.

Endotracheal tube for providing ventilatory assistance, suctioning, and use of end-tidal CO$_2$ monitor.

Central venous or Swan-Ganz catheter for monitoring central venous pressure, pulmonary artery pressure, temperature, SVO$_2$. Can be used for determining cardiac output, for venous and pulmonary artery blood sampling, and for fluid and medication administration.

ECG electrodes for monitoring heart rate and rhythm.

SpO$_2$ monitor for measuring arterial oxygen saturation.

Assess peripheral pulses: radial, posterior tibial, dorsalis pedis.

Neurological assessment:
- Level of responsiveness
- Hand grasp
- Pupils
- Pain
- Movement

Assess skin color and temperature, color of lips, and color and capillary refill of nail beds.

Epicardial pacing electrodes to temporarily pace the heart.

Mediastinal and pleural chest tubes attached to suction; drainage and wound healing are monitored.

Radial arterial line; used for monitoring arterial blood pressure and for blood sampling.

Indwelling catheter to closed drainage system for accurate measurement of urine output; a temperature probe may be part of the indwelling catheter.

FIGURE 14-9 Postoperative care of the cardiac surgical patient requires the nurse to be proficient in interpreting hemodynamics, correlating physical assessments with laboratory results, sequencing interventions, and evaluating progress toward desired outcomes.

may exhibit behavior that reflects denial or depression, or may experience postcardiotomy delirium. Characteristic signs of delirium include transient perceptual illusions, visual and auditory hallucinations, disorientation, and paranoid delusions.

Diagnosis

Appropriate nursing diagnoses of the patient recovering from cardiac surgery may include:

- Decreased cardiac output/tissue perfusion
- Fluid volume and electrolyte imbalance
- Impaired gas exchange
- Impaired cerebral circulation

Planning

The goal after CABG surgery is to maintain hemodynamic stability, adequate gas exchange, fluid volume balance, and cerebral perfusion. As the patient progresses toward hospital discharge, patient education and activity progression must be included in the plan of care.

Nursing Interventions

Restoring Cardiac Output

To evaluate the patient's cardiac status, the nurse primarily determines the effectiveness of cardiac output through clinical observations and routine measurements: serial readings of blood pressure, heart rate, CVP, arterial pressure, and pulmonary artery pressures.

Renal function is related to cardiac function, as blood pressure and heart rate drive glomerular filtration; therefore, urinary output is measured and recorded. Urine output of less than 30 mL/hr or .5 mL/kg/hr may indicate a decrease in cardiac output. Body tissues depend on adequate cardiac output to provide a continuous supply of oxygenated blood to meet the changing demands of the organs and body systems. Because the buccal mucosa, nail beds, lips, and earlobes are sites with rich capillary beds, they should be observed for cyanosis or duskiness as possible signs of reduced cardiac output. The nurse notes distention of the neck veins, along with an elevated CVP signaling right-sided heart failure. Generally, if cardiac output has decreased, the skin becomes cool, moist, and cyanotic or mottled.

Arrhythmias may develop when perfusion of the heart is poor. The most common arrhythmias encountered during the postoperative period are atrial fibrillation, bradycardias, tachycardias, and ectopic beats. Epicardial pacing wires are typically placed during the surgery, and the nurse and physician work collaboratively if pacing is needed postoperatively to stabilize a rhythm. Continuous observation of the cardiac monitor for arrhythmias is essential.

Any indications of decreased cardiac output are reported promptly to the provider. These assessment data and results of diagnostic tests are used to determine the cause of the problem. After a diagnosis has been made, the physician

and the nurse work together to restore cardiac output and prevent further complications.

Maintaining Adequate Tissue Perfusion

Thromboemboli formation also can result from injury to the intima of the blood vessels, dislodging a clot from a damaged valve, loosening of mural thrombi, or coagulation problems. Air embolism can result from CPB or central venous cannulation. Symptoms of embolization vary according to site. The usual embolic sites are the lungs, coronary arteries, mesentery, spleen, extremities, kidneys, and brain. The patient is observed for onset of the following:

- Chest pain and respiratory distress from pulmonary embolus or MI
- Abdominal or back pain from mesenteric emboli
- Pain, cessation of pulses, blanching, numbness, or coldness in an extremity
- Decreased urine output from renal emboli
- One-sided weakness and pupillary changes, as occur in stroke

All such symptoms are promptly reported to the provider. After surgery, the following measures are taken to prevent venous stasis, which can cause deep venous thrombosis and subsequent pulmonary embolism:

- Applying elastic bandage wraps, elastic stocking, and/or sequential pneumatic compression wraps
- Discouraging crossing of legs
- Early and frequent ambulation

Inadequate renal perfusion can occur as a complication of cardiac surgery. One possible cause is low cardiac output. Trauma to blood cells during CPB can cause hemolysis of red blood cells, which then occlude the renal glomeruli. Additionally, use of vasopressor agents to increase blood pressure may constrict the renal arterioles and reduce blood flow to the kidneys.

Nursing management includes accurate measurement of urine output. An output of less than 30 mL/hr or .5 mL/kg/hr may indicate hypovolemia or renal insufficiency. Fluids may be prescribed to increase cardiac output and renal blood flow. IV diuretics may be administered to increase urine output. The nurse should be aware of the patient's BUN, serum creatinine, and urine and serum electrolyte levels. Abnormal levels are reported promptly because it may be necessary to adjust fluids and the dose or type of medication administered. If efforts to maintain renal perfusion are ineffective, the patient may require continuous renal replacement therapy or dialysis (refer to Chapter 44).

Maintaining Normal Body Temperature

Patients are usually hypothermic when admitted to the critical care unit following the cardiac surgical procedure if their surgery was done using CPB. The patient must be

gradually warmed to a normal temperature. This is accomplished partially by the patient's own basal metabolic processes and often with the assistance of warmed ventilator air, warm air or warm blankets, or heat lamps. While the patient is hypothermic, the clotting process is less efficient, the heart is prone to arrhythmias, and oxygen does not readily transfer from the hemoglobin to the tissues. Because anesthesia and hypothermia suppress normal basal metabolism, oxygen supply usually meets the cellular demand.

Monitoring and Managing Potential Complications

INFECTION. Common sites of infection postoperatively include the lungs, urinary tract, incisions, and intravascular catheters. Foley catheters should be removed as early as possible to prevent infection (post-op Day 1 if possible). Dressings applied in the operating room should remain intact for 24 to 48 hours to protect the nonepithelialized tissue (Ackley, Ladwig, Swan et al., 2007). There is no evidence that wound dressings after 48 hours are protective against infection. Aseptic technique is used when changing dressings and when providing endotracheal tube and catheter care. Closed systems are used to maintain all IV and arterial lines. All invasive equipment is discontinued as soon as possible after surgery.

Clearance of pulmonary secretions is accomplished by frequently repositioning the patient, suctioning, and chest physical therapy, as well as teaching and encouraging the patient to breathe deeply, cough, and use the incentive spirometer frequently. Prevention of atelectasis is achieved through these interventions. Postpericardiotomy syndrome may occur in patients who undergo cardiac surgery (Porth & Matfin, 2009). The syndrome is characterized by fever, pericardial pain, pleural pain, dyspnea, pericardial effusion, pericardial friction rub, and arthralgia. These signs and symptoms may occur in combination. Leukocytosis (elevated WBCs) occurs, along with elevation of the erythrocyte sedimentation rate. These signs frequently appear after the patient is discharged from the hospital. Anti-inflammatory agents often produce a dramatic improvement in symptoms.

FLUID VOLUME AND ELECTROLYTE IMBALANCE. Fluid and electrolyte imbalance may occur after cardiac surgery. Nursing assessment includes monitoring of intake and output, weight, hemodynamic parameters, hematocrit levels, distention of neck veins, edema, breath sounds, and electrolyte levels. Changes in serum electrolytes are reported promptly, so that treatment can be instituted. Especially important are high or low levels of potassium, magnesium, sodium, and calcium. Elevated blood glucose levels are common in the postoperative period. Administration of insulin may be required in patients both with and without diabetes to achieve the glycemic control necessary for promoting wound healing.

IMPAIRED GAS EXCHANGE. Impaired gas exchange is another possible complication after cardiac surgery. All body tissues require an adequate supply of oxygen for survival. To achieve this after surgery, an endotracheal tube (ETT) with ventilator assistance will be needed initially postop (for an

average of about 6 hours). The assisted ventilation is continued until the patient's blood gas measurements are acceptable and the patient demonstrates the ability to breathe independently. To ensure adequate gas exchange, the nurse assesses and maintains the patency of the ETT. The patient is suctioned when necessary. Because a patent airway is essential for oxygen and carbon dioxide exchange, the ETT must be secured to prevent it from slipping into the right mainstem bronchus or accidental dislodgment. The patient is weaned from the ventilator and extubated as soon as possible, usually within 6 hours of CABG. Physical assessment and ABG results guide the process. Before being extubated, the patient should have cough and gag reflexes and stable vital signs; be able to lift the head off the bed or give firm hand grasps; have adequate vital capacity, negative inspiratory force, and minute volume appropriate for body size; and have acceptable ABG levels while breathing without the assistance of the ventilator. Refer to Chapter 55 for additional information related to ventilators and weaning.

During this time, the nurse assists with the weaning process and eventually with removal of the ETT. Deep breathing and coughing are encouraged at least every 1 to 2 hours after extubation to open the alveolar sacs and provide for increased ventilation, and to clear secretions (preventing atelectasis).

The patient is continuously assessed for signs of impaired gas exchange: restlessness, anxiety, cyanosis of mucous membranes and peripheral tissues, and tachycardia. Breath sounds are assessed frequently, as well as ABGs, oxygen saturation, and end-tidal CO_2. Following extubation, aggressive pulmonary interventions, such as turning, coughing of secretions, using incentive spirometer, and deep breathing, are necessary to prevent atelectasis and pneumonia.

When the patient's condition stabilizes, body position is changed every 1 to 2 hours. Frequent changes of patient position provide for optimal pulmonary ventilation and perfusion by allowing the lungs to expand more fully.

IMPAIRED CEREBRAL CIRCULATION. Brain function depends on a continuous supply of oxygenated blood. The brain does not have the capacity to store oxygen and must rely on adequate continuous perfusion by the heart. Hypoperfusion or microemboli may produce central nervous system injury after cardiac surgery.

It is important to observe the patient for any symptoms of hypoxia: restlessness, headache, confusion, dyspnea, hypotension, and cyanosis. An assessment of the patient's neurologic status includes level of consciousness, response to verbal commands and painful stimuli, pupil size and reaction to light, facial symmetry, movement of the extremities, and hand grip strength. Any indication of a change in status is documented, and abnormal findings are reported to the provider.

Minimizing Sensory-Perception Imbalance

Some patients exhibit abnormal behaviors that occur with varying intensity and duration. In the early years of cardiac surgery, this phenomenon occurred more frequently than it

(continued on page 416)

does today. Advances in surgical techniques and in the delivery of anesthetic agents have significantly decreased the incidence of postoperative delirium. When it occurs today, it is thought to be caused by anxiety, sleep deprivation, increased sensory input, medications, and physiologic problems such as hypoxemia. Delirium may appear after a 2- to 5-day stay in an intensive care environment and is associated with increased morbidity and mortality, including postoperative complications of respiratory insufficiency and sternal instability, prolonged length of stay, higher nursing home placement, and reduced cognitive and functional recovery, making early recognition and response crucial (Koster, Hensens, Oosterveld et al., 2009).

Careful explanations of all procedures and of the need for cooperation help keep the patient oriented throughout the postoperative course. Continuity of care is desirable; a familiar face and a nursing staff with a consistent approach help the patient feel safe. The patient's family should be welcomed at the bedside. Some patients have difficulty learning and retaining information after cardiac surgery. Many patients have difficulties in cognitive function after cardiac surgery, a phenomenon that does not occur after other types of major surgery. The patient may experience recent memory loss, short attention span, difficulty with simple math, poor handwriting, and visual disturbances. Patients with these difficulties often become frustrated when they try to resume normal activities and learn how to care for themselves at home. The patient and family are reassured that the difficulty is almost always temporary and will subside, usually in 6 to 8 weeks. A well-designed plan of nursing care can assist the nursing team in coordinating their efforts for the emotional well-being of the patient. A plan of nursing care for a patient with an uncomplicated MI is available online at http://thePoint.lww.com/Pellico1e.

Relieving Pain

Deep pain may not be felt in the peri-incisional area but may occur in a broader, more diffuse area. Patients who have had cardiac surgery experience pain caused by the interruption of intercostal nerves along the incision route and irritation of the pleura by the chest catheters. Incisional pain may also be experienced from peripheral vein or artery graft harvest sites. IV and oral NSAIDs decrease the amount of opioids required for pain relief and increase patient comfort. Patients report the most pain during coughing, turning, and moving (Bainbridge, Cheng, Martin et al., 2009). Physical support of the incision with a folded bath blanket or small pillow during deep breathing and coughing helps to minimize pain. The patient should then be able to participate in respiratory exercises and to increase self-care progressively. Patient comfort improves after removal of the chest tubes. The patient is observed for any adverse effects of opioids, which may include respiratory depression, hypotension, ileus, or urinary retention. If serious side effects occur, an opioid antagonist (e.g., naloxone [Narcan]) may be used.

Evaluation

Expected patient outcomes may include:

- Maintains adequate cardiac output
- Maintains adequate gas exchange
- Maintains fluid and electrolyte balance
- Experiences decreased symptoms of sensory-perception disturbances
- Experiences relief of pain
- Maintains adequate tissue perfusion
- Maintains normal body temperature
- Incisions are well healed
- Performs self-care activities
- Engages in follow-up care with health care providers and cardiac rehabilitation services
- Adheres to recommendations for diet and lifestyle changes to maintain optimal future health
- Exhibits no complications

MYOCARDIAL INFARCTION

Coronary occlusion, heart attack, and MI are terms used synonymously, but the preferred term is MI.

Pathophysiology

In an MI, an area of the myocardium is permanently destroyed. MI is usually caused by reduced blood flow in a coronary artery due to rupture of an atherosclerotic plaque and subsequent occlusion of the artery by a thrombus. In unstable angina, the plaque ruptures, but the artery is not completely occluded. Because unstable angina and acute MI are considered to be the same process but occurring at different points along a continuum, the term **acute coronary syndrome** may be used in lieu of these diagnoses. Other causes of MI include vasospasm (sudden constriction or narrowing) of a coronary artery, decreased oxygen supply (e.g., from acute blood loss, anemia, or low blood pressure), and increased demand for oxygen (e.g., from a rapid heart rate, thyrotoxicosis, or ingestion of cocaine). In each case, a profound imbalance exists between myocardial oxygen supply and demand.

The area of infarction develops over minutes to hours. As the cells are deprived of oxygen, ischemia develops, cellular injury occurs, and the lack of oxygen results in infarction, or the death of cells. The expression "time is muscle" reflects the urgency of appropriate treatment to improve patient outcomes. Each year in the United States, nearly 900,000 people have acute MIs; one-fourth of these people die of MI (AHA, 2008). Half of those who die never reach a hospital.

Various descriptions are used to further identify an MI: the type of MI (ST-segment elevation, non–ST-segment elevation), the location of the injury to the ventricular wall (anterior, inferior, posterior, or lateral wall), the point in time within the process of infarction (acute, evolving, or old), and

the extent of the damage to the myocardium caused by the MI (partial or full thickness). Partial infarcts are associated with severely narrow coronary arteries and present as non–ST-segment elevation, while full thickness infarcts commonly occur with obstruction of a single coronary artery and present as ST elevation on ECG readings (Porth & Matfin, 2009).

The ECG usually identifies the type and location, and other ECG indicators such as a Q wave and patient history identify the timing. Regardless of the location of the infarction of cardiac muscle, the goal of medical therapy is to prevent or minimize myocardial tissue death and to prevent complications.

Risk Factors

Risk factors for MI are the same as those described for atherosclerosis and angina.

Clinical Manifestations and Assessment

Chest pain that occurs suddenly and continues despite rest and medication is the presenting symptom in most patients with an MI. Some of these patients have prodromal (early nonspecific) symptoms or a previous diagnosis of CAD, but about half report no previous symptoms (AHA, 2008). Box 14-4 discusses assessment parameters. In many cases, the signs and symptoms of MI cannot be distinguished from those of unstable angina. The diagnosis of MI is generally based on the presenting symptoms, physical findings, ECG, and laboratory test results (e.g., serial cardiac biomarker values). The prognosis depends on the severity of coronary artery obstruction and the extent of myocardial damage.

NURSING ALERT
Women often present with symptoms different from those seen in men, therefore a high level of suspicion is associated with vague complaints such as fatigue, shoulder blade discomfort, and/or shortness of breath (O'Keefe-McCarthy, 2008).

Patient History

The patient history has two parts: the description of the presenting symptom(s) (e.g., pain) and the history of previous illnesses and family history of heart disease. The patient's risk factors for heart disease should also be evaluated.

Electrocardiogram

The ECG provides information that assists in diagnosing acute MI. It should be obtained within 10 minutes from the time a patient reports pain or arrives in the emergency department. By monitoring serial ECG changes over time, the location, evolution, and resolution of an MI can be identified and monitored. The ECG changes that occur with an MI are seen in the leads that view the involved surface of the heart. The extent of ischemia and resultant injury through

---

BOX 14-4 **Focused Assessment**

Acute Myocardial Infarction (MI) or Acute Coronary Syndrome (ACS)

Be alert for the following signs and symptoms:

Cardiovascular
- Chest pain or discomfort, palpitations
- S_3, S_4, and new onset of a murmur
- Increased jugular venous distention (may be seen if the MI has caused heart failure)
- Elevated blood pressure (because of sympathetic stimulation) or decreased blood pressure (because of decreased contractility, impending cardiogenic shock, or medications)
- Pulse deficit indicating atrial fibrillation
- In addition to ST-segment and T-wave changes, tachycardia, bradycardia, or arrhythmias on electrocardiogram (ECG)

Respiratory
- Shortness of breath, dyspnea, tachypnea, and crackles if MI has caused pulmonary congestion
- Pulmonary edema

Gastrointestinal
- Nausea and vomiting

Genitourinary
- Decreased urinary output (may indicate cardiogenic shock)

Skin
- Cool, clammy, diaphoretic, and pale appearance (due to sympathetic stimulation may indicate cardiogenic shock)

Neurologic
- Anxiety, restlessness, and light-headedness (may indicate increased sympathetic stimulation or a decrease in contractility and cerebral oxygenation or cardiogenic shock)

Psychological
- Fear with feeling of impending doom
- Denial

---

the various layers of the heart determine the type of ECG changes seen. The classic ECG changes are T-wave inversion, ST-segment elevation, and development of an abnormal Q wave (Fig. 14-10). The first ECG signs of an acute MI occur as a result of myocardial ischemia and injury. As the area becomes ischemic, myocardial repolarization is delayed, causing the T wave (represents ventricular depolarization) to invert. The ischemic region may remain depolarized while adjacent areas of the myocardium return to the resting state. As ischemia progresses to injury, the T wave becomes

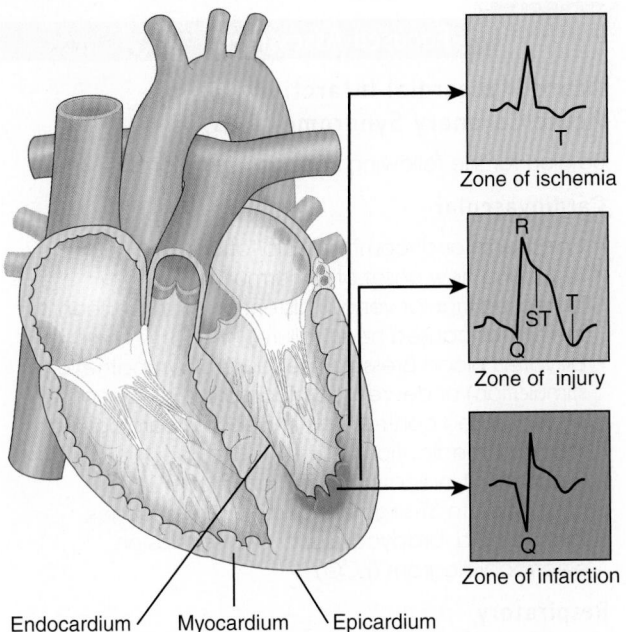

FIGURE 14-10 Effects of ischemia, injury, and infarction on an electrocardiogram (ECG) recording. Ischemia causes inversion of the T wave because of altered repolarization. Cardiac muscle injury causes elevation of the ST segment and tall, symmetrical T waves. Later, Q waves develop because of the absence of depolarization current from the necrotic tissue and opposing currents from other parts of the heart.

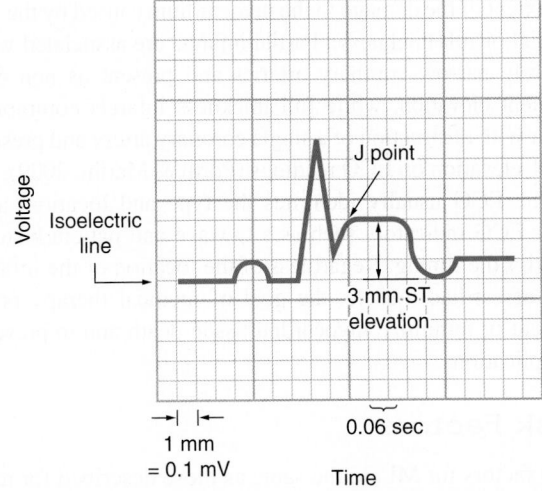

FIGURE 14-11 Using the electrocardiogram (ECG) to diagnose acute myocardial infarction (MI). (ST-segment elevation is measured 0.06 to 0.08 seconds after the J point. An elevation of more than 1 mm in contiguous leads is indicative of acute MI.)

enlarged and symmetric. Myocardial injury also causes ST-segment changes. The ST segment may rise at least 1 mm above the isoelectric line (area between the T wave and the next P wave is used as the reference for the isoelectric line), or there may be non–ST-segment elevation. Remember that there may be a combination of ischemia, injury, and infarction occurring simultaneously, thus resulting in mixed ECG patterns.

The beginning of the ST segment is usually identified by a change in the thickness or angle of the terminal portion of the QRS complex and is called the *J point* (Fig. 14-11). The J point is the end of ventricular depolarization (QRS) and the beginning of the ventricular repolarization (ST segment) and is identified by a change from an essentially vertical angle (QRS) to a more horizontal angle (ST segment). This J point is normally on the baseline, and elevation in the ST segment in two contiguous leads is a key diagnostic indicator for MI. The nurse assesses for ST elevation, as it relates to the isoelectric line, at a point 0.08 seconds past the J point.

The appearance of abnormal Q waves is another indication of MI. A Q wave is a negative deflection that signals the beginning of ventricular depolarization; however, abnormal Q waves represent myocardial necrosis and can develop within 1 to 3 days of an MI. A pathological Q wave is identified by an abnormal depth and duration of the Q wave or the appearance of "new" Q waves not previously seen in ECG tracings. The pathological Q wave therefore reflects the conduction from other parts of the heart, because of

necrotic tissue. An abnormal Q wave is 0.04 seconds or longer, 25% of the R-wave depth (provided the R wave exceeds a depth of 5 mm), or did not exist before the event. An acute MI may also cause a significant decrease in the height of the R wave. During an acute MI, injury and ischemic changes are usually present. An abnormal Q wave may be present without ST-segment and T-wave changes, which indicates an old, not acute, MI. For some patients, there are no persistent ECG changes, and the MI is diagnosed by blood levels of cardiac biomarkers.

Using the above information, patients are diagnosed with one of the following forms of ACS:

- *Unstable angina*: The patient has clinical manifestations of coronary ischemia, but ECG or cardiac biomarkers show no evidence of acute MI.
- *ST-segment elevation MI (STEMI)*: The patient has ECG evidence of acute MI with characteristic changes in two contiguous leads on a 12-lead ECG. In this type of MI, significant damage to the myocardium occurs.
- *Non–ST-segment elevation MI (non-STEMI)*: The patient has elevated cardiac biomarkers but no definite ECG evidence of acute MI.

During recovery from an MI, the ST segment often is the first ECG indicator to return to normal (1 to 6 weeks). The T wave becomes large and symmetric for 24 hours, and it then inverts within 1 to 3 days for 1 to 2 weeks. Q-wave alterations are usually permanent. An old ST-segment elevation MI is usually indicated by an abnormal Q wave or decreased height of the R wave without ST-segment and T-wave changes.

Echocardiogram

The echocardiogram is used to evaluate ventricular function. It may be used to assist in diagnosing an MI, especially when

TABLE
14-5 Biomarkers of Acute Myocardial Infarction

Serum Test	Earliest Increase (hr)	Test Running Time (min)	Peak (hr)	Return to Normal
Total creatinine kinase (CK)	3–6	30–60	24–36	3 days
CK-MB:isoenzyme	4–8	30–60	12–24	3–4 days
mass assay	2–3	30–60	10–18	3–4 days
Myoglobin	1–3	30–60	4–12	12 hr
Troponin T or I	3–4	30–60	4–24	1–3 wk

the ECG is nondiagnostic. The echocardiogram can detect hypokinetic and akinetic wall motion, can determine the ejection fraction, and can also assess valvular function.

Laboratory Tests

Laboratory tests called *cardiac biomarkers* are used to diagnose an MI (Table 14-5). Newer laboratory tests with faster results, and thus producing earlier diagnosis, include troponin analysis. These tests are based on the release of cellular contents into the circulation when myocardial cells die.

Creatine Kinase and Its Isoenzymes

Creatinine kinase-myocardial band (CK-MB) is the cardiac-specific isoenzyme; CK-MB is found mainly in cardiac cells and therefore increases only when there has been damage to these cells. Elevated CK-MB assessed by mass assay is an indicator of acute MI; its level begins to increase within a few hours and peaks within 24 hours of an MI. A normal CK-MB is 0 to 3 ng/mL or 1 to 3 μg/L. If the patient has cardiac complaints and negative CK-MB for more than 48 hours, then etiologies for the symptoms outside of an MI will be assessed.

Myoglobin

Myoglobin is a heme protein that helps transport oxygen. Like CK-MB enzyme, myoglobin is found in cardiac and skeletal muscle. A normal level is 5 to 70 ng/mL or 5 to 70 μg/L. The myoglobin level starts to increase within 1 to 3 hours and peaks within 12 hours after the onset of symptoms. An increase in myoglobin is not very specific in indicating an acute cardiac event; however, negative results are an excellent parameter for ruling out an acute MI.

Troponin

Troponin, a protein found in the myocardium, regulates the myocardial contractile process. There are three isomers of troponin: C, I, and T. Troponins I and T are specific for cardiac muscle, and these tests are currently recognized as reliable and critical markers of myocardial injury. A normal troponin I level is less than 0.5 ng/dl. An increase in the level of troponin in the serum can be detected within a few hours during acute MI. It remains elevated for a long period, often as long as 3 weeks, and it therefore can be used to detect recent myocardial damage.

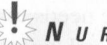 **NURSING ALERT**
Troponin I levels of greater than 1.5 ng/mL or greater than 1.5 μg/L are critical.

Medical Management

The goal of medical management is to minimize myocardial damage, preserve myocardial function, and prevent complications. These goals are facilitated by the use of guidelines developed by the American College of Cardiology and American Heart Association (Box 14-5). They may be achieved by reperfusing the area with the emergency use of thrombolytic medications or by PCI. Minimizing myocardial damage is also accomplished by reducing myocardial

---

BOX 14-5

Medical Treatment Guidelines for Acute Myocardial Infarction

Use rapid transit to the hospital.
Obtain 12-lead electrocardiogram (ECG) to be read within 10 minutes.
Obtain laboratory blood specimens of cardiac biomarkers, including troponin.
Obtain other diagnostics to clarify the diagnosis.
Begin routine medical interventions:
• Supplemental oxygen
• Nitroglycerin
• Morphine
• Aspirin 162–325 mg
• Beta blocker
• Angiotensin-converting enzyme inhibitor or angiotensin receptor blocker within 24 hours
Evaluate for indications for reperfusion therapy:
• Percutaneous coronary intervention
• Thrombolytic therapy
Continue therapy as indicated:
• IV heparin or low-molecular-weight heparin
• Clopidogrel (Plavix) or ticlopidine (Ticlid)
• Glycoprotein IIb/IIIa inhibitor
• Bed rest for a minimum of 12 to 24 hours

Pearle et al. (2008). Focused update of the ACC/AHA Guidelines for the management of patients with ST-elevation myocardial infarction. *Journal of the American College of Cardiology, 51,* 210–247.

oxygen demand and increasing oxygen supply with medications, oxygen administration, and bed rest. The resolution of pain and ECG changes indicate that demand and supply are in equilibrium; they may also indicate reperfusion. Visualization of blood flow through an open vessel in the catheterization laboratory is evidence of reperfusion.

Pharmacologic Therapy

The patient with suspected MI is given aspirin, nitroglycerin, morphine, a beta blocker, and other medications as indicated while the diagnosis is being confirmed. Patients should receive a beta blocker initially, throughout the hospitalization, and upon discharge. Also on discharge, there needs to be documentation that the patient was discharged on a statin, an **angiotensin-converting enzyme (ACE)** inhibitor or an **angiotensin receptor blocking agent (ARB)**, and aspirin. These are "quality indicators" for ACS treatment, and are now publicly reported measures. Remember **SAAB:** *s*tatin, *a*ce or arb, *a*spirin, *b*eta blocker. If any of these are not prescribed, clear documentation as to why not must be provided.

Thrombolytics

The purpose of **thrombolytics** is to dissolve and lyse the thrombus in a coronary artery (thrombolysis), allowing blood to flow through the coronary artery again (reperfusion), minimizing the size of the infarction, and preserving ventricular function. Hospitals monitor their ability to administer these medications within 30 minutes from the time the patient arrives in the emergency department. This is called *door-to-needle time*. The thrombolytic agents used most often are alteplase (t-PA, Activase) and reteplase (r-PA, TNKase). Box 14-6 discusses administration of thrombolytics.

Analgesics

The analgesic of choice for acute MI is morphine sulfate administered in IV boluses to reduce pain and anxiety. It reduces preload and afterload, which decreases the workload of the heart. Morphine also relaxes bronchioles to enhance oxygenation. The cardiovascular response to morphine is monitored carefully, particularly the blood pressure, which can decrease, and the respiratory rate, which can be depressed. Because morphine decreases the sensation of pain, ST-segment monitoring may be a better indicator of subsequent ischemia than assessment of pain.

Angiotensin-Converting Enzyme Inhibitors

ACE inhibitors prevent the conversion of angiotensin I to angiotensin II. In the absence of angiotensin II, the blood pressure decreases and the kidneys excrete sodium and fluid (diuresis), decreasing the oxygen demand of the heart. Use of ACE inhibitors in patients after MI decreases mortality rates and prevents remodeling of myocardial cells, which is associated with the onset of heart failure. It is important to ensure that the patient is not hypotensive, hyponatremic, hypovolemic, or hyperkalemic before administering ACE inhibitors. Blood pressure, urine output, and serum sodium,

---

BOX 14-6 | **Administration of Thrombolytic Therapy**

Indications
- Chest pain for longer than 20 minutes, unrelieved by nitroglycerin
- ST-segment elevation in at least two leads that face the same area of the heart
- Less than 6 hours from onset of pain

Absolute Contraindications
- Active bleeding
- Known bleeding disorder
- History of hemorrhagic stroke
- History of intracranial vessel malformation
- Recent major surgery or trauma
- Uncontrolled hypertension
- Pregnancy

Nursing Considerations
- Minimize the number of times the patient's skin is punctured.
- Avoid intramuscular injections.
- Draw blood for laboratory tests when starting the IV line.
- Start IV lines before thrombolytic therapy; designate one line to use for blood draws.
- Avoid continual use of noninvasive blood pressure cuff.
- Monitor for acute arrhythmias and hypotension.
- Monitor for reperfusion; resolution of angina or acute ST-segment changes.
- Check for signs and symptoms of bleeding: decrease in hematocrit and hemoglobin values, decrease in blood pressure, increase in heart rate, oozing or bulging at invasive procedure sites, back pain, muscle weakness, changes in level of consciousness, complaints of headache.
- Treat major bleeding by discontinuing thrombolytic therapy and any anticoagulants; apply direct pressure and notify the provider immediately.
- Treat minor bleeding by applying direct pressure if accessible and appropriate; continue to monitor for bleeding.

---

potassium, and creatinine levels need to be monitored closely. An ARB can be used in lieu of an ACE inhibitor.

 *D R U G A L E R T*
The nurse remembers the mnemonic MONA when treating potential MI patients: morphine, oxygen, nitrates, aspirin.

Reperfusion Procedures

Reperfusion procedures may be used to restore the blood supply to the myocardium. These include PCI procedures (e.g., PTCA, intracoronary stents, and atherectomy), and CABG. See discussion under "angina pectoris" section for detailed descriptions.

Cardiac Rehabilitation

After the MI patient is free of symptoms, an active rehabilitation program is initiated. Cardiac rehabilitation is a program that targets risk reduction by means of education, individual and group support, and physical activity. Most insurance programs, including Medicare, cover the cost of cardiac rehabilitation. The nurse needs to encourage the patient and ensure that referral from the hospital for outpatient cardiac rehabilitation is accomplished.

Cardiac rehabilitation is categorized in three phases. Phase I begins with the diagnosis of atherosclerosis, which may occur when the patient is admitted to the hospital for ACS (e.g., unstable angina or acute MI). It includes any postprocedure activity that occurs during the hospitalization. Phase I consists of low-level activities and initial education for the patient and family.

Phase II occurs after the patient has been discharged. It usually lasts for 4 to 6 weeks but may extend to 6 months. This outpatient program consists of supervised, often ECG-monitored, exercise training that is individualized based on the results of an exercise stress test.

Phase III focuses on maintaining cardiovascular stability and long-term conditioning. The patient is usually self-directed during this phase and does not require a supervised program, although it may be offered. The goals of each phase build on the accomplishments of the previous phase. Health promotion is discussed in Box 14-7.

Nursing Management

Relieving Pain and Other Signs and Symptoms of Ischemia

Balancing myocardial oxygen supply with demand (e.g., as evidenced by the relief of chest pain) is the top priority in the care of the patient with an acute MI. Although medication therapy is required to accomplish this goal, nursing interventions are also important.

The recommended treatment for acute MI is reperfusion with thrombolytic therapy or emergent PCI for patients who present to the health care facility immediately and who have no major contraindications. These therapies are important because, in addition to relieving symptoms, they aid in

---

BOX 14-7

Health Promotion

Promoting Health After Myocardial Infarction and Other Acute Coronary Syndromes

To extend and improve the quality of life, a patient who has had an MI must learn to adjust his or her lifestyle to promote heart-healthy living. With this in mind, the nurse and patient develop a program to help the patient achieve desired outcomes.

Changing Lifestyle During Convalescence and Healing

Adaptation to an MI is an ongoing process and usually requires some modification of lifestyle. Some specific modifications include:

- Avoiding any activity that produces chest pain, extreme dyspnea, or undue fatigue
- Avoiding extremes of heat and cold and walking against the wind
- Losing weight, if indicated
- Stopping smoking and use of tobacco; avoiding second-hand smoke
- Using personal strengths to support lifestyle changes
- Developing heart-healthy eating patterns and avoiding large meals and hurrying while eating
- Modifying meals to align with the Therapeutic Lifestyle Changes (TLC) or the Dietary Approaches to Stopping Hypertension (DASH) diet
- Adhering to medical regimen, especially in taking medications
- Following recommendations that ensure blood pressure and blood glucose are in control
- Pursuing activities that relieve and reduce stress

Adopting an Activity Program

Additionally, the patient needs to undertake an *orderly* program of increasing activity and exercise for long-term rehabilitation as follows:

- Engaging in a regimen of physical conditioning with a gradual increase in activity duration and then a gradual increase in activity intensity
- Walking daily, increasing distance and time as prescribed
- Monitoring pulse rate during physical activity until the maximum level of activity is attained
- Avoiding activities that tense the muscles: isometric exercise, weight-lifting, any activity that requires sudden bursts of energy
- Avoiding physical exercise immediately after a meal
- Alternating activity with rest periods (some fatigue is normal and expected during convalescence)
- Participating in a daily program of exercise that develops into a program of regular exercise for a lifetime

Managing Symptoms

The patient must learn to recognize and take appropriate action for possible recurrences of symptoms as follows:

- Call 911 if chest pressure or pain (or anginal equivalent) is not relieved in 15 minutes by nitroglycerin.
- Contact the provider if any of the following occur: shortness of breath, fainting, slow or rapid heartbeat, swelling of feet and ankles.

minimizing or avoiding permanent injury to the myocardium. With or without reperfusion, administration of aspirin, an IV beta blocker, and nitroglycerin is indicated. Use of a GPIIb/IIIa agent or heparin may also be indicated. The nurse administers morphine to relieve pain and anxiety and to promote vasodilation, reducing preload and afterload.

Oxygen should be administered along with medication therapy to assist with relief of symptoms. Administration of oxygen, even in low doses, raises the circulating level of oxygen to reduce pain associated with low levels of myocardial oxygen. The route of administration, usually by nasal cannula, and the oxygen flow rate are documented. A flow rate of 2 to 4 L/min is usually adequate to maintain oxygen saturation levels of 96% to 100% if no other disease is present.

Vital signs are assessed frequently as long as the patient is experiencing pain and other signs or symptoms of acute ischemia. Physical rest in bed with the backrest elevated (semi-Fowler's position) helps decrease chest discomfort and dyspnea. Elevation of the head and torso is beneficial for the following reasons:

- Tidal volume improves because of reduced pressure from abdominal contents on the diaphragm and better lung expansion and gas exchange.
- Drainage of the upper lung lobes improves.
- Venous return to the heart (preload) decreases, reducing the work of the heart.

Improving Respiratory Function

Regular and careful assessment of respiratory function can help the nurse detect early signs of pulmonary complications.

Scrupulous attention to fluid volume status prevents overloading the heart and lungs.

Promoting Adequate Tissue Perfusion

Limiting the patient to bed or chair rest during the initial phase of treatment is particularly helpful in reducing myocardial oxygen consumption. This limitation should remain until the patient is pain-free and hemodynamically stable. Checking skin temperature and peripheral pulses frequently is important in monitoring tissue perfusion.

Reducing Anxiety

Alleviating anxiety and decreasing fear are important nursing functions that reduce the sympathetic stress response. Decreased sympathetic stimulation decreases the workload of the heart, which may relieve pain and other signs and symptoms of ischemia.

Monitoring and Managing Potential Complications

Complications that can occur after acute MI are caused by the damage that occurs to the myocardium and to the conduction system as a result of the reduced coronary blood flow. Because these complications can be life-threatening, close monitoring for and early identification of their signs and symptoms are critical.

The nurse closely monitors and reports changes in cardiac rate/rhythm, heart and lung sounds, blood pressure, pain, respiratory status, urinary output, skin color/temperature, level of consciousness (LOC), ECG changes, and laboratory values. The nurse institutes emergency measures when necessary.

Chapter Review

Critical Thinking Exercises

1. You are working in a cardiology office and you receive a phone call from a patient who had an MI 2 years ago. She reports that she is experiencing some shortness of breath and mild back pain. What evidence base is there to suggest that symptoms of an MI may be different for women than men? Discuss the strength of this evidence and its significance in determining assessment criteria to be used for women and men. What questions would you ask this patient? What would you instruct her to do? Provide rationale for your instructions.

2. You are taking over the care of a patient who returned from the catheterization laboratory 2 hours ago following a successful PCI. He was reported to be stable on bed rest, with no bleeding from the right femoral site. The patient appears very pale and complains of right flank pain. Identify the key parameters that need to be assessed. Describe the actions you would take and state why.

3. You are caring for a patient who has been hospitalized awaiting CABG surgery. As you deliver his morning medications, he states that he is feeling "pressure" in the lower sternal area, but he thinks it is just "nerves." What questions would you ask and what would you assess? What would your next actions be?

NCLEX-Style Review Questions

1. A patient arrives in the emergency room complaining of nausea, diaphoresis, shortness of breath, and squeezing substernal chest pain that radiates to the left shoulder and jaw. The nurse should perform which interventions?
   A. Complete admission registration, alert the catheter laboratory team, establish an IV access, and record all vital signs
   B. Alert the catheter laboratory team, administer oxygen, obtain blood work, and notify the health care provider

C. Establish an IV, give sublingual nitroglycerin as ordered, insert a Foley catheter, and alert the catheter laboratory team.

D. Administer oxygen, apply a cardiac monitor, record patient's vital signs, and give sublingual nitroglycerin as ordered.

2. Which of the following is an absolute contraindication for thrombolytic therapy?
A. Active bleeding
B. Current anticoagulant therapy
C. Over age 75
D. Severe hepatic disease

3. The nurse is caring for a nonsmoking female patient with the diagnosis of coronary atherosclerosis who has been admitted to the hospital with angina. The patient states that she never experiences chest pain going down her arm or in the middle of her chest. The nurse is not surprised at this statement and explains to the patient that:
A. Women who have ischemia are usually totally asymptomatic.
B. Women have been found to have more atypical symptoms such as dyspnea, nausea, and weakness.
C. Chest pain occurs only with strenuous exercise.
D. Cigarette smoking is usually the contributing factor to chest pain.

4. Two hours after cardiac catheterization that was accessed via the right femoral artery route, an adult client complains of numbness and pain in the right foot. What action should the nurse take first:
A. Call the physician immediately.
B. Check the client's peripheral pulses (pedal/posterior tibial).
C. Take the client's blood pressure.
D. Recognize that this is an expected response and reassess the patient in 1 hour.

5. A 54-year-old man comes to triage complaining of severe, left-sided, pressure-like chest pain and left arm numbness. The pain began 2 hours ago and is unrelieved by rest. The patient is anxious, diaphoretic, and complaining of nausea. Cardiac monitoring is begun, and oxygen is given at 2 L/min. An intermittent infusion device (IID) is in place, and vital signs are as follows: BP of 128/68 mm Hg; pulse, 76 beats/minute; respirations easy and regular at 20 breaths/minutes. ECG reveals normal sinus rhythm with occasional unifocal premature ventricular contractions (PVCs).

A MI is suspected because of elevation in the following lab studies:
A. CK-MB and LDH
B. LDH and troponin I
C. CK-MB and troponin I
D. Troponin I and SGPT

Try these additional resources to enhance your learning and understanding of this chapter:
- thePoint online resource available at **http://thepoint.lww.com/Pellico1e**
- *Handbook for Focus on Adult Health: Medical-Surgical Nursing*
- *Study Guide for Focus on Adult Health: Medical-Surgical Nursing*

References and Selected Readings

References and selected readings associated with this chapter can be found on the website that accompanies the book. Visit http://thepoint.lww.com/Pellico1e to access the references and other additional resources associated with this chapter.

Nursing Management: Patients With Complications From Heart Disease

STEPHANIE L. CALCASOLA

Learning Objectives

After reading this chapter, you will be able to:

1. Compare and contrast diastolic and systolic heart failure (HF), including pathophysiology and clinical manifestations.

2. Describe the management of patients with HF.

3. Develop a teaching plan for patients with HF.

4. Describe the assessment and management of patients with pulmonary edema.

5. Describe the management of patients with cardiogenic shock.

6. Describe the management of patients with pericardial effusion.

7. Describe emergency management of patients with cardiac arrest.

Today, patients with heart disease can be assisted to live longer and achieve a higher quality of life than they could even a decade ago. Through advances in diagnostic procedures that allow earlier and more accurate diagnoses, treatment can begin well before significant debilitation occurs. Newer treatments, technologies, and pharmacotherapies are being developed rapidly. However, heart disease remains a chronic condition, and complications may develop. This chapter presents the complications most often resulting from heart diseases and the treatments provided by the health care team for these complications.

HEART FAILURE

Heart failure (HF) is the inability of the heart to pump sufficient blood to meet the needs of the tissues for oxygen and nutrients. In the past, HF was often referred to as **congestive heart failure** (CHF), because many patients experience pulmonary or peripheral congestion. Currently HF is recognized as a clinical syndrome characterized by signs and symptoms of fluid overload or of inadequate tissue perfusion. Fluid overload and decreased tissue perfusion result when the heart cannot generate a cardiac output (CO) sufficient to meet the body's demands (see Chapter 12 for a review of cardiac hemodynamics). The term *heart failure* indicates myocardial disease in which there is a problem with contraction of the heart (systolic dysfunction) or filling of the heart (diastolic dysfunction) that may or may not cause pulmonary or systemic congestion. Some cases of HF are reversible, depending on the cause. Most often, HF is a progressive, life-long diagnosis that is managed with lifestyle changes and medications to prevent acute congestive episodes.

CHRONIC HEART FAILURE

As with coronary artery disease (CAD), the incidence of HF increases with age. Over 5 million people in the United States have HF, and 550,000 new cases are diagnosed each year (American Heart Association [AHA], 2009). Although HF can affect people of all ages, the prevalence in people older than 75 years of age is about 10%, and as the U.S. population ages, HF has become an epidemic that challenges the country's health care resources (AHA, 2009). HF is the most common reason for hospitalization

of people older than 65 years of age and the second most common reason for visits to a health care provider. The rate of hospital readmission remains staggeringly high. The economic burden caused by HF is estimated to be more than $25 billion in direct and indirect costs and is expected to increase (AHA, 2009).

The increase in the incidence of HF reflects the increased number of elderly people and improvements in treatment of cardiac diseases, resulting in increased survival rates. Many hospitalizations could be prevented by appropriate outpatient care. Prevention and early intervention to arrest the progression of HF are major health initiatives in the United States.

Types and Classification

There are two types of HF, which are identified by assessment of left ventricular functioning, usually by echocardiogram. The more common type is an alteration in ventricular contraction called **systolic heart failure**, which is characterized by a weakened heart muscle. The less common alteration is **diastolic heart failure**, which is characterized by a stiff and noncompliant heart muscle, making it difficult for the ventricle to fill. An assessment of the **ejection fraction (EF)** is performed to assist in determining the type of HF. EF, an indication of the volume of blood ejected with each contraction, is calculated by subtracting the amount of blood at the end of systole from the amount at the end of diastole and calculating the percentage of blood that is ejected. A normal EF is 55% to 65% of the ventricular volume; the ventricle does not completely empty between contractions. The EF is normal in diastolic HF but severely reduced in systolic HF.

Although a low EF is a hallmark of HF, the severity of HF is frequently classified according to the patient's symptoms. The American College of Cardiology and the American Heart Association (Schocken et al., 2008) developed a new HF classification system that incorporates a patient's clinical status and pathophysiology of the disease in its classification. Stages of HF (A–D) have been created to understand and manage the progression of HF including risk factors for HF and primary prevention strategies. Additionally, Figure 15-1 considers the natural history and progressive nature of HF. Treatment guidelines have been developed for each stage.

Pathophysiology

HF results from a variety of cardiovascular conditions (including chronic hypertension, CAD, valvular disease, congenital heart defects, and arrhythmias), as well as from conditions such as diabetes mellitus, fever, infection, thyrotoxicosis, iron overload, hypoxia, anemia, and pulmonary embolus (Burke et al., 2006). These conditions can result in decreased contraction (systole), decreased filling (diastole), or both. Significant myocardial dysfunction most often occurs before the patient experiences signs and symptoms of HF, such as shortness of breath, edema, or fatigue.

As HF develops, the body activates neurohormonal compensatory mechanisms. These mechanisms represent the body's attempt to cope with the HF and are responsible for the signs and symptoms that eventually develop. Understanding these mechanisms is important because the treatment of HF is aimed at relieving them (Fig. 15-2).

Systolic HF results in decreased blood volume being ejected from the ventricle. The decreased ventricular stretch is sensed by baroreceptors (sensors in blood vessels that respond to perfusion pressure of blood flow) in the aortic and carotid bodies (Lee & Tkacs, 2008). The sympathetic nervous system is then stimulated to release epinephrine and norepinephrine. The purpose of this initial response is to increase heart rate and **contractility** and support the failing myocardium, but the continued response has multiple negative effects. Sympathetic stimulation causes vasoconstriction of the skin, gastrointestinal tract, and kidneys. A decrease in renal perfusion due to low CO and vasoconstriction then causes the release of renin by the kidney. Renin promotes the formation of angiotensin I, a benign, inactive substance. Angiotensin-converting enzyme (ACE) in the lumen of pulmonary blood vessels converts angiotensin I to angiotensin II, a potent vasoconstrictor, which then increases the blood pressure and **afterload** (see alert below). Angiotensin II also stimulates the release of aldosterone from the adrenal cortex, resulting in sodium and fluid retention by the renal tubules and stimulating the thirst center. This leads to the fluid volume overload commonly seen in HF. Angiotensin, aldosterone, and other neurohormones (e.g., endothelin, prostacyclin) lead to an increase in **preload** and afterload, which increases stress on the ventricular wall, causing an increase in the workload of the heart. A counterregulatory mechanism is attempted through the release of natriuretic peptides. Atrial natriuretic peptide (ANP) and B-type natriuretic peptide (BNP) are released from the overdistended cardiac chambers (Fig. 15-3, p. 428). These substances promote vasodilation and diuresis. However, their effect is usually not strong enough to overcome the negative effects of the other mechanisms.

⚡ NURSING ALERT

Preload should be considered as the stretching of the cardiac muscle prior to contraction. Ventricular preload is determined by the volume of blood in the ventricle prior to the onset of systole and is a function of both venous return and end systolic volume of the chamber. For example, when venous return or volume of blood entering the heart is increased, preload increases. In contrast, if there is a loss of blood due to hemorrhage, less blood returns to the atria and this leads to decreased ventricular filling and reduced preload. Regardless of the chamber (atria or ventricle), preload is related to the volume just prior to contraction. Afterload should be considered as resistance to flow (the pressure gradient that the ventricles must overcome to pump blood out the ventricles to either the lungs or systemic circulation).

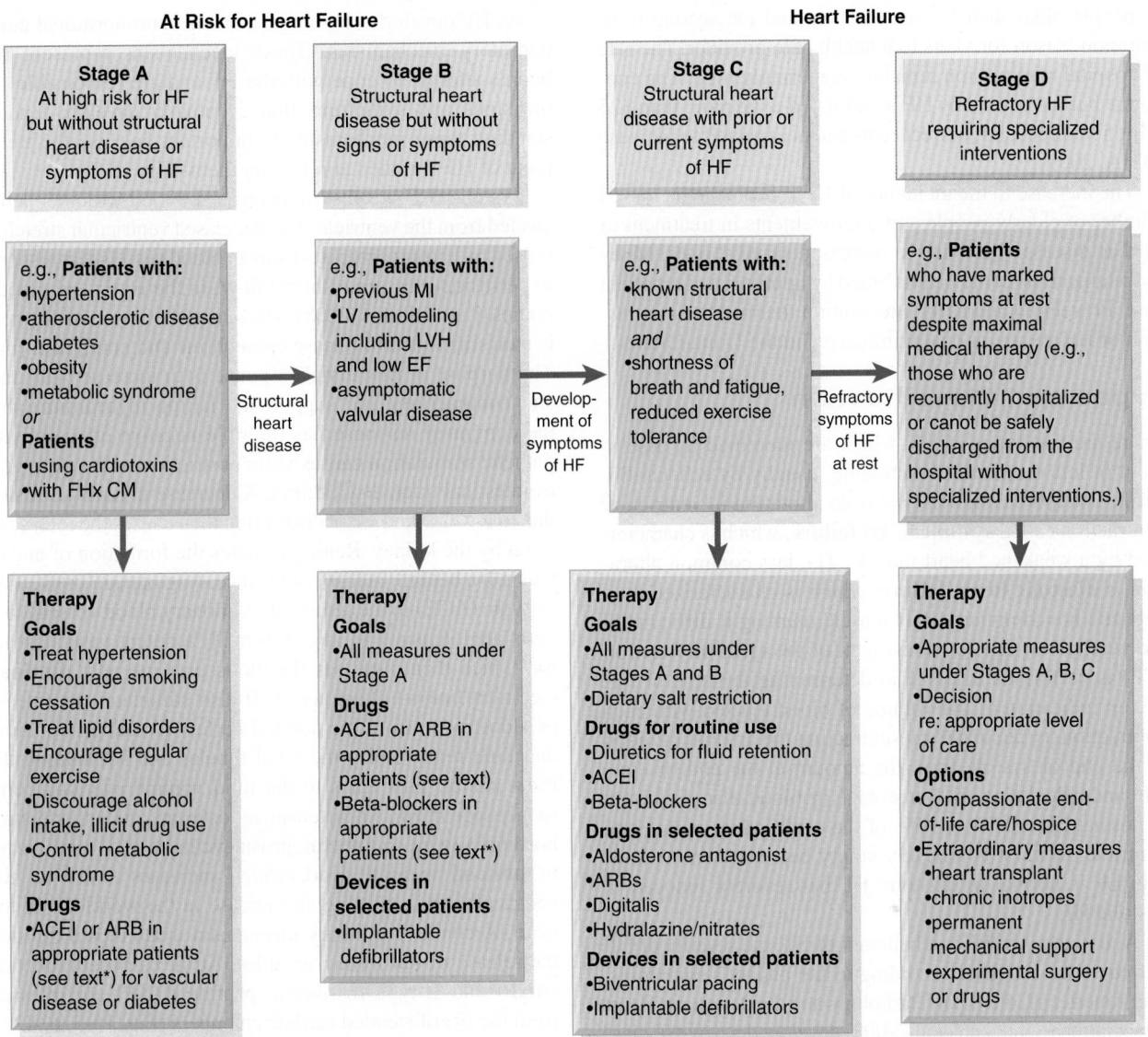

At Risk for Heart Failure

Heart Failure

Stage A
At high risk for HF but without structural heart disease or symptoms of HF

Stage B
Structural heart disease but without signs or symptoms of HF

Stage C
Structural heart disease with prior or current symptoms of HF

Stage D
Refractory HF requiring specialized interventions

e.g., **Patients with:**
•hypertension
•atherosclerotic disease
•diabetes
•obesity
•metabolic syndrome
or
Patients
•using cardiotoxins
•with FHx CM

→ Structural heart disease →

e.g., **Patients with:**
•previous MI
•LV remodeling including LVH and low EF
•asymptomatic valvular disease

→ Develop-ment of symptoms of HF →

e.g., **Patients with:**
•known structural heart disease *and*
•shortness of breath and fatigue, reduced exercise tolerance

→ Refractory symptoms of HF at rest →

e.g., **Patients** who have marked symptoms at rest despite maximal medical therapy (e.g., those who are recurrently hospitalized or canot be safely discharged from the hospital without specialized interventions.)

Therapy
Goals
•Treat hypertension
•Encourage smoking cessation
•Treat lipid disorders
•Encourage regular exercise
•Discourage alcohol intake, illicit drug use
•Control metabolic syndrome
Drugs
•ACEI or ARB in appropriate patients (see text*) for vascular disease or diabetes

Therapy
Goals
•All measures under Stage A
Drugs
•ACEI or ARB in appropriate patients (see text)
•Beta-blockers in appropriate patients (see text*)
Devices in selected patients
•Implantable defibrillators

Therapy
Goals
•All measures under Stages A and B
•Dietary salt restriction
Drugs for routine use
•Diuretics for fluid retention
•ACEI
•Beta-blockers
Drugs in selected patients
•Aldosterone antagonist
•ARBs
•Digitalis
•Hydralazine/nitrates
Devices in selected patients
•Biventricular pacing
•Implantable defibrillators

Therapy
Goals
•Appropriate measures under Stages A, B, C
•Decision re: appropriate level of care
Options
•Compassionate end-of-life care/hospice
•Extraordinary measures
  •heart transplant
  •chronic inotropes
  •permanent mechanical support
  •experimental surgery or drugs

© 2009, American Heart Association, Inc.

FIGURE 15-1 Stages in the development of heart failure. ACEI, angiotensin-converting enzyme inhibitor; ARB, angiotensin receptor blocker; FHx cm, family history of cardiomyopathy; LV, left ventricle; LVH, left ventricular hypertrophy; MI, myocardial infarction. From © American Heart Association (AHA). 2009. *Circulation*, 119, 1977–2016. Reprinted with permission.

As the heart's workload increases, contractility of the myocardial muscle fibers decreases. Decreased contractility results in an increase in end-diastolic blood volume (preload) in the ventricle, stretching the myocardial muscle fibers and increasing the size of the ventricle (ventricular dilation). The increased size of the ventricle further increases the stress on the ventricular wall, adding to the workload of the heart. One way the heart compensates for the increased workload is to increase the thickness of the heart muscle (ventricular hypertrophy). However, hypertrophy results in an abnormal proliferation of myocardial cells, a process known as *ventricular remodeling*. Under the influence of neurohormones (e.g., angiotensin II), large myocardial cells are produced that are dysfunctional and die early, leaving the other normal myocardial cells to struggle to maintain CO (Lee & Tkacs, 2008). The heart does not pump sufficient blood to the body, which causes the body to stimulate the heart to work harder; the heart cannot respond and failure becomes worse. This cycle repeats itself, thus contributing to an ongoing process of further cardiac decline.

Diastolic HF develops because of continued increased workload on the heart, which responds by increasing the number and size of myocardial cells (i.e., ventricular hypertrophy and altered cellular functioning). These responses cause resistance to ventricular filling, which increases ventricular filling pressures despite a normal or reduced blood volume. Less blood in the ventricles causes decreased CO. The low CO and high ventricular filling pressures can cause

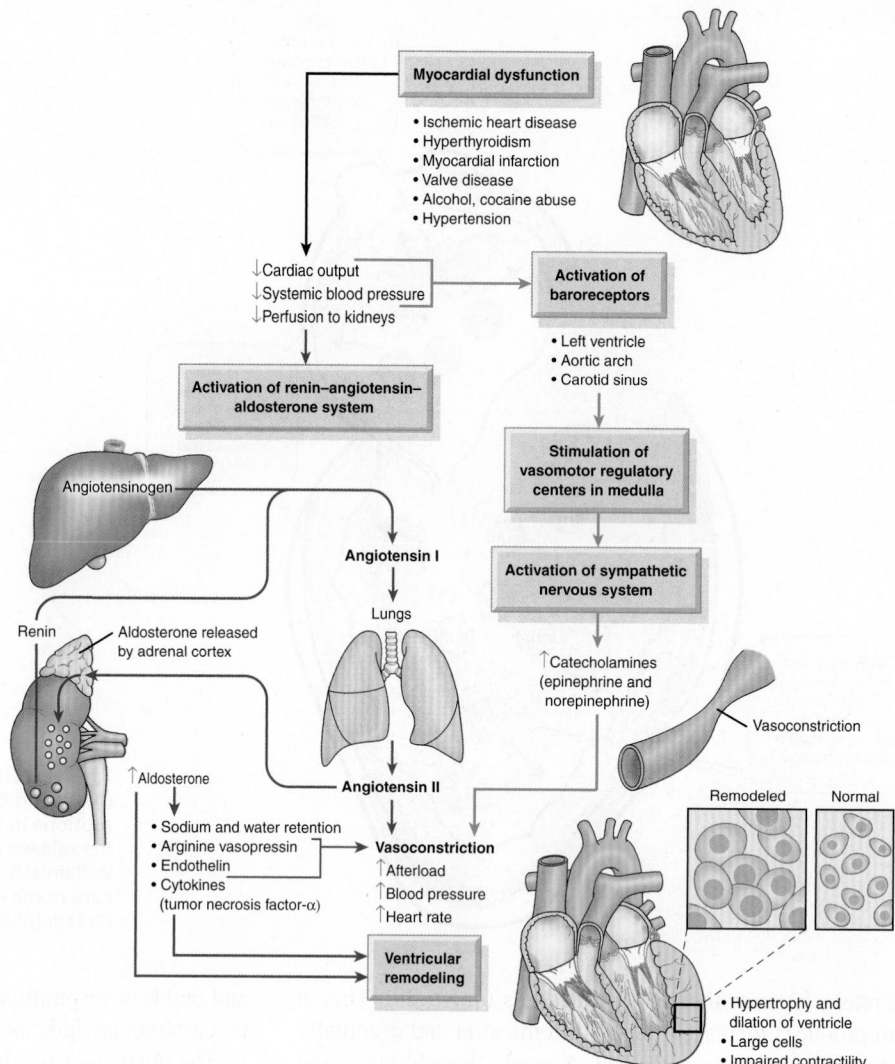

FIGURE 15-2 The pathophysiology of heart failure. A decrease in cardiac output activates multiple neurohormonal mechanisms that ultimately result in the signs and symptoms of HF.

the same neurohormonal responses as described for systolic HF. Table 15-1 provides a comparison of systolic and diastolic HF.

Additionally, HF may present as right-sided versus left-sided (Table 15-2).

Risk Factors

Risk factors for acquiring HF can be divided into two categories: major and minor. Major risk factors include: age (>65), male sex, hypertension, left ventricular hypertrophy, myocardial infarction, valvular heart disease, and obesity. Minor risk factors include: excessive alcohol consumption, smoking, high cholesterol (dyslipidemia), diabetes, toxins (chemotherapeutic agents), sleep-disordered breathing, chronic kidney disease, low socioeconomic status, psychological stress, sedentary lifestyle, and genetics (Schocken et al., 2008).

Clinical Manifestations and Assessment

Systolic and diastolic share similar clinical findings. Overt signs of HF, include resting dyspnea, cyanosis, and cachexia (physical wasting) resulting from longstanding heart disease. A baseline height and weight should be documented on admission, and weight rechecked each morning. Obtaining daily weights and tracking trends in weight, along with an accurate intake and output log provide an easy and accurate way to monitor fluid balance. Fluid balance is an important surveillance strategy in controlling HF symptoms.

A thorough cardiovascular assessment is performed, which includes blood pressure measurement in sitting and standing position in order to detect orthostatic hypotension.

Tachycardia (heart rate >120 bpm) may signal worsening HF. When the heart rate is rapid, the stroke volume (SV)

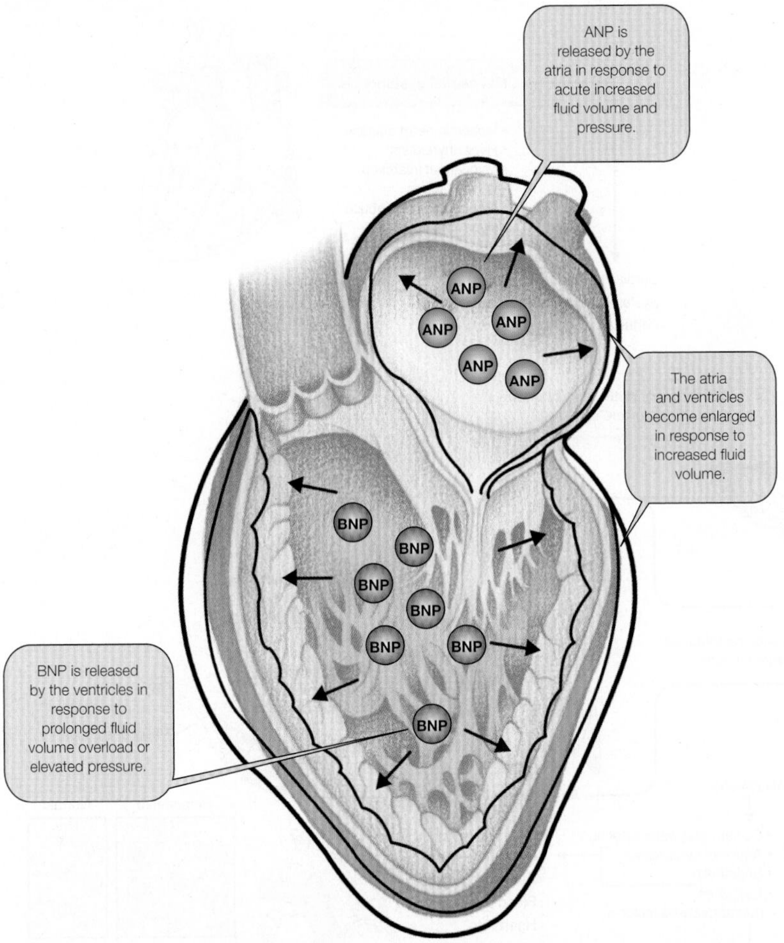

ANP is released by the atria in response to acute increased fluid volume and pressure.

The atria and ventricles become enlarged in response to increased fluid volume.

BNP is released by the ventricles in response to prolonged fluid volume overload or elevated pressure.

FIGURE 15-3 A-type natriuretic peptide (ANP) and B-type natriuretic peptide (BNP). Disruptions in intravascular fluid balance trigger the release of ANP and BNP. From Lippincott Williams & Wilkins. (2010). *Cardiovascular care made incredibly visual* (2nd ed., p. 50). Philadelphia: Lippincott Williams & Wilkins.

decreases because the ventricle has less time to fill. This in turn produces increased pressure in the atria and eventually in the pulmonary vascular bed. A weak, thready pulse and *pulsus alternans* (pulse is regular but force of amplitude varies with alternating beats from large to small) are signs of decreased left ventricular function.

Left ventricular hypertrophy (LVH) may displace the apical pulse left and downward from its normal location at the fifth intercostal space at the midclavicular line. Right-sided HF may present with an elevation in jugular venous pressure greater than 4 cm above the sternal angle. This is an estimate, not a precise measurement, of central venous pressure.

An S_3 heart sound is a sign that the heart is beginning to fail and that increased blood volume fills the ventricle with each beat. Other sounds may include mitral and tricuspid regurgitation murmurs. The nurse may detect an S_4 sound if the patient has increased resistance to ventricular filling because of increased stiffness of the ventricular myocardium.

The nurse assesses the lungs. Crackles, which are produced by the sudden opening of edematous small airways and alveoli that have adhered together by exudate, may be heard at the end of inspiration and are not cleared with coughing. Wheezing may also be heard in some patients. The rate

and depth of respirations are also documented. Dullness to percussion may indicate pleural effusions due to HF.

The nurse assesses dependent parts of the patient's body for perfusion and edema. With significant decreases in **stroke volume** (SV), there is a decrease in perfusion to the periphery, causing the skin to feel cool and appear pale or cyanotic. If the patient is sitting upright, the feet and lower legs are examined for edema; if the patient is supine in bed, the sacrum and back are also assessed for edema. Fingers and hands may also become edematous. The nurse notes the location and extent of the edema and assesses for evidence of pitting edema (refer to Chapter 12).

Hepatomegaly, hepatojugular reflux, and ascites can occur with venous congestion due to right-sided HF. To assess for hepatojugular reflux, the patient is positioned in bed so that the nurse can observe the blood column of the jugular veins above the clavicle (LeBlond, Brown, & DeGowin, 2009). The patient is asked to breathe normally while manual pressure is applied over the right upper quadrant of the abdomen for at least 15 seconds. If the top of the jugular venous column in the neck rises and persists as long as the abdominal pressure is continued, it is considered positive hepatojugular reflux, which is associated with right HF and constrictive pericarditis.

TABLE
15-1 Comparison of Systolic and Diastolic Heart Failure

	Systolic Failure	Diastolic Failure
Pathophysiology	• Impaired ventricular pumping of blood during systole • Characterized by reduced stroke volume, incomplete ventricular emptying, cardiac dilation, and elevated left ventricular diastolic pressure • Reduced cardiac output evokes compensatory neurohormonal responses that increase heart rate, sodium and water retention, and vasoconstriction.	• Impaired ventricular relaxation filling during diastole • Characterized by a stiffened left ventricle that can't relax and fill sufficiently at normal diastolic pressure • The result is either decreased left ventricular end-diastolic volume (leading to decreased cardiac output) or a compensatory rise in left ventricular filling pressure, which can lead to pulmonary venous hypertension.
Causes/Etiology	Usually caused by ischemic or idiopathic dilated cardiomyopathy, when the left ventricle cannot adequately contract or squeeze out its contents, so that preload increases and stroke volume decreases	Usually caused by hypertensive, hypertrophic, or restrictive cardiomyopathy

Sensorium and level of consciousness must be evaluated. As the volume of blood ejected by the heart decreases, so does the amount of oxygen transported to the brain. Patients may complain of dizziness or lightheadedness. Box 15-1 compares and contrasts assessment findings in left- and right-sided HF.

Diagnostic evaluation includes:

• A chest X-ray can determine the presence and extent of cardiac enlargement or pulmonary congestion and can help identify pulmonary disease. Cardiomegaly indicates systolic dysfunction; a normal heart size suggests diastolic dysfunction.

• A 12-lead electrocardiogram (ECG) determines the presence of cardiac arrhythmias, left ventricular hypertrophy, and previous or current myocardial infarction (MI). If the patient has left ventricular dysfunction, the ECG usually indicates a left ventricular electrical abnormality specific to ventricular dilation or hypertrophy.

• A two-dimensional echocardiogram with Doppler flow study is a noninvasive test to look for structural cardiac abnormalities and to measure EF. An EF of less than 40% indicates systolic dysfunction; an EF of greater than 40% with signs and symptoms of HF and impaired ventricular relaxation indicates diastolic dysfunction.

• Laboratory tests that may help diagnose HF include complete blood cell count, electrolyte levels (including calcium and magnesium), blood urea nitrogen, creatinine, serum glucose, serum albumin, liver function tests, thyroid-stimulating hormone, urinalysis, and BNP levels.

TABLE
15-2 Symptom Comparison of Left- vs. Right-Sided Heart Failure

	Left-Sided HF	Right-Sided HF
Pathophysiology	• Pulmonary congestion from impaired left ventricle (LV) function • LV cannot pump blood out of the ventricle effectively into the aorta and the systemic circulation. • Pulmonary venous blood volume and pressure increase, forcing fluid from the pulmonary capillaries into the pulmonary tissues and alveoli, causing pulmonary interstitial edema and impaired gas exchange.	• Right ventricle pump failure leading to congestion in the peripheral tissues and the viscera • Right side of the heart cannot eject blood and cannot accommodate all the blood that normally returns to it from the venous circulation. • Increased venous pressure leads to jugular vein distension (JVD) and increased hydrostatic pressure throughout the venous system. Normal central venous pressure is 2–8 mm Hg. A CVP >8 mm Hg indicates hypervolemia (excessive fluid circulating in the body) or right-sided HF.

Focus on Assessment

Left-Sided vs. Right-Sided Heart Failure

Be alert for the following signs and symptoms:

Left-Sided HF
- Dyspnea, orthopnea, paroxysmal nocturnal dyspnea (PND)
- Cough
- Pulmonary crackles
- Decrease O_2 saturation levels.
- S_3 ventricular gallop
- Oliguria if renal perfusion is diminished (Note: Nocturia may occur when perfusion improves with sleeping due to improved perfusion at rest.)
- Decreased perfusion to other systemic organs (advanced failure):
  - Sluggish GI motility
  - Dizziness, lightheadedness, confusion, restlessness
  - Anxiety
  - Skin cool and clammy
  - Decrease in EF
  - Tachycardia and/or weak/thready pulse
  - Fatigue or activity intolerance

Right-Sided HF
- Lower extremity dependent edema (dependent edema is swelling that follows the position of the body):
  - Legs and feet
  - May progress to thighs, external genitalia, lower trunk, abdomen, and sacral edema (in a bed-bound patient)
  - Pitting edema (indentations in the skin remain after even slight compression with the fingertips)
- Hepatomegaly (enlargement of the liver)
- Ascites (accumulation of fluid in the peritoneal cavity)
- Anorexia and nausea
- Weight gain due to retention of fluid.
- Weakness/fatigue from reduced CO and impaired cognition
- Decreased perfusion to other systemic organs (advanced failure)

High BNP levels (>100 pg/mL) indicate abnormal ventricular function or symptomatic HF.
- A right-sided heart catheterization also can be performed to determine the heart's preload pressures and pulmonary pressures to determine the degree of HF and the need for further intervention. A patient with angina who is a candidate for coronary revascularization may undergo a full cardiac catheterization with coronary arteriography.

Medical Management

Treatment begins with prevention. Identifying patients at risk is the first step in the care and treatment of HF.

The overall goals of management of HF are to relieve patient symptoms, improve functional status and quality of life, and extend survival. Treatment is based on the type, severity, and cause of HF. Specific objectives include the following:

- Eliminate or reduce any etiologic contributory factors, especially those that may be reversible (e.g., atrial fibrillation, excessive alcohol ingestion, uncontrolled hypertension).
- Reduce the workload on the heart by reducing afterload and preload.
- Optimize all therapeutic regimens.
- Prevent exacerbations of HF.

Treatment options vary according to the severity of the patient's condition (see Fig.15-1).

Lifestyle Changes

Managing the patient with HF includes providing general education and counseling to the patient and family. It is important that the patient and family understand the nature of HF and the importance of their participation in the treatment regimen. Lifestyle recommendations include restriction of dietary sodium; avoidance of excessive fluid intake, alcohol, and smoking; weight reduction when indicated; and regular exercise. The patient must know how to recognize signs and symptoms that need to be reported to the health care professional such as weight gain, increasing shortness of breath, fatigue, and edema.

Pharmacologic Therapy

Several medications (Table 15-3) are routinely prescribed for systolic HF, including ACE inhibitors, beta blockers, diuretics, and digitalis. Medications for diastolic failure depend on the underlying condition, such as hypertension or valvular dysfunction.

Additional Therapies

Additional therapy and surgical treatment are described in Table 15-4. Box 15-2 discusses the psychological impact of these therapies.

Nursing Management

Despite advances in medical and surgical approaches to HF, mortality remains high. Nurses can make a major difference in promoting positive outcomes. Caring for patients with HF requires a collaborative, interdisciplinary team approach. Nurses play a pivotal role in the care and ongoing teaching of this patient population.

Assessing the Patient

The nursing assessment for the patient with HF focuses on observing for effectiveness of therapy and for the patient's ability to understand and implement self-management strategies. Signs and symptoms of pulmonary and systemic fluid

TABLE
15-3 **Pharmacological Treatment of Heart Failure**

Drug Class	Pharmacokinetics	Indications and Nursing Implications
Diuretics	Diuretics prompt the kidneys to excrete sodium, chloride, and water, reducing fluid volume. They are a preload reducer.	• Diuretics should never be used alone to treat HF because they don't prevent further myocardial damage. • Loop diuretics, such as furosemide, bumetanide, and torsemide, are the preferred first-line diuretics because of their efficacy in patients with and without renal impairment. • Low-dose spironolactone may be added to a patient's regimen if he or she has recent or recurrent symptoms at rest despite therapy with ACE inhibitors, beta-blockers, digoxin, and diuretics.
Inotropes	Inotropes affect the force of myocardial contraction. Positive inotropes increase force of myocardial contraction and also increase workload of heart and oxygen demand. Negative inotropes decrease force of myocardial contraction and decrease workload of heart and oxygen demand.	• Digoxin increases the heart's ability to contract and improves HF symptoms and exercise tolerance in patients with mild to moderate HF. • Positive inotrope major adverse reactions include arrhythmias; gastrointestinal problems, such as anorexia; and neurologic symptoms, such as confusion. • IV positive inotropes such as dobutamine, dopamine, and milrinone, are IV positive inotropes. They can also be used for long-term support (e.g., patients awaiting cardiac transplant) via a tunneled central venous catheter or peripherally inserted central catheter.
ACE inhibitors	Angiotensin-converting enzyme (ACE) inhibitors, such as captopril and enalapril, block the conversion of angiotensin I to angiotensin II, a vasoconstrictor that can raise blood pressure. These drugs alleviate HF symptoms by causing vasodilation and decreasing myocardial workload. They are preload and afterload reducers. Provide renal protection.	• The most common adverse reaction to ACE inhibitors is a dry cough. Other adverse reactions include hypotension, worsening renal function, and potassium retention.
Angiotensin II receptor blockers	Angiotensin-II receptor antagonists selectively block the binding of angiotensin II to specific tissue receptors in vascular smooth muscle and the adrenal glands. Overall effects include: blocking the vasoconstricting effect of the renin–angiotensin system; blocking aldosterone release, leading to a reduction in sodium and water retention; little effect on potassium. They are preload and afterload reducers.	• Patients who cannot take ACE inhibitors may be prescribed angiotensin receptor blockers instead. This therapy reduces the effects of sodium and water retention, vasoconstriction, and myocardial remodeling.
Aldosterone receptor antagonists	Aldosterone receptor antagonists, such as eplerenone, block aldosterone from binding to receptors in the kidneys. This allows the kidneys to eliminate excess sodium and water. They are a preload reducer.	• Similar to ACE inhibitors for nursing implications. Evidence suggests patients may not exhibit the side effect of a cough, as they do with ACE inhibitors.
Beta blockers	Beta-adrenergic blockers, such as bisoprolol, metoprolol, and carvedilol, block the effects of catecholamines, resulting in reduction in heart rate, peripheral vasoconstriction, and myocardial ischemia. Beta blockers can interfere with the passage of air into the lungs. However selective beta blockers avoid this problem. They are a negative inotrope.	• Long-term therapy reduces HF symptoms and improves the patient's functional status.
Nesiritide	Nesiritide (Natrecor), a preparation of human B-type natriuretic peptide (BNP) that mimics the action of endogenous BNP, causing diuresis and vasodilation, reducing BP, and improving cardiac output. It is a preload and afterload reducer.	• It is given via the IV route only.
Vasodilators/ nitrates	Arterial and venous smooth muscle relaxation They are preload and afterload reducers.	• The combination of hydralazine and nitrates is recommended to improve outcomes for patients self-described as African American (Jessup, Abraham, Casey et al., 2009) with moderate-severe HF symptoms who are on optimal ACE inhibitors, beta blockers, and diuretics.

TABLE
15-4 Modalities for Treatment of Heart Failure

Modality	Indications	Description/Procedure
Ultrafiltration (UF)	Eases symptoms for patients in decompensated HF and can help some patients to respond again to conventional drug therapy; it is a low-volume extracorporeal process that removes fluid from the intravascular compartment.	• Uses a mechanical pump and a hemofilter to remove a specified amount of fluid with each treatment, alleviating the patient's symptoms • Treatment time varies depending on patient needs. • During treatment, the intravascular fluid volume remains stable, since fluid shifts from the interstitial space to replace fluid lost in treatment, which reduces edema and third-spacing. Typically, patients do not become hypotensive or hypovolemic with this treatment (Soat, 2008; Bartone, Saghir, Menon et al., 2008).
Cardiac resynchronization therapy	In the patient with HF who does not improve with standard therapy, cardiac resynchronization therapy (CRT) may be beneficial. CRT involves the use of a biventricular pacemaker to treat electrical conduction defects. Left bundle branch block is a feature of delayed conduction that is frequently seen in patients with HF that results in dyssynchronous conduction and contraction of the right and left ventricles, which can further decrease EF (Hunt, 2009).	• Use of a pacing device with leads placed in the right atrium, right ventricle, and left ventricular cardiac vein can synchronize the contractions of the right and left ventricles. This intervention has been shown to improve cardiac output, optimize myocardial energy consumption, reduce mitral regurgitation, and slow the ventricular remodeling process. For selected patients, this results in fewer symptoms and increased functional status (Hunt, 2009). For patients who require CRT and an implantable cardiac defibrillator (ICD), combination devices are available.
Implantable cardiac defibrillators (icds)	Patients with HF are at high risk for arrhythmias. In patients with life-threatening arrhythmias, placement of an ICD can prevent sudden cardiac death and extend survival.	• ICDs can provide a range of therapies that include cardioversion, defibrillation, and pacing. A lead or leads are placed in the appropriate chambers endocardium and attached to a generator box that can be implanted in right or left chest, under the clavicle.
Ventricular access devices/destination therapy	Patients with end-stage HF may require a ventricular assist device (VAD) for greater support for the failing ventricle(s). A VAD can reduce myocardial ischemia and workload, limit permanent cardiac damage, and restore adequate organ perfusion. Indications for use include: as a bridge to myocardial recovery in acute ventricular failure (e.g. shock, acute MI, etc.), as a bridge to heart transplantation in chronic ventricular failure, and for permanent therapy for end-stage chronic HF; also known as *destination therapy*.	• VADs are mechanical blood pumps that work by augmenting or replacing the function of either the left or right ventricle. • Most currently available devices are surgically implanted and require cardiopulmonary bypass to implant. Percutaneous assist devices are in development, and one is commercially available called Tandem Heart; this therapy may be a bridge to heart transplant (Kale & Fang, 2008).
Heart transplant	For some patients with end-stage HF, cardiac transplantation is the only option for long-term survival (Garratti, 2008). Some of these patients require mechanical circulatory assistance with an implanted ventricular assist device as a bridge therapy to cardiac transplantation. Research continues toward perfection of a totally implantable artificial heart that may be used as an alternative to transplantation.	Heart transplantation involves replacing a person's diseased heart with a donor heart. This is an option for advanced HF patients when all other therapies have failed.

BOX 15-2
Nursing Research

Bridging the Gap to Evidence-Based Practice

What Does the Evidence Suggest for Helping Patients Adjust to Living With Ventricular Assist Devices or Who Have Undergone Heart Transplantation?

Hallas, C., Banner, N. R., Wray, J. (2009). A qualitative study of the psychological experience of patients during and after mechanical cardiac support. *Journal of Cardiovascular Nursing, 24*(1), 31–39.

Purpose

Evidence indicates mortality has decreased in patients requiring surgical intervention (ventricular assist device (VAD) implantation or heart transplant) for HF treatment when compared to patients only receiving medical therapy. To date, little published research is available to address the psychological adjustment of patients requiring a VAD to manage their HF.

Design

A cross-sectional study design using a grounded theory methodology was used. Twenty-four patients were invited to participate in this study. A total of 11 patients (eight men and three women) agreed to be interviewed. From this sample, four patients were interviewed while living with a VAD, four patients were being medically managed on HF medications after explant from a VAD, and three patients were interviewed after receiving a cardiac transplant, after having been supported

on a VAD prior to transplant. The age of the participants ranged from 18 to 60 years. All participants were clinically stable at the time of the study.

Analyses of the interview transcripts indicated that there was one core category related to psychological adjustment, with six conceptual categories associated with the core category. All patients identified perceived control as the core category of their cognitive construction of quality of life. Additionally, three conceptual categories were identified that directly related to control: patient's construction of their normality, their emotional state, and thoughts and feelings regarding uncertainty about the future. For patients currently with a VAD, impact of the VAD and the illness/VAD identity was also identified as conceptual categories.

Nursing Implications

This was a small study with a cross-sectional sample of patients with end-stage HF. Caution must be taken not to generalize these findings to patients with less severe HF. Nurses can use these findings to help plan care around inclusion of the patient to optimize control. For example, assisting patients with normal routines, providing care maps of their day, and supportive communication can foster a sense of control.

---

overload are recorded and reported immediately, so that adjustments can be made in therapy. The nurse also explores the patient's emotional response to the diagnosis of HF, a chronic and often progressive condition.

The health history focuses on the signs and symptoms of HF, such as shortness of breath, **dyspnea on exertion (DOE)**, shortness of breath that occurs with exertion, and cough. Sleep disturbances, particularly sleep suddenly interrupted by shortness of breath termed *paroxysmal nocturnal dyspnea* (PND), may be reported. The nurse also asks about the number of pillows needed for sleep (an indication of **orthopnea**—shortness of breath while lying flat), edema, abdominal symptoms, altered mental status, activities of daily living, daily weight, and the activities that cause fatigue. The nurse explores the patient's understanding of HF, self-management strategies, and the desire to adhere to those strategies. The nurse helps patients identify the impact the illness has had on their quality of life and successful coping skills that they have used. Family and significant others are often included in these discussions.

Monitoring Intake and Output

If the patient is hospitalized, the nurse measures output carefully to establish a baseline against which to assess the

effectiveness of diuretic therapy. Intake and output records are rigorously maintained. It is important to know whether the patient has ingested more fluid than he or she has excreted (positive fluid balance), which is then correlated with a gain in weight. The patient must be monitored for **oliguria** (diminished urine output, >400 mL/24 hours) or anuria (urine output >100 mL/24 hours).

The patient is weighed daily in the hospital or at home, at the same time of day, with the same type of clothing, and on the same scale. If there is a significant change in weight (i.e., 2- to 3-lb increase in a day or 5-lb increase in a week), the patient is instructed to notify his or her provider or to adjust the medications (e.g., increase the diuretic dose) per provider's directions.

ACUTE HEART FAILURE AND PULMONARY EDEMA

Pulmonary edema is the abnormal accumulation of fluid in the lungs. The fluid may accumulate in the interstitial spaces and in the alveoli. Pulmonary edema can be categorized into two subsets depending on the etiology: cardiogenic and noncardiogenic. (Bashore, Granger, Hranitzky, & Patel, 2010).

Pathophysiology

Cardiogenic pulmonary edema is an acute event that results from HF. It can occur acutely, such as with MI, or it can occur as an exacerbation of chronic HF. Myocardial scarring as a result of ischemia can limit the distensibility of the ventricle and render it vulnerable to a sudden increase in workload. With increased resistance to left ventricular filling, blood backs up into the pulmonary circulation. The patient quickly develops pulmonary edema, sometimes called *flash pulmonary edema*, from the blood volume overload in the lungs. Pulmonary edema can also be caused by noncardiac disorders, such as renal failure, liver failure, and oncologic conditions that cause the body to retain fluid. The pathophysiology is similar to that seen in HF, in that the left ventricle cannot handle the volume overload, and blood volume and pressure build up in the left atrium. The rapid increase in atrial pressure results in an acute increase in pulmonary venous pressure, which produces an increase in hydrostatic pressure that forces fluid out of the pulmonary capillaries into the interstitial spaces and alveoli.

Impaired lymphatic drainage also contributes to the accumulation of fluid in the lung tissues. The fluid within the alveoli mixes with air, creating "bubbles" that are expelled from the mouth and nose, producing the classic symptom of pulmonary edema: frothy pink (blood-tinged) sputum. Because of the fluid within the alveoli, air cannot enter, and gas exchange is impaired. The result is hypoxemia, which is often severe. The onset may be preceded by premonitory symptoms of pulmonary congestion, but it also may develop quickly in the patient with a ventricle that has little reserve to meet increased oxygen needs.

Clinical Manifestations and Assessment

As a result of decreased cerebral oxygenation, the patient becomes increasingly restless and anxious. Clinical manifestations include a sudden onset of breathlessness, sense or suffocation, cough that produces a large amount of frothy sputum (may be blood-tinged), cold and moist skin, cyanotic (bluish) nail beds, a weak and rapid pulse, pulmonary rales, expiratory wheezing, and distended neck veins.

Additionally oxygen demand increases, yet oxygen saturation is significantly decreased. The patient, nearly suffocated by the blood-tinged, frothy fluid filling the alveoli, is literally drowning in secretions. The situation demands immediate action.

Medical and Nursing Management

Although the etiology of pulmonary edema may vary, management of symptoms follows the similar clinical management plan for treating acute decompensated HF (oxygen, diuretics, pharmacologic preload and afterload reduction, and possibly hemodynamic monitoring). Additional therapies may include early rescue with noninvasive mask ventilation and bronchodilator therapy with select beta$_2$ agonist medications like albuterol (Johnson, 2009).

CARDIOGENIC SHOCK

Cardiogenic shock occurs when decreased CO leads to inadequate tissue perfusion and initiation of the shock syndrome. Cardiogenic shock may occur following MI, when a large area of myocardium becomes ischemic, necrotic, and hypokinetic (slow or diminished muscle motion). It also can occur as a result of end-stage HF, cardiac tamponade, pulmonary embolism (PE), cardiomyopathy, and arrhythmias. Cardiogenic shock is a life-threatening condition with a high mortality rate.

Pathophysiology

The signs and symptoms of cardiogenic shock reflect the circular nature of the pathophysiology of HF. The degree of shock is proportional to the extent of left ventricular dysfunction. The heart muscle loses its contractile power, resulting in a marked reduction in SV and CO. The decreased CO in turn reduces arterial blood pressure and tissue perfusion in the vital organs (heart, brain, lung, kidneys). Flow to the coronary arteries is reduced, resulting in decreased oxygen supply to the myocardium, which increases ischemia and further reduces the heart's ability to pump. Inadequate emptying of the ventricle also leads to increased pulmonary pressures, pulmonary congestion, and pulmonary edema, exacerbating the hypoxia, causing ischemia of vital organs, and setting a vicious cycle in motion.

Clinical Manifestations and Assessment

The classic signs of cardiogenic shock are those of tissue hypoperfusion, and result from HF and the overall shock state. They include cerebral hypoxia (restlessness, confusion, agitation), low blood pressure, rapid and weak pulse, cold and clammy skin, tachypnea with respiratory crackles, and decreased urinary output. Initially, arterial blood gas (ABG) analysis may show respiratory alkalosis. Arrhythmias are common and result from myocardial ischemia.

The patient with cardiogenic shock is managed in an intensive care unit. A pulmonary artery catheter may be inserted to measure CO and other hemodynamic parameters that are used to assess the severity of the problem and to guide patient management. The pulmonary artery wedge pressure (indirect estimate of left atrial pressure) is elevated and the CO is decreased as the left ventricle loses its ability to pump. The systemic vascular resistance is elevated because of the sympathetic nervous system stimulation that occurs as a compensatory response to the decrease in blood pressure. The decreased blood flow to the kidneys causes a hormonal response (i.e., activation of

the renin–angiotensin–aldosterone system) that causes fluid retention and further vasoconstriction. Increases in HR, circulating volume, and vasoconstriction occur to maintain circulation to the brain, heart, kidneys, and lungs, but at a cost: an increase in the workload of the heart.

The reduction in blood volume delivered to the tissues results in an increase in the amount of oxygen extracted from the blood that is delivered to the tissues (to try to meet the cellular demand for oxygen). The increased systemic oxygen extraction results in decreased venous (mixed and central) oxygen saturation. When the cellular oxygen needs cannot be met, anaerobic metabolism and buildup of lactic acid occurs. Continuous central venous oximetry and measurement of blood lactic acid levels may help assess the severity of the shock as well as the effectiveness of treatment. Refer to Chapter 55 for further discussion on lactic acid levels.

Continued cellular hypoperfusion eventually results in organ failure. The patient becomes unresponsive, severe hypotension ensues, and the patient develops shallow respirations and cold, cyanotic, or mottled skin. ABG analysis shows metabolic acidosis, and all laboratory test results indicate organ dysfunction.

Medical Management

The most important approach to treating cardiogenic shock is to correct the underlying problem, reduce any further demand on the heart, improve oxygenation, and restore tissue perfusion. For example, if the ventricular failure is the result of an acute MI, emergency percutaneous coronary intervention may be indicated. Major arrhythmias are corrected because they may have caused or contributed to the shock. If the patient has hypervolemia, diuresis is indicated. Diuretics, vasodilators, and mechanical therapies, such as continuous renal replacement therapy, have been used to reduce the circulating blood volume. If hypovolemia (low intravascular volume) is suspected or detected through hemodynamic pressure readings, the patient is given IV volume expanders (e.g., normal saline solution, lactated Ringer's solution, albumin) to increase the amount of circulating fluid. The patient is placed on strict bed rest to conserve energy. If the patient has hypoxemia, as detected by pulse oximetry or ABG analysis, oxygen administration is increased, often under positive pressure when regular flow is insufficient to meet tissue demands. Intubation and sedation may be necessary to maintain oxygenation. The settings for mechanical ventilation are adjusted according to the patient's oxygenation status and the need for conserving energy. Ventilator management is discussed in Chapter 55.

PERICARDIAL EFFUSION AND CARDIAC TAMPONADE

Pericardial effusion (accumulation of fluid in the pericardial sac) may accompany pericarditis, advanced HF, metastatic carcinoma, cardiac surgery, or trauma.

Pathophysiology

Normally, the pericardial sac contains less than 50 mL of fluid, which is needed to decrease friction for the beating heart. An increase in pericardial fluid raises the pressure within the pericardial sac and compresses the heart. This has the following effects:

- Increased right and left ventricular end-diastolic pressures
- Decreased venous return
- Inability of the ventricles to distend and fill adequately

Pericardial fluid may accumulate slowly without causing noticeable symptoms until a large amount accumulates. However, a rapidly developing effusion can stretch the pericardium to its maximum size and, because of increased pericardial pressure, venous return to the heart is obstructed and the amount of blood pumped out with each contraction is reduced, which decreases CO. The result is cardiac tamponade (e.g., compression of the heart).

Clinical Manifestations and Assessment

The patient may report a feeling of fullness within the chest or may have substantial or ill-defined pain. The feeling of pressure in the chest may result from stretching of the pericardial sac. Because of increased pressure within the pericardium, venous pressure tends to increase, as evidenced by engorged neck veins. If hemodynamic pressures are monitored, the nurse will note diastolic pressures equilibrate in all chambers, so that right and left atrial pressures, right ventricular end diastolic pressure (RVEDP), left ventricular end diastolic pressure (LVEDP), and pulmonary artery diastolic pressures become equal or nearly equal (<3- to 5-mm Hg difference) (Belenkie, 2005). Other signs include dyspnea, cough, and labile or low blood pressure. Systolic blood pressure that is markedly lower during inhalation is called **pulsus paradoxus**. The difference in systolic pressure between the point that is heard during exhalation and the point that it is heard during inhalation is measured. Pulsus paradoxus exceeding 10 mm Hg is abnormal. A pericardial friction rub may be heard. The cardinal signs of cardiac tamponade are falling systolic blood pressure, narrowing pulse pressure, rising venous pressure (increased JVD), and distant (muffled) heart sounds (Fig. 15-4). If untreated, shock and death can result.

A chest X-ray shows a large pericardial effusion. An echocardiogram is performed to confirm the diagnosis.

Medical and Nursing Management
Pericardiocentesis

If cardiac function becomes seriously impaired as a result of pericardial effusion, **pericardiocentesis** (puncture of the pericardial sac to aspirate pericardial fluid) is performed to remove fluid from the pericardial sac (Fig. 15-5). The major

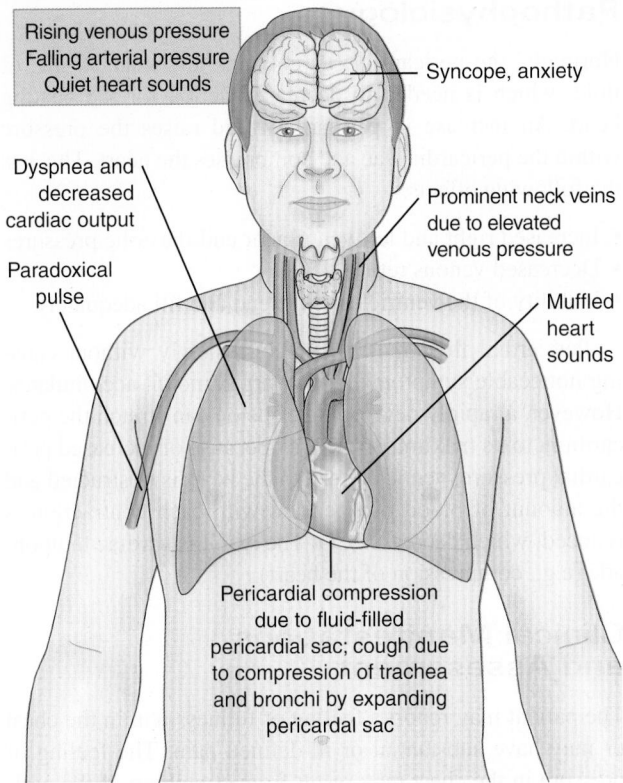

Rising venous pressure
Falling arterial pressure
Quiet heart sounds

Syncope, anxiety

Dyspnea and decreased cardiac output

Prominent neck veins due to elevated venous pressure

Paradoxical pulse

Muffled heart sounds

Pericardial compression due to fluid-filled pericardial sac; cough due to compression of trachea and bronchi by expanding pericardal sac

FIGURE 15-4 Assessment findings in cardiac tamponade resulting from pericardial effusion include feelings of faintness, shortness of breath, and anxiety from decreased cardiac output, cough from pressure created in the trachea from swelling of the pericardial sac, distended neck veins from rising venous pressure, paradoxical pulse, and muffled or distant heart sounds.

goal of this procedure is to prevent cardiac tamponade, which restricts normal heart filling and contraction.

During the procedure, vital signs, oxygen saturation, ECG and, if applicable, hemodynamic pressures are measured. Emergency resuscitation equipment should be readily available. The head of the bed is elevated to 45 to 60 degrees, placing the heart in proximity to the chest wall so that the needle can be inserted into the pericardial sac more easily. If a peripheral IV line is not already in place, one is inserted, and a slow IV infusion is started in case it becomes necessary to administer emergency medications or blood products.

The pericardial aspiration needle is attached to a 50-mL syringe by a three-way stopcock. Several possible sites are used for pericardial aspiration. Typically, ultrasound imaging is used to guide placement of the needle into the pericardial space. The needle is advanced slowly until it has entered the pericardium and fluid is obtained.

A resulting decrease in central venous pressure and an associated increase in blood pressure after withdrawal of pericardial fluid indicate that the cardiac tamponade has been relieved. The patient almost always feels immediate relief. If there is a substantial amount of pericardial fluid, a small catheter may be left in place to drain recurrent accumulation of blood or fluid. Pericardial fluid is sent to the laboratory for examination for tumor cells, bacterial culture, chemical and serologic analysis, and differential blood cell count.

Complications of pericardiocentesis include ventricular or coronary artery puncture, arrhythmias, pleural laceration, gastric puncture, and myocardial trauma. After pericardiocentesis, the patient's heart rhythm, blood pressure, venous pressure, and heart sounds are monitored to detect

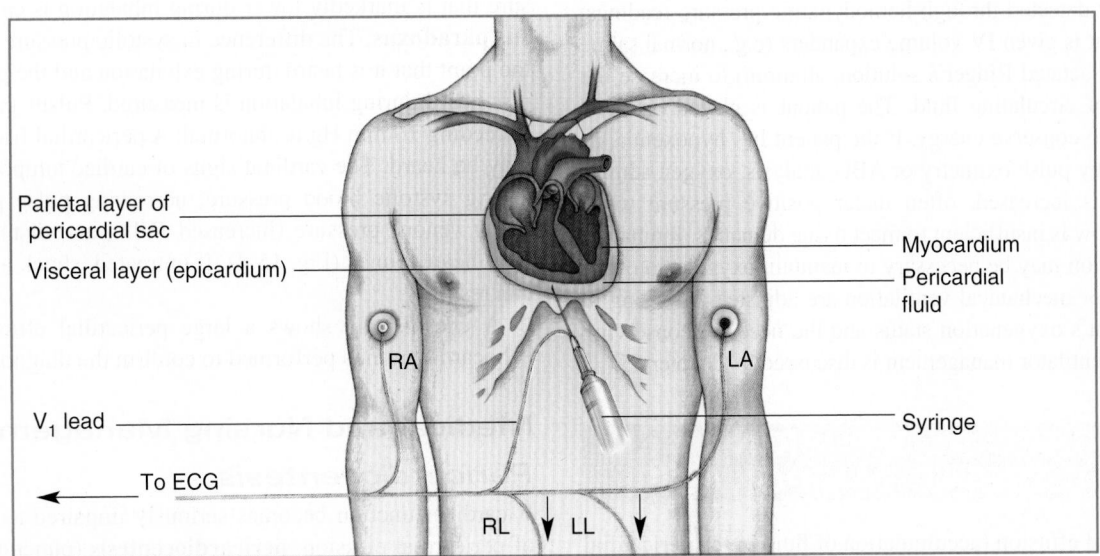

Parietal layer of pericardial sac

Visceral layer (epicardium)

Myocardium

Pericardial fluid

RA

LA

V_1 lead

Syringe

To ECG

RL   LL

FIGURE 15-5 Pericardiocentesis. From Lippincott Williams & Wilkins. (2010). *Cardiovascular care made incredibly visual* (2nd ed., p. 231). Philadelphia: Lippincott Williams & Wilkins.

possible recurrence of cardiac tamponade. If it recurs, repeated aspiration is necessary. Cardiac tamponade may require surgical treatment by open pericardial drainage called a pericardiotomy.

Pericardiotomy

Recurrent pericardial effusions, usually associated with neoplastic disease, may be treated by a **pericardiotomy** (pericardial window). Under general anesthesia, a portion of the pericardium is excised to permit the pericardial fluid to drain into the lymphatic system. The nursing care is the same as that for other cardiac surgery (see Chapter 14).

CARDIAC ARREST

Cardiac arrest occurs when the heart ceases to produce an effective pulse and circulate blood.

Pathophysiology

Cardiac arrest may be caused by a cardiac electrical event such as ventricular fibrillation, progressive profound bradycardia, or when there is no heart rhythm at all (asystole). Cardiac arrest may follow respiratory arrest; it may also occur when electrical activity is present but there is ineffective cardiac contraction or circulating volume, which is called **pulseless electrical activity (PEA)**. PEA can be caused by hypovolemia (e.g., with excessive bleeding), hypoxia, hypothermia, hyperkalemia, massive PE, MI, and medication overdose (e.g., beta blockers, calcium channel blockers).

Clinical Manifestations and Assessment

In cardiac arrest, consciousness, pulse, and blood pressure are lost immediately. Ineffective respiratory gasping may occur. The pupils of the eyes begin dilating within 45 seconds. Seizures may or may not occur.

The risk of irreversible brain damage and death increases with every minute from the time that circulation ceases. The interval varies with the age and underlying condition of the patient. During this period, the diagnosis of cardiac arrest must be made, and measures must be taken immediately to restore circulation.

Emergency Management: Cardiopulmonary Resuscitation

Cardiopulmonary resuscitation (CPR) provides blood flow to vital organs until effective circulation can be re-established. The ABCDs of basic CPR are *a*irway, *b*reathing, *c*irculation, and *d*efibrillation (Box 15-3, p. 438). Once loss of consciousness has been established, the resuscitation priority for the adult in most cases is placing a phone call to activate the code team or the emergency medical system (EMS). Exceptions to this include near drowning, drug or medication overdose, and respiratory arrest situations, for which 2 minutes of CPR should be performed before activating the EMS.

Resuscitation of adults consists of the following steps:

1. *Airway*: Maintaining an open airway
2. *Breathing*: Providing artificial ventilation by rescue breathing
3. *Circulation*: Promoting artificial circulation by external cardiac compression; administering medication therapy (e.g., epinephrine for asystole)
4. *Defibrillation*: Shocking with standard defibrillator or automatic external defibrillator (AED) for ventricular tachycardia and ventricular fibrillation

If the patient is already being monitored or is immediately placed on the monitor using the multifunction pads or the quick-look paddles (found on most defibrillators) and the ECG shows ventricular tachycardia or ventricular fibrillation, immediate defibrillation rather than CPR is the treatment of choice. In this scenario, CPR is performed initially only if the defibrillator is not immediately available. The survival rate decreases for every minute that defibrillation is delayed (Hazinski, 2010). If the patient has not been defibrillated within 10 minutes, the chance of survival is close to zero. Refer to Chapter 17 for more details on defibrillation.

Recent research on CPR performed in the field for persons in out-of-hospital cardiac arrest by bystanders supports eliminating mouth-to-mouth or rescue breathing and using "hands-only" cardiac compression only. No differences in patient survival were seen when bystanders received emergency-dispatcher instructions for compression-only versus compression-plus rescue breathing CPR. National guidelines on how bystanders should perform CPR will likely be updated to reflect current findings. These findings do not apply to health care professionals.

BOX 15-3

Performing One-Person CPR

1. After initiating the emergency response team or calling for a defibrillator when a patient is unresponsive, position the patient supine on a hard surface and open the airway. Check for adequate breathing for 10 seconds.

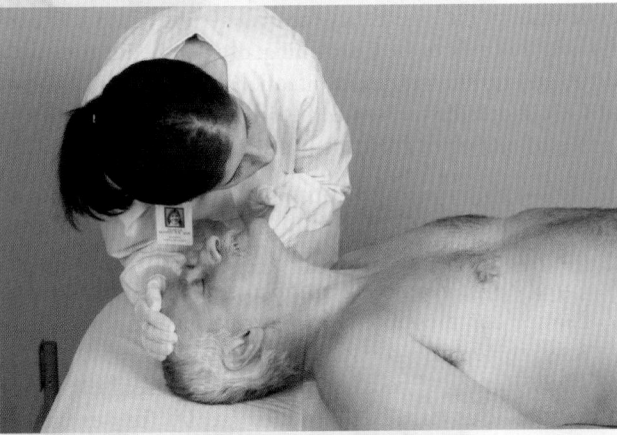

2. Perform ventilation with 2 breaths that make the chest rise at 1 second per breath. If ineffective, reposition the airway and retry.

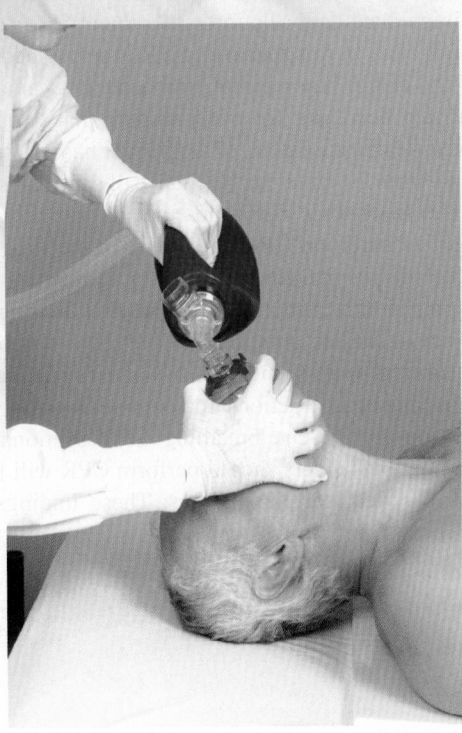

3. Palpate the carotid pulse for no more than 10 seconds. Unless a definite pulse is felt, initiate chest compressions.

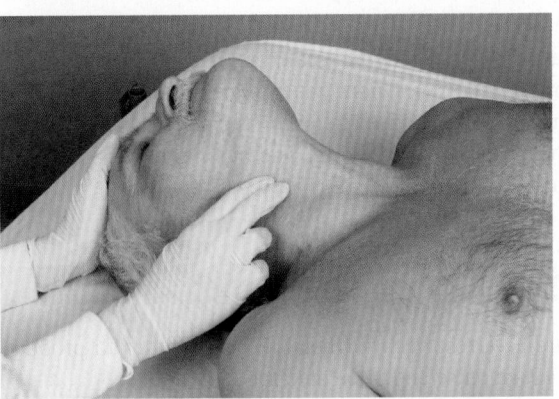

4. Place hands one on top of the other on the lower half of the sternum between the nipples, with elbows locked. Compress the chest 1½ to 2 inches (or one-third the depth of the chest) at a rate of 100 compressions per minute, keeping your hands on the chest. Allow equal time for compressions and full chest recoil. Continue for 30 compressions, then give 2 ventilations and resume compressions quickly for five cycles (2 minutes) before rechecking the pulse.

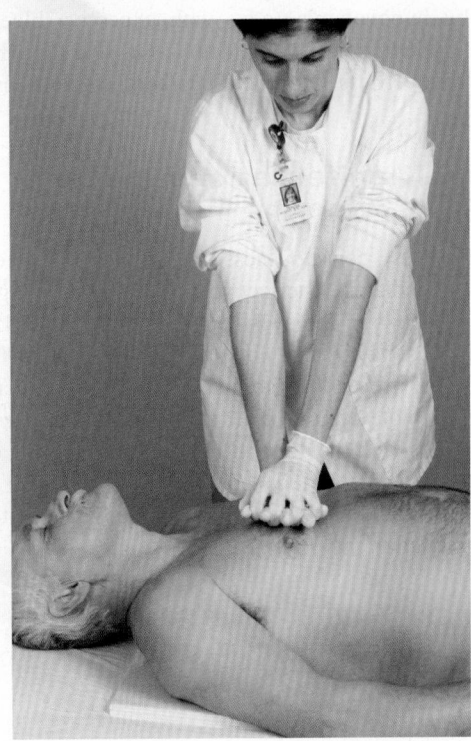

Chapter Review

Critical Thinking Exercises

1. Compare the pathophysiology of systolic and diastolic failure.
2. Describe the affect of ACE inhibitors and angiotensin receptor blockers on the renin–angiotensin–aldosterone system (RAAS) and its therapeutic effect for HF.

NCLEX-Style Review Questions

1. The effectiveness of treatment for a patient with right ventricular failure is best demonstrated by which of the following?
   A. Clear breath sounds
   B. Oxygen saturation greater than 96%
   C. Moist mucous membranes
   D. Central venous pressure of 4 mmHg
2. Mr. S. has right ventricular failure. The nurse should expect which of the following symptoms?
   A. Crackles on auscultation
   B. Jugular vein distention
   C. Pulmonary edema
   D. Normal CVP
3. When being discharged home, to assess fluid balance, a patient with CHF should be instructed to do which of the following?
   A. Monitor blood pressure.
   B. Assess radial pulses.
   C. Monitor weight daily.
   D. Monitor bowel movements.
4. Jugular vein distention, muffled heart sounds, and decreasing systolic pressure are classic signs and symptoms of which of the following conditions?
   A. HF
   B. Pericardial tamponade
   C. Pulmonary edema
   D. Cardiogenic shock
5. Which of the following medications is commonly used to treat cardiogenic shock related to hypervolemia?
   A. Diuretics
   B. Beta blockers
   C. Vasoconstrictors
   D. Inotropes

Try these additional resources to enhance your learning and understanding of this chapter:
- thePoint online resource available at **http://thepoint.lww.com/Pellico1e**
- *Handbook for Focus on Adult Health: Medical-Surgical Nursing*
- *Study Guide for Focus on Adult Health: Medical-Surgical Nursing*

References and Selected Readings

References and selected readings associated with this chapter can be found on the website that accompanies the book. Visit http://thepoint.lww.com/Pellico1e to access the references and other additional resources associated with this chapter.

JEANINE L. MAY

Nursing Management: Patients With Structural, Inflammatory, and Infectious Cardiac Disorders

After reading this chapter, you will be able to:

1. Differentiate valvular disorders of the heart and discuss their management.

2. Describe the pathophysiology, clinical manifestations, and management of patients with mitral and aortic regurgitation and stenosis.

3. Describe types of cardiac valve repair and replacement procedures used to treat valvular problems and the care needed by patients who undergo these procedures.

4. Describe the pathophysiology, clinical manifestations, and management of patients with cardiomyopathy.

5. Describe the pathophysiology, clinical manifestations, and management of patients with infections of the heart.

6. Describe the rationale for prophylactic antibiotic therapy for patients with valvular heart disease, rheumatic heart disease, and infective endocarditis.

Disorders of the heart present many challenges for the patient, family, and health care team. Dysfunctional heart valves, intracardiac septal defects, cardiomyopathies, and infectious diseases of the heart muscle alter cardiac output. Nursing care for patients with these disorders requires an understanding of cardiac anatomy, the structure and function of heart valves, and knowledge of the causes and management of each.

VALVULAR DISEASE

Acquired valvular heart disease is most often a chronic, progressive disorder that develops slowly, although it can occur acutely in certain conditions. Compensatory mechanisms often maintain equilibrium for an extended period of time, and it can be years before the disease progresses to the degree that symptoms become evident and treatment is required. Common causes include degenerative disease, rheumatic heart disease, and infective endocarditis.

Progression of valvular heart disease can result in sudden death, heart failure (HF), arrhythmias, and stroke. Interventions for the management and treatment of acquired valvular heart disease are aimed at preventing the sequelae of thromboembolism, atrial fibrillation, HF, and pulmonary artery hypertension.

A detailed review of normal cardiac valvular anatomy is found in Chapter 12 and shown in Figure 16-1. When the heart valves do not close or open properly, blood flow is affected. **Stenosis** occurs when the opening of the valve is narrowed, and the forward flow of blood through the valve is reduced. **Regurgitation** occurs when valves do not close completely and blood flows backward through the valve. Mitral valve **prolapse** (MVP) occurs when the **mitral valve** doesn't close properly and the valve leaflets balloon back into the left atrium during systole. An understanding of the structure and function of heart valves and the causes and management of valvular disorders is necessary to provide appropriate nursing care for patients with valvular heart disease. Figure 16-2 on page 422 illustrates the pathophysiology and Box 16-1 examines the nursing management of valvular disorders. Valvular disorders may require surgical repair or replacement of the valve to correct the problem, depending on severity of symptoms.

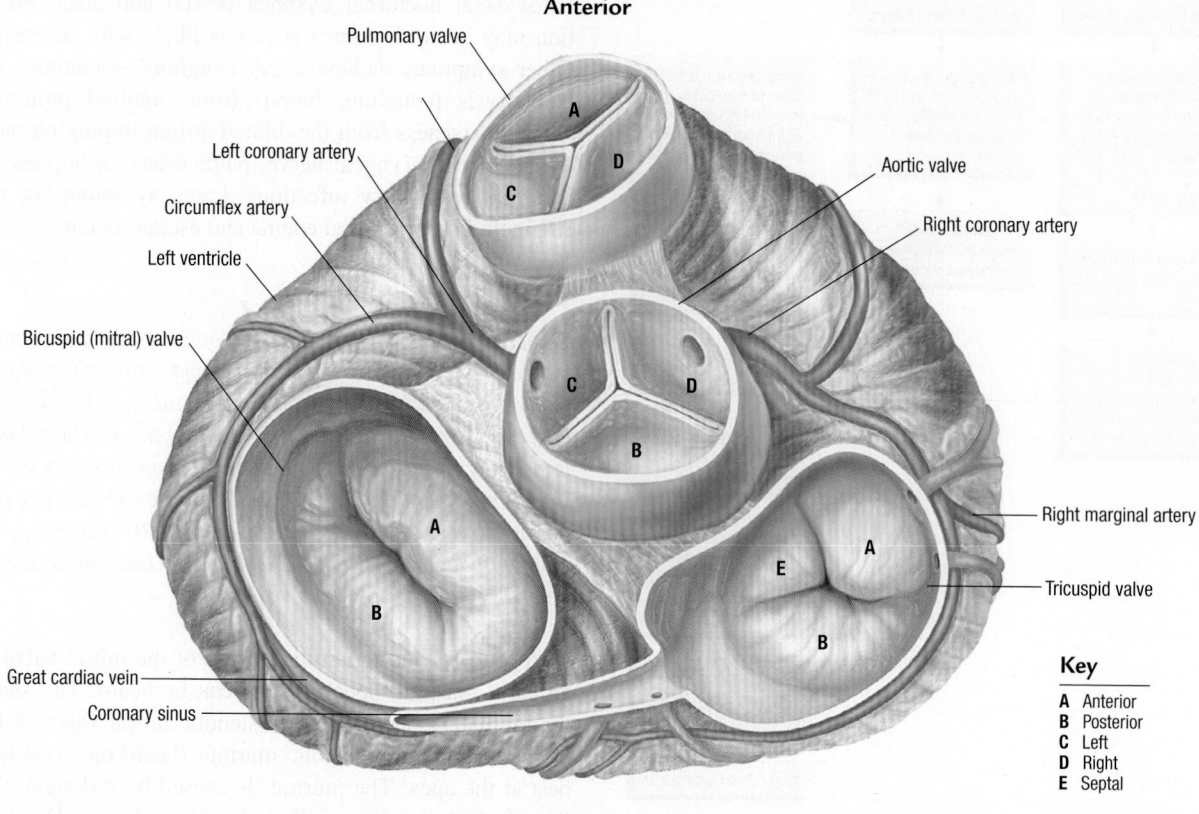

Anterior

Pulmonary valve

Left coronary artery

Circumflex artery

Left ventricle

Bicuspid (mitral) valve

Aortic valve

Right coronary artery

Right marginal artery

Tricuspid valve

Great cardiac vein

Coronary sinus

Key

A Anterior
B Posterior
C Left
D Right
E Septal

Posterior

FIGURE 16-1 The heart contains four valves: two atrioventricular (AV) valves (the bicuspid [mitral] and tricuspid) and two semilunar valves (the pulmonary and aortic).

BOX 16-1

Nursing Management of Valvular Heart Disorders

Heart and lung sounds are auscultated and peripheral pulses palpated. The nurse assesses the patient with valvular heart disease for signs and symptoms of HF, arrhythmias, and other symptoms such as dizziness, syncope, weakness, or chest pain. The nurse teaches the patient about the diagnosis, its progressive nature and treatment, and also teaches the patient to report new symptoms or changes in symptoms to the health care provider. In addition, the nurse collaborates with the patient to develop a medication schedule and teaches about the name, dosage, actions, adverse effects, and any drug–drug or drug–food interactions of the medications for HF, arrhythmias, or other symptoms. Specific precautions are emphasized, such as the risk to patients with aortic stenosis (AS) who experience angina pectoris and take nitroglycerin. Venous dilation that results from nitroglycerin decreases blood return to the heart, thus decreasing cardiac output and increasing the risk of syncope and decreased coronary artery blood flow.

The nurse teaches the patient about the importance of attempting to relieve chest pain with rest before taking nitroglycerin and to anticipate the potential adverse effects.

Pulmonic and **tricuspid valve** disorders also occur, although with less frequency and usually with fewer symptoms and complications. Tricuspid regurgitation usually occurs with mitral stenosis because of the increased volume and pressure load on the right side of the heart. It can also result from infective endocarditis. Tricuspid valve repair is only done if there is severe regurgitation. Tricuspid valve replacement is uncommon. Multivalvular disease is possible: Regurgitation and stenosis may occur at the same time in the same or different valves, or one disease may occur in two or more valves.

MITRAL STENOSIS

In mitral stenosis (MS), the valve orifice is narrowed and blood flow from the left atrium into the left ventricle (LV) is impaired. Generally, MS follows a slow, progressive course that may be accelerated later in life.

Pathophysiology

Normally, the mitral valve opening is as wide as the diameter of three fingers. In cases of marked stenosis, the opening narrows to the width of a pencil. Left atrial pressure increases because of the slowed blood flow into the LV through the narrowed orifice. The left atrium dilates and hypertrophies because of

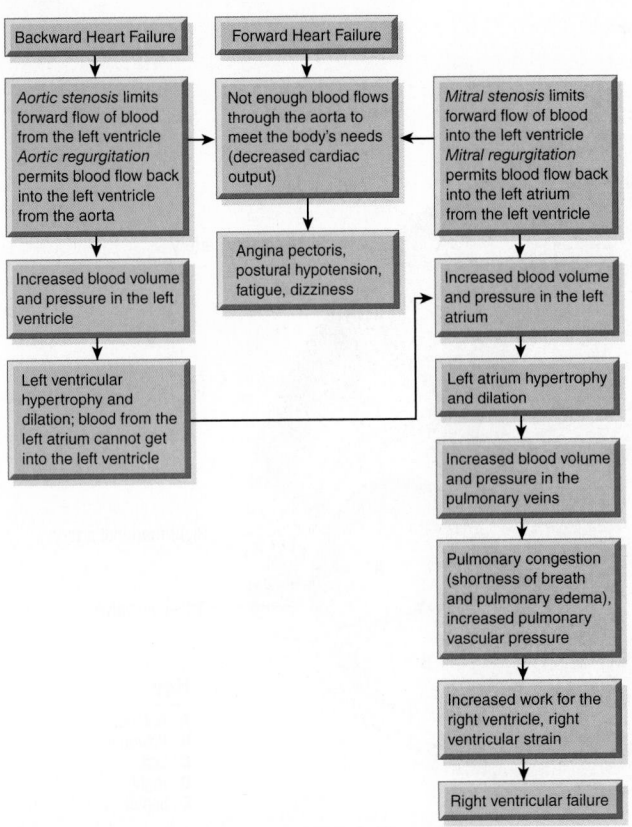

FIGURE 16-2 Pathophysiology: left-sided HF as a result of aortic and mitral valvular heart disease and the development of right ventricular failure.

the increased blood volume. Sluggish atrial blood flow can lead to clot formation and thromboembolism. Because there is no functional valve to protect the pulmonary veins from the backward flow of blood from the atrium, pulmonary venous pressure rises and circulation becomes congested. As a result, the right ventricle (RV) must contract against an abnormally high pulmonary pressure, and the RV and right atrium become enlarged. Eventually, the ventricle fails.

Risk Factors

The most significant risk factor for MS is rheumatic fever, which gradually causes the mitral valve leaflets to thicken and can result in leaflet fusion. Typically, MS occurs 20 to 40 years after rheumatic fever, and symptoms do not develop for another 10 years. Radiation therapy to the chest area can also result in MS.

Clinical Manifestations and Assessment

Symptoms usually develop after the valve opening is reduced by one-third to one-half its usual size. Dyspnea on exertion (DOE) results from pulmonary congestion. Patients become progressively fatigued as a result of low cardiac output.

Paroxysmal nocturnal dyspnea (PND) and atrial fibrillation may occur. Dyspnea at rest is likely with severe MS. Other symptoms include heavy coughing, sometimes with hemoptysis (coughing blood) from ruptured pulmonary veins, hoarseness from the dilated atrium impinging on the left recurrent laryngeal nerve, palpitations, orthopnea, and recurrent respiratory infections. Later, symptoms of right HF, including peripheral edema and ascites, occur.

NURSING ALERT

S_1 represents systole (pumping of blood to body) and is made by the closing of the mitral and tricuspid heart valves. Normally the openings of valves are not heard. S_2 or the second heart sound represents diastole (filling of the ventricles) and is made by closing of the pulmonary and aortic valves. Recall the sounds heard represent "closure" of the valves. There is normally synchrony of the tricuspid and mitral valve (S_1) and pulmonary and aortic valve (S_2), thus only two sounds are heard (S_1 and S_2) for four valves.

A loud S1 due to abrupt closure of the mitral valve and an early diastolic opening snap can be heard. The snap is the premature opening of the stenotic mitral valve. A low-pitched, rumbling, diastolic murmur (heard on S_2) is heard best at the apex. The murmur is caused by turbulent blood flow through the abnormally tight valve opening. Due to the increased blood volume and pressure, the atrium dilates, hypertrophies, and becomes electrically unstable, leading to atrial arrhythmias. The pulse can be weak and irregular because of atrial fibrillation. Echocardiography is the most sensitive and specific noninvasive method to diagnose MS. Cardiac catheterization is not indicated unless clinical findings and echo results are discordant.

Medical and Nursing Management

Medical therapy is aimed at symptom management only; it will not alter the stenotic valve. Antiarrhythmics and electrical cardioversion are utilized to restore sinus rhythm, and anticoagulation is usually initiated if atrial fibrillation is persistent. Digoxin, beta blockers, and calcium channel blockers are used for rate control with atrial fibrillation. Diuretics may be used to reduce pulmonary congestion.

Symptoms may appear or worsen when the heart rate increases, such as during exercise. They may also be triggered by pregnancy or other stress on the body, such as a pulmonary infection. Patients with MS are advised to avoid strenuous activities and competitive sports, as both increase heart rate. MS decreases blood flow from the left atrium to the LV during diastole. When heart rate increases, diastole is shortened, and the amount of time for forward flow is lessened; cardiac output decreases and pulmonary pressure increases, with blood backing up from the left atrium into the pulmonary veins. Over time, symptoms will worsen and percutaneous intervention or surgery must be considered.

Percutaneous Mitral Valvuloplasty

Percutaneous mitral balloon **valvuloplasty** treats symptomatic mitral valve stenosis when the leaflets are not heavily calcified. Use of this procedure instead of surgery is dependent upon the severity of the obstruction. The procedure is contraindicated for patients with left atrial thrombus, significant mitral valve regurgitation, and other cardiac conditions that require open heart surgery.

A guide wire is advanced percutaneously from the femoral vein to the right atrium, through a puncture in the septum, across the mitral valve, as shown in Figure 16-3. One or two balloon catheters are placed over the guide wire and positioned with the balloon across the mitral valve. When two balloons are used, they are inflated simultaneously. The advantage of two balloons is that they are each smaller than one large balloon, making smaller atrial septal defects. As the balloons are inflated, they split the fused commissures. Patients have some mitral regurgitation (MR) after the procedure. Other potential complications include left-to-right atrial shunts through an atrial septal defect caused by the procedure and emboli from dislodged left atrial thrombus.

Mitral Valve Replacement

Surgical valve replacement is indicated when the stenosis is not amenable to a percutaneous procedure or if there is concomitant MR. Rarely, open mitral **commissurotomy** is performed to separate fused leaflets to increase the size of the mitral valve orifice, when the valve is not calcified. Although some valves can be repaired by commissurotomy, most require replacement because of significant calcification, and a mechanical valve is commonly used as these patients are often already receiving anticoagulation for atrial fibrillation.

MITRAL VALVE PROLAPSE

In mitral valve prolapse (MVP), a portion of one or both mitral valve leaflets bulges back into the left atrium during systole, usually with little or no MR. Rarely, the leaflet stretches to the point at which the valve does not remain closed during systole, and blood then flows from the LV back into the left atrium.

Pathophysiology

Myxomatous degeneration (pathological weakening of connective tissue) can cause enlargement of one or both of the valve leaflets, with subsequent billowing into the left atrium during systole. Over time, as the leaflets prolapse, they can stretch to a degree at which the leaflet edges do not fully coapt, or close, resulting in MR.

Risk Factors

Family history and female gender are associated with MVP.

Clinical Manifestations and Assessment

MVP is commonly asymptomatic. However, over time, fatigue, dyspnea, lightheadedness, palpitations, and chest pain may develop. Chest pain is not correlated to activity and may be caused by abnormal stress placed on the chordae tendineae and papillary muscles. Shortness of breath is not correlated with activity levels or pulmonary function.

Cardiac auscultation may reveal a mitral midsystolic click. This is a sign that a valve leaflet is ballooning into the left atrium. A late systolic murmur may be heard if progressive valve leaflet stretching and regurgitation have occurred. Echocardiography is used to diagnose and monitor the progression of MVP.

Medical and Nursing Management

No treatment is required for asymptomatic patients. If symptoms develop, management is aimed at symptomatic control. Beta blockers and calcium channel blockers may be used to relieve chest pain and palpitations.

Elimination of caffeine and alcohol may help reduce symptoms, and the nurse encourages the patient to read labels on over-the-counter products, such as cough medicine, because these products may contain alcohol, caffeine, ephedrine, and epinephrine, which may produce arrhythmias and other symptoms. Treatment of arrhythmias, HF, or other complications of MVP is described in Chapters 15 and 17.

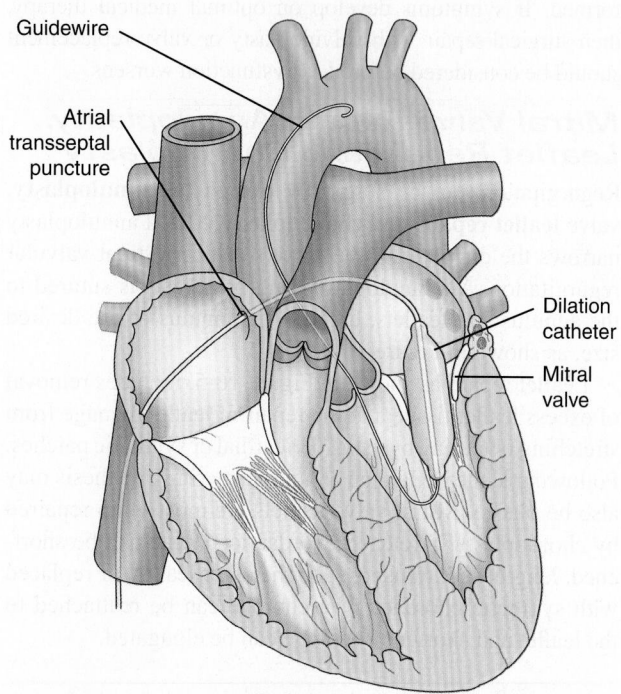

Guidewire

Atrial transseptal puncture

Dilation catheter

Mitral valve

FIGURE 16-3 Balloon valvuloplasty: cross-section of heart illustrating the guide wire and dilation catheter placed through an atrial transseptal puncture and across the mitral valve. The guide wire is extended out from the aortic valve into the aorta for catheter support.

MITRAL REGURGITATION

MR, also termed *mitral insufficiency*, is the backward flow of blood from the LV into the left atrium during systole because the valve fails to close completely. Disease processes that alter valve leaflets, mitral annulus, chordae tendineae, and the papillary muscle may result in MR.

Pathophysiology

When the mitral valve leaflets thicken, fibrose, and contract, they cannot close completely. With each heartbeat, blood is forced backward into the left atrium during systole. Regurgitation of blood into the left atrium causes left atrial pressure to rise. Because this blood is added to the blood flowing in from the lungs, the left atrium must stretch to accommodate the increased volume, and left atrial hypertrophy and dilatation occur. During diastole, regurgitant blood from the atrium increases volume load in the LV. Over time, compensatory left ventricular hypertrophy occurs to maintain a normal cardiac output. Eventually this leads to left ventricular failure. The backward flow of blood from the LV reduces blood volume flowing into the atrium from the lungs and pulmonary venous pressure increases. Pulmonary congestion results, elevating pulmonary artery pressure; this adds further strain on the right ventricle causing enlargement and right ventricular failure.

Risk Factors

Having MVP or mitral valve stenosis may lead to the development of chronic MR, although most people with MVP never develop severe regurgitation. While it is more common with advancing age, due to natural deterioration of the valve, MR causes symptoms in only a small percentage of older adults. Infections such as endocarditis or rheumatic fever can damage the mitral valve, causing MR.

Papillary muscle rupture, a complication of acute myocardial infarction (MI), may result in acute MR. Prosthetic valve malfunction and rupture of the chordae tendineae can lead to acute MR.

Clinical Manifestations and Assessment

Chronic MR may be asymptomatic for years; then, symptoms gradually develop. As cardiac output diminishes, fatigue, tachycardia, and weakness can occur. Orthopnea, DOE, and PND result from pulmonary congestion. Palpitations are related to a hyperdynamic LV and/or atrial fibrillation. Peripheral edema and ascites occur when the right ventricle fails. Acute MR manifests as severe left-sided HF. Patients may report a sudden inability to breathe accompanied by chest pain.

Physical examination may reveal a hyperdynamic point of maximal impulse, displaced leftward and downward because of the hypertrophied LV. A holosystolic murmur (heard on S_1) is heard as a high-pitched, blowing sound at the apex; radiation to the axilla is possible. An S_3 or S_4 gallop may be present because of increased, rapid blood flow into the ventricle during diastole. Signs of left- and right-sided HF are seen in acute MR: tachycardia, crackles, and hypotension, as well as peripheral edema, jugular venous distention, and ascites.

Chest X-ray may reveal left ventricular and left atrial enlargement. A transthoracic echocardiogram (TTE) is used to monitor the severity and progression of MR, as well as the anatomy of the valve. It also provides information regarding left ventricular size and function, left atrial size, and pulmonary artery pressures. A transesophageal echocardiogram (TEE) provides the best images of the mitral valve, and may be done if the TTE is inconclusive. Cardiac catheterization may be done preoperatively, and it may also be used if there is a discrepancy between clinical and noninvasive findings to determine the severity of MR.

Medical and Nursing Management

Management is aimed at decreasing regurgitant volume into the left atrium, increasing cardiac output, and reducing pulmonary congestion. Patients with chronic MR benefit from afterload reduction with angiotensin-converting enzyme (ACE) inhibitors, nitrates, or hydralazine. Vasodilators, diuretics, and sodium restriction are used to reduce preload. Less commonly, digoxin is given to increase contractility and slow rapid rates to allow for improved ventricular filling. Anticoagulation is initiated if atrial fibrillation is present. In acute, severe MR, IV vasodilators and intra-aortic balloon counterpulsation may be employed for afterload reduction until surgery can be performed. If symptoms develop on optimal medical therapy, then surgical repair with valvuloplasty or valve replacement should be considered before LV dysfunction worsens.

Mitral Valve Repair: Annuloplasty, Leaflet Repair, and Chordoplasty

Regurgitation can be surgically treated by **annuloplasty**, valve **leaflet repair**, and **chordoplasty**. Mitral annuloplasty narrows the diameter of the valve's orifice to treat valvular regurgitation. An annuloplasty ring prosthesis is sutured to the annulus and leaflets, creating an annulus of the desired size, as shown in Figure 16-4.

Leaflet repair, as shown in Figure 16-5, includes removal of excess leaflet tissue and the repair of leaflet damage from stretching or tearing by using pericardial or synthetic patches. Following leaflet repair, an annuloplasty ring prosthesis may also be placed. Mitral valve leaflets are most often repaired by chordoplasty. Stretched chordae tendineae can be shortened, lengthened, transposed to the other leaflet, or replaced with synthetic chordae. Torn chordae can be reattached to the leaflet and shortened chordae can be elongated.

AORTIC STENOSIS

Aortic stenosis (AS) is narrowing of the valve opening between the LV and the aorta, resulting in obstruction of blood flow across the valve.

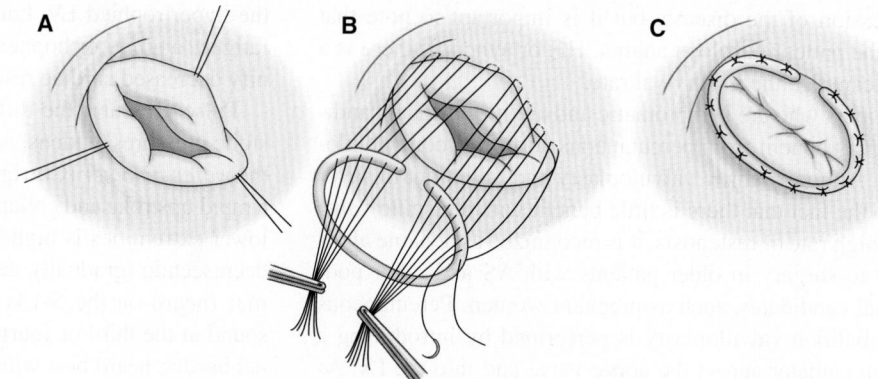

FIGURE 16-4 Annulo-plasty ring insertion. **(A)** Mitral valve regurgitation; leaflets do not close. **(B)** Insertion of an an-nuloplasty ring. **(C)** Completed valvuloplasty; leaflets close.

Pathophysiology

Progressive narrowing of the valve orifice usually occurs over several years to several decades. The LV overcomes this by contracting more slowly and more strongly than normal, forcibly squeezing the blood through the smaller orifice. This increases left ventricular pressure, and the ventricular wall hypertrophies and dilates. Left ventricular failure ensues. This leads to elevated left atrial pressure, then pulmonary congestion, and ultimately right HF.

Risk Factors

Having a congenital bicuspid **aortic valve** is a major risk factor. AS is more common with advancing age. Degenerative calcification, the buildup of calcium deposits on heart valves, hypercholesterolemia, and a history of rheumatic valve disease can lead to AS.

Clinical Manifestations and Assessment

Aortic stenosis can be asymptomatic for decades. A triad of symptoms is associated with AS: angina due to LV hypertrophy and diminished coronary blood flow; dyspnea due to increased pulmonary venous pressure from LV failure; and syncope, usually with exertion, due to fixed cardiac output.

On physical examination, a thrill, or a vibration may be felt in the aortic area (second intercostal space right sternal border). The vibration is caused by turbulent blood flow across the narrowed valve orifice. A loud, systolic ejection murmur (heard on the S_1) may be heard over the aortic area, and may radiate into the neck. This is caused by blood flowing through the narrowed opening of the stenotic valve. The patient should be instructed to lean forward during auscultation, especially upon exhalation, to accentuate the murmur. An S_3 or S_4 gallop may be heard.

Echocardiography is used to diagnose and monitor the progression of AS, and will demonstrate calcification of the valve or decreased mobility of valve cusps, and left ventricular hypertrophy. Patients with symptoms usually have echocardiograms every 6 to 12 months, and those without symptoms have echocardiograms every 2 to 5 years. Cardiac catheterization can measure the severity of AS when noninvasive testing is inconclusive.

Medical and Nursing Management

Most patients remain asymptomatic for years without intervention. The goal of medical therapy is to prevent complications. Nitrates may be prescribed for the treatment of angina, but must be used with caution due to the risk of orthostatic hypotension and syncope. With critical AS, strenuous exercise should be avoided. Digoxin may be used to treat LV dysfunction and diuretics may be prescribed for dyspnea.

Aortic Valve Repair and Replacement

Surgical replacement of the aortic valve is definitive treatment for AS and is recommended for all patients with severe symptoms. Timing of surgery is based on the natural

FIGURE 16-5 Valve leaflet resection and repair with a ring annuloplasty. **(A)** Mitral valve regurgitation; the section indicated by dashed lines is excised. **(B)** Approximation of edges and suturing. **(C)** Completed valvuloplasty, leaflet repair, and annuloplasty ring.

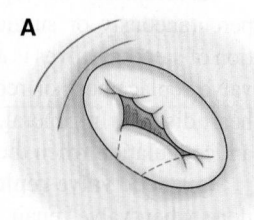
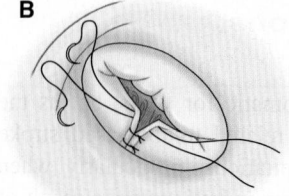
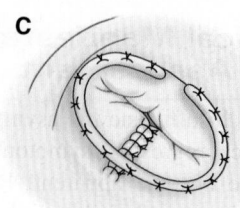

progression of the disease, but it is important to note that once the patient develops angina, HF, or syncope, there is a significant decline in survival rate.

Patients who are symptomatic and are not surgical candidates may benefit from percutaneous aortic balloon valvuloplasty. Although aortic valvuloplasty had fallen out of favor due to the fact that there is little benefit with a calcific valve and a high rate of restenosis, it is recognized as a viable alternative to surgery in older patients with AS and other poor surgical candidates, such as pregnant women. Percutaneous aortic balloon valvuloplasty is performed by introducing a balloon catheter across the aortic valve and into the LV. As the balloon is inflated, the commissures are split open and the valve ring is stretched. Potential complications include aortic regurgitation, emboli, ventricular perforation, rupture of the aortic valve annulus, ventricular arrhythmias, mitral valve damage, and bleeding from the catheter insertion sites.

AORTIC REGURGITATION

Aortic regurgitation (AR), also referred to as *aortic insufficiency*, is the backward flow of blood into the LV from the aorta during diastole.

Pathophysiology

When the aortic valve is incompetent, blood from the aorta returns to the LV during diastole, in addition to the blood normally delivered by the left atrium. The LV dilates in an attempt to accommodate blood volume overload, causing hypertrophy. Dilatation and hypertrophy allow the LV to expel more blood with above-normal force, increasing afterload and as a result, systolic blood pressure, while maintaining a normal ejection fraction. The arteries attempt to compensate for the higher pressures by reflex vasodilation; the peripheral arterioles relax, reducing peripheral resistance and diastolic blood pressure. Although compensatory mechanisms allow patients to remain asymptomatic despite pressure and volume overload, when left ventricular dysfunction develops, symptoms appear.

Risk Factors

Because they affect the valve leaflets, rheumatic heart disease and infective endocarditis can cause AR. Disorders affecting the aortic root, such as Marfan's syndrome and dissecting aortic aneurysms, can lead to AR. A bicuspid aortic valve is a risk factor for AR.

Clinical Manifestations and Assessment

Aortic insufficiency is asymptomatic for years, but as the disease progresses, symptoms related to increased stroke volume become apparent. Palpitations, particularly when lying down, and visible neck vein pulsations are a result of the increased force and volume of the blood ejected from the hypertrophied LV. Later symptoms, including dyspnea, fatigue, angina, orthopnea and pulmonary congestion, signify decreased cardiac reserve, and LV failure.

Pulse pressure, the difference between systolic and diastolic pressures, widens. Another characteristic sign of AR is the *water-hammer* (Corrigan's) *pulse*, in which the pulse has a rapid upstroke and collapses. Systolic blood pressure in the lower extremities is higher than in the upper extremities. A decrescendo (gradually decreasing loudness) diastolic murmur (heard on the S_2) is heard as a high-pitched blowing sound at the third or fourth intercostal space at the left sternal border, heard best with the patient sitting up and leaning forward.

Diagnosis is confirmed by echocardiography; valve morphology, degree of LV hypertrophy, and functional capacity are determined. Cardiac catheterization is not necessary in most patients with AR. Patients with symptoms usually have echocardiograms every 4 to 6 months, and those without symptoms have annual echocardiograms. Exercise stress testing will assess functional capacity and symptom response.

Medical and Nursing Management

Slowing disease progression, preventing complications, and optimizing the timing of surgery are the goals of medical management. Vasodilators are used for after-load reduction to lower the volume and pressure overload of the LV. Calcium channel blockers are contraindicated due to their negative inotropic effects (decreases the strength of the contraction) and the potential to cause bradycardia. Beta blockers should be avoided to allow for compensatory tachycardia. Intra-aortic balloon counterpulsation is contraindicated because it increases regurgitation. Aortic valve replacement surgery is advised for chronic AS when symptoms appear or if LV function begins to decrease. Acute AR is a surgical emergency.

VALVE REPAIR AND REPLACEMENT PROCEDURES

Most patients with valvular heart disease are managed medically until symptoms appear or the ventricles begin to fail. However, medication cannot cure valve disease. If the condition worsens, or if medication fails to control symptoms, a percutaneous intervention or surgery is indicated to repair or replace diseased heart valves.

Valvuloplasty, the repair of a cardiac valve, can be done percutaneously or surgically. Percutaneous balloon dilatation of stenotic valves is an appropriate alternative to surgical valve replacement or repair in some patients with valvular heart disease. In general, patients do not require continuous anticoagulation when they undergo valvuloplasty.

Prosthetic **valve replacement**, as seen in Figure 16-6, is done when valve repair is not an alternative, such as when the annulus or leaflets of the valve are immobilized by

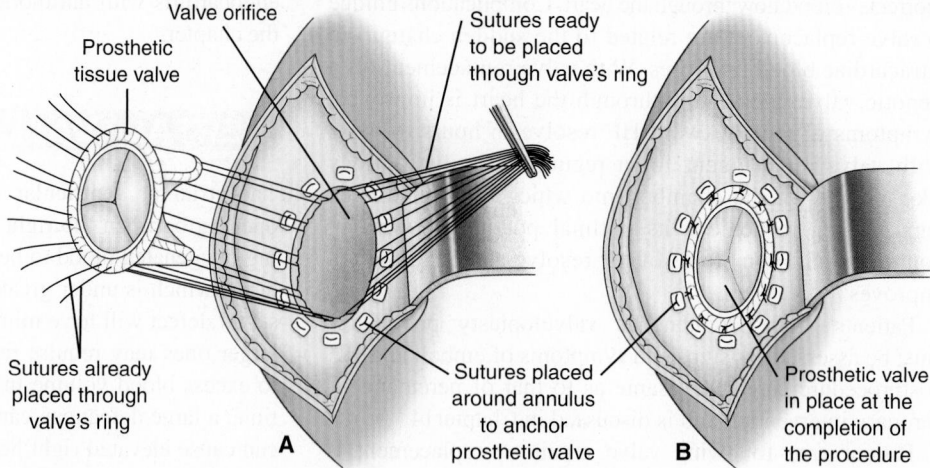

FIGURE 16-6 Valve replacement. (A) The native valve is trimmed, and the prosthetic valve is sutured in place. (B) Once all sutures are placed through the ring, the surgeon slides the prosthetic valve down the sutures and into the natural orifice. The sutures are then tied off and trimmed.

calcifications. More surgeries are performed for regurgitation than stenosis.

Types of Valve Prostheses

Two types of valve prostheses are available: mechanical and tissue (biological, bioprosthetic); these are depicted in Figure 16-7. The advantage of a mechanical valve is durability. The major disadvantage is the need for anticoagulation. Bioprosthetic valves have the advantage that they do not require anticoagulation; however, they are less durable. Age, lifestyle, medical history, and valve location are factors that determine whether a mechanical or biologic valve is used.

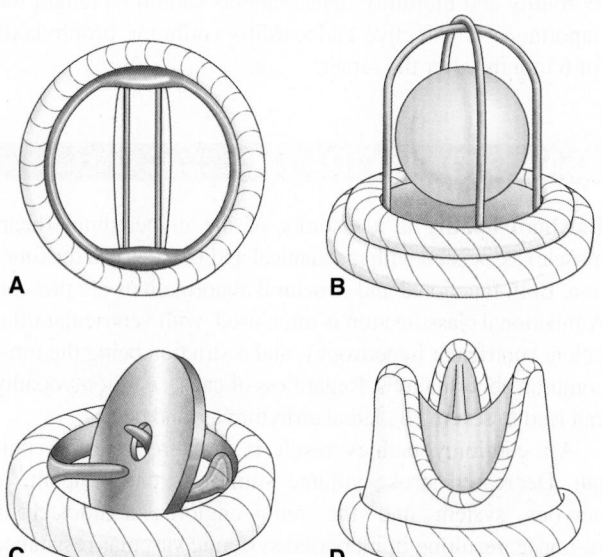

FIGURE 16-7 Common mechanical and tissue valve replacements. (A) Bi-leaflet valve (St. Jude, mechanical) (B) Caged ball valve (Starr-Edwards, mechanical). (C) Tilting-disk valve (Medtronic-Hall, mechanical). (D) Porcine heterograft valve (Carpenter-Edwards, tissue).

Mechanical Valves

Three major types of mechanical valves exist: (1) bi-leaflet valve, (2) tilting disk, and (3) caged-ball. The bi-leaflet and tilting disk are generally used today; the caged-ball valve is less frequently used in the United States. Because they are more durable than tissue valves, mechanical valves are often used for younger patients with a life expectancy of 15 years or more. They may also be used for patients with renal failure, endocarditis, or sepsis who require valve replacement, as they do not deteriorate or become infected as easily as tissue valves. Significant complications associated with mechanical valves are thromboemboli, and they require long-term use of anticoagulants. Some hemolysis also occurs with mechanical valves; usually it is not clinically significant.

Tissue Valves

Tissue valves, although less durable than mechanical valves, are used when anticoagulation is contraindicated or should be avoided, such as in women of childbearing age, because of potential risks of anticoagulation to the fetus. They also are used for patients older than 70 years of age, children, patients who are nonadherent with medications and follow-up, patients with a history of bleeding disorders, and others who cannot tolerate long-term anticoagulation. The major disadvantage of tissue valves is that they lack longevity.

Allograft (homograft) valves are preserved human cadaver valves. They are particularly advantageous in patients with active endocarditis because rates of thrombosis are extremely low without anticoagulation. **Xenograft** (heterograft) valves are bovine and porcine. Newer tissue valves demonstrate improved hemodynamics compared with older models.

Nursing Management

Before surgery, compensatory mechanisms allowed the heart to gradually adjust to the valvular pathology; surgery abruptly

"corrects" blood flow through the heart. Complications unique to valve replacement are related to the sudden changes in intracardiac blood pressures. With valve replacement for a stenotic valve, blood flow through the heart is improved. Symptoms of the backward HF resolve in hours to days. With valve replacement for a regurgitant valve, it may take months for the chamber into which blood had been regurgitating to achieve its optimal postoperative function. Signs and symptoms of HF resolve as heart function improves.

Patients with percutaneous valvuloplasty procedures must be assessed for signs and symptoms of emboli and HF. Postprocedure care is the same as to that of percutaneous coronary intervention and is discussed in Chapter14.

Patient care following valve repair or replacement is similar to that of a patient recovering from coronary artery bypass surgery, and is discussed in Chapter 14. In the immediate postoperative phase, attention is given to hemodynamic stabilization: augmenting preload, reducing afterload, and enhancing contractility, and recognizing that the heart is adjusting to improved function. Patients are at risk for postoperative complications including thromboembolism, infection, arrhythmias, and hemolysis.

Thromboembolism is the most common complication of prosthetic valves, and long-term anticoagulation with warfarin is initiated 48 hours after surgery. Thrombosis can lead to hemodynamic compromise by impeding the valve mechanisms or occluding the valve orifice. Embolic events and HF may be signs of valve thrombus, and urgent valve replacement is warranted for a large thrombus. To reduce the risk of thrombosis in patients with porcine or bovine tissue valves, warfarin is required for 6 to 12 weeks, followed by aspirin therapy. For homografts, anticoagulation is not necessary. The nurse educates the patient about long-term anticoagulant therapy, explaining the need for frequent follow-up appointments and blood laboratory studies. Patients receiving warfarin usually have individualized goal International Normalized Ratios (INRs) between 2 and 3.5.

Prosthetic valve endocarditis occurs more often with tissue valves. It can occur early, within the first 60 days after surgery or later. Signs include fever, HF, embolic events, and new murmur. Hemolytic anemia results from the destruction of red blood cells by movement of the prosthetic valve disk or caged ball.

Conduction disturbances and atrial arrhythmias occur frequently following valve surgery, likely due to circulating catecholamines, myocardial inflammation, and electrolyte imbalances. Digoxin, beta blockers, and calcium channel blockers may be used for treatment of arrhythmias.

The nurse provides teaching about all prescribed medications: the name of the medication, dosage, its actions, prescribed schedule, potential adverse effects, and any drug–drug or drug–food interactions. Patients with mechanical valve prostheses require education to prevent infective endocarditis with antibiotic prophylaxis, discussed later in the chapter.

SEPTAL WALL DEFECTS

The atrial or ventricular septum may have an abnormal opening between the right and left sides of the heart causing oxygenated blood to be shunted from the left side of the heart, which is under greater pressure, to the right. A small septal defect will have minimal effect on heart function, but larger ones may require repair to prevent problems related to excess blood volume in the right side of the heart. Over time, a large defect can cause pulmonary congestion, which can cause elevated right heart pressure; this may eventually cause right HF and pulmonary hypertension.

Most large septal defects are congenital and are repaired during infancy or childhood to prevent later problems. A patent foramen ovale (PFO) is a small atrial septal defect (ASD) that may not be detected in an adult until the patient presents with symptoms of a transient ischemic attack (TIA) or a stroke. Normally if there is a thrombus, it is filtered out of the blood by the lungs. With an ASD, however, there is a risk that the clot could bypass the lungs and travel directly to the brain, causing a TIA or stroke. Atrial fibrillation is common in patients with ASDs and further increases risk of stroke. Closure of the PFO is usually a percutaneous procedure to implant a device to plug the opening. Anticoagulation with aspirin is often prescribed. Small VSDs are rarely closed in adults, unless there is evidence of endocarditis or if valve function is compromised. A stitch or pericardial or synthetic patch is used to close the opening. ASD repairs have low morbidity and mortality rates. Patients should be taught the importance of infective endocarditis antibiotic prophylaxis for 6 months after the repair.

CARDIOMYOPATHY

Cardiomyopathy is a disorder of the myocardium (heart muscle) associated with mechanical and/or electrical dysfunction. Both functional and structural abnormalities are present. A functional classification is often used, with ventricular dilatation, ventricular hypertrophy, and restriction being the most common abnormalities. Regardless of cause, cardiomyopathy can lead to severe HF, lethal arrhythmias, and death.

All cardiomyopathies result in impaired cardiac output. Decreased stroke volume stimulates the sympathetic nervous system and the renin–angiotensin–aldosterone response, resulting in increased systemic vascular resistance and increased sodium and fluid retention, which places an increased workload on the heart. These alterations lead to HF, myocardial destruction, and death. A description of the five most common cardiomyopathies (dilated cardiomyopathy [DCM], hypertrophic cardiomyopathy [HCM],

restrictive cardiomyopathy, arrhythmogenic right ventricular cardiomyopathy [ARVC], and stress-induced cardiomyopathy), including pathophysiology and clinical manifestations is shown in Table 16-1.

Medical Management

Patients with cardiomyopathy may remain stable and asymptomatic for many years. As the disease progresses, so do symptoms. Treatment is specific to the type of cardiomyopathy, but often overlaps. It is directed toward determining and managing possible precipitating causes; specific treatment for the underlying cause is given if it is known. The echocardiogram is one of the most helpful diagnostic tools because the structure and function of the ventricles can be observed easily. Supportive care with standard HF therapy including ACE inhibitors, aldosterone antagonists, and diuretics should be administered for all cardiomyopathies. Beta blockers should be avoided in the early phases of decompensated HF but have proven mortality benefit after the patient stabilizes. Beta blockers and calcium channel blockers are used to reduce catecholamine response to minimize the risk of left ventricular outflow tract obstruction in patients with HCM. Nitrates and dehydration should be avoided in HCM to maintain cardiac output.

Antiarrhythmic medications may be initiated to prevent and treat arrhythmias. Embolization from venous thrombosis can occur, especially in patients on bed rest, and systemic anticoagulation is needed to prevent thromboembolic events. *Mural thrombi* (clot that is attached to the endocardium or wall of the blood vessel) are also a risk, and the patient's neurologic status should be monitored carefully.

Myocardial biopsy may be performed to analyze myocardial tissue cells. Because genetic factors may be involved, echocardiography and electrocardiography (ECG) should be used to screen all first-degree blood relatives (e.g., parents, siblings, and children) for HCM and for idiopathic DCM and ARVC, as early diagnosis and treatment can prevent or delay significant symptoms and sudden cardiac death.

If the patient presents with heart block, a pacemaker may be necessary to alter the electrical stimulation of the muscle and prevent the forceful hyperdynamic contractions that occur with HCM. Atrial-ventricular and biventricular pacing have been used to improve symptoms of HCM and RCM. Implantable defibrillators are recommended if there is persistent cardiac dysfunction and/or ventricular arrhythmias, particularly with ARVC. Intra-aortic balloon pump (IABP), left **ventricular assist devices** (VADs), and consideration of heart transplantation may be necessary in the most severe cases.

For stress-induced cardiomyopathy, accurate diagnosis and differentiation from ST-segment elevation MI (STEMI) is critical to avoid unnecessary treatments, such as administration of fibrinolytics, which can cause harm to the patient. Diuretics, ACE inhibitors, and beta blockers are frequently prescribed. Unstable patients may require positive inotropic medications, vasopressors, and IABPs. Overall prognosis is favorable. Recurrence can occur, although it is uncommon.

Nursing management includes careful cardiovascular assessment for signs of worsening HF, particularly, dyspnea, congested lungs, peripheral edema, and the presence of abnormal heart sounds. Arrhythmias occur frequently; continuous cardiac monitoring is recommended, with personnel and equipment readily available to treat life-threatening arrhythmias. Bed rest is maintained to decrease cardiac workload. Physical activity is increased slowly, and the patient is asked to report symptoms that occur with increasing activity. For stress-induced cardiomyopathy, the nurse must evaluate the presence of anxiety and guide stress management practices.

Surgical Management

When HF progresses and medical treatment is no longer effective, surgical intervention, including heart transplantation, is considered. There were fewer than 2,300 donors in 2007 (American Heart Association [AHA], 2009), and an estimated 80,000 to 150,000 persons who could benefit from a transplant (Stevenson & Couper, 2007). Because of the limited number of organ donors, many patients die waiting for transplantation. In some cases, a VAD is implanted to support the failing heart until a suitable donor heart becomes available (bridge to transplant). Increasingly, VADs are being used as destination therapy (DT) in persons who are ineligible for transplantation and for whom ventricular recovery is not possible. (Mechanical circulatory assist devices are discussed later in this chapter.)

Heart Transplantation

A multidisciplinary team screens the candidate before recommending the transplantation procedure. Age, pulmonary status, chronic health conditions, infections, history of other transplantations, psychosocial status, family support, compliance, and current health status are considered. Transplant candidates cannot have fixed, irreversible pulmonary hypertension, as this would lead to right ventricular failure of the transplanted heart. Other contraindications include malignancy, severe cerebrovascular disease, and severe peripheral vascular disease.

The use of tacrolimus, an immunosuppressant drug that significantly decreases the body's rejection of transplanted organs, along with improved methods for monitoring rejection have greatly improved survival rate and expanded selection criteria. In 2008, the 1-year survival rate after cardiac transplantation was more than 87.5% for men and 85.5% for women (AHA, 2009). Typical candidates have advanced HF, severe symptoms, and functional limitations uncontrolled by medical therapy, no other surgical options, and a poor life expectancy from heart disease.

TABLE
16-1 **Cardiomyopathies**

Type	Description	Etiology	Pathophysiology	Clinical Manifestations
Dilated Cardiomyopathy (DCM)	Significant, irreversible dilation of the ventricles Systolic dysfunction without hypertrophy Increased ventricular systolic and diastolic volumes with decreased left ventricular (LV) function Impaired contractility may result in HF, ventricular arrhythmias, and sudden cardiac death.	Can be ischemic, hypertensive, alcoholic, toxic, autoimmune, or idiopathic 15% to 45% of patients who had a myocardial infarction (MI) develop an enlarged LV and reduced ejection fraction; extent of myocardial damage cannot be explained by degree of ischemic damage. The anthracycline class of anticancer drugs, particularly daunorubicin and doxorubicin, is known to cause DCM. Peri- or postpartum DCM occurs in the last trimester or within the first 6 months of childbirth. As much as 50% of all DCM is thought to be familial.	Reduced ventricular wall thickness and increased myocardial mass result in poor systolic function. Decreased blood volume ejected from the ventricle during systole increases blood volume remaining in the ventricle after contraction. Less blood is then able to enter the ventricle during diastole, increasing end-diastolic pressure and eventually increasing pulmonary and systemic venous pressures. Valvular regurgitation can result from an enlarged stretched ventricle. Poor blood flow through the ventricle may cause ventricular or atrial thrombi, which may embolize to other locations in the body.	Symptoms are progressive and include dyspnea, fatigue, volume overload, weight gain, chest pain due to coronary artery disease or pulmonary embolism, abdominal discomfort from hepatomegaly. Signs include: holosystolic murmur (heard on S_1) due to MR, thromboembolism, ventricular arrhythmias, and sudden cardiac death. HF may be the initial presentation.
Hypertrophic Cardiomyopathy (HCM)	Hypertrophied, nondilated LV leads to obstruction of left ventricular outflow, without cardiac or systemic disease.	HCM is familial; 50% of the children of those with HCM will inherit the disorder.	Heart muscle asymmetrically increases in mass, especially along the septum, and increased thickness reduces the size of the ventricular cavities, taking longer to relax after systole. During diastole, ventricular filling is impaired; atrial contraction at the end of diastole becomes critical for filling and systolic contraction. Smaller-than-normal LV cavity creates high-velocity blood flow from the LV into the aorta. Left ventricular outflow tract obstruction causes high systolic pressure in the LV that leads to prolonged ventricular relaxation and diminished cardiac output, resulting in diastolic dysfunction. Systolic function is normal or high, resulting in an above-normal ejection fraction.	Most patients with HCM are asymptomatic but some present with ventricular arrhythmias, sudden cardiac death, or other symptoms: syncope, dyspnea, chest pain. Atrial fibrillation commonly occurs from atrial enlargement. Systolic ejection murmurs (heard on S_1) become more pronounced when the patient moves from standing to a squatting position. Mitral murmurs result from regurgitation.

Increased chamber size

Thin left ventricular muscle

Decreased chamber size

Thickened intraventricular septum

Type	Description	Etiology	Pathophysiology	Clinical Manifestations
Restrictive (RCM)	Characterized by diastolic dysfunction that negatively affects or "restricts" the heart's ability to fill with blood Uncommon cardiomyopathy Stiff ventricular walls	Frequently idiopathic Associated with amyloidosis and endomyocardial fibrosis (scarring of the heart) Often occurs after a heart transplant	Stiff ventricular walls lack ventricular stretch (flexibility to expand as they fill with blood). This impairs diastolic filling, resulting in diastolic HF. Normal, or slightly increased, ventricular wall thickness and atrial enlargement with normal systolic function is characteristic. Atrioventricular block and symptomatic bradycardia can occur.	Symptoms are similar to constrictive pericarditis: dyspnea, nonproductive cough, chest pain, and exercise intolerance. Signs may include jugular venous distention, edema, ascites, anasarca, pulmonary edema, and an S_3 and S_4 can be heard with auscultation.
Arrhythmogenic Right Ventricular Cardiomyopathy (ARVC) Fibrofatty replacement of right ventricular myocardium	Rare but increasingly recognized condition ARVC should be suspected in patients with ventricular tachycardia originating in the right ventricle (i.e., left bundle branch block on ECG) or sudden cardiac death, especially among previously symptom-free athletes.	Familial in more than 50% of patients and usually occurs in early adulthood	ARVC occurs when right ventricle is progressively infiltrated and replaced with fibrous scar and adipose tissue. Initially, localized areas of the right ventricle are affected, but as the disease progresses, the entire heart is affected. Eventually, the right ventricle dilates and develops poor contractility, and arrhythmias occur.	Symptoms are consistent with right HF. Supraventricular arrhythmias may occur. Ventricular arrhythmias and sudden cardiac death may be the initial presentation, and diagnosis is often made postmortem. Family history, ECG, and a history of arrhythmias can help establish a diagnosis of ARVC.
Stress-Induced (Takotsubo) Cardiomyopathy Akinesis (absence of or decreased movement) with sparing of the base and left ventricular apical ballooning	Recently identified syndrome of transient LV dysfunction. Ventricular function fully returns within weeks. LV morphology, seen with echocardiography or ventriculogram, demonstrates apical akinesis (absence of or decreased movement) with sparing of the base, and resultant ballooning of the ventricle. It has been identified predominantly in white, postmenopausal women. Noncardiac comorbidities, such as anxiety, chronic pulmonary disease, and thyroid disease are associated.	Precipitated by emotional or physical distress	The pathophysiology of stress-induced cardiomyopathy remains unclear. One theory gaining acceptance is catecholamine excess triggered by activation of sympathetic system.	Clinical presentation is identical to that of acute ST-segment elevation MI: acute substernal pain and shortness of breath following an emotionally or physically stressful trigger. ST-segment elevation may be present on ECG, and cardiac enzymes may be mildly elevated, disproportionate to levels seen with acute MI. Acute presentation may be severe; arrhythmias, HF, pulmonary edema, and cardiogenic shock have been reported in the absence of significant coronary artery disease. Ballooning of the LV, with rapid and complete recovery, is the hallmark feature.

BOX 16-2 Nursing Research

Bridging the Gap to Evidence-Based Practice

Caring for Patients and Families Awaiting a Donor Heart

Haugh, K., & Sayler, J. (2007). Needs of patients and families during the wait for a donor heart. *Heart and Lung: The Journal of Acute and Critical Care, 36* (5), 319–329.

Purpose

Waiting time to receive a donor heart is unpredictable, and research has documented that this is a source of stress for patients and families. Research regarding how the nurse may influence patients' and families' perceptions of this wait is lacking. The purpose of this study was to explore patients' and family members' perceptions of what interventions were being used during their wait for a donor heart, the perceived benefit of those interventions, and what other interventions not used that may be beneficial.

Design

Videotaped focus group interviews were used in this qualitative study to determine the perceptions of patients and their families regarding time spent waiting for a donor heart and their interactions with the health care team. Content analysis was used to determine themes concerning time spent waiting.

Findings

Tolerating uncertainty was the main theme describing perception of wait time. Five subthemes were interventions provided by the health care team: sharing information, being sensitive to the family, maintaining dignity and respect, doing "extra little things," and facilitating coping.

Nursing Implications

Nurses caring for patients awaiting transplantation must be aware that time waiting for a donor heart is stressful, and that sharing information was perceived as helpful by participants. Maintaining the patients' dignity, facilitating patients' control, and doing "extra things" such as taking the patient outside for fresh air, facilitating a visit to the chapel, or allowing a visit by a pet helped make them "feel normal" and was greatly appreciated by the patients. Coping mechanisms, such as the use of humor, spirituality, and peer support were perceived as useful by the patients. Informal, friendly nursing interactions, beyond the formal professional relationship, such as sitting and talking with the patient can be therapeutic for the patient and positively impact the patients' perception of time waiting for a donor heart.

Waiting for a donor heart is stressful for the patient and family. Much unpredictability and uncertainty exists regarding whether or when a donor heart will become available. Nurses may be able to influence the patient's perception of wait time, as seen in Box 16-2.

Orthotopic Transplantation

Orthotopic transplantation, as depicted in Figure 16-8, is the most common surgical procedure for cardiac transplantation. The recipient's heart is removed, leaving a portion of the recipient's atria with the vena cava and pulmonary veins in place. The donor heart, which usually has been preserved in ice, is prepared for implant by cutting away a small section of the atria that corresponds with the sections of the recipient's heart that were left in place. The donor heart is implanted by suturing the donor atria to the residual atrial tissue of the recipient's heart. After the venous or atrial anastomoses are complete, the recipient's pulmonary artery and aorta are sutured to those of the donor heart.

Postoperative Course

Patients who have had heart transplants constantly balance the risk of rejection with the risk of infection. They must adhere to a complex regimen of diet, medications, activity, follow-up laboratory studies, biopsies of the transplanted heart (to diagnose rejection), and clinic visits. Commonly, patients receive cyclosporine or tacrolimus, azathioprine or

mycophenolate mofetil (CellCept), and corticosteroids to minimize rejection.

The transplanted heart is denervated; it has no nerve connections to the recipient's body, and the sympathetic

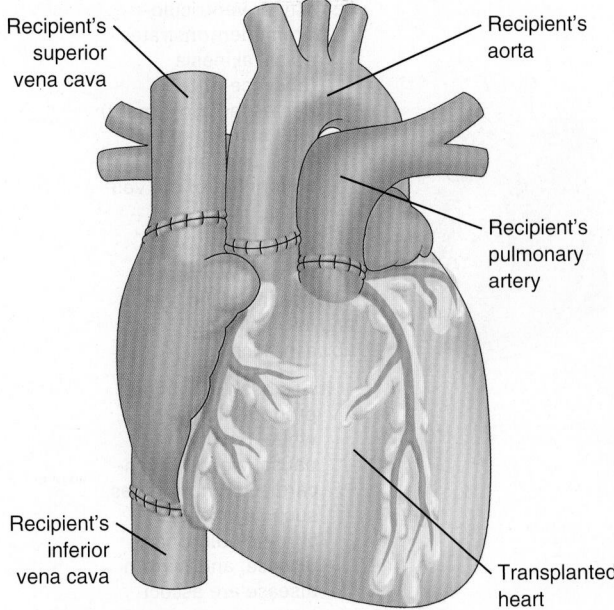

FIGURE 16-8 Orthotopic method of heart transplantation.

and vagus nerves do not affect the transplanted heart. The resting rate of the transplanted heart is approximately 70 to 90 beats per minute, but it increases gradually if catecholamines are in the circulation. Patients must gradually increase and decrease their exercise (i.e., extended warm-up and cool-down periods), because 20 to 30 minutes may be required to achieve the desired heart rate. Atropine does not increase the heart rate of transplanted hearts.

In addition to rejection and infection, complications include *cardiac allograft vasculopathy*, an accelerated, diffuse atherosclerosis of the coronary arteries. This can result in coronary lumen loss, ischemia, infarction, and sudden death (Woods, Froelicher, Motzer et al., 2010). Hypertension may occur in patients taking cyclosporine or tacrolimus; the cause has not been identified. Osteoporosis frequently occurs as a side effect of the anti-rejection medications and pretransplantation dietary insufficiency and medications, as well as the long-term sedentary lifestyle. Posttransplantation lymphoproliferative disease and cancer of the skin and lips are the most common malignancies after transplantation, likely caused by immunosuppression. Immunosuppressants and corticosteroids can cause weight gain, diabetes, dyslipidemia, renal failure, and central nervous system and GI disturbances, and toxicity from immunosuppressants can occur.

Transplant recipients face a number of stressors including:

- Coping with complications, such as graft rejection
- Managing a complex posttransplant regimen consisting of multiple medications, exercise and dietary prescriptions, regular medical follow-up evaluations and laboratory tests, lifestyle restrictions related to smoking, alcohol, and other potentially harmful substances
- Transitioning from their roles as critically ill or dying patients to roles and lifestyles that are less illness-focused
- Psychological acceptance of the transplant and the fact that someone lost their life when they regained theirs
- Coping with financial issues, such as the cost of surgery and medications

Mechanical Circulatory Assist Devices

The use of mechanical circulatory assist devices has increased dramatically since the late 1960s, when IABPs were first used. In addition to balloon pumps, VADs and total artificial hearts are increasingly used to support circulation when the heart is unable to generate adequate cardiac output. Circulatory assist devices have three main functions: (1) reduce or assume the workload of the heart, (2) support systemic circulation, completely or partially, and (3) improve myocardial oxygenation. Patients who cannot be weaned from cardiopulmonary bypass, patients in cardiogenic shock, and patients with refractory HF may benefit from mechanical heart assistance while the patient's own heart recovers, or until a donor heart becomes available for transplantation.

Increasingly, some devices are being used long term, while investigation continues for permanent use devices.

Intra-aortic Balloon Pump Counterpulsation

The most commonly used device is the IABP. This pump decreases the workload of the heart by reducing left ventricular afterload. Additionally, it improves coronary artery blood flow by increasing coronary artery perfusion pressure. The IABP is used pre- and postoperatively in patients with severely compromised left ventricular function, in patients with myocardial ischemia undergoing complex percutaneous coronary interventions, and in patients with complications resulting from acute MI, such as papillary muscle rupture, awaiting surgical repair. Bleeding, limb ischemia, infection, and vascular injury are potential complications of IABP, and monitoring the patient for compromised circulation and hemodynamic instability is a priority for nursing management.

Ventricular Assist Devices

More complex devices that can perform some or all of the pumping function for the heart also are increasingly being used. VADs can support a failing heart by generating blood flow to the systemic circulation and unloading the ventricle. Initially used for patients with difficulty weaning from cardiopulmonary bypass following cardiothoracic surgery, VADs were a bridge to recovery (BTR). The short-term use indications include support of the heart during high-risk percutaneous intervention to off-load the heart, cardiogenic shock, acute myocarditis, acute, reversible HF, and a bridge to an alternate device, such as a more permanent VAD.

Usage has expanded, and VAD therapies are also categorized as a bridge to decision (BTD), bridge to bridge (BTB), bridge to transplant (BTT), and DT. VADs used for a BTD allow time to evaluate whether a transplant or other treatment is most suited to a patient. Similarly, a BTB VAD is used when emergent stabilization is necessary, with a plan to transition to a longer-term device when the patient becomes more clinically stable. Long-term indications include using a VAD as a BTT in patients failing on maximal medical therapy, or for DT in patients with end-stage HF who are not transplant candidates. See Figure 16-9 for an example of a long-term use VAD.

These devices can have pumps that are outside the body (extracorporeal) or implantable, and can be broadly classified as volume-displacement (pulsatile, pneumatic) or continuous flow (axial-flow, centrifugal). Most are surgically inserted via sternotomy, but some short-term use VADs can be inserted percutaneously. First-generation volume-displacement pumps have a chamber that fills passively or by suction. The chamber is compressed by pressure to generate a pulsatile blood flow that is similar to systole and diastole, and depends on the patient's pre-load for filling. They can be extracorporeal or implanted, for short- and long-term use, and may be removed if heart function recovers.

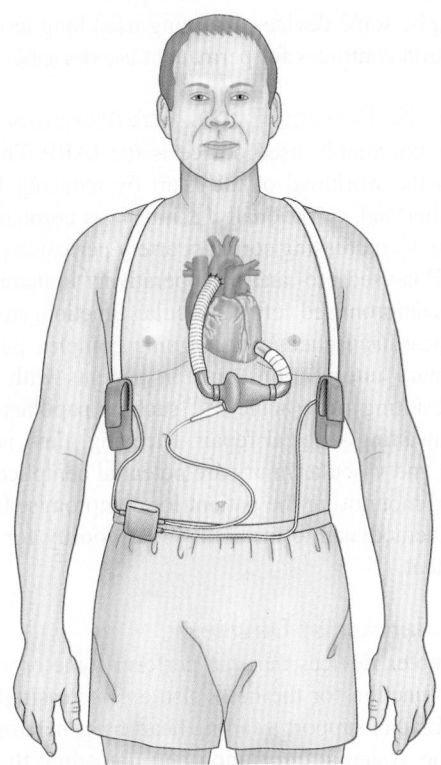

FIGURE 16-9 Left ventricular assist device.

Second-generation continuous flow pumps return blood to the aorta at a constant rate. Axial-flow devices contain a spinning impeller that generates a continuous flow by a rotor spinning around a central shaft; these may be used both short and long term. Centrifugal VADs are used short term (less than 1 week) to reduce pressure in the ventricles. A centrifugal force is generated from a spinning cone-shaped rotor resulting in a nonpulsatile flow of blood.

Total Artificial Hearts

Total artificial hearts (TAHs) are designed to replace both ventricles. Two devices are currently FDA approved. The SynCardia temporary Cardio West Total Artificial Heart is a pneumatic TAH approved for use in 2004 as a BTT in patients waiting for a donor heart who have biventricular failure unresponsive to other therapies and are at imminent risk of death (Chen, 2010). The AbioCor manufactured by Abiomed was approved in 2006 for DT under the humanitarian use device exemption (Morris, 2008).

Complications

Complications of VADs and TAHs include infection, ventricular arrhythmias, thrombus, thromboemboli, hemolysis, hemorrhage, right HF, multisystem failure, and mechanical failure (Chen, 2010). Appropriate anticoagulation to reduce the risk of thrombus formation and thromboembolism, while avoiding the risk of bleeding, is a challenge, and anticoagulation therapy depends on device type, patient history, and

platelet responsiveness. Infection is another major complication, particularly with extracorporeal devices, as the percutaneous driveline exit site commonly becomes infected. Infection at this site can quickly spread through the entire system causing *sepsis*, a systemic infection.

Nursing care for patients with mechanical assist devices focuses on the assessment of and minimization of complications, as well as providing emotional support and education about the mechanical assist device and the underlying cardiac disease. If a longer-term VAD is being considered, the patient's ability to manage the VAD should be assessed.

INFECTIOUS DISEASES OF THE HEART

Any of the heart's three layers may be affected by an infectious process. The diseases are named for the layer of the heart most involved in the infectious process: endocarditis (endocardium), myocarditis (myocardium), and pericarditis (pericardium). These diseases may significantly impact cardiac function and indirectly, quality of life. The ideal management for all infectious diseases is prevention.

INFECTIVE ENDOCARDITIS

Endocarditis is an infection of the endocardium. Prosthetic heart valves, structural cardiac defects, and IV drug use account for the majority of infectious endocarditis (IE). Nosocomial (hospital-acquired) infective endocarditis occurs most often in patients with bacteremia and an indwelling catheter, and in patients who are receiving prolonged IV fluid or antibiotic therapy. Patients taking immunosuppressive medications or corticosteroids are susceptible to fungal endocarditis.

Pathophysiology

Staphylococci and streptococci account for most IE. These pathogens colonize at the site of an abnormality or injury of the endocardium, such as a prosthetic valve site. Inflammation and infection result in endothelial damage; then platelets, fibrin, blood cells, and microorganisms cluster as *vegetations* on the endocardium. The vegetations can embolize to other tissues throughout the body. The infection may erode through the endocardium into the underlying structures (e.g., valve leaflets), causing tears or deformities of valve leaflets, dehiscence of prosthetic valves, deformity of the chordae tendineae, or paravalvular abscesses.

Acute IE is often caused by *Staphylococcus* infection and its onset is rapid, occurring within days to weeks. Subacute IE, usually caused by *Streptococcus*, occurs more slowly and its course is prolonged. Often, the onset of IE is insidious, and signs and symptoms develop from the infection, destruction of the heart valves, and embolization of the vegetative growths on the heart. Systemic emboli occur with left-sided

BOX 16-3
Risk Factors for Infective Endocarditis

- Acquired valvular dysfunction
- Atrial septal defect (unrepaired or repaired)
- Bicuspid aortic valve
- Body piercing
- Coarctation of the aorta
- Complex cyanotic congenital malformations
- Degenerative valve disease
- History of infective endocarditis
- Indwelling, long-term hemodialysis catheters
- IV drug use
- Mitral regurgitation
- Mitral valve prolapse with valvular regurgitation or thickened leaflets
- Nosocomial endocarditis
- Parenteral nutrition lines or IV lines into the right atrium
- Patent ductus arteriosus
- Prosthetic cardiac valves
- Ventricular septal defect

heart IE; pulmonary emboli can occur when the right heart is infected, typically from IV drug use.

Risk Factors

A cardiac valve with epithelial damage will attract bacteria to its surface and this can result in endocardial infection. This injury may be the result of a prosthetic valve; a congenital abnormality, such as a bicuspid aortic valve; structural abnormality such as MVP; or may be from age-related, degenerative valvular changes. IV drug use, long-term indwelling catheters and body piercing are also risk factors for IE, and a comprehensive list is provided in Box 16-3.

Clinical Manifestations and Assessment

The clinical presentation of IE varies, and diagnosis may be difficult as symptoms are often vague, such as anorexia, myalgias, fever, chills, weight loss, back and joint pain, and night sweats. Fever is common, but may be intermittent or absent, especially in patients who are receiving antibiotics or corticosteroids, in those who are elderly, or those who have heart or renal failure. A heart murmur may be absent initially but develops in almost all patients. Murmurs that worsen over time are indicative of progressive damage from vegetations or perforation of the valve or chordae tendineae.

In addition to fever and heart murmur, Osler nodes, Janeway lesions, and Roth spots are distinguishing signs of IE, and are the result of microembolization. Osler nodes, painful, erythematous nodules, may be present on the pads of fingers or toes. Janeway lesions are painless, red or purple macules found on the palms and soles. Roth spots, seen on funduscopic exam, are oval retinal hemorrhages with pale centers. Splinter hemorrhages may be seen under the fingernails and toenails, and petechiae may appear on the neck, chest, abdomen, conjunctiva, and mucous membranes. Central nervous system manifestations of IE include headache, transient cerebral ischemia, and strokes, which may be caused by emboli to the cerebral arteries. Embolization may be a presenting symptom; it may occur at any time and may involve other organ systems. Cardiomegaly, HF, tachycardia, or splenomegaly may occur.

Positive blood cultures are highly sensitive for diagnosis; however, negative blood cultures do not definitely rule out IE, especially if a patient has received antibiotics or if slow-growing bacteria are present. Three sets of blood cultures should be obtained before administration of any antimicrobial agents.

Echocardiography is used widely in the diagnosis and can detect the presence or absence of vegetations or abscesses, prosthetic valve dehiscence, new regurgitation, or HF. Other abnormal findings include anemia, elevated white blood cell (WBC) counts, elevated erythrocyte sedimentation rate (ESR), and elevated C-reactive protein. Abnormal electrocardiographic (ECG) findings include atrioventricular blocks, bundle branch blocks, and fascicular blocks.

Prevention

Prevention is critical. Since 1955, antibiotic prophylaxis has been recommended for prevention of IE in patients at risk for its development (i.e., those with rheumatic heart disease, mitral valve prolapse, or prosthetic heart valves) prior to dental, respiratory, genitourinary, and GI procedures. However, in 2008, significant changes were made for antibiotic prophylaxis recommendations by the American Heart Association, as described in Box 16-4. Antibiotic prophylaxis is no longer recommended prior to dental procedures unless patients are at highest risk of adverse outcomes. In addition, antibiotic prophylaxis is no longer recommended prior to respiratory tract procedures, unless it involves an incision, such as a tonsillectomy, and is in a high-risk patient, or prior to GI and genitourinary procedures regardless of patients' level of risk (Nishimura, Carabello, Faxon et al., 2008).

Medical and Nursing Management

The objective of treatment is to eradicate the infection and prevent complications. The cornerstone of treatment is long-term, parenteral antibiotic therapy. It is administered in doses that produce a high serum concentration and for a significant period, often for upward of 6 weeks to ensure eradication of the dormant bacteria within the dense vegetations.

Surgery is indicated when there is a persistent or recurrent infection, if HF occurs, or if patients have more than one serious systemic embolic episode, valve obstruction, valvular or myocardial abscess, or fungal endocarditis. Most

Infective Endocarditis Antibiotic Prophylaxis

Indications for Prophylaxis
- Previous infective endocarditis
- Prosthetic valve
- Congenital heart disease with persistent risk of IE (unrepaired cyanotic congenital abnormalities, completely repaired congenital defects with prosthetic material, during first 6 months after surgery, and repaired congenital defects with residual defect adjacent to prosthetic material)
- Cardiac transplant recipients with cardiac valve diseases.

Conditions for Which Prophylaxis Is No Longer Required
- Mitral valve prolapse
- Rheumatic heart disease
- Bicuspid valve disease
- Physiologic, functional, or innocent murmurs
- Echocardiographic evidence of physiologic MR, tricuspid regurgitation or pulmonary regurgitation in the absence of murmur and structurally normal valves

Rationale for Change in Antibiotic Prophylaxis Recommendations for Infective Endocarditis
- No randomized clinical trials have demonstrated a proven benefit.
- IE is less likely to be caused by a dental, GI, or genitourinary procedure than from frequent exposure to random bacteremias from daily activities.
- Prophylaxis may prevent only a small number of cases of IE, if any, in patients undergoing dental, GI, or genitourinary procedures.
- Risk of adverse events for antibiotic use outweighs the benefit (if any) from prophylaxis.
- Good oral health and hygiene is more important than antibiotic prophylaxis in preventing IE.

patients who have prosthetic valve endocarditis require valve replacement, and this greatly improves the prognosis for patients with severe symptoms. The nurse monitors the patient for fever, which can persist for weeks. Heart sounds are assessed. A new or worsening murmur may indicate dehiscence of a prosthetic valve, rupture of an abscess, or injury to valve leaflets. The nurse monitors for signs and symptoms of systemic embolization, and end-organ damage that may result, such as cerebrovascular accident, meningitis, HF, MI, pulmonary embolism, glomerulonephritis, and splenomegaly.

Patient care is directed toward management of infection. Antibiotics are initiated as soon as blood cultures have been obtained. Long-term IV antimicrobial therapy is often necessary, and many patients have peripherally inserted central catheters or other long-term IV access. All invasive lines and wounds must be assessed daily for redness, tenderness, warmth, swelling, drainage, or other signs of infection.

The patient and family are instructed about medications, and signs and symptoms of infection. The nurse instructs the highest-risk patients and family about the need for prophylactic antibiotics before certain dental procedures. For patients with low to moderate risk of developing IE, especially those who have previously received antibiotic prophylaxis, education must be provided regarding the updated recommendations. Rationale, as described in Box 16-4, must be provided for no longer providing prophylaxis for genitourinary and GI procedures, as well as for most respiratory and dental procedures, except in highest-risk individuals.

Blood cultures are taken periodically to monitor the effect of therapy, and serum levels of the selected antibiotic are monitored to ensure the serum demonstrates bactericidal activity. The nurse provides the patient and family with emotional support and facilitates coping strategies during the prolonged course of the infection and antibiotic treatment. If the patient has undergone surgical treatment, the nurse provides postoperative care and instructions.

Complications

Even if the patient responds to therapy, endocarditis can be destructive to the heart and other organs. HF and cerebral vascular complications, such as stroke, may occur before, during, or after therapy. HF can occur from perforation of a valve leaflet, rupture of chordae, blood flow obstruction due to vegetations, or intracardiac shunts from dehiscence of prosthetic valves. Valvular stenosis or regurgitation, myocardial damage, and mycotic (fungal) aneurysms are potential cardiac complications. First-, second-, and third-degree atrioventricular blocks may occur and are often a sign of a valve ring abscess (refer to Chapter 17 for descriptions of heart blocks). Septic or nonseptic emboli can lead to splenic abscess, cerebritis, hemodynamic deterioration, or complications in other organs.

MYOCARDITIS

Myocarditis is an inflammation of the heart muscle, commonly resulting from viral infection. It may also be caused by bacterial infections, immune-mediated mechanisms, and toxic agents. Frequently, the cause is unknown. It can be acute or chronic. Mortality varies with the severity of symptoms. Mild cases with few symptoms may resolve without treatment, while more serious cases result in cardiogenic shock and death.

Pathophysiology

Cardiac muscle inflammation that results in myocyte necrosis (e.g., cardiac cell death) is the hallmark of myocarditis. Acute myocarditis is characterized by myocyte damage from viral infection, autoimmunity, or other precipitating

event. Myocyte antigens and cytokines are released. In the subacute phase (days 4 to 14), T and B lymphocytes infiltrate the myocardium, and the virus is cleared. The immune response continues and infected myocytes are lysed. During the chronic phase, myocyte injury continues and can lead to dilated cardiomyopathy.

Clinical Manifestations and Assessment

The symptoms of myocarditis depend on the type of infection, the degree of myocardial damage, and the capacity of the myocardium to recover. Diagnosis is difficult. Clinical presentation can vary widely; symptoms can range from mild systemic findings of fever, myalgias, fatigue, and dyspnea to ventricular arrhythmias, cardiogenic shock, and DCM. Other signs and symptoms include an S_3 gallop, tachycardia, tachypnea, jugular venous distention, edema, ECG abnormalities, orthopnea, and palpitations. Fulminant HF or sudden cardiac death can quickly develop.

A minority will have elevated cardiac enzymes and WBC count. ESR will be elevated approximately 60% of the time. Echocardiography may show impaired heart muscle function or pericardial effusion. Myocardial biopsy may be used to confirm diagnosis.

Medical and Nursing Management

For patients with myocarditis, supportive care is of primary importance, with the goals of care focused on maintaining hemodynamic stability and improvement of symptoms. Treatment of HF symptoms with standard medical therapy and surgical options, such as the placement of a VAD or TAH, or heart transplantation, should be considered when there is no improvement in symptoms or hemodynamic status despite maximal medical therapy.

Nursing care of the patient with myocarditis includes an assessment of whether the patient's symptoms are improving or worsening. In addition to monitoring vital signs, heart sounds, lung sounds, and peripheral perfusion, the nurse must assess hemodynamic, oxygenation, and fluid status. Nurses should be prepared to use emergency equipment, as the risk of life-threatening ventricular arrhythmias is great. Nurses must also provide emotional support to the patient and family; myocarditis can be particularly stressful due to its variable presentation and course.

PERICARDITIS

Pericarditis is an inflammation of the pericardium, the membranous sac surrounding the heart. Causes are numerous, but it is most frequently caused by viral illness, and may also occur following certain medical problems or after some surgical procedures. A list of the most frequently occurring causes of pericarditis is provided in Box 16-5. Pericarditis

BOX 16-5 Causes of Pericarditis

- Acute MI
- Bacterial infection (e.g., streptococci, staphylococci, meningococci)
- Chest trauma: chest injury, cardiac surgery, implantation of pacemaker or defibrillator (ICD)
- Connective tissue disorders (e.g., lupus, rheumatic fever, rheumatoid arthritis, scleroderma)
- Disorders of adjacent structures: dissecting aneurysm, pulmonary disease (e.g., pneumonia)
- Fungal infection (e.g., aspergillus, candida, histoplasma)
- Idiopathic or nonspecific causes
- Medications (e.g., procainamide, hydralazine, and isoniazid)
- Neoplasm: metastasis from lung or breast tumors or lymphoma
- Radiation therapy of chest and upper torso (peak occurrence 5 to 9 months after treatment)
- Renal failure and uremia
- Tuberculosis
- Viral infection (e.g., coxsackie, hepatitis B, influenza, mononucleosis, mumps, varicella)

can develop after an acute MI or following pericardectomy (opening of the pericardium) during cardiac surgery.

Pathophysiology

The pericardial sac consists of two layers, the parietal (outer) layer and the visceral (inner) layer that is affixed to the heart. A small amount of fluid (15 to 50 mL) separates the layers. Pericarditis may lead to an accumulation of fluid in this space called *pericardial effusion*. This may result in increased pressure on the heart, leading to cardiac tamponade (refer to Chapter 15). Pericarditis may be acute or chronic. Acute pericarditis develops rapidly, causing an inflammatory reaction, while chronic progresses slowly and can be accompanied by effusion.

Frequent or prolonged episodes of pericarditis can lead to thickening and decreased elasticity of the pericardium, and scarring may fuse the visceral and parietal pericardium. These conditions restrict the heart's ability to fill with blood (constrictive pericarditis). The pericardium may become calcified, further restricting ventricular expansion during diastole. With less filling, the ventricles pump less blood, leading to decreased cardiac output and signs and symptoms of HF. Restricted diastolic filling may result in increased systemic venous pressure, causing peripheral edema and hepatic failure.

Risk Factors

Men between the ages of 20 and 50 are more likely to develop pericarditis. It can occur following a MI or recent viral

illness or bacterial infection. Lupus, scleroderma, rheumatoid arthritis, or other autoimmune disorders are risk factors for the development of pericarditis. In about half of all cases, the cause is unknown (idiopathic).

Clinical Manifestations and Assessment

Pericarditis may be asymptomatic; however, the most characteristic symptom is chest pain. Because of this and the ST-segment elevation that is often present, acute pericarditis can mimic acute MI. The pain is typically persistent, sharp, pleuritic, and usually felt in the mid-chest, although it also may be located beneath the clavicle, in the neck, or in the left trapezius region. The discomfort is usually fairly constant, but is aggravated by deep inspiration, coughing, lying down, or turning. It may be relieved with a forward-leaning or sitting position. Although not heard in all patients with pericarditis, a common finding is a creaky or scratchy friction rub.

> ! **NURSING ALERT**
>
> *A pericardial friction rub is diagnostic of pericarditis. It has a creaky or scratchy sound and is louder at the end of exhalation. Nurses can assess for the presence of a pericardial friction rub by placing the diaphragm of the stethoscope tightly against the thorax and auscultating the left lower sternal border in the fourth intercostal space, the site where the pericardium comes into contact with the left chest wall. The rub is best heard when the patient is sitting and leaning forward. The friction rub is caused by the inflamed layers of the pericardium rubbing against each other, and is often intermittent.*

Other signs may include a mild fever, increased WBC count, anemia, and an elevated ESR or C-reactive protein level. Patients may have a nonproductive cough. Dyspnea unrelated to exertion is typical of pericarditis; shortness of breath occurs as a result of pericardial compression due from cardiac tamponade.

The diagnosis is most often made on the basis of the history, signs, and symptoms. A 12-lead ECG may show diffuse concave ST elevation without reciprocal changes or T-wave inversion, and ST-segment elevation may persist for weeks. ECG may also reveal depressed PR segments or atrial arrhythmias. Echocardiography is done to assess for pericardial effusion or tamponade.

Medical and Nursing Management

The goals of management are to determine the cause, administer therapy for treatment and symptom relief, and detect signs and symptoms of cardiac tamponade. Nonsteroidal anti-inflammatory medications (NSAIDs) are prescribed for pain relief during the acute phase. Corticosteroids may be prescribed if the pericarditis is severe or if the patient does not respond to NSAIDs. Corticosteroids and NSAIDs, however, should not be given to patients who develop pericarditis following an acute MI because they can cause rupture of the infarcted area. In cases of constrictive pericarditis, surgical removal of the pericardium (pericardectomy) may be necessary to provide relief from restrictive inflammation and scarring.

Patients with acute pericarditis require pain management with analgesics, positioning, and psychological support. Patients with chest pain often benefit from education and reassurance that the pain is not a heart attack. The nurse monitors the patient for HF, and treats patients with hemodynamic instability or pulmonary congestion as if they had HF.

Complications

Nurses caring for patients with pericarditis must be aware of the potential of serious complications. The two major complications of pericarditis are pericardial effusion, the accumulation of fluid in the pericardial sac, and cardiac tamponade, compression of the heart from excessive fluid build-up (refer to Chapter 15).

NURSING PROCESS

The Patient with Pericarditis

Assessment

Pain is the primary symptom of the patient with pericarditis, and it is assessed while repositioning the patient. The nurse tries to identify whether the pain is influenced by inspiration or expiration; breath holding; flexion, extension, or rotation of the spine and neck; by movements of the shoulders and arms, and by coughing or swallowing. Recognizing that deep inspiration or coughing intensifies pain may help to differentiate the pain of pericarditis from the pain of MI. To distinguish a pericardial friction rub from a pleural friction rub, the patient is asked to hold his or her breath; a pericardial friction rub will continue. A pericardial friction rub occurs when the pericardial surfaces lose their lubricating fluid because of inflammation. The rub is audible on auscultation and is synchronous with the heartbeat, but is often intermittent and does not always occur. The patient's temperature and other vital signs are monitored frequently. Pericarditis may cause an abrupt onset of fever in a patient who has been afebrile.

Diagnosis

Based on the assessment data, a major nursing diagnosis may be:

• Acute pain related to inflammation of the pericardium

Planning

The nursing plan focuses on two goals: pain relief and absence of complications.

Nursing Interventions

Relieving Pain

Certain techniques can assist patients with pericarditis to conserve energy and reduce fatigue. Relief of pain is achieved by chair rest because sitting upright and leaning forward is the posture that tends to relieve pain. It is important to instruct the patient to restrict activity until the pain subsides. As the chest pain and friction rub abate, activities of daily living may be resumed gradually. If the patient is taking analgesics, antibiotics, or corticosteroids for the pericarditis, his or her responses are monitored and recorded. Patients taking NSAIDs are assessed for GI effects. If chest pain and friction rub recur, bed rest or chair rest is resumed.

Reducing the patient's anxiety can provide relief. Patients may confuse the pain of pericarditis with heart attack pain. Frequent rest periods and distraction techniques may also provide comfort. Patients should be taught to adhere to their medication schedule and to recognize signs and symptoms of recurrence: chest pain, malaise, and fever.

Monitoring and Managing Potential Complications

PERICARDIAL EFFUSION. Fluid that accumulates between the pericardial linings or in the pericardial sac, is called pericardial effusion (see Chapter 15). The fluid can constrict the myocardium and impair its ability to pump. Cardiac output declines with each contraction. Failure to identify and treat this problem can lead to cardiac tamponade and possible sudden death, so patients must be assessed for signs of decreasing cardiac output.

CARDIAC TAMPONADE. The first symptoms of cardiac tamponade are often shortness of breath, chest tightness, dizziness, or restlessness. Assessment of blood pressure may reveal a *pulsus paradoxus*, a decrease of 10 mm Hg or more in the systolic blood pressure during inspiration. Usually, the systolic pressure decreases and the diastolic pressure remains stable; hence, pulse pressure narrows. The patient may have tachycardia, and the ECG voltage may be decreased or the QRS complexes may alternate in height (electrical alternans). Heart sounds may progress from distant to imperceptible. Neck vein distention and other signs of rising central venous pressure develop. These signs occur as the fluid-filled pericardial sac compresses the myocardium. Blood continues to return to the heart from the periphery but cannot flow into the heart to be pumped back into the circulation. The nurse notifies the provider immediately and prepares to assist with diagnostic echocardiography and pericardiocentesis (see Chapter 15). The nurse stays with the patient and continues to assess and record signs and symptoms while intervening to decrease patient anxiety.

Evaluation

Expected patient outcomes include:

1. Freedom from pain:
   a. Performs activities of daily living without pain, fatigue, or shortness of breath
   b. Temperature returns to normal range
   c. Exhibits no pericardial friction rub

2. Absence of complications:
   a. Sustains blood pressure in normal range
   b. Has heart sounds that are strong and can be auscultated
   c. No evidence of effusion or tamponade

Chapter Review

Critical Thinking Exercises

1. A friend tells you she does not like to take drugs and does not plan to adhere to advice from her health care providers to use antibiotics before routine dental checkups. You know your friend has had a heterograft mitral valve replacement. How would you respond to your friend? On what evidence do you base your response? What is the strength of that evidence?

2. A 19-year-old man with HCM is being discharged from the hospital. He lives alone and states that he really needs to get back to the gym to resume his weight training. Based on your knowledge about the developmental tasks of 19-year-olds, what do you anticipate his psychosocial needs would be? His family came to the hospital during the first 2 days of his hospital stay, but they live out of town and have returned home. Should they be included in the plan of care? The cardiologist has requested a consult with transplant services. How will this consult be included in the plan of care?

3. A 68-year-old man with atrial fibrillation, who is recovering from an aortic valve replacement for aortic stenosis and three coronary artery bypass grafts, has been prescribed a beta blocker, an ACE inhibitor, digoxin, and warfarin. The cardiologist advises the patient to continue to carry nitroglycerin spray for treatment of angina, should it occur. What are the teaching and discharge planning needs? As you care for the patient on the

(continued on page 460)

Chapter Review (continued)

third postoperative day, you assess that the patient has short-term memory deficits. What are your plans to achieve discharge as expected on postoperative day 5 to 7?

NCLEX-Style Review Questions

1. A patient has been diagnosed with cardiac tamponade. Upon assessment, the nurse may expect to find which of the following?
   A. Widened pulse pressure
   B. Pulsus paradoxus
   C. Bradycardia
   D. Systolic pressure increase

2. The nurse is aware that severe aortic stenosis is consistent with which of the following? Select all that apply.
   A. Pulmonary edema
   B. Increased cardiac output
   C. Right-sided HF
   D. Left ventricular hypertrophy

3. The physician has ordered IE antibiotic prophylaxis for a high-risk patient undergoing dental work in a week.

The nurse identifies the need for IE antibiotic prophylaxis for which disease process?
   A. Mitral valve prolapse
   B. Rheumatic heart disease
   C. Prosthetic valve
   D. Bicuspid valve disease

4. Management of patients with cardiomyopathy is directed at preventing and treating HF. The treatment of HF includes which of the following? Select all that apply.
   A. Reducing circulating blood volume
   B. Reducing myocardial oxygen needs
   C. Increasing cardiac output by improving contractility or reducing peripheral resistance.
   D. Increasing preload

5. A patient with chest pain is under the nurse's care. Acute MI is excluded, and the patient is diagnosed with pericarditis. Which of the following medications would the physician be most likely to prescribe initially?
   A. Acetaminophen (Tylenol)
   B. Ibuprofen (Motrin)
   C. Ticarcillin (Ticar)
   D. Colchicine

Try these additional resources to enhance your learning and understanding of this chapter:
- thePoint online resource available at **http://thepoint.lww.com/Pellico1e**
- *Handbook for Focus on Adult Health: Medical-Surgical Nursing*
- *Study Guide for Focus on Adult Health: Medical-Surgical Nursing*

References and Selected Readings

References and selected readings associated with this chapter can be found on the website that accompanies the book. Visit http://thepoint.lww.com/Pellico1e to access the references and other additional resources associated with this chapter.

PRISCILLA K. GAZARIAN

Nursing Management: Patients With Arrhythmias and Conduction Problems

Learning Objectives

After reading this chapter, you will be able to:

1. Describe methods to diagnose and treat arrhythmias.

2. Analyze elements of an electrocardiogram (ECG) rhythm strip: ventricular and atrial rate, ventricular and atrial rhythm, QRS complex and shape, QRS duration, P wave and shape, PR interval, and QT interval.

3. Identify the ECG criteria, causes, and management of several arrhythmias, including conduction disturbances.

4. Use the nursing process as a framework for care of patients with arrhythmias.

5. Compare the different types of electrical therapies, their uses, possible complications, and nursing implications.

6. Describe the key points of using a defibrillator.

Arrhythmias (also called *dysrhythmias*) are disorders of the electrical impulse within the heart that cause disturbances of heart rate, heart rhythm, or both. Without a normal rate and regular rhythm, the heart does not perform efficiently as a pump to circulate oxygenated blood. Arrhythmias may initially produce symptoms related to the hemodynamic effect they cause, such as a decrease in cardiac output. Refer to Table 17-1 for signs and symptoms of a decreased cardiac output. In addition to decreasing the cardiac output, some arrhythmias increase the risk of clot formation within the chambers of the heart. Arrhythmias are named according to the site of origin of the impulse (e.g., atria or ventricular) and the mechanism of formation or **conduction** involved (e.g., bradycardia [too slow], tachycardia [too fast], premature [early], etc.). Their presence is confirmed by electrocardiography.

THE ELECTROCARDIOGRAM

The electrical impulse that travels through the heart can be viewed by means of an electrocardiogram (ECG). Each phase of the cardiac cycle is reflected by specific waveforms (discussed later in the chapter). The number and placement of the electrodes used depend on the type of ECG needed. The electrodes record waveforms that appear on the paper or monitor and represent the electrical current in relation to the two electrodes (Fig. 17-1, p. 463). Heart rate and rhythm may be effectively monitored through only two electrodes; however, the use of 10 electrodes (resulting in 12 leads) provides more detailed information and is the basis for understanding other types of electrocardiographic monitoring. The difference between electrodes, wires, and leads is described in Box 17-1.

THE 12-LEAD ELECTROCARDIOGRAM

The 12-lead ECG is a diagnostic tool that uses 10 electrodes, one placed on each limb and six placed on the chest (precordial). In combination, these 10 electrodes produce 12 different waveforms (or leads). These 12 leads include 3 bipolar leads (I, II, III) and 9 unipolar leads (aVR, aVL, aVF, V_1–V_6). Bipolar leads measure electrical activity traveling between a positive and negative electrode, while unipolar leads record electrical activity from a single reference point. Together, the 12 leads show electrical

TABLE
17-1 Signs and Symptoms of Decreased Cardiac Output

System	Signs and Symptoms of Decreased Cardiac Output
Respiratory	Tachypnea, shortness of breath (SOB), orthopnea, dyspnea on exertion, hypoxemia, crackles on lung auscultation, wheeze, dry or productive cough
Cardiac and peripheral vascular	Edema, jugular vein distention (JVD), displaced point of maximum impulse (PMI), S_3 gallop rhythm, tricuspid and/or mitral regurgitation murmurs, hypotension, decreased mean arterial pressure (MAP), narrow pulse pressure, cool skin and extremities, delayed capillary refill, tachycardia
Renal	Decreased urinary output, oliguria, rising creatinine
Gastrointestinal	Abdominal distention, ascites, liver engorgement, positive abdominojugular reflex
Central nervous	Dizziness, decreased sensorium, syncope, fatigue
Behavioral/emotional	Anxiety, restlessness

BOX 17-1 Understanding Electrodes, Wires, and Leads

Electrodes

Electrodes are electrical contacts that are placed on the patient's skin. They come in various shapes. Today's electrodes are disposable for single patient use. They all contain conductive gel and a connector for a wire.

Wires

The electrode is connected to a recording device by a set of wires or cables. The wires are colored coded, although the coding system is not internationally consistent. For 12-lead ECGs, there are 10 wires, one for each electrode. For continuous monitoring, there may be anywhere from three to five wires. Three- and four-wire systems allow monitoring of limb leads only, whereas five-wire systems allow monitoring of limb leads plus a chest lead. Some wires come preattached to the electrodes and are disposable; others need to be attached to the electrode and are reusable.

Leads

Leads are the images the nurse sees on paper or monitor. They represent an examination of the heart from a specific viewpoint. The direction of the ECG complex varies depending on which lead is viewed. The direction of the electric current determines how the waveforms appear on paper.

activity in both a frontal plane and a transverse plane. When viewed together, these two planes provide important diagnostic information beyond heart rate and rhythm, including conduction abnormalities such as bundle branch block (BBB), heart chamber enlargement, localization of ischemia or infarction, and even noncardiac conditions such as electrolyte imbalances (Wagner, 2007). Consider taking a picture of a statue from 12 different angles: When merged, a composite picture of the entire statue is achievable, but the viewer is also capable of analyzing unique details of the picture when selecting to view a specific angle—thus it is for ECG monitoring. The 12-lead ECG produces a picture of the heart, whereas particular leads view specific areas of the heart.

Electrode placement for a 12-lead ECG must be accurate and consistent, as misplacement can result in altered waveforms. Electrode placement is important in arrhythmia identification and is crucial in identifying changes related to ischemia (decreased blood flow often due to atherosclerosis), infarction (cellular damage or death because of limited blood supply), and many arrhythmias (American Association of Critical Care Nurses, 2008).

The four limb electrodes are placed on the lower legs, near the ankles, and on the arms, near the wrists. The remaining six electrodes are placed across the left side of the chest. Locating the specific anatomical landmark is critical for correct chest electrode placement (Box 17-2, p. 464). If the patient needs a series of ECGs, consistency of electrode placement is also important. In some cases, the chest electrodes are left in place or the correct location is marked with an indelible pen to ensure the identical placement for follow-up ECGs.

The specific locations for electrode placement are shown in Figure 17-2 on page 464.

V_1 Right side of the sternum, fourth intercostal space
V_2 Left side of the sternum, fourth intercostal space
V_3 Midway between V_2 and V_4.
V_4 Mid-clavicular line, fifth intercostal space
V_5 Left anterior axillary line, same level as V_4
V_6 Left midaxillary line, same level as V_4 (Aehlert, 2007)

The precordial (anterior surface over the heart) leads reflect the electrical activity primarily in the left ventricle. In some circumstances, an alternative electrode placement may be required. For example, in patients with suspected right-sided heart damage, right-sided chest leads are required to evaluate the right ventricle (see Fig. 17-2). Electrodes for V_1R (R refers to the right chest) through V_6R

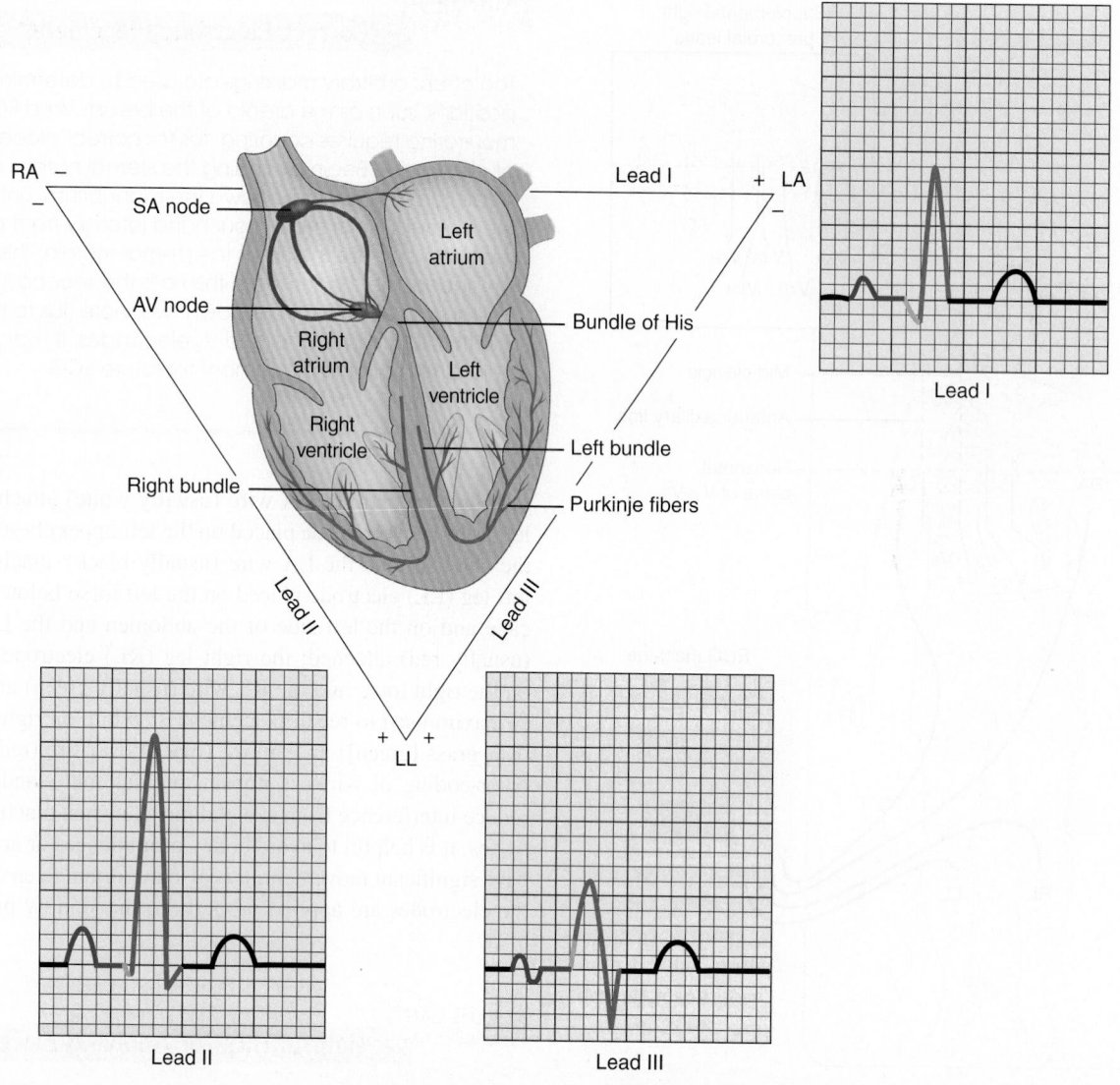

FIGURE 17-1 Relationship of electrocardiogram (ECG) complex, lead system, and electrical impulse. The heart conducts electrical activity, which the ECG measures and records. The configurations of electrical activity displayed on the ECG vary depending on the lead (or view) of the ECG and on the rhythm of the heart. Therefore, the configuration of a normal rhythm tracing from lead I will differ from the configuration of a normal rhythm tracing from lead II, lead II will differ from lead III, and so on. The same is true for abnormal rhythms and cardiac disorders. To make an accurate assessment of the heart's electrical activity or to identify where, when, and what abnormalities occur, the ECG needs to be evaluated from every lead, not just from lead II. Here the different areas of electrical activity are identified by color. RA, right arm; LA, left arm; SA, sinoatrial; AV, atrioventricular; LL, left arm.

are placed in the mirror image of the left chest electrodes as detailed here:

V_1R Left side of the sternum, fourth intercostal space
V_2R Right side of the sternum, fourth intercostal space
V_3R Midway between V_2 and V_4
V_4R Mid-clavicular line, fifth intercostal space
V_5R Right anterior axillary line, same level as V_4
V_6R Right midaxillary line, same level as V_4

CONTINUOUS MONITORING

ECG monitoring systems vary in sophistication, but in general can do the following:

- Monitor one limb lead or one limb lead plus one chest lead
- Monitor ST segments (ST-segment depression is a marker of myocardial ischemia; ST-segment elevation provides evidence of an evolving myocardial infarction [MI])
- Provide graded visual and audible alarms (based on priority, asystole would be highest)
- Provide computerized rhythm monitoring (arrhythmias are interpreted and stored in memory)
- Produce a graphical recording

Continuous monitoring systems have anywhere from three to five electrodes with capability of viewing two to

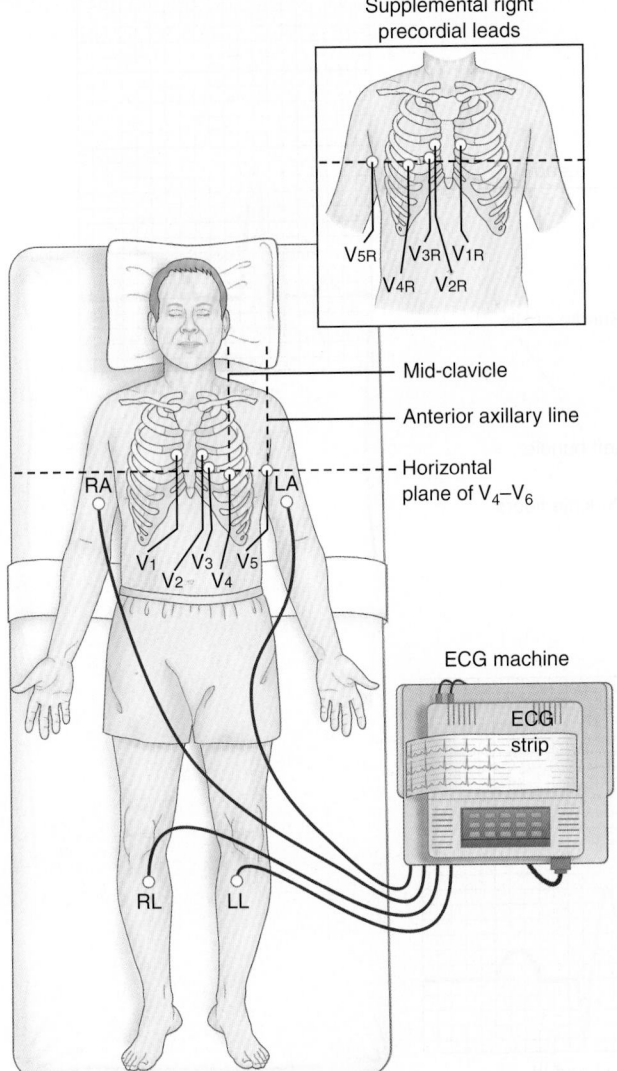

Supplemental right precordial leads

V5R V3R V1R
V4R V2R

Mid-clavicle
Anterior axillary line
Horizontal plane of V₄–V₆

RA   LA

V₁ V₃ V₅
V₂ V₄

ECG machine

ECG strip

RL   LL

FIGURE 17-2 ECG electrode placement. The standard left precordial leads are V₁—fourth intercostal space, right sternal border; V₂—fourth intercostal space, left sternal border; V₃—diagonally between V₂ and V₄; V₄—fifth intercostal space, left midclavicular line; V₅—same level as V₄, anterior axillary line; V₆ (not illustrated)—same level as V₄ and V₅, midaxillary line. The right precordial leads, placed across the right side of the chest, are the mirror opposite of the left leads. RA, right arm; LA, left arm; RL, right leg; LL, left leg. Adapted from Molle, E. A., Kronenberger, J., West-Stack, C., & Durham, L. S. (2005). *Lippincott Williams & Wilkins' Pocket Guide to Medical Assisting* (2nd ed.). Philadelphia: Lippincott Williams & Wilkins.

ten leads. Box 17-3 provides helpful hints on how to apply these electrodes. In continuous monitoring, although limb electrodes are still used, they are positioned on the torso as opposed to the lower legs and arms, as in a 12-lead ECG. This allows for greater patient movement and comfort and reduced interference from skeletal muscle artifact. The four disposable electrodes are positioned on the patient's chest in specific locations and a cable is connected to the monitor or telemetry device in the following arrangement: the right arm (RA) electrode placed on the right upper chest (below

Correct Electrode Placement

Too often, arbitrary markings are used to determine rib positions, such as the areola of the breast. Valid ECG monitoring requires counting ribs for correct placement of electrodes. Begin by finding the sternal notch and slowly move your finger down the manubrium, until a rise is noted. Next, move your hand laterally from the rise until you note the rib at the sternal margin; this is the second rib. Underneath this rib is the second intercostal space (ICS). Count down two more ribs to the fourth ICS and place V₁ and V₂ electrodes. It may be helpful to mark this placement for future ECG placements.

the clavicle) and the RA wire (usually white) attached; the left arm (LA) electrode placed on the left upper chest (below the clavicle) and the LA wire (usually black) attached; the left leg (LL) electrode placed on the left torso below the rib cage and on the left side of the abdomen and the LL wire (usually red) attached; the right leg (RL) electrode placed on the right torso and the RL wire (usually green) attached. A maxim used to recall placement is "white on right (snow over grass [green]) and smoke (black) over fire (red)." The color-coding of wires is not an international standard. To reduce interference from skeletal muscle when placing electrodes, it is helpful to avoid bony prominences or areas that have significant movement. It is also important to ensure that the electrodes are applied properly to the skin by prepping

Helpful Hits for Applying Electrodes

These guidelines optimize skin adherence and the conduction of electrical currents.
- Débride the skin surface of dead cells with soap and water and dry well.
- Clip (do not shave) hair from around the electrode site if needed.
- If the patient is diaphoretic, apply a small amount of benzoin to the skin, avoiding the area under the center of the electrode.
- Connect the electrodes to the lead wires prior to placing them on the chest; peel the backing off the electrode and make sure the center is moist with electrode gel.
- Locate the landmarks for lead placement and use light pressure to secure the electrode.
- Change the electrodes every 24 to 48 hours (or as recommended by the manufacturer), examine the skin for irritation, and apply the electrodes to different locations.
- If the patient is sensitive to the electrodes, use hypoallergenic electrodes.

the skin according to manufacturer's directions and removing excessive chest hair.

The signals are transmitted either directly to a bedside monitor (hardwire) or by radio waves from a small transmitter box to central monitoring station (telemetry).

The most basic monitoring system uses three electrodes to allow monitoring in one of three bipolar limb leads. Leads that can be monitored are lead I (positive electrode on the LA, negative electrode on the RA), lead II (positive electrode on the LL and negative electrode on the RA), and lead III (positive electrode on the LL and negative electrode on the LA). These are useful for heart rate and basic rhythm recognition. They are inadequate for accurately identifying many arrhythmias, especially tachycardias (increased heart rate) with a wide QRS. Bipolar limb lead monitoring systems are often found on portable monitors, defibrillators, and some telemetry ECG devices.

Five-electrode monitoring systems use four electrodes placed as above, in the LA, RA, LL, and RL positions, as well as one chest electrode that can be placed in any one of the precordial locations (V_1–V_6). Monitoring systems with five electrodes permit the nurse to decide which leads will be monitored based on the patient's diagnosis and condition. Five-electrode systems have a display that allows two leads to be monitored simultaneously; typically, the nurse chooses one limb lead and one precordial lead to be viewed. The ability to monitor a limb lead and precordial lead simultaneously is often necessary for accurate identification of many arrhythmias, including arrhythmias with a wide QRS complex (bundle-branch blocks, ventricular pacemaker rhythms, and wide QRS tachycardias). Two leads commonly used for continuous monitoring are leads II and V_1. Lead II provides the best visualization of atrial depolarization (represented by the P wave) and is preferred for monitoring atrial activity and heart rate. Lead V_1 best records ventricular depolarization and is most helpful when monitoring the patient for patients with tachycardias. V_1 is the preferred lead to monitor for wide QRS complex tachycardia (American Association of Critical Care Nurses, 2008; Drew, Califf, Funk, et al., 2004).

Ambulatory Electrocardiography

Ambulatory ECG is a continuous form of monitoring used in the outpatient setting to identify the etiology of distressing symptoms (syncope, palpitations) that may be caused by arrhythmias, myocardial ischemia, or pacemaker dysfunction. The patient wears a portable recording device (i.e., Holter monitor) that is connected to the chest by electrodes and lead wires. The patient keeps a diary while wearing this device, noting the type and time of symptoms or performance of unusual activities.

Transtelephonic Monitoring

Transtelephonic monitoring, a form of outpatient ECG monitoring, transmits ECG signals via the telephone. Chest electrodes are connected to a transmitter box. To send the ECG, the telephone mouthpiece is placed over transmitter box, and the ECG is evaluated at another location. This method is used for diagnosing arrhythmias and evaluating permanent cardiac pacemakers.

Wireless Mobile Cardiac Monitoring Systems

This outpatient monitoring system uses a small sensing device worn by the patient; it transmits the ECG signal to a small monitor. When an arrhythmia is detected, the system transmits the ECG to a monitoring center via a telephone line or a wireless communications system. This system enhances detection and early treatment of arrhythmias.

INTERPRETING THE ELECTROCARDIOGRAM

ECG waveforms are printed on graph paper that is divided by light and dark vertical and horizontal lines at standard intervals (Fig. 17-3). Time and rate are measured on the horizontal axis of the graph, and amplitude or voltage is measured on the vertical axis. Each small block on the graph paper equals **0.04** second, and five small blocks form a large block, which equals **0.2** second. When an ECG waveform moves toward the top of the paper, it is called a *positive deflection*. When it moves toward the bottom of the paper, it is called a *negative deflection*.

The ECG is composed of waveforms (including the P wave, the QRS complex, the T wave, and possibly a U wave) and of segments or intervals (PR interval, the ST segment, and the QT interval) (see Fig. 17-3).

The **P wave** represents the electrical impulse starting in the sinus node and spreading through the atria (atrial **depolarization** leading to atrial contraction).

The **QRS complex** represents ventricular depolarization. Not all QRS complexes have all three waveforms. The Q wave is the first negative deflection after the P wave. The R wave is the first positive deflection after the P wave, and the S wave is the first negative deflection after the R wave. The QRS complex is normally less than 0.10 seconds in duration (2½ small boxes).

The **T wave** represents ventricular repolarization or electrical recovery. It follows the QRS complex and is usually in the same direction as the QRS complex. Atrial repolarization also occurs but is not visible on the ECG because it occurs at the same time as the QRS.

The **U wave** may or may not be present, and is thought to represent repolarization of the Purkinje fibers; it is, however, sometimes seen in patients with hypokalemia (low potassium levels), hypertension, or heart disease. If present, the U wave follows the T wave and is usually smaller than the P wave. If tall, it may be mistaken for an extra P wave.

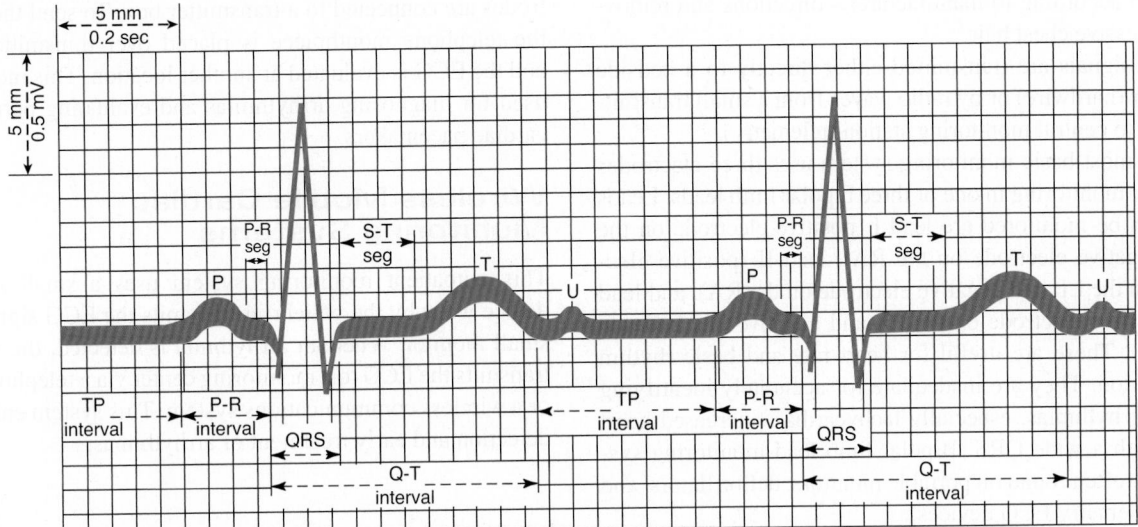

FIGURE 17-3 ECG and commonly measured components. Each small box represents 0.04 seconds on the horizontal axis and 1 mm or 0.1 millivolt on the vertical axis. The PR interval is measured from the beginning of the P wave to the beginning of the QRS complex; the QRS complex is measured from the beginning of the Q wave to the end of the S wave; the QT interval is measured from the beginning of the Q wave to the end of the T wave; and the TP interval is measured from the end of the T wave to the beginning of the next P wave.

The **PR interval** is measured from the beginning of the P wave to the beginning of the QRS complex and represents the time needed for sinus node stimulation, atrial depolarization, and conduction through the AV node before ventricular depolarization. In adults, the normal range for the PR is 0.12 to 0.20 seconds.

The **ST segment**, which represents early ventricular repolarization, lasts from the end of the QRS complex to the beginning of the T wave. The beginning of the ST segment is usually identified by a change in the thickness or angle of the terminal portion of the QRS complex and is called the *J point*. The end of the ST segment may be more difficult to identify because it merges into the T wave. The ST segment is analyzed to identify whether it is above or below the **isoelectric line**, which may be, among other signs and symptoms, a sign of cardiac ischemia (see Chapter 14).

> ⚠ **NURSING ALERT**
> *Nurses should note ST segment changes, as they may indicate:*
> - *ST segment depression is seen with ischemia*
> - *ST segment elevation is seen with injury*
> - *Q waves are seen with necrosis and infarction*

The **QT interval**, which represents the total time for ventricular depolarization and repolarization, is measured from the beginning of the QRS complex to the end of the T wave. The QT interval varies with heart rate, gender, and age. If the QT interval becomes prolonged, the patient may be at risk for a lethal ventricular arrhythmia called *torsades de pointes*. The corrected QT (QTc) is calculated based on heart rate and

is a more determinant of risk for torsades de pointes arrhythmia. The nurse should measure the QT interval every 8 to 12 hours and calculate the QTc on printouts of rhythm strips from the bedside or telemetry monitor for patients at risk for torsades de pointes. A QTc greater than 0.47 second for males or greater than 0.48 second for females is indicative of increased risk of torsades de pointes, and a QTc of more than 0.50 second is considered dangerously prolonged (Sommargren & Drew, 2007).

The PP and RR intervals are measured from the beginning of one P or R wave to the beginning of the next P or R wave. The PP interval is used to determine atrial rate and rhythm. The RR interval is measured from one QRS complex to the next QRS complex. The RR interval is used to determine ventricular rate and rhythm (Fig. 17-4).

ANALYZING THE ELECTROCARDIOGRAM RHYTHM STRIP

The ECG must be analyzed in a systematic manner to determine the patient's cardiac rhythm and to detect arrhythmias and conduction disorders. If continuous ST segment monitoring is in use, evidence of myocardial ischemia, injury, and infarction may also be detected (Flanders, 2007). Box 17-4 is an example of a method that can be used to analyze the patient's rhythm.

Normal **sinus rhythm** occurs when the electrical impulse starts at the sinus node and travels through the normal conduction pathway. Normal sinus rhythm serves as a baseline

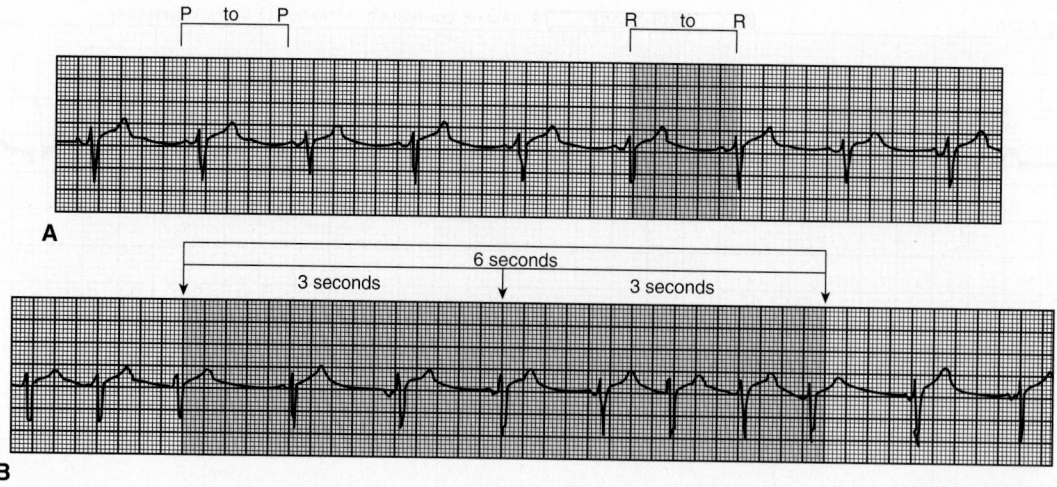

FIGURE 17-4 **(A)** Ventricular and atrial heart rate determination with a regular rhythm: 1,500 divided by the number of small boxes between two P waves (atrial rate) or between two R waves (ventricular rate). In this example, there are 25 small boxes between both the R waves and the P waves, so the heart rate is 60 bpm. **(B)** Heart rate determination if the rhythm is irregular. There are approximately seven RR intervals in 6 seconds, so there are about 70 RR intervals in 60 seconds ($7 \times 10 = 70$). The ventricular heart rate is 70 bpm.

BOX 17-4

Interpreting Arrhythmias: Systematic Analysis of the Electrocardiogram

Step 1: Determine the heart rate

The heart rate is usually visible on the monitor display or on the printed rhythm strip. However, the monitor will also record "artifact," which may alter the heart rate. The heart rate should always be confirmed by one of the following methods.

Six-second method

Locate the 3-second markers along the top or bottom of the ECG paper. Count the number of R waves (ventricular rate) or P waves (atrial rate) occurring between two 3-second markers (thus total time is 6 seconds) and multiply by 10 (thus, 60 seconds or 1 minute).

Large box method

Count the number of large boxes between two consecutive R waves (ventricular rate) or P waves (atrial rate) and divide into 300. If, for example, there are four large boxes between two R waves, the heart rate is 300/4, or 75.

Small box method

Count the number of small boxes between two consecutive R (ventricular rate) or P waves (atrial rate) waves and divide into 1,500. If, for example, there are 10 small boxes between two R waves, the heart rate is 1500/10, or 150 (see Fig. 17-4).

The normal heart rate is between 60 and 100. The term *bradycardia* is used when the heart rate is below 60, whereas *tachycardia* refers to rates above 100.

Step 2: Determine the rhythm regularity

Measure the distance between two consecutive R waves (ventricular regularity) or between two consecutive P waves (atrial regularity). Compare the distance between other R-R or P-P intervals. If the distance is consistent, the rhythm is regular; if the distance varies, the rhythm is irregular. The normal rhythm is regular.

Step 3: Determine if the rhythm originated in the SA node

Look for a P wave and determine if there is one P wave for every QRS. Determine if the size and shape of the P wave is consistent. The normal rhythm has one P wave for every QRS complex. Because P waves represent the contraction across both atria, irregularities in shape are noted with conduction defect within the atrium, atrial enlargement, or hypertrophy.

Step 4: Evaluate conduction

Measure the PR interval, the QRS duration. The normal PR interval is between 0.12 (3 small boxes) and 0.20 (5 small boxes) seconds. The normal QRS interval is less than .10 seconds (2½ small boxes). QRS duration of more than 0.10 is termed "wide QRS" and is indicative of abnormal ventricular conduction, such as BBBs or ventricular tachycardia.

Step 5: Evaluate the appearance of the rhythm

Look for premature beats or elevated or depressed ST segments. ST elevation/depression is associated with ventricular injury/ischemia.

Step 6: Interpret the rhythm

Compare the findings to the defining characteristics of specified arrhythmias.

Step 7: If a change is noted from the patient's baseline, evaluate the patient, consider obtaining a 12-lead ECG, and report the change to the provider as appropriate.

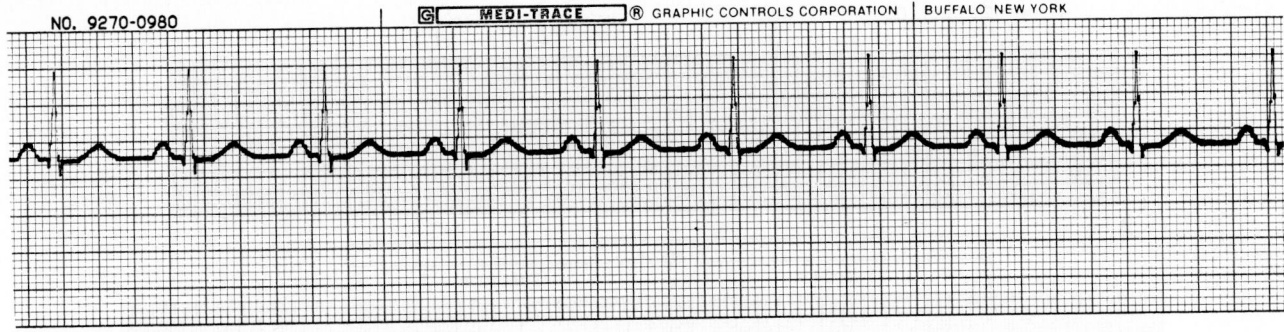

FIGURE 17-5 Normal sinus rhythm in lead II.

for comparison in identifying all other arrhythmias. ECG characteristics are as follows:

Rate: 60 to 100 in the adult
Rhythm: Regular
P wave: Normal and consistent shape; always in front of the QRS
PR interval: Consistent interval between 0.12 and 0.20 seconds
QRS duration: Less than 0.10 seconds

See Figure 17-5 above.

ARRHYTHMIAS

SINUS NODE ARRHYTHMIAS

SINUS ARRHYTHMIA

Sinus arrhythmia occurs when the sinus node creates an impulse at an irregular rhythm. Sometimes the irregularity is associated with the respiratory cycle. The rate increases with inspiration and decreases with expiration because the SA node fires more quickly with inspiration. Sinus arrhythmia does not cause any significant hemodynamic effect and is not clinically significant. It occurs frequently in the young and decreases with age.

SINUS BRADYCARDIA

Pathophysiology

Sinus bradycardia occurs when the sinus node creates an impulse at a slower-than-normal rate. Causes include lower metabolic needs (e.g., sleep, athletic training, hypothyroidism), vagal stimulation (e.g., from vomiting, suctioning, severe pain, extreme emotions), medications (e.g., calcium channel blockers, amiodarone, beta blockers), increased intracranial pressure (ICP), and myocardial infarction (MI), especially of the inferior wall.

Clinical Manifestations and Assessment

Sinus bradycardia often does not cause symptoms. The patient is assessed to determine the hemodynamic effect, if any, and the possible cause of the arrhythmia.

ECG characteristics are:

Rate: Less than 60 beats per minute (bpm)
Rhythm: Regular
P wave: Present before each QRS and consistent in size and shape
PR interval: Normal
QRS duration: Normal

See Figure 17-6 below.

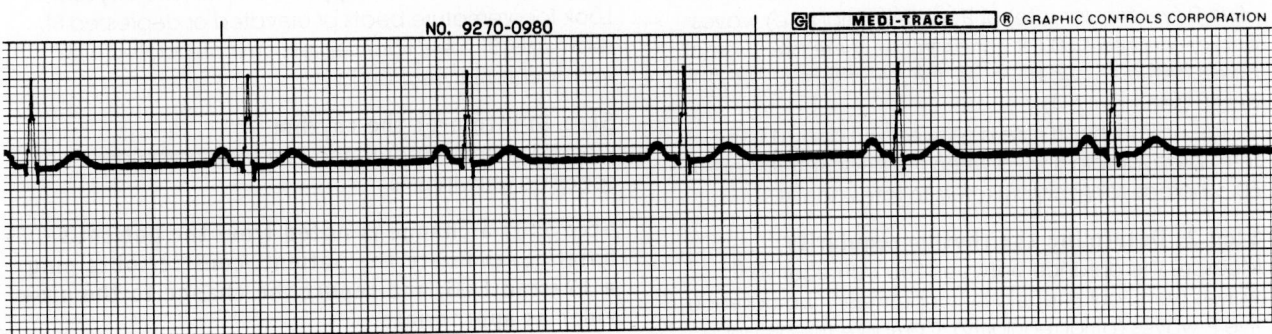

FIGURE 17-6 Sinus bradycardia in lead II.

Medical and Nursing Management

Only bradycardias that cause serious signs and symptoms (altered mental status, ongoing chest pain, hypotension, or shock) require immediate treatment. Treatment of symptomatic bradycardia includes transcutaneous pacing and atropine. If pacing is unavailable or ineffective, a dopamine or epinephrine infusion may be considered (Field, 2008). If significant bradycardia is due to medications, they should be held, and their necessity is reevaluated.

SINUS TACHYCARDIA

Pathophysiology

Sinus tachycardia occurs when the sinus node creates an impulse at a faster-than-normal rate. Causes may include the following:

- Physiologic or psychological stress (e.g., acute blood loss, anemia, shock, hypervolemia, hypovolemia, heart failure, pain, hypermetabolic states, fever, exercise, anxiety)
- Medications that stimulate the sympathetic response (e.g., catecholamines, aminophylline, atropine), stimulants (e.g., caffeine, alcohol, nicotine), and illicit drugs (e.g., amphetamines, cocaine, Ecstasy)

Clinical Manifestations and Assessment

Sinus tachycardia often does not cause symptoms. As the heart rate increases, the diastolic filling time decreases, possibly resulting in reduced cardiac output and associated symptoms (refer to Table 17-1). If the rapid rate persists and the heart can no longer compensate for the decreased ventricular filling, the patient may develop acute pulmonary edema or cardiac ischemia.

ECG characteristics are:

Rate: Greater than 100 bpm
Rhythm: Regular
P wave: Present before each QRS and consistent in size and shape

PR interval: Normal
QRS duration: Normal

See Figure 17-7 below.

Medical and Nursing Management

Treatment of sinus tachycardia is usually determined by the severity of symptoms and directed at identifying and treating its cause. For example, tachycardia caused by acute blood loss would be treated with IV fluid replacement and blood transfusion.

ATRIAL ARRHYTHMIAS

PREMATURE ATRIAL COMPLEX

Pathophysiology

A premature atrial complex (PAC) is a single ECG complex that occurs when an electrical impulse starts in the atrium before the next normal impulse of the sinus node. The PAC may be caused by caffeine, alcohol, nicotine, stretched atrial myocardium (e.g., as in hypervolemia), anxiety, hypokalemia (low potassium level), hypermetabolic states (e.g., with pregnancy), hypoxemia, or atrial ischemia, injury, or infarction.

Clinical Manifestations and Assessment

PACs are common ECG findings, often found without cardiac pathology. The patient may report, "My heart skipped a beat"; however, many times the patient is asymptomatic.

ECG characteristics are:

Rate: Depends on the underlying rhythm
Rhythm: Irregular
P wave: Size and shape of the P wave associated with the premature beat is different from sinus node generated P wave
PR interval: The PR interval of the premature beat is greater than 0.12 seconds but shorter than the sinus generated PR interval
QRS duration: Normal

See Figure 17-8 on page 470.

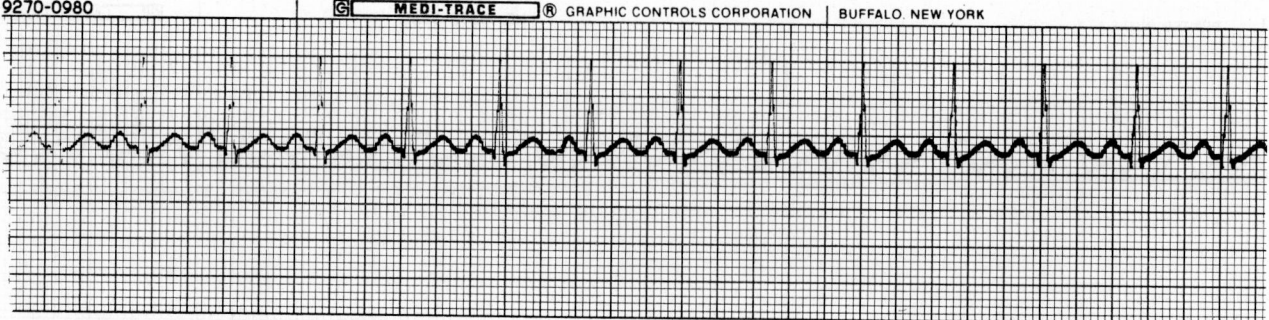

9270-0980 | MEDI-TRACE ® GRAPHIC CONTROLS CORPORATION | BUFFALO, NEW YORK

FIGURE 17-7 Sinus tachycardia in lead II.

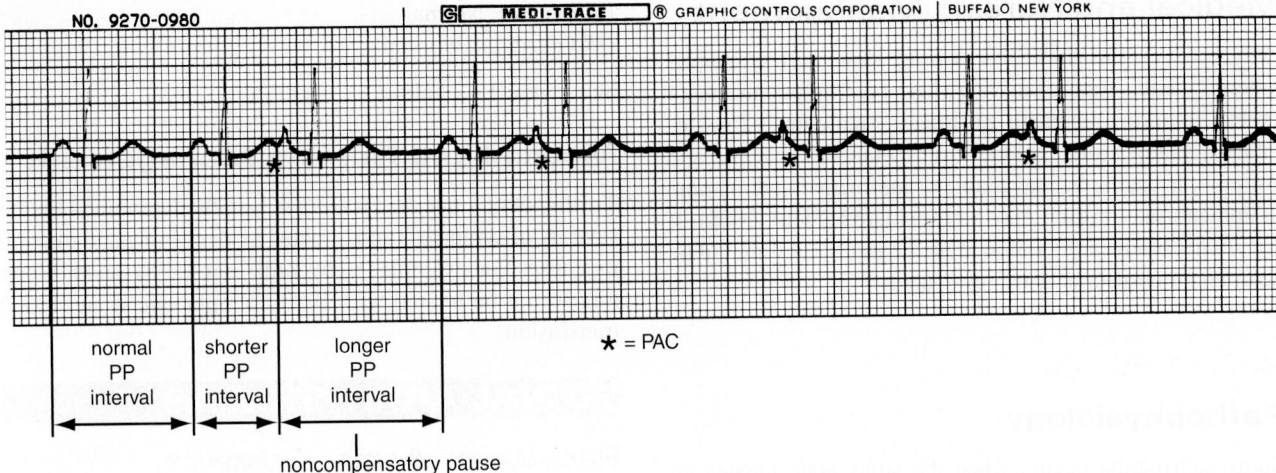

NO. 9270-0980   MEDI-TRACE ® GRAPHIC CONTROLS CORPORATION | BUFFALO NEW YORK

normal PP interval | shorter PP interval | longer PP interval

★ = PAC

noncompensatory pause

FIGURE 17-8 Premature atrial complexes (PACs) in lead II. Note that the pause following the PAC is longer than the normal PP interval but shorter than twice the normal PP interval.

Medical and Nursing Management

If PACs are infrequent, no treatment is necessary since hemodynamic stability is maintained. If they are frequent (more than six per minute), this may be a sign of a worsening condition or the onset of more serious arrhythmias, such as atrial fibrillation.

ATRIAL FLUTTER

Pathophysiology

Atrial flutter occurs in the atrium and creates impulses at a rapid but regular atrial rate between 220 and 350 times per minute. Because the atrial rate is faster than the AV node can conduct, not all atrial impulses are conducted into the ventricle. This is an important feature of this arrhythmia because if all atrial impulses were conducted to the ventricle, the ventricular rate would also be 220 to 350, which would result in a life-threatening arrhythmia. Causes include CAD, hypertension, mitral valve disease, hyperthyroidism, chronic lung disease, cor pulmonale (right ventricular failure), and cardiomyopathy. Occurrence of atrial flutter increases the patient's risk for developing atrial fibrillation (Ng, Altemose, Wu et al., 2008).

Clinical Manifestations and Assessment

Atrial flutter may not cause symptoms or can cause serious signs and symptoms, such as fatigue, lightheadedness, chest pain, shortness of breath, and low blood pressure. The risk of mural (wall) emboli forming in the atria increases with this arrhythmia because without a strong atrial contraction, stasis of blood occurs; therefore the nurse is alert for signs of pulmonary or systemic emboli.

ECG characteristics are:

Rate: Atrial rate ranges between 220 and 350 bpm; ventricular rate usually ranges between 75 and 150 depending on AV node conduction.

Rhythm: Usually regular, but may be irregular because of a change in the AV conduction.

P wave: Flutter waves in a characteristic "sawtooth" pattern

PR interval: Not measurable

QRS duration: Normal

See Figure 17-9 below.

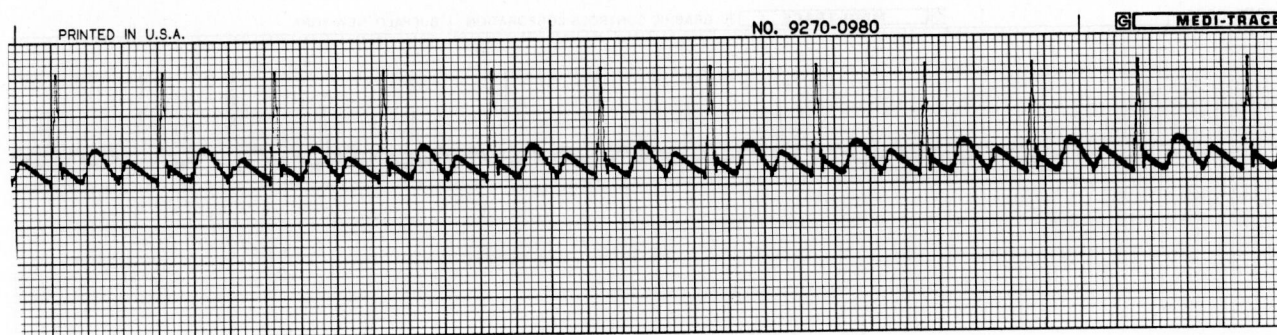

PRINTED IN U.S.A.   NO. 9270-0980   MEDI-TRACE

FIGURE 17-9 Atrial flutter in lead II.

Medical and Nursing Management

If the patient is unstable, urgent electrical **cardioversion** is usually indicated (discussed later in this chapter). If the patient is stable, the QRS is narrow, and the RR interval is regular, adenosine (Adenocard) may be rapidly administered IV. If the adenosine fails to convert the rhythm or if the RR interval is irregular, pharmacologic cardioversion with class IA, class IC, or class III antiarrhythmic agents (Table 17-2) may be administered IV to slow conduction through the AV node.

🜸 DRUG ALERT

Adenosine (Adenocard) 6 mg may be ordered as this agent slows conduction time through the AV node. The dose is administered by rapid IV push (1 to 2 seconds), followed with a rapid saline flush. Vital signs should be monitored. Side effects include nausea, headache, facial flushing, and shortness of breath but are short-lived owing to the drug's short duration of action (seconds). Cardiac effects include bradycardia, hypotension, and sinus arrest. If the initial dose is ineffective in breaking the flutter within 1 to 2 minutes, 12 mg may be ordered as a rapid IV bolus.

If medication therapy is unsuccessful, electrical cardioversion is often successful. If the arrhythmia has lasted for longer than 48 hours, anticoagulation may be indicated before cardioversion. Once conversion has occurred, an antiarrhythmic agent may be given to prevent a recurrence (see Table 17-2).

ATRIAL FIBRILLATION

Pathophysiology

Atrial fibrillation causes a rapid, disorganized, and uncoordinated electrical activity within the atria. Atrial fibrillation may be transient, starting and stopping suddenly and occurring for a very short time (**paroxysmal**), or it may be persistent, requiring treatment to terminate the rhythm or to control the ventricular rate. The erratic atrial contraction promotes formation of thrombi within the atria, increasing the risk for an embolic event such as stroke (brain attack). Atrial fibrillation is usually associated with advanced age, valvular heart disease, CAD, hypertension, heart failure, cardiomyopathy, diabetes, hyperthyroidism, pulmonary disease, chronic lung disease, and surgery (especially open heart surgery). Physiological stressors such as hypoxia, infection, and hypoglycemia, as well as caffeine and sympathomimetic drugs are also associated with atrial fibrillation. Sometimes atrial fibrillation occurs in people without any underlying pathophysiology.

TABLE
17-2 Summary of Antiarrhythmic Medications*

Class	Action	Drugs Generic (Trade) Names
IA	Moderate depression of depolarization; prolongs repolarization Treats and prevents atrial and ventricular arrhythmias	quinidine (Quinaglute, Quinidex, Cardioquin) procainamide (Pronestyl) disopyramide (Norpace)
IB	Minimal depression of depolarization; shortened repolarization Treats ventricular arrhythmias	lidocaine (Xylocaine) mexiletine (Mexitil) tocainide (Tonocard)
IC	Marked depression of depolarization; little effect on repolarization Treats atrial and ventricular arrhythmias	flecainide (Tambocor) propafenone (Rythmol)
II	Decreases automaticity and conduction Treats atrial and ventricular arrhythmias	atenolol (Tenormin) bisoprolol/HCTZ (Ziac, Zebeta) esmolol (Brevibloc) labetalol (Trandate) metoprolol (Lopressor, Toprol) propranolol (Inderal, Innopran)
III	Prolongs repolarization Treats and prevents ventricular and atrial arrhythmias, especially in patients with ventricular dysfunction	amiodarone (Cordarone, Pacerone) dofetilide (Tikosyn) ibutilide (Corvert) sotalol (Betapace; Sorine)
IV	Blocks calcium channel Treats atrial arrhythmias	verapamil (Calan, Isoptin) diltiazem (Cardizem, Dilacor, Tiazac, Diltia, Cartia) bepridil (Vascor)

*Based on Vaughn-Williams classification.

Clinical Manifestations and Assessment

People with atrial fibrillation may be asymptomatic. A rapid ventricular response reduces the time for ventricular filling, resulting in a smaller stroke volume. Additionally, loss of the atrial contraction (sometimes referred to as *atrial kick*) reduces ventricular filling volume and reduces cardiac output by 25%. This leads to symptoms of fatigue and malaise. The shorter time in diastole reduces the time available for coronary artery perfusion, thereby increasing the risk for myocardial ischemia.

ECG characteristics are:

Rate: Atrial rate is 300 to 400, with a variable ventricular response rate (typically rapid)
Rhythm: Irregular
P wave: No discernible P waves; irregular undulating waves may be seen and are referred to as *fibrillatory waves*
PR interval: Not measurable
QRS duration: Normal

See Figure 17-10 below.

Medical and Nursing Management

Treatment of atrial fibrillation depends on its cause and duration and the patient's symptoms, age, and comorbidities. The management of atrial fibrillation includes controlling the ventricular rate and achieving rhythm conversion to sinus rhythm if possible. Electrical cardioversion is indicated for atrial fibrillation that is hemodynamically unstable (Cordina, & Mead, 2008). Because of the high risk for embolization of atrial thrombi, cardioversion of atrial fibrillation that has lasted longer than 48 hours should be avoided unless the patient has received anticoagulants. For atrial fibrillation of acute onset (usually defined as that with an onset within 48 hours), IV adenosine (Adenocard) has been used to achieve cardioversion to sinus rhythm as well as to assist in the diagnosis.

> **NURSING ALERT**
> *If the QRS is wide and the ventricular rhythm is irregular, atrial fibrillation with an accessory pathway such as Wolff-Parkinson White syndrome, should be suspected. Medications that block AV conduction (e.g., adenosine [Adenocard], digoxin, diltiazem [Cardizem], and verapamil [Calan]) should be avoided because they may actually cause an increase in ventricular rate given that conduction is via an alternative pathway, not via the AV node. Expert consultation may be required to determine appropriate treatment.*

Warfarin is indicated if the patient with atrial fibrillation is at high risk for stroke (i.e., >75 years of age or has hypertension, diabetes, heart failure, or history of stroke). If immediate anticoagulation is necessary, the patient may be placed on heparin until the warfarin level is therapeutic. Pacemaker implantation or catheter ablation is sometimes indicated for patients who are unresponsive to medications. Catheter ablation is an invasive procedure during which high-frequency radio waves are applied to destroy the tissue at the site of the arrhythmia. Ablation procedures are usually performed in electrophysiologic labs and are similar to other types of heart catheterization. During a catheter ablation, long, thin, flexible tubes are placed in the heart via the vascular system. A diagnostic catheter determines where the abnormal tissue that is causing the arrhythmia is located. High-frequency energy is sent into the tissue, creating a lesion or scar. The area is now ablated (destroyed), thus facilitating normal electrical conduction.

Several approaches are effective in preventing the occurrence of postoperative atrial fibrillation, including preoperative administration of a beta blocker or immediate postoperative administration of IV amiodarone (Kern, McRae, & Funk, 2007).

JUNCTIONAL ARRHYTHMIAS

JUNCTION RHYTHM

Pathophysiology

Junctional rhythm occurs when the AV node, instead of the sinus node, becomes the pacemaker of the heart. When the sinus node slows (e.g., from increased vagal tone) or when the impulse cannot be conducted through the AV node

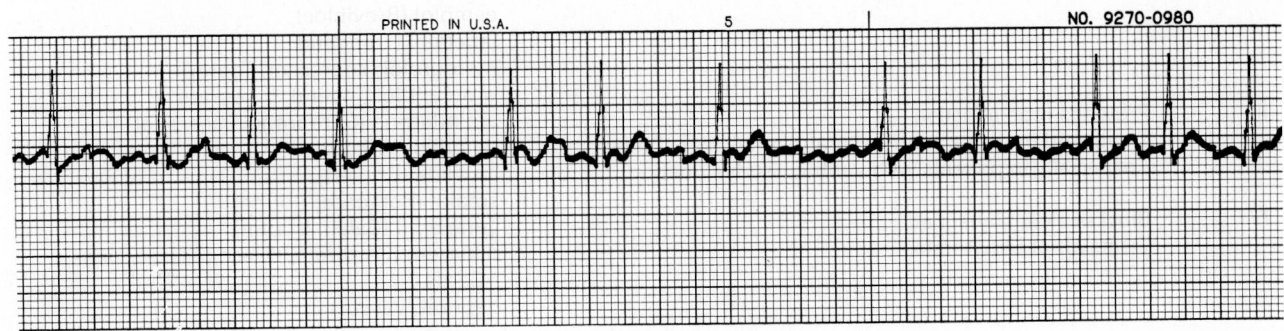

FIGURE 17-10 Atrial fibrillation in lead II.

(e.g., because of complete heart block), the AV node automatically discharges an impulse. Junctional escape rhythm may be caused by acute coronary syndromes, valvular disease, hypoxia, increased parasympathetic tone or the effects of medication including digoxin, beta blockers, and calcium channel blockers.

Clinical Manifestations and Assessment

The patient may be asymptomatic or experience signs and symptoms associated with a decreased cardiac output.

ECG characteristics are:

Rate: 40–60 bpm
Rhythm: Regular
P wave: If visible, may be before, during or after the QRS
PR interval: If a P wave is visible, less than 0.12 seconds
QRS duration: Normal

See Figure 17-11 below.

Medical and Nursing Management

If symptomatic, the treatment is the same as for bradycardia; the patient may be treated with pacing (temporary or permanent), or IV atropine, or epinephrine.

VENTRICULAR ARRHYTHMIAS

ABNORMAL VENTRICULAR CONDUCTION (BUNDLE BRANCH BLOCK)

Pathophysiology

If there is a delay or defect in the conduction system within the ventricles (right and left bundle branches), the QRS complex will be prolonged or widened (>0.12 seconds). BBB may be described as right or left and complete or incomplete. BBB may occasionally be present in otherwise healthy individuals but it may also be caused by ventricular enlargement (ventricular hypertrophy or cardiomyopathy) or anteroseptal myocardial ischemia or infarction. BBB may be clinically insignificant, however can be serious when associated with an acute MI.

Medical and Nursing Management

The goal is to treat the underlying cause of the BBB when possible, such as by maximizing medical management of CAD or cardiomyopathy. However, in the presence of an acute MI, BBB may progress to complete heart block, which may require temporary pacing.

PREMATURE VENTRICULAR COMPLEX

Pathophysiology

A premature ventricular complex (PVC) is an impulse that starts in a ventricle and is conducted through the ventricles before the next normal sinus impulse. PVCs can occur in healthy people, especially with intake of caffeine, nicotine, or alcohol. They are also caused by cardiac ischemia or infarction, increased workload on the heart (e.g., exercise, fever, hypervolemia, heart failure, tachycardia), digitalis toxicity, hypoxia, acidosis, or electrolyte imbalances, especially hypokalemia.

Clinical Manifestations and Assessment

The patient may be asymptomatic or complain that their heart "skipped a beat." The effect of a PVC depends on its timing in the cardiac cycle and how much blood was in the ventricles when they contracted. *Bigeminy* is a rhythm in which every other complex is a PVC. In *trigeminy*, every third complex is a PVC, and in *quadrigeminy*, every fourth complex is a PVC.

ECG characteristics are:

Rate: Depends on the underlying rhythm
Rhythm: Regular
P wave: Visibility of P wave depends on the timing of the PVC; may be absent (hidden in the QRS or T wave) or in front of the QRS. If the P wave follows the QRS, the shape of the P wave may be different.

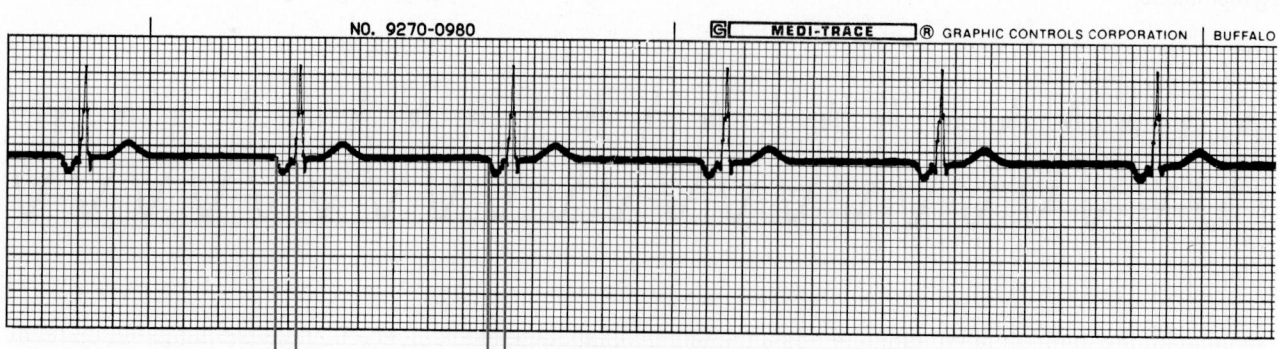

NO. 9270-0980   MEDI-TRACE ® GRAPHIC CONTROLS CORPORATION | BUFFALO

FIGURE 17-11 Junctional rhythm in lead II; note short PR intervals.

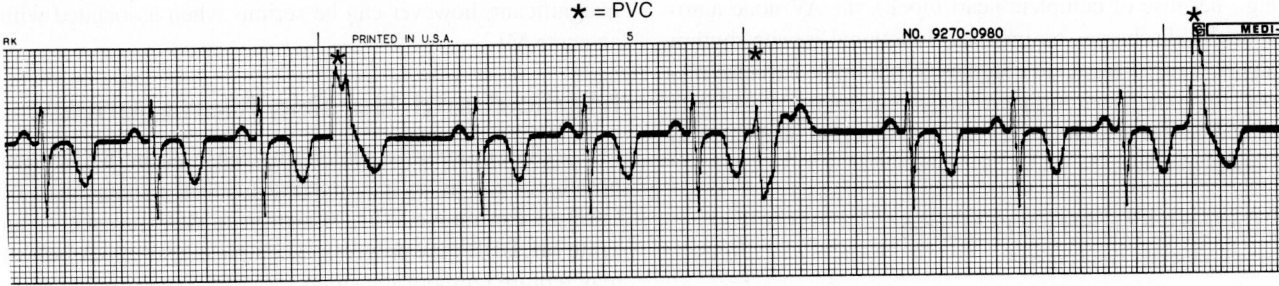

FIGURE 17-12 Multifocal premature ventricular complexes (PVCs) in quadrigeminy in lead V₁.

PR interval: If the P wave is in front of the QRS, the PR interval is less than 0.12 seconds.

QRS duration: Duration of the QRS in a PVC is 0.12 seconds or longer (wide); shape is bizarre and abnormal.

See Figure 17-12 above.

Medical and Nursing Management

Initial treatment is aimed at correcting the cause. Long-term pharmacotherapy for PVCs is not indicated unless the patient is symptomatic. In the absence of disease, PVCs usually are not serious. In the patient with an acute MI, PVCs may be more frequent and reflect the underlying heart disease.

VENTRICULAR TACHYCARDIA

Pathophysiology

Ventricular tachycardia (VT) is defined as three or more consecutive ventricular beats, occurring at a rate exceeding 100 bpm. The causes are similar to those of PVC. Ventricular tachycardia is usually associated with CAD and may precede ventricular fibrillation. Untreated ventricular tachycardia can deteriorate into ventricular fibrillation, a lethal arrhythmia.

Clinical Manifestations and Assessment

The patient can experience a range of symptoms related to decreased cardiac output, such as hypotension or syncope, pulselessness, and unresponsiveness. Some patients may be asymptomatic.

ECG characteristics are:

Rate: 100–250 bpm
Rhythm: Regular
P wave: Usually not visible; if visible are not associated with the QRS complex (called *dissociation*).
PR interval: None
QRS duration: Greater than 0.12 seconds

See Figure 17-13 below.

Medical and Nursing Management

The patient's tolerance for this rapid rhythm depends on the ventricular rate and underlying disease. Several factors determine the initial treatment, including the following: identifying the rhythm as monomorphic (having a consistent QRS shape and rate) or polymorphic (having varying QRS shapes and rhythms); determining the existence of a prolonged QT interval before the initiation of VT; and ascertaining the patient's heart function. If the patient is stable, continuing the assessment, especially obtaining a 12-lead ECG, may be the only action necessary. Amiodarone administered IV is the antiarrhythmic medication of choice for a stable patient with VT. Cardioversion is the treatment of choice for monophasic VT in a symptomatic patient. Atrial fibrillation should be suspected as the cause of a wide complex tachycardia with an irregular rhythm, and it should be treated appropriately.

Torsades de pointes (Fig. 17-14) is a polymorphic VT usually preceded by a prolonged QT interval (Sommargren &

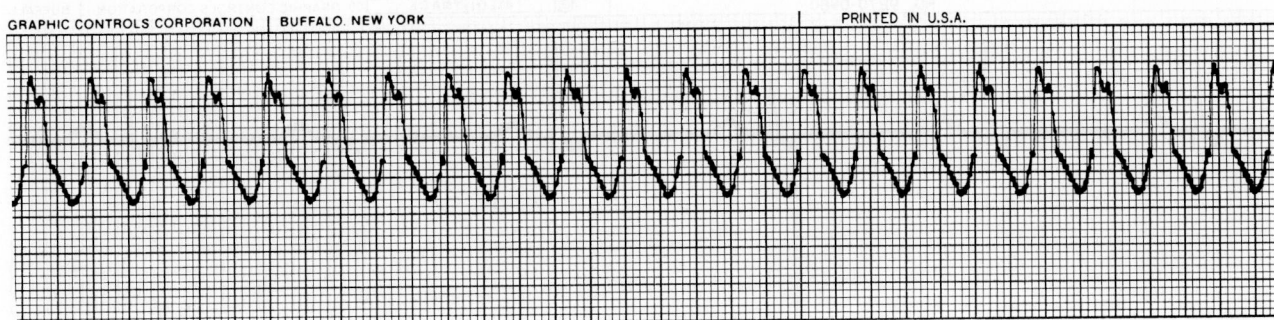

FIGURE 17-13 Ventricular tachycardia in lead V₁.

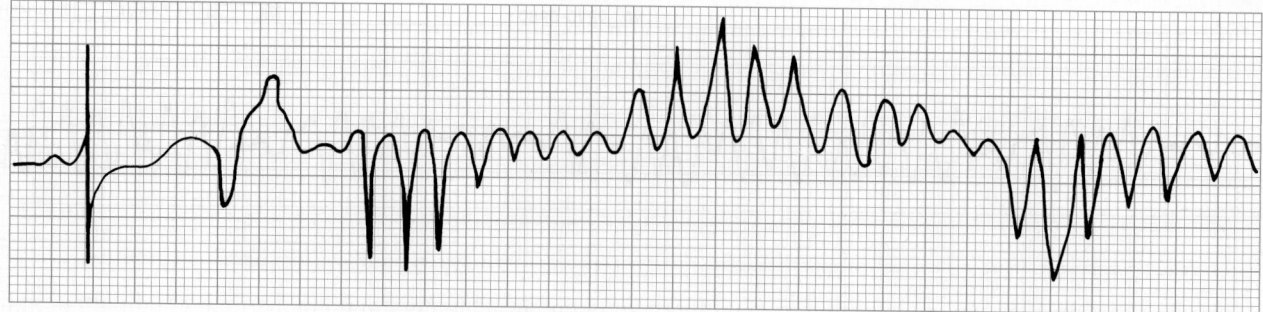

FIGURE 17-14 Torsades de Pointes. From Lippincott. (2005). *Just the Facts: ECG Interpretation*. Philadelphia: Lippincott Williams & Wilkins.

Drew, 2007). Risk factors for torsades de pointes are described in Box 17-5. Because this rhythm is likely to cause the patient to deteriorate and become pulseless, immediate treatment is usually required. Magnesium has frequently been used to treat torsades, but its use has not been proven effective (American Heart Association [AHA], 2010). Any type of VT in a patient who is unconscious and without a pulse is treated in the same manner as ventricular fibrillation: immediate **defibrillation** is the action of choice.

NURSING ALERT

When caring for a patient experiencing an emergent cardiac arrhythmia.

1. *Assess the patient's condition.*
2. *If patient has a loss of respirations, a loss of pulse, a decrease in their level of consciousness, or significant change in blood pressure, call a cardiac arrest code. If the patient is alert without a significant change in vital signs, call for a rapid response team or alert provider stat to the patient's change in condition.*
3. *While awaiting arrival of the medical team, continue to assess the patient, apply supplemental oxygen, ensure adequate IV access, and bring emergency equipment and bedside monitor to the patient's bedside.*

VENTRICULAR FIBRILLATION

Pathophysiology

Ventricular fibrillation is a rapid, disorganized ventricular rhythm that causes ineffective quivering of the ventricles. No atrial activity is seen on the ECG. Causes of ventricular fibrillation are the same as for VT; it may also result from untreated or unsuccessfully treated VT.

Clinical Manifestations and Assessment

Clinical manifestations include absence of an audible heartbeat, a palpable pulse, and respirations. Cardiac arrest and death are imminent.

ECG characteristics are:

Rate: Often cannot be determined, but is greater than 220 bpm
Rhythm: Irregular
P wave: Not visible
PR interval: Not visible
QRS duration: Not visible

See Figure 17-15 on page 476.

Medical and Nursing Management

Treatment of choice is immediate defibrillation if available, immediate cardiopulmonary resuscitation (CPR), and activation of emergency services. After the initial defibrillation, five cycles of CPR, alternating with a rhythm check and defibrillation, are used to convert ventricular fibrillation to an electrical rhythm that produces a pulse. Vasoactive medications (epinephrine, vasopressin, or both) should be administered as soon as possible after the second rhythm check (immediately before or after the second defibrillation). Antiarrhythmic medications (amiodarone, lidocaine, or possibly

---

BOX 17-5 **Risk Factors for Torsades de Pointes**

- Drugs that prolong the QT interval: *Antiarrhythmics* (Disopyramide, dofetilide, ibutilide, procanamide, quinidine, sotalol)*; *antipsychotics* (chlorpromazine, haloperidol, thioridazine); *antibiotics* (pentamidine, clarithromycin, erythromycin), *opiate agonists* (methadone).
- Heart disease: Ischemia/infarction, severe bradycardia, cardiomyopathy
- Electrolyte imbalances: Hypokalemia (serum potassium <3.5 mEq/L), hypomagnesia (serum magnesium <1.8 mEq/L)
- Starvation diet

*Amiodarone may cause a prolonged QTc interval, but does not increase risk of torsades de pointes. From Sommargren, C. E., & Drew, B. J. (2007). Preventing torsades de pointes by careful monitoring in hospital settings. *AACN Advanced Critical Care, 18*(3), 285–293.

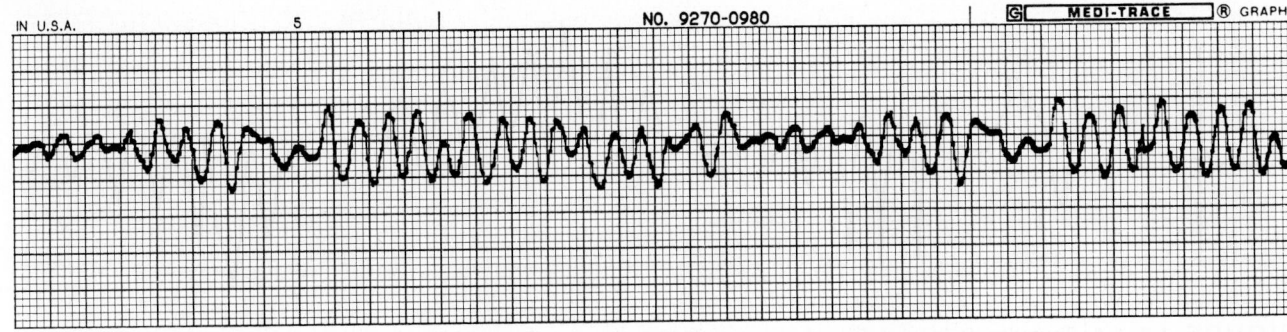

FIGURE 17-15 Ventricular fibrillation in lead II.

magnesium) should be administered as soon as possible after the third rhythm check (immediately before or after the third defibrillation). Once the patient is intubated, CPR should be administered continuously with one breath every 6 to 8 seconds, not in cycles of 30 compressions to two ventilations, and the rhythm check and medication administration should occur every 2 minutes. In addition, underlying and contributing factors are identified and eliminated throughout the event (AHA, 2005).

Idioventricular Rhythm

Pathophysiology

Idioventricular rhythm, also called *ventricular escape rhythm*, occurs when the impulse starts in the conduction system below the AV node. When the sinus node fails to create an impulse (e.g., from increased vagal tone) or when the impulse is created but cannot be conducted through the AV node (e.g., due to complete AV block), the Purkinje fibers automatically discharge an impulse.

Clinical Manifestations and Assessment

Idioventricular rhythm commonly causes the patient to lose consciousness and experience other signs and symptoms of reduced cardiac output.

ECG characteristics are:

Rate: 20 to 40; if the rate exceeds 40, the rhythm is known as *accelerated idioventricular rhythm* (AIVR)
Rhythm: Regular
P wave: Not visible
PR interval: Not visible
QRS duration: Duration is 0.12 seconds or more

See Figure 17-16 below

Medical and Nursing Management

If the patient is in cardiac arrest, treatment is the same as for asystole (absence of electrical activity and pulse); if the patient is not in cardiac arrest, treatment is the same as for bradycardia. Interventions include identifying the underlying cause, administering IV atropine and vasopressor medications, and initiating emergency pacing. In some cases, idioventricular rhythm may cause no symptoms of reduced cardiac output.

Ventricular Asystole

Pathophysiology

Commonly called *flatline*, ventricular asystole is characterized by absent QRS complexes confirmed in two different leads. Asystole is seen in the absence of cardiac electrical activity; because there is no contraction, there is no perfusion.

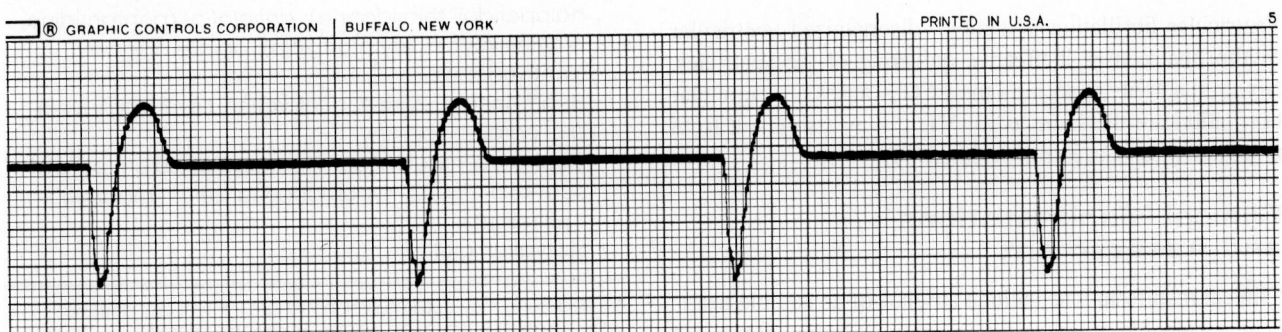

FIGURE 17-16 Idioventricular rhythm in lead V₁.

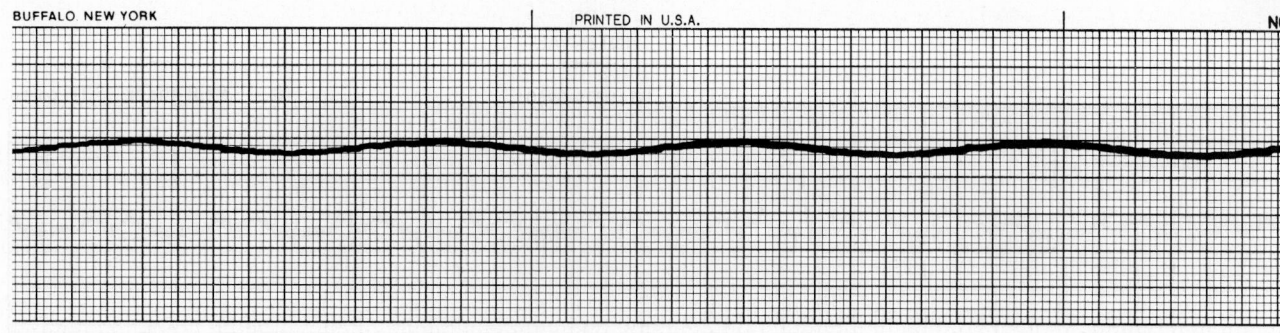

BUFFALO, NEW YORK | PRINTED IN U.S.A. | NO

FIGURE 17-17 Asystole. Always check two different leads to confirm rhythm.

Clinical Manifestations and Assessment

There is no heartbeat, no palpable pulse, and no respiration. Without immediate treatment, ventricular asystole is fatal.
ECG characteristics are:

Rate: Not measurable
Rhythm: Not measurable
P wave: Usually not visible
PR interval: Not measurable
QRS duration: Absent

See Figure 17-17 above.

Medical and Nursing Management

Asystole is treated by focusing on high-quality CPR with minimal interruptions and identifying underlying and contributing factors. The guidelines for advanced cardiac life support (AHA, 2005) state that the key to successful treatment is rapid assessment to identify a possible cause, which may be hypoxia, acidosis, severe electrolyte imbalance, drug overdose, hypovolemia, cardiac tamponade, tension pneumothorax, coronary or pulmonary thrombosis, trauma, or hypothermia. After the initiation of CPR, intubation and establishment of IV access are the next recommended actions, with no or minimal interruptions in chest compressions. After 2 minutes or five cycles of CPR, a bolus of IV epinephrine is administered and repeated at 3- to 5-minute intervals. One dose of vasopressin may be administered for the first or second dose of epinephrine. A 1 mg bolus of IV atropine may also be administered as soon as possible after the rhythm check (AHA, 2005). Because of the poor prognosis associated with asystole, if the patient does not respond to these actions and others aimed at correcting underlying causes, resuscitation efforts are usually ended ("the code is called") unless special circumstances (e.g., hypothermia, transportation to a hospital is required) exist.

PULSELESS ELECTRICAL ACTIVITY

In some situations, the patient may have an organized electrical rhythm visible on the monitor display, but is unresponsive, not breathing, and pulseless. This is termed *pulseless*

electrical activity (PEA) and is considered a cardiac arrest. The patient should receive immediate CPR and life support.

CONDUCTION ABNORMALITIES

AV blocks occur when the conduction of the impulse through the AV nodal area is decreased or stopped. These blocks can be caused by medications (e.g., digitalis, calcium channel blockers, beta blockers), myocardial ischemia and infarction, valvular disorders, or myocarditis.

The clinical signs and symptoms of a heart block vary with the ventricular rate and the severity of any underlying disease processes. Whereas first-degree AV block rarely causes any hemodynamic effect, the other blocks may result in decreased heart rate, causing a decrease in perfusion to vital organs, such as the brain, heart, kidneys, lungs, and skin. A patient with third-degree AV block caused by digitalis toxicity may be stable; another patient with the same rhythm caused by acute MI may be unstable. Health care providers must always keep in mind the need to treat the patient, not the rhythm. The treatment is based on the hemodynamic effect of the rhythm.

FIRST-DEGREE ATRIOVENTRICULAR BLOCK

First-degree AV block occurs when atrial conduction is delayed through the AV node resulting in a prolonged PR interval.

Pathophysiology

First-degree block may occur without an underlying pathophysiology or may be the result of medications such as beta blockers, calcium channel blockers, or digoxin. It can also result from conditions that increase parasympathetic (vagal) tone such as vomiting or Valsalva maneuver.

Clinical Manifestations and Assessment

The patient is usually asymptomatic.

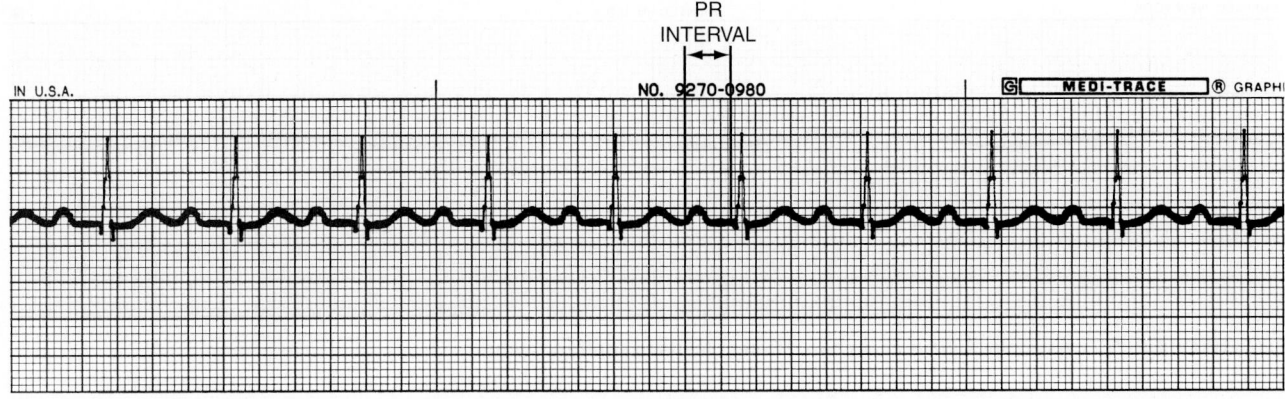

FIGURE 17-18 Sinus rhythm with first-degree AV block in lead II. Note that PR is constant but greater than 0.20 seconds.

ECG characteristics are:

Rate: Depends on underlying rhythm
Rhythm: Regular
P wave: Present before each QRS and consistent in size and shape
PR interval: Greater than 0.20 seconds
QRS duration: Normal

See Figure 17-18 above.

Medical and Nursing Management

The patient with first-degree AV block is only treated if symptoms related to bradycardia are present. If the AV block is new, the patient should be observed for potential progression to second-degree block.

SECOND-DEGREE ATRIOVENTRICULAR BLOCK, TYPE I (WENCKEBACH)

Second-degree AV block, type I, occurs when there is a repeating pattern in which all but one of a series of atrial impulses are conducted through the AV node into the ventricles (e.g.,

every four of five atrial impulses are not conducted). Each atrial impulse takes a longer time for conduction than the one before, until one impulse is fully blocked, thus an increasing PR interval is seen with each successive beat until a P wave is seen without a resulting QRS. Because the AV node is not depolarized by the blocked atrial impulse, the AV node has time to fully repolarize, so that the next atrial impulse can be conducted within the shortest amount of time.

Pathophysiology

Second-degree AV block, type I is caused by a gradual and progressive conduction delay through the AV node. It may be related to increased parasympathetic (vagal) tone, ischemia, or medications that slow conduction, such as beta blockers, calcium channel blockers, and digoxin.

Clinical Manifestations and Assessment

Signs and symptoms are related to bradycardia and may include chest discomfort, dyspnea, and hypotension.

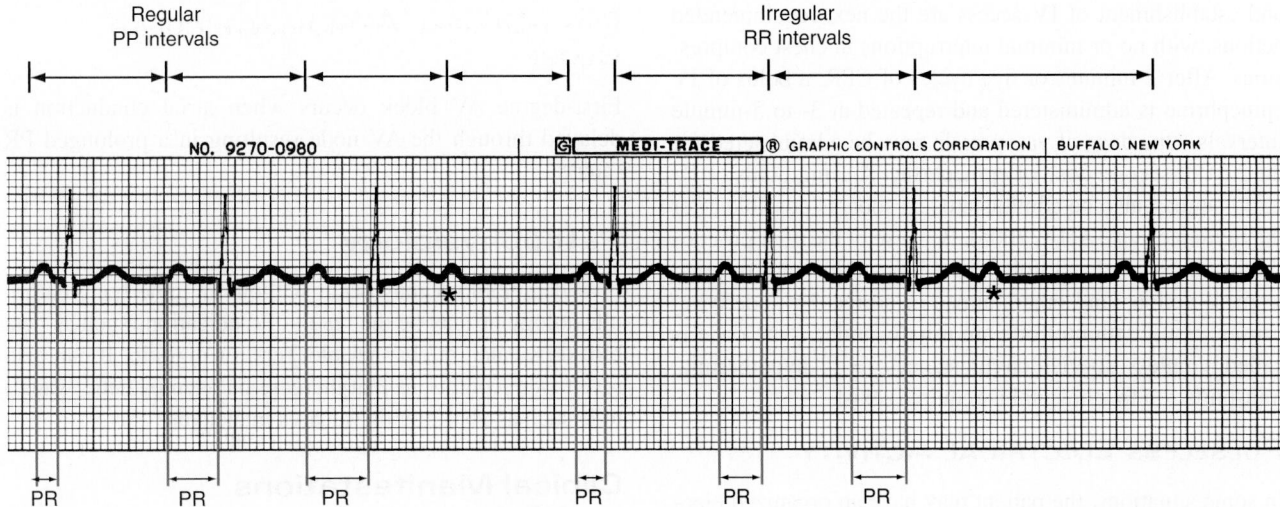

FIGURE 17-19 Sinus rhythm with second-degree AV block, type I in lead II. Note progressively longer PR durations until there is a nonconducted P wave, indicated by the asterisk.

ECG characteristics are:

Rate: Atrial rate faster than ventricular rate

Rhythm: The atrial rhythm is usually regular, the ventricular rhythm is usually irregular.

P wave: Size and shape normal

PR interval: PR interval becomes longer with each succeeding ECG complex until there is a P wave not followed by a QRS.

QRS duration: Normal

See Figure 17-19 on page 478.

Medical and Nursing Management

If the patient has symptomatic bradycardia, treatment with atropine or transcutaneous pacing is indicated.

SECOND-DEGREE ATRIOVENTRICULAR BLOCK, TYPE II

Second-degree AV block, type II, occurs when only some of the atrial impulses are conducted through the AV node into the ventricles. The ECG will reveal P waves not followed by a QRS. It is less common but more severe as it can progress to complete third-degree heart block.

Pathophysiology

Conduction is blocked below the AV node. It is caused by ischemia, usually due to blockage of the left coronary artery.

Clinical Manifestations and Assessment

Signs and symptoms are related to bradycardia and may include chest discomfort, dyspnea, and hypotension.

ECG characteristics are:

Rate: Atrial rate 60–100 bpm; ventricular rate less than atrial rate

Rhythm: Atrial rhythm is regular (constant P-P interval), ventricular rhythm is irregular.

P wave: Normal

PR interval: Constant, no progressive prolongation with conducted beats

QRS duration: Normal or wide depending on the location of the block relative to the AV node

See Figure 17-20 below.

Medical and Nursing Management

If the patient has symptomatic bradycardia, treatment with atropine or pacing is indicated.

THIRD-DEGREE ATRIOVENTRICULAR BLOCK

Third-degree AV block occurs when no atrial impulse is conducted through the AV node into the ventricles. In third-degree AV block, two separate impulses stimulate the heart: one stimulates the atria, represented by the P wave, and one stimulates the ventricles, represented by the QRS complex, but there is no relationship or synchrony between the atrial and the ventricular contraction. Each is beating at its own inherent rate and independently of each other, thus the cardiac output is affected. P waves may be seen, but the atrial electrical activity is not conducted down into the ventricles. This is called *AV dissociation*.

Pathophysiology

Complete heart block is caused by injury to the conduction system, so that there is no conduction between the atria and the ventricles.

Clinical Manifestations and Assessment

Signs and symptoms are related to bradycardia and may include syncope, chest discomfort, angina, dyspnea, and hypotension.

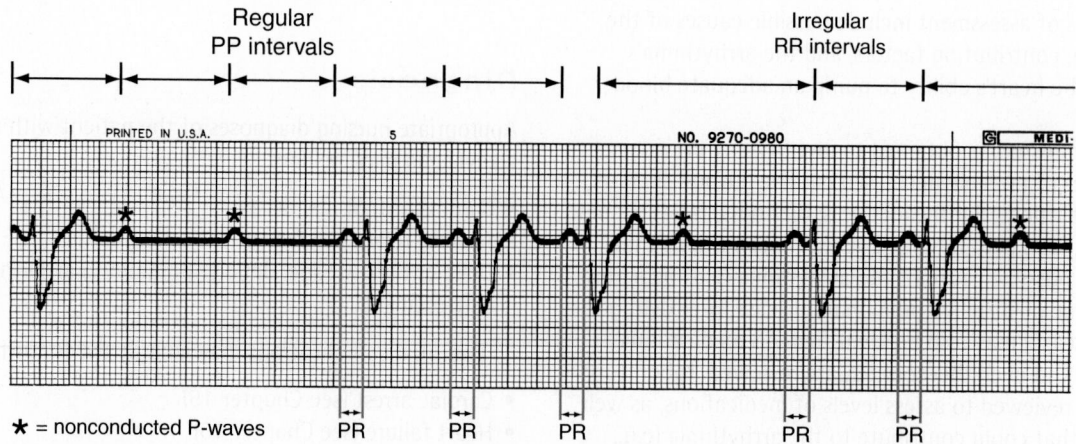

FIGURE 17-20 Sinus rhythm with second-degree AV block, type II in lead V$_1$; note constant PR interval and presence of more P waves than QRS complexes.

Regular PP intervals   Regular RR intervals

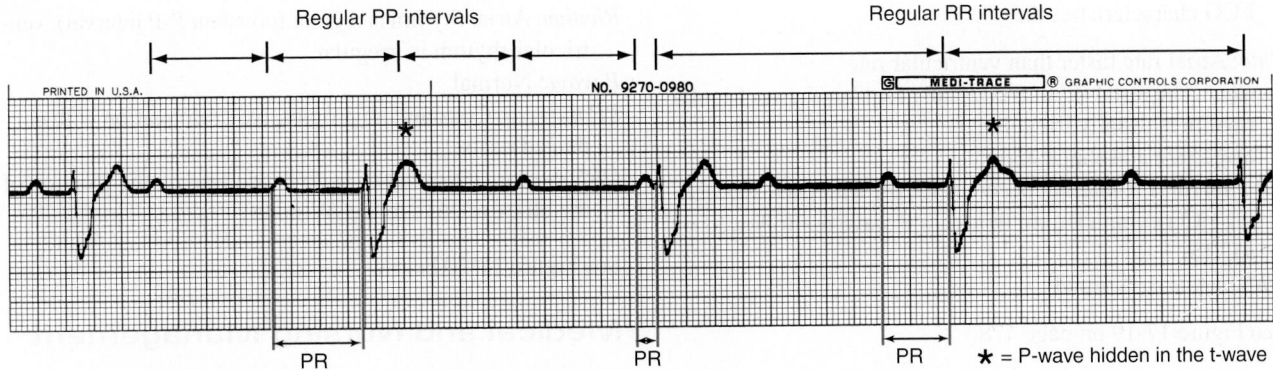

PR   PR   PR   ★ = P-wave hidden in the t-wave

FIGURE 17-21 Sinus rhythm with third-degree AV block and idioventricular rhythm in lead V₁; note irregular PR intervals.

ECG characteristics are:

Rate: Atrial rate 60–100 bpm, ventricular rate 20–40 bpm
Rhythm: Atrial and ventricular rhythms are both regular, but independent of each other.
P wave: Normal, more P waves than QRS complexes
PR interval: Not present; no relationship between the P wave and the R wave
QRS duration: Normal or wide depending on the location of the block relative to the AV node

See Figure 17-21 above.

Medical and Nursing Management

If the patient has symptomatic bradycardia, treatment with atropine or pacing is indicated.

NURSING PROCESS

The Patient With an Arrhythmia

Assessment

Major areas of assessment include possible causes of the arrhythmia, contributing factors, and the arrhythmia's effect on the heart's ability to pump an adequate blood volume.

A health history is obtained to identify any previous occurrences of possible decreased cardiac output, such as syncope (fainting), lightheadedness, dizziness, fatigue, chest discomfort, and palpitations. Coexisting conditions that could be a possible cause of the arrhythmia (e.g., heart disease, chronic obstructive pulmonary disease, preexisting thyroid disease) may also be identified. All medications, prescribed and over-the-counter, are reviewed. Laboratory results are reviewed to assess levels of medications, as well as factors that could contribute to the arrhythmia (e.g., anemia). A psychosocial assessment is performed to identify the possible effects of the arrhythmia, the patient's

perception of the arrhythmia, and whether anxiety is a significant contributing factor.

During physical assessment, the nurse assesses the patient's skin, which may be pale and cool. Signs of fluid retention, such as neck vein distention and crackles and wheezes auscultated in the lungs, may be detected. The presence of peripheral edema is assessed, its extent, and whether it is pitting or not. The rate and rhythm of apical and peripheral pulses are also assessed, and any pulse deficit (see Chapter 12) is noted. The nurse auscultates for extra heart sounds (especially S₃ and S₄) and for heart murmurs, evaluates blood pressure, and assesses the patient's usual versus current weight.

NURSING ALERT

Cardiac output is calculated as heart rate (HR) × stroke volume (SV). SV is the amount of blood ejected by the left ventricle with each contraction. If an arrhythmia occurs, the HR and SV can be affected, decreasing the filling times for the ventricle and ultimately causing a decreased cardiac output. The nurse is alert for patient complaints of dizziness, syncope, shortness of breath, weight gain, crackles, fatigue, chest pain, or discomfort.

Diagnosis

Appropriate nursing diagnoses of the patient with an arrhythmia may include:

- Cardiac output, decreased
- Anxiety related to fear of the unknown
- Deficient knowledge, deficient regarding arrhythmia and its treatment

Potential complications may include the following:

- Cardiac arrest (see Chapter 15)
- Heart failure (see Chapter 15)
- Thromboembolic event, especially with atrial fibrillation (see Chapter 15)

Planning

The major goals for the patient may include eliminating or decreasing the occurrence of the arrhythmia, minimizing anxiety, and acquiring knowledge about the arrhythmia and its treatment.

Nursing Interventions

Monitoring and Managing the Arrhythmia

The nurse regularly evaluates the patient's blood pressure, pulse rate and rhythm, rate and depth of respirations, breath sounds, and daily weights. The nurse also asks the patient about episodes of chest pain, syncope, lightheadedness, dizziness, or fainting as part of the ongoing assessment. If a patient with an arrhythmia is hospitalized, the nurse may obtain a 12-lead ECG, continuously monitor the patient, and analyze rhythm strips to track the arrhythmia. The patient should have vascular access and supplemental oxygen at the bedside.

The nurse assesses and observes for the beneficial and adverse effects of each **antiarrhythmic** medication. The nurse also manages medication administration carefully, so that a constant serum blood level of the medication is maintained.

In addition to medication, the nurse assesses for factors that contribute to the arrhythmia, such as caffeine and stress, and assists the patient in developing a plan to make lifestyle changes that eliminate or reduce these factors.

Minimizing Anxiety

When the patient experiences episodes of arrhythmia, the nurse maintains a calm and reassuring attitude. This assists in reducing anxiety (reducing the sympathetic response) and fosters a trusting relationship with the patient. In addition, the nurse can help the patient develop a system to identify possible causative, influencing, and alleviating factors (e.g., keeping a diary). The nursing goal is to maximize the patient's control and to make the episode less threatening.

Teaching Patients Self-Care

The nurse explains the importance of maintaining therapeutic serum levels of antiarrhythmic medications, so that the patient understands why medications should be taken regularly each day. If the patient has a potentially lethal arrhythmia, it is also important to establish with the patient and family a plan of action to take in case of an emergency. Family members should be encouraged to learn CPR. The patient and family should also be taught about potential effects of the arrhythmia and their signs and symptoms. This information allows the patient and family to feel more in control and better prepared for possible events.

Continuing Care

Home care is warranted if the patient has significant comorbidities, socioeconomic issues, or limited self-management skills that could increase the risk for nonadherence to the therapeutic regimen.

Evaluation

Expected patient outcomes may include:

1. Maintains cardiac output:
   a. Demonstrates heart rate, blood pressure, respiratory rate, and level of consciousness within normal ranges
   b. Demonstrates no or decreased episodes of arrhythmia
2. Experiences reduced anxiety:
   a. Expresses a positive attitude about living with the arrhythmia
   b. Expresses confidence in ability to take appropriate actions in an emergency
3. Expresses understanding of the arrhythmia and its treatment:
   a. Explains the arrhythmia and its effects
   b. Describes the medication regimen and its rationale
   c. Explains the need to maintain a therapeutic serum level of the medication
   d. Describes a plan to eliminate or limit factors that contribute to the arrhythmia
   e. States actions to take in the event of an emergency

ADJUNCTIVE MODALITIES AND MANAGEMENT

Acute arrhythmias may be treated with medications or with electrical therapy (emergency defibrillation, cardioversion, or pacing). Many antiarrhythmic medications are used to treat atrial and ventricular tachyarrhythmias (see Table 17-2, p. 471) (Mitchell, 2008). The choice of medication depends on the specific arrhythmia and its duration, the presence of heart failure and other diseases, and the patient's response to previous treatment. Electrical therapies include cardioversion and defibrillation for acute tachyarrhythmia, and implantable devices (pacemakers for bradycardias and internal cardiodefibrillators for chronic tachyarrhythmias). Catheter ablation is also available. The nurse is responsible for assessing the patient's understanding of and response to therapy, as well as the patient's self-management abilities.

CARDIOVERSION AND DEFIBRILLATION

Cardioversion and defibrillation are used to treat tachyarrhythmias by delivering an electrical current that depolarizes a critical mass of myocardial cells. When the cells repolarize, the sinus node is usually able to recapture its role as the heart's pacemaker. One major difference between cardioversion and defibrillation is the timing of the delivery of

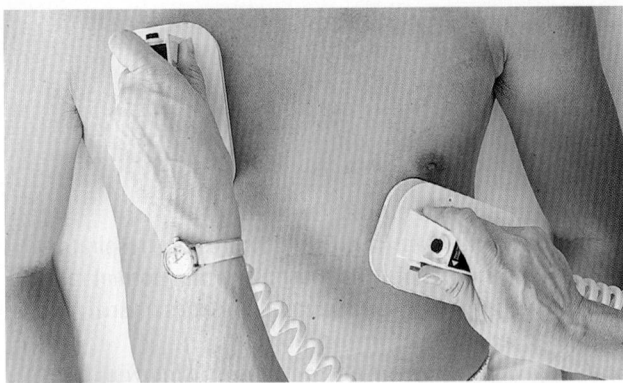

FIGURE 17-22 Standard paddle placement for defibrillation.

electrical current. In cardioversion, the delivery of the electrical current is synchronized with the patient's electrical events; in defibrillation, the delivery of the current is unsynchronized.

The electrical current may be delivered externally through the skin with the use of paddles or with conductor pads, or may be delivered internally as part of open heart surgery. The paddles or pads may be placed on the front of the chest (Fig. 17-22) (standard paddle placement), or one paddle may be placed on the front of the chest and the other connected to an adapter with a long handle and placed under the patient's back (anteroposterior placement) (Fig. 17-23). Whether using pads or paddles, the nurse must observe two safety measures. First, good contact must be maintained between the pads or paddles and the patient's skin (with a conductive medium in between them) to prevent electrical current from leaking into the air (arcing) when the defibrillator is discharged. Second, no one is to be in contact with the patient or with anything that is touching the patient when the defibrillator is discharged, to minimize the chance that electrical current will be conducted to anyone other than the patient. Box 17-6 lists key points for assisting with cardioversion or defibrillation.

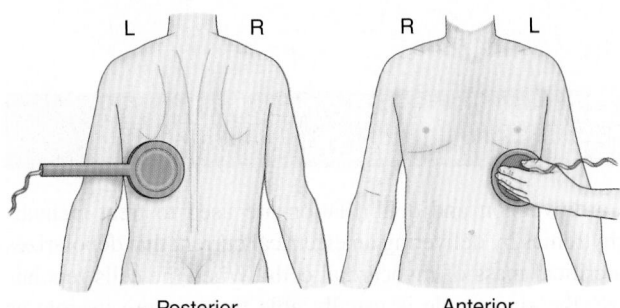

Posterior   Anterior

FIGURE 17-23 Anteroposterior paddle placement for defibrillation.

NURSING ALERT
When using paddles, the appropriate conductant is applied between the paddles and the patient's skin. Any other type of conductant, such as ultrasound gel, should not be substituted.

Electrical Cardioversion

Electrical cardioversion involves the delivery of a "timed" electrical current to terminate a tachyarrhythmia. In cardioversion, the defibrillator is set to synchronize with the ECG on a cardiac monitor, so that the electrical impulse discharges during ventricular depolarization (QRS complex). The synchronization prevents the discharge from occurring during the vulnerable period of repolarization (T wave), which could result in VT or ventricular fibrillation. When the synchronizer is on, no electrical current is delivered if the defibrillator does not discern a QRS complex. Because there may be a short delay until recognition of the QRS, the discharge buttons of an external defibrillator must be held down until the shock has been delivered.

If the cardioversion is elective and the arrhythmia has lasted longer than 48 hours, anticoagulation for a few weeks

before cardioversion may be indicated. Digoxin is usually withheld for 48 hours before cardioversion to ensure the resumption of sinus rhythm with normal conduction. The patient is instructed not to eat or drink for at least 4 hours before the procedure. Before cardioversion, the patient receives IV moderate sedation as well as an analgesic medication or anesthesia. The amount of voltage used varies, depending on the defibrillator's technology and the type of arrhythmia.

! **N U R S I N G   A L E R T**
When the heart returns to a normal sinus rhythm after cardio-version, the atria beat forcefully. If a clot has formed in the atria, systemic emboli may result, thus anticoagulation is needed if the arrhythmia has lasted over 48 hours. The nurse is alert for systemic signs of embolization such as sudden onset shortness of breath with pulmonary emboli or neurolog-ical changes (visual, motor, sensory, headache etc.; refer to Chapter 47) with cerebral emboli.

Defibrillation

Defibrillation is used in emergency situations as the treatment of choice for ventricular fibrillation and pulseless VT. Defibrillation is not used on patients who are conscious or have a pulse. It has been established that early defibrillation is the major determinant of survival in cardiac arrest (Field, 2008).

The electrical voltage required to defibrillate the heart is usually greater than that required for cardioversion and may cause more myocardial damage. Defibrillators are classified as monophasic or biphasic. Monophasic defibrillators deliver current in only one direction and require increased energy loads. Newer biphasic defibrillators deliver the electrical charge to the positive paddle, which then reverses back to the originating paddle. The recommended energy levels for defibrillation vary according to the type of waveform and the manufacturer of the defibrillator (Finamore & Turris, 2008). Following defibrillation, CPR is immediately initiated if a perfusable rhythm was not initiated, and other advanced life support treatments are begun. This treatment with continuous CPR, medication administration, and defibrillation continues until a stable rhythm resumes or until it is determined that the patient cannot be revived.

Implantable Cardioverter Defibrillator

The **implantable cardioverter defibrillator (ICD)** is a device that detects and terminates life-threatening episodes of tachycardia or fibrillation. ICDs are used for patients who have survived sudden cardiac death syndrome, usually caused by ventricular fibrillation, or have experienced symptomatic ventricular tachycardia. Other people at risk

of sudden cardiac death include those with dilated cardiomyopathy, hypertrophic cardiomyopathy, arrhythmogenic (capable of inducing an arrhythmia) right ventricular dysfunction, and prolonged QT syndrome. In addition, patients with moderate to severe left ventricular dysfunction, with or without nonsustained VT, are at high risk for cardiac arrest; therefore, prophylactic implantation may be indicated. ICDs may also be implanted in patients with symptomatic, recurrent, medication-refractory atrial fibrillation.

An ICD consists of a generator and at least one lead that can sense intrinsic electrical activity and deliver an electrical impulse. The device is usually implanted much like a pacemaker (Fig. 17-24). ICDs are designed to respond to two criteria: a rate that exceeds a predetermined level, and a change in the isoelectric line segments. When an arrhythmia occurs, the device automatically charges and delivers the programmed charge through the lead to the heart. ICD surveillance is similar to that of the pacemaker; however, it includes information about the number and frequency of shocks that have been delivered. Each device offers a different delivery sequence, but all are capable of delivering high-energy defibrillation to treat a tachycardia (atrial or ventricular). Antiarrhythmic medication usually is administered with this technology to minimize the occurrence of the tachyarrhythmia and to reduce the frequency of ICD discharge (Ferreira-Gonzalez, Dos-Subira, & Guyatt, 2007).

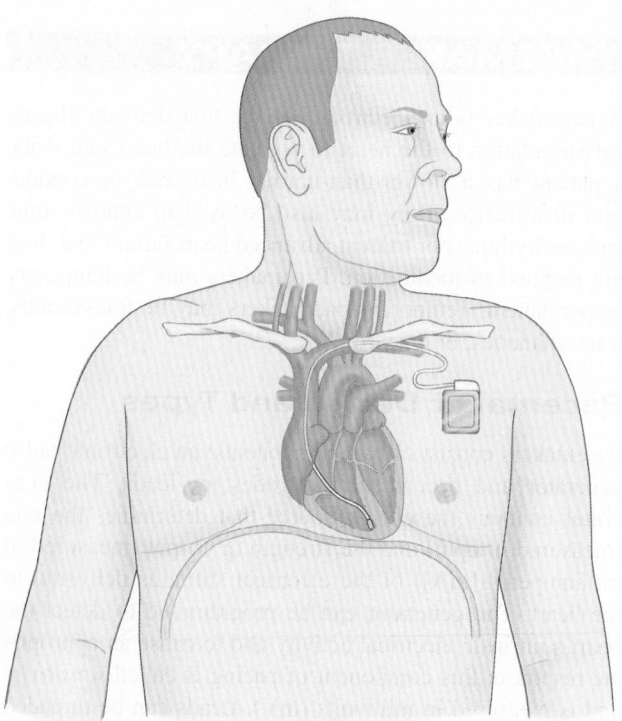

FIGURE 17-24 The implantable cardioverter defibrillator (ICD) consists of a generator and a sensing/pacing/defibrillating electrode.

Some ICDs can respond with antitachycardia pacing, in which the device delivers electrical impulses at a fast rate in an attempt to disrupt the tachycardia by: low-energy (low-intensity) cardioversion, by defibrillation, or by all three. Anti-tachycardia pacing is used to terminate tachycardias caused by a conduction disturbance called *reentry*. Some ICDs also have pacemaker capability if the patient develops bradycardia, which sometimes occurs after treatment of the tachycardia.

Which device is used and how it is programmed depend on the patient's arrhythmia. A universal code has been adopted to provide a means of safe communication about ICD function referred to as the NASPE-BPEG code (Bernstein, Daubert, Fletcher et al., 2002). The first letter represents the chamber or chambers shocked (O = none, A = atrium, V = ventricle, D = both atrium and ventricle). The second letter represents the chamber that can be antitachycardia paced (O, A, V, D, meaning the same as the first letter). The third letter indicates the method used by the generator to detect a tachycardia (E = electrogram, H = hemodynamics). The last letter represents the chambers that have antibradycardia pacing (O, A, V, D, meaning the same as the first and second letters of the ICD code).

The primary complication associated with the ICD is surgery-related infection. A few complications are associated with the technical aspects of the equipment, such as premature battery depletion and dislodged or fractured leads. Support may need to be provided to assist individuals with adjustment to the uncertainty and psychological distress related to ICD firing (Mauro, 2008).

PACEMAKER THERAPY

A pacemaker is an electronic device that delivers electrical stimulation to the heart to regulate the heart rate when a patient has a slower-than-normal heart rate or conduction disturbance. They may also be used to control some tachyarrhythmias or to treat advanced heart failure that does not respond to medication. Pacemakers may be temporary or permanent. Temporary pacemakers may be transvenous, transcutaneous, or epicardial.

Pacemaker Design and Types

Pacemakers consist of two components: an electronic pulse generator and pacemaker electrodes, or leads. The generator contains the energy source that determines the rate (measured in bpm) and the strength or output (measured in milliamperes [mA]) of the electrical stimulus delivered to the heart. The generator can be programmed to detect the heart's intrinsic electrical activity and to cause an appropriate response; this component of pacing is called *sensitivity* and is measured in millivolts (mV). Leads can be threaded through a major vein into the right ventricle (endocardial leads), or they can be lightly sutured onto the outside of the heart and brought through the chest wall during open

heart surgery (epicardial wires). The endocardial leads may be temporarily placed with catheters through a great vessel (transvenous wires), usually guided by fluoroscopy. The endocardial and epicardial wires are connected to a temporary external generator.

Endocardial leads may also be placed permanently, usually through the external jugular vein, and connected to a permanent generator. The generator is implanted in a subcutaneous pocket created in the pectoral region below the clavicle (Fig. 17-25). The procedure usually takes about 1 hour, and it is performed in a cardiac catheterization laboratory using a local anesthetic. Batteries need replacement after approximately 10 years; and battery replacement is usually performed using a local anesthetic.

If a patient suddenly develops a symptomatic bradycardia, emergency pacing may be started with transcutaneous pacing. Large pacing ECG electrodes (pads) are placed on the patient's chest and back. The electrodes are connected to the temporary pacemaker generator (Fig. 17-26). Because the impulse must travel through the patient's skin and tissue before reaching the heart, transcutaneous pacing can cause significant discomfort and is intended to be used only in emergencies. If the patient is alert, sedation and analgesia may be administered.

Pacemaker Generator Functions

As with ICDs, a universal code has been adopted to provide a means of safe communication about pacemaker function referred to as the NASPE-BPEG code. The complete code consists of five letters and was revised in 2002 (Bernstein et al., 2002):

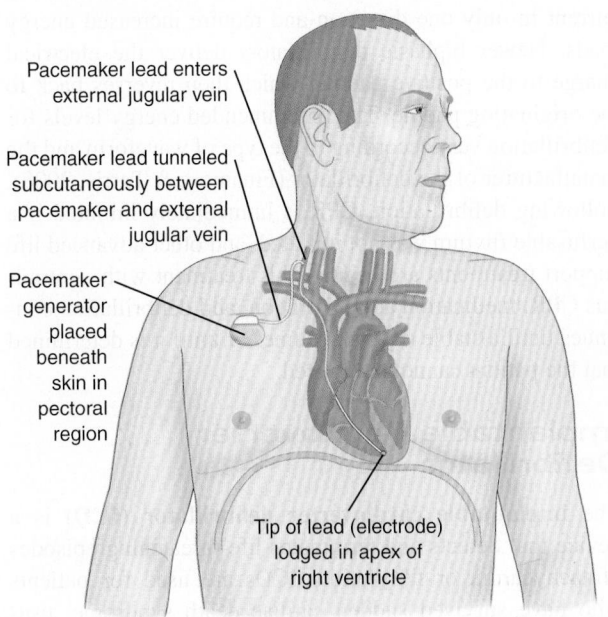

Pacemaker lead enters external jugular vein

Pacemaker lead tunneled subcutaneously between pacemaker and external jugular vein

Pacemaker generator placed beneath skin in pectoral region

Tip of lead (electrode) lodged in apex of right ventricle

FIGURE 17-25 Implanted transvenous pacing lead (with electrode) and pacemaker generator.

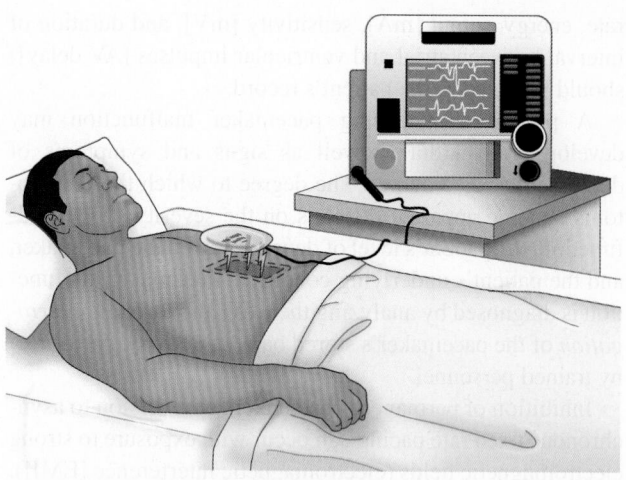

FIGURE 17-26 Transcutaneous pacemaker with electrode pads connected to the anterior and posterior chest walls.

- The first letter of the code identifies the chamber or chambers being paced (i.e., the chamber containing a pacing electrode). The letter characters for this code are A (atrium), V (ventricle), or D (dual, meaning both A and V).
- The second letter identifies the chamber or chambers being sensed by the pacemaker generator. Information from the electrode within the chamber is sent to the generator for interpretation and action by the generator. The letter characters are A (atrium), V (ventricle), D (dual), and O (indicating that the sensing function is turned off).
- The third letter of the code describes the type of response that will be made by the pacemaker to what is sensed. The letter characters used to describe this response are I (**inhibited**), T (**triggered**), D (dual, inhibited and triggered), and O (none). *Inhibited response* means that the response of the pacemaker is controlled by the activity of the patient's heart; that is, when the patient's heart beats, the pacemaker will not function, but when the heart does not beat, the

pacemaker will function. In contrast, *triggered response* means that the pacemaker will respond (pace the heart) when it senses an absence of intrinsic heart activity.

- The fourth and fifth letters are used only with permanent pacemakers. The fourth letter of the code is related to a permanent generator's ability to vary the heart rate. The possible letters are O, indicating no rate responsiveness, or R, indicating that the generator has rate modulation (i.e., the pacemaker has the ability to automatically adjust the pacing rate from moment to moment based on parameters such as physical activity, acid–base changes, temperature, rate and depth of respirations, or oxygen saturation). A pacemaker with rate-responsive ability is capable of improving cardiac output during times of increased cardiac demand, such as during exercise.
- The fifth letter of the code indicates that the permanent generator has multisite pacing capability. The letters are A (atrium), V (ventricle), D (dual), and O (none).

The type of generator and its selected settings depend on the patient's arrhythmia, underlying cardiac function, and age (Gregoratos, Abrams, Epstein, et al., 2002). When pacing is initiated, the ECG tracing will display a straight vertical line, called a *pacemaker spike*, with each pacemaker impulse. The appropriate ECG complex should immediately follow the pacing spike; therefore, a P wave should follow an atrial pacing spike and a QRS complex should follow a ventricular pacing spike. Because the impulse starts in a different place than the patient's normal rhythm, the QRS complex or P wave that responds to pacing looks different from the patient's normal ECG complex. *Capture* is a term used to denote that the appropriate complex followed the pacing spike (Fig. 17-27). *Synchronized biventricular pacing*, also called *cardiac resynchronized therapy* (CRT), has been found to modify the intraventricular, interventricular, and atrial-ventricular conduction defects identified with symptomatic moderate to severe (New York Heart Association Functional Class III and IV) left ventricular dysfunction and

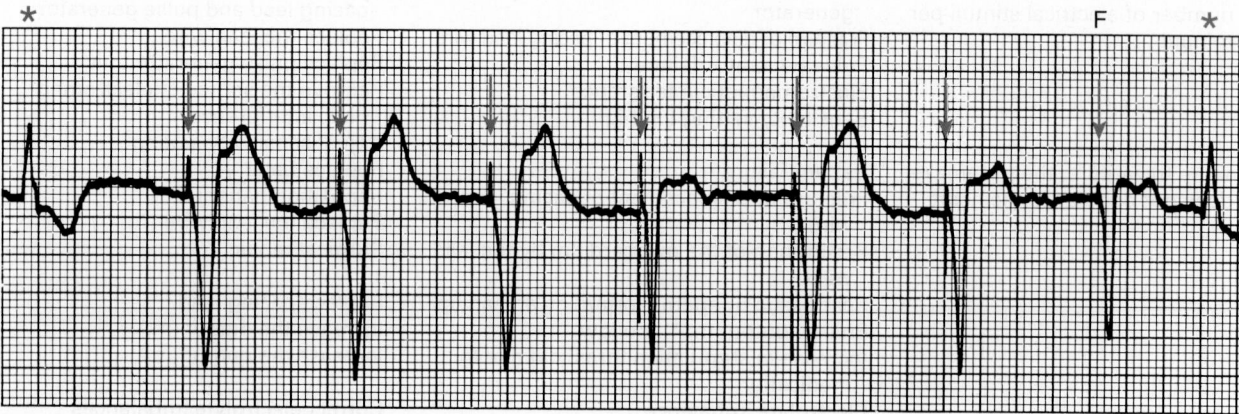

FIGURE 17-27 Pacing with appropriate sensing (on-demand pacing) in lead V₁. Arrows denote pacing spike. Asterisk (*) denotes intrinsic (patient's own) beats, therefore no pacing.

heart failure (Trupp, 2004). The generator for biventricular pacing has three leads: one for the right atrium; one for the right ventricle, as with most standard pacemaker generators; and one for the left ventricle, usually placed in the left lateral wall. Studies have shown that this therapy improves cardiac function, resulting in decreased heart failure symptoms and an improved quality of life (Trupp, 2004).

Complications of Pacemaker Use

Complications associated with pacemakers relate to their presence within the body and improper functioning. The following complications may arise from a pacemaker:

- Local infection
- Bleeding and hematoma
- Hemothorax
- Ventricular ectopy and tachycardia
- Movement or dislocation of the lead placed
- Phrenic nerve stimulation (hiccuping may be a sign)
- Rarely, cardiac tamponade

In the initial hours after a temporary or permanent pacemaker is inserted, the most common complication is dislodgment of the pacing electrode. Minimizing patient activity can help prevent this complication. If a temporary electrode is in place, the extremity through which the catheter has been advanced is immobilized. With a permanent pacemaker, the patient is instructed initially to restrict activity on the side of the implantation.

The ECG is monitored very carefully to detect pacemaker malfunction. Improper pacemaker function, which can arise from failure in one or more components of the pacing system, is outlined in Table 17-3. Pacer settings (e.g.,

rate, energy output [mA], sensitivity [mV], and duration of interval between atrial and ventricular impulses [AV delay]) should be noted in the patient's record.

A patient experiencing pacemaker malfunction may develop bradycardia as well as signs and symptoms of decreased cardiac output. The degree to which these symptoms become apparent depends on the severity of the malfunction, the patient's level of dependency on the pacemaker, and the patient's underlying condition. Pacemaker malfunction is diagnosed by analyzing the ECG and through *interrogation* of the pacemaker's stored bank of activity, performed by trained personnel.

Inhibition of permanent pacemakers or reversion to asynchronous fixed rate pacing can occur with exposure to strong electromagnetic fields (electromagnetic interference [EMI]). However, recent pacemaker technology allows patients to safely use most household electronic appliances and devices (e.g., microwave ovens, electric tools). Objects that contain magnets (e.g., the earpiece of a phone; large stereo speakers; portable media players; magnet therapy products, such as mattresses, jewelry, and wraps) should not be near the generator for longer than a few seconds. Patients are advised to keep digital cellular phones at least 6 to 12 inches away from (or on the side opposite of) the pacemaker generator and not to carry them in a shirt pocket.

Pacemaker Surveillance

Pacemaker clinics have been established to monitor patients and to test pulse generators for impending pacemaker battery failure. A computerized device is held over the generator to interrogate it with painless radio signals; it detects the generator's settings, battery status, pacing threshold, sensing function,

TABLE
17-3 Assessing Pacemaker Malfunction

Problem	Possible Cause	Intervention
Failure to pace; the pacemaker fails to deliver the correct number of electrical stimuli per minute	Battery failure	Replace the pulse generator battery
	Loose connection between lead wire and generator	Tighten the connections between pacing lead and pulse generator
	Fracture or displacement of pacing lead wire	Replace the lead wire
	Pulse generator failure	Replace pulse generator unit
	Electromagnetic interference	Remove the source of electromagnetic interference
	Sensitivity setting too high	Adjust sensitivity setting
Failure to capture; the pacemaker does not depolarize the heart	Battery failure	Replace battery
	Fracture or displacement of pacing lead wire	Reposition patient
		Replace the lead wire
	Perforation of the myocardium by the lead wire	Surgical repair
	Scar tissue or edema formation at lead tip	Replace pacing lead
	Energy output (mA) too low	Increase the output (mA)
	Increase in stimulation threshold due to medication	Increase the output (mA)
	Electrolyte imbalance	Correct electrolyte imbalances

From Aehlert, B. (2007). *ACLS Study Guide* (3rd ed.). Phoenix: Mosby JEMS.

lead integrity, and other stored information. Several factors, such as lead fracture, muscle inhibition, and insulation disruption, also may be assessed. If indicated, the pacemaker is turned off for a few seconds, using a magnet or a programmer, while the ECG is recorded to assess the patient's underlying cardiac rhythm. Transtelephonic transmission of the generator's information is another follow-up method. Special equipment is used to transmit information about the patient's pacemaker over the telephone to a receiving system at a pacemaker clinic. The information is converted into tones; equipment at the clinic converts these tones to an electronic signal and records them on an ECG strip. The pacemaker rate and other data concerning pacemaker function are obtained and evaluated by a cardiologist. This simplifies the diagnosis of a failing generator, reassures the patient, and improves management when the patient is physically remote from pacemaker testing facilities.

ELECTROPHYSIOLOGIC STUDIES

An electrophysiology (EP) study is an invasive procedure used to evaluate and treat significant arrhythmias. It also is indicated for patients with symptoms that suggest an arrhythmia that has gone undetected and undiagnosed by other methods. An EP study is used to do the following:

- Identify the impulse formation and propagation through the cardiac electrical conduction system
- Assess the function or dysfunction of the SA and AV nodal areas
- Identify the location (called *mapping*) and mechanism of dysrhythmogenic foci
- Assess the effectiveness of antiarrhythmic medications and devices for the patient with an arrhythmia
- Treat certain arrhythmias through the destruction of the causative cells (**ablation**)

An EP procedure is a type of cardiac catheterization that is performed in a specially equipped cardiac catheterization laboratory by an electrophysiologist. One of the main purposes of programmed stimulation is to assess the ability of the area of the myocardium to cause an arrhythmia. If the arrhythmia can be reproduced by programmed stimulation, it is called *inducible*. Once an arrhythmia is induced, a treatment plan is determined and implemented. If, on the follow-up EP study, the tachyarrhythmia cannot be induced, then the treatment is determined to be effective. Different medications may be administered and combined with electrical devices (pacemaker, ICD) to determine the most effective treatment to suppress the arrhythmia.

Patient care, patient teaching, and associated complications of an EP study are the same as those associated with cardiac catheterization (see Chapter 14). The study is usually about 2 hours in length; however, if the electrophysiologist conducts not only a diagnostic procedure but also treatment, the study can take up to 6 hours.

Patients who are to undergo an EP study may be anxious about the procedure and its outcome. Before the procedure, the patient should receive instructions, including its usual duration, the environment where the procedure is performed, and what to expect. Although an EP study is not painful, it does cause discomfort and can be tiring. It may also cause feelings that were experienced when the arrhythmia occurred in the past. In addition, patients are taught what will be expected of them (e.g., lying very still during the procedure, reporting symptoms or concerns).

The patient should also know that the arrhythmia may occur during the procedure. It often stops on its own; if it does not, treatment is given to restore the patient's normal rhythm. The arrhythmia may have to be terminated using cardioversion or defibrillation, but this is performed under more controlled circumstances than if performed in an emergency. Postprocedural care is similar to that for cardiac catheterization.

CARDIAC CONDUCTION SURGERY

Atrial tachycardias and ventricular tachycardias that do not respond to medications and are not suitable for antitachycardia pacing may be treated by methods that include a maze procedure and ablation. The *maze procedure* is an open heart surgical procedure for refractory atrial fibrillation.

Catheter ablation destroys specific cells that are the cause or central conduction route of a tachyarrhythmia. It is performed with or after an EP study. Usual indications for ablation are recurrent atrial arrhythmias or VT unresponsive to previous therapy (or for which the therapy produced significant side effects) (Noheria, Kumar, Wylie et al., 2008).

Chapter Review

Critical Thinking Exercises

1. You are caring for a 79-year-old woman who was admitted for control of heart failure 3 days ago. Today, her telemetry monitor alarmed and displayed a new sustained tachycardia with a wide QRS (0.14 sec). What are some of the possible causes of this arrhythmia? Identify some of the key factors that would need to be included in your assessment to assist in identification of the arrhythmia. What nursing interventions are needed?

2. You are caring for a 40-year-old man who recently had a DDD pacemaker inserted, with the rate set at 72 bpm.

(continued on page 488)

Chapter Review (continued)

When taking his pulse, you note that his heart rate is 66 bpm. Describe the possible causes of this difference in heart rates and the nursing actions that are needed.

3. The wife of this same patient tells you that her husband has informed her that now that he has a pacemaker, they must get rid of their microwave oven. What would you say to the wife? How would you discuss this with the patient? What other education would you provide to this patient and his wife about safety in relation to the pacemaker? What is the evidence base that supports this education? Discuss the strength of the evidence and the criteria used to evaluate the strength of the evidence.

NCLEX-Style Review Questions

1. In interpreting a patient's rhythm strip, the nurse is most concerned with which of the following findings?
   A. PR interval of 0.22 seconds
   B. Progressively lengthening PR interval
   C. A premature and short PR interval
   D. A PR interval of 0.10 seconds

2. The nurse is observing the central monitoring station and notes the following rhythm alarms. Which alarm should the nurse respond to first?
   A. Atrial fibrillation rate of 110
   B. SR with multifocal PVCs
   C. Ventricular tachycardia (monomorphic)
   D. Torsades des pointes (polymorphic)

3. A patient presents to the emergency room in atrial fibrillation. The nurse understands that the treatment plan for this patient will be determined based on which of the following?
   A. Whether or not the patient has a do not resuscitate prescription
   B. How long the patient has been in atrial fibrillation
   C. The number of episodes of atrial fibrillation the patient has experienced in the past year
   D. The rate of atrial contractions

4. The nurse notes a new wide complex tachycardia on the telemetry monitor. Upon assessing the patient, the nurse finds the patient is not arousable and has gasping respirations. The nurses next action is to:
   A. Call a code
   B. Notify the provider stat
   C. Document the findings in the telemetry record
   D. Defibrillate the patient at 100 joules

5. The nurse notes that her patient has a new second-degree type I block (Wenckebach). The patient denies chest pain or other symptoms, and the blood pressure is 90/60. After paging the provider stat, the nurse would perform which of the following set of interventions first?
   A. Apply oxygen, assess IV access, bring the portable monitor/external pacemaker to the bedside
   B. Administer nitroglycerin as ordered p.r.n. for chest discomfort and obtain a 12-lead ECG
   C. Call for stat labs to be drawn and prepare to the patient for surgical pacemaker implantation
   D. Ask the nurse's aide to stay with the patient and monitor the blood pressure every 5 minutes

---

Try these additional resources to enhance your learning and understanding of this chapter:
- thePoint online resource available at **http://thepoint.lww.com/Pellico1e**
- *Handbook for Focus on Adult Health: Medical-Surgical Nursing*
- *Study Guide for Focus on Adult Health: Medical-Surgical Nursing*

References and Selected Readings

References and selected readings associated with this chapter can be found on the website that accompanies the book. Visit http://thepoint.lww.com/Pellico1e to access the references and other additional resources associated with this chapter.

MARY SIEGGREEN

Nursing Management: Patients With Vascular Disorders and Problems of Peripheral Circulation

Learning Objectives

After reading this chapter, you will be able to:

1. Identify factors that affect peripheral blood flow and tissue oxygenation.

2. Identify clinical manifestations, management, and prevention of arterial disorders.

3. Describe prevention and management of deep venous thrombosis.

4. Describe medical and nursing management of venous and arterial ulcers.

5. Describe nursing management of lymphedema.

Conditions of the vascular system include arterial disorders, venous disorders, lymphatic disorders, and cellulitis. Nursing management depends on an understanding of the structure and function of the vascular and lymphatic system.

Intact, patent, and responsive blood vessels are necessary to deliver adequate amounts of oxygen to tissues and to remove metabolic wastes. Reduced blood flow through blood vessels characterizes all peripheral vascular diseases. Perfusion is about supply versus demand. If tissue needs are high, even modestly reduced blood flow may be inadequate to maintain tissue integrity. When blood flow decreases, ischemia follows, and tissues become malnourished and ultimately die unless blood flow is restored. Thus, the effect of decreased blood flow depends on the extent to which tissue demands exceed the supply of oxygen.

Nurses are in key positions to help patients with vascular disorders learn about the disease and their personal risk factors. Learning to modify the risk factors and manage their disorders may increase the lifespan of the vascular patient.

ARTERIAL DISORDERS

Arteries become damaged or obstructed as a result of atherosclerotic plaque, thromboemboli, chemical or mechanical trauma, infections or inflammatory processes, vasospastic disorders, and congenital malformations. A sudden arterial occlusion causes profound and often irreversible tissue ischemia and tissue death. When arterial occlusions develop gradually, there is less risk of sudden tissue death because **collateral** circulation may develop (the rerouting of blood vessels, in which new blood vessels join to take over some of the circulation of blocked vessels), giving that tissue the opportunity to adapt to gradually decreased blood flow. However, over time, continued decreased perfusion results in ischemia and tissue death.

PERIPHERAL ARTERIAL DISEASE

Peripheral artery disease (PAD) refers to any disease process that affects the arteries. Various peripheral arterial diseases result in ischemia and produce the signs and symptoms described in Box 18-1. The type and

Focused Assessment

Peripheral Arterial Disease

Be alert for the following signs and symptoms:

- Structural changes, resulting from chronic lack of oxygen and nutrient delivery to the tissues:
  - Hair loss distal to the occlusion
  - Thick, opaque nails; shiny, dry skin
  - Skeletal muscle atrophy
- Skin color changes:
  - Elevational pallor
  - Dependent rubor (red color when limb dependent from dilated damaged vessels)
- Pulse changes:
  - Pulses diminished or absent below area of stenosis/obstruction-pedal, posterior tibial, popliteal, femoral
  - Cool extremity distal to occlusion
- Sensation changes:
  - Paresthesias
  - Numbness
  - Tingling of extremities
- Ulceration/gangrene (traumatic or spontaneous on onset; located at tips of toes, between toes, over areas of pressure like heel or areas susceptible to trauma like the shin; defined punched out (circular), necrotic/yellow ulcer base, dry, pale in appearance; usually very painful; poor healing of injuries on the extremities)
- Edema, although usually absent, may be present and related to dependency

severity of symptoms depend in part on the type, stage, and extent of the disease process and on the speed with which the disorder develops. Arterial insufficiency of the extremities is a common cause of disability. The legs frequently are more affected than the upper extremities.

Clinical recognition varies in individuals; it is a slow process that begins in early adulthood and increases with age. PAD is one manifestation of **atherosclerosis**, thus systemic diseases that affect arteries of the brain, heart, kidneys, mesentery, and limbs should be suspected. Patients with PAD have an increased risk of mortality, myocardial infarction (MI), and cerebrovascular disease. Many patients with PAD are not receiving any treatment for their disease because they do not realize they have the condition (Hirsch et al., 2005).

Pathophysiology

As the lumen narrows, ischemia occurs, progressing to infarction. In PAD, obstructive lesions are predominantly confined to segments of the arterial system extending from the aorta below the renal arteries to the popliteal artery. Distal occlusive disease is frequently seen in patients with diabetes mellitus and in elderly patients.

Arteriosclerosis, the most common disease of the arteries, is a diffuse process whereby muscle fibers and endothelial linings of the walls of small arteries and arterioles become thickened. Atherosclerosis involves changes of the intima consisting of accumulation of lipids, calcium, blood components, complex carbohydrates, and fibrous tissue, referred to as *atheromas* or *plaques*. Atherosclerosis causes arterial **stenosis**, obstruction by thrombosis, **aneurysm**, ulceration, and vessel rupture.

Arterial bifurcations are more vulnerable to atherosclerosis than other areas of the arteries (Fig. 18-1). These include the distal abdominal aorta, the common iliac arteries, the orifice of the superficial femoral and *profunda femoris* arteries, and the superficial femoral artery in the adductor canal, which is particularly narrow, and anywhere along the arteries distal to the knee. Gradual narrowing of the arterial lumen stimulates the development of collateral circulation (Fig. 18-2) from preexisting vessels.

Risk Factors

Risk factors for developing PAD are similar to those for developing coronary artery disease (Box 18-2). The age of onset and disease severity are influenced by the type and number of atherosclerotic risk factors. Risk factors include modifiable and nonmodifiable (e.g., race and age) factors. Evidence indicates modification may slow the disease process. Of those that can be modified, tobacco use is one of the most important in atherosclerotic lesion development. Nicotine decreases blood flow, increases heart rate and blood pressure, and increases the risk for clot formation by increasing platelet aggregation. According to the TASC report (Norgren, Hiatt, Dormandy et al., 2007), smokers have a fourfold higher risk of developing pain from arterial disease than do nonsmokers.

Hyperhomocysteinemia is considered an independent risk factor for atherosclerosis. Homocysteine is a protein that promotes coagulation. Elevated homocysteine levels are

Risk Factors for Peripheral Arterial Disease (PAD)

- Family history
- Age (20% of adults >70 have PAD)
- Obesity
- Smoking
- Preexisting health conditions:
  - Coronary artery disease
  - Cerebral artery disease
  - Diabetes
  - Hypertension
  - Dyslipidemia
  - Clotting disorders
  - Hyperhomocysteinemia

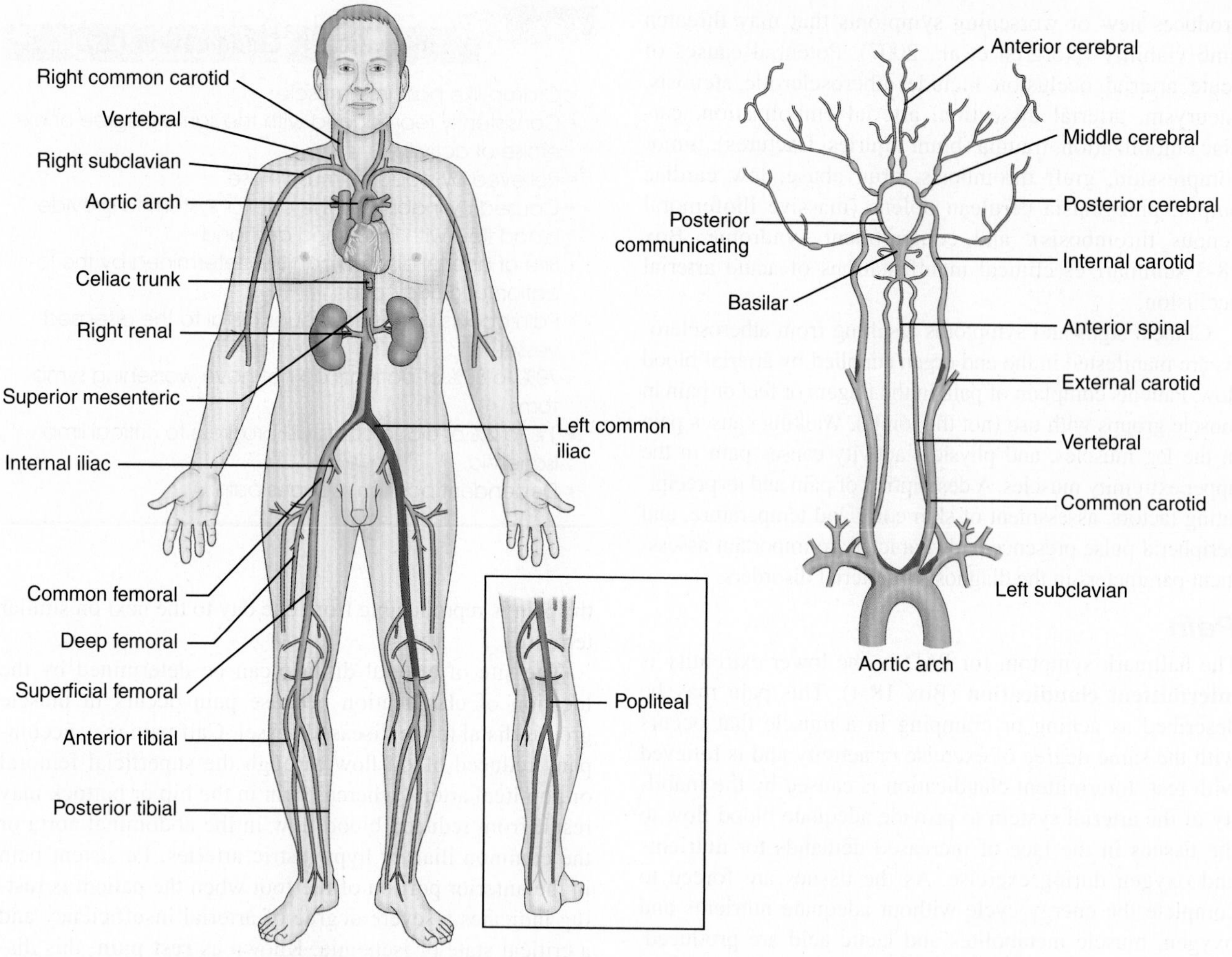

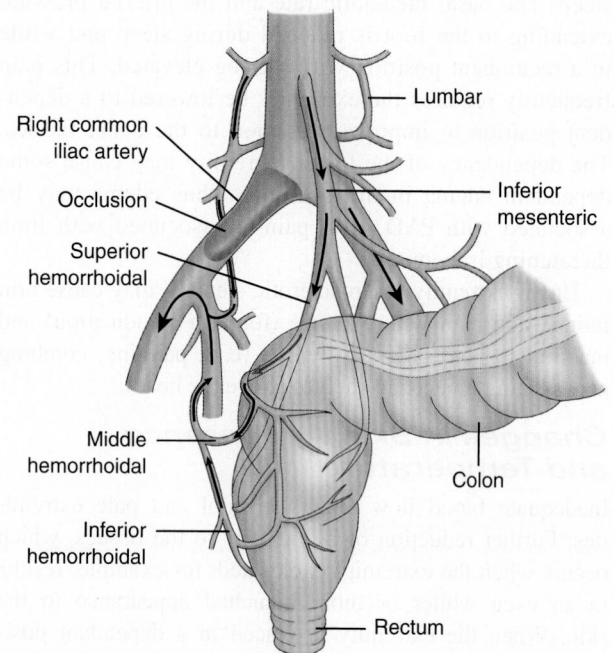

Right common carotid

Vertebral

Right subclavian

Aortic arch

Celiac trunk

Right renal

Superior mesenteric

Internal iliac

Common femoral

Deep femoral

Superficial femoral

Anterior tibial

Posterior tibial

Left common iliac

Popliteal

Anterior cerebral

Middle cerebral

Posterior cerebral

Internal carotid

Posterior communicating

Basilar

Anterior spinal

External carotid

Vertebral

Common carotid

Left subclavian

Aortic arch

FIGURE 18-1 Common sites of atherosclerotic obstruction in major arteries.

Lumbar

Right common iliac artery

Occlusion

Superior hemorrhoidal

Inferior mesenteric

Middle hemorrhoidal

Colon

Inferior hemorrhoidal

Rectum

FIGURE 18-2 Development of channels for collateral blood flow in response to occlusion of the right common iliac artery and the terminal aortic bifurcation.

associated with genetic factors and a diet low in folic acid, vitamin B_6, and vitamin B_{12}. Treatment includes vitamins B_6, B_{12}, and folate, which often lowers homocysteine levels (refer to Chapter 12 for more details on homocysteine levels).

Hypertension also accelerates the rate at which atherosclerotic lesions form in high-pressure vessels, and is a major PAD risk factor. Patients with diabetes have about five to ten times the amputation rate of those without diabetes. Obesity, stress, and lack of exercise also have been identified as contributing to the disease process.

Clinical Manifestations and Assessment

Most patients with PAD are asymptomatic. Studies have demonstrated that for every patient who has symptomatic disease, approximately three to four patients have no symptoms (Norgren et al., 2007). Approximately 1% to 5% of patients with PAD have **critical limb ischemia** (CLI), with either chronic ischemic pain at rest or ulcers or gangrene. A small number of patients with PAD have **acute limb ischemia** (ALI), a sudden decrease in limb perfusion, which

produces new or worsening symptoms that may threaten limb viability (Norgren et al., 2007). Potential causes of acute arterial occlusion include atherosclerotic stenosis, aneurysm, arterial dissection, arterial embolization, cardiac embolization, trauma (blunt injuries, fractures), tumor compression, graft thrombosis, drug abuse, low cardiac output, phlegmasia cerulean dolens (massive iliofemoral venous thrombosis), and compartment syndrome. Box 18-3 summarizes clinical manifestations of acute arterial occlusion.

Clinical signs and symptoms resulting from atherosclerosis are manifested in the end organ supplied by arterial blood flow. Patients complain of pain in the fingers or feet or pain in muscle groups with use (not the joints). Walking causes pain in the leg muscles, and physical activity causes pain in the upper extremity muscles. A description of pain and its precipitating factors, assessment of skin color and temperature, and peripheral pulse presence and character are important assessment parameters in the diagnosis of arterial disorders.

Pain

The hallmark symptom for PAD in the lower extremity is **intermittent claudication** (Box 18-4). This pain may be described as aching or cramping in a muscle that occurs with the same degree of exercise or activity and is relieved with rest. Intermittent claudication is caused by the inability of the arterial system to provide adequate blood flow to the tissues in the face of increased demands for nutrients and oxygen during exercise. As the tissues are forced to complete the energy cycle without adequate nutrients and oxygen, muscle metabolites and lactic acid are produced. Pain is experienced as the metabolites aggravate the nerve endings of the surrounding tissue. When the patient stops muscle activity and thereby decreases the metabolic needs of the muscles, the pain subsides. If the patient must sit to relieve the pain, the pain may be caused by a nerve injury to the back or a noncirculatory etiology. Progression of arterial disease can be monitored by documenting the ambulatory distance before pain is felt. Because the pain is associated with decreased perfusion, it is important to consider that

---

BOX 18-4 | Intermittent Claudication (IC)

- Cramp-like pain in a muscle
- Consistently reproduced with the same degree of exercise or activity
- Relieved by stopping muscle use
- Caused by inability of the arterial system to provide blood flow with increased demand
- Site of arterial disease can be determined by the location of claudication.
- Pain occurs in muscle groups distal to the diseased vessel
- 70% to 80% of patients do not have worsening symptoms.
- 1% to 2% of claudicants will progress to critical limb ischemia.
- Dependent position reduces pain.

---

the pain is reproducible from one day to the next on similar terrain.

The site of arterial disease can be determined by the location of claudication because pain occurs in muscle groups distal to the diseased vessel. Calf pain may accompany reduced blood flow through the superficial femoral or popliteal artery, whereas pain in the hip or buttock may result from reduced blood flow in the abdominal aorta or the common iliac or hypogastric arteries. Persistent pain in the anterior portion of the foot when the patient is resting indicates a severe degree of arterial insufficiency and a critical state of ischemia. Known as **rest pain**, this discomfort is often worse at night and may interfere with sleep. The basal metabolic rate and the arterial pressure extending to the foot is reduced during sleep and while in a recumbent position with the leg elevated. This pain frequently requires the extremity be lowered to a dependent position to improve perfusion to the distal tissues. The dependency of the lower extremity may cause some dependent edema in the extremity, thus edema may be associated with PAD. Rest pain is associated with limb threatening ischemia.

Upper extremity atherosclerotic stenosis may cause arm fatigue and pain with exercise (forearm claudication) and inability to hold or grasp objects (e.g., painting, combing hair, placing objects on shelves above the head).

Changes in Skin Appearance and Temperature

Inadequate blood flow results in cool and pale extremities. Further reduction of blood flow to the tissues, which occurs when the extremity is elevated, for example, results in an even whiter or more blanched appearance to the skin. When the extremity is placed in a dependant position after elevation, it becomes a reddish-blue color called **rubor**. This color change suggests severe peripheral arterial

---

BOX 18-3 | Focused Assessment

Acute Arterial Occlusion

Be alert for the following signs and symptoms, known as the "Six Ps":
- Pain (severe, shooting, stabbing, or burning sensation)
- Pallor (lighter color than rest of skin)
- Pulselessness (no palpable pulse)
- Poikilothermia (cool temperature to palpation)
- Paresthesia (numbness, tingling, hot/cold sensations)
- Paralysis (immobility (late sign), indicates severe tissue damage)

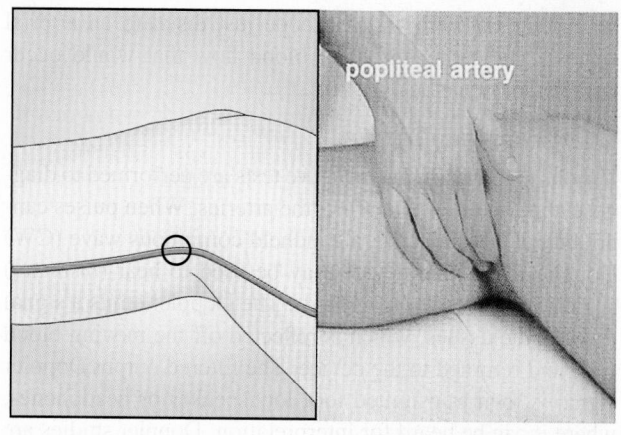

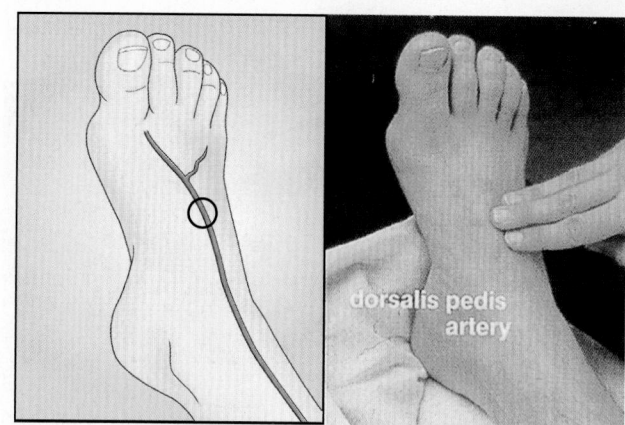

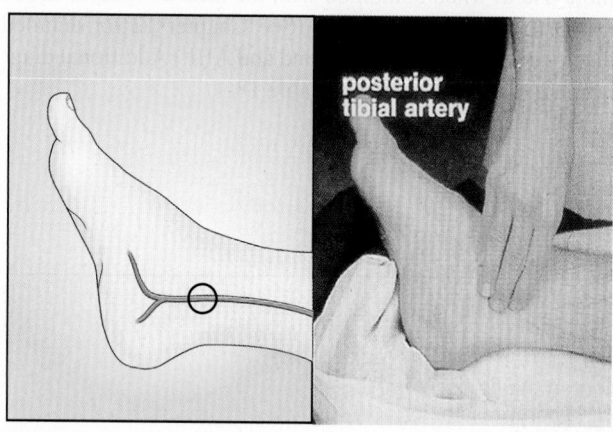

FIGURE 18-3 Assessing peripheral pulses. (*Left*) Popliteal pulse. (*Right*) Dorsalis pedis pulse. (*Bottom*) Posterior tibial pulse.

damage, in which vessels that cannot constrict remain dilated. *Cyanosis*, a bluish tint of the skin, is manifested when the amount of oxygenated hemoglobin contained in the blood is reduced. Skin color changes may be more subtle in darkly pigmented individuals. Comparing the contralateral limb is the best way to discern color changes. Capillary refill time (CRT) is frequently used as an assessment of peripheral perfusion. The nurse depresses the nail bed of the finger or toe between his or her fingers until it blanches. After releasing the pressure, the skin color in normal tissue is expected to return in less than 2 seconds. However, recent research findings call into question the efficacy of this test in assessing circulatory volume and because poor intraobserver agreement has been observed. The nurse considers this test not as a definitive marker for impaired perfusion but rather as an adjunctive tool to consider when clustering other manifestations of peripheral perfusion (Lewin & Maconochie, 2008; Sevransky, 2009).

Additional changes resulting from a chronically reduced nutrient supply include loss of hair, brittle nails, dry or scaling skin, atrophy, and ulcerations. Skin and nail changes, ulcers, gangrene, and muscle atrophy may be evident in chronic arterial disease but cannot be relied on for diagnosis of acute arterial insufficiency.

Pulses

Unequal pulses between extremities or the absence of a normally palpable pulse is a sign of PAD. Palpation of pulses (Fig. 18-3) is subjective. Box 18-5 provides tips for palpating pulses. The presence of good foot pulses does not exclude the possibility of PAD, and further investigation is required in the presence of leg pain. After exercise, the pulses may not be palpable. This is consistent with the distance the patient walks before experiencing claudication. **Bruits** may

---

BOX 18-5

Tips for Palpating Peripheral Pulses

- Use tips of fingers to palpate. To avoid mistaking your own pulse for that of the patient, use light touch and avoid using only the index finger for palpation because this finger has the strongest arterial pulsation of all the fingers. The thumb should not be used for the same reason.
- Palpate bilaterally and simultaneously.
- Compare both sides for symmetry in rate, rhythm, and quality.
- Document as present, absent, or bounding (if aneurysmal).

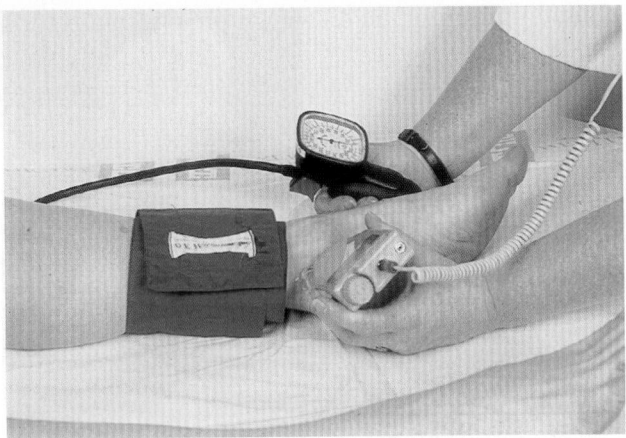

FIGURE 18-4 Continuous-wave (CW) Doppler ultrasound detects blood flow in peripheral vessels.

be auscultated with a stethoscope just distal to an arterial stenosis, indicating turbulent blood flow that would occur with vessel stenosis.

Diagnostic Tests

Various noninvasive and invasive tests are performed to diagnose abnormalities that affect the arteries. When pulses cannot be reliably palpated, a handheld continuous wave (CW) Doppler ultrasound device may be used to hear (*insonate*) signals in the vessels (Fig.18-4). The Doppler emits a signal through the tissues, which is reflected off the moving blood cells and returned to the device. The filtered output Doppler signal is then transmitted to a loudspeaker or headphones, where it can be heard for interpretation. Doppler studies are more useful when combined with the **ankle-brachial index (ABI)** (Grenon et al., 2009). (See Chapter 12 for detailed discussion of Doppler ultrasound and ABI.) Additional diagnostic tools are discussed in Table 18-1.

TABLE
18-1 **Noninvasive and Invasive Vascular Tests**

Test	Purpose
Doppler Ultrasound Flow Studies	Evaluation of arterial signals Blood pressure measurement in the limbs Assessment of vessel size and compressibility Assessment for presence of thrombus Assessment of valve function
Exercise Testing	Assessment of ankle systolic blood pressure in response to walking on treadmill (normal response is little or no drop in ankle systolic pressure after exercise) Assessment for claudication (a drop in ankle pressure correlates with claudication distance reported by the patient)
Duplex Ultrasonography	Localization of vascular obstruction Evaluation of stenosis Assessment for vascular reflux Provides both image and audible signal
Computed Tomography Angiography (CTA) (spiral or helical CT provides a series of images in continuous spiral)	Demonstration of cross-sectional images of soft tissue Diagnoses of abdominal aneurysms, graft infections or occlusions, hemorrhage
Magnetic Resonance Angiography (MRA)	Standard magnetic resonance imaging (MRI) scanner with software programmed to isolate blood vessels and reassemble images in three dimensions Detection of changes, aneurysms, DVT Useful in poor renal function or contrast agent allergy
Air Plethysmography	Measurement of volume, ejection fraction, and residual volume Quantification of venous reflux and calf muscle pump ejection
Venous Duplex	Assessment of venous reflux Manual compression of the veins
Angiography	Confirmation of occlusive arterial disease when considering interventions Patient may report sensation of warmth during injection and may have immediate or delayed allergic reaction to the iodine in the contrast agent Digital subtraction angiography (DSA) has bony structures removed from the image
Venography	Radiopaque contrast agent injected into the venous system produces an image showing unfilled segment of vein Used to outline vein for thrombolytic therapy Infrequently used (duplex ultrasound is standard for diagnosing venous thrombosis)
Vascular Endoscopy (Angioscopy)	Use of fiberoptics to visualize the vessel lumen Used to identify plaque, thrombus, hemorrhage, ulcers Used to remove debris or remove venous valves

Medical Management

Medical management includes exercise, pharmacologic treatment, and invasive options. Revascularization is recommended if there is a reasonable likelihood of symptomatic improvement and there has been an inadequate response to pharmacologic or exercise therapy. Invasive methods include surgery and percutaneous endoscopic procedures.

Management of Intermittent Claudication

Treatment goals for patients with intermittent claudication are to relieve symptoms, improve exercise performance, and improve functional abilities. Generally, patients with intermittent claudication feel better when on an exercise program. Initial treatment should be focused on a structured exercise program and pharmacotherapy. Patients are advised to "walk into the pain" of claudication, pause until the pain subsides, and continue walking. If this program is combined with weight reduction and tobacco cessation, patients may improve their activity tolerance and experience pain relief without further intervention.

Pharmacologic Therapy

Cilostazol is a phosphodiesterase III inhibitor that is a vasodilator and interferes with platelet aggregation. It is prescribed in combination with an exercise program to improve walking distance (Norgren et al., 2007). Guidelines recommend a 3- to 6-month course of cilostazol as first-line pharmacotherapy treatment for patients with intermittent claudication (Robless et al., 2008).

Antiplatelet agents, such as aspirin or clopidogrel, help prevent the formation of thromboemboli, which can lead to MI and stroke. Aspirin has been shown to reduce the risk of MI, stroke, and death in patients with vascular disease. Clopidogrel is indicated for the prevention of cardiovascular ischemic events in patients with PAD but not for treatment of claudication.

Thrombolysis

A thrombotic stenosis or occlusion may be treated by **thrombolysis**. After catheter insertion into the affected vessel, the thrombolytic agent is injected directly into the thrombus. It will lyse the thrombus (clot). The patient is admitted to a special or critical care unit for continuous monitoring. Vital signs are taken frequently, according to a protocol. The patient is closely monitored for any signs of bleeding, as this is the most common side effect of thrombolytic therapy. The nurse minimizes the number of punctures for IV lines and obtaining blood samples, avoids intramuscular injections, prevents tissue trauma, and applies pressure at least twice as long as usual after any puncture performed. Patients will have follow-up images to determine treatment effectiveness. Refer to Table 18-2 for discussion of thrombolytic agents.

Surgical Management

Disabling claudication or risk for amputation is an indication for surgical or percutaneous intervention. The initial treatment goal for ALI is to prevent worsening ischemia and thrombus propagation, manage pain, and preserve tissue. Anticoagulation is started immediately upon recognizing the acute ischemia. Revascularization or **arterial bypass** is the first-line intervention used in ALI treatment.

Vascular surgical procedures are divided into two groups: inflow procedures, which improve blood supply from the aorta into the femoral artery, and outflow procedures, which provide blood supply to vessels below the femoral artery. The type of procedure performed depends on the degree and location of the stenosis or occlusion. When diffuse disease is present, an inflow procedure is performed first. The restoration of arterial flow may be sufficient after this procedure, so that other procedures may not be needed. The overall health of the patient and the ability to tolerate a procedure factors into the decision as to what approach is best for each patient. For some patients who are at high risk or in a life-threatening situation, a primary amputation may be the best choice (Cronenwett et al., 2010).

Bypass grafts are performed to reroute blood flow around the stenosis or occlusion. Grafts below the knee require the use of native vein (i.e., autologous; the patient's own vein) to ensure patency; however, synthetic grafts may be used for bypass procedures on larger vessels above the knee. Several synthetic materials are available for use as a peripheral bypass graft. Cryopreserved saphenous veins and umbilical veins are also available, but usually do not last as long as native veins or synthetic grafts. Graft patency is determined by the size of the graft, graft type, and location. Great care is taken to prevent graft infection as the graft must be removed if infected. Vein grafts may be reversed before creating the graft conduit to prevent the valves from causing an occlusion, or they are left in place (*in situ*) and the valves are removed with a special instrument (valvulotome).

Doppler evaluation of the graft and the proximal vessels beyond the graft is usually performed for postprocedure vascular patients. Patients may have arterial studies, ABI, and arterial wave form analysis performed in the vascular laboratory after arterial reconstructive procedures and prior to discharge. Disappearance of a pulse or a Doppler signal that was previously present may indicate an occluded graft.

Endovascular Intervention

Several percutaneous interventional techniques are available to remove plaque and dilate vessels. **Angioplasty**, also called percutaneous transluminal **balloon angioplasty** (PTA), may be performed with or without a **stent**. Balloons are inserted into the vessels via a catheter and expanded at the stenotic site within the vessel. The expanding balloon cracks the atherosclerotic plaque and opens the vascular lumen. Stents may be inserted to support the vessel wall and maintain patency. Complications from PTA include hematoma, embolization, dissection of the vessel, bleeding, intimal damage (dissection), and stent migration. The advantage of angioplasty, stents, and **stent-grafts** compared to open surgical procedures is the decreased length of hospital stay required for the treatment and less physical trauma to the patient than open

TABLE
18-2 Arterial and Venous Thrombolysis

Indications (Arterial and Venous)	Drug	Suggested Dosage (Arterial)	Suggested Dosage (Venous)	Advantages (All Drugs in Arterial and Venous Thrombosis)	Disadvantages (All Drugs in Arterial and Venous Thrombosis)
In situ thrombosis of <14 days.	Alteplase	Standard regimen: 0.05–0.1 mg/kg/h intra-arterially High-dose regimen: 3 doses of 5 mg over 30 min, then 3.5 mg/h for up to 4 h	A catheter-directed infusion of 1–1.5 mg/h for 12–24 hours has been used; depends on local expertise.	Clot lysis between 6 and 72 hours Preferred choice for clot removal if no contraindications Avoidance of invasive surgical operations May be repeated if needed.	Limited in DVT lysis by long infusion times and risks of hemorrhagic complications associated with large doses
Non–life-threatening limb ischemia (arterial)	Reteplase	0.5 U/h by intra-arterial infusion	A catheter-directed infusion of 1 U/h is maintained for 18–36 hours. It is a non–FDA-approved indication for lysis of venous thrombus. It has been labeled by the FDA for acute MI, but it is widely used for acute DVT/PE.		Risk factors for hemorrhagic complications: older age, lower body weight, elevated pulse pressure, uncontrolled hypertension, recent stroke, recent operation, bleeding disorder, congestive heart failure
Initial treatment for many patients with acute peripheral arterial occlusions	Urokinase	4,000 U/min until initial recanalization, then 1,000–2,000 U/min until complete lysis, all given intra-arterially	Systemic dose: 4,400 U/kg IV bolus, with maintenance drip: 4,400 U/kg/h, continued for 1–3 days, until thrombus resolution. Intra-thrombus urokinase dose is a loading dose of 250,000 U IV, with an infusion of 500 U/kg/h The rate can be increased up to 2,000 U/kg/h.		Complications: hemorrhage, allergic reactions, embolism, stroke, reperfusion arrhythmias

Sources: Alteplase (Activase) [2005 package insert]. South San Francisco, CA: Genentech, Inc.
Reteplase [2006 package insert]. Fremont, CA: PDL BioPharma, Inc.
Urokinase (Abbokinase, Kinlytic) [2007 package insert]. Tucson, Arizona: ImaRx Therapeutics, Inc.
Grunwald, M.R., & Hofmann, L.V. Comparison of urokinase, alteplase and reteplase for catheter-directed thrombolysis of deep venous thrombosis. *J Vasc Interv Radiol.* Apr 2004;15(4):347–52. [Medline].
Sobel, M., & Verhaeghe, R. Antithrombotic therapy for peripheral artery occlusive disease: American College of Chest Physicians Evidence-Based Clinical Practice Guidelines (8th Edition). *Chest.* Jun 2008;133(6 Suppl):815S–843S. [Medline].

surgical procedures. Often percutaneous catheter procedures are performed in an outpatient setting (Moore, 2006).

Nursing Management

A plan of nursing care for a patient with peripheral vascular problems is available online at http://thePoint.lww.com/Pellico1e.

Providing Postoperative Care

In the postoperative period, the nurse collaborates with the surgeon about the patient's appropriate activity level based on the patient's condition. Generally, every effort is made to encourage patients to move the extremity and be active. The primary objective in the postprocedure period is to maintain adequate circulation. Anticoagulant therapy may be continued after surgery to prevent thrombosis of the

graft. Metabolic abnormalities, renal failure, and **compartment syndrome** are potential complications after arterial occlusions or operations (refer to Chapter 42 for details of compartment syndrome). The nurse assesses for evidence of local complications, such as hemorrhage or thrombosis, by performing neurovascular checks of the limb and systemic complications, by monitoring vital signs, intake and output, physical assessment parameters (e.g., pulmonary, cardiac, PV, GI, mental status), and laboratory data. Any evidence of deterioration is reported to the surgical team immediately (cool, dusky, weakened pulses, delayed capillary refill, decreased sensory/motor function).

Providing Pain Relief

Narcotics often are needed to manage rest pain until circulation can be restored. After interventions, pain management is similar to other postoperative patient care, keeping in mind that the patient may have been taking large doses of narcotics and may need more pain medication to relieve symptoms.

Maintaining Tissue Integrity

Poorly perfused tissues are susceptible to damage and infection. When lesions develop, healing may be delayed or inhibited because of the poor blood supply to the area. Infected, nonhealing ulcerations of the extremities can be debilitating and may require prolonged and often expensive treatments. Measures to prevent tissue loss and amputation are a high priority. Patients are taught to avoid trauma; wear sturdy, well-fitting shoes or slippers; and use neutral soaps and body lotions. Patients with vascular disease are taught the same precautions that diabetics are taught for foot care (see Chapter 30, Box 30-9). Patients who have an open arterial or venous ulcer are given detailed wound care instructions. Risk factor modification is the most effective intervention for preventing progression of vascular disease.

Patients and their families are educated on environmental and behavioral risk factors associated with ischemia. For example, excess heat may increase the metabolic rate of the extremities and increase the need for oxygen beyond that provided by the reduced arterial flow through the diseased artery. Cold temperature is associated with vasoconstriction, which decreases perfusion to the extremities. Nicotine from tobacco products causes vasospasm and can dramatically reduce circulation to the extremities. Tobacco smoke also impairs transport and cellular use of oxygen and increases blood viscosity. Patients with arterial insufficiency who use tobacco must be fully informed of the effects of nicotine on circulation and encouraged to stop using tobacco. Secondhand smoke is also harmful to the vascular system.

Emotional upsets cause vasoconstriction by stimulating the sympathetic nervous system. This can be minimized to some degree by avoiding stressful situations or by following a stress-management program. Counseling services or relaxation training may be indicated for people who cannot cope effectively with situational stressors.

Constrictive clothing and accessories are avoided, as are heating pads and hot water bottles. The temperature of bath water should also be evaluated, and the water temperature in the home decreased to prevent scalding. Tight socks, panty girdles, belts, and shoe laces impede arterial circulation to the extremities and promote venous congestion and edema. Finally, crossing of the legs is avoided to prevent vessel compression.

> **NURSING ALERT**
> *Elevation of the lower extremities is associated with decreased flow, which lessens perfusion and increases pain. A dependent position improves flow and decreases pain.*

UPPER EXTREMITY ARTERIAL OCCLUSIVE DISEASE

Arterial occlusions from atherosclerosis occur less frequently in the upper extremities than in the legs.

Pathophysiology

Upper extremity arterial symptoms and occlusive disease are more likely to be caused by vasospasm, trauma, or arterial constrictive disorders than by atherosclerosis.

Stenosis may occur at the origin of the subclavian artery proximal to the vertebral artery. Arterial blood flows to the brain via the carotid and the vertebral arteries. If there is diminished flow to the arm from the subclavian artery due to the stenosis, there will be preferential reverse flow down the vertebral artery to the arm when the arm is being used. This is called *subclavian steal syndrome* as the arm is "stealing" blood from the brain.

Clinical Manifestations and Assessment

The patient may complain of arm fatigue and pain when using the arm to paint or comb hair, and may occasionally report difficulty when driving. Patients also report dizziness, vertigo, ataxia, syncope, or bilateral visual changes when using the arm.

Assessment findings in the ischemic upper extremity may include coolness and pallor of the affected extremity, decreased capillary refill, a decreased amplitude and delay in radial artery pulse on the affected side, and a difference in arm blood pressures of more than 20 mm Hg (affected limb pressure is lower). Noninvasive studies performed to evaluate for upper extremity arterial occlusions include upper and forearm blood pressure determinations and duplex ultrasonography to identify the anatomic location of the lesion and to evaluate the hemodynamics of the blood flow.

Medical and Nursing Management

Surgical bypass or a PTA procedure may be indicated. If the stenosis involves the subclavian artery with siphoning of blood from the intracranial circulation, a carotid-to-subclavian artery bypass or reimplantation of the subclavian to the carotid artery may be performed.

INFLAMMATORY DISORDERS

Various inflammatory diseases affect the arterial system. Examples of these are Takayasu's arteritis, Behçet's disease, and giant cell arteritis. The inflammatory response creates granuloma formation and causes vessel destruction. Initial treatment for active vascular inflammatory diseases is high-dose corticosteroids. Revascularization, if indicated, is delayed until the inflammatory process in under control.

RAYNAUD'S DISEASE AND RAYNAUD'S PHENOMENON

Primary *Raynaud's disease* refers to vasospasm that occurs with cold or stress. Patients with scleroderma or systemic lupus erythematosus may have the same signs and symptoms. This is called *Raynaud's phenomenon.*

Pathophysiology

Raynaud's disease is of unknown etiology. While its exact cause is unknown, it may be associated with immunologic disorders. Emotional factors or cold may trigger episodes.

It usually occurs in women of between 16 and 40 years, and occurs more frequently in cold climates and during the winter. It may cause skin and muscle atrophy.

Prognosis varies; patients may slowly improve, become progressively worse, or show no change.

Clinical Manifestations and Assessment

The patient's skin becomes cyanotic due to vasospasm, then vasodilation causes redness (rubor). Numbness, tingling, and burning pain occur.

Medical and Nursing Management

With appropriate patient teaching and lifestyle modifications, the disorder is generally benign and self-limiting. The patient is instructed to avoid the stimuli (e.g., cold, tobacco) that provoke vasoconstriction. The patient may be prescribed calcium channel blockers to relieve symptoms. Sympathectomy (interrupting the sympathetic nerves) may help some patients.

THROMBOANGIITIS OBLITERANS (BUERGER'S DISEASE)

Buerger's disease is characterized by recurring inflammation of the intermediate and small arteries and vein, resulting in thrombus formation and vessel occlusion. It occurs in both upper and lower extremities. It is differentiated from vessel diseases by microscopic appearance.

Buerger's disease is an autoimmune disease. While its etiology is unknown, it is believed to be an autoimmune **vasculitis** (inflammation of a blood vessel). It most often occurs in men between 20 and 35 years and is reported in all races. Tobacco use is a causative factor, and continued use interferes with healing. Pain is generally bilateral and symmetric with focal lesions.

Treatment is essentially the same as atherosclerotic PAD; sympathetic block may dilate vessels and increase blood flow. Tobacco cessation is mandatory for healing to occur.

ANEURYSMS

An aneurysm is a localized out-pouching, sac, or dilation formed at a weak point in the artery wall (Fig. 18-5). It may be classified by its shape or form. The most common forms of aneurysms are saccular and fusiform. A *saccular aneurysm* projects from one side of the vessel only. If an entire arterial segment becomes dilated, a *fusiform aneurysm* develops. Very small aneurysms due to localized infection are called *mycotic aneurysms. Aortic aneurysms* occur in the abdominal and thoracic aorta and are characterized by disruption and loss of elastic fibers, resulting in degeneration of the medial vessel wall. It is thought to be an inflammatory process.

ABDOMINAL AORTIC ANEURYSM

Historically, the cause of abdominal aortic aneurysm (AAA), the most common type of degenerative aneurysm, has been attributed to atherosclerotic changes in the aorta. Most AAA are asymptomatic and are found on routine examinations or during a workup for another condition. Aneurysms are serious because they can rupture, leading to hemorrhage and death. If the AAA ruptures, mortality rates as high as 80% are seen (Lederie & Simel, 2009).

Pathophysiology

All aneurysms involve a damaged media layer of the vessel. This may be caused by congenital weakness, trauma, or disease. The degradation of the medial elastin fibers and collagen (which gives the vessel strength) leads to the weakening and dilation of the aorta and the development of aneurysm. After an aneurysm develops, it tends to enlarge, growing at

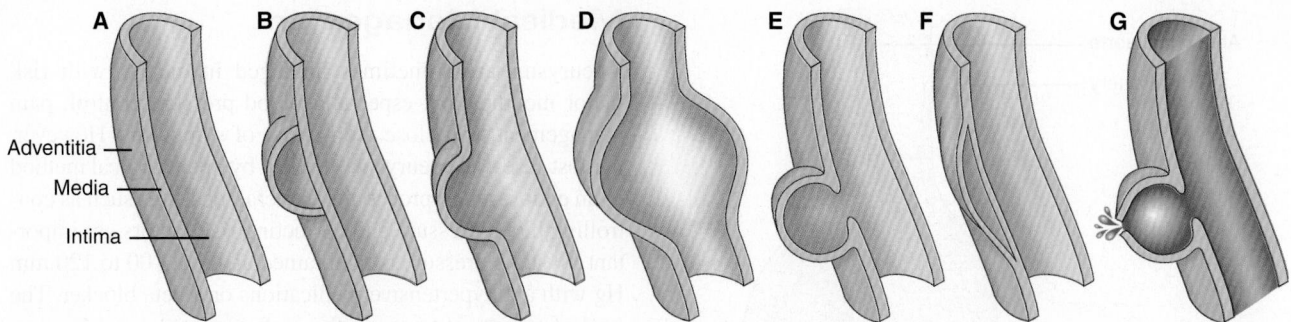

FIGURE 18-5 Characteristics of arterial aneurysm. **(A)** Normal artery. **(B)** False aneurysm (pseudoaneurysm); actually a pulsating hematoma. The clot and connective tissue are outside the arterial wall. **(C)** True aneurysm. One, two, or all three layers of the artery may be involved. **(D)** Fusiform aneurysm; symmetric, spindle-shaped expansion of entire circumference of involved vessel. **(E)** Saccular aneurysm; a bulbous protrusion of one side of the arterial wall. **(F)** Dissecting aneurysm; this usually is a hematoma that splits the layers of the arterial wall. **(G)** Ruptured aneurysm.

a rate of 0.4 cm per year on average; however, there is no predictable pattern (Lumsden, Peden, Bush et al., 2008).

Risk Factors

Risk factors include age (>50), male sex, tobacco use, family history, and hypertension. Many types of aneurysms have a genetic basis. Patient education includes advising family members to be evaluated for aneurysms.

Clinical Manifestations and Assessment

Not all patients with AAA have symptoms. Some patients complain that they can feel their heart beating in their abdomen when lying down, or they may say they feel an abdominal mass or abdominal throbbing. If the AAA is associated with thrombus, a major vessel may be occluded or smaller distal occlusions may result from emboli. Small **cholesterol**, platelet, or fibrin emboli may lodge in the digital arteries, causing cyanosis and mottling of the toes.

Signs of impending aneurysm rupture include severe back or abdominal pain, which may be persistent or intermittent. Abdominal pain is often localized in the middle or lower abdomen to the left of the midline. Low back pain may be present because of pressure of the aneurysm on the lumbar nerves. This is a significant symptom, usually indicating that the aneurysm is expanding rapidly and is about to rupture. Indications of a rupturing abdominal aortic aneurysm include constant, intense back pain; falling blood pressure; and decreasing hematocrit. Rupture into the peritoneal cavity is rapidly fatal, and surgical repair is the only chance for survival. A retroperitoneal rupture of an aneurysm may result in hematomas in the scrotum, perineum, flank, or penis.

The most important diagnostic indication of an abdominal aortic aneurysm is a pulsatile mass in the abdomen. These aneurysms can be palpated if the patient is not obese. A systolic bruit may be heard over the mass. Duplex ultra-sonography or computed tomography (CT) is used to determine the size, length, and location of the aneurysm.

Medical Management

When the aneurysm is small, ultrasonography is conducted at 6-month intervals. Some aneurysms remain stable over many years of observation.

Pharmacological Therapy

If an aneurysm is stable in size based on serial duplex ultrasound scans, the blood pressure is closely monitored over time. There is an association between increased diastolic blood pressure, size increase, and rupture. Antihypertensive agents, including diuretics, beta blockers, angiotensin-converting enzyme (ACE) inhibitors, angiotensin II receptor antagonists, and calcium channel blockers, may be prescribed to maintain the patient's blood pressure within acceptable limits.

Surgical Management

An expanding or enlarging AAA is likely to rupture. Surgery is the treatment of choice for AAAs more than 5.5 cm wide or those that are enlarging. An alternative for treating an infrarenal (below the renal arteries) AAA is endovascular grafting, which involves percutaneous transluminal placement and attachment of an aortic graft prosthesis across the aneurysm (Fig. 18-6). This procedure is performed under local or regional anesthesia. Potential complications are similar to other endograft procedures (discussed later). It is important to consider that the overall surgical mortality rate associated with a ruptured aneurysm is 50% to 75%, therefore early intervention is warranted. Nursing management after surgery can be found after the discussion of other types of aneurysms (see *Nursing Management After Surgical Interventions*, p. 501).

THORACIC AORTIC ANEURYSM

Approximately 85% of all cases of thoracic aortic aneurysm are caused by atherosclerosis. They occur most frequently in

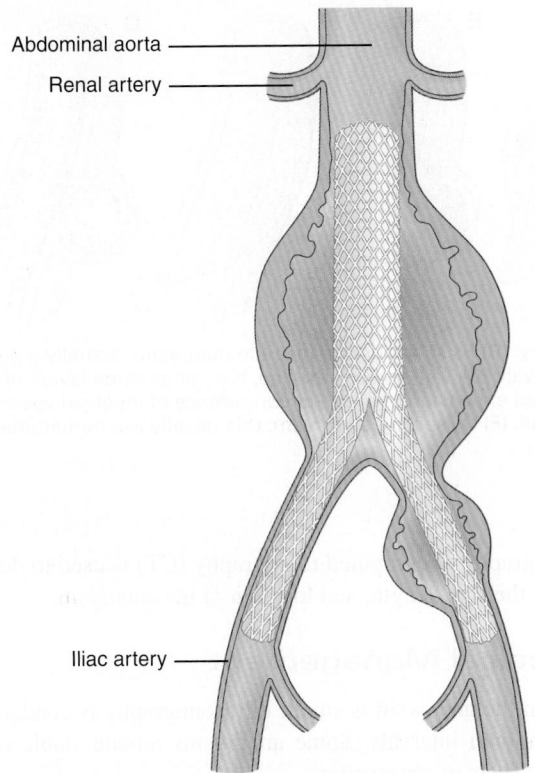

Abdominal aorta

Renal artery

Iliac artery

FIGURE 18-6 AneuRx Endograft repair of an abdominal aortic aneurysm (Medtronic).

men between the ages of 40 and 70 years. The thoracic area is the most common site for a dissecting aneurysm. About one-third of patients with thoracic aneurysms die of rupture of the aneurysm.

Clinical Manifestations and Assessment

Symptoms are variable and depend on how rapidly the aneurysm dilates and how the pulsating mass affects surrounding intrathoracic structures. Some patients are asymptomatic. In most cases, pain is the most prominent symptom. The pain is usually constant and of a boring quality, but may occur only when the person is supine. Other symptoms are dyspnea, the result of pressure of the aneurysm sac against the trachea, a main bronchus, or the lung itself; cough, frequently paroxysmal and with a brassy quality; hoarseness, stridor, or weakness or complete loss of the voice (aphonia), resulting from pressure against the laryngeal nerve; and dysphagia (difficulty in swallowing) due to impingement on the esophagus by the aneurysm.

When large veins in the chest are compressed by the aneurysm, the superficial veins of the chest, neck, or arms become dilated; edematous areas on the chest wall and cyanosis are often evident. Pressure against the cervical sympathetic chain can result in unequal pupils. Diagnosis of a thoracic aortic aneurysm is principally made by chest X-ray, transesophageal echocardiography (TEE), and CT.

Medical Management

Aneurysms are sometimes managed medically with risk factor modification, especially blood pressure control, pain management, and close monitoring of symptoms. However, in most cases, an aneurysm is treated by open surgical method or an endovascular procedure. General measures such as controlling blood pressure and correcting risk factors are important. Systolic pressure is maintained at about 100 to 120 mm Hg with antihypertensive medications or a beta blocker. The goal of surgery is to repair the aneurysm and restore vascular continuity with a vascular graft. Intensive monitoring is usually required after an open surgical procedure, and the patient is cared for in the critical care unit. Endovascular graft repair of thoracic aneurysms decrease postoperative recovery time and decrease complications compared with traditional surgical techniques. These endovascular grafts are inserted into the thoracic aorta via various vascular access routes, including the femoral or iliac artery. Because a large incision is not necessary to gain vascular access, the overall patient recovery time is shorter with endograft intervention than with open surgical repair. Postoperatively the immediate concern is blood pressure control and a device-related complication termed an *endoleak* from the endovascular graft. An endoleak is a persistent leaking of blood out of the graft and into the aneurysm sac. Early leaks have the potential to rupture within the first 30 postoperative days (primary endoleaks), but late endoleaks (secondary endoleaks) can occur as late as 7 years after the procedure. An endoleak is screened by CT scanning and duplex ultrasound. The nurse considers that during the operative procedure, necessary vessel clamping can have profound effect on the mesentery circulation (gut), renal circulation (kidneys), and artery of Adamkiewicz (supplies the lower two-thirds of the spinal cord). Postoperatively, regardless of type of procedure performed, the patient is assessed for changes in mentation, vision, speech, or motor strength, as well as pain in the abdomen or flank, vomiting, or bloody diarrhea, which may indicate embolization to cerebral vessels or other organs and should be reported to the surgeon immediately. Additionally, depending on length of time the aorta was clamped during the surgery, concerns include spinal cord ischemia with resultant paraplegia and renal insufficiency—thus, renal function and sensory/motor function is assessed post operatively. Patients undergoing open surgical procedures go the intensive care unit and are on mechanical ventilation postoperatively. Endovascular procedures may not require intensive care unit monitoring post procedure (Lumsden et al., 2008).

PERIPHERAL ANEURYSMS

Aneurysms may also arise in the peripheral vessels, most often as a result of atherosclerosis. These may involve the renal artery, femoral artery, or (most frequently) popliteal artery. Between 50% and 60% of popliteal aneurysms are bilateral and may be associated with abdominal aortic aneurysms.

The aneurysm produces a pulsating mass and disturbs peripheral circulation distal to it. Pain and swelling develop because of pressure on adjacent nerves and veins. Diagnosis is made by duplex ultrasonography and CT to determine the size, length, and extent of the aneurysm. Arteriography may be performed to evaluate the level of proximal and distal involvement.

DISSECTING ANEURYSM

Occasionally, in an aorta diseased by arteriosclerosis, a tear develops in the intima or the media degenerates, resulting in a dissection (refer to Fig. 18-5, p. 499). Dissections may be treated medically or surgically.

Pathophysiology

Arterial dissections are commonly associated with poorly controlled hypertension, blunt force chest trauma, and cocaine use. Dissection is caused by rupture in the intimal layer. A rupture may occur through adventitia or into the lumen through the intima, allowing blood to reenter the main channel, resulting in chronic dissection or occlusion of branches of the aorta.

As the separation progresses, the arteries branching from the involved area of the aorta shear and occlude. The tear occurs most commonly in the region of the aortic arch, with the highest mortality rate associated with ascending aortic dissection. The dissection of the aorta may progress toward the heart, obstructing the orifices of the coronary arteries, producing hemopericardium (effusion of blood into the pericardial sac), or aortic insufficiency, or it may extend distally, occluding the arteries supplying the GI tract, kidneys, spinal cord, and legs.

Clinical Manifestations and Assessment

Onset of symptoms is usually sudden. Severe and persistent pain, described as tearing or ripping, may be reported. The pain is in the anterior chest or back and extends to the shoulders, epigastric area, or abdomen. Aortic dissection may be mistaken for an acute MI, which could confuse the clinical picture and initial treatment. Cardiovascular, neurologic, and GI symptoms are responsible for other clinical manifestations, depending on the location and extent of the dissection. The patient may appear pale. Sweating and tachycardia may be detected. Blood pressure may be elevated or markedly different from one arm to the other if dissection involves the orifice of the subclavian artery on one side. Because of the variable clinical picture associated with this condition, early diagnosis is difficult.

Nursing Management After Surgical Interventions

Surgical repair of the aorta is performed for dissection, rupture, and aneurysm. General postoperative nursing assessment involves frequent vital signs; recording of intake and output; assessment of oxygen saturation; bilateral comparison of upper arm blood pressures and peripheral pulses; and assessment of motor and sensory function, temperature of extremities, color changes, and capillary refill. The patient who has had an endovascular repair must lie supine according to a protocol. The patient needs to use a bedpan or urinal while on bed rest. The access site (usually the femoral or iliac artery) is assessed when vital signs and pulses are monitored. The nurse assesses for bleeding, pulsation, swelling, pain, and hematoma formation. Additionally, the patient is monitored for signs of embolization to the lower extremities, therefore skin changes of the lumbar area, buttocks, and lower extremity (plantar area of the feet or toes are often affected) are assessed for extremely tender, irregularly shaped, cyanotic areas.

The patient's temperature should be monitored according to a protocol, and any signs of postimplantation syndrome should be reported. Postimplantation syndrome typically begins within 24 hours of stent-graft placement and consists of a spontaneously occurring fever, leukocytosis, and, occasionally, transient thrombocytopenia. The exact etiology is unknown, but the symptoms are thought to be related to the activation of cytokines, which results from thrombosis in the repaired aneurysm that occurs because of the release of coagulation proteins and platelets. These symptoms can be managed with mild analgesics or anti-inflammatory agents, such as acetaminophen or ibuprofen, and usually subside within a week.

Because of the increased risk for hemorrhage, the surgeon is notified of persistent coughing, sneezing, vomiting, or systolic blood pressure greater than 180 mm Hg. Most patients can resume their preprocedure diet and are encouraged to drink fluids. An IV infusion may be continued until the patient can drink normally. Fluids are important to maintain blood flow through the arterial repair site and to assist the kidneys with excreting IV contrast agent and other medications used during the procedure. According to a protocol, after a procedure that involves a catheter in the groin, the patient may be able to roll from side to side and may be able to ambulate with assistance to the bathroom. After the patient can take adequate fluids orally, the IV infusion may be discontinued and the IV access converted to a saline lock. Postoperative care requires intense monitoring of pulmonary, cardiovascular, renal, and neurologic status. Pulmonary complications include the potential development of acute respiratory distress syndrome (ARDS), particularly if large quantities of blood were required intraoperatively (refer to Chapter 10 for discussion of ARDS). MI and arrhythmias are potential cardiac complications and are discussed in Chapters 14 and 17, respectively. GI complications include a risk for ischemic colitis, and symptoms include bloody diarrhea, abdominal distention, leukocytosis, fever, and abdominal pain. Because acute renal failure is a potential complication, urine output is monitored hourly and laboratory parameters

are monitored (blood urea nitrogen [BUN] and creatinine values) for significant changes. Potential injury to the spinal cord with resultant paraplegia requires that the nurse assess the patient's sensory motor function postoperatively. Additionally, since it is important that perfusion to the spinal cord be maintained, the nurse frequently assesses blood pressure measurements and the surgeon is alerted upon evidence of decreasing parameters.

Before discharge, the patient is assisted in developing and implementing a plan to stop using tobacco and to manage pain. The patient may need to be encouraged to make the lifestyle changes necessary to adequately manage a chronic disease, including modifications in diet, activity, and hygiene. The nurse assesses the patient's resources, including family and friends to assist as needed. The nurse ensures that the patient has the knowledge and ability to assess for disease progression and postoperative or postprocedure complications as needed.

VENOUS DISORDERS

Venous blood flow is reduced by a thrombus or **embolus** obstructing a vein, by incompetent venous valves, or by a reduction of the pumping action effectiveness of surrounding muscles. Decreased venous blood flow causes increased venous pressure, which increases capillary hydrostatic pressure, facilitating filtration of fluid out of the capillaries into the interstitial space, with resultant development of tissue edema. Edematous tissue does not receive adequate nutrition from the blood and is more susceptible to breakdown, injury, and infection. Thus, the nurse is aware that edematous tissue is fragile tissue.

VENOUS THROMBOSIS

The terms *venous thrombosis, deep vein thrombosis* (DVT), *thrombophlebitis,* and *phlebothrombosis* do not necessarily reflect identical disease processes, but they are grouped together for clinical purposes.

Pathophysiology

The exact cause of venous thrombosis remains unclear. Three factors, known as *Virchow's triad* (Box 18-6), are believed to play a significant role in the development of venous thrombosis. Some hypercoagulable states are hereditary. Patients with these states should have a hematology consult.

Upper extremity venous thrombosis is not as common as lower extremity thrombosis. However, it may occur in patients with IV catheters (IV lines or wires from pacemaker leads, chemotherapy ports, dialysis catheters, or parenteral nutrition lines) or in patients with an underlying hypercoagulation disorder. Effort thrombosis is caused by repetitive motion (as in competitive swimmers, tennis players, and construction workers) that irritates the vessel wall, causing inflammation and subsequent thrombosis.

BOX 18-6 **Virchow's Triad**

1. *Stasis of blood*: Caused by immobility (bed rest, long plane/car/train rides, obesity, constrictive devices, paralysis, paresis, recent surgery, varicose veins, pregnancy).
2. *Vessel wall injury*: Caused by trauma (fractures, contusions), central venous catheterization, vascular devices (PICC, central lines, pacemaker wires), IV medications, cancer therapy (hormonal, chemotherapy, or radiotherapy).
3. *Altered coagulation*: Caused by estrogen-containing oral contraception or hormone replacement, cancer (secretes procoagulants), smoking, dehydration, hypercoagulable states, late pregnancy, and the postpartum period

---

Venous thrombi are aggregates of platelets attached to the vein wall that have a tail-like appendage containing fibrin, white blood cells, and many red blood cells. The thrombus can propagate as successive layers of thrombus form. A propagating venous thrombosis is dangerous because it is often the source of a pulmonary embolism (PE). Thrombus fragmentation can occur spontaneously or in association with an elevated venous pressure, as when a person stands suddenly or engages in muscular activity after prolonged inactivity. After an episode of acute DVT, recanalization of the lumen of the vessel occurs. However, the venous valves remain open and are ineffective. Reverse venous flow contributes to chronic venous insufficiency. Over time, postphlebitic syndrome (Box 18-7) occurs, manifested by skin and tissue changes.

Clinical Manifestations and Assessment

A major problem associated with recognizing DVT is that the signs and symptoms are nonspecific. The exception is

---

BOX 18-7 **Focus on Pathophysiology**

Postphlebitic Syndrome

Post phlebitic syndrome develops as follows:
1. Venous valve injury results in an incompetent valve and reverse venous flow.
2. Fluid, plasma, and red blood cells leak into the interstitial tissue.
3. Edema forms around ankles, lower legs.
4. Internal staining of skin occurs as red blood cells break down, releasing hemosiderin.
5. Subcutaneous tissue becomes firm, fibrotic.
6. Loss of elasticity in skin and subcutaneous tissue results.
7. Tissue becomes vulnerable to trauma and ulcer formation.

phlegmasia cerulea dolens (massive iliofemoral venous thrombosis), in which the entire extremity becomes massively swollen, tense, painful, and cool to the touch. Despite this variability, clinical signs should always be investigated.

Deep venous obstruction is associated with edema of the extremity due to inhibition of venous outflow. Swelling can be measured by obtaining the circumference of the affected extremity at specific levels and comparing one extremity with the other at the same level. The affected extremity may feel warmer than the unaffected extremity.

Tenderness, which usually occurs later, is produced by inflammation of the vein wall, and a cord may be detected in the involved veins by gently palpating the affected extremity. *Homans' sign* (pain in the calf after the foot is sharply dorsiflexed) used to be considered a sign of DVT, but is not reliable and is not used anymore. In some cases, signs and symptoms of a PE are the first indication of DVT.

Superficial vein thrombosis produces pain or tenderness, redness, and warmth in the involved area. Many of them dissolve spontaneously. This condition can be treated at home with bed rest, limb elevation, analgesics, and anti-inflammatory medication. It should be noted that while nonsteroidal anti-inflammatory drugs (NSAIDs) provide analgesia, they may obscure clinical evidence of thrombus propagation (Creager & Loscalzo, 2008).

Careful assessment is the key in detecting early signs of lower extremity venous disorders. Patients with a history of varicose veins, hypercoagulation, neoplastic disease, cardiovascular disease, or recent major surgery or injury are at high risk. Other patients at high risk include those who are obese, immobile, or elderly, and women taking oral contraceptives. Differences in leg circumference bilaterally from thigh to ankle; increase in the surface temperature of the leg, particularly the calf or ankle; and areas of tenderness or superficial thrombosis should be noted. Asymmetry of extremities (calf swelling at least 3 cm larger than asymptomatic leg, measured 10 cm below the tibial tuberosity, should alert the nurse to a potential DVT. In addition, the nurse should assess for the presence of a low-grade fever.

⚡ N U R S I N G   A L E R T

The D-dimer blood assay is a marker of coagulation activity. When a clot lyses, fibrin degradation occurs and a D-dimer is positive. When positive, it is associated with clot breakdown, such as the presence of DVT or PE, but it is also associated with a variety of nonthrombotic disorders including recent surgery, hemorrhage, trauma, cancer, MI, pneumonia, and sepsis. Thus, D-dimers are frequently elevated due to some systemic illness; however, a negative D-dimer decreases the likelihood of a DVT or PE.

Prevention

Preventive measures should be instituted for patients at risk for DVT. These might include physical interventions such as elastic compression stockings, intermittent pneumatic compression devices, and body positioning and exercise. Medications to prevent thrombosis include anticoagulant therapy, such as subcutaneous unfractionated or low-molecular-weight heparin (LMWH).

Medical Management

The objectives of treatment for DVT are to prevent the thrombus from growing and fragmenting (risking PE) and to prevent recurrent thromboemboli. Interventions to prevent thrombus formation are indicated in patients with thrombophlebitis, recurrent embolus formation, persistent leg edema from heart failure, and in any patients who may require lengthy immobilization.

Pharmacologic Therapy
Heparin

Anticoagulant therapy is effective prophylaxis; however, anticoagulants do not dissolve a thrombus that has already formed.

UNFRACTIONATED HEPARIN. Unfractionated heparin is administered subcutaneously to prevent development of DVT. In the event of a DVT, although heparin can be administered subcutaneously, common practice will be administered via an IV drip to prevent the extension of a thrombus and the development of new thrombi. IV heparin produces an immediate anticoagulant effect, and therefore is used when rapid anticoagulant effects are desired. Unfractionated heparin is administered via an infusion pump to carefully control the rate. Dosage is based on the patient's weight, and any possible bleeding tendencies are detected by a pre-treatment clotting profile. If renal insufficiency exists, lower doses of heparin are required. Periodic coagulation tests and hematocrit levels are obtained. Heparin is in the effective, or therapeutic, range when the activated partial thromboplastin time (aPTT) is 1.5 times to 2.5 times the baseline control. Normal aPTT level is 21 to 35 seconds (Fischbach & Dunning, 2009). If the PTT is greater than 100 seconds, the risk for hemorrhage is significant! The nurse is aware that heparin has a half-life of about 60 minutes; therefore, in an emergency, the heparin is discontinued for a period of at least 1 hour.

Coumadin, an oral anticoagulant, is administered soon after initiating heparin therapy, since Coumadin may require 3 to 5 days to achieve a therapeutic effect. Until a therapeutic international normalized ratio (INR) is achieved, both medications are administered concurrently. Medication dosage is regulated by monitoring the aPTT for heparin, the INR for Coumadin, and the platelet count, to assess for potential complications of heparin therapy (discussed later in this chapter) (Rawat et al., 2008).

LOW-MOLECULAR-WEIGHT HEPARIN (LMWH) Subcutaneous LMWH is an effective treatment for some cases of

DVT. These agents have longer half-lives than unfractionated heparin, so doses can be given in one or two subcutaneous injections each day. Doses are adjusted according to patient weight. LMWH prevents the extension of a thrombus and development of new thrombi, and they are associated with fewer bleeding complications and lower risks of heparin-induced thrombocytopenia (HIT) than is unfractionated heparin. Because there are several preparations, the dosing schedule must be based on the product used and the protocol at each institution. Because LMWH is cleared almost entirely by the kidneys, clearance can be variable in patients with renal insufficiency, thus a longer half-life may be expected. The cost of LMWH is higher than that of unfractionated heparin; however, LMWH may be used safely in pregnant women.

Thrombolytic Therapy

Unlike heparin, thrombolytic (fibrinolytic) therapy lyses and dissolves thrombi. Thrombolytic therapy is most effective if given within the first 3 days after acute thrombosis. The advantages of thrombolytic therapy is less long-term damage to the venous valves and less likelihood of post-thrombotic syndrome and chronic venous insufficiency. However, there is an increase in bleeding complications with thrombolytics than with heparin. If bleeding occurs, the thrombolytic agent may be discontinued. See Table 18-2 for thrombolytic therapy.

Oral Anticoagulants

Warfarin is a vitamin K antagonist that is frequently used for extended anticoagulant therapy. Routine coagulation monitoring is essential to ensure that a therapeutic response is obtained and maintained over time. Interactions with a range of other medications and various foods with vitamin K can reduce or enhance the anticoagulant effects of warfarin. Warfarin has a narrow therapeutic window, and there is a slow onset of action. Oral anticoagulants, such as warfarin (Coumadin), are monitored by the INR. Because the full anticoagulant effect of warfarin is delayed for 3 to 5 days, treatment is initially supported with concomitant parenteral anticoagulation with heparin until the warfarin demonstrates anticoagulant effectiveness; then the heparin can be discontinued and the patient maintained on oral Coumadin. A normal INR is approximately 1. The target INR depends on why the person is being anticoagulated. If for example, it is related to atrial fibrillation or DVT, the INR range will be 2 to 3, with a goal of 2.5. Once INR is stable, levels are checked weekly for 2 to 4 weeks, progressing to monthly thereafter (Rawat, Huynh, Peden et al., 2008). Refer to Table 18-3 for list of therapeutic goals for INR.

Surgical Management

Surgery is necessary for DVT when anticoagulant or thrombolytic therapy is contraindicated, the danger of PE is likely, or the venous drainage is so severely compromised that permanent damage to the extremity is likely. A thrombectomy

TABLE
18-3 Therapeutic Context

	INR	Target
Non–hip surgery	1.5–2.5	2.0
Hip surgery	2.0–3.0	2.5
Primary and secondary prevention of deep vein thrombosis	2.0–3.0	2.5
Prevention of systemic embolism in patients with atrial fibrillation	2.0–3.0	2.5
Recurrent systemic embolism	3.0–4.5	3.5
Prevention of recurrent deep vein thrombosis (two or more episodes)	2.5–4.0	3.0
Cardiac stents	3.0–4.5	3.5
Prevention of arterial thrombosis, including patients with mechanical heart valves	3.0–4.5	3.5

Fischbach, F., & Dunning, M. (2009). Manual of laboratory and diagnostic tests (8th ed.). Philadelphia: Wolters Kluwer Health | Lippincott Williams & Wilkins. Reprinted with permission.

(removal of the thrombosis) is the procedure of choice. A vena cava filter may be placed at the time of the thrombectomy; this filter traps large emboli and prevents PE (see Chapter 10, Fig. 10-8). The filter does not prevent other thrombi from forming. Balloon angioplasty and stent placement are being used in the iliac veins of patients with acute and chronic venous disease.

Nursing Management

Monitoring Drug Therapy

When the patient is receiving anticoagulant therapy, the nurse frequently monitors the aPTT, prothrombin time (PT), INR, activated coagulation time (ACT), hemoglobin and hematocrit values, platelet count, and fibrinogen level, depending on which medication is being given.

Nurses must watch for potential complications; the principal one is spontaneous bleeding anywhere in the body. Bleeding from the kidneys is detected by microscopic examination of the urine and is often the first sign of excessive dosage. Bruises, nosebleeds, and bleeding gums are also early signs. To promptly reverse the effects of heparin, protamine sulfate may be administered. Risks of protamine administration include bradycardia and hypotension, which can be minimized by slow administration. Protamine sulfate can be used in patients receiving LMWH, but it is less effective with LMWH than with unfractionated heparin. Reversing the anticoagulation effects of warfarin is more difficult, but effective measures may include administration of vitamin K and/or infusion of fresh-frozen plasma or prothrombin concentrate. Oral vitamin K significantly reduces the INR within 24 hours. Low-dose IV vitamin K is also effective.

HIT may be another complication of therapy, which is defined as a sudden decrease in the platelet count by at least 30% of baseline levels in patients receiving heparin.

Patients at greatest risk for bleeding are those who receive unfractionated heparin for a long period of time (i.e., several days or weeks). Therefore, it is preferable not to anticoagulate patients with unfractionated heparin over the long term. Beginning warfarin concomitantly with heparin can provide a stable INR by day 5 of heparin treatment, at which time the heparin may be discontinued.

The administration of LMWH is less frequently associated with HIT. The thrombocytopenia is thought to result from an autoimmune mechanism that causes destruction of platelets. If the process is not arrested, platelets may aggregate, initiating inappropriate clotting, and thrombosis may occur. This serious complication results in thromboembolic manifestations throughout the body, and the prognosis is extremely guarded.

Prevention of thrombocytopenia depends on regular monitoring of platelet counts. Early signs of complications associated with anticoagulants include a decreasing platelet count, the need for increasing doses of heparin to maintain the therapeutic level, and thromboembolic or hemorrhagic complications, such as skin necrosis at the injection site and at distal sites of thromboses, and skin discoloration consisting of hemorrhagic areas, hematomas, purpura, and blistering. If thrombocytopenia does occur, platelet aggregation studies are conducted, the heparin is discontinued, and alternate anticoagulant therapy is rapidly initiated because the continued prothrombotic state poses an ongoing threat of continuous clot development.

Lepirudin (Refludan) and argatroban are direct thrombin inhibitors approved for treatment of HIT. Lepirudin has a half-life of 1.3 hours, is excreted by the kidneys, and can be monitored using the aPTT. An initial IV bolus infusion followed by a continuous infusion with subsequent adjustments to maintain the aPTT between 1.5 and 2.5 times baseline has been recommended. Strict dosage adjustment in renal failure is required, because the clearance of lepirudin is proportional to the patient's creatinine clearance. Argatroban has a half-life of 30 to 45 minutes, is metabolized by the liver, and is unaffected by renal function. The anticoagulant effect of argatroban is predictable, with low variability between patients, but it is dose-dependent and requires monitoring with either the aPTT or ACT. There is no safe, rapidly acting antidote if the patient develops bleeding complications from direct thrombin inhibitors. Recombinant factor VIIa may reverse the anticoagulant effects, but it may not be available in all hospitals, and it is very expensive.

Because oral anticoagulants interact with many other medications and herbal and nutritional supplements, close monitoring of the patient's medication schedule is necessary. Many medications and supplements potentiate or inhibit oral anticoagulants; it is always wise to check to see if any medications or supplements the patient is taking are contraindicated with warfarin.

Providing Comfort

Elevation of the affected extremity, elastic compression stockings, and analgesics for pain relief are adjuncts to therapy. They help improve circulation and increase comfort. Depending on the extent and location of a venous thrombosis, bed rest may be required for a few days after the diagnosis. This allows the thrombus to adhere to the vein wall, preventing embolization. However, a research review suggests that early ambulation also decreases the risk of thrombus extension without increasing the risk of PE (Kahn, Shrier, & Kearon, 2008). Thus, the use of bed rest versus activity after diagnosis of a DVT is not conclusive at this time, and the nurse should follow institutional protocol until additional research is conducted to evaluate the safety of exercise in early diagnosis of DVT.

Warm, moist packs applied to the affected extremity reduce the discomfort associated with DVT, as do mild analgesics prescribed for pain control. When the patient begins to ambulate, elastic compression stockings are used. Walking is better than standing or sitting for long periods.

Applying Compression Therapy

Increased venous pressure causes the long-term negative effects of venous disease. Treatment for venous insufficiency is external compression, which counteracts this pressure and protects the tissues from further damage.

Elastic compression stockings are prescribed for patients with chronic venous insufficiency. These stockings exert a sustained, graduated compression over the extremity, compressing the superficial veins, minimizing venous blood pooling, and resulting in increased flow toward the deep veins. They also prevent the sequelae of postphlebitic syndrome (fibrosis, ulceration). Stockings are available in knee-high, thigh-high, or waist-high lengths.

Short stretch elastic wraps may be applied from the toes to the knee in a 50% spiral overlap. These wraps are available in two, three, or four-layer systems, which include an inner layer of soft padding. Other types of compression include the Unna boot, which consists of a gauze roll impregnated with glycerin, gelatin, and sometimes zinc oxide or calamine. It is applied without tension in a circular fashion from the base of the toes to the tibial tuberosity with a 50% spiral overlap. This type of compression may remain in place for as long as 1 week. Other manufactured rigid dressings are available to effectively augment the calf muscle pump

during ambulation. Patients may find these dressings easier to wear than the Unna boot or a compression stocking (O'Meara et al., 2010).

Intermittent pneumatic compression devices can be used with elastic compression stockings to prevent DVT and to reduce edema. They consist of an electric motor attached to plastic knee-high or thigh-high sleeves, with single-chamber or multiple sequential chamber air bladders. These devices mimic muscle contraction and apply pressure to the veins, increasing blood velocity during bed rest.

Body Positioning and Exercise

When the patient is on bed rest, the feet and lower legs should be elevated periodically above the level of the heart. This position allows the veins to empty rapidly. Active and passive leg exercises, particularly those involving calf muscles, should be performed to increase venous flow. Early ambulation is most effective in preventing venous stasis. Deep-breathing exercises produce increased negative pressure in the thorax, which assists in emptying the large veins. Once ambulatory, the patient is instructed to avoid sitting for more than 2 hours at a time and to perform active and passive leg exercises during long car, train, and plane trips when ambulation is not possible.

VARICOSE VEINS

Varicose veins (varicosities) are abnormally dilated, tortuous, superficial veins caused by incompetent venous valves. They occur more frequently in the lower extremities, the saphenous veins, or the lower trunk, but can occur elsewhere in the body.

Pathophysiology

Varicose veins may be primary (without involvement of deep veins) or secondary (resulting from obstruction of deep veins). A reflux of venous blood in the veins results in venous stasis. If the superficial veins are affected without deep vein involvement, the patient may be asymptomatic but may be troubled by the appearance of the distended veins.

Risk Factors

Varicose veins are more common in women than men and in people whose occupations require prolonged standing, such as salespeople, hair stylists, teachers, nurses and ancillary medical personnel, and construction workers. A hereditary weakness of the vein wall may contribute to the development of varicosities, and it commonly occurs in several members of the same family. Varicose veins are rare before puberty. Pregnancy may cause varicosities because of hormonal effects related to distensibility, increased pressure by the gravid uterus, and increased blood volume.

Clinical Manifestations and Assessment

Symptoms, if present, may include dull aches, muscle cramps, increased muscle fatigue in the lower legs, ankle edema, and a feeling of heaviness of the legs. Nocturnal cramps are common. When deep venous obstruction results in varicose veins, the patient may develop the signs and symptoms of chronic venous insufficiency: edema, pain, pigmentation, and ulcerations. Susceptibility to injury and infection is increased.

Diagnostic tests for varicose veins include the duplex scan, which documents the anatomic site of reflux and provides a quantitative measure of the severity of valvular reflux. Air plethysmography measures the changes in venous blood volume. Venography is not routinely performed to evaluate for valvular reflux.

Prevention

The patient should avoid activities that increase venous hypertension, such as wearing constricting clothing, crossing the legs at the thighs, and sitting or standing for long periods. Changing position frequently, elevating the legs when they are tired, and getting up to walk for several minutes of every hour promote circulation. The patient is encouraged to walk 1 or 2 miles each day if there are no contraindications. Walking up the stairs rather than using the elevator or escalator is helpful, and swimming is good exercise. Walking must incorporate the heel–toe step rather than a shuffle to elicit the calf muscle pump effect. Overweight patients should be encouraged to begin a weight-reduction plan.

Surgical Management

Ligation and Stripping

Surgery for varicose veins requires that the deep veins be patent and functional. The saphenous vein is ligated and divided. The vein is ligated high in the groin, where the saphenous vein meets the femoral vein. Pressure and elevation minimize bleeding during surgery. Vein stripping, which used to be a common surgical procedure, has been replaced by the venous ablation techniques.

Ablation Procedures

Thermal ablation is a nonsurgical approach using thermal energy. Radiofrequency ablation uses an electrical contact inside the vein. As the device is withdrawn, the vein is sealed. Laser ablation uses a laser fiber tip that seals the vein (decompresses it). Topical gel may be used first to numb the skin along the course of the saphenous vein. To protect the surrounding tissue, a series of small punctures are made along the vein, and 100 to 200 mL of dilute lidocaine is delivered to the perivenous space using ultrasound guidance. The goal of this tumescent anesthesia (i.e., anesthesia that causes localized swelling) is to provide analgesia,

thermal protection (the cuff of fluid surrounds the veins and accompanying nerves), and extrinsic compression of the vein. The saphenous vein is entered percutaneously near the knee using ultrasound guidance. The device is then activated and withdrawn, sealing the vein. Small bandages and compression stockings are applied after the procedure. The patient is asked not to remove the stockings for at least 48 hours and then to rewrap the legs and wear the compression stockings while ambulatory for a period of time according to a protocol. Patients are ambulatory prior to being discharged from the outpatient facility and have no activity restrictions, except that swimming is discouraged for 3 weeks. Nonsteroidal anti-inflammatory drugs NSAIDs, such as ibuprofen or acetaminophen, are used as needed for pain. The patient is informed that bruising along the course of the vein, and that leg cramps (for a few days) and difficulty straightening the knees (for up to 1.5 weeks) may be experienced postprocedure.

Sclerotherapy

Sclerotherapy involves injection of an irritating chemical into a vein to produce localized phlebitis and fibrosis, thereby obliterating the lumen of the vein. This treatment may be performed alone for small varicosities or may follow vein ablation or ligation. Sclerosing is palliative rather than curative. Sclerotherapy is typically performed in an examination or procedure room and does not require any sedation. After the sclerosing agent is injected, elastic compression bandages are applied to the leg and are worn according to a protocol, followed by elastic compression stockings. Walking activities are encouraged to maintain blood flow and to dilute the sclerosing agent within the deep venous system.

Postprocedure Nursing Management

After venous ablation procedures bed rest is discouraged; the nurse encourages the patient to become ambulatory as soon as sedation has worn off. The patient is instructed to walk according to an individual protocol and to increase walking and activity as tolerated. Elastic compression stockings are worn continuously for 1 to 2 weeks after vein procedures. The nurse assists the patient in performing exercises and moving the legs. The foot of the bed should be elevated. Standing and sitting are discouraged. Jogging and hard-impact exercises are avoided according to individual protocols.

Analgesics are prescribed to help the patient move the affected extremities more comfortably. Dressings are inspected for bleeding, particularly at the groin, where the risk of bleeding is greatest. The nurse is alert for reported sensations of "pins and needles." Hypersensitivity to touch in the involved extremity may indicate a temporary or permanent nerve injury resulting from the procedure because the saphenous vein and nerve are close to each other in the leg.

Usually, the patient may shower after the first 24 hours. The patient is instructed to dry the incisions well with a clean towel, using a patting technique, rather than rubbing. Application of skin lotion is avoided until the incisions are completely healed to avoid infection. The patient is instructed to apply sunscreen or zinc oxide to the incisional area prior to sun exposure for 6 months; otherwise, hyperpigmentation of the incision, scarring, or both may occur. The nurse may encourage the use of a mild analgesic as prescribed and walking to provide relief.

CHRONIC VENOUS INSUFFICIENCY

Venous insufficiency results from obstruction of the venous valves in the legs and a reflux of blood. Both superficial and deep leg veins can be involved. A prolonged increase in venous pressure causes venous hypertension. Because the walls of veins are thinner and more elastic than arterial walls, they distend readily when venous pressure is consistently elevated. In this state, leaflets of the venous valves are stretched and prevented from closing completely, allowing a backflow or reflux of blood in the veins (Fig. 18-7). Duplex ultrasonography confirms the obstruction and identifies incompetent venous valves.

Clinical Manifestations and Assessment

Classic signs of venous disease are edema and pigmentation of the skin termed *hemosiderosis*. Because of the poor venous return, there is extravasation of red blood cells, which break down and deposit hemosiderin (a pigment that gives red blood cells their color), staining the skin a gray-brown.

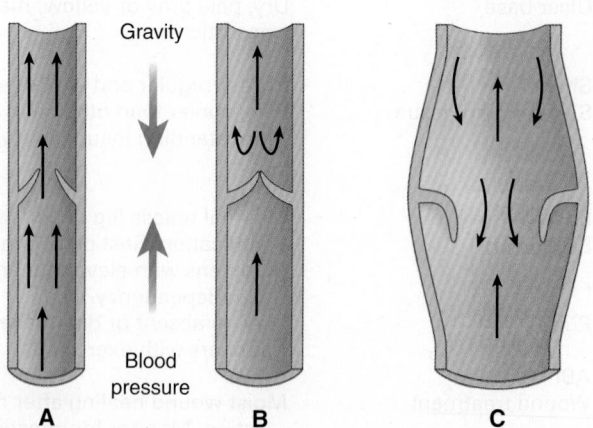

FIGURE 18-7 Competent valves showing blood flow patterns when the valve is open (**A**) and closed (**B**), allowing blood to flow against gravity. (**C**) With faulty or incompetent valves, the blood cannot move toward the heart.

Varicosities and telangiectasias are also commonly noted. The extremity is warm, and pulses are present (assuming there is no concomitant arterial disease) but may be difficult to feel due to the extensive edema.

Postthrombotic syndrome is the long-term result of an incompetent venous system and venous hypertension. Venous obstruction or poor calf muscle pumping, in addition to valvular reflux, also contributes to the development of severe postthrombotic syndrome. It is characterized by chronic edema, altered pigmentation, pain, and stasis dermatitis. This is called *dermatosclerosis*. The patient may notice aching and heaviness less in the morning after rest and elevation and more in the evening. The disorder is longstanding, difficult to treat, and often disabling.

Medical and Nursing Management

Management of the patient with venous insufficiency is directed at reducing venous stasis and preventing ulcerations (see additional discussion below). Measures that increase venous blood flow are antigravity activities, such as elevating the leg, and compression of superficial veins with elastic compression stockings.

Elevating the legs decreases edema, promotes venous return, and provides symptomatic relief. The legs should be elevated frequently throughout the day. At night, the patient should sleep with the foot of the bed elevated. Prolonged sitting or standing in one position is detrimental; walking should be encouraged.

VASCULAR ULCERS

Vascular ulcers include arterial ischemic ulcers, venous ulcers, and ulcers on the lymphatic limb (Table 18-4). Treatment is different for each of these ulcers because treatment is based on etiology, and it varies for each type of ulcer. Ulcers are not common on lymphatic limbs. When they occur, usually, associated venous disease or trauma to the already compromised tissue is present.

Pathophysiology

Venous ulceration is the most serious complication of chronic venous insufficiency and can be associated with other conditions affecting the circulation of the lower extremities. Cellulitis or dermatitis may complicate the care of chronic venous insufficiency and venous ulcer. Venous ulcers develop as a result of increased venous pressure or external trauma.

Atherosclerosis, the most common cause of peripheral arterial occlusive disease, primarily affects the superficial femoral and popliteal vessels, reducing blood flow to the lower extremities (Boike, Maier, & Logan, 2010). Ulceration will develop as a result of ischemia.

TABLE
18-4 Arterial and Venous Ulcer Characteristics

	Arterial	**Venous**
Location	Distal to arterial stenosis, heels, toes, over bony prominences, metatarsals, malleoli, between toes, trauma points	Around ankle, lower third of leg, more often on medial side
Ulcer base	Dry, pale gray or yellow; may be necrotic	Generally shallow but may be deep. Pink, but may be beefy red with granulation tissue. Ulcer bed usually moist. May have copious drainage
Shape	Border regular and well-demarcated	Irregular border
Surrounding tissue	Pale; cooler than other skin areas. In longstanding insufficiency, skin is thin.	Darkened color in gaiter area. Temperature higher than other skin areas. Brawny edema. Skin may be thick and fibrotic (woody). May be oozing and crusted
Edema	Minimal unless leg dependent often	May be severe
Pain	Claudication. Rest pain; continuous pain worsens with elevation, and eases with dependency.	Aching, throbbing, heaviness. Superficial stinging when open to air during dressing changes
Pulses	May be absent or diminished; often disappears with exercise	Usually present with only venous etiology but may be difficult to palpate with edema
ABI	<0.80	>0.90
Wound treatment	Moist wound healing after revascularization. Monitor for infection. Keep dry gangrene dry.	Compression. Elevation above heart. Absorptive dressings
Operative procedures	Arterial bypass. Angioplasty. Stent placement	Vein ligation/stripping. Valve grafts. Sclerotherapy. Laser or Radiofrequency ablation

Clinical Manifestations and Assessment

Venous ulcers occur in the lower part of the extremity, in the area of the medial malleolus of the ankle, called the *gaiter area*, and range from small to large in size, are superficial, irregular in shape, highly exudative, and associated with peri-ulcer hemosiderin staining of the skin. The skin becomes dry, cracked, and pruritic; subcutaneous tissues fibrose and atrophy. The risk for injury and infection of the extremities is increased (Fronek et al., 2008).

Typically, arterial ulcers are small lesions on the tips of toes or in the web spaces between the toes. Ulcers often occur on the medial side of the hallux or lateral fifth toe and may be caused by a combination of ischemia and pressure.

Arterial insufficiency may result in gangrene of the toe (digital gangrene), which may be precipitated by trauma (Box 18-8) (Sieggreen & Kline, 2008).

BOX 18-8

Gangrene of the Toe

Gangrene of the toes resulting from severe arterial ischemia causes the digits to turn black. Débridement is contraindicated in these instances. Although the toes are gangrenous, this is the dry form of gangrene. Managing dry gangrene is preferable to débriding and creating an open wound that will not heal because of insufficient circulation. A distal amputation requires adequate circulation to heal. Without it, further amputation, such as below the knee or above the knee may be necessary. A higher-level amputation in an elderly person often results in loss of independence and possibly the need for institutional care. Dry gangrene of the toe(s) in an elderly person with poor circulation, who is asymptomatic, is usually left undisturbed. The toes are kept clean and dry until they separate from the viable tissue. Soaking is avoided.

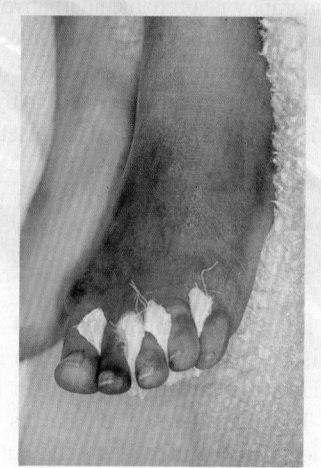

Medical and Nursing Management

Patients with ulcers can be effectively managed by advanced practice nurses or wound-ostomy-continence nurses in collaboration with health care providers. The nurse is aware that all ulcers have the potential to become infected.

Pharmacologic Therapy

All ulcers are colonized with superficial bacteria. Most leg ulcers do not need antibiotics. Antibiotic therapy is prescribed when the ulcer is infected; the specific antibiotic agent is based on culture and sensitivity test results. Oral antibiotics usually are prescribed because topical antibiotics have not proven to be effective for leg ulcers.

Wound Cleansing and Débridement

As a general rule, arterial ulcers are kept dry and necrotic tissue is not débrided until revascularization procedures are performed because of the risk of infection associated with poor peripheral perfusion.

Venous ulcers with necrotic tissue should be débrided. To promote healing, the wound is kept clean of drainage. The wound is cleaned with each dressing change using normal saline solution or a noncytotoxic wound-cleansing agent. The cleansing agent should be applied to the wound with enough force to wash the surface debris away. If there is necrotic tissue at the base of the wound, debridement, or removal of nonviable tissue, may be necessary. Removing the dead tissue is important to promote wound healing. There are several methods of debridement.

- *Surgical debridement*: This is the fastest method and can be performed by a physician, skilled advanced practice nurse, or wound-ostomy-continence nurse in collaboration with the physician.
- *Wet to dry or nonselective debridement*: This method can be accomplished by applying saline-impregnated gauze to the ulcer. When the dressing dries, it is removed, along with the debris adhering to the gauze. Pain management is usually necessary.
- *Enzymatic debridement*: This method involves application of enzyme ointments prescribed to treat the ulcer. The ointment is applied to the lesion but not to normal surrounding skin. Most enzymatic ointments are covered with saline-soaked gauze that has been thoroughly wrung out. A dry gauze dressing and a loose bandage are then applied. The enzymatic ointment is discontinued when the necrotic tissue has been débrided, and an appropriate wound dressing is applied.
- *Autolytic debridement*: With this method, an occlusive absorptive dressing, such as a hydrocolloid, is placed over the wound and left in place for a few (3 to 7) days to allow enzymes from the body to liquify the necrotic tissue and separate it from the viable tissue. The wound is irrigated copiously during dressing changes to cleanse away the necrotic tissue. This type of dressing promotes granulation tissue growth (Sieggreen & Kline, 2008).

Wound Dressings

After the circulatory status has been assessed and determined to be adequate for healing, surgical dressings can be used to promote a moist environment. The simplest method is to use a wound contact material next to the wound bed and cover it with gauze. Other available options that promote the growth of granulation tissue and reepithelialization include the *hydrocolloids*. These materials also provide a barrier for protection because they adhere to the wound bed and surrounding tissue. However, these dressings may not be effective treatment for deep wounds and infected wounds. Patient and family education is necessary before beginning and throughout the wound care program (Nelson, 2010). See Chapter 52 for further information about wound care.

Stimulated Healing

Tissue-engineered human skin equivalent is a skin product cultured from human dermal fibroblasts and keratinocytes used in combination with therapeutic compression. When applied, it seems to react to factors in the wound and may interact with the patient's cells to stimulate the production of growth factors. Application is not difficult, no suturing is involved, and the procedure is painless.

Hyperbaric Oxygenation

Hyperbaric oxygenation (HBO) may be beneficial as an adjunct treatment in patients with diabetes who evidence no signs of wound healing after standard wound treatment. HBO is accomplished by placing the patient into a chamber that increases barometric pressure while the patient is breathing 100% oxygen. The process by which HBO is thought to work involves several factors. The edema in the wound area is decreased because high oxygen tension facilitates vasoconstriction and enhances the ability of leukocytes to phagocytize and kill bacteria. In addition, HBO is thought to increase diffusion of oxygen to the hypoxic wound, thereby enhancing epithelial migration and improving collagen production.

Compression

Leg elevation helps to promote edema reduction. Venous ulcers require external compression. The Unna boot or commercial two- and three-layer compression bandages are available for this treatment. An Unna boot is a gauze dressing impregnated with a paste of glycerin, zinc oxide, and sometimes calamine. It is layered on the leg like a cast, from the tips of the toes to just below the knee. Extra padding is used if there is copious wound drainage, and an elastic bandage is placed over the dressing. Once the dressing dries, it becomes rigid. The boot is changed weekly. Its effectiveness depends on healthy calf muscle and the ability to ambulate.

LYMPHATIC DISORDERS

The lymphatic system consists of a set of vessels that start as lymph capillaries, which drain unabsorbed plasma from the interstitial spaces (spaces between the cells). The lymphatic capillaries unite to form the lymph vessels, which pass through the lymph nodes and then empty into progressively larger channels, most of which drain into the thoracic duct that joins the jugular vein on the left side of the neck.

Fluid drained from the interstitial space by the lymphatic system is called *lymph*. Lymph flow depends on the intrinsic contractions of the lymph vessels, the contraction of muscles, respiratory movements, and gravity. The lymphatic vessels of the extremities empty into nodes of the axillae and the groin. Under certain abnormal conditions, the fluid filtered out of the capillaries may greatly exceed the amounts reabsorbed and carried away by the lymphatic vessels. This imbalance can result from a variety of etiologies including damage to capillary walls and subsequent increased permeability, obstruction of lymphatic drainage, elevation of venous pressure, or decrease in plasma protein osmotic force. Accumulation of excess interstitial fluid that results from these processes is known as **edema**. In general, the nurse is aware that edema usually represents accumulation of 2.5 to 3 L of interstitial fluid. If the edema is *pitting*—that is, when the nurse presses the thumb into the edematous area for 5 seconds an imprint of the finger is noted—it is estimated that approximately 4.5 kg (10 lb) of fluid has accumulated (Leblond, DeGowin, & Brown, 2009). Refer to Chapter 12 for more details on assessing pitting edema.

Lymphangiography and lymphoscintigraphy are two diagnostic tests to assess lymphatic function. Lymphangiography involves injecting a contrast agent into a lymphatic vessel in each foot (or hand), followed by taking a series of X-rays at the conclusion of the injection, 24 hours later, and periodically thereafter. Failure to identify subcutaneous lymphatic collection of contrast agent and the persistence of contrast agent in the tissue for days afterward help confirm a diagnosis of lymphedema.

Lymphoscintigraphy is a reliable alternative to lymphangiography. A radioactively labeled colloid is injected subcutaneously in the second interdigital space. The extremity is then exercised to facilitate the uptake of the colloid by the lymphatic system, and serial images are obtained at preset intervals.

LYMPHANGITIS AND LYMPHADENITIS

Lymphangitis is an acute inflammation of the lymphatic channels. It arises most commonly from an infection in an extremity. Usually, the infectious organism is a hemolytic streptococcus. The characteristic red streaks that extend up the arm or the leg from an infected wound outline the course of the lymphatic vessels as they drain.

The lymph nodes located along the course of the lymphatic channels also become enlarged, red, and tender (acute lymphadenitis). They can also become necrotic and form an abscess (suppurative lymphadenitis). The nodes involved most often are those in the groin, axilla, or cervical region. Because these infections are nearly always caused by organisms that are sensitive to antibiotics, it is unusual to see abscess formation. Recurrent episodes of lymphangitis are often associated with progressive lymphedema. After acute attacks, and if the edema has subsided, an elastic compression stocking or sleeve should be worn on the affected extremity for several months to prevent long-term edema.

LYMPHEDEMA AND ELEPHANTIASIS

Lymphedema is swelling in the extremities due to an accumulation of lymph from blocked lymphatic vessels.

Pathophysiology

Lymphedemas are classified as primary (congenital malformations) or secondary (acquired obstructions). Tissue swelling occurs in the extremities because of an increased quantity of lymph that results from obstruction of lymphatic vessels. It is especially marked when the extremity is in a dependent position. Initially, the edema is soft and pitting. As the condition progresses, the edema becomes firm, non-pitting, and unresponsive to treatment. The most common type is congenital lymphedema (*lymphedema praecox*), which is caused by hypoplasia (underdevelopment) of the lymphatic system of the lower extremity.

The obstruction may be in the lymph nodes and the lymphatic vessels. Sometimes, it is seen in the arm after an axillary node dissection (e.g., for breast cancer) and in the leg in association with varicose veins or chronic thrombophlebitis. In the latter case, the lymphatic obstruction usually is caused by chronic lymphangitis. Lymphatic obstruction caused by a parasite (filaria) is seen frequently in the tropics. When chronic swelling is present, there may be frequent bouts of acute infection characterized by high fever and chills and increased residual edema after the inflammation has resolved. These lead to chronic fibrosis, thickening of the subcutaneous tissues, and hypertrophy of the skin. This condition, in which chronic swelling of the extremity recedes only slightly with elevation, is referred to as *elephantiasis*.

Clinical Manifestations and Assessment

The diagnosis of lymphedema is made by clinical evaluation and exclusion of other causes of edema. In the early stages, the tissue is soft and pliable but in advanced lymphedema the tissue becomes firm and thick, often with overlapping folds of tissue. Early diagnosis is important to prevent tissue destruction.

Medical Management

Treatment is focused on reducing the edema and preventing increased edema, infections, and tissue damage. Treatment may consist of comprehensive decongestant therapy provided by a certified therapist, use of a pump to reduce the edema, and elastic compression garments to maintain the edema reduction.

Care must be taken to avoid any break in the skin that would allow bacteria to enter the tissue. Antibiotics are prescribed for infection and often for prophylaxis when chronic infections are common. Patients need support and must be taught that lymphedema requires life-long vigilance. The individual needs to learn as much as possible about the condition and how to manage it (Box 18-9).

Pharmacologic Therapy

As initial therapy, the diuretic furosemide (Lasix) may be prescribed to prevent fluid overload while the extracellular fluid is mobilized. The use of diuretics alone has little benefit, because their main action is to limit capillary filtration by decreasing the circulating blood volume. If lymphangitis or cellulitis is present, antibiotic therapy is initiated.

Exercise and Compression

Active and passive exercises assist in moving lymphatic fluid into the bloodstream. External compression devices move the fluid proximally from the foot to the hip or from the hand to the axilla. When the patient is ambulatory, custom-fitted elastic compression stockings or sleeves are worn; those with the highest compression strength, exceeding 40 mm Hg, are required. When the leg is affected, continuous bed rest with the leg elevated may aid in mobilizing the fluids. Manual lymphatic drainage is a highly specialized massage technique designed to direct or shift the congested lymph

---

BOX 18-9   **Patient Education for Lymphedema**

- Keep skin clean and dry.
- Wear compression support garments as prescribed.
- Avoid blood pressure cuffs, needle sticks, injections, or procedures on affected limb.
- Report new swelling, redness, pain, heat, rash, blisters, or fever to physician/nurse.
- Avoid tight clothing.
- Check feet with a mirror for sores, rashes, or cracks in skin.
- Avoid trauma: Pet scratches, insect bites, burns, sports injuries, bruising.
- Clean cuts or insect bites with soap and water and apply antibiotic ointment.
- Elevate limb whenever possible.

through functioning lymphatics that have preserved drainage. Manual lymphatic drainage used in combination with compression bandages, exercises, skin care, pressure gradient sleeves, and sometimes, pneumatic pumps, depending on the severity and stage of the lymphedema.

Surgical Management

Surgery is performed if the edema is severe and uncontrolled by medical therapy, if mobility is severely compromised, or if infection persists. One surgical approach involves the excision of the affected subcutaneous tissue and fascia, with skin grafting to cover the defect. Another procedure involves the surgical relocation of superficial lymphatic vessels into the deep lymphatic system by means of a buried dermal flap to provide a conduit for lymphatic drainage. Surgery is rarely performed in these patients in most hospitals. Patients who would benefit from surgery are referred to specialized centers.

Nursing Management

After surgery, the management of skin grafts and flaps is the same as when these therapies are used for other conditions. Antibiotics are prescribed. Constant elevation of the affected extremity and observation for complications are essential. Complications may include flap necrosis, hematoma or abscess under the flap, and cellulitis. The nurse instructs the patient or caregiver to inspect the dressing daily. Unusual drainage or any inflammation around the wound margin suggests infection and should be reported to the surgeon. The patient is informed that there may be a loss of sensation in the skin graft area. The patient is also instructed to avoid the application of heating pads or exposure to sun to prevent burns or trauma to the area. The patient is taught to inspect the skin for evidence of infection.

CELLULITIS

Cellulitis is the most common infectious cause of limb swelling. Cellulitis can occur as a single isolated event or a series of recurrent events. It is often misdiagnosed, usually as recurrent thrombophlebitis or chronic venous insufficiency. It occurs when an entry point through normal skin barriers allows bacteria to enter. Cellulitis is a frequent complication in tissues with lymphedema. It is also diagnosed in otherwise healthy tissue.

Pathophysiology

Cellulitis occurs when there is an entry point through normal skin barrier. This allows bacteria to enter the subcutaneous tissue.

Clinical Manifestations and Assessment

The acute onset of swelling, localized redness, and pain is frequently associated with systemic signs of fever, chills, and sweating. The redness may not be uniform and often skips areas. Dimpling in the skin may be seen when the edema surrounds hair follicles. Regional lymph nodes may also be tender and enlarged.

Medical Management

Mild cases of cellulitis can be treated on an outpatient basis with oral antibiotic therapy. If the cellulitis is severe, the patient is treated with IV antibiotics. The key to preventing recurrent episodes of cellulitis lies in adequate antibiotic therapy for the initial event and in identifying the site of bacterial entry. The most commonly overlooked areas are the cracks and fissures that occur in the skin between the toes. Other possible locations are drug use injection sites, contusions, abrasions, ulcerations, ingrown toenails, and hangnails.

Nursing Management

The patient is instructed to elevate the affected area above heart level and apply warm, moist packs to the site. Patients with sensory and circulatory deficits, such as those caused by diabetes and paralysis, should use caution when applying warm packs because burns may occur; it is advisable to use a thermometer or have a caregiver ensure that the temperature is not more than lukewarm. Education should focus on preventing a recurrent episode. The patient with peripheral vascular disease or diabetes mellitus should receive education or reinforcement about skin and foot care.

Chapter Review

Critical Thinking Exercises

1. A 75-year-old male patient has been diagnosed with a stenosis of his external iliac artery and is scheduled for an angiogram with a possible balloon angioplasty and stent placement. What factors should be considered when planning his postprocedure and continuing care? If the patient is taking warfarin for atrial fibrillation and has renal insufficiency (creatinine of 1.8 mg/dL) as a complication of diabetes, how would these factors be addressed in the plan of care?

2. A 96-year-old patient presents with a 2-year history of chronic stasis ulceration of the left lower extremity requiring weekly placement of an Unna boot. The patient lives alone, six blocks from any mass transit or shopping area, and no longer drives a vehicle. The patient wants to continue living at his current location. What options and plan of care should be discussed with the patient?

3. One of your patients has been diagnosed with a recurrent DVT of the femoral vein. The patient has been treated previously with unfractionated heparin and developed HIT. Discuss strategies for DVT prophylaxis that you will include in your teaching plan with this patient.

NCLEX–Style Review Questions

1. The nurse is caring for a patient diagnosed with peripheral arterial disease. Based on assessment, which of the following clinical manifestations would be inconsistent with acute arterial occlusion?
   A. Pallor
   B. Paresthesia
   C. Hyperthermia
   D. Poikilothermia

2. A new postsurgical patient has been prescribed unfractionated heparin to prevent DVT. Which of the following is a true statement regarding the use of heparin?
   A. Heparin has a half-life of approximately 60 minutes.
   B. Therapeutic aPTT level is 3 times the baseline control.
   C. If renal insufficiency exists, higher doses of heparin are needed.
   D. Heparin is administered by gravity drip.

3. Using a hydrocolloid dressing, a patient is undergoing autolytic debridement of a necrotic venous ulcer. The nurse understands that this type of debridement is which of the following?
   A. Accomplished by applying enzymatic ointment to the lesion
   B. Left in place for 3 to 7 days
   C. The fastest method of debridement
   D. Accomplished by applying saline impregnated gauze to the ulcer

4. The nurse is assessing the lower extremities of a patient with a possible DVT. Which of the following is not a reliable indicator of a possible DVT?
   A. Calf tenderness
   B. Edema of the extremity
   C. Homan's sign
   D. Increased circumference of affected extremity

5. When assessing for an arterial and venous ulcer, which of the following characteristics are consistent with a arterial ulcer?
   A. Pink or beefy red with granulation tissue
   B. May have severe edema
   C. Darkened color tissue in gaiter area
   D. Pale and cool extremity

Try these additional resources to enhance your learning and understanding of this chapter:
- thePoint online resource available at **http://thepoint.lww.com/Pellico1e**
- *Handbook for Focus on Adult Health: Medical-Surgical Nursing*
- *Study Guide for Focus on Adult Health: Medical-Surgical Nursing*

References and Selected Readings

References and selected readings associated with this chapter can be found on the website that accompanies the book. Visit http://thepoint.lww.com/Pellico1e to access the references and other additional resources associated with this chapter.

Problems Related to Hematologic Function

A 65-YEAR-OLD woman has been diagnosed with chronic myeloid leukemia (CML). Previously she had been complaining of fatigue. She has lost 10 pounds in the last month. She is very apprehensive about starting chemotherapy and being hospitalized.

➡ What is the only curative treatment for CML?
➡ Discuss the three phases of the disease.
➡ Discuss important nursing considerations of the patient undergoing chemotherapy (Gleevec).

515

Nursing Assessment: Hematologic Function

LISA M. BARBAROTTA

Unlike many other body systems, the hematologic system truly encompasses the entire human body. Patients with hematologic disorders often have significant abnormalities in blood tests but few or no symptoms. Therefore, the nurse must have an understanding of the pathophysiology of the patient's condition and the ability to make a thorough assessment that relies heavily on the interpretation of laboratory tests. It is equally important for the nurse to anticipate potential patient needs and to target nursing interventions accordingly. A basic appreciation of blood cells and bone marrow function is critical to the understanding of most hematologic diseases.

ANATOMIC AND PHYSIOLOGIC OVERVIEW

The hematologic system consists of the blood and the sites where blood is produced, including the bone marrow and the **reticuloendothelial system** (RES). Blood is a specialized organ that differs from other organs in that it exists in a fluid state. Blood is composed of plasma and various types of cells. **Plasma** is the fluid portion of blood; it is thin and colorless and contains various proteins, such as albumin, globulin, **fibrinogen**, and other factors necessary for clotting, as well as electrolytes, waste products, and nutrients. Approximately 55% of blood volume is plasma, and 45% consists of various cellular components.

Blood

The cellular component of blood consists of three primary cell types (Table 19-1): **erythrocytes (red blood cells [RBCs])**, **leukocytes (white blood cells [WBCs])**, and **thrombocytes (platelets)**. As noted above, these cellular components of blood normally make up approximately 45% of the blood volume. Because most blood cells have a short lifespan, the need for the body to replenish its supply of cells is continuous; this process is termed **hematopoiesis**. RBCs generally live for 120 days, WBCs live from days to years depending on the type, and platelets live 7 to 10 days. The primary site for hematopoiesis (formation and production of blood cells) is the bone marrow. During embryonic development and in other conditions, the liver and spleen may also be involved.

TABLE 19-1 Blood Cells

Cell Type	Major Function
WBC (Leukocyte)	Fights infection
Neutrophil	Essential in preventing or limiting bacterial infection via phagocytosis
Monocyte	Enters tissue as macrophage; highly phagocytic, especially against fungus
Eosinophil	Involved in allergic reactions (neutralizes histamine); digests foreign proteins
Basophil	Contains histamine; integral part of hypersensitivity reactions
Lymphocyte	Integral component of immune system
T lymphocyte	Responsible for cell-mediated immunity; recognizes material as "foreign"
B lymphocyte	Responsible for humoral immunity; many mature into plasma cells to form antibodies
Plasma cell	Secretes immunoglobulin (Ig, antibody); most mature form of B lymphocyte
RBC (erythrocyte)	Carries hemoglobin to provide oxygen to tissues; average lifespan is 120 days
Platelet (thrombocyte)	Fragment of megakaryocyte; provides basis for coagulation to occur; maintains hemostasis; average lifespan is 7 days

Under normal conditions, the adult bone marrow produces approximately 175 billion erythrocytes, 70 billion **neutrophils** (a mature type of WBC), and 175 billion platelets each day. When the body needs more blood cells, as in infection (when neutrophils are needed to fight the invading pathogen) or in bleeding (when more RBCs and platelets are needed), the marrow increases its production of the cells required. Thus, under normal conditions, the marrow responds to increased demand and releases adequate numbers of cells into the circulation.

Blood makes up approximately 7% to 10% of the normal body weight and amounts to 5 L to 6 L of volume. Circulating through the vascular system and serving as a link among body organs, blood carries oxygen absorbed from the lungs and nutrients absorbed from the GI tract to the body cells for cellular metabolism. Blood also carries proteins such as hormones, antibodies, and other substances to their sites of action or use. In addition, blood carries waste products produced by cellular metabolism to the lungs, skin, liver, and kidneys for elimination.

To prevent blood loss as a result of trauma or injury, an intricate clotting mechanism is activated to seal any leak in the blood vessels. Excessive clotting is equally as dangerous as excessive blood loss because it can obstruct blood flow

to vital tissues. To prevent this, the body has a fibrinolytic mechanism that eventually dissolves clots (thrombi) formed within blood vessels. The balance between these two systems, clot (thrombus) formation and clot (thrombus) dissolution, or **fibrinolysis**, is called **hemostasis**.

Bone Marrow

The bone marrow is the site of hematopoiesis, or blood cell formation (Fig. 19-1). In children, blood formation involves all skeletal bones, but with aging, marrow activity is usually limited to the pelvis, ribs, vertebrae, and sternum.

Marrow, which accounts for up to 4% to 5% of total body weight, consists of islands of cellular components (red marrow) separated by fat (yellow marrow). As the adult ages, the proportion of active marrow is gradually replaced by fat; however, in the healthy person, the fat can again be replaced by active marrow when more blood cell production is required. In adults with disease that causes marrow destruction, fibrosis, or scarring, the liver and spleen can

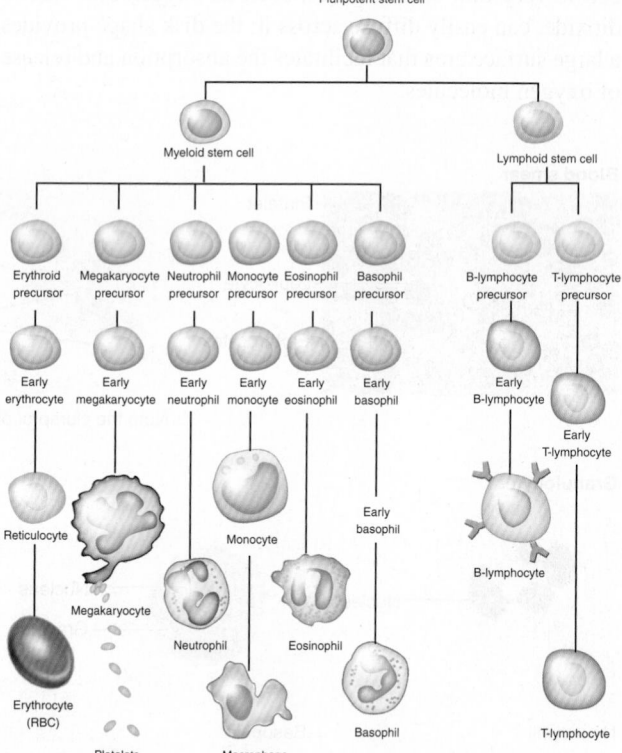

FIGURE 19-1 Hematopoiesis. Uncommitted (pluripotent) stem cells can differentiate into myeloid or lymphoid stem cells. These stem cells then undergo a complex process of differentiation and maturation into normal cells that are released into the circulation. The myeloid stem cell is responsible not only for all nonlymphoid white blood cells (WBCs) but also for the production of red blood cells (RBCs) and platelets. Each step of the differentiation process depends in part on the presence of specific growth factors for each cell type. When the stem cells are dysfunctional, they may respond inadequately to the need for more cells, or they may respond excessively, sometimes uncontrollably, as in leukemia.

also resume production of blood cells by a process known as *extramedullary hematopoiesis.*

The marrow is highly vascular. Within it are primitive cells called **stem cells**, which have the ability to self-replicate, thereby ensuring a continuous supply of stem cells throughout the lifecycle. When stimulated, stem cells can begin a process of **differentiation** into either **myeloid** or **lymphoid** stem cells. Lymphoid stem cells produce either T or B **lymphocytes**, whereas myeloid stem cells differentiate into three broad cell types: erythrocytes, leukocytes, and platelets. Thus, with the exception of lymphocytes, all blood cells are derived from myeloid stem cells. A defect in a myeloid stem cell can cause problems with erythrocyte, leukocyte, and platelet production. Many complex mechanisms are involved in hematopoiesis, many at the molecular level.

Erythrocytes (Red Blood Cells)

The normal erythrocyte has a biconcave disk shape (Fig. 19-2). It has a diameter of approximately 8 μm and is so flexible that it can pass easily through capillaries that may be as small as 2.8 μm in diameter. The membrane of the red cell is very thin so that gases, such as oxygen and carbon dioxide, can easily diffuse across it; the disk shape provides a large surface area that facilitates the absorption and release of oxygen molecules.

Mature erythrocytes consist primarily of **hemoglobin**, which contains iron and makes up 95% of the cell mass. Mature erythrocytes have no nuclei, and they have many fewer metabolic enzymes than do most other cells. The presence of a large amount of hemoglobin enables the red cell to perform its principal function of oxygen transport. Occasionally, the marrow releases slightly immature forms of erythrocytes, called **reticulocytes**, into the circulation. An elevation in the reticulocyte count may occur as a normal response to an increased demand for erythrocytes (as in bleeding) or in some disease states.

The oxygen-carrying hemoglobin molecule is made up of four subunits, each containing a heme portion attached to a globin chain. Iron is present in the heme component of the molecule. An important property of heme is its ability to bind to oxygen loosely and reversibly. Oxygen readily binds to hemoglobin in the lungs and is carried as **oxyhemoglobin** in arterial blood. Oxyhemoglobin is a brighter red than hemoglobin that contains lesser amounts of oxygen (reduced hemoglobin), which is why arterial blood is a brighter red than venous blood. The oxygen readily dissociates (detaches) from hemoglobin in the tissues, where the oxygen is needed for cellular metabolism. In venous blood, hemoglobin combines with hydrogen ions produced by cellular metabolism and thus buffers excessive acid. Whole

Blood smear

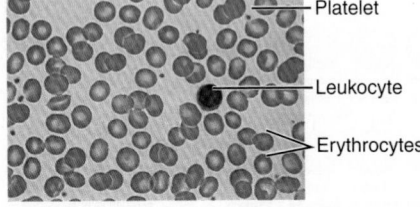

- Platelet
- Leukocyte
- Erythrocytes

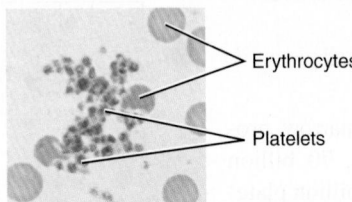

- Erythrocytes
- Platelets

Note the clump of platelets

Granulocytes

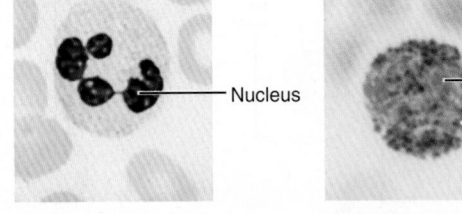

Neutrophil — Nucleus

Basophil — Nucleus — Granules

Eosinophil — Granules — Nucleus

Agranulocytes

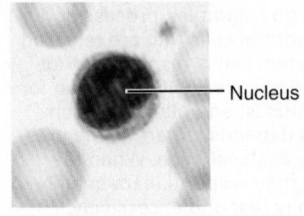

Lymphocyte — Nucleus

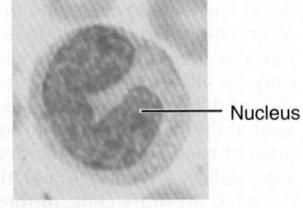

Monocyte — Nucleus

FIGURE 19-2 Normal types of blood cells. From Cohen, B. J. (2005). *Memmler's the human body in health and disease* (10th ed.). Philadelphia: Lippincott Williams & Wilkins.

blood normally contains approximately 15 g of hemoglobin per 100 mL of blood.

Erythropoiesis

Erythroblasts arise from the primitive myeloid stem cells in bone marrow. The erythroblast is an immature nucleated cell that accumulates hemoglobin and then gradually loses its nucleus. At this stage, the cell is known as a *reticulocyte*. Further maturation into an erythrocyte entails the loss of the dark-staining material within the cell and slight shrinkage. The mature erythrocyte is then released into the circulation.

Differentiation of the primitive myeloid stem cell of the marrow into an erythroblast is stimulated by **erythropoietin**, a hormone produced primarily by the kidney. If the kidney detects low levels of oxygen (as would occur in **anemia**, in which fewer red cells are available to bind oxygen, or with people living at high altitudes), the release of erythropoietin is increased. The increased erythropoietin then stimulates the marrow to increase production of erythrocytes. The entire process typically takes 5 days.

For normal erythrocyte production, the bone marrow also requires iron, vitamin B_{12}, folic acid, pyridoxine (vitamin B_6), protein, and other factors. A deficiency in any one of these factors during erythropoiesis can result in decreased red cell production and anemia.

IRON STORES AND METABOLISM. The average daily diet in the United States contains 10 to 15 mg of elemental iron, but only 0.5 to 1 mg of ingested iron is normally absorbed from the small intestine daily. The rate of iron absorption is regulated by the amount of iron already stored in the body and by the rate of erythrocyte production. Additional amounts of iron, up to 2 mg daily, must be absorbed by women of childbearing age to replace that lost during menstruation. Total body iron content in the average adult is approximately 3 g, most of which is present in hemoglobin or in one of its breakdown products.

The concentration of iron in blood is normally about 75 to 175 µg/dL (13 to 31 µmol/L) for men and 65 to 165 µg/dL (11 to 29 µmol/L) for women. With iron deficiency, bone marrow iron stores are rapidly depleted; hemoglobin synthesis is depressed, and the erythrocytes produced by the marrow are small and low in hemoglobin. This is known as *microcytic anemia* (characterized by small red blood cells). Part of a standard complete blood count (CBC) includes the mean corpuscular volume (MCV), which measures the size of the RBCs. In microcytic anemia, a small ($< 82 \ \mu m^3$) MCV is seen. Causes of microcytic anemia include iron deficiency related to dietary inadequacy, malabsorption, increased iron loss, and increased iron requirement (Fischbach & Dunning, 2009, p. 100). In the adult, lack of dietary iron is rarely the sole cause of iron deficiency anemia. Iron deficiency in the adult generally indicates that blood has been lost from the body (e.g., from bleeding in the GI tract or heavy menstrual flow). The source of iron deficiency should be investigated promptly, because iron deficiency in an adult may be a sign of bleeding in the GI tract or colon cancer.

VITAMIN B_{12} AND FOLIC ACID METABOLISM. Vitamin B_{12} and folic acid are required for the synthesis of DNA in many tissues. Deficiencies of either of these vitamins have the greatest effect on erythropoiesis. Both vitamin B_{12} and folic acid are derived from the diet and depend on a functioning intestinal mucosa for absorption. Vitamin B_{12} combines with intrinsic factor produced in the stomach, and is absorbed in the distal ileum. It is important for nurses to recall that patients who have had a partial or total gastrectomy may have limited amounts of intrinsic factor, and therefore the absorption of vitamin B_{12} may be diminished, leading to anemia. The effects of either decreased absorption or decreased intake of vitamin B_{12} are not apparent for 2 to 4 years.

Red Blood Cell Destruction

Aged erythrocytes lose their elasticity and become trapped in small blood vessels and the spleen. They are removed from the blood by the reticuloendothelial cells, particularly in the liver and the spleen. As the erythrocytes are destroyed, most of their hemoglobin is recycled. Some hemoglobin also breaks down to form bilirubin and is secreted in the bile. Most of the iron is recycled to form new hemoglobin molecules within the bone marrow; small amounts are lost daily in the feces and urine and monthly in menstrual flow.

Leukocytes (White Blood Cells)

Leukocytes are divided into two general categories: granulocytes and agranulocytes. In normal blood, the total leukocyte count is 5,000 to 10,000 cells per cubic millimeter. Of these, approximately 60% to 70% are granulocytes, and 30% to 40% are lymphocytes. Both of these types of leukocytes primarily protect the body against infection and tissue injury.

Granulocytes

Granulocytes are defined by the presence of granules in the cytoplasm of the cell. Granulocytes are divided into three main subgroups (see Fig. 19-2): eosinophils, basophils, and neutrophils. **Neutrophils** are the most numerous cells of this class. Neutrophils are also called polymorphonuclear neutrophils (PMNs, or polys) or segmented neutrophils (segs).

The nucleus of the mature neutrophil has multiple lobes (usually two to five), or a "segmented" nucleus. The somewhat less mature granulocyte has a single-lobed, elongated nucleus, and is called a **band cell**. Ordinarily, band cells account for only a small percentage of circulating granulocytes, although their percentage can increase greatly under conditions in which neutrophil demand increases, such as infection. An increased number of band cells is sometimes called a **bandemia**.

Fully mature neutrophils result from the gradual differentiation of myeloid stem cells, specifically myeloid **blast cells**. The process, called **myelopoiesis**, takes an average of 10 days (see Fig. 19-1). Once the neutrophil is released into the circulation from the marrow, it stays there for only about

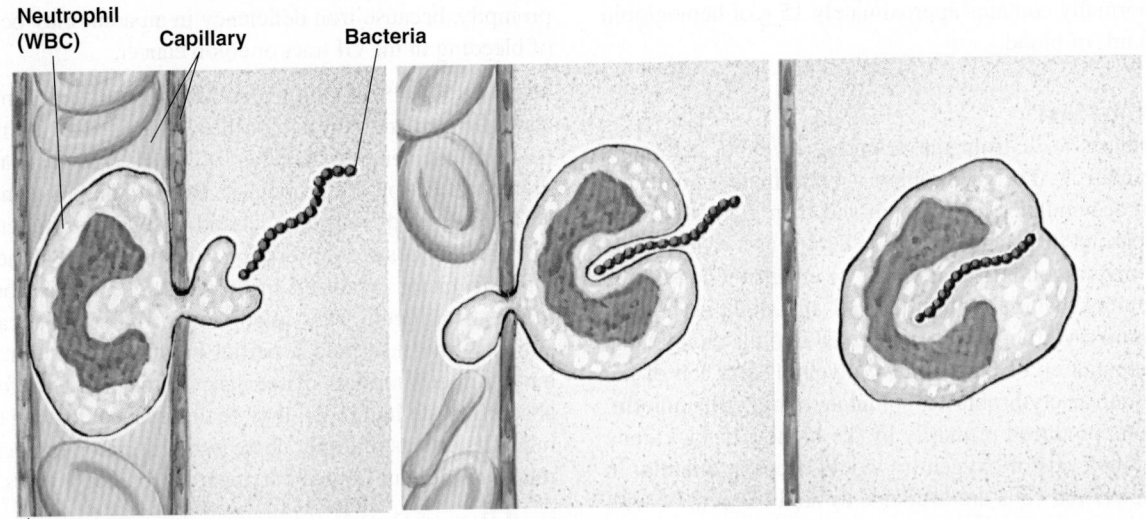

Neutrophil (WBC)   Capillary   Bacteria

Endothelial cell

FIGURE 19-3 Phagocytosis. In order for phagocytosis to occur, a foreign body (such as bacteria, parasites, or cellular debris) must adhere to the cell wall of the phagocyte. The phagocyte then extends around the foreign body by projecting out pseudopods, engulfing the foreign body. Once inside the phagocyte, the engulfed material is left in a vacuole, where enzymes within the cell destroy the foreign material.

6 hours before it migrates into the body tissues to perform its function of **phagocytosis** (ingestion and digestion of bacteria and particles; Fig. 19-3). Here, neutrophils last no more than 1 to 2 days before they die.

Eosinophils play a key role in response to parasitic and allergic diseases. The presence of certain microbes (such as parasites) results in the release of the granular contents of the eosinophil, allowing for destruction and phagocytosis of the organism.

Basophils are the least numerous of the circulating leukocytes and have characteristically large, dark-purple granules. The granules contain heparin and histamine and are released in response to exposure to allergens.

The number of circulating granulocytes found in the healthy person is relatively constant. An elevation in the total number of WBCs may indicate infection, trauma, or tissue injury, or may be a side effect of certain medications, such as corticosteroids. A WBC count that is below normal may be related to viral infections, the result of side effects from medications such as antiviral medications, or may hint of a more serious condition such as leukemia or myelodysplastic syndrome.

Agranulocytes

Monocytes and lymphocytes are leukocytes with granule-free cytoplasm—hence the term *agranulocyte* (see Fig. 19-2).

MONOCYTES. Monocytes (also called *mononuclear leukocytes*) have a single-lobed nucleus. They are the largest of the leukocytes. In normal adult blood, monocytes account for approximately 5% of the total leukocyte count. When released from the marrow, monocytes spend a short time in the circulation (approximately 24 hours) and then enter the body tissues. Within the tissues, the monocytes continue to differentiate into **macrophages**, which can survive for months. Macrophages are particularly active in the spleen, liver, peritoneum, and the alveoli; they remove debris from these areas and phagocytize bacteria within the tissues (see discussion of the Reticuloendothelial System, below).

LYMPHOCYTES. Mature lymphocytes are small cells with scanty cytoplasm (see Fig. 19-2). Immature lymphocytes are produced in the marrow from the lymphoid stem cells. A second major source of production is the cortex of the thymus. Cells derived from the thymus are known as T lymphocytes (or T cells); those derived from the marrow can also be T cells but are more commonly B lymphocytes (or B cells). Lymphocytes complete their differentiation and maturation primarily in the lymph nodes and in the lymphoid tissue of the intestine and spleen after exposure to a specific antigen. Mature lymphocytes are the principal cells of the immune system, producing antibodies and identifying other cells and organisms as "foreign."

Function of Leukocytes

Granulocytes protect the body from invasion by bacteria and other foreign entities. Neutrophils arrive at a given site within 1 hour after the onset of an inflammatory reaction and initiate phagocytosis, but they are short-lived. An influx of monocytes follows; these cells continue their phagocytic activities for long periods as macrophages. This process constitutes a second line of defense for the body against inflammation and infection. Although neutrophils can often work adequately against bacteria without the help of macrophages, macrophages are particularly effective against fungi and viruses.

The primary function of lymphocytes is to produce substances that aid in attacking foreign material. T lymphocytes kill foreign cells directly or release a variety of *lymphokines*,

substances that enhance the activity of phagocytic cells. T lymphocytes are responsible for delayed allergic reactions, rejection of foreign tissue (e.g., transplanted organs), and destruction of tumor cells. This process is known as *cellular immunity*. B lymphocytes are capable of differentiating into plasma cells. Plasma cells, in turn, produce antibodies called immunoglobulin (Ig), which are protein molecules that destroy foreign material by several mechanisms. This process is known as *humoral immunity*.

The increase in eosinophil levels in allergic states indicates that these cells are involved in the hypersensitivity reaction since they neutralize histamine. Thus, eosinophil counts are examined in allergic reactions and parasitic infections and to monitor response to treatment (Fischbach & Dunning, 2009, p. 78). Basophils play a large part in hypersensitivity reactions and are used to study chronic inflammation (Fischbach, 2009, p. 80).

Platelets (Thrombocytes)

Platelets, or thrombocytes, are not technically cells; rather, they are granular fragments of giant cells in the bone marrow, called *megakaryocytes*. Platelet production in the marrow is regulated in part by the hormone thrombopoietin, which stimulates the production and differentiation of megakaryocytes from the myeloid stem cell.

Platelets play an essential role in the control of bleeding. They circulate freely in the blood in an inactive state, where they nurture the endothelium of the blood vessels, maintaining the integrity of the vessel. When vascular injury occurs, platelets collect at the site and are activated. They adhere to the site of injury and to each other, forming a platelet plug that temporarily stops bleeding. Substances released from platelet granules activate coagulation factors in the blood plasma and initiate the formation of a stable clot composed of **fibrin**, a filamentous protein.

Plasma and Plasma Proteins

After cellular elements are removed from blood, the remaining liquid portion is called *plasma*. More than 90% of plasma is water. The remainder consists primarily of plasma proteins, clotting factors (particularly fibrinogen), and small amounts of other substances such as nutrients, enzymes, waste products, and gases. If plasma is allowed to clot, the remaining fluid is called **serum**. Serum has essentially the same composition as plasma, except that fibrinogen and several clotting factors have been removed in the clotting process.

Plasma proteins consist primarily of albumin and the globulins. The globulins can be separated into three main fractions (alpha, beta, and gamma), each of which consists of distinct proteins that have different functions. Important proteins in the alpha and beta fractions are the transport globulins and the clotting factors that are made in the liver. The transport globulins carry various substances in bound

form in the circulation. For example, thyroid-binding globulin carries thyroxin, and transferrin carries iron. The clotting factors, including fibrinogen, remain in an inactive form in the blood plasma until activated by the clotting cascade. The gamma globulin fraction refers to the immunoglobulins, or antibodies. These proteins are produced by the well-differentiated lymphocytes and plasma cells. The actual fractionation of the globulins can be measured on a specific laboratory test (serum protein electrophoresis).

Albumin is particularly important for the maintenance of fluid balance within the vascular system. Capillary walls are impermeable to albumin, so its presence in the plasma creates an osmotic force that keeps fluid within the vascular space. Albumin, which is produced by the liver, has the capacity to bind to several substances that are transported in plasma (e.g., certain medications, bilirubin, and some hormones). People with poor hepatic function may have low concentrations of albumin, with a resultant decrease in osmotic pressure and the development of edema.

Reticuloendothelial System

The RES (also called the *mononuclear phagocytic system*, or MPS) is a system of phagocytic cells, including monocytes and macrophages. The RES is divided into primary and secondary lymphoid systems. The primary lymphoid system is the site of RES cell production and includes the bone marrow and thymus. The secondary lymphoid system is the site of RES cell function and includes the liver, spleen, and lymph nodes. In the liver, spleen, lymph nodes, and other areas throughout the body, these cells function to recognize foreign cells and trigger an immune response.

The spleen has a number of additional functions including recycling of iron, pooling of platelets, and blood volume regulation. It also acts as a filter for bacteria. In addition, the spleen is a major source of fetal hematopoiesis. It can resume hematopoiesis later in adulthood if necessary, particularly when marrow function is compromised (e.g., in bone marrow fibrosis).

Hemostasis

Hemostasis is the process of preventing blood loss from intact vessels and of stopping bleeding from a severed vessel. The prevention of blood loss from intact vessels requires adequate numbers of functional platelets. Platelets nurture the endothelium and thereby maintain the structural integrity of the vessel wall. Two processes are involved in arresting bleeding: primary and secondary hemostasis (Fig. 19-4).

In primary hemostasis, the severed blood vessel constricts. Circulating platelets aggregate at the site and adhere to the vessel and to one another. An unstable hemostatic plug is formed. For the coagulation process to be correctly activated, circulating inactive coagulation factors must be converted to active forms. This process occurs on the surface of the aggregated platelets at the site of vessel injury. The end

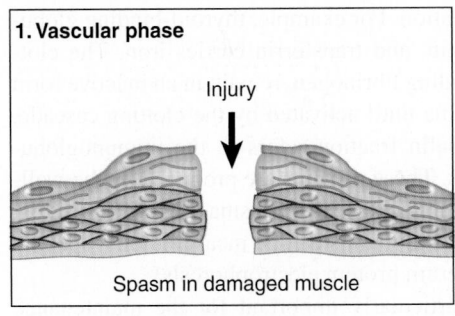

1. Vascular phase

Injury

Spasm in damaged muscle

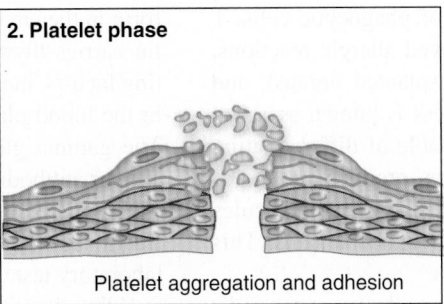

2. Platelet phase

Platelet aggregation and adhesion

3. Coagulation phase

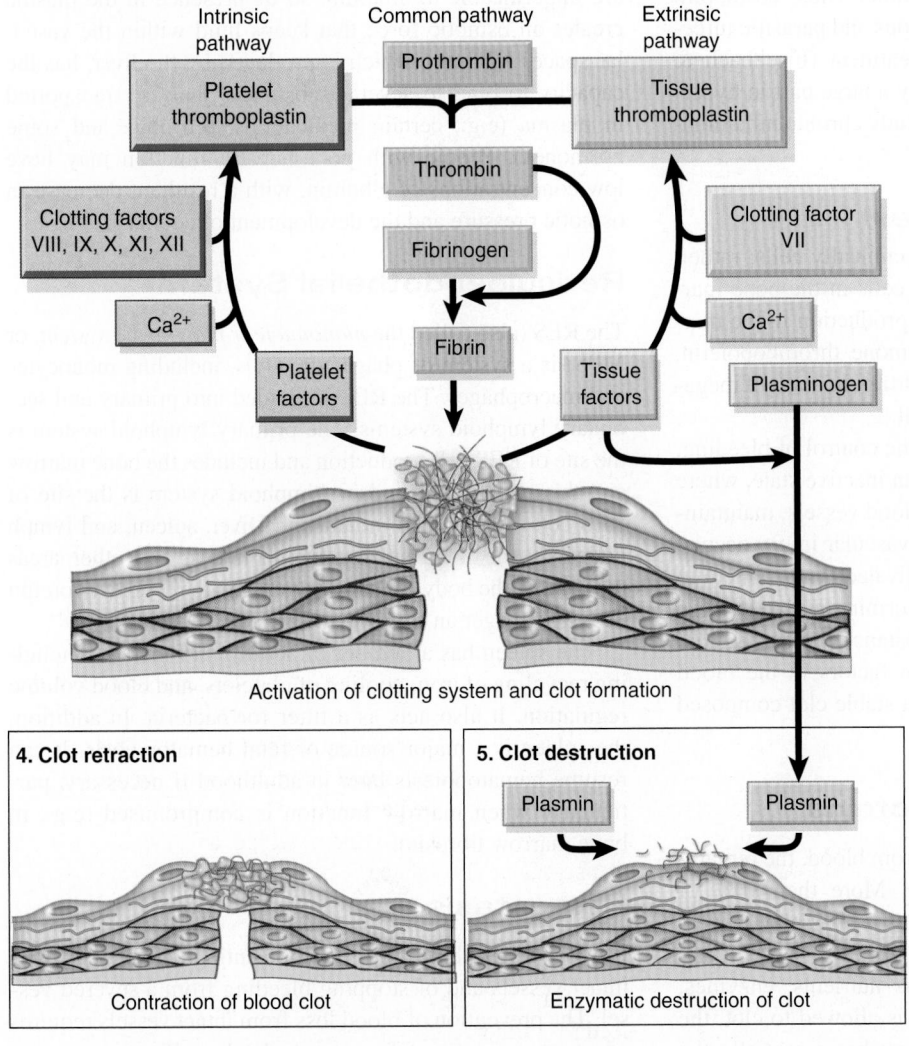

Intrinsic pathway

Common pathway

Extrinsic pathway

Platelet thromboplastin

Prothrombin

Tissue thromboplastin

Clotting factors VIII, IX, X, XI, XII

Thrombin

Clotting factor VII

Ca^{2+}

Fibrinogen

Ca^{2+}

Platelet factors

Fibrin

Tissue factors

Plasminogen

Activation of clotting system and clot formation

4. Clot retraction

Contraction of blood clot

5. Clot destruction

Plasmin

Plasmin

Enzymatic destruction of clot

FIGURE 19-4 Hemostasis. When the endothelial surface of a blood vessel is injured, several processes occur. In primary hemostasis, platelets within the circulation are attracted to the exposed layer of collagen at the site of injury. They adhere to the site of injury, releasing factors that stimulate other platelets to aggregate at the site, forming an unstable platelet plug. In secondary hemostasis, based on the type of stimulus, one of two clotting pathways is initiated—the intrinsic or extrinsic pathway—and the clotting factors within that pathway are activated. The end result from either pathway is the conversion of prothrombin to thrombin. Thrombin is necessary for fibrinogen to be converted into fibrin, the stabilizing protein that anchors the fragile platelet plug to the site of injury to prevent further bleeding and permit the injured vessel or site to heal. Modified from www.irvingcrowley.com/cls/clotting.gif.

result is the formation of fibrin, which reinforces the platelet plug and anchors it to the injury site. This process is termed *secondary hemostasis*. The process of blood coagulation is highly complex. It can be activated by the intrinsic or the extrinsic pathway. Both pathways are needed for maintenance of normal hemostasis.

Many factors are involved in the coagulation cascade that forms fibrin. When tissue is injured, the extrinsic pathway is activated by the release of thromboplastin from the tissue. As

the result of a series of reactions, prothrombin is converted to **thrombin**, which in turn catalyzes the conversion of fibrinogen to fibrin. Clotting by the intrinsic pathway is activated when the collagen that lines blood vessels is exposed. Clotting factors are activated sequentially until, as with the extrinsic pathway, fibrin is ultimately formed.

As the injured vessel is repaired and again covered with endothelial cells, the fibrin clot is no longer needed. The fibrin is digested via two systems: the plasma fibrinolytic

system and the cellular fibrinolytic system. The substance **plasminogen** is required to lyse (break down) the fibrin. Plasminogen, which is present in all body fluids, circulates with fibrinogen and is therefore incorporated into the fibrin clot as it forms. When the clot is no longer needed (e.g., after an injured blood vessel has healed), the plasminogen is activated to form plasmin. Plasmin digests the fibrinogen and fibrin. The by-products of clot digestion, called *fibrin degradation products*, are released into the circulation. Through this system, clots are dissolved as tissue is repaired, and the vascular system returns to its normal baseline state.

Gerontologic Considerations

In elderly patients, the bone marrow's ability to respond to the body's need for blood cells (erythrocytes, leukocytes, and platelets) may be decreased. This decreased ability is a result of many factors, including diminished production of the growth factors necessary for hematopoiesis by stromal cells within the marrow or a diminished response to the growth factors (in the case of erythropoietin). In addition, in elderly patients, the bone marrow may be more susceptible to the myelosuppressive effects of medications. As a result of these factors, when an elderly person needs more blood cells (e.g., leukocytes in infection, erythrocytes in anemia), the bone marrow may not be able to increase production of these cells adequately. **Leukopenia** (a decreased number of circulating leukocytes) or anemia can result.

Anemia is the most common hematologic condition affecting elderly patients; with each successive decade of life, the incidence of anemia increases. Anemia frequently results from iron deficiency (in the case of blood loss) or from a nutritional deficiency, particularly folate or vitamin B_{12} deficiency or protein–calorie malnutrition; it may also result from inflammation or chronic disease. Management of the disorder varies, depending on the etiology. Therefore, it is important to identify the cause of the anemia rather than to consider it an inevitable consequence of aging. Elderly people with concurrent cardiac or pulmonary problems may not tolerate anemia very well, and a prompt, thorough evaluation is warranted.

ASSESSMENT AND DIAGNOSTIC EVALUATION

Most hematologic diseases reflect a defect in the hematopoietic or hemostatic systems, or in the RES. The defect can be quantitative (e.g., increased or decreased production of cells), qualitative (e.g., the cells that are produced are defective in their normal functional capacity), or both.

Initially, many hematologic conditions cause few symptoms. Therefore, extensive laboratory tests are often required to diagnose a hematologic disorder. For most hematologic conditions, continued monitoring via specific blood tests is

TABLE 19-2 Normal Complete Blood Count With Differential		
	Example: 42-Year-Old Man	
WBC	5,000–10,000/µL Absolute neutrophil count >1,800/ µL	5, 300/ µL
Segments	38%–71% of total WBC	61%
Bands	0%–10% of total	5%
Monocytes	2%–15% of total	11%
Basophils	0%–1% of total	0%
Eosinophils	0%–5% of total	1%
Lymphocytes	20%–40% of total	22%
Hemoglobin	male: 14–18 g/dL (female: 12–16 g/dL)	17 g/dL
Hematocrit	male: 40%–52% (female: 37–47%)	51%
Platelets	150–400,000/ mm³	200,000/ mm³
Red blood cells (RBC)	4.5–5.5 ($\times 10^6$/mm³)	

required. In general, it is important to assess trends in blood counts because these trends help the clinician decide whether the patient is responding appropriately to interventions.

Hematologic Studies

The most common tests used to assess bone marrow function are the CBC and the peripheral blood smear. Blood for the CBC and peripheral blood smear is typically obtained by venipuncture. The CBC identifies the total number of blood cells (leukocytes, erythrocytes, and platelets) as well as the hemoglobin, **hematocrit** (percentage of blood volume consisting of erythrocytes), and RBC indices (Table 19-2). Because cellular morphology (shape and appearance of the cells) is particularly important in most hematologic disorders, the blood cells involved must be examined. This process is referred to as the *manual examination of the peripheral smear*, which may be part of the CBC. In this test, a drop of blood is spread on a glass slide, stained, and examined under a microscope. The shape and size of the erythrocytes and platelets, as well as the actual appearance of the leukocytes, provide useful information in identifying hematologic conditions. Increases or decreases in any one parameter of the CBC may indicate a hematologic disorder and indicate the need for further testing (refer to Chapter 20). Nurses must be familiar with the normal CBC parameters and be aware of potential implications of hematologic alterations.

NURSING ALERT

A falsely elevated hematocrit is noted in conditions of fluid volume loss. Since no single test confirms hemoconcentration, the nurse must assess for signs of fluid deficit, such as weight loss, dry mucous membranes, delayed skin turgor, orthostatic hypotension, decreased pulse pressure (difference between the systolic and diastolic pressure), decreasing urinary output

with elevated urine specific gravity, and vital sign changes (increasing heart rate and decreasing blood pressure as volume is lost). Regardless of the etiology, a hematocrit of greater than 60% is associated with spontaneous clotting (Fischbach & Dunning, 2009, p. 94). Likewise, in times of hemodilution (i.e., fluid gain), a falsely lower hematocrit is noted. The nurse assesses for weight gain, moist mucous membranes, edema, hypertension, crackles in the lung fields, an S_3 gallop over the mitral area, increased urinary output with decreased specific gravity, and distended neck veins. A hematocrit of less than 20% is associated with cardiac failure and death (Fischbach, 2009, p. 94).

Assessing the Patient With Low Hemoglobin and Hematocrit

Patients with mild to moderately lowered hemoglobin and hematocrit levels may be asymptomatic due to effective compensatory mechanisms. However, a careful history may uncover the following: fatigue, dyspnea, palpitations, poor activity tolerance, headaches, tinnitus, anorexia, indigestion, irritability, difficulty sleeping or concentrating, abnormal menstruation in females, impotence in males, loss of libido, chest pain, and shortness of breath. On physical examination, pallor is the most common and obvious sign of anemia. Pallor can be most easily assessed in the oral mucous membranes, nail beds, conjunctiva, and creases of the palms. Other findings may include tachycardia and flow murmurs. Patients with hemolytic anemia may exhibit jaundice and splenomegaly.

Assessing the Patient With a Low White Blood Cell Count

The most critical factors influencing an individual's risk for infection are the severity and duration of neutropenia. Nurses caring for a patient with a low WBC count should calculate the absolute neutrophil count (ANC; Box 19-1). Neutropenia severity is classified using the following guidelines: ANC 1,500 to 1,000/mm^3 indicates mild neutropenia; ANC 999 to 500/mm^3 indicates moderate neutropenia; ANC of less than 500/mm^3 indicates severe neutropenia. Patients with severe neutropenia are at significantly increased risk for developing opportunistic infections and sepsis and should be assessed carefully for the following:

- *Skin*: Check for tenderness, erythema, edema, breaks in skin integrity, moisture, drainage, lesions (especially under breasts, axillae, groin, skin folds, bony prominences, perineum, and peri rectum); check all puncture sites (e.g., IV sites) and central venous access device sites for erythema, tenderness, induration, and drainage.
- *Oral mucosa*: Check for moisture, lesions, color (check palate, tongue, buccal mucosa, gums, lips, oropharynx); assess level of pain and taste changes, which may precede objective signs of mucosal damage by 3 to 5 days.

BOX 19-1 **Calculating the Absolute Neutrophil Count (ANC)**

Normally, the neutrophil count is greater than 2,000/mm^3. The actual (or absolute) neutrophil count (ANC) is calculated using this formula:

Total WBC × (%segs + %bands) = ANC

For example, if the total white blood cell (WBC) count is 3,000/mm^3 with 72% neutrophils and 3% bands, the ANC would be calculated as follows:

3,000 × (72% + 3%) = 2,250/mm^3

This result is not indicative of neutropenia, because the ANC is greater than 2,000/mm^3 despite the low total WBC count (3,000/mm^3).

Conversely, in the following example, neutropenia is evident despite a normal WBC count (5500/mm^3) with 8% neutrophils and 0% bands:

5,500 × (8% + 0%) = 440/mm^3

Here, the ANC is severely low (440/mm^3) despite the normal total WBC count (5,500/mm^3).

When evaluating neutropenia, it is important to calculate the ANC and not to rely solely on the total WBCs and percentage of neutrophils alone.

- *Respiratory*: Check for presence of cough, sore throat, tachypnea; auscultate breath sounds. Note color, amount, and consistency of sputum.
- *Gastrointestinal*: Check for abdominal discomfort and distention, nausea, change in bowel pattern; auscultate bowel sounds.
- *Genitourinary*: Check for dysuria, urgency, frequency; check urine for color, clarity, and odor.
- *Neurologic*: Check for complaints of headache, neck stiffness, visual disturbances; assess level of consciousness, orientation, and behavior.
- *Temperature*: Check for elevation (>38°C [>100.4°F]).

Patients with neutropenia are often not able to manifest the classic signs of infection, such as pus, because pus is comprised of WBCs; therefore, the presence of fever may be the only sign that the patient has an infection and should be addressed immediately.

NURSING ALERT
Agranulocytosis or marked neutropenia and leukopenia place the patient at significant risk for infection. The nurse is aware that handwashing is critical to prevent infection. Reverse isolation procedures, such as the use of mask, gown, and gloves to prevent infection, has not been demonstrated to decrease infection rates and are no longer routinely implemented (Nirenberg, Bush, Davis et al., 2006; Zitella, Friese, Hauser et al., 2006).

Assessing the Patient at Risk for Bleeding

Signs and symptoms of bleeding disorders vary depending on the type and severity of the defect. Thrombocytopenia severity can be described as follows: excess bleeding may occur as a result of injury, trauma, or surgery, with a platelet count of 50,000 to 100,000/ mm^3; platelet counts of 20,000/ mm^3 or less increase the risk for spontaneous bleeding; and platelet counts of 10,000/ mm^3 or less are associated with serious episodes of spontaneous bleeding, including intracranial hemorrhage. Bleeding precautions are recommended for patients with a platelet count of less than 50,000/mm^3.

A careful history and physical examination can be very useful in determining the source of the hemostatic defect. Abnormalities of the vascular system give rise to local bleeding, usually into the skin. Because platelets are primarily responsible for hemostasis in small vessels, patients with platelet defects develop petechiae, often in clusters; these are most often seen first on the extremities and then the mucous membranes. With prolonged thrombocytopenia, petechiae may be seen on the trunk and throughout the body.

Other pertinent assessment findings include ecchymoses or hematomas, conjunctival hemorrhages, bleeding gums, bleeding at puncture sites (venipuncture, lumbar puncture, bone marrow); hypotension, tachycardia, dizziness, epistaxis (nose bleed); respiratory distress, tachypnea, hemoptysis (coughing of blood); hematemesis (vomiting blood), abdominal distention, rectal bleeding; vaginal or urethral bleeding; and headache, blurred vision, and mental status changes.

! NURSING ALERT

Because of the risk of spontaneous intracranial bleeding, patients with very severe thrombocytopenia must be monitored closely for subtle changes in mental status including irritability and restlessness, and educated to report even mild headaches immediately.

The nursing care and patient education required to safely care for patients with thrombocytopenia are outlined in Box 19-2.

In contrast to platelet defects, coagulation factor defects do not tend to cause superficial bleeding because the primary hemostatic mechanisms are still intact. Instead, bleeding occurs deeper within the body (e.g., subcutaneous or intramuscular hematomas, hemorrhage into joint spaces). External bleeding diminishes very slowly when local pressure is applied; it often recurs several hours after pressure is removed. For example, severe bleeding may start several hours after a tooth extraction.

BOX 19-2

Nursing Interventions for Patients With Thrombocytopenia (Platelet Count <50,000/mm^3)

Prevent Complications: Implement Bleeding Precautions

- Avoid giving aspirin and aspirin-containing medications or other medications known to inhibit platelet function (NSAIDS), if possible.
- Do not give intramuscular injections.
- Do not insert indwelling catheters.
- Do not use the rectal route for taking temperatures or administering medications.
- Use stool softeners and oral laxatives to prevent constipation.
- Use the smallest possible needles when performing venipuncture.
- Apply pressure to venipuncture sites for 5 minutes or until bleeding has stopped.
- Use only soft-bristled toothbrush for mouth care.
- Do not permit wearing of restrictive clothing; avoid tourniquets or overinflation of blood pressure cuffs.
- Lubricate lips with water-soluble lubricant every 2 hours while patient is awake.
- Avoid suctioning if at all possible; if unavoidable, use only gentle suctioning.
- Discourage vigorous coughing or blowing of the nose.
- Use only electric razor for shaving.
- Pad side rails as needed.

- Prevent falls by ambulating with patient as necessary and keeping the environment safe.
- Teach patient to avoid contact sports and sports with risk for falling or injury (such as biking or roller-blading).
- Teach patient to avoid sexual intercourse (both vaginal and anal) until platelet count is over 50,000/mm^3.

Control Bleeding

- Apply direct pressure.
- Use manual pressure with gauze over the source of bleeding.
- For epistaxis, position patient in high Fowler's position with body tilted forward and the mouth open so that the blood can be spit out instead of swallowed; apply ice pack to the bridge of the nose and direct pressure to nose.
- Hemostatic agents such as thromboplastin, absorbable gelatin, fibrin sealants, collagen, and alginate can be used for hemostasis at wound sites and central venous access device sites that are bleeding.
- Notify health care provider for prolonged bleeding (e.g., unable to stop within 10 minutes).
- Administer platelets, fresh frozen plasma, packed red blood cells, as prescribed.

Nirenberg et al., 2006.

Bone Marrow Aspiration and Biopsy

The bone marrow aspiration and biopsy are crucial when additional information is needed to assess how a person's blood cells are being formed and to assess the quantity and quality of each type of cell produced within the marrow. These tests are also used to document infection or tumor within the marrow.

Normal bone marrow is in a semifluid state and can be aspirated through a special hollow core, large-bore needle. In adults, bone marrow is usually aspirated from the posterior iliac crest and rarely from the sternum. The aspirate provides only a sample of cells. Aspirate alone may be adequate for evaluating certain conditions, such as anemia. However, when more information is required, a biopsy is also performed. Biopsy samples are taken from the posterior iliac crest; occasionally, an anterior approach is required. A marrow biopsy shows the architecture of the bone marrow as well as its degree of cellularity.

Most patients need no more preparation than a careful explanation of the procedure and the sensations that will be experienced, but for some very anxious patients, an antianxiety agent may be useful. The risks, benefits, and alternatives are also discussed. A signed informed consent is needed before the procedure is performed.

Before aspiration, the skin is cleansed as for any minor surgery, using aseptic technique. Then a small area is anesthetized with a local anesthetic through the skin and subcutaneous tissue to the periosteum of the bone. It is not possible to anesthetize the bone itself. The bone marrow needle is introduced with a stylet in place. When the needle is felt to go through the outer cortex of bone and enter the marrow cavity, the stylet is removed, a syringe is attached, and a small volume (5 to 10 mL) of blood and marrow is aspirated. Patients typically feel a sensation of pressure as the needle is advanced into position. The aspiration of fluid causes a sudden and sharp but brief pain, resulting from the suction exerted as the marrow is aspirated into the syringe; the patient should be warned about this. Taking deep breaths or using relaxation techniques often helps ease the discomfort.

If a bone marrow biopsy is necessary, it is best performed after the aspiration and in a slightly different location, because the marrow structure may be altered after aspiration. A special biopsy needle is used. Because these needles are large, the skin is punctured first with a surgical blade to make a 3- or 4-mm incision. The biopsy needle is advanced well into the marrow cavity. When the needle is properly positioned, a portion of marrow is cored out, using a twisting or gentle rocking motion to free the sample and permit its removal within the biopsy needle. The patient feels a pressure sensation but should not feel actual pain. The nurse should instruct the patient to inform the provider if pain occurs so that an additional anesthetic can be administered.

Hazards of either bone marrow aspiration or biopsy include bleeding and infection. The risk for bleeding is somewhat increased if the patient's platelet count is low or if the patient has been taking a medication (e.g., aspirin) that alters platelet function. After the marrow sample is obtained, pressure is applied to the site for several minutes. The site is then covered with a sterile dressing. Most patients have no discomfort after a bone marrow aspiration, but the site of a biopsy may ache for 1 or 2 days. Patients should be instructed not to submerge in a bath for 24 hours, until the site heals. A mild analgesic (e.g., acetaminophen) may be useful. Aspirin-containing analgesics should be avoided because they can aggravate or potentiate bleeding.

Chapter Review

Critical Thinking Exercises

1. You are caring for a patient with acute leukemia and sepsis who has a declining platelet count of 10,000/ mm³. On assessment, you observe oozing blood from the Hickman catheter site, petechiae to the upper and lower extremities, and epistaxis. What are the potential causes of this patient's bleeding? What other lab results would you assess? What further assessments would you perform? What nursing interventions would you implement? What medical interventions would you anticipate?

2. You are working in a hematology–oncology clinic. The laboratory reports a critical laboratory result for one of your patients with possible acute leukemia: the leukocyte count is 1,200/mm³ with 10% neutrophils. What other laboratory results would be important to review or consider? The patient is also anemic (hemoglobin 8.2 mg/dL) and platelets are 110,000/mm³. What observations will you include in your assessment of this patient? Determine the extent to which this patient is neutropenic. What medical treatments would you anticipate? How would you educate the patient about neutropenia precautions? What information do you need to obtain about the patient's home setting that will assist you in determining the patient's risk of developing an infection at home? How will you modify this education if the patient has mild dementia? Lives alone? Does not understand or speak English well?

NCLEX-Style Review Questions

1. A nurse is caring for a patient who is 73 years old with a platelet count of 5,000/mm^3 resulting from myelodysplastic syndrome. At 10 p.m., the patient complains of a headache. What should be the nurse's immediate action to take?

A. Administer aspirin per p.r.n. order.

B. Administer acetaminophen per p.r.n. order.

C. Notify the health care provider.

D. Administer a nonpharmacologic intervention, such as a cool compress.

2. Mrs. S. presented to her primary care provider with a complaint of a "cold that just won't go away." She has a CBC drawn, revealing the following: WBC 4.5: segs 5, bands 0, lymphs 45, eosinophils 5, basophils 5, monocytes 5, blasts 35. What is the patient's absolute neutrophil count?

A. 500

B. 250

C. 225

D. 2,250

3. What is the priority nursing diagnosis for a client experiencing anemia?

A. Risk for injury related to poor blood clotting

B. Fatigue related to decreased cellular oxygenation

C. Risk of infection related to decreased leukocytes

D. Imbalanced nutrition; less than body requirements related to anorexia

4. A patient with thrombocytopenia due to chemotherapy develops a nose bleed (epistaxis). What is the nurse's expected response?

A. Apply ice to the anterior surface of the nose and place the patient in a supine position

B. Apply pressure to the nares and position the patient in a high Fowler's position, leaning slightly forward

C. Squeeze the nares together firmly and position the patient in prone position with mouth open

D. Ask the patient to blow the nose vigorously as the nurse applies firm pressure to the nares

5. The nurse recognizes which of the following as the most common hematological condition associated with aging?

A. Thrombocytopenia

B. Leukopenia

C. Agranulocytosis

D. Anemia

Try these additional resources to enhance your learning and understanding of this chapter:

- thePoint online resource available at **http://thepoint.lww.com/Pellico1e**
- *Handbook for Focus on Adult Health: Medical-Surgical Nursing*
- *Study Guide for Focus on Adult Health: Medical-Surgical Nursing*

 References and Selected Readings

References and selected readings associated with this chapter can be found on the website that accompanies the book. Visit http://thepoint.lww.com/Pellico1e to access the references and other additional resources associated with this chapter.

Nursing Management: Patients With Hematologic Disorders

LISA BARBAROTTA

Hematologic disorders include both benign and malignant conditions. These disorders can impact every system in the body. Nursing care of these patients requires an understanding of the anatomy and physiology of hematopoiesis and immunology, as well as astute assessment skills.

ANEMIA

Anemia, a condition in which the **hemoglobin** concentration is lower than normal, reflects the presence of fewer than normal **erythrocytes** within the circulation. As a result, the amount of oxygen delivered to body tissues is also diminished. Anemia is not a specific disease state per se but a sign of an underlying disorder. It is by far the most common hematologic condition. A common occurrence among all age groups, it is particularly prevalent among the elderly, with prevalence rates of anemia in elderly residents living in skilled nursing facilities as high as 48% (Landi, Russo, Danese et al., 2007; Robinson, Arttz, Culleton et al., 2007).

OVERVIEW

Anemia, a decrease in the number of red blood cells (RBCs), has a number of different etiologies. The treatment varies based on the cause. The different classifications of anemia, as well as the nursing management of each, will be discussed here.

Classification of Anemias

Anemia can be classified by cellular morphology (shape) or by physiologic process. Morphologic classification is the most common approach and includes the cell size, color, and shape. Changes in the size of the RBC are described as normocytic (normal or average size), macrocytic (larger than normal), or microcytic (smaller than normal). Changes in the color of the RBC are described as normochromic (normal in color), hyperchromic (darker cellular contents), or hypochromic (pale or lighter cellular contents) (see Table 20-1). A physiologic approach (see Table 20-2, p. 530) classifies anemia according to whether the deficiency in erythrocytes is caused by a defect in their production (hypoproliferative anemia), by their destruction (hemolytic anemia), or by their loss (e.g., bleeding) (Fig. 20-1).

Learning Objectives

After reading this chapter, you will be able to:

1. Differentiate between the different types of anemias, and compare and contrast the physiologic mechanisms, clinical manifestations, medical management, and nursing interventions for each.

2. Compare the leukemias in terms of their incidence, physiologic alterations, clinical manifestations, management, and prognosis.

3. Discuss nursing management of patients with lymphoma or multiple myeloma.

4. Discuss nursing management of patients with bleeding or thrombotic disorders.

5. Identify therapies for blood disorders, including the nursing implications for the administration of blood components.

TABLE
20-1 Classification of Anemia by Morphology

Type of Anemia	Morphology	Examples	Laboratory Values Expected
Normocytic, normochromic	Cells of normal size with normal hemoglobin content	Aplastic anemia Acute blood loss Hemolytic anemia Anemia of chronic disease Sickle cell anemia	Normal MCV Normal MCHC ↓ Hemoglobin ↓ Hematocrit
Microcytic, hypochromic	Small, reduced amount of hemoglobin	Iron deficiency anemia Sideroblastic anemia Thalassemia	↓ MCV ↓ MCHC ↓ Hemoglobin ↓ Hematocrit
Macrocytic, normochromic	Large in size, thickness, and volume.	Folic acid deficiency Vitamin B_{12} deficiency	↑ MCV Normal MCHC ↓ Hemoglobin ↓ Hematocrit

In hypoproliferative anemias, the marrow cannot produce adequate numbers of erythrocytes. The reticulocyte count reflects bone marrow production of RBCs. In anemia due to blood loss, a healthy bone marrow compensates for losses and increases RBC production, reflected as an increased reticulocyte count. In hypoproliferative anemias, the bone marrow cannot mount an adequate response to anemia, and this lack of RBC production is reflected as a low reticulocyte count.

Inadequate production of erythrocytes may result from marrow damage due to medications (e.g., chloramphenicol) or chemicals (e.g., benzene), or from a lack of factors (e.g.,

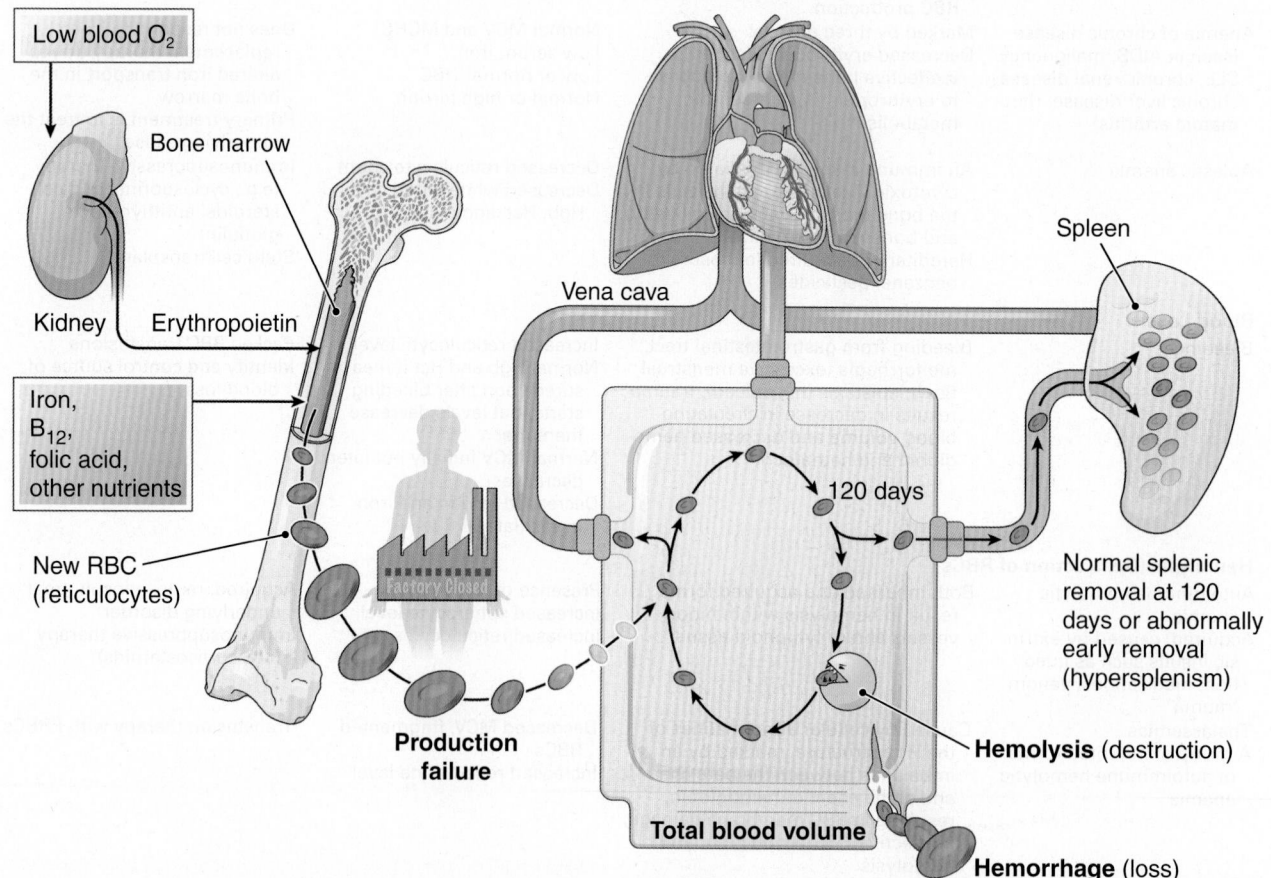

FIGURE 20-1 Production, circulation, and death of red blood cells. Every anemia is caused by at least one of three problems: (1) decreased red cell production, (2) loss of red cells by hemorrhage, or (3) early death (destruction) of RBCs. From McConnell, T. H. (2007). *The nature of disease pathology for the health professions.* Philadelphia: Lippincott Williams & Wilkins.

TABLE
20-2 Anemia Classification by Etiology

Type of Anemia	Pathophysiology	Lab Findings	Treatment
Hypoproliferative (Decreased Production)			
Pernicious, megaloblastic	Vitamin B_{12} deficiency; lack of intrinsic factor required for B_{12} absorption	Decreased vitamin B_{12} level; increased MCV Elevated methylmalonic acid and homocysteine levels Low reticulocyte count	B_{12} replacement Cyanocobalamin 1,000 µg IM monthly
Folate deficiency	Decreased folic acid intake; impaired absorption; alcohol impairs folate metabolism in the liver, causing a significant depletion in folate reserves Decreases in folate impair DNA synthesis and increase erythroblast cell deaths	Decreased folate levels Increased MCV	Oral folic acid 1 to 5 mg/day PO
Iron deficiency	Chronic blood loss, failure to recapture iron from recycled RBCs Demands for iron exceed iron intake. Decreased iron intake results in use and depletion of iron stores, resulting in decreased Hgb production	Decreased reticulocytes, iron, ferritin, iron saturation, MCV Increased TIBC	Iron replacement therapy: ferrous sulfate 325 mg PO t.i.d. Parenteral iron therapy reserved for those who cannot take oral replacement due to intolerance, poor enteral absorption, or continued blood loss IV iron therapy requires careful monitoring for signs of hypersensitivity
Decreased erythropoietin production	Renal disease can impair erythropoietin production (due to renal disease, malignancy), which in turn decreases RBC production	Decreased erythropoietin level; normal MCV and MCH; increased creatinine level	Erythropoietin replacement
Anemia of chronic disease (seen in AIDS, malignancy, SLE, chronic renal disease, chronic liver disease, rheumatoid arthritis)	Marked by three defects: Decreased erythrocyte lifespan, ineffective bone marrow response to erythropoietin, altered iron metabolism	Normal MCV and MCHC Low serum iron Low or normal TIBC Normal or high ferritin	Does not respond to iron replacement therapy due to altered iron transport in the bone marrow Primary treatment is to treat the underlying cause
Aplastic anemia	An immune response mediated by cytotoxic T cells; targets the cells in the bone marrow, causing cell death and bone marrow failure Hereditary or acquired (exposure to benzene, pesticides)	Decreased reticulocyte count Decreased white blood cells, Hgb, Hct, and platelets	Immunosuppressive therapy (e.g., cyclosporine, corticosteroids, antithymocyte globulin) Stem cell transplant
Blood Loss			
Bleeding	Bleeding from gastrointestinal tract, menorrhagia (excessive menstrual flow), epistaxis (nosebleed), trauma results in decrease in circulating blood volume and decreased hemoglobin and hematocrit	Increased reticulocyte level Normal Hgb and Hct if measured soon after bleeding starts, but levels decrease thereafter Normal MCV initially but later decreases Decreased ferritin and iron levels (later)	Packed RBC transfusions Identify and control source of blood loss
Hemolysis (Destruction of RBCs)			
Autoimmune hemolytic anemia Acquired; caused by extrinsic insults such as infection, medications, venom, trauma	Both inherited and acquired forms result in hemolysis within blood vessels and/or lymphoid tissue	Presence of schistocytes Increased spherocyte level Increased reticulocytes	Acquired: remove insult, treat underlying disorder Immunosuppressive therapy (i.e., corticosteroids)
Thalassemias A group of inherited forms of autoimmune hemolytic anemia	Caused by cellular abnormalities of the Hgb structure, marked by an imbalance between the beta chain and alpha chain of hemoglobin, resulting in RBC membrane damage, ineffective RBC production, and hemolysis	Decreased MCV; fragmented RBCs Increased reticulocyte level	Transfusion therapy with PRBCs

MCV, mean corpuscular volume; MCHC, mean corpuscular hemoglobin concentration; TIBC, total iron binding capacity; Hgb, hemoglobin; Hct, hematocrit; AIDS, acquired immune deficiency syndrome; SLE, systemic lupus erythematosus; RBC, red blood cells; PRBCs, packed RBCs.

iron, vitamin B$_{12}$, folic acid, **erythropoietin**) necessary for erythrocyte formation.

In hemolytic anemias, premature destruction of erythrocytes results in the liberation of hemoglobin from the erythrocytes into the plasma. The increased erythrocyte destruction leads to tissue hypoxia, which in turn stimulates erythropoietin production. This increased production is reflected in an increased reticulocyte count as the bone marrow responds to the destruction of erythrocytes. The released hemoglobin is converted in large part to bilirubin; therefore, the bilirubin concentration rises. **Hemolysis** can result from an abnormality within the erythrocyte itself (e.g., sickle cell anemia, glucose-6-phosphate dehydrogenase [G-6-PD] deficiency) or within the plasma (e.g., immune hemolytic anemias), or from direct injury to the erythrocyte within the circulation (e.g., hemolysis caused by mechanical heart valve).

To determine whether the presence of anemia in a given patient is caused by destruction or by inadequate production of erythrocytes, consider the following factors:

- The marrow's ability to respond to decreased erythrocytes (as evidenced by an increased reticulocyte count in the circulating blood)
- The degree to which young erythrocytes (**nucleated RBCs**) proliferate in the bone marrow and the manner in which they mature (as observed on bone marrow biopsy)
- The presence or absence of end products of erythrocyte destruction within the circulation (e.g., increased bilirubin level, decreased haptoglobin [a protein produced by the liver] level)

Clinical Manifestations and Assessment

Aside from the severity of the anemia itself, several factors influence the development of anemia-associated symptoms:

- The rapidity with which the anemia has developed
- The duration of the anemia (i.e., chronicity)
- The metabolic requirements of the patient
- Other concurrent disorders or disabilities (e.g., cardiopulmonary disease)

In general, the more rapidly an anemia develops, the more severe its symptoms. An otherwise healthy person can often tolerate as much as a 50% gradual reduction in hemoglobin without pronounced symptoms or significant incapacity, whereas the rapid loss of as little as 30% may precipitate profound vascular collapse in the same person. A person who has become gradually anemic, with hemoglobin levels between 9 and 11 g/dL, may have few or no symptoms other than slight tachycardia on exertion and fatigue.

People who usually are very active or who have significant demands on their lives (e.g., a single, working mother of small children) are more likely to experience symptoms. Patients with hypothyroidism with decreased oxygen needs may be completely asymptomatic, without tachycardia or

increased cardiac output, at a hemoglobin level of 10 g/dL. Similarly, patients with coexistent cardiac, vascular, or pulmonary disease may develop more pronounced symptoms of anemia (e.g., dyspnea, chest pain, muscle pain or cramping) at a higher hemoglobin level than those without these concurrent health problems.

The most common signs and symptoms of anemia are discussed in Box 20-1. A careful and thorough assessment is essential in identifying potential complications and targeting nursing interventions.

A variety of hematologic studies are performed to determine the type and cause of the anemia (see Chapter 19 for a detailed overview). In an initial evaluation, the hemoglobin, **hematocrit**, reticulocyte count, and RBC indices, particularly the mean corpuscular volume (MCV) and red cell distribution width (RDW), are particularly useful. Iron studies (**serum iron level**, total iron-binding capacity [TIBC], % saturation, and ferritin), as well as serum vitamin B$_{12}$ and folate levels, are also frequently obtained. Other tests include haptoglobin and erythropoietin levels. The remaining complete blood count (CBC) values are useful in determining whether the anemia is an isolated problem or part of another hematologic condition, such as **leukemia** or myelodysplastic syndrome (MDS) (a group of disorders where the bone marrow does not produce enough healthy blood cells). Bone marrow aspiration may be performed. In addition, other diagnostic studies may be performed to determine the presence of underlying chronic illness, such as malignancy, or the source of any blood loss, such as polyps or ulcers within the gastrointestinal (GI) tract.

Medical Management

Management of anemia is directed toward correcting or controlling the cause of the anemia; if the anemia is severe, the erythrocytes that are lost or destroyed may be replaced with a transfusion of packed RBCs (PRBCs). The management of the various types of anemia is covered in the discussions that follow.

Nursing Management

Managing Fatigue

The most common symptom and complication of anemia is fatigue. This distressing symptom is too often minimized by health care providers. Fatigue is often the symptom that has the greatest negative impact on a patient's level of functioning and consequent quality of life. Patients often describe the fatigue from anemia as oppressive. Fatigue can interfere with a person's ability to work, both inside and outside the home. It can disrupt relationships with family and friends. Patients often lose interest in hobbies and activities, including sexual activity. The severity of distress from fatigue is often related to a person's responsibilities and life demands, as well as the amount of assistance and support received from others.

Nursing interventions can focus on assisting the patient to prioritize activities and to establish a balance between

Focused Assessment: Anemia

Be alert for the following signs and symptoms:

General:
- Weakness, fatigue
- Dizziness
- Pica (craving unusual items including: ice, starch, or dirt)

Neurologic:
- Numbness and tingling (paresthesias), irritability
- Weakness
- Headache
- Poor coordination, confusion
- Gait disturbances
- Reflex abnormalities
- Loss of position (proprioception) and vibration sense
- Spasticity
- Roaring, rushing, ringing, or pounding sensation in the ears

Integumentary:
- Pallor of the skin and mucous membranes
- Jaundice (hemolytic anemia)
- Brittle, ridged, concave nails
- Impaired wound healing
- Loss of elasticity
- Early thinning and graying of hair
- Dry skin
- Painful mouth sores

- Beefy red, sore tongue (megaloblastic anemia)
- Smooth and red tongue (iron deficiency anemia)
- Ulcerated corners of the mouth (angular cheilosis)

Cardiovascular:
- Palpitations
- Chest pain
- Tachycardia
- Hypotension
- Peripheral edema
- Murmurs

Respiratory:
- Dyspnea
- Orthopnea
- Tachypnea

Gastrointestinal:
- Anorexia, nausea, vomiting
- Dysphagia
- Abdominal pain
- Flatulence
- Diarrhea
- Hepatomegaly
- Splenomegaly

Musculoskeletal:
- Muscle pain (claudication)

*Neurologic signs and symptoms are most commonly seen in pernicious anemia.

activity and rest that is realistic and feasible from the patient's perspective. Patients with chronic anemia need to maintain some physical activity and exercise to prevent the deconditioning that results from inactivity. Short periods of daily exercise can also decrease the severity of fatigue (Mitchell, Beck, Hood et al., 2007).

Maintaining Adequate Nutrition

Inadequate intake of essential nutrients, such as iron, vitamin B_{12}, and folic acid can cause some anemias. The symptoms associated with anemia (e.g., fatigue, anorexia) can in turn interfere with maintaining adequate nutrition. A healthy diet should be encouraged. The nurse should inform the patient that alcohol interferes with the utilization of essential nutrients and should advise the patient to avoid alcoholic beverages or to limit intake. Dietary teaching sessions should be individualized and culture-sensitive to food preferences and food preparation. The involvement of family members enhances compliance with dietary recommendations. Dietary supplements (e.g., vitamins, iron, folate, protein) may be prescribed as well.

Equally important, the patient and family must understand the underlying cause of the anemia because many forms of anemia are not the result of a nutritional deficiency. In such cases, even an excessive intake of nutritional supple-

ments will not improve the anemia. A potential problem in patients with chronic transfusion requirements occurs with the indiscriminate use of iron supplements. These individuals are at risk for iron overload from their transfusions. The addition of an iron supplement will only exacerbate the situation and necessitates the use of iron chelation therapy (the administration of agents that remove metals such as iron).

Maintaining Adequate Perfusion

Patients with acute blood loss or severe hemolysis may have decreased tissue perfusion from decreased blood volume or reduced circulating erythrocytes (decreased hematocrit). Lost volume is replaced with transfusions or IV fluids, based on the symptoms and the laboratory test results. Supplemental oxygen may be necessary, but it is rarely needed on a long-term basis unless there is underlying severe cardiac or pulmonary disease. The nurse monitors the patient's vital signs and pulse oximeter readings closely; other medications, such as antihypertensive agents, may need to be adjusted or withheld.

Complications

General complications of severe anemia include heart failure, paresthesias, and confusion. At any given level of

anemia, patients with underlying heart disease are far more likely to have angina or symptoms of heart failure than those without heart disease.

HYPOPROLIFERATIVE ANEMIAS

IRON DEFICIENCY ANEMIA

The development of iron deficiency anemia occurs when the body's iron stores are depleted and there is no iron available for hemoglobin synthesis. The volume of individual iron stores is dependent upon sex, age, rate of growth, and the balance between dietary iron absorption and losses. Iron is stored primarily in the liver, spleen, and bone marrow. The remainder of iron exists as hemoglobin and proteins.

Iron deficiency anemia is the most common type of anemia in all age groups, and it is the most common anemia in the world. It is particularly prevalent in developing countries, where inadequate iron stores can result from inadequate intake of iron (seen with vegetarian diets) or from blood loss (e.g., from intestinal hookworm). Iron deficiency is also common in the United States. In children, adolescents, and pregnant women, the cause is typically inadequate iron in the diet to keep up with increased growth. However, for most adults with iron deficiency anemia, the cause is blood loss. In fact, in adults, the cause of iron deficiency anemia should be considered to be bleeding until proven otherwise.

The most common cause of iron deficiency anemia in men and postmenopausal women is bleeding (from ulcers, gastritis, inflammatory bowel disease, or GI tumors). The most common cause of iron deficiency anemia in premenopausal women is menorrhagia (excessive menstrual bleeding) and pregnancy with inadequate iron supplementation. Patients with chronic alcoholism often have chronic blood loss from the GI tract, which causes iron loss and eventual anemia. Other causes include iron malabsorption, as is seen after gastrectomy or with celiac disease.

Medical Management

Except in the case of pregnancy, the cause of iron deficiency should be investigated. Anemia may be a sign of a curable GI cancer or of uterine fibroid tumors. Stool specimens should be tested for occult blood. People 50 years of age or older should have periodic colonoscopy and endoscopy to detect ulcerations, gastritis, polyps, or cancer.

Several oral iron preparations—ferrous sulfate, ferrous gluconate, and ferrous fumarate—are available for treating iron deficiency anemia. The hemoglobin level may increase in only a few weeks, and the anemia can be corrected in a few months. Iron store replenishment takes much longer, so it is important that the patient continue taking the iron for as long as 6 to 12 months. Vitamin C facilitates the absorption of iron. Therefore, iron supplements should be taken with a glass of orange juice or a vitamin C tablet to maximize absorption.

In some cases, oral iron is poorly absorbed or poorly tolerated, or iron supplementation is needed in large amounts. In these situations, IV or intramuscular (IM) administration of iron dextran may be needed. Before parenteral administration of a full dose, a small test dose should be administered parenterally to avoid the risk of anaphylaxis with either IV or IM injections. Emergency medications (e.g., epinephrine) should be close at hand. If no signs of allergic reaction have occurred after 30 minutes, the remaining dose of iron may be administered. Several doses are required to replenish the patient's iron stores.

Nursing Management

Preventive education is important, because iron deficiency anemia is common in menstruating and pregnant women. Food sources high in iron include organ meats (beef or calf's liver, chicken liver), other red meats, beans (black, pinto, and garbanzo), leafy green vegetables, raisins, and molasses. Taking iron-rich foods with a source of vitamin C (e.g., orange juice) enhances the absorption of iron.

The nurse helps the patient select a healthy diet. Nutritional counseling can be provided for those whose usual diet is inadequate. Patients with a history of eating fad diets or strict vegetarian diets are counseled that such diets often contain inadequate amounts of absorbable iron. The nurse encourages the patient to continue iron therapy as long as it is prescribed, even if the symptoms of anemia resolve.

Because iron is best absorbed on an empty stomach, the patient is instructed to take the supplement an hour before meals. Iron supplements are usually given in the oral form, typically as ferrous sulfate. Most patients can use the less expensive, more standard forms of ferrous sulfate. Tablets with enteric coating may be poorly absorbed and should be avoided. Many patients have difficulty tolerating iron supplements because of GI side effects (primarily constipation, but also cramping, nausea, and vomiting). Some iron formulations are designed to limit GI side effects by the addition of a stool softener or use of sustained-release formulations to limit nausea or gastritis. Specific patient teaching aids (Box 20-2) can assist patients with the use of iron supplements.

IV supplementation may be used when the patient's iron stores are completely depleted, the patient cannot tolerate oral forms of iron supplementation (see Medical Management), or both. IM supplementation is used infrequently. The volume of iron required when administered IM may be excessive. The IM injection causes some local pain and can stain the skin. These side effects are minimized by using the Z-track technique for administering iron dextran deep into the gluteus maximus muscle (buttock). The nurse avoids vigorously rubbing the injection site after the injection to limit staining of the skin. Because of the problems with IM administration, the IV route is preferred for administration of iron dextran.

BOX 20-2 **Patient Education**

Taking Oral Iron Supplements

- Take iron on an empty stomach (1 hour before or 2 hours after a meal). Because iron absorption is reduced with food, especially dairy products and antacids, avoid taking iron with these items.
- To prevent gastrointestinal distress, the following schedule may work better if more than one tablet a day is prescribed: Start with only one tablet per day for a few days, then increase to two tablets per day, then three tablets per day. This method permits the body to adjust gradually to the iron.
- Increase the intake of vitamin C (citrus fruits and juices, strawberries, tomatoes, broccoli), to enhance iron absorption.
- Eat foods high in fiber to minimize problems with constipation.
- Remember that stools will become dark in color.
- To prevent staining the teeth with a liquid preparation, use a straw or place a spoon at the back of the mouth to take the supplement. Rinse the mouth thoroughly afterward.

ANEMIA IN RENAL DISEASE

The degree of anemia in patients with end-stage renal disease (ESRD) varies greatly, but in general patients do not become significantly anemic until the serum creatinine level exceeds 3 mg/100 mL.

Pathophysiology

This anemia is caused by both a mild shortening of erythrocyte lifespan and a deficiency of erythropoietin (necessary for **erythropoiesis**). As renal function decreases, erythropoietin, which is produced by the kidney, also decreases. Because erythropoietin is also produced outside the kidney, some erythropoiesis continues, even in patients whose kidneys have been removed. However, the number of RBCs produced is small and the degree of erythropoiesis is inadequate.

Patients undergoing long-term hemodialysis lose blood into the dialyzer and therefore may become iron deficient. Folic acid deficiency develops because this vitamin passes into the dialysate. Therefore, patients who receive hemodialysis and who have anemia should be evaluated for iron and folate deficiency and treated appropriately.

Clinical Manifestations and Assessment

For patients with ESRD, the symptoms of anemia including fatigue and decreased activity tolerance, are often the most disturbing. If untreated, the hematocrit usually falls to between 20% and 30%, although in rare cases it may fall to less than 15%. The erythrocytes appear normal on the peripheral smear.

Medical and Nursing Management

The availability of recombinant erythropoietin (epoetin alfa [Epogen, Procrit]; darbepoetin alfa [Aranesp]) has dramatically altered the management of anemia in ESRD by decreasing the need for RBC transfusion, with its associated risks. Erythropoietin, in combination with oral iron supplements, can raise and maintain hematocrit levels to between 33% and 38%. This treatment has been successful with dialysis patients. Hypertension is the most serious side effect in this patient population when the hematocrit rapidly increases to a high level. Therefore, the hematocrit and blood pressure should be checked frequently when a patient with renal disease begins erythropoietin therapy. The dose of erythropoietin should be titrated to the hematocrit. In some patients, the elevated hematocrit and associated hypertension may necessitate antihypertensive therapy.

ANEMIA OF CHRONIC DISEASE

The term "anemia of chronic disease" is a misnomer in that only the chronic diseases of inflammation, infection, and malignancy cause this type of anemia. Many chronic inflammatory diseases are associated with a **normochromic, normocytic** anemia (i.e., the erythrocytes are normal in color and size). These disorders include rheumatoid arthritis; severe, chronic infections; and many cancers. It is therefore imperative that the "chronic disease" be diagnosed when this form of anemia is identified so that it can be appropriately managed.

The anemia is usually mild to moderate and non- progressive. It develops gradually over 6 to 8 weeks and then stabilizes at a hematocrit seldom less than 25%. The hemoglobin level rarely falls below 9 g/dL, and the bone marrow has normal cellularity with increased stores of iron as the iron is diverted from the serum.

Most of these patients have few symptoms and do not require treatment for the anemia. With successful treatment of the underlying disorder, the bone marrow iron is used to make erythrocytes and the hemoglobin level rises.

APLASTIC ANEMIA

Aplastic anemia is a rare disease caused by a decrease in or damage to marrow **stem cells**, damage to the microenvironment within the marrow, and replacement of the marrow with fat. Evidence suggests that cytotoxic T cells produce substances that inhibit **hematopoiesis**, resulting in a fatty, hypocellular bone marrow (Mansen & McCance, 2006). Therefore, in addition to severe anemia, significant **neutropenia** (decreased **neutrophils**) and thrombocytopenia (a deficiency of **platelet**s) are also seen.

Pathophysiology

Aplastic anemia can be congenital or acquired, but most cases are idiopathic (i.e., without apparent cause). Infections and pregnancy can trigger it, or it may be caused by certain medications, chemicals, or radiation damage. Agents that regularly produce marrow aplasia include benzene and benzene derivatives (e.g., airplane glue). Certain toxic materials, such as inorganic arsenic and several pesticides (including dichlorodiphenyltrichloroethane [DDT], which is no longer used or available in the United States), have also been implicated as potential causes.

Clinical Manifestations and Assessment

The manifestations of aplastic anemia are often insidious. Complications resulting from bone marrow failure may occur before the diagnosis is established including infection (due to neutropenia) and bleeding (due to thrombocytopenia). Symptoms of anemia including fatigue, shortness of breath, and decreased activity tolerance are usually present at the time of diagnosis. Purpura (bruising) may develop later and should trigger a CBC and hematologic evaluation if these were not performed initially.

Medical Management

It is presumed that the lymphocytes of patients with aplastic anemia destroy the stem cells and consequently impair the production of erythrocytes, **leukocytes**, and platelets. Despite its severity, aplastic anemia can be treated in most people. Those who are younger than 60 years, who are otherwise healthy, and who have a compatible donor can be cured of the disease by a bone marrow transplant (BMT) or peripheral blood stem cell transplant (PBSCT). In others, the disease can be managed with immunosuppressive therapy, commonly using a combination of antithymocyte globulin (ATG) and cyclosporine. ATG, a purified gamma globulin solution, is obtained from horses or rabbits immunized with human T lymphocytes. Side effects during the infusion are common and may include fever and chills. The sudden onset of a rash or bronchospasm may herald anaphylaxis and requires prompt management (see Chapter 38). Serum sickness, a delayed immune response, evidenced by fever, rash, arthralgias, and pruritus, may develop in some patients; it may take weeks to resolve. Steroids are used to provide additional immunosuppression, but also to decrease the risk of serum sickness (Afable & Lyon, 2008). The average overall response rate for ATG plus cyclosporine is 60% to 70% with a 20% to 30% rate of relapse (Young, Scheinberg, & Calado, 2008). Response rates and survival are lower for patients over the age of 60 (Marsh, Ball, Cavenagh et al., 2009).

Immunosuppressants, including cyclosporine, corticosteroids, ATG, and cyclophosphamide, prevent the patient's lymphocytes from destroying the stem cells. If relapse occurs

(i.e., the patient becomes pancytopenic [reduction of RBCs, white blood cells [WBCs], and platelets] again), reinstitution of the same immunologic agents may induce another remission. Corticosteroids are useful as immunosuppressive agents; however, they have significant side effects including bone complications (i.e., avascular necrosis) and infection.

Supportive therapy plays a major role in the management of aplastic anemia. Any offending agent is discontinued. The patient is supported with transfusions of PRBCs and platelets as necessary. Growth factors, such as growth-colony stimulating factor (i.e., Filgrastim) may be used to decrease the duration and severity of neutropenia (Afable & Lyon, 2008). Death is most commonly caused by hemorrhage or infection.

Nursing Management

Patients with aplastic anemia are vulnerable to problems related to erythrocyte (RBC), leukocyte (WBC), and platelet deficiencies. They should be assessed carefully for signs of infection and bleeding. Specific nursing interventions are outlined in the sections on neutropenia and thrombocytopenia.

MEGALOBLASTIC ANEMIAS

In the anemias caused by deficiencies of either vitamin B_{12} or folic acid, identical bone marrow and peripheral blood changes occur because both vitamins are essential for normal DNA synthesis. In either anemia, the erythrocytes that are produced are abnormally large and are called *megaloblastic red cells*. Other cells derived from the **myeloid** stem cell (nonlymphoid leukocytes, platelets) are also abnormal, resulting in low leukocyte and platelet counts in advanced stages of disease. A bone marrow analysis reveals **hyperplasia** (abnormal increase in the number of cells), and the precursor erythroid and myeloid cells are large and bizarre in appearance.

Pathophysiology
Folic Acid Deficiency

Folic acid is stored as compounds referred to as *folates*. The folate stores in the body are much smaller than those of vitamin B_{12}, and they are quickly depleted when the dietary intake of folate is deficient (within 4 months). Folate is found in green vegetables and liver. Folate deficiency occurs in people who rarely eat uncooked vegetables. Alcohol increases folic acid requirements; patients with alcoholism usually have a diet that is deficient in the vitamin. Folic acid requirements are also increased in patients with chronic hemolytic anemias and in women who are pregnant, because the need for erythrocyte production is increased in these conditions. Some patients with malabsorptive diseases of the small bowel, such as sprue, may not absorb folic acid normally.

Vitamin B₁₂ Deficiency

A deficiency of vitamin B_{12} can occur in several ways. Inadequate dietary intake is rare but can develop in strict vegans (who consume no meat or dairy products). Faulty absorption from the GI tract is a more common cause. This occurs in conditions such as Crohn's disease, or after ileal resection or gastrectomy. Another cause is the absence of intrinsic factor, as in pernicious anemia. Intrinsic factor is normally secreted by cells within the gastric mucosa; normally, it binds with the dietary vitamin B_{12} and travels with it to the ileum, where the vitamin is absorbed. Without intrinsic factor, orally consumed vitamin B_{12} cannot be absorbed, and erythrocyte production is eventually diminished. Even if adequate vitamin B_{12} and intrinsic factor are present, a deficiency may occur if disease involving the ileum or pancreas impairs absorption. Pernicious anemia, which tends to run in families, is primarily a disorder of adults, particularly the elderly. The abnormality is in the gastric mucosa: the stomach wall atrophies and fails to secrete intrinsic factor. Therefore, the absorption of vitamin B_{12} is significantly impaired.

The body normally has large stores of vitamin B_{12}, so years may pass before the deficiency results in anemia. Because the body compensates so well, the anemia can be severe before the patient becomes symptomatic. For unknown reasons, patients with pernicious anemia have a higher incidence of gastric cancer than the general population; these patients should have endoscopies at regular intervals (every 1 to 2 years) to screen for early gastric cancer.

Clinical Manifestations and Assessment

Assessment of patients who have or are at risk of megaloblastic anemia includes inspection of the skin and mucous membranes. Mild jaundice may be apparent and is best seen in the sclera without using fluorescent lights. Vitiligo (patchy loss of skin pigmentation) and premature graying of the hair are often seen in patients with pernicious anemia. The tongue is smooth, red, and sore.

Symptoms of folic acid and vitamin B_{12} deficiencies are similar, and the two anemias may coexist. However, the neurologic manifestations of vitamin B_{12} deficiency do not occur with folic acid deficiency, and they persist if vitamin B_{12} is not replaced. Therefore, careful distinction between the two anemias must be made. Serum levels of both vitamins can be measured. In the case of folic acid deficiency, even small amounts of folate increase the serum folate level. Measuring the amount of folate within the red cell itself (red cell folate) is therefore a more sensitive test in determining true folate deficiency.

After the body stores of vitamin B_{12} are depleted, the patient may begin to show signs and symptoms of the anemia. However, because the onset and progression of the anemia are so gradual, the body can compensate very well until the anemia is severe, so that the typical manifestations of anemia (weakness, listlessness, fatigue) may not be apparent initially. The hematologic effects of deficiency are accompanied by effects on other organ systems, particularly the GI tract and nervous system (see Box 20-1). These symptoms are progressive, although the course of illness may be marked by spontaneous partial remissions and exacerbations. Without treatment, patients can die after several years, usually from heart failure secondary to anemia.

Medical Management

Folate deficiency is treated by increasing the amount of folic acid in the diet and administering 1 to 5 mg of folic acid daily. Folic acid is administered IM only to those with malabsorption problems. With the exception of the vitamins administered during pregnancy, most proprietary vitamin preparations do not contain folic acid, so it must be administered as a separate tablet. After the hemoglobin level returns to normal, the folic acid replacement can be stopped. However, patients with alcoholism should continue receiving folic acid as long as they continue to consume alcohol.

Vitamin B_{12} deficiency is treated by vitamin B_{12} replacement. Vegetarians can prevent or treat deficiency with oral supplements, vitamins, or fortified soy milk. When the deficiency is due to the more common defect in absorption or the absence of intrinsic factor, replacement by monthly IM injections of vitamin B_{12} is necessary. Even in the absence of intrinsic factor, a small amount of an oral dose of vitamin B_{12} can be absorbed by passive diffusion, but large doses (2 mg/day) are required if vitamin B_{12} is to be replaced orally.

As vitamin B_{12} is replaced, the reticulocyte count rises within 1 week, and in several weeks the blood counts are all normal. The characteristic beefy red, sore tongue feels better and appears less red in several days. However, the neurologic manifestations require more time for recovery; if there is severe neuropathy, the patient may never recover fully. To prevent recurrence of pernicious anemia, vitamin B_{12} therapy must be continued for life.

⚡ NURSING ALERT

Even when the megaloblastic anemia is severe, RBC transfusions may not be used because the patient's body has compensated over time by expanding the total blood volume. Administration of blood transfusions to such patients, particularly those who are elderly or who have cardiac dysfunction, can precipitate pulmonary edema. If transfusions are required, the RBCs should be transfused slowly, with careful attention to signs and symptoms of fluid overload.

Nursing Management

The nurse needs to pay particular attention to ambulation and should assess the patient's gait and stability as well as the need for assistive devices (e.g., canes, walkers) and for assistance in managing daily activities. Of particular

concern is ensuring safety when position sense, coordination, and gait are affected. Physical and occupational therapy referrals may be needed. If sensation is altered, the patient needs to be instructed to avoid excessive heat and cold.

Because mouth and tongue soreness may restrict nutritional intake, the nurse advises the patient to eat small amounts of bland, soft foods frequently and educates the patient on routine mouth care. The nurse also may explain that other nutritional deficiencies, such as alcohol-induced anemia, can induce neurologic problems.

HEMOLYTIC ANEMIAS

In hemolytic anemias, the erythrocytes have a shortened lifespan; thus, their number in the circulation is reduced. Fewer erythrocytes result in decreased available oxygen, causing hypoxia, which in turn stimulates an increase in erythropoietin release from the kidney. The erythropoietin stimulates the bone marrow to compensate by producing new erythrocytes and releasing some of them into the circulation somewhat prematurely as reticulocytes. If the red cell destruction persists, the hemoglobin is broken down excessively; about 80% of the heme is converted to bilirubin, conjugated in the liver, and excreted in the bile.

The mechanism of erythrocyte destruction varies, but all types of hemolytic anemia share certain laboratory features: the reticulocyte count is elevated, the fraction of indirect (unconjugated) bilirubin is increased, and the supply of haptoglobin (a binding protein for free hemoglobin) is depleted as more hemoglobin is released. As a result, the plasma haptoglobin level is low. The severity of anemia will increase if the marrow does not compensate by replacing the hemolyzed erythrocytes (poor response indicated by a decreased reticulocyte count). Causes of hemolytic anemia are discussed in Box 20-3.

THALASSEMIA

The thalassemias are a group of hereditary anemias characterized by **hypochromia** (an abnormal decrease in the hemoglobin content of erythrocytes), extreme **microcytosis** (smaller-than-normal erythrocytes), destruction of blood elements (hemolysis), and variable degrees of anemia. The thalassemias occur worldwide, but the highest prevalence is found in people of Mediterranean, African, and Southeast Asian ancestry.

Thalassemias are classified into two major groups according to which hemoglobin chain is diminished: alpha or beta. The alpha thalassemias occur mainly in people from Asia and the Middle East, and the beta thalassemias are most prevalent in people from Mediterranean regions but also occur in those from the Middle East or Asia. The alpha thalassemias are milder than the beta forms and often occur without symptoms; the erythrocytes are extremely microcytic, but the anemia, if present, is mild.

The severity of beta thalassemia varies depending on the extent to which the hemoglobin chains are affected. Patients with mild forms have a microcytosis and mild anemia. If left untreated, severe beta thalassemia (*thalassemia major*, or *Cooley's anemia*) can be fatal within the first few years of life. PBSCT offers a chance of cure, but when this is not possible, the disease is usually treated with transfusion of PRBCs. Patients may survive into their 20s and 30s. Patient teaching during the reproductive years should include preconception counseling about the risk of thalassemia major.

IMMUNE HEMOLYTIC ANEMIA

Hemolytic anemias can result from exposure of the erythrocyte to antibodies. Alloantibodies (i.e., antibodies against the host, or "self") result from the immunization of a person with foreign antigens (e.g., the immunization of an Rh-negative person with Rh-positive blood). Alloantibodies tend to

---

BOX 20-3   **Causes of Hemolytic Anemias**

Inherited Hemolytic Anemia
- Abnormal hemoglobin:
  - Sickle cell anemia
  - Thalassemia
- Red blood cell membrane abnormality:
  - Hereditary spherocytosis
  - Hereditary elliptocytosis
  - Acanthocytosis
  - Stomatocytosis
- Enzyme deficiencies:
  - Glucose-6-phosphate dehydrogenase (G-6-PD) deficiency

Acquired Hemolytic Anemia
- Antibody-related:
  - Iso-antibody/transfusion reaction
  - Autoimmune hemolytic anemia (AIHA)

- Cold agglutinin disease
- Not antibody-related:
  - RBC membrane defects
  - Paroxysmal nocturnal hemoglobinuria (PNH)
  - Liver disease
  - Uremia
  - Trauma
  - Mechanical heart valve
  - Microangiopathic hemolytic anemia
  - Infection
  - Bacterial
  - Parasitic
  - Disseminated intravascular coagulation (DIC)
  - Toxins
  - Hypersplenism

be large (IgM type) and cause immediate destruction of the sensitized erythrocytes, either within the blood vessel (intravascular hemolysis) or within the liver. The most common type of alloimmune hemolytic anemia in adults results from a hemolytic transfusion reaction.

Pathophysiology

Autoantibodies may develop for many reasons. In many instances, the person's immune system is dysfunctional, so that it falsely recognizes its own erythrocytes as foreign and produces antibodies against them. This mechanism is seen in people with chronic lymphocytic leukemia (CLL). Another mechanism is a deficiency in suppressor lymphocytes, which normally prevent antibody formation against a person's own antigens. Autoantibodies tend to be of the IgG type. The erythrocytes are sequestered in the spleen and destroyed by the **macrophages** outside the blood vessel (extravascular hemolysis).

Autoimmune hemolytic anemias can be classified based on the body temperature involved when the antibodies react with the RBC antigen. Warm-body antibodies bind to erythrocytes most actively in warm conditions (37°C); cold-body antibodies react in cold conditions (0°C). Most autoimmune hemolytic anemias are the warm-body type. Autoimmune hemolytic anemia is associated with other disorders in most cases (e.g., medication exposure, lymphoma, CLL, other malignancy, collagen vascular disease, autoimmune disease, infection). In idiopathic autoimmune hemolytic states, the etiology of autoantibody production is not known. All ages and both genders are equally vulnerable to this form, whereas the incidence of secondary forms is greater in people older than 45 years of age and in females.

Medical Management

Any possible offending medication should be immediately discontinued. The treatment consists of high doses of corticosteroids until hemolysis decreases. Corticosteroids decrease the macrophage's ability to clear the antibody-coated erythrocytes. If the hemoglobin level returns to normal, usually after several weeks, the corticosteroid dose can be lowered or, in some cases, tapered and discontinued. However, corticosteroids rarely produce a lasting remission. In severe cases, blood transfusions may be required. Because the antibodies may react with all possible donor cells, careful blood typing is necessary, and the transfusion should be administered slowly and cautiously.

Splenectomy (removal of the spleen) removes the major site of erythrocyte destruction; therefore, splenectomy may be performed if corticosteroids do not produce a remission. If neither corticosteroid therapy, nor splenectomy is successful, or in cases where splenectomy is contraindicated, immunosuppressive agents may be administered. The two immunosuppressive agents most frequently used are cyclophosphamide (Cytoxan), which has a more rapid effect but more toxicity,

and azathioprine (Imuran), which has a less rapid effect but less toxicity. The synthetic androgen danazol can be useful in some patients, particularly in combination with corticosteroids. The mechanism for this success is unclear. If corticosteroids or immunosuppressive agents are used, the taper must be very gradual to prevent a rebound "hyperimmune" response and exacerbation of the hemolysis. Immunoglobulin administration is effective in about one-third of patients, but the effect is transient and the medication is expensive. Transfusions may be necessary if the anemia is severe; it may be extremely difficult to cross-match samples of available units of PRBCs with that of the patient. The monoclonal antibody Rituximab has been used with success in 45% to 60% of patients with autoimmune hemolytic anemia, and studies are ongoing to determine the duration of remission following Rituximab therapy (Berensten, 2007).

For patients with cold-antibody hemolytic anemia, no treatment may be required other than to advise the patient to keep warm; relocation to a warm climate may be necessary.

Nursing Management

Patients may have great difficulty understanding the pathologic mechanisms underlying the disease and may need repeated explanations in terms they can understand. Patients who have had a splenectomy should be vaccinated against pneumococcal infections (e.g., Pneumovax) and informed that they are permanently at greater risk for infection. Patients receiving long-term corticosteroid therapy, particularly those with concurrent diabetes or hypertension, need careful monitoring. They must understand the need for the medication and the importance of never abruptly discontinuing it. A written explanation and a tapering schedule should be provided, and adjustments based on hemoglobin levels should be emphasized. Similar teaching should be provided when immunosuppressive agents are used. Corticosteroid therapy is not without significant risk, and patients need to be monitored closely for complications. The short- and long-term complications of corticosteroid therapy are presented in Chapter 31.

POLYCYTHEMIA

Polycythemia, literally meaning "too many cells in the blood," refers to an increased number of erythrocytes. It is a term used when the hematocrit is elevated (to >55% in males, >50% in females). Dehydration (decreased volume of plasma) can cause an elevated hematocrit, but not typically to the level to be considered polycythemia (relative polycythemia). Polycythemia is classified as either primary or secondary (Tefferi, 2008).

POLYCYTHEMIA VERA

Polycythemia vera (PV), or primary polycythemia, is a myeloproliferative disorder in which the myeloid stem cells

have escaped normal control mechanisms. The bone marrow is hypercellular, and the erythrocyte, leukocyte, and platelet counts in the peripheral blood are elevated. The erythrocyte elevation is predominant; the hematocrit can exceed 60%. This phase can last for an extended period (10 years or longer). Over time, the spleen resumes its embryonic function of hematopoiesis and enlarges. Splenomegaly is a hallmark of PV. Eventually, the bone marrow may become fibrotic, with a resultant inability to produce as many cells ("burnt out" or spent phase). The disease evolves into myeloid metaplasia with myelofibrosis, MDS, or acute myeloid leukemia (AML) in 5% to 10% of patients within 15 years of diagnosis and in 50% of patients within 20 years; this form of AML is usually refractory to standard treatments (Mansen & McCance, 2006; Tefferi, 2008). The incidence of polycythemia has been estimated at 0.5 to 2.6 per 100,000 people. The median age at onset is 60 years (Tefferi, 2008). Median survival exceeds 10 years with appropriate treatment but is only 6 to 18 months without treatment (Mansen & McCance, 2006).

Clinical Manifestations and Assessment

Patients typically have a ruddy complexion and splenomegaly (enlarged spleen). Symptoms result from increased blood volume (headache, dizziness, tinnitus, fatigue, paresthesias, and blurred vision) or from increased blood viscosity (angina, claudication, dyspnea, and thrombophlebitis), particularly if the patient has atherosclerotic blood vessels. For this reason, blood pressure is often elevated. Uric acid may be elevated, resulting in gout and renal stone formation. Another common and bothersome problem is generalized pruritus, which may be caused by histamine release due to the increased number of basophils. A hallmark feature of PV is severe and painful itching that is triggered by exposure to water (aquagenic pruritus) (Mansen & McCance, 2006). Erythromelalgia a syndrome of painful burning, warmth, and redness in a localized distal area of the extremities; it most commonly occurs in the fingers and toes and is only partially relieved by cooling.

Patients who present with an elevated hemoglobin and hematocrit should be assessed for the presence of PV. A diagnosis of PV requires the presence of an elevated Hgb (>18.5 g/dL in men and >16.5 g/dL in women) or evidence of increased RBC volume and the presence of a *JAK 2* genetic mutation; additional criteria include a hypercellular bone marrow and low serum erythropoietin levels (Tefferi, 2008). More than 95% of patients with PV have mutations to *JAK 2*, and patients with suspected PV should be screened for these mutations. A test that is positive for the mutation supports the diagnosis of PV. Causes of secondary erythrocytosis should not be present (see later discussion). Patients typically have a normal oxygen saturation level and splenomegaly.

Complications

Patients with PV are at increased risk for thromboses resulting in a cerebrovascular accident (CVA or stroke) or myocardial infarction (MI); thrombotic complications are the most common cause of death. Bleeding is also a complication, possibly because the platelets (often very large) are somewhat dysfunctional. The bleeding can be significant and can occur in the form of nosebleeds, ulcers, frank GI bleeding, hematuria, and intracranial hemorrhage.

Medical Management

The objective of management is to reduce the high blood cell mass. Phlebotomy is a critical part of therapy and is the only treatment that has demonstrated improved survival (Tefferi, 2008). It involves removing enough blood (initially 500 mL once or twice weekly) to diminish the blood viscosity, maintain the hematocrit below 45% in men and 42% in women, and deplete the patient's iron stores, thereby rendering the patient iron deficient and consequently unable to continue to manufacture erythrocytes excessively. Many patients are managed by routine phlebotomy on an intermittent basis. In addition, high-risk patients (patients >60 years or patients with a history of thrombotic events) should receive additional therapy, such as hydroxyurea or alfa interferon. Patients receiving hydroxyurea appear to have a lower incidence of thrombotic complications than do those treated by phlebotomy alone; this may result from a more effectively controlled platelet count. Myelosuppressive therapy increases the risk for leukemic transformation; however, of the agents used to treat PV, hydroxyurea carries a lower risk for this complication (Tefferi, 2008). Interferon alfa-2b (Intron-A) is also an effective treatment for managing the pruritus associated with polycythemia vera (Landolfi, Nicolazzi, Porfidia et al., 2010) but may be difficult for patients to tolerate because of its frequent side effects (e.g., flu-like syndrome, depression). Antihistamines, including histamine-2 blockers, are not particularly effective in controlling itching. Allopurinol (Zyloprim) is used to prevent gout in patients with elevated uric acid concentrations.

The use of aspirin to prevent thrombotic complications is controversial. Antiplatelet therapy should be used with caution secondary to the underlying risk of bleeding in these patients. A double-blind, placebo-controlled, randomized study of patients with PV who did not have contraindications to aspirin therapy (i.e., history of GI bleeding, hemorrhagic stroke) demonstrated that low-dose aspirin (100 mg/day) is effective in preventing thromboembolic events without increasing the risk for bleeding (Landolfi, Marchioli, Kutti et al., 2004; Vannucchi et al., 2010). Aspirin is also useful in reducing the pain associated with erythromelalgia (a symptom that affects the extremities causing redness, warmth, and burning pain).

Nursing Management

The nurse's role is primarily that of educator. Risk factors for thrombotic complications, particularly smoking, obesity, and poorly controlled hypertension, should be assessed, and the patient should be instructed about risk reduction as well as the signs and symptoms of thrombosis. To reduce the likelihood of deep vein thrombosis (DVT), activity should be promoted, and crossing the legs and use of restrictive clothing should be avoided. The nurse instructs patients to walk around frequently on long flights. Patients with a history of bleeding are usually advised to avoid aspirin and aspirin-containing medications because these medications alter platelet function. The nurse encourages minimizing alcohol intake to further diminish the risk of bleeding. The patient needs to be instructed to avoid iron supplements, including those within multivitamin supplements, because the iron can further stimulate RBC production. For pruritus, the nurse may recommend bathing in tepid or cool water (hot water can exacerbate the symptom), limiting bathing time to 30 minutes or extending to every other day, and avoiding vigorous toweling-off after bathing. Use of mild soaps, application of emollient lotions, adding colloidal oatmeal treatment to bath water, use of cotton blankets and clothing, and washing sheets, clothing, and undergarments with baby detergent may also decrease pruritus. Aspirin has also been shown to reduce pruritus (National Cancer Institute [NCI], 2010).

SECONDARY POLYCYTHEMIA

Pathophysiology

Secondary polycythemia is caused by excessive production of erythropoietin. This may occur in response to a reduced amount of oxygen, which acts as a hypoxic stimulus, as in cigarette smoking, chronic obstructive pulmonary disease, or cyanotic heart disease, or in nonpathologic conditions such as living at a high altitude. It can also result from certain hemoglobinopathies (e.g., hemoglobin Chesapeake), in which the hemoglobin has an abnormally high affinity for oxygen. Secondary polycythemia can also occur from neoplasms (e.g., renal cell carcinoma) that stimulate erythropoietin production.

Medical and Nursing Management

Management of secondary polycythemia may not be necessary; when management is necessary, the goal is to treat the primary conditions. If the cause cannot be corrected (e.g., by treating the renal cell carcinoma or improving pulmonary function), therapeutic phlebotomy may be necessary in symptomatic patients to reduce blood viscosity and volume.

LEUKEMIA

Hematopoiesis is characterized by a rapid, continuous turnover of cells. Normally, production of specific blood cells from their stem cell precursors is carefully regulated according to the body's needs. If the mechanisms that control the production of these cells are disrupted, the cells can proliferate excessively. Hematopoietic malignancies are often classified by the cells involved. **Leukemia**, literally "white blood," is a term used to describe neoplastic proliferation of one particular hematopoietic cell type (**granulocyte**s, **monocyte**s, lymphocytes, or infrequently erythrocytes or megakaryocytes). The defect originates in the hematopoietic stem cell, either the myeloid or the **lymphoid** stem cell.

The common feature of the leukemias is an unregulated proliferation of leukocytes in the bone marrow. The bone marrow becomes packed with cells and ultimately begins to prematurely release these cells into the circulation. The increase in the number of leukocytes in the circulation is referred to as *leukocytosis*. Typically, only one specific type of leukocyte is increased, most commonly either the neutrophils or the lymphocytes. In acute forms (or late stages of chronic forms), the proliferation of leukemic cells leaves little room for normal cell production, resulting in **pancytopenia**. There can also be a proliferation of cells in the liver and spleen (extramedullary hematopoiesis). With acute forms, there can be infiltration of other organs, such as the meninges, lymph nodes, gums, and skin (leukemia cutis).

The cause of leukemia is not fully known, but there is some evidence that genetic influences and viral pathogenesis may be involved. Bone marrow damage from radiation exposure or from chemicals such as benzene and alkylating agents (e.g., cyclophosphamide [Cytoxan], melphalan [Alkeran]) can cause leukemia.

The leukemias are commonly classified according to the stem cell line involved, either lymphoid (relating to lymphatic tissue) or myeloid (relating to bone marrow). They are also classified as either acute or chronic, based on the phase of cell development that is halted, with few leukocytes differentiating beyond that phase.

In acute leukemia, the onset of symptoms is abrupt, often occurring within a few weeks. Leukocyte development is halted at the blast phase, so that most leukocytes are undifferentiated, immature cells (blasts). Acute leukemia progresses very rapidly; death can occur within weeks to months without aggressive treatment.

In chronic leukemia, symptoms evolve over a period of months to years. Most of the leukocytes produced mature and retain some ability to function normally. Chronic leukemia progresses more slowly; the disease trajectory can extend for years.

ACUTE MYELOID LEUKEMIA

AML results from a defect in the hematopoietic stem cell that differentiates into all myeloid cells: monocytes, granulocytes (neutrophils, basophils, eosinophils), erythrocytes, and platelets. All age groups are affected; the incidence rises

with age, with a peak incidence at age 60 years. AML is the most common nonlymphocytic leukemia.

The prognosis is highly variable. The strongest risk factors for resistant disease, early relapse, and decreased survival included advanced age, poor functional status, and complex cytogenetic abnormalities. Patients over the age of 65 have a poorer response to treatment and a worse prognosis than younger patients. The 5-year survival rate for patients with AML who are 65 years or younger is 33%; it drops to 4% for those older than 65 years (American Cancer Society, 2006). Those who have leukemia stemming from preexisting myelodysplastic syndrome (MDS) or who previously received alkylating agents for cancer (secondary AML) have a much worse prognosis; the leukemia tends to be more resistant to treatment, resulting in a much shorter duration of remission. With treatment, patients with secondary AML survive an average of less than 1 year, with death usually a result of infection or hemorrhage. Patients receiving supportive care also usually survive less than 1 year, dying of infection or bleeding.

Clinical Manifestations and Assessment

Most signs and symptoms of AML result from insufficient production of normal blood cells. Fever and infection result from neutropenia, weakness and fatigue from anemia, and bleeding tendencies from thrombocytopenia. The proliferation of leukemic cells within organs leads to a variety of additional symptoms: pain from an enlarged liver or spleen, hyperplasia of the gums, and bone pain from expansion of the bone marrow.

AML develops without warning, with symptoms occurring over a period of weeks to months. The CBC may show a decrease in both erythrocytes and platelets. Although the total leukocyte count can be low, normal, or high, the percentage of normal cells is usually vastly decreased. The differential may reveal the presence of circulating blasts and a decreased neutrophil count. A bone marrow analysis shows an excess of immature **blast cell**s (>20%). AML can be further classified into eight different subgroups (M0–M7), based on cytogenetics, histology, and morphology (appearance) of the blasts. The actual prognosis varies somewhat between subgroups; however, the clinical course and treatment are similar with one exception. Patients with acute promyelocytic leukemia (APL, or AML-M3) often have significantly more problems with bleeding due to an underlying coagulopathy and a higher incidence of disseminated intravascular coagulation (DIC), however, they also have a significantly higher rate of cure (discussed later in the chapter).

Complications

Complications of AML include bleeding and infection, the major causes of death. The risk of bleeding correlates with the level of platelet deficiency (thrombocytopenia). The

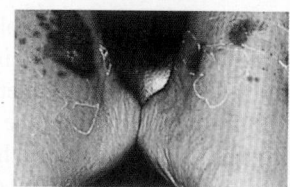

low platelet count can result in **ecchymoses** (bruises) and **petechiae** (pinpoint red or purple hemorrhagic spots on the skin) (Fig. 20-2). Major spontaneous hemorrhages also may develop when the platelet count drops to less than 10,000/ mm^3. The most common sites of bleeding are GI, pulmonary, and intracranial. Fever increases platelet consumption and therefore may increase the likelihood of bleeding.

Because of the lack of mature and normal granulocytes, infection is the most common cause of death in patients with acute leukemia. The likelihood of infection increases with the degree and duration of neutropenia; neutrophil counts that persist at less than 100/mm^3 make the chances of systemic infection extremely high. As the duration of severe neutropenia increases, the patient's risk of developing fungal infection also increases.

Medical Management

The overall objective of treatment is to achieve complete remission, in which there is no evidence of residual leukemia in the bone marrow. Attempts are made to achieve remission by the aggressive administration of chemotherapy, called *induction therapy*, which usually requires hospitalization for several weeks. Induction therapy typically involves IV administration of cytarabine (Cytosar, Ara-C) and an anthracycline such as idarubicin (Idamycin). The choice of agents is based on the patient's performance status and history of prior antineoplastic treatment.

The aim of induction therapy is to eradicate the leukemic cells, but this is often accompanied by the eradication of normal types of myeloid cells. Thus, the patient becomes severely neutropenic (an **absolute neutrophil count** [ANC] of 0 is not uncommon), anemic, and thrombocytopenic (a platelet count of <10,000/mm^3 is common). (Refer to Chapter 33 for calculation of the ANC.) During this time, the patient is typically very ill and hospitalized. Common complications include bacterial, fungal, and occasionally viral infections, bleeding, and severe mucositis, which can cause mouth pain and diarrhea, as well as a marked decline in the ability to eat and meet nutritional demands. Supportive care consists of administering blood products (PRBCs and platelets) and promptly treating infections. Prophylactic use of granulocytic growth factors (GCSF or Filgrastim) to minimize the risk of neutropenic fever and infection have not demonstrated the same effects on survival in patients with

AML compared to patients with nonhematologic malignancies; therefore, widespread use of GCSF in patients with AML is not encouraged (Wang, An, Chen, et al., 2009).

When the patient has recovered from the induction therapy (i.e., the neutrophil and platelet counts have returned to normal and any infection has resolved), he or she typically receives *consolidation therapy* (postremission therapy) to eliminate any residual leukemia cells that are not clinically detectable and to reduce the chance for recurrence. Multiple treatment cycles of various agents are used, usually containing some form of high-dose cytarabine (e.g., Cytosar, Ara-C).

Following consolidation therapy, the next step is determined based on the patient's risk for recurrence. Patients with low- or intermediate-risk leukemia may not require further treatment after they complete consolidation therapy. Patients with high-risk leukemia, or patients who have been treated for a relapse, are often candidates for peripheral blood stem cell transplant (PBSCT). When a suitable donor can be obtained, the patient embarks on an even more aggressive regimen of chemotherapy (sometimes in combination with total body radiation therapy), with the treatment goal of destroying the hematopoietic function of the patient's bone marrow. The patient is then "rescued" with the infusion of the donor stem cells to reinitiate hematopoiesis. In addition to providing a "rescue" and a healthy source of hematopoiesis, infusion of donor cells also provides protection against disease recurrence. The healthy immune system of the donor kills residual cancer cells and prevents cancer recurrence, this is know as the *graft versus leukemia* or *graft versus lymphoma* effect. Patients who undergo PBSCT have a significant risk for infection, graft-versus-host disease (GVHD, in which the donor's lymphocytes [graft] recognize the patient's body as "foreign" and attack the "foreign" host), and other complications. Refer to Chapter 6 for a detailed discussion of PBSCT.

Another important option for the patient to consider is supportive care alone. In fact, supportive care may be the only option if the patient has significant comorbidity, such as extremely poor cardiac, pulmonary, renal, or hepatic function; advanced age; or poor performance status. In such cases, aggressive antileukemia therapy is not used; occasionally, hydroxyurea (Hydrea) may be used to control the number of blast cells. Patients are supported with antimicrobial therapy and transfusions as needed. This treatment approach provides the patient with some additional time at home; however, death frequently occurs within months, typically from infection or bleeding. (Refer to Chapter 3 for a discussion of end-of-life care.)

Nursing Management

The priority nursing interventions for the patient with AML include infection prevention, bleeding prevention, promoting comfort, and patient education. Nursing care to prevent infection and bleeding are discussed in detail in Chapters 6 and 19. Patients with a new diagnosis of AML are experiencing a crisis and require an overwhelming amount of education about their disease, self-care, and treatment strategies. The role of the nurse is critical in alleviating anxiety by providing information tailored to the patient's readiness and educational level.

The nurse also assesses for complications of treatment. Massive leukemic cell destruction from chemotherapy results in the release of intracellular electrolytes and fluids into the systemic circulation. Increases in uric acid levels, potassium, and phosphate are seen; this process is referred to as **tumor lysis** syndrome (see Chapter 6). Patients require a high fluid intake and prophylaxis with allopurinol to prevent crystallization of uric acid and subsequent stone formation. Anorexia, nausea, vomiting, diarrhea, and severe mucositis are common. Because of the profound myelosuppressive effects of chemotherapy, significant neutropenia and thrombocytopenia typically result in serious infection and increased risk of bleeding.

CHRONIC MYELOID LEUKEMIA

Chronic myeloid leukemia (CML) arises from a mutation in the myeloid stem cell. Normal myeloid cells continue to be produced, but there is a pathologic increase in the production of blast cells. Therefore, a wide spectrum of cell types exists within the blood, from blast forms through mature neutrophils. Because there is an uncontrolled proliferation of cells, the marrow expands into the cavities of long bones (e.g., the femur), and cells are also formed in the liver and spleen (extramedullary hematopoiesis), resulting in enlargement of these organs that is sometimes painful. In 90% to 95% of patients with CML, a section of DNA is missing from chromosome 22 (the Philadelphia chromosome [Ph1]); it is translocated onto chromosome 9. The specific location of these changes is on the *BCR* gene of chromosome 22 and the *ABL* gene on chromosome 9. When these two genes fuse (*BCR-ABL* gene), they produce an abnormal protein (a tyrosine kinase protein) that causes leukocytes to divide rapidly. This *BCR-ABL* gene is present in virtually all patients with this disease. There are three phases of the disease: the chronic phase, during which there is usually adequate numbers of healthy cells to fight infection; the accelerated phase, in which the numbers of abnormal cells are being produced at a faster rate; and blast crisis, in which the predominant cell type is immature. Most patients are diagnosed in the chronic phase.

CML is uncommon in people younger than 20 years; the incidence increases with age. Median age of onset varies by race. In the white population, median age is 75 years, whereas blacks demonstrate a bimodal age distribution at 40

years and 70 years (Mendizabal, Anderson, Garcia-Gonzalez et al., 2010).

Clinical Manifestations and Assessment

The clinical picture of CML varies based on the phase of the disease. During the chronic phase, patients have few symptoms and complications from the disease itself. Problems with infections and bleeding are rare. At the time of diagnoses, many patients are asymptomatic, and leukocytosis is detected by a CBC performed for some other reason. The most common symptoms include fatigue, bleeding, or weight loss (Giles, DeAngelo, Baccarani et al., 2008). Once the disease transforms to the acute phase (blast crisis), the overall survival rarely exceeds several months.

In both the chronic and acute phases of CML, the leukocyte count may exceed 100,000/mm^3. Patients with extremely high leukocyte counts may be short of breath or slightly confused due to decreased capillary perfusion to the lungs and brain from leukostasis (the excessive volume of leukocytes slows and inhibits blood flow through the capillaries). The patient may have an enlarged, tender spleen. The liver may also be enlarged. Some patients have insidious symptoms, such as malaise, anorexia, and weight loss. Lymphadenopathy is rare. Patients develop more symptoms and complications as the disease progresses.

Medical and Nursing Management

Advances in understanding of the pathology of CML at a molecular level have led to dramatic changes in its treatment. The tyrosine kinase inhibitors (TKIs), such as imatinib mesylate (Gleevec) dasatinib, and nilotinib, work by blocking signals within the leukemia cells that express the *BCR-ABL* protein, thus preventing a series of chemical reactions that cause the cell to grow and divide. These drugs have revolutionized the care of CML and significantly prolonged survival. The 5-year survival rate for patients diagnosed in the chronic phase and treated with TKIs is 80%. The treatment of CML in the accelerated and blast phases is more challenging, as many patients in advanced stages of disease have developed resistance to TKIs (Giles et al., 2008). The nurse must educate the patient that antacids and grapefruit juice may limit drug absorption, and large doses of acetaminophen can cause hepatotoxicity. The patient should be monitored for other side effects including fluid retention (manifested as pleural effusions, pericardial effusions, peripheral edema) and hepatotoxicity. The long-term effects of TKIs, the optimal length of treatment, and their role in combination therapy are currently being studied.

Therapy depends on the stage of disease. In the chronic phase, the expected outcome is correction of the chromosomal abnormality (i.e., conversion of the malignant stem cell population back to normal) and the standard therapy is

a TKI. An alternate approach focuses on reducing the leukocyte count to a more normal level but does not alter cytogenetic changes. This goal can be achieved by using oral chemotherapeutic agents, typically hydroxyurea (Hydrea) or busulfan (Myleran). In the case of an extreme leukocytosis at diagnosis (e.g., leukocyte count >300,000/mm^3), a more emergent treatment may be required. In this instance, *leukapheresis* (in which the patient's blood is removed and separated, with the leukocytes withdrawn, and the remaining blood returned to the patient) can temporarily reduce the number of leukocytes.

The accelerated or transformation phase can be insidious or rapid; it marks the process of evolution (or transformation) to the acute form of leukemia (blast crisis). In the accelerated phase, the patient may complain of bone pain and may report fevers (without any obvious sign of infection) and weight loss. Even with treatment, the spleen may continue to enlarge. The patient may become more anemic and thrombocytopenic.

In the acute form of CML (blast crisis), treatment may resemble induction therapy for acute leukemia, using the same medications as for AML or acute lymphocytic leukemia (ALL). Patients whose disease evolves into a "lymphoid" blast crisis are more likely to reenter a chronic phase after induction therapy. For those whose disease evolves into AML, therapy is largely ineffective in achieving a second chronic phase. Life-threatening infections and bleeding occur frequently in this phase.

Allogeneic stem cell transplantation remains the only curative treatment for CML. However, the efficacy of imatinib in first-line treatment and the treatment-related mortality of stem cell transplant limits use of transplant to patients with high-risk or relapsed disease, or in those patients who did not respond to therapy with a TKI (Venepalli, Rezvani, Mielke et al., 2010). Human leukocyte antigen (HLA)-matched, related donor stem cell transplants result in long-term survival in 45% to 70% of recipients. Patients over age 50 have a slightly lower survival rate (Liesveld & Lichtman, 2010b).

ACUTE LYMPHOCYTIC LEUKEMIA

ALL results from an uncontrolled proliferation of immature cells (lymphoblasts) derived from the lymphoid stem cell. The cell of origin is the precursor to the B lymphocyte in approximately 75% of ALL cases; T-lymphocyte ALL occurs in approximately 25% of ALL cases. The *BCR-ABL* translocation (see earlier discussion) is found in 20% of ALL blast cells. ALL is most common in young children, with boys affected more often than girls; the peak incidence is 4 years of age. After 15 years of age, ALL is relatively uncommon. Increasing age appears to be associated with diminished

survival; the 5-year event-free survival rate is almost 80% for children with ALL but drops to 48% for adults (Marks, Paietta, Moorman et al., 2009).

Clinical Manifestations and Assessment

Immature lymphocytes proliferate in the marrow and impede the development of normal myeloid cells. As a result, normal hematopoiesis is inhibited, resulting in reduced numbers of leukocytes, erythrocytes, and platelets. Leukocyte counts may be either low or high, but there is always a high proportion of immature cells. Manifestations of leukemic cell infiltration into other organs are more common with ALL than with other forms of leukemia and include pain from an enlarged liver or spleen and bone pain. The testes and central nervous system (CNS) are sanctuary sites where leukemic cells may infiltrate. The patient may exhibit testicular swelling or discomfort, or headache, visual changes, vomiting, and neurologic deficits from CNS invasion.

Medical and Nursing Management

The expected outcome of treatment is complete remission. Lymphoid blast cells are typically very sensitive to corticosteroids and to vinca alkaloids; therefore, these medications are an integral part of the initial induction therapy. Because ALL frequently invades the CNS, prophylaxis with cranial irradiation or intrathecal (injection of medications into the subarachnoid space [cerebral spinal fluid]), chemotherapy (e.g., methotrexate), or both is also a key part of the treatment plan (Vitale, Guarini, Chiaretti et al., 2006).

Treatment protocols for ALL tend to be complex, using a wide variety of chemotherapeutic agents given over a protracted period of time. Treatment includes an induction phase, followed by a consolidation phase, followed by a maintenance phase, when lower doses of medications are given for up to 3 years. Despite the complexity, treatment can often be provided in the outpatient setting until severe complications develop.

Imatinib is highly effective in those with Philadelphia chromosome–positive ALL and can be used alone or in combination with chemotherapy, with remission rates exceeding 90% (Ottmann & Pfeifer, 2009). Monoclonal antibodies, in which the antibody specific for the antigens expressed on the ALL blast cell—including CD20, CD22, CD33, and CD52—are a type of targeted therapy used to treat ALL. For example, the CD52 antigen is expressed on approximately 70% of ALL cells; thus, alemtuzumab (Campath), a monoclonal antibody with specific affinity for the CD52 antigen, is effective therapy for this subset of patients.

Infections, especially viral infections, are common. The use of corticosteroids to treat ALL increases the patient's susceptibility to infection. Patients with ALL often require prophylactic antimicrobials to decrease the risk of certain types of infection. Patients with ALL tend to have a better response to treatment than do patients with AML. PBSCT offers a chance for prolonged remission, or even cure, if the illness recurs after therapy.

Nursing Management

Nursing management of the patient with ALL is similar to the care of patients with AML. The nursing priorities include the prevention of infection and bleeding, and management of symptoms such as nausea and pain, often resulting from mucositis. As ALL is a disease that most commonly affects children and young adults, fertility preservation should also be discussed prior to the initiation of treatment.

CHRONIC LYMPHOCYTIC LEUKEMIA

CLL is a common malignancy of older adults; 81% of all patients with CLL are older than 60 years at diagnosis (Yee & Obrien, 2006). It is the most common form of leukemia in the United States and Europe, affecting more than 120,000 people. The average survival for patients with CLL ranges from 20 years (early stage) to 2 years (late stage), with a median survival time of 10 years. CLL occurs more often in males (2:1 male-to-female ratio) (Kipps, 2010).

Pathophysiology

CLL is typically derived from a malignant clone of B lymphocytes (T-lymphocyte CLL is rare). In contrast to the acute forms of leukemia, most of the leukemia cells in CLL are fully mature. It appears that these cells can escape **apoptosis** (programmed cell death), resulting in an excessive accumulation of the cells in the marrow and circulation. The antigen CD52 is prevalent on the surface of many of these leukemic B cells.

Two classification systems are in regular use to stage CLL; the disease is classified into three (Binet system; Stage A, B, C) or five stages (Rai system; Stage 0–IV). Both staging systems help to estimate prognosis and assist with treatment stratification (Elphee, 2007). In the early stage, an elevated lymphocyte count is seen; it can exceed 100,000/mm^3. Because the lymphocytes are small, they can easily travel through the small capillaries within the circulation, and the pulmonary and cerebral complications of leukocytosis (as seen with myeloid leukemias) typically are not found in CLL.

Lymphadenopathy occurs as the lymphocytes are trapped within the lymph nodes. The nodes can become very large and are sometimes painful. Hepatomegaly and splenomegaly then develop.

In later stages, anemia and thrombocytopenia may develop. Treatment is typically initiated in the later stages; earlier treatment does not appear to increase survival, so treatment for limited-stage disease is only employed if the

patient is symptomatic (Elphee, 2007). Autoimmune complications can also occur at any stage, as either autoimmune hemolytic anemia or idiopathic thrombocytopenic purpura (ITP). ITP of unknown causes (idiopathic) is characterized by the destruction of blood platelets due to the presence of antiplatelet autoantibodies, in which antibodies are directed against the patient's own platelets. As the term implies, the platelet level decreases (thrombocytopenia) resulting in visible bruising (purpura) in the skin and mucous membranes. Simply put, in the autoimmune process, the **reticuloendothelial system** (RES) destroys the body's own erythrocytes (hemolytic anemia) or platelets (ITP).

Clinical Manifestations and Assessment

Many patients are asymptomatic and are diagnosed incidentally during routine physical examinations or during treatment for another disease. At the time of diagnosis, lymphadenopathy (enlarged lymph nodes) is seen in 80% and splenomegaly (enlarged spleen) in 50% of patients (Kipps, 2010). An increased lymphocyte count (lymphocytosis) is always present. The erythrocyte and platelet counts may be normal or, in later stages of the illness, decreased.

Approximately 15% of patients with CLL present with "B symptoms," a constellation of symptoms including fevers, fatigue, drenching sweats (especially at night), and unintentional weight loss (Elphee, 2007). Patients with CLL have defects in their humoral and cell-mediated immune systems; therefore, infections are common. The defect in cellular immunity is evidenced by an absent or decreased reaction to skin sensitivity tests (e.g., *Candida,* mumps), which is known as **anergy**. Life-threatening infections are common. Viral infections, such as herpes zoster, can become widely disseminated.

Medical Management

In early stages, CLL may require no treatment. When symptoms are severe (drenching night sweats, painful lymphadenopathy) or when the disease progresses to later stages (with resultant anemia and thrombocytopenia), chemotherapy with fludarabine (Fludara) or corticosteroids and chlorambucil (Leukeran) is often used. The major side effect of fludarabine is prolonged bone marrow suppression, manifested by prolonged periods of neutropenia, lymphopenia, and thrombocytopenia. Patients are then at risk of infections such as *Pneumocystis jiroveci, Listeria,* mycobacteria, herpes viruses, and cytomegalovirus (CMV).

The use of monoclonal antibodies is gaining popularity; these are effective and less toxic than traditional chemotherapy (Elphee, 2007; Jaglowski, Alinari, Lapalombella et al., 2010). The monoclonal antibody rituximab (Rituxan) has efficacy in CLL therapy and is often used in combination with other chemotherapeutic medications. The monoclonal antibody alemtuzumab (Campath) targets the CD52

antigen commonly found on CLL cells and is effective in clearing the marrow and circulation of these cells without affecting the stem cells. Because CD52 is present on both B and T lymphocytes, patients receiving alemtuzumab are at significant risk for infection; prophylactic use of antiviral agents and antibiotics (e.g., Acyclovir; trimethoprim/sulfamethoxazole [Bactrim, Septra]) is important and needs to continue for at least 2 months after treatment ends. Bacterial infections are common in patients with CLL, and treatment with IV immunoglobulin (IVIG) may be given to selected patients to decrease the risk for infection.

The disease trajectory of CLL is variable; thus, it is difficult to determine the best time to initiate treatment. Patients with early-stage disease are often monitored without treatment. In contrast, patients with signs of more aggressive disease or those who have developed an associated autoimmune disorder (autoimmune hemolytic anemia or ITP) are treated promptly. Five to 10% of patients will experience a transformation from CLL to a more aggressive form of lymphoma. The median survival in this population is 5 months, and aggressive therapy is often employed.

Nursing Management for Acute Myeloid Leukemia and Acute Lymphocytic Leukemia

Although the clinical picture varies with the type of leukemia as well as the treatment implemented, the health history may reveal a range of subtle symptoms reported by the patient before the problem is detectable on physical examination. Weakness and fatigue are common manifestations, not only of the leukemia, but also of the resulting complications of anemia and infection. If the patient is hospitalized, the assessments should be performed daily, or more frequently as warranted. Because the physical findings may be subtle initially, a thorough, systematic assessment incorporating all body systems is essential. For example, a dry cough, mild dyspnea, and diminished breath sounds may indicate a pulmonary infection. However, the infection may not be seen initially on the chest X-ray; the absence of neutrophils delays the inflammatory response against the pulmonary infection, and it is the inflammatory response that produces the X-ray changes. The platelet count can become dangerously low, leaving the patient at risk for significant bleeding. The specific body system assessments are delineated in the neutropenic precautions and bleeding precautions found in Chapters 6 and 19, respectively. When serial assessments are performed, current findings are compared with previous findings to evaluate improvement or worsening.

The nurse also must closely monitor the results of laboratory studies. Flow sheets are particularly useful in tracking the leukocyte count, ANC, hematocrit, platelet, creatinine and electrolyte levels, and hepatic function tests. During initial treatment for acute leukemia, the ANC often drops below $100/mm^3$, placing the patient at very high risk for infection

(Liesveld & Lichtman, 2010b). Empiric antibiotics are used to preemptively treat infection when the patient has a fever of 100.4° F or greater. Culture results need to be reported immediately, so that antimicrobial therapy can be modified appropriately based on microbial sensitivity.

LYMPHOMA

The lymphomas are neoplasms (abnormal growth of tissue) of lymphoid tissue, usually derived from B lymphocytes. These tumors usually start in lymph nodes but can involve lymphoid tissue in the spleen, the GI tract (e.g., the wall of the stomach), the liver, or the bone marrow. They are often classified according to the degree of cell **differentiation** and the origin of the predominant malignant cell. Lymphomas can be broadly classified into two categories: Hodgkin's lymphoma and non-Hodgkin's lymphoma (NHL).

HODGKIN'S LYMPHOMA

Hodgkin's lymphoma is a relatively rare malignancy that has an impressive cure rate.

Pathophysiology

Unlike other lymphomas, Hodgkin's lymphoma is unicentric in origin in that it initiates in a single node. The disease spreads by contiguous extension along the lymphatic system. The malignant cell of Hodgkin's lymphoma is the Reed-Sternberg cell, a large tumor cell that is morphologically unique and is thought to be of immature lymphoid origin. It is the pathologic hallmark and essential diagnostic criterion for Hodgkin's disease. However, the tumor is very heterogeneous and may actually contain few Reed-Sternberg cells. Repeated biopsies may be required to establish the diagnosis.

The cause of Hodgkin's lymphoma is unknown but a viral etiology is suspected. In fact, fragments of the Epstein-Barr virus (EBV) have been found in some Reed-Sternberg cells. Rates of EBV found in Hodgkin's lymphomas have been shown to vary between 20% and 50% (Cader, Kearns, Young et al., 2010).

There are five sub-types of Hodgkin's lymphoma. The nodular-sclerosing subtype accounts for up to 70% of cases (Horning, 2010). The majority of these patients present with limited disease, or at an early stage. Hodgkin's lymphoma is classified into four stages, I through IV. If patients present with B symptoms, a B is added to the stage.

Risk Factors

Hodgkin's lymphoma is somewhat more common in men than women and has two peaks of incidence: one in the early 20s and the other after 50 years of age. Disease occurrence has a familial pattern: first-degree relatives have a higher-than-normal frequency of disease, but the actual incidence of this pattern is low. Hodgkin's lymphoma is seen more commonly in patients receiving chronic immunosuppressive therapy (e.g., for renal transplant) and in woodworkers. It is also seen in veterans of the military who were exposed to the herbicide Agent Orange.

Clinical Manifestations and Assessment

Hodgkin's lymphoma usually begins as a painless enlargement of one or more lymph nodes above the diaphragm. The individual nodes are painless and rubbery or firm but not hard. Seventy five percent of patients present with painless, enlarged cervical lymph nodes (Cader et al., 2010). A mediastinal mass may be seen on chest X-ray; occasionally, the mass is large enough to compress the trachea and cause dyspnea and cough. Pruritus is common; it can be extremely distressing, and the cause is unknown. Less than 10% of patients experience brief but severe pain after drinking alcohol, usually at the site of the tumor (Horning, 2010). Again, the cause of this is unknown.

All organs are vulnerable to invasion by Hodgkin's lymphoma. The symptoms result from compression of organs by the tumor, such as cough and pulmonary effusion (from pulmonary infiltrates), jaundice (from hepatic involvement or bile duct obstruction), abdominal pain (from splenomegaly or retroperitoneal adenopathy), or bone pain (from skeletal involvement). Herpes zoster infections are common. A cluster of constitutional symptoms has important prognostic implications. Referred to as "B symptoms," they include fever (without chills), drenching sweats (particularly at night), and unintentional weight loss of more than 10%. B symptoms are found in 40% of patients and are more common in advanced disease. An elevated **erythrocyte sedimentation rate** (ESR) represents a poor prognostic indicator (Hoppe et al., 2010).

A mild anemia is the most common hematologic finding. The leukocyte count may be elevated or decreased. The platelet count is typically normal, unless the tumor has invaded the bone marrow, suppressing hematopoiesis. Patients with Hodgkin's lymphoma have impaired cellular immunity, as evidenced by an absent or decreased reaction to skin sensitivity tests (e.g., *Candida*, mumps).

Because many manifestations are similar to those occurring with infection, diagnostic studies are performed to rule out an infectious origin for the disease. The diagnosis is made by means of an excisional lymph node biopsy and the finding of the Reed-Sternberg cell. Once the diagnosis is confirmed and the histologic type is established, it is necessary to assess the extent of the disease, a process referred to as *staging*.

In addition to a careful physical exam, a chest X-ray, computed tomography (CT) scan of the chest, abdomen, and pelvis, and a positron emission tomography (PET) scan are all obtained to assist with staging. The PET scan may be the

most sensitive imaging test in identifying residual disease. Laboratory tests include CBC, platelet count, ESR, lactate dehydrogenase (LDH), and liver and renal function studies. A bone marrow biopsy is performed if there are signs of marrow involvement, and some physicians routinely perform bilateral biopsies. Bone scans may be performed to identify any involvement in these areas.

Medical Management

The general goal in treatment of Hodgkin's lymphoma, regardless of stage, is cure. Treatment is determined primarily by the stage of the disease, not the histologic type; however, extensive research is ongoing to target treatment regimens to histologic subtypes or prognostic features. Traditionally, early Hodgkin's disease was treated by a staging laparotomy followed by radiation therapy. This treatment method has commonly been replaced by a short course (2 to 4 months) of chemotherapy followed by radiation therapy in early-stage disease (I and II). Combination therapy prevents relapse and improve 5-year overall survival (Herbst, Rehan, Brillant et al., 2010). Some patients with early-stage disease and good prognostic features may receive radiation therapy alone. Combination chemotherapy, for example with doxorubicin (Adriamycin), bleomycin (Blenoxane), vinblastine (Velban), and dacarbazine (DTIC), referred to as ABVD, is now the standard treatment for more advanced disease (stages III and IV and all B stages).

Radiation therapy is still very useful for patients with extensive adenopathy (often termed bulky disease). In this group, residual disease often persists after the chemotherapy treatment is finished; radiation therapy to the areas of remaining adenopathy has been shown to improve survival.

Even when Hodgkin's lymphoma does recur, the use of high doses of chemotherapeutic agents, followed by autologous PBSCT, can be very effective in controlling the disease and extending survival time.

Nursing management is similar to that of NHL and is discussed in that section.

Long-Term Complications of Therapy

Much is now known about the long-term effects of chemotherapy and radiation therapy, primarily from the large numbers of people who were cured of Hodgkin's lymphoma by these treatments. Long-term complications include hypothyroidism, immune dysfunction, dental caries, cardiomyopathy, and secondary malignancies. Risk factors for other cancers should be assessed, and long-term surveillance is crucial. Lung cancer is the most common type of secondary malignancy in patients with Hodgkin's disease, particularly following combination chemotherapy and radiation (Kiserud, Loge, Fosså et al., 2010).

Breast cancer is the most common secondary malignancy in female survivors, particularly in those who were treated before age 20 years (O'Brien, Donaldson, Balise et al., 2010). The risks for secondary malignancies must be explained to the patient prior to initiation of therapy, as part of informed consent. Patients should be encouraged to reduce other factors that increase the risk of developing secondary cancers, such as use of tobacco and alcohol and exposure to environmental carcinogens. Revised treatment approaches are aimed at diminishing the risk for complications without sacrificing the potential for cure.

NON-HODGKIN'S LYMPHOMAS

The NHLs are a heterogeneous group of cancers that originate from the neoplastic growth of lymphoid tissue. As in CLL, the neoplastic cells are thought to arise from a single clone of lymphocytes; however, in NHL, the cells may vary morphologically. Most NHLs involve malignant B lymphocytes; only 5% involve T lymphocytes. In contrast to Hodgkin's lymphoma, the lymphoid tissues involved are largely infiltrated with malignant cells. The spread of these malignant lymphoid cells occurs unpredictably, and true localized disease is uncommon. Lymph nodes from multiple sites may be infiltrated, as may sites outside the lymphoid system (extranodal tissue).

While the incidence of NHL continues to rise in the United States, there has been a significant decline in NHL-related deaths in the last 10 years. It is now the sixth most common type of cancer diagnosed in the United States, the eighth most common cause of cancer death in men, and the sixth most common cause of cancer death in women (Jemal, Siegal, Xu et al., 2010). The incidence increases with each decade of life; the average age at diagnosis is 50 to 60 years. Although no common etiologic factor has been identified, the incidence of NHL has increased in people with immunodeficiencies or autoimmune disorders; prior treatment for cancer; prior organ transplant; viral infections (including Epstein-Barr virus and HIV); and exposure to pesticides, solvents, dyes, or defoliating agents, including Agent Orange. Prognosis varies greatly among the various types of NHL. Long-term survival (>10 years) is commonly achieved in low-grade, localized lymphomas. Even with aggressive disease forms, cure is possible in at least one-third of patients who receive aggressive treatment.

Clinical Manifestations and Assessment

Symptoms are highly variable, reflecting the diverse nature of the NHLs. Lymphadenopathy is most common (66%); however, in more indolent (less aggressive) types of lymphomas, the lymphadenopathy can wax and wane. With early-stage disease, or with the types that are considered more indolent, there may be no symptoms, and the illness typically is not diagnosed until it progresses to a later stage,

when the patient becomes symptomatic. At these stages (III or IV), lymphadenopathy is distinctly noticeable. One-third of patients with NHLs have "B symptoms" (recurrent fever, drenching night sweats, and unintentional weight loss of 10% or more). Lymphomatous masses can compromise organ function. For example, a mass in the mediastinum can cause respiratory distress; abdominal masses can compromise the ureters, leading to renal dysfunction; and splenomegaly can cause abdominal discomfort, nausea, early satiety, anorexia, and weight loss. Less than 10% of patients will experience CNS involvement at some point in their disease. Certain populations have higher rates of CNS involvement including patients with HIV, or with testicular, breast, epidural, or sinus involvement.

The actual diagnosis of NHL is categorized into a highly complex classification system based on histopathology, immunophenotyping, and cytogenetic analyses of the malignant cells. The specific histopathologic type of the disease has important prognostic implications. Treatment also varies and is based on these features. Staging, also an important factor, is typically based on data obtained from CT and PET scans, bone marrow biopsies, and occasionally cerebrospinal fluid analysis. The stage is based on the site of disease and its spread to other sites. For example, in stage I disease, only one area of involvement is detected; thus, stage I disease is highly localized and may respond well to localized therapy (e.g., radiation therapy). In contrast, in stage IV disease, at least one extranodal site is detected.

Medical Management

Treatment is based on the actual classification of disease, the stage of disease, prior treatment (if any), and the patient's ability to tolerate therapy. If the disease is not an aggressive form and is truly localized, radiation alone may be the treatment of choice.

Low-grade lymphomas may not require treatment until the disease progresses to a later stage, but historically they have also been relatively unresponsive to treatment, and in most cases, use of therapeutic modalities did not improve overall survival. More aggressive types of NHL (e.g., lymphoblastic lymphoma, Burkitt's lymphoma) require prompt initiation of chemotherapy; however, these types tend to be more responsive to treatment.

With aggressive types of NHL, aggressive combinations of chemotherapeutic agents are given even in early stages. More intermediate forms are commonly treated with combination chemotherapy and radiation therapy for stage I and II disease. The advent of the monoclonal antibody, Rituximab, which targets the CD20 antigen on the surface of B cells has significantly improved survival in patients with NHL. The combination of rituximab with conventional chemotherapy (Cytoxan, doxorubicin, vincristine, and prednisone [CHOP]) is now considered standard treatment for common, aggressive B cell lymphomas (Molina, 2008). Unfor-

tunately, more than 30% of patients with diffuse large B cell NHL will experience a relapse. Treatment for relapsed disease includes Rituximab and combination chemotherapy followed by high-dose chemotherapy with stem cell support (Tilly & Dreyling, 2009). CNS involvement may occur with some aggressive forms of NHL; in this situation, intrathecal chemotherapy is used in addition to systemic chemotherapy. Radiation may be used for palliation of symptoms.

Nursing Management

Lymphoma is a highly complex constellation of diseases. When caring for patients with lymphoma, it is extremely important to know the specific disease type, stage of disease, treatment history, and current treatment plan. Most of the care for patients with Hodgkin's lymphoma or NHL takes place in the outpatient setting, unless complications occur (e.g., infection, respiratory compromise due to mediastinal mass). The most commonly used treatment methods are chemotherapy and radiation therapy. Chemotherapy causes systemic side effects (e.g., myelosuppression, nausea, hair loss, risk of infection), whereas radiation therapy causes specific effects that are limited to the area being irradiated. For example, patients receiving abdominal radiation therapy may experience nausea and diarrhea but not hair loss. Regardless of the type of treatment, all patients experience fatigue.

The risk for infection is significant for these patients, not only from treatment-related myelosuppression but also from the defective immune response that results from the disease itself. Patients need to be taught to minimize the risks of infection, to recognize signs of possible infection, and to contact the health care professional should such signs develop (see Chapters 6 and 19). Additional complications depend on the location of the lymphoma. Therefore, it is important for the nurse to know the tumor location, so that assessments can be targeted appropriately. For example, patients with lymphomatous masses in the upper chest should be assessed for superior vena cava obstruction or airway obstruction, if the mass is near the bronchus or trachea.

Many lymphomas can be cured with current treatments. However, as survival rates increase, the incidence of second malignancies, particularly AML or MDS, also increases. Therefore, survivors should be screened regularly for the development of second malignancies.

MULTIPLE MYELOMA

Multiple myeloma is a malignant disease of the most mature form of B lymphocyte, the plasma cell. It is not classified as a lymphoma. Plasma cells secrete immunoglobulins, proteins necessary for antibody production to fight infection. The incidence of multiple myeloma is decreasing (Altekruse, Kosary, Krapcho et al., 2009). Multiple myeloma most commonly affects people over 70 years of age with only 1% to 2% of patients diagnosed under age 40. The incidence rate is more than twice as high in the black population as

compared to white populations. Median survival time for patients with multiple myeloma is 3 years with standard therapy and 5 years with dose-intense treatment (Lin, 2009). Death usually results from infection.

Pathophysiology

In multiple myeloma, the malignant plasma cells produce an increased amount of a specific immunoglobulin that is nonfunctional. Functional types of immunoglobulin are still produced by nonmalignant plasma cells, but in lower-than-normal quantity. The specific immunoglobulin secreted by the myeloma cells is detectable in the blood or urine and is referred to as the *monoclonal protein*, or *M protein*. This protein serves as a useful marker to monitor the extent of disease and the patient's response to therapy. In addition, the presence of light chains (antibodies are made up of light chains and heavy chains) in the urine (sometimes referred to as *Bence-Jones protein*) is considered to be a major criterion in the diagnosis of multiple myeloma. It is commonly measured by serum or urine protein electrophoresis. Moreover, the patient's total protein level is typically elevated, again due to the production of M protein. The diagnosis of myeloma can also be confirmed by bone marrow biopsy; the presence of more than 10% plasma cells in the bone marrow is another hallmark diagnostic criterion.

Malignant plasma cells also secrete certain substances to stimulate the creation of new blood vessels to enhance the growth of these clusters of plasma cells; this process is referred to as **angiogenesis**. Occasionally, the plasma cells infiltrate other tissue, in which case they are referred to as *plasmacytomas*. Plasmacytomas can occur in the sinuses, spinal cord, and soft tissues.

Clinical Manifestations and Assessment

As many as 90% of patients with multiple myeloma develop bone lesions. Although patients can have asymptomatic bone involvement, the most common presenting symptom of multiple myeloma is bone pain, usually in the back or ribs. Unlike arthritic pain, the bone pain associated with myeloma increases with movement and decreases with rest; patients may report that they have less pain on awakening, but the pain intensity increases during the day. In myeloma, a substance secreted by the plasma cells, osteoclast activating factor, and other substances (e.g., interleukin-6 [IL-6]) are involved in stimulating osteoclasts. Both mechanisms appear to be involved in the process of bone breakdown. Thus, lytic lesions as well as osteoporosis may be seen on bone X-rays. (They are not well visualized on bone scans.) The bone destruction can be severe enough to cause vertebral collapse and fractures, including spinal fractures, which can impinge on the spinal cord and result in spinal cord compression. It is this bone destruction that causes significant pain.

If the bone destruction is fairly extensive, excessive ionized calcium is lost from the bone and enters the serum; hypercalcemia may therefore develop (frequently manifested by excessive thirst, dehydration, constipation, altered mental status, confusion, and rarely coma). Renal failure may also occur; the configuration of the circulating immunoglobulin molecule (particularly the shape of lambda light chains) can damage the renal tubules.

As more and more malignant plasma cells are produced, the marrow has less space for erythrocyte production, and anemia may develop. This anemia is also caused to a great extent by a diminished production of erythropoietin by the kidney. The patient may complain of fatigue and weakness due to the anemia. In the late stage of the disease, a reduced number of leukocytes and platelets may also be seen because the bone marrow is infiltrated by malignant plasma cells.

> **NURSING ALERT**
> *Any elderly patient whose chief complaint is back pain and who has an elevated total protein level should be evaluated for possible myeloma.*

Medical Management

There is no cure for multiple myeloma. Even autologous PBSCT is considered to extend remission rather than provide a cure. However, for many patients, it is possible to control the illness and maintain their level of functioning quite well for several years. Initial treatment is often dictated by patient age, with younger patients being driven toward high-dose chemotherapy and autologous transplant, and older patients being treated with immunomodulatory agents and steroids (Reece, 2009). Corticosteroids are the mainstay of treatment, particularly dexamethasone (Decadron); steroids are often combined with immunomodulatory agents such as thalidomide, lenalidomide, or bortezomib. Corticosteroids inhibit the expression of **cytokines**, such as IL-6, which are primary growth factors for the development of multiple myeloma. Steroids also reduce the activity of nuclear factor-kappa B, which encourages apoptosis of myeloma cells (Faiman, Bilotti, Mangan et al., 2008). More recently, the use of a proteasome inhibiting agent, bortezomib (Velcade), has been approved by the U.S. Food and Drug Administration (FDA) for use in refractory disease (Dave & Dunbar, 2010). Side effects include transient thrombocytopenia, orthostatic hypotension, nausea and vomiting, skin rash, and neuropathy.

Recent advances in the understanding of the process of angiogenesis have resulted in new therapeutic options. The sedative thalidomide (Thalomid), initially used as an antiemetic, and the newer agent, Lenalidomide, have significant antimyeloma effects. These agents inhibit the cytokines necessary for new vascular generation, such as vascular endothelial growth factor, and for myeloma cell growth and survival, such as IL-6 and tumor necrosis factor, by

boosting the body's immune response against the tumor and by creating favorable conditions for apoptosis (programmed cell death) of the myeloma cells. Thalidomide is effective in refractory myeloma and in "smoldering" disease states, and may prevent progression to a more active state. Thalidomide and lenalidomide are not typical chemotherapeutic agents and have unique side-effect profiles. Thalidomide commonly causes fatigue, dizziness, constipation, rash, and peripheral neuropathy. Lenalidomide's side-effect profile is quite different from that of thalidomide: myelosuppression is common, whereas sedation, neuropathy, and constipation are not. Patients who have progressed on thalidomide can still be treated with lenalidomide; lenalidomide is thought to exhibit more antimyeloma activity than thalidomide. Lenalidomide is often used in combination with bortezomib; together, the two drugs are synergistic and may improve outcomes without increasing toxicity (Laubach, Colson, Harvey et al., 2010).

Multiple myeloma increases the risk for the development of venous thromboembolism (VTE). Drugs such as thalidomide and lenalidomide are also thrombogenic; the risk for VTE increases when these agents are used in combination with dexamethasone. To minimize the risk for VTE, patients are educated to maintain an active lifestyle including daily exercise. In addition, some patients are given prophylaxis using aspirin or a combination of aspirin and Plavix (Talamo, Ibrahim, Claxton et al., 2009).

Both thalidomide and lenalidomide are contraindicated in pregnancy because of associated severe birth defects. Additionally, due to the risks for birth defects, use of either agent requires registry into a monitoring program that ensures routine pregnancy testing, contraception, and control of drug distribution. Patients must be counseled and agree to use approved methods of birth control prior to taking these drugs.

Radiation therapy is very useful in strengthening the bone at a specific lesion, particularly one at risk for bone fracture or spinal cord compression. It is also useful in relieving bone pain and reducing the size of plasma cell tumors that occur outside the skeletal system. However, because it is a nonsystemic form of treatment, it does not diminish the source of the bone conditions (i.e., the production of malignant plasma cells). Therefore, radiation therapy is typically used in combination with systemic treatment such as chemotherapy.

When lytic lesions result in vertebral compression fractures, vertebroplasty is often performed. This procedure is performed under fluoroscopy. A hollow needle is positioned within the fractured vertebra, and when the precise location is confirmed, an orthopedic cement is injected into the vertebra to stabilize the fracture and strengthen the vertebra. For most patients, relief from pain is almost immediate. This procedure has been enhanced by concomitant kyphoplasty, the use of a special inflatable balloon inserted into the vertebra to increase the height of the vertebra prior to injecting the cement.

All patients with one or more lytic lesions or a compression fracture should start on bisphosphonate therapy. Newer forms of bisphosphonates, such as pamidronate (Aredia) and zoledronic acid (Zometa), have been shown to strengthen bone in multiple myeloma by diminishing the secretion of osteoclast-activating factor, thus controlling bone pain and potentially preventing bone fracture. These agents are also effective in managing and preventing hypercalcemia. Some evidence suggests that bisphosphonates may actually have activity against the myeloma cells themselves by inhibiting a growth factor necessary for myeloma cell survival (Guenther, Gordon, Tiemann et al., 2010; Terpos, Sezer, Croucher et al., 2009). However, a complication associated primarily with IV bisphosphonates is osteonecrosis of the jaw, which can result in intractable pain, swallowing difficulty, sinusitis, soft-tissue abscesses, and extraoral fistulas (a permanent abnormal passageway between the mouth and exterior of the body). Estimates of incidence are from 1% to 12% of patients receiving IV bisphosphonates. A recent review of bisphosphonate-induced osteonecrosis of the jaw revealed that 89% of cases were associated with the treatment of a malignant condition, particularly multiple myeloma (Filleul, Crompot, & Saussez, 2010). Patients should receive a comprehensive dental exam and appropriate dental interventions as needed prior to initiation of bisphosphonate therapy. Throughout the duration of treatment, careful assessment for this complication should be performed (Laubach et al., 2010; Lipton, 2010).

Hyperviscosity may result from elevations in the M protein levels. When patients have signs and symptoms of hyperviscosity, such as mental status changes or blurred vision, plasmapheresis may be used to lower the immunoglobulin level. Symptoms may be more useful than serum viscosity levels in determining the need for this intervention.

Nursing Management

Pain management is very important in patients with multiple myeloma. Nonsteroidal anti-inflammatory drugs (NSAIDs) can be very useful for mild pain or can be administered in combination with opioid analgesics. Because NSAIDs can cause gastritis and renal dysfunction, renal function must be carefully monitored. The patient needs to be educated about activity restrictions (e.g., lifting no more than 10 pounds, use of proper body mechanics). Braces are occasionally needed to support the spinal column.

Peripheral neuropathy is a common side effect of the immunomodulatory agents used to treat multiple myeloma, occurring in as many as 80% of patients. Peripheral neuropathy can significantly impact the patient's quality of life and ability to perform activities of daily living (ADLs). The physical exam should include an assessment of neuropathy using a neurotoxicity assessment tool, as well as a subjective assessment of the patient's discomfort. Management of

peripheral neuropathy may include decreasing the dose of thalidomide or lenalidomide, holding therapy, treating discomfort with medications such as gabapentin, and involving other disciplines such as occupational and physical therapy to maximize and restore function (Tariman, Love, McCullagh et al., 2008).

The patient also needs to be instructed about the signs and symptoms of hypercalcemia. Maintaining mobility and hydration are important to diminish exacerbations of this complication; however, the primary cause is the disease itself. Renal function should also be monitored closely. Renal failure can become severe, and dialysis may be needed. Maintaining high urine output (3 L/day) can be very useful in preventing or limiting this complication.

Because antibody production is impaired, infections, particularly bacterial infections, are common and can be life-threatening. The patient needs to be instructed in appropriate infection prevention measures such as hand hygiene and avoiding sick individuals, and should be advised to contact the health care provider immediately if he or she has a fever or other signs and symptoms of infection. The patient should receive pneumonia (Pneumovax) and influenza vaccines. Prophylactic antibiotics are sometimes used. IVIG can be useful for patients with recurrent infections and low levels of immunoglobulins.

Many patients with multiple myeloma are treated with high doses of corticosteroids for protracted periods of time. Patients must be monitored for potential short- and long-term effects of steroids including hyperglycemia and insomnia (short-term), and osteopenia, osteoporosis, cataracts, and diabetes (long-term).

Gerontologic Considerations

The incidence of multiple myeloma increases with age; the disease rarely occurs in patients younger than 40 years of age. Because of the increasing older population, more patients are seeking treatment for this disease. Back pain, which is often a presenting symptom in this disease, should be closely investigated in older patients. In addition, any patient over 40 presenting with anemia should also undergo a workup for myeloma, primarily through an evaluation of the serum protein electrophoresis (SPEP). Autologous PBSCT is an option that can prolong remission and potentially cure some patients, but it is unavailable to many older people because of age limitations, poor performance status, and comorbidities.

BLEEDING DISORDERS

OVERVIEW

Normal hemostatic mechanisms can control bleeding from vessels and prevent spontaneous bleeding. The bleeding vessel constricts and platelets aggregate at the site, forming an unstable hemostatic plug. Circulating coagulation factors are activated on the surface of these aggregated platelets, forming **fibrin**, which anchors the platelet plug to the site of injury.

The failure of normal hemostatic mechanisms can result in bleeding, which is severe at times. This bleeding is commonly provoked by trauma, but in certain circumstances it can occur spontaneously. When the source is platelet or coagulation factor abnormalities, the site of bleeding can be anywhere in the body. When the source is vascular abnormalities, the site of bleeding may be more localized to the involved blood vessels. Some patients have defects in more than one hemostatic mechanism simultaneously.

In a variety of situations, the bone marrow may be stimulated to increase platelet production (thrombopoiesis). The increased production may be a reactive response, as in a compensatory response to significant bleeding, or as a result of a myeloproliferative disorder, such as essential thrombocythemia. Sometimes, the increase in platelets does not result from increased production but from a loss in platelet pooling within the spleen. The spleen typically holds about one-third of the circulating platelets at any time. If the spleen is absent (e.g., splenectomy), the platelet reservoir is lost, and an abnormally high number of platelets enters the circulation. In time, the rate of thrombopoiesis slows to reestablish a more normal platelet level.

Clinical Manifestations and Assessment

Signs and symptoms of bleeding disorders vary depending on the type of defect. A careful history and physical examination can be very useful in determining the source of the hemostatic defect. Abnormalities of the vascular system give rise to local bleeding, usually into the skin. Because platelets are primarily responsible for **hemostasis** in small vessels, patients with platelet defects develop petechiae, often in clusters; these are seen on the skin, most commonly the extremities, and mucous membranes but can also occur throughout the body, particularly in individuals who have had prolonged thrombocytopenia. Bleeding from platelet disorders can be significant. Unless the platelet disorder is severe, bleeding can often be stopped promptly when local pressure is applied; it does not typically recur when the pressure is released.

In contrast, coagulation factor defects do not tend to cause superficial bleeding because the primary hemostatic mechanisms are still intact. Instead, bleeding occurs deeper within the body (e.g., subcutaneous or IM hematomas, hemorrhage into joint spaces). External bleeding diminishes very slowly when local pressure is applied; it often recurs several hours after pressure is removed. For example, severe bleeding may start several hours after a tooth extraction.

Medical Management

Management varies based on the underlying cause of the bleeding disorder. If bleeding is significant, transfusions

of blood products are indicated. The specific blood product used is determined by the underlying defect. If **fibrinolysis** (breakdown of a fibrin clot) is excessive, indicated by an increase in fibrin degradation products (FDPs) in the blood, hemostatic agents such as aminocaproic acid (Amicar) can be used to inhibit this process. This agent must be used with caution because excessive inhibition of fibrinolysis can result in thrombosis.

Nursing Management

Patients who have bleeding disorders or who have the potential for development of such disorders as a result of disease or therapeutic agents must be taught to observe themselves carefully and frequently for bleeding and understand self-care strategies to minimize bleeding risk (Chapter 19, Box 19-3). They need to understand the importance of avoiding activities that increase the risk of bleeding, such as contact sports. The skin is observed for petechiae and ecchymoses (bruises) and the nose and gums for bleeding. Hospitalized patients may be monitored for bleeding by testing all drainage and excreta (feces, urine, emesis, and gastric drainage) for occult as well as obvious blood. Outpatients are often given fecal occult blood screening cards to detect occult blood in stools (see Chapter 19 for additional assessment and patient education information).

PRIMARY THROMBOCYTHEMIA

Primary thrombocythemia (also called essential thrombocythemia) is a stem cell disorder within the bone marrow. It affects men and women equally and tends to occur in late middle age. The median survival exceeds 10 years.

Pathophysiology

A marked increase in platelet production occurs, with the platelet count consistently greater than 600,000/mm³. Platelet size may be abnormal, but platelet survival is typically normal. Occasionally, the platelet increase is accompanied by an increase in erythrocytes, leukocytes, or both; however, these cells are not increased to the extent that they are in PV, CML, or myelofibrosis. Although the exact cause is unknown, primary thrombocythemia is similar to other myeloproliferative disorders, particularly PV. However, unlike the other myeloproliferative disorders, it rarely evolves into acute leukemia.

Clinical Manifestations and Assessment

Many patients with primary thrombocythemia are asymptomatic; the illness is diagnosed as the result of finding an elevated platelet count on a CBC. Symptoms, when they do occur, result primarily from hemorrhage or vasoocclusion in

the microvasculature. Symptoms occur most often when the platelet count exceeds 1 million/mm³. However, symptoms do not always correlate with the extent to which the platelet count is elevated. Thrombosis is common and can be either arterial or venous; arterial thrombosis is more common (Hoffman, 2008). Common sites of large vessel arterial occlusion include the arteries of the legs, the coronary arteries, and the renal arteries. Vasomotor symptoms occur in approximately 40% of patients and can include visual disturbances, lightheadedness, headaches, palpitations, and atypical chest pain (Shenoy, Robyn, & Sloand, 2010). Headache is the most common neurologic complication, followed by transient ischemic attacks, dizziness, syncope, and seizures. More common forms of venous thrombosis include DVT and pulmonary embolism; less commonly, stroke and MI occur. Small vessel vasoocclusive manifestations cause symptoms of erythromelalgia (described earlier).

Because these platelets can be dysfunctional, minor or major hemorrhage can also occur. The GI tract is the most common site of bleeding, followed by the skin, eyes, urinary tract, gums, tooth socket and gums, joints, or brain. Bleeding typically does not occur unless the platelet count exceeds 1 million/mm³. The spleen may be enlarged but usually not to a clinically significant extent.

The diagnosis of primary thrombocythemia is made by ruling out other potential disorders—either other myeloproliferative disorders or underlying illnesses that cause a reactive or secondary thrombocytosis (see below). Iron deficiency should be excluded, because a reactive increase in the platelet count often accompanies this deficiency. Occult malignancy should be excluded. The CBC shows markedly large and abnormal platelets. Analysis of the bone marrow (by aspiration and biopsy) does not impact management decisions and therefore is not a standard part of the workup.

No data reliably predict the development of complications. Risk factors for the development of thrombotic complications are age older than 60 years, gender (men are at greater risk than women), smoking, prior thrombotic or bleeding events, and preexisting cardiac risk factors (Hoffman, 2008).

Medical Management

The management of primary thrombocythemia is highly controversial. The risk for significant thrombotic or hemorrhagic complications may not be increased until the platelet count exceeds 1.5 million/mm³. A careful assessment of other risk factors, such as history of peripheral vascular disease, history of tobacco use, atherosclerosis, and prior thrombotic events, should be used in making the decision as to when to initiate therapy.

In younger, asymptomatic patients (<60 years) with none of the above risk factors, observation alone is sufficient. Alternatively, low-dose aspirin may be used to prevent thrombotic complications. Aspirin can also be used to relieve the neurologic symptoms (e.g., headache), erythromelalgia, and visual symptoms of primary thrombocythemia.

However, the use of aspirin can increase the risk of hemorrhagic complications and is typically a contraindication in patients with a history of GI bleeding or if platelet counts exceeds 1.5 million/mm^3 (Shenoy et al., 2010; Tefferi, 2008).

In older patients with an increased risk for thrombosis, more aggressive measures may be necessary. Hydroxyurea (Hydrea), a chemotherapeutic medication, is effective in lowering the platelet count. This agent is taken orally and causes minimal side effects other than dose-related leukopenia. However, use of hydroxyurea increases the risk of developing leukemia. The medication anagrelide (Agrylin) is more specific in lowering the platelet count than is hydroxyurea but has more side effects. Severe headaches cause many patients to stop taking the medication. Tachycardia and chest pain may also occur, and anagrelide is contraindicated in patients with concurrent cardiac problems. Interferon-alfa-2b (Intron-A) has been shown to lower platelet counts by an unknown mechanism. The medication is administered subcutaneously at varying frequency, commonly three times per week. Significant side effects, such as fatigue, depression, weakness, memory deficits, dizziness, anemia, and liver dysfunction, limit its usefulness. These medications should be used in combination with low-dose aspirin in the high-risk groups.

Rarely, the occlusive symptoms are so great that the platelet count must be reduced immediately. When necessary, platelet pheresis (see later discussion) can reduce the amount of circulating platelets, but only transiently. The extent to which symptoms and complications (e.g., thromboses) are reduced by pheresis remains unclear.

Nursing Management

Patients with primary thrombocythemia need to be instructed about the accompanying risks of hemorrhage and thrombosis. The patient is informed about signs and symptoms of thrombosis, particularly the neurologic manifestations, such as visual changes, numbness, tingling, and weakness. Risk factors for thrombosis are assessed, and measures to diminish risk factors (particularly cessation of tobacco use) are encouraged. Patients receiving aspirin therapy should be informed about the increased risk of bleeding. Patients who are at risk for bleeding should be instructed about medications (e.g., aspirin, NSAIDs) and other substances (e.g., alcohol) that can alter platelet function and should therefore be avoided. Patients receiving interferon therapy are taught to self-administer the medication and manage side effects (primarily fatigue, flu-like symptoms, and depression).

SECONDARY THROMBOCYTOSIS

Increased platelet production is the primary mechanism of secondary, or reactive, **thrombocytosis**. The platelet count is above normal, but, in contrast to primary thrombocythe-

mia, an increase to more than 1 million/mm^3 is rare. Platelet function is normal; the platelet survival time is normal or decreased. Consequently, symptoms associated with hemorrhage or thrombosis are rare. Many disorders or conditions can cause a reactive increase in platelets, including infection, chronic inflammatory disorders, iron deficiency, malignant disease, acute hemorrhage, and splenectomy (see previous discussion of primary thrombocythemia). Treatment is aimed at the underlying disorder. With successful management, the platelet count usually returns to normal.

THROMBOCYTOPENIA

Thrombocytopenia (low platelet level) can result from various factors: decreased production of platelets within the bone marrow, increased destruction of platelets, or increased consumption of platelets. There are numerous causes of thrombocytopenia including malignancy, infection, medications, and DIC. The primary strategy for managing thrombocytopenia is correction or treatment of the underlying cause, or removal of the offending agent.

Clinical Manifestations and Assessment

Bleeding and petechiae usually do not occur with platelet counts greater than 50,000/mm^3, although excessive bleeding can follow surgery or trauma. When the platelet count drops to less than 20,000/mm^3, petechiae can appear, along with nasal and gingival bleeding, excessive menstrual bleeding, and excessive bleeding after surgery or dental extractions. When the platelet count is less than 10,000/mm^3, spontaneous, potentially fatal CNS or GI hemorrhage can occur. If the platelets are dysfunctional due to disease (e.g., MDS) or medications (e.g., aspirin), the risk for bleeding may be much greater even when the actual platelet count is not significantly reduced.

A platelet deficiency that results from decreased production (e.g., leukemia, MDS) can usually be diagnosed by examining the bone marrow via aspiration and biopsy. Infections, either viral or bacterial, as well as alcoholism can also suppress platelet production. Lab tests should include testing for HIV and hepatitis B and C.

When platelet destruction is the cause of thrombocytopenia, the marrow shows increased megakaryocytes (the cells from which the platelets originate) and normal or even increased platelet production as the body attempts to compensate for the decreased platelets in circulation. Another cause of thrombocytopenia is sequestration. Approximately one-third of the circulating platelets are within the spleen, and a greatly enlarged spleen results in increased sequestration of platelets. Many medications (e.g., sulfa drugs, methotrexate) can either decrease platelet production or shorten their lifespan. Numerous genetic causes of thrombocytopenia

have been discovered, including autosomal dominant, autosomal recessive, and X-linked mutations (Diz-Küçükkaya, Chen et al., 2010).

An important cause to exclude is *pseudothrombocytopenia*. Here, platelets aggregate and clump in the presence of ethylenediamine tetra-acetic acid (EDTA), the anticoagulant present in the tube used for CBC collection. This clumping accounts for up to 20% of instances of isolated thrombocytopenia (Diz-Küçükkaya et al., 2010). A manual examination of the peripheral smear can easily determine platelet clumping as the cause of thrombocytopenia; newer cell counter machines can also detect this.

Medical Management

The management of thrombocytopenia is usually treatment of the underlying disease. If platelet production is impaired, platelet transfusions may increase the platelet count and stop bleeding or prevent spontaneous hemorrhage. If excessive platelet destruction occurs, transfused platelets are also destroyed, and the platelet count does not increase. The most common cause of excessive platelet destruction is ITP (see the following discussion). In some instances, splenectomy can be a useful therapeutic intervention, but often it is not an option; for example, in patients in whom the enlarged spleen is due to portal hypertension related to cirrhosis, splenectomy may cause more bleeding disorders.

Nursing Management

Nursing interventions for patients with thrombocytopenia are listed in Chapter 19, Box 19-3.

IMMUNE THROMBOCYTO-PENIC PURPURA

ITP is the most common autoimmune blood disorder, affecting people of all ages, although it is more common among children and young women. Historically, this disorder was referred to as "idiopathic" thrombocytopenia purpura because in many cases the underlying causes were unknown. In recent years, scientists have uncovered a number of etiologies leading to our current understanding of ITP as an autoimmune process, thus leading to the change in terminology from *idiopathic* to *immune* (Ahn, 2010). There are two forms of ITP: acute and chronic. Acute ITP, which occurs predominantly in children, often appears 1 to 6 weeks after a viral illness. This form is self-limited; remission often occurs spontaneously within 6 months. Chronic ITP is often diagnosed by exclusion of other causes of thrombocytopenia.

Pathophysiology

Although the precise cause of ITP remains unknown, the platelet count is decreased by a combination of autoantibody

mediated platelet destruction and impaired platelet production secondary to autoantibody effects on the megakaryocyte. Additionally, there is a decreased rise in serum thrombopoietin, a hormone that stimulates platelet production (Rice, 2009). Normally, in the presence of a low platelet count, the serum thrombopoietin rises to stimulate platelet production. In ITP, there is a low platelet count and an inappropriately low thrombopoietin level. Antiplatelet autoantibodies that bind to the patient's platelets are found in the blood of patients with ITP. When the platelets are bound by the antibodies, the RES or tissue macrophage system ingests the platelets, destroying them. The production of autoantibodies may be triggered by medications or infections. Viral infections sometimes precede the disease in children. Occasionally medications such as sulfa drugs can induce ITP. Other conditions, such as systemic lupus erythematosus or pregnancy, can also induce ITP.

Clinical Manifestations and Assessment

Many patients have no symptoms, and the low platelet count (often <20,000/mm^3; <5,000/mm^3 is not uncommon) is an incidental finding. Common physical manifestations are easy bruising, heavy menses, and petechiae on the extremities or trunk. Patients with simple bruising or petechiae, termed "dry purpura," tend to have fewer complications from bleeding than do those with bleeding from mucosal surfaces, such as the GI tract (including the mouth) and pulmonary system (e.g., hemoptysis), termed "wet purpura." Patients with wet purpura have a greater risk of intracranial bleeding than do those with dry purpura. Despite low platelet counts, the platelets are young and very functional. They adhere to endothelial surfaces and to one another, so that spontaneous bleeding does not always occur. Thus, treatment may not be initiated unless bleeding becomes severe or life-threatening, the platelet count is extremely low (<10,000/mm^3), or in those with risk factors for bleeding, such as uncontrolled hypertension or peptic ulcer disease (Diz-Küçükkaya et al., 2010).

Medical Management

The primary goal of treatment is a "safe" platelet count. Because the risk for bleeding typically does not increase until the platelet count is less than 10,000/mm^3, a patient whose count exceeds 30,000/mm^3 to 50,000/mm^3 may be carefully observed without additional intervention. However, if the count is less than 20,000/mm^3 or if bleeding occurs, the goal is to improve the patient's platelet count rather than to cure the disease. The decision to treat should not be made merely on the basis of the patient's platelet count, but also on his or her lifestyle and activity level. A person with a sedentary lifestyle can tolerate a low platelet count more safely than one with a more active lifestyle.

Treatment for ITP usually involves several approaches. If the patient is taking a medication known to cause ITP

(e.g., quinine, sulfa-containing medications), the medication must be stopped immediately. The mainstay of short-term therapy is the use of immunosuppressive agents. These agents block the binding receptors on macrophages, so that the platelets are not destroyed. Prednisone is the agent typically used, and it is effective in about 80% of patients (Rice, 2009). Other immunosuppressive agents such as azathioprine, danazol, cyclosporine, or mycophenolate mofetil may be used if steroids fail to induce a response (Rice, 2009). Platelet counts typically begin to rise within a few days after institution of corticosteroid therapy in 90% of patients; this effect takes longer with azathioprine. Because of the associated side effects, patients cannot take high doses of corticosteroids indefinitely. It is not unusual for the platelet count to drop once the corticosteroid dose is tapered. Some patients can be successfully maintained on low doses of prednisone.

IVIG is also commonly used to treat ITP. The timing of IVIG in the treatment of ITP is controversial. IVIG works by binding receptors on the macrophages; however, high doses are required, the drug is very expensive, and the effect is transient (Rice, 2009). Splenectomy is an alternative treatment but results in a sustained normal platelet count only 50% of the time; however, many patients can maintain a "safe" platelet count of more than 30,000/mm^3 after removal of the spleen. Even those who do respond to splenectomy may have recurrences of severe thrombocytopenia months or years later. Patients who have undergone splenectomy are permanently at risk for sepsis; these patients should receive pneumonia (Pneumovax), *Haemophilus influenzae* B, and meningococcal vaccines, preferably 2 to 3 weeks before the splenectomy is performed (Diz-Küçükkaya et al., 2010). The Pneumovax vaccine should be repeated at 5- to 10-year intervals.

Rituximab, a monoclonal antibody that targets the CD 20 marker on B cells, has been used successfully to treat ITP following treatment with steroids. Rituxan depletes the B cells that produce platelet-destroying autoantibodies, effectively increasing the platelet count. Rituxan is well tolerated and has few side effects. Studies have demonstrated a 43% complete response rate by the third week of weekly therapy, when many of the patients treated were refractory to other therapies (Arnold, Dentali, Crowther et al., 2007).

The treatment of ITP has been changed dramatically with the discovery of drugs that target the point of platelet production. Romiplostim (Nplate®) and Eltrombopag (Promacta®) are thrombopoietin-like agents that stimulate platelet production. Romiplostim is administered weekly via subcutaneous injection and Eltrombopag is a pill given once daily. Both medications have demonstrated efficacy in increasing the platelet count to more than 50,000/mm^3 within 2 weeks of initiation (Bussel, Kuter, Pullarkat et al., 2009; Bussel, Cheng, Saleh et al., 2007). Response rates are similar with both romiplostim and eltrombopag (Rice, 2009).

Despite the extremely low platelet count, platelet transfusions are usually avoided. Transfusions tend to be ineffective because the patient's antiplatelet antibodies bind with the transfused platelets, causing them to be destroyed. Platelet counts can actually drop after platelet transfusion. Occasionally, transfusion of platelets may protect against catastrophic bleeding in patients with severe wet purpura.

Nursing Management

Nursing care includes an assessment of the patient's lifestyle to determine the risk of bleeding from activity. A careful medication history is also obtained, including use of over-the-counter medications, herbs, and nutritional supplements. The nurse must be alert for sulfa-containing medications and others that alter platelet function (e.g., aspirin-based or other NSAIDs) (see Box 20-4). The nurse assesses for any history of recent viral illness and for risk factors for hepatitis and HIV. Reports of headache or visual disturbances should be reported to the licensed provider immediately as these symptoms can signal intracranial bleeding. Patients who are admitted to the hospital with wet purpura and low platelet counts should have a neurologic assessment incorporated into their routine vital sign measurements. All injections or rectal medications should be avoided, and rectal temperature measurements should not be performed because they can stimulate bleeding.

Patient teaching addresses signs of exacerbation of disease (petechiae, ecchymoses), how to contact appropriate health care personnel; the name and type of medication inducing ITP (if appropriate), current medical treatment (medications, tapering schedule if relevant, side effects), and the frequency of monitoring the platelet count. The patient is instructed to avoid all agents that interfere with platelet function (see Box 20-4). The patient should avoid constipation, as well as the Valsalva maneuver (straining to have a bowel movement). Electric razors should be used for shaving, and soft-bristled toothbrushes should replace stiff-bristled ones. The patient is also counseled to refrain from sexual intercourse when the platelet count is less than 50,000/mm^3. Patients who are receiving corticosteroids long term are at risk for complications including osteoporosis, proximal muscle wasting, cataract formation, and dental caries. Bone mineral density should be monitored, and these patients may benefit from calcium and vitamin D supplementation and bisphosphonate therapy to prevent significant bone disease.

PLATELET DEFECTS

Quantitative platelet defects are relatively common (thrombocytopenia), but qualitative defects can also occur. With qualitative defects, the number of platelets may be normal, but the platelets do not function normally. Currently, there are no tests with sufficient sensitivity and specificity to evaluate platelet function, so the patient history and presentation are critical to identifying the underlying defect.

Medications and Substances That Impair Platelet Function

- Anesthetic Agents:
  - Local anesthetics
  - Halothane
- Antibiotics:
  - Beta-lactam antibiotics
  - Penicillins
  - Cephalosporins
  - Nitrofurantoin
  - Sulfonamides
- Anticoagulation Agents:
  - Heparin
  - Fibrinolytic agents
- Anti-inflammatory Agents (Nonsteroidal):
  - Aspirin
  - Ibuprofen
  - Naproxen
- Antineoplastic Agents:
  - Carmustine
  - Daunorubicin
  - Mithramycin
- Cardiovascular Drugs:
  - Beta blockers
  - Calcium channel blockers
  - Isosorbide
  - Nitroglycerine
  - Nitroprusside
  - Quinidine
- Medications That Increase Platelet cAMP:
  - Dipyridamole
  - Prostacyclin
  - Theophylline
- Food and Food Additives:
  - Caffeine
  - Chinese black tree fungus
  - Clove
  - Cumin
  - Ethanol
  - Fish oils
  - Garlic
  - Onion extract
  - Turmeric
- Plasma Expanders:
  - Dextrans
  - Hydroxyethyl starch
- Psychotropic Agents:
  - Tricyclic antidepressants
  - Phenothiazines
- Miscellaneous:
  - Antihistamines
  - Clofibrate
  - Furosemide
  - Heroin
  - Contrast agents
  - Ticlopidine
  - Vitamin E
- Herbal Supplements:
  - Feverfew
  - Ginger
  - Gingko
  - Ginseng
  - Kava kava

An important functional platelet disorder is that induced by aspirin. Even small amounts of aspirin reduce normal platelet aggregation, and the prolonged bleeding time lasts for several days after aspirin ingestion. Although this does not cause bleeding in most people, patients with a coagulation disorder (e.g., hemophilia) or thrombocytopenia can have significant bleeding after taking aspirin, particularly if invasive procedures or trauma has occurred.

NSAIDs can also inhibit platelet function, but the effect is not as prolonged as with aspirin (about 5 days versus 7 to 10 days). Other causes of platelet dysfunction include ESRD, possibly from metabolic products affecting platelet function; MDS; multiple myeloma (due to abnormal proteins interfering with platelet function); cardiopulmonary bypass; and other medications (see Box 20-4).

Clinical Manifestations and Assessment

Bleeding may be mild or severe. The extent is not necessarily correlated with the platelet count or with tests that measure coagulation (prothrombin time [PT], partial thromboplastin time [PTT]). Ecchymoses are common, particularly on the extremities. Patients with platelet dysfunction may be at risk for significant bleeding after trauma or invasive procedures (e.g., biopsy, dental extraction).

Medical Management

If the platelet dysfunction is caused by medication, use of the offending medication should be stopped, if possible, particularly when bleeding occurs or prior to an invasive procedure. If platelet dysfunction is marked, bleeding can often be prevented by transfusion of normal platelets before or during invasive procedures. Aminocaproic acid (EACA, Amicar) may be required to prevent significant bleeding after such procedures.

Nursing Management

Patients with significant platelet dysfunction need to be instructed to avoid substances that can diminish platelet function, such as certain over-the-counter medications, herbs, nutritional supplements, and alcohol. They also need

to serve as their own advocates and inform their health care providers (including dentists) of the underlying condition before any invasive procedure is performed, so that appropriate steps can be initiated to diminish the risk of bleeding. Bleeding precautions should be initiated as appropriate (see Chapter 19, Box 19-3).

VON WILLEBRAND'S DISEASE

Von Willebrand's disease is the most common inherited bleeding disorder in humans. The disease affects males and females equally. The prevalence of this disease is estimated to be 1%; thus, it is 50 times more prevalent than hemophilia (Fogarty, 2010; Johnsen & Ginsberg, 2010). The disease is a result of deficiency, dysfunction, or absence of von Willebrand Factor (vWF) (James, Manco-Johnson, Yawn et al., 2009). vWF is necessary for factor VIII activity and is essential for platelet adhesion at the site of vascular injury. Although synthesis of factor VIII is normal in vWD, its half-life is shortened; therefore, factor VIII levels are mildly low (15% to 50% of normal).

There are three types of von Willebrand's disease. Type 1, the most common, is characterized by decreases in structurally normal vWF and is inherited in an autosomal dominant pattern. Type 2 shows variable qualitative defects based on the specific vWF subtype involved. Type 3 is very rare and is characterized by a severe vWF deficiency, as well as by a significant deficiency of factor VIII. Types 2 and 3 are inherited in an autosomal recessive pattern (Johnsen & Ginsberg, 2010).

Clinical Manifestations and Assessment

The history should include questions related to bleeding following a procedure, such as a dental procedure; need for blood transfusions following surgery or childbirth; history of heavy menses; and easy bruising (James et al., 2009). Patients commonly have nosebleeds and prolonged bleeding from cuts, although they do not have massive soft tissue or joint hemorrhages. Laboratory test results show a normal platelet count but a prolonged bleeding time and a normal or slightly prolonged PTT. These defects are not static, and laboratory test results can vary widely within the same patient over time. As the laboratory values can vary over time, so can the history and extent of bleeding. For example, a careful history of prior bleeding may show little problem with postoperative bleeding on one occasion but significant bleeding from a dental extraction at another time. More important laboratory tests include the vWF ristocetin cofactor activity, vWF antigen, factor VIII, and, for patients with suspected type 2 defects, vWF multimers (James et al., 2009).

Medical Management

The goal of treatment is to replace the deficient protein (e.g., vWF or factor VIII) at the time of spontaneous bleeding or prior to an invasive procedure to minimize postprocedural bleeding. There are two general strategies to meet this goal. The first is administration of a synthetic form of the hormone vasopressin, called desmopressin (DDAVP). Desmopressin causes the release of vWF stored within the endothelium, resulting in a temporary increase in circulating vWF and factor VIII (Johnsen & Ginsberg, 2010). Desmopressin can be administered intranasally or intravenously. With major surgery or invasive procedures, IV administration is preferable. DDAVP is contraindicated in patients with unstable coronary artery disease, because it can induce platelet aggregation and cause a MI. Side effects include headache, facial flushing, tachycardia, hyponatremia, and rarely seizures.

The second strategy is the administration of replacement products such as Humate-P, a commercial concentrate of vWF and factor VIII, and Alphanate, which contains similar amounts of these factors; both require at least once daily dosing (Batlle, Lópes-Fernández, Fraga et al., 2009). Replacement continues for several days to ensure correction of the factor VIII deficiency. Treatment should continue for 4 days following minor surgery, and up to 14 days of treatment may be necessary after major surgery. The dosage and frequency of administration depend on factor VIII levels; doses may need regular adjustment based on trough levels. Antibody (inhibitor) formation is usually seen only in patients with type 3 von Willebrand's disease, when large amounts of replacement products have been administered.

Other agents may be effective in reducing the bleeding. Aminocaproic acid (EACA, Amicar) is useful in managing mild forms of mucosal bleeding. Hormonal contraceptives, such as the levonorgestrel-releasing intrauterine device, have demonstrated efficacy in reducing menorrhagia in women with bleeding disorders (American College of Obstetrics and Gynecology [ACOG], 2009). Platelet transfusions may be useful when significant bleeding is present.

ACQUIRED COAGULATION DISORDERS

The most common causes of acquired coagulation disorders include vitamin K deficiency, liver disease, and DIC, all of which can result in abnormal bleeding.

LIVER DISEASE

With the exception of factor VIII, most blood coagulation factors are synthesized in the liver. Therefore, hepatic dysfunction (due to cirrhosis, tumor, or hepatitis; see Chapter 25) can result in diminished amounts of the factors needed to maintain coagulation and hemostasis. Prolongation of the PT, unless it

is caused by vitamin K deficiency, may indicate severe hepatic dysfunction. Although minor bleeding is common (e.g., ecchymoses), these patients are also at risk for significant bleeding, related especially to trauma or surgery. Transfusion of fresh frozen plasma may be required to replace clotting factors and to prevent or stop bleeding. Patients may also have life-threatening hemorrhage from peptic ulcers or esophageal varices. In these cases, replacement with fresh frozen plasma, PRBCs, and platelets is usually required.

VITAMIN K DEFICIENCY

The synthesis of many coagulation factors depends on vitamin K. Vitamin K deficiency is common in malnourished patients, and some antibiotics decrease the intestinal flora that produce vitamin K, depleting vitamin K stores. Administration of vitamin K (phytonadione [Mephyton]), either orally or as a subcutaneous injection, can correct the deficiency quickly; adequate synthesis of coagulation factors is reflected by normalization of the PT.

COMPLICATIONS OF ANTICOAGULANT THERAPY

Anticoagulants are used in the treatment or prevention of thrombosis. These agents, particularly warfarin or heparin, can cause bleeding. If the PT or PTT is longer than desired, and bleeding has not occurred, the medication can be stopped or the dose decreased. Vitamin K is administered as an antidote for warfarin toxicity. Protamine sulfate is rarely needed for heparin toxicity, because the half-life of heparin is very short. With significant bleeding, fresh frozen plasma is needed to replace the vitamin K–dependent coagulation factors.

DISSEMINATED INTRAVASCULAR COAGULATION

DIC is not a disease but a sign of an underlying condition. DIC may be triggered by sepsis, trauma, cancer, shock, abruptio placentae, toxins, or allergic reactions. The severity of DIC is variable, but it is potentially life-threatening. The mortality rate can exceed 80% of patients who develop severe DIC with ischemic thrombosis and frank hemorrhage. Identification of patients who are at risk for DIC and recognition of the early clinical manifestations of this syndrome can result in earlier medical intervention, which may improve the prognosis. However, the primary prognostic factor is the ability to treat the underlying condition that precipitated DIC.

Pathophysiology

Normal hemostatic mechanisms are altered in DIC, so that a massive amount of tiny clots forms in the microcirculation. Initially, the coagulation time is normal. However, as the platelets and clotting factors are consumed to form the microthrombi, coagulation fails. Thus, the paradoxical result of excessive clotting is bleeding. The clinical manifestations of DIC are reflected in the organs, which are affected either by excessive clot formation (with resultant ischemia to all or part of the organ) or by bleeding. The excessive clotting triggers the fibrinolytic system to release fibrin degradation products, which are potent anticoagulants, furthering the bleeding. The bleeding is characterized by consumption of platelets and clotting factors thus low platelet and fibrinogen levels (due to the consumption of fibrinogen); prolonged PT, PTT, and **thrombin** time are seen; and elevated fibrin degradation products (**D-dimers**) (see Table 20-3 for an overview of laboratory values commonly found in DIC).

Clinical Manifestations and Assessment

Patients with frank DIC may bleed from mucous membranes, venipuncture sites, and the GI and urinary tracts. The bleeding can range from minimal occult internal bleeding to profuse hemorrhage from all orifices. The patient may also develop organ dysfunction, such as renal failure and pulmonary and

TABLE
20-3 Laboratory Values Commonly Found in Disseminated Intravascular Coagulation (DIC)*

Test	Function Evaluated	Normal Range	Changes in DIC
Platelet count	Platelet number	150,000 to 450,000/mm³	↓
Prothrombin time (PT)	Extrinsic pathway	11 to 12.5 sec	↑
Partial thromboplastin time (PTT)	Intrinsic pathway	23 to 35 sec	↑
Thrombin time (TT)	Clot formation	8 to 11 sec	↑
Fibrinogen	Amount available for coagulation	170 to 340 mg/dL	↓
D-dimer	Local fibrinolysis	0 to 250 ng/mL	↑
Fibrin degradation products (FDPs)	Fibrinolysis	0 to 5 µg/mL	↑
Euglobulin clot lysis	Fibrinolytic activity	≥2 hours	≤1 hour

*Because DIC is a dynamic condition, the laboratory values measured will change over time. Therefore, a progressive increase or decrease in a given laboratory value is likely to be more important than the actual value of a test at a single point in time.

TABLE
20-4 Assessing for Thrombosis and Bleeding in Disseminated Intravascular Coagulation (DIC)*

System	Signs and Symptoms of Microvascular Thrombosis	Signs and Symptoms of Microvascular and Frank Bleeding
Integumentary system (skin)	↓ Temperature, sensation; ↑ pain; cyanosis in extremities, nose, earlobes; focal ischemia, superficial gangrene	Petechiae, including periorbital and oral mucosa; bleeding: gums, oozing from wounds, previous injection sites, around catheters (IVs, tracheostomies); epistaxis; diffuse ecchymoses; subcutaneous hemorrhage; joint pain
Circulatory system	↓ Pulses; capillary filling time >3 sec	Tachycardia
Respiratory system	Hypoxia (secondary to clot in lung); dyspnea; chest pain with deep inspiration; ↓ breath sounds over areas of large embolism	High-pitched bronchial breath sounds; tachypnea; ↑ consolidation; signs and symptoms of acute respiratory distress syndrome
Gastrointestinal system	Gastric pain; "heartburn"	Hematemesis (heme⊕† NG output) melena (heme⊕ stools → tarry stools → bright-red blood from rectum) retroperitoneal bleeding (abdomen firm and tender to palpation; distended; ↑ abdominal girth)
Renal system	↓ Urine output; ↑ creatinine, ↑ blood urea nitrogen	Hematuria
Neurologic system	↓ Alertness and orientation; ↓ pupillary reaction; ↓ response to commands; ↓ strength and movement ability	Anxiety; restlessness; ↓ mentation, altered level of consciousness; headache; visual disturbances; conjunctival hemorrhage

*Signs of microvascular thrombosis are the result of an inappropriate activation of the coagulation system, causing thrombotic occlusion of small vessels within all body organs. As the clotting factors and platelets are consumed, signs of microvascular bleeding appear. This bleeding can quickly extend into frank hemorrhage. Treatment must be aimed at the disorder underlying the DIC; otherwise, the stimulus for the syndrome will persist.
†heme⊕, positive for hemoglobin.

multifocal CNS infarctions, as a result of microthromboses, macrothromboses, or hemorrhages.

During the initial process of DIC, the patient may have no new symptoms, the only manifestation being a progressive decrease in the platelet count. As the thrombosis becomes more extensive, the patient exhibits signs and symptoms of thrombosis in the organs involved. Then, as the clotting factors and platelets are consumed to form these thrombi, bleeding occurs. Initially, the bleeding is subtle, but it can develop into frank hemorrhage. Signs and symptoms, which depend on the organs involved, are listed in Table 20-4.

Medical Management

The most important management factor in DIC is treating the underlying cause; until the cause is controlled, the DIC will persist. Correcting the secondary effects of tissue ischemia by improving oxygenation, replacing fluids, correcting electrolyte imbalances, and administering vasopressor medications is also important. If serious hemorrhage occurs, the depleted coagulation factors and platelets may be replaced to reestablish the potential for normal hemostasis and thereby diminish bleeding. Cryoprecipitate is given to replace fibrinogen and factors V and VII; fresh frozen plasma is administered to replace other coagulation factors.

A controversial treatment strategy is to interrupt thrombosis through the use of heparin infusion. Heparin may

inhibit the activation of the coagulation pathway in sepsis, inhibiting microthrombi formation and thereby correcting perfusion of the organs. However, a beneficial effect of heparin on outcomes in patients with DIC has never been demonstrated in controlled trials and may increase the incidence and risk for bleeding in patients with DIC. Heparin is only indicated in patients with clinically evident thromboembolism in a large blood vessel or with evidence of tissue damage secondary to thromboemboli; extreme caution must be used due to the high risk for bleeding (Levi & Seligsohn, 2010).

Other therapies include recombinant activated protein C (APC; drotrecogin alfa [Xigris®]), which is effective in diminishing inflammatory responses on the surface of the vessels, and has anticoagulant properties. APC has been used in the setting of DIC secondary to sepsis and has demonstrated improvement in coagulation abnormalities and a lower incidence of organ failure (Levi & Seligsohn, 2010). However, APC is contraindicated in patients with bleeding and increases the risk for bleeding in patients with low platelet counts (<30,000/mm³) or an international normalized ratio (INR) of more than 3.0. Bleeding is common, can occur at any site, and can be significant. Antithrombin (AT) infusions can also be used for their anticoagulant and anti-inflammatory properties. Bleeding can be significant, particularly when administered in association with heparin.

Nursing Management

Nurses need to be aware of which patients are at risk of DIC. Sepsis and acute promyelocytic leukemia are the most common causes of DIC. Patients need to be assessed thoroughly and frequently for signs and symptoms of thrombi and bleeding and monitored for any progression of these signs. Timely recognition of symptoms and prompt reporting to the medical team can help facilitate early intervention and improve outcomes (see Table 20-4).

In addition, the nurse monitors and manages potential complications. Assessment and interventions should target potential sites of end-organ damage (see Table 20-4). As organs are inadequately perfused because of occlusion by microthrombi, organ function diminishes; the kidneys, lungs, brain, and skin are particularly vulnerable, and renal dysfunction is common. Lack of renal perfusion may result in acute tubular necrosis and renal failure, sometimes requiring dialysis. Placement of a large-bore dialysis catheter is extremely hazardous for this patient population and should be accompanied by adequate platelet and plasma transfusions. Hepatic dysfunction is also relatively common, reflected in altered liver function tests, depleted albumin stores, and diminished synthesis of clotting factors. Respiratory function warrants careful monitoring and aggressive measures to diminish alveolar compromise, such as incentive spirometry. Suctioning (if required) should be performed as gently as possible to diminish the risk for additional bleeding. CNS involvement can be manifested as headache, visual changes, and alteration in level of consciousness. A plan of nursing care for the patient with DIC is available online at http://thePoint.lww.com/Pellico1e.

THROMBOTIC DISORDERS

As in many bleeding disorders, several conditions can alter the balance within the normal hemostatic process and cause excessive thrombosis. Abnormalities that predispose a person to thrombotic events include decreased clotting inhibitors within the circulation (which enhances coagulation), altered hepatic function (which may decrease production of clotting factors or clearance of activated coagulation factors), and lack of fibrinolytic enzymes, and tortuous vessels (which promote platelet aggregation). Thrombosis can be caused by more than one predisposing factor. Several conditions can result from thrombosis, such as MI (see Chapter 14), CVA (brain attack or stroke; see Chapter 47), and peripheral arterial occlusion (see Chapter 18). Several inherited or acquired deficiency conditions, including hyperhomocysteinemia, AT III deficiency, protein C deficiency, APC resistance, factor V Leiden, and protein S deficiency, can predispose a patient to repeated episodes of thrombosis; these are referred to as hypercoagulable states or thrombophilia. Table 20-5 lists these disorders, their abnormal laboratory values, and the need for family testing.

Thrombosis requires anticoagulation therapy. The duration of therapy varies with the location and extent of the thrombosis,

TABLE
20-5 Hypercoagulable States

Disorder	Abnormal Laboratory Value*
Inherited Disorders (Family Testing Necessary)	
Hyperhomocysteinemia	Homocysteine ↑ after methionine load
Antithrombin III (AT III) deficiency	AT III ↓
Protein C deficiency	Protein C activity ↓ (must be measured off warfarin [Coumadin])
Activated protein C (APC) resistance	Must be measured off anticoagulant; <2× prolongation of PTT when APC added. Patients with APC resistance have a smaller increase in clotting time than normal (i.e., the prolongation of clotting time is less than normal).
Factor V Leiden	Positive
Protein S deficiency	Protein S activity ↓; must be measured off warfarin (Coumadin)
Dysfibrinogenemia	↑ thrombin time; ↑ reptilase time; ↓ functional fibrinogen; often requires special fibrinogen assays
Acquired Disorders (Family Testing Unnecessary)	
Anticardiolipin antibody	Positive
Cancer	Varied, depending on disorder
Lupus anticoagulant	Positive
Hyperhomocysteinemia	Homocystine ↑ after methionine load
AT III deficiency	AT III ↓
Paroxysmal nocturnal hemoglobinuria	+ Hamm's test; acid hemolysis
Myeloproliferative disorders	Varied, depending on disorder
Nephrotic syndrome	Varied, depending on disorder
Cancer chemotherapy	Varied, depending on specific agent

*Protein C and protein S are vitamin K–dependent proteins. Warfarin (Coumadin) interferes with the hepatic synthesis of vitamin K-dependent factors, which may decrease levels of protein C or protein S; therefore, protein C and protein S should be measured while the patient is off warfarin.

precipitating events (e.g., trauma, immobilization), and concurrent risk factors (e.g., use of oral contraceptives, tortuous blood vessels, history of thrombotic events). With some conditions, life-long anticoagulant therapy is necessary.

THERAPIES FOR BLOOD DISORDERS

SPLENECTOMY

The surgical removal of the spleen (splenectomy) is sometimes necessary after trauma to the abdomen. Because the spleen is very vascular, severe hemorrhage can result if the

spleen is ruptured. Under such circumstances, splenectomy becomes an emergency procedure.

Splenectomy is also a possible treatment for other hematologic disorders. For example, an enlarged spleen may be the site of excessive destruction of blood cells. If the destruction is life-threatening, surgery may be life-saving. This is the case in autoimmune hemolytic anemia and ITP when these disorders do not respond to more conservative measures, such as corticosteroid therapy. Some patients with grossly enlarged spleens develop severe thrombocytopenia due to the platelets being sequestered in the spleen; splenectomy removes the "trap," and platelet counts may normalize over time.

In general, the mortality rate after splenectomy is low. Laparoscopic splenectomy can be performed in selected patients, with a resultant decrease in postoperative morbidity. The most common complications in patients following splenectomy include infection, thrombosis, and bleeding (Kyaw, Holmes, Toolis et al., 2006; Mesa, Nagorney, Schwager et al., 2006). Although young children are at the highest risk after splenectomy, all age groups are vulnerable to overwhelming, lethal infections and should receive the pneumonia vaccine (Pneumovax) before undergoing splenectomy, if possible.

The patient is instructed to seek prompt medical attention if even relatively minor symptoms of infection occur. Often, patients with high platelet counts have even higher counts after splenectomy (>1 million/mm³), which can predispose them to serious thrombotic or hemorrhagic problems. However, this increase is transient and usually does not warrant additional treatment.

THERAPEUTIC APHERESIS

Apheresis is a Greek word meaning separation. In therapeutic apheresis (or pheresis), blood is taken from the patient and passed through a centrifuge, in which a specific component is separated from the blood and removed. The remaining blood is then returned to the patient. The entire system is closed, so the risk of bacterial contamination is extremely low. When platelets or leukocytes are removed, the decrease in these cells within the circulation is temporary. However, the temporary decrease provides a window of time until suppressive medications (e.g., chemotherapy) can have therapeutic effects. Sometimes plasma is removed rather than blood cells—typically so that specific, abnormal proteins within the plasma are transiently lowered until a long-term therapy can be initiated.

Apheresis is also used to obtain larger amounts of platelets from a donor than can be provided from a single unit of whole blood. A unit of platelets obtained in this way is equivalent to six to eight units of platelets obtained from six to eight separate donors via standard blood donation methods. Platelet donors can have their platelets apheresed as often as every

14 days. Leukocytes can be obtained similarly, typically after the donor has received growth factors (G-CSF, GM-CSF) to stimulate the formation of additional leukocytes and thereby increase the leukocyte count. The use of these growth factors also stimulates the release of stem cells within the circulation. Apheresis is used to harvest these stem cells (typically over a period of several days) for use in PBSCT.

THERAPEUTIC PHLEBOTOMY

Therapeutic phlebotomy is the removal of a certain amount of blood under controlled conditions. Patients with elevated hematocrits (e.g., those with polycythemia vera) or excessive iron absorption (e.g., hemochromatosis) can usually be managed by periodically removing 1 unit (about 500 mL) of whole blood; however, the elderly, small individuals, or women may only be able to tolerate 250 mL (Edwards, 2009). Eventually, this process can produce iron deficiency, leaving the patient unable to produce as many erythrocytes. The actual procedure for therapeutic phlebotomy is similar to that for blood donation (see later discussion).

BLOOD COMPONENT THERAPY

A single unit of whole blood contains 450 mL of blood and 50 mL of an anticoagulant. A unit of whole blood can be processed and dispensed for administration. However, it is more appropriate, economical, and practical to separate that unit of whole blood into its primary components: erythrocytes, platelets, and plasma (leukocytes are rarely used; see later discussion). Because the plasma is removed, a unit of PRBCs is very concentrated (hematocrit approximately 70%). Each component must be processed and stored differently to maximize the longevity of the viable cells and factors within it; each individual blood component has a different storage life. PRBCs are stored at 4°C. With special preservatives, they can be stored safely for up to 42 days before they must be discarded. In contrast, platelets must be stored at room temperature because they cannot withstand cold temperatures, and they last for only 5 days before they must be discarded. To prevent clumping, platelets are gently agitated while stored. Plasma is immediately frozen to maintain the activity of the clotting factors within; it lasts for 1 year if it remains frozen. Alternatively, plasma can be further pooled and processed into blood derivatives, such as albumin, immune globulin, factor VIII, and factor IX. Table 20-6 describes each blood component and how each is commonly used.

Blood transfusion is discussed in detail on page 563.

Special Preparations

Factor VIII concentrate (antihemophilic factor) is a lyophilized, freeze-dried concentrate of pooled fractionated human

TABLE
20-6 Blood and Blood Components Commonly Used in Transfusion Therapy*

	Composition	Indications and Considerations
Whole blood	Cells and plasma, hematocrit about 40%	Volume replacement and oxygen-carrying capacity; usually used only in significant bleeding (>25% blood volume lost)
Packed red blood cells (PRBCs)	RBCs with little plasma (hematocrit about 75%); some platelets and WBCs remain	↑ RBC mass Symptomatic anemia: platelets in the unit are not functional; WBCs in the unit may cause reaction and are not functional
Platelets—random	Platelets (5.5×10^{10} platelets/unit) Plasma; some RBCs, WBCs	Bleeding due to severe ↓ platelets Prevent bleeding when platelets <5,000 to 10,000/mm^3 Survival ↓ in presence of fever, chills, infection Repeated treatment → ↓ survival due to alloimmunization
Platelets—single donor	Platelets (3×10^{11} platelets/unit) 1 unit is equivalent to 6 to 8 units of random platelets	Used for repeated treatment: ↓ alloimmunization risk by limiting exposure to multiple donors
Plasma	Plasma; all coagulation factors Complement	Bleeding in patients with coagulation factor deficiencies; plasmapheresis
Granulocytes	Neutrophils (>1×10^{10}/unit); lymphocytes; some RBCs and platelets	Severe neutropenia in selected patients; controversial
Lymphocytes (white blood cells [WBCs])	Lymphocytes (number varies)	Stimulate graft-versus-disease effect
Cryoprecipitate	Fibrinogen ≥150 mg/bag, AHF (VIII:C) 80 to 110 units/bag, von Willebrand factor; fibronectin	von Willebrand's disease Hypofibrinogenemia Hemophilia A
Antihemophilic factor (AHF)	Factor VIII	Hemophilia A
Factor IX concentrate	Factor IX	Hemophilia B (Christmas disease)
Factor IX complex	Factors II, VII, IX, X	Hereditary factor VII, IX, X deficiency; hemophilia A with factor VII inhibitors
Albumin	Albumin 5%, 25%	Hypoproteinemia; burns; volume expansion by 5% to ↑ blood volume; 25% → ↓ hematocrit
IV gamma globulin	IgG antibodies	Hypogammaglobulinemia (in CLL, recurrent infections); ITP; primary immunodeficiency states
Antithrombin III concentrate (AT III)	AT III (trace amounts of other plasma proteins)	AT III deficiency with or at risk for thrombosis

*The composition of each type of blood component is described, as well as the most common indications for using a given blood component. RBCs, platelets, and fresh frozen plasma are the blood products most commonly used. When transfusing these blood products, it is important to realize that the individual product is always "contaminated" with very small amounts of other blood products (e.g., WBCs mixed in a unit of platelets). This contamination can cause some difficulties, particularly isosensitization, in certain patients.
AHF, antihemophilic factor; CLL, chronic lymphocytic leukemia; ITP, idiopathic thrombocytopenic purpura.

plasma. It is used in treating hemophilia A. Factor IX concentrate (prothrombin complex) is similarly prepared and contains factors II, VII, IX, and X. It is used primarily for treatment of factor IX deficiency (hemophilia B). Factor IX concentrate is also useful in treating congenital factor VII and factor X deficiencies. Recombinant forms of factor VIII, such as Humate-P or Alphanate, are also useful. Because they contain vWF, these agents are used in von Willebrand's disease as well as in hemophilia A, particularly when patients develop acquired factor VIII inhibitors (e.g., antibodies).

Plasma albumin is a large protein molecule that usually stays within vessels and is a major contributor to plasma oncotic pressure. This protein is used to expand the blood volume of patients in hypovolemic shock and, rarely, to increase the concentration of circulating albumin in patients with hypoalbuminemia.

Immunoglobulin is a concentrated solution of the antibody IgG; it contains very little IgA or IgM. It is prepared from large pools of plasma. The IV form (IVIG) is used in various clinical situations to replace inadequate amounts of IgG in patients who are at risk for recurrent bacterial infection (e.g., those with CLL, those receiving BMT or PBSCT). It is also used in certain autoimmune disorders, such as ITP. IVIG, in contrast to all other fractions of human blood, cells, or plasma, can survive being subjected to heating at 60°C (140°F) for 10 hours to free it of the viral contaminants that may be present.

PHARMACOLOGIC ALTERNATIVES TO BLOOD TRANSFUSIONS

Pharmacologic agents that stimulate production of one or more types of blood cells by the marrow are commonly used (Box 20-5).

Researchers continue to seek a blood substitute that is practical and safe (Katz, 2009). Manufacturing artificial blood is problematic, given the myriad functions of blood components. Recent research has focused on the role of blood in oxygen transport or its role as an oxygen carrier and the manufacturing of a suitable RBC substitute. Current artificial RBC products undergoing clinical trials have distinct advantages and disadvantages compared with human RBCs. These products can be rendered essentially sterile, resulting in fewer immunity-related transfusion problems. They require no refrigeration, have approximately 12 times the shelf-life of PRBCs, and require no cross-matching. Their most significant disadvantage is their short half-life: approximately 1 day, versus the normal 120-day lifespan of a normal erythrocyte. Therefore, the usefulness of these products would likely be limited to situations in which the need is short term (e.g., surgery or trauma).

BOX 20-5 Pharmacologic Alternatives to Blood Transfusions

Growth Factors

Recombinant technology has provided a means to produce hematopoietic growth factors necessary for the production of blood cells within the bone marrow. By increasing the body's production of blood cells, transfusions and complications resulting from diminished blood cells (e.g., infection from neutropenia or transfusions) may be avoided. However, the successful use of growth factors requires functional bone marrow.

Erythropoietin

Erythropoietin (epoetin alpha/EPO (e.g., Epogen, Procrit)) is an effective alternative treatment for patients with chronic anemia secondary to diminished levels of erythropoietin, as in chronic renal disease. This medication stimulates erythropoiesis. It also has been used for patients who are anemic from chemotherapy or zidovudine (AZT) therapy and for those who have diseases involving bone marrow suppression, such as myelodysplastic syndrome (MDS). Recent studies have shown that exceeding the recommended Hgb goal of 12 g/dL results in increased risk for cardiovascular events, including stroke and MI. Additionally, use of erythropoietin has been associated with decreased survival in certain types of cancer. EPO has been safely used in the preoperative setting to decrease the need for allogeneic blood transfusions. In this setting, erythropoietin can also enable a patient to donate several units of blood for future use (e.g., preoperative autologous donation). The medication can be administered intravenously or subcutaneously, although plasma levels are better sustained with the subcutaneous route. Side effects are rare, but erythropoietin can cause or exacerbate hypertension. If the anemia is corrected too quickly or is overcorrected, the elevated hematocrit can cause headache, hypertension, and, potentially, seizures. These adverse effects are rare except for patients with renal failure. Serial CBCs should be performed to evaluate the response to the medication. The dose and frequency of administration are titrated to the hematocrit.

Granulocyte-Colony Stimulating Factor (G-CSF)

G-CSF (filgrastim (Neupogen)) is a cytokine that stimulates the proliferation and differentiation of myeloid stem cells; a rapid increase in neutrophils is seen within the circulation. G-CSF is effective in improving transient but severe neutropenia after chemotherapy or in some forms of MDS. It is particularly useful in preventing bacterial infections that would be likely to occur with neutropenia. G-CSF is administered subcutaneously on a daily basis. The primary side effect is bone pain; this probably reflects the increase in hematopoiesis within the marrow. Serial CBCs should be performed to evaluate the response to the medication and to ensure that the rise in white blood cells is not excessive. The effect of G-CSF on myelopoiesis is short; the neutrophil count drops once the medication is stopped.

Granulocyte-Macrophage Colony Stimulating Factor (GM-CSF)

GM-CSF (sargramostim (Leukine)) is a cytokine that is naturally produced by a variety of cells, including monocytes and endothelial cells. It works either directly or synergistically with other growth factors to stimulate myelopoiesis. GM-CSF is not as specific to neutrophils as is G-CSF; thus, an increase in erythroid (RBC) and megakaryocytic (platelet) production may also be seen. GM-CSF serves the same purpose as G-CSF. However, it may have a greater effect on macrophage function and therefore may be more useful against fungal infections, whereas G-CSF may be better used to fight bacterial infections. GM-CSF is also administered subcutaneously. Side effects include bone pain, fevers, and myalgias.

Thrombopoietin

Thrombopoietin (TPO) is a cytokine that is necessary for the proliferation of megakaryocytes and subsequent platelet formation. Unfortunately, clinical studies have not consistently demonstrated the effectiveness of TPO in the setting of chemotherapy-induced thrombocytopenia, but it is effective in facilitating platelet collection via apheresis (Kaushansky & Kipps, 2006). Further research is currently under way in the development of smaller molecular mimics of TPO (Kaushansky & Kipps, 2006).

Hemoglobin-based oxygen carriers, made from animal or human hemoglobin or synthetic materials, are currently being studied as alternatives to blood transfusion. Further study is needed to establish safety and efficacy (Katz, 2009).

Stem cell transplant is covered in Chapter 6.

PROCURING BLOOD AND BLOOD PRODUCTS AND BLOOD TRANSFUSIONS

BLOOD DONATION

To protect both the donor and the recipients, all prospective donors are examined and interviewed before they are allowed to donate their blood. The intent of the interview is to assess the general health status of the donor and to identify risk factors that might harm a recipient of the donor's blood. Donors should be in good health and meet a number of specific criteria (Box 20-6).

Potential donors should be asked whether they have consumed any aspirin or aspirin-containing medications within the past 3 days. Although aspirin use does not render the donor ineligible, the platelets obtained would be dysfunctional and therefore not useful; aspirin usage within 48 to 72 hours contraindicates platelet donation. Aspirin does not affect the erythrocytes or plasma obtained from the donor.

Directed Donation

At times, friends and family of a patient wish to donate blood for that person. These blood donations are termed directed donations. These donations are not any safer than those provided by random donors, because directed donors may not be as willing to identify themselves as having a history of any of the risk factors that disqualify a person from donating blood.

Standard Donation

Phlebotomy consists of venipuncture and blood withdrawal. Standard precautions are used. Donors are placed in a semi-recumbent position and venipuncture with a large bore IV is performed. Withdrawal of 450 mL of blood usually takes less than 15 minutes. After the needle is removed, donors are asked to hold the involved arm straight up, and firm pressure is applied with sterile gauze for 2 to 3 minutes or until bleeding stops. A firm bandage is then applied. The donor remains recumbent until he or she feels able to sit up, usually within a few minutes.

The donor is instructed to leave the dressing on and to avoid heavy lifting for several hours, to avoid smoking for 1 hour, to avoid drinking alcoholic beverages for 3 hours, to increase fluid intake for 2 days, and to eat healthy meals for 2 weeks. Specimens from this donated blood are tested to detect infections and to identify the specific blood type (see later discussion).

Autologous Donation

A patient's own blood may be collected for future transfusion; this method is useful for many elective surgeries in which the potential need for transfusion is high (e.g., orthopedic surgery). Preoperative donations are ideally collected 4 to 6 weeks before surgery. Iron supplements are prescribed

---

BOX 20-6　Eligibility Requirements for Blood Donation

All donors are expected to meet the following minimal requirements:
- Be at least 17 years old in most states
- Body weight should exceed 50 kg (110 pounds) for a standard 450-mL donation.
- The oral temperature should not exceed 37.5°C (99.6°F) with vital signs within normal limits.
- The hemoglobin level should be at least 12.5 g/dL.

Contraindications to Blood Donation
- A history of viral hepatitis at any time in the past
- A history of receiving a blood transfusion or an infusion of any blood derivative (other than serum albumin) within 12 months
- A history of untreated syphilis or malaria, because these diseases can be transmitted by transfusion even years later
- A history or evidence of IV drug abuse
- A history of possible exposure to HIV

- A history of recent tattoo within the last 12 months, because of the risk of blood-borne infections (e.g., hepatitis, HIV)
- A recent history of asthma, urticaria, or allergy to medications, because hypersensitivity can be transferred passively to the recipient
- Pregnancy, because of the nutritional demands of pregnancy on the mother
- A history of tooth extraction or oral surgery within 72 hours, because such procedures are frequently associated with transient bacteremia
- Recent immunizations, because of the risk of transmitting live organisms (2-week waiting period for live, attenuated organisms; 1 month for rubella, mumps, varicella; 1 year for rabies)
- A diagnosis of cancer, hemochromatosis, sickle cell disease, or active skin infections
- A history of whole blood donation within the past 56 days

American Red Cross (2009).

during this period to prevent depletion of iron stores. Occasionally, erythropoietin (epoetin-alfa [Epogen, Procrit]) is given to stimulate erythropoiesis, so that the donor's hematocrit remains high enough to be eligible for donation. Typically, 1 unit of blood is drawn each week; the number of units obtained varies with the type of surgical procedure to be performed (i.e., the amount of blood anticipated to be transfused). Phlebotomies are not performed within 72 hours of surgery.

The primary advantage of autologous transfusions is the prevention of viral infections from another person's blood. It is the policy of the American Red Cross that autologous blood be transfused only to the donor. If the blood is not required, it can be frozen until the donor needs it in the future (for up to 10 years). The blood is never returned to the general donor supply of blood products to be used by another person.

The disadvantage of autologous donation is that it may be performed even when the likelihood that the anticipated procedure will necessitate a transfusion is small. Needless autologous donation is expensive, takes time, and uses resources inappropriately. Furthermore, although autologous transfusion can eliminate the risk of viral contamination, the risk for bacterial contamination is the same as that in transfusion from random donors.

Contraindications to donation of blood for autologous transfusion are acute infection, severely debilitating chronic disease, hemoglobin level of less than 12.5 g/dL, hematocrit less than 38%, unstable angina, and acute cardiovascular or cerebrovascular disease.

Intraoperative Blood Salvage

This transfusion method provides replacement for patients who cannot donate before surgery and for those undergoing vascular, orthopedic, or thoracic surgery. During a surgical procedure, blood lost into a sterile cavity (e.g., hip joint) is suctioned into a cell-saver machine. The whole blood or PRBCs are washed, often with saline solution, filtered, and then returned to the patient as an IV infusion. The goal of intraoperative salvage is to reduce the need for allogeneic blood transfusions. Studies have demonstrated that intraoperative blood salvage safely and effectively decreases the need for transfusions of donated blood without causing adverse outcomes (Carless, Henry, Moxey et al., 2010). The intraoperative blood salvage is returned to the patient when the bag is full or within 4 hours of the start of collection to prevent bacterial overgrowth (Cushing & Ness, 2008).

Hemodilution

This transfusion method may be initiated before or after induction of anesthesia. About 1 to 2 units of blood are removed from the patient through a venous or arterial line and simultaneously replaced with a colloid or crystalloid solution. The blood obtained is then reinfused after surgery.

The advantage of this method is that the patient loses fewer erythrocytes during surgery, because the added IV solutions dilute the concentration of erythrocytes and lower the hematocrit. However, patients who are at risk of myocardial injury should not be further stressed by hemodilution.

Complications of Blood Donation

The overall incidence of complications secondary to blood donation is very low. The most common complications include bleeding secondary to needle injury (such as hematoma formation or inadvertent arterial puncture) and vasovagal reactions (Sorenson, Johnsen, & Jorgensen, 2007). Excessive bleeding at the donor's venipuncture site is sometimes caused by a bleeding disorder in the donor but more often results from a technique error: laceration of the vein, excessive tourniquet pressure, or failure to apply enough pressure after the needle is withdrawn. A donor who appears pale or complains of faintness should immediately lie down or sit with the head lowered below the knees. He or she should be observed for another 30 minutes.

BLOOD PROCESSING

Samples of the unit of blood are always taken immediately after donation, so that the blood can be typed and tested. Each donation is tested for antibodies to HIV 1 and 2, hepatitis B core antibody (anti-HBc), hepatitis C virus (HCV), West Nile virus, and human T-cell lymphotropic virus, type I (anti-HTLV-I/II). The blood is also tested for hepatitis B surface antigen (HbsAG) and for syphilis. Negative reactions are required for the blood to be used, and each unit of blood is labeled to certify the results. New testing methods have increased the sensitivity and therefore increased the safety of blood transfusions (Gorgas, 2009). Blood is also screened for CMV; if it tests positive for CMV, it can still be used, except in recipients who are negative for CMV and who are immunocompromised (e.g., BMT or PBSCT recipients).

Equally important to viral testing is accurate determination of the blood type. More than 200 antigens have been identified on the surface of RBC membranes. Of these, the most important for safe transfusion are the ABO and Rh systems. The ABO system identifies which sugars are present on the membrane of a person's erythrocytes: A, B, both A and B, or neither A nor B (type O). To prevent a significant reaction, the same type of PRBCs should be transfused. In an emergency situation in which the patient's blood type is not known, type O blood may be safely transfused.

The Rh antigen (also called D) is present on the surface of erythrocytes in 85% of the population (Rh-positive). Those who lack the D antigen are called Rh-negative. PRBCs are routinely tested for the D antigen as well as ABO. Patients should receive PRBCs with a compatible Rh type.

The majority of transfusion reactions (other than those due to procedural error) are due to the presence of donor leukocytes within the blood component unit (PRBCs or platelets); the recipient may form antibodies to the antigens present on these leukocytes. PRBC components typically have 1 to 3 × 10^9 leukocytes remaining in each unit. Leukocytes from the blood product are frequently filtered to diminish the likelihood of developing reactions and refractoriness to transfusions, particularly in patients who have chronic transfusion needs. Filtration can occur at the time the unit is collected from the donor and processed, which achieves better results but is more expensive, or at the time the blood component is transfused by attaching a leukocyte filter to the blood administration tubing. Many centers advocate routinely using leukopoor filtered blood components for people who have or are likely to develop chronic transfusion requirements.

When a patient is extremely immunocompromised, as in the case of bone marrow or stem cell transplant, any donor lymphocytes must be removed from the blood components. In this situation, the blood component is exposed to low amounts of radiation (25 Gy) that kill any lymphocytes within the blood component. Irradiated blood products are highly effective in preventing transfusion-associated GVHD, which is fatal in most cases. Irradiated blood products have a shorter shelf life.

> **NURSING ALERT**
> *It can be difficult to cross-match blood when antibodies are present. If imperfectly cross-matched RBCs must be transfused, the nurse should begin the infusion very slowly (10 to 15 mL over 20 to 30 minutes) and monitor the patient very closely for signs and symptoms of a hemolytic transfusion reaction.*

TRANSFUSION

Administration of blood and blood components requires knowledge of correct administration techniques and possible complications. It is very important to be familiar with the agency's policies and procedures for transfusion therapy.

Setting

Although most blood transfusions are performed in the acute care setting, patients with chronic transfusion requirements often can receive transfusions in other settings, including free-standing infusion centers, ambulatory care clinics, physicians' offices, and occasionally even patients' homes (Benson, 2006). Typically, patients who need chronic transfusions but are otherwise stable physically are appropriate candidates for outpatient therapy. Verification and administration of the blood product are performed as in a hospital setting. Although most blood products can be transfused in the outpatient setting, the home is typically limited to the

transfusion of PRBCs and factor components (e.g., factor VIII for patients with hemophilia) (Benson, 2006).

Method

Transfusing blood components are presented in Box 20-7.

Nursing Management

Nursing responsibilities include pretransfusion and posttransfusion assessment.

Pretransfusion Assessment

Patient history is an important component of the pretransfusion assessment to determine the history of previous transfusions as well as previous reactions to transfusion. The history should include the type of reaction, its manifestations, the interventions required, and whether any preventive interventions were used in subsequent transfusions. It is important to assess the number of pregnancies a woman has had, because a high number can increase her risk for reaction due to antibodies developed from exposure to fetal circulation. Patients with blood disorders such as sickle cell anemia or CLL, and patients who have received a stem cell transplant may also be at increased risk for transfusion reactions based on the number of previous transfusions. Other concurrent health problems should be noted, with careful attention to cardiac (particularly congestive heart failure with a decreased left ventricular ejection fraction), pulmonary, and vascular disease.

A systematic physical assessment and measurement of baseline vital signs are important before transfusing any blood product. The respiratory system should be assessed, including careful auscultation of the lungs and the patient's use of accessory muscles. Cardiac system assessment should include careful inspection for any edema as well as other signs of cardiac failure (e.g., jugular venous distention). The skin should be observed for rashes, petechiae, and ecchymoses. The sclera should be examined for icterus. In the event of a transfusion reaction, a comparison of findings can help differentiate between types of reactions.

> **NURSING ALERT**
> *To evaluate a patient's response to therapy, the nurse is aware that when administering PRBCs it is expected that one unit of PRBCs will raise the hemoglobin by 1 g and HCT by 3%, if the patient is not bleeding or hemolyzing. If administering platelets (which consists of 4 to 6 pooled platelets from random donors [random donor platelets or RDP]), the count should increase by approximately 7,000 to 10,000/mm³ for each RDP given, or 30,000 to 60,000/ mm³ for each single donor platelets (SDP) given (American Red Cross [ARC], 2007).*

Providing Patient Teaching

Reviewing the signs and symptoms of a transfusion reaction is crucial for patients who have not received a transfusion

Transfusion of Packed Red Blood Cells (PRBCs)

Preprocedure
- Confirm that the transfusion has been prescribed.
- Check that patient's blood has been typed and cross-matched.
- Verify that patient has been provided informed consent per institution or agency policy.
- Explain the procedure to the patient. Instruct patient in signs and symptoms of transfusion reaction (itching, hives, swelling, shortness of breath, fever, chills).
- Take patient's temperature, pulse, respiration, and blood pressure to establish a baseline for comparing vital signs during transfusion.
- Perform hand hygiene and wear gloves in accordance with Standard Precautions.
- Use a 20-gauge or larger needle for insertion in a large vein. Use special tubing that contains a blood filter to screen out fibrin clots and other particulate matter. Do not vent the blood container.

Procedure
- Obtain the PRBCs from the blood bank *after* the IV line is started and vital signs are assessed. (Institution policy may limit release to only 1 unit at a time.)
- Double-check the labels with another nurse or physician to make sure that the ABO group and Rh type agree with the compatibility record. Check to see that the number and type on the donor blood label and on the patient's chart are correct. Check the patient's identification by using two forms of identification (can include the patient's name, date of birth, and medical record number) comparing the blood product label to the patient. Also ask the patient to confirm his or her name.
- Check the blood for gas bubbles and any unusual color or cloudiness. (Gas bubbles may indicate bacterial growth. Abnormal color or cloudiness may be a sign of hemolysis.)
- Make sure PRBC transfusion is initiated within 30 minutes after removal of the PRBCs from the blood bank refrigerator.
- For first 15 minutes, run the transfusion slowly—no faster than 5 mL/min. Observe the patient carefully for adverse effects. If no adverse effects occur during the first 15 minutes increase the flow rate unless the patient is at high risk for circulatory overload.
- Monitor closely for 15 to 30 minutes to detect signs of reaction. Monitor vital signs at regular intervals per institution or agency policy; compare results with baseline measurements. Increase frequency of measurements based on patient's condition. Observe the patient frequently throughout the transfusion for any signs of adverse reaction, including restlessness, hives, nausea, vomiting, torso or back pain, shortness of breath, flushing, hematuria, fever, or chills. Should any adverse reaction occur, stop infusion immediately, notify physician, and follow the agency's transfusion reaction standard.
- Note that administration time does not exceed 4 hours because of the increased risk for bacterial proliferation.
- Be alert for signs of adverse reactions: circulatory overload, sepsis, febrile reaction, allergic reaction, and acute hemolytic reaction.
- Change blood tubing after every 2 units transfused, to decrease chance of bacterial contamination.

Postprocedure
- Obtain vital signs and compare with baseline measurements.
- Dispose of used materials properly.
- Document procedure in patient's medical record, including patient assessment findings and tolerance to procedure.
- Monitor patient for response to and effectiveness of the procedure.

Note: Never add medications to blood or blood products; if blood is too thick to run freely, normal saline may be added to the unit. If blood must be warmed, use an in-line blood warmer with a temperature monitoring system.

Note: Fresh frozen platelets (FFP) requires ABO but not Rh compatibility. Platelets are not typically cross-matched for ABO compatibility. Never add medications to blood or blood products. Both platelets and FFP can be infused as rapidly as the patient can tolerate, based on fluid status and cardiac function.

---

before. Even for patients who have received prior transfusions, a brief review of the signs and symptoms of transfusion reactions is essential. Signs and symptoms of a reaction include fever, chills, itching, hives, respiratory distress, low back pain, nausea, pain at the IV site, or anything "unusual." Although a thorough review is very important, it is also important to reassure the patient that the blood is carefully tested against the patient's own blood (cross-matched) to diminish the likelihood of any adverse reaction. Such assurance can be extremely beneficial in allaying anxiety.

Monitoring and Managing Potential Complications

Any patient who receives a blood transfusion may develop complications from that transfusion. When explaining the reasons for the transfusion, it is important to include the risks and benefits and what to expect during and after the transfusion. Patients must be informed that the supply of blood is not completely risk-free, although it has been tested carefully (Box 20-8). Nursing management is directed toward preventing complications, promptly recognizing complications if they develop, and promptly initiating measures to

BOX 20-8 **Diseases Transmitted by Blood Transfusion**

Hepatitis (Viral Hepatitis B, C)
- Greater risk from pooled blood products and blood of paid donors than from volunteer donors
- Screening test detects most hepatitis B and C
- Transmittal risk estimated at 1:10,000

AIDS (HIV and HTLV)
- Donated blood screened for antibodies to HIV
- Transmittal risk estimated at 1:670,000
- People with high-risk behaviors (multiple sex partners, anal sex, IV/injection drug use) and people with signs and symptoms that suggest AIDS should not donate blood

Cytomegalovirus (CMV)
- Transmittal risk greater for premature newborns with CMV antibody-negative mothers and for immunocompromised recipients who are CMV-negative (e.g., those with acute leukemia, organ or tissue transplant recipients).
- Blood products rendered "leukocyte-reduced" help reduce transmission of virus.

Graft-Versus-Host Disease (GVHD)
- Occurs only in severely immunocompromised recipients (e.g., leukemia, bone marrow and stem cell transplantation).
- Transfused lymphocytes engraft in recipient and attack host lymphocytes or body tissues; signs and symptoms are fever, diffuse reddened skin rash, nausea, vomiting, diarrhea.
- Preventive measures include irradiating blood products to inactivate donor lymphocytes (no known radiation risks to transfusion recipient) and processing donor blood with leukocyte reduction filters.

Creutzfeldt–Jakob Disease (CJD)
- Rare, fatal disease causing irreversible brain damage
- No evidence of transmittal by transfusion, but hemophiliacs and others are concerned that transmittal is possible
- All blood donors must be screened for positive family history of CJD.
- Potential donors who spent 6 months or more in the United Kingdom (or Europe) from 1980 to 1996 cannot donate blood; blood products from a donor who develops CJD are recalled.

control complications. The following sections describe the most common or potentially severe transfusion-related complications. Table 20-7 summarizes potential long-term complications.

Febrile Nonhemolytic Reaction
A febrile nonhemolytic transfusion reaction (FNHTR) is defined by a 1°C increase in temperature, into the febrile range, during or shortly following a transfusion. An FNHTR is caused by antibodies to donor leukocytes that remain in the unit of blood or blood component; it is the most common type of transfusion reaction, accounting for more than 90% of reactions. It occurs more frequently in patients who have had previous transfusions (exposure to multiple antigens from previous blood products) and in Rh-negative women who have borne Rh-positive children (exposure to an Rh-positive fetus raises antibody levels in the mother). These reactions occur in 1% of PRBC transfusions and 20% of platelet transfusions. Rates have declined since the standardization of leukocyte reduction, which significantly decreases the number of leukocytes in a transfused product, thus decreasing the risk of an antibody-antigen reaction (Hendrickson & Hillyer, 2009). More than 10% of patients with chronic transfusion requirements develop this type of reaction.

The diagnosis of a febrile nonhemolytic reaction is made by excluding other potential causes, such as a hemolytic reaction, sepsis, or bacterial contamination of the blood product. The signs and symptoms of a febrile nonhemolytic transfusion reaction are chills (minimal to severe) followed by fever. The fever typically begins within 2 hours after the transfusion is begun. Although the reaction is not life-threatening, the fever, and particularly the chills and muscle stiffness, can be frightening to the patient.

This reaction can be diminished, even prevented, by further depleting the blood component of donor leukocyte through filtration. Antipyretics can be given to prevent fever, but routine premedication is not advised because it can mask the beginning of a more serious transfusion reaction.

Acute Hemolytic Reaction
The most dangerous, and potentially life-threatening, type of transfusion reaction occurs when the donor blood is incompatible with that of the recipient. Antibodies already present in the recipient's plasma rapidly combine with antigens on donor erythrocytes, and the erythrocytes are hemolyzed (destroyed) in the circulation (intravascular hemolysis). The most rapid hemolysis occurs in ABO incompatibility. This reaction can occur after transfusion of as little as 10 mL of PRBCs. Rh incompatibility often causes a less severe reaction. The most common causes of acute hemolytic reaction are errors in blood component labeling and patient misidentification that result in the administration of an ABO-incompatible transfusion.

Symptoms consist of fever, chills, low back pain, nausea, chest tightness, dyspnea, hypotension, hematuria, oliguria, bleeding, and anxiety. As the erythrocytes are destroyed, the hemoglobin is released from the cells and excreted by the kidneys; therefore, hemoglobin appears in the urine (hemoglobinuria) (Lerner, Refaai, & Blumberg, 2010). Hypotension, bronchospasm, and vascular collapse may result. Diminished renal perfusion results in acute renal failure, and DIC may also occur.

The reaction must be recognized promptly and the transfusion discontinued immediately. Blood and urine

TABLE
20-7 Common Complications Resulting From Long-Term Packed Red Blood Cell (PRBC) Transfusion Therapy*

	Manifestation	Management
Infection	Hepatitis (B,C)	May immunize against hepatitis B; give alpha-interferon for hepatitis C; monitor hepatic function
	Cytomegalovirus (CMV)	WBC filters to protect against CMV
Iron overload	Heart failure	Prevent by chelation therapy
	Endocrine failure (diabetes, hypothyroidism, hypoparathyroidism, hypogonadism)	
Transfusion reaction	Sensitization	Diminish by RBC phenotyping, using WBC-filtered, leukocyte reduced products
	Febrile reactions	Diminish by using WBC-filtered, leukocyte reduced products

*Patients with long-term transfusion therapy requirements are at risk not only for the transfusion reactions discussed in the text but also for the complications noted above. In many cases, the use of WBC-filtered (e.g., leukocyte-poor) blood products is standard for patients who receive long-term PRBC transfusion therapy. Blood product irradiation, which more effectively reduces the leukocytes in the product, is reserved for patients at highest risk for infection, alloimmunization, and graft versus host disease. An aggressive chelation program initiated early in the course of therapy can prevent problems with iron overload.
PRBC, packed RBCs; WBC, white blood cell; RBC, red blood cell.

specimens must be obtained and analyzed for evidence of hemolysis. Treatment goals include maintaining blood volume and renal perfusion and preventing and managing DIC. Acute hemolytic transfusion reactions are preventable. Meticulous attention to detail in labeling blood samples and blood components and accurately identifying the recipient cannot be overemphasized.

Delayed Hemolytic Reaction

Delayed hemolytic reactions usually occur within 14 days after transfusion, when the level of antibody has been increased to the extent that a reaction can occur. The hemolysis of the erythrocytes is extravascular via the RES and occurs gradually.

Signs and symptoms of a delayed hemolytic reaction are fever, anemia, increased bilirubin level, decreased or absent haptoglobin, and possibly jaundice. Rarely is there hemoglobinuria. Generally, these reactions are not dangerous, but it is useful to recognize them, because subsequent transfusions with blood products containing these antibodies may cause a more severe hemolytic reaction. However, recognition is also difficult, because the patient may not be in a health care setting to be tested for this reaction, and even if the patient is hospitalized, the reaction may be too mild to be recognized clinically. Because the amount of antibody present can be too low to detect, it is difficult to prevent delayed hemolytic reactions. Fortunately, the reaction is usually mild and requires no intervention.

Allergic Reaction

Allergic reactions occur in 1% to 3% of transfusions. An allergic reaction is marked by the development of urticaria (hives) or generalized itching during a transfusion (Hendrickson & Hillyer, 2009). The cause of these reactions is thought to be a sensitivity reaction to a plasma protein within the blood component being transfused. Symptoms of an allergic reaction are urticaria, itching, and flushing. The reactions are usually mild and respond to antihistamines. If the symptoms resolve after administration of an antihistamine (e.g., diphenhydramine [Benadryl]), the transfusion may be resumed. Rarely, the allergic reaction is severe, with bronchospasm, laryngeal edema, and shock. These reactions are managed with epinephrine, corticosteroids, and pressor support, if necessary.

Giving the patient antihistamines before the transfusion may prevent future reactions. For severe reactions, future blood components are washed to remove any remaining plasma proteins. Leukocyte filters are not useful to prevent such reactions, because the offending plasma proteins can pass through the filter.

Circulatory Overload

If too much blood is infused too quickly, hypervolemia can occur. This condition can be aggravated in patients who already have increased circulatory volume (e.g., those with heart failure). PRBCs are safer to use than whole blood. If the administration rate is sufficiently slow, circulatory overload may be prevented. For patients who are at risk of, or already in, circulatory overload, diuretics are administered after the transfusion or between units of PRBCs. Patients receiving fresh frozen plasma or even platelets may also develop circulatory overload. The infusion rate of these blood components must also be titrated to the patient's tolerance.

Signs of circulatory overload include dyspnea, orthopnea, tachycardia, and sudden anxiety. Jugular vein distention, crackles at the base of the lungs, and an increase in blood pressure can also occur. If the transfusion is continued, pulmonary edema can develop, as manifested by severe dyspnea and coughing of pink, frothy sputum.

If fluid overload is mild, the transfusion can often be continued after slowing the rate of infusion and administering diuretics. However, if the overload is severe, the patient is placed in an upright position with the feet in a dependent position, the transfusion is discontinued, and the provider is notified. The IV line is kept patent with a very slow infusion of normal saline solution or a saline or heparin lock device to maintain access to the vein in case IV medications are necessary. Oxygen and morphine may be needed to treat severe dyspnea.

Bacterial Contamination

The incidence of bacterial contamination of blood components is very low; however, administration of contaminated products puts the patient at great risk. Gram-negative bacteria, including *Pseudomonas*, *Yersinia*, *Enterobacter*, are the most common organism found in contaminated RBC products (Wu, Mantha, & Snyder, 2009). Contamination can occur at any point during procurement or processing but is usually due to organisms on the donor's skin (Wu et al., 2009). Many bacteria cannot survive in the cold temperatures used to store PRBCs, but some organisms can survive cold temperatures. Platelets are at greater risk of contamination because they are stored at room temperature. Since 2004, blood centers have developed rapid methods of culturing the platelet unit to decrease the risk of using a contaminated platelet unit for transfusion. Despite bacterial testing, this complication has not been eradicated, thus mandating that nurses remain vigilant for this complication.

Preventive measures include meticulous care in the procurement and processing of blood components. When PRBCs or whole blood is transfused, it should be administered within a 4-hour period, because warm room temperatures promote bacterial growth. A contaminated unit of blood product may appear normal, or it may have an abnormal color.

The signs of bacterial contamination are fever, chills, and hypotension, which most commonly occur during the transfusion. Occasionally, the signs of a reaction may occur hours after the transfusion is complete. If the condition is not recognized and treated immediately with fluids and broad-spectrum antibiotics, shock can occur. While these reactions are rare, they can be fatal (Wu et al., 2009). The following steps are taken to determine the type and severity of the reaction:

- Stop the transfusion. Maintain the IV line with normal saline solution through new IV tubing, administered at a slow rate.
- Assess the patient carefully. Compare the vital signs with baseline. Assess the patient's respiratory status carefully. Note the presence of adventitious breath sounds, use of accessory muscles, extent of dyspnea, and changes in mental status, including anxiety and confusion, and changes in oxygen saturation. Note any chills, diaphoresis, jugular vein distention, and reports of back pain or urticaria.
- Notify the physician of the assessment findings, and implement any treatments prescribed. Continue to monitor the patient's vital signs and respiratory, cardiovascular, and renal status.
- Notify the blood bank that a suspected transfusion reaction has occurred.
- Send the blood container and tubing to the blood bank for repeat typing and culture. The identifying tags and numbers are verified.

If a hemolytic transfusion reaction or bacterial infection is suspected, the nurse does the following:

- Obtain appropriate blood specimens from the patient (this usually includes blood cultures, a CBC and a type and screen).
- Collect a urine sample as soon as possible for a hemoglobin determination.
- Document the reaction according to the institution's policy.

Chapter Review

Critical Thinking Exercises

1. You are working in a hematology-oncology clinic. The laboratory reports a critical laboratory result for one of your patients with possible acute leukemia: the leukocyte count is 1,200/mm³ with 10% neutrophils. What other laboratory results would be important to review or consider? The patient is also anemic (hemoglobin 8.2 mg/dL) and platelets are 30,000/mm³. What observations will you include in your assessment of this patient? Determine the extent to which this patient is neutropenic. What medical treatments would you anticipate?

How would you educate the patient about neutropenia and bleeding precautions? What information do you need to obtain about the patient's home setting that will assist you in determining the patient's risk of developing an infection at home?

2. You are caring for a man with a chronic transfusion requirement (typically 2 to 3 units of PRBCs each month). He asks you how he should modify his diet so that "I don't need so much blood." How would you respond? What role do iron supplements play in patients with chronic transfusion needs? How would you assess this patient for iron overload?

3. You are caring for a patient who is septic and is now receiving a transfusion of 2 units of PRBCs. The patient's temperature spikes to 101.3°F (38.5°C) after half of the second unit has been transfused. What are the possible causes of the fever? What are the appropriate nursing interventions?

4. You are caring for a patient with acute leukemia and sepsis who has a declining platelet count of 10,000/mm³. On assessment, you observe oozing blood from the Hickman catheter site, petechiae to the upper and lower extremities, and epistaxis. What are the potential causes of this patient's bleeding? What other lab results would you assess? What further assessments would you perform? What nursing interventions would you implement? What medical interventions would you anticipate?

NCLEX-Style Review Questions

1. A patient's 18-year-old son would like to donate blood. The nurse educates him regarding eligibility requirements for blood donation. Which of the following statements demonstrates that he does not understand the education provided?
   A. "I am so glad that I am old enough to donate."
   B. "Because I just got a tattoo a week ago, I am unable to donate."
   C. "Because I live with a friend with HIV, I cannot donate."
   D. "Because my girlfriend has hepatitis, and we are sexually active, I cannot donate."

2. The nurse is explaining the potential signs and symptoms of a transfusion reaction to a patient who is receiving his first blood transfusion. The nurse explains that she will do which of the following to ensure safe blood product administration? Select all that apply.
   A. Check ABO compatibility by comparing the blood product label to the patient's medical record.
   B. Use two patient identifiers, such as the patient's date of birth and name to verify the blood product.
   C. Administer the blood product slowly for the first 15 minutes.

D. Administer acetaminophen and diphenhydramine, which are standard premedications used in all transfused patients.

3. Mrs. Jones is being treated for sepsis. On the second day caring for her, she experiences epistaxis and persistent bleeding from a venipuncture site. The nurse suspects DIC. Which of the following lab results supports the nurse's suspicion?
   A. Increased fibrinogen, decreased PTT, decreased platelets
   B. Decreased fibrinogen, increased PTT, increased platelets
   C. Decreased fibrinogen, increased PTT, decreased platelets
   D. Increased fibrinogen, increased PTT, increased platelets

4. The nurse provides patient education related to the management of iron deficiency anemia. Which of the following statements made by the patient signifies understanding of the education provided?
   A. "I should take my iron pills with a glass of orange juice."
   B. "I should take my iron pills with breakfast to decrease stomach upset."
   C. "Iron pills often cause constipation, so I should decrease my fluid and fiber intake."
   D. "I will only need to take these pills for a few days and then my problem will be fixed."

5. The nurse is caring for a patient diagnosed with ALL receiving initial treatment. The patient has been complaining of a dry cough. She also has diminished breath sounds upon auscultation. Which of the following should the nurse monitor as priority with regards to potential complications in this patient?
   A. Hemoglobin
   B. Absolute neutrophil count (ANC)
   C. Hematocrit
   D. Urine

Try these additional resources to enhance your learning and understanding of this chapter:
- thePoint online resource available at **http://thepoint.lww.com/Pellico1e**
- *Handbook for Focus on Adult Health: Medical-Surgical Nursing*
- *Study Guide for Focus on Adult Health: Medical-Surgical Nursing*

References and Selected Readings

References and selected readings associated with this chapter can be found on the website that accompanies the book. Visit http://thepoint.lww.com/Pellico1e to access the references and other additional resources associated with this chapter.

Problems Related to Digestive, Gastrointestinal, and Metabolic Function

A 55-YEAR-OLD woman is undergoing bariatric surgery to treat morbid obesity. She is 120 pounds over her ideal body weight. The patient also has comorbidities of diabetes and hypertension.

➡ Discuss patient selection for bariatric surgery.
➡ What lifestyles changes might the patient expect?
➡ What complications should the patient be aware of regarding the surgical procedure?

ROSE A. HARDING

Nursing Assessment: Digestive, Gastrointestinal, and Metabolic Function

After reading this chapter, you will be able to:

1. Describe the anatomy and physiology of the gastrointestinal (GI) tract.

2. Identify the metabolic functions of the liver.

3. Discuss important physical assessment findings of the GI tract.

4. Identify the assessment parameters used to determine the status of the upper and lower GI tract.

The gastrointestinal (GI) system performs the functions of ingestion, digestion, and elimination. Liver function is complex. An understanding of the structure and function of the biliary tract and pancreas is essential to providing clinical care. Interruption of any of these functions can quickly affect the patient nutritionally and cause myriad fluid, electrolyte, and acid–base imbalances. When performing the GI assessment, the nurse must remember that the majority of people have preexisting problems and that these problems can be exacerbated or new conditions can develop when illness in other systems occurs.

ANATOMIC AND PHYSIOLOGIC OVERVIEW OF THE DIGESTIVE SYSTEM

Anatomy of the Gastrointestinal Tract

The GI tract is a 23- to 26-foot-long (7 m to 7.9 m) pathway that extends from the **mouth** to the esophagus, stomach, small and large intestines, and rectum, to the terminal structure, the **anus** (Fig. 21-1). The **esophagus** is located in the mediastinum, anterior to the spine and posterior to the trachea and heart. This hollow muscular tube, which is approximately 10 inches (25 cm) long, passes through the diaphragm at an opening called the *diaphragmatic hiatus.*

The remaining portion of the GI tract is located within the peritoneal cavity. The **stomach** is situated in the left upper portion of the abdomen under the left lobe of the liver and the diaphragm, overlaying most of the pancreas (see Fig. 21-1). A hollow muscular organ with a capacity of approximately 1,500 mL, the stomach stores food during eating, secretes digestive fluids, and propels the partially digested food into the small intestine. The gastroesophageal junction is the inlet to the stomach. The stomach has four anatomic regions: the cardia (entrance), fundus, body, and pylorus (outlet). Circular smooth muscle in the wall of the pylorus forms the pyloric sphincter and controls the opening between the stomach and the small intestine.

The **small intestine** is the longest segment of the GI tract, accounting for about two-thirds of the total length. It folds back and forth on itself, providing approximately 7,000 cm of surface area for secretion and **absorption**, the process by which nutrients enter the bloodstream through

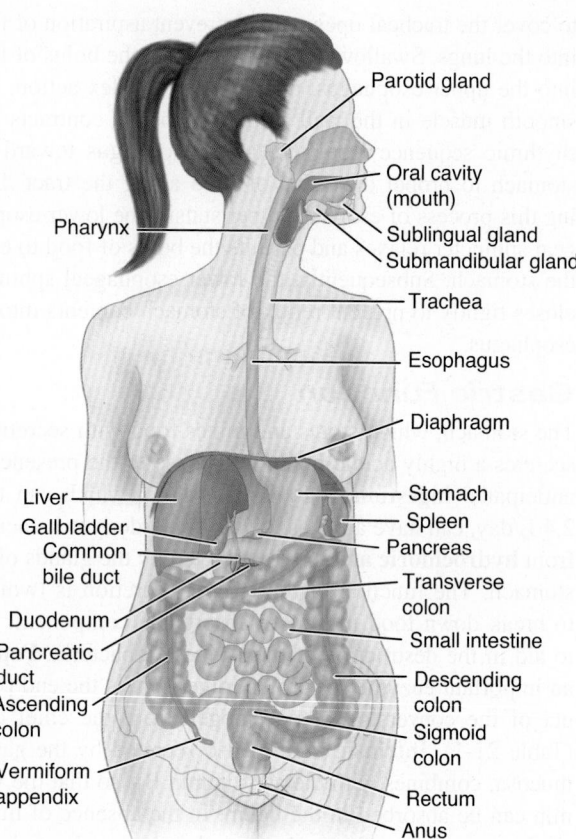

FIGURE 21-1 Organs of the digestive system and associated structures.

Parotid gland
Oral cavity (mouth)
Pharynx
Sublingual gland
Submandibular gland
Trachea
Esophagus
Diaphragm
Liver
Stomach
Gallbladder
Spleen
Common bile duct
Pancreas
Transverse colon
Duodenum
Pancreatic duct
Small intestine
Descending colon
Ascending colon
Sigmoid colon
Vermiform appendix
Rectum
Anus

the intestinal walls. It has three sections: the most proximal section is the duodenum, where the common bile duct and pancreatic duct enter at the ampulla of Vater, which allows for the passage of both bile and pancreatic secretions. The middle section of the small intestine is the jejunum, and the distal section is the ileum. They terminate at the ileocecal valve. This valve, or sphincter, controls the flow of digested material from the ileum into the cecal portion of the large intestine and prevents reflux of bacteria into the small intestine. Attached to the cecum is the vermiform appendix, an appendage that has little or no physiologic function.

The **large intestine** consists of an ascending segment on the right side of the abdomen, a transverse segment that extends from right to left in the upper abdomen, and a descending segment on the left side of the abdomen. Completing the terminal portion of the large intestine are the sigmoid colon, the rectum, and the anus. Regulating the anal outlet is a network of striated muscle, which forms both the internal and the external anal sphincters.

NURSING ALERT
Since the sigmoid colon lies on the left side of the lower abdomen, the nurse understands that the best position for administration of an enema is left lateral position.

The GI tract receives blood from arteries that originate along the entire length of the thoracic and abdominal aorta and veins that return blood from the digestive organs and the spleen. This portal venous system is composed of five large veins: the superior mesenteric, inferior mesenteric, gastric, splenic, and cystic veins, which eventually form the vena portae that enters the liver. Once in the liver, the blood is distributed throughout and collected into the hepatic veins that then terminate in the inferior vena cava. Of particular importance are the gastric artery and the superior and inferior mesenteric arteries. Oxygen and nutrients are supplied to the stomach by the gastric artery and to the intestine by the mesenteric arteries (Fig. 21-2). Venous blood is returned from the small intestine, cecum, and the ascending and transverse portions of the colon by the superior mesenteric vein, which corresponds with the distribution of the branches of the superior mesenteric artery. Blood flow to the GI tract is approximately 20% of the total cardiac output and increases significantly after eating.

The internal abdominal cavity is lined with peritoneum, which is the largest serous membrane in the body and which has a surface area similar to that of skin. The peritoneum is a single sheet that has visceral and parietal components. The visceral peritoneum covers the abdominal organs, and the parietal peritoneum lines the walls of the abdominal pelvic cavity. Between these two layers is a potential space containing fluid secreted by the serous membranes (Porth & Maftin, 2009). This space is sometimes accessed for diagnostic procedures, such as peritoneal tap to assess for internal injuries or catheter insertion for peritoneal dialysis. Structures that

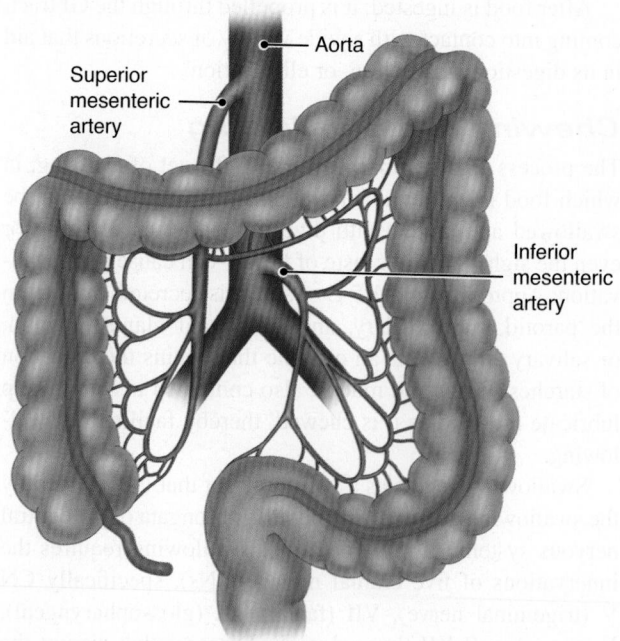

Aorta
Superior mesenteric artery
Inferior mesenteric artery

FIGURE 21-2 Anatomy and blood supply of the large intestine.

lie between the parietal peritoneum and the body wall are said to be *retroperitoneal*. A *mesentery* is a double layer of peritoneum that encircles internal organs such as the intestines and contains blood vessels, nerves, and lymphatic vessels. An *omentum* is a fold of mesentery that passes from the stomach to organs in the abdominal cavity. It is a sheet that has mobility, cushions the abdominal organs against injury, and provides insulation against loss of body heat.

Both the sympathetic and parasympathetic portions of the autonomic nervous system innervate the GI tract. In general, sympathetic nerves exert an inhibitory effect on the GI tract, decreasing gastric secretion and motility and causing the sphincters and blood vessels to constrict. Parasympathetic nerve stimulation causes peristalsis and increases secretory activities. The sphincters relax under the influence of parasympathetic stimulation except for the sphincter of the upper esophagus and the external anal sphincter, which are under voluntary control.

Function of the Digestive System

All cells of the body require nutrients. These nutrients are derived from the diet and need the GI system for digestion, absorption via blood or lymphatic channels, and elimination. Primary functions of the GI tract are the following:

- The breakdown of food particles into the molecular form for **digestion**
- The absorption into the bloodstream of small nutrient molecules produced by digestion
- The **elimination** of undigested unabsorbed foodstuffs and other waste products

After food is ingested, it is propelled through the GI tract, coming into contact with a wide variety of secretions that aid in its digestion, absorption, or elimination.

Chewing and Swallowing

The process of digestion begins with the act of chewing, in which food is broken down into small particles that can be swallowed and mixed with digestive enzymes. Eating—or even the sight, smell, or taste of food—can cause reflex salivation. Approximately 1.5 L of saliva is secreted daily from the parotid, submaxillary, and sublingual glands. Ptyalin, or salivary amylase, is an enzyme that begins the digestion of starches. Water and mucus, also contained in saliva, help lubricate the food as it is chewed, thereby facilitating swallowing.

Swallowing begins as a voluntary act that is regulated by the swallowing center in the medulla oblongata of the central nervous system (CNS). The act of swallowing requires the innervations of five cranial nerves (CNs), specifically CN V (trigeminal nerve), VII (facial), IX (glossopharyngeal), X (vagus), and XII (hypoglossal). Diseases that disrupt the brain centers or cranial nerves predispose the patient to aspiration. As a bolus of food is swallowed, the epiglottis moves to cover the tracheal opening and prevent aspiration of food into the lungs. Swallowing, which propels the bolus of food into the upper esophagus, thus ends as a reflex action. The smooth muscle in the wall of the esophagus contracts in a rhythmic sequence from the upper esophagus toward the stomach to propel the bolus of food along the tract. During this process of esophageal peristalsis, the lower esophageal sphincter relaxes and permits the bolus of food to enter the stomach. Subsequently, the lower esophageal sphincter closes tightly to prevent reflux of stomach contents into the esophagus.

Gastric Function

The stomach, which stores and mixes food with secretions, secretes a highly acidic fluid in response to the presence or anticipated **ingestion** of food. This fluid, which can total 2.4 L/day, can have a pH as low as 1 and derives its acidity from **hydrochloric acid** (HCl) secreted by the glands of the stomach. The function of this gastric secretion is twofold: to break down food into more absorbable components and to aid in the destruction of most ingested bacteria. **Pepsin**, an important enzyme for protein digestion, is the end product of the conversion of pepsinogen from the chief cells (Table 21-1). **Intrinsic factor**, also secreted by the gastric mucosa, combines with dietary vitamin B_{12} so that the vitamin can be absorbed in the ileum. In the absence of intrinsic factor, vitamin B_{12} cannot be absorbed and pernicious anemia results.

Peristaltic contractions in the stomach propel the stomach's contents toward the pylorus. Because large food particles cannot pass through the pyloric sphincter, they are churned back into the body of the stomach. In this way, food in the stomach is agitated mechanically and broken down into smaller particles. Food remains in the stomach for a variable length of time, from 30 minutes to several hours, depending on the volume, osmotic pressure, and chemical composition of the gastric contents. Peristalsis in the stomach and contractions of the pyloric sphincter allow the partially digested food to enter the small intestine at a rate that permits efficient absorption of nutrients. This partially digested food mixed with gastric secretions is called **chyme**. Hormones, neuroregulators, and local regulators found in the gastric secretions control the rate of gastric secretions and influence gastric motility (Table 21-2, p. 578).

Small Intestine Function

The digestive process continues in the duodenum. Duodenal secretions come from the accessory digestive organs—the pancreas, liver, and gallbladder—and the glands in the wall of the intestine itself. These secretions contain digestive enzymes: amylase, lipase, and bile. Pancreatic secretions have an alkaline pH due to their high concentration of bicarbonate. This alkalinity neutralizes the acid entering the duodenum from the stomach. Digestive enzymes secreted by the pancreas include **trypsin**, which aids in digesting protein;

TABLE
21-1 The Major Digestive Enzymes and Secretions

Enzyme/Secretion	Enzyme Source	Digestive Action
Action of Enzymes That Digest Carbohydrates		
Ptyalin (salivary amylase)	Salivary glands	Starch → dextrin, maltose, glucose
Amylase	Pancreas and intestinal mucosa	Starch → dextrin, maltose, glucose
		Dextrin → maltose, glucose
Maltase	Intestinal mucosa	Maltose → glucose
Sucrase	Intestinal mucosa	Sucrose → glucose, fructose
Lactase	Intestinal mucosa	Lactose → glucose, galactose
Action of Enzymes/Secretions That Digest Protein		
Pepsin	Gastric mucosa	Protein → polypeptides
Trypsin	Pancreas	Proteins and polypeptides → polypeptides, dipeptides, amino acids
Aminopeptidase	Intestinal mucosa	Polypeptides → dipeptides, amino acids
Dipeptidase	Intestinal mucosa	Dipeptides → amino acids
Hydrochloric acid	Gastric mucosa	Protein → polypeptides, amino acids
Action of Enzymes Secretions That Digest Fat (Triglyceride)		
Pharyngeal lipase	Pharynx mucosa	Triglycerides → fatty acids, diglycerides, monoglycerides
Steapsin	Gastric mucosa	Triglycerides → fatty acids, diglycerides, monoglycerides
Pancreatic lipase	Pancreas	Triglycerides → fatty acids, diglycerides, monoglycerides
Bile	Liver and gallbladder	Fat emulsification

amylase, which aids in digesting starch; and **lipase**, which aids in digesting fats. These secretions drain into the pancreatic duct, which empties into the duodenum along with the common bile duct at a short dilated tube called the *hepatopancreatic ampulla,* or ampulla of Vater. Bile, secreted by the liver and stored in the gallbladder, aids in emulsifying ingested fats, making them easier to digest and absorb. The sphincter of Oddi (muscle tissue at the confluence of the common bile duct and the duodenum), controls the flow of bile. When this sphincter is closed, bile will move back into the common bile duct and gallbladder. Hormones, neuroregulators, and local regulators found in these intestinal secretions control the rate of intestinal secretions and also influence GI motility. Intestinal secretions total approximately 1 L/day of pancreatic juice, 0.5 L/day of bile, and 3 L/day of secretions from the glands of the small intestine. Tables 21-1 and 21-2 give further information about the actions of digestive enzymes and GI regulatory substances.

Two types of contractions occur regularly in the small intestine: segmentation contractions and intestinal peristalsis. *Segmentation contractions* produce mixing waves that move the intestinal contents back and forth in a churning motion. *Intestinal peristalsis* propels the contents of the small intestine toward the colon. Both movements are stimulated by the presence of chyme.

Food, initially ingested in the form of fats, proteins, and carbohydrates, is broken down into absorbable particles (constituent nutrients) by the process of digestion. Carbohydrates are broken down into disaccharides (e.g., sucrose, maltose, and galactose) and monosaccharides (e.g., glucose, fructose). Glucose is the major carbohydrate that tissue cells use as fuel. Proteins are a source of energy after they are broken down into amino acids and peptides. Ingested fats become monoglycerides and fatty acid by the process of emulsification, which makes them smaller and therefore easier to absorb. Chyme stays in the small intestine for 3 to 6 hours, allowing for continued breakdown and absorption of nutrients.

Small, finger-like projections called villi are present throughout the entire intestine and function to produce digestive enzymes as well as to absorb nutrients. Absorption is the primary function of the small intestine. Vitamins and minerals are not digested but rather absorbed essentially unchanged. The process of absorption begins in the jejunum and is accomplished by both active transport and diffusion across the intestinal wall into the circulation. Nutrients are absorbed at specific locations throughout the small intestine and duodenum, whereas fats, proteins, carbohydrates, sodium, and chloride are absorbed in the jejunum. Vitamin B_{12} and bile salts are absorbed in the ileum. Magnesium, phosphate, and potassium are absorbed throughout the small intestine.

Colon Function

Within 4 hours after eating, residual waste material passes into the terminal ileum and slowly into the proximal portion

TABLE
21-2 The Major Gastrointestinal Regulatory Substances

Substance	Stimulus for Production	Target Tissue	Effect on Secretions	Effect on Motility
Neuroregulators				
Acetylcholine	Sight, smell, chewing food, stomach distention	Gastric glands, other secretory glands, gastric and intestinal muscle	Increased gastric acid	Generally increased; decreased sphincter tone
Norepinephrine	Stress, other various stimuli	Secretory glands, gastric and intestinal muscle	Generally inhibitory	Generally decreased; increased sphincter tone
Hormonal Regulators				
Gastrin	Stomach distention with food	Gastric glands	Increased secretion of gastric juice, which is rich in HCl	Increased motility of stomach, decreased time required for gastric emptying Relaxation of ileocecal sphincter Excitation of colon Constriction of gastro-esophageal sphincter
Cholecystokinin	Fat in duodenum	Gallbladder	Release of bile into duodenum	
		Pancreas	Increased production of enzyme-rich pancreatic secretions	
		Stomach	Inhibits gastric secretion somewhat	
Secretin	pH of chyme in duodenum below 4–5	Stomach	Inhibits gastric secretion somewhat	Inhibits stomach contractions
		Pancreas	Increased production of bicarbonate-rich pancreatic juice	
Local Regulator				
Histamine	Unclear; substances in food	Gastric glands	Increased gastric acid production	

of the right colon through the ileocecal valve. With each peristaltic wave of the small intestine, the valve opens briefly and permits some of the contents to pass into the colon.

It is estimated that there are over 500 different species of intestinal anaerobic (without oxygen) and aerobic bacteria in the large intestine. This bacteria assists in completing the breakdown of waste material, especially of undigested or unabsorbed proteins and bile salts, vitamin synthesis, and in the absorption of calcium, magnesium, and iron (Porth & Matfin, 2009). This intestinal flora also provides a critical resistance to potential invading pathogens. The nurse is aware that broad-spectrum antibiotics have the potential to disrupt this normal intestinal flora and place the patient at risk for overgrowth of pathogens such as *Clostridium difficile*. Probiotics, such as lactobacilli, are live organisms considered healthy for the host organisms and are often administered to restore the microbial balance in the intestines.

Two types of colonic secretions are added to the residual material: an electrolyte solution and mucus. The electrolyte solution is chiefly a bicarbonate solution that acts to neutralize the end products formed by the colonic bacterial action, whereas the mucus protects the colonic mucosa from the interluminal contents.

Slow, weak peristaltic activity moves the colonic contents along the tract. This slow transport allows for efficient reabsorption of water and electrolytes, which is the primary purpose of the colon. Approximately 9 L of fluid is sent through the GI track daily and all but 100 mL is reabsorbed, thus the nurse is aware that any process or pathology that increases peristalsis will result in decreased fluid, nutrient, and electrolyte reabsorption, resulting in malnutrition, profound dehydration, and electrolyte depletion. The waste materials from a meal eventually reach and distend the rectum, usually in about 12 hours. As much as 25% of the waste materials

from a meal may still be in the rectum 3 days after the meal was ingested.

Waste Products of Digestion

Feces consist of undigested food, inorganic materials, water, and bacteria. Fecal matter is approximately 75% fluid and 25% solid material. The composition is relatively unaffected by alterations in diet because a large portion of the fecal mass is of nondietary origin, derived from the secretions of the GI tract. The brown color of the feces results from the breakdown of bile by the intestinal bacteria. Chemicals formed by intestinal bacteria are responsible in large part for the fecal odor. Gases formed contain methane, hydrogen sulfide, and ammonia, among others. The GI tract normally contains approximately 150 mL of these gases, which are either absorbed into the portal circulation and detoxified by the liver or expelled from the rectum as flatus.

Elimination of stool begins with distention of the rectum, which reflexively initiates contractions of the rectal musculature and relaxes the normally closed internal anal sphincter. The internal sphincter is controlled by the autonomic nervous system; the external sphincter is under the conscious control of the cerebral cortex. During defecation, the external anal sphincter voluntarily relaxes to allow colonic contents to be expelled. Normally, the external anal sphincter is maintained in a state of tonic contraction. Thus, defecation is seen to be a spinal reflex (involving the parasympathetic nerve fibers) that can be inhibited voluntarily by keeping the external anal sphincter closed. Contracting the abdominal muscles (straining) facilitates emptying of the colon. The average frequency of defecation in humans is once daily, but this varies among people.

ACCESSORY DIGESTIVE ORGANS

Liver

The liver, the largest gland of the body, can be considered a chemical factory that manufactures, stores, alters, and excretes a large number of substances involved in metabolism. The location of the liver is essential in this function, because it receives nutrient-rich blood directly from the GI tract and then either stores or transforms these nutrients into chemicals that are used elsewhere in the body for metabolic needs. The liver is especially important in the synthesis of glucose, protein, and blood-clotting factors.

An important and unique characteristic of the liver is its ability to regenerate. The normal liver maintains a constant mass regulated by the metabolic needs and size of the person. After removal or injury of liver tissue, hepatocytes proliferate to replace the mass of the liver to its original size. This physiologic feature is important in the event of partial

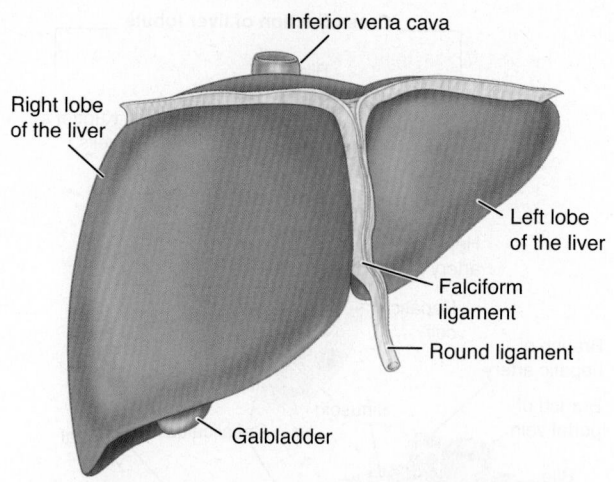

FIGURE 21-3 The liver and biliary system.

hepatectomy (removal of tumors or other lesions) and in liver transplant (Schiff, Sorrell, & Maddrey, 2007).

The major functions of the liver include glucose metabolism, conversion of ammonia to urea, protein metabolism, fat metabolism, vitamin and iron storage, drug metabolism, bile formation, and bilirubin excretion.

Bile, which is manufactured by the liver and plays a major role in the digestion and absorption of fats in the GI tract, is stored temporarily in the gallbladder until it is needed for digestion, at which time the gallbladder empties and bile enters the intestine (Fig. 21-3). Waste products removed by the liver are secreted into bile. The smallest bile ducts, called *canaliculi*, are located between the lobules of the liver. The canaliculi receive secretions from the hepatocytes and carry them to larger bile ducts, which eventually form the hepatic duct. The hepatic duct from the liver and the cystic duct from the gallbladder join to form the common bile duct, which empties into the small intestine. The sphincter of Oddi, located at the junction where the common bile duct enters the duodenum, controls the flow of bile into the intestine.

The liver is located behind the ribs in the upper right portion of the abdominal cavity, and under normal conditions cannot be palpated as it lies within the rib cage. It weighs approximately 1,800 g in men and 1,400 g in women and is divided into two large lobes and two smaller lobes. A thin layer of connective tissue surrounds each lobe, extending into the lobe itself and dividing the liver mass into small, functional units called *lobules* (Porth & Maftin, 2009).

The circulation of the blood into and out of the liver is of major importance to liver function. The blood that perfuses the liver comes from two sources. Approximately 75% of the blood supply comes from the portal vein, which drains the GI tract and is rich in nutrients. The remainder of the blood supply enters by way of the hepatic artery and is rich in oxygen. Terminal branches of these two blood vessels join to form common capillary beds, which constitute the sinusoids of the liver (Fig. 21-4). Thus, a mixture of venous and

Cross Section of liver lobule

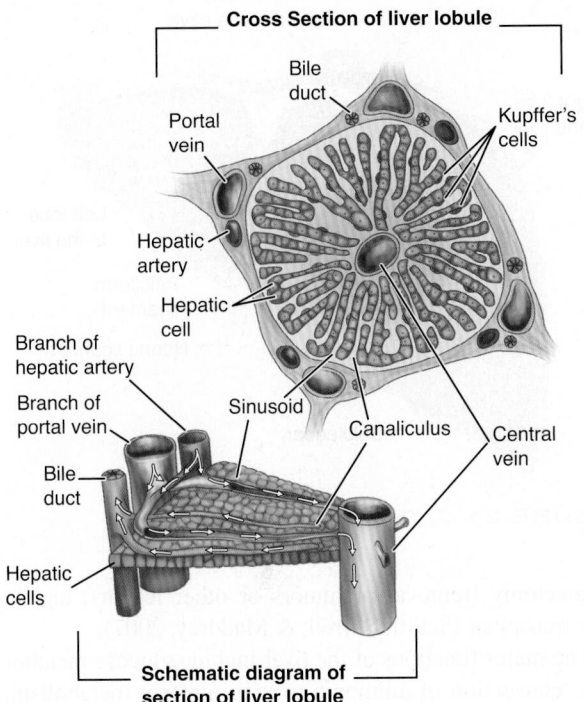

Schematic diagram of section of liver lobule

FIGURE 21-4 A section of liver lobule showing the location of hepatic veins, hepatic cells, liver sinusoids, and branches of the portal vein and hepatic artery.

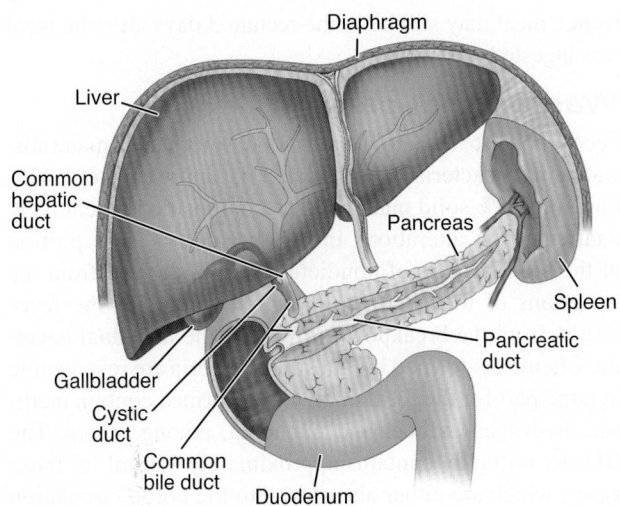

FIGURE 21-5 The liver, biliary system, and pancreas.

arterial blood bathes the liver cells (hepatocytes). The sinusoids empty into venules that occupy the center of each liver lobule and are called the *central veins*. The central veins join to form the hepatic vein, which constitutes the venous drainage from the liver and empties into the inferior vena cava, close to the diaphragm. Thus, there are two sources of blood flowing into the liver and only one exit pathway. Because of the pressure differences between the hepatic and portal veins, the liver normally stores approximately 450 mL of blood (Porth & Maftin, 2009), which can be available in times of hypovolemia. However, in conditions such as right heart failure, in which blood flows back up in the vena cava, additional blood accumulates in the liver.

In addition to hepatocytes, phagocytic cells belonging to the reticuloendothelial system (RES) are present in the liver. Other organs that contain reticuloendothelial cells are the spleen, bone marrow, lymph nodes, and lungs. In the liver, these cells are called *Kupffer cells*. As the most common phagocyte in the human body, their main function is to engulf particulate matter (e.g., bacteria) that enters the liver through the portal blood.

The Gallbladder

The gallbladder, a pear-shaped, hollow, saclike organ, 7.5 to 10 cm (3 to 4 in) long, lies in a shallow depression on the inferior surface of the liver, to which it is attached by loose connective tissue. The capacity of the gallbladder is 30 to

50 mL of bile. Its wall is composed largely of smooth muscle. The gallbladder is connected to the common bile duct by the cystic duct (Fig. 21-5).

The gallbladder functions as a storage area for bile. Between meals, when the sphincter of Oddi is closed, bile produced by the hepatocytes enters the gallbladder. During storage, a large portion of the water in bile is absorbed through the walls of the gallbladder, so that gallbladder bile is five to ten times more concentrated than that originally secreted by the liver. When food enters the duodenum, the gallbladder contracts and the sphincter of Oddi relaxes, which allows the bile to enter the intestine. This response is mediated by secretion of the hormone **cholecystokinin-pancreozymin (CCK-PZ)** from the intestinal wall.

Bile is composed of water and electrolytes (sodium, potassium, calcium, chloride, and bicarbonate) along with significant amounts of lecithin, fatty acids, cholesterol, bilirubin, and bile salts. The bile salts, together with cholesterol, assist in emulsification of fats in the distal ileum. They are then reabsorbed into the portal blood for return to the liver, after which they are once again excreted into the bile. This pathway from hepatocytes to bile to intestine and back to the hepatocytes is called the *enterohepatic circulation*. Because of the enterohepatic circulation, only a small fraction of the bile salts that enter the intestine are excreted in the feces. This decreases the need for active synthesis of bile salts by the liver cells.

Approximately half of the bilirubin, a pigment derived from the breakdown of red blood cells, is converted by the intestinal flora into urobilinogen, a highly soluble substance. Urobilinogen is either excreted in the feces or returned to the portal circulation, where it is re-excreted into the bile. About 5% is normally absorbed into the general circulation and then excreted by the kidneys (Porth & Maftin, 2009).

If the flow of bile is impeded (e.g., by gallstones in the bile ducts), bilirubin does not enter the intestine. As a result,

blood levels of bilirubin increase and cause a characteristic yellow hue to the skin termed jaundice and yellowing of the sclera, termed *icterus*. Increased levels of bilirubin cause increased renal excretion of urobilinogen, resulting in dark colored urine, which, since bile is a soap, will be frothy when agitated. If the bile is prevented from entering the small intestine, clay-colored stool will be noted. Bile salts are also irritating to the skin, thus the nurse is alert for complaints of itchy skin or pruritus. These changes produce many of the signs and symptoms seen in gallbladder disorders.

The Pancreas

The pancreas, located in the upper abdomen, has **endocrine** as well as **exocrine** functions (see Fig. 21-5). The exocrine functions include secretion of pancreatic enzymes into the GI tract through the pancreatic duct. The endocrine functions include secretion of insulin, glucagon, and somatostatin directly into the bloodstream.

The Exocrine Pancreas

The secretions of the exocrine portion of the pancreas are collected in the pancreatic duct, which joins the common bile duct and enters the duodenum at the ampulla of Vater. Surrounding the ampulla is the sphincter of Oddi, which partially controls the rate at which secretions from the pancreas and the gallbladder enter the duodenum.

The secretions of the exocrine pancreas are digestive enzymes high in protein content and an electrolyte-rich fluid; they include amylase, trypsin, and lipase. The secretions, which are very alkaline because of their high concentration of sodium bicarbonate, are capable of neutralizing the highly acid gastric juice that enters the duodenum. Hormones originating in the GI tract stimulate the secretion of these exocrine pancreatic juices. The hormone **secretin** is the major stimulus for increased bicarbonate secretion from the pancreas, and the major stimulus for digestive enzyme secretion is the hormone CCK-PZ. The vagus nerve also influences exocrine pancreatic secretion.

The Endocrine Pancreas

The islets of Langerhans, the endocrine part of the pancreas, are collections of cells embedded in the pancreatic tissue. They are composed of alpha, beta, and delta cells. The hormone produced by the beta cells is called *insulin*. The alpha cells secrete glucagon, and the delta cells secrete somatostatin. Refer to Chapter 30 for details on insulin and glucagon secretion.

Somatostatin is a hormone secreted in the pancreas, the stomach, and the small intestine. It decreases GI activity after ingestion of food and also acts in the islets of Langerhans to inhibit the release of insulin and glucagon (Porth & Maftin, 2009). By decreasing the transit time and inhibiting insulin and glucagon it is proposed that absorption of foodstuffs and nutrients is enhanced.

Spleen

The spleen is a large lymphoid organ located in the left upper abdominal cavity near ribs nine and eleven (posterior to the midaxillary line), and rib fractures in this region should alert the nurse to potential splenic laceration. The spleen is highly vascular because it filters antigens from the blood. It is responsible for immune response to infection because it is rich with B- and T-cell lymphocytes. The spleen in a healthy adult is approximately 9 to 13 cm (3.5 to 5.1 in) in length. It cannot be palpated unless significantly enlarged.

Gerontologic Considerations

Although an increased prevalence of several common GI disorders occurs in the elderly population, aging per se appears to have minimal direct effect on most GI functions, in large part because of the functional reserve of the GI tract (Table 21-3).

ASSESSMENT

Health History

A focused GI assessment begins with a complete history. Information about abdominal pain, appetite changes, dyspepsia, gas, nausea and vomiting, diarrhea, constipation, fecal incontinence, and previous GI disease is investigated. Past and current medication use and any previous diagnostic studies, treatments, and surgery are noted.

The initial presentation of a patient with liver disease varies greatly and can range from elevated liver enzymes on routine screening with no clinical signs or symptoms of disease, to the patient who presents in liver failure with **jaundice**, **hepatic coma**, or esophageal bleeding. A comprehensive and complete health history is critical to determine exposure to hepatoxic substances (including alcohol) or infectious agents causing liver dysfunction and to distinguish between acute and chronic hepatic dysfunction.

Current History

Current nutritional status is ascertained. The nurse and patient discuss changes in appetite or eating patterns and any unexplained weight gain or loss over the past year. A complete metabolic panel, including liver function studies, triglyceride levels, iron studies, and complete blood count (CBC) are obtained.

Questions are raised about the use of tobacco and alcohol and include details about type, amount, length of use, and the date of discontinuation, if any. It is also important to include questions about psychosocial, spiritual, or cultural factors that may be affecting the patient.

If liver disease is suspected because of clinical manifestations or abnormal liver function tests, the health history focuses on previous exposure of the patient to hepatotoxic

TABLE
21-3 — **GERONTOLOGIC CONSIDERATIONS** / Age-Related Changes of the Gastrointestinal System

Component	Structural Changes	Implications
Oral Cavity and Pharynx	• Injury/loss or decay of teeth • Atrophy of taste buds • Decreased saliva production • Reduced ptyalin and amylase in saliva • Atrophy of gingival tissue	Difficulty chewing and swallowing
Esophagus	• Decreased motility and emptying • Weakened gag reflex • Decreased resting pressure of lower esophageal sphincter • Decreased muscle tone and weakness in lower esophageal sphincter	Reflux and heartburn Dysphagia (difficulty swallowing) Dyspepsia (indigestion)
Stomach	• Degeneration and atrophy of gastric mucosal surfaces with decreased production of HCl • Decreased secretion of gastric acids and most digestive enzymes • Decreased motility and emptying	Delayed gastric emptying Food intolerances Malabsorption Decrease in iron and vitamin B_{12} absorption Anorexia Anemia
Small Intestine	• Atrophy of muscle and mucosal surfaces • Thinning of villi and epithelial cells	Decreased motility and transit time, which lead to complaints of indigestion and constipation
Large Intestine	• Decrease in mucus secretion • Decrease in elasticity of rectal wall • Decreased tone of internal anal sphincter • Slower and duller nerve impulses in rectal area	Decreased absorption of nutrients (dextrose, fats, calcium, and iron), leading to decreased sensation to defecate and increased constipation Fecal incontinence from decrease or loss of sphincter control
Liver	• Decrease in size and weight • Decrease in total hepatic blood flow • Decreased phagocytosis by the Kupffer cells • Decreased drug metabolism, leading to drug toxicity	Decreases proportional to decreases in body size and weight Increased incidence of hepatitis B Increased incidence of liver abscesses

substances or infectious agents. Lifestyle behaviors that increase the risk for exposure to infectious agents are identified. The patient's history of alcohol and drug use, including but not limited to the use of IV injection drugs, provides additional information about exposure to toxins and infectious agents. The patient's occupational, recreational, and travel history may assist in identifying exposure to hepatotoxins (e.g., industrial chemicals, other toxins). Travel to endemic areas such as Mexico, Africa, India, or Latin America may indicate ingestion of contaminated food or water and raw shellfish. Sexual practices may be a potential risk factor for liver disease. The amount and type of alcohol consumption are identified using screening questionnaires that have been developed for this purpose. Men who consume 60 to 80 g of alcohol per day (approximately four glasses of beer, wine, or mixed drinks) and women whose alcohol intake is 40 to 60 g/day are estimated to be at high risk for cirrhosis (10 g of alcohol is equivalent to 1 oz bourbon, 12 ounces beer, or 4 ounces of red wine). The nurse is aware that the impact of alcohol induced liver injury or disease is increased in the presence of other risk factors such as hepatitis C (Bacon, O'Grady, Dibisceglie et al., 2007; Schiff et al., 2007).

Many medications (including acetaminophen, ketoconazole, and valproic acid) are responsible for hepatic dysfunction and disease. Acetaminophen overdose can result in **fulminant hepatic failure**, while chronic liver disease is commonly caused by alcohol and viruses such as hepatitis B or C. A prior history of inflammatory bowel disease or ulcerative colitis may lead to the diagnosis of primary sclerosing cholangitis. Patients with nonalcoholic fatty liver disease (NAFLD) may frequently have a prior medical history of diabetes, hyperlipidemia, and obesity.

A thorough medication history to assess hepatic dysfunction should address all current and past prescription medications, over-the-counter medications, herbal remedies, and dietary supplements.

Past History

The history also includes an evaluation of the client's past medical history to identify risk factors for liver disease. Current and past medical conditions, including those of a psychological or psychiatric nature, are identified. The family history includes questions about familial liver disorders that may have their origin in alcohol abuse or gallstone disease,

as well as other familial or genetic diseases, such as hemochromatosis, Wilson's disease, or alpha$_1$-antitrypsin disease. A positive family history of hepatitis B may indicate vertical transmission (Bacon et al., 2007).

Common Complaints

Pain

Pain can be a major symptom of GI disease. Pain may be described as visceral; that is, nocioreceptors in the abdominal organs are stimulated and the pain is often described by patients as cramping, aching, squeezing, or colicky and difficult to pinpoint. Parietal pain occurs when the parietal peritoneum is inflamed, as occurs with appendicitis. It is a steady, severe pain that may be localized. Referred pain is pain that travels to a more distant site, where it localizes or presents. The character, duration, pattern, frequency, location, and distribution of referred pain (Fig. 21-6) vary greatly depending on the underlying cause. Other factors such as meals, rest, activity, and defecation patterns may directly affect this pain.

Dyspepsia

Dyspepsia, which is upper abdominal discomfort or distress associated with eating (commonly called *indigestion*) is the most common symptom of clients with GI dysfunction. Indigestion is an imprecise term that refers to a host of upper abdominal or epigastric symptoms such as pain, discomfort, fullness, bloating, early satiety, belching, heartburn, and regurgitation; it occurs in approximately 25% of the adult population. Typically, fatty foods cause the most discomfort because they remain in the stomach for digestion longer than proteins or carbohydrates. Salads and coarse vegetables, as well as highly seasoned foods, may also cause considerable GI distress.

Intestinal Gas

The accumulation of gas in the GI tract may result in belching (expulsion of gas from the stomach through the mouth) or flatulence (expulsion of gas from the rectum). Usually, gases in the small intestine pass into the colon and are released as flatus. Patients often complain of bloating, distention, or feeling "full of gas," with excessive flatulence as a symptom of food intolerance or gallbladder disease.

Nausea and Vomiting

Nausea is a vague, intensely unsettling sensation of sickness or "queasiness" that may or may not be followed by vomiting. It can be triggered by odors, activity, medications, or food intake. The emesis, or vomitus, may vary in color and content and may contain undigested food particles, blood (hematemesis), or bilious material mixed with gastric juices. The causes of nausea and vomiting are many. Nausea and vomiting may result from visceral afferent stimulation (i.e., dysmotility, peritoneal irritation, infections, hepatobiliary or pancreatic disorders, mechanical obstruction); CNS disorders (i.e., vestibular disorders, increased intracranial pressure, infections, psychogenic conditions); and irritation of the chemoreceptor trigger zone from radiation therapy, systemic disorders, and antitumor chemotherapy medications.

Change in Bowel Habits and Stool Characteristics

Changes in bowel habits may signal colonic dysfunction or disease. Diarrhea, an abnormal increase in the frequency of bowel movements and liquidity of the stool or in daily stool weight or volume, commonly occurs when the contents move so rapidly through the intestine and colon that there is inadequate time for the GI secretions and oral contents to be absorbed. This physiologic function is typically associated with abdominal pain or cramping and nausea or vomiting. Constipation, a decrease in the frequency of bowel movements, or stools that are hard, dry, and of smaller volume than normal, may be associated with anal discomfort and rectal bleeding.

The characteristics of the stool can vary greatly. Stool is normally light to dark brown; however, specific disease

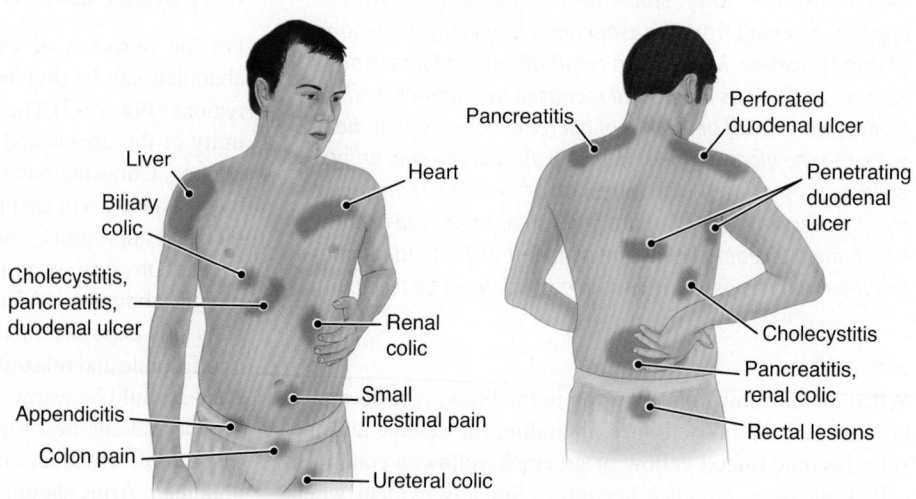

FIGURE 21-6 Common sites of referred abdominal pain.

Liver
Biliary colic
Cholecystitis, pancreatitis, duodenal ulcer
Appendicitis
Colon pain
Heart
Renal colic
Small intestinal pain
Ureteral colic

Pancreatitis
Perforated duodenal ulcer
Penetrating duodenal ulcer
Cholecystitis
Pancreatitis, renal colic
Rectal lesions

TABLE
21-4 Foods and Medications That Alter Stool Color

Altering Substance	Color
Meat protein	Dark brown
Spinach	Green
Carrots and beets	Red
Cocoa	Dark red or brown
Senna	Yellow
Bismuth, iron, licorice, and charcoal	Black
Barium	Milky white

processes and ingestion of certain foods and medications may change the appearance of stool (Table 21-4). Blood in the stool can present in various ways and must be investigated. If blood is shed in sufficient quantities into the upper GI tract, it produces a tarry-black color (melena), whereas blood entering the lower portion of the GI tract or passing rapidly through will cause the stool to appear bright or dark red. Lower rectal or anal bleeding is suspected if there is streaking of blood on the surface of the stool or if blood is noted on toilet tissue. Other common abnormalities in stool characteristics described by the patient may include:

- Bulky, greasy, foamy stools that are foul in odor and may or may not float
- Light-gray or clay-colored stool, caused by a decrease or absence of conjugated bilirubin
- Stool with mucus threads or pus that may be visible on gross inspection of the stool
- Small, dry, rock-hard masses occasionally streaked with blood
- Loose, watery stool that may or may not be streaked with blood

☀ N U R S I N G   A L E R T

Melena, or black "tarry" stools, occurs in association with upper GI bleeding from the esophagus, stomach, duodenum, or small intestine. Melena can result after blood loss in an amount as small as 60 mL and is caused by stomach acid (hydrochloric acid) or intestinal bacterial conversion of hemoglobin to the black pigment hematin. Pseudomelena, or false melena, is associated with ingestion of iron. The term hematochezia refers to stools that are maroon or bright red in color, signifying a bleeding below the ligament of Treitz (duodenum level) but may be associated with a rapid upper GI bleed.

Jaundice

When the bilirubin concentration in the blood is abnormally elevated, all the body tissues, including the sclerae and the skin, become tinged yellow or greenish-yellow, a condition called jaundice. Jaundice becomes clinically evident when the serum bilirubin level exceeds 2.5 mg/dL (43 μmol/L). The elevated bilirubin stains tissues and fluid, but jaundice is most intense in the face, trunk, and sclera (LeBlond, DeGowin, & Brown, 2009). Increased serum bilirubin levels and jaundice may result from impairment of hepatic uptake, conjugation of bilirubin, or excretion of bilirubin into the biliary system. There are several types of jaundice: hemolytic, hepatocellular, and obstructive jaundice, and jaundice due to hereditary hyperbilirubinemia. Hepatocellular and obstructive jaundice are the two types commonly associated with liver disease (refer to Chapter 25).

Ascites

Ascites is an increased accumulation of peritoneal fluid in the abdomen caused by a variety of disorders associated with the liver. One factor associated with development of ascites is portal hypertension and the resulting increase in capillary pressure and obstruction of venous blood flow through the damaged liver. **Portal hypertension** causes an increased pressure gradient (a difference in pressure between the portal vein and the hepatic veins), facilitating fluid accumulation in the peritoneal cavity. Another factor is the decreased synthesis of albumin in liver disease. The hypoalbuminemia results in decreased plasma oncotic pressure, which facilitates fluid accumulation in the abdominal cavity. An obstruction of the normal lymphatic drainage can cause fluid accumulation in the peritoneum, as can cancers or inflammatory processes that stimulate increased production of peritoneal fluid. Ascites can also be associated with nonhepatic etiologies such as renal failure and heart failure.

Engorged Veins

Under normal conditions, the veins in the abdominal wall are barely noted unless the skin and subcutaneous fat are thin. When venous pressure increases as a result of obstruction, as in portal hypertension, vessels distal to the inferior vena cava engorge, and distended veins can be seen on the abdomen, chest, and extremities.

Physical Examination

For the purposes of examination and documentation, the abdomen can be divided into either four quadrants or nine regions (Fig. 21-7). The nurse must know the physical proximity of the organs and blood vessels to these quadrants or regions. Choosing one of these mapping methods and using it consistently will ensure a thorough evaluation of the abdomen and appropriate corresponding documentation.

The physical examination includes assessment of the mouth, abdomen, and rectum. Good lighting is necessary, as is full exposure of the abdomen. The patient should be comfortable and relaxed, with an empty bladder. The nurse's hands should be warm, and the fingernails short.

The patient lies supine with knees flexed slightly for inspection, auscultation, palpation, and percussion of the abdomen. Arms should not be raised over the head because

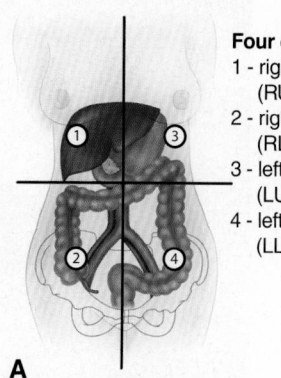

Four quadrants
1 - right upper quadrant (RUQ)
2 - right lower quadrant (RLQ)
3 - left upper quadrant (LUQ)
4 - left lower quadrant (LLQ)

Nine regions
1 - epigastric region
2 - umbilical region
3 - hypogastric or suprapubic region
4 - right hypochondriac region
5 - left hypochondriac region
6 - right lumbar region
7 - left lumbar region
8 - right inguinal region
9 - left inguinal region

FIGURE 21-7 Division of the abdomen into (**A**) four quadrants or (**B**) nine regions.

A

B

the abdominal muscles tense in this position. A small pillow may be placed behind the patient's head for comfort. The patient's breasts are covered with a gown and sheets are rolled down to above the symphysis pubis. Examination of the abdomen is performed with the nurse standing on the patient's right side

Inspection

The mouth, tongue, buccal mucosa, teeth, and gums are inspected, noting any ulcers, nodules, swelling, discoloration, or inflammation. Dentures should be removed to allow good visualization of the entire oral cavity.

The nurse inspects the abdominal skin for nodules, lesions, masses, scarring, discolorations, inflammation, bruising, increased vascularity of the abdominal skin, and striae (stretch marks). In the presence of liver disease, the nurse inspects the skin, mucosa, and sclera for jaundice. The extremities are assessed for muscle atrophy, edema, and skin excoriation secondary to scratching. The nurse observes the skin for petechiae or ecchymotic areas (bruises), spider angiomas, and palmar erythema (a diffuse reddening of the palm, particularly near the base of the thumb (thenar eminence) and base of the little finger (hypothenar eminence). Additionally, a male patient is assessed for unilateral or bilateral gynecomastia and testicular atrophy due to hormonal changes associated with liver disease. The patient's cognitive status (recall, memory, abstract thinking) and neurologic status are assessed. The nurse observes for general tremor, asterixis (flapping of the hands when wrists dorsiflexed), weakness, and slurred speech related to elevated ammonia levels secondary to liver failure, and notes the patient's breath for **hepatic fetor** a sweet, mildly fecal breath odor associated with encephalopathy. The contour and symmetry of the abdomen are noted, and any localized bulging, distention, or peristaltic waves are identified. Under normal circumstances, peristalsis is not noted on the abdominal wall and if present is usually associated with early intestinal obstruction. Expected contours of the anterior abdominal wall can be described as flat, rounded, or scaphoid (hollowed or shaped like a boat). The umbilicus is assessed for color, position, and shape. The umbilicus may be everted with

increased intra-abdominal pressure. Ecchymoses around the umbilical area is termed *Cullen's sign* and is associated with a retroperitoneal bleed due to any cause. Ecchymoses noted on either flank, the groin, or the abdomen, termed *Grey-Turner's sign*, is also associated with a retroperitoneal bleed (see Chapter 27, Fig. 27-10). A hernia is a protrusion on the abdominal wall and may be noted anywhere in the abdomen. If ascites is suspected, the nurse notes bulging flanks when the patient is in the supine position as the weight of the fluid flows dependently to the sides.

 NURSING ALERT
If abdominal distention is noted, the nurse assesses for common causes described as the 6 F's: fetus (pregnancy), feces (constipation), flatulence, fat (obesity), fluid (ascites), and fibroids or fatal growth.

Auscultation

Auscultation always precedes percussion and palpation since manipulation of the abdomen may alter the frequency and intensity of bowel sounds. The nurse listens to determine the character, location, and frequency of bowel sounds and to identify vascular sounds. Bowel sounds are assessed in all four quadrants using the diaphragm of the stethoscope, which affords greatest auscultation of high-pitched and gurgling sounds. The frequency and character of the sounds are usually heard as clicks and gurgles that occur irregularly and range from 5 to 35 per minute. The terms *normoactive* (sounds heard about every 2 to 12 seconds), *hypoactive* (<5 clicks or gurgles per minute), *hyperactive* (>35 per minute), or *absent* (no sounds in 3 to 5 minutes) are frequently used in documentation, but these assessments are highly subjective. Hypoactive bowel sounds are associated with decreased bowel function, as occurs in postoperative patients, patients with myxedema, peritonitis, hypokalemia, or mesentery ischemia, and in patients on medications such as opioid and anticholinergic agents. The nurse must listen for 5 minutes before documenting the absence of bowel sounds, which is suggestive of ileus and can be due to a variety of causes.

Hyperactive bowel sounds are associated with diarrhea or gastroenteritis. High-pitched, high-frequency bowel sounds and abdominal cramping are suggestive of a partial intestinal obstruction.

Bruits in the aortic, renal, iliac, and femoral arteries are noted using the bell of the stethoscope. Bruits are associated with turbulent blood flow in an artery. Friction rubs are high-pitched grating sounds heard over the liver or spleen during respiration. These are rare findings but are associated with pathology. Borborygmi or "stomach growling" is heard as a loud prolonged gurgle.

Percussion

Percussion is used to assess the size and density of the abdominal organs and to detect the presence of air-filled, fluid-filled, or solid masses. Percussion is used either independently or concurrently with palpation because it can validate palpation findings. All quadrants are percussed for a sense of overall tympany and dullness. Tympany is the predominant sound that results from the presence of air in the stomach and small intestines; dullness is heard over organs and solid masses.

If ascites is suspected, the nurse will note tympany at the top of the abdomen and dullness laterally, with the patient in a supine position. Shifting dullness is noted as the fluid flows to the dependent regions when the patient moves to a lateral position.

The nurse estimates the size of the liver by percussing its upper and lower borders. The normal liver span is 6 to 12 cm in the midclavicular line (MCL), and it decreases with age. A hollow tympanic note over the stomach in the left upper quadrant (LUQ) should be expected. A full bladder elicits dullness above the suprapubic area, whereas abdominal distention increases the area of tympany. If the spleen is enlarged, dullness may be percussed in the LUQ over the lower ribs. Percussion that elicits pain, especially pain remote to the immediate site of the percussion, is suggestive of peritoneal inflammation (LeBlond et al., 2009).

Palpation

If a patient complains of abdominal pain, it is important to assess the area of tenderness last. Use of light palpation is appropriate for identifying areas of tenderness or muscular resistance, and deep palpation is used to identify masses. If a mass is noted, the nurse assesses its size, shape, location, consistency, pulsatility, mobility, and tenderness.

A palpable liver has a firm, sharp ridge and a smooth surface (Fig. 21-8). If the liver is palpable, the examiner notes and records its size, its consistency, any tenderness, and whether its outline is regular or irregular. If the liver is enlarged, the degree to which it descends below the right costal margin is recorded to provide some indication of its size. The nurse determines whether the liver's edge is sharp and smooth or blunt, and whether the enlarged liver is nodular or smooth. The liver of a patient with cirrhosis is small

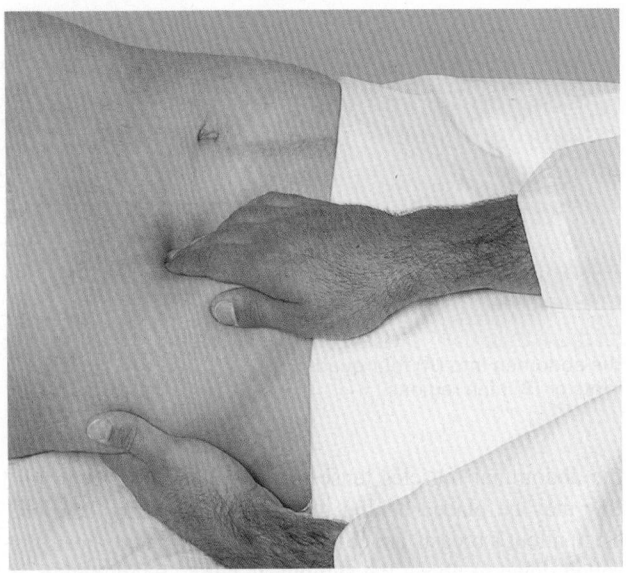

FIGURE 21-8 Technique for palpating the liver. The examiner places one hand under the right lower rib cage and presses downward with light pressure with the other hand.

and hard, whereas the liver of a patient with acute hepatitis is soft, and the hand easily moves the edge (Bickley, 2008).

Tenderness of the liver indicates recent acute enlargement with consequent stretching of the liver capsule. The absence of tenderness may imply that the enlargement is of long-standing duration. The liver of a patient with viral hepatitis is tender, whereas that of a patient with alcoholic hepatitis is not. Enlargement of the liver is an abnormal finding that requires evaluation (Bickley, 2008).

The fluid wave test can be conducted if ascites is suspected. A fluid wave can be demonstrated by tapping the patient's flank sharply with one hand while the other hand receives the impulse against the opposite flank. There is a perceptible time lag between the tap and reception of the impulse. Since mesentery fat may produce a similar wave, the patient or an assistant presses the ulnar surface of his or her hand into the midline of the abdomen. A wave passing this hand barrier is usually caused by free fluid. It is estimated that at least 500 mL of peritoneal fluid must accumulate to note a positive wave test (LeBlond et al., 2009).

Cholecystitis, acute inflammation of the gallbladder, causes pain and tenderness, and makes it difficult for the nurse to palpate and percuss the abdomen. The nurse should observe for Murphy's sign (the patient's inability to take a deep breath when the examiner's fingers are pressed below the right costal margin).

Testing for rebound tenderness is not performed by many examiners because it can cause severe pain; light percussion is used instead to produce a mild localized response when peritoneal irritation is present. If testing for rebound tenderness is undertaken, it is done at the end of the examination

since the patient's pain will interfere with the remaining examination. Using palpation, the nurse's places his or her hand in the painful quadrant and then releases it quickly. Pain upon releasing is termed *Blumberg's sign* and is associated with peritonitis, such as appendicitis.

NURSING ALERT
Guarding, rigidity, and rebound tenderness (Blumberg's sign) are reliable indicators of peritonitis.

Rectal Examination

The final part of the physical examination is evaluation of the terminal portions of the GI tract, the rectum, perianal region, and anus. The anal canal is approximately 2.5 to 4 cm in length and opens into the perineum. Concentric rings of muscle, the internal and external sphincters, normally keep the anal canal securely closed. Gloves, water-soluble lubrication, a penlight, and drapes are necessary tools for the evaluation. Although the rectal examination is generally uncomfortable and often embarrassing for the patient, it is a mandatory part of every thorough examination. For women, the rectal examination may be part of the gynecologic examination. Positions for the rectal examination include knee–chest, left lateral with hips and knees flexed, and standing with hips flexed and upper body supported by the examination table. External examination includes inspection for lumps, rashes, inflammation, excoriation, tears, scars, pilonidal dimpling, and tufts of hair at the pilonidal area. The discovery of tenderness, inflammation, or both should alert the examiner to the possibility of a pilonidal cyst, perianal abscess, or anorectal fistula or fissure. The patient's buttocks are carefully spread and visually inspected until the patient has relaxed the external sphincter control. The patient is asked to bear down, thus allowing the ready appearance of fistulas, fissures, rectal prolapse, polyps, and internal hemorrhoids. Internal examination is performed with a lubricated index finger inserted into the anal canal while the patient bears down. The tone of the sphincter is noted, as are any nodules or irregularities of the anal ring. Because this is an uncomfortable part of the examination for most people, the patient is encouraged to focus on deep breathing during the brief examination.

Diagnostic Evaluation

Initial diagnostic tests begin with serum laboratory studies, including but not limited to CBC, a complete metabolic panel, prothrombin time/partial thromboplastin time, triglycerides, liver function tests, amylase, and lipase, with the possibility of more specific studies such as carcinoembryonic antigen (CEA), cancer antigen (CA) 19-9, and alphafetoprotein, indicating sensitivity and specificity for colorectal and hepatocellular carcinomas, respectively. CEA is a protein that is normally not detected in the blood of a healthy

person; therefore, when detected it indicates that cancer is present, but not what type of cancer is present. Practitioners can use CEA results to determine the stage and extent of the disease and the prognosis for patients with cancer, especially GI and, in particular, colorectal cancer (Porth & Maftin, 2009). CA 19-9 is also a protein that exists on the surface of certain cells and is shed by tumor cells, making it useful as a tumor marker to follow the course of the cancer. CA 19-9 levels are elevated in most patients with advanced pancreatic cancer, but it may also be elevated in other conditions such as colorectal, lung, and gallbladder cancers, gallstones, **pancreatitis**, cystic fibrosis, and liver disease.

Many other modalities are available for diagnostic assessment of the GI tract. Table 21-5 identifies various procedures and their diagnostic uses.

The majority of these tests and procedures are performed on an outpatient basis in special settings designed for this purpose (e.g., endoscopy suite or GI laboratory). In the past, frequently, patients who required such tests were elderly; however, within the past 5 years, in part due to heightened media exposure and early diagnosis of colorectal cancer, the median age of patients evaluated for colorectal cancer has decreased significantly. Preparation for many of these studies includes clear liquid diets, fasting, ingestion of a liquid bowel preparation, the use of laxatives or enemas, and ingestion or injection of a contrast agent or a radiopaque dye. These measures are poorly tolerated by some patients and are especially problematic in the elderly population or in patients with comorbidities because bowel preparations significantly alter the internal fluid and electrolyte balance. If further assessment or treatment is needed after any outpatient procedure, the patient may be admitted to the hospital. Specific interventions for each diagnostic test are listed in Table 21-6 on page 589.

General nursing interventions for the patient who is undergoing a GI diagnostic evaluation include:

- Establishing the possible nursing diagnosis
- Providing needed information about the test and the activities required of the patient
- Providing instructions about postprocedure care and activity restrictions
- Providing health information and procedural teaching to patients and significant others
- Helping the patient cope with discomfort and alleviating anxiety
- Informing the physician or nurse practitioner of known medical conditions or abnormal laboratory values that may affect the procedure
- Assessing for adequate hydration before, during, and immediately after the procedure, and providing education about maintenance of hydration

Stool Tests

Basic examination of the stool includes inspecting the specimen for consistency, color, and occult (not visible) blood.

TABLE
21-5 Additional Laboratory Studies for Digestive, Gastrointestinal, and Metabolic Function

Study	Clinical Functions
Abdominal X-ray	To determine gross liver size, assess for intestinal obstruction, fecal impaction
Angiography	To visualize hepatic circulation and detect presence and nature of hepatic masses
Barium study of esophagus	To identify varices, which indicate increased portal blood pressure
Celiac axis arteriography	To visualize liver and pancreas
Cholecystogram and cholangiogram	To visualize gallbladder and bile duct
Cholesterol levels	Elevated in biliary obstruction; decreased in parenchymal liver disease
Computed tomography (CT scan)	To detect hepatic neoplasms; diagnose cysts, abscesses, and hematomas; and distinguish between obstructive and nonobstructive jaundice. Detects cerebral atrophy in hepatic encephalopathy
Electroencephalogram	To detect abnormalities that occur with hepatic coma
Endoscopic retrograde cholangiopancreatography (ERCP)	To visualize biliary structures and pancreas via endoscopy
Esophagoscopy/endoscopy	To search for esophageal varices and other abnormalities
Gamma-glutamyl (GGT), gamma-glutamyl transpeptidase (GGTP), lactate dehydrogenase (LDH)	Markers for biliary stasis; also elevated in alcohol abuse
Laparoscopy	To directly visualize anterior surface of liver, gallbladder, and mesentery through a trocar
Liver biopsy (percutaneous or transjugular)	To determine anatomic changes in liver tissue
Liver scan with radio-tagged iodinated rose bengal, gold, technetium, or gallium	To show size and shape of liver; to show replacement of liver tissue with scars, cysts, or tumor
Magnetic resonance imaging (MRI)	To detect hepatic neoplasms; diagnose cysts, abscesses, and hematomas. Detects cerebral atrophy in encephalopathy
Measurement of portal pressure	To detect increased portal pressure which occurs with cirrhosis of the liver
Serum alkaline phosphatase	In absence of bone disease, to measure biliary tract obstruction
Splenoportogram (splenic portal venography)	To determine adequacy of portal blood flow
Ultrasonography	To show size of abdominal organs and presence of masses

Additional studies, including fecal urobilinogen, fecal fat, nitrogen, *Clostridium difficile,* fecal leukocytes, calculation of stool osmolar gap, parasites, pathogens, food residues, and other substances, require laboratory evaluation.

Stool samples are usually collected on a random basis unless a quantitative study (e.g., fecal fat, urobilinogen) is to be performed. Random specimens should be sent promptly to the laboratory for analysis; however, the quantitative 24- to 72-hour collections must be kept refrigerated until transported to the laboratory. Some stool collections require the patient to follow a specific diet or refrain from taking certain medications before the collection. Thorough and accurate patient education regarding a specific stool study prior to collection greatly increases the accuracy of study results.

Fecal occult blood testing (FOBT) is one of the most commonly performed stool tests. It can be useful in initial screening for several disorders, although it is used most frequently in early cancer detection programs. FOBT can be performed at the bedside, in the laboratory, or at home.

Probably the most widely used in-office or at-home occult blood test is the Hemoccult II. It is inexpensive, noninvasive, and carries minimal risk to the patient.

Breath Tests

The hydrogen breath test was developed to evaluate carbohydrate absorption, in addition to aiding in the diagnosis of bacterial overgrowth in the intestine (anaerobic bacteria in the colon are capable of producing hydrogen) and diagnosis of short bowel syndrome. This test determines the amount of hydrogen expelled in the breath. Hydrogen is produced in the colon (on contact of galactose with fermenting bacteria), absorbed into the blood, and circulated to the lungs, where the hydrogen is released and exhaled in the breath, where it can be measured. Urea breath tests detect the presence of *Helicobacter pylori*, the bacteria that can live in the mucosal lining of the stomach and cause peptic ulcer disease (Porth & Maftin, 2009).

Abdominal Ultrasonography

Ultrasonography is a noninvasive diagnostic technique in which high-frequency sound waves are passed into internal body structures and the ultrasonic echoes are recorded on an oscilloscope as they strike tissues of different densities. A clear, water-based conducting gel is applied to the skin over the abdomen, which helps with the transmission of the

TABLE
21-6 Gastrointestinal Laboratory Tests

Test	Nursing Implications
Abdominal ultra-sonography	• The patient is instructed to fast for 8 to 12 hours before the test to decrease the amount of gas in the bowel. • If gallbladder studies are to be performed, the patient should eat a fat-free meal the evening before the test. • If barium studies are to be performed, they should be scheduled after ultrasonography; otherwise, the barium could interfere with the transmission of the sound waves.
Anoscopy, proctos-copy, and sig-moidoscopy	• Preparation varies according to providers. Patients may receive an enema until the returns are clear. • During the procedure, the nurse monitors vital signs, skin color and temperature, pain tolerance, and vagal response. • After the procedure, the nurse monitors the patient for rectal bleeding and signs of intestinal perforation (i.e., fever, rectal drainage, abdominal distention, and pain). On completion of the examination, the patient can resume regular activities and diet.
Breath tests	• The patient ingests a capsule of carbon-labeled urea, and a breath sample is obtained 10 to 20 minutes later. Because *Helicobacter pylori* metabolizes urea rapidly, the labeled carbon is absorbed quickly; it can then be measured as carbon dioxide in the expired breath to determine whether *H. pylori* is present. • The patient is instructed to avoid antibiotics and loperamide (Pepto Bismol) for 1 month before the test; sucralfate (Carafate) and omeprazole (Prilosec) for 1 week before the test; and cimetidine (Tagamet), famotidine (Pepcid), and ranitidine (Zantac) for 24 hours. • *H. pylori* also can be detected by assessing serum antibody levels.
Blood chemistry	• Many electrolytes are altered in GI dysfunction. Calcium is absorbed in GI tract and may be measured to detect malabsorption. Excessive vomiting or diarrhea causes electrolyte depletion, thus requiring replacement. • Assays of serum enzymes are important in the evaluation of liver damage. AST and ALT are two enzymes found in most liver and other organs. These enzymes are elevated in most liver disorders, but they are highest in conditions that cause necrosis (viral hepatitis). • Conjugated (direct) and unconjugated (indirect) bilirubin are important measurements in the diagnosis of jaundice. • Serum ammonia level is measured to evaluate hepatic function. • CA19-9 and CEA are evaluated to diagnose, monitor the success of cancer therapy, and assess for the recurrence of cancer in the GI tract (Pagana & Pagana, 2006).
Cholecystography	• The patient is asked about allergies to iodine or seafood. If no allergy is identified, the patient receives the oral form of the contrast agent the evening before (10 to 12 hours) the X-rays are obtained. • After the contrast agent is administered, the patient is permitted nothing by mouth, to prevent contraction and emptying of the gallbladder. • An X-ray of the right upper abdomen is obtained. If the gallbladder is found to fill and empty normally and to contain no stones, gallbladder disease is ruled out. • If gallbladder disease is present, the gallbladder may not be visualized because of obstruction by gallstones. If the gallbladder is not visualized on the first attempt, a repeat of the oral cholecystography with a second dose of the contrast agent may be necessary.
CT	• CT may be performed with or without an oral or IV contrast agent, but the enhancement of the study is far superior with the administration of a contrast agent. • Any allergies to contrast agents, iodine, or shellfish, the patient's current serum creatinine level, and urine levels of human chorionic gonadotropin must be determined before administration of a contrast agent. Patients allergic to the contrast agent may be premedicated with IV prednisone 24 hours, 12 hours, and 1 hour before the scan. • In addition, renal protective measures include the administration of IV sodium bicarbonate 1 hour before and 6 hours after IV contrast and oral acetylcysteine (Mucomyst) before or after the study. Both sodium bicarbonate and Mucomyst are free radical scavengers that sequester the contrast byproducts that are destructive to renal cells.
Endoscopy through ostomy	• Nursing interventions are similar to those for other endoscopic procedures.
ERCP	• Before the procedure, the patient is given an explanation of the procedure and his or her role in it. • The patient is NPO for several hours before the procedure. • Moderate sedation is used, and the sedated patient must be monitored closely. • It may be necessary to administer medications, such as glucagon or anticholinergics, to make cannulation easier by decreasing duodenal peristalsis. • The nurse observes closely for signs of respiratory and CNS depression, hypotension, oversedation, and vomiting (if glucagon is administered).

(continued on page 590)

TABLE
21-6 **Gastrointestinal Laboratory Tests** (continued)

Test	Nursing Implications
	• During the procedure, the nurse monitors IV fluids, administers medications, and positions the patient.
	• After the procedure, the nurse monitors the patient's condition, observing vital signs and monitoring for signs of perforation or infection.
	• The nurse monitors the patient for side effects of any medications received during the procedure and for return of the gag and cough reflexes after the use of local anesthetics.
Fiberoptic colonoscopy	• Adequate colon cleansing provides optimal visualization and decreases the time needed for the procedure. The physician may prescribe a laxative for two nights before the examination and a Fleet's or saline enema until the return is clear the morning of the test. More commonly, polyethylene glycol electrolyte lavage solutions (Go-LYTELY, CoLyte, and Nu-Lytely) are used as intestinal lavages for effective cleansing of the bowel.
	• The patient maintains a clear liquid diet starting at noon the day before the procedure. Then the patient ingests the lavage solution orally at intervals over 3 to 4 hours. If necessary, the nurse can give the solution through a feeding tube if the patient cannot swallow.
	• Patients with a colostomy receive this same bowel preparation.
	• The use of lavage solutions is contraindicated in patients with intestinal obstruction or inflammatory bowel disease.
	• Side effects of the electrolyte solutions include nausea, bloating, cramping or abdominal fullness, fluid and electrolyte imbalance, and hypothermia.
	• The side effects are especially problematic for elderly patients, and sometimes they have difficulty ingesting the required volume of solution. Monitoring elderly patients after a bowel prep is especially important because their physiologic ability to compensate for fluid loss is diminished.
	• Many elderly people take multiple medications each day; therefore, the nurse's knowledge of their daily medication regimen can prompt assessment for and prevention of potential problems and early detection of physiologic changes.
Gastric analysis, gastric acid stimulation test	• The patient is NPO for 8 to 12 hours before the procedure.
	• Any medications that affect gastric secretions are withheld for 24 to 48 hours before the test.
	• Smoking is not allowed on the morning of the test, because it increases gastric secretions.
Laparoscopy (peritoneoscopy)	• The patient is NPO 12 hours prior to the procedure. An empty stomach lowers the chance of vomiting during or after the procedure.
	• An enema may be prescribed the day before or several hours prior to the procedure to empty the colon.
	• The patient should ask the primary care provider if daily medicines should be taken the day of the laparoscopy.
Lower GI series (Barium enema)	• Preparation includes emptying and cleansing the lower bowel. This often necessitates a low-residue diet 1 to 2 days before the test, a clear liquid diet and a laxative the evening before, NPO after midnight, and cleansing enemas until returns are clear the following morning.
	• The nurse makes sure that barium enemas are scheduled before any upper GI studies.
	• If the patient has active inflammatory disease of the colon, enemas are contraindicated. Barium enemas also are contraindicated in patients with signs of perforation or obstruction; instead, a water-soluble contrast study may be performed.
	• Active GI bleeding may prohibit the use of laxatives and enemas.
	• Postprocedural patient education includes information about increasing fluid intake, evaluating bowel movements for evacuation of barium, and noting increased number of bowel movements, because barium, due to its high osmolarity, may draw fluid into the bowel, thus increasing the intraluminal contents and resulting in greater output.
MRI	• The patient should be NPO 6 to 8 hours before the study.
	• Any ferromagnetic objects (metals that contain iron) can be attracted to the magnet and cause injury. Items that can be problematic or dangerous include jewelry, pacemakers, dental implants, paperclips, pens, keys, IV poles, clips on patient gowns, and oxygen tanks.
	• The patient and family are informed that the study may take 60 to 90 minutes; during this time, the technician will instruct the patient to take deep breaths at specific intervals.
	• The close-fitting scanners used in many MRI facilities may induce feelings of claustrophobia, and the machine will make a knocking sound during the procedure. Patients may choose to wear a headset and listen to music or to wear a blindfold during the procedure. Open MRIs that are less close-fitting eliminate the claustrophobia that many patients experience
	• MRI is contraindicated for patients with permanent pacemakers, artificial heart valves and defibrillators, implanted insulin pumps, or implanted transcutaneous electrical nerve stimulation devices, because the magnetic field could cause malfunction.
	• MRI is also contraindicated for patients with internal metal devices (e.g., aneurysm clips) or intraocular metallic fragments. Foil-backed skin patches (e.g., NicoDerm, nitroglycerine [Transderm-Nitro], scopolamine [Transderm- Scop], clonidine [Catapres-TTS]) should be removed before an MRI because of the risk of burns; however, the patient's physician should be consulted before the patch is removed to determine whether an alternate form of the medication should be provided.

Test	Nursing Implications
PET	• The patient should be NPO for 4 hours on the day of the test.
	• The patient should refrain from alcohol, caffeine, and tobacco for 24 hours.
	• Diabetic patients should take their pretest dose of insulin with a meal 3 to 4 hours before the test.
	• The patient should be informed that an IV line may be inserted.
	• After the PET, the patient should change position slowly from lying to standing to avoid postural hypotension.
	• The patient should be encouraged to drink fluids and urinate frequently to aid in the removal of the radioisotope from the bladder.
pH monitoring	• The patient is NPO for 6 hours before the test.
	• All medications affecting gastric secretions are withheld for 24 to 36 hours before the test.
Small-bowel enteroscopy	• The patient must be NPO for 8 to 10 hours before the test and be NPO for the first 2 hours of the testing.
	• At the time of the procedure, the patient's abdomen is marked for the location of the sensors, and the eight-lead sensors are applied. The patient wears an abdominal belt that houses a recorder to capture the transmitted images.
	• After the capsule is taken with a glass of water, the patient may return to normal activity for the remainder of the study. The patient can resume a normal diet 4 hours after the ingestion of the capsule.
	• During the procedure, the patient may receive a mild sedative and pain medication for comfort. At the end of the procedure, the patient returns to the facility with the receiver for downloading to a central computer.
	• The procedure lasts approximately 8 hours (Nakamura & Terano, 2008).
	• The capsule endoscopy is a single-use device that is propelled through the GI tract by peristalsis and excreted naturally. The patient should be informed that the capsule will be excreted in the stool.
Stool tests	• Should not be performed if there is hemorrhoidal bleeding.
	• Careful assessment of the patient's diet and medication regimen is essential to avoid incorrect interpretation of results. Red meats, fish, turnips, horseradish, and NSAIDs, should be avoided for 72 hours prior to the study because they may cause a false-positive result. Ingestion of vitamin C from supplements or foods can cause a false-negative result.
	• A small amount of the specimen is applied to the guaiac-impregnated paper slide. If the test is performed at home, the patient mails the slide to the health care provider or laboratory in an envelope provided for that purpose.
	• Other occult blood tests that may yield more specific and more sensitive readings include Hematest II SENSA and HemoQuant.
Ultrasonography	• No fasting is required for ultrasonography of the abdominal aorta, kidney, liver, spleen, or pancreas, but is preferred before ultrasonography of the gallbladder and biliary tree.
	• During the procedure, the patient is lying down. The patient may be asked to change position so that the healthcare provider can examine different areas.
	• The patient may also be asked to hold his or her breath for short periods of time during the examination.
Upper GI fibros-copy/esophago-gastroduodeno-scopy	• The patient should be NPO for 8 hours prior to the examination.
	• A sedative that provides moderate sedation and relieves anxiety during the procedure, may be administered at the initiation of the study.
	• Atropine may be administered to reduce secretions, and glucagon may be administered to relax smooth muscle.
	• Before the introduction of the endoscope, the patient is given a local anesthetic gargle or spray.
	• The patient is placed in the left lateral position to facilitate clearance of pulmonary secretions and provide smooth entry of the scope.
	• After gastroscopy, assessment includes level of consciousness, vital signs, oxygen saturation, pain level, and monitoring for signs of perforation (i.e., pain, bleeding, unusual difficulty swallowing, and rapidly elevated temperature).
	• After the patient's gag reflex has returned, lozenges, saline gargle, and oral analgesics may be offered to relieve minor throat discomfort.
	• Patients who were sedated for the procedure must remain in bed until fully alert.
Upper GI series (Barium swallow)	• The patient is instructed to fast after midnight the day before the test.
	• Smoking, chewing gum, and using mints can stimulate gastric motility; therefore, the nurse advises against these practices.
	• Typically, oral medications are withheld on the morning of the study and resumed that evening, but each patient's medication regimen should be evaluated on an individual basis.
	• Follow-up care is provided after the upper GI procedure to ensure that the patient has eliminated most of the ingested barium. Fluids may be increased to facilitate evacuation of stool and barium.

(continued on page 592)

TABLE
21-6 Gastrointestinal Laboratory Tests (continued)

Test	Nursing Implications
Urine tests	• Amylase can be detected in the urine. There is an increased renal clearance of amylase in patients with acute pancreatitis. Amylase levels in the urine remain high even after serum levels return to normal. • Urine urobilinogen is a form of bilirubin that is converted by the intestinal flora and excreted in the urine. Its measurement is useful in the evaluation of hepatic and biliary obstruction. The presence of bilirubin in urine often precedes the development of jaundice (Pagana & Pagana, 2006). For the urine urobilinogen test, some laboratories require keeping the patient NPO after midnight the day of the test, except for water.

ALT, alanine aminotransferase; AST, aspartate aminotransferase; CA19-9, carbohydrate antigen 19-9; CEA, carcinoembryonic antigen; CT, computed tomography; ERCP, endoscopic retrograde cholangiopancreatography; GI, gastrointestinal tract; IV, intravenous; MRI, magnetic resonance imaging; NSAIDs, nonsteroidal anti-inflammatory drugs; NPO (*nil per os*), nothing by mouth; PET, positron emission tomography.

sound waves. A handheld probe called a transducer is then moved over the abdomen. Ultrasonography is particularly useful in the detection of an enlarged gallbladder or pancreas, the presence of gallstones, an enlarged ovary, an ectopic pregnancy, or appendicitis. Most recently this technique has proved useful in diagnosing acute colonic diverticulitis.

Ultrasonography is the diagnostic procedure of choice for gallbladder disease because it is rapid and accurate and can be used in patients with liver dysfunction and jaundice. It does not expose patients to ionizing radiation. The procedure is most accurate if the patient fasts overnight so that the gallbladder is distended. Ultrasound studies are based on analysis of reflected sound waves. Ultrasonography can detect with over 90% accuracy calculi in the gallbladder or a dilated common bile duct (Schiff et al., 2007). Ultrasound findings include gallbladder sludge, gallbladder wall thickening, and pericholecystic fluid, which are diagnostic for acute cholecystitis. Cholecystography, which uses radiotracer to visualize the gallbladder to determine cystic duct obstruction, is used if ultrasound findings are inconclusive (Elwood, 2008).

Endoscopic ultrasonography (EUS) is a specialized enteroscopic procedure that aids in the diagnosis of GI disorders by providing direct imaging of a target area. A small, high-frequency ultrasonic transducer is mounted at the tip of the fiberoptic scope, which displays an image that enables tumor staging and visualization of marginal structures. This procedure delivers results with higher-quality resolution and definition in comparison with regular ultrasonic imaging. EUS may be used for evaluating submucosal lesions, specifically determining their location and depth of penetration. In addition, EUS may aid in the evaluation of Barrett's esophagus, portal hypertension, chronic pancreatitis, suspected pancreatic neoplasm, biliary tract disease, and changes in the bowel wall that occur in ulcerative colitis. Intestinal gas, bone, and thick layers of adipose tissue (all of which hamper conventional ultrasonography) are not problematic when EUS is used.

DNA Testing

Researchers have refined methods for genetics risk assessment, preclinical diagnosis, and prenatal diagnosis to identify people who are at risk for certain GI disorders (e.g., gastric cancer, lactose deficiency, inflammatory bowel disease, colon cancer). In some cases, DNA testing allows providers to prevent (or minimize) disease by intervening before its onset, and to improve therapy; however, it is imperative to seek advice from genetics counselors routinely, given the exponential growth of genetics information (Hodgson & Loannides, 2009). People who are identified as at risk of certain GI disorders may choose to undergo genetic counseling to learn about the disease, to understand options for preventing and treating the disease, and to receive support in coping with the situation. Ethical and legal issues are involved in genetic testing, and there are legal protections for clients against discrimination. For instance, false-positive results can create unnecessary worry, alarm, and further testing, typically at the expense of the patient and the family, with potential effects on health-related quality of life (Aronson, 2009).

Imaging Studies

Many minimally invasive and noninvasive imaging studies, including X-ray and contrast studies, computed tomography (CT), magnetic resonance imaging (MRI), positron emission tomography (PET), and virtual endoscopy, are available today to aid in the accurate assessment of the many possible causes of GI abnormalities.

Upper Gastrointestinal Tract Study

An upper GI study delineates the entire GI tract after the introduction of a contrast agent. A radiopaque liquid (e.g., barium sulfate) is commonly used; however, thin barium, Hypaque, and, at times, water are used due to their low associated risks. The GI series enables the examiner to detect or exclude anatomic or functional derangement of the upper GI organs or sphincters. It also aids in the diagnosis of ulcers, varices, tumors, regional enteritis, and malabsorption

syndromes. The procedure may be extended to examine the duodenum and small bowel (small bowel follow-through). As the barium descends into the stomach, the position, patency, and caliber of the esophagus are visualized, enabling the examiner to detect or exclude any anatomic or functional derangement of that organ. Fluoroscopic examination next extends to the stomach as its lumen fills with barium, allowing observation of stomach motility, thickness of the gastric wall, the mucosal pattern, patency of the pyloric valve, and the anatomy of the duodenum. Multiple X-ray films are obtained during the procedure, and additional images may be taken at intervals for up to 24 hours to evaluate the rate of gastric emptying. Small-bowel X-rays taken while the barium is passing through that area allow for observation of the motility of the small bowel. Obstructions, ileitis, and diverticula can be detected if present.

Variations of the upper GI study include double-contrast studies and enteroclysis (defined below). The double-contrast method of examining the upper GI tract involves administration of a thick barium suspension to outline the stomach and esophageal wall, after which tablets that release carbon dioxide in the presence of water are administered. This technique has the advantage of showing the esophagus and stomach in finer detail, permitting signs of early superficial neoplasms to be noted.

Enteroclysis is a very detailed, double-contrast study of the entire small intestine that involves the continuous infusion, through a duodenal tube, of 500 to 1,000 mL of a thin barium sulfate suspension; after this, methylcellulose is infused through the tube. The barium and methylcellulose fill the intestinal loops and are observed continuously by fluoroscopy and viewed at frequent intervals as they progress through the jejunum and the ileum. This process (even with normal motility) can take up to 6 hours and can be quite uncomfortable for the patient. The procedure aids in the diagnosis of partial small-bowel obstructions or diverticula.

Lower Gastrointestinal Tract Study

Visualization of the lower GI tract is obtained after rectal installation of barium. The barium enema can be used to detect the presence of polyps, tumors, or other lesions of the large intestine and demonstrate any anatomic abnormalities or malfunctioning of the bowel. After proper preparation and evacuation of the entire colon, each portion of the colon may be readily observed. The procedure usually takes about 15 to 30 minutes, during which time X-ray images are obtained.

Other means for visualizing the colon include double-contrast studies and a water-soluble contrast study. A double-contrast, or air-contrast, barium enema involves the instillation of a thicker barium solution, followed by the instillation of air. The patient may feel some cramping or discomfort during this process. This test provides a contrast between the air-filled lumen and the barium-coated mucosa, allowing easier detection of smaller lesions.

If active inflammatory disease, fistulas, or perforation of the colon is suspected, a water-soluble iodinated contrast agent (e.g., Gastrografin) can be used. The procedure is the same as for a barium enema, but the patient must be assessed for allergy to iodine or contrast agent. The contrast agent is eliminated readily after the procedure, so there is no need for postprocedure laxatives. Some diarrhea may occur in a few patients until the contrast agent has been totally eliminated.

Computed Tomography

CT provides cross-sectional images of abdominal organs and structures. Multiple X-ray images are taken from numerous angles, digitized in a computer, reconstructed, and then viewed on a computer monitor. The procedure is completely painless, but radiation doses are considerable. New continuous-motion (helical or spiral), three-dimensional CT, which provides very detailed pictures of the GI organs and vasculature, has been developed.

Magnetic Resonance Imaging

MRI is used in gastroenterology to supplement ultrasonography and CT. This noninvasive technique uses magnetic fields and radio waves to produce an image of the area being studied. The use of oral contrast agents to enhance the image has increased the application of this technique for the diagnosis of GI diseases. It is useful in evaluating abdominal soft tissues as well as blood vessels, abscesses, fistulas, neoplasms, and other sources of bleeding.

Positron Emission Tomography

PET produces images of the body by detecting the radiation emitted from radioactive substances. The radioactive substances are injected into the body intravenously and are usually tagged with a radioactive atom, such as carbon-11, fluorine-18, oxygen-15, or nitrogen-13. The atoms decay quickly, do not harm the body, have lower radiation levels than a typical X-ray or CT scan, and are eliminated in the urine or feces. The scanner essentially "captures" where the radioactive substances are in the body, transmits information to a scanner, and produces a scan with "hot spots" for evaluation by the radiologist or oncologist.

Endoscopic Procedures

Endoscopy procedures are performed for a variety of reasons and are associated with a variety of psychological reactions from the patients. Many patients avoid the recommended endoscopies out of fear of the procedure or what the procedure may find. In recent years, propofol has been used increasingly during endoscopy procedures instead of sedation with the combination of an opiate and benzodiazepine. Box 21-1 details nursing responsibilities associated with the use of propofol during a GI endoscopy procedure.

Upper Gastrointestinal Fibroscopy/ Esophagogastroduodenoscopy

Fibroscopy of the upper GI tract allows direct visualization of the esophageal, gastric, and duodenal mucosa through a

BOX 21-1
Sedation and Anesthesia in Gastrointestinal Endoscopy

Endoscopy is direct visualization of the GI tract using a flexible fiberoptic endoscope. Visualization of the esophagus, stomach, biliary system, and bowel is possible with an endoscope. Sedation is given to reduce anxiety and diminish the patient's memory of this uncomfortable event. The level of sedation required to perform an endoscopy ranges from minimal sedation to general anesthesia.

In recent years, studies have identified advantages of using propofol during endoscopy procedures oversedation with the combination of an opiate and benzodiazepines. Propofol during GI endoscopy procedures can lead to patient and physician satisfaction, improved patient cooperation, faster recovery, and mild antiemetic properties. However, there are some disadvantages, including the potential to induce general anesthesia, respiratory depression, and the fact that there is no pharmacologic antagonist.

The patient should be monitored to detect any changes in pulse, blood pressure, ventilator status, cardiac electrical activity, and neurological status. An individual with skills sets including certification in basic and advanced cardiac life support should be present to monitor and interpret the patient's status throughout the procedure. A study suggests the use of an anesthesiologist in the following situations: endoscopic procedures requiring deep sedation, anticipated intolerance to standard sedatives, multiple comorbidities, and increased risk for airway obstruction because of anatomical variation.

Additional studies are needed to determine the adequacy of using propofol for GI endoscopies instead of the commonly used benzodiazepine and opioid combination.

Source: American Society for Gastrointestinal Endoscopy. (2008). Sedation and anesthesia in GI endoscopy. *Gastrointestinal Endoscopy, 68*(5), 815–826.

lighted endoscope (gastroscope; Fig. 21-9). Esophagogastroduodenoscopy (EGD) is especially valuable when esophageal, gastric, or duodenal abnormalities or inflammatory, neoplastic, or infectious processes are suspected. This procedure also can be used to evaluate esophageal and gastric motility and to collect secretions and tissue specimens for further analysis.

In EGD, the gastroenterologist views the GI tract through a viewing lens and can take still or video photographs through the scope to document findings. Electronic video endoscopes also are available that attach directly to a video processor, converting the electronic signals into pictures on a television screen. This allows larger and continuous viewing capabilities, as well as the simultaneous recording of the procedure.

PillCam ESO, a pill-sized instrument equipped with two cameras, is available. Each camera takes seven photographs per second and transmits them wirelessly to a nearby storage device (Nakamura & Terano, 2008). This technique is gaining popularity with patients and practitioners alike as a comfortable, convenient alternative to endoscopy. Two major drawbacks to this method of endoscopy are that it evaluates only the esophagus and that it may become lodged in a previously anastomosed section of bowel and require further endoscopic or surgical intervention for removal.

Side-viewing flexible scopes are used to visualize the common bile duct and the pancreatic and hepatic ducts through the ampulla of Vater in the duodenum. This procedure, called **endoscopic retrograde cholangiopancreatography (ERCP)**, uses the endoscope in combination with X-ray techniques to view the ductal structures of the biliary tract (Vitale, Davis, Zavaleta et al., 2009). ERCP is helpful

in evaluating jaundice, pancreatitis, pancreatic tumors, common bile duct stones, and biliary tract disease. ERCP is described further later in this chapter.

Upper GI fibroscopy also can be a therapeutic procedure when it is combined with other procedures. Therapeutic endoscopy can be used to remove common bile duct stones, dilate strictures, and treat gastric bleeding and esophageal varices. Laser-compatible scopes can be used to provide laser therapy for upper GI neoplasms. Sclerosing solutions can be injected through the scope in an attempt to control upper GI bleeding.

Fiberoptic Colonoscopy
Historically, direct visualization of the bowel was the only means to evaluate the colon, but virtual colonoscopy (also

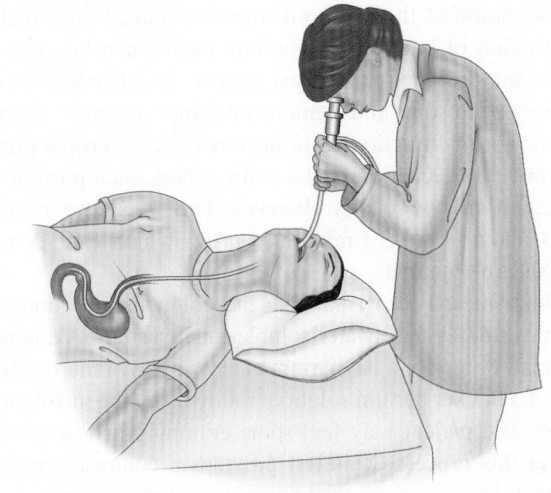

FIGURE 21-9 Client undergoing gastroscopy.

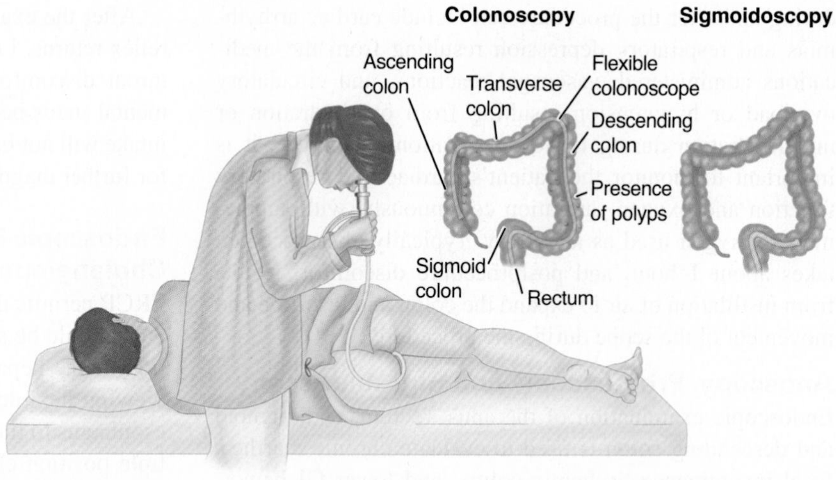

FIGURE 21-10 Colonoscopy. The flexible scope is passed through the rectum and sigmoid colon into the descending, transverse, and ascending colon.

known as CT colonography) has brought a more patient-friendly approach to this study. First described by Vining in 1994, virtual colonoscopy provides a computer-simulated endoluminal perspective of the air-filled distended colon using conventional spiral or helical CT scanning (Johnson, 2009).

Direct visual inspection of the large intestine (anus, rectum, sigmoid, transcending and ascending colon) is possible by means of a flexible fiberoptic colonoscope (Fig. 21-10). These scopes have the same capabilities as those used for EGD but are larger in diameter and longer. Still and video recordings can be used to document the procedure and findings.

This procedure is used commonly as a diagnostic aid and screening device. It is most frequently used for cancer screening (Box 21-2) and for surveillance in patients with previous colon cancer or polyps. In addition, tissue biopsies can be obtained as needed, and polyps can be removed and evaluated. Other uses of colonoscopy include the evaluation of patients with diarrhea of unknown cause, occult bleeding, or anemia; further study of abnormalities detected on barium enema; and diagnosis, clarification, and determination of the extent of inflammatory or other bowel disease.

Therapeutically, the procedure can be used to remove all visible polyps with a special snare and cautery through the colonoscope. Many colon cancers begin with adenomatous polyps of the colon; therefore, one goal of colonoscopic polypectomy is early detection and prevention of colorectal cancer. This procedure also can be used to treat areas of bleeding or stricture. Use of bipolar and unipolar coagulators, use of heater probes, and injections of sclerosing agents or vasoconstrictors are all possible during this procedure. Laser-compatible scopes provide laser therapy for bleeding lesions or colonic neoplasms. Bowel decompression (removal of intestinal contents to prevent gas and fluid from distending the coils of the intestine) can also be completed during the procedure.

Colonoscopy is performed while the patient is lying on the left side with the legs drawn up toward the chest. The

patient's position may be changed during the test to facilitate advancement of the scope. Biopsy forceps or a cytology brush may be passed through the scope to obtain specimens for histology and cytology examinations. Complications

---

BOX 21-2 | **Health Promotion**

Guidelines for Colon and Rectal Cancer Screening

Beginning at age 50, both men and women should follow one of these five testing schedules:
- Fecal occult blood test (FOBT)* or fecal immuno-chemical test (FIT) every year
- Flexible sigmoidoscopy every 5 years
- Yearly FOBT or FIT, plus flexible sigmoidoscopy every 5 years†
- Double-contrast barium enema every 5 years
- Colonoscopy every 10 years

All positive tests should be followed up with colonoscopy.

Individuals should talk to their providers about starting colorectal cancer screening earlier and/or undergoing screening more often if they have any of the following colorectal cancer risk factors:
- A personal history of colorectal cancer or adenomatous polyps
- A strong family history of colorectal cancer or polyps (cancer or polyps in a first-degree relative <60 or in two first-degree relatives of any age)‡
- A personal history of chronic inflammatory bowel disease
- A family history of an hereditary colorectal cancer syndrome (familial adenomatous polyposis or hereditary nonpolyposis colon cancer)

*For FOBT, the take-home multiple sample method should be used.
†The combination of yearly FOBT or FIT flexible sigmoidoscopy every 5 years is preferred over either of these options alone.
‡A first-degree relative is defined as a parent, sibling, or child.
Reprinted by the permission of The American Cancer Society, Inc. from www.cancer.org. All rights reserved.

during and after the procedure can include cardiac arrhythmias and respiratory depression resulting from the medications administered, vasovagal reactions, and circulatory overload or hypotension resulting from overhydration or underhydration during bowel preparation. Therefore, it is important to monitor the patient's cardiac and respiratory function and oxygen saturation continuously, with supplemental oxygen used as necessary. Typically, the procedure takes about 1 hour, and postprocedure discomfort results from instillation of air to expand the colon and insertion and movement of the scope during the procedure.

Anoscopy, Proctoscopy, and Sigmoidoscopy

Endoscopic examination of the anus, rectum, and sigmoid and descending colon is used to evaluate chronic diarrhea, fecal incontinence, ischemic colitis, and lower GI hemorrhage and to observe for ulceration, fissures, abscesses, tumors, polyps, and other pathologic processes.

Flexible scopes have largely replaced the rigid scopes used in the past for routine examinations. The flexible fiberoptic sigmoidoscope (see Fig. 21-10) permits the colon to be examined up to 40 to 50 cm (16 to 20 inches) from the anus, much more than the 25 cm (10 inches) that can be visualized with the rigid sigmoidoscope. It has many of the same capabilities as the scopes used for the upper GI study, including the use of still or video images to document findings.

For flexible scope procedures, the patient assumes a comfortable position on the left side with the right leg bent and placed anteriorly. It is important to keep the patient informed throughout the examination and to explain the sensations associated with the examination. Biopsies and polypectomies can be performed during this procedure. Biopsy is performed with small biting forceps introduced through the endoscope; one or more small pieces of tissue may be removed. If rectal or sigmoid polyps are present, they may be removed with a wire snare, which is used to grasp the pedicle, or stalk. An electrocoagulating current is then used to sever the polyp and prevent bleeding. It is extremely important that all excised tissue be placed immediately in moist gauze or in an appropriate receptacle, labeled correctly, and delivered without delay to the pathology laboratory for examination.

Endoscopy for Esophageal Varices

Esophageal varices are varicosities that develop from elevated pressure in the veins that drain into the portal system. Varices are associated with cirrhosis of the liver. They are prone to rupture and often are the source of massive hemorrhages from the upper GI tract. Immediate endoscopy is indicated to identify the cause and the site of bleeding; at least 30% of patients with suspected bleeding from esophageal varices are actually bleeding from another source (gastritis, ulcer). Nursing support can be effective in relieving anxiety during this often stressful experience. Careful monitoring can detect early signs of cardiac arrhythmias, perforation, and hemorrhage.

After the examination, fluids are not given until the gag reflex returns. Lozenges and gargles may be used to relieve throat discomfort if the patient's physical condition and mental status permit. If the patient is actively bleeding, oral intake will not be permitted, and the patient will be prepared for further diagnostic and therapeutic procedures.

Endoscopic Retrograde Cholangiopancreatography

ERCP permits direct visualization of structures that previously could be seen only during laparotomy. The examination of the hepatobiliary system is carried out via a side-viewing flexible fiberoptic endoscope inserted through the esophagus to the descending duodenum (Fig. 21-11). Multiple position changes are required to pass the endoscope during the procedure, beginning in the left semiprone position.

Fluoroscopy and multiple X-rays are used during ERCP to evaluate the presence and location of ductal stones. Careful insertion of a catheter through the endoscope into the common bile duct is the most important step in sphincterotomy (division of the muscles of the biliary sphincter) for gallstone extraction via this technique.

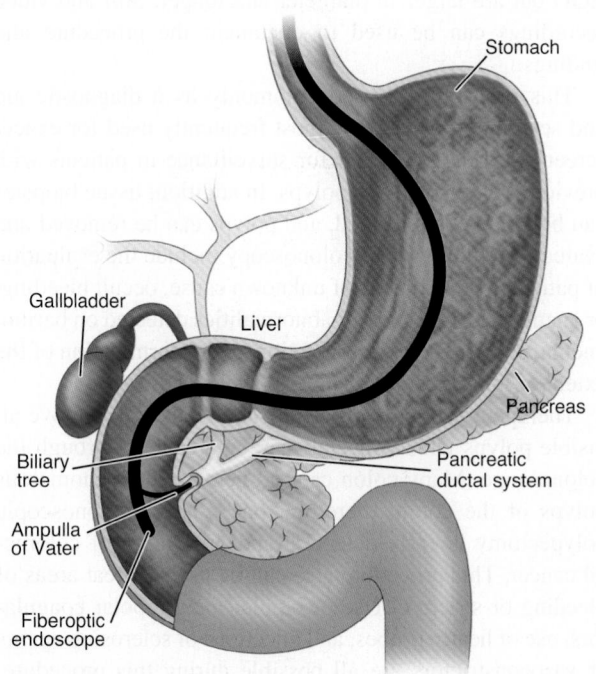

FIGURE 21-11 Endoscopic retrograde cholangiopancreatography (ERCP). A fiberoptic duodenoscope, with side-viewing apparatus, is inserted into the duodenum. The ampulla of Vater is catheterized, and the biliary tree is injected with contrast agent. The pancreatic ductal system is also assessed, if indicated. This procedure is of special value in visualizing neoplasms of the ampulla area and extracting a biopsy specimen.

Laparoscopy (Peritoneoscopy)

With the tremendous advances in minimally invasive surgery, diagnostic laparoscopy is efficient, cost-effective, and useful in the diagnosis of GI disease. After creating a pneumoperitoneum (gas, usually carbon dioxide, is insufflated into the peritoneal cavity to separate the intestines from the pelvic organs, creating a working space for visualization), a small incision is made lateral to the umbilicus, allowing for the insertion of the fiberoptic laparoscope. This permits direct visualization of the organs and structures within the abdomen, permitting visualization and identification of any growths, anomalies, and inflammatory processes. In addition, biopsy samples can be taken from the structures and organs as necessary. This procedure can be used to evaluate peritoneal disease, chronic abdominal pain, abdominal masses, and gallbladder and liver disease. However, laparoscopy has not become an important diagnostic modality in patients with acute abdominal pain because less invasive tools (i.e., CT and MRI) are readily available. Laparoscopy usually requires general anesthesia and sometimes requires that the stomach and bowel be decompressed. One of the benefits of this procedure is that after visualization of a problem, excision (e.g., removal of the gallbladder) can then be performed at the same time, if appropriate.

Small-Bowel Enteroscopy

Capsule endoscopy is a noninvasive enteroscopy that visualizes the entire small bowel, including the distal ileum. It is used to evaluate the source of GI bleeding. Prior to the development of the capsule endoscopy, visualization of the small intestine was inadequate and physicians relied primarily on barium X-rays for diagnosing disorders of the small intestine (Tukey, Pleskow, Legnani et al., 2009). The technique consists of the patient swallowing a capsule approximately the size of a vitamin pill that has embedded in it a wireless miniature camera, a light source, and an image transmission system. The capsule is propelled through the intestines by peristalsis and is excreted naturally in the stool in 1 to 2 days. During the procedure, images are transmitted from the capsule to a data recorder housed in an abdominal belt worn by the patient. This is a diagnostic procedure that does not allow the retrieval of tissue samples for histology nor does it provide for endoscopic therapy, thus limiting its use (Cellier, 2008).

Another procedure used to visualize the entire mucosa of the small bowel, as well as to enable diagnostic and therapeutic interventions, is double-balloon enteroscopy (DBE), also known as the push-and-pull method (Pohl, May, Nachbar, & Ell, 2007). This endoscope has two balloons, one attached to the distal end of the scope and the other attached to the transparent overtube that slides over the endoscope. The endoscope is advanced using a push-and-pull technique that involves inflating and deflating the balloons alternatively. This process causes the telescoping of the small intestine onto the overtube, which enables the endoscope to visualize much more of the small intestine than the length of the scope itself. The procedure takes 1 to 3 hours and requires moderate sedation (Cellier, 2008).

Endoscopy Through Ostomy

Endoscopy using a flexible endoscope through an ostomy stoma is useful for visualizing a segment of the small or large intestine and may be indicated to evaluate the anastomosis for recurrent disease, or to visualize and treat bleeding in a segment of the bowel.

Gastric Analysis, Gastric Acid Stimulation Test, and pH Monitoring

Analysis of the gastric juice yields information about the secretory activity of the gastric mucosa and the presence or degree of gastric retention in patients thought to have pyloric or duodenal obstruction. It is also useful for diagnosing **Zollinger-Ellison syndrome**, or atrophic gastritis.

A small nasogastric tube with a catheter tip marked at various points is inserted through the nose. When the tube is at a point slightly less than 50 cm (21 inches), it should be within the stomach, lying along the greater curvature. Once in place, the tube is secured to the patient's cheek, and the patient is placed in a semi-reclining position. The entire stomach contents are aspirated by gentle suction into a syringe.

The gastric acid stimulation test usually is performed in conjunction with gastric analysis. Histamine or pentagastrin is administered subcutaneously to stimulate gastric secretions. It is important to inform the patient that this injection may produce a flushed feeling. The nurse monitors the patient's blood pressure and pulse frequently to detect hypotension. Gastric specimens are collected after the injection every 15 minutes for 1 hour and are labeled to indicate the time of specimen collection after histamine injection. The volume and pH of the specimen are measured; in certain instances, cytologic study by the Papanicolaou technique may be used to determine the presence or absence of malignant cells.

Esophageal reflux of gastric acid may be diagnosed by ambulatory pH monitoring. A probe that measures pH is inserted through the nose and into position about 5 inches above the lower esophageal sphincter. It is connected to an external recording device and is worn for 24 hours while the patient continues his or her normal daily activities. At the end of the test, there is a computer analysis and graphic display of the results. This test allows for the direct correlation between chest pain and reflux episodes (Wolfe, Davis, Farraye et al., 2009).

A Bernstein test may be performed to evaluate complaints of acid-related chest or epigastric pain. HCl is instilled through a small feeding tube positioned in the esophagus to try to elicit the reported chest pain. Resultant signs and symptoms are compared with the patient's usual symptoms. However, since the advent of ambulatory pH monitoring,

this previously popular evaluation tool is used infrequently (Wolfe et al., 2009).

The Bravo pH monitoring system is a newer procedure that offers the advantage of pH monitoring of the esophagus without the transnasal catheter. The Bravo system involves a pH capsule about the size of a gel cap, which is temporarily attached to the wall of the esophagus. The Bravo pH capsule measures pH levels in the esophagus and transmits readings via radio telemetry to the pager-sized receiver worn on the patient's belt or waistband. Data are collected for up to 48 hours and then downloaded and analyzed. Normal patient activities such as swallowing, eating, and drinking should cause the disposable pH capsule to spontaneously detach from the esophagus and pass through the digestive tract in 7 to 10 days (Pandolfino & Kwiatek, 2008).

Liver Function Tests

Early recognition and assessment of hepatic dysfunction is critical to provide timely and appropriate care for the patient with acute or chronic liver disease. More than 70% of the parenchyma of the liver may be damaged before liver function test results become abnormal. Function is generally measured in terms of serum enzyme activity (i.e., serum aminotransferases, alkaline phosphatase [ALP], lactic dehydrogenase) and serum concentrations of proteins (albumin and globulins), bilirubin, ammonia, clotting factors, and lipids. Several of these tests may be helpful for assessing patients with liver disease. However, the nature and extent of hepatic dysfunction cannot be determined by these tests alone, because other disorders can affect test results.

Serum aminotransferases (also called transaminases) are enzymes that reflect varying degrees of hepatocellular injury or inflammation of the liver and are useful in detecting acute liver disease such as hepatitis. Alanine aminotransferase (ALT), aspartate aminotransferase (AST), and gamma-glutamyl transferase (GGT; also called G-glutamyl transpeptidase) are the most frequently used tests for liver damage. ALT levels increase primarily in liver disorders and may be used to monitor the course of hepatitis or cirrhosis or the effects of treatments that may be toxic to the liver. AST is present in tissues that have high metabolic activity; therefore, the level may be increased if there is damage to or death of tissues of organs such as the heart, liver, skeletal muscle, and kidney. Although not specific to liver disease, levels of AST may be increased in cirrhosis, hepatitis, and liver cancer. Abnormal aminotransferases may occur in the absence of any clinical indication of liver disease and this finding requires further investigation to determine if it is incidental or if hepatic injury is present. A ratio of AST to ALT greater than 2.0 may reflect chronic alcoholic liver disease, however, it is not diagnostic (Bacon et al., 2007).

Increased GGT levels are associated with cholestasis but can also be due to alcoholic liver disease. Although the kidney has the highest level of the enzyme, the liver is considered the source of normal serum activity. Alkaline

phosphatase (ALP) elevations may indicate injury to the biliary tree (i.e., biliary obstruction), presence of tumors, primary biliary cirrhosis, and primary sclerosing cholangitis. Elevations of both ALP and GGT indicate disease of the liver or biliary system. Elevation of ALP with normal GGT levels should initiate evaluation for possible bone disease, as this enzyme is also present in bone tissue.

Other important tests to determine the extent of liver dysfunction are serum bilirubin, serum albumin, and prothrombin time as measured by the international normalized ratio (INR). These tests represent the synthetic function of the liver and are used as a prognostic tool to determine the severity of liver disease (Bacon et al., 2007). Common liver function tests are summarized in Table 21-7.

Liver Biopsy

Liver biopsy is considered the gold standard for the diagnosis of liver disease. A small sample of liver tissue is obtained, usually through needle aspiration, for microscopic evaluation of liver cells and architecture. The most common indication is to evaluate diffuse disorders of the parenchyma and to diagnose space-occupying lesions. Liver biopsy is especially useful when clinical findings and laboratory tests are not diagnostic. Bleeding and bile peritonitis after liver biopsy are the major complications; therefore, coagulation studies are obtained, their values are noted, and abnormal results are treated before liver biopsy is performed. Other techniques for liver biopsy are preferred if ascites or coagulation abnormalities exist. A liver biopsy can be performed percutaneously with ultrasound guidance or transvenously through the right internal jugular vein to right hepatic vein under fluoroscopic control. Liver biopsy can also be performed laparoscopically. Guidelines for assisting with a liver biopsy are found in Box 21-3 on page 600.

Paracentesis

Paracentesis is the removal of fluid (ascites) from the peritoneal cavity through a puncture or a small surgical incision through the abdominal wall under sterile conditions. Ultrasound guidance may be indicated in some patients who are at high risk for bleeding because of an abnormal coagulation profile and in those who have had previous abdominal surgery and may have adhesions. Paracentesis was once considered a routine form of treatment for ascites. However, it is now performed primarily for diagnostic examination of ascitic fluid; for treatment of massive ascites that is resistant to nutritional and diuretic therapy and causing severe problems for the patient; to assess for trauma, infection in the peritoneal fluid, and pathology (e.g., cancer); and to remove fluid in renal and cardiac disease. A sample of the ascitic fluid may be sent to the laboratory for cell count, albumin and total protein levels, culture, and other tests.

Large-volume (5 to 6 L) paracentesis has been shown to be a safe method for treating patients with severe ascites. This technique, in combination with the IV infusion

TABLE
21-7 Common Laboratory Tests to Assess Liver Function

Test	Normal	Clinical Functions
Pigment Studies		
Serum bilirubin, direct	0–0.3 mg/dL (0–5.1 μmol/L)	These studies measure the ability of the liver to conjugate and excrete bilirubin. Results are abnormal in liver and biliary tract disease and are associated with jaundice clinically.
Serum bilirubin, total	0–0.9 mg/dL (1.7–20.5 μmol/L)	
Urine bilirubin	0(0)	
Urine urobilinogen	0.05–2.5 mg/24 h (0.09–4. Ehrlich U /24 h)	
Fecal urobilinogen (infrequently used)	50–300 mg/24 h (100–400 Ehrlich U /100 g)	
Protein Studies		
Total serum protein	7.0–7.5 g/dL (70–75 g/L)	Proteins are manufactured by the liver. Their levels may be affected in a variety of liver impairments: albumin is affected in cirrhosis, chronic hepatitis, edema, and ascites; globulins are affected in cirrhosis, liver disease, chronic obstructive jaundice, and viral hepatitis.
Serum albumin	4.0–5.5 g/dL (40–55 g/L)	
Serum globulin	1.7–3.3 g/dL (17–33 g/L)	
Serum protein electrophoresis		
Albumin	4.0–5.5 g/dL (40–55 g/L)	
Alpha$_1$-Globulin	0.15–0.25 g/dL (1.5–2.5 g/L)	
Alpha$_2$-Globulin	0.43–0.75 g/dL (4.3–7.5 g/L)	
Beta-Globulin	0.5–1.0 g/dL (5–10 g/L)	
Gamma-Globulin	0.6–1.3 g/dL (6–13 g/L)	
Albumin/globulin (A/G) ratio	A > G or 1.5:1–2.5:1	A/G ratio is reversed in chronic liver disease (decreased albumin and increased globulin).
Prothrombin Time	100% or 12–16 seconds	Prothrombin time may be prolonged in liver disease. It will not return to normal with vitamin K in severe liver cell damage.
Serum Alkaline Phosphatase	Varies with method: 2–5 Bodansky units 30–50 U/L at 34°C (17–142 U/L at 30°C) (20–90 U/L at 30°C)	Serum alkaline phosphatase is manufactured in bones, liver, kidneys, and intestine and excreted through biliary tract. In absence of bone disease, it is a sensitive measure of biliary tract obstruction.
Serum Aminotransferase Studies		The studies are based on release of enzymes from damaged liver cells. These enzymes are elevated in liver cell damage.
AST	10–40 units (4.8–19 U/L)	
ALT	5–35 units (2.4–17 U/L)	
GGT, GGTP	10–48 IU/L	Elevated in alcohol abuse. Marker for biliary cholestasis.
LDH	100–200 units (100–225 U/L)	
Ammonia (plasma)	15–45 μg/dL (11–32 μmol/L)	Liver converts ammonia to urea. Ammonia level rises in liver failure.
Cholesterol		
Ester	60% of total (fraction of total cholesterol: 0.60)	Cholesterol levels are elevated in biliary obstruction and decreased in parenchymal liver disease.
HDL (high-density lipoprotein)	HDL Male: 35–70 mg/dL, Female: 35–85 mg/dL	
LDL (low-density lipoprotein)	LDL <130 μg/dL	

of salt-poor albumin or other colloid, has become a standard management strategy yielding an immediate effect. Refractive, massive ascites is unresponsive to multiple diuretics and sodium restriction for 2 weeks or more and can result in severe sequelae, such as respiratory distress, which requires rapid intervention. Albumin infusions help to correct decreases in effective arterial blood volume that lead to sodium retention. Use of this colloid reduces the incidence of hyponatremia and renal dysfunction associated with decreased effective arterial volume (Greenberger, Blumberg, & Burakoff, 2009). The beneficial effects of albumin administration on hemodynamic stability and renal functional status may be related to an improvement in

cardiac function, as well as to a decrease in the degree of arterial vasodilation (Greenberger et al., 2009). Although the patient with cirrhosis has greatly increased extracellular blood volume, the kidney incorrectly senses that the effective volume has decreased. The renin–angiotensin–aldosterone axis is stimulated, and sodium is reabsorbed. In addition, antidiuretic hormone (ADH) secretion increases, which leads to increased retention of free water and sometimes to the development of dilutional hyponatremia (Reddy & Mooradian, 2009). Therapeutic paracentesis provides only temporary removal of fluid; ascites rapidly recurs, necessitating repeated fluid removal. Guidelines for assisting with paracentesis are found in Box 21-4 on page 601.

BOX 21-3

GUIDELINES FOR NURSING CARE

Assisting With Percutaneous Liver Biopsy

Equipment

- Liver biopsy tray (contains needles, scalpel, specimen tubes, etc.)
- Sterile gloves
- Antiseptic solution
- Local anesthetic
- Sterile dressing
- Sphygmomanometer to monitor BP

Implementation

NURSING ACTION	RATIONALE
Preprocedure	
1. Ascertain that results of coagulation tests (prothrombin time, partial thromboplastin time, and platelet count) are available and that compatible donor blood is available.	1. Many patients with liver disease have clotting defects and are at risk for bleeding.
2. Check for signed consent; confirm that informed consent has been provided.	2. Ensure that the patient consents to this invasive procedure.
3. Measure and record the patient's pulse, respirations, and blood pressure immediately before biopsy.	3. Prebiopsy values provide a basis on which to compare the patient's vital signs and evaluate status after the procedure.
4. Describe to the patient in advance: steps of the procedure; sensations expected; after-effects anticipated; restrictions of activity and monitoring procedures to follow.	4. Explanations allay fears and ensure cooperation.
During Procedure	
1. Support the patient during the procedure.	1. Encouragement and support of the nurse enhance comfort and promote a sense of security.
2. Expose the right side of the patient's upper abdomen (right hypochondriac).	2. The skin at the site of penetration will be cleansed and a local anesthetic will be infiltrated.
3. Instruct the patient to inhale and exhale deeply several times, finally to exhale, and to hold breath at the end of expiration. The physician promptly introduces the biopsy needle by way of the transthoracic (intercostal) or transabdominal (subcostal) route, penetrates the liver, aspirates, and withdraws.	3. Holding the breath immobilizes the chest wall and the diaphragm; penetration of the diaphragm thereby is avoided, and the risk of lacerating the liver is minimized.
4. Instruct the patient to resume breathing.	4. The patient often continues holding his or her breath because of anxiety.

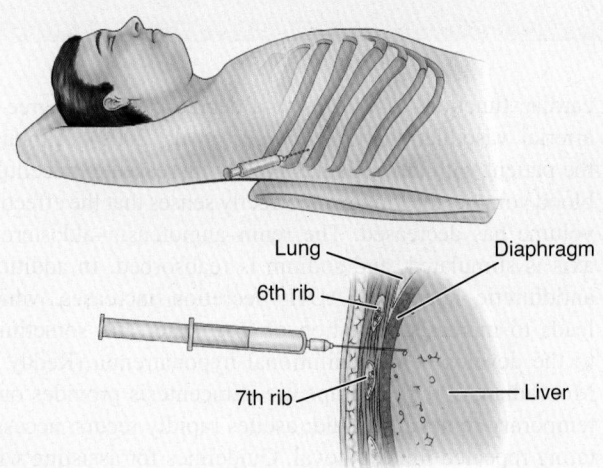

Lung — Diaphragm
6th rib
7th rib — Liver

NURSING ACTION (continued)	RATIONALE (continued)
Postprocedure	
1. Immediately after the biopsy, assist the patient to turn onto the right side; place a pillow under the costal margin, and caution the patient to remain in this position, recumbent and immobile, for several hours. Instruct the patient to avoid coughing or straining.	1. In this position, the liver capsule at the site of penetration is compressed against the chest wall, and the escape of blood or bile through the perforation is prevented.
2. Measure and record the patient's pulse, respiratory rate, and blood pressure at 10- to 15-minute intervals for the first hour, then every 30 minutes for the next 1 to 2 hours or until the patient's condition stabilizes.	2. Changes in vital signs may indicate bleeding, severe hemorrhage, or bile peritonitis, the most frequent complications of liver biopsy.
3. If the patient is discharged after the procedure, instruct the patient to avoid heavy lifting and strenuous activity for 1 week.	3. Activity restriction reduces the risk of bleeding at the biopsy puncture site.

BOX 21-4

GUIDELINES FOR NURSING CARE

Assisting With a Paracentesis

Equipment

- Paracentesis tray (contains trocar, syringe, needles, drainage tube)
- Sterile gloves
- Antiseptic solution
- Local anesthetic
- Sterile dressing
- Drainage collection bottles, receptacles
- Sphygmomanometer to monitor BP

Implementation

NURSING ACTION	RATIONALE
Preprocedure	
1. Check for signed consent form.	1. Ensure that patient has agreed to procedure.
2. Prepare the patient by providing the necessary information and instructions and by offering reassurance.	2. Having information increases the patient's understanding of the procedure and the reason for it.
3. Instruct the patient to void.	3. An empty bladder minimizes the risk of inadvertent puncture of the bladder and minimizes discomfort from a full bladder.
4. Gather appropriate sterile equipment and collection receptacles.	4. Sterility of equipment is essential to minimize risk of infection; having equipment available enables the procedure to be performed smoothly.
5. Place the patient in upright position on the edge of the bed or in a chair with feet supported on a stool. Fowler's position should be used by the patient confined to bed.	5. An upright position results in movement of the peritoneal fluid close to the abdominal wall and promotes easier puncture and removal of fluid.
6. Place the sphygmomanometer cuff around patient's arm.	6. This allows the nurse to monitor the patient's blood pressure during procedure.
During Procedure	
1. The physician, using aseptic technique, inserts the trocar through a puncture below the umbilicus. The trocar, or needle, is connected to a drainage tube, the end of which is inserted into a collecting receptacle. (See Figure, p. 602.)	1. Sterile technique minimizes the risk of infection. Bleeding at the puncture site is minimal at this location. The fluid drains by gravity or mild siphon into the container.
2. Help the patient maintain position throughout the procedure.	2. The patient who is fatigued or weak may have difficulty maintaining an optimal position for drainage of fluid.

(continued on page 602)

BOX 21-4

GUIDELINES FOR NURSING CARE (continued)

NURSING ACTION	RATIONALE

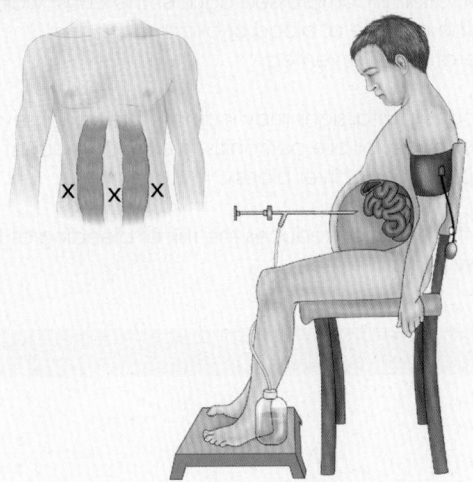

Figure on left shows possible sites for insertion of trocar.

3. Measure and record blood pressure at frequent intervals throughout the procedure.

4. Monitor the patient closely for signs of vascular collapse: pallor, increased pulse rate, or decreased blood pressure.

Postprocedure

1. Return the patient to bed or to a comfortable sitting position.
2. Measure, describe, and record the fluid collected.

3. Label samples of fluid and send to laboratory.

4. Monitor vital signs every 15 minutes for 1 hour, every 30 minutes for 2 hours, every hour for 2 hours, and then every 4 hours.
5. Measure the patient's temperature.

6. Assess for hypovolemia, electrolyte shifts, changes in mental status, and encephalopathy.

7. When taking vital signs, check puncture site for leakage or bleeding.

8. Provide patient teaching regarding need to monitor for bleeding or excessive drainage from puncture site, importance of avoiding heavy lifting or straining, the need to change position slowly, and frequency of monitoring for fever.

3. Decreased blood pressure may occur with vascular collapse, which can result from removal of the fluid from the peritoneal cavity and fluid shifts.
4. Vascular collapse (hypovolemia) may occur as fluid moves from the vascular system to replace fluid drained from peritoneal cavity.

1. The weak or fatigued patient may have difficulty resuming a comfortable position without assistance.
2. The volume of fluid removed may range from small to very large, and its removal may affect fluid and vascular status; volume should be included in input and output records. The characteristics of the fluid (clear vs. cloudy, red vs. colorless) may be helpful in diagnostic evaluation.
3. Peritoneal fluid is analyzed as part of the diagnostic workup.
4. Vital signs (blood pressure, pulse rate) may change as fluid shifts occur after removal of fluid, especially if a large volume of fluid has been removed.
5. An elevated temperature is a sign of infection and should be reported to the patient's provider.
6. Changes in fluid and electrolyte states and mental and cognitive status may occur with removal of fluid and fluid shifts, and should be reported.
7. Leakage of fluid may occur because of changes in abdominal pressure and may contribute to further loss of fluid if undetected. Leakage suggests a possible site for infection, and bleeding may occur in patients with altered clotting secondary to liver disease.
8. The patient (or family members) need to monitor the patient and puncture site for bleeding and excessive drainage if the patient is discharged home after the procedure. Heavy lifting or straining is avoided to enable the puncture site to close. Slow changes in position are recommended because of the risk of hypovolemia related to fluid removal. Monitoring for fever is needed to detect infection.

Cholecystography

Although cholecystography has been replaced by ultrasonography as the test of choice for gallstones, it is still used if ultrasound equipment is not available or if the ultrasound results are inconclusive. Oral cholecystography may be performed to detect gallstones and to assess the ability of the gallbladder to fill, concentrate its contents, contract, and empty. An iodide-containing contrast agent that is excreted by the liver and concentrated in the gallbladder is administered to the patient. The normal gallbladder fills with this radiopaque substance. If gallstones are present, they appear as shadows on the X-ray film.

The patient is asked about allergies to iodine or seafood. If no allergy is identified, the patient receives the oral form of the contrast agent the evening before the X-rays are obtained.

Cholecystography in the obviously jaundiced patient is not useful because the liver cannot excrete the radiopaque dye into the gallbladder in the presence of jaundice. Oral cholecystography is likely to continue to be used as part of the evaluation of the few patients who have been treated with gallstone **dissolution therapy** or lithotripsy.

Chapter Review

Critical Thinking Exercises

1. While taking blood pressure measurements at the adult day care center, one of the patients tells the nurse that this morning after he had a bowel movement, he noticed bright red blood on the toilet tissue. What further data would the nurse need to gather?
2. A 50-year-old female patient is seen in the emergency department complaining of right upper quadrant (RUQ) abdominal pain and cramping for the last 2 days. The symptoms usually began 1 to 2 hours after eating a dinner of fried or spicy foods. As a marketing specialist, she travels extensively and her usual dietary pattern consists of eating at restaurants several times weekly.
   A. For what aspect of the patient's history should the nurse seek additional information or clarification?
   B. What physical assessment findings would the nurse be most likely to find during the abdominal assessment?

NCLEX Style Review Questions

1. Which assessment finding does the nurse expect as a normal consequence of aging?
   A. Increased salivation and drooling
   B. Hyperactive bowel sounds and loose stools
   C. Increased gastric production and heartburn
   D. Decreased sensation to defecate and constipation

2. Which of the following foods could give a false-positive result on the fecal occult blood test (FOBT)? *Select all that apply.*
   A. Red meats
   B. Pasta
   C. Turnips
   D. Fish
   E. Whole-grain bread
3. Which question will best assist the nurse in the assessment of a patient with acute diarrhea?
   A. "Have you had a colonoscopy in the last 3 months?"
   B. "Have you traveled outside the country recently?"
   C. "Do you have any trouble swallowing?"
   D. "Do you have any allergies?"
4. The nurse recognizes that most nutrients and electrolytes are absorbed by which of the following?
   A. Esophagus
   B. Stomach
   C. Colon
   D. Small intestine
5. When performing an abdominal assessment on a patient with suspected cholecystitis, in what sequence does the nurse palpate the patient's abdomen?
   A. Palpate the right lower quadrant only
   B. Palpate the upper quadrants only
   C. Defer palpation and use percussion only
   D. Palpate the right upper quadrant last

References and Selected Readings

References and selected readings associated with this chapter can be found on the website that accompanies the book. Visit http://thepoint.lww.com/Pellico1e to access the references and other additional resources associated with this chapter.

Nursing Management: Patients With Oral and Esophageal Disorders and Patients Receiving Gastrointestinal Intubation, Enteral, and Parenteral Nutrition

ZACHARY R. KROM

Learning Objectives

After reading this chapter, you will be able to:

1. Describe nursing management of patients with conditions of the oral cavity.

2. Use the nursing process as a framework for care of patients undergoing neck dissection.

3. Describe the various conditions of the esophagus and their clinical manifestations and management.

4. Describe the purposes and types of gastrointestinal intubation.

5. Discuss nursing management of the patient who has a nasogastric or nasoenteric tube.

6. Identify the purposes and uses of parenteral nutrition.

Digestion begins in the mouth; adequate nutrition is closely related to good dental health and the general condition of the mouth. Any discomfort or adverse condition in the oral cavity can affect a person's nutritional status, influencing the type and amount of food ingested as well as the degree to which food particles are exposed to salivary enzymes. Given the close relationship between adequate nutritional intake and the structures of the upper gastrointestinal (GI) tract (lips, mouth, teeth, pharynx, esophagus), nursing assessment and health teaching related to food and fluid intake, general nutritional health, speech, and self-image is warranted. In some patients, certain pathologies impede the function of the GI system, and artificial devices must be placed to support nutritional intake. It is important for the nurse to be familiar with the placement procedures, function, and associated complications when caring for patients receiving supplemental enteral or parenteral nutrition.

ORAL DISORDERS

ORAL CARE

The nurse understands that oral health is a very important component of a person's physical and psychological well-being; common oral problems include dental plaque and caries. Healthy teeth must be conscientiously and effectively cleaned on a daily basis. Brushing and flossing are particularly effective in mechanically breaking up the bacterial plaque that collects around teeth. The level of mouth care performed on or by patients is dependent upon patient condition and tolerance of the procedure, with the ideal situation being when patients are able to brush and floss their teeth as they normally would at home. The American Dental Society recommends brushing twice a day and flossing once a day (2010). The primary focus of mouth care is to lessen the amount of bacterial film that accumulates on teeth, around gums, and in saliva (Box 22-1). Normal mastication (chewing) and the normal flow of saliva also aid greatly in keeping the teeth clean. Because many ill patients do not eat adequate amounts of food, they produce less saliva, which in turn reduces this natural tooth cleaning process. The nurse may need to assume the responsibility for brushing the patient's teeth. A soft-bristled toothbrush is more effective than a sponge or

Health Promotion

Preventive Oral Hygiene

Instruct patients to:

- Brush teeth using a soft toothbrush at least twice daily. Hold toothbrush at a 45-degree angle against the gums and teeth. A small brush is better than a large brush. Gums and tongue surface should be brushed.
- Floss at least once daily.
- Use an anti-plaque mouth rinse.
- Visit a dentist at least every 6 months, or when you have a chipped tooth, a lost filling, an oral sore that persists longer than 2 weeks, or a toothache.
- Avoid alcohol and tobacco products, including smokeless tobacco.
- Maintain adequate nutrition and avoid sweets.
- Replace toothbrush at first signs of wear, usually every 2 months.

---

foam stick. If brushing is not possible, the nurse should wipe the teeth with a gauze pad, then have the patient swish an antiseptic mouthwash several times before expectorating into an emesis basin. To prevent drying, the lips may be coated with a water-based gel.

Not only is the bacterial film detrimental to the tooth surface and gums, it can also potentially create problems in the respiratory system. This film can translocate to the lungs and cause an infection. Research supports oral care in patient's requiring mechanical ventilation to decrease the likelihood of ventilator-associated pneumonia (VAP) (Coffin, Klompas, Classen et al., 2008). The following combination of interventions is recommended for preventing VAP in patients at risk: oral moisturizing 6 to 12 times a day; brushing teeth, gums, and tongue twice a day; and using oral chlorhexidine gluconate (0.12%) twice a day in patients having cardiac surgery (AACN, 2010a). For more information on VAP, refer to Chapter 10.

TEMPOROMANDIBULAR JOINT DISORDERS

Disorders of the temporomandibular joint (TMJ) can originate within the joint capsule itself or involve the muscle tissue that surrounds and supports the joint. Osteoarthritis, rheumatoid arthritis, and disruption of the joint structures, such as dislocation or disc displacement, occur within the joint.

Clinical Manifestations and Assessment

Pain with mastication and/or pain in the joint itself are the two most common manifestations of a TMJ disorder. Patients have pain ranging from a dull ache to throbbing, debilitating pain that can radiate to the ears, teeth, neck muscles, and facial sinuses. They often have restricted jaw motion and

locking of the jaw. There also may be a sudden change in the way the upper and lower teeth fit together. The patient may hear clicking and grating noises, and chewing and swallowing may be difficult (National Institute of Dental & Craniofacial Research, 2009).

Diagnosis is based on the patient's report of pain, limitations in range of motion (ROM), dysphagia, difficulty chewing, difficulty with speech, or hearing difficulties. Magnetic resonance imaging (MRI), X-ray studies, and an arthrogram may be performed.

Medical Management

Conservative and reversible treatment is recommended. If irreversible surgical options are recommended, the patient is encouraged to seek a second opinion.

Nonsurgical Management

Although some practitioners think the role of stress in TMJ disorders is overrated, patient education in stress management may be helpful (to reduce grinding and clenching of teeth). Occlusal guards are often used in conjunction with stress management to prevent further deterioration of the tooth surface and irritation of the joint. The patient may also benefit from ROM exercises without overextension of the joint. Pain management measures may include nonsteroidal anti-inflammatory drugs (NSAIDs), with the possible addition of opioids, muscle relaxants, or mild antidepressants. Occasionally, intra-oral orthotics (a plastic guard worn over the upper and lower teeth) may be worn to reposition the condyle head in the joint space to a more normal position, which in turn relieves the stress and pressure on the tissues of the joint. This allows the tissues to heal.

Surgical Management

Correction of mandibular structural abnormalities may require surgery involving repositioning or reconstruction of the jaw. Simple fractures of the mandible without displacement, resulting from a blow on the chin, and planned surgical interventions, as in jaw repositioning (orthognathic) surgical correction to remedy cosmetic and functional jaw problems may require treatment by these means. Jaw reconstruction may also be necessary in the aftermath of trauma from a severe injury or cancer, both of which can cause tissue and bone loss.

Mandibular fractures are usually closed fractures. Rigid plate fixation (insertion of metal plates and screws into the bone to approximate and stabilize the bone) is the current treatment of choice in many cases of mandibular fracture and in some mandibular reconstructive surgery procedures. In some instances, the fracture repair involves wiring the patient's jaw shut for a number of weeks. Bone grafting may be performed to replace structural defects using bones from the patient's own ilium, ribs, or cranial sites. Rib tissue may also be harvested from cadaver donors.

Nursing Management

The patient who has had rigid fixation should be instructed not to chew food in the first 1 to 4 weeks after surgery. A liquid diet is recommended, and dietary counseling should be obtained to ensure optimal caloric and protein intake. To prevent aspiration, these patients should have wire cutters (for rigid fixation) or scissors (for rubber band fixation) at the bedside to release the jaw if the patient begins to vomit. The patient and family members should be instructed before discharge by the surgeon on where and how to cut the wires or rubber bands in an emergency before the patient is discharged. Rigid fixation remains for approximately 6 weeks depending upon the age of the patient, condition of bone, and the extent of the mandible injury.

The patient needs specific guidelines for mouth care and feeding. Any irritated areas in the mouth should be reported to the surgeon. The importance of keeping scheduled appointments to assess the stability of the fixation appliance is emphasized.

Consultation with a dietitian may be indicated, so that the patient and family can learn about foods that are high in essential nutrients and ways in which these foods can be prepared so that they can be consumed through a straw or spoon while remaining palatable. Nutritional supplements may also be recommended.

DISORDERS OF THE SALIVARY GLANDS

About 1,200 mL of saliva is produced daily and swallowed. The three main functions of saliva are lubrication, protection against harmful bacteria, and digestion. The glands that can be affected include the parotids, the submandibulars, and the sublinguals.

Sialadenitis refers to the bacterial or viral infection of the salivary glands. Infection may be caused by dehydration, radiation therapy, stress, malnutrition, salivary gland calculi (stones), or improper oral hygiene. Patients having a bacterial infection have significant inflammation, pain, swelling, and purulent discharge. Treatment includes antibiotics, massage, hydration, warm compresses, and corticosteroids. Chronic sialadenitis with uncontrolled pain is treated by surgical drainage of the gland or excision of the gland and its ducts.

Parotitis (inflammation of the parotid gland) is the most common inflammatory condition of the salivary glands. The parotids are the largest of the salivary glands. Mumps (epidemic parotitis), a communicable disease caused by viral infection and most commonly affecting children, is an inflammation of a salivary gland, usually the parotid.

Elderly, acutely ill, or debilitated people with decreased salivary flow from general dehydration or medications are at high risk for parotitis. The infecting organisms travel from the mouth through the salivary duct. The organism is usually *Staphylococcus aureus* (except in mumps). The onset of this complication is sudden, with an exacerbation of both the fever and the symptoms of the primary condition. The gland swells and becomes tense and tender. The patient feels pain in the ear, and swollen glands interfere with swallowing. The swelling increases rapidly, and the overlying skin soon becomes red and shiny. The patient may have purulent drainage from the site as well.

Medical management includes maintaining adequate nutritional and fluid intake, good oral hygiene, and discontinuing medications (e.g., tranquilizers, diuretics) that can diminish salivation. Antibiotic therapy is necessary, and analgesics may be prescribed to control pain. If antibiotic therapy is not effective, the gland may need to be drained by extraoral pressure applied to the area or by surgical removal of the gland parotidectomy. Surgery may also be necessary to treat chronic parotitis. The patient is advised to have any necessary dental work performed prior to surgery.

ORAL AND OROPHARYNGEAL CANCER

Cancers of the oral cavity, which can occur in any part of the mouth or throat, are curable if discovered early. Approximately 35,000 to 40,000 new cases of oral cavity and oropharyngeal cancer occur annually in the United States (American Cancer Society, 2009). In 2009, almost 8,000 people died from oral cancer in the United States (American Cancer Society, 2009).

Pathophysiology

Malignancies of the oral cavity are usually squamous cell cancers. Any area of the oropharynx can be a site of malignant growths, but the lips, the lateral aspects of the tongue, and the floor of the mouth are most commonly affected.

Risk Factors

Oral cancers are often associated with the use of alcohol and all types of tobacco products, which, if used together, have a synergistic carcinogenic effect. Other factors include dietary deficiency, smoked meat ingestion, and prolonged exposure to sun and wind for cancer of the lip.

Cancer of the oral cavity affects men more often than women; however, the incidence of oral cancer in women is increasing, possibly because of increased tobacco and alcohol use. Cancers of the oral cavity and oropharynx occur more often in African Americans than in Caucasians.

Clinical Manifestations and Assessment

Many oral cancers produce few or no symptoms in the early stages. Later, the most frequent symptom is a painless sore or mass that will not heal. A typical lesion in oral cancer is a painless indurated (hardened) ulcer with raised edges. Tissue from any ulcer of the oral cavity that does not heal in 2 weeks should be examined through biopsy. As the cancer progresses, the patient may complain of tenderness; difficulty in chewing, swallowing, or speaking; coughing of blood-tinged sputum; or enlarged cervical lymph nodes.

Diagnostic evaluation consists of an oral examination as well as an assessment of the cervical lymph nodes to detect possible metastases. Biopsies are performed on suspicious lesions (those that have not healed in 2 weeks). High-risk areas include the buccal mucosa and gingiva in people who use snuff or smoke cigars or pipes. For those who smoke cigarettes and drink alcohol, high-risk areas include the floor of the mouth, the ventrolateral tongue, and the soft palate complex (soft palate, anterior and posterior tonsillar area, uvula, and the area behind the molar and tongue junction).

Medical Management

Management varies with the nature of the lesion, the preference of the physician, and patient choice. Surgical resection, radiation therapy, chemotherapy, or a combination of these therapies may be effective.

In cancer of the lip, small lesions are usually excised liberally. Radiation therapy may be more appropriate for larger lesions involving more than one-third of the lip because of superior cosmetic results. The choice depends on the extent of the lesion and what is necessary to cure the patient while preserving the best appearance. Tumors larger than 4 cm often recur.

In cancer of the tongue, treatment with radiation therapy and chemotherapy may preserve organ function and maintain quality of life. A combination of radioactive interstitial implants (surgical implantation of a radioactive source into the tissue adjacent to or at the tumor site) and external beam radiation may be used. Surgical procedures include hemiglossectomy (surgical removal of half of the tongue) and total glossectomy (removal of the tongue).

Neck Dissection

Often cancer of the oral cavity has metastasized through the extensive lymphatic channel in the neck region (Fig. 22-1),

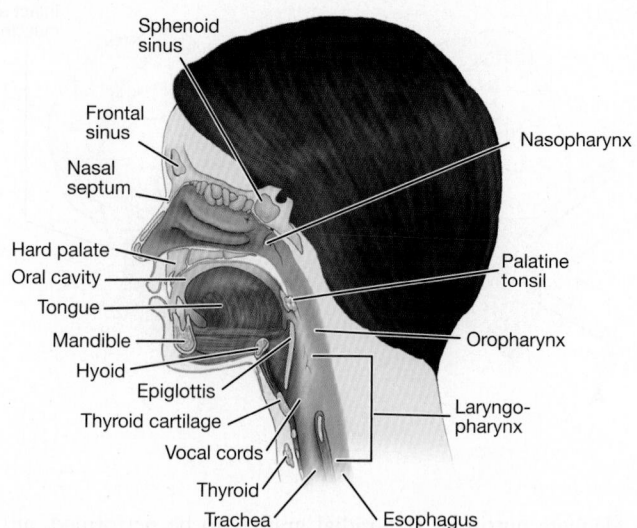

FIGURE 22-2 Anatomy of the head and neck.

requiring a neck dissection and reconstructive surgery of the oral cavity. Other malignancies of the head and neck that may metastasize into the lymphatic channel include those of the, oropharynx, hypopharynx, nasopharynx, nasal cavity, paranasal sinus, and larynx (Fig. 22-2). A radical neck dissection involves removal of all cervical lymph nodes from the mandible to the clavicle and removal of the sternocleidomastoid muscle, internal jugular vein, and spinal accessory muscle on one side of the neck. The associated complications include shoulder drop and poor cosmesis (visible neck depression). Modified radical neck dissection, which preserves one or more of the nonlymphatic structures, is used more often. A selective neck dissection (in comparison to a radical dissection) preserves one or more of the lymph node groups, the internal jugular vein, the sternocleidomastoid muscle, and the spinal accessory nerve (Fig. 22-3).

Reconstructive techniques may be performed with a variety of grafts. A cutaneous flap (skin and subcutaneous tissue), such as the deltopectoral flap, may be used. A myocutaneous flap (subcutaneous tissue, muscle and skin) is a more frequently used graft; the pectoralis major muscle is also used. For large grafts, a microvascular free flap may be used. This involves the transfer of muscle, skin, or bone with an artery and vein to the area of reconstruction, using microinstrumentation. Areas used for a free flap include the scapula, the radial area of the forearm, or the fibula. The fibula, which provides a larger bone area, may be used if mandibular reconstruction is involved. Neck dissection is further discussed below in the nursing process section.

Nursing Management

The nurse assesses the patient's nutritional status preoperatively, and a dietary consultation may be necessary. The patient may require enteral (through the GI tract) or parenteral (IV) feedings before and after surgery to maintain

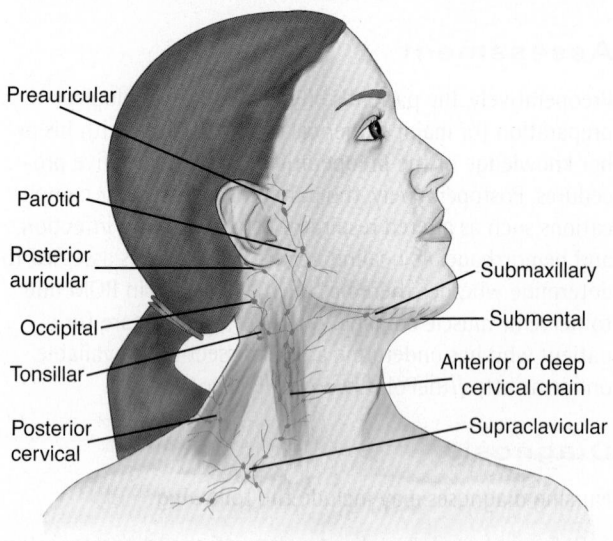

FIGURE 22-1 Lymphatic drainage of the head and neck.

Intact sternocleidomastoid
muscle

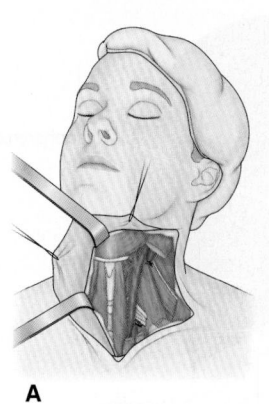 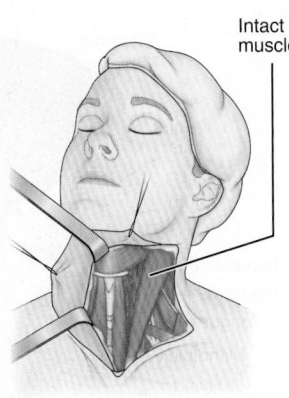 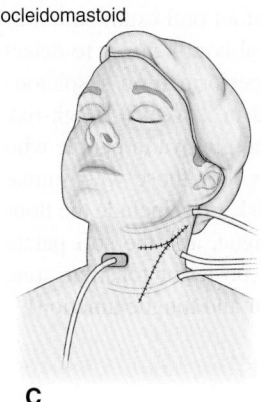

A B C

FIGURE 22-3 (**A**) A classic radical neck dissection in which the sternocleidomastoid and smaller muscles are removed. All tissue is removed, from the ramus of the jaw to the clavicle. The jugular vein has also been removed. (**B**) The selective neck dissection is similar but preserves the sternocleidomastoid muscle, internal jugular vein, and spinal accessory nerve. The wound is closed (**C**), and portable suction drainage tubes are in place.

adequate nutrition. If a radial graft is to be performed, an Allen test on the donor arm must be performed to ensure that the ulnar artery is patent. Refer to Chapter 12 for details on the Allen test.

Postoperatively, the nurse monitors the patient's ability to protect the airway by assessing the ability to swallow and manage oral secretions. Suctioning of oral secretions may be necessary, and the patient can be instructed on use of a Yankauer suction device (tonsil tip suction) to remove oral secretions if appropriate. If grafting was part of the surgery, suctioning must be performed with care to prevent damage to the graft. The graft is assessed postoperatively for viability. Although color should be assessed (white may indicate arterial occlusion, and blue mottling may indicate venous congestion), it can be difficult to assess the graft by looking into the mouth. An intermittent Doppler ultrasound device or fiberoptic monitoring device (producing a continuous audible pulse of the graft site), may be used to assess the graft perfusion.

Xerostomia, dryness of the mouth, is a frequent sequela of oral cancer, particularly when the salivary glands have been exposed to radiation or major surgery. It is also seen in patients receiving psychopharmacologic agents, patients with HIV infection, patients who cannot close the mouth, patients having endotracheal or tracheostomy tubes, and in patients with poor oral food intake.

The patient's mouth appears red, dry, and tender to palpation. Cracks in the dry oral mucosa may occur in which infection could develop. To minimize this problem, the patient is advised to avoid dry, bulky, and irritating foods and fluids, as well as alcohol and tobacco. The patient is also encouraged to increase intake of fluids (when not contraindicated) and to use a humidifier during sleep. The use of synthetic saliva, a moisturizing antibacterial gel such as Oral Balance, or a saliva production stimulant such as Salagen may be helpful.

Stomatitis, or mucositis, which involves inflammation and breakdown of the oral mucosa, is often a side effect of chemotherapy or radiation therapy. Prophylactic mouth care is started when the patient begins receiving treatment;

however, mucositis may become so severe that a break in treatment is necessary. If a patient receiving radiation therapy has poor dentition, extraction of the teeth before radiation treatment in the oral cavity is often preformed to prevent infection. As a result, many radiation therapy centers recommend the use of fluoride treatments for patients receiving radiation to the head and neck.

People with cancer of the head and neck frequently have used alcohol or tobacco before surgery; postoperatively, the patient is encouraged to abstain from these substances. Treatment to decrease the likelihood of alcohol and nicotine withdrawal is recommended. Depression is also common in this patient population, with the highest prevalence rates at diagnosis and during treatment (Haisfield-Wolfe, McGuire, Soeken et al., 2009).

NURSING PROCESS

The Patient Undergoing a Neck Dissection

Assessment

Preoperatively, the patient's physical and psychological preparation for major surgery is assessed, along with his or her knowledge of the preoperative and postoperative procedures. Postoperatively, the patient is assessed for complications such as altered respiratory status, wound infection, and hemorrhage. As healing occurs, neck ROM is assessed to determine whether there has been a decrease in ROM due to nerve or muscle damage. A plan of nursing care for a patient who has undergone a neck dissection is available online at http://thePoint.lww.com/Pellico1e.

Diagnosis

Nursing diagnoses may include the following:

• Deficient knowledge about preoperative and postoperative procedures

- Ineffective airway clearance related to obstruction by mucus, hemorrhage, or edema
- Acute pain related to surgical incision
- Risk for infection related to surgical intervention secondary to decreased nutritional status, or immunosuppression from chemotherapy or radiation therapy
- Impaired tissue integrity secondary to surgery and grafting
- Imbalanced nutrition, less than body requirements, related to disease process or treatment
- Situational low self-esteem related to diagnosis or prognosis
- Impaired verbal communication secondary to surgical resection
- Impaired physical mobility secondary to nerve injury

Potential postoperative complications that may develop include the following:

- Hemorrhage
- Chyle fistula
- Nerve injury

Planning

The major goals for the patient include participation in the treatment plan, maintenance of respiratory status, attainment of comfort, absence of infection, viability of the graft, maintenance of adequate intake of food and fluids, effective coping strategies, effective communication, maintenance of shoulder and neck motion, and absence of complications.

Nursing Interventions

Before surgery, the patient should be informed about the nature and extent of the surgery, and what the postoperative period will be like (see Chapter 5 for preoperative education).

For the patient who has had extensive neck surgery, specific postoperative interventions include maintenance of a patent airway and continuous assessment of respiratory status, wound care and oral hygiene, maintenance of adequate nutrition, and observation for hemorrhage or nerve injury.

Maintaining the Airway

After the endotracheal tube or airway has been removed and the effects of the anesthesia have worn off, the patient may be placed in Fowler's position to facilitate breathing and promote comfort. This position also increases lymphatic and venous drainage, facilitates swallowing, and decreases venous pressure on the skin flaps.

In the immediate postoperative period, the nurse assesses for stridor (coarse, high-pitched sound on inspiration) by listening frequently over the trachea with a stethoscope. This finding must be reported immediately because it indicates obstruction of the airway. Signs of respiratory distress, such as dyspnea, cyanosis, changes in mental status, and changes in vital signs, are assessed because they may suggest edema, hemorrhage, inadequate oxygenation, or inadequate drainage.

Pneumonia may occur in the postoperative phase if pulmonary secretions are not removed. To aid in the removal of secretions, coughing and deep breathing are encouraged. The patient should assume a sitting position, with the nurse supporting the neck so that the patient can bring up excessive secretions. If this is ineffective, the patient's respiratory tract may have to be suctioned. Care is taken to protect the suture lines during suctioning. If a tracheostomy tube is in place, suctioning is performed through the tube. The patient may also be instructed on use of Yankauer suction (tonsil tip suction) to remove oral secretions. Temperature should not be taken orally.

Relieving Pain

Pain and the patient's fear of pain are assessed and managed. Patients with head and neck cancer often report less pain than do patients with other types of cancer; however, the nurse needs to be aware that each person's pain experience is individual. The nurse administers analgesics as prescribed and assesses their effectiveness.

Providing Wound Care

Wound drainage tubes are usually inserted during surgery to prevent the subcutaneous collection of fluid. The drainage tubes are connected to a portable suction device (e.g., Jackson-Pratt), and the container is emptied periodically. Between 80 and 120 mL of serosanguineous secretions may drain over the first 24 hours. Excessive drainage may be indicative of a chyle fistula or hemorrhage (see later discussion). If dressings are present, they may need to be reinforced periodically. Dressings are observed for evidence of hemorrhage and constriction, which impairs respiration and perfusion of the graft. A graft, if present, is assessed for color and temperature, and for the presence of a pulse if applicable, to determine viability. The graft should be pale pink and warm to the touch. The surgical incisions are also assessed for infection, which is reported immediately. Prophylactic antibiotics may be prescribed.

Maintaining Adequate Nutrition

Nutritional status is assessed preoperatively; early intervention to correct nutritional imbalances may decrease the risk of postoperative complications. Frequently, nutrition is less than optimal because of inadequate intake, and the patient often requires enteral or parenteral supplements preoperatively and postoperatively to attain and maintain a positive nitrogen balance.

The patient who can chew may take food by mouth; the level of the patient's chewing ability determines whether some diet modification (e.g., soft, puréed, or liquid foods) is necessary. Food preferences should also be discussed with the patient. Oral care before eating may enhance the patient's appetite, and oral care after eating is important to prevent infection and dental caries. Most patients can maintain and gain weight.

(continued on page 610)

Supporting Coping Measures

Preoperatively, information about the planned surgery is given to the patient and family. Postoperatively, psychological nursing interventions are aimed at supporting the patient who has had a change in body image or who has major concerns regarding the prognosis. The patient may have difficulty communicating and may be concerned about his or her ability to breathe and swallow normally. The nurse supports the patient's family and friends in encouraging and reassuring the patient that adjusting to the results of this surgery will take time.

The person who has had extensive neck surgery often is sensitive about his or her appearance. This can occur when the operative area is covered by bulky dressings, when the incision line is visible, or later after healing has occurred and the appearance of the neck and possibly the lower face has been significantly altered. If the nurse accepts the patient's appearance and expresses a positive, optimistic attitude, the patient is more likely to be encouraged. The patient also needs an opportunity to express concerns regarding the success of the surgery and the prognosis. The American Cancer Society may be a resource to provide a volunteer to meet with the patient either preoperatively or postoperatively.

Promoting Effective Communication

If a laryngectomy was performed, the nurse explores other methods of communicating with the patient and obtains a consultation with a speech/language therapist. Alternatives to verbal communication may include use of a pencil and paper or pointing to needed items on a picture pad. Alternative speech techniques, such as an electrolarynx (a mechanical device held against the neck) or esophageal speech, may be taught by a speech/language therapist.

Maintaining Physical Mobility

Excision of muscles and nerves results in weakness at the shoulder that can cause *shoulder drop,* a forward curvature of the shoulder. Many problems can be avoided with a conscientious exercise program. These exercises are usually begun after the drains have been removed and the neck incision is sufficiently healed. Physical therapists and occupational therapists can assist patients in performing these exercises.

Monitoring and Managing Potential Complications

HEMORRHAGE. Hemorrhage may occur from carotid artery rupture as a result of necrosis of the graft or damage to the artery itself from tumor or infection. The following measures are indicated:

- Vital signs are assessed. Tachycardia, tachypnea, and hypotension may indicate hemorrhage and impending hypovolemic shock.
- The patient is instructed to avoid the Valsalva maneuver (bearing down activities such as having a bowel movement) to prevent stress on the graft and carotid artery.

- Signs of impending rupture, such as high epigastric pain or discomfort, are reported.
- Dressings and wound drainage are observed for excessive bleeding.
- If hemorrhage occurs, assistance is summoned immediately.
- Hemorrhage requires the continuous application of pressure to the bleeding site or major associated vessel.
- Although some advocate placing the patient in supine position and elevating the legs to maintain blood pressure, others recommend that the head of the patient's bed be elevated to maintain airway patency and prevent **aspiration**.
- A controlled, calm manner allays the patient's anxiety.
- The surgeon is notified immediately, because a vascular or ligature tear requires surgical intervention.

CHYLE FISTULA. A chyle fistula (milk-like drainage from the thoracic duct into the thoracic cavity) may develop as a result of damage to the thoracic duct during surgery. The diagnosis is made if there is excess drainage that has a 3% fat content and a specific gravity of 1.012 or greater. Treatment of a small leak ($\leq$500 mL) includes application of a pressure dressing and a diet of medium-chain fatty acids or parenteral nutrition. Surgical intervention to repair the damaged duct is necessary for larger leaks.

NERVE INJURY. Nerve injury can occur if the cervical plexus or spinal accessory nerves are severed during surgery. Because lower facial paralysis may occur as a result of injury to the facial nerve, this complication is observed for and reported. Likewise, if the superior laryngeal nerve is damaged, the patient may have difficulty swallowing liquids and food because of the partial lack of sensation of the glottis. Speech therapy may be indicated to assist with the problems related to nerve injury.

Teaching Patients Self-Care

The patient and caregiver require instructions about management of the wound, the dressing, and any drains that remain in place. Patients who require oral suctioning or who have a tracheostomy may be very anxious about their care at home; the transition to home can be eased if the caregiver is given several opportunities to demonstrate the ability to meet the patient's needs. The patient and caregiver are also instructed about possible complications, such as bleeding and respiratory distress, and when to notify the health care provider of signs and symptoms of these complications.

If the patient cannot take food by mouth, detailed instructions and demonstration of enteral or parenteral feedings will be required. Education in techniques of effective oral hygiene is also important.

A referral for home care nursing may be necessary in the early period after discharge. The nurse assesses healing, ensures that feedings are being administered properly, and

monitors for any complications. The home care nurse assesses the patient's adjustment to changes in physical appearance and status, and ability to communicate and to eat normally. Physical and speech therapy also may be continued at home.

The patient is given information regarding local support groups such as "I Can Cope" or "New Voice Club," if indicated. The local chapter of the American Cancer Society may be contacted for information and equipment needed for the patient.

Evaluation

Expected patient outcomes may include:

1. Discusses expected course of treatment
2. Demonstrates good respiratory exchange:
   a. Lungs are clear to auscultation
   b. Breathes easily with no shortness of breath
   c. Demonstrates ability to use suction effectively
3. Remains free of infection:
   a. Maintains normal laboratory values
   b. Is afebrile
4. Graft is pink and warm to touch
5. Maintains adequate intake of foods and fluids:
   a. Accepts altered route of feeding
   b. Is well hydrated
   c. Maintains or gains weight
6. Demonstrates ability to cope:
   a. Discusses emotional responses to the diagnosis
   b. Attends support group meetings
7. Verbalizes comfort
8. Attains maximal mobility:
   a. Adheres to physical therapy exercises
   b. Attains maximal ROM
9. Exhibits no complications:
   a. Vital signs stable
   b. No excessive bleeding or discharge
   c. Able to move muscles of lower face

DISORDERS OF THE ESOPHAGUS

The esophagus is a mucus-lined, muscular tube that carries food from the mouth to the stomach. It begins at the base of the pharynx and ends about 4 cm below the diaphragm. Its ability to transport food and fluid is facilitated by two sphincters. The upper esophageal sphincter, also called the *hypopharyngeal sphincter*, is located at the junction of the pharynx and the esophagus. The lower esophageal sphincter, also called the *gastroesophageal sphincter* or *cardiac sphincter*, is located at the junction of the esophagus and the stomach. The lower esophageal sphincter prevents reflux (backward flow) of gastric contents. There is no serosal layer

of the esophagus; therefore, if surgery is necessary, it is more difficult to perform suturing or anastomosis.

Disorders of the esophagus include motility disorders (achalasia, diffuse spasm), hiatal hernias, diverticula, perforation, foreign bodies, chemical burns, gastroesophageal reflux disease, Barrett's esophagus, and carcinoma. **Dysphagia** (difficulty swallowing), the most common symptom of esophageal disease, may vary from an uncomfortable feeling that a bolus of food is caught in the upper esophagus to acute pain on swallowing (**odynophagia**). Obstruction of food (solid and soft) and even liquids may occur anywhere along the esophagus. Often, the patient indicates that the problem is located in the upper, middle, or lower third of the esophagus.

ACHALASIA

Achalasia is absent or ineffective **peristalsis** of the distal esophagus, accompanied by failure of the esophageal sphincter to relax in response to swallowing. Narrowing of the esophagus just above the stomach results in a gradually increasing dilation of the esophagus in the upper chest. Achalasia may progress slowly and occurs most often in people 40 years or older.

Clinical Manifestations and Assessment

The primary symptom is difficulty in swallowing both liquids and solids. The patient has a sensation of food sticking in the lower portion of the esophagus. As the condition progresses, food is commonly regurgitated either spontaneously or intentionally by the patient to relieve the discomfort produced by prolonged distention of the esophagus by food that will not pass into the stomach. The patient may also report chest pain and heartburn (**pyrosis**) that may or may not be associated with eating. Secondary pulmonary complications may result from aspiration of gastric contents.

X-ray studies show esophageal dilation above the narrowing at the gastroesophageal junction. Barium swallow, computed tomography (CT) of the chest, and endoscopy may be used for diagnosis; however, *manometry*, a process in which the esophageal pressure is measured by a radiologist or gastroenterologist, confirms the diagnosis.

Medical and Nursing Management

The patient is instructed to eat slowly and to drink fluids with meals. As a temporary measure, calcium channel blockers and nitrates have been used to decrease esophageal pressure and improve swallowing. Injection of botulinum toxin (Botox) to quadrants of the esophagus via endoscopy has been helpful because it inhibits the contraction of smooth muscle. Periodic injections are required to maintain remission.

Achalasia may be treated conservatively by pneumatic dilation to stretch the narrowed area of the esophagus (Fig. 22-4). Pneumatic dilation has a high success rate. Although

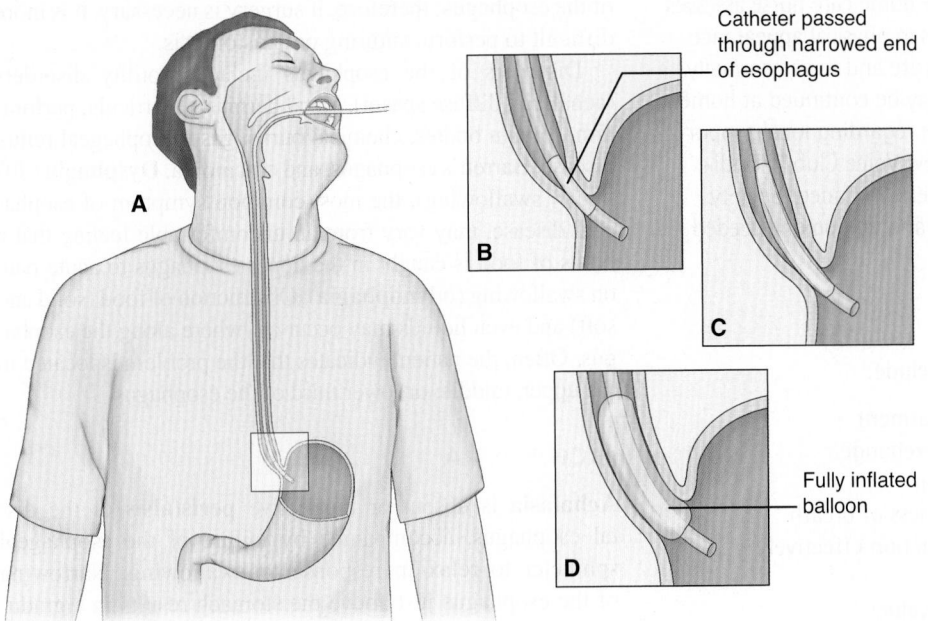

FIGURE 22-4 Treatment of achalasia by pneumatic dilation. (A–C) The dilator is passed, guided by a previously inserted guide wire. (D) When the balloon is in proper position, it is distended by pressure sufficient to dilate the narrowed area of the esophagus.

perforation is a potential complication, its incidence is low. The procedure can be painful; therefore, moderate sedation in the form of an analgesic or tranquilizer, or both, is administered for the treatment. The patient is monitored for perforation. Abdominal tenderness and fever may indicate perforation (see later discussion).

Achalasia may be treated surgically by esophagomyotomy. The procedure usually is performed laparoscopically, either with a complete lower esophageal sphincter myotomy and an antireflux procedure, or without an antireflux procedure. The esophageal muscle fibers are separated to relieve the lower esophageal stricture.

HIATAL HERNIA

In the condition known as hiatus (or hiatal) **hernia**, the opening in the diaphragm through which the esophagus passes becomes enlarged, and part of the upper stomach tends to move up into the lower portion of the thorax. Hiatal hernia occurs more often in women than in men. There are two types of hiatal hernias: sliding and paraesophageal. Sliding, or type I, hiatal hernia occurs when the upper stomach and the gastroesophageal junction are displaced upward and slide in and out of the thorax (Fig. 22-5A). About 90% of patients with esophageal hiatal hernia have a sliding hernia. A paraesophageal hernia occurs when all or part of the stomach pushes through the diaphragm beside the esophagus (see Fig. 22-5B). Paraesophageal hernias are further classified as types II, III, or IV, with type IV having the greatest degree of herniation.

Clinical Manifestations and Assessment

The patient with a sliding hernia may have heartburn, regurgitation, and dysphagia, but at least 50% of patients are asymptomatic. Sliding hiatal hernia is often implicated in

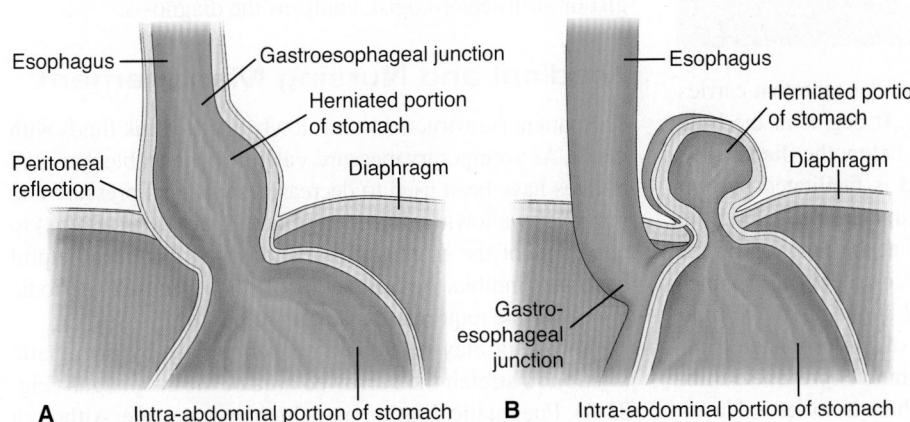

FIGURE 22-5 (A) Sliding esophageal hernia. The upper stomach and gastroesophageal junction have moved upward and slide in and out of the thorax. (B) Paraesophageal hernia. All or part of the stomach pushes through the diaphragm next to the gastroesophageal junction.

reflux. The patient with a paraesophageal hernia usually feels a sense of fullness after eating or chest pain, or there may be no symptoms. Reflux usually does not occur, because the gastroesophageal sphincter is intact. Hemorrhage, obstruction, and strangulation can occur with any type of hernia.

Diagnosis is confirmed by X-ray studies, barium swallow, and fluoroscopy.

Medical and Nursing Management

Management for a sliding hernia includes frequent, small feedings that can pass easily through the esophagus. The patient is advised not to recline for 1 hour after eating, to prevent reflux or movement of the hernia, and to elevate the head of the bed on 4- to 8-inch (10- to 20-cm) blocks to prevent the hernia from sliding upward. Surgery is indicated when a patient has significant esophageal injury or when he or she does not respond to medical management. Medical and surgical management of a paraesophageal hernia is similar to that for gastroesophageal reflux; however, people with paraesophageal hernias may require emergency surgery to correct torsion (twisting) of the stomach that can lead to restriction of blood flow to the area.

DIVERTICULUM

A diverticulum is an outpouching of mucosa and submucosa that protrudes through a weak portion of the musculature that can occur at any location in the esophagus.

The most common type of diverticulum, which is found three times more frequently in men than in women, is *Zenker's diverticulum* (also known as pharyngoesophageal pulsion diverticulum or a pharyngeal pouch). It occurs posteriorly through the cricopharyngeal muscle in the midline of the neck. It is usually seen in people older than 60 years. Other types of diverticula include midesophageal (rare), epiphrenic (large), and intramural diverticula (numerous and small; related to stricture).

Clinical Manifestations and Assessment

Symptoms experienced by the patient with a pharyngoesophageal pulsion diverticulum include difficulty swallowing, fullness in the neck, belching, regurgitation of undigested food, and gurgling noises after eating. The diverticulum, or pouch, becomes filled with food or liquid. When the patient assumes a recumbent position, undigested food is regurgitated, and coughing may be caused by irritation of the trachea. Halitosis and a sour taste in the mouth are also common because of the decomposition of food retained in the diverticulum.

Symptoms produced by midesophageal diverticula are less acute. Due to the difficulty these patients have with food passing through their upper GI tract, they often have chest pain and difficulty with swallowing. Some patients experience regurgitation of undigested food, and some do not experience any symptoms at all.

A barium swallow may determine the exact nature and location of a diverticulum. Pressure studies are often performed for patients with epiphrenic diverticula to rule out a motor disorder. Esophagoscopy usually is contraindicated because of the danger of perforation of the diverticulum. Blind insertion of a nasogastric (NG) tube should be avoided.

Medical and Nursing Management

Because pharyngoesophageal pulsion diverticulum is progressive, the only means of cure is surgical removal of the diverticulum. During surgery, care is taken to avoid trauma to the common carotid artery and internal jugular veins. The sac is dissected free and amputated flush with the esophageal wall. In addition to a diverticulectomy, a myotomy of the cricopharyngeal muscle is often performed to relieve spasticity of the musculature, which otherwise seems to contribute to a continuation of the previous symptoms. An NG tube may be inserted at the time of surgery. Postoperatively, the surgical incision must be observed for evidence of leakage from the esophagus and a developing fistula. Food and fluids are withheld until radiographic studies indicate there is no leakage at the surgical site. The diet begins with liquids and is progressed as tolerated.

Surgery is indicated for epiphrenic and midesophageal diverticula only if the symptoms are troublesome and becoming worse. Treatment consists of a diverticulectomy and long myotomy. Intramural diverticula usually regress after the esophageal stricture is dilated.

PERFORATION

The esophagus is a common site of injury. Perforation may result from stab or bullet wounds of the neck or chest, trauma from a motor vehicle crash, caustic injury from a chemical burn, or inadvertent puncture during a surgical procedure or esophageal dilatation.

Clinical Manifestations and Assessment

The patient has persistent pain, followed by dysphagia, fever, leukocytosis, and severe hypotension may be noted. In some instances, signs of pneumothorax are observed. X-ray studies and fluoroscopy by either a barium swallow or esophagram are used to identify the site of the injury.

Medical and Nursing Management

Because of the high risk of infection, broad-spectrum antibiotic therapy is initiated. If the perforation is small enough and without symptoms, medical intervention may not be necessary. Nothing is given by mouth; nutritional needs are met by administering nutrition into the intestine, bypassing the stomach, or by the parenteral route. The type of nutritional support depends on the location and the extent of the

The smaller the French size, the smaller the lumen of the tube. Contraindications to placement of NG tubes include facial and head trauma, severe coagulopathy, deviated septum, esophageal strictures or diverticula, and a history of alkali ingestion (Roberts & Hedges, 2009). Caution is used when inserting NG tubes in patients with esophageal varices, and post-gastric bypass and lap banding procedures (Roberts & Hedges, 2009).

A gastric or Salem sump tube (SST) is a double-lumen tube, available in 12 to 18 Fr (although typically a 16 to 18 Fr is used for adults); it is marked from the distal end at particular distances indicated by the manufacturer. The larger main lumen tube is intended for suction, and the smaller lumen or *pigtail*, which is typically blue in color, is termed the *venting tube*. The venting port ensures that the suction at the distal end of the tube maintains a safe level to preserve the mucosa of the stomach by allowing atmospheric air to enter the blue lumen to prevent invagination of stomach into the multiple distal openings. An **antireflux valve** can be placed in the venting port of the tube if gastric fluid leaks through the air vent. The venting tube (blue pigtail) must be higher than the stomach level to prevent the siphoning of gastric contents out via this lumen. In the event that leakage has occurred, the larger lumen is irrigated with 30 mL of normal saline, after which air is injected to reestablish a buffer of air between the lumens, and an antireflux valve applied to the venting lumen. The antireflux valve is a one-way valve that prevents gastric fluid from exiting the SST via the vent lumen (Fig. 22-7). If an SST is used, it must be on continuous low suction.

In the event that gastric decompression is no longer needed, an SST can be used to administer intermittent medications, intermittent liquid feedings, or continuous liquid feedings. However, to do so, the venting tube must be plugged to prevent the instillation fluid from leaking out via this lumen. Residual volumes of stomach contents in patients receiving continuous tube feedings can be easily assessed with these large-bore tubes (residual volumes are discussed later in the chapter).

Postpyloric Tubes

Tubes that continue past the stomach and enter the duodenum and jejunum are longer, smaller-bore, single-lumen tubes. Duodenal and jejunal tubes are commonly 8 to 10 Fr and 110 to 140 cm long. Postpyloric tubes are most often inserted into the nares and are primarily designed for continuous feeding into the small intestine when gastric feeding is not desired. Examples of contraindications for gastric feedings include patients with a high risk of aspiration and those undergoing gastric surgery. Patients having pancreatic surgery may have jejunal tubes placed to rest the pancreas by bypassing the hepatopancreatic ampulla, thereby avoiding the release of digestive enzymes into the duodenum.

Postpyloric tubes can be inserted before or during surgery, by interventional radiologists assisted by fluoroscopy, or at

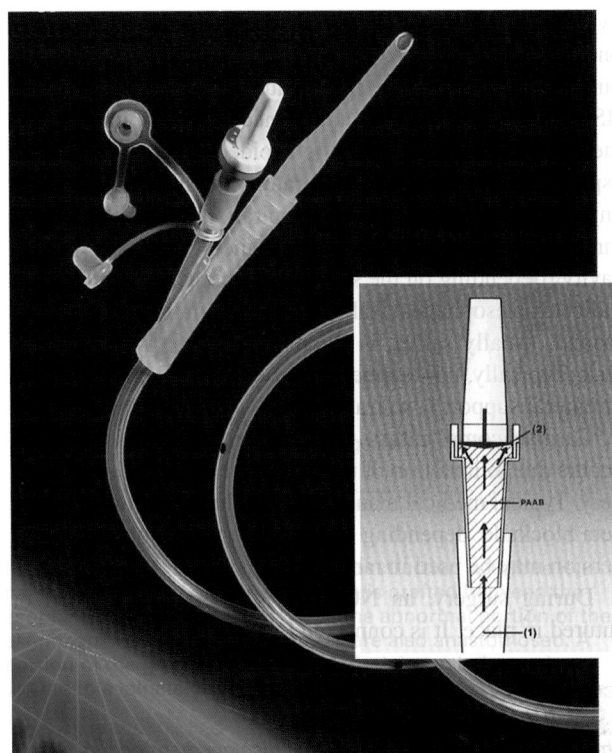

FIGURE 22-7 Gastric sump tube (Salem) equipped with a one-way valve that allows air to enter and can prevent reflux of gastric contents. The antireflux valve is designed with a pressure activated air buffer (PAAB). The buffer is activated (**1**) and the valve closes (**2**) when pressure from gastric contents enters the tubing. Argyle Silicone Salem Sump Tube with pre-attached Argyle Salem Sump Anti-Reflux Valve, courtesy of Sherwood Medical, St. Louis, Missouri.

the bedside by a trained nurse or health care provider. At the bedside, the tube is advanced past the stomach actively, using a combination of air bolusing and peristalsis-enhancing medications such as metoclopramide. Metoclopramide, which increases gastric and small intestinal motility, aids in the insertion of nasointestinal tubes and, if ordered, should be administered (typically a dose of 10 mg, IV) 10 minutes before the procedure (Rohm, Boldt, & Piper, 2009). Passive advancement involves waiting for the peristaltic movement of the stomach and intestine to facilitate the migration of the tube into the small intestine. Placing the patient on his or her right side may be helpful in advancing the tube because gravity may assist the tube in passing through the pyloric sphincter and into the small intestine.

Nursing Management

Assessing Patient Before Tube Placement

When gastric or enteric/postpyloric intubation is ordered for a patient, it is important for the nurse to review the patient's history to check for contraindications for tube placement. Examples of contraindications include oral or nasal surgery,

esophageal varices, esophageal diverticula, and esophageal or gastric surgery such as a gastric pullup or gastric bypass. Such patients would have a greater risk for perforation, and an altered anatomy would make tube placement difficult if the details of the procedure were not known. It also important to consider the nutritional status of the patient before a tube is inserted into his or her GI tract; serum prealbumin levels should be assessed. Prealbumin is an excellent marker for malnutrition because it has a shorter half-life (2 days) than does albumin (21 days), and is not influenced fluid balance. A normal prealbumin level is 19 to 38 mg/dL with values of 0 to 5, 5 to 10, and 10 to 15 mg/dL reflecting a severe, moderate, and mild protein depletion, respectively (Fischbach & Dunning, 2009). The likelihood of perforation is higher in patients with severe nutritional deficiencies due to poor tissue integrity.

Passage of an NG tube carries risk for patients with known or suspected cervical injuries and may exacerbate hemorrhage in patients with penetrating neck injuries if coughing and gagging occur during insertion (Roberts & Hedges, 2009). Serious complications include pulmonary misplacement of the NG tube and intracranial placement. Patients with head trauma should be evaluated for basilar skull fracture before an NG tube is placed. The tube could be inadvertently inserted into the cranial vault, if the fracture communicates.

Preparing the Patient

Before the patient is intubated, the nurse explains the purpose of the tube; this information may assist the patient in being cooperative and tolerant of what is often an unpleasant

procedure. The general activities related to inserting the tube are then reviewed, including the fact that the patient may have to breathe through the mouth and that the procedure may cause gagging until the tube has passed the area of the gag reflex.

Inserting the Tube

Before inserting the tube, the nurse determines the length of tubing that will be needed to reach the stomach or the small intestine. A mark is made on the tube to indicate the desired length. This length is determined by measuring the distance from the tip of the Nose to the Earlobe and from the earlobe to the Xiphoid process for gastric placement or NEX (Figure 22-8). A common error in inserting NG tubes is to incorrectly estimate the proper length of the tube that should be inserted, thus NG tubes may be inserted too short (in the lower esophagus) or coiled in the stomach. Two additional measurements are noted in the literature: Adding 2 to 6 inches (or ~5.1 to 15 cm) to the NEX measurement to prevent high NG tube placement in tall patients (Kowalak, 2009; Roberts & Hedges, 2009), and the length of NG tube should equal ([NEX − 50 cm]/2) + 50 cm to prevent coiling in the stomach (Ellett, Beckstrand, Flueckiger et al., 2005). The average measurement for adults is 22 to 26 inches or 56 to 66 cm. (Kowalak, 2009).

Insertion of the tube is not a sterile procedure; the nurse and other staff involved should follow Universal Precaution procedures as designated by their facility. While the tube is being inserted, the patient usually sits upright with a towel

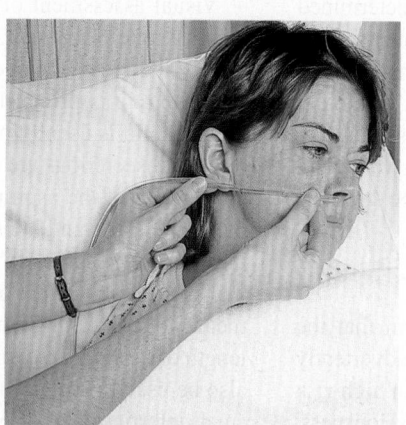

Measuring distance from nostril to tip of earlobe.

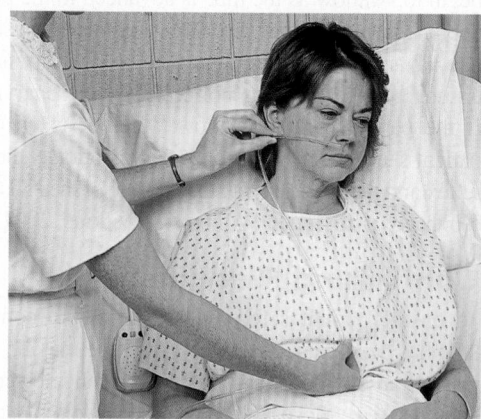

Measuring distance from earlobe to tip of xiphoid process.

Have the patient sit in a neutral position with head facing forward. Place the distal tip of the tubing at the tip of the patient's nose (N); extend tube to the tragus (tip) of the ear (E), and then extend the tube straight down to the tip of the xiphoid (X). The tube is placed 6–10 cm beyond that measured length.

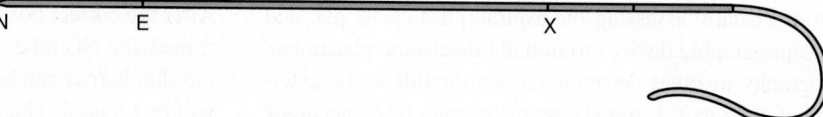

N   E   X

FIGURE 22-8 Measuring length of nasogastric tube for placement into stomach.

or some type of protective barrier spread bib-fashion over the chest. Tissue wipes are made available. Privacy and adequate light are provided. The provider may swab the nostril and spray the oropharynx with tetracaine/benzocaine (Cetacaine) at least 5 minutes before the procedure to numb the nasal passage and suppress the gag reflex. This makes the entire procedure more tolerable. Having the patient gargle with a liquid anesthetic or hold ice chips in the mouth for a few minutes can have a similar effect. Encouraging the patient to breathe through the mouth or to pant often helps, as does swallowing water, if permitted.

A polyurethane tube may need to be warmed to make it more pliable. To make the tube easier to insert, it should be lubricated with a water-soluble lubricant unless it has a dry coating (called *hydromer*), which, when moistened, provides its own lubrication.

The patient is placed in Fowler's position, and the nostrils are inspected for any obstruction. The more patent nostril is selected for use. The tip of the patient's nose is tilted, and the tube is aligned to enter the nostril, following the floor of the nose (under the inferior turbinate), not upward toward the nasal bridge. The tube is advanced slowly to avoid pressure on the nasal turbinates until the posterior pharynx is reached. If significant resistance is encountered, the other nostril is tried rather than forcing the tube, which can cause complications of bleeding or dissection into retropharyngeal tissue (Roberts & Hedges, 2009). When the tube reaches the posterior pharynx, the patient is allowed to rest for a few minutes before proceeding. Unless contraindicated, the patient is instructed to flex the neck to facilitate passage into the esophagus and to begin to swallow as the tube is advanced to the predetermined depth. The patient may also sip water through a straw to facilitate advancement of the tube. The oropharynx is inspected to ensure that the tube has not coiled in the pharynx or mouth. If the patient cannot swallow water or is unconscious, the patient's neck can be stroked to encourage the swallowing reflex and thereby facilitate the passage of the NG tube down the esophagus (Lippincott Williams & Wilkins, 2007).

Confirming Placement

To ensure patient safety, it is essential to confirm that the tube has been placed correctly: the tube may be inadvertently inserted in the lungs, and this may go undetected in high-risk patients (e.g., those with decreased levels of consciousness, confused mental states, poor or absent cough and gag reflexes, or agitation during insertion). The gold standard for verifying placement of a blindly inserted tube is radiographic or X-ray confirmation (AACN, 2010b). X-ray confirmation is necessary if the patient will be receiving feedings or medications through the tube. When a tube is to be used for removal of air or fluid and not instillation, the nurse can use a combination of visually assessing the aspirate, testing its pH, and using capnographic devices to initially determine placement. Capnography involves detecting carbon dioxide at the external end of NG tubes. Limited research reveals 100% accuracy

in ascertaining respiratory placement; however, only patient's on mechanical ventilators were involved (Araujo-Preza, Melhado, Gutierrez et al., 2003; Phillips & Nay, 2007), thus additional research is ongoing about this technique.

Placement must also be ensured at regular intervals once the device is placed. These times include when medications or fluids are given, and every 4 hours for patients receiving continuous tube feedings. The traditional method has been to inject air through the tube while auscultating the epigastric area with a stethoscope to detect air insufflation. However, studies indicate that this auscultatory method is not particularly accurate in determining whether the tube has been inserted into the stomach, intestines, or respiratory tract (AACN, 2010b). Instead of the auscultation method, a combination of four methods is recommended: assessment of the patient's tolerance to medication and feeding administration, measurement of tube length, visual assessment of aspirate, and assessing the pH measurement of aspirate.

To determine tolerance of the feeding to ascertain placement, the nurse assesses the patient's respiratory status. Coughing, gagging, and decreased pulse oximetry could indicate that the tube has migrated. The nurse also inspects the oral cavity to visualize the tube in the back of the patient's throat. It is possible for a patient to regurgitate the tube into the mouth with frequent gagging and coughing. After the tube is inserted, the exposed portion of the tube is measured and the length is documented. The nurse measures the exposed tube length every shift and compares it with the original measurement. An increase in the length of exposed tube may indicate dislodgement.

Visual assessment of the color of the aspirate may help identify tube placement. Gastric aspirate is most frequently cloudy and green, tan or off-white, or bloody or brown. Intestinal aspirate is primarily clear and yellow to bile-colored. Pleural fluid is usually pale yellow and serous, and tracheobronchial secretions are usually tan or off-white mucus. The appearance of the aspirate may be helpful in distinguishing between gastric and intestinal placement but is of little value in ruling out respiratory placement.

Determining the pH of the tube aspirate is a more accurate method of confirming tube placement than is maintaining tube length or visually assessing tube aspirate. The pH method can also be used to monitor the advancement of the tube into the small intestine. The pH of gastric aspirate is acidic (1 to 5), typically less than 4. The pH of intestinal aspirate is approximately 6 or higher, and the pH of respiratory aspirate is more alkaline (≥ 6). pH testing is best suited for distinguishing between gastric and intestinal placement, and remains an area of ongoing research to determine best practice.

Securing the Tube

After the correct position of the tip of the tube has been confirmed, the NG tube is secured to the nose (Fig. 22-9). A liquid skin barrier can be applied to the skin where the NG tube will be secured. The prepared area is covered with a strip of

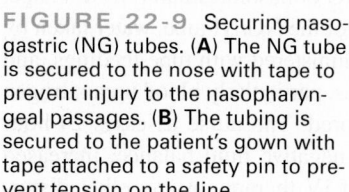
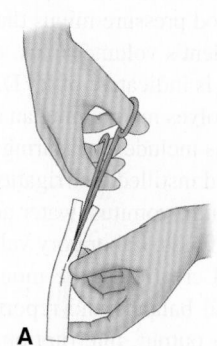
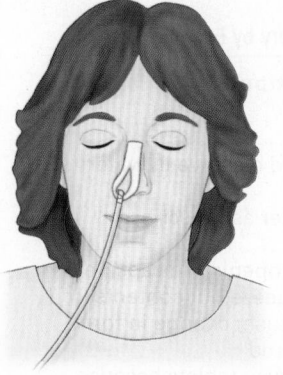
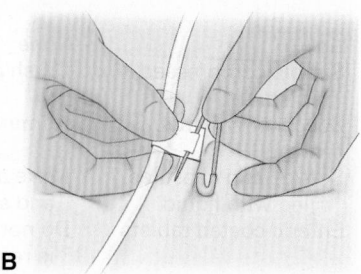

FIGURE 22-9 Securing naso-gastric (NG) tubes. (**A**) The NG tube is secured to the nose with tape to prevent injury to the nasopharyn-geal passages. (**B**) The tubing is secured to the patient's gown with tape attached to a safety pin to prevent tension on the line.

hypoallergenic tape or Op-Site, and the tube is then placed over the tape and secured with a second piece of tape. Instead of tape, a number of companies have feeding tube device holders that can be placed. A nasal bridle can be used in patients who have a history of tube dislodgment. Bridling, which involves the insertion of a loop of strong but flexible material through one nares, around the nasal septum, and out the other nares as a "bridle" to which the nasoenteric tube is secured, has demonstrated success in preventing tube dislodgment in 85.6% of cases (Power, Smyth, Duggan et al., 2010). Additionally, it is wise to secure the NG tube to the patient's gown or pajamas with an elastic band and safety pin or with adhesive tape loops, so that a tug on the tube will not pull on the nares. It is crucial that the NG tube is secured without putting undue pressure on the medial or lateral nares, to prevent tissue necrosis. Additionally, the tape securing the tube should be changed daily and the nares inspected for complications such as erosion (Lippincott Williams & Wilkins, 2007). The tube must be looped loosely to prevent tension and dislodgement.

> **NURSING ALERT**
> *If the patient is ambulatory and has an SST, the blue pigtail must be above the level of the stomach to prevent gastric fluid leaking out via this port. The pigtail can be fitted into the larger suction lumen to seal off the NG tube, while ambulating.*

Monitoring the Patient and Maintaining Tube Function

It is important to keep an accurate record of all fluid intake, feedings, and irrigation. To maintain patency, the tube is irrigated every 4 to 6 hours with normal saline to avoid electrolyte loss through gastric drainage. Tap water may be used during medication administration or tube feedings. The nurse records the amount, color, and type of all drainage every 8 hours.

When double- or triple-lumen tubes are used, each lumen is labeled according to its intended use: aspiration, feeding, or balloon inflation (refer to Sengstaken-Blakemore tube in Chapter 25).

When feedings or medications are ordered for administration through a GI tube, it is the nurse's responsibility to maintain the patency of the device as well as to assess the patient's tolerance of the feeding or meds. Liquid nutritional solutions are commonly administered at a continuous rate via programmable electronic pump or by syringe in intermittent boluses. With continuous feedings, it is important for the nurse to assess the volume of feed in the bag to ensure it does not run dry.

Administering Medication

When medications are administered through GI tubes, flushing with 20 to 30 mL of tap water with a 60 mL bulb syringe may decrease the risk of tube occlusion (Kowalak, 2009; Philips & Nay, 2007). With NG tubes and small-diameter nasoenteric tubes, thorough crushing of medications in pill form is a necessity. A nurse should collaborate with the medical team and pharmacy to convert medications to liquid forms if possible. The nurse should also be aware that administering extended-release tablets that would require crushing through such tubes is prohibited since overdosage can result. However, occasionally, time-released capsules are permitted to be opened (not crushed) and administered, and pharmacy staff should be consulted if any questions or concerns exist related to whether medications can be crushed or opened. The medical team should be notified to have the medications changed to liquid form whenever possible. Table 22-1 discusses administering medications.

Unclogging Tubes

When a tube becomes clogged with feedings or medications, a number of methods can be used to regain patency of the tube without having to replace it. Smaller-diameter postpyloric tubes can clog if feedings are stopped and the tube is not properly flushed. Warm water can be administered through the tube with caution, using varying sizes of syringes; smaller syringes having greater force to dislodge the clog. Cola and cranberry juice have historically been recommended as an effective, noninvasive means of unclogging tubes; however, a more consistently effective method involves instilling a mixture of pancreatic enzymes and sodium bicarbonate into the tube for 20 minutes to digest the clog. The nurse is aware that correct placement of the NG tube must be confirmed before any mixture is injected to unclog the tube.

TABLE
22-1 Preparing Medication for Delivery by Feeding Tube

Medication Form	Preparation
Liquid	None
Simple compressed tablets	Crush and dissolve in water
Buccal or sublingual tablets	Administer as prescribed
Soft gelatin capsules filled with liquid	Make an opening in capsule and squeeze out contents
Enteric-coated tablets	Do not crush; change in form is required
Timed-release tablets	Do not crush tablets because doing so may release too much drug too quickly (overdose); check with pharmacist for alternative formulation
Timed-release capsules or sustained-release capsules	Some can be opened and contents added to tube-feeding formula; *always* check with pharmacist before doing this

NURSING ALERT

Currently, a paucity of research literature evaluates the nursing considerations and interventions relating to the administration of medications via enteral tubes. The nurse should read current literature and access databases such as the Cochrane library for the most current evidence.

Providing Oral and Nasal Hygiene

Regular and conscientious oral and nasal hygiene is a vital part of patient care, because the tube causes discomfort and pressure and may be in place for several days. Moistened cotton-tipped swabs can be used to clean the nose, followed by cleansing with a water-soluble lubricant. Frequent mouth care is comforting for the patient. The nasal tape is changed daily, and the nose is inspected for skin irritation. If the nasal and pharyngeal mucosa is excessively dry, steam or cool vapor inhalations may be beneficial. Throat lozenges, an ice collar, chewing gum, or sucking on hard candies (if permitted), and limiting talking also assist in relieving patient discomfort. These activities keep the mucous membranes moist and help prevent inflammation of the parotid glands.

Monitoring and Managing Potential Complications

Patients with NG or nasoenteric intubation are susceptible to a variety of problems, including fluid volume deficit, pulmonary complications, and tube-related irritations. These potential complications require careful ongoing assessment.

Symptoms of fluid volume deficit (FVD) include dry skin and mucous membranes, decreased urinary output, lethargy, orthostatic hypotension, and increased heart rate. A nurse can also calculate the patient's pulse pressure (systolic blood pressure minus diastolic blood pressure) to predict the patient's volume status. A pulse pressure of less than 30 mm Hg is indicative of FVD. Assessment of fluid volume deficit involves maintaining an accurate record of intake and output. This includes measuring NG or nasointestinal (NI) drainage, fluid instilled by irrigation of the NG/NI tube, water taken by mouth, vomitus, water administered with tube feedings, and IV fluids. Laboratory values, particularly blood urea nitrogen and creatinine, are monitored. The nurse assesses 24-hour fluid balance and reports negative fluid balance, increased NG output, interruption of IV therapy, or any other disturbance in fluid intake or output.

Pulmonary complications from NG intubation occur because coughing and clearing of the pharynx are impaired, because gas buildup can irritate the phrenic nerve, and because tubes may become dislodged, retracting the distal end above the esophagogastric sphincter (which places the patient at risk for aspiration, or breathing fluids or foods into the trachea and lungs). Medications (e.g., antacids, simethicone [Gaviscon], and metoclopramide [Reglan]) can be administered to decrease potential problems. Signs and symptoms of complications include coughing during the administration of foods or medications, difficulty clearing the airway, tachypnea, and fever. Assessment includes regular auscultation of lung sounds and routine assessment of vital signs. It is important to encourage the patient to cough and to take deep breaths regularly. The nurse also carefully confirms the proper placement of the tube by assessing tube length before instilling any fluids or medications.

Irritation of the mucous membranes is a common complication of NG/NI intubation. The nostrils, oral mucosa, esophagus, and trachea are susceptible to irritation and necrosis. Visible areas are inspected frequently, and the adequacy of hydration is assessed. When providing oral hygiene, the nurse carefully inspects the mucous membranes for signs of irritation or excessive dryness. The nurse palpates the area around the parotid glands to detect any tenderness or enlarged nodes, indicating parotitis, and observes for any irritation or skin breakdown at the insertion site (e.g., nares) or of the mucous membranes. In order to preserve the skin integrity of the nares, the nurse should rotate the position of the tube on the wall of the nares once every 24 hours. In addition, it is important to assess the patient for esophagitis and tracheitis; symptoms include sore throat and hoarseness.

NURSING ALERT

The nurse alerts the health provider when new frank bleeding is noted in the NG tube drainage, if or "coffee ground material" is noted because it may indicate bleeding. Gastroccult testing is available to assess the presence of blood in gastric drainage. The nurse is aware that Hemoccult test for stool cannot be used for evaluation of gastric drainage.

Removing the Tube

Before removing a tube, the nurse may intermittently clamp and unclamp it for a trial period of several hours to ensure that the patient does not experience nausea, vomiting, or distention. Before the tube is removed, it is flushed with 10 mL of water or normal saline to ensure that it is free of debris and away from the gastric lining; then the balloon (if present) is deflated. Gloves are worn to remove the tube and a towel or disposable pad placed on the patient's chest. The tube is withdrawn gently and slowly for 15 to 20 cm (6 to 8 in) until the tip reaches the esophagus; the remainder is withdrawn rapidly from the nostril. If the tube does not come out easily, force should not be used, and the problem should be reported to the provider. As the tube is withdrawn, it is concealed in the disposable pad or towel to prevent secretions from soiling the patient or nurse. After the tube is removed, the nurse provides oral hygiene.

Administering Tube Feedings With Nasogastric and Nasoenteric Devices

Enteral nutrition feedings are given to meet nutritional requirements when oral intake is inadequate or not possible and the GI tract is functioning normally. Tube feedings have several advantages over parenteral nutrition: they are low in cost, safe, well tolerated by the patient, and easy to use both in extended-care facilities and in the patient's home. Other advantages include:

- Preserving GI integrity by delivery of nutrients and medications intraluminally
- Preserving the normal sequence of intestinal and hepatic metabolism
- Maintaining fat metabolism and lipoprotein synthesis
- Maintaining normal insulin/glucagon ratios

Tube feedings are delivered to the stomach (in the case of NG intubation or gastrostomy) or to the distal duodenum or proximal jejunum (in the case of **nasoduodenal** or **nasojejunal tube** feeding). Nasoduodenal or nasojejunal feeding is indicated when the esophagus and stomach need to be bypassed or when the patient is at risk for aspiration. For long-term feedings (longer than 4 weeks), gastrostomy or jejunostomy tubes are preferred for administration of medications or food. The numerous conditions requiring enteral nutrition are summarized in Table 22-2.

Reducing the Risk of Aspiration

To decrease the risk of aspiration, the head of the bed must remain elevated to 30 degrees at all times (Metheny, Davis-Jackson, & Stewart, 2010). If the patient is on bedrest, the tube feeding must be shut off when bed making, bathing, or anytime the head of the bed must be lowered to below 30 degrees. Additionally, newest research demonstrates the use of a small-bowel feeding site (past the first portion of the duodenum) reduces the incidence of aspiration (Metheny, Schallom, Oliver et al., 2008).

TABLE
22-2 Conditions Requiring Enteral Therapy

Condition or Need	Examples
Preoperative bowel preparation	—
GI problems	Fistula, short-bowel syndrome, mild pancreatitis, Crohn's disease, ulcerative colitis, nonspecific maldigestion or malabsorption
Cancer therapy	Radiation, chemotherapy
Convalescent care	Surgery, injury, severe illness
Coma, semiconsciousness*	Stroke, head injury, neurologic disorder, neoplasm
Hypermetabolic conditions	Burns, trauma, multiple fractures, sepsis, AIDS, organ transplantation
Alcoholism, chronic depression, anorexia nervosa*	Chronic illness, psychiatric or neurologic disorder
Debilitation*	Disease or injury
Maxillofacial or cervical surgery	Disease or injury
Oropharyngeal or esophageal paralysis*	Disease or injury, neoplasm, inflammation, trauma, respiratory failure

*Because some of these patients are at risk for regurgitating or vomiting and aspirating administered formula, each condition must be considered individually.

Residual Assessment

Patient tolerance of liquid enteral nutrition is determined by residual measurement and the presence or absence of nausea and vomiting. Residual measurement or volume of aspiration is most easily assessed with large-bore GI tubes. Smaller diameter nasojejunal tubes and duodenal tubes often collapse when suction is applied. The volume of aspirate indicates the rate at which the patient is digesting the feedings and how quickly the chyme is passing into the small intestine. The volume of the stomach is approximately 1 L, with an ability to stretch with increased intake depending on the size of the patient.

To assess gastric residuals, a 60-mL syringe is used to measure volumes from feeding tubes every 4 hours. It is recommended that the nurse instill approximately 30 mL of air into the feeding tube before withdrawing contents from the tube, to prevent inaccurate measurement of fluid within the lumen of the tube as residual (Methany et al., 2010). The nurse then slowly applies a steady pressure on the plunger and aspirates the residual volume until no more fluid can be withdrawn into the syringe. Policies vary according to institutions, and the nurse should follow unit guidelines. Research demonstrates, however, that residual volumes of less than 200 mL appear to be well tolerated without risk of aspiration (Metheny et al., 2008, 2010). In general, if less than this amount is noted, the residual fluid is returned to the patient; if over 200 mL, it is discarded.

Osmosis, Osmolality, and Dumping Syndrome

Osmolality is an important consideration for patients receiving tube feedings through the duodenum or jejunum because feeding formulas with a high osmolality may lead to undesirable effects, such as dumping syndrome.

Fluid balance is maintained by **osmosis**, the process by which water moves through membranes from a dilute solution of lower **osmolality** (ionic concentration) to a more concentrated solution of higher osmolality until both solutions are of nearly equal osmolality. The osmolality of normal body fluids is approximately 300 mOsm/kg. The body attempts to keep the osmolality of the contents of the stomach and intestines at approximately this level.

Highly concentrated solutions and certain foods can upset the normal fluid balance in the body. Individual amino acids and carbohydrates are small particles that have great osmotic effect. Electrolytes, such as sodium and potassium, are comparatively small particles; they have a great effect on osmolality and consequently on the patient's ability to tolerate a given solution.

When a concentrated solution of high osmolality is taken in large amounts, water moves to the stomach and intestines from fluid surrounding the organs and the vascular compartment. The patient has a feeling of fullness, nausea, and diarrhea; this causes dehydration, hypotension, and tachycardia, collectively termed **dumping syndrome**. Patients vary in the degree to which they tolerate the effects of high osmolality; usually, debilitated patients are less tolerant. The nurse needs to be knowledgeable about the osmolality of the patient's formula and needs to observe for and take steps to prevent undesired effects. Dumping syndrome can be prevented by the following interventions: using room-temperature feedings (gastric emptying will be faster if temperature of the fluid is too hot or too cold), changing from **bolus** to continuous feedings if appropriate, having the patient remain in a semi-Fowler's position for 1 hour after eating to gradually allow the feedings to pass into the intestine, and slowing the rate of feedings to allow more time for digestion.

In the event that a tube feeding uses a high-osmolality formula, the nurse observes the patient's sodium level and expects that free water may be ordered by diluting the tube feeding or by periodic instillation of water by the health care team if rising sodium levels are seen. Response to the free water (either dilution of tube feeding or tap water instilled via the NG/NI tube) is assessed with subsequent electrolyte levels.

Tube Feeding Formulas

The choice of formula to be delivered by tube feeding is influenced by the status of the GI tract and the nutritional needs of the patient. Dietitians collaborate with providers and nurses to determine the best formula for the individual patient. The formula characteristics that are considered prior to selection include the chemical composition of the nutrient source (protein, carbohydrates, fat), caloric density, osmolality, residue, bacteriologic safety, vitamins, minerals, and cost.

Various major formula types for tube feedings are available commercially. Commercially prepared polymeric formulas (formulas with high molecular weight) are composed of protein, carbohydrates, and fats in a high-molecular-weight form (e.g., Boost Plus, TwoCal HN, Isosource). Chemically defined formulas (e.g., Peptamen 1.5 or Vivonex) contain predigested and easy-to-absorb nutrients. Modular products contain only one major nutrient, such as protein (Beneprotein). Disease-specific formulas are available for various conditions. For patients with renal failure, a formula such as Nepro, which is high in calories and low in electrolytes, is ideal because it is formulated to maintain electrolyte and fluid balance. For patients with severe chronic obstructive pulmonary disease, a formula such as Pulmocare may be selected because it is high in fat and low in carbohydrates, has a high density (1.5 calories/mL) that helps maintain fluid restriction, and reduces carbon dioxide production. Excess carbohydrates may increase production of CO_2, and this impacts negatively respiratory status. Fiber is added to some formulas (e.g., Jevity) to decrease the occurrence of diarrhea in some at-risk patients. Blenderized formulas can also be used. They can be made by the patient's family or obtained in a ready-to-use form that is carefully prepared according to directions. Some feedings are given as supplements, and others are designed to meet the patient's total nutritional needs.

Administration Methods and Frequency

The frequency of tube feeding and administration method depends on the location of the tube in the GI tract, patient tolerance, convenience, and cost. Intermittent bolus feedings are administered into the stomach (usually by gastrostomy tube) in large amounts at designated intervals and may be given four to eight times per day. The intermittent gravity drip, another method for administering tube feedings into the stomach, is commonly used when the patient is at home. In this instance, the tube feeding is administered over 30 minutes at designated intervals. Both of these tube feeding methods are practical and inexpensive. However, the feedings delivered at variable rates may be poorly tolerated and time-consuming.

The continuous infusion method is often used when feedings are administered into the small intestine. This method is preferred for patients who are at risk for aspiration or who tolerate tube feedings poorly (Methany et al., 2010). The feedings are given continuously at a constant rate by means of a pump. This method decreases abdominal distention, gastric residuals, and the risk of aspiration. However, pumps are expensive, and they allow the patient less flexibility than intermittent feedings.

An alternative to the continuous infusion method is **cyclic feeding**. The infusion is given at a faster rate over a shorter time (usually 8 to 12 hours). Feedings may be infused at night to avoid interrupting the patient's lifestyle. Cyclic continuous infusions may be appropriate for patients who are being weaned from tube feedings to an oral diet, as supplements for patients who cannot eat enough, and for patients at

home who need daytime hours free from the pump. Whichever method is chosen, the head of the bed must be maintained at a minimum of 30 degrees to decrease the risk of aspiration. A wide variety of containers, feeding tubes and catheters, delivery systems, and pumps are available for use with tube feedings.

Complications of Tube Feedings

Diarrhea, the most common complication associated with liquid feedings, is commonly due to the hyperosmolality of the feedings and/or the decreased serum osmolality of the patient's serum. Changing the concentration or type of formula often decreases or stops this complication.

Aspiration pneumonia is an important mechanical complication. Aspiration can occur due to improperly placed tubes or when the patient vomits the formula into the airway. When aspiration occurs or is suspected, it is important for the nurse to stop the feeding, suction the pharynx and trachea, and closely assess the patient's respiratory status while contacting the provider. Aspiration prevention involves keeping the patient's head of bed elevated to at least 30 degrees and verifying the tube placement on insertion, before food or medication administration and periodically throughout a 24-hour shift.

Patients may have an increased blood glucose as a metabolic complication of tube feedings. Carbohydrate content varies between the different types of formula used and should be considered if the patient is hyperglycemic. The nurse should frequently assess the patient's blood sugar especially when initiating a tube feeding. Additional complications of enteral therapy can be found in Table 22-3 on page 626.

GASTROSTOMY

A **gastrostomy** is a surgical procedure in which an opening is created into the stomach for the purpose of administering foods and fluids via a feeding tube.

Clinical Indications

Gastrostomy is preferred for prolonged enteral nutrition support when the patient's diagnosis makes it difficult to support the nutritional requirements, such as patients with traumatic brain injury and patients with neurodegenerative diseases (Alzheimer's disease). Gastrostomy is also preferred over NG feedings in the patient who is comatose because the gastroesophageal sphincter remains intact. Regurgitation and aspiration are less likely to occur with a gastrostomy than with NG feedings.

Types

Different types of feeding gastrostomies may be used, including the Stamm (temporary and permanent), Janeway

(permanent), and **percutaneous endoscopic gastrostomy (PEG)** tube (temporary) systems. The Stamm and Janeway gastrostomies require either an upper abdominal midline incision or a left upper quadrant transverse incision. The Stamm procedure requires the use of concentric pursestring sutures to secure the tube to the anterior gastric wall. To create the gastrostomy, an exit wound is created in the left upper abdomen. The Janeway procedure necessitates the creation of a tunnel (called a gastric tube) that is brought out through the abdomen to form a permanent **stoma**.

Insertion of a PEG requires the services of two physicians (or a physician and a nurse with specialty skills). After administering a local anesthetic, one health care provider inserts a cannula into the stomach through an abdominal incision and then threads a nonabsorbable suture through the cannula; the second provider inserts an endoscope via the patient's upper GI tract and uses the endoscopic snare to grasp the end of the suture and guide it up through the patient's mouth. The suture is knotted to the dilator tip at the end of the PEG tube. The endoscopist then advances the dilator tip through the patient's mouth while the first provider pulls the suture through the cannula site. The attached PEG tube is guided down the esophagus, into the stomach, and out through the abdominal incision (Fig. 22-10, p. 627). The mushroom catheter tip and internal crossbar secure the tube against the stomach wall. An external crossbar or bumper keeps the catheter in place. A tubing adaptor is in place between feedings, and a clamp or plug is used to close or open the tubing.

The initial PEG device can be removed and replaced once the tract is well established (10 to 14 days after insertion). Replacement of the PEG device is indicated to provide long-term nutritional support, to replace a clogged or migrated tube, or to enhance patient comfort. The PEG replacement device should be fitted securely to the stoma to prevent leakage of gastric acid and is maintained in place through traction between the internal and anchoring devices.

An alternative to the PEG device is a **low-profile gastrostomy device (LPGD)** (see Fig. 22-10). The LPGD may be inserted 3 to 6 months after initial gastrostomy tube placement. These devices are inserted flush with the skin; they eliminate the possibility of tube migration and obstruction and have antireflux valves to prevent gastric reflux. Two types of devices may be used—obturated or nonobturated. The obturated devices (G-button) have a dome tip that acts as an internal stabilizer. Only a physician may obturate (insert a tube that is larger than the actual stoma). The nonobturated device (MIC-KEY) has an external skin disk and is inserted into the stoma without force; a balloon is inflated to secure placement. A nurse in the home setting may insert these nonobturated devices. The drawbacks of both types of LPGDs are the inability to assess residual volumes (one-way valve) and the need for a special adaptor to connect the device to the feeding container.

TABLE
22-3 Complications of Enteral Therapy

Complications	Causes	Selected Nursing Interventions	
		Treatment	**Prevention**
Gastrointestinal			
Diarrhea (most common)	Hyperosmolar feedings Rapid infusion/bolus feedings Bacteria-contaminated feedings Lactase deficiency Medications/antibiotic therapy Decreased serum osmolality level Food allergies Cold formula	Assess fluid balance and electrolyte levels; report findings Implement changes in tube feeding formula or rate	Assess rate of infusion and temperature of formula Replace formula every 4 hours; change tube feeding container and tubing daily
Nausea/vomiting	Change in formula or rate Hyperosmolar formula Inadequate gastric emptying	Review medications	Check residuals; if <200 mL continue feeding and recheck; report if residual is still high
Gas/bloating/cramping	Air in tube	Notify physician if persistent	Keep tubing free of air
Dumping syndrome	Bolus feedings/rapid rate Cold formula	Check fiber and water content; report findings Check rate and temperature of formula	Avoid rapid infusion of feeding Administer feeding at or near room temperature
Constipation	High milk (lactose) content Lack of fiber Inadequate fluid intake/dehydration Opioid use	Check fiber and water content; report findings	Administer adequate amount of hydration as flushes
Mechanical			
Aspiration pneumonia	Improper tube placement Vomiting with aspiration of tube feeding Flat in bed Use of large tube	Assess respiratory status and notify physician	Implement reliable method for checking small-bore enteral tube placement (i.e., measuring length of exposed tube) Keep head of bed elevated 30 degrees continuously
Tube displacement	Excessive coughing/vomitus Tension on the tube or unsecured tube Tracheal suctioning Airway intubation	Stop feeding and notify provider	Check tube placement before administering feeding
Tube obstruction	Inadequate flushing/formula rate	Follow policy for declogging feeding tubes	Obtain liquid medications when possible
Residue	Inadequate crushing of medications and flushing after administration		Flush tube and crush medications adequately
Nasopharyngeal irritation	Tube position/improper taping Use of large tubes	Assess nasopharyngeal mucous membranes every 4 hours	Tape tube to prevent pressure on nares
Metabolic			
Hyperglycemia	Glucose intolerance High carbohydrate content of the feeding	Check blood glucose levels periodically Request dietary consult to reevaluate choice of feeding product	
Dehydration and azotemia (excessive urea in the blood)	Hyperosmolar feedings with insufficient fluid intake	Report signs and symptoms of dehydration Implement changes in tube feeding formula, rate, or ratio to water	Provide adequate hydration through flushes or dilution of tube feeding

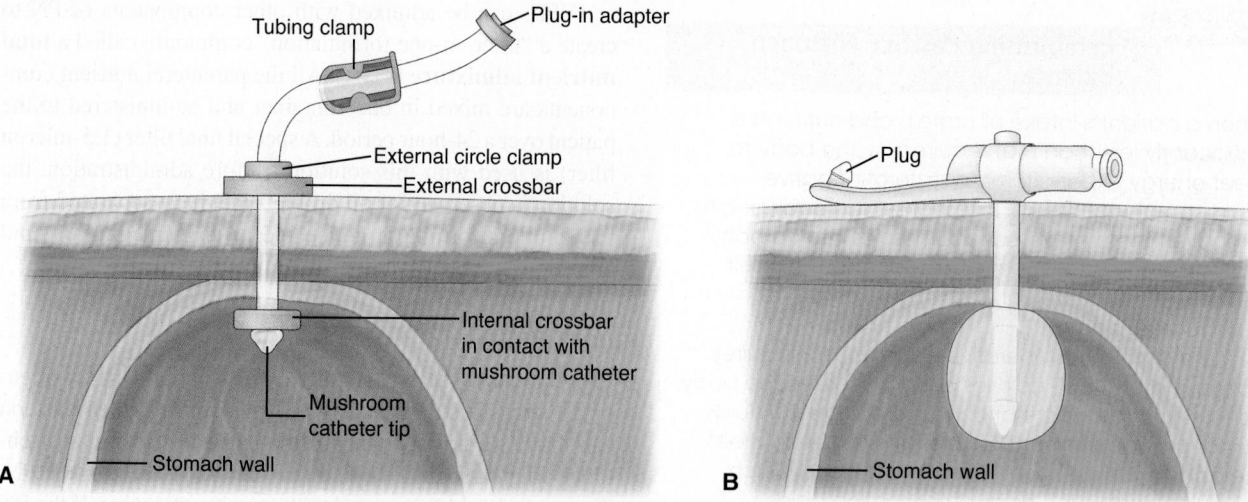

FIGURE 22-10 (**A**) A detail of the abdomen and the percutaneous endoscopic gastrostomy (PEG) tube, showing catheter fixation. (**B**) A detail of the abdomen and the nonobturated low-profile gastrostomy device (LPGD), showing balloon fixation.

Complications

Reflux from stomach feedings can result in aspiration pneumonia. Therefore, patients at risk for aspiration pneumonia are not ideal candidates for a gastrostomy. A jejunostomy is preferred, or jejunal feeding through a nasojejunal tube may be recommended.

Other complications of gastrostomy tube placement include premature removal, infection, and leakage around the insertion site. To prevent premature removal, a loosely taped dressing can be placed over the top of the tube flange. A fenestrated drape (split dressing) often used for tracheotomy care works well. In addition, a tube-securing device can be placed on the patient's abdomen or flank to further decrease the tension on the insertion site. These devices use adhesives and Velcro to temporarily fix the gastrostomy tube to the patient's skin. The nurse should educate the patient on how much mobility he or she has with the gastrostomy tube, to aid in preventing tension on the device. If the tube is inadvertently removed, the nurse should clean the site, place a dressing, and notify the provider as soon as possible.

Infection is prevented by assessing and cleansing the site daily. Soap and water can be used around the general area. To remove hardened feedings that may accumulate around the insertion site, the nurse can use normal saline. The area should be dried before a dressing is reapplied. Redness, tenderness, and skin breakdown should be documented and the provider notified.

PARENTERAL NUTRITION

Parenteral nutrition (PN) is a method of providing nutrients to the body by a peripheral or central IV route. The solution is composed of a very complex admixture containing proteins, carbohydrates, fats, electrolytes, vitamins, trace minerals, and sterile water in a single container. The goals of PN are to improve nutritional status, establish a positive nitrogen balance (Box 22-2), maintain muscle mass, promote weight maintenance or gain, and support the healing process.

Clinical Indications

In both the home and hospital setting, PN is indicated in the following situations:

- The patient is exhibiting signs and symptoms of protein calorie malnutrition: a weight loss of greater than 10% to 15% or a weight of less than 90% of the ideal body weight (McClave, Martindale, Vanek et al., 2009).
- The patient's intake is insufficient to maintain an anabolic state (e.g., severe burns, malnutrition, short bowel syndrome, AIDS, sepsis, cancer).
- The patient's ability to ingest food orally or by tube is impaired (e.g., paralytic ileus, Crohn's disease with obstruction, postradiation enteritis, severe hyperemesis gravidarum in pregnancy).
- The patient is unwilling or unable to ingest adequate nutrients (e.g., anorexia nervosa, postoperative elderly patients).
- The underlying medical condition precludes being fed orally or by tube (e.g., acute pancreatitis, high enterocutaneous fistula).
- Preoperative and postoperative nutritional needs are prolonged (e.g., extensive bowel surgery).

Preoperatively malnourished patients who are not candidates for enteral feedings should have PN initiated for nutrient resuscitation a week before surgery if possible. PN therapy lasting less than 7 days has been shown to have no effect on nutritional status or was linked to poor outcomes (McClave et al., 2009).

BOX 22-2 Establishing Positive Nitrogen Balance

When a patient's intake of protein and nutrients is significantly less than that required by the body to meet energy expenditures, a state of negative nitrogen balance results. In response, the body begins to convert the protein found in muscles into carbohydrates to be used to meet energy needs. The result is muscle wasting, weight loss, fatigue, and, if left uncorrected, death.

The average postoperative adult patient requires approximately 1,500 calories per day to keep the body from using its own store of protein. Traditional IV fluids do not provide sufficient calories or nitrogen to meet the body's daily requirements. PN solutions, which supply nutrients such as dextrose, amino acids, electrolytes, vitamins, minerals, and fat emulsions, provide enough calories and nitrogen to meet the patient's daily nutritional needs. In general, PN usually provides 25 to 35 kcal/kg of ideal body weight and 1.0 to 1.5 g of protein/kg of ideal body weight.

The patient with fever, trauma, burns, major surgery, or hypermetabolic disease requires additional daily calories. The volume of fluid necessary to provide these calories would surpass fluid tolerance and lead to pulmonary edema or heart failure. To provide the required calories in a small volume, it is necessary to increase the concentration of nutrients and use a route of administration (i.e., a large, high-flow vein, such as the subclavian) that rapidly dilutes incoming nutrients to the proper levels of body tolerance.

When highly concentrated dextrose is administered, caloric requirements are satisfied and the body uses amino acids for protein synthesis rather than for energy. Additional potassium is added to the solution to maintain proper electrolyte balance and to transport glucose and amino acids across cell membranes. To prevent deficiencies and fulfill requirements for tissue synthesis, other elements, such as calcium, phosphorus, magnesium, and sodium chloride, are added.

Parenteral Formulas

A total of 2 to 3 L of solution is administered over a 24-hour period using a filter (1.2-micron particulate filter). Before administration, the PN infusion must be inspected for clarity and any precipitate. The label is compared with the provider's order, noting the expiration date. **IV fat emulsions** (IVFEs, Intralipids) may be infused simultaneously with PN through a Y-connector close to the infusion site and *should not* be filtered. Before administration, the IVFE is inspected for frothiness, separation, or oily appearance. If any of these are present, the solution is not used. Usually 500 mL of a 10% emulsion or 250 mL of 20% emulsion is administered over 6 to 12 hours, one to three times a week. IVFEs can provide up to 30% of the total daily calorie intake.

IVFEs can be admixed with other components of PN to create a "three-in-one formulation" commonly called a **total nutrient admixture** (TNA). All the parenteral nutrient components are mixed in one container and administered to the patient over a 24-hour period. A special final filter (1.5-micron filter) is used with this solution. Before administration, the solution is observed for oil droplets that have separated from the solution, forming a noticeable layer ("cracking of lipid emulsion"); such a solution should be discarded.

Initiating Therapy

PN solutions have a higher glucose concentration than do regular IV fluids. As a result, PN is a medium in which bacteria can thrive. In is important for the nurse to use aseptic technique when assessing the catheter port to be used for the PN. The ports should be prepped with an antiseptic wipe. If the PN bag does not come with preprimed tubing from the pharmacy, the nurse must take great care not to contaminant the bag or tubing. The dressing on the catheter should also be changed in accordance with the institution's policy to prevent infection at the insertion site. PN solutions are initiated slowly and advanced gradually each day to the desired rate as the patient's fluid and glucose tolerance permits. If the solution is administered too rapidly, the patient could become fluid overloaded. If this occurs, the rate should be decreased, and the patient's respiratory status should be monitored. The patient's laboratory test results and response to PN therapy are monitored on an ongoing basis by the provider and licensed nutrition provider. Standing orders are initiated for weighing the patient; monitoring intake, output, and blood glucose; and baseline and periodic monitoring of complete blood count, platelet count, and chemistry panel, including serum carbon dioxide, magnesium, phosphorus, triglycerides, and prealbumin. A 24-hour urine nitrogen determination may be performed for analysis of nitrogen balance. In most hospitals, the provider prescribes PN solutions on a daily standard PN order form. The formulation of the PN solutions is calculated carefully each day to meet the complete nutritional needs of the individual patient.

Administration Methods

Peripheral Method

A peripheral parenteral nutrition formula is prescribed when a patient's oral intake requires supplementation. This type of solution is not as hypertonic as PN or total parenteral nutrition (TPN) so it can be administered peripherally. PPN formulas are not nutritionally complete: there is typically less dextrose content.

> **NURSING ALERT**
> Any formula with a dextrose concentration of more than 10% should not be administered through peripheral veins because they irritate the intima (innermost walls) of small veins, causing a chemical phlebitis.

Lipids are administered simultaneously to buffer the PPN and to protect the peripheral vein from irritation. For PPN solutions, the amino acids are usually limited to 5% to prevent phlebitis (Diepenbrock, 2008). These solutions use a *dedicated line*; that is, no other medication or IV solution can be infused other than the PPN solution through this peripheral IV.

Central Method

Because TPN solutions have five or six times the solute concentration of blood (and exert an osmotic pressure of about 2,000 mOsm/L), they are injurious to the intima of peripheral veins. Therefore, to prevent phlebitis and other venous complications, these solutions are administered into the vascular system through a catheter inserted into a high-flow, large blood vessel such as the subclavian vein. Concentrated solutions are then very rapidly diluted to isotonic levels by the blood in this vessel.

Four types of **central venous access devices (CVADs)** can be used to administer TPN: nontunneled (or percutaneous) central catheters, peripherally inserted central catheters, tunneled catheters, and implanted ports. Whenever one of these catheters is inserted, catheter tip placement should be confirmed by X-ray studies before PN therapy is initiated. The optimal position is the midproximal third of the superior vena cava at the junction of the right atrium.

Nontunneled Central Catheters

Nontunneled central catheters are used for short-term (<6 weeks) IV therapy in acute-care, long-term care, and home-care settings. The provider inserts these catheters. Examples of nontunneled central catheters are Vas Cath, percutaneous subclavian Arrow, and Hohn catheters. The subclavian vein is the most common vessel used, because the subclavian area provides a stable insertion site to which the catheter can be anchored, allows the patient freedom of movement, and provides easy access to the dressing site. The jugular vein should be avoided and only be considered for cannulation if the patient has no other points of access. Jugular access should be used temporarily for approximately 1 to 2 days.

To ensure accessibility in a patient with limited IV access, a triple-lumen subclavian catheter can be used, because it offers three ports for various uses (Fig. 22-11). The 16-gauge distal lumen can be used to infuse blood or other viscous fluids. The 18-gauge middle lumen is reserved for PN infusion. The 18-gauge proximal port can be used for administration of blood or medications. A port not being used for fluid administration can be used for obtaining blood specimens if indicated. The nurse may temporarily stop an IV solution or medication drip (if warranted—some solutions cannot be stopped even for brief periods of time, such as a nitroglycerine drip with the acute MI patient) when drawing blood from another lumen on the triple-lumen catheter. Otherwise, these infusions can contaminate the studies ordered and alter the results. The nurse may also waste 5 to 10 cc of blood from

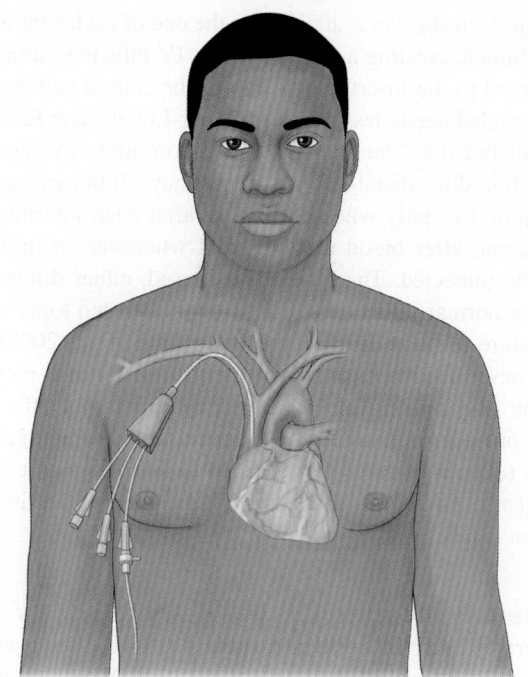

FIGURE 22-11 Subclavian triple-lumen catheter used for parenteral nutrition and other adjunctive therapy. The catheter is threaded through the subclavian vein into the vena cava. Each lumen is an avenue for solution administration. The lumens are secured with threaded needleless adapters or Luer-Lok–type caps when the device is not in use.

the patient before drawing the actual specimen for analysis as an additional method for getting a clean sample.

If a single-lumen central catheter is used for administering TPN, various restrictions apply:

- Blood cannot be drawn from the catheter, and transfusions of blood products cannot be given through the main line because red blood cells may coat the lumen of the catheter, thereby reducing the flow of the nutritional solution.
- Medications cannot be administered through it because the medication may be incompatible with the components of the nutritional solution (insulin is an exception). If medications must be given, they must be infused through a separate peripheral IV line, not by piggyback into the TPN line.

Once the catheter's position is confirmed, the prescribed TPN solution is started. The initial rate of infusion is usually 50 mL/hour, and the rate is gradually increased to the maintenance rate or predetermined dose (e.g., 100 to 125 mL/hour). An infusion pump is always used for administration of TPN.

NURSING ALERT

If, for any reason, there is a delay in the infusion rate, this solution is never increased beyond the hourly ordered rate. There is no "playing catch up" with TPN (Diepenbrock, 2008).

An injection site cap is attached to the end of each central catheter lumen, creating a closed system. IV infusion tubing is connected to the insertion site cap of the central catheter with a threaded needleless adapter or Luer-Lok device. Each lumen is labeled by the manufacturer according to location (proximal, middle, distal). To ensure patency, all lumens are flushed initially, daily when not in use, after each intermittent infusion, after blood drawing, and whenever an infusion is disconnected. The type of flush used, either diluted heparin or normal saline remains a strongly debated topic in the literature (Bishop, Dougherty, Bodenham et al., 2007). Force is never used to flush the catheter. If resistance is met, aspiration may restore lumen patency; if this is not effective, the provider is notified. Low-dose tissue plasminogen activator (alteplase) may be prescribed to dissolve a clot or fibrin sheath. If attempts to clear the lumen are ineffective, the lumen is labeled as "clotted off" and not used again.

Peripherally Inserted Central Catheters

Peripherally inserted central catheters (PICCs) are used for intermediate-term (several days to months) IV therapy in the hospital, long-term care, or home setting. These catheters may be inserted by a specially trained nurse at the bedside or in the outpatient setting. They can also be inserted using fluoroscopy by an interventional radiologist. PICC lines are placed in the arm, specifically the basilic or cephalic vein, via the antecubital space. The catheter is then threaded to a designated location, depending on the type of solution to be infused (superior vena cava for TPN, which allows dilution of this hypertonic solution). Blood drawing and blood pressure measurement are avoided in the accessed arm.

Tunneled Central Catheters

Tunneled central catheters are for long-term use and may remain in place for many years. These catheters are cuffed and can have single or double lumens; examples are the Hickman, Groshong, and PermCath. These catheters are inserted surgically. They are threaded under the skin (reducing the risk of ascending infection) to the subclavian vein,

and the distal end of the catheter is advanced into the superior vena cava.

Implanted Ports

Implanted ports are also used for long-term home IV therapy; examples include the Port-A-Cath, Mediport, Hickman Port, and P.A.S. Port. Instead of exiting from the skin, as do the Hickman and Groshong catheters, the end of the catheter is attached to a small chamber that is placed in a subcutaneous pocket, either on the anterior chest wall or on the forearm. The subcutaneous port requires minimal care and allows the patient complete freedom of activity. Implanted ports are more expensive than the external catheters, and access requires passing a special noncoring needle (Huber-tipped) through the skin into the chamber to initiate IV therapy.

Discontinuing Parenteral Nutrition

The PN solution is discontinued gradually to allow the patient to adjust to decreased levels of glucose. A patient's blood sugar must be very closely followed when weaning a patient off of PN, while on a continuous insulin infusion, or when concurrently increasing enteral feedings. If the PN solution is abruptly terminated, a 5% or 10% dextrose solution is administered for a period of hours to protect against rebound hypoglycemia. Specifically, a 5% solution is administered for PPN, while a 10% solution is administered for TPN at the same rate, owing to the approximate glucose concentration in the two solutions. Providing oral carbohydrates can shorten the tapering time. Specific symptoms of rebound hypoglycemia include weakness, faintness, diaphoresis, shakiness, feeling cold, confusion, and increased heart rate. Once all IV therapy is completed, the nontunneled central venous catheter or PICC can be removed and an occlusive dressing is applied to the exit site. Once a decision is made to discontinue the line, physicians or nurses who have been deemed competent in the removal procedure and are aware of the potential complications may remove central and PICC lines. Tunneled catheters and implanted ports are removed only by the physician.

Chapter Review

Critical Thinking Questions

1. You are the night shift nurse in the intensive care unit and have been assigned a new postoperative patient who has undergone a radical neck dissection. Which form of nutritional support would you most likely see being used, and why? What nursing measures would be used to facilitate breathing and promote comfort? Describe the potential complications of radical neck dissection and the assessment parameters that are used to detect the earliest signs and symptoms of these complications.

2. An elderly woman is brought to the emergency department by the rescue squad. Her daughter found her on the kitchen floor. A bottle of cleaning fluid with a poison label was open next to the kitchen sink. On admission, the patient was in respiratory distress. Burns were observed around her mouth. What emergency care would be provided for this patient to prevent further trauma to the GI and respiratory tracts? Identify the evidence that supports this care, and evaluate the strength of the evidence.

3. You prepare to administer feedings through a patient's newly placed naso-jejunal feeding tube. What methods

would you consider to confirm the location of the tube before you initiate feedings? What patients would require postpyloric feedings rather than gastric and why? Before administering medications through the tube, how would you prepare them, and which types of medications would you pay particular attention to?

NCLEX-Style Review Questions

1. A confused patient prematurely removes her NG tube. The nurse knows to observe for which of the following complications?
   A. Constipation
   B. Flatulence
   C. Abdominal distention
   D. Gastric bleeding

2. The nurse is administering liquids to a patient who has recently been changed from NPO to a clear liquid diet. The patient coughs and occasionally gags with sips of water. Which health care team member would the nurse consult?
   A. Physical therapist
   B. Respiratory therapist
   C. Dietician
   D. Speech pathologist

3. A nurse is caring for a patient who is on strict bowel rest and will need IV nutrition. The nurse knows the following devices are appropriate for TPN. Select all that apply.
   A. PICC line
   B. Triple-lumen catheter
   C. Large-bore IV line
   D. Implantable venous assess device (Port-A-Cath)

4. A nurse receives report on a patient experiencing dumping syndrome. The nurse knows that the patient would be displaying which of the following symptoms 30 minutes after eating?
   A. Difficulty swallowing
   B. Heartburn
   C. Nausea
   D. Cramping in the abdomen

5. The nurse recognizes which of the following as a cause of xerostomia? Select all that apply.
   A. HIV infection
   B. Oral hypoglycemic medications
   C. Tracheostomy tube
   D. Inability to close the mouth

Try these additional resources to enhance your learning and understanding of this chapter:
- thePoint online resource available at **http://thepoint.lww.com/Pellico1e**
- *Handbook for Focus on Adult Health: Medical-Surgical Nursing*
- *Study Guide for Focus on Adult Health: Medical-Surgical Nursing*

References and Selected Readings

References and selected readings associated with this chapter can be found on the website that accompanies the book. Visit http://thepoint.lww.com/Pellico1e to access the references and other additional resources associated with this chapter.

Nursing Management: Patients With Gastric and Duodenal Disorders

JANCEE PUST-MARCONE

Learning Objectives

After reading this chapter, you will be able to:

1. Compare the etiology, clinical manifestations, and management of acute gastritis, chronic gastritis, and peptic ulcer.

2. Describe the management of the patient with gastritis.

3. Describe the dietary, pharmacologic, and surgical treatment of peptic ulcer.

4. Describe the nursing management of patients who undergo surgical procedures to treat obesity.

5. Use the nursing process as a framework for care of patients undergoing gastric surgery.

6. Identify the complications of gastric surgery and their prevention and management.

A person's nutritional status depends not only on the type and amount of intake but also on the functioning of the gastric and intestinal portions of the gastrointestinal (GI) system. This chapter describes disorders of the stomach and duodenum, their treatment, and related nursing care.

GASTRITIS

Gastritis (inflammation of the **gastric** or stomach mucosa) is a common GI problem. Gastritis may be acute, lasting several hours to a few days, or chronic, resulting from repeated exposure to irritating agents or recurring episodes of acute gastritis.

Acute gastritis is often caused by dietary indiscretion—the person eats food that is irritating, too highly seasoned, or contaminated with disease-causing microorganisms. Other causes of acute gastritis include overuse of aspirin and other nonsteroidal anti-inflammatory drugs (NSAIDs), excessive alcohol intake, bile reflux, and radiation therapy. A more severe form of acute gastritis is caused by the ingestion of strong acid or alkali, which may cause the mucosa to become gangrenous or to perforate. Scarring can occur, resulting in **pyloric stenosis** or obstruction. Acute gastritis also may develop in acute illnesses, especially when the patient has had major traumatic injuries; burns; severe infection; hepatic, renal, or respiratory failure; or major surgery. Gastritis may be the first sign of an acute systemic infection.

Chronic gastritis and prolonged inflammation of the stomach may be caused either by benign or malignant ulcers of the stomach or by the bacteria *Helicobacter pylori* (*H. pylori*). Chronic gastritis is sometimes associated with autoimmune diseases such as pernicious anemia; dietary factors such as caffeine; the use of medications such as NSAIDs, bisphosphonate (e.g., alendronate [Fosamax], risedronate [Actonel]) or ibandronate [Boniva]; alcohol; smoking; or chronic reflux of pancreatic secretions and bile into the stomach.

Pathophysiology

In gastritis, the gastric mucous membrane becomes edematous and hyperemic (congested with fluid and blood) and undergoes superficial erosion (Fig. 23-1). It secretes a scanty amount of gastric juice, containing very

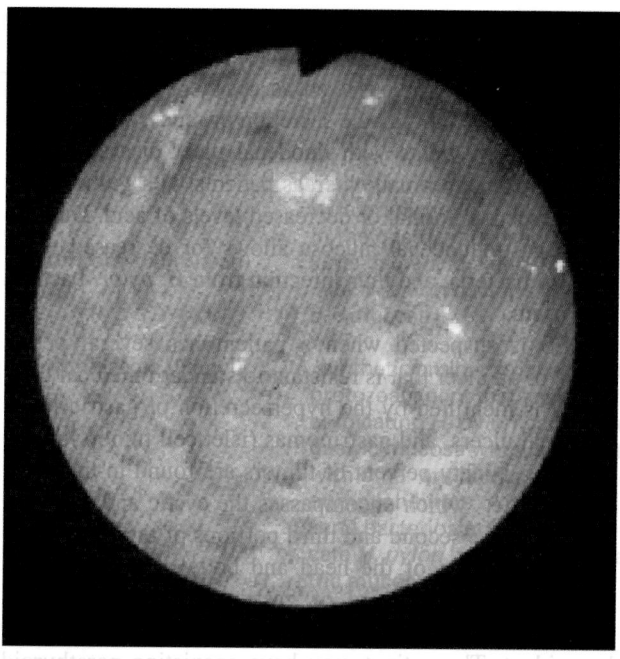

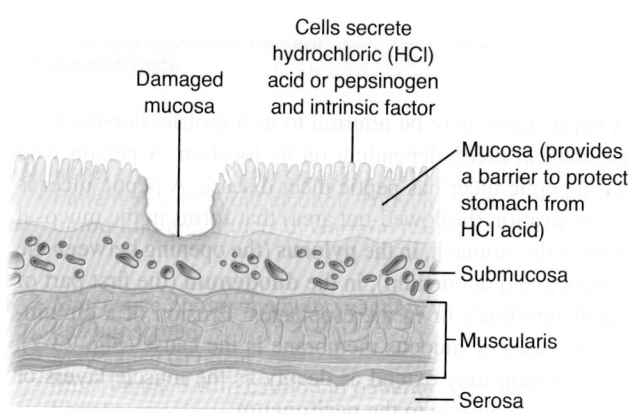

Damaged mucosa

Cells secrete hydrochloric (HCl) acid or pepsinogen and intrinsic factor

Mucosa (provides a barrier to protect stomach from HCl acid)

Submucosa

Muscularis

Serosa

FIGURE 23-1 Endoscopic view of erosive gastritis (*left*). Damage from irritants (*right*) results in increased intracellular pH, impaired enzyme function, disrupted cellular structures, ischemia, vascular stasis, and tissue death. Reproduced with permission from Porth, C.M., & Matfin, G. (2009). *Pathophysiology: Concepts of altered health states* (8th ed.). Philadelphia: Lippincott Williams & Wilkins.

little acid but much mucus. Superficial ulceration may occur and can lead to hemorrhage.

Clinical Manifestations and Assessment

The patient with acute gastritis may have a rapid onset of symptoms, such as abdominal discomfort, headache, lassitude, and nausea, anorexia, vomiting, and hiccupping, which can last from a few hours to a few days. The patient with chronic gastritis may complain of anorexia, heartburn after eating, belching, a sour taste in the mouth, or nausea and vomiting. Some patients may have only mild epigastric discomfort or report intolerance to spicy or fatty foods or slight pain that is relieved by eating. Patients with chronic gastritis from vitamin deficiency usually have evidence of malabsorption of vitamin B_{12} caused by the production of antibodies that interfere with the binding of vitamin B_{12} to intrinsic factor. However, some patients with chronic gastritis have no symptoms.

Gastritis is sometimes associated with **achlorhydria** or hypochlorhydria (absence or low levels of hydrochloric acid [HCl]) or with hyperchlorhydria (high levels of HCl). Diagnosis can be determined by an upper GI X-ray series or endoscopy and histologic examination of a tissue specimen obtained by biopsy. Diagnostic measures for detecting *H. pylori* infection may be used and are discussed in the section on peptic ulcers.

Medical and Nursing Management

The gastric mucosa is capable of repairing itself after a bout of gastritis. As a rule, the patient recovers in about 1 day, although the appetite may be diminished for an additional 2 or 3 days. Acute gastritis is also managed by instructing the patient to refrain from alcohol and food until symptoms subside. When the patient can take nourishment by mouth, a nonirritating diet is recommended. If the symptoms persist, IV fluids may need to be administered. If bleeding is present, management is similar to the procedures used to control upper GI tract hemorrhage, discussed later in this chapter.

If gastritis is caused by ingestion of strong acids or alkalis, emergency treatment consists of diluting and neutralizing the offending agent. To neutralize acids, common antacids (e.g., aluminum hydroxide) are used; to neutralize an alkali, diluted lemon juice or diluted vinegar is used. If corrosion is extensive or severe, emetics and lavage are avoided because of the danger of perforation and damage to the esophagus.

Therapy is supportive and may include nasogastric (NG) intubation (see Chapter 22), analgesic agents and sedatives, antacids, and IV fluids. Fiberoptic endoscopy may be necessary. In extreme cases, emergency surgery may be required to remove gangrenous or perforated tissue. A gastric resection or a gastrojejunostomy (anastomosis of jejunum to stomach to detour around the pylorus) may be necessary to treat pyloric obstruction, a narrowing of the pyloric orifice that cannot be relieved by medical management.

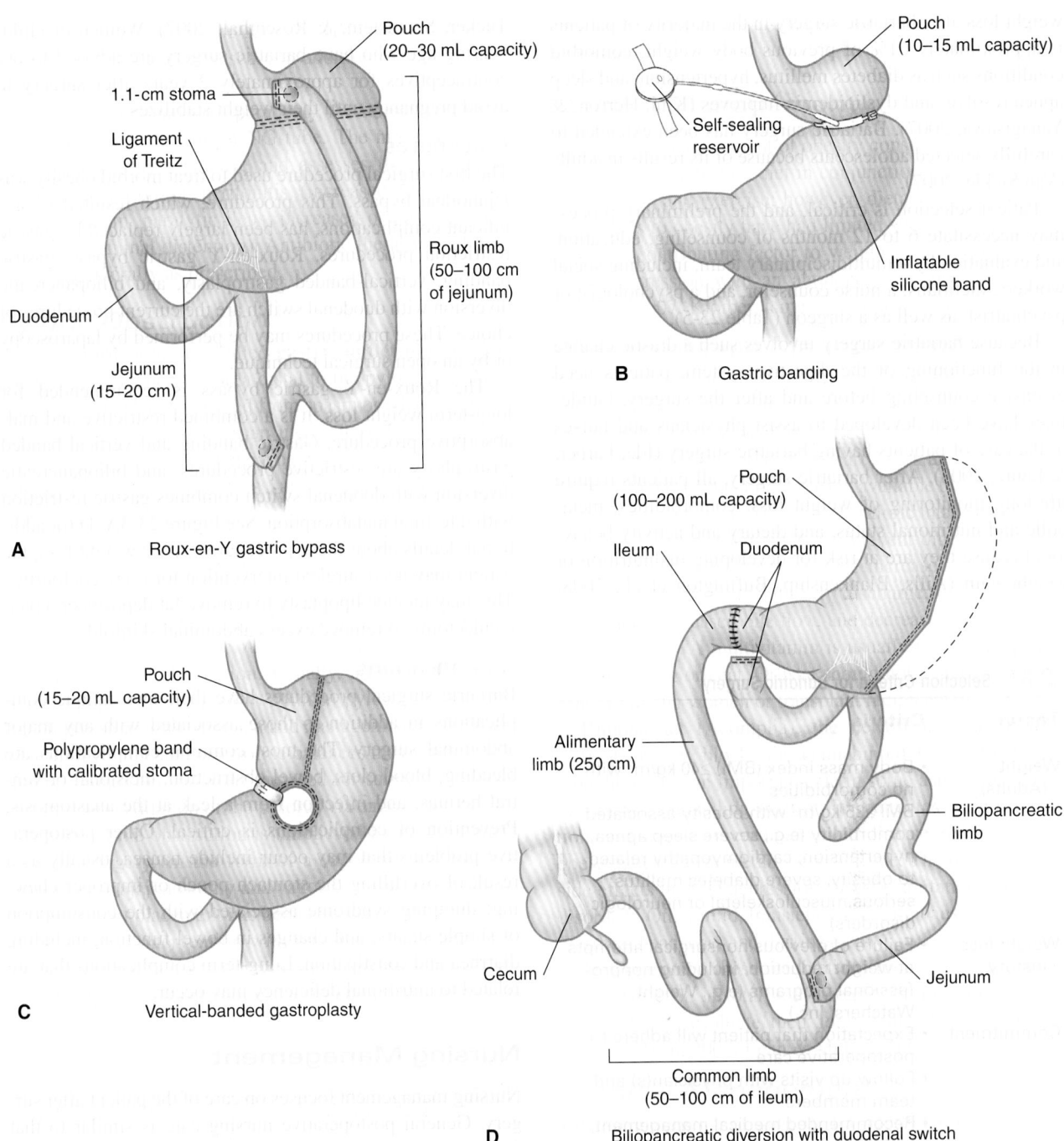

A Roux-en-Y gastric bypass

- Pouch (20–30 mL capacity)
- 1.1-cm stoma
- Ligament of Treitz
- Duodenum
- Jejunum (15–20 cm)
- Roux limb (50–100 cm of jejunum)

B Gastric banding

- Pouch (10–15 mL capacity)
- Self-sealing reservoir
- Inflatable silicone band

C Vertical-banded gastroplasty

- Pouch (15–20 mL capacity)
- Polypropylene band with calibrated stoma

D Biliopancreatic diversion with duodenal switch

- Pouch (100–200 mL capacity)
- Ileum
- Duodenum
- Alimentary limb (250 cm)
- Biliopancreatic limb
- Jejunum
- Cecum
- Common limb (50–100 cm of ileum)

FIGURE 23-3 Surgical procedures for morbid obesity. (**A**) Roux-en-Y gastric bypass. A horizontal row of staples across the fundus of the stomach creates a pouch with a capacity of 20 to 30 mL. The jejunum is divided distal to the ligament of Treitz, and the distal end is anastomosed to the new pouch. The proximal segment is anastomosed to the jejunum. (**B**) Gastric banding. A prosthetic device is used to restrict oral intake by creating a small pouch of 10 to 15 mL that empties through the narrow outlet into the remainder of the stomach. (**C**) Vertical-banded gastroplasty. A vertical row of staples along the lesser curvature of the stomach creates a new, smaller stomach pouch of 10 to 15 mL. (**D**) Biliopancreatic diversion with duodenal switch. Half of the stomach is removed, leaving a small area that holds about 60 mL. The entire jejunum is excluded from the rest of the gastrointestinal tract. The duodenum is disconnected and sealed off. The ileum is divided above the ileocecal junction, and the distal end of the jejunum is anastomosed to the first portion of the duodenum. The distal end of the biliopancreatic limb is anastomosed to the ileum.

Patient Education

Dietary Guidelines for the Patient Who Has Had Bariatric Surgery

- Eat three meals per day (containing protein and fiber).
- Include two protein snacks per day.
- Restrict total meal size to less than 1 cup.
- Eat slowly.
- Chew thoroughly.
- Eat only foods packed with nutrients (e.g., peanut butter, cheese, chicken, fish, beans).
- Do not eat and drink at the same time.
- Drink plenty of water, from 90 minutes after each meal to 15 minutes before the next meal.
- Avoid liquid calories, such as alcoholic beverages, fruit drinks, and regular soda (cola).
- Walk for at least 30 minutes per day.

From Tucker, O., Szomstein, S., & Rosenthal, R. (2007). Nutritional consequences of weight-loss surgery. *Medical Clinics of North America, 91*(3), 499–514; Allis, L., Blankenship, J., Buffington, C., et al. (2008). ASMBS Allied Health Nutritional Guidelines for the Surgical Weight Loss Patient. *Surgery For Obesity and Related Diseases, 4*, S73–S108.

detailed dietary instructions (Box 23-2). The nurse instructs the patient to report excessive thirst or concentrated urine, both of which are indications of dehydration. Psychosocial interventions are also essential for these patients. Efforts are directed at helping them modify their eating behaviors and cope with changes in body image. The nurse explains that noncompliance by eating too much or too fast, or eating high-calorie liquids and soft foods results in vomiting and painful esophageal distention. The nurse discusses dietary instructions before discharge and emphasizes the importance of routine follow-up outpatient appointments. Long-term side effects may include increased risk of gallstones, nutritional deficiencies (Table 23-6), and potential to regain weight. Nutritional deficits tend to stabilize by 2 years postprocedure (Dalcanale, Oliveira, Faintuch et al., 2010).

GASTRIC CANCER

The incidence of gastric or stomach cancer continues to decrease in the United States; however, it still accounts for almost 11,000 deaths annually (American Cancer Society, 2009). The prognosis is generally poor: the diagnosis is usually made late because most patients are asymptomatic during the early stages of the disease. Most cases of gastric cancer are discovered only after local invasion has advanced or metastases are present (Correia, Machado, & Ristimaki, 2009).

Pathophysiology

Most gastric cancers are adenocarcinomas; they can occur anywhere in the stomach. The tumor infiltrates the surrounding mucosa, penetrating the wall of the stomach and adjacent organs and structures. The liver, pancreas, esophagus, and duodenum are often affected at the time of diagnosis. Metastasis through lymph to the peritoneal cavity occurs later in the disease.

Risk Factors

The typical patient with gastric cancer is between 40 and 70 years of age, but gastric cancer can occur in people younger than 40 years of age. Men have a higher incidence of gastric cancer than women. Native Americans, Hispanic Americans, and African Americans are twice as likely as Caucasian Americans to develop gastric cancer. The incidence of gastric cancer is much greater in Japan, which has instituted mass screening programs for earlier diagnosis. Diet appears to be a significant factor: a diet high in smoked, salted, or pickled foods and low in fruits and vegetables may increase

TABLE
23-6 Nutritional Deficiencies After Bariatric Surgery

Deficiency	Signs and Symptoms
Decreased magnesium	Muscle cramps, muscle pain, constipation, headaches, insomnia, anxiety, hyperactivity
Decreased zinc	Delayed wound healing, altered immune function, mental lethargy, perhaps association with alopecia
Decreased hemoglobin	Anemia
Decreased iron	Fatigue, anemia, lethargy, pallor, and loss of hair
Decreased ferritin	Anemia
Decreased vitamin B_{12}	Macrocytic anemia, pernicious anemia, leukopenia, thrombocytopenia, paresthesia, neuropathy, muscular pains, weakness, fatigue, dizziness, and brittle nails.
Decreased vitamin D_3	Late symptoms may include osteopenia, muscle pain, bone fractures
Decreased β-carotene	Reducing the fat-soluble antioxidant capacity, neuropathy
Decreased calcium	Osteopenia, bone fractures

From Dalcanale, L., Oliveira, C. P. M. S., Faintuch, J., Nogueira, M. A., Rondó, P., Lima, V. M. R., et al. (2010), Long-term nutritional outcome after gastric bypass. *Obesity Surgery, 20*(2), 181–187.

the risk of gastric cancer. Other factors related to the incidence of gastric cancer include chronic inflammation of the stomach, *H. pylori* infection, pernicious anemia, smoking, achlorhydria, gastric ulcers, previous subtotal gastrectomy (>20 years ago), and genetics.

Clinical Manifestations and Assessment

Symptoms of early disease, such as pain relieved by antacids, resemble those of benign ulcers and are seldom definitive, because most gastric tumors begin on the lesser curvature of the stomach, where they cause little disturbance of gastric function. Symptoms of progressive disease include dyspepsia (indigestion), early satiety, weight loss, abdominal pain just above the umbilicus, loss or decrease in appetite, bloating after meals, nausea and vomiting, and symptoms similar to those of peptic ulcer disease.

The physical examination is usually not helpful in detecting the cancer because most early gastric tumors are not palpable. Advanced gastric cancer may be palpable as a mass. Ascites and hepatomegaly (enlarged liver) may be apparent if the cancer cells have metastasized to the liver. Palpable nodules around the umbilicus, called Sister Mary Joseph's nodules, are a sign of a GI malignancy, usually a gastric cancer. Esophagogastroduodenoscopy for biopsy and cytologic washings is the diagnostic study of choice, and a barium X-ray examination of the upper GI tract may also be performed. Endoscopic ultrasound is an important tool to assess tumor depth and any lymph node involvement. Computed tomography (CT) completes the diagnostic studies, particularly to assess for surgical resectability of the tumor before surgery is scheduled. CT of the chest, abdomen, and pelvis is valuable in staging gastric cancer.

Medical and Nursing Management

There is no successful treatment for gastric carcinoma except removal of the tumor. If the tumor can be removed while it is still localized to the stomach, the patient may be cured. If the tumor has spread beyond the area that can be excised, cure is less likely. In many patients, effective palliation to prevent discomfort caused by obstruction or dysphagia may be obtained by resection of the tumor (see Gastric Surgery). A diagnostic laparoscopy may be the initial surgical approach to evaluate the gastric tumor, obtain tissue for pathologic diagnosis, and detect metastasis. The patient with a tumor that is deemed resectable undergoes an open surgical procedure to resect the tumor and appropriate lymph nodes. The patient with an unresectable tumor and advanced disease would undergo chemotherapy.

A total gastrectomy may be performed for a resectable cancer in the midportion or body of the stomach. The entire stomach is removed, along with duodenum, the section of esophagus attached to the stomach, supporting mesentery, and lymph nodes. Reconstruction of the GI tract is performed by anastomosing the end of the jejunum to the end of the esophagus, a procedure called an *esophagojejunostomy*.

A radical subtotal gastrectomy is performed for a resectable tumor in the middle and distal portions of the stomach. A Billroth I or Billroth II operation (see Table 23-4) is performed. The Billroth I involves a limited resection and offers a lower cure rate than the Billroth II. The Billroth II procedure is a wider resection that involves removing approximately 75% of the stomach and decreases the possibility of lymph node spread or metastatic recurrence.

A proximal subtotal gastrectomy may be performed for a resectable tumor located in the proximal portion of the stomach or cardia. A total gastrectomy or an esophagogastrectomy is usually performed in place of this procedure to achieve a more extensive resection. A palliative surgical procedure may be required for patients with gastric cancer to achieve a better quality of life (QOL).

Common problems of advanced gastric cancer that often require surgery include pyloric obstruction, bleeding, and severe pain. Gastric perforation is an emergency situation requiring surgical intervention. A gastric resection may be the most effective palliative procedure for advanced gastric cancer. Palliative procedures such as gastric or esophageal bypass, gastrostomy, or jejunostomy may temporarily alleviate symptoms such as nausea and vomiting. Palliative rather than radical surgery may be performed if there is metastasis to other vital organs, such as the liver, or to achieve a better QOL.

If surgical treatment does not offer cure, treatment with chemotherapy may offer further control of the disease or palliation. Commonly used single-agent chemotherapeutic medications include 5-fluorouracil (5-FU), cisplatin (Platinol), doxorubicin (Adriamycin), etoposide (Etopophos), and mitomycin-C (Mutamycin). For improved response rates, it is more common to administer combination therapy, primarily 5-FU–based therapy, with other agents. Studies are being conducted to assess the use of chemotherapy before surgery. Radiation therapy is mainly used for palliation in patients with obstruction, GI bleeding secondary to tumor, and significant pain. Assessment of tumor markers (blood analysis for antigens indicative of cancer), such as carcinoembryonic antigen (CEA), carbohydrate antigen (CA 19–9), and CA 50, may help determine the effectiveness of treatment. If these values were elevated before treatment, they should decrease if the tumor is responding to the treatment (Gao, Zhang, Du et al., 2007). Box 23-3 discusses the relationship between home health care and QOL for patients with cancer.

GASTRIC SURGERY

Gastric surgery may be performed on patients with peptic ulcers who have life-threatening hemorrhage, obstruction, perforation, or penetration, or whose condition does not

BOX 23-3 | Nursing Research

Bridging the Gap to Evidence-Based Practice

What Are the Effects of Home Health Care on QOl in Patients Diagnosed With Gastrointestinal Cancer?

Nural, N., Hintistan, S., Gürsoy, A.A., & Duman, E.N. (2009). *Gastroenterology Nursing, 32(4)*, 273–283.

Purpose

Cancer is a malignant disease characterized by a metastatic phase. Depending on treatment, it is either eradicated or forced into remission. Patients undergoing cancer treatment experience physical, psychosocial, psychological, and economic stressors that may in turn affect their quality of life (QOL) and lifespan. Cancer's impact on physical QOL may result in complaints of fatigue, nausea, pain, and diarrhea. Psychologically, cancer patients experience anxiety, depression and hopelessness, social isolation, and loneliness. Economically, the patient may encounter economic issues if he or she is unable to work. As cancer treatment improves and lifespan increases, improvement in a patient's QOL and health becomes a focused outcome.

QOL has different meaning for different individuals, reflecting personal values and characteristics. QOL may be seen as the sum of a whole life or episodic, a measure of their current state of health and function. Scales to measure QOL reflect this individual diversity, incorporating the physical, psychological, and social dimensions in addition to symptoms of illness and treatment modalities. Many studies have documented the importance of QOL in patients with cancer.

Home health care is the provision of medical, nursing, emotional, and social care in the patient's home. Home care services enable the patient and family to participate in the health care plan, shorten the hospitalization period, decrease costs, and provide for continuity of care. Many more treatments and care for oncology patients are provided in the ambulatory/outpatient setting. Patients may only require hospitalization for complications of their disease or treatment. Nurses play a vital role in improving the QOL for the patient with cancer in the home health care setting. Interventions include prevention and early detection of complications, symptom management, and patient education about the disease and living with it.

Design

This study was undertaken to evaluate the effect of home health care on QOL in patients diagnosed with gastrointestinal (GI) cancer. The study used a cross-sectional, quasi-experimental design. Patients had to have a life expectancy of more than 1 year. Eligible patients attending a pain control clinic over a 6-month period were invited to participate. The final sample size consisted of 42 subjects: 21 assigned to the control group (usual care) and 21 assigned to the experimental group (enhanced home health care visits). Patients were randomly assigned to groups.

Data collected included demographic information, pain assessment, cancer disease progression, symptoms experienced by the patient, and QOL. Pain was measured via a visual analog scale, 0 to 10, with patients being asked to rate their pain on a line measured in centimeters, with the value registered as the pain severity. Cancer disease progression was measured using the Eastern Cooperative Oncology Group (ECOG) Performance Status, a 6-point scale evaluating the effect of the disease in daily life. The Rotterdam Symptom Checklist was used to measure symptoms in two subscales, psychological and physical distress. QOL was measured with the Rolls-Royce Quality of Life Scale, a 42-item scale divided into eight categories. A guideline for homecare of the GI cancer patient was developed by the researchers to establish a standard for problems most frequently occurring in GI cancer; dyspnea, fatigue, pain, lack of appetite, nausea, vomiting, mouth sores, constipation, diarrhea, bleeding, infection, skin sores, inability to perform self-care, sleep pattern disorders, alterations in body image, change in sexual functioning, and mood instability. The guideline included evidence-based nursing interventions for these problems that are practical to implement in a homecare setting.

Patients of the pain clinic who met the study criteria and agreed to participate provided written informed consent. The experimental group received three homecare visits, and the control group received two visits. All patients received their first visit 1 day after being seen at the pain control clinic. The experimental group received visits at 20 and 40 days, the control group received a second, final visit at the 40-day mark.

Results

The sample consisted of 42 patients with GI cancer divided between two groups. The study had 24 women, 13 assigned to the experimental group and 11 to the control group. There were 18 men in the study, 8 in the experimental group, and 10 in the control group. The subjects had a variety of GI cancers, and all but two had a surgical intervention. Symptoms experienced by the patients, as measured by the Rotterdam Symptom checklist, recorded physiological and psychological symptoms and total stress for the experimental group, and these decreased by the final homecare visit when compared to the first visit; however, there was an increase in these measures for the control group. The pain levels of the experimental group also decreased compared to the control group as the visits progressed. The measures of performance status and QOL indicators increased for the experimental group from baseline to final visit. It appears that the care given at home contributed positively to decrease physical symptoms and increase the activities of the patient.

(continued on page 648)

BOX 23-3 **Nursing Research** (continued)

Nursing Implications

Cancer and cancer treatment affect the QOL of patients, and it is the responsibility of the health care team to evaluate the effects of the illness on each individual patient. The results of this study provide more knowledge into the relationship between symptom management, home health care, and QOL in patients with GI cancer. It was able to show a positive relationship among pain management, activity performance, symptom management, and QOL measures when the patient with gastroenterological cancer participates in a

homecare program with nurses providing evidenced-based interventions.

The role of professional homecare is important for not only physiologic care but also for psychological and emotional support. Emotional support has been found to be of utmost importance to improve the QOL in these patients. The role of the nurse and other members of the health care team in palliative care at home is to provide appropriate interventions and symptom management in patients with life-limiting illness, with the goal to improve QOL.

---

respond to medication. It also may be indicated for patients with gastric cancer or trauma. Surgical procedures include a vagotomy and **pyloroplasty** (transecting nerves that stimulate acid secretion and opening the pylorus), a partial gastrectomy, or a total gastrectomy (see Table 23-4).

NURSING PROCESS

The Patient Undergoing Gastric Surgery

Assessment

Before surgery, the nurse assesses the patient's and family's knowledge of pre- and postoperative surgical routines and the rationale for surgery. The nurse also assesses the patient's nutritional status: Has the patient lost weight? How much? Over how much time? The nurse is aware that a 5% weight loss in 30 days, a 7.5% weight loss in 90 days, or a greater than 10% weight loss in 180 days is associated with significant health risks (DeLegge & Drake, 2008). Does the patient have nausea and vomiting? Has the patient had hematemesis? The nurse assesses for the presence of bowel sounds and palpates the abdomen to detect masses or tenderness.

After surgery, the nurse assesses the patient for complications secondary to the surgical intervention, such as hemorrhage, infection, abdominal distention, atelectasis, or impaired nutritional status.

Diagnosis

Nursing diagnoses may include the following:

- Anxiety related to surgical intervention
- Acute pain related to surgical incision
- Deficient knowledge about surgical procedure and postoperative course
- Imbalanced nutrition, less than body requirements, related to poor nutrition before surgery and altered GI system after surgery

Planning

The major goals for the patient undergoing gastric surgery may include reduced anxiety, increased knowledge and understanding about the surgical procedure and postoperative course, optimal nutrition and management of the complications that can interfere with nutrition, relief of pain, avoidance of hemorrhage and steatorrhea, and enhanced self-care skills at home.

Nursing Interventions

Reducing Anxiety

An important part of the preoperative nursing care involves allaying the patient's fears and anxieties about the impending surgery and its implications. The nurse encourages the patient to verbalize fears and concerns, and answers the patient's and family's questions. If the patient has an acute obstruction, a perforated bowel, or an active GI hemorrhage, adequate psychological preparation may not be possible. In this event, the nurse caring for the patient after surgery should anticipate the concerns, fears, and questions that are likely to surface, and should be available for support and further explanations.

Relieving Pain

After surgery, analgesics may be administered as prescribed to relieve pain and discomfort. It is important to provide adequate pain relief so the patient can perform pulmonary care activities (deep breathing and coughing) and leg exercises, turn from side to side, and ambulate. The nurse assesses the effectiveness of analgesic intervention and consults with other members of the health care team if pain is not adequately controlled. Positioning the patient in the Fowler's position promotes comfort and allows emptying of the stomach after gastric surgery.

The nurse maintains functioning of the NG tube to prevent distention and secures the tube to prevent dislocation, which may result in increased pain and tension on the suture line. Normally, the amount of NG drainage after a total

gastrectomy is minimal, as there is no reservoir where secretions can collect.

Providing Teaching

The nurse explains routine pre- and postoperative procedures to the patient, which include preoperative medications, NG intubation, IV fluids, abdominal dressings, and the possible need for a feeding tube, pain management, and pulmonary care. These explanations need to be reinforced after surgery, especially if the patient had emergency surgery.

Resuming Enteral Intake

The patient's nutritional status is evaluated before surgery. If surgery is performed for gastric cancer, the patient is often malnourished and may require preoperative enteral or, more often, parenteral nutrition. After surgery, parenteral nutrition may be continued to meet caloric needs, to replace fluids lost through drainage and vomiting, and to support the patient metabolically until oral intake is adequate.

After the return of bowel sounds and removal of the NG tube, the nurse may give fluids, followed by food in small portions. Foods are gradually added until the patient is able to eat six small meals a day and drink 120 mL of fluid between meals. The key to increasing the dietary content is to offer food and fluids gradually, as tolerated, and to recognize that each patient's tolerance is different.

Recognizing Obstacles to Adequate Nutrition

DYSPHAGIA AND GASTRIC RETENTION. Dysphagia may occur in patients who have had a truncal vagotomy, a surgical procedure that may result in trauma to the lower esophagus. Gastric retention may be evidenced by abdominal distention, nausea, and vomiting. Regurgitation may also occur if the patient has eaten too much or too quickly. It also may indicate that edema along the suture line is preventing fluids and food from moving into the intestinal tract. If gastric retention occurs, it may be necessary to reinstate NPO status and NG suction; pressure must be low in the remaining portion of the stomach to avoid disrupting the sutures.

BILE REFLUX. Bile reflux gastritis and esophagitis may occur with the removal of the pylorus, which acts as a barrier to the reflux of duodenal contents. Burning epigastric pain and vomiting of bilious material manifest this condition. Eating or vomiting does not relieve the situation. Agents that bind with bile acid, such as cholestyramine (Questran), may be helpful. Aluminum hydroxide gel (an antacid) and metoclopramide hydrochloride (Reglan) have been used with limited success.

DUMPING SYNDROME. **Dumping syndrome** is an unpleasant set of vasomotor and GI symptoms that sometimes occur in patients who have had gastric surgery or a form of vagotomy. It may be the mechanical result of surgery in which a small gastric remnant is connected to the jejunum through a large opening. Foods high in carbohydrates and electrolytes must be diluted in the jejunum before absorption can take place, but the passage of food from the stomach remnant into the jejunum is too rapid to allow this to happen. The hypertonic intestinal contents draw extracellular fluid from the circulating blood volume into the jejunum to dilute the high concentration of electrolytes and sugars. The ingestion of fluid at mealtime is another factor that causes the stomach contents to empty rapidly into the jejunum (Pedrazzani, Marrelli, Rampone et al., 2007).

Early symptoms include a sensation of fullness, weakness, faintness, dizziness, palpitations, diaphoresis, cramping pains, and diarrhea. These symptoms resolve once the intestine has been evacuated. Later, there is a rapid elevation of blood glucose, followed by increased insulin secretion. This results in a reactive hypoglycemia, which also is unpleasant for the patient. Vasomotor symptoms that occur 10 to 90 minutes after eating are pallor, perspiration, palpitations, headache, and feelings of warmth, dizziness, and even drowsiness. Anorexia may also be a result of the dumping syndrome, as the person may be reluctant to eat.

Steatorrhea (excess fat in feces) also may occur in the patient with gastric surgery. It is partially the result of rapid gastric emptying, which prevents adequate mixing with pancreatic and biliary secretions. In mild cases, reducing the intake of fat and administering an antimotility medication (e.g., loperamide [Imodium]) may control steatorrhea.

VITAMIN AND MINERAL DEFICIENCIES. Other dietary deficiencies that the nurse should be aware of include malabsorption of organic iron, which may require supplementation with oral or parenteral iron, and a low serum level of vitamin B_{12}, which may require supplementation by the intramuscular route. Total gastrectomy results in lack of intrinsic factor, a gastric secretion required for the absorption of vitamin B_{12} from the GI tract. Unless this vitamin is supplied by parenteral injection after gastrectomy, the patient inevitably will suffer vitamin B_{12} deficiency, which eventually leads to a condition identical to pernicious anemia. All manifestations of pernicious anemia, including macrocytic anemia (few, fragile, and larger than normal red blood cells) and combined system disease (neurologic disorders of the central and peripheral nervous systems), may be expected to develop within a period of 5 years or less; they progress in severity thereafter and, in the absence of therapy, are fatal. This complication is avoided by the regular monthly intramuscular injection of vitamin B_{12}. This regimen should be started without delay after gastrectomy. Weight loss is a common long-term problem because the patient experiences early fullness, which suppresses the appetite.

Teaching Dietary Self-Management

Because the patient may experience any of the described conditions affecting nutrition, nursing intervention includes

(continued on page 650)

BOX 23-4 Patient Education

Dietary Management After Gastric Surgery

- To delay stomach emptying and dumping syndrome, assume a low Fowler's position (head of bed (HOB) elevated 30 degrees) during mealtime; after the meal, the patient should lie down for 20 to 30 minutes.
- Take antispasmodics as prescribed to aid in delaying the emptying of the stomach.
- Do not drink fluids with meals; instead, drink fluids up to 1 hour before or 1 hour after mealtime.
- Create meals containing more dry items than liquid items.
- Eat fat as tolerated, but keep carbohydrate intake low and avoid concentrated sources of carbohydrates (sugared soda, pastries).
- Eat smaller but more frequent meals.
- Take dietary supplements of vitamins and medium-chain triglycerides and injections of vitamin B_{12} and iron as prescribed.

proper dietary instruction (Box 23-4). The nurse also gives instructions regarding enteral or parenteral supplementation if it is needed.

Monitoring and Managing Potential Complications

Occasionally, hemorrhage complicates gastric surgery. The patient has the usual signs of rapid blood loss and shock (see Chapter 54) and may vomit considerable amounts of bright red blood. The nurse assesses NG drainage for type and amount; some bloody drainage for the first 12 hours is expected, but excessive bleeding should be reported. The nurse also assesses the abdominal dressing for bleeding. Because this situation is upsetting to the patient and family, the nurse should remain calm. The nurse performs emergency measures, such as NG lavage and administration of blood and blood products, along with vigilant hemodynamic monitoring.

Teaching Patients Self-Care

Patient teaching is based on the assessment of the patient's physical and psychological readiness to participate in self-care. The nurse provides information about nutrition, enteral or parenteral nutrition if required, nutritional supplements, pain management, and the symptoms of dumping syndrome and measures to prevent or minimize these symptoms.

The patient and caregivers benefit from a team approach to discharge planning. The team members include the patient and caregiver along with the nurse, physician, dietitian, and social worker. Written or video instructions about meals, activities, medications, and follow-up care are helpful. After the patient is discharged from the hospital, the home care nurse helps with the transition to home by

supervising the administration of any enteral or parenteral feedings, emphasizing information about detection and prevention of untoward effects or complications related to feedings. Information about community support groups and end-of-life care is provided to the patient, family, or significant other when indicated.

Evaluation

Expected patient outcomes may include:

1. Reports decreased anxiety; expresses fears and concerns about surgery
2. Demonstrates knowledge regarding postoperative course by discussing the surgical procedure and postoperative course
3. Attains optimal nutrition:
   a. Maintains a reasonable weight
   b. Does not have excessive diarrhea
   c. Tolerates six small meals a day
   d. Does not experience dysphagia, gastric retention, bile reflux, dumping syndrome, or vitamin and mineral deficiencies
4. Attains optimal level of comfort
5. Exhibits no complications

DUODENAL TUMORS

Tumors of the duodenum are uncommon and are usually benign and asymptomatic. They are most often discovered at autopsy. Malignant tumors are more likely to cause specific signs and symptoms leading to diagnosis. Unfortunately, malignant tumors are often not discovered until they have metastasized to distant sites. Benign tumors may place patients at an increased risk for malignancy. The relative rarity of tumors of the duodenum and the nonspecific nature of their manifestations complicate their diagnosis and treatment.

Clinical Manifestations and Assessment

Duodenal tumors often present insidiously with vague, nonspecific symptoms. Most benign tumors are discovered incidentally on an X-ray study, during surgery, or at autopsy. When the patient is symptomatic, benign tumors often present with intermittent pain. The next most common presentation is occult bleeding. Malignant tumors often result in symptoms that lead to their diagnosis, although these symptoms may reflect advanced disease. Most patients have sustained weight loss and are malnourished at diagnosis. Bleeding and pain are common. Perforation of the bowel occurs in approximately 10% of patients (Kostakou, Khaldi, Flossos et al., 2007; Ramakrishnan & Salinas, 2007).

An upper GI X-ray series with small bowel follow-through using oral water-insoluble contrast with frequent and detailed X-rays to follow the contrast through the small bowel is the

traditional approach to diagnosis. A more sensitive examination is an **enteroclysis**, in which a nasogastric tube is advanced into the small bowel to a position above the area in question; the area is then studied by single-contrast and double-contrast techniques. Abdominal CT is used to determine the extent of disease outside the lumen of the duodenum.

Medical and Nursing Management

Benign tumors of the duodenum include adenomas, lipomas, hemangiomas, and hamartomas (a focal malformation that resembles a neoplasm, but unlike a neoplasm does not result in compression of adjacent tissue). These tumors may be treated endoscopically by excision/resection or electrocautery if the patient is symptomatic. Routine surveillance may be recommended to assess for malignant transformation.

The most common primary malignant tumor of the duodenum is adenocarcinoma; the second and third portions of the duodenum are most often involved. These tumors may present with bleeding or duodenal obstruction (Chestovich, Schiller, Sasu et al., 2007). If the tumor is located at the ampulla of Vater, obstructive jaundice is likely. Other rare malignant tumors of the duodenum include carcinoid tumors, lymphoma, and GI stromal tumors. Specialized abdominal surgery may be required to remove these rare tumors. Chemotherapy and radiation therapy may also be part of the treatment regimen.

Nursing care of the patient with a duodenal tumor is similar to that of the patient with gastric cancer. Each patient requires specialized care, astute assessment for complications, prompt interventions, and individualized teaching for self-care.

Chapter Review

Critical Thinking Exercises

1. A 45-year-old woman with a history of rheumatoid arthritis and gastritis related to her medication is admitted with abdominal discomfort, headache, lassitude, and nausea and vomiting. What questions should you ask the patient? What signs should be noted during the physical examination? What diagnostic studies should you anticipate for this patient? Describe your nursing interventions, including teaching. How would you modify teaching for this patient if she does not understand English?

2. A 27-year-old morbidly obese woman has tried conservative medical management (weight loss diet, behavior modification, exercise, medications for obesity) of her weight condition. She is scheduled for a vertical-banded gastroplasty. Describe the dietary modifications, along with nutritional needs, for this patient during the immediate postoperative period, after discharge from the hospital, and for long-term maintenance. What is the evidence base that supports the use of specific dietary modifications to meet her nutritional needs after surgical procedures to treat obesity? Describe the strength of this evidence and identify the criteria used to evaluate the strength of the evidence that supports the appropriateness of the dietary modifications.

3. A 54-year-old business executive has been admitted with the diagnosis of peptic ulcer disease. As you enter his room, he is vomiting bright red blood. What are the nursing interventions for managing and monitoring this complication? If the bleeding cannot be controlled, what invasive measures may need to be performed? How would you prepare your patient for these? What other complications may occur with a peptic ulcer, and how should they be managed? What teaching interventions are warranted for this patient?

NCLEX-Style Review Questions

1. A 47-year-old man with epigastric pain is being admitted to the hospital. During the admission assessment and interview, what specific information should the nurse obtain from the patient, who is suspected of having peptic ulcer disease?
   A. Any allergies to food or medications
   B. Use of nonsteroidal anti-inflammatory drugs (NSAIDs)
   C. Past medical history of two generations
   D. History of side effects of all medications

2. What assessment finding supports the client's diagnosis of gastric ulcer?
   A. Presence of blood in the client's stool for the past month
   B. Complaints of sharp pain in the abdomen after eating a heavy meal
   C. Periods of pain shortly after eating any food.
   D. Complaints of epigastric burning that moves like a wave

3. Which medication should the nurse question before administering it to a patient with peptic ulcer disease?
   A. E-mycin, an antibiotic
   B. Prilosec, a PPI
   C. Flagyl, an antimicrobial agent
   D. Tylenol, a nonnarcotic analgesic

4. The nurse is planning for the discharge of a client with peptic ulcer disease. Which outcome must be included in the plan of care?
   A. The client's pain is controlled with NSAIDs.
   B. The client understands and maintains lifestyle modifications.
   C. The client takes antacids around the clock.
   D. The client has no episodes of GI bleeding.

Chapter Review (continued)

5. The client with a peptic ulcer is admitted to the hospital's intensive care unit with obvious gastric bleeding. What is the priority intervention for the nurse?

A. Keep an accurate record of intake and output.
B. Provide for quiet environment, restrict visitors.
C. Prepare the client for an endoscopy.
D. Insert a nasogastric tube and begin saline lavage.

Try these additional resources to enhance your learning and understanding of this chapter:
- thePoint online resource available at **http://thepoint.lww.com/Pellico1e**
- *Handbook for Focus on Adult Health: Medical-Surgical Nursing*
- *Study Guide for Focus on Adult Health: Medical-Surgical Nursing*

References and Selected Readings

References and selected readings associated with this chapter can be found on the website that accompanies the book. Visit http://thepoint.lww.com/Pellico1e to access the references and other additional resources associated with this chapter.

PHILIP R. MARTINEZ, JR.

Nursing Management: Patients With Intestinal and Rectal Disorders

Learning Objectives

After reading this chapter, you will be able to:

1. Describe the health care needs of patients with constipation, diarrhea, or fecal incontinence.

2. Compare the conditions of malabsorption with regard to their pathophysiology, clinical manifestations, and management.

3. Describe diverticular disease and the care of patients with diverticulitis.

4. Compare and contrast regional enteritis and ulcerative colitis regarding their pathophysiology, and medical, surgical, and nursing management.

5. Identify the care needs of the patient with inflammatory bowel disease.

6. Describe the responsibilities of the nurse in meeting the needs of the patient with an ileostomy.

7. Describe the various types of intestinal obstructions, as well as their medical and nursing management.

8. Describe the pathophysiology, assessment, and management in regards to cancer of the colon or rectum.

9. Describe anorectal conditions including fissures, fistulas, hemorrhoids, and sexually transmitted anorectal diseases.

At least 60 million people in the United States are diagnosed with some type of disease of the gastrointestinal (GI) tract (National Institutes of Health [NIH], 2009). These diseases account for more than 104.7 million office visits and approximately 13.5 million hospital admissions annually. GI diseases cost the American public more than $141 billion each year and account for approximately 9% of all deaths each year (Everhart, 2008). The types of diseases and disorders that affect the lower GI tract are many and varied.

In all age groups, a fast-paced lifestyle, high levels of stress, irregular eating habits, insufficient intake of fiber and water, and lack of daily exercise contribute to GI disorders. There is a growing understanding of the biopsychosocial implications of GI disease. Nurses can have an impact on these GI disorders by identifying behavior patterns that put patients at risk, by educating the public about prevention and management, and by helping those affected to improve their condition and prevent complications.

DISORDERS RELATED TO FECAL ELIMINATION

CONSTIPATION

Constipation is considered an abnormal infrequency or irregularity of defecation, an abnormal hardening of stools that makes their passage difficult and sometimes painful, a decrease in actual stool volume, or retention of stool in the rectum for a prolonged period. Any variation from normal habits may be considered a problem. Physician visits for constipation are more common in people 65 years and older (Rao & Go, 2010). The most common complaint is the need to strain in order to pass stool.

Perceived constipation can also be a problem. This subjective problem occurs when a person's bowel elimination pattern is not consistent with what he or she perceives as normal. Chronic laxative use may contribute to this problem and is a major health concern in the United States.

Pathophysiology

The pathophysiology of constipation is poorly understood, but it is thought to include interference with one of three major functions of the colon: mucosal transport (i.e., mucosal secretions facilitate the movement of

colon contents), myoelectric activity (i.e., mixing of the rectal mass and propulsive actions), or the processes of defecation.

The urge to defecate is stimulated normally by rectal distention, which initiates a series of four actions: stimulation of the inhibitory rectoanal reflex, relaxation of the internal sphincter muscle, relaxation of the external sphincter muscle and muscles in the pelvic region, and increased intra-abdominal pressure. Interference with any of these processes can lead to constipation.

If all organic causes are eliminated, idiopathic constipation is diagnosed. When the urge to defecate is ignored, the rectal mucous membrane and musculature become insensitive to the presence of fecal masses, and consequently a stronger stimulus is required to produce the necessary peristaltic rush for defecation. The initial effect of fecal retention is irritability of the colon, which at this stage frequently goes into spasm, especially after meals, giving rise to colicky midabdominal or low abdominal pains. After several years of this process, the colon loses muscular tone and becomes essentially unresponsive to normal stimuli. **Atony** or decreased muscle tone occurs with aging. This also leads to constipation because the stool is retained for longer periods.

Risk Factors

Constipation can be caused by certain medications (i.e., tranquilizers, anticholinergics, antidepressants, antihypertensives, bile acid sequestrants, opioids, aluminum-based antacids, iron preparations); rectal or anal disorders (e.g., hemorrhoids, fissures); obstruction (e.g., bowel tumors); metabolic, neurologic, and neuromuscular conditions (e.g., Hirschsprung's disease, Parkinson's disease, multiple sclerosis); endocrine disorders (e.g., diabetes mellitus, hypothyroidism, pheochromocytoma); lead poisoning; and connective tissue disorders (e.g., scleroderma, systemic lupus erythematosus).

Diseases of the colon, such as irritable bowel syndrome (IBS) and diverticular disease, are commonly associated with constipation. Constipation can also occur with any acute disease process in the abdomen (e.g., appendicitis or cholecystitis) or with any abdominal surgery.

Older adults tend to have decreased food intake, reduced mobility, weak abdominal and pelvic muscles, and multiple chronic illnesses requiring medications that can cause constipation. The astute nurse will always check a patient's medication list for those that may exacerbate constipation.

Low-fiber convenience foods are widely used by people who have lost interest in eating. Dentition is important to consider as people with ill-fitting dentures or poor dentition have increased difficulty chewing and frequently will choose softer, processed foods that are lower in fiber. Some older people reduce their fluid intake if they are not eating regular meals. Depression, weakness, or prolonged bedrest also contribute to constipation by decreasing intestinal motility and anal sphincter tone. Nerve impulses are dulled, and there is a decreased urge to defecate. Prolonged bedrest

is also a risk factor in constipation; therefore, nursing care for these patients should include ambulation when possible. Many older people overuse laxatives in an attempt to have a daily bowel movement and become dependent on them, which paradoxically can increase the risk of constipation.

Other causes of constipation may include weakness, immobility, debility, fatigue, and an inability to increase intra-abdominal pressure to facilitate the passage of stools, as may occur in patients with emphysema, for instance. Many people develop constipation because they do not take the time to defecate or they ignore the urge to defecate.

Clinical Manifestations and Assessment

Clinical manifestations of constipation include fewer than three bowel movements per week, abdominal distention, pain and pressure, decreased appetite, headache, fatigue, indigestion, a sensation of incomplete evacuation, straining at stool, and the elimination of small-volume, lumpy, hard, dry stools. Due to the wide range of normal bowel function in people, it is extremely difficult to accurately identify constipation in all patients.

The nurse elicits information about the onset and duration of constipation, current and past elimination patterns, the patient's expectation of normal bowel elimination, and lifestyle information (e.g., exercise and activity level, occupation, food and fluid intake, and stress level) during the health history interview. Past medical and surgical history, current medications, and laxative and enema use are important, as is information about the sensation of rectal pressure or fullness, abdominal pain, excessive straining at defecation, and flatulence.

Medical and Nursing Management

Treatment is aimed at the underlying cause of constipation and includes education, bowel habit training, increased fiber and fluid intake, and judicious use of laxatives. Management may also include discontinuing laxative abuse. Routine exercise to strengthen abdominal muscles is encouraged. Biofeedback is a technique that can be used to help patients learn to relax the sphincter mechanism to expel stool (Byrne, Solomon, Young et al., 2007).

Daily dietary intake of 6 to 12 teaspoonfuls of unprocessed bran is recommended, especially for the treatment of the elderly. If laxative use is necessary, one of the following may be prescribed: bulk-forming agents, saline and osmotic agents, lubricants, stimulants, or fecal softeners. The physiologic action and patient education information related to these laxatives are given in Table 24-1. Enemas and rectal suppositories are generally not recommended for treating constipation; they should be reserved for the treatment of impaction. If long-term laxative use is necessary, a bulk-forming agent may be prescribed in combination with an osmotic laxative.

TABLE
24-1 Laxatives: Classification, Agent, Action, and Patient Education

Classification	Sample Agent	Action	Patient Education
Bulk forming	Psyllium hydrophilic mucilloid (Metamucil)	Polysaccharides and cellulose derivatives mix with intestinal fluids, swell, and stimulate peristalsis.	Take with 8 oz water and follow with 8 oz water; do not take dry. Report abdominal distention or unusual amount of flatulence.
Saline agent	Magnesium hydroxide (Milk of Magnesia)	Nonabsorbable magnesium ions alter stool consistency by drawing water into the intestines by osmosis; peristalsis is stimulated. Action occurs within 2 hours.	The liquid preparation is more effective than the tablet form. Only short-term use is recommended because of toxicity (CNS or neuromuscular depression, electrolyte imbalance). Magnesium laxatives should not be taken by patients with renal insufficiency.
Lubricant	Mineral oil	Nonabsorbable hydrocarbons soften fecal matter by lubricating the intestinal mucosa; the passage of stool is facilitated. Action occurs within 6 to 8 hours.	Do not take with meals, because mineral oils can impair the absorption of fat-soluble vitamins and delay gastric emptying. Swallow carefully, because drops of oil that gain access to the pharynx can produce a lipid pneumonia.
Stimulant	Bisacodyl (Dulcolax)	Irritates the colon epithelium by stimulating sensory nerve endings and increasing mucosal secretions. Action occurs within 6 to 8 hours.	Catharsis may cause fluid and electrolyte imbalance, especially in the elderly. Tablets should be swallowed, not crushed or chewed. Avoid milk or antacids within 1 hour of taking the medication, because the enteric coating may dissolve prematurely.
Fecal softener	Dioctyl sodium sulfosuccinate (Colace)	Hydrates the stool by its surfactant action on the colonic epithelium (increases the wetting efficiency of intestinal water); aqueous and fatty substances are mixed. Does not exert a laxative action.	This can be used safely by patients who should avoid straining (cardiac patients, patients with anorectal disorders).
Osmotic agent	Polyethylene glycol and electrolytes (Colyte)	Cleanses colon rapidly and induces diarrhea	This is a large-volume product. It takes time to consume it safely. It can cause considerable nausea and bloating.

Specific medications may be prescribed to enhance colonic transit by increasing propulsive motor activity. These may include cholinergic agents (e.g., bethanechol [Urecholine]), cholinesterase inhibitors (e.g., neostigmine [Prostigmin]), or prokinetic agents (e.g., metoclopramide [Reglan]).

Patient education and health promotion are important functions of the nurse. Patient education should include establishing a bowel routine, providing dietary information, and reducing patient anxiety. After the health history is obtained, the nurse sets specific goals for teaching. Goals for the patient include restoring or maintaining a regular pattern of elimination by responding to the urge to defecate, ensuring adequate intake of fluids and high-fiber foods, learning methods to avoid constipation, relieving anxiety about bowel elimination patterns, and avoiding complications.

Complications

Complications of constipation include hypertension, fecal impaction, hemorrhoids (dilated portions of anal veins), fissures (tissue folds), and **megacolon** (abnormal enlargement of the colon). Increased arterial pressure can occur with defecation. Straining at stool, which results in the **Valsalva maneuver** (i.e., forcibly exhaling with the glottis closed), has a striking effect on arterial blood pressure. During active straining, the flow of venous blood in the chest is temporarily impeded because of increased intrathoracic pressure. This pressure tends to collapse the large veins in the chest. The atria and the ventricles receive less blood, and consequently less blood is ejected by the left ventricle. Cardiac output is decreased, and there is a transient drop in arterial pressure. Almost immediately after this period of hypotension, an increase in arterial pressure occurs; the pressure is elevated momentarily to a point far exceeding the original level (i.e., *rebound phenomenon*).

NURSING ALERT
In patients with hypertension, the compensatory rebound phenomenon reaction may be exaggerated greatly, and the peak pressure attained may be dangerously high—sufficient to rupture a major artery in the brain or elsewhere.

Fecal impaction occurs when an accumulated mass of dry feces cannot be expelled. The mass may be palpable on digital examination, may produce pressure on the colonic mucosa that results in ulcer formation, and frequently causes seepage of liquid stools.

Hemorrhoids and anal fissures can develop as a result of constipation. Hemorrhoids develop as a result of perianal vascular congestion caused by straining. Anal fissures may result from the passage of the hard stool through the anus, tearing the lining of the anal canal.

Megacolon is caused by a fecal mass that obstructs the passage of colon contents. Symptoms include constipation, liquid fecal incontinence, and abdominal distention. Megacolon can lead to perforation of the bowel.

DIARRHEA

Diarrhea is defined as an increased frequency of bowel movements of more than three per day, an increased amount of stool (>200 g/day), or abnormally liquid stool. It is usually associated with increased urgency, perianal discomfort, or incontinence. Diarrhea lasting less than 2 weeks is considered acute; conversely, diarrhea lasting more than 4 weeks is considered chronic. Acute diarrhea is most often associated with infection and is usually self-limiting; chronic diarrhea persists for a longer period and may return sporadically. Any condition that causes increased intestinal secretions, decreased mucosal absorption, or altered motility can produce diarrhea. IBS, inflammatory bowel disease, and lactose intolerance are frequently the underlying disease processes that cause diarrhea.

Pathophysiology

Types of diarrhea include secretory, osmotic, and mixed diarrhea. Secretory diarrhea is usually high-volume diarrhea and is caused by increased production and secretion of water and electrolytes by the intestinal mucosa into the intestinal lumen. Osmotic diarrhea occurs when water is pulled into the intestines by the osmotic pressure of unabsorbed particles, slowing the reabsorption of water. Mixed diarrhea is caused by increased **peristalsis** (usually from inflammatory bowel disease) and a combination of increased secretion and decreased absorption in the bowel.

Risk Factors

Diarrhea can be caused by certain medications (e.g., thyroid hormone replacement, stool softeners and laxatives, antibiotics, chemotherapy, magnesium-based antacids), certain tube-feeding formulas, metabolic and endocrine disorders (e.g., diabetes, Addison's disease, thyrotoxicosis), and viral or bacterial infectious processes (e.g., dysentery, shigellosis, food poisoning). Other disease processes associated with diarrhea include nutritional and malabsorptive disorders (e.g., celiac disease), anal sphincter defect, Zollinger-Ellison syndrome, paralytic ileus, intestinal obstruction, and AIDS.

Clinical Manifestations and Assessment

In addition to the increased frequency and fluid content of stools, the patient usually has abdominal cramps, distention, intestinal rumbling (**borborygmus**), anorexia, and thirst. Painful spasmodic contractions of the anus and ineffective straining (**tenesmus**) may occur with defecation. Other symptoms depend on the cause and severity of the diarrhea but are related to dehydration and to fluid and electrolyte imbalances.

Watery stools are characteristic of disorders of the small bowel, whereas loose, semisolid stools are associated more often with disorders of the large bowel. Large, greasy stools suggest intestinal malabsorption, and the presence of mucus and pus in the stools suggests inflammatory enteritis or colitis. Oil droplets on the toilet water are almost always diagnostic of pancreatic insufficiency. Nocturnal diarrhea may be a manifestation of diabetic neuropathy.

Typically, when the source of the diarrhea is not clear, the following diagnostic tests may be performed: complete blood cell count (CBC); serum chemistries; urinalysis; routine stool examination; and stool examinations for infectious or parasitic organisms, bacterial toxins, blood, fat, and electrolytes. Endoscopy or barium enema may assist in identifying the cause.

☀ NURSING ALERT

Elderly patients can become dehydrated quickly and develop low potassium levels (i.e., hypokalemia) as a result of diarrhea. The nurse observes for clinical manifestations of muscle weakness, arrhythmias, or decreased peristaltic motility that may lead to paralytic ileus. The older patient taking digitalis (e.g., digoxin [Lanoxin]) must be aware of how quickly dehydration and hypokalemia can occur with diarrhea. The nurse teaches the patient to recognize the symptoms of hypokalemia because low levels of potassium intensify the action of digitalis, leading to digitalis toxicity.

Medical and Nursing Management

Primary management is directed at controlling symptoms, preventing complications, and eliminating or treating the underlying disease. Medications such as antibiotics and anti-inflammatory agents may be used to reduce the severity of the diarrhea and treat the underlying disease.

The nurse's role includes assessing and monitoring the characteristics and pattern of diarrhea. A health history should address the patient's medication therapy, medical and surgical history, and dietary patterns and intake. Reports of recent exposure to an acute illness or recent travel to another geographic area are important as treatment can change depending on the patient's illness and travel history. Assessment includes abdominal inspection, auscultation (for

hyperactive bowel sounds), and palpation for abdominal tenderness. Vital signs are assessed for fever and evidence of fluid volume deficit (weak pulse, hypotension, narrow pulse pressure). Inspection of the mucous membranes and skin is important to determine hydration status. Stool samples are obtained for testing.

During an episode of acute diarrhea, the nurse encourages bedrest and intake of liquids and foods low in bulk until the acute attack subsides. When the patient is able to tolerate food intake, the nurse recommends a bland diet of semisolid and solid foods. The patient should avoid caffeine, carbonated beverages, and very hot and very cold foods due to stimulation of intestinal motility. It may be necessary to restrict milk products, fat, whole-grain products, fresh fruits, and vegetables for several days. Antidiarrheal medications such as diphenoxylate (Lomotil) or loperamide (Imodium) may be administered as prescribed to reduce the frequency and amount of stools. IV fluid therapy may be necessary for rapid rehydration in some patients, especially in elderly patients and in patients with preexisting GI conditions such as inflammatory bowel disease. It is important to monitor serum electrolyte levels closely as imbalances such as hypokalemia (K^+ <3.5 mEq/L) can occur. The nurse immediately reports evidence of arrhythmias, muscular weakness, fatigue or flaccid paralysis, and hyporeflexia (associated with a K^+ <2.5 mEq/L).

NURSING ALERT
Decreased potassium levels cause cardiac arrhythmias (i.e., atrial and ventricular tachycardia, ventricular fibrillation, premature ventricular contractions) that can lead to death.

The perianal area may become excoriated because diarrheal stool contains digestive enzymes that can irritate the skin. Older individuals have decreased skin turgor and reduced subcutaneous fat layers, therefore care should be taken to follow a structured perianal skin care routine to reduce irritation and excoriation.

FECAL INCONTINENCE

Fecal incontinence describes the involuntary passage of stool from the rectum. It is estimated that over 40% of extended-care facility residents and more than 10% of adults in the community have fecal incontinence. A substantial number of extended-care facility residents have what is termed "double incontinence," or difficulties with both urine and stool continence (Landefeld, Bowers, Feld et al., 2008). Factors that influence fecal continence include the ability of the rectum to sense and accommodate stool, the amount and consistency of stool, the integrity of the anal sphincters and musculature, and rectal motility. It is an embarrassing and socially incapacitating problem that requires a many-tiered approach to treatment and much adaptation on the patient's part.

Pathophysiology

Continence is maintained by tonic contraction of the muscles around the rectum. During defecation, nerves relax the muscles, causing a straightening of the rectoanal angle. Distension of the rectum causes relaxation of the sphincter. Fecal incontinence is a failure of this process and can occur for a variety of reasons.

Risk Factors

Fecal incontinence can result from trauma (e.g., after surgical procedures involving the rectum), neurologic disorders (e.g., stroke, multiple sclerosis, diabetic neuropathy, dementia), inflammation, infection, chemotherapy, radiation treatment, fecal impaction, pelvic floor relaxation, laxative abuse, medications, or advancing age (i.e., weakness or loss of anal or rectal muscle tone).

Clinical Manifestations and Assessment

Patients may have minor soiling, occasional urgency and loss of control, or complete incontinence. Patients may also experience poor control of flatus, diarrhea, or constipation.

The nurse obtains a thorough health history, including information about previous surgical procedures, chronic illnesses, dietary patterns, bowel habits and problems, and current medication regimen. The nurse also completes both a visual and digital examination of the rectal area checking for abnormalities (fecal impaction, hemorrhoids, fissures, and fistulas) that may be contributing to the incontinence.

Diagnostic studies are necessary because the treatment of fecal incontinence depends on the cause. A rectal examination and other endoscopic examinations, such as a flexible sigmoidoscopy, are performed to rule out tumors, inflammation, or fissures. X-ray studies such as barium enema, computed tomography (CT), anorectal manometry, and transit studies may be helpful in identifying alterations in intestinal mucosa and muscle tone or in detecting other structural or functional problems.

Medical and Nursing Management

Specific management techniques can help the patient achieve a better quality of life. If fecal incontinence is related to diarrhea, the incontinence may disappear when diarrhea is successfully treated. Fecal incontinence is frequently a symptom of a fecal impaction. After the impaction is removed and the rectum is cleansed, normal functioning of the anorectal area can resume. If the fecal incontinence is related to a more permanent condition, other treatments are initiated. Biofeedback therapy can be of assistance if the problem is decreased sensory awareness or sphincter control. Bowel training programs can also be effective. Surgical procedures include surgical reconstruction, sphincter repair, or fecal diversion.

The nurse initiates a bowel training program that involves setting a schedule to establish bowel regularity. The goal is to help the patient achieve fecal continence. If this is not possible, the goal should be to manage the problem so the person can have predictable, planned elimination. Sometimes, it is necessary to use suppositories to stimulate the anal reflex. After the patient has achieved a regular schedule, the suppository can be discontinued.

Complications

Fecal incontinence may cause problems with perineal skin integrity. Maintaining skin integrity is a priority, especially in the debilitated or elderly patient. Incontinence briefs, although helpful in containing the fecal material, allow for increased skin contact with the feces and may cause excoriation of the skin. The nurse encourages and teaches meticulous skin hygiene, and in the hospital setting, interventions such as turning the patient every 2 hours and applying barrier creams or sprays to protect the skin may be warranted.

Continence sometimes cannot be achieved, and the nurse assists the patient and family to accept and cope with this chronic situation. The patient can use fecal incontinence devices, which include external collection devices and internal drainage systems. External devices are special, drainable pouches. They are attached to a synthetic adhesive skin barrier specially designed to conform to the buttocks. Internal drainage systems can be used to eliminate fecal skin contact and are especially useful when there is extensive excoriation or skin breakdown. A rectal catheter is inserted into the rectum and is connected to a drainage system and stool is collected in order to preserve skin integrity. Rectal catheters are contraindicated in patients who are postoperative from rectal or prostate surgery, recent myocardial infarction, rectal mucosal disease, bleeding dyscrasia, and impaired immune status. It is important to consider that at present, long-term consequences of indwelling fecal collectors have not yet been studied, although some research suggests that some commercially available catheters may be safe for upwards of 30 days. A provider's order is required to place these devices.

IRRITABLE BOWEL SYNDROME

IBS is one of the most common GI conditions. Approximately 15% of adults in the United States report classic symptoms of IBS (Friedrich, Grady, & Wall, 2010).

Pathophysiology

IBS results from a functional disorder of intestinal motility. The change in motility may be related to neuroendocrine dysregulation, infection or irritation, or a vascular or metabolic disturbance. The peristaltic waves are affected at specific segments of the intestine and in the intensity with which they propel the fecal matter forward. There is no evidence of inflammation or tissue changes in the intestinal mucosa.

Risk Factors

Although no anatomic or biochemical abnormalities have been found that account for the common symptoms, various factors are associated with the syndrome: heredity, a diet high in fat and stimulating or irritating foods, alcohol consumption, smoking, and psychological stress or conditions such as depression and anxiety. As many as 90% of people diagnosed with IBS present with symptoms of major depression, and it is now suggested that some antidepressant medications may in fact help with symptoms of IBS (Friedrich et al., 2010).

IBS occurs more commonly in women than in men (Friedrich et al., 2010).

Clinical Manifestations and Assessment

There is a wide variability in symptom presentation. Symptoms range in intensity and duration from mild and infrequent to severe and continuous. The primary symptom is an alteration in bowel patterns—constipation, diarrhea, or a combination of both. Pain and abdominal distention often accompany changes in bowel pattern. The abdominal pain is sometimes precipitated by eating and is frequently relieved by defecation.

A definite diagnosis of IBS requires tests that confirm the absence of structural or other disorders. Stool studies, contrast X-ray studies, and proctoscopy may be performed to rule out other colon diseases. Barium enema and colonoscopy may reveal spasm, distention, or mucus accumulation in the intestine (Fig. 24-1). Manometry and electromyography (EMG) are used to study intraluminal pressure changes generated by spasticity.

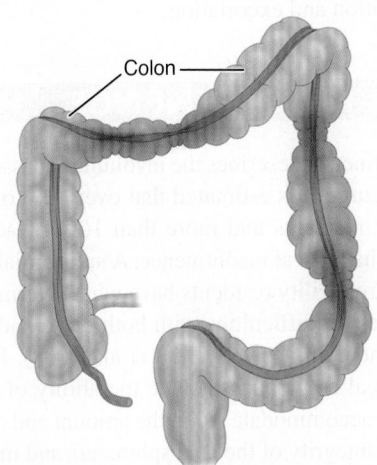

Colon

FIGURE 24-1 In irritable bowel syndrome (IBS), the spastic contractions of the bowel can be seen on X-ray contrast studies.

Medical and Nursing Management

The goals of treatment are relieving abdominal pain, controlling the diarrhea or constipation, and reducing stress. Restriction and then gradual reintroduction of foods that are possibly irritating may help determine what types of food are acting as irritants (e.g., beans, caffeinated products, fried foods, alcohol, and spicy foods). A high-fiber diet is prescribed to help control the diarrhea and constipation. Exercise can assist in reducing anxiety and increasing intestinal motility. Patients often find it helpful to participate in a stress reduction or behavior modification program. Hydrophilic colloids (i.e., bulk) and antidiarrheal agents (e.g., loperamide [Imodium]) may be given to control the diarrhea and fecal urgency. Antidepressants can assist in treating underlying anxiety and depression. Anticholinergics (e.g., propantheline [Pro-Banthine]) may be taken to decrease smooth muscle spasm, thus decreasing cramping and constipation.

Tegaserod (Zelnorm) may be prescribed to treat women with IBS whose chief complaint is chronic constipation. Tegaserod increases the effects of serotonin in the intestines, thereby increasing intestinal motility. The most commonly reported side effect of this medication is diarrhea, which typically subsides after the first week of treatment. Research has shown that some women with IBS who take tegaserod develop diarrhea with hypovolemia and hypotension (Chey, Paré, Viegas et. al., 2008). Thus, women who take tegaserod must be taught to discontinue the drug and contact their primary health care provider if they develop severe diarrhea, particularly if it is accompanied by dizziness or orthostatic hypotension.

The nurse's role is to provide patient and family education. The nurse emphasizes teaching and reinforces good dietary habits. Patients are encouraged to eat at regular times and to chew food slowly and thoroughly. They should understand that although adequate fluid intake is necessary, fluid should not be taken with meals because this results in abdominal distention. Alcohol use and cigarettes should be avoided.

MALABSORPTION

Malabsorption is the inability of the digestive system to absorb one or more of the major vitamins (especially A and B_{12}), minerals (i.e., iron and calcium), and nutrients (i.e., carbohydrates, fats, and proteins). Interruptions in the complex digestive process may occur anywhere in the digestive system and cause decreased absorption.

Pathophysiology

The conditions that cause malabsorption can be grouped into the following categories:

- Mucosal (transport) disorders causing generalized malabsorption (e.g., celiac sprue, regional enteritis, radiation enteritis)

- Infectious diseases causing generalized malabsorption (e.g., small bowel bacterial overgrowth, tropical sprue)
- Luminal disorders causing malabsorption (e.g., bile acid deficiency, Zollinger-Ellison syndrome, pancreatic insufficiency)
- Postoperative malabsorption (e.g., after gastric or intestinal resection)
- Disorders that cause malabsorption of specific nutrients (e.g., disaccharidase deficiency leading to lactose intolerance)

Table 24-2 lists the clinical and pathologic aspects of malabsorptive diseases.

Risk Factors

Risk factors predisposing people to malabsorption include any process that interferes with the body's ability to absorb nutrients. These can include pathologic factors including abdominal diseases or deformities, surgery, radiation therapy, and certain medications that inhibit bacterial growth within the intestine (antibiotics). Finally, use of medications such as mineral oil or laxatives can decrease absorption by increasing peristalsis.

Clinical Manifestations and Assessment

The hallmarks of malabsorption syndrome are diarrhea or frequent, loose, bulky, foul-smelling stools that have increased fat content and are often grayish in color. Patients often have associated abdominal distention, pain, increased flatus, weakness, weight loss, and a decreased sense of well-being. The chief result of malabsorption is malnutrition, manifested by weight loss and other signs of vitamin and mineral deficiency (e.g., easy bruising [vitamin K deficiency], osteoporosis [calcium deficiency], anemia [iron, vitamin B_{12} deficiency]).

Patients with a malabsorption syndrome, if untreated, become weak and emaciated because of starvation and dehydration. Failure to absorb the fat-soluble vitamins A, D, and K causes a corresponding avitaminosis.

Several diagnostic tests may be prescribed, including stool studies for quantitative and qualitative fat analysis, lactose tolerance tests, D-xylose absorption tests (absorption of sugar), and Schilling tests (B_{12} deficiency). The hydrogen breath test that is used to evaluate carbohydrate absorption is performed if carbohydrate malabsorption is suspected. Endoscopy with biopsy of the mucosa is the best diagnostic tool. Biopsy of the small intestine is performed to assay enzyme activity or to identify infection or destruction of mucosa. Ultrasound studies, CT scans, and X-ray findings can reveal pancreatic or intestinal tumors that may be the cause. A CBC is used to detect anemia. Pancreatic function tests can assist in the diagnosis of specific disorders.

TABLE
24-2 Characteristics of Diseases of Malabsorption

Diseases/Disorders	Physiologic Pathology	Clinical Features
Gastric resection with gastro-jejunostomy	Decreased pancreatic stimulation because of duodenal bypass; poor mixing of food, bile, pancreatic enzymes; decreased intrinsic factor	Weight loss, moderate steatorrhea, anemia (combination of iron deficiency, vitamin B_{12} malabsorption, folate deficiency)
Pancreatic insufficiency (chronic pancreatitis, pancreatic carcinoma, pancreatic resection, cystic fibrosis)	Reduced intraluminal pancreatic enzyme activity, with maldigestion of lipids and proteins	History of abdominal pain followed by weight loss; marked steatorrhea, azotorrhea (excess of nitrogenous matter in the feces or urine); also frequent glucose intolerance (70% in pancreatic insufficiency)
Ileal dysfunction (resection or disease)	Loss of ileal absorbing surface leads to reduced bile-salt pool size and reduced vitamin B_{12} absorption; bile in colon inhibits fluid absorption	Diarrhea, weight loss with steatorrhea, especially when >100 cm resection, decreased vitamin B_{12} absorption
Stasis syndromes (surgical strictures, blind loops, enteric fistulas, multiple jejunal diverticula, scleroderma)	Overgrowth of intraluminal intestinal bacteria, especially anaerobic organisms, to >10^6/mL results in deconjugation of bile salts, leading to decreased effective bile-salt pool size, also bacterial utilization of vitamin B_{12}	Weight loss, steatorrhea; low vitamin B_{12} absorption; may have low D-xylose absorption
Zollinger-Ellison syndrome	Hyperacidity in duodenum inactivates pancreatic enzymes	Ulcer diathesis, steatorrhea
Lactose intolerance	Deficiency of intestinal lactase results in high concentration of intraluminal lactose with osmotic diarrhea	Varied degrees of diarrhea and cramps after ingestion of lactose-containing foods; positive lactose intolerance test, decreased intestinal lactase
Celiac disease (gluten enteropathy)	Toxic response to a gluten fraction by surface epithelium results in destruction of absorbing surface	Weight loss, diarrhea, bloating, anemia (low iron, folate), osteomalacia, steatorrhea, azotorrhea, low D-xylose absorption; folate and iron malabsorption
Tropical sprue	Unknown toxic factor results in mucosal inflammation, partial villous atrophy	Weight loss, diarrhea, anemia (low folate, vitamin B_{12}); steatorrhea; low D-xylose absorption, low vitamin B_{12} absorption
Whipple's disease	Bacterial invasion of intestinal mucosa	Arthritis, hyperpigmentation, lymphadenopathy, serous effusions, fever, weight loss, steatorrhea, azotorrhea
Certain parasitic diseases (giardiasis, strongyloidiasis, coccidiosis, capillariasis)	Damage to or invasion of surface mucosa	Diarrhea, weight loss; steatorrhea; organism may be seen on jejunal biopsy or recovered in stool
Immunoglobulinopathy	Decreased local intestinal defenses, lymphoid hyperplasia, lymphopenia	Frequent association with *Giardia*: hypogammaglobulinemia or isolated IgA deficiency

Medical and Nursing Management

Intervention is aimed at avoiding dietary substances that aggravate malabsorption and at supplementing nutrients that have been lost. Common supplements are water-soluble vitamins (e.g., B_{12}, folic acid), fat-soluble vitamins (e.g., A, D, and K), and minerals (e.g., calcium, iron). Primary disease states may be managed surgically or medically. Dietary therapy is aimed at reducing gluten intake in patients with celiac sprue. Folic acid supplements are prescribed for patients with tropical sprue. Antibiotics (e.g., tetracycline [Tetracap, Tetracyn], ampicillin [Polycillin]) are sometimes needed in the treatment of tropical sprue and bacterial over-growth syndromes. Antidiarrheal agents may be used to decrease intestinal spasms. Parenteral fluids may be necessary to treat dehydration.

The nurse provides patient and family education regarding diet and the use of nutritional supplements. It is important to monitor patients with diarrhea for fluid and electrolyte imbalances. The nurse conducts ongoing assessments to determine whether the clinical manifestations related to the nutritional deficits have abated. Patient education includes information about the risk of osteoporosis related to malabsorption of calcium (refer to Chapter 41 for information on osteoporosis).

Complications

Medical management may include the administration of corticosteroids, which may cause a host of adverse effects such as hypertension, hypokalemia, insomnia, and euphoria. Antibiotics may reduce vitamin K–producing intestinal flora, resulting in a prolonged prothrombin time (PT) and international normalized ratio (INR) if the patient is concurrently taking warfarin (Coumadin). Urinary retention, altered mental status, or glaucoma may occur as adverse effects of anticholinergic drug therapy in older people.

ACUTE INFLAMMATORY CONDITIONS

APPENDICITIS

The appendix is a small, finger-like appendage about 10 cm (4 in) long that is attached to the cecum just below the ileocecal valve. The appendix fills with food and empties regularly into the cecum. Because it empties inefficiently and its lumen is small, the appendix is prone to obstruction and is particularly vulnerable to infection (i.e., appendicitis).

Approximately 325,000 people in the United States are hospitalized each year for appendicitis, and an estimated 1 in 15 people will get appendicitis in their lifetime, according to the National Institute of Diabetes and Digestive and Kidney Diseases (Everhart, 2008). The disease is most common between the ages of 10 and 30. Appendicitis is the most frequent intra-abdominal emergency, resulting in approximately 250,000 appendectomies in the United States every year (Sporn, Petroski, Mancini et al., 2009).

Pathophysiology

The appendix becomes inflamed and edematous as a result of becoming kinked or occluded by a fecalith (i.e., hardened mass of stool), tumor, or foreign body. The inflammatory process increases intraluminal pressure, initiating a progressively severe, generalized or periumbilical pain that becomes localized to the right lower quadrant of the abdomen within a few hours. Eventually, the inflamed appendix fills with pus.

Risk Factors

Appendicitis is most prevalent in the young, but can occur at any age. Most cases appear in the winter months; however, no clear reason as to why has been established. Having a family history of appendicitis may increase a child's risk for the illness, especially in males, and having cystic fibrosis also seems to put a child at higher risk.

Clinical Manifestations and Assessment

Vague epigastric or periumbilical pain progresses to right lower quadrant pain and is usually accompanied by a low-grade

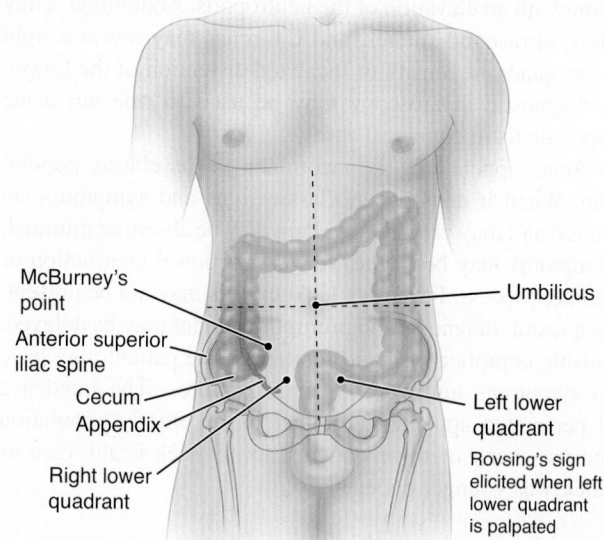

FIGURE 24-2 When the appendix is inflamed, tenderness can be noted in the right lower quadrant at McBurney's point, which is between the umbilicus and the anterior superior iliac spine. Rovsing's sign is pain felt in the right lower quadrant after the left lower quadrant has been palpated.

fever and nausea and sometimes by vomiting. Loss of appetite is common. In up to 50% of presenting cases, local tenderness is elicited at McBurney's point when pressure is applied (Fig. 24-2). Rebound tenderness (production or intensification of pain when pressure is released) may be present. The extent of tenderness and muscle spasm and the existence of constipation or diarrhea depend not so much on the severity of the appendiceal infection as on the location of the appendix. If the appendix curls around behind the cecum, pain and tenderness may be felt in the lumbar region. If its tip is in the pelvis, these signs may be elicited only on rectal examination. Pain on defecation suggests that the tip of the appendix is resting against the rectum; pain on urination suggests that the tip is near the bladder or impinges on the ureter. Some rigidity of the lower portion of the right rectus muscle may occur. Rovsing's sign may be elicited by palpating the left lower quadrant; this paradoxically causes pain to be felt in the right lower quadrant (see Fig. 24-2). If the appendix has ruptured, the pain becomes more diffuse; abdominal distention develops as a result of paralytic ileus, and the patient's condition worsens.

> **NURSING ALERT**
>
> *Constipation can also occur with an acute process, such as appendicitis. Laxatives administered in this instance may result in perforation of the inflamed appendix. In general, a laxative or cathartic should never be given when a person has fever, nausea, or pain.*

Diagnosis is based on results of a complete physical examination and on laboratory findings and imaging studies. The CBC demonstrates an elevated white blood cell (WBC)

count with an elevation of the neutrophils. Abdominal X-ray films, ultrasound studies, and CT scans may reveal a right lower quadrant density or localized distention of the bowel. A diagnostic laparoscopy may be used to rule out acute appendicitis in equivocal cases.

Acute appendicitis is uncommon in the elderly population. When it does occur, classic signs and symptoms are altered and may vary greatly. Pain may be absent or minimal. Symptoms may be vague, suggesting bowel obstruction or another process. Fever and leukocytosis may not be present. As a result, diagnosis and prompt treatment may be delayed, causing complications and mortality. The patient may have no symptoms until the appendix ruptures. The incidence of perforated appendix is higher in the elderly population because many of these patients do not seek health care as quickly as younger patients.

Medical and Nursing Management

Immediate surgery is typically indicated if appendicitis is diagnosed. To correct or prevent fluid and electrolyte imbalance, dehydration, and sepsis, antibiotics and IV fluids are administered until surgery is performed. Appendectomy (i.e., surgical removal of the appendix) is performed as soon as possible to decrease the risk of perforation. It may be performed using general or spinal anesthesia with a low abdominal incision (laparotomy) or by laparoscopy. Both laparotomy and laparoscopy are safe and effective in the treatment of appendicitis with perforation. However, recovery after laparoscopic surgery is generally quicker.

When perforation of the appendix occurs, an **abscess** may form. If this occurs, the patient may be initially treated with antibiotics, and the surgeon may place a drain in the abscess during the operative procedure to facilitate drainage. Subsequent surgical procedures may be performed to ensure complete drainage of the abscess. The postoperative care of the patient with a perforated appendix is more complex and complicated due to the risk of developing sepsis and organ damage.

The nurse prepares the patient for surgery, which includes an IV infusion to replace fluid loss and promote adequate renal function, and antibiotic therapy to prevent infection. If there is evidence or likelihood of paralytic ileus, a nasogastric tube is inserted. An enema is not administered because it can lead to perforation.

After surgery, the nurse places the patient in a high Fowler's position. This position reduces the tension on the incision and abdominal organs, helping to reduce pain. An opioid, usually morphine sulfate, is prescribed to relieve pain. When tolerated, oral fluids are administered. Any patient who was dehydrated before surgery receives IV fluids. Food is provided as desired and tolerated on the day of surgery, once normal bowel sounds are present.

The patient may be discharged on the day of surgery if the temperature is within normal limits, there is no undue discomfort in the operative area, and the appendectomy was uncomplicated. Discharge teaching for the patient and family is imperative. The nurse instructs the patient to make an appointment to have the surgeon remove the sutures between the fifth and seventh days after surgery. Incision care and activity guidelines are discussed; normal activity can usually be resumed within 2 to 4 weeks.

If there is a possibility of **peritonitis**, a drain is left in place at the area of the incision. Patients at risk for this complication may be kept in the hospital for several days and are monitored carefully for signs of intestinal obstruction or secondary hemorrhage. Secondary abscesses may form in the pelvis, under the diaphragm, or in the liver, causing elevation of the temperature, pulse rate, and WBC count.

When the patient is ready for discharge, the nurse teaches the patient and family to care for the incision and perform dressing changes and irrigations as prescribed. A home care nurse may be needed to assist with this care and to monitor the patient for complications and wound healing.

Complications

The major complication of appendicitis is perforation of the appendix, which can lead to peritonitis, abscess formation (collection of purulent material), or portal pylephlebitis, which is septic thrombosis of the portal vein caused by vegetative emboli that arise from septic intestines. Perforation generally occurs 24 hours after the onset of pain if no intervention has occurred. Symptoms include a fever of 37.7°C (100°F) or greater, a toxic appearance, and continued abdominal pain or tenderness. Other complications of appendectomy are listed in Table 24-3.

DIVERTICULAR DISEASE

A diverticulum is a sac-like herniation of the lining of the bowel that extends through a defect in the muscle layer. Diverticula may occur anywhere in the small intestine or colon but occur most commonly in the distal sigmoid colon. Diverticular disease of the colon is very common in developed countries, accounting for over 300,000 admissions and 1.5 million days of inpatient care annually (Etzioni, Mack, Beart et al., 2009). It is estimated that more than 50% of Americans older than 80 years have **diverticulosis** (Etzioni et al., 2009).

Pathophysiology

Diverticula form when the mucosa and submucosal layers of the colon herniate through the muscular wall because of high intraluminal pressure, low volume in the colon (i.e., fiber-deficient contents), and decreased muscle strength in the colon wall (e.g., muscular hypertrophy from hardened fecal masses). Bowel contents can accumulate in the diverticulum and decompose, causing inflammation and infection. The

TABLE
24-3 Potential Complications and Nursing Interventions After Appendectomy

Complication	Nursing Interventions
Peritonitis	Observe for abdominal tenderness, fever, vomiting, abdominal rigidity, and tachycardia.
	Employ nasogastric suction.
	Correct dehydration as prescribed.
	Administer antibiotic agents as prescribed.
Pelvic abscess	Evaluate for anorexia, chills, fever, and diaphoresis.
	Observe for diarrhea, which may indicate pelvic abscess.
	Prepare patient for rectal examination.
	Prepare patient for surgical drainage procedure.
Subphrenic abscess (abscess under the diaphragm)	Assess patient for chills, fever, and diaphoresis.
	Prepare for X-ray examination.
	Prepare for surgical drainage of abscess.
Ileus (paralytic and mechanical)	Assess for bowel sounds.
	Employ nasogastric intubation and suction.
	Replace fluids and electrolytes by intravenous route as prescribed.
	Prepare for surgery, if diagnosis of mechanical ileus is established.

diverticulum can also become obstructed and then inflamed if the obstruction continues. Inflammation and subsequent infection of the diverticulum (i.e., **diverticulitis**), can cause the development of abscesses, which may eventually perforate, leading to peritonitis and erosion of the arterial blood vessels, resulting in bleeding.

Diverticulosis exists when multiple diverticula are present without inflammation or symptoms. A low intake of dietary fiber is considered a predisposing factor, but the exact cause has not been identified. Most patients with diverticular disease are asymptomatic, so its exact prevalence is unknown.

Diverticulitis results when food and bacteria retained in a diverticulum produce infection and inflammation that can impede drainage and lead to perforation or abscess formation. Diverticulitis may occur as an acute attack or may persist as a continuing, smoldering infection. The symptoms manifested generally result from complications: abscess, fistula formation, obstruction, perforation, peritonitis, and hemorrhage.

Risk Factors

It is estimated that 10% to 25% of people with diverticulosis have diverticulitis at some point in their lives (Everhart,

2008). A congenital predisposition is suspected when the disorder occurs in those younger than 40 years.

Clinical Manifestations and Assessment

Chronic constipation often precedes the development of diverticulosis, sometimes by many years. Frequently, no problematic symptoms occur with diverticulosis. Signs and symptoms of diverticulosis are relatively mild and include bowel irregularity with intervals of diarrhea, nausea, anorexia, and abdominal distention. With repeated local inflammation of the diverticula, the large bowel may narrow with fibrotic strictures, leading to cramps, narrow stools, and increased constipation or at times intestinal obstruction. Weakness, fatigue, and anorexia are common symptoms. With diverticulitis, the patient reports an acute onset of mild to severe pain in the lower left quadrant, accompanied by nausea, vomiting, fever, chills, and leukocytosis. The condition, if untreated, can lead to septicemia.

Diverticulosis is typically diagnosed by colonoscopy, which permits visualization of the extent of diverticular disease and allows the clinician to biopsy tissue to rule out other diseases as needed. Until recently, barium enema had been the preferred diagnostic test, but it is now used less frequently than colonoscopy. If there are symptoms of peritoneal irritation when the diagnosis is diverticulitis, barium enema is contraindicated because of the potential for perforation.

CT scan is the diagnostic test of choice if the suspected diagnosis is diverticulitis; it can also reveal one or more abscesses. Abdominal X-rays may demonstrate free air under the diaphragm if a perforation has occurred from the diverticulitis, which causes peritonitis. Laboratory tests that assist in diagnosis include a CBC, revealing an elevated WBC count, and elevated erythrocyte sedimentation rate (ESR).

Gerontologic Considerations

The incidence of diverticular disease increases with age because of degeneration and structural changes in the circular muscle layers of the colon and because of cellular hypertrophy. The symptoms are less pronounced in the elderly than in other adults. The elderly may not have abdominal pain until infection occurs. They may delay reporting symptoms because they fear surgery or are afraid that they may have cancer. Blood in the stool is overlooked frequently, especially in the elderly, because of a failure to examine the stool or the inability to see changes if vision is impaired.

Medical and Nursing Management

Diverticulitis can usually be treated on an outpatient basis with diet and medication. When symptoms occur, rest, analgesics, and antispasmodics are recommended. Initially, the diet is clear liquid until the inflammation subsides; then a high-fiber, low-fat diet is recommended. This type of diet

helps increase stool volume, decrease colonic transit time, and reduce intraluminal pressure. Antibiotics are prescribed for 7 to 10 days. A bulk-forming laxative also is prescribed.

In acute cases of diverticulitis with significant symptoms, hospitalization is required. Hospitalization is often indicated for those who are elderly, immunocompromised, or taking corticosteroids. Measures taken to rest the bowel include withholding oral intake, administering IV fluids, and instituting nasogastric suctioning if vomiting or abdominal distention are present. Broad-spectrum antibiotics are prescribed for 7 to 10 days. An opioid is prescribed for pain relief. Historically, morphine was considered to be contraindicated because of a claim that it can increase intraluminal pressure in the colon, thus exacerbating symptoms; however, no research evidence is available to support this claim. Nonsteroidal anti-inflammatory drugs (NSAIDs), however, are associated with increased risk of perforation and should be avoided. Oral intake is increased as symptoms subside. A low-fiber diet may be necessary until signs of infection decrease.

Antispasmodics such as propantheline bromide (Pro-Banthine) and oxyphencyclimine (Daricon) may be prescribed. Often, it is not possible for patients to consume the 20 to 30 g of daily fiber that is recommended. Normal stools can be achieved by supplementing dietary fiber by using bulk preparations (psyllium [Metamucil]) or stool softeners (docusate [Colace]), by instilling warm oil into the rectum, or by inserting a suppository (bisacodyl [Dulcolax]). Such a prophylactic plan can reduce the bacterial flora of the bowel, diminish the bulk of the stool, and soften the fecal mass so that it moves more easily through the area of inflammatory obstruction.

More often than not, acute diverticulitis will subside with medical management. Immediate surgical intervention is necessary if complications (e.g., perforation, peritonitis, hemorrhage, obstruction) occur. In cases of abscess formation without peritonitis, hemorrhage, or obstruction, CT-guided percutaneous drainage may be performed to drain the abscess, and IV antibiotics are administered. Stabilization of the patient by drainage of the abscess and resolution of the inflammation is complete after approximately 6 weeks; surgery may be recommended to prevent repeated episodes. Two types of surgery are typically considered either to treat acute complications or prevent further episodes of inflammation:

- One-stage resection, in which the inflamed area is removed and a primary end-to-end anastomosis is completed
- Multiple-stage procedures for complications such as obstruction or perforation (Fig. 24-3)

The type of surgery performed depends on the extent of complications found during surgery. When possible, the area of diverticulitis is taken out and the remaining bowel is joined end-to-end (i.e., primary resection and end-to-end anastomosis). This is performed through traditional surgical or laparoscopically assisted colectomy. A two-stage resection may be performed in which the diseased colon is removed (as in a one-stage procedure) but no anastomosis is

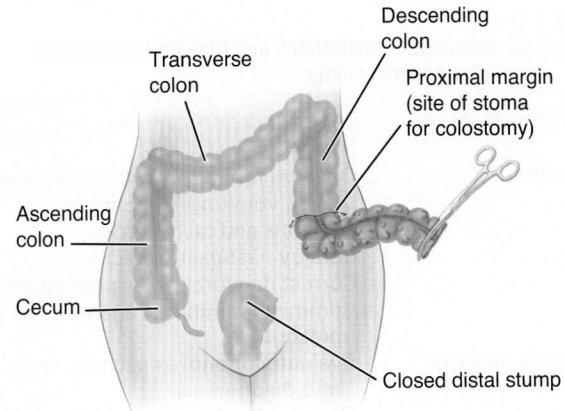

FIGURE 24-3 The Hartmann procedure for diverticulitis: primary resection for diverticulitis of the colon. The affected segment (*clamp attached*) has been divided at its distal end. In a primary anastomosis, the proximal margin (*dotted line*) is transected and the bowel attached end-to-end. In a two-stage procedure, a colostomy is constructed at the proximal margin with the distal stump oversewn (Hartmann procedure, as shown) or brought to the outer surface as a mucous fistula. The second stage consists of colostomy takedown and anastomosis.

performed; both ends of the bowel are brought out onto the abdomen as stomas. This "double-barrel" temporary colostomy is then reanastomosed in a later procedure. Fecal diversion procedures are discussed later in this chapter.

Complications

Complications of diverticulitis include peritonitis (see below), abscess formation, and bleeding. If an abscess develops, the associated findings are tenderness, a palpable mass, fever, and leukocytosis. An inflamed diverticulum that perforates results in abdominal pain localized over the involved segment, usually the sigmoid; local abscess or peritonitis follows. Abdominal pain, a rigid board-like abdomen, loss of bowel sounds, and signs and symptoms of shock occur with peritonitis. Noninflamed or slightly inflamed diverticula may erode areas adjacent to arterial branches, causing massive rectal bleeding.

PERITONITIS

Peritonitis is inflammation of the peritoneum, the serous membrane lining the abdominal cavity and covering the viscera. Peritonitis is typically a life-threatening emergency that requires prompt surgical intervention, and typically involves postoperative critical care monitoring due to the risk of sepsis, organ failure, and subsequent infections.

Pathophysiology

Peritonitis is caused by leakage of contents from abdominal organs into the abdominal cavity, usually as a result of inflammation, infection, ischemia, trauma, or tumor perforation. Bacterial proliferation occurs. Edema of the tissues ensues, and

exudation of fluid develops in a short time. Fluid in the peritoneal cavity becomes turbid with increasing amounts of protein, WBCs, cellular debris, and blood. The immediate response of the intestinal tract is hypermotility, soon followed by paralytic ileus with an accumulation of air and fluid in the bowel.

Risk Factors

Usually, peritonitis is a result of bacterial infection; the organisms come from diseases of the GI tract or, in women, from the internal reproductive organs. Peritonitis can also result from external sources such as injury or trauma (e.g., gunshot wound, stab wound) or an inflammation that extends from an organ outside the peritoneal area, such as the kidney. The most common bacteria implicated are *Escherichia coli, Klebsiella, Proteus,* and *Pseudomonas.* Inflammation and paralytic ileus are the direct effects of the infection. Other common causes of peritonitis are appendicitis, perforated ulcer, diverticulitis, and bowel perforation (Fig. 24-4). Peritonitis may also be associated with abdominal surgical procedures and peritoneal dialysis.

Clinical Manifestations and Assessment

Symptoms depend on the location and extent of the inflammation. The early clinical manifestations of peritonitis frequently are the symptoms of the disorder causing the condition, aptly nicknamed an "acute abdomen." At first, a diffuse type of pain is felt. The pain tends to become constant, localized, and more intense near the site of the inflammation. Movement usually aggravates it. The affected area of the abdomen becomes extremely tender and distended, and the muscles become rigid. Rebound tenderness and paralytic

ileus may be present. Diminished perception of pain in peritonitis can occur in people receiving corticosteroids or analgesics. Patients with diabetes who have symptoms of advanced neuropathy and patients with cirrhosis who have signs of ascites may not experience pain during an acute bacterial episode. Usually, nausea and vomiting occur, and peristalsis is diminished. A temperature of 100° to 101°F (37.8° to 38.3°C) can be expected, along with an increased pulse rate.

The WBC count is almost always elevated. The hemoglobin and hematocrit levels may be low if blood loss has occurred. Serum electrolyte studies may reveal altered levels of potassium, sodium, and chloride.

An abdominal X-ray study may show air and fluid levels, as well as distended bowel loops. A CT scan of the abdomen may show abscess formation, acute inflammation or infection of one of the major abdominal organs, or a perforation of the small or large bowel. Peritoneal aspiration and culture and sensitivity studies of the aspirated fluid may reveal infection and identify the causative organisms.

Medical and Nursing Management

Fluid, colloid, and electrolyte replacement is the major focus of medical management. The administration of several liters of an isotonic solution is emergently prescribed. Hypovolemia occurs because massive amounts of fluid and electrolytes move from the intestinal lumen into the peritoneal cavity and deplete the fluid in the vascular space.

Analgesics are prescribed for pain. Antiemetics are administered as prescribed for nausea and vomiting. Placement of nasogastric tube is warranted, and suction is maintained to assist in relieving abdominal distention. Fluid in the abdominal cavity can cause pressure that restricts expansion of the lungs and causes respiratory distress. Oxygen therapy by nasal cannula or mask generally promotes adequate oxygenation, but airway intubation and ventilatory assistance occasionally are required due to the patient's inability to compensate for the metabolic acidosis that typically occurs with peritonitis.

Antibiotic therapy is initiated early in the treatment of peritonitis. Large doses of a broad-spectrum antibiotic and antifungicide are administered IV until the specific organism causing the infection is identified and appropriate antibiotic therapy can be initiated.

Surgical objectives include removing the infected material and correcting the cause. Surgical treatment is directed toward excision (i.e., appendix), resection with or without anastomosis (i.e., intestine), repair (i.e., perforation), and/or drainage (i.e., abscess). With sepsis accompanying the peritonitis, a fecal diversion may need to be created.

The two most common postoperative complications are wound evisceration and abscess formation. Any suggestion from the patient that an area of the abdomen is tender or painful or "feels as if something just gave way" must be reported. The sudden occurrence of serosanguineous

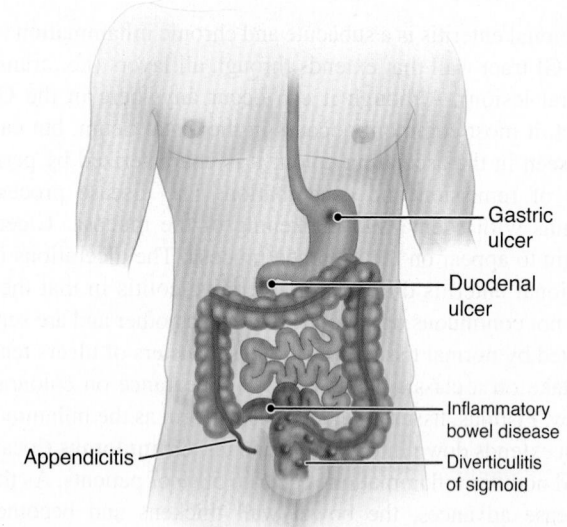

Gastric ulcer

Duodenal ulcer

Inflammatory bowel disease

Diverticulitis of sigmoid

Appendicitis

FIGURE 24-4 Common gastrointestinal causes of peritonitis.

wound drainage strongly suggests wound dehiscence and is a surgical emergency that must be promptly reported to the on-call provider.

Intensive care is often needed. The blood pressure is monitored by arterial line if shock is present. Accurate recording of all intake and output and central venous pressures and/or pulmonary artery pressures assist in calculating fluid replacement. The nurse administers and closely monitors IV fluids response.

In addition, ongoing assessment of pain, GI function, and fluid and electrolyte balance is important. Bladder pressure is also routinely measured to identify abdominal compartment syndrome (refer to Chapter 53, Fig 53-4). The nurse reports the nature of the pain, its location in the abdomen, and any changes in location. Administering analgesic medication and positioning the patient for comfort are helpful in decreasing pain. The patient is placed on the side with knees flexed; this position decreases tension on the abdominal organs.

Signs that indicate that peritonitis is subsiding include a decrease in temperature and pulse rate, softening of the abdomen, return of peristaltic sounds, and passing of flatus and bowel movements. The nurse increases fluid and food intake gradually and reduces parenteral fluids as prescribed. A worsening clinical condition may indicate a complication, and the nurse must prepare the patient for emergency surgery.

Drains are frequently inserted during the surgical procedure, and the nurse must observe and record the character of the drainage postoperatively. Care must be taken when moving and turning the patient to prevent the drains from being dislodged. It is prudent to safety pin the drains to the patient's gown to limit the chance of accidental dislodgement. It is also important for the nurse to prepare the patient and family for discharge by teaching the patient to care for the incision and drains, if the patient will be sent home with the drains still in place. Referral for home care or rehabilitation may be indicated for further monitoring and patient and family teaching.

Complications

Frequently, the inflammation is not localized, and the entire abdominal cavity shows evidence of widespread infection. Sepsis is the major cause of death from peritonitis. Shock may result from septicemia or hypovolemia. The inflammatory process may cause intestinal obstruction, primarily from the development of bowel adhesions, and care must be made to closely monitor the patient's nasogastric tube drainage and input and output. The patient is also at high risk of developing pulmonary emboli, and compression stockings, sequential-compression boots, and subcutaneous anticoagulation may be prescribed.

INFLAMMATORY BOWEL DISEASE

Inflammatory bowel disease (IBD) refers to two chronic inflammatory GI disorders: regional enteritis (i.e., Crohn's disease) and ulcerative colitis. Both disorders have striking similarities but also several differences (Tab 24-4); medical and nursing management for both types is similar and discussed jointly.

The incidence of IBD in the United States has increased to well over 1 million cases (Kappelman, Rifas-Shiman, Porter et al., 2008). Typically IBD presents during childhood or later in life and is attributed with a high morbidity and a decreased quality of life (Kappleman et al., 2008). Women and men tend to be equally affected, and family history appears to predispose people to develop IBD, particularly if a first-degree relative has the disease.

Despite extensive research, the cause of IBD is still unknown. Researchers theorize that it is triggered by environmental agents such as pesticides, food additives, tobacco, and radiation (Kasper, Braunwald, Fauci et al., 2008). NSAIDs have been found to exacerbate IBD. Allergies and immune disorders have also been suggested as causes. Abnormal response to dietary or bacterial antigens has been studied extensively, and genetic factors also are being examined.

REGIONAL ENTERITIS (CROHN'S DISEASE)

Regional enteritis is usually first diagnosed in adolescents or young adults but can appear at any time of life. Histopathologic changes consistent with regional enteritis most commonly occur in the distal ileum and colon but can occur anywhere along the GI tract. The incidence of regional enteritis has risen to over 1.1 million ambulatory care visits a year (Everhart, 2008). The most popular theory is that the body's immune system reacts abnormally in people with Crohn's disease, mistaking bacteria, foods, and other substances for dangerous foreign substances (NIH, 2009).

Pathophysiology

Regional enteritis is a subacute and chronic inflammation of the GI tract wall that extends through all layers (i.e., transmural lesion). Although it can occur anywhere in the GI tract, it most commonly occurs in the distal ileum, but can be seen in the ascending colon. It is characterized by periods of remission and exacerbation. The disease process begins with edema and thickening of the mucosa. Ulcers begin to appear on the inflamed mucosa. The ulcerations in regional enteritis differ from ulcerative colitis in that they are not continuous or in contact with each other and are separated by normal tissue. Hence, these clusters of ulcers tend to take on a classic "cobblestone" appearance on colonoscopy. Fistulas, fissures, and abscesses form as the inflammation extends down into the peritoneum. **Granulomas** (localized nodular inflammation) occur in 50% of patients. As the disease advances, the bowel wall thickens and becomes fibrotic, and the intestinal lumen narrows. Diseased bowel loops sometimes stick to other loops surrounding those developing adhesions.

TABLE
24-4 Comparison of Regional Enteritis and Ulcerative Colitis

Factor	Regional Enteritis	Ulcerative Colitis
Course	Prolonged, variable	Exacerbations, remissions
Pathology		
Early	Transmural thickening	Mucosal ulceration
Late	Deep, penetrating granulomas	Minute, mucosal ulcerations
Clinical Manifestations		
Location	Ileum, ascending colon (usually)	Rectum, descending colon
Bleeding	Usually not, but if it occurs, tends to be mild	Common—severe
Perianal involvement	Common	Rare—mild
Fistulas	Common	Rare
Rectal involvement	About 20%	Almost 100%
Diarrhea	Less severe	Severe
Diagnostic Study Findings		
Barium series	Regional, discontinuous lesions	Diffuse involvement
		No narrowing of colon
	Narrowing of colon	No mucosal edema
	Thickening of bowel wall	Stenosis rare
	Mucosal edema	Shortening of colon
	Stenosis, fistulas	
Sigmoidoscopy	May be unremarkable unless accompanied by perianal fistulas	Abnormal inflamed mucosa
Colonoscopy	Distinct ulcerations separated by relatively normal mucosa in ascending colon	Friable mucosa with pseudopolyps or ulcers in descending colon
Therapeutic Management	Corticosteroids, sulfonamides (sulfasalazine [Azulfidine])	Corticosteroids, sulfonamides; sulfasalazine useful in preventing recurrence
	Antibiotics	
	Parenteral nutrition	Bulk hydrophilic agents
	Partial or complete colectomy, with ileostomy or anastomosis	Antibiotics
		Proctocolectomy, with ileostomy
	Rectum can be preserved in some patients	Rectum can be preserved in only a few patients "cured" by colectomy
	Recurrence common	
Systemic Complications	Small bowel obstruction	Toxic megacolon
	Right-sided hydronephrosis	Perforation
	Nephrolithiasis	Hemorrhage
	Cholelithiasis	Malignant neoplasms
	Arthritis	Pyelonephritis
	Retinitis, iritis	Nephrolithiasis
	Erythema nodosum	Cholangiocarcinoma
		Arthritis
		Retinitis, iritis
		Erythema nodosum

Clinical Manifestations and Assessment

The onset of symptoms is usually insidious in regional enteritis, with prominent lower right quadrant abdominal pain unrelieved by defecation, and diarrhea. Scar tissue and the formation of granulomas interfere with the ability of the intestine to transport products of the upper intestinal digestion through the constricted lumen, resulting in crampy abdominal pains. There is abdominal tenderness and spasm. Because eating stimulates intestinal peristalsis, the crampy pain typically occurs after meals. The patient will tend to

limit food intake in order to reduce the crampy pain, and in fact can reduce the amount and type of food to such a degree that normal nutritional requirements are often not met.

As a result, weight loss, malnutrition, and secondary anemia occur. Ulcers in the membranous lining of the intestine and other inflammatory changes result in a weeping, edematous intestine that continually empties a colonic- and skin-irritating discharge. Disrupted absorption causes chronic diarrhea and nutritional deficits. The result is a person who is thin and emaciated from inadequate food intake and constant fluid loss. In some patients, the inflamed intestine may

perforate, leading to intra-abdominal and anal abscesses. Fever and leukocytosis may occur. Chronic symptoms of regional enteritis may include **steatorrhea** (i.e., excessive fat in the feces).

Abscesses, fistulas, and fissures are common. Manifestations may extend beyond the GI tract and commonly include joint disorders (e.g., arthritis), skin lesions (e.g., erythema nodosum), ocular disorders (e.g., conjunctivitis), and oral ulcers. The clinical course and symptoms can vary; in some patients, periods of remission and exacerbation occur, but in others, the disease follows a fulminating course.

A proctosigmoidoscopy is usually performed initially to determine whether the rectosigmoid area is inflamed. A stool examination is also performed; the result may be positive for occult blood and steatorrhea. The most conclusive diagnostic aid for regional enteritis is a barium study of the upper GI tract that shows the classic "string sign" on an X-ray film of the terminal ileum, indicating the constriction of a segment of intestine. Endoscopy, colonoscopy, and intestinal biopsies may be used to confirm the diagnosis. A barium enema may show ulcerations (the cobblestone appearance described earlier), fissures, and fistulas. A CT scan may show bowel wall thickening and fistula formation.

A CBC is performed to assess hematocrit and hemoglobin levels (usually decreased) as well as the WBC count (may be elevated). The ESR is usually elevated in relation to the inflammation. Albumin (the long-term marker of nutrition) and protein levels may be decreased, indicating malnutrition.

Complications

Complications of regional enteritis include intestinal obstruction or stricture formation, perianal disease, fluid and electrolyte imbalances, malnutrition from malabsorption, and fistula and abscess formation. The most common type of small bowel fistula caused by regional enteritis is the enterocutaneous fistula (i.e., an abnormal opening between the small bowel and the skin). Abscesses can be the result of an internal fistula that results in fluid accumulation and infection. Patients with regional enteritis are also at increased risk of colon cancer.

ULCERATIVE COLITIS

Ulcerative colitis is a recurrent ulcerative and inflammatory disease of the mucosal and submucosal layers of the colon and rectum. The prevalence of ulcerative colitis is highest in Caucasians and people of Jewish heritage (Baumgart & Carding, 2007). It is a serious disease, accompanied by systemic complications and a high mortality rate. Approximately 5% of patients with ulcerative colitis develop colon cancer (NIH, 2009).

Pathophysiology

Ulcerative colitis affects the superficial mucosa of the colon and is characterized by multiple ulcerations, diffuse inflammations, and desquamation or shedding of the colonic epithelium.

Bleeding occurs as a result of the ulcerations. The mucosa becomes edematous and inflamed. The lesions are contiguous, occurring one after the other. Abscesses form, and infiltrate is seen in the mucosa and submucosa, with clumps of neutrophils found in the lumens of the crypts (i.e., crypt abscesses) that line the intestinal mucosa (Porth & Matfin, 2009). The disease process usually begins in the rectum and spreads proximally to involve the entire colon. Eventually, the bowel narrows, shortens, and thickens because of muscular hypertrophy and fat deposits.

Clinical Manifestations and Assessment

The clinical course is usually one of intermittent exacerbations and remissions. The predominant symptoms of ulcerative colitis include diarrhea, lower left quadrant abdominal pain, intermittent tenesmus, and rectal bleeding. The bleeding may be mild or severe, and pallor, anemia, and fatigue result. The patient may have anorexia, weight loss, fever, vomiting, and dehydration, as well as cramping, the feeling of an urgent need to defecate, and the passage of 10 to 20 liquid stools each day. The disease is classified as mild, severe, or fulminant, depending on the severity of the symptoms. Hypocalcemia and anemia frequently develop. Rebound tenderness may occur in the right lower quadrant. Extraintestinal manifestations include skin lesions (e.g., erythema nodosum), eye lesions (e.g., uveitis), joint abnormalities (e.g., arthritis), and liver disease.

The patient should be assessed for tachycardia, hypotension, tachypnea, fever, and pallor. Other assessments address level of hydration and nutritional status. The abdomen is examined for bowel sounds, distention, and tenderness. These findings assist in determining the severity of the disease.

The stool can be positive for blood, and laboratory test results reveal low hematocrit and hemoglobin levels in addition to an elevated WBC count, low albumin levels, and an electrolyte imbalance. Abdominal X-ray studies are useful for determining the cause of symptoms. Free air in the peritoneum and bowel dilation or obstruction should be excluded as a source of the presenting symptoms, as peritonitis can also occur.

Sigmoidoscopy or colonoscopy and barium enema are valuable in distinguishing this condition from other diseases of the colon with similar symptoms. A barium enema may show mucosal irregularities, focal strictures or fistulas, shortening of the colon, and dilation of bowel loops. Colonoscopy may reveal friable, inflamed mucosa with exudate and ulcerations. This procedure assists in defining the extent and severity of the disease. CT scanning, magnetic resonance imaging (MRI), and ultrasound studies can identify abscesses and perirectal involvement. Leukocyte scanning, in which samples of the patient's own WBCs are isolated, labeled with a radiopharmaceutical agent, and reinjected, is used for localization of acute abscess formation, and is useful when severe colitis prohibits the use of colonoscopy

to determine the extent of inflammation (Fischbach & Dunning, 2009).

Careful stool examination for parasites and other microbes is performed to rule out dysentery caused by common intestinal organisms, especially *Entamoeba histolytica* and *Clostridium difficile*.

Complications

Complications of ulcerative colitis include toxic megacolon, perforation, and bleeding as a result of ulceration, vascular engorgement, and highly vascular granulation tissue. In toxic megacolon, the inflammatory process extends into the muscularis, inhibiting its ability to contract and resulting in colonic distention. Symptoms include fever, abdominal pain and distention, vomiting, and fatigue. If the patient with toxic megacolon does not respond within 24 to 72 hours to medical management with nasogastric suction, IV fluids with electrolytes, corticosteroids, and antibiotics, then surgery is required. Total colectomy is then indicated. For many patients, surgery becomes necessary to relieve the effects of the disease and to treat these serious complications; an ileostomy usually is performed. The surgical procedures involved and the care of patients with this type of fecal diversion are discussed later in this chapter.

Patients with IBD also have a significantly increased risk of osteoporotic fractures due to decreased bone mineral density. Corticosteroid therapy may also contribute to the diminished bone density.

MEDICAL AND NURSING MANAGEMENT OF INFLAMMATORY BOWEL DISEASE

Medical treatment for regional enteritis and ulcerative colitis is aimed at reducing inflammation, suppressing inappropriate immune responses, providing rest for a diseased bowel so that healing may take place, improving quality of life (Box 24-1), and preventing or minimizing complications. Most patients have long periods of well-being interspersed with short intervals of illness, and management depends on the disease location, severity, and complications.

Oral fluids and a low-residue, high-protein, high-calorie diet with supplemental vitamin therapy and iron replacement are prescribed to meet nutritional needs, reduce inflammation, and control pain and diarrhea. Fluid and electrolyte imbalances from dehydration caused by diarrhea are corrected by IV therapy as necessary if the patient is hospitalized or by oral fluids if the patient is managed at home. Any foods that exacerbate diarrhea are avoided. Milk may contribute to diarrhea in those with lactose intolerance. Cold foods and smoking are avoided because both increase intestinal motility. Parenteral nutrition may be indicated (see Chapter 22).

Sedatives and antidiarrheal and antiperistaltic medications are used to minimize peristalsis to rest the inflamed

---

BOX 24-1 | **Nursing Research**

Bridging the Gap to Evidence-Based Practice

Factors Influencing Patient's Quality of Life Living With Crohn's Disease

What does the evidence suggest can be done to improve the therapeutic relationship between the nurse and the individual living with Crohn's Disease?

Pihl-Lesnovska, K., Hjortswang, H., Ek, A. C., & Frisman, G. H. (2010). Patients' perspective of factors influencing quality of life while living with Crohn's disease. *Gastroenterology Nursing, 33*(1), 37–44.

Purpose

Crohn's disease is a chronic inflammatory illness that produces a variety of physical, emotional, and social stressors. Identification of the definition of quality of life in relation specifically to this patient population is limited in the research. The goal of the study was to identify issues and provide support to patients, so that they can maintain a daily life that they perceive as normal.

Design

A qualitative cross-sectional study utilizing grounded theory and symbolic interactionism was used. Patients were identified at an outpatient gastroenterology clinic at a university hospital. A total of 11 patients (six men and five women) fit criteria and agreed to be interviewed.

Analysis of the interviews identified five categories. These categories were: self-image, confirmatory relations, powerlessness, attitude toward life, and sense of well-being. All participants described limitations and symptoms as barriers to their quality of life. Individuals tended to hold themselves to high expectations; however, many described feelings of "failure" due the inability to engage in activities with others of the same age. The need for not letting others down was a prevalent theme by the participants.

Nursing Implications

This was a small study of patients afflicted with Crohn's disease. While one must not generalize treatment based only on a study with a limited sample size such as this one, the main themes identified provide valuable resources to the bedside nurse. Reduction of limitations and improvement of self-esteem were perceived goals by all participants. Identifying the specific needs of each patient, developing an effective communication process, and offering the right kind of support by letting patients participate in their health care decisions may help patients achieve a greater sense of control over their situation.

bowel. They are continued until the patient's stools approach normal frequency and consistency.

Aminosalicylate formulations such as sulfasalazine (Azulfidine) are often effective for mild or moderate inflammation and are used to prevent or reduce recurrences in long-term maintenance regimens. Sulfa-free aminosalicylates (e.g., mesalamine [Asacol, Pentasa]) are effective in preventing and treating recurrence of inflammation. Antibiotics (e.g., metronidazole [Flagyl]) are used for secondary infections, particularly for purulent complications such as abscesses, perforation, and peritonitis.

Corticosteroids are used to treat severe and fulminant disease and can be administered orally (e.g., prednisone [Deltasone]) in outpatient treatment or parenterally (e.g., hydrocortisone [Solu-Cortef]) in hospitalized patients. Topical (i.e., rectal administration) corticosteroids (e.g., hydrocortisone enema, budesonide [Entocort]) are also widely used in the treatment of distal colon disease. When the dosage of corticosteroids is reduced or stopped, the symptoms of disease may return. If corticosteroids are continued, adverse sequelae such as hypertension, fluid retention, cataracts, hirsutism (i.e., abnormal hair growth), adrenal suppression, steroid-induced diabetes mellitus (secondary to the hyperglycemia associated with glucocorticoid therapy), poor wound healing, and loss of bone density may occur.

Immunomodulators (e.g., azathioprine [AZA], 6- mercaptopurine [6-MP], methotrexate, and cyclosporine) have been used to alter the immune response. The exact mechanism of action of these medications in treating IBD is unknown. They are used for patients with severe disease who have not responded favorably to other therapies. These medications are useful in maintenance regimens to prevent relapses. Newer biologic therapies using monoclonal antibodies are being studied, including natalizumab (Tysabri) for treating Crohn's disease (Edula & Picco, 2009) and infliximab (Remicade) for treating ulcerative colitis (Sandborn, Rutgeerts, & Feagan, 2009). Initial reports from clinical trials appear promising for both these agents (Sandborn et al., 2009; Edula & Picco, 2009), although the use of natalizumab is currently limited to patients who have not tolerated or failed treatment with other biological agents (Edula & Picco, 2009).

When nonsurgical measures fail to relieve the severe symptoms of IBD, surgery may be necessary. Approximately 30% of all patients with regional enteritis require surgery. Fortunately, this number has been steadily decreasing with the increased use of infliximab therapy (Sandborn et al., 2009). The most common indications for surgery are medically intractable disease, poor quality of life, or complications from the disease or its treatment. Recurrence of inflammation and disease after surgery in regional enteritis is inevitable. Sandborn et al. (2009) found that patients with moderate to severe ulcerative colitis who were treated with infliximab therapy were less likely to have colectomy at 1 year.

A common procedure performed for strictures of the small intestines is laparoscope-guided strictureplasty, in which the blocked or narrowed sections of the intestines are widened, leaving the intestines intact. In some cases, a small bowel resection is performed: diseased segments of the small intestines are resected, and the remaining portions of the intestines are anastomosed. Surgical removal of up to 50% of the small bowel usually can be tolerated. In cases of severe regional enteritis of the colon, a total colectomy and ileostomy may be the procedure of choice.

A newer surgical procedure developed for patients with severe regional enteritis is intestinal transplant. This technique is now available to children and to young and middle-aged adults who have lost intestinal function from disease. Although this procedure is not a cure, it may eventually provide improvement in quality of life for some patients. The associated technical and immunologic problems remain formidable, and the costs and mortality rates remain high.

At least 25% of patients with ulcerative colitis eventually have total colectomies (NIH, 2009). When the colon is surgically removed, the patient is considered "cured," in that extraintestinal manifestations subside and the disease process is otherwise limited to the colon. Indications for surgery include lack of improvement and continued deterioration, profuse bleeding, perforation, continued stricture formation, and cancer. Surgical excision usually improves quality of life. Proctocolectomy with ileostomy (i.e., complete excision of colon, rectum, and anus) is recommended when the rectum is severely diseased. If the rectum can be preserved, restorative proctocolectomy with ileal pouch anal anastomosis (IPAA) is the procedure of choice.

ILEOSTOMY

Procedures

An **ileostomy**, the surgical creation of an opening into the ileum or small intestine (usually by means of an ileal stoma on the abdominal wall), is commonly performed after a total colectomy (i.e., excision of the entire colon). It allows for drainage of fecal matter (i.e., effluent) from the ileum to the outside of the body. The drainage is typically loose to semi-formed and may occur at frequent intervals.

Another procedure involves the creation of a continent ileal reservoir (i.e., **Kock pouch**) by diverting a portion of the distal ileum to the abdominal wall and creating a stoma. This procedure eliminates the need for an external fecal collection bag. Approximately 30 cm of the distal ileum is reconstructed to form a reservoir with a nipple valve that is created by pulling a portion of the terminal ileal loop back into the ileum. GI effluent can accumulate in the pouch for several hours and then be removed by means of a catheter inserted through the nipple valve. In many patients, a total colectomy is also performed with the Kock pouch. Possible indications for a total colectomy with Kock pouch placement (rather than a restorative proctocolectomy with IPAA) include a badly diseased rectum, lack of rectal sphincter tone, or inability to achieve fecal continence post-IPAA.

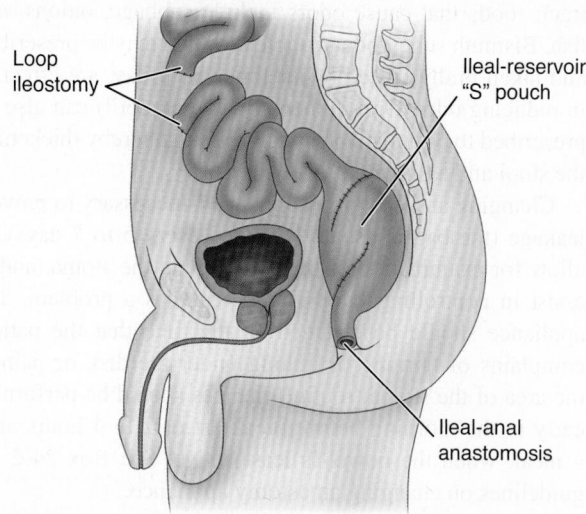

Loop
ileostomy

Ileal-reservoir
"S" pouch

Ileal-anal
anastomosis

FIGURE 24-5 A mucosal proctectomy precedes anastomosis of the ileal reservoir. A temporary loop ileostomy diverts effluent for several months to allow healing.

The major problem with the Kock pouch is malfunction of the nipple valve. Surgical research is currently focused on developing valves that may slip less frequently than the nipple valve.

A restorative proctocolectomy with IPAA is the surgical procedure of choice in cases in which the rectum can be preserved, in that it eliminates the need for a permanent ileostomy. It establishes an ileal reservoir, and anal sphincter control of elimination is retained. The procedure involves connecting a portion of the ileum to the anus (i.e., ileoanal anastomosis) in conjunction with removal of the colon and the rectal mucosa (i.e., total abdominal colectomy and mucosal proctectomy) (Fig. 24-5). A temporary diverting loop ileostomy is constructed at the time of surgery and closed about 3 months later.

With ileoanal anastomosis, the diseased colon and rectum are removed, voluntary defecation is maintained, and anal continence is preserved. The ileal reservoir decreases the number of bowel movements by 50%, from approximately 14 to 20 per day to 7 to 10 per day. Nighttime elimination is gradually reduced to one bowel movement. Complications of ileoanal anastomosis include irritation of the perianal skin from leakage of fecal contents, stricture formation at the anastomosis site, and small bowel obstruction.

Nursing management of patients with IBD may be medical, surgical, or both. Patients in the community setting or those recently diagnosed may require education about diet and medications, and referral to support groups. Hospitalized patients with longstanding or severe disease also require careful monitoring, parenteral nutrition, fluid replacement, and possibly emergent surgery. The surgical procedures may involve a fecal diversion, with attendant needs for physical care, emotional support, and extensive teaching about management of the ostomy.

Nursing Management

Some patients with IBD eventually require a permanent fecal diversion, with creation of an ileostomy to manage symptoms and to treat or prevent complications. Ileostomy education can be started while the patient is still in the hospital, and with a small amount of planning and care the patient lives a very normal life. A plan of nursing care for a patient undergoing ostomy surgery is available online at http://thePoint.lww.com/Pellico1e.

Providing Preoperative Care

A period of preparation with intensive replacement of fluid, blood, and protein is necessary before surgery is performed. Antibiotics may be prescribed. If the patient has been taking corticosteroids, they will be continued during the surgical phase to prevent steroid-induced adrenal insufficiency. Usually, the patient is given a low-residue diet, provided in frequent, small feedings. All other preoperative measures are similar to those for general abdominal surgery. The abdomen is marked for the proper placement of the stoma by the surgeon or the enterostomal therapist. Care is taken to ensure that the stoma is conveniently placed—usually in the right lower quadrant about 2 inches below the waist, in an area away from previous scars, bony prominences, skin folds, or fistulas.

The patient must have a thorough understanding of the surgery to be performed and what to expect after surgery. Information about an ileostomy is presented to the patient by means of written materials, models, and discussion. Preoperative teaching includes management of drainage from the stoma, the nature of drainage, and the need for nasogastric intubation, parenteral fluids, and possibly perineal packing.

Providing Postoperative Care

General abdominal surgery wound care is required. The nurse observes the stoma for color and size. It should be pink to bright red and shiny. Typically, a temporary plastic bag with an adhesive facing is placed over the ileostomy in the operating room and firmly pressed onto the surrounding skin. The nurse monitors the ileostomy for fecal drainage, which should begin about 72 hours after surgery. The drainage is a continuous liquid from the small intestine because the stoma does not have a controlling sphincter. The contents drain into the plastic bag and are thus kept from coming into contact with the skin. They are collected and measured when the bag becomes full. If a continent ileal reservoir was created, as described for the Kock pouch, continuous drainage is provided by an indwelling reservoir catheter for 2 to 3 weeks after surgery. This allows the suture lines to heal.

As with other patients undergoing abdominal surgery, the nurse encourages those with an ileostomy to engage in early ambulation. It is important to administer prescribed pain medications as required.

Because these patients lose much fluid in the early postoperative period, an accurate record of fluid intake, urinary output, and fecal discharge is necessary to help gauge the

fluid needs of the patient. There may be up to 1L of fluid lost each day, in addition to expected fluid loss through urine, perspiration, respiration, and other sources. With this loss, sodium and potassium are depleted. The nurse monitors laboratory values and administers electrolyte replacements as prescribed. Fluids are administered IV for 4 to 5 days to replace lost fluids.

Nasogastric suction is also a part of immediate postoperative care, with the tube requiring frequent irrigation, as prescribed. The purpose of nasogastric suction is to prevent a buildup of gastric contents. After the tube is removed, the nurse offers sips of clear liquids and gradually progresses the diet. It is important to immediately report nausea and abdominal distention, which may indicate intestinal obstruction.

By the end of the first week, rectal packing is removed. Because this procedure may be uncomfortable, the nurse may administer an analgesic an hour before its removal. After the packing is removed, the perineum is irrigated two or three times daily until full healing takes place.

The patient with a traditional ileostomy cannot establish regular bowel habits because the contents of the ileum are fluid and are discharged continuously. The patient must wear a pouch at all times. Stomal size and pouch size vary initially; the stoma should be rechecked 3 weeks after surgery, when the edema has subsided. The final size and type of appliance is selected in 3 months, after the patient's weight has stabilized and the stoma shrinks to a stable shape.

The location and length of the stoma are significant in the management of the ileostomy by the patient. The surgeon positions the stoma as close to the midline as possible and at a location where even an obese patient with a protruding abdomen can care for it easily. Usually, the ileostomy stoma is about 2.5 cm (1 in) long, which makes it convenient for the attachment of an appliance.

Skin excoriation around the stoma can be a persistent problem. Peristomal skin integrity may be compromised by several factors, such as an allergic reaction to the ostomy appliance, skin barrier, or paste; chemical irritation from the effluent; mechanical injury from the removal of the appliance; and infection. If irritation and yeast growth occur, nystatin powder (Mycostatin) is dusted lightly on the peristomal skin.

Changing an Appliance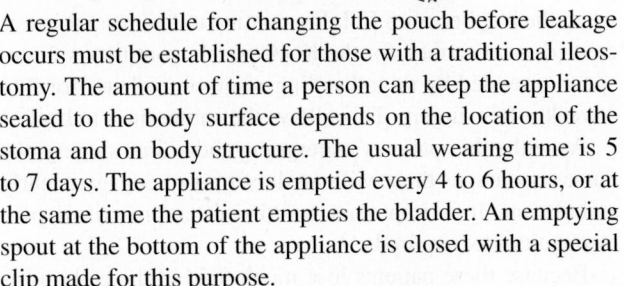

A regular schedule for changing the pouch before leakage occurs must be established for those with a traditional ileostomy. The amount of time a person can keep the appliance sealed to the body surface depends on the location of the stoma and on body structure. The usual wearing time is 5 to 7 days. The appliance is emptied every 4 to 6 hours, or at the same time the patient empties the bladder. An emptying spout at the bottom of the appliance is closed with a special clip made for this purpose.

Most pouches are disposable and odor-proof. Foods such as spinach and parsley act as deodorizers in the intestinal tract; foods that cause odors include cabbage, onions, and fish. Bismuth subcarbonate tablets, which may be prescribed and taken orally three or four times each day, are effective in reducing odor. Oral diphenoxylate (Lomotil) can also be prescribed to diminish intestinal motility, thereby thickening the stool and assisting in odor control.

Changing an ileostomy appliance is necessary to prevent leakage (the bag is usually changed every 5 to 7 days), to allow for examination of the skin around the stoma, and to assist in controlling odor if this becomes a problem. The appliance should be changed at any time that the patient complains of burning or itching under the disk or pain in the area of the stoma; routine changes should be performed early in the morning before breakfast or 2 to 4 hours after a meal, when the bowel is least active. See Box 24-2 for guidelines on changing an ostomy appliance.

Managing Dietary and Fluid Needs

A low-residue diet is followed for the first 6 to 8 weeks. Strained fruits and vegetables are given. These foods are important sources of vitamins A and C. Later, there are few dietary restrictions, except for avoiding foods that are high in fiber or hard-to-digest kernels, such as celery, popcorn, corn, poppy seeds, caraway seeds, and coconut. Foods are reintroduced one at a time. The nurse assesses the patient's tolerance for these foods and reminds him or her to chew food thoroughly.

Fluids may be a problem during the summer, when fluid lost through perspiration adds to the fluid loss through the ileostomy. Fluids such as Gatorade are helpful in maintaining electrolyte balance.

Preventing Complications

Monitoring for complications is an ongoing activity for the patient with an ileostomy. Peristomal skin irritation, which results from leakage of effluent, is the most common complication of an ileostomy. A drainable pouching system that does not fit well is often the cause. Components of the drainable pouching system include the pouch, a solid skin barrier, and adhesive. The enterostomal therapist typically recommends the appropriate drainable pouching system. The solid skin barrier is the component of this system that is most important in ensuring healthy peristomal skin. Solid skin barriers are typically shaped as rectangular or elliptical wafers and are composed of polymers and hydrocolloids. They protect the skin around the stoma from effluent from the stoma and provide a stable interface between the stoma and the pouch.

Other common complications include fluid volume deficit, stomal stenosis, urinary calculi, and cholelithiasis. Even in the presence of a properly fitted drainable pouching system, loose watery effluent can be problematic, often filling the pouch (every hour or sooner), which can quickly lead to dehydration and electrolyte losses. Supplemental

BOX 24-2

GUIDELINES FOR NURSING CARE

Changing an Ileostomy Appliance

Equipment Needed

- Mild soap
- Clean cloths or towels
- Skin barrier (stoma adhesive, Convatec)
- Cutting guide
- Appliance pouch

Optional Equipment
- Barrier powder
- Antifungal spray or powder
- Barrier washer

Implementation

NURSING ACTION	RATIONALE

1. Promote patient comfort and involvement in the procedure.
  a. Have the patient assume a relaxed position.
  b. Provide privacy.
  c. Explain details of the procedure.
  d. Expose the ileostomy area; remove the ileostomy belt (if worn)
	1. Providing a relaxed atmosphere and adequate explanations help the patient to become an active participant in the procedure.

2. Remove the appliance.
  a. Have the patient sit on the toilet or on a chair facing the toilet. A patient who prefers to stand should face the toilet.
  b. The appliance (pouch) can be removed by gently pushing the skin away from the adhesive.
	2. These positions facilitate disposal or drainage.

3. Cleanse the skin:
  a. Wash the skin gently with a soft cloth moistened with tepid water and mild soap; the patient may prefer to bathe before putting on a clean appliance.
  b. Rinse the soap and dry the skin thoroughly after cleansing.
	3. The patient may shower with or without the pouch.
	  a. Micropore or waterproof tape applied to the sides of the faceplate keeps it secure during bathing.
	  b. Moisture or soap residue interferes with appliance adhesion.

Pouching options

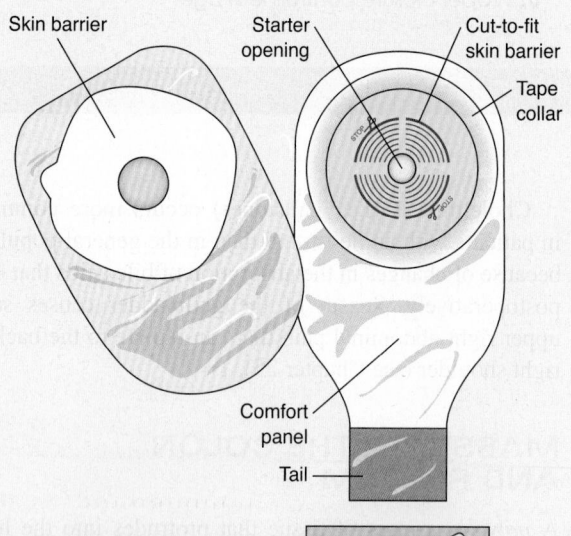

One-piece systems

In a one-piece system, the pouch and skin barrier are a single unit.

Tail clip

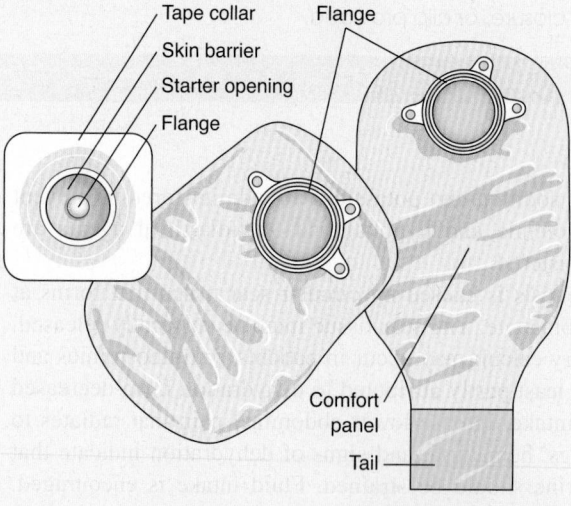

Two-piece systems

In a two-piece system, the pouch attaches to a skin barrier with flange.

Tail clip

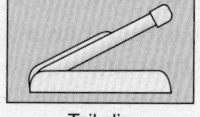

(continued on page 674)

BOX 24-2

GUIDELINES FOR NURSING CARE (continued)

NURSING ACTION	RATIONALE
4. Apply appliance: When there is no skin irritation: **a.** An appropriate skin barrier is applied to the peristomal skin before the appliance is applied. **b.** Remove cover from adherent surface of disk of disposable plastic appliance and apply directly to the skin. **c.** Press firmly in place for 30 seconds to ensure adherence. When there is skin irritation: **a.** Cleanse the skin thoroughly but gently; pat dry. Apply barrier powder. **b.** If more irritation developed, apply Kenalog spray; blot excess moisture with a cotton pledget and dust lightly with nystatin (Mycostatin) powder. OR Place the sizing guide directly on the skin around the stoma, leaving as little skin as possible around the stoma uncovered. Then, using the guide, cut the appropriate hole in the disk. At times, the stoma site is irregular; if this is the case, the hole should be cut approximating the stoma site as closely as possible. Apply as an alternative a wafer or barrier (Stomahesive, ConvaTec), which is commercially available. The stomal opening should be the same size as the stoma; use a cutting guide (supplied with appliance as indicated). The wafer is applied directly to the skin. Barrier powder can be used to dry irritated skin before barrier application. **c.** Another alternative is to apply a special barrier washer (eg, Eakin's Seal). The special barrier adheres well to irritated skin. **d.** The pouch is then applied to the treated skin. 5. Check the pouch bottom for closure; use clamp, Velcro closure, or clip provided.	4. Many appliances have a built-in skin barrier. The skin should be thoroughly dried before applying the appliance. **a.** Cleansing removes debris and protects irritated skin under wafer **b.** The corticosteroid preparation (Kenalog) helps decrease inflammation. The antifungal agent (nystatin) treats those types of infections that are common around stomas. A prescription is required for either medication. A skin barrier is a substance that facilitates healing of excoriated skin. It adheres well even to moist, irritated skin. **c.** A special barrier protects skin from effluent, promotes healing and helps with adherence. **d.** This allows skin to heal while the appliance is in place. 5. Proper closure controls leakage.

water, sodium, and potassium are administered to prevent hypovolemia and hypokalemia. Antidiarrheal agents are administered.

Stenosis is caused by circular scar tissue that forms at the stoma site. The scar tissue must be surgically released. Urinary calculi may occur in patients with ileostomies and are at least partly attributed to dehydration from decreased fluid intake. Intense lower abdominal pain that radiates to the legs, hematuria, and signs of dehydration indicate that the urine should be strained. Fluid intake is encouraged. Sometimes, small stones are passed during urination; otherwise, treatment is necessary to crush or remove the calculi (see Chapter 28).

Cholelithiasis (i.e., gallstones) occurs more commonly in patients with an ileostomy than in the general population because of changes in the absorption of bile acids that occur postoperatively. Spasm of the gallbladder causes severe upper right abdominal pain that can radiate to the back and right shoulder (see Chapter 25).

MASSES IN THE COLON AND RECTUM

A *polyp* is a mass of tissue that protrudes into the lumen of the bowel. Polyps can occur anywhere in the intestinal tract and rectum. They can be classified as neoplastic (i.e.,

adenomas and carcinomas) or non-neoplastic (i.e., mucosal and hyperplastic).

NON-NEOPLASTIC POLYPS

Although most polyps do not develop into invasive neoplasms, they must be identified and followed closely.

Risk Factors

Non-neoplastic polyps, which are benign epithelial growths, are common in the Western world. They occur more commonly in the large intestine than in the small intestine. Adenomatous (benign) polyps are more common in men. The proportion of these polyps arising in the proximal part of the colon increases with age (after 50 years of age). Prevalence rates vary from 25% to 60%, depending on age. Non-neoplastic polyps occur in 80% of the population, and their frequency increases with age.

Clinical Manifestations and Assessment

Clinical manifestations depend on the size of the polyp and the amount of pressure it exerts on intestinal tissue. The most common symptom is rectal bleeding. Lower abdominal pain may also occur. If the polyp is large enough, symptoms of obstruction occur. The diagnosis is based on history and digital rectal examination, barium enema studies, sigmoidoscopy, or colonoscopy.

Medical and Nursing Management

After a polyp is identified, it should be removed. There are several methods: colonoscopy with the use of special equipment (i.e., biopsy forceps and snares), laparoscopy, or colonoscopic excision with laparoscopic visualization. The latter technique enables immediate detection of potential problems and allows laparoscopic resection and repair of the major complications of perforation and bleeding that may occur with polypectomy. Microscopic examination of the polyp then identifies the type of polyp and indicates what further surgery is required, if any.

COLORECTAL CANCER

Tumors of the colon and rectum are relatively common; the colorectal area (the colon and rectum combined) is now the third most common site of new cancer cases and deaths in the United States. Colorectal cancer is the second most common cause of cancer death among men ages 40 to 79 years (Jemal, Siegel, Xu et al., 2010). Improved screening strategies have helped reduce the number of deaths from colon cancer in recent years. Of the approximately 150,000 people

diagnosed each year, fewer than half that number dies annually (American Cancer Society [ACS], 2010).

Early diagnosis and prompt treatment could save almost three of every four people. If the disease is detected and treated at an early stage, the 5-year survival rate is 90%; however, only 34% of colorectal cancers are detected at an early stage (ACS, 2010). Survival rates after late diagnosis are very low. Most people are asymptomatic for long periods and seek health care only when they notice a change in bowel habits or rectal bleeding. Prevention and early screening are the keys to detection and reduction of mortality rates.

Pathophysiology

Cancer of the colon and rectum is predominantly (95%) adenocarcinoma (i.e., arising from the epithelial lining of the intestine) (ACS, 2010). It may start as a benign polyp but may become malignant, invade and destroy normal tissues, and extend into surrounding structures. Cancer cells may migrate away from the primary tumor and spread to other parts of the body (most often to the liver).

Risk Factors

Colorectal cancer is a disease of Western cultures. The incidence increases with age (the incidence is highest in people >85 years) and is higher in people with a family history of colon cancer and those with IBD or polyps. In men, only the incidence of prostate cancer and lung cancer exceeds that of colorectal cancer. In women, only the incidence of breast and lung cancer exceeds that of colorectal cancer.

Colon cancer in the elderly has been closely associated with dietary carcinogens. Lack of fiber is a major causative factor because the passage of feces through the intestinal tract is prolonged, which extends exposure to possible carcinogens. Excess dietary fat, high alcohol consumption, and smoking all increase the incidence of colorectal tumors. Physical activity and dietary folate have protective effects (Jemal et al., 2010).

Clinical Manifestations and Assessment

Symptoms are often insidious. Patients with colorectal cancer usually report fatigue, which is caused primarily by iron-deficiency anemia. In early stages, minor changes in bowel patterns and occasional bleeding may occur. The later symptoms most commonly reported by the elderly are abdominal pain, obstruction, tenesmus, and rectal bleeding.

The symptoms are greatly determined by the location of the cancer, the stage of the disease, and the function of the intestinal segment in which it is located. The most common presenting symptom is a change in bowel habits. The passage of blood in the stools is the second most common symptom. Symptoms may also include unexplained anemia, anorexia, weight loss, and fatigue.

The symptoms most commonly associated with right-sided lesions are dull abdominal pain and melena (black, tarry stools). The symptoms most commonly associated with left-sided lesions are those associated with obstruction (abdominal pain and cramping, narrowing stools, constipation, distention), as well as bright red blood in the stool. Symptoms associated with rectal lesions are tenesmus (ineffective, painful straining at stool), rectal pain, the feeling of incomplete evacuation after a bowel movement, alternating constipation and diarrhea, and bloody stool.

Along with an abdominal and rectal examination, the most important diagnostic procedures for cancer of the colon are fecal occult blood testing, barium enema, proctosigmoidoscopy, and colonoscopy (see Chapter 21). The majority of colorectal cancer cases can be identified by colonoscopy with biopsy or cytology smears.

Carcinoembryonic antigen (CEA) studies may also be performed. Although CEA may not be a highly reliable indicator in diagnosing colon cancer because not all lesions secrete CEA, studies show that CEA levels are reliable prognostic predictors. With complete excision of the tumor, the elevated levels of CEA should return to normal within 48 hours. Elevations of CEA at a later date suggest recurrence.

Medical and Nursing Management

The patient with symptoms of intestinal obstruction is treated with IV fluids and nasogastric suction. If there has been significant bleeding, blood component therapy may be required.

Treatment for colorectal cancer depends on the stage of the disease and consists of surgery to remove the tumor, supportive therapy, and adjuvant therapy. Patients who receive some form of adjuvant therapy, which may include chemotherapy, radiation therapy, immunotherapy, or multimodality therapy, typically demonstrate delays in tumor recurrence and increases in survival time.

Radiation therapy is used before, during, and after surgery to shrink the tumor, to achieve better results from surgery, and to reduce the risk of recurrence. For inoperative or unresectable tumors, radiation is used to provide significant relief from symptoms. Intracavitary and implantable devices are used to deliver radiation to the site. The response to adjuvant therapy varies.

Surgery is the primary treatment for most colon and rectal cancers. It may be curative or palliative. Advances in surgical techniques can enable the patient with cancer to have sphincter-saving devices that restore continuity of the GI tract. The type of surgery recommended depends on the location and size of the tumor. Cancers limited to one site can be removed through the colonoscope. Laparoscopic colotomy with polypectomy minimizes the extent of surgery needed in some cases. A laparoscope is used as a guide in making an incision into the colon; the tumor mass is then excised. Use of the neodymium/yttrium-aluminum-garnet (Nd:YAG) laser has proved effective with some lesions as well.

Surgical procedures include the following:

- Segmental resection with anastomosis (i.e., removal of the tumor and portions of the bowel on either side of the growth, as well as the blood vessels and lymphatic nodes) (Fig. 24-6)
- Abdominoperineal resection with permanent sigmoid colostomy (i.e., removal of the tumor and a portion of the sigmoid and all of the rectum and anal sphincter) (Fig. 24-7)
- Temporary colostomy followed by segmental resection and anastomosis and subsequent reanastomosis of the colostomy, allowing initial bowel decompression and bowel preparation before resection
- Permanent colostomy or ileostomy for palliation of unresectable obstructing lesions
- Construction of a coloanal reservoir called a *colonic J pouch*, which is performed in two steps. A temporary loop ileostomy is constructed to divert intestinal flow, and the

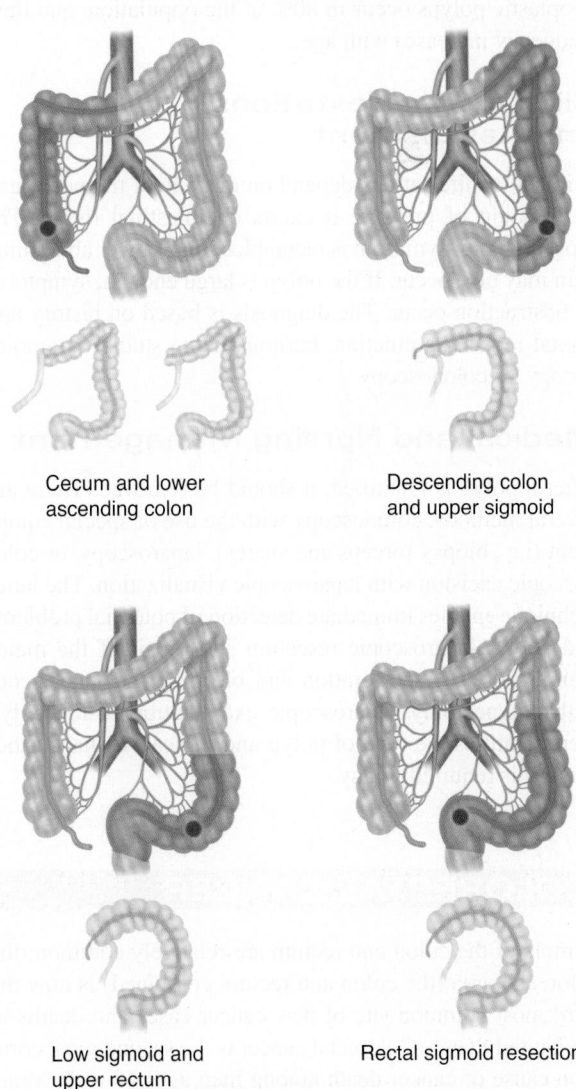

Cecum and lower
ascending colon

Descending colon
and upper sigmoid

Low sigmoid and
upper rectum

Rectal sigmoid resection

FIGURE 24-6 Examples of areas where cancer can occur, the area that is removed, and how the anastomosis is performed (*small diagrams*).

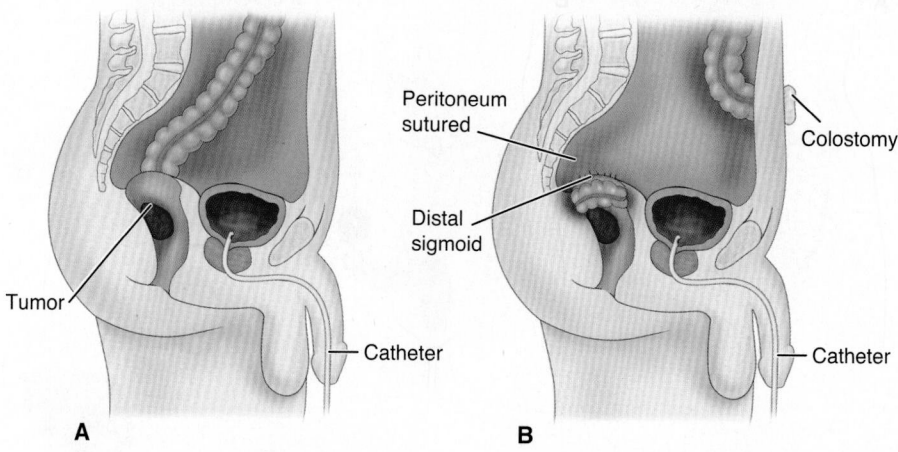

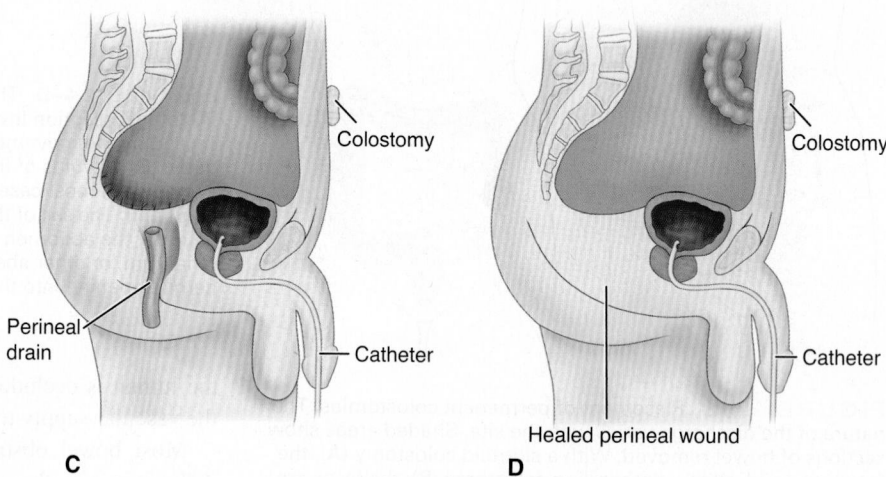

FIGURE 24-7 Abdominoperineal resection for carcinoma of the rectum. (**A**) Prior to surgery. Note tumor in rectum. (**B**) During surgery, the sigmoid is removed and the colostomy is established. The distal bowel is dissected free to a point below the pelvic peritoneum, which is sutured over the closed end of the distal sigmoid and rectum. (**C**) Perineal resection includes removal of the rectum and free portion of the sigmoid from below. A perineal drain is inserted. (**D**) The final result after healing. Note the healed perineal wound and the permanent colostomy.

newly constructed J pouch (made from 6 to 10 cm of colon) is reattached to the anal stump. About 3 months after the initial stage, the ileostomy is reversed and intestinal continuity is restored. The anal sphincter and therefore continence are preserved.

A colostomy is the surgical creation of an opening (i.e., stoma) into the colon. It can be created as a temporary or permanent fecal diversion. It allows the drainage or evacuation of colon contents to the outside of the body. The consistency of the drainage is related to the placement of the colostomy, which is dictated by the location of the tumor and the extent of invasion into surrounding tissues (Fig. 24-8). With improved surgical techniques, colostomies are performed in less than one-third of patients with colorectal cancer.

Complications

Tumor growth may cause partial or complete bowel obstruction. Extension of the tumor and ulceration into the surrounding blood vessels result in hemorrhage. Perforation, abscess formation, peritonitis, sepsis, and shock may occur.

The elderly are at increased risk of complications after surgery and may have difficulty managing colostomy care. Some elderly patients may have decreased vision, impaired hearing, and difficulty with fine motor coordination. It may be helpful for patients to handle ostomy equipment and simulate cleaning the peristomal skin and irrigating the stoma before surgery. Skin care is a major concern in older patients with a colostomy because of the skin changes that occur with aging—the epithelial and subcutaneous fatty layers become thin, and the skin is irritated easily. To prevent skin breakdown, special attention is paid to skin cleansing and the proper fit of an appliance. Arteriosclerosis causes decreased blood flow to the wound and stoma site. As a result, transport of nutrients is delayed, and healing time may be prolonged. Some patients have delayed elimination after irrigation because of decreased peristalsis and mucus production. Most patients require 6 months before they feel comfortable with their ostomy care.

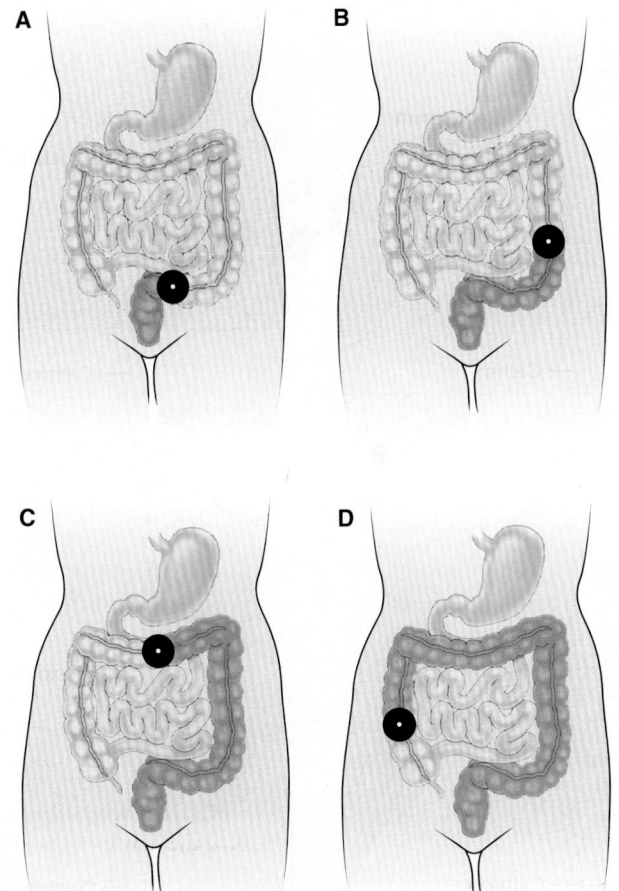

FIGURE 24-8 Placement of permanent colostomies. The nature of the discharge varies with the site. Shaded areas show sections of bowel removed. With a sigmoid colostomy (**A**), the feces are solid. With a descending colostomy (**B**), the feces are semiformed. With a transverse colostomy (**C**), the feces are unformed. With an ascending colostomy (**D**), the feces are fluid.

INTESTINAL OBSTRUCTION

Intestinal obstruction exists when blockage prevents the normal flow of intestinal contents through the intestinal tract. In mechanical obstruction, and intraluminal or mural obstructions secondary to pressure on the intestinal wall occur. Examples are intussusception (telescoping of a portion of the intestine within another immediately adjacent portion of intestine), polypoid tumors and neoplasms, stenosis, strictures, adhesions, hernias, and abscesses. Figure 24-9 depicts additional causes of obstruction. In functional obstruction, intestinal musculature cannot propel the contents along the bowel thereby causing a blockage within the intestine. Examples are amyloidosis, muscular dystrophy, endocrine disorders such as diabetes mellitus, or neurologic disorders such as Parkinson's disease. The blockage also can be temporary and the result of the manipulation of the bowel during surgery.

The obstruction can be partial or complete. Its severity depends on the region of bowel affected, the degree to which

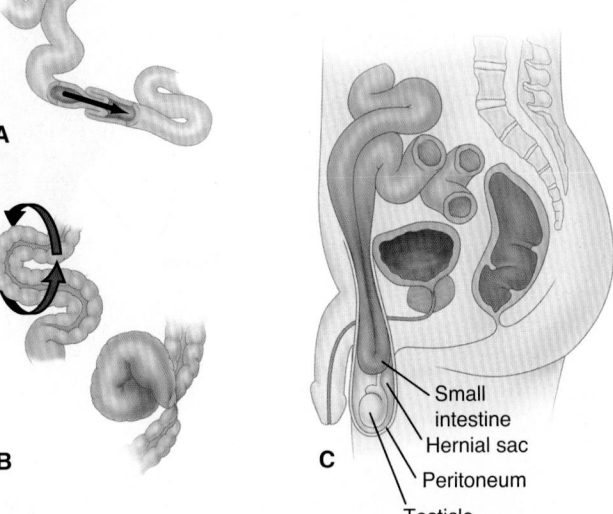

FIGURE 24-9 Three causes of intestinal obstruction. (**A**) Intussusception invagination or shortening of the colon caused by the movement of one segment of bowel into another. (**B**) Volvulus of the sigmoid colon; the twist is counterclockwise in most cases. Note the edematous bowel. (**C**) Hernia (inguinal). The sac of the hernia is a continuation of the peritoneum of the abdomen. The hernial contents are intestine, omentum, or other abdominal contents that pass through the hernial opening into the hernial sac.

the lumen is occluded, and especially the degree to which the vascular supply to the bowel wall is disturbed.

Most bowel obstructions occur in the small intestine. Adhesions are the most common cause of small bowel obstruction, followed by hernias and neoplasms. Other causes include intussusception, **volvulus** (i.e., twisting of the bowel), and paralytic ileus. Most obstructions in the large bowel occur in the sigmoid colon. The most common causes are carcinoma, diverticulitis, inflammatory bowel disorders, and benign tumors. Table 24-5 and Figure 24-9 list mechanical causes of obstruction and describe how they occur.

SMALL BOWEL OBSTRUCTION

Pathophysiology

Intestinal contents, fluid, and gas accumulate above the intestinal obstruction. The abdominal distention and retention of fluid reduce the absorption of fluids and stimulate more gastric secretion. With increasing distention, pressure within the intestinal lumen increases, causing a decrease in venous and arteriolar capillary pressure. This causes edema, congestion, necrosis, and eventual rupture or perforation of the intestinal wall, with resultant peritonitis.

Reflux vomiting may be caused by abdominal distention. Vomiting results in loss of hydrochloric acid (HCl) and

TABLE
24-5 Mechanical Causes of Intestinal Obstruction

Cause	Course of Events	Result
Adhesions	Loops of intestine become adherent to areas that heal slowly or scar after abdominal surgery.	After surgery, adhesions produce a kinking of an intestinal loop.
Intussusception	One part of the intestine slips into another part located below it (like a telescope shortening).	The intestinal lumen becomes narrowed.
Volvulus	Bowel twists and turns on itself.	Intestinal lumen becomes obstructed. Gas and fluid accumulate in the trapped bowel.
Hernia	Protrusion of intestine through a weakened area in the abdominal muscle or wall.	Intestinal flow may be completely obstructed. Blood flow to the area may be obstructed as well.
Tumor	A tumor that exists within the wall of the intestine extends into the intestinal lumen, or a tumor outside the intestine causes pressure on the wall of the intestine.	Intestinal lumen becomes partially obstructed; if the tumor is not removed, complete obstruction results.

potassium from the stomach, leading to reduction of chlorides and potassium in the blood and to metabolic alkalosis. Dehydration develops from loss of water and sodium. With acute fluid losses, hypovolemic shock may occur.

Clinical Manifestations and Assessment

The initial symptom is usually crampy pain that is wavelike and colicky. The patient may pass blood and mucus but no fecal matter and no flatus. Vomiting occurs. If the obstruction is complete, the peristaltic waves initially become extremely vigorous and eventually assume a reverse direction, with the intestinal contents propelled toward the mouth instead of toward the rectum. If the obstruction is in the ileum, fecal vomiting takes place. First, the patient vomits the stomach contents, then the bile-stained contents of the duodenum and the jejunum, and finally, with each paroxysm of pain, the darker, fecal-like contents of the ileum. The signs of dehydration become evident: intense thirst, drowsiness, generalized malaise, aching, and a parched tongue and mucous membranes. The abdomen becomes distended. The lower the obstruction is in the GI tract, the more marked the abdominal distention. If the obstruction continues uncorrected, hypovolemic shock occurs from dehydration and loss of plasma volume.

Diagnosis is based on the symptoms described previously and on imaging studies. Abdominal X-ray and CT findings include abnormal quantities of gas, fluid, or both in the intestines. Laboratory studies (i.e., electrolyte studies and a CBC) reveal a picture of dehydration, loss of plasma volume, and possible infection.

Medical and Nursing Management

Decompression of the bowel through a nasogastric tube (see Chapter 22) is successful in most cases. When the bowel is completely obstructed, the possibility of strangulation warrants surgical intervention. Before surgery, IV therapy is necessary to replace the depleted water, sodium, chloride, and potassium.

The surgical treatment of intestinal obstruction depends largely on the cause of the obstruction. In the most common causes of obstruction, such as hernia and adhesions, the surgical procedure involves repairing the hernia or dividing the adhesion to which the intestine is attached. In some instances, the portion of affected bowel may be removed and an anastomosis performed. The complexity of the surgical procedure for intestinal obstruction depends on the duration of the obstruction and the condition of the intestine.

Nursing management of the nonsurgical patient with a small bowel obstruction includes maintaining the function of the nasogastric tube, assessing and measuring the nasogastric output, assessing for fluid and electrolyte imbalance, monitoring nutritional status, and assessing improvement (e.g., return of normal bowel sounds, decreased abdominal distention, subjective improvement in abdominal pain and tenderness, passage of flatus or stool). The nurse reports discrepancies in intake and output, worsening of pain or abdominal distention, and increased nasogastric output. If the patient's condition does not improve, the nurse prepares him or her for surgery. The exact nature of the surgery depends on the cause of the obstruction. Nursing care of the patient after surgical repair of a small bowel obstruction is similar to that for other abdominal surgeries (see Chapter 23).

LARGE BOWEL OBSTRUCTION

Pathophysiology

As in small bowel obstruction, large bowel obstruction results in an accumulation of intestinal contents, fluid, and gas proximal to the obstruction. Obstruction in the large

bowel can lead to severe distention and perforation unless some gas and fluid can flow back through the ileal valve. Large bowel obstruction, even if complete, may be without catastrophic issue if the blood supply to the colon is not disturbed. However, if the blood supply is cut off, intestinal strangulation and necrosis (i.e., tissue death) occur; this condition is life threatening. In the large intestine, dehydration occurs more slowly than in the small intestine because the colon can absorb its fluid contents and can distend to a size considerably beyond its normal full capacity.

Adenocarcinoid tumors account for the majority of large bowel obstructions. Most tumors occur beyond the splenic flexure, making them accessible with a flexible sigmoidoscope.

Clinical Manifestations and Assessment

Large bowel obstruction differs clinically from small bowel obstruction in that the symptoms develop and progress relatively slowly. In patients with obstruction in the sigmoid colon or the rectum, constipation may be the only symptom for months. The shape of the stool is altered as it passes the obstruction that is gradually increasing in size. Blood in the stool may result in iron deficiency anemia. The patient may experience weakness, weight loss, and anorexia. Eventually, the abdomen becomes markedly distended, loops of large bowel become visibly outlined through the abdominal wall, and the patient has crampy lower abdominal pain. Finally, fecal vomiting develops. Symptoms of shock may occur.

Diagnosis is based on symptoms and on imaging studies. Abdominal X-ray and abdominal CT or MRI findings reveal a distended colon and pinpoint the site of the obstruction. Barium studies are contraindicated because of risk of perforation.

Medical and Nursing Management

Restoration of intravascular volume, correction of electrolyte abnormalities, and nasogastric aspiration and decompres-

sion are instituted immediately. A colonoscopy may be performed to untwist and decompress the bowel. A cecostomy, in which a surgical opening is made into the cecum, may be performed in patients who are poor surgical risks and urgently need relief from the obstruction. The procedure provides an outlet for releasing gas and a small amount of drainage. A rectal tube may be used to decompress an area that is lower in the bowel. However, the usual treatment is surgical resection to remove the obstructing lesion. A temporary or permanent colostomy may be necessary. An ileoanal anastomosis may be performed if it is necessary to remove the entire large bowel.

The nurse's role is to monitor the patient for symptoms that indicate that the intestinal obstruction is worsening and to provide emotional support and comfort. The nurse administers IV fluids and electrolytes as prescribed. If the patient's condition does not respond to nonsurgical treatment, the nurse prepares the patient for surgery. This preparation includes preoperative teaching as the patient's condition indicates. After surgery, general abdominal wound care and routine postoperative nursing care are provided.

DISEASES OF THE ANORECTUM

Diseases of the anorectum include anal fistulas and fissures, hemorrhoids, sexually transmitted anorectal diseases, and pilonidal cysts. Nursing management of these conditions is discussed in Box 24-3.

ANAL FISTULA

An anal fistula is a tiny, tubular, fibrous tract that extends into the anal canal from an opening located beside the anus (Fig. 24-10A). Fistulas usually result from an infection. They may also develop from trauma, fissures, or regional

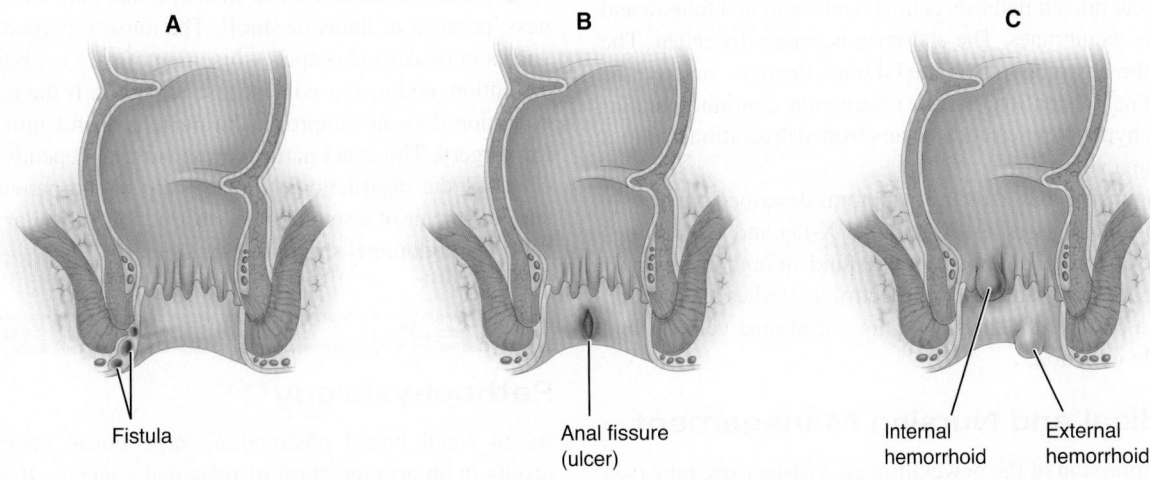

A   B   C

Fistula   Anal fissure   Internal   External
                   (ulcer)   hemorrhoid   hemorrhoid

FIGURE 24-10 Various types of anal lesions. (**A**) Fistula. (**B**) Fissure. (**C**) External and internal hemorrhoids.

BOX 24-3

Nursing Management of Anorectal Disorders

Relieving Constipation

The nurse encourages intake of at least 2 L of water daily to provide adequate hydration and recommends high-fiber foods to promote bulk in the stool and to make it easier to pass fecal matter through the rectum. In patients with preexisting cardiopulmonary or renal disease, consultation with the patient's provider regarding fluid intake should occur. Bulk laxatives such as psyllium (Metamucil) and stool softeners (e.g., docusate (Colace)) are administered as prescribed. The patient is advised to set aside a time for bowel movements and to heed the urge to defecate as promptly as possible. It may be helpful to have the patient perform relaxation exercises before defecating to relax the abdominal and perineal muscles, which may be constricted or in spasm. Administering an analgesic before a bowel movement is beneficial.

Reducing Anxiety

Patients facing rectal surgery may be upset and irritable because of discomfort, pain, and embarrassment. The nurse identifies specific psychosocial needs and individualizes the plan of care. The nurse maintains the patient's privacy while providing care and limits visitors, if the patient desires. Soiled dressings are removed from the room promptly to prevent unpleasant odors; room deodorizers may be needed if dressings are foul smelling.

Relieving Pain

During the first 24 hours after rectal surgery, painful spasms of the sphincter and perineal muscles may occur. Control of pain is a prime consideration. The patient is encouraged to assume a comfortable position. Flotation pads under the buttocks when sitting help decrease the pain, as may ice and analgesic ointments. Warm compresses may promote circulation and soothe irritated tissues. Sitz baths taken three or four times each day can relieve soreness and pain by relaxing sphincter spasm. Twenty-four hours after surgery, topical anesthetic agents may be beneficial in relieving local irritation and soreness. Medications may include topical anesthetics (i.e., suppositories), astringents, antiseptics, tranquilizers, and antiemetics. Patients are more compliant and less apprehensive if they are free of pain.

Wet dressings saturated with equal parts of cold water and witch hazel help relieve edema. When wet compresses are being used continuously, petrolatum is applied around the anal area to prevent skin maceration. The patient is instructed to assume a prone position at intervals because this position reduces edema of the tissue.

Promoting Urinary Elimination

Voiding may be a problem after surgery because of a reflex spasm of the sphincter at the outlet of the bladder and a certain amount of muscle guarding from apprehension and pain. The nurse tries all methods to encourage voluntary voiding (i.e., increasing fluid intake, listening to running water, and pouring warm water over the urinary meatus) before resorting to catheterization. After rectal surgery, urinary output is closely monitored.

Monitoring and Managing Complications

The operative site is examined frequently for rectal bleeding. The nurse assesses the patient for systemic indicators of excessive bleeding (i.e., tachycardia, hypotension, restlessness, and thirst). After hemorrhoidectomy, hemorrhage may occur from the veins that were cut. If a tube has been inserted through the sphincter after surgery, blood may be visible on the dressings. If bleeding is obvious, direct pressure is applied to the area, and the surgeon is notified. It is important to avoid using moist heat because it encourages vessel dilation and bleeding.

Promoting Home and Community-Based Care
Teaching Patients Self-Care

Most patients with anorectal conditions are not hospitalized. Those who undergo surgical procedures to correct the condition often are discharged directly from the outpatient surgical center. If they are hospitalized, it is for a short time, usually only 24 hours.

The nurse instructs the patient to keep the perianal area as clean as possible by gently cleansing with warm water and then drying with absorbent cotton wipes. The patient should avoid rubbing the area with toilet tissue. Instructions are provided about how to take a sitz bath and how to test the temperature of the water.

Continuing Care

Sitz baths may be given in the bathtub or plastic sitz bath unit three or four times each day. Sitz baths should follow each bowel movement for 1 to 2 weeks after surgery. The nurse encourages the patient to respond quickly to the urge to defecate to prevent constipation. The diet is modified to increase fluids and fiber. Moderate exercise is encouraged, and the patient is taught about the prescribed diet, the significance of proper eating habits and exercise, and the laxatives that can be taken safely.

---

enteritis. Pus or stool may leak constantly from the cutaneous opening. Other symptoms may be the passage of flatus or feces from the vagina or bladder, depending on the fistula tract. Untreated fistulas may cause systemic infection with related symptoms.

Surgery is always recommended, because few fistulas heal spontaneously. A fistulectomy (i.e., excision of the fistulous tract) is the recommended surgical procedure. The lower bowel is evacuated thoroughly with several prescribed enemas. The fistula is dissected out or laid open by

an incision from its rectal opening to its outlet. The wound is packed with gauze.

ANAL FISSURE

An anal fissure is a longitudinal tear or ulceration in the lining of the anal canal (see Fig. 24-10B). Fissures are usually caused by the trauma of passing a large, firm stool or from persistent tightening of the anal canal because of stress and anxiety (leading to constipation). Other causes include childbirth, trauma, and overuse of laxatives.

Extremely painful defecation, burning, and bleeding characterize fissures. Bright red blood may be seen on the toilet tissue after a bowel movement.

Most fissures heal if treated by conservative measures, which include dietary modification with addition of fiber supplements, stool softeners and bulk agents, an increase in water intake, sitz baths, and emollient suppositories. A suppository combining an anesthetic with a corticosteroid helps relieve the discomfort. Anal dilation under anesthesia may be required.

If fissures do not respond to conservative treatment, surgery is indicated. Most surgeons consider the procedure of choice to be the lateral internal sphincterotomy with excision of the fissure.

HEMORRHOIDS

Hemorrhoids are dilated portions of veins in the anal canal. They are very common: by 50 years of age, about 50% of people have hemorrhoids (NIH, 2009). Shearing of the mucosa during defecation results in the sliding of the structures in the wall of the anal canal, including the hemorrhoidal and vascular tissues. Increased pressure in the hemorrhoidal tissue due to pregnancy may initiate hemorrhoids or aggravate existing ones. Hemorrhoids are classified as one of two types: those above the internal sphincter are called *internal hemorrhoids*, and those appearing outside the external sphincter are called *external hemorrhoids* (see Fig. 24-10C).

Hemorrhoids cause itching and pain and are the most common cause of bright red bleeding with defecation. External hemorrhoids are associated with severe pain from the inflammation and edema caused by thrombosis (i.e., clotting of blood within the hemorrhoid). This may lead to ischemia of the area and eventual necrosis. Internal hemorrhoids are not usually painful until they bleed or prolapse when they become enlarged.

Hemorrhoid symptoms and discomfort can be relieved by good personal hygiene and by avoiding excessive straining during defecation. A high-residue diet that contains fruit and bran along with an increased fluid intake may be all the treatment necessary to promote the passage of soft, bulky stools to prevent straining. If this treatment is not successful, the

addition of hydrophilic bulk-forming agents such as psyllium (Metamucil) may help. Warm compresses, sitz baths, analgesic ointments and suppositories, astringents (e.g., witch hazel), and bed rest allow the engorgement to subside.

There are several types of nonsurgical treatments for hemorrhoids. Infrared photocoagulation, bipolar diathermy, and laser therapy are used to affix the mucosa to the underlying muscle. Injection of sclerosing agents is also effective for small, bleeding hemorrhoids. These procedures help prevent prolapse.

A conservative surgical treatment of internal hemorrhoids is the rubber-band ligation procedure. The hemorrhoid is visualized through the anoscope, and its proximal portion above the mucocutaneous lines is grasped with an instrument. A small rubber band is then slipped over the hemorrhoid. Tissue distal to the rubber band becomes necrotic after several days and sloughs off. Fibrosis occurs; the result is that the lower anal mucosa is drawn up and adheres to the underlying muscle. Although this treatment has been satisfactory for some patients, it has proven painful for others and may cause secondary hemorrhage. It has also been known to cause perianal infection.

Cryosurgical hemorrhoidectomy, another method for removing hemorrhoids, involves freezing the hemorrhoid for a sufficient time to cause necrosis. Although it is relatively painless, this procedure is not widely used because the discharge is very foul smelling and wound healing is prolonged. The Nd:YAG laser is useful in excising hemorrhoids, particularly external hemorrhoidal tags. The treatment is quick and relatively painless. Hemorrhage and abscess are rare postoperative complications.

The previously described methods of treating hemorrhoids are not effective for advanced thrombosed veins, which must be treated by more extensive surgery. Hemorrhoidectomy, or surgical excision, can be performed to remove all the redundant tissue involved in the process. During surgery, the rectal sphincter is usually dilated digitally and the hemorrhoids are removed with a clamp and cautery or are ligated and then excised. After the surgical procedures are completed, a small tube may be inserted through the sphincter to permit the escape of flatus and blood; pieces of Gelfoam or Oxycel gauze may be placed over the anal wounds.

SEXUALLY TRANSMITTED ANORECTAL DISEASES

Three infectious syndromes that are related to sexually transmitted infections (STIs) have been identified: proctitis, proctocolitis, and enteritis. Proctitis involves the rectum. It is commonly associated with recent anal-receptive intercourse with an infected partner. Symptoms include a mucopurulent discharge or bleeding, pain in the area, and diarrhea. The pathogens most frequently involved are *Neisseria gonorrhoeae, Chlamydia,* herpes simplex virus, and *Treponema*

pallidum. Proctocolitis involves the rectum and lowest portion of the descending colon. Symptoms are similar to proctitis but may also include watery or bloody diarrhea, cramps, and abdominal tenderness. Enteritis involves more of the descending colon, and symptoms include watery, bloody diarrhea; abdominal pain; and weight loss. The most common pathogens causing enteritis are *E. histolytica, Giardia lamblia, Shigella,* and *Campylobacter.*

Sigmoidoscopy is performed to identify portions of the anorectum involved. Samples are taken with rectal swabs, and cultures are obtained to identify the pathogens involved. Antibiotics (i.e., cefixime [Suprax], doxycycline [Vibramycin], and penicillin G) are the treatment of choice for bacterial infections. Acyclovir [Zovirax] is given to patients with viral infections. Antiamebic therapy (i.e., metronidazole [Flagyl]) is appropriate for infections with *E. histolytica* and *G. lamblia.* Ciprofloxacin (Cipro) is effective for *Shigella.* The antibiotics erythromycin (E-Mycin) and ciprofloxacin are the treatment of choice for *Campylobacter* infection.

PILONIDAL SINUS OR CYST

A pilonidal sinus or cyst is found in the intergluteal cleft on the posterior surface of the lower sacrum (Fig. 24-11). Current theories suggest that it results from local trauma, causing the penetration of hairs into the epithelium and subcutaneous tissue. It may also be formed congenitally by an infolding of epithelial tissue beneath the skin, which may communicate with the skin surface through one or several small sinus openings. Hair frequently is seen protruding from these openings, and this gives the cyst its name, *pilonidal* (i.e., a nest of hair). The cysts rarely cause symptoms

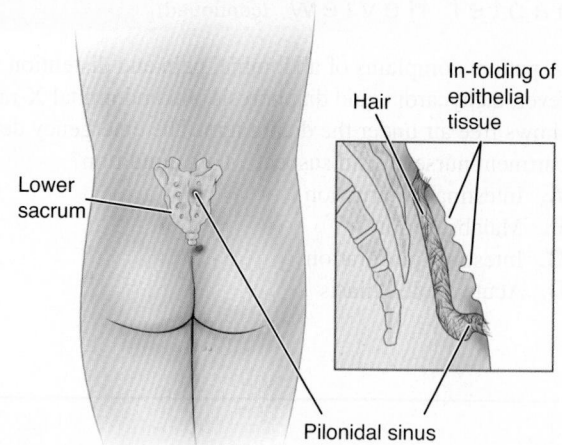

FIGURE 24-11 (**A**) Pilonidal sinus on lower sacrum about 5 cm (2 in) above the anus in the intergluteal cleft. (**B**) Hair particles emerge from the sinus tract, and localized indentations (pits) can appear on the skin near the sinus openings.

until adolescence or early adult life, when infection produces an irritating drainage or an abscess. Perspiration and friction easily irritate this area.

In the early stages of the inflammation, the infection may be controlled by antibiotic therapy, but after an abscess has formed, surgery is indicated. The abscess is incised and drained under local anesthesia. After the acute process resolves, further surgery is performed to excise the cyst and the secondary sinus tracts. The wound is allowed to heal by granulation. Gauze dressings are placed in the wound to keep its edges separated while healing occurs.

Chapter Review

Critical Thinking Exercises

1. Discuss the antibiotic choices for spontaneous bacterial peritonitis using the current evidence-based practice.
2. Compare and contrast the pathophysiologic differences between Crohn's disease and ulcerative colitis in their presentation, course of disease, and treatment regimens.

NCLEX-Style Review Questions

1. A patient returns to his room following a diagnostic colonoscopy after radiological evidence of diverticulosis. He reports an increase in abdominal pain, fever, and chills. Which clinical condition is most concerning to the nurse?
   A. Colon cancer
   B. Hemorrhoids
   C. Bowel perforation
   D. Anal fissure
2. A patient is complaining of right lower quadrant pain, fever, and decreased appetite. The nurse knows that which of the following is the most likely cause?
   A. Diverticulitis
   B. Appendicitis
   C. Small bowel obstruction
   D. Sigmoid colon cancer
3. A patient complains of abdominal pain that typically occurs after meals, along with diarrhea that is unrelieved by defecation. The nurse recognizes that which of the following is the most likely diagnosis?
   A. Ulcerative colitis
   B. Regional enteritis
   C. Cholecystitis
   D. Diverticulosis

Chapter Review (continued)

4. A patient complains of abdominal pain and distention, fever, tachycardia, and diaphoresis. An abdominal X-ray shows free air under the diaphragm. The emergency department nurse should suspect which condition?
   A. Intestinal obstruction
   B. Malabsorption
   C. Intestinal perforation
   D. Acute cholelithiasis

5. A patient has a bowel perforation from a recent surgery and has now been diagnosed with peritonitis. He has hypoactive bowel sounds, a temperature of 100.5°F, and an elevated WBC count. To which of the following should the nurse be alert as the most serious potential complication of peritonitis?
   A. Nausea
   B. Diarrhea
   C. Sepsis
   D. Abdominal tenderness

Try these additional resources to enhance your learning and understanding of this chapter:
- thePoint online resource available at **http://thepoint.lww.com/Pellico1e**
- *Handbook for Focus on Adult Health: Medical-Surgical Nursing*
- *Study Guide for Focus on Adult Health: Medical-Surgical Nursing*

References and Selected Readings

References and selected readings associated with this chapter can be found on the website that accompanies the book. Visit http://thepoint.lww.com/Pellico1e to access the references and other additional resources associated with this chapter.

Nursing Management: Patients With Hepatic and Biliary Disorders

SYLVIA M. LEMPIT

Learning Objectives

After reading this chapter, you will be able to:

1. Relate jaundice, portal hypertension, ascites, varices, nutritional deficiencies, and hepatic coma to pathophysiologic alterations of the liver.

2. Describe the medical, surgical, and nursing management of patients with esophageal varices.

3. Compare the various types of hepatitis and their causes, prevention, clinical manifestations, management, prognosis, and home health care needs.

4. Discuss medical and nursing management of patients with cancer of the liver.

5. Describe the postoperative nursing care of the patient undergoing liver transplantation.

6. Discuss management of cholelithiasis.

7. Differentiate between acute and chronic pancreatitis.

8. Discuss nursing management of patients with acute pancreatitis.

Liver function is complex, and liver dysfunction affects all body systems. Liver disorders are common and may result from a virus, exposure to toxic substances such as alcohol, or tumors. Disorders of the biliary tract and pancreas are also common and include gallbladder stones and pancreatic dysfunction. An understanding of how biliary tract disorders are closely linked with liver disease is necessary to adequately care for patients.

HEPATIC DISORDERS

Understanding and managing liver disorders requires expert clinical assessment and management skills. Box 25-1 highlights important considerations for hepatic assessment.

MANIFESTATIONS OF HEPATIC DYSFUNCTION

JAUNDICE

Yellowing of the skin and sclerae of the eyes is caused by impairment of the liver's ability to metabolize and secrete bilirubin. Jaundice is apparent when the serum bilirubin level exceeds 3 mg/dL. Elevations of serum bilirubin levels can result from either acute or chronic liver injury. The differential diagnosis of jaundice can result from the following causes:

- Hepatocellular jaundice caused by viral hepatitis, hepatotoxins (including drugs, alcohol) metabolic disorders, ischemia, autoimmune hepatitis, or pregnancy
- Obstructive jaundice caused by obstruction of the bile ducts; gallstones; inflammation of bile ducts caused by primary sclerosing cholangitis, biliary strictures, malignancies of the biliary system, pancreatic cancer, liver cancer, or pancreatitis
- Hemolytic jaundice caused by increased production of bilirubin due to hemolysis, hematological disorders, resorption of a hematoma, or multiple transfusions
- Hereditary hyperbilirubinemia caused by the inherited disorders of bilirubin metabolism, including various syndromes, some which may require transplantation

BOX 25-1 Review of Hepatic Assessment

The initial presentation of a patient with liver disease varies greatly and can range from elevated liver enzymes on routine screening with no clinical signs or symptoms of disease to the patient who presents in liver failure with jaundice, hepatic coma, or esophageal bleeding. A comprehensive and complete health history is critical to determine exposure to hepatoxic substances (including alcohol) or infectious agents causing liver dysfunction and to distinguish between acute and chronic hepatic dysfunction.

Health History Findings
Common Symptoms
- General: Lethargy, weakness, fatigue, fever, jaundice, pruritus (itching)
- Neurological: Changes in mental acuity, personality changes, sleep disturbances, confusion, and outright coma in advanced chronic liver disease or acute failure
- Cardiopulmonary: Dyspnea resulting from increased fluid retention
- GI: Abdominal pain, increasing abdominal girth, anorexia, nausea, vomiting, hematemesis (vomiting blood), melena (black, tarry stool), hematochezia (stool that contains blood)
- Hematologic/Circulatory: Increased bruising, spontaneous bleeding, dependent and or/pedal edema
- Endocrine: Decreased libido in both men and women

Past Medical History
A prior history of inflammatory bowel disease or ulcerative colitis may lead to the diagnosis of primary sclerosing cholangitis (inflammation of the bile ducts). Chronic liver disease is commonly caused by alcohol and viruses such as hepatitis B or C. Patients with nonalcoholic fatty liver disease (NAFLD) may frequently have prior medical history of diabetes, hyperlipidemia, and obesity.

Family History
Wilson's disease, hemochromatosis, and autoimmune liver disease are genetically based. A positive family history of hepatitis B may indicate vertical transmission (Schiff et al., 2007).

Social History
- Lifestyle: Current and prior drug use (i.e., IV drug abuse, inhalation of drugs), sexual practices, tattoos, piercings, blood transfusions, needlestick injury, shared razors, toothbrushes
- Occupational: Exposure to toxins in workplaces, health care worker exposure to patients in trauma areas, operating rooms, renal dialysis units

- Travel History: Recent travel to endemic areas such as Mexico, Africa, India, or Latin America with ingestion of contaminated food or water, and raw shellfish
- Alcohol Use: Information regarding current and prior alcohol use should be obtained from both patient and family (i.e., amount of alcohol ingested daily). Intake of 60 g/day for men and 30 g/d for women (10 g of alcohol is equivalent to 1 oz bourbon, or 12 ounces beer, or 4 ounces of red wine) is sufficient to cause liver injury. The impact of alcohol-induced liver injury or disease is increased in the presence of other risk factors such as hepatitis C (Schiff et al., 2007).
- Medications: Review all prescription medications, over-the-counter, herbal supplements or home remedies, intake of vitamins (especially vitamin A). Medications are frequent culprits in acute hepatic dysfunction and may lead to fulminant hepatic failure (e.g., acetaminophen overdose).

Physical Examination Findings
- Integumentary and oral: Jaundice, ecchymosis, spider angiomas and palmar erythema, scleral icterus or yellowing of the sclerae, leukonychia of the nails (white spots on nails), and clubbing of the fingers
- Oral: Hepatic fetor, a sweet, mildly fecal breath odor associated with encephalopathy
- Neurological: Impairment of the patient's neurological or cognitive status (slurred speech, confusion, poor recall or slowed responses)
- Musculoskeletal: Muscle wasting; tremors or asterixis (flapping of the hands when wrists dorsiflexed) with altered mental status indicate hepatic encephalopathy.
- Abdominal: Signs of abdominal distention indicating ascites, or prominent dilated veins visible through the skin. Umbilical hernia or ventral hernias may also be observed. The patient with liver disease may also show striae, excoriations, or petechiae of the abdominal skin. Palpation of the liver important to determine its size, shape, and consistency, and percussion is necessary to assess for ascites. The normal liver has a sharp, smooth edge, is firm but not hard, with a nonpalpable left lobe. Presence of an enlarged liver indicates liver disease (Schiff et al., 2007).
- Other: Pitting edema of the lower extremities; males may demonstrate gynecomastia and testicular atrophy (Schiff et al., 2007).

Diagnostic Evaluation
Diagnostic evaluation includes liver biopsy, liver function tests, and ultrasound (see Chapter 21).

PORTAL HYPERTENSION

Portal hypertension is caused by increased resistance to blood flow through the liver and increased blood flow due to vasodilatation in the splanchnic circulation. The two major complications of portal hypertension are **ascites** and gastroesophageal varices (discussed below) (Runyon, 2009).

ASCITES

In ascites, fluid accumulates in the peritoneal cavity. Increased blood flow in the veins draining the portal system results in dilation and the development of varicose veins.

Pathophysiology

The mechanisms responsible for the development of ascites are not completely understood. Portal hypertension and the resulting increase in capillary pressure and obstruction of venous blood flow through the damaged liver are contributing factors. The vasodilation that occurs in the splanchnic circulation is also a suspected causative factor. The failure of the liver to metabolize aldosterone increases sodium and water retention by the kidney. Sodium and water retention, increased intravascular fluid volume, increased lymphatic flow, and decreased synthesis of albumin by the damaged liver all contribute to

the movement of fluid from the vascular system into the peritoneal space. The process becomes self-perpetuating, as loss of fluid into the peritoneal space causes further sodium and water retention by the kidney in an effort to maintain the vascular fluid volume. As a result of liver damage, large amounts of albumin-rich fluid, 15 L or more, may accumulate in the peritoneal cavity as ascites (Schiff, Sorrell, & Maddrey, 2007). Figure 25-1 illustrates the pathogenesis of ascites.

Clinical Manifestations and Assessment

Common symptoms of the patient presenting with ascites include increased abdominal girth, weight gain, and swelling of the lower extremities (pedal edema). Dyspnea may be present as the result of abdominal distention or pleural effusions. Abdominal hernias due to increased intra-abdominal pressure may be visible, as well as visible collateral veins and striae (stretch marks). The patient may also experience early satiety, anorexia and general weakness (Schiff et al., 2007).

The detection of ascites by physical examination can be assessed by percussion for shifting dullness. With the patient supine, the free fluid in the abdomen will accumulate in the flanks; percussion of the abdomen will reveal tympany over the anterior abdomen and dullness over the flanks. Turning the patient to one side with repeat percussion will reveal shifting dullness (the uppermost area will sound tympanic while the lower area will sound dull to percussion). Assessing for abdominal fluid wave also detects ascites (Fig. 25-2).

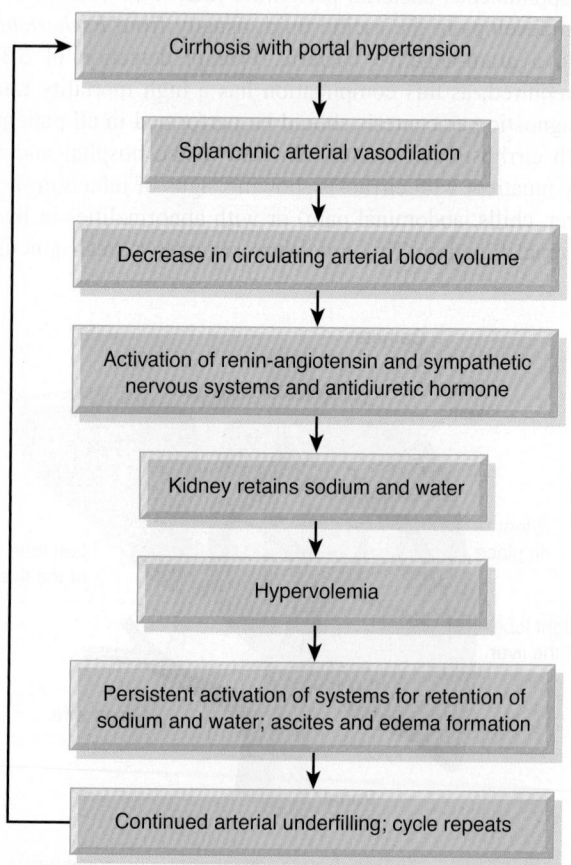

FIGURE 25-1 Pathogenesis of ascites (arterial vasodilation theory).

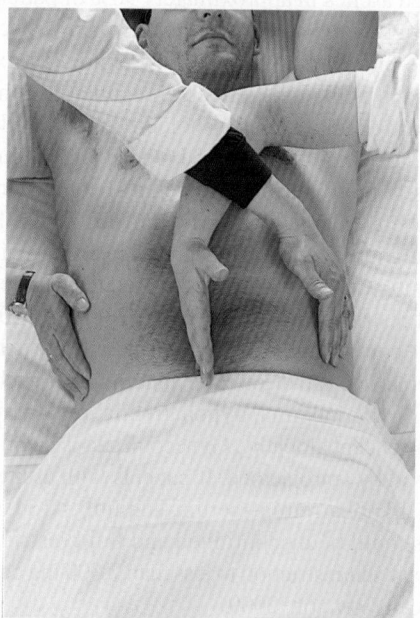

FIGURE 25-2 Assessing for abdominal fluid wave. The examiner places the hands along the sides of the patient's flanks, then strikes one flank sharply, detecting any fluid wave with the other hand. An assistant's hand is placed (ulnar side down) along the patient's midline to prevent the fluid wave from being transmitted through the tissues of the abdominal wall.

Bulging flanks may also reveal the presence of ascites. Accurate physical assessment of ascites through examination may be decreased if ascitic fluid is less than 1,500 mL or if the patient is obese (Runyon, 2009).

Ultrasonography of the liver and abdomen will definitively confirm the presence of ascites (Runyon, 2009; Shiff et al., 2007). Diagnostic paracentesis (discussed in Chapter 21) is routinely performed on patients presenting with ascites upon hospital admission to detect the presence of spontaneous bacterial peritonitis (SBP). This complication of cirrhosis has a high mortality rate and will be discussed later in the chapter (Younossi, 2008).

Medical and Nursing Management

Dietary Modification

Dietary restriction of salt intake is the mainstay of treatment of ascites to achieve a negative sodium balance to reduce fluid retention. The recommended daily sodium intake of patients with ascites should be 2,000 mg or less (Runyon, 2009; Younossi, 2008). Patients on sodium-restricted diets should receive nutritional education and guidance on foods that contain high sodium content (i.e., all processed foods, frozen and canned foods not indicated as low sodium) and avoid the use of added salt in meals and food preparation. Ongoing patient education and referral to a licensed nutritionist will facilitate dietary adherence.

Diuretics

The addition of diuretics with sodium restriction will result in decreased ascites in approximately 90% of patients. Combination drug therapy using spironolactone (Aldactone), an aldosterone-blocking agent, and furosemide (Lasix), a loop diuretic agent, is the most effective regimen to control ascites and pedal edema. Patients should be monitored for daily weight changes (not to exceed .5 kg/day (1.1 lbs) gain or loss in patients without peripheral edema, 1 kg/day in patients with peripheral edema (2.2 lbs) (Runyon, 2009). Failure to achieve weight reduction and decrease in ascites with the use of therapeutic doses of diuretics is frequently due to insufficient salt restriction (Runyon, 2009; Younossi, 2008).

Possible complications of diuretic therapy are dehydration, volume depletion, and electrolyte abnormalities such as hypokalemia or hyperkalemia, hyponatremia, renal impairment, and hepatic encephalopathy. Gynecomastia is a common side effect caused by spirolactone. If patients with ascites develop dilutional hyponatremia (serum sodium <134 mmol/L), diuretics should be discontinued and fluid restriction initiated. Dietary salt restriction to less than 2,000 mg daily should be reinforced (Runyon, 2009).

Paracentesis

Paracentesis is the removal of fluid (ascites) from the peritoneal cavity through a puncture or a small surgical incision through the abdominal wall under sterile conditions. Therapeutic paracentesis provides only temporary removal of fluid; ascites rapidly recurs, necessitating repeated fluid removal. See Chapter 21 for detailed discussion of paracentesis.

Transjugular Intrahepatic Portosystemic Shunt

Transjugular intrahepatic portosystemic shunt (TIPS) is a method of treating ascites in which a cannula is threaded into the portal vein by the transjugular route (Fig. 25-3). To reduce portal hypertension, an expandable stent is inserted to serve as an intrahepatic shunt between the portal circulation and the hepatic vein. This diverts blood flow from a high-pressure vascular bed (portal) to a lower-pressure vascular bed (hepatic veins /inferior vena cava), allowing for the return of blood to the heart and decompressing portal hypertension (Boyer & Haskal, 2010). It is extremely effective in decreasing sodium retention, improving the renal response to diuretic therapy, and preventing recurrence of fluid accumulation (Schiff et al., 2007).

Although TIPS is an effective treatment for patients with refractory ascites, it does not increase survival benefit and it increases hepatic encephalopathy (Boyer & Haskal, 2010).

Complications

An important complication of ascites is the development of spontaneous bacterial peritonitis (SBP), in which infection develops in the ascitic fluid, usually from *Escherichia coli,* a gram-negative bacteria. Prompt detection of SBP is required, as this complication has a high mortality rate. Diagnostic paracentesis should be performed in all patients with cirrhosis and ascites admitted to the hospital and in any inpatient with cirrhosis showing signs of infection (i.e., fever, chills, abdominal pain) or with abnormalities in liver or renal function. This procedure removes a small amount

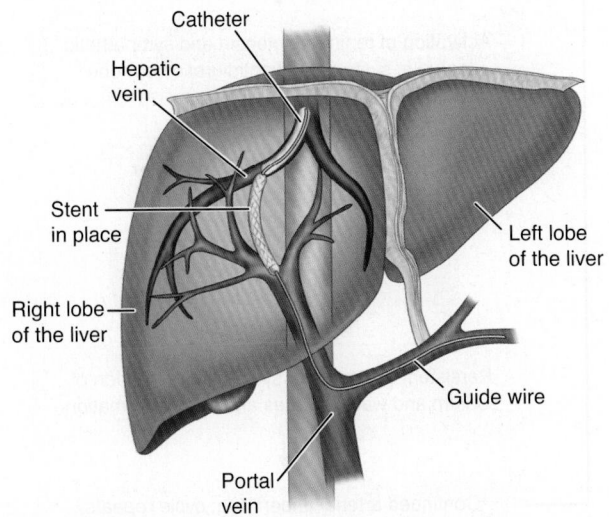

FIGURE 25-3 Transjugular intrahepatic portosystemic shunt (TIPS). A stent is inserted via catheter to the portal vein to divert blood flow and reduce portal hypertension.

of ascitic fluid from the abdomen percutaneously and can be performed at the bedside. The specimen is analyzed for cell count and differential, albumin, total protein, and susceptible organisms (Runyon, 2009; Younossii, 2008). The treatment of spontaneous bacterial peritonitis includes the use of IV antibiotics or oral treatment if tolerated. Long-term prophylaxis with oral antibiotic therapy is recommended to prevent future infection in patients who have had a diagnosis of SBP (Runyon, 2009).

ESOPHAGEAL VARICES

Gastroesophageal varices is present in 50% of patients with cirrhosis and is the most life-threatening complication in patients with chronic liver disease. Bleeding or hemorrhage from esophageal varices is associated with significantly decreased overall life with a mortality rate as high as 20% within the first 6 weeks of initial bleeding episode (Garcia-Tsao, Sanyal, Grace et al., 2007).

Pathophysiology

Esophageal varices are dilated, tortuous veins that are usually found in the submucosa of the lower esophagus but may develop higher in the esophagus or extend into the stomach. Portal hypertension is the primary mechanism by which collateral circulation develops.

Because of increased obstruction of the portal vein, venous blood from the intestinal tract and spleen seeks an outlet through collateral circulation (new pathways for return of blood to the right atrium). The effect is increased pressure, particularly in the vessels in the submucosal layer of the lower esophagus and upper part of the stomach. These collateral vessels are not very elastic; rather, they are tortuous and fragile, and they bleed easily (Schiff et al., 2007). Gastroesophageal bleeding (Fig. 25-4) is due to high portal pressure and increased collateral blood flow causing dilation and thinning of varices. Any additional increase in pressure or defect in the varices will cause rupture and hemorrhage. Factors that may precipitate hemorrhage are alcohol intake, physical exercise, and any activity that would increase intra-abdominal pressure (e.g., lifting, straining at stool, vomiting, coughing) (Schiff et al., 2007).

Bleeding esophageal varices are life-threatening and can result in hemorrhagic shock that produces decreased cerebral, hepatic, and renal perfusion. In turn, there is an increased nitrogen load from bleeding into the GI tract and an increased serum ammonia level, increasing the risk for encephalopathy.

Clinical Manifestations and Assessment

The patient with bleeding esophageal varices may present with hematemesis, melena, or general deterioration in mental or physical status and often has a history of alcohol abuse. Signs and symptoms of shock (cool clammy skin, hypoten-

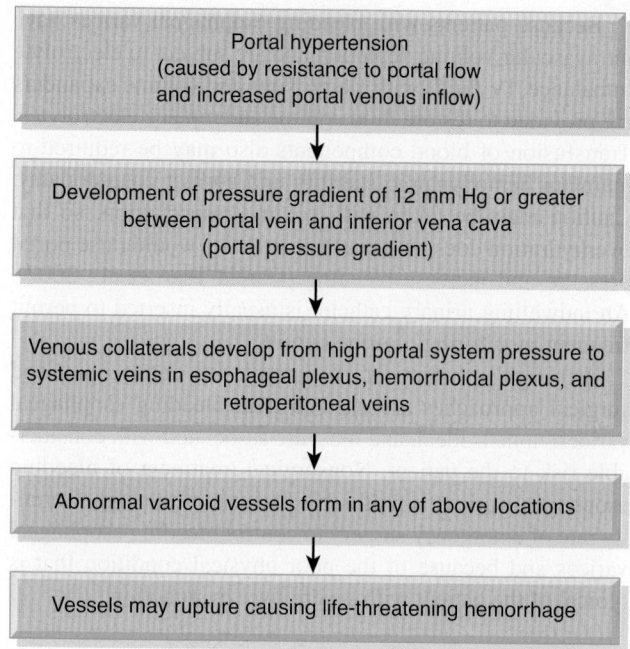

FIGURE 25-4 Pathogenesis of bleeding esophageal varices.

sion, tachycardia) may be present. Endoscopic evaluation (or esophagogastroduodenoscopy [EGD]) is used in the diagnosis and treatment of varices, in both the acute and outpatient setting. Assessment of variceal size, location, and features are used to predict the risk of bleeding. Variceal size is an important factor that determines both pharmacological and endoscopic therapies to prevent and manage risk of bleeding. In the acute setting, endoscopy should take place within 12 hours after stabilization of the patient (Garcia-Tsao et al., 2007).

Medical Management

Acute bleeding from esophageal varices is an emergency that can quickly lead to hemorrhagic shock. The patient is critically ill, requiring aggressive medical care and expert nursing care, and he or she should be transferred to the intensive care unit (ICU) for close monitoring and management. Assessment and protection of the patient's airway and peripheral venous access is required. Endotracheal intubation may be necessary to prevent aspiration of blood (Garcia-Tsao et al., 2007).

The extent of bleeding is evaluated, and vital signs are monitored continuously if hematemesis and melena are present. Signs of potential hypovolemia are noted, such as cold clammy skin, tachycardia, a drop in blood pressure, decreased urine output, restlessness, and weak peripheral pulses. The volume of circulating blood is estimated and monitored with a central venous catheter or pulmonary artery catheter. Blood pressure is monitored noninvasively or via an arterial catheter. Oxygen is administered to prevent hypoxia and to maintain adequate blood oxygenation, which is evaluated via pulse oximetry or arterial blood gases (ABGs).

Because patients with bleeding esophageal varices have intravascular volume depletion and are subject to electrolyte imbalance, IV fluids with electrolytes and volume expanders are provided to restore fluid volume and replace electrolytes. Transfusion of blood components also may be required to maintain hemodynamic stability and correct coagulopathy. Caution must be taken with volume resuscitation, so that overhydration does not occur because this would raise portal pressure and increase bleeding (Garcia-Tsao et al., 2007). An indwelling urinary catheter is usually inserted to permit frequent monitoring of urine output.

Although a variety of pharmacologic, endoscopic, and surgical approaches are used to treat bleeding esophageal varices, none is ideal, and most are associated with considerable risk to the patient. Nonsurgical treatment of bleeding esophageal varices is preferable because of the high mortality rate of emergency surgery to control bleeding esophageal varices and because of the poor physical condition that is typical of the patient with severe liver dysfunction.

Pharmacologic Therapy

In an actively bleeding patient, medications are administered initially because other therapies take longer to initiate. Vasopressin (Pitressin) may be the initial mode of therapy, because it produces constriction of the splanchnic arterial bed and decreases portal pressure. It may be administered by IV infusion. Stable vital signs and the decreasing presence or absence of blood in the gastric aspirate indicate the effectiveness of vasopressin. Monitoring of fluid intake and output and electrolyte levels is necessary, because hyponatremia may develop, and vasopressin may have an antidiuretic effect.

The use of vasopressin may be used in conjunction with nitroglycerin (IV) to prevent the side effects of vasoconstriction including cardiac ischemia, arrhythmias, and hypertension.

💊 D R U G   A L E R T

Vasopressin is administered in acute esophageal bleed because of its vasoconstrictive properties in the splanchnic, portal, and intrahepatic vessels. This medication also causes coronary artery constriction that may dispose patients with coronary artery disease to cardiac ischemia, therefore the nurse observes the patient for evidence of chest pain, electrocardiogram (ECG) changes, and vital sign changes. A high degree of suspicion is maintained, as many patients may have silent ischemia. A nitroglycerine drip may therefore be administered concurrently with vasopressin.

The medical management of the patient with acute variceal hemorrhage includes the use of antibiotic therapy (IV ciprofloxacin, or ceftriaxone in patients with advanced cirrhosis) to prevent infection and improve survival. Initial pharmacological therapy is vasopressin and nitroglycerin for the first 24 hours, after which somastatin or octreotide

is administered. Nonselective beta blockers are used for the prevention of variceal bleeding in patients with cirrhosis and also to reduce episodes of rebleeding after an initial episode (Garcia-Tsao et al., 2007).

Endoscopic Therapies

Esophageal Banding Therapy (Variceal Band Ligation)

In **variceal banding** (Fig. 25-5), also referred to as esophageal variceal ligation (EVL), a modified endoscope loaded with an elastic rubber band is passed through an overtube directly onto the varix (or varices) to be banded. After the bleeding varix is suctioned into the tip of the endoscope, the rubber band is slipped over the tissue, causing necrosis, ulceration, and eventual sloughing of the varix. Complications include superficial ulceration and dysphagia (difficulty swallowing), transient chest discomfort, and, rarely, esophageal strictures.

EVL is the most effective therapy to treat acute hemorrhage. After an acute episode of bleeding, the combination of beta-blocker therapy and EVL is the treatment of choice and has been shown to effectively prevent rebleeding and improve survival.

Endoscopic Injection Sclerotherapy

In endoscopic injection **sclerotherapy** (EIS), a sclerosing agent is injected through a fiberoptic endoscope into the bleeding esophageal varices to promote thrombosis and eventual sclerosis (Fig. 25-6). This therapy is only used to

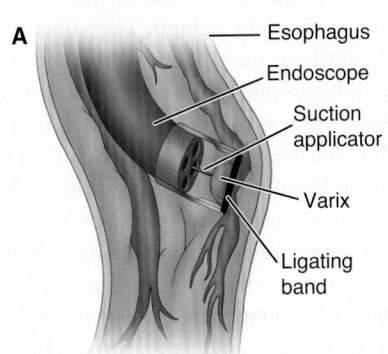
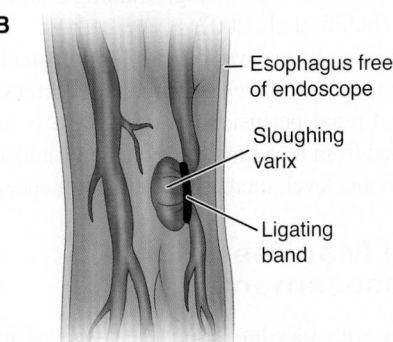

FIGURE 25-5 Esophageal banding. (**A**) A rubber band–like ligature is slipped over an esophageal varix via an endoscope. (**B**) Necrosis results, and the varix eventually sloughs off.

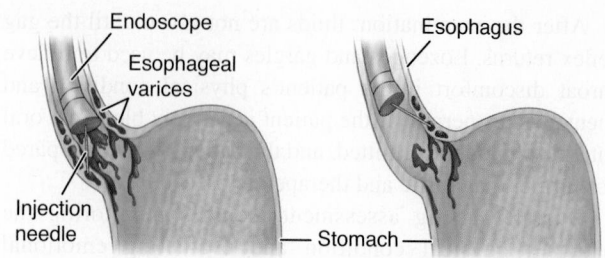

FIGURE 25-6 Endoscopic or injection sclerotherapy. Injection of sclerosing agent into esophageal varices through an endoscope promotes thrombosis and eventual sclerosis, thereby obliterating the varices.

treat an acute variceal bleed if EVL is not feasible. Because of unproven efficacy and a high incidence of complications, endoscopic variceal sclerotherapy use is limited (Garcia-Tsao et al., 2007).

Balloon Tamponade

Balloon tamponade may be used as a temporary measure to control bleeding in an active hemorrhage. In this procedure, pressure is exerted on the cardia (upper orifice of the stomach) and against the bleeding varices by a double-balloon tamponade (Sengstaken-Blakemore tube) (Fig. 25-7). The tube has four openings, each with a specific purpose: gastric aspiration, esophageal aspiration, gastric balloon inflation, and esophageal balloon inflation. This method is effective in controlling bleeding in 80% of patients; however, it is associated with

lethal complications including esophageal rupture, aspiration, and rebleeding, and it carries a high mortality risk. Its use is restricted to patients with uncontrolled bleeding and as a temporary bridge to other treatment such as TIPS or endoscopy (Boyer & Haskel, 2010; Garcia-Tsao et al., 2007).

> **NURSING ALERT**
> *The patient being treated with balloon tamponade must remain under close observation in the ICU because of the risk for serious complications. The patient must be monitored closely and continuously. Precautions must be taken to ensure that the patient does not pull on or inadvertently displace the tube.*

Transjugular Intrahepatic Portosystemic Shunting

A TIPS procedure is indicated for the treatment of an acute episode of variceal bleeding refractory to pharmacologic or endoscopic therapy. In 10% to 20% of patients for whom urgent band ligation and medications are not successful in eradicating bleeding, a TIPS procedure can effectively control acute variceal hemorrhage by rapidly lowering portal pressure. TIPS is also indicated for those patients who rebleed after pharmacologic or endoscopic prophylaxis has failed. This technique is also used as a bridge to liver transplantation. Potential complications include bleeding, sepsis, increased hepatic encephalopathy, heart failure, organ perforation, shunt

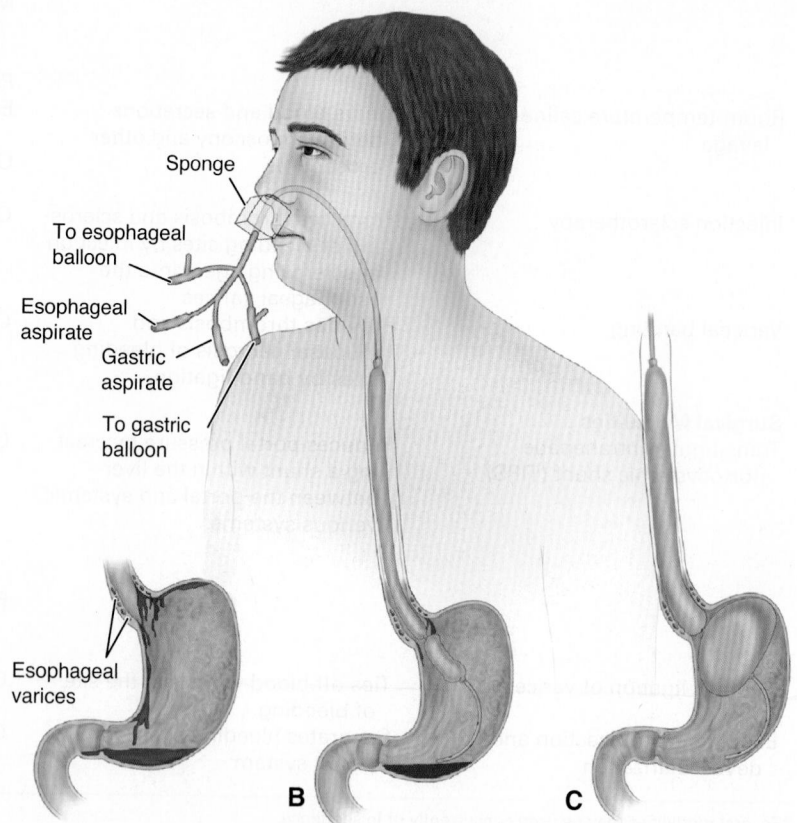

FIGURE 25-7 Balloon tamponade to treat esophageal varices. (**A**) Dilated, bleeding esophageal veins (varices) of the lower esophagus. (**B**) A four-lumen esophageal tamponade tube with balloons (uninflated) in place. (**C**) Compression of bleeding esophageal varices by inflated esophageal and gastric balloons. The gastric and esophageal outlets permit the nurse to aspirate secretions.

A   B   C

thrombosis, and progressive liver failure. (Boyer & Haskel, 2010; Garcia-Tsao et al., 2007).

Nursing Management

After treatment for acute hemorrhage, the patient must be observed for bleeding, perforation of the esophagus, aspiration pneumonia, and esophageal stricture. Antacids, histamine-2 antagonists such as cimetidine (Tagamet), or proton pump inhibitors such as pantoprazole (Protonix) may be administered after the procedure.

After the examination, fluids are not given until the gag reflex returns. Lozenges and gargles may be used to relieve throat discomfort if the patient's physical condition and mental status permit. If the patient is actively bleeding, oral intake will not be permitted, and the patient will be prepared for further diagnostic and therapeutic procedures.

Overall nursing assessment includes monitoring the patient's physical condition and evaluating emotional responses and cognitive status. The nurse monitors and records vital signs and assesses the patient's nutritional and neurologic status. This assessment assists in identifying

TABLE
25-1 Management Modalities and Nursing Care for the Patient With Bleeding Esophageal Varices

Treatment Modality*	Action	Nursing Priorities
Nonsurgical Modalities		
Pharmacologic Agents		
Vasopressin (Pitressin)	Reduces portal pressure by constricting splanchnic arteries	Observe response to therapy. Monitor for side effects: *vasopressin*—angina; nitroglycerin may be prescribed to prevent or treat angina.
Propranolol (Inderal)/nadolol (Corgard)	Reduces portal pressure by beta-adrenergic blocking action	*Propranolol* and *nadolol*—decreased pulse pressure, impaired cardiovascular response to hemorrhage.
Somatostatin/octreotide (Sandostatin)	Reduces portal pressure by selective vasodilation of portal system	Support patient during treatment.
Balloon tamponade	Exerts pressure directly to bleeding sites in esophagus and stomach	Explain procedure to patient briefly to obtain cooperation with insertion and maintenance of esophageal/gastric tamponade tube and reduce patient's fear of the procedure. Monitor closely to prevent inadvertent removal or displacement of tube, subsequent airway obstruction, and aspiration. Provide frequent oral hygiene.
Room-temperature saline lavage	Clears blood and secretions before endoscopy and other procedures	Ensure patency of the nasogastric tube to prevent aspiration. Observe gastric aspirate for blood and cessation of bleeding.
Injection sclerotherapy	Promotes thrombosis and sclerosing of bleeding sites by injection of sclerosing agent into the esophageal varices	Observe for aspiration, perforation of the esophagus, and recurrence of bleeding after treatment.
Variceal banding	Provides thrombosis and mucosal necrosis of bleeding sites by band ligation	Observe for recurrence of bleeding, esophageal perforation.
Surgical Modalities		
Transjugular intrahepatic portosystemic shunt (TIPS)	Reduces portal pressure by creating a shunt within the liver between the portal and systemic venous systems.	Observe for rebleeding and signs of infection. Observe for development of portal-systemic encephalopathy (altered mental status, neurologic dysfunction), hepatic failure, hypertension due to increased volume after surgery, and coagulopathy. Requires intensive, expert nursing care for prolonged period. Follow-up may include ultrasound with Doppler to evaluate for shunt patency.
Surgical ligation of varices	Ties off blood vessels at the site of bleeding	Observe for rebleeding.
Esophageal transection and devascularization	Separates bleeding site from portal system	Observe for rebleeding.

*Several modalities may be used concurrently or in sequence.

hepatic encephalopathy, which results from the breakdown of blood in the GI tract and a rising serum ammonia level. Manifestations range from drowsiness to encephalopathy and coma.

If complete rest of the esophagus is indicated because of bleeding, parenteral nutrition is initiated. Gastric suction usually is initiated to keep the stomach as empty as possible and to prevent straining and vomiting. The patient often complains of severe thirst, which may be relieved by frequent oral hygiene and moist sponges to the lips. The nurse closely monitors the blood pressure. Vitamin K therapy and multiple blood transfusions often are indicated because of blood loss and coagulation abnormalities. A quiet environment and calm reassurance may help to relieve the patient's anxiety and reduce agitation.

Bleeding anywhere in the body is anxiety-provoking, resulting in a crisis for the patient and family. If the patient has been a heavy user of alcohol, delirium secondary to alcohol withdrawal can complicate the situation. The nurse provides support and explanations about medical and nursing interventions. Close monitoring of the patient helps in detecting and managing complications. Management modalities and nursing care of the patient with bleeding esophageal varices are summarized in Table 25-1.

HEPATIC ENCEPHALOPATHY AND COMA

Hepatic encephalopathy coma, a life-threatening complication of liver disease, occurs with profound liver failure and may result from the accumulation of ammonia and other toxic metabolites in the blood. Hepatic coma represents the most advanced stage of hepatic encephalopathy.

Pathophysiology

Ammonia is produced in the liver as a by-product of protein and amino acid breakdown. The colon and small intestine are also sites of ammonia production resulting from bacterial action. The liver converts ammonia into urea, which is then excreted into the urine. In normal liver function, this process prevents the toxic buildup of ammonia in the blood (Schiff et al., 2007). Damaged liver cells fail to detoxify and convert the ammonia to urea, and the elevated ammonia enters the bloodstream.

Circumstances that increase serum ammonia levels tend to aggravate or precipitate hepatic encephalopathy. The largest source of ammonia is the enzymatic and bacterial digestion of dietary and blood proteins in the GI tract. Ammonia from these sources increases as a result of GI bleeding (i.e., bleeding esophageal varices, chronic GI bleeding), a high-protein diet, bacterial infection, or uremia. In the presence of alkalosis or hypokalemia, increased amounts of ammonia are absorbed from the GI tract and from the renal tubular fluid. Conversely, serum ammonia is decreased by elimination of protein from the diet and by the administration of antibiotic agents, such as neomycin sulfate, that reduce the number of intestinal bacteria capable of converting urea to ammonia (Schiff et al., 2007). Other factors unrelated to increased serum ammonia levels that can cause hepatic encephalopathy in susceptible patients include excessive diuresis, dehydration, infections, constipation, surgery, fever, and some medications (sedatives, tranquilizers, analgesics, and diuretics that cause potassium loss) (Younossi, 2008). The increased ammonia concentration in the blood causes brain dysfunction and damage, resulting in hepatic encephalopathy. Table 25-2 presents the stages of hepatic

TABLE
25-2 Stages of Hepatic Encephalopathy and Possible Nursing Diagnoses*

Stage	Clinical Symptoms	Clinical Signs	Electroencephalogram (EEG) Changes	Selected Potential Nursing Diagnoses
1	Normal level of consciousness with periods of lethargy and euphoria; reversal of day–night sleep patterns	Asterixis; impaired writing and ability to draw line figures	Normal EEG	Activity intolerance Self-care deficit Disturbed sleep pattern
2	Increased drowsiness; disorientation; inappropriate behavior; mood swings; agitation	Asterixis; fetor hepaticus	Abnormal EEG with generalized slowing	Impaired social interaction Ineffective role performance Risk for injury
3	Stuporous; difficult to rouse; sleeps most of time; marked confusion; incoherent speech	Asterixis; increased deep tendon reflexes; rigidity of extremities	EEG markedly abnormal	Imbalanced nutrition Impaired mobility Impaired verbal communication
4	Comatose; may not respond to painful stimuli	Absence of asterixis; absence of deep tendon reflexes; flaccidity of extremities	EEG markedly abnormal	Risk for aspiration Impaired gas exchange Impaired tissue integrity Disturbed sensory perception

*Nursing diagnoses are likely to progress, so that most nursing diagnoses present at earlier stages will occur during later stages as well.

encephalopathy, common signs and symptoms, and potential nursing diagnoses for each stage.

Clinical Manifestations and Assessment

The earliest symptoms of hepatic encephalopathy include minor mental changes and motor disturbances. The patient appears slightly confused and unkempt and has alterations in mood and sleep patterns. The patient tends to sleep during the day and have restlessness and insomnia at night. As hepatic encephalopathy progresses, the patient may become difficult to awaken, eventually resulting in coma (Younossi, 2008).

Asterixis (flapping tremor of the hands) may occur (Fig. 25-8). Simple tasks, such as handwriting, become difficult. A handwriting or drawing sample (e.g., star figure), taken daily, may provide graphic evidence of progression or reversal of hepatic encephalopathy; *constructional apraxia* is the inability to reproduce a simple figure (Fig. 25-9). In the early stages of hepatic encephalopathy, the deep tendon reflexes are hyperactive; with worsening of the encephalopathy, these reflexes disappear and the extremities may become flaccid.

The electroencephalogram (EEG) shows generalized slowing, an increase in the amplitude of brain waves, and characteristic triphasic waves. Occasionally, **fetor hepaticus**, a sweet, slightly fecal odor to the breath that is presumed to be of intestinal origin, may be noticed. The odor has also been described as similar to that of freshly mowed grass, acetone, or old wine. Fetor hepaticus is prevalent with extensive collateral portal circulation in chronic liver disease. In a more advanced stage, there are gross disturbances of consciousness and the patient is completely disoriented with respect to time and place (Schiff et al., 2007).

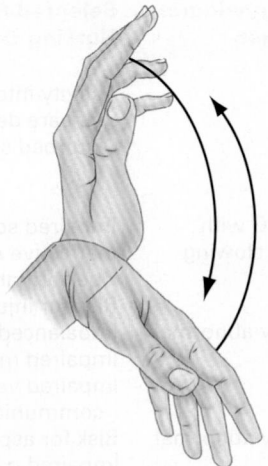

FIGURE 25-8 Asterixis or "liver flap" may occur in hepatic encephalopathy. The patient is asked to hold the arm out with the hand held upward (dorsiflexed). Within a few seconds, the hand falls forward involuntarily and then quickly returns to the dorsiflexed position.

FIGURE 25-9 Effects of constructional apraxia. Deterioration of handwriting and inability to draw a simple star figure occurs with progressive hepatic encephalopathy. With permission from Sherlock, S. & Dooley, J. (2002). *Diseases of the liver and biliary system* (11th ed.). Oxford, UK: Blackwell Scientific Ltd.

Medical Management

Medical management of hepatic encephalopathy focuses on identifying and correcting the precipitating cause if possible. Lactulose (Cephulac) is administered to reduce serum ammonia levels. It acts by several mechanisms that promote the excretion of ammonia in the stool:

- Ammonia is kept in the ionized state, resulting in a decrease in colon pH, reversing the normal passage of ammonia from the colon to the blood.
- Evacuation of the bowel takes place, which decreases the ammonia absorbed from the colon.
- Fecal flora are changed to organisms that do not produce ammonia from urea.

Two or three soft stools per day are desirable; this indicates that lactulose is performing as intended.

Possible side effects include intestinal bloating and cramps, which usually disappear within a week. To mask the sweet taste, which some patients dislike, lactulose can be diluted with fruit juice. The patient is closely monitored for hypokalemia (due to GI loss of potassium) and dehydration. Other laxatives are not prescribed during lactulose administration because their effects disturb dosage regulation. Lactulose may be administered by nasogastric tube or enema for patients who are comatose or for those in whom oral administration is contraindicated or impossible (Younossi, 2008).

☀ N U R S I N G A L E R T

The patient receiving lactulose is monitored closely for the development of watery diarrheal stools, because they indicate a medication overdose.

The addition of antibiotic therapy to alter the intestinal flora and reduce nitrogenous waste from the gut can be used as adjunct therapy to lactulose. Agents such as neomycin and

rifaximin have been used; only short-term use (<2 weeks) of neomycin is recommend due to possible auditory loss and nephrotoxicity (Younossi, 2008).

Other aspects of management include IV administration of glucose to minimize protein breakdown, administration of vitamins to correct deficiencies, and correction of electrolyte imbalances (especially potassium). Additional principles of management of hepatic encephalopathy include the following:

- Therapy is directed toward treating or removing the cause.
- Neurologic status is assessed frequently.
- Mental status is monitored by keeping a daily record of handwriting and arithmetic performance.
- Fluid intake and output and body weight are recorded each day.
- Vital signs are measured and recorded every 4 hours.
- Potential sites of infection (peritoneum, lungs) are assessed frequently, and abnormal findings are reported promptly.
- Serum ammonia level is monitored.
- Protein intake is moderately restricted in patients who are comatose or who have encephalopathy that is refractory to lactulose and antibiotic therapy (Box 25-2).
- Reduction in the absorption of ammonia from the GI tract is accomplished by the use of gastric suction, enemas, or oral antibiotics.
- Electrolyte status is monitored and corrected if abnormal.
- Sedatives, tranquilizers, and analgesic medications are discontinued.
- Benzodiazepine antagonists such as flumazenil (Romazicon) may be administered to improve encephalopathy, whether or not the patient has previously taken benzodiazepines.

Nursing Management

The nurse is responsible for maintaining a safe environment to prevent injury, bleeding, and infection. The nurse admin-

BOX 25-2
Nutrition Alert

Management of Hepatic Encephalopathy

- Prevent the formation and absorption of toxins, principally ammonia, from the intestine.
- Keep daily protein intake between 1.0 and 1.5 g/kg, depending on the degree of decompensation.
- Avoid protein restriction if possible, even in those with encephalopathy. If necessary, implement temporary restriction of 0.5 to 0.8 g/kg.
- For patients who are truly protein-intolerant, provide additional nitrogen in the form of an amino acid supplement. Use of branched-chain amino acids is still controversial.
- Provide small, frequent meals and an evening snack of complex carbohydrates to avoid protein loading.
- Substitute vegetable protein for animal protein in as high a percentage as possible.

isters the prescribed treatments and monitors the patient for the numerous potential complications. The nurse also communicates with the patient's family, to inform them about the patient's status, and supports them by explaining the procedures and treatments that are part of the patient's care. If the patient recovers from hepatic encephalopathy and coma, rehabilitation is likely to be prolonged. Therefore, the patient and family will require assistance to understand the causes of this severe complication and to recognize that it may recur.

VITAMIN DEFICIENCY

Decreased production of several clotting factors may be partially due to deficient absorption of vitamin K from the GI tract. This probably is caused by the inability of liver cells to use vitamin K to make prothrombin. Absorption of the other fat-soluble vitamins (vitamins A, D, and E) as well as dietary fats may also be impaired because of decreased secretion of bile salts into the intestine.

Another group of problems common to patients with severe chronic liver dysfunction results from inadequate intake of sufficient vitamins. These include the following:

- Vitamin A deficiency, resulting in night blindness and eye and skin changes
- Thiamine deficiency, leading to beriberi, polyneuritis, and Wernicke-Korsakoff psychosis
- Riboflavin deficiency, resulting in characteristic skin and mucous membrane lesions
- Pyridoxine deficiency, resulting in skin and mucous membrane lesions and neurologic changes
- Vitamin C deficiency, resulting in the hemorrhagic lesions of scurvy
- Vitamin K deficiency, resulting in hypoprothrombinemia, characterized by spontaneous bleeding and ecchymosis
- Folic acid deficiency, resulting in macrocytic anemia

Because of these avitaminoses (vitamin deficiencies), the diet of every patient with chronic liver disease (especially if alcohol-related) is supplemented with ample quantities of vitamins A, B complex, C, and K, and folic acid.

OTHER MANIFESTATIONS

The patient with advanced chronic liver disease and cirrhosis frequently will develop other systemic complications such as altered respiratory or cardiac function resulting from hepatopulmonary syndrome (HPS) and renal function hepatorenal syndrome (HRS). Hematologic abnormalities in patients with cirrhosis is common due to decrease in clotting factors resulting from vitamin K deficiency, decreased platelets (thrombocytopenia), anemia, and decreased white cells (neutropenia). The patient with cirrhosis will demonstrate easy bruising and bleeding, and increased susceptibility to infection (Schiff et al., 2007). Endocrine dysfunction in the regulation of glucose control and altered synthesis of sex hormones by the liver results in gynecomastia,

testicular atrophy, and decreased libido and impotence in men. Women may have irregular or absent menstrual cycles and decreased sexual function as well.

VIRAL HEPATITIS

Viral hepatitis is a systemic, viral infection in which necrosis and inflammation of liver cells produce a characteristic cluster of clinical, biochemical, and cellular changes. To

date, six types of viral hepatitis have been identified: hepatitis A, B, C, D, E, and G (Schiff et al., 2007) (Table 25-3). These viruses infect the liver and can result in either acute or chronic liver dysfunction and disease. Initial presentation of viral hepatitis may be asymptomatic or result in fulminant liver failure or chronic liver disease. Patients may have nonspecific symptoms of malaise, GI distress, or present with frank jaundice and elevations of aminotransferases (Younossi, 2008). Terms associated with viral hepatitis are listed in Box 25-3.

TABLE 25-3 Comparison of Major Forms of Viral Hepatitis

	Hepatitis A	Hepatitis B	Hepatitis C	Hepatitis D	Hepatitis E
Previous names	Infectious hepatitis	Serum hepatitis	Non-A, non-B hepatitis		
Epidemiology					
Cause	Hepatitis A virus (HAV)	Hepatitis B virus (HBV)	Hepatitis C virus (HCV)	Hepatitis D virus (HDV)	Hepatitis E virus (HEV)
Mode of transmission	Fecal–oral route; poor sanitation. Person-to-person contact Waterborne; food-borne Transmission possible with oral–anal contact during sex	Parenterally; by intimate contact with carriers or those with acute disease; sexual and oral–oral contact Perinatal transmission from mothers to infants An important occupational hazard for health care personnel	Transfusion of blood and blood products; exposure to contaminated blood through equipment or drug paraphernalia Transmission possible with sex with infected partner; risk increased with STD	Same as HBV; HBV surface antigen necessary for replication; pattern similar to that of hepatitis B	Fecal–oral route; person-to-person contact may be possible, although risk appears low
Incubation (days)	15–50 days Average: 30 days	28–160 days Average: 70–80 days	15–160 days Average: 50 days	21–140 days Average: 35 days	15–65 days Average: 42 days
Immunity	Homologous	Homologous	Second attack may indicate weak immunity or infection with another agent.	Homologous	Unknown
Nature of Illness					
Signs and symptoms	May occur with or without symptoms; flulike illness *Preicteric phase:* Headache, malaise, fatigue, anorexia, fever *Icteric phase:* Dark urine, jaundice of sclera and skin, tender liver	May occur without symptoms May develop arthralgias, rash	Similar to HBV; less severe and anicteric	Similar to HBV	Similar to HAV; very severe in pregnant women
Outcome	Usually mild with recovery. Fatality rate: <1% No carrier state or increased risk of chronic hepatitis, cirrhosis, or hepatic cancer	May be severe. Fatality rate: 1%–10%. Carrier state possible Increased risk of chronic hepatitis, cirrhosis, and hepatic cancer	Frequent occurrence of chronic carrier state and chronic liver disease Increased risk of hepatic cancer	Similar to HBV but greater likelihood of carrier state, chronic active hepatitis, and cirrhosis	Similar to HAV except very severe in pregnant women

Hepatitis Terms and Abbreviations

Hepatitis A

HAV	Hepatitis A virus; etiologic agent of hepatitis A (formerly infectious hepatitis)
Ig G anti-HAV	Antibody to hepatitis A virus; appears in serum soon after onset of symptoms; persists indefinitely,
IgM anti-HAV	indicates life-long immunity: IgM antibody to HAV; indicates recent infection with HAV; positive up to 6 months after infection

Hepatitis B

HBV	Hepatitis B virus; etiologic agent of hepatitis B (formerly serum hepatitis)
HBsAG	Hepatitis B surface antigen (Australian antigen); indicates acute or chronic hepatitis B or carrier state; indicates infectious state
Anti-HBs	Antibody to hepatitis B surface antigen; indicates prior exposure and immunity to hepatitis; may indicate passive antibody from HBIG or immune response from hepatitis B vaccine
HBeAg	Hepatitis B e-antigen; present in serum early in course; indicates highly infectious stage of hepatitis B; persistence in serum indicates progression to chronic hepatitis
Anti-HBe	Antibody to hepatitis B e-antigen; suggests low titer of HBV
HBcAg	Hepatitis B core antigen; found in liver cells; not easily detected in serum
Anti-HBc	Antibody to hepatitis B core antigen; most sensitive indicator of hepatitis B; appears late in the acute phase of the disease; indicates infection of HBV at some time in the past
IgM anti-HBc	IgM antibody to HBcAg; present for up to 6 months after HBV infection

Hepatitis C

HCV	Hepatitis C virus (formerly non-A, non-B virus); may be more than one virus

Hepatitis D

HDV	Hepatitis D virus (delta agent); etiologic agent to hepatitis D; HBV required for replication
HDAg	Hepatitis delta antigen; detectable in early acute HDV infection
Anti-HDV	Antibody to HDV; indicates past or present infection with HDV

Hepatitis E

HEV	Hepatitis E virus; etiologic agent of hepatitis E

Hepatitis G

HGV	Hepatitis G virus; also known as GB virus C or GB-C

HEPATITIS A VIRUS

Pathophysiology

The mode of transmission of hepatitis A virus (HAV) occurs through the fecal–oral route, primarily through person-to-person contact and/or ingestion of fecally contaminated food or water. Uncooked food or poor food handling practices are common methods of transmission of HAV.

HAV replicates in the liver, is excreted in bile, and sheds in the stool. The incubation period averages 28 days, with signs and symptoms typically lasting less than 2 months (although in some patients, these can extend up to 6 months). The peak period for transmission of HAV from one person to another occurs in the 2-week period prior to development of jaundice or symptoms, when the concentration of virus in the stool is highest (Schiff et al., 2007). Typically, persons infected with HAV spontaneously recover; however, adults over 50 years of age or with chronic liver disease may progress to fulminant liver failure (Schiff et al., 2007).

Clinical Manifestations and Assessment

Infection by HAV can present either asymptomatically or with acute symptoms such as fever, malaise, anorexia, nausea, diarrhea, vomiting, abdominal pain, and jaundice. Jaundice presents in over 70% of patients, primarily in adults. Serologic testing is required for accurate diagnosis of hepatitis A infection. A positive anti-HAV (IgM) signifies serum IgM antibodies that are reactive to the hepatitis A virus and confirms an acute infection.

Anti-HAV (Ig G) becomes positive shortly after the onset of infection, will remain positive throughout the person's life, and confers immunity. Total anti-HAV positivity and negative anti-HAV (IgM) indicates immunity to HAV infection either through exposure or vaccination (Younossi, 2008).

Prevention

Current recommendations to prevent the transmission of HAV are to routinely vaccinate all children, to identify and vaccinate persons at high risk for contracting HAV, and to vaccinate any person who wishes to prevent HAV.

At risk persons who should be vaccinated include:

- Travelers or visitors to countries with increased incidence of HAV (Mexico, Latin America, Africa, Middle East, Asia, India)
- Men having sex with men
- Illicit drug users

BOX 25-4
Community Prevention of Hepatitis A

- Proper community and home sanitation
- Conscientious individual hygiene
- Safe practices for preparing and dispensing food
- Effective health supervision of schools, dormitories, extended care facilities, barracks, and camps
- Community health education programs
- Mandatory reporting of viral hepatitis to local health departments
- Vaccination for travelers to developing countries, illegal drug users (injection and noninjection drug users), men who have sex with men, and persons with chronic liver disease
- Vaccination to interrupt community-wide outbreaks

- Persons with occupational risk (e.g., research with primates or HAV in laboratory settings)
- Persons with clotting factor disorders
- Persons with chronic liver disease

Active immunization for HAV is through vaccination with hepatitis A antigen in two dose schedules and is administered intramuscularly in the deltoid muscle. Passive immunization is achieved through administration of immune globulin containing hepatitis A antibodies to persons for prophylaxis after exposure to the virus. Its use is indicated for patients with no evidence of immunity (Advisory Committee on Immunization Practices [ACIP], 2010).

Box 25-4 discusses community prevention of hepatitis A.

Medical Management

Acute HAV infection in most patients is managed with supportive care. The patient may experience decreased appetite due to alterations in GI function. Dehydration should be prevented; if necessary, IV fluids may be administered. Patients can participate in physical activity as tolerated. Signs and symptoms indicating possible fulminant liver failure, such as altered mental status or severe vomiting, should be promptly identified with referral to a liver transplant center (Younossi, 2008).

Nursing Management

Management usually occurs in the home unless symptoms are severe. Therefore, the nurse assists the patient and family in coping with the temporary disability and fatigue that are common in hepatitis and instructs them to seek additional health care if the symptoms persist or worsen. The patient and family also need specific guidelines about diet, rest, follow-up blood work, and the importance of avoiding alcohol, as well as sanitation and hygiene measures (particularly hand washing after bowel movements and before eating) to prevent spread of the disease to other family members, environmental sanitation (safe food and water supply, effective

sewage disposal), proper food storage, and thorough cooking of foods to recommended temperatures.

HEPATITIS B VIRUS

Hepatitis B virus (HBV) infection is an important public health problem with as many as 350 million people worldwide with chronic infection (Lok & McMahon, 2009). Hepatitis B virus (HBV) is highly prevalent in Asia, Africa, Middle East, parts of Europe, the Caribbean, and Central and South America (Lok & McMahon, 2009).

Pathophysiology

HBV is transmitted primarily through blood (percutaneous and mucosal routes). HBV can be found in blood, saliva, and semen, and can be transmitted through mucous membranes and breaks in the skin. HBV is also transferred from carrier mothers to their babies, especially in areas with a high incidence (Lok & McMahon, 2007). HBV is primarily transmitted by perinatal, percutaneous, sexual exposure, and close person-to-person contact via contact with open cuts or sores or by use of shared razors or toothbrushes. HBV-contaminated surfaces are also possible sources of infection as the virus can survive outside of the body for extended periods (Lok & McMahon, 2009).

HBV has a long incubation period. It replicates in the liver and remains in the serum for relatively long periods, allowing transmission of the virus. Most people (>95%) who contract HBV infection develop antibodies and recover spontaneously (Lok & McMahon, 2007). The risk of developing chronic HBV infection is significantly higher in persons from endemic countries. Acute HBV infection can result in fulminant liver failure or progress to chronic infection. Patients with chronic HBV infection may eventually develop cirrhosis, end-stage liver disease, and cancer of the liver (Lok & McMahon, 2009).

Risk Factors

Those at risk for development of hepatitis B include individuals born in areas with high rates of HBV infection. Risk factors for HBV infection are summarized in Box 25-5 (Lok & McMahon, 2007, 2009).

Clinical Manifestations and Assessment

Signs and symptoms of acute hepatitis B may be insidious and variable. The patient may have anorexia, fevers, dyspepsia, abdominal pain, generalized aching, malaise, and weakness. Jaundice may or may not be evident. Skin rashes and arthralgias (pain in the joints) may occur (CDC, 2006). Chronic hepatitis B may remain largely asymptomatic until the development of cirrhosis and signs of hepatic decompensation (Younossi, 2008).

Risk Factors for Hepatitis B

- Frequent exposure to blood, blood products, or other body fluids
- Being a health care worker: hemodialysis staff, oncology and chemotherapy nurses, personnel at risk for needle sticks, operating room staff, respiratory therapists, surgeons, dentists
- Hemodialysis
- Male homosexual and bisexual activity
- IV/injection drug use
- Close contact with carrier of HBV
- Travel to or residence in area with uncertain sanitary conditions
- Multiple sexual partners
- Recent history of sexually transmitted disease
- Receipt of blood or blood products (e.g., clotting factor concentrate)

The evaluation of a patient with HBV infection includes a complete history and physical examination, a family history of liver disease, and potential risk factors for disease transmission.

Laboratory testing should include complete blood counts (CBC with platelets), hepatic function panel, and prothrombin time and international normalized ratio (INR). Lab tests to detect hepatitis B replication and other viral co-infections (HAV, HCV, HIV) should be included in the assessment (Lok & McMahon, 2007).

Prevention

The goals of prevention are to interrupt the chain of transmission, to protect people who are at high risk by active immunization through the use of hepatitis B vaccine, and to use passive immunization for unprotected people exposed to HBV.

Preventing Transmission

Recommendations to prevent transmission of hepatitis B include vaccination of sexual contacts of individuals with chronic hepatitis B, use of barrier protection during sexual intercourse, avoidance of sharing toothbrushes and razors with others, and covering of open sores or skin lesions. Blood spills should be cleaned with bleach diluted to a 10:1 concentration. Persons with HBV infection should be advised to avoid donation of blood, organs, or sperm.

Active Immunization: Hepatitis B Vaccine

The most effective strategy to prevent hepatitis B infection is through vaccination. Current prevention recommendations include:

- Universal vaccination of infants at birth
- Screening of pregnant women for hepatitis B surface antigen (HBsAg)

- Prophylaxis of infants with HBsAg-positive mothers or with unknown HBsAg status
- Vaccination of unvaccinated children and adolescents
- Vaccination of unvaccinated adults at risk for HBV infection (i.e., health care workers, sexual or household contacts of HBV carriers) (Lok & McMahon, 2009)

The hepatitis B vaccine series is administered in three doses intramuscularly at 0, 1-month, and 6-month intervals for adults (ACIP, 2010).

NURSING ALERT
The U.S. Food and Drug Administration (FDA) has approved a combined hepatitis A and B vaccine (Twinrix) for vaccination of people 18 years of age and older with indications for both hepatitis A and B vaccination. Vaccination consists of three doses, on the same schedule as that used for single-antigen hepatitis B vaccine (ACIP, 2010).

Passive Immunity: Hepatitis B Immune Globulin

Hepatitis B immune globulin (HBIG) provides passive immunity to hepatitis B and is indicated for people exposed to HBV who have never had hepatitis B and have never received hepatitis B vaccine. It has demonstrated efficacy in the prevention of HBV infection in high-risk persons (hemodialysis patients, sexual partners of patients with hepatitis B, and newborn infants of HBsAg-positive mothers) (Perrillo, 2010).

Medical Management

The goals of treatment for hepatitis B are to prevent replication of active hepatitis B virus (viral suppression) and reduce the effects of chronic liver inflammation. The ultimate goal of medical management of hepatitis B is to prevent cirrhosis, liver failure, and hepatocellular carcinoma (Lok & McMahon, 2007). Multiple antiviral therapies are available to treat hepatitis B; of these, pegylated interferon alfa, adefovir, entecavir, telbivudine, and tenofovir are the preferred medications, either as single agents or in combination. Patients with HBV infection should have periodic laboratory testing to assess elevations in hepatic function, and replication of HBV DNA. Patients at high risk for hepatocellular carcinoma (discussed later in this chapter), including patients with cirrhosis, should receive ultrasound screening every 6 months (Lok & McMahon, 2007, 2009).

Nursing Management

In patients with acute hepatitis B, management of the symptoms of malaise, anorexia, nausea, vomiting, and fever are primarily supportive to maintain nutrition, fluid intake, and adequate rest during recovery. The nurse must be vigilant for signs of progression to fulminant liver failure (discussed later in the chapter); however, alterations in mental status, severe vomiting, and increasing jaundice should initiate

referral to a tertiary care center or liver transplant center. In patients with chronic hepatitis B, the nursing role is geared to patient education in the prevention of transmission and avoidance of lifestyle factors that may exacerbate existing liver disease.

HEPATITIS C VIRUS

Hepatitis C virus (HCV) infection is the leading cause of liver disease and is the primary indication for liver transplantation.

Pathophysiology

HCV is a blood-borne RNA virus and is avidly replicated in the liver. Transmission of hepatitis C occurs primarily through injection of drugs and through pre-1992 transfusion of blood products. Its route is through parenteral contact with blood. Sexual transmission may also occur, with high risk associated with multiple sex partners. Other less common modes of transmission include via hemodialysis, health care worker exposure to needlestick injury or contaminated blood, and tattooing (Ghany, Strader, Thomas, & Seeff, 2009). Box 25-6 summarizes risk factors for hepatitis C.

Patients infected with this virus spontaneously clear the acute infection in only 15% of cases; the majority of individuals will develop chronic infection, with evidence of hepatitis C RNA viremia. Unlike other hepatitis viruses, the acute stage of hepatitis C often is asymptomatic for decades. Hepatitis C infection with progression to cirrhosis occurs in up to 20% of patients over a period of 20 years or longer. Factors contributing to the severity of liver disease include increased alcohol use, male gender, older age at infection, HIV or HBV coinfection, and obesity (Younossi, 2008). Individuals with HCV cirrhosis are at higher risk of developing hepatic decompensation and hepatocellular carcinoma (Ghany et al., 2009).

Clinical Manifestations and Assessment

Most patients with acute or chronic hepatitis C are asymptomatic. Some patients will develop jaundice, nausea, vomit-

ing, and malaise during the acute stage (Box 25-7). Patients with chronic hepatitis C will frequently be diagnosed incidentally during routine lab testing, or not until cirrhosis develops. Extrahepatic signs of hepatitis C are common, such as skin rashes, joint aches, and purpura (small blood vessels leaking under the skin and causing purple bruising) (Schiff et al., 2007).

The diagnosis of HCV infection is confirmed by serology with anti-HCV antibodies present and measurement of viremia through HCV RNA. Genotype testing and liver biopsy will provide information to assist in the management and treatment of hepatitis C, and to stage the severity of disease. Other tests to assess the extent of liver disease include laboratory tests (i.e., bilirubin, albumin, aminotransferases, prothrombin time, and INR). Ultrasound or other imaging may be used to assess for cirrhosis or the presence of lesions (Ghany et al., 2009).

Medical and Nursing Management

Treatment of hepatitis C aims to prevent the progression of fibrosis and evolution to cirrhosis by reducing HCV RNA levels to nondetectable levels. A nondetectable viral load or HCV RNA 6 months after completion of therapy is considered curative. This is called a *sustained viral response*. Current antiviral therapy consists of pegylated interferon alfa injected subcutaneously once weekly and ribavirin taken orally daily. The duration of treatment is based upon genotype; most patients undergo therapy for 48 weeks or longer (Schiff et al., 2007). Antiviral therapy for treatment of hepatitis C has significant side effects and commonly causes patients to stop treatment (Box 25-7). Side effects include moderate to severe flu-like symptoms, skin rashes, pruritus, insomnia, irritability, decreased concentration, and depression. The patient requires close monitoring of hematological function for evidence of anemia, neutropenia, and/or thrombocytopenia (Ghany et al., 2009; Younossi, 2008). Ribavirin is highly teratogenic; females of childbearing age should be advised to use reliable contraception, and female partners of men undergoing therapy should also use contraception (Ghany et al., 2009).

HEPATITIS D VIRUS

Hepatitis D virus (delta agent) (HDV) infection occurs in some cases of hepatitis B. Because the virus requires hepatitis B surface antigen for its replication, only individuals with hepatitis B are at risk for hepatitis D. Anti-HDV antibodies (IGg) in patients with chronic hepatitis B confirms the diagnosis (Younossi, 2008).

The symptoms of hepatitis D are similar to those of hepatitis B, except that patients are more likely to develop fulminant hepatitis and to progress to chronic active hepatitis and cirrhosis. Current treatment for hepatitis D is the use of interferon or pegylated interferon alfa for 12 months (Lok & McMahon, 2007).

BOX 25-6 **Risk Factors for Hepatitis C**

- Receiving blood products or organ transplant before 1992 or clotting factor concentrates before 1987
- Being a health care or public safety worker (needle stick injuries or mucosal exposure to blood)
- Being a child born to woman infected with hepatitis C virus
- Past/current illicit IV/injection drug use
- Past treatment with chronic hemodialysis
- Multiple sex partners, history of sexually transmitted disease, unprotected sex

BOX 25-7

Nursing Research

Bridging the Gap to Evidence-Based Practice

An Intervention to Prevent Symptoms Associated With Hepatitis C

Zucker, D.M. (2010). An Intervention to Prevent Symptoms Associated With Hepatitis C: A pilot study. *Applied Nursing Research, 23,* 116–120.

Purpose

The purpose of this pilot study was to assess the impact a home walking intervention would have on patients with hepatitis C of undergoing antiviral therapy with interferon and ribavirin. Fatigue is a major symptom for patients with hepatitis C and those undergoing therapy. This pilot was designed to determine if this intervention would decrease fatigue, facilitate completion of therapy, and assess quality of life and walking distance. Over 3 million U.S. citizens have chronic hepatitis C infection, with increased morbidity and mortality as disease progresses. Cirrhosis, end-stage liver failure requiring transplantation, and hepatocellular carcinoma are sequelae of this disease.

Design

The study recruited 20 participants and employed a two group pretest–posttest design. Patients were randomly assigned to an exercise or control group. Prior to randomization, the subjects completed questionnaires and a 12-minute walk test. The patients assigned to the exercise group started a home walking program 3 weeks prior to the start of therapy for hepatitis C and ended at completion of therapy either at 24 weeks or 48 weeks. Pretest and posttest measures of fatigue were assessed

by the Schwartz Cancer Fatigue scale and the Hepatitis Quality of Life Questionnaire. Sample characteristics were evenly matched, with 80% males in each group, and 50% of study subjects having Genotype 1a.

Findings

Thirty percent of the control group and 40% of the exercise group did not complete the study due to termination of therapy for adverse side effects, loss to follow-up, and nonspecified reasons.

The author determined at the conclusion of the study that a larger sample size of 30 or more participants is necessary to achieve sufficient power of .80 or more. Both the Schwartz Cancer Fatigue Scale and Hepatitis Quality of Life Questionnaire were determined to be reliable instruments to assess fatigue and quality of life factors in this group. Those who completed the exercise program felt well. Over all, the author concluded that a larger sample was necessary to determine if an exercise intervention was sufficient to decrease symptoms of fatigue and improve therapy adherence and outcomes.

Nursing Implications

Both hepatitis C and antiviral therapy to treat this disease negatively impact quality of life with chronic fatigue. This is a frequent reason for patient's to discontinue treatment. Nursing interventions to improve therapeutic outcomes and mitigate the side effects of treatment are necessary to support patient's undergoing this therapy. Additional research is necessary with larger groups to determine best approaches for patient management.

HEPATITIS E VIRUS

It is believed that hepatitis E virus (HEV) is transmitted by the fecal–oral route, principally through contaminated water in endemic areas with poor sanitation. This form of hepatitis usually is self-limiting, with acute onset and subsequent recovery with no chronicity. HEV is responsible for most cases of fulminant hepatitis in India. Pregnant women infected with hepatitis E infection have a high mortality rate (up to 25%); this is increased during the last trimester (Schiff et al., 2007). Currently, there is no vaccine or specific treatment for HEV; however, research in vaccine development may be promising in the near future.

Prevention of transmission is focused on improvement of sanitation, development of clean water supplies in endemic countries, and safe food handling practices (Schiff et al., 2007).

HEPATITIS G VIRUS AND GB VIRUS-C

The hepatitis G virus (HGV) is a RNA virus that has recently been identified; however, controversy exists as to its role in the pathogenesis of liver disease.

NONVIRAL HEPATITIS

Liver inflammation and disease can be caused by nonviral etiologies such as toxins, infections, alcoholic overuse, and autoimmune disorders.

ALCOHOLIC LIVER DISEASE (ALCOHOLIC HEPATITIS)

Excessive ingestion or abuse of alcohol is a common cause of acute hepatitis, and chronic use results in cirrhosis. Alcoholic liver disease (ALD) is a major public health problem and accounts for approximately 40% of deaths related to cirrhosis of the liver. The risk of developing hepatocellular carcinoma (HCC) increases fivefold from ALD and is responsible for approximately one-third of all cases of HCC in the United States.

The impact of alcohol ingestion upon the liver is dose-dependent; females will develop advanced liver disease at lower amounts of alcohol than will men. Other cofactors contributing to the development of cirrhosis in ALD is hepatitis C infection, smoking, and obesity. The amount of alcohol

consumed to result in significant liver disease is more than 20 g of alcohol daily over a 10-year period in females, and 60 to 80 g of alcohol daily in men (O'Shea, Dasarathy, & McCullough, 2010).

Pathophysiology

Ethanol (alcohol) is metabolized by the liver by alcohol dehydrogenases, cytochrome P450, and catalase. The resultant product, acetaldehyde, is toxic to the liver, resulting in impairment of liver function and cells. Other factors contributing to the pathogenesis of ALD are oxidative stress, hypoxia or oxygen depletion of cells, and mitochondrial injury. Fatty infiltration of liver cells (hepatic steatosis) is a common finding in liver biopsies of patients with ALD (O'Shea et al., 2010).

Clinical Manifestations and Assessment

Patients presenting with alcoholic hepatitis are universally jaundiced. The patient may have symptoms of anorexia, nausea, vomiting, and abdominal pain. Fever, muscle wasting, and *stigmata*—such as spider angiomas (Fig. 25-10) or palmar erythema (redness of the palm)—are common findings. The liver may be enlarged, or hard and small. The spleen will be enlarged, and late signs of hepatic decompensation may be evident such as ascites, pedal edema, and hepatic encephalopathy (O'Shea et al., 2010).

There is no specific evaluation or test for the diagnosis of ALD; the clinical history and physical presence of liver disease correlated with information regarding alcohol overuse is diagnostic. An AST/ALT ratio of greater than three indicates ALD in over 70% of cases (O'Shea et al., 2010).

A complete history and physical examination is important in the assessment of patients with ALD. Patients should be screened for frequency, amount of alcohol use, type of alcohol, and patterns of alcohol use. Additional information regarding the negative impact of alcohol abuse upon employment, health

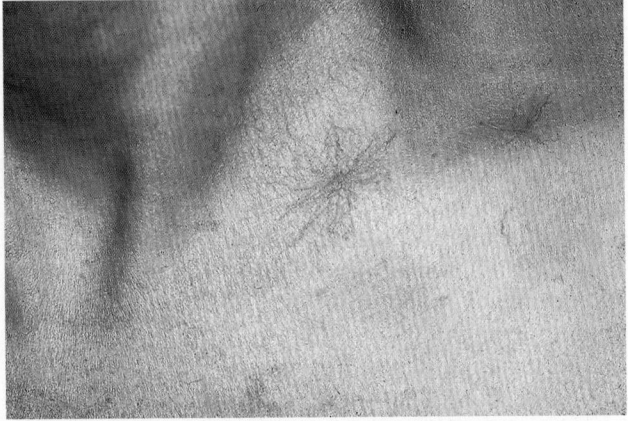

FIGURE 25-10 Spider angioma. This vascular (arterial) spider appears on the skin. Beneath the elevated center and radiating branches, the blood vessels are looped and tortuous.

BOX 25-8 **Nutrition Alert**

Dietary Management of Viral or Drug-Related Hepatitis

- Recommend small, frequent meals.
- Provide intake of 2,000 to 3,000 kcal/d during acute illness.
- Although early studies indicate that a high-protein, high-calorie diet may be beneficial; advise patient not to force food and to restrict fat intake.
- Carefully monitor fluid balance.
- If anorexia and nausea and vomiting persist, enteral feedings may be necessary.
- Instruct patient to abstain from alcohol during acute illness and for at least 6 months after recovery.
- Advise patient to avoid substances (medications, herbs, illicit drugs, and toxins) that may affect liver function.

(i.e., falls, fractures), or driving status provides more data to assess the extent of alcohol use (O'Shea et al., 2010).

Medical Management

The mainstay of treatment for ALD is abstinence and either oral or enteral nutritional therapy. Patients with ALD frequently are malnourished, with depleted protein stores and vitamin deficiencies; the complex nutritional management of these patients is best suited to clinical nutritionists with expertise in this area. In patients with severe alcoholic hepatitis, prednisolone may be used; however, this remains controversial and is contraindicated in the presence of infection, bleeding, or renal impairment (O'Shea et al., 2010). Box 25-8 reviews dietary management appropriate for patients with hepatitis.

General management includes supportive care with adequate rest, correction of bleeding abnormalities, treatment of infection, and management of fluid overload. Trained providers in alcohol addiction should be employed once the patient is able to engage in therapy to maintain abstinence.

DRUG-INDUCED LIVER DISEASE (DRUG-RELATED HEPATITIS)

Drug-induced hepatotoxicity is very common and can range from mild elevations in aminotransferases to fulminant liver failure. It is the most common cause of acute liver failure, accounting for more than 50% of all cases in the United States and the United Kingdom (Chun, Tong, Busuttil et al., 2009; Ichai & Samuel, 2008).

Pathophysiology

Although any medication can affect liver function, use of acetaminophen (found in many over-the-counter medications

used to treat fever and pain) has been identified as the leading cause of acute liver failure (Chun et al., 2009). Other medications commonly associated with liver injury include anesthetic agents, medications used to treat rheumatic and musculoskeletal disease, antidepressants, psychotropic medications, anticonvulsants, and antituberculosis agents (Ichai & Samuel, 2008).

Clinical Manifestations and Assessment

Manifestations of sensitivity to a medication may occur on the first day of its use or not until several months later, depending on the medication. Usually the onset is abrupt, with chills, fever, rash, pruritus, arthralgia, anorexia, and nausea. Later, there may be jaundice, dark urine, and an enlarged and tender liver. After the offending medication is withdrawn, symptoms may gradually subside. However, reactions can be severe, or even fatal, even if the medication is stopped. If fever, rash, or pruritus occurs from any medication, its use should be stopped immediately. A thorough history of all medications, over-the-counter medications, and supplements should be obtained from all patients presenting with signs or symptoms of acute or chronic liver disease.

Medical and Nursing Management

The management of drug-induced liver injury includes discontinuation of the suspected medication or medications; evaluation of liver damage, including hospitalization if jaundice or impaired hepatic function is present; and in cases of fulminant or acute liver failure, referral to a liver transplant center.

Although its efficacy is uncertain, a short course of high-dose corticosteroids may be used in patients with severe hypersensitivity (Younossi, 2008).

🔹 D R U G   A L E R T

The liver metabolizes many medications, such as barbiturates, opioids, sedative agents, anesthetics, and amphetamines. Metabolism generally results in inactivation of the medication, although in some cases activation of the medication may occur. One of the important pathways for medication metabolism involves conjugation (binding) of the medication with a variety of compounds to form more soluble substances that may be excreted in the feces or urine, similar to bilirubin excretion. Bioavailability is the fraction of the administered medication that actually reaches the systemic circulation. The bioavailability of an oral medication (absorbed from the GI tract) can be decreased if the medication is metabolized to a great extent by the liver before it reaches the systemic circulation; this is known as first-pass effect. Some medications have such a large first-pass effect that their use is essentially limited to the parenteral route, or oral doses must be substantially larger than parenteral doses to achieve the same effect. If medications are administered that have a high hepatic metabolism, bioavailability increases and hepatic clearance decreases in liver disease. It is important for the nurse to understand the clearance of medications and to observe patients for signs of further deterioration.

FULMINANT HEPATIC FAILURE

Fulminant hepatic failure is the clinical syndrome of sudden and severely impaired liver function in a previously healthy person.

Pathophysiology

Fulminant liver failure is caused by many different etiologies. Viral hepatitis caused by A, B, and E is a common culprit worldwide. Acetaminophen overdoses accounts for over 50% of fulminant liver failure cases in the United States, and is the leading cause for acute liver failure (ALF) in Great Britain, and parts of Europe (Chun et al., 2009).

Other causes of fulminant liver failure include drug overdoses or reactions, viruses such as herpes simplex and varicella zoster, toxins, metabolic disorders such as Wilson's disease, poisonous mushroom ingestion, and obstruction to hepatic blood flow (**Budd-Chiari syndrome**) (Ichai & Samual, 2008).

Clinical Manifestations and Assessment

The clinical manifestations of fulminant liver failure are **hepatic encephalopathy**, jaundice, nausea, anorexia, vomiting, and coagulopathy in a patient with no history of prior liver disease (Chun et al., 2009). The onset is abrupt, and the patient or family may or may not be able to identify the precipitating event.

Medical and Nursing Management

The clinical decision whether a patient will recover from acute liver injury with intense medical management or require liver transplantation is typically made on a case-by-case basis after careful evaluation of the patient (Schilsky, Honiden, Arnott et al., 2009). Multiple selection criteria have been developed to determine survival outcome (i.e., risk of death with or without transplant) and assist in the selection of patients appropriate for liver transplant, including time from jaundice to encephalopathy, prothrombin time, and levels of bilirubin, arterial pH, and creatinine (Ichai & Samuel, 2008).

Currently, in the United States, the United Network for Organ Sharing (UNOS) has defined criteria to determine which patients qualify for urgent transplant listing for fulminant liver failure:

- Onset of hepatic encephalopathy within 8 weeks of first symptoms of liver disease

- Absence of preexisting liver disease
- Transaminases ALT/AST of greater than 3,000
- INR greater than 2.0

Patients may require one of the following interventions:

- Ventilator dependence
- Dialysis or continuous veno-venous hemofiltration (CVVH) or continuous veno-venous hemofiltration with dialysis (CVVD)
- Patient requires care within a ICU

Patients with fulminant liver failure have a life expectancy of less than 7 days without liver transplant (United Network of Organ Sharing [UNOS], 2009).

The key to optimized treatment is rapid recognition of acute liver failure and intensive intervention. Supporting the patient in the ICU and assessing the indications for and feasibility of liver transplantation are hallmarks of management in this population. Fulminant hepatic failure is often accompanied by coagulation defects, renal failure and electrolyte disturbances, cardiovascular abnormalities, infection, hypoglycemia, encephalopathy, and cerebral edema. The use of antidotes for certain conditions may be indicated, such as *N*-acetylcysteine for acetaminophen toxicity.

In patients who have fulminant liver failure with stage three (somnolent but can be aroused) or four (coma) encephalopathy, or elevated serum ammonia, there is a high risk for cerebral edema, a life-threatening complication. These patients may require intracranial pressure monitoring, although its use remains controversial. Measures to promote adequate cerebral perfusion include careful fluid balance and hemodynamic assessments, a quiet environment, and diuresis with mannitol, an osmotic diuretic. Use of barbiturate anesthesia or pharmacologic paralysis and sedation is indicated to prevent surges in intracranial pressure related to agitation. Other support measures include monitoring for and treating hypoglycemia, coagulopathy, renal impairment, and infection. Despite these treatment modalities, the mortality rate remains high. Consequently, liver transplantation (discussed later) has become the treatment of choice for fulminant hepatic failure (Schilsky et al., 2009).

CIRRHOSIS

The most common causes of chronic liver disease are viral hepatitis B and C, ALD, nonalcoholic fatty liver disease (NAFLD), primary biliary cirrhosis, and autoimmune disorders of the liver. Acute forms of liver dysfunction and failure can occur from viral agents, drug hepatotoxicity, toxins, parasites, or metabolic disorders such as Wilson's disease (Younossi, 2008). The development of cirrhosis is the final stage of all chronic liver disease and is one of the leading causes of death in the United States (Younossi, 2008).

Pathophysiology

Cirrhosis of the liver occurs when the normal liver tissue is replaced by fibrotic tissue in response to damage to liver cells resulting in accumulation of extracellular matrix or "scar." The progression from fibrosis to cirrhosis results in the loss of normal structure and function in the liver (Schiff et al., 2007). The progression and severity of chronic liver disease can be classified as either compensated or decompensated cirrhosis.

Clinical Manifestations and Assessment

Compensated cirrhosis is typically asymptomatic. The transition from compensated cirrhosis to decompensated cirrhosis results in the development of jaundice, ascites, GI bleeding from esophageal varices, and hepatic encephalopathy. Box 25-9 provides guidelines for assessing cirrhosis. The development of any of these complications of hepatic dysfunction signals that the patient has progressed to decompensated cirrhosis. The hallmarks of decompensated cirrhosis are the development of jaundice, ascites (fluid collection in the peritoneum), pedal edema, gastroesophageal varices, and hepatic

---

BOX 25-9 | **Focused Assessment**

Cirrhosis

Be alert for the following signs and symptoms:

Compensated Cirrhosis
- Intermittent mild fever
- Vascular spiders
- Palmar erythema (reddened palms)
- Unexplained epistaxis
- Ankle edema
- Vague morning indigestion
- Flatulent dyspepsia
- Abdominal pain
- Firm, enlarged liver
- Splenomegaly

Decompensated Cirrhosis
- Ascites
- Jaundice
- Weakness
- Muscle wasting
- Weight loss
- Continuous mild fever
- Clubbing of fingers
- Purpura (due to decreased platelet count)
- Spontaneous bruising
- Epistaxis
- Hypotension
- Sparse body hair
- White nails
- Gonadal atrophy

encephalopathy. Other complications, such as spontaneous bacterial peritonitis, hepatorenal syndrome (renal dysfunction), and hepatopulmonary syndrome (causes symptoms such as shortness of breath and hypoxemia) may occur as well (Garcia-Tsao et al., 2007; Runyon, 2009).

Medical Management

NURSING PROCESS

The Patient With Cirrhosis

Assessment

Nursing assessment focuses on the onset of symptoms and the history of precipitating factors, particularly long-term alcohol abuse, as well as dietary intake and changes in the patient's physical and mental status. The patient's past and current patterns of alcohol use (duration and amount) are assessed and documented. It is also important to document any exposure to toxic agents encountered in the workplace or during recreational activities. The nurse documents and reports exposure to potentially hepatotoxic substances, including medications, illicit IV/injection drugs, inhalants, and general anesthetic agents.

The nurse assesses the patient's mental status during the interview and other interactions with the patient; orientation to person, place, and time is noted. The patient's ability to carry out a job or household activities provides some information about physical and mental status. The patient's relationships with family, friends, and coworkers may give some indication about incapacitation secondary to alcohol abuse and cirrhosis. Abdominal distention and bloating, GI bleeding, bruising, and weight changes are noted.

The nurse assesses nutritional status, which is of major importance in cirrhosis, by obtaining daily weights and monitoring plasma proteins, transferrin, and creatinine levels. A plan of nursing care for a patient with impaired liver function is available online at http://thePoint.lww.com/Pellico1e.

Diagnosis

Nursing diagnoses may include the following:

- Activity intolerance related to fatigue, general debility, muscle wasting, and discomfort
- Imbalanced nutrition, less than body requirements, related to chronic gastritis, decreased GI motility, and anorexia
- Impaired skin integrity related to compromised immunologic status, edema, and poor nutrition
- Risk for injury and bleeding related to altered clotting mechanisms

Potential complications may include the following:

- Bleeding and hemorrhage
- Hepatic encephalopathy
- Fluid volume excess

Planning

The goals for the patient may include increased participation in activities, improvement of nutritional status, improvement of skin integrity, decreased potential for injury, improvement of mental status, and absence of complications.

Nursing Interventions

Promoting Rest

The patient with active liver disease requires rest and other supportive measures to permit the liver to reestablish its functional ability. If the patient is hospitalized, weight and fluid intake and output are measured and recorded daily. The nurse adjusts the patient's position in bed for maximal respiratory efficiency, which is especially important if ascites is marked, because it interferes with adequate thoracic excursion. Oxygen therapy may be required in liver failure to oxygenate the damaged cells and prevent further cell destruction.

Rest reduces the demands on the liver and increases the liver's blood supply. Because the patient is susceptible to the hazards of immobility, efforts to prevent respiratory, circulatory, and vascular disturbances are initiated, such as range-of-motion exercises, turning every 2 hours, and the use of an incentive spirometer (IS) every hour while awake. These measures may help prevent such problems as pneumonia, thrombophlebitis, and pressure ulcers. After nutritional status improves and strength increases, the nurse encourages the patient to increase activity gradually. Activity and mild exercise, as well as rest, are planned.

Improving Nutritional Status

The patient with cirrhosis who has no ascites or edema and exhibits no signs of impending hepatic coma should receive a nutritious, high-protein diet, if tolerated, supplemented by vitamins of the B complex and others as indicated (including vitamins A, C, K, and folic acid). Because proper nutrition is so important, the nurse makes every effort to encourage the patient to eat. Proper nutrition is as important as any medication. Often, small, frequent meals are better tolerated than three large meals because of the abdominal pressure exerted by ascites. Protein supplements may also be indicated.

Patient preferences are considered. Patients with prolonged or severe anorexia and those who are vomiting or eating poorly for any reason may receive nutrients by the enteral or parenteral route.

Patients with fatty stools (steatorrhea) should receive water-soluble forms of fat-soluble vitamins—A, D, and E (Aquasol A, D, and E). Folic acid and iron are prescribed to prevent anemia. If the patient shows signs of impending or advancing coma, the amount of protein in the diet is decreased temporarily. In the absence of hepatic encephalopathy, a moderate-protein, high-calorie intake is provided, with protein foods of high biologic value. A diet containing

(continued on page 706)

1 to 1.5 g of protein per kilogram of body weight per day is required unless the patient is malnourished. Protein is restricted if encephalopathy develops. Incorporating vegetable protein to meet protein needs may decrease the risk for encephalopathy. Sodium restriction is also indicated to prevent ascites.

Providing Skin Care

Providing careful skin care is important because of subcutaneous edema, the patient's immobility, jaundice, and increased susceptibility to skin breakdown and infection. Frequent changes in position are necessary to prevent pressure ulcers. It is important to avoid irritating soaps and the use of adhesive tape, to prevent trauma to the skin. Lotion may be soothing to irritated skin; the nurse takes measures to minimize scratching by the patient.

Reducing Risk of Injury

The nurse protects the patient with cirrhosis from falls and other injuries. The side rails should be in place and padded with blankets or other materials in case the patient becomes agitated or restless. To minimize agitation, the nurse orients the patient to time and place and explains all procedures. The nurse instructs the patient to ask for assistance to get out of bed. The nurse carefully evaluates any injury because of the possibility of internal bleeding.

Because of the risk for bleeding from abnormal clotting, the patient should use an electric razor rather than a safety razor. A soft-bristled toothbrush helps minimize bleeding gums, and pressure applied to all venipuncture sites helps minimize bleeding.

Monitoring and Managing Potential Complications

BLEEDING AND HEMORRHAGE. The patient is at increased risk for bleeding and hemorrhage because of decreased production of prothrombin and decreased ability of the diseased liver to synthesize the necessary substances for blood coagulation. Precautionary measures include protecting the patient with padded side rails, applying pressure to injection sites, and avoiding injury from sharp objects. The nurse observes for melena and assesses stools for blood (signs of possible internal bleeding). Vital signs are monitored regularly. Precautions are taken to minimize rupture of esophageal varices by avoiding further increases in portal pressure (see earlier discussion). Dietary modification and appropriate use of stool softeners may help prevent straining during defecation. The nurse closely monitors the patient for GI bleeding and keeps readily available equipment (e.g., balloon tamponade tube), IV fluids, and medications needed to treat hemorrhage from esophageal and gastric varices.

If hemorrhage occurs, the nurse helps the physician initiate measures to halt the bleeding and administers fluid and blood component therapy and medications. The patient with massive hemorrhage from bleeding esophageal or gastric varices is transferred to the ICU and requires emergency surgery or other treatment modalities. The patient and family require explanations about the event and the necessary treatment.

HEPATIC ENCEPHALOPATHY. Hepatic encephalopathy and coma, possible complications of cirrhosis, may manifest as deteriorating mental status and dementia or as physical signs such as abnormal voluntary and involuntary movements. Hepatic encephalopathy is mainly caused by the accumulation of ammonia in the blood and its effect on cerebral metabolism. Many factors predispose the patient with cirrhosis to hepatic encephalopathy. Therefore, the patient may require extensive diagnostic testing to identify hidden sources of bleeding and increased ammonia production.

Treatment may include the use of lactulose and nonabsorbable intestinal tract antibiotics to decrease ammonia levels, modification of medications to eliminate those that may precipitate or worsen hepatic encephalopathy, and bedrest to minimize energy expenditure.

Monitoring is an essential nursing function to identify early deterioration in mental status. The nurse monitors the patient's mental status closely and reports changes, so that treatment of encephalopathy can be initiated promptly. Because electrolyte disturbances can contribute to encephalopathy, serum electrolyte levels are carefully monitored and corrected if abnormal. Oxygen is administered if oxygen desaturation occurs. The nurse monitors for fever or abdominal pain, which may signal the onset of bacterial peritonitis or other infection (see earlier discussion of hepatic encephalopathy).

FLUID VOLUME EXCESS. Patients with advanced chronic liver disease develop cardiovascular abnormalities. These occur due to an increased cardiac output and decreased peripheral vascular resistance, possibly resulting from the release of vasodilators. A hyperdynamic circulatory state develops in patients with cirrhosis, and plasma volume increases. The greater the degree of hepatic decompensation, the more severe the hyperdynamic state. Close assessment of cardiovascular and respiratory status is of key importance for the care of patients with this disorder. Pulmonary compromise, which is always a potential complication of ESLD because of plasma volume excess, makes prevention of pulmonary complications an important role for the nurse. Administering diuretics, implementing fluid restrictions, and enhancing patient positioning can optimize pulmonary function. Fluid retention may be noted in the development of ascites, lower extremity swelling, and dyspnea. Monitoring of intake and output, daily weight changes, changes in abdominal girth, and edema formation is part of nursing assessment in the hospital or in the home setting. Patients are also monitored for any changes in renal function.

Promoting Home and Community-Based Care

During the hospital stay, the nurse and other health care providers prepare the patient with cirrhosis for discharge,

focusing on dietary instruction. Of greatest importance is the exclusion of alcohol from the diet. The patient may need referral to Alcoholics Anonymous, psychiatric care, or counseling, or may benefit from support from a spiritual advisor. The patient should also avoid the consumption of raw shellfish.

Sodium restriction will continue for a considerable time, if not permanently. The patient will require written instructions, teaching, reinforcement, and support from the staff as well as family members.

Successful treatment depends on convincing the patient of the need to adhere completely to the therapeutic plan. The nurse also instructs the patient and family about symptoms of impending encephalopathy, possible bleeding tendencies, and susceptibility to infection.

Recovery is neither rapid nor easy; there are frequent setbacks and apparent lack of improvement. Many patients find it difficult to refrain from using alcohol for comfort or escape. The nurse plays a significant role in offering support and encouragement to the patient.

Evaluation

Expected patient outcomes may include the following:

1. Participates in activities:
   a. Plans activities and exercises to allow alternating periods of rest and activity
   b. Reports increased strength and well-being
   c. Participates in hygiene care
2. Increases nutritional intake:
   a. Demonstrates intake of appropriate nutrients and avoidance of alcohol as reflected by diet log
   b. Gains weight without increased edema and ascites formation
   c. Reports decrease in GI disturbances and anorexia
   d. Identifies foods and fluids that are nutritious and allowed on or restricted from the diet
   e. Adheres to vitamin therapy regimen
   f. Describes the rationale for small, frequent meals
3. Exhibits improved skin integrity:
   a. Has intact skin without evidence of breakdown, infection, or trauma
   b. Demonstrates normal turgor of skin of the extremities and trunk, and decreased edema
   c. Changes position frequently and inspects bony prominences daily
   d. Uses lotions to decrease pruritus
4. Avoids injury
   a. Is free of ecchymotic areas or hematoma formation
   b. States rationale for side rails and asks for assistance to get out of bed
   c. Uses measures to prevent trauma (e.g., uses electric razor and soft toothbrush, blows nose gently, arranges furniture to prevent bumps and falls, avoids straining during defecation)
5. Is free of complications:
   a. Reports absence of frank bleeding from the GI tract (i.e., absence of melena and hematemesis)
   b. Is oriented to time, place, and person and demonstrates normal attention span
   c. Has a serum ammonia level within normal limits
   d. Identifies early, reportable signs of impaired thought processes

HEPATOCELLULAR CARCINOMA

Hepatocellular carcinoma (HCC) is the fifth leading cause of cancer and is responsible for a high incidence of mortality relating to cancer (Schiff et al., 2007).

Risk Factors

HCC is strongly linked to cirrhosis and chronic hepatitis B and C infections. ALD, nonalcoholic steatohepatitis (inflammation and fat accumulation of the liver), primary biliary cirrhosis, and hemochromatosis (excessive retained iron in the body) are also thought to increase risk for HCC. An age of greater than 50 years and male gender also increase the likelihood of HCC developing in patients with cirrhosis (Schiff et al., 2007). HCC may arise in patients without cirrhosis; typically these are individuals with chronic hepatitis B infection.

Clinical Manifestations and Assessment

The clinical manifestations of hepatocellular carcinoma are usually found in the context of the patient with known cirrhosis: jaundice, ascites, varices, and the stigmata of chronic liver disease are common features. Unintentional weight loss, anorexia, and right upper quadrant pain may be additional presenting signs. In late cases, the patient may present with intra-abdominal bleeding from tumor rupture. In patients deemed high risk, routine screening with abdominal ultrasound and measurement of alpha fetoprotein levels has improved the detection of liver cancer (El-Serag, Marrero, Rudolph et al., 2008).

The diagnosis of liver cancer is based on clinical signs and symptoms, the history and physical examination, and the results of laboratory and imaging studies. Increased serum levels of bilirubin, alkaline phosphatase, GGT, and alpha fetoprotein may occur. Anemia is a common finding, and leukocytosis (increased white blood cells [WBCs]), hypercalcemia, hypoglycemia, and hypocholesterolemia may also be seen on laboratory assessment.

Confirmation of the diagnosis of HCC is made radiologically with use of computed tomography (CT) scan imaging

or magnetic resonance imaging (MRI) to determine the number, size, and location of tumors and if vascular invasion has occurred. In equivocal cases, liver biopsy may be used to obtain tissue samples of the lesion to determine malignancy (El-Serag et al., 2008).

Medical and Nursing Management

Currently there are multiple treatment options for the patient with HCC. Surgical resection is the preferred treatment for patients without cirrhosis and with adequate hepatic reserve; 5-year survival outcomes after resection now exceed 50% (Bruix & Sherman, 2010). In patients with HCC and cirrhosis, liver transplantation (discussed in detail below) is the treatment of choice. Liver transplantation is curative for patients with both HCC and ESLD; however, careful patient selection is critical to achieve good outcomes (El-Serag et al., 2008).

Other treatments for HCC are percutaneous ethanol injection (PEI) and radiofrequency ablation (RFA), which directly induce tumor necrosis Transarterial chemoembolization (TACE) is used to block the hepatic blood flow feeding the tumor and is used in combination with chemotherapeutic agents (El-Serag et al., 2008; Schiff et al., 2007). Systemic chemotherapy includes sorafenib and other agents; multiple clinical trials are currently under way to study the effectiveness of chemotherapeutic agents to treat HCC (El-Serag et al., 2008).

LIVER TRANSPLANTATION

With recent advances in surgical techniques, immunosuppressant medications, and increased knowledge of immunology, liver transplantation has become the treatment of choice for patients with ESLD and acute liver failure. Because liver transplantation is now recognized as an established therapeutic modality, rather than an experimental procedure to treat these disorders, the number of liver transplantation centers is increasing. Patients requiring transplantation are often referred from distant hospitals to these sites. To prepare the patient and family for liver transplantation, nurses in all settings must understand the processes and procedures of liver transplantation.

The transplantation procedure involves total surgical removal of the diseased liver and replacement with a healthy donor organ in the same anatomic location (**orthotopic liver transplantation** [OLT]). The efficacy of this therapeutic modality is demonstrated by survival outcomes of over 85% at 1 year and 75% at 5 years (Koffron & Stein, 2008). The important benefit of this option for patients with ESLD or fulminant liver failure is limited by the shortage of cadaveric donor organs. As of 2009, over 16,000 patients were on the national UNOS transplant list awaiting liver transplant (HRSA/OPTN, 2011).

Indications and Contraindications

Indications for liver transplantation include:

- Advanced chronic liver disease
- Fulminant hepatic failure
- Metabolic liver diseases
- HCC
- Hepatocellular liver diseases (e.g., viral hepatitis, drug- or alcohol-induced liver disease, Wilson's disease)
- Cholestatic diseases (interruption in bile flow seen in primary biliary cirrhosis, sclerosing cholangitis, and biliary atresia)

Other less common diseases requiring liver transplantation are polycystic liver disease, vascular disease (Budd-Chiari), and rare metabolic disorders (Koffron & Stein, 2008).

Medical contraindications for liver transplant include uncontrolled infection, extrahepatic malignancy or advanced hepatobiliary metastatic disease, irreversible brain damage, anatomic difficulties, and multiorgan failure. Psychosocial contraindications include active substance use, medical nonadherence, and severe psychiatric instability (Koffron & Stein, 2008). Other factors that may present obstacles to successful transplant are comorbidities such as advanced cardiac or pulmonary disease, and poor psychosocial support.

Selection and Evaluation for Liver Transplant

The selection and evaluation of a patient for liver transplantation is a multidisciplinary process that requires a complete assessment of the patient, including etiology and stage of liver disease, and evaluation of comorbidities and/or contraindications, psychosocial status, and any medical or surgical issues. The patient being considered for liver transplantation frequently has many systemic problems that influence preoperative and postoperative care. The medical condition of the patient must be optimized as well as possible to prevent complications and to ensure good outcomes. Patients must undergo complete medical, surgical, and psychosocial testing to determine if liver transplant is feasible, and for organ matching.

Once the patient is evaluated and deemed appropriate for liver transplant by the transplant center, he or she is placed on the national transplant wait-list administered by the United Network for Organ Sharing (UNOS). The priority for obtaining a cadaveric liver organ is determined by the Model of End Stage Liver Disease (MELD) score, which stratifies the level of illness of those awaiting a liver transplant. The MELD score is derived from a complex formula incorporating bilirubin levels, prothrombin time (reported as INR), and creatinine levels. The MELD score is an indicator of short-term mortality for those with ESLD. Additional priority beyond the patient's physiologic MELD score may be provided for selected diseases that increase the patient's mortality risk such as HCC, hepatopulmonary syndrome, and metabolic diseases of the liver. The highest priority on

the transplant wait-list is provided to patients with acute or fulminant liver failure (HRSA/OPTN, 2010).

Surgical Procedure

The transplant operation involves total removal of the diseased liver or hepatectomy, replacement with the donor organ, vascular anastomoses of the donor liver to the recipient, and biliary reconstruction. The stages of this complex surgical procedure are divided in three phases: hepatectomy, anhepatic (no liver) phase, and reperfusion phase.

The first stage involves the total removal of the diseased liver. Vascular clamps are placed on the portal vein and the inferior vena cava above and below the liver, and the native liver is dissected from the recipient. Hemostasis is maintained using sutures and cauterization of bleeding vessels. After preparation of the donor liver, anastomoses of the suprahepatic inferior vena cava, infrahepatic inferior vena cava, and portal vein surgically connect the donor liver to the recipient. Reperfusion of the new donor liver is achieved by removal of vascular clamps and perfusion of portal venous blood. Hepatic artery anastomosis is then performed and last, biliary reconstruction.

Multiple surgical innovations have been developed to prevent complications such as bleeding, bile leaks, and reperfusion injury of the new graft to improve outcomes (Schiff et al., 2007; Younossi, 2008).

Liver transplantation is a long surgical procedure, partly because the patient with liver failure often has portal hypertension that requires the ligation of many venous collateral vessels. Blood loss during the surgical procedure may be extensive. If the patient has adhesions from previous abdominal surgery, lysis of adhesions is often necessary. If a shunt procedure was performed previously, it must be surgically reversed to permit adequate portal venous blood supply to the new liver. During the lengthy surgery, it is helpful to provide regular updates to the family about the progress of the operation and the patient's status.

Complications

Immediate postoperative complications may include bleeding, infection, rejection, and delayed graft function. Other complications include biliary leaks and obstruction, hepatic artery thrombosis, and portal vein thrombosis (Koffron & Stein, 2008).

Primary Graft Nonfunction

Primary graft nonfunction is the most severe complication of liver transplant and occurs in 5% to 10% of cases. Ongoing encephalopathy, coagulopathy, jaundice, metabolic acidosis, and hemodynamic instability are clinical indications of primary graft nonfunction (Younossi, 2008). Transplant recipients with primary graft nonfunction require immediate retransplantation and receive priority on the transplant wait-list (HRSA/OPTN, 2010).

Bleeding

Bleeding is common in the postoperative period and may result from coagulopathy, portal hypertension, and fibrinolysis (breakdown of fibrin clots) caused by ischemic injury to the donor liver. Hypotension may occur in this phase, secondary to blood loss. Administration of platelets, fresh-frozen plasma, or other blood products may be necessary. Hypertension is more common, although its cause is uncertain. Blood pressure elevation that is significant or sustained is treated.

Infection

Infection is the leading cause of death after liver transplantation. Pulmonary and fungal infections are common; susceptibility to infection is increased by the immunosuppressive therapy that is needed to prevent rejection (Schiff et al., 2007). Therefore, precautions must be taken to prevent health care–associated infections. The nurse uses strict asepsis when manipulating central venous catheters, arterial lines, and urine, bile, and other drainage systems; when obtaining specimens; and when changing dressings. Meticulous hand hygiene and contact precautions is crucial to prevent infection in the liver transplant recipient.

Rejection

Rejection is a primary concern. A transplanted liver is perceived by the immune system as a foreign antigen. This triggers an immune response, leading to the activation of T lymphocytes that attack and destroy the transplanted liver. Immunosuppressive agents are used as long-term therapy to prevent this response and rejection of the transplanted liver. These agents inhibit the activation of immunocompetent T lymphocytes to prevent the production of effector T cells. Most transplant centers use two or three immunosuppressants in combination to prevent rejection (Younossi, 2008). The liver transplant recipient requires intensive education in dosing, side effects, and the drug interactions of these medications and will require life-long immunosuppression.

Although the 1- and 5-year survival rates have increased dramatically with the use of new immunosuppressive therapies, these advances are not without side effects. Both cyclosporine and tacrolimus have important side effects such as renal dysfunction, hypertension, hyperlipidemia, and hyperkalemia. Neurotoxicity may occur with use of tacrolimus, and patients may experience tremors to more severe complications such as psychosis or seizures. Optimal dosing of immunosuppression must be carefully monitored to prevent rejection and to reduce side effects (Younossi, 2008).

Despite the success of immunosuppression in reducing the incidence of rejection of transplanted organs, liver transplantation is not routine and may be accompanied by complications related to the lengthy surgical procedure, immunosuppressive therapy, infection, and the technical difficulties encountered in reconstructing the blood vessels and biliary tract.

Nursing Management

The patient considering transplantation, together with the family, must make difficult choices about treatment, use of financial resources, and relocation to another area to be closer to the medical center. They must also cope with the patient's longstanding health problems and any social and family problems associated with behaviors that may have caused the patient's liver failure. As a result, considerable emotional stress occurs while the patient and family consider liver transplantation and wait for an available liver. The nurse must be aware of these issues and attuned to the emotional and psychological status of the patient and family. Referral to a psychiatric liaison nurse, psychologist, psychiatrist, or spiritual advisor may help them cope with the stressors associated with ESLD and liver transplantation.

Preoperative Nursing Interventions

The nurse, surgeon, hepatologist, and other health care team members provide the patient and family with full explanations about the procedure, the chances of success, and the risks, including the side effects of long-term immunosuppression. The need for close follow-up and life-long compliance with the therapeutic regimen, including immunosuppression, is explained to the patient and family.

The nurse coordinator is an integral member of the transplant team and plays an important role in preparing the patient for liver transplantation. The nurse serves as advocate for the patient and family and assumes the important role of liaison between the patient and the other members of the transplant team. The nurse also serves as a resource to other nurses and health care team members involved in evaluating and caring for the patient.

Postoperative Nursing Interventions

The patient is maintained in an environment as free from bacteria, viruses, and fungi as possible, because immunosuppressive medications reduce the body's natural defenses. In the immediate postoperative period, cardiovascular, pulmonary, renal, neurologic, and metabolic functions are monitored continuously. Mean arterial and pulmonary artery pressures are also monitored. Ventilator support and airway management are priorities. Cardiac output (CO), central venous pressure (CVP), pulmonary artery pressures (PAPs), pulmonary capillary wedge pressure (PCWP), arterial and mixed venous blood gases, oxygen saturation, oxygen demand and delivery, urine output, heart rate, and blood pressure are used to evaluate the patient's hemodynamic status and intravascular fluid volume. Liver function tests, electrolyte levels, the coagulation profile, chest X-ray, electrocardiogram, and fluid output (including urine, bile from the T tube, and output from nasogastric [NG] and drainage tubes) are monitored closely. Because the liver is responsible for the storage of glycogen and the synthesis of protein and clotting factors, these substances need to be monitored and replaced in the immediate postoperative period. The nurse monitors for signs of excess bleeding in the immediate postoperative period and notifies the provider immediately if bleeding is suspected (hypotension, tachycardia, tachypnea, decreasing CO, CVP, PAPs, PCWP, melena, increasing abdominal girth, bloody nasogastric drainage, etc.).

There is a high risk for atelectasis and an altered ventilation–perfusion ratio, caused by insult to the diaphragm during the surgical procedure, prolonged anesthesia, immobility, and postoperative pain. Because of this risk, the patient will have an endotracheal tube in place and will require mechanical ventilation during the initial postoperative period. Suctioning is performed as required, and sterile humidification is provided.

As the vital signs and condition stabilize, efforts are made to assist the patient to recover from the trauma of this complex surgery. After removal of the endotracheal tube, the nurse encourages the patient to use an IS to decrease the risk for atelectasis. Once the arterial lines and the urinary catheter are removed, the patient is assisted to get out of bed, to ambulate as tolerated, and to participate in self-care to prevent the complications associated with immobility. Close monitoring for signs and symptoms of liver dysfunction and rejection continue throughout the hospital stay. Plans are made for close follow-up after discharge as well. Teaching is initiated during the preoperative period and continues after surgery.

Promoting Home and Community-Based Care

Teaching the patient and family about long-term measures to promote health is crucial for the success of transplantation and represents an important role of the nurse. The patient and family must understand why they need to adhere continuously to the therapeutic regimen, with special emphasis on the methods of administration, rationale, and side effects of the prescribed immunosuppressive agents. The nurse provides written as well as verbal instructions about how and when to take the medications. To avoid running out of medication or skipping a dose, the patient must make sure that an adequate supply of medication is available. Instructions are also provided about the signs and symptoms that indicate problems necessitating consultation with the transplant team.

The nurse emphasizes the importance of follow-up blood tests and appointments with the transplant team. Trough blood levels of immunosuppressive agents are obtained, along with other blood tests that assess the function of the liver and kidneys. During the first months, the patient is likely to require blood tests two or three times a week. As the patient's condition stabilizes, blood studies and visits to the transplant team are less frequent. The importance of routine ophthalmologic examinations is emphasized because of the increased incidence of cataracts and glaucoma associated with the long-term corticosteroid therapy used with transplantation. Regular oral hygiene and follow-up dental care, with administration of prophylactic antibiotics before dental examinations and treatments, are recommended because of the immunosuppression.

The nurse reminds the patient that preventing rejection and infection leads to a successful transplantation and increases the chances for survival and living a more normal life than before transplantation. Many patients have lived successful and productive lives after receiving a liver transplant.

DISORDERS OF THE GALLBLADDER

Several disorders affect the biliary system and interfere with normal drainage of bile into the duodenum. These disorders include inflammation of the biliary system and carcinoma that obstructs the biliary tree. Gallbladder disease with gallstones is the most common disorder of the biliary system. Although not all occurrences of gallbladder inflammation (**cholecystitis**) are related to gallstones (**cholelithiasis**), more than 90% of patients with acute cholecystitis have gallstones. However, most of the 20 million Americans with gallstones have no pain and are unaware of the presence of stones.

CHOLELITHIASIS

Calculi, or gallstones, usually form in the gallbladder from the solid constituents of bile; they vary greatly in size, shape, and composition (Fig. 25-11).

Pathophysiology

There are two major types of gallstones: those composed predominantly of pigment and those composed primarily of cholesterol. Pigment stones form when unconjugated pigments in the bile precipitate to form stones. The risk of developing such stones is increased in patients with cirrhosis, hemolysis, and infections of the biliary tract. Pigment stones cannot be dissolved and must be removed surgically.

Cholesterol stones account for over 50% of gallbladder disease in the United States. Cholesterol, a normal constituent of bile, is insoluble in water. Its solubility depends on bile acids and lecithin (phospholipids) in bile. In gallstone-prone patients, there is decreased bile acid synthesis and increased cholesterol synthesis in the liver, resulting in bile supersaturated with cholesterol, which precipitates out of the bile to form stones. The cholesterol-saturated bile predisposes to the formation of gallstones and acts as an irritant that produces inflammatory changes in the gallbladder (Schiff et al., 2007).

Risk Factors

Gallstones are uncommon in children and young adults but become increasingly prevalent after 40 years of age, especially in women (Box 25-10).

Clinical Manifestations and Assessment

Gallstones may be silent, producing no pain and only mild GI symptoms. Such stones may be detected incidentally during surgery or evaluation for unrelated problems.

The patient with gallbladder disease resulting from gallstones may develop two types of symptoms: those due to

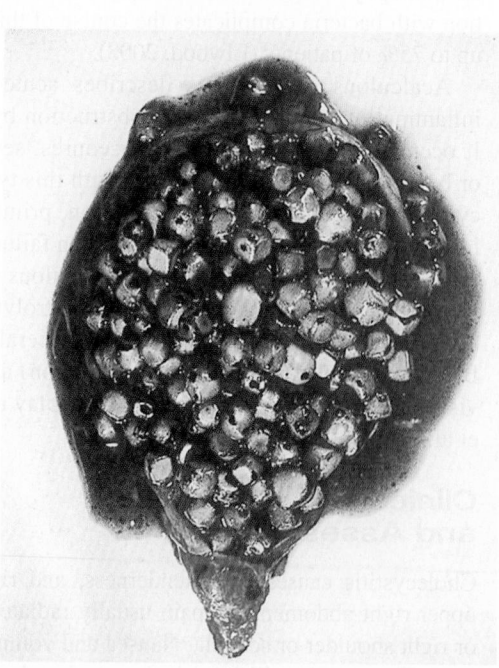 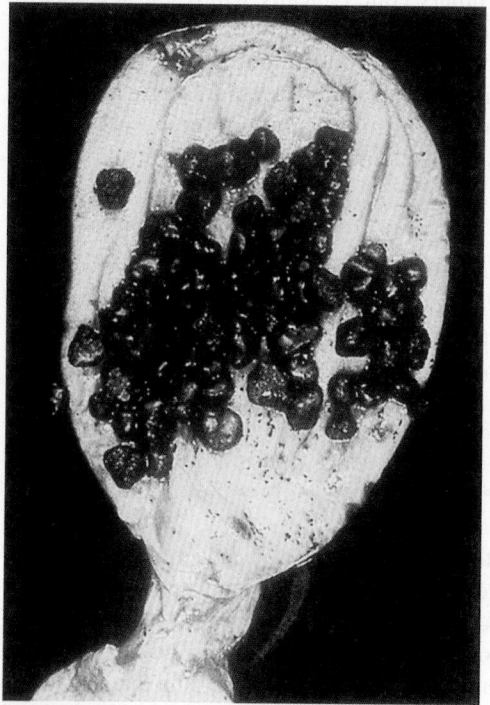

FIGURE 25-11 Examples of cholesterol gallstones (*left*) made up of a coalescence of multiple small stones and pigment gallstones (*right*) composed of calcium bilirubinate. From Rubin, R. & Strayer, D. S. (2008). *Rubin's Pathology* (5th edition). Philadelphia: Lippincott Williams & Wilkins.

Risk Factors for Cholelithiasis

- Obesity
- Female gender, especially women who have had multiple pregnancies or who are of Native American or U.S. Southwestern Hispanic ethnicity
- Frequent changes in weight
- Rapid weight loss (leads to rapid development of gallstones and high risk of symptomatic disease)
- Treatment with high-dose estrogen (e.g., in prostate cancer)
- Low-dose estrogen therapy; a small increase in the risk of gallstones
- Ileal resection or disease
- Gastric bypass
- Total parental nutrition
- Cystic fibrosis
- Diabetes mellitus
- Family history

disease of the gallbladder itself, and those due to obstruction of the bile passages by a gallstone. The symptoms may be acute or chronic. Epigastric distress, such as fullness, abdominal distention, and vague pain in the right upper quadrant of the abdomen, may occur. This distress may follow a meal rich in fried or fatty foods. Clinical manifestations of gallstones are largely asymptomatic; however, 15% to 20% of patients with gallstones will develop pain and biliary colic with repeated episodes of obstruction. Increased frequency of biliary colic typically will result in cholecystitis. If the gallstone is dislodged and no longer obstructs the cystic duct, the gallbladder drains and the inflammatory process subsides after a relatively short time. If the gallstone continues to obstruct the duct, abscess, necrosis, and perforation with generalized peritonitis may result.

! NURSING ALERT

The nurse is alert to the signs and symptoms of peritonitis, including abdominal pain that initially may be vague and generalized but becomes increasingly severe and constant; abdominal distention and tenderness with rebound tenderness; anxiety, paleness, and diaphoresis; anorexia; nausea; vomiting; inability to pass feces and flatus; rigidity of the abdomen; an absence of bowel sounds; cautious movement; and knee–chest position for comfort.

If a gallstone obstructs the cystic duct, the gallbladder becomes distended, inflamed, and eventually infected (acute cholecystitis). The patient develops a fever and may have a palpable abdominal mass. The patient may have biliary colic with excruciating upper right abdominal pain that radiates to the back or right shoulder. Biliary colic is usually associated with nausea and vomiting, and is noticeable several hours after a heavy meal. The patient moves about restlessly, unable to find a comfortable position. The pain will fluctuate, lasting from 30 minutes to up to 6 hours. The patient may experience other symptoms including nausea, chills, and gastric distress including belching and bloating.

Such a bout of biliary colic is caused by contraction of the gallbladder, which cannot release bile because of obstruction by the stone. This produces marked tenderness in the right upper quadrant on deep inspiration and prevents full inspiratory excursion when the examiner's fingers are under the liver border, known as *Murphy's sign* (Elwood, 2008). See management under cholecystitis.

CHOLECYSTITIS

Cholecystitis is acute inflammation of the gallbladder. An empyema of the gallbladder develops if the gallbladder becomes filled with purulent fluid (pus). Repeated episodes of cystic duct obstruction by gallstones will cause cholecystitis.

Pathophysiology

Calculous cholecystitis is the cause of more than 90% of cases of acute cholecystitis (Schiff et al., 2007). In calculous cholecystitis, a gallbladder stone obstructs bile outflow. Bile remaining in the gallbladder initiates a chemical reaction; autolysis and edema occur. The gallbladder becomes inflamed and distended due to increased pressure and vascular compromise resulting in ischemia and necrosis. The release of inflammatory agents additionally plays a role in the pathophysiology of acute cholecystitis. Secondary infection with bacteria complicates the course of this disorder in up to 75% of patients (Elwood, 2008).

Acalculous cholecystitis describes acute gallbladder inflammation in the absence of obstruction by gallstones. It occurs after major surgical procedures, severe trauma, or burns. Other factors associated with this type of cholecystitis include cystic duct obstruction, primary bacterial infections of the gallbladder, multiorgan failure, and acute renal failure. It is speculated that acalculous cholecystitis is caused by alterations in fluids and electrolytes and alterations in regional blood flow in the visceral circulation. Bile stasis (lack of gallbladder contraction) and increased viscosity of the bile are also thought to play a role (Schiff et al., 2007).

Clinical Manifestations and Assessment

Cholecystitis causes pain, tenderness, and rigidity of the upper right abdomen; the pain usually radiates to the back or right shoulder or scapula. Nausea and vomiting are common. The patient will have leukocytosis (elevated WBCs), and physical examination may reveal a positive Murphy's sign (right subcostal tenderness) (Schiff et al., 2007).

Medical Management

The major objectives of medical therapy are to reduce the incidence of acute episodes of gallbladder pain and cholecystitis by supportive and dietary management and, if possible, to remove the cause of cholecystitis by pharmacologic therapy, endoscopic procedures, or surgical intervention. Asymptomatic cholelithiasis can be treated with ursodiol (URSO), a bile acid that dissolves gallstones and decreases biliary cholesterol formation. This treatment is limited to patients with small stones who demonstrate no complications. Initial management of cholecystitis involves bowel rest (i.e., nothing by mouth), management of fluids and electrolyte balance, pain management, and antibiotic coverage (Elwood, 2008).

Pharmacologic Therapy

Ursodeoxycholic acid (UDCA) and chenodeoxycholic acid (chenodiol or CDCA) have been used to dissolve small, radiolucent gallstones composed primarily of cholesterol. UDCA has fewer side effects than chenodiol and can be administered in smaller doses to achieve the same effect. It acts by inhibiting the synthesis and secretion of cholesterol, thereby desaturating bile. Treatment with UDCA can reduce the size of existing stones, dissolve small stones, and prevent new stones from forming. Six to 12 months of therapy is required in many patients to dissolve stones, and monitoring of the patient for recurrence of symptoms or the occurrence of side effects is required during this time. The effective dose of medication depends on body weight. This method of treatment is generally indicated for patients who refuse surgery or for whom surgery is considered too risky.

Patients with significant, frequent symptoms; cystic duct occlusion; or pigment stones are not candidates for this therapy.

Surgical Management

Laparoscopic or open cholecystectomy is more appropriate for symptomatic patients with acceptable operative risk. Removal of the gallbladder (**cholecystectomy**) through traditional surgical approaches was considered the standard treatment for more than 100 years. There is now widespread use of **laparoscopic cholecystectomy** (removal of the gallbladder through a small incision through the umbilicus). As a result, surgical risks have decreased, along with the length of hospital stay and the long recovery period required after standard surgical cholecystectomy (Schiff et al., 2007).

Laparoscopic Cholecystectomy

Laparoscopic cholecystectomy (Fig. 25-12) has dramatically changed the approach to the management of cholecystitis. It has become the new standard for therapy of symptomatic gallstones. Approximately 700,000 patients in the United States require surgery each year for removal of the gallbladder, and 80% to 90% of them are candidates for laparoscopic cholecystectomy.

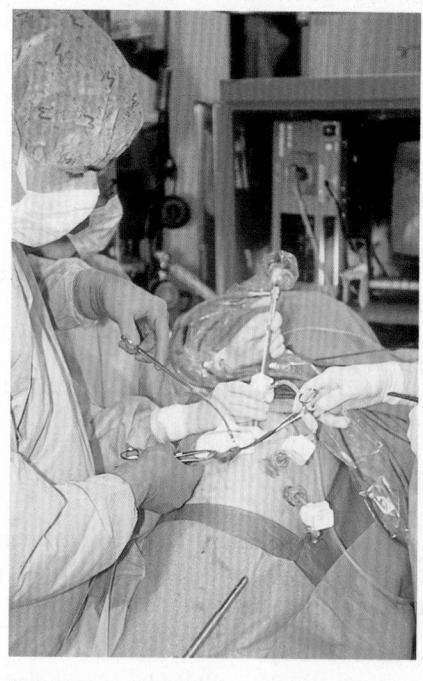

A

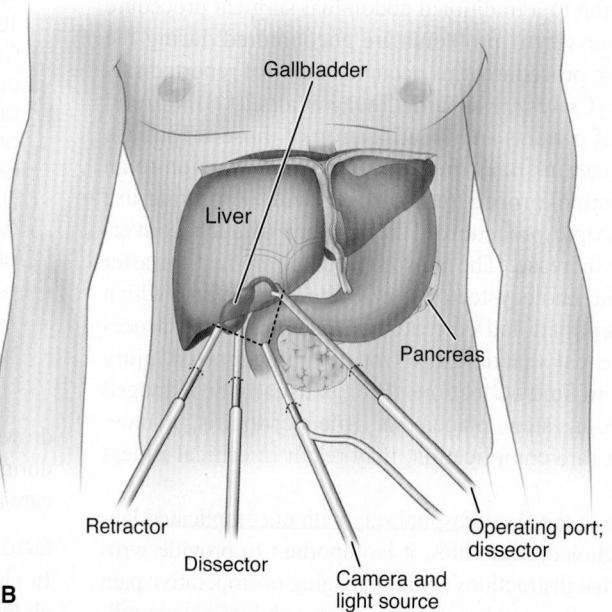

B

FIGURE 25-12 In laparoscopic cholecystectomy (**A**), the surgeon makes four small incisions (less than 12 inches each) in the abdomen (**B**) and inserts a laparoscope with a miniature camera through the umbilical incision. The camera apparatus displays the gallbladder and adjacent tissues on a screen, allowing the surgeon to visualize the sections of the organ for removal.

Before the procedure, the patient is informed that an open abdominal procedure may be necessary, and general anesthesia is administered. Laparoscopic cholecystectomy is performed through a small incision or puncture made through the abdominal wall at the umbilicus. The abdominal cavity is insufflated with carbon dioxide (pneumoperitoneum) to assist in inserting the laparoscope and to aid in visualizing the abdominal structures. The fiberoptic scope is inserted through the small umbilical incision. Several additional punctures or small incisions are made in the abdominal wall to introduce other surgical instruments into the operative field. The surgeon visualizes the biliary system through the laparoscope; a camera attached to the scope permits a view of the intra-abdominal field to be transmitted to a television monitor. After the cystic duct is dissected, the common bile duct can be visualized by ultrasound or cholangiography (imaging of the bile ducts with contrast medium) to evaluate the anatomy and identify stones. The cystic artery is dissected free and clipped. The gallbladder is separated from the hepatic bed and dissected. The gallbladder is then removed from the abdominal cavity after bile and small stones are aspirated. Stone forceps also can be used to remove or crush larger stones.

Advantages of the laparoscopic procedure are that the patient does not experience the paralytic ileus that occurs with open abdominal surgery and has less postoperative abdominal pain. Early laparoscopic cholecystectomy (within 24 to 48 hours of symptoms) is the preferred intervention for treatment of acute cholecystitis and results in reduced length of stay, fewer surgical complications, and faster recovery for the patient (Castillas, Yegiyants, Collins et al., 2008; Elwood, 2008).

Conversion to a traditional abdominal surgical procedure may be necessary if problems are encountered during the laparoscopic procedure; this occurs in 9.5% of reported surgical cases (Csikesz, Ricciardi, Tseng et al., 2008). Careful screening of patients and identification of those at low risk for complications limit the frequency of conversion to an open abdominal procedure. However, with increasing use of laparoscopic procedures, the number of such conversions may increase. The most serious complication after laparoscopic cholecystectomy is a bile duct injury, which may be identified and corrected at the time of the procedure. A bile leak that develops from an unrecognized injury may result in fluid collections that can usually be managed by endoscopic stent placement. Bile peritonitis, a more serious but rare complication, may result in critical illness or death.

Because of the short hospital stay with uncomplicated laparoscopic cholecystectomies, it is important to provide written and verbal instructions about managing postoperative pain and reporting signs and symptoms of intra-abdominal complications, including loss of appetite, vomiting, pain, distention of the abdomen, and temperature elevation. Although recovery from laparoscopic cholecystectomy is rapid, patients are

---

BOX 25-11 Patient Education

Managing Self-Care After Laparoscopic Cholecystectomy

Resuming Activity
- Begin light exercise (walking) immediately.
- Take a shower or bath after 1 or 2 days.
- Wait to drive a car for 3 or 4 days.
- Avoid lifting objects exceeding 5 pounds after surgery, usually for 1 week.
- Resume sexual activity when desired.

Caring for the Wound
- Check puncture site daily for signs of infection.
- Wash puncture site with mild soap and water.
- Allow special adhesive strips on the puncture site to fall off. Do not pull them off.

Resuming Eating
- Resume your normal diet.
- If you had fat intolerance before surgery, gradually add fat back into your diet in small increments.

Managing Pain
- You may experience pain or discomfort in your right shoulder from the gas used to inflate your abdominal area during surgery. Sitting upright in bed or a chair, walking, or use of a heating pad may ease the discomfort.
- Take analgesics as needed and as prescribed. Report to surgeon if pain is unrelieved even with analgesic use.

Managing Follow-Up Care
- Make an appointment with your surgeon for 7 to 10 days after discharge.
- Call your surgeon if you experience any signs or symptoms of infection at or around the puncture site: redness, tenderness, swelling, heat, or drainage.
- Call your surgeon if you experience a fever of 37.7°C (100°F) or more for 2 consecutive days.
- Call your surgeon if you develop nausea, vomiting, or abdominal pain.

---

drowsy afterward. The patient must have assistance at home during the first 24 to 48 hours. Box 25-11 details patient self-care after a laparoscopic cholecystectomy.

Cholecystectomy

In cholecystectomy, the gallbladder is removed through an abdominal incision (usually right subcostal) after the cystic duct and artery are ligated. The procedure is performed for acute and chronic cholecystitis. In some patients, a drain is placed close to the gallbladder bed and brought out through

a puncture wound if there is a bile leak. A small leak should close spontaneously in a few days, with the drain preventing accumulation of bile. Usually, only a small amount of serosanguineous fluid drains in the initial 24 hours after surgery; afterward, the drain is removed. The drain is typically maintained if there is excess oozing or bile leakage. Bile duct injury is a serious complication of cholecystectomy, but it occurs less frequently than with the laparoscopic approach. Patients with multiple comorbidities or with high surgical risk may be treated with the open cholecystectomy (Csikesz et al., 2008).

DISORDERS OF THE PANCREAS
PANCREATITIS

Pancreatitis (inflammation of the pancreas) is a serious disorder. The most basic classification system used to describe or categorize the various stages and forms of pancreatitis divides the disorder into acute and chronic forms. Acute pancreatitis can be a medical emergency associated with a high risk for life-threatening complications and mortality, whereas chronic pancreatitis often goes undetected until 80% to 90% of the **exocrine** and endocrine tissue is destroyed. Acute pancreatitis does not usually lead to chronic pancreatitis unless complications develop. However, chronic pancreatitis can be characterized by acute episodes. Common causes for pancreatitis are frequently due to alcohol abuse or gallstones; however drugs, trauma, infection, autoimmune disease, or infection may also result in pancreatitis (Toskes & Greenberger, 2008).

Although the mechanisms causing pancreatic inflammation are unknown, pancreatitis is commonly described as autodigestion of the pancreas. It is believed that the pancreatic duct becomes temporarily obstructed, accompanied by hypersecretion of the exocrine enzymes of the pancreas. These enzymes enter the bile duct, where they are activated and, together with bile, back up (reflux) into the pancreatic duct, causing pancreatitis.

ACUTE PANCREATITIS

Acute pancreatitis ranges from a mild, self-limited disorder to a severe, rapidly fatal disease that does not respond to any treatment. Mild acute pancreatitis is characterized by edema and inflammation confined to the pancreas. Minimal organ dysfunction is present, and return to normal function usually occurs within 6 months. Although this is considered the milder form of pancreatitis, the patient is acutely ill and at risk for hypovolemic shock, fluid and electrolyte disturbances, and sepsis. A more widespread and complete enzymatic digestion of the gland characterizes severe acute pancreatitis. Enzymes damage the local blood vessels, and bleeding and thrombosis can occur. The tissue may become necrotic, with damage extending into the retroperitoneal tissues. Local complications consist of pancreatic cysts or abscesses and acute fluid collections in or near the pancreas. Patients who develop systemic complications with organ failure, such as pulmonary insufficiency with hypoxia, shock, renal failure, and GI bleeding, are also characterized as having severe acute pancreatitis. This disorder is seen in approximately 20% of all patients with acute pancreatitis and has a mortality rate of over 30% (Bakker, van Santvoort, Besselink et al., 2009). The severity of acute pancreatitis and its outcomes can be predicted based on clinical and laboratory data (Box 25-12).

Pathophysiology

Self-digestion of the pancreas by its own proteolytic enzymes, principally **trypsin**, causes acute pancreatitis. Activation of the enzymes can lead to vasodilation, inflammation, increased vascular permeability, necrosis, erosion, and hemorrhage. This cascade of events may also result in multiorgan failure (Toskes & Greenberger, 2008).

Long-term use of alcohol is commonly associated with acute episodes of pancreatitis, but the patient usually has had undiagnosed chronic pancreatitis before the first episode of acute pancreatitis occurs.

Other, less common causes of pancreatitis include bacterial or viral infection, with pancreatitis occasionally developing as a complication of mumps virus. Spasm and edema of the ampulla of Vater, caused by duodenitis (inflammation of duodenum), can probably produce pancreatitis. Blunt abdominal trauma, peptic ulcer disease, ischemic vascular disease, hyperlipidemia, hypercalcemia, and the use of corticosteroids, thiazide diuretics, oral contraceptives, and other medications have also been associated with an increased

---

BOX 25-12 | **Criteria for Predicting Severity of Pancreatitis***

Criteria on Admission to Hospital
Age >55 years
WBC >16,000 mm^3
Serum glucose >200 mg/dL (>11.1 mmol/L)
Serum LDH >350 IU/L (>350 U/L)
AST >250 U/mL (120 U/L)

Criteria Within 48 Hours of Hospital Admission
Fall in hematocrit >10% (>0.10)
Blood urea nitrogen (BUN) increase >5 mg/dL (>1.7 mmol/L)
Serum calcium <8 mg/dL (<2.0 mmol/L)
Base deficit >4 mEq/L (>4 mmol/L)
Fluid retention or sequestration >6 L
PO$_2$ <60 mm Hg
Two or fewer signs, 1% mortality; 3 or 4 signs, 15% mortality; 5 or 6 signs, 40% mortality; >6 signs, 100% mortality

*Note: The more risk factors a patient has, the greater the severity and likelihood of complications or death.

incidence of pancreatitis. Acute pancreatitis may develop after surgery on or near the pancreas or after instrumentation of the pancreatic duct. Acute idiopathic pancreatitis accounts for up to 15% of the cases of acute pancreatitis. In addition, there is a small incidence of hereditary pancreatitis (Rickes & Uhle, 2009).

Clinical Manifestations and Assessment

Severe abdominal pain is the major symptom of pancreatitis that causes the patient to seek medical care. Typically, the pain occurs in the midepigastrium. Pain is frequently acute in onset, occurring 24 to 48 hours after a very heavy meal or alcohol ingestion, and it may be diffuse and difficult to localize. It is generally more severe after meals and is unrelieved by antacids. Pain may be accompanied by abdominal distention; a poorly defined, palpable abdominal mass; and decreased peristalsis. Pain caused by pancreatitis is accompanied frequently by vomiting that fails to relieve the pain or nausea.

The patient appears acutely ill. Abdominal guarding is present. A rigid or board-like abdomen may develop and is generally an ominous sign; the abdomen may remain soft in the absence of peritonitis. Ecchymosis (bruising) in the flank (Grey-Turner sign) or around the umbilicus (Cullen sign) may indicate severe pancreatitis with retroperitoneal hemorrhage (see Chapter 27, Fig. 27-10). Nausea and vomiting are common in acute pancreatitis. The emesis is usually gastric in origin but may also be bile-stained. Fever, jaundice, mental confusion, and agitation may also occur.

Hypotension is typical and reflects hypovolemia and shock caused by the loss of large amounts of protein-rich fluid into the tissues and peritoneal cavity. In addition to hypotension, the patient may develop tachycardia, cyanosis, and cold, clammy skin. Respiratory distress and peritonitis are also associated with acute pancreatitis (Rickes & Uhle, 2009).

The diagnosis of acute pancreatitis is based on a history of abdominal pain, the presence of known risk factors, physical examination findings, and diagnostic findings. Serum **amylase** and **lipase** levels are used in making the diagnosis of acute pancreatitis. Serum amylase and lipase levels will be elevated three times the upper limit of normal in most cases. A history of gallstones, alcohol use, and viral infection is used to diagnose acute pancreatitis. The WBC count is usually elevated; hypocalcemia is present in many patients and correlates well with the severity of pancreatitis. Transient hyperglycemia and glucosuria and elevated serum bilirubin levels occur in some patients with acute pancreatitis. Plasma lipids and calcium are additional laboratory tests used to diagnose acute pancreatitis.

Ultrasound and contrast-enhanced CT scans are used to identify an increase in the diameter of the pancreas and to detect pancreatic cysts, abscesses, or pseudocysts. CT imaging is the modality of choice for the assessment of both acute and chronic pancreatitis. (Rickes & Uhle, 2009; Toskes & Greenberger, 2008).

Medical Management

The overall mortality rate of patients with acute pancreatitis is high because of shock, anoxia, hypotension, or fluid and electrolyte imbalances. Attacks of acute pancreatitis may result in complete recovery, may recur without permanent damage, or may progress to chronic pancreatitis. The patient who is admitted to the hospital with a diagnosis of pancreatitis is acutely ill and needs expert nursing and medical care (Rickes & Uhle, 2009).

Management of acute pancreatitis is directed toward relieving symptoms and preventing or treating complications. All oral intake is withheld, to inhibit stimulation of the pancreas and its secretion of enzymes. The current recommendation is that, whenever possible, the enteral route should be used to meet nutritional needs in patients with pancreatitis. This strategy also has been found to prevent infectious complications, safely and cost effectively (Bakker et al., 2009).

The mainstay of therapy for acute pancreatitis is analgesic management of pain, IV fluids to maintain intravascular volume, and elimination of oral intake. In cases of severe or necrotizing acute pancreatitis the use of antibiotics is recommended (Toskes & Greenberger, 2008).

Although surgery is often risky because the acutely ill patient is a poor surgical risk, it may be performed to assist in the diagnosis of pancreatitis (diagnostic laparotomy), to establish pancreatic drainage, or to resect or débride a necrotic pancreas (Bakker et al., 2009; Toskes & Greenberger, 2008).

Nursing Management

A plan of nursing care for a patient with acute pancreatitis is available online at http://thePoint.lww.com/Pellico1e.

Relieving Pain and Discomfort

Because the pathologic process responsible for pain is autodigestion of the pancreas, the objectives of therapy are to relieve pain and decrease secretion of pancreatic enzymes. The pain of acute pancreatitis is often very severe, necessitating the liberal use of analgesics. The current recommendation for pain management in this population is parenteral opioids, preferably morphine (Twedel & Pfrimmer, 2009). Alternatively, hydromorphone may be used (Berkley & Klamut, 2009). Oral feedings are withheld to decrease the formation and secretion of **secretin**. The patient is maintained on parenteral fluids and electrolytes to restore and maintain fluid balance. Nasogastric (NG) suction may be used to relieve nausea and vomiting or to treat abdominal distention and paralytic ileus (refer to Chapter 22 for care of NG tube). The nurse provides frequent oral hygiene and care to decrease discomfort from the nasogastric tube and relieve dryness of the mouth.

The acutely ill patient is maintained on bedrest to decrease the metabolic rate and reduce the secretion of pancreatic and gastric enzymes. If the patient experiences increasing severity of pain, the nurse reports this to the provider, because the patient may be experiencing hemorrhage of the pancreas or the dose of analgesic may be inadequate.

The patient with acute pancreatitis often has a clouded sensorium because of severe pain, fluid and electrolyte disturbances, and hypoxia. Therefore, the nurse provides frequent and repeated but simple explanations about the need for withholding fluids, maintenance of gastric suction, and bed rest.

Improving Breathing Pattern

The nurse maintains the patient in a semi-Fowler's position to decrease pressure on the diaphragm by a distended abdomen and to increase respiratory expansion. Frequent changes of position are necessary to prevent atelectasis and pooling of respiratory secretions. Pulmonary assessment and monitoring of pulse oximetry or ABGs are essential to detect changes in respiratory status so that early treatment can be initiated. The nurse instructs the patient in techniques of deep breathing and in the use of an IS to improve respiratory function, and encourages and assists the patient to perform these activities every hour. Intubation may be necessary to support ventilation.

Improving Nutritional Status

The patient with acute pancreatitis has generally not been permitted food or oral fluid intake. However, recent studies suggest enteral feedings with naso-jejunum tubes, thereby preventing pancreatic enzyme release, and maintaining nothing by mouth (NPO) maintains gut integrity, enhances immune system functioning, and demonstrate lower complication rates when compared to parenteral feedings (Siow, 2008). It is important to assess the patient's nutritional status and to note factors that alter the patient's nutritional requirements (e.g., temperature elevation, surgery, drainage). Laboratory test results and daily weights are useful to monitor the nutritional status.

In addition to administering enteral or parenteral nutrition, the nurse monitors serum glucose levels every 4 to 6 hours. As the acute symptoms subside, the nurse gradually reintroduces oral feedings. Between acute attacks, the patient receives a diet that is high in carbohydrates and low in fats and proteins. The patient should avoid heavy meals and alcoholic beverages.

Improving Skin Integrity

The patient is at risk for skin breakdown because of poor nutritional status, enforced bedrest, and restlessness, which may result in pressure ulcers and breaks in tissue integrity. In addition, the patient who has undergone surgery may have multiple drains or an open surgical incision and is at risk for skin breakdown and infection. The nurse carefully assesses

the wound, drainage sites, and skin for signs of infection, inflammation, and breakdown. The nurse carries out wound care as prescribed and takes precautions to protect intact skin from contact with drainage. Consultation with an **enterostomal therapist** (also referred to as a wound care specialist or wound-ostomy-continence nurse) is often helpful in identifying appropriate skin care devices and protocols. It is important to turn the patient every 2 hours; use of specialty beds may be indicated to prevent skin breakdown.

Monitoring and Managing Potential Complications

Fluid and electrolyte disturbances are common complications because of nausea, vomiting, movement of fluid from the vascular compartment to the peritoneal cavity, diaphoresis, fever, and the use of gastric suction. The nurse assesses the patient's fluid and electrolyte status by noting skin turgor and moistness of mucous membranes. The nurse weighs the patient daily and carefully measures fluid intake and output, including urine output, nasogastric secretions, and diarrhea. In addition, it is important to assess for other factors that may affect fluid and electrolyte status, including increased body temperature and wound drainage. Inflammation can lead to significant fluid depletion, and extravasation of fluid into the retroperitoneal space and abdominal cavity.

The nurse assesses the patient for ascites and measures abdominal girth daily if ascites is suspected.

Fluids are administered intravenously and may be accompanied by infusion of blood or blood products to maintain the blood volume and to prevent or treat hypovolemic shock. It is important to keep emergency medications readily available because of the risk for circulatory collapse and shock. The nurse promptly reports decreased blood pressure and reduced urine output, because these signs may indicate hypovolemia and shock or renal failure. Low serum calcium and magnesium levels may occur and require prompt treatment.

Pancreatic necrosis is a major cause of morbidity and mortality in patients with acute pancreatitis. The patient who develops necrosis is at risk for hemorrhage, septic shock, and multiple organ failure. The patient may undergo diagnostic procedures to confirm pancreatic necrosis; surgical débridement or insertion of multiple drains may be performed. The patient with pancreatic necrosis is usually critically ill and requires expert medical and nursing management, including hemodynamic monitoring in the ICU.

In addition to carefully monitoring vital signs and other signs and symptoms, the nurse is responsible for administering prescribed fluids, medications, and blood products; assisting with supportive management, such as use of a ventilator; preventing additional complications; and attending to the patient's physical and psychological care.

Shock and multiple organ failure may occur with acute pancreatitis. Hypovolemic shock may occur as a result of hypovolemia and sequestering of fluid in the peritoneal

cavity. Hemorrhagic shock may occur with hemorrhagic pancreatitis. Septic shock may occur with bacterial infection of the pancreas. Cardiac dysfunction may occur as a result of fluid and electrolyte disturbances, acid–base imbalances, and release of toxic substances into the circulation.

The nurse closely monitors the patient for early signs of neurologic, cardiovascular, renal, and respiratory dysfunction. The nurse must be prepared to respond quickly to rapid changes in the patient's status, treatments, and therapies. In addition, it is important to inform the family about the status and progress of the patient and to allow them to spend time with the patient.

Promoting Home and Community-Based Care

The patient who has survived an episode of acute pancreatitis has been acutely ill. A prolonged period is needed to regain strength and return to the previous level of activity. The patient is often still weak and debilitated for weeks or months after an acute episode of pancreatitis. Because of the severity of the acute illness, the patient may not recall many of the explanations and instructions given during the acute phase. Teaching often needs to be repeated and reinforced. The nurse instructs the patient about the factors implicated in the onset of acute pancreatitis and about the need to avoid high-fat foods, heavy meals, and alcohol. It is important to give the patient and family verbal and written instructions about signs and symptoms of acute pancreatitis and possible complications that should be reported promptly to the provider.

If acute pancreatitis is a result of biliary tract disease, such as gallstones and gallbladder disease, additional explanations are needed about required dietary modifications. If the pancreatitis is a result of alcohol abuse, the nurse reminds the patient of the importance of eliminating all alcohol.

A referral for home care is often indicated. This enables the nurse to assess the patient's physical and psychological status and adherence to the therapeutic regimen. The nurse also assesses the home situation and reinforces instructions about fluid and nutrition intake and avoidance of alcohol. The nurse provides specific information about resources and support groups that may be of assistance in avoiding alcohol in the future. Referral to Alcoholics Anonymous or other appropriate support groups is essential.

CHRONIC PANCREATITIS

Chronic pancreatitis is an inflammatory disorder that is characterized by progressive anatomic and functional destruction of the pancreas.

Pathophysiology

As cells are replaced by fibrous tissue with repeated attacks of pancreatitis, pressure within the pancreas increases. The end result is mechanical obstruction of the pancreatic and common bile ducts and the duodenum. Additionally, there is atrophy of the epithelium of the ducts, inflammation, and destruction of the secreting cells of the pancreas.

Alcohol consumption in Western societies and malnutrition worldwide are the major causes of chronic pancreatitis. Excessive and prolonged consumption of alcohol accounts for most cases of chronic pancreatitis (Tattersall, Apte, Wilson et al., 2008). Long-term alcohol consumption causes hypersecretion of protein in pancreatic secretions, resulting in protein plugs and calculi within the pancreatic ducts. Alcohol also has a direct toxic effect on the cells of the pancreas. Some research suggests that smoking, dyslipidemia, and diet may also contribute to the development of chronic pancreatitis. Less common causes of chronic pancreatitis are due to genetic mutations, autoimmune pancreatitis, duct obstruction, and idiopathic pancreatitis. Patients with chronic pancreatitis are at increased risk for the development of pancreatic cancer (Tattersall et al., 2008).

Clinical Manifestations and Assessment

Chronic pancreatitis is characterized by recurring attacks of severe upper abdominal and back pain, accompanied by vomiting. Attacks are often so painful that opioids, even in large doses, do not provide relief. As the disease progresses, recurring attacks of pain are more severe, more frequent, and of longer duration. Some patients experience continuous severe pain; others have a dull, nagging constant pain. The risk of opioid dependence is increased in pancreatitis because of the chronic nature and severity of the pain.

Weight loss is a major problem in chronic pancreatitis: more than 75% of patients experience significant weight loss, usually caused by decreased dietary intake secondary to anorexia or fear that eating will precipitate another attack. Malabsorption occurs late in the disease due to decreases in lipase production. As a result, digestion, especially of proteins and fats, is impaired. The stools become frequent, frothy, and foul-smelling because of impaired fat digestion, which results in stools with a high fat content. This is referred to as **steatorrhea**. As the disease progresses, calcification of the gland may occur, and calcium stones may form within the ducts. Diabetes mellitus occurs due to loss of pancreatic beta cells.

Endoscopic retrograde cholangiopancreatography (ERCP) is the most useful study in the diagnosis of chronic pancreatitis (refer to Chapter 21 for details). It provides detail about the anatomy of the pancreas and the pancreatic and biliary ducts. It is also helpful in obtaining tissue for analysis and differentiating pancreatitis from other conditions, such as carcinoma. Various imaging procedures, including MRI, CT scans, and ultrasound, have been useful in the diagnostic evaluation of patients with suspected pancreatic disorders. A CT scan or ultrasound study is also helpful to detect pancreatic cysts. Steatorrhea can be confirmed by laboratory analysis of fecal fat content and determination of exocrine pancreatic insufficiency via the secretin-cholecystokinin test. In most cases,

the diagnosis of chronic pancreatitis is based upon clinical findings, history, and imaging modalities such as ERCP, CT, and MRI to detect abnormalities of the pancreas (Tattersall et al., 2008).

Medical Management

Nonsurgical Management

Nonsurgical approaches are primarily focused on complete abstinence of alcohol, pain management, nutritional management, and treatment of diabetes mellitus. Pain management is achieved through use of analgesics as first-line therapy, and for refractory pain. Pancreatic enzyme replacement is indicated for the patient with malabsorption and steatorrhea. A proton pump inhibitor (omeprazole [Prilosec], lansoprazole [Prevacid]) is administered with enzyme therapy to reduce gastric acid inactivation of enzymes. Supplementation of fat-soluble vitamins is also indicated. Improved nutrition and resolution of steatorrhea usually are indicators of clinical improvement in the patient with chronic pancreatitis.

Diabetes mellitus resulting from dysfunction of the pancreatic islet cells is treated with diet, insulin, or oral antidiabetic agents. Use of insulin is the preferred therapy; however, administration should be carefully adjusted to avoid hypoglycemic events (Tattersall et al., 2008).

Surgical Management

Surgery or interventional therapies are used primarily to address complications of pancreatitis and to relieve abdominal pain and discomfort, restore drainage of pancreatic secretions, and reduce the frequency of acute attacks of pancreatitis. The type of surgery that is performed depends on the anatomic and functional abnormalities of the pancreas, including the location of disease within the pancreas, the presence of diabetes, exocrine insufficiency, biliary stenosis, and pseudocysts of the pancreas.

Pancreaticojejunostomy (also referred to as Roux-en-Y), with a side-to-side anastomosis or joining of the pancreatic duct to the jejunum, allows drainage of the pancreatic secretions into the jejunum. Other surgical procedures may be performed for different degrees and types of underlying disorders. These procedures include revision of the sphincter of the ampulla of Vater, internal drainage of a pancreatic cyst into the stomach, insertion of a stent, and wide resection or removal of the pancreas. A Whipple resection (pancreaticoduodenectomy) can be carried out to relieve the pain of chronic pancreatitis. Endoscopic therapy is used for pancreatic duct stones and strictures. The use of surgical and endoscopic treatment is based upon patient presentation, complications, and the availability of surgical expertise (Tattersall et al., 2008).

PANCREATIC CANCER

Pancreatic cancer is the fourth leading cause of cancer death in the United States. Cancer may develop in the head, body, or tail

of the pancreas; most pancreatic cancers originate in the head of the pancreas. Patients usually do not seek medical attention until late in the disease; most patients have advanced, unresectable tumor when first detected. In fact, pancreatic carcinoma has only a 5% survival rate at 5 years regardless of the stage of disease at diagnosis or treatment (Chua & Cunningham, 2008).

Risk Factors

Most pancreatic cancers are diagnosed between the ages of 65 and 84, with higher prevalence in men and African Americans. Use of tobacco, obesity, and nonhereditary chronic pancreatitis are risk factors for pancreatic cancer. Diabetes mellitus is also associated with pancreatic cancer; however, whether it is a cause or a result of pancreatic cancer is unclear. Genetic predisposition may also play a role; up to 10% of patients with this cancer have a first-degree relative diagnosed with pancreatic cancer.

Clinical Manifestations and Assessment

Pain, jaundice, or both are present in more than 80% of patients and, along with weight loss, are considered classic signs of pancreatic carcinoma. However, they often do not appear until the disease is far advanced. Other signs include rapid, profound, and progressive weight loss as well as vague upper or midabdominal pain or discomfort that is unrelated to any GI function and is often difficult to describe. Such discomfort radiates as a boring pain in the midback and is unrelated to posture or activity. It is often progressive and severe, requiring the use of opioids. The formation of ascites is common. An important sign, if it is present, is the onset of symptoms of insulin deficiency: glucosuria, hyperglycemia, and abnormal glucose tolerance. Therefore, diabetes may be an early sign of carcinoma of the pancreas. Meals often aggravate epigastric pain, which usually occurs before the appearance of jaundice and pruritus. Diarrhea and steatorrhea are also commonly present in pancreatic cancer (Chua & Cunningham, 2008).

Spiral (helical) CT has more than 90% accuracy in the diagnosis and staging of pancreatic cancer and is currently the most useful preoperative imaging technique. CT can accurately image pancreatic masses, show dilatation of pancreatic duct, and indicate if metastases are present in the liver or peritoneum. ERCP and magnetic resonance cholangiopancreatography (MRCP) are also used to diagnose pancreatic cancer. Cells obtained during ERCP are sent to the laboratory for histologic analysis. Although cancer-associated antigen (CA 19-9) serum levels may be elevated, this tumor marker is used primarily to monitor disease progression and treatment efficacy.

Medical Management

Only 10% to 15% of patients with pancreatic cancer benefit from surgical resection; the majority of patients present at a

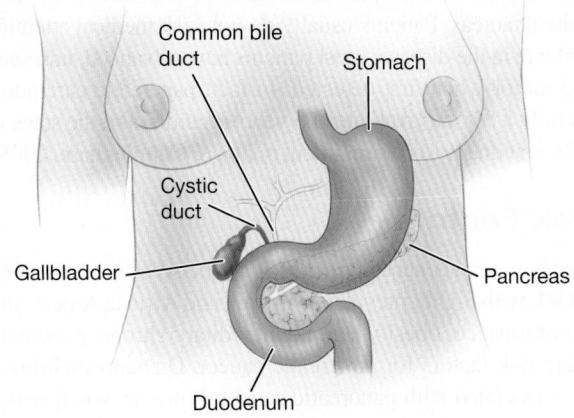

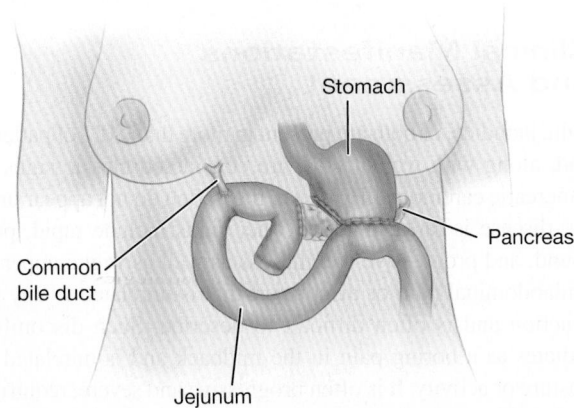

FIGURE 25-13 Pancreatoduodenectomy (Whipple's procedure or resection). End result of resection of carcinoma of the head of the pancreas or the ampulla of Vater. The common duct is sutured to the end of the jejunum, and the remaining portion of the pancreas and the end of the stomach are sutured to the side of the jejunum.

late stage, frequently with metastatic spread to other organs or vascular invasion. In patients with early-stage disease, the Whipple procedure (pancreaticoduodenectomy) is used to remove the pancreatic head, duodenum, part of the jejunum, common bile duct, and gallbladder (Fig. 25-13). Use of adjuvant therapy (i.e., chemotherapy) continues to be controversial and nonstandard in this small group of surgical patients, with ongoing clinical trials to evaluate potential benefits of treatment. The chemotherapy agent gemcitabine alone or in combination with other chemotherapeutic agents remains the treatment of choice for most patients with pancreatic cancer. Overall, patients with pancreatic cancer have a high mortality rate and poor survival outcomes even with chemotherapy or surgical treatment. Palliative measures to address symptoms of pancreatic cancer include nutritional support and pain management (Chua & Cunningham, 2008; Li & Saif, 2009).

Nursing Management

Pain management and attention to nutritional requirements are important nursing measures that improve the level of patient comfort. Skin care and nursing measures are directed toward relief of pain and discomfort associated with jaundice, anorexia, and profound weight loss. Specialty mattresses are beneficial and protect bony prominences from pressure. Pain associated with pancreatic cancer may be severe and may require liberal use of opioids; patient-controlled analgesia should be considered for the patient with severe, escalating pain.

Because of the poor prognosis and likelihood of short survival, end-of-life preferences are discussed and honored. If appropriate, the nurse refers the patient to hospice care (see Chapter 3 for further discussion).

The postoperative management of patients who have undergone a pancreaticoduodenectomy is similar to the management of patients after extensive GI or biliary surgery. The patient's physical status is often suboptimal, increasing the risk for postoperative complications. Hemorrhage, vascular collapse, and hepatorenal failure remain the major complications of these extensive surgical procedures. The mortality rate associated with these procedures has improved because of advances in nutritional support and improved surgical techniques. A nasogastric tube with suction, NPO status, and nutrition that allows the GI tract to rest while promoting adequate nutrition is anticipated (Fig. 25-14).

Preoperatively and postoperatively, nursing care is directed toward promoting patient comfort, preventing complications, and assisting the patient to return to and maintain as normal and comfortable a life as possible. The nurse closely monitors the patient in the ICU after surgery; in the

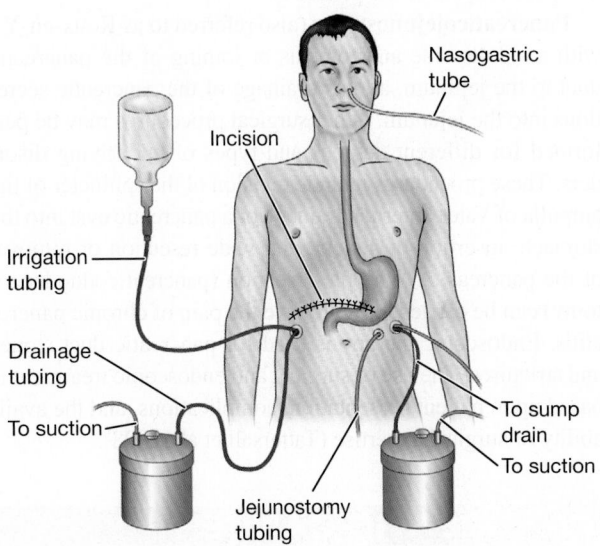

FIGURE 25-14 Multiple sump tubes are used after pancreatic surgery. Triple-lumen tubes consist of ports that provide tubing for irrigation, air venting, and drainage.

immediate postoperative period, multiple IV and arterial lines are used for fluid and blood replacement and hemodynamic monitoring, and a mechanical ventilator is used. It is important to note and report changes in vital signs, arterial blood gases and pressures, pulse oximetry, laboratory values, and urine output. The nurse must also consider the patient's compromised nutritional status and risk for bleeding. Depending on the type of surgical procedure performed, malabsorption syndrome and diabetes mellitus are likely; the nurse must address these issues during acute and long-term patient care.

Although the patient's physiologic status is the focus of the health care team in the immediate postoperative period, the patient's psychological and emotional state must be considered, along with that of the family. The patient has undergone a major high-risk surgery and is critically ill; anxiety and depression may affect recovery. The immediate and long-term outcomes of this extensive surgical resection are uncertain, and the patient and family require emotional support and understanding in the critical and stressful preoperative and postoperative periods.

Promoting Home and Community-Based Care

The specific teaching for the patient and family varies with the stage of disease and the treatment choices made by the patient. The patient who has undergone this extensive surgery requires careful and thorough preparation for self-care at home. The nurse instructs the patient and family about the need for modifications in the diet because of malabsorption and hyperglycemia resulting from the surgery. It is important to instruct the patient and family about the continuing need for pancreatic enzyme replacement, a low-fat diet, and vitamin supplementation.

The nurse teaches the patient and family strategies to relieve pain and discomfort, along with strategies to manage drains, if present, and to care for the surgical incision. The patient and family members may require instruction about use of patient-controlled analgesia, enteral/parenteral nutrition, wound care, skin care, and management of drainage. It is important to describe, verbally and in writing, the signs and symptoms of complications, and to teach the patient and family about indicators of complications that should be reported promptly.

Discharge of the patient to a long-term care or rehabilitation facility may be warranted after surgery as extensive as a pancreaticoduodenectomy, particularly if the patient's preoperative status was not optimal. Information about the teaching that has been provided is shared with the long-term care staff so that instructions can be clarified and reinforced.

If the patient elects to receive chemotherapy, the nurse focuses teaching on prevention of side effects and complications of the agents used. If surgery is performed to relieve obstruction and establish biliary drainage, teaching addresses management of the drainage system and monitoring for complications. The nurse instructs the family about changes in the patient's status that should be reported to the provider.

A referral for home care may be indicated when the patient returns home. The home care nurse assesses the patient's physical status, fluid and nutritional status, and skin integrity and the adequacy of pain management. The nurse teaches the patient and family strategies to prevent skin breakdown and relieve pain, pruritus, and anorexia. The home care nurse assesses the patient's physical and psychological status and the ability of the patient and family to manage needed care. The home care nurse provides needed physical care and monitors the adequacy of pain management. In addition, it is important to assess the patient's nutritional status and monitor the use of parenteral nutrition. The nurse discusses the use of hospice services with the patient and family and makes a referral if indicated.

Chapter Review

Critical Thinking Exercises

1. A 28-year-old African woman came to the United States from Nigeria 3 years ago to live with relatives. She is being treated for end-stage liver disease (ESLD) with cirrhosis related to hepatitis B and is undergoing evaluation for liver transplantation. The sequelae of ESLD that she was experiencing included encephalopathy and ascites. What would you anticipate this patient's treatment regimen to include? What medications would be most appropriate for her? What would you include in your cultural assessment when you develop a preoperative teaching plan for this patient? What alternative therapies might be employed preoperatively? Once the patient receives a liver transplant, what medications would you expect to be prescribed for her in addition to an immunosuppressant regimen?

2. A 64-year-old man is admitted to the hospital with end-stage liver disease (ESLD), ascites, and impending hepatic encephalopathy. Dietary modifications and lactulose (Cephulac) are prescribed to minimize hepatic encephalopathy. What is the evidence base for use of dietary measures and lactulose in reducing or reversing hepatic encephalopathy? What is the strength of that evidence? What are the nursing implications associated with prescribed dietary modifications, lactulose, and other measures to reduce the severity and progression of hepatic encephalopathy?

(continued on page 722)

Chapter Review (continued)

3. A 34-year-old woman is scheduled for a cholecystectomy. Since undergoing bariatric surgery a year ago, she has lost 150 pounds. What postoperative care is indicated for this patient? What impact, if any, does her previous surgical procedure have on her postoperative recovery?

4. A 56-year-old man with a history of alcoholism and cirrhosis is admitted to your unit with a diagnosis of pancreatitis. He is complaining of severe epigastric pain, vomiting, and diarrhea. What medications and laboratory tests would you expect to see prescribed for this patient? What physical assessment findings will you see? Describe nursing care for this patient, and compare and contrast care with and without the diagnosis of cirrhosis. What issues would be of high priority in caring for this patient during his hospital stay? What issues would be of high priority in preparing him for hospital discharge?

NCLEX-Style Review Questions

1. The nurse is caring for a patient diagnosed with ascites. The nurse would expect which of the following to be restricted from the patient's diet?
   A. Potassium
   B. Calcium
   C. Sodium
   D. Magnesium

2. A patient diagnosed with hepatic encephalopathy is receiving lactulose (Cephulac). When preparing to administer this medication, the nurse understands that it is used to decrease which of the following serum levels?
   A. Calcium
   B. Ammonia
   C. Potassium
   D. Sodium

3. Patients with severe chronic liver dysfunction often have problems related to inadequate intake of sufficient vitamins. Which of the following vitamin deficiencies would result in hemorrhagic lesions of scurvy?
   A. Riboflavin
   B. Vitamin C
   C. Vitamin A
   D. Vitamin K

4. A patient with hepatitis A is admitted to a general medical-surgical floor. The nurse knows that this type of hepatitis is spread through which of the following modes of transmission?
   A. Injection of drugs
   B. Blood
   C. Semen
   D. Fecal–oral

5. A patient is being seen in the clinic to rule out pancreatitis. The nurse expects that which of the following diagnostic tests will be performed to diagnose this disease process?
   A. MRI
   B. CT
   C. Abdominal X-ray
   D. Lumbar puncture

Try these additional resources to enhance your learning and understanding of this chapter:
- thePoint online resource available at **http://thepoint.lww.com/Pellico1e**
- *Handbook for Focus on Adult Health: Medical-Surgical Nursing*
- *Study Guide for Focus on Adult Health: Medical-Surgical Nursing*

References and Selected Readings

References and selected readings associated with this chapter can be found on the website that accompanies the book. Visit http://thepoint.lww.com/Pellico1e to access the references and other additional resources associated with this chapter.

Problems Related to Urinary Tract Function

A NURSE is caring for a patient diagnosed with renal failure. He is currently receiving hemodialysis three times a week. He is very anxious about the lifestyle change that is occurring due to his health problems.

⇒ What areas of teaching would be important for the nurse to emphasize for this patient?

⇒ Explain the various treatment modalities available for this patient population.

⇒ Discuss areas of nursing management that would apply to this patient.

SUSANNE A. QUALLICH
AND MICHELLE
J. LAJINESS

Nursing Assessment: Renal and Urinary Tract Function

After reading this chapter, you will be able to:

1. Describe the anatomy and physiology of the renal and urinary systems.

2. Discuss the role of the kidney in regulating fluid and electrolyte balance, acid–base balance, and blood pressure.

3. Identify the assessment parameters used for determining the status of upper and lower urinary tract function.

4. Describe the diagnostic studies used to determine upper and lower urinary tract function.

Proper function of the renal and urinary systems is essential to life. Dysfunction of the kidneys and lower urinary tract is common and may occur at any age and with varying degrees of severity. Assessment of upper and lower urinary tract function is part of every health examination and necessitates an understanding of the anatomy and physiology of the urinary system, as well as of the effects of changes in the system on other physiologic functions.

ANATOMIC AND PHYSIOLOGIC OVERVIEW

The primary function of the renal and urinary systems is to maintain the body's state of homeostasis by carefully regulating fluid and electrolytes, removing wastes, and providing hormones that are involved in red blood cell production, bone metabolism, and blood pressure. A thorough understanding of the renal and urinary systems is necessary for assessing people with acute or chronic dysfunction and implementing appropriate nursing care.

Anatomy of the Renal and Urinary Systems

The renal and urinary systems include the kidneys, ureters, bladder, and urethra. Urine is formed by the kidney and flows through the other structures to be eliminated from the body.

Kidneys

The kidneys are a pair of bean-shaped, brownish-red structures located retroperitoneally (behind and outside the peritoneal cavity) on the posterior wall of the abdomen—from the twelfth thoracic vertebra to the third lumbar vertebra in the adult (Fig. 26-1A). The average adult kidney weighs approximately 113 to 170 g (about 4.5 oz), and is 10 to 12 cm long, 6 cm wide, and 2.5 cm thick (Porth & Matfin, 2009). The right kidney is slightly lower than the left due to the location of the liver.

The kidneys are well protected by the ribs and by the muscles of the abdomen and back. Internally, fat deposits surround each kidney, providing protection against jarring. The kidneys and surrounding fat are suspended from the abdominal wall by renal fascia made of connective

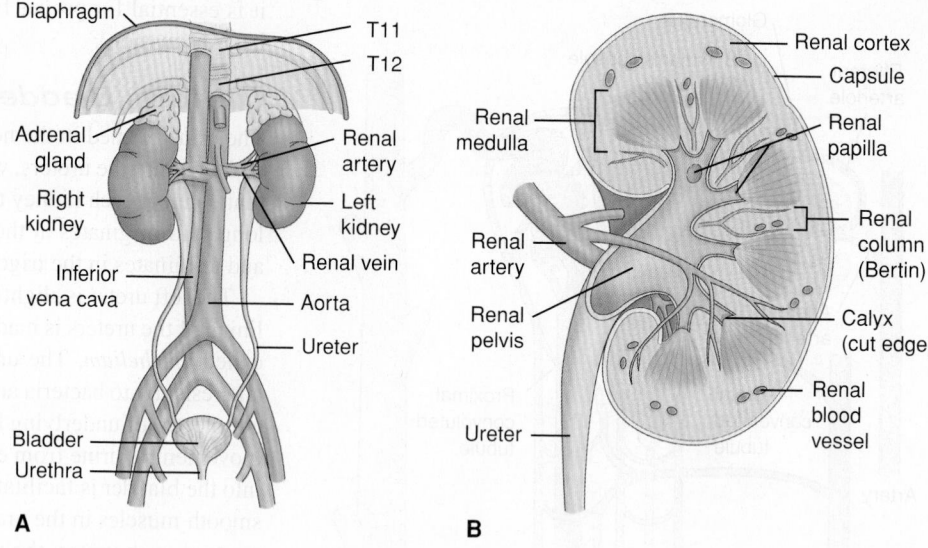

FIGURE 26-1 (**A**) Kidneys, ureters, and bladder. (The right kidney is usually lower than the left.) (**B**) Internal structure of the kidney. Redrawn from Porth, C. M. & Matfin, G. (2009). *Pathophysiology: Concepts of altered health states* (8th ed.). Philadelphia: Lippincott Williams & Wilkins.

tissue. The fibrous connective tissue, blood vessels, and lymphatics surrounding each kidney are known as the *renal capsule* (Fig. 26-1B).

An adrenal gland lies on top of each kidney. Each organ is independent in terms of its function, blood supply, and innervation.

The renal parenchyma (organ tissue) is divided into two parts: the cortex and the medulla. The medulla is the inner portion of the kidney. It contains the loops of Henle, the vasa recta, and the collecting ducts of the juxtamedullary nephrons. The collecting ducts from both the juxtamedullary and the cortical nephrons connect to the renal pyramids, which are triangular and are situated with the base facing the concave surface of the kidney and the point (papilla) facing the hilum, or pelvis. Each kidney contains approximately 8 to 18 pyramids. The pyramids drain into 4 to 13 minor calices, which drain into 2 to 3 major calices that open directly into the renal pelvis. The renal pelvis is the beginning of the collecting system and is composed of structures that are designed to collect and transport urine. Once the urine leaves the renal pelvis, the composition or amount of urine does not change.

The cortex, which is approximately 1 cm wide, is located farthest from the center of the kidney and around the outermost edges. It contains the **nephrons** (the functional units of the kidney), which are discussed below.

Blood Supply to the Kidneys

The hilum, or pelvis, is the concave portion of the kidney through which the renal artery enters and the ureters and renal vein exit. The kidneys receive 20% to 25% of the total cardiac output; all of the body's blood circulates through the kidneys approximately 12 times per hour. The renal artery arises from the abdominal aorta and divides into smaller and smaller vessels, eventually forming the afferent arterioles. Each afferent arteriole branches to form a **glomerulus**, which is the capillary bed responsible for glomerular filtration. Blood leaves the glomerulus through the efferent arteriole

and flows back to the inferior vena cava through a network of capillaries and veins.

NURSING ALERT

The nurse auscultates for renal artery bruits, which indicate turbulent blood flow and are associated with a narrowing of the blood vessel or increased flow. Any patient with hypertension should be evaluated for bruits. They are typically noted with renal artery stenosis just above (2 cm) and to the right or left of the umbilicus. A whooshing sound is indicative of a bruit.

Nephrons

Each kidney has 1 million nephrons, which usually allows for adequate renal function even if the opposite kidney is damaged or becomes nonfunctional. The nephrons are the structures located within the renal parenchyma that are responsible for the initial formation of urine. If the total number of functioning nephrons is less than 20% of normal, renal replacement therapy needs to be considered.

There are two kinds of nephrons. The cortical nephrons, making up 80% to 85% of the total number, are located in the outermost part of the cortex. The juxtamedullary nephrons, distinguished by long loops of Henle, make up the remaining 15% to 20%, are located deeper in the cortex, and are surrounded by long capillary loops called vasa recta that dip into the medulla of the kidney. The length of the tubular component of the nephron is directly related to its ability to concentrate urine.

Nephrons are made up of two basic components: a filtering element composed of an enclosed capillary network (the glomerulus) and the attached tubule (Fig. 26-2). The glomerulus is a unique network of capillaries suspended between the afferent and efferent blood vessels, which are enclosed in an epithelial structure called Bowman's capsule. The glomerular membrane is composed of three filtering layers: the

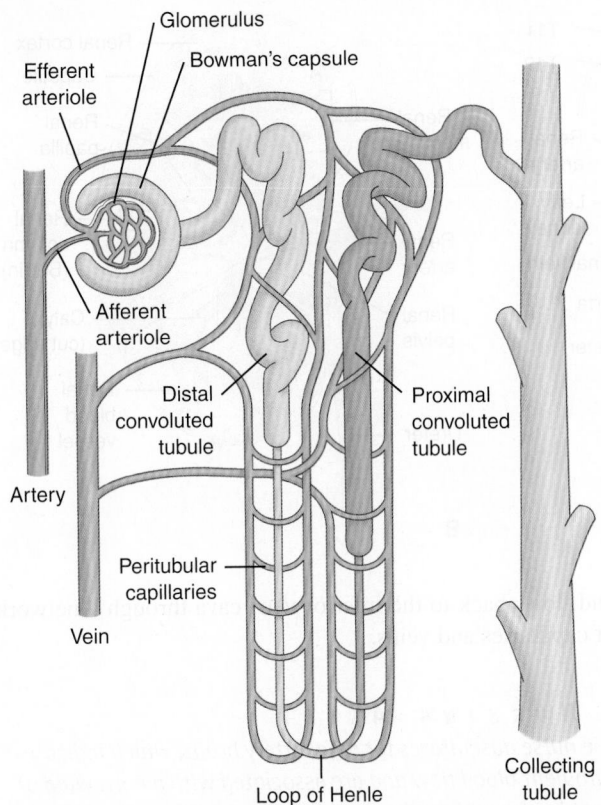

FIGURE 26-2 Representation of a nephron. Each kidney has about 1 million nephrons, which take two forms: cortical and juxtamedullary. Cortical nephrons are located in the cortex of the kidney; juxtamedullary nephrons are adjacent to the medulla.

capillary endothelium, the basement membrane, and the epithelium. This membrane normally allows filtration of fluid and small molecules yet limits passage of larger molecules, such as blood cells and albumin. Pressure changes and the permeability of the glomerular membrane of Bowman's capsule facilitate the passage of fluids and various substances from the blood vessels, filling the space within Bowman's capsule with this filtered solution.

The tubular component of the nephron begins in the Bowman's capsule. The filtrate created in the Bowman's capsule travels first into the proximal tubule, then the loop of Henle, the distal tubule, and either the cortical or medullary collecting ducts. Changes are continually made as the filtrate travels through the tubules until it enters the collecting system and is expelled as urine from the body (see Fig. 26-2).

The structural arrangement of the tubule allows the distal tubule to lie in close proximity to where the afferent and efferent arteriole respectively enter and leave the glomerulus. The distal tubular cells located in this area, known as the *macula densa*, function with the adjacent afferent arteriole and create what is known as the juxtaglomerular apparatus. This is the site of renin production. Renin is a hormone directly involved in the control of arterial blood pressure;

it is essential for proper functioning of the glomerulus (see later discussion).

Ureters, Bladder, and Urethra

The urine formed in the nephrons flows into the renal pelvis and then into the ureters, which are long fibromuscular tubes that connect each kidney to the bladder. Each is 24 to 30 cm long, and originates at the lower portion of the renal pelvis and terminates in the trigone of the bladder wall.

The left ureter is slightly shorter than the right ureter. The lining of the ureters is made up of transitional cell epithelium called *urothelium*. The urothelium is impermeable to urine and resistant to bacteria and foreign substances and serves as a protector of underlying bladder tissue (Lazzeri, 2006). The movement of urine from each renal pelvis through the ureter into the bladder is facilitated by peristaltic contraction of the smooth muscles in the ureter wall. There are three narrowed areas of each ureter: the ureteropelvic junction, the ureteral segment near the sacroiliac junction, and the ureterovesical junction. These three areas of the ureters have a propensity for obstruction by renal calculi (kidney stones) or stricture. Obstruction of the ureteropelvic junction is the most serious because of its close proximity to the kidney and the risk of associated kidney dysfunction.

The urinary bladder is a muscular, hollow sac located just behind the pubic bone. The capacity of the adult bladder is about 300 to 500 mL. The bladder has two inlets (the ureters) which are angled to prevent retrograde flow of urine into the ureters and one outlet (the urethra). The area surrounding the bladder neck is called the *urethrovesical junction*.

The wall of the bladder contains four layers. The outermost layer is the adventitia, which is made up of connective tissue. Beneath the adventitia is a smooth muscle layer known as the *detrusor*; beneath the detrusor is a submucosal layer of loose connective tissue that serves as an interface between the detrusor and the innermost layer, a mucosal lining. This inner layer contains specialized transitional cell epithelium, a membrane that is impermeable to water and prevents reabsorption of urine stored in the bladder.

When the detrusor muscle contracts, urine is released from the bladder; thus, the detrusor is responsible for **micturition** (voiding). This muscle is continuous with the bladder neck, which forms a portion of the urethral sphincter often referred to as the *internal urethral sphincter*. When the bladder is relaxed, the muscle fibers are closed and functions as a sphincter (Porth & Matfin, 2009). The sphincteric mechanism helps maintain continence. Another muscle involved in continence is the external urinary sphincter at the anterior urethra, the segment most distal from the bladder (Porth & Matfin, 2009). During micturition, increased intravesical pressure keeps the ureterovesical junction closed and keeps urine within the ureters. As soon as micturition is completed, intravesical pressure returns to its normal low baseline value, allowing efflux of urine to resume. The only time that the bladder is completely empty is in the last seconds of micturition, before efflux of urine resumes.

The urethra arises from the base of the bladder: In the male, it passes through the penis; in the female, it opens just anterior to the vagina. In the male, the prostate gland, which lies just below the bladder neck, surrounds the urethra posteriorly and laterally.

Function of the Upper and Lower Urinary Tracts

Urine Formation

The healthy human body is composed of approximately 60% water. Water balance is regulated by the kidneys and results in the formation of urine. Urine is formed in the nephrons through a complex three-step process: glomerular filtration, **tubular reabsorption**, and **tubular secretion** (Fig. 26-3). The various substances normally filtered by the glomerulus, reabsorbed by the tubules, and excreted in the urine include sodium, chloride, bicarbonate, potassium, glucose, urea, creatinine, and uric acid. Within the tubule, some of these substances are selectively reabsorbed into the blood to maintain electrolyte and acid–base balance. Others are secreted from the blood into the filtrate as it travels down the tubule.

Amino acids and glucose are usually filtered at the level of the glomerulus and reabsorbed so that neither is excreted in the urine. Normally, glucose does not appear in the urine. However, glycosuria occurs if the amount of glucose in the blood and glomerular filtrate exceeds the amount that the tubules are able to reabsorb. **Renal glycosuria** occurs in diabetes and is the most common clinical expression of a blood glucose level exceeding the kidney's reabsorption capacity. In general, the serum glucose level is greater than 180 to 200 mg/dL when glycosuria is seen.

Protein molecules also are not usually found in the urine; however, low-molecular-weight proteins (globulins and albumin) may periodically be excreted in small amounts. Recall that the glomerulus filters the blood, similar to a strainer. Therefore, when significant **proteinuria** is found, glomerular disease is suspected. Levels of greater than 3.5 g/day are indicative of severe proteinuria and are associated with nephrotic syndrome as well as a variety of glomerular disorders (see Chapter 27).

Glomerular Filtration

The normal blood flow through the kidneys is about 1,200 mL/min. As blood flows into the glomerulus from an afferent arteriole, filtration occurs. The filtered fluid enters the renal tubules. Under normal conditions, about 20% of the blood passing through the glomeruli is filtered into the nephron, amounting to about 180 L/day of filtrate. The filtrate normally consists of water, electrolytes, and other small molecules, whereas larger molecules stay in the bloodstream. Efficient filtration depends on adequate blood flow that maintains a consistent pressure through the glomerulus. Many factors can alter this blood flow and pressure, including hypotension, decreased oncotic pressure in the blood, and increased pressure in the renal tubules from an obstruction.

Tubular Reabsorption and Tubular Secretion

The second and third steps of urine formation occur in the renal tubules. In tubular reabsorption, a substance moves from the filtrate back into the peritubular capillaries or vasa recta. In tubular secretion, a substance moves from the peritubular capillaries or vasa recta into tubular filtrate. Of the 180 L (45 gallons) of filtrate that the kidneys produce each day, 99% is reabsorbed into the bloodstream, resulting in the formation of 1,000 to 1,500 mL of urine each day. Although most reabsorption occurs in the proximal tubule, reabsorption occurs along the entire tubule. Reabsorption and secretion in the tubule frequently involve passive and active transport. Filtrate becomes concentrated in the distal tubule and collecting ducts under hormonal influence and becomes urine, which then enters the renal pelvis.

Osmolarity and Osmolality

Osmolarity and osmolality refer to the ratio of solute (examples include sodium, chloride, potassium, urea and glucose) to water in blood or urine. While osmolarity refers to measuring the amount of solutes (milliosmoles) to water using liters (expressed as mOsm/L), osmolality calculates the amount of solutes (milliosmoles) to water using weight or kilograms and is expressed as mOsm/kg. The terms are confusing and often misused; what is important to remember is that clinicians are attempting to determine the concentration of blood or urine. Because 1 liter is roughly equivalent to 1 kilogram, they are generally similar. The regulation of salt and water is paramount for control of the extracellular volume and both serum and urine osmolarity. Controlling either the amount of water or the amount of solute can change the concentration of blood

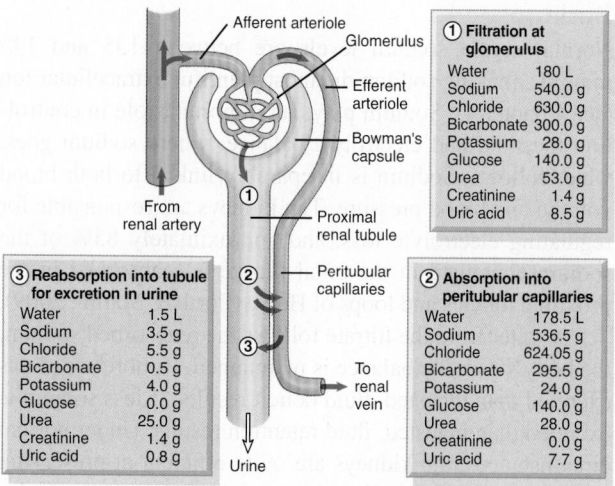

① Filtration at glomerulus

Water	180 L
Sodium	540.0 g
Chloride	630.0 g
Bicarbonate	300.0 g
Potassium	28.0 g
Glucose	140.0 g
Urea	53.0 g
Creatinine	1.4 g
Uric acid	8.5 g

② Absorption into peritubular capillaries

Water	178.5 L
Sodium	536.5 g
Chloride	624.05 g
Bicarbonate	295.5 g
Potassium	24.0 g
Glucose	140.0 g
Urea	28.0 g
Creatinine	0.0 g
Uric acid	7.7 g

③ Reabsorption into tubule for excretion in urine

Water	1.5 L
Sodium	3.5 g
Chloride	5.5 g
Bicarbonate	0.5 g
Potassium	4.0 g
Glucose	0.0 g
Urea	25.0 g
Creatinine	1.4 g
Uric acid	0.8 g

FIGURE 26-3 Urine is formed in the nephrons in a three-step process: filtration, reabsorption, and excretion. Water, electrolytes, and other substances, such as glucose and creatinine, are filtered by the glomerulus; varying amounts of these substances are reabsorbed in the renal tubule or excreted in the urine. Approximate normal volumes of these substances during the steps of urine formation are shown at the top. Wide variations may occur in these values depending on diet.

and urine. Osmolarity and ionic composition are maintained by the body within very narrow limits. As little as an elevation of 1% to 2% change in the serum osmolarity (increased number of solute atoms or molecules) can cause a conscious desire to drink and conservation of water by the kidneys (Ropper & Samuels, 2009). It is important for nurses to recognize that cognitive impairments can interfere with recognition of cues of thirst and predispose a patient to dehydration.

> **! NURSING ALERT**
>
> *The terms* isotonic, hypotonic, *and* hypertonic *refer to the osmolarity of body fluids (measure of the number of dissolved particles). A serum osmolality test measures the amount of chemicals dissolved in the fluid portion of blood (serum). It could be imagined visually as the total number of molecules floating in the fluid. Normal osmolality = 275 to 295 mOsm/ kg of body weight (Porth & Matfin, 2009). Therefore, isotonic solutions are equal to normal osmolarity; hypotonic solutions have less molecules and more water in the solution (<275 mOsm/L); and hypertonic solutions have a higher number of molecules and are more concentrated solutions (>295 mOsm/L) (Springhouse, 2008).*

Regulation of Water Excretion

Regulation of the amount of water excreted is an important function of the kidney. **Antidiuretic hormone (ADH)**, also known as vasopressin, plays a key role in the regulation of extracellular fluid by excreting or retaining water. ADH is secreted by the posterior portion of the pituitary gland and acts on the kidney in response to changes in osmolality of the blood; that is, ADH is secreted or suppressed depending on blood concentration or dilution respectively. Blood osmolality increase is seen with decreased water intake or increased water loss stimulating ADH release. Consequently, a small volume of concentrated urine is excreted. ADH increases reabsorption of water and returns the osmolality of the blood to normal. With excess water intake or increased retention of water, as occurs in many disease states such as renal failure, the blood becomes dilute, resulting in suppression of ADH secretion, causing less water to be reabsorbed by the kidney tubule. Assuming maintenance of kidney function, this would result in increased urine volume (diuresis).

A person normally ingests about 1,500 mL of oral liquids and 700 mL of water in food per day, while an additional 250 mL per day is generated with oxidative metabolism. Of the fluid ingested, approximately 700 mL is lost through the skin and lungs (called *insensible loss*), 100 mL through sweat, and 200 mL through feces (Candela & Yucha, 2004; Metheny, 2000). Normal urine output in 24 hours ranges from 1 to 2 L/day or more specifically a range between .5 to 2 mL/ kg/hr (Metheny, 2000). Thus, intake is roughly equivalent to output in a healthy person (see Table 26-1). It is important to consider all fluid gained and lost when evaluating total fluid status. Daily weight measurements are a reliable means of

TABLE 26-1 24-hour Balance of Intake and Output for Adults

Water Input	Input Volume	Output	Output Volume
Liquid	800–1500 mL	Urine	800–1,500 mL
Solid	500–700 mL	Lung / Skin	600–700 mL
Oxidative Metabolism	150–250 mL	Sweat	0–100 mL
		Stool	100–200 mL
TOTAL ~1,500–2,500 mL per day		**Total ~ 1,500–2,500 mL**	

determining overall fluid status. One pound equals approximately 500 mL, so a weight change of as little as 1 lb could suggest an overall fluid gain or loss of 500 mL. The nurse is aware that edema is not present until 2.5 L of interstitial fluid has been retained (Porth & Matfin, 2009).

> **! NURSING ALERT**
>
> *It is important to maintain consistency when assessing daily weight: the nurse uses the same scale, with the patient wearing the same clothes at the same time daily.*

Regulation of Electrolyte Excretion

When the kidneys are functioning normally, the volume of electrolytes excreted per day is equal to the amount ingested. For example, the average American daily diet contains 6 to 8 g each of sodium chloride (salt) and potassium chloride, and approximately the same amounts are excreted in the urine.

Sodium

Normal serum sodium levels are between 135 and 145 mmol/L, making sodium the most plentiful extracellular ion (see Chapter 4). Sodium plays an important role in controlling the fluid and electrolyte balance: where sodium goes, water follows. Sodium is inseparably linked to both blood volume and blood pressure. The kidneys are responsible for regulating electrolyte loss, and approximately 85% of the sodium contained in the renal filtrate is reabsorbed in the proximal tubules and loops of Henle (Porth & Matfin, 2009).

As water from the filtrate follows the reabsorbed sodium, the body's osmotic balance is maintained. If more sodium is excreted than ingested, fluid deficit results; if less sodium is excreted than ingested, fluid retention results. Under normal circumstances, the kidneys are quite efficient at preserving or excreting sodium depending on its loss via the gastrointestinal (GI) tract, skin, sodium intake via diet, medications, or IV therapy.

The regulation of sodium volume excreted depends on **aldosterone**, a hormone synthesized and released from the adrenal cortex. With increased aldosterone in the blood, less sodium is excreted in the urine, as aldosterone causes

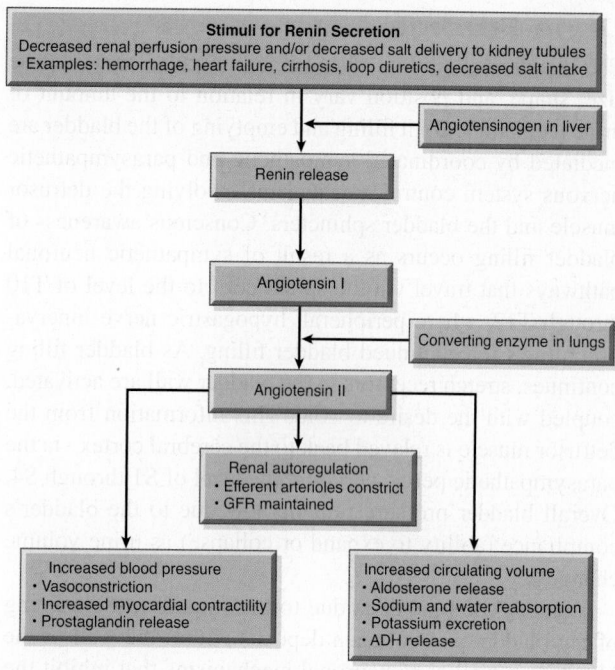

FIGURE 26-4 The renin–angiotensin system. ADH, antidiuretic hormone; GFR, glomerular filtration rate.

renal reabsorption of sodium. Release of aldosterone from the adrenal cortex is largely under the control of angiotensin II, the most powerful vasoconstrictor known. Angiotensin II levels are controlled by renin, an enzyme that is released from specialized cells in the kidneys (Fig. 26-4). This complex system is activated when pressure in the renal arterioles falls below normal levels, as occurs with shock, dehydration, or decreased sodium chloride delivery to the tubules. Activation of this system increases the retention of water and expansion of the intravascular fluid volume, thereby maintaining enough pressure within the glomerulus to ensure adequate filtration.

Potassium

Potassium is the most abundant intracellular ion; about 98% of the total body potassium is located intracellularly. To maintain a normal serum potassium balance (see Chapter 4), the kidneys are responsible for excreting more than 90% of the total daily potassium intake. Aldosterone causes the kidneys to excrete potassium, in contrast to its effects on sodium. The acid–base balance, the amount of dietary potassium intake, and the flow rate of the filtrate in the distal tubule also influence the amount of potassium secreted into the urine. Retention of potassium is the most life-threatening effect of renal failure.

Regulation of Acid–Base Balance

The normal serum pH is about 7.35 to 7.45 and must be maintained within this narrow range for optimal physiologic function. The kidney reabsorbs and returns bicarbonate from the urinary filtrate to the body's circulation. It also excretes acid in the urine. Because bicarbonate is a small ion, it is freely filtered at the glomerulus, and reabsorbed in the urinary filtrate. To replace any lost bicarbonate, new bicarbonate is generated by the renal tubular cells, and then reabsorbed by the tubules and returned to the body.

The body's acid production is the result of the breakdown of proteins, which produces acid compounds. The normal daily diet also includes a certain amount of acid materials. Unlike carbon dioxide (CO_2), the phosphoric and sulfuric acids produced are nonvolatile (solid) and cannot be eliminated by the lungs. If these acids were not excreted in the urine, accumulation of these acids in the blood would lower its pH and inhibit cell function. A person with normal kidney function excretes about 70 mEq of acid each day. The kidney is able to excrete some of this acid directly into the urine until the urine pH reaches 4.5, which is 1,000 times more acidic than blood.

More acid may need to be eliminated from the body than can be secreted directly as free acid in the urine. These excess acids are bound to chemical buffers so that they can be excreted in the urine. Two important chemical buffers are phosphate ions and ammonia (NH_3). Through the buffering process, the kidney is able to excrete large quantities of acid in a bound form, without further lowering the pH of the urine.

Autoregulation of Blood Pressure

Regulation of blood pressure is also a function of the kidney. Specialized vessels of the kidney, called the *vasa recta*, constantly monitor blood pressure as blood begins its passage into the kidney. When the vasa recta detect a decrease in blood pressure, specialized juxtaglomerular cells near the afferent arteriole, distal tubule, and efferent arteriole secrete the hormone renin. Renin does not affect blood pressure directly. It converts a circulating plasma protein named angiotensinogen to angiotensin I, which is then converted to angiotensin II, and causes the blood pressure to increase by its vasoconstrictor properties and secretion of aldosterone (Porth & Matfin, 2009). Aldosterone causes renal reabsorption of sodium and water by the distal tubules and collecting ducts, thus volume is returned to systemic circulation. Any etiology that results in poor perfusion or increasing serum osmolality, such as hemorrhage or diarrhea, will cause activation of renin, which leads to activation of angiotensin II and aldosterone secretion. The result is an increase in blood pressure. When the vasa recta recognize the increase in blood pressure, renin secretion stops. Failure of this feedback mechanism is one of the primary causes of hypertension.

Renal Clearance

Renal clearance refers to the ability of the kidneys to clear solutes from the plasma. A 24-hour collection of urine is the primary test of renal clearance. Renal clearance depends on several factors: how quickly the substance is filtered across the glomerulus, how much of the substance is reabsorbed

along the tubules, and how much of the substance is secreted into the tubules. It is possible to measure the renal clearance of any substance, but the one measure that is particularly useful is the creatinine clearance: as renal function declines, creatinine clearance decreases.

Creatinine is an endogenous waste product of skeletal muscle that is filtered at the glomerulus, passed through the tubules with minimal change, and excreted in the urine, making creatinine clearance is a good measure of the **glomerular filtration rate (GFR)**. To calculate creatinine clearance, a 24-hour urine specimen is collected. Midway through the collection, the serum creatinine level is measured.

The adult GFR can vary from a normal of approximately 125 mL/min (1.67 to 2.0 mL/sec) to a high of 200 mL/min (Porth & Matfin, 2009).

Regulation of Red Blood Cell Production

When the kidneys sense a decrease in the oxygen tension in renal blood flow, they release erythropoietin. Erythropoietin stimulates the bone marrow to produce red blood cells, thereby increasing the amount of hemoglobin available to carry oxygen. Some conditions, such as chronic kidney disease, require that patients receive exogenous erythropoietin in order to maintain red blood cell production.

Vitamin D Synthesis

The kidneys are also responsible for the final conversion of inactive vitamin D to its active form, 1,25-dihydroxycholecalciferol. Vitamin D is necessary for maintaining normal calcium balance in the body.

Secretion of Prostaglandins

The kidneys also produce prostaglandin E and prostacyclin, which have a vasodilatory effect and are important in maintaining renal blood flow.

Excretion of Waste Products

The kidney functions as the body's main excretory organ, eliminating the body's metabolic waste products. The major waste product of protein metabolism is urea, of which about 25 to 30 g are produced and excreted daily. All of this urea must be excreted in the urine; otherwise it accumulates in body tissues. Other waste products of metabolism that must be excreted are creatinine, phosphates, and sulfates. Uric acid, formed as a waste product of purine metabolism, is also eliminated in the urine. The kidneys serve as the primary mechanism for excreting drug metabolites.

❉ N U R S I N G   A L E R T

The kidneys are responsible for excretion of waste products that account for a daily solute load of approximately 600 mOsm. It is approximated that 500 cc of urine is required daily to excrete that solute load. Without that excretion of 500 cc, toxins and waste products will rise in the serum or blood value.

Urine Storage

The bladder is a hollow, distensible, muscular organ whose size, shape, and position vary in relation to the amount of urine it contains. Both filling and emptying of the bladder are mediated by coordinated sympathetic and parasympathetic nervous system control mechanisms involving the detrusor muscle and the bladder sphincters. Conscious awareness of bladder filling occurs as a result of sympathetic neuronal pathways that travel via the spinal cord to the level of T10 through T12, where peripheral, hypogastric nerve innervation allows for continued bladder filling. As bladder filling continues, stretch receptors in the bladder wall are activated, coupled with the desire to void. This information from the detrusor muscle is relayed back to the cerebral cortex via the parasympathetic pelvic nerves at the level of S1 through S4. Overall bladder pressure remains low due to the bladder's compliance (ability to expand or collapse) as urine volume changes.

Bladder compliance is due to the smooth muscle lining of the bladder and collagen deposits within the wall of the bladder, as well as to neuronal mechanisms that inhibit the detrusor muscle from contracting (specifically, adrenergic receptors that mediate relaxation). To maintain adequate kidney filtration rates, bladder pressure during filling must remain lower than 40 cm H_2O. This low pressure allows the urine to freely leave the renal pelvis and enter the ureters. The bladder is capable of holding 1,500 to 2,000 mL of urine. This is referred to as the *anatomic capacity* of the bladder. The sensation of bladder fullness is transmitted to the central nervous system when the bladder has reached about 150 to 250 mL in adults, and an initial desire to void occurs (Porth & Matfin, 2009). A marked sense of fullness and discomfort with a strong desire to void usually occurs when the bladder contains 350 mL or more of urine, referred to as the *functional capacity*. Neurologic changes to the bladder at the level of the supraspinal nerves, the spinal nerves, or the bladder wall itself can cause abnormally high volumes of urine to be stored due to a decreased or absent urge to void.

Under normal circumstances with average fluid intake of approximately 1,500 to 2,000 mL/day, the bladder should be able to store urine for periods of 2 to 4 hours at a time during the day. At night, the release of vasopressin in response to decreased fluid intake causes a decrease in the production of urine and makes it more concentrated. It allows the bladder to continue filling for periods of 6 to 8 hours in adolescents and adults, making them able to sleep for longer periods before needing to void. This process, which is less pronounced in the elderly, coupled with decreasing bladder compliance and decreased vasopressin levels often causes **nocturia**.

Bladder Emptying

Micturition normally occurs approximately eight times in a 24-hour period. It is activated via the micturition reflex arc

within the sympathetic and parasympathetic nervous system, which causes a coordinated sequence of events. Initiation of voiding occurs when the efferent pelvic nerve, which originates at S1 to S4, stimulates the bladder to contract, resulting in complete relaxation of the striated urethral sphincter. This is followed by a decrease in urethral pressure, contraction of the detrusor muscle, opening of the vesicle neck and proximal urethra, and flow of urine. This coordinated effort by the parasympathetic system is mediated by muscarinic and, to a lesser extent, cholinergic receptors within the detrusor muscle. The pressure generated in the bladder during micturition is about 20 to 40 cm H_2O in females. It is somewhat higher and more variable in males 45 years of age and older due to the normal hyperplasia of the lobes of the prostate gland, which surround the proximal urethra. Any obstruction of the bladder outlet, such as in advanced benign prostatic hyperplasia (BPH), results in a high voiding pressure. High voiding pressures make it more difficult to start urine flow and maintain it.

If the spinal pathways from the brain to the urinary system are destroyed (e.g., after a spinal cord injury), reflex contraction of the bladder is maintained, but voluntary control over the process is lost. In both situations, the detrusor

muscle can contract and expel urine, but the contractions are generally insufficient to empty the bladder completely, so residual urine (urine left in the bladder after voiding) remains. Normally, residual urine amounts to no more than 50 mL in the middle-aged adult and less than 50 to 100 mL in the older adult.

!NURSING ALERT
Residual urine volumes of more than 100 mL are significantly associated with the risk of infection (LeBlond, Brown, & DeGowin, 2009).

Gerontologic Considerations

Upper and lower urinary tract function changes with age (Table 26-2). The GFR decreases, starting between 35 and 40 years of age, and a yearly decline of about 1 mL/min continues thereafter. The elderly are more susceptible to acute and chronic renal failure due to the structural and functional changes in the kidney. Examples include sclerosis of the glomerulus and renal vasculature, decreased blood flow, decreased GFR, altered tubular function, and acid–base imbalance. Although renal function usually remains

TABLE 26-2 GERONTOLOGIC CONSIDERATIONS / Age-Related Changes in the Renal System

Component	Structural and Functional Changes	History & Physical Findings
Kidney	Kidney weight and volume (primarily of the cortex) declines after age 40.	Progressive decline of renal reserve (the ability to respond to changes in water or electrolyte imbalances)
Renal blood flow	Blood flow decreases approximately 10% per decade. Renal arteries thicken (similar to other vascular changes). Sclerosis of the glomerulus results in atrophy of the afferent and efferent arteriole.	Increased risk for renal failure due to polypharmacy, comorbidities, and decreased renal function
Nephron	The number of nephrons declines after the age of 40 and is associated with decline in GFR. The glomerular basement membrane thickens.	Yearly decline in GFR of 1 mL per minute (after age of 40). The elderly are at risk for altered drug excretion and drug–drug interaction.
Tubule system	Degeneration of the tubule system, replaced with connective tissue. Decrease in the length of the proximal tubule	Ability to conserve sodium or excrete hydrogen is decreased, predisposing the elderly to fluid and electrolyte and acid–base disturbances.
Bladder	Reduced bladder tone. Decreased bladder capacity. In women, decreased estrogen causes changes to the urethral sphincter.	Increased sense of urgency. In women, increased risk of urinary incontinence. Incomplete emptying of bladder, leading to urinary tract infection
Prostate	Enlargement of the prostate	Obstruction to urine flow, leading to frequency, oliguria, anuria
General	Decrease in muscle mass results in decreased production of creatinine. Decreased vitamin D synthesis	Serum creatinine levels remain constant; creatinine clearance is a better indicator of renal function. Osteomalacia

From Criddle, L. (2009). Caring for the critically ill elderly patient. In Carlson, K., *Advanced Critical Care Nursing*, American Association of Critical-Care Nursing. St. Louis: Saunders, Elsevier; and from Porth & Matfin (2009).

adequate despite these changes, renal reserve is decreased and may reduce the kidneys' ability to respond effectively to drastic or sudden physiologic changes. This steady decrease in glomerular filtration, combined with the use of multiple medications in which metabolites are cleared by the kidneys, puts the older person at higher risk for adverse drug effects and drug–drug interactions (Criddle, 2009).

The elderly are more prone to develop hypernatremia and fluid volume deficit, because increasing age is also associated with diminished osmotic stimulation of thirst (Criddle, 2009). Thirst is a subjective sensory symptom that is defined as an awareness of the desire to drink. The sense of thirst is so protective that hypernatremia almost never occurs in adults younger than 60 years of age.

Structural or functional abnormalities that occur with aging may also prevent complete emptying of the bladder. This may be due to decreased bladder wall contractility; secondary to myogenic or neurogenic factors, or it may be related to bladder outlet obstruction, such as in BPH (Porth & Matfin, 2009). Vaginal and urethral tissues atrophy (become thinner) in aging women due to decreased estrogen levels, resulting in decreased blood supply to the urogenital tissues, with subsequent urethral and vaginal irritation and possible urinary incontinence.

Urinary incontinence is the most common reason for admission to skilled nursing facilities. Many older people and their families are unaware that urinary incontinence stems from many causes. The nurse needs to inform the patient and family that, with appropriate evaluation, urinary incontinence can often be managed at home, and in most cases it can be eliminated. Many treatments are available for urinary incontinence in the elderly, including noninvasive, behavioral interventions that the patient or caregiver can carry out (Roe, Milne, Ostaszhiewicz, & Wallace, 2006; Roe, Ostaszhiewicz, Milne, & Wallace, 2006). Treatment modalities for urinary incontinence are described in further detail in Chapter 28.

Preparation of the elderly patient for diagnostic tests must be managed carefully to prevent dehydration, which might precipitate renal failure in a patient with marginal renal reserve. Limitations in mobility may affect an elderly patient's ability to void adequately or to consume an adequate volume of fluids, usually considered six to eight 8-ounce glasses daily. The patient may limit fluid intake to minimize the frequency of voiding or the risk of incontinence. Teaching the patient and family about the dangers of an inadequate fluid intake is an important role of the nurse caring for the elderly incontinent patient.

ASSESSMENT

Obtaining a comprehensive health history is the first step in assessing a patient with upper or lower urinary tract dysfunction.

Health History

Obtaining a urologic health history requires excellent communication skills, because many patients are embarrassed or uncomfortable discussing genitourinary function or symptoms. It is important to use language the patient can understand and to avoid medical jargon while reviewing risk factors, particularly for those patients who are at high risk.

When obtaining the health history specific to the renal and urinary systems, the nurse should inquire about the following:

- The patient's chief concern or reason for seeking health care, the onset of the problem, and its effect on the patient's quality of life
- The location, character, and duration of pain, if present, and its relationship to voiding; factors that precipitate pain, and those that relieve it
- History of urinary tract infections (UTIs), including past treatment or hospitalization for UTI
- Fever or chills
- Previous renal or urinary diagnostic tests
- Use of indwelling urinary catheters, suprapubic tubes, condom catheters or intermittent catheterization
- Dysuria (painful urination) and when during voiding (i.e., at initiation or at termination of voiding) it occurs
- Hesitancy, straining, or pain during or after urination
- Urinary incontinence (stress incontinence, urge incontinence, overflow incontinence, or functional incontinence)
- **Hematuria** (blood in urine) or change in color or volume of urine
- The presence of nocturia and number of episodes nightly
- Renal calculi (kidney stones), passage of stones or gravel in urine
- Female patients: Number and type (vaginal or cesarean) of deliveries; use of forceps; vaginal infection, discharge, or irritation; contraceptive practices
- History of anuria (<50 cc of urine a day) or other renal problem
- Presence or history of genital lesions or sexually transmitted diseases
- Use of tobacco, alcohol, or recreational drugs
- Any prescription and over-the-counter medications (including those prescribed for renal or urinary problems)

Common Complaints

Fatigue, pain, changes in voiding, and GI symptoms are particularly suggestive of urinary tract disease. Dysfunction of the kidney can produce a complex array of symptoms throughout the body.

Fatigue

Gradual kidney dysfunction can be insidious in its presentation, although fatigue is a common symptom. Fatigue, shortness of breath, and exercise intolerance all result from the condition known as *anemia of chronic disease*. Although

TABLE
26-3 Identifying Characteristics of Genitourinary Pain

Type	Location	Character	Associated Signs and Symptoms	Possible Etiology
Kidney	Costovertebral angle, may extend to umbilicus	Dull constant ache; if sudden distention of capsule, pain is severe, sharp, stabbing, and colicky in nature	Nausea and vomiting, diaphoresis, pallor, signs of shock	Acute obstruction, kidney stone, blood clot, acute pyelonephritis, trauma
Bladder	Suprapubic area	Dull, continuous pain, may be intense with voiding, may be severe if bladder full	Urgency, pain at end of voiding, painful straining	Overdistended bladder, infection, interstitial cystitis; tumor
Ureteral	Costovertebral angle, flank, lower abdominal area, testis, or labium	Severe, sharp, stabbing pain, colicky in nature	Nausea and vomiting, paralytic ileus	Ureteral stone, edema or stricture, blood clot
Prostatic	Perineum and rectum	Vague discomfort, feeling of fullness in perineum, vague back pain	Suprapubic tenderness, obstruction to urine flow; frequency, urgency, dysuria, nocturia	Prostatic cancer, acute or chronic prostatitis
Urethral	Male: along penis to meatus; female: urethra to meatus	Pain variable, most severe during and immediately after voiding	Frequency, urgency, dysuria, nocturia, urethral discharge	Irritation of bladder neck, infection of urethra, trauma, foreign body in lower urinary tract

historically hematocrit has been the blood test of choice when assessing a patient for anemia, use of the hemoglobin level rather than hematocrit is currently recommended because that measurement is a better assessment of the oxygen transport ability of the blood.

Pain

Genitourinary pain is usually caused by distention of some portion of the urinary tract as a result of obstructed urine flow or inflammation and swelling of tissues. Severity of pain is related to the sudden onset rather than the extent of distention.

Table 26-3 lists the various types of genitourinary pain, characteristics of the pain, associated signs and symptoms, and possible causes. Kidney disease, however, does not always involve pain. It tends to be diagnosed because of other symptoms that cause a patient to seek health care, such as pedal edema, shortness of breath, and changes in urine elimination (Stanley, Blair, & Beare, 2005).

Changes in Voiding

Micturition is normally a painless function that occurs approximately eight times in a 24-hour period. The average person voids 1,200 to 1,500 mL of urine in 24 hours, although this amount varies depending on fluid intake, sweating, environmental temperature, vomiting, or diarrhea. Common problems associated with voiding include **frequency**, urgency, dysuria, hesitancy, incontinence, enuresis (bed wetting), **polyuria** (>2.5 L/day of urine), **oliguria** (<500 mL/day), and hematuria (Table 26-4). Increased urinary urgency and frequency coupled with decreasing urine

volumes strongly suggest urine retention. Depending on the acuity of the onset of these symptoms, immediate bladder emptying via catheterization and evaluation are necessary to prevent kidney dysfunction (Newman, 2003).

Gastrointestinal Symptoms

GI symptoms may occur with urologic conditions because of shared autonomic and sensory innervation and renointestinal reflexes. The most common signs and symptoms are nausea, vomiting, diarrhea, abdominal discomfort, and abdominal distention. Urologic symptoms can mimic such disorders as appendicitis, peptic ulcer disease, and cholecystitis, making diagnosis difficult, especially in the elderly, who have decreased neurologic innervation to this area (Goshorn, 2005).

Past History

Various diseases or clinical situations can increase a patient's risk for renal and urinary tract dysfunction. Data collection about previous health problems or diseases provides the health care team with useful information for evaluating the patient's current urinary status. For example, the nurse needs to be aware that multiparous women delivering their children vaginally have a high risk for stress **urinary incontinence**. Elderly women and people with neurologic disorders such as diabetic neuropathy, multiple sclerosis (MS), or Parkinson's disease often have incomplete emptying of the bladder and urinary stasis, which may result in UTI or increasing bladder pressure, leading to overflow incontinence, hydronephrosis, pyelonephritis, or renal insufficiency. People with diabetes who have consistent hypertension and those with primary hypertension are at risk for renal dysfunction, as are those

26-4 Problems Associated With Changes in Voiding

Problem	Definition	Possible Etiology
Frequency	Frequent voiding; more than every 3 hours	Infection, obstruction of lower urinary tract leading to residual urine and overflow, anxiety, diuretics, benign prostatic hyperplasia, urethral stricture, diabetic neuropathy, interstitial cystitis (IC), neurologic conditions
Urgency	Strong desire to void	Infection, chronic prostatitis, urethritis, obstruction of lower urinary tract leading to residual urine and overflow, anxiety, diuretics, benign prostatic hyperplasia, urethral stricture, diabetic neuropathy, IC, neurologic conditions
Dysuria	Painful or difficult voiding	Lower urinary tract infection, inflammation of bladder or urethra, acute prostatitis, stones, foreign bodies, tumors in bladder, IC
Hesitancy	Delay, difficulty in initiating voiding	Benign prostatic hyperplasia, compression of urethra, outlet obstruction, neurogenic bladder, DSD (detrusor sphincter dyssynergia: the sphincter and bladder do not coordinate)
Nocturia	Wakening from sleep to void more than twice a night (Newman, 2009)	Decreased renal concentrating ability, heart failure, diabetes mellitus, incomplete bladder emptying, excessive fluid intake at bedtime, nephrotic syndrome, cirrhosis with ascites
Incontinence	Involuntary loss of urine	External urinary sphincter injury, obstetric injury, lesions of bladder neck, detrusor dysfunction, infection, neurogenic bladder, medications, neurologic abnormalities
Enuresis	Involuntary voiding during sleep	Delay in functional maturation of central nervous system (bladder control usually achieved by 5 years of age), obstructive disease of lower urinary tract, genetic factors, failure to concentrate urine, urinary tract infection, psychological stress, neurologic conditions
Polyuria	Increased volume of urine voided (generally >3 L/d)	Diabetes mellitus, diabetes insipidus, use of diuretics, excess fluid intake, lithium toxicity, some forms of kidney disease (hypercalcemic and hypokalemic nephropathy)
Oliguria	Urine output <400 mL/d	Acute or chronic renal failure (see Chapter 27), inadequate fluid intake
Anuria	Urine output <50 mL/d	Acute or chronic renal failure (see Chapter 27), complete obstruction
Hematuria	Red blood cells in the urine	Cancer of genitourinary tract, acute glomerulonephritis, renal stones, renal tuberculosis, blood dyscrasia, trauma, extreme exercise, rheumatic fever, hemophilia, leukemia, sickle cell trait or disease
Proteinuria	Abnormal amounts of protein in the urine	Acute and chronic renal disease, nephrotic syndrome, vigorous exercise, heat stroke, severe heart failure, diabetic nephropathy, multiple myeloma

who suffer from autoimmune diseases such as systemic lupus erythematosus (SLE). Older men are at risk for prostatic enlargement, which causes urethral obstruction and can result in UTIs and renal failure.

Risk factors for specific disorders and kidney and lower urinary tract dysfunction are summarized in Table 26-5 and discussed in Chapters 27 and 28.

Family History

People with a family history of urinary tract problems are at increased risk for renal disorders, such as autosomal-dominant polycystic kidney disease (which occurs in 1 of 400 to 1,000 people) heredity nephritis, or urolithiasis (Schrier, 2006).

Social History

It is especially important to obtain a thorough medication history when assessing elderly patients, for whom the increased occurrence of chronic illness often leads to polypharmacy (concurrent use of multiple medications). Aging affects the way the body absorbs, metabolizes, and excretes drugs, placing the elderly patient at risk for adverse reactions. Aging

also affects the genitourinary system, leading to compromise and dysfunction in the renal and urinary systems.

Other key information to obtain includes an assessment of the patient's psychosocial status, level of anxiety, perceived threats to body image, available support systems, and sociocultural patterns. Obtaining this information during the initial and subsequent nursing assessments enables the nurse to uncover special needs, misunderstandings, lack of knowledge, and need for patient teaching.

Physical Examination

Several body systems can affect upper and lower urinary tract dysfunction, and that dysfunction can affect several end organs; therefore, a head-to-toe assessment is indicated. Areas of emphasis include the abdomen, suprapubic region, genitalia, lower back, and lower extremities.

Palpation of the Kidneys

The kidneys are not usually palpable; it is uncommon to palpate kidneys except in very thin patients. However, palpation of the kidneys may detect an enlargement that could prove

TABLE
26-5 Risk Factors for Selected Renal or Urologic Disorders

Risk Factor	Possible Renal or Urologic Disorder
Childhood diseases: "strep throat" impetigo, nephrotic syndrome	Chronic renal failure
Advanced age	Incomplete emptying of bladder, leading to urinary tract infection
Instrumentation of urinary tract, cystoscopy, catheterization	Urinary tract infection, incontinence
Immobilization	Kidney stone formation
Occupational, recreational, or environmental exposure to chemicals (plastics, pitch, tar, rubber)	Acute renal failure
Diabetes mellitus	Chronic renal failure, neurogenic bladder
Hypertension	Renal insufficiency, chronic renal failure
Multiple sclerosis	Incontinence, neurogenic bladder
Parkinson's disease	Incontinence, neurogenic bladder
Systemic lupus erythematosus	Nephritis, chronic renal failure
Gout, hyperparathyroidism, Crohn's disease, ileostomy	Kidney stone formation
Sickle cell anemia, multiple myeloma	Chronic renal failure
Benign prostatic hyperplasia	Obstruction to urine flow, leading to frequency, oliguria, anuria
Radiation therapy to pelvis	Cystitis, fibrosis of ureter, or fistula in urinary tract, frequency, hematuria
Recent pelvic surgery	Inadvertent trauma to ureters or bladder
Pregnancy	Proteinuria, frequent voiding
Obstetric injury, tumors	Incontinence, fistulas
Spinal cord injury	Neurogenic bladder, urinary tract infection, incontinence

to be very important (Bickley, 2009). The correct technique for palpation is illustrated in Figure 26-5. Renal dysfunction may produce tenderness over the costovertebral angle, which is the angle formed by the lower border of the twelfth rib and the spine (Fig. 26-6).

Inspection, Palpation, Percussion, and Auscultation of the Abdomen

The abdomen (just slightly to the right and left of midline in both upper quadrants) is auscultated to assess for bruits (low-pitched murmurs that indicate renal artery stenosis or an aortic aneurysm). The abdomen is also assessed for the presence of ascites (accumulation of fluid in the peritoneal cavity), which may occur with kidney as well as liver dysfunction. On inspection, with the patient lying down, a distended abdomen is noted with bulging flanks (sides) due to the weight of fluid accumulation pressing against the flanks. On percussion, dullness is noted on the flank area (where the water is), whereas tympanic sounds are heard on the upper abdomen as the gas-filled intestines rise above the ascites fluid (refer to Chapter 21 for further details and techniques).

Percussion of the Bladder

To check for residual urine, the bladder should be percussed after the patient voids. Percussion of the bladder begins at the midline just above the umbilicus and proceeds downward. The sound changes from tympanic to dull when percussing over the bladder. The bladder, which can be palpated only if it is moderately distended, feels like a smooth, firm, round mass rising out of the abdomen, usually at midline

(Fig. 26-7). Dullness to percussion of the bladder after voiding indicates incomplete bladder emptying.

Palpation of the Prostate and Inguinal Area

In older men, BPH or prostatitis can cause difficulty with urination. The prostate gland is palpated by digital rectal examination (DRE) as part of the yearly physical examination in men 50 years of age and older (see Chapter 34). In addition, a blood specimen is obtained to test the prostate-specific antigen (PSA) level annually; the results of the DRE and PSA are then correlated. Blood is drawn for PSA before the DRE, because manipulation of the prostate can cause the PSA level to increase temporarily. The inguinal area is examined for enlarged nodes, or an inguinal or femoral hernia.

Inspection and Palpation of the Female Genitalia

In women, the vulva, urethral meatus, and vagina are examined; refer to Chapter 33 for additional details regarding the vaginal examination. The urethra is palpated for diverticula, and the vagina is assessed for adequate estrogen effect and any evidence of herniation. A *urethrocele* is the bulging of the anterior vaginal wall into the urethra. When the pelvic floor muscles, fascia, or supporting ligaments fail, pelvic organs may fall through the vagina. A *cystocele* is the herniation of the bladder wall into the anterior vaginal vault. Urinary stasis with a cystocele is a risk factor for the development of UTIs. A *rectocele* is herniation of the terminal

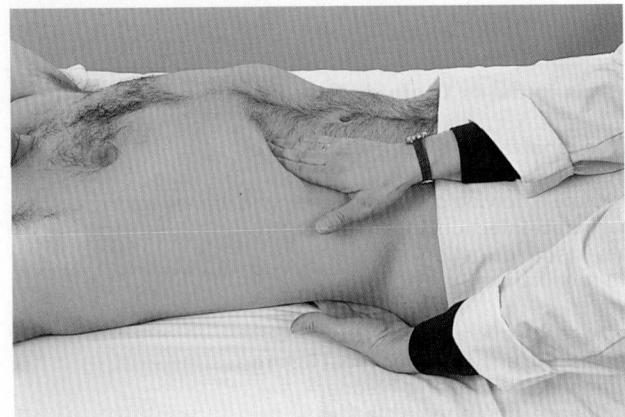

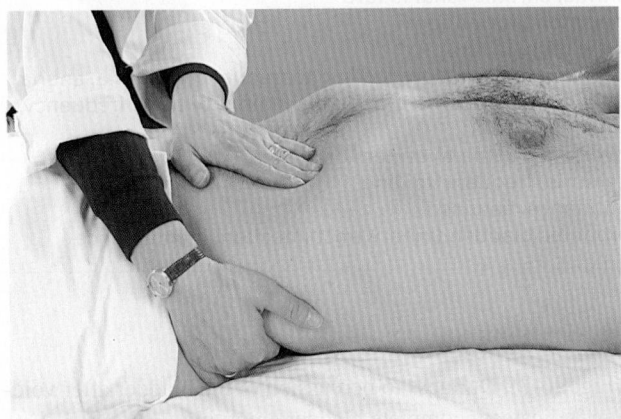

FIGURE 26-5 Technique for palpating the right kidney (*top*). Place one hand under the patient's back with the fingers under the lower rib. Place the palm of the other hand anterior to the kidney with fingers above the umbilicus. Push the hand on top forward as the patient inhales deeply. The left kidney (*bottom*) is palpated similarly by reaching over to the patient's left side and placing the right hand beneath the patient's lower left rib. From Weber, J. W., & Kelley, J. (2007). *Health assessment in nursing* (3rd ed.). Philadelphia: Lippincott Williams & Wilkins.

rectum into the posterior vagina. Complaints of constipation and incomplete rectal evacuation may be noted with a rectocele (LeBlond, Brown & DeGowin, 2009).

Assessment for Edema and Body Weight

The patient is assessed for edema and changes in body weight. Edema may be observed, particularly in the face and dependent parts of the body, such as the ankles and sacral areas, and suggests fluid retention. An increase in body weight commonly accompanies edema. A 1 kg weight gain equals approximately 1,000 mL of fluid (1 lb ≈ 500 mL).

Assessment of Lower Extremities

The deep tendon reflexes of the knee are assessed for quality and symmetry. This is an important part of testing for neurologic causes of bladder dysfunction, because the sacral area, which innervates the lower extremities, is the same peripheral nerve area responsible for urinary continence. The gait pattern

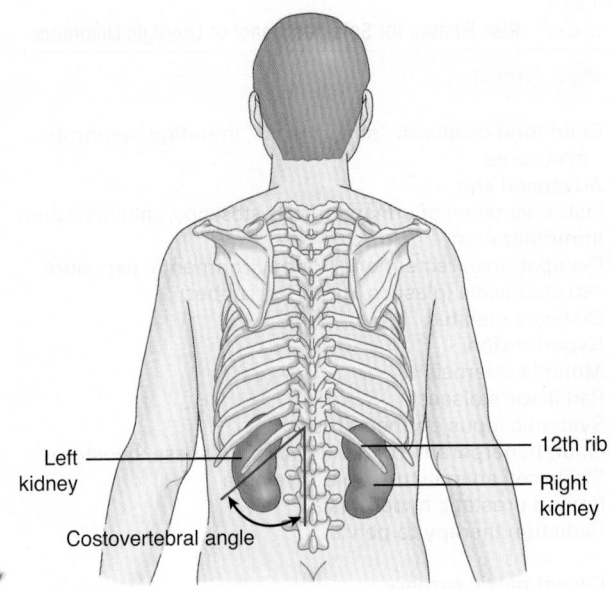

FIGURE 26-6 Location of the costovertebral angle.

of the person with bladder dysfunction is also noted, as well as the patient's ability to walk toe-to-heel. These tests evaluate possible supraspinal causes for urinary incontinence.

Diagnostic Evaluation

A comprehensive health history and physical examination are used to determine the appropriate laboratory and diagnostic

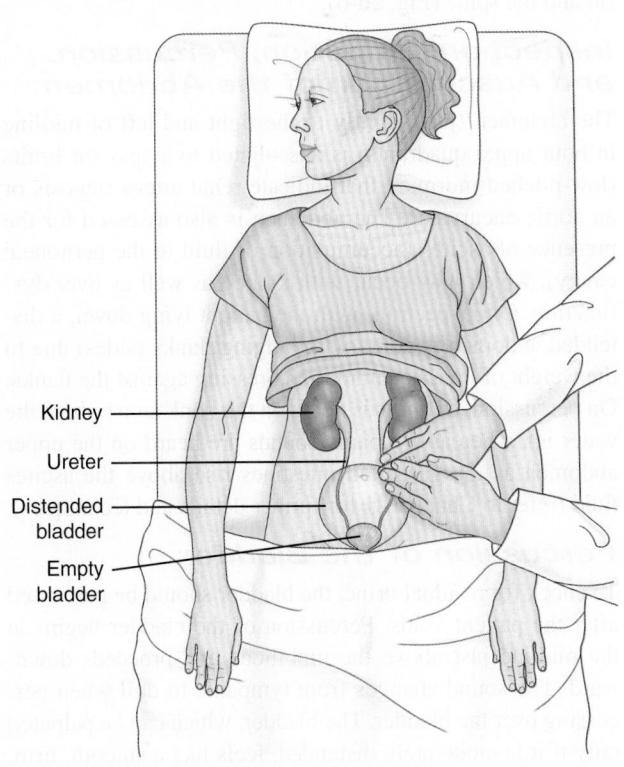

FIGURE 26-7 Palpation of the bladder.

tests. Most patients undergoing urologic testing or imaging studies are apprehensive, even those who have had these tests in the past. Patients frequently feel discomfort and embarrassment about such a private and personal function as voiding. Voiding in the presence of others can frequently cause guarding, a natural reflex that inhibits voiding due to situational anxiety. Because the outcomes of these studies determine the plan of care, the nurse must help the patient relax by providing as much privacy and explanation about the procedure as possible. The following sections review some of the tests that might be used.

Urinalysis and Urine Culture

The urinalysis provides important clinical information about kidney function and helps diagnose other diseases, such as diabetes. The urine culture determines whether bacteria are present in the urine, as well as their strains and concentration. Urine culture and sensitivity also identify the antimicrobial therapy that is best suited for the particular strains identified, taking into consideration the antibiotics that have the best rate of resolution in that particular geographic region. Appropriate evaluation of any abnormality can assist in detecting serious underlying diseases. Refer to Table 26-6

TABLE
26-6 Select Urinalysis Components

Component	Discussion

Color	Colorless to pale yellow
	  (Possible causes: Dilute urine due to diuretics, alcohol consumption, diabetes insipidus, glycosuria, excess fluid intake, renal disease)
	Yellow to milky white
	  (Possible causes: Pyuria, infection, vaginal cream)
	Bright yellow
	  (Possible causes: Multiple vitamin preparations)
	Pink to red
	  (Possible causes: Hemoglobin breakdown, red blood cells, gross blood, menses, bladder or prostate surgery, beets, blackberries, medications [phenytoin, rifampin, phenothiazine, cascara, senna products])
	Blue, blue green
	  (Possible causes: Dyes, methylene blue, *Pseudomonas* species organisms, medications [amitriptyline, triamterene, phenyl salicylate])
	Orange to amber
	  (Possible causes: Concentrated urine due to dehydration, fever, bile, excess bilirubin or carotene, medications [phenazopyridium HCl, nitrofurantoin, sulfasalazine, docusate calcium, thiamine])
	Brown to black
	  (Possible causes: Old red blood cells, urobilinogen, bilirubin, melanin, porphyrin, extremely concentrated urine due to dehydration, medications [cascara, metronidazole, iron preparations, quinine, senna products, methyldopa, nitrofurantoin]; myoglobinuria)

Specific gravity	Evaluates ability of kidneys to concentrate solutes in urine, and is altered by the presence of blood, protein, and casts in the urine. (Disorders or conditions that cause *decreased* urine specific gravity (that is, dilute urine) include diabetes insipidus, glomerulonephritis, and severe renal damage, which may cause a fixed specific gravity of 1.010. Glucose, protein, or dyes excreted in the urine *increase* the specific gravity (concentrated urine); therefore, etiologies include diabetes mellitus, patients who recently received high-density radiopaque dyes, and fluid deficit.
Osmolality	Concentrating ability is lost early in kidney disease; these test findings may disclose early defects in renal function.
Red blood cells (hematuria)	Can develop from an abnormality anywhere along the genitourinary tract and is more common in women than in men. Common causes include acute infection (cystitis, urethritis, or prostatitis), renal calculi, and neoplasm. Other causes include systemic disorders, such as bleeding disorders; malignant lesions; and medications, such as warfarin and heparin.
White blood cells	Should be very few; increased numbers indicate infection or inflammation
Protein	Occasional loss of up to 150 mg/day of protein in the urine primarily is considered normal and usually does not require further evaluation. Urine concentration, pH, hematuria, and radiocontrast materials all affect the results. Microalbuminuria (excretion of 20 to 200 mg/dL of protein in the urine) is an early sign of diabetic nephropathy. Common benign causes of transient proteinuria are fever, strenuous exercise, and prolonged standing. Causes of persistent proteinuria include glomerular diseases, malignancies, collagen diseases, diabetes mellitus, preeclampsia, urinary tract infection, hyperthyroidism, hypertension, heart failure, and use of a wide variety of medications (Fischbach & Dunning, 2009).
Glucose	Should be absent; its presence is suspicious for diabetes.

for the details regarding urinalysis components and potential significance.

Renal Function Tests

Renal function tests are used to evaluate the severity of kidney disease and to assess the status of the patient's kidney function. These tests also provide information about the effectiveness of the kidney in carrying out its excretory function. Renal function test results may be within normal limits until the GFR is reduced to less than 50% of normal. Renal function can be assessed most accurately if several tests are performed and their results are analyzed together. Common tests of renal function include renal concentration tests, creatinine clearance, and serum creatinine and blood **urea nitrogen** levels. Table 26-7 describes the purpose and gives the normal range for each test. Other tests for evaluating renal function that may be helpful include serum electrolyte levels (see Chapter 4). A plan of nursing care for a patient undergoing diagnostic testing of the renal/urologic system is available online at http://thePoint.lww.com/Pellico1e.

Imaging Modalities

Several imaging modalities play a vital role in the evaluation of renal and urologic disease.

X-ray: Kidneys, Ureters, Bladder (KUB)

This X-ray delineates the size, shape, and position of the kidneys and reveals abnormalities, such as calculi in the kidneys or urinary tract, hydronephrosis, cysts, tumors, or kidney displacement by abnormalities in surrounding tissues.

Computed Tomography and Magnetic Resonance Imaging

Computed tomography (CT) scans and magnetic resonance imaging (MRI) are noninvasive techniques that provide excellent cross-sectional views of the kidney and urinary tract. They are used to evaluate genitourinary masses, nephrolithiasis, chronic renal infections, renal or urinary tract trauma, metastatic disease, and soft tissue abnormalities. Occasionally, an oral or IV radiopaque contrast agent is used in CT scanning to enhance visualization, although the use of a CT scan should take into account the patient's previous exposures to radiation via imaging studies.

Intravenous Urography

This test shows the kidneys, ureters, and bladder via X-ray imaging as a radiopaque contrast agent that is administered intravenously moves through the upper and then the lower urinary system. It may be used as the initial assessment of many suspected urologic problems, especially lesions in the kidneys and ureters and provides an approximate estimate of renal function.

Retrograde Pyelography

If an IV urography provides inadequate visualization of the collecting systems, a retrograde pyelography may be performed. It involves advancing catheters through the ureters into the renal pelvis by means of cystoscopy, followed by injection of a contrast agent.

Cystography

In cystography, a catheter is inserted into the bladder, and a contrast agent is instilled to outline the bladder wall. This study aids in evaluating vesicoureteral reflux (backflow of urine from the bladder into one or both ureters) and in assessing for bladder injury.

Voiding Cystourethrography

In a voiding cystourethrography, a urethral catheter is inserted, and a contrast agent is instilled into the bladder.

TABLE
26-7 Additional Tests of Renal Function

Test	Description	Normal Range		
Creatinine clearance	Detects and evaluates progression of renal disease. Test measures volume of blood cleared of endogenous creatinine in 1 minute, which provides an approximation of the glomerular filtration rate. Sensitive indicator of renal disease used to follow progression of renal disease.	Measured in mL/min/1.73 m^2		
		Age	**Male**	**Female**
		<30	88–146	81–134
		30–40	82–140	75–128
		40–50	75–133	69–122
		50–60	68–126	64–116
		60–70	61–120	58–110
		70–80	55–113	52–105
Creatinine level	Measures effectiveness of renal function. In normal function, the level of creatinine remains fairly constant in body.	0.6–1.2 mg/dL (50–110 mmol/L)		
Urea nitrogen (blood urea nitrogen [BUN])	Serves as index of renal function. Urea is nitrogenous end product of protein metabolism. Test values are affected by protein intake, tissue breakdown, and fluid volume changes.	7–18 mg/dL Patients >60 y: 8–20 mg/dL		
BUN to creatinine ratio	Evaluates hydration status. An elevated ratio is seen in hypovolemia; a normal ratio with an elevated BUN and creatinine is seen with intrinsic renal disease.	About 10:1		

TABLE
26-8 Common Urologic Procedures

Procedure	Description	Purpose
Cystoscopy	Cystoscope is inserted through the urethra into the bladder.	Used to directly visualize the urethra and bladder, as well as the urethral orifices and prostatic urethra. Calculi may be removed from the urethra, bladder, and ureter.
Renal and ureteral brush biopsy	Ureteral catheter is introduced via cystoscope, followed by a biopsy brush that is passed through the catheter.	Suspected lesion is brushed back and forth to obtain cells and surface tissue fragments for histologic analysis.
Kidney biopsy	Small section of renal cortex is obtained either percutaneously (needle biopsy) or by open biopsy through small flank incision.	Helps diagnose and evaluate the extent of kidney disease. Indications for biopsy include unexplained acute renal failure, persistent proteinuria/hematuria, transplant rejection, glomerulopathies.

When the bladder is full and the patient feels the urge to void, the catheter is removed, and the patient voids. This study uses fluoroscopy to visualize the lower urinary tract and assess urine storage in the bladder. It is used as a diagnostic tool to identify vesicoureteral reflux. Retrograde urethrography, in which a contrast agent is injected retrograde into the urethra, is always performed before urethral catheterization if urethral trauma is suspected.

Nuclear Scans

A nuclear scan requires injection of a radioisotope into the circulatory system; the isotope is then monitored as it moves through the blood vessels of the kidneys. The test provides information about kidney perfusion and function. It is used to evaluate acute and chronic renal failure, renal masses, and blood flow before and after kidney transplantation.

Renal Angiography

In renal angiography, a catheter is threaded up through the femoral and iliac arteries into the aorta or renal artery. A contrast agent is injected to opacify the renal arterial supply. Angiography is used to evaluate renal blood flow, to differentiate renal cysts from tumors, to evaluate hypertension, and preoperatively, for renal transplantation.

Bladder Ultrasonography

Ultrasonography is a noninvasive procedure that uses sound waves passed into the body through a transducer to detect abnormalities of internal tissues and organs. A bladder ultrasonography is a noninvasive method of measuring urine volume in the bladder; it automatically calculates and displays urine volume. The test requires a full bladder; therefore, fluid intake should be encouraged before

the procedure. This test also can be used to determine if a patient is emptying the bladder after urination.

Urologic Endoscopic Procedures

Endourology, or urologic endoscopic procedures, can be performed in one of two ways: using a cystoscope (Fig. 26-8) inserted into the urethra, or percutaneously, through a small incision (Table 26-8).

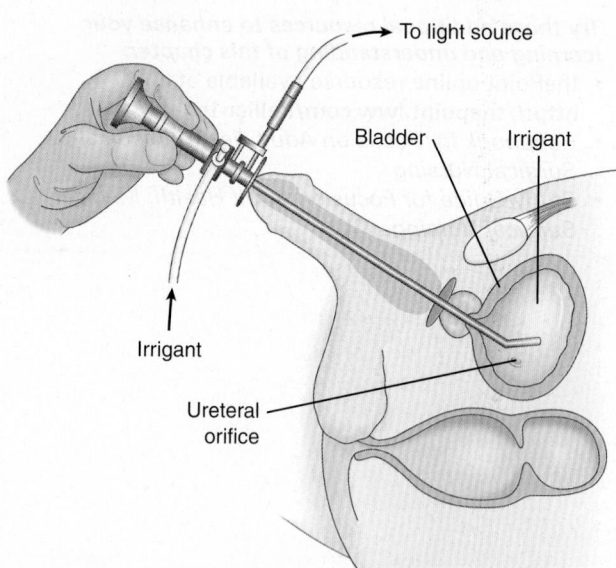

FIGURE 26-8 Cystoscopic examination. A rigid or semi-rigid cystoscope is introduced into the bladder. The upper cord is an electric line for the light at the distal end of the cystoscope. The lower tubing leads from a reservoir of sterile irrigant that is used to inflate the bladder.

Chapter Review

Critical Thinking Exercises

1. Discuss the changes to renal function in an otherwise healthy 28-year-old female patient who becomes dehydrated during a marathon.
2. Discuss some of the changes that are likely to be seen when examining the urine of a diabetic patient with poor control of his or her blood sugar. How do you explain each finding?

NCLEX-Style Review Questions

1. A client has been diagnosed with a small kidney stone. He has been told to increase his fluid intake and is asking why. Which of the following is the nurse's best response?
   A. This will decrease his pain
   B. This will increase urine production and help move the stone from his system
   C. This will help pain medications to work more quickly.
   D. This will help prevent any nausea he is having
2. A male client is concerned about changes to his urinary stream. Which of the following are associated with lower urinary tract symptoms? Select all that apply.
   A. Urgency
   B. Incontinence
   C. Frequency
   D. Dribbling
3. The nurse recognizes that which of the following hormones must be replaced in chronic kidney disease?
   A. Anterior pituitary
   B. Parathyroid
   C. Erythropoietin
   D. Corticotropin-releasing
4. The nurse knows that white blood cells (WBCs) in the urine indicate which of the following?
   A. Prostate enlargement
   B. Kidney dysfunction
   C. Bladder cancer
   D. Genitourinary infection
5. A 42-year-old male patient complains of nausea, vomiting, and right flank pain. What is the most likely cause of these symptoms?
   A. Interstitial cystitis
   B. Renal colic
   C. Ureterocele
   D. Nephritic syndrome

Try these additional resources to enhance your learning and understanding of this chapter:
- thePoint online resource available at **http://thepoint.lww.com/Pellico1e**
- *Handbook for Focus on Adult Health: Medical-Surgical Nursing*
- *Study Guide for Focus on Adult Health: Medical-Surgical Nursing*

References and Selected Readings

References and selected readings associated with this chapter can be found on the website that accompanies the book. Visit http://thepoint.lww.com/Pellico1e to access the references and other additional resources associated with this chapter.

Nursing Management: Patients With Renal Disorders

ANDREA ROTHMAN MANN

Learning Objectives

After reading this chapter, you will be able to:

1. Compare and contrast the pathophysiology, assessment, nursing management, and medical management of the glomerular diseases.

2. Identify the causes of acute and chronic renal failure.

3. Summarize the nursing management of the patient with renal failure.

4. Describe renal replacement therapies.

5. Provide patient education for the patient undergoing kidney transplantation.

6. Describe care for the patient sustaining renal trauma.

7. Evaluate outcomes of care for the patient with renal disorders.

The renal system is an important regulator of the body's internal environment and is essential for the maintenance of life. The kidneys regulate fluid volume, electrolyte balance, play a role in acid–base balance, excrete waste products, regulate blood pressure (BP) and blood osmolarity, and contribute to red blood cell (RBC) production and vitamin D metabolism. Kidney dysfunction may be acute or chronic and can affect all body systems. Various factors contribute to kidney dysfunction; Box 27-1 on page 742 addresses gerontologic considerations. This chapter addresses glomerular dysfunction, acute and chronic renal failure, and treatment options, as well as kidney trauma and transplant.

GLOMERULAR DISEASES

ACUTE GLOMERULONEPHRITIS

Glomerulonephritis is an inflammation of the glomerular capillaries. Acute glomerulonephritis is more common in children older than 2 years of age, but it can occur at any age.

Pathophysiology

Primary glomerulonephritis and primary glomerular diseases are disorders in which the glomerulus is the predominant or sole tissue involved (Molzahn & Butera, 2006). Examples of primary diseases are postinfectious glomerulonephritis, rapidly progressive glomerulonephritis, membrane proliferative glomerulonephritis, and membranous glomerulonephritis. Acute nephritic syndrome is the clinical manifestation of glomerular inflammation. In acute glomerulonephritis, the kidneys become large, edematous, and congested. All renal tissues, including the glomeruli, tubules, and blood vessels, are affected to varying degrees. Box 27-2 on page 743 depicts the pathophysiology of glomerulonephritis.

Risk Factors

Risk factors include a family history of glomerulonephritis; a preexisting history of known diseases, such as a streptococcal infection of the upper respiratory tract; other infections with organisms including staphylococci, such as impetigo; and viral infectious diseases, such as hepatitis, mumps, and varicella zoster. Additionally, other diseases such as Goodpasture's

Gerontologic Considerations

Kidney Dysfunction

Changes in kidney function with normal aging increase the susceptibility of elderly patients to kidney dysfunction and renal failure. In addition, the incidence of systemic diseases, such as atherosclerosis, hypertension, heart failure, diabetes, and cancer, increases with advancing age, predisposing older adults to renal disease associated with these disorders. Therefore, acute problems need to be prevented if possible or recognized and treated quickly to avoid kidney damage, and nurses in all settings need to be alert for signs and symptoms of renal dysfunction in elderly patients.

Because alterations in renal perfusion, glomerular filtration, and renal clearance increase the risk for medication-associated changes in renal function or toxicities, precautions and surveillance are warranted (Noor & Usmani, 2008). When elderly patients undergo diagnostic testing or when new medications (e.g., diuretic agents) are added, precautions must be taken to prevent dehydration, which can compromise marginal renal function and lead to renal failure.

With aging, the kidney is less able to respond to acute fluid and electrolyte changes. Elderly patients may develop atypical and nonspecific signs and symptoms of disturbed renal function and fluid and electrolyte imbalances. Recognition of these problems is further hampered by their association with preexisting disorders and the misconception that they are normal changes of aging.

---

syndrome, Wegener's granulomatosis, systemic lupus erythematosus (SLE), subacute bacterial endocarditis, and sepsis have been implicated as risk factors.

Clinical Manifestations and Assessment

The primary presenting features of acute glomerulonephritis are hematuria, edema, **azotemia** (excessive nitrogenous wastes in the blood), and proteinuria (>3 to 5 g/day) (Broscious & Castagnola, 2006; Corwin, 2007). The hematuria may be microscopic or macroscopic (visible to the eye). The urine may appear cola-colored because of RBCs and casts; RBC casts indicate glomerular injury. Glomerulonephritis may be mild, and the hematuria may be discovered incidentally through a routine microscopic urinalysis, or the disease may be severe, with acute renal failure (ARF) and oliguria.

Some degree of edema and hypertension is present in most patients. Marked proteinuria due to the increased permeability of the glomerular membrane may also occur, with associated pitting edema, and hypoalbuminemia. Blood urea nitrogen (BUN) and serum creatinine levels may increase as urine output decreases. In addition, anemia may be present.

In the more severe form of the disease, patients also complain of headache, malaise, and flank pain. Elderly patients may experience circulatory overload with dyspnea, engorged neck veins, cardiomegaly, and pulmonary edema. Atypical symptoms include confusion, somnolence, and seizures, which are often confused with the symptoms of a primary neurologic disorder.

If the patient improves, the amount of urine increases and the urinary protein and sediment diminish. The percentage of adults who recover is not well known. Some patients develop severe **uremia** within weeks and require dialysis for survival. Others, after a period of apparent recovery, insidiously develop chronic glomerulonephritis.

Medical and Nursing Management

Management consists primarily of treating symptoms, attempting to preserve kidney function, and treating complications promptly. Dietary protein is restricted when renal insufficiency and nitrogen retention (elevated BUN) develop. Sodium is restricted when the patient has hypertension, edema, or heart failure. Loop diuretic and antihypertensive medications may be prescribed to control hypertension.

Pharmacologic therapy is focused on the cause of acute glomerulonephritis. If residual streptococcal infection is suspected, penicillin is the agent of choice; however, other antibiotic agents may be prescribed. Corticosteroids and immunosuppressant medications may be prescribed for patients with rapidly progressive acute glomerulonephritis. Carbohydrates are given liberally to provide energy and reduce the catabolism of protein. Intake and output are carefully measured and recorded. Fluids are given according to the patient's fluid losses and daily body weight. Insensible fluid loss of approximately 1 liter (lungs and skin) is considered when estimating fluid loss. Diuresis usually begins about 1 week after the onset of symptoms, with a decrease in edema and BP. Proteinuria and microscopic hematuria may persist for many months, and some patients may develop chronic glomerulonephritis.

NURSING ALERT

The most accurate indicator of fluid loss or gain in an acutely ill patient is weight, as accurate intake and output and assessment of insensible losses may be difficult. A 1 kg weight gain is equal to 1,000 mL of retained fluid (Porth & Matfin, 2009).

Nursing interventions focus on patient education about the disease process, explanations of laboratory and other diagnostic tests, and preparation for safe and effective self-care at home. Patient education is directed toward symptom management and monitoring for complications. Fluid and diet restrictions must be reviewed with the patient to avoid worsening of edema and hypertension. The patient is instructed to notify the primary care provider if symptoms of renal failure occur including fatigue, nausea, vomiting, diminishing urine output, or at the first sign of any infection. Information is given verbally and in writing.

BOX 27-2

Focus on Pathophysiology

Acute Glomerulonephritis

Acute glomerulonephritis is an inflammatory disease of the glomeruli associated with an antigen–antibody response to infection. Postinfectious causes are group A beta-hemolytic streptococcal infection of the throat that precedes the onset of glomerulonephritis by 2 to 3 weeks. It may also follow impetigo (infection of the skin), visceral abscesses, and acute viral infections (upper respiratory tract infections, mumps, varicella zoster virus,

Epstein-Barr virus, hepatitis, and HIV infection). In some patients, antigens outside the body (e.g., medications, foreign serum) initiate the process, resulting in antigen–antibody complexes being deposited in the glomeruli. In other patients, the kidney tissue itself serves as the inciting antigen.

From the antigen, the below sequence occurs and results in decreased glomerular filtration rate (GFR).

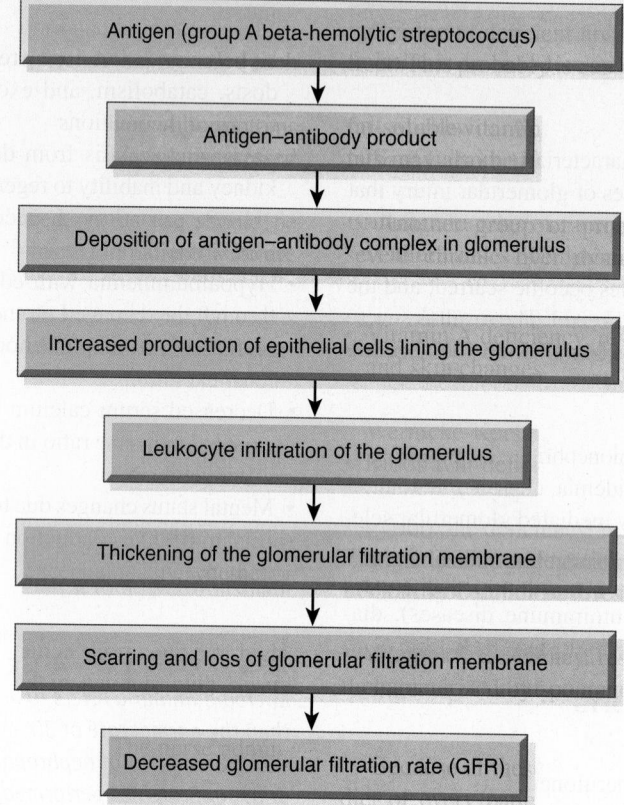

Antigen (group A beta-hemolytic streptococcus)

↓

Antigen–antibody product

↓

Deposition of antigen–antibody complex in glomerulus

↓

Increased production of epithelial cells lining the glomerulus

↓

Leukocyte infiltration of the glomerulus

↓

Thickening of the glomerular filtration membrane

↓

Scarring and loss of glomerular filtration membrane

↓

Decreased glomerular filtration rate (GFR)

The nurse educates the patient on the importance of follow-up evaluations of BP, urinalysis for protein, and serum BUN and serum creatinine levels to evaluate for disease progression in the patient. A referral for home care may be indicated, giving the nurse an opportunity for assessment and detection of early signs and symptoms of renal insufficiency. If corticosteroids, immunosuppressant agents, or antibiotic medications are prescribed, the nurse uses the opportunity to review the dosage, desired actions, and adverse effects of medications and the precautions to be taken.

Complications

Complications of acute glomerulonephritis include hypertensive encephalopathy, heart failure, and pulmonary edema.

Hypertensive encephalopathy is a medical emergency, and therapy is directed toward reducing the BP without impairing renal function. Rapidly progressive glomerulonephritis is characterized by a rapid decline in renal function. Without treatment, **end-stage renal disease (ESRD)** develops in a matter of weeks or months. Signs and symptoms are similar to those of acute glomerulonephritis (hematuria and proteinuria), but the course of the disease is more severe and rapid. Crescent-shaped cells accumulate in Bowman's space, disrupting the filtering surface. Plasma exchange (plasmapheresis) and treatment with high-dose corticosteroids and cytotoxic agents have been used to reduce the inflammatory response. Dialysis is initiated in acute glomerulonephritis if signs and symptoms of uremia are severe. The prognosis for patients with acute glomerulonephritis is favorable, with

most patients recovering; however, 20% may have protein-uria for up to 1 year (Porth & Matfin, 2009).

> ! **N U R S I N G   A L E R T**
>
> *Azotemia refers to the accumulation of nitrogen combining compounds (BUN, creatinine) in the blood. It usually occurs before symptoms are noted. Uremia describes the clinical manifestations of renal failure (altered fluid, electrolyte, acid-base balance, impaired body function [hypertension, anemia, pruritus, osteodystrophy etc]).*

CHRONIC GLOMERULONEPHRITIS

Pathophysiology

Chronic glomerulonephritis is characterized by proteinuria, usually caused by repeated episodes of glomerular injury that results in renal destruction. The kidneys are reduced to as little as one-fifth their normal size, consisting largely of fibrous tissue. The glomeruli and their tubules become scarred, and the branches of the renal artery are thickened. The result is severe glomerular damage that can progress to ESRD.

Risk Factors

Risk factors include acute glomerulonephritis, diabetes, hypertensive **nephrosclerosis**, hyperlipidemia, chronic tubulointerstitial injury, or hemodynamically mediated glomerular sclerosis (Corwin, 2007). Secondary glomerular diseases that can have systemic effects include systemic lupus erythematosus and Goodpasture's syndrome (autoimmune diseases), diabetic glomerulosclerosis, and amyloidosis.

Clinical Manifestations and Assessment

The symptoms of chronic glomerulonephritis vary. Some patients with severe disease are asymptomatic for many years. Their condition may be discovered when hypertension is found, elevated BUN and serum creatinine levels are detected, or during a routine eye examination when vascular changes or retinal hemorrhages are discovered. The first indication of disease may be a sudden, severe nosebleed, a stroke, or a seizure. Many patients report that their feet are slightly swollen (edematous) at night. Most patients also have general symptoms, such as loss of weight and strength, increasing irritability, and an increased need to urinate at night (nocturia). Headaches, dizziness, and digestive disturbances are common.

As chronic glomerulonephritis progresses, signs and symptoms of chronic renal failure may develop. The patient appears poorly nourished, with a yellow-gray pigmentation of the skin due to uremia. Periorbital and peripheral (dependent) edema with a normal or severely elevated BP may be noted. Mucous membranes are pale due to anemia. Cardiomegaly, a gallop rhythm, distended neck veins, and other signs and symptoms of heart failure may be present. Crackles can be heard in the lungs.

Peripheral neuropathy with diminished deep tendon reflexes and neurosensory changes occur late in the disease. The patient becomes confused and demonstrates a limited attention span. An additional late finding includes evidence of pericarditis with or without a pericardial friction rub.

A number of laboratory abnormalities occur. Urinalysis reveals a fixed specific gravity of about 1.010, variable proteinuria, and **urinary casts**, which are proteins secreted by damaged kidney tubules. As renal failure progresses and the glomerular filtration rate (GFR) falls, the following changes occur:

- Hyperkalemia due to decreased potassium excretion, acidosis, catabolism, and excessive potassium intake from food and medications
- Metabolic acidosis from decreased acid secretion by the kidney and inability to regenerate and reabsorb bicarbonate
- Anemia secondary to decreased erythropoiesis (production of RBCs)
- Hypoalbuminemia with edema secondary to protein loss through the damaged glomerular membrane.
- Increased serum phosphorus level due to its decreased renal excretion
- Decreased serum calcium level (calcium and phosphorus exist in an inverse ratio in the body) and decreased vitamin D activation
- Mental status changes due to build up of nitrogenous wastes
- Impaired nerve conduction due to electrolyte abnormalities and uremia

> ! **N U R S I N G   A L E R T**
>
> *Microalbuminuria refers to urinary albumin excretion greater than the normal rate of 30 mg/24 hours and may precede the development of nephropathy by 5 to 7 years. A 24-hour urine for protein is performed; dipsticks are not accurate until more than 300 to 500 mg/day protein are excreted.*

The signs and symptoms of common fluid and electrolyte disturbances that can occur in patients with renal disorders and their general management strategies are listed in Table 27-1.

Chest X-rays may show cardiac enlargement and pulmonary edema. The electrocardiogram (ECG) may be normal or may indicate left ventricular hypertrophy associated with hypertension. Signs of electrolyte disturbances, such as tall, tented (or peaked) T waves associated with hyperkalemia or dysrhythmia may appear. Computed tomography (CT) and magnetic resonance imaging (MRI) scans reveal a decrease in the size of the renal cortex.

Medical and Nursing Management

Treatment is directed toward reversing the renal impairment and eliminating the underlying cause if possible. Changes in

TABLE
27-1 Common Fluid and Electrolyte Disturbances in Renal Disorders

Disturbance	Manifestations	General Management Strategies
Fluid volume excess	Acute weight gain ≥5%, edema, crackles, shortness of breath, decreased BUN, decreased hematocrit, distended neck veins	Fluid and sodium restriction, diuretics, dialysis
Sodium deficit (often dilutional)	Nausea, malaise, lethargy, headache, abdominal cramps, apprehension, seizures	Low-sodium diet, fluid restriction, normal saline or hypertonic saline solutions during dialysis
Sodium excess	Dry, sticky mucous membranes, thirst, rough dry tongue, fever, restlessness, weakness, disorientation	Fluids, diuretics, dietary restriction
Potassium excess	Diarrhea, colic, nausea, irritability, muscle weakness, ECG changes	Dietary restriction, diuretics, IV glucose, insulin and sodium bicarbonate, cation exchange resin, calcium gluconate, dialysis
Calcium deficit	Abdominal and muscle cramps, stridor, hyperactive reflexes, tetany, positive Chvostek's or Trousseau's sign, tingling of fingers and around mouth, electrocardiogram (ECG) changes	Diet, phosphate binders, oral or parenteral calcium salt replacement
Bicarbonate deficit	Headache, confusion, drowsiness, increased respiratory rate and depth, nausea and vomiting, warm flushed skin	Citric acid-sodium citrate, bicarbonate replacement (rare), dialysis
Protein deficit	Chronic weight loss, emotional depression, pallor, fatigue, soft flabby muscles	Diet, dietary supplements, total parenteral nutrition, albumin
Magnesium excess	Facial flushing, nausea and vomiting, sensation of warmth, drowsiness, depressed deep tendon reflexes, muscle weakness, respiratory depression, cardiac arrest	Calcium gluconate, mechanical ventilation, dialysis
Phosphorus excess	Tetany, tingling of fingers and around mouth, muscle spasms, soft tissue calcification	Diet restriction, phosphate binders

fluid and electrolyte status and in cardiac and neurologic status are reported promptly to the primary care provider. Anxiety levels are often extremely high for both the patient and family. Throughout the course of the disease and treatment, the nurse gives emotional support by providing opportunities for the patient and family to verbalize their concerns, have their questions answered, and explore their options for treatment if the kidneys fail.

Instructions to the patient include explanations and scheduling for follow-up evaluations of BP, urinalysis for protein and casts, serum BUN and creatinine levels. If long-term dialysis is needed, the patient and family are taught about the procedure, how to care for the access site, dietary restrictions, and other necessary lifestyle modifications. These topics are discussed later in this chapter.

The nurse uses each encounter in the hospital and community setting to educate the patient and reinforce notifying the health care provider for worsening signs and symptoms of renal failure, such as nausea, vomiting, and diminished urine output. Specific teaching includes explanations about recommended diet and fluid modifications and medications (purpose, desired effects, adverse effects, dosage, and administration schedule). The patient is instructed to inform all health care providers about the diagnosis of glomerulonephritis, so that all medical management, including pharmacologic therapy, is based on altered renal function.

Complications

The major complication of chronic glomerulonephritis is chronic renal failure or ESRD. It is the third most common disease of patients requiring hemodialysis (U.S. Renal Data System [USRDS], 2008).

NEPHROTIC SYNDROME

Nephrotic syndrome is a cluster of clinical findings reflecting underlying organ damage. Nephrotic syndrome can occur with almost any intrinsic renal disease or systemic disease that affects the glomerulus (Corwin, 2007). Although generally considered a disorder of childhood, nephrotic syndrome also occurs in adults, including the elderly.

Pathophysiology

Nephrotic syndrome is a disorder that causes structural changes in the glomerulus resulting in renal loss of protein (proteinuria), hypoalbuminemia, hyperlipidemia, and edema.

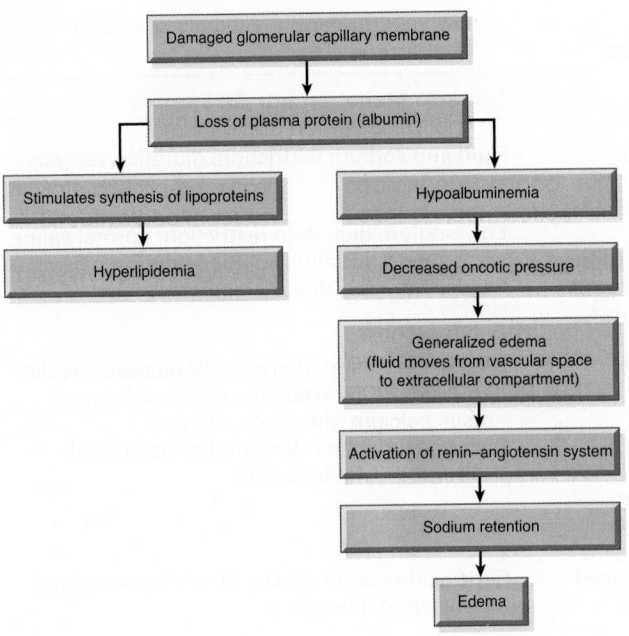

FIGURE 27-1 Sequence of events in nephrotic syndrome.

Figure 27-1 depicts the pathophysiology of nephrotic syndrome.

Risk Factors

Diabetic nephropathy is the most common cause; however, other glomerular diseases may cause nephrotic syndrome (Corwin, 2007). Causes include chronic glomerulonephritis, diabetes mellitus with intercapillary glomerulosclerosis, amyloidosis of the kidney, SLE, multiple myeloma, and renal vein thrombosis.

Clinical Manifestations and Assessment

Proteinuria, predominately in the form of albuminuria, in which albumin excretion exceeds 3.5 g/day, is the hallmark of the diagnosis of nephrotic syndrome (Corwin, 2007). Hypoalbuminuria results leading to edema, periorbital edema, or anasarca. The urine may also contain increased white blood cells (WBCs) as well as granular and epithelial casts. Hypoimmunoglobulinemia places the patient at risk for infections. Hyperlipidemia with increased high-density lipoproteins (HDL) occurs and places the patient at risk for cardiovascular disease. Hypertension, irritability, headache, and malaise occur.

⚡ N U R S I N G   A L E R T
Decreased serum albumin level presents decreased protein binding sites for medications, therefore the nurse is aware that patients must be observed closely for signs of drug toxicity as the amount of free or unbound drug is increased (Porth & Matfin, 2009).

A needle biopsy of the kidney may be performed for histologic examination of renal tissue to confirm the diagnosis.

Medical and Nursing Management

Patients with nephrotic syndrome need instruction about the importance of following medication and dietary regimens, so that their condition can remain stable as long as possible. The patient who does not have hyperkalemia may be placed on a low-sodium diet containing liberal amounts of potassium. This type of diet enhances the sodium–potassium pump mechanism and assists in elimination of sodium to reduce edema. Reduced dietary cholesterol and saturated fats help with lipidemia. Protein intake should be moderate, sufficient to meet protein needs while avoiding excessive intake, which may accelerate renal deterioration and increase urinary protein losses. An intake of 0.7 to 1.0 g/kg/day, a level close to the RDA, is recommended (Dudek, 2009).

The patient is taught to report any signs of acute infection promptly, such as a respiratory tract infection to prevent further glomerular damage. Diuretics may be prescribed for the patient with severe edema; however, caution must be used because of the risk of reducing the plasma volume to the point of impaired circulation with subsequent prerenal ARF (discussed later in the chapter). The use of angiotensin-converting enzyme (ACE) inhibitors in combination with loop diuretics often reduces the degree of proteinuria but may take 4 to 6 weeks to be effective.

Other medications used in treating nephrotic syndrome include corticosteroids, antineoplastic agents (cyclophosphamide [Cytoxan]) or immunosuppressant medications (azathioprine [Imuran], chlorambucil [Leukeran], or cyclosporine [Neoral]). It may be necessary to repeat treatment with corticosteroids if relapse occurs. Patients should be taught to protect themselves from infection and to report any infections promptly due to immunosuppression. Treatment of the associated hyperlipidemia is controversial. The usual medications used to treat hyperlipidemia are often ineffective or have side effects of muscle injury or rhabdomyolysis (syndrome associated with rapid destruction of striated muscle fibers), which can damage the kidney.

Complications

Complications of nephrotic syndrome include infection secondary to loss of immunoglobulins, accelerated atherosclerosis secondary to hyperlipidemia, and a hypercoagulable state owing to a loss of coagulation and anticoagulation factors that may result in thromboembolism of the renal vein and pulmonary embolism (Porth & Matfin, 2009). Body image may be altered due to anasarca and edema causing a change in appearance.

RENAL FAILURE

Renal failure results when the kidneys cannot remove the body's metabolic wastes or perform their regulatory functions.

This process may be acute, developing over hours to days or chronic, developing over months to years. Renal failure results in azotemia, metabolic derangements, acid–base disturbances, and electrolyte imbalances. Renal failure is a systemic disease and is a final common pathway of many different kidney and urinary tract diseases. Each year, the number of deaths from irreversible renal failure increases (USRDS, 2008).

ACUTE RENAL FAILURE

ARF is a typically reversible clinical syndrome in which there is an abrupt loss of kidney function and GFR over a period of hours to days. ARF occurs in 5% to 7% of hospitalized patients and up to 20% of critically ill patients. The mortality rate of 40% to 60% has not appreciably changed over the last several decades due to an aging population with increased comorbidities (Morton & Fontaine, 2009).

Manifestations of ARF include oliguria or anuria with resulting azotemia (increased serum creatinine, BUN, and other nitrogenous waste products). Acidemia, fluid excess, alterations in calcium and phosphorus balance and failure of BP regulation and erythropoiesis with resulting anemia develop rapidly.

Pathophysiology

Although the exact pathogenesis of ARF is not always known, this condition may be reversible if identified and treated before kidney function is permanently impaired.

ARF is classified by its etiology, which helps to focus the treatment.

Categories of Acute Renal Failure

The major categories of ARF are prerenal azotemia caused by hypoperfusion of the kidney; intrarenal causes, in which the renal parenchyma or nephron is damaged; and postrenal causes, in which outflow of urine is obstructed. Common causes of each type of ARF are summarized in Box 27-3.

Prerenal ARF, which occurs in 60% of cases of ARF, is caused by reduced blood flow to the kidney with resulting decrease in the GFR and urine output (Perrin, 2009). Common clinical situations are volume-depletion states, which include dehydration, hemorrhage or gastrointestinal (GI) losses, decreased cardiac output such as occurs with myocardial infarction, heart failure, or cardiogenic shock, and vasodilated states such as sepsis or anaphylaxis. Although no specific target mean arterial pressure (MAP) has been defined to maintain renal perfusion, many protocols will suggest maintaining a MAP of 60 to 65 mm Hg. However, it is understood that for patients with a history of hypertension and/or renal vascular diseases, higher pressures may be required to maintain renal perfusion (Venkatraman & Kellum, 2007).

Intrarenal ARF is the result of actual parenchymal damage to the glomeruli or kidney tubules. **Acute tubular necrosis (ATN)** is the most common cause of intrarenal ARF in the hospitalized patient. Nephrotoxic agents, such as aminoglycosides and radiocontrast agents, account for 12% of cases of ATN (Kohtz & Thompson, 2007). Ischemia, due

---

BOX 27-3   Causes of Acute Renal Failure

Prerenal Failure
- Volume depletion resulting from:
  - Hemorrhage
  - Renal losses (diuretics, osmotic diuresis)
  - GI losses (vomiting, diarrhea, nasogastric suction)
- Impaired cardiac efficiency resulting from:
  - Myocardial infarction
  - Heart failure
  - Dysrhythmias
  - Cardiogenic shock
- Vasodilation resulting from:
  - Sepsis
  - Anaphylaxis
  - Antihypertensive medications or other medications that cause vasodilation

Intrarenal Failure
- Prolonged renal ischemia resulting from:
  - Pigment nephropathy (associated with the breakdown of blood cells containing pigments that occlude kidney structures)
  - Myoglobinuria (trauma, crush injuries, burns)

- Hemoglobinuria (transfusion reaction, hemolytic anemia)
- Rhabdomyolysis
- Nephrotoxic agents such as:
  - Aminoglycoside antibiotics (gentamicin, tobramycin)
  - Radiopaque contrast agents
  - Heavy metals (lead, mercury)
  - Solvents and chemicals (ethylene glycol, carbon tetrachloride, arsenic)
  - NSAIDs
  - ACE inhibitors
- Infectious processes such as:
  - Acute pyelonephritis
  - Acute glomerulonephritis

Postrenal Failure
- Urinary tract obstruction, including:
  - Calculi (stones)
  - Tumors
  - Benign prostatic hyperplasia (BPH)
  - Strictures
  - Blood clots

to decreased renal perfusion, accounts for more than 50% of cases of ATN. Conditions such as burns, crush injuries, infections, and severe blood transfusion reactions can lead to **myoglobinuria** or rhabdomyolysis. With burns and crush injuries, myoglobin (a protein released from muscle when injury occurs) and hemoglobin are liberated, causing obstruction, renal toxicity, and ischemia. The term **rhabdomyolysis**, in which breakdown of skeletal muscle is seen, may be used to describe this event. Severe transfusion reactions may also cause intrarenal failure; hemoglobin released through hemolysis filters through the glomeruli and becomes concentrated in the kidney tubules to such a degree that precipitation of hemoglobin occurs. Certain medications, especially nonsteroidal anti-inflammatory drugs (NSAIDs) and ACE inhibitors, may also predispose a patient to intrarenal damage. These medications interfere with the normal autoregulatory mechanisms of the kidney and may cause hypoperfusion and eventual ischemia.

Postrenal ARF is the result of an obstruction that develops anywhere from the collecting ducts of the kidney to the urethra. This results from ureteral blockage, such as from bilateral renal calculi or benign prostatic hyperplasia (BPH) (Morton & Fontaine, 2009). Pressure rises in the kidney tubules and hydronephrosis occurs, compressing normal renal tissue and resulting in a decrease in the GFR. Any sudden or complete cessation of urine output with an indwelling catheter should alert the nurse to possible obstruction. The catheter should be inspected, kinks removed, or the catheter irrigated or changed to reestablish urine flow.

Phases of Acute Renal Failure

There are four clinical phases of ARF: initiation or onset, oliguric, diuretic, and recovery. The initiation period begins with the initial insult and ends when cellular injury and oliguria develops. A small incidence of patients develop non-oliguric renal failure, usually associated with nephrotoxic agents; it may also occur with burns, traumatic injury, and the use of halogenated anesthetic agents.

The oliguric period is accompanied by an increase in the serum concentration of wastes such as urea, creatinine, organic acids, and the electrolytes potassium, phosphorous, and magnesium. The average time period for oliguria is 7 to 14 days. Because the minimum amount of urine needed to rid the body of fluid and metabolic waste products is 400 mL in 24 hours, renal replacement therapy such as dialysis may be needed until kidney function returns.

The diuretic phase is marked by a gradual increase in urine output, which signals that glomerular filtration has started to recover. Urine output may be normal, or the patient may excrete large amounts of dilute urine and should be observed closely for dehydration, which may damage the kidney further. Laboratory values plateau and begin to decline.

The recovery period signals the improvement of renal function and energy level and may take 6 to 12 months (Perrin, 2009). If residual damage to the glomerular basement membrane occurs, residual renal impairment may result.

Clinical Manifestations and Assessment

Almost every system of the body is affected when there is failure of the renal regulatory mechanisms. The patient may appear critically ill and lethargic. Table 27-2 summarizes common clinical findings in all three categories of ARF.

Assessment of the patient with ARF includes evaluation for changes in the urine output, diagnostic tests that evaluate the kidney contour and function, and a variety of laboratory values. See Chapter 26 for information about the normal characteristics of urine, diagnostic findings, and laboratory values in the renal system.

TABLE **27-2** Comparing Clinical Findings Among Categories of Acute Renal Failure

| | Categories | | |
Characteristics	Prerenal	Intrarenal	Postrenal
Etiology	Hypoperfusion	Parenchymal damage	Obstruction
Blood urea nitrogen value	Increased >20:1 proportion blood urea nitrogen (BUN) to creatinine	Increased	Increased
Creatinine	Normal or slightly increased	Increased	Increased
Urine output	Decreased	Varies, often decreased	Varies, may be decreased, or sudden anuria
Urine sodium	Decreased to <20 mEq/L	Increased to >40 mEq/L	Varies, often decreased to ≤20 mEq/L
Urinary sediment	Normal, few hyaline casts	Abnormal casts and debris	Usually normal
Urine osmolality	Increased to 500 mOsm	~350 mOsm similar to serum	Varies, increased or equal to serum
Urine specific gravity	Increased	Low normal	Varies

In ARF, oliguria (<500 mL a day) is typically present. Hematuria may be present, and the urine has a low specific gravity due to the kidney's inability to concentrate the urine (Porth & Matfin, 2009). Patients with ARF have decreased urine sodium levels and urinary casts, and other cellular debris may be present.

The BUN level increases steadily at a rate dependent on the degree of protein catabolism, renal perfusion, and fluid or protein intake. Nausea, vomiting, lethargy, headache, muscle twitching, and seizures may occur. Serum creatinine, a more sensitive indicator of renal function than BUN, increases with glomerular damage and is used to monitor kidney function and disease progression.

Patients with oliguria and **anuria** (<50 mL/day) are at high risk for hyperkalemia, a potassium value of more than 5.5 mEq/L (5.5 mmol/L). Hyperkalemia develops as the damaged kidney cannot excrete potassium; protein catabolism and acidosis result in the release of intracellular potassium into the serum, worsening hyperkalemia. The ECG may reveal changes such as tall, tented, or peaked T waves, absent P wave, widened QRS, or bradydysrhythmia. Symptoms of hyperkalemia may include weakness, diarrhea, dysrhythmias, and cardiac arrest. The nurse should be aware of exogenous sources of potassium, such as IV infusions or medications such as potassium penicillin, as well as dietary sources.

As metabolic acidosis develops, normal renal buffering mechanisms fail resulting in hyperventilation. The patient may breathe more rapidly and deeply to "blow off" CO_2 in an attempt to restore normal serum pH. Hyperventilation as compensation for acidosis may lead to respiratory fatigue or failure requiring mechanical ventilation.

Serum phosphate levels increase. Calcium levels may decrease in response to decreased absorption of calcium from the intestine as well as a compensatory mechanism for the elevated blood phosphate levels. Anemia is another common laboratory finding in ARF, as a result of reduced erythropoietin production, uremic GI lesions, reduced RBC lifespan, and blood loss, usually from the GI tract.

Prevention

Prevention of ARF is essential, as ARF has mortality rates as high as 60% or more, especially in patients with multisystem failure (Morton & Fontaine, 2009) (Box 27-4).

The nurse assesses for use of potentially nephrotoxic agents and exposure to environmental toxins. Patients taking nephrotoxic medications such as amphotericin B, vancomycin, cyclosporine, aminoglycosides (gentamicin, tobramycin, neomycin), certain antineoplastics or anesthetics, heavy metals such as cisplatin or bismuth, or radiological contrast agents, should be monitored closely for changes in renal function. BUN and serum creatinine levels should be obtained at baseline, during treatment, and after therapy is complete, if indicated.

BOX 27-4 **Health Promotion**

Preventing Acute Renal Failure

- Provide adequate hydration to patients at risk of dehydration:
  - Perioperative patients
  - Patients on fluid restriction
  - Patients undergoing diagnostic studies with or requiring contrast agents (e.g., barium enema, intravenous pyelograms, angiography), especially elderly patients who may have marginal renal reserve
  - Patients with neoplastic disorders or disorders and those receiving chemotherapy
  - Patients with metabolic disorders such as gout, glycosuria
- Prevent and treat hypotension or shock promptly with blood and fluid replacement.
- Monitor hourly urine output of critically ill patients to detect the onset of renal failure as early as possible. When available, monitor central venous and arterial pressures.
- Continually assess renal laboratory values.
- Properly identify patients to prevent transfusion reactions, which can precipitate myoglobinuria.
- Prevent and treat infections promptly. Infections can lead to sepsis and renal damage.
- Intervene promptly with wounds, burns, and other precursors of sepsis.
- To prevent infections from ascending in the urinary tract, give meticulous care to patients with indwelling catheters. Remove catheters as soon as possible.
- To prevent toxic drug effects, closely monitor dosage, duration of use, and blood levels of all medications metabolized or excreted by the kidneys.

Chronic use of analgesics, particularly NSAIDs, may cause **interstitial nephritis** (inflammation within the renal tissue) and papillary necrosis. Patients with heart failure or cirrhosis with ascites are at particular risk for NSAID-induced renal failure. Increased age, preexisting renal disease, and the coadministration of nephrotoxic agents increase the risk for kidney damage.

Radiocontrast-induced nephropathy is a major cause of hospital-acquired ARF (Sinert & Peacock, 2006), therefore patients at risk for this complication should be identified before procedures in which contrast media is used. Patients with creatinine levels greater than 2 mg/dL are at risk and should receive preprocedure hydration and acetylcysteine (Mucomyst) the day prior to the test. The action of acetylcysteine is not fully understood, but it is thought to be an antioxidant that works by scavenging free radicals (Perrin, 2009). The nurse should withhold Metformin prior to procedures requiring IV contrast. While metformin is not nephrotoxic, if ARF occurs after a procedure, acidosis may be worsened.

Medical and Nursing Management

The kidneys have a remarkable ability to recover from insult. Management includes maintaining fluid and electrolyte balance, avoiding fluid excesses, and supporting the patient until repair of renal tissue and restoration of function occur. Dialysis may be used on a temporary basis to restore homeostasis.

The underlying cause is identified, treated, and eliminated when possible (Morton & Fontaine, 2009). Treatment of prerenal azotemia consists of optimizing renal perfusion with fluids or treating decreased cardiac output. Treatment of postrenal failure is relieving the obstruction. Surgery such as prostatectomy, nephrostomy tubes, or indwelling catheters may be used. Intrarenal azotemia is treated with supportive therapy, removal of causative agents, and aggressive management of shock and infection.

The nurse observes for fluid excess manifested by dyspnea, crackles, tachycardia, hypertension, and distended neck veins, as well as generalized edema in the presacral and pretibial areas. The central venous pressure (CVP), where measured, will be elevated. Fluid restriction becomes important to prevent fluid overload and pulmonary edema. Diuretics, such as furosemide (Lasix), may be prescribed to initiate diuresis and maintain renal perfusion.

Adequate blood flow to the kidneys in patients with prerenal causes of ARF may be restored by IV fluids or transfusions of blood products. If ARF is caused by hypovolemia secondary to hypoproteinemia, an infusion of albumin may be prescribed. Dialysis or continuous renal replacement therapy may be used to maintain homeostasis when hyperkalemia, metabolic acidosis, pericarditis, fluid volume excess, and pulmonary edema occur. While this is expected to be a temporary intervention, a small portion of patients (5% to 19%) do not recover kidney function and may develop chronic renal failure (Perrin, 2009).

Pharmacologic Therapy

Hyperkalemia may be reduced by administering sodium polystyrene sulfonate [Kayexalate] orally, via NG tube, or by retention enema. Kayexalate, a cation-exchange resins works by exchanging sodium ions for potassium ions in the intestinal tract. Sorbitol is typically combined with Kayexalate to draw water into the bowel, thus inducing diarrhea and excretion of potassium. The patient should retain the Kayexalate enema for 30 to 45 minutes. To facilitate retention, a rectal catheter with a balloon may be inserted. Current research questions that cation-exchange resins do in fact lower potassium levels in the short-term and do carry significant risk of bowel ischemia; therefore, this practice has begun to fall out of favor among health care providers. For symptomatic hyperkalemia, IV dextrose, insulin, and calcium replacement may be administered to shift potassium back into the cells. Albuterol sulfate (Ventolin HFA) by nebulizer can lower plasma potassium concentration by 0.5 to 1.5 mEq/L.

Acidosis may require sodium bicarbonate therapy—if the serum bicarbonate concentration is below 15 mmol/L or arterial PH is less than 7.2 (Fauci, Braunwald, Kasper et al., 2008)—or dialysis. Phosphate-binding agents such as calcium acetate (PhosLo) or aluminum hydroxide gel (short term only) are given to decrease the absorption of phosphate from the intestinal tract.

Drugs with renal excretion require dosage adjustment for patients with ARF. Commonly used agents requiring adjustment are antibiotics, especially aminoglycosides, digoxin, ACE inhibitors, and magnesium-containing agents.

Nutritional Therapy

ARF causes impaired glucose use and protein synthesis and increased tissue catabolism. Azotemia may cause nausea and vomiting. Weight loss may result from negative nitrogen balance. Dietary proteins are restricted (Dudek, 2009), and caloric requirements are met with high-carbohydrate meals, due to their protein-sparing effect. Dietary restrictions include foods and fluids containing potassium such as bananas citrus, tomatoes, melons, or those with phosphorus, as is found in dairy products, beans, nuts, legumes, and carbonated beverages. Caffeine is also restricted. The patient may require enteral or parenteral nutrition. Suspect fluid retention if the patient develops hypertension, crackles, edema, or weight gain. Administering fluids (PO or IV) may require replacing both sensible and insensible loss. Insensible loss is estimated at 1 liter. Fluid replacement in renal disease may be based on urine output, any GI losses (gastric drainage or diarrhea), plus insensible losses, thus meticulous attention is paid to accurate intake and output. Metabolism and the oxidation process produce about 200 to 500 mL of fluid per day, which may decrease the fluid requirements, whereas fever may increase the fluid requirement (Dudek, 2009). As ARF resolves, results of blood chemistry tests are used to determine the amounts of sodium, potassium, and water needed for replacement. Following the diuretic phase, the patient is placed on a high-carbohydrate diet with sufficient protein to promote nitrogen balance. The patient is encouraged to resume activities gradually.

⚠ NURSING ALERT

If the caloric intake is insufficient to prevent the breakdown of body protein, additional nitrogenous waste accumulation develops, which may increase uremic symptoms.

The nurse monitors for complications, participates in emergency treatment of fluid and electrolyte imbalances, assesses the patient's progress and response to treatment, and provides physical and emotional support. Additionally, the nurse keeps family members informed about the patient's condition, helps them understand the treatments, and provides psychological support. ARF is a serious problem; however, the nurse must continue to provide interventions for the underlying disorder (e.g., burns, shock, trauma, obstruction of the urinary tract, etc.).

Reducing Metabolic Rate

Bedrest may be indicated to reduce exertion and the metabolic rate during the most acute stage of the disorder. Fever and infection, both of which increase the metabolic rate and catabolism, are prevented or treated promptly.

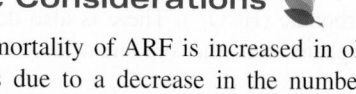

N U R S I N G   A L E R T
Fever increases the insensible loss by about 13% for each degree of Celsius temperature elevation (Metheny, 2000).

Promoting Pulmonary Function

Attention is given to pulmonary function, and the patient is assisted to turn, cough, and deep breathe frequently to prevent atelectasis and respiratory tract infection. Drowsiness and lethargy may prevent the patient from moving and turning without encouragement and assistance. Maintaining a patent airway through oral or endotracheal suction may be necessary.

Preventing Infection

Asepsis is essential with invasive lines and catheters to minimize the risk of infection and subsequent increased metabolism. An indwelling urinary catheter is avoided whenever possible because of the high risk of urinary tract infection (UTI) associated with its use.

Providing Skin Care

The skin may be dry or susceptible to breakdown as a result of edema; therefore, meticulous skin care is important. Additionally, excoriation and itching of the skin may result from the deposit of uremic toxins in the patient's tissues. Turning the patient frequently, bathing him or her with cool water, and keeping the skin clean and well moisturized and the fingernails trimmed to avoid excoriation are often comforting and prevent skin breakdown (Morton & Fontaine, 2009).

Providing Support

While ARF is considered potentially reversible, the length of time that the patient is ill and duration of treatment varies. The patient and family need assistance, explanation, and support during this period. The nurse provides frequent explanations of the purpose and rationale of the treatments, as rising BUN leads to confusion and lethargy. The patient and family are included in teaching to allay anxiety and fear.

Gerontologic Considerations

The incidence and mortality of ARF is increased in older, hospitalized patients due to a decrease in the number of functional nephrons and renal blood flow, and to atherosclerosis of the renal arteries.

Nurses need to be aware of the risk of ARF in elderly patients, especially those undergoing diagnostic testing or procedures that can result in dehydration. Suppression of thirst, decreased mobility with lack of access to drinking water, and confusion contribute to the older patient's failure to consume adequate fluids, which may lead to dehydration and further compromise of already decreased renal function.

Muscle mass and GFR can decrease with age; therefore, even small elevated changes in creatinine may indicate significant renal impairment in the elderly and should be investigated.

CHRONIC RENAL FAILURE AND END-STAGE RENAL DISEASE

Chronic renal failure is a progressive and irreversible deterioration in renal function taking place over months to years. Chronic renal failure results in the body's inability to maintain metabolic and fluid and electrolyte balance, resulting in azotemia and subsequent uremia. In ESRD, renal replacement therapy with dialysis or renal transplant is needed to sustain life. The incidence of ESRD has increased by almost 8% per year for the past 5 years. In the United States, more than 280,000 patients with chronic renal failure (65%) are receiving hemodialysis; more than 120,000 patients (28%) have functioning renal transplants, and more than 24,000 patients (7%) are receiving peritoneal dialysis (PD; USRDS, 2008). Total cost for chronic kidney disease programs in the United States was $25.2 billion in 2002 (Broscious & Castagnnola, 2008).

Pathophysiology

As renal function declines, the end products of protein metabolism, normally excreted in urine, accumulate in the blood. Uremia develops and adversely affects every system in the body. The greater the buildup of waste products, the more severe the symptoms. Box 27-5 outlines stages of chronic kidney disease. The disease tends to progress more rapidly in patients who excrete significant amounts of protein or have elevated BP than in those without these conditions.

Risk Factors

Healthy People 2010 identifies five risk factors for ESRD: diabetes, hypertension, proteinuria, family history, and

---

BOX 27-5   **Stages of Chronic Kidney Disease**

Stages are based on the GFR. The normal GFR is 120 to 130 mL/min corrected for body size (per 1.73 m²).
Stage 1: GFR ≥90 mL/min; kidney damage with normal or increased GFR
Stage 2: GFR = 60–89 mL/min; diminished renal reserve; nephrons highly susceptible to failure
Stage 3: GFR = 30–59 mL/min; renal insufficiency
Stage 4: GFR = 15–29 mL/min; severe decrease in GFR
Stage 5: GFR <15 mL/min/1.73 m²

Source: Corwin, E. J. (2007).

increasing age. It also identifies diabetes (36%) and hypertension (24%) as the two major causes. Other causes include chronic glomerulonephritis, **pyelonephritis**, obstruction of the urinary tract, hereditary lesions such as in polycystic kidney disease, vascular and autoimmune disorders (such as SLE), infections, medications, or toxic agents. Comorbid conditions that develop during chronic renal disease contribute to the high morbidity and mortality among patients with ESRD (Broscious & Castagnnola, 2008). Environmental and occupational agents that have been implicated in chronic renal failure include lead, cadmium, mercury, and chromium.

The incidence of ESRD is higher in African Americans, Hispanics, and Native Americans. The nurse must consider this evidence when targeting health education for prevention. Increasing evidence reveals that early detection and treatment of chronic kidney disease may prevent or a least delay the progression of chronic renal failure to ESRD. ACE inhibitors or angiotensin receptor blockers (ARBs) are used to slow the progression of renal failure. The Diabetes Control and Complications Trial (DCCT) found that strict blood glucose control delayed and possibly even prevented the progression of diabetic nephropathy (Morton & Fontaine, 2009).

Clinical Manifestations and Assessment

Virtually every body system is affected by chronic renal failure. Severity of signs and symptoms depends on the degree of uremia and renal impairment, other underlying conditions, and the patient's age.

Systemic Manifestations

- *Neurologic manifestations:* Neurologic changes include altered level of consciousness, inability to concentrate, muscle twitching, agitation, confusion, and seizures. Peripheral neuropathy is present in some patients. Restless leg syndrome and pain or burning feet can occur in the early stage of uremic peripheral neuropathy (Broscious & Castagnola, 2006).
- *Cardiovascular manifestations:* Hypertension results from sodium and water retention due to activation of the renin–angiotensin–aldosterone system; fluid volume excess causes heart failure and pulmonary edema. Pericarditis is caused by irritation of the pericardium by uremic toxins and may require dialysis. Cardiovascular disease is the predominant cause of death in patients with ESRD (Martchev, 2009). In patients receiving chronic hemodialysis, approximately 45% of overall mortality is attributable to cardiac disease, and about 20% of these cardiac deaths are due to acute myocardial infarction (USRDS, 2008).
- *GI manifestations:* GI signs and symptoms are common and include anorexia, nausea, vomiting, and hiccups. The patient's breath may have the odor of ammonia or urine

(uremic fetor), or the patient may complain of a metallic taste in the mouth.

- *Immunologic manifestations:* Defective granulocytes, B- and T-cell function, and impaired phagocytosis can lead to impaired immune and inflammatory response (Broscious & Castagnola, 2006).
- *Genitourinary manifestations:* Erectile dysfunction, decreased libido, pain during intercourse (women), and amenorrhea may result.
- *Dermatologic manifestations:* Pruritus is common. Uremic frost, the deposit of urea crystals on the skin, is uncommon today because of early and aggressive treatment of ESRD with dialysis. The skin may be bronze or waxy yellow or gray, particularly in dark-skinned individuals. The precise mechanisms for many of these diverse signs and symptoms have not been identified.

Box 27-6 summarizes the signs and symptoms seen in chronic renal failure.

Glomerular Filtration Rate

As glomerular filtration decreases, the serum creatinine and BUN levels increase; the creatinine clearance decreases. Serum creatinine is the more sensitive indicator of renal function because of its constant production in the body. The BUN is affected not only by renal disease but also by protein intake in the diet, tissue catabolism, fluid intake, parenteral nutrition, and medications such as corticosteroids. Calculation of GFR is discussed in Chapter 26, and the stages of chronic kidney disease based on GFR can be found in Box 27-5 on page 751.

Sodium and Water Retention

Some patients retain sodium and water, thus increasing the risk for edema, heart failure, and hypertension. Dilutional hyponatremia typically occurs. Hypertension may also result from activation of the renin–angiotensin–aldosterone system and the concomitant increased aldosterone secretion. Episodes of vomiting and diarrhea may cause sodium and water depletion, which worsens the uremic state.

Acidosis

In advanced renal disease, metabolic acidosis occurs because the kidneys are unable to excrete hydrogen ions (H^+). Decreased acid secretion results from the inability of the kidney tubules to excrete ammonia (NH_3^-) and to reabsorb bicarbonate (HCO_3^-). There is also decreased excretion of phosphates and other organic acids.

Anemia

Inadequate production of erythropoietin by the damaged kidney causes anemia. Erythropoietin, normally produced by the kidneys, stimulates bone marrow to produce RBCs. Anemia is further exacerbated by the shortened lifespan of RBCs due to uremia, nutritional deficiencies, and the patient's tendency to bleed, particularly from the GI tract.

BOX 27-6
Focused Assessment

Chronic Renal Failure

Be alert for the following signs and symptoms:

Neurologic
- Weakness and fatigue
- Confusion or behavior changes
- Inability to concentrate
- Disorientation
- Tremors
- Seizures
- Asterixis
- Restlessness leg syndrome
- Burning of soles of feet

Integumentary
- Gray-bronze skin color
- Dry, flaky skin
- Pruritus
- Ecchymosis or purpura
- Thin, brittle nails
- Coarse, thinning hair

Cardiovascular
- Hypertension
- Pitting edema (feet, hands, sacrum)
- Periorbital edema
- Engorged neck veins
- Pericarditis/pericardial friction rub
- Pericardial effusion or tamponade
- Hyperkalemia
- Hyperlipidemia

Pulmonary
- Crackles
- Thick, tenacious sputum

- Depressed cough reflex
- Pleuritic pain
- Shortness of breath
- Tachypnea
- Kussmaul-type respirations
- Uremic pneumonitis

Gastrointestinal
- Ammonia odor to breath ("uremic fetor")
- Metallic taste
- Mouth ulcerations and bleeding
- Anorexia, nausea, and vomiting
- Hiccups
- Constipation or diarrhea
- Bleeding from GI tract

Hematologic
- Anemia
- Thrombocytopenia

Reproductive
- Erectile dysfunction
- Amenorrhea
- Testicular atrophy
- Infertility
- Decreased libido

Musculoskeletal
- Muscle cramps
- Loss of muscle strength
- Renal osteodystrophy
- Bone pain
- Bone fractures
- Foot drop

The nurse should assess for fatigue, shortness of breath, and chest pain.

Calcium and Phosphorus Imbalance

Hyperphosphatemia with resulting hypocalcemia develops in renal failure. The decreased serum calcium level causes increased secretion of parathormone from the parathyroid glands, causing calcium to leave the bone. Bone weakness and fractures may result. The active metabolite of vitamin D (1,25-dihydroxycholecalciferol), normally manufactured by the kidney, decreases as renal failure progresses impairing calcium absorption. Uremic bone disease or renal osteodystrophy develops from the complex changes in calcium, phosphate, and parathormone balance.

Medical Management

The goal of management is to maintain kidney function and homeostasis for as long as possible while continuing to treat the underlying disorder(s). Management is accomplished primarily with medications and diet therapy. **Renal replacement therapy** is planned for in stage 4 kidney disease and is discussed in detail later in the chapter.

Pharmacologic Therapy

Complications can be prevented or delayed by administering prescribed phosphate-binding agents, calcium supplements, antihypertensive and cardiac medications, antiseizure medications, and erythropoietin (Epogen/Procrit).

Calcium and Phosphorus Binders

Hyperphosphatemia and hypocalcemia are treated with medications that bind dietary phosphorus in the GI tract. Binders such as calcium carbonate (Os-Cal) or calcium acetate (PhosLo) are prescribed, but there is a risk of hypercalcemia. If calcium is high or the calcium–phosphorus product exceeds 55 mg/dL, a polymeric phosphate binder such as sevelamer hydrochloride (Renagel) may be used

(Zonderman & Doyle, 2006). The nurse plans to administer phosphate binders with food for them to be effective.

Antihypertensive and Cardiovascular Agents

Hypertension is managed by sodium and fluid restriction and antihypertensive agents. Diuretics and inotropics, such as digoxin (Lanoxin) or dobutamine (Dobutrex) may be used.

Agents to Treat Metabolic Acidosis

Bicitra (Shohl's solution/sodium citrate and citric acid) or sodium bicarbonate supplements (rarely used) is given to correct acidosis. Dialysis may be needed as kidney disease worsens (Molzahn & Butera, 2006).

Antiseizure Agents

IV diazepam (Valium), lorazepam (Ativan), or phenytoin (Dilantin) is usually administered to control seizures, which may develop as azotemia worsens. The side rails of the bed should be raised and padded to protect the patient. The nursing management of the patient with seizures is discussed in Chapter 46.

Erythropoietin

Anemia associated with chronic renal failure is treated with recombinant human erythropoietin (e-poietin, Epogen/Procrit). Therapy is initiated to achieve a hematocrit of 33% to 38% and a target hemoglobin of 11 to 12 g/dL, to alleviate the symptoms of anemia and the need for blood transfusions (Carter & Keen, 2007). Hemoglobin values above 12 g increase the risk of death and serious thromboembolic and cardiovascular events. Erythropoietin is administered intravenously at the end of dialysis or subcutaneously. Blood transfusions are indicated for chest pain or extreme dyspnea. Adverse effects seen with erythropoietin therapy include headache, arthralgia, nausea, hypertension, increased clotting of vascular access sites, seizures, and depletion of body iron stores (Carter & Keen, 2007; Zonderman & Doyle, 2006). The expected outcome for patients receiving e-poietin is decreased levels of fatigue, increased feelings of well-being, better tolerance of dialysis, higher energy levels, and improved exercise tolerance.

Iron, in the form of iron sucrose (Venofer) and ferric gluconate (Ferrlecit), may be prescribed to promote an adequate response to erythropoietin. Hypertension that cannot be controlled is a contraindication to recombinant erythropoietin therapy.

Nutritional Therapy

The renal diet includes limiting protein, fluid restriction, and sodium, potassium, and phosphorus restrictions. Restricting protein to 0.7 to 1.0 g/kg of ideal body weight can slow the progression of renal disease and improve the symptoms of uremia including nausea and vomiting. The allowed protein must be of high biologic value including eggs, meats, and plant-based proteins. Protein restriction is difficult for most patients; positive feedback and confidence in the patient's ability to adhere to the eating plan results in patients making

better choices (Dudek, 2009). Dietary protein is increased slightly during dialysis to compensate for loss of protein and amino acids in the dialysate. At the same time, adequate caloric intake and vitamin supplementation must be ensured because a protein-restricted diet does not provide the necessary complement of vitamins, and dialysis results in loss of water-soluble vitamins. Calories are supplied by carbohydrates and fat to prevent wasting.

The patient must adhere to a daily fluid allowance of approximately 500 to 800 mL plus the previous day's 24-hour urine output. The nurse teaches the patient strategies to control intake and thirst: such as sucking on hard candies or mints, chewing gum, rinsing the mouth with refrigerated water, sucking on a lemon wedge, using small glasses instead of large ones, and moisturizing the lips (Dudek, 2009).

Potassium restriction involves limiting citrus, tomatoes, melons, and potatoes. Phosphorus is also restricted and is contained in dairy, peas, beans, nuts (including peanut butter), and cola products. Sodium is contained in many canned and processed, and in smoked foods lunchmeats, as well as in MSG.

Dialysis

The patient with increasing symptoms of chronic renal failure is referred to a dialysis and transplantation center early in the course of progressive renal disease. Dialysis is initiated when the patient cannot maintain homeostasis with conservative treatment, and is discussed in detail later in the chapter.

Nursing Management

The patient with chronic renal failure requires astute nursing care to avoid the complications of reduced renal function and the stresses and anxieties of dealing with a life-threatening illness.

Nursing care and education are directed toward fluid and electrolyte imbalance, dietary management, and promoting positive feelings by encouraging increased self-care and greater independence. It is extremely important to provide frequent, clear explanations and information to the patient and family concerning ESRD, treatment options, and potential complications. A plan of nursing care for a patient with chronic renal failure is available online at http://thePoint. lww.com/Pellico1e.

Teaching Patients Self-Care

Encouraging self-management is an essential role of the nurse when caring for patients with renal failure. Nurses in home care, dialysis center, hospital, and outpatient settings all provide ongoing education and reinforcement while monitoring the patient's progress and adherence to the treatment regimen. The nurse includes the patient's beliefs, values, and concerns in the treatment regimen to improve patient outcomes (Costantin, 2006).

The nurse and dietician reinforce the renal diet and explain the correlation between symptoms and nonadherence. The patient can be encouraged to take BP measurements at home to illustrate the effect of prescribed antihypertensives and fluid restriction with BP elevations or SOB (Kammerer, Garry, & Hartigan, 2007).

The patient and family should report the following symptoms of worsening renal function to the health care provider:

- Worsening signs and symptoms of renal failure including nausea, vomiting, change in usual urine output, or ammonia/urine odor to the breath
- Signs and symptoms of hyperkalemia including muscle weakness, diarrhea, abdominal cramps
- If receiving dialysis, signs and symptoms of access problems such as clotted fistula or graft or signs of infection at the site

Continuing Care

The nurse teaches the patient to follow-up with examinations and treatments to prevent progression of renal disease or to detect progression, and the nurse reinforces care for the primary disorder. The patient and family should be alerted to symptoms of worsening condition, have treatment options explained, and be offered psychoemotional support. The home care nurse has the opportunity to assess the patient's environment, emotional status, and the coping strategies used by the patient and family to deal with the changes in family roles often associated with chronic illness. Assessment, ongoing education, and reinforcement of the renal diet are performed. Reminders about the need for health promoting activities and health screening, particularly cardiovascular health, are important when caring for the patient with renal failure.

Gerontologic Considerations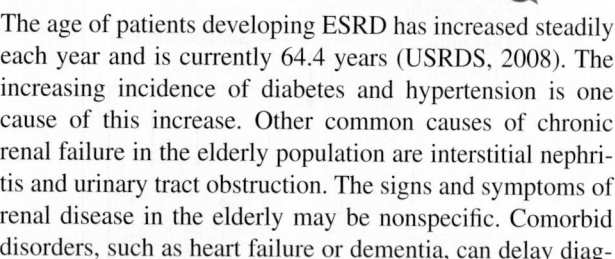

The age of patients developing ESRD has increased steadily each year and is currently 64.4 years (USRDS, 2008). The increasing incidence of diabetes and hypertension is one cause of this increase. Other common causes of chronic renal failure in the elderly population are interstitial nephritis and urinary tract obstruction. The signs and symptoms of renal disease in the elderly may be nonspecific. Comorbid disorders, such as heart failure or dementia, can delay diagnosis and treatment.

Hemodialysis and PD have been used effectively in treating elderly patients. The number of patients 75 years and older being treated for ESRD has doubled. Although there is no specific age limitation for renal transplantation, concomitant disorders such as coronary artery disease or peripheral vascular disease have made it a less common treatment for the elderly. When an elderly patient refuses dialysis or transplantation, conservative management with nutritional therapy, fluid control, and medications may be used. Advanced directives and end-of-life care based on quality of life should be explored.

Complications

Complications of chronic renal failure necessitate a collaborative approach to care and include the following:

- Hyperkalemia due to decreased excretion, metabolic acidosis, catabolism, and excessive intake (diet, medications, fluids)
- Pericarditis, pericardial effusion, and pericardial tamponade due to retention of uremic waste products and inadequate dialysis
- Hypertension due to sodium and water retention and malfunction of the renin–angiotensin–aldosterone system
- Anemia due to decreased erythropoietin production, decreased RBC lifespan, bleeding in the GI tract from irritating toxins and ulcer formation, and blood loss during hemodialysis
- Bone disease and metastatic and vascular calcifications due to retention of phosphorus, low serum calcium levels, abnormal vitamin D metabolism, and elevated aluminum levels

RENAL REPLACEMENT THERAPIES

Renal replacement therapy is a term used to encompass life-supporting treatments for renal failure including hemodialysis, PD, hemofiltration, and renal transplantation.

While these treatment modalities are discussed within the context of ESRD, hemodialysis and PD may be employed to restore homeostasis in patients with ARF as well.

DIALYSIS

Dialysis is used to remove fluid and uremic waste products from the body when the kidneys are unable to do so. Methods of therapy include hemodialysis, PD, and continuous renal replacement therapy (CRRT).

Whether kidney disease is acute or chronic, dialysis becomes necessary in uremia when hyperkalemia, fluid overload, or impending pulmonary edema, acidosis, pericarditis, or severe confusion/encephalopathy develop. It may also be used to remove certain medications or other toxins due to poisoning or medication overdose.

The decision to initiate dialysis is reached after thoughtful discussion with the patient, family, providers, and others, as appropriate. Many potentially life-threatening issues are associated with the need for dialysis. The nurse can assist the patient and family by answering their questions, clarifying the information provided, and supporting their decision. The lifestyle changes that patients requiring long-term hemodialysis need to make are often overwhelming.

Although the costs of dialysis are usually reimbursable, limitations on the patient's ability to work resulting from illness and dialysis usually impose a great financial burden on the patient and family.

HEMODIALYSIS

Hemodialysis is the most common method of dialysis. More than 280,000 Americans receive chronic hemodialysis (Martchev, 2008). Treatments usually occur three times a week and take about 3 to 5 hours per treatment. The trend in managing ESRD is to initiate treatment before the signs and symptoms associated with uremia become severe.

Description

Hemodialysis functions as an artificial kidney, removing toxic nitrogenous substances from the blood and excess water. The patient's blood is diverted to a machine, where toxins are removed and the blood is returned to the patient. Hemodialysis requires a semipermeable membrane found in the hollow fiber **dialyzer** or artificial kidney, to replace the function of the impaired kidneys. The dialyzer contains thousands of tiny cellophane tubules through which the blood flows; a **dialysate** solution circulates around the tubules. The exchange of wastes from the blood to the dialysate occurs through the semipermeable membrane by way of **osmosis**, **diffusion**, and **ultrafiltra-tion** (Fig. 27-2). The toxins and wastes in the blood are removed by diffusion, in which particles move from an area of higher concentration in the blood to an area of lower concentration in the dialysate. The dialysate is a solution made up of electrolytes in their ideal extracellular concentrations. The electrolyte level in the patient's blood can be brought under control by adjusting the dialysate. The semipermeable membrane impedes the diffusion of large molecules, such as RBCs and proteins, keeping them in the bloodstream.

Excess water is removed from the blood by osmosis, in which water moves from an area of higher solute concentration in the blood toward an area of lower solute concentration in the dialysate. In ultrafiltration, water moves under high pressure to an area of lower pressure to facilitate water removal. This process is accomplished by applying negative pressure or a suctioning force to the dialysis membrane.

The anticoagulant heparin is administered to keep blood from clotting in the dialysis circuit. When this is dangerous to the patient, such as with thrombocytopenia, saline flushes may be used. At the end of the treatment, the dialysate, excess fluid, and waste products are discarded.

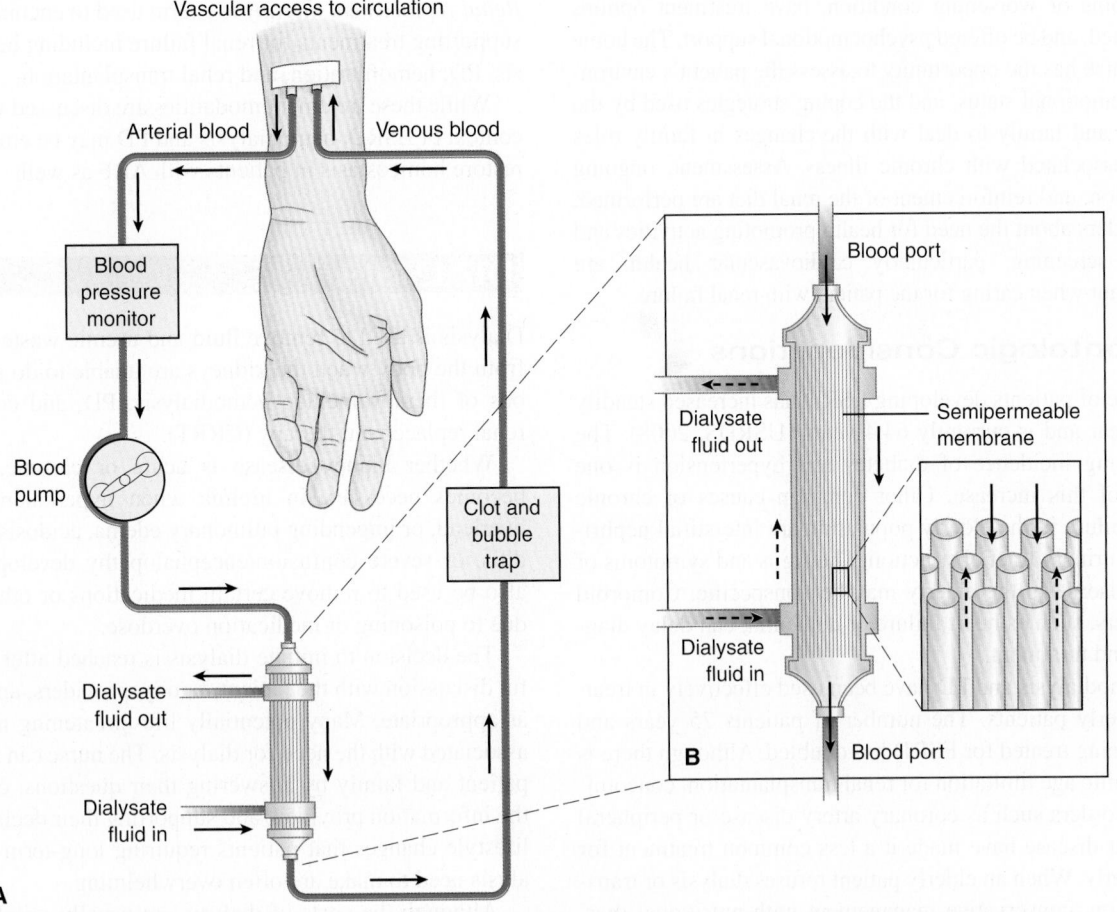

FIGURE 27-2 Hemodialysis system. (**A**) Blood from an artery is pumped into (**B**) a dialyzer where it flows through the cellophane tubes, which act as the semipermeable membrane (*inset*). The dialysate, which has the same chemical composition as the blood except for urea and waste products, flows in around the tubules. The waste products in the blood diffuse through the semipermeable membrane into the dialysate.

Vascular Access

Access to the patient's vascular system must be established to allow blood to be removed, cleansed, and returned to the patient's vascular system at rates between 300 and 550 mL/minute. Several types of access are available.

Temporary Vascular Access Devices

Immediate access to the patient's circulation for emergency hemodialysis is achieved by inserting a double-lumen large-bore catheter into the subclavian, internal jugular, or femoral vein (Fig. 27-3). This method of vascular access involves some risk, such as hematoma, pneumothorax, infection, thrombosis of the subclavian vein, or inadequate flow. For the patient with ESRD, the nurse should emphasize that these are "bridge" catheters and not permanent access; they are used while a permanent vascular access is created and matures.

The goal of the Fistula First Project (National Vascular Access Improvement Initiative) is to increase permanent access with AV fistula placement in 66% of long-term dialysis patients by 2009.

Arteriovenous Fistula

The gold standard for permanent access is a surgically created **arteriovenous fistula**, usually placed in the forearm. The fistula is created by joining (anastomosing) an artery to a vein (Fig. 27-4). The venous segment of the fistula will

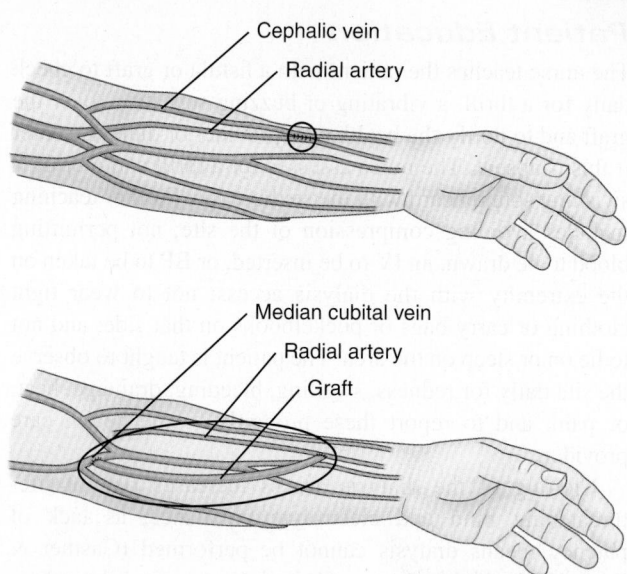

FIGURE 27-4 An internal arteriovenous fistula (*top*) is created by a side-to-side anastomosis of the artery and vein. A graft (*bottom*) can also be established between the artery and vein.

dilate in response to increased arterial pressure to provide for rapid removal and return of blood. When performing dialysis, two large-bore (14- to 16-gauge) needles are inserted into the fistula; the arterial segment of the fistula is used for flow to the dialyzer and the venous segment for reinfusion of the dialyzed blood. The fistula should be allowed at least 14 days to heal and mature although 4 to 6 weeks is preferable. The patient is encouraged to perform exercises, such as squeezing a rubber ball, to help the access mature and to increase the size of these vessels.

Arteriovenous Graft

An **arteriovenous graft** can be created by subcutaneously inserting synthetic graft material between an artery and vein (see Fig. 27-4). The most commonly used synthetic graft material is expanded polytetrafluoroethylene (Gortex). Usually, a graft is created when the patient's vessels are not suitable for creation of a fistula, such as in the diabetic patient. Infection and thrombosis are the most common complications of arteriovenous grafts.

Ideally, the surgical access should be created 2 to 6 months before the need for renal replacement therapy (Murigai, Noble, McGowan et al., 2008; ESRDnetwork. org). Patients should be given information about the access and about potential changes in body image, which can trigger noncompliance or depression.

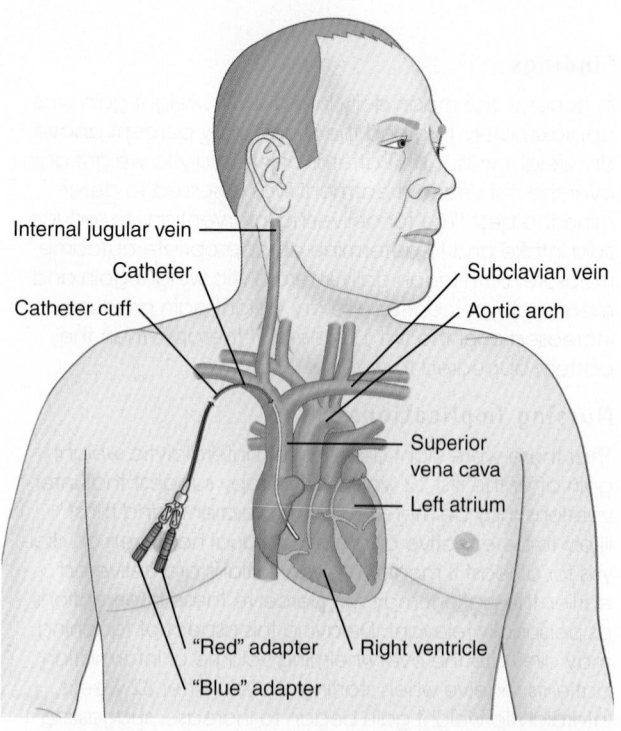

FIGURE 27-3 Double-lumen, cuffed hemodialysis catheter used in acute hemodialysis. The red adapter is attached to a blood line through which blood is pumped from the patient to the dialyzer. After the blood passes through the dialyzer (artificial kidney), it returns to the patient through the blue adapter.

> **! NURSING ALERT**
> *Failure of the permanent dialysis access (fistula or graft) accounts for most hospital admissions of patients undergoing chronic hemodialysis. Thus, protection of the access is of high priority.*

Patient Education

The nurse teaches the patient with a fistula or graft to check daily for a thrill, a vibrating or buzzing sensation, over the graft and to notify the health care provider or dialysis center if this is absent. The nurse assesses for a thrill and a bruit, a swishing sound heard with the stethoscope. Further teaching includes avoiding compression of the site; not permitting blood to be drawn, an IV to be inserted, or BP to be taken on the extremity with the dialysis access; not to wear tight clothing or carry bags or pocketbooks on that side; and not to lie on or sleep on the area. The patient is taught to observe the site daily for redness, swelling, bleeding, drainage, heat, or pain, and to report these promptly to the health care provider.

Clotting of the dialysis access increases risk of life-threatening fluid and electrolyte imbalance, as lack of patency means dialysis cannot be performed (Castner & Ball, 2007). If this occurs, fibrinolysis, surgical thrombectomy, or revision is indicated.

Medical and Nursing Management

During dialysis, the patient, the dialyzer, and the dialysate bath require constant monitoring for complications. The dialysis nurse uses this time for assessing, monitoring, supporting, and educating the patient. The nurse may use this time to discuss the renal diet or reinforce fluid restriction, which may cause interdialytic weight gain (Box 27-7). The nurse palpates the fistula or graft for a thrill and auscultates for a bruit or swishing sound, indicating patency of the access.

Pharmacologic Therapy

Just as many medications are excreted wholly or in part by the kidneys, many medications are removed from the blood during hemodialysis; therefore, the provider may need to adjust the dosage. Metabolites of drugs that are bound to protein are not removed during dialysis. Removal of other drug metabolites depends on the weight and size of the molecule.

Patients undergoing hemodialysis who require medications, for example, cardiac glycosides, antibiotic agents, antiarrhythmic medications, or antihypertensive agents, are monitored closely to ensure that the blood and tissue levels of these medications are maintained without toxic accumulation. The nurse plans to administer these medications after dialysis to avoid their removal.

Evaluating for medications that may promote complications during dialysis is part of nursing care. For example, if

---

BOX 27-7 | **Nursing Research**

Bridging the Gap to Evidence-Based Practice

Patterns of Interdialytic Weight Gain During the First Year of Hemodialysis

Welch, J., et al. (2006). Patterns of interdialytic weight gain during the first year of hemodialysis. *Nephrology Nursing Journal, 33*(5), 493–498.

Purpose

More than 450,000 people in the United States have chronic renal failure, with 60% being treated by dialysis. Fluid restriction of approximately 1 L per day is particularly difficult for these patients and compliance is poor. Not only must patients consider the intake of actual liquids but they also must consider foods with high water content, such as fruits, gelatins, or soups. Failure to adhere to this restriction increases interdialytic weight gain and symptoms such as shortness of breath and hypertension.

Design

A retrospective descriptive design was used to follow 27 patients. Pre- and postdialysis weights were retrieved in addition to age, gender, race, estimated dry weight, and changes in estimated dry weight during the first year of hemodialysis. The participants had a mean age of 58.5 years; gender makeup was 55.6% male and 54.2% female. Interdialytic weight gain was assessed by mean daily interdialytic weight gain and percentage above dry weight. Scales were zeroed prior to each weight and calibrated monthly to ensure accuracy.

Findings

In general, the mean daily interdialytic weight gain was approximately 1 kg and the mean daily percent above dry weight was 1.3%. Patterns of interdialytic weight gain over the first year of treatment was assessed to determine the best time for delivering interventions to reduce fluid intake and to determine an appropriate outcome measure. Both mean daily interdialytic weight gain and mean daily percent above dry weight gain gradually increased over the first 12 weeks of therapy, then the pattern appeared to reverse.

Nursing Implications

That there were slight decreases in interdialytic weight gain after the first 12 weeks of therapy suggest that interventions may be more relevant to patients and most likely to be effective after an individual has been on dialysis for at least 3 months. If interventions are delivered earlier, the patient may not perceive these interventions as personally relevant. Delaying this aspect of teaching may alleviate the overwhelming volume of information patients receive when starting dialysis. After 32 weeks, interdialytic weight gain began to increase, suggesting self-management of fluid intake becomes more difficult over time. Increased intervention may be needed at this time.

an antihypertensive agent is taken prior to dialysis, hypotension may occur during dialysis, causing dangerously low BP. Many medications that are taken once daily can be held until after the dialysis treatment.

Nutritional and Fluid Therapy

Diet is an important factor for patients on hemodialysis because of the effects of uremia. With the initiation of hemodialysis, the patient usually requires restriction of dietary protein, sodium, potassium, phosphorous, and fluid. Protein intake is more liberal during hemodialysis but still restricted to about 1.2 to 1.3 g/kg/day ideal body weight; therefore, protein must be of high biologic quality and consist of the essential amino acids to prevent poor protein use and to maintain a positive nitrogen balance. Examples of foods high in biologic protein content include eggs, soy, meat, milk, poultry, and fish. Sodium is usually restricted to 2 to 3 g/day; fluids are restricted to an amount equal to the daily urine output plus approximately 500 to 800 mL/day to replace insensible losses (Porth & Matfin, 2009). The goal for patients on hemodialysis is to keep their interdialytic weight gain under 1.5 kg.

Dietary restriction is a difficult lifestyle change for many patients with chronic renal failure. Patients often feel stigmatized in social situations because they may feel there are few food choices available for their diet. If the restrictions are ignored, life-threatening complications, such as hyperkalemia, hypertension, and pulmonary edema, may result. The nurse who cares for a patient with symptoms or complications resulting from dietary indiscretion should avoid harsh, judgmental, or punitive tones when communicating with the patient. Rather, the nurse emphasizes the correlation between dietary indiscretion and the outcome, such as hypertension or dyspnea, and promotes self-management of the disease (Costantini, 2006).

Providing Psychosocial Care

Patients requiring long-term hemodialysis are often concerned about the unpredictability of the illness and the disruption to their lives. Financial problems, difficulty working, waning sexual desire and impotence, depression from chronic illness, and fear of dying may occur. Younger patients have concerns about marriage, having children, and the burden on their families. Dialysis treatments and restrictions in food and fluid intake often impose challenges to the patient and family. Earlier hospital discharge increases the expectation on the individual and family to assist with care (Beanlands, Horsburgh, Fox et al., 2005). The time required for dialysis and physician visits, low energy, and chronic illness can create conflict, frustration, guilt, and depression. The nurse can encourage caregivers and patients to express concerns, anger, or negative feelings; if not expressed, anger may be directed inward and lead to depression, despair, or suicide. If anger is projected outward to other people, it may destroy already threatened family relationships.

Depression may require counseling, therapy, and pharmacologic treatment. A mental health provider with expertise in the care of patients receiving dialysis may also be helpful. The sense of loss that the patient experiences cannot be underestimated because every aspect of a "normal life" is disrupted.

Some patients use denial to deal with the overwhelming array of medical issues. Labeling a patient "noncompliant" does not consider the impact of renal failure and its treatment on the patient and family, nor does it encourage positive coping strategies. Nurses and dialysis personnel should rethink the ideal of insisting on perfect compliance and instead work with the patient to share difficulties, such as indiscretion in fluid intake, so it can be dealt with during dialysis.

Patients and their families should be encouraged to discuss end-of-life options. Only between 21% and 25% of patients on hemodialysis have an advanced directive or living will. The ANNA Ethics Committee has developed an end-of-life module to foster the nurse's role in these discussions (Rabetoy & Bahr, 2007).

Teaching Self-Care

The diagnosis of chronic renal failure and the need for dialysis may be overwhelming. Many patients with ESRD have depressed mentation, a shortened attention span, a decreased level of concentration, and altered perception. Therefore, teaching must occur in brief, 10- to 15-minute sessions, with time added for clarification, repetition, reinforcement, and questions from the patient and family. The nurse needs to convey a nonjudgmental attitude to enable the patient and family to discuss feelings about those treatment options and the material taught.

One study indicated that higher levels of knowledge and greater degree of self-management were associated with significant improvement of function and well-being. Teaching materials at all reading levels are available on the National Kidney Foundation and National Institute of Health web sites (Martchev, 2008).

Home Hemodialysis

Although most patients who require hemodialysis undergo the procedure in an outpatient setting, home hemodialysis is an option for some. Patients delivering their own hemodialysis have been shown to increase emotional wellness, energy level, and social functioning (Costantini, 2006). Home hemodialysis lets the patient set the schedule, decreases travel and wait times at the dialysis center, and if done slowly through the night, increases removal of more phosphorus and wastes. Thus, the patient may not require as much dietary restriction or antihypertensive therapy (http://kidney.niddk.nih.gov/kudiseases/pubs/homehemodialysis/).

According to the National Institute of Diabetes and Digestive and Kidney Diseases (NIDDK), a patient learns to perform treatments at the dialysis center, working with a

dialysis nurse. Most people who do home hemodialysis have helpers, such as a family member, neighbor, or close friend, who train with them at the clinic. The dialysis center supplies the machine and equipment, such as dialysis solution, that will be delivered to the home once or twice a month. The training staff makes sure the patient is confident about performing each task before doing home HD. Someone from the clinic will be available to answer phone calls 24 hours a day. The health care team never forces a patient to use home hemodialysis, because this treatment requires significant changes in the home and family. Home hemodialysis must be the patient's and family's decision. During training, the patient and assistant learn to:

- Prepare equipment and supplies
- Place the needle in the vascular access
- Monitor the machine
- Check BP and pulse
- Keep records of the treatments
- Clean the equipment and the room where dialysis is done
- Order supplies

In addition training includes how to prepare, operate, and disassemble the dialysis machine; maintain and clean the equipment; administer medications (e.g., heparin) into the machine lines; and handle emergency problems such as hemodialysis dialyzer rupture, electrical or mechanical problems, hypotension, shock, and seizures.

Before home hemodialysis is initiated, the home environment, household, and community resources are assessed. The home is surveyed to see if electrical outlets, plumbing facilities, and storage space are adequate. The home must have room for the HD machine, supplies, and in some cases, a water purification machine. Modifications may be needed to enable the patient and assistant to perform dialysis safely and to deal with emergencies.

Once home dialysis is initiated, the home care nurse visits periodically to evaluate adherence with the recommended techniques, to assess the patient for complications, to reinforce previous teaching, and to provide reassurance. The patient may report to the dialysis center monthly to see the nephrologist, dialysis nurse, and dietitian. Blood tests will be done to evaluate and adjust hemodialysis treatments.

Continuing Care

The health care team's goal in treating patients undergoing hemodialysis is to maximize their vocational potential, functional status, and quality of life. Many patients can resume relatively normal lives, doing the things that are important to them: traveling, exercising, working, or actively participating in family activities. Outcome goals for renal rehabilitation include employment for those able to work, improved physical functioning of all patients, improved understanding about adaptation and options for living well, increased control over the effects of kidney disease and dialysis, and resumption of activities enjoyed before dialysis. Nurses

must shift patient care away from the traditional paradigm to one of self-management, which lessens the patient's negativity toward treatment (Costantini, 2006).

Complications

Although hemodialysis can prolong life indefinitely, it does not alter the natural course of the underlying kidney disease, nor does it completely replace kidney function. The patient is subject to a number of problems and complications. A leading cause of death among patients undergoing maintenance hemodialysis is atherosclerotic cardiovascular disease (USRDS, 2008). Disturbances of lipid metabolism (hypertriglyceridemia) appear to be accentuated by hemodialysis. Heart failure, coronary heart disease, and anginal pain, stroke, and peripheral vascular insufficiency may occur and may incapacitate the patient (Broscious & Castagnola, 2006). Anemia and fatigue contribute to diminished physical and emotional well-being, lack of energy and drive, and apathy, although the use of erythropoietin (Epogen/Procrit) before the start of dialysis has been shown to have a significant positive effect on hematocrit levels for the first 19 months after starting dialysis.

Gastric ulcers and other GI problems result from the physiologic stress of chronic illness, medication, and related problems. Disturbed calcium metabolism leads to renal osteodystrophy that produces bone pain and fractures. Other problems include fluid overload associated with heart failure, malnutrition, infection, neuropathy, and pruritus.

Up to 85% of people undergoing hemodialysis experience major sleep problems that further complicate their overall health status. Early-morning or late-afternoon dialysis may be a risk factor for developing sleep disturbances. Interventions, such as changing the temperature of the dialysate bath, may prevent temperature elevation, and limiting napping during dialysis may reduce sleep problems in people receiving hemodialysis. Some centers are offering nocturnal dialysis for 6 to 8 hours nightly (Martchev, 2008). Home dialysis may offer more freedom and promotes the self-management paradigm (Thomas, Chan, Hunks et al., 2007).

Other complications during dialysis may include:

- Hypotension associated with nausea and vomiting, diaphoresis, tachycardia, and dizziness due to fluid shifting
- Painful muscle cramping, usually late in dialysis, as fluid and electrolytes rapidly leave the extracellular space
- Exsanguination if blood lines separate or dialysis needles become dislodged
- Dysrhythmias resulting from electrolyte and pH changes or from removal of antidysrhythmic medications during dialysis
- Air embolism, a rare circumstance, but can occur if air enters the vascular system
- Chest pain, particularly in patients with anemia or arteriosclerotic heart disease

- Dialysis disequilibrium resulting from cerebral fluid shifts. Signs and symptoms include headache, nausea and vomiting, restlessness, decreased level of consciousness, and seizures. It is more likely to occur in ARF or when BUN levels are very high.
- Dialyzer clotting, which can be prevented by adjusting heparin doses

CONTINUOUS RENAL REPLACEMENT THERAPIES

CRRT, a process similar to hemodialysis, is used with patients demonstrating hemodynamic instability, such as hypotension, or in those who cannot tolerate rapid fluid shifts. CRRT (Fig. 27-5) circulates the blood outside the body through a filter similar to the hemodialysis filter. A pump is used to assist blood flow. The types of CRRT include **continuous venovenous hemofiltration (CVVH)** and **continuous venovenous hemofiltration with dialysis (CVVHD)**. Continuous arteriovenous hemofiltration (CAVH) is being replaced by the venous filtration techniques (Morton & Fontaine, 2009). Slow continuous ultrafiltration (SCUF) is performed primarily to remove fluid.

Continuous Venovenous Hemofiltration

CVVH is used to manage ARF. Blood from a double-lumen venous catheter is pumped through a hemofilter and then returned to the patient through the same catheter. CVVH provides continuous, slow fluid removal (ultrafiltration);

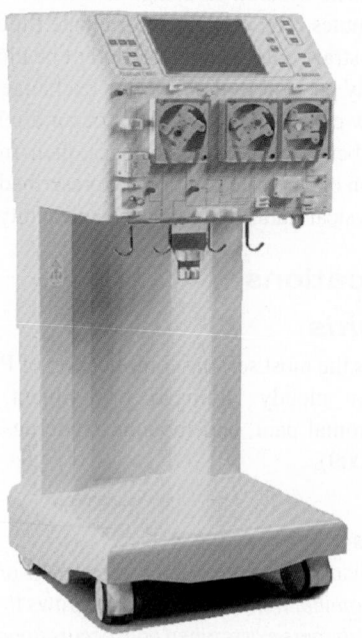

FIGURE 27-5 Diapact® CRRT System.

therefore, hemodynamic effects are mild and better tolerated by patients with unstable conditions. CVVH does not require arterial access, and critical care nurses can set up, initiate, maintain, and terminate the system.

Continuous Venovenous Hemodialysis

CVVHD is similar to CVVH. Blood is pumped from a double-lumen venous catheter through a hemofilter and returned to the patient through the same catheter. In addition to the benefits of ultrafiltration, CVVHD uses a dialysate to create a concentration gradient, thus facilitating the removal of uremic toxins and fluid. The access required is the same as for emergency hemodialysis (Morton & Fontaine, 2009). Critical care nurses perform this procedure after competency has been validated.

PERITONEAL DIALYSIS

The goals of PD are to remove toxic substances and metabolic wastes and to re-establish normal fluid and electrolyte balance. PD may be performed chronically on an outpatient basis or for acutely ill patients, although the latter is falling out of favor. Patients who are unable or unwilling to undergo hemodialysis or renal transplantation, or who do not have access to the bloodstream can benefit from PD. In addition, patients who do not tolerate the rapid fluid, electrolyte, and metabolic changes that occur during hemodialysis experience fewer of these problems with the slower rate of PD. Therefore, patients with diabetes or cardiovascular disease, many older patients, and those who may be at risk for adverse effects of systemic heparin are likely candidates for PD. Additionally, severe hypertension, heart failure, and pulmonary edema not responsive to usual treatment regimens have been successfully treated with PD.

During PD, the thin, serous peritoneal membrane that covers the abdominal organs and lines the abdominal wall serves as the semipermeable or dialyzing membrane (Morton & Fontaine, 2009). Sterile dialysate fluid is introduced into the peritoneal cavity through a peritoneal or Tenckhoff catheter (Fig. 27-6). Diffusion across the semipermeable membrane removes urea creatinine and metabolic end-products normally excreted by the kidneys. Excess fluid is removed through osmosis as water moves from an area of lower particle concentration in the patient's blood to an area of higher concentration across a semipermeable membrane into the dialysate. Dialysis solutions are available in concentrations of 1.5%, 2.5%, and 4.25% dextrose. This concentration gradient for fluid removal is created by varying concentrations of glucose; the higher the dextrose concentration, the greater the osmotic gradient and the more water will be removed. PD is a slower process than hemodialysis; therefore, it takes longer to reach equilibrium.

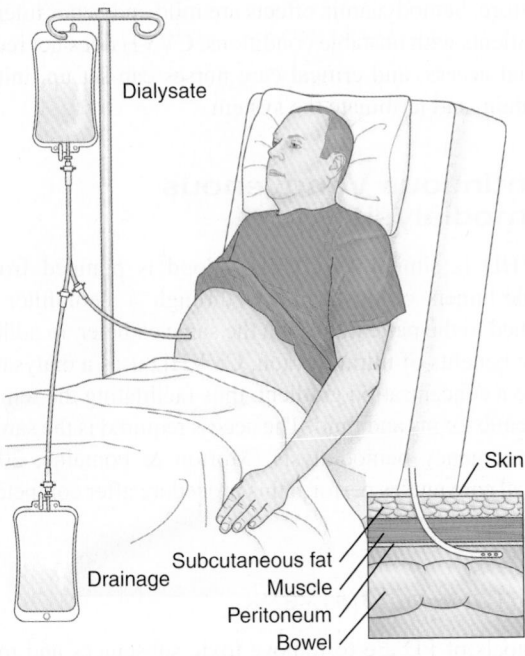

FIGURE 27-6 In peritoneal dialysis (PD) and in acute intermittent PD, dialysate is infused into the peritoneal cavity by gravity, after which the clamp on the infusion line is closed. After a dwell time (when the dialysate is in the peritoneal cavity), the drainage tube is unclamped and the fluid drains from the peritoneal cavity, again by gravity. A new container of dialysate is infused as soon as drainage is complete. The duration of the dwell time depends on the type of PD.

Procedure

Preparing the Patient

Insertion of the peritoneal catheter may be performed at the bedside or in the operating room, depending on acuity of the patient. A broad-spectrum antibiotic may be administered prior to the procedure to prevent postoperative infection. The patient is encouraged to empty the bladder and bowel prior to catheter insertion to reduce the risk of puncturing internal organs. Baseline vital signs, weight, and serum electrolyte levels are recorded. The nurse also assesses the patient's anxiety about the procedure and provides support and instruction.

Preparing the Equipment

Aseptic technique is imperative during PD. The nurse assembles the equipment, including the dialysate and any medications to be added. Heparin may be added to prevent occlusion of the peritoneal catheter, potassium chloride to prevent hypokalemia, and antibiotics to prevent or treat **peritonitis**. The osmotic agent in the dialysate is glucose, which may be absorbed, therefore regular insulin may be added. All medications are added immediately before the solution is instilled.

NURSING ALERT

It is important to remember that peritoneal solutions contain varying concentrations of glucose. Because 30% to 40% of patients receiving PD are diabetic, glycemic monitoring is critical.

Before medications are added, the dialysate is warmed to body temperature to prevent abdominal discomfort and to dilate the vessels of the peritoneum to increase urea clearance. Dry heating with a heating cabinet or incubator is recommended. Microwave heating of the fluid is *not* recommended because of the danger of burning the peritoneum. The nurse primes the PD tubing with the dialysate to prevent air from entering the peritoneal cavity.

Catheters used for long-term PD (i.e., Tenckhoff) are usually made of silicone and are radiopaque to permit visualization on X-ray. The catheter has two cuffs, which stabilize the catheter, limit movement, prevent leaks, and provide a barrier against microorganisms. One cuff is placed just distal to the peritoneum, and the other cuff is placed subcutaneously. The subcutaneous tunnel (5 to 10 cm long) further protects against bacterial infection (Fig. 27-7).

Performing the Exchange

PD involves a series of exchanges or cycles. An exchange is defined as the infusion, dwell, and drainage of the dialysate. This cycle is repeated throughout the course of the dialysis. The dialysate is infused by gravity into the peritoneal cavity. A period of about 5 to 10 minutes is usually required to infuse 2 L of fluid. The prescribed dwell, or equilibration time allows diffusion and osmosis to occur. At the end of the dwell time, the drainage portion of the exchange begins. The solution drains from the peritoneal cavity by gravity through a closed, sterile system. Drainage is usually completed in 10 to 30 minutes. The effluent or drainage fluid is normally colorless or straw-colored and should not be cloudy. Bloody drainage may be seen in the first few exchanges after insertion of a new catheter but should not occur after that time.

The number of cycles or exchanges, their frequency, and concentration of dialysate solution are prescribed based on the patient's physical status, fluid balance and acuity of illness.

Complications

Peritonitis

Peritonitis is the most serious complication of PD. The nurse assesses for cloudy drainage or effluent, low grade fever, abdominal pain, and rebound tenderness (Morton & Fontaine, 2009).

NURSING ALERT

To detect rebound tenderness, the nurse presses one hand firmly into the abdominal wall and quickly withdraws the hand. Rebound tenderness exists when pain occurs upon removal and is associated with inflammation of the peritoneal cavity.

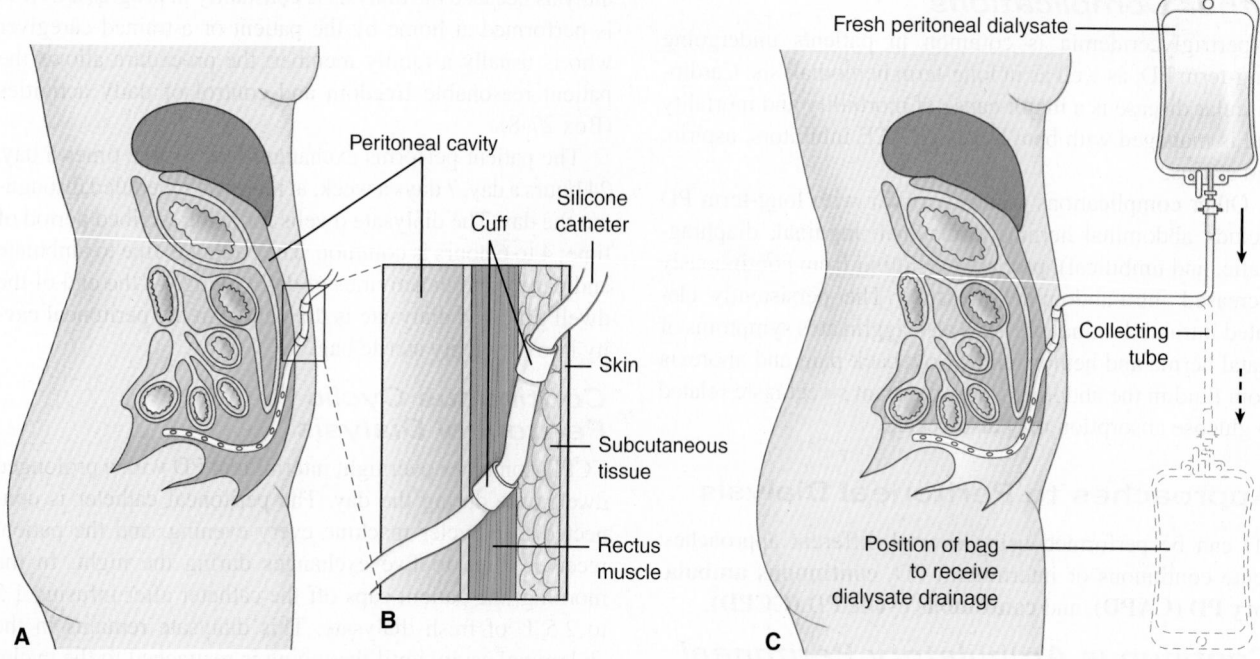

FIGURE 27-7 Continuous ambulatory peritoneal dialysis. **(A)** The peritoneal catheter is implanted through the abdominal wall. **(B)** Dacron cuffs and a subcutaneous tunnel provide protection against bacterial infection. **(C)** Dialysate flows by gravity through the peritoneal catheter into the peritoneal cavity. After a prescribed period of time, the fluid is drained by gravity and discarded. New solution is then infused into the peritoneal cavity until the next drainage period. Dialysis thus continues on a 24-hour-a-day basis during which the patient is free to move around and engage in his or her usual activities.

Treatment is based on culture and sensitivity of the peritoneal fluid. Antimicrobial therapy with a cephalosporin or aminoglycoside may be administered intravenously and/or added to the dialysate. Hypotension and other signs of shock may occur. Regardless of which organism causes peritonitis, the patient with peritonitis loses large amounts of protein through the peritoneum. Acute malnutrition and delayed healing may result. Therefore, attention must be given to detecting and promptly treating peritonitis.

Leakage

Leakage of dialysate around the catheter site must be corrected because the area acts as a pathway for bacteria to enter the peritoneal cavity. Usually, the leak stops spontaneously if dialysis is withheld for several days to give the incision and exit site time to heal. If necessary, leakage of dialysate around the catheter site may be managed with extra sutures and a decrease in the amount of dialysate used. Increases in intra-abdominal pressure such as vomiting, coughing, and straining during bowel movements should be avoided as these may delay healing. Leakage through the exit site or into the abdominal wall can occur for months or years after catheter placement.

Bleeding

A bloody effluent (drainage) may be expected in the initial outflow or observed occasionally in young, menstruating women. Bleeding is common during the first few exchanges after a new catheter insertion because some blood enters the abdominal cavity following insertion. During menstruation, the hypertonic fluid pulls blood from the uterus, through the opening in the fallopian tubes, into the peritoneal cavity. Some patients have had bloody effluent after an enema or from minor trauma. Invariably, bleeding stops in 1 to 2 days and requires no specific intervention. More frequent exchanges during this time may be necessary to prevent blood clots from obstructing the catheter. Gross bleeding at any time indicates a more serious problem and must be investigated immediately.

Incomplete Recovery of Fluid

If the fluid drains slowly or the volume drained is less than the amount inserted, the nurse turns the patient from side to side, elevates the head of the bed, or repositions the patient to facilitate drainage. If fibrin or clots prevent outflow, heparin may be added to the dialysate (Morton & Fontaine, 2009). The nurse should ensure the patient empties the colon through regular bowel movements, as the tip of the catheter may come up against the bowel, preventing adequate drainage. The catheter itself should never be repositioned.

Other measures to promote drainage include checking the patency of the catheter by inspecting for kinks, closed clamps, or an air lock. The nurse must ensure that the PD catheter remains secure and that the dressing remains dry.

Other Complications

Hypertriglyceridemia is common in patients undergoing long-term PD, as well as in long-term hemodialysis. Cardiovascular disease is a major cause of morbidity and mortality and is managed with beta blockers, ACE inhibitors, aspirin, and statins.

Other complications that may occur with long-term PD include abdominal hernias (incisional, inguinal, diaphragmatic, and umbilical), probably resulting from continuously increased intra-abdominal pressure. The persistently elevated intra-abdominal pressure also aggravates symptoms of hiatal hernia and hemorrhoids. Low back pain and anorexia from fluid in the abdomen and a constant sweet taste related to glucose absorption may also occur.

Approaches to Peritoneal Dialysis

PD can be performed using several different approaches: acute continuous or intermittent PD, **continuous ambulatory PD (CAPD)**, and **continuous cyclic PD (CCPD)**.

Continuous Ambulatory Peritoneal Dialysis

CAPD works on the same principles as other forms of PD; however, less extreme fluctuations in the patient's laboratory values occur with CAPD than with intermittent PD or hemo-

dialysis because the dialysis is constantly in progress. CAPD is performed at home by the patient or a trained caregiver who is usually a family member; the procedure allows the patient reasonable freedom and control of daily activities (Box 27-8).

The patient performs exchanges four or five times a day, 24 hours a day, 7 days a week, at intervals scheduled throughout the day. The dialysate dwells for the prescribed period of time; 4 to 6 hours is common. The patient is free to ambulate and participate in activities of daily living. At the end of the dwell time, the dialysate is drained from the peritoneal cavity into the empty sterile bag.

Continuous Cyclic Peritoneal Dialysis

CCPD combines overnight intermittent PD with a prolonged dwell time during the day. The peritoneal catheter is connected to a cycler machine every evening, and the patient receives three to five exchanges during the night. In the morning, the patient caps off the catheter after infusing 1.5 to 2.5 L of fresh dialysate. This dialysate remains in the abdominal cavity until the tubing is reattached to the cycler machine at bedtime.

CCPD has a lower infection rate than other forms of PD because there are fewer opportunities for contamination with bag changes and tubing disconnections. It also allows the

---

BOX 27-8 **Assessing Suitability for Continuous Ambulatory Peritoneal Dialysis**

Although CAPD is not suitable for all patients with ESRD, it is a viable therapy for those who can perform self-care and exchanges and who can fit therapy into their own routines. Often, patients report having more energy and feeling healthier once they begin CAPD. Nurses can be instrumental in helping patients with ESRD find the dialysis therapy that best suits their lifestyle. Those considering CAPD need to investigate the advantages and disadvantages, along with the indications and contraindications for this form of therapy.

Advantages
- Freedom from a dialysis machine
- Control over daily activities
- Opportunities to avoid dietary restrictions, increase fluid intake, raise serum hematocrit values, improve BP control, avoid venipuncture, and gain a sense of well-being

Disadvantages
- Continuous dialysis 24 hours a day, 7 days a week

Indications
- Patient's willingness, motivation, and ability to perform dialysis at home
- Strong family or community support system (essential for success), particularly if the patient is an older adult

- Special problems with long-term hemodialysis, such as dysfunctional or failing vascular access devices, excessive thirst, severe hypertension, postdialysis headaches, and severe anemia requiring frequent transfusion
- Interim therapy while awaiting kidney transplantation
- ESRD secondary to diabetes because hypertension, uremia, and hyperglycemia is easier to manage with CAPD than with hemodialysis

Contraindications
- Adhesions from previous surgery (adhesions reduce clearance of solutes) or systemic inflammatory disease
- Chronic backache and preexisting disk disease, which could be aggravated by the continuous pressure of dialysis fluid in the abdomen
- Risk of complications, for example, in patients receiving immunosuppressive medications, which impede healing of the catheter site, and in patients with a colostomy, ileostomy, nephrostomy, or ileal conduit because of the risk of peritonitis. The risk for complications is not an absolute contraindication for CAPD therapy.
- Diverticulitis, because CAPD has been associated with rupture of the diverticulum
- Severe arthritis or poor hand strength, necessitating assistance in performing the exchange; however, blind or partially blind patients and those with other physical limitations can learn to perform CAPD.

BOX 27-9

Nursing Management for Continuous Ambulatory Peritoneal Dialysis

Caring for the Catheter Site

To reduce the risk of peritonitis in the patient using peritoneal dialysis (PD), the patient must use meticulous care to avoid contaminating the catheter, fluid, or tubing and to avoid accidentally disconnecting the catheter from the tubing. Excess manipulation is avoided, and meticulous care of the catheter entry site is provided using a standardized protocol. The patient and significant others present wear a mask and use strict aseptic technique for preparation of the dialysate and dressing changes.

The nurse uses every opportunity to assess catheter care technique and correct the patient's technique. Recommended daily or three or four times weekly routine catheter site care is typically performed during showering or bathing. The exit site should not be submerged in bath water. The most common cleaning method is soap and water; liquid soap is recommended. During care, the nurse and patient need to make sure that the catheter remains secure to avoid tension and trauma. The patient may wear a gauze or semitransparent dressing over the exit site.

Meeting Psychosocial Needs

In addition to the complications of PD previously described, patients who elect to use continuous ambulatory peritoneal dialysis (CAPD) may experience altered body image because of the abdominal catheter and the bag and tubing. Waist size increases from 1 to 2 inches (or more) with fluid in the abdomen. This affects clothing selection and may make the patient feel "fat." Body image may be so altered that patients do not want to look at or care for the catheter for days or weeks. The nurse may arrange for the patient to talk with other patients who have adapted well to CAPD. Although some patients have no psychological problems with the catheter—they think of it as their lifeline and as a life-sustaining device—other patients feel they are doing exchanges all day long and have no free time, particularly in the beginning. They may experience depression because they feel overwhelmed with the responsibility of self-care.

Patients undergoing CAPD may also experience altered sexuality patterns and sexual dysfunction. The patient and partner may be reluctant to engage in sexual activities, partly because of the catheter being

psychologically "in the way" of sexual performance. The peritoneal catheter, drainage bag, and about 2 L of dialysate may interfere with the patient's sexual function and body image as well. Although these problems may resolve with time, some problems may warrant special counseling. Questions by the nurse about concerns related to sexuality and sexual function often provide the patient with a welcome opportunity to discuss these issues and provide a first step toward their resolution.

Teaching Patients Self-Care

Patients are taught to perform PD according to their own learning ability and knowledge level, and are given only as much information at one time as they can handle without feeling uncomfortable or becoming overwhelmed.

Because protein loss is higher with PD than with hemodialysis, the patient is instructed to eat a high-protein, well-balanced diet. The patient is also encouraged to increase his or her daily fiber intake to help prevent constipation, which can impede the flow of dialysate into or out of the peritoneal cavity. Many patients gain 3 to 5 lb within a month of initiating CAPD, so they may be asked to limit their carbohydrate intake to avoid excessive weight gain. Potassium, sodium, and fluid restrictions are not usually needed. Patients commonly lose about 2 to 3 L of fluid over and above the volume of dialysate infused into the abdomen during a 24-hour period, permitting a more normal fluid intake.

Continuing Care

The nurse assesses that strict aseptic technique is being followed. Blood chemistry values are followed closely to make certain the therapy is adequate for the patient. The home care nurse assesses the home environment and suggests modifications to accommodate the equipment and facilities needed to carry out CAPD. Additional assessments include checking for changes related to renal disease, complications such as peritonitis, and treatment-related problems such as heart failure, inadequate drainage, and weight gain or loss. The nurse continues to reinforce and clarify teaching about renal failure and renal disease while assessing the patient's and family's progress in coping with the procedure.

---

patient to be free from exchanges throughout the day, making it possible to engage in work and activities of daily living more freely. Box 27-9 provides nursing management for CAPD.

KIDNEY TRANSPLANTATION

Kidney transplantation has become the treatment of choice for most patients with ESRD. In 2006, 18,000 transplants

were performed in the United States. While the number of transplantations increased by 4% in 2006, the number of patients on the kidney transplant waiting list has grown by 8%. At the conclusion of 2006, approximately 46,000 active candidates were waiting for a kidney. Waiting times across the country continue to increase, with the median time to transplant projected to be nearly 4 years for candidates added to the list in 2008 (USRDS, 2008). Healthy People 2010 calls for the number of dialysis patients registered on the transplant waiting list to increase to 66% by 2010 and the

BOX 27-10
Kidney Donation

An inadequate number of available kidneys remains the greatest limitation to treating patients with end-stage renal disease successfully. For those interested in donating a kidney, the National Kidney Foundation provides written information describing the organ donation program and a card specifying the organs to be donated in the event of death.

The organ donation card is signed by the donor and two witnesses and should be carried by the donor at all times. Procurement of an adequate number of kidneys for potential recipients is still a major problem, despite national legislation that requires relatives of deceased patients or patients declared brain-dead to be asked if they would consider organ donation.

In some states in the United States, drivers can indicate their desire to be organ donors on their driver's license application or renewal.

proportion of dialysis patients waiting to receive a transplant within 3 years to increase to 30% (Scandling, 2005).

Patients choose kidney transplantation for various reasons, such as the desire to avoid dialysis or to improve their sense of well-being and the wish to lead a more normal life. Additionally, the cost of maintaining a successful transplantation is one-third the cost of dialysis treatment.

Kidney transplantation involves transplanting a kidney from a living donor or heartbeat-only donor (one who has been pronounced brain dead but whose cardiopulmonary system is artificially maintained) to a recipient who has ESRD (Box 27-10). Kidney transplant donors have traditionally been blood relatives; however, living donors such as spouses, friends, and those on organ registries have produced results

comparable with those of living, blood-related donors (Morton & Fontaine, 2009). The success rate increases if kidney transplantation from a living donor is performed before dialysis is initiated (Danovitch, 2005; Scandling, 2005).

Depending on the cause and symptoms of renal failure, a nephrectomy of the patient's own native kidneys may be performed before transplantation. The transplanted kidney is placed in the patient's iliac fossa anterior to the iliac crest. The renal artery of the donor is anastomosed to the hypogastric, renal, or iliac artery of the recipient. The ureter of the newly transplanted kidney is anastomosed to the ureter of the recipient and the renal vein anastomosed to the renal vein of the recipient (Fig. 27-8). The left donor kidney is preferred because the left renal vein is longer than the right (Morton & Fontaine, 2009).

Medical and Nursing Management
Preoperative Management

Preoperative management goals include bringing the patient's metabolic state to a level as close to normal as possible, making sure that the patient is free of infection, and preparing the patient for surgery and the postoperative course. Preoperatively, immunosuppressant medication is initiated prior to the transplant to prevent rejection of the new kidney.

A complete physical examination is performed to detect and treat any conditions that could cause complications after transplantation. Tissue typing, blood typing, and antibody screening are performed to determine compatibility of the tissues and cells of the donor and recipient. Other diagnostic tests must be completed to identify conditions requiring treatment before transplantation. The lower urinary tract is studied to assess bladder neck function and to detect urethral reflux.

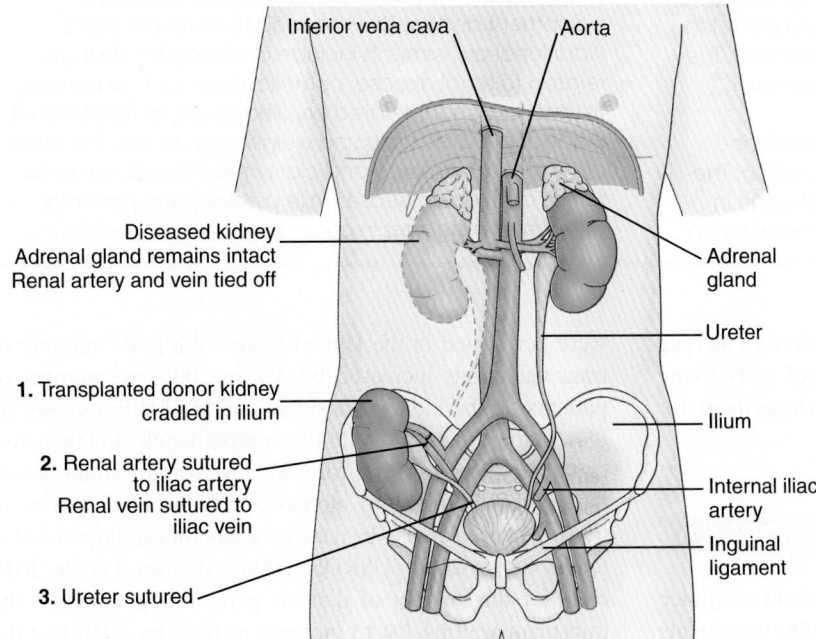

FIGURE 27-8 Renal transplantation: (1) The diseased kidney may be removed and the renal artery and vein tied off. (2) The transplanted kidney is placed in the iliac fossa. (3) The renal artery of the donated kidney is sutured to the iliac artery, and the renal vein is sutured to the iliac vein. (4) The ureter of the donated kidney is sutured to the bladder or to the patient's ureter.

The patient must be free of infection and cancers at the time of renal transplantation because medications to prevent transplant rejection suppress the immune response, leaving the patient at risk for infection. Therefore, the patient is evaluated and treated for any infections, including gingival (gum) disease and dental caries.

A psychosocial evaluation is conducted to assess the patient's ability to adjust to the transplant, coping styles, social history, social support available, and financial resources. A history of psychiatric illness is important to obtain because psychiatric conditions are often aggravated by the corticosteroids needed for immunosuppression after transplantation. If a dialysis routine has been established, hemodialysis is often performed the day before the scheduled transplantation procedure to optimize the patient's physical status. However, immediate transplant prior to initiation of dialysis results in better graft survival (Resende, Guerra, Santana et al., 2009).

The nursing aspects of preoperative care for the patient undergoing renal transplant are similar to those for patients undergoing other types of elective abdominal surgery. Preoperative teaching addresses postoperative pulmonary hygiene, pain management options, dietary restrictions, IV and arterial lines, tubes, such as an indwelling catheter and possibly a nasogastric tube, and early ambulation. The patient who receives a kidney from a living related donor may be concerned about the donor and how the donor will tolerate the surgical procedure.

Most patients have been on dialysis for months or years before transplantation. Many have waited months to years for a kidney transplant and are anxious about the surgery, possible rejection, and the need to return to dialysis. Helping the patient to deal with these concerns is part of the nurse's role in preoperative management, as is teaching the patient about what to expect after surgery. A plan of nursing care for a patient undergoing kidney surgery is available online at http://thePoint.lww.com/Pellico1e.

Postoperative Management

The goal of care is to maintain homeostasis until the transplanted kidney is functioning well. The patient whose kidney functions immediately has a more favorable prognosis than does the patient whose kidney does not.

Administering Drug Therapy

The survival of a transplanted kidney depends on the ability to prevent the body's immune response to the transplanted kidney. To overcome or minimize the body's defense mechanism, immunosuppressive agents are administered. Corticosteroids are initially part of the immunosuppression regimen, but are frequently tapered due to long-term side effects (Matas, 2007). Cyclosporine is available in a microemulsion form (Neoral) that delivers the medication reliably, thus producing a steady-state serum concentration. Tacrolimus (Prograf) is similar to cyclosporine and about 100 times

more potent. Mycophenolate mofetil (CellCept), sirolimus (Rapamune), and antithymocyte globulin (Thymoglobulin), as well as tacrolimus, are used in various combinations to prevent transplant rejection. Treatment with combinations of these new agents has dramatically improved survival rates (Aschenbrenner & Venable, 2009).

Doses of corticosteroid agents are gradually tapered over a period of several weeks, depending on the patient's immunologic response to the transplant. Corticosteroids may be discontinued; however, the patient is required to take some form of immunosuppressive therapy for the entire time that he or she has the transplanted kidney.

The side effects and risks associated with these medications include nephrotoxicity, hypertension, hyperlipidemia, hirsutism, tremor, and several types of cancers (Ashenbrenner & Venable, 2009).

Assessing the Patient for Transplant Rejection

After kidney transplantation, the nurse assesses the patient for signs and symptoms of transplant rejection: oliguria, edema, fever, increasing BP, weight gain, and swelling or tenderness over the transplanted kidney or graft. Leukocytosis, and increasing BUN and creatinine levels should be evaluated. Patients receiving cyclosporine may not exhibit the usual signs and symptoms of acute rejection. In these patients, the only sign may be an asymptomatic rise in the serum creatinine level (a >20% rise is considered acute rejection). Box 27-11 discusses renal transplant rejection and infection.

Preventing Infection

The patient is closely monitored for infection because of susceptibility to impaired healing and infection related to immunosuppressive therapy and complications of renal failure. Clinical manifestations of infection include shaking chills, fever, tachycardia, and tachypnea, as well as either an increase or a decrease in WBCs (leukocytosis or leukopenia).

Infection may be introduced through the urinary tract, the respiratory tract, the surgical site, or other sources. Urine cultures are performed frequently because of the high incidence of bacteriuria during early and late stages of transplantation. Any type of wound drainage should be viewed as a potential source of infection because drainage is an excellent culture medium for bacteria. Catheter and drain tips should be cut with sterile scissors, placed in a sterile container, and sent to the laboratory for culture.

The nurse ensures that the patient is protected from exposure to infection by hospital staff, visitors, and other patients with active infections. Careful hand hygiene by all who come in contact with the patient is imperative.

Monitoring Urinary Function

A kidney from a living donor related to the patient usually begins to function immediately after surgery and may produce large quantities of dilute urine. A kidney from a cadaver

BOX 27-11 **Renal Transplant Rejection and Infection**

Renal graft rejection and failure may occur immediately (hyperacute), within the first 2 weeks, or later. Failure is potentially reversible (acute), or the transplanted kidney may steadily lose function after many years (chronic). It is not uncommon for rejection to occur during the first year after transplantation.

Detecting Rejection
Ultrasonography may be used to detect enlargement of the kidney; percutaneous renal biopsy (most reliable) and X-ray techniques are used to evaluate transplant rejection. If the body rejects the transplanted kidney, the patient needs to return to dialysis. The rejected kidney might not be removed, depending on the risk for infection if the kidney is left in place.

Potential Infection
About 75% of kidney transplant recipients have at least one episode of infection in the first year after transplantation because of immunosuppressant therapy. Immunosuppressants of the past made the transplant recipient more vulnerable to opportunistic infections (candidiasis, cytomegalovirus, *Pneumocystis* pneumonia) and infection with other relatively nonpathogenic viruses, fungi, and protozoa, which can be a major hazard. Cyclosporine therapy has reduced the incidence of opportunistic infections because it selectively exerts its effect, sparing T cells that protect the patient from life-threatening infections. In addition, combination immunosuppressant therapy and improved clinical care have produced 1-year patient survival rates approaching 100% and graft survival exceeding 90%. Infections, however, remain a major cause of death at all points in time for kidney transplant recipients (Danovitch, 2005).

donor may undergo acute tubular necrosis and therefore may not function for 2 or 3 weeks, during which time anuria, oliguria, or polyuria may be present. During this stage, the patient may experience significant changes in fluid and electrolyte status. Therefore, careful monitoring of hourly urine output should be performed. IV fluids are administered on the basis of urine volume and serum electrolyte levels and as prescribed by the provider. Hemodialysis may be necessary postoperatively to maintain homeostasis until the transplanted kidney is functioning well.

Addressing Psychological Concerns

The rejection of a transplanted kidney remains a matter of great concern to the patient, the family, and the health care team. The fears of kidney rejection and the complications of immunosuppressive therapy, which include Cushing's syndrome, diabetes, capillary fragility, osteoporosis, glaucoma, cataracts, acne, and nephrotoxicity, place tremendous psychological stresses on the patient. Anxiety and uncertainty about the future and difficult post-transplantation adjustment are often sources of stress for the patient and family.

An important nursing function is the assessment of the patient's stress and coping. The nurse uses each visit with the patient to determine if the patient and family are coping effectively and that the patient is adhering to the prescribed medication regimen. If indicated or requested, the nurse refers the patient for counseling.

Monitoring and Managing Potential Complications

The patient undergoing kidney transplantation is at risk for the postoperative complications that are associated with any surgical procedure. In addition, the patient's physical condition may be compromised because of the complications associated with longstanding renal failure and its treatment. Therefore, careful assessment for the complications related to renal failure and corticosteroid use, such as poor wound healing, are important aspects of nursing care.

GI ulceration and corticosteroid-induced bleeding may occur. Fungal colonization of the GI tract, especially the mouth and urinary bladder, may occur secondary to corticosteroid and antibiotic therapy. Closely monitoring the patient and notifying the provider about the occurrence of these complications are important nursing interventions. In addition, the patient is monitored closely for signs and symptoms of adrenal insufficiency if the treatment has included use of corticosteroids.

Teaching Patients Self-Care

The nurse works closely with the patient and family to be sure that they understand the need for continuing immunosuppressive therapy as prescribed. Additionally, the patient and family are instructed to assess for and report signs and symptoms of transplant rejection, infection, or significant adverse effects of the immunosuppressive regimen. These include decreased urine output; weight gain; malaise; fever; respiratory distress; tenderness over the transplanted kidney; anxiety; depression; changes in eating, drinking, or other habits; and changes in BP. The patient is instructed to inform other health care providers (e.g., dentist) about the kidney transplant and the use of immunosuppressive agents.

Continuing Care

Follow-up care with the transplant team is a life-long necessity. Individual verbal and written instructions are provided concerning diet, medication, fluids, daily weight, daily measurement of urine, management of intake and output, prevention of infection, resumption of activity, and avoidance of contact sports in which the transplanted kidney may be injured. Cardiovascular disease is the major cause of morbidity and mortality after transplantation, due in part to the increasing age of patients with transplants.

Malignancy develops more frequently in patients receiving long-term immunosuppressive. Post-transplant patients are at risk for skin cancers; risk for malignant melanoma is up to 8 times higher, and for squamous cell carcinoma, up to 250 times higher than in the general population (Feuerstein & Geller, 2008). The patient is reminded of the importance of health promotion activities such as using sunscreen and health screenings, including regular PAP smears, mammogram, colonoscopy, and breast or testicular self-examination as appropriate.

The American Association of Kidney Patients (see Resources) is a nonprofit organization that serves the needs of those with kidney disease. It can provide many helpful suggestions for patients and family members learning to cope with dialysis and transplantation.

RENAL TRAUMA

The kidneys are protected by the rib cage and musculature of the back posteriorly and by a cushion of abdominal wall and viscera anteriorly. They are highly mobile and are fixed only at the renal pedicle (stem of renal blood vessels and the ureter). With traumatic injury, the kidneys can be thrust against the lower ribs, resulting in contusion and rupture. Renal trauma occurs in approximately 10% of abdominal injuries, and 90% of renal trauma is due to blunt injury. The nurse should suspect renal injury when the patient presents with blunt abdominal or penetrating flank and back wounds; up to 80% of patients with renal trauma have associated injuries of other internal organs (Perrin, 2009).

Injuries may be blunt (automobile and motorcycle collisions, falls, athletic injuries, assaults) or penetrating (gunshot wounds, stabbings). Blunt renal trauma accounts for 80% to 90% of all renal injuries; penetrating renal trauma accounts for the remaining 10% to 20% (McQuillan, Makic, & Whalen, 2009). Blunt renal trauma is classified into one of four groups, as follows:

- *Contusion:* Bruises or hemorrhages under the renal capsule; capsule and collecting system intact
- *Minor laceration:* Superficial disruption of the cortex; renal medulla and collecting system are not involved
- *Major laceration:* Parenchymal disruption extending into cortex and medulla, possibly involving the collecting system
- *Vascular injury:* Tears of renal artery or vein

The most common renal injuries are contusions, lacerations, ruptures, and renal pedicle injuries or small internal lacerations of the kidney (Fig. 27-9). The kidneys receive half of the blood flow from the abdominal aorta; therefore, even a fairly small renal laceration can produce massive bleeding. The nurse should consider hemorrhage is present when gross hematuria or microscopic hematuria with a BP of less than 90 mm HG is present (McQuillan et al., 2009).

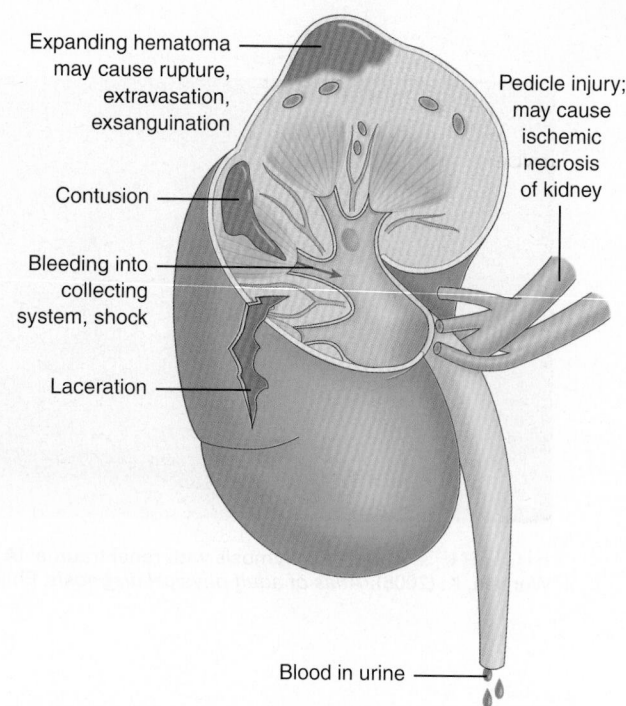

FIGURE 27-9 Types and pathophysiologic effects of renal injuries: contusions, lacerations, rupture, and pedicle injury.

Clinical Manifestations and Assessment

Clinical manifestations renal injury includes pain, renal colic (due to blood clots or fragments obstructing the collecting system), hematuria, mass or swelling in the flank, ecchymosis, and lacerations or wounds of the lateral abdomen and flank. While hematuria is the most common manifestation of renal trauma, there is no relationship between the degree of hematuria and the degree of injury.

The nurse assesses for ecchymosis over the flank (Grey-Turner's sign) and periumbilical area (Cullen's sign), as well as flank tenderness with palpation and gross hematuria (Fig. 27-10).

! NURSING ALERT
Grey-Turner's sign and Cullen's sign are associated with retroperitoneal bleeds.

Microscopic hematuria may be present, therefore evaluation of hemoglobin and hematocrit is critical. A CT scan of the abdomen may be done to assess penetrating trauma. Free air, injury to the kidney, or a penetrating object is assessed. Any patient with gross hematuria will most likely require surgery (Perrin, 2009).

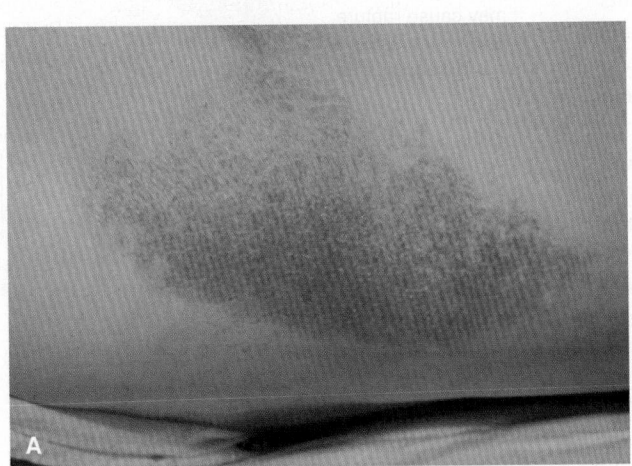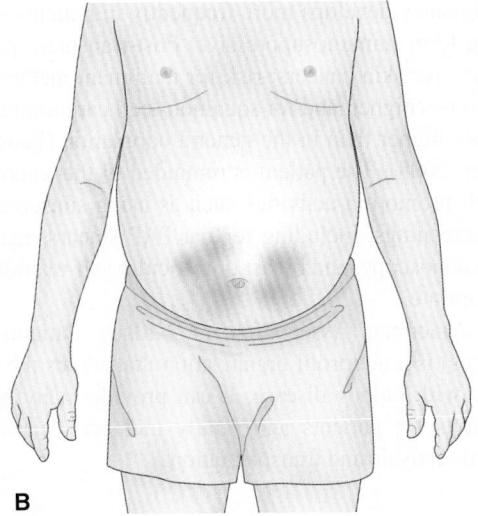

FIGURE 27-10 Ecchymosis with renal trauma. **(A)** Grey-Turner's sign. **(B)** Cullen's sign. **A** from Berg, D., & Worzala, K. (2006). *Atlas of adult physical diagnosis.* Philadelphia: Lippincott Williams & Wilkins.

Medical and Nursing Management

The goals of management in patients with renal trauma are to control hemorrhage, pain, prevent infection as well as to preserve and restore renal function. The patient is monitored for oliguria and signs of hemorrhagic shock, because a pedicle injury or shattered kidney can lead to rapid exsanguination and death. An expanding hematoma may cause rupture of the kidney capsule. A palpable flank or abdominal mass with local tenderness, swelling, and ecchymosis suggests renal hemorrhage. The area of the original mass can be outlined with a marking pen so that the examiner can evaluate the area for change.

Renal trauma is often associated with other injuries to nearby organs; therefore, the patient is assessed for skin abrasions, lacerations, and entry and exit wounds of the upper abdomen and lower thorax because these may be associated with renal injury. Trauma to the right kidney may be associated with liver injury while trauma to the left kidney may involve injury to the spleen. In rare cases, damage to the adrenal gland may result in adrenal insufficiency and death. The nurse should consider adrenal insufficiency when a patient receiving treatment for shock does not respond to fluid administration (McQuillan et al., 2009).

With a contusion of the kidney, healing may take place with conservative measures. If the patient has microscopic hematuria and a normal IV urogram, bedrest will allow the contusion to resolve with time (Perrin, 2009), and outpatient management is possible. If gross hematuria or a minor laceration is present, the patient is hospitalized and kept on bed rest until the hematuria clears. Antimicrobial medications may be prescribed to prevent infection from perirenal hematoma or urinoma (a cyst containing urine). Patients with retroperitoneal hematomas may develop low-grade fever as absorption of the clot takes place.

Surgical Management

In renal trauma, any sudden change in the patient's condition suggests hemorrhage and requires rapid surgical intervention within 12 hours to reestablish blood flow to the ischemic kidney (Perrin, 2009). The patient is often in shock and requires aggressive fluid resuscitation. The damaged kidney may have to be removed (nephrectomy).

Early postoperative complications (within 6 months) include rebleeding, perinephritic abscess formation, sepsis, urine extravasation, and fistula formation. Other complications include stone formation, infection or abscess, cysts, chronic pyelonephrosis, vascular aneurysms, and loss of renal function. Hypertension can be a complication of any renal surgery but usually is a late complication of renal injury.

The patient who has undergone surgery is instructed about care of the incision and the importance of an adequate fluid intake. In addition, instructions about changes that should be reported to the provider, such as fever, hematuria, flank pain, or any signs and symptoms of decreasing kidney function, are provided. Guidelines for gradually increasing activity, lifting, and driving are also provided in accordance with the provider's prescription.

Follow-up nursing care includes monitoring the BP to detect hypertension and advising the patient to restrict activities for about 1 month after trauma to minimize the incidence of delayed or secondary bleeding. The patient should be advised to schedule periodic follow-up assessments of renal function (creatinine clearance, BUN, and serum creatinine analyses). If a nephrectomy was necessary, the patient is advised to wear medical identification.

Gerontologic Considerations

Care for this population is essentially the same; however, the elderly may have chronic disease processes that must be considered. Older adults often have higher mortality follow-ing traumatic injury than do younger adults, including alter-ations in cardiac and respiratory systems that reduce physi-ologic reserve needed to respond to shock and hypoxia (Kaplow & Hardin, 2007; Perrin, 2009).

Chapter Review

Critical Thinking Exercises

1. As primary nurse for a 50-year-old man with renal fail-ure secondary to poorly controlled diabetes, develop a teaching plan to explain the different types of renal re-placement therapies. Include the level of involvement on the part of the patient and family for self management required for each. How would you modify the approach if the patient is distraught and does not seem to hear what you are saying?

2. A 45-year-old married woman with three teenage chil-dren visits the nephrology department to discuss options for dealing with her ESRD. Her healthy twin sister wants to donate her kidney, and the preliminary reports show that a match is possible. The patient states that she does not want her sister to go through the process of kidney donation if dialysis is possible. Identify the pros and cons of her wishes based on current evidence regarding out-comes of dialysis compared to kidney transplantation.

3. You are treating a 35-year-old woman who is in the emergency department following a motor vehicle crash; she is complaining of severe left-sided flank pain. Iden-tify possible causes of her pain and laboratory tests that would be indicated. What nursing assessment and inter-ventions should you make at this time? What explana-tions would you give the patient while awaiting the results of laboratory tests?

NCLEX–Style Review Questions

1. Which of the following assessment findings would the nurse anticipate in a patient with ARF?
   A. Hypomagnesemia
   B. Hypercalcemia
   C. Hyperkalemia
   D. Hyperchloremia

2. When caring for the patient with chronic renal failure, the nurse teaches the patient to manage his diet by avoiding which of the following foods?
   A. Green leafy vegetables and citrus
   B. Apples and pears
   C. Proteins of high biologic value
   D. Oat-, wheat-, and rye-containing products

3. The nurse recognizes the patient will recognize the signs and symptoms of renal transplant rejection when the patient states he will monitor for which of the following?
   A. Thrill and bruit over the fistula
   B. Weight gain and fever
   C. Palpitations and thirst
   D. Flank pain and pyuria

4. When planning care for the patient with kidney trauma, the nurse notifies the physician immediately for which of the following?
   A. Laboratory reports microscopic hematuria
   B. Tachycardia and hypotension
   C. Patient is upset and crying
   D. Scar noted on patient's left flank

5. Which of the following reflects appropriate teaching to prevent long-term complications for the patient with nephrotic syndrome?
   A. Observe for dark urine and clay-colored stool.
   B. Void every 2 hours on schedule.
   C. Avoid driving at night.
   D. Minimize your intake of saturated fat.

Try these additional resources to enhance your learning and understanding of this chapter:
- thePoint online resource available at **http://thepoint.lww.com/Pellico1e**
- *Handbook for Focus on Adult Health: Medical-Surgical Nursing*
- *Study Guide for Focus on Adult Health: Medical-Surgical Nursing*

References and Selected Readings

References and selected readings associated with this chapter can be found on the website that accompanies the book. Visit http://thepoint.lww.com/Pellico1e to access the references and other additional resources associated with this chapter.

Nursing Management: Patients With Urinary Disorders

SUSANNE A. QUALLICH
MICHELLE J. LAJINESS

Learning Objectives

After reading this chapter, you will be able to:

1. Identify factors contributing to upper and lower urinary tract infections (UTIs).

2. Describe nursing care of the patient with a UTI.

3. Differentiate between the various adult dysfunctional voiding patterns.

4. Develop a patient education plan for a patient who has mixed (stress and urge) urinary incontinence.

5. Identify potential causes of an obstruction of the urinary tract, and management of the patient with this condition.

6. Develop a teaching plan for the patient undergoing treatment for renal calculi (kidney stones).

7. Discuss the available options for management of urinary cancers.

8. Identify issues relevant to the initial management of trauma to the urinary tract.

9. Identify issues important to patient self-care of urinary diversions.

The urinary system is responsible for providing the route for drainage of urine formed by the kidneys. Nursing requires an understanding of the anatomy, physiology, diagnostic testing, nursing care, and rehabilitation of patients with the multiple processes that interfere with the urinary system. This chapter focuses on the nursing management of patients with common urinary conditions.

INFECTIONS OF THE URINARY TRACT

Urinary tract infections (UTIs) are caused by pathogenic microorganisms in the urinary tract (the normal urinary tract is sterile above the urethra). Lower UTIs include bacterial **cystitis** (inflammation of the bladder), bacterial **prostatitis** (inflammation of the prostate), and bacterial **urethritis** (inflammation of the urethra). Acute or chronic nonbacterial causes of inflammation in any of these areas can be misdiagnosed as bacterial infections. Upper UTIs are much less common and include acute or chronic **pyelonephritis** (inflammation of the kidney and renal pelvis), interstitial nephritis (inflammation of the spaces between the kidney tubules), and renal abscesses (pus-filled cavity of the kidney). Upper and lower UTIs are further classified as uncomplicated or complicated, depending on other patient-related conditions (Box 28-1) (e.g., whether the UTI is recurrent and the duration of the infection). Most uncomplicated UTIs are community-acquired, while complicated UTIs usually occur in people with urologic abnormalities, comorbidities such as diabetes, or recent catheterization.

A UTI is the second most common reason patients seek health care (Porth & Matfin, 2009). Most cases occur in women; one out of every five women in the United States will develop a UTI sometime during her lifetime. The urinary tract is the most common site of nosocomial infection, accounting for greater than 3% of the total number reported by hospitals each year (Centers for Disease Control and Prevention [CDC], 2009). In most of these hospital-acquired UTIs, instrumentation of the urinary tract or catheterization is the precipitating cause. Approximately 7 million patients are diagnosed with UTIs in the United States annually, representing an expenditure over $1 billion in direct heath care costs (Gray & Moore, 2009). This amount does not include the indirect costs associated with time lost from work and the negative impact on the person's lifestyle.

Classifying Urinary Tract Infections

Urinary tract infections (UTIs) are classified by location: the lower urinary tract (which includes the bladder and structures below the bladder) or the upper urinary tract (which includes the kidneys and ureters). They can also be classified as uncomplicated or complicated UTIs.

Lower UTIs
Cystitis, prostatitis, urethritis

Upper UTIs
Acute pyelonephritis, chronic pyelonephritis, renal abscess, interstitial nephritis, perirenal abscess

Uncomplicated Lower or Upper UTIs
Community-acquired infection; common in young women and not usually recurrent

Complicated Lower or Upper UTIs
Often nosocomial (acquired in the hospital) and related to catheterization; occur in patients with urologic abnormalities, pregnancy, immunosuppression, diabetes mellitus, and obstructions and are often recurrent

LOWER URINARY TRACT INFECTIONS

Pathophysiology

For infection to occur, bacteria must gain access to the bladder, attach to and colonize the epithelium of the urinary tract, evade host defense mechanisms, and initiate inflammation. Many UTIs result from fecal organisms that ascend from the perineum to the urethra and the bladder and then adhere to the mucosal surfaces.

Bacterial Invasion of the Urinary Tract

By increasing the normal slow shedding of bladder epithelial cells (resulting in bacteria removal), the bladder can clear even large numbers of bacteria. Glycosaminoglycan (GAG), a hydrophilic protein, normally exerts a nonadherent protective effect against various bacteria by attracting water molecules and forming a water barrier that serves as a defensive layer between the bladder and the urine. GAG may be impaired by certain agents (cyclamate, saccharin, aspartame, and tryptophan metabolites). The normal bacterial flora of the vagina and urethral area also interfere with adherence of *Escherichia coli*.

Reflux

An obstruction to free-flowing urine is a problem known as **urethrovesical reflux**, which is the reflux of urine from the urethra into the bladder (Fig. 28-1). With coughing, sneezing, or straining, the bladder pressure increases, which may force urine from the bladder into the urethra. When the pressure returns to normal, the urine flows back into the bladder, bringing into the bladder bacteria from the anterior portions of the urethra. Urethrovesical reflux is also caused by dysfunction of the bladder neck or urethra. The urethrovesical angle and urethral closure pressure may be altered with menopause, increasing the incidence of infection in postmenopausal women.

Ureterovesical or **vesicoureteral reflux** refers to the backward flow of urine from the bladder into one or both ureters (see Fig. 28-1). The ureters tunnel into the bladder wall, so that the bladder musculature compresses a small portion of the ureter during normal voiding. When the ureterovesical valve is impaired by congenital causes or ureteral abnormalities, the bacteria may reach the kidneys (Porth & Matfin, 2009).

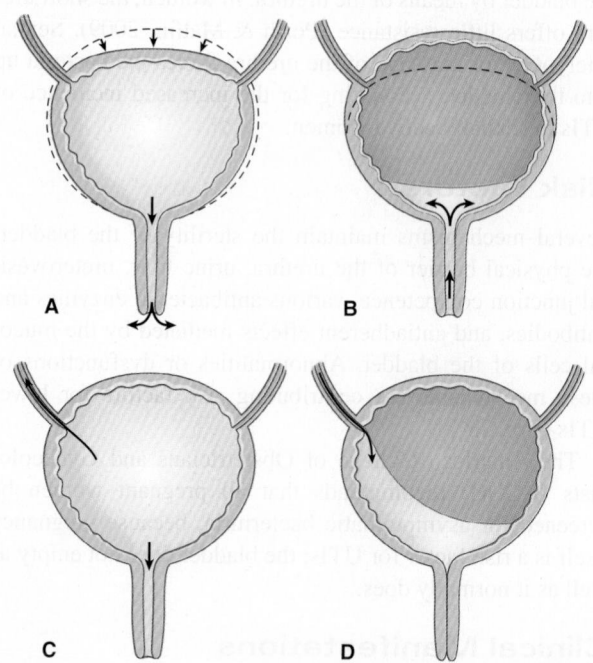

FIGURE 28-1 Mechanisms of urethrovesical and ureterovesical reflux may cause urinary tract infection. Urethrovesical reflux: With coughing and straining, bladder pressure rises, which may force urine from the bladder into the urethra. **(A)** When bladder pressure returns to normal, the urine flows back to the bladder **(B)**, which introduces bacteria from the urethra to the bladder. Ureterovesical reflux: With failure of the ureterovesical valve, urine moves up the ureters during voiding **(C)** and flows into the bladder when voiding stops **(D)**. This prevents complete emptying of the bladder. It also leads to urinary stasis and contamination of the ureters with bacteria-laden urine.

Uropathogenic Bacteria

Bacteriuria is generally defined as more than 10^5 colonies of bacteria per milliliter of urine, which distinguishes true bacteriuria from contamination, and is a major criterion for infection (Porth & Matfin, 2009). Because urine samples (especially in women) are commonly contaminated by the bacteria normally present in the urethral area, a bacterial count exceeding 10^5 colonies/mL of clean-catch midstream urine is the measure that distinguishes true bacteriuria from contamination. In men, contamination of the collected urine sample occurs less frequently. The organisms most frequently responsible for UTIs are those normally found in the lower gastrointestinal (GI) tract. In a large-scale study of the types and prevalence of organisms of patients with UTIs in both the community and hospital, *E. coli* was responsible for 54.7% of UTIs (Porth & Matfin, 2009).

Routes of Infection

Bacteria enter the urinary tract in three well-recognized ways: by the transurethral route (ascending infection), through the bloodstream (hematogenous spread), or by means of a fistula (direct extension). The most common route of infection is transurethral, in which bacteria (often from fecal contamination) colonize the periurethral area and subsequently enter the bladder by means of the urethra. In women, the short urethra offers little resistance (Porth & Matfin, 2009). Sexual intercourse or massage of the urethra forces the bacteria up into the bladder, accounting for the increased incidence of UTIs in sexually active women.

Risk Factors

Several mechanisms maintain the sterility of the bladder: the physical barrier of the urethra, urine flow, ureterovesical junction competence, various antibacterial enzymes and antibodies, and antiadherent effects mediated by the mucosal cells of the bladder. Abnormalities or dysfunctions of these mechanisms are contributing risk factors for lower UTIs (Box 28-2).

The American College of Obstetricians and Gynecologists (ACOG) recommends that all pregnant women be screened for asymptomatic bacteriuria, because pregnancy itself is a risk factor for UTIs; the bladder does not empty as well as it normally does.

Clinical Manifestations and Assessment

Signs and Symptoms

A variety of signs and symptoms are associated with UTI but about half of all patients with bacteriuria have no symptoms. Signs and symptoms of an uncomplicated lower UTI include **dysuria** (painful or difficult urination), burning on urination, **frequency**, urgency, **nocturia** (excessive urination at night), incontinence, and suprapubic or pelvic pain. Hematuria (bloody urine) and back pain may also be

BOX 28-2

Risk Factors for Urinary Tract Infection

- Inability or failure to empty the bladder completely
- Obstructed urinary flow:
  Congenital abnormalities
  Urethral strictures
  Contracture of the bladder neck
  Bladder tumors
  Calculi (stones) in the ureters or kidneys
  Compression of the ureters
  Neurologic abnormalities
- Decreased natural host defenses or immunosuppression
- Instrumentation of the urinary tract (e.g., catheterization, cystoscopic procedures)
- Inflammation or abrasion of the urethral mucosa
- Contributing conditions:
  Diabetes mellitus (increased urinary glucose levels create an infection-prone environment in the urinary tract)
  Pregnancy
  Neurologic disorders
  Gout
  Altered states caused by incomplete emptying of the bladder and urinary stasis

present (Bickley, 2009). In older people, these symptoms are less common.

> **NURSING ALERT**
> *Elderly patients often lack the typical symptoms of UTI and sepsis. Although frequency, urgency, and dysuria may occur, nonspecific symptoms, such as altered sensorium, lethargy, anorexia, new incontinence, hyperventilation, and low-grade fever, may be the only clues.*

In patients with complicated UTIs, such as those with indwelling catheters, manifestations can range from asymptomatic bacteriuria to gram-negative sepsis with shock. Complicated UTIs often are due to a broader spectrum of organisms, have a lower response rate to treatment, and tend to recur. Many patients with catheter-associated UTIs are asymptomatic; however, any patient with a catheter who suddenly develops signs and symptoms of septic shock should be evaluated for **urosepsis**. The kidneys receive approximately 25% of the cardiac output every minute. When a patient has pyelonephritis, the infection is in the kidney parenchyma and can travel from the kidney into the bloodstream, which is termed *bacteremia*. *Septicemia* is the clinical syndrome associated with the bacteremia that results in vasodilatation, microvascular permeability, and massive inflammatory response. Nurses should be alert for signs and symptoms of urosepsis, including hypothermia or hyperthermia, tachycardia, tachypnea, leukocytosis or leukopenia, and

greater than 10% immature (band) forms (bands are immature neutrophils that contain a nucleus, indicating infection). Under normal circumstances only 1% to 3% of neutrophils are band forms (Fishbach & Dunning, 2009). Refer to Chapter 54 for further discussion of sepsis and septic shock.

Diagnostic Tests

Results of various tests such as urine cultures and sensitivities help confirm the diagnosis of UTI. In an uncomplicated UTI, the strain of bacteria determines the antibiotic of choice. Urine cultures are useful for documenting a UTI and can identify the specific organism present. UTI and subsequent sepsis can occur with lower bacterial colony counts. About one-third of women with symptoms of acute infections have negative midstream urine culture results and may go untreated if 10^5 colony-forming unit (CFU)/mL is used as the only criterion for infection. The presence of any bacteria in specimens obtained by catheterization (insertion of a tube into the urinary bladder) is considered indicative of infection.

The following groups of patients may need urine cultures when bacteriuria is present:

- All men (because of the likelihood of structural or functional abnormalities)
- Women with a history of compromised immune function or renal problems
- Patients with diabetes mellitus
- Patients who have undergone recent instrumentation (including catheterization) of the urinary tract
- Patients who have been recently hospitalized or who live in long-term care facilities

- Patients with prolonged or persistent symptoms
- Patients with three or more UTIs in the past year
- Pregnant women
- Postmenopausal women

A multiple-test dipstick often includes testing for white blood cells (WBCs), known as the *leukocyte esterase test*, and nitrite testing (Griess nitrate reduction test). If the leukocyte esterase test is positive, it is assumed that the patient has pyuria (pus in the urine), since esterase is an enzyme released from WBCs; a UTI is suspected and should be treated. The Griess nitrate reduction test is considered positive if bacteria that reduce normal urinary nitrates to nitrites are present.

Tests for sexually transmitted diseases infections (STIs) may be performed (see Chapter 35) because acute urethritis caused by sexually transmitted organisms or acute vaginitis infections may be responsible for symptoms similar to those of UTIs.

Imaging studies are rarely indicated for the evaluation of UTIs, except with suspected anatomic issues or if additional pathology, such as renal lithiasis (stone formation or calculi) or fistula (a false track or abnormal passageway), is suspected.

Medical and Nursing Management

Management of UTIs typically involves pharmacologic therapy and patient education. The nurse teaches the patient about medication regimens and infection prevention measures (Box 28-3).

BOX 28-3 **Patient Education**

Preventing Recurrent Urinary Tract Infections

Hygiene

- Shower rather than bathe in tub because bacteria in the bath water may enter the urethra.
- After each bowel movement, clean the perineum and urethral meatus from front to back. This will help reduce concentrations of pathogens at the urethral opening and, in women, the vaginal opening.

Fluid Intake

- Drink liberal amounts of fluids daily to flush out bacteria.
- Avoid coffee, tea, colas, alcohol, and other fluids that are urinary tract irritants.

Voiding Habits

- Void every 2 to 3 hours during the day and completely empty the bladder. This prevents overdistention of the bladder and compromised blood supply to the bladder wall. Both predispose the patient to UTI. Precautions expressly for women include voiding immediately after sexual intercourse.

Therapy

- Take medication *exactly* as prescribed.
- If bacteria continue to appear in the urine, long-term antimicrobial therapy may be required to prevent colonization of the periurethral area and recurrence of infection.
- Special timing of administration may be required.
- For recurrent infection, consider acidification of the urine through ascorbic acid (vitamin C), 1,000 mg daily, or cranberry juice.
- If prescribed, test urine for presence of bacteria following manufacturer's and health care provider's instructions.
- Notify the primary health care provider if fever occurs or if signs and symptoms persist.
- Consult the primary health care provider regularly for follow-up.

Initial Pharmacologic Therapy

The ideal medication for treatment of UTI is an antibacterial agent that eradicates bacteria from the urinary tract with minimal effects on GI and vaginal flora, minimizing the incidence of vaginal yeast infections. (Yeast vaginitis occurs in as many as 25% of patients treated with antimicrobial agents that affect vaginal flora, causes more symptoms, and is more difficult and, thus, more costly to treat than the UTI). The antibacterial agent should be affordable, have few adverse effects, and produce low resistance in the targeted organisms. Because the organism in initial, uncomplicated UTIs is most likely *E. coli* or other fecal flora, the agent should be effective against these organisms.

Various treatment regimens have been successful in treating uncomplicated lower UTIs in women: single-dose administration, short-course (3 to 4 days) regimens, or 7- to 10-day regimens. The trend is toward a shortened course of antibiotic therapy for uncomplicated UTIs, because most cases are cured after 3 days of treatment (Zonderman & Doyle, 2006). Phenazopyridine, a urinary analgesic, may be prescribed to relieve the discomfort associated with the infection (Zonderman & Doyle, 2006). Patients should be informed that their urine will turn dark orange with this medication. Regardless of the regimen prescribed, the patient is instructed to take all the doses prescribed, even if relief of symptoms occurs promptly.

A fluoroquinolone is a routine choice for short-course therapy of uncomplicated, mild to moderate UTIs. There is high patient adherence (95.6%) to the 3-day regimen and a high eradication rate (96.4%) for all pathogens. Before using a fluoroquinolone in patients with complicated UTIs, the causative pathogen should be identified; fluoroquinolone is used only when generic and less costly antibiotics are likely to be ineffective (Zonderman & Doyle, 2006).

Nitrofurantoin should not be used in patients with renal insufficiency because it is ineffective at glomerular filtration rates of less than 50 mL/min, and may cause peripheral neuropathy.

In a complicated UTI (i.e., pyelonephritis), the general treatment of choice is usually a cephalosporin or an ampicillin/aminoglycoside combination; ideally, the choice is based on culture results. Patients in institutional settings may require 7 to 10 days of medication for the treatment to be effective. Medications such as ampicillin or amoxicillin can be used, but *E. coli* has developed resistance. Because of this problem of resistance, the fluoroquinolone ciprofloxacin is often used as a first-line agent (Tanagho & McAninch, 2007). Longer medication courses are indicated for men, pregnant women, and women with pyelonephritis and other types of complicated UTIs. Hospitalization and IV antibiotics are occasionally needed.

Long-Term Pharmacologic Therapy

Although brief pharmacologic treatment of UTIs for 3 days is usually adequate in women, infection recurs in about 20% of women treated for uncomplicated UTIs. Infections that recur within 2 weeks of therapy do so because organisms of the original offending strain remain in the vagina. Relapses suggest that the source of bacteriuria may be the upper urinary tract or that initial treatment was inadequate or administered for too short a time. Recurrent infections in men are usually due to persistence of the same organism; further evaluation and treatment are indicated.

If infection recurs after completing antimicrobial therapy, another short course (3 to 4 days) of full-dose antimicrobial therapy, followed by a regular bedtime dose of an antimicrobial agent may be prescribed. In addition, continuous prophylaxis via a 4- to 12-month course of antibiotics may be considered, either nightly or every other night (Tanagho & McAninch, 2007). Long-term use of antimicrobial agents decreases the risk of reinfection and may be indicated in patients with recurrent infections. Choice of antibiotic will be based upon the organism involved, previous UTI strains, and allergic drug history of the patient. Development of microbial resistance to prolonged antibiotic administration is always a concern, therefore the nurse is alert for signs and symptoms of a UTI despite antibiotic therapy.

Reinfection with new bacteria is the reason for more than 90% of recurrent UTIs in women. If the diagnostic evaluation reveals no structural abnormalities in the urinary tract, the woman with recurrent UTIs may be instructed to begin treatment on her own whenever symptoms occur and to contact her health care provider only when symptoms persist, fever occurs, or the number of treatment episodes exceeds four in a 6-month period (Guay, 2009).

If recurrence is caused by persistent bacteria from preceding infections, the cause (i.e., kidney stone, abscess) must be treated. After treatment and sterilization of the urine, low-dose preventive therapy (trimethoprim with or without sulfamethoxazole) each night at bedtime may be prescribed. Finally, for those women who develop UTI after sexual intercourse, postcoital prophylaxis with low-dose antimicrobials may be prescribed.

The patient is encouraged to drink liberal amounts of fluids (water is the best choice) to promote renal blood flow and to flush the bacteria from the urinary tract. Current evidence about the effectiveness of daily intake of cranberry juice to prevent UTIs is inconclusive (Jepson & Craig, 2008). Patients who like cranberry juice can be encouraged to include it in their increased fluid intake that will assist to flush bacteria (Dudek, 2006). Urinary tract irritants (e.g., coffee, tea, citrus, spices, colas, alcohol) are avoided.

The pain associated with UTI is quickly relieved once effective antimicrobial therapy is initiated. Analgesic agents and the application of heat to the perineum help relieve pain and spasm. Frequent voiding (every 2 to 3 hours) is encouraged to empty the bladder completely because this can significantly lower urine bacterial counts, reduce urinary stasis, and prevent reinfection.

Gerontologic Considerations

The incidence of bacteriuria in the elderly differs from that in younger adults. Bacteriuria increases with age and disability, and women are affected more frequently than men. UTI is the most common cause of acute bacterial sepsis in patients older than 65 years, in whom gram-negative sepsis carries a mortality rate exceeding 50%. Urologists see many asymptomatic older patients with bacteriuria, and 20% are women older than 65 years. In long-term care facilities, up to 50% of females have asymptomatic bacteriuria (Newman & Wein, 2009). When indwelling catheters are used, the risk for UTI increases dramatically.

In the elderly population at large, structural abnormalities secondary to decreased bladder tone and neurogenic bladder secondary to stroke or autonomic neuropathy of diabetes may prevent complete emptying of the bladder and increase the risk for UTI (Newman & Wein, 2009). Elderly women often have incomplete emptying of the bladder and urinary stasis. In the absence of estrogen, postmenopausal women are susceptible to colonization and increased adherence of bacteria to the vagina and urethra. Oral or topical estrogen has been used to restore the glycogen content of vaginal epithelial cells and an acidic pH for some postmenopausal women with recurrent cystitis.

The antibacterial activity of prostatic secretions that protect men from bacterial colonization of the urethra and bladder decreases with aging. Although UTIs are rare in men, the prevalence of infection in men older than 50 years approaches that of women in the same age group. The increase of UTIs in men as they age is due largely to prostatic hyperplasia, strictures of the urethra, and neuropathic bladder. Catheterization may also contribute to the higher incidence of UTI in this group. The incidence of bacteriuria increases in men with confusion, dementia, or bowel or bladder incontinence. The most common cause of recurrent UTIs in elderly males is chronic bacterial prostatitis. In institutionalized elderly patients, such as those in long-term care facilities, infecting pathogens are often resistant to many antibiotics.

Diligent hand hygiene, careful perineal care, and frequent toileting may decrease the incidence of UTIs seen in patients in long-term care facilities. The organisms responsible for UTIs in the institutionalized elderly may differ from those found in patients residing in the community; this may be due to the frequent use of antibiotic agents by patients in long-term care facilities. *E. coli* is the most common organism seen in elderly patients in the community or hospital. However, patients with indwelling catheters are more likely to be infected with *Proteus, Klebsiella, Pseudomonas,* or *Staphylococcus* species. Patients who have been previously treated with antibiotics may be infected with *Enterococcus* species. Controversy continues about the need for treatment of asymptomatic bacteriuria in institutionalized elderly patients, because resulting antibiotic-resistant organisms and sepsis may be greater threats to patients. Treatment reg-

imens are generally the same as those for younger adults, although age-related changes in the intestinal absorption of medications and decreased renal function and hepatic flow may necessitate alterations in dose.

UPPER URINARY TRACT INFECTIONS

Pyelonephritis is a bacterial infection of the renal pelvis, tubules, and interstitial tissue of one or both kidneys. Causes involve either the ascending spread of bacteria from the bladder or proliferation of bacteria from systemic sources reaching the kidney via the bloodstream. It is not uncommon for bacteria that are causing a bladder infection to ascend into the kidney, causing pyelonephritis. An incompetent ureterovesical valve or obstruction occurring in the urinary tract increases the susceptibility of the kidneys to infection (see Fig. 28-1) because static urine provides a good medium for bacterial growth. Bladder tumors, strictures, benign prostatic hyperplasia (BPH), and urinary stones are some potential causes of obstruction that can lead to infections.

Pyelonephritis may be acute or chronic. Acute pyelonephritis is usually manifested by enlarged kidneys with interstitial infiltrations of inflammatory cells. Abscesses may be noted on the renal capsule and at the corticomedullary junction. Atrophy and destruction of tubules and the glomeruli may result. When pyelonephritis becomes chronic, the kidneys become scarred, contracted, nonfunctional, and cause chronic kidney disease that can result in the need for therapies such as transplantation or dialysis.

ACUTE PYELONEPHRITIS

More than 250,000 cases of acute pyelonephritis occur in the United States each year, with 100,000 patients requiring hospitalization.

Clinical Manifestations and Assessment

The patient with acute pyelonephritis is acutely ill with chills, fever, leukocytosis (elevated WBCs), bacteriuria, and pyuria. Low back pain, flank pain, nausea and vomiting, headache, malaise, and painful urination are common findings. Physical examination reveals pain and tenderness in the area of the costovertebral angle (see Chapter 26, Fig. 26-6). In addition, symptoms of lower urinary tract involvement, such as dysuria and frequency, are common. An ultrasound study or a computed tomography (CT) scan may be performed to locate any obstruction in the urinary tract. Relief of obstruction is essential to prevent the complications and eventual kidney damage. Urine culture and sensitivity tests are performed to determine the causative organism so that appropriate antimicrobial agents can be prescribed.

Medical and Nursing Management

Patients with acute uncomplicated pyelonephritis are treated on an outpatient basis if they are not exhibiting dehydration, nausea or vomiting, or symptoms of sepsis. A 2-week course of antibiotics is recommended because renal parenchymal disease is more difficult to eradicate than mucosal bladder infections. Commonly prescribed agents include TMP-SMZ, ciprofloxacin, gentamicin with or without ampicillin, or a third-generation cephalosporin (Zonderman & Doyle, 2006). These medications must be used with great caution if the patient has renal or liver dysfunction. Pregnant women may be hospitalized for 2 or 3 days of parenteral antibiotic therapy. Oral antibiotic agents may be prescribed once the patient is afebrile and showing clinical improvement. Hydration is essential in all patients with UTIs when there is adequate kidney function; this helps facilitate "flushing" of the urinary tract and reduces pain and discomfort.

A possible issue in acute pyelonephritis treatment is a chronic or recurring symptomless infection persisting for months or years. After the initial antibiotic regimen, the patient may need antibiotic therapy for up to 6 weeks if evidence of a relapse is seen. A follow-up urine culture is obtained 2 weeks after completion of antibiotic therapy to document clearing of the infection.

CHRONIC PYELONEPHRITIS

Repeated bouts of acute pyelonephritis may lead to chronic pyelonephritis.

Clinical Manifestations and Assessment

The patient with chronic pyelonephritis usually has no symptoms of infection unless an acute exacerbation occurs. Noticeable signs and symptoms may include fatigue, headache, poor appetite, polyuria, excessive thirst, and weight loss. Persistent and recurring infection may produce progressive scarring of the kidney resulting in renal failure (see Chapter 27).

The extent of the disease is assessed by an IV urogram and degree of renal dysfunction via measurements of creatinine clearance, blood urea nitrogen, and creatinine levels. Bacteria, if detected in the urine, are eradicated if possible.

Medical and Nursing Management

Long-term use of prophylactic antimicrobial therapy may help limit recurrence of infections and renal scarring (Tanagho & McAninch, 2007). Impaired renal function alters the excretion of antimicrobial agents and necessitates careful monitoring of renal function, especially if the medications are potentially toxic to the kidneys.

The patient may require hospitalization or may be treated as an outpatient. When the patient requires hospitalization, fluid intake and output are carefully measured and recorded.

Unless contraindicated, 3 to 4 L of fluids per day is encouraged to dilute the urine, decrease burning on urination, and prevent dehydration. The nurse assesses the patient's temperature every 4 hours and administers antipyretic and antibiotic agents as prescribed. Symptomatic patients are often more comfortable on bedrest. Patient teaching focuses on prevention of further infection by consuming adequate fluids, emptying the bladder regularly, and performing recommended perineal hygiene. The importance of taking antimicrobial medications exactly as prescribed is stressed, as is the need for keeping follow-up appointments.

Complications

Complications of chronic pyelonephritis include end-stage renal disease (ESRD) from progressive loss of nephrons secondary to chronic inflammation and scarring.

ADULT VOIDING DYSFUNCTION

Both neurogenic and non-neurogenic disorders can cause adult voiding dysfunction (Table 28-1). The **micturition** process involves several highly coordinated neurologic responses that mediate bladder function. A functional urinary system allows for appropriate bladder filling and complete bladder emptying (see Chapter 26). If voiding dysfunction goes undetected and untreated, the upper urinary system may be compromised. Chronic incomplete bladder emptying from poor detrusor pressure results in recurrent bladder infection. Incomplete bladder emptying due to bladder outlet obstruction (such as BPH), causing high-pressure detrusor contractions, can result in hydronephrosis from the high detrusor pressure that radiates up the ureters to the renal pelvis.

OVERACTIVE BLADDER

It is estimated that over 33 million Americans have overactive bladder (OAB). OAB is a condition in which a person has urgency, frequency, and nocturia that may or may not be associated with urinary incontinence (Newman & Wein, 2009). Normal frequency is seven voids per day and once at night up until the age of 70. Overactive bladder can have a significant impact on quality of life indicators. Treatment for OAB is similar to urge incontinence, discussed later in the chapter.

URINARY INCONTINENCE

More than 17 million adults in the United States are estimated to have **urinary incontinence**, with most of them experiencing OAB syndrome, making this disorder more prevalent than diabetes or ulcer disease. Despite widespread media coverage, urinary incontinence remains under-diagnosed and under-reported. Patients may be too embarrassed to seek help, causing them to ignore or conceal symptoms. Many

TABLE
28-1 Conditions Causing Adult Voiding Dysfunction

Condition	Voiding Dysfunction	Treatment
Neurogenic Disorders		
Cerebellar ataxia	Incontinence or dyssynergia	Timed voiding; anticholinergics
Cerebrovascular accident	Retention or incontinence	Anticholinergics; bladder retraining
Dementia	Incontinence	Prompted voiding
Diabetes mellitus	Incontinence and/or incomplete bladder emptying	Timed voiding; electromyelogram (EMG)/biofeedback; pelvic floor nerve stimulation; anticholinergics/antispasmodics; well-controlled blood glucose levels
Multiple sclerosis	Incontinence or incomplete bladder emptying	Timed voiding; EMG/biofeedback to learn pelvic muscle exercises and urge inhibition; pelvic floor nerve stimulation; antispasmodics
Parkinson's disease	Incontinence	Anticholinergics/antispasmodics
Spinal Cord Dysfunction		
Acute injury	Urinary retention	Indwelling catheter
Degenerative disease	Incontinence and/or incomplete bladder emptying	EMG/biofeedback; pelvic floor nerve stimulation; anticholinergics
Nonneurogenic Disorders		
"Bashful bladder"	Inability to initiate voiding in public bathrooms	Relaxation therapy; EMG/biofeedback
Overactive bladder	Urgency, frequency, and/or urge incontinence	EMG/biofeedback; pelvic floor nerve stimulation; anticholinergics
Post general surgery	Acute urine retention	Catheterization
Post-prostatectomy	Incontinence	*Mild:* biofeedback; pelvic floor nerve stimulation *Moderate/severe:* surgery—artificial sphincter
Stress incontinence	Incontinence with cough, laugh, sneeze, position change	*Mild:* biofeedback: periurethral bulking with collagen *Moderate/severe:* surgery

patients resort to using absorbent pads or other devices without having their condition properly diagnosed and treated. Health care providers must be alert to subtle cues of urinary incontinence and stay informed about current management strategies. Subtle cues include avoidance of social situations, perineal dermatitis, and depression (Newman & Wein, 2009). The costs of care for patients with urinary incontinence include cost of absorbent products, medications, and surgical or nonsurgical treatment modalities, as well as the psychosocial costs of urinary incontinence, including embarrassment, loss of self-esteem, and social isolation.

Risk Factors

Urinary incontinence affects people of all ages but is particularly common among the elderly and can decrease an elderly person's ability to maintain an independent lifestyle. This increases dependence on caregivers and may lead to institutionalization. More than half of all nursing home residents have urinary incontinence. Although urinary incontinence is not a normal consequence of aging, age-related changes in the urinary tract predispose the older person to incontinence.

Although it is commonly regarded as a condition that occurs in older multiparous women, it is also seen in young nulliparous women, especially during vigorous high-impact activity. Age, gender, and number of vaginal deliveries are established risk factors (Box 28-4) that explain, in part, the increased incidence in women.

Types of Incontinence

Only with appropriate recognition of the problem, assessment, and referral for diagnostic evaluation and treatment can the outcome of incontinence be determined. All patients with incontinence should be considered for evaluation and treatment. Urinary incontinence may be transient or reversible if the underlying cause is successfully treated and the voiding pattern reverts to normal (Box 28-5).

Stress incontinence is the involuntary loss of urine through an intact urethra as a result of sneezing, coughing, or changing position. It predominantly affects women who have had vaginal deliveries and is thought to be the result of decreasing ligament and pelvic floor support (pelvic floor dysfunction) of the urethra and decreasing or absent estrogen levels within the urethral walls and bladder base. In men, stress incontinence is often experienced after a radical prostatectomy for prostate cancer because of the loss of urethral compression that the prostate had supplied before the surgery.

Risk Factors for Urinary Incontinence

- Pregnancy: vaginal delivery, episiotomy
- Menopause
- Genitourinary surgery
- Pelvic muscle weakness
- Incompetent urethra due to trauma or sphincter relaxation
- Immobility
- High-impact exercise
- Diabetes mellitus
- Stroke
- Age-related changes in the urinary tract
- Morbid obesity
- Cognitive disturbances: dementia, Parkinson's disease
- Medications: diuretics, sedatives, hypnotics, opioids
- Caregiver or toilet unavailable

Urge incontinence is the involuntary loss of urine associated with a strong urge to void that cannot be suppressed. The patient is aware of the need to void but is unable to reach a toilet in time. An uninhibited detrusor contraction is the precipitating factor. This can occur in a patient with neurologic dysfunction that impairs inhibition of bladder contraction or in a patient without overt neurologic dysfunction.

Reflex incontinence is the involuntary loss of urine due to hyperreflexia in the absence of normal sensations usually associated with voiding. This commonly occurs in patients with spinal cord injury because they have neither neurologically mediated motor control of the detrusor nor sensory awareness of the need to void (see Chapter 45).

Overflow incontinence is the involuntary loss of urine associated with overdistention of the bladder. Such overdistention results from the bladder's inability to empty normally, despite frequent urine loss. Both neurologic abnormalities (e.g., spinal cord lesions) and factors that obstruct

Causes of Transient Incontinence: DIAPPERS

Delirium
Infection of urinary tract
Atrophic vaginitis, urethritis
Pharmacologic agents (anticholinergics, sedatives, alcohol, analgesics, diuretics, muscle relaxants, adrenergic agents)
Psychological factors (depression, regression)
Excessive urine production (increased intake, diabetes insipidus, diabetic ketoacidosis)
Restricted activity
Stool impaction

the outflow of urine (e.g., tumors, strictures, and prostatic hyperplasia) can cause overflow incontinence.

Functional incontinence refers to those instances in which lower urinary tract function is intact but other factors, such as severe cognitive impairment (e.g., Alzheimer's dementia), make it difficult for the patient to identify the need to void or physical impairments make it difficult or impossible for the patient to reach the toilet in time for voiding.

Iatrogenic incontinence refers to the involuntary loss of urine due to extrinsic medical factors, predominantly medications. One such example is the use of alpha-adrenergic agents to decrease blood pressure. In some people with an intact urinary system, these agents adversely affect the alpha receptors responsible for bladder neck closing pressure; the bladder neck relaxes to the point of incontinence with a minimal increase in intra-abdominal pressure, thus mimicking stress incontinence. As soon as the medication is discontinued, the apparent incontinence resolves.

Some patients have several types of urinary incontinence. This mixed incontinence is usually a combination of stress and urge incontinence (Newman & Wein, 2009).

Clinical Manifestations and Assessment

Once incontinence is recognized, a thorough history is necessary. This includes a detailed description of the problem and a history of medication use, noting those associated with urinary incontinence such as loop diuretics, calcium channel blockers, narcotics, sedatives, and alcohol (Resnick & Yalla, 1985). The patient's voiding history, a diary of fluid intake and output, and bedside tests (e.g., residual urine, stress maneuvers) may be used to help determine the type of urinary incontinence involved. Extensive urodynamic tests may be performed. In addition, urinalysis and urine culture are performed to identify infection.

Medical Management

Management depends on the type of urinary incontinence and its causes. Strategies for promoting urinary continence can be found in Box 28-6. Management of urinary incontinence may be behavioral, pharmacologic, or surgical in nature.

Behavioral Therapy

Behavioral therapies are the first choice to decrease or eliminate urinary incontinence and or symptoms of OAB (Box 28-7, p. 782). In using these techniques, health care professionals help patients avoid potential adverse effects of pharmacologic or surgical interventions.

Pharmacologic Therapy

Pharmacologic therapy works best when used as an adjunct to behavioral interventions. Anticholinergic agents inhibit bladder contraction and are considered first-line medications for urge incontinence. Oxybutynin (Ditropan) is frequently

Patient Education

Strategies for Promoting Urinary Continence

- Increase your awareness of the amount and timing of all fluid intake.
- Avoid taking diuretics after 4 p.m.
- Avoid bladder irritants, such as caffeine, alcohol, and aspartame (NutraSweet).
- Take steps to avoid constipation: Drink adequate fluids, eat a well-balanced diet high in fiber, exercise regularly, and take stool softeners if recommended.
- Void regularly, 5 to 8 times a day (about every 2 to 3 hours):
  First thing in the morning
  Before each meal
  Before retiring to bed
  Once during night if necessary
- Perform all pelvic floor muscle exercises as prescribed, every day.
- Stop smoking (smokers usually cough frequently, which increases incontinence).

prescribed and has dual actions of relaxing the detrusor muscle and inhibiting bladder contraction. Hormone therapy (e.g., estrogen) taken orally, transdermally, or topically was once the treatment of choice for urinary incontinence in postmenopausal women. Estrogen is believed to decrease obstruction to urine flow by restoring the mucosal, vascular, and muscular integrity of the urethra (Herbruck, 2008). However, the results of the Women's Health Initiative (Mennick, 2005) and the Nurses' Health study II (Townsend, Curhan, Resnick et al., 2009) revealed that urinary incontinence increased in women taking estrogen, leading researchers to examine the relationship of estrogen replacement therapy and urinary incontinence.

Surgical Management

Surgical correction may be indicated in patients who have not achieved continence using behavioral and pharmacologic therapy. Surgical options vary according to the underlying anatomy and the physiologic problem. Most procedures involve lifting and stabilizing the bladder or urethra to restore the normal urethrovesical angle or to lengthen the urethra (Newman & Wein, 2009). Women with stress incontinence may undergo an anterior vaginal repair, retropubic suspension, or needle suspension to reposition the urethra. Procedures to compress the urethra and increase resistance to urine flow include sling procedures and placement of periurethral bulking agents such as artificial collagen.

Periurethral bulking is a semipermanent procedure in which small amounts of artificial collagen (or other substances) are placed within the walls of the urethra to enhance the closing pressure of the urethra. This procedure takes only 10 to 20 minutes and may be performed under local anesthe-

sia or moderate sedation. A cystoscope is inserted into the urethra, and a small amount of collagen is injected into the urethral wall. The patient is usually discharged home after voiding. More than one collagen bulking session may be necessary if the initial procedure did not halt the stress urinary incontinence. Periurethral bulking with collagen offers an alternative to surgery, as in a frail, elderly person. It is also an option for people who are seeking help with stress urinary incontinence who prefer to avoid surgery and who do not have access to behavioral therapies.

An artificial urinary sphincter can be used to close the urethra and promote continence. Two types of artificial sphincters are a periurethral cuff and a cuff inflation pump. This therapy is approved for men only and is often used after treatment for prostate cancer (Fig. 28-2).

Men with overflow and urge incontinence may undergo a transurethral resection to relieve symptoms of prostatic enlargement.

Nursing Management

Nursing management is based on the premise that incontinence is not inevitable with illness or aging and that it is often reversible and treatable. The nursing interventions are determined by the type of treatment that is undertaken. For behavioral therapy to be effective, the nurse must provide support and encouragement because it is easy for the patient to become discouraged if therapy does not quickly improve the level of continence. Patient teaching is important and should be provided verbally and in writing (see Box 28-6). The patient should be taught to develop and use a log or diary to record timing of pelvic floor muscle exercises, frequency of voiding, any changes in bladder function, and any episodes of incontinence (Newman & Wein, 2009).

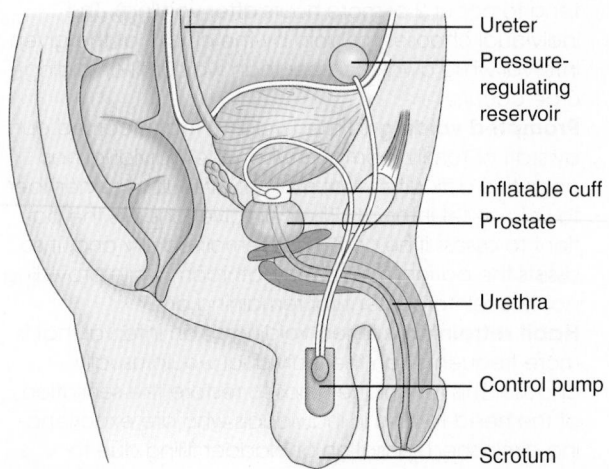

FIGURE 28-2 Male artificial urinary sphincter. An inflatable cuff is inserted surgically around the urethra or neck of the bladder. To empty the bladder, the cuff is deflated by squeezing the control pump located in the scrotum.

BOX 28-7 Behavioral Interventions for Urinary Incontinence

Behavioral strategies are largely carried out, coordinated, and monitored by the nurse. These interventions may or may not be augmented by the use of medications.

Fluid Management

One of the most common approaches is fluid management because adequate daily fluid intake of approximately 50 to 60 ounces (1,500 to 1,800 mL), taken as small increments between breakfast and the evening meal, helps to reduce urinary urgency related to concentrated urine production, decreases the risk of urinary tract infection, and maintains bowel functioning. (Constipation, resulting from inadequate daily fluid intake, can increase urinary urgency and/or urine retention.) The best fluid is water. Fluids containing caffeine, carbonation, alcohol, or artificial sweetener should be avoided because they irritate the bladder wall, thus resulting in urinary urgency. Some patients who have coexisting medical diagnoses, such as heart failure or end-stage renal disease, need to discuss their daily fluid limit with their primary health care provider.

Weight Management

Obesity is associated with OAB and urinary incontinence, thus weight control should be considered as a first line intervention, particularly when the body mass index (BMI) is greater than 27 (Newman & Wein, 2009).

Standardized Voiding Frequency

After establishing a patient's natural voiding and urinary incontinence tendencies, voiding on a schedule can be very effective in those with and without cognitive impairment, although patients with cognitive impairment may require assistance with this technique from nursing personnel or family members. The object is to purposely empty the bladder before the bladder reaches the critical volume that would cause an urge or stress incontinence episode. This approach involves the following:

- **Timed voiding** involves establishing a set voiding frequency (such as every 2 hours if incontinent episodes tend to occur 2 or more hours after voiding). The individual chooses to "void by the clock" at the given interval while awake, rather than wait until a voiding urge occurs.
- **Prompted voiding** is timed voiding that is carried out by staff or family members when the individual has cognitive difficulties that make it difficult to remember to void at set intervals. The caregiver checks the patient to assess if he or she has remained dry and, if so, assists the patient to use the bathroom while providing positive reinforcement for remaining dry.
- **Habit retraining** is timed voiding at an interval that is more frequent than the individual would usually choose. This technique helps to restore the sensation of the need to void in individuals who are experiencing diminished sensation of bladder filling due to various medical conditions such as a mild cerebrovascular accident (CVA).
- **Bladder retraining** incorporates a timed voiding schedule and urinary urge inhibition exercises to inhibit voiding, or leaking urine, in an attempt to remain dry for a set time. When the first timing interval is easily reached on a consistent basis without urinary urgency or incontinence, a new voiding interval, usually 10 to 15 minutes beyond the last, is established. Again, the individual practices urge inhibition exercises to delay voiding or avoid incontinence until the next preset interval arrives. When an acceptable voiding interval is reached, the patient continues that timed voiding sequence throughout the day.

Pelvic Muscle Exercise

Pelvic muscle exercise (PME) aims to strengthen the voluntary muscles that assist in bladder and bowel continence in both men and women. Research shows that written and/or verbal instruction alone is usually inadequate to teach an individual how to identify and strengthen the pelvic floor for sufficient bladder and bowel control. Biofeedback-assisted PME uses either electromyography or manometry to help the individual identify the pelvic muscles as he or she attempts to learn which muscle group is involved when performing PME. The biofeedback method also allows assessment of the strength of this muscle area.

PME involves gently tightening the same muscles used to stop flatus or the stream of urine for 5- to 10-second increments, followed by 10-second resting phases. To be effective, these exercises need to be performed 2 or 3 times a day for at least 6 weeks. Depending on the strength of the pelvic musculature when initially evaluated, anywhere from 10 to 30 repetitions of PME are prescribed at each session. Elderly patients may need to exercise for an even longer time to strengthen the pelvic floor muscles. Pelvic muscle exercises are helpful for women with stress, urge, or mixed incontinence and for men who have undergone prostate surgery.

Vaginal Cone Retention Exercises

Vaginal cone retention exercises are an adjunct to the pelvic muscle (Kegel) exercises. Vaginal cones of varying weight are inserted intravaginally twice a day. The patient tries to retain the cone for 15 minutes by contracting the pelvic muscles.

Transvaginal or Transrectal Electrical Stimulation

Commonly used to treat urinary incontinence, electrical stimulation is known to elicit a passive contraction of the pelvic floor musculature, thus re-educating these muscles to provide enhanced levels of continence. This modality is often used with biofeedback-assisted pelvic muscle exercise training and voiding schedules. At high frequencies, it is effective for stress incontinence. At low frequencies, electrical stimulation can also relieve symptoms of urinary urgency, frequency, and urge incontinence. Intermediate ranges are used for mixed incontinence.

Neuromodulation

Neuromodulation via transvaginal or transrectal nerve stimulation of the pelvic floor inhibits detrusor overactivity and hypersensory bladder signals and strengthens weak sphincter muscles.

If pharmacologic treatment is used, it is important to educate patients who have mixed incontinence (both stress and urge incontinence) that anticholinergic and antispasmodic agents can help decrease urinary urgency and frequency and urge incontinence, but they do not decrease the urinary incontinence related to stress incontinence. If surgical correction is undertaken, the procedure and its desired outcomes are described to the patient and family. Follow-up contact with the patient enables the nurse to answer the patient's questions and to provide reinforcement and encouragement.

Gerontologic Considerations

Many older people experience transient episodes of incontinence that tend to be abrupt in onset. When this occurs, the nurse should question the patient, as well as the family if possible, about the onset of symptoms and any signs or symptoms of a change in other organ systems. Acute UTI, infection elsewhere in the body, constipation, stool impaction, a change in a chronic disease pattern, such as elevated blood glucose levels in patients with diabetes or decreased estrogen levels in menopausal women, can provoke the onset of urinary incontinence.

Dehydration is the most common fluid and electrolyte problem among older adults and may mask the urge sensation causing urinary incontinence. When hydration occurs, urinary incontinence may resolve (Newman & Wein, 2009). If the cause is identified and modified or eliminated early at the onset of incontinence, the incontinence itself may be eliminated. Although the bladder of the older person is more vulnerable to altered detrusor activity, age alone is not a risk factor for urinary incontinence (Newman & Wein, 2009). Decreased bladder muscle tone is a normal age-related change found in the elderly. This leads to decreased bladder capacity, increased residual urine, and an increase in urgency (Newman & Wein, 2009).

URINARY RETENTION

Urinary retention is the inability to empty the bladder completely during attempts to void. Acute urinary retention is frequently associated with obstruction such as BPH or acute prostatitis. Chronic urine retention often leads to overflow incontinence (from the pressure of the retained urine in the bladder). **Residual urine** is urine that remains in the bladder after voiding. In a healthy adult younger than 60 years, complete bladder emptying should occur with each voiding. In adults older than 60 years, 50 to 100 mL of residual urine may remain after each voiding because of the decreased contractility of the detrusor muscle.

Urinary retention can occur postoperatively in any patient who received spinal or general anesthesia. General anesthesia reduces bladder muscle innervation and suppresses the urge to void, impeding bladder emptying (Tanagho & McAninch,

2007). A number of medications have been implicated in the development of urinary retention and are briefly discussed below. Other etiologies that should be considered in acute urinary retention are trauma, infection (prostatitis, cystitis), and neurological and psychiatric disorders.

Pathophysiology

Urinary retention may result from diabetes, prostatic enlargement, urethral pathology (infection, urethral strictures, tumor, calculus), trauma (pelvic injuries), pregnancy, or neurologic disorders such as stroke, spinal cord injury, multiple sclerosis (MS), Guillain-Barré syndrome, or Parkinson's disease.

Some medications cause urinary retention, either by inhibiting bladder contractility or by increasing bladder outlet resistance, namely anticholinergics and sympathomimetic agents. Medications that cause retention by inhibiting bladder contractility include antispasmodic agents (oxybutynin chloride, belladonna, and opioid suppositories) and tricyclic antidepressant medications (imipramine, doxepin). Medications that cause urine retention by increasing bladder outlet resistance include alpha-adrenergic agents (ephedrine sulfate, pseudoephedrine), beta-adrenergic blockers (propranolol), and estrogens.

Sympathomimetics "mimic" the sympathetic nervous system and therefore have the anticipated result of increasing heart rate and contractility, dilating bronchioles and pupils, and—pertinent to this chapter—relaxing the bladder wall and thus closing the sphincter, affecting urinary retention. Anticholinergics work by blocking the parasympathetic nervous system response, which causes contraction of the bladder and relaxation of the sphincter. Thus since this response is blocked, clinically the effects are similar to the sympathomimetics; hence, both drugs are implicated in urinary retention.

Clinical Manifestations and Assessment

The assessment of a patient for urinary retention is multifaceted because the signs and symptoms may be easily overlooked. The following questions serve as a guide in assessment:

- What was the time of the last voiding, and how much urine was voided?
- Is the patient voiding small amounts of urine frequently?
- Is the patient dribbling urine?
- Does the patient complain of pain or discomfort in the lower abdomen? (Discomfort may be relatively mild if the bladder distends slowly).
- Is the pelvic area rounded and swollen, indicating urine retention and a distended bladder?
- Does percussion of the suprapubic region elicit dullness, possibly indicating urine retention and a distended bladder?

- Are other indicators of urinary retention present, such as restlessness and agitation?
- Does a postvoid bladder ultrasound test reveal residual urine?

The patient may verbalize an awareness of bladder fullness and a sensation of incomplete bladder emptying. Signs and symptoms of UTI (hematuria, urgency, frequency, nocturia, and dysuria) may be present. A series of urodynamic studies, described in Chapter 26, may be performed to identify the type of bladder dysfunction and to aid in determining appropriate treatment. The patient may complete a voiding diary to provide a written record of the amount of urine voided and the frequency of voiding. Postvoid residual urine may be assessed either using straight catheterization or an ultrasound bladder scanner and is considered diagnostic of urinary retention if there is more than 100 mL of residual urine.

Medical Management

Management strategies are instituted to prevent overdistention of the bladder and to treat infection or correct underlying etiology for the retention. Immediate management involves decompression of the bladder via catheterization, which is discussed later in this chapter.

Nursing Management

Many problems can be prevented with careful assessment and appropriate nursing interventions. The nurse explains why normal voiding is not occurring and monitors urine output closely. The nurse also provides reassurance about the temporary nature of retention and successful management strategies.

In the case of acute urinary retention, decompression with a urethral catheter is commonly required. Nurses need to assess, however, if the patient recently underwent surgery, such as a radical prostatectomy or urethral reconstruction, since catheterization via urethra would be contraindicated. Barring no contraindications to urinary catheterization, the nurse chooses a 14- to 18-French Foley catheter, and if the patient has a past history of prostatic disease a *coude* catheter is recommended to facilitate passage through the posterior urethra. A complication associated with emergent catheterization for urinary retention is hypotension and hematuria. In the past, it has been suggested to clamp the catheter after 1 L of urine was released to prevent profound hypotension. However, limited data suggest no benefit for gradual urinary decompression via clamping the catheter versus rapid decompression (Curtis, Sullivan Dolan, & Cespedes, 2001; Nyman, Schwenk, & Silverstein, 1997; Oberst, Graham, Geller et al., 1981).

Promoting Urinary Elimination

Nursing measures to encourage normal voiding patterns include providing privacy, ensuring an environment and a position conducive to voiding, and assisting the patient with the use of the bathroom or bedside commode, rather than a bedpan, to provide a more natural setting for voiding. The male patient may stand beside the bed while using the urinal; most men find this position more comfortable and natural.

Additional measures include applying warmth to relax the sphincters (i.e., sitz baths, warm compresses to the perineum, showers), giving the patient hot tea, and offering encouragement and reassurance. Simple trigger techniques, such as turning on the water faucet while the patient is trying to void, may also be used. After surgery or childbirth, prescribed analgesics should be administered because pain in the perineal area can make voiding difficult.

When the patient cannot void, catheterization is used to prevent overdistention of the bladder (see later discussion of neurogenic bladder and catheterization). Rarely is a suprapubic tube used for BPH. After urinary drainage is restored, bladder retraining is initiated for the patient who cannot void spontaneously.

Promoting Home Care

Modifications to the home environment can provide simple and effective ways to assist in treating urinary incontinence and retention. For example, the patient may need to remove obstacles, such as throw rugs or other objects, to provide easy, safe access to the bathroom. Other modifications that the nurse may recommend include installing support bars in the bathroom; placing a bedside commode, bedpan, or urinal within easy reach; leaving lights on in the bedroom and bathroom; and wearing clothing that is easy to remove quickly.

Complications

Urine retention can lead to chronic infection and, if left unresolved, predispose the patient to renal calculi (urolithiasis or nephrolithiasis), pyelonephritis, and sepsis. Acute or chronic renal failure may develop secondary to renal obstruction (refer to Chapter 27). If hydronephrosis has occurred due to large volumes of retained urine, renal insufficiency may develop and progress to renal failure.

NEUROGENIC BLADDER

Neurogenic bladder is a dysfunction that results from a lesion of the nervous system and leads to urinary incontinence. It may be caused by spinal cord injury, spinal tumor, herniated vertebral disk, MS, congenital disorders (spina bifida or myelomeningocele), infection, or diabetes mellitus.

Pathophysiology

The two types of neurogenic bladder are spastic (or reflex) bladder and flaccid bladder. Spastic bladder is more common and is caused by any spinal cord lesion above the voiding reflex arc (upper motor neuron lesion). The result is a

loss of conscious sensation and cerebral motor control. A spastic bladder empties on reflex, with minimal or no controlling influence to regulate its activity.

Flaccid bladder is caused by a lower motor neuron lesion, commonly resulting from trauma, but increasingly recognized in patients with diabetes mellitus. The bladder continues to fill and becomes greatly distended, and overflow incontinence occurs. The bladder muscle does not contract forcefully at any time. Because sensory loss may accompany a flaccid bladder, the patient feels no discomfort. This can also occur in men with BPH with obstructive component.

Clinical Manifestations and Assessment

Evaluation for neurogenic bladder involves measurement of fluid intake, urine output, and residual urine volume, urinalysis, and assessment of sensory awareness of bladder fullness and degree of motor control. Comprehensive urodynamic studies are also performed.

Medical Management

The problems resulting from neurogenic bladder disorders vary considerably from patient to patient. Several long-term objectives are appropriate for all types of neurogenic bladders:

- Preventing overdistention of the bladder
- Emptying the bladder regularly and completely
- Maintaining urine sterility with no stone formation
- Maintaining adequate bladder capacity with no reflux

Specific interventions include continuous or intermittent self-catheterization, use of an external condom-type catheter, a diet low in calcium to prevent calculi, and encouragement of mobility and ambulation. A liberal fluid intake is encouraged to reduce the urinary bacterial count, reduce stasis, decrease the concentration of calcium in the urine, and minimize the precipitation of urinary crystals and subsequent stone formation.

A bladder retraining program may be effective in treating a spastic bladder or urine retention. Use of a timed voiding schedule may be established. The patient may be taught to "double void": after each voiding, the patient is instructed to remain on the toilet, relax for 1 to 2 minutes, and then attempt to void again in an effort to further empty the bladder.

Pharmacologic Therapy

Alpha blockers were originally developed for hypertension; these drugs block the adrenergic system and help patients with BPH by relaxing smooth muscle tissue found in the prostate and the bladder neck, thereby facilitating urine outflow. The four alpha medications approved by the U.S. Food and Drug Administration (FDA) are: terazosin (Hytrin), doxazosin (Cardura), tamsulosin (Flomax) and alfuzosin (Uroxatral).

Surgical Management

In some cases, surgery may be carried out to correct bladder neck contractures, prostatic obstruction, vesicoureteral reflux, or to perform some type of urinary diversion procedure.

Catheterization

In patients with a urologic disorder or with marginal kidney function, care must be taken to ensure that urinary drainage is adequate and that kidney function is preserved. When urine cannot be eliminated naturally and must be drained artificially, catheters may be inserted directly into the bladder, the ureter, or the renal pelvis. Catheters vary in size, shape, length, material, and configuration. The type of catheter used depends on its purpose, and catheterization is performed to achieve the following:

- Relieve urinary tract obstruction
- Assist with postoperative drainage in urologic and other surgeries
- Provide a means to monitor accurate urine output in critically ill patients
- Promote urinary drainage in patients with neurogenic bladder dysfunction or urine retention
- Prevent urinary leakage in patients with stage III to IV pressure ulcers (see Chapter 52)

A patient should be catheterized only if necessary, because instrumentation can lead to UTI. Catheters impede most of the natural defenses of the lower urinary tract by obstructing the periurethral ducts, irritating the bladder mucosa, and providing an artificial route for organisms to enter the bladder. Organisms may be introduced from the urethra into the bladder during catheterization, or they may migrate along the epithelial surface of the urethra or external surface of the catheter.

Indwelling Catheters

Approximately 50,000 long-term care patients each year have an indwelling catheter (CDC, 2009). When an indwelling catheter cannot be avoided, a closed drainage system is essential. This drainage system is designed to prevent any disconnections, thereby reducing the risk of contamination. The spout (or drainage port) of any urinary drainage bag can become contaminated when opened to drain the bag. Bacteria enter the urinary drainage bag, multiply rapidly, and then migrate to the drainage tubing, catheter, and bladder. By keeping the drainage bag lower than the patient's bladder and not allowing urine to flow back into the bladder, this risk is minimized.

Triple-lumen catheters are commonly used after transurethral prostate surgery (TURP) (see Chapter 34). This system has a triple-lumen indwelling urethral catheter attached to a closed sterile drainage system. With the triple-lumen catheter, urinary drainage occurs through one channel. The retention balloon of the catheter is inflated with water or air

through the second channel, and the bladder is continuously irrigated with sterile irrigating solution through the third channel.

> ⚡ **NURSING ALERT**
>
> *After a patient undergoes a TURP, he will have a three-way catheter system in place that fulfills several roles: irrigation, tamponade, drainage, and traction. Precise intake and output records must be maintained, especially if total resection time was greater than 90 minutes. These men are at risk for TUR syndrome, a result of the absorption of irrigation fluid intra-operatively, which can lead to hyponatremia, bradycardia, and confusion (Gray & Moore, 2009).*

Accurate intake and output and patient assessment are essential to avoid the complication of hyponatremia and volume overload associated with instillation of large volumes of irrigating solution. Solutions used for urinary irrigation are electrolyte-free, thus hypo-osmotic and in general are glycine, sorbitol, and mannitol (Tanagho & McAninch, 2007). During a TURP, the hypotonic solution can be absorbed into the prostatic veins with resultant volume overload and dilutional hyponatremia. The nurse is alert for signs of fluid overload such as dyspnea, decreasing O_2 saturation, jugular vein distention, development of S_3 gallop, hypertension or hypotension (with the development of congestive heart failure [CHF]), and arrhythmias. Early signs of dilutional hyponatremia are mental status changes, headache, nausea and vomiting, muscle twitching, and respiratory distress. The provider is notified of any change in patient condition. The rate of irrigant infusion is aimed at maintaining clear to pink-colored urine. When clots are present, the rate of infusion is increased to prevent clot retention. Since the draining irrigant and urine are both returning to the urinary drainage bag, the nurse must keep an accurate record of amount of irrigant solution instilled and subtract the volume of the irrigant from the total drainage amount in the urinary drainage bag, which is recorded as urine. Thus, if 2 L were instilled over the past 4 hours and the urinary drainage bag contained 2,150 mL, the urine output for the past 4 hours is recorded as 150 mL.

Suprapubic Catheters

Suprapubic catheterization allows bladder drainage by inserting a catheter or tube into the bladder through a suprapubic (above the pubis) incision or puncture (Fig. 28-3). The catheter or suprapubic drainage tube is then threaded into the bladder and secured with sutures or tape, and the area around the catheter is covered with a sterile dressing. The catheter is connected to a sterile closed drainage system, and the tubing is secured to prevent tension on the catheter. This may be a temporary or permanent measure to divert the flow of urine from the urethra when the urethral route is impassable (because of injuries, strictures, prostatic obstruction), after gynecologic or other abdominal surgery when bladder dysfunction is likely to occur, and occasionally after pelvic

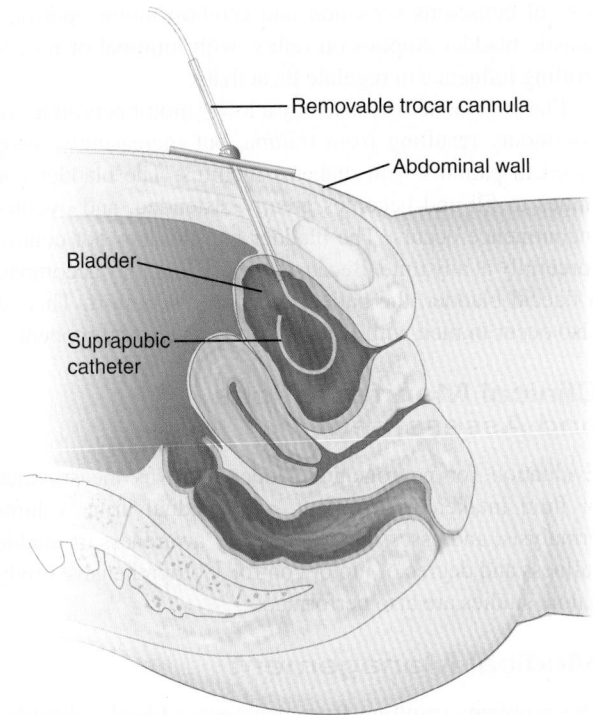

FIGURE 28-3 Suprapubic bladder drainage. A trocar cannula is used to puncture the abdominal and bladder walls. The catheter is threaded through the trocar cannula, which is then removed, leaving the catheter in place. The catheter is secured by tape or sutures to prevent unintentional removal.

fractures. Suprapubic bladder drainage may be maintained continuously for several weeks.

Suprapubic drainage offers certain advantages. Patients can usually void sooner after surgery than can those with urethral catheters, and they may be more comfortable. The catheter allows greater mobility, permits measurement of residual urine without urethral instrumentation, and presents less risk of bladder infection. The suprapubic catheter is removed when it is no longer required, and a sterile dressing is placed over the site.

The patient requires liberal amounts of fluid to prevent encrustation around the catheter. Other potential problems include the formation of bladder stones, acute and chronic infections, and problems collecting urine. A **wound care specialist**/enterostomal therapist, also referred to as a wound-ostomy-continence nurse, may be consulted to assist the patient and family in selecting the most suitable urine collection system and to teach them about its use and care.

Nursing Management During Catheterization

Assessing the Patient and the System

For patients with indwelling catheters, the nurse assesses the drainage system to ensure that it provides adequate

urinary drainage. The color, odor, and volume of urine are also monitored. An accurate record of fluid intake and urine output provides essential information about the adequacy of renal function and urinary drainage. The nurse observes the catheter to make sure that it is properly anchored, to prevent pressure on the urethra at the meatus in male patients, and to prevent tension and traction on the tubing in both male and female patients. Care is taken to ensure that the catheter position permits leg movement. In male patients, the drainage tube (not the catheter) is taped laterally to the thigh to prevent pressure on the urethra at the penoscrotal junction, which can eventually lead to formation of an urethrocutaneous fistula. In female patients, the drainage tubing attached to the catheter is taped to the thigh to prevent tension and traction on the bladder.

Patients at high risk for UTI from catheterization need to be identified and monitored carefully. These include women, older adults, and patients who are debilitated, malnourished, chronically ill, immunosuppressed, or have diabetes. The nurse observes these patients for signs and symptoms of UTI that have been discussed previously. The area around the urethral orifice is observed for drainage and excoriation.

The elderly patient with an indwelling catheter or patients with neurological conditions (MS, stroke, spinal cord injury) may not exhibit the typical signs and symptoms of infection. Any subtle change in physical condition or mental status must be considered a possible indication of infection and promptly investigated because sepsis may occur before the infection is diagnosed. Figure 28-4 summarizes the sequence of events leading to infection and leakage of urine that often follow long-term use of an indwelling catheter in an elderly patient.

Preventing Infection

Certain principles of care are essential to prevent infection in patients with a closed urinary drainage system (Box 28-8). The catheter is a foreign body in the urethra and produces a reaction in the urethral mucosa with some urethral discharge.

Bacteriuria is considered inevitable in patients with indwelling catheters. Continual observation for fever, chills, and other signs and symptoms of systemic infection is necessary; these symptoms are generally treated aggressively.

Minimizing Trauma

Trauma to the urethra during catheterization can be minimized by:

- Using an appropriate-sized catheter
- Lubricating the catheter adequately with a water-soluble lubricant during insertion
- Inserting the catheter far enough into the bladder to prevent trauma to the urethral tissues when the retention balloon of the catheter is inflated

Manipulation of the catheter is the most common cause of trauma to the bladder mucosa in the catheterized patient.

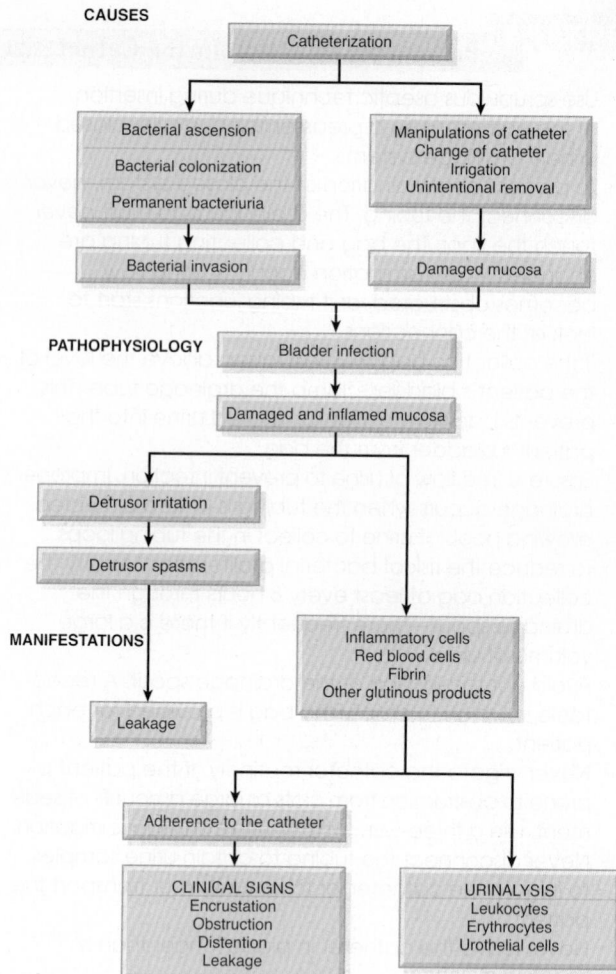

FIGURE 28-4 Pathophysiology and manifestations of bladder infection in long-term catheterized patients.

Infection can occur when urine invades the damaged mucosa. Special care should be taken to ensure that any patient who is confused does not remove the catheter with the retention balloon still inflated, because this could cause bleeding and considerable injury to the urethra.

Retraining the Bladder

When an indwelling urinary catheter is in place, the detrusor muscle does not actively contract the bladder wall to stimulate emptying because urine is continuously draining from the bladder. The detrusor may not immediately respond to bladder filling when the catheter is removed, resulting in either urine retention or urinary incontinence. This condition, known as *postcatheterization detrusor instability*, can be managed with bladder retraining (Box 28-9).

Immediately after the indwelling catheter is removed, the patient is placed on a timed voiding schedule, usually every 2 to 3 hours. After voiding, the bladder is scanned using a portable ultrasonic bladder scanner. If 100 mL or more of urine remains in the bladder, straight catheterization may be performed for complete bladder emptying. After a few

Preventing Infection in the Catheterized Patient

- Use scrupulous aseptic technique during insertion of the catheter. Use a preassembled, sterile, closed urinary drainage system.
- To prevent contamination of the closed system, *never* disconnect the tubing. The drainage bag must *never* touch the floor. The bag and collecting tubing are changed if contamination occurs, if urine flow becomes obstructed, or if tubing junctions start to leak at the connections.
- If the collection bag *must* be raised above the level of the patient's bladder, clamp the drainage tube. This prevents backflow of contaminated urine into the patient's bladder from the bag.
- Ensure a free flow of urine to prevent infection. Improper drainage occurs when the tubing is kinked or twisted, allowing pools of urine to collect in the tubing loops.
- To reduce the risk of bacterial proliferation, empty the collection bag at least every 8 hours through the drainage spout—more frequently if there is a large volume of urine.
- Avoid contamination of the drainage spout. A receptacle in which to empty the bag is provided for each patient.
- Never irrigate the catheter routinely. If the patient is prone to obstruction from clots or large amounts of sediment, use a three-way system with continuous irrigation.
- Never disconnect the tubing to obtain urine samples, to irrigate the catheter, or to ambulate or transport the patient.
- Never leave the catheter in place longer than is necessary.

- Avoid routine catheter changes. The catheter is changed only to correct problems such as leakage, blockage, or encrustations.
- To remove obvious encrustations from the external catheter surface, the area can be washed gently with soap during the daily bath. Using silicone catheters results in significantly less crust formation. A liberal fluid intake, within the limits of the patient's cardiac and renal reserve, and an increased urine output must be ensured to flush the catheter and to dilute urinary substances that might form encrustations.
- Avoid unnecessary handling or manipulation of the catheter by the patient or staff.
- Carry out hand hygiene before and after handling the catheter, tubing, or drainage bag.
- Wash the perineal area with soap and water at least twice a day; avoid a to-and-fro motion of the catheter. Vigorous cleansing of the meatus while the catheter is in place is discouraged because the cleansing action can move the catheter back and forth, increasing the risk of infection. Dry the area well, but avoid applying powder because it may irritate the perineum.
- Monitor the patient's voiding when the catheter is removed. The patient must void within 8 hours; if unable to void, the patient may require catheterization with a straight catheter.
- Urine cultures are obtained as prescribed or indicated when monitoring the patient for infection; many catheters have an aspiration (puncture) port from which a specimen can be obtained.

---

days, as the nerve endings in the bladder wall become aware of bladder filling and emptying, bladder function usually returns to normal. If the person has had an indwelling catheter in place for an extended period, bladder retraining will take longer.

Assisting With Intermittent Self-Catheterization

Intermittent self-catheterization (ISC) provides periodic drainage of urine from the bladder. By promoting drainage and eliminating excessive residual urine, intermittent catheterization protects the kidneys, reduces the incidence of UTIs, and improves continence. It is the treatment of choice in patients with spinal cord injury and other neurologic disorders, such as MS, when the ability to empty the bladder is impaired. Self-catheterization promotes independence, results in few complications, and enhances self-esteem and quality of life.

When teaching the patient how to perform self-catheterization, the nurse must use aseptic technique to minimize the risk of cross-contamination. However, the patient may use a "clean" (nonsterile) technique at home, where the risk of cross-contamination is reduced. In teaching the patient, the

nurse emphasizes the importance of frequent catheterization and emptying the bladder at the prescribed time. The average daytime clean intermittent catheterization schedule is every 4 to 6 hours and just before bedtime. If the patient is awakened at night with an urge to void, catheterization may be performed after an attempt is made to void normally. Refer to Box 28-10 for details regarding ISC teaching.

Complications

The most common complication of neurogenic bladder is infection resulting from urinary stasis and catheterization. Long-term complications include urolithiasis (stones in the urinary tract), vesicoureteral reflux, and hydronephrosis, all of which can lead to destruction of the kidney.

UROLITHIASIS AND NEPHROLITHIASIS

Urolithiasis and nephrolithiasis refer to stones (calculi) in the urinary tract and kidney, respectively. Urinary stones account for more than 320,000 hospital admissions each year (Tanagho & McAninch, 2007).

BOX 28-9
Bladder Retraining After Indwelling Catheterization

- Instruct the patient to drink a measured amount of fluid from 8 a.m. to 10 p.m. to avoid bladder overdistention. Offer no fluids (except sips) after 10 p.m.
- At specific times, ask the patient to void by applying pressure over the bladder, tapping the abdomen, or stretching the anal sphincter with a finger to trigger the bladder.
- Immediately after the voiding attempt, assess the postvoid residual (PVR) urine either using straight catheterization or an ultrasound bladder scanner. Residual urine of more than 100 mL is considered diagnostic of urinary retention.
- Measure the volumes of urine voided and obtained by catheterization if indicated.
- Palpate the bladder at repeated intervals to assess for distention. If there is suspicion of urinary retention, percuss the bladder (refer to Chapter 26).
- Instruct the patient who has no voiding sensation to be alert for any signs that indicate a full bladder, such as perspiration, cold hands or feet, or feelings of anxiety.
- Lengthen the intervals between catheterizations as the volume of residual urine decreases. Catheterization is usually discontinued when the volume of residual urine is less than 100 mL.

BOX 28-10
Patient Education

Intermittent Self-Catheterization

Females:
- Assume a sitting position.
- Use a mirror to help locate the urinary meatus once, and then after that feel for the appropriate location.
- Insert the lubricated catheter 7.5 cm (3 in) into the urethra, in a downward and backward direction until urine begins to flow.
- After removal, discard the catheter.
- Consult a primary health care provider at regular intervals to assess urinary function and to detect complications.

Males:
- Assume a Fowler's or sitting position.
- Lubricate the catheter.
- Retract the foreskin of the penis (if necessary) with one hand.
- Grasp the penis and hold it at a right angle to the body. (This maneuver straightens the urethra and makes it easier to insert the catheter.)
- Insert the catheter 15 to 25 cm (6 to 10 in) until urine begins to flow.
- After removal, discard the catheter.
- Consult a primary health care provider at regular intervals to assess urinary function and to detect complications.

*If the patient cannot perform intermittent self-catheterization, a family member may be taught to carry out the procedure at regular intervals during the day.

Pathophysiology

Stones are formed in the urinary tract when urinary concentrations of substances such as calcium oxalate, calcium phosphate, and uric acid increase. Referred to as *supersaturation,* this is dependent on the amount of the substance, ionic strength, and pH of the urine (an acid environment promotes calcium excretion). Stones may be found anywhere from the kidney to the bladder (Fig. 28-5) and may vary in size from minute granular deposits, called sand or gravel, to bladder stones as large as an orange.

Stone formation is not clearly understood, and there are a number of theories about their causes. One theory is that there is a deficiency of substances that normally prevent crystallization in the urine, such as citrate, magnesium, nephrocalcin, and uropontin (Porth & Matfin, 2009). Another theory relates to fluid volume status of the patient (stones tend to occur more often in dehydrated patients). Certain factors favor the formation of stones; however, in many patients, no cause may be found.

Risk Factors

Urinary stones occur predominantly in the third to fifth decades of life and affect men more than women. About half of patients with a single renal stone have another episode within 5 years. Anatomical structure of the upper and lower urinary tract may pose a risk as urinary tract infections (struvite calculi) or stasis is associated with stone formation. Metabolic defects such as hyperparathyroidism and hyperuricemia (gout) are also associated with stone formation. Genetic predisposition, such as familial renal tubule acidosis, is strongly associated with nephrolithiasis. Spring and summer season are associated with a higher incidence of stone formation, most likely due to dehydration.

Clinical Manifestations and Assessment

Signs and symptoms of stones in the urinary system depend on the presence of obstruction, infection, and edema. When stones block the flow of urine, obstruction develops, producing an increase in hydrostatic pressure and distending the renal pelvis and proximal ureter. Infection (pyelonephritis and UTI with chills, fever, and dysuria) can be a contributing factor with struvite stones (Porth & Matfin, 2009). Some stones cause few symptoms while slowly destroying the nephrons of the kidney; others cause excruciating pain and discomfort.

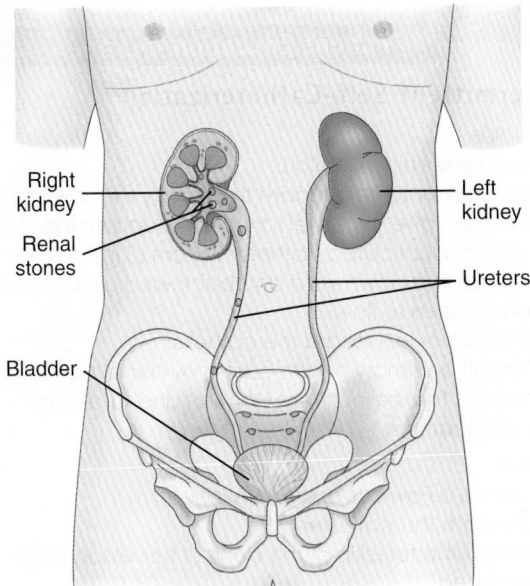

FIGURE 28-5 Examples of potential sites of calculi formation (urolithiasis) in the urinary tract.

Stones in the renal pelvis may be associated with an intense, deep ache in the costovertebral region (see Fig. 26-6). Hematuria is often present; pyuria may also be noted. Pain originating in the renal area radiates anteriorly and downward toward the bladder in the female and toward the testis in the male. If the pain suddenly becomes acute, with tenderness over the costovertebral area, and nausea and vomiting appear, the patient is having an episode of renal colic. Diarrhea and abdominal discomfort may occur. Stones lodged in the ureter (ureteral obstruction) cause ureteral colic: acute, excruciating, colicky, wavelike pain, radiating down the thigh and to the genitalia. Often, the patient has a desire to void, but little urine is passed, and it usually contains blood because of the abrasive action of the stone. In general, the patient spontaneously passes stones 0.5 to 1 cm in diameter. Stones larger than 1 cm in diameter usually must be removed or fragmented so that they can be removed or passed spontaneously. Stones lodged in the bladder usually produce symptoms of irritation and may be associated with UTI and hematuria. If the stone obstructs the bladder neck, urinary retention occurs.

The diagnosis is confirmed by X-rays of the kidneys, ureters, and bladder (KUB) or by ultrasonography, IV urography, or retrograde pyelography. Blood chemistries and a 24-hour urine test for measurement of calcium, uric acid, creatinine, sodium, pH, and total volume are part of the diagnostic workup. Dietary and medication histories and family history of renal stones are obtained to identify factors predisposing the patient to the formation of stones.

When stones are recovered (stones may be freely passed by the patient or removed through special procedures),

chemical analysis is carried out to determine their composition. Stone analysis can provide a clear indication of the underlying disorder (Table 28-2, p. 792).

Medical Management

The goals of management are to eradicate the stone, determine the stone type, prevent nephron destruction, control infection, and relieve any obstruction that may be present. The immediate objective of treatment of renal or ureteral colic is to relieve the pain until its cause can be eliminated. Opioid analgesics are administered; nonsteroidal anti-inflammatory drugs (NSAIDs) also have demonstrated efficacy in treating renal stone pain. In addition, NSAIDs also inhibit the synthesis of prostaglandin E, reducing swelling and facilitating passage of the stone. Hot baths or moist heat to the flank areas may also be useful. Fluids are encouraged to increase the hydrostatic pressure behind the stone, assisting it in its downward passage.

Nutritional Therapy

Nutritional therapy plays an important role in preventing renal stones (Dudek, 2006). Fluid intake is the mainstay of most medical therapy for renal stones. Unless fluids are contraindicated, patients with renal stones should drink eight to ten 8-ounce glasses of water daily or have IV fluids prescribed to keep the urine dilute. A urine output exceeding 2 L a day is advisable.

Procedures for Treatment of Stone Disease

If the stone does not pass spontaneously or if complications occur, common interventions include endoscopic or other procedures—for example, ureteroscopy, extracorporeal shock wave lithotripsy (ESWL), or endourologic (percutaneous) stone removal (Fig. 28-6). Refer to discussion of surgical treatment in Table 28-3 on page 793.

Open surgical removal was the major mode of therapy before the advent of lithotripsy and improved endoscopic techniques. Today, open procedures are performed in only 1% to 2% of patients. Surgical intervention is indicated if the stone does not respond to other forms of treatment, and to correct anatomic abnormalities within the kidney to improve urinary drainage. If the stone is in the kidney, the surgery performed may be a nephrolithotomy (incision into the kidney with removal of the stone) or a nephrectomy, if the kidney is nonfunctional secondary to infection or hydronephrosis. Stones in the kidney pelvis are removed by a pyelolithotomy, those in the ureter by ureterolithotomy, and those in the bladder by cystotomy. If the stone is in the bladder, an instrument may be inserted through the urethra into the bladder, and the stone is crushed in the jaws of this instrument. Such a procedure is called a cystolitholapaxy. Nursing management following kidney surgery is discussed in Chapter 27.

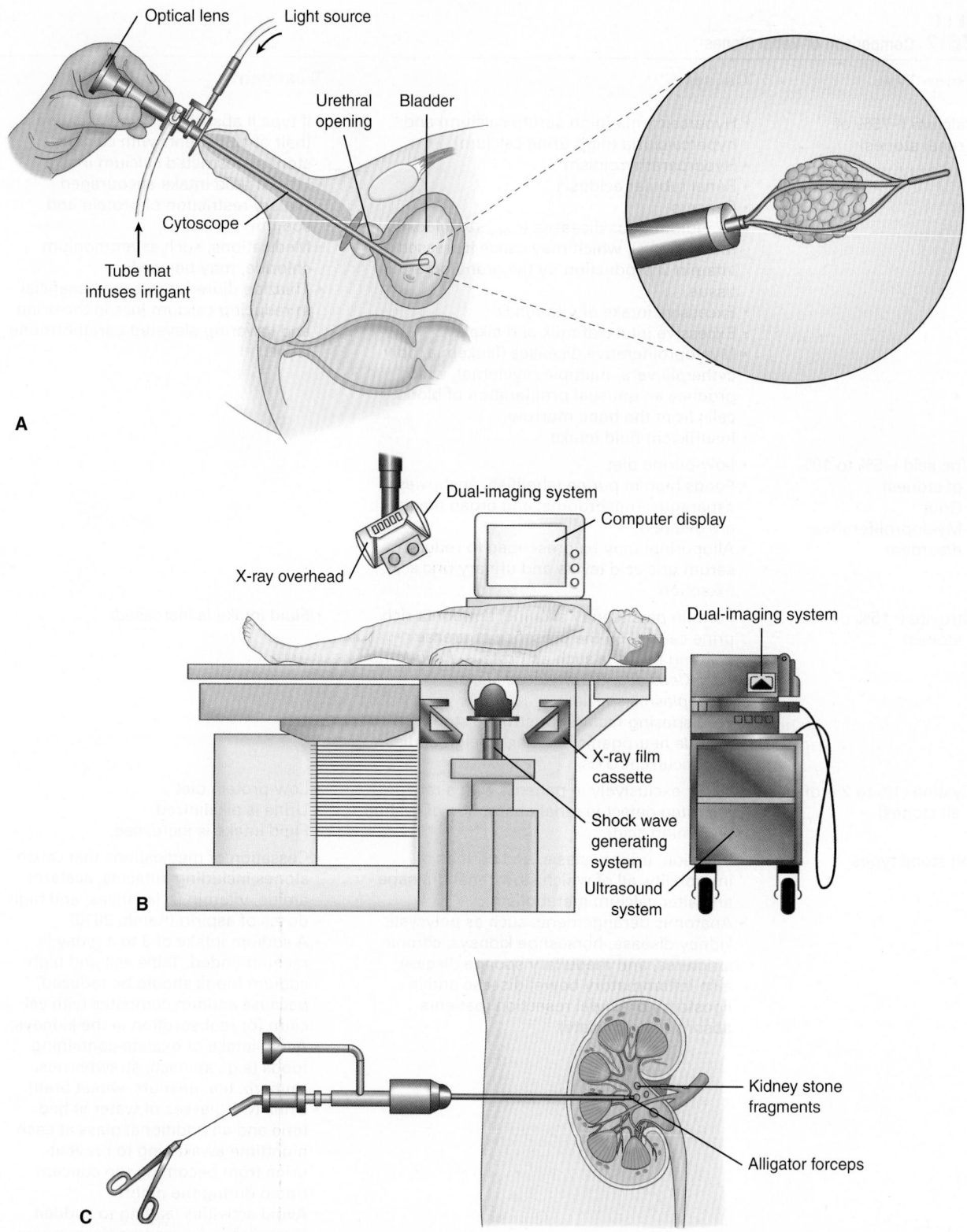

FIGURE 28-6 Methods of treating renal stones. (**A**) During a cystoscopy, which is used for removing small stones located in the ureter close to the bladder, a ureteroscope is inserted into the ureter to visualize the stone. The stone is then fragmented or captured and removed. (**B**) Extracorporeal shock wave lithotripsy (ESWL) may be used for symptomatic, non-passable upper urinary tract stones. Electromagnetically generated shock waves are focused over the area of the renal stone. The high-energy dry shock waves pass through the skin and fragment the stone. (**C**) Percutaneous nephrolithotomy is used to treat larger stones. A percutaneous tract is formed and a nephroscope is inserted through it. Then the stone is extracted or pulverized.

TABLE
28-2 Comparison of Renal Stones

Stone Type	Causes	Treatment
Calcium (~75% of renal stones)	• Hypercalcemia (high serum calcium) and hypercalciuria (high urine calcium) • Hyperparathyroidism • Renal tubular acidosis • Cancers • Granulomatous diseases (e.g., sarcoidosis, tuberculosis), which may cause increased vitamin D production by the granulomatous tissue • Excessive intake of vitamin D • Excessive intake of milk and alkali • Myeloproliferative diseases (leukemia, polycythemia vera, multiple myeloma), which produce an unusual proliferation of blood cells from the bone marrow • Insufficient fluid intake	• If type II absorptive hypercalciuria (half of all patients with calcium stones), restricted calcium intake • Liberal fluid intake encouraged • Dietary restriction of protein and sodium • Medications, such as ammonium chloride, may be used. • Thiazide diuretics may be beneficial in reducing calcium loss in the urine and lowering elevated parathormone levels.
Uric acid (~5% to 10% of stones) • Gout • Myeloproliferative disorders	• Low-purine diet • Foods high in purine (shellfish, anchovies, asparagus, mushrooms, and organ meats) are avoided. • Allopurinol may be prescribed to reduce serum uric acid levels and urinary uric acid excretion.	
Struvite (~15% of stones)	• Form in persistently alkaline, ammonia-rich urine caused by the presence of urease-splitting bacteria such as *Proteus, Pseudomonas, Klebsiella, Staphylococcus,* or *Mycoplasma* species • Predisposing factors for struvite stones include neurogenic bladder, foreign bodies, and recurrent UTIs.	• Fluid intake is increased.
Cystine (1% to 2% of all stones)	• Occur exclusively in patients with a rare inherited defect in renal absorption of cystine (an amino acid)	• Low-protein diet • Urine is alkalinized. • Fluid intake is increased.
All stone types	• Infection, urinary stasis, and periods of immobility, all of which slow renal drainage and alter calcium metabolism • Anatomic derangements such as polycystic kidney disease, horseshoe kidneys, chronic strictures, and medullary sponge disease; also inflammatory bowel disease and in ileostomy or bowel resection (patients absorb more oxalate).	• Cessation of medications that cause stones including antacids, acetazolamide, vitamin D, laxatives, and high doses of aspirin (Karch, 2010). • A sodium intake of 3 to 4 g/day is recommended. Table salt and high-sodium foods should be reduced, because sodium competes with calcium for reabsorption in the kidneys. • Avoid intake of oxalate-containing foods (e.g., spinach, strawberries, rhubarb, tea, peanuts, wheat bran). • Drink two glasses of water at bedtime and an additional glass at each nighttime awakening to prevent urine from becoming too concentrated during the night. • Avoid activities leading to sudden increases in environmental temperatures that may cause excessive sweating and dehydration. • Contact your primary healthcare provider at the first sign of a urinary tract infection.

TABLE
28-3 Surgical Treatment of Renal Stones

Procedure	Description	Postprocedure Care
Ureteroscopy (See Fig. 28-6A)	Access to the stone is accomplished by inserting a ureteroscope into the ureter and then, depending on the size of the stone, either basketing or inserting a laser, electrohydraulic lithotriptor, or ultrasound device through the ureteroscope to fragment and remove the stones. A stent may be inserted and left in place for 48 hours or more after the procedure to keep the ureter patent.	*For all procedures:* • Increase fluid intake to assist in the passage of stone fragments. • Monitor for signs and symptoms that indicate complications, such as fever, decreasing urine output, and pain. *For all procedures except electrohydraulic lithotripsy:* • Expect hematuria (it is anticipated in all patients), but it should disappear within 4 to 5 days.
Extracorporeal shock wave lithotripsy (ESWL) (See Fig. 28-6B)	A high-energy amplitude of pressure, or shock wave, is generated by the abrupt release of energy and transmitted through water and soft tissues; noninvasive procedure used to break up stones in the calyx of the kidney. After the stones are fragmented to the size of grains of sand, the remnants of the stones are spontaneously voided. The patient is observed for obstruction and infection resulting from blockage of the urinary tract by stone fragments.	
Endourologic methods (See Fig. 28-6C) percutaneous nephrostomy; percutaneous nephrolithotomy	A nephroscope is introduced through a percutaneous route into the renal parenchyma. Depending on its size, the stone may be extracted with forceps or by a stone retrieval basket.	
Electrohydraulic lithotripsy	An electrical discharge is used to create a hydraulic shock wave to break up the stone. A probe is passed through the cystoscope, and the tip of the lithotriptor is placed near the stone. After the stone is extracted, the percutaneous nephrostomy tube is left in place for a time to ensure that the ureter is not obstructed by edema or blood clots.	

NURSING PROCESS

The Patient With Kidney Stones

Assessment

The patient with suspected renal stones is assessed for pain and discomfort as well as associated symptoms, such as nausea, vomiting, diarrhea, and abdominal distention. The severity and location of pain are determined, along with any radiation of the pain. Nursing assessment also includes observing for signs and symptoms of UTI and obstruction. The urine is inspected for blood and is strained for stones or gravel. The history focuses on factors that predispose the patient to urinary tract stones or that may have precipitated the current episode of renal or ureteral colic. The patient's knowledge about renal stones and measures to prevent their occurrence or recurrence is also assessed.

Diagnosis

Appropriate nursing diagnoses of the patient with kidney stones may include:

• Acute pain related to inflammation, obstruction, and abrasion of the urinary tract

(continued on page 794)

- Deficient knowledge regarding prevention of recurrence of renal stones
- Deficient knowledge regarding the role of diet in the treatment of renal stones
- Impaired urinary elimination due to presence of renal stones

Potential complications may include the following:

- Infection and urosepsis (from UTI and pyelonephritis)
- Obstruction of the urinary tract by a stone or edema with subsequent acute renal failure

Planning

The major goals for the patient may include relief of pain and discomfort, prevention of recurrence of renal stones, and absence of complications.

Nursing Interventions

Relieving Pain

Severe and acute pain is often the presenting symptom of a patient with renal and urinary calculi and requires immediate attention. Opioid analgesic agents (IV or intramuscular) may be prescribed and administered to provide rapid relief along with an IV NSAID. The patient is encouraged and assisted to assume a position of comfort. If activity brings pain relief, the patient is assisted to ambulate. The pain level is monitored closely, and an increase in severity is reported promptly so that relief can be provided and additional treatment initiated.

Monitoring and Managing Potential Complications

Increased fluid intake is encouraged to prevent dehydration and increase hydrostatic pressure within the urinary tract to promote passage of the stone. If the patient cannot take adequate fluids orally, IV fluids are prescribed. The total urine output and patterns of voiding are monitored. Ambulation is encouraged as a means of moving the stone through the urinary tract.

All urine is strained because uric acid stones may crumble. Any blood clots passed in the urine should be crushed and the sides of the urinal and bedpan inspected for clinging stones. Because renal stones increase the risk of infection, sepsis, and obstruction of the urinary tract, the patient is instructed to report decreased urine volume and bloody or cloudy urine.

Patients with calculi require frequent nursing observation to detect the spontaneous passage of a stone. The patient is instructed to immediately report any sudden increases in pain intensity because of the possibility of a stone fragment obstructing a ureter. Vital signs, including temperature, are monitored closely to detect early signs of infection. UTIs may be associated with renal stones due

to an obstruction from the stone or from the stone itself. All infections should be treated with the appropriate antibiotic agent before efforts are made to dissolve the stone.

Because the risk of recurring renal stones is high, the nurse provides education about the causes of kidney stones and recommendations to prevent their recurrence (see Table 28-2). The patient is encouraged to follow a regimen to avoid further stone formation, including maintaining a high fluid intake because stones form more readily in concentrated urine. A patient who has shown a tendency to form stones should drink enough fluid to excrete greater than 2,000 mL.

Continuing Care

The patient is monitored closely in follow-up care to ensure that treatment has been effective and that no complications, such as obstruction, infection, renal hematoma, or hypertension, have developed.

The patient's ability to monitor urinary pH and interpret the results is assessed during follow-up visits to the clinic or health care provider's office. Because of the high risk of recurrence, the patient with renal stones needs to understand the signs and symptoms of stone formation, obstruction, and infection, and the importance of reporting these signs promptly. If medications are prescribed for the prevention of stone formation, the actions and importance of the medications are explained to the patient.

Evaluation

Expected patient outcomes may include:

1. Reports relief of pain
2. States increased knowledge of health-seeking behaviors to prevent recurrence:
   a. Consumes increased fluid intake (at least eight 8-ounce glasses of fluid per day)
   b. Participates in appropriate activity
   c. Consumes diet prescribed to reduce dietary factors predisposing to stone formation
   d. Recognizes symptoms (fever, chills, flank pain, hematuria) to be reported to health care provider
   e. Monitors urinary pH as directed
   f. Takes prescribed medication as directed to reduce stone formation
3. Experiences no complications:
   a. Reports no signs or symptoms of infection or urosepsis
   b. Voids 200 to 400 mL per voiding of clear urine without evidence of bleeding
   c. Experiences absence of dysuria, frequency, and hesitancy
   d. Maintains normal body temperature

tube. Urine collects in the pouch until a catheter is inserted and the urine is drained (Tanagho & McAninch, 2007).

The pouch must be drained at regular intervals by a catheter to prevent absorption of metabolic waste products from the urine, reflux of urine to the ureters, and UTI. Postoperative nursing care of the patient with a continent ileal urinary pouch is similar to nursing care of the patient with an ileal conduit. These patients usually have additional drainage tubes (cecostomy catheter from the pouch, stoma catheter exiting from the stoma, ureteral stents, Penrose drain, as well as a urethral catheter). All drainage tubes must be carefully monitored for patency and amount and type of drainage. In the immediate postoperative period, the cecostomy tube is irrigated two or three times daily to remove mucus and prevent blockage.

Other variations of continent urinary reservoirs include the Kock pouch (U-shaped pouch constructed of ileum, with a nipple-like one-way valve; see Fig. 28-8B C) and the Charleston pouch (uses the ileum and ascending colon as the pouch, with the appendix and colon junction serving as the one-way valve mechanism).

URETEROSIGMOIDOSTOMY

Ureterosigmoidostomy, another form of continent urinary diversion, is an implantation of the ureters into the sigmoid colon (see Fig. 28-8D). It is usually performed in patients who have had extensive pelvic irradiation, previous small bowel resection, or coexisting small bowel disease.

After surgery, voiding occurs from the rectum (for life), and an adjustment in lifestyle will be necessary because of urinary frequency. Drainage has a consistency equivalent to watery diarrhea, and the patient has some degree of nocturia. Patients usually need to plan activities around the frequent need to urinate, which in turn may affect the patient's social life. However, this provides the advantage of urinary control without having to wear an external appliance.

Chapter Review

Critical Thinking Exercises

1. As the head nurse in a long-term care facility, you are approached by the daughter of one of the residents. She requests that her mother, who can ambulate with assistance, undergo bladder retraining in order to increase her level of independence. What should your response be to this request? What is the evidence base that supports your response? Identify the criteria used to evaluate the strength of the evidence.

2. As one of the nurses in a busy urology practice, you are performing telephone triage. A 62-year-old man who underwent a ureteroscopy for stone disease 2 days ago complains of increasing urinary frequency, dysuria, and increasing abdominal pain. Explain the instructions you would provide. What medical and nursing interventions would you anticipate?

NCLEX-Style Review Questions

1. A sexually-active, 23-year-old woman presents with a history of three UTIs in the past 12 months. What is the first step in her evaluation?
   A. A urine culture
   B. An intravenous pyelogram to look for an anatomic abnormality
   C. A history and physical examination
   D. A 3-day course of antibiotics

2. A 55-year-old woman reports stress incontinence when sneezing and playing tennis. She asks what she can do to prevent this from happening. Which of the following is the nurse's best response?

   A. Start an anticholinergic medication.
   B. Void immediately prior to playing tennis to try and decrease urine loss while playing.
   C. Decrease overall fluid intake so this is unlikely to happen at any time.
   D. Restrict intake of calcium-containing foods.

3. Mrs. Andersen has an indwelling catheter after an open cholecystectomy. She develops cramping in the suprapubic area and urinary leakage. What is the nurse's first intervention?
   A. Make certain the catheter is not kinked.
   B. Evaluate for incisional pain.
   C. Explain that her symptoms are due to peristalsis.
   D. Irrigate the urinary catheter to assess for blockage of flow.

4. Traci, a 29-year-old married woman, frequently experiences a UTI after sexual intercourse. In addition to instruction regarding voiding after intercourse, her initial management may include which of the following?
   A. A recommendation for abstinence
   B. Testing for anatomic abnormalities
   C. A prescription for antibiotics to be used post-coitus
   D. Boric acid suppositories

5. When being instructed on methods for managing the mucous in their urinary diversion, patients should be reminded to do which of the following?
   A. Increase fiber intake.
   B. Consume high levels of citrus fruits and juices.
   C. Increase consumption of cranberry juice.
   D. Avoid caffeine consumption.

> **Try these additional resources to enhance your learning and understanding of this chapter:**
> - thePoint online resource available at
>   **http://thepoint.lww.com/Pellico1e**
> - *Handbook for Focus on Adult Health: Medical-Surgical Nursing*
> - *Study Guide for Focus on Adult Health: Medical-Surgical Nursing*

References and Selected Readings

References and selected readings associated with this chapter can be found on the website that accompanies the book. Visit http://thepoint.lww.com/Pellico1e to access the references and other additional resources associated with this chapter.

Problems Related to Endocrine Function

A 70-YEAR-OLD patient with type 1 diabetes is being seen in the endocrinology clinic because of a foot wound that will not heal. The patient states that his blood sugar levels have been ranging from 78 to 350 mg/dL and that he eats "sweets" at every meal. A culture of the wound was sent to the laboratory.

➡ What questions are pertinent to ask the patient regarding his fluctuating blood sugar levels?

➡ What teaching areas would you reinforce regarding wound healing in this patient?

➡ What would help the patient keep an accurate record of his blood sugar times and levels?

Nursing Assessment: Endocrine Function

HAVOVI D. PATEL

After reading this chapter, you will be able to:

1. Identify the major endocrine glands of the body, their anatomic location, and the hormones they secrete.

2. Summarize the major action of the hormones secreted from each of the glands.

3. Describe the negative feedback mechanism and its importance in the regulation of the biologic processes.

4. Summarize the role of the hypothalamus and the pituitary in regulation of hormone secretion from the thyroid and the adrenal glands.

5. Name the disorders produced by over and under secretion of the endocrine glands.

6. Describe components of a heath history and physical examination of the endocrine system.

7. Identify the diagnostic tests used to assess altered function of the endocrine glands.

Understanding the function of the endocrine glands and the consequences of dysfunction enables the health care professional to anticipate physiologic changes. Symptoms of endocrine disorders usually manifest according to hormone oversecretion or undersecretion. The assessment of the endocrine system is not as straightforward as the other systems because it is difficult to inspect and palpate these glands due to their anatomic location, and patients present with a wide variety of symptoms. The health care professional must understand the function of endocrine hormones and attentively assess patient's symptoms and diagnostic findings to detect an endocrine disorder.

ANATOMIC AND PHYSIOLOGIC OVERVIEW

Function and Regulation of Hormones

The **endocrine** system consists of groups of organs that regulate the complex processes involved in metabolism, tissue function, reproduction, growth, and development by synthesizing and releasing specific hormones. The **hormones** released have specific "target" tissue, where the hormone binds and impacts the cells functions/reactions. The endocrine system maintains optimal internal functional cell integrity, thus its influence impacts almost every cell, organ, and function of the body. The endocrine glands include the pituitary, thyroid, parathyroids, adrenals, pancreatic islets, ovaries, and testes (Fig. 29-1). Endocrine glands secrete their hormones directly into the bloodstream, which differentiates them from **exocrine** glands, such as sweat glands, which secrete their products through ducts onto epithelial surfaces of the skin, or the salivary glands, which secrete directly into the digestive tract. The endocrine glands are composed of secretory cells arranged in minute clusters known as *acini*. No ducts are present, but the glands have a rich blood supply, so the hormones they produce enter the bloodstream rapidly. The hypothalamus is the link between the nervous system and the endocrine system. The hypothalamus controls the pituitary, which influences the target gland through the action of the secreting hormones. Table 29-1 on page 806 lists the major hormones, their target tissue, and some of their properties.

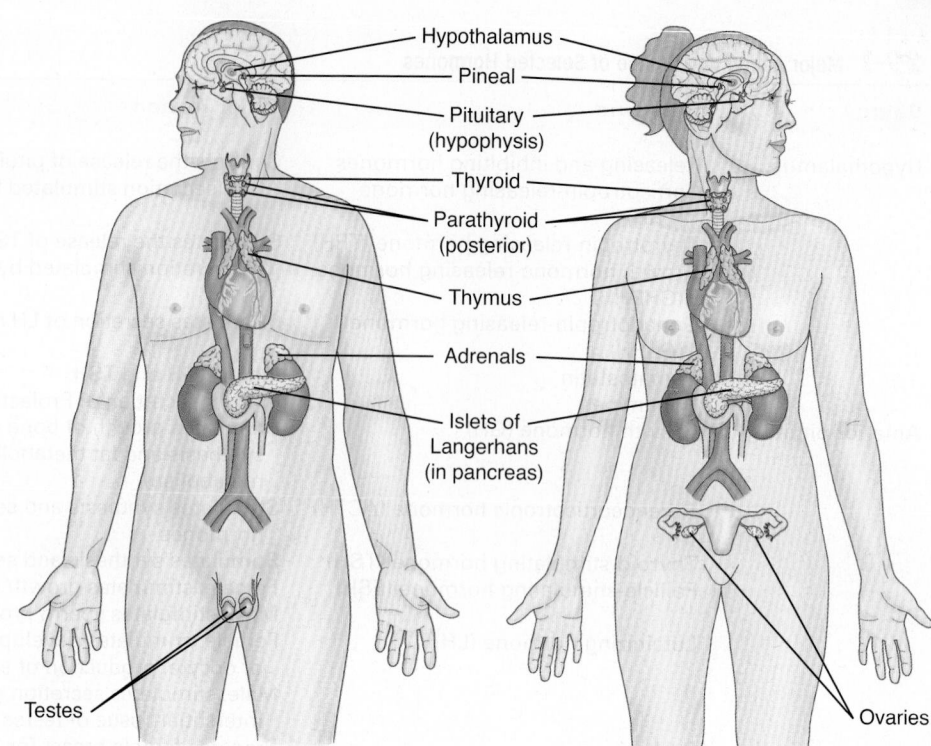

Hypothalamus
Pineal
Pituitary (hypophysis)
Thyroid
Parathyroid (posterior)
Thymus
Adrenals
Islets of Langerhans (in pancreas)
Testes
Ovaries

FIGURE 29-1 Major hormone-secreting glands of the endocrine system.

In the healthy physiologic state, hormone concentration in the bloodstream is maintained at a relatively constant level. When the hormone concentration increases, further production of that hormone is inhibited. When the hormone concentration decreases, the rate of production of that hormone increases. This mechanism for regulating hormone concentration in the bloodstream is called **negative feedback**, and is important in the regulation of many biologic processes.

Glands of the Endocrine System

Pituitary Gland

The pituitary gland, or hypophysis, is a round structure about 1.27 cm (½ inch) in diameter located on the inferior aspect of the brain. Commonly referred to as the *master gland*, the pituitary secretes hormones that control the secretion of additional hormones by other endocrine glands (Fig. 29-2, p. 807). The pituitary itself is controlled by the hypothalamus, an adjacent area of the brain that is connected to the pituitary by the pituitary stalk. The pituitary gland is divided into the anterior and posterior lobes.

Anterior Pituitary Gland

The major hormones of the anterior pituitary gland are follicle-stimulating hormone (FSH), luteinizing hormone (LH), prolactin, **adrenocorticotropic hormone** (ACTH), **thyroid-stimulating hormone** (TSH), and growth hormone (also referred to as somatotropin). Releasing factors secreted by the hypothalamus control the secretion of these major hormones. These releasing factors reach the anterior pituitary by way of the bloodstream in a special circulation called the pituitary

portal blood system. Other hormones secreted by the anterior pituitary include melanocyte-stimulating hormone and beta-lipotropin; the function of lipotropin is poorly understood.

The hormones released by the anterior pituitary enter the general circulation and are transported to their target organs. The main function of TSH, ACTH, FSH, and LH is the release of hormones from other endocrine glands. Prolactin acts directly on the breast to stimulate milk production. Hormones that stimulate other organs and tissues are discussed in conjunction with their target organs.

Posterior Pituitary

Important hormones secreted by the posterior lobe of the pituitary gland (called the *neurohypophysis*) include **vasopressin**, also termed antidiuretic hormone or ADH, and **oxytocin**. These hormones are synthesized in the hypothalamus and travel from the hypothalamus to the posterior pituitary gland for storage via nerve tracks. Vasopressin (ADH) release will result in re-absorption of water into the bloodstream rather than excretion by the kidneys; its secretion is stimulated by an increase in the osmolality of the blood (concentrated blood) or by a decrease in blood pressure as additional water is needed to return to the blood stream. Oxytocin secretion is stimulated during pregnancy and at childbirth. It facilitates milk ejection during lactation and increases the force of uterine contractions during labor and delivery.

Thyroid Gland

The thyroid gland is a butterfly-shaped organ located in the lower neck, anterior to the trachea. It consists of two lateral lobes connected by an isthmus. The gland is about 5 cm long

TABLE
29-1 Major Action and Source of Selected Hormones

Source	Hormone	Major Action
Hypothalamus	Releasing and inhibiting hormones	Controls the release of pituitary hormones
	Corticotropin-releasing hormone (CRH)	ACTH secretion stimulated by CRH
	Thyrotropin-releasing hormone (TRH)	Stimulates the release of TSH
	Growth hormone-releasing hormone (GHRH)	GH secretion stimulated by GHRH
	Gonadotropin-releasing hormone (GnRH)	Stimulates secretion of LH and FSH
	Somatostatin	Inhibits GH and TSH
	Dopamine	Inhibits secretion of Prolactin
Anterior pituitary	Growth hormone (GH)	Stimulates growth of bone and muscle, promotes protein synthesis and fat metabolism, decreases carbohydrate metabolism
	Adrenocorticotropic hormone (ACTH)	Stimulates synthesis and secretion of adrenal cortical hormones
	Thyroid-stimulating hormone (TSH)	Stimulates synthesis and secretion of thyroid hormone
	Follicle-stimulating hormone (FSH)	Female: stimulates growth of ovarian follicle, ovulation Male: stimulates sperm production
	Luteinizing hormone (LH)	Female: stimulates development of corpus luteum, release of oocyte, production of estrogen and progesterone Male: stimulates secretion of testosterone, development of interstitial tissue of testes
	Prolactin	Prepares female breast for breast-feeding
Posterior pituitary	Antidiuretic hormone (ADH)	Increases water reabsorption by kidney
	Oxytocin	Stimulates contraction of pregnant uterus, milk ejection from breasts after childbirth
Adrenal cortex	Mineralocorticosteroids, mainly aldosterone	Increases sodium absorption, potassium loss by kidney
	Glucocorticoids, mainly cortisol	Affects metabolism of all nutrients; regulates blood glucose levels, affects growth, has anti-inflammatory action, and decreases effects of stress
	Adrenal androgens, mainly dehydro-epiandrosterone (DHEA) and androstenedione	Have minimal intrinsic androgenic activity; they are converted to testosterone and dihydrotestosterone in the periphery
Adrenal medulla	Epinephrine Norepinephrine	Serve as neurotransmitters for the sympathetic nervous system; the flight or fight response specifically increases heart rate, blood flow to skeletal muscle and production of glucose
Thyroid (follicular cells)	Thyroid hormones: triiodothyronine (T_3), thyroxine (T_4)	Increase the metabolic rate; increase protein and bone turnover; increase responsiveness to catecholamines; necessary for fetal and infant growth and development
Thyroid C cells	Calcitonin	Lowers blood calcium and phosphate levels
Parathyroid glands	Parathormone (PTH, parathyroid hormone)	Regulates serum calcium
Pancreatic islet cells	Insulin	Lowers blood glucose by facilitating glucose transport across cell membranes of muscle, liver, and adipose tissue
	Glucagon	Increases blood glucose concentration by stimulation of glycogenolysis and glyconeogenesis
	Somatostatin	Delays intestinal absorption of glucose
Kidney	1,25-Dihydroxyvitamin D	Stimulates calcium absorption from the intestine
	Renin	Activates renin-angiotensin-aldosterone system
	Erythropoietin	Increases red blood cell production
Ovaries	Estrogen	Affects development of female sex organs and secondary sex characteristics
	Progesterone	Influences menstrual cycle; stimulates growth of uterine wall; maintains pregnancy
Testes	Androgens, mainly testosterone	Affect development of male sex organs and secondary sex characteristics; aid in sperm production

Adapted with permission from Porth, C. M., & Matfin, G. (2009), *Pathophysiology: Concepts of altered health states* (8th ed.) Philadelphia: Lippincott Williams & Wilkins.

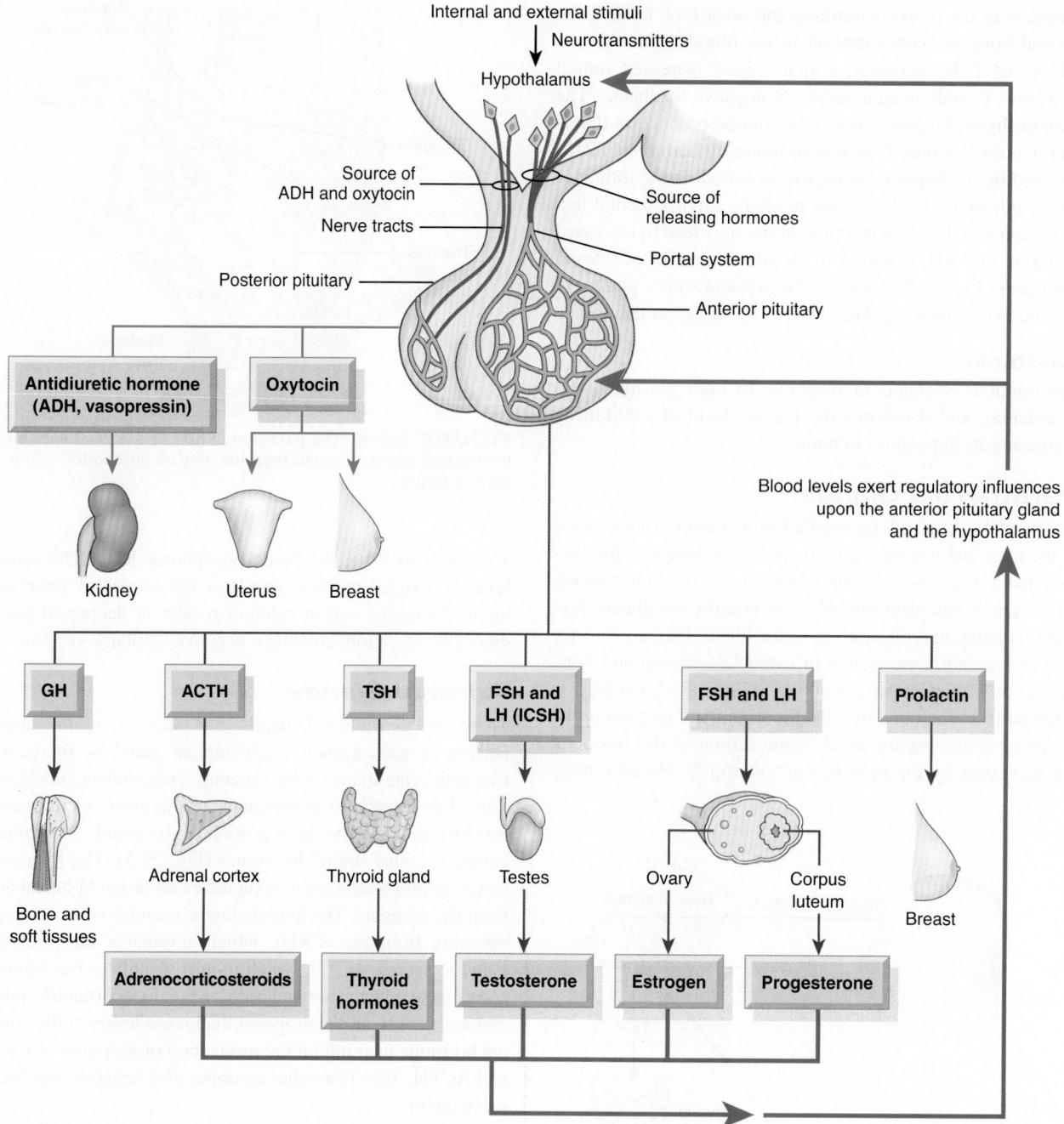

FIGURE 29-2 The pituitary gland, the relationship of the brain to pituitary action, and the hormones secreted by the anterior and posterior pituitary lobes.

and 3 cm wide and weighs about 30 g. Blood flow to the thyroid is very high (about 5 mL/min per gram of thyroid tissue), approximately five times the blood flow to the liver. This reflects the high metabolic activity of the thyroid gland. The thyroid gland produces three hormones: **thyroxine (T_4), triiodothyronine (T_3),** and **calcitonin.** T_4 and T_3 are referred to collectively as *thyroid hormone.* Iodine is essential to the thyroid gland for synthesis of its hormones.

Thyroid Hormone

The primary function of thyroid hormone is to control cellular metabolic activity. T_4, a relatively weak hormone, main-

tains body metabolism in a steady state. T_3 is about five times as potent as T_4 and has a more rapid metabolic action. These hormones accelerate all bodily processes that contribute to oxygen consumption and altering the responsiveness of tissues to other hormones. The thyroid hormones influence cell replication, are important in brain development, and are necessary for normal growth. The thyroid hormones, through their widespread effects on cellular metabolism, influence every major organ system. The secretion of T_3 and T_4 by the thyroid gland is controlled by TSH (also called *thyrotropin*) from the anterior pituitary gland. TSH controls the rate of thyroid hormone release. In turn, the level of thyroid

hormone in the blood determines the release of TSH. If the thyroid hormone concentration in the blood decreases, the release of TSH increases, which causes increased output of T_3 and T_4 (this is an example of negative feedback). The term **euthyroid** refers to thyroid hormone production that is within normal limits. Thyrotropin-releasing hormone (TRH), secreted by the hypothalamus, exerts a modulating influence on the release of TSH from the pituitary. Environmental factors, such as a decrease in temperature, may lead to increased secretion of TRH, resulting in elevated secretion of thyroid hormones. Figure 29-3 shows the hypothalamic–pituitary–thyroid axis, which regulates thyroid hormone production.

Calcitonin

Calcitonin is secreted in response to high plasma levels of calcium, and it reduces the plasma level of calcium by increasing its deposition in bone.

Parathyroid Glands

The parathyroid glands (normally four in number) are situated in the neck and embedded in the posterior aspect of the thyroid gland (Fig. 29-4). Parathormone (parathyroid hormone), the protein hormone produced by the parathyroid glands, regulates calcium and phosphorus metabolism. Increased secretion of parathormone results in osteoclast growth and bone resorption. When bone resorption is increased, calcium is released from the bone into the blood thereby increasing the serum or blood calcium level. Some actions of this hormone are increased by the presence of vitamin D. Parathormone

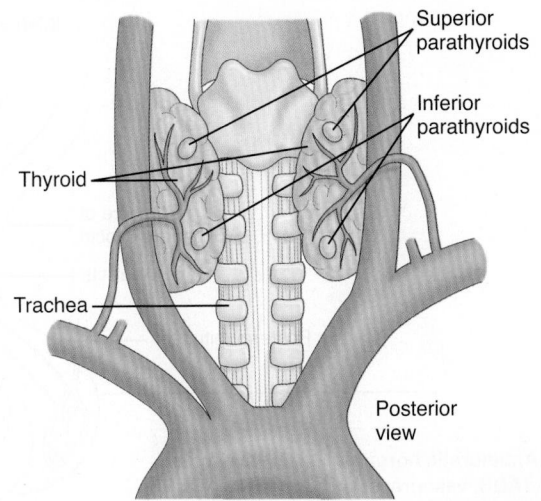

FIGURE 29-4 The parathyroid glands are located behind the thyroid gland. The parathyroids may be embedded in the thyroid tissue.

also tends to lower the blood phosphorus level. The serum level of ionized calcium regulates the output of parathormone. Increased serum calcium results in decreased parathormone secretion, creating a negative feedback system.

Adrenal Glands

There are two adrenal glands, one attached to the upper portion of each kidney. Each adrenal gland is, in reality, two endocrine glands with separate, independent functions. The adrenal medulla at the center of the gland secretes catecholamines, and the outer portion of the gland, the adrenal cortex, secretes steroid hormones (Fig. 29-5). The hypothalamic–pituitary–adrenal axis regulates secretion of hormones from the adrenals. The hypothalamus secretes corticotropin-releasing hormone (CRH), which stimulates the pituitary gland to secrete ACTH, which in turn stimulates the adrenal cortex to secrete the adrenal hormones (glucocorticoids, mineralocorticoids, and androgens). Increased levels of the adrenal hormone then inhibit the production or secretion of CRH and ACTH. This is another example of a negative feedback mechanism.

Adrenal Medulla

The adrenal medulla functions as part of the autonomic nervous system. Stimulation of preganglionic sympathetic nerve fibers, which travel directly to the cells of the adrenal medulla, causes release of the catecholamine hormones epinephrine and norepinephrine. About 90% of the secretion of the human adrenal medulla is epinephrine (also called *adrenaline*). The major effects of epinephrine release are to prepare to meet a challenge (fight-or-flight response). Secretion of epinephrine causes decreased blood flow to tissues that are not needed in emergency situations, such as the gastrointestinal (GI) tract, and increased blood flow to tissues that are important for effective fight or flight, such

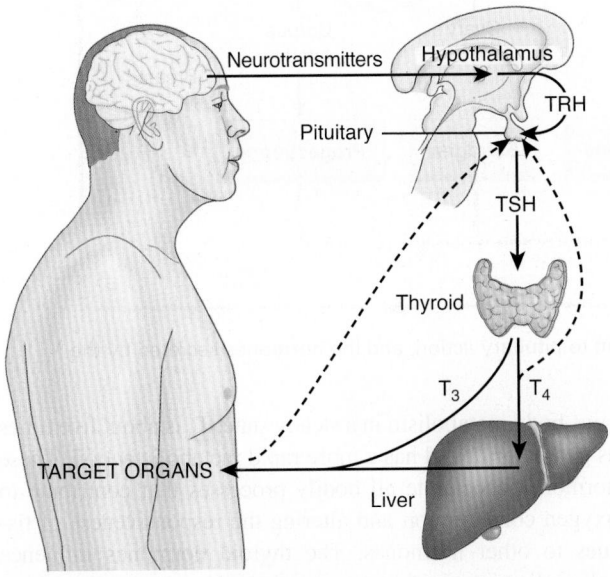

FIGURE 29-3 The hypothalamic–pituitary–thyroid axis. Thyroid-releasing hormone (TRH) from the hypothalamus stimulates the pituitary gland to secrete thyroid-stimulating hormone (TSH). TSH stimulates the thyroid to produce thyroid hormone (T_3 and T_4). High circulating levels of T_3 and T_4 inhibit further TSH secretion and thyroid hormone production through a negative feedback mechanism (*dashed lines*).

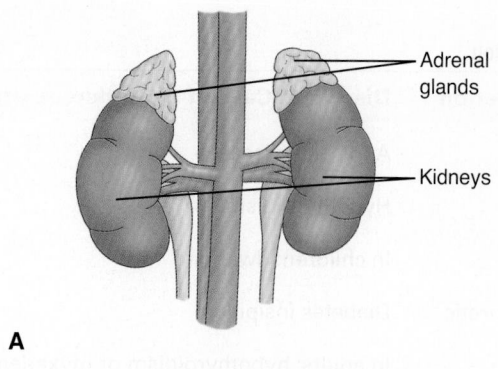

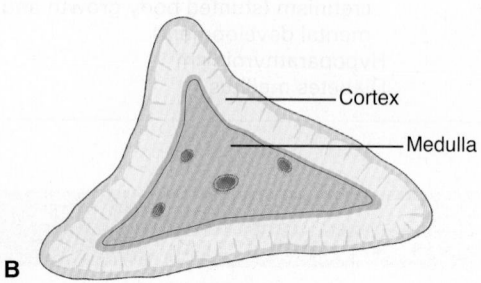

FIGURE 29-5 **(A)** The adrenal glands sit on top of the kidneys. **(B)** Each gland is composed of an outer cortex and an inner medulla. Each area secretes specific hormones. The adrenal medulla secretes catecholamines—epinephrine and norepinephrine; the adrenal cortex secretes glucocorticoids, mineralocorticoids, and sex hormones.

as cardiac and skeletal muscle. Catecholamines regulate metabolic pathways to promote catabolism of stored fuels to meet caloric needs from endogenous sources, induce the release of free fatty acids, increase the basal metabolic rate, and elevate the blood glucose level.

Adrenal Cortex

A functioning adrenal cortex is necessary for life; adrenocortical secretions make it possible for the body to adapt to stress of all kinds. With primary adrenal hypofunction or insufficiency (Addison's disease), the problem originates in the adrenal gland itself and is characterized by decreased secretion of the three types of steroid hormones produced by the adrenal cortex: **glucocorticoids**, the prototype of which is hydrocortisone; **mineralocorticoids**, mainly aldosterone; and sex hormones, mainly **androgens** (male sex hormones). Secondary hypofunction is associated with low ACTH, which may occur in panhypopituitarism and is characterized by decreased glucocorticoid secretion; aldosterone secretion is unaffected.

GLUCOCORTICOIDS. The adrenal cortex secretes glucocorticoids in response to the release of ACTH from the anterior lobe of the pituitary gland. Glucocorticoids have major effects on the metabolism of almost all organs because of their influence on glucose metabolism (elevation of blood glucose

levels), and their ability to inhibit the inflammatory response to tissue injury and suppress allergic manifestations. Without the adrenal cortex, severe stress would cause peripheral circulatory failure, circulatory shock, and prostration. Survival in the absence of a functioning adrenal cortex is possible only with nutritional, electrolyte, fluid, and appropriate exogenous adrenocortical hormone replacement.

MINERALOCORTICOIDS. **Mineralocorticoids** exert their major effects on electrolyte metabolism. They act principally on the renal tubular and GI epithelium to cause increased sodium ion absorption in exchange for excretion of potassium or hydrogen ions. Aldosterone is primarily secreted in response to the presence of angiotensin II in the bloodstream. Angiotensin II is a substance that elevates the blood pressure by constricting arterioles. Its concentration is increased when renin is released from the kidney in response to decreased perfusion pressure. The resultant increased aldosterone levels promote sodium reabsorption by the kidney and the GI tract, which tends to restore blood pressure to normal, and increases renal excretion of potassium. The release of aldosterone can therefore also be increased in the presence of hyperkalemia. Aldosterone is the primary hormone for the long-term regulation of sodium balance.

SEX HORMONES. Androgens, the third major type of steroid hormones produced by the adrenal cortex, exert effects similar to those of male sex hormones. The adrenal gland may also secrete small amounts of some estrogens, or female sex hormones. ACTH controls the secretion of adrenal androgens. When secreted in normal amounts, the adrenal androgens appear to have little effect, but when secreted in excess, as in certain inborn enzyme deficiencies, masculinization may result. This is termed the **adrenogenital syndrome**.

Pancreatic Islets

The pancreas lies transversely in the upper abdomen with the head of the pancreas resting at the curve of the duodenum and the body beneath the stomach. The beta cells of the pancreas secrete insulin. Insulin facilitates glucose transport into body cells, thus lowering the blood glucose levels. The alpha cells of the pancreas secrete the hormone glucagon. It promotes gluconeogenesis, thus increasing the blood glucose level. Because its action is opposite to insulin, it may be termed a *counter-regulatory hormone*. The delta cells of the pancreas secrete somatostatin, which reduces the rate food is absorbed from the GI tract. See Chapter 30 for more detailed discussion of insulin.

Hormone Oversecretion and Undersecretion

Oversecretion and undersecretion of hormones result in many disorders. Table 29-2 summarizes disorders associated

TABLE
29-2 Disorders Associated With Hormone Oversecretion and Undersecretion

Hormone	Disorders Caused by Oversecretion	Disorders Caused by Undersecretion
Adrenocorticotropic hormone (ACTH)	Cushing's syndrome	Addison's disease
Thyroid-stimulating hormone (TSH)	Hyperthyroidism	Hypothyroidism
Growth hormone	In adults: acromegaly In children: gigantism	In children: dwarfism
Antidiuretic hormone (ADH; vasopressin)	Syndrome of inappropriate antidiuretic hormone (SIADH) secretion	Diabetes insipidus
Thyroid hormone	Hyperthyroidism	In adults: hypothyroidism or myxedema During fetal and neonatal development: cretinism (stunted body growth and mental development)
Parathormone	Hyperparathyroidism	Hypoparathyroidism
Insulin	Hypoglycemia	Diabetes mellitus

with hormone over- and undersecretion; additional information is found in Chapters 30 and 31.

Gerontologic Considerations

As a result of aging, the endocrine glands have decreased ability to cause secretion of the hormones, or the target organs lose their ability to respond to the hormones produced by the different glands.

These gerontological changes are summarized in Table 29-3.

ASSESSMENT OF THE ENDOCRINE SYSTEM

Health History

The nurse assesses the patient's history for the presence of preexisting endocrine disorders, compliance with medications and the presence of coexisting medical problems.

Endocrine disorders often manifest with nonspecific, atypical symptoms, or common complaints that can be attributed to a variety of disorders. The range of symptoms

TABLE
29-3 GERONTOLOGICAL CONSIDERATIONS / Age-Related Changes to the Endocrine System

Endocrine Gland	Age-Related Changes	History and Physical Findings
Thyroid	Atrophy and fibrosis of the thyroid gland with decreased thyroid gland activity resulting in decreased basal metabolic rate Reduced radioactive iodine uptake and decreased secretion and release of thyrotropin Increased nodularity of the thyroid	Cold intolerance Decreased appetite Decreased vital signs
Parathyroid gland	Decreased absorption and activation of vitamin D, which can lead to increased bone mineral loss and decreased bone mass	Increased risk for fractures
Adrenal gland	Decreased adrenal function adrenocorticotropic hormone (ACTH) secretion decreases with age with resultant decreased estrogen, progesterone, androgen and glucocorticoids	Increased incidence of osteoporosis Perineal and vaginal dryness Fragile skin tissue
Pituitary gland	The volume of the pituitary decreases Decreased ACTH, thyroid-stimulating hormone (TSH), follicle stimulating hormone (FSH), luteinizing hormone (LH)	Decreased muscle mass Decreased strength and energy tolerance Thin and dry skin
Pancreas	Decreased insulin secretion and decreased sensitivity to circulating insulin, resulting in reduced ability to metabolize glucose	

Adapted from Elipoulos, C. (2010). *Gerontological nursing* (7th ed.). Philadelphia: Lippincott Williams and Wilkins.

spans a wide trajectory including weight gain or loss, constipation or diarrhea, tachycardia or bradycardia, hypotension or hypertension, depression or anxiety, heat or cold intolerance, etc. Additionally, endocrine disease may be masked or associated with other comorbidities. For example, the symptoms of an elderly patient admitted with congestive heart failure (CHF) may be attributed to preexisting cardiac disease, without consideration of possible diagnosis of hyperthyroidism. Thus, because the endocrine system impacts nearly all cells and organs, the nurse must have a suspicion of potential endocrine disorders in all hospitalized patients. Additionally, it is the clustering of signs and symptoms, correlated with the nurse's knowledge of normal physiological endocrine function, that will alert the nurse to an underlying endocrine disorder. Clinical presentations of endocrine disorders are discussed below, according to specific endocrine glands.

Pituitary Dysfunction

A number of hormonal imbalances may be seen as the pituitary secretes numerous hormones including FSH, LH, ACTH, growth hormone (somatotropin), TSH, melanocyte stimulating hormone (MSH), and prolactin from the anterior pituitary, and ADH and oxytocin (stimulates uterine contractions and milk-ejection reflex) from the posterior pituitary.

During the health history, the nurse asks the patient about history of weakness, lethargy, muscular weakness, changes in sexual function (loss of libido) and secondary sex characteristics, as well as any menstrual disturbances in the females. In addition, assessment for galactorrhea (spontaneous, inappropriate flow of milk from male or female breast in absence of pregnancy or breastfeeding) is indicated, as prolactinomas (excessive prolactin) are the most common form of pituitary tumor. The nurse asks about changes in weight, height, enlargement of peripheral body parts, changes in the texture of the skin or hair, and any changes in urination or body temperature. Owing to the proximity of the pituitary to the optic chiasm, complaints of headaches and visual disturbances are not uncommon and should be evaluated. Neurological assessment data should consider the patient's level of consciousness, orientation, ability to obey commands, and appropriate response to stimuli. The nurse also inquires about symptoms of hyper/hypotension, palpitations, tremors, and mood changes.

Thyroid Gland Dysfunction

During the health history, the nurse asks the patient about changes in weight and appetite, bowel movements, heart rate and respiration, any marked tremors, nervousness, excitability, apprehension or impaired memory, decreased initiative, and slow thought processes. The nurse also asks about changes in the patient's tolerance of heat and cold. Also noted are excessive sweating or feeling very cold, lethargy or apathy, and changes in hair and skin. Exophthalmos,

which is an abnormal protrusion of one or both eyeballs that produces a startled expression, should be evaluated.

Parathyroid Dysfunction

During the health history, the nurse considers that hypofunction of the parathyroids is associated with hypocalcemia, while hyperfunction results in hypercalcemia (Mosekilde, 2008). If hypofunction is suspected, the nurse assesses for neuromuscular irritability since nerve cells become excited and overstimulate muscle cells in the presence of hypocalcemia. Clinical manifestations include complaints of paresthesias (perioral, extremities), and fasciculations (muscle twitching); therefore, the nurse asks the patient about neuromuscular manifestations. In addition, hypocalcemia has an impact on cardiac function and can prolong the QT interval and cause cardiac arrhythmias, hypotension, and potential cardiac failure. The nurse inquires about complaints of palpitations, shortness of breath, dizziness, and presence of peripheral edema. In addition, since chronic hypocalcemia is associated with cataract formation, the nurse asks about visual changes.

If hyperfunction of the parathyroid is suspected, with its resulting effects of hypercalcemia, the nurse understands that symptoms may be vague and include GI (anorexia, nausea, vomiting, bowel hypomotility, and constipation), musculoskeletal (muscle weakness, bone pain), neurological (fatigue, decreased concentration), renal (polyuria as hypercalcemia decreases the concentrating ability in the distal tubule), or more severe complaints. For example, hyperparathyroidism is associated with an increased incidence of peptic ulcer disease; therefore, the nurse should ask about presence of melena. Additionally, the patient is asked about cardiac complaints since hypercalcemia is associated with shortened QT interval, bradycardia, and hypertension. Finally, the formation of stones in one or both kidneys may cause symptoms due to renal calculi such as back or flank pain, nausea, vomiting, and dysuria.

Adrenal Dysfunction

The nurse asks the patient about symptoms of fluid imbalance (related to aldosterone), symptoms of hyper/hypoglycemia (related to cortisol), and changes in voice, hair, and sexual drive (related to androgens). With hypersecretion of the adrenal cortex (Cushing's disease), the nurse should inquire about problems with acne or hirsutism (related to hypersecretion of androgens), muscle weakness and paresthesia (hypersecretion of aldosterone), or history of fractures (hypersecretion of cortisol). When considering failure of the adrenal cortex, the nurse asks about symptoms of weakness, fatigue, poor appetite, and weight loss as they are prominent features of Addison's disease. If a problem with the adrenal medulla is suspected, the nurse assesses the patient's level of stress (related to catecholamines), such as headache, anxiety, nervousness, complaints of a racing heart, and sweating.

Physical Examination

General Appearance

The nurse notes the appearance of facial features, presence of hair, skin condition, and overall proportion. Excessive adrenocortical hormones may cause facial hair in women, "moon face" (swollen and round face), "buffalo hump"(accumulation of fatty deposits at the base of the neck), thinning of the skin, obesity of the trunk and thinness of the extremities, purple striae (stretch marks), and slow healing of minor cuts and bruises. Masculinization (in females) and truncal obesity may be seen in basophilic tumors giving rise to Cushing's syndrome. When a bronze skin color is noted, particularly in the creases of the hands or over the metacarpophalangeal (finger) joints, elbows, and knees, primary adrenal hypofunction or Addison's disease is suspected. This increased pigmentation is associated with excessive melanocyte-stimulating hormone. In acromegaly, growth occurs in the soft tissues and bones of the face, jaw, nose, chin, feet, and hands. Diabetes insipidus may cause dry mucous membranes and delayed skin turgor.

Vital Signs

The nurse performs a thorough cardiac assessment, including vital signs, noting rate and rhythm of the heart and auscultation of heart sounds. Bradycardia is associated with hypothyroidism; tachycardia is associated with hyperthyroidism (see Box 29-1 for additional information on hypothyroidism and hyperthyroidism). Diabetes insipidus, which causes profound polyuria, may cause clinical signs of volume depletion, such as tachycardia and hypotension.

Parathyroid problems may cause calcium derangements, which profoundly impact the cardiac system. Hypocalcemia decreases myocardial contractility, prolongs the QT interval (predisposing patients to ventricular arrhythmias), and is associated with hypotension secondary to reduced cardiac output. Hypercalcemia alters myocardial function; causes rhythm disturbances, such as bradycardia, first-, second-, and third-degree heart blocks, and a shortened QT interval; and is associated with hypertension.

Pheochromocytoma, a tumor of the adrenal medulla that causes excess secretion of catacholamines, results in episodic severe hypertension and tachycardia.

Thyroid

The nurse inspects and palpates the thyroid gland routinely in all patients. Inspection begins with identification of landmarks. The nurse inspects the lower neck region between the sternocleidomastoid muscles for swelling or asymmetry. The nurse instructs the patient to extend the neck slightly and swallow. Thyroid tissue rises normally with swallowing. The thyroid is palpated for size, shape, consistency, symmetry, and the presence of tenderness. Each of the lobes is palpated in detail. The nurse may examine the thyroid from an anterior or a posterior position (Fig. 29-6). If palpation

---

BOX 29-1 **Focused Assessment**

Hyperthyroidism Versus Hypothyroidism

Be alert for the following signs and symptoms of hyperthyroidism:

- Weight loss
- Warm, moist, flushed skin
- Tremors, emotionally hyperexcitable
- Tachycardia, irregular pulse
- Heat intolerance, hyperthermia
- Increased GI function
- Thinning of hair
- Exophthalmos (visual protrusion of the eye), corneal ulcerations
- Systolic murmur, thrill, bruit

Be alert for the following signs and symptoms of hypothyroidism:

- Weight gain
- Dry skin, nonpitting edema
- Fatigue, mental and physical sluggishness
- Bradycardia
- Cold intolerance, hypothyroidism
- Constipation
- Coarse hair, loss of eyebrows
- Carpal tunnel syndrome
- Pleural and pericardial effusions

---

discloses an enlarged thyroid gland, check for thrills and auscultate both lobes using the diaphragm of the stethoscope to identify any bruits (Box 29-2).

Eyes and Vision

Assess central vision and visual fields. Loss of color discrimination, diplopia (double vision), or blindness in a portion of a field of vision may be related to pressure of a pituitary tumor on the optic chiasm (located anterior to the pituitary stalk). See Chapter 49 for information on assessing vision and extraocular movements (EOM). Exophthalmos or

---

BOX 29-2 **Physical Assessment of an Enlarged Thyroid**

In Graves' disease, hypertrophy (enlarged cells) and hyperplasia (increased number of cells) of the thyroid may cause the gland to grow to two to three times its normal size. If the thyroid is retrosternal, goiters may not be visual, so it is important to assess for difficulty in swallowing. When the nurse places the hands on the thyroid, she or he feels increased blood flow to the thyroid (thrills). Thrills are often described as sensation of a purring cat. Auscultation using a stethoscope assesses for a bruit (blowing or whooshing sound), which signifies turbulent blood flow and may be found on one side or on the entire gland.

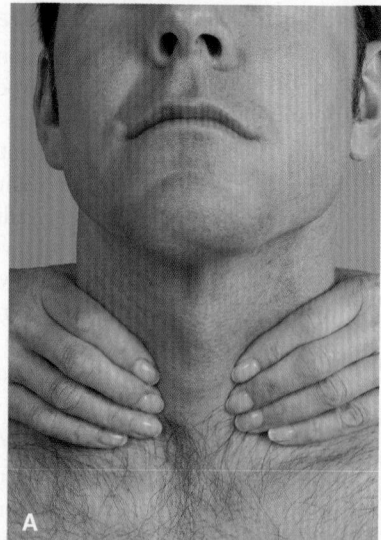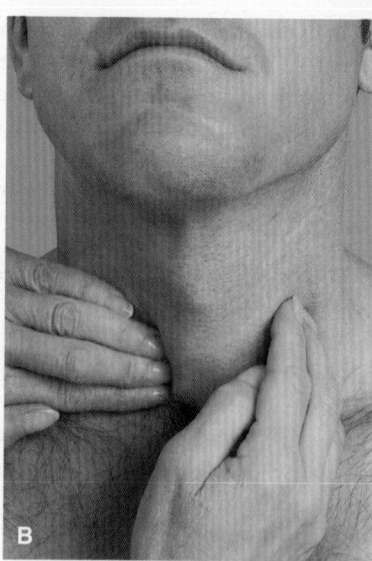

FIGURE 29-6 Palpating the thyroid. **(A)** Posterior approach. **(B)** Anterior approach. From Rhoads, J. (2006). *Advanced health assessment and diagnostic reasoning.* Philadelphia: Lippincott Williams & Wilkins.

proptosis is an anterior bulging of the eyeballs associated with hyperthyroidism.

Other Assessments

When a parathyroid problem is suspected, check for any pathologic fractures or symptoms due to renal calculi. Assess for neuromuscular irritability (tetany) related to hypocalcemia (refer to chapter 32 for assessment cues).

Diagnostic Evaluation

Diagnostic evaluation is described related to the glands.

Anterior Pituitary Gland Tests

Computed tomography (CT) scan and magnetic resonance imaging (MRI) can be done to identify the presence or extent of tumors. Serum levels of pituitary hormones, along with hormones of target glands may be indicated to evaluate for increased or decreased activity of each gland. For example, an increased thyrotropic hormone-releasing factor (TRF), which targets the thyroid, is associated with hyperthyroidism. An increase in ACTH, which targets the adrenal cortex, will result in Cushing's disease, whereas a decrease in ACTH will be seen in adrenal insufficiency or Addison's disease.

Posterior Pituitary Gland Tests

Plasma levels of ADH can indicate increased or decreased levels. A fluid deprivation test may be indicated for diabetes insipidus. In this test, plasma and urine osmolality are measured, and these levels may be altered in disease. Refer to Chapter 31 for more details on this test.

Urine osmolality is assessed for syndrome of inappropriate secretion of antidiuretic hormone (SIADH). Because SIADH patients do not excrete dilute urine, the urine osmolality will be increased. Also serum sodium levels will show low levels because of the retention of water.

Thyroid Gland Tests

Several tests can be performed to test the functioning of the thyroid gland. Serum TSH is the best screening test for thyroid disorders and helps differentiate between disorder of the thyroid gland itself and disorders of the pituitary and hypothalamus. High levels of serum TSH will indicate normal or hypothyroidism, whereas low values indicate hyperthyroidism. This is an example of the negative feedback system. If the thyroid hormones (T_3 and T_4) are not secreted by the thyroid, TSH is increased to help stimulate the thyroid to produce these hormones. If T_3 and T_4 are excreted in large amounts, as occurs in hyperthyroidism, TSH is decreased. TSH is also used to monitor thyroid replacement regimen.

Free T_4 levels measure the unbound thyroxine levels in the blood that is free to enter cells and produce its effects (Porth & Matfin, 2009). More than 99% of T_3 and T_4 are bound to proteins. Thus, serum free T_4 levels will be increased in hyperthyroidism. T_4 decreases in hypothyroidism. Total T_3 or T_4-T_3 levels increase in hyperthyroidism.

Antithyroid antibodies will be seen in autoimmune thyroid disease, like Hashimoto's thyroiditis and Graves' disease. A radioactive iodine uptake test can also be done. This indicates the rate of iodine uptake by thyroid gland. It increases in hyperthyroidism and decreases in hypothyroidism. Needle aspiration biopsy can be done to check thyroid cell structure.

Thyroid imaging can be used in the differential diagnosis of masses. Increased functioning of nodules or "hot" nodules are often associated with benign adenomas, whereas "cold" areas refer to decreased functioning. Cancer of the thyroid often manifest as a "cold" area.

Parathyroid Tests

Serum calcium levels and serum PTH levels, as well as bone density tests, may be ordered.

In hyperparathyroidism, the serum calcium increases and serum PTH decreases. Phosphate levels may be decreased but in general are in the lower range of normal. Bone density tests may reveal decreased density owing to the increased osteoclast activity.

In hypoparathyroidism, the serum calcium levels will be lower and phosphate levels elevated.

Adrenal Medulla Tests

With pheochromocytoma, a rare tumor of the adrenal medulla, urine and plasma levels of catecholamine and metanephrine and serum levels of epinephrine and norepinephrine will be increased.

A urine vanillylmandelic acid (VMA) level test is performed when pheochromocytoma is suspected. A 24-hour urine specimen will show levels of urine VMA as high as 2 times the normal.

Clonidine suppression test, CT, MRI, ultrasound, and scintigraphy are other tests that can be ordered.

Adrenal Cortex Tests

In Addison's disease (adrenal insufficiency), the adrenal glands produce too little cortisol, thus serum cortisol levels are decreased, as is blood glucose. Addison's often causes insufficient levels of aldosterone, which results in decreased serum sodium and increased potassium levels. A patient with primary adrenal insufficiency will present with a low serum cortisol level and a simultaneously high serum ACTH level. A patient with secondary adrenal insufficiency (pituitary disease) will reveal low serum cortisol and ACTH levels. Refer to Chapter 31 for more details of primary versus secondary adrenal insufficiency.

Adrenal Cortex Tests

To assess for Cushing's syndrome, overnight dexamethasone suppression test, plasma ACTH, plasma and urinary cortisol, and 24-hour urinary free cortisol level tests may be ordered to evaluate the functioning of adrenal cortex.

Chapter Review

Critical Thinking Exercises

1. Explain the mechanism by which the hypothalamic–pituitary–thyroid axis regulates thyroid hormone production.
2. Summarize the functions of the three major types of hormones secreted by the adrenal cortex.

NCLEX-Style Review Questions

1. A client complains of nervousness and palpitations. Upon assessing the heart rate, the nurse notes a heart rate of 120 bpm. Which of the following endocrine disorders is associated with palpitations and increased heart rate?
   A. Hypothyroidism
   B. Hyperthyroidism
   C. SIADH
   D. Hypoparathyroidism
2. While assessing a client with Cushing's syndrome, the nurse should expect high blood glucose reading due to which of the following?
   A. Increased secretion of the thyroid gland
   B. Increased secretion of the parathyroid glands
   C. Increased secretion of the adrenal glands
   D. Increased secretion of the pituitary gland
3. An elderly woman complaining of weight gain, depression, and lethargy, is diagnosed with hypothyroidism, and thyroid replacement is prescribed. During initiation of thyroid replacement therapy for the patient, the priority assessment for the nurse is to evaluate which of the following?
   A. Mental status
   B. Nutritional status
   C. Cardiovascular function
   D. Bowel function
4. A 47-year-old woman presents to her primary care provider complaining of bone pain. Routine laboratory studies reveal a high serum calcium of 12.0 mg/dL and increased PTH levels. Which of the following is the most likely diagnosis?
   A. Graves disease
   B. Cushing's disease
   C. Addison's disease
   D. Hyperparathyroidism
5. The nurse is assessing a client for acromegaly at the clinic. Besides asking about changes in shoe size and facial features, the nurse should also inquire about which of the following?
   A. Changes in hearing
   B. Changes in bowel habits
   C. Changes in vision
   D. Changes in taste of foods

References and Selected Readings

References and selected readings associated with this chapter can be found on the website that accompanies the book. Visit http://thepoint.lww.com/Pellico1e to access the references and other additional resources associated with this chapter.

PATRICIA DALE CORK

Nursing Management: Diabetes Mellitus

Learning Objectives

After reading this chapter, you will be able to:

1. Differentiate between type 1 and type 2 diabetes.

2. Describe etiologic factors associated with diabetes.

3. Relate the clinical manifestations of diabetes to the associated pathophysiologic alterations.

4. Identify the diagnostic and clinical significance of blood glucose test results.

5. Explain the dietary modifications used for management of people with diabetes.

6. Describe the relationships among diet, exercise, and medication for people with diabetes.

7. Develop a plan for teaching insulin self-management.

8. Identify the role of oral antidiabetic agents in diabetic therapy.

9. Differentiate between hyperglycemia with diabetic ketoacidosis and hyperosmolar nonketotic syndrome.

Diabetes mellitus is a group of metabolic diseases characterized by elevated levels of glucose in the blood (**hyperglycemia**). Diabetes is a chronic illness that requires medical care and patient self-management to prevent or decrease the risk of complications (American Diabetes Association [ADA], 2008a). It affects many body systems and has potentially far-reaching and devastating physical, social, and economic consequences. It is a significant cause of hypertension and death from heart disease and stroke, and is the leading cause of nontraumatic amputations, blindness in working-age adults, and end-stage renal disease (ESRD) (Centers for Disease Control and Prevention [CDC], 2007).

The economic cost of diabetes continues to rise because of increasing health care costs and an aging population. Costs related to diabetes are estimated to be $174 billion annually, including direct medical care expenses and indirect costs attributable to disability and premature death (CDC, 2007).

Nursing management of patients with diabetes can involve treatment of a wide variety of physiologic disorders, depending on the patient's health status and whether the patient is newly diagnosed or seeking care for an unrelated health problem. Because all patients with diabetes must master the concepts and skills necessary for long-term management and avoidance of potential complications of diabetes, patient education is necessary for competent self-care and is an ongoing focus of nursing care.

DIABETES MELLITUS

Diabetes affects nearly 24 million people in the United States, or approximately 8% of the population. Of this number, 17.9 million are diagnosed with diabetes and an estimated 5.7 million are undiagnosed. As many as 57 million people are thought to have **prediabetes**, a condition that puts people at increased risk for the development of diabetes (ADA, 2008b). The occurrence of diabetes, especially type 2 diabetes, is increasing in all age groups. Diabetes is especially prevalent in persons over the age of 60 (CDC & National Institutes for Health [NIH], 2008).

Classification

The major classifications of diabetes are type 1 diabetes, type 2 diabetes, and gestational diabetes. Other types of diabetes, comprising 1% to 5%

Learning Objectives *(continued)*

10. Describe management strategies for a person with diabetes to use during "sick days."

11. Describe the major macrovascular, microvascular, and neuropathic complications of diabetes.

12. Use the nursing process as a framework for care of hospitalized patients with diabetes.

of all diagnosed cases, are caused by genetic conditions, surgery, medications, pancreatic disease, and other illnesses (ADA, 2007a).

Table 30-1 summarizes the major classifications of diabetes, current terminology, and major clinical characteristics. This classification system is dynamic in two ways. First, there can be many differences among individuals within each category. Second, except for people with type 1 diabetes, patients may move from one category to another. For example, a woman with gestational diabetes may, after delivery, move into the type 2 category. Older terms such as "insulin-dependent diabetes" and "non–insulin-dependent diabetes," "juvenile diabetes," "adult-onset diabetes," and others have been eliminated to reduce confusion.

Pathophysiology

Insulin is a hormone produced by the pancreas that controls blood glucose levels by regulating the production, use, and storage of glucose. It is secreted by beta cells, in the islets of Langerhans of the pancreas. In diabetes, cells may stop responding to insulin or the pancreas may decrease insulin secretion or stop insulin production completely. Insulin is an anabolic, or storage hormone. When a person eats a meal, insulin secretion increases and moves glucose from the blood into muscle, liver, and fat cells. Once inside the cells, insulin functions in the following ways:

- Transports and metabolizes glucose for energy
- Stimulates storage of glucose as glycogen in the liver and muscle cells
- Signals liver cells to stop the release of glucose
- Enhances storage of dietary fat in adipose tissue
- Accelerates transport of amino acids into cells
- Facilitates the transport of potassium into the cells (Porth & Matfin, 2009)
- Inhibits the breakdown of stored glucose, protein, and fat

During fasting periods, for example, between meals and overnight, the pancreas continuously releases a small amount of "basal" insulin. If the blood sugar becomes too low, another pancreatic hormone, *glucagon,* is secreted by the alpha cells of the islets of Langerhans. Glucagon stimulates the liver to release stored glucose, thereby increasing the blood sugar. In short, insulin promotes hypoglycemia; glucagon promotes hyperglycemia. They work in tandem to maintain a constant level of glucose in the blood.

⚡ NURSING ALERT

Fifty percent of the total insulin secreted daily by the pancreas is secreted under basal conditions and the remainder in response to meals. The estimated adult (assume a weight of 70 Kg) basal insulin secretion rates range from 18 to 32 U/24 hours (0.7 to 1.3 mg) (Kahn, King, Moses et al., 2005). Minutes after eating, the serum insulin level rises, peaking in 3 to 5 minutes and returning to baseline within 2 to 3 hours (Porth & Matfin, 2009). To attain glycemic control, nurses may be required to manage insulin drips based upon the basal insulin secretion rates.

The liver assists with glucose control by storing glucose in the form of glycogen. When the blood sugar becomes too low, the liver produces glucose through the breakdown of glycogen (glycogenolysis). After 8 to 12 hours without food, the liver forms glucose from the breakdown of noncarbohydrate substances, including amino acids (gluconeogenesis).

TABLE
30-1 Classification of Diabetes Mellitus and Related Glucose Intolerances

Current Classification	Previous Classifications	Clinical Characteristics and Clinical Implications
Type 1 (5% to 10% of all diabetes)	Juvenile diabetes Juvenile-onset diabetes Ketosis-prone diabetes Brittle diabetes Insulin-dependent diabetes mellitus (IDDM)	Onset any age, but usually young (<30 years) Usually thin at diagnosis; recent weight loss Etiology includes genetic, immunologic, and environmental factors (e.g., virus) Often have islet cell antibodies Often have antibodies to insulin even before insulin treatment Little or no endogenous insulin Need insulin to preserve life Ketosis-prone when insulin absent Acute complication of hyperglycemia: diabetic ketoacidosis
Type 2 (90% to 95% of all diabetes: obese—80% of type 2; nonobese—20% of type 2)	Adult-onset diabetes Maturity-onset diabetes Ketosis-resistant diabetes Stable diabetes Non–insulin-dependent diabetes (NIDDM)	Onset any age, usually over 30 years Usually obese at diagnosis Causes include obesity, heredity, and environmental factors No islet cell antibodies Decrease in endogenous insulin, or increased with insulin resistance Most patients can control blood glucose through weight loss if obese Oral antidiabetic agents may improve blood glucose levels if dietary modification and exercise are unsuccessful May need insulin on a short- or long-term basis to prevent hyperglycemia Ketosis uncommon, except in stress or infection Acute complication: hyperglycemic hyperosmolar nonketotic syndrome
Diabetes mellitus associated with other conditions or syndromes	Secondary diabetes	Accompanied by conditions known or suspected to cause the disease: pancreatic diseases, hormonal abnormalities, medications such as corticosteroids and estrogen-containing preparations Depending on the ability of the pancreas to produce insulin, the patient may require treatment with oral antidiabetic agents or insulin
Gestational diabetes	Gestational diabetes	Onset during pregnancy, usually in the second or third trimester Due to hormones secreted by the placenta, which inhibit the action of insulin Above-normal risk for perinatal complications, especially macrosomia (abnormally large babies) Treated with diet and, if needed, insulin to strictly maintain normal blood glucose levels Occurs in about 2% to 5% of all pregnancies Glucose intolerance transitory but may recur: • In subsequent pregnancies • 30% to 40% will develop overt diabetes (usually type 2) within 10 years (especially if obese) Risk factors include obesity, age >30 years, family history of diabetes, previous large babies (>9 lb) Screening tests (glucose challenge test) should be performed on all pregnant women between 24 and 28 weeks of gestation
Impaired glucose tolerance	Borderline diabetes Latent diabetes Chemical diabetes Subclinical diabetes Asymptomatic diabetes	Oral glucose tolerance test value between 140 mg/dL (7.7 mmol/L) and 200 mg/dL (11 mmol/L) Impaired fasting glucose is defined as a fasting plasma glucose between 110 mg/dL (6 mmol/L) and 126 mg/dL (7 mmol/L) 29% eventually develop diabetes Above-normal susceptibility to atherosclerotic disease Renal and retinal complications usually not significant May be obese or nonobese; obese should reduce weight Should be screened for diabetes periodically

Current Classification	Previous Classifications	Clinical Characteristics and Clinical Implications
Prediabetes	Previous abnormality of glucose tolerance (PrevAGT)	Current normal glucose metabolism Previous history of hyperglycemia (e.g., during pregnancy or illness) Periodic blood glucose screening after age 40 if there is a family history of diabetes or if symptomatic Encourage ideal body weight, because loss of 10 to 15 lb may improve glycemic control
Prediabetes	Potential abnormality of glucose tolerance (PotAGT)	No history of glucose intolerance Increased risk of diabetes if: • Positive family history • Obesity • Mother of babies over 9 lb at birth • Member of certain Native American (e.g., Pima) tribes with high prevalence of diabetes Screening and weight advice as in PrevAGT

Type 1 Diabetes

Type 1 diabetes affects approximately 5% to 10% of people with the disease. It is characterized by an acute onset and most commonly affects children and young adults, but it can occur at any age (CDC, 2007). Type 1 diabetes is characterized by destruction of the pancreatic beta cells. Combined genetic, immunologic, and environmental factors are thought to contribute to beta cell destruction. Although the events that lead to beta cell destruction are not fully understood, it is generally accepted that genetic susceptibility is a common underlying factor in the development of type 1 diabetes. People do not inherit type 1 diabetes itself, but rather a genetic predisposition, or tendency, toward development of the disease.

Type 1 diabetes is an autoimmune disease. Autoimmune diseases are caused by abnormal immune responses in which antibodies are directed against normal tissues of the body, responding to those tissues as if they were foreign. Immune destruction of the beta cells, caused by autoantibodies against islet cells and insulin, is associated with certain human leukocyte antigen (HLA) types. It is believed that immune system destruction of the beta cells is initiated by environmental factors, such as viruses or toxins. The risk of developing type 1 diabetes is three to five time higher in people with certain HLA types.

Regardless of the specific cause, beta cell destruction results in decreased insulin production, unchecked glucose production by the liver, and fasting hyperglycemia. In addition, glucose derived from food cannot be stored in the liver but instead remains in the blood and contributes to postprandial (after meals) hyperglycemia. If the concentration of glucose in the blood exceeds the renal threshold for glucose, usually 180 to 200 mg/dL, the kidneys cannot reabsorb all of the filtered glucose; glucose then appears in the urine (glycosuria). Glucose is an osmotic agent; water follows it. As the glucose is excreted in the urine, it is accompanied by excessive loss of fluids and electrolytes. This is termed *osmotic diuresis.*

Because insulin normally inhibits glycogenolysis (breakdown of stored glucose) and gluconeogenesis (production of new glucose from amino acids and other substrates), these processes occur unrestrained in people with insulin deficiency and contribute further to hyperglycemia. In addition, fat breakdown occurs, resulting in an increased production of **ketones**, which are organic acids. If excessive amounts of ketones are present in the blood, ketoacidosis develops.

Type 2 Diabetes

Type 2 diabetes affects approximately 90% to 95% of people with the disease. Although type 2 diabetes is commonly associated with older age and obesity, its incidence is increasing in younger people because of the growing epidemic of obesity in children, adolescents, and young adults (CDC, 2007). The two main problems related to insulin in type 2 diabetes are insulin resistance and impaired insulin secretion. Insulin resistance refers to decreased tissue sensitivity to insulin. Normally, insulin binds to special receptors on cell surfaces and initiates a series of reactions involved in glucose metabolism. In type 2 diabetes, these intracellular reactions are diminished, making insulin less effective in stimulating glucose uptake by the cells and at regulating glucose release by the liver (Fig. 30-1). The exact mechanisms that lead to insulin resistance and impaired insulin secretion in type 2 diabetes are unknown, although genetic factors are thought to play a role (ADA, 2007a).

To overcome insulin resistance and prevent the buildup of glucose in the blood, increased amounts of insulin must be secreted to maintain the glucose level. However, if the beta cells cannot keep up with the increased demand for insulin, the glucose level rises, and type 2 diabetes develops.

Despite the impaired insulin secretion that is characteristic of type 2 diabetes, there is enough insulin present to prevent

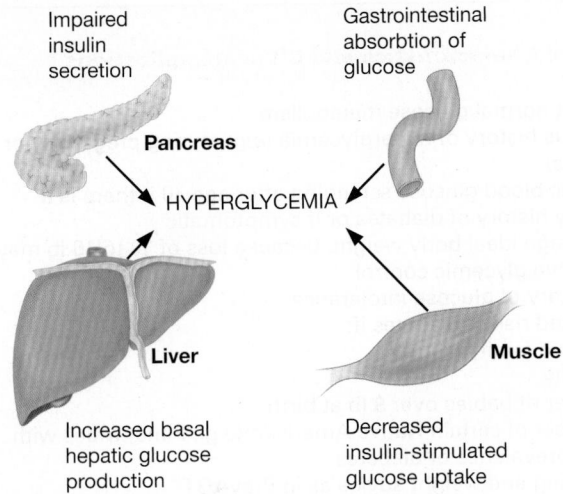

FIGURE 30-1 Pathogenesis of type 2 diabetes.

the breakdown of fat and the accompanying production of ketone acids. Therefore, diabetic ketoacidosis (DKA) does not typically occur in type 2 diabetes. However, uncontrolled type 2 diabetes may lead to *hyperglycemic hyperosmolar nonketotic syndrome*, another acute complication of diabetes.

Because type 2 diabetes is associated with a slow, progressive glucose intolerance, its onset may go undetected for many years. If the patient experiences symptoms, they are frequently mild and may include fatigue, irritability, increased urination, increased thirst, poor wound healing, frequent infections, or changes in vision.

Many patients with type 2 diabetes are diagnosed as a result of routine laboratory tests or during ophthalmoscopic examinations. One consequence of undetected diabetes is that long-term microvascular (diabetic retinopathy, neuropathy, and nephropathy) and macrovascular complications (peripheral vascular, coronary disease, and stroke) may have developed before the actual diagnosis of diabetes is made (ADA, 2008c).

Gestational Diabetes

Gestational diabetes mellitus (GDM) is any degree of glucose intolerance with onset occurring during pregnancy. Hyperglycemia can develop during pregnancy because of the secretion of placental hormones, which causes insulin resistance. It can also develop when the physiologic stress of pregnancy reveals glucose tolerance abnormalities that were not apparent prior to pregnancy. Gestational diabetes occurs in as many as 14% of pregnant women and increases their risk for hypertensive disorders and other complications during pregnancy (ADA, 2007b).

Risk assessment for gestational diabetes should be completed during the first prenatal visit. Women at high risk for GDM include those with marked obesity, personal history of GDM, glycosuria, or a strong family history of diabetes. Those at high risk should have their blood glucose tested as soon as possible and retested between 24 and 28 weeks

of gestation, if initial glucose was normal. Women at low to moderate risk for gestational diabetes are initially tested between 24 and 28 weeks of pregnancy (ADA, 2008d).

Initial management of gestational diabetes includes diet, exercise, and blood glucose monitoring. If hyperglycemia persists, insulin is prescribed. Goals for blood glucose levels during pregnancy are 95 mg/dL or less before meals, less than 130 to 140 mg/dL 1 hour after meals, and less than 120 mg/dL 2 hours after meals (ADA, 2008d).

After delivery, blood glucose levels in women with GDM usually return to normal. However, many women who have had GDM develop type 2 diabetes later in life. Therefore, a woman who has had GDM should be counseled to maintain her ideal body weight and to exercise regularly to reduce her risk for type 2 diabetes.

Risk Factors

Because diabetes is frequently not diagnosed until complications are present, screening is recommended for overweight adults and children with risk factors for type 2 diabetes. Box 30-1 summarizes risk factors for diabetes mellitus.

Because of the increased incidence of type 2 diabetes in children, screening is recommended for at-risk children beginning at age 10 (ADA, 2008c).

Ethnic groups and minority populations are disproportionately affected by diabetes. Age-adjusted population differences demonstrate the highest incidence among Native Americans and Alaska Natives (16.5%), followed by blacks (11.8%) and Hispanics (10.4%), compared with 7.5% for Asian Americans and 6.6% for whites (CDC, 2008). By 2050, nearly half of the population in the United States will be other than white. Because the above racial and ethnic groups are at greater risk for diabetes, and because of increasing obesity and inactivity in the general population, the incidence of diabetes is expected to continue to rise well into the 21st century (CDC & NIH, 2008).

BOX 30-1 **Risk Factors for Diabetes Mellitus**

- Family history of diabetes (i.e., parents or siblings with diabetes)
- Obesity (i.e., BMI ≥25 kg/m²)
- Ethnicity (e.g., African Americans, Latino, Native American, Asian American, Pacific Islanders)
- Age ≥45 years
- Previously identified impaired glucose tolerance or impaired fasting glucose
- Hypertension (≥140/90 mm Hg)
- HDL cholesterol level ≤35 mg/dL (0.90 mmol/L) and/or triglyceride level ≥250 mg/dL (2.82 mmol/L)
- History of gestational diabetes or delivery of babies over 9 pounds

Adapted from American Diabetes Association (2007). Standards of medical care in diabetes. *Diabetes Care, 30*(S1), S6.

Clinical Manifestations and Assessment

Clinical manifestations depend on the patient's level of hyperglycemia. Classic clinical manifestations of all types of diabetes include the "three Ps": polyuria, polydipsia, and polyphagia. Polyuria (increased urination) and polydipsia (increased thirst) occur as a result of the excess loss of fluid associated with osmotic diuresis. Patients may experience polyphagia (increased appetite) resulting from the catabolic state induced by insulin deficiency and the breakdown of proteins and fats. Other symptoms include dehydration, weight loss, fatigue and weakness, vision changes, tingling or numbness in the hands or feet, dry skin, skin lesions or wounds that are slow to heal, and recurrent infections.

! NURSING ALERT

Hyperglycemia impairs immune function (decreases white blood cell function), promotes inflammation, increases blood viscosity, favors the growth of yeast organisms, and is associated with blood vessel wall changes resulting in increased risk for infection, microvascular, macrovascular complications and foot ulcers.

An abnormally high blood glucose level is the basic criterion for the diagnosis of diabetes. Fasting plasma glucose (FPG) levels of 126 mg/dL or higher or random plasma glucose levels exceeding 200 mg/dL on more than one occasion are diagnostic for diabetes. Normal fasting glucose for a nondiabetic is 80 to 90 mg/dL with a range of 70 to 120 mg/dL. Prediabetes is diagnosed with fasting plasma glucose of 100 to 125 mg/dL. The oral glucose tolerance test (OGTT) is no longer recommended for routine clinical use in nonpregnant adults. See Box 30-2 for American Diabetes Association (ADA) diagnostic criteria for diabetes mellitus (ADA, 2007a).

In addition to assessment and diagnostic evaluation to diagnose diabetes, ongoing specialized assessment of patients with known diabetes and evaluation for complications in patients with newly diagnosed diabetes are important components of care. Parameters that should be regularly assessed are shown in Box 30-3.

Gerontologic Considerations

The overall incidence of diabetes is increasing, with the greatest increase occurring in the aging population (CDC, 2008), necessitating assessment in the elderly. The cause of age-related changes in carbohydrate metabolism is not clear. Possibilities include poor diet, physical inactivity, altered insulin secretion, and insulin resistance.

Elevated blood glucose levels commonly appear in the fifth decade of life and increase in frequency with advancing age. Approximately 20% of people over the age of 65, have age-related hyperglycemia, not including those with overt diabetes; this number is expected to grow (ADA, 2008e).

BOX 30-2
Criteria for the Diagnosis of Diabetes Mellitus

1. Symptoms of diabetes plus casual plasma glucose concentration equal to or greater than 200 mg/dL (11.1 mmol/L). "Casual" is defined as any time of day without regard to time since last meal. The classic symptoms of diabetes include polyuria, polydipsia, and unexplained weight loss.

or

2. Fasting plasma glucose greater than or equal to 126 mg/dL (7.0 mmol/L). Fasting is defined as no caloric intake for at least 8 hours.

or

3. Two-hour postload glucose equal to or greater than 200 mg/dL (11.1 mmol/L) during an oral glucose tolerance test. The test should be performed as described by the World Health Organization, using a glucose load containing the equivalent of 75 g anhydrous glucose dissolved in water.

In the absence of unequivocal hyperglycemia with acute metabolic decompensation, these criteria should be confirmed by repeat testing on a different day. The third measure is not recommended for routine clinical use.

Used with permission of American Diabetes Association (2007). Report of the Expert Committee on the Diagnosis and Classification of Diabetes Mellitus. *Diabetes Care, 30*(1), S46.

Because people with diabetes are living longer, both type 1 and type 2 diabetes are seen more frequently in the elderly population.

Older patients with diabetes are likely to have coexisting illnesses such as hypertension, heart disease, stroke, and other health care problems that complicate diabetes management. Normal physiologic changes of aging may mask the symptoms of diabetes, making diagnosis more difficult. Finally, age-related health problems such as polypharmacy, depression, cognitive impairment, urinary incontinence, falls, and chronic pain increase the risk for complications of diabetes (ADA, 2008e).

Regardless of the type or duration of diabetes, the goals of diabetes treatment may need to be altered when caring for elderly patients. The focus is on quality-of-life issues, such as maintaining independent functioning and promoting general well-being. Although striving for strict control of blood glucose levels may not be safe or appropriate, prolonged hyperglycemia should be avoided. Box 30-4 presents age-related changes that may affect diabetes and its management.

Medical Management

The therapeutic goal for diabetes management is to achieve normal blood glucose levels (euglycemia) without

BOX 30-3 Assessing the Patient With Diabetes

History

- Symptoms related to the diagnosis of diabetes:
  Symptoms of hyperglycemia
  Symptoms of hypoglycemia
  Frequency, timing, severity, and resolution
- Results of blood glucose monitoring
- Status, symptoms, and management of chronic complications of diabetes:
  Eye, kidney, nerve, genitourinary and sexual, bladder, and gastrointestinal
  Cardiac, peripheral vascular, foot complications associated with diabetes:
- Adherence to/ability to follow prescribed dietary management plan
- Adherence to prescribed exercise regimen
- Adherence to/ability to follow prescribed pharmacologic treatment (insulin or oral antidiabetic agents)
- Use of tobacco, alcohol, and prescribed and over-the-counter medications/drugs
- Lifestyle, cultural, psychosocial, and economic factors that may affect diabetes treatment
- Effects of diabetes or its complications on functional status (e.g., mobility, vision)

Physical Examination

- Blood pressure (sitting and standing to detect orthostatic changes)

- Body mass index (height and weight)
- Funduscopic examination and visual acuity
- Foot examination (lesions, signs of infection, pulses)
- Skin examination (lesions and insulin-injection sites)
- Neurologic examination:
  Vibratory and sensory examination using monofilament
  Deep tendon reflexes
- Oral examination

Laboratory Examination

- HgbA$_{1C}$ (A1C)
- Fasting lipid profile
- Test for microalbuminuria
- Serum creatinine level
- Urinalysis
- Electrocardiogram

Need for Referrals

- Ophthalmology
- Podiatry
- Dietitian
- Diabetes educator
- Others if indicated

BOX 30-4 Gerontologic Considerations

Age-Related Changes That May Affect Diabetes and Its Management

Sensory Changes

- Decreased vision
- Decreased smell
- Taste changes
- Decreased proprioception
- Diminished thirst

Gastrointestinal Changes

- Dental problems
- Appetite changes
- Delayed gastric emptying
- Decreased bowel motility

Activity/Exercise Pattern Changes

- More sedentary

Renal Function Changes

- Decreased function
- Decreased drug clearance

Affective/Cognitive Changes

- Medications/meals omitted or taken erratically

Socioeconomic Factors

- Fad diets
- Loneliness/living alone
- Lack of money/lack of support system

Chronic Diseases

- Hypertension
- Arthritis
- Neoplasms
- Acute/chronic infections

Potential Drug Interactions

- Use of another person's medications
- Consulting multiple health providers for different illnesses
- Alcohol use/abuse

hypoglycemia while maintaining a high quality of life. Diabetes management has five components:

- Nutrition
- Exercise
- Monitoring
- Medication
- Education

Patients with type 1 diabetes produce little or no insulin and require daily insulin injections to control blood glucose levels. Because insulin resistance is associated with obesity, the primary treatment of type 2 diabetes is weight loss. Exercise is also important in enhancing the effectiveness of insulin. Oral antidiabetic agents may be added if meal planning, diet therapy, and exercise are not successful in controlling blood glucose levels. If maximum doses of a single category of oral agents fail to reduce glucose to satisfactory levels, additional oral agents may be used. Insulin may be added to oral agent therapy, or the patient may be moved to insulin therapy entirely. Some patients require insulin on an ongoing basis; others require insulin on a temporary basis during periods of acute physiologic stress, such as illness or surgery. A patient's treatment depends on the severity of the hyperglycemia at the time of diagnosis.

Treatment varies because of changes in lifestyle and physical and emotional status, as well as because of advances in treatment methods. Therefore, diabetes management involves ongoing assessment and modification of the treatment plan as needed. Although the health care team directs treatment, it is the individual patient who must manage the complex therapeutic regimen. For this reason, patient and family education is an essential component of diabetes treatment.

Nutrition

Nutrition is the foundation of diabetes management. Nutrition management alone is often associated with reversal of hyperglycemia in type 2 diabetes. The most important objectives in the dietary management of diabetes are control of total caloric intake to attain or maintain a reasonable body weight, control of blood glucose levels, and normalization of lipids and blood pressure to prevent heart disease. However, achieving these goals is not always easy. Because medical nutrition therapy (nutritional therapy) for diabetes is complex, a registered dietitian who understands diabetes management has the primary responsibility for designing and teaching this aspect of the therapeutic plan. Nurses and other members of the health care team must be knowledgeable about nutrition therapy and supportive of patients who need to implement diet and lifestyle changes. Nutrition management of diabetes includes the following guidelines (ADA, 2002):

- Provide all essential food constituents necessary for optimal nutrition.
- Meet and maintain energy needs.
- Achieve and maintain a reasonable weight.

- Prevent wide daily fluctuations in blood glucose levels, with blood glucose levels as close to normal as is safe and practical to prevent or reduce the risk for complications.
- Decrease serum lipid levels, if elevated, to reduce the risk for macrovascular disease (coronary artery, cerebrovascular and peripheral vascular disease).

For patients who require insulin to help control blood glucose levels, maintaining as much consistency as possible in the amount of calories and carbohydrates ingested at each meal is essential. In addition, consistency in the approximate time intervals between meals, with the addition of snacks if necessary, helps prevent hypoglycemic reactions and maintain overall blood glucose control.

For overweight patients with type 2 diabetes, weight loss is the key to treatment. A weight loss as small as 10% of total weight may significantly improve blood glucose levels (Diabetes Prevention Program Research Group, 2002). Some patients with type 2 diabetes who require insulin or oral agents to control blood glucose levels may be able to reduce or eliminate the need for medication through weight loss.

For obese patients with diabetes who do not take insulin or oral agents, consistent meal content or timing is important but not as critical. Rather, decreasing overall caloric intake is most important. However, meals should not be skipped. Pacing food intake throughout the day places more manageable demands on the pancreas. Consistently following a meal plan is one of the most challenging aspects of diabetes management.

Meal Planning

For all patients with diabetes, the meal plan must consider the patient's food preferences, lifestyle, usual eating times, and ethnic and cultural background. Recent advances in diabetes management and insulin therapy allow greater flexibility in the timing and content of meals. This contrasts with the older concept of maintaining a constant dose of insulin, which required patients to adjust their schedule to the actions and duration of the insulin.

When teaching about meal planning, clinical dietitians use various educational tools, materials, and approaches. Initial education addresses the importance of consistent eating habits, the relationship of food and insulin, and the provision of an individualized meal plan. In-depth follow-up education then focuses on management skills, such as eating at restaurants, reading food labels, and adjusting the meal plan for exercise, illness, and special occasions. The nurse plays an important role in communicating pertinent information to the dietitian and reinforcing the patient's understanding.

For some patients, certain aspects of meal planning may be difficult to learn. This may be related to limitations in the patient's intellectual level or to emotional issues, such as difficulty accepting the diagnosis of diabetes or feelings of deprivation. In any case, it helps to emphasize that nutritional management of diabetes provides a new way of thinking about food, rather than a new way of eating. It also is

important to simplify information as much as possible and to provide opportunities for the patient to practice and repeat activities and information.

CALORIC REQUIREMENTS AND DISTRIBUTION. Calorie-controlled diets are planned by first calculating a person's energy needs and caloric requirements based on age, gender, height, and weight. An activity element is then factored in to provide the actual number of calories required for weight maintenance. To promote a 1- to 2-pound weight loss per week, 500 to 1,000 calories are subtracted from the daily total. The calories are distributed into carbohydrates, proteins, and fats, and a meal plan is developed with consideration of the patient's lifestyle and food preferences. Currently, the ADA and the American Dietetic Association recommend that, for all levels of caloric intake, 50% to 60% of calories should be derived from carbohydrates, 20% to 30% from fat, and the remaining 10% to 20% from protein (ADA, 2004a).

CARBOHYDRATES. Carbohydrates are an important source of energy. In general, carbohydrates have the greatest effect on blood glucose levels because they are more quickly digested than other foods and are rapidly converted into glucose.

Sources of carbohydrates include grains, fruits, vegetables, and milk. The majority of carbohydrate selections in the diabetic diet should come from whole grains. Foods containing sucrose (sugar) may be included in the diabetic diet. However, because they are typically high in fat and lack vitamins, minerals, and fiber, sucrose-containing foods should be limited. All carbohydrates should be eaten in moderation to avoid high postprandial (after meal) blood glucose levels (ADA, 2008f).

FATS. The recommendations regarding fat content of the diabetic diet include reducing the total percentage of calories from fat sources to less than 30% of total calories and limiting the amount of saturated fats to less than 7% of total calories. Additional recommendations include limiting the total intake of dietary cholesterol to less than 200 mg/day. This approach may help reduce risk factors such as increased serum cholesterol levels, which are associated with the development of coronary artery disease, the leading cause of death and disability among people with diabetes (ADA, 2008f).

PROTEIN. To help reduce saturated fat and cholesterol intake, the meal plan for diabetes should include the use of some non-animal sources of protein (e.g., legumes and whole grains). The amount of protein may be reduced in patients with early signs of renal disease (ADA, 2008f).

FIBER. Dietary fiber helps lower total cholesterol and low-density lipoprotein (LDL) cholesterol in the blood. Increased fiber in the diet may also improve blood glucose levels and decrease the need for exogenous insulin (ADA, 2008f).

There are two types of dietary fibers: soluble and insoluble. Soluble fiber in foods such as legumes, oats, and some fruits appears to lower blood glucose and lipid levels more than insoluble fiber. The potential glucose-lowering effect of fiber may be caused by a slower rate of glucose absorption from foods that contain soluble fiber. Insoluble fiber is found in whole-grain breads and cereals and in some vegetables. This type of fiber is important in increasing stool bulk and preventing constipation. Both insoluble and soluble fibers increase satiety, which is helpful for weight loss.

One risk involved in suddenly increasing fiber intake is that it may require adjusting the dosage of insulin or oral agents to prevent hypoglycemia. Other problems may include abdominal fullness, nausea, diarrhea, increased flatulence, and constipation if fluid intake is inadequate. If fiber is added to or increased in the meal plan, it should be done gradually and in consultation with a dietitian.

FOOD CLASSIFICATION SYSTEMS. To teach diet principles and to help patients with meal planning, several systems have been developed in which foods are organized into groups with common characteristics, such as number of calories, composition of foods, or effect on blood glucose levels. Food intake can be managed several ways, including carbohydrate counting, exchange lists, food lists, and calorie counting.

CARBOHYDRATE INTAKE. Because carbohydrates are the main nutrients in food that influence blood glucose, monitoring carbohydrate intake by carbohydrate counting, exchange lists, or experienced-based estimation can be effective ways to achieve blood glucose control.

Carbohydrate counting provides flexibility in food choices and can be less complicated to understand than other systems. It also allows for more accurate management with medication and exercise. For patients who take insulin, 1 unit of insulin for every 10 to 15 grams of carbohydrate may be prescribed. All food sources of carbohydrates should be considered when developing a diabetic meal plan using carbohydrate counting. Patients who can manage insulin-to-carbohydrate calculations have the potential to enjoy a more flexible lifestyle and more predictable diabetes control.

Exchange lists also are used for the nutritional management of diabetes. The Exchange Lists for Meal Planning (ADA, 1995) consist of six main exchange lists: (1) starch, (2) fruit, (3) milk (4) vegetable, (5) meat, and (6) fat. Foods included on each list, in the amounts specified, contain equal numbers of calories and are approximately equal in grams of protein, fat, and carbohydrate. Meal plans are based on a recommended number of choices from each exchange list. Foods on one list may be interchanged with one another, allowing the patient to choose a variety while maintaining as much consistency as possible in the nutrient content of foods eaten. Table 30-2 presents three sample lunch menus that are interchangeable in terms of carbohydrate, protein, and fat content.

DIABETES FOOD GUIDE PYRAMID. The Diabetes Food Guide Pyramid consists of the following food groups: (1) grains and starches, (2) vegetables, (3) fruits, (4) milk and other dairy products, and (5) meats and beans. The smallest group, fats,

TABLE
30-2 Selected Sample Lunch Menus From Exchange Lists

Exchanges	Sample Lunch #1	Sample Lunch #2	Sample Lunch #3
2 starch	2 slices bread	Hamburger bun	1 cup cooked pasta
3 meat	2 oz sliced turkey and 1 oz low-fat cheese	3 oz lean beef patty	3 oz boiled shrimp
1 vegetable	Lettuce, tomato, onion	Green salad	½ cup plum tomatoes
1 fat	1 tsp mayonnaise	1 Tbsp salad dressing	1 tsp olive oil
1 fruit	1 medium apple	1¼ cup watermelon	1¼ cup fresh strawberries
"Free" items (optional)	Unsweetened iced tea	Diet soda	Ice water with lemon
	Mustard, pickle, hot pepper	1 Tbsp catsup, pickle, onions	Garlic, basil

sweets, and alcohol, is at the top of the pyramid. Starches, fruits, and vegetables, which are lowest in calories and fat and highest in fiber, should make up the basis of the diet (ADA, 2008g). For those with diabetes, as well as for the general population, 50% to 60% of the daily caloric intake should be from those three food groups. Foods higher in fat, particularly saturated fat, should account for a smaller percentage of the daily caloric intake. Fats, oils, and sweets should be used sparingly by people with diabetes to obtain weight and blood glucose control and to reduce the risk for cardiovascular disease. Calorie counting or point systems are methods that can be used for weight management in type 2 diabetes.

Other Dietary Concerns

ALCOHOL. Patients with diabetes do not need to give up alcoholic beverages entirely, but must be aware of the potential adverse effects of alcohol specific to diabetes. Alcohol is absorbed before other nutrients and does not require insulin for absorption. Large amounts can be converted to fats, increasing the risk for diabetic ketoacidosis (DKA). In general, the same precautions regarding the use of alcohol by people without diabetes should be applied to patients with diabetes.

A major danger of alcohol consumption by the patient with diabetes is hypoglycemia, especially for patients who take insulin. Alcohol may decrease the normal physiologic reactions in the body that produce glucose (gluconeogenesis). Therefore, if a patient with diabetes consumes alcohol on an empty stomach, there is an increased likelihood of hypoglycemia. In addition, excessive alcohol intake may impair the patient's ability to recognize and treat hypoglycemia or to follow a prescribed meal plan to prevent hypoglycemia. To reduce the risk of hypoglycemia, the patient should be cautioned to consume food with alcohol.

Alcohol consumption can lead to excessive weight gain from the high caloric content of alcohol, as well as to hyperlipidemia and elevated glucose levels. Patient teaching about alcohol intake must emphasize moderation in the amount of alcohol consumed. Moderate intake is considered to be one alcoholic beverage per day for women and two per day for men (ADA, 2008f). Lower-calorie or less sweet drinks (e.g., light beer, dry wine) and food intake

with alcohol consumption are advised. It is especially important that patients with type 2 diabetes who wish to control their weight include calories from alcohol in the overall meal plan.

SWEETENERS. Use of sweeteners is acceptable for patients with diabetes, especially if it assists in overall dietary adherence. Moderation in the amount of sweetener used is encouraged, to avoid potential adverse effects. There are two main types of sweeteners: nutritive and non-nutritive. Nutritive sweeteners contain calories; non-nutritive sweeteners have few or no calories in the amounts normally used.

MISLEADING FOOD LABELS. Food manufacturers are required to include the nutrition content of foods on package labels. Reading food labels is an important skill for patients to learn and use when food shopping.

Foods labeled "sugarless" or "sugar-free" may still provide calories equal to those of the equivalent sugar-containing products if they are made with nutritive sweeteners. Therefore, for weight loss, these products may not always be useful. In addition, patients must not consider them "free" foods to be eaten in unlimited quantity, because they can elevate blood glucose levels.

Foods labeled "dietetic" are not necessarily reduced-calorie foods. They may be lower in sodium or have other special dietary uses. Patients are advised that foods labeled "dietetic" may still contain significant amounts of sugar or fat.

Patients must also be taught to read the labels of "health foods"—especially snacks—because they often contain carbohydrates such as honey, brown sugar, and corn syrup. In addition, these supposedly healthy snacks frequently contain saturated vegetable fats (e.g., coconut or palm oil), hydrogenated vegetable fats, or animal fats, which may be contraindicated in people with elevated blood lipid levels.

Exercise

Benefits

Exercise is extremely important in diabetes management because of its effects on lowering blood glucose and reducing cardiovascular risk factors. Exercise lowers blood glucose levels by increasing the uptake of glucose by body

muscles and by improving insulin utilization. Moderate to vigorous aerobic activities help with weight control and improve cardiovascular health. Resistance exercises, such as weight lifting, increase lean muscle mass, thereby increasing the resting metabolic rate (ADA, 2007c). These effects are useful in diabetes in relation to losing weight, easing stress, and maintaining a feeling of well-being. Exercise also alters blood lipid concentrations, increasing levels of high-density lipoproteins (HDLs) and decreasing total cholesterol and triglyceride levels. This is especially important for people with diabetes because of their increased risk of cardiovascular disease.

Exercise Precautions

Patients with blood glucose levels exceeding 250 mg/dL and ketones in the urine should not begin exercising until urine test results are negative for ketones and the blood glucose level is closer to normal (ADA, 2007c). Exercising with elevated blood glucose levels increases the secretion of glucagon, growth hormone, and catecholamines. The liver then releases more glucose, resulting in a further increase in the blood glucose level.

Since exercising facilitates glucose uptake intracellularly, patients should also be instructed to avoid unexpected hypoglycemia. Patients who require insulin should be taught to eat a 15 g carbohydrate snack or a snack of complex carbohydrates with a protein before engaging in moderate exercise. The exact amount of food needed varies from person to person and should be determined by blood glucose monitoring. Another potential problem for patients who take insulin is hypoglycemia that occurs many hours after exercise. To avoid post exercise hypoglycemia, especially after strenuous or prolonged exercise, the patient may need to eat a snack at the end of the exercise session and at bedtime, and to monitor the blood glucose level more frequently. Other participants or observers should be aware that the person exercising has diabetes, and they should know how to assist if hypoglycemia occurs.

Ideally, a person with diabetes should exercise at the same time and in the same amount each day. Regular daily exercise, rather than sporadic exercise, should be encouraged. Exercise recommendations must be altered as necessary for patients with diabetic complications such as retinopathy, autonomic neuropathy, sensorimotor neuropathy, and cardiovascular disease (ADA, 2004b). Increased blood pressure associated with exercise may aggravate diabetic retinopathy and increase the risk of a hemorrhage into the vitreous or retina. Patients with ischemic heart disease risk triggering angina or a myocardial infarction. Avoiding trauma to the lower extremities is especially important in patients with numbness related to neuropathy.

In general, a slow, gradual increase in the exercise period is encouraged. For many patients, walking is a safe and beneficial form of exercise that, other than proper shoes, requires no special equipment and can be performed anywhere. People

with diabetes should discuss exercise with their health care providers and undergo medical evaluation before starting an exercise program (ADA, 2007c).

Monitoring Glucose Levels and Ketones

Self-Monitoring of Blood Glucose

Blood glucose monitoring is a cornerstone of diabetes management. **Self-monitoring of blood glucose (SMBG)** levels by patients has dramatically altered diabetes care. Using frequent SMBG and learning how to respond to the results enable people with diabetes to adjust their treatment regimen to obtain optimal blood glucose control. This allows for detection and prevention of hypoglycemia and hyperglycemia and plays a crucial role in normalizing blood glucose levels, which in turn may reduce the risk of long-term diabetic complications.

SMBG is a key component of treatment for any intensive insulin therapy regimen and for diabetes management during pregnancy. It is also recommended for patients with unstable diabetes, those with a tendency to develop severe ketosis or hypoglycemia, and for patients who experience hypoglycemia without warning symptoms.

For patients not taking insulin, SMBG is helpful for monitoring the effectiveness of exercise, diet, and oral antidiabetic agents. It can also help motivate patients to continue with treatment. For patients with type 2 diabetes, SMBG is recommended during periods of suspected hyperglycemia (e.g., illness) or hypoglycemia (e.g., unusual increased activity levels) and when the medication or dosage of medication is modified (ADA, 2007c).

Various methods for SMBG are available. Most involve applying a drop of blood to a special reagent strip and allowing the blood to stay on the strip for the amount of time specified by the manufacturer. Blood glucose meters give a digital readout of the blood glucose value.

ADVANTAGES AND DISADVANTAGES OF SMBG SYSTEMS. Methods for SMBG must match the skill level of patients. Factors affecting SMBG performance include visual acuity, fine motor coordination, cognitive ability, comfort with technology and willingness to use it, and cost.

The use of meters to monitor blood glucose is recommended because meters have become much less expensive and less dependent on technique, making the results more accurate. Referral to a social worker may be needed to assist a patient who is without the financial means to purchase a meter. Most insurance companies cover some or all of the costs of meters and strips.

Nurses play an important role in providing initial teaching about SMBG techniques. Equally important is evaluating the techniques of patients who are experienced in self-monitoring. Patients should be discouraged from purchasing SMBG products from stores or catalogs that do not provide direct education. Every 6 to 12 months, patients should

conduct a comparison of their meter result with a simultaneous laboratory-measured blood glucose level in their primary care provider's office. The accuracy of the meter and strips should also be assessed with control solutions specific to that meter whenever a new vial of strips is used and whenever the validity of the reading is in doubt.

FREQUENCY. For most patients who require insulin, SMBG is recommended two to four times daily, usually before meals and at bedtime. For patients with type 1 diabetes and pregnant women taking insulin, SMBG is recommended three or more times daily (ADA, 2007c). Patients not receiving insulin may be instructed to assess their blood glucose levels at least two or three times a week, including a 2-hour postprandial test. For all patients, testing is recommended whenever hypoglycemia or hyperglycemia is suspected. Patients should increase the frequency of SMBG with changes in medications, activity, or diet and with stress or illness. Patients are asked to keep a record or logbook of blood glucose levels so that patterns can be detected. SMBG instruction should include parameters for contacting the primary care provider.

Continuous Glucose Monitoring System

A **continuous glucose monitoring system (CGMS)** uses new technology capable of continuously monitoring blood glucose. A sensor inserted subcutaneously and attached to an infusion set is capable of detecting high or low glucose levels. Information from the CGMS is especially useful for patients using insulin pumps and can also be used to identify patterns of diabetes control over a 24- to 72-hour period. Figure 30-2 shows a CGMS.

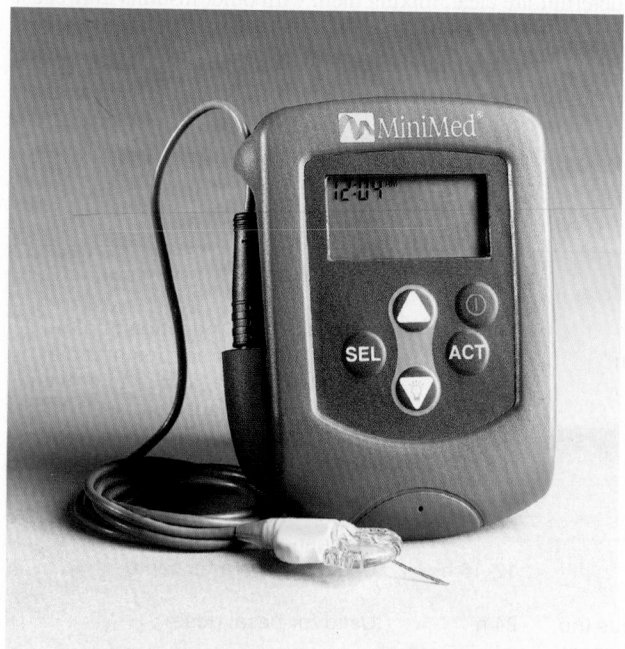

FIGURE 30-2 MiniMed CGMS System Gold Continuous Glucose Monitoring System (Medtronic, Northridge, CA).

Measuring Glycated Hemoglobin

Glycated hemoglobin (also referred to as glycosylated hemoglobin, $HgbA_{1C}$, or A1C) is a blood test that reflects average blood glucose levels over a period of approximately 2 to 3 months (ADA, 2007c). When blood glucose levels are elevated, glucose molecules attach to hemoglobin in red blood cells. The longer the amount of glucose in the blood remains above normal, the more glucose binds to hemoglobin and the higher the glycated hemoglobin level becomes. The glucose remains attached to the hemoglobin for the life of the individual red blood cell, approximately 120 days. If near-normal blood glucose levels are maintained, with only occasional increases, the overall value will not be greatly elevated. However, if the blood glucose values are consistently high, then the test result also is elevated. If the patient reports mostly normal SMBG results but the glycated hemoglobin is high, there may be errors in the methods used for glucose monitoring, errors in recording results, or frequent elevations in glucose levels at times during the day when the patient is not usually monitoring blood sugar levels. Normal values differ slightly from test to test and from laboratory to laboratory, but typically range from 4% to 6%. Values within the normal range indicate consistently near-normal blood glucose concentrations, a goal made easier by SMBG.

Urine Glucose Testing

Before SMBG was available, urine glucose testing was the only way to monitor diabetes on a daily basis. Its advantages are that it is less expensive than SMBG, noninvasive, and painless. However, urine glucose testing is no longer recommended because the results do not accurately reflect blood glucose level at the time of the test and because they are unpredictable. Also, the renal threshold for glucose, 180 to 200 mg/dL, is far above target blood glucose levels.

Furthermore, because age and renal function can affect the renal threshold, it is not an accurate measure of blood glucose control. Finally, a potentially dangerous outcome of urine testing for glucose is that it cannot detect or measure hypoglycemia.

Testing for Ketones

Ketones (or ketone bodies) are by-products of fat breakdown that accumulate in the blood and urine. Ketones in the urine signal that control of type 1 diabetes is deteriorating and that the risk of DKA is high. When there is little or no effective insulin available, the body starts to break down stored fat for energy. Urine testing is the most common method used for self-testing of ketone bodies by patients. A urine dipstick (Ketostix or Chemstrip uK) is used to detect ketonuria. The reagent pad on the strip turns purplish when ketones are present. Other strips are available for measuring both urine glucose and ketones (Keto-Diastix or Chemstrip uGK).

Urine ketone testing should be performed whenever patients with type 1 diabetes have glycosuria or persistently elevated blood glucose levels, as well as during illness and pregnancy.

Pharmacologic Therapy

As previously stated, insulin is secreted by the beta cells of the islets of Langerhans and works to lower the blood glucose level after meals by facilitating the uptake and utilization of glucose by muscle, fat, and liver cells. In the absence of adequate insulin, pharmacologic therapy is essential.

Insulin Therapy

In type 1 diabetes, exogenous insulin must be administered daily for life because the body has lost its ability to produce insulin. In type 2 diabetes, insulin may be necessary on a long-term basis to control glucose levels if meal planning and oral agents are ineffective. In addition, some patients with type 2 diabetes who usually are controlled by meal planning alone, or by meal planning and an oral antidiabetic agent, may require insulin temporarily during illness, infection, pregnancy, surgery, or other stressful events. In many cases, insulin injections are administered two or more times daily to control blood glucose levels.

SOURCES OF INSULIN. In the past, all insulins were obtained from pork and beef pancreas. Now, recombinant DNA technology or genetic engineering is used to create "human" insulin. Modification of the amino acid sequence of the human insulin molecule has produced new, rapid-acting insulin analogues. Human source insulin, which is designed to act more like insulin from the human pancreas, is now standard therapy (Adams, Holland, & Bostwick, 2008).

INSULIN PREPARATIONS. Insulin is available in the following preparations: rapid-acting, short-acting, intermediate-acting, and long-acting. In general, the rapid- and short-acting insulins are expected to cover the increase in glucose levels after meals soon after injection; the intermediate-acting insulins are expected to cover

subsequent meals; and the long-acting insulins provide a relatively constant (or basal) level of insulin. Table 30-3 summarizes categories of insulin.

Rapid-acting insulins such as insulin lispro (Humalog), insulin aspart (NovoLog), and insulin glulisine (Apidra) produce a more rapid effect that is of shorter duration than regular insulin. Because of their rapid onset, the patient should be instructed to eat no more than 15 minutes after injection. The short duration of action of these insulins usually requires that patients with type 1 diabetes and some patients with type 2 or gestational diabetes receive additional longer-acting insulin to maintain glucose control.

Short-acting insulin, called regular insulin and marked "R" on the vial, is an unmodified clear solution that usually is administered 20 to 30 minutes before a meal. Regular insulin is the only insulin that can be given intravenously. It can be given either alone or in combination with modified longer-acting insulins. Regular insulin is used to treat DKA and may also be used on a supplemental basis, sometimes called a "sliding scale." Humulin R and Novolin R are examples of regular insulin.

Intermediate-acting insulin is NPH insulin, marked "N" on the vial. Intermediate-acting insulin is cloudy and white in appearance and is frequently used in combination with a shorter-acting insulin. To avoid hypoglycemia, it is important that patients eat around the time of the onset and peak of intermediate-acting insulin. Humulin N and Novolin N are examples of NPH insulins.

Insulin glargine (Lantus) and insulin detemir (Levemir) are long-acting "basal" insulins that are absorbed very slowly over 24 hours. They are given subcutaneously, once a day, and do not have a peak time of effect. Although both glargine and determir are clear, mixing them with other insulins may cause a dangerous precipitation or diminish the effect of the insulin. Lantus was originally approved to be given once a day at bedtime; however, it is now approved to be given once a day at

TABLE
30-3 Categories of Subcutaneous Insulin

Time Course	Agent	Onset	Peak	Duration	Indications
Rapid-acting	Lispro (Humalog) Aspart (Novolog) Glulisine (Apidra)	15 min 15 min 15 min	1 h 40–50 min 1 h	 3–5 h 3–5 h	Used for rapid reduction of glucose level, to treat postprandial hyperglycemia, and/or to prevent nocturnal hypoglycemia "Mealtime insulin"
Short-acting	Regular (Humulin-R, Novolin-R)	½–1 h	2–3 h	4–6 h	Usually administered 20–30 minutes before a meal; may be taken alone or in combination with longer-acting insulin
Intermediate-acting	NPH (Humulin N, Novolin N)	2–4 h	6–8 h	12–16 h	Usually taken after food
Long acting	Glargine (Lantus) Detemir (Levemir)	2 h	Continuous (no defined onset or peak)	24 h	Used for basal dose

any time of the day but must be given at the same time each day to prevent overlap of action.

Exubera, an inhaled insulin, was approved in 2006 for use in adults. This insulin is used as a pre-meal dose and is delivered through an inhaler device. It is the first insulin not given parenterally. Although the drug was discontinued by the manufacturer in 2007 because of poor sales, the noninjection route of administration remains an attractive alternative for the future. Exubera was successfully used in combination with other insulin for type 1 diabetes and as monotherapy for type 2 diabetes. No adverse effects on the lungs were noted during short-term use; further study on long-term effects is needed. Use of inhaled insulin is contraindicated for patients who smoke and those with lung disease (Adams et al., 2008).

In general, the rapid- and short-acting insulins are expected to cover the increase in glucose levels after meals soon after injection; the intermediate-acting insulins are expected to cover subsequent meals; and the long-acting insulins provide a relatively constant (or basal) level of insulin.

INSULIN REGIMENS. Insulin regimens vary from one to four injections a day. Usually there is a combination of short-acting insulin and longer-acting insulin. The normally functioning pancreas continuously secretes small amounts of insulin during the day and night. In addition, whenever blood glucose increases after ingestion of food, there is a rapid burst of insulin secretion in proportion to the glucose-raising effect of the food. The goal of all but the simplest, one-injection insulin regimens is to mimic this normal pattern of insulin secretion in response to food intake and activity patterns. Table 30-4 illustrates several insulin regimens, including the advantages and disadvantages of each.

Some patients can learn to use SMBG results and carbohydrate counting to vary insulin doses. This allows the patient more flexibility in timing and content of meals and exercise periods. Complex insulin regimens require a strong level of commitment, intensive education, and close follow-up by the health care team. In addition, patients aiming for normal blood glucose levels run the risk of more hypoglycemic reactions. There are two general approaches to insulin therapy: conventional and intensive.

CONVENTIONAL INSULIN THERAPY. One approach is to simplify the insulin regimen as much as possible, with the goal of avoiding acute complications of diabetes (hypoglycemia and symptomatic hyperglycemia). Conventional insulin therapy involves one or more injections a day of a mixture of short- and intermediate-acting insulins. The patient using the conventional regimen should not vary meal patterns or activity levels.

INTENSIVE INSULIN THERAPY. A second approach is to use a more complex insulin regimen to achieve as much control of blood glucose levels as is safe and practical. An intensive insulin therapy regime involves three to four injections of insulin a day. Although intensive treatment is beneficial in

reducing the risk of complications, not all people with diabetes are candidates for this approach to diabetes management.

NURSING ALERT

When administering insulin, it is very important to read the label carefully and to be sure that the correct type of insulin is administered. Take care to avoid mistaking Lantus insulin for Lispro insulin because both begin with "L," or Lantus for regular insulin because both are clear.

TEACHING PATIENTS TO SELF-ADMINISTER INSULIN. Insulin injections are self-administered into the subcutaneous tissue with the use of special insulin syringes. A variety of syringes and injection-aid devices are available.

STORING INSULIN. All insulin, including spare vials not in use, should be refrigerated. Extremes of temperature should be avoided; insulin should not be allowed to freeze and should not be kept in direct sunlight or in high temperatures. The insulin vial in use should be kept at room temperature to reduce local irritation at the injection site, which may occur if cold insulin is injected. Vials of insulin that will be used within 1 month may be kept at room temperature. The patient should be instructed to always have a spare vial of the type or types of insulin used.

Vials of intermediate-acting insulin should also be inspected for flocculation, which is a frosted, whitish coating inside the bottle. If a frosted, adherent coating is present, some of the insulin is bound, and should not be used. Vials of insulin that have been open for several weeks, or those that have passed the expiration date also should be discarded.

SELECTING SYRINGES. Syringes must be matched with the insulin concentration (e.g., U-100). Currently, three sizes of U-100 insulin syringes are available:

- 1 mL syringes that hold 100 units
- 0.5 mL syringes that hold 50 units
- 0.3 mL syringes that hold 30 units

The concentration of insulin used most often in the United States is U-100; that is, there are 100 units of insulin per milliliter (mL). Small syringes allow patients who require small amounts of insulin to measure and draw up the amount of insulin accurately. Patients who require large amounts of insulin use larger syringes. A U-500 (500 U/mL) concentration of insulin is available by special order for patients who have severe insulin resistance and require massive doses of insulin.

Most insulin syringes have a disposable 27- to 29-gauge needle that is approximately 0.5 inch long. The smaller syringes are marked in 1-unit increments and may be easier for patients with visual deficits and those taking very small doses of insulin. The 1-mL syringes are marked in 1- and 2-unit increments.

PREPARING THE INJECTION: MIXING INSULINS. When rapid- or short-acting insulins are given with longer-acting insulins,

TABLE
30-4 Insulin Regimens

Schematic Representation	Description	Advantages	Disadvantages
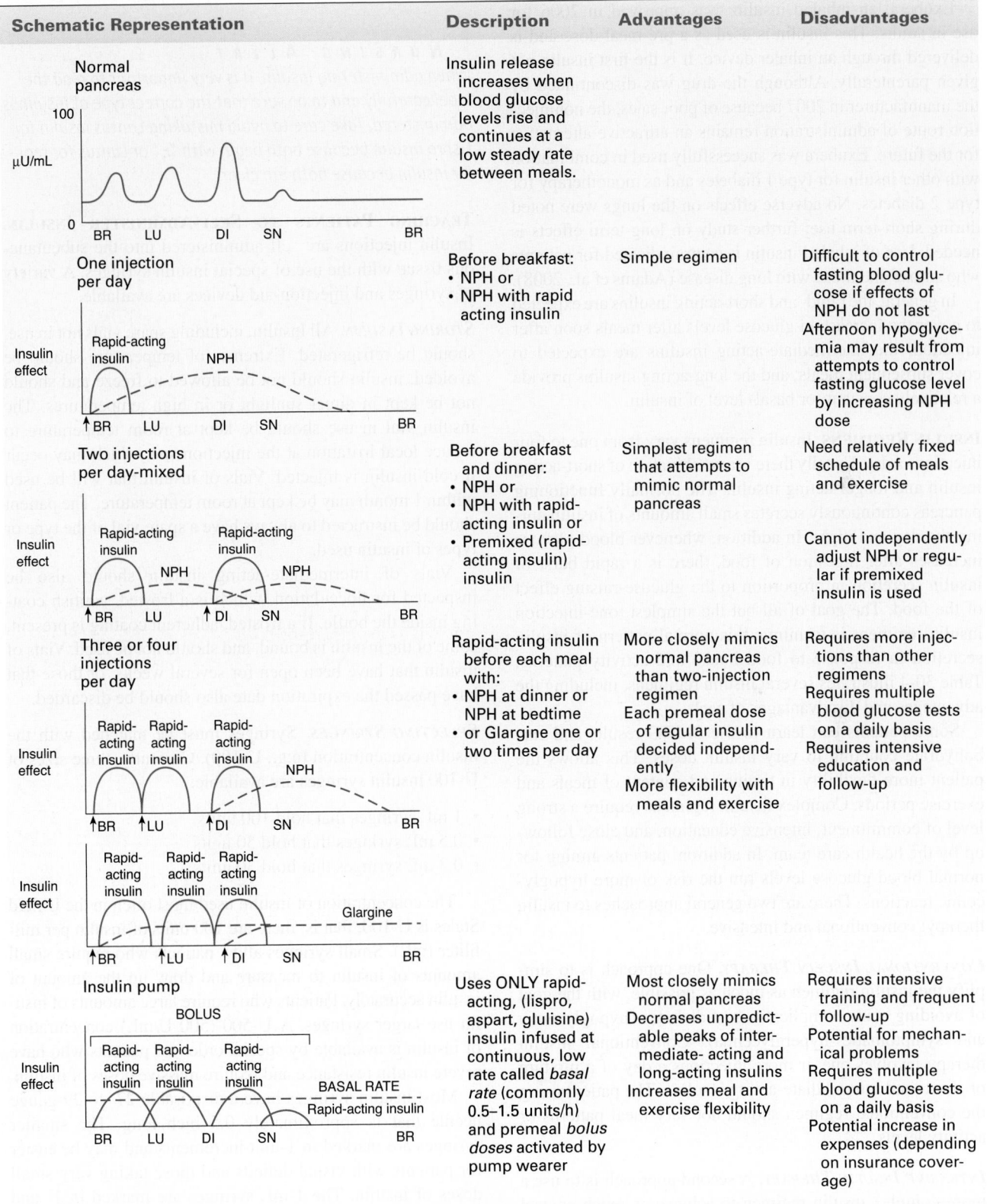 Normal pancreas	Insulin release increases when blood glucose levels rise and continues at a low steady rate between meals.		
One injection per day	Before breakfast: • NPH or • NPH with rapid acting insulin	Simple regimen	Difficult to control fasting blood glucose if effects of NPH do not last Afternoon hypoglycemia may result from attempts to control fasting glucose level by increasing NPH dose
Two injections per day-mixed	Before breakfast and dinner: • NPH or • NPH with rapid-acting insulin or • Premixed (rapid-acting insulin) insulin	Simplest regimen that attempts to mimic normal pancreas	Need relatively fixed schedule of meals and exercise Cannot independently adjust NPH or regular if premixed insulin is used
Three or four injections per day	Rapid-acting insulin before each meal with: • NPH at dinner or NPH at bedtime • or Glargine one or two times per day	More closely mimics normal pancreas than two-injection regimen Each premeal dose of regular insulin decided independently More flexibility with meals and exercise	Requires more injections than other regimens Requires multiple blood glucose tests on a daily basis Requires intensive education and follow-up
Insulin pump	Uses ONLY rapid-acting, (lispro, aspart, glulisine) insulin infused at continuous, low rate called *basal rate* (commonly 0.5–1.5 units/h) and premeal *bolus doses* activated by pump wearer	Most closely mimics normal pancreas Decreases unpredictable peaks of intermediate- acting and long-acting insulins Increases meal and exercise flexibility	Requires intensive training and frequent follow-up Potential for mechanical problems Requires multiple blood glucose tests on a daily basis Potential increase in expenses (depending on insurance coverage)

BR, breakfast; LU, lunch; DI, dinner; SN, snack; REG, regular; T indicates insulin injections. Rapid acting insulin; lispro, aspart, or glulisine [Apidra].

they usually are mixed together in the same syringe. Regular insulin must be inspected for clarity and not used unless it is crystal clear. Modified insulins will be cloudy and should be carefully mixed by gently rolling the vial. The regular insulin is drawn into the syringe first, followed by the modified insulin. Injecting cloudy insulin into a vial of clear insulin contaminates the entire vial of clear insulin and alters its action.

Patients who have difficulty mixing insulins have two options. They may use premixed insulin in a vial or in a prefilled syringe. Fig. 30-3 shows a prefilled syringe; it is also discussed in detail below. Premixed insulins are available in different ratios of NPH insulin to regular insulin. The ratio of 70/30 (70% NPH and 30% regular insulin in one vial) is most common; this combination is available as Novolin 70/30 (Novo-Nordisk) and Humulin 70/30 (Lilly). Humulin also is available in a 50/50 ratio of NPH to regular (Humulin 50/50).

For patients who can inject insulin but who have difficulty drawing up a single or mixed dose, syringes may be prefilled with the help of home care nurses or family and friends. A 3-week supply of insulin syringes may be prepared and kept in the refrigerator. Prefilled syringes should be stored with the needle in an upright position to avoid clogging of the needle. Like insulin in vials, prefilled syringes should be rotated gently between the hands to mix and warm the insulin before injection.

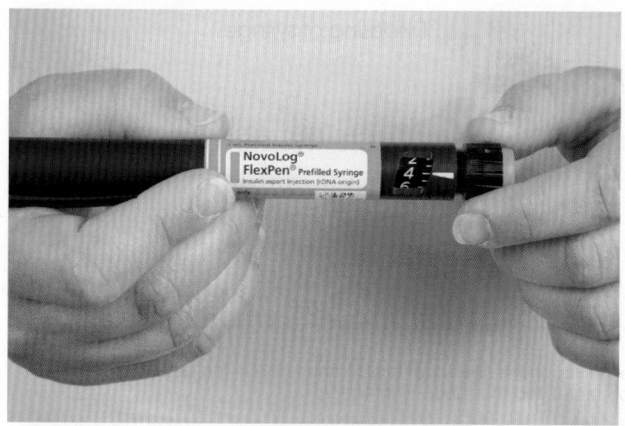

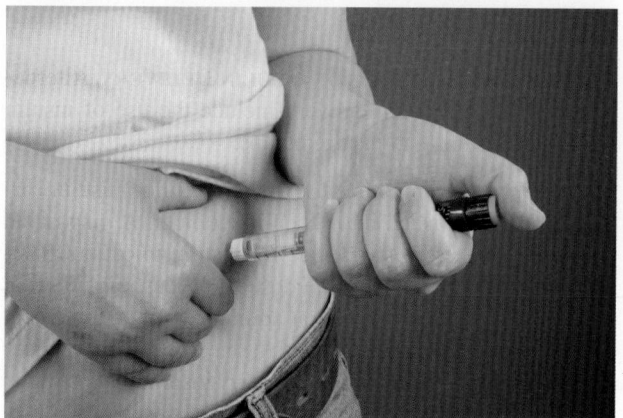

FIGURE 30-3 Prefilled insulin syringe.

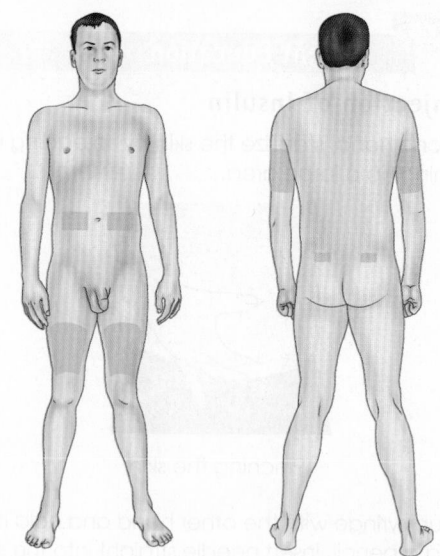

FIGURE 30-4 Suggested areas for insulin injection.

SELECTING AND ROTATING THE INJECTION SITE. As shown in Figure 30-4, the four main areas for injection are the abdomen, the posterior surface of the upper arms, the anterior surface of the thighs, and the hips. Insulin is absorbed faster in some areas of the body than others. The rate of absorption is greatest in the abdomen and decreases progressively in the arm, thigh, and hip, respectively.

Systematic rotation of injection sites within an anatomic area is recommended to prevent localized changes in fatty tissue (lipodystrophy). To promote consistency in insulin absorption, the patient should be encouraged to use all available injection sites within one area rather than randomly rotating sites from area to area (ADA, 2004d). For example, some patients almost exclusively use the abdominal area, administering each injection 0.5 to 1 inch away from the previous injection. Another approach to site rotation is always to use the same area at the same time of day. For example, patients may inject morning doses into the abdomen and evening doses into the arms or legs. If the patient plans to exercise, insulin should not be injected into the limb that will be exercised because this will cause faster absorption and may result in hypoglycemia.

INSULIN INJECTION. The injection site is cleansed prior to insertion of the needle. To inject insulin, the skin is gently pinched and the needle inserted at a 90-degree angle. For small patients, a 45-degree angle is used. Injection sites should be about 1 inch apart. Injection that is too deep or too shallow may affect the rate of absorption. Because insulin is injected into subcutaneous tissue, routine aspiration to assess for blood being drawn into the syringe is not necessary. Following injection, gentle pressure is applied; the injection site should not be massaged because massaging can interfere with insulin absorption. Box 30-5 illustrates patient education

BOX 30-5
Patient Education

Self-Injection of Insulin

1. With one hand, stabilize the skin by spreading it or pinching up a large area.

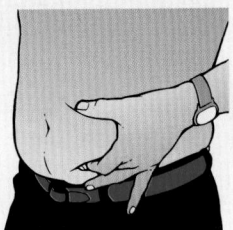

Pinching the skin

2. Pick up syringe with the other hand and hold it as you would a pencil. Insert needle straight into the skin.*

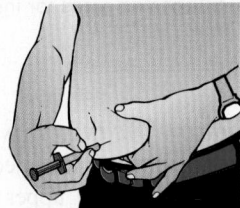

Inserting the needle into the skin

3. To inject the insulin, push the plunger all the way in.

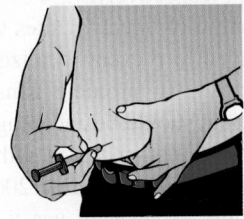

Injecting the insulin

4. Pull needle straight out of skin. Press cotton ball over injection site for several seconds.

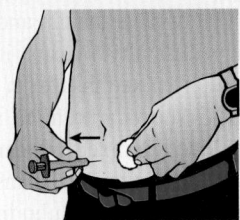

Removing the needle and holding cotton ball over site

5. Use disposable syringe *only once* and discard into hard plastic container (with a tight-fitting top) such as an empty bleach or detergent container.† Follow state regulations for disposal of syringes and needles.

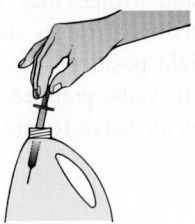

Disposing of syringe

---

*Some patients may be taught to insert the needle at a 45-degree angle.
†Although some studies suggest that reusing disposable syringes may be safe, it is recommended that this be done only in the absence of poor personal hygiene, an acute concurrent illness, open wounds on the hands, or decreased resistance to infection.

---

for insulin injection. Box 30-6 details how to evaluate the effectiveness of self-injection of insulin education.

DISPOSING OF SYRINGES AND NEEDLES. Insulin syringes and pens, needles, and lancets should be disposed of according to local regulations. Some areas have special needle disposal programs to prevent sharps from being discarded in the main waste disposal system. If community disposal programs are unavailable, used sharps should be placed in a puncture-resistant container. The patient should contact local authorities for instructions about proper disposal of filled containers; they should never be mixed with containers to be recycled.

ALTERNATIVE METHODS OF INSULIN DELIVERY. Alternative methods of insulin delivery include the use of insulin pens, jet injectors, and insulin pumps.

INSULIN PENS. Insulin pens use small, prefilled insulin cartridges that are loaded into a pen-like holder. A disposable needle is attached to the device for insulin injection. Insulin is delivered by dialing in a dose or by pushing a button for every 1- or 2-unit increment administered. People using these devices still need to insert the needle for each injection; however, they do not need to carry insulin vials or draw up insulin before each injection. These devices are most useful for patients who need to inject only one type of insulin at

BOX 30-6

Outcome Criteria for Determining Effectiveness of Self-Injection of Insulin Education

Equipment

Insulin

1. Identifies information on label of insulin bottle:
   - Type (e.g., NPH, regular, 70/30)
   - Species (human, biosynthetic, pork)
   - Manufacturer (Lilly, Novo Nordisk)
   - Concentration (e.g., U-100)
   - Expiration date
2. Checks appearance of insulin:
   - Clear or milky white
   - Checks for flocculation (clumping, frosted appearance)
3. Identifies where to purchase and store insulin:
   - Indicates approximately how long bottle will last (1,000 units per bottle U-100 insulin)
   - Indicates how long opened bottles can be used

Syringes

1. Identifies concentration (U-100) marking on syringe; U-100 = 100 units per 1 mL
2. Identifies size of syringe (e.g., 500-unit 100-unit, 50-unit, 30-unit). The most common syringe used for insulin administration is a U-100. However, in the event that very small or large doses of insulin are required syringes may be varied. For example, a U-30 syringe = 30 units per mL allowing for accurate withdrawal of small dosages; whereas a U-500 syringe= 500 units per 1 mL, which may be required with insulin resistance.
3. Describes appropriate disposal of used syringe

Preparation and Administration of Insulin Injection

1. Draws up correct amount and type of insulin
2. Properly mixes two insulins if necessary
3. Inserts needle and injects insulin
4. Describes site rotation:
   - Demonstrates injection with all anatomic areas to be used
   - Describes pattern for rotation, such as using abdomen only or using certain areas at the same time of day
   - Describes system for remembering site locations, such as horizontal pattern across the abdomen as if drawing a dotted line

Knowledge of Insulin Action

1. Lists prescription:
   - Type and dosage of insulin
   - Timing of insulin injections
2. Describes approximate time course of insulin action:
   - Identifies long- and short-acting insulins by name.
   - States approximate time delay until onset of insulin action.

- Identifies need to delay food until 5 to 15 minutes after injection of rapid-acting insulin (lispro, aspart).

Incorporation of Insulin Injections Into Daily Schedule

1. States proper order of premeal diabetes activities:
   - May use mnemonic device such as the word "tie," which helps the patient remember the order of activities ("t" = test (blood glucose), "i" = insulin injection, "e" = eat).
   - Describes daily schedule, such as test, insulin, eat before breakfast and dinner; test and eat, before lunch and bedtime.
2. Describes information regarding hypoglycemia:
   - Symptoms: shakiness, sweating, nervousness, hunger, weakness
   - Causes: too much insulin, too much exercise, not enough food
   - Treatment: 15 g concentrated carbohydrate, such as two or three glucose tablets, 1 tube glucose gel, or ½ cup of juice
   - After initial treatment, follow with snack including starch and protein, such as cheese and crackers, milk and crackers, half sandwich.
3. Describes information regarding prevention of hypoglycemia:
   - Avoids delays in meal timing.
   - Eats a meal or snack approximately every 4 to 5 hours (while awake).
   - Does not skip meals.
   - Increases food intake before exercise if blood glucose level is less than 100 mg/dL.
   - Checks blood glucose regularly.
   - Identifies safe modification of insulin doses consistent with management plan.
   - Carries a form of fast-acting sugar at all times.
   - Wears a medical identification bracelet.
   - Teaches family, friends, co-workers about signs and treatment of hypoglycemia.
   - Has family, roommates, traveling companions learn to use injectable glucagon for severe hypoglycemic reactions.
4. Maintains regular follow-up for evaluation of diabetes control:
   - Keeps written record of blood glucose, insulin doses, hypoglycemic reactions, variations in diet.
   - Keeps all appointments with health professionals.
   - Sees health care provider regularly (usually two to four times per year).
   - States how to contact health care provider in case of emergency.
   - States when to call health care provider to report variations in blood glucose levels.

a time or who use premixed insulins. They are convenient for those who administer insulin before dinner when eating out or traveling. They are also useful for patients with impaired manual dexterity, vision, or cognitive function that makes the use of traditional syringes difficult.

JET INJECTORS. Jet injection devices deliver insulin through the skin under pressure in an extremely fine stream. These devices are more expensive than other methods of insulin administration and require thorough training and supervision when first used. In addition, patients should be cautioned that absorption rates, peak insulin activity, and insulin levels may be different when using a jet injector.

CONTINUOUS SUBCUTANEOUS INSULIN INFUSION (CSSI): INSULIN PUMPS. Continuous subcutaneous insulin infusion (CSII) involves the use of small, externally worn devices that closely mimic the functioning of the normal pancreas (Skyler, Ponder, Kruger et al., 2007). Insulin pumps contain a 3-mL syringe connected to a subcutaneous needle by a thin, narrow-lumen tube with a needle or Teflon catheter attached to the end. The patient inserts the needle or catheter into subcutaneous tissue, usually on the abdomen, and secures it with tape or a transparent dressing. The needle or catheter is changed at least every 2 to 3 days. Figure 30-5 illustrates CSSI equipment.

The pump is programmed to deliver rapid- or short-acting insulin by subcutaneous infusion at a constant (basal) rate (e.g., 0.5 to 2.0 U/hour) over a 24-hour period. This allows flexibility for meal times and food choices. The pump can easily be disconnected for limited periods for showering, exercise, or sexual activity (Skyler et al., 2007).

A disadvantage of insulin pumps is that unexpected disruptions in the flow of insulin from the pump may happen if the tubing or needle becomes occluded, if the supply of

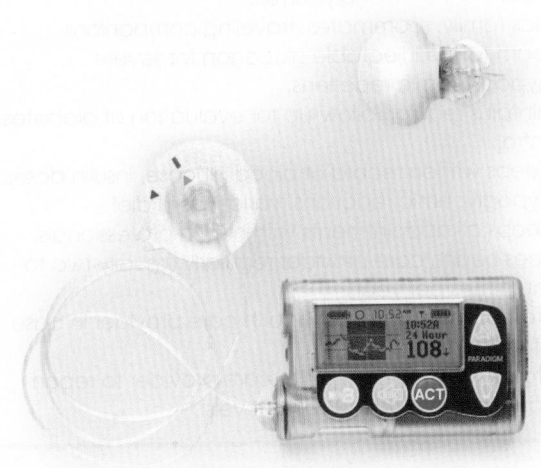

FIGURE 30-5 Medtronic (Northridge, CA) insulin pump system.

insulin runs out, or if the battery is depleted. These occurrences increase the risk of DKA. Another disadvantage is the potential for infection at needle insertion sites. Effective patient teaching minimizes both of these risks. Hypoglycemia also may occur with insulin pump therapy; however, this usually is related to the lowered blood glucose levels many patients achieve, rather than to a specific problem with the pump itself.

Candidates for the insulin pump must be willing to assess their blood glucose level several times daily. In addition, they must be psychologically stable and open about having diabetes because the insulin pump is a visible sign to others and a constant reminder to patients that they have diabetes. Most important, patients using insulin pumps must have extensive education in the use of the pump and in self-management of blood glucose and insulin doses. Many insurance policies cover the cost of pump therapy. If not, the extra expense of the pump and associated supplies may be a deterrent for some patients. Medicare now covers insulin pump therapy for patients with type 1 diabetes (Skyler et al., 2007).

Research into mechanical delivery of insulin includes implantable insulin pumps that can be externally programmed according to blood glucose test results. Clinical trials with these devices are continuing.

COMPLICATIONS OF INSULIN THERAPY. Reactions to insulin therapy and other complications may occur.

LOCAL ALLERGIC REACTIONS. A local allergic reaction (redness, swelling, tenderness, and induration) may appear at an injection site 1 to 2 hours after insulin administration. These reactions are becoming rare because of the increased use of human insulins.

SYSTEMIC ALLERGIC REACTIONS. Systemic allergic reactions to insulin also are rare. When they do occur, there is an immediate local skin reaction that gradually spreads into generalized urticaria (hives). Treatment is desensitization with small doses of purified pork or human insulin administered in gradually increasing amounts. These rare reactions are occasionally associated with generalized edema or anaphylaxis.

INSULIN LIPODYSTROPHY. Lipodystrophy refers to a localized reaction at the insulin injection site, in the form of either lipoatrophy or lipohypertrophy. Lipoatrophy is loss of subcutaneous fat; it appears as slight dimpling or pitting of subcutaneous fat. Lipohypertrophy is the development of a fibrofatty mass; it appears as raised, hardened tissue. Because injection into a damaged site may delay insulin absorption, use of these areas should be delayed until the lipodystrophy is resolved. The use of human insulin, site rotation, and administration of insulin at room temperature decreases the risk of lipodystrophy.

RESISTANCE TO INJECTED INSULIN. Many patients have some degree of insulin resistance at one time or another for various reasons, the most common being obesity, which can be overcome by weight loss. Clinical insulin resistance has

TABLE
30-5 Causes of Morning Hyperglycemia

Characteristic	Treatment
Insulin Waning Progressive rise in blood glucose from bedtime to morning	Increase evening (predinner or bedtime) dose of intermediate- or long-acting insulin, or institute a dose of insulin before the evening meal if one is not already part of the treatment regimen.
Dawn Phenomenon Relatively normal blood glucose until about 3 AM, when the level begins to rise	Change time of injection of evening intermediate-acting insulin from dinnertime to bedtime.
Somogyi Effect Normal or elevated blood glucose at bedtime, a decrease at 2 to 3 AM to hypoglycemic levels, and a subsequent increase caused by the production of counterregulatory hormones	Decrease evening (predinner or bedtime) dose of intermediate-acting insulin, or increase bedtime snack.

been defined as a daily insulin requirement of 200 units or more. Treatment consists of administering a more concentrated insulin preparation, such as U-500, which is available by special order.

MORNING HYPERGLYCEMIA. An elevated blood glucose level on arising in the morning is caused by an insufficient level of insulin, which may be caused by several factors: the dawn phenomenon, the Somogyi effect, or insulin waning. The *dawn phenomenon* is characterized by a relatively normal blood glucose level until approximately 3 a.m., when blood glucose levels begin to rise. This phenomenon is thought to result from nocturnal surges in growth hormone secretions, which create a greater need for insulin in the early morning hours in patients with type 1 diabetes. The dawn phenomenon must be distinguished from *insulin waning* (the progressive increase in blood glucose from bedtime to morning) and from the *Somogyi effect* (nocturnal hypoglycemia followed by rebound hyperglycemia).

It may be difficult to tell from a patient's history which of the above causes is responsible for morning hyperglycemia. To determine the cause, the patient must be awakened once or twice during the night to test blood glucose levels. Testing at bedtime, at 3 a.m., and on awakening provides information that can be used to make adjustments in insulin to avoid morning hyperglycemia. Table 30-5 summarizes the differences among insulin waning, the dawn phenomenon, and the Somogyi effect.

Oral Antidiabetic Agents

Oral antidiabetic agents may be effective for patients with type 2 diabetes who cannot be treated effectively with diet and exercise alone. Oral antidiabetic agents include sulfonylureas, biguanides, alpha-glucosidase inhibitors, nonsulfonylurea insulin secretagogues (meglitinides and phenylalanine derivatives), and thiazolidinediones (glitazones). Sulfonylureas and meglitinides are known as *insulin secretagogues* because their action increases the secretion of insulin by the pancreatic beta

cells. Table 30-6 on page 836 provides a summary of oral antidiabetic agents with nursing implications.

Patients must understand that oral agents are prescribed as an addition to, not as a substitute for, diet and exercise. Use of oral antidiabetic medications may need to be temporarily stopped and insulin prescribed during illness, pregnancy, or hospitalization.

In time, as beta cells continue to decline, oral antidiabetic agents may no longer be effective in controlling type 2 diabetes. In such cases, the patient is treated with insulin. Approximately half of all patients who initially use oral antidiabetic agents eventually require insulin. Because mechanisms of action vary, use of multiple oral medications with different actions is common. For some patients with type 2 diabetes, the use of oral agents in combination with insulin is indicated. Mechanisms of action for oral antidiabetic agents are shown in Figure 30-6 on page 838.

SULFONYLUREAS. The sulfonylureas exert their primary action by directly stimulating the pancreas to secrete insulin. Therefore, a functioning pancreas is necessary for these agents to be effective; they cannot be used in patients with type 1 diabetes. Sulfonylureas improve insulin action at the cellular level and may also directly decrease glucose production by the liver.

The most common side effect of sulfonylureas is hypoglycemia. Second-generation sulfonylureas (glipizide, glyburide, glimepiride) have fewer side effects and drug interactions than do first-generation sulfonylureas since they are excreted by both the liver and the kidneys, thus making them safer to use in the elderly. However, if renal or hepatic insufficiency is suspected, patients must be monitored for hypoglycemia. Because the second-generation drugs are a better option, first-generation sulfonylureas are seldom used today.

NONSULFONYLUREA INSULIN SECRETAGOGUES. Repaglinide (Prandin) and naglitinide (Starlix) act similarly to sulfonylureas, but have a different chemical structure. Both

TABLE
30-6 Antidiabetic Agents

Generic (Trade) Name	Action/Indications	Side Effects	Implications
Sulfonylureas **First- and Second-Generation Sulfonylureas**	Used in type 2 diabetes to control blood glucose levels Stimulate beta cells of the pancreas to secrete insulin; may improve binding between insulin and insulin receptors or increase the number of insulin receptors	Hypoglycemia Mild GI symptoms Weight gain Drug–drug interactions (nonsteroidal anti-inflammatory drugs, warfarin, sulfonamides) Sulfa allergy	Monitor patient for hypoglycemia Monitor blood glucose and urine ketone levels to assess effectiveness of therapy Patients at high risk for hypoglycemia: advanced age, renal insufficiency When taken with beta-adrenergic blocking agents may mask usual warning signs and symptoms of hypoglycemia Instruct patients to avoid use of alcohol
Second-Generation Sulfonylureas Glipizide (Glucatrol, Glucatrol XL) Glyburide (Micronase, Glynase, Dia-Beta) Glimepiride (Amaryl) **First-Generation Sulfonylureas** Chlorpropamide (Diabinese) Tolazamide (Tolinase) Tolbutamide (Orinase)	Have more potent effects than first-generation sulfonylureas May be used in combination with metformin or insulin to improve glucose control Used infrequently in U.S. today	Same as above	Same as above
Biguanides Metformin (Glucophase, Glucophage XL, Fortamet) Metformin with glyburide (Glucovance)	Inhibit production of glucose by the liver Increase body tissues' sensitivity to insulin Decrease hepatic synthesis of cholesterol Used in type 2 diabetes to control blood glucose levels Metformin has been effective in preventing type 2 diabetes related to obesity in young adults	Lactic acidosis Hypoglycemia if metformin is used in combination with insulin or other antidiabetic agents Drug–drug interactions GI disturbances Contraindicated in patients with impaired renal or liver function, respiratory insufficiency, severe infection, or alcohol abuse	Monitor for lactic acidosis and hypoglycemia Patients taking metformin are at increased risk of acute renal failure and lactic acidosis with use of iodinated contrast material for diagnostic studies; metformin should be stopped 48 hours prior to and for 48 hours after use of contrast agent or until renal function is evaluated and normal.
Alpha-Glucosidase Inhibitors Acarbose (Precose) Miglitol (Glyset)	Delay absorption of complex carbohydrates in the intestine and slow entry of glucose into systemic circulation Do not increase insulin secretion Used in type 2 diabetes to control blood glucose levels Can be used alone or in combination with sulfonylureas, metformin, or insulin to improve glucose control	Hypoglycemia (risk increased if used with insulin or other antidiabetic agents) GI side effects (abdominal discomfort or distention, diarrhea, flatulence) Drug–drug interactions	Must be taken with first bite of food to be effective Monitor for GI side effects (diarrhea, abdominal distention) Monitor for blood glucose levels to assess effectiveness of therapy Monitor liver function studies every 3 months for 1 year, then periodically Contraindicated in patients with GI or renal dysfunction, or cirrhosis

Generic (Trade) Name	Action/Indications	Side Effects	Implications
Nonsulfonylurea Insulin Secretagogues			
Repaglinide (Prandin) categorized as a meglitinide Neteglide (Starlix) categorized as a D-phenylalanine derivative	Stimulate rapid and short insulin secretion from the pancreas Used in type 2 diabetes to control blood glucose levels by decreasing postprandial increases in blood glucose Can be used alone or in combination with metformin or thiazolidinediones to improve glucose control	Hypoglycemia/weight gain less likely than sulfonylureas Drug–drug interactions (with ketoconazole, fluconazole, erythromycin, rifampin, isoniazid)	Monitor blood glucose levels to assess effectiveness of therapy Has rapid action and short half-life Monitor patients with impaired liver function and renal impairment Has no effect on plasma lipids Is taken before each meal
Thiazolidinediones (or Glitazones)			
Pioglitazone (Actos) Rosiglitazone (Avandia)	Sensitize body tissue to insulin; stimulate insulin receptor sites to lower blood glucose and improve action of insulin May be used alone or in combination with sulfonylurea, metformin or insulin	Hypoglycemia (risk increased with use of insulin or other antidiabetic agents) Anemia Weight gain, edema Decrease effectiveness of oral contraceptives Possible liver dysfunction Drug–drug interactions Hyperlipidemia (has variable effect on lipids; pioglitazone may be preferred choice in patients with lipid abnormalities) Impaired platelet function	Monitor blood glucose levels to assess effectiveness of therapy Monitor liver function Arrange dietary teaching to establish weight control program
DPP-4 Inhibitors/Incretin Enhancers			
Sitagliptin (Januvia) Saxaglipton (Onglyza) Exenatide (Byetta)	Used in type 2 diabetes to control blood glucose levels. Stimulates release of insulin; prevents secretion of glucagon; slows postprandial gastric emptying; may promote weight loss.	GI disturbances (nausea and diarrhea) Mild to moderate hypoglycemia Possible acute pancreatitis	Used with metformin or sulfonylureas to achieve improved blood glucose control

lower the blood glucose level by stimulating insulin release from the pancreatic beta cells. These drugs have a very rapid onset and a short duration and *must be taken with meals*; they should not be taken if a meal is skipped.

BIGUANIDES. Metformin (Glucophage), the most commonly used biguanide, produces its antidiabetic effects by decreasing hepatic production of glucose and facilitating the action of insulin on peripheral receptor sites. Biguanides have no effect on pancreatic beta cells. Biguanides used with a sulfonylurea may enhance the glucose-lowering effect more than either medication alone. Metformin is contraindicated in patients with renal impairment and in those at risk for renal dysfunction. Metformin-induced lactic acidosis is a serious complication of biguanide therapy. Metformin should not be administered for 2 days before any diagnostic testing that may require use of a contrast agent.

An extended-release form and combination forms (Glucophage XR, Metaglip) combine metformin with a sulfonylurea, such as glyburide or glipizide. The combination provides two mechanisms of action and results in increased efficacy and improved patient compliance, but increases the risk for hypoglycemia.

ALPHA-GLUCOSIDASE INHIBITORS. Acarbose (Precose) and miglitol (Glyset) are alpha-glucosidase inhibitors. They work by delaying the absorption of glucose in the intestines, which results in a lower postprandial blood glucose level. Plasma glucose reduction results in improved diabetes control and lower hemoglobin A1C levels.

The advantage of alpha-glucosidase inhibitors is that they are not systemically absorbed, making them safer to use. Side effects include diarrhea and flatulence. These effects may be minimized by starting at a very low dose and increasing the dose gradually. Because acarbose and miglitol affect food absorption, they must be taken immediately before a meal, making therapeutic adherence a potential problem.

THIAZOLIDINEDIONES (TZDs). Rosiglitazone (Avandia) and pioglitazone (Actos) are oral antidiabetic medications

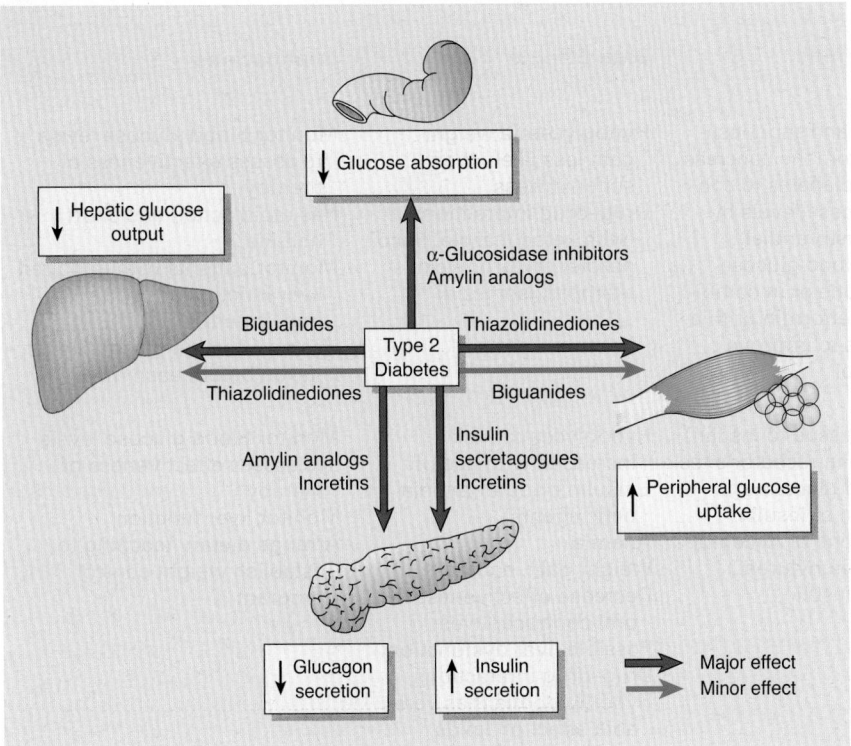

FIGURE 30-6 Sites of action of oral antidiabetic

categorized as thiazolidinediones (TZDs). These drugs enhance insulin action at receptor sites without increasing insulin secretion from the beta cells of the pancreas. They can be used alone or in combination with sulfonylureas, metformin, or insulin. These medications may impair liver function and also may increase the risk of myocardial infarction and congestive heart failure. Liver function studies must be performed at baseline and at frequent intervals throughout treatment.

Other Pharmacologic Therapy

Pramlintide (Symlin) is a synthetic analogue of human amylin, a hormone that is secreted by the beta cells of the pancreas. It is used as an adjunct in the treatment of type 1 and type 2 diabetes when insulin alone cannot control blood glucose levels. Pramlintide is used with insulin, not in the place of insulin.

Exenatide (Byetta) is given subcutaneously to treat type 2 diabetes in combination with metformin or sulfonylureas. It is derived from the hormone incretin, which is produced in the small intestine and is deficient in people with type 2 diabetes. Exenatide delays gastric emptying and enhances insulin secretion, resulting in a slower rise in postprandial blood glucose levels and increased satiety. Dipeptidyl peptidase (DPP-4) inhibitors stimulate insulin production, suppress glucagon secretion, and slow gastric emptying time (Adams et al., 2008).

Transplantation of Pancreatic Cells

Transplantation of the whole pancreas or a segment of the pancreas is being performed on a limited population, mostly patients with diabetes who are receiving kidney transplantation simultaneously. The main issue involves weighing the risks of antirejection medications against the advantages of pancreas transplantation. **Islet cell transplantation**, the implantation of insulin-producing pancreatic islet cells, is another approach that is under investigation (ADA, 2004c). The latter approach involves a less extensive surgical procedure and a potentially lower incidence of immunogenic problems.

Nursing Management

Nursing management of patients with diabetes can involve treatment of a wide variety of physiologic disorders, depending on the patient's health status and whether the patient is newly diagnosed or seeking care for an unrelated health problem. Because all patients with diabetes must master the concepts and skills necessary for long-term management and avoidance of potential complications of diabetes, a solid educational foundation is necessary for competent self-care and is an essential component of nursing care.

Diabetes mellitus is a chronic illness that requires a lifetime of special self-management behaviors. Because diet, physical activity, and physical and emotional stress affect diabetic control, patients must learn to balance a multitude of factors. They must learn daily self-care skills to prevent acute fluctuations in blood glucose, and they must also incorporate into their lifestyle many preventive behaviors for avoidance of long-term diabetic complications. Patients must become knowledgeable about nutrition, medication effects and side effects, exercise, disease progression, prevention strategies,

blood glucose monitoring techniques, and medication adjustment. In addition, they must learn the skills associated with monitoring and managing diabetes and must incorporate many new activities into daily routines. An understanding of the knowledge and skills that patients with diabetes must acquire helps nurses provide effective patient education and counseling.

Developing a Diabetic Teaching Plan

Changes in the health care system as a whole have had a major impact on diabetes education and training. Patients with new-onset type 1 diabetes are hospitalized for much shorter periods or may be managed completely on an outpatient basis. Patients with new-onset type 2 diabetes are rarely hospitalized for initial care. Because many patients with diabetes are admitted to the hospital for reasons other than diabetes or its complications, all nurses play a vital role in identifying patients with diabetes, assessing self-care skills, providing basic education, reinforcing teaching, and referring patients for follow-up care after discharge. Regardless of the setting, all encounters with patients with diabetes are opportunities for reinforcement of self-management skills.

Patients with newly diagnosed diabetes and those who have had diabetes for several years should be assessed for self-care needs. The American Diabetes Association recommends that teaching include three levels of care. The first, survival skills, provides the patient with basic knowledge and skills for diabetes management. An outline of survival information includes the following:

1. Simple pathophysiology:
   a. Basic definition of diabetes
   b. Normal blood glucose ranges and target blood glucose levels
   c. Effect of insulin and exercise
   d. Effect of food and stress, including illness and infections
   e. Basic treatment approaches
2. Treatment modalities:
   a. Administration of insulin and oral medications
   b. Meal planning
   c. Monitoring of blood glucose and urine ketones
3. Recognition, treatment, and prevention of acute complications:
   a. Hypoglycemia
   b. Hyperglycemia
4. Practical information:
   a. Where to buy and store insulin, syringes, and glucose monitoring supplies
   b. When and how to contact the primary care provider

When patients have mastered basic skills and information, they are ready for home management, the second level of teaching. This level involves providing the patient with detailed information, beyond basic survival skills, to foster self-reliance and independence for diabetes management at home.

More advanced patient education includes skills and information to improve lifestyle and individualization of diabetes self-management. The degree of advanced diabetes education provided depends on the patient's interest and ability.

Assessing Readiness to Learn

Before initiating diabetes education, the nurse assesses the patient's readiness to learn. When patients are first diagnosed with diabetes, or first told of the need for insulin, they often go through various stages of the grieving process. The amount of time it takes for the patient and family members to accept the realities of living with diabetes varies.

Once the patient's questions have been answered and possible misconceptions are corrected, the nurse focuses attention on concrete survival skills. Because of the immediate need for multiple new skills, teaching is initiated as soon as possible after diagnosis. Nurses whose patients are in the hospital rarely have the luxury of waiting until the patient feels ready to learn; short hospital stays necessitate initiation of survival skill education as early as possible. This gives the patient the opportunity to practice skills with supervision by the nurse before discharge. Follow-up by home health nurses is often necessary for reinforcement of survival skills.

Determining Teaching Methods

Patient teaching must be flexible and planned to meet individual patient needs. Teaching skills and providing information in a logical sequence is not always the most helpful approach for patients. For example, many patients fear self-injection. Before they learn how to prepare insulin, patients should be taught to insert the needle and inject insulin. Once they have actually performed injections, most patients are better prepared to hear and to comprehend other information necessary for insulin administration. Ample opportunity should be provided for patients and families to practice skills under supervision.

Implementing the Plan
Teaching Experienced Patients

Nurses should continue to assess the skills and self-care behaviors of patients who have had diabetes for many years. Assessment of experienced patients must include direct observation of skills, not just the patient's self-report of self-care behaviors. In addition, these patients must be fully aware of preventive measures related to foot care, eye care, and risk factor management.

Teaching Patients Self-Care

Patient teaching and support for diabetes self-management is an important nursing responsibility. Patients who are having difficulty following the diabetes treatment plan must be approached with care and understanding. If problems with glucose control or with the development of preventable complications exist, the nurse should assess the patient to determine possible reasons. Often problems can be corrected simply by providing complete information and ensuring that the patient understands the information. The focus of diabetes education

is on patient empowerment, highlighting the knowledge, skills, and attitudes needed to maintain and improve one's health.

If knowledge deficit is not the problem, certain physical or emotional factors may be impairing the patient's ability to perform self-care skills. For example, decreased visual acuity may interfere with the patient's ability to administer insulin accurately, measure the blood glucose level, or inspect the skin and feet. Decreased joint mobility or other disability also may impair a patient's ability to inspect the bottom of the feet. Emotional factors, such as denial of the diagnosis or depression, may impair the patient's ability to carry out multiple daily self-care measures. Sometimes family, personal, or work problems are given priority over diabetes management. It is also important to assess the patient for infection or emotional stress, which can lead to elevated blood glucose levels despite adherence to the treatment regimen.

> **NURSING ALERT**
> *When stressed the "flight-or-flight" response elevates catecholamine release, which stimulates glucose production and inhibits insulin release, elevating serum glucose levels.*

Providing Continuing Care

Continuing care of patients with diabetes is critical in managing and preventing complications. The degree to which patients interact with health care providers to obtain ongoing care depends on many factors. Age, socioeconomic level, existing complications, type of diabetes, and other health problems all may influence the frequency of follow-up visits. Many patients with diabetes are seen by home health nurses for diabetes education, wound care, insulin preparation, or assistance with glucose monitoring. Even patients who achieve excellent glucose control and have no complications should see their primary health care provider at least twice a year for ongoing evaluation. In addition, the nurse should remind the patient about the importance of participating in other health promotion activities such as immunizations and recommended age-appropriate health screenings. Participation in support groups is encouraged for patients who have had diabetes for many years, as well as for those who are newly diagnosed. Those who participate in support groups often have an opportunity to share valuable information and experiences and to learn from others.

ACUTE COMPLICATIONS OF DIABETES

The three major acute complications of diabetes are caused by short-term imbalances in blood glucose levels. They are hypoglycemia, DKA, and hyperglycemic hyperosmolar nonketotic syndrome (HHNS), also called hyperglycemic hyperosmolar syndrome (HHS).

HYPOGLYCEMIA (INSULIN REACTION)

Hypoglycemia (low blood glucose) occurs when the blood glucose falls to less than 50 to 60 mg/dL.

Pathophysiology

Hypoglycemia can be caused by too much insulin or oral hypoglycemic agents, too little food, or excessive physical activity. Hypoglycemia may occur at any time of the day or night. It often occurs before meals, especially if meals are delayed or snacks are omitted. For example, midmorning hypoglycemia may occur when the morning regular insulin is peaking, while hypoglycemia that occurs in the late afternoon often coincides with the peak of the morning NPH insulin. Middle-of-the-night hypoglycemia may occur because of peaking late afternoon NPH insulin, especially in patients who have not eaten a bedtime snack.

Clinical Manifestations and Assessment

The clinical manifestations of hypoglycemia are grouped into two categories: autonomic nervous system (ANS) and central nervous system (CNS) symptoms.

At the onset of hypoglycemia, the parasympathetic system is activated causing hunger (Porth, 2009). This is followed by sympathetic nervous system activation, resulting in a surge of epinephrine and norepinephrine. This causes symptoms such as sweating, tremor, tachycardia, palpitation, anxiety, and hunger.

In moderate hypoglycemia, the fall in blood glucose level deprives the brain cells of needed fuel for functioning. Signs of impaired function of the CNS may include inability to concentrate, headache, lightheadedness, confusion, memory lapses, numbness of the lips and tongue, slurred speech, impaired coordination, emotional changes, irrational or combative behavior, double vision, and drowsiness. Any combination of these symptoms may occur.

In severe hypoglycemia, CNS function is so impaired that the patient needs the assistance of another person for treatment of hypoglycemia. Symptoms may include disoriented behavior, seizures, difficulty arousing from sleep, or loss of consciousness.

> **NURSING ALERT**
> *The brain relies almost entirely on glucose for energy. Since the brain cannot synthesize or store more than a few minutes supply of glucose, symptoms of cerebral function deterioration are noted with hypoglycemia (Porth, 2009).*

Symptoms of hypoglycemia may occur suddenly and unexpectedly and vary considerably from person to person. To some degree, this may be related to the actual level to which the blood glucose falls or to the rate at which it falls. For example, patients who usually have a blood glucose level

in the hyperglycemic range (e.g., 200 mg/dL or greater) may feel hypoglycemic symptoms when the blood glucose falls rapidly to 120 mg/dL or less. Conversely, patients who frequently have a glucose level in the low range of normal (e.g., 80 to 100 mg/dL) may be asymptomatic when the blood glucose falls slowly to less than 50 mg/dL. Some patients who have had diabetes for many years experience hypoglycemic unawareness. This condition occurs when the normal compensatory response to low blood sugar fails to cause symptoms, thus the patient is unaware of the problem and may experience profound hypoglycemia.

Medical and Nursing Management

Giving Carbohydrates

Immediate treatment must be given when hypoglycemia occurs. The usual recommendation is that 15 g of a fast-acting concentrated source of carbohydrate be taken orally. Sources of carbohydrate for the treatment of hypoglycemia include:

- Three or four commercially prepared glucose tablets
- 4 to 6 oz of fruit juice or regular soda
- 6 to 10 hard candies
- 2 to 3 teaspoons of sugar or honey

Sugar should *not* be added to juice, even if it is labeled as unsweetened juice. Adding table sugar to fruit juice may cause a sharp increase in the blood glucose level, causing prolonged hyperglycemia.

The blood glucose level should be retested in 15 minutes and retreated with 15 grams of carbohydrate if it is less than 70 to 75 mg/dL. If the symptoms persist for longer than 15 minutes after initial treatment, the treatment is repeated even if blood glucose testing is not possible. Once the symptoms resolve, a snack containing protein and starch (e.g., milk or cheese and crackers) is recommended unless the patient plans to eat a regular meal or snack within 30 to 60 minutes (ADA, 2007d). It is important that people with diabetes, especially those receiving insulin or oral hypoglycemic agents, have a source of carbohydrate readily available at all times.

NURSING ALERT
If a patient with hypoglycemia is unresponsive, a glucagon injection or bolus of D$_{50}$W via IV push is administered rather than risking aspiration with carbohydrates by mouth.

Initiating Emergency Measures

For adult patients experiencing hypoglycemia who are unconscious and unable to swallow, an injection of glucagon 1 mg can be administered either subcutaneously or intramuscularly. **Glucagon** is a hormone produced by the alpha cells of the pancreas that stimulates the liver to convert glycogen to glucose. Because of glycogen's short duration of action,

a concentrated source of carbohydrate followed by a snack should be given when the patient regains consciousness. This will prevent recurrence of hypoglycemia and replenish the liver's stores of glucose.

Glucagon is sold by prescription only and should be part of the emergency supplies available to patients with diabetes who require insulin. Family members, friends, and co-workers should be instructed in the use of glucagon, especially for patients who have little or no warning of hypoglycemic episodes.

Hospitalized patients experiencing severe hypoglycemia are given 25 to 50 mL of 50% dextrose in water (D$_{50}$W) via IV push at a rate of 10 mL/minute. This intervention is effective in achieving an increase in the blood glucose within minutes.

DIABETIC KETOACIDOSIS

DKA is caused by an absence or markedly inadequate amount of insulin. This deficit of insulin results in disorders in the metabolism of carbohydrates, proteins, and fats. The primary clinical features of DKA are hyperglycemia, ketosis, dehydration, electrolyte loss, and acidosis.

Pathophysiology

Without insulin, the amount of glucose entering the cells is reduced, and production and release of glucose by the liver is increased. Both factors lead to hyperglycemia. In an attempt to rid the body of the excess glucose, the kidneys excrete excess glucose causing an osmotic diuresis, leading to dehydration and marked electrolyte loss. The hyperosmolality of the extracellular fluid leads to the stimulation of thirst with resulting polydipsia, and fluid shifting from intracellular to extracellular space. This fluid shifting results in low or normal serum sodium levels despite water losses with polyuria. This low serum sodium level is referred to as *pseudohyponatremia*.

Another effect of insulin deficiency is the breakdown of fat (lipolysis) into free fatty acids and glycerol. The free fatty acids are converted into ketone bodies by the liver. In DKA, the excessive production of ketoacids leads to the development of metabolic acidosis. A characteristic response to this acidemia is for the respiratory center to blow off its respiratory acid, leading to rapid deep respirations known as **Kussmaul respirations**.

NURSING ALERT
Since ketones are a volatile acid, as they are exhaled, an acetone breath may be noted that has a fruity odor similar to overripe apples.

Causes of DKA include insufficient or missed doses of insulin, physical or emotional stress, and illness or infection. An insulin deficit may result from an insufficient dosage of insulin prescribed or from insufficient insulin being administered by the patient. Physical and emotional stress increases

the level of the counterregulatory ("stress") hormones—glucagon, epinephrine, norepinephrine, and cortisol—all of which cause an increase in blood glucose. Finally, illness and infection are associated with insulin resistance, which puts the patient at risk for hyperglycemia. If insulin is not increased during times of stress, illness, and infection, hyperglycemia may progress to DKA. For some patients with undiagnosed or untreated type 1 diabetes, DKA is the initial manifestation of diabetes.

Clinical Manifestations and Assessment

The hyperglycemia of DKA leads to polyuria and polydipsia, weakness, and malaise. In addition, the patient may experience blurred vision due to osmotic changes on the lens related to hyperglycemia. Clinical manifestation of DKA are depicted in Figure 30-7. Patients with marked intravascular volume depletion may present with orthostatic hypotension, warm, dry skin, decreased skin turgor, flat neck veins, and dry mucous membranes. Volume depletion may also lead to frank hypotension and a weak, rapid pulse.

The ketosis and acidosis of DKA lead to gastrointestinal (GI) symptoms such as anorexia, nausea, vomiting, and abdominal pain. The patient may have acetone breath (a fruity odor), and Kussmaul respirations representing the body's attempt to decrease the acidosis, counteracting the effect of ketone accumulation. Mental status changes in DKA vary widely; the patient may be alert, lethargic, or comatose, usually depending on the plasma osmolality.

⚡ NURSING ALERT

Ketone bodies are acids that disturb the acid–base balance of the body when they accumulate in excessive amounts. The resulting DKA may cause signs and symptoms such as abdominal pain, nausea, vomiting, hyperventilation, a fruity breath odor, and, if left untreated, altered level of consciousness, coma, and death. Initiation of insulin treatment, along with fluid and electrolytes as needed, is essential to treat hyperglycemia and DKA and rapidly improves the metabolic abnormalities.

Diagnostic findings include:

- Blood glucose levels greater than 250 mg/dL.
- Low serum pH (6.8 to 7.3)

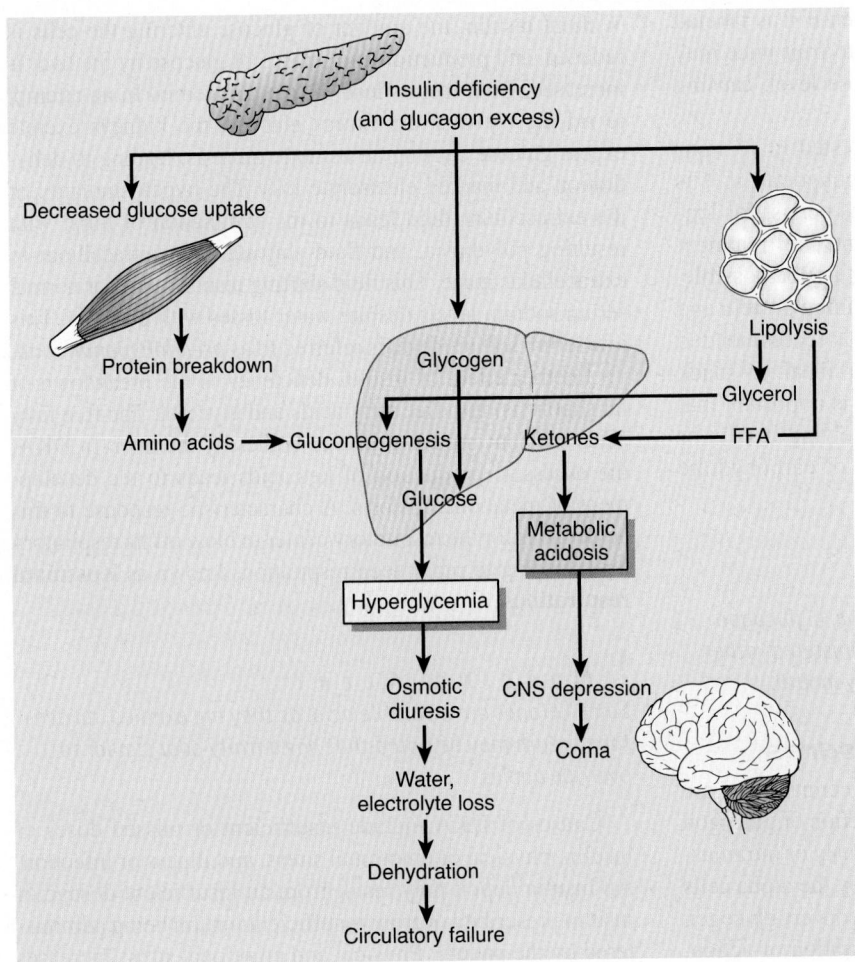

FIGURE 30-7 Mechanisms of diabetic ketoacidosis. Diabetic ketoacidosis is associated with very low insulin levels and extremely high levels of glucagon, catecholamines, and other counter-regulatory hormones. Increased levels of glucagon and the catecholamines lead to mobilization of substrates for gluconeogenesis and ketogenesis by the liver. Gluconeogenesis in excess of that needed to supply glucose for the brain and other glucose-dependent tissues produces a rise in blood glucose levels. Mobilization of free fatty acids from triglyceride stores in adipose tissue leads to accelerated ketone production and ketosis. FFA, free fatty acids; CNS, central nervous system. From Porth, C.M. (2009). *Pathophysiology: Concepts of altered health states.* Philadelphia: Lippincott Williams and Wilkins.

Patient Education

Guidelines to Follow During Periods of Illness ("Sick Day Rules")

- Take insulin or oral antidiabetic agents as usual.
- Test blood glucose and test urine ketones every 3 to 4 hours.
- Report elevated glucose levels (>300 mg/dL (16.6 mmol/L) or as otherwise specified) or urine ketones to your health care provider.
- If you take insulin, you may need supplemental doses of regular insulin every 3 to 4 hours.
- If you cannot follow your usual meal plan, substitute soft foods (e.g., ⅓ cup regular gelatin, 1 cup cream soup, ½ cup custard, 3 squares graham crackers) six to eight times per day.
- If vomiting, diarrhea, or fever persists, take liquids (e.g., ½ cup regular cola or orange juice, ½ cup broth, 1 cup Gatorade) every ½ to 1 hour to prevent dehydration and to provide calories.
- Report nausea, vomiting, and diarrhea to your health care provider, because extreme fluid loss may be dangerous.
- If you are unable to retain oral fluids, you may require hospitalization to avoid diabetic ketoacidosis and possibly coma.

- Low serum bicarbonate (0 to 15 mEq/L)
- Accumulation of serum and urine ketones
- Presence of glucose in the urine
- Abnormal serum electrolyte levels (sodium, potassium, and chloride)

Prevention

For prevention of DKA related to illness, patients must be taught "sick day" rules for managing their diabetes when ill. Box 30-7 lists sick day rules. The most important concept to teach patients is not to eliminate insulin doses when nausea and vomiting occur. Instead, the patient should take the usual insulin dose, or previously prescribed special "sick day" doses, and then attempt to consume frequent small portions of carbohydrates. Drinking fluids every hour is important to prevent dehydration. Blood glucose and urine ketones must be assessed every 3 to 4 hours.

If the patient cannot take fluids without vomiting, or if elevated glucose or ketone levels persist, the primary care provider must be contacted. After the acute phase of DKA has been resolved, the patient should be assessed for the underlying cause.

Medical and Nursing Management

In addition to treating hyperglycemia, management of DKA is directed toward correcting dehydration, electrolyte loss, and acidosis.

Rehydration

In dehydrated patients, rehydration is important for maintaining tissue perfusion. In addition, fluid replacement enhances the excretion of excessive glucose by the kidneys. The patient may need as much as 6 to 10 L of IV fluid to replace fluid losses caused by polyuria, hyperventilation, diarrhea, and vomiting.

Initially, 0.9% sodium chloride (normal saline) solution is administered at a rapid rate, usually 0.5 to 1 L/hour for 2 to 3 hours. Subsequent fluid replacement will depend on the sodium level and level of dehydration and typically will be either normal saline or half-strength normal saline solution. Moderate to high rates of infusion (200 to 500 mL/hour) may continue for several more hours depending on the patient's vital signs, physical assessment findings, and urinary output. Too rapid administration of IV fluid increases the risk of cerebral edema, and while the patient clinically may present with hypovolemic shock it is essential to monitor the patient closely to avoid cerebral edema while correcting the fluid volume deficit. When the blood glucose level reaches 250 mg/dL or less, change to IV solutions containing glucose (D5NS, D5.45NS) to prevent a precipitous decline in the blood glucose level with insulin administration (Kitabchi, Guillermo, Murphy et al., 2006).

DRUG ALERT

The onset of regular insulin administered intravenously is faster than subcutaneous administration. In general, when regular insulin is administered IV, its half-life is about 9 minutes, and steady state is reached in approximately 45 minutes. Therefore, when monitoring blood glucose levels, the nurse is aware that the IV regular insulin is continuing to exert its action. When the blood glucose level reaches 250 mg/dL or less, prevention of hypoglycemia necessitates changing IV solutions to those containing glucose. Typically, the insulin dose for continuous IV infusion is 4 to 10 U/hr or 0.1 U/kg/hr (Metheny, 2005).

Monitoring of fluid volume status involves frequent measurements of vital signs; respiratory, cardiac, and neurological assessment; and evaluation of intake and output. Monitoring for signs of fluid overload is especially important for patients who are older, have renal impairment, or who are at risk for heart failure. Signs include crackles, distended neck veins, edema, weight gain, shortness of breath, orthopnea, paroxysmal nocturnal dyspnea, hypertension, moist mucous membranes, and a full and bounding pulse.

Restoring Electrolytes

The major electrolyte of concern during treatment of DKA is potassium. The initial plasma concentration of potassium may be low because of renal loss due to osmotic diuresis. Conversely, it may be normal or high because of the shifting of potassium out of the cell with hydrogen movement into the cells because of acidemia. If high, the nurse is aware that potassium replacement is withheld until serum K^+ levels

The specific causes and pathogenesis of each type of complication are not thoroughly understood. However, it appears that increased levels of blood glucose predispose patients with diabetes to neuropathic disease, microvascular complications, and risk factors contributing to macrovascular complications. Hypertension is most likely another contributing factor, especially in macrovascular and microvascular diseases.

Long-term complications are seen in both type 1 and type 2 diabetes. Because patients with type 2 diabetes often are undiagnosed for many years, evidence of complications may be present at the time of diagnosis. Renal (microvascular) disease is more prevalent in patients with type 1 diabetes; cardiovascular (macrovascular) complications are more prevalent in older patients with type 2 diabetes.

MACROVASCULAR COMPLICATIONS

Diabetic macrovascular (macroangiopathy) complications result from changes in medium to large blood vessels. Blood vessel walls thicken, sclerose, and become occluded by plaque that adheres to the vessel walls. Eventually, blood flow is blocked. These atherosclerotic changes tend to occur more often and at an earlier age in patients with poorly controlled diabetes. Coronary artery disease, cerebrovascular disease, and peripheral vascular disease are the three main types of macrovascular complications that occur frequently in the diabetic population.

Cardiovascular disease is the major cause of illness and death for people with diabetes (ADA, 2008h). One unique feature of coronary artery disease in patients with diabetes is that typical ischemic symptoms may be absent. Therefore, the patient may not experience the early warning signs of decreased coronary blood flow and may have a "silent" myocardial infarction. This lack of ischemic symptoms may be secondary to autonomic neuropathy. Cardiac disease is discussed in detail in Chapter 14.

Cerebral blood vessels are similarly affected by accelerated atherosclerosis. Occlusive changes or an embolus elsewhere in the vasculature that lodges in a cerebral blood vessel can lead to transient ischemic attacks and strokes. People with diabetes have twice the risk of developing cerebrovascular disease and a greater likelihood of death. Recovery from a stroke is likely to be more difficult for patients with elevated blood glucose levels at the time of, and immediately after, a stroke. Because symptoms of cerebrovascular disease may be similar to symptoms of acute diabetic complications (HHNS or hypoglycemia), it is very important to assess the blood glucose level and treat abnormal levels rapidly, so that testing and treatment of cerebrovascular disease can be initiated promptly, if indicated.

Atherosclerotic changes in the large blood vessels of the lower extremities are responsible for a two to three times higher incidence of occlusive peripheral arterial disease in people with diabetes. Signs and symptoms of peripheral vascular disease include diminished peripheral pulses and intermittent claudication (pain in the buttock, thigh, or calf during walking). Severe arterial occlusive disease in the lower extremities is largely responsible for the increased incidence of gangrene and subsequent amputation in patients with diabetes. Refer to Chapter 12 for assessment of ankle-brachial index (ABI).

Medical and Nursing Management

The focus of management is aggressive modification and reduction of risk factors. Diet and exercise are important in managing obesity, hypertension, and hyperlipidemia. Smoking cessation is essential. If blood pressure goals are not met within 3 months of lifestyle changes, angiotensin-converting enzyme (ACE) inhibitors or angiotensin receptor blockers (ARBs) are recommended for blood pressure control. Antilipidemic medications (e.g., statins) may be added. It is also recommended that 81 mg of enteric coated aspirin be taken daily to reduce the possibility of atherosclerosis (ADA, 2008h).

When macrovascular complications do occur, patients may require increased amounts of insulin or may need to change from oral antidiabetic agents to insulin.

MICROVASCULAR COMPLICATIONS

Diabetic microvascular disease (microangiopathy) is characterized by capillary basement membrane thickening. The basement membrane surrounds the endothelial cells of the capillary. Increased blood glucose levels react through a series of biochemical responses to thicken the basement membrane to several times its normal thickness. Two areas affected by these changes are the retina and the kidneys.

Diabetic Retinopathy

Diabetic retinopathy is the leading cause of blindness in the United States among people between 20 and 74 years of age; it occurs in both type 1 and type 2 diabetes. Glaucoma, cataracts, and other disorders of the eye occur earlier and more frequently in people with diabetes (ADA, 2008h). Table 30-8 summarizes the complications of diabetes that affect vision.

Diabetic retinopathy is caused by changes in the small blood vessels in the retina, the area of the eye that receives images and sends information about the images to the brain. The retina is richly supplied with blood vessels of all kinds: small arteries and veins, arterioles, venules, and capillaries. Figure 30-8 shows the difference between a healthy retina and a retina affected by diabetes.

The risk for retinopathy increases with the length of time a person has had diabetes. Chronic hyperglycemia and hypertension also increase the risk for retinopathy (ADA, 2008h). Changes in the microvasculature include microaneurysms, intraretinal hemorrhage, hard exudates, and focal capillary closure.

TABLE
30-8 Ocular Complications of Diabetes

Eye Disorder	Characteristics
Retinopathy	Deterioration of the small blood vessels that nourish the retina
Nonproliferative (Background)	Early stage, asymptomatic retinopathy. Blood vessels within the retina develop microaneurysms that leak fluid, causing swelling and forming deposits (exudates). In some cases, macular edema causes distorted vision.
Preproliferative	Represents increased destruction of retinal blood vessels
Proliferative	Abnormal growth of new blood vessels on the retina. New vessels rupture, bleeding into the vitreous and blocking light. Ruptured blood vessels in the vitreous form scar tissue, which can pull on and detach the retina.
Cataracts	Opacity of the lens of the eye; cataracts occur at an earlier age in patients with diabetes.
Lens changes	The lens of the eye can swell when blood glucose levels are elevated. For some patients, visual changes related to lens swelling may be the first symptoms of diabetes. It may take up to 2 months of improved blood glucose control before hyperglycemic swelling subsides and vision stabilizes. Therefore, patients are advised not to change eyeglass prescriptions during the 2 months after discovery of hyperglycemia.
Glaucoma	Results from occlusion of the outflow channels by new blood vessels. Glaucoma may occur with slightly higher frequency in the diabetic population.

Retinopathy has three stages: nonproliferative, preproliferative, and proliferative.

- *Stage I:* Nonproliferative retinopathy is characterized by macular edema and occurs in approximately 10% of people with type 1 or type 2 diabetes. It may lead to visual distortion and loss of central vision.
- *Stage II:* Preproliferative retinopathy involves more widespread vascular changes and loss of nerve fibers. Approximately 10% to 50% of patients with preproliferative retinopathy develop proliferative retinopathy in a short time, some within a year.
- *Stage III:* Proliferative retinopathy is characterized by production of new blood vessels and formation of scar tissue. The new vessels are prone to bleeding. Fibrous scar tissue places traction on the retina that may cause hemorrhage or retinal detachment, with subsequent loss of vision.

Clinical Manifestations and Assessment

Retinopathy is a painless process. In nonproliferative and preproliferative retinopathy, blurry vision secondary to macular edema occurs in some patients, although many patients are asymptomatic. Even patients with a significant degree of proliferative retinopathy and some hemorrhaging may not experience major visual changes. Symptoms indicative of hemorrhaging include floaters or cobwebs in the visual field, sudden visual changes including spotty or hazy vision, or complete loss of vision.

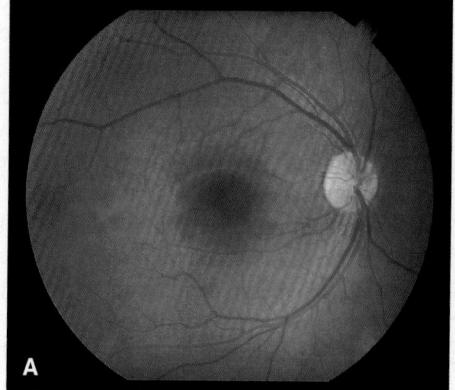 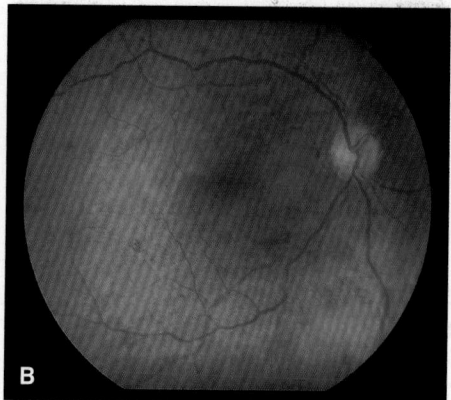

FIGURE 30-8 Diabetic retinopathy. **(A)** In the fundus photograph of a normal eye, the light circular area over which a number of blood vessels converge is the optic disc, where the optic nerve meets the back of the eye. **(B)** The fundus photograph of a patient with diabetic retinopathy shows characteristic waxy-looking retinal lesions, microaneurysms of the vessels, and hemorrhages. (Courtesy of American Optometric Association).

Diagnosis of retinopathy is made by direct visualization of the retina through dilated pupils with an ophthalmoscope by an ophthalmologist or optometrist.

Medical Management

The primary focus of the management of retinopathy is prevention through blood glucose control. Other strategies that may slow the progression of diabetic retinopathy include control of hypertension and smoking cessation. An important reason for screening for diabetic retinopathy is the effectiveness of laser photocoagulation surgery in preventing vision loss (ADA, 2008h).

Nursing Management

Nursing management of patients with diabetic retinopathy or other eye disorders focuses on patient education about the importance of prevention through regular ophthalmologic examinations and blood glucose control. The effectiveness of early diagnosis and prompt treatment is emphasized. If vision loss occurs, nursing care must also address the patient's adjustment to impaired vision and use of adaptive devices for diabetes self-care as well as activities of daily living. Nursing care for patients with low vision or loss of vision is discussed in detail in Chapter 49.

Diabetic Nephropathy

Diabetic nephropathy, or renal disease secondary to microvascular changes in the kidney occurs in 20% to 40% of patients with diabetes and is the single leading cause of ESRD. It is characterized by albuminuria (albumin in the urine), hypertension, and progressive renal insufficiency. Many patients eventually require dialysis or renal transplantation (ADA, 2008h).

Patients with type 1 diabetes frequently show initial signs of renal disease after 10 to 15 years, while patients with type 2 diabetes may develop renal disease within 10 years after diagnosis. However, because many patients with type 2 diabetes have had diabetes for many years before diagnosis, there can be evidence of nephropathy at the time of diagnosis.

Pathophysiology

If blood glucose levels are elevated consistently for a significant period of time, the kidney's filtration mechanism is stressed, allowing blood proteins to leak into the urine. As a result, the pressure in the blood vessels of the kidney increases. It is thought that this elevated pressure serves as the stimulus for the development of nephropathy.

Clinical Manifestations and Assessment

Most of the signs and symptoms of renal dysfunction in patients with diabetes are similar to those seen in patients without diabetes. For patients with diabetes, as renal failure progresses, the catabolism (breakdown) of both exogenous and endogenous insulin decreases, causing frequent hypoglycemic episodes. Insulin needs change as a result of changes in the catabolism of insulin, changes in diet related to the treatment of nephropathy, and changes in insulin clearance that occur with decreased renal function. As renal function decreases, patients commonly have multiple-system failure.

Nephropathy is characterized by the presence of albumin in the urine. Although small amounts of albumin may leak undetected for years, its presence in the urine (microalbuminuria) is an early sign of nephropathy. People with diabetes should have their urine checked annually for the presence of microalbumin (ADA, 2008h).

Hypertension often develops in patients who are in the early stages of renal disease. However, because essential hypertension occurs in many people with diabetes, this symptom may or may not be due to renal disease.

Medical Management

In addition to achieving and maintaining near-normal blood glucose levels, management for all patients with diabetes should include careful attention to control of hypertension to decrease or delay the onset of early albuminuria. Other concerns include prevention or vigorous treatment of urinary tract infections and avoidance of nephrotoxic medications. As renal function changes, adjustment of medications and introduction of a low-sodium, low-protein diet will be necessary.

For patients who have developed microalbuminuria, an ACE inhibitor should be prescribed. ACE inhibitors lower blood pressure and reduce microalbuminuria, thereby protecting the kidney. Alternatively, ARB agents may be prescribed. This preventive strategy should be part of the standard of care for all people with diabetes. In chronic or end-stage renal failure, two types of treatment are available: dialysis (hemodialysis or peritoneal dialysis) and kidney transplantation (ADA, 2008h).

Diabetic Neuropathy

Diabetic neuropathy refers to a group of diseases that affect all types of nerves, including peripheral (sensorimotor) and autonomic nerves. The disorders are clinically diverse and depend on the location of the affected nerve cells. They may be focal or diffuse (ADA, 2008h).

The etiology of neuropathy appears to be related to elevated blood glucose levels over a period of years. The pathogenesis of neuropathy may be attributed to either vascular or metabolic mechanisms, or both. Capillary basement membrane thickening and capillary closure disrupt blood supply to nerves. Also, demyelinization of nerves, thought to be related to hyperglycemia, and accumulation of sorbitol in nerve cells slow nerve conduction.

The two most common types of diabetic neuropathy are sensorimotor polyneuropathy and autonomic neuropathy. Sensorimotor polyneuropathy, also called peripheral neuropathy, most commonly affects the distal portions of the nerves, especially the nerves of the lower extremities. Mononeuropathies (e.g., cranial neuropathies affecting the

oculomotor nerve) affect a single nerve. Autonomic neuropathies cause a variety of clinical manifestations, depending on the area involved.

Peripheral Neuropathy

Clinical Manifestations and Assessment

Initial symptoms may include paresthesias (numbness or tingling) and aching or burning sensations, especially at night. A decrease in proprioception (awareness of posture and movement of the body and of position and weight of objects in relation to the body) and a decreased sensation of light touch may lead to an unsteady gait. Decreased sensations of pain and temperature place patients with neuropathy at increased risk for injury and undetected foot infections. Joint deformities may result from abnormal weight distribution on joints resulting from lack of proprioception.

On physical examination, a decrease in deep tendon reflexes and vibratory sensation is found. For patients who have few or no symptoms of neuropathy, these physical findings may be the only indication of neuropathic changes.

Medical and Nursing Management

Pain, particularly of the lower extremities, is a disturbing symptom for many people with neuropathy secondary to diabetes. The first step in pain management is to achieve optimal blood glucose control. Pharmacologic treatment of pain may include nonopioid analgesics, antidepressants, and antiseizure medications, as well as use of transcutaneous electrical nerve stimulation (TENS).

Autonomic Neuropathies

Neuropathy of the autonomic nervous system can result in a broad range of dysfunctions affecting many organ systems. Three manifestations of autonomic neuropathy are related to the cardiac, GI, and renal systems. Cardiovascular symptoms may range from resting tachycardia, exercise intolerance, and orthostatic hypotension to silent, or painless, myocardial ischemia and infarction.

GI symptoms of early satiety, bloating, nausea, vomiting, and constipation or diarrhea may occur as a result of delayed gastric emptying. Decreased gastric motility may result in poor blood glucose control caused by delayed absorption of glucose from ingested foods.

Urinary retention, a decreased sensation of bladder fullness, and other urinary symptoms of neurogenic bladder may result from autonomic neuropathy. The patient with a neurogenic bladder is predisposed to development of urinary tract infections because of the inability to empty the bladder completely. This is especially true of patients with poorly controlled diabetes, because hyperglycemia impairs resistance to infection.

Sexual dysfunction, especially erectile dysfunction and ejaculatory changes in men, is a complication of diabetes. Impotence occurs with greater frequency in men with diabetes. Some men with autonomic neuropathy have normal erectile function and can experience orgasm but do not ejaculate

normally. The effects of autonomic neuropathy on female sexual functioning include reduced vaginal lubrication, decreased libido, and lack of orgasm. Vaginal infection, which is more common in women with diabetes, may be associated with decreased lubrication, itching, and tenderness.

Medical and Nursing Management

Management strategies depend on symptoms and focus on modification and management of risk factors. Early recognition and appropriate management of neuropathy is important. Effective treatment options for symptomatic diabetic neuropathy are available and may relieve symptoms.

For example, treatment of delayed gastric emptying includes a low-fat diet, frequent small meals, close blood glucose monitoring, and use of agents that increase gastric motility (e.g., metoclopramide and bethanechol). Treatment of diabetic diarrhea may include bulk-forming laxatives or antidiarrheal agents. Constipation is treated with a high-fiber diet and adequate hydration; medications, laxatives, and enemas may be necessary if constipation is severe. Treatment of erectile dysfunction may include medication (e.g., sildenafil citrate) and mechanical devices (ADA, 2008h).

COMPLICATIONS OF THE FEET AND LEGS

Amputation and foot ulcers, consequences of diabetic neuropathy and/or peripheral artery disease, are common and major causes of death and disability in people with diabetes. Early recognition and management of risk factors can prevent or delay these complications of diabetes (ADA, 2008h).

As shown in Figure 30-9, the typical sequence of events in the development of a diabetic foot ulcer begins with a soft tissue injury of the foot, formation of a fissure between the toes or in an area of dry skin, or formation of a callus. Patients with an insensitive foot do not feel injuries, which may be thermal (e.g., from using heating pads, walking barefoot on

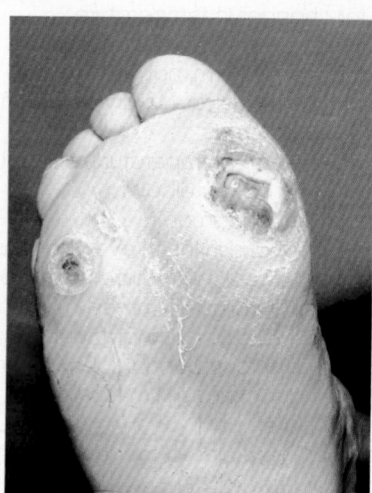

FIGURE 30-9 Neuropathic ulcers occur on pressure points in areas with diminished sensation in diabetic polyneuropathy. Because pain is absent, the ulcer may go unnoticed.

hot concrete, testing bath water with the foot), chemical (e.g., burning the foot while using caustic agents on calluses, corns, or bunions), or traumatic (e.g., injuring skin while cutting nails, walking with an undetected foreign object in the shoe, or wearing ill-fitting shoes and socks).

If the patient is not in the habit of thoroughly inspecting both feet on a daily basis, the injury or fissure may go unnoticed until a serious infection has developed. Drainage, swelling, redness of the leg, or gangrene may be the first sign of foot problems that the patient notices. Treatment of foot ulcers involves antibiotics and debridement. In addition, controlling glucose levels, which tend to increase when infections occur, is important for promoting wound healing, as is smoking cessation. In patients with peripheral vascular disease, foot ulcers may not heal because of the decreased ability of oxygen, nutrients, and antibiotics to reach the injured tissue. Amputation may be necessary to prevent the spread of infection.

The risk of amputation and other problems involving the lower extremities is especially high for patients who have had diabetes for more than 10 years, those with poor blood glucose control, and those with peripheral vascular disease and peripheral neuropathy. Foot assessment and foot care

instructions are vitally important for patients who are at high risk for foot infections.

Medical and Nursing Management

Teaching patients proper foot care is a nursing intervention that can prevent costly and painful complications that result in disability. Box 30-8 provides foot care tips for patient education. Preventive foot care begins with careful daily assessment of the feet. The feet must be inspected for redness, blisters, fissures, calluses, ulcerations, changes in skin temperature, or development of foot deformities. For patients with visual impairment or decreased joint mobility, use of a mirror to inspect the bottoms of both feet or the help of a family member for foot inspection may be necessary. The interior surfaces of shoes should also be inspected for any rough spots or foreign objects. In addition to daily visual and manual inspection of the feet, the feet should be examined during every health care visit or at least once a year. Patients with neuropathy also should undergo evaluation of neurologic status by an experienced examiner using a monofilament device, shown in Figure 30-10. Patients with pressure areas, such as calluses, or thick toenails should be treated by a podiatrist.

BOX 30-8	Patient Education

Foot Care Tips

- Take care of your diabetes:
  - Work with your health care team to keep your blood glucose level within a normal range.
- Inspect your feet every day:
  - Look at your bare feet every day for cuts, blisters, red spots, and swelling.
  - Use a mirror to check the bottoms of your feet or ask a family member for help if you have trouble seeing.
  - Check for changes in temperature.
- Wash your feet every day:
  - Wash your feet in warm, not hot, water.
  - Dry your feet well. Be sure to dry between the toes.
  - Do not soak your feet.
  - Do not check water temperature with your feet; use a thermometer or your elbow.
- Keep the skin soft and smooth:
  - Rub a thin coat of skin lotion over the tops and bottoms of your feet, but not between your toes.
  - Have corns and calluses trimmed by a podiatrist.
- Inspect toenails. All diabetic individuals should seek a qualified podiatrist for foot and nail maintenance.
- Wear shoes and socks at all times:
  - Never walk barefoot.
  - Wear comfortable closed-toe shoes that fit well and protect your feet.
  - Stockings should fit well (without folds, wrinkles, or seams), be comfortable, and changed daily

- Feel inside your shoes before putting them on each time to make sure the lining is smooth and there are no objects inside.
  - Wear sandals in public showers.
- Protect your feet from hot and cold:
  - Wear shoes at the beach or on hot pavement.
  - Wear socks at night if your feet get cold.
- Keep the blood flowing to your feet:
  - Put your feet up when sitting.
  - Wiggle your toes and move your ankles up and down for 5 minutes, two or three times a day.
  - Do not cross your legs for long periods of time.
  - Do not smoke.
- Check with your health care provider:
  - Have your health care provider check your bare feet and find out whether you are likely to have serious foot problems. Remember that you may not feel the pain of an injury.
  - Call your health care provider right away if a cut, sore, blister, or bruise on your foot does not begin to heal after one day.
  - Follow your health care provider's advice about foot care.
  - Do not self-medicate or use home remedies or over-the-counter agents to treat foot problems.

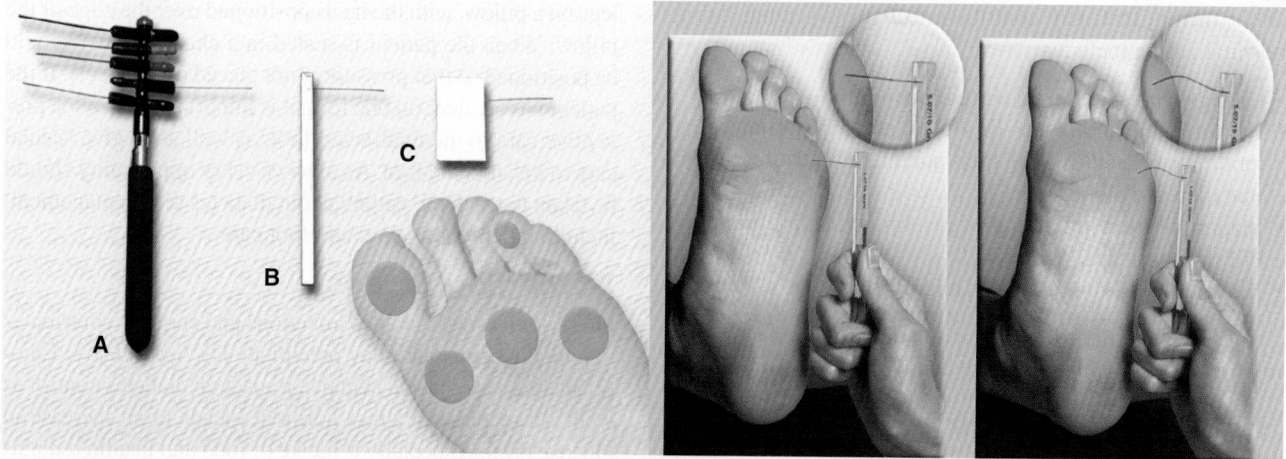

FIGURE 30-10 The monofilament test is used to assess the sensory threshold in patients with diabetes. The test instrument—a monofilament—is gently applied to about five pressure points on the foot (as shown in image on *left*). (**A**) Example of a monofilament used for advanced quantitative assessment. (**B**) Semmes-Weinstein monofilament used by clinicians. (**C**) Disposable monofilament used by patients. The examiner applies the monofilament to the test area to determine whether the patient feels the device. Adapted with permission from Cameron, B. L. (2002). Making diabetes management routine. *American Journal of Nursing, 102*(2), 26–32.

Blood glucose control is important for avoiding decreased resistance to infections and for preventing diabetic neuropathy. The patient may be referred by the health provider to a wound care center for management of persistent wounds of the feet or legs.

SPECIAL ISSUES IN DIABETES CARE

Patients With Diabetes Who Are Undergoing Surgery

During periods of physiologic stress, such as surgery, blood glucose levels tend to increase, because levels of stress hormones increase. If hyperglycemia is not controlled during surgery, the resulting osmotic diuresis may lead to excessive loss of fluids and electrolytes. Patients with type 1 diabetes also risk developing ketoacidosis during periods of stress.

Hypoglycemia also is a concern in patients with diabetes who are undergoing surgery. For example, this is a special concern during the preoperative period if surgery is delayed beyond the morning when the patient received a morning injection of intermediate-acting insulin.

There are various approaches to managing glucose control during the perioperative period. Frequent blood glucose monitoring is essential throughout the preoperative and postoperative periods, regardless of the method used for glucose control.

During the postoperative period, patients with diabetes also must be closely monitored for cardiovascular complications because of the increased prevalence of atherosclerosis, wound infection, and skin breakdown.

Patients With Diabetes Who Are Hospitalized

At any one time, 10% to 20% of hospitalized general medical-surgical patients have diabetes. This number may increase as elderly patients make up an increasing proportion of the hospitalized population.

Often, diabetes is not the primary medical diagnosis, yet problems with control of diabetes frequently result from changes in the patient's normal routine or from surgery or illness. Some of the main issues pertinent to nursing care of hospitalized patients with diabetes are presented below.

Self-Care Issues

All patients admitted to the hospital must relinquish control of some aspects of their daily care to the hospital staff. For patients with diabetes who are actively involved in diabetes self-management, relinquishing control over meal timing, insulin timing, and insulin dosage can be particularly difficult.

It is important for the nurse to acknowledge the patient's concerns and involve the patient in the plan of care as much as possible. If the patient disagrees with certain aspects of nursing or medical care related to diabetes, the nurse must communicate this to other members of the health care team and, where appropriate, make changes in the plan to meet the patient's needs.

Hyperglycemia During Hospitalization

Hyperglycemia may occur in hospitalized patients as a result of the original illness that led to the need for hospitalization.

Other factors that may contribute to hyperglycemia during hospitalization include:

- Changes in usual treatment regimen
- Use of medications and IV fluids, such as partial parenteral nutrition (PPN) and total parenteral nutrition (TPN), that increase blood sugar
- Inappropriate withholding of insulin or inappropriate use of "sliding scales"
- Mismatched timing of meals and insulin

Nursing actions to correct or manage these factors are important for avoiding hyperglycemia.

Hypoglycemia During Hospitalization

Hypoglycemia in hospitalized patients is usually the result of too much insulin or delays in eating. Causes of hypoglycemia in hospitalized patients include:

- Overuse of "sliding scale" regular insulin
- Lack of change in insulin dosage when dietary intake is changed
- Overly vigorous treatment of hyperglycemia
- Delayed meal after insulin administration

The nurse must assess the pattern of glucose values and avoid giving doses of insulin that repeatedly lead to hypoglycemia. Successive doses of subcutaneous regular insulin should be administered no more frequently than every 3 to 4 hours. For patients receiving NPH insulin before breakfast and dinner, the nurse must use caution in administering supplemental doses of regular insulin at lunch and bedtime since hypoglycemia may occur when two insulins peak at similar times. To avoid hypoglycemic reactions caused by delayed food intake, the nurse should arrange for snacks to be given to the patient if meals are postponed because of procedures, physical therapy, or other activities.

Assisting With Hygiene

Nurses caring for hospitalized patients with diabetes must focus attention on oral hygiene and skin care. Because these patients are at increased risk for periodontal disease, it is important for the nurse to assist the patient with daily dental care. The patient may also require assistance in keeping the skin clean and dry, especially in the groin and axillary areas and under the breasts, where chafing and fungal infections tend to occur.

For patients who are confined to bed, nursing care must emphasize the prevention of skin breakdown at pressure points. The heels are particularly susceptible to breakdown because of loss of sensation of pain and pressure associated with sensory neuropathy.

Feet should be cleaned, dried, lubricated with lotion, and inspected frequently. If the patient is in the supine position, pressure on the heels can be alleviated by elevating the lower legs on a pillow, with the heels positioned over the edge of the pillow. When the patient is seated in a chair, the feet should be positioned so that pressure is not placed on the heels. If the patient has an ulcer on one foot, it is important to provide preventive care to the unaffected foot, as well as to give special care to the affected foot. As always, every opportunity should be taken to teach the patient about diabetes self-management, including daily oral, skin, and foot care.

Managing Stress

Physiologic stress, such as infections and surgery, contributes to hyperglycemia and may precipitate DKA or HHNS. Emotional stress can have a negative impact on diabetes control as well. An increase in stress hormones leads to an increase in glucose levels, especially if intake of food and insulin remains unchanged. In addition, during periods of emotional stress, people with diabetes may alter their usual pattern of meals, exercise, and medication. This can contribute to hyperglycemia or hypoglycemia.

People with diabetes must be made aware of the potential deterioration in diabetic control that can accompany emotional stress. They must be encouraged to follow the diabetes treatment plan as much as possible during times of stress. In addition, learning strategies for minimizing stress and coping with stress are important aspects of diabetes education.

NURSING PROCESS

The Patient With Diabetes as a Secondary Diagnosis

Patients with diabetes frequently seek medical attention for problems not directly related to blood glucose control. However, during the course of treatment for the primary medical diagnosis, blood glucose control may worsen. Therefore, it is important for nurses caring for patients with diabetes to focus attention on the diabetes, as well as on the primary health issue.

Nursing Assessment

Assessment of patients with diabetes is the same as that for all patients and is described in other chapters. In addition to nursing assessment for the primary problem, assessment of the patient with diabetes must also focus on hypoglycemia and hyperglycemia, skin assessment, and diabetes self-care skills, including survival skills and measures for prevention of long-term complications. In addition, the nurse should ask about the use of alternative and complementary therapies.

Assessment for hypoglycemia and hyperglycemia involves frequent blood glucose monitoring, usually before meals and at bedtime, and monitoring for signs and symptoms of hypoglycemia or prolonged hyperglycemia, including DKA or HHNS.

Careful assessment of the skin, especially at pressure points and on the lower extremities, is important. The skin is

assessed for dryness, cracks, skin breakdown, and redness. The patient is asked about symptoms of neuropathy, such as tingling and pain or numbness of the feet. Deep tendon reflexes are assessed.

The nurse should assess the patient's diabetes self-care skills as soon as possible to determine whether further diabetes teaching is required. The nurse observes the patient preparing and injecting the insulin, monitoring blood glucose, and performing foot care. The patient's knowledge about diet can be assessed with the help of a dietitian through direct questioning and review of the patient's menu choices. The patient is asked about signs and symptoms, treatment, and prevention of hypoglycemia and hyperglycemia. The patient's knowledge of risk factors for microvascular and macrovascular disease, including hypertension, increased lipids, and smoking is assessed. In addition, the patient is asked the date of the last eye examination, which included dilation of the pupils. It is also important to assess the patient's use of preventive health measures such as an annual influenza vaccination, date of the most recent pneumonia vaccination, and a daily dose of aspirin, unless contraindicated, as well as current medication regimen.

Nursing Diagnosis

Appropriate nursing diagnoses may include:

- Imbalanced nutrition related to increase in stress hormones secondary to the primary medical problem and imbalances in insulin, food, and physical activity
- Risk for impaired skin integrity related to immobility and decreased sensation
- Deficient knowledge about diabetes self-care skills related to new diagnosis, lack of basic diabetes education or lack of continuing in-depth diabetes education

Potential complications from inadequate control of blood glucose may include:

- Hyperglycemia, hypoglycemia
- DKA or HHNS

Planning and Goals

The major goals for the patient may include improved nutritional status, maintenance of skin integrity, ability to perform basic diabetes self-care skills as well as preventive care for the avoidance of chronic complications of diabetes and absence of complications.

Nursing Interventions

Improving Nutritional Status

The patient's food intake is planned with the primary goal of glucose control. The dietary prescription must also consider the primary health problem in addition to lifestyle, cultural background, activity level, and food preferences.

Alterations may be required because of the patient's primary health problem. The patient may be NPO in preparation for diagnostic or surgical procedures. Other common alterations for the hospitalized patient include special diets, tube feedings, and parenteral fluids. All of these treatments require special consideration for the patient with diabetes. The patient's nutritional intake is monitored carefully along with blood glucose and daily weight.

Maintaining Skin Care

The skin is assessed daily for dryness or breaks. The feet are cleaned with warm water and soap. Excessive soaking of the feet is avoided. The feet are dried thoroughly, especially between the toes, and lotion is applied to the entire foot, except between the toes. For patients who are confined to bed, the heels are elevated off the bed with a pillow placed under the lower legs and the heels resting over the edge of the pillow. Dermal ulcers are treated as indicated and prescribed. The nurse promotes optimal blood glucose control in the patient with skin breakdown.

Addressing Knowledge Deficits

Hospital admission of the patient with diabetes provides an ideal opportunity for the nurse to assess the patient's level of knowledge about diabetes and its management. The nurse uses this opportunity to assess the patient's understanding of diabetes management, including blood glucose monitoring, administration of medications, meal planning, exercise, and strategies to prevent long- and short-term complications of diabetes. The nurse also assesses the adjustment of the patient and family to diabetes and its management and identifies any misconceptions they may have.

Monitoring and Managing Potential Complications

Inadequate control of blood glucose levels may hinder recovery from the primary health problem. Blood glucose levels are monitored and insulin is administered as prescribed. It is important for the nurse to ensure that prescribed insulin dosage is modified as needed to compensate for changes in the patient's schedule or eating pattern. Treatment is given for hypoglycemia or hyperglycemia. Blood glucose records are assessed for patterns of hypoglycemia and hyperglycemia at the same time of day, and findings are reported to the primary care provider. In the patient with prolonged elevations in blood glucose, laboratory values and the patient's physical condition are monitored for signs and symptoms of DKA or HHNS.

Development of acute complications of diabetes secondary to inadequate control of blood glucose levels may be associated with other health care problems because of changes in activity level and diet, and physiologic alterations related to the primary health problem itself. Therefore, the patient must be monitored for hyperglycemia and

(continued on page 854)

hypoglycemia, and measures must be implemented for their prevention and early treatment.

Providing Continuing Care

A patient who is hospitalized for another health problem may require referral for home care for that problem or if gaps in knowledge about self-care are found. The home care nurse reinforces the teaching provided during hospitalization and assesses the home care environment to determine its adequacy for self-care and safety.

Evaluation

Expected patient outcomes may include the following:

1. Achieves optimal control of blood glucose:
   a. Avoids extremes of hypoglycemia and hyperglycemia
   b. Takes steps to resolve rapidly any hypoglycemic episodes
2. Maintains skin integrity:
   a. Demonstrates intact skin without dryness and cracking
   b. Avoids ulcers caused by pressure and neuropathy
3. Demonstrates/verbalizes diabetes survival skills and preventive care
4. Exhibits understanding of treatment modalities:
   a. Demonstrates correct technique for administering insulin or oral antidiabetic medications and assessing blood glucose
   b. Demonstrates appropriate knowledge of diet through proper menu selections and identification of pattern used for selecting foods at home
   c. Verbalizes signs, appropriate treatment, and prevention of hypoglycemia and hyperglycemia
5. Demonstrates proper foot care:
   a. Inspects feet, including inspection for cracks or infections between toes
   b. Washes feet with warm water and soap; dries feet thoroughly
   c. Applies lotion to entire foot, except between toes
   d. Identifies strategies that decrease the risk of foot ulcers, including wearing shoes at all times; using hand or elbow, not foot, to test temperature of bath water; avoiding use of heating pad on feet; avoiding constrictive shoes; wearing new shoes for brief periods only; avoiding home remedies for treatment of corns and calluses; having feet examined at every appointment with the health care provider; and consulting a podiatrist for regular nail care if necessary
6. Takes steps to prevent eye disease:
   a. Verbalizes need for yearly or more frequent thorough dilated eye examinations by an ophthalmologist
   b. Verbalizes that retinopathy usually does not cause change in vision until serious damage to the retina has occurred
   c. States that early laser treatment along with good control of blood glucose and blood pressure may prevent visual loss from retinopathy
   d. Identifies hypoglycemia and hyperglycemia as two causes of temporary blurred vision
7. States measures to control risk factors:
   a. Smoking cessation
   b. Limitation of fats and cholesterol
   c. Control of hypertension
   d. Exercise
   e. Regular monitoring of renal function
8. Reports absence of acute complications:
   a. Maintains blood glucose and urine ketones within normal limits
   b. Experiences no signs or symptoms of hypoglycemia or hyperglycemia
   c. Identifies signs and symptoms of hypoglycemia or hyperglycemia
   d. Reports appearance of symptoms so that treatment can be initiated

Chapter Review

Critical Thinking Exercises

1. A 65-year-old man with type 2 diabetes is scheduled for surgical repair of an abdominal aortic aneurysm. What modifications in nursing assessment and care before, during, and after surgery are indicated because of the diagnosis of type 2 diabetes? How would these differ if the patient had type 1 diabetes?

2. You are providing discharge instructions for a patient being discharged from the hospital after coronary artery bypass surgery. The 52-year-old man was overweight before surgery and smoked two packs of cigarettes daily for 20 years. He states that he neglected his health and his type 2 diabetes for two reasons: (1) the stress of his work, and (2) his belief that he did not consider his diabetes serious because he never required insulin. Identify the areas of patient teaching you would provide for this patient and the rationale for each topic as it relates to the complications of diabetes.

3. A 28-year-old patient is newly diagnosed with type 1 diabetes. Identify the major nursing assessment issues and nursing interventions in each of the following situations: (1) the patient is in the first trimester of pregnancy; (2) the patient has a phobia about use of needles; (3) the patient has been blind from birth; and (4) the patient speaks very little English.

4. A 48-year-old woman is brought to the emergency department by her coworkers because she has become drowsy and has had slurred speech for the past hour. Her coworkers report that she lives alone and has no family nearby. They state that they think she has diabetes but can provide no additional information, including the type of diabetes or the name of her health care provider. What would be your initial actions? What assessment data would you initially obtain? What diagnostic tests and treatments would you anticipate? Provide the rationale for those tests and treatments.

5. A 45-year-old man who has three children has had diabetes for 5 years and has not followed the prescribed treatment regimen. He says, "My father and grandfather both died from diabetes. I don't see any point in modifying my life if I'm going to die from diabetes anyway." How would you approach this patient? What resources would you use? How would you alter your approach if your first efforts to convince him of the benefits of treatment were unsuccessful? How would you modify your teaching plan if the patient understands little English?

6. You are caring for a patient with diabetes, for whom self-blood glucose monitoring is recommended. Identify teaching approaches to instruct the patient about blood glucose monitoring. What is the evidence base for the teaching approach or strategy that you selected? What is the strength of the evidence, and what criteria do you use to select the approach? How would you evaluate the effectiveness of your teaching to this patient? Explain how the results of monitoring are used in the management of type 1 and type 2 diabetes.

NCLEX–Style Review Questions

1. Which should be included when teaching a newly diagnosed patient about the dietary management of diabetes?

    A. Food intake should be decreased before exercise.
    B. Consistency between food intake and activity is important.
    C. Carbohydrates are strictly limited.
    D. Insulin and oral antidiabetic agents decrease the need for dietary management.

2. A morning dose of NPH insulin is given at 7:30 a.m. What is the timeframe in which the nurse can expect it to peak?

    A. 11:30 a.m. and 1:30 p.m.
    B. 1:30 p.m. and 3:30 p.m.
    C. 3:30 p.m. and 9:30 p.m.
    D. 5:30 p.m. and 11:30 p.m.

3. For which of the following patients would the nurse expect that insulin may be substituted for oral antidiabetic agents?

    A. In a patient hospitalized for an infection
    B. In a patient having difficulty with weight management
    C. In a patient experiencing hypoglycemia
    D. In a newly diagnosed patient

4. The nurse anticipates that during the initial treatment of diabetic ketoacidosis, the provider will order which solution?

    A. D_5W
    B. $D_5$0.45% saline
    C. Lactated Ringer's solution
    D. 0.9% saline

5. Which does the nurse recognize as an early indicator of nephropathy?

    A. Hematuria
    B. Glycosuria
    C. Albuminuria
    D. Polyuria

Try these additional resources to enhance your learning and understanding of this chapter:

- thePoint online resource available at **http://thepoint.lww.com/Pellico1e**
- *Handbook for Focus on Adult Health: Medical-Surgical Nursing*
- *Study Guide for Focus on Adult Health: Medical-Surgical Nursing*

References and Selected Readings

References and selected readings associated with this chapter can be found on the website that accompanies the book. Visit http://thepoint.lww.com/Pellico1e to access the references and other additional resources associated with this chapter.

ELAINE SIOW

Nursing Management: Patients With Endocrine Disorders

After reading this chapter, you will be able to:

1. Identify the disorders associated with each of the endocrine glands.

2. Describe the underlying pathophysiology of each of the endocrine disorders.

3. Identify the risk factors associated with each of the endocrine disorders.

4. Describe the clinical manifestations and assessment of each of the endocrine disorders.

5. Summarize the medical and nursing management of each of the endocrine disorders.

Disorders of the endocrine system are common and have the potential to affect the function of every organ system in the body. When considering pathology of the endocrine system it is helpful to consider that disorders commonly reflect either too little hormone (undersecretion), too much hormone (oversecretion) or tumors.

PITUITARY DISORDERS

Oversecretion (hypersecretion) is the most common cause of pituitary disorders. It usually involves hypersecretion of adrenocorticotropic hormone (ACTH) that leads to Cushing's syndrome or oversecretion of growth hormone leading to **acromegaly** or gigantism. Acromegaly, an excess of growth hormone in adults (after the epiphyseal plates are fused), results in bone and soft tissue deformities and enlargement of the viscera without an increase in height. Undersecretion (hyposecretion) usually involves all of the anterior pituitary hormones and is termed *panhypopituitarism*. In this condition, the thyroid gland, the adrenal cortex, and the gonads atrophy because of loss of the trophic-stimulating (influencing the activity of a gland) hormones. Hypopituitarism can result from destruction of the anterior lobe of the pituitary gland.

Too little antidiuretic hormone (ADH), secreted by the posterior lobe of the pituitary gland, results in diabetes insipidus, while too much ADH leads to **syndrome of inappropriate ADH** (SIADH).

PITUITARY TUMORS

Pathophysiology

Pituitary tumors are usually benign, although their location and effects on hormone production by target organs can cause life-threatening effects. Although local symptoms such as headache and visual changes may be seen as the tumor causes pressure within the brain, systemic effects are varied depending on the over/undersecretion of particular hormones. Three principal types of pituitary tumors represent an overgrowth of (1) eosinophilic cells, (2) basophilic cells, or (3) chromophobic cells (i.e., cells with no affinity for either eosinophilic or basophilic stains). Prolactinomas are the most common form of pituitary tumor causing a hypersecretion of prolactin. Excessive prolactinomas can lead to amenorrhea (loss of menstruation), galactorrhea

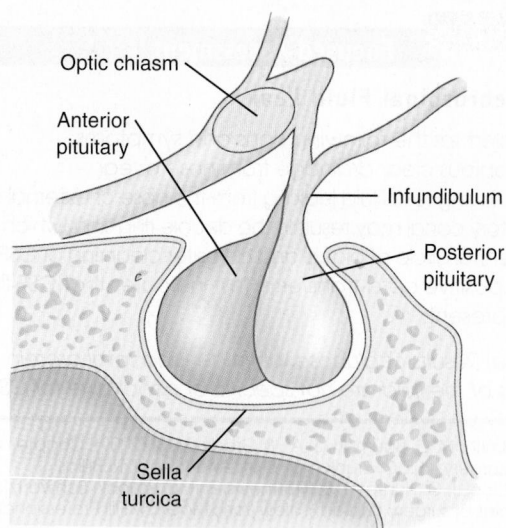

FIGURE 31-1 Relationship of the pituitary gland to the optic chiasm.

(spontaneous, inappropriate flow of milk from male or female breasts in absence of pregnancy/breast-feeding), and infertility in females. In males, these tumors can cause hypogonadism, decreased libido, and impotence. Because the disorder is not diagnosed early, the tumor is generally large; therefore, visual complaints from pressure on the optic chiasm (Fig. 31-1) and headaches are common findings.

Risk Factors

Multiple endocrine neoplasia, type 1 (MEN1), is a hereditary condition that is strongly associated with developing pituitary tumors (American Cancer Society, 2010).

Clinical Manifestations and Assessment

Eosinophilic tumors that develop early in life result in gigantism. The affected person may be more than 7 feet tall and large in all proportions, but the person may be so weak and lethargic that he or she can hardly stand. If the disorder begins during adult life, the excessive skeletal growth occurs only in the feet, the hands, the superciliary ridge, the molar eminences, the nose, and the chin, which is called *acromegaly*. Enlargement also involves all tissues and organs of the body. Patients typically suffer from severe headaches and visual disturbances because the tumors exert pressure on the optic nerves (Porth & Matfin, 2009). Assessment of central vision and visual fields may indicate loss of color discrimination, diplopia (double vision), or blindness in a portion of a field of vision. These tumors promote protein synthesis, which stimulates the growth of all organs; liver gluconeogenesis, causing hyperglycemia; decalcification of the skeleton; muscular weakness; and endocrine disturbances.

Basophilic tumors give rise to Cushing's disease; manifestations are associated with excessive secretion of ACTH

in the pituitary gland. This can lead to masculinization and amenorrhea in females, truncal obesity, hypertension, thin skin, moon face, purple skin striae, and osteoporosis.

Chromophobic tumors represent 90% of pituitary tumors. These tumors usually produce no hormones but destroy the rest of the pituitary gland, causing hypopituitarism. Because the pituitary gland releases growth hormone, thyroid-releasing hormone, ADH, adrenocorticotropic hormone, luteinizing hormone, follicle-stimulating hormone, and prolactin, signs and symptoms vary depending on specific deficient hormones, but may include weight loss; somnolence; fine, scant hair; dry, soft skin; a pasty complexion; short stature; and small bones. Patients also experience headaches, loss of libido, and visual defects progressing to blindness. Other signs and symptoms include polyuria, polyphagia, a lowering of the **basal metabolic rate**, and a subnormal body temperature.

Diagnosis requires a careful history and physical examination, including assessment of visual acuity and visual fields. Computed tomography (CT) and magnetic resonance imaging (MRI) reveal the presence and extent of pituitary tumors. If other information is inconclusive, serum levels of pituitary hormones may be obtained, along with measurements of hormones of target organs (e.g., thyroid and adrenal) to assist in diagnosis.

Medical Management

Hypophysectomy using a transsphenoidal approach is the treatment of choice for patients with pituitary tumor. Tumors within the sella turcica and small adenomas of the pituitary can be removed through a transsphenoidal approach: an incision is made beneath the upper lip (sublabial) or via an endonasal approach, in which entry is gained successively into the nasal cavity, sphenoidal sinus, and sella turcica. Microsurgical techniques used in the transsphenoidal approach provide improved illumination, magnification, and visualization so that nearby vital structures can be avoided. The transsphenoidal approach offers direct access to the sella turcica with minimal risk of trauma and hemorrhage. The approach avoids the risks of craniotomy, and the postoperative discomfort is similar to that of other transnasal surgical procedures.

Preoperatively, the patient undergoes a series of endocrine tests such as rhinologic evaluation (to assess the status of the sinuses and nasal cavity) and neuroradiologic studies (Lubbe & Semple, 2008). Funduscopic and visual field examination are performed because sometimes the pituitary tumor may create localized pressure on the optic nerve or chiasm. In addition, the nasopharyngeal secretions are cultured to detect a sinus infection, which is a contraindication to using the transsphenoidal approach.

Corticosteroids may be administered before and after surgery because the pituitary is the source of ACTH. In addition, the absence of the pituitary gland can alter the function of many body systems. For instance, cessation of menstruation and infertility can occur after total or near-total ablation

of the pituitary gland. Corticosteroid replacement therapy and thyroid hormone replacement is necessary. In addition, prior to surgery, octreotide may be used to shrink the pituitary tumor and inhibit the production or release of growth hormone, improving the patient's clinical condition.

The postoperative management focuses on preventing infection and promoting healing because the procedure disrupts the oral and nasal mucous membranes. Medications include antimicrobial agents (continued until removal of the nasal packing), corticosteroids, analgesic agents for discomfort, and agents for the control of diabetes insipidus (Comerford, 2007).

Nursing Management

Preoperative nursing care of patients undergoing transsphenoidal removal of the pituitary tumor includes teaching deep-breathing exercises before surgery and instructing the patient to avoid vigorous coughing, blowing the nose, sucking through a straw, or sneezing, because these actions may place increased pressure at the surgical site and cause a cerebrospinal fluid (CSF) leak. A leak represents a tear in the tough outermost meningeal dura, the membrane that surrounds the brain and spinal cord that contains CSF. If CSF can descend and escape via the nares, so too can bacteria ascend into the meninges. Therefore, the nurse assesses for signs of meningeal irritation such as nuchal rigidity, temperature elevation, and changes in mental status. The nurse teaches patients to avoid activities such as bending over or straining during urination or defecation because they can raise intracranial pressure (ICP).

Postoperative nursing care includes monitoring vital signs such as hemodynamic, cardiac, and respiratory status. The nurse assesses visual acuity and visual fields at regular intervals because of the anatomic proximity of the pituitary gland to the optic chiasm. One method is to ask the patient to count the number of fingers held up by the nurse. Evidence of decreasing visual acuity may suggest an expanding hematoma. In addition, the nurse raises the head of the bed to 15 to 30 degrees with head in the midline position to limit neck vein compression, decrease pressure on the sella turcica, and promote cerebral venous drainage (reducing potential for elevated ICP). Measurement of the patient's serum electrolytes and intake and output guide fluid and electrolyte replacement and assess for diabetes insipidus. The urine specific gravity is measured after each voiding. The patient's daily weight is monitored to determine fluid status. Fluids are usually given after nausea ceases, following which, the patient may be able to progress to a regular diet.

The nurse should check the nasal packing inserted during surgery frequently for blood or CSF drainage (Box 31-1). Patients are often instructed to breathe through their mouth instead of the nose. The nurse provides oral care to the patient every 4 hours or less because the patient can experience excessive mouth dryness. In addition, the patient is advised

---

BOX 31-1 **Focused Assessment**

Cerebrospinal Fluid Leak

Be alert for the following signs and symptoms:
- Copious clear drainage from nose or ear
- Halo ring test: Fluid leaking from the nose or external auditory canal may result in the double ring sign, which is a central circle of blood and an outer clear ring of CSF.
- A positive beta-transferrin test indicates that CSF fluid is present.

Note: Results of glucose, chloride, and total protein tests of the fluid are not specific or conclusive for CSF.

From Smith, M. L., Bauman, J. A., & Grady, M. S. (2009). Chapter 42: Neurosurgery. In F. C. Brunicardi, D. K. Andersen, T. R. Billiar, D. L. Dunn, J. G. Hunter, J. B. Matthews, & R. E. Pollock. Schwartz's principles of surgery (9th ed.). New York: McGraw Hill Professional.

not to brush his or her teeth until the incision above the teeth has been healed if a sublabial approach is used. Measures to help patient maintain oral care and maintaining moist mucous membranes include offering warm saline mouth rinses, using a mist vaporizer, applying lip balm, and using a room humidifier. The nasal packing is often removed 3 to 4 days postoperatively, and only then can the area around the nares be cleaned with the prescribed solution to remove crusted blood and moisten the mucous membranes (Hickey, 2009). In addition, IV antibiotics are administered as ordered to protect the patient from infection.

DIABETES INSIPIDUS

Diabetes insipidus is a disorder of the posterior lobe of the pituitary gland that is characterized by a deficiency of ADH, also known as vasopressin. This disorder is generally characterized by excessive thirst (polydipsia) and large volumes of dilute urine. It is helpful to remember the three D's: **d**iabetes insipidus, **d**ecreased ADH, and **d**iuresis. There are three types of diabetes insipidus: neurogenic, nephrogenic, and psychogenic polydipsia.

Pathophysiology

Neurogenic diabetes insipidus is characterized by an acute onset resulting from the destruction of the posterior pituitary gland, resulting in a lack of vasopressin. Nephrogenic diabetes insipidus generally results from drug-related damage to the renal tubules resulting in the inability to conserve water. Psychogenic diabetes insipidus is caused by excessive water intake.

Risk Factors

Diabetes insipidus may develop as a result of head trauma, brain tumor, surgical ablation, or irradiation of the pituitary. It may also occur with infections of the central nervous

system (e.g., meningitis, encephalitis, or tuberculosis) or with tumors (e.g., metastatic disease and lymphoma of the breast or lung). Another cause of diabetes insipidus is failure of the renal tubules to respond to ADH. This nephrogenic form of diabetes insipidus may be related to hypokalemia, hypercalcemia, and a variety of medications (e.g., lithium, demeclocycline [Declomycin] that impair the kidneys ability to reabsorb water). The incidence of acute diabetes insipidus in severe head injury is high, especially in penetrating injuries. Independent risk factors for diabetes insipidus include a Glasgow Coma Scale (GCS) of 8 or less, cerebral edema, and a head Abbreviated Injury Score (AIS) of 3 or more. Acute diabetes insipidus is associated with significantly increased mortality (Hadjizacharia, Beale, Inaba et al., 2008).

Clinical Manifestations and Assessment

Without the action of ADH on the distal nephron of the kidney, an enormous daily output of very dilute urine (3 to 20 L) with nocturia, frequency, and a specific gravity of 1.001 to 1.005 occurs. Signs and symptoms of fluid volume deficit that occur as patients are unable to compensate for the massive urinary loss include:

• Weight loss
• Poor skin turgor
• Dry mucous membranes
• Increased heart rate
• Hypotension

Due to intense thirst, the patient tends to drink 2 to 20 L of fluid daily and often prefers cold water. The onset of diabetes insipidus may be abrupt or insidious. The disease cannot be controlled by limiting fluid intake because the high-volume loss of urine continues even without fluid replacement. Fluid restriction can cause the patient to experience an insatiable craving for fluid and to develop hypernatremia and severe dehydration.

There is no one diagnostic test for diabetes insipidus. To diagnose diabetes insipidus, an accurate 24-hour urine collection is obtained to measure for volume and creatinine. A urine volume of less than 2 L/24 hours (without hypernatremia) rules out diabetes insipidus.

If central diabetes insipidus is suspected, a *vasopressin challenge test* may be used. Desmopressin (DDAVP; desamino-arginine vasopressin) is administered intranasally, subcutaneously, or intravenously with subsequent measurement of urine volumes, specific gravity, and/or urine osmolality. If diabetes insipidus is secondary to central or neurogenic diabetes insipidus, administration of ADH results in an elevation of the urine osmolality by greater than 50% (urine is becoming more concentrated). However, if the etiology is nephrogenic, there is a small or absent subsequent increase in the urine osmolality, as the kidneys are not responsive to ADH. In addition, serum plasma levels are obtained to

screen for diabetes mellitus (glucose), dehydration and azotemia (urea nitrogen), hypercalcemia (calcium), hypokalemia (potassium), and hyperuricemia (uric acid).

Other diagnostic procedures include concurrent measurements of plasma levels of ADH and plasma and urine osmolality. Table 31-1 summarizes laboratory findings. A fluid deprivation test may also be considered; however, it is contraindicated if the patient's serum sodium is elevated. This test involves withholding fluids for 8 to 12 hours or until 3% to 5% of the body weight is lost. The patient is weighed frequently during the test. Plasma and urine osmolality studies are performed at the beginning and end of the test. The inability to increase the specific gravity and osmolality of the urine is characteristic of diabetes insipidus. The patient continues to excrete large volumes of urine with low specific gravity and experiences weight loss, increasing serum osmolality, and elevated serum sodium levels. During the deprivation test, ADH or vasopressin can be given subcutaneously as described previously. The patient's condition needs to be monitored frequently due to the risk of severe dehydration. The test will be terminated if tachycardia, excessive weight loss, or hypotension develops.

Once the diagnosis is confirmed, but the cause (e.g., head injury) is unclear, the patient will be further assessed for presence of tumors that may be causing the disorder.

Medical Management

The objectives of medical therapy are to replace ADH (which is usually a long-term therapeutic program), to ensure adequate fluid replacement, and to identify and correct the underlying intracranial pathology.

Desmopressin/DDAVP, a synthetic vasopressin is used to control fluid balance and prevent dehydration. Desmopressin does not have the vascular effects of natural ADH. Thus, it is particularly valuable due to its longer duration of action and fewer adverse effects compared to other preparations previously used to treat the disease. It is administered intranasally using a flexible calibrated plastic tube. One or two administrations daily (every 12 to 24 hours) is usually needed to control the symptoms (Fitzgerald, 2007).

Other medications that are used in the treatment of patients with diabetes insipidus include intramuscular administration of vasopressin, chlorpropamide (Diabinese), thiazide diuretics (potentiate the action of vasopressin), and/or prostaglandin inhibitors (e.g., ibuprofen, indomethacin, and aspirin). Intramuscular administration of ADH, vasopressin tannate in oil, is used if the intranasal route is not possible. The medication is administered every 24 to 96 hours. The vial of medication should be warmed or shaken vigorously before administration. The injection is administered in the evening so that maximum results are obtained during sleep. Abdominal cramps are a side effect of this medication. Rotation of injection sites is necessary to prevent lipodystrophy. The patient receiving chlorpropamide should be warned of the

TABLE
31-1 Laboratory Tests for Diabetes Insipidus

Test	Normal Values	Critical Values	Nursing Implications
Serum osmolality Urine osmolality Urine specific gravity	288–291 mOsm/Kg 700–1400 mOsm/Kg ≥1.015	>295 mOsm/kg <200 mOsm/kg 1.001–1.005	Patients will not be given fluid intake for 4 to 18 hours. The nurse will measure hourly urine osmolality, urine specific gravity, and weigh patient. If patient loses >3% of body weight, measure serum osmolality.
Plasma sodium	135–145 mEq/L	>145 mEq/L	Patient will be monitored for hypernatremia due to hypothalamic lesions that cause impaired osmotic regulation but intact volume regulation of antidiuretic hormone (ADH) secretion.
Serum ADH levels	1.3–4.1 pg/mL (Values may vary slightly among different laboratories)	Look for low serum ADH levels in diabetes insipidus; e.g. in central diabetes insipidus look for values <1.1 pg/mL.	If three successive hourly urine osmolality indicates no change, administer 5 units of vasopressin and measure urine osmolality 1 hour later. Serum ADH is used to determine type of diabetes insipidus; e.g., primary diabetes insipidus ranges from 3 to 7.5 pg/mL and nephrogenic diabetes insipidus ranges from 12 to 13 pg/mL. The nurse should be aware that serum ADH levels are always interpreted relative to serum osmolality.

From Wallach, J. (2007). *Interpretation of diagnostic tests* (8th ed.). Philadelphia: Lippincott Williams & Wilkins.

possibility of hypoglycemic reactions. If the diabetes insipidus is renal in origin, the previously described treatments are ineffective. Thiazide diuretics, mild salt depletion, and prostaglandin inhibitors (ibuprofen, indomethacin, and aspirin) are used to treat the nephrogenic form of diabetes insipidus. There is no effective treatment for psychogenic diabetes insipidus (Jameson & Weetman, 2008).

Nursing Management

The nursing management of the patient with diabetes insipidus includes maintaining adequate fluid volume, monitoring patient's weight, administering vasopressin, monitoring vital signs, and monitoring patient's intake and output. Due to vasoconstrictive properties, vasopressin should be avoided in patients with preexisting coronary artery disease or vascular disease. The patient with possible diabetes insipidus needs support while undergoing studies for a possible cranial lesion. The nurse informs the patient and family about follow-up care and emergency measures, provides specific verbal and written instructions, demonstrates how to administer the medications, and observes return demonstrations as appropriate. The nurse should provide instructions on measuring daily weights to determine how much body fluid has been gained or lost. This information will allow the provider to titrate the dosage of vasopressin accordingly to avoid too high or too low doses. For instance, high dose of vasopressin will lead to fluid retention and weight gain. On the other

hand, insufficient or low dose of vasopressin will lead to excess urine production (polyuria) and weight loss. In addition, the nurse should advise the patient to wear a medical identification bracelet and to carry medication and information about this disorder at all times.

SYNDROME OF INAPPROPRIATE ANTIDIURETIC HORMONE

Pathophysiology

SIADH secretion includes excessive ADH secretion from the pituitary gland even in the face of subnormal serum osmolality. Patients with this disorder cannot excrete diluted urine. They retain water and develop a subsequent sodium deficiency known as **dilutional hyponatremia**.

Risk Factors

SIADH is often of nonendocrine origin. For instance, the syndrome may occur in patients with carcinomas (lung, pancreas, and lymphoma) that synthesize and release ADH. SIADH has occurred in patients with pulmonary disease such as severe pneumonia, pneumothorax, and other disorders of the lungs (Porth & Matfin, 2009). Central nervous system disorders, such as head injury, brain surgery or tumor, and infection, can produce SIADH by direct stimulation of the pituitary gland. HIV infection is also associated with the development of SIADH and may be related to an underlying pulmonary

(pneumocystic pneumonia), central nervous system infection, or malignancy (Porth & Matfin, 2009). Medications such as vincristine, phenothiazines, tricyclic antidepressants, thiazide diuretics, and nicotine can cause SIADH, either directly stimulating the pituitary gland or increase the sensitivity of renal tubules to circulating ADH.

Clinical Manifestations and Assessment

The clinical manifestations of SIADH include hyponatremia (sodium <134 mEq/L), decreased serum osmolality (<280 mOsm/kg) with inappropriately increased urine osmolality, and urine sodium over 20mEq/L (Fukagawa, Kurokawa, & Papadakis, 2007). Obtain a detailed history to rule out other causes of hyponatremia, such as heart failure, adrenal insufficiency, and renal failure. On assessment, patients usually present with normal vital signs, moist mucous membranes, normal skin turgor, and no edema. The reabsorbed water tends to be intracellular rather than interstitial and therefore patients appear euvolemic (normal volume). Patients with SIADH resulting in severe hyponatremia often exhibit more acute symptoms, such as confusion, lethargy, weakness, myoclonus, asterixis, depressed reflexes, generalized seizures, and coma related to ensuing cerebral edema.

Medical Management

Medical management includes identifying and eliminating the underlying cause. Diuretics such as furosemide (Lasix) may be used, along with fluid restriction (<1 to 2 L water daily). If severe hyponatremia is present, an IV of 3% sodium chloride along with fluid restriction and furosemide may be required for patients. Because retained water is excreted slowly through the kidneys, the extracellular fluid volume contracts and the serum sodium concentration gradually increases toward normal.

Nursing Management

Nursing management includes close monitoring of fluid intake and output, daily weight, urine and blood chemistries, and neurological status. The nurse assesses for neurological signs caused by hyponatremia, such as confusion, seizures and delirium.

NURSING ALERT
As appropriate, use seizure precautions to protect the patient from injury and prevent aspiration. Keep oxygen and suctioning equipment at the bedside. Ensure side rails are padded.

In the event of a seizure, lower the head of the bed and place the patient on his side to prevent aspiration and protect the airway.

If ordered, the nurse carefully monitors hypertonic saline administration, as a complication of overaggressive treatment

BOX 31-2 | **Focus on Pathophysiology**

Central Pontine Myelinolysis

Central pontine myelinolysis (CMP) is a serious complication that develops after aggressive treatment of hyponatremia. The rapid rise in serum sodium with resultant change in serum osmolality causes water to be pulled from the brain cells. The changes in the brain cell volume (shift in water out of brain cells) causes injury to the myelin sheath (myelin sheath protects the nerves). These changes can result in significant neurological morbidity and mortality. The most common presentation of CPM is a decreased level of consciousness.

with 3% saline is central pontine myelinolysis (CMP) (Box 31-2). Providing supportive measures and explanations of procedures helps the patient with this disorder.

DISORDERS OF THE THYROID GLAND

HYPOTHYROIDISM

Hypothyroidism results from insufficient levels of thyroid hormone. Thyroid deficiency can affect all body functions and can range along a spectrum from mild, subclinical forms to myxedema coma, a life-threatening hypothyroidism.

Patients with hypothyroidism may often have primary or thyroidal hypothyroidism, which refers to dysfunction of the thyroid gland itself. If the cause of the thyroid dysfunction is failure of the pituitary gland, the hypothalamus, or both, the hypothyroidism is known as *central hypothyroidism*. If the cause is entirely a pituitary disorder, it may be referred to as *pituitary* or *secondary hypothyroidism*. If the cause is a disorder of the hypothalamus resulting in inadequate secretion of TSH due to decreased stimulation by TRH, it is referred to as *hypothalamic* or *tertiary hypothyroidism*. If thyroid deficiency is present at birth, the hypothyroidism is known as *cretinism*. In such instances, the mother may also have thyroid deficiency.

Pathophysiology

In hypothyroidism, the decreased thyroxine (T_4) production leads to the stimulation of TSH in the pituitary gland. Subsequently, TSH stimulates the secretion of triiodothyronine (T_3) to increase production of T_4, leading to hypertrophy of the thyroid gland. Laboratory findings include decreased T_3 and T_4 and an increased TSH.

Risk Factors

The most common cause of hypothyroidism in adults is autoimmune thyroiditis (**Hashimoto's disease**), in which the

immune system attacks the thyroid gland. Hypothyroidism can occur in patients with previous hyperthyroidism that has been treated with radioiodine or antithyroid medications or **thyroidectomy**. There is an increased incidence of hypothyroidism in patients who have undergone radiation therapy for head and neck cancer. Therefore, thyroid function tests are recommended for all patients who receive such treatment.

Hypothyroidism has been shown to affect women five times more frequently than men and occurs most often between the ages of 30 and 60 years. Additionally longstanding mild to moderate hypothyroidism is often seen in the elderly. The explanation for the higher prevalence of hypothyroidism among elderly people may be related to alterations in immune function with age. Subclinical disease is common among the older women and can be asymptomatic or mistaken for other medical conditions. For instance, subtle symptoms of hypothyroidism, such as fatigue, muscle aches, and mental confusion, may be attributed to the normal aging process by the patient, family, and health care provider. Hence, screening of TSH levels is recommended for women older than 50 years of age presenting with one or more symptoms (U.S. Preventive Services Task Force, 2004). Gerontological considerations are discussed in Box 31-3.

Clinical Manifestations and Assessment

Clinical manifestations of hypothyroidism are divided into early and late symptoms and represent slowing of the metabolic process. The early symptoms of hypothyroidism are nonspecific and can range from fatigue to somnolence, loss of libido to amenorrhea, apathy to mental and physical sluggishness, nonpitting edema to pleural and pericardial effusions. Reports of hair loss, brittle nails, and dry skin are common. The patient frequently complains of constipation. Paresthesia (numbness and tingling of the fingers) and nerve entrapment syndrome has been linked with endocrine disorders such as hypothyroidism, but the etiology is poorly understood. Hearing loss may also occur.

Late symptoms include slow speech, subdued emotional responses, apathy, absence of sweating, cold intolerance, constipation, thickening of skin (due to accumulation of mucopolysaccharides in subcutaneous tissues), dyspnea, weight gain, thinning of hair, alopecia, and deafness. On assessment, patients usually present with swelling of eyelids, pitting edema, bradycardia, hypotension, and hypothermia. Figure 31-2 illustrates clinical manifestations of hypothyroidism.

Advanced hypothyroidism may produce personality and cognitive changes that are characteristic of dementia. Respiratory manifestations include pleural effusion, respiratory muscle weakness, inadequate ventilation, and sleep apnea.

Severe hypothyroidism is associated with an elevated serum cholesterol level, atherosclerosis, coronary artery disease, poor left ventricular function, and pericardial effusion. In addition, the patient with severe hypothyroidism often presents with subnormal temperature and pulse rate. The patient usually begins to gain weight even without an increase in food intake, although he or she may be cachectic. The hair thins and falls out, and the face becomes expressionless and mask

---

BOX 31-3   Gerontologic Considerations

Hypothyroidism

The elderly often present atypical signs and symptoms of hypothyroidism. For instance, the elderly patient may have few or no symptoms until the dysfunction is severe. Depression, apathy, and decreased mobility are major initial symptoms that may be accompanied by significant weight gain despite a poor appetite. In addition, constipation is common and affects one-fourth of elderly patients with hypothyroidism. In the elderly patient with mild to moderate hypothyroidism, thyroid hormone replacement must be started with low dosages and increased gradually to prevent serious cardiovascular and neurologic side effects. (Remember "start low and go slow.") In general, thyroid replacement begins at one-fourth to one-half the expected dose and is increased in small increments no sooner than 4 to 6 weeks apart. Angina may occur with rapid thyroid replacement in the presence of coronary artery disease secondary to the hypothyroid state or preexisting atherosclerosis. Heart failure and tachyarrhythmias may worsen during the transition from the hypothyroid state to the normal metabolic state. Dementia may become more apparent during early thyroid hormone replacement in the elderly patient.

Elderly patients with severe hypothyroidism and atherosclerosis may become confused and agitated if their metabolic rate is increased too quickly. Marked clinical improvement follows the administration of hormone replacement; such medication must be continued for life. The elderly patient requires periodic follow-up monitoring of serum TSH levels. In addition, the elderly should be reminded that the failure to comply with current therapy may lead to complications. A careful history can identify the need for further teaching about the importance of safe medication administration.

Complications such as myxedema and myxedema coma usually occur exclusively in patients older than 50 years of age. The high mortality rate of myxedema coma mandates immediate IV administration of thyroid hormone, as well as supportive care and monitoring for cardiac complications, particularly in patients with ischemic heart disease.

hospital on the day of surgery. Preoperative teaching i
demonstrating to the patient how to support the ne
the hands after surgery to prevent stress on the incisi
involves raising the elbows and placing the hands beh
neck to provide support and reduce strain and tensior
neck muscles and the surgical incision.

Assessing the Postoperative Patient

Postoperatively, the nurse periodically assesses the
cal dressings and reinforces them if necessary. Th
observes the sides and the back of the neck, as wel
anterior dressing for bleeding. In addition to mor
the pulse and blood pressure for any indication of
bleeding, it is important to be alert for complaints of a
tion of pressure or fullness at the incision site, freque
lowing or choking. Such symptoms may indicate sub
ous hemorrhage and hematoma formation. In addit
nurse notes vocal changes or hoarseness, as this ma
cate injury to the laryngeal nerve or laryngeal edema
may develop postoperatively. If drains are inserted int
atively, the nurse records the color, amount, and cons
of the drainage and maintains function of the device.

Maintaining the Airway

Respiratory difficulties can occur as a result of ed
the glottis, hematoma formation, or injury to the re
laryngeal nerve. This complication requires insertio
airway. It is vital to have a tracheostomy set by the
at all times because in the event of significant edema
ment of an endotracheal tube is unlikely because of
ing of the airway. If the respiratory distress is cau
hematoma, a surgical evacuation is required.

Managing Pain

The nurse assesses the intensity of pain and administe
gesic agents as prescribed. The nurse should anticipate
hension in the patient and inform the patient that oxy
assist breathing. When moving and turning the pati
nurse must carefully support the patient's head and av
sion on the sutures. The most comfortable patient po
the semi-Fowler's position, with the head elevated a
ported by pillows.

Administering Hydration Therap

IV fluids are administered during the immediate po
tive period. Nurses can anticipate that when PO flu
allowed, patients report little difficulty in swallowin
ing cold fluids and ice is recommended.

Managing Safety

The nurse advises the patient to talk as little as
to reduce edema to the vocal cords. Items that are
frequently are kept within easy reach, so the patie
not need to turn the head to reach for them. An
table provides easy access to items, such as tissues,

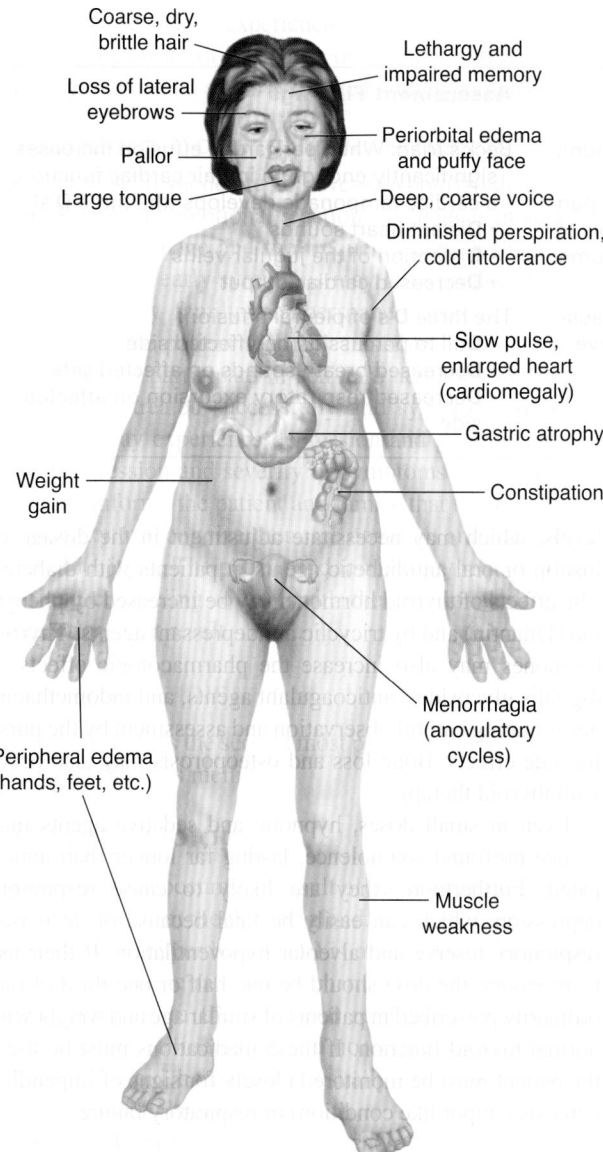

FIGURE 31-2 Dominant clinical features of hypothyroidism. From Porth, C. M. & Matfin, G. (2009). *Pathophysiology: Concepts of altered health states* (8th ed.). Philadelphia: Lippincott Williams & Wilkins.

like. The patient often complains of being cold even in a warm environment.

DRUG ALERT
The patient with advanced hypothyroidism is profoundly hypothermic (91°F to 95°F) and abnormally sensitive to sedatives, opioids, and anesthetic agents. Therefore, these medications are administered only with extreme caution. If these medications are used, closely monitor the patient's vital signs (heart rate, blood pressure, body temperature, and respiration rate).

Myxedema refers to the accumulation of mucopolysaccharides in subcutaneous and other interstitial tissues; this

causes nonpitting edema. The fluid accumulation causes a characteristic puffy appearance to the face and eyes (periorbital edema). Myxedematous fluid can cause pericardial and pleural effusions (Porth, 2007). Myxedema coma describes the most extreme, severe stage of hypothyroidism, in which the patient is hypothermic and unconscious. Increasing lethargy may progress to stupor and then coma. Myxedema coma may also develop with undiagnosed hypothyroidism and may be precipitated by infection or other systemic disease or by use of sedatives or opioid analgesic agents. The patient's respiratory drive is depressed, resulting in alveolar hypoventilation, progressive carbon dioxide retention, narcosis, and coma. These symptoms, along with cardiovascular collapse and shock, require aggressive and intensive therapy if the patient is to survive. Myxedema coma is a medical emergency; even with early vigorous therapy, mortality rate is high.

Medical Management
Hormone Replacement

The primary objective in the medical management of hypothyroidism is to restore a normal metabolic state by replacing the missing hormone, levothyroxine (thyroxine; T_4). Synthetic levothyroxine (Synthroid or Levothroid) is the preferred preparation for treating hypothyroidism and suppressing nontoxic **goiters** (enlargements of the thyroid gland). The dosage for hormone replacement is based on the patient's serum TSH concentration. If replacement therapy is adequate, the symptoms of myxedema disappear and normal metabolic activity is resumed.

Cardiac Management

The patient who has hypothyroidism for long periods is likely to have coronary-related diseases, such as elevated serum cholesterol, atherosclerosis, and coronary artery disease (CAD). As long as metabolism is subnormal and the tissues, including the myocardium, require relatively little oxygen, a reduction in blood supply is tolerated without overt symptoms of CAD. When thyroid hormone is administered, the myocardial oxygen demand increases without increasing the myocardial oxygen supply, therefore patients should be monitored for cardiac complications, such as chest pain and congestive heart failure. Patients may also be treated for angina or arrhythmias due to the release of catecholamines that may be activated during thyroid replacement therapy. In the event of angina or arrhythmias, the nurse should immediately notify the primary care provider and discontinue the thyroid hormone administration. The thyroid hormone replacement can be resumed at a later time at a lower prescribed starting dosage under the close observation of the prescribing provider and the nurse.

Nursing Management

A plan of nursing care for a patient with hypothyroidism is available online at http://thePoint.lww.com/Pellico1e.

glands. These substances include excessive amount or lithium, often used in the treatment of bipolar Too much iodine can cause enlargement of the thyr ing in the development of excess thyroid hormone Keep in mind that many patients receive IV iodine pital as a result of diagnostic studies that require cor as cardiac catheterization and CT scans.

Simple goiter represents a compensatory h of the thyroid gland, caused by stimulation by th gland. Such goiters usually cause no symptoms, the swelling in the neck, which may result in trac pression when excessive. Many goiters of this t after the iodine imbalance is corrected. Supp iodine, such as SSKI, is prescribed to suppress the thyroid-stimulating activity.

Some thyroid glands are nodular because c hyperplasia (overgrowth). No symptoms may ar these nodules increase in size and descend into where local pressure symptoms may manifest. Sor become malignant, and some are associated with a roid state. The patient with many thyroid nodules tually require surgery.

Clinical Manifestations and Assessment

Most patients with simple goiters are asymptomat complain of pressure in the neck. On assessment, may present with a soft diffusely enlarged nodule ov As the goiter progresses, the patient may experience such as difficulty breathing and swallowing. Patic present in euthyroid state with normal TSH and T_4

On the other hand, lesions that are single, hard on palpation or associated with cervical lymph suggest malignancy. Although thyroid function te helpful in evaluating thyroid nodules and masses are rarely conclusive. Fine-needle biopsy (FNB) of gland is often used to establish the diagnosis of thy The purpose of the biopsy is to differentiate cancer nodules from noncancerous nodules and to stage if detected. The procedure is safe and usually req local anesthetic. Another type of aspiration or bi large-bore needle rather than the fine needle. Thi often used to detect rapid growing tumors or whe of the FNB are inconclusive. Other diagnostic stu ultrasound, MRI, CT, thyroid scans, radioactive ic studies, and thyroid suppression tests.

Medical Management

Most patients with small simple goiters and euth do not require treatment. Patients with large goite receive exogenous thyroid hormones and iodine to roid growth. Surgery is not required unless the g ues to grow (1) despite pharmacological treatment airway difficulties, and (3) leading to suspected n

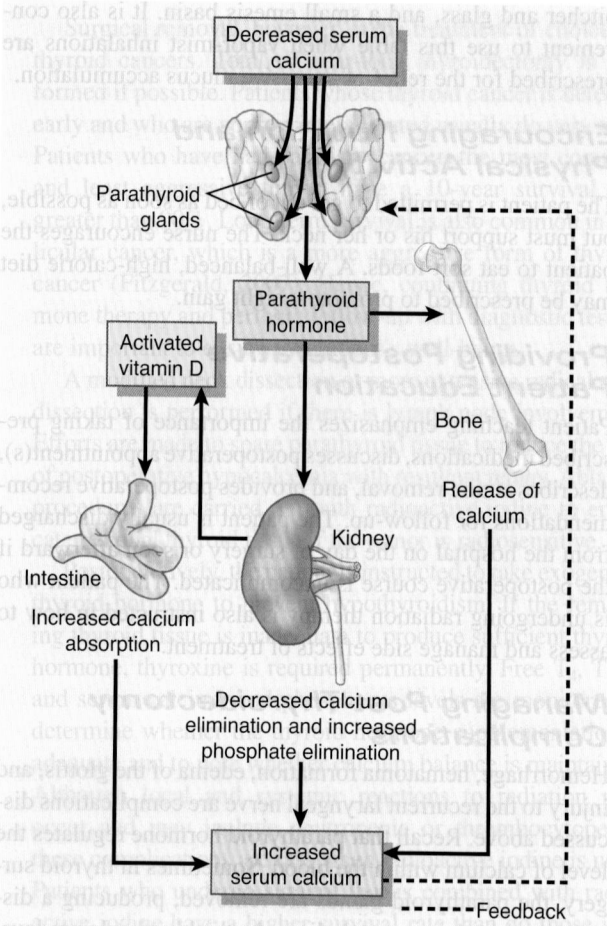

FIGURE 31-4 Regulation of serum calcium concentration by parathyroid hormone. From Porth, C. M. & Matfin, G. (2009). *Pathophysiology: Concepts of altered health states* (8th ed.). Philadelphia: Lippincott Williams & Wilkins.

The actions of PTH are increased by the presence of vitamin D. The serum level of ionized calcium regulates the output of parathormone (Fig. 31-4). Increased serum calcium leads to a decreased parathormone secretion, thus creating a negative feedback system. When the product of serum calcium and serum phosphorus rises, calcium phosphate may precipitate and calcify in various organs of the body such as the kidneys.

Risk Factors

About 100,000 new cases of hyperparathyroidism are detected each year in the United States. The incidence of this disorder increases tenfold between 15 and 65 years. Primary hyperparathyroidism (tumor or hyperplasia of the parathyroids) occurs two to four times more often in women than in men and is most common in people between 60 and 70 years. Secondary hyperparathyroidism is most often seen in patients with chronic renal failure (Box 31-6).

Renal Failure and Secondary Hyperparathyroidism

Phosphate excretion becomes impaired when renal function deteriorates, resulting in an elevated serum phosphate level. There is an inverse relationship between calcium and phosphorus: As the phosphate serum level rises, the serum calcium level falls.

This hypocalcemia stimulates PTH release with resultant increase in calcium release from the bone. In renal failure, the kidneys ability to synthesize vitamin D becomes impaired, which leads to decreased intestinal absorption of calcium. Hypocalcemia in this situation will stimulate the release of PTH, leading to hyperparathyroidism.

Clinical Manifestations and Assessment

Half of the people diagnosed with hyperparathyroidism are asymptomatic. Secondary hyperparathyroidism manifests signs and symptoms similar to those of primary hyperparathyroidism.

The patient may experience signs and symptoms resulting from involvement of several body systems; Box 31-7 summarizes symptoms of hypercalcemia. Apathy, fatigue, muscle weakness, nausea, vomiting, and constipation may occur due to the increased concentration of calcium in the blood. The direct effect of calcium on the brain and nervous system can cause psychological manifestations such as irritability, neurosis, or psychoses. Cardiac responses to elevated serum calcium levels include increased cardiac contractility and the development of ventricular arrhythmias. It is important for the nurse to assess patients on digitalis as this drug accentuates the cardiac response of hypercalcemia.

The formation of stones in one or both kidneys, related to the increased urinary excretion of calcium and phosphorus, occurs in 55% of patients with primary hyperparathyroidism. Renal damage results from the precipitation of calcium

Hypercalcemia

Be alert for the following signs and symptoms:
- **Stones:** Renal
- **Bones:** Bone pain, osteoporosis, pathological fractures
- Abdominal **Moans:** Nausea, vomiting, and abdominal pains (hypercalcemia can lead to peptic ulcer development and acute pancreatitis)
- Psychic **Groans:** Mental irritability, neurosis, confusion

phosphate in the renal pelvis and parenchyma, which causes renal calculi (kidney stones), obstruction, pyelonephritis, and renal failure.

Musculoskeletal symptoms accompanying hyperparathyroidism—such as skeleton pain and tenderness, especially of the back and joints, pain on weight bearing, pathologic fractures, deformities, and shortening of body stature—may be caused by demineralization of the bones or by bone tumors composed of benign giant cells resulting from overgrowth of osteoclasts. Oversecretion of PTH causes excessive osteoclast growth, which in turn promotes bone resorption. The resultant loss of calcium from the bone or demineralization causes kyphosis, compression fractures, and bony cysts that produce fragile bones, increasing the risk for fracture. Hypercalcemia may stimulate gastric secretions, causing an increased incidence of peptic ulcer and abdominal pain. Pancreatitis may develop as a result of stones in the pancreatic ducts.

Primary hyperparathyroidism is diagnosed by persistent elevation of serum calcium levels and an elevated concentration of PTH. **Radioimmunoassay** for PTH is sensitive and differentiates primary hyperparathyroidism from other causes of hypercalcemia in more than 90% of patients with elevated serum calcium levels. An elevated serum calcium level alone is a nonspecific finding because serum levels may be altered by diet, medications, and renal and bone changes. Bone changes on X-ray or bone scans indicates advanced disease. The double-antibody parathyroid hormone test distinguishes between primary hyperparathyroidism and malignancy as a cause of hypercalcemia. Ultrasound, MRI, thallium scan, and FNB evaluate the parathyroid functions and localize parathyroid cysts, adenomas, or hyperplasia.

Medical and Nursing Management

The recommended treatment of primary hyperparathyroidism is the surgical removal of abnormal parathyroid tissue (parathyroidectomy). In some patients who are without symptoms and have only mildly elevated serum calcium concentrations and normal renal function, surgery may be delayed, and the patient is monitored closely for worsening of hypercalcemia, bone deterioration, renal impairment, or the development of kidney stones. Nursing management involves providing hydration, encouraging mobility, administering nutrition and medications, providing emotional support, and observing for and managing hypercalcemic crisis.

Providing Hydration Therapy

Patients with hyperparathyroidism are at risk for renal calculi because kidney involvement is possible. Strict intake and output measurements are monitored in hospitalized patients. The nurse encourages a daily fluid intake of 2,000 mL or more to help prevent calculus formation; cranberry juice is suggested, because it may lower the urinary pH. Cranberry extract tablets are an alternative. The nurse instructs the patient to report symptoms of renal calculi, such as abdominal

pain and hematuria. Thiazide diuretics are avoided, because they decrease the renal excretion of calcium and further elevate serum calcium levels. Because of the risk for hypercalcemic crisis, the nurse should instruct the patient to avoid dehydration and to seek immediate health care if conditions that commonly produce dehydration (e.g., vomiting and diarrhea) occur.

Encouraging Mobility

The nurse encourages the patient to ambulate using a walker. For those with limited mobility, use a rocking chair because bones that are subjected to normal stress give up less calcium. Bedrest increases calcium excretion and the risk for renal calculi. Oral phosphates lower the serum calcium level in some patients; however, long-term use is not recommended due to the risk of ectopic calcium phosphate deposition into the soft tissues.

Administering Nutrition and Medication

Dietary calcium will be restricted or increased, depending on the patient's serum calcium level. If the patient has a coexisting peptic ulcer, prescribed antacids and protein feedings are necessary. Measures to prevent constipation (a common occurrence postoperatively) include offering prune juice, stool softeners (e.g. Colace or Sena), and increasing physical activity, and increasing fluid intake.

Providing Emotional Support

The insidious and chronic onset of hyperparathyroidism together with diverse and vague symptoms may lead to depression and frustration. The family may have considered the patient's illness to be psychosomatic. Increasing awareness of the course of the disorder with patient education may help the patient and family deal with their reactions and feelings.

Managing Hypercalcemic Crisis

Acute hypercalcemic crisis can occur with extreme elevation of serum calcium levels. Serum calcium levels of greater than 15 mg/dL (3.7 mmol/L) result in neurologic, cardiovascular, and renal symptoms that can be life-threatening. Treatment involves rehydration with large volumes of IV fluids (normal saline expands volume and inhibits calcium resorption), diuretic agents (to promote renal excretion of excess calcium), and phosphate therapy (to correct hypophosphatemia and decrease serum calcium levels by promoting calcium deposition in bone and reducing the GI absorption of calcium). Cytotoxic agents (e.g., mithramycin), calcitonin, and dialysis may be used in emergency situations to decrease serum calcium levels quickly. Effective results occur within 24 hours but last only about 1 to 2 weeks. A combination of calcitonin and corticosteroids has been administered in emergencies to reduce the serum calcium level by increasing calcium deposition in bone. Other agents that may be administered to decrease serum calcium levels include bisphosphonates (e.g., etidronate [Didronel], pamidronate [Aredia]).

may be excessive in patients with adrenal insufficiency. During the acute crisis, the nurse maintains a quiet, nonstressful environment and performs all activities (e.g., bathing, turning) for the patient. Maintaining communication and explaining all procedures to the patient and family can help reduce their anxiety. During stressful procedures or significant illnesses, additional supplementary therapy with glucocorticoids is required to prevent an addisonian crisis.

Maintaining Self-Care

Because of the need for life-long replacement of adrenal cortex hormones to prevent addisonian crises, the patient and family members receive explicit verbal and written instructions about the rationale for replacement therapy and proper dosage. In addition, they learn about how to modify the medication dosage and increase salt intake in times of illness, very hot weather, and other stressful situations. The patient also learns how to modify diet and fluid intake to help maintain fluid and electrolyte balance.

The patient and family are prescribed preloaded, single-injection syringes of corticosteroid for use in emergencies. Specific instructions on how and when to use the injection are also provided. It is important to instruct the patient to inform other health care providers, such as dentists, about the use of corticosteroids, to wear a medical alert bracelet, and to carry information at all times about the need for corticosteroids. Patient and family need to know the signs of excessive or insufficient hormone replacement. The development of edema or weight gain may signify too high dose; postural hypotension and weight loss frequently signify too low dose.

Monitoring and Managing Addisonian Crisis

Physical and psychological stressors must be avoided, since the patient with Addison's disease is at risk for addisonian crisis, which presents as complete circulatory collapse and shock. Triggers include exposure to cold, overexertion, infection, and emotional distress. The patient with addisonian crisis requires immediate treatment with IV administration of fluid, glucose, and electrolytes, especially sodium; replacement of missing steroid hormones; and vasopressors. Additionally, the patient must avoid exertion; therefore, the nurse must anticipate the patient's needs and take measures to meet them. Careful monitoring of symptoms, vital signs, weight, and fluid and electrolyte status is essential to assess the patient's progress and return to a precrisis state. To reduce the risk of future episodes of addisonian crisis, efforts are made to identify and reduce the factors that may have led to the crisis.

CUSHING'S SYNDROME/DISEASE

Pathophysiology

Cushing's syndrome, or hypercortisolism, is a disorder characterized by high levels of serum cortisol. Three important causes of Cushing's syndrome are:

- A pituitary tumor that overproduces ACTH, termed Cushing's disease
- An adrenal tumor that overproduces ACTH, termed Cushing's syndrome
- Long-term glucocorticoid pharmacological therapy, termed iatrogenic

Pathophysiology

Cushing's syndrome is commonly caused by use of synthetic corticosteroid medications and is infrequently due to excessive corticosteroid production secondary to hyperplasia or tumor of the adrenal cortex. Overproduction of endogenous corticosteroids may be caused by several mechanisms, including a tumor of the pituitary gland that produces ACTH and stimulates the adrenal cortex to increase its hormone secretion despite production of adequate amounts (as noted earlier, technically termed Cushing's disease). Primary hyperplasia of the adrenal glands in the absence of a pituitary tumor is less common. Another less common cause of Cushing's syndrome is the ectopic production of ACTH by malignancies; bronchogenic carcinoma is the most common type of these malignancies. Regardless of the cause, the normal feedback mechanisms that control the function of the adrenal cortex become ineffective, and the usual diurnal pattern of cortisol is lost.

Risk Factors

The chronic use of corticosteroids is a common risk factor of developing Cushing's syndrome. In addition, women between the ages of 20 and 40 years are five times more likely than men to develop Cushing's syndrome. Other less common risk factors that may result in Cushing's syndrome include primary hyperplasia of the adrenal glands in the absence of a pituitary tumor and ectopic production of ACTH by malignancies.

Clinical Manifestations and Assessment

The signs and symptoms of Cushing's syndrome are primarily due to oversecretion of glucocorticoids and androgens (sex hormones), although mineralocorticoid secretion also may be affected. Overproduction of the adrenal cortical hormone leads to an arrest of height, obesity, musculoskeletal changes, and glucose intolerance. The altered fat metabolism results in a classic picture of Cushing's syndrome in the adult: central-type obesity, a protruding abdomen, with a fatty "buffalo hump" in the neck and supraclavicular areas, and a round "moon-faced" appearance (Fig. 31-5). The skin is thin, fragile, and easily traumatized; ecchymoses (bruises) and purple striae develop (secondary to stretching of the weakened skin). The patient complains of weakness and lassitude. Sleep is disturbed due to altered diurnal secretion of cortisol.

Muscle weakness, wasting, and thin extremities are caused by protein wasting. Excessive bone protein catabolism can

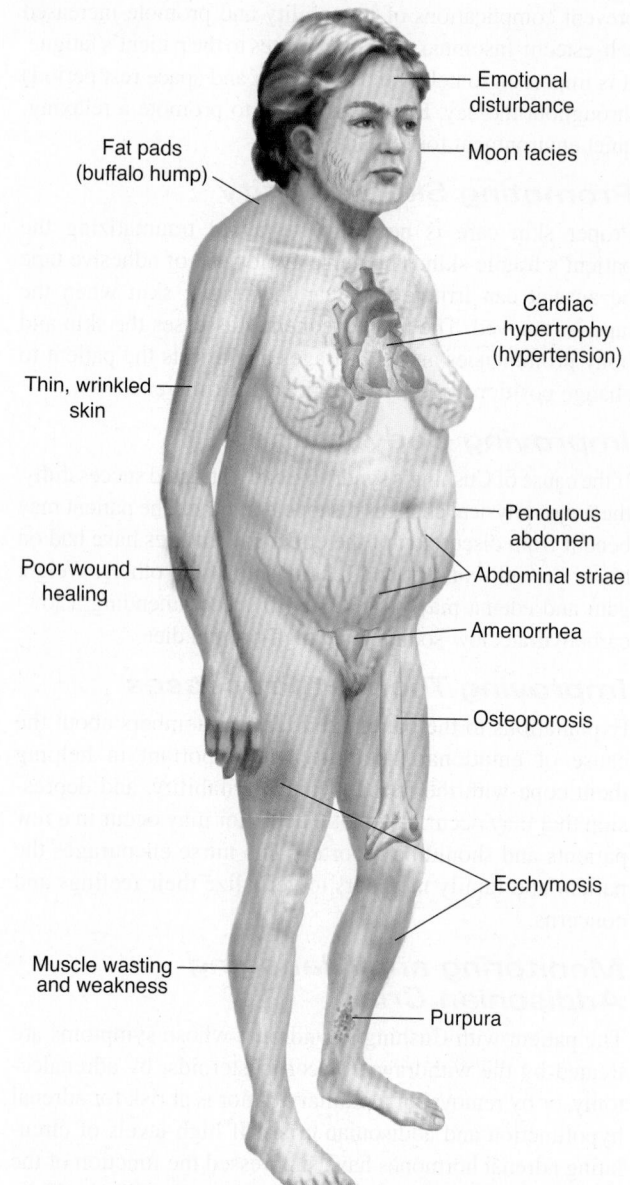

Emotional disturbance

Moon facies

Fat pads (buffalo hump)

Cardiac hypertrophy (hypertension)

Thin, wrinkled skin

Pendulous abdomen

Abdominal striae

Poor wound healing

Amenorrhea

Osteoporosis

Ecchymosis

Muscle wasting and weakness

Purpura

FIGURE 31-5 Major clinical manifestations of Cushing syndrome. From Porth, C. M. & Matfin, G. (2009). *Pathophysiology: Concepts of altered health states* (8th ed.). Philadelphia: Lippincott Williams & Wilkins.

result in osteoporosis. Kyphosis, backache, and compression fractures of the vertebrae may result.

Retention of sodium and water occurs as a result of increased mineralocorticoid activity, producing hypertension, hypokalemia, and heart failure. Hyperglycemia or overt diabetes may develop. The patient may report weight gain, increased susceptibility to infection, and slow healing of minor cuts.

In females of all ages, virilization may occur as a result of excess androgens. Virilization is characterized by the appearance of masculine traits and the recession of feminine traits. There is an excessive growth of hair on the face (hirsutism),

the breasts atrophy, menses cease, the clitoris enlarges, and the voice deepens. Libido is lost in men and women.

Changes occur in mood and mental activity, and psychosis may develop. Distress and depression are common and are increased by the severity of the physical changes that occur with this syndrome. If Cushing's disease is a consequence of pituitary tumor, visual disturbances may occur because of pressure of the growing tumor on the optic chiasm.

Diagnostic assessment involves an overnight dexamethasone suppression test (the most widely used and most sensitive screening) for the diagnosis of pituitary and adrenal causes of Cushing's disease (Porth, 2011). Generally, 1 mg of dexamethasone is administered orally at 11:00 p.m., and a plasma cortisol level is obtained at 8:00 a.m. the next morning. Suppression of cortisol to less than 5 mg/dL indicates that the hypothalamic–pituitary–adrenal axis is functioning properly. Stress, obesity, depression, and medications such as antiseizure agents, estrogen (during pregnancy or as oral medications), and rifampin can falsely elevate cortisol levels. Studies have shown that nighttime salivary cortisol levels shows promise in effectively screening for Cushing's syndrome. Although not a routine diagnostic test in the United States, salivary cortisol concentrations are shown to be reflective of active free cortisol in plasma. In addition, saliva samples can easily be obtained in a nonstressful environment (e.g., at home); the test is relatively safe and easy to administer, with a sensitivity of 92% to 100% and a specificity of 93% to 100% (Carroll, Raff, & Findling, 2008).

Indicators of Cushing's syndrome include an increase in serum sodium and blood glucose levels and a decrease in serum potassium, a reduction in the number of blood eosinophils, and disappearance of lymphoid tissue. Measurements of plasma and urinary cortisol levels are obtained. Several blood samples may be collected to determine whether the normal diurnal variation in plasma levels is present; this variation is frequently absent in adrenal dysfunction. If several blood samples are required, they must be collected at the times specified, and the time of collection must be noted on the requisition slip. Other diagnostic studies include a 24-hour urinary free cortisol level and a low-dose dexamethasone suppression test. Low-dose suppression tests are similar to the overnight test but vary in dosage and timing.

Radioimmunoassay measurement of plasma ACTH is used together with the high-dose suppression test to distinguish pituitary tumors from ectopic sites of ACTH production. Elevation of ACTH and cortisol indicates pituitary or hypothalamic disease. Low ACTH with high cortisol level indicates adrenal disease. CT, ultrasound, or MRI is performed to localize adrenal tissue and detect tumors of adrenal gland.

Medical Management

Treatment is directed at the pituitary gland if Cushing's is caused by pituitary tumors rather than tumors of the adrenal

cortex. Surgical removal of the tumor by transsphenoidal hypophysectomy is the treatment of choice and has an 78% success removal rate (Tabafe, Anand, Barron et al., 2009). In addition, radiation of the pituitary gland has been successful, but may take several months for control of the symptoms. **Adrenalectomy** is the treatment of choice in patients with primary adrenal hypertrophy.

Postoperatively, symptoms of adrenal insufficiency may begin to appear 12 to 48 hours after surgery because of the reduction of high levels of circulating adrenal hormones. Temporary replacement therapy with hydrocortisone may be necessary for several months, until the adrenal glands begin to respond normally to the body's needs. If both adrenal glands have been removed (bilateral adrenalectomy), a lifetime replacement of adrenal cortex hormones is necessary.

Adrenal enzyme inhibitors such as metyrapone, aminoglutethimide, mitotane, and ketoconazole are used to reduce hyperadrenalism if the syndrome is caused by ectopic ACTH secretion by a tumor that cannot be eradicated. Close monitoring is necessary, because symptoms of inadequate adrenal function may result due to possible side effects of these medications.

If Cushing's syndrome is a result of the administration of corticosteroids, an attempt is made to reduce or taper the medication to the minimum dosage needed to treat the underlying disease process (e.g., autoimmune, allergic disease, or rejection of transplanted organ). Frequently, alternate-day therapy decreases the symptoms of Cushing's syndrome and allows recovery of the adrenal glands' responsiveness to ACTH.

Nursing Management

Decreasing Risk of Injury

Establishing a protective environment helps prevent falls, fractures, and other injuries to bones and soft tissues. The patient who is very weak may require assistance in ambulating to avoid falling or bumping into sharp corners of furniture. Foods high in protein, calcium, and vitamin D are recommended to minimize muscle wasting and osteoporosis. Referral to a dietitian may assist the patient in selecting appropriate foods that are also low in sodium and calories.

Decreasing Risk of Infection

The patient should avoid unnecessary exposure to others with infections. The nurse frequently assesses the patient for subtle signs of infection because the anti-inflammatory effects of corticosteroids may mask the common signs of inflammation and infection.

Encouraging Rest and Activity

Weakness, fatigue, and muscle wasting make it difficult for the patient with Cushing's syndrome to carry out normal activities; however, the nurse encourages moderate activity to prevent complications of immobility and promote increased self-esteem. Insomnia often contributes to the patient's fatigue. It is important to help the patient plan and space rest periods throughout the day. Efforts are made to promote a relaxing, quiet environment for rest and sleep.

Promoting Skin Integrity

Proper skin care is necessary to avoid traumatizing the patient's fragile skin. The nurse avoids use of adhesive tape because it can irritate and tear the fragile skin when the tape is removed. The nurse frequently assesses the skin and bony prominences and encourages and assists the patient to change positions frequently to prevent skin breakdown.

Improving Body Image

If the cause of Cushing's syndrome can be treated successfully, the major physical changes disappear in time. The patient may benefit from discussion of the effect the changes have had on his or her self-concept and relationships with others. Weight gain and edema may be modified by recommending a low-carbohydrate, low-sodium, and high-protein diet.

Improving Thought Processes

Explanations to the patient and family members about the cause of emotional instability are important in helping them cope with the mood swings, irritability, and depression that may occur. Psychotic behavior may occur in a few patients and should be reported. The nurse encourages the patient and family members to verbalize their feelings and concerns.

Monitoring and Managing Addisonian Crisis

The patient with Cushing's syndrome whose symptoms are treated by the withdrawal of corticosteroids, by adrenalectomy, or by removal of a pituitary tumor is at risk for adrenal hypofunction and addisonian crisis. If high levels of circulating adrenal hormones have suppressed the function of the adrenal cortex, atrophy of the adrenal cortex is likely. If the circulating hormone level is decreased rapidly because of surgery or abrupt cessation of corticosteroid agents, manifestations of adrenal hypofunction and addisonian crisis may develop. The nurse monitors the patient closely for hypotension, rapid weak pulse, rapid respiratory rate, pallor, and extreme weakness. Efforts are made to identify factors that may have led to the crisis. The patient may require IV administration of fluid and electrolytes and corticosteroids before, during, and after treatment or surgery. The nurse assesses fluid and electrolyte status by monitoring laboratory values and daily weights. Sodium and water retention may result in the development of edema and hypertension, therefore assessment of vital signs and fluid volume excess are warranted. In addition, observe for signs and symptoms of hypokalemia (K^+ <3.5 MEq/L), which can have profound impact on cardiac and neurological function. Blood

glucose monitoring should be closely followed because of the increased risk for glucose intolerance and hyperglycemia with Cushing's syndrome and hypoglycemia if patient is now at risk for adrenal hypofunction due to interventions to treat Cushing's syndrome. If addisonian crisis occurs, the patient is treated for circulatory collapse and shock.

Teaching Self-Care Measures

Upon discharge, the patient and family should understand that stopping the corticosteroid use abruptly and without medical supervision is likely to result in acute adrenal insufficiency as well as reappearance of the underlying symptoms of the chronic disease. The nurse emphasizes the need to ensure an adequate supply of the corticosteroid because running out of the medication or skipping doses can precipitate adrenal insufficiency and addisonian crisis. The need for dietary modifications to ensure adequate calcium intake without increasing the risks for hypertension, hyperglycemia, and weight gain is stressed. The patient and family may be taught to monitor blood pressure, blood glucose levels, and weight. Wearing a medical alert bracelet and notifying health care providers (e.g., dentist) of the patient's condition are important.

PRIMARY ALDOSTERONISM

Pathophysiology

Primary aldosteronism, also known as *Conn's syndrome*, is a condition in which the adrenal glands produce too much aldosterone because of hyperplasia or tumor. The principal action of aldosterone is to conserve body sodium. Too much aldosterone, however, will result in increased renal reabsorption of sodium that will in turn lead to an increase in extracellular fluids and blood pressure.

Risk Factors

Excessive production of aldosterone occurs in some patients with functioning tumors of the adrenal gland. Other risk factors for primary aldosteronism include bilateral adrenal hyperplasia (caused by overactivity of both adrenal glands), familial hyperaldosteronism, and cancerous tumor of the adrenal gland (Stewart & Young, 2007).

Clinical Manifestations and Assessment

Patients with aldosteronism exhibit a profound decline in the serum levels of potassium (hypokalemia) and hydrogen ions (alkalosis), as demonstrated by an increase in pH and serum bicarbonate concentration. The serum sodium level is normal or typically elevated, depending on the amount of water reabsorbed with the sodium or water loss in the urine. Hypertension is the most prominent and almost universal sign of aldosteronism and affects up to

5% to 13% of individuals with hypertension (Fogari, Preti, Zoppi et al., 2007).

Hypokalemia leads to muscle weakness, cramping, and fatigue, as well as an inability on the part of the kidneys to acidify or concentrate the urine. Accordingly, the urine volume is excessive, leading to polyuria. Serum sodium becomes abnormally concentrated, contributing to excessive thirst (polydipsia) and arterial hypertension. A secondary increase in blood volume and possible direct effects of aldosterone on nerve receptors, such as the carotid sinus, result in hypertension.

Hypokalemic alkalosis may decrease the ionized serum calcium level and predispose the patient to tetany and paresthesias. Glucose intolerance may occur, because hypokalemia interferes with insulin secretion from the pancreas.

In addition to a high or normal serum sodium level and a low serum potassium level, diagnostic studies indicate high serum aldosterone and low serum renin levels. The measurement of the aldosterone excretion rate after salt loading is a useful diagnostic test for primary aldosteronism. The renin–aldosterone stimulation test and bilateral adrenal venous sampling are useful in differentiating the cause of primary aldosteronism. Antihypertensive medication may be discontinued up to 2 weeks before testing.

Medical Management

Treatment of primary aldosteronism usually involves surgical removal of the adrenal tumor through adrenalectomy. Adrenalectomy is performed through an incision in the flank or the abdomen. In general, the postoperative care resembles that for other abdominal surgery. The patient is susceptible to fluctuations in adrenocortical hormones and requires administration of corticosteroids, fluids, and other agents to maintain blood pressure and prevent acute complications. If the adrenalectomy is bilateral, lifetime replacement of corticosteroids will be necessary. If one adrenal gland is removed, the replacement therapy may only be temporary because of the suppression of the remaining adrenal gland by high levels of adrenal hormones. A normal serum glucose level is maintained with insulin, IV fluids, and dietary modifications. Hypokalemia resolves for all patients after surgery, but hypertension may persist. Spironolactone (potassium-sparing diuretic) may be prescribed to control hypertension and minimize hypokalemia.

Nursing Management

The nursing management during the postoperative period includes frequent assessment of vital signs to detect early signs and symptoms of adrenal insufficiency and crisis or hemorrhage. Explaining all treatments and procedures, providing comfort measures, and providing rest periods can reduce the patient's stress and anxiety level.

Chapter Review

Critical Thinking Exercises

1. A 68-year-old woman has just been diagnosed with thyroid cancer. She is scheduled for a total thyroidectomy in 1 week. What preoperative and postoperative nursing care is important for her? What long-term follow-up would you anticipate and discuss with the patient and her family?

2. A 70-year-old man has a diagnosis of bronchogenic carcinoma. He is being evaluated for possible SIADH secretion. The patient and his family are asking for explanations about the syndrome and about methods of managing it. What nursing interventions and patient and family teaching are warranted when caring for this patient? Contrast the clinical picture and symptoms of SIADH with those of diabetes insipidus.

3. A 14-year-old girl was recently diagnosed with Addison's disease. The patient is overly concerned that she will not be able to lead a normal life as a result of this disease. What advice/patient education should the nurse give to the patient? Describe and provide rationale on how each advice will benefit the patient.

NCLEX-Style Review Questions

1. Upon evaluation of the patient's laboratory data and clinical signs and symptoms, the nurse suspects that the patient may have pheochromocytoma. Which of the following is directly related with pheochromocytoma? Select all that apply.
   A. Severe headache. Pain score 9 out of 10
   B. Perspiration
   C. Blood pressure 80/90 mmHg
   D. Pallor

2. A patient admitted to the unit is exhibiting signs of Graves' disease. What nursing intervention is indicated for Graves' disease?
   A. Providing blanket to patient
   B. Instilling eye ointment
   C. Providing a warm bath to patient
   D. Serving coffee to patient during breakfast

3. A patient presented to the unit with an ADH-secreting tumor. Upon diagnostic and physical evaluation, the nurse finds that the patient may be having SIADH. Which of the following is a clinical manifestation finding of SIADH?
   A. Hyponatremia
   B. Hypernatremia
   C. Increased osmolality
   D. Dry mucus membranes

4. The nursing management of a patient who underwent transsphenoidal removal of the pituitary tumor yesterday includes which of the following actions? Select all that apply.
   A. Maintaining oral care
   B. Removing nasal pack to check for bleeding and CSF leak
   C. Giving fluid after nausea, then slowly progressing to diet
   D. Raising head of bed to promote normal drainage

5. What is the first line of treatment for an 85-year-old patient who is newly diagnosed with Graves' disease?
   A. Thyroidectomy
   B. Angiotensin-converting enzyme (ACE) inhibitors to control hypertension
   C. Methimazole and propylthiouracil
   D. Radioactive iodine therapy

Try these additional resources to enhance your learning and understanding of this chapter:
- thePoint online resource available at **http://thepoint.lww.com/Pellico1e**
- *Handbook for Focus on Adult Health: Medical-Surgical Nursing*
- *Study Guide for Focus on Adult Health: Medical-Surgical Nursing*

References and Selected Readings

References and selected readings associated with this chapter can be found on the website that accompanies the book. Visit http://thepoint.lww.com/Pellico1e to access the references and other additional resources associated with this chapter.

Problems Related to Reproductive Function

A 40-YEAR-OLD single mother of three children has been diagnosed with squamous cell carcinoma of the cervix following an abnormal Pap smear and colposcopy. She is being seen in the gynecologist office for follow-up treatment. She is very worried about her prognosis.

➡ Discuss risk factors associated with this type of cancer.

➡ What clinical manifestations may this patient have had prior to this diagnosis?

➡ What is the purpose of a colposcopy?

➡ Discuss medical management of cervical cancer.

Nursing Assessment: Female and Male Reproductive Function

LIANNE F. HERBRUCK
SUSANNE A. QUALLICH

Learning Objectives

After reading this chapter, you will be able to:

1. Describe female reproductive function.

2. Discuss components of female reproductive assessment.

3. Identify the diagnostic examinations and tests used to determine alteration in female reproductive function and breast disorders.

4. Describe structures and function of the male reproductive system.

5. Discuss nursing assessment of the male reproductive system and identify diagnostic tests that complement assessment.

FEMALE REPRODUCTIVE SYSTEM

Women utilize the health care system more often than do men (Owens, 2008; Robinson, 2008; Smith, Braunack-Mayer, & Wittert, 2006), often seeking health care during the changes involving the reproductive system from the onset of menarche to menopause. An understanding of the normal anatomy and physiology of the female reproductive system is a necessary and important function of the nurse. It is integral to recognizing the complex issues that can occur within the female reproductive system.

ANATOMIC AND PHYSIOLOGIC OVERVIEW

Anatomy of the Female Reproductive System

The female reproductive system consists of the external and internal genital structures, as well as the mammary glands located in the female breast. Hormonal influences on the female reproductive system are driven by the hypothalamus and pituitary gland. These influences cause the cyclical changes throughout the reproductive life of women, and their cessation results in menopause.

External Genitalia

The external genital structures, referred to as the vulva, consist of the mons pubis; labia majora; labia minora; clitoris; and the vestibule of the vagina, which contains the hymen, the urethral and vaginal orifice, and the paraurethral (Skene's) and Bartholin's glands (Fig. 32-1). The mons pubis is the fatty tissue at the junction of the thighs and torso, while the labia majora are two thick folds of tissue that forms the outer border of the vulva. Both are covered by pubic hair after puberty. The upper portions of the labia minora unite anteriorly to form a partial covering for the clitoris, a highly sensitive organ composed of erectile tissue. The labia minora are thinner folds of tissue internal to the majora that cover the urethral meatus and vaginal **introitus**. The urethral meatus lies below and posterior to the clitoris, and the vaginal introitus lies just posterior to the urethral meatus. The mucus secreting structures that are set in the wall of the urethra are termed Skene's glands. The Bartholin's glands, bean-sized structures that

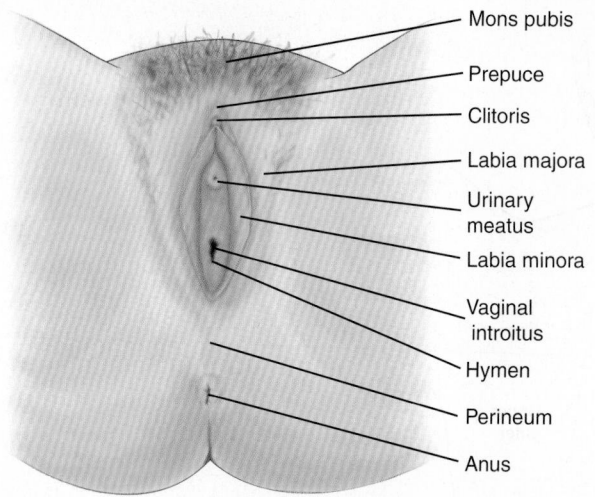

FIGURE 32-1 External female genitalia.

secrete mucus, lie on each side of the vaginal orifice. The area between the vagina and rectum is called the perineum.

Internal Reproductive Structures

The internal structures are the vagina, uterus, ovaries, and fallopian tubes (Fig. 32-2).

The vagina is a mucous membrane–lined canal that extends from the vulva to the cervix. The upper part of the vagina, the **fornix**, surrounds the **cervix** (the inferior part of the uterus).

The uterus is a pear-shaped, muscular organ, which can vary in size depending on parity (number of viable births) and uterine abnormalities (e.g., fibroids). The uterus lies posterior to the bladder and is held in position by several ligaments. The uterus consists of the cervix, which projects into the vagina, and the **fundus** or body. The triangular inner portion of the fundus narrows to a small canal in the cervix that has constrictions at each end, referred to as the *external os* and *internal os.* The upper lateral parts of the uterus are called the *cornua.* From here, the oviducts, or fallopian tubes, extend outward to meet the ovaries.

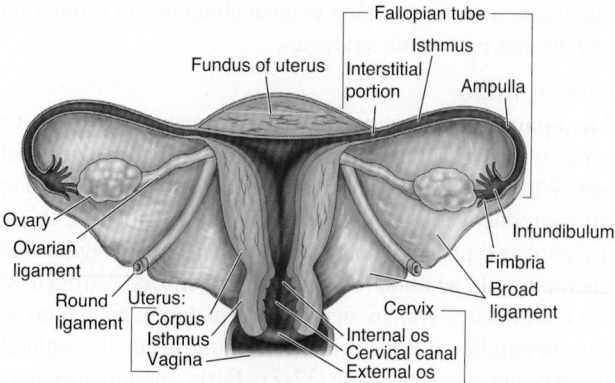

FIGURE 32-2 Internal female reproductive structures.

The **ovaries** lie behind, and below, the fallopian tubes. They are oval bodies about 3 cm long. At birth, they contain thousands of tiny egg cells, or ova. The ovaries and the fallopian tubes together are referred to as the **adnexa**.

Breasts

The breasts lie over the pectoralis muscle from the sternum to the midaxillary line. An area of breast tissue, called the tail of Spence, extends into the axilla. Cooper's ligaments support the breast on the chest wall. During puberty, estrogen and other hormones in the female stimulate breast development. This development usually occurs from 10 to 16 years of age, although the range can vary from 9 to 18 years.

Each fully developed breast (Fig. 32-3) is made up of glandular lobules and ducts bound and separated by fibrous tissue and fat. Approximately 15 to 20 lobules group together to form cone-shaped lobes. Fibrous tissue surrounds the lobes and ducts. Fatty tissue fills the spaces between lobes and ducts and gives the breast a soft texture. During lactation, milk is produced in the lobules and is carried through the ducts to the nipple.

Function of the Female Reproductive System

The main function of the female reproductive system is to prepare the woman's body each month to be ready to accept a fertilized egg and provide a nourishing environment for growth of a fetus. The monthly changes in the woman of reproductive age—the menstrual cycle—is a complex process involving the reproductive and endocrine systems. In girls, this usually begins when they reach puberty between 12 and 14 years of age, although it may occur from 9 to 16 years of age (Carrol, 2009). The first menstrual cycle is termed **menarche**. Normal cycles average 28 days during the reproductive years, although cycles can vary from 21 to 42 days.

The woman's reproductive cycle consists of a complex series of interactions between the hypothalamic–pituitary system, the ovarian system, the endometrial system, and the various hormones they secrete.

The Menstrual Cycle

Estrogen and progesterone are two hormones integral to proper functioning of the female reproductive system. The ovaries produce several types of **estrogen**, as well as progesterone. Estrogen is responsible for development and maintenance of the female reproductive organs, secondary sex characteristics of the adult female, breast development, and the monthly uterine changes associated with menstruation. **Progesterone** plays a role in regulating uterine changes during the menstrual cycle, preparing the **endometrium** (via the **corpus luteum**) for implantation of a fertilized ovum and maintaining (via the placenta) a normal pregnancy. Together, progesterone and estrogen help prepare the breasts for

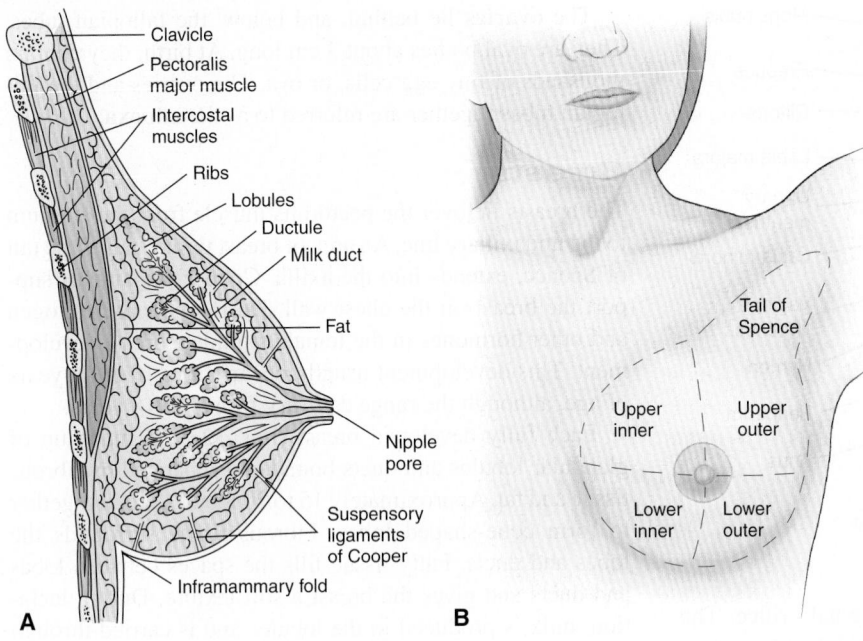

FIGURE 32-3 **(A)** Anatomy of the breast. **(B)** Areas of breast, including the tail of Spence.

lactation. **Androgens** are hormones that are produced by the ovaries in small amounts; they influence early follicular development as well as the female libido (Carroll, 2009).

The female pituitary gland releases the gonadotropic hormones **follicle-stimulating hormone** (FSH) and **luteinizing hormone** (LH). FSH is primarily responsible for stimulating the ovaries to secrete estrogen and triggers follicles in the ovary to mature into eggs, while LH is primarily responsible for stimulating progesterone production, as well as encouraging release of mature eggs through the mid-cycle LH surge. Feedback mechanisms help to regulate FSH and LH secretion. Elevated estrogen levels in the blood inhibit FSH secretion but promote LH secretion. FSH and LH release is also influenced by gonadotropin-releasing hormone (GnRH), which is secreted from the hypothalamus.

This complex feedback system results in the cyclic changes in the uterine endometrium, ovaries, and menstruation (Table 32-1).

In the beginning of the menstrual cycle, low estrogen levels signal the hypothalamus to release FSH and begin follicular maturation. Maturing follicles release estrogen, which stimulates the release of LH. This surge of LH encourages **ovulation**, which is the release of the mature egg from the ovary. Ovulation generally occurs mid-way (14 days) through a typical 28-day menstrual cycle. The egg is released into the fallopian tubes, where it awaits fertilization. If fertilization does not occur, hormone levels decrease and the menstrual phase of the cycle begins.

Menstruation is the cyclic shedding of the uterine lining that occurs when pregnancy has not been established. This menstrual flow is discharged through the cervix and into the vagina, and usually lasts 4 to 5 days. Women lose 60 to 150 mL

of blood and tissue. After the menstrual flow stops, the cycle begins anew (Carroll, 2009).

Perimenopause

Perimenopause is the period of transition from normal periods to the complete cessation of menses for 1 year. It involves a range of hormonal adjustments as the reproductive organs prepare to shut down. This transition can begin as early as 35 years of age, and often takes up to 10 years. Women experience a wide range of symptoms, from none at all to irregular periods, heavy bleeding, hot flashes, vaginal dryness, sleep disturbances, and emotional distress (Pick, 2009). Women should understand that, until menstruation has ceased for 1 full year, they can still get pregnant. Women often have varied beliefs about aging, so nurses caring for or educating perimenopausal patients should be sensitive to their individual needs. Perimenopausal women often benefit from information about the subtle physiologic changes they are experiencing. Perimenopause has been described as an opportune time for teaching women about health promotion and disease prevention strategies.

Menopause

Menopause marks the end of a woman's reproductive capacity and generally occurs between 45 and 52 years of age. With menopause, the ovaries are no longer active and the reproductive organs become smaller. Menopause is not a pathologic phenomenon but a normal part of aging and maturation. In addition to the effects of reduced estrogen on the reproductive system, neuroendocrinologic, biochemical, and metabolic changes related to aging occur throughout the woman's body (Table 32-2). Early menopause may occur if the ovaries are surgically removed, are destroyed

TABLE
32-1 Hormonal Influences and Menstrual Cycle

(Times approximate) Phase	Menstrual	Follicular	Ovulation	Luteal	Premenstrual
Days	1 2 3 4 5 6 7 8 9	10 11 12 13 14 15	16 17 18 19 20	21 22 23 24 25	26 27 28 1 2
Ovary	Degenerating corpus luteum; beginning follicular development	Growth and maturation of follicle	Ovulation	Active corpus luteum	Degenerating corpus luteum
Estrogen Production	Low	Increasing	High	Declining, then a secondary rise	Decreasing
Progesterone Production	None	Low	Low	Increasing	Decreasing
FSH Production	Increasing	High, then declining	Low	Low	Increasing
LH Production	Low	Low, then increasing	High	High	Decreasing
Endometrium	Degeneration and shedding of superficial layer. Coiled arteries dilate, then constrict again.	Reorganization and proliferation of superficial layer	Continued growth	Active secretion and glandular dilation; highly vascular; edematous	Vasoconstriction of coiled arteries; beginning degeneration

by radiation or chemotherapy, or because of an unknown etiology. This transition offers an opportunity for health promotion and disease prevention teaching and counseling, as women experiencing bothersome symptoms of menopause may be more likely to seek health care (Williams, Kalilani, DiBenedetti et al., 2007). Box 32-1 on page 892 discusses nursing care of patients experiencing menopause.

ASSESSMENT

Nurses obtaining health history information and performing physical assessments are in ideal positions to discuss women's general health issues, health promotion, and health-related concerns. Relevant topics include fitness, nutrition, cardiovascular risks, health screening, sexuality, menopause,

TABLE
32-2   **GERONTOLOGIC CONSIDERATIONS / Age-Related Changes in the Female Reproductive System**

Structural Change	Functional Change	History and Physical Findings
Cessation of ovarian function and decreased estrogen production; thinning of urinary and genital tracts; thinning of pubic hair and shrinking of labia	Decreased ovulation Onset of menopause Vasomotor instability and hormonal fluctuations Decreased bone formation Decreased vaginal lubrication Increased pH of vagina	Decreased/loss of ability to conceive; increased infertility Irregular menses with eventual cessation of menses Hot flashes or flushing; night sweats, sleep disturbances; mood swings; fatigue Bone loss and increased risk for osteoporosis and osteoporotic fractures; loss of height Dyspareunia, resulting in lack of interest in sex Increased risk for urinary tract infection Increased incidence of inflammation (atrophic vaginitis) with discharge, itching, and vulvar burning
Relaxation of pelvic musculature	Prolapse of uterus, cystocele, rectocele	Dyspareunia, incontinence, feelings of perineal pressure

BOX 32-1

Management During Menopause

Clinical Manifestations and Assessment

Long before menopause occurs, hormonal changes contribute to common symptoms of menopause including irregular menses, breast tenderness, mood changes, hot flashes, and night sweats. Thought to be due to hormonal changes, hot flashes denote vasomotor instability and vary in intensity from a barely perceptible warm feeling to a sensation of extreme warmth accompanied by profuse sweating, causing discomfort, sleep disturbances, and subsequent fatigue. **Osteoporosis** can also be a manifestation of menopause.

Reduced estrogen levels affect the entire genitourinary system. Changes in the vulvovaginal area include gradual thinning of pubic hair and a shrinking of the labia. Vaginal secretions decrease, and women may report dyspareunia (discomfort during intercourse). The vaginal pH increases during menopause, predisposing women to bacterial infections and atrophic vaginitis. Some women report fatigue, forgetfulness, weight gain, irritability, feeling "blue," and feelings of panic. Menopausal complaints need to be evaluated carefully, because they may also indicate other disorders.

Women's reactions and feelings related to loss of reproductive capacity may vary. Some women may experience role confusion, whereas others experience a sense of sexual and personal freedom. Each woman's experience must be considered on an individual basis, and nurses need to be sensitive to all possibilities.

Medical Management

Women approaching menopause often have many concerns about their health. Some have concerns based on a family history of heart disease, osteoporosis, or cancer. Each woman needs to be as knowledgeable as possible about her options and should be encouraged to discuss her concerns with her primary health care provider in order to make an informed decision about managing menopausal symptoms and maintaining her health. Postmenopausal bleeding, or bleeding 1 year after menses cease at menopause, must be investigated, as a malignant condition must be considered until proved otherwise.

Until recently, hormone therapy (HT) was prescribed to prevent hot flashes, reduce the risk of osteoporotic fractures, and decrease the risk for cardiovascular disease. Although HT decreases hot flashes and reduces the risk for osteoporotic fractures and colorectal cancer, HT was found to increase the risk for breast cancer, heart attack, stroke, and blood clots (Women's Health Initiative (WHI), 2002). The benefits of HT were determined to be inadequate given the increased risk of breast cancer and other disorders. Due to these findings, many women discontinued, or elected not to start HT.

There are several different treatment methods for those women who do elect to take HT. Both estrogen and progestin pills are prescribed for women who still have a uterus. Progestin prevents proliferation of the uterine lining and hyperplasia, which are factors that increase the risk for uterine cancer. Women without a uterus can take estrogen without progestin (unopposed estrogen), although there is a slight increase of risk of stroke in women taking estrogen alone (WHI, 2002).

Patches are another option. Estrogen patches are replaced once or twice weekly, but will require a progestin pill along with them if the woman still has a uterus. Another type of patch provides estrogen and progestin treatment. Vaginal symptoms can be treated with an estrogen cream or suppository, or an estradiol vaginal ring may be used for vaginal dryness or atrophic vaginitis.

HT is contraindicated in women with a history of breast cancer, vascular thrombosis, impaired liver function, some cases of uterine cancer, and undiagnosed abnormal vaginal bleeding. Because HT increases the risk for thromboembolic phenomena, women who elect to take HT must be taught the signs and symptoms of deep vein thrombosis and pulmonary embolism (i.e., unilateral leg redness, tenderness, and edema; chest pain, and sudden onset shortness of breath) and told to report these signs and symptoms immediately.

Although the results of the Women's Health Initiative (WHI) study may make the decision about use of HT easy for some women, it remains a difficult decision for those who could benefit from it because of the disruptive symptoms of menopause and evidence of bone loss. HT may be useful for women for short periods of time when no other therapy has been able to reduce their vasomotor symptoms, but even this use must be taken with caution as it may increase risk for breast cancer (Bernstein, 2009). Women often seek information about alternatives to HT use, but these therapies are often not regulated or research-proven methods and must be used with caution. Assessment of menopausal patients should address their use of complementary and alternative therapies and supplements.

The decisions women make related to HT use must be individualized, and based on their current health, risk factors, family history, and severity of symptoms.

Nursing Management

Nurses can encourage women to view menopause as a natural change resulting in freedom from symptoms related to menses and pregnancy. Measures should be taken to promote general health. The nurse can explain to the patient that cessation of menses is normal and is rarely accompanied by illness. Many symptoms can even be controlled with lifestyle factors. The current expected lifespan after menopause for the average woman is 30 to 35 years, and women retain their usual response to sex long after menopause. The individual woman's evaluation of herself and her worth, now, and in the future, is likely to affect her emotional reaction to menopause. Patient teaching and counseling regarding healthy lifestyles, health promotion, and health screening are of paramount importance.

TABLE
32-3 Summary of Health Screening and Counseling Issues for Women*

Component	Screening and Counseling		
	Ages 19–39	Ages 40–64	Ages 65+
Sexuality and reproductive issues	Annual pelvic examination Annual clinical breast exam Contraceptive options High-risk sexual behaviors	Annual pelvic examination Annual clinical breast exam Contraceptive options High-risk sexual behaviors Menopausal concerns	Annual pelvic examination Annual clinical breast exam High-risk sexual behaviors
Health and risk behaviors	Hygiene Injury prevention Nutrition Exercise patterns Risk for domestic abuse Use of tobacco, drugs, and alcohol Life stresses Immunizations	Hygiene Bone loss and injury prevention Nutrition Exercise patterns Risk for domestic abuse Use of tobacco, drugs, and alcohol Life stresses Immunizations	Hygiene Injury prevention Nutrition Exercise patterns Risk for domestic abuse Use of tobacco, drugs, and alcohol Life stresses Immunizations
Diagnostic testing	Pap smear Sexually transmitted disease (STD) screening as indicated	Pap smear Mammography** Cholesterol and lipid profile Colorectal cancer screening Bone mineral density testing Thyroid-stimulating hormone testing Hearing and eye examinations	Pap smear Mammography Cholesterol and lipid profile Colorectal cancer screening Bone mineral density testing Thyroid-stimulating hormone testing Hearing and eye examinations

*Each individual's risks (family history, personal history) influence the need for specific assessments and their frequency.
**Recent recommendations include regular screening with mammography at age 50, and every 2 years through the age of 74 (http://www.ahrq.gov/clinic/uspstf09/breastcancer/brcanrs.htm#update).

abuse, health risk behaviors, and immunizations. Recommendations for health screening are summarized in Table 32-3. Many problems can be corrected if treated early, while allowing them to go untreated may result in serious health problems.

Although sexuality and sexual function are more often discussed with gynecologic or women's health care providers, any nurse caring for women should consider these issues part of a routine health assessment.

Health History

In addition to obtaining a general health history, information related to past illnesses and experiences specific to women's health are necessary. In addition to basic medical and surgical history information, data should be collected about the following:

- Menstrual history (including menarche, length of cycles, length and amount of flow, presence of cramps or pain, bleeding between periods or after intercourse, bleeding after menopause), pain with menses, pain with intercourse, pelvic pain
- Sexual history, including past and present contraceptive use
- Pregnancy history (number of pregnancies, outcomes of pregnancies)

- Exposure to medications (diethylstilbestrol [DES], immunosuppressive agents, others) and present medication use (vitamins, prescriptions, herbs)
- History of vaginal discharge and odor or itching
- History of problems with urinary function, including frequency, urgency, and incontinence
- History of bowel problems
- History of sexually transmitted diseases (STDs) and methods of treatment
- History of fertility treatments or hormone therapy
- History of breast health, including family history of breast disease
- History of sexual or physical abuse
- History of surgery or other procedures on reproductive tract structures (including female genital mutilation (FGM) or female circumcision)
- History of chronic illness or disability that may affect health status, reproductive health, need for health screening, or access to health care
- Psychosocial information (availability of resources and support)

Sexual History

Incorporation of the sexual history into the general health history can provide the opportunity to clarify myths and explore

areas of concern that the patient may not have felt comfortable discussing in the past. The nurse can begin by explaining the purpose of obtaining a sexual history. History taking includes gathering data about present, and past, sexual activity, sexual orientation, and possible sexual dysfunction. Sexual problems may be related to medication, life changes, disability, or the onset of physical or emotional illness. By initiating an assessment about sexual concerns, the nurse can provide a safe environment for discussing sensitive topics, as well as validation that these topics are appropriate for discussion.

Sexually Transmitted Infections

Individual risk for sexually transmitted infections (STIs) can be assessed by determining the number of partners a patient has had in the past year, or in her lifetime, as well as whether or not she is taking proper protective precautions with their partner(s). Women must understand that certain STIs (e.g., chlamydia and gonorrhea), especially if left untreated, can affect a woman's fertility and ability to become pregnant (Centers for Disease Control and Prevention [CDC], 2008). (For further details refer to Chapter 35.)

Female Genital Mutilation

FGM refers to partial or total removal of the external female genitalia or other injury to female organs, and occurs when a girl is between 4 and 10 years of age. More than 140 million girls and women worldwide have undergone FGM. In some cultures, such as in Africa and the Middle East, FGM is a rite of passage to womanhood and is an acceptable practice as it is believed to promote hygiene, protect virginity and family honor, prevent promiscuity, improve female attractiveness and male sexual pleasure, and enhance fertility (World Health Organization [WHO], 2008). There are four types of FGM (Table 32-4).

Short-term complications of FGM include hemorrhage, cellulitis, lacerations, urinary dysfunction, and infection. Long-term complications include urinary dysfunction, chronic vaginitis and pelvic infections, inability to undergo pelvic examination, painful intercourse, impaired sexual response, anemia, increased risk of HIV infection due to tearing of scar tissue, and psychological and psychosexual sequelae. Women who have undergone FGM may not think of themselves as mutilated. Nurses who care for these women must be sensitive, knowledgeable, culturally competent, and nonjudgmental. Respect for others' health beliefs, practices, behaviors, and recognition of the complexity of issues involved is crucial (WHO, 2008).

Domestic Violence

Domestic violence is a broad term that includes child abuse, elder abuse, and abuse of women and men. Abuse can be emotional, physical, sexual, or economic, and it involves fear of one partner by another and control by threats, intimidation, and physical abuse. As many as one in three women will experience domestic violence in her lifetime—approximately

TABLE
32-4 Female Genital Mutilation (FGM) Types

Type	Description
Type 1 FGM (Clitoridectomy)	Partial or total removal of the clitoris (a small, sensitive, and erectile part of the female genitals) and, rarely, the prepuce (the fold of skin surrounding the clitoris) as well
Type II FGM (Excision)	Clitoridectomy with partial or total excision of the labia minora, with or without excision of the labia majora
Type III FGM (Infibulation)	Clitoridectomy, excision of the labia, and stitching or narrowing of the vaginal opening through the creation of a covering seal, formed by cutting and repositioning the inner, and sometimes outer, labia Type III is more likely to result in infertility than other types of FGM.
Type IV, or unclassified, FGM	Pricking, piercing, or incision of the clitoris, the labia, or both, stretching of the clitoris or surrounding tissues, and introduction of corrosive substances into the vagina

From World Health Organization (2008). *Female genital mutilation.* Retrieved from http://www.who.int/mediacentre/factsheets/fs241/en/

three-quarters of a million annually—and battered women are encountered daily in nursing practice (Box 32-2) (Hathaway, Zimmer, Willis et al., 2008; Woods, Hall, Campbell et al., 2008). Violence is rarely a one-time occurrence in a relationship; it usually continues and escalates in severity.

All women should be asked directly about violence in their lives during every health assessment (Koziol-McLain, Giddings, Rameka et al., 2008; McCool & Durain, 2004). Manifestations of abuse may involve abuse of drugs and alcohol, frequent emergency department visits, vague pelvic pain, somatic complaints, depression, and even suicide attempts (Chan, Straus, Brownridge et al., 2008).

Incest and Childhood Sexual Abuse

Incest and sexual abuse are under-reported crimes as children are often abused by someone they trust (National Center for Victims of Crime [NCVC], 2008). It has been reported that female survivors of sexual abuse have more health problems than do women who were not victims of abuse. They are reported to experience more chronic depression, posttraumatic stress disorder, eating disorders, low self-esteem, gastrointestinal problems, and self-destructive behaviors than people who were not victims, with more severe symptoms seen in survivors of incest (NCVC, 2008). Posttraumatic stress disorder is a major concern as it may surface as self-inflicted injury or suicide attempts (Seng, Sperlich, & Low, 2008). The nurse should also plan to offer these women

BOX 32-2

GUIDELINES FOR NURSING CARE

Managing Domestic Violence

Equipment

- Appropriate documentation forms
- Camera
- Appropriate patient teaching materials

Procedure

ACTIONS	RATIONALE
1. Reassure the woman that she is not alone.	**1.** Women often believe that they are alone in experiencing abuse at the hands of their partners.
2. Express your belief that no one should be hurt, that abuse is the fault of the batterer and is against the law.	**2.** Lets the woman know that no one deserves to be abused and that she has not caused the abuse.
3. Assure the woman that her information is confidential, although it does become part of her medical record. *If children are suspected of being abused or are being abused, the law requires that this be reported to the authorities.* Some states require reporting of spousal or partner abuse. Domestic violence agencies and medical and nursing groups disagree with this policy and are trying to have it changed. Serious opposition is based on the fact that reporting does not and cannot currently guarantee a woman's safety and may place her in more danger. It may also interfere with a patient's willingness to discuss her personal life and concerns with care providers. This places a serious barrier in the way of comprehensive nursing care. If nurses are in doubt about laws on reporting abuse, they need to check with their local or state domestic violence agency.	**3.** Women are often afraid that their information will be reported to the police or protective services and their children may be taken away.
4. Document the woman's statement of abuse and take photographs of any visible injuries if written formal consent has been obtained. (Emergency departments usually have a camera available if one is not on the nursing unit).	**4.** Provides documentation of injuries that may be needed for later legal or criminal proceedings.
5. Provide teaching: • Inform the woman that shelters are available to ensure safety for her and her children. (Lengths of stay in shelters vary by state but are often up to 2 months. Staff often assist with housing, jobs, and the emotional distress that accompanies the break-up of the family). Provide list of shelters. • Inform the woman that violence gets worse, not better. • If the woman chooses to go to a shelter, let her make the call. • If the woman chooses to return to the abuser, remain nonjudgmental and provide information that will make her safer than she was before disclosing her situation. • Make sure that the woman has a 24-hour hotline telephone number that provides information and support (Spanish translation and a device for the deaf are also available), police number, and 911. • Assist her to set up a safety plan in case she decides to return home. (A safety plan is an organized plan for departure with packed bags and important papers hidden in a safe spot).	**5.** These options may be life-saving for the woman and her children.

support and referral to psychologists, community resources, and self-help groups.

Rape and Sexual Assault

In 2007, there were more than 248,300 victims of rape, attempted rape, or sexual assault, amounting to approximately one assault every two minutes (Rape, Abuse & Incest National Network [RAINN], 2011). Screening for abuse, rape, and violence should be part of routine assessment because women often do not report or seek treatment for assault. Often, the assailant is a partner, husband, or date. Nurses may encounter women with infections or pregnancies related to sexual assault who require support, understanding, and comprehensive care. Women who have experienced rape or sexual abuse may be very anxious about pelvic examinations, labor, pelvic or breast irradiation, or any treatment or examination that involves hands-on treatment or requires removal of clothing.

Physical Assessment

The nurse can use the physical assessment time to educate patients on their reproductive health, including normal physiologic processes, like menstruation and menopause, and to assess possible abnormalities. This section focuses on physical assessment gynecologic and breast examinations. Annual breast and pelvic examinations are important for all women 18 years of age or older and for those who are sexually active, regardless of age. Most women have a gynecological examination as part of their annual physical. The gynecological portion is often the last portion of the physical examination, as care providers tend to move from less sensitive areas to more sensitive ones. This also gives the patient a chance to become comfortable with the examination and her provider.

Pelvic Examination

The pelvic portion of the assessment consists of external and internal inspection and palpation or structures and organs. Gynecologic examinations may be uncomfortable or even distressing for some women. It is important, then, that the nurse employ assessment techniques that help their patients feel more comfortable and less vulnerable. Patient education is essential as appropriate and accurate information can help to minimize the fear and negative feelings that some women associate with gynecologic examinations (Box 32-3).

Before the examination begins, the patient should be asked to empty her bladder. This can ease the examination as a full bladder can make palpation of pelvic organs difficult for the examiner, which may increase discomfort to the patient.

Positioning

Although several positions may be used for the pelvic examination, the supine lithotomy position is used most commonly. In this position, the patient lies on the table with her feet in stirrups, buttocks at the edge of the table, and thighs spread as widely apart as possible. Supine lithotomy offers several advantages as it is more comfortable for most women

---

BOX 32-3 **Patient Education**

Pelvic Examination

A pelvic examination includes assessment of the appearance of the vulva, vagina, and cervix and the size and shape of the uterus and ovaries to ensure reproductive health and absence of illness. The following should make the examination proceed more smoothly:

- You may have a feeling of fullness or pressure during the examination, but you should not feel pain. It is important to relax, because if you are very tense, you may feel discomfort.
- It is normal to feel uncomfortable and apprehensive.
- A narrow, warmed speculum will be inserted to visualize the cervix.
- A Papanicolaou (Pap) smear will be obtained and should not be uncomfortable.
- You may watch the examination with a mirror if you choose.
- The examination usually takes no longer than 5 minutes.
- Draping will be used to minimize exposure and reduce embarrassment.

---

and allows better eye contact between patient and examiner. It may also facilitate the bimanual exam as well. However, it may be uncomfortable for some women, and some patients may need to be reminded to keep their legs in the proper position. Sims' position (patient on left side with her right leg bent at a 90-degree angle), may be used with a patient who is unable to maintain the supine lithotomy position due to acute illness or disability. The presence of a disability does not justify skipping any parts of the physical assessment, including the pelvic examination.

Inspection

After the patient is positioned, the examiner inspects the external genitalia. Lesions of any type are evaluated. In the nulliparous woman, the labia minora come together at the opening of the vagina. In a woman who has delivered children vaginally, the labia minora may gape and vaginal tissue may protrude. Structural changes from childbirth include **cystocele** (bulging of bladder into the vagina), **rectocele** (bulging of rectum into the vagina), or **uterine prolapse** (uterus falling out of normal position). The examiner may ask the patient to bear down in order to visualize these changes.

Palpation

Using the fingers of a gloved hand, the examiner gently separates the labia and palpates the lower part of the vagina. In many women who have not had vaginal intercourse, the **hymen** can be palpated within the vaginal opening. In the sexually active woman, remnants of the hymen may be palpated as a rim of scar tissue. The greater vestibular glands

(Bartholin's glands) lie between the labia minora and the hymenal ring and should be free of abscess and drainage.

Speculum Examination

The speculum is an instrument used to open the vaginal walls for internal inspection of the vagina and cervix, as well as for performance of the Papanicolaou (Pap) smear. Warming the speculum prior to insertion can be more comfortable for the patient. Current practice discourages the use of lubricants to ease insertion of the speculum for fears the gel may contaminate cervical cytology. While studies have shown that using gel does not, in fact, contaminate cervical samples, it also has not been found to significantly increase tolerance of the procedure (Gilson, Desai, Cardoza-Favorato et al., 2006). When the speculum is properly positioned, it is slowly opened to visualize the cervix and then tightened to hold it in place for inspection of the cervix (Fig. 32-4). The examiner inspects the cervical surface for any lesions or anomalies. The cervix typically is 2 to 3 cm wide, pink in color with a smooth appearance. Discharge from the cervical os may be cultured to rule out infection or disease.

While withdrawing the speculum, the nurse inspects the vagina. Vaginal discharge, which may be normal or may result from vaginitis, may be present (Table 32-5). Purulent material appearing at the cervical os is obtained for culture with a sterile applicator. In patients with high risk for infection, routine cultures for gonococcal and chlamydial organisms are recommended.

While the speculum is in place, a **Papanicolaou** (Pap) smear is obtained (this test is discussed in detail under diagnostic evaluation).

Bimanual Palpation

After the internal inspection, a bimanual examination of the pelvic organs may be conducted. The practitioner inserts two lubricated fingers from one hand into the vagina of the patient, while the other hand compresses from the outside to assess the reproductive organs. The practitioner assesses size and position of the uterus and ovarian structures while looking for any tenderness upon movement of the organs. Some mild discomfort is not unusual when palpating the ovaries. Many practitioners also perform a rectal exam at this time.

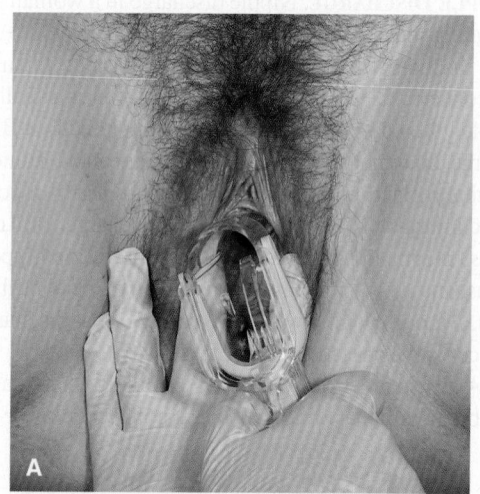

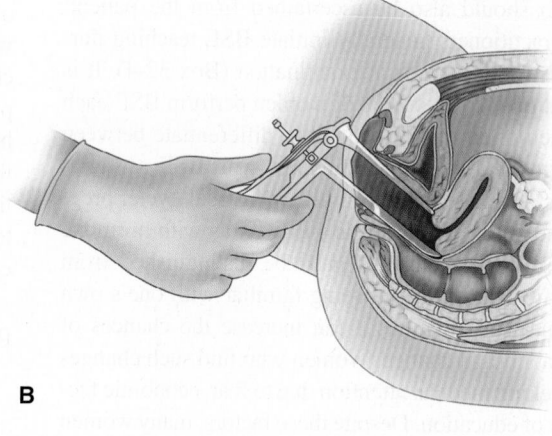

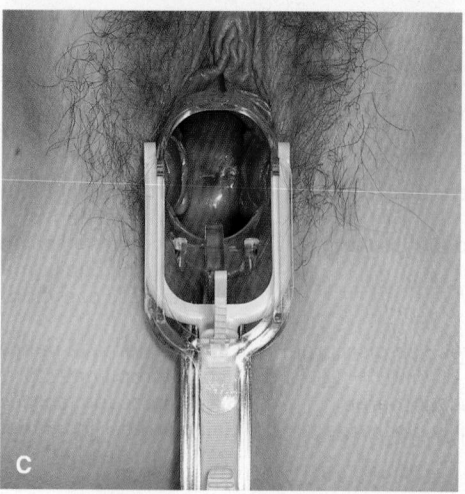

FIGURE 32-4 Technique for speculum examination of the vagina and cervix. (**A**) The labia are spread apart with a gloved left hand, while the speculum is grasped in the right hand and turned counterclockwise before being inserted into the vagina. Once the speculum is inserted, the blades are then spread apart (**B**) to reveal the cervical os (**C**).

TABLE
32-5 Vaginal Discharge Characteristics

Cause of Discharge	Symptoms	Odor	Consistency/Color
Physiologic	None	None	Mucus/white
Candida infection	Itching, irritation	Yeast odor or none	Thin to thick, curd-like/white
Bacterial vaginosis	Odor	Fishy, often noticed after intercourse	Thin/grayish or yellow
Trichomonas infection	Irritation, odor	Malodorous	Copious, often frothy/yellow-green
Atrophic	Vulvar or vaginal dryness	Occasional mild malodor	Usually scant and mucoid/may be blood-tinged

Breast Examination

The American Cancer Society (ACS) recommends that women at average risk for breast cancer undergo a clinical breast examination at least every 3 years while in their 20s and 30s and then annually thereafter (see Chapter 33). In the normal progression of a general physical examination, the breasts would be examined before the genitals as the provider moves from "head to toe." Before the examination, the patient should be asked if she has any known, palpable masses and if there is any associated pain, swelling, redness, nipple discharge, or skin changes.

Knowledge and comfort in practicing breast self-examination (BSE) should also be ascertained from the patient; health care practitioners generally initiate BSE teaching during a patient's routine physical examination (Box 32-4). It is estimated that only 25% to 30% of women perform BSE each month. Women often find it difficult to differentiate between normal changes and worrisome findings with BSE as variations in breast tissue occur during the menstrual cycle, pregnancy, and the onset of menopause, as well as with hormone therapy. These normal changes must be distinguished from those that may signal disease. Being familiar with one's own tissue ("normal abnormalities") can increase the chances of detecting an abnormal change. Women who find such changes may delay seeking medical attention due to fear, economic factors, and lack of education. Despite these factors, many women discover their own breast cancers (Lam, Chan, Chan et al., 2008). The nurse should discuss proper timing for BSE, how normal breast tissue feels, and the identification of changes.

Inspection

Examination begins with inspection. The patient disrobes to the waist and sits in a comfortable position facing the examiner. The breasts are inspected for size and symmetry. A slight variation in size between the breasts is common and generally normal. Inspect the skin for color, venous pattern, thickening, or edema. Nipple inversion of one or both breasts is not uncommon and is significant only when of recent origin. Ulceration or rashes require evaluation. The breasts are then inspected while the patient raises both arms overhead and again while she places her hands on her waist, pushing her shoulders in. These movements cause contraction

of the pectoral muscles and should not alter the breast contour or nipple direction. Dimpling or retraction observed during these position changes suggests an underlying mass. The nurse observes for deep pin-point dimpling of the skin similar to an orange's skin (termed *peau d'orange*), which is associated with carcinoma. The clavicular and axillary regions are visually inspected before palpation.

Two of the more common issues providers may find affecting the nipple are nipple discharge and fissures.

NIPPLE DISCHARGE. Nipple discharge in a woman who is not lactating may be related to many causes (Table 32-6), although any discharge that is spontaneous, persistent, or unilateral is of concern. Clear discharge on expression is usually normal, while green discharge could indicate an infection. Bloody discharge does not always indicate malignancy. Tumors of the pituitary gland or brain, encephalitis (a brain infection), and head injuries can also cause a nipple discharge. Oral contraceptives, pregnancy, hypertension, chlorpromazine-type medications, and frequent breast stimulation may be contributing factors. Among women who have an abnormal discharge, breast cancer is the cause in fewer than 10%.

A discharge from one breast is likely to be caused by a problem with that breast, such as a noncancerous or cancerous

TABLE
32-6 Nipple Discharge and Associated Causes

Description of Discharge	Associated Conditions
Clear discharge	Galactorrhea, blunt injury, fibrocystic changes
Bloody discharge	Noncancerous breast tumor (intraductal papilloma), breast cancer (less common), blunt injury
Greenish discharge	Fibroadenoma (a noncancerous solid lump), galactorrhea
Pus discharge	Breast infection, abscess
Milky discharge	Galactorrhea (in women who are not breastfeeding)

BOX 32-4
Patient Education

Breast Self-Examination (BSE)

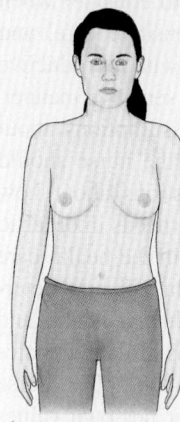

Step 1

1. Stand in front of a mirror.
2. Check both breasts for anything unusual.
3. Look for discharge from the nipple, puckering, dimpling, or scaling of the skin.

The next two steps are done to check for any changes in the contour of your breasts. As you do them, you should be able to feel your muscles tighten.

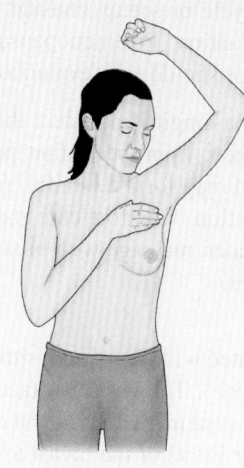

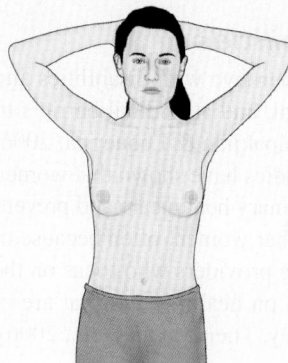

Step 2

1. Watch closely in the mirror as you clasp your hands behind your head and press your hands forward.
2. Note any change in the contour of your breasts.

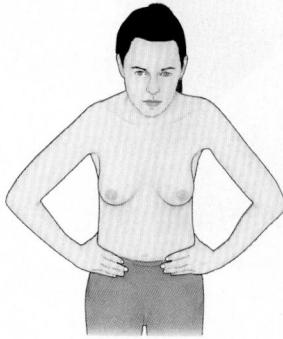

Step 3

1. Next, press your hands firmly on your hips and bow slightly toward the mirror as you pull your shoulders and elbows forward.
2. Note any change in the contour of your breasts.

Some women do the next part of the examination in the shower. Your fingers will glide easily over soapy skin, so you can concentrate on feeling for changes inside the breast.

Step 4

1. Raise your left arm.
2. Use three or four fingers of your right hand to feel your left breast firmly, carefully, and thoroughly.
3. Beginning at the outer edge, press the flat part of your fingers in small circles, moving the circles slowly around the breast.
4. Gradually work toward the nipple.
5. Be sure to cover the whole breast.
6. Pay special attention to the area between the breast and the underarm, including the underarm itself.
7. Feel for any unusual lumps or masses under the skin.
8. If you have any spontaneous discharge during the month—whether or not it is during your BSE—see your health care provider.
9. Repeat the examination on your right breast.

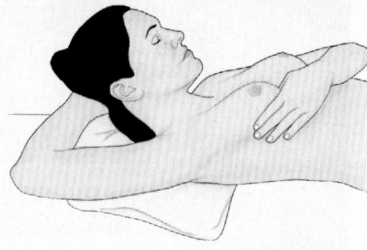

Step 5

1. Step 4 should be repeated lying down.
2. Lie flat on your back with your left arm over your head and a pillow or folded towel under your left shoulder. (This position flattens your breast and makes it easier to check).
3. Use the same circular motion described above.
4. Repeat on your right breast.

Adapted from U.S. Department of Health and Human Services, Public Health Service, *What you need to know about breast cancer.* Bethesda, MD: National Institutes of Health.

breast tumor. A discharge from both breasts is more likely to be caused by a problem outside the breast, such as a pituitary tumor, or by drugs. If a nipple discharge persists for more than one menstrual cycle or seems unusual to the woman, she should seek evaluation. Postmenopausal women who have a nipple discharge should seek evaluation promptly.

FISSURE. A fissure is a longitudinal ulcer that may develop in breastfeeding women. Improper infant positioning may irritate the nipple, and may form a painful, raw area, which can be a site of infection. Comfort care measures include daily washing with water, massage with breast milk or lanolin, and exposure to air.

Palpation

Both breasts are palpated with the patient sitting up (upright) and lying down (supine). The entire surface of the breasts and axillary tails are systematically palpated in dime-sized circles, from the outer limits of the breast toward the nipple in a clockwise direction (Fig. 32-5). If a mass is detected, it is described by its location (e.g., left breast, 2 cm from the nipple at 2 o'clock position). Size, shape, consistency, border delineation, and mobility are included in the description. Different phases of the menstrual cycle cause changes in the breast tissue.

Special Considerations in Health Assessment

Cultural Considerations

The health care system is an area in which cultural divisions are notable. Cultural views and beliefs differ, and traditional cultural beliefs can affect women's health care encounters. Practitioners can increase cooperation and compliance by providing culturally sensitive care to all their patients. (Tombros & Jordan, 2007). There are many facets to consider when engaging in culturally competent and sensitive care, and nurses are in a position to provide women with reproductive health facts in an accepting and culturally sensitive manner. The nurse should refrain from making assumptions about patients from any ethnic group. Instead, the nurse should feel comfortable asking the patient questions about how she perceives her health care and what she needs in order to make her feel comfortable and confident in the health care setting. Religious, ethnic, and cultural influence may determine how women care for their own reproductive health, and women may have individual interpretations of the mandates set forth by those influences (Berkowitz, 2008). The nurse should also be willing to recognize his or her own values and biases and how they impact care of women from other cultures (Tombros & Jordan, 2007).

Women With Disabilities

Approximately 19 million women live with disabilities and encounter physical, architectural, and attitudinal barriers to full participation in society (Kalpakjian & Lequerica, 2006; U.S. Census Bureau, 2008). Studies have shown that women with disabilities receive less primary health care and preventive health screening than do other women, often because of access problems and health care providers who focus on the causes of disability rather than on health issues that are of concern to all women (Chevarley, Theirry, Gill et al., 2006).

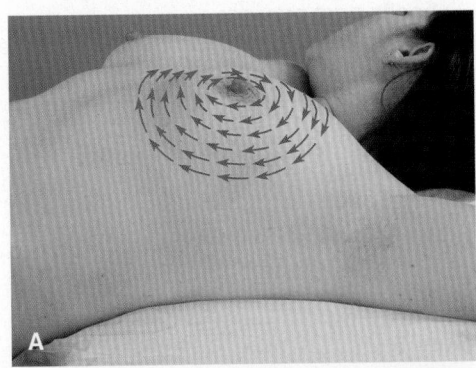
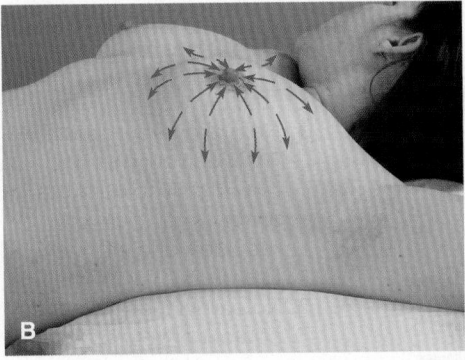
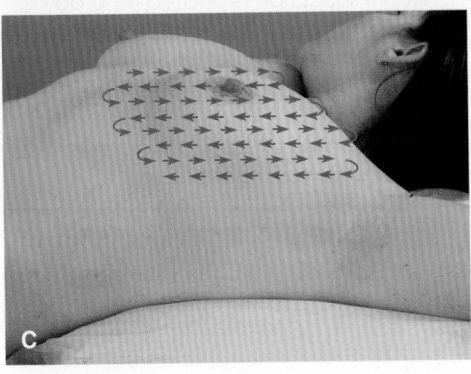

FIGURE 32-5 Breast examination with the woman in a supine position. The entire surface of the breast is palpated from the outer edge of the breast to the nipple; palpation patterns are circular or clockwise, wedge, and vertical strip.

BOX 32-5

Assessment of Women with Disabilities

Health History

Address questions directly to the woman herself rather than to people accompanying her. Ask about:

- Self-care limitations resulting from her disability (ability to feed and dress self, use of assistive devices, transportation requirements, other assistance needed)
- Sensory limitations (lack of sensation, low vision, deaf or hard of hearing)
- Accessibility issues (ability to get to health care provider, transfer to examination table, accessibility of office/clinic of health care provider, previous experiences with health care providers, health screening practices; her understanding of physical examination)
- Cognitive or developmental changes that affect understanding
- Limitations secondary to disability that affect general health issues and reproductive health and health care
- Sexual function and concerns (those of all women and those that may be affected by the presence of a disabling condition)
- Menstrual history and menstrual hygiene practices
- Physical, sexual, or psychological abuse (including abuse by care providers; abuse by neglect, withholding or withdrawing assistive devices or personal health care)
- Presence of secondary disabilities (i.e., those resulting from the patient's primary disability: pressure ulcers, spasticity, osteoporosis, etc.)
- Health concerns related to aging with a disability

Physical Assessment

Provide instructions directly to the woman herself rather than to people accompanying her; provide written or audiotaped instructions.

Ask the woman what assistance she needs for the physical examination and provide assistance if needed:

- Undressing and dressing
- Providing a urine specimen
- Standing on scale to be weighed (provide alternative means of obtaining weight if she is unable to stand on scale)
- Moving on and off the examination table
- Assuming, changing, and maintaining positions

Consider the fatigue experienced by the woman during a lengthy exam and allow rest.

Provide assistive devices and other aids/methods needed to allow adequate communication with the patient (interpreters, signers, large-print written materials).

Complete the examination as it would be indicated for any other woman; having a disability is *never* justification for omitting parts of the physical examination, including the pelvic examination.

Nurses assessing women with disabilities may require additional time to complete an assessment (Box 32-5) in a sensitive and unhurried manner.

Women with disabilities tend to undergo tests like mammography less often than recommended. It may be that they may lack transportation to the imaging facility, or they may be unable to undress, stand, or maintain positioning for a mammogram without assistance (Ahmed, Smith, Haber et al., 2009). Reminding women of the need for recommended and regular checkups, clinical breast examinations, and mammograms is an important part of nursing care.

Gerontologic Considerations

Women represent the majority of the population 65 years and over. Women live longer than men and, therefore, encounter and live with more physical and medical limitations with aging (Robinson, 2007). Elderly women are more likely to place value on screening services, such as mammography, instead of preventative health care counseling regarding things like diet and exercise on longevity. While diagnostic screening measures are appropriate, preventative health issues may be more likely to positively impact quality and longevity of life in the elderly woman and may,

therefore, be appropriate for the practitioner to discuss with elderly patient (Schonberg, York, Davis et al., 2008). Nurses should, however, encourage all aging women to undergo an annual gynecological exam, and they should use this time to educate and reassure their aging patients.

Caring for older women with gynecologic concerns requires the nurse to be prepared for a wide spectrum of issues. The aging woman may be bright, energetic, and ambitious, or she may be coping with multiple family crises, including her own health. Health disparities, cultural competency, and end-of-life issues also need to be considered (Rousseau, 2004). The optimal treatment modality for the elderly patient should not be based on age alone. Many older women, regardless of advancing chronological age, remain in excellent health. Therefore, the woman's treatment preferences must play a role in the decision-making process and this should include making her aware of preventative health activities that may be just as important to her continued health as diagnostic procedures (Schonberg et al., 2008).

Abnormal gynecologic findings in the elderly woman include perineal pruritus, which may indicate a disease process, and vulvar dystrophy, characterized by thickened or whitish discoloration of tissue. With relaxing pelvic

Follow-Up According to Pap Test Results

- If the Pap test shows atypical cells, but no high-risk for human papilloma virus (HPV), the next Pap is performed in 1 year.
- If a specific infection is causing inflammation, it is treated appropriately, and the Pap test is repeated after treatment.
- If the repeat Pap smear reveals atypical squamous cells with high-risk HPV types, colposcopy is indicated.
- Pap smears that indicate low-grade squamous intraepithelial lesion (LSIL) should be repeated in 4 to 6 months and colposcopy performed if the LSIL has not resolved.
- Patients with Pap smears that indicate high-grade squamous intraepithelial lesion (HGSIL) and carcinoma in situ (CIS) require prompt colposcopy

Adapted from International Agency for Research on Cancer Websites (2008). The Bethesda System. http://screening.iarc.fr/atlasclassifbethesda.php

musculature, uterine prolapse and relaxation of the vaginal walls can occur. Performance of Kegel exercises to strengthen the pelvic floor is frequently recommended. Refer to Chapter 33, Box 33-9 for details regarding Kegel exercises.

Diagnostic Evaluation

Papanicolaou (Pap) Test Cytologic Test for Cervical Cancer

The Pap test is a very effective tool used to screen for cervical cancer. Before the introduction of the Pap test by Papanicolaou in the 1930s, cervical cancer was the most common cause of cancer death in women; when diagnosed at an early stage, cervical cancer is one of the most treatable cancers (Martin, 2008). Incorporation of the Pap test into routine well-woman care has decreased the incidence of cervical cancer to levels lower than that of breast or ovarian cancer.

During the Pap test, secretions are gently removed from the cervix and cervical os. This test should not be performed when a patient is menstruating, as blood can interfere with interpretation. Although the Pap test is an excellent screening

Diagnostic Testing Indicated by Abnormal Pap Test Results

Colposcopy
All suspicious Pap smears should be evaluated by colposcopy. Nurse practitioners and gynecologists require special training in this diagnostic technique.

The colposcope is a portable microscope used to visualize the cervix and obtain samples of abnormal tissue for analysis. The examiner applies acetic acid to the cervix to outline suspect areas.

A cervical biopsy or endocervical curettage may be performed during colposcopy. Tissue analysis is used to determine whether abnormal changes have occurred. If these biopsy specimens show premalignant cells, cervical dysplasia, or cervical intraepithelial neoplasia (CIN), the patient usually requires further intervention (cryotherapy, laser therapy, or a cone biopsy).

Cervical Biopsy
Abnormal colposcopy findings indicating the need for biopsy include leukoplakia (white plaque visible before applying acetic acid), acetowhite tissue (white epithelium after applying acetic acid), punctation (dilated capillaries occurring in a dotted or stippled pattern), mosaicism (a tile-like pattern), and atypical vascular patterns.

Biopsy involves taking a sample of tissue from the cervix for further analysis.

Cryotherapy and Laser Therapy
Both are outpatient procedures. Cryotherapy is the freezing of suspect cervical tissue with nitrous oxide. It is good for small areas of mild to moderate dysplasia.

Cryotherapy may result in cramping and occasional feelings of faintness (vasovagal response). A watery discharge is normal for a few weeks after the procedure as the cervix heals. It is not precisely controlled, so abnormal cells may be left behind.

Laser treatment uses a tiny beam of light to vaporize abnormal cervical cells. The laser beam is directed through a colposcope, is more precise than cryosurgery, and has the benefit of targeting only the diseased cervical tissues. Healing is much faster than with freezing. Not all offices have lasers, thus increasing costs to patient if treatment is carried out in the hospital.

Cone Biopsy and Loop Electrosurgical Excision Procedure
If endocervical curettage findings indicate abnormal changes or if the lesion extends into the canal, the patient may undergo a cone biopsy. The cone biopsy can be performed surgically or with a procedure called loop electrosurgical excision procedure (LEEP).

LEEP can be performed in the outpatient setting and has a high success rate in removal of abnormal cervical tissue. The provider uses a fine wire loop with electrical energy flowing through it to remove abnormal cervical tissue. Samples are sent to pathology.

Cone biopsy is usually done in an operating room with a laser or conventional surgical instruments (cold-cone). A cone- or cylinder-shaped piece of the cervix is removed. A diagnostic cone may also treat the problem.

system, both false-positive and false-negative results may occur. The Bethesda Classification system has been developed to promote consistency in reporting Pap results.

Although patients may incorrectly assume an abnormal Pap smear signifies cancer, this is not generally the case (National Cervical Cancer Coalition, 2008). Abnormal Pap results require prompt notification and follow-up as abnormalities detected in a Pap test may signify cellular changes that may lead to cancer if left untreated (Box 32-6). Factors associated with nonadherence to recommendations or lack of follow-up include young age, low socioeconomic status, coping difficulty, no social support, fear, lack of understanding, and negative gynecologic experience (Martin, 2008). The nurse should provide clear explanations and emotional support designed to meet the needs of the specific patients that may encourage appropriate and timely follow-up (Box 32-7).

Uterine Diagnostics

Certain uterine conditions, such as dysfunctional uterine bleeding, may require diagnostic testing as well. Diagnostic tests performed on uterine and peritoneal tissues include endometrial (aspiration) biopsy, dilation and curettage (D&C), laparoscopy, hysteroscopy, and **endometrial ablation**. For information on these procedures, refer to Table 32-7.

Mammography

Mammography is a 15-minute breast-imaging technique performed in a hospital radiology department or independent imaging center that can detect nonpalpable lesions and assist in diagnosing palpable masses. The breast is mechanically compressed from top to bottom (craniocaudal view) and side to side (mediolateral oblique view) (Fig. 32-6). Experiences of slight discomfort are due to the maximum compression necessary for proper visualization. Although

TABLE 32-7 Uterine Diagnostic Tests

Test	Description
Endometrial (aspiration) biopsy	Method of obtaining endometrial tissue by placing a flexible suction tube through the cervix into the uterus. This tissue sample permits diagnosis of cellular changes in the endometrium. Indicated in cases of midlife irregular bleeding, postmenopausal bleeding, and irregular bleeding while taking hormone therapy or tamoxifen.
Dilation and curettage (D&C)	Can be used as a diagnostic or therapeutic tool. Cervical canal is dilated and the endometrium is scraped. Can be used to gather endometrial tissue for cytologic examination, control abnormal uterine bleeding, and as therapeutic measure for incomplete miscarriage.
Laparoscopy (pelvic peritoneoscopy)	Involves inserting laparoscope into peritoneal cavity through small incision below the umbilicus to allow visualization of the pelvic structures. Used for diagnostic purposes (e.g., in cases of pelvic pain when no cause can be found), as well as for surgical procedures, including tubal ligation, ovarian biopsy, hysterectomy and adhesion lysis.
Hysteroscopy (transcervical intrauterine endoscopy)	Allows direct visualization of all parts of the uterine cavity by means of a lighted optical instrument. Under a local anesthetic, the hysteroscope is passed into the cervical canal and advanced 1 or 2 cm under direct vision. Uterine-distending fluid is infused through the instrument to dilate the uterine cavity and enhance visibility.
Endometrial ablation (destruction of the uterine lining)	Performed in cases of severe bleeding not responsive to other therapies. Performed in an outpatient setting under general, regional, or local anesthesia, the uterus is distended with a fluid infusion. Providers use a hysteroscope and resector (cutting loop), roller ball (a barrel-shaped electrode), or laser beam to destroy the lining of the uterus. Hemorrhage, perforation, and burns can occur. This rapid procedure is an alternative to hysterectomy for some patients.
Hysterosalpingography (HSG)	Radiographic study of the uterus and fallopian tubes performed to evaluate infertility or tubal patency and to detect abnormal conditions in the uterine cavity. With the patient in lithotomy position, and the cervix is exposed with a speculum, a cannula is inserted into the cervix and a contrast agent is injected into the uterine cavity and the fallopian tubes. X-rays are then taken to show the path and the distribution of the contrast agent.
Ultrasonography (ultrasound, US)	Useful adjunct to the physical examination for patients with abnormal pelvic findings. Based on pulsed ultrasonic sound wave transmission via a transducer that is either placed on the abdomen (abdominal scan) or through a vaginal probe (vaginal US). The entire procedure takes usually less than 10 minutes and involves no ionizing radiation.
Computed tomography (CT)	More effective than US for obese patients or for those with a distended bowel; demonstrates tumor and any extension into the retroperitoneal lymph nodes and skeletal tissue. Does expose the patient to radiation. More costly then US procedures.
Magnetic resonance imaging (MRI)	Produces patterns that are finer and more definitive than other imaging procedures; does not expose patients to radiation. High cost is the major drawback.

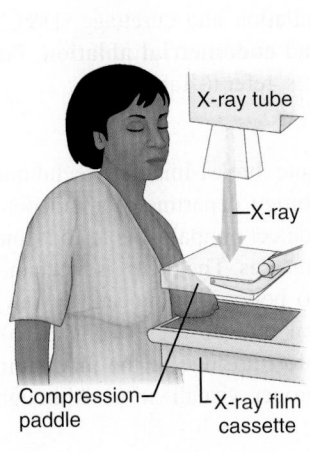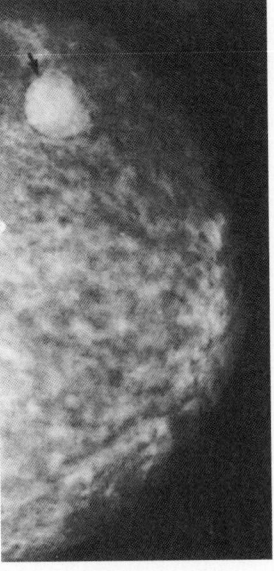

X-ray tube

X-ray

Compression paddle

X-ray film cassette

A

B

FIGURE 32-6 The mammography procedure (**A**) relies on X-ray imaging to produce the mammogram (**B**), which in this case reveals a breast lump.

mammography may detect a breast tumor before it is clinically palpable (i.e., smaller than 1 cm), it has limitations. The false-negative rate ranges between 5% and 10%. It also may be more difficult to detect lesions with mammography in younger women or those taking hormone therapy (HT) as they have denser breast tissue.

Current screening guidelines of the ACS recommend a mammogram every year beginning at 40 years of age. The ACS also has guidelines for older women and women at increased risk of breast cancer. Three other diagnostic tests to detect/view breast masses are galactography, ultrasound (US), and magnetic resonance imaging (MRI) (Box 32-8).

Breast Tissue Analysis

Diagnostic tests performed on breast tissue are described in Table 32-8.

MALE REPRODUCTIVE SYSTEM

In the male, several organs serve as parts of both the urinary tract and the reproductive system. Disorders in the male reproductive organs may interfere with the functions of one or both of these systems. As a result, diseases of the male reproductive system are usually treated by a urologist.

ANATOMIC AND PHYSIOLOGIC OVERVIEW

The structures in the male reproductive system include the testes, the vas deferens (ductus deferens) and seminal vesicles, the penis, and certain accessory glands, such as the prostate gland and Cowper's gland (bulbourethral gland) (Fig. 32-7).

The testes are formed in the embryo, within the abdominal cavity, near the kidney. During the last month of fetal life, they descend posterior to the peritoneum, pierce the abdominal wall in the groin, and progress along the inguinal canal into the scrotum. In this descent, they are accompanied by blood vessels, lymphatics, nerves, and ducts, all of which support the tissue and make up the spermatic cord. This cord extends from the internal inguinal ring through the abdominal wall and the inguinal canal to the scrotum. As the testes descend into the scrotum, a tubular extension of peritoneum accompanies them. This tissue is obliterated during fetal development; the only remaining portion is that which covers the testes, the tunica vaginalis.

The testes are encased in the scrotum, which keeps them at a slightly lower temperature than the rest of the body to

---

BOX 32-8 **Other Radiologic Tests for Breasts Masses**

Galactography is a diagnostic procedure that involves a small injection of radiopaque material through a cannula inserted into a ductal opening on the areola, which is followed by a mammogram. It evaluates abnormalities within the duct when the patient has bloody nipple discharge on expression, spontaneous nipple discharge, or a solitary dilated duct noted on mammography.

Ultrasonography (US) is a diagnostic adjunct to mammography to help distinguish fluid-filled cysts from other lesions. No radiation is emitted during the procedure.

The technique diagnoses cysts with great accuracy but cannot definitively rule out malignant lesions. Ultrasonography is useful for screening women with dense breasts.

Magnetic Resonance Imaging (MRI) of the breast is a highly sensitive technology that is a useful diagnostic

adjunct to mammography, and creates detailed images of the breast without exposure to radiation. The procedure cannot always accurately distinguish between malignant and benign breast conditions.

MRI is most useful when assessing for multifocal (more than one tumor in the same quadrant of the breast) or multicentric (more than one tumor in different quadrants of the breast) disease, chest wall involvement, tumor recurrence, or response to chemotherapy.

MRI can also identify occult (undetectable) breast cancer and determine the integrity of saline or silicone breast implants.

Disadvantages of MRI include high cost, variations in technique and interpretation, and the potential for patient claustrophobia.

32-8 Procedures for Breast Tissue Analysis

Procedure	Description
Percutaneous biopsy	Samples palpable and nonpalpable lesions via needle or core biopsy that obtains tissue by making a small puncture in the skin. It is less invasive than a surgical biopsy.
Fine-needle aspiration (FNA)	Small-gauge needle with a syringe is inserted into the mass or area of nodularity. Cellular material obtained during the procedure is spread on a glass slide or placed in a preservative and sent for analysis.
Core needle biopsy	Similar to FNA, except that a larger gauge needle is used (usually 14-gauge). It allows for a more definitive diagnosis than FNA, because actual tissue, not just cells, is removed. Often performed for relatively large tumors that are close to the skin surface.
Stereotactic core biopsy	Performed on nonpalpable lesions detected by mammography. After using digital mammography to determine the exact coordinates of the lesion, a core needle is inserted to retrieve samples of the tissue for pathologic examination. Stereotactic biopsy often allows the patient to avoid a surgical biopsy.
Ultrasound-guided core biopsy	Performed on nonpalpable lesions found by ultrasound; does not use radiation and is faster and less expensive than stereotactic core biopsy.
Excisional biopsy (lumpectomy)	Standard procedure for complete pathological assessment of a palpable breast mass. The entire mass, plus a margin of surrounding tissue, is removed.
Incisional biopsy	Surgical removal of a portion of a mass when complete excision of the area may not be possible or immediately beneficial to the patient. Incisional biopsy is becoming less common as pathological information can be obtained from core needle biopsy.
Wire needle localization	Technique used to precisely locate nonpalpable masses detected on a mammogram, ultrasound, or MRI that require an excisional biopsy. A long, thin wire is inserted through a needle, and guided into the area of abnormality using X-ray or ultrasound. The needle is withdrawn and the wire is left in place to ensure the precise location.

facilitate spermatogenesis. The **testes** have a dual function: **spermatogenesis** (production of sperm) and secretion of the male sex hormone **testosterone**, which induces and preserves the male sex characteristics. The testes consist of numerous seminiferous tubules in which the spermatozoa form. Collecting tubules transmit the spermatozoa into the epididymis, a hood-like structure lying on the testes and containing winding ducts that lead into the vas deferens. This firm, tubular structure passes upward through the inguinal canal as part of the spermatic cord, to enter the abdominal cavity behind the peritoneum. It then extends downward toward the base of the bladder. An outpouching from this structure is the seminal vesicle. The tract is continued as the ejaculatory duct, which passes through the prostate gland to enter the urethra. Secretions from the seminal vesicles join secretions from the prostate and exit the penis during ejaculation.

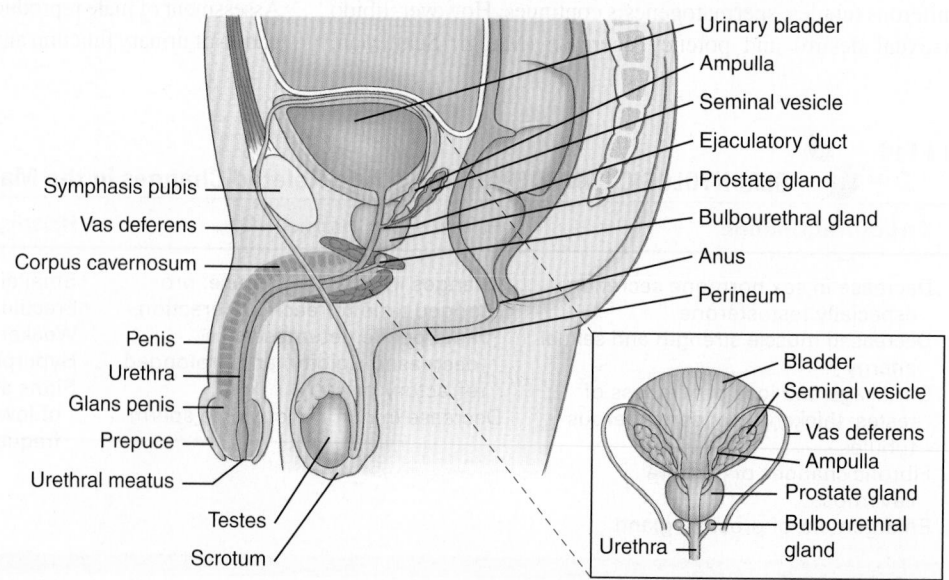

FIGURE 32-7 Structures of the male reproductive system.

The **penis** has a dual function: it is the organ for copulation and for urination. Anatomically, it consists of the glans penis, the body, and the root. The glans penis is the soft, rounded portion at the distal end of the penis. The urethra opens at the tip of the glans. The glans is naturally covered or protected by elongated penile skin—the foreskin—which may be retracted to expose the glans. However, many men have had the foreskin removed (circumcision) as newborns. The body of the penis is composed of erectile tissues containing numerous blood vessels that become distended, leading to an erection during sexual excitement. The urethra, which passes through the penis, extends from the bladder through the prostate to the distal end of the penis, ending at the meatal opening.

The **prostate gland** lies just below the neck of the bladder. It surrounds the urethra and is traversed by the ejaculatory duct, a continuation of the vas deferens. This gland produces a secretion that is chemically and physiologically suitable to the needs of the spermatozoa in their passage from the testes. The Cowper's gland lies below the prostate, within the posterior aspect of the urethra. This gland empties its secretions into the urethra during ejaculation, providing lubrication.

Gerontologic Considerations

As men age, the prostate gland enlarges, prostate secretion decreases, the scrotum hangs lower, the testes become smaller and less firm, and pubic hair becomes sparser. Changes in gonadal function include a decline in plasma testosterone levels and reduced production of progesterone (Table 32-9). Other potential changes include decreased sexual function, slowed sexual responses, an increased incidence of genitourinary tract cancer, and possible urinary incontinence.

Male reproductive capability is maintained with advancing age. Although degenerative changes occur in the seminiferous tubules, spermatogenesis continues. However, libido (sexual desire) and potency decrease (Maggi, Schulman,

Quinton et al., 2007). Vascular problems cause about half of the cases of impotence in men older than 50 years of age (Tanagho & McAninch, 2007).

Hypogonadism occurs in up to one-fourth of older men. This decline is more evident in men older than 60 years of age (Maggi et al., 2007). In older men, the sexual response slows, attaining an erection takes longer, and full erections may not be attained until climax. Sexual function can be affected by several factors, such as psychological problems, comorbidities, and medications. In older men, if the erection is partially lost, there may be difficulty in attaining a full erection again, and resolution may occur without orgasm. Sexual activity is closely correlated with the man's sexual history; if he was more active than average as a young man, he will most likely continue to be more active than average in his later years (Tanagho & McAninch, 2007).

Cancers of the kidney, bladder, prostate, and penis all have increased incidence in men older than 50 years of age. Digital rectal examination (DRE) and screening tests for hematuria may uncover a higher percentage of malignancies at earlier stages and lead to lower morbidity associated with treatment, as well as a lower mortality rate.

Urinary incontinence in the elderly man may have many causes, including medications and age-related conditions such as neurologic disease or benign prostatic hyperplasia (BPH). Diagnostic tests are performed to exclude reversible causes of urinary incontinence.

ASSESSMENT

Health History

Male sexuality is a complex phenomenon that is strongly influenced by personal, cultural, and social factors. Sexuality and male reproductive function become concerns in the presence of illness (Emmelot-Vonk, Verhaar, Nakhai Pour et al., 2008). Assessment of male reproductive function begins with an evaluation of urinary function and symptoms. This assessment also

TABLE
32-9 **GERONTOLOGIC CONSIDERATIONS** / Age-Related Changes in the Male Reproductive System

Structural Change	Functional Change	History and Physical Findings
Decrease in sex hormone secretion, especially testosterone Decreased muscle strength and sexual energy Shrinkage and loss of firmness of testes; thickening of seminiferous tubules Fibrotic changes of corpora cavernosa Enlargement of prostate gland	Changes in sexual response: prolonged time to reach full erection, rapid penile detumescence (decreased rigidity) and prolonged refractory period Decrease in number of viable sperm	Smaller testes Erectile dysfunction Weakening of prostatic contractions Hyperplasia of prostate gland Signs and symptoms of obstruction of lower urinary tract (urgency, frequency, nocturia)

includes a focus on sexual function, as well as on manifestations of sexual dysfunction.

The patient is asked about his usual state of health and any recent change in general physical and sexual activity. Any symptoms or changes in function are explored fully and described in detail. These symptoms may include those associated with an obstruction caused by an enlarged prostate gland: increased urinary frequency, decreased force of urine stream, "double" voiding (the patient needs to urinate two or three times over a period of several minutes to completely empty his bladder). The patient is also assessed for dysuria (painful urination) and hematuria (blood in the urine).

Assessment of sexual function is an essential part of every health history. The extent of the history depends on the patient's presenting symptoms and the presence of factors that may affect sexual function: chronic illnesses (e.g., diabetes, multiple sclerosis, stroke, cardiac disease), use of medications that affect sexual function (e.g., many antihypertensive and anticholesterolemic medications, psychotropic agents), stress, and alcohol use.

Patients are often embarrassed to initiate a discussion about sexual issues with their health care providers (Tanagho & McAninch, 2007). By initiating an assessment about sexual concerns, the nurse demonstrates that changes in sexual functioning are valid topics for discussion and provides a safe environment for discussing these sensitive topics.

Physical Assessment

Physical assessment includes penis and scrotal examination, the DRE, and assessment if the male breast.

Penis and Scrotal Examination

The male genitalia are inspected for abnormalities and palpated for masses. The scrotum is palpated carefully for nodules, masses, or inflammation. Examination of the scrotum can reveal such disorders as hydrocele (accumulation of serous fluid in the scrotal sac), varicocele (enlargement of the veins of the spermatic cord), or tumor of the testis. The penis is inspected and palpated for ulcerations, plaques, inflammation, and discharge. The testicular examination provides an excellent opportunity to instruct the patient about techniques for testicular self-examination (TSE) and its importance in early detection of testicular cancer (see Chapter 34). TSE could begin during adolescence, although recently this practice has been called into question, with recommendations that TSE not be emphasized (U. S. Preventive Services Task Force [USPSTF], 2008) due to the low incidence of testicular cancer and the high rate of anxiety associated with self-examination.

Digital Rectal Examination

The DRE is recommended as part of the regular health checkup for every man older than 50 years of age; it is invaluable in screening for cancer of the prostate gland. The DRE enables the examiner to estimate the size, shape, and con-

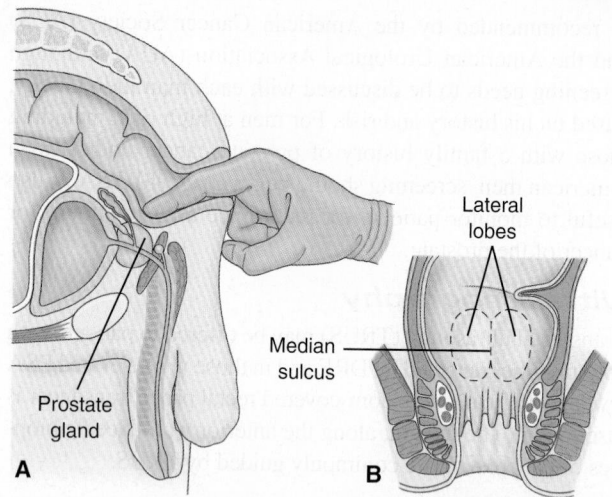

FIGURE 32-8 (**A**) Palpation of the prostate gland during digital rectal examination (DRE) enables the examiner to assess the size, shape, and texture of the gland. (**B**) The prostate is round, with a palpable median sulcus or groove separating the lateral lobes. It should feel rubbery and free of nodules and masses.

sistency of the prostate gland (Fig. 32-8). Tenderness of the prostate gland on palpation and the presence and consistency of any nodules are noted. Although this examination may be embarrassing for the patient, it is an important screening tool.

Assessment of the Male Breast

Breast cancer can occur in men. Examination of the male breast and axillae should be included in a physical examination. The nipple and areola are inspected for masses and nipple discharge.

Gynecomastia is the firm enlargement of glandular tissue beneath and immediately surrounding the areola of the male. This is different from the enlargement of soft, fatty tissue, which is caused by obesity.

Diagnostic Evaluation

Prostate-Specific Antigen Test

The prostate gland produces a substance known as prostate-specific antigen (PSA). It can be measured in a blood specimen, and levels increase with certain pathologies: prostate cancer, BPH, acute urinary retention, and acute prostatitis are the most common examples. In most laboratories, the range of values generally considered normal is 0.2 to 4.0 ng/mL, with levels greater than 4.0 considered elevated. The use of age-specific reference ranges for populations helps minimize unnecessary biopsies (American Urological Association [AUA], 2009).

Prostate cancer screening with serum PSA testing has become common practice (AUA, 2009) although its overall utility has recently come into question (USPSTF, 2008). An annual PSA test beginning at age 50, along with DRE,

is recommended by the American Cancer Society (ACS) and the American Urological Association (AUA), although screening needs to be discussed with each man individually, based on his history and risk. For men at high risk, including those with a family history of prostate cancer and African American men, screening should begin at age 40. PSA is also useful to monitor patients for recurrence after treatment for cancer of the prostate.

Ultrasonography

Transrectal ultrasound (TRUS) may be offered to patients with abnormalities detected by DRE and in those with elevated PSA levels; a lubricated, condom-covered rectal probe transducer is inserted into the rectum, along the anterior wall. Needle biopsies of the prostate are commonly guided by TRUS.

Prostate Fluid or Tissue Analysis

Specimens of prostate fluid or tissue may be obtained for culture if disease or inflammation of the prostate gland is suspected, but this is uncommonly performed.

Tests of Male Sexual Function

If the patient cannot engage in sexual intercourse to his satisfaction, a detailed history is obtained. A Rigiscan® test may be ordered, or nocturnal penile tumescence tests may be conducted in a sleep laboratory, to monitor changes in penile circumference during sleep. The results help identify the cause of erectile dysfunction. Additional tests, including penile Doppler studies or psychological evaluations, can be also part of the diagnostic workup and are usually conducted by a specialized team of health care providers.

Chapter Review

Critical Thinking Exercises

1. While preparing a male patient to be evaluated by his provider, he confides that his interest in sexual activity and overall energy level have lessened. Explain the information you would provide. What medical and nursing interventions would you anticipate?

2. A 55-year-old, post-menopausal woman comes to you with concerns regarding vaginal bleeding. She has not had a period in 3 years and is not currently on HR therapy. Vaginal bleeding is noted most significantly after intercourse. What lifestyle questions would you ask this patient? How would you prioritize her plan of care? What types of tests might you order to rule out disease processes?

NCLEX-Style Review Questions

1. A 51-year-old male patient who has been given written information asks why it has been recommended he have a PSA test. What is the nurse's best response?
   A. It will measure his sperm count.
   B. It will measure his response to testosterone replacement.
   C. It is a useful test to screen for cancer of the prostate.
   D. It is a useful test to screen for sexual function.

2. A 21-year-old man asks how long he will continue to produce sperm, since he "knows that women can't have babies after they're 43." What is the nurse's best response?
   A. "That is correct, men and women lose their reproductive capacity at roughly the same time."
   B. "Men continue to produce sperm despite advanced age."

   C. "Current literature does not provide this information for men."
   D. "Men stop sperm production at age 60."

3. A 19-year-old girl comes to you complaining of vaginal irritation. She says she was out for an evening a week ago at a club with friends, but doesn't remember leaving the club. She states that she has never been sexually active, but is afraid she may have been assaulted. What are the appropriate steps you, as the nurse, might take?
   A. Tell her you are sure nothing bad happened to her if she left willingly with a man. If he was a bad guy, her friends would not have let her leave with him.
   B. Tell her you believe her, that this is not her fault, and you want to help her.
   C. Tell her she probably decided to have sex with a man, now she has an STD, and she needs to accept the responsibility for her own actions.
   D. Offer emotional support and referral for counseling, but medical treatment at this time is not necessary as it has been too long since the incident.

4. A 21-year-old is in your office for a routine physical examination. She tells you that she has been in a monogamous relationship for 1 year and is sexually active. She is using the rhythm method of birth control to avoid pregnancy. Which of these statements indicates that she understands this method of birth control?
   A. I am only fertile for 1 day of my cycle every month, so I avoid sexual intercourse on that day.
   B. I use a regular thermometer to check my basal body temperature, but I only need to do that once or twice a week.

C. My cycle is 28 to 29 days long and midway through, around day 14 or 15, I note that my cervical mucus becomes very slippery and stretchy. I definitely avoid intercourse on this day, and for 2 days after.

D. I like the rhythm method because I don't need to use a condom and I cannot acquire STDs.

5. A 35-year-old woman has an abnormal Pap test. She will undergo cryotherapy for treatment of moderate dysplasia. Which of the following should be included in the teaching plan for this patient?

A. All abnormal cells will be removed.

B. It involves freezing of cervical tissue.

C. Discharge following the procedure is considered abnormal.

D. A tiny beam of light is used to vaporize abnormal cervical cells.

Try these additional resources to enhance your learning and understanding of this chapter:
- thePoint online resource available at **http://thepoint.lww.com/Pellico1e**
- *Handbook for Focus on Adult Health: Medical-Surgical Nursing*
- *Study Guide for Focus on Adult Health: Medical-Surgical Nursing*

References and Selected Readings

References and selected readings associated with this chapter can be found on the website that accompanies the book. Visit http://thepoint.lww.com/Pellico1e to access the references and other additional resources associated with this chapter.

JULIA MERRILL JONES
VANESSA POMARICO-
DENINO

Nursing Management: Patients With Breast and Female Reproductive Disorders

Learning Objectives

After reading this chapter, you will be able to:

1. Describe common benign breast problems.

2. Identify risk factors for breast cancer.

3. Identify screening and diagnostic tests used to detect breast disorders.

4. Describe different treatment modalities for breast cancer.

5. Use the nursing process as a framework for care of the patient undergoing breast cancer treatment.

6. Describe the various types of menstrual disorders and their management.

7. Differentiate between vaginitis and candidiasis.

8. Identify factors associated with pelvic organ prolapse.

9. Understand risk factors for gynecological cancers.

10. Describe differences between the types of hysterectomies.

11. Identify appropriate care for the transgendered client.

The breast and female reproductive organs play a significant role in a woman's sexuality and body image. Disorders of the breast or reproductive system, whether minor or serious, can cause great anxiety. Some disorders require only simple treatment, while others require significant intervention and may be life-threatening. All disorders necessitate nurses to have knowledge, understanding, and skill in patient teaching.

BREAST DISORDERS

BENIGN CONDITIONS OF THE BREAST

Most benign breast disorders are the results of normal physiologic processes. They represent a spectrum of problems that receive clinical attention as imaging abnormalities or as palpable lesions or irregularities found on physical examination. Once a benign diagnosis has been confirmed, treatment typically focuses on symptom management and patient education. Benign epithelial breast lesions are classified in three categories: nonproliferative, proliferative without atypia, and **atypical hyperplasia**. The latter may confer a mild to moderate increase in a patient's risk for developing breast cancer and should indicate a need for counseling, screening recommendations, and any potential risk reduction strategies (Sabel, 2009). The nurse should work as an integral member of the interdisciplinary team to ensure a thorough history and physical exam, and that all diagnostic and treatment options are made available to the patient. Table 33-1 compares various breast masses.

BREAST PAIN

Mastalgia, or breast pain, is one of the most common breast complaints. Cyclical breast pain, the most common type of breast pain, accounts for nearly 75% of all complaints. It is usually related to hormonal fluctuations during the **luteal phase** of the menstrual cycle that stimulate the proliferation of normal glandular tissue and cause pain. Noncyclical pain is far less common and does not vary with the menstrual cycle. Women who experience injury or trauma to the breast or those who had a breast biopsy may experience noncyclical pain. Patients should be reassured that breast pain is rarely indicative of cancer. A patient should seek attention from her primary care provider for persistent pain. Elimination of methylxanthines, including, caffeine, theophylline, and theobromine may alleviate breast pain. These are found in coffee, tea, chocolate, and cola

TABLE
33-1 Comparison of Various Breast Masses

The most common breast masses are due to cysts, fibroadenomas, or malignancy. Biopsy is usually needed for confirmation, but the following characteristics are diagnostic clues:

Characteristics	Cysts	Fibroadenomas	Malignancy
Age	30–55 years, regress after menopause except with use of estrogen therapy	Puberty to menopause	30–90 years; most common, 40–80 years
Number	Single or multiple	Usually single	Usually single
Shape	Round	Round, disk, or lobular	Irregular or stellate
Consistency	Soft to firm, usually elastic	Usually firm	Firm or hard
Mobility	Mobile	Mobile	May be fixed to skin or underlying tissues
Tenderness	Usually tender	Usually nontender	Usually nontender
Retraction signs	Absent	Absent	May be present

beverages. Lowering dietary fat may also improve cyclic tenderness and swelling, and nonsteroidal anti-inflammatory drugs (NSAIDs) may be implemented. There is some evidence that evening primrose oil may provide some relief for women who have abnormal blood levels of some essential fatty acids. The attenuated androgen danazol may be implemented for severe, persistent pain and is effective due to its antiestrogenic effects. The nurse may recommend that the patient wear a supportive bra both day and night, decrease her salt and caffeine intake, and take ibuprofen as needed for breast pain (Bland & Copeland, 2009; Sabel, 2009).

BREAST CYSTS

Cysts are the most common nonproliferative breast lesions. They do not increase a woman's risk for developing breast cancer. They are fluid-filled round or ovoid masses, derived from the terminal duct lobular unit, that develop as breast ducts dilate. Cysts occur most commonly in women 30 to 55 years of age and may be exacerbated during perimenopause. Acute enlargement of cysts, which may occur immediately prior to menses, may cause sudden-onset severe, localized pain.

Simple Cysts

Simple cysts are benign by definition and do not require intervention. On ultrasound, they are well circumscribed, anechoic (low degree of sound reverberation), have posterior acoustic enhancement, and an absence of solid components. Aspiration is often performed to relieve discomfort, but simple, nonpainful cysts identified incidentally on ultrasound do not require aspiration.

Complicated Cysts

Complicated cysts meet most but not all criteria for simple cysts on ultrasound examination. They may have internal echoes, fluid or debris levels, septations, a perceptible wall, or lack of posterior acoustic enhancement. They are very rarely malignant but should be aspirated to confirm diagnosis or followed with imaging (Daly, Bailey, Klein et al., 2008).

Complex Cysts

Complex cysts have a mixed cystic and solid component or an intracystic solid mass and do require core biopsy to rule out malignancy. These lesions are more likely than simple or complicated cysts to be malignant. The nurse should educate the patient as to the diagnostic workup process and provide support to alleviate anxiety.

FIBROCYSTIC BREAST CHANGES

Breast pain is often attributed to **fibrocystic breast changes**, or fibrocystic breast disease. However, breast discomfort and

breast nodularity are very common and are often a normal response to hormonal changes during the menstrual cycle. From a clinical standpoint, it is more accurate to describe a breast as nodular and sensitive, or tender. By the same token, pathologists historically used the term "fibrocystic" to refer to histologic findings such as fibrosis, adenosis, and hyperplasia (Sabel, 2009).

FIBROADENOMAS

Fibroadenomas are proliferative lesions without atypia (cell abnormalities). They usually present as firm, round, movable, benign tumors that contain glandular and fibrous tissue. In many cases, multiple fibroadenomas will occur in the same breast or bilaterally. They can occur from puberty to menopause and are most common from the late teens through the early 30s. Diagnosis is best confirmed through the "triple test": clinical examination, imaging, and nonsurgical tissue biopsy. Fibroadenomas larger than 2 cm are more likely to recur and should be excised. Fibroadenomas are sometimes completely excised when they are painful or when the presence of a palpable mass is too anxiety-provoking for the patient. Patients with a "triple negative test" (negative clinical examination, benign appearance on imaging, and benign pathology results demonstrating fibroadenoma) should have short-term interval follow-up with clinical examination and age-appropriate imaging (Bland & Copeland, 2009; Grady, Gorsuch, & Wilburn-Bailey, 2008; Sklair-Levy, Sella, Alwess et al., 2008).

ATYPICAL DUCTAL HYPERPLASIA

Atypical ductal hyperplasia requires a pathologic diagnosis and is usually an incidental finding from biopsy of a radiographic abnormality or palpable mass. It is characterized by an abnormal increase in the ductal cells in the breast and the presence of atypia without either the cytologic or architectural criteria necessary for a diagnosis of ductal carcinoma in situ. Atypical ductal hyperplasia increases a woman's risk for breast cancer to three to four times that of the general population. Multifocal lesions, especially those with associated microcalcifications, can present an even higher risk for developing breast cancer (Bland & Copeland, 2009; Worsham, Raju, Lu et al., 2009).

LOBULAR CARCINOMA IN SITU

Lobular carcinoma in situ (LCIS) is characterized by a proliferation of cells within the breast lobules. LCIS is usually found incidentally because it cannot be seen on mammography and does not form a palpable lump. The term is misleading because this is not a carcinoma. Historically, LCIS was considered a premalignant condition but is now considered a marker of increased risk for invasive carcinoma. The invasive carcinoma can be either ductal or lobular in origin and can develop in either breast. LCIS increases a woman's

risk of breast cancer about eight to ten times compared with that of the general population (National Cancer Institute [NCI], 2009; Sabel, 2009). Patients with lobular carcinoma in situ should be referred to a specialist for full discussion of treatment options due to their significantly higher risk for breast cancer. These options include observation alone, tamoxifen to reduce the risk for subsequent breast cancer, breast cancer prevention trials, and bilateral **prophylactic mastectomy** without axillary node dissection (NCI, 2009; Sabel, 2009).

MALIGNANT CONDITIONS OF THE BREAST

Breast cancer occurs when cells in the breast change and grow out of control. Some breast cancers are in situ, meaning confined to the ducts of the breast, but most are invasive or infiltrating. These cancers have extended through the ducts or glandular walls and invaded the surrounding breast tissue. The expected prognosis for invasive breast cancer depends largely on the extent to which is has spread when it is first diagnosed. Breast cancer is the most commonly diagnosed malignancy in women, except for nonmelanoma skin cancer. The ACS estimates that 207,090 new cases of invasive breast cancer will be diagnosed in the United States in 2010, as well as an additional estimated 54,010 cases of in situ breast cancer; 39,840 women are expected to die from breast cancer in the United States in 2010. Lung cancer is the only cancer that causes more deaths in women. In 2010, it is estimated that 1,970 men will be diagnosed with breast cancer, accounting for about 1% of all breast cancer diagnoses. Approximately 390 men are expected to die from breast cancer in 2010; this accounts for about 1% of breast cancers. The NCI estimates that, in January 2006, approximately 2.5 million women were alive with a history of breast cancer. Most were free of disease, while others were still undergoing treatment and had evidence of breast cancer (American Cancer Society [ACS], 2010).

Risk Factors

The two most significant risk factors for developing breast cancer are being a woman and growing older. Eighty-five percent of women who develop breast cancer have no risk factors other than age and gender. About 5% to 10% of women with breast cancer may have a germ-line mutation of the genes *BRCA1* and/or *BRCA2*. Women who carry these mutations have a 40% to 85% lifetime risk of developing breast cancer. Box 33-1 lists other risk factors for developing breast cancer.

Screening and Prevention

Breast cancer is a disease of early detection, not one of prevention (however, there are preventative strategies for the

BOX 33-1

Risk Factors for Breast Cancer

- Being a woman
- Increasing age
- Inherited genetic mutation for breast cancer, such as BRCA1 and/or BRCA2
- Family history of breast cancer, particularly first-degree relatives diagnosed with breast cancer at an early age
- Personal history of breast cancer
- History of benign proliferative breast disease, such as atypical hyperplasia
- History of high-dose radiation therapy to the chest, such as patients who have undergone treatment for Hodgkin's disease or non-Hodgkin lymphoma
- Hormonal factors:
  - Early menarche (<12 years)
  - Late menopause (>55 years)
  - Nulliparity or no full-term pregnancies
  - Late age at first full-term pregnancy (>30 years)
  - Recent contraceptive use
  - Long-term use of estrogen and progestin (hormone replacement therapy)
- History of ovarian cancer or endometrial cancer
- Obesity, particularly postmenopausal
- Alcohol consumption
- Ashkenazi Jewish ethnicity

high-risk patient, see below). The two greatest risk factors, being female and growing older, are not modifiable. This is why screening mammograms and prompt attention for any breast problem are extremely important.

Men can experience breast cancer as well, but the disease is 100 times more likely to occur in women. Since it is so rare in men, they are not routinely screened, and male breast cancer is not addressed in detail in this chapter. Any breast lump or abnormality should be evaluated in men, however, and male breast cancer is treated similarly to breast cancer in females (ACS, 2010).

Protective Factors

Women can choose to maximize their overall health by avoiding weight gain, particularly after menopause, engaging in regular physical activity, and avoiding excessive alcohol consumption. Women who breastfeed for an extended period of time (at least a year) may have some added protection. Women at high risk for breast cancer may take medications such as tamoxifen or raloxifene to reduce their risk (ACS, 2010).

Screening Recommendations

The American Cancer Society recommends that women begin annual screening mammography at age 40. Women may have a baseline mammogram at age 35, and return at age 40 provided they receive normal results. Women should

also have a clinical breast exam every 3 years beginning at age 20 and annually at age 40, and should practice breast self-awareness. Women who are at increased risk for breast cancer should talk with their care provider to establish the optimal age to begin screening mammography. A general guideline is to begin screening 10 years earlier than the age at which the youngest family member developed breast cancer, but not before 25 years of age.

Prevention Strategies in the High-Risk Patient

By identifying the population of women who are at highest risk for breast cancer, earlier detection is possible. Women who have multiple risk factors should talk with their healthcare provider to implement an individualized surveillance plan. The decision whether or not to undergo genetic testing and the risks and benefits of prevention strategies should be discussed in detail, weighing the potential benefits with the demonstrated morbidities of the interventions.

Long-Term Surveillance

Some high-risk women choose a conservative approach, with more frequent or earlier screening and additional imaging tests such as magnetic resonance imaging (MRI). Frequent clinical breast exams and breast self-awareness are emphasized. The National Comprehensive Cancer Network Clinical Practice Guidelines in Oncology offer patient-specific recommendations for screening in this population (2010).

Chemoprevention

Chemoprevention with tamoxifen has demonstrated significant reduction in breast cancer in high-risk women. The National Surgical Adjuvant Breast and Bowel Project (NSABP) Breast Cancer Prevention Trial showed that treatment with tamoxifen resulted in a 49% decrease in short-term risk for breast cancer in healthy women at increased risk (Fisher, Constantino, Wickerham et al., 2005). Raloxifene has also demonstrated effectiveness in risk reduction and has a lower side-effect profile than tamoxifen (Vogel, Constantino, Wickerham et al., 2006). The risks and benefits of chemoprevention should be carefully weighed by the patient and her health care provider.

Prophylactic Mastectomy

Prophylactic bilateral **total mastectomy** and bilateral salpingo-oophorectomy are an option for carefully selected women with significant breast cancer risk and/or extreme anxiety associated with potential diagnosis. This surgery as a method of breast cancer prevention has demonstrated a significant risk reduction in women who are known to have *BRCA1* or *BRCA2* mutations (Domcheck, Friebel, Singer et al., 2010). The decision to undergo prophylactic mastectomy should be made carefully and with the input of the multidisciplinary team. All breast tissue should be removed, but lymph node dissection is not necessary unless breast cancer is detected upon pathologic examination of the tissue (NCCN, 2010).

Clinical Manifestations

Breast cancers can occur anywhere in the breast but are usually found in the upper outer quadrant, where the most breast tissue is located. Generally, the lesions are nontender, fixed rather than mobile, and hard with irregular borders. Complaints of diffuse breast pain and tenderness with menstruation are usually associated with benign breast disease.

With the increased use of mammography, more women are seeking treatment at earlier stages of the disease. These women often have no signs or symptoms other than a mammographic abnormality. Unfortunately, some women with advanced disease seek initial treatment after ignoring symptoms. Advanced signs may include skin dimpling, nipple retraction, or skin ulceration.

Breast Imaging

Breast imaging includes all of the radiographic imaging modalities used to detect and diagnose breast abnormalities and diseases. Mammography is the most common imaging modality and has dramatically improved since its inception in the 1930s. Other common imaging procedures include ultrasound and MRI (Bland & Copeland, 2009).

Mammography

Mammography is a specific type of radiographic imaging that utilizes low dose X-ray for examination of the breasts. Mammography is the best and most universally accepted screening tool available to detect breast cancer at its earliest and most treatable stages, and is currently the only imaging modality recommended for routine breast cancer screening in the general population.

There are two types of mammograms: screening and diagnostic. Screening mammograms are for routine use at recommended intervals to detect unanticipated breast cancer in asymptomatic women. Screening mammography must be performed on a regular basis in order to reduce breast cancer mortality. Diagnostic mammograms are performed either when a radiographic abnormality is detected on a screening mammogram or when the patient or her care provider notice a change or a problem in her breast. Mammography is also used to assist in interventional breast procedures, such as stereotactic breast biopsy and needle localization (Bland & Copeland, 2009; Silverstein, Recht, Lagios et al., 2009).

Newer, digital mammography techniques provide dramatic improvements in the visualization of lesions for interpreting physicians and greater ease of examination for the patient.

The mammography examination takes only a few minutes and has only minimal radiation exposure. During a mammogram, the breast is manually compressed in the mammography unit by a registered mammography technologist in two different views: the craniocaudal view (compression from top to bottom) and the mediolateral oblique view (from side to side). Other views may be obtained when a patient has a palpable or image-detected abnormality requiring more focused or directed examination. The nurse should educate the patient on the importance of regular screening mammography, immediate pursuit of attention upon discovery of any palpable abnormality, and the availability of comfort options such as disposable foam pads to ease discomfort during compression.

Ultrasound

Ultrasonography (ultrasound) is used as a diagnostic adjunct to mammography to help distinguish fluid-filled cysts from other lesions. A thin coating of lubricating jelly is spread over the area to be imaged. A transducer is then placed on the breast. The transducer transmits high-frequency sound waves through the skin toward the area of concern. The sound waves that are reflected back form a two-dimensional image, which is then displayed on a computer screen. No radiation is emitted during the procedure. The technique diagnoses cysts with great accuracy but cannot definitively rule out malignant lesions. Due to its limited specificity, ultrasound should not be used for routine screening (Silverstein, Recht, Lagios et al., 2009).

Magnetic Resonance Imaging

MRI of the breast produces very detailed cross-sectional images using magnetic fields rather than X-rays. An IV injection of gadolinium, a contrast dye, is given to improve visibility. The patient lies face down and the breast is placed through a depression in the table. A coil is placed around the breast, and the patient is placed inside the MRI machine. The entire procedure takes about 30 to 40 minutes.

MRI is most useful in patients with proven breast cancer, when assessing for multifocal (more than one tumor in the same quadrant of the breast) or multicentric (more than one tumor in different quadrants of the breast) disease, chest wall involvement, tumor recurrence, or response to chemotherapy. The procedure can also identify occult (undetectable) breast cancer and determine the integrity of saline or silicone breast implants. It is not recommended for routine screening in the general population, but may be appropriate for individuals who have a lifetime risk of 15% to 20% based on predictive models, who have a personal history of invasive breast cancer or ductal carcinoma in situ, or other elevating risk factors. The risks of false-positive and false-negative exam results should be discussed, and MRI screening should be performed at the discretion of the patient and care provider (Silverstein, Recht, Lagios et al., 2009).

Some disadvantages of MRI include high cost, variations in technique and interpretation, and the potential for patient claustrophobia. The procedure cannot always accurately distinguish between malignant and benign breast conditions. MRI is contraindicated in patients with implantable metal devices such as aneurysm clips, pacemakers, and ports of tissue expanders because of the magnetic force acting on metallic objects. Foil-backed medication patches should be removed prior to MRI to avoid burns to the skin.

Breast Biopsy

Percutaneous needle biopsy, or minimally invasive breast biopsy, is as accurate as open **surgical biopsy** and should always be the first modality for breast tissue sampling. This type of biopsy allows for definitive diagnosis with lower morbidity than surgical biopsy and lower cost for the procedure (Silverstein, Recht, Lagios et. al., 2009). The nurse educates the patient prior to the procedure, answers questions, and offers emotional support.

Fine-Needle Aspiration

Fine-needle aspiration (FNA) is a noninvasive biopsy technique that is generally well tolerated by most women. A local anesthetic may or may not be used. For palpable masses, a surgeon performs the procedure. A small-gauge needle (25- or 22-gauge) attached to a syringe is inserted into the mass or area of nodularity. Suction is applied to the syringe, and multiple passes are made through the mass. A simple cyst often disappears on aspiration, and the fluid is usually discarded. If no fluid is obtained, any cellular material obtained in the hub of the needle is spread on a glass slide or placed in a preservative and sent to the laboratory for analysis. For nonpalpable masses, the same procedure can be performed by a radiologist or surgeon using ultrasound guidance.

FNA is less expensive than other diagnostic methods, and results are usually available quickly; however, due to lower sensitivity and specificity, close clinical correlation is necessary.

Ultrasound-Guided Breast Biopsy

Ultrasound-guided breast biopsy is a minimally invasive procedure wherein the physician uses the ultrasound to visualize the lesions and guide the needle for sampling (Fig. 33-1). It is the preferred biopsy modality for all lesions visible by ultrasound (Silverstein, Recht, Lagios et al., 2009). The patient lies supine on a table and, after thoroughly cleaning the skin, injecting subcutaneous analgesia such as lidocaine, and making a small nick in the skin, the physician inserts a needle to

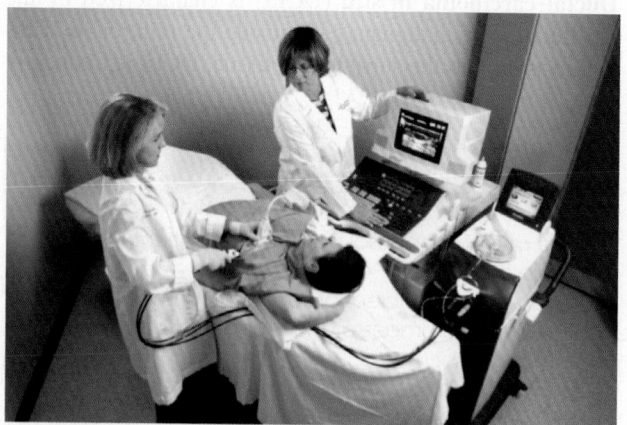

FIGURE 33-1 Ultrasound-guided breast biopsy. Courtesy of Mammotome.

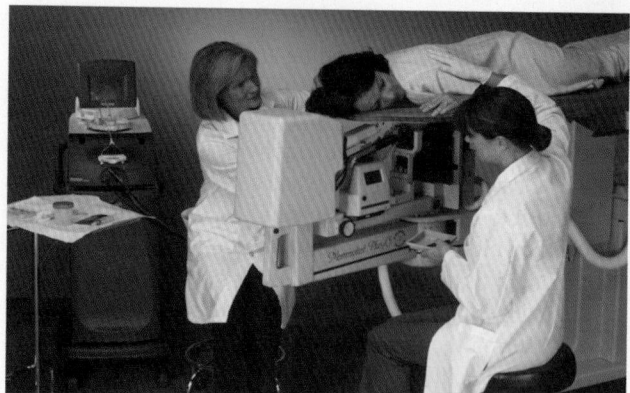

FIGURE 33-2 Stereotactic breast biopsy. Courtesy of Mammotome.

obtain specimens. The needle may or may not have vacuum-assistance to help obtain adequate specimens. The biopsy needle is typically 12- to 18-gauge without vacuum assistance, and 7- to 12-gauge with vacuum assistance. Several tissue samples are obtained and sent to the lab for analysis. A small titanium clip should be placed in the biopsy cavity for documentation of correct sampling site, for future mammogram evaluation, and for locating the site should further treatment be warranted.

Stereotactic Breast Biopsy

Stereotactic core biopsy is another minimally invasive procedure that uses X-ray guidance to obtain breast tissue samples (Fig. 33-2). It is the preferred biopsy modality for microcalcifications and lesions not visible by ultrasound. The patient lies prone on the stereotactic table, and the breast is suspended through an opening and compressed between two X-ray plates. Digital mammography images are obtained, and the exact coordinates of the lesion to be sampled are located with the aid of a computer. After sterilizing the skin, a local anesthetic is injected into the entry site on the breast. A small nick is made in the skin, a core needle is inserted, and samples of the tissue are taken for pathologic examination. Often, several passes are taken to ensure adequate tissue sampling. Clip placement is necessary for this type of biopsy as well.

Magnetic Resonance Imaging–Guided Breast Biopsy

MRI-guided breast biopsy is logistically similar to **stereotactic biopsy** and is used increasingly for lesions that cannot be visualized under mammography or ultrasound. Special concern is necessary for equipment safety in the magnetic field, and MRI-specific biopsy equipment is used.

Surgical Biopsy

When minimally invasive breast biopsy is not feasible, an excisional or surgical biopsy may be used to remove an entire lesion and a surrounding margin of normal appearing breast tissue. This type of biopsy may also be referred to as a *lumpectomy*. Depending on the clinical situation, a frozen section analysis of the specimen may be performed

at the time of the biopsy by the pathologist, who does an immediate intraoperative reading and provides a provisional diagnosis. Surgical biopsy is usually performed using local anesthesia and IV sedation and often follows *wire needle localization*, wherein mammography or ultrasonography are used to locate the lesion and place a guide wire through the skin and into the area of suspicion. The surgeon may then follow the guide wire down to the lesion for precise removal and minimal tissue loss.

The nurse plays an important role in surgical breast biopsy. During the preoperative visit, the nurse assesses the patient for specific educational, physical, or psychosocial needs. The nurse should review medical and psychosocial history and facilitate conversation regarding fears, concerns, and questions. Patients are often worried not only about the procedure but also about the potential implications of the pathology results. The nurse should provide a thorough explanation and written materials to reinforce education.

The patient should discontinue any anticoagulant therapy prior to the procedure. The patient may be instructed not to eat or drink for several hours or after midnight the night before the procedure, depending on the type of biopsy planned. Most breast biopsy procedures today are performed with the use of moderate sedation and local anesthesia.

Immediate postoperative assessment includes monitoring the effects of the anesthesia and inspecting the surgical dressing for any signs of bleeding. Once the sedation has worn off, the nurse reviews the care of the biopsy site, pain management, and activity restrictions with the patient. Prior to discharge from the ambulatory surgical center or the office, the patient must be able to tolerate fluids, ambulate, and void. The patient must have someone to drive her home. The dressing covering the incision is usually removed after 48 hours, but the Steri-Strips, which are applied directly over the incision, should remain in place for approximately 7 to 10 days. The use of a supportive bra following surgery is encouraged to limit movement of the breast and reduce discomfort. A follow-up telephone call from the nurse 24 to 48 hours after the procedure can provide the patient with the opportunity to ask any questions and can be a source of great comfort and reassurance.

Most women return to their usual activities the day after the procedure but are encouraged to avoid jarring or high-impact activities for 1 week to promote healing of the biopsy site. Discomfort is usually minimal, and most women find acetaminophen sufficient for pain relief, although a mild opioid may be prescribed if needed. Follow-up after the biopsy includes a return visit to the surgeon for discussion of the final pathology report and assessment of the healing of the biopsy site.

Staging

There are two primary staging systems for cancer. The American Joint Committee on Cancer (AJCC) classifies tumors using information on the size of the tumor and the extent of spread within the breast and nearby organs (T), involvement in lymph nodes (N), and spread to distant organs (M). This staging system is very commonly used in clinical settings and assigns a stage of I, II, III, or IV according to the determined T, N, and M classification. Stage I indicates an early stage breast cancer, and IV indicates the most advanced (Edge, Byrd, Compton et al., 2009). The SEER Summary Stage system is another classification that is more commonly used in data reporting and tumor registries. This system classifies tumors as local-stage (confined to the breast), regional-stage (spread to surrounding tissue or regional lymph nodes), and distant-stage (metastasized or spread to distant organs) (Johnson & Adamo, 2008).

Prognosis

The two most important prognostic factors associated with breast cancer are tumor size and axillary lymph node involvement.

In general, a smaller tumor is associated with a better prognosis. Prognosis also depends on the extent of spread of the breast cancer. Women who have more advanced stage at diagnosis have a lower 5-year relative survival rate, as do women with larger tumor size at diagnosis. The 5-year relative survival rate for localized disease is 98%, for regional disease is 84%, and for distant-stage disease is 23% (Horner, Ries, Krapcho et al., 2009). The most common route of regional spread is to the axillary lymph nodes. Other sites of lymphatic spread include the internal mammary and supraclavicular nodes. Distant metastasis can affect any organ, but the most common sites are bone, lung, liver, pleura, adrenals, skin, and brain. Amplification of certain genes such as *HER2/neu* (discussed later in this chapter) or excessive amounts of their protein product may represent a poorer prognosis. Box 33-2 lists other prognostic factors.

Types

Ductal Carcinoma In Situ

Ductal carcinoma in situ (DCIS) is characterized by the proliferation of malignant cells inside the milk ducts without invasion into the surrounding tissue. DCIS is frequently

---

BOX 33-2 **Factors Affecting Prognosis for Breast Cancer**

- Age and menopausal status of the patient
- Stage of disease
- Histologic and nuclear grade of the primary tumor
- Estrogen and progesterone receptor status of the primary tumor
- Proliferative capacity of the tumor
- *HER2/neu* gene amplification

From Breast Cancer Treatment, NCI.

manifested on a mammogram with the appearance of calcifications, and it is considered breast cancer stage 0. Treatment options include breast-conserving surgery and radiation therapy with or without tamoxifen, total mastectomy with or without tamoxifen, and breast-conserving surgery without radiation therapy (NCI, 2009).

Infiltrating Ductal Carcinoma

Infiltrating ductal carcinoma, the most common histologic type of breast cancer, accounts for 75% of all cases. The tumors arise from the duct system and invade the surrounding tissues. They often form a solid irregular mass in the breast.

Infiltrating Lobular Carcinoma

Infiltrating lobular carcinoma accounts for 5% to 10% of breast cancers. The tumors arise from the lobular epithelium and typically occur as an area of ill-defined thickening in the breast. They are often multicentric and can be bilateral.

Medullary Carcinoma of the Breast

Medullary carcinoma accounts for about 5% of breast cancers, and it tends to be diagnosed more often in women younger than 50 years. The tumors grow in a capsule inside a duct. They can become large and may be mistaken for a fibroadenoma. The prognosis is often favorable.

Medical and Nursing Management

A multidisciplinary team approach to treatment for breast cancer allows for an individualized plan of care based upon careful consideration of the optimal treatment for the stage and biological characteristics of the tumor; the patient's personal preference, performance status, and age; and the potential risks and benefits of all treatment options. Treatment decisions should be made by the patient and her physician. Most women who are diagnosed with breast cancer will undergo some type of surgery, and many will also have radiation therapy, chemotherapy, hormone therapy, and/or biologic therapy. The treatment guidelines for breast cancer are available via free registration from the National Comprehensive Cancer Network at nccn.org/professionals/physician_gls/PDF/breast.pdf (ACS, 2010).

Surgical Management

The primary goal of surgery is to obtain local control of the disease by removing the cancer from the breast, and to determine the stage and extent of disease. Because breast cancer is now diagnosable at earlier stages, options for less invasive surgical procedures are available.

Procedures

LUMPECTOMY. In a lumpectomy, the surgeon removes the cancerous tissue and a border of normal tissue. This usually follows a wire needle localization procedure to mark the tumor or the metallic clip left from the biopsy. Patients who undergo lumpectomy almost always undergo 5 to 7 weeks of radiation therapy afterward. Patients who have a lumpectomy

or breast conservation surgery followed by radiation therapy have the same predicted long-term survival as patients who choose to undergo mastectomy. Appropriate patient selection is critical when planning surgical intervention (Khan & Eladoumikdachi, 2010). A woman who undergoes lumpectomy may also have regional lymph nodes removed to determine if the cancer has spread beyond the breast.

SIMPLE MASTECTOMY. In a simple or total mastectomy, the entire breast and nipple-areola complex are removed, without axillary lymph node dissection (ALND). Total mastectomy may be performed for patients with noninvasive breast cancer, or DCIS, which does not have a tendency to spread to the lymph nodes. It may also be performed prophylactically for patients who are at high risk for breast cancer. A total mastectomy may also be performed in conjunction with **sentinel lymph node** biopsy (SLNB) for patients with invasive breast cancer.

MODIFIED RADICAL MASTECTOMY. **Modified radical mastectomy** is performed to treat invasive breast cancer. The procedure involves removal of the entire breast tissue, including the nipple-areola complex. In addition, a portion of the axillary lymph nodes is also removed in ALND. Box 33-3 discusses hand and arm care after ALND.

If immediate breast reconstruction is desired, the patient is referred to a plastic surgeon prior to the mastectomy, so that she has the opportunity to explore all available options. In modified radical mastectomy, the pectoralis major and pectoralis minor muscles are left intact, unlike in radical mastectomy, in which the muscles are removed.

RADICAL MASTECTOMY. Radical mastectomy includes removal of the entire breast and lymph nodes under the arm,

---

BOX 33-3 | **Patient Education**

Hand and Arm Care After Axillary Lymph Node Dissection

- Avoid blood pressures, injections, and blood draws in affected extremity.
- Use sunscreen (>15 SPF) for extended exposure to sun.
- Apply insect repellent to avoid insect bites.
- Wear gloves for gardening.
- Use cooking mitt for removing objects from oven.
- Avoid cutting cuticles; push them back during manicures.
- Use electric razor for shaving armpit.
- Avoid lifting objects greater than 5 to 10 pounds.
- If a trauma or break in the skin occurs, wash the area with soap and water, and apply an OTC antibacterial ointment (Bacitracin or Neosporin).
- Observe the area and extremity for 24 hours; if redness, swelling, or a fever occurs, call the surgeon or nurse.

and removal of the underlying pectoralis major and minor muscles. This technique is currently very rarely used due to the proven effectiveness and significantly decreased morbidity associated with less aggressive procedures such as modified radical mastectomy, total mastectomy, and lumpectomy.

BREAST CONSERVATION THERAPY. The goal of **breast conservation treatment**, including lumpectomy, wide excision, partial or segmental mastectomy, and quadrantectomy, is to excise the tumor in the breast completely and obtain clear margins while achieving an acceptable cosmetic result. If the procedure is being performed to treat a noninvasive breast cancer, lymph node removal is not necessary. For an invasive breast cancer, lymph node removal is indicated. The lymph nodes are removed through a separate semicircular incision in the axilla. Breast conservation along with radiation therapy in stage I and stage II breast cancer has demonstrated survival rates equal to that of modified radical mastectomy.

SENTINEL LYMPH NODE BIOPSY. SLNB is used for pathologic axillary staging for patients with breast cancer. The sentinel lymph nodes are the first nodes in the lymphatic basin to receive drainage from the primary tumor in the breast and are identified by injecting a radioactive tracer, blue dye, or both around the tumor in the breast. The tracer travels via the lymphatic pathways to the sentinel nodes. The surgeon locates the nodes, excises them, and sends them for pathologic analysis. If cancer cells are present in the sentinel nodes, the likelihood of cancer in other lymph nodes is high, so the surgeon performs a complete ALND. If the sentinel lymph nodes are free of cancer, ALND is not necessary. Sentinel lymph node biopsy is considered best practice, and is the standard of care for staging invasive breast cancer as it is accurate and spares patients considerable morbidity and sequelae associated with complete dissection. Figure 33-3 shows the lymphatic drainage of the breast.

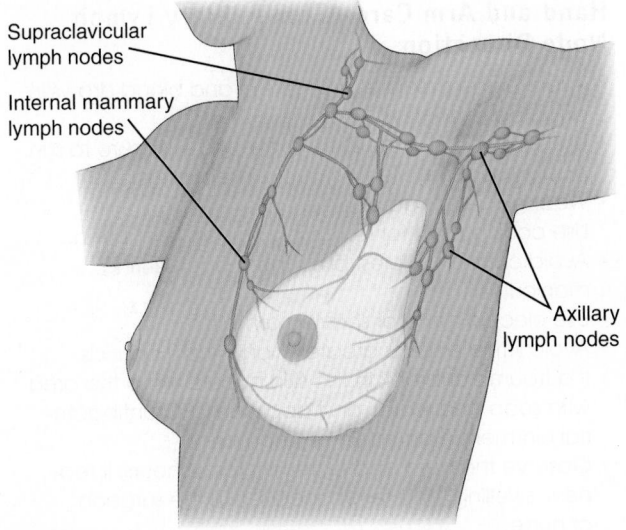

Supraclavicular lymph nodes

Internal mammary lymph nodes

Axillary lymph nodes

FIGURE 33-3 Lymphatic drainage of the breast.

Although SLNB is a less invasive procedure than ALND and results in a shorter recovery period, a patient who has undergone SLNB also has many difficult issues surrounding her breast cancer diagnosis and treatment. The nurse must listen, provide emotional support, and refer the patient to appropriate specialists when indicated.

Complications for the Surgical Patient

LYMPHEDEMA. Lymphedema results from impaired lymph fluid flow through the draining lymphatic vessels after lymph node dissection. An accumulation of lymph fluid develops in the surrounding and dependent tissues, leading to swelling, fibrosis of the soft tissues, neurologic complications such as pain and paresthesias, and infection. Continuous assessment and early identification of signs and symptoms of lymphedema should be integral in the care of patients undergoing therapy for breast cancer. Risk for lymphedema depends on the type of therapy received, and is more common with patients who undergo axillary lymph node dissection. Referral to a lymphedema specialist is key to management of this complication (Lawenda, Mondry, & Johnstone, 2009).

> ! **NURSING ALERT**
> *To prevent lymphedema or lymphangitis (infection of the lymph vessels), nurses should place a sign above the bed of a patient following mastectomy or node dissection not to perform blood pressures, blood draws, injections, or IV insertions on the operated side. Lymphatic drainage is altered due to node dissection, causing the potential for fluid to accumulate in the affected extremity. Complications of infiltration, phlebitis, or trauma can result if the affected extremity is used. Some patients will obtain a medical alert bracelet with this warning.*

HEMATOMA AND SEROMA FORMATION. Hematoma, a collection of blood inside the surgical cavity, may occur after either mastectomy or breast conservation and usually develops within the first 12 hours after surgery. The nurse assesses for signs and symptoms of hematoma at the surgical site, which may include swelling, tightness, pain, and bruising of the skin. The surgeon should be notified immediately for gross swelling or increased bloody output from the drain. While most hematomas are small and resolve without intervention, some must be surgically evacuated. Refer to Box 33-4 for drain care.

A seroma, a collection of serous fluid, may accumulate under the breast incision after mastectomy or breast conservation or in the axilla. Signs and symptoms include swelling, heaviness, discomfort, and a sloshing of fluid. Seromas may develop temporarily after the drain is removed or if the drain is in place and becomes obstructed. Seromas rarely pose a threat and may be treated by unclogging the drain or manually aspirating the fluid with a needle and syringe.

INFECTION. Infection is a risk after any surgical procedure. This risk may be higher in patients with accompanying

BOX 33-4

Surgical Breast Cancer Patient With a Drainage Device

A drain is placed in the surgical wound at the time of surgery to evacuate drainage from the surgical site. The tubing has multiple perforations on the distal end (in the wound site) and the tubing is attached to a device externally that collects the drainage. Suction is maintained by compression of the device. The drain is usually sutured to the skin. The typical device used for breast surgery is called a *Jackson Pratt* (JP), a bulb-like device (see Figure).

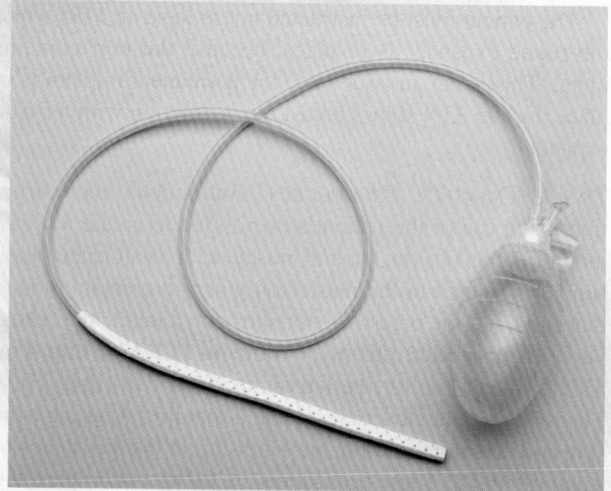

The nurse and patient or care provider are aware that the device must be compressed to maintain suction at the wound bed. If the device is fully inflated, it must be emptied to maintain the vacuum necessary to facilitate drainage away from the wound bed.

The nurse explains the procedure to the patient and/or care provider, brings a measuring device such as an ounce medicine cup (if limited drainage is expected) or a graduated cylinder, and explains the importance of hand washing before the procedure (maximum capacity of the JP is ~100 mL). Nonsterile gloves are donned.

The JP drainage device is unclipped from the patient's gown, and using sterile technique, the spout plug is opened on the JP bulb. The device will fully expand since the suction has been released (image above reveals fully expanded JP; no vacuum exists).

The nurse is careful not to touch the inside of the spout or plug and teaches this to patient and/or caregiver. The device is emptied by turning the bulb over and squeezing the bulb, so that contents can escape from the device. The amount and appearance of the drainage is recorded. The JP bulb is NEVER squeezed unless the spout plug is released.

An alcohol wipe can be used to clean the spout and plug. Maintaining sterile technique, the JP is completely compressed flat with one hand and, while compression is maintained, the plug is reattached with the other hand.

The nurse is aware that the system must be airtight to function. If rapid reinflation is noted after plugging the spout, an air leak should be suspected; the nurse attempts to compress and plug the device again and if the device remains inflated, the provider should be notified. The nurse secures the device to the patient's gown, below the wound (to facilitate drainage), to prevent pulling on the wound site and/or potential dislodgment. The nurse removes and discards gloves and washes hands thoroughly.

If multiple drains are used, they are labeled numerically (1, 2) or alphabetically (a, b) and drainage per drain is recorded as deemed by institutional policy or surgeon protocol.

Depending on surgeon preference and quality of the drainage, the patient may be instructed on how to "milk clots" through the tubing of the drainage device, which requires gentle compression of the tubing between the thumb and index finger, while stabilizing the exit site to prevent dislodgment of the tubing with the nondominant hand. Holding the tube securely above the obstruction is necessary to avoid pulling the tube out of the incision. *Note: This is only done depending on surgeon preference.*

The nurse teaches the patient and/or care providers observations of the drain site that require contacting the physician or nurse (e.g., sudden change in color of drainage, sudden cessation of drainage, signs or symptoms of an infection) as per surgeon's recommendation.

The nurse reinforces that the drain is typically ready for removal by the surgeon when draining <30 mL for a 24-hour period.

---

conditions such as diabetes, immune disorders, and advanced age, as well as in those with poor hygiene. Patients are taught to monitor for signs and symptoms of infection such as redness, warmth around the incision, tenderness, foul-smelling drainage, temperature greater than 100.4°F, and chills, and to contact the surgeon or nurse for evaluation should they notice any of these. For more severe infections, treatment consists of oral or IV antibiotics for 1 or 2 weeks.

Nursing management for patients undergoing surgery is discussed in the nursing process section later in this chapter.

Reconstructive Surgery

A variety of reconstructive options are available today for women who desire a correction in the size or the shape of the breast, including reduction **mammoplasty**, augmentation mammoplasty, and mastopexy (discussed shortly). Several options are also available to reconstruct the breast after a mastectomy.

RECONSTRUCTIVE SURGERIES FOR LUMPECTOMY. Reconstructive surgeries include reduction mammoplasty, augmentation mammoplasty, and mastopexy.

Reduction mammoplasty is usually performed on women who have large breasts. It is an outpatient procedure that is performed under general anesthesia. Most commonly, an anchor-shaped incision that circles the areola is made, extending downward and following the natural curve of the inframammary fold. Depending on the size of the breast, the nipple may be moved up to a higher position while still attached to the breast tissue, or it may be separated and transplanted to a new location. Drains are placed in the incision and remain for 2 to 5 days.

Augmentation mammoplasty is usually performed on women who desire larger or fuller breasts. The procedure is usually performed by placing a saline breast implant under the pectoralis muscle. The incision line can be placed in the inframammary fold, in the axilla, or around the areola. The procedure is performed as an outpatient procedure under general anesthesia. A drain is not necessary.

Mastopexy is performed when the patient is content with the size of her breasts but wishes to have the shape improved and a lift performed. The procedure is also an outpatient surgery.

RECONSTRUCTIVE PROCEDURES AFTER MASTECTOMY. Breast reconstruction can provide a significant psychological benefit for women who are already struggling with the emotional distress of losing a breast. A consultation with a plastic surgeon can help the patient understand procedures for which she is a candidate and the pros and cons of each. Factors to consider include body size and shape; comorbidities such as hypertension, diabetes mellitus, or obesity; personal habits such as smoking; and patient preference. The patient must be informed that although breast reconstruction can provide a good cosmetic result, it will never precisely duplicate the natural breast. Realistic preparation can help the patient avoid unrealistic expectations. Reconstruction is considered an integral component in the surgical treatment of breast cancer and is usually covered by insurance companies.

Many women elect immediate reconstruction at the time of the mastectomy operation. Delayed reconstruction is preferable in women who are having a difficult time deciding on the type of reconstruction they desire. It may also be preferable in patients with advanced disease, as in inflammatory breast cancer, in which the breast cancer treatments should be given without delay. Delays in healing after immediate reconstruction may interfere with the initiation of treatment.

TISSUE EXPANDER FOLLOWED BY PERMANENT IMPLANT. Breast reconstruction using a tissue expander followed by a permanent implant is commonly used. To accommodate an implant, the skin remaining after a mastectomy and the underlying muscle must gradually be stretched by a process called *tissue expansion*. The surgeon places a balloon-like device through the mastectomy incision underneath the pectoralis muscle. A small amount of saline is injected through a metal port intraoperatively to partially inflate the expander, followed by additional saline injections through the port at weekly intervals until the expander is fully inflated. It remains fully expanded for about 6 weeks to allow the skin to loosen. The expander is then exchanged for a permanent implant.

Advantages are a shorter operating time and a shorter recuperation period than for autologous reconstruction. A disadvantage is a tendency for the implant to feel firm and round, with little natural ptosis, or sag. Women with a small to medium opposite breast with little ptosis are good candidates for this procedure. Women who have had radiation or who have connective tissue disease are not good candidates because of the decreased elasticity of the skin.

The patient must be instructed not to have an MRI while the tissue expander is in place, because the port contains metal. This is not an issue once the permanent implant is in place. Figure 33-4 shows breast reconstruction with a tissue expander.

TISSUE TRANSFER PROCEDURES. Autologous reconstruction is the use of the patient's own tissue to create a breast mound. A flap of skin, fat, and muscle with its attached blood supply is rotated to the mastectomy site to create a mound that simulates the breast. Donor sites may include the **transverse rectus abdominis myocutaneous (TRAM) flap** (Fig. 33-5), gluteal flap, or the latissimus dorsi flap (Fig. 33-6). The results more closely resemble a real breast because the skin and fat from the donor sites are similar in consistency to a natural breast. These procedures are far more complex and involve longer recuperation than a tissue expander procedure. The risk for potential complications such as infection, bleeding, and flap necrosis is also greater.

The TRAM flap is the most commonly performed tissue transfer procedure. This involves completely detaching the skin, fat, muscle, and blood supply from the body and then transplanting them to the mastectomy site using microvascular surgery. Postoperatively, patients who have undergone TRAM procedures often face a lengthy recovery of 8 to 10 weeks and have incisions both at the mastectomy site and at the donor site in the abdomen. The nurse must assess the newly constructed breast site for changes in color, circulation, and temperature, because flap loss is a potential complication. Mottling or an obvious decrease in skin temperature is reported to the surgeon immediately. Breathing and leg exercises are essential, because the patient is more limited in her activity and is at greater risk for respiratory complications and deep vein thrombosis. Measures to help the patient reduce tension on the abdominal incision during the first postoperative week include elevating the head of the bed 45 degrees and flexing the patient's knees. Once the patient is able to ambulate, she can protect the surgical incision by splinting it and will gradually achieve a more upright position. The patient is instructed to avoid high-impact activities and lifting to prevent stress on the incision.

NIPPLE–AREOLAR RECONSTRUCTION. After the breast mound has been created and the site has healed, some women choose to have nipple–areola reconstruction. This is a minor surgical

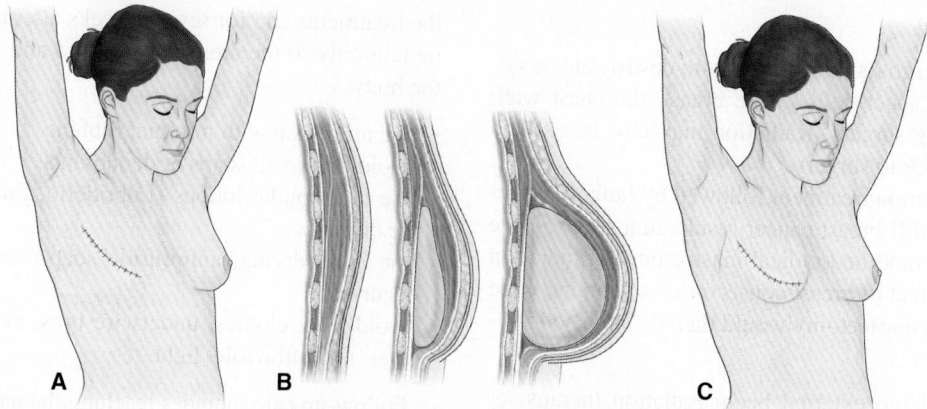

FIGURE 33-4 Breast reconstruction with tissue expander. (**A**) Mastectomy incision line prior to tissue expansion. (**B**) The expander is placed under the pectoralis muscle and is gradually filled with saline solution through a port to stretch the skin enough to accept a permanent implant. (**C**) The breast mound is restored. Although permanent, scars will fade with time. The nipple and areola are reconstructed later. Adapted from American Society of Plastic and Reconstructive Surgeons. *Breast reconstruction*. Arlington Heights, IL: Author.

procedure carried out either in the physician's office or at an outpatient surgical facility. The most common method of creating a nipple is with the use of local flaps of skin and fat from the center of the new breast mound, which are wrapped around each other to create a projecting nipple. The areola is created using a skin graft. The most common donor site is the upper inner thigh, because this skin has darker pigmentation than the skin on the reconstructed breast. After the nipple graft has healed, micropigmentation or tattooing can be performed to achieve a more natural color. The surgeon can usually match the reconstructed nipple–areola complex with that of the contralateral breast for an acceptable cosmetic result.

PROSTHETICS. A breast prosthesis, an external form that simulates the breast, is an option for women who are not candidates for or do not desire breast reconstruction. Prosthetics are available in different shapes, sizes, colors, and materials, and can be placed inside a bra.

Prior to discharge from the hospital, the nurse usually provides the patient with a temporary, lightweight, cotton-filled form that can be worn until the surgical incision is well healed. Then the patient can be fitted for a prosthesis. Insurance companies generally cover the cost of the prosthesis and the special bras that hold it in place. A breast prosthesis can provide a psychological benefit and assist the woman in resuming proper posture by balancing the weight of the remaining breast.

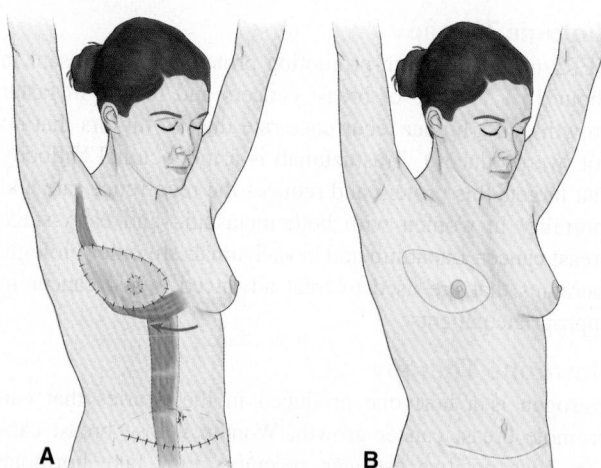

FIGURE 33-5 Breast reconstruction: transverse rectus abdominis myocutaneous (TRAM) flap. (**A**) A breast mound is created by tunneling abdominal skin, fat, and muscle to the mastectomy site. (**B**) Final location of scars. Adapted from American Society of Plastic and Reconstructive Surgeons. *Breast reconstruction*. Arlington Heights, IL: Author.

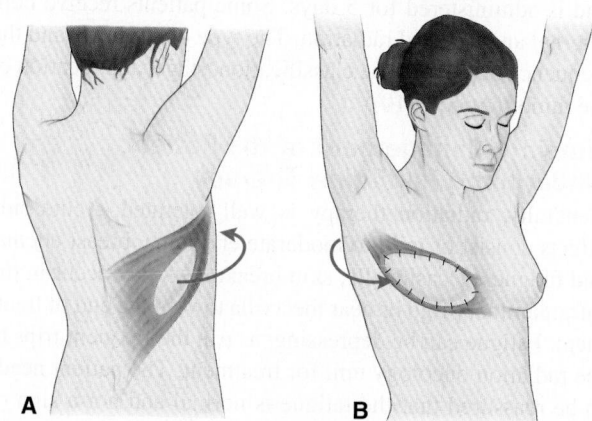

FIGURE 33-6 Breast reconstruction: latissimus dorsi flap. (**A**) The latissimus muscle with an ellipse of skin is rotated from the back to the mastectomy site. (**B**) Because the flap is usually not bulky enough to provide an adequate breast mound, an implant is often also required. Adapted from American Society of Plastic and Reconstructive Surgeons. *Breast reconstruction*. Arlington Heights, IL: Author.

Radiation

Patients may undergo radiation therapy to destroy any residual microscopic cancer cells in the breast, the chest wall, or axilla following surgery. Radiation may also be used to shrink a tumor prior to surgery.

Breast conservation treatment followed by radiation therapy for stage I and II breast cancer results in a survival rate equal to that of a modified radical mastectomy. If radiation therapy, a component of breast conservation treatment, were contraindicated, a mastectomy would then be indicated.

Types

Patients may undergo external beam radiation therapy, or internal radiation, also known as **brachytherapy**.

EXTERNAL BEAM RADIATION. External beam radiation typically begins about 6 weeks after breast conservation surgery to allow the surgical site to heal. If systemic chemotherapy is indicated, radiation therapy usually begins after its completion. Before radiation begins, the patient undergoes a planning session called a *simulation*, in which the anatomic areas to be treated are mapped out and then identified with small permanent ink markings. External beam radiation delivers high-energy photons from a linear accelerator and is usually administered to the entire breast region. Each treatment lasts only a few minutes and is generally given 5 days a week for 5 to 7 weeks. After completion of radiation to the entire breast, many patients receive a "boost," a dose of radiation to the lumpectomy site where the cancer cells were located. The boost consists of the same dose of radiation but is less penetrating and directed to a smaller area. The treatments are not painful.

INTERNAL RADIATION THERAPY. Internal radiation therapy, or brachytherapy, involves inserting a radioactive substance sealed in needles, seeds, catheters, or wires directly into the breast. MammoSite is one form of internal radiation and is administered for 5 days. Some patients receive both internal and external radiation. The type of radiation and the frequency depend on the classification, stage, and location of the tumor (ACS, 2010).

Nursing Management of the Patient Undergoing Radiation Therapy

Generally, radiation therapy is well tolerated. Acute side effects consist of mild to moderate erythema, breast edema, and fatigue. Occasionally, skin breakdown may occur in the inframammary fold or near the axilla toward the end of treatment. Fatigue can be depressing, as can the frequent trips to the radiation oncology unit for treatment. The patient needs to be reassured that the fatigue is normal and not a sign of recurrence. Side effects usually resolve within a few weeks to a few months after treatment is completed. Rare long-term effects of radiation therapy include pneumonitis, rib fracture, and breast fibrosis.

Self-care instructions for patients receiving radiation are provided to assist in the maintenance of skin integrity during the treatments and for several weeks after completion. They pertain only to the area being treated and not to the rest of the body.

- Use mild soap with minimal rubbing.
- Avoid perfumed soaps or deodorants.
- Use hydrophilic lotions (Lubriderm, Eucerin, Aquaphor) for dryness.
- Use a nondrying, antipruritic soap (Aveeno) if pruritus occurs.
- Avoid tight clothes, underwire bras, excessive temperatures, and ultraviolet light.

Follow-up care includes teaching the patient to minimize sun exposure to the treated area, such as using sunblock with an SPF of 15 or above, and reassuring the patient that minor twinges and shooting pain in the breast are normal after radiation treatment.

Systemic Therapy

Systemic treatment uses anticancer, or antineoplastic, drugs that are given by vein or taken by mouth and travel throughout the body in the bloodstream. Chemotherapy, hormonal therapy, and biologic therapy are types of systemic treatment. **Neoadjuvant therapy** (drug treatment given prior to surgery) is used to shrink a tumor before removing it. Adjuvant therapy (agents that modify the effects of other agents) is administered after surgery and is used to eradicate any microscopic metastases or residual cancer cells in the body. The type of systemic therapy used depends on the tumor type, size, and the presence or absence of lymph node metastases, as well as the age and performance status of the patient.

For some patients who have metastatic disease, or breast cancer that has traveled beyond the breast and into other organs or parts of the body, surgery is no longer an option, and systemic therapy is the primary treatment choice.

Biologic Therapy

HER2/neu is a growth-promoting protein that is present in about 15% to 30% of breast cancers and results in faster growth and a higher recurrence rate than in tumors that do not overproduce it. Trastuzumab is a monoclonal antibody that targets this protein and reduces the recurrence rate and mortality in women with both metastatic and early-stage breast cancer. Lapatinib and bevacizumab are other biologic therapies that are used to treat advanced breast cancer in appropriate patients.

Hormone Therapy

Estrogen is a hormone produced in the ovaries that can promote breast cancer growth. Women whose breast cancers have positive estrogen receptors may take hormone therapy to block the effects of estrogen on tumor growth. Both premenopausal and postmenopausal women may take tamoxifen if their tumors test positive for hormone receptors. Tamoxifen is recommended for 5 years and has demonstrated significant reduction in the recurrence rate and in

TABLE 33-2 Adverse Reactions Associated With Adjuvant Hormonal Therapy Used to Treat Breast Cancer

Therapeutic Agent	Adverse Reactions/Side Effects
Selective Estrogen Receptor Modulator Tamoxifen	Hot flashes, vaginal dryness/ discharge/bleeding, irregular menses, nausea, mood disturbances; increased risk for endometrial cancer; increased risk for thromboembolic events (deep vein thrombosis, pulmonary embolism, superficial phlebitis)
Aromatase Inhibitors Anastrozole Letrozole Exemestane	Musculoskeletal symptoms (arthritis, arthralgia [joint pain], myalgia [muscle pain]), increased risk of osteoporosis/ fractures, nausea/vomiting, hot flashes, fatigue, mood disturbances

mortality. Sequelae of tamoxifen include endometrial cancer and blood clots.

Aromatase inhibitors such as letrozole, anastrozole, and exemestane are another hormone therapy option for postmenopausal women. These drugs block the production of an enzyme that makes small amounts of estrogen. They are not effective in premenopausal women because they do not stop the ovaries from creating estrogen. They have a lower side-effect profile than tamoxifen but can cause osteoporosis, bone fractures, and musculoskeletal problems (ACS, 2010). Table 33-2 lists potential adverse effects of different hormonal therapies for breast cancer. Box 33-5 addresses side-effect management of hormonal agents.

Chemotherapy

The indication for chemotherapy depends on the size of the tumor, lymph node involvement, the presence or absence of hormone receptors in the tumor, and the amount of HER2/neu present in the breast cancer cells. Combination chemotherapy, or the use of more than one drug, has proven to be more effective than single-drug regimens. The most common drugs recommended for use in early stage breast cancer are cyclophosphamide, docetaxel, doxorubicin, epirubicin, fluorouracil, methotrexate, and paclitaxel. Most chemotherapy regimens are given for 3 to 6 months, and the full cycle should be implemented and completed as soon as possible to maximize effectiveness (ACS, 2010).

Nursing Management of the Patient Undergoing Chemotherapy

Common physical side effects of chemotherapy for breast cancer vary with the type of treatment given and may include nausea, vomiting, bone marrow suppression, taste changes, alopecia (hair loss), mucositis (painful inflammation and

---

BOX 33-5 Patient Education

Managing Side Effects of Adjuvant Hormonal Therapy in Breast Cancer

Hot Flashes
- Wear breathable, layered clothing.
- Avoid caffeine and spicy foods.
- Perform breathing exercises (paced respirations).
- Consider medications (vitamin E, antidepressants) or acupuncture.

Vaginal Dryness
- Use vaginal moisturizers for everyday dryness (e.g., Replens, Vitamin E suppository).
- Apply vaginal lubrication during intercourse (e.g., Astroglide, K-Y jelly).

Nausea and Vomiting
- Consume a bland diet.
- Try to take medication in the evening.

Musculoskeletal Symptoms
- Take nonsteroidal analgesics as recommended.
- Take warm baths.

Risk of Endometrial Cancer
- Report any irregular bleeding to a gynecologist for evaluation.

Risk for Thromboembolic Events
- Report any redness, swelling, or tenderness in the lower extremities, or any unexplained shortness of breath.

Risk for Osteoporosis or Fractures
- Undergo a baseline bone density scan.
- Perform regular weight-bearing exercises.
- Take calcium supplements with vitamin D.
- Take bisphosphonates (e.g., alendronate) or calcitonin as prescribed.

ulcerations of the mucous membranes in the digestive tract), skin changes, and fatigue. A weight gain of more than 10 pounds occurs in about half of all patients; the cause is unknown. Premenopausal women may also experience temporary or permanent **amenorrhea** (absence of menstrual period) leading to sterility. Nurses play an important role in helping patients manage the physical and psychosocial sequelae of chemotherapy. Instructing the patient about the use of antiemetics and reviewing the optimal dosage schedule can help minimize nausea and vomiting. Measures to ease the symptoms of mucositis may include rinsing with normal saline or sodium bicarbonate solution, avoiding hot and spicy foods, and using a soft toothbrush. Some patients may require hematopoietic growth factors to minimize the effects of chemotherapy-induced neutropenia and anemia. Granulocyte colony-stimulating factors (G-CSFs) boost the white blood cell count, helping reduce the incidence of neutropenic fever and infection. Erythropoietin growth factor increases the production of red blood cells, thus decreasing the symptoms of anemia. The nurse instructs the patient and family on proper injection technique of hematopoietic growth factors and about symptoms that require follow-up with their provider.

The nurse may assist the patient in finding a wig prior to hair loss to alleviate the stress associated with alopecia. The nurse may provide a list of wig suppliers in the patient's geographic region. Familiarity with creative ways to use scarves and turbans may also help minimize the patient's distress. The patient needs reassurance that new hair will grow back when treatment is completed, although the color and texture may be different. The ACS offers a program called "Look Good, Feel Better" that provides useful tips for applying cosmetics during chemotherapy.

Chemotherapy may negatively affect the patient's self-esteem, sexuality, and sense of well-being. This, combined with the stress of a potentially life-threatening disease, can be overwhelming. Providing support and promoting open communication are important aspects of nursing care. Referring the patient to the dietitian, social worker, psychiatrist, or spiritual advisor can provide additional support. Numerous community support and advocacy groups are available for patients and their families. Complementary therapies, such as guided imagery, meditation, and relaxation exercises, can also be used in conjunction with conventional treatments. Refer to Chapter 6 for details on cancer care.

Treatment for Recurrent or Metastatic Breast Cancer

Breast cancer may recur locally (on the chest wall or in the conserved breast), regionally (in the remaining lymph nodes), or systemically (in distant organs). In metastatic disease, the bone, usually the hips, spine, ribs, or pelvis, is the most common site of spread. Other sites of metastasis include the lungs, liver, pleura, and brain.

The overall prognosis and optimal treatment are determined by a variety of factors, such as the site and extent of recurrence, the time to recurrence from the original diagnosis, history of prior treatments, the patient's performance status, and any existing comorbid conditions. Patients with bone metastases generally have a longer overall survival compared with metastases in visceral organs.

Local recurrence in the absence of systemic disease is treated aggressively with surgery, radiation, and hormonal therapy. Chemotherapy may also be used for tumors that are not hormonally sensitive. Local recurrence may be an indicator that systemic disease will develop in the future, particularly if it occurs within 2 years of the original diagnosis.

Metastatic breast cancer involves control of the disease rather than cure. Treatment includes hormonal therapy, chemotherapy, and targeted therapy. Surgery or radiation may be indicated in select situations. Premenopausal women who have hormonally dependent tumors may eliminate the production of estrogen by the ovaries through **oophorectomy** or suppression of estrogen synthesis by luteinising hormone releasing hormone (LHRH) agonists such as leuprolide or goserelin.

Patients with advanced breast cancer are monitored closely for signs of disease progression. Baseline studies are obtained at the time of recurrence. These may include complete blood count; comprehensive metabolic panel; tumor markers; bone scan; CT of the chest, abdomen, and pelvis; and MRI of symptomatic areas. Additional X-rays may be performed to evaluate areas of pain or abnormal areas seen on bone scan. These studies are repeated at regular intervals to assess for effectiveness of treatment and to monitor progression of disease.

Nursing Management of the Patient With Recurrent or Metastatic Breast Cancer

Nurses play an important role in not only educating patients and managing their symptoms but in providing emotional support. Many patients find that recurrence of the disease is more distressing than the initial cancer diagnosis. They not only have to deal with another round of treatments but are faced with a greater uncertainty about their future and long-term survival. The nurse can help the patient identify coping strategies and set priorities to optimize quality of life (QOL). Family members and significant others should be included in the treatment plan and follow-up care. Referrals to support groups, psychiatry, social work, and complementary medicine programs, such as guided imagery, meditation, and yoga, should be made as indicated.

Nurses are also key members of the interdisciplinary team providing palliative care. The highest priorities should include alleviating pain and providing comfort measures. A frank discussion with the patient and family regarding their preferences for end-of-life care should occur before the need arises, to ensure a smooth transition without disruption of care. Referrals to hospice and home health care should be initiated as necessary.

Survivorship and Quality of Life

With increased early detection and improved treatment modalities, women with breast cancer have become the largest group of cancer survivors. Sequelae of diagnosis and treatment may affect the patient and her family for a long time. It is important that nurses learn about these effects and intervene appropriately to optimize QOL. The nurse can be pivotal in providing education and support to the patient as she makes very difficult and emotional decisions. The patient should be prepared early for the potential long-term effects of the disease and its treatments, so that she has realistic expectations and can make informed decisions.

Many breast cancer survivors have difficulty with issues pertaining to sexuality and menopausal symptoms. Estrogen withdrawal from chemotherapy-induced menopause and hormonal treatments can also lead to a variety of symptoms, including hot flashes, vaginal dryness, urinary tract infections (UTIs), weight gain, decreased sex drive, and increased risk for osteoporosis. Some of these symptoms can also lead to fatigue and sleep disturbances. Hormone therapy to alleviate symptoms is contraindicated in women with breast cancer. Certain chemotherapeutic agents can cause long-term cardiac effects and impaired cognitive functioning, such as difficulty concentrating. Rare long-term effects of radiation can include pneumonitis and rib fractures. Long-term sequelae after breast surgery may include lymphedema (mainly after ALND), pain, and sensory disturbances.

Long-term psychosocial sequelae may include anxiety, depression, uncertainty about the future, and fear of recurrence. Many of these sequelae may affect the patient's partner and children. In the workplace, the patient may suffer from fear of discrimination, concern over coworkers' reactions, fear of losing benefits, and lack of physical stamina. The nurse should facilitate open conversation with the patient about her fears and concerns.

NURSING PROCESS

The Patient Undergoing Surgery for Breast Cancer

Assessment

The health history is a valuable tool to assess the patient's reaction to the diagnosis and her ability to cope with it. Pertinent questions include the following:

- How is the patient responding to the diagnosis?
- What coping mechanisms does she find most helpful?
- What psychological or emotional supports does she have and use?
- Is there a partner, family member, or friend available to assist her in making treatment choices?
- What are her educational needs?
- Is she experiencing any pain or discomfort?

Diagnosis

Major preoperative nursing diagnoses may include the following:

- Deficient knowledge about the planned surgical treatments
- Anxiety related to the diagnosis of cancer
- Fear related to specific treatments and body image changes
- Risk for ineffective coping (individual or family) related to the diagnosis of breast cancer and related treatment options
- Decisional conflict related to treatment options

Major postoperative nursing diagnoses may include the following:

- Pain and discomfort related to surgical procedure
- Disturbed sensory perception related to nerve irritation in affected arm, breast, or chest wall
- Disturbed body image related to loss or alteration of the breast
- Risk for impaired adjustment related to the diagnosis of cancer and surgical treatment
- Self-care deficit related to partial immobility of upper extremity on operative side
- Risk for sexual dysfunction related to loss of body part, change in self-image, and fear of partner's responses
- Deficient knowledge:
  - Drain management after breast surgery
  - Arm exercises to regain mobility of affected extremity
  - Hand and arm care after an axillary lymph node dissection (ALND)

Potential complications may include the following:

- Lymphedema
- Hematoma/seroma formation
- Infection

Planning

The major goals may include increased knowledge about the disease and its treatment; reduction of preoperative and postoperative fear, anxiety, and emotional stress; improvement of decision-making ability; pain management; improvement in coping abilities; improvement in sexual function; and the absence of complications.

Interventions

Both pre- and postoperative nursing care greatly impact the patient's surgical experience.

Preoperative Nursing Interventions

PROVIDING EDUCATION AND PREPARATION ABOUT SURGICAL TREATMENTS. Patients with newly diagnosed breast cancer are expected to absorb an abundance of new information during a very emotionally difficult time. The nurse plays a

(continued on page 926)

key role in reviewing treatment options by reinforcing information provided to the patient and answering any questions. The nurse fully prepares the patient for what to expect before, during, and after surgery. Patients undergoing breast conservation with ALND, or a total or modified radical mastectomy, generally remain in the hospital overnight (or longer if they have immediate reconstruction). Surgical drains will be inserted in the mastectomy incision and in the axilla if the patient undergoes an ALND. The patient should be informed that she will go home with the drain(s) and that complete

instructions about drain care will be provided prior to discharge. In addition, the patient should be informed that she will often have decreased arm and shoulder mobility after an ALND and that she will be shown range-of-motion exercises prior to discharge. Refer to Box 33-6 for exercises after breast surgery. The patient should also be reassured that appropriate analgesia and comfort measures will be provided to alleviate any postoperative discomfort.

REDUCING FEAR AND ANXIETY AND IMPROVING COPING ABILITY. The nurse must help the patient cope with the physical as

---

BOX 33-6 **Patient Education**

Exercise After Breast Surgery

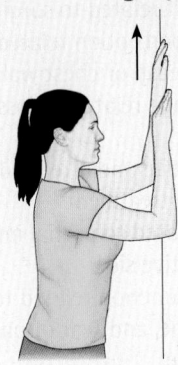

1. *Wall handclimbing.* Stand facing the wall with feet apart and toes as close to the wall as possible. With elbows slightly bent, place the palms of the hand on the wall at shoulder level. By flexing the fingers, work the hands up the wall until arms are fully extended. Then reverse the process, working the hands down to the starting point.

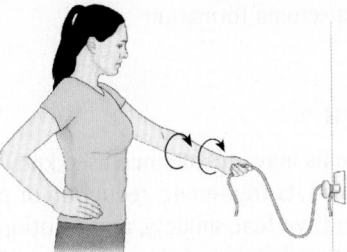

2. *Rope turning.* Tie a light rope to a doorknob. Stand facing the door. Take the free end of the rope in the hand on the side of surgery. Place the other hand on the hip. With the rope-holding arm extended and held away from the body (nearly parallel with the floor), turn the rope, making as wide swings as possible. Begin slowly at first; speed up later.

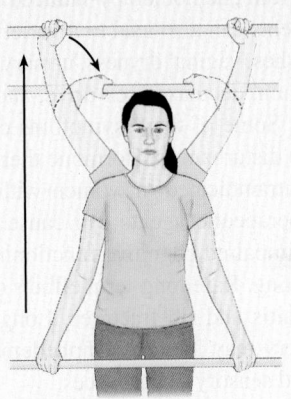

3. *Rod or broomstick lifting.* Grasp a rod with both hands, held about 2 feet apart. Keeping the arms straight, raise the rod over the head. Bend elbows to lower the rod behind the head. Reverse maneuver, raising the rod above the head, then return to the starting position.

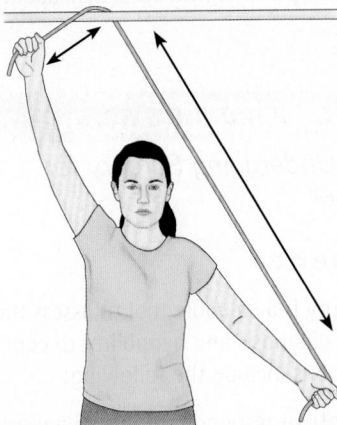

4. *Pulley tugging.* Toss a light rope over a shower curtain rod or doorway curtain rod. Stand as nearly under the rope as possible. Grasp an end in each hand. Extend the arms straight and away from the body. Pull the left arm up by tugging down with the right arm, then the right arm up and the left down in a see-sawing motion.

well as the emotional effects of surgery. Many fears may emerge during the preoperative phase. These can include fear of pain, mutilation (after mastectomy), and loss of sexual attractiveness; concern about inability to care for oneself and one's family; concern about taking time off from work; and coping with an uncertain future. Providing the patient with realistic expectations about the healing process and expected recovery can help alleviate fears. Maintaining open communication and assuring the patient that she can contact the nurse at any time with questions or concerns can be a source of comfort. The patient should also be made aware of available resources at the treatment facility, as well as in the breast cancer community, such as social workers, psychiatrists, and support groups. Some women find it helpful and reassuring to talk to a breast cancer survivor who has undergone similar treatments.

PROMOTING DECISION-MAKING ABILITY. Choosing the optimal treatment can be very overwhelming for patients. The nurse can be instrumental in ensuring that the patient and family members truly understand their options and can weigh the risks and benefits of each option. The patient may be presented with the option of having breast conservation treatment followed by radiation or a mastectomy. The nurse can explore the issues with the individual patient by asking questions such as the following:

- How would you feel about losing your breast?
- Are you considering breast reconstruction?
- If you choose to retain your breast, would you consider undergoing radiation treatments 5 days a week for 5 to 6 weeks?

Questions such as these can help the patient focus. Once the patient's decision is made, it is very important to support it.

Postoperative Nursing Interventions

RELIEVING PAIN AND DISCOMFORT. Many patients tolerate the breast surgery quite well and have minimal pain during the postoperative period. Patients who have had more invasive procedures, such as a modified radical mastectomy with immediate reconstruction, may have considerably more pain. All patients are discharged home with analgesic and are encouraged to take it if needed. Sometimes patients complain of a slight increase in pain after the first few days of surgery as they regain sensation around the surgical site and become more active. Patients who report severe pain must be evaluated to rule out any potential complications. Alternative methods of pain management, such as taking warm showers and using distraction methods such as guided imagery, may also be helpful.

MANAGING POSTOPERATIVE SENSATIONS. Because nerves in the skin and axilla are often cut or injured during breast surgery, patients experience a variety of sensations such as tenderness, soreness, numbness, tightness, pulling, and twinges

along the chest wall, in the axilla, and along the inside aspect of the upper arm. After mastectomy, some patients experience phantom sensations and report a feeling that the breast and/or nipple are still present. Sensations usually persist for several months and then begin to diminish. Patients should be reassured that this is a normal part of healing and that these sensations are not indicative of a problem.

PROMOTING POSITIVE BODY IMAGE. Patients who have undergone mastectomy often find it very difficult to view the surgical site for the first time. No matter how prepared the patient may think she is, the appearance of an absent breast can be very emotionally distressing. Some patients who have undergone breast conservation treatment may find it difficult to view their surgical incisions, although this is rare. Ideally, the patient sees the incision for the first time when she is with the nurse or another health care provider who is available for support. The nurse first assesses the patient's readiness and provides gentle encouragement and a private setting.

PROMOTING POSITIVE ADJUSTMENT AND COPING. Providing ongoing assessment of how the patient is coping with her diagnosis of breast cancer and her surgical treatment is important in determining her overall adjustment. Assisting the patient in identifying and mobilizing her support systems can be beneficial to her well-being. The patient's spouse or partner may need guidance, support, and education as well. The patient and partner may benefit from a wide network of available community resources, including the Reach to Recovery program of the ACS, advocacy groups, or a spiritual advisor. Encouraging the patient to discuss issues and concerns with other patients who have had breast cancer may help her to understand that her feelings are normal and that other women who have had breast cancer can provide invaluable support and understanding.

The patient may also have considerable anxiety about the treatments that will follow surgery and their implications. Providing her with information about the plan of care and referring her to the appropriate members of the health care team also promote coping during recovery. Some women require additional support to adjust to their diagnosis and the changes that it brings. Box 33-7 lists talking points for patients and partners.

IMPROVING SEXUAL FUNCTION. Once discharged from the hospital, most patients are physically allowed to engage in sexual activity. However, any change in the patient's body image, self-esteem, or the response of her partner may increase her anxiety level and affect sexual function. Some partners may have difficulty looking at the incision, whereas others may be completely unaffected. Encouraging the patient to openly discuss how she feels about herself and about possible reasons for a decrease in libido such as fatigue, anxiety, and self-consciousness may help clarify issues for her. Helpful suggestions for the patient may include varying the time of day for sexual activity, such as

(continued on page 928)

BOX 33-7

Talking With Patients and Partners

For patients in the diagnostic phase: We've talked about your recent breast cancer diagnosis. It's natural for you to be full of feelings, concerns, and fears for yourself and your family. Sometimes it's hard to find someone to speak freely with. Would you share what you've been thinking, feeling, and worrying about recently?

For partners in the diagnostic phase: We've talked about your partner's recent breast cancer diagnosis. It's natural for you to have a lot of feelings, concerns, and fears for your partner, yourself, and your family. Partners often feel that they have to be strong for the patient or for others and that they aren't entitled to express their own concerns. Would you share what you've been thinking about, feeling, or worrying about recently?

For patients in the postsurgical phase: Many women who have had breast surgery, especially mastectomy or extensive lumpectomy, are concerned not only with their own loss, but with how their partner will accept it. How have you felt about losing (part of) your breast? How has it changed your body image? Your sense of your sexuality? Your desire for intimacy?

For partners in the postsurgical phase: Many partners of women who have had breast surgery are concerned, as are the women themselves, about how they'll respond to the loss. How have you felt about your partner's losing (part of) her breast? How has it changed

her attractiveness for you? Your sexual feelings toward her? Your desire for intimacy?

For patients in the adjuvant therapy phase: Given the type of therapy (radiation, chemotherapy, hormone therapy) you're going to have, what side effects do you anticipate? What do you know about them? Let's talk about ways to reduce and handle potential side effects.

For partners in the adjuvant therapy phase: Given the type of therapy (radiation, chemotherapy, hormone therapy) your partner is going to have, what side effects do you anticipate? What do you know about them? Let's talk about ways to reduce and handle potential side effects, and how it might help you to be familiar with them.

For patients in the ongoing recovery phase: As you plan your return to a full work schedule, what measures—setting priorities, delegating responsibility, managing stress—might help you make the necessary physical and emotional adjustments? What have you learned about balancing work, family, and play in your life?

For partners in the ongoing recovery phase: As your partner plans her return to a full work schedule, what strategies have you thought about using to make your own physical and emotional adjustments, so that you don't continue to be overburdened at work and at home?

From Hoskins, C. N., & Haber, J. (2000). Adjusting to breast cancer. *American Journal of Nursing, 100*(4), 26–32.

when the patient is less tired, assuming positions that are more comfortable, and expressing affection using alternative measures such as hugging, kissing, and manual stimulation.

Most patients and their partners adjust with minimal difficulty if they openly discuss their concerns. However, if issues cannot be resolved, a referral may be helpful. The ambulatory care nurse in the outpatient clinic or hospital should inquire whether the patient is having difficulty with sexuality issues, because many patients are reluctant or embarrassed to bring it up themselves.

Evaluation

Expected preoperative patient outcomes may include:

1. Exhibits knowledge about diagnosis and surgical treatment options:
   a. Asks relevant questions about diagnosis and available surgical treatments
   b. States rationale for surgery
   c. Describes advantages and disadvantages of treatment options
2. Verbalizes willingness to deal with anxiety and fears related to the diagnosis and the effects of surgery on self-image and sexual functioning

3. Demonstrates ability to cope with diagnosis and treatment:
   a. Verbalizes feelings appropriately and recognizes normalcy of mood lability
   b. Proceeds with treatment in timely fashion
   c. Discusses impact of diagnosis and treatment on family and work
4. Demonstrates ability to make decisions regarding treatment options in timely fashion

Expected postoperative patient outcomes may include:

1. Reports that pain has decreased, and states that pain and discomfort management strategies are effective
2. Identifies postoperative sensations and recognizes that they are a normal part of healing
3. Exhibits clean, dry, and intact surgical incisions without signs of inflammation or infection
4. Lists the signs and symptoms of infection to be reported to the nurse or surgeon
5. Verbalizes feelings regarding change in body image
6. Discusses meaning of the diagnosis, surgical treatment, and fears appropriately
7. Participates actively in self-care activities:
   a. Performs exercises as prescribed
   b. Participates in self-care activities as prescribed

8. Discusses issues of sexuality and resumption of sexual relations

9. Demonstrates knowledge of postdischarge recommendations and restrictions:
   a. Describes follow-up care and activities
   b. Demonstrates appropriate care of incisions and drainage system
   c. Demonstrates arm exercises and describes exercise regimen and activity limitations during postoperative period
   d. Describes care of affected arm and hand and lists indications to contact the surgeon or nurse

10. Experiences no complications:
    a. Identifies signs and symptoms of reportable complications (e.g., redness, heat, pain, edema)
    b. Explains how to contact appropriate health care providers in case of complications

REPRODUCTIVE DISORDERS

MENSTRUAL DISORDERS

Menstrual disorders consist of any irregularity within the menstrual cycle: **amenorrhea** (absence of menses), **dysmenorrhea** (painful menses), **menorrhagia** (excessive menstrual bleeding), **metrorrhagia** (excessive and prolonged menstrual bleeding), irregular bleeding patterns, **premenstrual syndrome** (PMS), and **premenstrual dysphoric disorder** (PMDD).

Any menstrual cycle changes should be discussed with the patient's health care provider, so that appropriate diagnosis, management, and treatment can occur.

AMENORRHEA

Amenorrhea is divided into two types: primary, which is the absence of menses until age 16 or absence of secondary sex characteristics and menarche by age 14; and secondary, which is more common and occurs after a regular pattern of menstrual cycles has already been established.

Pathophysiology

Primary amenorrhea is caused by hypothyroidism, **Turner's syndrome**, pituitary disorders, or in-utero exposure to DES (diethylstilbestrol). Those with Turner's syndrome have only one normal "X" chromosome and have absence of breast or pubic hair development. DES was a drug given to pregnant women between 1940 and 1970 to help prevent miscarriages. It was later discovered that the drug affected the reproductive organs of the female offspring, causing infertility. These patients will have secondary sex characteristics but incomplete development of reproductive organs.

When menses do not occur for 6 months or more after a regular pattern of cycles has been established, it is considered **secondary amenorrhea**. Pathologic causes of secondary amenorrhea include eating disorders, pregnancy, excessive weight loss, low body mass index (BMI) of less than 22% of average, excessive exercise, endocrine dysfunction, medications, or anatomical deviations such as **cervical stenosis** or **imperforate hymen**.

This type of amenorrhea is common among athletes and those with rapid weight loss due to bariatric surgery or starvation dieting. Amenorrhea may also be caused by hormonal contraceptives such as oral contraception, Depo-Provera, or Implanon.

Clinical Manifestations and Assessment

Patients who have an established menstrual cycle pattern will report a history of the absence of menstruation or other symptoms that are associated with the underlying cause of amenorrhea. Those patients 16 years of age who have developed secondary sex characteristics will generally seek medical evaluation if they have not experienced any menstruation, as will 14-year-olds who have not developed any secondary sex characteristics. A detailed menstrual history is critical in determining abnormality in menstrual patterns, and should be accompanied by pregnancy and sexual histories, contraception use, medications, exercise patterns, and weight history.

Once pregnancy has been excluded, appropriate labs should include thyroid stimulating hormone (TSH) and prolactin levels, Follicle-stimulating hormone (FSH), luteinizing hormone (LH, also known as lutropin), dehydroepiandrosterone sulfate (DHEAS), and serum testosterone. Physical examination of the external and internal genitalia by a health care provider will determine any anatomical deviations that may cause obstruction of the vaginal outlet.

Medical and Nursing Management

A withdrawal bleed occurs with the administration of medroxyprogesterone acetate (Provera) 10 mg for 7 to 10 days. An oral contraceptive pill can then be initiated to assist with regulation of the menstrual cycle. Alternatively, the patient can take progesterone the first week of each month or every 3 months for a withdrawal bleed. It is important to instruct the patient that if she has not had a menstrual period for several months, she can expect a heavy flow after taking Provera and may experience severe cramping as a result. Therapies for painful menstruation are listed below.

DYSMENORRHEA

Painful menstruation has two classifications: primary and secondary. Primary dysmenorrhea occurs at the onset of menarche and the early following years after establishing a cycle. It is estimated that 40% to 50% of women suffer from dysmenorrhea, resulting in loss of time from school or work (Altman & Wolcyzk, 2010).

Pathophysiology

The classic characterization of primary dysmenorrhea is crampy abdominal and/or lower back pain just before the onset of bleeding and persisting for the first few days into the menstrual flow. It is due to an excessive production of **prostaglandins** in the lining of the uterus, which causes smooth muscle contractions.

Secondary dysmenorrhea begins well after the menstrual cycle has been established, usually after age 20, and is suggestive of an underlying pathology such as **endometriosis** (most common cause) or a pelvic infection. It may be related to intrauterine devices (IUDs), congenital anomalies, ovarian cysts, or benign or malignant tumors.

Clinical Manifestations and Assessment

Primary dysmenorrhea is often characterized by sharp, intermittent abdominal pain that is accompanied by headache, fatigue, backache, nausea, diarrhea, or constipation. The gastrointestinal (GI) symptoms are caused by prostaglandins. Symptoms for secondary dysmenorrhea begin earlier in the cycle and last longer. There is also a change in bowel habits, rectal pressure, and painful defecation due to the influence production of prostaglandins. Table 33-3 compares primary and secondary dysmenorrhea.

Medical Management

Nonsteroidal anti-inflammatories (NSAIDs) and hormonal contraceptives are the mainstay of treating primary dysmenorrhea due to their antiprostaglandin effect.

Ibuprofen and naproxen are available over the counter (OTC). Other NSAIDs available by prescription include mefenamic acid (Ponstel), prescription-strength ibuprofen and naproxen and cyclooxygenase (COX)-2 inhibitors (Celebrex). By blocking the prostaglandin production, pain usually will not occur or will be mild in comparison.

While effective, NSAIDs can have a negative impact on the GI system, therefore care must be taken to avoid long-term use of these medications. Combined oral contraceptives (COCs) are very beneficial in treatment for this condition as the combined hormones inhibit ovulation as well as

decrease uterine flow and thereby decrease uterine contractility. COCs are a good choice for sexually active women who desire birth control as well as relief from dysmenorrhea.

Management of secondary dysmenorrhea is aimed at the causative factor through the use of the appropriate diagnostic tests. The same medications listed above may also be used to alleviate pain.

Nursing Management

Nurses can teach patients how to accurately keep a menstrual diary that will assist in tracking patterns of menstrual discomfort and pain (Fig. 33-7). Advising the patient to take an OTC NSAID 1 to 2 days prior to the onset of menses will help to inhibit prostaglandin production and help to decrease the amount of abdominal pain and cramping. Patients who take OTC proton pump inhibitors (PPIs), such as Prevacid OTC or a prescription PPI, need to be instructed on the proper administration of these drugs, which will help to protect the lining of the stomach from the effects of the NSAIDs. It is recommended that PPIs be taken on an empty stomach. The patient should eat something 30 to 60 minutes after taking the PPI to allow the medication to start working. Also, taking the NSAID with food will help to minimize stomach upset.

Nonpharmacological therapy includes supplementation with magnesium, calcium, and vitamins B and E, but further studies are needed to accurately define appropriate dosages and outcomes (Borgelt, O'Connell, Smith et al., 2010). Low-level localized heat, such as a heating pad or wrap, for 15 to 20 minutes intermittently can be beneficial in easing uterine contractility. It is important to instruct the patient not to use too high heat or to use heat for prolonged periods of time due to the risk of burns.

ABNORMAL UTERINE BLEEDING

Any uterine bleeding that deviates from a patient's usual pattern is considered abnormal uterine bleeding (AUB).

Bleeding that occurs at regular intervals but is in excessive amounts and/or duration is known as menorrhagia. Bleeding that occurs frequently but irregularly is known as metrorrhagia. Menometrorrhagia is heavy bleeding of prolonged duration occurring at irregular intervals. Any persistent abnormal uterine bleeding can lead to iron-deficiency anemia if left

TABLE
33-3 Comparing Primary and Secondary Dysmenorrhea

Aspect	Primary Dysmenorrhea	Secondary Dysmenorrhea
Quality of Pain	Sharp, intermittent pain	
Timing	Begins with onset of menarche	Symptoms begin earlier in cycle and last longer
Age of onset	Occurs with menarche	Occurs between ages 30 and 40
Additional symptoms	Headache, fatigue, backache, dizziness, nausea, diarrhea, and constipation	Change in bowel habits, rectal pressure, painful defecation, dyspareunia

Menstrual Cycle Log

Month and Date	Bleeding Y/N	Symptoms	Lenght of time	Intensity	Treatment	Impact
1						
2						
3						
4						
5						
6						
7						
8						
9						
10						
11						
12						
13						
14						
15						
16						
17						
18						
19						
20						
21						
22						
23						
24						
25						
26						
27						
28						
29						
30						
31						

KEY:
Symptoms:
NS-no symptoms
N/V-nausea/vomiting
TS-trouble sleeping
S-sensitive to light, sight or sound
D-disturbances in sight/vision
B-bleeding: heavy, moderate, light
GI-diarrhea or constipation
BE-binge eating
FC-food cravings
Intensity:
Mild
Moderate
Severe

I-irritable
FN-feeling nervous
T-tired

C-abdominal cramping or pain
H-headache
M-mood: depressed, anxious

Treatment:
M-medicine
BR-bed rest
HCP-contacted healthcare professional

FIGURE 33-7 Menstrual log.

undiagnosed and untreated. Cycles greater than 35 days are known as **oligomenorrhea**, and cycles occurring less than 21 days are known as **polymenorrhea**.

Causes

Coagulation disorders such as thrombocytopenia or Von Willebrand's disease are causes of AUB and should be ruled out as an underlying factor. Women who take unopposed estrogen are likely to develop AUB, as well as those with liver diseases that impair fibrinogen synthesis. Certain endocrine disorders, including Cushing's syndrome, Addison's disease, thyroid disorders, and polycystic ovarian syndrome (PCOS) can cause irregular uterine bleeding.

Other causes include pelvic infections caused by sexually transmitted infections (STIs; gonorrhea, *Chlamydia*, trichomonas), endometriosis, trauma, benign tumors, or lesions. Pregnancy can also cause irregular bleeding and must be ruled out. Refer to Chapter 35 for details on STIs.

Medical and Nursing Management

Menstrual pad counts assist the health care provider in determining the approximate amount of blood loss through the description of the saturation of sanitary pads or tampons on an hourly basis. Characteristics of the flow, such as the color of blood and presence of clots are to be noted as well. Physical examination of the genitalia and a Pap smear are

performed. It is important that the patient undergo appropriate diagnostic testing to determine underlying pathology of AUB prior to treatment. This may include a pelvic ultrasound and endocrine tests, as described earlier.

Once any pathology has been ruled out, it is appropriate for the patient to be treated with hormonal contraception that will regulate the menstrual cycle, decrease bleeding and cramping associated with heavy bleeding, and decrease any incidence of anemia associated with excessive blood loss. Progestin-releasing IUDs reduce blood flow, as does implanted progesterone.

PREMENSTRUAL SYNDROME AND PREMENSTRUAL DYSPHORIC DISORDER

PMS is a cluster of behavioral, emotional, and physical symptoms that typically occur the week prior to menstruation and may continue into the first week of the menstrual cycle. Symptoms usually resolve with the onset of menstrual flow but can persist for the first few days of bleeding. PMDD is a more severe form of PMS and is recognized by diagnostic criteria developed by the American Psychiatric Association (APA). Symptoms must be present consistently during the luteal phase (second half of the menstrual cycle) and have a negative impact to some degree on the woman's life.

It is estimated that approximately 75% to 80% of women of reproductive age are affected by symptoms related to menstrual cycle changes that interfere with daily lifestyle and relationships. There is no known cause of PMS/PMDD, although research indicates these symptoms are most likely due to fluctuating levels of estrogen, progesterone, and serotonin.

Clinical Manifestations and Assessment

More than 100 physical and behavioral symptoms are associated with PMS/PMDD and range from mild to severely disabling (Box 33-8).

Symptoms may be misdiagnosed as menopause, anxiety, bipolar disorder, metabolic disorders (such as diabetes), chronic fatigue syndrome, or rheumatological diseases. It is important that health care providers perform a comprehensive, systematic approach to properly diagnosing patients with PMS/PMDD, so that appropriate therapy may be initiated.

Medical Management

Menstrual cycle diaries (see Fig. 33-7, p. 931) are kept for two to three menstrual cycles. Presence or absence of symptoms are noted daily, with their impact on daily activities. Providers are able to view trends of symptoms based on these logs. Nurses can encourage lifestyle changes that will impact on the severity of symptoms. These lifestyle changes include regular exercise, which promotes increased circulation of endorphins released from exercise; avoidance of excessive caffeine (coffee, soda, tea, energy drinks, and chocolate) and

---

BOX 33-8 **Focused Assessment**

Premenstrual Syndrome

Be alert for the following signs and symptoms:
Physical:
- Weight gain
- Abdominal bloating
- Constipation or diarrhea
- Breast tenderness
- Acne
- Headache
- Heart palpitations

Behavioral:
- Irritability
- Depression
- Mood swings
- Increased appetite
- Overwhelming fatigue
- Insomnia
- Crying spells

Cognitive:
- Decreased concentration
- Paranoia
- Indecision
- Sensitivity to rejection
- Suicidal ideation

---

sodium-rich foods; decreased alcohol intake, and smoking cessation. Randomized trials of increased complex carbohydrates during the luteal phase have revealed a decrease in the severity of PMS symptoms (Medhurst, 2010). Low serum calcium can cause muscle irritability, therefore it is recommended that the patient ensure a daily intake of 1,200 to 1,600 mg of calcium daily.

Vitamin B_6 50 to 500 mg/day has been met with mixed success. Other nonpharmacological therapies include oral magnesium, vitamin E supplements, and evening primrose oil. Due to flaws in recent studies of evening primrose oil, results are preliminary and do not appear to provide any significant improvement of symptoms (Bayles & Usatine, 2009).

A single-blind, randomized, placebo-controlled study of the use of *Ginkgo biloba* L revealed a significant decrease in the severity of PMS symptoms among the *Ginkgo* control group (Ozgoli, Selselei, Mojab et al., 2009). Further studies on complementary and alternative therapies are warranted.

For women who do not respond to nonpharmacological therapy, pharmacological management is considered. The use of oral contraceptives has proven to be of great benefit for those with physical and emotional symptoms of PMS. Continuous contraception for 3 months' duration or longer often alleviates PMS symptoms.

Selective serotonin reuptake inhibitors (SSRIs) and serotonin-norepinephrine reuptake inhibitors (SNRI) have

shown efficacy in mood stabilization. Pulsed or cyclical dosing of SSRIs can also be used during the 2 weeks prior to and including the week of menstrual flow.

Gonadotropin-releasing hormone (GnRH) agonists (Lupron or Depo-Provera) suppress the menstrual cycle, but long-term use can produce consequences of menopause due to the lack of estrogen, which may lead to irreversible osteoporosis. NSAIDs are beneficial for physical symptoms including headache and dysmenorrhea.

Nursing Management

Nurses take accurate and detailed health and nutritional histories and screen for symptoms of anxiety and/or depression, and suicidal and homicidal ideation.

If the nurse recognizes any signs of an inability to manage anger, suicide/homicide ideation, depression, or anxiety, he or she should encourage the patient to seek evaluation by the appropriate health care provider. They also help patients with stress management techniques, compliance with medication, and therapeutic lifestyle changes (such as smoking cessation, regular exercise, and eating a low-fat, low-cholesterol, low-sodium diet). Pain management is similar to that discussed under dysmenorrhea (NSAIDs, PPIs, and heat pad use).

VULVOVAGINAL INFECTIONS

Fungal and bacterial infections in the vagina are common, self-limited gynecological conditions that occur in women of all ages due to a disruption in the normal pH of the vagina. The pH of the vagina is 3.5 to 4.5 and provides the normal environment for *Lactobacillus acidophilus* to exist. This is a healthy bacterium that thrives in the vaginal ecosystem and provides protection against infections by inhibiting growth of anaerobes.

Lactobacillus metabolizes glycogen to lactic acid in the vagina and maintains normal vaginal pH. Antibiotics, menopause (or estrogen deficiency), oral contraceptives, spermicides, and diabetes are known to decrease the number of healthy lactobacilli.

Without the lactobacillus, there is a proliferation of anaerobic activity, the pH of the vagina is altered, and an overgrowth of bacteria is produced. Table 33-4 summarizes types of vaginal infections and vaginitis. **Bacterial vaginosis** (BV) and **vulvovaginal candidiasis** (VVC) are discussed in detail below.

Nurses play a vital role in helping patients to understand the mode of infection, treatment, and self-care modalities. Although not considered STIs, BV and VVC can coexist with STIs; therefore, appropriate screening for these infections is important. It is also important to note that the creams and suppositories used in the treatment of VVC and BV weaken latex condoms, diaphragms, and cervical caps; therefore,

caution should be taken to avoid sexual intercourse during treatment.

BACTERIAL VAGINOSIS

The most common vaginal infection is BV or Gardnerella, occurring in approximately 40% to 50% of all cases of vaginitis.

Risk Factors

Risk factors for developing BV include new or multiple sexual partners, douching, an increase in sexual activity, and coexisting STIs. BV may also be present after a menstrual cycle due to the increase in the vaginal pH. If left untreated in pregnancy patients, BV is a risk factor for premature labor as well as postabortion endometritis and cuff cellulitis (infection) after hysterectomy.

Clinical Manifestations and Assessment

Many patients who have BV are asymptomatic. Patients with symptomatic BV will report an increased malodorous, vaginal discharge or leukorrhea that is grayish white in color. Amines commonly found in the vagina become unstable when the pH is altered and release the characteristic "fishy" odor. The odor is generally more noticeable after sexual intercourse, sexual activity, or menses. Unprotected intercourse will produce the malodorous discharge due to the interaction of semen and normal vaginal amines. Women will sometimes report vaginal itching, dysuria, or pelvic pressure similar to that of a UTI due to the localized irritation of the urinary meatus from the discharge.

A swab of vaginal discharge taken from the vaginal walls and applied to two glass slides is known as a *wet mount*. One slide has saline added and the other has potassium hydroxide (KOH) added then is viewed under a microscope. The presence of *clue cells* (vaginal epithelial cells that are coated with bacteria) on the saline slide is a hallmark for diagnosing BV. The KOH-prepared slide will release amines and is known as a "whiff test." The presence of a fishy odor on the whiff test suggests BV. Nitrazine paper determines the pH, which will be greater than 4.5 for BV.

Medical and Nursing Management

The preferred medication for treatment of BV is metronidazole 500 mg twice daily for 7 days. If the patient is noncompliant, a single 2-g dose may be administered, although higher cure rates occur with the 7-day dose (Glass, 2009). The Centers for Disease Control and Prevention (CDC) no longer recommend the single-dose therapy due to its low efficacy. Metronidazole gel 0.75%, one 5-g applicator vaginally at bedtime for 7 nights is an alternative and is preferred to avoid any GI upset caused by oral medications. If an allergy to metronidazole exists, alternative therapies are oral

TABLE
33-4 Vaginal Infections and Vaginitis

Infection	Cause	Clinical Manifestations	Management Strategies
Candidiasis	Candida albicans, glabrata, or tropicalis	Inflammation of vaginal epithelium, producing itching, reddish irritation White, cheese-like discharge clinging to epithelium	Eradicate the fungus by administering an antifungal agent. Frequently used brand names of vaginal creams and suppositories are Monistat, Femstat, Terazol, and Gyne-Lotrimin. Review other causative factors (e.g., antibiotic therapy, nylon underwear, tight clothing, pregnancy, oral contraceptives). Assess for diabetes and HIV infection in patients with recurrent monilia.
Gardnerella-associated bacterial vaginosis	Gardnerella vaginalis and vaginal anaerobes	Usually no edema or erythema of vulva or vagina Gray-white to yellow-white discharge clinging to external vulva and vaginal walls	Administer metronidazole (Flagyl), with instructions about avoiding alcohol while taking this medication. If infection is recurrent, may treat partner.
Trichomonas vaginalis vaginitis (STD)	Trichomonas vaginalis	Inflammation of vaginal epithelium, producing burning and itching Frothy yellow-white or yellow-green vaginal discharge	Relieve inflammation, restore acidity, and reestablish normal bacterial flora; provide oral metronidazole for patient and partner.
Bartholinitis (infection of greater vestibular gland)	Escherichia coli Trichomonas vaginalis Staphylococcus Streptococcus Gonococcus	Erythema around vestibular gland Swelling and edema Abscessed vestibular gland	Drain the abscess; provide antibiotic therapy; excise gland of patients with chronic bartholinitis.
Cervicitis: acute and chronic	Chlamydia Gonococcus Streptococcus Many pathogenic bacteria	Profuse purulent discharge Backache Urinary frequency and urgency	Determine the cause: perform cytologic examination of cervical smear and appropriate cultures. Eradicate the gonococcal organism, if present: penicillin (as directed) or spectinomycin or tetracycline, if patient is allergic to penicillin. Tetracycline, doxycycline (Vibramycin) to eradicate chlamydia. Eradicate other causes.
Atrophic vaginitis	Lack of estrogen; glycogen deficiency	Discharge and irritation from alkaline pH of vaginal secretions	Provide topical vaginal estrogen therapy; improve nutrition if necessary; relieve dryness through use of moisturizing medications.

clindamycin 300 mg twice daily for 7 days; clindamycin 2% cream, one 5-g application vaginally at bedtime for 7 days, or clindamycin ovules 100 mg intravaginally once at bedtime for 3 days. Tinidazole, a newer-generation medication that is chemically related to metronidazole, was approved in 2007 by the U.S. Food and Drug Administration (FDA) for treatment of BV. Improved patient adherence due to once-a-day dosing and shorter duration of therapy is observed.

It is extremely important that the nurse educate the patient on avoidance of all alcoholic use while taking metronidazole and for 3 days after the last dose due to the disulfiram (Antabuse)-type reaction that is induced; this causes nausea, vomiting, flushing of the skin, chest pain, blurred vision, mental confusion, sweating, breathing difficulty, and anxiety.

CANDIDIASIS

VVC is predominantly caused by *Candida albicans*. Other non-albicans species that cause VVC include *C. tropicalis* and *C. glabrata*. It is estimated that approximately 25% of all vaginal infections are VVC, but that number is difficult to determine because it is not a reportable condition and because the availability of OTC treatments makes it hard to determine how many women are affected.

Risk Factors

Risk factors include use of broad-spectrum antibiotics (such as penicillins, cephalosporins, and tetracyclines), exogenous hormones, and corticosteroids. Other risk factors for

VVC include uncontrolled diabetes, obesity, and diets high in sugars or artificial sweeteners. New sexual partners, contaminated sex toys, or an increase in sexual activity may also change the pH of the vagina, making it more susceptible to infection. Some resources have suggested that wearing tightly fitted clothing and undergarments that are not made of a breathable material promote an environment for fungus to grow (Kruger & Botha, 2007). Males who are uncircumcised and do not practice good hygiene may harbor yeast and pass the infection onto their partners.

Clinical Manifestations and Assessment

The most common chief complaint is vulvar pruritus. Patients also complain of dysuria related to inflammation of the urinary meatus by the vulvar discharge. A urine specimen should be obtained to rule out any other source of infection. **Dyspareunia** or pain with intercourse may also be reported.

VVC differs from BV in that the discharge is generally thick, white and curd-like much like the appearance of cottage cheese and is odorless. It is adherent to the vaginal walls on speculum exam. On physical examination, the external genitalia is erythematous and adherent white discharge may be noted. Diagnosis is established based on a wet mount (a swab of the vaginal discharge on a glass slide that has been mixed with KOH). Under microscopic exam, the presence of hyphae is visible and Nitrazine will reveal a normal pH of 4.0 to 4.5. If there are clue cells or trichomonads present, it is indicative of a coexisting BV or trichomonas infection. A 48-hour culture will definitively diagnose the predominant causative factor.

Medical Management

Many women will self-diagnose and treat based on symptoms with OTC topical preparations containing azole (Monistat or Gyne-Lotrimin). This practice is not encouraged as patients may be self-treating for an infection that may not be VVC. It is important to educate patients to seek evaluation by a health care professional who can appropriately diagnose and treat any vaginal infection.

Topical antifungal agents that are used vaginally offer the most rapid relief. Terconazole (Terazol) cream is available in both 3- and 7-day preparations. This medication covers all three species of yeast, whereas the OTC preparations only cover *C. albicans*. Fluconazole (Diflucan) is a single dose oral medication that is effective against *Candida*, but there is a delay in symptom relief for up to 3 days. It is however, an effective treatment, particularly when treating a patient with coexisting BV who is using a vaginal preparation of metronidazole.

Nursing Management

The nurse's role in educating a patient with BV or VVC includes assessing for high-risk behaviors such as multiple sexual partners and unprotected sexual intercourse. If a patient is having recurrent vaginal infections, it is important for the patient to be evaluated by a health care professional to determine the cause.

Recurrent infections can be caused by nonadherence with medication therapy and poor hygiene. It is important to also assess any cross-contamination with sexual toys. Teaching patients and their partners about proper hygiene in addition to sterilization of sex toys can decrease recurrent infections.

If the cause is determined to be from diabetes, the nurse can assist the patient with compliance with dietary guidelines, proper blood glucose management, and hygienic practices.

STRUCTURAL DISORDERS

Physical strain or hormone deficiencies compromise the ability of the pelvic musculature to support pelvic organs. Weakening of this musculature causes pelvic organs to displace downward into the pelvic cavity to varying degrees.

PROLAPSE

The pelvic organs are supported by a complex system of ligaments and muscles that are protected by the bony pelvis. The bony pelvis serves as an attachment site for these ligaments and muscles. The uterus is located deep within the bony pelvis but is freely movable during physical examination. A series of muscles known as the pubococcygeal muscles extend from the pubic bone to the coccyx, encompassing the urethra, vagina, anus, and rectum.

If the muscles and ligaments are weakened, the uterus and bladder **prolapse** into the vaginal canal. Patients may or may not be aware of these structural defects until they become symptomatic or are discovered on physical examination. Types of prolapse include:

- *Cystocele:* The herniation of the bladder into the anterior vagina (Fig. 33-8A)
- *Rectocele:* The extrusion of the rectum into the posterior vagina (Fig. 33-8B)
- *Enterocele:* The descent of the small intestine into the vaginal vault (Fig. 33-8C)
- *Uterine prolapse:* Downward descent of the uterus into the vagina (Fig. 33-9)
- *Vault prolapse:* Top of the vagina prolapses after a hysterectomy

Pelvic organ prolapse increases with age. More than 300,000 surgical procedures are performed annually to correct these defects (Blandon, Bharucha, Melton et al., 2009). Up to 60% of these patients will have a history of a previous gynecological surgery, such as a hysterectomy.

Risk Factors

Increased pressure on the abdomen and pelvic floor from pregnancy or obesity causes the pelvic floor ligaments to

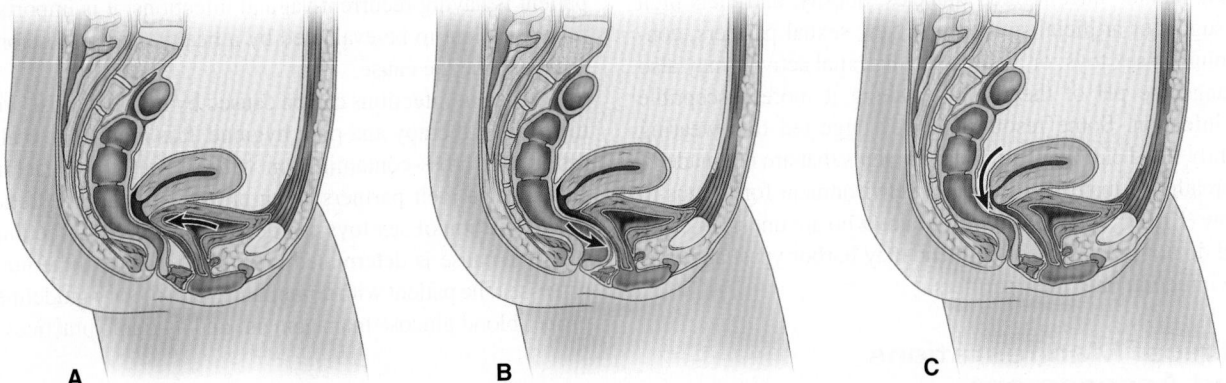

A **B** **C**

FIGURE 33-8 Diagrammatic representation of the three most common types of pelvic floor relaxation: (**A**) cystocele, (**B**) rectocele, and (**C**) enterocele. *Arrows* depict sites of maximum protrusion.

weaken. Direct injury to the levator ani or the stretching of the pudendal nerves during childbirth impairs the elasticity of the pelvic floor muscles (Storey, Aston, Price et al., 2009). Women who have more than one vaginal birth are at higher risk for developing prolapse, with risk increasing with each subsequent vaginal delivery. Estrogen helps with maintaining pelvic structure, therefore patients who are menopausal are more likely to develop a prolapse due to lack of estrogen. Smokers are at a higher risk of developing a prolapse; although the exact mechanism is unknown, it is thought to be due to the effects of smoking-related lifestyle factors (Miedel, Tegerstedt, Mæhle-Schmidt et al., 2009). Recreational or occupational activities such as repeated heavy lifting, runners, or jumpers actually have a decreased prevalence of prolapse (Miedel et al., 2009). This is related to a strengthening effect of exercise on those core and abdominal muscles that prevent the pelvic organs from displacement.

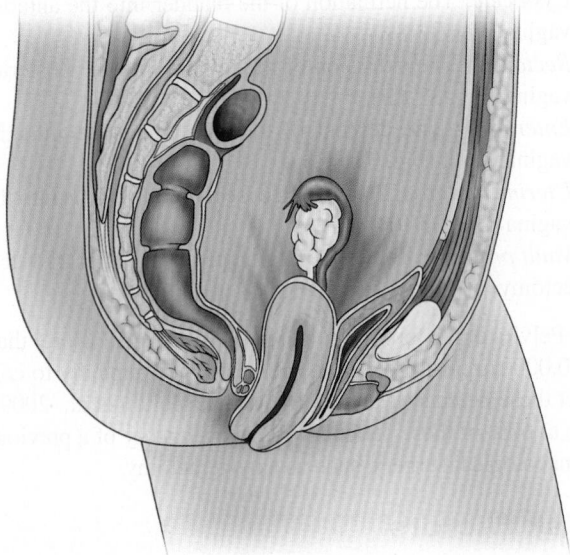

FIGURE 33-9 Complete prolapse of the uterus through the introitus.

Regardless of age, straining from constipation and increased intra-abdominal pressure from coughing are other risk factors for prolapse.

Clinical Manifestations and Assessment

Many patients who have a uterine or bladder prolapse will be asymptomatic, while others may seek evaluation by a health care provider because of a noticeable "bulge" in the vaginal area. Back pain in the absence of trauma may be present. Urinary incontinence is a common complaint with a bladder prolapse accompanied by pelvic pressure. Women will frequently complain of a UTI when, in fact, it is the prolapse that is producing the symptoms. Patients may also report difficulty having a bowel movement and will often need to place pressure on their perineal or vaginal areas in order to facilitate a bowel movement. Incomplete rectal evacuation may occur as a result of prolapse.

Medical and Nursing Management

Treatment depends upon the severity of the symptoms and degree of prolapse involved. Patients' general state of health and activity is also of concern if considering surgical intervention. Urodynamic testing evaluates bladder function. Electromyography (EMG) determines the type and severity of incontinence but also evaluates bladder filling and ability to store and release urine (McGovern, 2009). For mild uterine prolapse, a **pessary** is the first line of treatment. Pessaries are removable devices made of silicone, latex, plastic, or rubber that are inserted into the vagina to provide support. A variety of styles are available (Fig. 33-10).

Pelvic floor rehabilitation or pelvic floor muscle training (PFMT) offers a nonsurgical approach to patients who are motivated to adhere to the exercise schedule. **Kegel exercises** are a form of PFMT (Box 33-9). Physical therapists or urogynecologists who are specifically trained in PFMT teach the patient exercises that increase the strength of the pelvic floor muscle. Biofeedback programs feature assisted

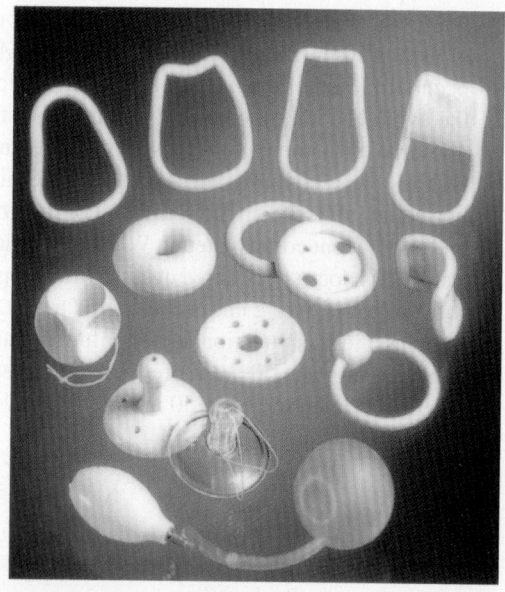
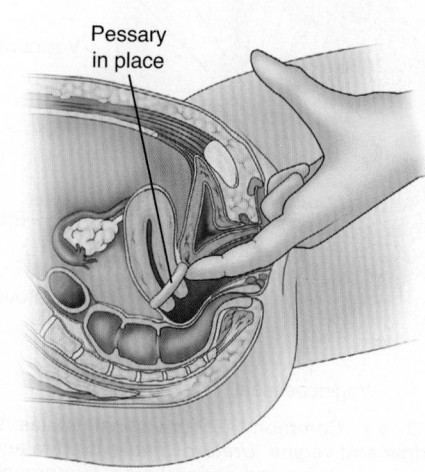

Pessary in place

FIGURE 33-10 Examples of pessaries. (**A**) Various shapes and sizes of pessaries available. (**B**) Insertion of one type of pessary.

pelvic floor exercises utilizing a functional electrical stimulator (FES) and are used to help patients contract the appropriate pelvic muscles. Nurses can become trained in PFMT and are able to effectively teach patients about proper use of FES equipment.

Reconstructive pelvic surgery depends upon the impact of the severity of symptoms on the patients' daily living. Sacrospinous fixation, also referred to as an anterior-posterior repair, utilizes the surrounding ligaments to tighten and attach lax musculature onto the bony pelvis.

Nurses provide important patient teaching. Educating the patient on weight loss, smoking cessation, and avoiding heavy lifting enables the patient to care for herself. Proper insertion, removal, and cleaning of pessary devices will help the patient to avoid vaginal infections. Nurses can discuss appropriate

ways to avoid unnecessary straining and constipation. Anticipatory guidance regarding procedures or surgery will help to alleviate any patient anxiety about the surgical process.

Nurses providing information to patients with pelvic organ prolapse helps to empower women in taking an active role in the decision-making process for self-care (Richardson, Hagen, Glazener et al., 2009).

FISTULAS

A fistula is an abnormal, tortuous opening between two internal organs or between an internal hollow organ and the exterior of the body. Figure 33-11 depicts vaginal fistulas. Rectovaginal fistulas are abnormal openings that occur between the vagina and the rectum, allowing fecal material and flatulence to leak into the vagina causing fecal incontinence. They may be simple or complex. Vesicovaginal fistulas occur between the bladder and the vagina and cause urinary incontinence. These conditions occur as a result of congenital anomalies, trauma due to childbirth or surgery, radiation therapy, Crohn's disease, diverticular diseases, or neoplasm of the rectum or vagina. Postpartum infections may also result in fistula formation due to third- and fourth-degree perineal tears or tissue breakdown. This condition causes discomfort and has social ramifications.

Clinical Manifestations and Assessment

Depending upon the type of fistula, symptoms will vary. If caused by an obstetric or surgical complication, fistulas may not be immediately apparent for up to 30 days after the initial injury. Urinary or fecal incontinence are the main reasons why women will seek evaluation by a health care provider.

BOX 33-9
Patient Education

Performing Kegel (Pelvic Muscle) Exercises

Purposes: To strengthen and maintain the tone of the pubococcygeal muscle, which supports the pelvic organs; reduce or prevent stress incontinence and uterine prolapse; enhance sensation during sexual intercourse; and hasten postpartum healing:

1. Become aware of pelvic muscle function by "drawing in" the perivaginal muscles and anal sphincter as if to control urine or defecation, but not contracting the abdominal, buttock, or inner thigh muscles.
2. Sustain contraction of the muscles for up to 10 seconds, followed by at least 10 seconds of relaxation.
3. Perform these exercises 30 to 80 times a day.

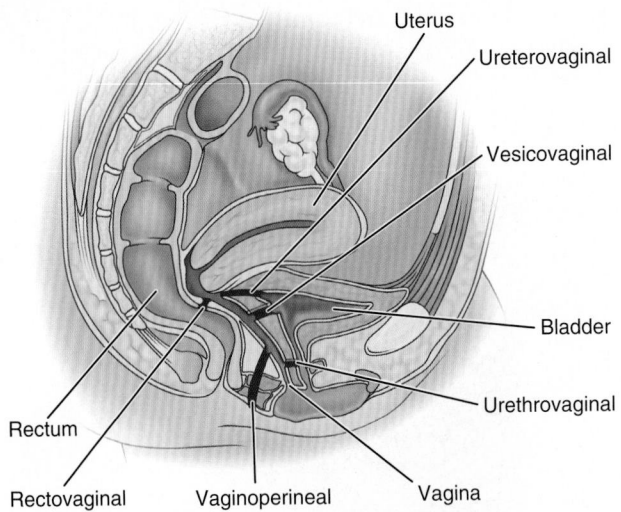

FIGURE 33-11 Common sites for vaginal fistulas: *Vesicovaginal*, bladder and vagina. *Urethrovaginal*, urethra and vagina. *Vaginoperineal*, vagina and perineal area. *Ureterovaginal*, ureter and vagina. *Rectovaginal*, rectum and vagina.

Fecal discharge through the vagina produces a malodorous discharge and may be mistaken for a vaginal infection. An accurate history of onset, timing, and location, along with symptoms the patient is experiencing, is important to help locate the structural abnormality. Physical assessment of the genital area will help to identify the affected area. The fistula may be palpable on digital rectal exam or vaginal exam. A sigmoidoscopy, colonoscopy, small bowel imaging, cystoscopy, or intravenous pyelography will aid in definitive diagnosis.

Medical and Nursing Management

If the fistula is due to Crohn's disease or diverticular disease, treatment is aimed at the causative disease and should be followed by a gastroenterologist.

Surgical repair is the only option if the fistula does not heal spontaneously. There is a high rate of recurrence of fistulas in spite of surgical repair. Nurses play an important role in helping the patient to understand the importance of cleanliness and hygiene and to understand the signs and symptoms of recurrent infection or surgical failure to repair the fistula. Regular sitz baths and changing of perineal pads help prevent infection. It is important for the nurse to inspect the patient's skin for any signs of erythema or breakdown.

BENIGN DISORDERS

OVARIAN CYSTS

Ovaries produce estrogen, progesterone, and a small amount of testosterone necessary for female reproductive function as well as formation of oocytes or eggs. Follicles are structures within the ovary containing a single ovum or egg. Follicular growth is stimulated by FSH once a month. After ovulation occurs (release of the egg), the graafian follicle that houses the ovum becomes the corpus luteum. This structure undergoes transformation and regresses with the onset of menses. Ovaries are a common site for cysts to form as a result of hormonal influence on the formation of the **graafian follicle** and subsequent corpus luteum. When this series of hormonal transitions does not occur, a cyst may develop. Any graafian follicle that is over 2 cm is considered a cyst. Ovarian cysts are classified as functional or nonfunctional. Statistically, women under age 50 are more likely to have a benign cyst, whereas women over age 50 are more likely to have a cyst that is malignant.

Types

Functional cysts are also known as *simple cysts* due to their appearance on ultrasound.

These types of cysts rupture and hemorrhage and occasionally cause pain. The condition is self-limiting. Pain that occurs during ovulation, known as **mittelschmerz**, also produces unilateral ovarian pain and is generally relieved with symptomatic treatment such as OTC NSAIDs. Ovarian follicles that rupture during ovulation release fluid, cause pain, and may be noted on ultrasound. Two-thirds of corpus luteum cysts typically rupture on days 20 through 26 of the menstrual cycle (Bottomley & Bourne, 2009).

Nonfunctional cysts, or endometriomas, are also known as "chocolate cysts" due to their characteristic appearance on ultrasound. The cysts develop as a result of sloughed off endometrial tissue that has formed a cystic mass on the ovary; they are brown in appearance. Dermoid cysts are nonfunctional and are comprised of embryonic cells containing hair, teeth, bone, and nails. Statistically, these types of cysts are almost always benign, but approximately 3% to 5% are malignant (Levine, De Los Santos, Fleming et al., 2010).

Patients with nonfunctional dermoid cysts are diagnosed by pelvic ultrasound after they have had a missed menstrual cycle and have a false-positive pregnancy test.

Ovaries with multiple cysts due to chronic anovulatory cycles are known as *polycystic ovaries*. PCOS is the most common endocrine disorder that affects women of reproductive age (DuRant & Leslie, 2007). It is a complex disorder of androgen excess, insulin resistance, and an imbalance in the ratios of luteinizing hormone and FSH causing **anovulation** (lack of ovulation). Androgen excess coupled with disproportionate amounts of LH and FSH, and decreased sex hormone-binding globulins (SHBG) causes the occurrence of anovulatory cycles. This fluctuation in the normal levels of hormones results in insulin resistance due to the influence of hormone production from the pituitary. Women affected by PCOS are at risk for developing type 2 diabetes, acne, endometrial cancer, hyperlipidemia, obesity, hirsutism, and infertility.

Clinical Manifestations and Assessment

Patients experiencing rupture of functional cysts present with a sudden onset of unilateral lower abdominal pain. Nausea and vomiting may be present. Pain typically increases with movement. A typical presentation of PCOS will include a history of irregular menstrual cycles (can be >35 day cycles or <8 menses annually). Characteristics of bleeding include heavy flow with increased abdominal cramping and may also include large clots. The patient may be hirsute on the face and chest or between the breasts and demonstrate mild to severe acne. Male pattern baldness or alopecia may be present. Fifty percent of women with PCOS have central obesity (Bartoszek, 2009). **Acanthosis nigricans** is a hyperpigmentation of the skin around the neck but also may be noted in the axilla, groin, or the dorsal aspect of hands, and the patient may also have an excessive number of skin tags around the neck, under the arms and breasts, or in the groin.

Pelvic ultrasound will reveal large edematous ovaries with follicles (Bottomley et al., 2009). Patients with unilateral right lower quadrant pain must be evaluated for the potential of appendicitis.

Medical and Nursing Management

Functional cysts are self-limiting and generally respond to the use of OTC NSAIDs, such as ibuprofen or naprosyn. Once a diagnosis of ovarian cysts is made, and depending upon the size of the cyst, combined oral contraceptives or medroxyprogesterone acetate (Depo-Provera) is recommended to induce suppression of FSH. This decreases the incidence of formation of ovarian follicles, limits or halts an increase in the size of any established cysts, and halts the future formation of cysts. COCs are not used to treat existing functional ovarian cysts larger than 5 to 8 cm (American Congress of Obstetricians and Gynecologists [ACOG], 2010). If pain persists longer than 48 hours, an exploratory laparoscopy may be performed to rule out the presence of ovarian torsion (twisting of the ovary, primarily affecting the right ovary).

Patients with PCOS require extensive blood work and a transvaginal ultrasound to rule out any other causative factors. Labs include FSH, LH, beta human chorionic gonadotropin (β-hCG), SHBG, free testosterone, prolactin, lipid panel, thyroid studies, and a fasting glucose. A 2-hour glucose tolerance test is useful in determining glucose intolerance. The LH-to-FSH ratio in patients with PCOS is usually greater than 2:1 or 3:1, but a normal ratio is not a diagnosis of exclusion.

It is important that blood work not be performed while the patient is currently taking oral contraceptives as this will alter the accuracy of results and delay diagnosis.

Treatment of PCOS is aimed at the primary concerns (acne, infertility, obesity). Due to the incidence of insulin resistance with PCOS, patients should follow a regular program of exercise and eat a low-fat diet. If, in spite of therapeutic lifestyle changes, the patient is unable to lose weight or ovulate, metformin or Glucophage is initiated to assist with decreasing insulin resistance and allow for spontaneous ovulation. Metformin is an insulin sensitizing agent that lowers testosterone levels and induces ovulation once hormone levels are balanced. The most common side effect of this medication is transient nausea and diarrhea (Ruby, 2008). Slowly tapering up the dosage of metformin and dosing at mealtime will help alleviate these side effects and increase patient compliance. Thirty percent of women with PCOS will develop type 2 diabetes over 2 to 3 years (Bartoszek, 2009). The method of birth control used while on metformin should be discussed with the patient because treatment can restore fertility. Patients with PCOS should be evaluated by a reproductive endocrinologist.

COCs help patients with PCOS regulate menstrual cycles and decrease blood flow with menses and the cramping associated with heavy menses. Additionally, COCs improve SHBG production, which helps bind free testosterone. This improves acne, hirsutism, and alopecia. Women who do not have regular menstrual cycles are at risk for endometrial cancer due to the prolonged exposure of estrogen and overgrowth of the endometrial lining, and therefore may need to have an endometrial biopsy if there has not been a menses in 1 year (Bartoszek, 2009).

Spironolactone is a blood pressure medication that has antiandrogenic effects that is beneficial to those who experience hirsutism. Because this is a potassium-sparing diuretic, PCOS patients should have their electrolytes monitored periodically, particularly the potassium level. Two COCs are available that contain *drospirenone*, a newer-generation progesterone that has the same antiandrogenic effects as spironolactone.

Nurses can assist patients with weight loss and exercise guidelines, as well as with adherence with medications. It is important to help patients understand the implications of this disease on QOL and infertility. Nurses play an important role in supporting patients with this disease and recognizing if patients need referral to a dietician or for psychological support.

UTERINE FIBROIDS

Leiomyomas or myomas are common, benign growths of the uterus (Fig. 33-12). They occur in approximately 70% to 80% or 1 in 3 women (Jolley, 2009). African American women have a three to nine times higher incidence of uterine fibroids (Pansky, Cowan, Frank et al., 2009). Women affected by fibroids have higher rates of time lost from work due to prolonged and heavy menstrual bleeding (Lerner, Mirza, Chang et al., 2008). Approximately 50% will require surgical intervention. Symptoms largely depend on the size and number of fibroids. The incidence of fibroids increases with age. Box 33-10 describes the types of uterine fibroids.

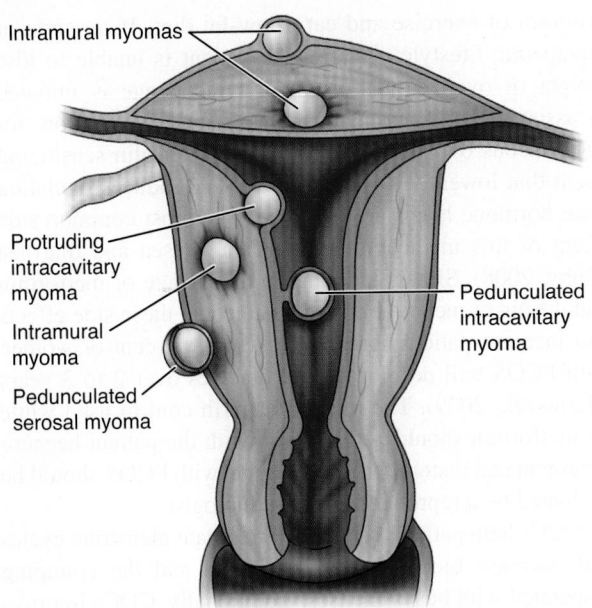

Intramural myomas

Protruding intracavitary myoma

Intramural myoma

Pedunculated serosal myoma

Pedunculated intracavitary myoma

FIGURE 33-12 Myomas (fibroids). Those that impinge on the uterine cavity are called intracavitary myomas.

Clinical Manifestations and Assessment

The majority of women with fibroids are asymptomatic until the fibroid has enlarged and is impeding on other organs. Fibroids cause increased uterine bleeding, dyspareunia, disabling pelvic pain, rectal pressure, and infertility. Diagnosis is made on pelvic ultrasound or felt on bimanual pelvic examination. The uterus is often enlarged as a result of the growth.

It is important to rule out pregnancy with a woman who is experiencing these signs and symptoms.

Medical Management

There are several treatments for fibroids. Only one uses GnRH agonists, such as Lupron, to decrease the size of the fibroid by effectively suppressing the hormonal production that feeds the fibroid. Hysterectomy is another treatment (see discussion later in the chapter). For patients who have fibroids and want to preserve their fertility, a **myomectomy** is performed. This is a surgical procedure that removes the

---

BOX 33-10
Types of Uterine Fibroids

- Subserosal fibroids lie underneath the outermost layer of the uterus and grow towards the pelvic cavity.
- Intramural fibroids grow within the wall of the uterine muscle and are the most common type.
- Submucosal fibroids grow immediately below the inner uterine surface and into the uterine cavity.
- Pedunculated fibroids arise from inside or outside the surface of the uterine muscle and project outward.

---

fibroid but leaves the uterus intact. Myomectomies can be performed laparoscopically or hysteroscopically (inspection of the uterine cavity by laparoscopy).

Uterine artery embolization (UAE) uses minimally invasive plastic or gelatin particles that are injected into the uterine arteries to occlude blood flow to the fibroid. The fibroid then shrinks over time. This type of procedure is only used on women who have completed childbearing. Magnetic resonance-guided high-frequency ultrasound energy (MRgFUS) uses high-intensity ultrasound with increased temperature to destroy fibroid cells. Cryoablation or radiofrequency of individual fibroids has not yet been FDA approved. Approximately 40% of patients undergoing UAE will develop postembolization syndrome: fever, pain, and leukocytosis due to the degenerating fibroid. This is a normal response to treatment but patients must be monitored for worsening symptoms.

Nursing Management

Patients experience heightened anxiety when diagnosed with a fibroid. Nurses can reassure patients of the benign nature of fibroids and the potential side effects of medications and surgical procedures. The use of GnRH agonists induces temporary menopause and vasomotor symptoms associated with menopause. The patient may experience hot flashes, sleep disruption, and vaginal dryness as a result of loss of estrogen. These symptoms are reversible once the medication has been discontinued. Due to the high level of bleeding associated with any myomectomy or surgical procedure, all aspirin and aspirin-containing products should be discontinued 3 to 4 weeks before the procedure is performed. Aggressive pain management is advised due to the increased amount of cramping from the infarction of the fibroid. Instructing patients on the patient-controlled analgesia (PCA) pumps and regular administration of NSAIDs and antiemetics will ensure adequate pain control (Bradley, 2009). Patients are not only coping with the physical loss but the psychological loss of fertility, so nurses need to address those concerns and offer referrals to therapists if needed.

ENDOMETRIOSIS

Endometriosis is a progressive, benign gynecological disorder affecting women in their childbearing years and causing chronic inflammation and formation of adhesions. It does not continue after menopause. Approximately 10% of women suffer from endometriosis, with as high as 80% of these reporting chronic pelvic pain (Mao & Anastasi, 2010). This disease may be disabling and chronic. It impacts the woman's sexual relations, as well as her physical, social, and psychological well-being (Mao & Anastasi).

Pathophysiology

Endometriosis is the presence of endometrial-like tissue that proliferates outside of the uterine cavity to cause persistent

pelvic pain and scarring that leads to infertility. The pathophysiology of this disease is largely unknown, but many theories exist (Mao & Anastasi, 2010). It is thought to be caused by the retrograde flow during menses of endometrial tissue through the fallopian tubes and into the peritoneal cavity, where this tissue seeds, forming adhesions in the pelvic, bladder, and bowel areas. The peritoneal endometrial tissues are influenced by the hormonal changes of the menstrual cycle and therefore swell, break down and bleed; typically, the patients' symptoms worsen during the premenstrual phase.

Clinical Manifestations and Assessment

Chronic pelvic pain is the most frequent presentation of endometriosis (Mousa, Bedaiwy, & Casper, 2007). Low back pain, dyspareunia, dysuria, **dyschezia** (pain with defecation), dysmenorrhea, and menorrhagia are among the common complaints. The level of pain associated with endometriosis is not necessarily correlated with the stage of endometriosis. The cyclical bowel and bladder symptoms of endometriosis are similar to those found in irritable bowel syndrome (IBS) or interstitial cystitis (IC), making it difficult to differentiate among the disorders.

A detailed health history regarding the patients' symptoms in relation to their menstrual cycle will help the health care provider establish a pattern. On physical examination, any tenderness of the fallopian tubes, ovaries, or uterus on bimanual exam is an indication for further evaluation. The most common finding is tenderness with palpation of the posterior vaginal fornix, but a definitive diagnosis cannot be established without further diagnostic testing. Transvaginal ultrasound visualizes the uterine cavity and endometrium for any adhesions. This examination is unable to visualize smaller lesions, therefore misdiagnosis may be made.

Medical and Nursing Management

The first line of treatment for endometriosis consists of the use of NSAIDs for pain and COCs to treat the condition. However, evidence for the efficacy of COCs is limited due to the small number of randomized studies performed (Brankin & Cackovic, 2010). The combined hormones in COCs suppress ovulation and growth of endometrial implants, thereby decreasing inflammation and pain. GnRH agonists (such as Lupron), androgenic agents (Danazol), and antiprogestogens (gestrinone) are considered second-line therapy (Mao & Anastasi, 2010). Any of these medications suppress ovulation and endometrial growth and reduces or eliminates menses, thus alleviating the chance of retrograde flow into the pelvic cavity (Mao & Anastasi, 2010). There are no differences in the outcomes of the use of COCs over GnRH, although GnRH agonists have higher incidence of complaints of hot flashes, vaginal dryness, and other vasomotor symptoms associated with menopause. These symptoms are reversible once GnRH therapy has been discontinued.

Use of continuous contraception has been found to significantly decrease pain and is considered effective treatment for women with symptomatic endometriosis (Brankin & Cackovic, 2010).

Surgical intervention is considered the last line of therapy. Exploratory laparoscopy with lysis of adhesions is considered the gold standard and temporarily decreases the pain and bleeding associated with endometriosis, although 40% to 60% of women will have a recurrence 2 years after surgery (Mao & Anastasi, 2010). Total abdominal hysterectomy remains the definitive therapy for those women who have completed their childbearing (Mousa et al., 2007). Those women who leave their ovaries intact have a 31% increased chance of recurrent symptoms 4 years after having surgery (Shakiba, Bena, McGill et al., 2008).

Complementary and alternative therapies are useful in women who suffer from endometriosis and should be a part of the plan of care for these women. Due to the issues surrounding loss of fertility with this disease, stress management should be included. Yoga may help with stress reduction and also increases core and abdominal strength, which will help patients who undergo surgical intervention have an easier recovery. Specifically trained physical therapists can help alleviate and manage the symptoms associated with chronic pelvic pain. Massage releases endorphins that can ease pain associated with endometriosis (Kaatz, Solari-Twadell, Cameron et al., 2010).

Educating the woman affected by endometriosis and her family and support network will help them to understand the significant impact of this disease on the woman and her physical and psychological health. Many women have sought the opinions of multiple medical providers regarding the treatment of endometriosis (Brankin & Cackovic, 2010), and many have had a negative experience; therefore, establishing trust between the patient and the health care provider is crucial. A collaborative effort between all members of the health care team, including the nurse, health care provider, pharmacist, pain management specialist, and social worker, must exist to help improve the patient's outcome.

MALIGNANT CONDITIONS

CANCER OF THE CERVIX

The most common reproductive cancer among women is cervical cancer; it is the second most common cancer among women. Approximately 11,000 new cases of cervical cancer are diagnosed annually, and approximately 4,000 women will die of cervical cancer each year (Tracy, Lydecker, & Ireland, 2010). The incidence and mortality of cervical cancer has dramatically decreased over the past 50 years due to the development and subsequent acceptance and use of the Pap smear.

TABLE
33-5 American Congress of Obstetricians and Gynecologists (ACOG) Cervical Cytology Screening Guidelines

Patient Population	Frequency
Ages 21 to 30	Every 2 years
Ages 30 to 65	Every 3 years, if 3 negative Pap tests
Ages 65 and older	Discontinue if no abnormal Pap tests for 10 years
Patients having had a hysterectomy for non-cancerous reasons	Discontinue after hysterectomy
Those patients with high risk factors: HIV, diethylstilbestrol (DES) exposure, or cervical intraepithelial neoplasm (CIN) 2 or 3	Every 6 months or as directed by health care provider

ACOG Practice Bulletin #109 December, 2009.

The most common type of cervical cancer is squamous cell carcinoma (SCC), accounting for approximately 80% of all cervical cancer cases. Scientists researching triggers to changes in the cervical tissue that lead to cancer have implicated human papilloma virus (HPV). Cervical cancer has a slow progression from certain strains of oncogenic HPV to invasive cervical cancer and may take years to progress (Rogers & Cantu, 2009). HPV comprises over 100 strains, some of which have oncogenic potential and are known to cause cervical abnormalities. Women are asymptomatic unless they have external genital warts, or **condyloma**. At least 50% of sexually active women will be infected with HPV by age 50 (CDC, 2010). Infection with HPV during the younger years is generally cleared spontaneously or is suppressed to undetectable levels.

Screening and Prevention

The Pap smear is a screening tool used to detect any abnormalities of the cervix (Table 33-5). In recent years, liquid-based cytology has been developed to improve specimen adequacy, making it superior to traditional glass slide specimens (ACOG Practice Bulletin, Dec., 2008).

Pap tests are the most effective preventative measure for invasive cervical cancer (Tracy et al., 2010).

Risk Factors

Lesbian women are at higher risk for cervical cancer due to misinformation, and insufficient knowledge and screening. Many have reported negative experiences with health care providers, so they do not routinely receive preventative care (Tracy et al., 2010). Box 33-11 lists other risk factors for cervical cancer.

BOX 33-11 | **Risk Factors for Cervical Cancer**

- Intercourse with an uncircumcised male
- Early age of first coitus
- Multiple sexual partners
- High parity
- STIs
- Cigarette smoking
- Exposure to human papillomavirus

Clinical Manifestations and Assessment

Routine screening for cervical cancer increases a woman's chances of being diagnosed at an earlier stage. Advanced disease will manifest itself with irregular vaginal bleeding, and pelvic pain and pressure. Malodorous vaginal discharge occurs as a result of tumor necrosis. Dyspareunia and rectal pressure is also common as the tumor increases in size and extent, invading surrounding tissue and causing other symptoms to develop. The standard of care for an abnormal Pap test is to follow-up with a **colposcopy** and directed biopsy. Colposcopy is a high-powered magnification of the cervix, which has had an acetic acid solution applied to it to help differentiate the cervical cells. Biopsies are taken in areas of visible abnormal vascular patterns.

Approximately 50% of newly diagnosed women with cervical cancer will present with stage 1 disease (Bansal Herzog, Shaw, Burke et al., 2009). Twenty-eight percent of women with low-grade squamous intraepithelial lesions (LGSIL) harbor cervical intraepithelial neoplasm (CIN) 2 or 3, which are precursors to cervical cancer (ACOG Practice Bulletin, Dec. 2008). High-risk HPV testing in women over age 30 will predict whether or not CIN 2 or 3 will develop.

Delayed diagnosis of cervical cancer will result in a more advanced disease state.

Staging is the next step, once the diagnosis for invasive cervical cancer has been made. Staging is performed on a scale of 0 to IVB. Stage 0 is known as carcinoma in situ (CIS). Stage IVB is consistent with distant metastasis. Treatment is dependant upon type of carcinoma and extent of disease. As the tumor size increases, so does the risk of treatment failure. Pelvic ultrasound is an easy and noninvasive way to evaluate any cervical pathology due to its ability to visualize the size and location of a cervical mass (Shenavi, 2008). A chest X-ray and abdominal/pelvic imagining, such as CT scan or MRI, are performed to rule out metastasis to other areas of the body.

Medical Management

Abnormal Pap smears that reveal high- or low-grade squamous intraepithelial lesions (HGSIL or LGSIL) are followed up with a colposcopy and cervical biopsy. Once diagnosis

has been established, a cervical conization or cone biopsy is performed. Cold knife conization and loop electrosurgical excision procedure (LEEP) are other procedures that may be performed to treat HGSIL or LGSIL, which are precursors to cervical cancer. These types of procedures remove cone-shaped wedges high in the cervical canal with enough surrounding tissue to ensure clear margins. This is accomplished using a surgical scalpel, laser, or electrocautery. Prognosis is excellent for these types of procedures. Cervical conization alone is adequate for those women who want to preserve childbearing ability (Wright, Nathavithrana, Lewin et al., 2010). Invasive cervical cancer is rare under the age of 20, but there has been a documented increased risk for premature births among women who have had excisional cervical procedures for dysplasia prior to conception.

Patients diagnosed with a stage 1B or IIA undergo a radical hysterectomy: removal of the uterus and upper one-third of the vagina, including the cervix, but sparing the ovaries. Bilateral pelvic lymph node sampling is also done. Pelvic radiation and chemotherapy may follow, but depends upon the size and extent of the tumor. Stage IB carries an increased risk of recurrence. Neoadjuvant chemotherapy has demonstrated success in decreasing tumor size and increasing survival when used prior to a radical hysterectomy (Goksedef, Kunos, Belinson et al., 2009).

Nursing Management

Nurses working in a variety of settings have the opportunity to educate women on cervical cancer screenings. Availability of access to care is prevalent with federally funded cervical cancer screening programs through public health departments, hospital-based primary care centers, and community health care clinics. Educating parents and young women about HPV vaccination is important when considering that vaccination is 94% to 98% effective against CIN lesions caused by HPV (Rogers & Cantu, 2009).

If a woman has undergone any cervical biopsy procedures, it is important to instruct her on the importance of pelvic rest, observing and reporting to her provider if fever, increased bleeding, pelvic pain, or malodorous vaginal discharge is noted. Ensure that the patient has the phone number of her health care provider or local hospital in the event that any of these symptoms occur after her procedure.

CANCER OF THE UTERUS

Cancer of the endometrium or uterus is the most commonly reported female reproductive cancer and comprises approximately 6% of all reproductive cancers in the United States (Diavolitsis, Boyle, Singh et al., 2009). The 5-year survival rate is 96% with localized disease. It is usually diagnosed early and better outcomes are reported with surgical intervention. It is rarely diagnosed in women under the age of 40 (ACS, 2010).

Most endometrial cancers are considered endometrioid. Less common are the nonendometrioid lesions, including

---

> **BOX 33-12**
>
> ## Risk Factors for Endometrial Cancer
>
> - Unopposed estrogen use
> - Early onset of menarche (<12) or late menopause (>50)
> - Nulliparous
> - Polycystic ovarian syndrome (PCOS)
> - Use of tamoxifen
> - Obesity
> - Diabetes
> - Prior pelvic radiation
> - Personal or family history of breast, uterine, ovarian, or colon cancer
> - Previous history of atypical hyperplasia

serous, clear cell, and carcinosarcomas. Nonendometrioid cancers are more aggressive, with an increased mortality rate (Holland, 2008).

Unopposed estrogen causes endometrial hyperplasia or an overgrowth of the uterine lining. Simple hyperplasia often spontaneously regresses, but complex hyperplasia and atypical hyperplasia are more likely to progress to cancer (Epplien, Reed, Voigh et al., 2008). Patients can be treated with progesterone prior to considering surgical hysterectomy.

Risk Factors

Risk factors are discussed in Box 33-12. Nurses should encourage those with hereditary nonpolyposis colorectal cancer (HNPCC) (Box 33-13) or who are high risk to begin annual screening with endometrial biopsies and transvaginal ultrasound beginning at age 25 (Sorosky, 2008).

Clinical Manifestations and Assessment

Abnormal vaginal bleeding is the most common early symptom of endometrial cancer; 90% of women will present with

---

> **BOX 33-13**
>
> ## Hereditary Nonpolyposis Colorectal Cancer Syndrome
>
> Hereditary nonpolyposis colorectal cancer (HNPCC) syndrome increases women's risk of developing ovarian, colon, endometrial, renal, bladder, brain, and stomach cancer.
>
> It is an inherited cancer susceptibility syndrome occurring in approximately 5% of all cancers.
>
> A woman is at higher risk for HNPCC if she has three or more first-degree relatives with colon or endometrial cancer, with at least two of them having been diagnosed with colon cancer at age 50 or younger.
>
> Genetic testing for HNPCC is available and recommended to those at risk.

abnormal vaginal bleeding as their chief complaint (Abraham, Allegra, Gulley et al., 2009). Postmenopausal women may also present with complaints of vaginal bleeding well after menses has ceased. Any unexplained vaginal bleeding or an irregularity in menstrual cycle should be evaluated by a health care professional.

Diagnosis has traditionally been made based on the tissue pathology from a dilation and curettage (D&C); however, endometrial biopsy is the preferred method since it is a simple procedure performed in the health care provider's office and does not involve anesthesia. If the biopsy is inconclusive or suggests endometrial cancer, a D&C is the gold standard. Hysteroscopic-directed biopsy is another alternative that is performed through the insertion of a scope through the cervix and directly into the uterus, allowing for complete visualization of the endometrium. A transvaginal ultrasound may be performed and measures the endometrial thickness. Greater than 16 mm is a predictor of abnormal pathology; in postmenopausal women, greater than 5 mm is considered pathologic (Sorosky, 2008).

Medical Management

Once the diagnosis has been established, the standard treatment is a total abdominal hysterectomy with bilateral salpingo-oophorectomy (removal of fallopian tubes and ovaries). There is questionable value in pelvic lymph node removal; it is a current source of debate (Goonatillake, Khong, & Hoskin, 2009). Type of hysterectomy has little bearing on outcome, although some believe that an open hysterectomy is optimal in visualizing the peritoneum over a laparoscopic-assisted vaginal hysterectomy, in which the peritoneum is not as well-visualized (Wright, Fiorelli, Kansler et al., 2009). Laparoscopic vaginal hysterectomy decreases morbidity in morbidly obese women or those with high rates of comorbid conditions (Holland, 2008). Surgical staging is the most precise method to determine metastasis to surrounding tissues and organs; it involves abdominal and pelvic washings and periaortic lymph node evaluation.

Stage I is curable by surgery alone as it is considered low risk and the disease is confined to the uterus (Diavolitsis et al., 2009). High risk stage I and some stage II cancers will require postoperative adjuvant radiation therapy as the disease has lymph node involvement, is outside of the uterus, or contains high-risk cell types (papillary or clear cell). Radiation affects the ability of cells to proliferate and decreases growth of cancer cells. Vaginal brachytherapy consists of a device containing sealed radioactive material placed into the vagina postoperatively for 3 to 4 days, then removed. This method is preferred over external beam radiation (EBR) due to its lessened side effects. It delivers low- or high-dose radiation directly into the tumor. Brachytherapy decreases the incidence of regional recurrence (Diavolitsis et al., 2009). During this time, the patient is on strict bedrest for the entire duration of therapy. Patients are isolated from other patients,

and a camera mounted on the wall of the room allows monitoring of the patient while minimizing caregivers' exposure to radiation. Lead absorbs more radiation than any other material, therefore a portable lead shield is placed at the bedside behind which all caregivers stand to administer medications, change IV bags, or deliver food trays.

Patients are kept on a clear liquid or low-residue diet to avoid stool formation. Stool softeners and medications to decrease peristalsis are administered. Nurses wear film badges or dosimeters to measure the amount of radiation exposure.

High-risk stages II and III will receive both radiation and chemotherapy. Those women who do not receive radiation therapy were 48% more likely to die from their tumors (Wright et al., 2009). High-risk features stage Ic or poorly differentiated adenocarcinoma, clear cell carcinoma, and papillary serous carcinoma.

Nursing Management

Educating women who have high risk factors and discussing strategies to reduce risk factors is considered primary prevention. Decreasing obesity and controlling diabetes are two ways to decrease the risk of the development of endometrial cancer.

Nurses can stress the importance of evaluation for any abnormal vaginal bleeding. Use of oral contraceptives as a younger adult also provides some protection against developing endometrial cancer.

Nurses caring for patients receiving brachytherapy must take precautions against occupational exposure to radioactive material. Time, distance, and shielding make up the rules for protecting against unnecessary exposure. A long-handled forceps and lead container are kept in the patients' room after the radioactive material has been placed into the patient. It is imperative that staff never pick up the radioactive source with their bare hands if it becomes displaced from the patient's vagina. The institution's radiation safety team should be notified in the event this occurs. Patients should also be made aware of the side effects of radiation therapy, including radiation enteritis, nausea, loss of appetite, bladder irritation, early menopause, vaginal dryness, and loss of interest in sexual intercourse (Lippincott Williams & Wilkins, 2008). Refer to Chapter 6 for more details on radiation therapy.

CANCER OF THE OVARY

Ovarian cancer is referred to as a cancer that "whispers" because its clinical manifestations are not apparent until the tumor has invaded surrounding structures and is causing symptoms. It carries a high fatality rate due to the aggressiveness of the malignancy. Five-year survivorship rate is not unforeseeable if the cancer is diagnosed at an early stage, but only 20% of women with ovarian cancer are diagnosed at that stage (ACS, 2010). Eighty-five percent of women diagnosed are over age 50; 15% have genetic links; 10% have *BRCA 1* and *BRCA 2* mutations, and 5% have HNPCC risk factors

Risk Factors for Cancer of the Ovary

- Age over 40 or postmenopausal
- Nulliparous
- Northern American or Northern European descent
- Personal history of breast, colon, or endometrial cancer
- Obesity (BMI >30)
- Use of fertility drugs
- Long-term use of hormone replacement therapy
- Genetic predisposition; positive family history of ovarian cancer

(Tate, 2009). See Box 33-14 for additional risk factors. Use of oral contraceptives has been proven to decrease risk of developing ovarian cancer by 50%, with long-term protection benefits (Tate, 2009). Hormonal contraception causes reversible anovulation, thus decreasing the cumulative cycles of the ovary over a woman's lifetime. The longer duration of oral contraceptive pill use decreases the risk of ovarian cancer 20% for every 5 years of use (Grimbizis & Tarlatzis, 2010).

Cancers of the ovary occur in epithelial cells lining the ovary. Malignant ovarian cells shed from the ovary implant onto the surfaces of the peritoneal cavity. These cancerous cells then undergo transformation into ovarian surface epithelium (Martin, 2007).

Clinical Manifestations and Assessment

Symptoms of ovarian cancer are subtle and start with persistent bloating, early satiety, or a change in bowel or bladder habits. Women will typically complain of weight gain confined to their abdominal area. Due to the close proximity of the ovaries to the intestines, patients will typically complain of GI symptoms and, as a result, this cancer carries a high rate of misdiagnosis, with patients commonly receiving treatment for a variety of disorders, including IBS, gastroesophageal reflux (GERD), menopause, or UTIs (Tate, 2009). Ascites (fluid accumulation in the peritoneal cavity) is considered a late-stage symptom and prognosis is poor (Bohenkamp, LeBaron, & Yoder, 2007).

No reliable screening tools are available for this disease. Treatment is hindered by late diagnosis, when the disease has already invaded peritoneal tissues and surrounding structures.

Bimanual examinations diagnose approximately one-third of ovarian masses. Pelvic ultrasounds and blood tests for CA 125, a tumor marker, are the first diagnostics performed when ruling out an ovarian mass. If either of these tests is suggestive of a tumor, an abdominal and pelvic CT scan is performed. Patients are always referred to a oncologic gynecologist for management of this disease.

Medical Management

Surgical staging identifies tumor histological grade and volume, which allows for the identification of treatment options and determines the prognosis based on tumor type (Table 33-6). During surgery, the suspicious tissue that is removed and sent to the lab for immediate analysis is known as a *frozen section*. If positive, the surgeon then performs extensive cytoreduction surgery or **debulking** to obtain clean tissue margins. This includes a total abdominal hysterectomy (TAH) with bilateral salpingo-oophorectomy (BSO), removal of the omentum, peritoneal washings, and partial colectomy if there is any colon involvement (Bohnenkamp et al., 2007).

Stage 1A or 1B tumors are considered low risk and favorable to treatment, if well or moderately well differentiated tumors are confined to the ovary. Absence of tumor on the external surfaces, absence of ascites, and negative peritoneal washings are also favorable signs. Stage 1A or 1B with poorly differentiated tumors, tumors notable on the external surface of the ovary, ruptured tumor capsule, and positive peritoneal washings are all considered high risk and unfavorable. Advanced stages III and IV require combination chemotherapy after surgical staging has been performed to determine tumor sensitivity to a particular chemotherapeutic agent.

Chemotherapy treats residual tumor and helps to control any metastatic disease. Advance tumors receive chemotherapy first to decrease the size of the tumor; the patient then undergoes surgical debulking to remove as much tumor as possible (Tate, 2009). First-line chemotherapy consists of platinum and paclitaxel. Seventy-five percent of women respond to initial treatment, but there is an 85% relapse rate with a median survival of 3 years after platinum therapy. Carboplatin and paclitaxel are considered the gold standard for treatment of ovarian cancer (Bettman, 2009). Carboplatin has recently replaced cisplatin due to its ability to be administered on an outpatient basis and its lesser toxicity. Patients undergo two or three cycles to evaluate their response and toxicity before proceeding with further treatment. Carboplatin combined with gemcitabine yields a higher response rate that has a longer median progression-free survival (Martin, 2007). Patients whose tumors are resistant to platinum receive single-agent therapy. CA 125 is a sensitive indicator of disease relapse.

TABLE
33-6 Stages of Ovarian Cancer

Stage	Description
Stage 1	Tumor confined to ovary
Stage 2	Involves 1 or both ovaries and extends into pelvis
Stage 3	1 or both ovaries, + peritoneal metastasis and/or lymph node involvement
Stage 4	Distant metastasis beyond peritoneal cavity including the liver

Nursing Management

Education and support begin preoperatively and continue through discharge (Bohenkamp et al., 2007). Care must be individualized based on the patient's psychological and physical status, stage of illness, and treatment plan. Patients will need anticipatory guidance regarding postoperative infections, pain management, and potential side effects from chemotherapeutic agents. Postoperatively, patients will need to be monitored for signs and symptoms of infection, **ileus**, deep vein thrombosis (DVT), pulmonary embolus (PE), and bleeding. Encouraging the regular use of incentive spirometry, as well as regular ambulation, will help to decrease the development of DVT and atelectasis.

Emotional support is extremely important as the patient recovers from surgery and has to cope with a diagnosis of cancer. Side effects from chemotherapy should be discussed with the patient and her support system. Hair loss, nutrition, neuropathies, nausea and vomiting, as well as self-image alterations, should be addressed regularly with the patient during her preoperative assessment and should be ongoing during her treatment (Bohenkamp et al., 2007). Refer to Chapter 6 for details on cancer care.

CANCER OF THE VULVA

Vulvar cancer is rare, with an incidence of only 2.2 out of 100,000 cases annually (Lanneau, Argenta, Lanneau et al., 2009). Its incidence has been slowly increasing since 1973, however, and this is thought to be due to its link with HPV. There is increased evidence of young women with HPV being diagnosed with vulvar intraepithelial neoplasia, but the disease has a high cure rate after surgical resection and radiotherapy. Women diagnosed with vulvar cancer are usually between the ages of 70 and 80. The majority of these women (approximately 80% to 90%) will be diagnosed in an early stage (I or II) (Likes, 2009).

The majority (90%) of vulvar cancer is SCC, which can be superficial but invasive. Vulvar intraepithelial neoplasia (VIN) is more complex, deeply invasive, and is considered the precancerous condition of HPV types 16, 18, 31, and 33. Women diagnosed with vulvar CIS are usually under the age of 65, but their risk of invasive vulvar cancer is increased (Lanneau et al., 2009). Women who have been treated for condyloma, HPV, or abnormal cervical cytology, and those who smoke cigarettes or have an increased number of sexual partners have increased risk of developing cancer of the vulva.

Clinical Manifestations and Assessment

Itching or burning of the external genitalia are early signs often self-treated by patients with OTC cortisone or anti-itch creams. Only about half of women will present with dyspareunia, vulvar edema, or pain. Later-stage manifestations include ulcerated lesions that are indicative of cancer (Likes, 2009). Lesions occur in the vulvar area but may extend into the perianal and rectal areas, and most commonly occur in areas that do not have hair. A Keyes punch biopsy or tissue biopsy is the gold standard for diagnosing vulvar cancer.

Medical Management

Vulvar colposcopy may be performed, but a wide excision of the affected area or a vulvectomy (removal of the vulva) with lymph node sampling for clear margins is dependant upon the size, depth, and focality of lesions. As a result, preservation of the clitoral area may or may not occur (McClurg & Hagen, 2009). An alternative to surgery for early-stage lesions is the use of imiquimod (Aldara), which is a topical immune-response modifier with antiviral and antitumor properties typically used for the treatment of external genital warts. The use of this medication for early vulvar cancer lesions is not FDA approved and is considered an off-label use (Likes, 2009). Depending upon the extent of the vulvectomy, chemotherapy and radiation treatments may also be indicated. There is a statistically significant correlation between extent of reconstructive surgery and disease outcomes, with local reconstructive surgery demonstrating a better prognosis with significant reduction in relapse rate.

Nursing Management

Patients are at higher risk for infection depending upon the size and extent of the surgical site. Monitoring patients postoperatively for wound infections, fever, discharge, and pain is a priority. Avoidance of cross-contamination of body fluids (such as urine or feces) will help to decrease infection. Foley care and assessment of skin are important in identifying any potential site of entry for infection.

It is also important to assess the patient for development of DVT and PE due to the prolonged bedrest necessary postoperatively to avoid tension on the surgical site and promote healing. Frequent position changes, and the use of compression stockings and intermittent pneumatic compression boots, along with regular use of incentive spirometry, will aid in avoiding the formation of DVTs and PEs.

Patients who have undergone a vulvectomy may suffer from distorted body images as a result of surgical resection. Decreased sensation affecting a woman's ability to enjoy sexual relations and pelvic floor dysfunction occur due to the severing of the delicate nerve supply in the vulvar area. Discussion with the surgeon regarding the extent of surgery will help the nurse to answer any questions the patient may have postoperatively. Partner involvement and a social work or mental health referral is beneficial to help patients and their partners understand what to expect after discharge from the hospital.

HYSTERECTOMY

Surgical removal of the female reproductive organs is performed for a variety of reasons: dysfunctional uterine

bleeding, benign or malignant masses, pelvic organ prolapse, pelvic pain, endometriosis, or trauma. Hysterectomies are the most common nonobstetric major surgery performed in the United States. Over 600,000 hysterectomies are performed annually (Forsgren, Lundholm, Johansson et al., 2009). The majority of hysterectomies are performed for benign uterine disorders that impact on the QOL for women suffering from uterine disease or menstrual disorder.

Hysterectomies consist of surgical removal of the uterus and fallopian tubes; however, conservation of the ovaries and cervix may be considered depending upon the patient's age and reason for surgery. Bilateral oophorectomy is associated with a decreased risk of breast and ovarian cancer, but an overall increased risk of mortality, fatal and nonfatal coronary artery disease, and lung cancer (Parker, Broder, Chang et al., 2009). Fifty percent of women who undergo hysterectomy between the ages of 40 and 44 will have both ovaries removed at the time of surgery. That percentage increases to 78% between the ages of 45 and 64. Surgical removal of the ovaries results in immediate cessation of estrogen and androgen production, causing surgical menopause. Retention of the cervix has become a recent trend, although there is no evidence currently that supports increased sexual function or decreased rates of urinary incontinence (Falcone & Walters, 2008). This is known as a **supracervical or subtotal hysterectomy**. It is important for women to know if they have not had their cervix removed; women with an intact cervix will need to continue to undergo annual Pap smear screening for cervical cancer.

Types

TAHs are the most frequent type of hysterectomy performed, followed by a total vaginal hysterectomy (TVH), which uses a vaginal approach to remove the organs. TVH allows for less blood loss, quicker recovery, shorter hospital stays, fewer infections, and less pain than the abdominal approach, which requires incisions through the abdominal musculature. TVH and laparoscopic-assisted vaginal hysterectomy (LAVH) can be done in a 1-day surgery center, whereas TAH and radical hysterectomies require a longer hospital stay. The use of laparoscopic and hysteroscopic (inspection of the uterine cavity by endoscopy) approaches are other alternatives to be considered and are dependent upon the surgeons' skill and experience with the equipment. LAVHs are more technically difficult to perform than are TVHs (Julian, 2008). Radical hysterectomies, performed for malignant conditions, consist of the complete removal of all the reproductive organs, including the surrounding tissue margins, the upper one-third of the vagina, and pelvic lymph node sampling. The number of hysterectomies performed overall are less now due to the development and use of endometrial ablation, progestin IUDs, and UAE. The mode of hysterectomy influences the development of fistulas due to injury to the bowel or bladder during surgery (Forsgren et al., 2009).

Nursing Management

All hysterectomy patients are surgical patients and therefore must be cared for like any other surgical patient. Attention to pain management; postoperative complications, such as DVT, PE, wound infections, and UTIs; and return of bowel function are the primary concerns for nurses. The nurse assesses the patients for breath sounds and encourages regular use of incentive spirometry. The nurse also monitors for return of bowel functions, as an ileus may occur due to manipulation of the bowel during surgery and the effects of anesthesia and analgesia on peristalsis.

Encouraging patients to walk with assistance as soon as the effects from general anesthesia have resolved helps with circulation and prevents blood clot formation. Many patients undergoing hysterectomy are also dealing with the loss of fertility and possibly a cancer diagnosis. The nurse allows patients to verbalize their concerns and feelings and makes referrals to mental health providers if needed.

Discharge planning should include pelvic rest for 4 to 6 weeks and teaching the patient wound care and signs and symptoms of infection. Patients are allowed to shower and should be encouraged to gradually resume regular activity as per the surgeon's recommendation. Patients who have had a TAH are generally not permitted to drive for 4 to 6 weeks. They should avoid any heavy lifting, pushing, or pulling (such as vacuum cleaning) until their surgeon clears them to resume those activities. It is normal for women who have had hysterectomies to have some vaginal discharge. Patients who have undergone TAH will normally have some vaginal bleeding for up to 1 week postoperatively; patients who have undergone TVH and LAVH may have some vaginal discharge consisting of blood and mucus for several weeks postoperatively. Any foul-smelling vaginal discharge, unusual pain, or fever should be reported to the surgeon immediately. If there is evidence of unilateral swelling of the lower extremities, shortness of breath, or any discharge or redness around their incision sites, patients should contact their health care provider.

TRANSGENDER HEALTH CARE

Health Care Disparities

There is an increasing awareness of **transgender** patients and their lack of access to health care. This patient population is largely uninsured, experience social stigmatization, and are at higher risk for PCOS, HIV exposure, interpersonal violence, and suicide (Dutton, Koenig, & Fennie, 2008).

Patients who are in transition do not qualify for health care insurance, nor will current insurance pay for any procedures related to patients' transitions. Many patients will purchase hormones via the Internet or from unreliable sources. If patients become hospitalized, they may be anxious that they will not receive their hormones. They are frequently discriminated against by those in the health care profession

due to lack of knowledge, training, or personal bias on the part of the provider. The patient's level of anxiety may be escalated, and he or she may be perceived as a "difficult" patient. A person who has had to turn to prostitution to survive, or who has been discriminated against repeatedly throughout life may turn to negative behaviors in times of crisis. These behaviors will dissipate once a relationship of trust with care providers has been formed. It is difficult to find culturally competent and compassionate providers who have experience with transgender clients. The nurse is reminded that Healthy People 2010 states "access to quality health care and related services is important in order to eliminate health disparities and increase the quality and years of healthy life for all persons in the United States" (Healthy People, 2010).

Nursing Management

It is important for nurses to be culturally diverse at all levels of practice. Nurses need to understand the specific needs of transgender patients and demonstrate acceptance with increased sensitivity and remain nonjudgmental while delivering care. It is equally as important for nurses to educate other members of the health care team who may not have experience with this population to avoid any compromise in patient care due to bias or ignorance.

Due to the historically poor treatment of the transgender population by the health care profession, many will seek care only in an emergency and when routine health conditions have exacerbated into a serious condition. It is vital that nurses treat the patient, not the gender, and accept and encourage involvement of the client's domestic partner, significant other, and any other person who is considered family by that patient. Nurses must also be familiar with individual institution policies regarding non–blood relatives as next of kin for patients.

Nurses are in a unique position to establish a trusting relationship with patients. It is important to use gender-neutral terms and ask the patient for the preferred name and pronoun (Williamson, 2010). Other important interventions for this patient population include:

- Assessing the patient for high-risk behaviors, including IV drug abuse, prostitution, or use of hormones obtained via the Internet, on the street, or from the patient's friends.
- Offering to help **female-to-male** (FTM) patients with their breast binder (if they wear one) after a shower, or assisting with padded bras and undergarments for **male-to-female** (MTF) patients.
- Offering support and reassurance for those undergoing invasive exams, such as a breast or pelvic exam, as transgender clients have a lot of emotional conflict between their actual body and what they perceive their body to be. The gynecological exam is considered mentally and physically traumatic for FTM patients (Trotsenburg, 2010).

Hysterectomies are routine gynecological procedures performed for specific medical and surgical needs, as previously discussed in this chapter. In order to be considered a surgical candidate for a hysterectomy, the client will need to undergo a gynecological exam. However, almost all transgender patients undergoing this surgery are either nulliparous or have never had vaginal penetration. The gynecological exam is considered mentally and physically traumatic for females becoming males (FTMs) (Trotsenburg, 2010). If the client has been using testosterone, a significant amount of vaginal atrophy will occur. If a client is taking estrogen therapy, penile and scrotal atrophy will be present. A digital rectal exam is still mandatory on any MTFs over the age of 50 due to the presence of the prostate gland. Any FTM who has not had a hysterectomy or has had a supracervical hysterectomy will need to continue with routine cervical screening.

Chapter Review

Critical Thinking Questions

1. A 60-year-old woman has a weak family history of breast cancer, including two great aunts, both postmenopausal at diagnosis. She would like to pursue *BRCA* testing. How would you address this request? What are the implications of genetic testing? What would you need to know about her history to determine the appropriateness of this test?

2. A 72-year-old woman with comorbidities of obesity and diabetes, who lives alone, is scheduled for a modified radical mastectomy for invasive breast cancer. Discuss the postoperative care of this patient, including discharge planning. How would you modify your care if she has a severe hearing impairment? How would you modify care if she has been noncompliant with her

medical care in the past? What appropriate resources are available for this patient?

3. When visiting the employee health center to obtain her annual influenza vaccine, a 48-year-old woman with a history of breast cancer and previous mastectomy reports that she has been experiencing vague abdominal discomfort, bloating, flatulence, and increased waist size over the last 6 months. Her next annual physical examination is 6 months from now. What additional information is it important to obtain from her? What recommendations for further follow-up and health care would you provide?

4. A 50-year-old woman is scheduled for a total hysterectomy to treat fibroids. She reports that she anticipates severe symptoms of menopause because her mother and

grandmother had severe symptoms. She asks you about medications and herbal substances that can prevent or minimize menopausal symptoms without increasing her risk of breast cancer or cardiac disease. What is the strength of evidence about medications, including estrogen, and herbal substances to reduce menopausal symptoms? What criteria would you use to determine the strength of that evidence?

NCLEX–Style Review Questions

1. A patient is concerned with developing breast cancer. The nurse recognizes which of the following as the greatest risk factor for developing breast cancer?
   A. Having a first-degree relative who developed breast cancer
   B. Being female and advancing age
   C. Beginning menses before age 12 and never having children
   D. Smoking and obesity

2. A patient asks the nurse when she should be screened for breast cancer. What is the nurse's best response, based on the American Cancer Society's recommendations for breast cancer screening?
   A. Annual screening mammography beginning at age 40, clinical breast exam every 3 years beginning at age 20 and annually beginning at age 40, and practicing breast self-awareness
   B. Annual screening mammography beginning at age 50, annual clinical breast exam beginning at age 50
   C. Screening mammography every other year beginning at age 50, annual clinical breast exam beginning at age 40, monthly breast self-exam

   D. Baseline screening mammogram at age 35, annual screening mammography beginning at age 40, breast MRI every 5 years beginning at age 40, annual clinical breast exam beginning at age 20, monthly breast self-exam

3. Which patient would be at highest risk for subsequent development of lymphedema?
   A. A 75-year-old woman with a single focus of biopsy-proven localized ductal carcinoma in situ
   B. A 65-year-old woman with a known benign cyst
   C. A 50-year-old woman with a biopsy-confirmed fibroadenoma
   D. A 62-year-old woman with biopsy-proven invasive ductal carcinoma with palpable axillary lymph nodes and positive node fine needle aspiration

4. A patient suspects that she may have PMS. The nurse should ask the patient about which of the following symptoms?
   A. Symptoms occur during the luteal phase of the menstrual cycle.
   B. Symptoms occur during the follicular phase of the menstrual cycle.
   C. Symptoms worsen during menopause.
   D. Symptoms persist throughout the entire menstrual cycle.

5. A patient has just been prescribed Lupron for her endometriosis. The nurse should include which of the following side effects while educating the patient about this drug?
   A. She may experience breakthrough bleeding.
   B. Reversible symptoms of menopause may occur.
   C. The medication will reduce the size of her fibroids.
   D. A form of back-up contraception should be used while taking this drug.

Try these additional resources to enhance your learning and understanding of this chapter:
- thePoint online resource available at **http://thepoint.lww.com/Pellico1e**
- *Handbook for Focus on Adult Health: Medical-Surgical Nursing*
- *Study Guide for Focus on Adult Health: Medical-Surgical Nursing*

References and Selected Readings

References and selected readings associated with this chapter can be found on the website that accompanies the book. Visit http://thepoint.lww.com/Pellico1e to access the references and other additional resources associated with this chapter.

SUSANNE A. QUALLICH

Nursing Management: Patients With Male Reproductive Disorders

Learning Objectives

After reading this chapter, you will be able to:

1. Discuss the causes and management of male sexual dysfunction.

2. Compare the types of prostatectomy with regard to advantages and disadvantages.

3. Use the nursing process as a framework for care of the patient undergoing prostatectomy.

4. Describe the various conditions affecting the penis, including pathophysiology, clinical manifestations, and management.

5. Describe the various conditions affecting the testes, including pathophysiology, clinical manifestations, and management.

Disorders of the male reproductive system involve the genitalia and, in some instances, sexuality; as a consequence, the patient may experience anxiety and embarrassment. The effects of trauma, chronic illness, and physical disability on sexual function can be profound. The nurse must recognize the patient's need for privacy as well as his need for education.

DISORDERS OF MALE SEXUAL FUNCTION

ERECTILE DYSFUNCTION

Erectile dysfunction (ED), also referred to as impotence, is the inability to achieve or maintain an erection sufficient for satisfactory sexual activity. Up to 50% of men age 40 and older may report some difficulty with erectile function (Jimbo, 2008).

Pathophysiology

The physiology of erection and ejaculation is complex and involves sympathetic and parasympathetic components. Erection involves the release of nitric oxide into the corpus cavernosum during sexual stimulation; this releases cyclic guanosine monophosphate (cGMP) and causes smooth muscle relaxation. This allows flow of blood into the corpus cavernosum, resulting in erection (Porth & Matfin, 2009).

ED has both psychogenic and organic causes. Psychogenic causes include anxiety, fatigue, depression, and pressure to perform sexually. Organic causes include occlusive vascular disease, endocrine disease (diabetes, hypogonadism, hyperthyroidism, and hypothyroidism), cirrhosis, chronic renal failure, postsurgical causes (retroperitoneal surgery), neurologic disorders (neuropathies, parkinsonism, spinal cord injury, and multiple sclerosis), trauma to the pelvic or genital area, alcohol, medications (Box 34-1), and drug abuse.

Clinical Manifestations and Assessment

The diagnosis of ED requires a sexual and medical history; an analysis of presenting symptoms; a physical examination, including a neurologic examination; a detailed assessment of all medications, alcohol, and drugs used;

Classes of Medications Associated With Erectile Dysfunction

- Antiadrenergics and antihypertensives
- Anticholinergics and phenothiazines
- Antiseizure agents
- Antifungals
- Antiandrogen medications (prostate cancer treatment)
- Antipsychotics
- Antispasmodics
- Anxiolytics, sedative–hypnotics, tranquilizers
- Beta blockers
- Calcium channel blockers
- Carbonic anhydrase inhibitors
- H_2 antagonists
- Thiazide diuretics
- Tricyclic antidepressants

and laboratory studies. Because ED can occur secondary to a variety of disorders and pharmacological agents, nurses are encouraged to ask the patient questions about erectile function. Numerous tools are available to help nurses introduce the topic of sexual health with their patients; the BETTER model is presented in Box 34-2 (Hordern, 2008; Katz, 2006).The man may report decreased frequency of erections, inability to achieve a firm erection, or rapid detumescence (subsidence of erection).

Nocturnal penile tumescence tests and Rigiscan® testing are options to evaluate actual erectile function and help to determine whether there is an organic or a psychological cause; these are ordered at the discretion of the provider. Arterial blood flow to the penis can be measured using a Doppler probe. Figure 34-1 describes the evaluation and treatment of ED.

BETTER Model for Assessing Sexuality

Bring up the topic.

Explain you are concerned with quality-of-life issues, including sexuality. Although you may not be able to answer all questions, you want to convey that patients can talk about any concerns they have.

Tell patients that you will find appropriate resources to address their concerns.

Timing might not seem appropriate now, but acknowledge that they can ask for information at any time.

Educate patients about the side effects of their medications, cancer treatments, or treatments for other comorbidities.

Record your assessment and interventions in patients' medical records.

Adapted from Mick, J., Hughes, M., & Cohen, M. (2004). Using the BETTER model to assess sexuality. *Clinical Journal of Oncology Nursing, 8*(1), 85.

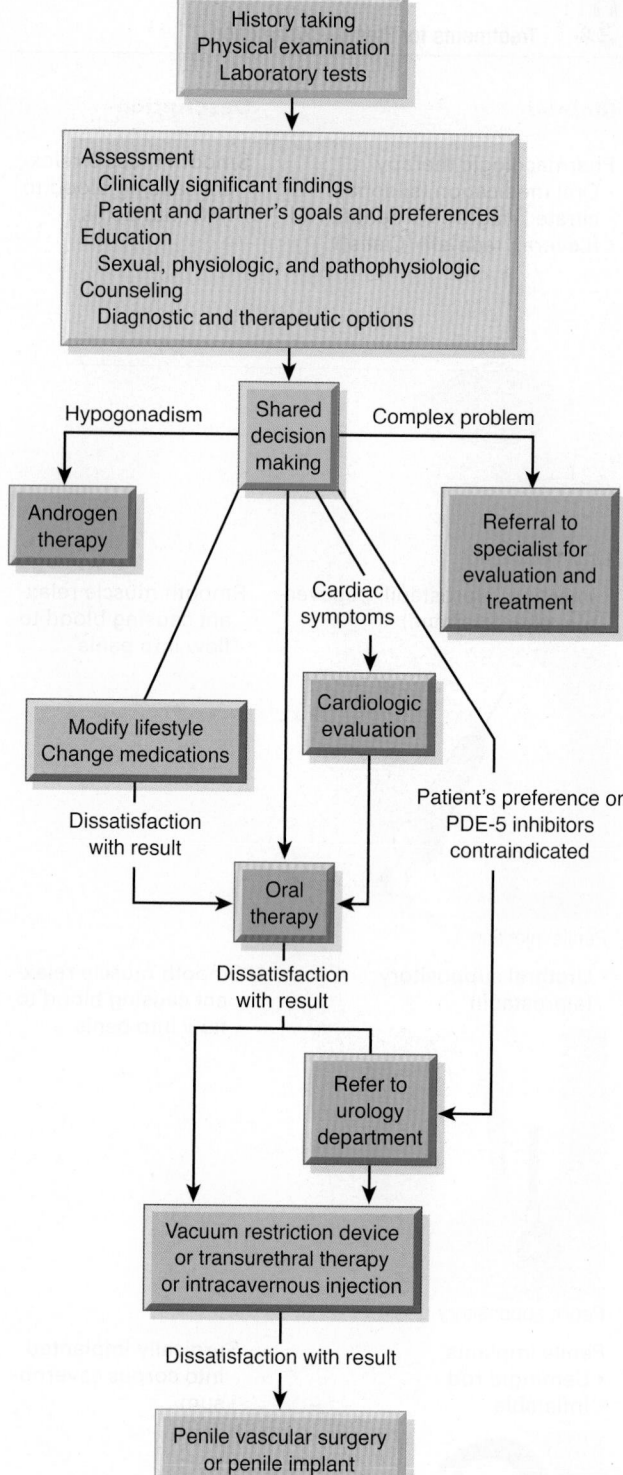

FIGURE 34-1 Evaluation and treatment of men with erectile dysfunction. From Lue, T. F. (2000). Erectile dysfunction. *New England Journal of Medicine, 342*(24), 1807. ©2000 Massachusetts Medical Society. All rights reserved. Used with permission.

TABLE
34-1 Treatments for Erectile Dysfunction

Method	Description	Advantages and Disadvantages	Duration
Pharmacologic therapy • Oral medication (sildenafil citrate [Viagra]; vardenafil HCl [Levitra]; tadalafil [Cialis])	Smooth muscle relaxant causing blood to flow into penis	Can cause headache and sinus stuffiness Contraindicated for men taking nitrate medications Used with caution in patients with retinopathy, or poor exercise tolerance	Taken orally 1 hour before intercourse Stimulation is required to achieve erection.

Oral medication

• Injection (alprostadil, papaverine, phentolamine)	Smooth muscle relaxant causing blood to flow into penis	Firm erections are achievable in more than 50% of cases Pain at injection site; plaque formation, risk of priapism	Injection 20 minutes before intercourse Erection can last up to 1 hour.

Penile injection

• Urethral suppository (alprostadil)	Smooth muscle relaxant causing blood to flow into penis	May be used twice a day Not recommended with pregnant partners, or if trying to become pregnant	Inserted 20 to 30 minutes before intercourse Erection can last up to 1 hour.

Penile suppository

Penile implants • Semirigid rod • Inflatable	Surgically implanted into corpus cavernosum	Reliable Requires surgery Healing takes up to 3 weeks Semirigid rod results in permanent semierection	Indefinite Inflatable prosthesis: Saline returns from penile receptacle to reservoir.

Penile implant

Method	Description	Advantages and Disadvantages	Duration
Negative-pressure (vacuum) devices Penile vacuum pump	Induction of erection with vacuum; maintained with constriction band around base of penis	Few side effects Patients may find it cumbersome to use Vasocongestion of penis can cause pain or numbness	To prevent penile injury, constriction band must not be left in place for longer than 1 hour.

Medical Management

Treatment can be medical, surgical, or both, depending on the cause (Table 34-1). Nonsurgical therapy includes treating associated conditions, such as diabetes, and adjusting antihypertensive agents or other medications. Endocrine therapy may reverse the condition. Patients with ED from psychogenic causes are referred to a sex therapist. Patients with ED secondary to organic causes may be candidates for penile implants.

Pharmacologic Therapy

Phosphodiesterase-5 (PDE-5) inhibitors are oral medications that are used to treat ED. Sildenafil citrate (Viagra), the first of these agents, was introduced in 1998 in the United States. Other PDE-5 inhibitors are vardenafil HCl (Levitra) and tadalafil (Cialis). PDE-5 is an enzyme that destroys cGMP, the nucleotide that causes the cavernosal relaxation necessary for erection to occur. By inhibiting PDE-5, cGMP is allowed to accumulate, thus facilitating corporeal smooth muscle relaxation in response to sexual stimulation (Porth & Matfin, 2009). When these PDE-5 inhibitors are taken about 1 hour before sexual activity, they are effective in producing, with stimulation, an erection that can last about 60 to 120 minutes (Li & Ralph, 2010). These medications have side effects and are contraindicated in men who take organic nitrates, because together these drugs can cause severe hypotension (Li & Ralph, 2010). Table 34-2 summarizes the dosing and nursing implications of these medications.

Other pharmacologic measures to induce erections include injecting vasoactive agents, such as alprostadil, papaverine, and phentolamine, directly into the penis. Complications include **priapism** (a persistent erection of the penis) and development of fibrotic plaques at the injection sites. Alprostadil is also formulated in a gel pellet that can be inserted into the urethra to promote an erection.

Penile Implants

Penile implants are available in two types: the semirigid rod and the inflatable prosthesis. The semirigid rod results in a permanent semierection, but is uncommonly used. The inflatable prosthesis simulates natural erections and natural flaccidity. Complications after implantation include infection and erosion of the prosthesis through the corpora (see Chapter 32, Fig. 32-7), which may require removal of the implant (Quallich & Ohl, 2002). Factors to consider in choosing a prosthesis include the expectations of the patient and his partner.

Vacuum Erection Devices

Negative-pressure (vacuum) devices may also be used to induce an erection. A plastic cylinder is placed over the flaccid penis, and negative pressure is applied. When an erection is attained, a constriction band is placed around the base of the penis to maintain the erection.

Nursing Management

Personal satisfaction and the ability to sexually satisfy a partner are common concerns of patients. Men with illnesses and disabilities may need the assistance of a sex therapist to find, implement, and integrate their sexual beliefs and behaviors into a healthy and satisfying lifestyle. The nurse should assess the patient's needs and make appropriate resources available, including information regarding referral to a specialized sex therapist, such as www.aasect.org.

DISORDERS OF EJACULATION

The spectrum of disorders of ejaculation responses ranges from occasional ejaculation through intercourse or self-stimulation to complete inability to ejaculate under any circumstances. For instance, premature ejaculation occurs when a man reaches climax before or shortly after intromission. Treatment modalities depend on the nature and severity of the ejaculation problem. Behavioral therapies may be indicated; these therapies often involve both sexual partners. In some cases, pharmacologic and behavioral therapy together may be effective.

TABLE
34-2 Pharmacologic Treatment of Erectile Dysfunction

	Sildenafil Citrate (Viagra)	Vardenafil HCl (Levitra)	Tadalafil (Cialis)
Recommended dose	Dosage range is 25 to 100 mg, based on individual response. Take only once in 24 hours.	Dosage range is 5 to 20 mg, based on individual response. Take only once in 24 hours.	Dosage range is 5 to 20 mg, based on individual response. Take only once in 24 hours. For patients with decreased liver or kidney function, the maximum dose is 10 mg every 48 hours.
When to take	Take the medication 30 minutes to 4 hours before intercourse. *There must be sexual stimulation to produce an erection.*	Follow the same directions as with sildenafil; take the medication 1 hour before intercourse. The peak action occurs in 30 to 120 minutes. *There must be sexual stimulation to produce an erection.*	Take the medication before sexual activity. Effect peaks at 30 minutes to 6 hours; effect may last up to 36 hours. *There must be sexual stimulation to produce an erection.*
Side effects	Side effects include headache, flushing, indigestion, nasal congestion, blue vision.	Side effects include headache, flushing, runny nose, indigestion, sinusitis. Tell your provider if you experience any of these effects.	Tadalafil may cause back pain and muscle aches. Tell your provider if you experience any of these side effects.
Contraindications	Do not take if you are taking nitrate medications such as nitroglycerine or isosorbide mononitrate. Do not take if you have high uncontrolled blood pressure, coronary artery disease, or have had a heart attack within the past 6 months. Do not take if you have been diagnosed with a cardiac arrythmia or kidney or liver dysfunction.		
Drug interactions	This medication can react with other medications that you may be taking. Provide your provider with a complete list of all prescribed as well as over-the-counter medications that you are using.		

Neurologic disorders (e.g., spinal cord injury, multiple sclerosis, neuropathy secondary to diabetes), surgery (prostatectomy), and medications are the most common causes of inhibited ejaculation. Chemical, vibratory, and electrical methods of stimulation have been used with some success.

CONDITIONS OF THE PROSTATE

PROSTATITIS

Prostatitis is an inflammation of the prostate gland that is caused by infectious agents or other conditions (e.g., urethral stricture, prostatic hyperplasia).

Pathophysiology

Escherichia. coli is the most commonly isolated organism. Microorganisms are usually carried to the prostate from the urethra. Prostatitis syndromes are classified as acute bacterial (type I), chronic bacterial (type II), chronic prostatitis/chronic pelvic pain syndrome (CP/CPPS) (type IIIa), inflammatory, chronic prostatitis/chronic pelvic pain syndrome (CP/CPPS) (type IIIb), and noninflammatory and asymptomatic inflammatory prostatitis (type IV) (National Institute of Health; National Institute of Diabetes and Digestive and Kidney Disease [NIH/NIDDK], 2008).

Clinical Manifestations and Assessment

The diagnosis of prostatitis requires a careful history and physical examination. Symptoms of prostatitis may include perineal discomfort, dysuria, urgency, frequency, and pain with or after ejaculation. Prostatodynia (pain in the prostate) is manifested by pain on voiding or perineal pain without evidence of inflammation or bacterial growth in the prostate fluid.

Acute bacterial prostatitis may produce sudden fever and chills and perineal, rectal, or low back pain. Urinary symptoms, such as dysuria (painful urination), frequency, urgency, and **nocturia** (awakening at night to urinate) may occur. Chronic bacterial prostatitis is a major cause of relapsing urinary tract infection (UTI) in men. Symptoms are usually mild, consisting of frequency, dysuria, and occasionally urethral discharge. Complications of prostatitis include swelling of the prostate gland, urinary retention, epididymitis, bacteremia, and pyelonephritis (discussed in Chapter 27).

If the patient does not have acute prostatitis, the provider performs a digital rectal examination (DRE) after collection of a urine sample, which commonly reveals many white blood cells. A DRE should not be performed if acute prostatitis is suspected because of the increased risk of causing bacteremia and septicemia.

Medical Management

The goal of therapy for acute bacterial prostatitis is to avoid the complications of abscess formation and septicemia. A complete blood count (CBC), and blood and urine culture may be ordered. A **prostate-specific antigen** (PSA) test may not be obtained since in many patients the acute inflammatory process causes elevation. However, it can also provide a means to track the success of treatment, as it should lessen with the use of antibiotics. A broad-spectrum antibiotic, frequently a fluoroquinolone, is administered for 14 to 30 days. Comfort is promoted with analgesic agents, antispasmodic medications, bladder sedatives (to relieve bladder irritability), sitz baths (to relieve pain and spasm), and stool softeners (to prevent pain from straining).

Chronic bacterial prostatitis can be difficult to treat because most antibiotics diffuse poorly from the plasma into the prostatic fluid. Treatment includes alpha-adrenergic blockers to promote relaxation of the bladder and prostate. Antibiotics such as trimethoprim-sulfamethoxazole or a fluoroquinolone may be prescribed.

The treatment of nonbacterial prostatitis is directed toward relief of symptoms.

Nursing Management

A patient experiencing symptoms of acute prostatitis may be hospitalized for IV antibiotic therapy. Nursing management includes administration of prescribed antibiotics and provision of comfort measures, including prescribed analgesic agents and sitz baths. In addition, the patient is cautioned to avoid activities that results in repetitive perineal trauma such as mountain biking.

The patient with chronic prostatitis is usually treated on an outpatient basis and needs to be instructed about the importance of continuing antibiotic therapy. The nurse instructs the patient to complete the prescribed course of antibiotics. Hot sitz baths (10 to 20 minutes) may be taken several times daily. Fluids are encouraged to satisfy thirst but are not "forced," because an effective medication level must be maintained in the urine. To minimize discomfort, the patient should avoid sitting for long periods.

BENIGN PROSTATIC HYPERPLASIA

In approximately one half of men 50 years and older, the prostate gland enlarges, and obstructs the outflow of urine. Benign prostatic hyperplasia (BPH), is evident in 80% of men 80 years of age and older.

Pathophysiology

The hypertrophied lobes of the prostate may obstruct the vesical neck or prostatic urethra, causing incomplete emptying of the bladder and urinary retention. As a result, a gradual dilation of the ureters (hydroureter) and kidneys (hydronephrosis)

can occur. UTIs may result from urinary stasis since retained urine serves as a medium for infective organisms.

Risk Factors

The cause of BPH is uncertain. Many African American men develop BPH at a much younger age (40 years) than Caucasian men do, whereas Asian men are unlikely to develop BPH (Peterson & Sesterhenn, 2009). Recent studies have identified smoking (both current and former smoking), heavy alcohol consumption, hypertension, heart disease, and diabetes as risk factors associated with BPH in African American men (Tanagho & McAninch, 2007). Other studies suggest that dietary factors may affect prostate growth and BPH (American Cancer Society [ACS], 2009).

Clinical Manifestations and Assessment

The obstructive and irritative symptoms associated with BPH include increased frequency of urination, nocturia, urgency, hesitancy in starting urination, abdominal straining with urination, a decrease in the volume and force of the urinary stream, interruption of the urinary stream, dribbling, a sensation of incomplete emptying, possible acute urinary retention, and recurrent UTIs.

DRE may reveal a large, rubbery, and nontender prostate gland, although the size of the prostate correlates poorly with symptom report. Diagnostic studies may be indicated to determine the degree to which the prostate is enlarged, the presence of any changes in the bladder wall, and the efficiency of renal function. These tests may include urinalysis, as well as urodynamic studies to assess urine flow and bladder function. Renal function tests, including serum creatinine levels, may be performed to determine whether renal impairment exists.

Medical Management

The treatment plan depends on the severity of the obstruction and the patient's condition. If the patient is admitted on an emergency basis because of urinary retention, an emergency catheterization is performed. The ordinary catheter may be too soft and pliable to advance through the urethra into the bladder. A Coude catheter is recommended to facilitate passage through the posterior urethra. If a catheter cannot be placed, an incision is made into the bladder (a suprapubic cystostomy) to provide drainage; however, this is rare. Further details are discussed in Chapter 28 under urinary retention.

Pharmacologic Therapy

Pharmacologic treatment for BPH includes use of alpha-adrenergic blockers and 5-alpha-reductase inhibitors (Karch, 2010). Alpha-adrenergic blockers relax the smooth muscle of the bladder neck and prostate, improve urine flow, and relieve

BPH symptoms (Karch, 2010). 5-alpha-reductase inhibitors interfere with the conversion of testosterone to dihydrotestosterone (DHT), which is associated with prostate growth. Decreased levels of DHT lead to decreased glandular cell activity and prostate size. Side effects may include gynecomastia, erectile dysfunction, and flushing.

Saw palmetto is an herbal product used to treat the symptoms associated with BPH. In theory, it functions by interfering with the conversion of testosterone to DHT. Research has shown that the efficacy of saw palmetto is similar to that of medications such as finasteride, and the herbal product may be better tolerated and less expensive (Tanagho & McAninch, 2007).

Other Therapies

Other treatment options for BPH include surgical options such as transurethral incision of the prostate (TUIP), balloon dilation, transurethral laser resection, transurethral needle ablation, and microwave thermotherapy (Tanagho & McAninch, 2007). The surgical approach of choice depends on the size of the gland, the severity of the obstruction, the age of the patient, any comorbidities, and the function of the bladder. "Watchful waiting" is another option chosen by many, in which patients are monitored periodically for severity of symptoms, physical findings, and laboratory tests, and may undergo diagnostic urologic tests.

CANCER OF THE PROSTATE

Prostate cancer is the most common cancer in men other than nonmelanoma skin cancer. It is the second most common cause of cancer death in American men, exceeded only by lung cancer, and is responsible for 10% of cancer-related deaths in men. Among men diagnosed with prostate cancer, 5 year-survival is nearly 100%, 93% survive at least 10 years, and 79% survive 15 years (ACS, 2009).

Risk Factors

Prostate cancer is common in the United States and northwestern Europe but is rare in Asia, Africa, Central America, and South America. The worldwide incidence of prostate cancer is highest in African American men; possible factors that may explain the increased mortality rate in African American men include their lower level of engagement in the health care system, disparities in health care, and cultural constraints (Tanagho & McAninch, 2007). Other risk factors for prostate cancer include increasing age; more than two-thirds of cases occur in men older than 65 years of age (ACS, 2009). A familial predisposition may occur in men who have a father or brother previously diagnosed with prostate cancer, especially if their relatives were diagnosed at a young age. Data suggest that men who consume a diet containing excessive amounts of red meat or high-fat dairy products are at increased risk for prostate cancer (ACS, 2009).

Clinical Manifestations and Assessment

Cancer of the prostate in its early stages rarely produces symptoms. If the neoplasm is large enough to encroach on the bladder neck, signs and symptoms of urinary obstruction occur (difficulty and frequency of urination, urinary retention, and decreased size and force of the urinary stream). Hematuria may result if the cancer invades the urethra or bladder, or both.

Prostate cancer can metastasize to bone and lymph nodes. Symptoms related to metastases include backache, hip pain, perineal and rectal discomfort, anemia, weight loss, weakness, nausea, and oliguria (<400 mL/day). These symptoms may be the first indications of prostate cancer.

The American Urological Association (AUA) (2009) recommends that "men who wish to be screened should have both a PSA test and a DRE." The AUA also recommends that men be counseled regarding their potential treatment options prior to screening (AUA, 2009).

In direct contrast, the American Cancer Society (2009) does not support routine PSA screening, but recommends that providers "*offer* for testing with the PSA blood test and digital rectal exam (DRE) yearly, beginning at age 50, to men who are at average risk of prostate cancer and have at least a 10-year life expectancy." These tests are recommended for younger men (40 to 45 years of age) if they are at high risk for prostate cancer; namely, African American men and men who have a first-degree relative (father, brother, or son) diagnosed with prostate cancer at an early age (<65) (ACS, 2009).

The level of PSA in the blood is proportional to the total prostatic mass and does not necessarily indicate malignancy. There are limitations in the relationship between serum PSA, prostate cancer volume, and higher stages of prostate cancer as measured by the Gleason score, which is the system used most often to grade prostate cancer and to guide the physician in determining the most appropriate treatment (Tanagho & McAninch, 2007). The combination of DRE and PSA testing appears to be a cost-effective method of detecting prostate cancer. If prostate cancer is detected early, the likelihood of cure is high. Unfortunately, the methods used to identify prostate cancer from abnormal findings on DRE and serum PSA elevations have limitations of both false-positive and false-negative results, and this adds to the continued lack of consensus regarding "best screening" tools.

Routine repeated rectal palpation of the gland (preferably by the same examiner) is important, because early cancer may be detected as a nodule within the substance of the gland. The diagnosis of prostate cancer is confirmed by a histologic examination of tissue. Cancer detected when transurethral resection of the prostate (TURP) is performed for benign prostatic enlargement and lower urinary tract symptoms occurs in about 1 out of 10 cases (Tanagho & McAninch, 2007).

Needle biopsies of the prostate are guided by transrectal ultrasound (TRUS), and may be indicated for men who have elevated PSA levels and abnormal DRE findings. Other tests

that may be used to establish the extent of disease include bone scans to detect metastasis to the bones, and computed tomography (CT) scan to identify metastases in the pelvic lymph nodes.

Medical and Nursing Management

Treatment is based on the stage of the disease and the patient's age and symptoms. Review of data from clinical assessment, laboratory and radiology tests, TRUS, and/or biopsy results assists in the treatment decision process.

Surgical Management

Radical prostatectomy is the complete surgical removal of the prostate, seminal vesicles, and often the surrounding fat, nerves, lymph nodes, and blood vessels. It is considered the standard first-line treatment for prostate cancer. Although ED commonly follows radical prostatectomy, Da Vinci prostatectomy or robotically assisted laparoscopic radical prostatectomy (RALP) offers advantages of low morbidity and more rapid discharge postprocedure (see below for discussion).

Radiation Therapy

If prostate cancer is detected in its early stage, the treatment may be curative radiation therapy. Two major forms of radiation therapy are used to treat cancer of the prostate: teletherapy (external) and brachytherapy (internal).

Teletherapy (external-beam radiation therapy) involves 6 to 7 weeks of daily (5 days/week) radiation treatments. Current technology sets a dose for the target volume and restricts the dose to adjacent structures. It is thought to be accurate within 1 to 3 millimeters.

Brachytherapy involves the implantation of interstitial radioactive seeds under anesthesia, via the perineum, into the prostate. Eighty to 100 seeds are placed directly into the prostate, and the patient returns home after the procedure. Exposure of others to radiation is minimal, but the patient should avoid close contact with pregnant women and infants for up to 2 months.

Side effects of teletherapy and brachytherapy include inflammation of the rectum, bowel, and bladder due to their proximity to the prostate and the radiation doses. Table 34-3 discusses nursing interventions to minimize side effects. Combination therapy (radiation therapy followed by hormonal therapy) may improve overall survival.

Hormonal Therapy

Hormonal therapy for advanced prostate cancer suppresses androgenic stimuli to the prostate by decreasing the level of circulating plasma testosterone or interrupting the conversion to or binding of DHT. As a result, the prostatic epithelium atrophies. This effect is accomplished either by surgical castration (**orchiectomy**) or by the administration of medications. Orchiectomy is associated with considerable emotional impact. The most appropriate choice, timing, and actual benefits of hormonal therapy are uncertain.

TABLE 34-3 Management of Radiation-Induced Symptoms

Symptom	Intervention
Cystitis	Maintain hydration. Encourage patient to take prescribed medications (bladder antispasmodics, alpha blockers, analgesics). Avoid known bladder irritants (see Chapter 28).
Diarrhea	Provide low-residue diet. Maintain hydration. Administer antidiarrheals as indicated. Give dietary bulking agents as indicated.
Erectile dysfunction	Assess for level of distress and suggest sexual therapist as appropriate. Provide education regarding appropriate medication.
Proctitis (inflammation of the rectum)	Offer sitz baths. Recommend water-based lubricants. Maintain hydration to avoid constipation. Adjust diet to avoid constipation.

Effective hormonal alternatives to orchiectomy include the nonsteroidal antiandrogen bicalutamide (Karch, 2010). Newer hormonal therapies include luteinizing hormone–releasing hormone (LHRH) agonists (leuprolide and goserelin) and antiandrogen agents, such as flutamide. LHRH suppresses testicular androgen, while flutamide causes adrenal androgen suppression. LHRH agonists are used for the following: (1) in the adjuvant and neoadjuvant setting (i.e., before use of hormonal suppressive agents), in combination with radiation therapy; (2) in combination with radical prostatectomy; and (3) in the treatment of recurrence indicated by an elevation in the PSA. Hot flashes can occur with orchiectomy or LHRH agonist therapy.

Second-Line Medical Treatment

The management of hormone-refractory cancer of the prostate remains somewhat controversial. Administration of second-line hormonal therapy using ketoconazole is an option that lowers testosterone by decreasing both testicular and endocrine production of androgens. There may be benefits in terms of survival with chemotherapy treatment that includes paclitaxel and docetaxel for non–androgen-dependent prostate cancer.

Other Therapies

Cryosurgery of the prostate is used to ablate prostate cancer in patients who cannot tolerate surgery and in those with recurrent prostate cancer. Transperineal probes are inserted into the prostate under ultrasound guidance to freeze the tissue directly.

Keeping the urethral passage patent may require repeated transurethral (TUR) resections. If this is impractical, catheter drainage is instituted by way of the suprapubic or transurethral route. For men with advanced prostate cancer, palliative measures such as pain management, complementary and alternative medicine (CAM), and androgen deprivation can be options. Although cure is unlikely with advanced prostate cancer, many men survive for a long period apparently free of metastatic disease.

Bone lesions resulting from metastasis of prostate cancer can be very painful. Opioid and nonopioid medications are used to control the pain. External-beam radiation therapy can be delivered to skeletal lesions to relieve pain, while radiopharmaceuticals can be injected IV to treat multiple sites of bone metastasis.

More than one-third of men with a diagnosis of prostate cancer elect to use some form of CAM. Because of lack of research on many forms of CAM, patients may be forced to rely on anecdotal information or information gained via the Internet to make decisions about its use.

Complications

Each treatment for prostate cancer has some incidence of sexual function issues (Box 34-3). With nerve-sparing radical prostatectomy, the likelihood of recovering the ability to have erections is better for men who are younger and in whom both neurovascular bundles are spared. Hormonal therapy also affects the central nervous system mechanisms that mediate sexual desire and arousability. PDE-5 inhibitors may be effective for treatment of ED in younger men after radical retropubic prostatectomy (discussed shortly), especially if the neurovascular bundles were preserved. They may improve erectile function in men with partial or moderate ED after radiation therapy for localized prostate cancer.

PROSTATE SURGERY

Prostate surgery may be indicated for the patient with BPH or prostate cancer. Prostate surgery should be performed before acute urinary retention develops and damages the upper urinary tract and collecting system or before cancer progresses.

Procedures

Several approaches can be used to remove the hypertrophied portion of the prostate gland: TURP, suprapubic prostatectomy, perineal prostatectomy, retropubic prostatectomy, TUIP, and robotic prostatectomy (Table 34-4). Hyperplastic tissue is removed, leaving behind the capsule of the prostate.

Transurethral Resection of the Prostate

TURP is carried out through endoscopy: the surgical instrument is introduced via the urethra to the prostate, which

---

BOX 34-3 | **Nursing Research Profile**

Bridging the Gap to Evidence-Based Practice

Effects of Radiation Therapy on Sexual Function and Quality of Life.

Howlett, K., Koetters, T., Edrington, J., West, C., Paul, S., Lee, K., et al. (2010) Changes in sexual function on mood and quality of life in patients undergoing radiation therapy for prostate cancer. *Oncology Nursing Forum, 37*(1), E58–66.

Purpose

The purpose of this study was to describe the percentages of men with and without changes in sexual function from the beginning to end of radiation therapy and to evaluate for differences in demographic and clinical characteristics, mood states, and quality of life (QOL) among patients who did and did not experience changes in sexual function.

Design

A descriptive, longitudinal study was conducted with 70 men with prostate cancer who underwent primary or adjuvant radiation therapy in radiation therapy departments in northern California. They completed several self-report questionnaires, including a demographic questionnaire, the Karnofsky Performance Status (KPS), the Center for Epidemiological Studies-Depression Scale (CES-D), the Spielberger State Anxiety Inventory (STAI-S), and the Quality of Life Scale-Patient Version (QOL-PV). In addition, medical record reviews were conducted. Data were analyzed using descriptive statistics, frequency distributions, and repeated measures analysis of variance.

Findings

About 50% had a problem with sexual function either at the beginning or end of radiation therapy. Overall, men without sexual problems at both the beginning and end of radiation therapy had significantly less anxiety and depression and higher QOL scores than did patients who developed a problem at the end and patients who had a problem at both time points. Findings from this relatively small sample of men suggest that changes in sexual function during the course of radiation therapy affect patients' mood and QOL.

Nursing Implications

Nurses should evaluate the effects of radiation therapy on sexual function and monitor patients with prostate cancer for depression and anxiety, as well as for changes in QOL.

TABLE 34-4 Surgical Approaches for Treatment of Prostate Disorders

Surgical Approach	Advantages	Disadvantages	Nursing Implications
Transurethral resection (TURP) (removal of prostatic tissue by instrument introduced through urethra)	Avoids abdominal incision Safer for surgical risk patient Shorter hospitalization and recovery periods Lower morbidity rate Causes less pain	Recurrent obstruction, urethral trauma, and stricture may develop Delayed bleeding may occur	Monitor for hemorrhage. Observe for symptoms of urethral stricture (dysuria, straining, weak urinary stream)
Open surgical removal (for prostate cancer; uncommonly used to treat enlarged prostate)			
Suprapubic approach	Technically simple Offers wide area of exploration Permits exploration for cancerous lymph nodes Allows more complete removal of obstructing gland Permits treatment of associated bladder lesions	Requires surgical approach through the bladder Control of hemorrhage difficult Urine may leak around the suprapubic tube Recovery may be prolonged and uncomfortable	Monitor for indications of hemorrhage and shock Provide meticulous aseptic care to the area around suprapubic tube
Perineal approach	Offers direct anatomic approach Permits gravity drainage of catheter Particularly effective for radical cancer therapy Allows hemostasis under direct vision Low mortality rate Low incidence of shock	Higher postoperative incidence of impotence and urinary incontinence Possible damage to rectum and external sphincter Restricted operative field	Avoid using rectal tubes or thermometers and enemas after perineal surgery Use drainage pads to absorb excess urinary drainage Possible urinary leakage around the wound after the catheter is removed
Retropubic approach	Avoids incision into the bladder Permits surgeon to see and control bleeding Shorter recovery period Less bladder sphincter damage	Cannot treat associated bladder disease Increased incidence of hemorrhage from prostatic venous plexus	Monitor for hemorrhage Anticipate urinary leakage for several days after removing the catheter
Transurethral incision (TUIP)	Results comparable to TURP Low incidence of erectile dysfunction and retrograde ejaculation No bladder neck contracture	Recurrent obstruction and urethral trauma Delayed bleeding	Monitor for hemorrhage
Robotic prostatectomy (Da Vinci prostatectomy)	Minimally invasive technique Improved patient satisfaction and quality of life Short convalescence More rapid return to normal activity Short indwelling catheter duration Decreased blood loss Improved magnification of operative field	Technically demanding skill set for surgeon Lack of tactile sensation available with open prostatectomy Inability to palpably assess for induration and palpable nodules Inability to delineate the proximity of involvement of the neurovascular bundles due to lack of palpation	Observe for symptoms of urethral stricture (dysuria, straining, weak urinary stream) Monitor for hemorrhage and shock Provide meticulous aseptic care to the area around suprapubic tube Avoid using rectal tubes or thermometers and enemas after perineal surgery Use drainage pads to absorb excess urinary drainage Anticipate urinary leakage after the catheter is removed

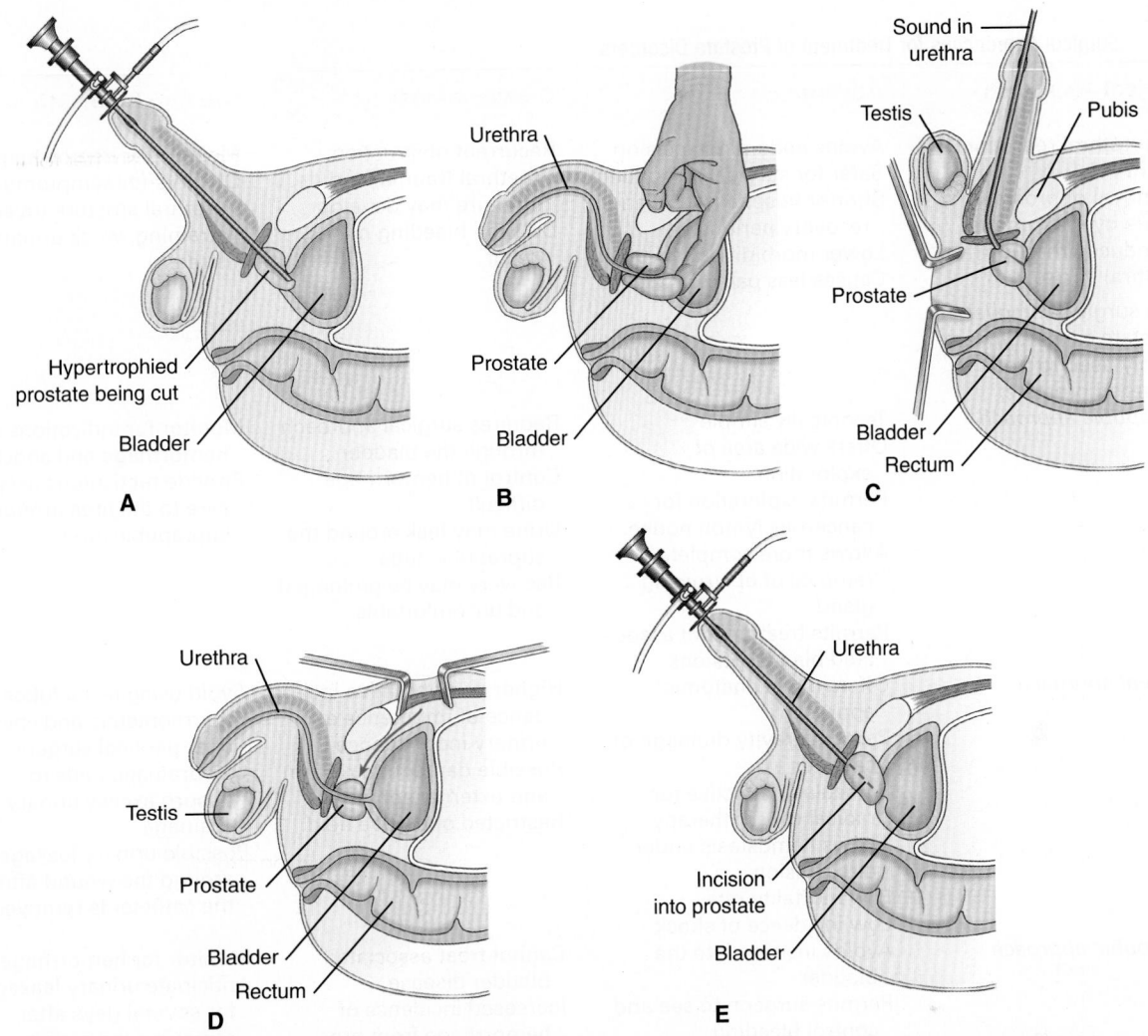

FIGURE 34-2 Prostate surgery procedures. (**A**) Transurethral resection (TUR). A loop of wire connected with a cutting current is rotated in the cystoscope to remove shavings of prostate at the bladder orifice. (**B**) Suprapubic prostatectomy. With an abdominal approach, the prostate is shelled out of its bed. (**C**) Perineal prostatectomy. Two retractors on the left spread the perineal incision to provide a view of the prostate. (**D**) Retropubic prostatectomy is performed through a low abdominal incision. Note two abdominal retractors and *arrow* pointing to the prostate gland. (**E**) Transurethral incision of prostate (TUIP) involves one or two incisions into the prostate to reduce pressure on the urethra.

can then be viewed directly. The gland is removed in small chips with an electrical cutting loop (Fig. 34-2A). This procedure may be used for glands of varying size and is ideal for patients who have small glands and for those who are considered poor surgical risks. Newer technology uses bipolar electrosurgery and reduces the risk of electrical shock and also eliminates the risk of TUR syndrome (Box 34-4), a rare complication of TURP that occurs in approximately 2% of men.

TURP usually requires an overnight hospital stay. Urethral strictures are more frequent than with non-transurethral procedures, and repeated procedures may be necessary because the residual prostatic tissue grows back. TURP may trigger retrograde ejaculation due to removal of prostatic tissue at the bladder neck, which causes the seminal fluid to flow backward into the bladder.

Suprapubic Prostatectomy

Suprapubic prostatectomy is one method of removing the gland through an abdominal incision. An incision is made into the bladder, and the prostate gland is removed from above (see Fig. 34-2B). Blood loss may be greater than with the other methods, and it requires an abdominal incision.

Perineal Prostatectomy

Perineal prostatectomy involves removal of the gland through an incision in the perineum (see Fig. 34-2C). Postoperatively, the wound may easily become contaminated

BOX 34-4

BOX 34-4 Transurethral Resection Syndrome (Symptomatic Dilutional Hyponatremia)

Transurethral resection (TUR) syndrome is a rare (<2%) but potentially serious complication of transurethral prostatectomy (TURP). Signs and symptoms are caused by neurologic, cardiovascular, and electrolyte imbalances associated with absorption of the solution used to irrigate the surgical site during the surgical procedure. Hyponatremia, hypo-osmolality, and hypervolemia are dominant findings. Symptoms usually are associated with a serum sodium level of 125 mEq or less (Leslie, 2006). The dilutional hyponatremia leads to cerebral edema; thus, the patient exhibits neurological symptoms, while the volume overload is noted in symptoms of hypertension, arrhythmias, and full, bounding pulse. Patients with poor left ventricular function may develop pulmonary edema. Given the age of many men undergoing TURP and possible comorbidities of cardiac disease, the nurse is aware that fluctuating intravascular volume and myocardial compromise may result in hypotension. Additionally, if the hyponatremia develops rapidly to less than 120 mEq/L, negative inotropic effects cause hypotension and electrocardiographic changes of widened QRS complexes, and ventricular ectopy (Mutlu, Titiz, & Göğüş, 2007).

Signs and Symptoms of TUR Syndrome
- Lethargy and confusion
- Hypertension
- Tachycardia
- Nausea and vomiting
- Visual disturbances, such as flashing lights if glycine is used as an irrigant, as it is a neurotransmitter for the retina (Gray & Moore, 2009)
- Headache
- Muscle spasms
- Seizures

Interventions
- During the operative procedure, normal saline cannot be used as it conducts electricity. If the patient displays the aforementioned signs and symptoms, the intraoperative irrigating solution of glycine, sorbitol/ mannitol, or water is discontinued and replaced with normal saline.
- Administer diuretics as prescribed to facilitate excretion of absorbed fluid.
- Monitor intake and output.
- Monitor the patient's vital signs and level of consciousness.
- Differentiate the lethargy and confusion of TUR syndrome from postoperative disorientation and hyponatremia.
- Maintain patient safety during times of confusion.
- Assess lung and heart sounds for indications of pulmonary edema, heart failure, or both (fluid already present in profound hyponatremia).

---

because the incision is near the rectum, and incontinence, erectile dysfunction, and rectal injury are more likely.

Retropubic Prostatectomy

Retropubic prostatectomy is more common than the suprapubic approach. A low abdominal incision is made, and the prostate gland can be reached between the pubic arch and the bladder without entering the bladder (see Fig. 34-2D). This has the advantage of allowing better control of blood loss and better visualization of the surgical site.

Transurethral Incision of the Prostate

TUIP is indicated when the prostate gland is small (≤30 g), and it is an effective treatment for many cases of BPH. An instrument is passed through the urethra (see Fig. 34-2E). Incisions are made in the prostate and prostate capsule to reduce the prostate's pressure on the urethra and to reduce urethral constriction. It is performed on an outpatient basis and has a low complication rate.

Robotic or Laparoscopic Prostatectomy

Laparoscopic prostatectomy provides better visualization of the surgical site and surrounding areas. Patients who undergo this procedure have been shown to experience less bleeding, shorter hospital stays, less postoperative pain, and more rapid return to normal activity compared to those who undergo open radical prostatectomy (Tanagho & McAninch, 2007).

Complications

Postoperative complications depend on the type of prostatectomy performed and may include hemorrhage, clot formation, catheter obstruction, and sexual dysfunction. All prostatectomies carry a risk of impotence because of potential damage to the pudendal nerves. The anatomic changes in the posterior urethra lead to retrograde ejaculation. For the patient with resulting ED that does not resolve, options are available to produce erections sufficient for sexual intercourse: prosthetic penile implants, vacuum devices, and pharmacologic interventions (see Table 34-1, p. 952).

NURSING PROCESS

Patient Undergoing Prostatectomy

Assessment

The nurse assesses how the underlying disorder (BPH or prostate cancer) has affected the patient's lifestyle. The

(continued on page 962)

nurse asks about the patient's family history of cancer and heart or kidney disease, including hypertension. In addition, the nurse observes for weight loss, pallor, ability to get in and out of bed without assistance, and ability to perform activities of daily living (ADL). This information helps determine how soon the patient will be able to return to normal activities after prostatectomy.

Diagnosis

Based on the assessment data, the patient's major nursing diagnoses may include the following:

Preoperative nursing diagnoses:
- Anxiety related to surgery and its outcome
- Acute pain related to bladder distention
- Deficient knowledge about factors related to the disorder and the treatment protocol

Postoperative nursing diagnoses:
- Acute pain related to the surgical incision, catheter placement, and bladder spasms
- Deficient knowledge about postoperative care and management

Based on the assessment data, the potential complications may include the following:

- Hemorrhage and shock
- Infection
- Deep vein thrombosis
- Catheter obstruction
- Sexual dysfunction

Planning

The major preoperative goals for the patient may include reduced anxiety and learning about his prostate disorder and the perioperative experience. The major postoperative goals may include maintenance of fluid volume balance, relief of pain and discomfort, ability to perform self-care activities, and absence of complications.

Preoperative Nursing Interventions

Reducing Anxiety

The nurse must establish communication with the patient to assess his understanding of the diagnosis and of the planned surgical procedure. The nurse clarifies the nature of the surgery and expected postoperative outcomes, familiarizes the patient with the preoperative and postoperative routines, and initiates measures to reduce anxiety. Because the patient may be sensitive and embarrassed discussing problems related to the genitalia and sexuality, the nurse provides privacy and establishes a trusting and professional relationship. He is encouraged to verbalize his feelings and concerns.

Relieving Discomfort

If the patient experiences discomfort before surgery, he is prescribed bedrest, and analgesic agents are administered. If he is hospitalized, the nurse monitors his voiding patterns, watches for bladder distention, and assists with catheterization if indicated. The catheter can help decompress the bladder gradually over several days, especially if the patient is elderly and hypertensive and has diminished renal function or urinary retention that has existed for many weeks. If the patient cannot tolerate a urinary catheter, he is prepared for a cystostomy (surgical creation of an opening into the bladder, usually with a catheter (e.g., suprapubic tube, see Chapter 28).

Providing Instruction

Before surgery, the nurse reviews with the patient the anatomy of the affected structures and their function in relation to the urinary and reproductive systems, using diagrams and other teaching aids if indicated. This instruction often takes place during the preadmission testing visit or in the urologist's office. The nurse explains what will take place as the patient is prepared for surgery (depending on the type of prostatectomy planned). The nurse also describes the type of incision, which varies with the surgery chosen, and informs the patient about the likely type of urinary drainage system and the recovery room procedure. The amount of information given is based on the patient's needs and questions.

Preparing the Patient

If the patient is scheduled for a prostatectomy, the preoperative preparation described in Chapter 5 is provided.

Postoperative Nursing Interventions

Maintaining Fluid Balance

During the postoperative period, the patient is at risk for imbalanced fluid volume due to irrigation of the surgical site during and after surgery. With irrigation of the urinary catheter to prevent its obstruction by blood clots, fluid may be absorbed through the open surgical site and retained, increasing the risk of excessive fluid retention, fluid imbalance, and water intoxication. The patient is observed for signs of fluid volume excess, such as jugular vein distention (JVD), the development of an S_3 gallop, and pulmonary crackles. The urine output and the amount of fluid used for irrigation must be closely monitored to determine whether irrigation fluid is being retained and to ensure an adequate urine output. An intake and output record, including the amount of fluid used for irrigation, must be closely maintained. The patient also is monitored for electrolyte imbalances (e.g., hyponatremia), increasing blood pressure, confusion, and respiratory distress. Additionally, since the prostate is a vascular organ, hemorrhage is an immediate danger

postoperatively; thus, the nurse monitors the patient for hypotension, tachycardia, tachypnea, gross hematuria, restlessness, pallor, and decreasing hemoglobin and hematocrit. If deterioration of patient condition occurs, the surgeon is notified immediately. The nurse anticipates fluid resuscitation with IV fluids and blood products.

NURSING ALERT

In assessing urinary output, the nurse anticipates at a minimum 0.5 mL/kg/hr; thus, if the patient weighs 70 kg, 35 mL of urine is expected hourly. To calculate the actual urine output, the nurse must consider all irrigating fluids instilled, against total urine collection bag drainage. If large amounts of irrigating solutions are required postoperatively, the nurse empties the collection bag frequently to prevent overfilling and creating back pressure within the bladder. Meticulous recording of the urinary output is required.

Relieving Pain

If pain is present, the cause and location are determined, and the severity of pain and discomfort is assessed using a pain scale. The pain may be incisional, referred to the flank area, or may be caused by bladder spasms. Patients experiencing bladder spasms typically describe the pain as severe cramping and spasmodic in the suprapubic region. They may note a feeling of pressure or fullness in the bladder, and leakage from the urethra around the catheter rather than through the catheter.

NURSING ALERT

Bladder spasms are associated with irritation to the detrusor muscle, causing spasm of the muscle. If spasms are present, the nurse ensures that the urinary drainage system is patent since obstruction is associated with spasms. In addition, the nurse administers antispasmodic medication as prescribed.

The nurse monitors the drainage tubing and irrigates the system as prescribed to relieve any obstruction that may cause discomfort. Usually, if clots impede urinary drainage, the catheter is irrigated with 50 to 60 mL of irrigating fluid at a time. It is important to make sure that the same amount is recovered in the drainage receptacle. Securing the catheter drainage tubing to the leg or the lower abdomen can help decrease tension on the catheter and prevent bladder irritation.

After the patient is ambulatory, he is encouraged to walk but not to sit for prolonged periods because this increases intra-abdominal pressure and the possibility of discomfort and bleeding.

Monitoring and Managing Potential Complications

After prostatectomy, the patient is monitored for major complications such as hemorrhage, infection, DVT, catheter obstruction, and sexual dysfunction.

HEMORRHAGE. The immediate dangers after a prostate surgery are bleeding and hemorrhagic shock. This risk is increased with BPH, because a hyperplastic prostate gland is very vascular. Bleeding may result in the formation of clots, which then obstruct urine flow. The drainage normally begins as reddish-pink and then clears to a light pink within 24 hours after surgery. Bright red bleeding with increased viscosity and numerous clots usually indicates arterial bleeding and requires surgical intervention. Venous bleeding, which is dark red in color, may be controlled by the provider via "over-inflating" the urinary catheter balloon and applying traction to the catheter, so that the balloon holding the urinary catheter in place applies pressure to the prostatic fossa. If, after 20 minutes, the bleeding is not controlled, surgical exploration may be considered. Since bleeding is increased in the sitting position, which increases bladder and venous pressure, the patient is encouraged to rest in bed with the head of the bed slightly elevated.

Nursing management includes assistance in implementing strategies to stop the bleeding and to prevent or reverse hemorrhagic shock. If hemorrhagic shock occurs, treatments described in Chapter 54 are initiated.

Nursing interventions include closely monitoring vital signs; administering medications, IV fluids, and blood component therapy as prescribed; maintaining an accurate record of intake and output; and carefully monitoring drainage to ensure adequate urine flow and patency of the drainage system.

INFECTION. After perineal prostatectomy, the surgeon usually changes the dressing on the first postoperative day. Careful aseptic technique is used, because the potential for infection is great. Rectal thermometers, rectal tubes, and enemas are avoided because of the risk of injury and bleeding in the prostatic fossa. Sitz baths are also used to promote healing.

UTIs and epididymitis (infection of the epididymis, discussed later in chapter) are possible complications after prostatectomy, and the patient is assessed for their occurrence. Because the risk for infection continues after discharge from the hospital, the patient and family need to be instructed to monitor for signs and symptoms of infection (fever, chills, sweating, myalgia, dysuria, urinary frequency, and urgency).

DEEP VEIN THROMBOSIS (DVT). Because patients undergoing prostatectomy have a high incidence of DVT and pulmonary embolism, the provider may prescribe prophylactic low-dose heparin therapy. The nurse assesses the patient frequently after surgery for manifestations of DVT and applies elastic compression stockings. Nursing and medical management of DVT and pulmonary embolism are described in Chapters 10 and 18, respectively.

OBSTRUCTED CATHETER. After any procedure involving the prostate in which a catheter is placed, the catheter must drain well. An obstructed catheter produces distention of the prostatic capsule and resultant hemorrhage. A diuretic may be prescribed to promote urination and initiate postoperative diuresis, thereby helping to keep the catheter

(continued on page 964)

patent. The nurse observes the lower abdomen for increasing distention to ensure that the catheter has not become blocked. On percussion, increased dullness will be noted in the suprapubic region.

The drainage bag, dressings, and incisional site are examined for bleeding. The color of the urine is noted and documented; a change in color from pink to amber indicates reduced bleeding. Blood pressure, pulse, and respirations are monitored and compared with baseline preoperative vital signs to detect hypotension. The nurse also observes the patient for restlessness, diaphoresis, pallor, any drop in blood pressure, and an increasing pulse rate.

Drainage of the bladder may be accomplished by gravity through a closed sterile drainage system. A three-way drainage system is useful in irrigating the bladder and preventing clot formation (Fig. 34-3). Continuous bladder irrigation (CBI) may be used after a TURP, to maintain the drainage of the urinary catheter, remove blood clots from the bladder that are the result of the procedure, and cleanse the surgical area to promote healing, as well as to prevent potentially obstructing clots. The amount of fluid recovered in the drainage bag must equal the amount of fluid infused. Overdistention of the bladder is avoided, because it can induce secondary hemorrhage by stretching the coagulated blood vessels in the prostatic capsule.

To prevent traction on the bladder, the drainage tube (not the catheter) is taped to the shaved inner thigh. If a cystostomy catheter is in place, it is taped to the abdomen.

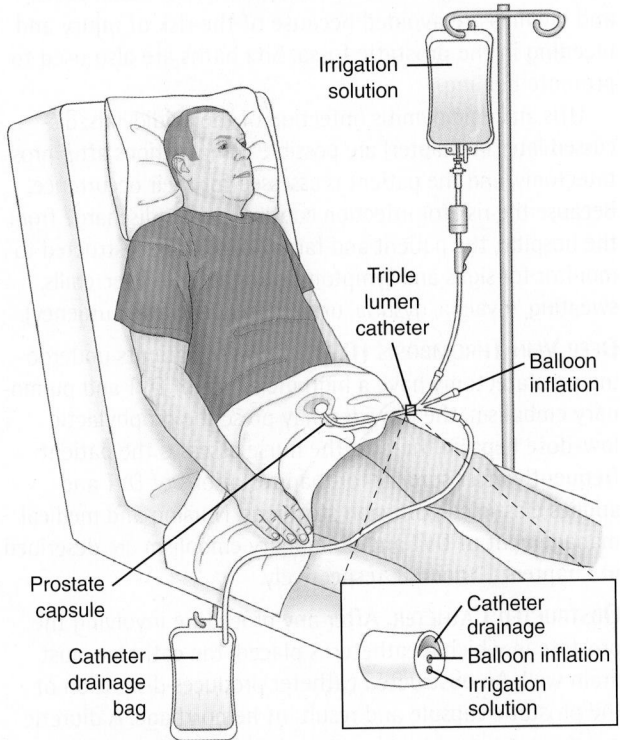

FIGURE 34-3 A three-way system for bladder irrigation.

Irrigation solution

Triple lumen catheter

Balloon inflation

Prostate capsule

Catheter drainage bag

Catheter drainage
Balloon inflation
Irrigation solution

SEXUAL DYSFUNCTION. The patient may experience sexual dysfunction related to ED, decreased libido, and fatigue. These issues may become a concern to the patient soon after surgery or in the weeks to months of rehabilitation. Options to restore erectile function may include medications, surgically placed implants, or vacuum devices. The patient should be aware that he may experience fatigue during rehabilitation from surgery, which may decrease his libido and alter his enjoyment of usual activities.

Nursing interventions include assessing for the presence of sexual dysfunction after surgery. Providing a private and confidential environment to discuss issues of sexuality is important. The emotional challenges of prostate surgery and its consequences need to be carefully explored with the patient and his partner.

Teaching Patients Self-Care

The patient undergoing prostatectomy may be discharged within several days. The length of the hospital stay depends on the type of prostatectomy performed. The patient and family require instructions about how to manage the urinary drainage system, how to assess for complications, and how to promote recovery. Verbal and written instructions should be provided, and the patient and family need to know about signs and symptoms that should be reported to the physician (e.g., blood in urine, decreased urine output, fever, change in wound drainage, calf tenderness) (Box 34-5).

After the catheter is removed (usually when the urine appears clear), urine may leak around the wound for several days. Some urinary incontinence may occur after catheter removal, and the patient is informed that this is likely to subside over time.

Continuing Care

Referral for home care may be indicated if the patient is elderly or has other health problems, if the patient and family cannot provide care in the home, or if the patient lives alone without available supports. The home care nurse assesses the patient's physical status and provides catheter and wound care. The home care nurse encourages the patient to ambulate and to carry out perineal exercises as prescribed. If the prostatectomy was performed to treat prostate cancer, the patient and family are also instructed about the importance of follow-up and monitoring with the urologist.

Evaluation

Expected postoperative patient outcomes may include the following:

1. Reports relief of discomfort
2. Exhibits fluid and electrolyte balance:
   a. Irrigation fluid and urinary output are within parameters determined by surgeon
   b. Experiences no signs or symptoms of fluid retention

Patient Education

Self-Care After a Prostatectomy

- Perform Kegel exercises, as they may help with regaining urinary control:
  - Tense the perineal muscles by pressing the buttocks together; hold this position; relax. This exercise can be performed 10 to 20 times each hour while sitting or standing.
  - Try to interrupt the urinary stream after starting to void; wait a few seconds and then continue to void.
- While the prostatic fossa heals (6 to 8 weeks), avoid activities that produce Valsalva effects (straining, heavy lifting), as this may increase venous pressure and produce hematuria.
- Avoid long motor trips and strenuous exercise, which increase the tendency to bleed.
- Note that spicy foods, alcohol, and coffee may cause bladder discomfort.
- Maintain fluid intake to avoid dehydration, which increases the tendency for a blood clot to form and obstruct the flow of urine.
- Report signs of complications, such as bleeding, passage of blood clots, a decrease in the urinary stream, urinary retention, or symptoms of UTI, to the urologist.

3. Participates in self-care measures:
   a. Increases activity and ambulation daily
   b. Produces urine output within normal ranges and consistent with intake
   c. Performs perineal exercises and interrupts urinary stream to promote bladder control
   d. Avoids straining and lifting heavy objects
4. Is free of complications:
   a. Maintains vital signs within normal limits
   b. Exhibits wound healing, without signs of inflammation or hemorrhage
   c. Maintains acceptable level of urinary elimination
   d. Maintains optimal drainage of catheter and other drainage tubes
   e. Reports understanding of changes in sexual function

CONDITIONS AFFECTING THE TESTES AND ADJACENT STRUCTURES

ORCHITIS AND EPIDIDYMITIS

Orchitis is an inflammation of the testes caused by a variety of factors (bacterial, viral, spirochetal, parasitic, traumatic, chemical, or unknown). Bacterial causes usually spread from an associated epididymitis, which usually descends from an infected prostate or urinary tract. Rest, elevation of the scrotum, ice packs to reduce scrotal edema, antibiotics, analgesic agents, and anti-inflammatory medications are recommended.

Pathophysiology

In men younger than 35 years of age, the major cause of epididymitis or orchitis is *Chlamydia trachomatis*. The infection passes upward through the urethra and the ejaculatory duct, and then along the vas deferens to the epididymis, and it can migrate to the testis as well.

Clinical Manifestations and Assessment

The patient complains of unilateral pain and soreness in the inguinal canal along the course of the vas deferens and can develop pain and swelling in the scrotum and the groin. The epididymis becomes swollen and extremely painful. Bacteriuria may be evident, and the patient may experience chills and fever, along with nausea, urinary frequency, urgency, or dysuria. Laboratory assessment includes urinalysis, and Gram stain of urethral drainage if there is suspicion of sexually transmitted infection (STI). If the epididymitis is untreated, it can progress to involve the testis.

Medical Management

Treatment of scrotal support, ice, and antibiotic therapy are anticipated, on an outpatient basis. If the epididymitis is caused by a chlamydial infection, the patient and his sexual partner must be treated with antibiotics. If no improvement occurs within 2 weeks, an underlying testicular tumor should be considered. An epididymectomy (excision of the epididymis from the testis) may be performed as a last resort for patients who have recurrent, incapacitating episodes of epididymitis or for those with chronic, painful conditions.

Nursing Management

The scrotum is elevated with a scrotal bridge or folded towel to prevent traction on the spermatic cord, to promote venous drainage, and to relieve pain. Antimicrobial agents are administered as prescribed until the acute inflammation subsides. Intermittent cold compresses to the scrotum may help ease the pain. Later, local heat or sitz baths may help resolve the inflammation. Analgesic medications are administered for pain relief.

The nurse instructs the patient to avoid straining, lifting, and sexual activity until the infection is resolved. He should continue taking analgesic agents and antibiotics as prescribed and using ice packs if necessary to relieve discomfort. He needs to know that it may take 2 to 3 months for the epididymis to return to normal.

TESTICULAR CANCER

Testicular cancer is the most common cancer in men between the ages of 15 and 40 years, although it can occur in males of any age. It is a highly treatable and usually curable

form of cancer, with a cure rate of greater than 90% for all stages of the disease (ACS, 2009).

Classification of Testicular Tumors

The testicles contain several types of cells, each of which may develop into one or more types of cancer. The type of cancer determines the appropriate treatment and affects the prognosis. Testicular cancers are classified as germinal, having their origins within the germ cells of the gonads (testes) or nongerminal (stromal).

Germinal Tumors

More than 90% of all cancers of the testicle are germinal and may be further classified as seminomas or nonseminomas. Seminomas are tumors that develop from the sperm-producing cells of the testes, and account for 50% of tumors. Seminomas tend to remain localized, whereas nonseminomatous tumors grow quickly. Nonseminomas tend to develop earlier in life than seminomas, usually occurring in men in their 20s. Many tumors are mixtures of at least two different tumor types.

Nongerminal Tumors

Testicular cancer may also develop in the supportive and hormone-producing tissues, or stroma, of the testicles. The two main types of stromal tumors are Leydig cell tumors and Sertoli cell tumors. These tumors infrequently spread beyond the testicle.

Risk Factors

Risk factors for testicular cancer include undescended testicles (**cryptorchidism**), a family history of testicular cancer, and cancer of one testicle, which increases the risk in the other testicle. Caucasian American men have a five times greater risk than that of African American men and more than double the risk of Asian American men (Tanagho & McAninch, 2007).

Clinical Manifestations and Assessment

The symptoms appear gradually, with a mass or lump on the testicle and usually painless enlargement of the testis. The patient may report heaviness in the scrotum, inguinal area, or lower abdomen. Backache (from retroperitoneal node extension), abdominal pain, weight loss, and general weakness may result from metastasis. Enlargement of the testis without pain is a significant diagnostic finding. Testicular tumors tend to metastasize early, spreading from the testis to the lymph nodes in the retroperitoneum and to the lungs.

Monthly testicular self-exams (TSEs) can detect testicular cancer (Box 34-6). Teaching men of all ages to perform TSE is an important health promotion intervention for early detection of testicular cancer, but recent recommendations argue against this practice in asymptomatic adolescent and adult males (USPSTF, 2008) due to the low incidence of finding testicular cancer via TSE and the high rate of anxiety associated with self-examination.

Human chorionic gonadotropin (hCG) and alpha-fetoprotein (AFP) are tumor markers that may be elevated. Tumor marker levels in the blood are used for diagnosis, staging, and monitoring the response to treatment. Other diagnostic tests include lactate dehydrogenase (LDH) levels, and ultrasound examination to determine the presence and size of the testicular mass.

A CT of the abdomen and pelvis is performed to determine the extent of the disease in the retroperitoneum and pelvis. A chest X-ray is also performed to assess for lung metastasis. Tissue biopsy is the only definitive way to determine whether cancer is present, and is performed at the time of surgery rather than as a part of the diagnostic workup, to reduce the risk of promoting spread of the cancer (Kovitz, Logothestis, & Millikan, 2006).

Medical Management

Testicular cancer is highly responsive to treatment. The goals of management are to eradicate the disease and achieve a cure. Treatment selection is based on the cell type and the anatomic extent of the disease. The testis is removed by orchiectomy through an inguinal incision with a high ligation of the spermatic cord. A retroperitoneal lymph node dissection (RPLND) may be performed after orchiectomy if there is evidence of lymph node metastasis. Although libido and climax are usually unimpaired after RPLND, the patient may develop ejaculatory dysfunction. Because men with testicular cancer demonstrate pretreatment subfertility, and treatment of the cancer itself can result in subfertility or infertility, cryopreservation of sperm before treatment should be offered (Tanagho & McAninch, 2007).

Seminomatous tumors are more sensitive to radiation therapy, and radiation therapy alone provides excellent results for the majority of patients. Postoperative irradiation of the lymph nodes from the diaphragm to the iliac region is used to treat seminomas. Radiation is delivered only to the affected side; the other testis is shielded from radiation to preserve fertility.

Chemotherapy is reserved for the treatment of stage IIC testicular cancer as well as more advanced stages (Motzer & Bosi, 2008). Chemotherapy with cisplatin-based regimens results in a high percentage of complete remissions. Even with disseminated testicular cancer, the prognosis is favorable. Follow-up studies may include chest X-rays, hCG levels (a tumor marker with nonseminomatous germ cell tumors), AFP levels (a tumor marker for some men with nonseminomatous germ cell tumors), and LDH levels (an enzyme found in many body tissues such as heart, skeletal muscle, liver, and kidney, but that may also be elevated in some men with testicular cancer), and serial CT scans to detect recurrent malignancy.

Nursing Management

Nursing management includes assessment of the patient's physical and psychological status and monitoring of the patient for response to and possible effects of surgery, chemotherapy,

BOX 34-6

Patient Education

Testicular Self-Examination

Testicular self-examination (TSE) is to be performed once a month. The test is neither difficult nor time-consuming. A convenient time is usually after a warm bath or shower when the scrotum is more relaxed.

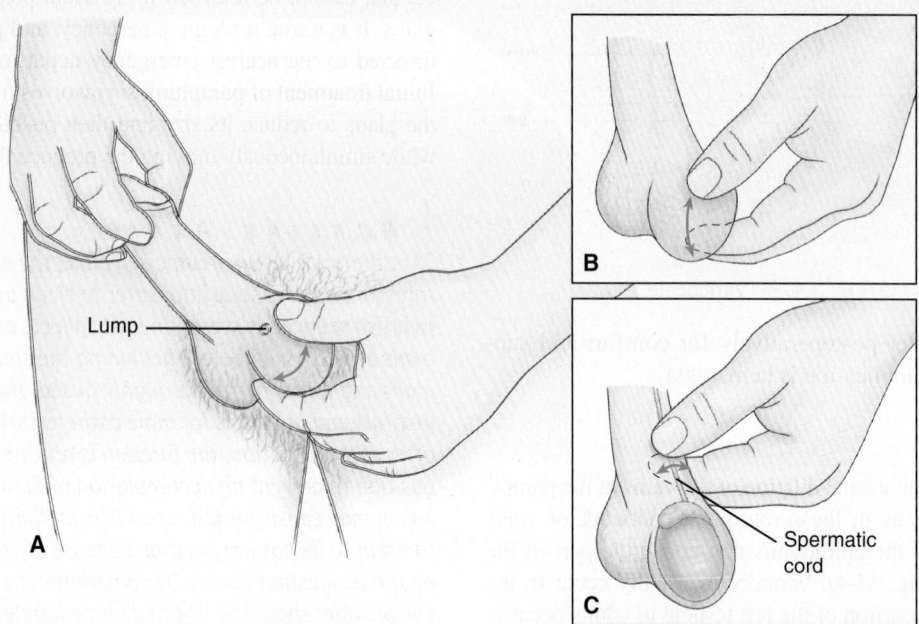

1. Use both hands to palpate the testis. The normal testicle is smooth and uniform in consistency.
2. With the index and middle fingers under the testis and the thumb on top, roll the testis gently in a horizontal plane between the thumb and fingers (**A**).
3. Feel for any evidence of a small lump or abnormality.
4. Follow the same procedure and palpate upward along the testis (**B**).
5. Locate and palpate the epididymis (**C**), a cordlike structure on the top and back of the testicle that stores and transports sperm. Also locate and palpate the spermatic cord.
6. Repeat the examination for the other testis, epididymis, and spermatic cord. It is normal to find that one testis is larger than the other.
7. If you find any evidence of a small, pealike lump or if the testis is swollen (possibly from an infection or tumor), consult your health care provider.

and radiation therapy (see Chapter 6). Operative care is described in Chapter 5. Because the patient may have difficulty coping with his condition, issues related to body image and sexuality are addressed; he also needs to know that radiation therapy will not necessarily prevent him from fathering children, and unilateral excision of a testis will not necessarily decrease virility.

Banking Sperm

Cryopreserving semen in a sperm bank is an option for men who are about to undergo a procedure or treatment (e.g., radiation therapy to the pelvis, chemotherapy, RPLND) that may affect his fertility. This requires visits to the facility, where the sperm is produced by masturbation and collected in a sterile container for storage.

HYDROCELE

A **hydrocele** is a collection of fluid, generally in the tunica vaginalis of the testis, although it may also collect within the spermatic cord. Hydrocele can be differentiated from a hernia by transillumination; the hydrocele will glow red, whereas dense tissue will not illuminate. Acute hydrocele may occur in association with acute infectious disease of the epididymis or as a result of local injury. Chronic hydrocele has an unknown cause.

Therapy is not required unless the hydrocele becomes tense, or if the scrotal mass becomes large, uncomfortable, or embarrassing. In the surgical treatment of hydrocele, an incision is made through the wall of the scrotum down to the distended tunica vaginalis. The sac is resected and, is sutured together to collapse the wall. The patient is advised to wear

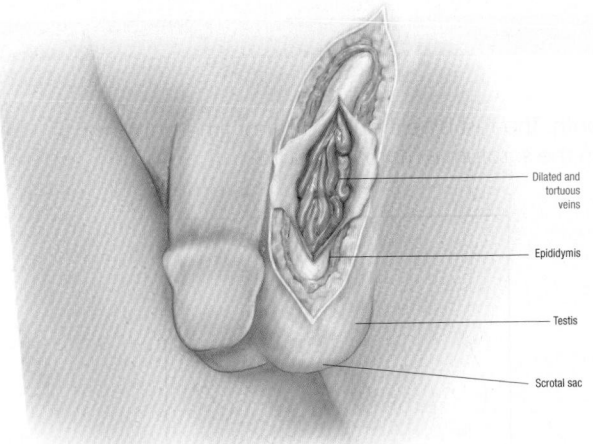

FIGURE 34-4 Varicocele.

an athletic supporter postoperatively for comfort and support. The major complication is hematoma.

VARICOCELE

A **varicocele** is an abnormal dilation of the veins of the pampiniform venous plexus in the scrotum (the network of veins from the testis and the epididymis that constitute part of the spermatic cord) (Fig. 34-4). Varicoceles usually occur in the veins on the upper portion of the left testicle in adults because of the angle in which the left spermatic cord inserts into the left renal vein, while the right spermatic cord enters the inferior vena cava. In some men, a varicocele has been associated with infertility. Few symptoms may be produced by the enlarged spermatic vein, and no treatment is required unless fertility is a concern or there is pain. It is corrected microsurgically by ligation of the external spermatic vein. An ice pack may be applied to the scrotum for the first few hours after surgery to relieve edema. The patient then wears a scrotal supporter.

CONDITIONS AFFECTING THE PENIS

PHIMOSIS AND PARAPHIMOSIS

Phimosis, a condition in which the foreskin is constricted so that it cannot be retracted over the glans, can occur congenitally or as a result of inflammation and edema. If the preputial area is not cleaned, normal secretions accumulate,

causing inflammation (balanitis), which can lead to adhesions and fibrosis. It is more commonly seen in adult men with poorly controlled diabetes. In elderly men, penile carcinoma may develop. Phimosis is corrected by circumcision.

Paraphimosis is a condition in which the foreskin is retracted behind the glans and, because of narrowness and subsequent edema, cannot be returned to its usual position covering the glans. It is a true urologic emergency, and patients should be directed to the nearest emergency department for treatment. Initial treatment of paraphimosis involves firmly compressing the glans to reduce its size and then pushing the glans back while simultaneously moving the prepuce forward.

☀ NURSING ALERT

To catheterize an uncircumcised male, the nurse retracts the foreskin and uses soap and water to clean away the smegma (whitish sebaceous secretion that collects between the glans penis and foreskin) before beginning the sterile procedure. The glans and foreskin are thoroughly rinsed. The nurse follows institutional protocols for male catheterization. Immediately after catheterization, the foreskin is returned to its normal position to prevent an accumulation of fluid within the glans, which may cause paraphimosis (the inability to retract the foreskin to its natural position because of venous and lymphatic congestion caused by constriction by the foreskin). The provider should be notified immediately if the nurse is unable to retract the foreskin.

PRIAPISM

Priapism is a persistent erection that causes the penis to become large, hard, and painful. It results from either neural or vascular causes, including sickle cell thrombosis, leukemic cell infiltration, and tumor invasion of the penis or its vessels. It may occur with use of medications that affect the central nervous system, antihypertensive agents, antidepressant medications, and substances injected into the penis to treat ED.

Priapism is a true urologic emergency. The goal of therapy is to improve venous drainage of the corpora cavernosa to prevent ischemia, fibrosis, and impotence. The corpora may be irrigated with an anticoagulant, which allows stagnant blood to be aspirated. Shunting procedures to divert the blood from the turgid corpora cavernosa to the venous system or into the corpus spongiosum–glans penis compartment may be attempted.

Chapter Review

Critical Thinking Exercises

1. A 58-year-old man with type 2 diabetes has undergone TURP. What immediate postoperative assessment is indicated when he arrives from the postanesthetic care unit and for the first 24 hours after surgery? What discharge teaching and preparation are indicated for this patient?

2. One of your patients, a 32-year-old man with a spinal cord injury, tells you that he has seen an advertisement on television for vardenafil HCl (Levitra). He wishes to

try this to improve his erectile function. What is the appropriate teaching for this patient?

3. A 21-year-old college athlete who describes his health as excellent comes to the student health clinic because he noticed a painless walnut-size mass in his testicle when showering. What would be your concerns, and what referrals would be warranted for him? What initial lab work would be indicated?

NCLEX–Style Review Questions

1. A 45-year-old man complains of a painless swelling in his scrotum. He should be assessed for which of the following conditions?
   A. Prostatitis
   B. Hydronephrosis
   C. Varicocele
   D. Cystitis

2. A 60-year-old patient is complaining of difficulty sustaining his erections. The nurse is aware that he suffered a myocardial infarction approximately 3 months ago. Which of the following teaching is relevant to his concern? Select all that apply.
   A. If he increases his physical activity, his function will improve.
   B. He is a candidate for a penile implant.
   C. He can use a vacuum erection device.
   D. Men with a heart attack in the preceding 6 months cannot use PDE medications.

3. A 55-year-old man has been diagnosed with prostate cancer. His treatment options depend on which of the following? Select all that apply.
   A. Staging of the tumor
   B. His preference
   C. His diet
   D. His age

4. A 50-year-old man is being treated presumptively for acute prostatitis. He asks the nurse why the course of antibiotics is so long. What is the nurse's best response?
   A. His infection is resistant to most antibiotics.
   B. Most antibiotics diffuse poorly from the plasma into the prostatic fluid.
   C. His liver is preventing the antibiotic from working effectively.
   D. Men of his age need a prolonged antibiotic course.

5. A 58-year-old patient has had a prostatectomy. The nurse is preparing him for discharge. Which of the following would be important to incorporate in the teaching plan?
   A. Do not interrupt stream after starting to void.
   B. Increased activity is permitted.
   C. Limit fluid intake to prevent hypervolemia.
   D. Note that spicy foods, alcohol, and coffee may cause bladder discomfort.

Try these additional resources to enhance your learning and understanding of this chapter:
- thePoint online resource available at **http://thepoint.lww.com/Pellico1e**
- *Handbook for Focus on Adult Health: Medical-Surgical Nursing*
- *Study Guide for Focus on Adult Health: Medical-Surgical Nursing*

References and Selected Readings

References and selected readings associated with this chapter can be found on the website that accompanies the book. Visit http://thepoint.lww.com/Pellico1e to access the references and other additional resources associated with this chapter.

CHRISTA PALANCIA
ESPOSITO

Nursing Management: Patients With Sexually Transmitted Infections

A sexually transmitted infection (STI), also known as a sexually transmitted disease (STD), is an infection acquired through sexual contact with an infected person. STIs are the most common infectious diseases in the United States and are epidemic in most parts of the world. To understand the pathophysiology of STIs, it is important to understand the infectious process.

THE INFECTIOUS PROCESS

An infectious disease is any disease caused by the growth of pathogenic microbes in the body. It may or may not be communicable (i.e., contagious). The nurse plays an important role in infection control and prevention. Educating patients can decrease their risk of becoming infected or decrease the sequelae of infection.

The Chain of Infection

A complete chain of events is necessary for infection to occur. The necessary elements for infection to occur are described in Box 35-1.

Colonization, Infection, and Infectious Disease

Relatively few anatomic sites (e.g., brain, blood, bone, heart, vascular system) are sterile. Bacteria found throughout the body usually provide beneficial **normal flora** to compete with potential pathogens, to facilitate digestion, or to work in other ways symbiotically with the host.

Colonization

The term *colonization* is used to describe microorganisms present without host interference or interaction. Organisms reported in microbiology test results often reflect colonization rather than infection. *Colony count* represents a visual count of microbes present in a sample. In general, clinicians use a colony count of greater than 100,000/mL or 10^5 bacteria/mL to represent an infection. However, astute clinicians will also consider other local and systemic signs of infection at lower colony counts, such as fever, leukocytosis (elevated white blood cells [WBCs]), erythema, purulent exudate, and the like.

BOX 35-1
Chain of Infection

The chain of infection requires the following elements:
- A causative organism
- A reservoir of available organisms
- A portal or mode of exit from the reservoir
- A mode of transmission from reservoir to host
- A susceptible host
- A mode of entry to host

Causative Organism

The types of microorganisms that cause infections are bacteria, rickettsiae (gram-negative bacteria carried by ticks, fleas and lice), viruses, protozoa, fungi, and helminths (parasitic worms).

Reservoir

Reservoir is the term used for any person, plant, animal, substance, or location that provides nourishment for microorganisms and enables their further dispersal.

Mode of Exit

The organism must have a mode of exit from a reservoir. An infected host must shed organisms to another or to the environment before transmission can occur. Organisms exit through the respiratory tract, the gastrointestinal tract, the genitourinary tract, the skin, or the blood.

Route of Transmission

A route of transmission is necessary and specific to each pathogen, to connect the infectious source with its new host. Organisms may be transmitted through sexual contact, skin-to-skin contact, percutaneous injection, or through infectious particles carried in the air. A person who carries or transmits an organism but does not have apparent signs and symptoms of infection is called a *carrier*.

Susceptible Host

For infection to occur, the host must be susceptible (not possessing immunity to a particular pathogen). Previous infection or vaccine administration may render the host immune (not susceptible) to further infection with an agent. Although exposure to potentially infectious microorganisms occurs essentially on a constant basis, our elaborate immune systems generally prevent infection from occurring. A person who is immunosuppressed has much greater susceptibility to infection than does a healthy person.

Portal of Entry

A portal of entry is needed for the organism to gain access to the host. For example, airborne *Mycobacterium tuberculosis* does not cause disease when it settles on the skin of an exposed host; the only entry route for *M. tuberculosis* is through the respiratory tract.

Infection

Infection indicates a host interaction with an organism. A patient colonized with *Staphylococcus aureus* may have staphylococci on the skin without any skin interruption or irritation. However, if the patient had an incision, *S. aureus* could enter the wound, be seen as foreign, and result in an immune system reaction of local inflammation and migration of WBCs to the site. Clinical evidence of erythema (redness), heat, and pain, and laboratory evidence of WBCs on the wound specimen smear suggest infection.

Infectious Disease

It is important to recognize the difference between infection and infectious disease. **Infectious disease** is the state in which the infected host displays a decline in wellness due to the infection. When the host interacts immunologically with an organism but remains symptom free, the definition of infectious disease has not been met. The microbiology laboratory report is the primary source of bacterial infection identification and should be viewed as a tool to be used along with clinical indicators to determine whether a patient is colonized, infected, or diseased. Microbiology reports from clinical specimens usually show three components: the smear and stain, the culture and organism identification, and the antimicrobial susceptibility (i.e., sensitivity). As a marker for the likelihood of infection, the smear and stain (referred to as *Gram stain*) generally provide the most helpful information because they describe the mix of cells present at the anatomic site at the time of specimen collection and are a guide to the choice of antibiotic pending the culture results. The Gram stain will classify organisms as either gram-positive or gram-negative. The culture will detail the exact organism(s), while the sensitivity will specify antimicrobials most likely to be effective against the organism(s).

SEXUALLY TRANSMITTED INFECTIONS

STIs are acquired through sexual contact with an infected person. Table 35-1 identifies infections that can be classified as STIs and their routes of transmission. Portals of entry of STI-causing microorganisms and sites of infection include the skin and mucosal linings of the urethra, cervix, vagina, rectum, and oropharynx.

Education about prevention of STIs includes information about risk factors and behaviors that can lead to infection. Refer to Box 35-2 for risk factors associated with STIs. The use of a condom or protective barrier (i.e., dental dam) placed before any sexual contact is imperative to help prevent the

TABLE
35-1 Conditions Classified as Sexually Transmitted Diseases (STDs) and Their Routes of Transmission

Disease	Route(s) of Transmission
Chlamydia	Sexual
Gonorrhea	Sexual
Herpes simplex	Sexual, percutaneous, perinatal
Human papillomavirus (HPV)	Sexual, percutaneous
Syphilis	Sexual, perinatal
Trichomoniasis	Sexual

acquisition or transmission of an STI. Refer to Box 35-3 for the application of male condom and Figure 35-1 for the application of a female condom.

✴ NURSING ALERT

Infection with one STI suggests the possibility of infection with other diseases as well. After one STI is identified, diagnostic evaluation for others should be performed.

SYPHILIS

Pathophysiology

Syphilis is an acute and chronic infectious disease caused by the spirochete *Treponema pallidum*. It is acquired primarily through sexual contact, although rarely may be congenital in origin; that is, it is passed from mother to child during pregnancy or childbirth.

Risk Factors

Risk factors include having unprotected sex and being infected with other STIs.

Clinical Manifestations and Assessment

In the untreated person, the course of syphilis can be divided into three stages: primary, secondary, and tertiary. These

---

BOX 35-2
Risk factors for Sexually Transmitted Disease

- Having unprotected sex
- Having multiple partners
- Being under 26 years of age
- Starting sex at an early age
- Using alcohol or illegal drugs
- Using IV drugs
- Having a history of STI
- Participating in prostitution
- Using oral contraceptives as only form of contraception

BOX 35-3
Patient Education

Use of Male Condoms

1. Put on a new condom before any kind of sex.
2. Hold the condom by the tip to squeeze out the air.

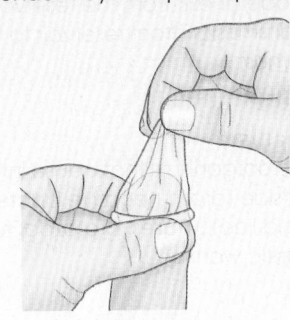

3. Unroll the condom all the way over the erect penis

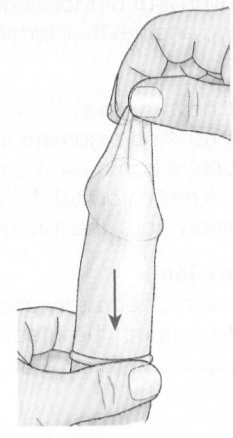

4. Have sex.
5. Hold the condom so it cannot come off the penis.
6. Pull out.
7. Use a new condom if you want to have sex again or if you want to have sex in a different place (eg, in the anus and then in the vagina).

   Keep condoms cool and dry. Never use skin lotions, baby oil, petroleum jelly, or cold cream with condoms. The oil in these products will cause the condom to break. Products made with water (such as K-Y jelly or glycerin) are safer to use.

---

stages reflect the time from infection and the clinical manifestations observed in that period and are the basis for treatment decisions.

Primary syphilis occurs 2 to 3 weeks after initial inoculation with the organism. A painless lesion at the site of infection is called a *chancre* (Figure 35-2). Untreated, these lesions usually resolve spontaneously within about 2 months.

Secondary syphilis occurs when the hematogenous spread of organisms from the original chancre leads to generalized infection. The rash of secondary syphilis occurs about 2 to 8 weeks after the chancre and involves the trunk and the

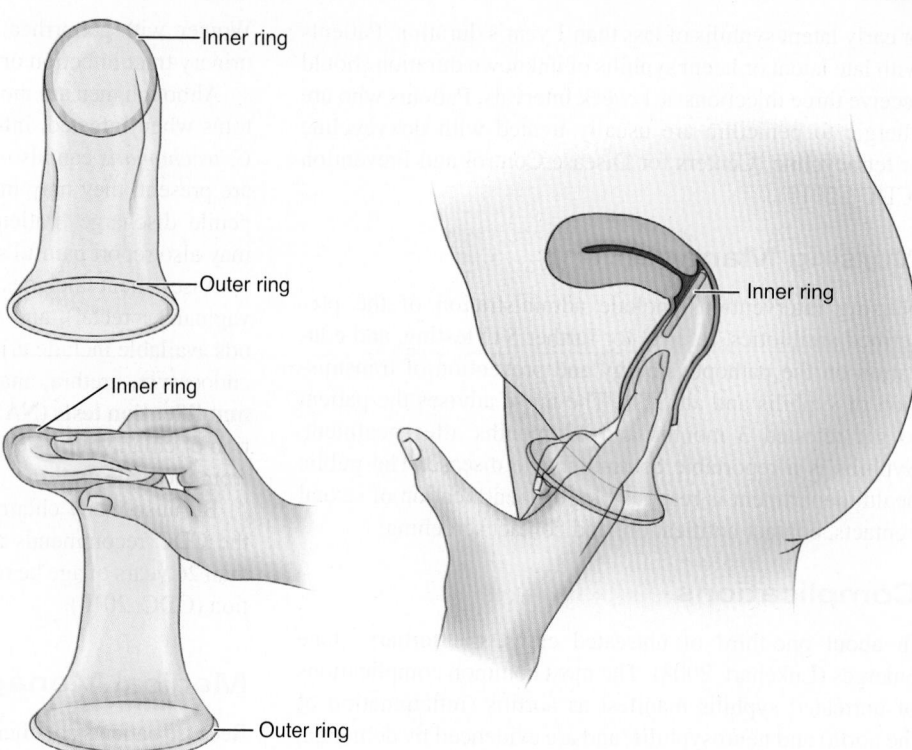

FIGURE 35-1 Female condom. To insert the female condom, hold the inner ring between the thumb and middle finger. Put the index finger on the pouch between the thumb and other fingers and squeeze the ring. Slide the condom into the vagina as far as it will go. The inner ring keeps the condom in place.

extremities, including the palms of the hands and the soles of the feet. Transmission of the organism can occur through contact with these lesions. Generalized signs of infection may include lymphadenopathy (abnormal enlargement of lymph nodes), arthritis, meningitis, hair loss, fever, malaise, and weight loss. After the secondary stage, there is a period of **latency**, when the infected person has no signs or symptoms of syphilis. Latency can be interrupted by a recurrence of secondary syphilis.

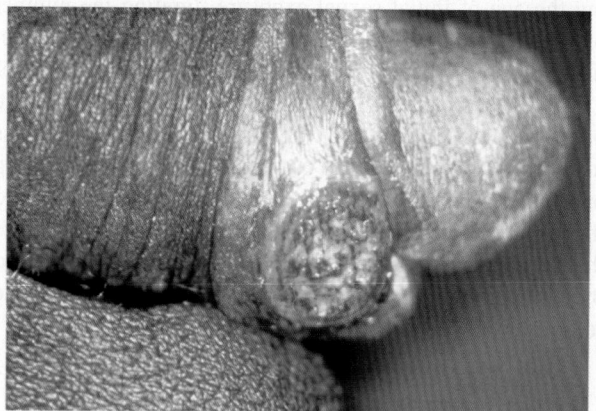

FIGURE 35-2 The first stage of a syphilis infection is the appearance of a chancre, a round, usually solitary, painless sore that appears on the glans penis, the shaft of the penis, or may lie within the urethra. If left untreated it will heal; however, secondary syphilis will develop. From Goodheart, H. (2003). *Goodheart's photoguide of common skin disorders.* Philadelphia: Lippincott Williams & Wilkins.

Tertiary syphilis is the final stage in the natural progression of the disease. It is estimated that between 20% and 40% of those infected do not exhibit signs and symptoms in this final stage. Tertiary syphilis presents as a slowly progressive inflammatory disease with the potential to affect multiple organs.

The conclusive diagnosis of syphilis can be made by direct identification of the spirochete obtained from the chancre lesions of primary syphilis. Serologic tests used in the diagnosis of secondary and tertiary syphilis require clinical correlation in interpretation. The serologic tests are summarized as follows:

- Nontreponemal or reagin tests, such as the Venereal Disease Research Laboratory (VDRL) or the rapid plasma reagin circle card test (RPR-CT), are generally used for screening and diagnosis. After adequate therapy, the test result is expected to decrease quantitatively until it is read as negative, usually about 2 years after therapy is completed.
- Treponemal tests, such as the fluorescent treponemal antibody absorption test (FTA-ABS) and the microhemagglutination test (MHA-TP), are used to verify that the screening test did not represent a false-positive result. Positive results usually are positive for life and therefore are not appropriate to determine therapeutic effectiveness.

Medical Management

Administration of antibiotics is the treatment of all stages of syphilis. A single dose of penicillin G benzathine intramuscular injection is the medication of choice for early syphilis

or early latent syphilis of less than 1 year's duration. Patients with late latent or latent syphilis of unknown duration should receive three injections at 1-week intervals. Patients who are allergic to penicillin are usually treated with doxycycline or tetracycline (Centers for Disease Control and Prevention [CDC], 2010).

Nursing Management

Nursing interventions include administration of the prescribed antibiotics, referral for further STI testing, and education on the pathophysiology and prevention of transmission of syphilis and all STIs. The nurse advises the patient to get retested 3 months and 12 months after treatment. Syphilis is a reportable communicable disease. The public health department is responsible for identification of sexual contacts, contact notification, and contact screening.

Complications

In about one-third of untreated cases, the tertiary stage emerges (Lukehart, 2008). The most common complications of untreated syphilis manifest as aortitis (inflammation of the aorta) and neurosyphilis, and are evidenced by dementia, psychosis, paresis, stroke, or meningitis.

CHLAMYDIA TRACHOMATIS AND NEISSERIA GONORRHOEAE

Pathophysiology

Chlamydia trachomatis and *Neisseria gonorrhoeae* are the most commonly reported STIs. Coinfection with *C. trachomatis* often occurs in patients infected with *N. gonorrhoeae*. *C. trachomatis* and *N. gonorrhoeae* are caused by bacteria that are transmitted during sexual relations or may be transmitted from mother to child during vaginal birth.

Risk Factors

Any sexually active person can be infected with *Chlamydia* or *N. gonorrhoeae*, and the risk increases with the number of sexual partners. The group with the greatest risk for *C. trachomatis* infection is young women 25 years and younger and may be associated with a cervix that has not fully matured (CDC, 2007). The risk for *N. gonorrhoeae* also includes sexually active young women but also men who have sex with men.

Clinical Manifestations and Assessment

Both *C. trachomatis* and *N. gonorrhoeae* infections frequently do not cause symptoms in women and thus are often referred to as "silent" related to clinical presentation. When symptoms are present, mucopurulent cervicitis with exudates in the endocervical canal is the most frequent finding.

Women with gonorrhea can also present with symptoms of urinary tract infection or vaginitis.

Although men are more likely than women to have symptoms when infected, infection with *N. gonorrhoeae* and/or *C. trachomatis* can also be asymptomatic. When symptoms are present, they may include burning during urination and penile discharge. Patients with *N. gonorrhoeae* infection may also report painful swollen testicles.

Assessment includes noting fever, discharge (urethral, vaginal, or rectal), and signs of arthritis. Diagnostic methods available include urine testing or swab specimens of the endocervix, urethra, anal canal, and pharynx. **Nucleic acid amplification tests (NAAT)** are most sensitive for the detection of chlamydia. The Gram stain best identifies gonorrhea from the male urethra.

Because many chlamydial infections are asymptomatic, the CDC recommends all sexually active women younger than 26 years of age be routinely tested for chlamydial infection (CDC, 2010).

Medical Management

Because patients are often coinfected with both gonorrhea and chlamydia, the CDC recommends dual therapy if chlamydia has not been ruled out by NAAT. The CDC-recommended treatment for chlamydia is either doxycycline (Adoxa) or azithromycin (Zithromax), and for gonorrhea ceftriaxone (Rocephin) or Suprax (2010).

Nursing Management

Gonorrhea and chlamydia are reportable communicable diseases. The target group for preventive patient teaching about gonorrhea and chlamydia is the adolescent and young adult population. Along with reinforcing the importance of abstinence, when appropriate, education should address postponing the age of initial sexual exposure, limiting the number of sexual partners, and use of condoms or barrier protection. Moreover, patient counseling includes abstinence for 1 week after treatment in addition to the completion of the partner's treatment. Test of cure is not recommended unless medication compliance is in question; however, the retesting of females 3 months post-treatment is recommended due to the possibility of reinfection. Education for males includes that they must inform their female partners of infection, and they must provide literature on STIs and the risk of **pelvic inflammatory disease** (PID) to them.

Complications

In women, PID, **ectopic pregnancy**, endometritis, and infertility are possible complications of either *N. gonorrhoeae* or *C. trachomatis* infection. Figure 35-3 demonstrates how microorganisms spread in pelvic infection.

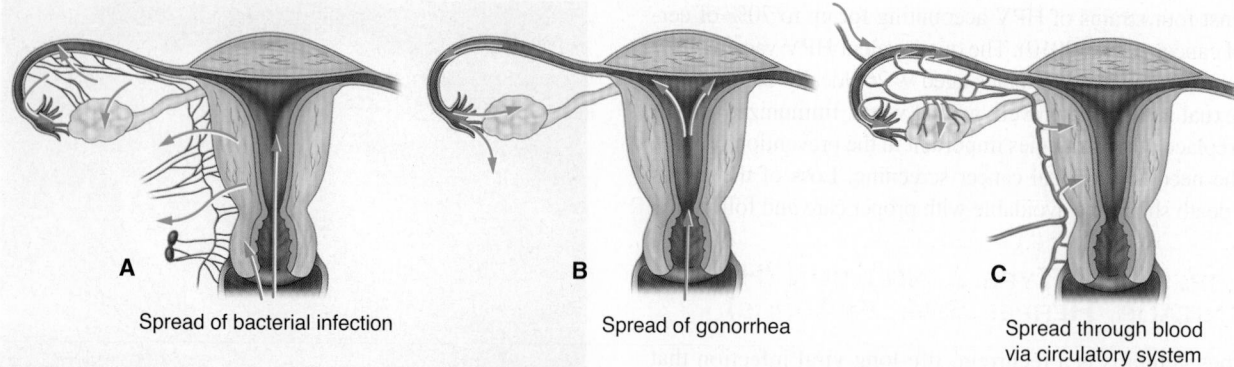

FIGURE 35-3 Pathway by which microorganisms spread in pelvic infections. (**A**) Bacterial infection spreads up the vagina into the uterus and through the lymphatics. (**B**) Gonorrhea spreads up the vagina into the uterus and then to the tubes and ovaries. (**C**) Bacterial infection can reach the reproductive organs through the bloodstream (hematogenous spread).

In men, epididymitis, a painful disease that may lead to infertility, may result from infection with either bacterium. In people of either gender, *N. gonorrhoeae* may cause arthritis or bloodstream infection.

HUMAN PAPILLOMAVIRUS

Human papillomavirus (HPV) infection is the most common STI among young, sexually active people. Millions of Americans are infected with HPV, many unaware they carry the virus. At least 50% of sexually active men and women acquire genital HPV infection at some point in their lives (CDC, 2010).

Pathophysiology

The virus affects the skin and mucous membranes through sexual contact (i.e., naked rubbing and vaginal/anal intercourse). At least 40 HPV types can infect the genitalia and perineum including the skin of the penis, vulva, anus, and the linings of the vagina, cervix, and rectum. Certain types of HPV can cause the cells of the cervix to become abnormal, contributing to approximately 70% of cervical cancer cases. Other strains of HPV cause genital warts. The virus can be present in the body for a long period of time before detection or symptoms occur (CDC, 2010). HPV is often self-limiting due to an effective immune system response; however, smoking has been associated with increased morbidity.

Risk Factors

Risk factors include being sexually active, having multiple sex partners, and having sex with a partner who has or has had multiple partners.

Clinical Manifestations and Assessment

More than 100 strains of HPV exist, and infection can be latent (asymptomatic and detected only by DNA hybridization tests for HPV), subclinical (visualized only after application of acetic acid followed by inspection under magnification), or clinical (visible warts).

The most common strains of HPV, 6 and 11, usually cause **condylomata** (genital warts) on the female and male genitalia and can be found in the mouth. These are often visible flesh-colored, flat, verrucous, or papillary lesions.

Some HPV strains (16, 18, 31, 33, and 45) affect the cervix, resulting in abnormal Papanicolaou (Pap) smears and are strongly associated with cervical cancer (CDC, 2010). Thus, the Pap smear is the detection vehicle identifying HPV DNA. **Colposcopy**-derived biopsies diagnose any cellular changes or dysplasia (changes in cervical cells).

Medical and Nursing Management

Treatment of external genital warts includes topical application of trichloroacetic acid, podophyllin (Podofin), and chemotherapeutic agents, and injections of interferon administered by a health care provider. Topical agents that can be applied by patients to external lesions include podofilox (Condylox) and imiquimod (Aldara). Electrocautery and laser therapy are alternative therapies that may be indicated for patients with a large number or area of genital warts (CDC, 2010).

Women with HPV should have annual Pap smears because of the potential of HPV to cause dysplasia. Use of condoms can reduce the likelihood of transmission, but transmission can also occur during skin-to-skin contact in areas not covered by condoms.

In many cases, patients are angry about having warts or HPV and do not know who infected them because the incubation period can be long and partners may have no symptoms. Acknowledging the emotional distress that occurs when an STI is diagnosed and providing support and facts are important nursing actions. Likewise, patient education about the likelihood of recurrence in the first 3 months after treatment is encouraged.

Complications

Preventatively, vaccination is recommended for girls and women ages 9 to 26, before the onset of sexual activity,

against four strains of HPV accounting for up to 70% of cervical cancer (CDC, 2010). The quadrivalent HPV vaccine may also be administered to males aged 9–26, ideally before onset of sexual activity, to prevent genital warts. Immunization will not replace other strategies important in the prevention of HPV or the need for cervical cancer screening. Loss of the uterus and death should be avoidable with proper care and follow-up.

HERPESVIRUS TYPE 2 INFECTION (HERPES GENITALIS, HERPES SIMPLEX VIRUS)

Herpes genitalis is a recurrent, life-long viral infection that causes herpetic lesions (blisters) on the vulva, vagina, and cervix in females and the penis in males. There are two types of herpes simplex virus (HSV): HSV-1 and HSV-2, which are clinically indistinguishable.

Pathophysiology

HSV-1 is known as the oral type and can be transmitted to the genitalia by oral sex or self-inoculation (i.e., touching a cold sore and then touching the genital area). HSV-2 is always sexually transmitted. The initial infection is usually very painful and lasts about 1 week, but it can also be asymptomatic. Most HSV infections occur via asymptomatic transmission when neither the carrier nor the recipient manifests lesions (Sen & Barton, 2007).

Recurrences are more common with HSV-2 than HSV-1, are less painful, and usually produce minor itching and burning. Some patients have few or no recurrences, whereas others have frequent bouts. Recurrences are often associated with stress, sunburn, dental work, or inadequate rest or nutrition—all situations that may tax the immune system.

When viral replication diminishes, the virus ascends the peripheral sensory nerves and remains inactive in the nerve ganglia.

Risk Factors

Risk factors include contact with an infected person by the mouth, oropharynx, mucosal surface, vagina, or cervix.

Clinical Manifestations and Assessment

Itching and pain accompany the process as the infected area becomes red and edematous. Primary infection may begin with macules and papules and progress to vesicles and ulcers. The vesicular state often appears as a blister, which later coalesces, ulcerates, and encrusts (Fig. 35-4). Influenza-like symptoms may occur 3 or 4 days after the lesions appear. Inguinal lymphadenopathy (enlarged lymph nodes in the groin), minor temperature elevation, malaise, headache, myalgia (aching muscles), and dysuria (pain on urination) are often noted. Pain is evident during the first week and then decreases. The lesions subside in about 2 weeks unless secondary infection occurs.

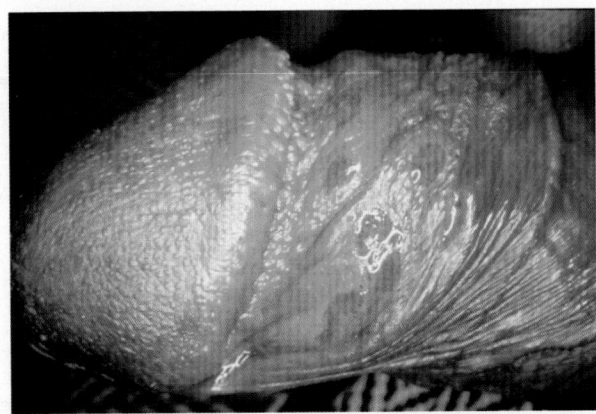

FIGURE 35-4 Herpes simplex may manifest as a painful open ulcer or cluster of superficial vesicles (fluid-filled) with an erythematous base. From Goodheart, H. (2003). *Goodheart's photoguide of common skin disorders.* Philadelphia: Lippincott Williams & Wilkins.

The gold standard for HSV diagnosis is a culture of the lesion. Serology may help determine new versus chronic infection when obtained concurrently with positive culture of a lesion.

Medical Management

There is currently no cure for HSV-2 infection, but treatment is aimed at relieving the symptoms. Antiviral dosing varies depending on primary, recurrent, or suppressive management. Management goals include preventing the spread of infection, making patients comfortable, decreasing potential health risks, and initiating a counseling and education program. The antiviral agents acyclovir (Zovirax), valacyclovir (Valtrex), and famciclovir (Famvir) are recommended to suppress the viral load and decrease recurrence and shedding (Gupta, Warren, & Wald, 2007).

Nursing Management

Patient education is paramount in preventing the transmission of HSV. Counseling regarding suppressive therapy should be offered at the initial diagnosis and has been shown to decrease the risk of recurrence by 70% to 80% and transmission to a partner by 48% (Sen & Barton, 2007). The nurse informs patients of their potential to transmit the virus without symptoms or lesions. In addition, patients have a potentially legal and moral obligation to disclose their diagnosis to sexual partners. Moreover, the importance of barrier methods to prevent the transmission is imperative. Emotional support of the newly HSV diagnosed patient is often needed (CDC, 2010).

Complications

Rarely, complications may arise from extragenital spread of HSV, such as to the buttocks, upper thighs, or even the eyes as a result of touching lesions and then touching other areas. Patients should be advised to wash their hands after contact

with lesions. Other potential problems are aseptic meningitis, neonatal transmission, and severe emotional stress related to the diagnosis.

FEMALE REPRODUCTIVE INFECTIONS ASSOCIATED WITH SEXUAL ACTIVITY

PELVIC INFLAMMATORY DISEASE

PID is an inflammatory condition of the pelvic cavity that may begin with cervicitis and may involve the uterus (endometritis), fallopian tubes (salpingitis), ovaries (oophoritis), pelvic peritoneum, or pelvic vascular system. Infection, which may be acute, subacute, recurrent, or chronic and localized or widespread, is usually caused by bacteria but may be attributed to a virus, fungus, or parasite. Gonorrheal and chlamydial organisms are the most likely causes.

Pathophysiology

PID arises from a polymicrobial infection that ascends upward from the vagina and into the uterus, fallopian tubes, and peritoneal cavity. In bacterial infections that occur after childbirth or abortion, pathogens are disseminated directly through the tissues that support the uterus by way of the lymphatics and blood vessels.

In gonorrheal infections, the gonococci pass through the cervical canal and into the uterus, where the environment, especially during menstruation, allows them to multiply rapidly and spread to the fallopian tubes and into the pelvis (see Figure 35-3B, p. 975). The infection is usually bilateral.

Pelvic infection is most commonly caused by sexual transmission but can also occur with invasive procedures such as endometrial biopsy, surgical abortion, hysteroscopy, or insertion of an intrauterine device. Bacterial vaginosis, a vaginal infection, may predispose women to pelvic infection.

Figures 35-3 and 35-5 illustrate the path organisms can travel from the vagina to the sterile peritoneum, resulting in peritonitis (inflammation of the peritoneum).

Risk Factors

Risk factors for PID include early age at first intercourse, multiple sexual partners, frequent intercourse, intercourse without condoms, intercourse with a partner with an STI, and a history of STIs or previous pelvic infection (CDC, 2010).

Clinical Manifestations and Assessment

Symptoms of pelvic infection usually begin with vaginal discharge, **dyspareunia** (painful sexual intercourse), lower abdominal pelvic pain, and tenderness that occurs after menses. Pain may increase with voiding or with defecation. The minimal criteria for diagnosis include lower abdominal tenderness, adnexal tenderness (adnexa are the "appendages" of the uterus, namely the ovaries, fallopian tubes, and ligaments that hold the uterus in place [Shiel & Stöppler, 2008]), and cervical motion tenderness. Other symptoms include fever,

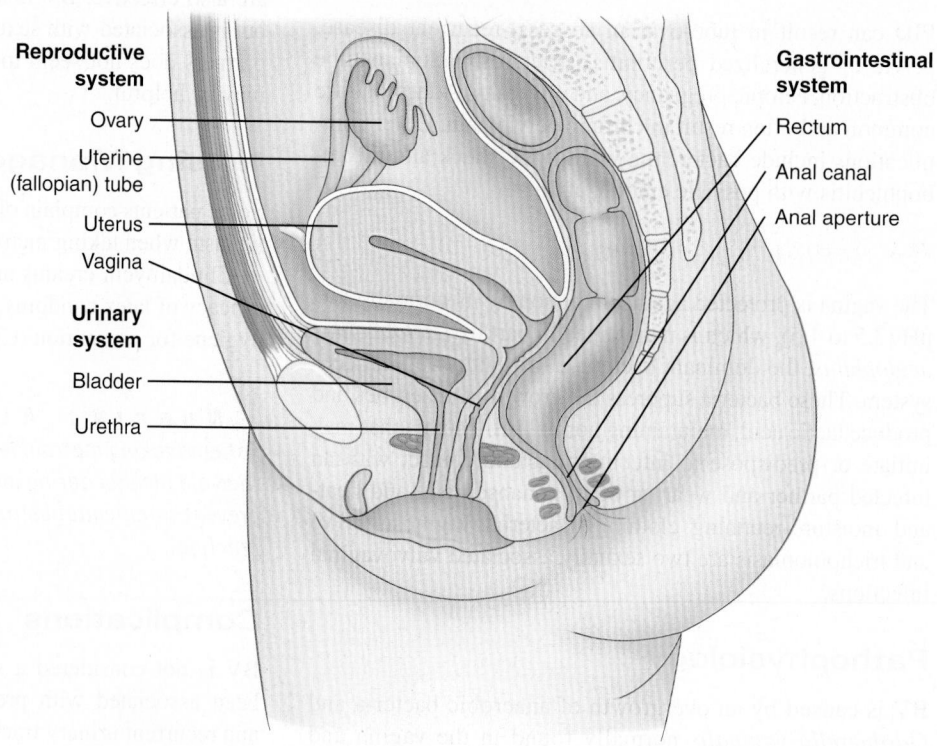

Reproductive system
- Ovary
- Uterine (fallopian) tube
- Uterus
- Vagina

Urinary system
- Bladder
- Urethra

Gastrointestinal system
- Rectum
- Anal canal
- Anal aperture

FIGURE 35-5 Female anatomy. Note the relationship of the reproductive organs to the pelvic peritoneum.

general malaise, anorexia, nausea, headache, and possibly vomiting (CDC, 2010).

Medical Management

Women with mild infections may be treated as outpatients with ofloxacin or levofloxacin with or without metronidazole, but hospitalization may be necessary (CDC, 2010). Intensive therapy includes bedrest, IV fluids, and IV antibiotic therapy. If the patient has abdominal distention or **ileus**, nasogastric intubation and suction are initiated. Careful monitoring of vital signs and symptoms assists in evaluating the status of the infection. Treatment of sexual partners is necessary to prevent reinfection.

Nursing Management

A hospitalized patient is maintained on bedrest and is usually placed in the semi-Fowler's position to facilitate dependent drainage. The nurse administers analgesic agents as prescribed for pain relief. Heat applied safely to the abdomen may also provide some pain relief and comfort. On an outpatient basis, confirming patient follow-up 3 days after treatment is imperative to assess symptom abatement.

Patient teaching consists of explaining how pelvic infections occur, how they can be controlled and avoided, and their signs and symptoms. All patients who have had PID need to be informed of the signs and symptoms of ectopic pregnancy (pain, abnormal bleeding, delayed menses, faintness, dizziness, and shoulder pain) because they are prone to this complication.

Complications

PID can result in tubo-ovarian abscess, recurrent disease, pelvic or generalized peritonitis, strictures, fallopian tube obstruction, ectopic pregnancy, and infertility. Adhesions are common and often result in chronic pelvic pain. Other complications include bacteremia with septic shock and thrombophlebitis with possible embolization.

BACTERIAL VAGINOSIS

The vagina is protected against infection by its normally low pH (3.5 to 4.5), which is maintained in part by *Lactobacillus acidophilus*, the dominant bacteria in a healthy vaginal ecosystem. These bacteria suppress the growth of anaerobes and produce lactic acid, maintaining normal pH. Factors that may initiate or predispose to infections include contact with an infected partner and wearing tight, nonabsorbent, and heat- and moisture-retaining clothing. Bacterial vaginosis (BV) and trichomoniasis are two sexually associated vulvovaginal infections.

Pathophysiology

BV is caused by an overgrowth of anaerobic bacteria and *Gardnerella vaginalis* normally found in the vagina and an absence of **lactobacilli**. It is characterized by a fish-like odor that is particularly noticeable after sexual intercourse or during menstruation as a result of an increase in vaginal pH. It is usually accompanied by a heavier-than-normal discharge.

Risk Factors

Douching after menses, smoking, multiple sex partners, other STIs, and increased sexual activity are risk factors for BV.

Clinical Manifestations and Assessment

BV can occur throughout the menstrual cycle and does not produce local discomfort or pain. Discharge is gray to yellowish white and smoothly coats the vaginal walls. The fish-like odor can be detected before or after adding a drop of potassium hydroxide to a glass slide with a sample of vaginal discharge. Under the microscope, vaginal cells are coated with bacteria and are described as *clue cells*. The pH of the discharge is usually greater than 4.7 because of the amines that result from enzymes from anaerobes. Lactobacilli, which serve as a natural host defense, are usually absent.

Medical Management

Metronidazole (Flagyl), administered orally twice a day for 1 week, is effective; a vaginal gel is also available. Clindamycin (Cleocin) vaginal cream or ovules (oval suppositories) are also effective. BV is not considered an STI exclusively but is associated with sexual activity. Treatment of patients' partners does not seem to be effective, but use of condoms may be helpful.

Nursing Management

Some patients complain of an unpleasant but transient metallic taste when taking metronidazole.

Clindamycin creams are oil-based and will decrease the efficacy of latex condoms. The nurse teaches proper perineal hygiene for prevention (CDC, 2010).

> **N U R S I N G   A L E R T**
> *Patients taking metronidazole (Flagyl) must be instructed to avoid alcohol during and for 24 hours after treatment to prevent significant gastrointestinal upset (disulfiram-like reaction).*

Complications

BV is not considered a serious condition; however, it has been associated with premature labor, endometritis, PID, and recurrent urinary tract infection (CDC, 2010).

TRICHOMONIASIS

Pathophysiology

Trichomonas vaginalis (aka "trich") is a flagellated proto-zoan that causes a common sexually transmitted vaginitis. It may be transmitted by an asymptomatic carrier who harbors the organism in the urogenital tract.

Clinical Manifestations and Assessment

Clinical manifestations include a vaginal discharge that is thin (sometimes frothy), yellow to yellow-green, malodorous, and very irritating. An accompanying vulvitis may result, with vulvovaginal burning and itching. Trich often causes urethritis in men. Diagnosis is made most often by microscopic detection of the causative organisms or by a specialized vaginal culture. Inspection with a speculum often reveals vaginal and cervical erythema (redness) with multiple small petechiae ("strawberry spots"). Testing of a trichomonal discharge demonstrates a pH greater than 4.5.

Medical and Nursing Management

The most effective treatment for trichomoniasis is metronidazole or tinidazole. Both partners receive a one-time loading dose. Test of cure is not needed unless symptoms recur.

Nursing education on abstaining from sexual activity until both partners are treated is imperative.

MALE REPRODUCTIVE INFECTIONS ASSOCIATED WITH SEXUAL ACTIVITY

Several infections affect the male genitourinary tract, including prostatitis (see Chapter 34), epididymitis, and orchitis often caused by STIs.

Epididymitis usually descends from an infected prostate or urinary tract. The infection passes upward through the urethra, ejaculatory duct, and vas deferens to the epididymis and commonly develops from STIs such as gonorrhea and chlamydia. In men younger than 35 years of age, the major cause of epididymitis is *C. trachomatis* (Tracy, Steers, & Costabile, 2008).

Orchitis is an inflammation of the testes (testicular congestion) caused by bacterial, viral, spirochetal, parasitic, traumatic, chemical, or unknown factors. Bacterial causes usually spread from an associated epididymitis in sexually active men. Causative organisms include *N. gonorrhoeae*, *C. trachomatis*, *Escherichia coli*, *Klebsiella*, *Pseudomonas aeruginosa*, *Staphylococcus* species, and *Streptococcus* species. Additionally, a more common cause of isolated orchitis is mumps. When postpubertal men contract mumps, about one in five develop some form of orchitis 4 to 7 days after the jaw and neck swell, and the testes may show some atrophy. Mumps vaccination is therefore recommended for postpubertal men who have not had mumps or previous mumps vaccination in childhood. Further details related to epididymitis and orchitis may be found in Chapter 34.

NURSING PROCESS

The Patient With a Sexually Transmitted Infection

Assessment

During the physical examination, the examiner looks for rashes, lesions, drainage, discharge, or swelling. Inguinal nodes are palpated to elicit tenderness and to assess swelling. Women are examined for abdominal or uterine tenderness.

Diagnosis

Appropriate nursing diagnoses of the patient with an STI may include:

- Deficient knowledge about the disease and risk for spread of infection and reinfection
- Anxiety related to anticipated stigmatization and to prognosis and complications
- Ineffective health maintenance related to high-risk sexual behaviors
- Risk for infection transmission related to lack of STI prevention measures
- Risk of infection transmission from mother to child during delivery

Planning and Goals

Major goals are increased patient understanding of the natural history and treatment of the infection, reduction in anxiety, increased compliance with therapeutic and preventive goals, and absence of complications.

Nursing Interventions

Increasing Knowledge and Preventing Spread of Disease
Education about STIs and prevention of the spread to others is often accomplished simultaneously. Explanation includes covering the causative organism, the usual course of the infection (including the interval of potential communicability to others), and possible complications. The nurse stresses the importance of following therapy as prescribed and the need to report any side effects or symptom progression. The nurse emphasizes that the same behaviors that led to infection with one STI increase the risk for any other STI. Methods used to contact sexual partners should be discussed. The patient should understand that until the partner has been treated, continued sexual exposure to the same person may lead to reinfection. The nurse discusses the relative value of condoms in reducing the risk for infection with STIs.

(continued on page 980)

Reducing Anxiety

When appropriate, the nurse encourages the patient to discuss anxieties and fear associated with the diagnosis, treatment, or prognosis. Patients may need help in planning discussion with partners. If the patient is especially apprehensive about this aspect, referral to a social worker or other specialist may be appropriate.

Increasing Compliance

In group settings or in a one-to-one setting, open discussion about STI information facilitates patient teaching. Discomfort can be reduced by factual explanation of causes, consequences, treatments, and prevention. Patients can

obtain more information by accessing the CDC web site (see Resources at the end of the chapter).

Evaluation

Expected patient outcomes may include the following:

1. Understands infection and treatment:
   a. Verbalizes understanding of infectious process
   b. Demonstrates medication, barrier, and behavior compliance
2. Absence of complications, such as ectopic pregnancy, infertility, neurosyphilis, gonococcal meningitis/arthritis, and prostatitis

Chapter Review

Critical Thinking Exercises

1. During a checkup, a 23-year-old woman tells you that she has a new boyfriend and is not concerned about sexual risks of STIs because she only plans on having oral sex. How would you address the educational needs of this patient? How would your teaching differ if her new partner is a woman?

2. A 28-year-old man is seeking treatment for urinary frequency. He informs you that he believes he has a urinary tract infection. When you are obtaining the health history, he reports that he has multiple sexual partners outside his marriage. He has undergone treatment for gonorrhea within the past 6 months. What are your major concerns regarding the patient's complaint of urinary frequency? Describe important aspects that must be addressed when teaching this patient about safer sex. What community resources should you make available to this patient and his wife?

NCLEX-Style Review Questions

1. A 22-year-old presents requesting STI testing after a recent encounter ended with a broken condom. She has cervical cultures but declined blood work done. Which of the following positive test results would lead the nurse to counsel the patient to seek further STI blood work?
   A. Candida yeast
   B. Group B *Streptococcus*
   C. Trichomoniasis
   D. Gardnerella

2. A 16-year-old girl presents with recurrent painful vulvar lesions. The nurse obtains subsequent test results from her pelvic evaluation and confirms the identification of HSV-2. What counseling is most appropriate for this patient?
   A. HSV-2 is self-limiting and will go away again on its own, no medication needed.

   B. HSV-2 can be transmitted and acquired without obvious symptoms or sores.
   C. A blood test can determine if this is a new infection or subsequent outbreak.
   D. Stress caused the sores; exercise and stress management will prevent them.

3. A 29-year-old woman presents with pelvic pain, fever, and irregular bleeding. She has been trying to get pregnant and fears she is having a miscarriage. Upon examination, the woman yells when her uterus is palpated bimanually and almost jumps off the table with cervical motion tenderness. The pregnancy test is negative. What nursing intervention is most appropriate for this patient?
   A. Administer the antibiotics as prescribed for PID.
   B. Reassure her she is not pregnant.
   C. Refer her to a fertility specialist.
   D. Counsel her on the signs of ectopic pregnancy.

4. A 24-year-old woman recently had a colposcopy detecting cervical dysplasia and HPV types 16 and 18, necessitating the removal of part of her cervix. The patient returns for her postoperative follow-up appointment saying, "I'm glad the cancer thing is over and I don't have to come back again for a long time." Which nursing response is most appropriate?
   A. "You are fortunate the cancer was caught early and you healed fast."
   B. "You still need to return for frequent Pap smears to monitor your cervix."
   C. "Good for you, not smoking helps keep the HPV away for good."
   D. "There will be a problem getting pregnant now after your surgery."

5. A 24-year-old man complains about an ulcer on the shaft of his penis along with complaints of fever and enlarged nodes in the inguinal region. He is diagnosed with syphilis and discharged after

receiving one dose of penicillin IM. Which comment made by the patient would alert the nurse of the need to review the management plan with this patient?

A. I am aware that all my sexual partners will need to be treated.

B. I know that my blood work (VDRL or RPR titer) may take 12 months to become negative.

C. This disease cannot be cured, and I will likely develop complications.

D. I am aware that I must wear a condom every time I have sex.

Try these additional resources to enhance your learning and understanding of this chapter:

- thePoint online resource available at **http://thepoint.lww.com/Pellico1e**
- *Handbook for Focus on Adult Health: Medical-Surgical Nursing*
- *Study Guide for Focus on Adult Health: Medical-Surgical Nursing*

References and Selected Readings

References and selected readings associated with this chapter can be found on the website that accompanies the book. Visit http://thepoint.lww.com/Pellico1e to access the references and other additional resources associated with this chapter.

Problems Related to Immunologic Function

A 45-YEAR-OLD patient with a history of leukemia has been diagnosed with secondary gout. She is complaining of pain in the wrist and fingers. She recently had a surgical procedure done and believes this is the cause of her current attack.

➡ What medications would the nurse expect the health care provider to order for this patient?

➡ Discuss the two phases of medical management.

➡ What are important components of nursing management for this patient?

➡ List two possible nursing diagnoses for this patient.

Nursing Assessment: Immune Function

MARY E. BARTLETT

After reading this chapter, you will be able to:

1. Discuss the body's general immune response.

2. Discuss the stages of the immune response.

3. Differentiate between cellular and humoral immune responses.

4. Complete an assessment on the function of the immune system.

The most basic abilities of the human body to protect itself from disease and illness derive from the various components of the immune system. The term *immunity* refers to the body's specific protective response to an invading foreign agent or organism. The immune system functions as the body's defense mechanism against invasion and allows a rapid response to foreign substances in a specific manner. Responses occur at the genetic and cellular levels.

Immune function is affected by a variety of factors, such as central nervous system integrity, emotional status, medications, and the stress of illness, trauma, or surgery. Dysfunctions involving the immune system occur across the lifespan. When the functions of the immune system are diminished or disturbed, autoimmune and other disorders may develop. Disorders of the immune system may stem from excesses or deficiencies of immunocompetent cells, alterations in the function of these cells, immunologic attack on self-antigens, or inappropriate or exaggerated responses to specific antigens (Table 36-1).

ANATOMIC AND PHYSIOLOGIC OVERVIEW

One of the most effective defense mechanisms is the body's capacity to equip itself rapidly with weapons (antibodies) individually designed to meet each new invader (antigens). Antibodies react with antigens:

- By coating antigens' surfaces
- By neutralizing the antigens if they are toxins
- By precipitating the antigens out of solution if they are dissolved

Although this system is normally protective, in some cases, the body produces inappropriate or exaggerated responses to specific antigens, and the result is an allergic or hypersensitivity reaction. Before looking at immunity and immune response more closely, it is helpful to understand the basic components of the immune system.

Anatomy of the Immune System

The immune system is composed of an integrated collection of various cell types, each with a designated functional role in defending against

TABLE
36-1 Immune System Disorders

Disorder	Description
Autoimmunity	Normal protective immune response paradoxically turns against or attacks the body, leading to tissue damage
Hypersensitivity	Body produces inappropriate or exaggerated responses to specific antigens
Gammopathies	Immunoglobulins are overproduced
Immune deficiencies	
Primary	Deficiency results from improper development of immune cells or tissues; usually congenital or inherited
Secondary	Deficiency results from some interference with an already developed immune system; usually acquired later in life

infection and invasion by other organisms. Supporting this system are molecules that are responsible for the interactions, modulations, and regulation of the system. These molecules and cells participate in specific interactions with immunogenic **epitopes** (antigenic determinants [a substance that, when introduced into the body, stimulates the production of an antibody]) present on foreign materials and initiate a series of actions in a host, including the inflammatory response, the lysis of microbial agents, and the disposal of foreign toxins. The major components of the immune system include the bone marrow, the white blood cells (WBCs), the lymphoid tissues (including the thymus gland, the spleen, the lymph nodes, and the tonsils and adenoids), and similar tissues in the gastrointestinal (GI), respiratory, and reproductive systems (Fig. 36-1).

Stem cells (undifferentiated cells) in the bone marrow generate lymphocytes (a type of WBC) (Fig. 36-2). There are two types of lymphocytes: **B lymphocytes (B cells)**, which mature in the bone marrow and enter the circulation as precursors to antibody-secreting cells or memory cells, and **T lymphocytes (T cells)**, which move from the bone marrow to the thymus, where they mature into several kinds of cells with different helper functions (Fig. 36-3).

The thymus is a double-lobed organ found in the upper mediastinum. The spleen is located in the left upper quadrant of the abdomen. It is composed of red pulp (where old and injured red blood cells [RBCs] are destroyed) and white pulp (which contains concentrations of lymphocytes), and it acts like a filter. Lymph nodes are distributed throughout the body and connected by lymph channels and capillaries. The lymph nodes remove foreign material from the lymph system before it enters the bloodstream. They are centers for immune cell proliferation.

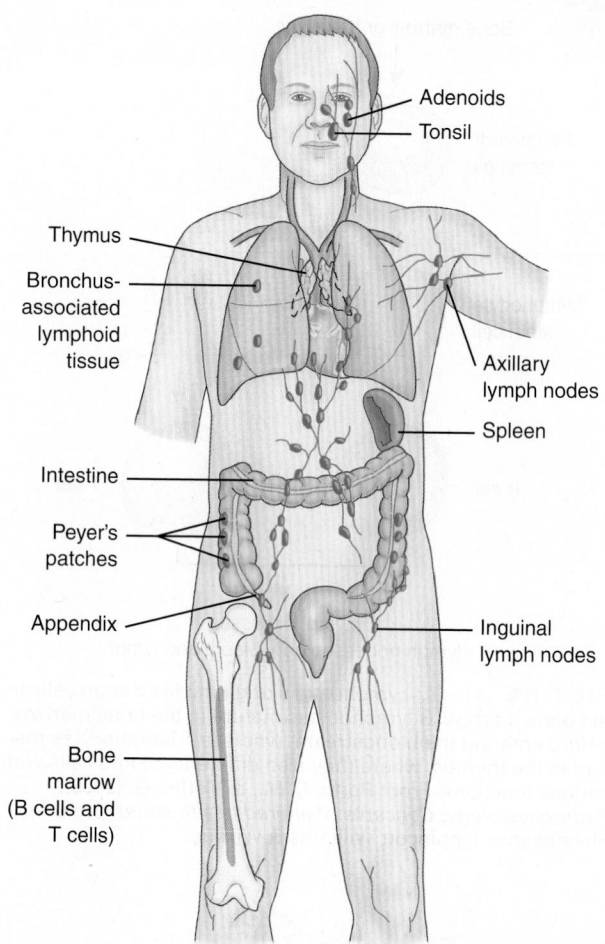

FIGURE 36-1 Central and peripheral lymphoid organs and tissues. From Porth, C. M., & Matfin, G. (2009). *Pathophysiology: Concepts of altered health states* (8th ed.). Philadelphia: Lippincott Williams & Wilkins.

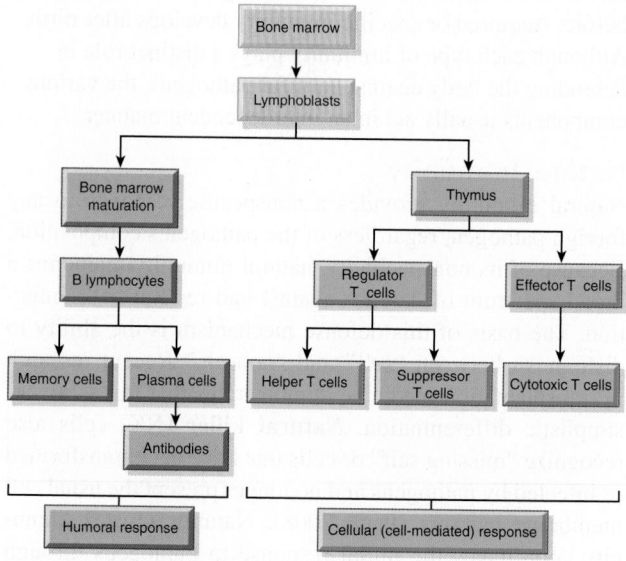

FIGURE 36-2 Development of cells of the immune system.

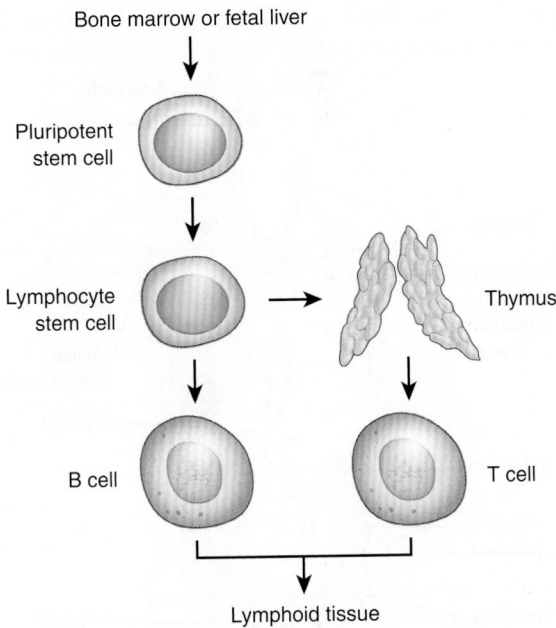

Bone marrow or fetal liver

Pluripotent
stem cell

Lymphocyte
stem cell

Thymus

B cell

T cell

Lymphoid tissue
(lymph nodes, spleen, blood, and lymph)

FIGURE 36-3 Lymphocytes originate from stem cells in the bone marrow. B lymphocytes mature in the bone marrow before entering the bloodstream, whereas T lymphocytes mature in the thymus, where they also differentiate into cells with various functions. From Porth, C. M., & Matfin, G. (2009). *Pathophysiology: Concepts of altered health states* (8th ed.). Philadelphia: Lippincott Williams & Wilkins.

Immune Function

Types of Immunity

There are two general types of immunity: natural (innate) and acquired (adaptive). Natural immunity is a nonspecific immunity present at birth that provides protection against an infectious agent without ever having encountered it before. Acquired or specific immunity develops after birth. Although each type of immunity plays a distinct role in defending the body against harmful pathogens, the various components usually act in an interdependent manner.

Natural Immunity

Natural immunity provides a nonspecific response to any foreign pathogen, regardless of the pathogen's composition. Because of its nonspecificity, natural immunity maintains a broad spectrum of defense against and resistance to infection. The basis of this defense mechanism is the ability to distinguish between "self" and "nonself." Recent research in transplantation medicine demonstrates that this is a very simplistic differentiation. **Natural killer** (NK) cells also recognize "missing self" or cells that have been transformed or infected by pathogens and no longer present the usual cell membrane markers (Paul, 2008). Natural (innate) immunity coordinates the initial response to pathogens through the production of cytokines (hormone-like molecules released by cells; they have profound impact on the growth,

development, and activation of immune system cells and inflammatory response), and other effector molecules, which either activate cells for control of the pathogen (by elimination) or promote the development of the acquired immune response. The cells involved in this response include macrophages, dendritic cells, and NK cells. These cells directly recognize and respond to a wide variety of pathogens long before the development of antigen-specific acquired immunity. The early events in this immune response are critical in determining the nature of the adaptive immune response. Innate immune mechanisms can be divided into two stages: immediate (generally occurring within 4 hours) and delayed (occurring between 4 and 96 hours after exposure).

The development of immunity occurs via physical and chemical barriers, inflammatory response, and immune response.

PHYSICAL AND CHEMICAL BARRIERS. Activation of the natural immunity response is enhanced by processes inherent in physical and chemical barriers. The processes prevent or delay the entry into the body of various pathogens before infection can develop. Physical surface barriers include intact skin, mucous membranes, and cilia of the respiratory tract, which prevent pathogens from gaining access to the body. The cilia of the respiratory tract, along with coughing and sneezing responses, filter and clear pathogens from the upper respiratory tract before they can invade the body further. Chemical barriers, such as mucus, acidic gastric secretions, enzymes in tears and saliva, and substances in sebaceous and sweat secretions, act in a nonspecific way to destroy invading bacteria and fungi. For example, hydrochloric acid in the stomach destroys pathogens present in food or swallowed mucus, as well as dissolving food (Munden, 2007). Viruses are countered by other means, such as interferon (IFN). **Interferon**, one type of biologic response modifier, is a nonspecific viricidal protein that is naturally produced by the body and is capable of activating other components of the immune system.

INFLAMMATORY RESPONSE. The inflammatory response is a major function of the natural immune system that is elicited in response to tissue injury or pathogens. Chemical mediators assist this response by minimizing blood loss, walling off the pathogen, activating phagocytes, and promoting formation of fibrous scar tissue and regeneration of injured tissue. The inflammatory response is facilitated by physical and chemical barriers inherent in the body.

IMMUNE RESPONSE. A successful immune response eliminates the responsible antigen. Regulation of the immune response involves balance and counterbalance. Dysfunction of the natural immune system can occur when the immune components are inactivated or when they remain active long after their effects are beneficial. Immunodeficiencies are characterized by inactivation or impairment of immune components (described further in Chapter 37). Disorders with an

inflammatory component (e.g., asthma, allergy, arthritis) are characterized by persistent inflammatory responses. In some cases, the body produces inappropriate or exaggerated responses to specific antigens, and the result is an allergic or hypersensitivity reaction (Box 36-1). The immune system's recognition of the body's own tissues as "foreign" rather than as self is the basis for many autoimmune disorders (refer to Chapter 38 and 39). Despite the fact that the immune response is critical to the prevention of disease, it must be well controlled to curtail immunopathology. Most microbial infections induce an inflammatory response mediated by T cells and cytokines, which, in excess, can cause tissue damage. Therefore, regulatory mechanisms must be in place to suppress or halt the immune response, to minimize tissue damage. This is mainly achieved by the production of cytokines and transformation of growth factors that inhibit macrophage activation. In some cases, T-cell activation is so overwhelming that these mechanisms fail and pathology results. Current cancer research focuses on NK T cells in the suppression of tumor growth (Terabe, 2007). Researchers in gene therapy are attempting to recruit natural components of the immune system to fight cancer through activation of these inhibitory factors (Wang & Balasundaram, 2010; Yoshimura, Olino, Edil et al., 2010).

Acquired Immunity

Acquired immunity—immunologic responses acquired during life but not present at birth—usually develops as a result of exposure to an antigen through immunization (vaccination) or by contracting a disease, both of which generate a protective immune response. Weeks or months after initial exposure to the disease or vaccine, the body produces an immune response that is sufficient to defend against the disease on re-exposure. In contrast to the rapid but nonspecific innate immune response, this form of immunity relies on the recognition of specific foreign antigens. The two components of the immune response are strongly interrelated. Events occurring early in infection dictate the direction of the adaptive response and activate the acquired immune effector mechanisms, which have a direct feedback on the cells of the innate (natural) system. The acquired immune response is broadly divided into two mechanisms: the cell-mediated response, involving T-cell activation, and effector mechanisms, involving B-cell maturation and the production of antibodies. With the combination of innate and acquired immune responses, the body is capable of protecting itself immediately as well as against future challenges to its integrity.

The two types of acquired immunity are known as active and passive. In active acquired immunity, the immunologic defenses are developed by the person's own body. This immunity typically lasts many years or even a lifetime. This response is best demonstrated by the response of the body to immunizations. Exposure to attenuated virus, such as the influenza vaccine, prompts the production of antibodies

against influenza. Re-exposure to influenza initiates a cascade of immune responses that are more rapid and capable of controlling the virus. Patients either eliminate the virus from their system or have a milder case of influenza. Passive acquired immunity is temporary immunity transmitted from a source outside the body that has developed immunity through previous disease or immunization. For example, immune globulin or antiserum, obtained from plasma of people with acquired immunity, is used in emergencies to provide temporary immunity to certain diseases, such as hepatitis, immediately after exposure. Immunity resulting from the transfer of antibodies from the mother to an infant in utero or through breastfeeding is another example of passive immunity. Active and passive acquired immunity involve humoral and cellular (cell-mediated) immunologic responses.

Response to Invasion

When the body is invaded or attacked by bacteria, viruses, or other pathogens, it has three means of defense:

- The phagocytic immune response
- The humoral or antibody immune response
- The cellular immune response

The first line of defense, the **phagocytic immune response**, involves the WBCs (granulocytes and macrophages), which have the ability to ingest foreign particles. These cells move to the point of attack, where they engulf and destroy the invading agents. Phagocytes also remove the body's own dying or dead cells. Dying cells in necrotic tissue release substances that trigger an inflammatory response. **Apoptosis**, or programmed cell death, is the body's way of destroying worn-out cells, such as blood or skin cells, or cells that need to be renewed. The cells that have been damaged by infection or genetic change, or cells that are simply in excess of the body's needs are targeted for removal and destruction by a subgroup of proteases called *caspase*. Once the process of apoptosis begins, it is generally irreversible (Paul, 2008).

Unlike macrophages, eosinophils are only weakly phagocytic. On activation, eosinophils probably kill parasites by releasing specific chemical mediators into the extracellular fluid. Additionally, eosinophils secrete leukotrienes (discussed later in the chapter), prostaglandins, and various cytokines (Paul, 2008).

A second protective response, the **humoral immune response** (sometimes called the **antibody** response), begins with the B lymphocytes, which can transform themselves into plasma cells that manufacture antibodies. These antibodies are highly specific proteins that are transported in the bloodstream and attempt to disable pathogens. The third mechanism of defense, the **cellular immune response**, also involves the T lymphocytes, which can turn into special cytotoxic (or killer) T cells that can attack the pathogens. Table 36-2 summarizes the types of cells involved in immune response.

BOX 36-1

Focus on Pathophysiology

Allergic Reaction

An allergic reaction is a manifestation of tissue injury resulting from interaction between an antigen and an antibody. Allergy is an inappropriate and often harmful response of the immune system to normally harmless substances. In this case, the inappropriate substance is termed an *allergen*.

Mast cells located in tissues throughout the body can be activated by a variety of stimuli, causing immediate allergic inflammation. The binding of the antigen and antibodies on the mast cells causes the release of mediators that effect blood vessel, smooth muscle, and glandular secretions. The powerful chemical mediators released from the mast cells cause a sequence of physiologic events resulting in symptoms of immediate hypersensitivity. There are two types of chemical mediators: primary and secondary. Primary mediators are preformed and are found in mast cells or basophils. Secondary mediators are inactive precursors that are formed or released in response to primary mediators (e.g., leukotrienes, bradykinin, and serotonin).

When in contact with an allergen, the body produces large amounts of IgE thus causing a hypersensitivity or allergic response (see figure on page 989). IgE-producing cells are located in the respiratory and intestinal mucosa. Two or more IgE molecules bind together to an allergen and trigger mast cells or basophils to release chemical mediators, such as histamine and leukotrienes. Maximal intensity of histamine release is reached within about 15 minutes after antigen contact. Effects of histamine release include erythema; localized edema in the form of wheals; pruritus; contraction of bronchial smooth muscle, resulting in wheezing and bronchospasm; dilation of small venules and constriction of larger vessels; and increased secretion of gastric and mucosal cells, resulting in diarrhea. Histamine action results from stimulation of histamine-1 (H_1) and histamine-2 (H_2) receptors found on different types of lymphocytes, particularly T lymphocyte suppressor cells and basophils. H_1 receptors are found predominantly on bronchiolar and vascular smooth muscle cells; H_2 receptors are found on gastric parietal cells.

Certain medications are categorized by their action at these receptors. Diphenhydramine (Benadryl) is an example of an antihistamine, a medication that displays an affinity for H_1 receptors. Cimetidine (Tagamet) and ranitidine (Zantac) target H_2 receptors to inhibit gastric secretions in peptic ulcer disease.

Leukotrienes, another chemical mediator released by mucosal mast cells causes smooth muscle contraction, bronchial constriction, mucus secretion in the airways, and the typical wheal-and-flare reaction of the skin.

Compared with histamine, leukotrienes are 100 to 1,000 times more potent in causing bronchospasm. Many manifestations of inflammation can be attributed in part to leukotrienes. Medications categorized as leukotriene antagonists or modifiers, such as zileuton (Zyflo), zafirlukast (Accolate), and montelukast (Singulair), block the synthesis or action of leukotrienes and prevent the signs and symptoms associated with asthma.

Hypersensitivity

A hypersensitivity reaction is an abnormal, heightened reaction to any type of stimulus. It usually does not occur with the first exposure to an allergen, but is a reflection of excessive or atypical immune responses. To promote understanding of the immunopathogenesis of disease, hypersensitivity reactions have been classified into four specific types of reactions: Anaphylactic (type 1) Hypersensitivity, Cytotoxic (type II) Hypersensitivity, Immune Complex (type III) Hypersensitivity, and Delayed-Type (type IV) Hypersensitivity. Most allergies are identified as either type I or type IV hypersensitivity reactions.

Anaphylactic (Type I) Hypersensitivity

The most severe form of hypersensitivity reaction or immune-mediated reaction is **anaphylaxis**. An unanticipated severe allergic reaction that is often explosive in onset, anaphylaxis is characterized by edema in many tissues, including the larynx, and is often accompanied by hypotension, bronchospasm, and cardiovascular collapse in severe cases. Type I or anaphylactic hypersensitivity is an immediate reaction beginning within minutes of exposure to an antigen. This reaction is mediated by IgE antibodies and typically occurs on re-exposure to a specific antigen. If chemical mediators continue to be released, a delayed reaction may occur up to 24 hours after allergen exposure.

Cytotoxic (Type II) Hypersensitivity

Type II, or cytotoxic, hypersensitivity occurs when the system mistakenly identifies a normal constituent of the body as foreign. This reaction may be the result of a cross-reacting antibody, possibly leading to cell and tissue damage. Several disorders are associated with type II hypersensitivity reactions, including myasthenia gravis, in which the body mistakenly generates antibodies against normal nerve ending receptors; Goodpasture's syndrome, in which antibodies are generated against lung and renal tissue, producing lung damage and renal failure; or associated with drug-induced immune hemolytic anemia, Rh-hemolytic disease of the newborn, and incompatibility reactions in blood transfusions.

Immune Complex (Type III) Hypersensitivity

Type III, or immune complex, hypersensitivity involves immune complexes that are formed when antigens bind to antibodies. These complexes are cleared from the circulation by phagocytic action. If these type III complexes are deposited in tissues or vascular endothelium, two factors contribute to injury: the increased amount of circulating complexes and the presence of vasoactive amines. As a result, there is an increase in vascular permeability and tissue injury. The joints and kidneys are particularly susceptible to this type of injury. Type III hypersensitivity is associated with systemic lupus erythematosus, rheumatoid arthritis, certain types of nephritis, and some types of bacterial endocarditis.

Delayed-Type (Type IV) Hypersensitivity

Type IV, or delayed-type hypersensitivity, also known as cellular hypersensitivity, occurs 24 to 72 hours after exposure to an allergen. It is mediated by sensitized T cells and macrophages. An example of this reaction is the effect of an intradermal injection of tuberculin antigen or purified protein derivative (PPD). Sensitized T cells react with the antigen at or near the injection site. Lymphokines are released and attract, activate, and retain macrophages at the site. These macrophages then release lysozymes, causing tissue damage. Edema and fibrin are responsible for the positive tuberculin reaction.

Another example of a type IV hypersensitivity reaction is contact dermatitis resulting from exposure to allergens such as cosmetics, adhesive tape, topical agents (e.g., povidone-iodine), medication additives, and plant toxins. The most common immune-mediated reaction to local anesthetics is a type IV hypersensitivity reaction. The primary exposure results in sensitization. Re-exposure causes a hypersensitivity reaction with resultant symptoms such as pruritus, erythema, and raised lesions.

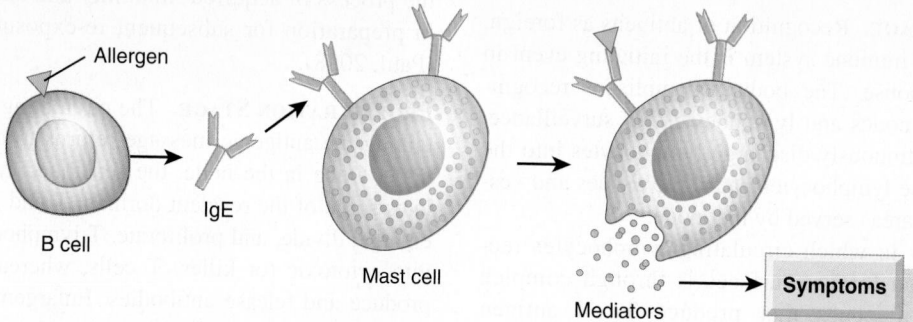

Allergen triggers the B cell to make IgE antibody, which attaches to the mast cell. When that allergen reappears; it binds to the IgE and triggers the mast cell to release its chemicals. Courtesy of the U.S. Department of Health and Human Services. National Institutes of Health.

TABLE
36-2 Lymphocytes Involved in Immune Responses

Type of Immune Response	Cell Type	Function
Humoral	B lymphocyte	Produces antibodies or immunoglobulins (IgA, IgD, IgE, IgG, IgM)
Cellular	T lymphocyte	Attacks foreign pathogens (antigens) directly
	Helper T	Initiates and augments inflammatory response
	Helper T$_1$	Increases activated cytotoxic T cells
	Helper T$_2$	Increases B-cell antibody production
	Suppressor T	Suppresses the immune response
	Memory T	Remembers contact with an antigen and on subsequent exposures mounts an immune response
	Cytotoxic T (killer T)	Lyses cells infected with virus; plays a role in graft rejection
Nonspecific	Non-T or non-B lymphocyte	
	Null cell	Destroys antigens already coated with antibody
	Natural killer (NK) cell (granular lymphocyte)	Defends against microorganisms and some types of malignant cells; produces cytokines

Basics of Immune Response

The structural part of the invading or attacking organism that is responsible for stimulating antibody production is called an **antigen** (or an immunogen). An antigen can be a small patch of proteins on the outer surface of a microorganism. Some antigens are naturally immunogenic or able to directly stimulate an immune response. Most antigens must be coupled to other molecules to stimulate the immune response. A single bacterium or large molecule, such as a diphtheria or tetanus toxin, may have several antigens, or markers, on its surface, thus inducing the body to produce a number of different antibodies. Once produced, an antibody is released into the bloodstream and carried to the attacking organism. There, it combines with the antigen, binding with it like an interlocking piece of a jigsaw puzzle (Fig. 36-4). There are four well-defined stages in an immune response: recognition, proliferation, response, and effector.

RECOGNITION STAGE. Recognition of antigens as foreign, or nonself, by the immune system is the initiating event in any immune response. The body accomplishes recognition using lymph nodes and lymphocytes for surveillance. Lymph nodes continuously discharge lymphocytes into the bloodstream. These lymphocytes patrol the tissues and vessels that drain the areas served by that node.

The exact way in which circulating lymphocytes recognize antigens on foreign surfaces is through complex rearrangements of genes that produce T-cell antigen receptors (TCR) during cell differentiation and maturation in the thymus. T-cells present in primary lymphoid tissue that have not been presented with an antigen are called *naïve* and are capable of responding to a vast array of antigens (Paul, 2008). Macrophages play an important role in helping the circulating lymphocytes process the antigens. Both macrophages and neutrophils have receptors for antibodies and complement (proteins found in normal blood plasma that combines with antibodies to destroy pathogens); as a result, they coat microorganisms with antibodies, complement, or both, enhancing phagocytosis. The engulfed microorganisms are then subjected to a wide range of toxic intracellular molecules. When foreign materials enter the body, circulating lymphocytes come into physical contact with the surfaces of these materials. Upon contact with the foreign material, naïve lymphocytes, with the help of macrophages, either remove the antigen from the surface or obtain an imprint of its structure, initiating the process of acquired immunity and antigen recognition in preparation for subsequent re-exposure to the antigen (Paul, 2008).

PROLIFERATION STAGE. The circulating lymphocyte containing the antigenic message returns to the nearest lymph node. Once in the node, the sensitized lymphocyte stimulates some of the resident dormant T and B lymphocytes to enlarge, divide, and proliferate. T lymphocytes differentiate into cytotoxic (or killer) T cells, whereas B lymphocytes produce and release antibodies. Enlargement of the lymph nodes in the neck in conjunction with a sore throat is one example of the inflammatory response during immune activation.

RESPONSE STAGE. In the response stage, the differentiated lymphocytes function in either a humoral or a cellular capacity. The production of antibodies by the B lymphocytes in response to a specific antigen begins the humoral response. *Humoral* refers to the fact that the antibodies are released into the bloodstream and therefore reside in the plasma (fluid fraction of the blood).

With the initial cellular response, the returning sensitized lymphocytes migrate to areas of the lymph node other than those areas containing lymphocytes programmed to become plasma cells. Here, they stimulate the residing lymphocytes to become cells that will attack microbes directly, rather than through the action of antibodies. These transformed lymphocytes are known as cytotoxic (killer) T cells. The T stands for *thymus*, signifying that, during embryologic development of the immune system, these T lymphocytes spent time in the thymus of the developing fetus. Viral rather than bacterial antigens induce a cellular response. This response is manifested by the increasing number of T lymphocytes (lymphocytosis) seen on the complete blood counts (CBC) of people with viral illnesses such as infectious mononucleosis (cellular immunity is discussed in further detail later in this chapter.)

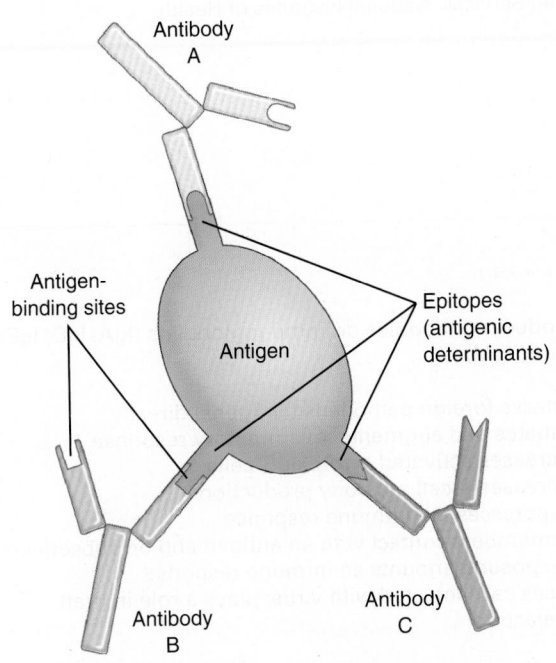

FIGURE 36-4 Complement-mediated immune responses. From Porth, C. M., & Matfin, G. (2009) *Pathophysiology: Concepts of altered health states* (8th ed.). Philadelphia: Lippincott Williams & Wilkins.

Examples of Humoral and Cellular Immune Responses

Humoral Responses (B Cells)
- Bacterial phagocytosis and lysis
- Anaphylaxis
- Allergic hay fever and asthma
- Immune complex disease
- Bacterial and some viral infections

Cellular Responses (T Cells)
- Transplant rejection
- Delayed hypersensitivity (tuberculin reaction)
- Graft-versus-host disease
- Tumor surveillance or destruction
- Intracellular infections
- Viral, fungal, and parasitic infections

Most immune responses to antigens involve both humoral and cellular responses, although one usually predominates. For example, during transplant rejection, the cellular response predominates, whereas in the bacterial pneumonias and sepsis, the humoral response plays the dominant protective role (Box 36-2).

EFFECTOR STAGE. In the effector stage, either the antibody of the humoral response or the cytotoxic (killer) T cell of the cellular response reaches and connects with the antigen on the surface of the foreign pathogen. The connection initiates a series of events that in most instances results in the total destruction of the invading microbes or the complete neutralization of the toxin. The events involve interplay of antibodies (humoral immunity), complement, and action by the cytotoxic T cells (cellular immunity). Figure 36-5 summarizes the stages of the immune response.

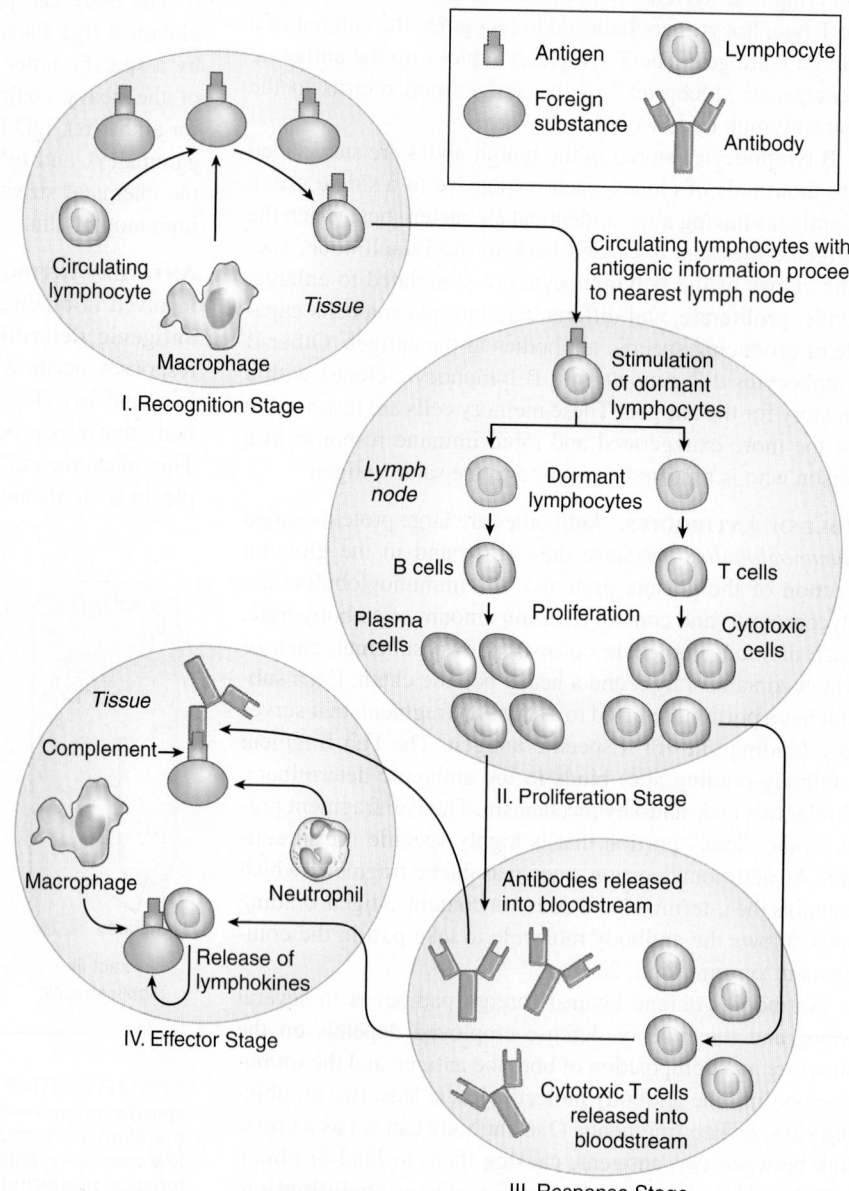

FIGURE 36-5 Stages of the immune response. (I) In the *recognition stage,* antigens are recognized by circulating lymphocytes and macrophages. (II) In the *proliferation stage,* the dormant lymphocytes proliferate and differentiate into cytotoxic (killer) T or B cells responsible for formation and release of antibodies. (III) In the *response stage,* the cytotoxic T cells and the B cells perform cellular and humoral functions, respectively. (IV) In the *effector stage,* antigens are destroyed or neutralized through the action of antibodies, complement, macrophages, and cytotoxic T cells.

Humoral Immune Response

The humoral response is characterized by the production of antibodies by B lymphocytes in response to a specific antigen. Although the B lymphocyte is ultimately responsible for the production of antibodies, both the macrophages of natural immunity and the special T-cell lymphocytes of cellular immunity are involved in recognizing the foreign substance and in producing antibodies.

ANTIGEN RECOGNITION. B lymphocytes recognize and respond to invading antigens in more than one way.

The B lymphocytes appear to respond to some antigens by directly triggering antibody formation; however, in response to other antigens, they need the assistance of T cells to trigger antibody formation. The T lymphocytes are part of a surveillance system that is dispersed throughout the body and recycles through the general circulation, tissues, and lymphatic system. With the assistance of macrophages, the T lymphocytes are believed to recognize the antigen of a foreign pathogen. The T lymphocyte picks up the antigenic message, or "blueprint," of the antigen and returns to the nearest lymph node with that message.

B lymphocytes stored in the lymph nodes are subdivided into thousands of clones, each responsive to a single group of antigens having almost identical characteristics. When the antigenic message is carried back to the lymph node, specific clones of the B lymphocyte are stimulated to enlarge, divide, proliferate, and differentiate into plasma cells capable of producing specific antibodies to the antigen. Other B lymphocytes differentiate into B-lymphocyte clones with a memory for the antigen. These memory cells are responsible for the more exaggerated and rapid immune response in a person who is repeatedly exposed to the same antigen.

ROLE OF ANTIBODIES. Antibodies are large proteins called *immunoglobulins* (because they are found in the globulin fraction of the plasma proteins). All immunoglobulins are glycoproteins and contain a certain amount of carbohydrate. Each antibody molecule consists of two subunits, each of which contains a light and a heavy peptide chain. Each subunit has a portion, referred to as the Fab fragment, that serves as a binding site for a specific antigen. The Fab fragment (antibody-binding site) binds to the antigenic determinant, similar to a lock-and-key mechanism. The Fab fragment provides the "lock" portion that is highly specific for an antigen. An additional portion, known as the Fc fragment, which contains the c-terminal and does not contain antigen-binding sites, allows the antibody molecule to take part in the complement system (Paul, 2008).

Antibodies defend against foreign pathogens in several ways, and the type of defense employed depends on the structure and composition of both the antigen and the immunoglobulin. The antibody molecule has at least two combining sites, or Fab fragments. One antibody can act as a cross-link between two antigens, causing them to bind or clump together. This clumping effect, referred to as **agglutination**,

helps clear the body of the pathogen by facilitating phagocytosis. Agglutination is used in several laboratory tests, such as those for syphilis, to recognize and enumerate the presence of antibody–antigen complexes, indicative of infection. Some antibodies assist in removal of offending organisms through **opsonization**. In this process, the antigen–antibody molecule is coated with a sticky substance that also facilitates phagocytosis.

Antibodies also promote the release of vasoactive substances, such as histamine and slow-reacting substance, two of the chemical mediators of the inflammatory response. Antibodies do not function in isolation; rather, they mobilize other components of the immune system to defend against the pathogen. The typical role of antibodies is to focus components of the natural immune system on the pathogen. This includes activation of the complement system and activation of phagocytosis (Paul, 2008).

The body can produce five different types of immunoglobulins (Ig). Each of the five types, or classes, is identified by a specific letter of the alphabet derived from the name of the heavy chain present on the immunoglobulin: IgA for alpha (α), IgD for delta (δ), IgE for epsilon (ϵ), IgG for gamma (γ), and IgM for mu (μ). Classification is based on the chemical structure and biologic role of the individual immunoglobulin.

ANTIGEN–ANTIBODY BINDING. The portion of the antigen involved in binding with the antibody is referred to as the **antigenic determinant**. The most efficient immunologic responses occur when the antibody and antigen fit like a lock and key (Fig. 36-6). Poor fit can occur with an antibody that was produced in response to a different antigen. This phenomenon is known as cross-reactivity. For example, in acute rheumatic fever, the antibody produced against

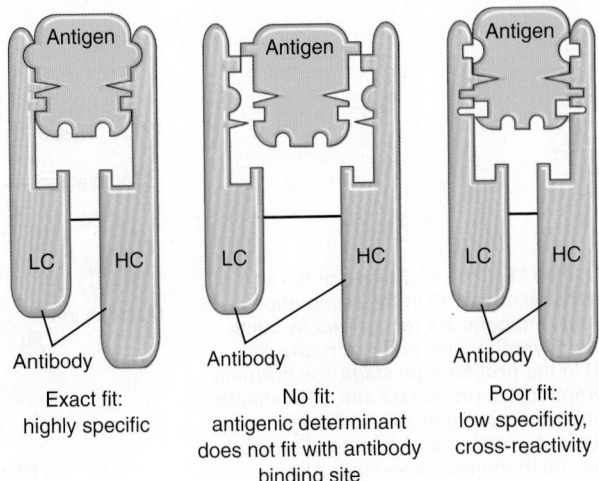

FIGURE 36-6 Antigen–antibody binding. (*Left*) A highly specific antigen–antibody complex. (*Middle*) No match and therefore, no immune response. (*Right*) Poor fit or match with low specificity; antibody reacts to antigen with similar characteristics, producing cross-reactivity.

Streptococcus pyogenes in the upper respiratory tract may cross-react with the patient's heart tissue, leading to mitral valve prolapse.

Cellular Immune Response

T lymphocytes are primarily responsible for cellular immunity. Several types of T cells exist, each with designated roles in the defense against bacteria, viruses, fungi, parasites, and malignant cells. T cells attack foreign pathogens directly rather than by producing antibodies. T cells are either naïve—capable of reacting to new antigens—or activated—having the memory of previous antigen exposure (Paul, 2008).

Cellular reactions are initiated by the binding of an antigen to an antigen receptor located on the surface of a naïve T cell. This may occur with or without the assistance of macrophages. The activated T cells then carry the antigenic message, or blueprint, to the lymph nodes, where the production of other T cells is stimulated. Some T cells remain in the lymph nodes and retain a memory for the antigen. Other T cells migrate from the lymph nodes into the general circulatory system and ultimately to the tissues, where they remain until they either come in contact with their respective antigens or die.

ROLE OF T LYMPHOCYTES. T cells include effector T cells, suppressor T cells, and memory T cells. Two major categories of effector T cells exist: helper T cells and cytotoxic T cells. These effector T cells participate in the destruction of foreign organisms. T cells interact closely with B cells, indicating that humoral and cellular immune responses are not separate, unrelated processes, but rather, branches of the immune response that interact.

Helper T cells are activated on recognition of antigens and stimulate the rest of the immune system. When activated, helper T cells secrete **cytokines**, which attract and activate B cells, cytotoxic T cells, NK cells, macrophages, and other cells of the immune system. Separate subpopulations of helper T cells produce different types of cytokines and determine whether the immune response will be the production of antibodies or a cell-mediated immune response. Helper T cells produce **lymphokines**, one category of cytokines. These lymphokines activate other T cells (e.g., interleukin-2 [IL-2]), natural and cytotoxic T cells (e.g., IFN-gamma), and other inflammatory cells (e.g., tumor necrosis factor). Helper T cells produce IL-4 and IL-5, lymphokines that activate B cells to grow and differentiate. Table 50-2 lists the functions of a few of the more than 35 types of interleukin discovered so far.

Cytotoxic T cells (killer T cells) attack the antigen directly by altering the cell membrane and causing cell lysis (disintegration) and by releasing cytolytic enzymes and cytokines. Lymphokines can recruit, activate, and regulate other lymphocytes and WBCs. These cells then assist in destroying the pathogen. Delayed-type hypersensitivity is an example of an immune reaction that protects the body from

antigens through the production and release of lymphokines (see later discussion).

Another type of cell, the **suppressor T cell**, has the ability to decrease B cell production, thereby keeping the immune response at a level that is compatible with health (e.g., sufficient to fight infection adequately without attacking the body's healthy tissues). **Memory cells** are responsible for recognizing antigens from previous exposure and mounting an immune response.

ROLES OF NULL LYMPHOCYTES AND NATURAL KILLER CELLS. Null lymphocytes and NK cells are other lymphocytes that assist in combating organisms. These cells are distinct from B and T cells and lack the usual characteristics of those cells. **Null lymphocytes**, a subpopulation of lymphocytes, destroy antigens already coated with antibody. These cells have special Fc receptor sites on their surface that allow them to connect with the Fc end of antibodies; this is known as antibody-dependent, cell-mediated cytotoxicity.

NK cells, another subpopulation of lymphocytes, defend against microorganisms and some types of malignant cells (Porth & Matfin, 2009). NK cells are capable of directly killing pathogens and producing cytokines. The helper T cells contribute to the differentiation of null and NK cells.

Complement System

Circulating plasma proteins, known as **complement**, are made in the liver and other sites and activated when an antibody connects with its antigen. There are more than 35 of these plasma or membrane proteins, and they are an important additional component of the immune system (Paul, 2008). Destruction of an invading or attacking organism or toxin is not achieved merely by the binding of the antibody and antigens; it also requires activation of complement, the arrival of killer T cells, or the attraction of macrophages. Complement has three major physiologic functions: defending the body against bacterial infection, bridging natural and acquired immunity, and disposing of immune complexes and the by-products associated with inflammation.

The proteins that comprise complement interact sequentially with one another in a cascading or "falling domino" effect. The complement cascade is important to modifying the effector arm of the immune system. Activation of complement allows important events, such as removal of infectious agents and initiation of the inflammatory response, to take place. These events involve active parts of the pathway that enhance chemotaxis of macrophages and granulocytes, alter blood vessel permeability, change blood vessel diameters, cause cells to lyse, alter blood clotting, and cause other points of modification. These macrophages and granulocytes continue the body's defense by devouring the antibody-coated microbes and by releasing antibacterial products.

Role of Interferons

IFNs are cytokines. They have antiviral and antitumor properties. In addition to responding to viral infection, IFNs are

produced by T lymphocytes, B lymphocytes, and macrophages in response to antigens. They modify the immune response by suppressing antibody production and cellular immunity. They also facilitate the cytolytic (cell destruction) role of lymphocytes, macrophages, and NK cells. Research continues on the pathways that IFNs use to transmit signals from cell membranes to the nucleus. IFNs are undergoing extensive testing to evaluate their effectiveness in treating tumors and AIDS (Macatangay, Zheng, Rinaldo et al., 2010). One IFN that is currently being used in therapy is pegylated IFN-alpha, for the treatment of chronic hepatitis C (Zoller & Vogel, 2006).

Advances in Immunology

Genetic Engineering

One of the more remarkable evolving technologies is **genetic engineering**, which uses recombinant DNA technology. Genetic engineering is used in everything from the production of insulin and human growth hormone to the production of experimental mice. One type of genetic engineering permits scientists to combine genes from one type of organism with genes of a second organism. This type of technology allows cells and microorganisms to manufacture proteins, monokines, and lymphokines that can alter and enhance immune system function. The second use of recombinant DNA technology involves gene therapy (Lackner & Behr-Gross, 2009). If a particular gene is abnormal or missing, experimental recombinant DNA technology may be capable of restoring normal gene function. For example, a recombinant gene is inserted onto a virus particle. When the virus particle splices its genes, the virus automatically inserts the missing gene, and theoretically corrects the genetic anomaly. Extensive research into recombinant DNA technology and gene therapy is ongoing, including phase III clinical trials of a recombinant DNA vaccine against lymphoma (Park, 2008).

Stem Cells

Stem cells are potentially immortal cells that are capable of self-renewal and differentiation; they continually replenish the body's entire supply of both RBCs and WBCs. Some stem cells, described as *totipotent cells*, have tremendous capacity to self-renew and differentiate. Embryonic stem cells, described as *pluripotent*, give rise to numerous cell types that are able to form tissues (Porth & Matfin, 2009). Research and clinical trials have shown that stem cells can restore an immune system that has been destroyed. Stem cell transplantation has been carried out in humans with certain types of immune dysfunction, such as severe combined immunodeficiency (SCID) and acute myeloid leukemia (Storb, 2009). Clinical trials using stem cells are under way in patients with a variety of disorders having an autoimmune component, including systemic lupus erythematosus (SLE), rheumatoid arthritis, scleroderma, multiple sclerosis, and heart disease, specifically in the repair of endothelial cells

(Sundin, Barrett, Ringdn et al., 2009). Currently, allogenic (transplantation from one person to another) stem cells are being cultured that will decrease the reaction in graft versus host disease (Van der Bogt, Schrepfer, Sheikh et al., 2009). On March 9, 2009 President Barack Obama issued an Executive Order that permits the National Institute of Health to "support and conduct responsible, scientifically worthy human stem cell research, including human embryonic stem cell research." This ended an almost 9-year ban in the United States, although research has continued abroad.

Gerontologic Considerations

People at the extremes of the lifespan are more likely to develop problems related to immune system functioning than are middle-aged adults (Table 36-3). The greatest impact of aging on the immune system is on cell-mediated immunity; age has a lesser but substantial impact on humoral immunity. The frequency and severity of infections are increased in elderly people, possibly due to a decreased ability to respond adequately to pathogens. Both the production and the function of T and B lymphocytes may be impaired. Responses to antigen stimulation may be altered, with increasing proportions of lymphocytes becoming unresponsive with age. An example of this is the recent development of a vaccine for older patients against herpes zoster and postherpetic neuralgia caused by the varicella virus. The antigen present in this vaccine is 14 times the amount of live attenuated virus present in the varicella vaccine for children (Paul, 2008). Aging has an impact on the immune system that can best be summarized as *immunosenescence*, a condition thought to be a result of involution of the thymus (Paul, 2008).

ASSESSMENT OF THE IMMUNE SYSTEM

Assessment of the immune system involves nearly every organ system of the body.

Health History

Common Complaints

Accurately assessing a patient's immune system can include nonspecific signs and symptoms such as fatigue, impaired wound healing, recurrent infections, weight loss, or lymphadenopathy; or it may be specific, such as a butterfly (malar) rash in SLE, joint deformities in rheumatoid arthritis, thrush in HIV, or erythema, hoarseness, and dyspnea with anaphylactic reaction.

Past History

The patient is asked about childhood and adult immunizations and the childhood diseases. Known past or present exposure to tuberculosis is assessed, and the dates and results of

TABLE
36-3 GERONTOLOGICAL CONSIDERATIONS / Age-Related Changes in Immunologic Function

Body System	Structural and Functional Changes	History and Physical Findings
Immune	Impaired function of B and T lymphocytes	Suppressed responses to pathogenic organisms with increased risk for infection
	Failure of lymphocytes to recognize mutant or abnormal cells	Increased incidence of cancers
	Decreased antibody production	Anergy (lack of response to antigens applied to the skin [PPD, allergens])
	Failure of immune system to differentiate "self" from "non-self"	
	Suppressed phagocytic immune response	Increased incidence of autoimmune diseases
		Absence of typical signs and symptoms of infection and inflammation
		Dissemination of organisms usually destroyed or suppressed by phagocytes (e.g., reactivation or spread of tuberculosis)
Gastrointestinal	Decreased gastric secretions and motility	Proliferation of intestinal organisms resulting in gastroenteritis and diarrhea
	Decreased phagocytosis by the liver's Kupffer cells	Increased incidence and severity of hepatitis B; increased incidence of liver abscesses
	Altered nutritional intake with inadequate protein intake	Suppressed immune response
Urinary	Decreased kidney function and changes in lower urinary tract function (enlargement of prostate gland, neurogenic bladder). Altered genitourinary tract flora.	Urinary stasis and increased incidence of urinary tract infections
Pulmonary	Impaired ciliary action due to exposure to smoke and environmental toxins	Impaired clearance of pulmonary secretions; increased incidence of respiratory infections
Integumentary	Thinning of skin with less elasticity; loss of adipose tissue	Increased risk of skin injury, breakdown and infection
Circulatory	Impaired microcirculation	Stasis and pressure ulcers
Neurologic function	Decreased sensation and slowing of reflexes	Increased risk of injury, skin ulcers, abrasions, and burns

any tuberculin tests (PPD or tine test) and chest X-rays are obtained. Recent exposure to any infections and the exposure dates are elicited. It is important for the nurse to assess whether the patient has been exposed to any sexually transmitted infections (STIs) or bloodborne pathogens, such as hepatitis A, B, or C viruses and HIV virus. A history of STIs such as gonorrhea, syphilis, HPV infection, and chlamydia can alert the nurse that the patient may have been exposed to HIV infection or to hepatitis. However, the Centers for Disease Control and Prevention (CDC) recommends universal HIV testing of all patients over the age of 13, with risk assessment determining the need for repeat testing. A history of past and present infections and the dates and types of treatments, along with a history of any multiple persistent infections, fevers of unknown origin, lesions or sores, or any type of drainage, are obtained.

Allergy

The patient is asked about any allergies, including types of allergens (e.g., pollens, dust, plants, cosmetics, food, medications, vaccines, latex), the symptoms experienced, and seasonal variations in occurrence or severity in the symptoms.

A history of testing and treatments, including prescribed and over-the-counter medications that the patient has taken or is currently taking for these allergies and the effectiveness of the treatments is obtained. All medication and food allergies are listed on an allergy alert sticker and placed on the front of the patient's health record or chart to alert others. Continued assessment for potential allergic reactions in the patient is vital.

Autoimmune Disorders

Autoimmune disorders affect people of both genders of all ages, ethnicities, and social classes. The patient is asked about any autoimmune disorders, such as lupus erythematosus, rheumatoid arthritis, or psoriasis. The onset, severity, remissions and exacerbations, functional limitations, treatments that the patient has received or is currently receiving, and the effectiveness of the treatments are described. Although most specific autoimmune disorders are rare, together they affect approximately 5% of the United States population. The occurrence of different autoimmune diseases within a family strongly suggests a genetic predisposition to more than one autoimmune disease (Paul, 2008).

Neoplastic Disease

If there is a history of cancer in the family, the type of cancer, age at onset, and relationship (maternal or paternal) of the patient to the affected family members is noted. Dates and results of any cancer screening tests for the patient are obtained. A history of cancer in the patient is also obtained, along with the type of cancer, date of diagnosis, and treatment modalities used. Immunosuppression contributes to the development of cancers; however, cancer itself is immunosuppressive. Hematologic cancers, such as leukemia and lymphoma, are associated with altered production and function of WBCs and lymphocytes (Paul, 2008).

All treatments that the patient has received or is currently receiving, such as radiation or chemotherapy, are recorded in the health history. Radiation destroys lymphocytes and decreases the ability to mount an effective immune response. The size and extent of the irradiated area determine the extent of immunosuppression. Whole-body irradiation may leave the patient totally immunosuppressed. Chemotherapy also affects bone marrow function, destroying cells that contribute to an effective immune response and resulting in immunosuppression.

Chronic Illness and Surgery

The nurse notes any history of chronic illness, such as diabetes mellitus, renal disease, chronic obstructive pulmonary disease (COPD), or fibromyalgia (Munden, 2006). The onset and severity of illnesses, as well as treatment that the patient is receiving for the illness, are obtained. Chronic illness may contribute to immune system impairments in various ways. Renal failure is associated with a deficiency in circulating lymphocytes. In addition, immune defenses may be altered by acidosis and uremic toxins. In diabetes, an increased incidence of infection has been associated with neuropathy, macrovascular disease, and microvascular dysfunction. Whether hyperglycemia causes increased infection or results from infection continues to be researched. Recurrent respiratory tract infections are associated with COPD as a result of altered inspiratory and expiratory function and ineffective airway clearance.

Special Problems

Conditions such as burns and other forms of injury and infection may contribute to altered immune system function. Major burns cause impaired skin integrity and compromise the body's first line of defense. Loss of large amounts of serum occurs with burn injuries and depletes the body of essential proteins, including immunoglobulins. The physiologic and psychological stressors associated with surgery or injury stimulate cortisol release from the adrenal cortex; increased serum cortisol also contributes to suppression of normal immune responses.

Social History

Poor nutritional status, poor sleep habits, smoking, excessive consumption of alcohol, illicit drug use, STIs, and occupa-

tional or residential exposure to environmental radiation and pollutants have been associated with impaired immune function and are assessed in a detailed patient history.

Nutrition

The importance of optimal nutrition in enhancing immunity is gaining greater recognition. Inadequate intake of vitamins that are essential for DNA and protein synthesis may lead to protein–calorie deficiency and subsequently to impaired immune function. Vitamins also help in the regulation of cell proliferation and maturation of immune cells. Excess or deficiency of trace elements (i.e., copper, iron, manganese, selenium, or zinc) in the diet generally suppresses immune function.

Fatty acids are the building blocks that make up the structural components of cell membranes. Lipids are precursors of vitamins A, D, E, and K, as well as cholesterol. Both excess and deficiency of fatty acids have been found to suppress immune function.

Depletion of protein reserves results in atrophy of lymphoid tissues, depression of antibody response, reduction in the number of circulating T cells, and impaired phagocytic function. As a result, susceptibility to infection is greatly increased. During periods of infection or serious illness, nutritional requirements may be further altered, potentially contributing to depletion of protein, fatty acid, vitamin, and trace elements and causing even greater risk of impaired immune response and sepsis. Patients whose nutritional status is compromised have a delayed postoperative recovery and often experience more severe infections and delayed wound healing. The nurse must assess the patient's nutritional status and caloric intake. The nurse is responsible for assuming a proactive role in ensuring the best possible nutritional intake for all patients as a vital step in preventing untoward treatment outcomes.

Box 36-3 discusses the role of probiotics.

Medications and Blood Transfusions

A list of past and present medications is obtained. In large doses, antibiotics, corticosteroids, cytotoxic agents, salicylates, nonsteroidal anti-inflammatory drugs (NSAIDs), and anesthetics can cause immune suppression (Table 36-4, p. 998).

A history of blood transfusions is obtained because previous exposure to foreign antigens through transfusion may be associated with abnormal immune function. Additionally, although the risk of HIV transmission through blood transfusion is extremely low in patients who received a transfusion after 1985 (the year that testing of blood for HIV was initiated in the United States), a small risk remains. The nurse also assesses for signs or symptoms of hepatitis in patients who have received blood products.

Travel and Occupation

Patients who are immunocompromised should be asked about travel history and occupational history to determine specific pathogen exposure. For example, patients from

BOX 36-3

Nursing Research

Bridging the Gap to Evidence-Based Practice

Are Probiotic Supplements Truly Beneficial to the Immune System?

Weichselbaum, E. (2009). Probiotics and health: A review of the evidence. *Nutrition Bulletin, 34*(4), 340–373.

Purpose

This study comprised a review of more than 100 articles to determine the actual benefits associated with *probiotics,* live microorganisms (usually bacteria) that are reported to enhance the host's health. Examples of probiotics include *Lactobacillus* species found in yogurt. Most of these articles research probiotic effects on the GI system, especially as they affect irritable bowel syndrome, diarrhea, and constipation. Other investigations focused on the effects of probiotics on the immune system's ability to fight common colds, influenza, allergies, or eczema.

Design

Using PubMed, the researchers gathered articles that were clinical trials, meta-analyses, or systematic reviews on probiotics and health benefits. Articles from clinical trials were included if their methodology was randomized, blinded, and placebo-controlled. Findings of these articles were then summarized and analyzed.

Findings

Limited research was reviewed about ulcerative colitis, but results are promising in the ability for probiotics to maintain remission at rates similar to gold standard therapies. *Pouchitis,* an inflammation of the ileal pouch created during surgical treatment for patients with ulcerative colitis, shows very promising results from the use of probiotics. The use of probiotics after surgery can prevent development of pouchitis in the postsurgical treatment of patients with ulcerative colitis. One of the most commonly recommended uses of probiotics is in the prevention of postantibiotic diarrhea. Clinical trials and meta-analyses showed this is an effective and safe treatment, but specific strains of probiotics need further analysis to determine the most effective. Analysis of articles and trials related to the common cold and allergic rhinitis show promise for probiotics to reduce the duration and severity of symptoms, but probiotics were not effective in prevention. One study that administered probiotics to pregnant women showed some reduction of the occurrence of eczema; further research is needed for confirmation.

Nursing Implications

The review of the research indicates potential benefits to the use of probiotics for several types of disorders. Patient education focuses on the multitude of strains of probiotics that are commercially available to consumers, from yogurt to nutritional supplements to miso and juice. There are no standards developed by the U.S. Food and Drug Administration (FDA) for additions of probiotics to food, nor are there recommended dosages. At this time, the research indicates that probiotics are safe and potentially beneficial.

---

the Southwest United States are more likely to be infected with certain types of fungi that are more prevalent in the desert.

Psychoneuroimmunological Factors

The patient assessment also addresses psychoneuroimmunological factors. The bidirectional pathway between the brain and immune system is referred to as *psychoneuroimmunology,* a field that has been the focus of research and discussion over the last several decades (Figueira, 2008). It is thought that the immune response is regulated and modulated in part by neuroendocrine influences. Lymphocytes and macrophages have receptors that are capable of responding to neurotransmitters and endocrine hormones. Lymphocytes can produce and secrete adrenocorticotropic hormone and endorphin-like compounds. Cells in the brain, especially in the hypothalamus, can recognize prostaglandins, IFNs, and interleukins, as well as histamine and serotonin, which are released during the inflammatory process. Like all other biologic systems functioning in the interest of homeostasis, the immune system is integrated with other psychophysiologic processes and is subject to regulation and modulation by the brain.

Conversely, the immune processes can affect neural and endocrine function, including behavior. Growing evidence indicates that a measurable immune system response can be positively influenced by biobehavioral strategies such as relaxation and imagery techniques, biofeedback, humor, hypnosis, and conditioning. Therefore, the assessment should address the patient's general psychological status and the patient's use of and response to these strategies.

Physical Assessment

Immune dysfunction may have manifestations in various body systems (Box 36-4, p. 999). In addition to the assessment components described below, the nurse assesses the patient's respiratory, cardiovascular, genitourinary, and neurosensory status for signs and symptoms indicative of immune dysfunction.

TABLE
36-4 Selected Medications and Effects on the Immune System

Drug Classification (and Examples)	Effects on the Immune System
Antibiotics (in large doses)	**Bone marrow suppression**
ceftriaxone (Rocephin)	Eosinophilia, hemolytic anemia, hypoprothrombinemia, neutropenia, thrombocytopenia
cefuroxime sodium (Ceftin)	Eosinophilia, hemolytic anemia, hypoprothrombinemia, neutropenia, thrombocytopenia
chloramphenicol (Chloromycetin)	Leukopenia, aplastic anemia
dactinomycin (Cosmegen)	Agranulocytosis, neutropenia
fluoroquinolones (Cipro, Levaquin, Tequin)	Hemolytic anemia, methemoglobinemia, eosinophilia, leukopenia, pancytopenia
gentamicin sulfate (Garamycin)	Agranulocytosis, granulocytosis
macrolides (erythromycin, Zithromax, Biaxin)	Neutropenia, leukopenia
penicillins	Agranulocytosis
streptomycin	Leukopenia, neutropenia, pancytopenia
vancomycin (Vancocin, Vancoled)	Transient leukopenia
Antithyroid drugs	
propylthiouracil (PTU)	Agranulocytosis, leukopenia
Nonsteroidal anti-inflammatory drugs (NSAIDs) (in large doses)	**Inhibit Prostaglandin Synthesis or Release**
aspirin	Agranulocytosis
COX-2 inhibitors	Anemia, allergy, no major other adverse affects to the immune system
ibuprofen (Advil, Motrin)	Leukopenia, neutropenia
indomethacin (Indocid, Indocin)	Agranulocytosis, leukopenia
phenylbutazone	Pancytopenia, agranulocytosis, aplastic anemia
Adrenal corticosteroids	**Immunosuppression**
prednisone	
Antineoplastic agents (cytotoxic agents)	**Immunosuppression**
alkylating agents	Leukopenia, bone marrow suppression
cyclophosphamide (Cytoxan)	Leukopenia, neutropenia
mechlorethamine HCl (Mustargen)	Agranulocytosis, neutropenia
cyclosporine	Leukopenia, inhibits T-lymphocyte function
Antimetabolites	**Immunosuppression**
fluorouracil (pyrimidine antagonist)	Leukopenia, eosinophilia
methotrexate (folic acid antagonist)	Leukopenia, aplastic bone marrow
mercaptopurine (6-MP) (purine antagonist)	Leukopenia, pancytopenia

Assessment of the Skin

The nurse assesses the skin and mucous membranes for lesions, dermatitis, purpura (subcutaneous bleeding), urticaria, inflammation, or any discharge. Purpura may indicate life-threatening infections like meningitis; urticaria indicates an acute or chronic response to allergens, pathogens, or autoimmune disorders.

Assessment for Signs of Infection

The nurse notes any signs of infection. The patient's temperature is recorded, and the patient is observed for chills and sweating. Fever often accompanies infection.

Assessment of the Lymph Nodes

The lymph nodes and thyroid are palpated for enlargement. If palpable nodes are detected, their location, size, consistency, and reports of tenderness on palpation are noted. Lymphadenopathy indicates immune system activation against pathogens.

Assessment of the Joints

Joints are assessed for tenderness, swelling, increased warmth, and limited range of motion. These findings indicate inflammation and infiltration by leukocytes, including macrophages and cytokines.

Diagnostic Evaluation

The nurse needs to be aware that patients undergoing evaluation for possible immune system disorders experience not only physical pain and discomfort with certain types of diagnostic procedures, but many psychological reactions as well. For example, patients may fear test results that demonstrate decreased immune function, because the diminished immune system can make them more prone to certain infections, cancers, and other disorders. It is the nurse's role to counsel, educate, and support patients throughout the diagnostic process. Further, many patients may be extremely

BOX 36-4
BOX 36-4   Focused Assessment

Immune Dysfunction

Be alert for the following signs and symptoms:

Respiratory System

- Changes in respiratory rate
- Cough (dry or productive)
- Abnormal lung sounds (wheezing, crackles, rhonchi)
- Rhinitis
- Hyperventilation
- Bronchospasm

Cardiovascular System

- Hypotension
- Tachycardia
- Arrhythmia
- Vasculitis
- Anemia

Gastrointestinal System

- Hepatosplenomegaly
- Colitis
- Vomiting
- Diarrhea

Genitourinary System

- Frequency and burning on urination
- Hematuria
- Discharge

Musculoskeletal System

- Joint mobility, edema, and pain

Skin

- Rashes
- Lesions
- Dermatitis
- Hematomas or purpura
- Edema or urticaria
- Inflammation
- Discharge

Neurosensory System

- Cognitive dysfunction
- Hearing loss
- Visual changes
- Headaches and migraines
- Ataxia
- Tetany

---

anxious about the results of diagnostic tests and the possible implications of those results for their employment, insurance, and personal relationships. This is an ideal time for the nurse to provide counseling and education, should these interventions be warranted.

Immune Competence Testing

A series of blood and skin tests and a bone marrow biopsy may be performed to evaluate the patient's immune competence. Specific laboratory and diagnostic tests are discussed in greater detail along with individual disease processes in subsequent chapters in this unit. Selected laboratory and diagnostic tests used to evaluate immune competence are summarized in Box 36-5.

Allergy Testing

Diagnostic evaluation of the patient with allergic disorders commonly includes blood tests, smears of body secretions (nasal, conjunctival, or sputum secretions), skin tests (intradermal injections of solutions at several sites that may provoke an allergic response), and the radioallergosorbent test (RAST).

Results of laboratory blood studies provide supportive data for various diagnostic possibilities; however, they are not the major criteria for the diagnosis of allergic disease.

NURSING ALERT

With allergic condition, the WBC count is usually normal, except with infection. Eosinophils, which are granular leukocytes, normally make up 1% to 3% of the total number of WBCs. A level between 5% and 15% is nonspecific but suggests an allergic reaction. Moderate eosinophilia is defined as 15% to 40% eosinophils and is found in patients with allergic disorders; in patients with malignancy, immunodeficiencies, parasitic infections, or congenital heart disease; and in patients receiving peritoneal dialysis. Severe eosinophilia is defined as 50% to 90% eosinophils and is found in the idiopathic hypereosinophilic syndrome.

Skin Tests

If a skin test is indicated, there is a reasonable suspicion that a specific allergen is producing symptoms in an allergic patient. However, several precautionary steps must be observed before skin testing with allergens is performed:

- Testing is not performed during periods of bronchospasm.
- Epicutaneous tests (scratch or prick tests) are performed before other testing methods, in an effort to minimize the risk of systemic reaction.
- Emergency equipment must be readily available to treat anaphylaxis.

BOX 36-5

Selected Tests for Evaluating Immunologic Status

Various laboratory tests may be performed to assess immune system activity or dysfunction. The studies assess leukocytes and lymphocytes, humoral immunity, cellular immunity, phagocytic cell function, complement activity, hypersensitivity reactions, specific antigen–antibodies, or HIV infection.

Leukocyte and Lymphocyte Tests
• White blood cell count and differential
• Bone marrow biopsy

Humoral (Antibody-Mediated) Immunity Tests
• B-cell quantification with monoclonal antibody
• In vivo immunoglobulin synthesis with T-cell subsets
• Specific antibody response
• Total serum globulins and individual immunoglobulins (by electrophoresis, immunoelectrophoresis, single radial immunodiffusion, nephelometry, isohemagglutinin techniques)

Cellular (Cell-Mediated) Immunity Tests
• Total lymphocyte count
• T-cell and T-cell subset quantification with monoclonal antibody
• Delayed hypersensitivity skin test
• Cytokine production
• Lymphocyte response to mitogens, antigens, and allogenic cells
• Helper and suppressor T-cell functions

Phagocytic Cell Function Tests
• Nitroblue tetrazolium reductase assay

Complement Component Tests
• Total serum hemolytic complement
• Individual complement component titrations
• Radial immunodiffusion
• Electroimmunoassay
• Radioimmunoassay
• Immunonephelometric assay
• Immunoelectrophoresis

Hypersensitivity Tests
• Scratch test
• Patch test
• Intradermal test
• Radioallergosorbent test (RAST)

Specific Antigen-Antibody Tests
• Radioimmunoassay
• Immunofluorescence
• Agglutination
• Complement fixation test

HIV Infection Tests
• Enzyme-linked immunosorbent assay (ELISA)
• Western blot
• CD4 and CD8 cell counts
• P24 antigen test
• Polymerase chain reaction (PCR)

Methods of **skin testing** include prick skin tests, scratch tests, and intradermal skin testing. After negative prick or scratch tests, intradermal skin testing is performed with allergens that are suggested by the patient's history to be problematic. The back is the most suitable area of the body for skin testing, because it permits the performance of many tests. The multitest applicator is a commercially available device with multiple test heads that allows simultaneous administration of antigens by multiple punctures at different sites. A negative response on a skin test cannot be interpreted as an absence of sensitivity to an allergen. Such a response may occur with insufficient sensitivity of the test or with use of an inappropriate allergen in testing. Therefore, it is essential to observe the patient undergoing skin testing for an allergic reaction, even if the previous response was negative.

The results of skin tests complement the data obtained from the history. They indicate which of several antigens are most likely to provoke symptoms and provide some clue to the intensity of the patient's sensitization. The dosage of the antigen (allergen) injected is also important. Most patients are hypersensitive to more than one allergen. Under testing conditions, they may not react (although they usually do) to the specific allergens that induce their attacks.

Familiarity with and consistent use of a grading system with skin tests are essential. The grading system used should be identified on a skin test sheet for later interpretation. A positive reaction, evidenced by the appearance of an urticarial wheal (round, reddened skin elevation) (Fig. 36-7), localized **erythema** (diffuse redness) in the area of inoculation or contact, or pseudopodia (irregular projection at the end of a wheal) with associated erythema is considered indicative of sensitivity to the corresponding antigen.

False-negative results may occur because of improper technique, outdated allergen solutions, or prior use of medications that suppress skin reactivity. Corticosteroids and antihistamines, including over-the-counter allergy medications, suppress skin test reactivity and are usually withheld for 48 to 96 hours before testing, depending on the duration of their activity. False-positive results may occur because of improper preparation or administration of allergen solutions.

Interpretation of positive or negative skin tests must be based on the history, physical examination, and other

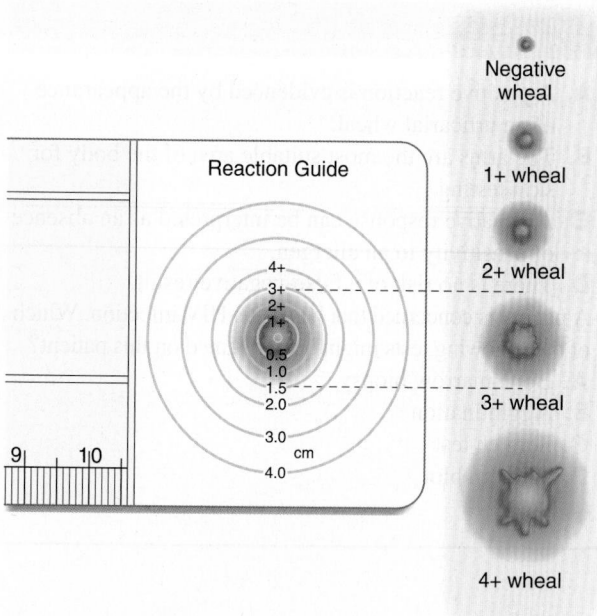

Negative wheal

1+ wheal

2+ wheal

Reaction Guide

4+
3+
2+
1+
0.5
1.0
1.5
2.0
3.0
cm
4.0

9 10

3+ wheal

4+ wheal

FIGURE 36-7 Interpretation of reactions: Negative = wheal soft with minimal erythema. 1+ = wheal present (5 to 8 mm) with associated erythema. 2+ = wheal (7 to 10 mm) with associated erythema. 3+ = wheal (9 to 15 mm), slight pseudopodia possible with associated erythema. 4+ = wheal (12 mm+) with pseudopodia and diffuse erythema.

laboratory test results. The following guidelines are used for the interpretation of skin test results:

- Skin tests are more reliable for diagnosing atopic sensitivity in patients with allergic rhinoconjunctivitis than in patients with asthma.
- Positive skin tests correlate highly with food allergy.

- The use of skin tests to diagnose immediate hypersensitivity to medications is limited because metabolites of medications, not the medications themselves, are usually responsible for causing hypersensitivity.

In cases of doubt about the validity of the skin tests, a RAST or a provocative challenge test may be performed.

Radioallergosorbent Testing

RAST is a radioimmunoassay that measures allergen-specific IgE in the patient's blood. In addition to detecting an allergen, RAST indicates the quantity of allergen necessary to evoke an allergic reaction. Values are reported on a scale from 0 to 5. Values of 2 or greater are considered significant. The major advantages of RAST over other tests include decreased risk of systemic reaction, stability of antigens, and lack of dependence on skin reactivity modified by medications. The major disadvantages include limited allergen selection and reduced sensitivity compared with intradermal skin tests, lack of immediate results, and higher cost.

Provocative Testing

Provocative testing involves the direct administration of the suspected allergen to the sensitive tissue, such as the conjunctiva, nasal or bronchial mucosa, or GI tract (by ingestion of the allergen), with observation of target organ response. This type of testing is helpful in identifying clinically significant allergens in patients who have a large number of positive tests. Major disadvantages of this type of testing are the limitation of one antigen per session and the risk of producing severe symptoms, particularly bronchospasm, in patients with asthma.

Chapter Review

Critical Thinking Exercises

1. A 36-year-old man was camping and hiking with his partner when he began to run a high temperature and developed a nonproductive cough. He is diagnosed with *Pneumocystis* pneumonia (PCP) and started on antibiotic therapy. He asks why he has developed this problem. How would you respond? What diagnostic tests would you expect to be ordered? Why?

2. A 68-year-old woman is hospitalized for a kidney transplantation, and immunosuppressant medications are prescribed. Describe the parameters you would use to assess her immune function. How would altered immune function affect the care that you provide?

NCLEX-Style Review Questions

1. In which stage of the immune response does the antibody of the humoral response or the cytotoxic (killer) T cell of the cellular response reach and connect with the antigen on the surface of the foreign pathogen?
   A. Recognition stage
   B. Proliferation stage
   C. Response stage
   D. Effector stage

2. A patient is exhibiting anaphylaxis after eating shellfish. Which of the following reactions is the patient experiencing?
   A. Type I
   B. Type II
   C. Type III
   D. Type IV

(continued on page 1002)

Chapter Review (continued)

3. Disorders of the immune system may stem from excesses or deficiencies of immunocompetent cells, alterations in the functions of these cells, immunologic attack on self-antigens, or inappropriate or exaggerated responses to specific antigens. Which type of immune system disorder is characterized by an overproduction of immunoglobulins?
   A. Autoimmunity
   B. Gammopathies
   C. Hypersensitivity
   D. Secondary immune deficiency

4. A patient is being seen in the dermatology clinic to have allergy testing performed. Which of the following statements is accurate regarding this type of testing?

A. A positive reaction is evidenced by the appearance of an urticarial wheal.
B. The arms are the most suitable area of the body for skin testing.
C. A negative response can be interpreted as an absence of sensitivity to an allergen.
D. There is no risk of a false-negative result.

5. A patient is concerned that he has an HIV infection. Which of the following tests might be performed on this patient?
   A. Bone marrow biopsy
   B. Agglutination
   C. Scratch test
   D. Western blot

Try these additional resources to enhance your learning and understanding of this chapter:
- thePoint online resource available at **http://thepoint.lww.com/Pellico1e**
- *Handbook for Focus on Adult Health: Medical-Surgical Nursing*
- *Study Guide for Focus on Adult Health: Medical-Surgical Nursing*

 ## References and Selected Readings

References and selected readings associated with this chapter can be found on the website that accompanies the book. Visit http://thepoint.lww.com/Pellico1e to access the references and other additional resources associated with this chapter.

Nursing Management: Patients With Immunodeficiency, HIV Infection, and AIDS

MARY E. BARTLETT

Learning Objectives

After reading this chapter, you will be able to:

1. Describe the basic aspects of primary immunodeficiency.

2. Describe the essential aspects of secondary immunodeficiency.

3. Summarize the epidemiology of HIV infection and AIDS.

4. Describe the pathophysiology, modes of transmission and prevention of HIV infection.

5. Explain postexposure prophylaxis for health care workers.

6. Explain the gerontological considerations of HIV/AIDS in the United States.

7. Summarize the clinical manifestations, assessment and treatment of patients of HIV infection.

8. Use the nursing process as a framework for care of the patient with AIDS.

Nurses have been at the forefront of human immunodeficiency virus (HIV) care even before the cause and infectious nature of the virus was known. Today, nurses work as clinicians, researchers, patient advocates, and educators. Nursing presence in positions of leadership related to HIV care are many, notably the selection of Deborah Parham Hopson, Ph.D., RN, FAAN, as the Assistant Surgeon General and Associate Director of the HIV/AIDS Bureau at Health Resources and Services Administration for the U.S. Department of Health and Human Services. Through the concerted effort of policy makers, researchers, and clinicians developing best practices and strategies, nursing is in a unique position to meet the challenges of HIV care. Because the field of HIV nursing and medicine changes rapidly, readers should refer to the most recent guidelines and recommendations at www.iasusa.org.

Immunodeficiency, or the inability for the body's natural defenses to protect itself from outside pathogens, presents in one of its most complicated forms in patients with the infection that causes **acquired immunodeficiency syndrome (AIDS).**

PRIMARY AND SECONDARY IMMUNODEFICIENCY

Immunodeficiencies are classified as either primary or secondary, and are further classified by the affected components of the immune system. Primary immunodeficiency diseases are genetic in origin and manifest most commonly in infancy and childhood as abnormally recurrent infections. About 80% of the patients with primary immunodeficiency are less than 20 years old. Many primary immunodeficiencies may occur alone or as part of a syndrome. More than 100 have been described that affect different components of the immune system. Transmission of these inborn errors is predominantly X-linked; therefore, more than 70% of affected patients are male. Primary immunodeficiencies, classified by the main component of the immune system that is dysregulated, include B lymphocytes (or IgG), T lymphocytes, natural killer (NK) cells, phagocytic cells, or complement proteins. More than 50% of primary immunodeficiency is caused by errors in B lymphocytes, causing immunoglobulin and antibody decreases. The most common B-cell disorder is selective IgA deficiency (McCutchan, 2009).

In contrast, secondary immunodeficiencies affect the normal immune system of the patient, resulting in increased susceptibility to infection and certain types of cancer. Extrinsic and intrinsic factors such as nonimmune systemic disorders like HIV infection, immunosuppressive therapy, prolonged illness or hospitalization, and aging trigger secondary immunodeficiency. These factors cause impaired immune response through loss or destruction of lymphocytes, such as CD4 cell depletion, or decreased production of lymphocytes, as in the effects of irradiation on bone marrow lymphocyte production (McCutchan, 2009). Patients with immunosuppression from secondary immunodeficiencies are referred to as *immunocompromised hosts*. The most common secondary immunodeficiency is AIDS.

HUMAN IMMUNODEFICIENCY VIRUS AND ACQUIRED IMMUNODEFICIENCY SYNDROME

The Centers for Disease Control and Prevention (CDC) estimate that more than 1 million persons are living with HIV/AIDS in the United States. The CDC estimates that there were 56,300 new infections in 2006. Every 9 ½ minutes, someone in the United States is infected with HIV. In July 2008, UNAIDS/WHO estimated that 33 million people are living with HIV/AIDS in the world, and 2.7 million new infections occur each year. While many advances have been made in the treatment and long-term survival of people living with HIV/AIDS, new infections continue. More than 21% of people infected with HIV are unaware of their diagnosis; these patients transmit most new infections. The recommendation by the CDC is for universal testing for all people between the ages of 13 and 64, to lead to early diagnosis and treatment of people infected with HIV and to slow the rate of new infections in the United States (Centers for Disease Control and Prevention [CDC], 2006).

Epidemiology

An analysis of persons with a diagnosis of HIV infection by race/ethnicity and risk factor underscores the disproportionate impact of HIV among communities of color and men who have sex with other men (MSM) of all races. By race/ethnicity, nearly half (49%) were African American. Although African Americans made up only 13% of the population of the 34 states surveyed, their rate of HIV infection was seven times that of Caucasians. The rate for African American women is 20 times that of Caucasian women. By transmission category, MSM continued to account for the largest number of diagnoses overall, followed by males and females exposed through high-risk heterosexual contact and injection drug use.

Worldwide, AIDS kills more than 2 million people every year, and 75% of those deaths occur in sub-Saharan Africa (UNAIDS, 2009). Since the beginning of the epidemic, 15 million children have been orphaned due to AIDS. The gender distribution of newly HIV infected adults in 2007 was approximately 50% men and 50% women; unsafe sex was the predominant mode of transmission. The earliest confirmed case of HIV infection was found in blood drawn from an African man in 1959. Most theories about the origin and spread of AIDS point to a mutated simian immunodeficiency virus (SIV) that crossed species to humans, similar to the changes seen with bird and swine influenza viruses today (AVERT, 2009).

New research finds that many patients live longer due to the use of antiretroviral (ARV) agents but are increasingly susceptible to age-associated non-AIDS diseases. The mechanism suspected is a chronic inflammatory process caused by HIV or the long-term use of medications. In resource-rich countries such as the United States, the epidemic has changed to one in which patients that are motivated can achieve long-term, if not life-long suppression of the virus with safe and tolerable medications. Patients who access and adhere to therapy rarely suffer AIDS-related complications. More likely, these patients will have many non–AIDS-defining cancers, cardiovascular disease, kidney disease, osteopenia/osteoporosis, liver failure, frailty, and neurologic decline. These normal age-related processes occur sooner and more severely in patients infected with HIV (Deeks & Phillips, 2009).

Gerontological Considerations

Of the 56,300 new HIV infections diagnosed in 2006, more than 10% of these were over the age of 50. HIV infection in middle-aged and older populations may be under-reported and under-diagnosed because health care professionals erroneously believe that older adults are not at risk for HIV infection. In addition, HIV-related dementia in the older adult may mimic Alzheimer's disease and may be misdiagnosed.

In fact, several factors put older adults at risk for HIV infection:

- Many older adults are sexually active but do not use condoms, viewing them only as a means of unneeded birth control.
- Many older adults do not consider themselves at risk for HIV infection.
- Older gay men may begin new relationships with younger men.
- Older adults may be IV/injection drug users.
- Older adults may have received HIV-infected blood through transfusions before 1985.
- Normal age-related changes include a reduction in immune system function, which puts the older adult at greater risk for infections, cancers, and autoimmune disorders. Many older adults also experience the loss of loved ones, resulting in depression and bereavement, factors that are associated with depressed immune function.

Physical strain and the number of comorbidities were significant predictors of the adequacy of social support in older adults with HIV.

Transmission

HIV is a bloodborne, sexually transmissible virus. **HIV-1** is transmitted in body fluids containing HIV or infected CD4+ T lymphocytes. These fluids include blood, seminal fluid, vaginal secretions, amniotic fluid, and breast milk. Mother-to-child transmission of HIV-1 may occur in utero, or through breastfeeding, but most perinatal infections are thought to occur after exposure during delivery (CDC, 2006a). Inflammation and breaks in the skin or mucosa result in the increased probability of exposure to HIV. HIV is not transmitted through casual contact. Because HIV is harbored within lymphocytes, a type of white blood cell (WBC), any exposure to infected blood results in a significant risk of infection. The amount of virus and infected cells in the body fluid, as well as other host factors, is associated with the risk of new infection after exposure to that fluid.

Blood and blood products can transmit HIV to recipients. However, the risk associated with transfusions has been virtually eliminated because of voluntary self-deferral, completion of a detailed health history, extensive testing, heat treatment of clotting factor concentrates, and more effective virus inactivation methods. Donated blood is tested for antibodies to HIV-1, **HIV-2**, and p24 antigen (an early marker for HIV infection); in addition, since 1999, nucleic acid amplification testing (NAAT) has been performed (CDC, 2006b). However, blood donated during the **window period** after infection is infectious, even though it tests negative for HIV antibodies. The window period is the period between initial infection with HIV and development of a positive antibody test for HIV. Development of a positive HIV antibody test generally occurs within 4 weeks and with few exceptions by 6 months (Sax, Cohen, & Kuritzkes, 2007).

Until an effective vaccine is developed, preventing HIV by eliminating or reducing risky behaviors is essential (Box 37-1). Primary prevention efforts through effective educational programs are vital for control and prevention. As noted earlier, HIV is not transmitted by casual contact.

<table>
<tr><td>BOX 37-1</td><td>**Risk Behaviors Associated With HIV Infection and AIDS**</td></tr>
</table>

- Sharing injection drug use equipment aka "works"
- Having sexual relations with infected individuals (both male and female)
- People who received HIV-infected blood or blood products (especially before blood screening was instituted in 1985)
- Infants born to mothers with HIV infection not taking antiretroviral medication

Prevention and Education

To reduce further the incidence of HIV infection, the CDC announced a new initiative, Advancing HIV Prevention (AHP), in 2003. This initiative comprises four strategies: making HIV testing a routine part of medical care, implementing new models for diagnosing HIV infections outside medical settings, preventing new infections by working with HIV-infected persons and their partners, and further decreasing perinatal HIV transmission (CDC, 2007).

Initiation of effective educational programs educates the public regarding safer sexual practices and decreases the risk of transmitting HIV-1 infection to sexual partners (Box 37-2). Other than abstinence, consistent and correct use of condoms is the only method proven to decrease the risk for sexual transmission of HIV infection (see Chapter 35, Box 35-2, Fig. 35-1). Latex condoms should be used during vaginal or anal intercourse. Nonlatex condoms made of natural materials such as lambskin are available for people with latex allergy but will not protect against HIV infection. A condom should be used for oral contact with the penis, and a dental dam (a piece of latex used by dentists to isolate a tooth for treatment) should be used for oral contact with the vagina or rectum.

<table>
<tr><td>BOX 37-2</td><td>**Health Promotion**</td></tr>
</table>

Safer Sexual Behaviors

- Encourage patients to be tested for HIV.
- Advise patients to abstain from sharing sexual fluids.
- Advise patients to reduce the number of sexual partners to one.
- Encourage patients to use latex condoms always. If the patient is allergic to latex, nonlatex condoms should be used.
- Advise patients to avoid using cervical caps or diaphragms without using a condom as well.
- Recommend patients always use dental dams for oral–genital or anal stimulation.
- Advise patients to avoid anal intercourse because this practice may injure tissues.
- Advise patients to avoid manual–anal intercourse.
- Encourage patients not to ingest urine or semen.
- Educate patients about nonpenetrative sexual activities, such as body massage, social kissing (dry), mutual masturbation, fantasy, and sex films.
- Advise patients to avoid sharing needles, razors, toothbrushes, sex toys, or blood-contaminated articles.
- Encourage HIV-positive patients to inform previous, present, and prospective sexual and drug-using partners of their HIV-positive status. If the patient is concerned for his or her safety, advise the patient that many states have anonymous partner notification programs through the public health department to notify exposed people.
- Advise HIV-positive patients to avoid donating blood, plasma, body organs, or sperm.

The use of a microbicide, nonoxynol-9 (N-9), was widely advocated to reduce the risk of HIV infection until a clinical trial conducted in almost 1,000 female commercial sex workers in African countries revealed that those who used N-9 intravaginally along with condoms were 50% more likely to be infected with HIV than those who did not use the N-9 gel. Based on these results, it is now recommended that intravaginal application of N-9 not be used as a means of HIV prevention. Further research throughout the world continues to investigate the use of other microbicides, especially since the female sex partner controls its use. The challenge lies in developing a microbicide that is antiviral yet not irritating to the genital mucosa.

Other topics important in preventive education include the importance of avoiding sexual practices that might cut or tear the lining of the rectum, penis, or vagina, and avoiding sexual contact with multiple partners or people who are known to be HIV positive or IV/injection drug users. In addition, people who are HIV positive or who use injection drugs should be instructed not to donate blood or share drug equipment with others.

Increasingly, needle exchange programs are available so that IV/injection drug users can obtain sterile drug equipment at no cost. Extensive research has demonstrated that needle exchange programs do not promote increased drug use; on the contrary, they have been found to decrease the incidence of bloodborne infections in people who use IV/injection drugs (CDC, 2007). In the absence of needle exchange programs, IV/injection drug users should be instructed on methods to clean their syringes and advised to avoid sharing cotton and other drug use equipment. Drug users interested in treatment programs should be referred to those programs.

Related Reproductive Education

Because HIV infection in women often occurs during the childbearing years, family planning issues need to be addressed. Attempts to achieve pregnancy by couples in which only one partner has HIV, referred to as *serodiscordant*, expose the unaffected partner to the virus. Efforts at artificial insemination using processed semen from an HIV-infected partner are under way. At a fertility clinic in Italy, 3,000 successful pregnancies occurred between serodiscordant couples in whom the male partner was HIV-positive through sperm washing. HIV-positive women considering pregnancy need to have adequate information about the risks for transmitting HIV infection to their partner and their future children, and about the benefits of taking ARV agents to reduce perinatal HIV transmission. The desire of women who are HIV-positive to bear children is strong, despite health risks to these women, their children, and society in general (Savasi, Parrilla, Ratti et al., 2008). Due to effective ARV medications and universal testing of pregnant women and newborns in the United States, mother-to-child transmission rates have dropped dramatically. Women who are HIV-positive should be instructed not to breastfeed their infants, because HIV is transmitted through breast milk. Through use of medications and not breastfeeding, the risk of transmission of HIV from mother to child dropped from 25% to less than 2% (Burr, 2011).

Certain contraceptive methods may pose additional health risks for women. The message to women must be that contraception and prevention of HIV or other sexually transmitted infections (STIs) are two separate considerations. Estrogen and progesterone may increase a woman's risk for HIV infection through changes in the cervical mucosa. In addition, women infected with HIV who use estrogen oral contraceptives have shown increased shedding of HIV in vaginal and cervical secretions. The intrauterine contraceptive device (IUD) may also increase the risk for HIV transmission through an inflammatory foreign body response (Burr, 2011). The female condom (see Chapter 35, Fig. 35-1) is as effective in preventing pregnancy as other barrier methods, such as the diaphragm and the male condom. Unlike the diaphragm, the female condom is also effective in preventing the transmission of HIV infection and STIs. The female condom has the distinction of being the first barrier method that can be controlled by the woman.

Postexposure Prophylaxis

Standard Precautions

In 1996, the CDC and its Hospital Infection Control Practices Advisory Committee (HICPAC) developed guidelines to reduce the risk for exposure of health care workers to HIV through the development of Standard Precautions. Standard Precautions incorporate the major features of Universal Precautions (designed to reduce the risk of transmission of blood borne pathogens) and Body Substance Isolation (designed to reduce the risk of transmission of pathogens from moist body substances); they are applied to all patients in health care facilities regardless of their diagnosis or presumed infectious status (Box 37-3). Standard Precautions apply to blood; all body fluids, secretions, and excretions (except sweat), regardless of whether they contain visible blood; nonintact skin; and mucous membranes (CDC, 2007). The primary purpose of Standard Precautions is to prevent the transmission of nosocomial infection. The first tier, referred to as Standard Precautions, reduces the risk for exposure from all recognized or unrecognized sources of infections in hospitals. New elements, such as Respiratory Hygiene/Cough etiquette, safe injection practices, and the use of masks during catheter placement, effectively address issues centered on patient protection.

Large-scale studies of exposed health care workers continue to be conducted by the CDC and other groups. In November 2000, the Needle-stick Safety and Prevention Act became law, mandating that health care facilities use devices to protect against sharps injuries. A plan of nursing care for a patient with an infectious disease is available online at http://thePoint.lww.com/Pellico1e.

BOX 37-3 Standard Precautions

The following guidelines prevent the transmission of infection during patient care for all patients, regardless of known or unknown infectious status. Barrier protection should be used at all times to prevent skin and mucous membrane contamination with blood, body fluids containing visible blood, or other body fluids (cerebrospinal, synovial, pleural, peritoneal, pericardial, and amniotic fluids, semen and vaginal secretions). Barrier protection should be used with *all* tissues. The type of barrier protection used should be appropriate for the type of procedures being performed and the type of exposure anticipated. Examples of barrier protection include disposable lab coats, gloves, and eye and face protection. Private rooms and rooms specially equipped with ventilation systems should be used as indicated.

- Gloves are to be worn when there is a potential for hand or skin contact with blood, other potentially infectious material, or items and surfaces contaminated with these materials.
  - Clean, nonsterile gloves can be used to protect the nurse's hands.
  - Change gloves after contact with materials that may contain a high concentration of microorganisms even when working with the same patient.
  - Remove gloves promptly after use, wash hands immediately before touching noncontaminated items and environmental surfaces, and before going to another patient.
- Face protection (face shield, mask, and eye protection) should be worn during procedures that are likely to generate droplets of blood or body fluid, to prevent exposure to mucous membranes of the mouth, nose, and eyes.
- Environmental control includes the following:
  - Ensure that the hospital has adequate procedures for the routine care, cleaning, and disinfection of environmental surfaces, beds, bed rails, bedside equipment, and other frequently touched surfaces.
  - Ensure that procedures are being followed.
  - Advocate for the purchase and correct use of the safest equipment.
- Patient care equipment:
  - Handle used patient care equipment soiled with blood, body fluids, secretions, and excretions in a manner that prevents skin and mucous membrane exposures, contamination of clothing, and transfer of microorganisms to other patients and environment.
  - Ensure that reusable equipment is not used for the care of another patient until it has been cleaned and reprocessed appropriately.
  - Ensure that single-use items are discarded properly.
  - Use mouthpieces, resuscitation bags, or other ventilation devices as an alternative to mouth-to-mouth resuscitation methods.

- Handle, transport, and process used linen soiled with blood, body fluids, secretions, and excretions in a manner that prevents skin and mucous membrane exposures and contamination of clothing and that avoids transfer of microorganisms to other patients and environments.
- **Protective body clothing** such as disposable laboratory coats should be worn whenever there is a potential for splashing of blood or body fluids:
  - Wear a clean, nonsterile gown to protect skin and prevent soiling of clothing during procedures and patient care activities that are likely to generate splashes or sprays of blood, body fluids, secretions, or excretions.
  - Remove a soiled gown promptly, avoiding contact with clean clothes, and wash hands/perform hand hygiene to prevent the transfer of microorganisms to other patients or environments.
- **Wash hands** thoroughly and immediately if contaminated with blood, body fluids containing visible blood, or other body fluids to which universal precautions apply:
  - Use soap and water or antimicrobial agent or waterless antiseptic agent.
  - Wash hands during procedures for the same patient to prevent cross-contamination of different body sites.
  - Wash hands immediately and other skin surfaces after gloves are removed.
- **Avoid accidental injuries** that can be caused by needles, scalpel blades, laboratory instruments, and so on when performing procedures, cleaning instruments, handling sharp instruments, disposing of used needles or pipettes, and similar activities. Used needles, disposable syringes, scalpel blades, pipettes, and other sharp items are to be placed in puncture-resistant containers marked with a biohazard symbol for disposal:
  - Use "needleless" systems correctly whenever possible.
  - Never recap used needles or otherwise manipulate them by using both hands or use any technique that involves directing the point of the needle toward any part of the body.
  - Use either a one-handed scoop technique or a mechanical device designed for holding the needle sheath.
  - Do not remove used needles from disposable syringes by hand and do not bend, break, or otherwise manipulate used needles by hand.
  - Place used disposable syringes and needles, scalpel blades, and other sharp items in appropriate puncture-resistant containers as close as practical to the area in which the items were used.
  - Place reusable syringes and needles in a puncture-resistant container for transport to the reprocessing area.

Adapted from: Siegel, J. D., et al. (2007). Guideline for Isolation Precautions: Preventing Transmission of Infectious Agents in Healthcare Settings. Accessed from http://www.cdc.gov/ncidod/dhqp/pdf/guidelines/Isolation2007.pdf.

Postexposure Prophylaxis for Health Care Providers

Postexposure prophylaxis in response to the exposure of health care personnel to blood or other body fluids reduces the risk for HIV infection. The CDC recommends that all health care providers who have sustained a significant exposure to HIV be counseled and offered anti-HIV postexposure prophylaxis, if appropriate (Box 37-4). Some clinicians are considering the use of postexposure prophylaxis for patients exposed to HIV because of high-risk sexual behavior or possible contact through IV/injection drug use. This use of postexposure prophylaxis is controversial because of concern that it may be substituted for safer sex practices and safer IV/injection drug use. Postexposure prophylaxis should not be considered an acceptable method of preventing HIV infection.

The medications recommended for postexposure prophylaxis are those used to treat established HIV infection. Ideally, prophylaxis needs to start immediately after exposure; therapy started more than 72 hours after exposure is thought

---

BOX 37-4 **Postexposure Prophylaxis for Health Care Providers**

If you sustain a puncture injury, such as a needle stick, take the following actions immediately:

• Wash the area thoroughly with soap and water.
• Alert your supervisor/nursing faculty and initiate the injury-reporting system used in the setting.
• Identify the source patient, who may need to be tested for HIV, hepatitis B, and hepatitis C. State laws will determine whether written informed consent must be obtained from the source patient before his or her testing. Rapid testing should be used, if possible, if the HIV status of the source patient is unknown, because results can be available within 20 minutes.
• Report as quickly as possible to the employee health services, the emergency department, or other designated treatment facility. This visit should be documented in the health care worker's confidential medical record.
• Give consent for baseline testing for HIV, hepatitis B, and hepatitis C. Confidential HIV testing can be performed up to 72 hours after the exposure but should be performed as soon as the health care worker can give informed consent for baseline testing.
• Get postexposure prophylaxis for HIV in accordance with CDC guidelines. Start the prophylaxis medications within 2 hours after exposure. Make sure that you are being monitored for symptoms of toxicity. Practice safer sex until follow-up testing is complete. Continue the HIV medications for 4 weeks.
• Follow up with postexposure testing at 1 month, 3 months, and 6 months.
• Document the exposure in detail for your own records, as well as for the employer.

---

to offer no benefit due to rapid increases in viral load upon initial infection.

The recommended course of therapy involves taking the prescribed medications for 4 weeks. Those who choose postexposure prophylaxis must be prepared for the side effects of the medications and must be adherent to treatment or face the possible long-term risks due to developing resistance. The cost is also of concern; the cost of a medication regimen ranges from $500 to more than $1,000, in addition to the costs of testing and counseling. Most health care employers and agencies provide access to treatment and medication through Occupational Health Services.

Pathophysiology

Because HIV infection is an infectious disease, it is important to understand how HIV integrates itself into a person's immune system and how immunity plays a role in the course of infection. This knowledge is also essential for understanding medication therapy and vaccine development.

Viruses are intracellular parasites. HIV belongs to a group of viruses known as **retroviruses**. These viruses carry their genetic material in the form of ribonucleic acid (RNA) rather than deoxyribonucleic acid (DNA). As shown in Figure 37-1, HIV consists of a viral core containing the viral RNA, surrounded by an envelope consisting of protruding glycoproteins (gp). For HIV to enter the targeted cell, the membrane of the viral envelope must be fused with the plasma membrane of the cell, a process mediated by the envelope glycoproteins of HIV and other coreceptors (National Institutes of Health [NIH], 2009).

All viruses target specific cells. Lymphocytes (type of WBC) consist of three major populations: T cells, B cells, and NK cells. Mature T cells are phenotypically (characteristics of the cells) composed of two major subpopulations, defined by cell surface reciprocal expression of CD4 or CD8. Approximately two-thirds of peripheral blood T cells are CD4$^+$ and approximately one-third is CD8$^+$. Most people have about 700 to 1,000 CD4$^+$ cells/mm^3, but as low as 500 cells/mm^3 can be considered "normal." HIV targets cells with the CD4 glycoprotein, expressed on the surface of T lymphocytes, **monocytes**, dendritic cells, and brain microglia. Most primary clinical isolates of HIV use the chemokine coreceptor **CCR5** for cell entry. HIV-1 isolates that appear later in the course of infection often use other chemokine receptors, such as CXCR4, in addition to CCR5 (Libman & Makadon, 2007). HIV must attach to both the CD4 and the CCR5 coreceptor binding sites in order to infect CD4$^+$ cells.

A mutation of CCR5 that is common among Caucasians but not other ethnic groups has been identified. About 1% of Caucasians lack functional CCR5 and are highly protected against HIV infection even if exposed (although protection is not absolute); about 18% are not markedly protected against infection but, if infected, demonstrate significantly slower rates of disease progression (Libman & Makadon,

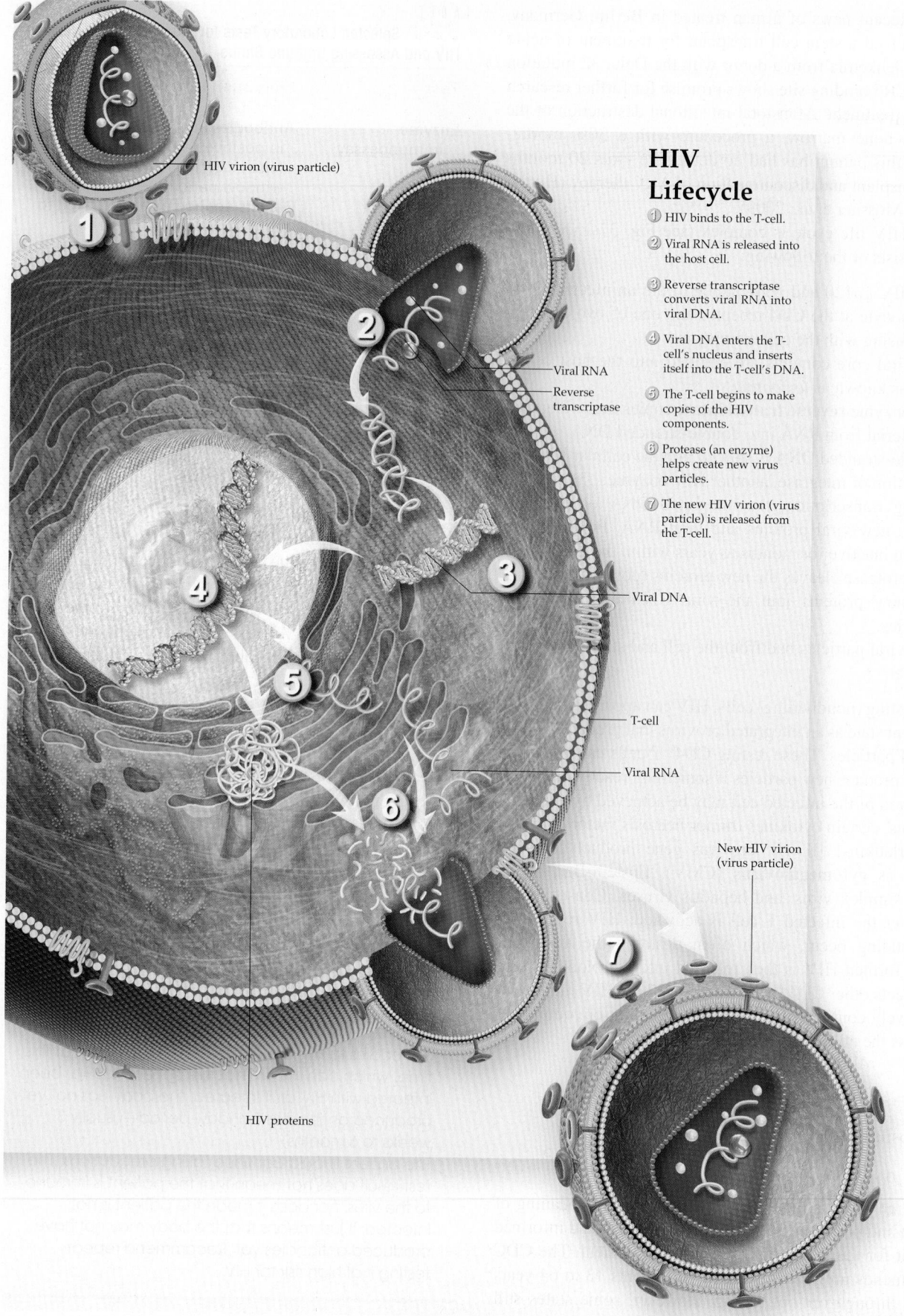

HIV Lifecycle

1. HIV binds to the T-cell.

2. Viral RNA is released into the host cell.

3. Reverse transcriptase converts viral RNA into viral DNA.

4. Viral DNA enters the T-cell's nucleus and inserts itself into the T-cell's DNA.

5. The T-cell begins to make copies of the HIV components.

6. Protease (an enzyme) helps create new virus particles.

7. The new HIV virion (virus particle) is released from the T-cell.

HIV virion (virus particle)

Viral RNA

Reverse transcriptase

Viral DNA

T-cell

Viral RNA

New HIV virion (virus particle)

HIV proteins

FIGURE 37-1 HIV life cycle. Courtesy of Anatomical Chart Company.

2007). Recent news of a man treated in Berlin, Germany, who received a stem cell transplant for treatment of acute myeloid leukemia from a donor with the Delta 32 mutation at the CCR5 binding site shows promise for further research for HIV treatment. After total intentional destruction of the patient's bone marrow, a procedure with a 30% mortality rate, this patient has had no detectable virus 20 months after transplant and discontinuation of ARV therapy (Hütter, Nowak, Mossner et al., 2009).

The HIV life cycle is complex (see Fig. 37-1, p. 1009) and consists of the following:

- The HIV gp120 and gp41 attach to the uninfected CD4+ lymphocyte at the CD4 receptor and one of two coreceptors, fusing with the cell membrane.
- The viral core contents are emptied into the host cell, a process known as *uncoating*.
- HIV enzyme **reverse transcriptase** copies the viral genetic material from RNA into double-stranded DNA.
- Double-stranded DNA is spliced into the cellular DNA by the action of integrase, another HIV enzyme.
- During transcription, the integrated DNA or **provirus** makes new viral proteins and viral RNA. Provirus may remain inactive for months to years within the CD4+ cell.
- HIV protease cleaves the new proteins (polyproteins).
- The new proteins join the viral RNA into new viral particles.
- New viral particles bud from the cell and start the process all over.

In resting (nondividing) cells, HIV can apparently survive in a latent state as an integrated provirus that produces few or no viral particles. These resting CD4+ T cells can be stimulated to produce new particles if something reactivates them. Activation of the infected cell may be achieved by antigens, mitogens, certain cytokines (tumor necrosis factor-α [TNF] or interleukin-1 [IL-1]), or virus gene products of such viruses as **cytomegalovirus** (CMV), Epstein-Barr virus, herpes simplex virus, and hepatitis viruses. Consequently, whenever the infected T cell is activated, HIV replication and budding occur, which often destroys the host cell. Newly formed HIV is then released into the blood plasma and infects other CD4+ cells (see Fig. 37-1). HIV mutates at a relatively constant rate, enabling it to blunt or completely suppress the effects of HIV medications.

Assessment and Diagnosis

Diagnostic tests are summarized in Table 37-1.

HIV Antibody Tests

Before an HIV antibody test is performed, the meaning of the test and possible test results are explained, and informed consent for the test is obtained from the patient. The CDC recommends universal testing of all patients 13 to 64 years of age through opt-out testing. However, some states still

TABLE 37-1 Selected Laboratory Tests for Diagnosing and Tracking HIV and Assessing Immune Status

Test	Findings in HIV Infection
Enzyme immunoassay (EIA)	Antibodies are detected, resulting in positive results. May have false-negative results within the window period.
Western blot	Detects antibodies to HIV; used to confirm EIA.
Viral load	Quantifies HIV RNA in the plasma. Measure monitors efficacy of ARV treatment through virological suppression. Goal is undetectable.
CD4/CD8 ratio	These are markers found on lymphocytes. HIV kills CD4+ cells, which results in a significantly impaired immune system. Measure determines initiation of ARV treatment and use of prophylactic medications.

require written informed consent and face-to-face results counseling. Consult state laws about specific requirements related to testing for HIV. When the result of the HIV antibody test is received, it is carefully explained to the patient in private (Box 37-5). All test results are kept confidential. Education and counseling about the test result and about

BOX 37-5 HIV Test Results: Implications for Patients

Interpretation of Positive Test Results
- Antibodies to HIV are present in the blood (the patient has been infected with the virus, and the body has produced antibodies).
- HIV is active in the body, and the patient can transmit the virus to others.
- Despite HIV infection, the patient does not necessarily have AIDS.
- The patient is not immune to HIV (the antibodies do not indicate immunity).

Interpretation of Negative Test Results
- Antibodies to HIV are not present in the blood at this time, which can mean that the patient has not been infected with HIV or, if infected, the body has not yet produced antibodies (window period—usually 3 weeks to 6 months).
- The patient should continue taking precautions. The test result does not mean that the patient is immune to the virus, nor does it mean the patient is not infected; it just means that the body may not have produced antibodies yet. Recommend repeat testing if at high risk for HIV.

preventing transmission are essential. The patient's psychological response to a seropositive test result may include feelings of panic, depression, and hopelessness. The social and interpersonal consequences of a positive test result can be devastating. The patient may lose his or her sexual partner and health insurance because of disclosure. The patient may experience discrimination in employment and housing, as well as social ostracism. For these reasons and others, a patient who tests positive may need ongoing counseling, as well as referrals for social, financial, medical, and psychological support services.

Patients whose test results are seronegative may develop a false sense of security, possibly resulting in continued high-risk behaviors or feelings that they are immune to the virus. These patients may need ongoing counseling to help modify high-risk behaviors and to encourage returns for repeated testing. Other patients may experience anxiety regarding the uncertainty of their status.

During initial infection with HIV, the immune system responds by producing antibodies against the virus, usually within 3 to 12 weeks after infection. In 1985, the U.S. Food and Drug Administration (FDA) licensed an HIV-1 antibody assay that used approximately 5 to 7 mL of blood. Samples are tested using two different laboratory techniques to determine the presence of antibodies to HIV. The **enzyme immunoassay (EIA)** test, formerly referred to as the enzyme-linked immunosorbent assay (ELISA) test, identifies antibodies directed specifically against HIV. The **Western blot assay** is used to confirm seropositivity when the EIA result is positive.

Home-based testing for HIV antibodies using a small amount of blood was first proposed in 1985 but was not approved by the FDA until 1995. Although home testing kits are commercially available, they raise concerns because of the lack of counseling and the possibility of inaccurate results, including both false-positive and false-negative results.

Viral Load Tests

Target amplification methods quantify HIV RNA or DNA levels in the plasma and have replaced p24 antigen capture assays. Target amplification methods include reverse transcriptase–**polymerase chain reaction** (RT-PCR) and nucleic acid sequence–based amplification (NASBA). A widely used **viral load test** measures plasma HIV RNA levels. Currently, these tests track viral load and response to treatment of HIV infection. RT-PCR is also used to detect HIV in high-risk seronegative people before antibodies are measurable, to confirm a positive EIA result, and to screen neonates. Viral load is a better predictor of the risk for HIV disease progression than the CD4+ count. The lower the viral load, the longer the time to AIDS diagnosis and the longer the survival time. Increased virus causes lymphoid dysfunction and other inflammatory responses that affect long-term survival (Deeks & Phillips, 2009).

Stages of HIV Disease

The stage of HIV disease is based on clinical history, physical examination, laboratory evidence of immune dysfunction, signs and symptoms, infections, and malignancies. The CDC standard case definition of AIDS categorizes HIV infection and AIDS in adults and adolescents based on clinical conditions associated with HIV infection and CD4+ T-cell counts. The classification system groups clinical conditions into one of three categories, denoted A, B, and C. Each category denotes clinical progression of HIV infection in the patient, from asymptomatic category A to "full blown" AIDS category C. Although a patient's health and immune status may improve, the CDC classification of their illness does not change.

Primary Infection (Acute HIV Infection, Acute HIV Syndrome)

The period from infection with HIV to the development of antibodies to HIV is known as **primary infection**. This period is characterized by intense viral replication and widespread dissemination of HIV throughout the body. During primary infection, a window period occurs, during which a person with HIV infection tests negative on the HIV antibody blood test. Although antibodies to the HIV envelope glycoproteins typically can be detected in the sera of HIV-infected individuals by 2 to 3 weeks after infection, most of these antibodies lack the ability to inhibit virus infection. By the time neutralizing antibodies can be detected, HIV-1 is firmly established in the host. During this period, there are high levels of viral replication and destruction of CD4+ T cells, resulting in high levels of HIV in the blood and a dramatic drop in CD4+ T-cell counts from the normal level of 500 to 1,500 cells/mm^3 of blood. Detectable levels of virus can occur as early as 72 hours after exposure; this provides the rationale for immediate initiation of prophylaxis.

About 3 weeks into this acute phase, the person may display symptoms similar to mononucleosis, such as fever, enlarged lymph nodes, rash, muscle aches, and headaches. These symptoms resolve within another 1 to 3 weeks as the immune system begins to recuperate. That is, the CD4+ T-cell population responds in ways that cause other immune cells, such as CD8+ lymphocytes, to increase their killing of infected, virus-producing cells. The body produces antibody molecules in an effort to contain the virus; they bind to free HIV particles (outside cells) and assist in their removal. This balance between the amount of HIV in the body and the immune response is referred to as the **viral set point**; it results in a steady state of infection that can last for years.

Primary HIV infection, the time during which the viral burden set point is achieved, includes the acute symptomatic and early infection phases. During this initial stage, viral replication is associated with dissemination in lymphoid tissue (lymph nodes, spleen, tonsils and adenoids, and the thymus) and a distinct immunologic response. The final level of the viral set point is inversely correlated with disease prognosis;

that is, the higher the viral set point, the poorer the prognosis. The primary infection stage is part of CDC category A.

HIV Asymptomatic (CDC Category A: More Than 500 CD4+ T Lymphocytes/mm³)

When a viral set point is reached, a chronic, clinically asymptomatic state begins. Despite its best efforts, the immune system rarely if ever fully eliminates the virus. By about 6 months, the rate of viral replication reaches a lower but relatively steady state that is reflected in the maintenance of viral levels at a set point. This set point varies greatly from patient to patient and dictates the subsequent rate of disease progression; on average, 8 to 10 years pass before a major HIV-related complication develops. In this prolonged, chronic stage, patients feel well and have few if any symptoms. Apparent good health continues because CD4+ T-cell levels remain high enough to preserve defensive responses to other pathogens.

HIV Symptomatic (CDC Category B: 200 to 499 CD4+ T Lymphocytes/mm³)

Over time, the number of CD4+ T cells gradually falls. Category B consists of symptomatic conditions in HIV- infected patients that are not included in the conditions listed in category C. These conditions must also meet one of the following criteria: (1) the condition is due to HIV infection or a defect in cellular immunity, or (2) the condition is considered to have a clinical course or to require management that is complicated by HIV infection.

AIDS (CDC Category C: Fewer Than 200 CD4+ T Lymphocytes/mm³)

When the CD4+ T-cell level drops below 200 cells/mm³ of blood, the person has AIDS. As levels decrease to fewer than 100 cells/mm³, the immune system is significantly impaired. Once a patient has had a category C condition, he or she remains in category C. This classification has implications for entitlements (i.e., disability benefits, housing, and food stamps), because these programs are often linked to an AIDS diagnosis. Although the revised classification emphasizes CD4+ T-cell counts, it allows for CD4+ percentages (percentage of CD4+ T cells compared with total lymphocytes). The CD4+ percentage is less subject to variation on repeated measurements than is the absolute CD4+ T-cell count. A CD4+ percentage of less than 14% of the total lymphocytes is consistent with an AIDS diagnosis. The percentage, as compared with the absolute number of CD4+ T cells, becomes particularly important when the patient has a heightened immune response to infections in addition to HIV.

Clinical Manifestations

During the first stage of HIV infection, the patient may be asymptomatic or may exhibit various signs and symptoms. The patient's health history should alert the health care provider about the need for HIV screening based on the patient's sexual practices, IV/injection drug use, and receipt of blood transfusions. Patients who are in later stages of HIV infection may have a variety of symptoms related to their immunosuppressed state. HIV often causes **opportunistic infections**. Opportunistic infections and other common manifestations are discussed below.

Respiratory Manifestations

Dyspnea (labored breathing), cough, chest pain, and fever are associated with various opportunistic infections, such as those caused by *P. jiroveci, Mycobacterium avium-intracellulare,* CMV, and *Legionella* species.

Pneumocystic Pneumonia

The most common infection in people with AIDS is *Pneumocystis* pneumonia (PCP). The current guidelines on treatment of opportunistic infections (Burr, 2011) refer to the causative organism as *P. jiroveci* instead of *P. carinii,* although the infection is still abbreviated as PCP. PCP was one of the first opportunistic infections described in association with AIDS, and it is the most common opportunistic infection resulting in the diagnosis of AIDS. Without prophylactic therapy, 80% of all people infected with HIV will develop PCP.

The clinical presentation of PCP in HIV infection is generally less acute than in people who are immunosuppressed because of other conditions. The time between the onset of symptoms and the actual documentation of disease may be weeks to months. Patients with AIDS initially develop nonspecific signs and symptoms, such as nonproductive cough, fever, chills, dyspnea, and occasionally chest pain. PCP may be present despite the absence of crackles. Arterial oxygen concentrations in patients who are breathing room air may be mildly decreased, indicating minimal hypoxemia. Pulse oximetry after exercise, such as walking up and down a flight of stairs is a simple, noninvasive test for outpatient use.

If left untreated, PCP eventually progresses and causes significant pulmonary impairment and respiratory failure. Some patients have a dramatic onset and a fulminating course involving severe hypoxemia, cyanosis, tachypnea, and altered mental status. Respiratory failure can develop within 2 to 3 days after the initial appearance of symptoms.

PCP can be diagnosed definitively by identifying the organism in lung tissue or bronchial secretions. This is accomplished by such procedures as sputum induction, bronchial-alveolar lavage, and transbronchial biopsy (by fiberoptic bronchoscope).

Tuberculosis

Mycobacterium tuberculosis tends to occur in IV/injection drug users and other groups with a preexisting high prevalence of tuberculosis (TB) infection. TB that occurs late in HIV infection is characterized by absence of an immune response to the tuberculin skin test. This is known as **anergy**, and it occurs because the compromised immune system can no longer respond to the TB antigen. For this reason, TB testing is essential upon initial diagnosis of

HIV, with appropriate treatment for patients demonstrating latent TB infection. Nurses administer the Mantoux test to determine infection with TB (refer to Chapter 10 for further discussion). In the later stages of HIV infection, TB may be associated with dissemination to extra pulmonary sites such as the central nervous system (CNS), bone, pericardium, stomach, peritoneum, and scrotum. Multidrug-resistant strains of the bacillus have emerged and are often associated with lack of adherence to antituberculosis medication regimens.

Immune reconstitution syndrome (also known as *paradoxical reactions*) seems to occur more often among patients with TB. Patients can experience high fevers, worsening lymphadenopathy, or transient to severe worsening of pulmonary infiltrates, and expanding CNS lesions. Reduction of HIV-1 RNA levels and marked increases in CD4+ T-lymphocyte counts have been associated with the occurrence of paradoxical reactions in patients with TB disease or mycobacterium avium complex (MAC). A common mycobacteria, MAC may cause infection in immunosuppressed patients. While affecting the lungs primarily, it can have extrapulmonary impact on the lymph nodes, bones, skin, and other tissues. However, a MAC infection cannot be passed from one person to another. Although the majority of reactions occur within the first few weeks after initiation of antiretroviral therapy (ART), some have occurred up to several months after the initiation of TB therapy or ART (Libman & Makadon, 2007).

Gastrointestinal Manifestations

The gastrointestinal (GI) manifestations of AIDS include loss of appetite, nausea, vomiting, oral and esophageal candidiasis, and chronic diarrhea. Diarrhea is a problem in 50% to 90% of all AIDS patients. GI symptoms may be related to the direct effect of HIV on the cells lining the intestines. Some of the enteric pathogens that occur most frequently, identified by stool cultures or intestinal biopsy, are *Cryptosporidium muris*, *Salmonella* species, *Isospora belli*, *Giardia lamblia*, CMV, *Clostridium difficile*, and *M. avium-intracellulare*. In patients with AIDS, the effects of diarrhea can be devastating in terms of profound weight loss (more than 10% of body weight), fluid and electrolyte imbalances, perianal skin excoriation, weakness, and inability to perform the usual activities of daily living.

Candidiasis

Candidiasis or *thrush*, a fungal infection, occurs in almost all patients with AIDS and AIDS-related conditions. It commonly precedes other life-threatening infections and is characterized by creamy-white patches in the oral cavity (Fig. 37-2). When left untreated, oral candidiasis progresses to involve the esophagus and stomach. Associated signs and symptoms include difficult, painful swallowing and retrosternal pain. Some patients also develop ulcerating oral lesions and are particularly susceptible to dissemination of candidiasis to other body systems.

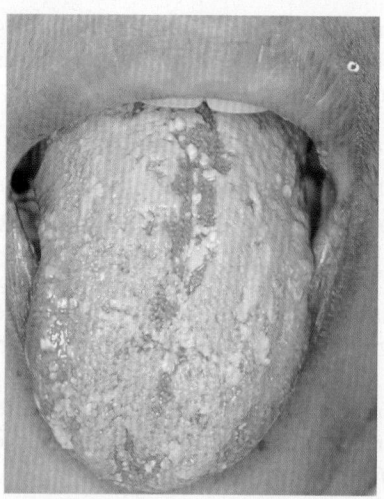

FIGURE 37-2 Oral candidiasis. From Goodheart, H. P. (2009). *Goodheart's photoguide of common skin disorders* (3rd ed., p. 452). Philadelphia: Lippincott Williams & Wilkins.

Wasting Syndrome

Wasting syndrome is part of the category C case definition for AIDS. Diagnostic criteria include profound involuntary weight loss exceeding 10% of baseline body weight and either chronic diarrhea for more than 30 days or chronic weakness and documented intermittent or constant fever in the absence of any concurrent illness that could explain these findings. This protein–energy malnutrition is multifactorial. In some AIDS-associated illnesses, patients experience a hypermetabolic state in which excessive calories are burned and lean body mass is lost. This state is similar to that seen in sepsis or trauma and can lead to organ failure. The distinction between cachexia (wasting) and malnutrition, or between cachexia and simple weight loss, is important, because the metabolic derangement seen in wasting syndrome may not be modified by nutritional support alone.

Progressive tissue wasting may occur with only modest GI involvement and without diarrhea. TNF and IL-1 are cytokines that play important roles in AIDS-related wasting syndrome. Both act directly on the hypothalamus to cause anorexia. Cytokine-induced fever accelerates the body's metabolism by 14% for every 1°F increase in temperature. TNF causes inefficient use of lipids by reducing enzymes that are needed for fat metabolism, whereas IL-1 triggers the release of amino acids from muscle tissue. It is believed that infections and sepsis lead to transient increases in TNF, IL-1, and other cell mediators above the chronically elevated levels that are often seen with AIDS (refer to Chapter 54 for discussion of sepsis). These transient increases in TNF and IL-1 trigger muscle wasting. People with AIDS generally experience increased protein metabolism in relation to fat metabolism, which results in significant decreases in lean body mass due to muscle and protein breakdown. Hypertriglyceridemia, seen in people with AIDS and attributed to chronically elevated cytokine levels, can persist for months

without tissue wasting and loss of lean body mass. It is also caused by **protease inhibitors** (PIs) and increases the risk for pancreatitis.

Oncologic Manifestations

Patients with AIDS have a higher than usual incidence of cancer, possibly related to HIV stimulation of developing cancer cells or to the immune deficiency that allows cancer-causing substances, such as viruses, to transform susceptible cells into malignant cells. Kaposi's sarcoma (KS), certain types of B-cell lymphomas, and invasive cervical carcinoma are included in the CDC classification of AIDS-related malignancies. Carcinomas of the skin, stomach, pancreas, rectum, and bladder also occur more frequently than expected in people with AIDS.

Kaposi's Sarcoma

KS, the most common HIV-related malignancy, is a disease that involves the endothelial layer of blood and lymphatic vessels. Since the introduction of ARVs, there has been a significant decrease in the incidence of KS. It is associated with human herpes virus 8 (HHV-8) transmission. Acquired KS occurs in patients who are treated with immunosuppressive agents and commonly in patients who have undergone organ transplantation. In such patients, KS usually resolves once the dose of the immunosuppressive medication is decreased or discontinued. In people with AIDS, epidemic KS is most often seen among male homosexuals and bisexuals. Although the histopathology of all forms of KS is virtually identical, the clinical manifestations differ: AIDS-related KS exhibits a more variable and aggressive course, ranging from localized cutaneous lesions to disseminated disease involving multiple organ systems. Cutaneous signs may be the first manifestation of HIV, appearing in more than 90% of HIV-infected patients as the immune functions deteriorate. These skin signs correlate to low CD4+ counts, usually less than 50. Cutaneous lesions can appear anywhere on the body and are brownish pink to deep purple. They may be flat or raised and surrounded by ecchymoses (hemorrhagic patches) and edema (Fig. 37-3). Rapid development of lesions involving large areas of skin is associated with extensive disfigurement. The location and size of some lesions can lead to venous stasis, lymphedema, and pain. Ulcerative lesions disrupt skin integrity and increase discomfort and susceptibility to infection. The most common sites of visceral involvement are the lymph nodes, GI tract, and lungs. Involvement of internal organs may eventually lead to organ failure, hemorrhage, infection, and death.

Proper identification of these lesions is difficult with darkly pigmented skin; biopsy confirms the diagnosis. Prognosis depends on the extent of the tumor, the presence of other symptoms of HIV infection, and the CD4+ count. Death may result from tumor progression.

B-Cell Lymphomas

B-cell lymphomas are the second most common malignancy occurring in people with AIDS. Lymphomas associated with

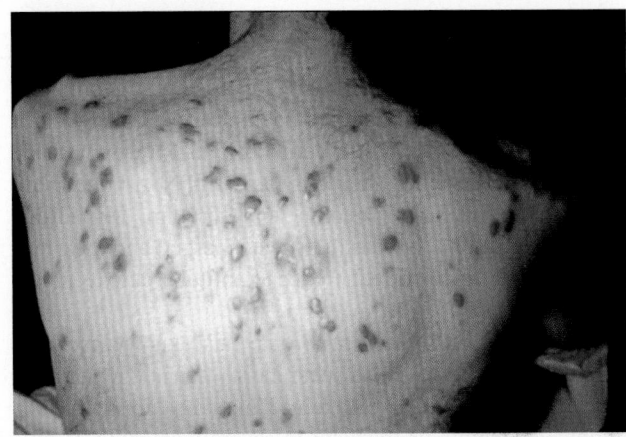

FIGURE 37-3 Lesions of AIDS-related Kaposi's sarcoma. Whereas some patients may have lesions that remain flat, others experience extensively disseminated, raised lesions with edema. From Hall J. C. (2000). *Sauer's manual of skin* (8th ed., p. 197). Philadelphia: Lippincott Williams & Wilkins.

AIDS usually differ from those occurring in the general population. Patients with AIDS are typically much younger than the usual population affected by non-Hodgkin lymphoma. In addition, AIDS-related lymphomas tend to develop outside the lymph nodes, most commonly in the brain, bone marrow, and GI tract. These types of lymphomas are characteristically of a higher grade, indicating aggressive growth and resistance to treatment.

The course of AIDS-related lymphomas includes multiple sites of organ involvement and complications related to opportunistic infections. Although aggressive combination chemotherapy is frequently successful in the treatment of non-Hodgkin lymphoma in the HIV negative patient, treatment is less successful in people with AIDS because of severe hematologic toxicity and complications of opportunistic infections.

Neurologic Manifestations

An estimated 80% of all patients with AIDS experience some form of neurologic involvement during the course of HIV infection. Many neuropathologic disorders are underreported because patients may have neurologic involvement without overt signs or symptoms. Neurologic complications involve central, peripheral, and autonomic functions. Neurologic dysfunction results from direct effects of HIV on nervous system tissue, opportunistic infections, primary or metastatic neoplasms, cerebrovascular changes, metabolic encephalopathies, or complications secondary to therapy. Immune system response to HIV infection in the CNS includes inflammation, atrophy, demyelination, degeneration, and necrosis.

HIV Encephalopathy

HIV encephalopathy or HIV-associated dementia (HAD) was formerly referred to as *AIDS dementia complex*. The clinical syndrome is characterized by a progressive decline

in cognitive, behavioral, and motor functions. Substantial evidence exists that HIV encephalopathy is a direct result of HIV infection. HIV has been found in the brain and cerebrospinal fluid (CSF) of patients with HIV encephalopathy. HIV infection is thought to trigger the release of toxins or lymphokines that result in cellular dysfunction or interference with neurotransmitter function rather than cellular damage.

Signs and symptoms may be subtle and difficult to distinguish from fatigue, depression, or the adverse effects of treatment for infections and malignancies. Early manifestations include memory deficits, headache, difficulty concentrating, progressive confusion, psychomotor slowing, apathy, and ataxia. Later stages include global cognitive impairments, delay in verbal responses, a vacant stare, spastic paraparesis (a slight weakness or paralysis of both lower extremities), hyperreflexia, psychosis, hallucinations, tremor, incontinence, seizures, mutism, and death.

Confirming the diagnosis of HIV encephalopathy can be difficult. Extensive neurologic evaluation includes a computed tomography scan, which may indicate diffuse cerebral atrophy and ventricular enlargement. Other tests that may detect abnormalities include magnetic resonance imaging, analysis of CSF through lumbar puncture, and brain biopsy.

Cytomegalovirus

Retinitis is the most common clinical manifestation of CMV. Before the use of ARVs, 30% of patients experienced CMV retinitis with a high incidence of blindness. The incidence of CMV retinitis has been reduced by 75% with these medications.

Peripheral retinitis might be asymptomatic or present with floaters, scotomata (a loss of vision within the visual field), or reduced visual acuity. CMV retinitis has characteristic fluffy yellow-white retinal lesions with or without intraretinal hemorrhage visual on funduscopic exam. Blood vessels near the lesions might appear to be sheathed. Patients with CD4+ counts of less than 50 should be examined by an ophthalmologist on a yearly basis (Burr, 2011).

Other Neurologic Disorders

Other common infections involving the nervous system include *T. gondii*, *M. tuberculosis*, and syphilis. Additional neurologic manifestations include both central and peripheral neuropathies. Vascular myelopathy is a degenerative disorder that affects the lateral and posterior columns of the spinal cord, resulting in progressive spastic paraparesis, ataxia (inability to coordinate body movements), and incontinence. HIV-related peripheral neuropathy is thought to be a demyelinating disorder. It is associated with pain and numbness in the extremities, weakness, diminished deep tendon reflexes, orthostatic hypotension, and impotence. Peripheral neuropathy is a common adverse effect of many HIV medications.

Depressive Manifestations

The prevalence of depression among people with HIV infection is three times higher than in the HIV-negative population (Treisman, Hsu, & Angelino, 2009). The causes of depression are multifactorial and may include a history of preexisting mental illness, neuropsychiatric disturbances, and psychosocial factors. Depression also occurs in people with HIV infection in response to the physical symptoms, including pain and weight loss, as well as isolation. People with HIV/AIDS who are depressed may experience irrational guilt and shame, loss of self-esteem, feelings of helplessness and worthlessness, and suicidal ideation.

Integumentary Manifestations

Cutaneous manifestations are associated with HIV infection and the accompanying opportunistic infections and malignancies. KS (described earlier) and opportunistic infections such as herpes zoster and herpes simplex are associated with painful vesicles that disrupt skin integrity. Molluscum contagiosum is a viral infection characterized by deforming plaque formation. Seborrheic dermatitis is associated with an indurated, diffuse, scaly rash involving the scalp and face (see Chapter 52). Patients with AIDS may also exhibit a generalized eosinophilic folliculitis associated with dry, flaking skin or atopic dermatitis, such as eczema or psoriasis. Up to 60% of patients treated with trimethoprim-sulfamethoxazole (TMP-SMZ) develop a drug-related rash that is pruritic with pinkish-red macules and papules. Regardless of the origin of these rashes, patients experience discomfort and are at increased risk for additional infection from disrupted skin integrity. See Chapter 51 for how to assess and describe rashes.

> **NURSING ALERT**
> *The viral exanthem associated with acute retroviral syndrome during initial infection with AIDS is one of the few rashes accurately described as maculopapular.*

Gynecologic Manifestations

Persistent, recurrent vaginal candidiasis or bacterial vaginosis may be the first sign of HIV infection in women. Past or present genital ulcer disease is a risk factor for the transmission of HIV infection. Women with HIV infection are more susceptible to and have increased rates of incidence and recurrence of genital ulcer disease and venereal warts. Ulcerative STIs such as chancroid, syphilis, and herpes are more severe in women with HIV infection. Human papillomavirus (HPV) causes venereal warts and is a risk factor for cervical intraepithelial neoplasia, a cellular change that is frequently a precursor to cervical cancer. Women with HIV are 10 times more likely to develop cervical intraepithelial neoplasia than are those not infected with HIV. HIV-seropositive women with cervical carcinoma present at a more advanced stage of disease and have more persistent and recurrent disease and a shorter interval to recurrence and death than women without HIV infection.

A significant percentage of women who require hospitalization for pelvic inflammatory disease (PID) have HIV

infection. Women with HIV are at increased risk for PID, and the associated inflammation may potentiate the transmission of HIV infection (see Chapter 35 for information related to PID). Moreover, women with HIV infection appear to have a higher incidence of menstrual abnormalities, including amenorrhea or bleeding between periods, than do women without HIV infection.

Immunological Manifestations

Immune reconstitution inflammatory syndromes (IRIS) have been described for mycobacterial infections, including disease caused by *M. avium* complex (MAC) and *M. tuberculosis*, PCP, toxoplasmosis, hepatitis B and hepatitis C, CMV infection, varicella-zoster virus infection, cryptococcal infection, and progressive multifocal leukoencephalopathy. Immune reconstitution syndromes are characterized by fever and worsening of the clinical manifestations of the opportunistic infection, or the appearance of new manifestations developing weeks after the initiation of ART. It is important to determine the absence or reappearance of the underlying opportunistic infection, new drug toxicity, or a new opportunistic infection. If the syndrome represents an immune reactivation syndrome, adding nonsteroidal anti-inflammatory agents (NSAIDs) or corticosteroids to alleviate the inflammatory reaction is appropriate. The inflammation might take weeks to months to subside (Page & Andrade, 2009). The nurse should be alert to signs of immune reconstitution syndrome and advise the patient to seek health care if he or she is feeling sicker with no clear explanation.

Medical and Nursing Management

Treatment Regimen

Protocols on treatment of HIV disease change frequently. The U.S. Department of Health and Human Services (DHHS) periodically convenes a team of HIV specialists from across the country to evaluate the latest evidence and make recommendations that are widely disseminated (Department of Health and Human Services [DHHS] Panel, 2008a). Treatment decisions are individualized based on a number of factors, including CD4+ T-cell count, HIV RNA (viral load), severe symptoms of HIV disease or AIDS, and willingness of the patient to adhere to a life-long treatment regimen. The CD4+ count is usually the most important consideration in decisions to initiate ART (DHHS Panel, 2008a). Treatment should be offered to all patients with primary infection (acute HIV syndrome, as previously described). In general, ARV medications should be offered to individuals with a CD4+ cell count of less than 350 cells/mm^3 or plasma HIV RNA levels exceeding 100,000 copies/mL (DHHS Panel, 2008a). Some clinicians and patients, however, are choosing not to start medications until the CD4+ cell count decreases to approximately 200 cells/mm^3. Currently, recommendations support the early use of ARVs with a CD4+ count around 500 to preserve immune function, reduce the risk of opportunistic infections, and maintain patient quality of life. New HIV medications are easier to take, have fewer adverse reactions, and are effective and potent. Monitoring the DHHS website for updates of the recommendations is essential before caring for patients with HIV/AIDS (DHHS Panel, 2008a).

The increasing number of ARV agents (Table 37-2) and the rapid evolution of new information have introduced extraordinary complexity into the treatment of HIV infection. ARV regimens may be complex, have major side effects, pose difficulties with regard to adherence, and carry serious potential consequences; these include viral resistance resulting from nonadherence to the medication regimen or suboptimal levels of ARV agents. The goals of treatment include maximal and sustained suppression of viral load, restoration or preservation of immunologic function, improved quality of life, and reduction of HIV-related morbidity and mortality. The DHHS Guidelines recommend viral load testing at the time of diagnosis of HIV disease and every 3 to 4 months thereafter in the untreated person; CD4+ cell counts should be measured at diagnosis and usually every 3 to 6 months thereafter (DHHS Panel, 2008b).

Medications

More than 20 approved ARV agents, belonging to six classes, are available for the design of combination regimens. Effective regimens contain at least three virologically active medications from at least two classes. The six classes currently approved by the FDA are the nucleoside/nucleotide reverse transcriptase inhibitors (NRTI), non-nucleoside reverse transcriptase inhibitors (NNRTI), protease inhibitors, fusion inhibitors, integrase inhibitors, and entry inhibitors (see Table 39-2, [DHHS Panel, 2008b]). Each of these medications attacks HIV at different stages of viral replication in the CD4+ lymphocyte.

As new medications are developed and research is completed, the number and types of recommended drug combinations continue to change (DHHS Panel, 2008). In addition, some pharmaceutical companies have combined two to three agents into one tablet or capsule (such as Kaletra, which is a combination of lopinavir and ritonavir), so that a patient may be taking one tablet or capsule that contains two different medications. With a decrease in the number of tablets or capsules that the patient must take ("pill burden"), the patient is more likely to adhere to prescribed regimens and achieve sustained viral suppression. Efforts are under way to develop additional combinations of ARV medications. One medication made available in 2006, Atripla, combines Sustiva (efavirenz), Emtriva (emtricitabine), and Viread (tenofovir disoproxil fumarate) in a single tablet for once-a-day use. It is anticipated that simplifying treatment regimens and decreasing the number of medications that must be taken each day may increase patients' adherence to therapy (DHHS Panel, 2008b).

TABLE
37-2 Commonly Used Antiretroviral Agents*

Generic Name (Abbreviation) and Trade Names	Food Effect	Adverse Events
Nucleoside Reverse Transcriptase Inhibitors (NRTIs)		
abacavir (ABC) Ziagen Trizivir (ABC + ZDV + 3TC) Epzicom (ABC + 3TC)	Can be taken without regard to meals. Alcohol increases abacavir levels 41%.	Hypersensitivity reaction, which can be fatal; symptoms may include fever, rash, nausea, vomiting, malaise or fatigue, loss of appetite, respiratory symptoms such as sore throat, cough, shortness of breath. HLA-B*5701 test identifies patients at risk for hypersensitivity.
didanosine (ddI) Videx Videx EC	Levels decrease 55%; take ½ hour before or 2 hours after meals.	Pancreatitis; peripheral neuropathy; nausea; diarrhea. Lactic acidosis with fatty degeneration of the liver (rare but potentially life-threatening toxicity associated with use of NRTIs)
emtricitabine (FTC) Emtriva Truvada (FTC + TDF)	Can be taken without regard to meals.	Minimal toxicity; lactic acidosis with hepatic steatosis (rare but potentially life-threatening toxicity with use of NRTIs)
lamivudine (3TC) Epivir Combivir (3TC + ZDV) Epzicom (3TC + ABC) Trizivir (3TC + ZDV + ABC)	Can be taken without regard to meals.	Minimal toxicity; lactic acidosis with hepatic steatosis (rare but potentially life-threatening toxicity with use of NRTIs)
tenofovir disoproxil fumarate (TDF) Viread Truvada (TDF + FTC)	Can be taken without regard to meals.	Asthenia (loss of strength and energy), headache, diarrhea, nausea, vomiting, and flatulence; renal insufficiency; lactic acidosis with hepatic steatosis (rare but potentially life-threatening toxicity with use of NRTIs)
zidovudine (AZT or ZDV) Retrovir Combivir (AZT + 3TC) Trizivir (AZT + 3TC + ABC)	Can be taken without regard to meals.	Bone marrow suppression; macrocytic anemia or neutropenia; GI intolerance, headache, insomnia, asthenia; lactic acidosis with hepatic steatosis (rare but potentially life-threatening toxicity with use of NRTIs)
Non-nucleoside Reverse Transcriptase Inhibitors (NNRTIs)		
efavirenz (EFV) Sustiva	High-fat/high-caloric meals increase peak plasma concentrations of capsules by 39% and tablets by 79%; take on an empty stomach.	Rash (rare cases of Stevens-Johnson syndrome have been reported); central nervous system symptoms (dizziness, somnolence, insomnia, abnormal dreams, confusion, abnormal thinking, impaired concentration, amnesia, agitation, depersonalization, hallucinations, and euphoria); increased transaminase levels; false-positive cannabinoid test; teratogenic in monkeys
nevirapine (NVP) Viramune	Take without regard to meals.	Rash including Stevens-Johnson syndrome, symptomatic hepatitis including fatal hepatic necrosis has been reported.
Protease Inhibitors (PIs)		
atazanavir (ATV) Reyataz	Administration with food increases bioavailability. Should be taken with food; avoid taking with antacids.	Indirect hyperbilirubinemia; prolonged PR interval—some patients experienced asymptomatic first-degree AV block; use with caution in patients with underlying conduction defects or on concomitant medications that can cause PR prolongation; hyperglycemia; fat maldistribution, possible increased bleeding episodes in patients with hemophilia
fosamprenavir (f-APV) Lexiva	Can be taken without regard to meals.	Skin rash (19%); diarrhea; nausea; vomiting; headache; hyperlipidemia; transaminase elevation; hyperglycemia; fat maldistribution; possible increased bleeding episodes in patients with hemophilia

(continued on page 1018)

TABLE
37-2 Commonly Used Antiretroviral Agents* (continued)

Generic Name (Abbreviation) and Trade Names	Food Effect	Adverse Events
lopinavir + ritonavir (LPV/r) Kaletra	Should be taken with food.	GI intolerance; nausea; vomiting; diarrhea; asthenia; hyperlipidemia (especially hypertri-glyceridemia) elevated serum transaminase; hyperglycemia; fat maldistribution; possible increased bleeding episodes in patients with hemophilia
nelfinavir (NFV) Viracept	Should be taken with a meal or snack.	Diarrhea; hyperlipidemia; hyperglycemia; fat maldistribution; possible increased bleeding episodes in patients with hemophilia; serum transaminase elevation
ritonavir (RTV) Norvir	Should be taken with food if possi-ble; may improve tolerability.	GI intolerance; nausea; vomiting; diarrhea; par-esthesias—circumoral and extremities; hyper-lipidemia, especially hypertriglyceridemia; hepatitis; asthenia; taste perversion; hypergly-cemia; fat maldistribution; possible increased bleeding in patients with hemophilia
Fusion Inhibitors enfuvirtide (T-20) Fuzeon	Injected subcutaneously	Local injection site reactions—almost 100% of patients (pain, erythema, induration, nodules and cysts, pruritus, ecchymosis); increased rate of bacterial pneumonia; hypersensitivity reaction—symptoms may include rash, fever, nausea, vomiting, chills, rigors, hypotension, or elevated serum transaminases; may recur on challenge
CCR5 Antagonists maraviroc (MVC) Selzentry	No food effect; take with or without food.	Abdominal pain; cough; dizziness; musculo-skeletal symptoms; pyrexia; rash; upper respi-ratory infections; hepatotoxicity; orthostatic hypotension
Integrase Inhibitors raltegravir (RAL) Isentress	Take with or without food.	Nausea, headache; diarrhea; pyrexia; CPK elevation

*Regimens should be individualized based on the advantages and disadvantages of each combination such as pill burden, dosing frequency, toxicities, drug–drug interaction potential, comorbid conditions, and level of plasma HIV-RNA.
From Department of Health and Human Services Panel on ARV Guidelines for Adults and Adolescents—A Working Group of the Office of AIDS Research Advisory Council (2008). *Guidelines for the use of ARV agents in HIV-1-infected adults and adolescents, November 3, 2008.* Available at http://aidsinfo.nih.gov

Adherence

It is difficult to predict which patients will adhere to medica-tion regimens. Adherence rates of 95% minimize the risks of developing resistant virus. Patients should understand that the first regimen prescribed is the best chance for long-term treatment success with minimal impact on daily functioning and prevention of resistance. Individualized plans of care that take into consideration housing and social support issues, in addition to health indicators, are essential. Adherence to the ARV treatment plan involves very complex behavior that can change over the duration of the medication regimen. Self-reported adherence measures can distinguish clini-cally meaningful patterns of medication-taking behaviors;

therefore, nurses should ask patients if they are taking their medications as prescribed on a scale of 1 to 6. Factors asso-ciated with nonadherence include active substance abuse, depression, lack of social support, and treatment fatigue. Gender, race, pregnancy, and history of past substance use have not been associated with nonadherence (DHHS Panel, 2008b). Box 37-6 summarizes various strategies that health care providers can use to encourage treatment regimen adherence. Every health care encounter should be used as an opportunity to briefly review the treatment regimen and identify any new issues.

Patients who elect to interrupt therapy should be coun-seled that the HIV viral load would increase, usually to

BOX 37-6

Patient Education

Adhering to the Medication Therapy for HIV

To help ensure adherence with the therapy regimen, you need to be able to:

- Correctly identify each medication, preferably by name.
- State the action of each medication.
- State the correct times that medication is to be taken.
- Identify special guidelines to follow when taking medications (e.g., with meals, on an empty stomach, medications that are not to be taken together).
- Demonstrate methods of tracking and storage of the medication regimen and use reminders such as beepers and/or pillboxes.
- Identify specific laboratory tests, such as viral load, that are necessary to monitor the effectiveness of the medication regimen.
- List expected side effects of each medication.
- Identify side effects reportable to health care providers.
- Explain the importance of and necessity for adherence.
- Demonstrate correct administration of intramuscular, subcutaneous, or IV medications.
- Demonstrate correct use and safe disposal of needles, syringes, and other IV equipment.
- Discuss episodes of nonadherence to the medication regimen.

pretreatment levels, resulting in an increased risk for transmission to others during risky behaviors such as unsafe sex and sharing needles. Because of drug toxicities, drug resistance, quality-of-life issues, and the high cost of medications, some patients may choose to take a "drug holiday" or structured treatment interruption. Through an open, honest partnership between the health care provider and the patient, these options can be explored and their effectiveness maximized. Structured intermittent therapy, characterized by alternating short periods on and off medication, appears to be ineffective and may increase mortality.

Evaluation of Therapy

Viral load tests evaluate the results of therapy (DHHS Panel, 2008b). Viral load levels should be measured immediately before initiation of ART and again after 2 to 8 weeks. In most patients, adherence to a regimen of potent ARV agents should result in a significant decrease in the viral load by 2 to 8 weeks. The viral load should continue to decline over the following weeks, and in most individuals, it will drop below detectable levels (currently defined as <50 RNA copies/mL) by 16 to 20 weeks. The rate of viral load decline toward undetectable levels is affected by the baseline T-cell

count, the initial viral load, the potency of the medication, adherence to the medication regimen, prior exposure to ARV agents, and the presence of any opportunistic infections. The confirmed absence of a viral load response in an adherent patient should prompt the health care team to reevaluate the regimen. The CD4+ count should increase by 100 to 150 cells/mm³ per year, with an accelerated response in the first 3 months (DHHS Panel, 2008b).

Side Effects

Many of the ARV agents that prolong life may simultaneously cause lipodystrophy syndrome and place the person at risk for early-onset hypercholesterolemia, heart disease, and diabetes. Fat redistribution syndrome, which consists of lipoatrophy (Fig. 37-4), lipohypertrophy, or both in localized areas, is also known as *lipodystrophy syndrome*. This syndrome is one of the most frequent systemic side effects associated with the use of ARV medications, especially protease inhibitors, and affects up to 58% of patients (Libman & Makadon, 2007). Many people who have lipodystrophy experience an increase in fat loss in the legs, arms, face, or a buildup of fat around the abdomen and at the base of the neck, or both. Patients may also experience an increase in breast size.

Facial wasting, characterized as a sinking of the cheeks, eyes, and temples caused by the loss of fat tissue under the skin, may be treated by injectable fillers such as poly-L-lactic acid (Sculptra).

Drug Resistance

Drug resistance can be broadly defined as the ability of pathogens to withstand the effects of medications that are intended to be toxic to them. Resistance develops because of spontaneous genetic mutation of the pathogens or in

FIGURE 37-4 Facial lipoatrophy.

response to exposure to the medication. Factors associated with the development of drug resistance include serial monotherapy (taking one medication at a time), common during early clinical trials, inadequate suppression of virus replication with suboptimal treatment regimens, difficulty with adherence to complex and toxic regimens, and initiation of therapy late in the course of HIV infection. HIV-1 may find refuge in organ sanctuaries, such as behind the blood–brain barrier, where diminished drug concentrations in the CNS might induce the development of drug-resistant mutants. HIV-1 persists in lymphoid tissue even in people who appear to have responded well to antiviral therapy (Libman & Makadon, 2007).

Resistance testing has a number of limitations and is more helpful in the elimination of ARV agents rather than in deciding which ones should be used. Deciding whether a medication regimen is effective or ineffective is a complex phenomenon. Some patients demonstrate inconsistent results on virologic, immunologic, and clinical parameters. In general, virologic failure occurs first, followed by immunologic failure, and finally by clinical progression. These events may be separated by months to years (DHHS Panel, 2008a). Genotypic testing allows detection of amino acid mutations that are either proved or suspected to be associated with phenotypic resistance. Phenotypic testing predicts the susceptibility of resistant virus to inhibition by a particular drug (Libman & Makadon, 2007).

In addition to resistance testing, several factors must be considered in choosing medications for a new regimen, once the prior regimen has failed. These factors include the patient's past treatment history, viral load, and medication tolerance; the likelihood of the patient's adhering to the medication regimen; and concomitant medical conditions or medications. Resistance testing is of greatest value when it is performed before drugs are discontinued or immediately afterward (within 4 weeks). Most HIV providers perform genotype testing during the initial diagnosis stage as some patients with HIV are infected with resistant virus. Drug resistance testing is not advised for patients with a viral load of less than 1,000 copies/mL because amplification of the virus is unreliable (DHHS Panel, 2008a).

Vaccines

Vaccine research for HIV has two potential areas of application: prevention of new infections, and therapy for those already infected with HIV (therapeutic vaccine). Since HIV-1 was discovered, researchers have been working to develop a vaccine. A vaccine is a substance that triggers the production of antibodies to destroy the offending organism. Creation of an HIV vaccine is feasible, but researchers have had difficulty finding an adequate animal model in which to test new vaccines. Because HIV can attack the human immune system as either cell-free or cell-associated virus, a vaccine against HIV must be capable of producing antibodies and cytotoxic lymphocytes (Libman & Makadon, 2007).

Treatment of Opportunistic Infections

Pneumocystis Pneumonia

In the past several years, many advances have been made in the treatment of PCP. TMP-SMZ (Bactrim, Septra), the treatment of choice for PCP in patients with AIDS and in immunocompromised patients without HIV infection, is available in both IV and oral preparations. TMP-SMZ is an antibacterial agent used to treat various organisms causing infection. People with HIV infection who have a T-cell count of less than 200 cells/mm^3 should receive chemoprophylaxis against PCP with TMP-SMZ. PCP prophylaxis can be safely discontinued in patients who are responding to highly active ART (HAART) with a sustained increase in T lymphocytes. TMP-SMZ also confers cross-protection against toxoplasmosis and some common respiratory bacterial infections. Patients with AIDS who are treated with TMP-SMZ experience a high incidence of adverse effects, such as fever, rashes, leukopenia (decreased WBC count), thrombocytopenia (decreased platelet count), and renal dysfunction. Reintroduction of TMP-SMZ using a gradually increasing dose (desensitization) may be successful in up to 70% of patients.

Pentamidine (Pentacarinat, Pentam 300, NebuPent), an antiprotozoal medication, is used as an alternative agent for combating PCP. Avoid intramuscular administration because of the potential for painful sterile abscess formation. In addition, IV pentamidine can cause severe hypotension if it is administered too rapidly. Other adverse effects include impaired glucose metabolism leading to the development of diabetes mellitus from damage to the pancreas, renal damage, hepatic dysfunction, and neutropenia. Initially, the success of aerosolized pentamidine led to its use as a treatment for mild to moderate PCP. However, it has proved to be less effective and more costly than TMP-SMZ, and early relapses are common. Because of these limitations, aerosolized pentamidine should not be used (DHHS Panel, 2008a).

Mycobacterium Avium Complex

Chemoprophylaxis against disseminated MAC disease is indicated for HIV-infected people with T-cell counts lower than 50 cells/mm^3. Treatment for MAC infections involves use of either clarithromycin (Biaxin) or azithromycin (Zithromax). Secondary prophylaxis for disseminated MAC may be discontinued in patients who have sustained increases in CD4 counts (>100 cells/mm^3) in response to HAART, have completed 12 months of MAC therapy, and have no signs or symptoms attributable to MAC. Primary prophylaxis for disseminated MAC may be discontinued in patients who have responded to HAART with CD4 counts of 100 cells/mm^3 or higher for at least 3 months and may be reintroduced if counts decrease to 50 to 100 cells/mm^3 (DHHS Panel, 2008a).

Cytomegalovirus Retinitis

Retinitis caused by CMV is a leading cause of blindness in patients with AIDS. Prophylaxis with oral ganciclovir may be considered for HIV-infected people who have CD4+ T-cell counts of less than 50 cells/mm³. Two antiviral agents, ganciclovir (DHPG, Cytovene, Vitrasert) and foscarnet (Foscavir), offer effective treatment but not a cure for CMV retinitis. Because ganciclovir and foscarnet do not kill the virus but rather control its growth, they must be taken for life. Relapse rates associated with the two agents are similar. Discontinuation of the medication is associated with the relapse of retinitis within 1 month.

A common adverse reaction to ganciclovir is severe neutropenia, which limits the concomitant use of zidovudine (AZT, Retrovir). Intravitreal injections of ganciclovir have been effective for patients who cannot tolerate systemic ganciclovir because of severe neutropenia, infection at the venous access site, or the need to take zidovudine. Zidovudine may be given with foscarnet (Foscavir). Common adverse reactions to foscarnet are nephrotoxicity, including acute renal failure, and electrolyte imbalances, including hypocalcemia, hyperphosphatemia, and hypomagnesemia, which can be life-threatening. Other common adverse effects include seizures, GI disturbances, anemia, phlebitis at the infusion site, and low back pain. Possible bone marrow suppression (producing a decrease in WBC and platelet counts), oral candidiasis, and liver and renal impairments require close patient monitoring.

Other Infections

Oral acyclovir, famciclovir, or valacyclovir may be used to treat infections caused by herpes simplex or herpes zoster. Patients coinfected with HSV and HIV are more likely to transmit and infect others if not treated for herpes. Esophageal or oral candidiasis is treated topically with clotrimazole (Mycelex) oral troches or nystatin suspension. Chronic refractory candidiasis (thrush) or esophageal involvement is treated with ketoconazole (Nizoral) or fluconazole (Diflucan).

Antidiarrheal Therapy

Although many forms of diarrhea respond to treatment, it is not unusual for this condition to recur and become a chronic problem for the HIV patient. Therapy with octreotide acetate (Sandostatin), a synthetic analogue of somatostatin, has been shown to be effective in managing chronic severe diarrhea. High concentrations of somatostatin receptors have been found in the GI tract and in other tissues. Somatostatin inhibits many physiologic functions, including GI motility and intestinal secretion of water and electrolytes.

Chemotherapy

Kaposi's Sarcoma

Management of KS is usually difficult because of the variability of symptoms and the organ systems involved. KS is rarely life-threatening except when there is pulmonary or GI involvement. The treatment goals are to reduce symptoms by decreasing the size of the skin lesions, to reduce discomfort associated with edema and ulcerations, and to control symptoms associated with mucosal or visceral involvement. No one treatment has been shown to increase survival. Localized treatment includes surgical excision of the lesions or application of liquid nitrogen to local skin lesions, and injections of intraoral lesions with dilute vinblastine. Injection of intraoral lesions has been associated with local pain and skin irritation. Radiation therapy is effective as a palliative measure to relieve localized pain due to tumor mass (especially in the legs) and for KS lesions that are in sites such as the oral mucosa, conjunctiva, face, and soles of the feet.

Interferon is known for its antiviral and antitumor effects. Patients with cutaneous KS treated with **alpha-interferon** have experienced tumor regression and improved immune system function. Positive responses have been observed in 30% to 50% of patients, with the best responses seen in those with limited disease and no opportunistic infections. Alpha-interferon is administered by the IV, intramuscular, or subcutaneous route. Patients may self-administer interferon at home or receive interferon in an outpatient setting.

Lymphoma

Successful treatment of AIDS-related lymphomas has been limited because of the rapid progression of these malignancies. Combination chemotherapy and radiation therapy regimens may produce an initial response, but it is usually short-lived. Because standard regimens for non-AIDS lymphomas have been ineffective, many clinicians suggest that AIDS-related lymphomas should be studied as a separate group in clinical trials.

Antidepressant Therapy

Treatment for depression in people with HIV infection involves psychotherapy integrated with pharmacotherapy. If depressive symptoms are severe and of sufficient duration, treatment with antidepressants may be initiated. Antidepressants such as imipramine (Tofranil), desipramine (Norpramin), and fluoxetine (Prozac) may be used, because these medications also alleviate the fatigue and lethargy associated with depression. A psychostimulant such as methylphenidate (Ritalin) may be used in low doses in patients with neuropsychiatric impairment. Electroconvulsive therapy may be an option for patients with severe depression who have not responded to pharmacologic interventions.

Nutrition Therapy

Malnutrition increases the risk for infection and may increase the incidence of opportunistic infections. Nutrition therapy should be integrated into the overall management plan and should be tailored to meet the nutritional needs of the patient, whether by oral diet, enteral tube feedings, or parenteral nutritional support, if needed. As with all patients, a healthy diet is essential for the patient with HIV infection.

For all patients with AIDS who experience unexplained weight loss, calorie counts should be obtained to evaluate nutritional status and initiate appropriate therapy. The goal is to maintain the ideal weight and, when necessary, to increase weight.

Appetite stimulants have been successfully used in patients with AIDS-related anorexia. Megestrol acetate (Megace), a synthetic oral progesterone preparation used to treat breast cancer, promotes significant weight gain and inhibits cytokine IL-1 synthesis. In patients with HIV infection, it increases body weight primarily by increasing body fat stores. Dronabinol (Marinol), which is a synthetic tetrahydrocannabinol (THC), the active ingredient in marijuana, has been used to relieve nausea and vomiting associated with cancer chemotherapy.

Oral supplements may be used to supplement diets that are deficient in calories and protein. Ideally, oral supplements should be lactose-free as many people with HIV infection are lactose intolerant. Parenteral nutrition is the final option because of its prohibitive cost and associated risks, including risk of infections.

Complementary and Alternative Modalities

Traditional Western or allopathic medicine focuses on the treatment of disease. These treatments or interventions are taught in medical and nursing schools and are used by health care providers in the care of patients. Complementary and alternative medicine (CAM) is often viewed as consisting of unconventional and unorthodox treatments or interventions. These modalities and therapies stress the need to treat the whole person, recognizing the interaction of the body, mind, and spirit. People with HIV infection report substantial use of CAM for symptom management. The use of CAM in HIV infection and AIDS often results because of disillusionment with standard medical treatment, which to date has provided no cure. Combined with traditional therapies, CAM may improve the patient's overall well-being. However, there can be adverse drug–drug interactions between certain CAM therapies (e.g., St. John's wort) and some ARV medications (DHHS Panel, 2008).

CAM can be divided into four categories:

- Spiritual or psychological therapies may include humor, hypnosis, faith healing, guided imagery, and positive affirmations.
- Nutritional therapies may include vegetarian or macrobiotic diets, vitamin C or beta-carotene supplements. Chinese herbs are also used, in addition to compound Q (a Chinese cucumber extract) and *Momordica charantia* (bitter melon).
- Drug and biologic therapies include medications and other substances not approved by the FDA. Examples are *N*-acetylcysteine, pentoxifylline (Trental), and 1-chloro-2, 4-dinitrobenzene.

- Treatment with physical forces and devices may include acupuncture, acupressure, massage therapy, reflexology, therapeutic touch, and yoga.

Although there is insufficient research on the effects of CAM, a growing body of literature reports benefits for modalities involving nutrition, exercise, psychosocial treatment, and Chinese medicine.

Many patients who use these therapies do not report use of CAM to their health care providers. To obtain a complete health history, the nurse should ask about the patient's use of alternative therapies, including all over-the-counter, nutritional supplements and vitamins. Patients may need to be encouraged to report their use of CAM to their primary health care provider. Problems may arise, for example, when patients are using CAM while participating in clinical drug trials; alternative therapies can have significant adverse side effects, making it difficult to assess the effects of the medications in the clinical trial. The nurse needs to become familiar with the potential adverse side effects of these therapies. The nurse who suspects that CAM is causing a side effect needs to discuss this with the patient, the alternative therapy provider, and the primary health care provider. It is important for the nurse to view CAM with an open mind and to try to understand the importance of this treatment to the patient. This approach will improve communication with the patient and reduce conflict.

NURSING PROCESS

The Patient with AIDS

The nursing care of patients with AIDS is challenging because of the potential for any organ system to be the target of infections or cancer. In addition, this disease is complicated by many emotional, social, and ethical issues.

Assessment

Nursing assessment includes identification of potential risk factors, including a history of risky sexual practices or IV/injection drug use. The nurse assesses the patient's physical and psychological status and should explore all factors affecting immune system and functioning.

Nutritional Status

The nurse assesses nutritional status by obtaining a dietary history and identifying factors that may interfere with oral intake, such as anorexia, nausea, vomiting, oral pain, or difficulty swallowing. In addition, the nurse evaluates the patient's ability to purchase and prepare food. Weight history (i.e., changes over time); anthropometric measurements; and blood urea nitrogen (BUN), serum protein, albumin, and transferrin levels provide objective measurements of nutritional status.

Transferrin, which is synthesized in the liver, is a transport protein that regulates iron absorption by transporting it from the intestines to the bloodstream; therefore, it may be monitored to evaluate iron saturation of the blood. Low levels of transferrin impair hemoglobin production, resulting in anemia. Transferrin levels also decrease with liver disease and poor protein intake, thus this lab test may be ordered to assess liver function and nutritional status. High levels of transferrin are associated with immune function and the ability to deal with infection. Normal transferrin levels for adults are 250 to 425 mg/dL or 2.5 to 4.2 g/L. Decreased transferrin levels are seen in microcytic (small red blood cells) anemia, protein calorie malnutrition, chronic infection, acute liver disease and nephrotic disease (protein loss in urine) (Fischbach & Dunning, 2009).

Skin Integrity

The nurse inspects the skin and mucous membranes daily for evidence of breakdown, ulceration, or infection. Monitoring the oral cavity for redness, ulcerations, and the presence of creamy-white adherent patches detects candidiasis. Assessment of the perianal area for excoriation and infection in patients with profuse diarrhea is important. Cultures of wounds may be indicated and performed by the nurse to identify infectious organisms, especially methicillin-resistant *Staphylococcus aureus* (MRSA).

Respiratory Status

The nurse assesses respiratory status by monitoring the patient for cough, sputum production (i.e., amount and color), shortness of breath, orthopnea, tachypnea, and chest pain. Auscultation detects the quality of breath sounds. Other measures of pulmonary function include chest X-ray results, arterial blood gas values, pulse oximetry, and pulmonary function tests.

Neurologic Status

The nurse determines neurologic status by assessing level of consciousness; orientation to person, place, and time; and memory lapses. Assessment of mental status as early as possible during initial care provides a baseline. The nurse assesses the patient for sensory deficits (visual changes, headache, or numbness and tingling in the extremities), motor involvement (altered gait, paresis [slight or partial paralysis], or paralysis), and seizure activity.

Fluid and Electrolyte Balance

Fluid and electrolyte status is determined by examining the skin and mucous membranes for turgor and dryness. Dehydration may be indicated by increased thirst, decreased urine output, postural hypotension, weak and rapid pulse, and urine specific gravity of 1.025 or more. Electrolyte imbalances, such as decreased serum sodium, potassium, calcium, magnesium, and chloride, typically result from profuse diarrhea. The nurse assesses the patient for signs and symptoms of electrolyte deficits, including decreased mental status, muscle twitching, muscle cramps, irregular pulse, nausea, vomiting, and shallow respirations.

Knowledge Level

The nurse evaluates the patient's level of knowledge about the disease and the modes of disease transmission. In addition, the nurse assesses the level of knowledge of family and friends. The patient's psychological reaction to the diagnosis of HIV infection or AIDS is important to explore. Reactions vary among patients and may include denial, anger, fear, shame, withdrawal from social interactions, and depression. The nurse should identify the patient's resources for support.

Diagnosis

The list of potential nursing diagnoses is extensive because of the complex nature of this disease. However, based on assessment data, major nursing diagnoses for the patient may include the following:

- Impaired skin integrity related to cutaneous manifestations of HIV infection, excoriation, and diarrhea
- Diarrhea related to enteric pathogens, HIV infection, or ARV medications
- Risk for infection related to immunodeficiency
- Activity intolerance related to weakness, fatigue, malnutrition, impaired fluid and electrolyte balance, and hypoxia associated with pulmonary infections
- Disturbed thought processes related to shortened attention span, impaired memory, confusion, and disorientation associated with HIV cognitive decline
- Ineffective airway clearance related to PCP, increased bronchial secretions, and decreased ability to cough related to weakness and fatigue
- Pain related to impaired perianal skin integrity secondary to diarrhea, KS, and peripheral neuropathy
- Imbalanced nutrition, less than body requirements, related to decreased oral intake
- Social isolation related to stigma of the disease, withdrawal of support systems, isolation procedures, and fear of infecting others
- Anticipatory grieving related to changes in lifestyle and roles and unfavorable prognosis
- Deficient knowledge related to HIV infection, means of preventing HIV transmission, and self-care

Based on the assessment data, possible complications may include the following:

- Opportunistic infections
- Impaired breathing or respiratory failure

(continued on page 1024)

- Wasting syndrome and fluid and electrolyte imbalance
- Adverse reaction to medications

Planning

Goals for the patient may include achievement and maintenance of skin integrity, resumption of usual bowel patterns, absence of infection, improved activity tolerance, improved thought processes, improved airway clearance, increased comfort, improved nutritional status, increased socialization, expression of grief, increased knowledge regarding disease prevention and self-care, and absence of complications.

Nursing Interventions

Promoting Skin Integrity

The nurse routinely assesses the skin and oral mucosa for changes in appearance, location and size of lesions, and evidence of infection and breakdown. The nurse assists immobile patients to change position every 1 to 2 hours. Devices such as alternating-pressure mattresses and low-air-loss beds are used to prevent skin breakdown. Patients should avoid scratching; use nonabrasive, nondrying soaps; and apply nonperfumed skin moisturizers to dry skin surfaces. Regular oral care is also encouraged.

The nurse applies medicated lotions, ointments, and dressings to affected skin surfaces as prescribed. Adhesive tape is avoided. Protect patient's skin from friction and rubbing by keeping bed linens free of wrinkles and avoiding tight or restrictive clothing. The nurse advises patients with foot lesions to wear cotton socks and shoes that do not cause the feet to perspire. Antipruritic, antibiotic, and analgesic agents are administered as prescribed.

The nurse assesses the perianal region frequently for impairment of skin integrity and infection. The patient should keep the area as clean as possible. The perianal area should be cleaned after each bowel movement with nonabrasive soap and water to prevent further excoriation and breakdown of the skin. If the area is very painful, soft cloths or cotton sponges may be less irritating than washcloths. In addition, sitz baths or gentle irrigation may facilitate cleaning and promote comfort. It is important to dry the area thoroughly after cleaning. Topical lotions or ointments may be prescribed to promote healing. If infection is suspected, wounds should be cultured to initiate the appropriate antimicrobial treatment. The nurse assists debilitated patients in maintaining hygienic practices.

Promoting Usual Bowel Patterns

The nurse assesses bowel patterns for diarrhea. The nurse monitors the frequency and consistency of stools and the patient's reports of abdominal pain or cramping associated with bowel movements. Factors that exacerbate frequent diarrhea should be avoided. The nurse measures the quantity and volume of liquid stools to document fluid volume losses and obtains stool cultures to identify pathogenic organisms.

The nurse counsels the patient about ways to decrease diarrhea. Recommendations may restrict oral intake to rest the bowel during periods of acute inflammation associated with severe enteric infections. As the patient's dietary intake is increased, the patient avoids foods that act as bowel irritants, such as raw fruits and vegetables, popcorn, carbonated beverages, and spicy foods. Small, frequent meals help to prevent abdominal distention. The nurse administers prescribed medications, such as anticholinergics, antispasmodics, or opioids, which decrease diarrhea by decreasing intestinal spasms and motility. Administering antidiarrheal agents on a regular schedule may be more beneficial than administering them on an as-needed basis. Antibiotics and antifungal agents may also be prescribed to combat pathogens identified by stool cultures. The nurse also assesses the self-care strategies being used by the patient to control diarrhea.

Preventing Infection

The nurse instructs the patient and caregivers to monitor for signs and symptoms of infection: fever; chills; night sweats; cough with or without sputum production; shortness of breath; difficulty breathing; oral pain or difficulty swallowing; creamy-white patches in the oral cavity; unexplained weight loss; swollen lymph nodes; nausea; vomiting; persistent diarrhea; frequency, urgency, or pain on urination; headache; visual changes or memory lapses; redness, swelling, or drainage from skin wounds; and vesicular lesions on the face, lips, or perianal area. The nurse monitors laboratory test results that indicate infection, such as the WBC count and differential. Culture specimens of wound drainage, skin lesions, urine, stool, sputum, mouth, and blood are obtained to identify pathogenic organisms and the most appropriate antimicrobial therapy. The nurse instructs the patient to avoid others with active infections such as upper respiratory infections.

Improving Activity Tolerance

The nurse assesses activity tolerance by monitoring the patient's ability to ambulate and perform activities of daily living. Patients may be unable to maintain their usual levels of activity because of weakness, fatigue, shortness of breath, dizziness, and neurologic involvement. Assistance in planning daily routines that maintain a balance between activity and rest may be necessary. In addition, patients benefit from instructions about energy conservation techniques, such as sitting while washing or while preparing meals. Personal items that are frequently used should be kept within the patient's reach. Measures such as relaxation and guided imagery may be beneficial because they decrease anxiety, which contributes to weakness and fatigue.

Collaboration with other members of the health care team may uncover other factors associated with increasing

fatigue and strategies to address them. For example, if fatigue is related to anemia, administering epoetin alfa (Epogen) as prescribed may relieve fatigue and increase activity tolerance.

Maintaining Thought Processes

The nurse assesses the patient for alterations in mental status that may be related to neurologic involvement, metabolic abnormalities, infection, side effects of treatment, and coping mechanisms. Manifestations of neurologic impairment may be difficult to distinguish from psychological reactions to HIV infection, such as anger and depression.

If the patient experiences altered mental or cognitive status, the nurse instructs family members to speak to the patient in simple, clear language and give the patient sufficient time to respond to questions. Family members orient the patient to the daily routine by talking about what is taking place during daily activities. They are encouraged to provide the patient with a regular daily schedule for medication administration, grooming, meal times, bedtimes, and awakening times. Posting the schedule in a prominent area (e.g., on the refrigerator), providing nightlights for the bedroom and bathroom, and planning safe leisure activities allow the patient to maintain a regular routine in a safe manner. The nurse encourages activities that the patient previously enjoyed. These should be easy to accomplish and fairly short in duration. Around-the-clock supervision may be necessary, and strategies can be implemented to prevent the patient from engaging in potentially dangerous activities, such as driving or using the stove. The nurse uses strategies for improving or maintaining functional abilities and for providing a safe environment for patients with HIV cognitive decline.

Improving Airway Clearance

At least daily, the nurse assesses respiratory status, including rate, rhythm, use of accessory muscles, and breath sounds; mental status; and skin color. Any cough and the quantity and characteristics of sputum is documented. The nurse obtains sputum specimens for infectious organism analysis as indicated. Pulmonary therapy (coughing, deep breathing, postural drainage, percussion, and vibration) as often as every 2 hours may be required to prevent stasis of secretions and promote airway clearance. Because of weakness and fatigue, many patients require assistance in attaining a position (such as a semi-Fowler's position) that facilitates breathing and airway clearance. The nurse evaluates fluid volume status so that adequate hydration can be maintained. Daily intake is 3 L of fluid unless contraindicated because of renal or cardiac disease. Humidified oxygen may be prescribed, and nasopharyngeal or tracheal suctioning, intubation, and mechanical ventilation may be necessary to maintain adequate ventilation.

Relieving Pain and Discomfort

The nurse assesses the patient for the quality and severity of pain associated with impaired perianal skin integrity, the

lesions of KS, and peripheral neuropathy. In addition, the nurse explores the effects of pain on elimination, nutrition, sleep, affect, and communication, along with exacerbating and relieving factors. Cleaning the perianal area, as previously described, can promote comfort. Topical anesthetics or ointments may be prescribed. The nurse increases patient comfort while sitting with the use of soft cushions or foam pads. If necessary, systemic analgesic agents may also be prescribed. Pain from KS is frequently described as a sharp, throbbing pressure and heaviness if lymphedema is present. Pain management may include use of NSAIDs and opioids, plus nonpharmacologic approaches such as relaxation techniques. When NSAIDs are administered to patients who are receiving zidovudine, the nurse is aware that hepatic and hematologic status are evaluated.

The patient with pain related to peripheral neuropathy frequently describes it as burning, numbness, and "pins and needles." Pain management approaches may include opioids, tricyclic antidepressants, and elastic compression stockings to equalize pressure. Tricyclic antidepressants potentiate the actions of opioids and can be used to relieve pain without increasing the dose of the opioid.

Improving Nutritional Status

The nurse assesses nutritional status by monitoring weight, dietary intake and output, serum albumin, BUN, protein, and transferrin levels. The patient is assessed for factors that interfere with oral intake, such as anorexia, candidal infection, nausea, pain, weakness, fatigue, and lactose intolerance. Based on the results of assessment, the nurse implements specific measures to facilitate oral intake. A dietitian helps to determine the patient's nutritional requirements.

Control of nausea and vomiting with antiemetic medications administered on a regular basis may increase the patient's dietary intake. Inadequate food intake resulting from pain caused by oral lesions or a sore throat may be managed by administering prescribed opioids and viscous lidocaine. Additionally, the nurse encourages the patient to eat foods that are easy to swallow and to avoid rough, spicy, or sticky food items and foods that are excessively hot or cold. The patient should perform oral hygiene before and after meals. If fatigue and weakness interfere with intake, the nurse encourages the patient to rest before meals. If the patient is hospitalized, meals should be scheduled so that they do not occur immediately after painful or unpleasant procedures. The nurse advises the patient with diarrhea and abdominal cramping to avoid foods that stimulate intestinal motility and abdominal distention, such as fiber-rich foods or lactose, if the patient is intolerant to lactose. The nurse instructs the patient about ways to enhance the nutritional value of meals. Supplements such as puddings, powders, milkshakes, and Advera (a nutritional product specifically designed for people with HIV infection or AIDS) may also be useful. Patients who cannot maintain their nutritional status through oral intake may require enteral feedings or parenteral nutrition.

(continued on page 1026)

Decreasing the Sense of Isolation

People with AIDS are at risk for double stigmatization. Judgments about disease acquisition and lifestyle choices isolate many HIV positive patients. Many people with AIDS are young adults at a developmental stage that is usually associated with establishing intimate relationships, personal goals, and career goals, as well as having and raising children. Their focus changes as they are faced with a disease that threatens their life expectancy with no cure. In addition, they may be forced to reveal hidden lifestyles or behaviors to family, friends, coworkers, and health care providers. As a result, people with HIV infection may be overwhelmed with emotions such as anxiety, guilt, shame, and fear. They also may be faced with multiple losses, such as loss of financial security, normal roles and functions, self-esteem, privacy, ability to control bodily functions, ability to interact meaningfully with the environment, and sexual functioning, as well as rejection by sexual partners, family, and friends. Some patients may harbor feelings of guilt because of their lifestyle or because they may have infected others in current or previous relationships. Other patients may feel anger toward sexual partners who transmitted the virus to them. Infection control measures used in the hospital or at home may further contribute to the patient's emotional isolation. Any or all of these stressors may cause the patient with AIDS to withdraw both physically and emotionally from social contact.

Nurses are in a key position to provide an atmosphere of acceptance and understanding for people with AIDS and their families and partners. The nurse assesses the patient's usual level of social interaction as early as possible to provide a baseline for monitoring changes in behaviors that suggest social isolation (e.g., decreased interaction with staff or family, hostility, noncompliance). Patients are encouraged to express feelings of isolation and loneliness, with the assurance that these feelings are not unique or abnormal.

Providing information about how to protect themselves and others may help patients avoid social isolation. The nurse reassures patients, family, and friends that AIDS is not spread through casual contact. Patient care conferences that address the psychosocial issues associated with AIDS may help sensitize the health care team to patients' needs.

Coping With Grief

The nurse helps the patient verbalize feelings and explore and identify resources for support and mechanisms for coping, especially when the patient is grieving anticipated losses. The patient is encouraged to maintain contact with family, friends, and coworkers, and to use local or national AIDS support groups and hotlines. If possible, losses are identified and addressed. The nurse encourages the patient to continue usual activities whenever possible. Consultations with mental health counselors are useful for many patients.

Monitoring and Managing Potential Complications

OPPORTUNISTIC INFECTIONS. Immunosuppressed patients are at risk for opportunistic infections. Therefore, anti-infective agents may be prescribed and laboratory tests obtained to monitor their effect. The nurse should report signs and symptoms of opportunistic infections, including fever, malaise, difficulty breathing, nausea or vomiting, diarrhea, difficulty swallowing, and any occurrences of swelling or discharge.

RESPIRATORY FAILURE. Impaired breathing is a major complication that increases the patient's discomfort and anxiety and may lead to respiratory and cardiac failure. The nurse monitors respiratory rate and pattern and auscultates the lungs for abnormal breath sounds. The patient should report shortness of breath and increasing difficulty in carrying out usual activities. The nurse monitors pulse rate and rhythm, blood pressure, and oxygen saturation. Suctioning, if indicated, and oxygen therapy ensure an adequate airway and prevent hypoxia. Mechanical ventilation may be necessary for the patient who cannot maintain adequate ventilation because of pulmonary infection, fluid and electrolyte imbalance, or respiratory muscle weakness. Arterial blood gas values will be obtained to guide ventilator management. Instruct intubated patients in methods to allow communication with the nurse and others. The patient receiving mechanical ventilation should be assessed regarding coping with the stress associated with intubation and ventilator assistance. The possible need for mechanical ventilation in the future should be discussed early in the course of the disease, when the patient is able to make known his or her preferences about treatment. The use of mechanical ventilation should be consistent with the patient's decisions about end-of-life treatment.

CACHEXIA AND WASTING. Wasting syndrome, and fluid and electrolyte disturbances, including dehydration, are common complications of HIV infection and AIDS. The nurse evaluates the patient's nutritional and electrolyte status by monitoring weight gains or losses, skin turgor, ferritin levels, hemoglobin, hematocrit, and electrolyte levels. Fluid and electrolyte status is monitored on an ongoing basis; fluid intake and output and urine specific gravity may be monitored daily if the patient is hospitalized with complications. The nurse assesses the skin for dryness and adequate turgor. Vital signs are monitored for decreased systolic blood pressure or increased pulse rate on sitting or standing. The nurse documents and reports signs and symptoms of electrolyte disturbances, such as muscle cramping, weakness, irregular pulse, decreased mental status, nausea, and vomiting to the provider. The nurse also monitors serum electrolyte values and reports abnormalities.

The nurse helps the patient select foods that will replenish electrolytes, such as oranges and bananas (potassium) and cheese and soups (sodium). Fluid intake is 3 L or more per day, unless contraindicated, to replace fluid lost with

diarrhea, and measures to control diarrhea are initiated. If fluid and electrolyte imbalances persist, the nurse administers IV fluids and electrolytes as prescribed. The nurse also monitors effects of parenteral therapy.

SIDE EFFECTS OF MEDICATIONS. Adverse reactions are of concern in patients who receive many medications to treat HIV infection or its complications. Many medications can cause severe toxic effects. The nurse provides information about the purpose of the medications, their correct administration, side effects, and strategies to manage or prevent side effects. Patients and their caregivers need to know which signs and symptoms of side effects should be reported immediately to their primary health care provider (see Table 37-2, p. 1017).

In addition to medications used to treat HIV infection, other medications that may be required include opioids, tricyclic antidepressants, and NSAIDs for pain relief; medications for treatment of opportunistic infections; antihistamines (diphenhydramine) for relief of pruritus; acetaminophen or aspirin for management of fever; and antiemetic agents for control of nausea and vomiting. Concurrent use of these medications can cause many drug interactions, resulting in hepatic and hematologic abnormalities. Therefore, careful monitoring of laboratory test results is essential.

During each contact with the patient, it is important for the nurse to ask not only about side effects but also about how well the patient is adhering to the medication regimen.

Teaching Patients Self-Care

The nurse instructs patients, families, and friends about the routes of transmission of HIV. As discussed earlier, the nurse discusses precautions the patient can use to avoid transmitting HIV sexually or through sharing of blood. Patients and their families or caregivers must receive instructions about how to prevent disease transmission, including hand washing techniques and methods for safely handling and disposing of items soiled with body fluids. Clear guidelines about avoiding and controlling infection, regular health care appointments, symptom management, nutrition, rest, and exercise are necessary. Emphasize the importance of personal and environmental hygiene. The nurse teaches caregivers the guidelines (Standard Precautions) described in Box 37-3. Patients and caregivers should clean kitchen and bathroom surfaces regularly with disinfectants to prevent growth of fungi and bacteria. Patients with pets should have another person clean area soiled by animals, such as birdcages and litter boxes. If this is not possible, patients should use gloves and should wash their hands after they clean the area. Patients should avoid exposure to others who are sick or who have recently received live vaccines. The nurse emphasizes the importance of avoiding smoking, excessive alcohol, and over-the-counter and street drugs. Instruct patients who are HIV positive or who inject drugs not to donate blood. IV/injection drug users who are unwilling to stop using should avoid sharing drug equipment with others.

The nurse teaches caregivers how to administer medications, including IV preparations, in the home. The medication regimens used for patients with HIV infection and AIDS are often complex and expensive. If the patient requires enteral or parenteral nutrition, provide instruction to the patient and family about how to administer nutritional therapies at home. Home care nurses provide ongoing teaching and support for the patient and family.

Providing Continuing Care

Many people with AIDS remain in their community and continue their usual daily activities, whereas others can no longer work or maintain their independence. Families or caregivers may need assistance in providing supportive care. Many community-based organizations provide a variety of services for people living with HIV infection and AIDS; nurses can help identify these services.

Nurses may refer patients to community programs that offer a range of services for patients, friends, and families, including help with housekeeping, hygiene, and meals; transportation and shopping; individual and group therapy; support for caregivers; telephone networks for the homebound; and legal and financial assistance. These services are typically provided by both professionals and nonprofessional volunteers. A social worker can identify sources of financial support, if needed.

Home care and hospice nurses are called on to provide physical and emotional support to patients and families as patients with AIDS enter the terminal stages of disease. This support takes on special meaning when people with AIDS lose friends and when family members fear the disease or feel anger concerning the patient's lifestyle. The nurse encourages the patient and family to discuss end-of-life decisions and to ensure that care is consistent with those decisions, all comfort measures are employed, and the patient is treated with dignity at all times.

Evaluation

Expected patient outcomes may include:

1. Maintains skin integrity
2. Resumes usual bowel habits
3. Experiences no infections
4. Maintains adequate level of activity tolerance
5. Maintains usual level of thought processes
6. Maintains effective airway clearance
7. Experiences increased sense of comfort and less pain
8. Maintains adequate nutritional status
9. Experiences decreased sense of social isolation
10. Progresses through grieving process
11. Reports increased understanding of AIDS and participates in self-care activities
12. Remains free of complications

A plan of nursing care for a patient with AIDS is available online at http://thePoint.lww.com/Pellico1e.

EMOTIONAL AND ETHICAL CONCERNS

Nurses in all settings provide care for patients with HIV infection. In doing so, they encounter not only the physical challenges of this epidemic but also emotional and ethical concerns. The concerns raised by health care professionals involve issues such as fear of infection, responsibility for giving care, values clarification, confidentiality, developmental stages of patients and caregivers, and poor prognostic outcomes.

Many patients with HIV infection have engaged in "stigmatized" behaviors. Because these behaviors challenge some traditional religious and moral values, nurses may feel reluctant to care for these patients. In addition, health care providers may still have fear and anxiety about disease transmission despite education concerning infection control and the low incidence of transmission to health care providers. Nurses are encouraged to examine their personal beliefs and to use the process of values clarification to approach controversial issues. The American Nurses Association's Code of Ethics for Nurses can also be used to help resolve ethical dilemmas that might affect the quality of care given to patients with HIV infection and AIDS (refer to Chapter 1).

Nurses are responsible for protecting the patient's right to privacy by safeguarding confidential information. Inadvertent disclosure of confidential patient information may result in personal, financial, and emotional hardships for the patient. The controversy surrounding confidentiality concerns the circumstances in which information may be disclosed to others. Many patients avoid necessary health care appointments due to confidentiality concerns. Health care team members need accurate patient information to conduct assessment, planning, implementation, and evaluation of patient care. Failure to disclose HIV status could compromise the quality of patient care. Sexual partners of HIV-infected patients should know about the potential for infection and the need to engage in safer sex practices, as well as the possible need for testing and health care. State health departments offer confidential partner notification services. In situations in which a patient cannot or will not inform others, duty to warn regulations varies by state. Nurses are advised to discuss concerns about confidentiality with nurse administrators and to consult professional nursing organizations such as the Association of Nurses in AIDS Care (ANAC) and legal experts in their state to identify the most appropriate course of action.

AIDS has had a high mortality rate, but advances in ARV and multidrug therapy have demonstrated promise in slowing or controlling disease progression. It is not known whether current treatment regimens will remain effective, because viral drug resistance has developed with many medications. However most experts agree that educated, adherent patients can expect to survive for decades. In spite of these advances, many young and middle-aged adults will experience serious illness and may die during the usual course of the disease process. Most nurses in the United States have never faced such an epidemic. Contributing to this stress is personal fears of contagion or disapproval of the patient's lifestyle and behaviors. Unlike cancer or other diseases, AIDS is associated with controversies challenging our legal and political systems as well as religious and personal beliefs. Nurses who feel stressed and overburdened may experience physical and mental distress in the form of fatigue, headache, changes in appetite and sleep patterns, helplessness, irritability, apathy, negativity, and anger.

Many strategies have been used by nurses to cope with the stress associated with caring for AIDS patients. Education and provision of up-to-date information help to alleviate apprehension and prepare nurses to deliver safe, high-quality patient care. Interdisciplinary meetings allow participants to support one another and provide comprehensive patient care. Staff support groups give nurses an opportunity to solve problems and explore values and feelings about caring for AIDS patients and their families; they also provide a forum for grieving. Other sources of support include nursing administrators, peers, and spiritual advisors.

Chapter Review

Critical Thinking Exercises

1. A 43-year-old man who has been injecting drugs for 20 years says that he is not going to stop his use of drugs but wants to reduce his risk for HIV infection. What would you teach him? What types of community agencies could provide resources to this patient?

2. During a code response in the intensive care unit (ICU), a nursing student was inadvertently stuck with a needle used on a homeless patient who has AIDS. The student states that he is not concerned about contracting any diseases as a result. As his clinical instructor or the nurse manager of the ICU, what actions should you take? What reporting and documentation are needed? What testing, treatment, and counseling are indicated for the student?

3. During a home visit to a family in which two adolescents are HIV positive, you are instructing the adolescents, their siblings, and their parents about strategies to protect the adolescents from other infections and to protect other family members from HIV transmission. What is the evidence for strategies that you plan to discuss with the adolescents and their family members? What is the strength of that evidence, and what criteria would you use to evaluate the strength of the evidence.

NCLEX–Style Review Questions

1. The patient with a CD4+ count of 100 cells/uL and not taking any antiretroviral medications is admitted to the hospital after a motor vehicle accident. In addition, the patient has a productive cough, fever, lymphadenopathy, and a history of night sweats. The patient's PPD test is negative. What is the nurse's best action?
   A. Use Standard Precautions alone because the patient does not have tuberculosis.
   B. Use Airborne Precautions alone because the patient has not started appropriate therapy for HIV.
   C. Use Standard Precautions and Airborne Precautions because the patient has tuberculosis.
   D. Use Standard and Airborne Precautions until the infectious disease providers verify the patient does not have tuberculosis, then continue using standard precautions.

2. The patient who just tested HIV positive has persistent lymphadenopathy. The patient asks, "When will I be capable of transmitting the virus to others?" What is the nurse's best response?
   A. At this stage, you can only transmit the virus through donation of blood or blood products.
   B. If your CD4+ T-cells drop below 200/uL, you would be considered infectious.
   C. You cannot transmit the virus as long as you take your prescribed drugs.
   D. The virus can be transmitted at all stages and categories of HIV infection.

3. Which finding in the patient with HIV disease who started HAART 3 months ago indicates that the treatment is effective?
   A. Increased CD4 cells
   B. Decreased CD4 cells
   C. Increased CD8 cells
   D. Decreased CD8 cells

4. The nurse suspects a patient has the early signs of an opportunistic infection with CMV. Which of the following is one of the early signs that may be present?
   A. Discolorations of the mucous membranes
   B. Cardiac arrythmias
   C. Hypotension
   D. Visual disturbances

5. Kaposi's sarcoma, once a common manifestation of AIDS before HAART was available, is seldom seen. A patient with AIDS wants to know what to expect. What is the nurse's best response?
   A. Thick, white exudate in the mouth
   B. A purple-red lesion on the body
   C. Weight loss
   D. An increase in respiratory secretions

Try these additional resources to enhance your learning and understanding of this chapter:
- thePoint online resource available at **http://thepoint.lww.com/Pellico1e**
- *Handbook for Focus on Adult Health: Medical-Surgical Nursing*
- *Study Guide for Focus on Adult Health: Medical-Surgical Nursing*

References and Selected Readings

References and selected readings associated with this chapter can be found on the website that accompanies the book. Visit http://thepoint.lww.com/Pellico1e to access the references and other additional resources associated with this chapter.

Nursing Management: Patients With Allergic Disorders

NICOLE C. GORA

After reading this chapter, you will be able to:

1. Describe the management of patients with allergic disorders.

2. Describe measures to prevent and manage anaphylaxis.

3. Discuss the different allergic disorders according to type.

Autoimmune reactions occur when self-antigens are recognized by the body's normal defense mechanisms as foreign. With the presence of these "foreign" antigens, B cells become hyperactive and increased amounts of immunoglobulin E (IgE) are produced, thus causing a hypersensitivity or allergic response. Hypersensitivity is an amplified or inappropriate response to an antigen (on second exposure), leading to inflammation and destruction of healthy tissue. The cause may result from genetic, hormonal, and environmental factors; many times, the etiology is unclear. The reaction time varies and can be within minutes to hours of exposure or may be delayed. Refer to Chapter 36 for details of types of allergic classifications. Symptoms will vary depending on the classification and may range from a local reaction to the life-threatening systemic response of anaphylaxis. It is important for nurses to recognize signs and symptoms of allergic reactions, understand the risk factors associated with reaction, and become familiar with treatment management.

There are two types of IgE-mediated allergic reactions: atopic and nonatopic disorders. Although the underlying immunologic reactions of the two types of disorders are the same, the predisposing factors and manifestations are different. The atopic disorders are characterized by a hereditary predisposition and production of a local reaction to IgE antibodies, which manifests in one or more of the following three atopic disorders: allergic rhinitis, asthma, and atopic dermatitis/eczema. The nonatopic disorders lack the genetic component and organ specificity of the atopic disorders (Porth & Matfin, 2009). Latex allergy (see later discussion) may be a type I or type IV **hypersensitivity** reaction, although true latex allergy is considered to be a type I hypersensitivity reaction. Contact dermatitis is considered to be a type IV hypersensitivity reaction.

ANAPHYLAXIS

Anaphylaxis is a clinical response to an immediate (type I hypersensitivity) immunologic reaction between a specific **antigen** and an **antibody**. The reaction results from a rapid release of IgE-mediated chemicals, which can induce a severe, life-threatening allergic reaction.

Pathophysiology

Anaphylaxis occurs when the body's immune system produces specific IgE antibodies toward a substance that is normally nontoxic (e.g., food such as a peanut) (Box 38-1). When the person first ingests the peanut, for example, there are no physical reactions manifested. Instead, antibodies are produced for that specific substance, and then those antibodies are stored in the immune system for future re-exposure. If the substance is ingested again, the body releases excess amounts of the protein **histamine**. Large amounts of histamine released into the body may then cause flushing, urticaria, angioedema, hypotension, and bronchoconstriction.

BOX 38-1

Focus on Pathophysiology

Anaphylaxis

The chain of events for anaphylaxis:

1. **Response to antigen.** IgM and IgG recognize and bind the antigen.

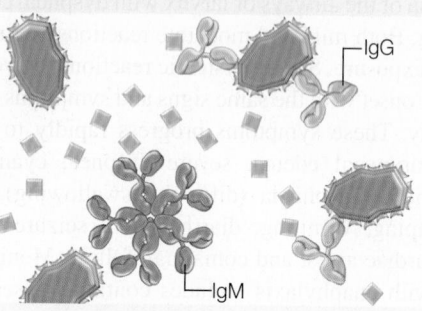

2. **Release of chemical mediators.** Activated IgE on basophils promotes release of mediators (histamine, serotonin, and leukotrienes).

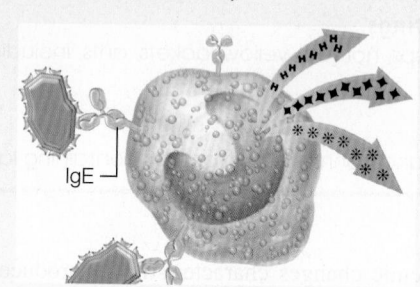

3. **Intensified response.** Mast cells release more histamine and eosinophil chemotactic factor of anaphylaxis (ECF-A), which create venule-weakening lesions.

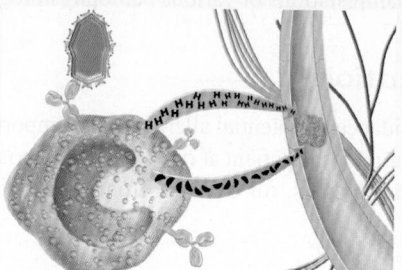

4. **Respiratory distress.** In the lungs, histamine causes endothelial cell destruction and fluid leakage into the alveoli.

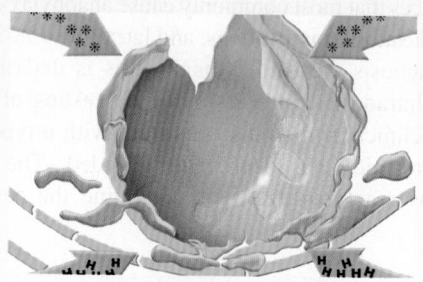

5. **Deterioration.** Meanwhile, mediators increase vascular permeability, causing fluid leak from the vessels.

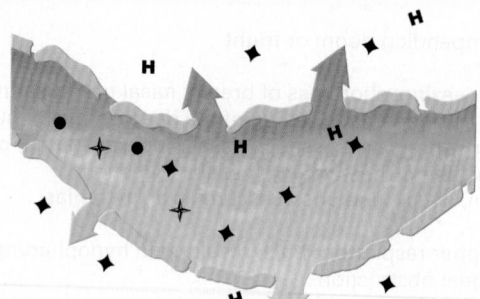

6. **Failure of compensatory mechanisms.** Endothelial cell damage causes basophils and mast cells to release heparin and mediator-neutralizing substances. However, anaphylaxis is now irreversible.

Key

Complement cascade	■	Serotonin	✦	Prostaglandins	✦
Histamine	H	Leukotrienes	✳	ECF-A	◖
				Bradykinin	●
				Heparin	▲

Common Causes of Anaphylaxis

Foods
Peanuts, tree nuts (e.g., walnuts, pecans, cashews, almonds), shellfish (e.g., shrimp, lobster, crab), fish, milk, eggs, soy, wheat

Medications
Antibiotics, especially penicillin and sulfa antibiotics, allopurinol, radiocontrast agents, anesthetic agents (lidocaine, procaine), vaccines, hormones (insulin, vasopressin, adrenocorticotropic hormone (ACTH), aspirin, nonsteroidal anti-inflammatory drugs (NSAIDs)).

Other Pharmaceutical/Biologic Agents
Animal serums (tetanus antitoxin, snake venom antitoxin, rabies antitoxin), antigens used in skin testing

Insect Stings
Bees, wasps, hornets, yellow jackets, ants, including fire ants

Latex
Medical and nonmedical products containing latex

These systemic changes characteristically produce clinical manifestations within seconds or minutes after antigen exposure. In severe cases, these symptoms may cause shock. If no medical intervention is sought, death may ensue (Porth & Matfin, 2009).

Substances that most commonly cause anaphylaxis include foods, medications, insect stings, and latex (Box 38-2).

The diagnosis of risk of anaphylaxis is determined by prick and intradermal skin testing. Skin testing of patients who have clinical symptoms consistent with a type I, IgE-mediated reaction has been recommended. The severity of previous reactions does not determine the severity of subsequent reactions, which could be the same, more, or less severe. The severity depends on the degree of **allergy** and the dose of **allergen** (Salzberg & Singer, 2007).

Clinical Manifestations and Assessment

Mild systemic reactions consist of peripheral tingling and a sensation of warmth, possibly accompanied by a sensation of fullness in the mouth and throat. Nasal congestion, periorbital swelling, pruritus, sneezing, and tearing of the eyes can also be expected.

Moderate systemic reactions may include flushing, warmth, anxiety, and itching in addition to any of the milder symptoms. More serious reactions include bronchospasm and edema of the airways or larynx with dyspnea, cough, and wheezing. Both mild and moderate reactions begin within 2 hours of exposure. Severe systemic reactions, however, have an abrupt onset with the same signs and symptoms described previously. These symptoms progress rapidly to bronchospasm, laryngeal edema, severe dyspnea, cyanosis, and hypotension. Dysphagia (difficulty swallowing), abdominal cramping, vomiting, diarrhea, and seizures can also occur. Cardiac arrest and coma may follow. Monitoring the patient with anaphylaxis includes continual assessment of the patient's respiratory rate and pattern, oxygen saturation, assessing for breathing difficulties or abnormal lung sounds, and monitoring for hemodynamic stability (pulse rate and rhythm, and blood pressure). Table 38-1 summarizes the clinical manifestations of various pathophysiologic changes.

Prevention

Strict avoidance of potential allergens is an important preventive measure for the patient at risk for anaphylaxis. Patients at risk for anaphylaxis, for example from insect stings, should

TABLE
38-1 Clinical Manifestations for Anaphylaxis

Change	Signs and Symptoms
Activation of IgE and subsequent release of chemical mediators	Feeling of impending doom or fright
Histamine release	Sweating; sneezing; shortness of breath; nasal pruritus, urticaria, and angioedema (swelling of the deep dermis or subcutaneous or submucosal tissues); nasal mucosal edema; profuse watery rhinorrhea; itching; nasal congestion
Increased vascular permeability, subsequent decrease in peripheral resistance and leakage of plasma fluids	Hypotension, shock, and possible cardiac arrhythmias
Increased capillary permeability and mast cell degranulation	Edema of upper respiratory tract, resulting in hypopharyngeal and laryngeal obstruction
Bronchiole smooth muscle contraction and increased mucus production	Hoarseness, stridor, wheezing, and accessory muscle use
Smooth muscle contraction of intestines and bladder	Severe stomach cramps, nausea, diarrhea; urinary urgency and incontinence

BOX 38-3

Nursing Research

Bridging the Gap to Evidence-Based Practice

Follow-Up Care After Anaphylaxis

Campbell, R.L., Luke, A., Weaver, A.L., St Sauver, J.L., Bergstralh, E.J., Li, J.T., Manivannan, V., & Decker, W.W. (2008). Prescriptions for self-injectable epinephrine and follow up referral in emergency department patients presenting with anaphylaxis. *Annals of Allergy Asthma & Immunology, 101*(6), 631–636.

Purpose

The purpose of the review was to evaluate how frequently patients dismissed from the emergency department after treatment for anaphylaxis received a prescription for self-injectable epinephrine or allergist referral.

Design

A retrospective medical record review identified patients with anaphylaxis in a community-based study from 1990 through 2000. Records of patients with *Hospital Adaptation of the International Classification of Diseases, Second Edition* or *International Classification of Diseases, Ninth Revision* codes representing anaphylaxis were reviewed, and a random sample of patients with associated diagnoses was also reviewed. Patients who met the criteria for diagnosis of anaphylaxis were included in the study.

Findings

Among 208 patients identified with anaphylaxis, 134 (64.4%) were seen in the emergency department and discharged home. On dismissal, 49 patients (36.6%; 95% confidence interval (CI), 28.4% to 44.7%) were prescribed self-injectable epinephrine, and 42 patients (31.3%; 95% CI, 23.5% to 39.2%) were referred to an allergist. Treatment with epinephrine in the emergency department (odds ratio, 3.6; 95% CI, 1.6 to 7.9; $P = .001$) and insect sting as the inciting allergen (odds ratio, 4.0; 95% CI, 1.6 to 10.5; $P = .004$) were significantly associated with receiving a prescription for self-injectable epinephrine. Patient age younger than 18 years was the only factor associated with referral to an allergist ($P = .007$).

Nursing Implications

Most patients dismissed after treatment for anaphylaxis did not receive a self-injectable epinephrine prescription or allergist referral. Emergency physicians may be missing an important opportunity to ensure prompt treatment of future anaphylactic reactions and specialized follow-up care.

---

avoid areas populated by insects and should use appropriate clothing, insect repellent, and caution to avoid further stings.

If avoidance of exposure to allergens is impossible, the patient should be instructed to carry and administer epinephrine to prevent an anaphylactic reaction in the event of exposure to the allergen. People who are sensitive to insect bites and stings, those who have experienced food or medication reactions, and those who have experienced idiopathic or exercise-induced anaphylactic reactions should always carry an emergency kit that contains epinephrine (Box 38-3). The EpiPen from Dey Pharmaceuticals (Napa, CA) is a commercially available first-aid device that delivers premeasured doses of 0.3 mg (EpiPen) or 0.15 mg (EpiPen Jr.) of epinephrine (Fig. 38-1). The autoinjection system requires no preparation, and the self-administration technique is uncomplicated. The patient must be given an opportunity to demonstrate the correct technique for use; an EpiPen training device can be used for teaching correct technique. Verbal and written information about the emergency kit, as well as strategies to avoid exposure to threatening allergens, must also be provided.

Screening for allergies before a medication is prescribed or first administered is an important preventive measure. A careful history of any sensitivity to suspected antigens must be obtained before administering any medication, particu-

larly in parenteral form, because this route is associated with the most severe anaphylaxis. Nurses caring for patients in any setting (hospital, home, outpatient diagnostic testing sites, long-term care facilities) must assess patients' risks for anaphylactic reactions. Patients are asked about previous exposure to contrast agents used for diagnostic tests and any allergic reactions, as well as reactions to any medications, foods, insect stings, and latex. People who are predisposed to anaphylaxis should wear some form of identification, such as a medical alert bracelet, which names allergies to medications, food, and other substances.

People who are allergic to insect venom may require venom immunotherapy, which is used as a control measure and not a cure. Immunotherapy administered after an insect sting is very effective in reducing the risk of anaphylaxis from future stings (Salzberg & Singer, 2007). Insulin-allergic

FIGURE 38-1 The EpiPen. Autoinjectors are commercially available first-aid devices that administer premeasured doses of epinephrine. An EpiPen training device is available for patients to practice correct self-injection technique. Courtesy of Dey L.P., Napa, CA.

patients with diabetes and those who are allergic to penicillin may require desensitization. Desensitization is based on controlled anaphylaxis, with a gradual release of mediators. Patients who undergo desensitization are cautioned that there should be no lapses in therapy, because this may lead to the reappearance of the allergic reaction when the use of the medication is resumed.

Medical Management

Management depends on the severity of the reaction. Initially, respiratory and cardiovascular functions are evaluated. If the patient is in cardiac arrest, cardiopulmonary resuscitation is instituted. Oxygen is provided in high concentrations during cardiopulmonary resuscitation or if the patient is cyanotic, dyspneic, or wheezing. Epinephrine, in a 1:1000 dilution, is administered subcutaneously in the upper extremity or thigh and may be followed by a continuous IV infusion. Most adverse events associated with administration of epinephrine (e.g., adrenaline) occur when the dose is excessive or it is given intravenously. Patients at risk for adverse effects include elderly patients and those with hypertension, arteriopathies (diseases of the arteries), or known ischemic heart disease (Anand & Routes, 2010).

Antihistamines and corticosteroids may also be administered to prevent recurrences of the reaction and to treat urticaria and angioedema. IV fluids (e.g., normal saline solution), volume expanders, and vasopressor agents are administered to maintain blood pressure and normal hemodynamic status. In patients with episodes of bronchospasm or a history of bronchial asthma or chronic obstructive pulmonary disease, aminophylline and corticosteroids may also be administered to improve airway patency and function. If hypotension is unresponsive to vasopressors, glucagon may be administered intravenously for its acute inotropic and chronotropic effects (Salzberg & Singer, 2007). Glucagon stimulates the enzyme adenylate cyclase and its activation results in the intracellular accumulation of the second messenger cyclic adenosine monophosphate (cAMP). Increased levels of cAMP improve the suppressive actions that epinephrine exerts on the biochemical events responsible for the anaphylactic response.

Patients who have experienced anaphylactic reactions and received epinephrine should be transported to the local emergency department for observation and monitoring because of the risk for a "rebound" reaction 4 to 10 hours after the initial allergic reaction. Patients with severe reactions are monitored closely for 12 to 14 hours in a facility that can provide emergency care, if needed. Because of the potential for recurrence, patients with even mild reactions must be informed about this risk (Anand & Routes, 2010).

Nursing Management

If a patient is experiencing an allergic response, the nurse's initial action is to assess the patient for signs and symptoms of anaphylaxis. The nurse assesses the airway, breathing pattern, and other vital signs. The patient is observed for signs of increasing edema and respiratory distress. Prompt notification of the provider and preparation for initiation of emergency measures (intubation, administration of emergency medications, insertion of IV lines, fluid administration, oxygen administration) are important to reduce the severity of the reaction and to restore cardiovascular function. The nurse documents the interventions used and the patient's vital signs and response to treatment.

The patient who has recovered from anaphylaxis needs an explanation of what occurred and instruction about avoiding future exposure to antigens and how to administer emergency medications to treat anaphylaxis. All patients who have experienced an anaphylactic reaction should receive a prescription for preloaded syringes of epinephrine. The nurse instructs the patient and family in their use and has the patient and family demonstrate correct administration of the medication (Box 38-4).

ALLERGIC RHINITIS

Allergic **rhinitis** (hay fever, seasonal allergic rhinitis) a type I hypersensitivity reaction, is the most common form of chronic respiratory allergic disease and is one of the most common reasons for visits to primary care practitioners. Symptoms are similar to those of viral rhinitis but are usually more persistent and demonstrate seasonal variation; rhinitis is considered to be the allergic form if the symptoms are caused by an allergen-specific IgE-mediated immunologic response. However, a sizable proportion of patients with rhinitis have mixed rhinitis, or coexisting allergic and nonallergic rhinitis (Brunton & Fromer, 2007).

The proportion of patients with the allergic form of rhinitis increases with age. It often occurs with other conditions, such as allergic conjunctivitis, sinusitis, and asthma. If symptoms are severe, allergic rhinitis may interfere with sleep, leisure, and school or work activities. If left untreated, many complications may result, such as allergic asthma, chronic nasal obstruction, chronic otitis media with hearing loss, anosmia (absence of the sense of smell), and, in children, orofacial dental deformities. Early diagnosis and adequate treatment are essential to reduce complications and relieve symptoms (Valovirta, Myrseth, & Palkonen, 2008).

Because allergic rhinitis is induced by airborne pollens or molds, it is characterized by the following seasonal occurrences:

- Early spring: Tree pollen (oak, elm, poplar), mold spores
- Early summer: Rose pollen (rose fever), grass pollen (timothy, red-top)
- Early fall: Weed pollen (ragweed), mold spores

Each year, attacks begin and end at about the same time. Airborne mold spores require warm, damp weather.

BOX 38-4
Patient Education

Self-Administration of Epinephrine

1. After removing the EpiPen autoinjector from its carrying tube, grasp the unit with the black tip (injecting end) pointing downward. Form fist around the unit with the black tip down and with your other hand, remove the gray safety release cap.

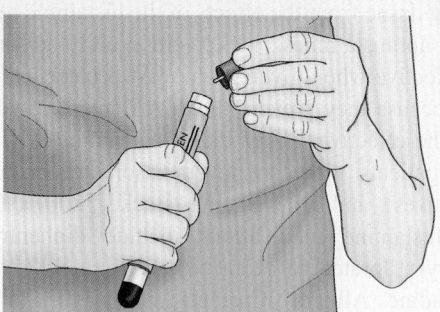

2. Hold black tip near outer thigh. Swing and **jab firmly** into outer thigh until a click is heard with the device perpendicular (90-degree angle) to the thigh.

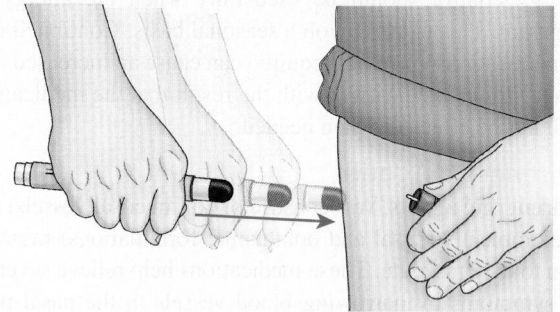

3. Hold firmly against the thigh for approximately 10 seconds. Remove the unit from the thigh and massage injection area for 10 seconds. Call 911 and seek immediate medical attention. Carefully place the used EpiPen, needle-end first, into the device storage tube without bending the needle. Screw on the storage tube completely, and take with you to the hospital emergency room.

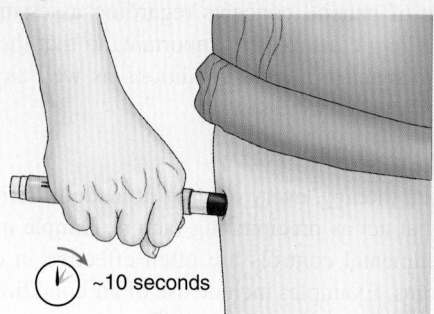

~10 seconds

Although there is no rigid seasonal pattern, these spores appear in early spring, are rampant during the summer, then taper off and disappear by the first frost.

Clinical Manifestations and Assessment

Typical signs and symptoms of allergic rhinitis include sneezing and nasal congestion; clear, watery nasal discharge; itchy eyes and nose; and lacrimation (Valovirta et al., 2008). Drainage of nasal mucus into the pharynx, otherwise known as *postnasal drip*, results in multiple attempts to clear the throat and results in a dry cough, hoarseness, or scratchy throat. Headache, pain over the paranasal sinuses, and epistaxis can accompany allergic rhinitis. The symptoms of this chronic condition depend on environmental exposure and intrinsic host responsiveness. Allergic rhinitis can affect quality of life by also producing fatigue, loss of sleep, and poor concentration (Becker, 2007).

Diagnosis of seasonal allergic rhinitis is based on history, physical examination, and diagnostic test results. On objective exam, a patient suffering with allergic rhinitis may appear fatigued (the patient may complain of not feeling well rested after a full nights sleep); present with allergic shiners (gray-black discoloration below lower eye lids that some refer to as "raccoon eyes"); puffy eyes; clear or cloudy fluid surrounding the tympanic membranes; nasal congestion or rhinorrhea; marked erythema of palpebral conjunctivae associated with increased tearing; enlarged nasal turbinates that are a pale-bluish color and boggy in texture; enlarged anterior cervical lymph nodes; cobblestoned appearance on posterior pharynx (due to chronic postnasal drip and nasal congestion); and sinus tenderness on palpation (Becker, 2007).

Diagnostic tests include nasal smears, peripheral blood counts, total serum IgE, epicutaneous and intradermal testing, radioallergosorbent test (RAST), food elimination and challenge, and nasal provocation tests. Results indicative of allergy as the cause of rhinitis include increased IgE and eosinophil levels and positive reactions on allergen testing. False-positive and false-negative responses to these tests,

particularly skin testing and provocation tests, may occur (Becker, 2007).

Medical Management

The goal of therapy is to provide relief from symptoms and encourage adherence to therapeutic regimens. Therapy may include one or all of the following interventions: avoidance therapy, pharmacotherapy, and immunotherapy. Verbal instructions must be reinforced by written information. Knowledge of general concepts regarding assessment and therapy in allergic diseases is important, so that the patient can learn to manage certain conditions as well as prevent severe reactions and illnesses.

Avoidance Therapy

In avoidance therapy, every attempt is made to remove the allergens that act as precipitating factors. Simple measures and environmental controls are often effective in decreasing symptoms. Examples include use of air conditioners, air cleaners, humidifiers, and dehumidifiers; keeping windows closed during periods of high pollen counts and windy conditions; using air conditioning as much as possible in the warmer months; sleeping with windows closed; removal of dust-catching furnishings (carpets, stuffed animals, feather bedding, window coverings); removal of pets from the home or bedroom; removal of cockroaches by professional extermination followed by regular cleaning of the infested area(s); use of pillow and mattress covers that are impermeable to dust mites; and maintaining a smoke-free environment (Perry, Wood, Matsui et al., 2006). Because multiple allergens are often implicated, multiple measures to avoid exposure to allergens are often necessary. High-efficiency particulate air (HEPA) purifiers and vacuum cleaner filters may also be used to reduce allergens in the environment. The patient is instructed to reduce exposure to people with upper respiratory tract infections. If an upper respiratory infection occurs, the patient is encouraged to take deep breaths and to cough frequently to ensure adequate gas exchange and prevent atelectasis. The patient is instructed to seek medical attention because the presence of allergy symptoms along with an upper respiratory tract infection may compromise adequate lung function.

Research has shown that multiple avoidance strategies tailored to a person's risk factors can reduce the severity of symptoms, the number of work or school days missed because of symptoms, and the number of unscheduled health care visits for treatment (Becker, 2007). In many cases, it is impossible to avoid exposure to all environmental allergens, so pharmacologic therapy or immunotherapy is needed.

Pharmacologic Therapy

Although allergen avoidance is clearly the safest and most effective means of treating symptoms associated with allergic rhinitis, some individuals may require pharmacologic therapy to further suppress the effects of histamine on the body. A few classes of medications are used to treat allergic rhinitis, the most common being **antihistamines**.

Antihistamines

Antihistamines, now classified as H_1-receptor antagonists (or H_1-blockers), are used in the management of mild allergic disorders. H_1-blockers bind selectively to H_1 receptors, preventing the actions of histamines at these sites. They do not prevent the release of histamine, but rather protect surrounding tissue from the effects of the histamine release.

Oral antihistamines, which are readily absorbed, are most effective when given at the first occurrence of symptoms, because they prevent the development of new symptoms. The effectiveness of these medications is limited to certain patients with hay fever, vasomotor rhinitis, **urticaria** (hives), and mild asthma (Becker, 2007). Examples of antihistamine medications include diphenhydramine (Benadryl), loratadine (Claritin), cetirizine (Zyrtec), and fexofenadine (Allegra). Currently, most antihistamines are available over-the-counter in local pharmacies. Refer to Table 38-2 for details.

Patients also need to understand that medications for allergy control should be used only when the allergy is apparent. This is usually on a seasonal basis. Continued use of medications when not required can cause an increased tolerance to the medication, with the result that the medication will not be effective when needed.

Adrenergic Agents

Adrenergic agents, vasoconstrictors of mucosal vessels, are used topically (nasal and ophthalmic formulations) in addition to the oral route. These medications help relieve severity of symptoms by narrowing blood vessels in the nasal passageways, but will not treat the underlying cause of nasal congestion, sinus pressure, etc. The most commonly used oral adrenergic agent is pseudoephedrine hydrochloride (Sudafed). Although considered safe if used as directed, some patients will complain of mild shakiness, heart palpitations, and anxiety shortly after ingestion. Pseudoephedrine is to be used cautiously or avoided in patients with underlying cardiac conditions, anxiety disorders, patients who are or plan on becoming pregnant, asthmatics, and those who use herbal supplements on a regular basis. Potential side effects include hypertension, arrythmias, palpitations, central nervous system stimulation, irritability, tremor, and tachyphylaxis (acceleration of hemodynamic status) (Brunton & Former, 2007).

The topical route (drops and sprays) causes fewer side effects than oral administration; however, the use of drops (e.g., tetrahydrozoline hydrochloride [Visine]) and sprays (e.g., oxymetazoline hydrochloride [Afrin]) should be limited to a few days to avoid rebound congestion. Adrenergic nasal decongestants are applied topically to the nasal mucosa for the relief of nasal congestion. They activate the alpha-adrenergic receptor sites on the smooth muscle of the nasal mucosal blood vessels, reducing local blood flow, fluid exudation, and mucosal edema. Topical ophthalmic drops

TABLE
38-2 Selected H₁-Antihistamines

H₁-Antihistamine	Contraindications	Major Side Effects	Nursing Implications and Patient Teaching
First-Generation H₁-Antihistamines (Sedating)			
Diphenhydramine (Benadryl)	Allergy to any antihistamines Third trimester of pregnancy Lactation Use cautiously with narrow-angle glaucoma, asthma, stenosing peptic ulcer, benign prostatic hypertrophy or bladder neck obstruction, pregnancy, elderly patients	Drowsiness, confusion, dizziness, dry mouth, nausea, vomiting, photosensitivity, urinary retention	Administer with food if gastrointestinal upset occurs. Caution patients to avoid alcohol, driving, or engaging in any hazardous activities until central nervous stimulation response to medication is stabilized. Suggest sucking on sugarless lozenges or ice chips for relief of dry mouth. Encourage use of sunscreen and hat while outdoors. Assess for urinary retention; monitor urinary output.
Chlorpheniramine (Chlor-Trimeton)	Allergy to any antihistamines Third trimester of pregnancy Lactation Use cautiously with narrow-angle glaucoma, asthma, stenosing peptic ulcer, BPH or bladder neck obstruction, pregnancy, elderly patients	Drowsiness, sedation, and dizziness, although less than other sedating agents; confusion, dry mouth, nausea, vomiting, urinary retention, epigastric distress, thickening of bronchial secretions	Caution patients to avoid alcohol, driving, or engaging in any hazardous activities until CNS response to medication is stabilized. Suggest sucking on sugarless lozenges or ice chips for relief of dry mouth. Recommend use of humidifier.
Hydroxyzine (Atarax)	Allergy to hydroxyzine or cetirizine (Zyrtec), pregnancy, lactation	Drowsiness, dry mouth, involuntary motor activity, including tremor and seizures	Caution patients to avoid alcohol, driving, or engaging in any hazardous activities until CNS response to medication is stabilized. Suggest sucking on sugarless lozenges or ice chips for relief of dry mouth. Instruct patients to report tremors.
Second-Generation H₁-Antihistamines (Nonsedating)			
Cetirizine (Zyrtec)	Allergy to any antihistamines Narrow-angle glaucoma Asthma Stenosing peptic ulcer BPH or bladder neck obstruction Lactation	Dry nasal mucosa, thickening of bronchial secretions	Can be taken without regard to meals. Instruct patients to use caution if driving or performing tasks that require alertness. Recommend use of humidifier.
Desloratadine (Clarinex)	Allergy to loratadine (Alavert, Claritin) Lactation Use cautiously with renal or hepatic impairment or with pregnancy	Somnolence, nervousness, dizziness, fatigue, dry mouth	Can be taken without regard to meals. Suggest sucking on sugarless lozenges or ice chips for relief of dry mouth. Recommend use of humidifier.
Loratadine (Alavert, Claritin)	Allergy to any antihistamines Narrow-angle glaucoma Asthma Stenosing peptic ulcer BPH or bladder neck obstruction	Headache, nervousness, dizziness, depression, edema, increased appetite	Instruct patients to take on empty stomach (1 hour before or 2 hour after meals or food). Instruct patients to avoid alcohol and to use caution if driving or performing tasks that require alertness. Suggest sucking on sugarless lozenges or ice chips for relief of dry mouth. Recommend use of humidifier.
Fexofenadine (Allegra)	Allergy to any antihistamines Pregnancy Lactation Use with caution with hepatic or renal impairment and in elderly patients	Fatigue, drowsiness, GI upset	Should not be administered within 15 minutes of ingestion of antacids. Instruct patients to use caution if driving or performing tasks that require alertness. Recommend use of humidifier.

are used for symptomatic relief of eye irritations caused by allergies. Common ocular complaints warranting use of ophthalmic drops include tearing, scleral and/or conjunctival erythemia, and itching.

Mast Cell Stabilizers

Mast cell stabilizers are used prophylactically (before exposure to allergens) to prevent the onset of symptoms and to treat symptoms once they occur. They are also used therapeutically in chronic allergic rhinitis. Intranasal cromolyn sodium (Nasal-Crom) is a spray that acts by stabilizing the mast cell membrane, thus reducing the release of histamine and other mediators of the allergic response (Anand & Routes, 2010). This spray is as effective as antihistamines but less effective than intranasal corticosteroids in the treatment of seasonal allergic rhinitis. The patient must be informed that the beneficial effects of the medication may take a week or so to manifest.

Corticosteroids

Intranasal **corticosteroids** are indicated in more severe cases of allergic and perennial rhinitis that cannot be controlled by more conventional medications such as decongestants, antihistamines, and intranasal cromolyn. Examples of these medications include beclomethasone (Beconase, Vancenase), budesonide (Rhinocort), dexamethasone (Decadron Phosphate Turbinaire), flunisolide (Nasalide), fluticasone (Cutivate, Flonase), and triamcinolone (Nasacort).

Because of their anti-inflammatory actions, these medications are equally effective in preventing or suppressing the major symptoms of allergic rhinitis.

Corticosteroids are administered by metered-spray devices. If the nasal passages are blocked, a topical decongestant may be used to clear the passages before the administration of the intranasal corticosteroid. Patients must be aware that full benefit may not be achieved for several days to 2 weeks. Adverse effects of intranasal corticosteroids are mild and include drying of the nasal mucosa potentially causing epistaxis (bloody nose), which is resolved with discontinuing the medication for a few days, and burning and itching sensations caused by the vehicle used to administer the medication (Brunton & Fromer, 2007). Recommended use of this medication is limited to 30 days.

Immunotherapy

Allergen desensitization (allergen immunotherapy, hyposensitization) is primarily used to treat IgE-mediated diseases by injections of allergen extracts. **Immunotherapy**, also referred to as allergy vaccine therapy, involves the administration of gradually increasing quantities of specific allergens to the patient until a dose is reached that is effective in reducing disease severity from natural exposure (Davis, 2009). This type of therapy provides an adjunct to symptomatic pharmacologic therapy and can be used when avoidance of allergens is not possible. Goals of immunotherapy include reducing the level of circulating IgE, increasing the level of blocking antibody IgG, and reducing mediator

---

BOX 38-5 **Immunotherapy: Indications and Contraindications**

Indications
- Allergic rhinitis, conjunctivitis, or allergic asthma
- History of a systemic reaction to *Hymenoptera* and specific IgE antibodies to *Hymenoptera* venom
- Desire to avoid the long-term use, potential adverse effects, or costs of medications
- Lack of control of symptoms by avoidance measures or use of medications

Contraindications
- Use of beta blocker or angiotensin-converting inhibitor therapy, which may mask early signs of anaphylaxis
- Presence of significant pulmonary or cardiac disease or organ failure
- Inability of the patient to recognize or report signs and symptoms of a systemic reaction
- Nonadherence of the patient to other therapeutic regimens and nonlikelihood that patient will adhere to immunization schedule (often weekly for an indefinite period)
- Inability to monitor the patient for at least 30 minutes after administration of immunotherapy
- Absence of equipment or adequate personnel to respond to allergic reaction if one occurs

---

cell sensitivity. Immunotherapy has been most effective for ragweed pollen; however, treatment for grass, tree pollen, cat dander, and house dust mite allergens has also been effective. Indications and contraindications for immunotherapy are presented in Box 38-5.

Unlike antiallergy medication, allergen immunotherapy has the potential to alter the allergic disease course after 3 to 5 years of therapy. Because it may prevent progression or development of asthma or multiple or additional allergies, it is also considered to be a potential preventive measure. The patient must understand what to expect and the importance of continuing therapy for several years before immunotherapy is accomplished. Specific treatment consists of injecting extracts of the allergens that cause symptoms in a particular patient. Injections begin with very small amounts and are gradually increased, usually at weekly intervals, until a maximum tolerated dose is attained. Maintenance booster injections are administered at 2- to 4-week intervals, frequently for a period of several years, before maximum benefit is achieved, although some patients will note early improvement in their symptoms. Long-term benefit seems to be related to the cumulative dose of vaccine given over time (Davis, 2009). Immunotherapy should not be initiated during pregnancy; for patients who have been receiving immunotherapy before pregnancy, the dosage should not be increased during pregnancy.

Although severe systemic reactions occur in fewer than 1% of patients receiving immunotherapy, the risk for systemic

and potentially fatal anaphylaxis exists. It tends to occur most frequently at the induction or "up-dosing" phase. Therefore, the patient must be monitored after administration of immunotherapy (Davis, 2009).

Because of the risk for anaphylaxis, injections should not be administered by a lay person or by the patient. The patient remains in the office or clinic for at least 30 minutes after the injection and is observed for possible systemic symptoms. If a large, local swelling develops at the injection site, the next dose should not be increased, because this may be a warning sign of a possible systemic reaction.

⚡ NURSING ALERT
Because the injection of an allergen may induce systemic reactions, such injections are administered only in a setting (e.g., physician's office, clinic) where epinephrine is immediately available.

Therapeutic failure is evident when a patient does not experience a decrease of symptoms within 12 to 24 months, fails to develop increased tolerance to known allergens, and cannot decrease the use of medications to reduce symptoms. Potential causes of treatment failure include misdiagnosis of allergies, inadequate doses of allergen, newly developed allergies, and inadequate environmental controls.

CONTACT DERMATITIS

Contact dermatitis, a type IV delayed hypersensitivity reaction, is an acute or chronic skin inflammation that results from direct skin contact with chemicals or allergens.

Types

There are four basic types: allergic, irritant, phototoxic, and photoallergic (Table 38-3). Eighty percent of cases are

TABLE 38-3 Types, Testing, and Treatment of Contact Dermatitis

Type	Etiology	Clinical Presentation	Diagnostic Testing	Treatment
Allergic	Results from contact of skin and allergenic substance. Has a sensitization period of 10 to 14 days.	Vasodilation and perivascular infiltrates on the dermis Intracellular edema Usually seen on dorsal aspects of hand	Patch testing (contraindicated in acute, widespread dermatitis)	Avoidance of offending material Burow's solution or cool water compress Systemic corticosteroids (prednisone) for 7 to 10 days Topical corticosteroids for mild cases Oral antihistamines to relieve pruritus
Irritant	Results from contact with a substance that chemically or physically damages the skin on a non-immunologic basis. Occurs after first exposure to irritant or repeated exposures to milder irritants over an extended time.	Dryness lasting days to months Vesiculation, fissures, cracks Hands and lower arms most common areas	Clinical picture Appropriate negative patch tests	Identification and removal of source of irritation Application of hydrophilic cream or petrolatum to soothe and protect Topical corticosteroids and compresses for weeping lesions Antibiotics for infection and oral antihistamines for pruritus
Phototoxic	Resembles the irritant type but requires sun and a chemical in combination to damage the epidermis.	Similar to irritant dermatitis	Photopatch test	Same as for allergic and irritant dermatitis
Photoallergic	Resembles allergic dermatitis but requires light exposure in addition to allergen contact to produce immunologic reactivity.	Similar to allergic dermatitis	Photopatch test	Same as for allergic and irritant dermatitis

caused by excessive exposure to or additive effects of irritants (e.g., soaps, detergents, plants, organic solvents). Skin sensitivity may develop after brief or prolonged periods of exposure, and the clinical picture may appear hours or weeks after the sensitized skin has been exposed.

Clinical Manifestations and Assessment

Symptoms include itching, burning, **erythema**, skin lesions (vesicles), and edema, followed by weeping, crusting, and finally drying and peeling of the skin. In severe responses, hemorrhagic bullae may develop. Repeated reactions may be accompanied by thickening of the skin and pigmentary changes. Secondary invasion by bacteria may develop in skin that is abraded by rubbing or scratching. Usually, there are no systemic symptoms unless the eruption is widespread.

The location of the skin eruption and the history of exposure aid in determining the condition (see Table 38-3). However, in cases of obscure irritants or an unobservant patient, the diagnosis can be extremely difficult, often involving many trial-and-error procedures before the cause is determined. Patch tests on the skin with suspected offending agents may clarify the diagnosis (Bourke, Coulson, & English, 2009). Management is discussed in Table 38-3.

ATOPIC DERMATITIS

Atopic dermatitis is a type I immediate hypersensitivity disorder characterized by inflammation and hyperreactivity of the skin often causing pruritus. Although most commonly seen in children, atopic dermatitis has an estimated lifetime prevalence between 10% and 20% (Lam & Friedlander, 2009). Other terms used to describe this skin disorder include *atopic eczema, atopic dermatitis/eczema,* and *atopic dermatitis/ eczema syndrome* (AEDS).

Clinical Manifestations and Assessment

Most patients with atopic dermatitis have significant elevations of serum IgE and peripheral eosinophilia. Pruritus and hyperirritability of the skin are the most consistent features of atopic dermatitis and are related to large amounts of histamine in the skin (Fig. 38-2). Excessive dryness of the skin with resultant itching is related to changes in lipid content, sebaceous gland activity, and sweating. In response to stroking of the skin, immediate redness appears on the skin and is followed in 15 to 30 seconds by pallor, which persists for 1 to 3 minutes. Years of chronically irritated skin resulting in excessive itching can cause lichenification, or a leathery hardened appearance to the affected area. Lesions develop secondary to the trauma of scratching and appear in areas of

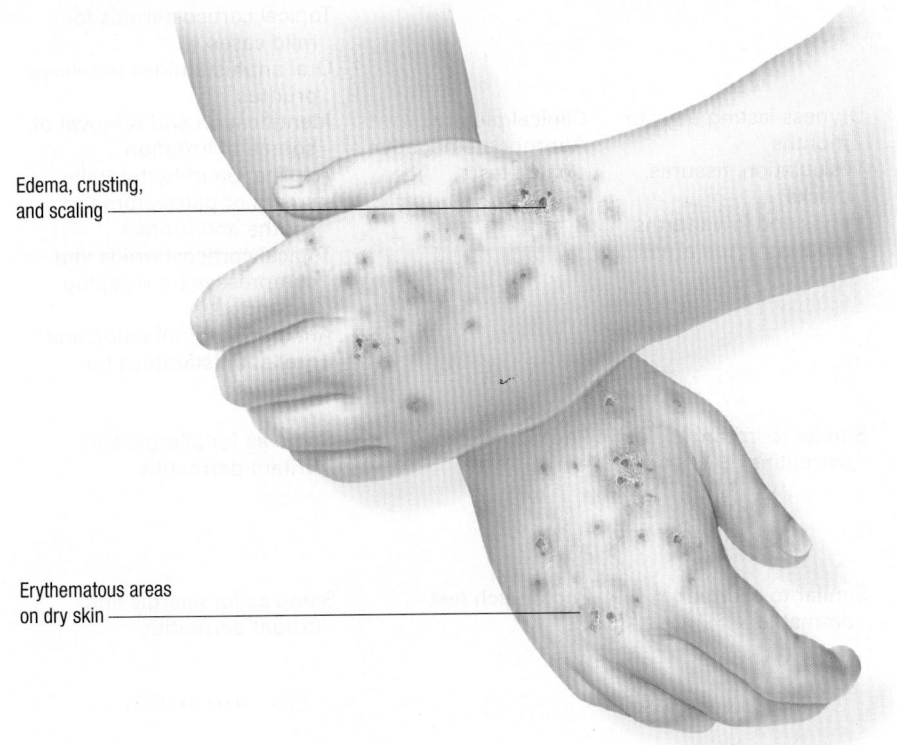

Edema, crusting, and scaling

Erythematous areas on dry skin

FIGURE 38-2 Atopic dermatitis. Courtesy of Anatomical Chart Company.

increased sweating and hypervascularity. Atopic dermatitis is chronic, with remissions and exacerbations. This condition has a tendency to recur, with remission from adolescence to age 20 (Lam & Friedlander, 2009).

It is important to note that atopic dermatitis is often the first step in a process that leads to asthma and allergic rhinitis, otherwise known as the "allergic/atopic triad" (Lan & Friedlander, 2009). It is the result of interactions between susceptibility genes, the environment, defective function of the skin barrier, and immunologic responses. Factors associated with more severe disease states or increased rates of exacerbations include familial history of atopic dermatitis, being the oldest or only child, having a severe case of dermatitis at a very early age, respiratory disease, early onset, and very high serum IgE levels (Peterson & Chan, 2006).

Medical Management

Treatment of patients with atopic dermatitis must be individualized. Guidelines for treatment include decreasing itching and scratching by wearing cotton fabrics; washing with a mild detergent; humidifying dry heat in winter; maintaining room temperature at 20°C to 22.2°C (68°F to 72°F); using antihistamines, such as diphenhydramine (Benadryl); and avoiding animals, dust, sprays, and perfumes. Keeping the skin moisturized with daily baths to hydrate the skin and the use of topical skin emollients is encouraged and remains the main treatment for atopic dermatitis (Lam & Friedlander, 2009). Topical corticosteroids are used to prevent inflammation, and any infection is treated with antibiotics to eliminate *Staphylococcus aureus* when indicated. Use of immunosuppressive agents, such as cyclosporine (Neoral, Sandimmune), tacrolimus (Prograf, Protopic), and pimecrolimus (Elidel), may be effective in inhibiting T cells and mast cells involved in atopic dermatitis (Bourke et al., 2009; Peterson & Chan, 2007).

Nursing Management

Patients who experience atopic dermatitis and their families require assistance and support from the nurse to cope with the disorder. The symptoms are often disturbing to the patient and disruptive to the family. The appearance of the skin may affect the patient's self-esteem and his or her willingness to interact with others. Instructions and counseling about strategies to incorporate preventive measures and treatments into the lifestyle of the family may be helpful. Instructions include counseling the patient and family on various triggers of atopic dermatitis (e.g., winter months, heat or exercise, emotional stress, hormonal fluxes in women, skin irritants [perfumes], and microorganisms [bacteria, fungi, viruses, and yeast]) that may lead to an exacerbation. The patient and family need to be aware of signs of secondary infection and of the need to seek treatment if infection occurs. The nurse also teaches the patient and family about the side effects of medications used in treatment.

To avoid the risk of developing eczema vaccinatum, which is a localized or generalized cutaneous dissemination of vaccinia virus, patients and close contacts of patients with atopic dermatitis should be cautioned to avoid vaccination with smallpox or contact with someone who has recently received smallpox vaccination. Although this illness is usually mild and self-limited, it can be severe or fatal (Buttaro, Trybulski, et al., 2008).

DERMATITIS MEDICAMENTOSA (DRUG REACTIONS)

Dermatitis medicamentosa, a type I hypersensitivity disorder, is the term applied to skin rashes associated with certain medications. Although people react differently to each medication, certain medications tend to induce eruptions of similar types. Rashes are among the most common adverse reactions to medications and occur in approximately 2% to 3% of hospitalized patients.

Clinical Manifestations and Assessment

In general, drug reactions appear suddenly, have a particularly vivid color, manifest with characteristics that are more intense than the somewhat similar eruptions of infectious origin, and, with the exception of bromide and the iodide rashes, disappear rapidly after the medication is withdrawn. Rashes may be accompanied by systemic or generalized symptoms, such as bronchospasm, urticaria, and significant angioedema.

Medical and Nursing Management

On discovery of a medication allergy, patients are warned that they have a hypersensitivity to a particular medication and are advised not to take it again. Patients should carry information identifying the hypersensitivity, and subsequent reaction experienced, with them at all times.

Skin eruptions related to medication therapy suggest more serious hypersensitivities. Frequent assessment and prompt reporting of the appearance of any eruptions are important so that early treatment can be initiated. Some cutaneous drug reactions may be associated with a clinical complex that involves other organs. These are known as complex drug reactions.

URTICARIA AND ANGIONEUROTIC EDEMA

Urticaria (hives) is a type I hypersensitive allergic reaction of the skin characterized by the sudden appearance of pinkish,

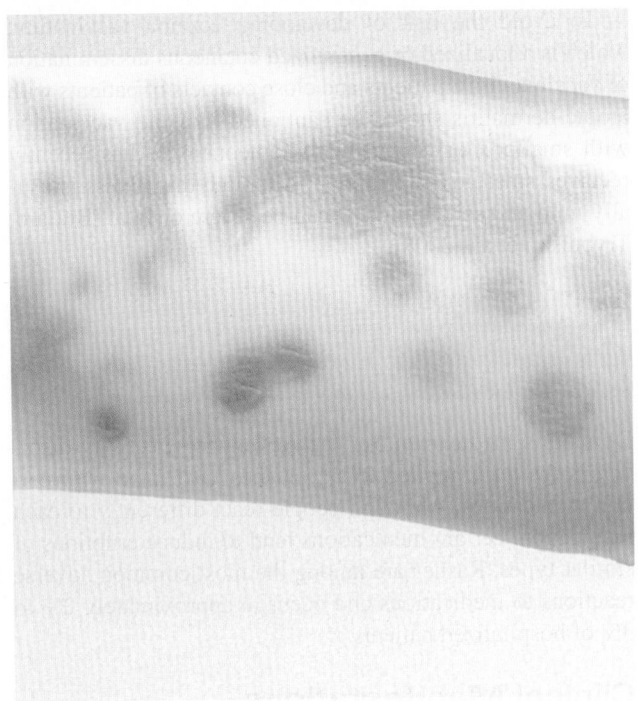

FIGURE 38-3 Hives.

edematous elevations that vary in size and shape, itch, and cause local discomfort (Fig. 38-3). They may involve any part of the body, including the mucous membranes (especially those of the mouth), the larynx (occasionally with serious respiratory complications), and the gastrointestinal (GI) tract.

Each hive remains for a few minutes to several hours before disappearing. For hours or days, clusters of these lesions may come, go, and return episodically. If this sequence continues for longer than 6 weeks, the condition is called chronic urticaria.

Angioneurotic edema involves the deeper layers of the skin, resulting in more diffuse swelling, rather than the discrete lesions characteristic of hives. On occasion, this reaction covers the entire back. The skin over the reaction may appear normal but often has a reddish hue. The skin does not pit on pressure, as ordinary edema does. The regions most often involved are the lips, eyelids, cheeks, hands, feet, genitalia, and tongue; the mucous membranes of the larynx, the bronchi, and the GI canal may also be affected, particularly in the hereditary type (see discussion in the following section). Swellings may appear suddenly, in a few seconds or minutes, or slowly, in 1 or 2 hours. In the latter case, their appearance is often preceded by itching or burning sensations. Seldom does more than a single swelling appear at one time, although one may develop while another is disappearing. Infrequently, swelling recurs in the same region. Individual lesions usually last 24 to 36 hours. On rare occasions, swelling may recur with remarkable regularity at intervals of 3 to 4 weeks.

FOOD ALLERGY

Pathophysiology

IgE-mediated food allergy, a type I hypersensitivity reaction, occurs in about 2% of the adult population; it is thought to occur in people who have a genetic predisposition combined with exposure to allergens early in life through the GI or respiratory tract or nasal mucosa. Researchers have also identified a second type of food allergy, a non-IgE–mediated food allergy syndrome in which T cells play a major role (Ozol & Mete, 2008).

Almost any food can cause allergic symptoms, some even resulting in anaphylaxis. The most common offenders are seafood (lobster, shrimp, crab, clams, fish), legumes (peanuts, peas, beans, licorice), seeds (sesame, cottonseed, caraway, mustard, flaxseed, sunflower seeds), tree nuts, berries, egg white, buckwheat, milk, and chocolate. Peanut and tree nut (e.g., cashew, walnut) allergies are responsible for most severe food allergy reactions and result in the highest patient death rate (Sicherer, 2009).

Clinical Manifestations and Assessment

The clinical symptoms are classic allergic symptoms (urticaria, dermatitis, wheezing, cough, laryngeal edema, angioedema) and GI symptoms (itching; swelling of lips, tongue, and palate; abdominal pain; nausea; cramps; vomiting; and diarrhea).

A careful diagnostic workup is required in any patient with a suspected food hypersensitivity. Included are a detailed allergy history, a physical examination, and pertinent diagnostic tests. Skin testing is used to identify the source of symptoms and is useful in identifying specific foods as causative agents.

Medical Management

Therapy for food hypersensitivity includes elimination of the food responsible for the hypersensitivity. Pharmacologic therapy is necessary for patients who cannot avoid exposure to offending foods and for patients with multiple food sensitivities not responsive to avoidance measures. Medication therapy involves the use of H_1-blockers, antihistamines, adrenergic agents, corticosteroids, and cromolyn sodium. An essential aspect of management is teaching patients and family members to recognize symptoms associated with an anaphylactic reaction, when and how to administer life-saving medication, and when to call for emergency help. Many food allergies disappear with time, particularly in children. About one-third of proven allergies disappear in 1 to 2 years if the patient carefully avoids the offending food. However, peanut allergy has been reported to persist throughout adulthood in some people (Sicherer, 2009).

Nursing Management

In addition to participating in management of the allergic reaction, the nurse focuses on preventing future exposure of the patient to the food allergen. If a severe allergic or anaphylactic reaction to food allergens has occurred, the nurse must instruct the patient and family about strategies to prevent its recurrence. The patient is instructed about the importance of carefully assessing foods prepared by others for obvious as well as hidden sources of food allergens and of avoiding locations and facilities where those allergens are likely to be present. This includes careful reading of food labels and monitoring the preparation of food by others to be sure that exposure to even minute amounts of allergenic foods is avoided. One of the dangers of food allergens is that they may be hidden in other foods and not apparent to people who are susceptible to the allergen. For example, peanuts and peanut butter are often used in salad dressings and Asian, African, and Mexican cooking and may result in severe allergic reactions, including anaphylaxis. Previous contamination of equipment with allergens (e.g., peanuts) during preparation of another food product (e.g., chocolate cake) is enough to produce anaphylaxis in people with severe allergy.

The patient and family must be knowledgeable about early signs and symptoms of allergic reactions and must be proficient in emergency administration of epinephrine if a reaction occurs. The nurse also advises the patient to wear a medical alert bracelet or to carry identification and emergency equipment at all times. Patients' food allergies should be noted on their medical records, because there may be risk of allergic reactions not only to food but also to some medications containing similar substances.

SERUM SICKNESS

Pathophysiology

Serum sickness is an immune-complex type III hypersensitivity. It has traditionally resulted from the administration of therapeutic antisera of animal sources for the treatment or prevention of infectious diseases such as tetanus, pneumonia, rabies, diphtheria, botulism, and venomous snake and black widow spider bites. With the advent of human antitetanus serum and antibiotics, classic serum sickness is much less common now. However, various medications (primarily penicillin) may cause a serum sickness–like reaction similar to that caused by foreign sera.

Clinical Manifestations and Assessment

Symptoms are caused by a reaction and immunologic attack on the serum or medication. Antibodies appear to be of the IgE and IgM classes. Early manifestations, beginning 6 to 10 days after administration of the medication, include an inflammatory reaction at the site of injection of the medication, followed by regional and generalized lymphadenopathy and fever. There is usually a skin rash, which may be urticarial or purpuric. Joints are frequently tender and swollen. Vasculitis may occur in any organ but is most commonly observed in the kidney, resulting in proteinuria and, occasionally, casts in the urine. There may be mild to severe cardiac involvement. Peripheral neuritis may cause temporary paralysis of the upper extremities or may be widespread, causing Guillain-Barré syndrome (Chen, 2010).

Medical and Nursing Management

The primary goal in serum sickness therapy is to treat the clinical syndrome symptomatically. This hypersensitivity reaction lasts for several days to a few weeks if untreated, but the patient responds promptly and completely if treated with antihistamines and corticosteroids (Chen, 2010). Aggressive therapy, including ventilator support, may be necessary if peripheral neuritis and Guillain-Barré syndrome occur. If symptoms are severe enough to warrant ventilator support or hemodynamic instability ensues, the patient is to be admitted to an intensive care unit (Buttaro, 2007). See Chapter 46 for nursing management of Guillain-Barré syndrome.

LATEX ALLERGY

Latex allergy, the allergic reaction to natural rubber proteins, has been implicated in rhinitis, conjunctivitis, contact dermatitis, urticaria, asthma, and anaphylaxis. Over the past 80 years, the numbers of individuals affected with this allergy have drastically dropped due to the processing of nonlatex materials and nonpowdered latex gloves used in health care settings. Despite numbers and studies confirming this, the severity of illness associated with a latex allergy remains a nursing priority.

Risk Factors

Populations at risk include health care workers, patients with atopic allergies or multiple surgeries, people working in factories that manufacture latex products, females, and patients with spina bifida. Because more food handlers, hairdressers, auto mechanics, and police officers are now wearing latex gloves, they may also be at risk for latex allergy. Latex is the second most common cause of anaphylactic reactions during the intraoperative period (due to repeated latex exposure), preceded only by muscle relaxants (Rolland & O'Hehir, 2008).

Food that has been handled by people wearing latex gloves may stimulate an allergic response. Cross-reactions

have been reported in people who are allergic to certain food products, such as kiwis, bananas, pineapples, mangos, passion fruit, avocados, and chestnuts (Rolland & O'Hehir, 2008).

Pathophysiology

Routes of exposure to latex products can be cutaneous, percutaneous, mucosal, parenteral, or aerosol. Allergic reactions are more likely with parenteral or mucous membrane exposure but can also occur with cutaneous contact or inhalation. The most frequent source of exposure is cutaneous, which usually involves the wearing of natural latex gloves. The powder used to facilitate putting on latex gloves can become a carrier of latex proteins from the gloves; when the gloves are put on or removed, the particles become airborne and can be inhaled or settle on skin, mucous membranes, or clothing. Mucosal exposure can occur from the use of latex condoms, catheters, airways, and nipples. Parenteral exposure can occur from IV lines or hemodialysis equipment. In addition to latex-derived medical devices, many household items also contain latex. Examples of medical and household items containing latex and a list of alternative products are found in Table 38-4.

Clinical Manifestations and Assessment

Several different types of reactions to latex are possible: irritant contact dermatitis, allergic dermatitis, and latex allergy. Table 38-5 lists the causes, symptoms, and management of each.

The diagnosis of latex allergy is based on the history and diagnostic test results. Sensitization is detected by

TABLE **38-4** **Selected Products Containing Natural Rubber Latex and Latex-Free Alternatives**

Products Containing Latex	Examples of Latex-Safe Alternatives*
Hospital Environment	
Ace bandage (brown)	Ace bandage, white all cotton
Adhesive bandages, Band-Aid dressing, Telfa	Cotton pads and plastic or silk tape, Active Strip (3M), Duoderm
Anesthesia equipment	Neoprene anesthesia kit (King)
Blood pressure cuff, tubing, and bladder	Clean Cuff, single-use nylon or vinyl blood pressure cuffs or wrap with stockinette or apply over clothing
Catheters	All-silicone or vinyl catheters
Catheter leg bag straps	Velcro straps
Crutch axillary pads and hand grips, tips	Cover with cloth, tape
ECG pads	Baxter, Red Dot 3M ECG pads
Elastic compression stockings	Kendall SCD stockings with stockinette
Gloves	Dermaprene, Neoprene, polymer, or vinyl gloves
IV catheters	Jelko, Deseret IV catheters
IV rubber injection ports	Cover Y-sites and ports; do not puncture. Use three-way stopcocks on plastic tubing.
Levin tube	Salem sump tube
Medication vials	Remove rubber stopper.
Penrose drains	Jackson-Pratt, Zimmer Hemovac drains
Prepackaged enema kits	Theravac, Fleet Ready-to-use
Pulse oximeters	Nonin oximeters
Resuscitation bags	Laerdal, Puritan Bennett, *certain* Ambu
Stethoscope tubing	PVC tubing; cover with latex-free stockinette
Syringes—single use (Monoject, B & D)	Terumo syringes, Abbott PCA Abboject
Suction tubing	PVC (Davol, Laerdal)
Tapes	Dermicel, Micropore
Thermometer probes	Diatec probe covers
Tourniquets	X-Tourn straps (Avcor)
Thera-Band	New Thera-band Exercisers, plastic tubing
Home Environment	
Balloons	Mylar balloons
Diapers, incontinence pads	Huggies, Always, *some* Attends
Condoms, diaphragms	Polyurethane products, Durex/Avanti and Reality products (female condom)
Feminine hygiene pad	Kimberly-Clark products
Wheelchair cushions	ROHO cushions, Sof Care bed/chair cushions

*Confirmation is essential to verify that all items are latex-free before using, especially if risk of latex allergy is present.

TABLE
38-5 Types of Reactions to Latex

Type of Reaction	Cause	Signs/Symptoms	Treatment
Irritant contact dermatitis	Damage to skin because of irritation and loss of epidermoid skin layer; not an allergic reaction. Can be caused by excessive use of soaps and cleansers, multiple handwashings, inadequate hand drying, mechanical irritation (e.g., sweating, rubbing inside powdered gloves), exposure to chemicals added during the manufacturing of gloves, and alkaline pH of powdered gloves. Reaction may occur with first exposure, is usually benign, and is not life-threatening.	Acute: redness, edema, burning, discomfort, itching Chronic: dry, thickened, cracked skin	Referral for diagnostic testing Avoidance of exposure to irritant Thorough washing and drying of hands Use of powder-free gloves with more frequent changes of gloves Changing glove types Use of water- or silicone-based moisturizing creams, lotions, or topical barrier agents Avoidance of oil- or petroleum-based skin agents with latex products, because they cause breakdown of the latex product
Allergic contact dermatitis	Delayed hypersensitivity (type IV) reaction. Usually affects only area in contact with latex; reaction is usually to chemical additives used in the manufacturing process rather than to latex itself. Cause of reaction is T cell–mediated sensitization to additives of latex. Reaction is not life-threatening and is far more common than a type I reaction. Slow onset; occurs 18 to 24 hours after exposure. Resolves within 3 to 4 days after exposure. More severe reactions may occur with subsequent exposures.	Pruritus, erythema, swelling, crusty thickened skin, blisters, other skin lesions	Referral for diagnosis (patch tests) and treatment Thorough washing and drying of hands Use of water- or silicone-based moisturizing creams, lotions, or topical barrier agents Avoidance of oil- or petroleum-based products unless they are latex compatible Avoidance of identified causative agent, because continued exposure to latex products in presence of breaks in skin may contribute to latex protein sensitization
Latex allergy	Type I IgE-mediated immediate hypersensitivity to plant proteins in natural rubber latex. In sensitized people, anti-latex IgE antibody stimulates mast cell proliferation and basophil histamine release. Exposure can be through contact with the skin, mucous membranes, or internal tissues, or through inhalation of traces of powder from latex gloves. Severe reactions usually occur shortly after parenteral or mucous membrane exposure. People with any type I reaction to latex are at high risk of anaphylaxis. Local swelling, redness, edema, itching, and systemic reactions, including anaphylaxis, occur within minutes after exposure.	Rhinitis, flushing, conjunctivitis, urticaria, laryngeal edema, bronchospasm, asthma, severe vasodilation angioedema, anaphylaxis, cardiovascular collapse, death	Immediate treatment of reaction with epinephrine, fluids, vasopressors, and corticosteroids, and airway and ventilator support, with close monitoring for recurrence for next 12 to 14 hours Prompt referral for diagnostic evaluation Treatment and diagnostic evaluation in latex-free environment Strict avoidance of allergy testing and management Assessment of all patients for symptoms of latex allergy Teaching of patients and family members about the disorder and about the importance of preventing future reactions by avoiding latex Encouraging wearing of a medical alert bracelet that identifies latex allergy for emergency situations Warning labels can be attached to car windows to alert police and paramedics about the driver's or passenger's latex allergy in case of a motor vehicle crash. Carrying an EpiPen at all times and being prepared and able to use it

skin testing, RAST, or enzyme-linked immunosorbent assay (ELISA). Skin tests should be performed only by clinicians who have expertise in their administration and interpretation, and who have the necessary equipment available to treat local or systemic allergic reactions to the reagent.

Medical Management

See Table 38-5 for medical management.

Nursing Management

The nurse can assume a pivotal role in the management of latex allergies in both patients and staff. All patients should be asked about latex allergy, although special attention should be given to those at particularly high risk (e.g., patients with spina bifida, patients who have undergone multiple surgical procedures). Every time an invasive procedure must be performed, the nurse should consider the possibility of latex allergies. Nurses working in operating rooms, intensive care units, short term procedure units, and emergency departments need to pay particular attention to latex allergy.

Although the type I reaction is the most significant of the reactions to latex, care must be taken in the presence of irritant contact dermatitis and delayed hypersensitivity reaction to avoid further exposure of the person to latex. Patients with latex allergy are advised to notify their health care providers and to wear a medical information bracelet. Patients must become knowledgeable about what products contain latex and what products are safe, nonlatex alternatives. They must also become knowledgeable about signs and symptoms of latex allergy and emergency treatment and self-injection of epinephrine in case of allergic reaction.

Nurses can be instrumental in establishing and participating in multidisciplinary committees to address latex allergy and to promote a latex-free environment. Latex allergy protocols and education of staff about latex allergy and precautions are important strategies to ensure assessment and prompt treatment of affected people.

Chapter Review

Critical Thinking Exercises

1. A 17-year-old girl has developed symptoms of asthma thought to be an allergic response to allergens in her environment. Develop an evidence-based plan for avoidance strategies for her while she is living at home and for her move next year to a college dormitory. Describe the strength of the evidence and criteria used to assess its strength. What instructional strategies and outcome measures will you use to educate her about avoidance strategies and to assess the effectiveness of their use?

2. A 72-year-old man is admitted for emergency surgery to treat a strangulated hernia. He reports that he has severe allergies but is unable to be specific about the nature of his allergies or the allergic reactions that he has experienced in the past. He reports that he has had to use emergency epinephrine on several occasions in the past because of severe allergic reactions. What precautions are needed preoperatively, intraoperatively, and postoperatively for this patient to prevent the occurrence of severe allergic reactions? What interventions and nursing management would be indicated if he developed a severe allergic reaction?

NCLEX-Style Review Questions

1. During a clinical postconference, the nursing instructor is discussing factors related to the risk of anaphylaxis. Which of the following statements made by the instructor would be inconsistent with the risk of anaphylaxis?
   A. The severity depends on the degree of allergy.
   B. The severity of previous reactions determines the severity of subsequent reactions.
   C. The severity depends on the dose of the allergen.
   D. The severity of previous reactions does not determine the severity of subsequent reactions.

2. Which of the following reactions would be consistent with a mild reaction to an allergen?
   A. Bronchospasm
   B. Warmth
   C. Periorbital swelling
   D. Throat tingling

3. When reviewing the chart of a patient diagnosed with allergic rhinitis, the nurse understands that this allergic disorder is caused by which type of hypersensitivity reaction?
   A. Type I
   B. Type II

C. Type III

D. Type IV

4. A patient is being seen in the dermatology clinic for urticaria. The nurse would expect which of the following medications to be prescribed for the patient?

A. Pseudoephedrine (Sudafed)

B. Diphenhydramine (Benadryl)

C. Dexamethasone (Decadron)

D. Cromolyn sodium (NasalCrom)

5. Which of the following is the most frequent source of exposure for a latex allergy?

A. Latex condoms

B. IV lines

C. Hemodialysis equipment

D. Latex gloves

Try these additional resources to enhance your learning and understanding of this chapter:

- thePoint online resource available at **http://thepoint.lww.com/Pellico1e**
- *Handbook for Focus on Adult Health: Medical-Surgical Nursing*
- *Study Guide for Focus on Adult Health: Medical-Surgical Nursing*

References and Selected Readings

References and selected readings associated with this chapter can be found on the website that accompanies the book. Visit http://thepoint.lww.com/Pellico1e to access the references and other additional resources associated with this chapter.

Nursing Management: Patients With Rheumatic Disorders

LINDA ALESSIE PODOLAK

Learning Objectives

After reading this chapter, you will be able to:

1. Explain the pathophysiology of rheumatic diseases or disorders.

2. Describe the assessment and diagnostic findings seen in patients with a suspected diagnosis of rheumatic disease or disorder.

3. Describe the systemic effects of a connective tissue disease.

4. Discuss the pharmacological, medical, and nursing management associated with rheumatic disorders.

5. Apply the nursing process as a framework for the care of the patient with a rheumatic disorder.

6. Identify appropriate nursing interventions based on nursing diagnoses that commonly occur with rheumatic disorders.

Rheumatic disorders affect the joints, bones, muscles, and connective tissues. These conditions can be minor illnesses, or they can be life-threatening. Systemic effects caused by rheumatic disorders or diseases result in obvious limitations in mobility and activities of daily living (ADL), and more subtle manifestations such as pain, fatigue, insomnia, and disturbed body image. Organ failure and death may be an end result for some rheumatic disorders. The rheumatic condition may be the patient's primary health problem or a secondary diagnosis. Thorough understanding of rheumatic conditions and their effects on a patient's function and well-being is key to developing an interdisciplinary plan of care.

OVERVIEW

Commonly called arthritis (inflammation of a joint) and thought of as one condition, the rheumatic diseases are actually more than 100 different types of disorders that primarily affect joints, bones, skeletal muscles, and connective tissues (Porth & Matfin, 2009). Some disorders are more likely to occur at a particular time of life or to affect one gender more than the other (see Box 39-1 for Gerontologic Considerations). The symptom that most commonly causes a person to seek medical attention is pain. Other common symptoms include joint swelling, limited movement, stiffness, weakness, and fatigue. The onset of these conditions may be acute or insidious, with a course possibly marked by periods of remission (a period when disease symptoms are reduced or absent) and exacerbation (a period when symptoms occur or increase).

Assessment includes a complete health history followed by a complete physical examination combined with a functional assessment. Inspection of the patient's general appearance occurs during initial contact. Gait, posture, and general musculoskeletal size and structure are observed. Gross deformities and abnormalities in movement are noted. The symmetry, size, and contour of other connective tissues, such as the skin and adipose tissue, are also noted and recorded. Observation of activities is made: the patient demonstrates what he or she can and cannot do, such as dressing and getting in and out of a chair. Observation also includes the adaptations and adjustments the patient may have made (sometimes without awareness); for example, with shoulder or elbow involvement, the person may bend over to reach a fork, rather than raising the fork to the mouth.

Gerontologic Considerations

Although people of all ages may be affected, rheumatic disease is commonly thought of by the patient, family, and society as a whole as an inevitable consequence of aging. Many older people expect and accept the immobility and self-care problems related to the rheumatic disorders and do not seek help, thinking that nothing can be done. Careful diagnosis and appropriate treatment is crucial and can improve the quality of life for older people. An adequate support system for the elderly is also a critical factor in the ability to follow an interdisciplinary plan of care that includes exercise, nutrition, general health maintenance, pharmacotherapy and nonpharmacologic management. However, the rheumatic disorders do have some special implications for the older adult.

Age alone causes changes in serologic studies (e.g., ESR, ANA), making interpretation of laboratory values more difficult. Decreased vision and altered balance, often present in elderly people, may be problematic if rheumatic disease in the lower extremities affects locomotion. Also, the combination of decreased hearing and visual acuity, memory loss, and depression contributes to failure to follow the treatment regimen in elderly patients.

Pharmacologic treatment of rheumatic disease in older patients is more difficult. Aging brings many physical and metabolic changes that may increase the elderly patient's sensitivity to both the therapeutic and toxic effects of some drugs, making overtreatment or inappropriate treatment possible. If therapeutic medications have an effect on the senses (hearing, cognition), this effect is intensified in the elderly. The cumulative effect of these medications is accentuated because of the physiologic changes of aging. For example, decreased renal function in the elderly alters the metabolism of certain medications, such as NSAIDs. Elderly patients are more prone to side effects associated with the use of multiple-drug therapy for various disorders (Lehne, 2010; Miller, 2009).

The history and physical assessment data are supplemented by supportive or confirming diagnostic test findings. Common serum laboratory tests used for patients with rheumatic disorders are described in Table 39-1. Radiological investigations facilitate early diagnosis, guide treatment, and ultimately impact prognosis. Scans, computed tomography (CT), and magnetic resonance imaging (MRI) are not the most cost-effective methods for detection of early disease and are not performed routinely at the time of diagnosis. In some instances, many tests are used to monitor the course of the disease. For example, contrast radiography and MRI play a role in diagnosing advancing systems affected in scleroderma; the erythrocyte sedimentation rate (ESR) reflects inflammatory activity and, indirectly, the progression

or remission of disease. Ultimately, the provider determines which tests are necessary based on the symptoms, stage of disease, cost, and likely benefit of the test.

NURSING ALERT
The ESR measures the rate in which red blood cells (RBCs) suspended in plasma fall in a test tube. Increased "sed" rates are often associated with inflammatory states. Normally, the distance a RBC falls in 1 hour is less than 15 mm/hr for men and slightly higher in women. The speed with which the RBC moves is related to the clumping of RBCs. The more clumping, the heavier and higher the speed that a RBC falls. Inflammatory states produce proteins that encourage this clumping, thus high ESR levels are associated with inflammation. The ESR does not diagnose a problem, but it is used to monitor status of a disease and response to therapy (Fischbach & Dunning, 2009).

Treatment can be simple, aimed at localized relief, or it can be complex, directed toward relief of systemic effects. The chronic nature of most of these disorders mandates that the patient understand the disease, have the information necessary to make good self-management decisions, be referred to appropriate community agencies (such as the Arthritis Foundation) for support, and be presented with a therapeutic program that is compatible with his or her lifestyle. The goals and strategies of basic rheumatic disease management are outlined in Table 39-2. The trend in management is toward a more aggressive pharmacologic approach earlier in the disease presentation.

Pharmacologic management of rheumatic disorders is used to manage symptoms, control pain and inflammation, and—in some diseases, such as rheumatoid arthritis (RA)—modify the disease course. However, disease typically advances steadily and, as a result, pharmacologic therapy is chronic; thus, success requires motivation and cooperation by the patient. Selection of medication is based on the patient's needs, the stage of disease, and the risk of side effects.

Antiarthritic drugs fall into three major groups: nonsteroidal anti-inflammatory drugs (NSAIDs) including salicylates (e.g., aspirin), disease-modifying antirheumatic drugs (DMARDs), and glucocorticoids (adrenal corticosteroids). These groups differ with reference to time course of effects, toxicity, and ability to slow disease progression. Table 39-3, on page 1052, reviews the medications commonly used in rheumatic disorders, particularly RA.

Nonpharmacologic treatment measures include the use of heat or cold, weight reduction, joint rest and avoidance of joint overuse, orthotic devices (e.g., splints, braces) to support inflamed joints, and an exercise regimen. Occupational and physical therapy can help the patient adopt self-management strategies. Other nonpharmacologic modalities such as massage, yoga, pulsed electromagnetic fields, transcutaneous electrical nerve stimulation (TENS), and music therapy, have been used in the treatment of arthritis. In addition,

TABLE
39-1 **Common Serum Laboratory Tests for Rheumatic Diseases**

Test	Normal Value	Implications
Serology *Erythrocyte Sedimentation Rate (ESR)* Measures the rate at which red blood cells settle out of unclotted blood in 1 hour	Westergren's Method *Men,* 0 to 15 mm/hr, over age 50 years: 0 to 20 mm/hr *Women,* 0 to 20 mm/hr, over age 50 years: 0 to 30 mm/hr	Increase is usually seen in inflammatory connective tissue diseases (e.g., RA, SLE, scleroderma), gout, can be seen in elderly An increase indicates rising inflammation; the higher the ESR, the greater the inflammatory activity
Uric Acid Measures level of uric acid in serum	*Men,* 3.4 to 7 mg/dL (202 to 416 µmol/L) *Women,* 2.4 to 6 mg/dL (143 to 357 µmol/L) *Biologic Crystallization Point,* ≥6.8 mg/dL (408 µmol/L)	Increase is seen with gout In gout, an overproduction of uric acids occurs when there is excessive cell breakdown and catabolism of nucleonic acids
Serum Immunology *Antinuclear Antibody (ANA)* Measures antibodies that react with a variety of nuclear antigens Usually the first step, if antibodies are present, further testing determines specific circulating antibodies to extractable nuclear antigens (anti-dsDNA, anti-RNP, anti Ro-SSA).	Screen: negative by ELISA and IFA methods If positive by IFA, specimen is titered. Titer: <1:160 Low titers are present in elderly and some healthy adults	Positive test is associated with systemic rheumatic disease such as mixed connective tissue disease, SLE, RA, scleroderma, CREST syndrome, can be seen in elderly The higher the titer, the greater the inflammation Some negative ANA findings have found to have positive anti-Ro (SSA)
Anticentromere Antibody Test A specific autoantibody, detected by using Hep-2 cells in various stages of cell division, centromere region of the cell chromosomes will stain if positive	Screen: negative by ELISA and IFA methods If positive by IFA, specimen is titered.	Positive test is associated with the CREST syndrome in scleroderma Present in 90% of those with CREST
Anticyclic Citrullinated Peptide (Anti-CCP) Disease-specific autoantibody, highly specific diagnostic and prognostic markers for RA Detects patients with early RA at baseline (after 3 to 6 months of symptoms) Second generation test: CCP2 assay, even higher sensitivity	Negative	Positive in RA Predictive of erosive disease Sensitivity of anti-CCP comparable to rheumatoid factor (RF), but has higher specificity (90% to 95%) Differentiates other entities that can resemble RA and at times be RF positive
Anti-double-stranded DNA (Anti-dsDNA) Specific autoantibody to extractable nuclear antigens; differentiates native (i.e., double-stranded) DNA antibodies from other nonnative antibodies; 95% specific for SLE, making it a valuable disease marker	Negative: <25 IU by ELISA	DNA-anti-dsDNA immune complexes play a role in SLE pathogenesis, found in 70% of SLE patients Positive: 31 to 200 IU; strongly positive: >200 IU Anti-dsDNA concentrations may decrease with successful therapy, may increase with exacerbation of SLE
Autoantibodies, Others Specific autoantibodies to extractable nuclear antigens (*Anti-RNA, Anti-Sm, Anti-Sci-70*); may reflect disease-specific immune mechanisms but not pathogenetic by themselves	Negative: <20 U/mL by ELISA	Positive: >26 U/mL *Anti-RNA:* mixed connective tissue disease (MCTD), 35% to 40% of SLE patients *Anti-Sm* (Smith): SLE, MCTD *Anti-Sci-70:* Scleroderma

Test	Normal Value	Implications
Complement Levels—C3, C4 Complement component levels: done if a reduction/consumption of complement component concentration is suspected C3 constitutes 70% of the total protein in the complement system (antigen–antibody complexes)	C3: 75 to 175 mg/dL (or 0.75 to 1.75 g/L) C4: 14 to 40 mg/dL (or 140 to 400 mg/L)	Decrease may be seen in active SLE, immune complex disease (i.e., RA) Decrease indicates autoimmune activity
C-Reactive Protein Test (CRP) Measures the presence of abnormal glycoprotein in response to inflammatory cytokines	<1 mg/dL (<10 mg/L)	A positive reading indicates active inflammation Often is positive for RA and SLE More sensitive than ESR test
Immunoglobulin Electrophoresis Measures the values of immunoglobulins	IgG: 700 to 1,500 mg/dL (7.0 to 15.0 g/L) IgM: 60 to 300 mg/dL (600 to 3,000 mg/L)	Increased levels of IgG occurs in RA, autoimmune disorders (i.e., SLE) Increased levels of IgM occurs in RA, SLE
Rheumatoid Factor (RF) Measures RFs, antibodies directed against the Fe fragment of IgG Determines the presence of abnormal antibodies seen in connective tissue disease	0 to 20 U/mL Negative titer	Positive titer >1:80 Present in 80% of those with RA; positive RF may also suggest SLE, MCTD Low titers can be seen in OA The higher the titer (number at right of colon), the greater the inflammation

iontophoresis can be used to deliver medication through the skin using direct electrical current. A combination of methods may be required, because different methods often work better at different times.

Common complementary and alternative medicine (CAM) choices used by rheumatologic patients include dietary supplements, herbal therapies, mind/body and spiritual practices, manual/manipulative therapies, biostimulation, and topical ointments. It is essential that health care practitioners remain informed on appropriate indications for use, risks, and limitations of such therapies or practices.

Nurses need to understand the classification of rheumatic diseases. One basic system is to classify disease as either monoarticular (affecting a single joint) or polyarticular (affecting multiple joints), and then to further classify it as either inflammatory (e.g., rheumatoid arthritis) or degenerative, noninflammatory (e.g., osteoarthritis). This chapter groups the conditions into those affecting the joints, bones, and muscles and those affecting the connective tissues.

CONDITIONS AFFECTING THE JOINTS, BONES, AND MUSCLES

Despite the diversity of rheumatic disorders, the joint is the area most commonly affected and involves some degree of

TABLE
39-2 Goals and Strategies for Rheumatic Diseases

Major Goals	Management Strategy
Suppress inflammation and the autoimmune response	Optimize pharmacologic therapy (anti-inflammatory and disease-modifying agents)
Control pain	Protect joints; ease pain with splints/orthoses, thermal modalities, relaxation techniques
Maintain or improve joint mobility	Implement exercise programs for joint motion and muscle strengthening and overall health
Maintain or improve functional status	Make use of adaptive devices and techniques
Increase patient's knowledge of disease process	Provide and reinforce patient teaching
Promote self-management by patient compliance with the therapeutic regimen	Promote social support and encouragement of change-based interventions compatible with therapeutic regimen and lifestyle

TABLE
39-3 Medications Used in Rheumatic Diseases

Medication	Action, Use, and Indication	Nursing Considerations

Salicylates
Acetylated
  Aspirin
Nonacetylated
  Choline salicylate (Arthropan, Trilisate), Salsalate (Disalcid), Sodium salicylate
	Action: anti-inflammatory, analgesic, antipyretic
	Acetylated salicylates are platelet aggregation inhibitors
	Anti-inflammatory doses will produce blood salicylate levels of 20 to 30 mg/dL
		Administer with meals to prevent gastric irritation
		Assess for tinnitus, gastric intolerance, gastrointestinal (GI) bleeding, and purpuric tendencies
		Monitor for possible confusion in the elderly

Nonsteroidal Anti-inflammatory Drugs (NSAIDs) *First-Generation (non salicylates)* Diclofenac (Voltaren), diflunisal (Dolobid), etodolac (Lodine), flurbiprofen (Ansaid), ibuprofen (Motrin), indomethacin (Indocin), ketoprofen (Orudis, Oruvail), meclofenamate (Meclomen), meloxicam (Mobic), nabumetone (Relafen), naproxen (Naprosyn), oxapro-zin (DayPro), piroxicam (Feldene), sulindac (Clinoril), tolmetin sodium (Tolectin)	*Action:* anti-inflammatory, analgesic, antipyretic, platelet aggregation inhibitor, inhibition of prostaglandin synthesis Anti-inflammatory effect occurs 2 to 4 weeks after initiation NSAIDs are alternative to salicylates for first-line therapy in several rheumatic diseases All NSAIDs are useful for short-term treatment of acute gout attack	Administer NSAIDs with food Monitor for GI, CNS, cardiovascular, renal, hematologic, and dermatologic adverse effects Avoid salicylates; use acetaminophen for additional analgesia Needs to be used regularly for maximal effect Watch for possible confusion in the elderly
Second-Generation: COX-2 Inhibitors Celecoxib (Celebrex)	*Action:* Selective prostaglandin inhibition, inhibit only cyclooxygenase (COX)-2 enzymes, which are produced during inflammation, and spare COX-1 enzymes, which can be protective to the stomach	Monitoring the same as for other NSAIDs Increased risk of cardiovascular events, including myocardial infarction and stroke Appropriate for the elderly and patients who are at high risk for gastric ulcers
Related Agent Acetaminophen (Tylenol)	*Action:* Inhibits the synthesis of prostaglandins; antipyretic, analgesic, no anti-inflammatory properties	Chronic excessive use of >4 g/day may lead to hepatotoxicity, renal or cardiac damage Concurrent NSAIDs increase the risk of adverse renal effects
Disease-Modifying Antirheumatic Drugs (DMARDs) *First-Choice DMARDs (Nonbiologic)* Immunosuppressives Methotrexate (Rheumatrex)	*Action:* Immune suppression, inhibits folic acid reductase, leading to inhibition of DNA synthesis and other cellular effects Acts faster than other DMARDs Methotrexate is gold standard for RA treatment; also useful in SLE	Assess for bone marrow suppression, GI ulcerations, skin rashes, alopecia, bladder toxicity, increased infections Monitor CBC, liver enzymes, creatinine every 2 to 4 weeks Caution with NSAID use Should be on folic acid Advise patient of contraceptive measures because of teratogenicity
Antimalarials Hydroxychloroquine (Plaquenil), chloroquine (Aralen)	*Action:* Anti-inflammatory, inhibits lysosomal enzymes Slow-acting, onset may take 2 to 4 months Useful in RA and SLE	Administer concurrently with NSAIDs Assess for visual changes, GI upset, skin rash, headaches, photosensitivity, bleaching of hair Retinopathy may occur; emphasize (every 6 to 12 months) ophthalmologic examinations
Sulfonamides sulfasalazine (Azulfidine)	*Action:* Anti-inflammatory, reduces lymphocyte response, inhibits angiogenesis Useful in RA, seronegative spondyloar-thropathies	Administer concurrently with NSAIDs Do not use in patients with allergy to sulfa medications or salicylates Emphasize adequate fluid intake Assess for GI upset, skin rash, headache, liver abnormalities, anemia

Medication	Action, Use, and Indication	Nursing Considerations
Biologic Agents (Immunomodulators)		
Tumor Necrosis Factor (TNF) Blocking Agents Adalimumab (Humira), etanercept (Enbrel), infliximab (Remicade), golimumab (Simponi), certolizumab pegol (Cimzia)	*Action:* Biologic response modifier that binds to TNF, a cytokine involved in inflammatory and immune responses Used in moderate to severe RA unresponsive to methotrexate Can be used alone or with methotrexate or other DMARDs Humira is administered every 1 to 2 weeks, and Enbrel is administered twice a week Simponi is the first once monthly treatment	Patient should be tested for tuberculosis before beginning this medication Teach patient subcutaneous self-injection of adalimumab (Humira) or etanercept (Enbrel) Infliximab (Remicade) is administered by IV over 2 hours or more Medication must be refrigerated Monitor for injection site reactions Educate patient about increased risk for serious infection and to withhold medication if fever occurs Contraindicated in CHF class III/IV, and may pose a risk for new onset of heart failure
Interleukin (IL)-1 Receptor Antagonist Anakinra (Kineret)	*Action:* Human IL-1 receptor antagonist; blocks IL-1 receptors, decreasing inflammatory and immunologic responses Used in moderate to severe RA unresponsive to methotrexate Can be used alone or with methotrexate or DMARDs, but not with TNF blockers	Administered daily by subcutaneous injection Teach patient subcutaneous self-injection to be administered daily Medication must be refrigerated Monitor for injection site reactions Educate patient about increased risk for infection and to withhold medication if fever occurs
T-Cell Activation Abatacept (Orencia)	*Action:* selectively modulates T-cell activation, altering immune response (costimulatory blocker) Can be used alone or with DMARDs, but not with TNF blockers	Contains maltose, may falsely elevate blood glucose High risk for infections Do not give live vaccines
B-Cell Target Rituximab (Rituxan)	*Action:* monoclonal antibody directed at the CD20 antigen expressed on mature B and pre-B cells B-cell depletion therapy: a course of two IV infusions, 2 weeks apart with a repeat treatment interval of 6 to 12 months	Patient is usually premedicated with acetaminophen and diphenhydramine to decrease fever, chills as associated with infusion Caution in patients with cardiac and pulmonary diseases
Newer, Small-Molecule DMARDs		
Pyrimidine Synthesis Inhibitor Leflunomide (Arava)	*Action:* Has anti-proliferative and anti-inflammatory effects, powerful immunosuppressant Used in moderate to severe RA May be used alone or in combination with other DMARDs (except methotrexate) About as equally effective as methotrexate but more adverse effects	Long half-life; requires loading dose followed by daily administration Assess for diarrhea, respiratory infection, alopecia, skin rash, mouth sores, nausea Monitor liver function tests Risk for serious infections Contraindicated in pregnancy and breastfeeding Administered orally
Cyclosporine (Neoral)	*Action:* Immune suppression by inhibiting T lymphocytes Used for severe, progressive RA, unresponsive to other DMARDs Used in combination with methotrexate	Assess slow dose titration upward until response noted or toxicity occurs Assess for toxic effects: bleeding gums, fluid retention, hair growth, tremors Monitor blood pressure and creatinine every 2 weeks until stable
Minor DMARDs		
Gold-Containing Compounds Aurothioglucose (Solganol), gold sodium thiomalate (Myochrysine), auranofin (Ridaura)	*Action:* Inhibits T- and B-cell activity, suppresses synovitis during active stage of rheumatoid disease Slow-acting, onset may take 3 to 6 months IM preparations are given weekly for about 6 months, then every 2 to 4 weeks	Administer concurrently with NSAIDs Assess for pruritus, stomatitis, diarrhea, dermatitis, proteinuria, hematuria, bone marrow suppression (decreased WBCs and/or platelets), profound hypotension CBC and urinalysis with every other injection

(continued on page 1054)

TABLE
39-3 Medications Used in Rheumatic Diseases (continued)

Medication	Action, Use, and Indication	Nursing Considerations
Penicillamine (Cuprimine, Depen)	*Action:* Anti-inflammatory, inhibits T-cell function, impairs antigen presentation Slow-acting, onset may take 2 to 3 months Useful in RA and systemic sclerosis	Administer concurrently with NSAIDs Assess for GI irritation, decreased taste, skin rash or itching, bone marrow suppression, proteinuria with CBC, and urinalysis every 2 to 4 weeks
Minor Immunosuppressants Azathioprine (Imuran), cyclophosphamide (Cytoxan)	*Action:* Immune suppression, affects DNA synthesis and other cellular effects Have teratogenic potential; azathioprine and cyclophosphamide reserved for more aggressive or unresponsive disease	Assess for bone marrow suppression, GI ulcerations, skin rashes, alopecia, bladder toxicity, increased infections Monitor CBC, liver enzymes, creatinine every 2 to 4 weeks Advise patient of contraceptive measures because of teratogenicity
Glucocorticoids *Adrenal Corticosteroids* Prednisone (Deltasone) hydrocortisone sodium succinate (Solu-Cortef) methylprednisolone sodium succinate (Solu-Medrol) methylprednisolone acetate (Depo-Medrol), intra-articular injection	*Action:* Anti-inflammatory Used for shortest duration and at lowest dose possible to minimize adverse effects Useful for unremitting RA, SLE Fast-acting; onset in days Intra-articular injections useful for joints unresponsive to NSAIDs	Assess for toxicity: cataracts, GI irritation, hyperglycemia, hypertension, fractures, avascular necrosis, hirsutism, psychosis Joints most amenable to injections include ankles, knees, hips, shoulders, and hands Repeated injections can cause joint damage

CBC, complete blood count; CNS, central nervous system; RA, rheumatoid arthritis; SLE, systemic lupus erythematosus; WBCs, white blood cells.
Adapted from Lehne, R.A. (2010). *Pharmacology for nursing care* (7th ed.). St. Louis: W. B. Saunders Elsevier.

inflammation and damage to the articular cartilages, which may occur simultaneously. Understanding normal anatomy and physiology of **articulations**, or joints, is the key to understanding the pathophysiology of the rheumatic disorders (Box 39-2).

OSTEOARTHRITIS

Osteoarthritis (OA), also known as degenerative joint disease, is a chronic, noninflammatory (even though inflammation may be present), progressive disorder that causes cartilage

---

BOX 39-2 **Focus on Pathophysiology**

Rheumatic Disorders

Each **synovial** joint has a given range of motion, and the synovial fluid within a joint has three primary functions: lubrication, nutrient distribution, and shock absorption. Inflammation is manifested in the joints as **synovitis**. Rheumatic disorders always involve damage to the articular cartilages. Because articular cartilages involve some degree of inflammation and degeneration, the rheumatic disorders can be classified as either inflammatory (e.g., RA) or degenerative, noninflammatory (e.g., OA).

In the inflammatory rheumatic disorder classification, the primary process starts with inflammation due to an altered immune function. The inflammatory reaction includes swelling, pain, and loss of function (see Chapter 36 for the inflammatory and immunologic processes). Degeneration then occurs as a secondary process, spreading to the articular surfaces. The cause of degeneration of the articular cartilage is poorly understood but

believed to be metabolically active and therefore is more accurately called *degradation*.

On the other hand, in the degenerative (noninflammatory) rheumatic disorder classification, inflammation occurs as a secondary process. The resultant secondary synovitis is usually milder, is more likely to be seen in advanced disease, and represents a reactive process. The synovitis is thought to result mainly from degeneration due to mechanical irritation of two bone surfaces. As the articular cartilage becomes damaged, the matrix (noncellular component of tissue) begins to break down; the exposed cartilage changes from a slick, smooth gliding surface to a rough fibrous network of collagen fibers. This network may later be converted to bone, locking the articulating elements into position. Fixation of a joint, called **ankylosis**, eliminates the friction, but at the drastic cost of immobility.

deterioration in synovial joints and vertebrae. It particularly affects the weight-bearing joints, knees and hips, and joints of the distal interphalangeal (DIP) and proximal interphalangeal (PIP) joints of the fingers. OA is the most common and most frequently disabling of the joint disorders; it is overdiagnosed and trivialized, and frequently over- or undertreated. The functional impact of OA on quality of life, especially for elderly patients, is often ignored.

OA has been classified as primary (idiopathic), with no prior event or disease related to the OA, and secondary, resulting from previous joint injury or inflammatory disease. The distinction between primary and secondary OA is not always clear, but the clinical presentation and symptoms are often similar.

Risk Factors

Risk factors for OA are summarized in Box 39-3. Age is the risk factor most strongly correlated with OA, while obesity is now well-recognized as an important contributing factor (Di Cesare, Abramson, & Samuels, 2009).

OA generally affects adults aged 50 and older (Nettina, 2010). Prevalence of arthritis in the United States for adults aged 25 and older having clinical OA of some joint was estimated at nearly 27 million (Lawrence, Felson, Helmick et al., 2008). Radiologic OA is more prevalent than symptomatic OA. According to the American College

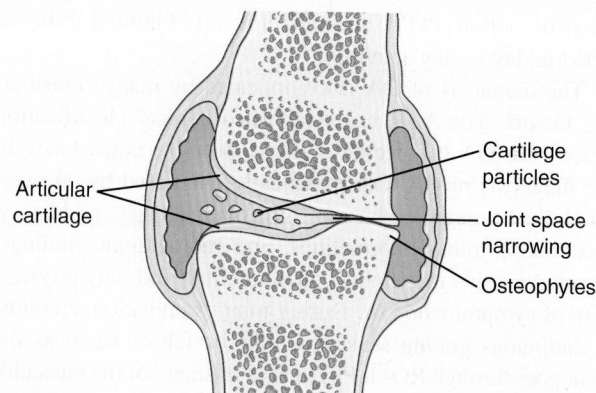

FIGURE 39-1 Osteoarthritic degenerative joint changes: hypertrophy of bone margins resulting in characteristic osteophytes (bone spurs) and joint space narrowing.

of Rheumatology (ACR), 70% of people over the age of 70 have X-ray evidence of OA; however, only half ever develop symptoms. OA of the hand, hip, and knee become more frequent with age, and more women are affected than men after age 50 (Sellam & Berenbaum, 2009).

Pathophysiology

OA may be thought of as the end result of many factors that, when combined, predispose the patient to the disease. In OA, changes in articular cartilage occur first; eventually, secondary soft tissue changes may occur. OA is characterized by erosion of the articular cartilage, combined with hypertrophy of bone at the joint margins, resulting in new bone formation known as **osteophytes** or bone spurs (Fig. 39-1) and subchondral (the bony plate that supports the articular cartilage) sclerosis. In addition, OA is characterized by a range of biochemical and morphological alterations of the synovial membrane and joint capsule. In general, a combination of cartilage degradation, bone stiffening, and reactive inflammation of the synovium occurs. Understanding of OA has been greatly expanded beyond what previously was thought of as simply "wear and tear" related to aging.

Clinical Manifestations and Assessment

The general clinical manifestations of OA are pain, stiffness, and loss of movement and function. Pain in one or more joints typically is worsened by activities and is alleviated by rest. Although osteoarthritic pain is unusual during the night or at rest, there are exceptions, including in patients with mild OA using joints for several hours, in advanced OA with destructive arthropathy, and in an acute inflammatory flare of OA. Stiffness may occur in the morning, after a period of inactivity, or particularly in the evening. Morning stiffness usually resolves after less than 10 minutes (no more than 30 minutes duration), in contrast to prolonged stiffness seen in inflammatory disorders. Functional impairment is reflected in limited

---

BOX 39-3

Risk Factors for Osteoarthritis (OA)

- Aging
- Obesity (greater body mass index is associated with an increased risk of knee OA; the link between OA and adipose-derived leptin is being investigated)
- Genetic predisposition
- Joint location (joint-specific, age-related articular cartilage changes, varying joint responsiveness to cytokines)
- Malalignment of joints (can lead to rapid development of OA; congenital and developmental disorders, e.g., poorly reduced intra-articular fractures, developmental dysplasia of the hip)
- Trauma (can also lead to rapid development of OA; overuse or abuse of joints, as occurs in high-impact sports; previous joint damage; excessive loading or forces such as pneumatic drill operators or frequent squatting position where up to 10 times body weight may be transmitted to the knee.)
- Gender (differences in incidence after age 50 may be result of postmenopausal estrogen deficiency; articular chondrocytes possess functional estrogen receptors)

Adapted from Di Cesare, P.E., Abramson, S.B., & Samuels, J. (2009). Pathogenesis of osteoarthritis. In G. S. Firestein, R.C. Budd, E. D. Harris, Jr., et al. (Eds.). *Kelley's textbook of rheumatology* (8th ed.). Philadelphia: Saunders Elsevier.

range of motion (ROM) and patient report of limited ability to perform day-to-day activities.

The diagnosis of OA is complicated by many contributing factors. The ACR has established clinical classification criteria for OA of specific joints to promote consistency in the diagnosis of OA. OA is typically diagnosed by an overall clinical impression based on the patient's age and history, location of joint abnormalities, and radiographic findings. Limited passive movement can be the first and only physical sign of symptomatic OA. During joint examination, crepitus, a continuous grating sensation, may be felt or heard as the joint goes through ROM. Physical assessment of the musculoskeletal system reveals joint enlargement, resulting from **joint effusion** or bony swelling or both. This is most easily detected in knees by the evidence of patellar tap or by the elicitation of a fluid thrill (wave test). Joint deformities reflect advanced disease with joint destruction, which then contributes to misalignment, joint instability (causing a sensation in the knees of "giving way" or "locking"), and limb shortening. Fingers also can be misaligned in the presence of Heberden's (enlargements of DIP joints) or Bouchard's nodes (enlargements of PIP joints) (Fig. 39-2).

Radiographic assessment can be helpful to diagnose OA and to establish severity of joint damage; to monitor disease activity, progression, and response to therapy; and to search for complications of the disorder or the treatment. Standard X-rays of affected joints show osteophytes, most characteristic feature of OA, and in more advanced disease, joint space narrowing and sclerosis. MRI can be used to assess the quantity and function of cartilage, synovium, and bone; however, it is not yet recommended for routine use. Arthroscopy is a more appropriate gold standard in the evaluation of OA, allowing direct visualization of cartilage surface integrity. Routine laboratory tests such as ESR and C-reactive protein

are usually normal, but can be helpful in ruling out other diseases. Low titers of rheumatoid factors can be found. Synovial fluid analysis can be done to differentiate OA from RA. No biochemical markers are currently examined; no single marker is yet adequate for predicting or monitoring OA.

Medical and Nursing Management

No treatment halts the degenerative process of OA; as a result, management focuses on managing pain and inflammation, preventing or limiting disability, and maintaining and improving joint function. Nonpharmacologic treatment measures mentioned earlier in the chapter are the core for OA management and should be maintained throughout the patient's course of the disease. Interventions mainly center around rest and joint protection, heat application with some use of cold, and weight reduction and exercise. CAM therapies for symptom management have become an increasingly popular avenue of treatment particularly movement therapies (e.g., T'ai chi, yoga) and nutritional supplements (e.g., glucosamine often in combination with chondroitin). More research is needed in the area of dietary supplements. Study findings on glucosamine are inconsistent as to the effectiveness of pain management in OA.

Pharmacologic therapy is used in conjunction with nonpharmacologic measures. In OA, the initial analgesic therapy is acetaminophen 650 mg to 1,000 mg every 6 hours, with the daily dose not to exceed 4,000 mg/day (Lehne, 2010; Porth & Matfin, 2009). However, current debate exists concerning decreasing the maximum dose of acetaminophen to 2,600 mg/day due to liver toxicity and unintentional overdosing. Adequate intake of water, at least 2,000 mL/day, is encouraged to promote excretion of the drug. For the patient who either fails to obtain adequate pain management with acetaminophen or has moderate to severe pain, an NSAID may provide greater relief. If the patient is at risk for or experiences gastrointestinal (GI) complications with an NSAID, supplemental treatment with a protective agent such as misoprostol (Cytotec) may be indicated. As an alternative to traditional NSAIDs, treatment with the cyclooxygenase (COX)-2 inhibitor celecoxib (Celebrex) may be considered in selected patients. The use of COX-2 inhibitors will be discussed later, in the management of RA.

Other medications that may be considered are the opioids, and topical analgesics such as capsaicin (Capsin, Zostrix) and methyl salicylate. Another therapeutic approach is the intra-articular injection of hyaluronic acid, referred to as viscosupplementation. Viscosupplementation is used in OA patients and thought to provide a short-term lubricant and biomechanical benefit as well as an analgesic effect by buffering synovial nerve endings directly; it may also have some anti-inflammatory effects, and it may stimulate synovial lining cells to produce hyaluronic acid.

For persistent, moderate to severe OA and erosive RA, reconstructive surgery and corticosteroids are often used. Reconstructive surgery is indicated when pain cannot be

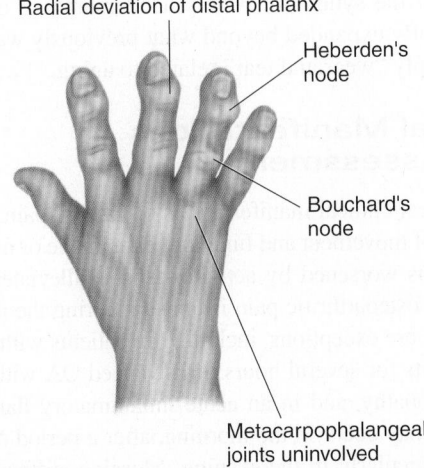

Radial deviation of distal phalanx

Heberden's node

Bouchard's node

Metacarpophalangeal joints uninvolved

FIGURE 39-2 Heberden's and Bouchard's nodes. From Bickley, L. S. (2009). *Bates' guide to physical examination and history taking* (10th ed.). Philadelphia: Lippincott Williams & Wilkins.

relieved by conservative measures and the threat of loss of independence is eminent. Surgical procedures include synovectomy (excision of the synovial membrane), arthrodesis (surgical fusion of the joint), tenorrhaphy (suturing of a tendon), and osteotomy (to alter the distribution of weight within the joint). The most commonly used procedure is **arthroplasty**, a surgical repair and replacement of the joint. Surgery is not performed during disease flares.

Tidal irrigation (lavage) of the knee involves the introduction of a large volume of saline into the joint through cannulas and then removal of this fluid. In some cases, this procedure provides pain relief for up to 6 months.

GOUT

Gout, one of the most common of the inflammatory arthritides, is a metabolic disorder marked by the deposition of monosodium urate crystals within joints and other tissues. Gout is a heterogeneous group of conditions related to a genetic defect of purine metabolism that results in hyperuricemia (excessive uric acid, a purine end product). The prevalence of gout is reported to be less than 1% to 15.3%, and it appears to be on the rise. It occurs more commonly in males (90%) than in females. The incidence increases with age, body mass index, and increasing serum uric acid (urate) levels (Montgomery, 2008; Wortmann, 2009). While hyperuricemia may indicate an increased risk of gout, the association between hyperuricemia and gout is unclear. Typically, the higher the uric acid level and longer the length of the elevation, the more likely that gout will occur and tophi (deposits of uric acid) will form. On the other hand, some patients with hyperuricemia do not develop gout, and other patients with repeated gout attacks have normal or low serum uric acid levels (laboratory population-based norm for men is up to 7 mg/dL and women is 6 mg/dL) (Fischbach & Dunning, 2009). Therefore, the exact level of uric acid that is considered pathological is controversial.

Primary gout is characterized by hyperuricemia caused by an overproduction of uric acid or a decreased urate excretion in the kidney. Primary gout is often caused by an inherited disorder in purine metabolism, with a 50% incidence (Montgomery, 2008). Secondary gout is related to a wide number of diseases or drugs that decrease the kidney's ability to excrete uric acid, increase the production of uric acid, or a combination of both. Conditions associated with secondary gout include diabetic ketoacidosis, severe dieting or starvation, and metabolic syndrome. Disorders such as multiple myeloma and leukemia result in increased production of uric acid because of a greater cell turnover and an increase in cell breakdown. Altered renal tubular function, either as a major action or as an unintended side effect of certain pharmacologic agents (e.g., diuretics such as thiazides and furosemide), low-dose salicylates, or ethanol, can contribute to uric acid underexcretion. An excessive intake of foods that are high in purines (shellfish, organ meats) may result in symptoms of gout in susceptible persons.

Pathophysiology

Hyperuricemia denotes an elevated level of uric acid (urate) in the blood, and in recent years, it has been recognized that the reference ranges are quite wide. The laboratory reference ranges of hyperuricemia are often reported based on population norms, and values vary depending on the population being evaluated. To define individuals with hyperuricemia, current evidence-based reviews recommend that it is more clinically relevant to use the biologic value of 6.8 mg/dL or 408 μmol/L, a level of serum uric acid above the saturation point for crystal formation (Chen & Schumacher, 2008; Malik, Schumacher, Dinnella, et al., 2009; Wortmann, 2009). Asymptomatic hyperuricemia is a laboratory finding, not a disease, but can lead to gout pathogenesis. Attacks of gout appear to be related to sudden increases or decreases of serum uric acid levels. When the uric acid precipitates and then deposits within a joint as urate crystals, an inflammatory response occurs, and an attack of gout begins. With repeated attacks, accumulations of sodium urate crystals, called **tophi**, are deposited in peripheral areas of the body, such as the great toe, the hands, and the ear (lower temperature areas). Renal urate lithiasis (kidney stones), with chronic renal disease secondary to urate deposition, may develop.

Clinical Manifestations and Assessment

Manifestations of the gout syndrome include acute gouty arthritis (recurrent attacks of severe articular and periarticular inflammation), tophi (crystalline deposits accumulating in articular tissue, osseous tissue, soft tissue, and cartilage), gouty nephropathy (renal impairment), and uric acid urinary calculi. Four stages (or phases) of gout can be identified: asymptomatic hyperuricemia, acute gouty arthritis, intercritical gout, and chronic tophaceous gout. Phase 1, asymptomatic hyperuricemia, is when the serum urate level is high, but gout manifested by arthritis or nephrolithiasis has not yet occurred. People can remain asymptomatic throughout their lifetimes. The subsequent development of gout is directly related to the duration and magnitude of the hyperuricemia. Therefore, the commitment to lifelong pharmacologic treatment of hyperuricemia is deferred until there is an initial attack of gout (phase 2).

Acute arthritis is the most common early clinical manifestation of gouty arthritis. The first attack usually occurs between age 40 and 60 years in men and after 60 in women (Wortmann, 2009). The patient experiences excruciating pain and inflammation in one or more small joints. The metatarsophalangeal joint of the big toe is the most commonly affected joint (90% of patients) and is referred to as **podagra** (Porth & Matfin, 2009). The tarsal area, ankle, or knee may also be affected. Less commonly, the wrists, fingers, and elbows may be affected. Trauma, alcohol ingestion, dieting, medications, surgical stress, or illness may trigger the acute attack. The abrupt onset often occurs at night, awakening the patient with severe

pain, redness, swelling, and warmth of the affected joint. Early attacks tend to subside spontaneously over 3 to 10 days even without treatment. The attack is followed by a symptom-free period (the intercritical stage or phase 3) until the next attack, which may not come for months or years. However, with time, attacks tend to occur more frequently, to involve more joints, last longer, and lead to long-term sequelae (phase 4).

Tophi are generally associated with more frequent and severe inflammatory episodes. Higher serum concentrations of uric acid are also associated with more extensive tophus formation. Tophi most commonly occur in the synovium, olecranon bursa, subchondral bone, infrapatellar and Achilles tendons, and subcutaneous tissue on the extensor surface of the forearms and overlying joints. They have also been found in the aortic walls, heart valves, nasal and ear cartilage, eyelids, cornea, and sclerae. Joint enlargement may cause a loss of joint motion. Uric acid deposits may cause renal stones and kidney damage.

A definitive diagnosis of gouty arthritis is established by polarized light microscopy of the synovial fluid of the involved joint (Malik et al., 2009). Uric acid crystals are seen within the polymorphonuclear leukocytes in the fluid. Although the gold standard for diagnosis is correct identification of crystals, clinical impressions are most frequently used.

Medical Management

Treatment of gout is managed in two major phases: management of acute gouty inflammation and long-term management to prevent flares and to control hyperuricemia. Prompt introduction of an anti-inflammatory agent is used to treat inflammatory episodes in gout. NSAIDS, such as indomethacin or ibuprofen, are considered agents of first choice; indomethacin or ibuprofen with colchicine as an alternative or in combination can be considered. Colchicine (in combination with uricosuric) was first approved by the U.S. Food and Drug Administration (FDA) in 1939, and in 2009, the FDA approved the first single-ingredient oral colchicine product, Colcrys, for the treatment of acute gout (Kesselheim & Soloman, 2010). Other agents prescribed to relieve an acute attack of gout are corticosteroids (oral or parenteral) or adrenocorticotropic hormones (ACTH) because of their anti-inflammatory properties.

Low-dose colchicine has been used for prophylaxis after resolution of attacks, but does not prevent accumulation of urate in joints and tophi. Management of hyperuricemia, tophi, joint destruction, and renal disorders is usually initiated after the acute inflammatory process has subsided. Allopurinol (Zyloprim), a xanthine oxidase inhibitor, is considered the drug of choice for preventing the precipitation of an attack and tophi formation and for promoting the regression of existing tophi. Uricosuric agents, such as probenecid (Benemid), correct hyperuricemia and dissolve deposited urate. Sulfinpyrazone (Anturane) is very similar to probenecid but it is more potent. Severe blood dyscrasias may occur with use, so

it is generally reserved for patients with symptoms resistant to other agents.

When reduction of the serum urate level is indicated, uricosuric agents are the medications of choice. The recommended target goal of therapy is a serum uric acid level of less than 6 mg/dL, a level below the saturation point of 6.8 mg/dL at which urate crystals precipitate from solution (Wortmann, 2009). Current practice trends have shown that reducing and maintaining the serum uric acid levels result in crystal dissolution from joints, a reduction in gout attacks (flares), and the prevention or reduction in tophaceous deposits. If the patient has, or is at risk for, renal insufficiency or renal calculi (kidney stones), allopurinol is also effective at a lowered adjusted dose. A new medication, febuxostat (Uloric), was approved by the FDA in 2009 for the treatment of gout that does not respond to usual treatment. Newer urate-lowering agents, such as uricase, are currently under investigation and show promise for successful gout treatment. Corticosteroids are useful for short-term therapy of acute gout and may be used in patients who have no response to other therapy. If the patient experiences several acute episodes or there is evidence of tophi formation, prophylactic treatment is considered. Specific treatment is based on the serum uric acid level, 24-hour urinary uric acid excretion, and renal function. Table 39-4 lists the common medications used in treating gout.

Nursing Management

Pain management is the primary concern during the acute phase of an attack. The joint should be rested and application of ice, not heat, may help with reducing discomfort. The management of the intercritical and chronic phases of gout involves teaching self-care measures to decrease the risk of attacks (e.g., avoidance of aspirin [because doses below 2 to 3 g/day impair renal excretion of uric acid retention and higher doses are associated with high renal excretion of uric acids], trauma, stress, alcohol) and to avoid long-term complications (e.g., importance of medication compliance). During the intercritical period, the patient feels well and may abandon preventive behaviors, which may result in an acute attack. Although special dietary restrictions are controversial, some health care providers recommend that patients restrict consumption of foods high in purines, especially organ meats and shellfish; others believe that limiting protein foods or avoiding trigger foods are sufficient. Patients should be taught to limit alcohol intake and to avoid fad starvation diets. It is important that patients drink plenty of fluids, at least 2,000 mL daily, to lessen renal involvement and the development of urinary stones (Montgomery, 2008). Maintenance of normal body weight should be encouraged. Also, dietary restriction of sodium, fat, and cholesterol can lead to a reduction in gout symptoms and decrease effects associated with coexisting metabolic syndrome. Although research is limited, first acute gout attacks may commonly precede the diagnosis of metabolic abnormalities and associated diseases.

TABLE
39-4 Medications Used to Treat Gout

Medication	Actions and Use	Nursing Implications
Colchicine	Lowers the deposition of uric acid and interferes with leukocyte infiltration, thus reducing inflammation; does not alter serum or urine levels of uric acid; used in acute and chronic management	*Acute management:* Administer when attack begins; dosage increased until pain is relieved or diarrhea develops *Chronic management:* Causes gastrointestinal upset in most patients
Probenecid (Benemid), sulfinpyrazone (Anturane)	Uricosuric agent; inhibits renal reabsorption of urates and increases the urinary excretion of uric acid; prevents tophi formation	Be alert for nausea and rash Risk of uric acid deposition in kidney, patient should ingest large volumes of fluids
Allopurinol (Zyloprim), febuxostat (Uloric)	Xanthine oxidase inhibitor; interrupts the breakdown of purines before uric acid is formed; inhibits xanthinoxidase because it blocks uric acid formation	Monitor for side effects, including bone marrow depression, vomiting, and abdominal pain

FIBROMYALGIA

Fibromyalgia (FM) is a chronic pain syndrome characterized by diffuse musculoskeletal achiness, stiffness, fatigue, and exaggerated tenderness at 18 specified tender points. The pain in FM is not due to tissue damage or inflammation, thus making it fundamentally different from other rheumatic disorders and many other pain conditions. FM affects between 2% and 4% worldwide, women more frequently than men (8:1 ratio) (Spaeth & Briley, 2009; Wolfe & Rasker, 2009). Although criteria for the classification of FM were identified in 1990 (Wolfe, Smythe, Yunus et al., 1990), controversy exists as to whether this diagnosis represents a unique syndrome. No consensus exists on the syndrome's cause and treatment. Theories have shifted from peripheral pathology (musculoskeletal changes) to central dysfunction (pain processing mechanisms) that results in central pain sensitization (Burkham & Harris, 2009; Wolfe & Rasker, 2009).

Clinical Manifestations and Assessment

The core features of pain and tenderness are almost invariably accompanied by a wide range of symptoms, the most common of which are sleep disturbances, fatigue, morning stiffness, muscle weakness, paresthesias, cognitive dysfunction ("fibro fog"), chronic headaches, and mood disturbances (Wolfe & Rasker, 2009). The patient complains of a widespread burning pain and is often unable to discriminate if pain occurs in the muscles, joints, or soft tissues. Physical examination typically reveals point tenderness at 11 or more of 18 identified sites (Fig. 39-3).

Medical Management

Treatment consists of attention to the specific symptoms reported by the patient. Patient education, exercise, and cognitive therapy, along with medication, are frequently used.

The pharmacotherapy of FM is mechanism-based; many have been tested to a greater or lesser extent. NSAIDs may be used to treat the diffuse muscle aching and stiffness. Tramadol is the only opiate shown to provide some relief. Many drugs have been used off-label to treat FM. Pregabalin (Lyrica), an analgesic, anxiolytic, and anticonvulsant ($\alpha_{2-\delta}$ receptor ligand agent), is the first to receive FDA approval for FM use. Psychotropic agents have been used to reduce pain centrally, even in the absence of depression: serotonin noradrenaline reuptake inhibitors or SNRIs (duloxetine, milnacipran), least selective serotonin reuptake inhibitors

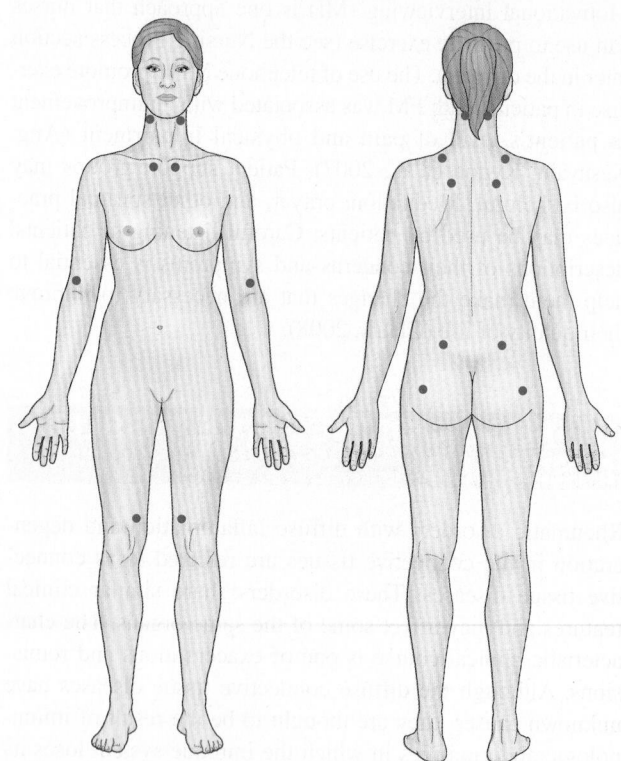

FIGURE 39-3 Fibromyalgia tender points.

(fluoxetine, paroxetine), dopaminergic agents (pramipexole), and antidepressants, particularly tricyclics (Clauw, 2008; Spaeth & Briley, 2009). Duloxetine (Cymbalta) has also been approved by the FDA for symptom relief in FM. Tricyclic antidepressants can also be used to improve or restore normal sleep patterns. Individualized programs of exercise (as a multicomponent treatment strategy) are used to decrease muscle weakness and discomfort and to improve the general deconditioning that occurs in affected patients (Burkham & Harris, 2009; Spaeth & Briley, 2009).

Nursing Management

Typically, patients with FM have endured their symptoms for a long period of time. They may feel as if their symptoms have not been taken seriously. Nurses need to pay special attention to supporting these patients and providing encouragement as they begin their program of therapy. The goal of FM treatment is to improve the physical and mental health of patients and their quality of life. Interventions or strategies should be developed to promote better functioning. Greater education, lower-intensity fatigue, and using aerobic or strength training exercises were predictors of physical functioning (Rutledge, Jones, & Jones, 2007). Nurses need to work with the patient to increase independence, avoiding complications of deconditioning, work disability, and the inability to fulfill social role. Nurses should also focus on patient safety: FM has found to be associated with impaired balance and falls (Jones, Horak, Winters-Stone et al., 2009). Stretching, aerobic exercise, and strength training should be in every patient's exercise plan. Motivational interviewing (MI) is one approach that nurses can use to promote exercise (see the Nursing Process section later in the chapter). The use of telephone MI to promote exercise in patients with FM was associated with an improvement in patient's level of pain and physical impairment (Ang, Kesavalu, Kydon et al., 2007). Patient support groups may also be helpful. Meditation, prayer, and other spiritual practices may be used by patients. Careful listening to patients' descriptions of their concerns and symptoms is essential to help them make the changes that are necessary to improve their quality of life (Clauw, 2008).

DIFFUSE CONNECTIVE TISSUE DISEASES

Rheumatic disorders with diffuse inflammation and degeneration in the connective tissues are referred to as connective tissue diseases. These disorders share similar clinical features and may affect some of the same organs. The characteristic clinical course is one of exacerbations and remissions. Although the diffuse connective tissue diseases have unknown causes, they are thought to be the result of immunologic abnormalities in which the immune system loses its ability to tell the difference between foreign invaders and the body's normal cells. The common connective tissue diseases, RA, systemic lupus erythematosus (SLE), and scleroderma are presented in detail.

RHEUMATOID ARTHRITIS

RA is the most common inflammatory arthritic disorder and serves as a prototype for the study of many inflammatory and immune-mediated diseases. RA affects 0.5% to 1% of the general population worldwide, with a female-to-male ratio of between 2:1 and 3:1 (Firestein, 2009).

Pathophysiology

In RA, numerous cell types are involved, including macrophages, T cells, B cells, fibroblasts, chondrocytes, and dendritic cells. The autoimmune reaction primarily occurs in the synovial tissue. Adaptive and innate immune responses in the synovium have been implicated in the pathogenesis of RA. Rheumatoid factor (RF) antibodies develop in the synovium against the immunoglobulin IgG to form immune complexes. The activation of the complement system and release of lysosomal enzymes from leukocytes leads to inflammation. It is unknown why the body produces an antibody (RF) against its own antibody (IgG) and, in consequence, transforms IgG to an antigen or foreign protein that must be destroyed. Phagocytosis produces enzymes (cytokines especially interleukin [IL]-1) within the joint. The enzymes break down collagen, causing edema, proliferation of the synovial membrane, and ultimately **pannus** formation (Fig. 39-4). Pannus, formation of vascular granulation tissue, is a characteristic of RA that differentiates it from other forms of inflammatory arthritis. Pannus has a destructive effect on the adjacent cartilage and bone. Research has found that the inflammatory chemical messenger, tumor necrosis factor (TNF), is produced by cells at the cartilage–pannus junction and may also lead to cartilage destruction. The consequences are loss of articular surfaces and joint motion. Muscle fibers also undergo degenerative changes. Tendon and ligament elasticity and contractile power are lost.

Clinical Manifestations and Assessment

Clinical manifestations of RA vary, usually reflecting the stage and severity of the disease. Physical signs of RA are associated with the pathophysiology of the disease. The manifestations of RA can be categorized as early or late disease, and as articular (joint) or extra-articular. Joint pain, swelling, warmth, erythema (redness), and lack of function are classic symptoms. Palpation of the joints reveals spongy or boggy tissue. Often, fluid can be aspirated from the inflamed joint. Characteristically, the pattern of joint involvement begins in the small joints of the hands, wrists, and feet. As the disease progresses, the knees, shoulders, hips, elbows, ankles, cervical

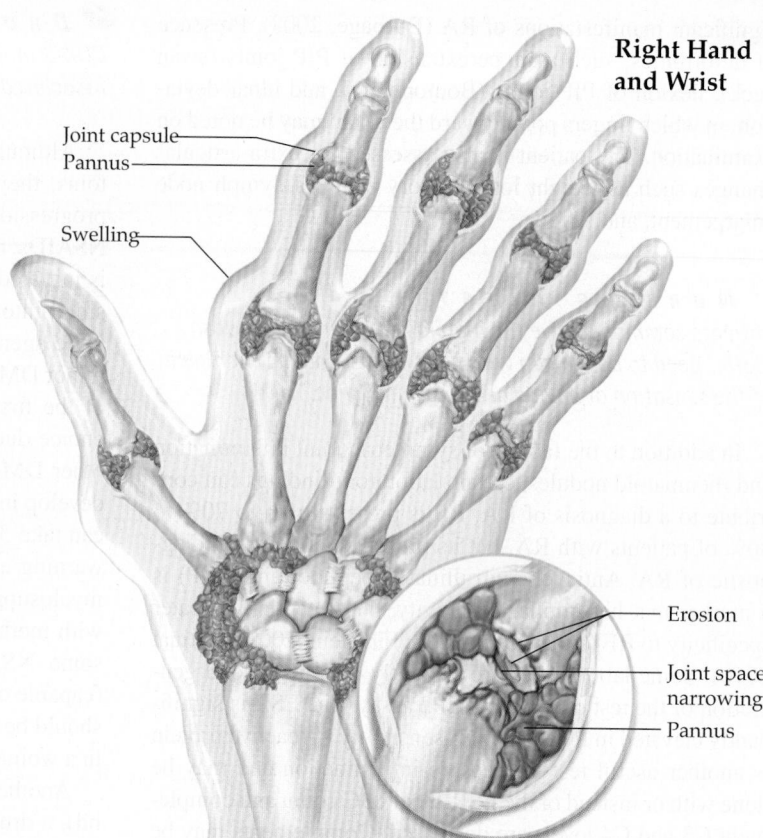

Right Hand and Wrist

Joint capsule

Pannus

Swelling

Erosion

Joint space narrowing

Pannus

FIGURE 39-4 Joints affected by rheumatoid arthritis.

spine, and temporomandibular joints are affected. The onset of symptoms is usually acute. Symptoms are usually bilateral and symmetric. In addition to joint pain and swelling, a cardinal sign of inflammatory arthritis that can appear even before pain is morning stiffness, lasting at least 30 to 45 minutes (Firestein, 2009).

Deformities of the hands and feet are common in RA (Fig. 39-5). Often the PIP and metacarpophalangeal (MCP) joints of the hands are involved initially. The deformity may be caused by misalignment resulting from swelling, progressive joint destruction, or the subluxation (partial dislocation)

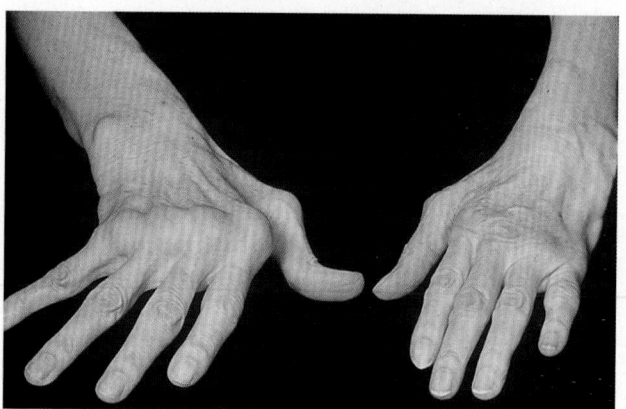

FIGURE 39-5 Rheumatoid arthritis.

that occurs when one bone slips over another and eliminates the joint space.

RA is a systemic disease with multiple extra-articular features. Most common are fever, weight loss, fatigue, anemia, lymph node enlargement, and Raynaud's phenomenon (cold- and stress-induced vasospasm causing episodes of digital blanching or cyanosis). Rheumatoid nodules may be noted in patients with more advanced RA, and they develop at some time in the course of the disease in about 15% to 20% of patients (Firestein, 2009). These nodules are usually nontender and movable in the subcutaneous tissue. They usually appear over bony prominences, most often on extensor surfaces or pressure points such as the elbow, are varied in size, and can disappear spontaneously. Nodules occur only in people who have RF. The nodules often are associated with rapidly progressive and destructive disease. Other extra-articular features include arteritis, neuropathy, scleritis, pericarditis, splenomegaly, and Sjögren's syndrome (dry eyes and dry mucous membranes).

A clinical examination of all synovial joints should be undertaken for evidence of tenderness, swelling, and range of movement. Evidence for synovitis should be seen by a rheumatologist, ideally within 6 weeks after the onset of symptoms to facilitate early diagnosis and clinical management and to achieve optimal outcomes for patients (Oliver, 2007). Swelling of three or more joints, involvements of the MCP or metatarsophalangeal joints, or early morning stiffness are

significant manifestations of RA (Burbage, 2008). Presence of deformities, such as hyperextension of PIP joints (swan neck), flexion of PIP joints (Boutonniere), and ulnar deviation, in which fingers point toward the ulnar, may be noted on examination. The patient is also assessed for extra-articular changes such as weight loss, sensory changes, lymph node enlargement, and fatigue.

☀ NURSING ALERT

Patients commonly have the inability to "wring out a wash cloth," need to hold a cup with both hands, and may complain of the sensation of having a "stone in my shoe."

In addition to the factors of symmetric joint inflammation and rheumatoid nodules, certain laboratory findings can contribute to a diagnosis of RA. RF is present in up to 70% to 80% of patients with RA, but its presence alone is not diagnostic of RA. Anticyclic citrullinated peptide (anti-CCP) is a marker that has similar sensitivity, but potentially greater specificity to RF (Brasington, 2008; Firestein, 2009; Nettina, 2010). Some laboratories are currently doing a second generation of the test called the CCP2 assay. The ESR is significantly elevated in RA. The high-sensitivity C-reactive protein is another useful test to measure inflammation and may be done with or instead of the ESR. The RBC count and complement C3 and C4 levels are decreased. Complements may be decreased as they are "used up" in some antigen-antibody reactions. Results of antinuclear antibody (ANA), the screening test for autoantibodies (antibodies that form against self), may also be positive. **Arthrocentesis** shows abnormal synovial fluid that is cloudy, milky, or dark yellow and contains numerous inflammatory components, such as leukocytes and complement. Synovial biopsy can detect inflammatory cells associated with RA. Radiological studies show characteristic bony erosions and narrowed joint spaces occurring later in the disease and help in diagnosing and monitoring the progression of disease.

Medical and Nursing Management

In most patients, NSAIDs usually are the first choice in the treatment of RA. The use of traditional NSAIDs and salicylates inhibit the production of prostaglandins and provide anti-inflammatory effects as well as analgesia. Effectiveness, side effects, cost, and dosing schedules are considered in the selection of an NSAID. The incidence of adverse reactions (e.g., gastric irritation, kidney damage, changes in liver function) to the NSAIDs increases with age and long-term use.

A new class or second-generation NSAID, the COX-2 inhibitors, has been shown to inhibit inflammatory processes, but do not inhibit the protective prostaglandin synthesis in the GI tract. Therefore, patients who are at increased risk for GI complications, especially GI bleeding, have been managed effectively with COX-2 inhibitors.

💊 DRUG ALERT

COX-2 inhibitors must be used with caution because of the associated risk of cardiovascular disease.

Although the NSAIDs may provide fast relief of symptoms, they do not prevent joint damage nor slow disease progression. In RA, if joint symptoms persist despite use of NSAIDs, the second major drug group, known as DMARDs, is initiated early in the disease. The DMARDs can be classified into: (1) first-choice DMARDs nonbiologic, (2) biologic agents, (3) newer, small-molecule DMARDs, and (4) minor DMARDs. Methotrexate (Rheumatrex, Trexall) is one of the first-choice DMARDs and has become the drug of choice due to its potency and time of action (faster than all other DMARDs). Therapeutic effects or improvement may develop in 3 to 6 weeks, compared to other DMARDs, which can take 3 to 4 months to work (Lehne, 2010). A black box warning exists for unexpected, severe, and sometimes fatal myelosuppression, aplastic anemia, and GI toxicity reported with methotrexate (usually high-dose) in combination with some NSAIDs. Additionally, methotrexate is teratogenic (capable of causing birth defects), therefore a pregnancy test should be performed if a decision is made to begin treatment in a woman of childbearing age.

Another preferred DMARD, hydroxychloroquine (Plaquenil), a drug with antimalarial actions, can be initiated early and used with mild symptoms, but as a rule is used in combination with methotrexate. By itself, hydroxychloroquine does not slow disease progression; however, early use can improve long-term outcomes.

Newer DMARDs—biologic and small-molecule agents—have revolutionized disease control for certain rheumatic, autoimmune conditions. Both are immunosuppressive agents that target specific components of the inflammatory process. These drugs are usually combined with methotrexate and are especially used for adults with moderately to severely active RA who have not responded adequately to one or more DMARDs. Biologic agents (also referred as *immunomodulators*) are expensive, whereas the small-molecule DMARDs cost much less and are easier to manufacture.

Some biologic agents or modifiers interfere with the action of TNF: etanercept (Enbrel), infliximab (Remicade), and adalimumab (Humira). Most recently, golimumab (Simponi) and certolizumab pegol (Cimzia) have been approved for use in RA. The immunosuppressant actions of TNF blockers can increase the patient's risk of serious infections, including bacterial sepsis, invasive fungal infection, and tuberculosis. As a result, prior to initiation of TNF blockers, patients should be tested for tuberculosis. A different biologic agent, anakinra (Kineret), interferes with IL-1, which modulates immune and inflammatory responses, and thus has efficacy with rheumatic disorders. Like the TNF blockers, anakinra poses a risk of serious infections; therefore, anakinra should not be used in combination with TNF blockers.

Do not give live vaccines to patients on a biologic agent. Nurses need to monitor for signs of infection (e.g., fever, cough, flu-like symptoms, open sores on body). Nurses should also monitor for heart failure in patients on etanercept (Enbrel) or infliximab (Remicade).

The emerging agents show that a new era in treatment has begun, newly targeting B cells, T-cell activation, and probably IL-6 in the future. These constitute new principles for interference with disease process.

Leflunomide (Arava), a small-molecule DMARD, is a relatively new and powerful immunosuppressant used for patients with RA. Compared with methotrexate, leflunomide is about equally as effective but more dangerous because of the incidence of liver failure; it is reserved for second-line use. Another small-molecule DMARD is cyclosporine (Neoral, Sandimmune). Although cyclosporine reduces symptoms of RA, it can cause kidney damage and other serious adverse effects; hence, its use is for severe RA patients or it is added in, in the case of an inadequate response to methotrexate.

The minor DMARDs, gold salts, penicillamine, and azathioprine have been available for many years. These have been frequently used in the past, but their use today is limited. The drugs are generally reserved for patients with severe progressive RA disease who have failed to respond to safer DMARDs.

The third major group of antiarthritic drugs is the glucocorticoids (adrenal corticosteroids). These are powerful anti-inflammatory drugs used in RA especially during exacerbations ("flares") of the disease or when needing a "bridging" medication while waiting for the slower DMARDs (e.g., methotrexate) to begin taking effect. Oral glucocorticoids, such as prednisone and prednisolone, are indicated for patients with generalized symptoms. Long-term therapy can cause serious toxicity (e.g., osteoporosis, gastric ulceration, adrenal suppression, diabetes), so glucocorticoids should be limited to patients with RA who have failed to respond adequately to all other treatment options. Intra-articular injections may be employed if only one or two joints are affected and are commonly used in severe RA. Antibiotics, the tetracycline derivatives minocycline (Minocin) and doxycycline (Vibramycin), are given to improve symptoms (morning stiffness, joint pain and tenderness, and activities of daily living) in patients with RA. These antibiotics have found to decrease the action of enzymes on cartilage degradation. Usage is seen in patients who have not responded to DMARDs.

The *Prosorba Column*, a blood filtration device used in apheresis, has been approved by the FDA for use in treating patients with more severe and longstanding RA who have had no response to or are intolerant of DMARDs. The device, a protein A immunoadsorption column, is used in 12 weekly 2-hour apheresis treatments to bind IgG (i.e., circulating immune complex). As the patient's blood passes through the column, RF is removed.

💊 D R U G   A L E R T
If the patient is on an angiotensin-converting enzyme (ACE) inhibitor, it should be discontinued prior to treatment using Prosorba Column, as the risk of serious hypotension exists with this treatment.

Through all stages of RA, depression and sleep deprivation may require the short-term use of low-dose antidepressant medications, such as amitriptyline (Elavil), paroxetine (Paxil), or sertraline (Zoloft), to reestablish an adequate sleep pattern and to manage chronic pain.

SYSTEMIC LUPUS ERYTHEMATOSUS

SLE is a chronic inflammatory autoimmune disease with variable presentations, course, and prognosis characterized by remissions and exacerbations. The overall prevalence of SLE is estimated to be 51 per 100,000 in the United States. Occurrence is nine times more frequent in women than in men, and African Americans and Hispanics are affected more frequently than are Caucasians (Fauci & Langford, 2010; Tassiulas & Boumpas, 2009).

Pathophysiology

SLE is a result of disturbed immune regulation that causes an exaggerated production of autoantibodies and antigens. The immune abnormalities that characterize SLE occur in five phases: susceptibility, abnormal innate and adaptive immune responses, autoantibodies immune complexes, inflammation, and damage. Interactions of predisposing factors (genes, female gender, and environment) result in abnormal immune responses, specifically in B cells and T cells. These responses produce pathogenic autoantibodies and immune complexes that activate complement, form in tissue, and cause inflammation. Inflammation stimulates antigens, which in turn stimulate additional antibodies. The cycle repeats and, over time, leads to irreversible organ damage. Some individuals do not progress through all phases.

💊 D R U G   A L E R T
Certain medications, such as hydralazine (Apresoline), procainamide (Pronestyl), isoniazid (INH), chlorpromazine (Thorazine), and some antiseizure medications, can trigger an exaggerated immune response and cause a chemical- or drug-induced SLE.

Clinical Manifestations and Assessment

The onset of SLE may be insidious or acute. For this reason, SLE may remain undiagnosed for many years. Systemic and musculoskeletal manifestations, particularly fatigue and myalgias/arthralgias, are most prevalent (95%) in the course of the disease (Fauci & Langford, 2010). SLE is an autoimmune systemic disease that can affect any body system. Clinical manifestations can resemble RA and may be mistaken

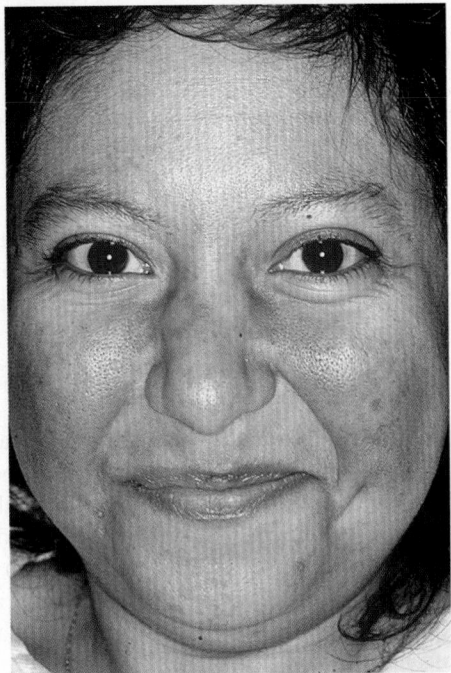

FIGURE 39-6 The characteristic butterfly rash of systemic lupus erythematosus.

for it, especially early in the course of the disease. Unlike RA, the arthritis is nonerosive and not seen on X-ray.

Several different types of skin manifestations are prevalent in 80% of patients with SLE. Photosensitivity rashes are most common; however, the most characteristic skin manifestation is an acute cutaneous lesion consisting of a butterfly-shaped rash across the bridge of the nose and cheeks (Pullen, Brewer, & Ballard, 2009) (Fig. 39-6). This malar rash manifests as an erythematous, flat or raised lesion, pruritic (itchy) or painful, and can be transient and heal without scarring. In some cases of discoid lupus erythematosus (DLE), only skin involvement occurs. Discoid (coinlike) lesions are scarring and ring-shaped that may result in erythematous, scaling plaques and alopecia (hair loss). In some patients with SLE, the initial skin involvement is the precursor to more systemic involvement. The lesions often worsen during exacerbations (flares) of the systemic disease and possibly are provoked by sunlight or artificial ultraviolet B light.

⚡ NURSING ALERT
The nurse should teach patients to avoid sunlight or ultraviolet (UV) exposure and to protect themselves with sunscreen, at least a sun protection factor of 30, and clothing.

Central nervous system involvement is widespread, encompassing the entire range of neurologic disease (60% prevalence). The varied and frequent neuropsychiatric presentations of SLE are now widely recognized. These are generally demonstrated by subtle changes in behavior patterns or cognitive ability. Mood disorder, depression, and psychosis

are common (Fauci & Langford, 2010; Nettina, 2010; Pullen et al., 2009).

Pericarditis and pleuritis are the most common cardiopulmonary disorders (refer to Chapters 16 and 10). Women who have SLE are also at risk for early atherosclerosis. About 50% of patients with SLE have renal disease, such as glomerulonephritis. Serum creatinine levels and urinalysis are used in screening for renal involvement. Early detection allows for prompt treatment, so that renal damage can be prevented. Renal involvement may lead to hypertension, which also requires careful monitoring and management.

Diagnosis of SLE is based on a complete history, physical examination, and diagnostic tests. SLE has an extreme range of clinical manifestations without classic presentation. Diagnosis is made difficult by the variable manifestations of the disease and relies on the overall clinical picture with the correlation of diagnostic laboratory and imaging studies, possibly including skin biopsy.

The presence of at least four of the criteria established by the ACR is required to make the diagnosis of SLE. Cutaneous manifestations comprise four of the 11 diagnostic ACR criteria (malar rash, discoid rash, photosensitivity and oral ulcers). When performing an assessment, it is critical to inspect skin for erythematous rashes. The nurse asks the patient about the existence of photosensitivity, fatigue, oral ulcers, or pain in joints. Additionally, systemic involvement may encompass several organ systems; therefore, the nurse must review laboratory values or findings that might suggest that the effects of inflammation are targeting organs (e.g., ESR, complete blood count- anemia or thrombocytopenia, creatinine, hematuria).

No single laboratory test confirms SLE. Most patients with SLE (>90%) demonstrate elevated serum levels of ANA, which is another ACR criterion for SLE diagnosis. A small percent of patients will test negative for ANA but will have antibodies to the nuclear antigen anti-Ro (SSA) (Nettina, 2010; Pullen et al., 2009). Other diagnostic immunologic tests that support SLE diagnosis in the presence of clinical manifestations are C-reactive protein, anti-double-stranded DNA (anti-ds DNA), anti-RNA, anti-Sm (Smith), and high-titer IgG antibodies. The double-stranded DNA test, C3, and C4 indicate whether there is a genetic component that is common in 50% to 60% of patients with SLE (Neal-Boylan, 2009).

Medical and Nursing Management

SLE can be life-threatening; however, advances in its treatment have led to improved survival and reduced morbidity. Treatment of SLE includes management of acute and chronic disease. The goals of treatment include preventing progressive loss of organ function, reducing the likelihood of acute disease, minimizing disease-related disabilities, and preventing complications from therapy.

NSAIDs, antimalarials, glucocorticoids, and in severe SLE cases, immunosuppressive agents (azathioprine, mycophenolate mofetil, methotrexate) are used in the management

of SLE. Corticosteroids are the single most important medication available for SLE. These drugs are used topically for cutaneous manifestations, in low oral doses for minor disease activity, and in high doses for major disease activity. IV administration of corticosteroids is an alternative to traditional high-dose oral use. Corticosteroid toxicity is a major problem, and tapering of the dosage is a primary concern.

Treatment of moderate to severe SLE consists of a period of intensive immunosuppressive therapy (induction therapy) followed by a longer period of less intensive maintenance therapy. The main objective of the induction therapy is to stop injury, recover function, and induce remission by managing immunologic activity. B-cell depleting therapies such as the monoclonal antibodies rituximab (Rituxan) and epratuzumab (humanized anti-CD22 antibody) are the newest form of treatment for SLE and are reserved for patients who have serious forms of SLE that have not responded to conservative therapies (Tassiulas & Boumpas, 2009).

SCLERODERMA

Scleroderma ("hard skin") is a relatively rare disease that is poorly understood; the cause is unknown. Exposure to certain environmental and occupational agents (e.g., silica dust, heavy metals, polyvinyl chloride) and drugs (e.g., bleomycin, cocaine, fenfluramine appetite suppressants), infection, and human cytomegalovirus (CMV) and other viruses have been implicated as a potential trigger. Scleroderma is classified into localized and systemic (systemic sclerosis), with subclassifications with each. Incidence estimates range from 9 to 19 people per million per year (Varga & Denton, 2009). Similar to other connective tissue diseases, scleroderma is more frequent in women than men.

Pathophysiology

Like other diffuse connective tissue diseases, scleroderma has a variable course, featuring remissions and exacerbations. Systemic scleroderma is a progressive, chronic, devastating, and debilitating disease with a prognosis not as optimistic as that of SLE. Pathogenesis integrates three cardinal features: vascular injury and damage, activation of innate and adaptive arms of the immune system autoimmunity, and generalized interstitial and vascular fibrosis.

Scleroderma commonly begins with skin involvement. Mononuclear cells cluster on the skin and stimulate lymphokines to stimulate procollagen. Insoluble collagen is formed and accumulates excessively in the tissues. Initially, the inflammatory response causes edema formation, with a resulting taut, smooth, and shiny skin appearance. The skin then undergoes fibrotic changes, leading to loss of elasticity and movement. Eventually, the tissue degenerates and becomes nonfunctional. This chain of events, from inflammation to degeneration, also occurs in blood vessels, synovium, skeletal muscles, and internal organ(s) of the heart, lungs, GI

tract, and kidneys (Babin, 2007; Harris-Akers & Ramirez, 2007; Nettina, 2010).

Clinical Manifestations and Assessment

Scleroderma starts insidiously with Raynaud's phenomenon and swelling in the hands. The hallmark of scleroderma is when the skin and the subcutaneous tissues become increasingly hard and rigid and cannot be pinched up from the underlying structures (fibrosis). Wrinkles and lines are obliterated. The skin is dry because sweat secretion over the involved region is suppressed. The extremities stiffen and lose mobility. The condition spreads slowly; for years, these changes may remain localized in the hands and the feet. The face appears masklike, immobile, and expressionless, and the mouth becomes rigid.

The changes within the body, although not visible directly, are vastly more important than the visible changes. The left ventricle of the heart is involved, resulting in heart failure. The esophagus hardens, interfering with swallowing. The lungs become scarred, impeding respiration. Digestive disturbances occur because of hardening (sclerosing) of the intestinal mucosa. Progressive renal failure may occur.

The patient may manifest a subset of limited cutaneous symptoms referred to as the CREST syndrome (Box 39-4).

Assessment focuses on the hallmark sclerotic changes in the skin, contractures in the fingers, and color changes or ulcerations in the fingertips due to poor circulation. Assessment of systemic involvement requires a systems review with special attention to GI, pulmonary, renal, and cardiac symptoms. Limitations in mobility and self-care activities should be assessed, along with the impact the disease has had (or will have) on body image.

There is no one conclusive test to diagnose scleroderma, and testing depends on the possibility or extent of organ involvement. A skin biopsy is performed to identify cellular changes specific to scleroderma. Pulmonary studies show ventilation–perfusion abnormalities. Echocardiography evaluates left ventricular function and pulmonary arterial pressure,

---

BOX 39-4 | **Focused Assessment**

Cutaneous Symptoms of Scleroderma

Be alert for the CREST symptoms:

- **C**alcinosis (calcium deposits in the tissues)
- **R**aynaud's phenomenon (spasm of blood vessels in response to cold or stress)
- **E**sophageal dysfunction (acid reflux and decrease in mobility of esophagus)
- **S**clerodactyly (thickening and tightening of skin on fingers and hands)
- **T**elangiectasia (capillary dilation that forms vascular red marks on surface of skin)

and identifies pericardial effusion (often present with cardiac involvement). Esophageal studies demonstrate reflux esophagitis (early discriminator) and dysmotility in most patients with scleroderma. Autoantibody testing, particularly ANA, is the most useful laboratory test, with a positive result common in more than 95% of patients with scleroderma and antisclerodermal antibody (anti-sci) 70 (Varga & Denton, 2009). In the presence of CREST syndrome, 90% have a positive anticentromere antibody test. Other autoantibodies demonstrate an association between scleroderma and a specific clinical pattern, such as anti-topoisomerase I antibodies and lung fibrosis, or anti-RNA polymerase I/III and scleroderma renal crisis.

Medical and Nursing Management

Management of scleroderma depends on the patient's clinical manifestations. In scleroderma, treatment includes management of acute and chronic disease. Acute conditions require interventions directed at controlling increased disease activity or exacerbations that can involve any organ system. Management of the more chronic condition involves periodic monitoring and recognition of meaningful clinical changes requiring adjustments in therapy. Because this is a life-altering disease that has no cure, all patients should receive counseling, during which realistic individual goals may be determined. As in the other rheumatic disorders, support measures include strategies to decrease pain, limit disability, maintain moderate exercise, and prevent joint contractures. No specific medication regimen has proved effective in modifying the disease process in scleroderma, but along with antiarthritic drugs, various medications are used to treat organ system involvement. Calcium channel blockers and other antihypertensive agents may provide improvement in symptoms of Raynaud's phenomenon.

In addition to the common problems of rheumatic disorders, nurses need to identify other patient difficulties or needs related to scleroderma and plan accordingly. For instance, patients with scleroderma have problems associated with impaired skin integrity and imbalanced nutrition, less than body requirements. The patient with advanced disease may also have impaired gas exchange, decreased cardiac output, impaired swallowing, and constipation.

Providing meticulous skin care and preventing the effects of Raynaud's phenomenon are major nursing challenges. Nurses teach patients to avoid the cold and to protect fingers with mittens. In addition, warm socks and properly fitting shoes are helpful in preventing ulcers. Careful, frequent inspection for early ulcers is important, and smoking cessation is critical.

NURSING PROCESS

The Patient With a Rheumatic Disorder

Assessment

The health history, and physical and psychological assessments focus on current and past symptoms, such as fatigue, weakness, pain, stiffness, fever, or anorexia, and the effects of these symptoms on the patient's lifestyle and self-image. The patient's social support systems are also assessed (Box 39-5), as well as his or her ability to participate in daily activities, comply with the treatment regimen, and manage self-care. Additional areas assessed include the patient's understanding, motivation, knowledge, coping abilities, past experiences, preconceptions, and fears. The impact of the rheumatic disorder on the patient must be assessed to understand the patient's problems, so that a plan of care specific to his or her issues can be developed. The nurse assesses the impact of the condition by asking, "Are there things that you cannot do now that you could do a year ago?" "What is it about your condition that you find most frustrating?" "What do you most enjoy doing?" "What things do you find difficult that you would like to be able to do?" and "How do you manage to get around the tasks that are difficult?" (Woolf, 2008). The nurse's assessment and patient response to these questions may lead to identifying issues and concerns that can be addressed by nursing interventions and, through collaboration with other team members, expected patient outcomes can be achieved.

Diagnosis

Nursing diagnoses for patients with rheumatic disorders may include, but are not limited to:

- Acute and chronic pain related to inflammation and/or progression of joint deterioration, tissue damage, fatigue, lowered tolerance level, or ineffective pain/comfort measures
- Fatigue related to inflammatory process and increased disease activity, pain, inadequate sleep/rest, impaired physical and psychosocial functioning (including emotional stress/depression), and inadequate nutrition
- Insomnia related to pain, anxiety/stress, depression, and medications
- Impaired physical mobility related to musculoskeletal impairment, decreased range of motion, muscle weakness, pain on movement, limited endurance, lack of or improper use of ambulatory devices
- Self-care deficits (specify) related to limitations secondary to progression of disease, pain, fatigue, contractures, or loss of motion
- Ineffective health self-management (formerly ineffective therapeutic regimen management) related to complexity of chronic health problem and medication compliance, decisional conflicts, economic difficulties, and deficient knowledge regarding disease management
- Disturbed body image related to physical (e.g., joint abnormalities) and psychological (e.g., depression) changes, loss of body function, and dependency imposed by chronic illness
- Ineffective coping related to actual or perceived lifestyle or role changes, chronicity of disease, poor prognosis, and sense of powerlessness

BOX 39-5 **Nursing Research**

Bridging the Gap to Evidence-Based Practice

What is the Evidence of the Relationship Between Physical Function, Knowledge of Disease, Social Support and Self-Care Behavior?

Chen, S. Y., & Wang, H. H. (2007). The relationship between physical function, knowledge of disease, social support and self-care behavior in patients with rheumatoid arthritis. *Journal of Nursing Research*, 15(3), 183–191.

Purpose

RA is a chronic, progressive, inflammatory disease of unknown etiology that causes disability as well as morbidity and mortality. A key factor in managing RA successfully is the engaging of patients in proper self-care behaviors. Therefore, it is important that health care providers have a greater understanding of the predictive factors related to self-care behavior. The purpose of this study was to explore the relationship between physical function, knowledge of disease, social support, and self-care behavior in patients with RA and to examine the predictive variables of self-care behavior.

Design

A cross-sectional design was developed using a convenience sampling method. Subjects were recruited from two hospitals located in southern Taiwan. Inclusion criteria consisted of patients who were positively diagnosed with RA in accordance with American Rheumatism Association standards, have suffered from RA for a period exceeding 6 months, and are free of other chronic diseases. Informed written consent was obtained from eligible participants and the completion of questionnaires—demographic, Health Assessment Questionnaire,

rheumatoid arthritis knowledge scale, social support scale, and self-care behavior—were done. A power analysis suggested a minimum of 88 subjects, 115 of the 117 subjects invited submitted valid questionnaires, giving a response rate of 98.3%.

Findings

Majority of the subjects were female (83.5%) and married (72.9%). The mean years with RA was 7.8 ($SD = 6.1$, range $= 0.5$ to 25); ages ranged from 23 to 77 years of age, with a mean age of 52.7 ($SD = 10.7$). Findings showed a significantly positive correlation between self-care behavior and age, physical function, and social support ($p < .01$, $p < .05$, respectively). Stepwise regression showed that age and social support represented the effective predictors of self-care behavior, explaining 13.4% of total variance in self-care behavior.

Nursing Implications

The results of this study indicate that patients with RA who are older and have higher level of social support have better self-care behavior. To alleviate and prevent problems associated with RA, nurses should emphasize health education regarding the signs and symptoms of joint problems in adults, especially for women above 30 years of age and with a family history of RA. Because RA is a chronic disease, a patient may live with the condition for 20 to 30 years. Motivating patients to make behavioral changes and promoting social support from family and friends are important nursing interventions in enhancing self-care behavior.

- Risk for injury related to adverse effects of medications and potential complications

Planning

The major goals for the patient may include relief of pain and discomfort, relief of fatigue, promotion of nutrition and restorative sleep, increased mobility and exercise, maintenance of self-care, motivation and adherence to therapeutic regimen, improved body image, effective coping, absence of complications, and promotion of home care.

Nursing Interventions

Pain management and optimal functional ability, including the promotion of a healthy, positive life course adaptation, are major goals of nursing intervention. Patient teaching is an essential nursing intervention in the care of the patient with a rheumatic disorder. Education is the key to successfully enabling the patient to maintain as much independence

as possible, to take medications accurately and safely, and to use adaptive devices correctly. Patient teaching focuses on the disorder itself, the possible changes related to the disorder, and the therapeutic regimen prescribed to treat it. Additional teaching is centered on the potential side effects of medications, strategies to maintain independence and function, and patient safety in the home. The diseases that usually present the greatest challenge are those with systemic manifestations, such as the diffuse connective tissue diseases. The patient and families are confronted with many psychosocial issues.

Relieving Pain and Discomfort

Pain has quite different effects on different patients. The response to pain and the degree to which it disrupts the patient's life give a more meaningful indication of severity. Does the pain affect their sleep? How has pain affected their mood? What specific functions or activities does it limit? Understanding the problems it causes can guide how to best manage the patient's pain.

(*continued on page 1068*)

The nurse teaches patients to differentiate between joint pain and stiffness. Medications are used on a short-term basis to relieve acute pain. Because the pain may be persistent, nonopioid analgesics such as acetaminophen are often used. After administering medications, the nurse needs to reassess pain levels and response to treatment. With persistent pain, assessment findings should be compared with baseline measurements; evaluations of additional measures include exploring coping skills and strategies that have worked in the past.

The nurse teaches patients self-administration of pharmacologic agents. The patient needs to understand the importance of taking medications, such as NSAIDs and DMARDs, exactly as prescribed to achieve maximum benefits. These benefits include relief of pain and anti-inflammatory action as the disease is brought under control. Because disease control and pain relief are delayed, the patient may mistakenly believe the medication is ineffective or may think of the medication as merely "pain pills," taking them only sporadically and failing to achieve control over the disease activity. Alternatively, the patient may not understand the need to continue the medication for its anti-inflammatory actions once pain control has been achieved.

Heat applications are also helpful in relieving pain, stiffness, and muscle spasm. Superficial heat may be applied in the form of warm tub baths or showers and warm moist compresses. Paraffin baths (dips), which offer concentrated heat, are helpful to patients with wrist and small-joint involvement. Therapeutic exercises can be carried out more comfortably and effectively after heat has been applied. However, in some patients, heat may actually increase pain, muscle spasm, and synovial fluid volume. If the inflammatory process is acute, cold applications in the form of moist packs or an ice bag may be tried. Both heat and cold are analgesic to nerve pain receptors and can relax muscle spasms (Brosseau, Yonge, Marchand et al., 2009). The nurse teaches safe use of heat and cold application, in 15 to 20 minute intervals, usually 3 to 4 times a day. The nurse checks temperature of warm soaks and covers cold packs with a towel, particularly for patients with impaired sensation. Further study of the effectiveness of these modalities is needed.

The nurse encourages measures to protect affected joints. There is no clear indication that the use of orthotic devices such as braces, splints, collars, and shoe modifications provide pain relief. However, there is preliminary evidence to support the use of extra-depth shoes, with or without semi-rigid insoles, to relieve pain on walking and weight-bearing (Egan, Brosseau, Farmer et al., 2009). Patients should be taught to avoid stooping, bending, or overreaching and to rest 5 to 10 minutes when trying to complete a task. The nurse educates the patient regarding other strategies for decreasing pain such as relaxation techniques, imagery, meditation, and distraction.

Decreasing Fatigue

Fatigue is a common problem for patients with rheumatic disorders. Fatigue related to rheumatic disorders can be both acute (brief and relieved by rest or sleep) and chronic. Chronic fatigue, related to the disease process, is persistent, cumulative, and not eliminated by rest but is influenced by biologic, psychological, social, and personal factors. The nurse discusses related causes of fatigue with patients. Disease-related factors that may influence the amount and severity of fatigue include persistent pain, sleep disturbance, impaired physical activity, and disease duration. Pain increases fatigue because additional physical and emotional energy is required to deal with it. It may also cause the patient to expend more energy to do tasks in a way that causes less pain. A plan of nursing care for a patient with a rheumatic disorder is available online at http://thePoint.lww.com/Pellico1e.

Promoting Nutrition

Dietary intake of high-quality food has declined for most Western cultures. Americans are eating an increased amount of processed animal products and foods (high in trans fatty acids, omega-6 free fatty acids), food additives, preservatives, and high-glycemic-index foods (Bonakdar & Leopold, 2009). These factors directly or indirectly stimulate inflammation by increasing levels of arachidonic acid, a key component of many inflammatory mediators. Evidence has suggested incorporating an anti-inflammatory diet to improve serologic and symptomatic markers of inflammation. Fish oil supplements, and omega-3 or omega-6 fatty acids, can be added to the diet.

An anti-inflammatory diet is a predominantly plant-based diet, avoiding excess and high-glycemic-load calories. There is a strong emphasis on avoidance of potentially pro-inflammatory foods (e.g., trans fats, refined sugars, high saturated fats, alcohol, and caffeine in excess). The majority of the diet should be derived from four areas: whole-grain products, fresh fruits and vegetables, legumes, and seeds and nuts. These sources provide several anti-inflammatory components such as fiber, isoflavones (e.g., soybeans and soy products), carotenoids, and omega-3 free fatty acids (e.g., flaxseed). Patients can be told to keep a journal to assist in monitoring ongoing diet and symptom changes and not to expect immediate results, allowing at least 12 weeks before reevaluating benefit. Consultation with a dietitian is highly recommended for understanding and meal planning suggestions.

NURSING ALERT

Some medications (i.e., oral corticosteroids) used in the treatment of rheumatic diseases stimulate the appetite and, when combined with decreased activity, may lead to weight gain. Therefore, patients may need to be counseled about eating a healthy, calorie-restricted diet.

Promoting Restorative Sleep

Restful sleep is important in helping the patient to cope with pain, minimize physical fatigue, and deal with the changes necessitated by a chronic disease. In patients with acute disease, sleep time is frequently reduced and fragmented by prolonged awakenings. Stiffness, depression, and medications may also compromise the quality of sleep and increase daytime fatigue. A sleep-inducing routine, medication, and comfort measures may help improve the quality of sleep. The nurse encourages patients to take a warm bath or shower before bedtime to relax muscles; showering first thing in the morning may be beneficial to reduce morning stiffness.

Teaching sleep hygiene strategies may be helpful in promoting restorative sleep. These strategies include establishing a set time to sleep and a regular wake-up time, creating a quiet sleep environment with a comfortable room temperature, avoiding factors that interfere with sleep (e.g., use of alcohol and caffeine), positioning of joints, using relaxation exercises, and getting out of bed and engaging in another activity (e.g., reading) if unable to fall asleep within 20 to 30 minutes (Gevirtz, 2007; Holcomb, 2007).

Increasing Mobility

Maintaining some degree of joint mobilization and load on the joints is essential to the preservation of articular cartilage integrity. If the patient is overweight, a weight reduction program is a critical element in relieving stress on painful joints. Proper body positioning is essential to minimize stress on inflamed joints and prevent deformities that limit mobility. All joints should be supported in a position of optimal function. When in bed, the patient should lie flat on a firm mattress, with feet positioned against a footboard and with only one pillow under the head because of the risk of dorsal kyphosis. A pillow should not be placed under the knees, because this promotes flexion contracture. It is best for the patient to lie prone several times daily to prevent hip flexion contracture.

Care must be taken so that splinting for comfort does not restrict mobility later. Regularly removing the splint and exercising the joint through a range of motion should be done to prevent joint "freezing." Splint modification may be needed when changes occur in joint structure.

In addition, assistive devices may be necessary for mobility. They should be properly fitted, and the patient should be instructed in their correct and safe use. A cane, long enough to allow for only a slight bend of the elbow, should be held in the hand opposite the affected side. Forearm-trough style crutches (platform crutches) may be needed to protect the upper extremities if the disease also involves the hands and wrists. This is especially important for the patient undergoing rehabilitation after lower extremity joint reconstructive surgery. Assistive devices can mean the difference between dependence and independence in mobility. However, keep in mind that use of assistive devices may also alter the patient's body image, which can become a barrier to adherence to the treatment regimen.

Encouraging Exercise

The ACR has identified exercise as a fundamental part in the management of rheumatic disorders. Active and active/self-assisted range-of-motion exercises are encouraged because they prevent joint stiffness and increase mobility (Macedo, Oakley, Panayi et al., 2009). Active/self-assisted exercises involve the use of overhead pulleys or wand exercises (shoulder exercises using a wand, stick, or cane). Measures to reinforce proper body posture and increase mobility include walking erect and using chairs with straight backs. When seated, the patient should rest the feet flat on the floor and the shoulders and hips against the back of the chair.

A formal program with occupational and physical therapy should be prescribed to educate the patient about principles of joint protection, pacing activities, work simplification, range of motion, and muscle-strengthening exercises. An individualized exercise program is crucial to movement. Exercises appropriate in promoting mobility in patients with rheumatic disorders are summarized in Table 39-5. Appropriate programs of exercise, including T'ai chi, have been shown to decrease pain, improve function, and improve quality of life (Conn, Hafdahi, & Brown, 2009; Flint-Wagner, Lisse, & Lohman, 2009; Macedo, Oakley, Panayi et al., 2009; McKnight, Kasle, Going et al., 2010; Wang, Schmid, Hibberd et al., 2009). The major challenge for the patient and the health care provider is the need to adjust all aspects of treatment according to the activity of the disease. Especially for the patient with an active diffuse connective tissue disease, such as RA or SLE, activity levels may vary from day to day and even within a single day.

Facilitating Self-Care

Self-care includes practices that patients undertake to promote their health and well-being despite having a chronic illness. Self-care practices must be taught and reinforced so the patient does not develop self-care deficits. The nurse needs to keep in mind that a patient's deformity does not necessarily equate with the severity of limitations or disability. For example, swollen (edematous) hands may be more limiting than deformed hands.

The nurse should assist the patient in identifying any self-care deficit and those factors that interfere with ability to perform self-care activities. The nurse in a hospital or extended care facility can help preserve the patient's independence by making available adaptive equipment for eating, toileting, bathing, and dressing. In the home, the nurse can encourage use of these devices. Also, the nurse should reemphasize the importance of relieving pain, stiffness, and fatigue and its impact on increasing the patient's ability to perform self-care.

(continued on page 1070)

Adapted from Levensky, E.R., Forcehimes, A., O'Donohue, W.T., et al. (2007). Motivational interviewing. *American Journal of Nursing, 107*(10), 50–58; and Rollnick, S., Miller, W.R. & Butler, C. C. (2008). *Motivational interviewing in health care: Helping patients change behavior.* New York: The Guilford Press.

BOX 39-6

Four Guiding Principles of Motivational Interviewing (Acronym RULE)

R: Reflect Resistance

When the nurse argues for change and the patient is resisting and arguing against it, the nurse should "roll with the patient resistance" (i.e., the nurse acknowledges that resistance to change is expected). The patient is the primary source of arguments and solutions. The nurse should reflect resistance nonjudgmentally.

U: Understand

The nurse expresses empathy and communicates acceptance of the patient's experience, including the patient's ambivalence about change. Be interested in the patient's own concerns, values, and motivations.

L: Listen

By listening to what patients say, the nurse can tell how likely they are to change. Listen for verbs in patient narrative indicating change talk, statements in relation to desire, ability, reasons, need, commitment, and taking action.

E: Empower

Nurses assist patients to explore how they can make a difference in their own health, emphasizing the patient's ability to choose and carry out a plan for change. Outcomes are best when patients take an active role in their own health care.

Improving Body Image and Coping

All aspects of the patient's life, including work role, social life, sexual function, financial status, and perception of self may be altered because of the impact and unpredictability of the course of a rheumatoid disorder. Body image changes can lead to social isolation and depression. Hence, the nurse and the family need to understand and be sensitive to the patient's emotional reactions to the disease and provide support and assistance when appropriate.

The nurse should encourage the patient and family to verbalize feelings, perceptions, and fears related to the disease. Additionally, the nurse facilitates communication and aids the patient and family in identifying areas in which they have some control over disease symptoms and treatment. By taking action and involving others, the patient develops or draws on coping skills and possibly community support. The nurse also assists the patient to identify past coping mechanisms, as well as use of effective coping strategies, which is a key to positive outcomes.

Monitoring and Managing Potential Complications

Medications used for treating rheumatic disorders have the potential for serious and adverse effects. Therefore, an important aspect of care is avoiding medication-induced complications. The clinician bases the prescribed medication regimen on clinical findings and past medical history, then monitors for side effects with periodic clinical assessments and laboratory testing. The nurse plays a major role in working with the primary care provider and pharmacist to help the patient recognize and deal with medication side effects. If side effects occur, the medication may need to be stopped or the dose reduced. The patient may experience an increase in symptoms while the complication is being resolved or a new medication is being initiated. In such cases, the nurse's counseling

regarding symptom management may relieve potential anxiety and distress.

Promoting Home Care

Depending on the severity of the disorder and the patient's resources and supports, referral for home care may or may not be warranted. The patient who is elderly or frail, has a rheumatic disorder that limits function significantly, and lives alone may need a referral for home care. A dietary consultation may be indicated to ensure that the patient is knowledgeable about dietary recommendations, given the increased risk of cardiovascular disease. The patient and family should be informed about support services such as Meals on Wheels and local Arthritis Foundation chapters.

During home visits, the nurse has the opportunity to assess the home environment and its adequacy for patient safety and management of the disorder. Adherence to the treatment program can be more easily monitored in the home setting, where physical and social barriers to adherence are more readily identified. For example, a patient with diabetes who requires insulin may be unable to fill the syringe accurately or be unable to administer the insulin because of impaired joint mobility. Appropriate adaptive equipment needed for increased independence is often identified more readily when the nurse sees how the patient functions in the home. Any barriers to adherence are identified, and appropriate referrals are made. Referrals to physical and occupational therapists may be made as problems are identified and limitations increase.

Furthermore, with each home visit the nurse assesses the patient's physical and psychological status, adequacy of symptom management, and adherence to the management plan. Previous teaching is reinforced, with emphasis on potential side effects of medications and changes in

(*continued on page 1072*)

physical status that indicate disease progression and the need to contact the health care provider for reevaluation. Because of the increased risk of involvement of multiple organ systems, the importance of follow-up appointments is emphasized to the patient and family. Additionally, the patient and family should be reminded about the importance of participating in other health promotion activities and health screening (e.g., immunizations, cholesterol screening, bone density testing, gynecologic examinations, mammography, colonoscopy) to avoid neglecting general health issues.

Evaluation

Expected patient outcomes may include the following:

1. Experiences relief of pain or improved comfort level:
   a. Identifies factors that cause or increase pain
   b. Identifies realistic goals for pain relief
   c. Uses pain management strategies safely and effectively
   d. Reports decreased pain and increased comfort level
2. Experiences reduction in level of fatigue:
   a. Identifies factors that contribute to fatigue
   b. Verbalizes the relationship of fatigue to disease activity
   c. Schedules periodic rest periods, and identifies and uses other measures to prevent or modify fatigue
   d. Reports decreased level of fatigue
   e. Practices energy conservation strategies
   f. Discusses the relationship of the inflammatory process to fatigue and nutrition
3. Improves sleep patterns:
   a. Reports fewer nighttime awakenings
   b. Adheres to sleep-inducing routine
   c. Reports feeling rested on awakening

4. Increases or maintains level of mobility:
   a. Identifies factors that impede mobility
   b. Demonstrates normal or acceptable body alignment and posture
   c. Uses assistive devices appropriately and safely
   d. Participates in activities and exercises that promote or maintain mobility
5. Maintains self-care activities:
   a. Participates in self-care activities within capabilities
   b. Uses adaptive equipment and alternative methods to increase participation in self-care activities
   c. Maintains self-care at highest possible level
6. Enhances motivation and health self-management:
   a. Self-initiates goal-directed behavior
   b. Expresses belief in ability to perform activities
   c. Develops contract for health management with mutually agreeable goals for treatment
   d. Performs self-care and health-related activities consistent with ability
   e. Balances treatment, exercise, work, leisure, rest, and nutrition
7. Experiences improved body image and coping:
   a. Verbalizes concerns about the impact of rheumatic disease on appearance and function
   b. Sets and achieves meaningful goals
   c. States acceptance of self-worth
   d. Adapts to body image changes caused by disease
   e. Identifies and uses effective coping strategies
8. Experiences absence of complications:
   a. Takes medications as prescribed
   b. States potential side effects of medications and names reportable side effects
   c. Verbalizes understanding of rationale for monitoring
   d. Complies with recommendations for monitoring
   e. Identifies strategies to reduce risks of side effects

Chapter Review

Critical Thinking Exercises

1. A 79-year-old woman with a 10-year history of OA of the right knee complains of pain every day and difficulty walking. Currently, she uses a walker to ambulate but needs to stop and rest every so often because of the pain. What treatment options are available? Develop an evidence-based plan of care for her.
2. A 20-year-old woman complains of alopecia, skin rash, joint pain, weight loss, and fatigue. Her family states that she does not "seem like herself" lately. A diagnosis of SLE is made. What can you explain to her about her diagnosis and her treatment options?
3. You are caring for a patient with a rheumatic disorder. NSAIDs, corticosteroids, and a biologic response

modifier have been prescribed. How do the actions, uses, and indications of these medications differ? What instructions and recommendations would you give to the patient to ensure their safe administration?

NCLEX-Style Review Questions

1. When assessing a patient, the nurse knows that which of the following clinical manifestations are shared by rheumatoid arthritis and OA?
   A. Joint space narrowing on X-ray and a decreased C4 level
   B. Symmetrical knee involvement and joint effusions
   C. Tophi, joint enlargement, and severe pain
   D. Joint swelling, stiffness, and pain

2. The nursing diagnosis identified for a patient with OA is Acute Pain. Which action by the patient warrants intervention by the visiting nurse?
   A. Acetaminophen (Tylenol) taken PO in doses no more than 4,000 mg/day
   B. Capsaicin (Capsin) applied topically as needed 3 to 4 times a day
   C. Cold application to localized area for 30 minutes 4 to 5 times a day
   D. Paraffin dips providing concentrated heat applied to wrist before bedtime
3. The nurse has finished the receiving shift report at 7:30 a.m. Which patient should the nurse assess first?
   A. The patient with scleroderma who had an episode of dyspnea during the night shift.
   B. The patient diagnosed with OA who complains of morning joint stiffness.
   C. The patient who needs to receive a scheduled 8 a.m. IV adrenal corticosteroid.
   D. The patient suspected of an acute gout attack who is scheduled for an arthrocentesis.
4. A patient with SLE is admitted to the hospital for evaluation and management of acute joint inflammation. Which information obtained in the admission laboratory testing results is of most concern to the nurse?
   A. Elevated blood urea nitrogen (BUN)
   B. Increased C-reactive protein
   C. Positive ANA
   D. Positive RF
5. Which statement indicates the patient requires further teaching regarding the nutritional management of gout?
   A. "I need to limit my alcohol intake."
   B. "I need to avoid fad starvation diets."
   C. "I need to follow a high-protein diet."
   D. "I need to eliminate trigger foods."

Try these additional resources to enhance your learning and understanding of this chapter:
- thePoint online resource available at **http://thepoint.lww.com/Pellico1e**
- *Handbook for Focus on Adult Health: Medical-Surgical Nursing*
- *Study Guide for Focus on Adult Health: Medical-Surgical Nursing*

References and Selected Readings

References and selected readings associated with this chapter can be found on the website that accompanies the book. Visit http://thepoint.lww.com/Pellico1e to access the references and other additional resources associated with this chapter.

Problems Related to Musculoskeletal Function

A 26-YEAR-OLD man is being seen in the orthopedic clinic for complaints of low back pain. He is employed as a construction worker. He complains of pain radiating down his left leg. He states that his back pain started after he lifted a steel beam at work.

⮕ Discuss evaluative data that would be important to gather on this patient.
⮕ Describe diagnostic procedures that would lead to a definitive diagnosis.
⮕ Discuss medical and nursing management for this patient.

Nursing Assessment: Musculoskeletal Function

GERIANN B. GALLAGHER

The musculoskeletal system includes the bones, joints, muscles, tendons, ligaments, and bursae of the body. The functions of these components are highly integrated; therefore, disease in or injury to one component adversely affects the others. For instance, an infection in a joint (septic arthritis) causes degeneration of the articular surfaces of the bones within the joint and local muscle atrophy.

Diseases and injuries that involve the musculoskeletal system are commonly implicated in disability and death. Falls account for more than 420,000 hospitalizations yearly among the elderly. Hip fracture is the most common musculoskeletal condition that necessitates hospitalization in patients who are at least 65 years of age (Agency for Healthcare Research and Quality [AHRQ], 2009). Musculoskeletal diseases and injuries can significantly affect overall productivity, independence, and quality of life in people of all ages. Nurses in all practice areas encounter patients with disruption in musculoskeletal function.

ANATOMIC AND PHYSIOLOGIC OVERVIEW

The health and proper functioning of the musculoskeletal system is interdependent with that of the other body systems. The musculoskeletal system has important functions, including providing protection for vital organs (e.g., brain, heart, liver, kidneys, lungs, spleen) and providing a sturdy framework to support body structures. It also makes mobility possible. Joints hold the bones together and allow the body to move. The muscles attached to the skeleton contract, moving the bones and producing heat that helps maintain body temperature. Movement facilitates the return of deoxygenated blood to the right side of the heart by massaging the venous vasculature. In addition, the musculoskeletal system serves as a reservoir for immature blood cells and essential minerals, including calcium, phosphorus, magnesium, and fluoride. More than 98% of total body calcium is present in bone. Additionally, the red bone marrow located within bone cavities produces red blood cells, white blood cells (WBCs), and platelets through a process referred to as **hematopoiesis**.

Structure and Function of the Skeletal System

The shape and construction of a specific bone are determined by its function and the forces exerted on it.

Bone Types and Tissue

Bones are constructed of two types of bone tissue: **cancellous** (trabecular) or **cortical** (compact). Cancellous bone, or spongy bone, is found in the interior of bones and forms a lattice-like pattern. Red or yellow bone marrow fills the lattice network. Cortical, or compact, bone forms the outer shell of a bone. It has a densely packed, calcified intercellular matrix, making the cortical bone more rigid than cancellous bone (Porth & Matfin, 2009). Varying amounts of both cancellous and cortical bone are found throughout the body in differing proportions depending on the function of the bone.

There are 206 bones in the human body, divided into four categories:

- Long bones (e.g., femur)
- Short bones (e.g., metacarpals)
- Flat bones (e.g., sternum)
- Irregular bones (e.g., vertebrae)

Long bones are shaped like rods or shafts with rounded ends (Fig. 40-1). The shaft, known as the **diaphysis**, is primarily cortical bone. The ends of the long bones, called **epiphyses**, are primarily cancellous bone. The epiphyseal plate separates the epiphyses from the diaphysis and is the center for longitudinal growth in children, thus it can be a critical indicator of potential growth problems if fractured in children. It is calcified in adults. The ends of long bones are covered at the joints by articular **cartilage**, which is tough, elastic, avascular tissue. Long bones are designed for weight-bearing and movement. Short bones consist of cancellous bone covered by a layer of compact bone. Flat bones are important sites of hematopoiesis and frequently provide vital organ protection. They are made of cancellous bone layered between compact bone. Irregular bones have unique shapes related to their function. An example of irregular shaped bones is the vertebrae.

Bone is composed of three basic cell types—**osteoblasts**, **osteocytes**, and **osteoclasts**. Osteoblasts function in bone formation by secreting bone matrix. The term *blast* refers to immature or precursor cell, thus it is foundational for bone formation (Stedman, 2006). The matrix consists of collagen and ground substances (glycoproteins and proteoglycans) that provide a framework in which inorganic mineral salts are deposited. These minerals are primarily composed of calcium and phosphorus. Osteocytes are mature bone cells involved in bone maintenance. Osteoclasts are multinuclear cells involved in dissolving and resorbing bone. The microscopic functioning unit of mature cortical bone is the **osteon** (Haversian system). The center of the osteon, the Haversian canal, contains blood vessels and nerve supply for the osteon.

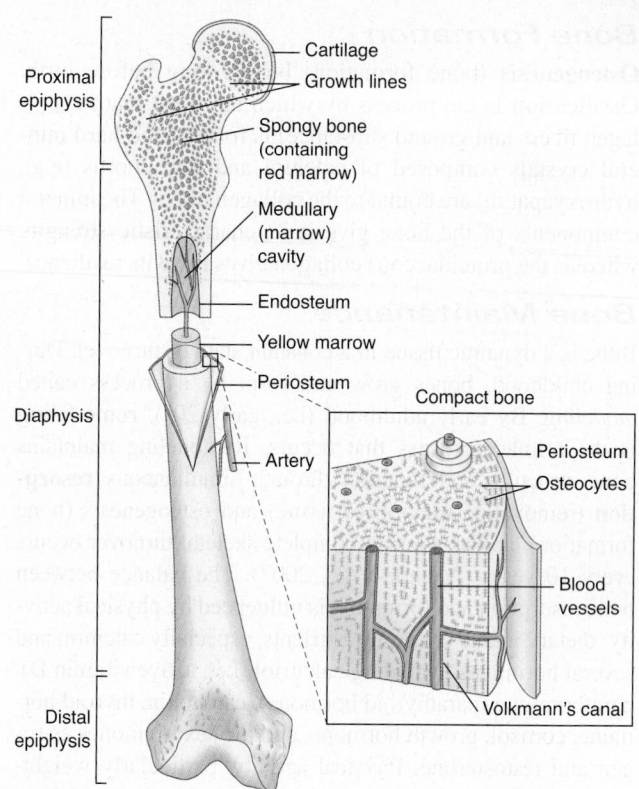

FIGURE 40-1 Structure of a long bone; composition of compact bone.

Around the canal are circles of mineralized bone matrix called **lamellae**. The lamellae follow along the shaft of the long bone to nourish the osteon. Covering the bone is a dense, fibrous membrane known as the **periosteum**. This membranous structure nourishes bone and facilitates its growth. The periosteum contains nerves, blood vessels, and lymphatics. It also provides for the attachment of tendons, which connect muscles to bones, and ligaments, which connect bones to bones. The **endosteum** is a thin, vascular membrane that covers the marrow cavity of long bones and the spaces in cancellous bone.

Bone marrow is a vascular tissue located in the medullary (shaft) cavity of long bones and in flat bones. Red bone marrow, located mainly in the sternum, ilium, vertebrae, and ribs in adults, is responsible for producing red blood cells, WBCs, and platelets. In adults, the long bone is filled with fatty, yellow marrow.

Bone tissue is well vascularized. Cancellous bone receives a rich blood supply through metaphyseal and epiphyseal vessels. Periosteal vessels carry blood to compact bone through minute openings called *Volkmann's canals*. In addition, nutrient arteries penetrate the periosteum and enter the medullary cavity through foramina (small openings). Nutrient arteries supply blood to the marrow and bone. The venous system may accompany arteries or may exit independently.

Bone Formation

Osteogenesis (bone formation) begins long before birth. **Ossification** is the process by which the bone matrix (collagen fibers and ground substance) is formed and hard mineral crystals composed of calcium and phosphorus (e.g., hydroxyapatite) are bound to the collagen fibers. The mineral components of the bone give it its characteristic strength, whereas the proteinaceous collagen gives bone its resilience.

Bone Maintenance

Bone is a dynamic tissue in a constant state of turnover. During childhood, bones grow and form by a process called *modeling*. By early adulthood (i.e., early 20s), **remodeling** is the primary process that occurs. Remodeling maintains bone structure and function through simultaneous **resorption** (removal/destruction of tissue) and osteogenesis (bone formation), and as a result, complete skeletal turnover occurs every 10 years (Allende-Vigo, 2007). The balance between bone resorption and formation is influenced by physical activity; dietary intake of certain nutrients, especially calcium; and several hormones, including calcitriol (i.e., active vitamin D), parathormone (parathyroid hormone), calcitonin, thyroid hormone, cortisol, growth hormone, and the sex hormones estrogen and testosterone. Physical activity, particularly weight-bearing activity, stimulates bone formation and remodeling. Bones subjected to continued weight bearing tend to be thick and strong. Conversely, people who are unable to engage in regular weight-bearing activities, such as those on prolonged bedrest or those with disabilities, have increased bone resorption from calcium loss, and their bones become osteopenic and weak. These weakened bones may fracture easily.

Good dietary habits are integral to bone health. In particular, absorption of daily calcium, approximately 1,200 mg for adults and 1,500 mg for postmenopausal women, is essential to maintaining adult bone mass. This may be achieved through ingesting calcium-rich foods on a daily basis (e.g., through drinking 16 to 24 ounces of milk daily) (Box 40-1).

Several hormones are vital in ensuring that calcium is properly absorbed and available for bone mineralization and matrix formation. Biologically active vitamin D (calcitriol)

BOX 40-1 **Nutrition Alert**

Bone Health

Calcium is important for bone health. Sources of calcium include:
- Milk, yogurt, and cheese (Use skim milk products to manage fat content.)
- Rhubarb, cooked collard greens, Chinese cabbage, kale, and broccoli
- Sardines, oysters, clams, canned salmon with bones
- Tofu
- Calcium-fortified fruit juices, fruit drinks, and cereals

---

functions to increase the amount of calcium in the blood by promoting absorption of calcium from the gastrointestinal tract. It also facilitates mineralization of osteoid tissue. A deficiency of vitamin D results in bone mineralization deficit, deformity, and fracture.

Parathormone and calcitonin are the major hormonal regulators of calcium homeostasis. Parathormone regulates the concentration of calcium in the blood, in part by promoting movement of calcium from the bone. In response to low calcium levels in the blood, increased levels of parathormone prompt the mobilization of calcium, the demineralization of bone, and the formation of bone cysts. Calcitonin is secreted by the thyroid gland in response to elevated blood calcium levels. It inhibits bone resorption (the breakdown of bone) and increases the deposit of calcium in bone.

Both thyroid hormone and cortisol have multiple systemic effects with specific effects on bones. Excessive thyroid hormone production in adults (e.g., Graves' disease) can result in increased bone resorption and decreased bone formation. Increased levels of cortisol have these same effects. Patients receiving long-term synthetic cortisol or corticosteroids (i.e., prednisone [Deltasone, Prednicot]) are at increased risk for steroid-induced osteopenia and fractures.

Growth hormone has direct and indirect effects on skeletal growth and remodeling. It indirectly stimulates the liver and, to a lesser degree, the bones to produce insulin-like growth factor-1 (IGF-I), which accelerates bone modeling in children and adolescents. Growth hormone also directly stimulates skeletal growth in children and adolescents. It is believed that the low levels of both growth hormone and IGF-I that occur with aging may be partly responsible for decreased bone formation and resultant osteopenia.

The sex hormones testosterone and estrogen have important effects on bone remodeling. Estrogen stimulates osteoblasts and inhibits osteoclasts; therefore, bone formation is enhanced and resorption is inhibited. Low levels of estrogen or increased levels of corticosteroids cause disruption in normal osteoclast and osteoblast homeostasis. Testosterone has both direct and indirect effects on bone growth and formation. It directly causes skeletal growth in adolescence and has continued effects on skeletal muscle growth throughout the lifespan. Increased muscle mass results in greater weight-bearing stress on bones, resulting in increased bone formation. In addition, testosterone converts to estrogen in adipose tissue, providing an additional source of bone-preserving estrogen for aging men.

Blood supply to the bone also affects bone formation. With diminished blood supply or hyperemia (congestion), osteogenesis and bone density decrease. Bone necrosis occurs when the bone is deprived of blood.

Bone Healing

When a bone is fractured, the bone fragments are not merely patched together with scar tissue. Instead, the bone regenerates itself.

Although the exact process of fracture healing is debated, stages of bone healing are identified below, each stimulated by the release and activation of biologic regulators and signaling molecules (Porth & Matfin, 2009).

1. *Hematoma and inflammation:* The body responds to a fracture by bleeding into the injured tissue and forming a fracture hematoma. The fracture fragment ends become devitalized because of the interrupted blood supply. This hematoma facilitates the formation of fibrin, which will become the framework upon which new bone will grow. The injured area is invaded by macrophages (large phagocytic WBCs), which débride the area. Inflammatory cells that migrate to the injured area release growth factors that stimulate osteoclast and osteoblast activity. Inflammation, swelling, and pain are present. The inflammatory stage lasts several days and resolves with a decrease in pain and swelling.

2. *Angiogenesis and cartilage formation:* New capillaries infiltrate the hematoma and fibroblasts (cells that produce collagen, the major protein of bone) from the periosteum, endosteum, and bone marrow produce a bridge between the fractured bones. This bridge made of tissue not yet ossified—termed a soft tissue **callus**—establishes a connection between the bone fragment and will in time become bone. Under the influence of signaling molecules, cell proliferation and differentiation occur.

3. *Cartilage calcification:* Chondrocytes (cartilage cells) in the cartilage callus form matrix vesicles, which regulate calcification of the cartilage. Enzymes within these matrix vesicles prepare the cartilage for calcium release and deposit.

4. *Cartilage removal:* The calcified cartilage, referred to as *bony callus,* is invaded by blood vessels and becomes resorbed by chondroblasts and osteoclasts. It is replaced by woven bone similar to that of the growth plate.

5. *Bone formation:* Minerals continue to be deposited until the bone is firmly reunited. With major adult long bone fractures, ossification (the making of bone) takes 3 to 4 months.

6. *Remodeling:* The final stage of fracture repair consists of remodeling the new bone into its former structural arrangement. Remodeling may take months to years, depending on the extent of bone modification needed, the function of the bone, and the functional stresses on the bone. Cancellous bone heals and remodels more rapidly than does compact cortical bone.

Serial X-rays are used to monitor the progress of bone healing. The type of bone fractured, the adequacy of blood supply, the surface contact of the fragments, and the age and general health of the person influence the rate of fracture healing. Adequate immobilization is essential until there is X-ray evidence of bone formation with ossification.

When fractures are treated with open rigid compression plate fixation techniques, the bony fragments can be placed in direct contact. Primary bone healing occurs through cortical bone (Haversian) remodeling. Little or no cartilaginous callus develops. Immature bone develops from the endosteum. There is an intensive regeneration of new osteons, which develop in the fracture line by a process similar to normal bone maintenance. Fracture strength is obtained when the new osteons have become established.

Structure and Function of the Articular System

The junction of two or more bones is called a **joint** (articulation). There are three basic kinds of joints: synarthrosis, amphiarthrosis, and diarthrosis joints. Synarthrosis joints are immovable (e.g., the skull sutures). Amphiarthrosis joints (e.g., the vertebral joints and the symphysis pubis) allow limited motion; the bones of amphiarthrosis joints are joined by fibrous cartilage. Diarthrosis joints are freely movable joints.

There are several types of diarthrosis joints:

- *Ball-and-socket* joints (e.g., the hip and the shoulder) permit full freedom of movement.
- *Hinge* joints permit bending in one direction only (e.g., the elbow and the knee) (Fig. 40-2).
- *Saddle* joints allow movement in two planes at right angles to each other. The joint at the base of the thumb is a saddle joint.
- *Pivot* joints are characterized by the articulation between the radius and the ulna. They permit rotation for such activities as turning a doorknob.
- *Gliding* joints allow for limited movement in all directions and are represented by the joints of the carpal bones in the wrist.

The ends of the articulating bones of a typical movable joint are covered with smooth hyaline cartilage. A tough, fibrous sheath called the **joint capsule** surrounds the articulating bones. The capsule is lined with a membrane, the **synovium,**

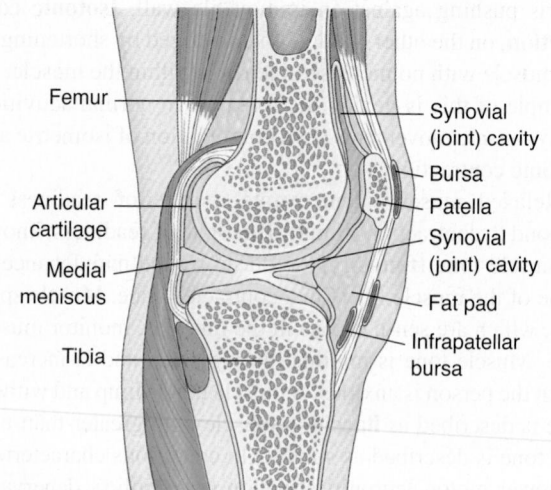

Femur
Articular cartilage
Medial meniscus
Tibia
Synovial (joint) cavity
Bursa
Patella
Synovial (joint) cavity
Fat pad
Infrapatellar bursa

FIGURE 40-2 Hinge joint of the knee.

which secretes the lubricating and shock-absorbing synovial fluid into the joint capsule. Therefore, the bone surfaces are not in direct contact. In some synovial joints (e.g., the knee), fibrocartilage disks (e.g., medial meniscus) are located between the articular cartilage surfaces. These disks provide shock absorption.

Ligaments (fibrous connective tissue bands) bind the articulating bones together. Ligaments and muscle tendons, which pass over the joint, provide joint stability. In some joints, interosseous ligaments (e.g., the cruciate ligaments of the knee) are found within the capsule and add stability to the joint.

A **bursa** is a sac filled with synovial fluid that cushions the movement of tendons, ligaments, and bones at a point of friction. Bursae are found at the elbow, shoulder, knee, and some other joints.

Structure and Function of the Skeletal Muscle System

Tendons (cords of fibrous connective tissue) or aponeuroses (broad, flat sheets of connective tissue) attach muscles to bones, connective tissue, other muscles, soft tissue, or skin. The muscles of the body are composed of parallel groups of muscle cells (fasciculi) encased in fibrous tissue called **fascia** (or epimysium). The more fasciculi contained in a muscle, the more precise the movements. Muscles vary in shape and size according to the activities for which they are responsible. Skeletal (striated) muscles are involved in body movement, posture, and heat-production functions. Muscles contract to bring the two points of attachment closer together, resulting in movement.

Muscle Tone

The contraction of muscle fibers can result in either isotonic or isometric contraction of the muscle. In **isometric contraction**, the length of the muscles remains constant but the force generated by the muscles is increased; an example of this is pushing against an immovable wall. **Isotonic contraction**, on the other hand, is characterized by shortening of the muscle with no increase in tension within the muscle; an example of this is flexing the forearm. In normal activities, many muscle movements are a combination of isometric and isotonic contraction.

Relaxed muscles demonstrate a state of readiness to respond to contraction stimuli. This state of readiness, known as muscle **tone (tonus)**, is produced by the maintenance of some of the muscle fibers in a contracted state. Muscle spindles, which are sense organs in the muscles, monitor muscle tone. Muscle tone is minimal during sleep and is increased when the person is anxious. A muscle that is limp and without tone is described as **flaccid**; a muscle with greater-than-normal tone is described as **spastic**. In conditions characterized by lower motor neuron destruction (e.g., polio), denervated muscle becomes **atonic** (soft and flabby) and atrophies.

Muscle Actions CONCEPTS IN ACTION

Muscles accomplish movement by contraction. Through the coordination of muscle groups, the body is able to perform a wide variety of movements (Fig. 40-3). The prime mover is the muscle that causes a particular motion. The muscles assisting the prime mover are known as *synergists*. The muscles causing movement opposite to that of the prime mover are known as *antagonists*. An antagonist must relax to allow the prime mover to contract, producing motion. For example, when contraction of the biceps causes flexion of the elbow joint, the biceps are the prime movers, and the triceps are the antagonists. A person with muscle **paralysis** (a loss of movement, possibly from nerve damage) may be able to retrain functioning muscles within the synergistic group to produce the needed movement. Muscles of the synergistic group then become the prime movers.

Exercise, Disuse, and Repair

Muscles need to be exercised to maintain function and strength. When a muscle repeatedly develops maximum or close to maximum tension over a long time, as in regular exercise with weights, the cross-sectional area of the muscle increases. This enlargement, known as **hypertrophy**, results from an increase in the size of individual muscle fibers without an increase in their number. Hypertrophy persists only if the exercise is continued. The opposite phenomenon occurs with disuse of muscle over a long period of time. Age and disuse cause loss of muscular function as fibrotic tissue replaces the contractile muscle tissue. The decrease in the size of a muscle is called **atrophy**. Bed rest and immobility cause loss of muscle mass and strength. When immobility is the result of a treatment modality (e.g., casting, traction), the patient can decrease the effects of immobility by isometric exercise of the muscles of the immobilized part.

Gerontologic Considerations

Multiple changes in the musculoskeletal system occur with aging (Table 40-1). Bone mass peaks by about 30 years of age, after which there is a universal gradual loss of bone. There is also a decrease in muscle mass and strength and an actual loss in the size and number of muscle fibers due to myofibril atrophy with fibrous tissue replacement. Numerous metabolic changes, including menopausal withdrawal of estrogen and decreased activity, contribute to **osteoporosis**. As a result, women lose more bone mass than men and are at higher risk for fractures. In the elderly, the articular cartilage degenerates in weight-bearing areas and heals less readily. Ultimately, ligaments become weak, and this contributes to the development of **osteoarthritis** (degenerative joint disease). Joints enlarge and range of motion (ROM) decreases causing a functional impairment in the elderly. Decreased activity, diminished neuron stimulation, and nutritional deficiencies also contribute to loss of muscle strength. In addition, remote musculoskeletal problems for

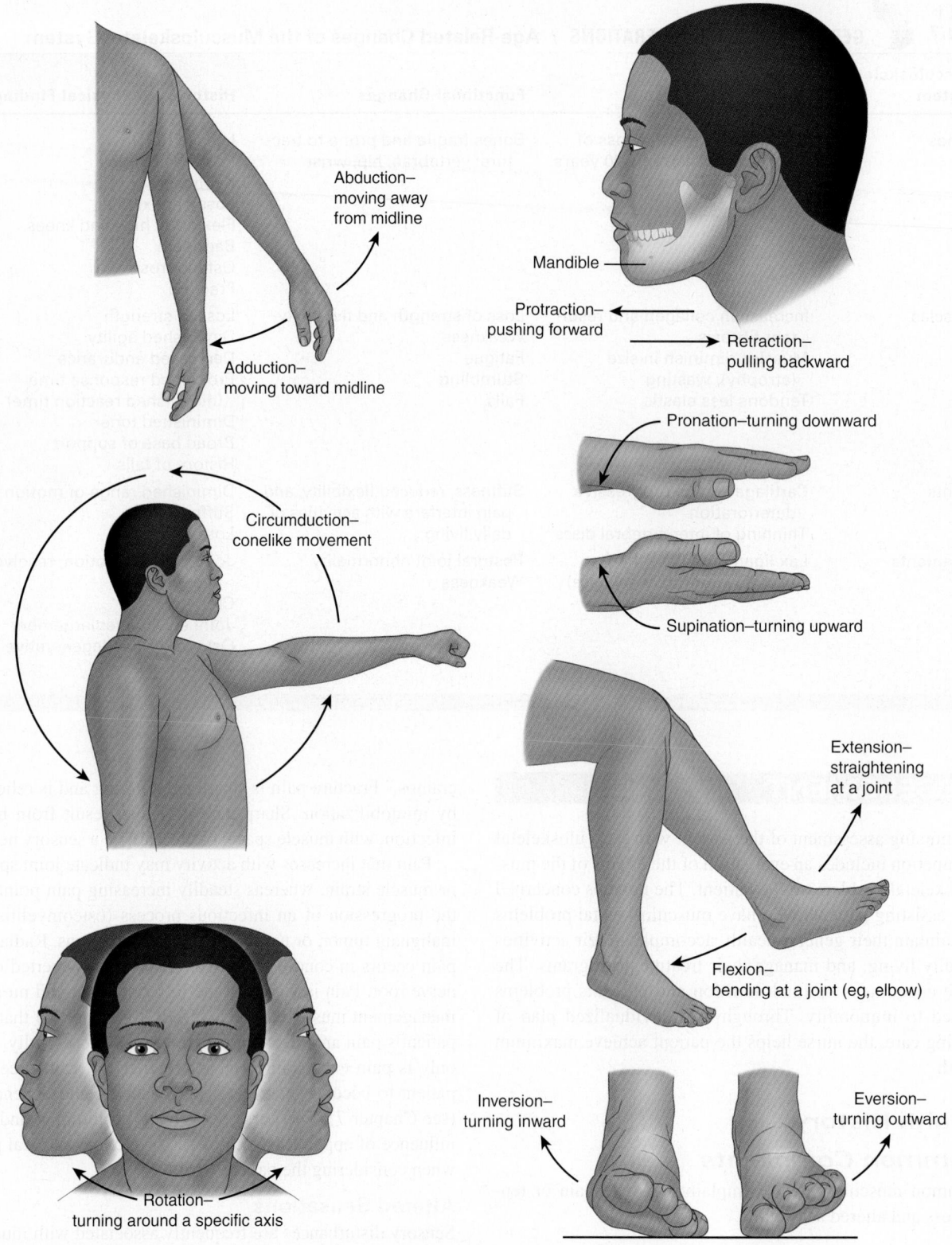

FIGURE 40-3 Body movements produced by muscle contraction.

which the patient has compensated may become new problems with age-related changes. For example, people who have had polio and who have been able to function normally by using synergistic muscle groups may discover increasing incapacity because of a reduced compensatory ability. However, many of the effects of aging can be slowed if the body is kept healthy and active through positive lifestyle behaviors.

TABLE
40-1 **GERONTOLOGIC CONSIDERATIONS** / Age-Related Changes of the Musculoskeletal System

Musculoskeletal System	Structural Changes	Functional Changes	History and Physical Findings
Bones	Gradual, progressive loss of bone mass after age 30 years Vertebrae collapse	Bones fragile and prone to fracture: vertebrae, hip, wrist	Loss of height Posture changes Kyphosis Loss of flexibility Flexion of hips and knees Back pain Osteoporosis Fracture
Muscles	Increase in collagen and resultant fibrosis Muscles diminish in size (atrophy); wasting Tendons less elastic	Loss of strength and flexibility Weakness Fatigue Stumbling Falls	Loss of strength Diminished agility Decreased endurance Prolonged response time (diminished reaction time) Diminished tone Broad base of support History of falls
Joints	Cartilage shows progressive deterioration Thinning of intervertebral discs	Stiffness, reduced flexibility, and pain interfere with activities of daily living	Diminished range of motion Stiffness Loss of height
Ligaments	Lax ligaments (less than normal strength; weakness)	Postural joint abnormality Weakness	Joint pain on motion; resolves with rest Crepitus Joint swelling/enlargement Osteoarthritis (degenerative joint disease)

ASSESSMENT

The nursing assessment of the patient with musculoskeletal dysfunction includes an evaluation of the effects of the musculoskeletal problem on the patient. The nurse is concerned with assisting patients who have musculoskeletal problems to maintain their general health, accomplish their activities of daily living, and manage their treatment programs. The nurse encourages optimal nutrition and prevents problems related to immobility. Through an individualized plan of nursing care, the nurse helps the patient achieve maximum health.

Health History

Common Complaints

Common musculoskeletal complaints include pain or tenderness and altered sensations.

Pain

Most patients with diseases and traumatic conditions or disorders of the muscles, bones, and joints experience pain. Bone pain is characteristically described as a dull, deep ache that is "boring" in nature, whereas muscular pain is described as soreness or aching and is referred to as "muscle

cramps." Fracture pain is sharp and piercing and is relieved by immobilization. Sharp pain may also result from bone infection, with muscle spasm or pressure on a sensory nerve.

Pain that increases with activity may indicate joint sprain or muscle strain, whereas steadily increasing pain points to the progression of an infectious process (osteomyelitis), a malignant tumor, or neurovascular complications. Radiating pain occurs in conditions in which pressure is exerted on a nerve root. Pain is variable, and its assessment and nursing management must be individualized. It is important that the patient's pain and discomfort be managed successfully. Not only is pain exhausting, but, if prolonged, it can force the patient to become increasingly preoccupied and dependent (see Chapter 7). The nurse notes body positioning, and the influence of appliances such as casts, traction, surgical pins when considering the patient's pain.

Altered Sensations

Sensory disturbances are frequently associated with musculoskeletal problems. The patient may describe **paresthesias**, which are burning, tingling sensations or numbness. Box 40-2 provides assessment questions related to altered sensation. These sensations may be caused by pressure on nerves or by circulatory impairment. Soft tissue swelling or direct trauma can impair function.

BOX 40-2

Assessing Altered Sensation

Questions that the nurse should ask regarding altered sensations include the following:
- Is the patient experiencing any abnormal sensations or numbness?
- If the abnormal sensation or feeling of numbness involves an extremity, how does this feeling compare to sensation in the unaffected extremity?
- When did the condition begin? Is it getting worse?
- Does the patient also have pain? (If the patient has pain, then the questions and assessments for pain discussed above should be included).
- If the affected part is an extremity, the nurse compares the overall appearance in relation to the unaffected extremity, noting size, shape, and symmetry.

- Can the patient move the affected part?
- What is the color of the part distal to the affected area? Is it pale? Dusky? Mottled? Cyanotic?
- Does rapid capillary refill occur? (The nurse can gently squeeze a nail until it blanches, then release the pressure. The amount of time for the color under the nail to return to normal is noted. Color normally returns within 2 seconds. The return of color is evidence of capillary refill.)
- Is a pulse palpable distal to the affected area? If the affected area is an extremity, how does the pulse compare to that felt in the unaffected extremity?
- Is edema present? If so, is it pitting?
- Is any constrictive device or clothing causing nerve or vascular compression?

Past, Family, and Social History

When taking the history, the nurse assesses for past history pertinent to the musculoskeletal system (e.g., broken bones or any history of musculoskeletal diseases such as rheumatoid arthritis). The nurse notes any history of family members who has had limitations that prevented them from functional activities. The nurse also assesses the patient's activity level. For example, does the patient do weight-bearing exercises on a regular basis? Are they involved in high-risk activities and sports that may put them at risk for injury? This may evolve into an opportunity for safety education, such as wearing a helmet when bicycle riding.

Physical Assessment

An examination of the musculoskeletal system ranges from a basic assessment of functional capabilities to sophisticated physical examination maneuvers that facilitate diagnosis of specific bone, muscle, and joint disorders. The extent of assessment depends on the patient's physical complaints, health history, and physical clues that warrant further exploration. The nursing assessment is primarily a functional evaluation, focusing on the patient's ability to perform activities of daily living.

Techniques of inspection and palpation are used to evaluate the patient's posture, gait, bone integrity, joint function, and muscle strength and size. In addition, assessing the skin and neurovascular status is an important part of a complete musculoskeletal assessment. When specific symptoms or physical findings of musculoskeletal dysfunction are apparent, the nurse carefully documents the examination findings and shares the information with the provider, who may decide that a more extensive examination and a diagnostic workup are necessary.

Special precautions must be taken when assessing a patient with a musculoskeletal injury (Box 40-3).

Posture

The normal curvature of the spine is convex through the thoracic portion and concave through the cervical and lumbar portions. Common deformities of the spine include **kyphosis**, an increased forward curvature of the thoracic spine; **lordosis**, an exaggerated curvature of the lumbar spine; and **scoliosis**, a lateral curving deviation of the spine (Fig. 40-4). Kyphosis is frequently seen in elderly patients with osteoporosis and in some patients with neuromuscular diseases. Scoliosis may be congenital, idiopathic (without an identifiable cause), or the result of damage to the paraspinal muscles, as in polio. Lordosis is frequently seen during pregnancy as the woman adjusts her posture in response to changes in her center of gravity.

BOX 40-3

The Patient With Musculoskeletal Injury

Special precautions must be taken when assessing a patient who has sustained trauma. If there is injury to an extremity, it is important to assess for soft tissue trauma, deformity, and neurovascular status. If the patient might have a cervical spine injury and is wearing a cervical collar, the collar must not be removed until the absence of spinal cord injury is confirmed by appropriate imaging studies. When the collar is removed, the cervical spine area is gently assessed for swelling, tenderness, deformity, and skin integrity. With pelvic trauma, abdominal organ injuries may occur. The patient is assessed for abdominal pain, tenderness, hematomas, distention, and the presence or absence of femoral pulses. If blood is present at the urinary meatus, the nurse should suspect bladder and urethral injury, and the patient should not be catheterized. Instead, such findings should be reported immediately to the emergency department physician or the surgeon.

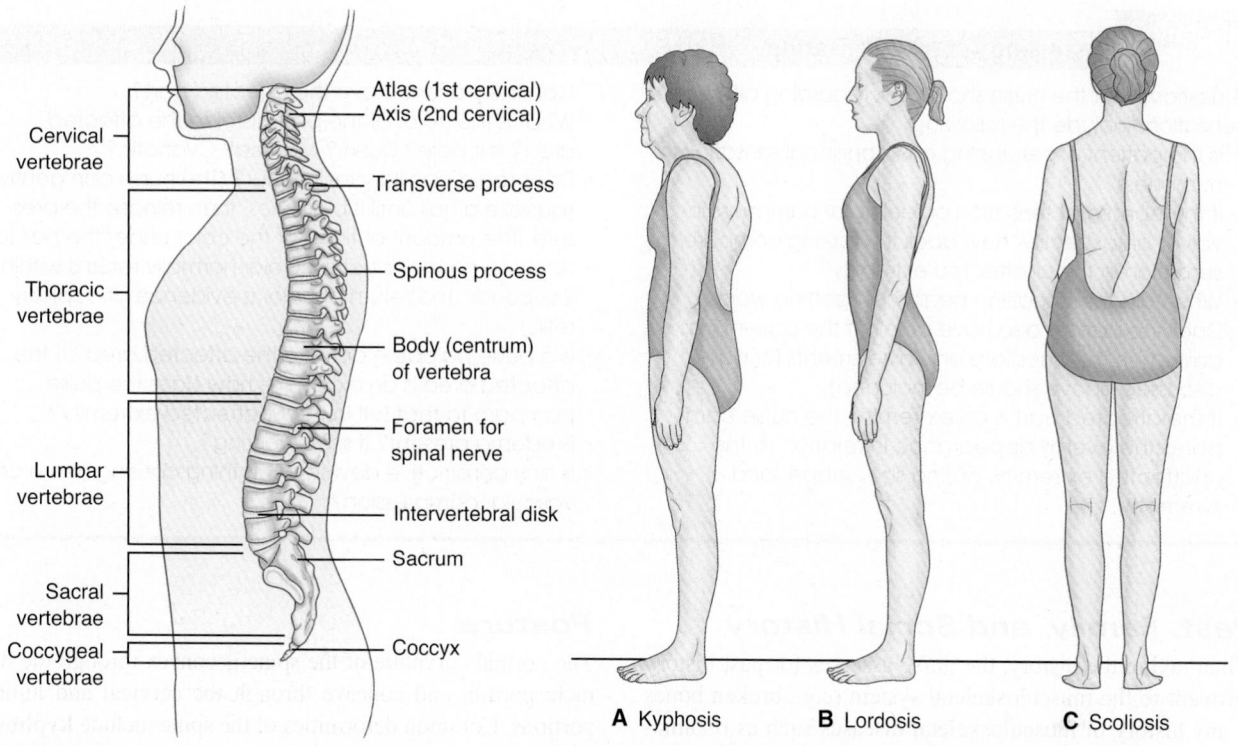

FIGURE 40-4 A normal spine and three abnormalities. (**A**) Kyphosis: an increased convexity or roundness of the spine's thoracic curve. (**B**) Lordosis: swayback; exaggeration of the lumbar spine curve. (**C**) Scoliosis: a lateral curvature of the spine.

Gait

Gait is assessed by having the patient walk away from the examiner for a short distance. The nurse observes the patient's gait for smoothness and rhythm. Any unsteadiness or irregular movements (frequently noted in elderly patients) are considered abnormal. Limited joint motion may affect gait. In addition, a variety of neurologic conditions are associated with abnormal gaits, such as a spastic hemiparesis gait (stroke), steppage gait (lower motor neuron disease), and shuffling gait (Parkinson's disease).

Bone Integrity

The bony skeleton is assessed for deformities, alignment, and symmetry. During the exam, body parts are compared from side to side. Shortened extremities, amputations, and body parts that are not in anatomic alignment are noted. Fracture findings may include abnormal angulation of long bones, motion at points other than joints, and crepitus (a grating sound) at the point of abnormal motion. Movement of fracture fragments must be minimized to avoid additional injury.

Joint Function

The articular system is evaluated by noting ROM, deformity, stability, and nodular formation. The tissues surrounding joints are examined for nodule formation, color changes, skin integrity, temperature, and injury. ROM is evaluated both actively (the joint is moved by the muscles surrounding the joint without assistance from the nurse) and passively (the joint is moved by the examiner). The nurse needs to be familiar with the normal ROM of major joints. Limited ROM may be the result of skeletal deformity, joint pathology, or **contracture** (shortening of surrounding joint structures) of the surrounding muscles, tendons, and joint capsule. In elderly patients, limitations of ROM associated with osteoarthritis may reduce their ability to perform activities of daily living.

If joint motion is compromised or the joint is painful, the joint is examined for **effusion** (excessive fluid within the capsule), swelling, and increased temperature that may reflect active inflammation. An effusion is suspected if the joint is swollen and the normal bony landmarks are obscured. The most common site for joint effusion is the knee. If inflammation or fluid is suspected in a joint, consultation with a provider is indicated.

Joint deformity may be caused by contracture, dislocation (complete separation of joint surfaces), subluxation (partial separation of articular surfaces), or disruption of structures surrounding the joint. Weakness or disruption of joint-supporting structures may result in a weak joint that requires an external supporting appliance (e.g., brace).

Palpation of the joint while it is passively moved provides information about the integrity of the joint. Normally, the joint moves smoothly. A snap or crack may indicate that a ligament is slipping over a bony prominence. Slightly roughened surfaces, as in arthritic conditions, result in **crepitus** (grating, crackling sound or sensation) as the irregular joint surfaces move across one another.

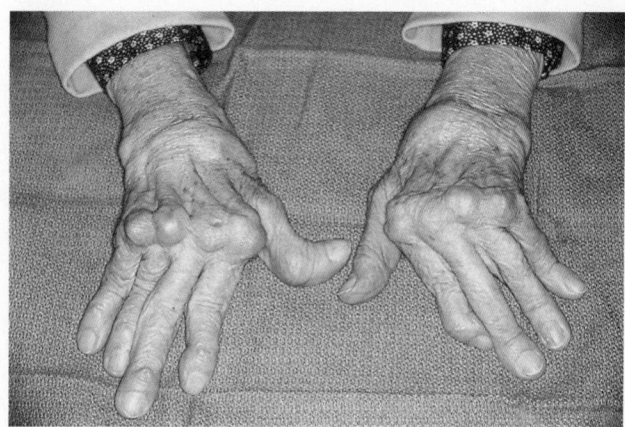

FIGURE 40-5 A patient with rheumatoid arthritis with involvement of the metacarpophalangeal joints. Note the severe ulnar drift of the fingers. From Koopman, W. J., & Moreland, L. W. (2005). *Arthritis and allied conditions: A textbook of rheumatology* (15th ed.). Philadelphia: Lippincott Williams & Wilkins.

Nodule formation is associated with rheumatoid arthritis (Fig. 40-5), gout, and osteoarthritis. While the subcutaneous nodules of rheumatoid arthritis are soft and occur within and along tendons, the nodules of gout are hard and lie within and immediately adjacent to the joint capsule itself. Osteoarthritic nodules are hard and painless and represent bony overgrowth that has resulted from destruction of the cartilaginous surface of bone within the joint capsule. They are frequently seen in older adults (refer to Chapter 39 for additional details).

Muscle Strength and Size

The muscular system is assessed by noting muscular strength and coordination, the size of individual muscles, and the patient's ability to change position. Weakness of a group of muscles might indicate a variety of conditions. By palpating the muscle while passively moving the relaxed extremity, the nurse can determine the muscle tone. The nurse assesses muscle strength by having the patient perform certain maneuvers with and without added resistance. For example, when the biceps are tested, the patient is asked to extend the arm fully and then to flex it against resistance applied by the nurse. A simple handshake may provide an indication of grasp strength.

The nurse may elicit muscle **clonus** (rhythmic contractions of a muscle) in the ankle or wrist by sudden, forceful, sustained dorsiflexion of the foot or extension of the wrist. **Fasciculation** (involuntary twitching of muscle fiber groups) may be observed.

The nurse measures the girth of an extremity to monitor increased size due to exercise, edema, or bleeding into the muscle. Girth may decrease due to muscle atrophy. The unaffected extremity is measured and used as the reference standard for the affected extremity. Measurements are taken at the maximum circumference of the extremity. It is important that the measurements be taken at the same location on the extremity, and with the extremity in the same position, with the muscle at rest. Distance from a specific anatomic landmark (e.g., 10 cm below the medial aspect of the knee for measurement of the calf muscle) should be indicated in the patient's record so that subsequent measurements can be made at the same point. For ease of serial assessment, the nurse may indicate the point of measurement by marking the skin. Variations in size are considered significant if greater than 1 cm for women and greater than 1.5 cm for men (Nettina, 2010).

Skin

In addition to assessing the musculoskeletal system, the nurse inspects the skin for edema, temperature, and color. Palpation of the skin can reveal whether any areas are warmer, suggesting increased perfusion or inflammation, whereas cooler skin suggests decreased perfusion or the presence of edema. Cuts, bruises, skin color, and evidence of decreased circulation or inflammation can influence nursing management of musculoskeletal conditions.

Neurovascular Status

It is important for the nurse to perform frequent neurovascular assessments of patients with musculoskeletal disorders (especially of those with fractures) because of the risk for tissue and nerve damage. Table 40-2 on page 1086 summarizes peripheral vascular assessment. One complication that the nurse needs to be alert for when assessing the patient is *compartment syndrome*, which is described in detail later in this unit. This major neurovascular problem is caused by pressure within a muscle compartment that increases to such an extent that microcirculation diminishes, leading to nerve and muscle anoxia and necrosis. Function can be permanently lost if the anoxic situation continues for longer than 6 hours. Assessment of neurovascular status is frequently referred to as assessment of CSM (circulation, sensation, and movement). Symptoms of neurovascular dysfunction are discussed in Box 40-4.

Diagnostic Evaluation

During the period of assessment, the patient requires support and nursing care, including physical and psychological

---

BOX 40-4

Indicators of Peripheral Neurovascular Dysfunction

Circulation
- *Color:* Pale, cyanotic, or mottled
- *Temperature:* Cool
- *Capillary refill:* More than 2 seconds

Motion
- Weakness
- Paralysis

Sensation
- Paresthesia
- Unrelenting pain
- Pain on passive stretch
- Absence of feeling

TABLE
40-2 Assessing for Peripheral Nerve Function

Assessment of peripheral nerve function has two key elements: evaluation of sensation and evaluation of motion. The nurse may perform one or all of the following during a musculoskeletal assessment.

Nerve	Test of Sensation	Test of Movement
Peroneal nerve	Stimulate the skin midway between the great and second toe.	Ask the patient to dorsiflex the foot and extend the toes.
Tibial nerve	Stimulate the medial and lateral surface of the sole.	Ask the patient to plantar flex toes and foot.
Radial nerve	Stimulate the skin midway between the thumb and second finger.	Ask the patient to stretch out the thumb, then the wrist, and then the fingers at the metacarpal joints.
Ulnar nerve	Stimulate the distal fat pad of the small finger.	Ask the patient to abduct all fingers.
Median nerve	Stimulate the top or distal surface of the index finger.	Ask the patient to touch the thumb to the little finger. Also observe whether the patient can flex the wrist.

preparation for examinations and tests. Patient education before the tests (what is to be done; why it is being done; what the patient can expect to experience, including tactile, visual, and auditory sensations; and what patient participation is expected) reduces anxiety and enables the patient to be an active participant in care. The resulting medical diagnosis and prescribed treatment regimen affect the nursing management of the patient.

Imaging Procedures
X-Ray Studies

X-ray studies are important in evaluating patients with musculoskeletal disorders. Bone X-rays determine bone density, texture, erosion, and changes in bone relationships. X-ray study of the cortex of the bone reveals any widening, narrowing, or signs of irregularity. Joint X-rays reveal fluid, irregularity, spur formation, narrowing, and changes in the joint structure. Multiple X-rays are needed for full assessment of the structure being examined. Serial X-rays may be indicated to determine if healing of a fractured bone is progressing normally or to determine if a bone affected by a degenerative disease (e.g., osteoarthritis) is responding to prescribed therapy. After being positioned for the study, the patient must remain still while the X-rays are taken.

Computed Tomography

A computed tomography (CT) scan shows in detail a specific plane of involved bone and can reveal tumors of the soft tissue or injuries to the ligaments or tendons. It is used to identify the location and extent of fractures in areas that are difficult to evaluate (e.g., acetabulum). CT studies, which may be performed with or without the use of contrast agents, last about 1 hour. The patient must remain still during the procedure.

Magnetic Resonance Imaging

Magnetic resonance imaging (MRI) is a noninvasive imaging technique that uses magnetic fields, radiowaves, and computers to demonstrate abnormalities (i.e., tumors or narrowing of tissue pathways through bone) of soft tissues such as muscle, tendon, cartilage, nerve, and fat. Because an electromagnet is used, patients with any metal implants, clips, or pacemakers are not candidates for MRI.

NURSING ALERT
Jewelry, hair clips, hearing aids, credit cards with magnetic strips, and other metal-containing objects must be removed before the MRI is performed; otherwise they can become dangerous projectile objects or cause burns. Credit cards with magnetic strips may be erased, and nonremovable cochlear devices can become inoperable. Also, transdermal patches (e.g., NicoDerm, Transderm-Nitro, Transderm Scopolamine, Catapres-TTS [clonidine]) that have a thin layer of aluminized backing must be removed before MRI because they can cause burns. The provider should be notified before the patches are removed.

To enhance visualization of anatomic structures, IV contrast agent may be used. During the MRI, the patient needs to lie still for 1 to 2 hours and hears a rhythmic knocking sound. Patients who experience claustrophobia may be unable to tolerate the confinement of closed MRI equipment without sedation. Open MRI systems are available but they use lower-intensity magnetic fields that reduce the quality of the imaging; thus, repeated imaging may be required. Advantages of open MRI include increased patient comfort, reduced problems with claustrophobic reactions, and reduced noise.

Arthrography

Arthrography is useful in identifying acute or chronic tears of the joint capsule or supporting ligaments of the knee, shoulder, ankle, hip, or wrist. A radiopaque contrast agent or air is injected into the joint cavity to outline soft tissue structures and the contour of the joint. The joint is put through its ROM to distribute the contrast agent while a series of X-rays is obtained. If a tear is present, the contrast agent leaks out of the joint and is evident on the X-ray image.

After an arthrogram, a compression elastic bandage is applied as prescribed and the joint is usually rested for 12 hours. The nurse provides additional comfort measures (mild analgesia, ice) as appropriate. The nurse explains to the patient that it is normal to experience clicking or crackling in the joint for a day or two after the procedure, until the contrast agent or air is absorbed.

If contrast agents will be used for CT scan, MRI, or arthrography, the nurse carefully assesses the patient for possible allergy. This includes previous experience with contrast studies and past reactions. In addition, the nurse is aware that risk factors for adverse reactions include a history of asthma, allergies, diabetes, renal insufficiency, and cardiac disease. Finally, the nurse assesses risk of pregnancy before decisions are made regarding the use of contrast materials.

Bone Densitometry

Bone densitometry is used to estimate bone mineral density (BMD). This can be performed through the use of X-rays or ultrasound. Dual-energy X-ray absorptiometry (DEXA) determines bone mineral density at the wrist, hip, or spine to estimate the extent of osteoporosis and to monitor a patient's response to treatment for osteoporosis. In particular, hip BMD is recommended as an osteoporosis screening for all Caucasian women older than 65 years and for other people at increased risk for osteoporosis-related fractures (Pham, Colon-Emeric, & Weber, 2009). See Chapter 41 for a further discussion of osteoporosis risks.

Bone Scan

A bone scan is performed to detect metastatic and primary bone tumors, osteomyelitis, certain fractures, and aseptic necrosis. A bone-seeking radioisotope is injected IV. The scan is performed 2 to 3 hours after the injection. At this point, distribution and concentration of the isotope in the bone are measured. The degree of nuclide uptake is related to

the metabolism of the bone. An increased uptake of isotope is seen in primary skeletal disease (osteosarcoma), metastatic bone disease, inflammatory skeletal disease (osteomyelitis), and certain types of fractures.

Before the patient undergoes an imaging study, the nurse assesses for conditions that may require special consideration during the study or that may be contraindications to the study (e.g., pregnancy; claustrophobia; inability to tolerate required positioning due to age, debility, or disability; metal implants). If contrast agents will be used for CT scan, MRI, bone scan, or arthrography, the nurse carefully assesses the patient for possible allergy.

Arthroscopy

Arthroscopy is a procedure that allows direct visualization of a joint to diagnose joint disorders. Treatment of tears, defects, and disease processes may be performed through the arthroscope. The procedure is performed in the operating room under sterile conditions; injection of a local anesthetic into the joint or general anesthesia is used. A large-bore needle is inserted, and the joint is distended with saline. The arthroscope is introduced, and joint structures, synovium, and articular surfaces are visualized. After the procedure, the puncture wound is closed with adhesive strips or sutures and covered with a sterile dressing. Complications are rare but may include infection, hemarthrosis (bleeding into the joint cavity), neurovascular compromise, thrombophlebitis, stiffness, effusion, adhesions, and delayed wound healing.

The joint is wrapped with a compression dressing to control swelling. In addition, ice may be applied to control edema and discomfort. Frequently, the joint is kept extended and elevated to reduce swelling. It is important to monitor neurovascular status. The nurse administers prescribed analgesics to control discomfort. The nurse explains when the patient can resume activity and what weight-bearing limits to follow, as prescribed by the orthopedic surgeon. The nurse also explains to the patient and family the symptoms (e.g., swelling, numbness, cool skin) to observe for in order to determine whether complications are occurring and the importance of notifying the surgeon of these observations. Finally, the nurse explains the surgeon's prescription for analgesic medication.

Other Studies

Arthrocentesis

Arthrocentesis (joint aspiration) is carried out to obtain synovial fluid for purposes of examination or to relieve pain due to effusion. Examination of synovial fluid is helpful in the diagnosis of septic arthritis and other inflammatory arthropathies and reveals the presence of hemarthrosis, which suggests trauma or a bleeding disorder. Normally, synovial fluid is clear, pale, straw-colored, and scanty in volume. Using aseptic technique, the physician inserts a needle into the joint and aspirates fluid. Anti-inflammatory medications may be injected into the joint. A sterile dressing is

applied after aspiration. There is a risk of infection after this procedure.

Electromyography

Electromyography (EMG) provides information about the electrical potential of the muscles and the nerves leading to them. The test is performed to evaluate muscle weakness, pain, and disability. The purpose of the procedure is to determine any abnormality of function and to differentiate muscle and nerve problems. Needle electrodes are inserted into selected muscles, and responses to electrical stimuli are recorded on an oscilloscope.

Biopsy

Biopsy may be performed to determine the structure and composition of bone marrow, bone, muscle, or synovium to help diagnose specific diseases. The nurse prepares the patient by providing teaching about the procedure and assuring the patient that analgesic agents will be provided. The nurse monitors the biopsy site for edema, bleeding, pain, and infection (fever, erythema, swelling, drainage, and tenderness at site). Ice is applied as prescribed to control bleeding and edema. In addition, analgesics are administered as prescribed for comfort.

Laboratory Studies

Examination of the patient's blood and urine can provide information about a primary musculoskeletal problem (e.g., Paget's disease), a developing complication (e.g., infection),

the baseline for instituting therapy (e.g., anticoagulant therapy), or the response to therapy. The complete blood count includes the hemoglobin level (which is frequently lower after bleeding associated with trauma and surgery) and the WBC count (which is elevated with any inflammatory condition, including acute infections, trauma, acute hemorrhage, and tissue necrosis). Before surgery, coagulation studies are performed to detect bleeding tendencies (because bone is very vascular tissue).

Blood chemistry studies provide data about a wide variety of musculoskeletal conditions. Serum calcium levels are altered in patients with osteomalacia, parathyroid dysfunction, Paget's disease, metastatic bone tumors, or prolonged immobilization. Serum phosphorus levels are inversely related to calcium levels and are diminished in osteomalacia associated with malabsorption syndrome. Acid phosphatase is elevated in Paget's disease and metastatic cancer. Alkaline phosphatase is elevated during early fracture healing and in diseases with increased osteoblastic activity (e.g., metastatic bone tumors). Bone metabolism may be evaluated through thyroid studies and determination of calcitonin, parathormone, and vitamin D levels. Serum enzyme levels of creatine kinase and aspartate aminotransferase become elevated with muscle damage. Serum myoglobin is also assessed to evaluate muscle trauma. Serum osteocalcin (bone GLA protein) indicates the rate of bone turnover. Urine calcium levels increase with bone destruction (e.g., parathyroid dysfunction, metastatic bone tumors, multiple myeloma).

Chapter Review

Critical Thinking Exercises

1. A 62-year-old Caucasian woman presents to the family practice clinic where you are the nurse manager for her annual wellness examination. She asks you if she should have "a type of bone scan" because her younger sister had recently had a hip fracture. What recommendations might be made for appropriate testing in this patient?
2. You are teaching a class at a senior center on age-associated changes in the musculoskeletal system. What age-related changes do you anticipate finding in this population?

NCLEX-Style Review Questions

1. A 78-year-old woman is complaining of neck and upper back pain. The nurse's assessment reveals an abnormal convex curvature of the cervical and thoracic area. What is the terminology for this finding?
   A. Kyphosis
   B. Lordosis
   C. Kyphoscoliosis
   D. Scoliosis

2. A 12-year-old girl complained to the school nurse about back pain. The nurse's assessment revealed a deviation of the vertebrae to the right, with a raised shoulder and hip. What is the terminology for this finding?
   A. Kyphosis
   B. Lordosis
   C. Osteoporosis
   D. Scoliosis

3. A patient had a fractured leg placed in a cast 4 hours ago. Which of the following findings is associated with neurovascular compromise?
   A. Capillary refill of 5 seconds
   B. Ability to move the toes without limitation
   C. Full sensation
   D. Toes warm to touch

4. What food would the nurse recommend for a patient with osteoporosis?
   A. Herbal tea
   B. Yogurt
   C. Liver
   D. Eggs

TABLE
39-5 Exercises to Promote Mobility

Type of Exercise	Purpose	Recommended Performance	Precautions
Range of motion	Maintain flexibility and joint motion	Active or active/self-assisted at least daily	Reduce number of repetitions when inflammation is present
Isometric exercise	Improve muscle tone, static endurance, and strength; prepare for dynamic and weight-bearing exercises	Perform at 70% of maximal voluntary contraction daily	Monitor blood pressure, isometric exercises may increase blood pressure and decrease blood flow to muscles
Dynamic exercise	Maintain or increase dynamic strength and endurance; increase muscle power; enhance synovial blood flow; promote strength of bone and cartilage	Start with repetitions against gravity and add progressive resistance; perform 2 to 3 days per week	May increase biomechanical stress on unstable or misaligned joints
Aerobic exercise	Improve cardiovascular fitness and endurance	Perform 3 to 5 days per week for 20 to 30 minutes of moderate-intensity exercise	Progress slowly as activity tolerance and fitness improve
Aquatic exercise	Water supports or resists movement; warm water may provide muscle relaxation	Provides buoyant medium for performance of dynamic or aerobic exercise	Heated swimming pool, warm water (84°F to 92°F); deep water to minimize joint compression; nonslip footwear for safety; receive appropriate instruction in a program designed for people with arthritis

Adapted from Oesch, P. R., & Bachmann, S. (2009). Introduction to physical medicine and rehabilitation. In G. S. Firestein, R. C. Budd, E. D. Harris, Jr., et al. (Eds.). *Kelley's textbook of rheumatology* (8th ed.). Philadelphia: Saunders Elsevier.

Promoting Motivation and Enhancing Health Management

Motivating patients to make behavioral changes is an important nursing intervention. Motivational interviewing (MI), proved effective in treating addictions, has been adapted for managing chronic illnesses. MI is a skillful clinical style for eliciting from patients their own good motivations for making behavior changes in the interest of their health. MI is an evidence-based counseling approach that can be used by nurses to help patients adhere to health regimens and can be applied in very brief, 10- to 15-minute patient encounters (Levensky, Forcehimes, O'Donohue et al., 2007). A key to understanding MI is knowing the phenomenon of ambivalence (Rollnick, Miller, & Butler, 2008). Patients may feel ambivalent about change. Conflicting motivations are normal and common, to simultaneously want and not want. "I want to exercise, but it hurts," "I mean to take my medicine, but I keep forgetting." Nurses need to recognize the tell-tale sign of ambivalence is the "but" in the middle of their narrative. The nurses' task is to elicit "change talk" rather than resistance from their patients. Resistance is the patient's way of trying to resolve the discomfort created by ambivalence. Resistance is best handled by restating, using a "but" statement. For example, "You say you want to exercise, but it hurts. What things can you do to help ease the pain with activity?" The nurse refrains from persuading and confronting, but guides the patient toward an acceptable resolution that triggers change. Patient motivation and readiness to change are dynamic states that can be greatly influenced by interactions between nurse and patient. By guiding the patient on what he or she sees as obstacles (the "buts"), nurses can play a vital role in motivating the patient toward change (Box 39-6).

As part of standard nursing practice, patient education is the cornerstone to effective health management. Nurses should use therapeutic skills, such as reflective listening and asking open questions, prior to informing. Ask the patient what she or he already knows about the topic before preceding—use the "ask–provide–ask–formula."

Educational topics should include information about the nature and treatment of the disease, pain management strategies, correct posture and body mechanics, correct use of assistive devices, principles of joint protection, energy conservation and pacing techniques, balanced nutrition, weight and stress management, and an individualized exercise program. In the spirit of motivation and enhancement, it is crucial to form a partnership (collaboration) between nurse and patient, listen and elicit information from client, understand patient's own perspectives (evocation), and recognize that the patient can and does make choices about the course of his or her life (autonomy). In the end, the patient should express confidence in his ability to make treatment decisions and to carry out a health regimen.

5. An MRI has been ordered for a patient with low back pain. Which of the following should be included in the teaching plan for this patient?
   A. The patient will need to lie still for 3 to 4 hours.
   B. A rhythmic rocking sound will be heard during the procedure.
   C. There is no risk of claustrophobia.
   D. It is an invasive technique.

Try these additional resources to enhance your learning and understanding of this chapter:
- thePoint online resource available at **http://thepoint.lww.com/Pellico1e**
- *Handbook for Focus on Adult Health: Medical-Surgical Nursing*
- *Study Guide for Focus on Adult Health: Medical-Surgical Nursing*

References and Selected Readings

References and selected readings associated with this chapter can be found on the website that accompanies the book. Visit http://thepoint.lww.com/Pellico1e to access the references and other additional resources associated with this chapter.

GERIANN B. GALLAGHER

Nursing Management: Patients With Musculoskeletal Disorders

Learning Objectives

After reading this chapter, you will be able to:

1. Describe the rehabilitation and health education needs of the patient with low back pain.

2. Describe common conditions and nursing care of the upper and lower extremities

3. Explain the pathophysiology, pathogenesis, prevention, and management of osteoporosis.

4. Describe management of the patient with Paget's disease.

5. Use the nursing process as a framework for care of the patient with osteomyelitis.

6. Describe medical and nursing management of the patient with a bone tumor.

Musculoskeletal disorders, particularly those affecting the back and spine, are leading health problems and causes of disability, mainly in people during their working years. The functional and psychological limitations imposed on the patient may be severe. The economic costs, in terms of loss of productivity, medical expenses, and other noncompensated costs, approaches 1% of the gross national product (GNP) per year (Yelin & Felts, 2005). Nurses must be aware of the clinical manifestations and management of these disorders.

ACUTE LOW BACK PAIN

Low back pain, one of the most common reasons for a visit to a provider, is primarily caused by one of many musculoskeletal problems, including acute lumbosacral strain, unstable lumbosacral ligaments and weak muscles, osteoarthritis of the spine, spinal stenosis, intervertebral disk problems, and unequal leg length.

Older patients may experience back pain associated with osteoporotic vertebral fractures or bone metastasis. Other causes include kidney disorders, pelvic problems, retroperitoneal tumors, and abdominal aortic aneurysms.

In addition, obesity, stress, and occasionally depression may contribute to low back pain. Back pain due to musculoskeletal disorders usually is aggravated by activity, whereas pain due to other conditions is not.

Pathophysiology

The spinal column can be considered as an elastic rod constructed of rigid units (vertebrae) and flexible units (intervertebral disks) held together by complex facet joints, multiple ligaments, and paravertebral muscles. Its unique construction allows for flexibility while providing maximum protection for the spinal cord. The abdominal and thoracic muscles help to stabilize the spine and are important in lifting activities, working together to minimize stress on the spinal units. Disuse weakens these supporting muscular structures. Obesity, postural problems, structural problems, and overstretching of the spinal supports may result in back pain.

The intervertebral disks change in character as a person ages. A young person's disks are mainly fibrocartilage with a gelatinous matrix. As a person ages, the fibrocartilage becomes dense and irregularly shaped. Disk

degeneration is a common cause of back pain. The lower lumbar disks, L4 to L5 and L5 to S1, are subject to the greatest mechanical stress and the greatest degenerative changes. Disk protrusion (herniated nucleus pulposus) or facet joint changes can cause pressure on nerve roots as they leave the spinal canal, which results in pain that radiates along the nerve.

Clinical Manifestations and Assessment

The initial evaluation of acute low back pain (lasting <3 months) includes a focused history and physical examination, including general observation of the patient, back examination, and neurologic testing (reflexes, sensory impairment, straight-leg raising, muscle strength, and assessment of muscle atrophy). The patient may report pain radiating down the leg, which is known as **radiculopathy** or **sciatica** (pain from irritation of the sciatic nerve, classically felt from the low back to behind the thigh and radiating down below the knee); presence of this symptom suggests nerve root involvement. The patient's gait, spinal mobility, reflexes, leg length, leg motor strength, and sensory perception may be affected. Physical examination may disclose paravertebral muscle spasm (greatly increased muscle tone of the back postural muscles) with a loss of the normal lumbar curve and possible spinal deformity. The findings suggest either nonspecific back symptoms or potentially serious problems, such as sciatica, spine fracture, cancer, infection, or a rapidly progressing neurologic deficit. If the initial examination does not suggest a serious condition, no additional testing is performed during the first 4 weeks of symptoms.

The diagnostic procedures described in Box 41-1 may be indicated for the patient with potentially serious or prolonged low back pain. The nurse prepares the patient for these studies, provides the necessary support during the testing period, and monitors the patient for any adverse responses to the procedures.

BOX 41-1 **Diagnostic Procedures for Low Back Pain**

X-ray of the spine: May demonstrate a fracture, dislocation, infection, osteoarthritis, or scoliosis

Bone scan and blood studies: May disclose infections, tumors, and bone marrow abnormalities

Computed tomography (CT): Useful in identifying underlying problems, such as obscure soft tissue lesions adjacent to the vertebral column and problems of vertebral disks

Magnetic resonance imaging (MRI): Permits visualization of the nature and location of spinal pathology

Electromyogram (EMG) and nerve conduction studies: Used to evaluate spinal nerve root disorders (radiculopathies)

Medical and Nursing Management

Management focuses on relief of pain and discomfort, activity modification, use of back-conserving techniques of body mechanics, improved self-esteem, and weight reduction. Most back pain is self-limited and resolves within 4 weeks with analgesics, rest, stress reduction, and relaxation.

Relieving Pain

To relieve pain, the nurse encourages the patient to reduce stress on the back muscles and to change position frequently. The patient is taught to control and modify the perceived pain through behavioral therapies that reduce muscular and psychological tension. Diaphragmatic breathing and relaxation help reduce muscle tension contributing to low back pain. Diverting the patient's attention from the pain to another activity (e.g., reading, conversation, watching television) may be helpful in some instances. Guided imagery, in which the relaxed patient learns to focus on a pleasant event, may be used along with other pain-relief strategies.

If medication is prescribed, the nurse assesses the patient's response to each medication. As the acute pain subsides, medication dosages are reduced as prescribed. Nonprescription analgesics are usually effective in achieving pain relief. At times, a patient may require the addition of muscle relaxants or opioids. Although heat or cold therapy frequently provides temporary relief of symptoms, further study of the effectiveness of heat or cold modalities is needed (French, Cameron, Walker et al., 2010). In the absence of symptoms of disease (radiculopathy of the roots of spinal nerves), spinal manipulation performed by a chiropractor or an osteopath may be helpful. Recent evidence suggests that massage, biofeedback, yoga, and acupuncture may be therapeutic (Tan, Craine, Bair et al., 2007). The nurse evaluates and notes the patient's response to various pain management modalities.

Improving Physical Mobility

Physical mobility is monitored through continuing assessments. The nurse assesses how the patient moves and stands. As the back pain subsides, self-care activities are resumed with minimal strain on the injured structures. Position changes should be made slowly and carried out with assistance as required. The patient should avoid twisting and jarring motions. The nurse encourages the patient to alternate lying, sitting, and walking activities frequently, and advises the patient to avoid sitting, standing, or walking for long periods. The patient may find that sitting in a chair with arm rests to support some of the body weight and a soft support at the small of the back provides comfort.

With severe pain, the nurse instructs the patient to limit activities for 1 to 2 days. Extended periods of inactivity are not effective and result in deconditioning. A firm, nonsagging mattress (a bed board may be used) is recommended. Lumbar flexion is increased by elevating the head and thorax 30 degrees using pillows or a foam wedge and slightly

flexing the knees supported on a pillow. Alternatively, the patient can assume a lateral position with knees and hips flexed (curled position) with a pillow between the knees and legs and a pillow supporting the head. A prone position should be avoided because it accentuates lordosis (inward curvature of the spine). The nurse instructs the patient to get out of bed by rolling to one side and placing the legs down while pushing the torso up, keeping the back straight.

As the patient achieves comfort, activities are gradually resumed, and an exercise program is initiated. Initially, low-stress aerobic exercises, such as short walks or swimming, are suggested. After 2 weeks, conditioning exercises for the abdominal and trunk muscles are started. The physical therapist designs an exercise program for the individual patient to reduce lordosis, increase flexibility, and reduce strain on the back. Exercise begins gradually and increases as the patient recovers.

The nurse encourages the patient to adhere to the prescribed exercise program. Erratic exercising is ineffective. For most exercise programs, it is suggested that the person exercise three to four times a week increasing the number of exercises gradually (Wong & Transfeldt, 2007). Some patients may find it difficult to adhere to a program of prescribed exercises for a long period. These patients are encouraged to improve their posture, use good body mechanics on a regular basis, and engage in regular exercise activities (e.g., walking, swimming) to maintain a healthy back. Activities should not cause excessive lumbar strain, twisting, or discomfort; for example, activities such as horseback riding, basketball, and weight-lifting should be avoided. If there is no improvement within 1 month, additional assessments for physiologic abnormalities are performed. Management is based on findings.

Using Proper Body Mechanics

Good body mechanics and posture are essential to avoid recurrence of back pain. The patient must be taught how to stand, sit, lie, and lift properly. Providing the patient with a list of suggestions helps in making these long-term changes (Box 41-2). If the patient wears high heels, the nurse encourages changing to low heels with good arch support. The patient who is required to stand for long periods should shift weight frequently and should rest one foot on a low stool, which decreases lumbar lordosis. Patients who stand in place for a long period of time (e.g., cashiers) should

---

BOX 41-2 **Health Promotion**

Activities to Promote a Healthy Back

Standing

Advise the patient to adhere to the following guidelines:
- Avoid prolonged standing and walking.
- When standing for any length of time, rest one foot on a small stool or box to relieve lumbar lordosis.
- Avoid forward flexion work positions.
- Avoid high heels.

Sitting

Discuss the following strategies with the patient:
- Avoid sitting for prolonged periods.
- Sit in a straight-back chair with back well supported and arm rests to support some of the body weight; use a footstool to position knees higher than hips if necessary.
- Eradicate the hollow of the back by sitting with the buttocks "tucked under."
- Maintain back support; use a soft support at the small of the back.
- Avoid knee and hip extension. When driving a car, have the seat pushed forward as far as possible for comfort.
- Guard against extension strains—reaching, pushing, sitting with legs straight out.
- Alternate periods of sitting with walking.

Lying

Encourage the patient to do the following:
- Rest at intervals; fatigue contributes to spasm of the back muscles.
- Place a firm bed board under the mattress.
- Avoid sleeping in a prone position.
- When lying on the side, place a pillow under the head and one between the legs, with the legs flexed at the hips and knees.
- When supine, use a pillow under the knees to decrease lordosis.

Lifting

Emphasize the importance of the following strategies:
- When lifting, keep the back straight and hold the load as close to the body as possible.
- Lift with the large leg muscles, not the back muscles.
- Use trunk muscles to stabilize the spine.
- Squat while keeping the back straight when it is necessary to pick something off the floor.
- Avoid twisting the trunk of the body, lifting above waist level, and reaching up for any length of time.

Exercising

Daily exercise is important in the prevention of back problems.
- Walk daily, and gradually increase the distance and pace of walking.
- Perform prescribed back exercises twice daily, increasing exercise gradually.
- Avoid jumping and jarring activities.

stand on a foot cushion made of foam or rubber. The proper posture can be verified by looking in a mirror to see whether the chest is up, the abdomen is tucked in, and the shoulders are down and relaxed (Fig. 41-1). The patient should avoid locking the knees when standing and bending forward for long periods.

When the patient is sitting, the knees and hips should be flexed, and the knees should be level with the hips or higher to minimize lordosis. The feet should be flat on the floor. The back needs to be supported, so the patient should avoid sitting on stools or chairs that do not provide firm back support.

The nurse instructs the patient in the safe and correct way to lift objects—using the strong quadriceps muscles of the thighs, with minimal use of weak back muscles. With feet placed hip-width apart to provide a wide base of support, the patient should bend the knees, tighten the abdominal muscles, and lift the object close to the body with a smooth

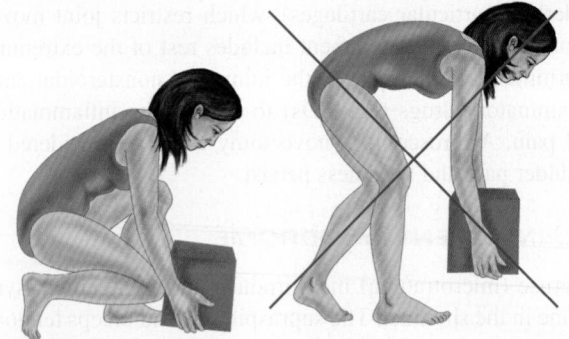

FIGURE 41-2 Proper and improper lifting techniques. (*Left*) Correct position for lifting. This person is using the long and strong muscles of the arms and legs and holding the object so that the line of gravity falls within the base of support. (*Right*) Incorrect position for lifting because pull is exerted on the back muscles and leaning causes the line of gravity to fall outside the base.

motion, avoiding twisting and jarring motions (Fig. 41-2). It takes about 6 months for a person to readjust postural habits. Practicing these protective and defensive postures, positions, and body mechanics results in natural strengthening of the back and diminishes the chance that back pain will recur.

Modifying Nutrition for Weight Reduction

Obesity contributes to back strain by stressing the relatively weak back muscles. Exercises are less effective and more difficult to perform when the patient is overweight. Weight reduction through diet modification may prevent recurrence of back pain. Weight reduction is based on a sound nutritional plan that includes a change in eating habits to maintain desirable weight. Monitoring weight reduction, noting achievement, and providing encouragement and positive reinforcement facilitate adherence. Frequently, back problems resolve as optimal weight is achieved.

COMMON UPPER EXTREMITY PROBLEMS

The structures in the upper extremities are frequently the sites of painful syndromes. The structures most frequently affected are the shoulder, wrist, and hand.

BURSITIS AND TENDINITIS

Bursitis and **tendinitis** are inflammatory conditions that commonly occur in the shoulder. Bursae are fluid-filled sacs that prevent friction between joint structures during joint activity. When inflamed, they are painful. Similarly, muscle tendon sheaths become inflamed with repetitive stretching. The inflammation causes proliferation of synovial membrane and pannus formation (inflammatory changes that destroy the

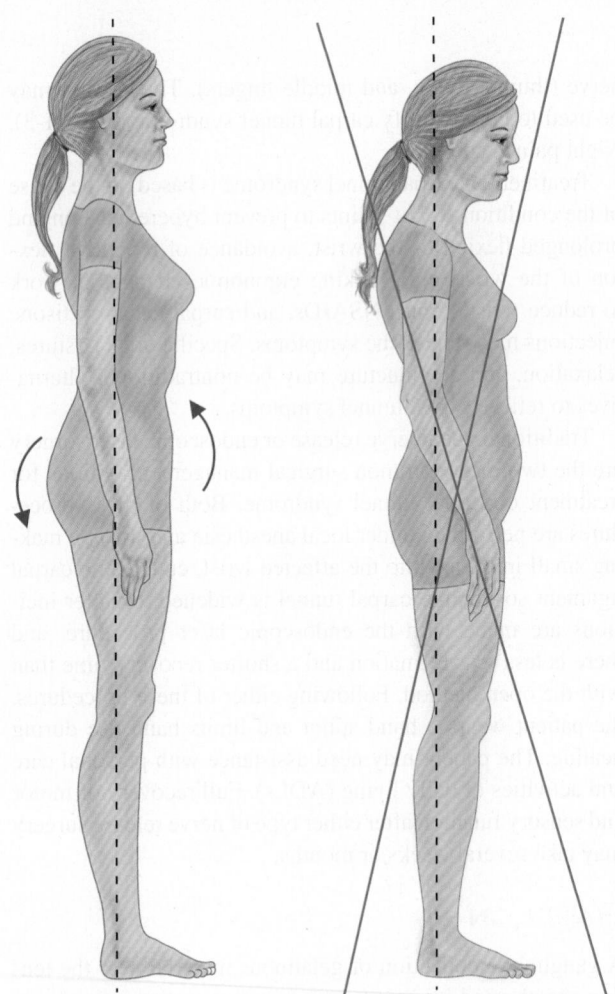

FIGURE 41-1 Proper and improper standing postures. (*Left*) Abdominal muscles contracted, giving a feeling of upward pull, and gluteal muscles contracted, giving a downward pull. (*Right*) Slouch position, showing abdominal muscles relaxed and body out of proper alignment.

underlying articular cartilages), which restricts joint movement. Conservative treatment includes rest of the extremity, intermittent ice and heat to the joint, and nonsteroidal anti-inflammatory drugs (NSAIDs) to control the inflammation and pain. Arthroscopic synovectomy may be considered if shoulder pain and weakness persist.

IMPINGEMENT SYNDROME

Overuse (microtrauma) may produce an impingement syndrome in the shoulder. The supraspinatus and biceps tendons become irritated and edematous and press against the acromion process, limiting shoulder motion. The patient experiences pain, shoulder tenderness, limited movement, muscle spasm, and atrophy. The process may progress to a rotator cuff tear (see Chapter 42). Conservative treatment includes rest, NSAIDs, joint injections, and physical therapy (Box 41-3 discusses patient education). Arthroscopic débridement (a minimally invasive surgical procedure that permits evacuation of joint debris) is used for persistent pain. Gentle joint motion is begun after surgery.

CARPAL TUNNEL SYNDROME

Carpal tunnel syndrome is an entrapment neuropathy that occurs when the median nerve at the wrist is compressed by a thickened flexor tendon sheath, skeletal encroachment, edema, or a soft tissue mass. The syndrome is commonly caused by repetitive hand and wrist movements, but it may also be associated with arthritis, hypothyroidism, or pregnancy. Patients who perform repetitive movements or those whose hands are repeatedly exposed to cold temperatures, vibrations, or extreme direct pressure are at a greater risk for carpal tunnel syndrome. The patient experiences pain, numbness, paresthesia, and possibly weakness along the median

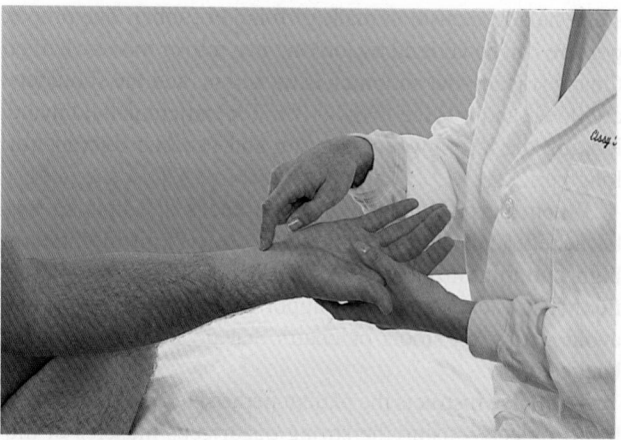

FIGURE 41-3 Tinel's sign may be elicited in patients with carpal tunnel syndrome by percussing lightly over the median nerve, located on the inner aspect of the wrist. If the patient reports tingling, numbness, and pain, the test for Tinel's sign is considered positive. From Weber, J. W., & Kelley, J. (2006). *Health assessment in nursing* (3rd ed.). Philadelphia: Lippincott Williams & Wilkins. ©B. Proud.

nerve (thumb, index, and middle fingers). Tinel's sign may be used to help identify carpal tunnel syndrome (Fig. 41-3). Night pain is common.

Treatment of carpal tunnel syndrome is based on the cause of the condition. Wrist splints to prevent hyperextension and prolonged flexion of the wrist, avoidance of repetitive flexion of the wrist (e.g., making ergonomic changes at work to reduce wrist strain), NSAIDs, and carpal canal cortisone injections may relieve the symptoms. Specific yoga postures, relaxation, and acupuncture may be nontraditional alternatives to relieve carpal tunnel symptoms.

Traditional open nerve release or endoscopic laser surgery are the two most common surgical management options for treatment of carpal tunnel syndrome. Both of these procedures are performed under local anesthesia and involve making small incisions into the affected wrist, cutting the carpal ligament so that the carpal tunnel is widened. Smaller incisions are made with the endoscopic laser procedure, and there is less scar formation and a shorter recovery time than with the open method. Following either of these procedures, the patient wears a hand splint and limits hand use during healing. The patient may need assistance with personal care and activities of daily living (ADLs). Full recovery of motor and sensory function after either type of nerve release surgery may take several weeks or months.

GANGLION

A ganglion, a collection of gelatinous material near the tendon sheaths and joints, appears as a round, firm, compressible, cystic swelling, usually on the dorsum of the wrist (60% to 70%). The ganglion may or may not be locally tender. The pain may be described as aching and can be aggravated by extreme flexion or extension. Often occurring between the

---

BOX 41-3

Patient Education

Measures to Promote Shoulder Healing of Impingement Syndrome

- Rest the joint in a position that minimizes stress on the joint structures, to prevent further damage and the development of adhesions.
- Support the affected arm on pillows while sleeping, to keep from turning onto the shoulder.
- For the first 24 to 48 hours of the acute phase, apply cold to reduce swelling and discomfort; then, according to the treatment plan, apply heat intermittently to promote circulation and healing.
- Gradually resume motion and use of the joint. Assistance with dressing and other ADLs may be needed.
- Avoid working and lifting above shoulder level or pushing an object against a "locked" shoulder.
- Perform the prescribed daily ROM and strengthening exercises.

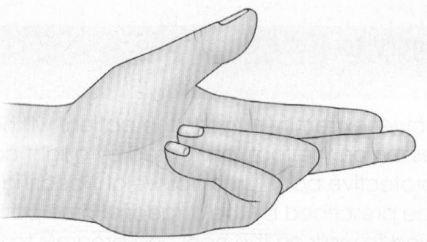

FIGURE 41-4 Dupuytren's contracture, a flexion deformity caused by an inherited trait, is a slowly progressive contracture of the palmar fascia, which severely impairs the function of the fourth, fifth, and sometimes, the middle finger.

second and third decade of life, they are three times more common in women than men (Bozentka, 2008). Asymptomatic ganglion are observed, since approximately 50% will resolve without treatment. Other treatments may include aspiration, corticosteroid injection, or surgical excision. After treatment, a compression dressing and immobilization splint are used.

DUPUYTREN'S DISEASE

Dupuytren's disease results in a slowly progressive **contracture** of the palmar fascia, called Dupuytren's contracture, which causes flexion of the fourth and fifth fingers, and frequently the middle finger (Fig. 41-4). This renders the fingers more or less useless. It is caused by an inherited autosomal dominant trait and occurs most frequently in men who are older than 50 years and who are of northern European descent. It is also associated with drug therapy for epilepsy, diabetes, and alcoholism (Thorne, 2007). It starts as a nodule of the palmar fascia. The nodule may not change, or it may progress so that the fibrous thickening extends to involve the skin in the distal palm and produces a contracture of the fingers. The patient may experience dull aching discomfort, morning numbness, cramping, and stiffness in the affected fingers. This condition starts in one hand, but eventually both hands are affected symmetrically. Initially, finger-stretching exercises may prevent contractures. With contracture development, palmar and digital fasciectomies are performed to improve function. Finger exercises are begun on postoperative day 1 or 2.

Box 41-4 on page 1096 discusses nursing interventions for patients undergoing surgery for upper extremity problems.

COMMON FOOT PROBLEMS

Disorders of the foot are commonly caused by poorly fitting shoes, which distort normal anatomy while inducing deformity and pain.

Several systemic diseases affect the feet. Patients with diabetes are prone to develop corns and peripheral neuropathies with diminished sensation, leading to ulcers at pressure points of the foot. Patients with peripheral vascular disease and arteriosclerosis complain of burning and itching feet, resulting in scratching and skin breakdown. Foot deformities may occur with rheumatoid arthritis. Dermatologic problems commonly affect the feet in the form of fungal infections and plantar warts.

The discomforts of foot strain are treated with rest, elevation, physiotherapy, and orthotic devices. The patient must inspect the foot and skin under pads and orthotic devices for pressure and skin breakdown daily. If a "window" is cut into shoes to relieve pressure over a bony deformity, the skin must be monitored daily for breakdown from pressure exerted at the window area. Active foot exercises promote circulation and help strengthen the feet. Walking in properly fitting shoes is considered the ideal exercise.

PLANTAR FASCIITIS

Plantar fasciitis, an inflammation of the foot-supporting fascia, presents as an acute onset of heel pain experienced with the first steps in the morning. The pain is localized to the anterior medial aspect of the heel and diminishes with gentle stretching of the foot and Achilles tendon. Management includes stretching exercises, wearing shoes with support and cushioning to relieve pain, orthotic devices (e.g., heel cups, arch supports), and NSAIDs. Unresolved plantar fasciitis may progress to fascial tears at the heel and eventual development of heel spurs.

HALLUX VALGUS

Hallux valgus (commonly called a bunion) is a deformity in which the great toe deviates laterally (Fig. 41-5A). Associated with this is a marked prominence of the medial aspect of the first metatarsophalangeal joint. There is also osseous enlargement (exostosis) of the medial side of the first

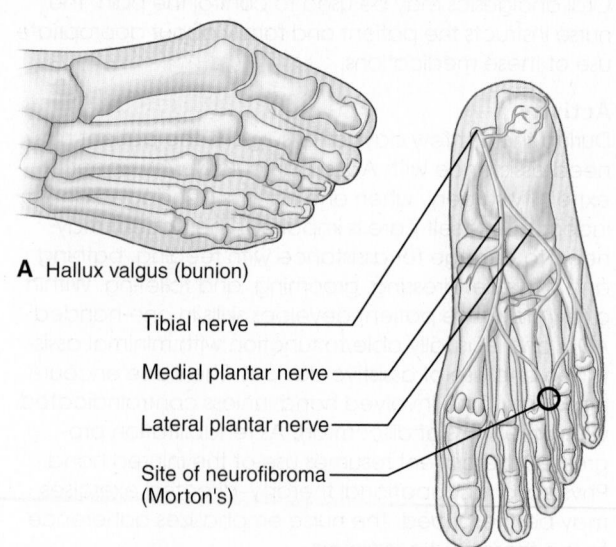

A Hallux valgus (bunion)

Tibial nerve

Medial plantar nerve

Lateral plantar nerve

Site of neurofibroma (Morton's)

B Neurofibroma (Morton's neuroma)

FIGURE 41-5 A & B Common foot deformities.

BOX 41-4

Nursing Interventions for Patient Undergoing Surgery to Treat Upper and Lower Extremity Conditions

Promoting Tissue Perfusion

Neurovascular assessment of the exposed digits every 1 to 2 hours for the first 24 hours after surgery is essential to monitor the function of the nerves and the perfusion of the tissues. The nurse compares the affected extremity with the unaffected one and the postoperative status with the documented preoperative status. Perfusion is assessed by temperature, color, capillary refill, and grading of peripheral pulses. The nurse asks the patient to describe the sensations in the affected extremity and to demonstrate mobility of the involved area. With tendon repairs and nerve, vascular, or skin grafts, motor function is tested as necessary. Dressings provide support but are nonconstrictive. If the patient is discharged within several hours after the surgery, the nurse teaches the patient and family how to assess for edema and neurovascular status (circulation, sensation, motion). Compromised neurovascular function can increase the patient's pain.

Relieving Pain

Pain experienced by patients who undergo hand and foot surgery is related to inflammation and edema. Formation of a hematoma may contribute to the discomfort. To control the edema, the extremity should be elevated on several pillows when the patient is sitting or lying. When higher elevation is prescribed for an upper extremity, an elevating sling may be attached to an IV pole or to an overhead frame. If the patient is ambulatory, the affected arm is elevated in a conventional sling with the hand at heart level.

Ice packs applied intermittently to the surgical area during the first 24 to 48 hours may be prescribed to control edema and provide some pain relief. Dependent positioning of an extremity is often uncomfortable. Simply elevating the extremity often relieves the discomfort. Oral analgesics may be used to control the pain. The nurse instructs the patient and family about appropriate use of these medications.

Activity

During the first few days after surgery, the patient may need assistance with ADLs, particularly with upper extremity surgery, when one hand is bandaged and independent self-care is impaired. The patient may need to arrange for assistance with feeding, bathing and hygiene, dressing, grooming, and toileting. Within a few days, the patient develops skills in one-handed ADLs and is usually able to function with minimal assistance and use of assistive devices. The nurse encourages use of the involved hand, unless contraindicated, within the limits of discomfort. As rehabilitation progresses, the patient resumes use of the injured hand. Physical or occupational therapy–directed exercises may be prescribed. The nurse emphasizes adherence to the therapeutic regimen.

After lower extremity surgery, the patient will have a bulky dressing on the foot, protected by a light cast or a special protective boot. Limits for weight-bearing on the foot will be prescribed by the surgeon. Some patients are allowed to walk on the heel and progress to weight-bearing as tolerated; other patients are restricted to non–weight-bearing activities. Assistive devices (e.g., crutches, walker) may be needed. The choice of the devices depends on the patient's general condition and balance and on the weight-bearing prescription. Safe use of the assistive devices must be ensured through adequate patient education and practice before discharge. Strategies to move around the house safely while using assistive devices are discussed with the patient. As healing progresses, the patient gradually resumes ambulation within prescribed limits. The nurse emphasizes adherence to the therapeutic regimen.

Preventing Infection

Any surgery carries a risk of infection. In addition, percutaneous pins may be used to hold bones in position, and these pins serve as potential sites for infection. Care must be taken to protect the surgical wound from dirt and moisture. When bathing, the patient can secure a plastic bag over the dressing to prevent it from getting wet. Patient instructions concerning aseptic wound care and pin care may be necessary. Refer to Chapter 42 for pin care.

The nurse teaches the patient to monitor for temperature changes and infection. Drainage on the dressing, a foul odor, or increased pain and swelling could indicate infection. The nurse instructs the patient to promptly report any of these findings to the provider. If prophylactic antibiotics are prescribed, the nurse provides instruction about their correct use.

Promoting Home and Community-Based Care

The nurse plans patient teaching for home care, focusing on neurovascular status, pain management, mobility, and wound care.

The nurse instructs the patient to report the following signs and symptoms, which indicate impaired circulation:
- Change in sensation
- Inability to move toes
- Digits or extremity cool to touch
- Color changes

The nurse also provides instructions for wound care, including:
- Keep the dressing or cast clean and dry.
- Report signs of wound infection (e.g., pain, drainage, fever) immediately.
- Follow the prescribed antibiotic regimen.
- Keep your appointment with the surgeon for the initial dressing change.

metatarsal head, over which a bursa may form (secondary to pressure and inflammation). Acute bursitis symptoms include a reddened area, edema, and tenderness.

Factors contributing to bunion formation include heredity, ill-fitting shoes, and gradual lengthening and widening of the foot associated with aging. Osteoarthritis is frequently associated with hallux valgus. Treatment depends on the patient's age, the degree of deformity, and the severity of symptoms. If a bunion deformity is uncomplicated, wearing a shoe that conforms to the shape of the foot or that is molded to the foot to prevent pressure on the protruding portions may be the only treatment needed. Corticosteroid injections control acute inflammation. Surgical removal of the bunion (exostosis) and osteotomies to realign the toe may be required to improve function and appearance. Complications related to bunionectomy include limited range of motion (ROM), paresthesias, tendon injury, and recurrence of deformity.

Postoperatively, the patient may have intense throbbing pain at the operative site, requiring liberal doses of analgesic medication. The foot is elevated to the level of the heart to decrease edema and pain. The neurovascular status of the toes is assessed by noting temperature, color, sensation, movement, and capillary refill of the affected toes. The duration of immobility and initiation of ambulation depend on the procedure used. Toe flexion and extension exercises are initiated to facilitate walking. Shoes that fit the shape and size of the foot are recommended.

MORTON'S NEUROMA

Morton's neuroma (plantar digital neuroma, neurofibroma) is a swelling of the third (lateral) branch of the median plantar nerve (see Fig. 41-5B). The third digital nerve, which is located in the third intermetatarsal (web) space, is most commonly involved. Microscopically, digital artery changes cause an ischemia of the nerve.

The result is a throbbing, burning pain in the foot that is usually relieved when the patient rests. Conservative treatment consists of inserting innersoles and metatarsal pads designed to spread the metatarsal heads and balance the foot posture. Local injections of hydrocortisone and a local anesthetic may provide relief. If these fail, surgical excision of the neuroma is necessary. Pain relief and loss of sensation are immediate and permanent.

See Box 41-4 for interventions for patients undergoing surgery for foot problems.

METABOLIC BONE DISORDERS

OSTEOPOROSIS

Osteoporosis is a costly disorder, not only in terms of health care dollars but also in terms of human suffering, pain, disability, and death. It is estimated that one in two women and one in five men over the age of 50 years will suffer a

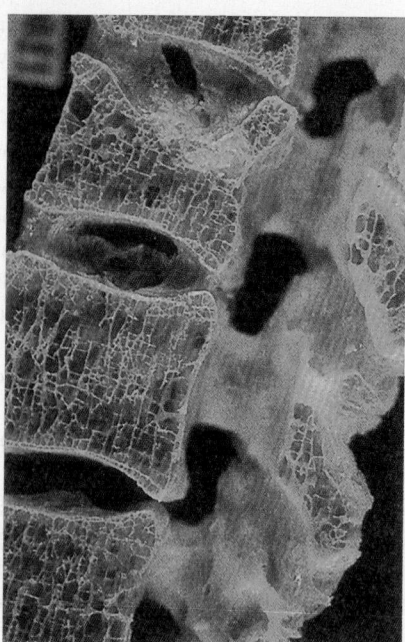

FIGURE 41-6 Progressive osteoporotic bone loss and compression fractures. From Rubin, E., Gorstein, F., Schwarting, R., et al. (2004). *Pathology* (4th ed.). Philadelphia: Lippincott Williams & Wilkins.

fracture due to osteoporosis (Compston, 2010). Characteristics of osteoporosis include a reduction of bone density and a change in bone structure. The bones become progressively porous, brittle, and fragile; they fracture easily under stresses that would not break normal bone. Osteoporosis frequently results in compression fractures (Fig. 41-6) of the thoracic and lumbar spine, fractures of the neck and intertrochanteric region of the femur, and Colles' fractures of the wrist (refer to Chapter 42). These fractures may be the first clinical manifestation of osteoporosis. Fracture risk increases with increasing age and is greatest in Caucasian women.

Pathophysiology

It is thought that 60% to 80% of a person's peak bone mass is genetically determined. Normally, bone mass increases steadily during childhood, reaching a peak in young adult years; however, at menarche in women (age 14), the rate of bone mass gain declines rapidly while males continue to gain mass until age 17 (Porth & Matfin, 2009; Rizzoli & Bonjour, 2010). Bone mass can be affected by factors such as diet, physical activity, and medications. The normal homeostatic bone turnover is altered; the rate of bone resorption (the lysis or breakdown of bone) is greater than the rate of bone formation, resulting in a reduced total bone mass. Primary osteoporosis occurs in women after menopause (usually between the ages of 45 and 55 years) and in men later in life. Loss of bone mass is a universal phenomenon associated with aging. Age-related loss begins soon after the peak bone mass is achieved (i.e., in the fourth decade). Calcitonin, which inhibits bone

resorption and promotes bone formation, is decreased. Estrogen, which inhibits bone breakdown, decreases with aging. On the other hand, parathyroid hormone (PTH) increases with aging, increasing bone turnover and resorption. The consequence of these changes is net loss of bone mass over time.

The withdrawal of estrogens at menopause or with oophorectomy causes an accelerated bone resorption that continues during the postmenopausal years. Women develop osteoporosis more frequently and more extensively than men because of lower peak bone mass and the effect of estrogen loss during menopause.

Primary osteoporosis is not merely a consequence of aging. Failure to develop optimal peak bone mass during childhood, adolescence, and young adulthood contributes to the development of osteoporosis without resultant bone loss. Early identification of at-risk teenagers and young adults, increased calcium intake, participation in regular weight-bearing exercise, and modification of lifestyle (e.g., reduced use of caffeine, cigarettes, carbonated soft drinks, and alcohol) are

interventions that decrease the risk of osteoporosis, fractures, and associated disability later in life. Calcium metabolism is illustrated in Figure 41-7.

Secondary osteoporosis is associated with many disease states, nutritional deficiencies, and medications. Coexisting medical conditions (e.g., malabsorption syndromes, lactose intolerance, alcohol abuse, renal failure, liver failure, Cushing's syndrome, hyperthyroidism, and hyperparathyroidism) contribute to bone loss and the development of osteoporosis. Medications (e.g., corticosteroids, antiseizure medications, heparin, tetracycline, aluminum-containing antacids, and thyroid supplements) affect the body's use and metabolism of calcium. The degree of osteoporosis is related to the duration of medication therapy. When the therapy is discontinued or the metabolic problem is corrected, the progression of osteoporosis is halted, but restoration of lost bone mass usually does not occur. Specific disease states (e.g., celiac disease, hypogonadism) and medications (e.g., corticosteroids, antiseizure medications) that place patients at risk need

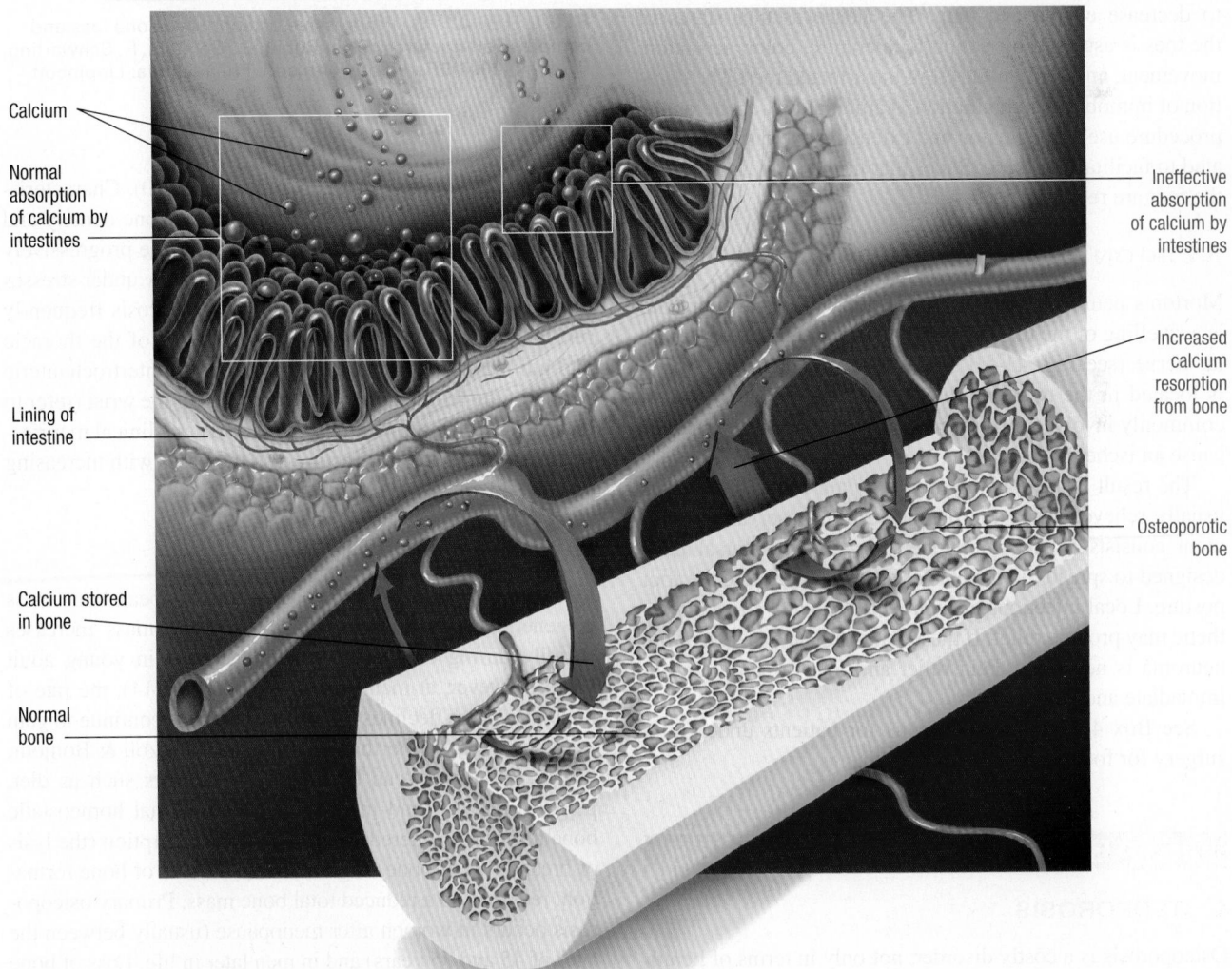

Calcium

Normal absorption of calcium by intestines

Lining of intestine

Calcium stored in bone

Normal bone

Ineffective absorption of calcium by intestines

Increased calcium resorption from bone

Osteoporotic bone

FIGURE 41-7 Calcium metabolism in osteoporosis. Normally, blood absorbs calcium from the digestive system and deposits it into bone. In osteoporosis, blood levels of calcium are reduced. To maintain blood calcium levels, reabsorption of calcium from the bones is increased.

to be identified and therapies instituted to reverse the development of osteoporosis.

Risk Factors

Small-framed, nonobese Caucasian women are at greatest risk for osteoporosis. Also, Asian women of slight build are at risk for low peak bone mineral density (BMD). African American women, who have a greater bone mass than Caucasian women, are less susceptible to osteoporosis. Men have a greater peak bone mass and do not experience sudden estrogen reduction. As a result, osteoporosis occurs in men at a lower rate and at an older age (about one decade later). It is believed that testosterone and estrogen are important in achieving and maintaining bone mass in men.

Nutritional factors contribute to the development of osteoporosis. A diet that includes adequate calories and nutrients needed to maintain bone, calcium, and vitamin D must be consumed. Vitamin D is necessary for calcium absorption and for normal bone mineralization. Dietary calcium and vitamin D must be adequate to maintain bone remodeling and body functions.

Bone formation is enhanced by the stress of weight and muscle activity. Resistance and impact exercises are most beneficial in developing and maintaining bone mass. Immobility contributes to the development of osteoporosis. When immobilized by casts, general inactivity, paralysis, or other disability, the bone is resorbed faster than it is formed, increasing the risk of osteoporosis (Sievänen, 2010). Risk factors for osteoporosis are summarized in Figure 41-8.

Gerontologic Considerations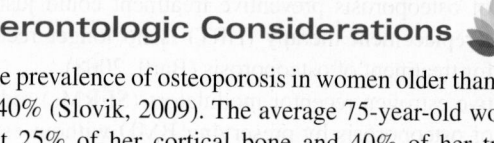

The prevalence of osteoporosis in women older than 80 years is 40% (Slovik, 2009). The average 75-year-old woman has lost 25% of her cortical bone and 40% of her trabecular bone (National Committee for Quality Assurance [NCQA], 2010). Furthermore, elderly people absorb dietary calcium less efficiently and excrete it more readily through their kidneys; therefore, postmenopausal women and the elderly need to consume liberal amounts of calcium. With the aging of the population, the incidence of fractures (more than 1.5 million osteoporotic fractures per year), pain, and disability associated with osteoporosis is increasing. Most residents of long-term care facilities have a low BMD and are at risk for bone fracture. Osteoporotic-related fractures account for more than 800,000 emergency department visits, more than 2,600,000 outpatient visits, and the placement of more than 180,000 people in long-term care facilities annually in the United States (NCQA, 2010).

Clinical Manifestations and Assessment

Osteoporosis may be undetectable on routine X-rays until there has been 25% to 40% demineralization, resulting in

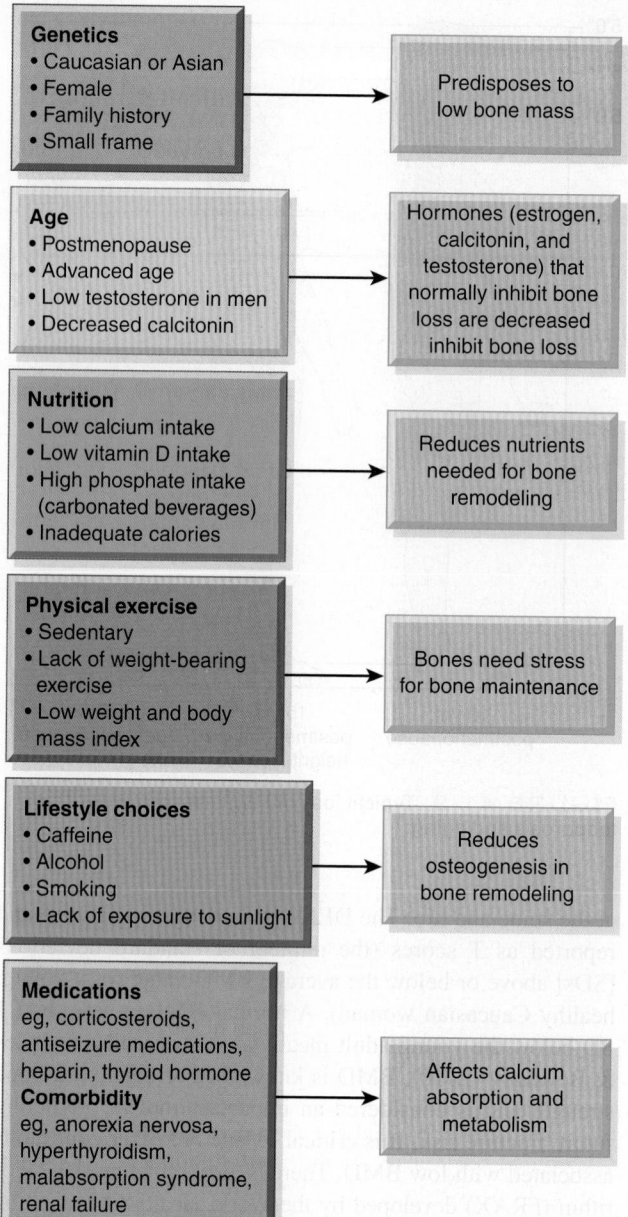

FIGURE 41-8 Risk factors for osteoporosis, and the effects of these factors on bone.

radiolucency of the bones. The gradual collapse of a vertebra may be asymptomatic; it is observed as progressive kyphosis. With the development of kyphosis ("dowager's hump"), there is an associated loss of height (Fig. 41-9). Multiple compression fractures of the vertebrae result in skeletal deformity.

Frequently, postmenopausal women lose height from vertebral collapse. The postural changes result in relaxation of the abdominal muscles and a protruding abdomen. The deformity may also produce pulmonary insufficiency. Many patients complain of fatigue.

Osteoporosis is diagnosed by dual-energy X-ray absorptiometry (DEXA), which provides information about BMD

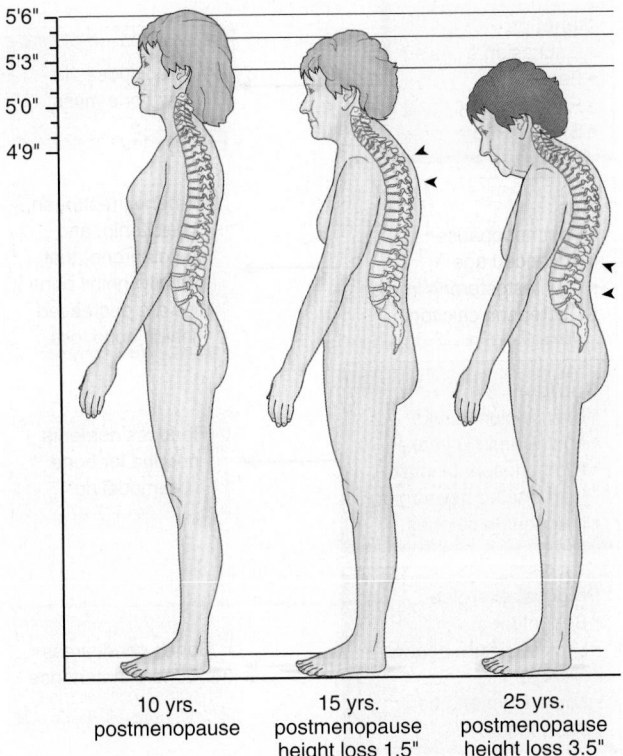

5'6"
5'3"
5'0"
4'9"

10 yrs.
postmenopause

15 yrs.
postmenopause
height loss 1.5"

25 yrs.
postmenopause
height loss 3.5"

FIGURE 41-9 Typical loss of height associated with osteoporosis and aging.

at the spine and hip. The DEXA scan data are analyzed and reported as T scores (the number of standard deviations [SDs] above or below the average BMD value for a young, healthy Caucasian woman). A normal BMD is less than 1 SD below the young adult mean value. According to Lyles & Beyzarov (2010), BMD is known to correlate with bone strength and is considered an important tool in predicting future fracture risk. It is critical to rule out other conditions associated with low BMD. There is also a fracture risk algorithm (FRAX) developed by the World Health Organization (WHO) to evaluated specific risk factors to assess the 10-year absolute fracture risk for all osteoporotic fractures. The WHO defines osteoporosis as being present when the T score is at least 2.5 SD below the young adult mean value on BMD scan (Lindsay & Cosman, 2008). Osteopenia is diagnosed when the BMD T score is between 1 and 2.5 SD below the young adult mean value. Fracture risk increases progressively as the SD of the T score falls below the mean value.

Quantitative ultrasound studies of the heel and DEXA of the wrist, hip, or spine are used to screen for osteoporosis and to predict the risk of hip and nonvertebral fracture. Current evidence-based guidelines recommend the use of hip BMD as the first-line screening test for osteoporosis (National Osteoporosis Foundation [NOF], 2010). In particular, hip BMD is recommended as a screening tool for all Caucasian women older than 65 years and for others thought to be at increased risk for osteoporotic fractures.

BMD studies are useful in identifying osteopenic and osteoporotic bone and in assessing response to therapy. Through early screening (using both assessment of risk factors and BMD scans), promotion of adequate dietary intake of calcium and vitamin D, encouragement of lifestyle changes, and early institution of preventive medications, bone loss and osteoporosis can be reduced, resulting in a reduced incidence of fracture.

Laboratory studies (e.g., serum calcium, serum phosphate, serum alkaline phosphatase [ALP], urine calcium excretion, urinary hydroxyproline excretion, hematocrit, erythrocyte sedimentation rate [ESR]) and X-ray studies are used to exclude other possible medical diagnoses (e.g., multiple myeloma, osteomalacia, hyperparathyroidism, malignancy) that contribute to bone loss.

Medical and Nursing Management

It is emphasized that all people continue to need sufficient calcium, vitamin D (Box 41-5), sunshine, and weight-bearing exercise to slow the progression of osteoporosis.

Pharmacologic Therapy

At natural or surgical menopause, hormone therapy with estrogen and progesterone had been the mainstay of therapy to retard bone loss and prevent occurrence of fractures. Estrogen replacement decreases bone resorption and increases bone mass, reducing the incidence of osteoporotic fractures. However, studies have demonstrated greater risks, including strokes, venous thromboemboli, and breast cancer, than the benefits of osteoporosis preventive treatment could justify. Hormone replacement therapy (HRT) is no longer recommended for treatment of osteoporosis (Bartl, 2008).

Selective estrogen receptor modulators (SERMs) reduce the risk of osteoporosis by preserving BMD without estrogenic effects on the uterus. They are indicated for both prevention and treatment of osteoporosis. Raloxifene is the only SERM approved for osteoporosis in postmenopausal women as it does not increase the risk of breast or uterine cancer, but it does come with an increased risk of thromboembolism.

Medications commonly prescribed to treat osteoporosis include bisphosphonates and calcitonin. Bisphosphonates reduce spine and hip fractures associated with osteoporosis through inhibiting osteoclast activity, reducing bone resorption and turnover. Adequate calcium and vitamin D intake is needed for maximum effect, and some bisphosphonates have formulations coupled with vitamin D or calcium (e.g., Fosamax plus D or Actonel with Calcium). Side effects of bisphosphonates include gastrointestinal (GI) symptoms (e.g., dyspepsia, nausea, flatulence, diarrhea, constipation), and some patients may develop esophageal ulcers, gastric ulcers, or osteonecrosis of the jaw related to bisphosphonate use. Patients must take these medications on an empty stomach, on arising in the morning, with a full glass of water, and must sit upright for 30 to 60 minutes after their

Nutrition Alert

Calcium and Vitamin D

A diet rich in calcium and vitamin D throughout life, with an increased calcium intake during adolescence, young adulthood, and the middle years, protects against skeletal demineralization. Such a diet includes three glasses of skim or whole vitamin D–enriched milk (a cup of milk or calcium-fortified orange juice contains about 300 mg of calcium) or other foods high in calcium (e.g., cheese and other dairy products, steamed broccoli, canned salmon with bones) daily. The recommended adequate intake (RAI) level of calcium for the age range of puberty through young adulthood (9 to 19 years of age) is 1,300 mg/day. The goal of this daily level of calcium is to maximize peak bone mass. The RAI level for adults 19 to 50 years of age is 1,000 mg/day, and the RAI level for adults 51 years of age and older is 1,200 mg/day. The actual estimated average daily intake for adults over 50 is only 600 to 700 mg (NOF, 2010).

NOF (2010) recommends an intake of 800 to 1,000 international units (IU) of vitamin D per day for adults age 50 and older. Inadequate intake of calcium or vitamin D over a period of years results in decreased bone mass and the development of osteoporosis.

To ensure adequate calcium intake, a calcium supplement with vitamin D may be prescribed and taken with meals or with a beverage high in vitamin C to promote absorption. The recommended daily dose should be split and not taken as a single dose. Common side effects of calcium supplements are abdominal distention and constipation. Because GI symptoms and abdominal distention are frequent side effects of calcium supplements, the nurse instructs the patient to take the calcium supplements with meals. Also, it is important to teach the patient to drink adequate fluids to reduce the risk of renal calculi.

administration. Other bisphosphonates are administered intravenously.

Calcitonin directly inhibits osteoclasts, thereby reducing bone loss and may increase osteoblast activity; it also helps to regulate calcium via bone, renal, and GI effects. Calcitonin is administered by nasal spray or by subcutaneous or intramuscular injection. Nasal calcitonin is administered daily, alternating the nares to prevent nasal mucosal dryness. It is approved only for postmenopausal osteoporosis (Wehmeier, 2008). Side effects include nasal irritation, flushing, GI disturbances, and urinary frequency.

Teriparatide (Forteo) is a subcutaneously administered medication that is given once daily for the treatment of osteoporosis. As a recombinant PTH, it stimulates osteoblasts to build bone matrix and facilitates overall calcium absorption.

Denosumab has recently been approved for treatment of postmenopausal women with osteoporosis who are at risk for fractures. It is a RANK ligand inhibitor that is considered a potent inducer of osteoclast formation. Denosumab has been shown to increase BMD at the lumbar spine, total hip, and femoral neck (Lyles & Beyzarov, 2010).

Improving Bowel Elimination

Constipation is a problem related to immobility and medications. Early institution of a high-fiber diet, increased fluids, and the use of prescribed stool softeners help prevent or minimize constipation. If the vertebral collapse involves the T10 to L2 vertebrae, the patient may develop a paralytic ileus. The nurse therefore monitors the patient's intake, bowel sounds, and bowel activity.

Preventing Injury

Physical activity is essential to strengthen muscles, improve balance, prevent disuse atrophy, and retard progressive bone demineralization. Regular weight-bearing exercise promotes bone formation. From 20 to 30 minutes of aerobic exercise (e.g., walking), 3 days or more a week, is recommended. Weight training stimulates an increase in BMD. In addition, exercise improves balance, reducing the incidence of falls and fractures. Isometric exercises can strengthen trunk muscles. The nurse encourages walking, good body mechanics, and good posture. Daily weight-bearing activity, preferably outdoors in the sunshine to enhance the body's ability to produce vitamin D, is encouraged. Sudden bending, jarring, and strenuous lifting are avoided.

Fracture Management

Fractures of the hip are managed surgically by joint replacement or by closed or open reduction with internal fixation (e.g., hip pinning). Surgery, early ambulation, intensive physical therapy, and adequate nutrition result in decreased morbidity and improved outcomes. In addition, patients need to be evaluated for osteoporosis and treated, if indicated.

Osteoporotic compression fractures of the vertebra are managed conservatively. Additional vertebral fractures and progressive kyphosis are common. Pharmacologic and dietary treatments are aimed at increasing vertebral bone density. Percutaneous vertebroplasty/kyphoplasty (injection of polymethylmethacrylate bone cement into the fractured vertebra, followed by inflation of a pressurized balloon to restore the shape of the affected vertebra) can provide rapid relief of acute pain and improve quality of life (QOL). The long-term effect of this procedure is unknown (Hakim & Grabo, 2007). Patients who have not responded to first-line approaches to the treatment of vertebral compression fracture can be considered for the procedure. It is contraindicated in the presence of infection, old fractures, uncorrected coagulopathies, and allergic sensitivity to any of the required components (Jensen & Evans, 2008). Refer to Chapter 42 for fracture care.

Box 41-6 discusses fall prevention. Box 41-7 discusses the impact of nurse practitioners on osteoporosis management.

Gerontologic Considerations

Fall Prevention

Elderly people fall frequently as a result of environmental hazards, neuromuscular disorders, diminished senses, cardiovascular responses, and responses to medications. The patient and family need to be included in planning for care and preventive management regimens. For example, the home environment should be assessed for safety and elimination of potential hazards (e.g., scatter rugs, cluttered rooms and stairwells, toys on the floor, pets underfoot). A safe environment can then be created (e.g., well-lighted staircases with secure hand rails, grab bars in the bathroom, properly fitting footwear).

PAGET'S DISEASE

Paget's disease (osteitis deformans) is a disorder of localized rapid bone turnover, most commonly affecting the skull, femur, tibia, pelvic bones, and vertebrae. The disease occurs in about 2% to 3% of the population older than 50 years. The incidence is slightly greater in men than in women and increases with aging. A family history has been noted, with siblings often developing the disease. The cause of Paget's disease is not known.

Pathophysiology

In Paget's disease, there is a primary proliferation of osteoclasts, which produces bone resorption. This is followed by a compensatory increase in osteoblastic activity that replaces the bone. As bone turnover continues, a classic mosaic (disorganized) pattern of bone develops. Because the diseased bone is highly vascularized and structurally weak, pathologic fractures occur. Structural bowing of the legs causes malalignment of the hip, knee, and ankle joints, which contributes to the development of arthritis and back and joint pain.

Clinical Manifestations and Assessment

Paget's disease is insidious; most patients never experience symptoms, but have skeletal deformity. A few patients have symptomatic deformity and pain. The condition is most frequently identified on X-ray studies performed during a routine physical examination or during a workup for another problem. Sclerotic changes, skeletal deformities (e.g., bowing of the femur and tibia, enlargement of the skull, deformity of pelvic bones), and cortical thickening of the long bones occur.

In most patients, skeletal deformity involves the skull or long bones. The skull may thicken, and the patient may report that a hat no longer fits. In some cases, the cranium, but not the face, is enlarged. This gives the face a small, triangular appearance. Most patients with skull involvement have impaired hearing from cranial nerve compression and dysfunction. Other cranial nerves may also be compressed.

The femurs and tibiae tend to bow, producing a waddling gait. The spine is bent forward and is rigid; the chin rests on the chest. The thorax is compressed and immobile on respiration. The trunk is flexed on the legs to maintain balance,

Nursing Research

Bridging the Gap to Evidenced-Based Practice

Nurse Practitioners Managing Osteoporosis

Greene, D., &. Dell, R. (2010). Outcomes of an osteoporosis disease-management program managed by nurse practitioners. *Journal of the American Academy of Nurse Practitioners, 22*(6), 326–329.

Purpose

The purpose of this study was to detail the outcomes of an osteoporosis disease-management program in which nurse practitioners (NPs) have taken a leadership role in screening, diagnosing, and treating patients at risk for osteoporosis.

Design

An electronic medical record (EMR) was used to collect demographic, pharmacy, DEXA scan, and fracture data from a population of over 625,000 patients with one or more risk factors for osteoporosis. Monthly reports were generated and distributed to the NPs to assist them in identifying patients who required screening or treatment.

Findings

Over a 6-year period, there was a 263% increase in the number of screening DEXA scans done each year, a 153% increase in the number of patients on antiosteoporosis medications each year, and a 38.1% decrease in the expected hip fracture rate.

Nursing Implications

NPs play an important leadership role in managing osteoporosis within a large health maintenance organization. The increased cost associated with obtaining more DEXA scans and having additional patients on antiosteoporosis medications was more than offset by the cost savings associated with the reduction seen in hip and other fragility fracture (38.1%). The screening and interventions used can be applied by any NP in any practice setting, on an individual basis, to reduce hip fracture rates in the United States.

and the arms are bent outward and forward and appear long in relation to the shortened trunk.

Pain, tenderness, and warmth over the bones may be noted. The pain is mild to moderate, deep, and aching; it increases with weight-bearing if the lower extremities are involved. Pain and discomfort may precede skeletal deformities of Paget's disease by years and are often wrongly attributed by the patient to old age or arthritis.

The temperature of the skin overlying the affected bone increases because of increased bone vascularity. Patients with large, highly vascular lesions may develop high-output cardiac failure because of the increased vascular bed and metabolic demands.

Elevated serum ALP concentration (conditions that affect bone growth or cause increased activity of bone cells affect serum ALP) and urinary hydroxyproline excretion reflect increased osteoblastic activity. Higher values suggest more active disease. Patients with Paget's disease have normal blood calcium levels.

X-rays confirm the diagnosis of Paget's disease. Local areas of demineralization and bone overgrowth produce characteristic mosaic patterns and irregularities. Bone scans demonstrate the extent of the disease. Bone biopsy may aid in the differential diagnosis.

Medical and Nursing Management

Pain usually responds to NSAIDs. Gait problems from bowing of the legs are managed with walking aids, shoe lifts, and physical therapy. Weight is controlled to reduce stress on weakened bones and malaligned joints. Asymptomatic patients may be managed with diets adequate in calcium and vitamin D and periodic monitoring.

Fractures, arthritis, and hearing loss are complications of Paget's disease. Fractures are managed according to location. Healing occurs if fracture reduction, immobilization, and stability are adequate. Severe degenerative arthritis may require total joint replacement. Loss of hearing is managed with hearing aids and communication techniques used with hearing-impaired people (e.g., speech reading, body language).

Patients with moderate to severe disease may benefit from specific antiosteoclastic therapy. Several medications reduce bone turnover, reverse the course of the disease, relieve pain, and improve mobility.

Calcitonin, a polypeptide hormone, retards bone resorption by decreasing the number and availability of osteoclasts. Calcitonin therapy facilitates remodeling of abnormal bone into normal lamellar bone, relieves bone pain, and helps alleviate neurologic and biochemical signs and symptoms. Calcitonin is administered subcutaneously or by nasal inhalation. Side effects include flushing of the face and nausea. The effect of calcitonin therapy is evident in 3 to 6 months through reduction of bone loss and pain.

Bisphosphonates produce rapid reduction in bone turnover and relief of pain. They also reduce serum ALP and urinary hydroxyproline levels. Food inhibits absorption of these medications. Adequate daily intake of calcium (1,500 mg in three divided doses of 500 mg) and vitamin D (400 to 800 IU) is required for patients with high bone turnover to prevent hypocalcemia during therapy (Favus & Vokes, 2008).

Plicamycin (Mithracin), a cytotoxic antibiotic, may be used to control the disease. This medication is reserved for severely affected patients with neurologic compromise and for those whose disease is resistant to other therapy. This medication has dramatic effects on pain reduction and on serum calcium, ALP, and urinary hydroxyproline levels. It is administered by IV infusion; hepatic, renal, and bone marrow function must be monitored during therapy. Clinical remissions may continue for months after the medication is discontinued.

Gerontologic Considerations

Because Paget's disease tends to affect elderly people, careful assessment of a patient's pain and discomfort is necessary. Patient teaching helps the patient understand the treatment regimen, the need for a diet with adequate calcium and vitamin D, and how to compensate for altered musculoskeletal functioning. The home environment is assessed for safety to prevent falls and to reduce the risk of fracture. Strategies for coping with a chronic health problem and its effect on QOL need to be developed.

MUSCULOSKELETAL INFECTIONS

OSTEOMYELITIS

Osteomyelitis is an infection of the bone. The bone becomes infected in one of three ways:

- Extension of soft tissue infection (e.g., infected pressure or vascular ulcer, incisional infection)
- Direct bone contamination from bone surgery, open fracture, or traumatic injury (e.g., gunshot wound)
- Hematogenous (bloodborne) spread from other sites of infection (e.g., infected tonsils, boils, infected teeth, upper respiratory infections). Osteomyelitis resulting from hematogenous spread typically occurs in a bone in an area of trauma or lowered resistance, possibly from subclinical (nonapparent) trauma.

Patients who are at high risk for osteomyelitis include those who are poorly nourished, elderly, or obese. Other patients at risk include those with impaired immune systems, those with chronic illnesses (e.g., diabetes, rheumatoid arthritis), and those receiving long-term corticosteroid therapy or immunosuppressive agents.

Postoperative surgical wound infections occur within 30 days after surgery. They are classified as incisional

(superficial, located above the deep fascia layer) or deep (involving tissue beneath the deep fascia). If an implant has been used, deep postoperative infections may occur within a year. Deep sepsis after arthroplasty (surgical procedure that replaces damaged joints) may be classified as follows:

- *Stage 1, acute fulminating:* Occurring during the first 3 months after orthopedic surgery; frequently associated with hematoma, drainage, or superficial infection
- *Stage 2, delayed onset:* Occurring between 4 and 24 months after surgery
- *Stage 3, late onset:* Occurring 2 or more years after surgery, usually as a result of hematogenous spread

Bone infections are more difficult to eradicate than are soft tissue infections because the infected bone is mostly avascular (without blood vessels) and not accessible to the body's natural immune response. Also, there is decreased penetration by antibiotics. Osteomyelitis may become chronic and may affect the patient's QOL.

Pathophysiology

Between 70% and 80% of bone infections are caused by *Staphylococcus aureus.* Other pathogenic organisms that are frequently found in osteomyelitis include *Proteus* and *Pseudomonas* species and *Escherichia coli.* The incidence of penicillin-resistant, nosocomial, gram-negative, and anaerobic infections is increasing.

The initial response to infection is inflammation, increased vascularity, and edema. After 2 or 3 days, thrombosis of the blood vessels occurs in the area, resulting in ischemia with bone necrosis. The infection extends into the medullary cavity and under the periosteum and may spread into adjacent soft tissues and joints. Unless the infective process is treated promptly, a bone abscess forms. The resulting abscess cavity contains dead bone tissue (the **sequestrum**), which does not easily liquefy and drain. Therefore, the cavity cannot collapse and heal, as it does in soft tissue abscesses. New bone growth (the **involucrum**) forms and surrounds the sequestrum (Fig. 41-10). Although healing appears to take

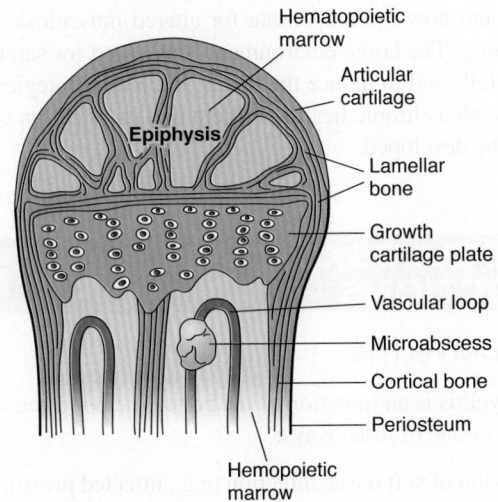

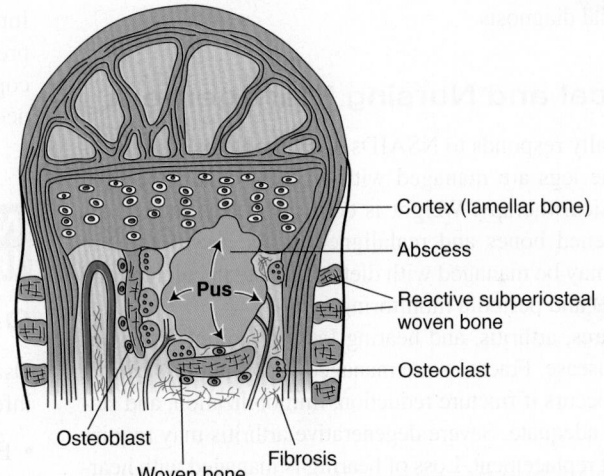

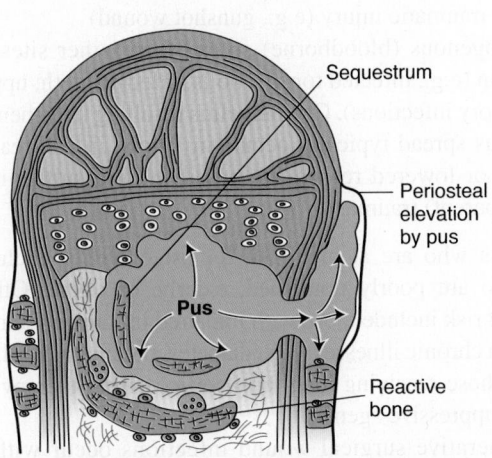

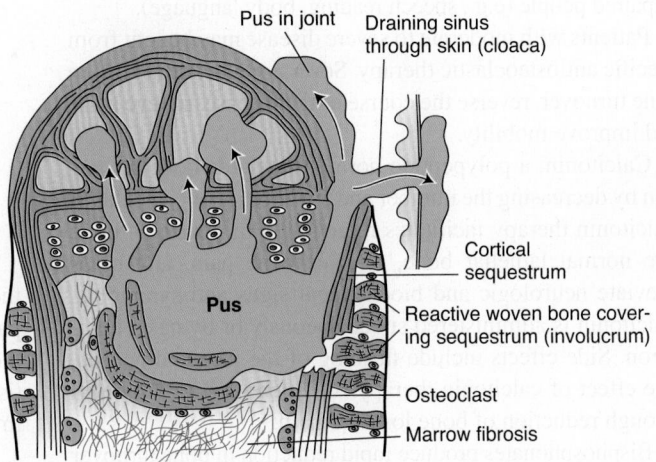

FIGURE 41-10 Stages of osteomyelitis.

place, a chronically infected sequestrum remains and produces recurring abscesses throughout the patient's life. This is referred to as chronic osteomyelitis.

Clinical Manifestations and Assessment

When the infection is bloodborne, the onset is usually sudden, occurring often with the clinical and laboratory manifestations of sepsis (e.g., chills, high fever, rapid pulse, general malaise). The systemic symptoms at first may overshadow the local signs. As the infection extends through the cortex of the bone, it involves the periosteum and the soft tissues. The infected area becomes painful, swollen, and extremely tender. The patient may describe a constant, pulsating pain that intensifies with movement as a result of the pressure of the collecting pus. When osteomyelitis occurs from spread of adjacent infection or from direct contamination, there may be symptoms of sepsis. The area is swollen, warm, painful, and tender to touch.

In acute osteomyelitis, early X-ray findings demonstrate soft tissue swelling. In about 2 weeks, areas of irregular decalcification, bone necrosis, periosteal elevation, and new bone formation are evident. Radioisotope bone scans, particularly the isotope-labeled white blood cell (WBC) scan, and magnetic resonance imaging (MRI) help with early definitive diagnosis. Blood studies reveal leukocytosis and an elevated ESR. Wound and blood culture studies are performed to identify appropriate antibiotic therapy.

With chronic osteomyelitis, large, irregular cavities, raised periosteum, sequestra, or dense bone formations are seen on X-ray. Bone scans may be performed to identify areas of infection. The ESR and the WBC count are usually normal. Anemia, associated with chronic infection, may be evident. The abscess is cultured to determine the infective organism and appropriate antibiotic therapy. While acute and chronic osteomyelitis are both associated with infections of the bone, they are differentiated by the presence of dead bone in the latter.

Prevention

Prevention of osteomyelitis is the goal. Elective orthopedic surgery should be postponed if the patient has a current infection (e.g., urinary tract infection, sore throat) or a recent history of infection. During orthopedic surgery, careful attention is paid to the surgical environment and to techniques to decrease direct bone contamination. Prophylactic antibiotics, administered to achieve adequate tissue levels at the time of surgery and for 24 hours after surgery, are helpful. Urinary catheters and drains are removed as soon as possible to decrease the incidence of hematogenous spread of infection.

Treatment of focal infections diminishes hematogenous spread. Aseptic postoperative wound care reduces the incidence of superficial infections and osteomyelitis. Prompt

management of soft tissue infections reduces extension of infection to the bone. When patients who have had joint replacement surgery undergo dental procedures or other invasive procedures (e.g., cystoscopy), prophylactic antibiotics are frequently recommended.

Medical Management

The initial goal of therapy is to control and halt the infective process. Antibiotic therapy depends on the results of blood and wound cultures. Frequently, the infection is caused by more than one pathogen. General supportive measures (e.g., hydration, diet high in vitamins and protein, correction of anemia) should be instituted. If necessary, the area affected with osteomyelitis is immobilized to decrease discomfort and to prevent pathologic fracture of the weakened bone.

Pharmacologic Therapy

As soon as the culture specimens are obtained, IV antibiotic therapy begins. The aim is to control the infection before the blood supply to the area diminishes as a result of thrombosis. Around-the-clock dosing is necessary to achieve a sustained high therapeutic blood level of the antibiotic. After results of the culture and sensitivity studies are known, an antibiotic to which the causative organism is sensitive is prescribed. IV antibiotic therapy continues for 3 to 6 weeks. After the infection appears to be controlled, the antibiotic may be administered orally for up to 3 months. To enhance absorption of the orally administered medication, antibiotics should not be administered with food.

Surgical Management

If the infection is chronic, surgical débridement may be indicated. The infected bone is surgically exposed, the purulent and necrotic material is removed, and the area is irrigated with sterile saline solution. Antibiotic-impregnated beads may be placed in the wound for direct application of antibiotics for 2 to 4 weeks. IV antibiotic therapy is continued.

In chronic osteomyelitis, antibiotics are adjunctive therapy to surgical débridement. A sequestrectomy (removal of enough involucrum to enable the surgeon to remove the sequestrum) is performed. In many cases, sufficient bone is removed to convert a deep cavity into a shallow saucer (saucerization). All dead, infected bone and cartilage must be removed before permanent healing can occur. A closed suction irrigation system may be used to remove debris. Wound irrigation using sterile physiologic saline solution may be performed for 7 to 8 days.

The wound is either closed tightly to obliterate the dead space or packed and closed later by granulation or possibly by grafting. The débrided cavity may be packed with cancellous bone graft to stimulate healing. With a large defect, the cavity may be filled with a vascularized bone transfer or muscle flap (in which a muscle is moved from an adjacent area with blood supply intact). These microsurgery techniques enhance

the blood supply. The improved blood supply facilitates bone healing and eradication of the infection. These surgical procedures may be staged over time to ensure healing. Because surgical débridement weakens the bone, internal fixation or external supportive devices may be needed to stabilize or support the bone to prevent pathologic fracture.

NURSING PROCESS

The Patient With Osteomyelitis

Assessment

The patient reports an acute onset of signs and symptoms (e.g., localized pain, edema, erythema, fever) or recurrent drainage of an infected sinus tract with associated pain, edema, and low-grade fever. The nurse assesses the patient for risk factors (e.g., older age, diabetes, long-term corticosteroid therapy) and for a history of previous injury, infection, or orthopedic surgery. The patient avoids pressure on the area and guards movement. In acute hematogenous osteomyelitis, the patient exhibits generalized weakness due to the systemic reaction to the infection.

Physical examination reveals an inflamed, markedly edematous, warm area that is tender. Purulent drainage may be noted. The patient has an elevated temperature. With chronic osteomyelitis, the temperature elevation may be minimal, occurring in the afternoon or evening.

Nursing Diagnoses

Appropriate nursing diagnoses may include:

- Acute pain related to inflammation and edema
- Impaired physical mobility related to pain, use of immobilization devices, and weight-bearing limitations
- Risk for extension of infection: bone abscess formation
- Deficient knowledge related to the treatment regimen

Planning

The patient's goals may include relief of pain, improved physical mobility within therapeutic limitations, control and eradication of infection, and knowledge of the treatment regimen.

Nursing Interventions

Relieving Pain

The affected part may be immobilized with a splint to decrease pain and muscle spasm. The nurse monitors the neurovascular status of the affected extremity. The wounds are frequently very painful, and the extremity must be handled with great care and gentleness. Elevation reduces swelling and associated discomfort. Pain is controlled with prescribed analgesics and other pain-reducing techniques.

Improving Physical Mobility

Treatment regimens may consist of activity restriction. The bone is weakened by the infective process and must be protected by immobilization devices and by avoidance of stress on the bone. The patient must understand the rationale for the activity restrictions. The nurse encourages full participation in ADLs within the physical limitations to promote general well-being.

Controlling the Infectious Process

The nurse monitors the patient's response to antibiotic therapy and observes the IV access site for evidence of phlebitis, infection, or infiltration. With long-term, intensive antibiotic therapy, the nurse monitors the patient for signs of superinfection (e.g., oral or vaginal candidiasis, loose or foul-smelling stools).

If surgery is necessary, the nurse takes measures to ensure adequate circulation to the affected area (wound suction to prevent fluid accumulation, elevation of the area to promote venous drainage, avoidance of pressure on the grafted area), to maintain needed immobility, and to ensure the patient's adherence to weight-bearing restrictions. The nurse changes dressings using aseptic technique to promote healing and to prevent cross-contamination.

The nurse continues to monitor the general health and nutrition of the patient. A diet high in protein and vitamin C promotes a positive nitrogen balance and healing. The nurse encourages adequate hydration as well.

Teaching Patients Self-Care

The patient and family are taught about the importance of strictly adhering to the therapeutic regimen of antibiotics and preventing falls or other injuries that could result in bone fracture. They need to learn to maintain and manage the IV access and IV administration equipment in the home. Teaching includes medication name, dosage, frequency, administration rate, safe storage and handling, adverse reactions, and necessary laboratory monitoring. In addition, aseptic dressing and warm compress techniques are taught.

The nurse carefully monitors the patient for the development of additional sites that are painful or for sudden increases in body temperature. The nurse instructs the patient and family to observe for and report elevated temperature, drainage, odor, signs of increased inflammation, adverse reactions, and signs of superinfection.

If warranted, the nurse completes a home assessment to determine the patient's and family's abilities regarding continuation of the therapeutic regimen. If the patient's support system is questionable, or if the patient lives alone, a home care nurse may be needed to assist with IV administration of the antibiotics. The nurse monitors the patient for response to the treatment, signs and symptoms of superinfections, and adverse drug reactions. The nurse stresses the importance of follow-up health care appointments and recommends age-appropriate health screening.

Evaluation

Expected patient outcomes may include:

1. Experiences pain relief:
   a. Reports decreased pain
   b. Experiences no tenderness at site of previous infection
   c. Experiences no discomfort with movement
2. Increases physical mobility:
   a. Participates in self-care activities
   b. Maintains full function of unimpaired extremities
   c. Demonstrates safe use of immobilizing and assistive devices
   d. Modifies environment to promote safety and to avoid falls
3. Shows absence of infection:
   a. Takes antibiotic as prescribed
   b. Reports normal temperature
   c. Exhibits no edema
   d. Reports absence of drainage
   e. Laboratory results indicate normal WBC count and ESR.
   f. Wound cultures are negative.
4. Adheres to therapeutic plan:
   a. Takes medications as prescribed
   b. Protects weakened bones
   c. Demonstrates proper wound care
   d. Reports signs and symptoms of complications promptly
   e. Consumes a diet high in protein and vitamin C
   f. Keeps follow-up health care appointments
   g. Reports increased strength
   h. Reports no elevation of temperature or recurrence of pain, edema, or other symptoms at the site

SEPTIC (INFECTIOUS) ARTHRITIS

Septic arthritis is an important medical emergency with high morbidity and mortality; inappropriate or delayed treatment can lead to joint damage and a mortality rate of about 11% (Mathews, Weston, Jones et al., 2010).

Pathophysiology

Joints can become infected through spread of infection from other parts of the body (hematogenous spread) or directly through trauma or surgical instrumentation. Previous trauma to joints, joint replacement, coexisting arthritis, and diminished host resistance contribute to the development of an infected joint. *S. aureus* causes most adult joint infections, followed by streptococci. IV drug abusers are at particular risk for unusual bacterial infection, and younger populations may present with a gonococcal infection (Mathews et al., 2010). Prompt recognition and treatment of an infected joint are important because accumulating purulent material results in chondrolysis (destruction of hyaline cartilage), which can cause destruction of the surface of the bones.

Clinical Manifestations and Assessment

The patient with acute septic arthritis usually presents with a warm, painful, swollen joint with decreased ROM. Systemic chills, fever, and leukocytosis are present. Risk factors include advanced age, diabetes mellitus, rheumatoid arthritis, and preexisting joint disease or joint replacement. Elderly patients and patients taking corticosteroids or immunosuppressive medications may not exhibit typical clinical manifestations of infection. Therefore, they require ongoing assessment to detect infection as early as possible in the infectious process. An assessment for the source and cause of infection is performed. Blood cultures, ESR, C-reactive protein, and complete blood count are evaluated. Diagnostic studies include aspiration, examination, and culture of the synovial fluid. Evaluation of the synovial fluid can be key when choosing the appropriate antibiotic and treatment plan for the patient. Computed tomography (CT) and MRI may reveal inflammation and damage to the joint lining but are not able to distinguish between infective and other causes of inflammatory arthritis (Mathews et al., 2010). MRI may be helpful in assessing osteomyelitis. Radioisotope scanning may be useful in localizing the infectious process.

Medical and Nursing Management

Prompt treatment is essential and may save a joint prosthesis for patients who have one. Broad-spectrum IV antibiotics are started promptly and then changed to organism-specific antibiotics after culture results are available. The IV antibiotics are continued until symptoms disappear. The synovial fluid is monitored for sterility and decrease in WBCs.

In addition to prescribing antibiotics, the provider may aspirate the joint with a needle to remove excessive joint fluid, exudate, and debris. This promotes comfort and decreases joint destruction caused by the action of proteolytic enzymes in the purulent fluid. Occasionally, arthrotomy (incision into a joint) or arthroscopy is used to drain the joint and remove dead tissue.

The inflamed joint is supported and immobilized in a functional position by a splint that increases the patient's comfort. Analgesics may be prescribed to relieve pain. The patient's nutrition and fluid status is monitored. Progressive ROM exercises are prescribed after the infection subsides.

If septic joints are treated promptly, recovery of normal function is expected. The patient is assessed periodically for recurrence. If the articular cartilage was damaged during the inflammatory reaction, joint fibrosis and diminished function may result.

The nurse describes the septic arthritis process to the patient and teaches the patient how to relieve pain using pharmacologic and nonpharmacologic interventions. The nurse also explains the importance of supporting the affected joint, adhering to the prescribed antibiotic regimen, and observing weight-bearing and activity restrictions. Additionally, the

nurse demonstrates and encourages the patient to practice safe use of ambulatory aids and assistive devices.

The nurse teaches the patient strategies to promote healing through aseptic dressing changes and proper wound care. The patient is then encouraged to perform ROM exercises after the infection subsides.

BONE TUMORS

Neoplasms of the musculoskeletal system are of various types, including osteogenic, chondrogenic, fibrogenic, muscle (rhabdomyogenic), and marrow (reticulum) cell tumors as well as nerve, vascular, and fatty cell tumors. They may be primary tumors or metastatic tumors from primary cancers elsewhere in the body (e.g., breast, lung, prostate, kidney). Metastatic bone tumors are more common than primary bone tumors.

BENIGN BONE TUMORS

Benign tumors of the bone and soft tissue are more common than malignant primary bone tumors. Benign bone tumors generally are slow-growing, well circumscribed, and encapsulated; present few symptoms; and are not a cause of death.

Benign primary neoplasms of the musculoskeletal system include osteochondroma, enchondroma, bone cyst (e.g., aneurysmal bone cyst), osteoid osteoma, rhabdomyoma, and fibroma. Some benign tumors, such as giant cell tumors, have the potential to become malignant.

Osteochondroma is the most common benign bone tumor. It usually occurs as a large projection of bone at the end of long bones (at the knee or shoulder). It develops during growth and then becomes a static bony mass. In fewer than 1% of patients, the cartilage cap of the osteochondroma may undergo malignant transformation after trauma, and a chondrosarcoma or osteosarcoma may develop.

Enchondroma is a common tumor of the hyaline cartilage that develops in the hand, femur, tibia, or humerus. Usually, the only symptom is a mild ache. Pathologic fractures may occur.

Bone cysts are expanding lesions within the bone. Aneurysmal (widening) bone cysts are seen in young adults, who present with a painful, palpable mass of the long bones, vertebrae, or flat bone. Unicameral (single cavity) bone cysts occur in children and cause mild discomfort and possible pathologic fractures of the upper humerus and femur, which may heal spontaneously.

Osteoid osteoma is a painful tumor that occurs in children and young adults. The neoplastic tissue is surrounded by reactive bone formation that can be identified by X-ray.

Giant cell tumors (osteoclastomas) are benign for long periods but may invade local tissue and cause destruction. They occur in young adults and are soft and hemorrhagic. Eventually, giant cell tumors may undergo malignant transformation and metastasize.

MALIGNANT BONE TUMORS

Primary malignant musculoskeletal tumors are relatively rare and arise from connective and supportive tissue cells (sarcomas) or bone marrow elements (multiple myeloma; see Chapter 20). Malignant primary musculoskeletal tumors include osteosarcoma, chondrosarcoma, and Ewing's sarcoma. Soft tissue sarcomas include liposarcoma, fibrosarcoma of soft tissue, and rhabdomyosarcoma, which arise in fat cells, fibrous connective tissue, or soft tissue, respectively. Bone tumor metastasis to the lungs is common.

Osteogenic sarcoma (osteosarcoma) is the most common and most often fatal primary malignant bone tumor. Prognosis depends on whether the tumor has metastasized to the lungs at the time the patient seeks health care. Osteogenic sarcoma appears most frequently in males between the ages of 10 and 25 years (in bones that grow rapidly), in older people with Paget's disease, and as a result of radiation exposure. Clinical manifestations include pain, edema, limited motion, and weight loss (which is considered an ominous finding). The bony mass may be palpable, tender, and fixed, with an increase in skin temperature over the mass and venous distention. The primary lesion may involve any bone, but the most common sites are the distal femur, the proximal tibia, and the proximal humerus.

Malignant tumors of the hyaline cartilage are called chondrosarcomas. These tumors are the second most common primary malignant bone tumor. They are large, bulky, slow-growing tumors that affect adults. The usual tumor sites include the pelvis, femur, humerus, spine, scapula, and tibia. Metastasis to the lungs occurs in fewer than half of patients. When these tumors are well differentiated, large bloc excision or amputation of the affected extremity results in increased survival rates. These tumors may recur. Refer to a pediatric text for details of the Ewing family of tumors.

METASTATIC BONE DISEASE

Metastatic bone disease (secondary bone tumor) is more common than any primary bone tumor. Tumors arising from tissues elsewhere in the body may invade the bone and produce localized bone destruction (lytic lesions) or bone overgrowth (blastic lesions). The most common primary sites of tumors that metastasize to bone are the kidney, prostate, lung, breast, ovary, and thyroid. Metastatic tumors most frequently attack the skull, spine, pelvis, femur, and humerus, and often involve more than one bone (polyostotic).

Pathophysiology

A tumor in the bone causes the normal bone tissue to react by osteolytic response (bone destruction) or osteoblastic response (bone formation). Primary tumors cause bone destruction, which weakens the bone, resulting in bone fractures. Adjacent normal bone responds to the tumor by altering its normal

pattern of remodeling. The bone's surface changes and the contours enlarge in the tumor area.

Malignant bone tumors invade and destroy adjacent bone tissue. Benign bone tumors, in contrast, have a symmetric, controlled growth pattern and place pressure on adjacent bone tissue. Malignant invading bone tumors weaken the structure of the bone until it can no longer withstand the stress of ordinary use; pathologic fracture commonly results.

Clinical Manifestations and Assessment

Patients with metastatic bone tumor may have a wide range of associated clinical manifestations. They may be symptom free or have pain (mild and occasional to constant and severe), varying degrees of disability, and, at times, obvious bone growth. Weight loss, malaise, and fever may be present. The tumor may be diagnosed only after pathologic fracture has occurred.

With spinal metastasis, spinal cord compression may occur. It can progress rapidly or slowly. Neurologic deficits (e.g., progressive pain, weakness, gait abnormality, paresthesia, paraplegia, urinary retention, loss of bowel or bladder control) must be identified early and treated with decompressive laminectomy to prevent permanent spinal cord injury.

The differential diagnosis is based on the history, physical examination, and diagnostic studies, including CT, bone scans, myelography, arteriography, MRI, biopsy, and biochemical assays of the blood and urine. Serum ALP levels are frequently elevated with osteogenic sarcoma. With metastatic carcinoma of the prostate, serum acid phosphatase levels are elevated. Hypercalcemia is present with bone metastases from breast, lung, or kidney cancer. Symptoms of hypercalcemia include muscle weakness, fatigue, anorexia, nausea, vomiting, polyuria, cardiac arrhythmias, seizures, and coma. Hypercalcemia must be identified and treated promptly. A surgical biopsy is performed for histologic identification. Extreme care is taken during the biopsy to prevent seeding and resultant recurrence after excision of the tumor.

Chest X-rays are performed to determine the presence of lung metastasis. Surgical staging of musculoskeletal tumors is based on tumor grade and site (intracompartmental or extracompartmental), as well as on metastasis. Staging is used for planning treatment.

During the diagnostic period, the nurse explains the diagnostic tests and provides psychological and emotional support to the patient and family. The nurse assesses coping behaviors and encourages use of support systems.

Medical Management

Primary Bone Tumors

The goal of primary bone tumor treatment is to destroy or remove the tumor. This may be accomplished by surgical excision (ranging from local excision to amputation and disarticulation), radiation therapy if the tumor is radiosensitive, and chemotherapy (preoperative [neoadjuvant], intraoperative, postoperative, and adjunctive for possible micrometastases). Preoperative imaging studies determine the extent of tumor penetration and impact on adjacent structures. Survival and QOL are important considerations in procedures that attempt to save the involved extremity (Yoon, Hornicet, Harmon et al., 2007).

Limb-sparing (salvage) procedures are used to remove the tumor and adjacent tissue. A customized prosthesis, total joint arthroplasty, or bone tissue from the patient (autograft) or from a cadaver donor (allograft) replaces the resected tissue. Soft tissue and blood vessels may need grafting because of the extent of the excision. Complications may include infection, loosening or dislocation of the prosthesis, allograft nonunion, fracture, devitalization of the skin and soft tissues, joint fibrosis, and recurrence of the tumor. Function and rehabilitation after limb salvage depend on positive encouragement and reducing the risk of complications.

Surgical removal of the tumor may require amputation of the affected extremity, with the amputation extending well above the tumor to achieve local control of the primary lesion (refer to Chapter 42). Because of the danger of metastasis with malignant bone tumors, combined chemotherapy is started before and continued after surgery in an effort to eradicate micrometastatic lesions. The goal of combined chemotherapy is greater therapeutic effect at a lower toxicity rate with reduced resistance to the medications. There is an improved long-term survival rate when a localized osteosarcoma is removed and chemotherapy is initiated. Soft tissue sarcomas are treated with radiation, limb-sparing excision, and adjuvant chemotherapy.

Secondary Bone Tumors

The treatment of metastatic bone cancer is palliative. The therapeutic goal is to relieve the patient's pain and discomfort while promoting QOL.

If metastatic disease weakens the bone, structural support and stabilization are needed to prevent pathologic fracture. At times, large bones with metastatic lesions are strengthened by prophylactic internal fixation. Internal fixation of pathologic fractures, arthroplasty, or methylmethacrylate (bone cement) reconstruction minimizes associated disability and pain. Patients with metastatic disease are at higher risk than other patients for postoperative pulmonary congestion, hypoxemia, deep vein thrombosis, and hemorrhage.

Hypercalcemia results from breakdown of bone. It needs to be recognized promptly. Treatment includes hydration with IV administration of normal saline solution; diuresis; mobilization; and medications such as bisphosphonates, pamidronate, and calcitonin. Because inactivity leads to loss of bone mass and increased calcium in the blood, the nurse assists the patient to increase activity and ambulation.

Hematopoiesis is frequently disrupted by tumor invasion of the bone marrow or by treatment (chemotherapy or

radiation). Blood component therapy restores hematologic factors. Pain can result from multiple factors, including the osseous metastasis, surgery, chemotherapy or radiation side effects, and arthritis. Pain must be assessed accurately and managed with adequate and appropriate opioid, nonopioid, and nonpharmaceutical interventions. External beam radiation to involved metastatic sites may be used. Patients with multiple bony metastases may achieve pain control with systemically administered "bone-seeking" isotopes (e.g., strontium-89). See Chapter 7 for more information about pain management.

Additional therapies are used to treat the original cancer. Radiation and hormonal therapy may be effective in promoting healing of osteolytic lesions. Chemotherapy is used to control the primary disease (see Chapter 6).

Nursing Management

The nursing care of a patient who has undergone excision of a bone tumor is similar in many respects to that of other patients who have had skeletal surgery. Vital signs are monitored; blood loss is assessed; and observations are made to assess for the development of complications such as deep vein thrombosis, pulmonary emboli, infection, contracture, and disuse atrophy. The affected part is elevated to reduce edema, and the neurovascular status of the extremity is assessed.

Providing Patient Education

Patient and family teaching about the disease process and diagnostic and management regimens is essential. Explanation of diagnostic tests, treatments (e.g., wound care), and expected results (e.g., decreased ROM, numbness, change of body contours) helps the patient deal with the procedures and changes. Cooperation and adherence to the therapeutic regimen are enhanced through understanding. The nurse can most effectively reinforce and clarify information provided by the provider by being present during these discussions.

Relieving Pain

Accurate pain assessment is the foundation for pain management. Pharmacologic and nonpharmacologic pain management techniques are used to relieve pain and increase the patient's comfort level. The nurse works with the patient in designing the most effective pain management regimen, thereby increasing the patient's control over the pain. Prescribed IV or epidural analgesics are used during the early postoperative period. Later, oral or transdermal opioid or nonopioid analgesics are indicated to alleviate pain. In addition, external radiation or systemic radioisotopes may be used to control pain. See Chapter 7 for further discussion of pain management.

Preventing Pathologic Fracture

Bone tumors weaken the bone to a point at which normal activities or even position changes can result in fracture. During nursing care, the affected extremities must be supported and handled gently. External supports (e.g., splints) may be used for additional protection. At times, the patient may elect to have surgery (e.g., open reduction with internal fixation, joint replacement) in an attempt to prevent pathologic fracture. Prescribed weight-bearing restrictions must be followed. The nurse and physical therapist teach the patient how to use assistive devices safely and how to strengthen unaffected extremities.

Promoting Coping Skills

The nurse encourages the patient and family to verbalize their fears, concerns, and feelings. They need to be supported as they deal with the impact of the malignant bone tumor. Feelings of shock, despair, and grief are expected. Referral to a psychiatric advanced practice nurse, psychologist, counselor, or spiritual advisor may be indicated for specific psychological help and emotional support.

Promoting Self-Care

Independence versus dependence is an issue for the patient who has a malignancy. Lifestyle is dramatically changed, at least temporarily. It is important to support the family in working through the adjustments that must be made. The nurse assists the patient in dealing with changes in body image due to surgery and possible amputation. It is helpful to provide realistic reassurance about the future and resumption of role-related activities and to encourage self-care and socialization. The patient participates in planning daily activities. The nurse encourages the patient to be as independent as possible. Involvement of the patient and family throughout treatment encourages confidence, restoration of self-concept, and a sense of being in control of one's life.

Monitoring and Managing Potential Complications
Delayed Wound Healing

Wound healing may be delayed because of tissue trauma from surgery, previous radiation therapy, inadequate nutrition, or infection. The nurse assesses the patient's nutritional status by monitoring weight, percentage of weight loss, and evaluating the serum albumin or prealbumin level. An unintentional weight loss of 10% of usual body weight in 3 months is a risk factor for malnutrition. Monitoring and reporting of laboratory findings facilitates the initiation of interventions that promote homeostasis and wound healing. Serum prealbumin has a shorter half-life (2 days) than albumin (21 days) and is not influenced by fluid balance, making it an excellent marker for malnutrition. A normal prealbumin level is 19 to 38 mg/dL with values of 0 to 5, 5 to 10, and 10 to 15 mg/dL reflecting a severe, moderate, and mild protein depletion, respectively (Fischbach & Dunning, 2009). It is expected that wound healing will increase the patient's requirements for calories, protein, vitamins, and minerals (Dudek, 2006).

The nurse minimizes pressure on the wound site to promote circulation to the tissues. Repositioning the patient at frequent intervals reduces the incidence of skin breakdown

and pressure ulcers. Special therapeutic beds may be needed to prevent skin breakdown and to promote wound healing after extensive surgical reconstruction and skin grafting.

Inadequate Nutrition

Because loss of appetite, nausea, and vomiting are frequent side effects of chemotherapy and radiation therapy, it is necessary to provide adequate nutrition for healing and health promotion. Antiemetics and relaxation techniques reduce the adverse GI effects of chemotherapy. Stomatitis is controlled with anesthetic or antifungal mouthwash (see Chapter 6). Adequate hydration is essential. Nutritional supplements, and enteral or parenteral nutrition may be prescribed to achieve adequate nutrition.

Osteomyelitis and Wound Infections

Prophylactic antibiotics and strict aseptic dressing techniques are used to diminish the occurrence of osteomyelitis

and wound infections. During healing, other infections (e.g., upper respiratory infections) need to be prevented so that hematogenous spread does not result in osteomyelitis. If the patient is receiving chemotherapy, it is important to monitor the WBC count and to instruct the patient to avoid contact with people who have colds or other infections.

Hypercalcemia

Hypercalcemia is a dangerous complication of bone cancer. The symptoms must be recognized and treatment initiated promptly. Symptoms include muscular weakness, incoordination, anorexia, nausea and vomiting, constipation, electrocardiographic changes (e.g., shortened QT interval and ST segment, bradycardia, heart blocks), and altered mental states (e.g., confusion, lethargy, psychotic behavior). See Chapter 6, Table 6-6 for a discussion of hypercalcemia and its management.

Chapter Review

Critical Thinking Exercises

1. At the general medical clinic where you are a nurse, a 64-year-old woman presents with acute onset of low back pain. You discover that she has a history of long-term alcohol use and has smoked one pack of cigarettes daily for the past 45 years. What musculoskeletal conditions is she at risk of developing? What specific questions would you ask her to determine the status of her bone health? Discuss the strength of the evidence that supports any risk factor reduction strategies you consider implementing.

2. You are a home care nurse who is about to visit a 26-year-old patient with osteomyelitis that occurred after a fracture to the left tibia and fibula sustained in a motorcycle crash. What is the strength of the evidence that identifies factors that affect bone healing? Discuss the significance of these factors in determining your health teaching strategies for this patient.

3. You are caring for an elderly patient who has advanced cancer. During the afternoon, she complains of muscle weakness, extreme fatigue, anorexia, and nausea. Her urinary output is also elevated. What laboratory value would you assess? What nursing interventions would you implement in light of her new symptoms? What might be the pathophysiology behind these new symptoms?

NCLEX-Style Review Questions

1. A 25-year-old woman experienced an open fracture of the right fibula with major soft tissue damage of her lower leg in a motor vehicle accident. Surgical reduction and fixation of the fibula were performed with débride-

ment of nonviable tissue and drain placement in the damaged soft tissue. Which of the following complications is this patient at risk for?
A. Osteoporosis
B. Osteomyelitis
C. Fat emboli
D. Compartment syndrome

2. Which of the following assessment findings may indicate to the nurse an acute peripheral neurovascular dysfunction for the patient recovering from surgery of the foot?
A. Pale skin, atrophy of the limb, with capillary refill of 2 seconds
B. Absence of feeling, capillary refill of 4 to 5 seconds, and cool skin
C. Atrophy of limb, increased motion, and thickened toe nails
D. Pale skin, weakness in motion, and loss of toe hairs.

3. Which assessment finding would the nurse expect in a client diagnosed with acute osteomyelitis?
A. Leukocytosis and localized bone pain
B. Leukopenia and elevated sedimentation (SED) rate
C. Leukopenia, and elevated fever
D. Petechiae over the chest and abnormal arterial blood gas (ABG) results

4. A client is diagnosed with osteoporosis. Which statements should the nurse include when teaching the client about the disease? Select all that apply.
A. Osteoporosis is common in females after menopause.
B. Osteoporosis is a degenerative disease characterized by a increase in bone density.

(continued on page 1112)

Chapter Review (continued)

C. Osteoporosis can increase the risk for fractures.

D. The recommended daily calcium dose should be taken as a single dose, and the patient should be instructed not to lie down for 30 minutes.

E. Weight-bearing exercise should be avoided.

F. The patient's T score is at least 2.5 SD below the young adult mean value on BMD scan.

5. Which of the following places the patient at risk for impaired wound healing after surgery for a primary bone cancer? Select all that apply.

A. Radiation therapy

B. Prealbumin level is 28 mg/dL

C. Weight loss of 18% over the previous 3 months

D. Anorexia

Try these additional resources to enhance your learning and understanding of this chapter:

- thePoint online resource available at **http://thepoint.lww.com/Pellico1e**
- *Handbook for Focus on Adult Health: Medical-Surgical Nursing*
- *Study Guide for Focus on Adult Health: Medical-Surgical Nursing*

References and Selected Readings

References and selected readings associated with this chapter can be found on the website that accompanies the book. Visit http://thepoint.lww.com/Pellico1e to access the references and other additional resources associated with this chapter.

Nursing Management: Patients With Musculoskeletal Trauma

LINDA HONAN PELLICO

Learning Objectives

After reading this chapter, you will be able to:

1. Differentiate between contusions, strains, sprains, and dislocations.

2. Specify the clinical manifestations of a fracture and the emergency management of the patient with a fracture.

3. Describe the principles and methods of fracture reduction, fracture immobilization, and management of open fractures.

4. Describe the prevention and management of complications of fractures.

5. Discuss nursing management of the patient with a cast.

6. Discuss nursing management of the patient undergoing joint replacement or amputation.

Injury to any part of the musculoskeletal system necessitates evaluation of the damaged area, along with assessment of the structures and organs that underlie the fracture. For example, if a bone is broken, the adjacent muscles cannot function, blood vessels and nerves may be injured with resultant neurovascular complications, and the organs that lie beneath the fracture may have damage secondary to the trauma.

Treatment of injury to the musculoskeletal system involves providing support to the injured part until healing is complete. Frequently, management includes the use of internal and/or external devices such as bandages, splints, casts, skin or skeletal traction, artificial joint replacement, pins, or a combination of these. Pharmacological treatment often includes anti-inflammatory agents, muscle relaxants, and analgesics. They may help diminish edema and relax muscles at risk for spasm that can cause further injury to inflamed muscles or to fractured bones. Pain relief is an important factor to facilitate healing.

Patient education is essential for optimal outcomes. Nursing care is planned to maximize the effectiveness of treatment modalities, prevent potential complications associated with interventions, and observe for the development of untoward signs and symptoms as soon as possible. After the immediate and painful effects of the injury have passed, treatment efforts are focused on preventing fibrosis and atrophy or degeneration of the injured muscles and joint structures, respectively.

COMMON MUSCULOSKELETAL INJURIES
CONTUSIONS, STRAINS, AND SPRAINS

Pathophysiology

A **contusion** is a soft tissue injury produced by blunt force, such as a blow, kick, or fall, that results in bleeding into soft tissues (ecchymosis, or bruising). A *hematoma* (collection of blood within tissues) develops when the bleeding is sufficient to form an appreciable solid swelling. A **strain**, or a "pulled muscle," is an injury to a musculotendinous unit caused by overuse, overstretching, or excessive stress. A tendon connects muscle to bone, whereas a ligament connects bone to bone. A **sprain** is an injury to the ligaments and supporting muscle fibers that surround a joint

often caused by a trauma, wrenching, or twisting motion. The injury can range from a mild stretching of the ligament to a complete tear. While a history and physical exam are important, diagnostic studies of the affected extremity may be ordered to determine diagnosis.

Risk Factors

The main risk factor for contusions, strains, or sprains is participation in sports and physical fitness activities. Strains and sprains occur after intense activity or are associated with overuse repetitive injuries, or trauma, whereas contusions can occur in any soft tissue that suffers blunt trauma. Ankles, knees, and wrists are vulnerable to sprains, while strains frequently occur in the neck, lower back, and hamstring muscle (back of the thigh). Previous injuries are a risk factor for reinjury.

Clinical Manifestations and Assessment

An important question for nurses to ask when assessing for musculoskeletal injury is, "What were you doing at the time of the injury?" For example, many ankle sprains occur because of inversion injury (turning ankle in while walking), while muscle strains occur because of a "pulled muscle" while exercising. The nurse assesses the threes "S's," size, shape and symmetry, of the involved area in comparison to the opposite region. It is important to note presence of **edema** (swelling), ecchymosis (bruising), tenderness, abnormal joint motion, and pain. Contusions, strains, and sprains can present with similar symptoms of pain, edema, and discoloration from the broken blood vessels. The patient may guard or protect the affected area, and he or she may have difficulty moving the affected area; increased warmth may be noted at the injury site.

With contusions, the nurse notes ecchymosis and edema of the injured area. The patient may complain initially of dull pain at the site that increases as edema develops and subsequent stiffness of the area, usually by the next day. Most contusions resolve in 1 to 2 weeks.

Strains are graded along a continuum based on symptoms and loss of function. A first-degree strain reflects tearing of few muscle fibers and is accompanied by minor edema, tenderness, and mild muscle spasm, without a noticeable loss of function. A second-degree strain involves a tearing of more muscle fibers and is manifested by edema, tenderness, muscle spasm, ecchymosis, and a notable loss of load-bearing strength of the involved extremity. A third-degree strain involves complete disruption of at least one musculotendinous unit that involves separation of muscle from muscle, muscle from tendon, or tendon from bone. Patients present with significant pain, muscle spasm, ecchymosis, edema, and loss of function. An X-ray should be obtained to rule out bone injury because an avulsion fracture (in which a bone fragment is pulled away from the bone by a tendon) may be associated with a third-degree strain.

Like strains, sprains are also graded to reflect the degree of injury. A mild sprain, termed first-degree sprain, may cause minor edema, tenderness, and mild muscle spasm, without a noticeable loss of function. Patients are able to bear weight with minimal pain. A second-degree sprain is an incomplete tear of the ligament (bone-to-bone); as blood vessels rupture, ecchymosis and edema are expected and movement of the joint becomes painful. The degree of disability and pain increases during the first 2 to 3 hours after the injury because of the associated swelling and bleeding. There is restricted motion of the affected limb, and weight bearing is painful. A third-degree sprain involves complete ligament tear with resultant complaints of significant pain, muscle spasm, ecchymosis, edema, and loss of function. Patients are unable to bear weight on the affected limb. Tenderness at the distal tibia (inner ankle) or fibula (outer ankle) is associated with an inversion or eversion injury may indicate a fracture.

Medical and Nursing Management

Treatment of contusions, strains, and sprains consists of resting and elevating the affected part, applying cold, and using a compression bandage (Box 42-1). Immobilization of the affected extremity until definite diagnosis is determined may be appropriate. It is important to monitor the **neurovascular status** of the injured extremity; this is termed **CSM: C**irculation, by way of pulses, color, temperature, and capillary refill; **S**ensation, by noting awareness of light touch; and **M**ovement, by range of motion (ROM) of the most distal digits. The nurse compares the injured limb in relation to the uninjured limb.

After the acute inflammatory stage (e.g., 24 to 48 hours after injury), intermittent heat application (for 15 to 30 minutes, four times a day) relieves muscle spasm and promotes vasodilation, absorption, and repair. Depending on the severity of injury, progressive passive and active exercises may begin in 2 to 5 days. Severe sprains and strains may require 1 to 3 weeks of immobilization before exercises are

---

BOX 42-1   **RICE**

The acronym **RICE—R**est, **I**ce, **C**ompression, **E**levation— is helpful for remembering treatment interventions for musculoskeletal injuries.

Rest prevents additional injury and promotes healing. Intermittent application of moist or dry cold packs for 20 to 30 minutes during the first 24 to 48 hours after injury produces vasoconstriction, which decreases bleeding, edema, and discomfort. Ensure care to avoid skin and tissue damage from excessive cold. An elastic compression bandage controls bleeding, reduces edema, and provides support for the injured tissues. Elevation controls the swelling.

initiated. Excessive exercise early in the course of treatment delays recovery. Strains and sprains take weeks or months to heal because ligaments and tendons are relatively avascular. Splinting may be used to prevent reinjury.

JOINT DISLOCATIONS

Pathophysiology

With **dislocation** of a joint, the articular surfaces of the bones forming the joint are no longer in anatomic alignment. The bones are literally "out of joint." Dislocations may be congenital, or present at birth; spontaneous or pathologic; or traumatic, resulting from injury in which the joint is disrupted by force. A **subluxation** is a partial dislocation of the articulating surfaces. Traumatic dislocations are orthopedic emergencies because the associated joint structures, blood supply, and nerves are distorted and severely stressed. If the dislocation is not treated promptly, **avascular necrosis** (AVN), tissue death due to anoxia and diminished blood supply, and nerve palsy may occur.

Clinical Manifestations and Assessment

Signs and symptoms of a traumatic dislocation include acute pain, change in contour of the joint, change in the length of the extremity (shortening of the affected limb), loss of normal mobility, and change in the axis of the dislocated bones. X-rays confirm the diagnosis and reveal any associated fracture.

Medical and Nursing Management

The affected joint needs to be immobilized while the patient is transported to the hospital. The dislocation is promptly reduced (i.e., displaced parts are brought into normal position) to preserve joint function. Analgesia, muscle relaxants, and possibly anesthesia are used to facilitate closed reduction (e.g., noninvasive or nonsurgical reduction). The joint is immobilized by bandages, splints, casts, or traction and is maintained in a stable position. Neurovascular status is monitored. After reduction, if the joint is stable, gentle, progressive, active and passive movement is begun to preserve ROM and restore strength. The joint is supported between exercise sessions.

SPECIFIC MUSCULOSKELETAL INJURIES

Common specific musculoskeletal injuries include **rotator cuff** tears, epicondylitis, and injury to the ligaments of the knee. Table 42-1 summarizes key findings and treatment for these common injuries.

FRACTURES

A **fracture** is a break in the continuity of bone caused by direct blows, crushing forces, sudden twisting motions, and extreme muscle contractions. When the bone is broken, adjacent structures are also affected, resulting in soft tissue edema and hemorrhage into the muscles and joints, with potential joint dislocations, ruptured tendons, severed nerves, and damaged blood vessels. Because body organs may be injured by the force that caused the fracture or by fracture fragments, it is important for nurses to have knowledge of the organs that lie beneath the fracture. For example, the nurse is alert for liver injuries with right rib fractures 6 through 12 and splenic injuries with left rib fractures 9 through 11.

Types of Fractures

Fractures are defined according to the bone involved (e.g., humerus, femur, tibia), and can be categorized in several ways, including the direction of the fracture. A *complete fracture* involves a break across the entire cross-section of the bone and is frequently displaced (removed from its normal position). An *incomplete fracture* (e.g., greenstick fracture) involves a break through only part of the cross-section of the bone. An *oblique fracture* runs across the bone at a diagonal angle of 45 to 60 degrees. A *comminuted* fracture is one that produces several bone fragments, while an *impacted* fracture is one whose ends are driven into each other. A *closed fracture* (simple fracture) is one that does not cause a break in the skin. An *open fracture* (compound, or complex, fracture) is one in which the skin or mucous membrane wound extends to the fractured bone. Some fractures have specific names, for example a fracture of the distal radius (wrist) is termed a *Colles' fracture*. *Stress fractures* occur with repeated bone trauma from athletic activities, most frequently involving the tibia and metatarsals. *Compression fractures* are caused by compression of vertebrae and are associated frequently with osteoporosis. Figure 42-1 on page 1117 depicts types of fractures.

Clinical Manifestations and Assessment

The diagnosis of a fracture is based on the patient's symptoms, the physical signs, and the X-ray findings. Usually, the patient reports having sustained an injury to the area. The clinical manifestations of a fracture include pain, loss of function, deformity, shortening, **crepitus**, swelling, and discoloration. These clinical manifestations do not all need to be present in every fracture.

Pain

The pain is immediate, continuous, and increases in severity until the bone fragments are immobilized. The muscle spasms that accompany a fracture begin within 20 minutes after the injury and result in increasing pain intensity and further bony fragmentation or malalignment.

TABLE
42-1 Specific Musculoskeletal Injuries

Injury	Description	Key Assessment Findings	Treatment
Rotator cuff tears	Tear results from an acute injury or from chronic joint stresses; it occurs when there is damage to one or more of the four muscles and their tendons in the shoulder.	• Acromioclavicular joint pain; in many cases, the patient with a rotator cuff tear experiences night pain and cannot sleep on the involved side). • Limited ROM; the patient cannot perform over-the-head activities or activities as simple as putting on a coat. • Muscle weakness	• Exercise regimens • Nonsteroidal anti-inflammatory drugs (NSAIDs) • Steroid injection into the shoulder joint or • Arthroscopic débridement (removal of devitalized tissue) • Arthroscopic or open acromioplasty with tendon repair
Epicondylitis (tennis elbow)	Chronic, painful condition that is caused by excessive, repetitive extension and flexion and/or pronation and supination activities of the forearm. These excessive, repetitious activities result in inflammation (**tendinitis**) and minor tears in the tendons at the origin of the muscles on the medial or lateral epicondyles.	• Pain that usually radiates down the extensor (dorsal) surface of the forearm and generally is relieved with rest and avoidance of the aggravating activity • Weakened grasp	• Application of ice after the activity for pain • NSAIDs for pain • In some instances, immobilization of arm in a molded splint or cast is necessary. • Local injection of a corticosteroid is generally reserved for patients with severe pain who do not respond to NSAIDs and immobilization because of its degenerative effects on tendons. • After pain subsides, rehabilitation exercises (including gentle and gradual increased stretching of the tendons) • Tennis elbow counterforce strap that limits extension of the elbow (may be prescribed when activity is resumed) • Occasionally, surgery to release strictures or to débride the joint
Knee injury	Injury to the anterior cruciate ligament (ACL) or the posterior cruciate ligament (PCL), which stabilize forward and backward motion of the femur and tibia, occurs when the foot is firmly planted and the knee is hyperextended and the person twists the torso and femur. Injury to the lateral or medial collateral ligaments of the knee, which provide stability lateral and medial to the knee, occurs when the foot is firmly planted and the knee is struck either medially or laterally.	• Acute onset of pain • Point tenderness (e.g., tenderness at the site of injury) • Joint instability and inability to walk without assistance. • Hemarthrosis (bleeding into the joint) may develop, contributing to the pain.	Treatment will depend on the severity of the injury, but may include: • RICE • Evaluation of the joint for fracture • Aspiration of joint fluid to relieve pressure • Limited weight bearing • Use of protective elastic bandaging or brace • Surgery; the operation is typically performed as ambulatory arthroscopic surgery, in which the surgeon uses an **arthroscope** to visualize and repair the damage.

Loss of Function

After a fracture, the extremity cannot function properly because normal function of the muscles depends on the integrity of the bones to which they are attached. Pain contributes to the loss of function. In addition, abnormal movement (false motion) may be present.

Deformity

Displacement, angulation, or rotation of the fragments in a fracture or soft tissue swelling causes a visible or palpable deformity. Movement may be noted at the fracture site, whereas under normal circumstances, movement of bones only occurs at joint.

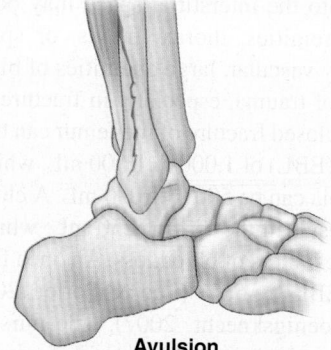

Avulsion
A fracture in which a fragment of bone has been pulled away by a tendon and its attachment

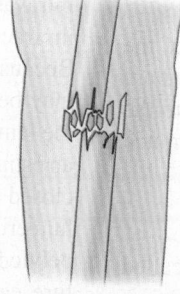

Comminuted
A fracture in which bone has splintered into several fragments

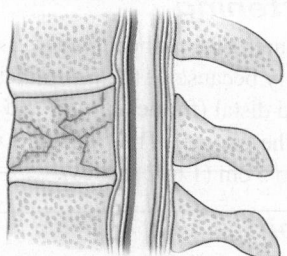

Compression
A fracture in which bone has been compressed (seen in vertebral fractures)

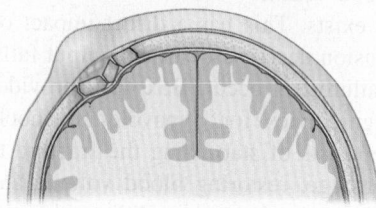

Depressed
A fracture in which fragments are driven inward (seen frequently in fractures of skull and facial bones)

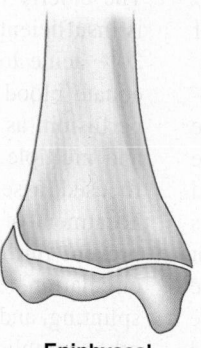

Epiphyseal
A fracture through the epiphysis

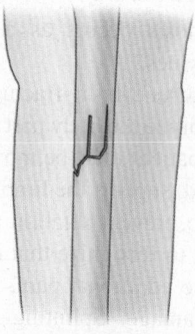

Greenstick
A fracture in which one side of a bone is broken and the other side is bent

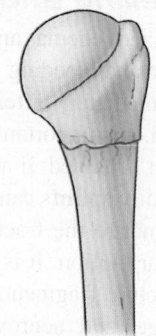

Impacted
A fracture in which a bone fragment is driven into another bone fragment

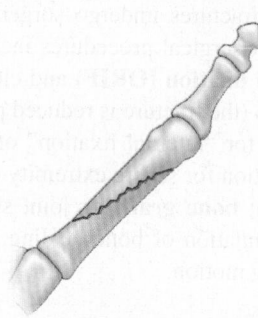

Oblique
A fracture occurring at an angle across the bone (less stable than a transverse fracture)

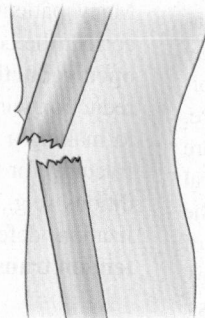

Open
A fracture in which damage also involves the skin or mucous membranes, also called a compound fracture

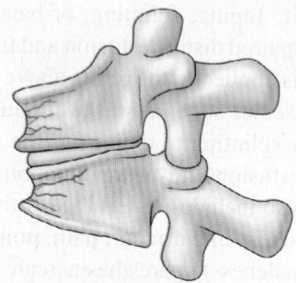

Pathologic
A fracture that occurs through an area of diseased bone (eg, osteoporosis, bone cyst, Paget's disease, bony metastasis, tumor); can occur without trauma or fall

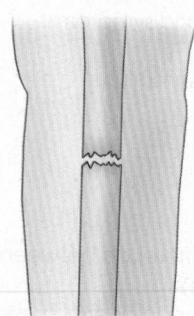

Simple
A fracture that remains contained, with no disruption of the skin integrity

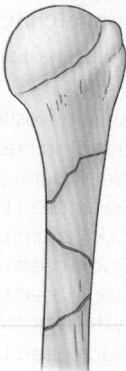

Spiral
A fracture that twists around the shaft of the bone

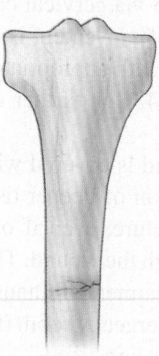

Stress
A fracture that results from repeated loading of bone and muscle

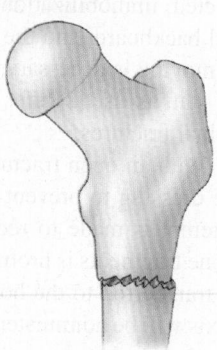

Transverse
A fracture that is straight across the bone shaft

FIGURE 42-1 Specific types of fractures.

Shortening

In fractures of long bones, there is actual shortening of the extremity because of the contraction of the muscles that are attached distal (furthest away) and proximal (nearest) to the site of the fracture. The fragments often overlap by as much as 2.5 to 5 cm (1 to 2 inches).

Crepitus

Palpation of the extremity reveals a grating sensation, called crepitus, caused by the rubbing of the bone fragments against each other.

Swelling and Discoloration

Localized edema and ecchymosis occurs as a result of trauma and bleeding into the tissues.

Immediately after injury, whenever a fracture is suspected, it is important to immobilize the body part before the patient is moved. If an injured patient must be moved before extremity **splint**s can be applied, support the limb distal and proximal to the fracture site to prevent rotation as well as angular motion. It is important to recognize that movement of fracture fragments can cause additional pain, soft tissue damage, and neurovascular damage. Splinting a fracture can include bandaging the legs together, with the unaffected extremity serving as a splint for the injured one. In an upper extremity injury, the arm can be bandaged to the chest, a forearm placed in a **sling**, or a finger can be taped to the adjacent digit. Taping, splinting, or bandaging too tightly may cause impaired distal perfusion and thus is avoided. Immobilization is applied to the joints above and below the fracture. Neurovascular status distal to the injury is assessed before and after splinting to determine the adequacy of peripheral tissue perfusion and nerve function. An assessment of the patient also includes observing for the five warning "P's" of neurovascular impairment: **p**ain, **p**oikilothermia (cold limb), **p**allor (paleness), **p**aresthesia (can range from numbness, "pins and needles," burning, itching, and/or tingling), and **p**ulselessness (weak pulses or delayed capillary refill; normal is <2 seconds).

If cervical and thoracolumbar spinal injuries are suspected, immobilization of the spine via cervical collar, spinal backboard, and the avoidance of movement is essential. If moving is necessary, log-rolling with appropriate number of staff is used. Refer to Chapter 45 for further details of spinal fractures.

With an open fracture, the wound is covered with a sterile dressing to prevent contamination of deeper tissues. No attempt is made to reduce the fracture, even if one of the bone fragments is protruding through the wound. The patient is transferred to the hospital for treatment. Tetanus prophylaxis will be administered in the emergency room (ER) if the last known booster was over 5 years ago.

An immediate priority is maintaining hemodynamic stability. Hypovolemic shock resulting from hemorrhage (both visible and nonvisible blood loss) and from loss of intravascular volume into the interstitial space may occur in fractures of the extremities, thorax, pelvis, or spine. Because the bone is very vascular, large quantities of blood may be lost as a result of trauma, especially in fractures of the femur and pelvis. A closed fracture of the femur can have an estimated blood loss (EBL) of 1,000 to 1,500 mL, while a closed fracture of the tibia can be 500 to 1,000 mL. A closed humerus fracture can result in the loss of 250 mL, while a pelvic fracture can cause 4 liters of blood loss. An open fracture can increase the EBL by 50% (Lee & Porter, 2005; Simon, Sherman, & Koenigsknecht, 2007). The nurse is aware that bleeding is a common problem with fractures. The elderly may be at increased risk if vasoconstriction is insufficient to maintain blood pressure. When a 15% to 20% acute loss of blood volume occurs, a state of inadequate blood volume exists. This has a direct impact on perfusion; as the perfusion decreases, cardiac output falls, and multiple organ failure can occur. Box 42-2 provides focused assessment guidelines for hypovolemic shock. Treatment of shock consists of stabilizing the fracture to prevent further hemorrhage, restoring blood volume and circulation, relieving the patient's pain, providing adequate splinting, and protecting the patient from further injury and other complications.

Surgical Management

Many patients with unstable fractures undergo surgery to correct the condition. Frequent surgical procedures include **open reduction with internal fixation (ORIF)** and closed reduction with internal fixation (the fracture is reduced prior to making a surgical incision for "internal fixation" of the fracture) for fractures; amputation for severe extremity conditions (e.g., massive trauma); **bone graft** for joint stabilization, defect filling, or stimulation of bone healing; and **tendon transfer** for improving motion.

BOX 42-2 **Focused Assessment**

Hypovolemic Shock

Be alert for the following signs and symptoms:
- Thirst
- Anxiety, restlessness, altered sensorium
- Elevated heart rate
- Weak pulse (thready)
- Decreased blood pressure
- Cool, clammy skin
- Decreased urine output
- Decreased pulse pressure (difference between the systolic and diastolic pressure)
- Decreased blood pressure; mean arterial pressure (MAP) below 60 mm Hg
- Rapid, shallow respirations
- Delayed capillary refill

Ongoing Management

Nursing goals include improving function by restoring motion and stability, and relieving pain and disability. The principles of fracture treatment include reduction, immobilization, and regaining of normal function and strength through rehabilitation.

Reduction

Reduction of a fracture ("setting" the bone) refers to restoration of the fracture fragments to anatomic alignment and rotation. Either closed reduction or **open reduction** may be used to reduce a fracture. Before **fracture reduction** and immobilization, the nurse prepares the patient for the procedure, assures permission for the procedure is obtained, and administers an analgesic as prescribed. The nurse gently handles the injured extremity to avoid additional damage.

CLOSED REDUCTION. In most instances, closed reduction is accomplished through manipulation and manual traction. The extremity is held in the desired position while the provider applies a cast, splint, or other device. Reduction under anesthesia with percutaneous pinning may be used. The immobilizing device maintains the reduction and stabilizes the extremity for bone healing. X-rays are obtained to verify that the bone fragments are correctly aligned.

Traction (skin or skeletal) may be used to effect fracture reduction and immobilization. Traction is discussed later in the chapter.

OPEN REDUCTION. With an open fracture, surgical intervention is needed to align the bone fragments. Internal fixation devices (metallic pins, wires, screws, plates, nails, or rods) are used to hold the bone fragments in position until bone healing occurs (Fig. 42-2). Internal fixation devices ensure firm approximation and fixation of the bony fragments. They are not designed to support the body's weight, and they can bend, loosen, or break if stressed. The estimated strength of the bone, the stability of the fracture, reduction and fixation, and the amount of bone healing are important considerations in determining weight-bearing limits. Although the incision may appear healed, the underlying bone requires more time to repair and regain normal strength. Some orthopedic procedures require weight-bearing restrictions. The orthopedic surgeon will prescribe the weight-bearing limits and the use of protective devices (orthoses), if necessary, after surgery.

Management of an Open Fracture

For patients with open fractures, prompt, thorough wound irrigation and **débridement** are necessary to remove foreign bodies, obvious debris, and bacteria. This is often performed in the operating room. Once the wound is cleaned, the fracture is carefully reduced and stabilized by internal and/or external fixation. All open fractures are considered contaminated and carry risks for osteomyelitis (bone infec-

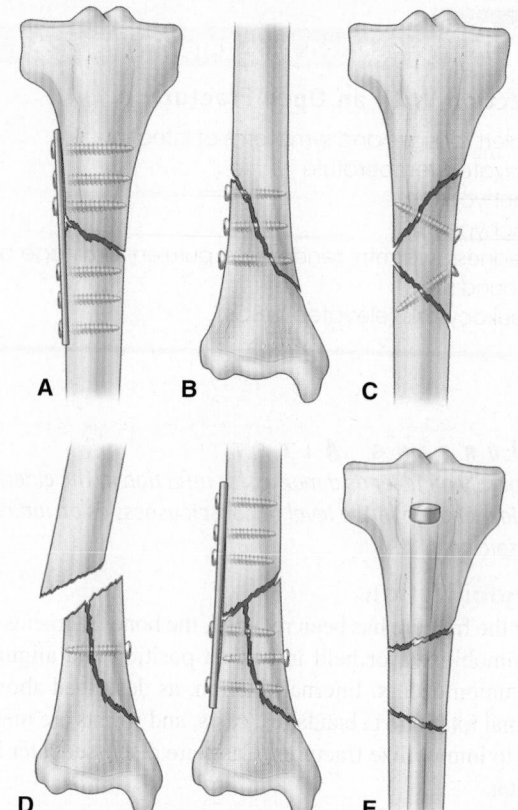

FIGURE 42-2 Techniques of internal fixation. (**A**) Plate and six screws for a transverse or short oblique fracture. (**B**) Screws for a long oblique or spiral fracture. (**C**) Screws for a long butterfly fragment. (**D**) Plate and six screws for a short butterfly fragment. (**E**) Medullary nail for a segmental fracture.

tion), tetanus, and gas gangrene. For this reason, systemic antibiotics are generally ordered and administered ideally within three hours of injury (Cross & Swiontkowski, 2008). The nurse is mindful that fixation of fractures carries a risk of infection. The objectives of management are to prevent infection of the wound, soft tissue, and bone, and to promote healing of soft tissue and bone. Options include sterile dressing changes to allow drainage of wound and edema from heavily contaminated injuries; the use of wound-vacuum assisted closure device; or reexploration of the wound with débridement, as necessary to remove infected and devitalized (dead) tissue and increasing vascularity in the region. After it has been determined that infection is not present, the wound is closed by grafting of autogenous (patient's own tissue) skin, or a flap, or healing by secondary intention (a full-thickness wound heals from the base upward, by laying down new tissue). The nurse instructs the patient or family to monitor temperature at regular intervals and report signs of infection to their provider (Box 42-3). Infections must be treated promptly. In 4 to 8 weeks, bone grafting may be necessary to bridge bone defects and to stimulate bone healing.

BOX 42-3 — Focused Assessment

Infection With an Open Fracture

Be alert for signs and symptoms of infection:
- Elevated temperature
- Tachycardia
- Tachypnea
- Redness, warmth, tenderness, purulent drainage at wound site
- Leukocytosis (elevated WBCs)

NURSING ALERT
Do not rely on fever as a marker for infection in the elderly. Consider change in the level of consciousness as an indication of suspicion.

Immobilization

After the fracture has been reduced, the bone fragments must be immobilized, or held in correct position and alignment, until union occurs. Internal fixation, as described above, or external fixation via bandages, casts, and splints are methods used to immobilize fractures. Casts are discussed later in the chapter.

Nursing Management

The major goals for the patient with a fracture include knowledge of the treatment regimen, relief of pain, improved physical mobility, achievement of maximum level of self-care, healing of any trauma-associated lacerations and abrasions, maintenance of adequate neurovascular function, and absence of complications.

Teaching Related to Treatment Regimen

Anticipatory guidance is provided to the patient and significant others by explaining the sights, sounds, and sensations (e.g., heat from the hardening reaction of the plaster) associated with application of internal or external device chosen to treat the fracture. Specific treatment modalities are discussed later in the chapter. Regardless of the treatment modality chosen for the fracture, patient teaching includes self-care, medication information, monitoring for potential complications, and the need for continuing health care supervision. Fracture healing and restoration of full strength and mobility may take many months.

Relieving Pain

The nurse must carefully evaluate pain associated with musculoskeletal conditions, asking the patient to indicate the exact site, character, and intensity of the pain to help determine its cause. Pain associated with the underlying condition (e.g., fracture) is frequently controlled by immobilization. Pain due to edema that is associated with trauma, surgery, or bleeding into the tissues can frequently be controlled by elevation and, if prescribed, intermittent application of cold packs. Ice bags (one-third to one-half full) or cold application devices are placed on each side of the cast or fixator, if prescribed, making sure not to indent the cast or put undue pressure on external pins. Analgesics are administered as prescribed.

Pain may also be indicative of complications. Unrelenting pain that is unresponsive to usual treatment measures (narcotics, elevation, cold) is associated with compartment syndrome. Severe pain over a bony prominence may warn of an impending pressure ulcer. Discomfort due to pressure on the skin may be relieved by elevation that controls edema or by positioning that alters pressure. However, the affected limb must be elevated no higher than heart level to ensure adequate arterial perfusion. If the fracture is casted, it may be necessary to modify the cast or to apply a new cast.

NURSING ALERT
The nurse must never ignore complaints of pain from the patient in a cast because of the possibility of problems such as impaired tissue perfusion or pressure ulcer formation.

Improving Mobility

Every joint and digit that is not immobilized should be exercised and moved through its ROM to maintain function. The nurse encourages the patient to assist in the repositioning, if not contraindicated, by use of the **trapeze** or bed rail. If a patient has a spica cast (a cast that stabilizes the hips and thighs, also known as a body cast), a stabilizing **abduction** bar may be incorporated into the cast to maintain the legs in an abducted position. This bar should never be used as a turning device. If internal fixation is required to stabilize the fracture, the provider determines weight-bearing activity.

Because deep vein thrombosis (DVT) is a significant risk for the immobilized patient, the nurse encourages the patient to do active flexion–extension foot and ankle exercises and isometric contraction of the calf muscles (calf-pumping exercises) every hour while awake to decrease venous stasis in the unaffected limb. In addition, elastic stockings, intermittent compression devices such as Venodyne boots, and anticoagulant therapy may be prescribed to help prevent thrombus formation. The nurse encourages the patient to move digits and joints distal to injury hourly when awake to prevent problems related to inactivity (Doenges, Moorhouse, & Murr, 2008; Whiteing, 2008).

Maintaining Adequate Neurovascular Function

The immobilized extremity's neurovascular status is assessed at least every hour initially and then every 4 hours, always comparing the affected to the noninjured extremity. The nurse assesses for the "five P's," as described previously. Edema is a natural response of the tissue to trauma. If the edema is significant, pressure can rise within the area compromising circulation,

BOX 42-4

GUIDELINES FOR NURSING CARE

Assessing the Radial, Medial, and Ulnar Nerves

Implementation

NURSING ACTION	RATIONALE
1. To assess the radial nerve, ask the patient to extend the forefinger against resistance. If you suspect radial nerve damage, check the sensation at the web space between the thumb and index finger by asking the patient to describe the sensation to light touch.	1. Inability to extend finger or lack of sensation suggests radial nerve abnormality.
2. To test for median nerve integrity, ask the patient to make the "OK" sign using the thumb and forefinger to make a ring. Check the strength of the "O" by trying to open it with your fingers. Assess sensation on the distal surface of the index finger.	2. Weakness indicates a median nerve abnormality.
3. To assess the ulnar nerve ask the patient to spread his fingers as widely as possible. Also check sensation to the little finger and the ulnar half of the ring finger by asking the patient to describe the sensation as you touch the area described.	3. Difficulty spreading fingers or lack of sensation suggests ulnar neuropathy.

nerve, and motor function. Early recognition of diminished circulation and nerve function therefore is essential to prevent loss of function. The affected extremity is adjusted so that it is no higher than heart level to control edema but not impede arterial perfusion. The surgeon is notified at once if signs of compromised neurovascular status are present. The nurse assesses the sensory and motor function of major nerves in the area of injury. Diminished circulation and nerve function must be treated promptly by release of constricting bandages. Refer to Box 42-4 for assessment of peripheral nerves of the upper extremities.

Normal findings of the fractured limb include minimal edema and discomfort, pink color, warm to touch, capillary refill less than 2 seconds, normal sensations, and ability to move fingers or toes. Numbness, tingling, and burning may be caused by nerve injury from pressure at the fracture site. The nurse instructs the patient to report any changes in sensation or movement immediately, so that they can be promptly evaluated.

Maintaining and Restoring Function

It is important to teach exercises to maintain the health of unaffected muscles and to increase the strength of muscles needed for transferring and for using assistive devices (e.g., crutches, walker, special utensils). The nurse and physical therapist teach patients how to use assistive devices safely. Isometric and muscle-setting exercises (discussed later in the chapter) are encouraged to minimize disuse atrophy and to promote circulation. Participation in activities of daily

living (ADLs) is encouraged to promote independent functioning and self-esteem. Gradual resumption of activities is promoted within the therapeutic prescription. With internal fixation, the surgeon determines the amount of movement and weight-bearing stress the extremity can withstand and prescribes the level of activity. Plans are made to help patients modify their home environment as needed and to secure personal assistance if necessary.

Monitoring and Managing Potential Complications

Fat Embolism Syndrome

An emboli is a clot that travels. In pelvic or long-bone fractures, or in trauma patients, the fat globules released when the bone was fractured may occlude the small blood vessels that supply the lungs, brain, kidneys, and other organs.

At the time of fracture, fat globules may diffuse into the vascular compartment because the marrow pressure is greater than the capillary pressure or because catecholamines elevated by the patient's stress reaction mobilize fatty acids and promote the development of fat globules in the bloodstream (Porth & Matfin, 2009). The onset of symptoms is rapid, usually within 24 to 72 hours of injury (Huang, Monu, & Wandtke, 2009). Risk factors for fat embolism syndrome (FES) include trauma, fracture of long bones or pelvic bones, multiple fractures, or crush injuries. FES occurs most frequently in young adults (typically in those 20 to 30 years of age) and in elderly adults who experience fractures of the proximal femur (hip fracture).

Presenting features of FES include a change in behavior and disorientation combined with respiratory compromise. The nurse observes for hypoxia, axillary, subconjunctival, or chest petechiae, tachypnea, tachycardia, and pyrexia. The respiratory distress response includes tachypnea, dyspnea, crackles, wheezes, and substernal chest pain. Occlusion of a large number of small vessels causes the pulmonary pressure to rise. Edema and hemorrhages in the alveoli impair oxygen transport, leading to hypoxia. Arterial blood gas values show the partial pressure of oxygen (PaO_2) to be less than 60 mm Hg, with an early respiratory alkalosis (hyperventilation) and later respiratory acidosis (hypoventilation). The chest X-ray reveals a typical "snowstorm" infiltrate. Without prompt, definitive treatment, acute pulmonary edema, acute respiratory distress syndrome (ARDS), and heart failure may develop.

The cerebral disturbances (due to hypoxia and the lodging of fat emboli in the brain) manifest by mental status changes varying from headache and mild agitation to confusion, delirium, and coma.

With systemic embolization, the patient appears pale. Petechiae, possibly due to a transient thrombocytopenia, are noted in the buccal membranes and conjunctival sacs, on the hard palate, and over the chest and anterior axillary folds. The patient develops a fever greater than 39.5°C (~103°F). Free fat may be found in the urine if emboli are filtered by the renal tubules. Acute tubular necrosis and renal failure may develop.

Immediate immobilization of fractures (including early surgical fixation), minimal fracture manipulation, adequate support for fractured bones during turning and positioning, and maintenance of fluid and electrolyte balance are measures that may reduce the incidence of fat emboli. The nurse monitors high-risk patients (adults between 20 and 30 years of age with long-bone, pelvic, or multiple fractures or crush injuries, and elderly patients with hip fractures) to identify this complication. Prompt initiation of respiratory support is essential to prevent respiratory failure and to correct homeostatic disturbances. Acute pulmonary edema and ARDS are the most common causes of death. Oxygen therapy, mechanical ventilation, and use of positive end-expiratory pressure (PEEP) may be used to maintain arterial oxygenation. Continuous monitoring of oxygen saturation is initiated. Corticosteroids may be administered IV to treat the inflammatory lung reaction and to control cerebral edema (Weinhouse, 2009). Vasopressor medications to support cardiovascular function are administered IV to prevent hypotension, shock, and interstitial pulmonary edema. Accurate fluid intake and output records facilitate adequate fluid replacement therapy. In addition, the nurse provides calm reassurance to allay apprehension.

Fat emboli are a major cause of death for patients with fractures. Therefore, the nurse must recognize early indications of FES and report them promptly to the provider.

! NURSING ALERT

Subtle personality changes, restlessness, irritability, or confusion in a patient who has sustained a fracture are indications for immediate reassessment of the patient (vitals, O_2 saturation, physical exam, and laboratory data).

Delayed Union, Malunion, and Nonunion

When prolonged healing for union of the fracture is noted, it is termed **delayed union**. The fracture eventually does heal. In **malunion**, there is flawed union of fractured bone, whereas **nonunion** results from failure of the ends of a fractured bone to unite in normal alignment.

Delayed union may be due to inadequate blood supply, infection, or incorrect immobilization of the fracture. It may be associated with a fracture that involved a significant loss of bone, a hematoma at the fracture site, or comorbidity (e.g., diabetes mellitus, autoimmune disease). Malunion is associated with inadequate reduction of the fracture, misalignment of the fracture at the time of immobilization, or infection at the fracture site, and it presents as a deformity at the site visually or on X-ray. In nonunion, fibrocartilage or fibrous tissue exists between the bone fragments; no bone salts have been deposited. Nonunion is associated with infection, inadequate circulation, malignancy, and noncompliance with activity restrictions. Cigarette smoking and poor nutrition place the patient at a higher risk of delayed healing or nonunion. Nonunion most commonly occurs with fractures of the middle third of the humerus, the lower third of the tibia, and, in elderly people, at the neck of the femur. Factors contributing to both nonunion and malunion include interposition of tissue between the bone ends, or manipulation that disrupts callus formation, excessive space between bone fragments (bone gap), limited bone contact, bone or soft tissue loss, and impaired blood supply resulting in AVN. Finally, a false joint (pseudarthrosis) often develops at the site of the fracture.

Steroids and older nonselective anti-cyclooxygenase (COX)-2 agents have been implicated in delayed fracture healing. If nonsteroidal anti-inflammatory drugs (NSAIDs) are used for analgesia with fractures, the literature suggests a preferred use of selective COX-2 inhibitors for short-term duration of 10 days. Additionally, these inhibitors should be avoided in smokers, diabetics, or those on corticosteroids to avoid nonunion (Boursinos, Karachalios, Poultsides et al., 2009).

Patient complaints of persistent discomfort and abnormal movement or instability at the fracture site indicate potential delayed union, malunion, or nonunion.

Nonunion is treated with internal fixation, bone grafting, electrical bone stimulation, or a combination of these therapies. Internal fixation stabilizes the bone fragments and ensures bone contact. A bone graft may be an **autograft** (tissue, frequently from the iliac crest, harvested from the patient for his or her own use) or an **allograft** (tissue harvested from

a donor for a recipient). The bone graft fills the bone gap, provides a lattice structure for invasion by bone cells, and actively promotes bone growth.

After grafting, immobilization and non–weight-bearing exercises are required while the bone graft becomes incorporated and the fracture or defect heals. Depending on the type of bone grafted, healing may take from 6 to 12 months or longer. Bone grafting problems include wound or graft infection, fracture of the graft, persistent pain, sensory loss, and nonunion (Waitayawinyu, Pfaeffle, McCallister et al., 2010).

Venous Thromboemboli

Venous thromboemboli, including DVT and pulmonary emboli (PE), are associated with reduced skeletal muscle contractions and bedrest. Patients with fractures of the lower extremities and pelvis are at high risk for venous thromboemboli. PEs may cause death several days to weeks after injury.

Depending on the size and location of the emboli, symptoms vary. A massive emboli can present as shock and loss of consciousness. The most frequent signs are sudden-onset shortness of breath, restlessness, increased respiratory rate, tachycardia, chest pain, and low-grade fever. Pleuritic pain that increases with inspiration is seen with pulmonary infarct. Moderate hypoxemia occurs, without retention of CO_2, and a cough that is productive of blood-tinged sputum may be seen.

Disseminated Intravascular Coagulation

Disseminated intravascular coagulation (DIC) is a systemic disorder that results in widespread hemorrhage and microthrombosis with ischemia. Its causes are diverse and can include massive tissue trauma. Early manifestations of DIC include unexpected bleeding after surgery, and bleeding from the mucous membranes, venipuncture sites, gastrointestinal and urinary tracts. The treatment of DIC is discussed in Chapter 20.

Avascular Necrosis of Bone

AVN occurs when the bone loses its blood supply and dies. It may occur after a fracture with disruption of the blood supply (especially of the femoral neck). It is also seen with dislocations, bone transplantation, prolonged high-dose corticosteroid therapy, excessive alcohol intake, cigarette smoking, chronic renal disease, systemic lupus erythematosus, and other diseases. The devitalized bone may collapse or reabsorb. The patient develops pain and experiences limited movement. X-rays reveal loss of mineralized matrix and structural collapse. Treatment generally consists of attempts to revitalize the bone with bone grafts, prosthetic replacement, or **arthrodesis** (joint fusion).

Reaction to Internal Fixation Devices

Internal fixation devices may be removed after bony union has taken place. However, in most patients, the device is not removed unless it produces symptoms. Pain and decreased function are the prime indications that a problem has developed. Problems may include mechanical failure (inadequate insertion and stabilization); material failure (faulty or damaged device); corrosion of the device, causing local inflammation; allergic response to the metallic alloy used; and osteoporotic remodeling adjacent to the fixation device, in which stress needed for bone strength is transferred to the device, causing a disuse osteoporosis (Bucholz, Heckman, Court-Brown et al., 2005). If the device is removed, the bone needs to be protected from refracture related to osteoporosis, altered bone structure, and trauma. Bone remodeling reestablishes the bone's structural strength.

Reaction to External Fixation Devices

Because the screws or pins are inserted externally (Fig. 42-3), infection is a complication for which nurses must be vigilant. Signs of infection include erythema, purulent drainage, warmth, leukocytosis, and fever. Pin care is performed according to hospital and provider protocol.

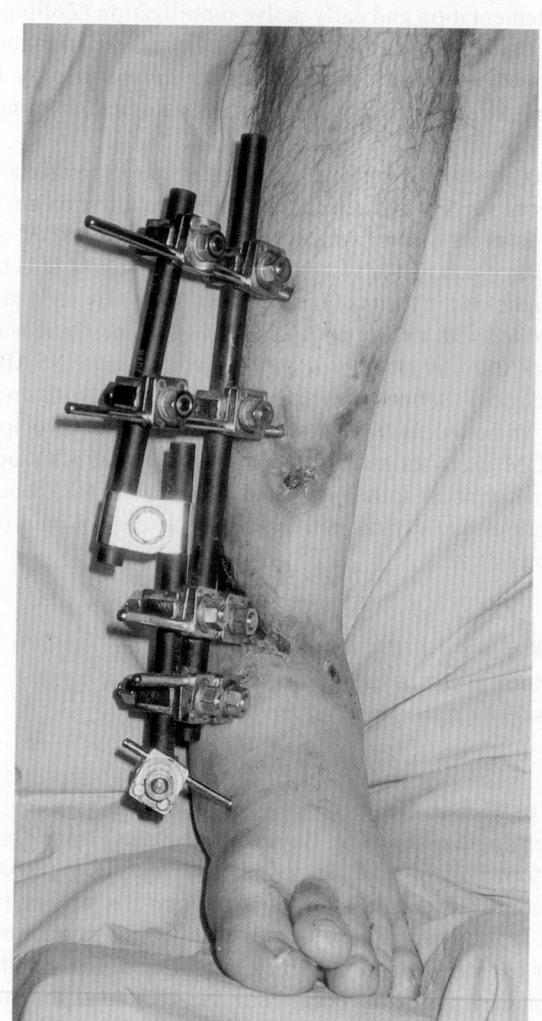

FIGURE 42-3 External fixation device. Pins are inserted into bone. The fracture is reduced and aligned and then stabilized by attaching the pins to a rigid portable frame. The device facilitates treatment of soft tissue damaged in complex fractures.

Complex Regional Pain Syndrome

Complex regional pain syndrome (CRPS), formerly called *reflex sympathetic dystrophy* or *RSD*, is a painful sympathetic nervous system problem. It occurs infrequently, with an estimated incidence of 5.46 to 26.2 per 100,000 person years (Van Eijs et al., 2011). When it does occur, it is most often in an upper extremity after trauma and is seen in 25% of patients with Colles' fracture, more often in women (Roberts & Heintzman, 2010).

Clinical manifestations of CRPS include severe burning pain, swelling, hyperesthesia, limited ROM, discoloration, vasomotor skin changes (i.e., fluctuating warm, red, dry and cold, sweaty, cyanotic), and abnormal nail and skin hair changes. This syndrome is frequently chronic, with extension of symptoms to adjacent areas of the body. Disuse muscle atrophy and bone deossification (osteoporosis) occur with persistence of CRPS. Patients may exhibit ineffective individual coping related to the chronic pain. The best treatment is prevention with vitamin C supplementation and early active mobilization (Zollinger, Tuinebreijer, Breederveld et al., 2007), imagery treatment with imagined hand movements and mirror therapy for upper extremity CRPS, and pharmacological treatment (Van Eijs, 2011).

Prevention may include elevation of the extremity after injury or surgery and selection of an immobilization device (e.g., external fixator) that allows for the greatest ROM and functional use of the rest of the extremity. Early effective pain relief is the focus of management. Pain may need to be controlled with a variety of agents including anesthetic nerve blocks, tricyclic antidepressants, anticonvulsants, NSAIDs, corticosteroids, muscle relaxants and, for those with severe pain, an opioid. With pain relief, the patient can participate in ROM exercises and functional use of the affected area. The nurse needs to help the patient cope with CRPS manifestations and explore multiple ways to control pain (see Chapter 7).

NURSING ALERT
The nurse avoids using the involved extremity for blood pressure measurements and venipunctures.

Heterotopic Ossification

Heterotopic ossification (myositis ossificans) is the abnormal formation of bone, near bones or in muscle, in response to soft tissue trauma after blunt trauma, fracture, or total joint replacement. The muscle is painful, and normal muscular contraction and movement are limited. Early mobilization may prevent its occurrence. NSAIDs (e.g., ibuprofen [Advil, Motrin]) may be used prophylactically if deep muscle contusion has occurred. Usually, the bone lesion resorbs over time, but the abnormal bone eventually may need to be excised if symptoms persist.

Fractures of Specific Sites

Injuries to the skeletal structure may vary from a simple linear fracture to a severe crushing injury. The type and location of the fracture and the extent of damage to surrounding structures determine the therapeutic management. Maximum functional recovery is the goal of management.

Clavicle

Fracture of the clavicle (collar bone) is a common injury that results from a fall or a direct blow to the shoulder. These injuries frequently are associated with equestrian sports and cycling, when a rider is thrown forward and lands on the unprotected shoulder. Head or cervical spine injuries may accompany these fractures. They are also seen in the geriatric population after a low-impact fall. When the clavicle is fractured, the patient assumes a protective position, slumping the shoulders and immobilizing the arm to prevent shoulder movements. A deformity of the clavicle may be observed, with obvious local tenderness. The treatment goal is to align the shoulder in its normal position by means of closed reduction and immobilization or, if displaced, an ORIF.

Depending on the site of the clavicular fracture, a figure-eight bandage (also called a *clavicular strap* or *broad arm sling*) may be used to pull the shoulders back, reducing and immobilizing the fracture (Fig. 42-4). Each treatment has advantages and disadvantages. When a clavicular strap is used, the axillae are well padded to prevent skin breakdown or a compression injury to the brachial plexus and the axillary artery. The nurse monitors the skin and circulation and nerve function of both arms. An arm sling may be used to support the arm and to relieve pain. A sling may cause the elbow to stiffen, so the patient is encouraged to perform elbow ROM exercises to maintain normal function and prevent stiffness. The patient may be permitted to use the arm for light activities within the range of comfort. In a Cochrane database review between the use of a simple sling or a figure-of-eight bandage for nonoperative management of clavicular fractures, no significant differences in functional or other outcomes were seen between the two groups (Lenza, Belloti, Andriolo et al., 2009).

With a clavicular fracture, the nurse cautions the patient not to elevate the arm above the shoulder level until the ends of the bone have united (about 6 weeks) but encourages the patient to exercise the elbow, wrist, and fingers as soon as possible. Vigorous activity is limited for 3 months. Complications of clavicular fractures include trauma to the nerves of the brachial plexus, injury to the subclavian vein or artery from a bony fragment, and malunion (faulty union of fractured bone).

Humeral Shaft

Fractures of the shaft of the humerus may injure the nerves and brachial blood vessels in the affected arm; therefore, neurovascular assessment is essential to identify when

immediate attention is required. Table 42-2 provides guidelines for neurovascular evaluation. A wrist drop is indicative of radial nerve injury. An ORIF of a fracture of the humerus is necessary if the patient has nerve palsy, blood vessel damage, comminuted fracture, or pathologic fracture.

If the fracture is uncomplicated, well-padded splints, overwrapped with an elastic bandage, are used to initially immobilize the upper arm and to support the arm in 90 degrees of flexion at the elbow. A sling or collar and cuff support the forearm (Fig. 42-5). The weight of the hanging arm and splints reduces the fracture. Functional bracing is another form of treatment used for these fractures. A contoured thermoplastic sleeve is secured in place with interlocking fabric (Velcro) closures around the upper arm, thus immobilizing the reduced fracture. As swelling decreases, the sleeve is tightened, and uniform pressure and bone stability is maintained. The forearm is supported with a collar and cuff sling. Functional bracing allows active use of muscles, shoulder and elbow motion, and good approximation of fracture fragments. Pendulum shoulder exercises are performed as prescribed to provide active movement of the shoulder, thereby preventing adhesions of the shoulder joint capsule. Isometric exercises may be prescribed to prevent muscle atrophy. Complications that are seen with humeral shaft fractures include delayed union and nonunion (failure of the ends of a fractured bone to unite).

Elbow

Fractures of the elbow result from motor vehicle crashes, falls on the elbow (in the extended or flexed position), or

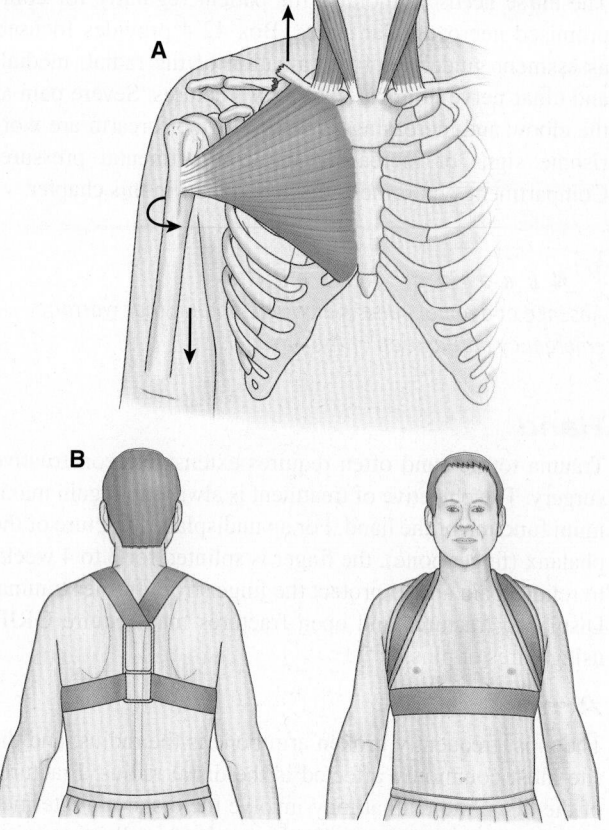

FIGURE 42-4 Fracture of the clavicle. (**A**) Anteroposterior view shows typical displacement in midclavicular fracture. (**B**) Immobilization is accomplished with a clavicular strap.

TABLE
42-2 Neurovascular Assessment and Expected Findings

Assessment Component	Technique	Normal Findings
Skin color	Evaluate the injured area in relation to noninjured area.	No change is noted compared to other parts of the body
Skin temperature	Palpate using the dorsum of the hand, as it is more sensitive to temperature.	No change is noted compared to other parts of the body
Pulses	Assess proximal and distal pulses. Grade as 0, absent; 1+, weaker than normal; 2+, normal; or 3+, full and bounding.	No change is noted compared to other extremity
Capillary refill	Depress the nail bed and note return of color.	Capillary refill is less than 2 seconds
Sensation	With his eyes closed, evaluate the patient's ability to feel light touch of the affected extremity (e.g., assess on the first web space of foot [between great toe and second toe] for the peroneal nerve, or base of thumb [radial nerve], or little finger [ulnar nerve]. Assess presence of numbness or tingling.	No sensory deficit is noted
Mobility	Observe the ROM in joints or digits distal to the injury.	Full movement of digits is noted.
	Note edema and tenseness of the injured area.	Minimal edema and ecchymosis is noted
	Mark and measure circumference if concerned.	In a nontraumatized limb, a difference of 1 cm at the ankles and 2 cm at mid-calf is expected.

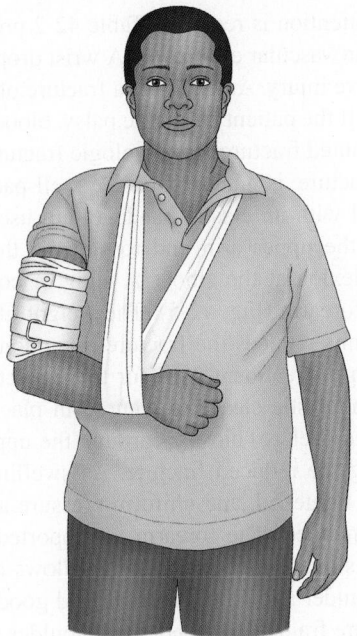

FIGURE 42-5 Humeral brace with collar and cuff sling.

a direct blow. Radial head fractures are the most common fractures involving the elbow; however, the distal humerus or proximal ulna are also commonly involved. These fractures may result in injury to the median, radial, or ulnar nerves. The patient is evaluated for paresthesia and signs of compromised circulation in the forearm and hand. The most serious complication is *Volkmann's contracture* (an acute compartment syndrome), which results from antecubital swelling or damage to the brachial artery (Fig. 42-6). Contracture of the fingers and wrist occurs as the result of obstructed arterial blood flow to the forearm and hand. The patient is unable to extend the fingers, describes abnormal sensation (e.g., unrelenting pain, pain on passive stretch), and exhibits signs of diminished circulation to the hand. Although the incidence of Volkmann's contracture is rare (0.5% of cases), its devastating complications are preventable if detected early (Marquis, Cheung, Dwyer et al., 2008). This serious complication warrants nursing vigilance to minimize limb loss.

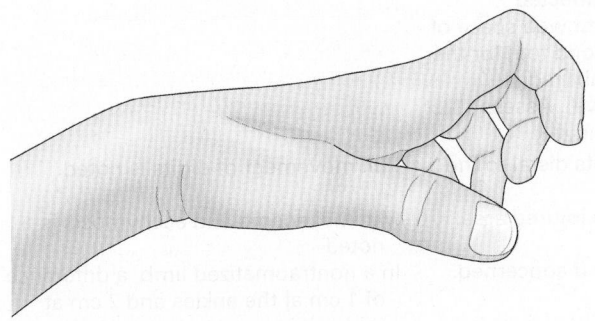

FIGURE 42-6 Volkmann's contracture.

The nurse needs to monitor the patient regularly for compromised neurovascular status. Box 42-4 provides focused assessment guidelines for evaluation of the radial, medial, and ulnar nerve in upper extremity fractures. Severe pain at the elbow and increasing tenseness of the forearm are worrisome signs of increasing intracompartmental pressure. Compartment syndrome is discussed later in this chapter.

NURSING ALERT
Absence of a radial pulse is a critical finding that warrants emergency notification of the provider.

Hand

Trauma to the hand often requires extensive reconstructive surgery. The objective of treatment is always to regain maximum function of the hand. For an undisplaced fracture of the phalanx (finger bone), the finger is splinted for 3 to 4 weeks to relieve pain and to protect the finger from further trauma. Displaced fractures and open fractures may require ORIF, using wires or pins.

Arm

The most frequently broken arm bone is the radius, and the site most commonly affected is the distal radius. Fractures of the distal radius that may involve the distal ulna, termed a Colles' fracture, are usually the result of a fall on an open, dorsiflexed hand (Altizer, 2008). This fracture is frequently seen in elderly women with osteoporotic bones and weak soft tissues that do not dissipate the energy of the fall, or in younger people involved in sports injuries. The patient presents with a deformed wrist, radial deviation, pain, swelling, weakness, limited finger ROM, and numbness.

Treatment usually consists of closed reduction and immobilization with a short-arm cast. For fractures with extensive comminution (bone is broken into a number of pieces) or impaction, ORIF, arthroscopic percutaneous pinning, or external fixation is used to achieve and maintain reduction and to allow for early functional rehabilitation. The wrist and forearm are elevated for 48 hours after reduction to control swelling, and active motion of the fingers and shoulder begins promptly. The nurse monitors for signs of neurovascular compromise comparing findings on affected limb to other limb.

Tibia and Fibula

The most common fractures below the knee are tibia and fibula fractures, and these tend to result from a direct blow, falls with the foot in a flexed position, or a violent twisting motion. The patient presents with pain, deformity, obvious hematoma, and considerable edema. Frequently, these fractures are open and involve severe soft tissue damage because there is little subcutaneous tissue in the area.

The peroneal nerve is assessed for damage that may result in foot drop (inability to lift the foot) by checking for sensation of the web between the great and second toes, and for

increased sensitivity of the dorsal surfaces of the foot (top). If nerve function is impaired, the patient cannot dorsiflex the great toe and has diminished sensation in the first web space (between first metatarsal and hallux [big toe]). As with all fractures, the patient is observed for signs of neurovascular complications. The development of acute compartment syndrome (see discussion later in this chapter) requires prompt recognition and resolution to prevent permanent functional deficit. Other complications include delayed union, infection, impaired wound edge healing due to limited soft tissue, and loosening of the internal fixation hardware (if ORIF is performed to repair fracture).

Most closed tibial fractures are treated with closed reduction and initial immobilization in a long-leg walking cast or a patellar tendon–bearing cast. Reduction must be relatively accurate in relation to angulation and rotation. Comminuted fractures may be treated with skeletal traction, internal fixation with intramedullary nails or plates and screws, or external fixation. External support may be used with internal fixation.

Pelvis

Falls, motor vehicle crashes, and crush injuries can cause pelvic fractures. Pelvic fractures are serious because at least two-thirds of affected patients have significant and multiple injuries. Management of severe, life-threatening pelvic fractures is coordinated with the trauma team. Hemorrhage and thoracic, intra-abdominal, and cranial injuries have priority over treatment of fractures. There is a high mortality rate associated with pelvic fractures related to hemorrhage, pulmonary complications, fat emboli, thromboembolic complications, and infection.

Signs and symptoms of pelvic fracture include ecchymosis; tenderness over the symphysis pubis, anterior iliac spines, iliac crest, sacrum, or coccyx (Fig. 42-7); local edema; numbness or tingling of the pubis, genitals, and proximal thighs; and inability to bear weight without discomfort. Neurovascular assessment of the lower extremities is performed to detect injury to pelvic blood vessels and nerves. The peripheral pulses of both lower extremities are palpated; absence of a pulse may indicate a tear in the iliac artery or one of its branches.

Hemorrhage and shock are two of the most serious consequences that may occur. Bleeding arises from the cancellous surfaces of the fracture fragments, from laceration of veins and arteries by bone fragments, and possibly from a torn iliac artery. Peritoneal lavage or abdominal CT may be performed to detect intra-abdominal hemorrhage. The patient is handled gently to minimize further bleeding and shock (Bodden, 2009).

Injuries to the bladder, rectum, intestines, other abdominal organs, and pelvic vessels and nerves are associated with pelvic fracture. To assess for urinary tract injury, the patient's urine is examined for blood (hematuria) or blood at the introitus, or if a male, observed for scrotal hematoma.

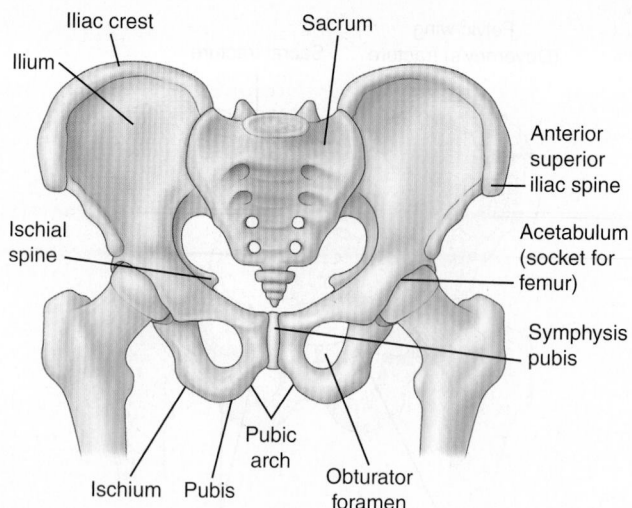

FIGURE 42-7 Pelvic bones.

A urinary drainage catheter should not be inserted until the status of the urethra is known. Ecchymosis of the anterior abdominal wall, flank, sacral, or gluteal region is suggestive of significant internal bleeding. Diffuse and intense abdominal pain, hyperactive or absent bowel sounds, and abdominal rigidity and hyper-resonance (free air) or dullness to percussion (blood) suggest injury to the intestines or abdominal bleeding. Additionally, the nurse is aware that the loss of dullness over the liver (normally percusses a dull sound) indicates the presence of free air, and that dullness over regions normally tympanic may indicate the presence of blood or fluid.

Numerous classification systems have been used to describe pelvic fractures in relation to pelvic anatomy, stability, and mechanism of injury. Some fractures of the pelvis do not disrupt the pelvic ring; others do—therefore the severity of pelvic fractures varies. Long-term complications of pelvic fractures include malunion, nonunion, residual gait disturbances, and back pain from ligament injury.

Stable Pelvic Fractures

Stable fractures of the pelvis (Fig. 42-8) heal rapidly because the pelvic bones are mostly cancellous bone, which has a rich blood supply. The fractures are treated with a few days of bedrest and symptom management until the pain and discomfort are controlled. The patient with a fractured sacrum is at risk for paralytic ileus, and bowel sounds should be monitored.

Unstable Pelvic Fractures

Unstable fractures of the pelvis may result in rotational instability (e.g., the "open book" type, in which a separation occurs at the symphysis pubis with sacral ligament disruption), vertical instability (e.g., the vertical shear type, with superior–inferior displacement), or a combination of both (Fig. 42-9).

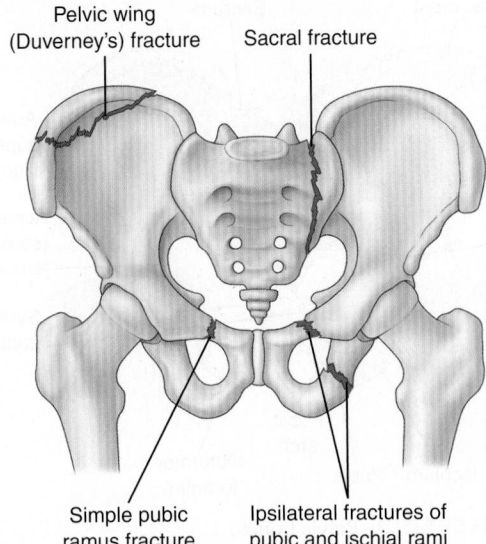

Pelvic wing
(Duverney's) fracture   Sacral fracture

Simple pubic
ramus fracture   Ipsilateral fractures of
                        pubic and ischial rami

FIGURE 42-8 Stable pelvic fractures.

Immediate treatment in the emergency department of a patient with an unstable pelvic fracture includes stabilizing the pelvic bones and tamponading or compressing bleeding vessels. A simple method of stabilizing the pelvis endorsed for use by the American College of Surgeons Committee on Trauma is the tying of a sheet circumferentially around the hips at the level of the greater trochanters. This is often done in the field, and this temporary measure applies pressure, closes the "open-book" pubic symphysis, and assists in controlling bleeding (Bodden, 2008).

If major vessels are lacerated, the bleeding may be stopped through emergent embolization using interventional radiology techniques prior to surgery. Patients with pelvic fractures can lose up to 4 to 5 liters of blood and therefore are at risk for exsanguination. Mortality rates for patients presenting with hypotension associated with pelvic fractures is approximately 50% (Coleman & Collins, 2008). Once the patient is hemodynamically stable, treatment generally involves external fixation or ORIF. These measures promote hemostasis, hemodynamic stability, comfort, and early mobilization.

Acetabular Fractures

Drivers and passengers sitting in the right front seat in motor vehicle crashes may forcibly propel their knees into the dashboard, injuring the knee-thigh-hip complex (Rupp & Schneider, 2004). The acetabulum (see Fig. 42-7) is particularly vulnerable to fracture with these types of injuries. Treatment depends on the pattern of fracture. Stable, nondisplaced fractures may be managed with traction and protective (toe-touch) weight bearing, so that the affected foot is only placed on the floor for balance. Displaced and unstable acetabular fractures are treated with open reduction, joint débridement, and internal fixation or arthroplasty (replacement of all or part of the joint surfaces). Internal fixation permits early non–weight-bearing ambulation and ROM exercise. Complications seen with acetabular fractures include nerve palsy, heterotopic ossification, and posttraumatic arthritis.

Femoral Shaft

Considerable force is required to break the shaft of the femur in adults. Most femoral fractures are seen in young adults who have been involved in a motor vehicle crash or who have fallen from a high place. Frequently, these patients have associated multiple injuries.

The patient presents with an enlarged, deformed, painful thigh and cannot move the hip or the knee. The fracture may be transverse, oblique, spiral, or comminuted. Frequently, the patient develops shock because the loss of 2 to 3 units of blood into the tissues is common with these fractures. An expanding diameter of the thigh may indicate continued bleeding.

The fracture is immobilized so that additional soft tissue damage does not occur. Generally, skeletal traction or splinting is used to immobilize fracture fragments until the patient is physiologically stable and ready for ORIF procedures.

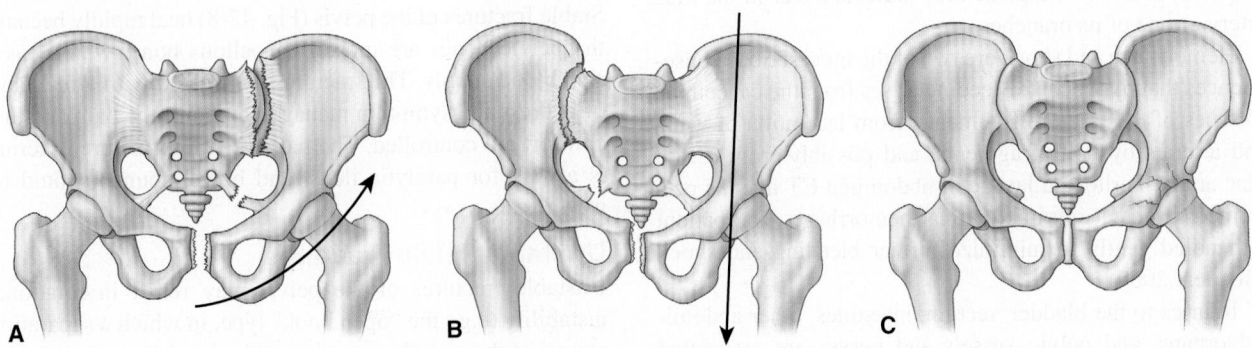

A   B   C

FIGURE 42-9 Unstable pelvic fracture. (**A**) Rotationally unstable fracture. The symphysis pubis is separated and the anterior sacroiliac, sacrotuberous, and sacrospinous ligaments are disrupted. (**B**) Vertically unstable fracture. The hemipelvis is displaced anteriorly and posteriorly through the symphysis pubis, and the sacroiliac joint ligaments is disrupted. (**C**) Undisplaced fracture of the acetabulum.

Internal fixation usually is carried out within a few days after injury. Intramedullary locking nail devices are used for midshaft (diaphyseal) fractures. Depending on the supracondylar fracture pattern, intramedullary nailing or screw plate fixation may be used. Internal fixation permits early mobilization. A thigh cuff orthosis may be used for external support. To preserve muscle strength, the patient is instructed to perform active exercises of the upper and lower extremities on a regular basis. Active muscle movement enhances healing by increasing blood supply and electrical potentials at the fracture site. Prescribed weight-bearing limits are based on the type of fracture. Physical therapy includes ROM and strengthening exercises, safe use of ambulatory aids, and gait training. Functional ambulation stimulates fracture healing. Healing time is 4 to 6 months.

A common complication after fracture of the femoral shaft is restriction of knee motion. Active and passive knee exercises begin as soon as possible, depending on the management approach and the stability of the fracture and knee ligaments.

Femur

Fracture of the proximal femur is termed a *hip fracture*. The fracture can include the femoral head, femoral neck, somewhere between the greater and lesser trochanter (termed a *intertrochanteric fracture*), and the shaft of the femur below the lesser trochanter (termed a *subtrochanteric fracture*) (Fig. 42-10). Fractures of the neck of the femur may damage the vascular system that supplies blood to the head and the neck of the femur, and the bone may become ischemic. For this reason, AVN is common in patients with femoral neck fractures. The elderly are particularly vulnerable to intertrochanteric fractures and generally have a much worse prognosis than do younger patients. It is important for the nurse to be aware that hip fractures are associated with a high incidence of DVT and PE (20% to 50%); the mortality rate the year after surgery is between 5% and 20% (Lindsay & Cosman, 2008).

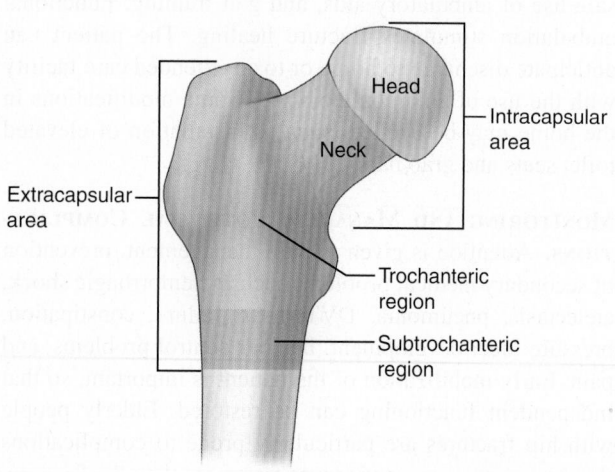

FIGURE 42-10 Regions of the proximal femur.

Clinical Manifestations and Assessment

With fractures of the femoral neck, the leg is shortened and externally rotated. The patient complains of pain in the hip and groin or knee. With most fractures of the femoral neck, the patient cannot move the leg without a significant increase in pain. Impacted intracapsular femoral neck fractures cause moderate discomfort (even with movement), may allow the patient to bear weight, and may not demonstrate obvious shortening or rotational changes. With extracapsular femoral fractures of the trochanteric or subtrochanteric regions, the extremity is significantly shortened, externally rotated to a greater degree than in intracapsular fractures, exhibits muscle spasm that resists positioning of the extremity in a neutral position, and has an associated large hematoma or area of ecchymosis. The diagnosis of fractured hip is confirmed with an X-ray.

Gerontologic Considerations

Elderly people (particularly women) who have brittle bones from osteoporosis and who tend to fall frequently have a high incidence of hip fracture. Weak quadriceps muscles, general frailty due to age, and comorbidities that produce decreased cerebral arterial perfusion (transient ischemic attacks, anemia, emboli, cardiovascular disease, and medication effects) contribute to the incidence of falls.

Often, a fractured hip is a catastrophic event that has a negative impact on the patient's lifestyle and quality of life. Hip fractures are a frequent contributor to death after 75 years of age. Many elderly people hospitalized with hip fractures exhibit delirium as a result of the stress of the trauma, unfamiliar surroundings, sleep deprivation, and medications. Preoperative predictors of postoperative delirium include age older than 70 years; a history of alcohol abuse; impaired cognitive status; poor functional status; and markedly abnormal serum sodium, potassium, or glucose concentrations. In addition, delirium that develops in some elderly patients may be caused by mild cerebral ischemia or mild hypoxemia. Other factors associated with delirium include responses to medications and anesthesia, malnutrition, dehydration, infectious processes, mood disturbances, and blood loss.

! N U R S I N G   A L E R T

When a patient presents with a change in the level of consciousness, the nurse recalls the mnemonic DOG: Drugs are reviewed to evaluate whether a medication could be associated with the altered sensorium, Oxygen saturation level is assessed for hypoxemia via pulse oximeter, and a Glucose level is obtained to evaluate for hypoglycemia/hyperglycemia via a finger stick since all are associated with altered LOC.

To prevent complications, the nurse must assess the elderly patient for chronic preexisting conditions as described above, including polypharmacy. Dehydration and poor nutrition may

be present, contributing to hemoconcentration, and this predisposes the patient to the development of venous thromboemboli. Therefore monitoring intake and output in the elderly and assessing for DVT are particularly important.

Muscle weakness and wasting, which may have initially contributed to the fall and fracture, will be further compromised by bed rest and immobility. The nurse encourages the patient to move all joints except the involved hip and knee. Strengthening of the arms and shoulders will facilitate walking with assistive devices. A plan of nursing care for an elderly patient with a fractured hip is available online at http://thePoint.lww.com/Pellico1e.

Medical Management

If surgery cannot be performed immediately, the fracture is immobilized, so that additional soft tissue damage does not occur. Temporarily, traction can either be applied as skin or skeletal (pins or wires inserted into bones) traction. Each carries risks. Skin traction can put undue pressure on skin for prolonged periods of time, is limited in the amount of weight that can be applied (5 to 7 lb or less), and as a result, has limited use (Smith & Giannoudis, 2008). Higher weights risk damage to the skin and neurovascular status of the involved extremity.

Skeletal traction is used more frequently to immobilize fracture fragments until the patient is physiologically stable and ready for surgical treatment. However, skeletal traction can increase the risk of infection since sterile pin(s) are drilled or wires are placed into the bone. The weight for skeletal traction is determined by body size and the extent of the injury. With either choice, continued neurovascular monitoring and assessment of the skin is needed.

Additionally, there are several types of traction. *Straight* or *running traction* applies the pulling force in a straight line with the body part resting on the bed. Buck's extension traction is an example of skin traction that is straight traction. It may be used for patients with fractures of the hip as a temporary measure to reduce muscle spasm, immobilize the extremity, and relieve pain. Another type of traction is *balanced suspension traction* (see Fig. 42-13 later in the chapter), in which the affected extremity "floats" or is suspended in the traction apparatus by the balanced weights. The line of traction on the extremity remains fairly constant despite patient movement, as long as the pull remains constant.

> ☀ **N U R S I N G   A L E R T**
> *The nurse must never remove weights from skeletal traction unless an emergency situation occurs. Removal of the weights completely defeats their purpose and may result in injury to the patient.*

The goal of surgical treatment of hip fractures is to obtain a satisfactory fixation, so that the patient can be mobilized quickly and avoid secondary medical complications. Surgical intervention is carried out as soon as possible after injury. Surgical treatment consists of one of the following:

- Open or closed reduction of the fracture and internal fixation; a thigh cuff orthosis may be used for external support
- Replacement of the femoral head with a prosthesis (**hemiarthroplasty**). This is usually reserved for fractures that cannot be satisfactorily reduced or securely nailed, or to avoid complications of nonunion and AVN of the head of the femur. It is similar to a total hip replacement, but only replaces the ball portion of the hip joint, not the socket (which is replaced in total hip replacement [discussed later in the chapter]).
- Closed reduction with percutaneous stabilization for an intracapsular fracture.

Nursing Management

The immediate postoperative care for a patient with a hip fracture is similar to that for other patients undergoing major surgery.

ENCOURAGING ACTIVITY. The patient is encouraged to exercise as much as possible by means of the overbed trapeze. This device helps strengthen the arms and shoulders in preparation for protected ambulation (e.g., toe touch, partial weight bearing). A common complication after fracture of the femoral shaft is restriction of knee motion. In general, active and passive knee exercises begin as soon as possible, depending on the management approach and the stability of the fracture and knee ligaments. To preserve muscle strength, the patient is instructed to exercise the noninjured hip and the lower leg, foot, and toes on a regular basis. The surgeon prescribes the degree of weight bearing and the rate at which the patient can progress to full weight bearing. On the first postoperative day, generally, the patient transfers to a chair with assistance and begins assisted ambulation. The amount of weight bearing that can be permitted depends on the stability of the fracture reduction. In general, hip flexion and internal rotation restrictions apply *only* if the patient has had a hemiarthroplasty (replacement of the ball of the hip). Physical therapists work with the patient on ROM and strengthening exercises, safe use of ambulatory aids, and gait training. Functional ambulation stimulates fracture healing. The patient can anticipate discharge to home or to an extended care facility with the use of an ambulatory aid. Some modifications in the home may be needed, such as installation of elevated toilet seats and grab bars.

MONITORING AND MANAGING POTENTIAL COMPLICATIONS. Attention is given to pain management, prevention of secondary medical problems such as hemorrhagic shock, atelectasis, pneumonia, DVT, heart failure, constipation, pressure ulcer development, bladder control problems, and pain. Early mobilization of the patient is important, so that independent functioning can be restored. Elderly people with hip fractures are particularly prone to complications that may require more vigorous treatment than the fracture. Frequently, the patient develops shock because the loss of

two to three units of blood into the tissues is common with these fractures. Achievement of homeostasis after injury and after surgery is accomplished through careful monitoring of vital signs, wound drainage from dressings and external drains (drains are typically removed 24 to 48 hours after surgery), laboratory results, and physical assessment findings, as well as through collaborative management, including adjustment of therapeutic interventions as indicated. Refer to Box 42-3 for signs and symptoms of hypovolemic shock.

Neurovascular complications may occur from direct injury to nerves and blood vessels or from increased tissue pressure. Assessment includes checking the neurovascular status of the extremity, especially circulatory perfusion of the lower leg and foot (popliteal, posterior tibial, and pedal pulses; toe capillary refill time; color; temperature; sensation and movement). A Doppler ultrasound device may be needed to assess blood flow. With hip fracture, bleeding into the tissues is expected. Excessive swelling may be observed and may further impair the neurovascular status. Patients may complain of increased pain at the site, and swelling may be noted in the thigh and buttock due to hematoma formation. Ice may be applied to decrease the swelling. The nurse marks the extent of drainage on the dressing by circling the extent and noting initials, date, and time. If excessive, the nurse should notify the provider.

DVT is a common postoperative complication contributing to significant morbidity and mortality in patients undergoing hip fracture surgery. To prevent DVT, the nurse encourages intake of fluids, and ankle and foot exercises. The nurse assesses the patient's legs for signs of DVT, which may include unilateral calf tenderness, warmth, redness, and swelling. The symptoms are related to inflammatory processes and therefore the nurse also assesses for low-grade fever, malaise, and elevated white blood cell (WBC) count and sedimentation rate (Porth & Matfin, 2009). The nurse administers the anticoagulant and mechanically based prophylaxis (e.g., elastic compression stockings, sequential compression devices, and prophylactic anticoagulant therapy) as prescribed.

Pulmonary complications, which commonly include atelectasis and pneumonia, are a threat to elderly patients undergoing hip surgery. Deep-breathing exercises, a change of position at least every 2 hours, and the use of an incentive spirometer help prevent respiratory complications. The nurse assesses breath sounds at least every 4 hours to detect adventitious or diminished sounds. Oxygen saturation should be assessed; supplemental oxygen may be ordered to keep the level above 95%. Pain must be treated with analgesic agents, typically opioids; otherwise, the patient may not be able to readily cough, deep breathe, or engage in prescribed activities. Out-of-bed (OOB) activities will be beneficial for lung function as well as muscle strength.

Heart failure is a frequent cause of mortality in elderly hip fracture patients. The cumulative effect of trauma, major surgery, and concurrent medical history place the patient at risk for heart failure. The nurse is alert for signs and symptoms associated with left-sided heart failure, including shortness of breath, cough, dyspnea on exertion (DOE), crackles, orthopnea, and paroxysmal nocturnal dyspnea. Right ventricular failure presents with peripheral edema (may be pitting), jugular vein distention, and abdominal distention. Edema will be in dependent areas, so the nurse assesses the sacral area as well as extremities. Accurate recording of intake and output (noting decreased urinary output), auscultation of heart (noting presence of S_3) and lung sounds (crackles), and monitoring O_2 saturation and vital signs (noting decreasing blood pressure, tachycardia, and tachypnea) are important nursing responsibilities. The nurse consults with the surgeon if signs and symptoms of excess fluid volume persist or worsen. The nurse expects fluid restriction and administers diuretics as ordered. Skin breakdown is often seen in elderly patients with hip fracture. Blisters caused by tape are related to the tension of soft tissue edema under the nonelastic tape. An elastic hip spica wrap dressing or elastic tape applied in a vertical fashion may reduce the incidence of tape blisters. In addition, patients with hip fractures tend to remain in one position and may develop pressure ulcers. Proper skin care, especially on the heels, back, sacrum, and shoulders, and turning and frequent repositioning helps to relieve pressure. Special mattress may provide protection by distributing pressure evenly.

Reduced GI motility, immobility, and the effects of anesthesia may result in constipation. Accurate intake and output, assessing bowel sounds, and noting distention of the abdomen are important nursing interventions, as prevention of constipation is the goal. A diet high in fiber and fluids may help stimulate gastric motility and since ambulation improves GI peristalsis, the nurse assists the patient in OOB activities and ambulation as prescribed. If constipation develops, therapeutic measures may include stool softeners, laxatives, suppositories, and enemas. To improve the patient's appetite, the nurse identifies and includes the patient's food preferences, as appropriate, within the prescribed therapeutic diet.

Loss of bladder control (incontinence or retention) may occur. In general, the routine use of an indwelling catheter is avoided because of the high risk for urinary tract infection. If a catheter is inserted at the time of surgery, it usually is removed on the morning of the first postoperative day. Because urinary retention is common after surgery, the nurse must assess the patient's voiding patterns and amounts, noting bladder distention and voiding of small amounts of urine (<100 mL) frequently. To ensure proper urinary tract function, the nurse monitors intake via IV route and/or by mouth if allowed and output. If no preexisting cardiac disease (e.g., heart failure, coronary artery disease) exists, then liberal intake of fluids are encouraged. The patient is informed to notify the nurse if complaints of bladder fullness or inability to void are noted.

Infection is suspected if the patient complains of persistent, moderate discomfort in the hip, experiences chills or malaise, and has an elevated WBC count and erythrocyte sedimentation rate (ESR). The nurse observes the surgical incision for erythema, warmth, tenderness, and notes color, amount, and consistency of wound drainage. In the elderly, symptoms of infection may be nonspecific (e.g., patients may be afebrile without complaints); an important marker is a decline in the patient's functional status and/or the presence of confusion. The closed-wound drainage system is observed for color and amount of drainage and functioning of the drainage device.

Delayed complications of hip fractures include malunion, delayed union or nonunion, AVN of the femoral head (particularly with femoral neck fractures), and fixation device problems (e.g., protrusion of the fixation device through the acetabulum, loosening of hardware) (discussed earlier in this chapter). Healing time is 4 to 6 months.

PROMOTING HEALTH. Osteoporosis screening of patients who have experienced hip fracture is important for prevention of future fractures (Box 42-5). Specific patient education regarding dietary requirements, lifestyle changes, and weight-bearing exercise to promote bone health is needed. Prevention of falls is also important and may be achieved through exercises to improve muscle tone and balance and through the elimination of environmental hazards such as throw rugs. Other environmental considerations are the use of hand rails on the stairs, nonskid surfaces in the bathroom, grab bars in the shower, raised toilet seats, well-fitting shoes with nonskid soles, and adequate home lighting.

BOX 42-5 **Risk Factors for Osteoporosis**

- Age
- Female
- Caucasian
- Small bone structure
- Postmenopausal
- Sedentary lifestyle
- Chronic obstructive pulmonary disease
- Smoking
- Steroid
- Family history
- Calcium deficiency
- High-protein diet
- Excessive alcohol intake
- Excessive caffeine intake
- Malignancy
- Hyperthyroidism
- Rheumatoid arthritis
- Diabetes mellitus
- Cushing's disease
- Gastrectomy (Lippincott, 2007)

TREATMENT MODALITIES

CAST

A **cast** is a rigid external immobilizing device that is applied for a variety of medical surgical disorders including fractures and deformities. Many injuries that were previously treated with casts may now be treated with other immobilization devices (e.g., immobilizers). In general, casts permit mobilization of the patient while restricting movement of a body part.

Casting Materials

Casts may be made of plaster or non-plaster materials. Refer to Box 42-6 for cast application.

Fiberglass

Nonplaster casts are generally referred to as fiberglass casts. These water-activated polyurethane materials are light in weight, strong, water resistant, and durable. They are made of nonabsorbent fabric impregnated with cool water–activated hardeners that bond and reach full rigid strength in minutes. The material does not soften when wet, which allows for hydrotherapy when appropriate. When wet, the casts are dried with a hair dryer on a cool setting; thorough drying is important to prevent skin breakdown.

Plaster

Traditional casts are made of rolls of plaster bandage that are wet in cool water and applied smoothly to the body. A crystallizing reaction occurs, and heat is given off (an exothermic reaction). The heat given off during this reaction can be uncomfortable, and the patient needs to be informed about the sensation of increasing warmth that generally dissipates after 15 minutes. Additionally, the nurse explains that the cast needs to be exposed to air (i.e., uncovered) to allow maximum dissipation of the heat and facilitate drying, which can take 24 to 72 hours. Because the plaster cast remains wet and somewhat soft, the cast needs to remain uncovered until it is completely dry. A wet plaster cast appears dull and gray, sounds dull on percussion, feels damp, and smells musty. A dry plaster cast is white and shiny, resonant to percussion, firm, and odorless.

Nursing Management

Monitoring and Managing Potential Complications

Compartment Syndrome

There are three types of compartment syndromes: acute compartment syndrome, chronic compartment syndrome, and crush compartment syndrome. *Acute compartment syndrome* involves a sudden and severe decrease in blood flow to the tissues distal to an area of injury that results in ischemic necrosis if prompt, decisive intervention does not occur. It is a potentially limb-threatening complication that occurs when increased pressure occurs within a limited space

BOX 42-6

GUIDELINES FOR NURSING CARE

Assisting with Cast Application

Equipment

Tubular stockinette, casting material as specified by provider (plaster rolls/plaster splints); sink equipped with plaster trap or bucket of water, gloves, padding, sponge or felt padding (if necessary)

Implementation

NURSING ACTIONS	RATIONALE
1. Support extremity or body part to be casted.	1. Minimizes movement; maintains reduction and alignment; increases comfort
2. Position and maintain part to be casted in position indicated by provider during casting procedure.	2. Facilitates casting; reduces incidence of complications (e.g., malunion, nonunion, contracture)
3. Drape patient.	3. Avoids undue exposure; protects other body parts from contact with casting materials
4. Wash and dry part to be casted.	4. Reduces incidence of skin breakdown
5. Place knitted material (e.g., stockinette) over part to be casted. • Apply in smooth and nonconstrictive manner.	5. Protects skin from casting materials Protects skin from pressure Folds over edges of cast when finishing application; creates smooth, padded edge; protects skin from abrasion
6. Wrap soft, nonwoven roll padding smoothly and evenly around part. Use additional padding around bony prominences to protect superficial nerves (e.g., head of fibula, olecranon process).	6. Protects skin from pressure of cast Protects skin at bony prominences Protects superficial nerves
7. Apply plaster or nonplaster casting material evenly on body part. • Choose appropriate width bandage. • Overlap preceding turn by half the width of the bandage. • Use continuous motion, maintaining constant contact with body part. • Use additional casting material (splints) at joints and at points of anticipated cast stress.	7. Creates smooth, solid, well-contoured cast Facilitates smooth application Creates smooth, solid, immobilizing cast Shapes cast properly for adequate support Strengthens cast.
8. "Finish" cast: • Smooth edges. • Trim and reshape with cast knife or cutter.	8. Protects skin from abrasion Allows full range of motion of adjacent joints
9. Remove particles of casting materials from skin.	9. Prevents particles from loosening and sliding underneath cast
10. Support cast during hardening. • Handle hardening casts with palms of hands. • Support cast on firm smooth surface. • Do not rest cast on hard surfaces or on sharp edges. • Avoid pressure on cast.	10. Casting materials begin to harden in minutes; maximum hardness of nonplaster cast occurs in minutes; maximum hardness of plaster cast occurs with drying (24 to 72 hours, depending on environment and thickness of cast) Avoids denting of cast and development of pressure areas
11. Promote drying of cast. • Leave cast uncovered and exposed to air. • Turn patient every 2 hours supporting major joints. • Fans may be used to increase air-flow and speed drying.	11. Facilitates drying

BOX 42-7 **Focus on Pathophysiology**

Rhabdomyolysis

A wide variety of etiologies are associated with rhabdomyolysis including: seizures, drug reactions, extreme exercise, soft tissue infections, burns, malignant hyperthermia, extended lithotomy position and lateral decubitus positions, use of pneumatic antishock garments, and electrical and crush injuries. With trauma injuries, the nurse is alert for rhabdomyolysis, in which the crushing injury causes the breakdown of skeletal muscle, resulting in the release of muscle cell contents including myoglobin (a protein released from muscle when injury occurs), creatine phosphokinase (CPK), and potassium into the systemic circulation. Myoglobin, which gives skeletal muscle its color, is released from the damaged muscle and filtered by the kidney, resulting in brown or tea-colored urine. Urine dipstick for blood may be positive because of the cross-reaction with myoglobin; however, microscopic examination of urine may reveal no red blood cells. The myoglobin threatens renal function due to renal tubular obstruction and direct toxic effects, resulting in acute renal failure. Goals of management are to prevent acute renal failure by countering the effects of myoglobin with the use of aggressive fluid resuscitation, bicarbonate administration (urine that is alkalized lessens myoglobin toxicity), and possibly the administration of mannitol (Osmitrol), an osmotic diuretic to "wash out" the myoglobin. In addition, management of hyperkalemia with insulin/dextrose is expected. The nurse assesses urine output hourly, monitors vital signs, maintains strict intake and output, and assesses for fluid volume deficit (secondary to the trauma) versus fluid volume excess (secondary to overhydration).

(e.g., cast, muscle compartment) that compresses the blood vessels and nerves within the area. The pressure within the confined space becomes so high that there is massive compromise to circulation and nerve transmission in the affected extremity. Permanent damage develops within a few hours if action is not taken.

Chronic compartment syndrome is characterized by pain, aching, and tightness in a muscle or muscle group that has been subjected to inordinate stress or exercise. In this instance, muscle volume increases by as much as 20% within a short time, resulting in stretching of the fascia and inflammation. *Crush compartment syndrome* is caused by massive external compression or crushing of a compartment; for instance, this may occur when a car jack fails and a car falls on a mechanic. This type of massive injury results in systemic effects that include rhabdomyolysis that causes acute renal failure and that may eventually lead to multiple organ dysfunction syndrome (MODS), further discussed in Chapter 54 (Box 42-7).

A specific type of compartment syndrome in the arm is Volkmann's contracture (discussed earlier in the chapter). It is frequently associated with supracondylar fractures of the humerus. The following discussion focuses on acute compartment syndrome.

Fascia is tough connective tissue that surrounds muscle groups, organs, nerves, blood vessels, bones, and internal structures. It does not expand readily. Therefore, if a compartment begins to swell, the pressure in the area rises, possibly compromising circulation and nerve and motor function to the point at which the limb may need to be amputated (Fig. 42-11).

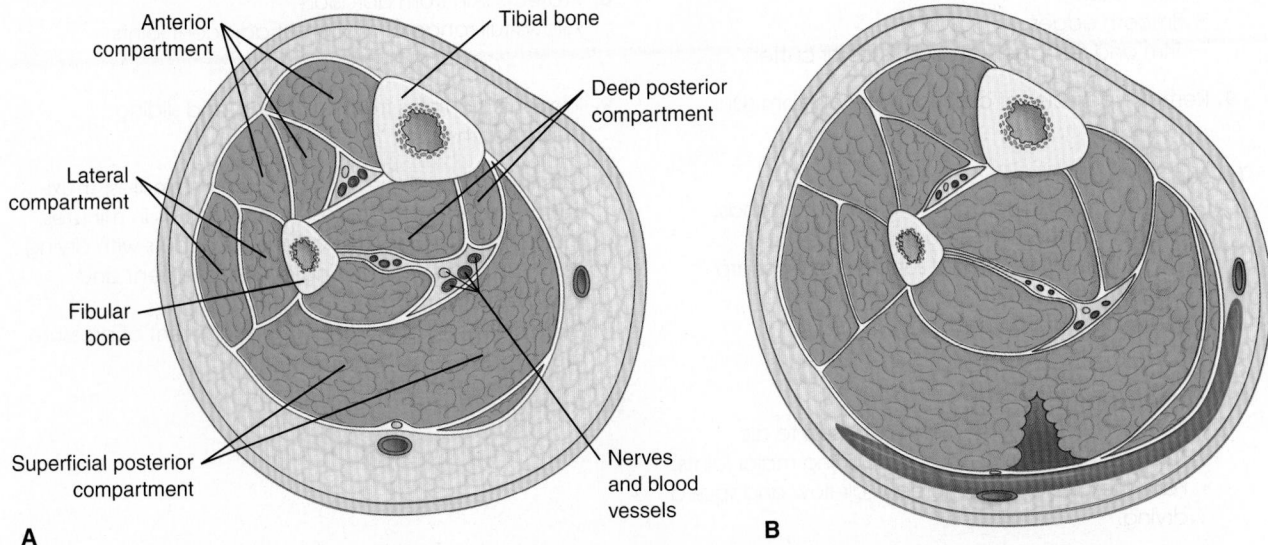

FIGURE 42-11 **(A)** Cross-section of normal lower leg with muscle compartments. **(B)** Cross-section of lower leg with compartment syndrome. Swelling of muscles causes compression of nerves and blood vessels.

Risk factors for this complication include trauma from accidents, surgery, or crushing injuries, in which massive edema and bleeding is expected. Casts and tight bandages are also associated with this complication as the external devices increase the pressure within the injured area. In addition, it may be caused by any condition that increases the risk of bleeding or edema in a confined space, including patients with soft tissue injury, without fractures, who are on anticoagulants, or have bleeding dyscrasias.

It is essential to detect this complication early. Clinical manifestations include paleness of limb, cool skin temperature, delayed capillary refill, weak pulsations, paresthesia (tingling/burning sensation in the involved muscle), decreased sensation and mobility, tight and full muscle, and pain (unrelenting pain not relieved by position changes, ice, or analgesia, or pain that is disproportional to the injury). A hallmark sign is pain that occurs or intensifies with passive ROM. If the nurse is concerned about neurovascular impairment, the provider is notified immediately.

❗ NURSING ALERT
It is important to note that late signs of compartment syndrome are pulselessness and pallor. The presence of a pulse does not rule out compartment syndrome (Murphy, Conway, McGrath et al., 2009).

If the complication is secondary to a tight bandage or cast, the nurse anticipates that the bandage would be loosened or removed and the cast bivalved (cut in half longitudinally) to release the constriction. While the surgeon is bivalving the cast, the nurse assists in maintaining limb alignment (Box 42-8). The affected limb must be elevated no higher than heart level to ensure arterial perfusion. Intracompart-

---

BOX 42-8

Procedure for Bivalving a Cast

The following procedure is followed when a cast is bivalved.
1. With a cast cutter, a longitudinal cut is made to divide the cast in half.
2. The under padding is cut with scissors.
3. The cast is spread apart with cast spreaders to relieve pressure and to inspect and treat the skin without interrupting the reduction and alignment of the bone.
4. After the pressure is relieved, the anterior and posterior parts of the cast are secured together with an elastic compression bandage to maintain immobilization.
5. To control swelling and promote circulation, the extremity is elevated (but no higher than heart level), to minimize the effect of gravity on perfusion of the tissues.

---

mental pressure monitoring may be required to diagnose compartment syndrome. A variety of commercial systems are available for the provider to measure intracompartmental pressure. The intracompartmental pressure of a normal muscle compartment at rest is less than 10 mmHg (Tzioupis, Cox, & Giannoudis, 2009). A high tissue pressure indicates compartment syndrome. Debate exists on the intracompartmental pressure that mandates fasciotomy, but pressures exceeding 30 mmHg suggest the need to consider a fasciotomy (Reurings & Verhofstad, 2007).

If pressure is not relieved by removing the bandage or cast, and circulation is not restored, a **fasciotomy** may be necessary to relieve the pressure within the muscle compartment. A fasciotomy is a surgical procedure in which the skin and affected compartments fascia are opened, allowing the pressure to be relieved and circulation restored. Patients who develop this complication unrelated to a cast or dressing undergo this sterile procedure. The fasciotomy area may be surgically repaired, or graft tissue may be used when the swelling subsides. Complications that may occur after fasciotomy include AVN and infection.

The nurse closely monitors the patient's response to conservative and surgical management of compartment syndrome. Limb assessment of circulation, sensation, and mobility continues as ordered, and the nurse promptly reports changes to the provider.

Pressure Ulcers

Pressure ulcers, also called *decubitus ulcers*, are breakdowns in the skin caused by prolonged pressure on a body part. Casts or bandages can put pressure on soft tissues, causing tissue anoxia and pressure ulcers. Susceptible sites in the lower extremity include the heel, malleoli, dorsum of the foot, head of the fibula, tibial tuberosity, and anterior surface of the patella (Fig. 42-12). Upper extremity sites are located at the medial and or lateral epicondyle of the humerus, olecranon, and the ulnar styloid.

The pathophysiology of and risk factors for pressure ulcers are discussed in Chapter 52. The nurse has a high degree of suspicion that a pressure ulcer is developing under a cast or dressing when the patient reports pain and tightness in a defined casted area. The area is inspected for drainage on the cast and any emitted odor. In addition, the nurse palpates the bandage or cast noting increasing warmth, which suggests underlying tissue erythema. Even if discomfort does not occur, there may be extensive loss of tissue with skin breakdown and tissue necrosis; therefore, any suspicious findings are reported to the provider.

The cast may be bivalved or an opening cut (window) in the cast in order to assess for pressure ulcer development. A window allows inspection of the affected area and possibly treatment. The portion of the cast is replaced and held in place by an elastic compression dressing or tape. The nurse assesses for "window edema"—that is, swelling of the underlying tissue through the window, which creates pressure

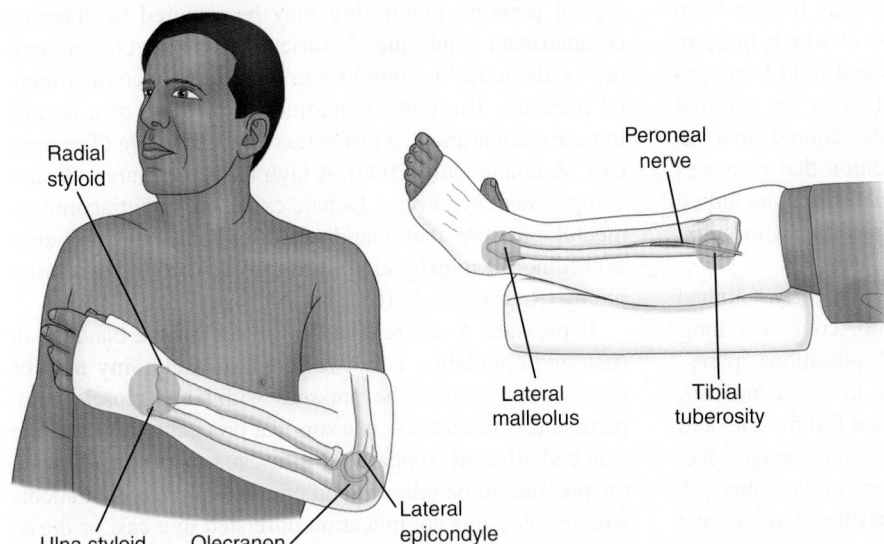

Radial styloid

Ulna styloid   Olecranon   Lateral epicondyle

Peroneal nerve

Lateral malleolus   Tibial tuberosity

FIGURE 42-12 Pressure areas in common types of casts. *Left,* long-arm cast. *Right,* short-leg cast.

areas around the window margins. Patients who have histories of impaired sensation due to neuropathy or neurologic injury are at high risk for ulcer development; thus, removable braces may be used for management of fractures with frequent skin assessments.

Disuse Syndrome

When a muscle is left inactive, it loses its strength and size. Disuse syndrome is the nursing diagnosis associated with musculoskeletal inactivity. Depending on the status of the patients and length of time since the initial trauma, strengthening exercises may be ordered. The nurse will teach the patient to tense or contract muscles (isometric muscle contraction) without moving the underlying bone. The internal or external devices stabilize the underlying bone. Isometric activity, such as teaching a patient in an arm cast to "make a fist," helps reduce muscle atrophy and maintain muscle strength. Muscle-setting exercises (e.g., quadriceps-setting and gluteal-setting exercises) are important in maintaining muscles essential for walking (Box 42-9). Isometric exercises should be performed hourly while the patient is awake. Physical therapy can assist in developing an exercise regimen for the patient.

Providing Initial Patient Teaching

The nurse teaches the patient and family that the casted extremity must be uncovered until it is completely dry, supported on pillows to the level of the heart to control swelling, and ice packs should be applied as prescribed over the fracture site for 1 or 2 days. The patient is taught to elevate the casted arm or leg when seated to promote venous return and control swelling. The patient needs to understand that the body part will be immobilized after casting.

Positioning

If a body cast is in place, the nurse turns the patient as a unit toward the uninjured side every 2 hours to relieve pressure and to allow the cast to dry. It is important to avoid twist-

ing the patient's body within the cast. Sufficient personnel (depending on the size of the patient and type of cast) are needed when the patient is turned, so that the fresh cast can be adequately supported with the palms of the hands at vulnerable points (i.e., body joints) to prevent cracking.

Teaching the Patient Self-Care

Self-care deficits occur when a portion of the body is immobilized. The nurse encourages the patient to participate actively in personal care and to use assistive devices safely. The nurse assists the patient in identifying areas of need and

---

BOX 42-9   **Muscle–Setting Exercises**

Isometric contractions of the muscle maintain muscle mass and strength and prevent atrophy.

Quadriceps-Setting Exercise
- Position patient supine with leg extended.
- Instruct patient to push knee back onto the mattress by contracting the anterior thigh muscles.
- Encourage patient to hold the position for 5 to 10 seconds.
- Let patient relax.
- Have the patient repeat the exercise 10 times each hour when awake.

Gluteal-Setting Exercise
- Position the patient supine with legs extended, if possible.
- Instruct the patient to contract the muscles of the buttocks.
- Encourage the patient to hold the contraction for 5 to 10 seconds.
- Let the patient relax.
- Have the patient repeat the exercise 10 times each hour when awake.

Patient Education

Cast Care

- Move about as normally as possible, but avoid excessive use of the injured extremity, and avoid walking on wet, slippery floors or sidewalks.
- If the cast is on an upper extremity, you may use a sling when you ambulate. To prevent pressure on the cervical spinal nerves, the sling should distribute the supported weight over a large area and not on the back of the neck. Remove the arm from the sling and elevate it frequently.
- Perform prescribed exercises regularly, as prescribed.
- Elevate the casted extremity to heart level frequently to prevent swelling. For example: when lying down, elevate the arm, so that each joint is positioned higher than the preceding proximal joint (e.g., elbow higher than the shoulder, hand higher than the elbow).
- Do not attempt to scratch the skin under the cast. This may cause a break in the skin and result in the formation of a skin ulcer. Cool air from a hair dryer may alleviate an itch. Do not insert objects such as coat hangers inside the cast to scratch itching skin. If itching persists, contact your provider.
- Cushion rough edges of the cast with tape.
- Keep the cast dry but do not cover it with plastic or rubber, because this causes condensation, which dampens the cast and skin. Moisture softens a plaster cast (a wet fiberglass cast must be dried thoroughly with a hair dryer on a cool setting to avoid skin burns).
- Report any of the following to the provider: persistent pain; swelling that does not respond to elevation; changes in sensation; decreased ability to move exposed fingers or toes; changes in capillary refill, skin color, and temperature.
- Note odors around the cast, stained areas, warm spots, and pressure areas. Report them to the provider.
- Report a broken cast to the provider; do not attempt to fix it yourself.

in developing strategies to achieve independence in ADLs. Patient teaching is discussed in Box 42-10.

Providing Continuing Care

The nurse prepares the patient for cast removal or cast changes by explaining that the cast is cut with a cast cutter, which vibrates. The cutter does not penetrate deeply enough to hurt the patient's skin. The cast padding is cut with scissors. Refer to Box 42-11.

The formerly casted body part is weak from disuse, stiff, and may appear atrophied. Therefore, support is needed when the cast is removed. The skin, which is usually dry and scaly from accumulated dead skin, is vulnerable to injury from scratching. The skin needs to be washed gently and lubricated with an emollient lotion.

The nurse and physical therapist teach the patient to resume activities gradually within the prescribed therapeutic regimen. Exercises prescribed to help the patient regain joint motion are explained and demonstrated. Because the muscles are weak from disuse, the body part that has been casted cannot withstand normal stresses immediately. In addition, the nurse teaches the patient with noticeable swelling of the affected extremity after cast removal to continue to elevate the extremity to control swelling until normal muscle tone and use are reestablished.

SKIN TRACTION

Skin traction is used to control muscle spasms and to immobilize an area before surgery. Skin traction is accomplished by using a weight to pull on traction tape or on a foam boot attached to the skin. The amount of weight applied must not exceed the tolerance of the skin. Adhesive tape and weights greater than 6 to 8 pounds (2.7 to 3.6 kg) are avoided as they may cause avulsion of the superficial skin layers (Simon & Koenigsknecht, 2007).

Buck's Extension Traction

Buck's extension traction (unilateral or bilateral) is skin traction to the lower leg. The pull is exerted in one plane when partial or temporary immobilization is desired. It is used to immobilize fractures of the proximal femur before surgical fixation.

Before the traction is applied, the nurse inspects the skin for abrasions and circulatory disturbances. The skin and circulation must be in healthy condition to tolerate the traction. The extremity should be clean and dry before the foam boot or traction tape is applied.

To apply Buck's traction, one nurse elevates and supports the extremity under the patient's heel and knee while another nurse places the foam boot under the leg, with the patient's heel in the heel of the boot. Next, the nurse secures Velcro straps around the leg. Traction tape overwrapped with elastic bandage in a spiral fashion may be used instead of the boot. Excessive pressure is avoided over the malleolus and proximal fibula during application to prevent pressure ulcers and nerve damage. The nurse then passes the rope affixed to the spreader or footplate over a pulley fastened to the end of the bed and attaches the weight—usually 5 pounds—to the rope.

Skin breakdown, nerve pressure, and circulatory impairment are complications that may develop as a result of skin traction. Skin breakdown results from irritation caused by contact of the skin with the tape or foam and shearing forces. Older adults are at greater risk for this complication because of their sensitive, fragile skin.

NURSING ALERT
The nurse must promptly investigate every report of discomfort expressed by the patient in traction.

BOX 42-11

GUIDELINES FOR NURSING CARE

Removing a Cast

Equipment

Cast scissors, cast saw, and cast spreader (if necessary); eye protection, Ace wraps, splints as indicated, adhesive tape (optional)

Implementation

NURSING ACTIONS	RATIONALE
1. Inform the patient about the procedure.	1. Facilitates cooperation and reduces fear about the procedure
2. Reassure patient that the electric saw or cast cutter will not cut skin. (Explain that blade oscillates to cut cast and vibrations will be felt.)	2. Reduces anxiety
3. Wear eye protection (patient and operator of the cast cutter).	3. Protects eyes from flying cast particles
4. Bivalve cast using a series of alternating pressures and linear movements of blade along the line to be cut.	4. Cuts cast in halves; avoids burning sensation from prolonged contact of oscillating blade with padding
5. Cut padding with scissors.	5. Releases all of the casting materials
6. Support body part as it is removed from the cast.	6. Reduces stresses on body part that has been immobilized
7. Gently wash and dry area that has been immobilized.* Apply emollient lotion.	7. Removes dead skin that has accumulated during immobilization; keeps skin supple
8. Teach patient to avoid rubbing and scratching skin.	8. Prevents skin breakdown
9. Collaborate with physical therapist to teach patient to resume active use of body part gradually within the guidelines of prescribed therapeutic regimen.	9. Protects weakened part from excessive stress; progressive exercises reduce stiffness, restore muscle strength, and function
10. Teach patient to control swelling by elevating the extremity or using elastic bandage if prescribed.	10. Facilitates circulation (i.e., venous return) and controls fluid pooling

*If a new cast is to be applied, follow guidelines for application of a cast and associated nursing care.

Nerve damage can result from pressure on the peripheral nerves. Foot drop may occur if pressure is applied to the peroneal nerve at the point at which it passes around the neck of the fibula just below the knee.

Circulatory impairment is manifested by cold skin temperature, decreased peripheral pulses, slow capillary refill time, and bluish skin. DVT, a serious circulatory impairment, may be manifested by unilateral calf tenderness, warmth, redness, and swelling (see Chapter 18).

SKELETAL TRACTION

The goals of skeletal traction are to maintain alignment of the injured limb and counteract the shortening of the injured limb from muscle spasm before definitive treatment can occur (Wood, Mahoney, & Cooper, 2009). Skeletal traction is applied directly to the bone. This method of traction is used occasionally to treat fractures of the femur, the tibia, and the cervical spine. The traction is applied directly to the bone by use of a metal pin or wire (e.g., Steinmann pin, or Kirschner wire), which is inserted through the bone distal to the fracture, avoiding nerves, blood vessels, muscles, tendons, and joints. Tongs applied to the head are fixed to the skull to apply traction that immobilizes cervical fractures.

After local anesthesia and skin preparation by the surgeon, using surgical asepsis, a small skin incision is made and sterile pin(s) are drilled or wire is placed through the bone. The patient feels pressure during this procedure and possibly some pain when the periosteum is penetrated.

After insertion, the pin or wire is attached to the traction bow or caliper. The ends of the pin or wire are covered

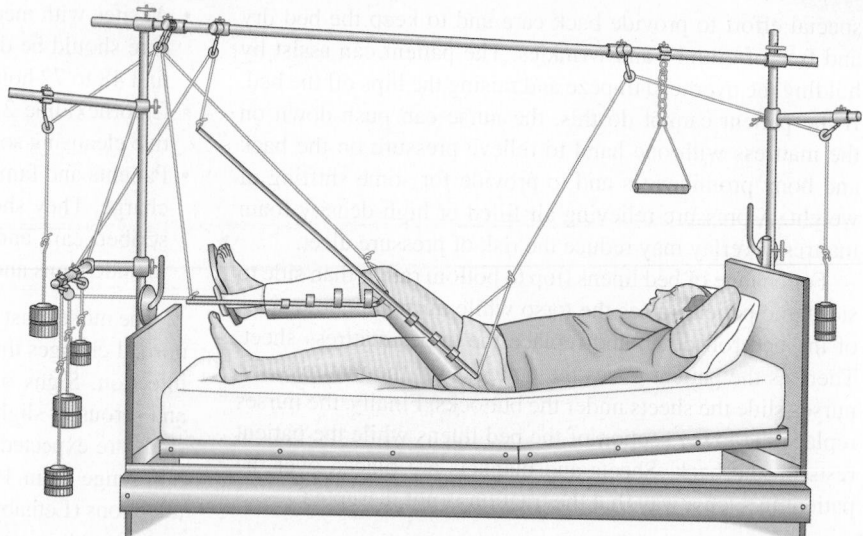

FIGURE 42-13 Balanced suspension skeletal traction with Thomas leg splint. The patient can move vertically as long as the resultant line of pull is maintained.

with corks or tape to prevent injury to the patient or caregivers. The weights are attached to the pin or wire bow by a rope-and-pulley system that exerts the appropriate amount and direction of pull for effective traction. Skeletal traction frequently uses 7 to 12 kg (15 to 25 lb) to achieve the therapeutic effect. The weights applied initially must overcome the spasms of the affected muscles that pull on the fractured bones and shorten the limb.

Often, skeletal traction is balanced traction, which supports the affected extremity, allows for some patient movement, and facilitates patient independence and nursing care while maintaining effective traction. The Thomas splint with a Pearson attachment (Fig. 42-13) is frequently used with skeletal traction for fractures of the femur. Because upward traction is required, an overbed frame is used.

When skeletal traction is discontinued, the extremity is gently supported while the weights are removed. The pin is cut close to the skin and removed by the physician. Internal fixation, casts, or splints are then used to immobilize and support the healing bone.

External fixators are often used to maintain position of unstable fractures when the use of a cast is prohibited or the patient's condition is unstable and precludes a surgical procedure to stabilize the fracture. They can also be used to manage open fractures with soft tissue damage or severe comminuted (crushed or splintered) fractures while permitting active treatment of damaged soft tissues. Complicated fractures of the humerus, forearm, femur, tibia, and pelvis are often managed with external skeletal fixators. The fracture is reduced, aligned, and immobilized by a series of pins or screws inserted directly into the bone above and below the fracture and secured with the use of a metal frame. Pin position is maintained through attachment to a portable frame. The fixator facilitates patient comfort, early mobility, and active exercise of adjacent uninvolved joints; thus, complications due to disuse and immobility are minimized.

> **NURSING ALERT**
> The nurse never adjusts the clamps on the external fixator frame. It is the physician's responsibility to do so.

Nursing Management

Maintaining Effective Traction

When skeletal traction is used, the nurse checks the traction apparatus at least once per shift to see that the ropes are in the wheel grooves of the pulleys, that the ropes are not frayed, that the weights hang freely, and that the knots in the rope are tied securely. The nurse also evaluates the patient's position because slipping down in bed results in ineffective traction.

Maintaining Positioning

The nurse must maintain alignment of the patient's body in traction as prescribed to promote an effective line of pull. The nurse positions the patient's foot to avoid footdrop (plantar flexion), inward rotation (inversion), and outward rotation (eversion). The patient's foot may be supported in a neutral position by orthopedic devices (e.g., foot supports).

Preventing Skin Breakdown

The patient's elbows frequently become sore, and nerve injury may occur if the patient repositions by pushing on the elbows. In addition, patients frequently push on the heel of the unaffected leg and elbows when they raise themselves in bed. Therefore, the nurse should protect the elbows and heels and inspect them for pressure ulcers. A trapeze can be suspended above the patient, to encourage movement without using the elbows or heels. Areas that are particularly vulnerable to pressure caused by a traction apparatus applied to the lower extremity include the ischial tuberosity, popliteal space, Achilles tendon, and heel. If the patient is not permitted to turn on one side or the other, the nurse must make a

special effort to provide back care and to keep the bed dry and free of crumbs and wrinkles. The patient can assist by holding the overhead trapeze and raising the hips off the bed. If the patient cannot do this, the nurse can push down on the mattress with one hand to relieve pressure on the back and bony prominences and to provide for some shifting of weight. A pressure-relieving air-filled or high-density foam mattress overlay may reduce the risk of pressure ulcer.

For change of bed linens (top to bottom rather than side to side), the patient raises the torso while nurses on both sides of the bed roll down and replace the upper mattress sheet. Then, as the patient raises the buttocks off the mattress, the nurses slide the sheets under the buttocks. Finally, the nurses replace the lower section of the bed linens while the patient rests on the back. Sheets and blankets are placed over the patient in such a way that the traction is not disrupted.

Providing Pin Site Care

The wound at the pin insertion site requires attention. The goal is to avoid infection and development of **osteomyelitis** (Box 42-12). Osteomyelitis is an acute or chronic inflammation of the bone caused by infection. There is wide variability on pin care, and research on outcomes is scarce, thus further studies are warranted (Lethaby, Temple, & Santy, 2008). However, the National Association of Orthopaedic Nurses Guidelines for Orthopaedic Nursing (Holmes & Brown, 2005) offers specific recommendations for pin care, which are as follows:

- Pins located in areas with considerable soft tissue should be considered at greatest risk for infection.

BOX 42-12   **Focus on Pathophysiology**

Osteomyelitis

Osteomyelitis is an infection in the bone caused by a variety of microorganisms, most commonly *Staphylococcus aureus*, that are introduced during injury, from the bloodstream, or during surgery. Once in the bone, the microorganisms proliferate and spread within the bone shaft, causing an inflammatory response that further destroys the bone. Wound cultures identify the organism and antibiotic sensitivity. Difficult to treat, IV therapy is needed in general for 6 weeks. Osteomyelitis may be classified as acute (an infection lasting <4 weeks) or chronic (>4 weeks). Pain over the affected bone is the dominant finding in osteomyelitis. Palpation of the involved bone usually elicits tenderness over the infected area. Increased warmth, erythema, and swelling may be seen at the affected segment, but are not always present. The ESR is commonly elevated, and elevated WBC levels may be seen in acute infections (but not always). The WBC count may be normal in chronic osteomyelitis.

- At sites with mechanically stable bone–pin interfaces, pin care should be done on a daily or weekly basis (after the first 48 to 72 hours, when drainage may be heavy).
- Chlorhexidine 2 mg/mL solution may be the most effective cleansing solution for pin site care.
- Patients and families should be taught pin care before discharge. They should be required to demonstrate the prescribed care and provided with written instructions that include signs and symptoms of infection.

The nurse must inspect the pin sites daily for reaction (i.e., normal changes that occur at the pin site after insertion) and infection. Signs of reaction may include redness, warmth, and serous or slightly sanguinous drainage at the site. These signs are expected to subside after 72 hours. Rates of infection range from 1% for major infections to 80% for minor infections (Lethaby et al., 2008). Signs of infection may mirror those of reaction but also include the presence of edema, purulent drainage, erythema, excessive warmth, tenderness, pin loosening, and odor. In addition, the nurse monitors the patient for fever. The frequency of pin care needs to be increased if mechanical looseness of pins or early signs of infection are present. Minor infections may be readily treated with antibiotics, whereas infections that result in systemic manifestations may additionally warrant pin removal until the infection resolves. When pins are mechanically stable (after 48 to 72 hours), weekly pin site care may be recommended. Crusting may occur at the pin site and uncertainties currently exist about whether scabs around the pin sites should be removed. Additional research is needed to determine best practice to prevent infection with external fixators. The nurse follows institutional protocol and teaches the patient and family to perform pin site care prior to discharge from the hospital. Written follow-up instructions that include the signs and symptoms of infection should be provided.

JOINT REPLACEMENT SURGERY

Joint surgery is one of the most frequently performed orthopedic surgeries. Joint disease, disability, or deformity may necessitate surgical intervention to relieve pain, improve stability, and improve function. Conditions contributing to joint degeneration include osteoarthritis (degenerative joint disease), rheumatoid arthritis, trauma, and congenital deformity. As noted previously, some fractures (e.g., femoral neck fracture) may cause disruption of the blood supply and subsequent avascular necrosis, and a **joint replacement** may be elected over an ORIF. Joints frequently replaced include the hip, knee (Fig. 42-14), and finger joints. Less frequently, more complex joints (shoulder, elbow, wrist, ankle) are replaced.

Timing of these procedures is important to ensure maximum function. Surgery should be performed before surrounding muscles become contracted and atrophied and

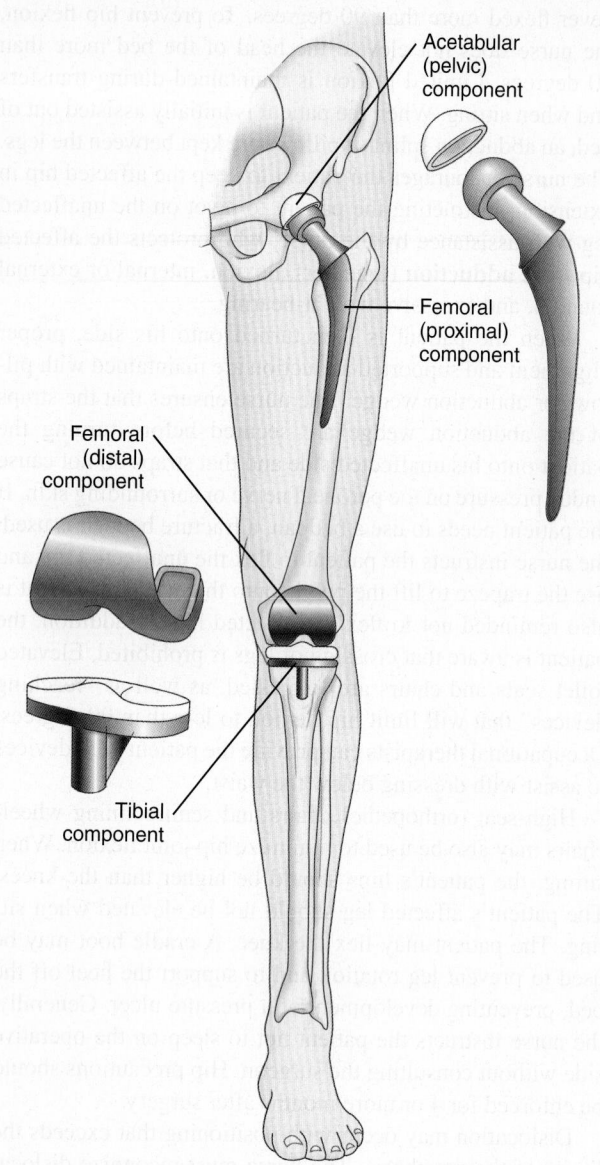

Acetabular
(pelvic)
component

Femoral
(proximal)
component

Femoral
(distal)
component

Tibial
component

FIGURE 42-14 Examples of hip and knee replacement.

serious structural abnormalities occur. The surgeon carefully evaluates the patient, so that the most appropriate procedure is performed.

Surgical procedures include excision of damaged and diseased tissue, repair of damaged structures (e.g., ruptured tendon), **arthroplasty** (replacement of all or part of the joint surfaces), and **arthrodesis** (immobilizing fusion of a joint).

Most joint replacements consist of metal and high-density polyethylene components. Porcelain may also be used. Finger prostheses are usually silastic. The joint implants may be cemented in the prepared bone with polymethyl methacrylate (PMMA), a bone-bonding agent that has properties similar to bone. Loosening of the prosthesis due to cement–bone interface failure is a common reason for prosthesis failure. Press-fit, ingrowth prostheses (porous-coated, cementless artificial

joint components) that allow the patient's bone to grow into and securely fix the prosthesis in the bone are alternatives to cemented prostheses. Accurate fitting and the presence of healthy bone with adequate blood supply are important in the use of cementless components. Much progress has been made in reducing the prosthesis failure rate through improved techniques, improved materials, and use of bone grafts.

With joint replacement, excellent pain relief is obtained in most patients. Return of motion and function depends on preoperative soft tissue condition, soft tissue reactions, and general muscle strength. Early failure of joint replacement is associated with excessive activity and preoperative joint and bone pathology.

Because these are elective procedures, many patients donate their own blood during the weeks preceding their surgery (autologous donation). This blood is used to replace blood lost during surgery. Autologous blood transfusions eliminate many of the risks of transfusion therapy.

TOTAL HIP REPLACEMENT

Total hip arthroplasty (TAH) or surgical replacement of the hip joint with an artificial prosthesis, is indicated for idiopathic osteoarthritis, acetabular dysplasia, rheumatoid arthritis, avascular necrosis, posttraumatic injury, and other causes (Schoen, 2009).

Preoperative Management

Assessment of the patient and preoperative management are aimed at having the patient in optimal health at the time of surgery. Preoperatively, it is important to evaluate cardiovascular, respiratory, renal, and hepatic functions. Additionally, the nurse considers factors such as age (>60), obesity, preoperative leg edema, a history of any venous thromboemboli, varicose veins, cancer, prolonged immobility, estrogens, and a wide variety of hematological conditions as they are indicators of risk for postoperative DVT and PE, the most common causes of postoperative mortality in those undergoing total hip replacement, and every effort is made to prevent them.

Preoperatively, it is important to also assess the neurovascular status of the extremity undergoing joint replacement. Postoperative assessment data are compared with preoperative assessment data to identify changes and deficits. For example, a sensory deficit postoperatively is of concern unless it was also noted preoperatively as nerve palsy can occur as a result of surgery. A plan of nursing care for a patient with a total hip replacement is available online at http://thePoint.lww.com/Pellico1e.

Providing Patient Education

Maintenance of the femoral head component in the acetabular cup is essential. The nurse teaches the patient about positioning the leg in **abduction**, which helps prevent dislocation of the prosthesis. The patient is aware that an abduction splint, a wedge pillow, or pillows will be placed between the

knees to keep the hip in abduction. In addition, raised toilet seats that will minimize hip joint flexion may be obtained for postoperative care.

NURSING ALERT
For total hip replacement surgery, the legs should be slightly abducted. Prevent hip flexion beyond 90 degrees to avoid dislocation of the hip after joint replacement surgery.

Preventing Infection

Preoperative assessment of the patient for infections (including skin, urinary tract, and pulmonary infection), is necessary because of the risk for postoperative infection. Any infection 2 to 4 weeks before planned surgery may result in postponement of surgery. Preoperative skin preparation frequently begins 1 or 2 days before the surgery. Prophylactic antibiotics are administered as a single preoperative or short perioperative course.

Intraoperative Management

Blood is conserved during surgery to minimize loss via a pneumatic tourniquet that produces a "bloodless field." Intraoperative blood salvage with reinfusion is used when a large volume of blood loss is anticipated, and this has shown to substantially reduce the need for allogeneic transfusions (transfusion of blood collected from someone other than the patient) (Keating, 2005).

Airborne bacteria that contaminate the wound at the time of surgery cause most deep infections. Therefore, as with any surgery, there is strict adherence to aseptic principles, and the operating area is controlled and made as bacteria-free as possible.

Culture of the joint during surgery, before intraoperative antibiotic therapy is begun, may be important in identifying and treating subsequent infections. If osteomyelitis develops, it is difficult to treat. Persistent infection at the site of the prosthesis usually requires removal of the implant and joint revision, which is a complex procedure. Also, it is not always possible to achieve a functional joint when the reconstruction procedure has to be repeated.

Postoperative Management

Repositioning the Patient and Preventing Dislocation

Depending on the surgical approach, the nurse may turn the patient onto the affected or unaffected extremity as prescribed by the surgeon. Dislocation is more common with the posterolateral approach and is seen when the hip is in full flexion, adducted (legs together), and internally rotated. For this reason, the patient will have a triangular abduction wedge placed between the legs or pillows placed between the patient's knees prior to positioning, to keep the affected leg in an abducted position and prevent internal rotation. The pillows between the legs are used when in a supine or side-lying position and when turning. The patient's hip is

never flexed more than 90 degrees. To prevent hip flexion, the nurse does not elevate the head of the bed more than 60 degrees. Limited flexion is maintained during transfers and when sitting. When the patient is initially assisted out of bed, an abduction splint or pillows are kept between the legs. The nurse encourages the patient to keep the affected hip in extension, instructing the patient to pivot on the unaffected leg with assistance by the nurse, who protects the affected hip from **adduction** (together), flexion, internal or external rotation, and excessive weight-bearing.

When the patient is then turned onto his side, proper alignment and supported abduction are maintained with pillows or abduction wedge. The nurse ensures that the straps of the abduction wedge are secured before turning the patient onto his unaffected side and that straps do not cause undue pressure on the peroneal nerve or surrounding skin. If the patient needs to use a bedpan, a fracture bedpan is used, the nurse instructs the patient to flex the unaffected hip and use the trapeze to lift the pelvis onto the pan. The patient is also reminded not to flex the affected hip. In addition, the patient is aware that crossing of legs is prohibited. Elevated toilet seats and chairs are suggested, as well as "reaching devices" that will limit hip flexion to less than 90 degrees. Occupational therapists can provide the patient with devices to assist with dressing below the waist.

High-seat (orthopedic) chairs and semireclining wheelchairs may also be used to minimize hip joint flexion. When sitting, the patient's hips should be higher than the knees. The patient's affected leg should not be elevated when sitting. The patient may flex the knee. A cradle boot may be used to prevent leg rotation and to support the heel off the bed, preventing development of a pressure ulcer. Generally, the nurse instructs the patient not to sleep on the operative side without consulting the surgeon. Hip precautions should be enforced for 4 or more months after surgery.

Dislocation may occur with positioning that exceeds the limits of the prosthesis. The nurse must recognize dislocation of the prosthesis. Indicators are as follows:

- Increased pain at the surgical site, swelling, and immobilization
- Acute groin pain in the affected hip or increased discomfort
- Shortening of the leg
- Abnormal external or internal rotation
- Restricted ability or inability to move the leg
- Reported "popping" sensation in the hip

If a prosthesis becomes dislocated, the nurse (or the patient, if at home) immediately notifies the surgeon, because the hip must be reduced and stabilized promptly, so that the leg does not sustain circulatory and nerve damage. After closed reduction, the hip may be stabilized with Buck's traction or a **brace** to prevent recurrent dislocation. As the muscles and joint capsule heal, the chance of dislocation diminishes. Stresses to the new hip joint should be avoided for the first 3 to 6 months.

BOX 42-13 Patient Education

Avoiding Hip Dislocation After Replacement Surgery

Until the hip prosthesis stabilizes after hip replacement surgery, it is necessary to follow instructions for proper positioning so that the prosthesis remains in place. Dislocation of the hip is a serious complication of surgery that causes pain and loss of function and necessitates reduction under anesthesia to correct the dislocation. Desirable positions include abduction, neutral rotation, and flexion of less than 90 degrees. When you are seated, the knees should be lower than the hip.

Methods for avoiding displacement include the following:
- Keep the knees apart at all times.
- Put a pillow between the legs when sleeping.
- Never cross the legs when seated.
- Avoid bending forward when seated in a chair.
- Avoid bending forward to pick up an object on the floor.
- Use a high-seated chair and a raised toilet seat.
- Do not flex the hip to put on clothing such as pants, stockings, socks, or shoes. Positions to avoid after total hip replacement are illustrated below.

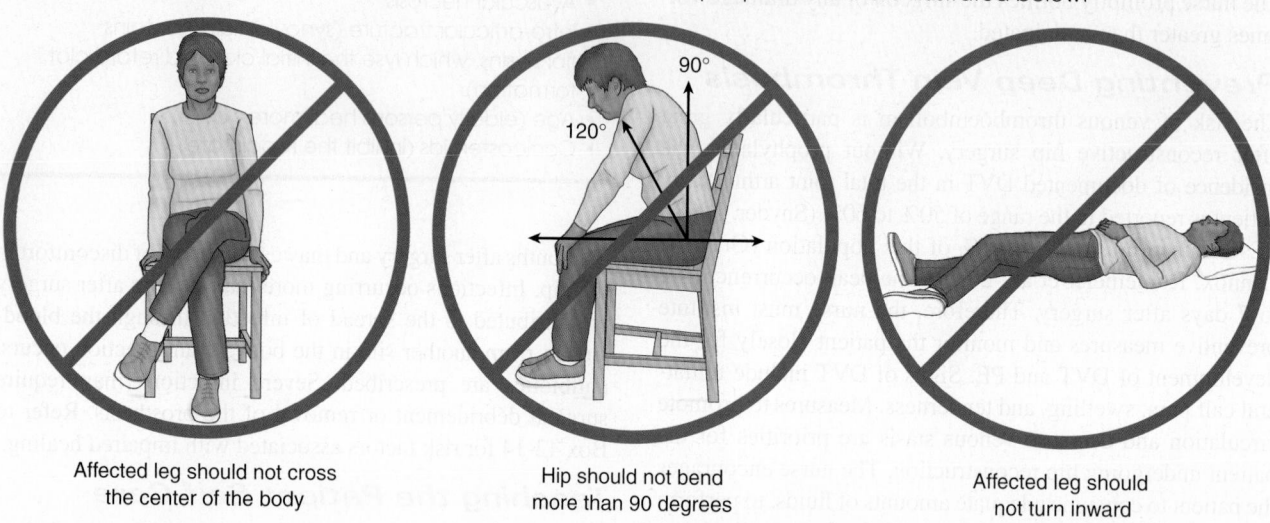

Affected leg should not cross the center of the body

Hip should not bend more than 90 degrees

Affected leg should not turn inward

Promoting Ambulation

Patients with total hip replacement begin ambulation with a physical therapist, generally within a day after surgery. The nurse and the physical therapist assist the patient in achieving the goal of independent ambulation. At first, the patient may be able to stand for only a brief period because of orthostatic hypotension.

⚡ NURSING ALERT
Orthostatic hypotension is an abnormal drop in blood pressure on change of position from lying to standing. Approximately 500 to 700 mL of blood momentarily shifts to the lower body when changing position to standing from supine, resulting in decreased venous return and arterial pressure. Complaints of dizziness may be noted. A drop of systolic pressure of 20 mm hg or a drop in diastolic pressure of 10 mm hg or more is diagnostic of orthostatic hypotension. It may be related to hypovolemia, dehydration, drug-induced hypotension, or prolonged bedrest. Patients should be encouraged to rise slowly and move their legs prior to rising to facilitate venous return from the extremities.

Specific weight-bearing limits on the prosthesis are determined by the surgeon and are based on the patient's condition, the procedure, and the fixation method. Usually, patients with cemented prostheses can proceed to weight-bearing as tolerated. If the patient has a press-fit, cementless, ingrowth prosthesis, weight-bearing immediately after surgery may be limited to minimize micromotion of the prosthesis in the bone. As the patient is able to tolerate more activity, the nurse encourages transferring to a chair several times a day for short periods and walking for progressively greater distances. Refer to Box 42-13 for patient education to prevent hip dislocation.

Monitoring for Complications

Complications that may occur include dislocation of the hip prosthesis, excessive wound drainage, thromboembolism, infection, and heel pressure ulcer. Other complications for which the nurse must monitor include those associated with immobility, heterotopic ossification, AVN, and loosening of the prosthesis.

Monitoring Wound Drainage

If extensive blood loss is anticipated after total joint replacement surgery, an autotransfusion drainage system (in which

the drained blood is filtered and reinfused into the patient during the immediate postoperative period) may be used to decrease the need for blood transfusions. Because of the risk of contamination, the blood should be administered within 6 hours of initiation of collection (Barden & Abran, 2007). The nurse should follow institutional protocol.

Fluid and blood accumulating at the surgical site are usually drained with a portable suction device. This prevents accumulation of fluid, which could contribute to discomfort and provide a site for infection. Drainage of 200 to 500 mL in the first 24 hours is expected; by 48 hours postoperatively, the total drainage in 8 hours usually decreases to 50 mL or less, and the suction device is then removed (Eby, 2008). The nurse promptly notifies the surgeon of any drainage volumes greater than anticipated.

Preventing Deep Vein Thrombosis

The risk of venous thromboembolism is particularly great after reconstructive hip surgery. Without prophylaxis, the incidence of documented DVT in the total joint arthroplasty patient is reported in the range of 50% to 60% (Snyder, 2008). PEs occur in up to 7% to 11% of this population (Gregory, Lennox, Kuhlemeier et al., 2005). The peak occurrence is 2 to 7 days after surgery. Therefore, the nurse must institute preventive measures and monitor the patient closely for the development of DVT and PE. Signs of DVT include unilateral calf pain, swelling, and tenderness. Measures to promote circulation and decrease venous stasis are priorities for the patient undergoing hip reconstruction. The nurse encourages the patient to consume adequate amounts of fluids, to perform ankle and foot exercises hourly while awake, to use elastic stockings and sequential compression devices as prescribed, and to transfer out of bed and ambulate with assistance beginning on the first postoperative day. Low-molecular-weight heparin (e.g., enoxaparin [Lovenox], dalteparin [Fragmin]) or sometimes unfractionated heparin is frequently prescribed as prophylaxis for DVT after hip replacement surgery.

Preventing Infection

Infection, a serious complication of total hip replacement, may necessitate removal of the implant. Patients who are elderly, obese, or poorly nourished, and patients who have diabetes, rheumatoid arthritis, concurrent infections (e.g., urinary tract infection, dental abscess), or large hematomas are at high risk for infection.

Because total joint infections are so disastrous, all efforts are made to prevent them. Potential sources of infection are avoided. Prophylactic antibiotics are prescribed. If indwelling urinary catheters or portable wound suction devices are used, they are removed as soon as possible to avoid infection. Prophylactic antibiotics are prescribed if the patient needs any future surgical or invasive procedures, such as tooth extraction or cystoscopic examination.

Acute infections may occur within 3 months after surgery and are associated with progressive superficial infections or hematomas. Delayed surgical infections may appear 4 to

---

BOX 42-14

Risk Factors for Delayed Healing

The nurse is aware that patients who present with the following factors are at risk for delayed healing of fractures:

- Extensive local trauma
- Malnutrition
- Bone loss
- Inadequate immobilization
- Space or tissue between bone fragments
- Infection
- Local malignancy
- Metabolic bone disease (e.g., Paget's disease)
- Irradiated bone (radiation necrosis)
- Avascular necrosis
- Intra-articular fracture (synovial fluid contains fibrolysins, which lyse the initial clot and retard clot formation)
- Age (elderly persons heal more slowly)
- Corticosteroids (inhibit the repair rate)

---

24 months after surgery and may cause return of discomfort in the hip. Infections occurring more than 2 years after surgery are attributed to the spread of infection through the bloodstream from another site in the body. If an infection occurs, antibiotics are prescribed. Severe infections may require surgical débridement or removal of the prosthesis. Refer to Box 42-14 for risk factors associated with impaired healing.

Teaching the Patient Self-Care

Before the patient prepares to leave the acute care setting, the nurse provides thorough teaching to promote continuity of the therapeutic regimen and active participation in the rehabilitation process. The nurse advises the patient of the importance of the daily exercise program in maintaining the functional motion of the hip joint and strengthening the abductor muscles of the hip, and reminds the patient that it will take time to strengthen and retrain the muscles.

Assistive devices (crutches, walker, or cane) are used for a time. After sufficient muscle tone has developed to permit a normal gait without discomfort, these devices are not necessary. In general, by 3 months, the patient can resume routine ADLs. Stair climbing is permitted as prescribed, but is kept to a minimum for 3 to 6 months. Frequent walks, swimming, and use of a high rocking chair are excellent for hip exercises. Sexual intercourse can be resumed based upon surgeon recommendation (typically 3 to 6 months postoperatively) and should be carried out with the patient in the dependent position (flat on the back) to avoid excessive adduction and flexion of the new hip. Sexual intercourse resumption is individualized by the surgeon based upon both the position of the hip that is most unstable and the degree of hip instability at the time of surgery. General considerations are to avoid positions of instability.

At no time during the first 4 months should the patient cross the legs or flex the hip more than 90 degrees. Assistance

in putting on shoes and socks may be needed. The patient should avoid low chairs and sitting for longer than 45 minutes at a time. These precautions minimize hip flexion and the risks of prosthetic dislocation, hip stiffness, and flexion **contracture**. Traveling long distances should be avoided unless frequent position changes are possible. Other activities to avoid include tub baths, jogging, lifting heavy loads, and excessive bending and twisting (e.g., lifting, shoveling snow, forceful turning).

TOTAL KNEE REPLACEMENT

Total knee replacement surgery is considered for patients who have severe pain and functional disabilities related to destruction of joint surfaces by arthritis (osteoarthritis, rheumatoid arthritis, posttraumatic arthritis) or bleeding into the joint (e.g., hemarthrosis), such as may result from hemophilia. Metal and acrylic prostheses designed to provide the patient with a functional, painless, stable joint may be used. If the patient's ligaments have weakened, a fully constrained (hinged) or semiconstrained prosthesis may be used to provide joint stability. A nonconstrained prosthesis depends on the patient's ligaments for joint stability.

Postoperative Management

Postoperatively, the knee is dressed with a compression bandage. Ice may be applied to control edema and bleeding. The nurse assesses the neurovascular status of the leg. It is important to encourage active flexion of the foot every hour when the patient is awake. Efforts are directed at preventing complications (thromboembolism, peroneal nerve palsy, infection, limited ROM).

A wound suction drain removes fluid accumulating in the joint. Drainage varies depending on operative event (cement vs. non-cement; use of drains, tourniquets) and patient comorbidities. In general, the surgeon can be expected to remove the drains within 24 hours. If extensive bleeding is anticipated, an autotransfusion drainage system may be used during the immediate postoperative period. The color, type, and amount of drainage are documented, and any excessive drainage or change in characteristics of the drainage is promptly reported to the surgeon.

Frequently, a **continuous passive motion (CPM) device** is used (Fig. 42-15). The patient's leg is placed in this device, which increases circulation and ROM of the knee joint. The rate and amount of extension and flexion are prescribed. Recent research suggests no statistically significant difference in flexion, edema or drainage, function, or pain when comparing the CPM device with physical therapy or physical therapy alone (Alkire & Swank, 2010). The physical therapist supervises exercises for strength and ROM. If satisfactory flexion is not achieved, gentle manipulation of the knee joint under general anesthesia may be necessary about 2 weeks after surgery.

The nurse assists the patient to get out of bed on the evening or the day after surgery. The knee is usually pro-

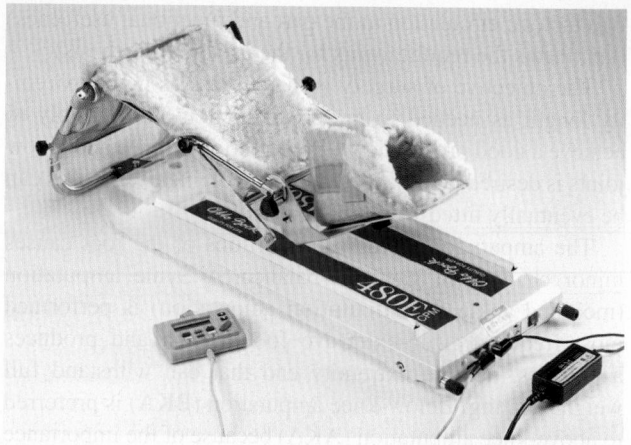

FIGURE 42-15 Lower-limb continuous passive motion (CPM) device. The Otto Bock 480E Knee CPM is 11 kg (24 lb) and combines durable construction with portability and ease of operation. CPM is best applied immediately after surgery and continued, uninterrupted, for up to 6 weeks, as prescribed by the provider. Photo courtesy of Otto Bock Healthcare, Minneapolis, Minnesota.

tected with a knee immobilizer (splint, cast, or brace) and is elevated when the patient sits in a chair. The physician prescribes weight-bearing limits. Progressive ambulation, using assistive devices and within the prescribed weight-bearing limits, begins on the day after surgery.

After discharge from the hospital, the patient may continue to use the CPM device at home and may undergo physical therapy on an outpatient basis. Late complications that may occur include infection and loosening and wear of prosthetic components. Patients usually can achieve a pain-free, functional joint and participate more fully in life activities than before the surgery.

AMPUTATION

Amputation is the removal of a body part, usually an extremity. Amputation of a lower extremity is often necessary because of progressive peripheral vascular disease (often a sequela of diabetes mellitus), fulminating gas gangrene, trauma (crushing injuries, burns, frostbite, electrical burns), congenital deformities, chronic osteomyelitis, or malignant tumor. Of all these causes, peripheral vascular disease accounts for most amputations of lower extremities. (See Chapter 18 for more information about peripheral vascular disease.) Amputation of an upper extremity occurs less frequently than amputation of a lower extremity and is most often necessary because of either traumatic injury or a malignant tumor. It is estimated that 1 of every 185 Americans has had an amputation (National Lower Limb Information Center, 2008).

Levels of Amputation

Amputation is performed at the most distal point that will heal successfully. The site of amputation is determined by

two factors: circulation in the part and functional usefulness (i.e., meets the requirements for the use of a prosthesis).

The objective of surgery is to conserve as much extremity length as needed to preserve function and possibly to achieve a good prosthetic fit. Preservation of knee and elbow joints is desired. Most amputations involving extremities can be eventually fitted with a prosthesis.

The amputation of toes and portions of the foot causes minor changes in gait and balance. A Syme amputation (modified ankle **disarticulation** amputation) is performed most frequently for extensive foot trauma and produces a painless, durable extremity end that can withstand full weight-bearing. Below-knee amputation (BKA) is preferred to above-knee amputation (AKA) because of the importance of the knee joint and the energy requirements for walking. Knee disarticulations are most successful with young, active patients who can develop precise control of the prosthesis. When AKAs are performed, all possible length is preserved, muscles are stabilized and shaped, and hip contractures are prevented for maximum ambulatory potential. Most people who have a hip disarticulation amputation must rely on a wheelchair for mobility.

Complications

Complications that may occur with amputation include hemorrhage, infection, skin breakdown, phantom limb pain, and joint contracture. Because major blood vessels have been severed, massive bleeding may occur. Infection is a risk with all surgical procedures. The risk of infection increases with contaminated wounds after traumatic amputation. Skin irritation caused by the prosthesis may result in skin breakdown. **Phantom limb pain** is caused by the severing of peripheral nerves. Joint contracture is caused by positioning and a protective flexion withdrawal pattern associated with pain and muscle imbalance.

Medical and Nursing Management

Dressings vary according to physician preference and may include a closed rigid cast dressing, a removable rigid dressing, or a soft dressing. A closed rigid cast dressing is frequently used to provide uniform compression, support soft tissues, control pain, and prevent joint contractures. Care is taken not to constrict circulation.

For the patient with a lower extremity amputation, the plaster cast may be equipped to attach a temporary prosthetic extension (pylon) and an artificial foot. This rigid dressing technique is used as a means of creating a socket for immediate postoperative prosthetic fitting. The length of the prosthesis is tailored to the individual patient. Early minimal weight bearing on the residual limb with a rigid cast dressing and a pylon attached produces little discomfort. The cast is changed in about 10 to 14 days. Elevated body temperature, severe pain, or a loose-fitting cast may necessitate earlier replacement.

A removable rigid dressing may be placed over a soft dressing to control edema, prevent joint flexion contracture, and protect the residual limb from unintentional trauma during transfer activities. This rigid dressing is removed several days after surgery for wound inspection and is then replaced to control edema. The dressing facilitates residual limb shaping.

A soft dressing with or without compression may be used if there is significant wound drainage and frequent inspection of the residual limb (stump) is desired. An immobilizing splint may be incorporated in the dressing. Stump (wound) hematomas are controlled with wound drainage devices to minimize infection.

NURSING ALERT
If the cast or elastic dressing inadvertently comes off, the nurse must immediately wrap the residual limb with an elastic compression bandage. If this is not done, excessive edema will develop in a short time, resulting in a delay in rehabilitation. The nurse notifies the surgeon if a cast dressing comes off, so that another cast can be applied promptly.

Promoting Rehabilitation

Patients who require amputation because of severe trauma are usually, but not always, young and healthy, heal rapidly, and are physically able to participate in a vigorous rehabilitation program. Because the amputation is the result of an injury, the patient needs psychological support in accepting the sudden change in body image and in dealing with the stresses of hospitalization, long-term rehabilitation, and modification of lifestyle. Patients who undergo amputation need support as they grieve the loss, and they need time to work through their feelings about their permanent loss and change in body image. Their reactions are unpredictable and can include anger, bitterness, and hostility.

The multidisciplinary rehabilitation team (patient, nurse, clinical nurse specialist, physician, social worker, physical therapist, occupational therapist, psychologist, prosthetist, vocational rehabilitation worker) helps the patient achieve the highest possible level of function and participation in life activities. Prosthetic clinics and amputee support groups facilitate this rehabilitation process. Vocational counseling and job retraining may be necessary to help patients return to work.

Psychological issues (e.g., denial, withdrawal) may be influenced by the type of support the patient receives from the rehabilitation team and by how quickly ADLs and use of the prosthesis are learned. Knowing the full options and capabilities available with the various prosthetic devices can give the patient a sense of control over the resulting disability.

Minimizing Altered Sensory Perceptions

A person who has had an amputation may experience phantom limb pain soon after surgery or 2 to 3 months later. It

occurs more frequently in patients who have had AKAs. The patient describes pain or unusual sensations, such as numbness, tingling, or muscle cramps, as well as a feeling that the extremity is present, crushed, cramped, or twisted in an abnormal position.

The pathogenesis of the phantom limb phenomenon is unknown. When a patient describes phantom pains or sensations, the nurse acknowledges these feelings and helps the patient modify these perceptions. Keeping the patient active helps decrease the occurrence of phantom limb pain. Early intensive rehabilitation and stump desensitization with kneading massage can sometimes bring relief. Phantom sensations may diminish over time. Transcutaneous electrical nerve stimulation (TENS), ultrasound, acupuncture, or local anesthetics may provide some relief for patients. In addition, beta blockers may relieve dull, burning discomfort; antiseizure medications control stabbing and cramping pain; and tricyclic antidepressants are used to modify pain signals and improve mood and coping ability. Newer treatment modalities include virtual reality in an attempt to extinguish maladaptive memory traces of the amputated limb and extinguish the pain (Flor, 2008).

Helping the Patient to Achieve Physical Mobility

Proper positioning prevents the development of hip or knee joint contracture in the patient with a lower extremity amputation. Abduction, external rotation, and flexion of the lower extremity are avoided. Depending on the surgeon's preference, the residual limb may be placed in an extended position or elevated for a brief period after surgery. Prolonged elevation (after initial 24 hours post operative) is not recommended as flexion contractions are to be avoided.

NURSING ALERT
The residual limb should not be placed on a pillow, because a flexion contracture of the hip may result.

A physical therapist will develop exercises if indicated for muscle strengthening and to prevent abduction and flexion contractures. The nurse encourages the patient to turn from side to side and to assume a prone position, if possible, to stretch the flexor muscles and to prevent flexion contracture of the hip. The nurse discourages sitting for prolonged periods, to prevent flexion contracture. The legs should remain close together to prevent an abduction deformity. The nurse encourages the patient to use assistive devices (e.g., reachers) to more readily perform self-care activities and to identify what home modifications should be made to perform these activities in the home environment

Postoperative ROM exercises are started early because contracture deformities develop rapidly. ROM exercises include hip and knee exercises for BKAs and hip exercises for AKAs. It is important that the patient understand the importance of exercising the residual limb.

The upper extremities, trunk, and abdominal muscles are exercised and strengthened. The extensor muscles in the arm and the depressor muscles in the shoulder play an important part in crutch walking. The major problems that can delay prosthetic fitting during this period are (1) flexion deformities, (2) nonshrinkage of the residual limb, and (3) abduction deformities of the hip.

The nurse also assesses for systemic indicators of infection (e.g., elevated temperature, leukocytosis [elevated WBCs] with an increase of >10% bands on the differential) and promptly reports indications of infection to the surgeon.

Chapter Review

Critical Thinking Exercises

1. You volunteer to provide field first aid for your neighborhood's softball league. Common injuries you expect include sprains, strains, and possibly dislocations and fractures. What specific assessment would you make to differentiate these problems? Describe the standard treatment for any of these common musculoskeletal disorders.

2. A 68-year-old man has had a repair of a fracture of his right tibia. During the evening of his second postoperative day, he complains of increasing pain and slight paresthesias of his right toes. Opioid analgesics have only moderately relieved his pain. The night-shift nurse documents her findings and asks you, as the oncoming day-shift nurse, to report these findings to the orthopedic surgeon when he makes his rounds. You assess the patient after report and find that he now describes his right lower leg as "feeling tight" and that he has sensations of "pins and needles." His right lower leg is shiny, capillary refill is longer than 3 seconds, and his right toes feel much cooler than the left toes. What additional assessments might you make at this time? What is your priority nursing diagnosis and intervention?

3. Mrs. Y, who is postoperative from total hip repair and has a history of ulcers, is complaining of abdominal pain. Her hematocrit this morning is 8/24. One unit of packed cells is administered. One hour after the unit has infused, you are asked to draw a repeat H/H. If Mrs. Y does not have any additional sources of blood loss, what do you expect her H/H to rise by in the repeat lab work?

(continued on page 1148)

Chapter Review (continued)

NCLEX-Style Review Questions

1. In the immediate postoperative period, which measure would best prevent a DVT?
   A. Adding a multivitamin to the patient's medication
   B. Early ambulation
   C. Measuring intake and output
   D. Lowering the legs below the level of the heart.

2. A 22-year-old man is admitted to the emergency department with a crush injury to both lower legs. He has been pinned under a car for 3 hours. On admission, his vital signs are stable; he is alert and oriented and complaining of extreme pain in his legs. Popliteal pulses are strong; pedal and posterior tibial pulses are weak. The ankle and feet appear dusky; the skin is tense, but the skin envelope is not broken. X-rays show no broken bones. Based upon these data, what interventions are most appropriate?
   A. Notify the provider and anticipate that a stat V̇/Q̇ scan will be performed to rule out fat emboli.
   B. Notify the provider and prepare to set up skin traction to decrease the pressure on the calf muscle.
   C. Notify the provider and anticipate that the provider will measure the pressure in the compartment and possibly perform a fasciotomy if elevated pressure is noted.
   D. Notify provider and prepare to give IV antibiotics stat to decrease the risk of osteomyelitis.

3. During assessment of the patient in the question above, he becomes semiconscious and continues moaning with pain. His blood pressure has dropped, and his pulse has increased. What is the most immediate life-threatening problem for this patient?
   A. Arrhythmias due to hypokalemia
   B. Hypovolemia
   C. Respiratory depression from pain medication
   D. Fat embolus to the lung

4. Mrs. L., age 73, is placed in skeletal traction prior to surgery for an ORIF of fractured femur. She develops chest pain, tachypnea, and tachycardia the second day in traction. What additional symptom would indicate her symptoms are related to a fat emboli rather than a pulmonary thromboembolic event?
   A. Hypotension
   B. Restlessness
   C. Petechiae of the anterior chest wall
   D. Warm, reddened areas in her leg

5. Richard S., age 23, experienced an open fracture of the left tibia with major soft tissue damage of his lower leg in a bicycle accident. Surgical reduction and fixation of the tibia were performed with debridement of nonviable tissue and drain placement in the damaged soft tissue. Which finding by the nurse would most likely indicate the development of the osteomyelitis?
   A. Tachycardia
   B. Elevated ESR
   C. Numbness in the left leg and toes
   D. Muscle spasms around the affected bone

Try these additional resources to enhance your learning and understanding of this chapter:
- thePoint online resource available at **http://thepoint.lww.com/Pellico1e**
- *Handbook for Focus on Adult Health: Medical-Surgical Nursing*
- *Study Guide for Focus on Adult Health: Medical-Surgical Nursing*

References and Selected Readings

References and selected readings associated with this chapter can be found on the website that accompanies the book. Visit http://thepoint.lww.com/Pellico1e to access the references and other additional resources associated with this chapter.

Problems Related to Neurologic Function

A 65-YEAR-OLD patient presents to the emergency department by ambulance. The paramedics state that his spouse witnessed the sudden onset of confusion, weakness in his right arm and leg, and difficulty speaking (he could not get the right words out). His symptoms occurred 2 hours prior to arrival at the hospital. He has a history of smoking, hypertension, atrial fibrillation, and prior transient ischemic attacks (TIAs). An initial non-contrast head CT was negative for intracerebral hemorrhage. An acute ischemic stroke in the left hemisphere is suspected.

→ Discuss emergency management of a stroke when a patient presents with suspected stroke symptoms.

→ What sub-type of ischemic stroke is the patient most likely experiencing?

→ Discuss nursing considerations for the patient receiving tPA.

→ Describe 3 of the 8 standardized performance measures that are considered for a patient with an ischemic stroke.

Nursing Assessment: Neurologic Function

DAWN K. BELAND
DONNA M. AVANECEAN

Learning Objectives

After reading this chapter, you will be able to:

1. Describe the structures and functions of the central and peripheral nervous systems.

2. Differentiate between pathologic changes that affect motor control and those that affect sensory pathways.

3. Compare the functioning of the sympathetic and parasympathetic nervous systems.

4. Describe changes in neurologic function associated with aging and their impact on neurologic assessment findings.

5. Describe the significance of physical assessment to the diagnosis of neurologic dysfunction.

6. Describe diagnostic tests used for assessment of suspected neurologic disorders and the related nursing implications.

Nurses in many practice settings encounter patients with altered neurologic function. Disorders of the nervous system can occur at any time during the lifespan and can vary from mild, self-limiting symptoms to devastating, life-threatening disorders. Nurses must be skilled in the assessment of the neurologic system, whether the assessment is generalized or focused on specific areas of function. In either case, assessment requires knowledge of the anatomy and physiology of the nervous system and an understanding of the array of tests and procedures used to diagnose neurologic disorders. Knowledge about the nursing implications and interventions related to assessment and diagnostic testing is also essential.

ANATOMIC AND PHYSIOLOGIC OVERVIEW

The function of the nervous system is control of all motor, sensory, autonomic, cognitive, and behavioral activities. The nervous system consists of two major divisions: the central nervous system (CNS), including the brain and spinal cord; and the peripheral nervous system (PNS), which includes cranial and spinal nerves that lie outside the brain and spinal cord. The PNS can be further divided into the somatic, or voluntary nervous system, and the autonomic, or involuntary nervous system.

Anatomy of the Nervous System

Cells and Neurotransmitters of the Nervous System

Cells of the brain link the motor and sensory pathways, monitor the body's processes, respond to the internal and external environment, maintain homeostasis, and direct all psychological, biologic, and physical activity through complex chemical and electrical messages. The basic functional unit of the brain is the neuron (Fig. 43-1). It is composed of a cell body, a dendrite, and an axon. The **dendrite** is a branch-type structure with synapses (a gap between two neurons, in which impulses jump from one neuron to another) for receiving electrochemical messages. The **axon** is a long projection that carries impulses away from the cell body. Nerve cell bodies occurring in clusters are called *ganglia* or *nuclei*. A

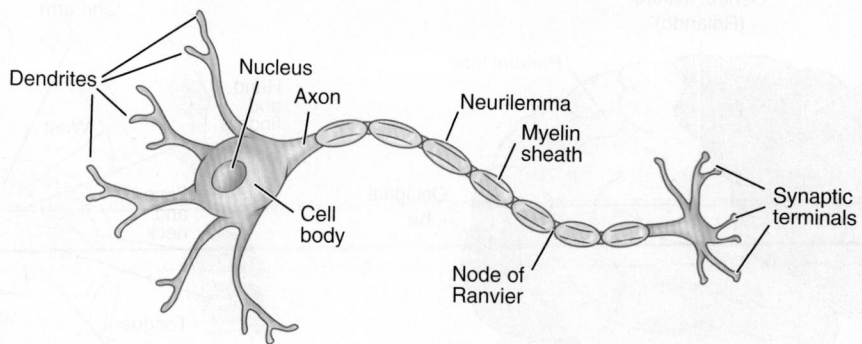

FIGURE 43-1 Neuron.

cluster of cell bodies with the same function is called a *center* (e.g., the respiratory center).

Neurotransmitters communicate messages from one neuron to another or from a neuron to a specific target tissue and are responsible for all types of brain activity. Each neurotransmitter has an affinity for specific receptors in the postsynaptic bulb. When released, neurotransmitters cross the synaptic cleft and bind to receptors in the postsynaptic cell membrane. The action of a neurotransmitter is to potentiate, terminate, or modulate a specific action, and it can either excite or inhibit the activity of the target cell. Usually, multiple neurotransmitters are at work in the neural synapse. Imbalances or deficiencies of a particular neurotransmitter may cause neurological dysfunction. Major neurotransmitters are described in Table 43-1.

The Central Nervous System

The Brain

The brain is divided into three major areas: the cerebrum, the brainstem, and the cerebellum. The cerebrum is composed of two hemispheres, the thalamus, the hypothalamus, and the basal ganglia. In addition, connections for the olfactory (cranial nerve I) and optic (cranial nerve II) nerves are found in the cerebrum. The brainstem includes the midbrain, pons, medulla, and connections for cranial nerves III through XII. The cerebellum is located under the cerebrum and behind the brainstem (Fig. 43-2).

CEREBRUM. The cerebrum consists of two hemispheres that are incompletely separated by the great longitudinal fissure. This sulcus (a depression or groove) separates the cerebrum

TABLE
43-1 Major Neurotransmitters

Neurotransmitter	Source	Action	Example of Dysfunction
Acetylcholine (major transmitter of the parasympathetic nervous system)	Many areas of the brain; autonomic nervous system	Usually excitatory; parasympathetic effects sometimes inhibitory (stimulation of heart by vagal nerve)	↓ Leads to Myasthenia gravis
Serotonin	Brainstem, hypothalamus, dorsal horn of the spinal cord	Inhibitory, helps control mood and sleep, inhibits pain pathways	↓ Leads to depression
Dopamine	Substantia nigra and basal ganglia	Usually inhibits, affects behavior (attention, emotions) and fine movement	↓ Leads to Parkinson's disease
Norepinephrine (major transmitter of the sympathetic nervous system)	Brainstem, hypothalamus, postganglionic neurons of the sympathetic nervous system	Usually excitatory; affects mood and overall activity	Seen rarely
Gamma-aminobutyric acid (GABA)	Spinal cord, cerebellum, basal ganglia, some cortical areas	Inhibitory	↓ Leads to seizures
Enkephalin, endorphin	Nerve terminals in the spine, brainstem, thalamus and hypothalamus, pituitary gland	Excitatory; pleasurable sensation, inhibits pain transmission	

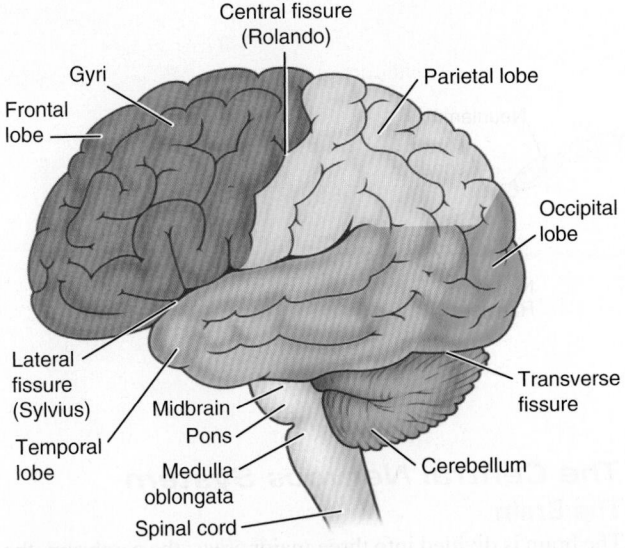

FIGURE 43-2 View of the external surface of the brain showing lobes, cerebellum, and brainstem.

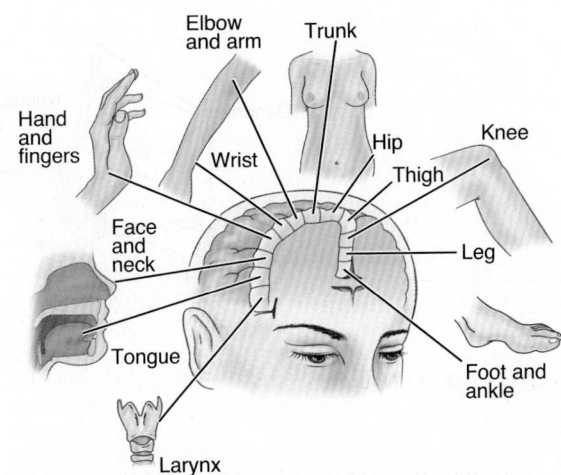

FIGURE 43-3 Diagrammatic representation of the cerebrum showing locations for control of motor movement of various parts of the body.

into the right and left hemispheres. The two hemispheres are joined at the lower portion of the fissure by the corpus callosum. The outside surface of the hemispheres has many folded layers or convolutions called *gyri,* which increase the surface area of the brain. The external or outer portion of the cerebrum (the cerebral cortex) is made up of gray matter, approximately 2 to 5 mm in depth. White matter makes up the innermost layer and is composed of nerve fibers and neuroglia (support tissue) that form tracts or pathways connecting various parts of the brain. The cerebral hemispheres are divided into pairs of frontal, parietal, temporal, and occipital lobes. The four lobes are as follows (see Fig. 43-2):

• Frontal: The frontal lobe is the largest lobe in the front of the skull. The major functions are concentration, abstract thought, information storage or memory, and motor function. The motor strip, which lies in the frontal lobe, anterior to the central sulcus, is responsible for muscle movement. Refer to Figure 43-3 for specific locations of control of motor movement. It also contains Broca's area (left frontal lobe region in most people), critical for motor control of speech. The frontal lobe is responsible in large part for a person's affect, judgment, personality, emotions, attitudes, and inhibitions, and contributes to the formation of thought processes.

• Parietal: The parietal lobe is the primary sensory cortex, which is located posterior to the motor strip, and is organized topographically similar to the motor strip. This lobe analyzes sensory information such as pressure, vibration, pain, and temperature, and relays the interpretation of this information to the thalamus from the sensory cortex. It is also essential to a person's awareness of the body in space, as well as orientation in space and spatial relations. For example, stereognosis or the ability to perceive an object using the sense of touch is processed in this area.

• Temporal: The temporal lobes contain the auditory receptive areas located around the temples. The interpretive area of the temporal lobe provides integration of visual and auditory areas and plays the most dominant role of any area of the cortex in thinking. Located in the posterior region of the temporal lobe is the area responsible for receptive speech referred to as *Wernicke's area.* For most people, whether right- or left-handed, Wernicke's area is in the left lobe. Long-term memory recall is also associated with this lobe.

• Occipital: The occipital lobe located in the posterior portion of the cerebral hemispheres is known as the primary visual cortex. The occipital lobe also assists in some visual reflexes, as well as allows for some involuntary eye movements.

The corpus callosum (Fig. 43-4) is a thick collection of nerve fibers that connects the two hemispheres of the brain and transmits the information from one side of the brain to the other. Right-handed people and some left-handed people have cerebral dominance on the left side of the brain for verbal, linguistic, arithmetical, calculating, and analytic functions. The nondominant hemisphere is responsible for geometric, spatial, visual, pattern, and musical functions.

The basal ganglia are masses of nuclei located deep in the white matter of the cerebral hemispheres and are responsible for control of fine motor movements. The thalamus lies on either side of the third ventricle and acts primarily as a relay station for all sensation except smell. All memory also passes through this section of the brain.

The hypothalamus (see Fig. 43-4) is anterior and inferior to the thalamus and lies next to the third ventricle. It includes the optic chiasm (where the two optic tracts cross) and the mamillary bodies (involved in olfactory reflexes

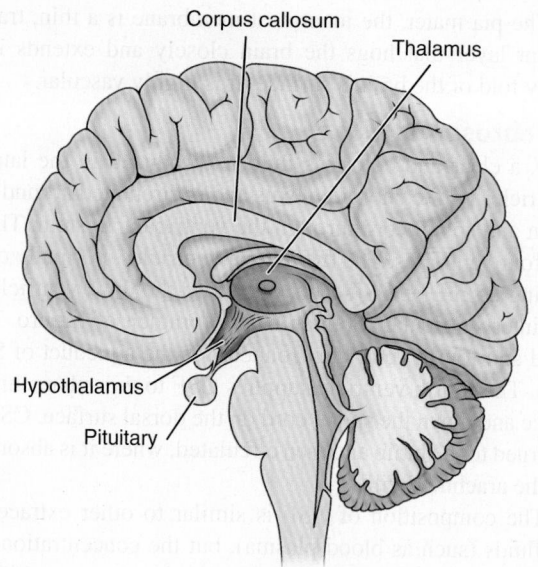

FIGURE 43-4 Medial view of the brain.

Corpus callosum
Thalamus
Hypothalamus
Pituitary

and emotional response to odors). The infundibulum of the hypothalamus connects to the posterior pituitary gland. The hypothalamus, important in the endocrine system, regulates the pituitary secretion of hormones influencing metabolism, reproduction, stress response, and urine production. It works with the pituitary to maintain fluid balance (refer to Chapter 29 for further detail). In addition, the hypothalamus, the site of the hunger center, is involved in appetite control. It contains centers that regulate the sleep–wake cycle, blood pressure, aggressive and sexual behavior, and emotional responses (i.e., blushing, rage, depression, panic, and fear). The hypothalamus also controls and regulates the autonomic nervous system and maintains temperature regulation by promoting vasoconstriction or vasodilatation.

The pituitary gland is located in the sella turcica at the base of the brain. The pituitary is a common site of brain tumors in adults, which are frequently detected by signs and symptoms traced to the pituitary, such as hormonal imbalance or visual disturbances due to pressure on the optic chiasm (see Chapter 31).

Nerve fibers from the cortex converge in each hemisphere and exit in a tight bundle of nerve fibers known as the *internal capsule*. After entering the pons and medulla, each bundle crosses to the corresponding bundle from the opposite side. Although the various cells in the cerebral cortex are quite similar in appearance, their functions vary widely, depending on location.

BRAINSTEM. The brainstem is responsible for automatic functions such as heart rate, breathing and swallowing. It consists of the **midbrain**, **pons**, and **medulla oblongata** and contains motor and sensory pathways (see Fig. 43-2). The midbrain connects the pons and cerebellum with the cerebral hemispheres and serves as the center for auditory and visual

reflexes. Cranial nerves III and IV originate in the midbrain. The pons is situated in front of the cerebellum, between the midbrain and the medulla, and acts as a bridge between the cerebrum, the cerebellum, and the medulla. Cranial nerves V through VIII connect to the brain in the pons. Portions of the pons also control the heart rate, respiration, and blood pressure.

The medulla oblongata contains motor fibers from the brain to the spinal cord and sensory fibers from the spinal cord to the brain. Most of these fibers cross, or *decussate* at this level. Cranial nerves IX through XII connect to the brain in the medulla. The medulla and pons are essential for respiratory function.

CEREBELLUM. The cerebellum is separated from the cerebral hemispheres by a fold of dura mater, the *tentorium cerebelli*. The cerebellum is largely responsible for coordination of all movement. It also controls fine movement, balance, **position (postural) sense** or proprioception (awareness of where each part of the body is), and integration of sensory input.

Structures Protecting the Brain

SKULL. The brain is contained in a rigid skull, protecting it from injury. The major bones of the skull are the frontal, temporal, parietal, and occipital bones (Fig. 43-5). These bones join at suture lines.

MENINGES. The meninges (fibrous connective tissues) cover the brain and spinal cord, and provide protection, support, and nourishment. The three layers of the meninges are the dura, arachnoid, and pia mater (Fig. 43-6). An easy way to remember the layers is to note that the meninges "PAD" the brain (*p*ia, *a*rachnoid, and *d*ura).

The dura mater, the outermost layer, covers the brain and the spinal cord. The dura mater is tough, thick, inelastic,

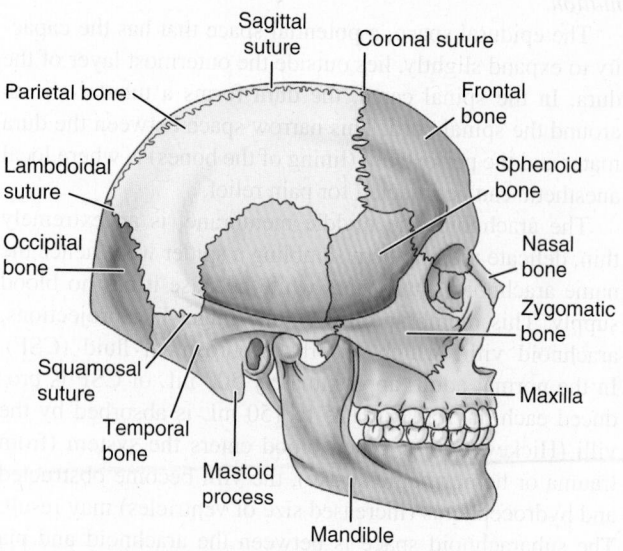

Sagittal suture
Coronal suture
Parietal bone
Frontal bone
Lambdoidal suture
Sphenoid bone
Occipital bone
Nasal bone
Zygomatic bone
Squamosal suture
Maxilla
Temporal bone
Mastoid process
Mandible

FIGURE 43-5 Bones and sutures of the skull.

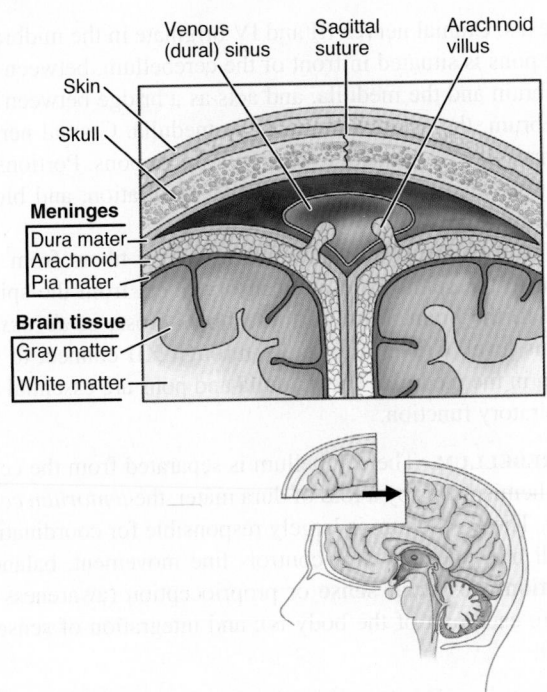

Skin
Skull

Meninges
Dura mater
Arachnoid
Pia mater

Brain tissue
Gray matter
White matter

Venous (dural) sinus
Sagittal suture
Arachnoid villus

FIGURE 43-6 Meninges and related structures.

fibrous, and gray. There are four extensions of the dura: the falx cerebri, which separates the two hemispheres in a longitudinal plane; the tentorium, which is an infolding of the dura that forms a tough, membranous shelf between the cerebrum and cerebellum; the falx cerebelli, which lies between the two lateral lobes of the cerebellum; and the diaphragm sellae, which provides a "roof" for the sella turcica. The tentorium supports the hemispheres and separates them from the lower part of the brain. When excess pressure occurs in the cranial cavity, brain tissue may be compressed against the tentorium or displaced downward, a process called *herniation.*

The epidural space, a potential space that has the capacity to expand slightly, lies outside the outermost layer of the dura. In the spinal canal, the dura forms a tubular sheath around the spinal cord. This narrow space between the dura mater and the periosteum (lining of the bones) is where local anesthetic can be injected for pain relief.

The arachnoid, the middle membrane, is an extremely thin, delicate membrane resembling a spider web (hence the name arachnoid). It appears white because it has no blood supply. This membrane has unique finger-like projections, arachnoid villi, which absorb cerebrospinal fluid (CSF). In the normal adult, approximately 500 mL of CSF is produced each day; all but 125 to 150 mL is absorbed by the villi (Hickey, 2009). When blood enters the system (from trauma or hemorrhagic stroke), the villi become obstructed and hydrocephalus (increased size of ventricles) may result. The subarachnoid space is between the arachnoid and pia layers and contains CSF.

The pia mater, the innermost membrane is a thin, transparent layer that hugs the brain closely and extends into every fold of the brain's surface. It is highly vascular.

Cerebrospinal Fluid

CSF, a clear and colorless fluid, is produced in the lateral ventricles by the choroid plexus and is circulated around the brain and spinal cord through the ventricular system. There are four ventricles. The two lateral ventricles, normally containing 25 mL of CSF each, open into the third ventricle at the interventricular foramen or the foramen of Monro. The third and fourth ventricles connect via the aqueduct of Sylvius. The fourth ventricle supplies CSF to the subarachnoid space and down the spinal cord on the dorsal surface. CSF is returned to the brain and then circulated, where it is absorbed by the arachnoid villi.

The composition of CSF is similar to other extracellular fluids (such as blood plasma), but the concentrations of the various constituents differ. The laboratory report of CSF analysis usually contains information on color, specific gravity, protein count, white blood cell count, glucose, and other electrolyte levels. Normal CSF contains a minimal number of white blood cells and no red blood cells. The intracranial pressure (ICP) within the skull results from a combination of brain tissue, blood flow and CSF. Normal CSF pressure is approximately 10 to 15 mm Hg, while pressures greater than 20 mm Hg indicate increased ICP.

NURSING ALERT

In the event of a skull fracture, the nurse should be alert for signs of CSF leakage. Suspect rhinorrhea (leakage of CSF via nares) with fractures involving the cribriform plates of the anterior cranial fossa, while otorrhea (leakage of CSF via ear) is suspected with fractures involving the basilar skull. Depending on the site of the fracture, the patient may present with raccoon eyes (bruising around the eyes) or Battle's sign (ecchymosis of the mastoid process of the temporal bone). Leakage of CSF places the patient at risk for meningitis. If a CSF leak is suspected, the nurse is aware that nothing is allowed into the patient's nose or ears (suction or nasogastric catheters, dressings, tissues etc.).

Cerebral Circulation

The cerebral circulation receives approximately 15% of the cardiac output, or 750 mL per minute. The brain does not store nutrients, has a high metabolic demand, and requires high blood flow. The brain's blood pathway is unique because it flows against gravity; its arteries fill from below, and the veins drain from above. The brain has poor collateral blood flow, which results in irreversible tissue damage when blood flow is occluded for even short time periods.

ARTERIES. Two internal carotid arteries and two vertebral arteries and their extensive system of branches provide blood supply to the brain (Fig. 43-7). The internal carotids

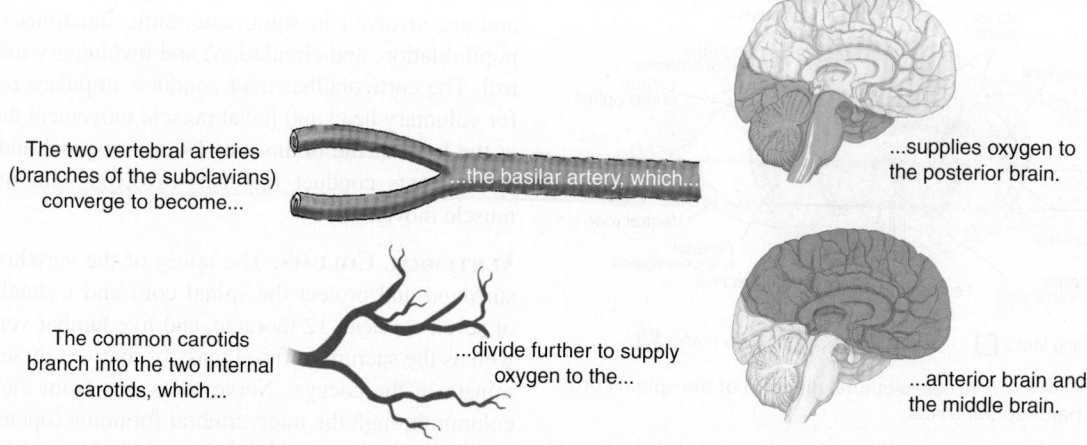

The two vertebral arteries (branches of the subclavians) converge to become...

...the basilar artery, which...

...supplies oxygen to the posterior brain.

The common carotids branch into the two internal carotids, which...

...divide further to supply oxygen to the...

...anterior brain and the middle brain.

FIGURE 43-7 Arterial circulation to the brain. From Lippincott (2009). *Anatomy and physiology made incredibly visual!* (p. 63). Philadelphia: Lippincott Williams & Wilkins.

arise from the bifurcation of the common carotid and supply much of the anterior circulation. The vertebral arteries branch from the subclavian arteries, flow back and upward on either side of the cervical vertebrae, and enter the cranium through the foramen magnum. The vertebral arteries join to become the basilar artery at the brainstem; then the basilar artery divides to form the two branches of the posterior cerebral arteries. The vertebrobasilar arteries supply most of the posterior circulation of the brain.

The circle of Willis is formed from the branches of the anterior circulation and posterior circulation connected by one anterior communicating artery and two posterior communicating arteries (Fig. 43-8). The arteries of the circle of Willis can provide collateral circulation if one or more of the four vessels supplying it become occluded.

The arterial bifurcations (branches) along the circle of Willis are frequent sites of aneurysm formation. Aneurysms may be congenital or result from changes in the vessel wall associated with atherosclerotic disease. If an artery with an aneurysm bursts, depending on its size and location, catastrophic effects can be seen. Additionally, if a blood vessel becomes constricted by vasospasm, it may lead to diminished blood flow, causing potential damage to neurons distal to the constriction leading to cell death. If not aggressively treated, this may result in an ischemic stroke. The effects of the constriction depend on which vessels are involved and the areas these vessels supply.

VEINS. Venous drainage for the brain does not follow the arterial circulation, as in other body structures. The veins reach the brain's surface, join larger veins, then cross the subarachnoid space, and empty into the dural sinuses, which are the vascular channels lying within the dura mater (see Fig. 43-6). The network of sinuses empties into the internal jugular vein, returning blood to the heart. Cerebral veins and sinuses are unique because, unlike other veins, they do not have valves to prevent blood from flowing backward and depend on both gravity and blood pressure.

Blood–Brain Barrier

The CNS and its neurons are inaccessible to many substances that circulate in the blood plasma (e.g., dyes, medications, and antibiotics) because of the blood–brain barrier. This barrier is formed by the tight junction of the endothelial cells in the brain's capillaries. All substances entering the CSF must filter through the capillary endothelial cells and astrocytes (Hickey, 2009). The blood–brain barrier has a protective function but can be altered by trauma, cerebral edema, and cerebral hypoxemia; this has implications in the treatment and selection of medication for CNS disorders.

Circle of Willis

Middle cerebral artery

Anterior cerebral artery

Anterior communicating artery

Internal carotid artery

Posterior communicating artery

Posterior cerebral artery

Basilar artery

Vertebral artery

Anterior spinal artery

FIGURE 43-8 Arterial blood supply of the brain, including the circle of Willis, as viewed from the ventral surface.

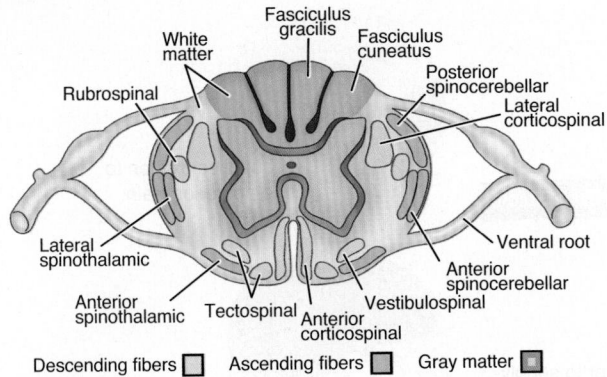

FIGURE 43-9 Cross-sectional diagram of the spinal cord showing major spinal tracts.

Spinal Cord

The spinal cord and medulla form a continuous structure extending from the cerebral hemispheres and serving as the connection between the brain and the periphery. Approximately 45 cm (18 in) long and about the thickness of a finger, it extends from the foramen magnum at the base of the skull to the lower border of the first lumbar vertebra, where it tapers to a fibrous band called the *conus medullaris*. Continuing below the second lumbar space are the nerve roots that extend beyond the conus, which are called the *cauda equina* because they resemble a horse's tail. Similar to the brain, the spinal cord consists of gray and white matter. Gray matter in the brain is external and white matter is internal; in the spinal cord, gray matter is in the center and is surrounded on all sides by white matter (Fig. 43-9). The spinal cord is an H-shaped structure with nerve cell bodies (gray matter) surrounded by ascending and descending tracts (white matter).

SENSORY AND MOTOR PATHWAYS: THE SPINAL TRACTS. The white matter of the cord is composed of myelinated and unmyelinated nerve fibers. The fast-conducting myelinated fibers form bundles that also contain glial cells. Fiber bundles with a common function are called *tracts*.

There are six ascending tracts (see Fig. 43-9). Two conduct sensation, principally the perception of touch, pressure, vibration, position, and passive motion from the same side of the body. Before reaching the cerebral cortex, these fibers cross to the opposite side in the medulla. The two spinocerebellar tracts conduct sensory impulses from muscle spindles, providing necessary input for coordinated muscle contraction. They ascend essentially uncrossed and terminate in the cerebellum. The last two spinothalamic tracts are responsible for conduction of pain, temperature, proprioception, fine touch, and vibratory sense from the upper body to the brain. They ascend, cross to the opposite side of the brain, and terminate in the thalamus.

There are eight descending tracts. The two corticospinal tracts conduct motor impulses to the anterior horn cells from the opposite side of the brain and control voluntary muscle

activity. The three vestibulospinal tracts descend uncrossed and are involved in some autonomic functions (sweating, pupil dilation, and circulation) and involuntary muscle control. The corticobulbar tract conducts impulses responsible for voluntary head and facial muscle movement and crosses at the level of the brainstem. The rubrospinal and reticulospinal tracts conduct impulses involved with involuntary muscle movement.

VERTEBRAL COLUMN. The bones of the vertebral column surround and protect the spinal cord and normally consist of seven cervical, 12 thoracic, and five lumbar vertebrae, as well as the sacrum (a fused mass of five vertebrae), and terminate in the coccyx. Nerve roots exit from the vertebral column through the intervertebral foramina (openings). The vertebrae are separated by disks, except for the first and second cervical, the sacral, and the coccygeal vertebrae. The vertebral body, arch, pedicles, and laminae all encase and protect the spinal cord.

The Peripheral Nervous System

The PNS includes the cranial nerves, the spinal nerves, and the autonomic nervous system.

Cranial Nerves

Twelve pairs of cranial nerves emerge from the lower surface of the brain and pass through the foramina in the skull (Fig. 43-10). Three are entirely sensory (I, II, VIII), five are motor (III, IV, VI, XI, and XII), and four are mixed (V, VII, IX, and X), because they have both sensory and motor functions. Most cranial nerves innervate the head, neck, and special sense structures. Table 43-2 lists the names and primary functions of the cranial nerves.

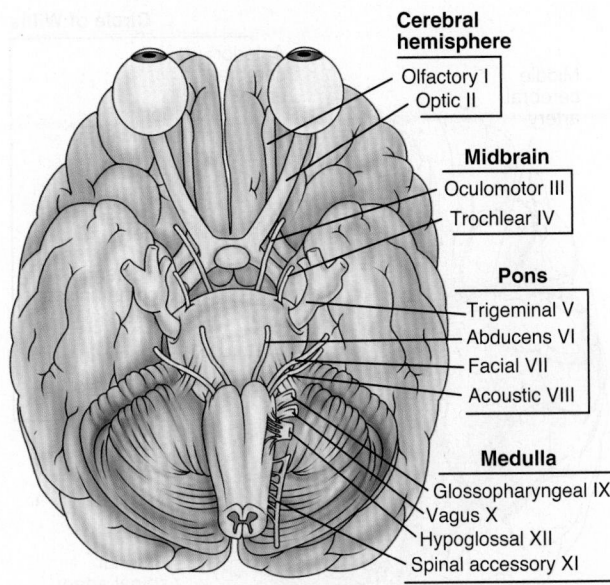

FIGURE 43-10 Diagram of the base of the brain showing entrance or exit of the cranial nerves. The right column shows the anatomic location of the connection of each cranial nerve to the central nervous system.

TABLE
43-2 Cranial Nerves

Cranial Nerve (CN)	Type	Assessment	Dysfunction
I (Olfactory)	Sensory	With eyes closed, ask the patient to identify two familiar odors (e.g., coffee, tobacco). Each nostril is tested separately. Avoid using strong odors such as ammonia as the trigeminal nerve may be stimulated. Testing of this CN is usually deferred.	Inability to identify odor, termed anosmia
II (Optic)	Sensory	Assess visual acuity using a portable eye chart or, if not available, grossly assess vision by having the patient read a card or newspaper from big print to small. Assess visual fields by testing peripheral vision: stand directly in front of the patient. Ask the patient to close one eye and focus on your nose as you assess the patient's ability to see your fingers that are positioned in four visual fields (upper right and left and lower right and left). In combination with CN III, assess the pupils (the light emitted into the pupil begins the process by which constriction is seen; constriction is the function of CN III).	Decreased visual acuity / Decreased visual fields
III (Oculomotor)	Motor	CN III controls most extraocular eye movement (EOM), eyelid elevation, and pupillary constriction. To assess EOM, ask the patient to follow your finger through the six cardinal positions (use the letter H as a guide to assess the ability of the eye to move to the left superior, left lateral, left inferior, right superior, right lateral, and right inferior). CN III is responsible for all movements except lateral movement (CN VI) and movement of the eye downward and in (CN IV). While the patient is looking in the six positions, hold the position briefly and assess for nystagmus (rotary oscillation of the eye). Test for pupillary reflexes (constriction of the pupil to light), and inspect eyelids for ptosis (drooping of the eyelid).	Inability to move the eyes in the visual field described / Ptosis of affected eye / Nonreactive or dilated pupil
IV (Trochlear)	Motor	This is assessed with EOM as described above. CN IV moves the eye down and in (as if looking toward the nose).	Inability to look down and in
V (Trigeminal)	Mixed	Assess facial sensation, corneal reflex (sensory aspect), and chewing or mastication. Have patient close the eyes. Touch cotton to forehead, cheeks, and jaw. Test sensitivity to superficial pain in these same three areas by using the sharp and dull ends of a broken tongue blade. Alternate between the sharp point and the dull end. Patient reports "sharp" or "dull" with each movement. If responses are incorrect, test for temperature sensation. Test tubes of cold and hot water are used alternately. To assess chewing, ask patient to jaw clench while palpating the temporal and masseter muscles. Corneal reflex may be assessed by having patient look up and away while brushing the cornea with a wisp of cotton; both eyes should blink (Note: use of contact lens decreases this response). Similar to the pupillary reaction (CN II and III), corneal reflexes are combination CN V and VII.	Absence of corneal reflex / Diminished sensation to forehead, maxillary and mandibular region / Weakness of muscles responsible for chewing
VI (Abducens)	Motor	Abducens moves the eye laterally (side to side or horizontally) and is assessed with EOMs.	Inability to look laterally, double vision
VII (Facial)	Mixed	Assess for symmetry of facial movement, ask patient to smile, raise eyebrows, keep eyes and lips closed while you try to open them, and puff out cheeks. Taste is also a function of this CN, although testing is often deferred. The motor response of closing the eye in response to stimuli is assessed with corneal reflex (combination of CN V and VII).	Facial paralysis / Facial asymmetry, droop of mouth / Absent nasolabial fold / Decreased ability to taste
VIII (Acoustic)	Sensory	Assess hearing by rubbing your fingers, place a ticking watch, or whispering near each ear. Equilibrium can be assessed with the Romberg test and is usually deferred.	Decreased hearing in affected ear

(continued on page 1158)

TABLE
43-2 Cranial Nerves (continued)

Cranial Nerve (CN)	Type	Assessment	Dysfunction
IX (Glossopha-ryngeal)	Mixed	This CN's function is primarily innervation of the pharynx and tongue, pharyngeal muscles, and swallowing. Ask the patient to open the mouth and say "Ah." Note symmetrical elevation of the upper palate and uvula in midline position. Assessing for the gag reflex tests this nerve and CN X, as they travel together. To test gag reflex, use a cotton swab or tongue blade and touch the posterior pharynx; note gag response.	Dysphagia Absence of gag reflex
X (Vagus)	Mixed	This CN is assessed by swallowing and gag reflex as noted above. In addition, the quality of the patient's voice is noted.	Hoarse or nasal quality to voice Slurred speech
XI (Spinal Accessory)	Motor	Have patient shrug shoulders and turn head from side to side; assess the sternocleidomastoid and trapezius muscles for symmetry.	Inability to shrug shoulders
XII (Hypoglossal)	Motor	Inspect the tongue for atrophy at rest. To assess movement of the tongue, have patient stick out tongue and move it internally from cheek to cheek.	Tongue weakness

Spinal Nerves

The spinal cord is composed of 31 pairs of spinal nerves: eight cervical, 12 thoracic, five lumbar, five sacral, and one coccygeal. Each spinal nerve has a ventral root and a dorsal root (Fig. 43-11).

The dorsal roots are sensory and transmit sensory impulses from specific areas of the body known as *dermatomes* (Fig. 43-12) to the dorsal ganglia. The sensory fiber may be somatic, carrying information about pain, temperature, touch, and position sense (proprioception) from the tendons, joints, and body surfaces; or visceral, carrying information from the internal organs.

The ventral roots are motor and transmit impulses from the spinal cord to the body, and these fibers are also either somatic or visceral. The visceral fibers include autonomic fibers that control the cardiac muscles and glandular secretions.

Autonomic Nervous System

The **autonomic nervous system** regulates activities of internal organs such as the heart, lungs, blood vessels, digestive organs, and glands. Maintenance and restoration of internal homeostasis is largely the responsibility of the autonomic nervous system. There are two major divisions: the **sympathetic nervous system**, with predominantly excitatory responses, most notably the "fight-or-flight" response, and the **parasympathetic nervous system**, which controls mostly visceral functions, known as "rest-and-digest."

The autonomic nervous system is regulated by centers in the spinal cord, brainstem, and hypothalamus. Its regulatory effects are exerted not on individual cells but on large expanses of tissue and on entire organs. The responses elicited do not occur instantaneously but after a lag period. These responses are sustained far longer than other neurogenic responses to ensure maximal functional efficiency on the part of receptor organs, such as blood vessels. The autonomic nervous system transmits its impulses by way of nerve pathways, enhanced by chemical mediators.

Sympathetic stimuli are mediated by norepinephrine, and parasympathetic impulses are mediated by acetylcholine. Both divisions produce stimulatory and inhibitory effects. Table 43-3 on page 1160 compares sympathetic and parasympathetic effects on different systems of the body.

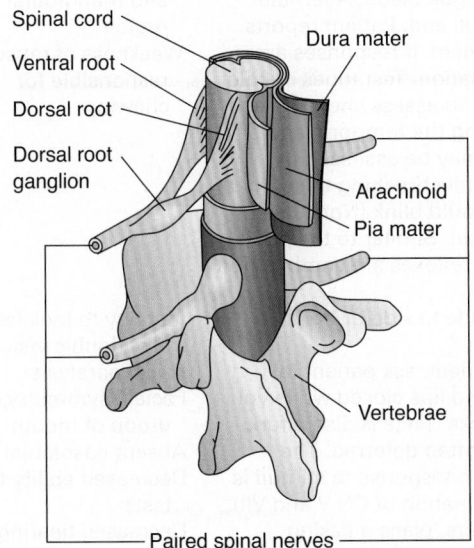

FIGURE 43-11 Spinal cord and meninges. From Porth, C. M. & Matfin, G. (2009). *Pathology: Concepts of altered health states* (8th ed.). Philadelphia: Lippincott Williams & Wilkins.

Spinal cord
Ventral root
Dorsal root
Dorsal root ganglion
Dura mater
Arachnoid
Pia mater
Vertebrae
Paired spinal nerves

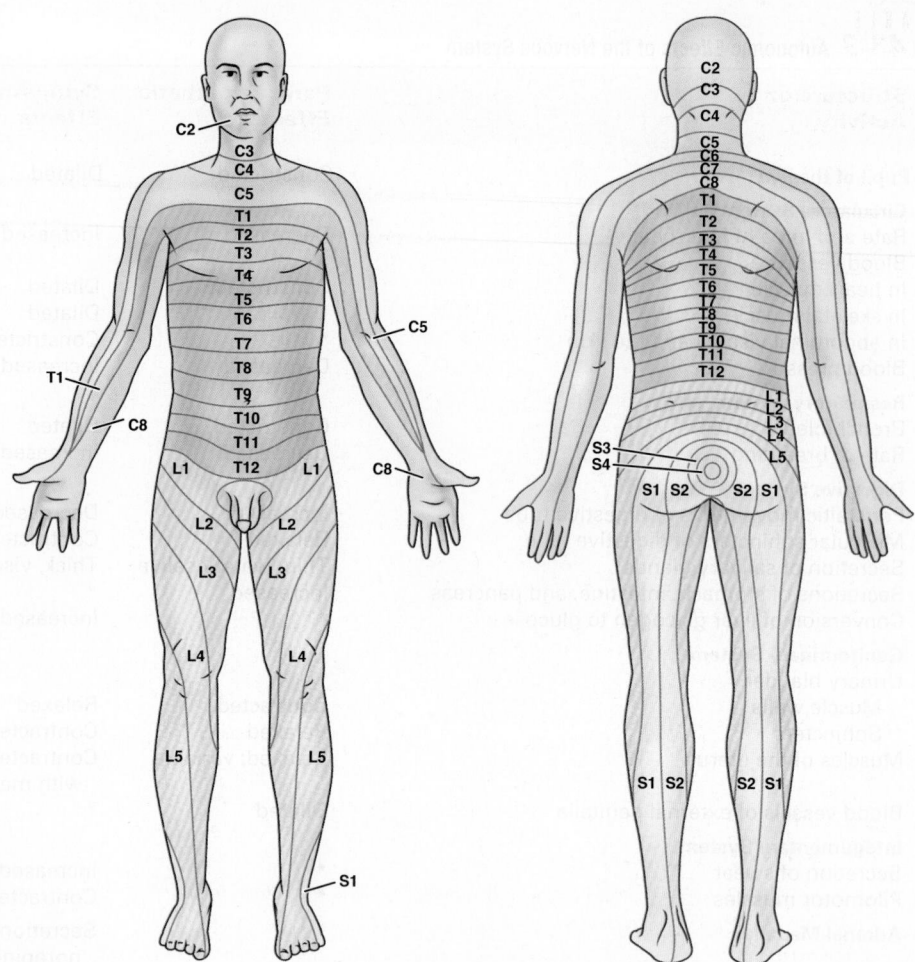

FIGURE 43-12 Dermatome distribution.

Motor and Sensory Functions of the Nervous System

Motor System Function

The motor cortex, a vertical band within each cerebral hemisphere, controls the voluntary movements of the body. The exact locations within the brain at which the voluntary movements of the muscles of the face, thumb, hand, arm, trunk, and leg originate are known (see Fig. 43-3). Stimulation of these cells results in muscle contraction. En route to the pons, the motor fibers converge into a tight bundle known as the *internal capsule*. A comparatively small injury to the capsule results in paralysis in more muscles than does a much larger injury to the cortex itself.

Within the medulla, the motor axons from the cortex form the corticospinal or pyramidal tracts. Here, most of the fibers cross (or decussate) to the opposite side. The remaining fibers enter the spinal cord on the same side as the direct pyramidal tract. All of the motor fibers of the spinal nerves represent extensions of the anterior horn cells, with each of these fibers communicating with only one particular muscle fiber. The motor system is complex, and motor function depends on the integrity of the corticospinal tracts, the extrapyramidal system, and cerebellar function.

Upper and Lower Motor Neurons

The voluntary motor system consists of two groups of neurons: upper motor neurons and lower motor neurons. Upper motor neurons originate in the cerebral cortex, the cerebellum, and the brainstem, where they cross over and descend throughout the corticospinal tract. Their fibers make up the descending motor pathways, are located entirely within the CNS, and modulate the activity of the lower motor neurons. Lower motor neurons are located either in the anterior horn of the spinal cord gray matter or within cranial nerve nuclei in the brainstem. Axons of lower motor neurons in both sites extend through peripheral nerves and terminate in skeletal muscle at the myoneural junction. Lower motor neurons are located in both the CNS and the PNS. The clinical features of lesions of upper and lower motor neurons are discussed in Table 43-4.

Coordination of Movement

The smoothness, accuracy, and strength that characterize muscular movements are attributable to the influence of the cerebellum and the basal ganglia.

The cerebellum (see Fig. 43-2) is responsible for the coordination, balance, and timing of all muscular movements. Through the action of the cerebellum, the contractions of

TABLE
43-3 Autonomic Effects of the Nervous System

Structure or Activity	Parasympathetic Effects	Sympathetic Effects
Pupil of the Eye	Constricted	Dilated
Circulatory System		
Rate and force of heartbeat	Decreased	Increased
Blood vessels		
In heart muscle	Constricted	Dilated
In skeletal muscle	*	Dilated
In abdominal viscera and the skin	*	Constricted
Blood pressure	Decreased	Increased
Respiratory System		
Bronchioles	Constricted	Dilated
Rate of breathing	Decreased	Increased
Digestive System		
Peristaltic movements of digestive tube	Increased	Decreased
Muscular sphincters of digestive tube	Relaxed	Contracted
Secretion of salivary glands	Thin, watery saliva	Thick, viscid saliva
Secretions of stomach, intestine, and pancreas	Increased	*
Conversion of liver glycogen to glucose	*	Increased
Genitourinary System		
Urinary bladder		
Muscle walls	Contracted	Relaxed
Sphincters	Relaxed	Contracted
Muscles of the uterus	Relaxed; variable	Contracted under some conditions; varies with menstrual cycle and pregnancy
Blood vessels of external genitalia	Dilated	*
Integumentary System		
Secretion of sweat	*	Increased
Pilomotor muscles	*	Contracted (goose-flesh)
Adrenal Medulla	*	Secretion of epinephrine and norepinephrine

*No direct effect.
From Hickey, J. (2009). *Clinical practice of neurological and neurosurgical nursing* (6th ed.). Philadelphia: Lippincott Williams & Wilkins.

opposing muscle groups are adjusted in relation to each other to maximal mechanical advantage.

The basal ganglia play an important role in planning and coordinating motor movements and posture. Complex neural connections link the basal ganglia with the cerebral cortex. The major effect of these structures is to inhibit unwanted

TABLE
43-4 Comparison of Upper Motor Neuron and Lower Motor Neuron Lesions

Upper Motor Neuron Lesions	Lower Motor Neuron Lesions
Loss of voluntary control	Loss of voluntary control
Increased muscle tone	Decreased muscle tone
Muscle spasticity	Flaccid muscle paralysis
No muscle atrophy	Muscle atrophy
Hyperactive and abnormal	Absent or decreased reflexes

muscular activity; disorders of the basal ganglia result in exaggerated, uncontrolled movements.

Impaired cerebellar function, which may occur as a result of an intracranial injury or some type of an expanding mass, results in loss of muscle tone, weakness, and fatigue. Cerebellar signs, such as ataxia and incoordination, as well as CSF obstruction and compression of the brainstem may be seen. Signs of increased ICP, including vomiting, headache, and changes in vital signs and level of consciousness (LOC), are especially common when CSF flow is obstructed.

Destruction or dysfunction of the basal ganglia leads not to paralysis but to muscle rigidity, with disturbances of posture and movement. The patient tends to have involuntary movements. These may take the form of coarse tremors, most often in the upper extremities, particularly in the distal portions; athetosis (movement of a slow, squirming, writhing, twisting type); or chorea (spasmodic, purposeless, irregular, uncoordinated motions of the trunk and the extremities,

and facial grimacing). Disorders due to lesions of the basal ganglia include Parkinson's disease, Huntington's disease, and spasmodic torticollis.

Sensory System Function

Integrating Sensory Impulses

The thalamus, a major receiving and transmitting center for the afferent sensory nerves, is a large structure connected to the midbrain (see Fig. 43-4). The thalamus integrates all sensory impulses except olfaction. It plays a role in the conscious awareness of pain and the recognition of variation in temperature and touch. The thalamus is responsible for the sense of movement and position and the ability to recognize the size, shape, and quality of objects.

Receiving Sensory Impulses

Afferent impulses travel from their points of origin to their destinations in the cerebral cortex via the ascending pathways directly, or they may cross at the level of the spinal cord or in the medulla, depending on the type of sensation that is registered. Sensory information may be integrated at the level of the spinal cord or may be relayed to the brain. Knowledge of these pathways is important for neurologic assessment and for understanding symptoms and their relationship to various lesions.

Sensory Losses

Destruction of a sensory nerve results in total loss of sensation in its area of distribution. Transection of the spinal cord yields complete anesthesia below the level of injury. Selective destruction or degeneration of the posterior columns of the spinal cord is responsible for a loss of position and vibratory sense in segments distal to the lesion, without loss of touch, pain, or temperature perception. A lesion, such as a cyst, in the center of the spinal cord causes dissociation of sensation—loss of pain at the level of the lesion. This occurs because the fibers carrying pain and temperature cross within the cord immediately on entering; thus, any lesion that divides the cord longitudinally divides these fibers. Other sensory fibers ascend the cord for variable distances, some even to the medulla, before crossing, thereby bypassing the lesion and avoiding destruction.

Lesions affecting the posterior spinal nerve roots may cause impairment of tactile sensation, including intermittent severe pain that is referred to the area of distribution. Tingling of the fingers and the toes can be a prominent symptom of spinal cord disease, presumably due to degenerative changes in the sensory fibers that extend to the thalamus (i.e., belonging to the spinothalamic tract).

Gerontologic Considerations

During the normal aging process, the nervous system undergoes many changes, and it is extremely vulnerable to general systemic illness. Changes throughout the nervous system that occur with age vary in degree. Nerve fibers that con-

TABLE
43-5  **GERONTOLOGICAL CONSIDERATIONS / Age-Related Changes in the Neurological System**

Structural changes	Brain weight decreases Loss of neurons in the brain Reduced cerebral blood flow Decreased myelin resulting in decreased nerve conduction in some nerves Decrease in muscle bulk Slowing in deep tendon reflexes Overall slowing of the autonomic and sympathetic nervous system Temperature regulation becomes less efficient Reduced pupillary response
Sensory changes	Atrophy of taste buds Degeneration of olfactory bulb Degeneration of nerve cells in vestibular system of inner ear, cerebellum, and proprioceptive pathways Stage IV sleep is decreased Presence of cataracts Dulling of tactile sensation

nect directly to muscles show little decline in function with age, as do simple neurologic functions that involve a number of connections in the spinal cord. Disease in the elderly often makes it difficult to distinguish normal from abnormal changes. It is important for clinicians not to attribute abnormality or dysfunction to aging without appropriate investigation. Pain in the absence of disease, for example, is not a normal part of aging and should be assessed, diagnosed, and treated. Table 43-5 summarizes structural changes.

Structural Changes

A number of alterations occur with increasing age. Brain weight decreases, as does the number of synapses. A loss of neurons occurs in select regions of the brain. Cerebral blood flow and metabolism are reduced. Temperature regulation becomes less efficient. In the PNS, myelin is lost, resulting in a decrease in conduction velocity in some nerves. There is an overall reduction in muscle bulk and the electrical activity within muscles. Taste buds atrophy, and nerve cell fibers in the olfactory bulb degenerate. Nerve cells in the vestibular system of the inner ear, cerebellum, and proprioceptive pathways also degenerate. Deep tendon reflexes can be decreased or in some cases absent. Hypothalamic function is modified such that stage IV sleep is reduced. There is an overall slowing of autonomic nervous system responses. Pupillary responses are reduced or may not appear at all in the presence of cataracts.

Motor Alterations

Changes in motor function often result in a flexed posture, shuffling gait, and rigidity of movement. These changes create difficulties for the older person in maintaining or recovering balance. Strength and agility are diminished, and reaction time and movement time are decreased. Repetitive movements and mild tremors may be noted during an examination and may be of concern to the person. Observation of gait may reveal a wide-based gait with balance difficulties.

Sensory Alterations

Sensory isolation due to visual and hearing loss can cause confusion, anxiety, disorientation, misinterpretation of the environment, and feelings of inadequacy. Sensory alterations may require modification of the home environment, such as large-print reading materials or sound enhancement for the telephone, as well as extra orientation to new surroundings. Simple explanations of routines, the location of the bathroom, and how to operate the call bell or light are just a few examples of information the elderly patient may need when hospitalized.

Temperature Regulation and Pain Perception

Other manifestations of neurologic changes are related to temperature regulation and pain. The elderly patient may feel cold more readily than heat and may require extra covering when in bed; a room temperature somewhat higher than usual may be desirable. Reaction to painful stimuli may be decreased with age. Because pain is an important warning signal, caution must be used when hot or cold packs are used. The older patient may be burned or suffer frostbite before being aware of any discomfort. Complaints of pain, such as abdominal discomfort or chest pain, may be more serious than the patient's perception might indicate and thus require careful evaluation. Two pain syndromes that are common in the neurological system in older adults are diabetic neuropathies and postherpetic neuropathies (refer to Chapters 30 and 52 for further information).

Taste and Smell Alterations

The acuity of the taste buds decreases with age; along with an altered olfactory sense, this may cause a decreased appetite and subsequent weight loss. Extra seasoning often increases food intake as long as it does not cause gastric irritation. A decreased sense of smell due to atrophy of olfactory organs may present a safety hazard, because elderly people living alone may be unable to detect household gas leaks or fires. Smoke and carbon monoxide detectors, important for all, are critical for the elderly.

Tactile and Visual Alterations

Another neurologic alteration in the elderly patient is the dulling of tactile sensation. There may be difficulty in identifying objects by touch, and because fewer tactile cues are received from the bottom of the feet, the person may become confused about body position and location.

These factors, combined with sensitivity to glare, decreased peripheral vision, and a constricted visual field, may result in disorientation, especially at night when there is little or no light in the room. Because the elderly person takes longer to recover visual sensitivity when moving from a light to dark area, night-lights and a safe and familiar arrangement of furniture are essential.

Mental Status

Mental status is evaluated when obtaining the history. Areas of judgment, intelligence, memory, affect, mood, orientation, speech, and grooming are assessed. Family members who bring the patient to the attention of the health care provider may have noticed changes in the patient's mental status. Drug toxicity should always be suspected as a causative factor when the patient has a change in mental status. **Delirium** (mental confusion, usually with delusions and hallucinations) is seen in elderly patients who have underlying CNS damage or are experiencing an acute condition such as infection, adverse medication reaction, or dehydration. Many elderly patients admitted to the hospital have delirium, and the cause is often reversible and treatable (e.g., drug toxicity, vitamin B deficiency, thyroid disease). Depression may produce impairment of attention and memory. In elderly patients, delirium, which is an acute change in mental status attributable to a treatable medical problem, must be differentiated from dementia, which is a chronic and irreversible deterioration of cognitive status.

Nursing Implications

Nursing care for patients with age-related changes to the nervous system and for patients with long-term neurologic disability who are aging should include the previously described modifications. In addition, the consequences of any neurologic deficit and its impact on overall function such as activities of daily living, use of assistive devices, and individual coping should be assessed and considered in planning patient care.

Patient teaching is also affected, because the nurse must understand the altered responses and the changing needs of the elderly patient before beginning to teach. When caring for the elderly patient, the nurse adapts activities such as preoperative teaching, diet therapy, and instruction about new medications, their timing, and doses to the patient's needs and capabilities. The nurse considers the presence of decline in fine motor movement and failing vision. When using visual materials for teaching or menu selection, adequate lighting without glare, contrasting colors, and large print are used to offset visual difficulties caused by rigidity and opacity of the lens in the eye and slower pupillary reaction.

Even with hearing loss, the elderly patient often hears adequately if the speaker uses a low-pitched, clear voice; shouting only makes it harder for the patient to understand

the speaker. Providing auditory and visual cues aids understanding; if the patient has a significant hearing or visual loss, assistive devices, a signer, or a translator may be needed.

Teaching at an unrushed pace and using reinforcement enhances learning and retention. Material should be short, concise, and concrete. Vocabulary is matched to the patient's ability, and terms are clearly defined. The elderly patient requires adequate time to receive and respond to stimuli, learn, and react. These measures allow comprehension, memory, and formation of association and concepts.

ASSESSMENT

Health History

The history-taking portion of the neurologic assessment is critical and, in many cases of neurologic disease, leads to an accurate diagnosis. The initial interview provides an excellent opportunity to systematically explore the patient's current condition and related events while simultaneously observing overall appearance, mental status, posture, movement, and affect. Depending on the patient's condition, the nurse may need to rely on yes-or-no answers to questions, a review of the medical record, or input from the family or a combination of these.

Common Complaints

An important aspect of the neurologic assessment is the history of the present illness. Neurologic disease may be acute or progressive, characterized by symptom-free periods as well as fluctuations in symptoms. The nurse therefore asks about the onset, character, severity, location, duration, and frequency of symptoms and signs; associated complaints; precipitating, aggravating, and relieving factors; progression, remission, and exacerbation; and the presence or absence of similar symptoms among family members.

The clinical manifestations of neurologic disease are as varied as the disease processes themselves. Symptoms may be subtle or intense, fluctuating or permanent, inconvenient or devastating. An introduction to some of the most common symptoms associated with neurologic disease is given in this chapter. Detailed discussions regarding how specific symptoms relate to a particular disorder are covered in later chapters in this unit.

Pain

Pain is considered an unpleasant sensory perception and emotional experience associated with actual or potential tissue damage or described in terms of such damage. Pain is therefore considered multidimensional and entirely subjective. Pain can be acute or chronic. In general, acute pain lasts for a relatively short period of time and remits as the pathology resolves. In neurologic disease, this type of pain is often associated with spinal disc disease, trigeminal neuralgia, or other neuropathic pathology (e.g., postherpetic neuralgia or

painful neuropathies). In contrast, chronic or persistent pain extends for long periods of time and may represent a low level of pathology. This type of pain can occur with many degenerative and chronic neurologic conditions (e.g., cerebral palsy).

Headache and Migraine

Headache, or cephalgia, is one of the most common of all human physical complaints. Headache is a symptom rather than a disease entity; it may indicate organic disease (neurologic or other disease), a stress response, vasodilation (migraine), skeletal muscle tension (tension headache), or a combination of factors. A **primary headache** is one for which no organic cause can be identified. These types of headache include migraine, tension-type, and cluster headaches. **Migraine headache** is characterized by periodic and recurrent attacks of severe headaches lasting from 4 to 72 hours in adults. The cause of migraine has not been clearly demonstrated, but it is primarily a vascular disturbance that occurs more commonly in women and has a strong familial tendency. The typical time of onset is at puberty, and the incidence is highest in adults 20 to 35 years of age. Migraine headaches may occur with or without an aura (a sensation that precedes the headache); however, most patients do not exhibit auras.

A **secondary headache** is a symptom associated with an organic cause, such as a brain tumor or an aneurysm. Although most headaches do not indicate serious disease, persistent headaches require further investigation. Serious disorders related to headache include brain tumors, subarachnoid hemorrhage, stroke, severe hypertension, meningitis, and head injuries.

Temporal arteritis is a cause of headache in the older population, reaching its greatest incidence in those older than 70 years of age. Inflammation of the cranial arteries is characterized by a severe headache localized in the region of the temporal arteries. The inflammation may be generalized (in which case temporal arteritis is part of a vascular disease) or focal (in which case only the cranial arteries are involved) and may be associated with visual loss.

Seizures

Seizures are the result of abnormal paroxysmal discharges in the cerebral cortex, which then manifest as an alteration in sensation, behavior, movement, perception, or consciousness. The alteration may be short, such as in a blank stare that lasts only a second, or of longer duration, such as a tonic-clonic seizure that can last several minutes. The type of seizure activity is a direct result of the area of the brain affected. Seizures can occur as isolated events, such as when induced by a high fever, alcohol or drug withdrawal, or hypoglycemia. A seizure may also be the first obvious sign of a brain lesion.

Dizziness and Vertigo

Dizziness is an abnormal sensation of imbalance or movement. It is fairly common in the elderly and one of the most

common complaints encountered by health professionals. Dizziness can occur as a result of a variety of medical conditions that include viral syndromes, hypotension, cardiac arrhythmia, hypoglycemia, and middle ear infections, to name a few. One difficulty confronting health care providers when assessing dizziness is the vague and varied terms patients use to describe the sensation.

About 50% of all patients with dizziness have **vertigo**, which is defined as an illusion of movement, usually rotation. Vertigo is usually a manifestation of vestibular dysfunction. It can be so severe as to result in spatial disorientation, light-headedness, loss of equilibrium (staggering), and nausea and vomiting.

Visual Disturbances

Visual defects that cause people to seek health care can range from the decreased visual acuity associated with aging to sudden blindness caused by acute glaucoma. Normal vision depends on functioning visual pathways through the retina and optic chiasm and the radiations into the visual cortex in the occipital lobes. Lesions of the eye itself (e.g., cataract), lesions along the pathway (e.g., tumor), or lesions in the visual cortex (from stroke) interfere with normal visual acuity. Abnormalities of eye movement can also compromise vision by causing diplopia or double vision.

Weakness

Weakness, specifically muscle weakness, is a common manifestation of neurologic disease. Weakness frequently coexists with other symptoms of disease and can affect a variety of muscles, causing a wide range of disability. Weakness can be sudden and permanent, as in stroke, or progressive, as in many neuromuscular diseases such as amyotrophic lateral sclerosis. Any muscle group can be affected.

Abnormal Sensation

Numbness, abnormal sensation, or loss of sensation is a neurologic manifestation of both central and PNS disease. Altered sensation can affect small or large areas of the body. It is frequently associated with weakness or pain and is potentially disabling. Both numbness and weakness can significantly affect balance and coordination.

Past History

A review of the medical history, including a system-by-system evaluation, is part of the health history. The nurse should be aware of any history of trauma or falls that may have involved the head or spinal cord.

Family History

The nurse may also use the interview to inquire about any family history of genetic diseases, such as Huntington's disease, dystonia, and epilepsy.

Social History

The nurse questions the patient regarding the use of alcohol, medications, and illicit drugs, and assesses for signs and symptoms of withdrawal. Additionally, the nurse is aware that certain agents, such as sedatives, analgesics, or neuromuscular blocking agents, may interfere with an accurate neurological assessment.

The nurse assesses the impact that any neurologic impairment has on the patient's lifestyle. Issues to consider include the limitations imposed on the patient by any deficit and the patient's role in society, including family and community roles. The plan of care that the nurse develops needs to address and support adaptation to the neurologic deficit and continued function to the extent possible within the patient's support system.

Physical Assessment

The neurologic examination is a systematic process that includes a variety of clinical tests, observations, and assessments designed to evaluate the neurologic status of a complex system. Although the neurologic examination is often limited to a simple screening, the examiner must be able to conduct a thorough neurologic assessment when the patient's history or other physical findings warrant it. An example of a simple screening tool for patients with head injury is the Glasgow Coma Scale (GCS; Table 43-6). A GCS score is based on three patient responses: eye opening, motor response, and verbal response. The patient receives a score for their best response in each of these areas, and the three scores are added together. The total score will range from 3 to 15; the higher the number, the better. A score of 8 or lower usually indicates coma.

The brain and spinal cord cannot be examined as directly as other systems of the body. Thus, much of the neurologic examination is an indirect evaluation that assesses the function of the specific body part or parts controlled or innervated

TABLE
43-6 Glasgow Coma Scale

Component	Response	Score
Best eye opening	Spontaneously	4
	To speech	3
	To pain	2
	No response	1
Best motor response	Obeys verbal command	6
	Localizes pain	5
	Nonpurposeful movement	4
	Flexion – abnormal	3
	Extension – abnormal	2
	No response	1
Best verbal response	Oriented	5
	Conversation – confused	4
	Speech – inappropriate	3
	Sounds – incomprehensible	2
	No response	1

by the nervous system. A neurologic assessment is divided into five components: cerebral function, cranial nerves, motor system, sensory system, and reflexes. As in other parts of the physical assessment, the neurologic examination follows a logical sequence and progresses from higher levels of cortical function, such as abstract thinking, to lower levels of function, such as the determination of the integrity of peripheral nerves.

Assessing Cerebral Function

Cerebral abnormalities may cause disturbances in mental status, intellectual functioning, and thought content, and in patterns of emotional behavior. There may also be alterations in perception, and motor and language abilities, as well as lifestyle.

Interpretation and documentation of neurologic abnormalities, particularly mental status abnormalities, should be specific and nonjudgmental. Lengthy descriptions and the use of terms such as *inappropriate* or *demented* should be avoided. Terms such as these often mean different things to different people and are therefore not useful when describing behavior. The examiner records and reports specific observations regarding orientation, LOC, emotional state, or thought content, all of which permit comparison by others over time. Analysis and the conclusions that may be drawn from these findings usually depend on the examiner's knowledge of neuroanatomy, neurophysiology, and neuropathology.

Level of Consciousness

The first cue to a change in the neurological function of a patient may be a change in the LOC, which is evaluated clinically as the patient's ability to respond appropriately to stimuli. It involves both wakefulness and cognition. The nurse compares current findings to previous patient baseline and notifies providers when any deterioration is noted. Rather than use terms like *stuporous* or *obtunded,* it is beneficial to describe the behavior in detail rather than use a broad term.

! NURSING ALERT

The major source of energy for the brain is glucose. Neurons of the brain are incapable of creating or storing glucose. The brain is therefore dependent on blood flow for brain glucose. When blood glucose drops because of insulin administration, patients exhibit signs of decreased mentation progressing to unconsciousness. If a patient has a history of diabetes or is receiving insulin treatment for other causes, the nurse should perform a glucose finger stick to assess blood glucose level when a change in the LOC is noted.

Mental Status

An assessment of mental status begins by observing the patient's appearance and behavior, noting dress, grooming, and personal hygiene. Posture, gestures, movements, facial expressions, speech, and motor activity often provide important information about the patient.

Assessing orientation to time, place, and person assists in evaluating mental status. Does the patient know what day it is, what year it is, and where he or she is? Is the patient aware of who the examiner is and of his or her purpose for being in the room?

Assessment of mental status also includes both long- and short-term memory, and the ability to concentrate and attend to tasks asked of them as well. A more detailed mental status assessment may also include assessment of an individual's ability to calculate as well as perform abstract reasoning such as "What would you do if you spotted a fire in your kitchen?"

Perception

The examiner may now consider more specific areas of higher cortical function. **Agnosia** is the inability to interpret or recognize objects seen through the special senses. The patient may see a pencil but not know what it is called or what to do with it. The patient may even be able to describe it but not interpret its function. The patient may experience auditory or tactile agnosia as well as visual agnosia. Each of the dysfunctions implicates a different part of the cortex (Table 43-7).

Screening for visual and tactile agnosia provides insight into the patient's cortical interpretation ability. The patient is shown a familiar object and asked to identify it by name. Placing a familiar object (e.g., key, coin) in the patient's hand and having him or her identify it with both eyes closed is an easy way to assess tactile interpretation.

Motor Ability

Nurses assess cortical motor integration by asking the patient to perform a skilled act (comb hair, brush teeth). Successful performance requires the ability to understand the activity desired and normal motor strength. Failure signals cerebral dysfunction.

Language Ability

The person with normal neurologic function can understand and communicate in spoken and written language. Does the patient answer questions appropriately? Can he or she read a sentence from a newspaper and explain its meaning? Can the patient write his or her name or copy a simple figure that the examiner has drawn? A deficiency in language function is called *aphasia.* Different types of aphasia result from injury to different parts of the brain (Table 43-8).

TABLE 43-7 Types of Agnosia and Corresponding Sites of Lesions

Type of Agnosia	Affected Cerebral Area
Visual	Occipital lobe
Auditory	Temporal lobe (lateral and superior portions)
Tactile	Parietal lobe
Body parts and relationships	Parietal lobe (posteroinferior regions)

TABLE
43-8 Types of Aphasia and Region of Brain Involved

Type of Aphasia	Brain Area Involved
Auditory-receptive	Temporal lobe
Visual-receptive	Parietal-occipital area
Expressive speaking	Inferior posterior frontal areas
Expressive writing	Posterior frontal area

Assessing the Cranial Nerves

See Table 43-2 for assessment of the cranial nerves. Opposite sides of the face and neck are compared throughout the examination. The assessment of multiple cranial nerves may be combined, such as eye movement (CN III, IV, VI) and **dysphagia**, difficulty swallowing (CN IX, X, XII).

Examining the Motor System

A thorough examination of the motor system includes an assessment of muscle size, tone, and strength, coordination, and balance. The muscles are inspected, and palpated if necessary, for their size and symmetry. Any evidence of atrophy or involuntary movements (tremors, tics) is noted. Muscle **tone** (the tension present in a muscle at rest) is evaluated by palpating various muscle groups at rest and during passive movement. Resistance to these movements is assessed and documented. Abnormalities in tone include **spasticity** (increased muscle tone), **rigidity** (resistance to passive stretch), and flaccidity.

Strength

Assessing the patient's ability to flex or extend the extremities against resistance tests muscle strength. The function of an individual muscle or group of muscles is evaluated by placing the muscle at a disadvantage. The evaluation of muscle strength compares the sides of the body to each other.

Clinicians use a five-point scale to rate muscle strength. A 5 indicates full power of contraction against gravity and resistance or normal muscle strength; 4 indicates fair but not full strength against gravity and a moderate amount of resistance or slight weakness; 3 indicates just sufficient strength to overcome the force of gravity or moderate weakness; 2 indicates the ability to move but not to overcome the force of gravity or severe weakness; 1 indicates minimal contractile power (weak muscle contraction can be palpated but no movement is noted) or very severe weakness; and 0 indicates no movement. Distal and proximal strength in both upper and lower extremities is recorded.

NURSING ALERT

There are occasional situations in which weakness of the upper extremities may be so subtle that the nurse is unsure if weakness is present. In these situations, the pronator drift can help assess for weakness. The patient holds her arms out in front of herself with palms facing the ceiling. The patient is asked to hold the position and close her eyes for approximately 20 seconds. If pronation (turning inward of the palm or the arm) or a downward drift of an arm is noted, the limb is weak. A positive pronator drift is associated with upper motor neurons in the brain and spinal cord that control voluntary movement.

Balance and Coordination

Cerebellar influence on the motor system is reflected in balance control and coordination. Coordination in the upper and lower extremities is tested by having the patient perform rapid, alternating movements and point-to-point testing. Speed, symmetry, and degree of difficulty are noted.

Point-to-point testing for coordination of the upper extremities is accomplished by having the patient touch the examiner's extended finger and then his or her own nose. This is repeated with each arm several times. Coordination in the lower extremities is tested by having the patient run the heel down the anterior surface of the tibia of the other leg. Each leg is tested in turn. **Ataxia** is defined as incoordination of voluntary muscle action, particularly of the muscle groups used in activities such as walking or reaching for objects. The presence of ataxia or tremors (rhythmic, involuntary movements) during these movements suggests cerebellar disease.

The **Romberg test** is a screening test for balance. The patient stands with feet together and arms at the side, first with eyes open and then with both eyes closed for 20 to 30 seconds. The examiner stands close to reassure the patient of support if he or she begins to fall. Slight swaying is normal, but a loss of balance is abnormal and is considered a positive Romberg test.

Examining the Reflexes

The motor reflexes are involuntary contractions of muscles or muscle groups in response to abrupt stretching near the site of the muscle's insertion. Common reflexes that may be tested include the deep tendon reflexes (biceps, brachioradialis, triceps, patellar, and ankle reflexes, Fig. 43-13) and superficial or cutaneous reflexes (abdominal reflexes and plantar or **Babinski reflex**).

Deep Tendon Reflexes

The tendon is struck directly with a reflex hammer or indirectly by striking the examiner's digit with the hammer, which is placed firmly against the patient's tendon. Testing these reflexes enables the examiner to assess involuntary reflex arcs that depend on the presence of afferent stretch receptors, spinal synapses, efferent motor fibers, and a variety of modifying influences from higher levels.

GRADING. The absence of reflexes is significant, although ankle jerks (Achilles reflex) may be normally absent in older people. Deep tendon reflex responses are often graded on a scale of 0 to 4+. Box 43-1 depicts how to document reflexes using this scale. As stated previously, scale ratings are highly

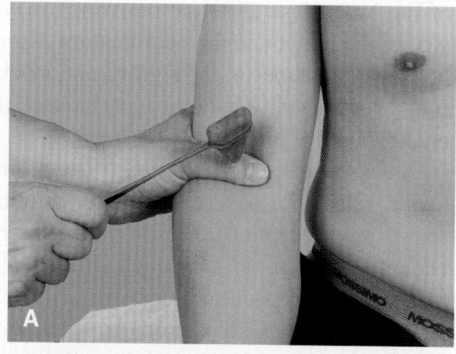
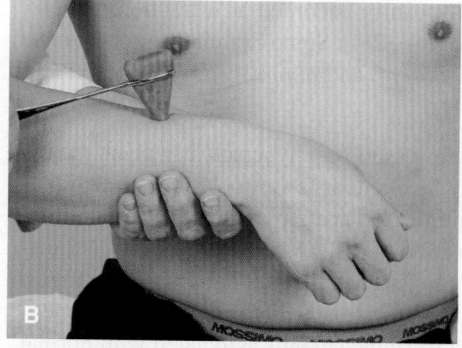
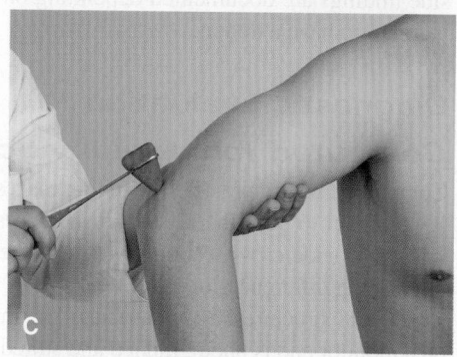
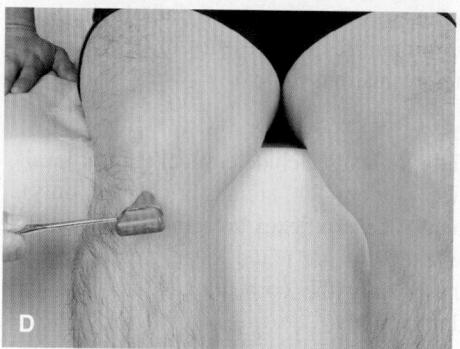
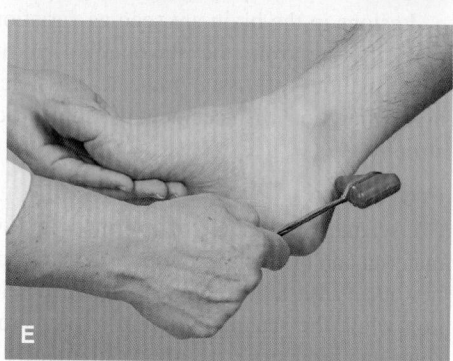

FIGURE 43-13 Deep tendon reflexes:
(**A**) biceps, (**B**) brachioradialis, (**C**) triceps,
(**D**) patellar, and (**E**) Ankles. From Rhoads, J.
(2006). *Advanced health assessment and
diagnostic reasoning.* Philadelphia: Lippincott
Williams & Wilkins.

Documenting Reflexes

Deep tendon reflexes are graded on a scale of 0 to 4:

0   No response
1+ Diminished (hypoactive)
2+ Normal
3+ Increased (may be interpreted as normal)
4+ Hyperactive (hyperreflexia)

The deep tendon responses and plantar reflexes are
commonly recorded on stick figures. The arrow points
downward if the plantar response is normal and upward
if the response is abnormal.

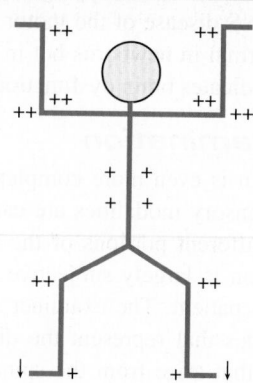

subjective. Findings can be recorded as a fraction, indicating the scale range (e.g., 2/4). Some examiners prefer to use the terms *present*, *absent*, and *diminished* when describing reflexes.

CLONUS. When reflexes are very hyperactive, a phenomenon called **clonus** may be elicited. If the foot is abruptly dorsiflexed, it may continue to "beat" two or three times before it settles into a position of rest. Occasionally, with CNS disease, this activity persists, and the foot does not come to rest while the tendon is being stretched but continues the repetitive activity. The unsustained clonus associated with normal but hyperactive reflexes is not considered pathologic. Sustained clonus always indicates the presence of CNS disease and requires further evaluation.

Superficial Reflexes

The major superficial reflexes include corneal, gag or swallowing, upper/lower abdominal, cremasteric (men only), plantar, and perianal. These reflexes are graded differently than the motor reflexes and are noted to be present (+) or absent (−). Of these, only the corneal, gag, and plantar reflexes are tested commonly.

The corneal reflex is tested carefully using a clean wisp of cotton and lightly touching the outer corner of each eye on the sclera. The reflex is present if the action elicits a blink. Conditions such as a stroke or coma might result in loss of this reflex, either unilaterally or bilaterally. Loss of this reflex indicates the need for eye protection and possible lubrication to prevent corneal damage.

The gag reflex is elicited by gently touching the back of the pharynx with a cotton-tipped applicator; first on one side of the uvula and then the other. Positive response is an equal elevation of the uvula and "gag" with stimulation. Absent response on one or both sides can be seen following a stroke and requires careful evaluation and treatment of the resultant swallowing dysfunction to prevent aspiration of food and fluids.

The plantar reflex, also known as the Babinski reflex, is elicited by stroking the lateral side of the foot with a tongue blade or the handle of a reflex hammer. In a person with an intact CNS, if the lateral aspect of the sole of the foot is stroked, the toes contract and draw together. However, in a person who has CNS disease of the motor system, the toes fan out. This is normal in newborns but in adults, the presence of babinski indicates brain dysfunction.

Sensory Examination

The sensory system is even more complex than the motor system, because sensory modalities are carried in different tracts located in different portions of the spinal cord. The sensory examination is largely subjective and requires the cooperation of the patient. The examiner should be familiar with dermatomes that represent the distribution of the peripheral nerves that arise from the spinal cord (see Fig. 43-12). Exceptions to this include major destructive lesions of the brain; loss of sensation, which may affect an entire side of the body; and the neuropathies associated with alcoholism, which occur in a glove-and-stocking distribution (i.e., over the entire hand or foot, in areas traditionally covered by a glove or sock).

Assessment of the sensory system involves tests for tactile sensation, superficial pain, vibration, and position sense (proprioception). During the sensory assessment, the patient's eyes are closed. Simple directions and reassurance that the examiner will not hurt or startle the patient encourage cooperation. Comparisons between the left- and right-side findings are documented depending on which modality is found to have a deficit.

Diagnostic Evaluation

Computed Tomography Scanning

Computed tomography (CT) scanning makes use of a narrow X-ray beam to scan the body part in successive layers. The images provide cross-sectional views of the brain, with distinguishing differences in tissue densities of the skull, cortex, subcortical structures, and ventricles. The image is displayed on a monitor and is photographed and stored digitally.

Lesions in the brain are seen as variations in tissue density differing from the surrounding normal brain tissue. Abnormalities of tissue indicate possible tumor masses, brain infarction, displacement of the ventricles, and cortical atrophy.

Procedure

CT scanning is usually performed first without contrast material and then with IV contrast enhancement. The patient lies on an adjustable table with the head held in a fixed position while the scanning system rotates around the head or spine and produces cross-sectional images. The patient must lie perfectly still without talking or moving, because motion distorts the image.

CT scanning is noninvasive and painless and has a high degree of sensitivity for detecting lesions. With advances in CT scanning, the number of disorders and injuries that can be diagnosed is increasing.

Nursing Interventions

Essential nursing interventions include preparation for the procedure and patient monitoring. Preparation includes teaching the patient about the need to lie quietly throughout the procedure. A review of relaxation techniques may be helpful for patients with claustrophobia.

Sedation can be used if agitation, restlessness, or confusion will interfere with a successful study. Ongoing patient monitoring during sedation is necessary. If a contrast agent is used, the patient must be assessed before the CT scan for an iodine/shellfish allergy, because the contrast agent is iodine-based. An IV line for injection of the contrast agent and a period of fasting (usually 4 hours) are required prior to the study. Patients who receive an IV or inhalation contrast

agent are monitored during and after the procedure for allergic reactions, kidney function, and other side effects, including flushing, nausea, and vomiting.

Positron Emission Tomography

Positron emission tomography (PET) is a computer-based nuclear imaging technique that produces images of actual organ functioning.

Procedure

The patient either inhales a radioactive gas or is injected with a radioactive substance that emits positively charged particles. When these positrons combine with negatively charged electrons (normally found in the body's cells), the resultant gamma rays can be detected by a scanning device that produces a series of two-dimensional views at various levels of the brain. This information is integrated by a computer and gives a composite picture of the brain at work.

PET permits the measurement of blood flow, tissue composition, and brain metabolism and thus indirectly evaluates brain function. The brain is one of the most metabolically active organs, consuming 80% of the glucose the body uses. PET measures this activity in specific areas of the brain and can detect changes in glucose use.

In addition, PET is useful in showing metabolic changes in the brain (Alzheimer's disease), locating lesions (brain tumor, epileptogenic lesions), identifying blood flow and oxygen metabolism in patients with strokes, evaluating new therapies for brain tumors, and revealing biochemical abnormalities associated with mental illness. The isotopes used have a very short half-life and are expensive to produce, requiring specialized equipment for production.

Nursing Interventions

Key nursing interventions include patient preparation, which involves explaining the test and teaching the patient about inhalation techniques and the sensations (e.g., dizziness, lightheadedness, and headache) that may occur. The IV injection of the radioactive substance produces similar side effects. Relaxation exercises may reduce anxiety during the test.

Single Photon Emission Computed Tomography

Procedure

Single photon emission computed tomography (SPECT) is a three-dimensional imaging technique that uses radionuclides and instruments to detect single photons. It is a perfusion study that captures a moment of cerebral blood flow at the time of injection of a radionuclide. Gamma photons are emitted from a radiopharmaceutical agent administered to the patient and are detected by a rotating gamma camera or cameras; the image is sent to a minicomputer. This approach allows areas behind overlying structures or background to be viewed, greatly increasing the contrast between normal and abnormal tissue. It is relatively inexpensive, and the duration is similar to that of a CT scan.

SPECT is useful in detecting the extent and location of abnormally perfused areas of the brain, thus allowing detection, localization, and sizing of stroke (before it is visible by CT scan); localization of seizure foci in epilepsy; detection of tumor progression; and evaluation of perfusion before and after neurosurgical procedures. Pregnancy and breastfeeding are contraindications to SPECT.

Nursing Interventions

The nursing interventions for SPECT primarily include patient preparation and patient monitoring. Teaching about what to expect before the test can allay anxiety and ensure patient cooperation during the test. Premenopausal women are advised to practice effective contraception before and for several days after testing, and the woman who is breastfeeding is instructed to stop nursing for the time period recommended by the nuclear medicine department.

The nurse may need to accompany and monitor the patient during transport to the nuclear medicine department for the scan. Patients are monitored during and after the procedure for allergic reactions to the radiopharmaceutical agent.

Magnetic Resonance Imaging

Procedure

Magnetic resonance imaging (MRI) uses a powerful magnetic field to obtain images of different areas of the body. This diagnostic test involves altering hydrogen ions in the body. Placing the patient into a powerful magnetic field causes the hydrogen nuclei (protons) within the body to align like small magnets in a magnetic field. In combination with radiofrequency pulses, the protons emit signals, which are converted to images. An MRI scan can be performed with or without a contrast agent and can identify a cerebral abnormality earlier and more clearly than other diagnostic tests. It can provide information about the chemical changes within cells, allowing the clinician to monitor a tumor's response to treatment. It is particularly useful in the diagnosis of multiple sclerosis and can describe the activity and extent of disease in the brain and spinal cord. MRI does not involve ionizing radiation. At present, MRI is most valuable in the diagnosis of nonacute conditions, because the test may take up to an hour to complete.

Several newer MRI scanning techniques, including magnetic resonance angiography (MRA), diffusion-weighted imaging (DWI), perfusion-weighted imaging (PWI), and fluid attenuation inversion recovery (FLAIR), are becoming more widely used. The use of MRA allows visualization of the cerebral vasculature without the administration of an arterial contrast agent, but the clarity of the images is enhanced when a contrast agent is used. If an agent is used, kidney function must be assessed.

Nursing Interventions

Patient preparation should include teaching relaxation techniques and informing the patient that he or she will be able to talk to the staff by means of a microphone located inside

the scanner. Many MRI suites provide headphones, so that patients can listen to the music of their choice during the procedure.

Before the patient enters the room where the MRI is to be performed, all metal objects and credit cards (the magnetic field can erase them) are removed. This includes medication patches that have a metal backing; these can cause burns if not removed. No metal objects may be brought into the room where the MRI is located; this includes oxygen tanks, traditional ventilators, or even stethoscopes. The magnetic field generated by the unit is so strong that any metal-containing items will be strongly attracted and literally can be pulled away with such force that they fly like projectiles toward the magnet. There is a risk of severe injury and death; furthermore, damage to a very expensive piece of equipment may occur. A patient history is obtained to determine the presence of any metal objects (e.g., aneurysm clips, orthopedic hardware, pacemakers, artificial heart valves, intrauterine devices). These objects could malfunction, be dislodged, or heat up as they absorb energy. Cochlear implants will be inactivated by MRI; therefore, other imaging procedures are considered.

The patient lies on a flat platform that is moved into a tube housing the magnet. The scanning process is painless, but the patient hears loud thumping of the magnetic coils as the magnetic field is being pulsed. Because the MRI scanner is a narrow tube, patients may experience claustrophobia; sedation may be prescribed in these circumstances. Newer versions of MRI machines (open MRI) are less claustrophobic than the earlier devices and are available in some locations. However, the images produced on these machines are not optimal, and traditional devices are preferable for accurate diagnosis.

⚠ NURSING ALERT

For patient safety, the nurse must make sure no patient care equipment (e.g., portable oxygen tanks) that contains metal or metal parts enters the room where the MRI is located. The patient must be assessed for the presence of medication patches with foil backing (such as nicotine) that may cause a burn.

Cerebral Angiography
Procedure

Cerebral angiography is an X-ray study of the cerebral circulation with a contrast agent injected into a selected artery. Cerebral angiography is a valuable tool to investigate vascular disease, aneurysms, and arteriovenous malformations and is still considered the gold standard for diagnosing these entities.

Most cerebral angiograms are performed by threading a catheter through the femoral artery in the groin and up to the desired vessel. After the groin is shaved and prepared, a local anesthetic is administered to prevent pain at the insertion site and to reduce arterial spasm. A catheter is introduced

into the femoral artery, flushed with heparinized saline, and filled with contrast agent. Fluoroscopy is used to guide the catheter to the appropriate vessels. During injection of the contrast agent, images are made of the arterial and venous phases of circulation through the brain.

Nursing Interventions

The patient should be well hydrated, and clear liquids are usually permitted up to the time of a regular arteriogram. Before going to the X-ray department, the patient is instructed to void. The locations of the appropriate peripheral pulses are marked with a felt-tip pen. The patient is instructed to remain immobile during the angiogram process and is told to expect a brief feeling of warmth in the face, behind the eyes, or in the jaw, teeth, tongue, and lips, and a metallic taste when the contrast agent is injected.

Nursing care after cerebral angiography includes observation for signs and symptoms of altered cerebral blood flow. In some instances, patients may experience major or minor arterial blockage due to embolism, thrombosis, or hemorrhage, producing a neurologic deficit. Signs of such an occurrence include alterations in the level of responsiveness and consciousness, weakness on one side of the body, motor or sensory deficits, and speech disturbances. Therefore, it is necessary to observe the patient frequently for these signs and to report them immediately if they occur.

The injection site is observed for hematoma formation (a localized collection of blood), and an ice bag may be applied intermittently to the puncture site to relieve swelling and discomfort. Because a hematoma at the puncture site or embolization to a distant artery affects the peripheral pulses, these pulses are monitored frequently. The color and temperature of the involved extremity are assessed to detect possible embolism.

Myelography
Procedure

A myelogram is an X-ray of the spinal subarachnoid space taken after the injection of a contrast agent through a lumbar puncture. It outlines the spinal subarachnoid space and shows any distortion of the spinal cord or spinal dural sac caused by tumors, cysts, herniated vertebral disks, or other lesions. Water-based agents have replaced oil-based agents, and their use has reduced side effects and complications; these agents disperse upward through the CSF. Myelography is performed less frequently today because of the sensitivity of CT and MRI scanning.

Nursing Interventions

Because many patients have misconceptions about myelography, the nurse clarifies the explanation given by the provider and answers questions. The patient is informed about what to expect during the procedure and should be aware that changes in position may be made during the procedure. The meal that normally would be eaten before the procedure is omitted. A sedative may be prescribed to help the patient

cope with this rather lengthy test. Patient preparation for lumbar puncture is discussed later in this chapter.

After myelography, the patient lies in bed with the head of the bed elevated 30 to 45 degrees. The patient is advised to remain in bed in the recommended position for 3 hours or as prescribed by the physician. The patient is encouraged to drink liberal amounts of fluid for rehydration and replacement of CSF. The blood pressure, pulse, respiratory rate, and temperature are monitored, as well as the patient's ability to void. Untoward signs include headache, fever, stiff neck, **photophobia** (sensitivity to light), seizures, and signs of chemical or bacterial meningitis.

Noninvasive Carotid Flow Studies
Procedure

Noninvasive carotid flow studies use ultrasound imagery and Doppler measurements of arterial blood flow to evaluate carotid and deep orbital circulation. The graph produced indicates blood velocity. Increased blood velocity can indicate stenosis or partial obstruction. These tests are often obtained before arteriography, which carries a higher risk of stroke or death. Carotid Doppler, carotid ultrasonography, oculoplethysmography, and ophthalmodynamometry are four common noninvasive vascular techniques that permit evaluation of arterial blood flow and detection of arterial stenosis, occlusion, and plaques. These vascular studies allow noninvasive imaging of extracranial and intracranial circulation.

Nursing Interventions

When a carotid flow study is scheduled, the procedure is described to the patient. The patient is informed that this is a noninvasive test, that a hand-held transducer will be placed over the neck or orbits of the eyes, and that some type of water-soluble jelly is used on the transducer.

Electroencephalography
Procedure

An electroencephalogram (EEG) represents a record of the electrical activity generated in the brain. It is obtained through electrodes applied on the scalp or through microelectrodes placed within the brain tissue. It provides a physiologic assessment of cerebral activity.

The EEG is a useful test for diagnosing and evaluating seizure disorders, coma, or organic brain syndrome. Tumors, brain abscesses, blood clots, and infection may cause abnormal patterns in electrical activity. The EEG is also used in making a determination of brain death.

For a baseline recording, the patient lies quietly with both eyes closed. The patient may be asked to hyperventilate for 3 to 4 minutes and then look at a bright, flashing light for photic stimulation. These activation procedures are performed to evoke abnormal electrical discharges, such as seizure potentials. A sleep EEG may be recorded after sedation because some abnormal brain waves are seen only when the patient is asleep.

Nursing Interventions

To increase the chances of recording seizure activity, it is sometimes recommended that the patient be deprived of sleep on the night before the EEG. Antiseizure agents, tranquilizers, stimulants, and depressants should be withheld 24 to 48 hours before an EEG because these medications can alter the EEG wave patterns or mask the abnormal wave patterns of seizure disorders (Hickey, 2009).

The patient is informed that the standard EEG takes 45 to 60 minutes (12 hours for a sleep EEG). The patient is assured that the procedure does not cause an electric shock and that the EEG is a diagnostic test, not a form of treatment. An EEG requires patient cooperation and ability to lie quietly during the test. Sedation is not advisable, because it may lower the seizure threshold in patients with a seizure disorder and it alters brain wave activity in all patients. The nurse needs to check with the physician regarding the administration of antiseizure medication prior to testing.

Routine EEGs use a water-soluble lubricant for electrode contact, which at the conclusion of the study can be wiped off and removed by shampooing. Sleep EEGs involve the use of collodion glue for electrode contact, which requires acetone for removal.

Electromyography
Procedure

An electromyogram (EMG) is obtained by inserting needle electrodes into the skeletal muscles to measure changes in the electrical potential of the muscles and the nerves leading to them. The electrical potentials are shown on an oscilloscope and amplified so that both the sound and appearance of the waves can be analyzed and compared simultaneously.

An EMG is useful in determining the presence of neuromuscular disorders and myopathies. It helps distinguish weakness due to neuropathy (functional or pathologic changes in the PNS) from weakness resulting from other causes.

Nursing Interventions

The procedure is explained, and the patient is warned to expect a sensation similar to that of an intramuscular injection as the needle is inserted into the muscle. The muscles examined may ache for a short time after the procedure.

Lumbar Puncture and Examination of Cerebrospinal Fluid
Procedure

A lumbar puncture (spinal tap) is carried out by inserting a needle into the lumbar subarachnoid space to withdraw CSF. The test may be performed to obtain CSF for examination, to measure and reduce CSF pressure, to assess for infection, and to determine the presence or absence of blood in the CSF. Antibiotics may be administered intrathecally (into the spinal canal) in certain cases of infection or contrast injected for diagnostic purposes.

The needle is usually inserted into the subarachnoid space between the third and fourth or fourth and fifth lumbar vertebrae. Because the spinal cord divides into a sheaf of nerves at the first lumbar vertebra, insertion of the needle below the level of the third lumbar vertebra prevents puncture of the spinal cord.

A successful lumbar puncture requires that the patient be relaxed; an anxious patient is tense, and this may increase the pressure reading. CSF pressure with the patient in a lateral recumbent position is normally 70 to 200 mm H_2O. Pressures of more than 200 mm H_2O are considered abnormal.

A lumbar puncture may be risky in the presence of an intracranial mass lesion because ICP is decreased by the removal of CSF, and the brain may herniate downward through the tentorium and the foramen magnum. To avoid this complication, a CT scan must be done prior to the procedure for patients with a suspected intracranial mass. See Box 43-2 for nursing guidelines for assisting with a lumbar puncture.

BOX 43-2

Assisting With a Lumbar Puncture

A needle is inserted into the subarachnoid space through the third and fourth or fourth and fifth lumbar interface to withdraw spinal fluid.

Preprocedure
1. Determine whether written consent for the procedure has been obtained.
2. Explain the procedure to the patient and describe sensations that are likely during the procedure (i.e., a sensation of cold as the site is cleansed with solution, a needle prick when local anesthetic is injected).
3. Determine whether the patient has any questions or misconceptions about the procedure; reassure the patient that the needle will not enter the spinal cord or cause paralysis.
4. Instruct the patient to void before the procedure.

Procedure
1. The patient is positioned on one side (knee to chest position) at the edge of the bed or examining table with back toward the provider; the legs are flexed as much as possible to increase the space between the spinous processes of the vertebrae, for easier entry into the subarachnoid space.
2. A small pillow may be placed under the patient's head to maintain the spine in a horizontal position; a pillow may be placed between the legs to prevent the upper leg from rolling forward.
3. The nurse assists the patient to maintain the position to avoid sudden movement, which can produce a traumatic (bloody) tap.
4. The patient is encouraged to relax and is instructed to breathe normally, because hyperventilation may lower an elevated pressure.
5. The nurse describes the procedure step by step to the patient as it proceeds.
6. Using an aseptic technique, the provider cleanses the puncture site with an antiseptic solution and drapes the site.
7. The provider injects local anesthetic to numb the puncture site, and then inserts a spinal needle into the subarachnoid space through the third and fourth or fourth and fifth lumbar interspace.

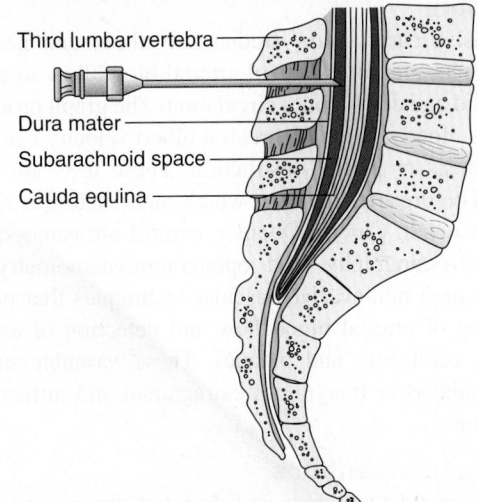

Third lumbar vertebra
Dura mater
Subarachnoid space
Cauda equina

8. A specimen of CSF is removed and usually collected in three test tubes, labeled in order of collection. A pressure reading may be obtained. The needle is withdrawn.
9. The provider applies a small dressing to the puncture site.
10. The tubes of CSF are sent to the laboratory immediately.

Postprocedure
1. Typically patients are instructed to rest in bed for a few hours after a lumbar tap, however a recent research review revealed no definite differences in the effects of bed rest of patients undergoing dural puncture (Sudlow & Warlow, 2010). The nurse should refer to institutional procedures for post procedure care.
2. Monitor the patient for complications of lumbar puncture; notify provider if complications occur:
   a. Common complications: Post–lumbar puncture headache, voiding difficulties, slight elevation of temperature, backache or spasms, stiffness of neck
   b. Rare complications: Herniation of intracranial contents, spinal epidural abscess, spinal epidural hematoma, meningitis
3. Encourage increased fluid intake to reduce the risk of postprocedure headache.

Cerebrospinal Fluid Analysis

The CSF should be clear and colorless. Pink, blood-tinged, or grossly bloody CSF may indicate a subarachnoid hemorrhage. Sometimes, with a difficult lumbar puncture, the CSF initially is bloody because of local trauma but then becomes clearer. Usually, specimens are obtained for cell count, culture, and glucose and protein testing. The specimens should be sent to the laboratory immediately because changes will take place and alter the result if the specimens are allowed to stand.

Post–Lumbar Puncture Headache

A post–lumbar puncture headache, ranging from mild to severe, may occur a few hours to several days after the procedure. This is the most common complication, occurring in 15% to 30% of patients. It is a throbbing bifrontal or occipital headache, dull and deep in character. It is particularly severe on sitting or standing but lessens or disappears when the patient lies down.

The headache is caused by CSF leakage at the puncture site. The fluid continues to escape into the tissues by way of the needle track from the spinal canal. It is then absorbed promptly by the lymphatics. As a result of this leak, the supply of CSF in the cranium is depleted to a point at which it is insufficient to maintain proper mechanical stabilization of the brain. This leakage of CSF allows settling of the brain when the patient assumes an upright position, producing tension and stretching the venous sinuses and pain-sensitive structures. Both traction and pain are lessened and the leakage is reduced when the patient lies down.

Post–lumbar puncture headache may be avoided if a small-gauge needle is used. If a patient complains of a headache post procedure, bedrest has demonstrated benefit (Sudlow & Warlow, 2010).

The postpuncture headache is usually managed by bed rest, analgesic agents, and hydration. Occasionally, if the headache persists, an epidural blood patch may be used. Blood is withdrawn from the antecubital vein and injected into the epidural space, usually at the site of the previous spinal puncture. The rationale is that the blood acts as a gelatinous plug to seal the hole in the dura, preventing further loss of CSF.

Other Complications of Lumbar Puncture

Herniation of the intracranial contents, spinal epidural abscess, spinal epidural hematoma, and meningitis are rare but serious complications of lumbar puncture. Other complications include temporary voiding problems, slight elevation of temperature, backache or spasms, and stiffness of the neck.

Chapter Review

Critical Thinking Exercises

1. A 68-year-old woman presents to your unit with complaints of weakness, headache, and lethargy. After completing the Glasgow coma scale, you are asked to perform assessment of her cranial nerves; identify what will be included in this assessment.

2. A 78-year-old patient with a history of chronic pain is admitted to the hospital to rule out an ischemic stroke and is scheduled for an MRI. Explain why the MRI is indicated and what, if any, precautions must be taken because this patient has chronic pain. What nursing observations and assessments are indicated because of the occurrence of these two disorders? What safety precautions are essential in the MRI suite, and why?

3. You are caring for a patient who is scheduled to undergo a lumbar puncture. How can you best assist and support the patient during the procedure? What laboratory studies would you expect to be ordered on the CSF sample? What postprocedure restrictions can you expect and prepare the patient for?

NCLEX-Style Review Questions

1. A patient is undergoing a cerebral angiography to rule out an aneurysm. When preparing the patient for the procedure, the nurse would include which of the following in her instructions?
   A. Expect a metallic taste when the contrast agent is injected.
   B. You will need a full bladder prior to the procedure.
   C. Maintain an NPO status.
   D. General sedation will be given prior to procedure.

2. The nurse is assisting with a lumbar puncture. The nurse understands that which of the following common complications can occur following the procedure?
   A. Post–lumbar puncture headache
   B. Herniation of intracranial contents
   C. Spinal epidural abscess
   D. Meningitis

3. A patient is scheduled for an EEG tomorrow. Which of the following information should the nurse provide to the patient prior to the procedure?
   A. Antiseizure medications need to be taken prior to procedure.
   B. Sedation will be given during the procedure.
   C. There is a slight chance of electric shock.
   D. Maintain a sleep-deprived state the night before procedure.

(continued on page 1174)

Chapter Review (continued)

4. A patient with Parkinson's disease is seen in the neurology clinic for treatment. The nurse identifies this disorder as being caused by a lack of which of the following neurotransmitters?
A. Acetylcholine
B. Dopamine
C. Serotonin
D. Gamma-aminobutyric acid (GABA)

5. The nurse is testing the cranial nerves of a patient diagnosed with myasthenia gravis. The nurse asks the patient to clench his jaw while she palpates the temporal and masseter muscles. The nurse is correctly testing which cranial nerve?
A. Abducens
B. Trigeminal
C. Acoustic
D. Hypoglossal

Try these additional resources to enhance your learning and understanding of this chapter:
- thePoint online resource available at **http://thepoint.lww.com/Pellico1e**
- *Handbook for Focus on Adult Health: Medical-Surgical Nursing*
- *Study Guide for Focus on Adult Health: Medical-Surgical Nursing*

References and Selected Readings

References and selected readings associated with this chapter can be found on the website that accompanies the book. Visit http://thepoint.lww.com/Pellico1e to access the references and other additional resources associated with this chapter.

JILL KELLER

Nursing Management: Patients With Oncologic Disorders of the Brain and Spinal Cord

Learning Objectives

After reading this chapter, you will be able to:

1. Describe the different types of brain and spinal cord tumors, including classification, clinical manifestations, diagnosis, and medical and nursing management.

2. Differentiate between primary and metastatic brain tumors.

3. Describe the symptoms and effects of increased intracranial pressure.

4. Describe the symptoms and effects of spinal cord compression.

PRIMARY BRAIN TUMORS

Primary brain tumors are localized intracranial lesions that begin in the brain and occupy space within the skull. The tumor is an abnormal growth of cells that forms a mass, but it also can grow diffusely. The effects of neoplasms (tumors or lesions), including seizure activity and focal neurologic signs, are caused by the compression or infiltration of tissue, or both. Tumors may be benign or malignant. Benign tumors are usually slow growing but can occur in a vital area, where they can grow large enough to cause serious effects. Malignant tumors are rapidly growing in nature, can spread into surrounding tissue, and are considered life-threatening. Primary brain tumors rarely spread to other areas of the body.

Oncologic (cancer) disorders of the brain include several types of neoplasms, each with its own biology, prognosis, and treatment options. Because of the unique anatomy and physiology of the central nervous system (CNS), this collection of neoplasms is challenging to diagnose and treat.

Types of Brain Tumors

There are many different types of brain tumors. They are classified into several groups: those originating within brain tissue (e.g., glioma), those arising from the coverings of the brain (e.g., dural meningioma), those developing in or on the cranial nerves (e.g., acoustic neuroma), and metastatic lesions originating from cancer elsewhere in the body. Tumors of the pituitary and pineal glands and of cerebral blood vessels are also considered types of brain tumors. Relevant clinical considerations when developing a plan of treatment include the location, size, histologic character of the tumor and if the tumor can be surgically removed.

Gliomas

Gliomas tumors are a type of intracerebral brain neoplasm. Gliomas are divided into many categories. (Box 44-1 lists the classification of these and other brain tumors). Glioblastoma multiforme (GBM) is the most common and aggressive malignant brain tumor (Chandana, Movva, Arora, & Sigh, 2008). In most all cases, a tissue biopsy, which can be obtained at the time of surgical removal, is needed to confirm the diagnosis. The grade of the tumor is based on cellular density, cell mitosis, and appearance. Usually,

Classification of Brain Tumors in Adults

I. Intracerebral Tumors
  A. Gliomas—infiltrate any portion of the brain:
   1. Astrocytomas (grades I and II)
   2. Glioblastoma multiforme (astrocytoma grades III and IV)
   3. Oligodendrocytoma (low and high grades)
   4. Ependymoma (grades I to IV)
   5. Medulloblastoma

II. Tumors Arising from Supporting Structures
  A. Meningiomas
  B. Neuromas (acoustic neuroma, schwannoma)
  C. Pituitary adenomas

III. Developmental Tumors
  A. Angiomas
  B. Dermoid, epidermoid, teratoma, craniopharyngioma

IV. Metastatic Lesions

these tumors form in the cerebrum and spread by infiltrating the surrounding neural connective tissue. Treatment for this type of tumor may include surgery, radiation therapy, and/or chemotherapy. Total surgical resection is difficult without causing considerable damage to vital structures, but it can improve survival time (Armstrong, 2009). The overall prognosis for this type of aggressive brain tumor is poor.

Meningiomas

Meningiomas are the most common brain tumor, representing 34% of all primary brain tumors (American Brain Tumor Association [ABTA], 2011). They are characterized as a benign, encapsulated, slow-growing tumor that occurs in people from 35 to 85 years of age. They are found more often in women (Central Brain Tumor Registry of the United States [CBTRUS], 2011). The tumor grows on the membrane covering of the brain, the meninges. Due to the slow-growing nature of this tumor, it is not uncommon that people die unaware they have a meningioma. Manifestations depend on the area involved and are the result of compression rather than invasion of brain tissue. Standard treatment is surgery with complete removal or partial dissection of the tumor.

Acoustic Neuromas

An acoustic neuroma (vestibular schwannoma) is a benign tumor of the eighth cranial nerve, the cranial nerve most responsible for hearing and balance. It usually arises within the internal auditory meatus. An acoustic neuroma may grow slowly and attain considerable size before it is correctly diagnosed. The patient usually experiences loss of hearing, tinnitus, episodes of vertigo and staggering gait. As the tumor becomes larger, painful sensations of the face may occur

on the same side, as a result of the tumor's compression of the fifth cranial nerve (trigeminal nerve) resulting in facial numbness (paresthesia) and pain. Diagnosis is suggested by unilateral sensorineural hearing loss; the Weber and Rinne test may be useful in assessing asymmetric hearing loss (refer to Chapter 48). Most acoustic neuromas can be surgically removed, or are suitable for stereotactic radiotherapy. When patients present with small tumors with limited symptomatology, treatment options may include observation over time since some tumors may not progress and may shrink in size.

Pituitary Adenomas

Pituitary tumors represent approximately 13% of all brain tumors (ABTA, 2011). They are slow growing in nature. A majority of these tumors are benign but, in rare cases, may be malignant. Pituitary tumors are classified as nonfunctioning and functioning. Nonfunctioning tumors do not produce hormones. Functioning tumors can produce one or more hormones, normally by the anterior pituitary. There are prolactin–secreting pituitary adenomas (prolactinomas), growth hormone–secreting pituitary adenomas that cause acromegaly in adults, and adrenocorticotropic hormone (ACTH)–producing pituitary adenomas that result in Cushing's disease. Pituitary adenomas are more common in women during the childbearing years. Amenorrhea is suggestive of a pituitary lesion (Khan, Turnbull, Rudralingam et al., 2009). Endocrine disorders resulting from these tumors are discussed in Chapter 31.

Pressure from a pituitary adenoma may be exerted on the optic nerves, optic chiasm, optic tracts, hypothalamus, or the third ventricle. Symptoms include headache, visual dysfunction, hypothalamic disorders (disorders of sleep, appetite, temperature, and emotions), and increased intracranial pressure (ICP). Surgery is the treatment of choice. However, depending on the tumor type, certain medications can be used to shrink the tumor. Radiation is used for recurring or persistent tumors.

Angiomas

Brain angiomas (masses composed largely of abnormal blood vessels) are found either in the brain or on its surface. They occur most often in the cerebellum. Some persist throughout life asymptomatically, while others cause symptoms of a brain tumor, such as seizures and headaches. Occasionally, the diagnosis is suggested by the presence of another angioma somewhere in the head or by a bruit (an abnormal sound) that is audible over the skull. Because the walls of the blood vessels in angiomas are thin, affected patients are at risk for hemorrhagic stroke. In fact, cerebral hemorrhage in people younger than 40 years of age should suggest the possibility of an angioma.

Cerebral Metastases

Metastatic (the spread of cancer cells from their primary site) lesions to the brain occur more often than do primary tumors (ABTA, 2011). Primary sites of cancer that commonly

metastasize to the brain include the lung and breast. This occurrence becomes important clinically as more patients with all forms of cancer live longer because of improved therapies.

Risk Factors

The cause of most primary brain tumors is unknown. The only known risk factors are exposure to ionizing radiation and cancer-causing chemicals. Additional possible risk factors that require further investigation include nonionizing radiation, physical and acoustic trauma, and dietary factors. There has been some suggestion that particular genetic syndromes may increase the risk for certain types of brain tumors (National Cancer Institute [NCI], 2009). However, the cause of the vast majority of brain tumors remains elusive.

The incidence of brain tumors appears to have increased in the past few decades. Epidemiologic data suggest that this is due to more aggressive and more accurate diagnosis rather than to an actual rise in incidence Better access to care and an increase in the aging population may contribute to the increase in rates. An estimated 64,530 new cases of primary brain (nonmalignant and malignant) and CNS tumors will be diagnosed in 2011. The incidence rate for primary brain

and CNS tumors is higher in females than males (CBTRUS, 2011).

Clinical Manifestations

Brain tumors can produce focal (localized) or generalized neurologic symptoms. Symptoms reflect either brain invasion, compression by the mass on adjacent structures, or increased ICP. The patient can experience seizures, nausea and vomiting, cognitive impairment, and visual disturbances. Additionally, specific signs and symptoms result from tumors that interfere with functions in specific brain regions. These focal symptoms may also include weakness, sensory loss, aphasia, visual dysfunction, and other manifestations related to specific neurological dysfunction because of localized involvement. Figure 44-1 indicates common tumor sites in the brain.

Increased Intracranial Pressure

Symptoms of increased ICP, which is discussed in Chapter 45, result from compression of the brain by the enlarging tumor or edema. Vasogenic (cerebral) edema plays a major role in symptoms related to an increase in mass. Edema can exceed the mass itself, creating increased pressure and disrupting local blood flow (Stummer, 2007). Symptoms often

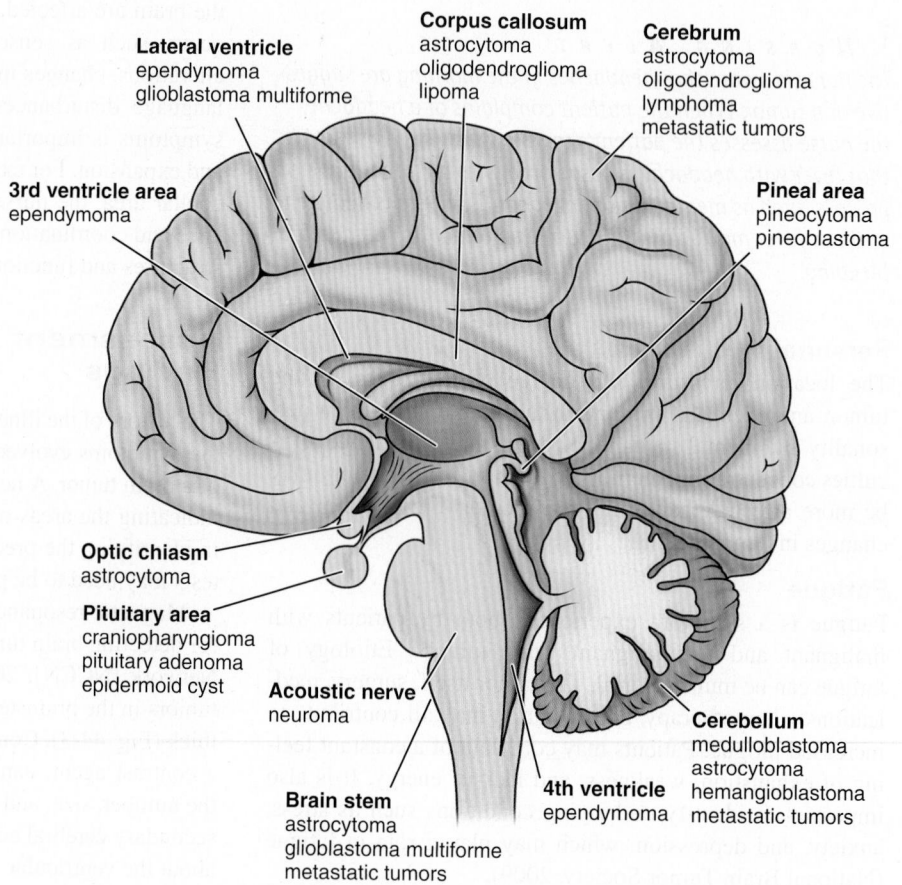

Lateral ventricle
ependymoma
glioblastoma multiforme

Corpus callosum
astrocytoma
oligodendroglioma
lipoma

Cerebrum
astrocytoma
oligodendroglioma
lymphoma
metastatic tumors

3rd ventricle area
ependymoma

Pineal area
pineocytoma
pineoblastoma

Optic chiasm
astrocytoma

Pituitary area
craniopharyngioma
pituitary adenoma
epidermoid cyst

Acoustic nerve
neuroma

Brain stem
astrocytoma
glioblastoma multiforme
metastatic tumors

4th ventricle
ependymoma

Cerebellum
medulloblastoma
astrocytoma
hemangioblastoma
metastatic tumors

FIGURE 44-1 Common brain tumor sites.

include headache, nausea with or without vomiting, and papilledema (edema of the optic disk) (Lee & Armstrong, 2008). Personality changes and a variety of focal deficits, including motor, sensory, and cranial nerve dysfunction, are common. The nurse remains alert for changes in the patient's level of consciousness (LOC) and notifies the primary care provider of any alterations in mental status. Late signs associated with rising ICP related to the vital signs include hypertension with a widening pulse pressure (the difference between systolic and diastolic pressure), bradycardia, and respiratory depression is termed Cushing's triad.

Headache

Headache, although not always present, is most common in the early morning and is made worse by coughing, straining, or sudden movement. Headaches may improve with vomiting. Headache is thought to be caused by the tumor's invading, compressing, or distorting the pain-sensitive structures or by edema that accompanies the tumor. Thus, headaches are related to intracerebral edema and increasing ICP; they do not appear to be directly related to tumor size (Palmieri, 2007). Headaches are usually described as deep or expanding or as dull but unrelenting. Frontal tumors usually produce a bilateral frontal headache; pituitary gland tumors produce pain radiating between the two temples (bitemporal); with cerebellar tumors, the headache may be located in the suboccipital region at the back of the head.

☀ N U R S I N G   A L E R T

The nurse is aware that headaches in the morning are suggestive of a tumor. When the patient complains of a headache, the nurse assesses the patient's temperature. The nurse knows that fever with headache is associated with an infectious process, such as meningitis or encephalitis, whereas headache without fever may be associated with a tumor or intracerebral bleeding.

Personality Changes

The location, pressure, and degree of infiltration of the tumor, and edema, if present, influence the changes in personality and mental status. The patient may experience difficulties concentrating, memory loss (short-term memory may be more affected than long-term memory), confusion, and changes in temperament.

Fatigue

Fatigue is a symptom experienced both by patients with malignant and nonmalignant brain tumors. Etiology of fatigue can be multifactorial. The tumor itself, surgery, medications, chemotherapy, and radiation may all contribute to increased fatigue. Patients may complain of a constant feeling of exhaustion, weakness, and lack of energy. It is also important to identify underlying conditions such as stress, anxiety, and depression, which may play a role in fatigue (National Brain Tumor Society, 2009).

Vomiting

Vomiting, seldom related to food intake, is usually the result of irritation of the vagal centers in the medulla. Forceful vomiting is described as *projectile vomiting.*

Visual Disturbances

Papilledema is associated with visual disturbances, such as decreased visual acuity, diplopia (double vision), and visual field deficits.

New Onset of Seizures

Seizures are episodes of abnormal motor, sensory, autonomic, or psychic activity (or a combination of these), which result from abnormal paroxysmal electrical discharges in the brain. They may be triggered by irritation of the brain directly by the tumor, by rising ICP, or by altered electrical potential in the brain (Palmieri, 2007). Approximately 50% of patients with brain tumors have seizures during their illness. Seizures may be the initial presenting symptom. The type and frequency of seizure vary, related to tumor size, site, and type. Simple partial seizures, complex partial seizures, and generalized tonic–clonic seizures are those more commonly seen (Palmieri, 2007).

Localized Symptoms

Common focal, or localized, symptoms are hemiparesis (weakness on one side of the body), seizures, and mental status changes (Palmieri, 2007). When specific regions of the brain are affected, additional local signs and symptoms occur, such as sensory and motor abnormalities, visual alterations, changes in hearing, alterations in cognition, and language disturbances. The progression of the signs and symptoms is important, because it indicates tumor growth and expansion. For example, if a tumor is present in the cerebellar area, the nurse might expect to see changes in balance and coordination. Figure 44-2 reviews specific cerebral structures and function.

Assessment and Diagnostic Findings

The history of the illness, the manner and time frame in which the symptoms evolved are key components in the diagnosis of a brain tumor. A neurologic examination can be helpful in indicating the areas of the CNS that are involved. To assist in identifying the precise location of the lesion, a battery of tests may need to be performed.

Magnetic resonance imaging (MRI) is the gold standard for detecting brain tumors (National Comprehensive Cancer Network [NCCN], 2009), particularly smaller lesions, and tumors in the brainstem and pituitary regions, where bone is thick (Fig. 44-3). Computed tomography (CT), enhanced by a contrast agent, can give specific information concerning the number, size, and density of the lesions and the extent of secondary cerebral edema. CT can also provide information about the ventricular system.

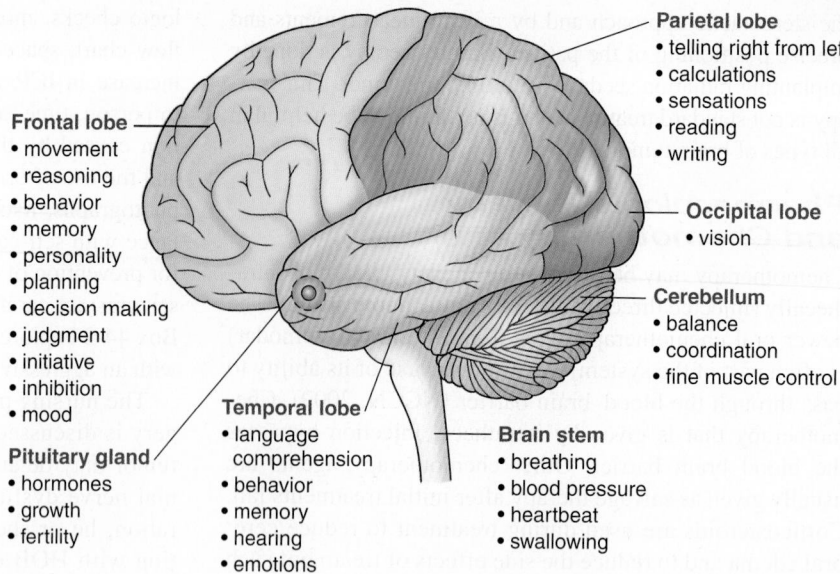

Frontal lobe
- movement
- reasoning
- behavior
- memory
- personality
- planning
- decision making
- judgment
- initiative
- inhibition
- mood

Pituitary gland
- hormones
- growth
- fertility

Temporal lobe
- language comprehension
- behavior
- memory
- hearing
- emotions

Parietal lobe
- telling right from left
- calculations
- sensations
- reading
- writing

Occipital lobe
- vision

Cerebellum
- balance
- coordination
- fine muscle control

Brain stem
- breathing
- blood pressure
- heartbeat
- swallowing

FIGURE 44-2 Brain structures and their function. Adapted with permission from *The essential guide to brain tumors*. National Brain Tumor Society (2010), page 9, http://www.braintumor.org/patients-family-friends/about-brain-tumors/publications/essentialguide.pdf.

Positron emission tomography (PET), which measures the brain's activity rather than simply its structure, is useful in differentiating tumor from scar tissue or radiation necrosis. Computer-assisted stereotactic (three-dimensional) biopsy is being used to diagnose deep-seated brain tumors. Cerebral angiography provides visualization of cerebral blood vessels and can localize most cerebral tumors.

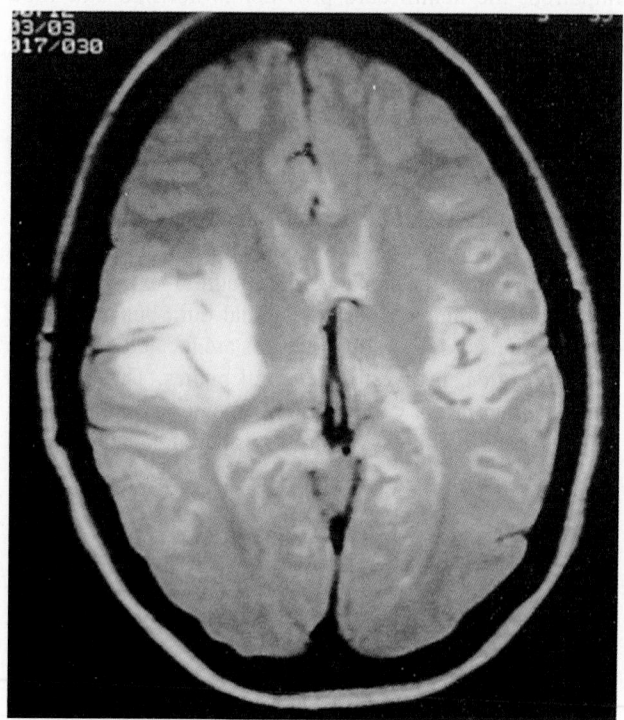

FIGURE 44-3 Low-grade glioma. Magnetic resonance imaging of the brain shows an abnormal density in the right temporal lobe. Courtesy of the Hospital of the University of Pennsylvania, Nuclear Medicine Section, Philadelphia, PA.

Cytologic studies of the CSF may be performed to detect malignant cells because CNS tumors can shed cells into the CSF.

Medical Management of Primary Brain Tumors

A variety of medical treatment modalities, including chemotherapy and external-beam radiation therapy, are used alone or in combination with surgical resection (Wen & Kesari, 2008). Depending on the type and the extent of the tumor, medical treatments may be done for symptom management purposes rather than to cure the patient of a brain tumor. This type of medical management is referred to as *palliative care* and will help improve the patient's quality of life when cure is not possible.

Surgical Management

Surgical intervention provides the best outcome for most tumor types. The objective of surgical management is removal of part of or the entire tumor without increasing the neurologic deficit. The surgical approach depends on the type of tumor, its location, and its accessibility. Options include stereotactic biopsy, open biopsy, craniotomy with debulking, and subtotal or gross total tumor resection (NCCN, 2009).

Radiation Therapy

Radiation therapy, the cornerstone of treatment for many brain tumors, decreases the incidence of recurrence of incompletely resected tumors. External-beam radiation therapy may be used alone or in combination with surgical resection. Stereotactic radiation therapy may be performed using a linear accelerator or gamma knife. These procedures allow treatment of deep, inaccessible tumors, often in a single session. Precise localization of the tumor is accomplished by

the stereotactic approach and by minute measurements and precise positioning of the patient. Brachytherapy is done by implanting radiation seeds close or into the tumor. This therapy is not standard treatment and is not found to be helpful in all types of brain tumors.

Pharmacologic Therapy and Chemotherapy

Chemotherapy may be given intravenously, orally, or intrathecally (injected directly into the subarachnoid space). The newer oral chemotherapy agent Temozolomide (Temodar) is often part of the systemic therapy because of its ability to pass through the blood–brain barrier (NCCN, 2009). Chemotherapy that is given by intrathecal injection bypasses the blood–brain barrier. Other chemotherapy agents are usually given as salvage therapy after initial treatments fail. Corticosteroids are used during treatment to reduce cerebral edema and to reduce the side effects of treatment such as nausea and vomiting. They are also helpful in relieving headache and alterations in level of consciousness. Antiseizure agents are used to treat seizures if they occur. Special consideration is given when managing seizures, related to a potential serious interaction between antiseizure medications and antineoplastic agents (Smith, 2010). Patients with brain tumors are at a higher risk for the development of deep vein thrombosis (DVT) and pulmonary embolism (PE). Careful consideration is taken when prescribing anticoagulant therapy due to the risk of CNS hemorrhage.

Pain is managed by means of a stepped progression with regard to the dosing, delivery method, and type of analgesic agents needed for relief. Headache is often a common complaint of pain in this population of patients. If the patient has severe pain, morphine can be infused into the epidural catheter placed as near as possible to the spinal segment where the pain is projected. Small doses of morphine are administered at prescribed intervals (refer to Chapter 7).

Medical Management of Metastatic Brain Cancer

The treatment of metastatic brain cancer is palliative and involves eliminating or reducing serious symptoms. Even when palliation is the goal, distressing signs and symptoms can be relieved, thereby improving the quality of life for both patient and family. The therapeutic approach includes radiation therapy, surgery (usually for a single intracranial metastasis), and chemotherapy. Gamma knife radiosurgery is considered if three or fewer lesions are present. Survival rates vary, depending the type and extent of the tumor at the time of diagnosis. The overall prognosis is poor in most cases.

Nursing Management

The effects of increased ICP caused by the tumor mass are reviewed in Chapter 45. The nurse performs neuro-

logic checks, monitors vital signs, maintains a neurologic flow chart, spaces nursing interventions to prevent a rapid increase in ICP, and reorients the patient when necessary to person, time, and place. Patients with changes in cognition caused by their lesions require frequent reorientation and the use of orienting devices (e.g., personal possessions, photographs, lists, and a clock). Supervision of and assistance with self-care, ongoing monitoring, and interventions for prevention of injury may be required. Patients who have seizures are carefully monitored and protected from injury. Box 44-2 explores the emotional impact of being diagnosed with an aggressive brain tumor.

The nursing process for patients undergoing neurosurgery is discussed in Chapter 45. The patient with a brain tumor may be at increased risk for aspiration due to cranial nerve dysfunction. If the patient is at risk for aspiration, he or she should be placed in a side-lying position with HOB elevated 10–30 degrees. The nurse must ensure that suction equipment is at the bedside. Preoperatively, the gag reflex and ability to swallow are evaluated by gently touching each side of the posterior pharyngeal wall with a cotton swab or suction catheter and noting the strength of the gag. The nurse expects to observe a simultaneous elevation of the uvula and "gag" with stimulation of the posterior pharynx. Function should be reassessed postoperatively because changes can occur because of alterations in cranial nerves IX (glossopharyngeal) and X (vagus) or the pons or medulla. If the gag reflex is impaired, the health care provider is notified and food and fluid are withheld until evaluation of swallowing is determined.

SPINAL CORD TUMORS

Tumors within the spine are classified according to their anatomic relation to the spinal cord. Intramedullary tumors arise from within the spinal cord. Intradural–extramedullary tumors are within or under the spinal dura but not on the actual spinal cord. Extradural tumors are located outside the dura and often involve the vertebral bodies. These tumors may be either primary or metastatic in nature. Spinal tumors causing cord compression are considered a neurological emergency.

Metastatic Spinal Cord Tumors

Cancer can spread to the spinal cord. The three most common cancers that metastasize to the spinal cord are breast, prostate, and lung. Cancer can invade the bone, causing vertebral metastases (Schiff, 2009).

Spinal Cord Compression

Spinal cord compression (SCC) occurs because of tumor extension into the epidural space. The cord can be compressed

BOX 44-2

Nursing Research

Bridging the Gap to Evidence-Based Practice

Identifying the Emotional Impact of Being Diagnosed With an Aggressive Brain Tumor

Lucas, M. R. (2010). Psychosocial implications for patients with a high-grade glioma. *Journal of Neuroscience Nursing, 42*(2), 104–108.

Purpose

Patients diagnosed with a high-grade glioma can experience a wide array of emotions— anxiety, fear of death, excessive worrying, insomnia, and difficulty concentrating. The purpose of this study was to identify the psychosocial implications experienced by patients to better educate providers and researchers about the patient's experience.

Design

The work was based on a qualitative study of data collected by a neuro-oncology social worker from hundreds of unstructured patient and group interviews between 2001 and 2008 in a large metropolitan outpatient brain tumor clinic. Interviews were conducted in the author's office or in an exam room to promote the least stressful environment in order to decrease anxiety. Reliability was measured by repetition of themes of loss.

Findings

The interviews identified three main themes: loss of independence, loss of self, and loss of relationship. Loss of independence included both physical and financial independence. The inability to drive, cognitive deficits, and weakness were identified as loss of independence. Patients who were no longer able to work and contribute income felt a loss of financial independence. Loss of self was defined as the loss of the qualities that defined the patient as an individual, which included loss of sense of humor and unique personality. Loss of relationships was expressed as the loss of ability to relate and share common interests with family and peers.

Nursing Implications

This study will help nurses working with this population of patients to identify not only the neurological changes that can occur in patients with high-grade brain tumors but also to be aware of the psychosocial implications that come with the diagnosis. Developing an understanding that patients may require psychological evaluations, counseling, and cognitive therapy will allow nurses to better recognize their patients' psychosocial needs.

---

at any area of the spine, resulting in permanent paralysis if not treated. Patients with myeloma or lymphoma, as well as those with breast, lung, prostate, or renal cancers, are at an increased risk for developing SCC. The nurse is alert for early complaints of back pain, which occurs in the region of the tumor. The pain typically increases when the patient is in the prone position (Colen, 2008). Early symptoms associated with SCC also include bladder and bowel dysfunction (urinary incontinence or retention; fecal incontinence or constipation). Later symptoms include evidence of motor weakness and sensory deficits progressing to paralysis. Radiological tests are used to diagnose SCC; MRI is considered the test of preference (Colen, 2008).

SCC is considered a medical emergency and requires immediate treatment to prevent permanent neurological damage. The treatment goal is to relieve cord compression with the use of IV steroids such as dexamethasone (Decadron) to reduce edema. Additionally, chemotherapy, radiation, or surgery to debulk the tumor is expected to preserve neurologic function. With early intervention, 75% to 100% of patients who were ambulatory before SCC remained so after therapy (Colen, 2008).

Assessment and Diagnostic Findings

Initial symptoms may present as radicular pain (pain that radiates along the dermatome [sensory distribution] of

a nerve), weakness, sphincter dysfunction, and sensory changes (Vaillant & Loghin, 2009). Neurologic examination and diagnostic studies are used to make the diagnosis. Neurologic examination includes assessment of pain, loss of reflexes above the tumor level, progressive loss of sensation or motor function, and the presence of weakness and paralysis. These changes in neurological function are related to the mass exerting pressure and compression of the nerve roots or spinal cord. MRI is the most commonly used diagnostic tool, detecting epidural SCC and metastases (Vaillant & Loghin, 2009).

Medical Management

Treatment of spinal cord tumors depends on the type, location of the tumor, the presenting symptoms, and physical status of the patient. Surgical intervention, if appropriate, is the primary treatment for most tumors. Other treatment modalities include partial removal of the tumor with decompression of the spinal cord. For metastatic lesions of the spine, radiation therapy can be used to decrease the size of the tumor. Because of the blood–brain barrier, chemotherapy for malignant spinal cord neoplasms is of limited benefit (Harrop & Ashwini, 2009). Dexamethasone is used temporarily to reduce edema and improve neurologic function until other treatments can take affect.

Tumor removal is desirable but not always possible. The goal is to remove as much tumor as possible while sparing

uninvolved portions of the spinal cord to avoid neurologic damage. Microsurgical techniques have improved the prognosis for patients with intramedullary tumors. Prognosis is related to the degree of neurologic impairment at the time of surgery, the speed with which symptoms occurred, and the origin of the tumor. Patients with extensive neurologic deficits before surgery usually do not make significant functional recovery, even after successful tumor removal.

Palliative care may be an option for the medical management of some patients. Relief from symptoms and pain control are the goal of care. Patients may receive palliative treatments such as radiation and then transition into hospice care when supportive treatments fail to control tumor growth. Other integrative (complementary/alternative) therapies consist of music, massage, Reiki, and guided imagery (Johnson & O'Brien, 2009).

Nursing Management

Providing Preoperative Care

The objectives of preoperative care include recognition of neurologic changes through ongoing assessments, pain control, and the management of altered activities of daily living (ADLs). The nurse assesses for weakness, muscle wasting, spasticity, sensory changes, bowel and bladder dysfunction, and potential respiratory problems, especially if a cervical tumor is present. The patient is also evaluated for coagulation deficiencies. Postoperative pain management strategies are discussed with the patient before surgery.

Assessing the Patient Postoperatively

The patient is monitored for deterioration in neurologic status. A sudden onset of neurologic deficit is an ominous sign and may be due to vertebral collapse associated with spinal cord infarction. Frequent neurologic checks are carried out, with emphasis on movement, strength, and sensation of the upper and lower extremities. Staining of the dressing may indicate leakage of CSF from the surgical site, which may lead to serious infection or to an inflammatory reaction in the surrounding tissues that can cause severe pain in the postoperative period (refer to Chapter 43 for evaluation of CSF leakage).

Managing Pain

The prescribed medication should be administered in adequate amounts and at appropriate intervals to relieve pain and prevent its recurrence. Early symptoms of spinal cord tumors include stiffness and pain that continues to worsen. Pain is the hallmark of spinal metastasis. Pain may increase in the recumbent position, which is not the case in degenerative joint disease (Huff, 2009). Bone pain at night is another concerning symptom for metastatic disease.

The bed is usually kept flat initially. The nurse turns the patient as a unit, keeping shoulders and hips aligned and the back straight. The side-lying position is usually the most comfortable, because this position imposes the least pressure on the surgical site. Placement of a pillow between the knees of the patient in a side-lying position helps to prevent extreme knee flexion.

Promoting Home and Community-Based Care

In preparation for discharge, the patient is assessed for the ability to function independently in the home and for the availability of resources such as family members to assist in care giving. Safety is a key component when arranging for home care. Patients with residual sensory involvement are cautioned about the dangers of extremes in temperature. They should be alerted to the dangers of heating devices (e.g., hot water bottles, heating pads, space heaters). The patient is taught to check skin integrity daily. Patients with impaired motor function related to motor weakness or paralysis may require training in ADLs and safe use of assistive devices, such as a cane, walker, or wheelchair.

The patient and family members are instructed about pain management strategies, bowel and bladder management, and assessment for signs and symptoms of neurologic dysfunction, which should be reported promptly.

Chapter Review

Critical Thinking Exercises

1. A 48-year-old man is married with two young children and has been newly diagnosed with a metastatic spinal cord tumor. The patient is scheduled to have surgery to debulk the tumor. What nursing assessments should be performed preoperatively? What postoperative nursing assessments should be performed? What assessments would alert the nurse of possible complications? What interventions can the nurse do to provide comfort pre- and postoperatively?

2. A 60-year-old patient with a history of lymphoma who has developed a new onset of low back pain is seen in the clinic. What pertinent questions should the nurse ask the patient that would aid in identifying the cause of the pain? Describe what nursing assessment is the priority. Identify deficits that would indicate that this is an urgent condition and why. What type of medication do you anticipate will be prescribed for this patient?

3. A 50-year-old patient has been recently diagnosed with a glioblastoma brain tumor. He had surgery several weeks ago and is now receiving chemotherapy. He is complaining of feeling exhausted and unable to do his normal work at home. What resources would you use to identify current guidelines for treatment of fatigue? How would this information help you develop a plan to educate your patient in lifestyle changes?

NCLEX-Style Review Questions

1. A patient admitted to the emergency room has a history of a spinal tumor. Which of the following signs and symptoms should alert the nurse to the possibility of SCC?
   A. Seizures
   B. Headache
   C. Back pain
   D. Diplopia

2. A patient with a decreased level of consciousness and an absent gag reflex was just admitted to the neurologic unit. In what position should the nurse place the patient?
   A. Prone
   B. Head of bed should be elevated 45–90 degrees
   C. Flat
   D. Side lying with head of bed elevated 10–30 degrees

3. Which of the following are late signs of rising ICP?
   A. Papilledema
   B. Change in the LOC
   C. Vomiting
   D. Hypertension

4. A nurse is caring for a patient who is 8 hours post surgery for a spinal cord tumor. Neurologic checks should include which of the following? Select all that apply.
   A. Movement of upper and lower extremities
   B. Monitoring sensation
   C. Bowel and bladder function
   D. Strength assessment

5. A patient has just been admitted to the hospital with a diagnosis of brain tumor. She makes a comment that drinking alcohol has caused her brain tumor. The nurse understands that which of the following is a cause of brain tumor?
   A. Smoking
   B. Ionizing radiation
   C. Diet high in fat
   D. Exposure to the sun

Try these additional resources to enhance your learning and understanding of this chapter:
- thePoint online resource available at
  http://thepoint.lww.com/Pellico1e
- *Handbook for Focus on Adult Health: Medical-Surgical Nursing*
- *Study Guide for Focus on Adult Health: Medical-Surgical Nursing*

References and Selected Readings

References and selected readings associated with this chapter can be found on the website that accompanies the book. Visit http://thepoint.lww.com/Pellico1e to access the references and other additional resources associated with this chapter.

TARA JENNINGS

Nursing Management: Patients With Neurologic Trauma

After reading this chapter, you will be able to:

1. Differentiate patients with head injuries according to mechanism of injury, clinical signs and symptoms, diagnostic testing, and treatment options.

2. Describe the multiple needs of the patient with altered level of consciousness.

3. Identify the early and late clinical manifestations of increased intracranial pressure (ICP).

4. Describe the management of the patient with increased ICP.

5. Identify the population at risk for spinal cord injury (SCI).

6. Identify common complications and management of complications in patients with SCI.

7. Use the nursing process as a framework for care of patients with SCI.

Trauma involving the central nervous system often can be life-threatening. Even when it is not life-threatening, brain and spinal cord injuries can result in major physical and psychological dysfunction and can alter the patient's life completely. Neurologic trauma affects the patient, the family, the health care system, and society as a whole because of its major sequelae and the costs of acute and long-term care of patients with trauma to the brain and spinal cord.

Ongoing assessment of the patient's neurologic function and health needs, identification of problems, mutual goal setting, development and implementation of care plans (including teaching, counseling, and coordinating activities), and evaluation of the outcomes of care are nursing actions integral to the recovery of the patient with neurologic trauma. The nurse also collaborates with other members of the health care team to provide essential care, offer a variety of solutions to problems, help the patient and family gain control of their lives, and explore the educational and supportive resources available in the community. The goals are to achieve as high a level of function as possible and to enhance the quality of life for the patient with neurologic trauma and his or her family.

HEAD INJURIES

Head injury is a broad classification that includes injury to the scalp, skull, or brain. It is the most common cause of death from trauma in the United States. Approximately 1.5 million people receive treatment for head injuries every year (Cekic & Stein, 2010). Of these, 1.1 million are treated and released by the emergency room, 235,000 are hospitalized, 80,000 have permanent disabilities, 60,000 develop seizure disorders, and 50,000 people die (Lettieri, 2008). Traumatic brain injury (TBI) is the most serious form of head injury. The most common causes of TBI are falls (28%), motor vehicle accidents (20%), collisions with stationary or moving objects (17%), and assaults (11%) (Brain Trauma Foundation, 2007). Males between 15 and 24 years old are at highest risk for TBI. The very young (<5 years) and the very old (>75 years) are also at increased risk. An estimated 5.3 million Americans today are living with a disability as a result of a TBI (Brain Trauma Foundation, 2007; Lettieri, 2008). Despite advances in care, only 40% of patients with severe TBI have good outcomes (Aarabi & Simard, 2009). The best approach to head injury is an emphasis on prevention (Box 45-1).

Health Promotion

Preventing Head and Spinal Cord Injuries

- Advise drivers to obey traffic laws, and to avoid speeding or driving when under the influence of drugs or alcohol.
- Advise all drivers and passengers to wear seat belts and shoulder harnesses.
- Caution passengers against riding in the back of pickup trucks.
- Advise motorcyclists, scooter riders, bicyclists, skateboarders, and roller-bladers to wear helmets.
- Promote educational programs that are directed toward violence and suicide prevention in the community.
- Provide water safety instruction.
- Teach patients steps that can be taken to prevent falls, particularly in the elderly.
- Advise athletes to use protective devices. Recommend that coaches be educated in proper coaching techniques.
- Advise owners of firearms to keep them locked in a secure area where children cannot access them.

Pathophysiology

Research has shown that not all brain damage occurs at the moment of impact. Damage to the brain from traumatic injury takes two forms: primary injury and secondary injury. Primary injury is the initial damage to the brain that results from the traumatic event. This may include contusions, lacerations, and torn blood vessels due to impact, acceleration/deceleration, or foreign object penetration (Porth & Matfin, 2008). Secondary injury evolves over the ensuing hours and days after the initial injury and can be due to cerebral edema, ischemia, seizures, infection, hyperthermia, hypovolemia, and hypoxia (Mittal, Vermani, Tweedie et al., 2009).

An injured brain is different from other injured body areas because of its unique characteristics. It resides within the skull, which is a rigid, closed compartment (Hickey, 2009). Unlike other areas of the body, the confines of the skull do not allow for the expansion of cranial contents. Any bleeding or swelling within the skull increases the volume of contents and therefore can cause increased **intracranial pressure** (ICP). If the increased pressure is high enough, it can cause **herniation** of the brain through or against the rigid structures of the skull. This causes restriction of blood flow to the brain, with resultant ischemia, infarction, irreversible brain damage, and, eventually, **brain death** (Box 45-2).

Skull Fractures

A skull fracture is a break in the continuity of the skull caused by forceful trauma. It may occur with or without damage to the brain. Skull fractures can be classified as simple, comminuted, depressed, or basilar. A simple (linear)

Focus on Pathophysiology

Traumatic Brain Injury

When the brain is injured, there is no room for swelling within the rigid cranial vault. Any bleeding or swelling causes an increase in the amount of intracranial contents, which in turn increases intracranial pressure (ICP). The increased pressure causes vasoconstriction and a decrease in blood flow to the brain. This causes hypoxia and ischemia of brain tissue. If ICP continues to rise, eventually the brain will herniate, causing brain death.

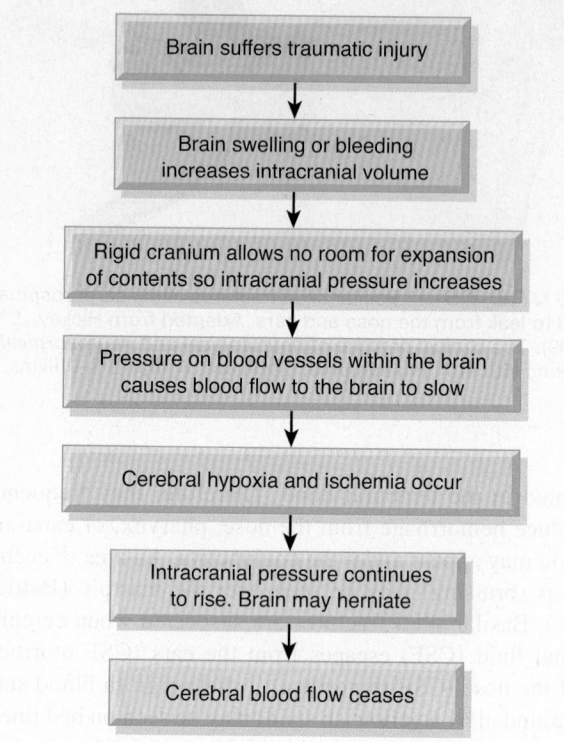

fracture is a break in the continuity of the bone. A comminuted skull fracture refers to a splintered fracture line. When bone fragments are embedded into brain tissue, the fracture is depressed. A fracture of the base of the skull is called a basilar or basal skull fracture (Fig. 45-1) (Porth & Matfin, 2008). A fracture may be open, indicating a scalp laceration or tear in the dura, or closed, in which case the dura is intact.

Clinical Manifestations

The symptoms, apart from those of the local injury, depend on the severity and the distribution of the underlying brain injury. Persistent, localized pain suggests that a fracture is present. Fractures of the cranial vault may or may not produce swelling in the region of the fracture.

Fractures of the base of the skull tend to traverse the paranasal sinus of the frontal bone or the middle ear

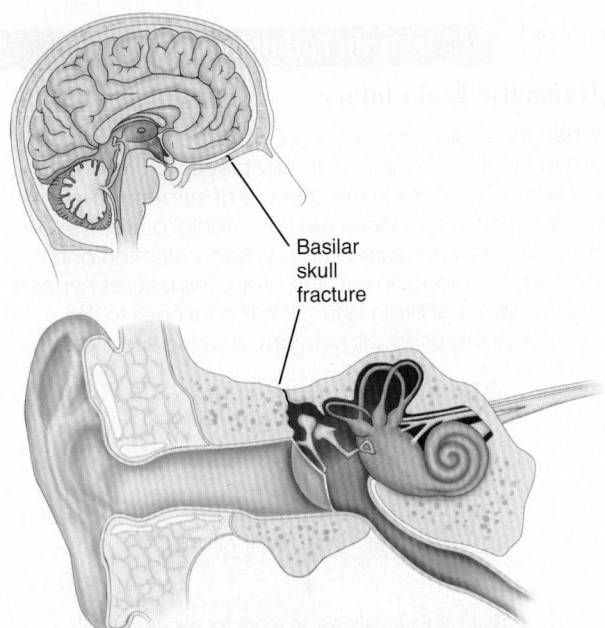

FIGURE 45-1 Basilar skull fractures allow cerebrospinal fluid to leak from the nose and ears. Adapted from Hickey, J. V. (2009). *The clinical practice of neurological and neurosurgical nursing* (6th ed.). Philadelphia: Lippincott Williams & Wilkins.

located in the temporal bone. Therefore, they frequently produce hemorrhage from the nose, pharynx, or ears, and blood may appear under the conjunctiva. An area of ecchymosis (bruising) may be seen over the mastoid (Battle's sign). Basilar skull fractures are suspected when cerebrospinal fluid (CSF) escapes from the ears (CSF otorrhea) and the nose (CSF rhinorrhea). A halo sign (a blood stain surrounded by a yellowish stain) may be seen on bed linens or on the head dressing and is highly suggestive of a CSF leak. Drainage of CSF is a serious problem, because meningeal infection can occur if organisms gain access to the cranial contents via the nose, ear, or sinus through a tear in the dura.

Assessment and Diagnostic Findings

Radiologic examination confirms the presence and extent of a skull fracture (Porth & Matfin, 2008). A rapid physical examination and evaluation of neurologic status detects obvious brain injuries, and a computed tomography (CT) scan uses high-speed X-ray scanning to detect less apparent abnormalities.

Magnetic resonance imaging (MRI) is used to evaluate patients with head injury when a more accurate picture of the anatomic nature of the injury is warranted and when the patient is stable enough to undergo this longer diagnostic procedure. See Chapter 43 for further discussion of CT and MRI.

Medical and Nursing Management

Nondepressed skull fractures generally do not require surgical treatment; however, close observation of the patient is essential. Nursing personnel may observe the patient in the hospital, but if no underlying brain injury is present, the patient may be allowed to return home. If the patient is discharged home, specific instructions must be given to the family.

Depressed skull fractures usually require surgery, particularly if contaminated or deformed fractures are present. Large defects can be repaired immediately with bone or artificial grafts; if significant cerebral edema is present, repair of the defect may be delayed for 3 to 6 months. Penetrating wounds require surgical débridement to remove foreign bodies and devitalized brain tissue and to control hemorrhage. IV antibiotic treatment is instituted immediately, particularly with a dural laceration, and blood products are administered if indicated.

As stated previously, fractures of the base of the skull are serious because they are usually open (involving the paranasal sinuses or the middle or external ear). CSF leakage is present in 15% to 20% of patients with skull base fractures (Mandrioli, Tieghi, Galie et al., 2008). Clear fluid that is draining from the nose or ears should be collected and tested for glucose. If the drainage is CSF, it will be positive for glucose. Suspicion of a CSF leak should be reported immediately to the provider.

The patient who is conscious is cautioned not to blow his or her nose if there is a CSF leak, as this can worsen the leak. The head is elevated 30 degrees to reduce ICP and promote spontaneous closure of the leak (Hickey, 2009). Early detection of a CSF leak may help avoid complications, including meningitis or pneumocephalus (air within the cranial vault). The patient with a basal skull fracture should not have the nose suctioned. Tears of the dura (protective covering directly on top of the brain) are commonly seen in basal skull fractures. A suction catheter is a potential source of infection and may lead to the development of meningitis. Early CSF rhinorrhea (resolving within 3 to 5 days) usually does not require surgery. Late-onset (7 or more days after the initial injury) and persistent CSF rhinorrhea usually requires surgical intervention to prevent development of meningitis. CSF otorrhea typically does not require surgical treatment (Mandrioli et al., 2008).

NURSING ALERT

Any patient with extensive facial fractures or suspected basilar skull fracture may also have a fracture of the cribriform plate (portion of the ethmoid bone that separates the roof of the nose from the cranial cavity). Attempted intubation with a nasogastric tube or nasotracheal tube or suctioning is prohibited to avoid intracranial penetration of the brain with the tube or catheter.

Focused Assessment

Traumatic Brain Injury

Be on alert for the following signs and symptoms:
- Altered LOC
- Confusion
- Pupillary abnormalities (changes in shape, size, and response to light)
- Sudden onset of neurologic deficits
- Changes in vital signs (altered respiratory pattern, widened pulse pressure, bradycardia, tachycardia, hypothermia or hyperthermia)
- Vision and hearing impairment
- Sensory dysfunction
- Headache
- Seizures

Patient and Family Education

Teaching Guidelines Following Concussion

Once the patient is discharged home, he or she should be closely observed for the next 24 hours, and awakened every 2 hours. The patient and family are instructed to observe for the following signs and symptoms and to notify the provider (or bring the patient to the emergency department) if they occur:
- Difficulty in awakening
- Difficulty speaking
- Confusion
- Seizures
- Severe headache
- Vomiting
- Weakness on one side of the body

The patient should also avoid playing contact sports, driving, drinking alcohol, and using heavy machinery until cleared by a health care provider.

BRAIN INJURY

The most important consideration in any head injury is whether or not the brain is injured. Even seemingly minor injury can cause significant brain damage secondary to obstructed blood flow and decreased tissue perfusion. The brain cannot store oxygen or glucose to any significant degree. Because neurons need an uninterrupted blood supply to obtain these nutrients, irreversible brain damage and cell death occur if the blood supply is interrupted for even a few minutes. Clinical manifestations of **brain injury** (injury to the brain that is severe enough to interfere with normal functioning) are listed in Box 45-3. Closed (blunt) brain injury occurs when the head accelerates and then rapidly decelerates or collides with another object (i.e. a wall, the dashboard of a car) and brain tissue is damaged but there is no opening through the skull and dura. Open brain injury occurs when an object penetrates the skull, enters the brain, and damages the soft brain tissue in its path (penetrating injury), or when blunt trauma to the head is so severe that it opens the scalp, skull, and dura to expose the brain.

Types of Brain Injury

Concussion

A **concussion** (also referred to as a mild TBI) involves an alteration in mental status that results from trauma, and may or may not involve loss of consciousness. This typically lasts no longer than 24 hours and may include symptoms such as headache, nausea, vomiting, photophobia (sensitivity to light), amnesia, and blurry vision (McConnell & Shubrook, 2009).

Treatment involves observing the patient for symptoms including headache, dizziness, lethargy, irritability, anxiety, photophobia, phonophobia, difficulty concentrating, and memory difficulties. The occurrence of these symptoms after the injury is referred to as *postconcussive syndrome* (Dischinger, Ryb, Kufera et al., 2009). Giving the patient information, explanations, and encouragement may reduce

some of the problems associated with postconcussive syndrome. The patient is advised to resume normal activities slowly; the exact recovery time is not known (McConnell & Shubrook, 2009). Once the patient is discharged home, he or she should be closely observed for the next 24 hours, and awakened every 2 hours in order to detect any changes in mental status. Box 45-4 provides complete instructions given to the patient and the family. Neuroimaging (CT and MRI) is generally not indicated in concussion.

Contusion

A **cerebral contusion** is a more severe injury than concussion, involving bruising of the brain, with possible surface hemorrhage. The patient is unconscious for more than a few seconds or minutes. Clinical signs and symptoms depend on the size of the contusion and the amount of associated swelling of the brain (cerebral edema). The patient may lie motionless, with a faint pulse, shallow respirations, and cool, pale skin. The patient may be aroused with effort but soon slips back into unconsciousness. Blood pressure and temperature are subnormal, and the clinical picture is somewhat similar to that of shock. Patients may recover consciousness but pass into a stage of cerebral irritability. In this stage, the patient is conscious and easily disturbed by any form of stimulation, such as noises, light, and voices; he or she may become hyperactive at times.

> **NURSING ALERT**
> *When the patient begins to emerge from unconsciousness, every measure that is available and appropriate for calming and quieting the patient should be used. Any form of restraint is likely to be countered with resistance, leading to self-injury or to a dangerous increase in ICP. Therefore, physical restraints should be avoided, if possible.*

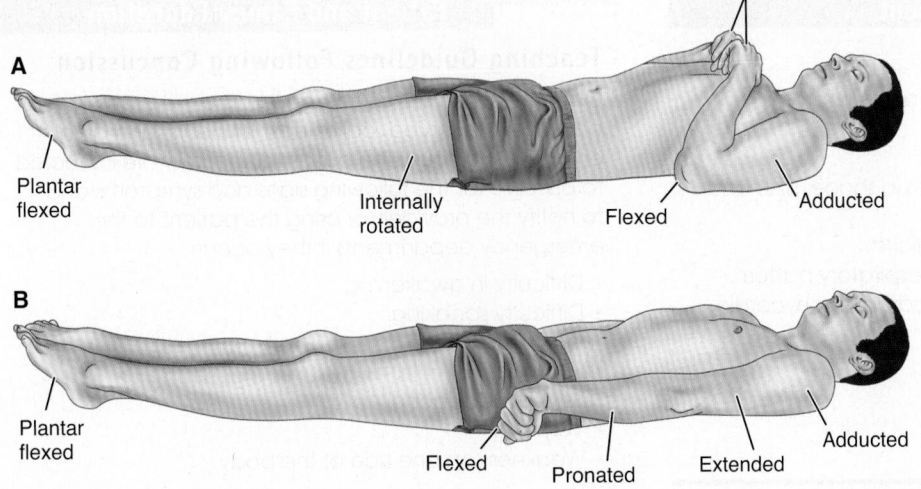

FIGURE 45-2 Abnormal posture response to stimuli. (**A**) Decorticate posturing, involving adduction and flexion of the upper extremities, internal rotation of the lower extremities, and plantar flexion of the feet. (**B**) Decerebrate posturing, involving extension and outward rotation of upper extremities and plantar flexion of the feet.

Gradually, the pulse, respirations, temperature, and other body functions return to normal, but full recovery can be delayed for months. Residual headache and vertigo are common, and impaired mental function or seizures may occur as a result of irreparable cerebral damage.

Diffuse Axonal Injury

Diffuse axonal injury involves widespread damage to axons in the cerebral hemispheres, corpus callosum, and brainstem. It can be seen with mild, moderate, or severe head trauma. The patient experiences immediate coma, global cerebral edema, decorticate and decerebrate rigidity, or *posturing* (Fig. 45-2). **Decorticate** posturing involves abnormal flexion of the upper extremities and extension of the lower extremities and indicates damage to the upper midbrain; **decerebrate** posturing involves extreme extension of the upper and lower extremities and indicates severe damage to the brain at the lower midbrain and upper pons (Barrett, Barman, Boitano et al., 2009). Diagnosis of diffuse axonal injury is made by clinical signs in conjunction with a CT or MRI scan. These tests are usually normal; a definitive diagnosis can only be made at autopsy. Recovery depends on the severity of the axonal injury.

Intracranial Hemorrhage (Intracranial Hematoma)

Hematomas (collections of blood) that develop within the cranial vault are the most serious type of brain injury (Hickey, 2009). A hematoma may be epidural (above the dura), subdural (below the dura), or intracerebral (within the brain) (Fig. 45-3). Major symptoms are frequently delayed until the hematoma is large enough to cause distortion of the brain and increased ICP. The signs and symptoms of cerebral ischemia resulting from compression by a hematoma are variable and depend on the speed with which vital areas are affected and the area that is injured (American Association of Neuroscience Nurses [AANN], 2005).

Epidural Hematoma (Extradural Hematoma or Hemorrhage)

After a head injury, blood may collect in the epidural (extradural) space between the skull and the dura. This can result from a skull fracture that causes a rupture or laceration of the middle meningeal artery, the artery that runs between the dura and the skull, inferior to a thin portion of temporal bone. Hemorrhage from this artery causes a rapid increase in pressure on the brain.

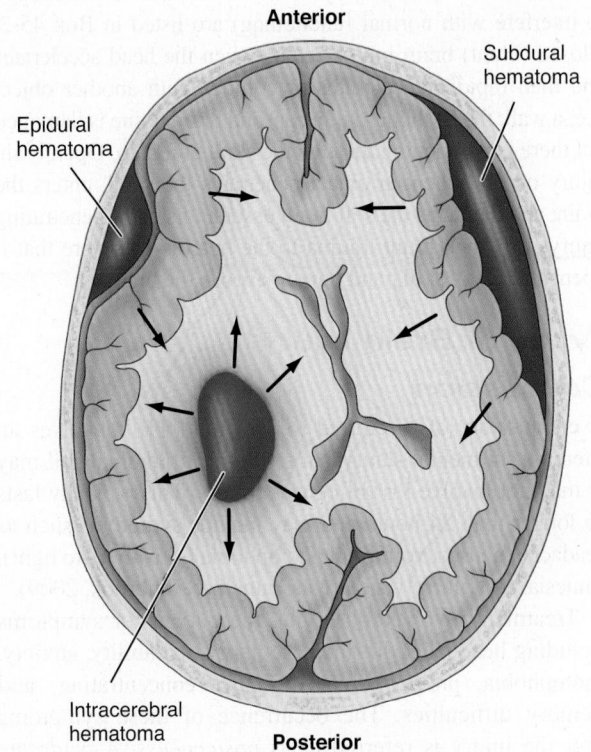

FIGURE 45-3 Location of epidural, subdural, intracerebral hematomas.

Symptoms are caused by the expanding hematoma. Usually a momentary loss of consciousness occurs at the time of injury, followed by an interval of apparent recovery (lucid interval). Although the lucid interval is considered a classic characteristic of an epidural hematoma, no lucid interval has been reported in many patients with this lesion (Hickey, 2009), and, therefore, it should not be considered a critical defining criterion. During the lucid interval, compensation for the expanding hematoma takes place by rapid absorption of CSF and decreased intravascular volume, both of which help maintain a normal ICP. When these mechanisms can no longer compensate, even a small increase in the volume of the hematoma produces a marked elevation in ICP. Then, often suddenly, signs of compression appear (usually deterioration of consciousness and signs of focal neurologic deficits, such as dilation and fixation of a pupil or paralysis of an extremity), and the patient's condition deteriorates rapidly.

An epidural hematoma is considered an extreme emergency; marked neurologic deficit and respiratory arrest can occur within minutes. Treatment consists of making openings through the skull (burr holes) to decrease ICP emergently, remove the clot, and control the bleeding. A craniotomy (surgical procedure that removes of part of the skull to gain access to the brain) may be required to remove the clot and control the bleeding. A drain may be inserted after creation of burr holes or a craniotomy to prevent reaccumulation of blood.

Subdural Hematoma

A subdural hematoma (SDH) is a collection of blood between the dura and the brain, a space normally occupied by a thin cushion of CSF (see Fig. 45-3). The most common cause of SDH is trauma, but it can also occur as a result of coagulopathies (bleeding disorders) or rupture of an aneurysm. The elderly are at increased risk for subdural hemorrhage secondary to whole brain atrophy. Box 45-5 is a discussion of the elderly and SDHs. SDHs can be acute, subacute, or chronic, depending on when the bleed occurred.

ACUTE AND SUBACUTE SUBDURAL HEMATOMA. Acute SDHs are associated with major head injury involving contusion or laceration. Clinical symptoms develop over 24 to 48 hours. Signs and symptoms include changes in the level of consciousness (LOC), changes in the reactivity of the pupils, and hemiparesis (weakness on one side of the body). There may be minor or even no symptoms, with small collections of blood. Coma, increasing blood pressure, decreasing heart rate, and slowing respiratory rate are all signs of a rapidly expanding mass requiring immediate intervention.

Subacute SDHs are the result of less severe contusions and head trauma. Clinical manifestations usually appear between 48 hours and 2 weeks after the injury. Signs and symptoms are similar to those of an acute SDH.

Subdural Hematomas

Subdural hematomas (SDHs) are more common in the elderly, occurring most often in patients in their 60s and 70s. SDHs represent a reversible cause of dementia, so their detection is vital to accurate diagnosis of dementia in the older adult.

Older adults are more prone to developing SDHs due to cerebral atrophy. This causes fragile bridging veins, which run between the dura and the brain, to tear as the atrophied brain pulls away from the dura. Trauma is the leading cause of SDHs, and will often be so trivial that the older adult does not remember it occurring. Alcoholics and patients taking anticoagulation are also at increased risk for developing a SDH.

Common presenting symptoms of SDHs in the older adult are gait disturbance, headache, aphasia (inability to speak), altered mental status, and hemiparesis (weakness on one side of the body). The initial presentation of a SDH is often very subtle, with the patient becoming confused and easily agitated. Diagnosis is made by obtaining a CT scan. Treatment typically consists of surgical evacuation of the hematoma.

When caring for the older adult, it is important to consider the risk for development of a SDH. SDHs represent a common cause of reversible dementia that is easily overlooked due to the subtlety of presenting signs and symptoms.

If the patient can be transported rapidly to the hospital, an immediate surgery may be performed to open the dura, allowing the subdural clot to be evacuated. Successful outcome also depends on the control of ICP and careful monitoring of respiratory function. The mortality rate for patients with acute or subacute SDH is high because of associated brain damage (Hickey, 2009).

CHRONIC SUBDURAL HEMATOMA. Chronic SDHs can develop from seemingly minor head injuries and are seen most frequently in the elderly. The time between injury and onset of symptoms can be lengthy (i.e., 3 weeks to many months), so the actual injury may be forgotten.

The treatment of a chronic SDH typically consists of surgical evacuation of the clot if the patient is symptomatic and the bleed is at least 1 cm in size. Smaller bleeds are monitored until the body has fully reabsorbed the blood (Hickey, 2009).

Intracerebral Hemorrhage and Hematoma

Intracerebral hemorrhage (ICH) is bleeding into the parenchyma of the brain. It is commonly seen in head injuries when force is exerted to the head over a small area (e.g., bullet wounds and stab injuries). These hemorrhages within the brain may also result from:

- Systemic hypertension, which causes degeneration and rupture of a vessel
- Rupture of a saccular aneurysm
- Vascular anomalies
- Intracranial tumors
- Bleeding disorders such as leukemia, hemophilia, aplastic anemia, and thrombocytopenia
- Complications of anticoagulant therapy

The onset may be insidious, beginning with the development of neurologic deficits followed by headache. Management includes supportive care, control of ICP, and careful administration of fluids, electrolytes, and antihypertensive medications. Surgical intervention by craniotomy permits removal of the blood clot and control of hemorrhage but may not be possible because of the inaccessible location of the bleeding or the lack of a clearly circumscribed area of blood that can be removed. Decompressive craniectomies that are performed up to 24 hours after the initial injury have been shown to improve outcomes. These procedures are performed to allow for swelling of the brain, which decreases ICP. The earlier the craniectomy can be done, the greater benefit it can have for the patient (Marinkovic, Strbian, Pedrono et al., 2009).

Management of Brain Injuries

Assessment and diagnosis of the extent of injury are accomplished by the initial physical and neurologic examinations. CT and MRI are the primary neuroimaging diagnostic tools of choice and are useful in evaluating the brain structure.

Cervical spine injuries occur in 5% to 10% of patients with TBI. Patients at highest risk for cervical spine injury are those involved in motorcycle accidents and those with lower Glasgow Coma Scale (GCS) scores (≤8) (Tian, Guo, Hu et al., 2009). The patient is transported from the scene of the injury on a board with the head and neck maintained in alignment with the axis of the body. A hard cervical collar should be applied and maintained until cervical spine X-rays have been obtained and the absence of cervical spinal cord injury (SCI) is documented.

All therapy is directed toward preserving brain homeostasis and preventing secondary brain injury. Common causes of secondary injury include cerebral edema, hypotension, and respiratory depression. Treatments to prevent secondary injury include stabilization of cardiovascular and respiratory function to maintain adequate cerebral perfusion, control of hemorrhage and hypovolemia, and maintenance of optimal blood gas values.

⚡ N U R S I N G A L E R T

Any patient with a head injury is presumed to have a cervical spine injury until ruled out; therefore, immobilization of the spine via cervical collar, spinal backboard, and the avoidance of movement is essential.

ALTERED LEVEL OF CONSCIOUSNESS AND INCREASED INTRACRANIAL PRESSURE

An **altered level of consciousness** is apparent in the patient who is not oriented, does not follow commands, or needs persistent stimuli to achieve a state of alertness. LOC is gauged on a continuum, with a normal state of alertness and full cognition (consciousness) on one end and coma on the other end. **Coma** is a clinical state of unarousable unresponsiveness in which there are no purposeful responses to internal or external stimuli, although nonpurposeful responses to painful stimuli and brainstem reflexes may be present (Hickey, 2009). The duration of coma is usually limited to 2 to 4 weeks. *Persistent vegetative state* is a condition in which the unresponsive patient resumes sleep–wake cycles after coma but is devoid of cognitive or affective mental function. **Locked-in syndrome** results from a lesion affecting the pons or midbrain and results in **tetraplegia** (formerly called quadriplegia) and inability to speak, but vertical eye movements and lid elevation typically remain intact and are used to indicate responsiveness (Hickey, 2009). The LOC is the most important indicator of the patient's condition.

The volume of the rigid cranial vault is approximately 1,700 mL, containing brain tissue (1,400 mL, or 80%), intravascular blood (150 mL, or 10%), and CSF (150 mL, or 10%). The volume and pressure of these three components are usually in a state of equilibrium, and together they produce the ICP. An alteration in LOC may be the result of increased ICP. Increased ICP is explained by the Monro-Kellie hypothesis. The **Monro-Kellie hypothesis** states that because of the limited space for expansion within the skull, an increase in any one of the components causes a change in the volume of the others. Because brain tissue has limited space to expand, compensation typically is accomplished by increasing absorption or diminishing production of CSF or decreasing cerebral blood volume. Without such changes, ICP will begin to rise. ICP is usually measured in the lateral ventricles, with normal pressure being 5 to 15 mm Hg. Treatment of increased ICP is generally initiated at a pressure of 20 mm Hg (Hickey, 2009).

Pathophysiology

Altered LOC is not a disorder itself; rather, it is the result of multiple pathophysiologic phenomena. The cause may be neurologic (head injury, stroke), toxicologic (drug overdose, alcohol intoxication), or metabolic (hepatic or renal failure, diabetic ketoacidosis). Increased ICP affects many patients with acute neurologic conditions. This is because pathologic conditions alter the relationship between intracranial volume and ICP. Elevated ICP is most commonly associated with head injury, although it may also be seen in other neurologic conditions, including brain tumors and subarachnoid

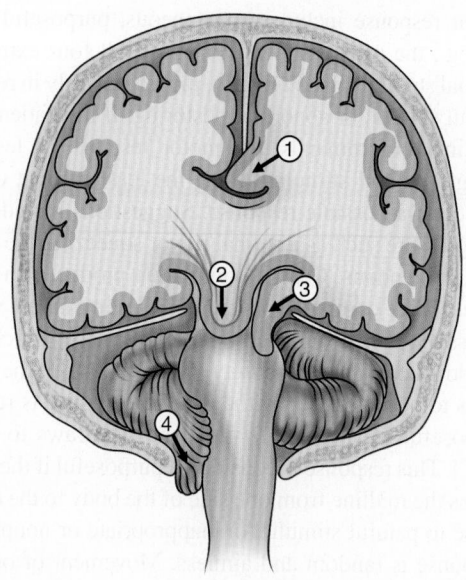

FIGURE 45-4 Brain with intracranial shifts from supratentorial lesions. **(1)** Herniation of the cingulate gyrus under the falx cerebri. **(2)** Central transtentorial herniation. **(3)** Uncal herniation of the temporal lobe into the tentorial notch. **(4)** Infratentorial herniation of the cerebral tonsils. Adapted from Porth, C.M., & Matfin, G. (2009). *Pathophysiology: Concepts of altered health states* (8th ed.). Philadelphia: Lippincott Williams & Wilkins.

hemorrhages. Increased ICP from any cause decreases cerebral perfusion, stimulates further swelling (edema), and may shift brain tissue through openings in the rigid dura, resulting in herniation (Fig. 45-4). The herniated brain tissue exerts pressure on the brain area into which it has shifted, which interferes with the blood supply in that area. Cessation of cerebral blood flow results in cerebral ischemia, infarction, and brain death. Herniation is often a dire, and frequently fatal event (Hickey, 2009).

Increased ICP may significantly reduce cerebral blood flow, resulting in ischemia and cell death. In the early stages of cerebral ischemia, the vasomotor centers are stimulated and the systemic pressure rises to maintain cerebral blood flow. This is typically accompanied by a slow, bounding pulse and respiratory irregularities. These changes in blood pressure, pulse, and respiration are important clinically because they suggest increased ICP.

Cerebral edema is defined as an abnormal accumulation of water or fluid in the intracellular space, extracellular space, or both, and is associated with an increase in the volume of brain tissue. Edema can occur in any part of the brain. As brain tissue swells within the rigid skull, several mechanisms attempt to compensate for the increasing ICP. These compensatory mechanisms include autoregulation and decreased production and flow of CSF. **Autoregulation** refers to the brain's ability to change the diameter of its blood vessels automatically to maintain a constant cerebral blood flow during alterations in systemic blood pressure.

This mechanism may be impaired in patients who are experiencing a pathologic and sustained increase in ICP.

A clinical phenomenon known as the **Cushing's response** (or Cushing's reflex) is seen when cerebral blood flow decreases significantly. When ischemic, the vasomotor center triggers an increase in arterial pressure in an effort to overcome the increased ICP. A sympathetically mediated response causes an increase in the systolic blood pressure, with a widening of the pulse pressure and cardiac slowing. It is a late sign requiring immediate intervention; however, perfusion may be recoverable if the Cushing's response is treated rapidly.

At a certain point, the brain's ability to autoregulate becomes ineffective and decompensation (ischemia and infarction) begins. When this occurs, the patient exhibits significant changes in mental status and vital signs. The bradycardia, hypertension, and bradypnea associated with this deterioration are known as **Cushing's triad**, a grave sign. At this point, herniation of the brainstem and occlusion of the cerebral blood flow occur if therapeutic intervention is not initiated immediately.

Clinical Manifestations

Alterations in LOC occur along a continuum, and the clinical manifestations depend on where the patient is along this continuum. As the patient's state of alertness and consciousness decreases, changes will ultimately occur in the pupillary response, eye opening response, verbal response, and motor response. However, initial alterations in LOC may be reflected by subtle behavioral changes, such as restlessness or increased anxiety. The pupils, normally round and briskly reactive to light, become sluggish (response is slower); as the patient becomes comatose, the pupils become fixed (no response to light). The patient in a coma does not open the eyes, respond verbally, or move the extremities in response to a request to do so.

It is important to be familiar with the patient's baseline status, as many early signs of increased ICP are subtle; they include sudden onset of restlessness (without apparent cause), confusion, and increasing drowsiness. As ICP increases, the patient becomes stuporous, reacting only to loud or painful stimuli. At this stage, serious impairment of brain circulation is likely taking place, and immediate intervention is required. As neurologic function deteriorates further, the patient becomes comatose and exhibits decorticate and decerebrate posturing or flaccidity (see Fig 45-2). If the coma is profound, with fixed and dilated pupils and impaired or absent respiration, death is usually inevitable.

Assessment and Diagnostic Findings

The patient with an altered LOC is at risk for alterations in every body system. A complete assessment is performed, with particular attention to the neurologic system. The neurologic examination should be as complete as the LOC

Focused Assessment

Glasgow Coma Scale

The Glasgow Coma Scale (GCS) is a tool for assessing a patient's response to stimuli. Scores range from 3 (deep coma) to 15 (normal).

Eye opening response	Spontaneous	4
	To voice	3
	To pain	2
	None	1
Best verbal response	Oriented	5
	Confused	4
	Inappropriate words	3
	Incomprehensible sounds	2
	None	1
Best motor response	Obeys command	6
	Localizes pain	5
	Withdraws	4
	Flexion	3
	Extension	2
	None	1
Total		3 to 15

allows (AANN, 2005). It includes an evaluation of mental status, cranial nerve function, cerebellar function (balance and coordination), reflexes, and motor and sensory function.

LOC, a sensitive indicator of neurologic function, can be assessed based on the criteria in the GCS, which include eye opening (E), verbal response (V), and motor response (M). The patient's responses are rated on a scale from 3 to 15. Box 45-6 provides the complete scoring of the GCS. The severity of TBI can be classified based upon the GCS score. A score of 13 to 15 is classified as mild TBI, 9 to 12 is moderate TBI, and 3 to 8 is severe TBI. (Hickey, 2009; Stiver & Manley, 2008). A score of 3 indicates severe impairment of neurologic function, deep coma, brain death, or pharmacologic inhibition of the neurologic response; a score of 8 or less typically indicates an unconscious patient; a score of 15 indicates a fully alert and oriented patient.

The patient's orientation to person, place, and time assesses verbal response. The patient is asked to identify his or her name, where he or she is, and the day, month, or season. Other questions such as "Who is the president?" may be helpful in determining the patient's processing of information in the environment. Verbal response cannot be evaluated if the patient is intubated or has a tracheostomy; this should be clearly documented.

Alertness is measured by the patient's ability to open the eyes spontaneously or in response to a vocal or noxious stimulus (pressure or pain). Patients with severe neurologic dysfunction cannot do this. The nurse assesses for periorbital edema (swelling around the eyes) or trauma, which may prevent the patient from opening the eyes, and documents any such condition that interferes with eye opening.

Motor response includes spontaneous, purposeful movement (e.g., the awake patient can move all four extremities with equal strength on command), movement only in response to painful stimuli, or abnormal posturing. If the patient is not responding to commands, the motor response is tested by applying a painful stimulus, using the least amount of pressure to elicit a possible response. Suggestions include using central pressure such as a sternal rub or squeezing the muscle masses and tendons. Central stimulation produces an overall body response, compared to peripheral stimulation via nail bed pressure, which can elicit a reflex response, which is not a true indicator of motor activity (Noah, 2004). If the patient attempts to push away or withdraw, the response is recorded as purposeful or appropriate ("patient withdraws to painful stimuli"). This response is considered purposeful if the patient can cross the midline from one side of the body to the other in response to painful stimuli. An inappropriate or nonpurposeful response is random and aimless. Movement of only one side is suggestive of hemiparesis, while withdrawal suggests purposeful behavior. The motor response cannot be elicited if the patient has been administered pharmacologic paralyzing agents. These must be shut and time must elapse for the effects to wear off before attempting to elicit a motor response.

In addition to LOC, the nurse monitors parameters such as respiratory status, pupillary response, and vital signs on an ongoing basis. Table 45-1 summarizes the assessment and the clinical significance of the findings. Body functions (circulation, respiration, elimination, fluid and electrolyte balance) are examined in a systematic and ongoing manner.

If the patient is comatose and has localized signs such as abnormal pupillary and motor responses, it is assumed that neurologic disease is present until proven otherwise. If the patient is comatose but pupillary light reflexes are preserved, a toxic or metabolic disorder is suspected. Common laboratory testing and diagnostic procedures performed on patients with decreased LOC and increased ICP are listed in Table 45-2 on page 1194.

Medical and Nursing Management

The first priority of treatment for the patient with altered LOC is to obtain and maintain a patent airway. The patient may be orally or nasally intubated (unless basilar skull fracture or facial trauma is suspected), or a tracheostomy may be performed. Until the ability of the patient to breathe on his or her own is determined, a mechanical ventilator is used to maintain adequate oxygenation and ventilation. The circulatory status (blood pressure, heart rate) is monitored to ensure adequate perfusion to the body and brain. An IV catheter is inserted to provide access for IV fluids and medications.

Increased ICP is a true emergency and must be treated promptly. Invasive monitoring of ICP is an important component of management. Immediate management to relieve increased ICP requires decreasing cerebral edema, lowering the volume of CSF, and decreasing cerebral blood volume

TABLE
45-1 Nursing Assessment of the Unconscious Patient

Examination	Clinical Assessment	Clinical Significance
Level of responsiveness or consciousness	Eye opening; verbal and motor responses; pupils (size, equality, reaction to light)	Obeying commands is a favorable response and demonstrates a return to consciousness.
Pattern of respiration	Respiratory pattern	Disturbances of respiratory center of brain may result in various respiratory patterns.
	Cheyne-Stokes respiration	Suggests lesions deep in both hemispheres; area of basal ganglia and upper brain stem
	Hyperventilation	Suggests onset of metabolic problem or brain stem damage
	Ataxic respiration with irregularity in depth/rate	Ominous sign of damage to medullary center
Eyes		
Pupils (size, equality, reaction to light)	Equal, normally reactive pupils	Suggests that coma is toxic or metabolic in origin
	Equal or unequal diameter	Helps determine location of lesion
	Progressive dilation	Indicates increasing intracranial pressure
	Fixed dilated pupils	Indicates injury at level of midbrain
Eye movements	Normally, eyes should move from side to side.	Functional and structural integrity of brain stem is assessed by inspection of extraocular movements; usually absent in deep coma.
Corneal reflex	When cornea is touched with a wisp of clean cotton, blink response is normal.	Tests cranial nerves V and VII; helps determine location of lesion if unilateral; absent in deep coma
Facial symmetry	Asymmetry (sagging, decrease in wrinkles)	Sign of paralysis
Swallowing reflex	Drooling versus spontaneous swallowing	Absent in coma
Paralysis of cranial nerves X and XII
Neck	Stiff neck	Subarachnoid hemorrhage, meningitis
	Absence of spontaneous neck movement	Fracture or dislocation of cervical spine
Response of extremity to noxious stimuli	Firm pressure on a joint of the upper and lower extremity	Asymmetric response in paralysis
	Observe spontaneous movements	Absent in deep coma
Deep tendon reflexes	Tap patellar and biceps tendons.	Brisk response may have localizing value
Asymmetric response in paralysis
Absent in deep coma
Pathologic reflexes	Firm pressure with blunt object on sole of foot, moving along lateral margin and crossing to the ball of foot	Flexion of the toes, especially the great toe, is normal except in newborn
Dorsiflexion of toes (especially great toe) indicates contralateral pathology of corticospinal tract (Babinski reflex)
Helps determine location of lesion in brain
Abnormal posture	Observation for posturing (spontaneous or in response to noxious stimuli)	Deep extensive brain lesion
	Flaccidity with absence of motor response	Seen with cerebral hemisphere pathology and in metabolic depression of brain function
	Decorticate posture (flexion and internal rotation of forearms and hands)	Decorticate posturing indicates damage to the upper midbrain
	Decerebrate posture (extension and external rotation)	Decerebrate posturing indicates deeper and more severe dysfunction than does decorticate posturing; implies brain pathology; poor prognostic sign.

TABLE
45-2 Laboratory and Diagnostic Tests for Patients With Traumatic Brain Injury

Test	Normal Values	Critical Values	Nursing Implications
Complete blood count	WBC: 4 to 10.5 (× 1,000/mm³) HCT: women: 37% to 47%; men: 42% to 52%	WBC: >10.5 (× 1,000/mm³) HCT: <32%	Assess for any signs or symptoms of infection with increased WBC; assess for any signs or symptoms of occult bleeding with decreased HCT.
Glucose	60 to 150 mg/dL	>150 mg/dL	Hyperglycemia may worsen outcomes; administer insulin if glucose is elevated.
Serum osmolality	278 to 300 mOsm/L	≥320 mOsm/L	Osmolality should be <320 mOsm/L to prevent renal failure in patients receiving mannitol.
Serum sodium	135 to 145 mEq/L	<130 mEq/L or >145 mEq/L	Hyponatremia may indicate cerebral salt wasting or SIADH. Hypernatremia may indicate diabetes insipidus or be due to mannitol therapy.
Urine specific gravity	1.005 to 1.015	<1.005 or >1.015	Low specific gravity can mean diabetes insipidus, while a high level may mean SIADH.
Chest radiograph	Negative for pneumonia or infiltrate	Presence of pneumonia or infiltrate	Ventilated patients are prone to aspiration and development of pneumonias.
Head CT without contrast	Negative for acute hemorrhage	Positive for epidural, subdural, or intracerebral hemorrhage	Observe for any signs or symptoms of intracranial bleeding.
Serum potassium	3.5 to 5.0 mEq/L	<3.5 mEq/L	Hypokalemia may be a consequence of mannitol therapy.
Magnesium	1.6 to 2.4 mg/dL	<1.6 mg/dL	Hypomagnesemia may lower the seizure threshold and cause secondary brain injury; low levels should be corrected.

WBC, white blood cell count; HCT, hematocrit; SIADH, syndrome of inappropriate antidiuretic hormone.

while maintaining cerebral perfusion. These goals are accomplished by administering osmotic diuretics, restricting fluids, draining CSF, controlling fever, maintaining systemic blood pressure and oxygenation, and reducing cellular metabolic demands. Corticosteroids are not recommended in cases of increased ICP resulting from TBI (Hickey, 2009).

Monitoring Intracranial Pressure

Nursing management focuses on detecting early signs of increasing ICP because medical interventions are usually ineffective once later signs develop. Frequent neurologic assessments and documentation and analysis of trends will reveal the subtle changes that may indicate increasing ICP.

Detecting Early Indications of Increasing Intracranial Pressure

The nurse assesses for and immediately reports any of the following early signs or symptoms of increasing ICP:

- Disorientation, restlessness, increased respiratory effort, purposeless movements, and mental confusion; these are early clinical indications of increasing ICP because the brain cells responsible for cognition are extremely sensitive to decreased oxygenation.
- Pupillary changes and impaired extraocular movements; these occur as the increasing pressure displaces the brain against the oculomotor and optic nerves (cranial nerves II, III, IV, and VI), which arise from the midbrain and brainstem (see Chapter 43).
- Weakness in one extremity or on one side of the body; this occurs as increasing ICP compresses the pyramidal tracts, which control motor function.
- Headache that is constant, increasing in intensity, and aggravated by movement or straining; this occurs as increasing ICP causes pressure and stretching of venous and arterial vessels in the base of the brain.

NURSING ALERT

The earliest sign of increasing ICP is a change in LOC. Any changes in LOC should be reported immediately.

Detecting Later Indications of Increasing Intracranial Pressure

As ICP increases, the patient's condition worsens and the following signs and symptoms may be observed:

- LOC continues to deteriorate until the patient is comatose.
- Respiratory rate decreases or becomes erratic, blood pressure and temperature increase. The pulse pressure widens and the pulse fluctuates rapidly, varying from bradycardia to tachycardia.
- Altered respiratory patterns develop, including Cheyne-Stokes breathing (rhythmic waxing and waning of rate and depth of respirations alternating with brief periods of apnea) and ataxic breathing (irregular breathing with a random sequence of deep and shallow breaths).
- Projectile vomiting may occur with increased pressure on the reflex center in the medulla.
- Hemiplegia or decorticate or decerebrate posturing may develop as pressure on the brainstem increases; bilateral flaccidity occurs before death.
- Loss of brainstem reflexes, including pupillary, corneal, gag, and swallowing reflexes, which is an ominous sign of impending death.

Because clinical assessment is not always a reliable guide in recognizing increased ICP, especially in comatose patients, monitoring of ICP is an essential part of management (Hickey, 2009). ICP is monitored closely for continuous elevation or significant increase over baseline. The trend of ICP measurements over time is an important indication of the patient's underlying status. Vital signs are assessed when an increase in ICP is noted.

ICP can be monitored with the use of an intraventricular catheter (ventriculostomy) or a subarachnoid bolt or screw (Fig. 45-5). When a **ventriculostomy** is used for monitoring ICP, a fine-bore catheter is inserted into a lateral ventricle, preferably in the nondominant hemisphere of the brain (Hickey, 2009). The catheter is connected by a fluid-filled system to a transducer, which records the pressure in the form of an electrical impulse. In addition to obtaining continuous ICP recordings, the ventricular catheter allows CSF to drain, particularly during acute increases in pressure. The ventriculostomy can also be used to drain blood from the ventricle. Continuous drainage of CSF under pressure control is an effective method of treating intracranial hypertension. Complications associated with its use include infection, meningitis, ventricular collapse, occlusion of the catheter by brain tissue or blood, and problems with the monitoring system (Gardner, Engh, Atteberry et al., 2009). CSF drainage is frequently performed because the removal of CSF with a ventriculostomy drain can dramatically reduce ICP and restore cerebral perfusion. Caution should be used in draining CSF, however, because excessive drainage may result in collapse of the ventricles and herniation.

The **subarachnoid bolt** or **screw** is a hollow device that is inserted through the skull and dura mater into the cranial

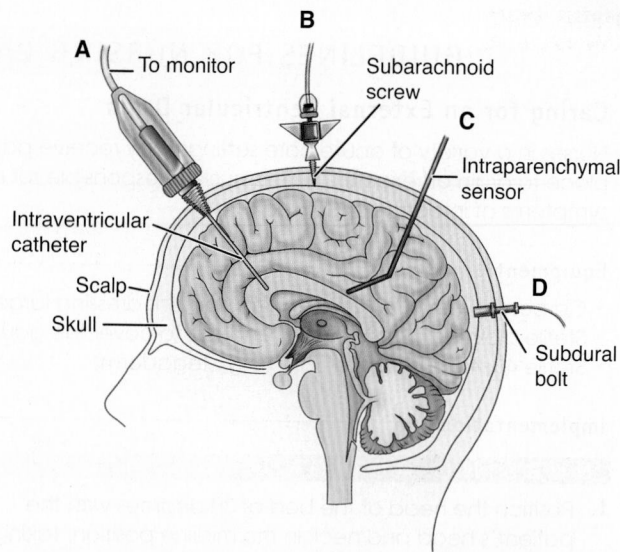

FIGURE 45-5 Intracranial pressure monitoring. A device may be placed in (**A**) the ventricle, (**B**) the subarachnoid space, (**C**) the intraparenchymal space, or (**D**) the subdural space.

subarachnoid space (Hickey, 2009). It has the advantage of not requiring a ventricular puncture. The subarachnoid bolt is attached to a pressure transducer, and the output is recorded on an oscilloscope. This technique also has the advantage of avoiding complications from brain shift and small ventricle size. One disadvantage to using a subarachnoid bolt is the inability to obtain CSF for analysis or drainage purposes. Complications include infection and blockage of the bolt by clot or brain tissue, which leads to a loss of pressure tracing and a decrease in accuracy at high ICP readings.

While ICP monitoring is only performed in an ICU setting, CSF drainage may be carried out in the operating room, emergency room, or intensive care unit. A ventriculostomy without the ICP monitoring catheter is known as an *external ventricular drain* (EVD). Box 45-7 provides guidelines on nursing care of the EVD.

Monitoring and Managing Complications

Potential complications for the patient with altered LOC include respiratory failure, pneumonia, pressure ulcers, and aspiration. Respiratory failure may develop shortly after the patient becomes unconscious. If the patient cannot maintain effective respirations, insertion of an airway and mechanical ventilation is initiated to provide adequate ventilation and to protect the airway. Pneumonia is common in patients receiving mechanical ventilation and in those who cannot maintain and clear the airway. The patient with altered LOC is subject to all the complications associated with immobility, such as pressure ulcers, venous stasis, musculoskeletal deterioration, and disturbed gastrointestinal functioning. Aspiration of gastric contents or feedings may occur, precipitating the development of aspiration pneumonia or airway occlusion.

BOX 45-7

GUIDELINES FOR NURSING CARE

Caring for an External Ventricular Drain

Nurses in a variety of acute care settings may receive patients who have an external ventricular drain (EVD) in place to drain off excess CSF. The nurse is responsible for maintaining the EVD while monitoring for any signs or symptoms of infection or CSF leak.

Equipment

- Carpenter's level
- Sterile gloves
- Sterile 4 × 4 gauze pad
- Transparent dressing large enough to cover the gauze (e.g., Tegaderm)

Implementation

NURSING ACTION	RATIONALE
1. Position the head of the bed at 30 degrees with the patient's head and neck in the midline position, taking care to avoid neck flexion.	1. Positioning the head of the bed at 30° helps promote venous return, which will assist in keeping ICP within normal limits. Keeping the head and neck in the midline position while avoiding flexion will help prevent any increases in ICP.
2. Using the carpenter's level, set the collection bag even with the EAM of the ear at the level that has been ordered by the physician (measured in cm either above or below the EAM).	2. The EAM is level with the foramen of Monro. A level below the EAM will increase drainage of CSF, while a level above the EAM will decrease drainage of CSF.
3. Documentation should include the position of the collection bag, the amount of CSF drainage, and the color and quality of the CSF (clear, cloudy, bloody, etc.).	3. Proper documentation of where the collection bag is placed and the amount of drainage is important for the neurosurgeons to evaluate when to make adjustments to the level and when the EVD is no longer needed. Any change in quality of the CSF may indicate infection or bleeding into the ventricles, which should be reported immediately.
4. If the patient needs to be turned, the head of the bed needs to be adjusted, or when the patient needs to be moved out of bed, the drainage system should be turned off until it can be returned to the ordered position. Once the patient is back in bed and the system has been re-leveled, the drainage system may be opened again.	4. If the drainage system is not turned off and the patient's head is moved, CSF may be forcefully pulled out of the ventricles, potentially causing herniation of the brain.
5. The EVD should always be handled with sterile technique when changing the dressing covering the insertion site. The dressing consists of a sterile 4 × 4 gauze pad that is folded in order to fully cover the insertion site, and then covered with a transparent dressing. The insertion site should be monitored for any sings or symptoms of infection and should be kept clean and dry. If the dressing becomes damp, it should be changed and the provider should be notified.	5. The EVD is a closed, sterile system. Risk for infection is high and all precautions should be taken to prevent any infection from entering the brain. The gauze needs to be covered with a clear dressing so that the gauze may be readily inspected for the presence of dampness and blood. If the dressing becomes damp with fluid, the fluid is presumed to be CSF. Presence of a damp dressing may indicate a CSF leak.

EAM, external auditory meatus; EVD, external ventricular drain; ICP, intracranial pressure; CSF, cerebrospinal fluid.

Endocrine abnormalities, including diabetes insipidus and syndrome of inappropriate antidiuretic hormone (SIADH), are common complications of TBI. Diabetes insipidus is the result of decreased secretion of antidiuretic hormone (ADH). The patient has excessive urine output, decreased urine osmolality, and serum hyperosmolarity. Therapy consists of administration of fluids, electrolyte replacement, and vasopressin (desmopressin, DDAVP) therapy. SIADH is the result of increased secretion of ADH. The patient becomes volume-overloaded, urine output diminishes, and serum sodium concentration becomes dilute (sodium <134 mEq/L). Treatment of SIADH includes fluid restriction (typically <1 L/day with no free water), which is usually sufficient to correct the hyponatremia. Severe cases call for judicious administration of a 3% hypertonic saline solution. Hyponatremia presents commonly with a change in mental status ranging from mild confusion to coma; seizures are associated with low sodium levels (<115 mEq/L). The more quickly this problem has developed, the more profound the signs and symptoms. Aggressive management may be required to correct hyponatremia as delaying treatment may result in irreversible brain damage. However, overcorrection of the sodium level predisposes the patient to central pontine myelinolysis, a disorder in which the white matter of the pons loses myelin (the protective sheath surrounding nerves); this results in tetraplegia with cranial nerve deficits (Rhoney & Parker, 2006). To prevent this complication, the nurse monitors results of sodium levels (initially, these may be ordered hourly), and the patient's response to hypertonic saline treatment. As a general guideline, the plasma sodium concentration should probably be raised by no more than 12 mEq during the first 24 hours.

Because the unconscious patient's protective reflexes are impaired, the quality of nursing care provided literally may mean the difference between life and death. The nurse must assume responsibility for the patient until the basic reflexes (coughing, blinking, and swallowing) return and the patient becomes conscious and oriented. Therefore, the major nursing goal is to compensate for the absence of these protective reflexes.

Potential complications include cerebra edema, high fever, alterations in blood pressure and oxygenation, increased metabolic demand, and seizures. The nurse must maintain oral hygiene, monitor for the presence of pressure ulcers, avoid any complications associated with the eyes, monitor urinary output and bowel function, and assess nutritional status. The nurse must always remember to be the patient's advocate, as an unconscious patient cannot advocate for him- or herself.

Decreasing Cerebral Edema: Osmotic Diuretics, Fluid Restriction, and Hypothermia

Cerebral edema is the leading cause of secondary brain injury (Mittal et al., 2009). Osmotic diuretics, such as mannitol, may be administered to dehydrate the brain tissue and reduce cerebral edema. Osmotic diuretics work by creating a gradient that draws water across intact membranes, thereby reducing the volume of the swollen brain. Secondarily they reduce blood viscosity and hematocrit and enhance cerebral blood flow (Rauen, Chulay, Bridges et al., 2008). If the patient is receiving osmotic diuretics, serum osmolality should be determined to assess hydration status.

⊘ DRUG ALERT
Mannitol becomes ineffective when the serum osmolality exceeds 320 mOsm.

Hypertonic saline is another medication that works to reduce cerebral edema. While mannitol is considered the gold standard in reducing increased ICP, hypertonic saline is gaining popularity as an effective osmotic diuretic (Infanti, 2008). Optimal concentration, dosing, timing and duration of hypertonic saline has yet to be determined (Rauen et al., 2008).

Another method for decreasing cerebral edema is fluid restriction. Limiting overall fluid intake leads to dehydration and hemoconcentration, which draws fluid across the osmotic gradient and decreases cerebral edema. Fluid needs are met initially by administering the required IV fluids.

⊘ DRUG ALERT
Hypotonic fluids should be avoided in patients with TBI as they can cause an increase in cerebral edema.

Researchers have long hypothesized that lowering body temperature decreases cerebral edema by reducing the oxygen and metabolic requirements of the brain, thus protecting the brain from continued ischemia. If body metabolism can be reduced by lowering the body temperature, the collateral circulation in the brain may be able to provide an adequate blood supply to the brain (Rupich, 2009). The effect of hypothermia on ICP requires more study; thus far, induced hypothermia has not consistently been shown to be beneficial for patients with brain injury. Current literature suggests it is beneficial, but only when maintained for at least 48 hours. Inducing and maintaining hypothermia is a major clinical treatment that requires knowledge and skilled nursing observation and management (Brain Trauma Foundation, 2007).

Controlling Fever

High fever in the unconscious patient may be caused by infection of the respiratory or urinary tract, drug reactions, or damage to the hypothalamic temperature-regulating center. Approximately one-fifth to one-half of fevers are never explained, despite extensive workup (Badjatia, 2009). Because of damage to the temperature center in the brain or severe intracranial infection, unconscious patients often develop very high temperatures. Such temperature elevations must be controlled, because the increased metabolic demands of the brain can exceed cerebral circulation and

oxygenation, resulting in cerebral deterioration (Hickey, 2009). Studies have shown that fever within the first week of injury is associated with poor outcomes and should be treated aggressively (Badjatia, 2009). Persistent hyperthermia with no identified clinical source of infection indicates brainstem damage and a poor prognosis.

Strategies for reducing fever include:

- Removing all bedding over the patient (with the possible exception of a light sheet or small drape)
- Administering acetaminophen as prescribed
- Giving cool sponge baths and allowing a fan to blow over the patient to increase surface cooling
- Using a hypothermia blanket

Frequent temperature monitoring is indicated to assess the patient's response to the therapy and to prevent an excessive decrease in temperature and shivering, which increases heat production.

Maintaining Blood Pressure, Oxygenation, and Hyperventilation

Patients with TBI may sustain a secondary insult if they become hypotensive or hypoxic. Due to ethical reasons, no randomized controlled trials have been done to study the effects of hypotension and hypoxia. However, a growing body of evidence shows deleterious effects if the patient experiences either of these conditions. It is recommended that systolic blood pressure be maintained at greater than 90 mm Hg and oxygen saturation be maintained at greater than 90% (Brain Trauma Foundation, 2007).

Hyperventilation, which results in vasoconstriction, was previously used in patients with increased ICP. Recent research has demonstrated that hyperventilation may not be as beneficial as once thought (Brain Trauma Foundation, 2007). The reduction in partial pressure of carbon dioxide ($PaCO_2$) may result in hypoxia, ischemia, and an increase in cerebral lactate levels (Hickey, 2009). Hyperventilation is an option for patients with ICP who are unresponsive to conventional therapies, but it should be used cautiously and should be avoided for the first 24 hours following the initial injury (Brain Trauma Foundation, 2007).

Reducing Metabolic Demands

Cellular metabolic demands may be reduced through the administration of high doses of barbiturates if the patient is unresponsive to conventional treatment. The mechanism by which barbiturates decrease ICP and protect the brain is through inhibition of free radicals, alterations in vascular tone, and suppression of metabolism (Hickey, 2009). Use of high-dose barbiturates should be reserved for patients with refractory increased ICP who do not respond to other medical or surgical treatments. Barbiturates should not be used as prophylaxis to prevent increased ICP (Brain Trauma Foundation, 2007).

Another method of reducing cellular metabolic demand and improving oxygenation is the administration of pharmacologic

paralyzing agents such as pancuronium, vecuronium, and cisatracurium. The patient who receives these agents cannot move; this decreases the metabolic demands and results in a decrease in cerebral oxygen demand. Because the patient cannot respond or report pain, sedation and analgesia must be provided, because the paralyzing agents do not provide either.

Patients receiving high doses of barbiturates or pharmacologic paralyzing agents require continuous cardiac monitoring, endotracheal intubation, mechanical ventilation, ICP monitoring, and arterial pressure monitoring.

The ability to perform serial neurologic assessments is lost with the use of barbiturates or paralyzing agents. Therefore, other monitoring tools are needed to assess the patient's status and response to therapy. Important parameters that must be assessed include ICP, blood pressure, heart rate, respiratory rate, and response to ventilator therapy (e.g., "bucking" or "fighting" the ventilator). Refer to Chapters 10 and 55 for ventilator considerations. Potential complications include hypotension due to decreased sympathetic tone and myocardial depression (Hickey, 2009).

Seizure Prophylaxis

Patients with severe TBI are at risk for developing seizures. Seizures that develop after head injury are known as posttraumatic seizures (PTS) and are classified according to when they occur. If they occur within 7 days of injury, they are known as early PTS; if they occur after 7 days after the injury, they are known as late PTS (Hickey, 2009). Box 45-8 lists risk factors for developing PTS. There is evidence to support the use of prophylactic anticonvulsants only for early PTS. It is not recommended that patients be started on seizure prophylaxis more than 1 week after the injury if they have not had any seizures. If the patient develops late PTS, the seizures should be managed in the same way as new-onset seizures (Brain Trauma Foundation, 2007). See Chapter 46 for further discussion on management of seizures.

Providing Mouth Care

The mouth is inspected for dryness, inflammation, and crusting. The unconscious patient requires conscientious oral care because there is a risk of parotitis (inflammation of the salivary glands) if the mouth is not kept scrupulously clean. The mouth is cleansed and rinsed carefully to remove secretions and crusts and to keep the mucous membranes moist. A thin coating of petrolatum on the lips prevents drying, cracking,

---

BOX 45-8 **Risk Factors for Developing Posttraumatic Seizures**

- Depressed skull fracture
- Penetrating head wound
- Epidural, subdural, or intracerebral hemorrhage
- GCS score <10
- Cortical contusion

and encrustations. If the patient has an endotracheal tube, the tube should be moved to the opposite side of the mouth daily to prevent ulceration of the mouth and lips.

Maintaining Skin and Joint Integrity

Preventing skin breakdown requires continuing nursing assessment and intervention. Special attention is given to unconscious patients because they cannot respond to external stimuli. Assessment includes a regular schedule of turning to avoid pressure, which can cause breakdown and necrosis of the skin. Turning also provides kinesthetic (sensation of movement), proprioceptive (awareness of position), and vestibular (equilibrium) stimulation. After turning, the patient is carefully repositioned to prevent ischemic necrosis over pressure areas.

Preserving Corneal Integrity

Unconscious patients may have their eyes open and have inadequate or absent corneal reflexes. The cornea may become irritated, dried out, or scratched, leading to ulceration. The eyes may be cleansed with cotton balls moistened with sterile normal saline to remove debris and discharge (Hickey, 2009). If artificial tears are prescribed, they may be instilled every 2 hours. Periorbital edema often occurs after cranial surgery. Cold compresses may be prescribed, and care must be exerted to avoid contact with the cornea. Eye patches should be used cautiously because of the potential for corneal abrasion from contact with the patch.

Managing Nutritional Needs

If the patient does not recover quickly and sufficiently enough to take adequate fluids and calories by mouth, a nasogastric tube or gastrostomy tube is inserted for the administration of enteral feedings. A nutritionist should be involved in the care of the unconscious patient. The nutritionist will determine the patient's caloric needs and will make recommendations for the amount and type of tube feeding that is appropriate. Daily intake and output should be recorded, as well as daily weights to ensure the patient has adequate caloric intake (Hickey, 2009). Box 45-9 gives nutritional considerations of the patient with decreased LOC and increased ICP.

Preventing Urinary Retention

The patient with an altered LOC is often incontinent or has urinary retention. The bladder is palpated or scanned at intervals to determine whether urinary retention is present. If the patient is not voiding, an indwelling urinary catheter is inserted and connected to a closed drainage system. A catheter may also be inserted during the acute phase of illness to monitor urinary output. Because catheters are a major factor in causing urinary tract infection (UTI), the patient is observed for fever and cloudy urine. The urinary catheter is usually removed if the patient has a stable cardiovascular system and if no diuresis, sepsis, or voiding dysfunction existed before the onset of coma. An intermittent catheterization program may be initiated to ensure complete emptying of the bladder at intervals, if indicated.

BOX 45-9 | **Nutrition Alert**

Nutritional Support Following Traumatic Brain Injury

- Patients with traumatic brain injury (TBI) have increased metabolic expenditure so they have high caloric needs.
- Full nutritional support should be begun no later than 72 hours after the injury to achieve full caloric replacement by post-injury day 7.
- Protein should comprise 15% of total calories.
- When feedings are initiated, glucose levels should be closely monitored as hyperglycemia is associated with worse outcomes.
- Consultation with a dietician is recommended to provide optimal nutritional support. (Brain Trauma Foundation, 2007)

Promoting Bowel Function

The abdomen is assessed for distention by listening for bowel sounds and measuring the girth of the abdomen with a tape measure. There is a risk for diarrhea from infection, antibiotics, and hyperosmolar fluids.

Immobility and lack of dietary fiber can cause constipation. The nurse monitors the number and consistency of bowel movements and performs a rectal examination for signs of fecal impaction. Stool softeners may be prescribed and can be administered with tube feedings. To facilitate bowel emptying, a glycerin suppository may be indicated. The patient may require an enema every other day to empty the lower colon (Hickey, 2009).

Protecting the Patient

Care should be taken to prevent injury from invasive lines and equipment, and other potential sources of injury should be identified, such as restraints, tight dressings, environmental irritants, damp bedding or dressings, and tubes and drains.

Protection also includes protecting the patient's dignity during altered LOC. Simple measures such as providing privacy and speaking to the patient during nursing care activities preserve the patient's dignity. Not speaking negatively about the patient's condition or prognosis is also important, because patients in a light coma may be able to hear. The comatose patient has an increased need for advocacy, and the nurse is responsible for seeing that these advocacy needs are met (Hickey, 2009).

New Therapies

New acute-stage treatments for TBI have not been developed for more than 30 years (Cekic & Stein, 2010). Current research has begun to focus more on novel treatments for TBI because as many as 30% of soldiers have suffered a TBI (Stein & Sayeed, 2009). One promising compound that

has shown substantial improvement in outcomes is the hormone progesterone. The National Institute of Neurological Disorders and Stroke (NINDS) recently sponsored a phase II clinical trial, the ProTECT trial, to evaluate the effectiveness of progesterone treatment in moderate to severe TBI. Patients who received 3 days of IV progesterone starting 6 to 8 hours after the initial injury showed a greater than 50% reduction in mortality when compared to controls at 30 days post-injury (Wright, Kellermann, Hertzberg et al., 2007). Further clinical trials are currently underway.

Intracranial Surgery

Decompressive craniectomy is a surgical procedure that can be used to help relieve increased ICP. A decompressive craniectomy involves removal of a bone flap from the skull to allow expansion of the brain. The bone flap is then implanted into the abdomen, so the bone remains viable. Once cerebral edema has decreased, the bone flap is replaced back on the skull. No randomized controlled trials have investigated the utility of decompressive craniectomy, although studies have suggested it is helpful (Hickey, 2009; Lettieri, 2008; Marinkovic et al., 2009).

BRAIN DEATH

When a patient has sustained a severe neurologic injury incompatible with life, the diagnosis of brain death should be considered. Often, it is the nurse who will first notice signs of decompensation and will begin the process of determining if the patient meets criteria for brain death. Approximately 5% to 10% of patients in ICUs who are comatose will be declared brain dead. The most common causes of brain death are ICH or SAH (39%), TBI (32%), and anoxic brain injury (11%) (Wijdicks, Rabinstein, Manno et al., 2008).

Brain death was formally defined by the Ad Hoc Committee at Harvard Medical School in 1968 as an "irreversible coma." In 1981, the President's Commission for the Study of Ethical Problems in Medicine and Biomedical and Behavioral Research published *Guidelines for the Determination of Death*. These guidelines clarified that patients who are considered brain dead must have confirmation of cessation of all brain function resulting from an irreversible cause. Reversible conditions such as shock, hypothermia, and drug intoxication must be excluded prior to diagnosis. This study served as the basis for the Uniform Death and Determination Act (UDDA), which is now recognized by all 50 states. The UDDA states that death will be determined with accepted medical standards and that death will indicate irreversible loss of all brain function.

The most recent practice parameters come from the Quality Standards Subcommittee of the American Academy of Neurology (1995) and include three cardinal findings: coma or unresponsiveness, absence of brainstem reflexes, and apnea. The current criteria for brain death are: the condition is irreversible with a known cause; the patient has apnea; the patient has no brainstem reflexes; the core body temperature

is greater than 90°F (32°C); and there is neuroimaging evidence of catastrophic CNS damage.

The nurse may assist in the clinical examination for determination of brain death and in the process of organ procurement. Often, there will be a meeting among the attending physician, nurse, social worker, and representative of the organ procurement organization to inform the family of the organ donation process. The family will often look to the nurse for answers about organ donation and an explanation of questions related to the determination of brain death (Peiffer, 2007).

SPINAL CORD INJURY

Spinal cord injury is a major health problem. An estimated 259,000 people in the United States live each day with a disability from SCI, and an estimated 12,000 new injuries occur each year (National Spinal Cord Injury Statistical Center [NSCISC], 2009). Males account for 80% of SCI in a reported national database (NSCISC, 2009). Young people between the ages of 16 and 30 years account for more than half of the new SCIs each year. The most common cause of SCI is motor vehicle accidents, which account for 42% of SCI. Violence-related injuries account for 15% of SCIs, with falls causing 26.7%, and sports-related injuries causing 7.6% of SCIs (NSCISC, 2009). The frequency of associated injuries and medical complications in SCI is high. The frequency with which these risk factors are associated with SCI serves to emphasize the importance of primary prevention. The same interventions suggested earlier in this chapter for head injury prevention serve to decrease the incidence of SCI as well (see Box 45-1, p. 1185).

Pathophysiology

Damage to the spinal cord ranges from transient concussion (from which the patient fully recovers) to contusion, laceration, and compression of the cord substance (either alone or in combination), to complete **transection** (severing) of the cord (which renders the patient paralyzed below the level of the injury).

SCIs, like head injuries, can be separated into two categories: primary injuries and secondary injuries (Porth & Matfin, 2008). Primary injuries are the result of the initial insult or trauma and are usually permanent. Secondary injuries are usually the result of a contusion or tear injury, in which the nerve fibers begin to swell and disintegrate. A secondary chain of events produces ischemia, hypoxia, edema, and hemorrhagic lesions, which in turn result in destruction of myelin and axons (Hickey, 2009). These secondary reactions, believed to be the principal causes of spinal cord degeneration at the level of injury, are now thought to be reversible during the first 4 to 6 hours after injury. Therefore, if the cord has not suffered irreparable damage, some method of early treatment is needed to prevent partial damage from developing into total and permanent damage (Hickey, 2009) (see later discussion).

The vertebrae most frequently involved in SCI are the fifth, sixth, and seventh cervical (neck) vertebrae (C5–C7), the twelfth thoracic vertebra (T12), and the first lumbar vertebra (L1). These vertebrae are most susceptible because there is a greater range of mobility in the vertebral column in these areas (Porth & Matfin, 2008).

Clinical Manifestations

Manifestations of SCI depend on the type and level of injury (Box 45-10). **Incomplete spinal cord lesions** (the sensory or motor fibers, or both, are preserved below the lesion) are classified according to the area of spinal cord damage: central, lateral, anterior, or peripheral. The American Spinal

---

BOX 45-10

Effects of Spinal Cord Injuries

Central Cord Syndrome
- Characteristics: Motor deficits (in the upper extremities compared to the lower extremities; sensory loss varies but is more pronounced in the upper extremities); bowel/bladder dysfunction is variable, or function may be completely preserved.
- Cause: Injury or edema of the central cord, usually of the cervical area. May be caused by hyperextension injuries.

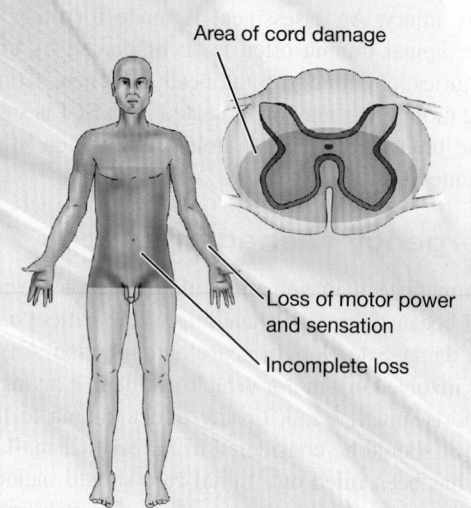

Central Cord Syndrome

Anterior Cord Syndrome
- Characteristics: Loss of pain, temperature, and motor function is noted below the level of the lesion; light touch, position, and vibration sensation remain intact.
- Cause: The syndrome may be caused by acute disk herniation or hyperflexion injuries associated with fracture-dislocation of vertebra. It also may occur as a result of injury to the anterior spinal artery, which supplies the anterior two-thirds of the spinal cord.

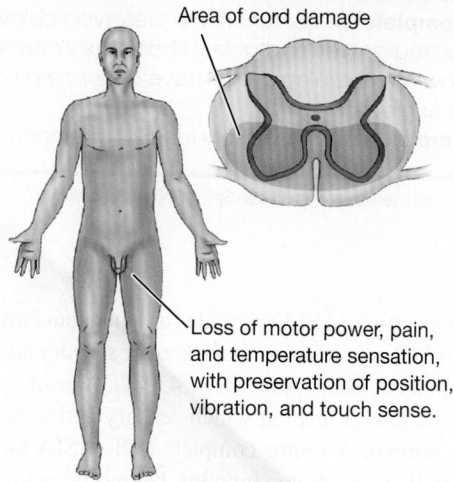

Anterior Cord Syndrome

Brown-Séquard Syndrome (Lateral Cord Syndrome)
- Characteristics: Ipsilateral paralysis or paresis is noted, together with ipsilateral loss of touch, pressure, and vibration and contralateral loss of pain and temperature.
- Cause: The lesion is caused by a transverse hemisection of the cord (half of the cord is transected from north to south), usually as a result of a knife or missile injury, fracture-dislocation of a unilateral articular process, or possibly an acute ruptured disk.

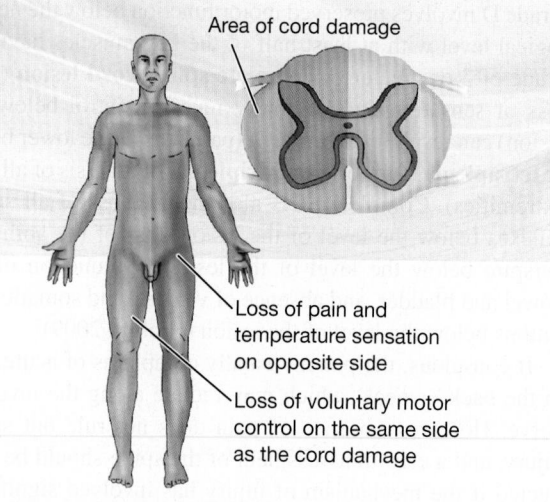

Brown-Séquard Syndrome

Adapted from Hickey, L. (2009). *The clinical practice of neurological and neurosurgical nursing* (6th ed., pp. 423–425). Philadelphia: Lippincott Williams & Wilkins.

ASIA Impairment Scale

A = Complete: No motor or sensory function is preserved in the sacral segments S4 to S5.

B = Incomplete: Sensory but not motor function is preserved below the neurologic level, and includes the sacral segments S4 to S5.

C = Incomplete: Motor function is preserved below the neurologic level, and more than half of key muscles below the neurologic level have a muscle grade of less than 3.

D = Incomplete: Motor function is preserved below the neurologic level, and at least half of key muscles below the neurologic level have a muscle grade of 3 or greater.

E = Normal: Motor and sensory function are normal.

Used with permission of American Spinal Injury Association.

Injury Association (ASIA) provides another standard classification of SCI according to the degree of sensory and motor function present after injury (Box 45-11). *Neurologic level* refers to the lowest level at which sensory and motor functions are normal. A motor complete SCI (ASIA Grades A and B) involves no motor function below the neurological level. ASIA Grade A involves no sensory or motor function all the way down to the sacral segments, S4 and S5. ASIA Grade B involves preserved sensory but not motor function below the neurological level and includes preservation of the sacral segments S4 and S5. A motor incomplete SCI (ASIA Grades C and D) involves preservation of motor function below the neurologic level. ASIA Grade C involves preserved motor function below the neurological level with at least half of the key muscles having a grade of less than 3 (see Chapter 43 for discussion of grading muscle strength). ASIA Grade D involves preserved motor function below the neurological level with at least half of the key muscles having a grade of 3 or greater. A **complete spinal cord lesion** (total loss of sensation and voluntary muscle control below the lesion) can result in **paraplegia** (paralysis of the lower body) or **tetraplegia** (formerly **quadriplegia**—paralysis of all four extremities). Complete SCIs also include loss of all spinal reflexes below the level of the lesion, loss of the ability to perspire below the level of the lesion, dysfunction of the bowel and bladder, and absence of visceral and somatic sensations below the level of the lesion (Hickey, 2009).

If conscious, the patient usually complains of acute pain in the back or neck, which may radiate along the involved nerve. However, absence of pain does not rule out spinal injury, and a careful assessment of the spine should be conducted if the mechanism of injury has involved significant force (i.e., concomitant head injury).

Respiratory dysfunction is related to the level of injury. The muscles contributing to respiration are the abdominals and intercostals (T1 to T11) and the diaphragm (C3 to C5). In high cervical cord injury, acute respiratory failure is the leading cause of death. Functional abilities by level of injury are described in Table 45-3.

NURSING ALERT

Ascending edema of the spinal cord in the acute phase of the injury may cause respiratory difficulty that requires immediate intervention. Therefore, the patient's respiratory status must be monitored frequently.

Assessment and Diagnostic Findings

A detailed neurologic examination is performed. Diagnostic X-rays (lateral cervical spine X-rays) and CT are usually performed initially. An MRI may be ordered as further workup if a ligamentous injury is suspected, because significant spinal cord damage may exist even in the absence of bony injury. An assessment is made for other injuries because spinal trauma often is accompanied by concomitant injuries, commonly to the head and chest. Continuous cardiac monitoring may be indicated if an SCI is suspected, because bradycardia and asystole are common in patients with acute SCIs.

Emergency Management

The immediate management at the scene of the injury is critical because improper handling of the patient can cause further damage and loss of neurologic function. Any patient who is involved in a motor vehicle accident, a diving or contact sports injury, a fall, or any direct trauma to the head and neck should be considered to have a SCI until such an injury has been ruled out. Initial care should include rapid assessment, immobilization, extrication, stabilization or control of life-threatening injuries, and transportation to the most appropriate medical facility (Haut, Kalish, Efron et al., 2010; Kattail, Furlan, & Fehlings, 2009).

At the scene of the injury, the patient should be immobilized on a spinal (back) board, with head and neck in a neutral position, to prevent an incomplete injury from becoming complete. Up to 25% of spinal cord injuries occur after the initial insult, during either transit to a care facility or during the early course of treatment (Hadley, Walters, Grabb et al., 2001). One member of the team must assume control of the patient's head to prevent flexion, rotation, or extension; this is done by placing the hands on both sides of the patient's head at about ear level to limit movement and maintain alignment while a spinal board or cervical immobilizing device is applied. If possible, at least four people should slide the patient carefully onto a board for transfer to the hospital. Any twisting movement may irreversibly damage the spinal cord by causing a bony fragment of the vertebra to cut into, crush, or sever the cord completely (Hickey, 2009).

TABLE
45-3 Functional Abilities by Level of Spinal Cord Injury

Injury Level	Segmental Sensorimotor Function	Dressing, Eating	Elimination	Mobility*
C1	Little or no sensation or control of head and neck; no diaphragm control; requires continuous ventilation	Dependent	Dependent	Limited. Voice or sip-n-puff controlled electric wheelchair
C2 to C3	Head and neck sensation; some neck control; independent of mechanical ventilation for short periods	Dependent	Dependent	Same as for C1
C4	Good head and neck sensation and motor control; some shoulder elevation; diaphragm movement	Dependent, may be able to eat with adaptive sling	Dependent	Limited to voice, mouth, head, chin, or shoulder-controlled electric wheelchair
C5	Full head and neck control; shoulder strength; elbow flexion	Independent with assistance	Maximal assistance	Electric or modified manual wheelchair, needs transfer assistance
C6	Fully innervated shoulder; wrist extension or dorsiflexion	Independent or with minimal assistance	Independent or with minimal assistance	Independent in transfers and wheelchair
C7 to C8	Full elbow extension; wrist plantar flexion; some finger control	Independent	Independent	Independent; manual wheelchair
T1 to T5	Full hand and finger control; use of intercostal and thoracic muscles	Independent	Independent	Independent; manual wheelchair
T6 to T10	Abdominal muscle control, partial to good balance with trunk muscles	Independent	Independent	Independent; manual wheelchair
T11 to L5	Hip flexors, hip abductors (L1 to L3); knee extension (L2 to L4); knee flexion and ankle dorsiflexion (L4 to L5)	Independent	Independent	Short distance to full ambulation with assistance
S1 to S5	Full leg, foot, and ankle control; innervation of perineal muscles for bowel, bladder, and sexual function (S2 to S4)	Independent	Normal to impaired bowel and bladder function	Ambulate independently with or without assistance

*Assistance refers to adaptive equipment, setup, or physical assistance.
From Porth, C. M., & Matfin, G. (2008). *Pathophysiology: Concepts of altered health states.* (8th ed.) Philadelphia: Lippincott Williams & Wilkins.

The standard of care is that the patient is referred to a regional spinal injury or trauma center because of the multidisciplinary personnel and support services required to counteract the destructive changes that occur in the first 24 hours after injury. During treatment in the emergency and X-ray departments, the patient is kept on the transfer board. The patient must always be maintained in an extended position. No part of the body should be twisted or turned, nor should the patient be allowed to sit up. Once the extent of the injury has been determined, the patient may be placed on a rotating bed or in a cervical collar. Later, if SCI and bone instability have been ruled out, the patient may be moved to a conventional bed or the collar may be removed without harm. If a rotating bed is needed but not available, the patient should be placed in a hard cervical collar and on a firm mattress.

Medical and Nursing Management

The goals of management are to prevent further SCI and to observe for symptoms of progressive neurologic deficits.

Many changes in the treatment of SCI have occurred during the past 20 years. Treatments such as hypothermia, corticosteroids, and naloxone were investigated and used during the 1980s; of these, high-dose corticosteroids have shown the most promise, but their use remains controversial. In the National Acute Spinal Cord Injury Studies (NASCIS) done in 1990 and 1997, the administration of high-dose corticosteroids, specifically methylprednisolone (Solu-Medrol), was found to improve motor and sensory outcomes at 6 weeks, 6 months, and 1 year if given within 8 hours after injury (Nicholas, Selassie, Lineberry et al., 2009). In 2001, The American Association of Neurological Surgeons/Congress of Neurological Surgeons conducted a review of available literature and noted that treatment for either 24 or 48 hours was recommended as an option. They noted, however, that there was more evidence to suggest harmful side effects than there was evidence that suggested clinical benefit (Hadley et al., 2001).

There remains a debate on whether high-dose methylprednisolone should be standard protocol. Despite current

literature, many centers continue using protocols for high-dose methylprednisolone in patients with acute SCI (Ito, Sugimoto, Tomioka et al., 2009). In a more recent review of available therapies for SCI, it was concluded that administration of high-dose methylprednisolone was justified in nondiabetic and nonimmunocomprised patients as there are no alternative therapies currently available (Hawryluk, Rowland, Kwon et al., 2008).

Biologic agents are currently being investigated for the acute and chronic phases of SCI. Cell-based therapies, including stem cells and glial cells, are showing promise in animal trials (Rowland, Hawryluk, Kwon et al., 2008).

Nonsurgical Management

Treatment of SCI attempts to achieve decompression, stabilization, and realignment of the spinal cord while preserving or improving neurologic function (Hickey, 2009). Cervical fractures are reduced, and the cervical spine is aligned with some form of skeletal traction, such as skeletal tongs or calipers, or with use of the halo device. A variety of skeletal tongs are available, all of which involve fixation in the skull in some manner. The Gardner-Wells tongs require no predrilled holes in the skull. Crutchfield and Vinke tongs are inserted through holes made in the skull with a special drill under local anesthesia.

A halo device may be used initially with traction, or may be applied after removal of the tongs. It consists of a stainless-steel halo ring that is fixed to the skull by four pins. The ring is attached to a removable **halo vest,** a device that suspends the weight of the unit circumferentially around the chest. A metal frame connects the ring to the chest. Halo devices provide immobilization of the cervical spine while allowing early ambulation (Fig. 45-6). Refer to Chapter 42 for nursing responsibilities related to pin care.

Thoracic and lumbar injuries are usually treated with surgical intervention followed by immobilization with a fitted brace. Traction is not indicated either before or after surgery, due to the relative stability of the spine in these regions.

Surgical Management

Surgery is indicated in any of the following instances:

- Compression of the cord
- Fragmented or unstable vertebral body
- Penetrating wound to the spinal cord
- Bone fragments in the spinal canal
- Deterioration of the patient's neurological status

Surgery is performed to decompress the spinal cord, reduce the spinal fracture or dislocation, or to stabilize the spinal column. Laminectomy is the most common surgical procedure used to decompress or stabilize the spinal column. A **laminectomy** involves excision of the lamina (a portion of the posterior arch) and spinous processes of a vertebra. Various techniques (i.e., fusion or fixation) are used to create a stable spinal column (Hickey, 2009).

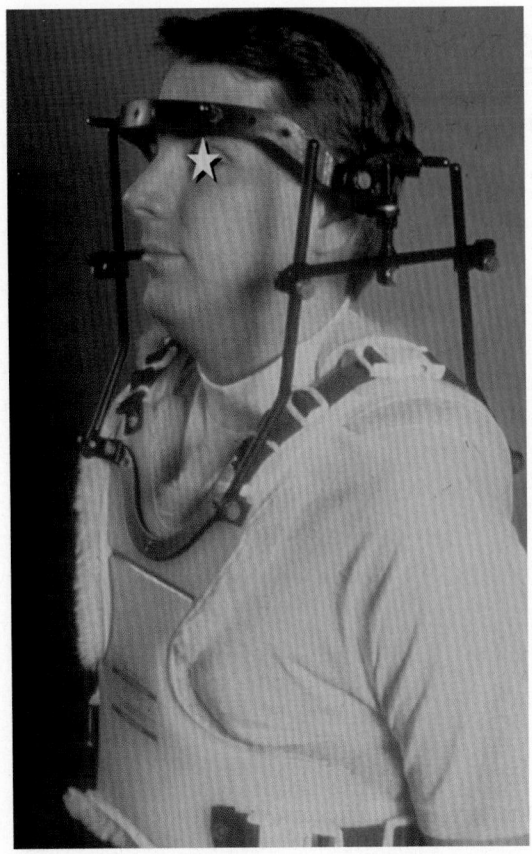

FIGURE 45-6 Halo vest.

Monitoring and Managing Acute Complications of Spinal Cord Injury

Spinal and Neurogenic Shock

The spinal shock associated with SCI reflects a sudden depression of reflex activity in the spinal cord (areflexia) below the level of injury. The muscles innervated by the part of the spinal cord segment below the level of the lesion are without sensation, paralyzed, and flaccid. In particular, the reflexes that initiate bladder and bowel function are affected. Bowel distention and paralytic ileus can be caused by depression of the reflexes and are treated with intestinal decompression by insertion of a nasogastric tube (Hickey, 2009).

Neurogenic shock develops due to the loss of autonomic nervous system function below the level of the lesion (Hickey, 2009). The vital organs are affected, causing the blood pressure and heart rate to decrease. This loss of sympathetic innervation causes a variety of other clinical manifestations, including a decrease in cardiac output, venous pooling in the extremities, and peripheral vasodilation resulting in mild hypotension, bradycardia, and warm skin. In addition, the patient does not perspire on the paralyzed portions of the body because sympathetic activity is blocked; therefore, close observation is required for early detection of an abrupt onset of fever.

Deep Vein Thrombosis

Thrombophlebitis, inflammation of a vein related to deep vein thrombosis (DVT) is a relatively common potential complication of immobility and is common in patients with SCI (Teasell, Hsieh, Abut et al., 2009). DVT occurs in a high percentage (67% to 100%) of SCI patients, placing them at risk for pulmonary embolism (PE), which is the third most common cause of death in patients with SCI (Ploumis, Ponnappan, Maltenfort et al., 2009). The patient must be assessed for symptoms both of DVT and PE. A low-grade fever may be the first sign of DVT. Manifestations of pulmonary embolism include pleuritic chest pain, anxiety, and shortness of breath.

Thigh and calf measurements should be made daily. The patient is evaluated for the presence of DVT if the circumference of one extremity increases significantly. Diagnostic studies used to detect DVT and PE include Doppler ultrasound, radiocontrast venography, and ventilation/perfusion lung scans (Hickey, 2009).

Anticoagulation therapy to prevent DVT and PE is initiated once head injury and other systemic injuries have been ruled out and there is low risk for bleeding. There is strong evidence to support the use of low-molecular-weight heparin as well as unfractionated heparin. This may be followed by long-term oral anticoagulation with a vitamin K antagonist (i.e., warfarin) or subcutaneous fractionated heparin injections (Teasell et al., 2009). In a review of the literature on treatments for thromboembolism, low-molecular-weight heparin was shown to be more effective at preventing DVT and had fewer bleeding complications than fractionated heparin. However, both are equally effective at preventing PE (Ploumis et al., 2009). Anticoagulant therapy should be continued for at least 6 to 12 weeks after injury.

Nonpharmacologic measures, including elastic compression stockings or pneumatic compression devices, as well as range-of-motion exercises, are important preventive measures that work to reduce venous pooling and promote venous return. Compression devices should be used for 2 weeks following injury. In some cases, permanent indwelling filters may be placed in the vena cava to prevent emboli (dislodged clots) from migrating to the lungs and causing PE in patients who have developed clots despite receiving anticoagulation. (Gorman, Qadri, & Rao-Patel, 2009).

Orthostatic Hypotension

For the first 2 weeks following SCI, blood pressure tends to be unstable and quite low. It gradually returns to preinjury levels, but periodic episodes of severe orthostatic hypotension frequently interfere with efforts to mobilize the patient. Orthostatic hypotension is defined as a drop in systolic blood pressure of at least 20 mm Hg or a drop in diastolic pressure of at least 10 mm Hg, regardless of the patient's symptoms (Krassioukov, Eng, Warburton et al., 2009). Patients with SCI are prone to orthostatic hypotension during position changes due to a loss of reflex vasoconstriction and pooling of blood in the lower extremities and abdominal viscera. This results in decreased venous return to the heart and decreased cardiac output. To compensate, patients develop reflex tachycardia, although this is rarely sufficient to raise blood pressure enough to return to normal levels (Krassioukov et al., 2009). Orthostatic hypotension is a particularly common problem for patients with lesions above T7 and those with tetraplegia (Hickey, 2009).

A number of techniques can be used to reduce the frequency of hypotensive episodes. Close monitoring of vital signs before and during position changes is essential. Vasopressor medication can be used to treat the profound vasodilation. Elastic compression stockings should be applied to improve venous return from the lower extremities. Abdominal binders may also be used to encourage venous return and provide diaphragmatic support when the patient is upright. Activity should be planned in advance, and adequate time should be allowed for a slow progression of position changes from recumbent to sitting and upright.

Autonomic Dysreflexia

Autonomic dysreflexia, also known as autonomic hyperreflexia, is an acute emergency that occurs as a result of exaggerated autonomic responses to stimuli that are harmless in normal people. It only occurs after spinal shock has resolved in patients with cord lesions above T6. This syndrome is characterized by a severe, pounding headache with paroxysmal hypertension, profuse diaphoresis (most often of the forehead), nausea, nasal congestion, and bradycardia (Hickey, 2009). The sudden increase in blood pressure may cause a rupture of one or more cerebral blood vessels or lead to increased ICP. Autonomic dysreflexia is more commonly seen in patients with complete spinal cord injuries and in the chronic stages of SCI (Krassioukov et al., 2009).

A number of stimuli may trigger this reflex: distended bladder (the most common cause); distention or contraction of the visceral organs, especially the bowel (from constipation, impaction); or stimulation of the skin (tactile, pain, thermal stimuli, pressure ulcer). Because this is an emergency situation, the objectives are to remove the triggering stimulus and to avoid the potentially serious complications.

The following measures are carried out:

- The head of the bed is raised, and the patient is placed immediately in a sitting position to lower blood pressure.
- Rapid assessment is performed to identify and alleviate the cause.
- The bladder is emptied immediately via a urinary catheter. If an indwelling catheter is not patent, it is irrigated or replaced with another catheter.
- The rectum is examined for a fecal mass. If one is present, a topical anesthetic such as lidocaine may be inserted 10 to 15 minutes before the mass is removed because visceral distention or contraction can worsen autonomic dysreflexia. The nurse observes for symptoms of flushing, sweating, nasal congestion, and headache while performing a digital

exam and ceases the procedure if symptoms appear and assesses blood pressure.

- The skin is examined for any areas of pressure, irritation, or broken skin.
- Any other stimulus that could be the triggering event, such as an object next to the skin or a draft of cold air, must be removed.
- If these measures do not relieve the hypertension and excruciating headache, a ganglionic blocking agent (hydralazine hydrochloride [Apresoline]) is prescribed and administered slowly by the IV route.
- The medical record or chart is labeled with a clearly visible note about the risk for autonomic dysreflexia.
- The patient is instructed about prevention and management measures.
- Any patient with a lesion above the T6 segment is informed that such an episode is possible and may occur even years after the initial injury.

NURSING PROCESS

The Patient With Acute Spinal Cord Injury

Assessment

The breathing pattern is observed, the strength of the cough is assessed, and the lungs are auscultated because paralysis of abdominal and respiratory muscles diminishes coughing and makes clearing of bronchial and pharyngeal secretions difficult.

The patient is monitored closely for any changes in motor or sensory function and for symptoms of progressive neurologic damage. In the early stages of SCI, determining whether the cord has been severed may be very difficult because signs and symptoms of cord edema are indistinguishable from those of cord transection. Edema of the spinal cord may occur with any severe cord injury and may further compromise spinal cord function.

Motor and sensory functions are assessed through careful neurologic examination. These findings are usually recorded on a flow sheet, so that changes in the baseline neurologic status can be monitored closely and accurately. The ASIA classification is commonly used to describe level of function for SCI patients. Box 45-10 gives examples of the effects of altered spinal cord function. At the minimum:

- Motor ability is tested by asking the patient to spread the fingers, squeeze the examiner's hand, and move the toes or turn the feet.
- Sensation is evaluated by gently pinching the skin or touching it lightly with an object such as a tongue blade, starting at shoulder level and working down both sides of the extremities. The patient should have both eyes closed, so that

the examination reveals true findings, not what the patient hopes to feel. The patient is asked where the sensation is felt.

- Any decrease in neurologic function is reported immediately.

The patient is also assessed for spinal shock, urinary retention, overdistention of the bladder, and paralytic ileus.

Diagnosis

Nursing Diagnoses

Based on the assessment data, the patient's major nursing diagnoses may include the following:

- Ineffective breathing patterns related to weakness or paralysis of abdominal and intercostal muscles and inability to clear secretions
- Ineffective airway clearance related to weakness of intercostal muscles
- Impaired bed and physical mobility related to motor and sensory impairments
- Disturbed sensory perception related to motor and sensory impairment
- Risk for impaired skin integrity related to immobility and sensory loss
- Impaired urinary elimination related to inability to void spontaneously
- Constipation related to presence of atonic bowel as a result of autonomic disruption
- Acute pain and discomfort related to treatment and prolonged immobility

Collaborative Problems/Potential Complications

Potential complications that may develop in patients with SCI include:

- DVT/PE (thrombophlebitis)
- Orthostatic hypotension
- Autonomic dysreflexia

Planning and Goals

The goals for the patient may include improved breathing pattern and airway clearance, improved mobility, improved sensory and perceptual awareness, maintenance of skin integrity, relief of urinary retention, improved bowel function, promotion of comfort, and absence of complications.

Nursing Interventions

Promoting Adequate Breathing and Airway Clearance

Oxygen is administered to maintain a normal saturation level because hypoxemia can create or worsen a neurologic deficit of the spinal cord. If endotracheal intubation is necessary, extreme care is taken to avoid flexing or extending the patient's neck, which can result in extension of a cervical injury.

Possible impending respiratory failure is detected by observing the patient, noting rate and depth of respirations, assessing lung sounds, accessory muscle use, monitoring oxygen saturation through pulse oximetry, and monitoring arterial blood gas values. Early and vigorous attention to clearing bronchial and pharyngeal secretions can prevent retention of secretions and atelectasis. Suctioning may be indicated, but caution must be used because this procedure can stimulate the vagus nerve, producing bradycardia, which can result in cardiac arrest.

If the patient cannot cough effectively because of decreased inspiratory volume and inability to generate sufficient expiratory pressure, chest physical therapy and assisted coughing may be indicated.

Improving Mobility

Proper body alignment is maintained at all times. The patient is repositioned frequently and is assisted out of bed as soon as the spinal column is stabilized. The feet are prone to footdrop; therefore, various types of splints are used to prevent it. When used, the splints are removed and reapplied every 2 hours. Trochanter rolls, applied from the crest of the ileum to the midthigh of both legs, help prevent external rotation of the hip joints.

Patients with lesions above the midthoracic level have loss of sympathetic control of peripheral vasoconstrictor activity, leading to hypotension. These patients may tolerate changes in position poorly and require monitoring of blood pressure when positions are changed. Usually, the patient is turned every 2 hours by log rolling. Log rolling ensures proper spinal alignment during turning of the patient. The patient should not be turned unless the spine is stable and the provider has indicated that it is safe to do so.

Contractures develop rapidly with immobility and muscle paralysis. A joint that is immobilized too long becomes fixed as a result of contractures of the tendon and joint capsule. Atrophy of the extremities results from disuse. Contractures and other complications may be prevented by range-of-motion exercises that help preserve joint motion and stimulate circulation. Passive range-of-motion exercises should be implemented as soon as possible after injury.

Promoting Adaptation to Sensory and Perceptual Alterations

The nurse assists the patient to compensate for sensory and perceptual alterations that occur with SCI. The intact senses above the level of the injury are stimulated through touch, aromas, flavorful food and beverages, conversation, and music. Additional strategies include the following:

- Providing prism glasses to enable the patient to see from the supine position
- Encouraging use of hearing aids, if indicated, to enable the patient to hear conversations and environmental sounds

- Providing emotional support to the patient
- Teaching the patient strategies to compensate for or cope with these deficits

Maintaining Skin Integrity

Because patients with SCI are immobilized and have loss of sensation below the level of the lesion, they have the highest prevalence of pressure ulcers in the United States. Up to 85% of patients with spinal cord disorders will develop pressure ulcers in their lifetime. In the spinal cord population, there is about an 8% mortality rate from pressure ulcers (Srivastava, Gupta, Taly et al., 2009). The most common sites for pressure ulcers are over the ischial tuberosity, the greater trochanter, the sacrum, the gluteal region, and the occiput (back of the head). Patients who wear cervical collars for prolonged periods may develop breakdown from the pressure of the collar under the chin, on the shoulders, and at the occiput. The nurse follows institutional policy regarding collar care, which typically may require changing of pads every 24 hours and inspecting and cleaning the skin every shift.

The patient is repositioned every 2 hours, and careful inspection of the skin is made every time the patient is turned. The skin over pressure points is assessed for redness or breakdown. The patient's skin should be kept clean by washing with a mild soap, rinsing well, and blotting dry. Pressure-sensitive areas should be kept well lubricated and soft with hand cream or lotion.

Maintaining Urinary Elimination

Immediately after SCI, the urinary bladder may become atonic and is unable to contract by reflex activity. Urinary retention typically results. Because the patient has no sensation of bladder distention, overstretching of the bladder and detrusor muscle may occur, delaying the return of bladder function.

Intermittent catheterization is carried out to avoid overdistention of the bladder and UTI. If this is not feasible, an indwelling catheter is inserted temporarily. At an early stage, family members are shown how to carry out intermittent catheterization and are encouraged to participate in this facet of care because they will be involved in long-term follow-up and must be able to recognize complications, so that treatment can be instituted.

The patient is taught to record fluid intake, voiding pattern, characteristics of urine, and any unusual sensations that may occur. The management of a neurogenic bladder (bladder dysfunction that results from a disorder or dysfunction of the nervous system) is discussed in detail in Chapter 28.

Improving Bowel Function

Immediately after SCI, a paralytic ileus may develop due to neurogenic paralysis of the bowel; therefore, a nasogastric

(continued on page 1208)

tube is often required to relieve distention and to prevent vomiting and aspiration.

Bowel activity usually returns within the first week following the injury. As soon as bowel sounds are heard on auscultation, the patient is given a high-calorie, high-protein, high-fiber diet, with the amount of food gradually increased. The nurse administers prescribed stool softeners to counteract the effects of immobility and analgesic agents. A bowel regimen is instituted as early as possible. Bowel dysfunction is more common in patients with a motor complete SCI but is also seen in those with motor incomplete SCI (Valles & Mearin, 2009).

Providing Comfort Measures

A patient who has had pins, tongs, or calipers placed for cervical stabilization may have a headache or discomfort for several days after the pins are inserted. Patients initially may be bothered by the rather startling appearance of these devices, but usually they readily adapt to it because the device provides comfort for the unstable neck. The patient may complain of being caged in and of noise created by any object coming in contact with the steel frame of a halo device, but he or she can be reassured that adaptation to this will occur.

The areas around the four pin sites of a halo device are cleaned daily and observed for redness, drainage, and pain. The pins are observed for loosening, which may contribute to infection. If one of the pins becomes detached, the head is stabilized in a neutral position by one person, while another notifies the neurosurgeon. A torque screwdriver should be readily available in case the screws on the frame need tightening.

The skin under the halo vest is inspected for excessive perspiration, redness, and skin blistering, especially on the bony prominences. The vest is opened at the sides to allow the torso to be washed. The liner of the vest should not become wet, because dampness causes skin excoriation. The liner should be changed periodically to promote hygiene and good skin care. If the patient is to be discharged with the vest, detailed instructions must be given to the family, with time allowed for them to demonstrate the necessary skills of halo vest care.

Promoting Home and Community-Based Care

TEACHING PATIENT SELF-CARE. In most cases, patients with SCI (i.e., patients with tetraplegia or paraplegia) need long-term rehabilitation. The process begins during hospitalization, as acute symptoms begin to subside or come under better control and the overall deficits and long-term effects of the injury become clear. The goals begin to shift from merely surviving the injury to learning strategies necessary to cope with the alterations that the injury imposes on activities of daily living (ADLs). The emphasis shifts from ensuring that the patient is stable and free of complications to specific assessment and planning designed to meet the patient's rehabilitation needs. Patient teaching may initially focus on the injury and its effects on mobility, dressing, and bowel, bladder, and sexual function. As the patient and family acknowledge the consequences of the injury and the resulting disability, the focus of teaching broadens to address issues necessary for carrying out the tasks of daily living and taking charge of their lives. Teaching begins in the acute phase and continues throughout rehabilitation. Interventions are aimed at increasing function, improving adjustment, increasing social integration, and reducing social stigma (Wilson, Huston, Koval et al., 2009).

Caring for the patient with SCI at home may at first seem a daunting task to the family. They will require dedicated nursing support to gradually assume full care of the patient. Although maintaining function and preventing complications will remain important, goals regarding self-care and preparation for discharge will assist in a smooth transition to rehabilitation and eventually to the community.

CONTINUING CARE. The ultimate goal of the rehabilitation process is independence. The nurse becomes a support to both the patient and the family, assisting them to assume responsibility for increasing aspects of patient care and management. Care for the patient with SCI involves members of all the health care disciplines, which may include nursing, medicine, rehabilitation, respiratory therapy, physical and occupational therapy, case management, and social services. The nurse often serves as coordinator of the management team and as a liaison with rehabilitation centers and home care agencies (Johnson, Bailey, Rundquist et al., 2008). Box 45-12 discusses another important role the nurse can assume in managing patients with SCI. The patient and family often require assistance in dealing with the psychological impact of the injury and its consequences; referral to a psychiatric clinical nurse specialist or other mental health care professional is often helpful. It is important to begin assessment of the patient's psychological state early in the rehabilitative process, as early intervention improves long-term patient satisfaction (van Koppenhagen, Post, van der Woude et al., 2009).

As more patients survive acute SCI, they face the changes associated with aging with a disability. Therefore, teaching in the home and community focuses on health promotion and addresses the need to minimize risk factors that increase the risk of mortality. Some risk factors that have been identified include cardiovascular disease, diabetes, psychiatric disorders, and alcohol or substance abuse (Krause, Zhai, Saunders et al., 2009). Home care nurses and others who have contact with patients with SCI are in a position to teach patients about healthy lifestyles, remind them of the need for health screenings, and make referrals as appropriate. Assisting patients to identify accessible health care providers, clinical facilities, and imaging centers may increase the likelihood that they will participate in health screening.

BOX 45-12

Nursing Research

Bridging the Gap to Evidence-Based Practice

How Can Registered Nurses Help Improve Patient and Physician Satisfaction in a Large Spine Center?

Crossley, L, Mueller, L., & Horstman, P. (2009). Software-assisted spine registered nurse care coordination and patient triage: One organization's approach. *Journal of Neuroscience Nursing, 41*(4), 217–224.

Purpose

Back disorders encompass a broad range of conditions, ranging from acute onset with a short duration to life-long disorders. Back pain patients typically have long waits for referrals to spine centers, poor communication among treating providers, and little coordination of care. The West Virginia University Spine Center is a multi-disciplinary regional spine referral center with a large number of new patient referrals. New patients were being booked to the first available appointment, without regard to the level of urgency. The result of this was high levels of patient and referring physician dissatisfaction. The WVU Spine Center then created a registered nurse (RN) care coordinator role, and developed software to assist the RN in triaging new referrals and coordinating care for patients.

Design

The role of the RN Care Coordinator was developed to improve triaging of referrals and to improve communication with both patients and referring providers. For each new patient, the RN reviews the patient's medical information, and, if there is no need for an immediate

appointment, a referral specialist will call the patient and complete a history intake. After the chart and appropriate radiologic films have been reviewed by the RN, a physician reviews the information and formulates an initial impression and treatment plan. The RN calls the patient as well as the referring physician to discuss the impression and plan, and to coordinate any additional testing that needs to be completed prior to the clinic appointment.

Findings

After implementing the role of the RN coordinator, both patient and referring physician satisfaction significantly improved. Patients appreciated having someone who could answer their questions in a timely manner and could explain complicated medical terminology, and the referring provider was able to receive feedback in a timely manner. Overall wait time was reduced from 9 to 12 weeks to 1 to 2 weeks. There was also a 17% increase in volume of surgical patients and a 21% increase in volume of referrals.

Nursing Implications

This study serves as a reminder of the vital role nurses play in the outpatient setting. This study shows that by implementing a RN care coordinator role, significant improvements were made in efficiency, productivity, and service in the clinic, as well as increased patient and provider satisfaction with the spine clinic.

Evaluation

Expected Patient Outcomes

Expected patient outcomes may include the following:

1. Demonstrates improvement in gas exchange and clearance of secretions, as evidenced by normal breath sounds on auscultation:
   a. Breathes easily without shortness of breath
   b. Performs hourly deep-breathing exercises, coughs effectively, and clears pulmonary secretions
   c. Is free of respiratory infection (i.e., has normal temperature, respiratory rate, and pulse, normal breath sounds, absence of purulent sputum)
2. Moves within limits of the dysfunction and demonstrates completion of exercises within functional limitations
3. Demonstrates adaptation to sensory and perceptual alterations:
   a. Uses assistive devices (i.e., prism glasses, hearing aids, computers) as indicated

   b. Describes sensory and perceptual alterations as a consequence of injury
4. Demonstrates optimal skin integrity:
   a. Exhibits normal skin turgor; skin is free of reddened areas or breakdown
   b. Participates in skin care and monitoring procedures within functional limitations
5. Regains control of urinary bladder function:
   a. Exhibits no signs of UTI (i.e., has normal temperature; voids clear, dilute urine)
   b. Has adequate fluid intake
   c. Participates in bladder training program within functional limitations
6. Regains control of bowel function:
   a. Reports regular pattern of bowel movement
   b. Consumes adequate dietary fiber and oral fluids
   c. Participates in bowel training program within functional limitations
7. Reports absence of pain and discomfort

(continued on page 1210)

8. Is free of complications:
   a. Demonstrates no signs of DVT or PE
   b. Exhibits no manifestations of PE (i.e., no chest pain or shortness of breath; arterial blood gas values are within normal limits)

c. Maintains blood pressure within normal limits
d. Reports no lightheadedness with position changes
e. Exhibits no manifestations of autonomic dysreflexia (i.e., absence of headache, diaphoresis, nasal congestion, bradycardia, or diaphoresis)

Chapter Review

Critical Thinking Exercises

1. A 70-year-old patient was brought to the emergency department after he fell and hit his head and was unconscious for about 2 minutes. He now seems alert and oriented. What type of injury has he most likely sustained? What discharge instructions are warranted for this patient's family or caregiver? How would you modify your discharge instructions if the patient lives alone?

2. Your 25-year-old patient with a TBI has early signs of increased ICP. Describe the medical management you would anticipate to control the ICP and the nursing measures that are indicated. How would you determine whether your interventions were effective in alleviating the increased ICP? What is the evidence base for these interventions?

3. A 47-year-old man with paraplegia secondary to SCI, diabetes, and obesity is admitted. For what complications is he at risk? What interventions would be appropriate to prevent these complications?

NCLEX-Style Review Questions

1. The nurse assesses the LOC of a patient who suffered a head injury and determines that the patient's GCS score is 15. Which of the following responses did the nurse assess to determine the GCS score? Select all that apply.
   A. Spontaneous eye opening
   B. Tachycardia, hypotension, bradycardia
   C. Ability to follow commands
   D. Unequal pupil size
   E. Orientation to person, place, and time

2. A patient sustained a C6 SCI 4 hours ago. Which of the following nursing diagnoses is a priority?
   A. Urinary retention
   B. Risk for impaired skin integrity

C. Ineffective breathing pattern
D. Powerlessness

3. The nurse notices clear fluid draining from the nose of a patient who sustained a head injury 2 hours ago. This may indicate the presence of which of the following conditions?
   A. Cerebral concussion
   B. Basal skull fracture
   C. Brain tumor
   D. Sinus infection

4. An 18-year-old man is admitted with a closed head injury that he sustained in a motorcycle accident. He has been showing an upward trend in his ICP measurements. Which of the following interventions should be the first action that a nurse takes?
   A. Administer 100 mg of IV pentobarbital as ordered
   B. Increase the ventilator settings to a respiratory rate of 20 breaths/min
   C. Administer 20 g of IV mannitol as ordered
   D. Reposition the patient to avoid neck flexion

5. Which interventions should the nurse's plan of care include to help prevent autonomic dysreflexia in a patient with SCI? Select all that apply.
   A. Check for fecal impactions.
   B. Monitor blood pressure for hypotension.
   C. Check the urinary drainage system for any obstruction.
   D. Monitor bowel movements.
   E. Instruct the patient to wear a medic alert bracelet.

Try these additional resources to enhance your learning and understanding of this chapter:
- thePoint online resource available at **http://thepoint.lww.com/Pellico1e**
- *Handbook for Focus on Adult Health: Medical-Surgical Nursing*
- *Study Guide for Focus on Adult Health: Medical-Surgical Nursing*

References and Selected Readings

References and selected readings associated with this chapter can be found on the website that accompanies the book. Visit http://thepoint.lww.com/Pellico1e to access the references and other additional resources associated with this chapter.

Nursing Management: Patients With Neurologic Disorders

CYNTHIA BAUTISTA

Learning Objectives

After reading this chapter, you will be able to:

1. Identify the various types and causes of seizures.

2. Use the nursing process to develop a plan of care for the patient experiencing seizures.

3. Differentiate among the infectious disorders of the nervous system according to causes, manifestations, medical care, and nursing management.

4. Describe the pathophysiology, clinical manifestations, and medical and nursing management of multiple sclerosis, myasthenia gravis, and Guillain–Barré syndrome.

5. Describe disorders of the cranial nerves, their manifestations, and indicated nursing interventions.

6. Use the nursing process as a framework for care of patients with degenerative neurologic disorders.

SEIZURE DISORDERS

SEIZURES, EPILEPSY, AND STATUS EPILEPTICUS

Seizures are temporary episodes of abnormal motor, sensory, autonomic, or psychic activity (or a combination of these) that result from sudden excessive electrical discharge from cortical neurons (Hickey, 2009). A part or all of the brain may be involved. The term *ictal* refers to an actual seizure or *ictal event*.

Epilepsy is a group of syndromes characterized by unprovoked, recurring seizures (Bazil & Pedley, 2010). Epileptic syndromes are classified by specific patterns of clinical features, including age at onset, family history, and seizure type. Types of epilepsies are differentiated by how the seizure activity manifests, usually detected in scalp electroencephalogram (EEG) recordings (Box 46-1). The most common syndromes are those with generalized seizures, which involve the brain diffusely, and those with partial-onset seizures, which are limited to one side of the cerebral hemisphere. Epilepsy can be idiopathic (formerly termed primary), in which no cause is identified, or symptomatic (formerly termed secondary), when the cause is known and the epilepsy is a symptom of another underlying condition, such as a brain tumor. Although some evidence suggests that susceptibility to some types of epilepsy may be inherited, the cause of seizures in many people is unknown. Epilepsy can follow birth trauma, asphyxia neonatorum, head injuries, some infectious diseases (bacterial, viral, parasitic), toxicity (carbon monoxide and lead poisoning), circulatory problems, fever, metabolic and nutritional disorders, and drug or alcohol intoxication (Criddle, Everley, Franges et al., 2008). It is also associated with brain tumors, abscesses, and congenital malformations. Most cases of epilepsy are idiopathic (i.e., the cause is unknown).

Epilepsy is not associated with intellectual level. People who have epilepsy without other brain or nervous system disabilities fall within the same intelligence ranges as the overall population. Epilepsy is not synonymous with mental retardation or illness. However, many people who have developmental disabilities because of serious neurologic damage also have epilepsy.

International Classification of Seizures

Partial Seizures (Seizures Beginning Locally)

Simple partial seizures (with elementary symptoms, generally without impairment of consciousness):
- With motor symptoms
- With special sensory or somatosensory symptoms
- With autonomic symptoms
- Compound forms (motor & sensory)

Complex partial seizures (with complex symptoms, generally with impairment of consciousness):
- With impairment of consciousness only
- With cognitive symptoms
- With affective symptoms
- With psychosensory symptoms
- With psychomotor symptoms (automatisms)
- Compound forms (motor & sensory)

Partial seizures secondarily generalized

Generalized Seizures (Convulsive or Nonconvulsive, Bilaterally Symmetric, Without Local Onset)

- *Tonic-clonic seizures:* Generalized seizures that affect the entire brain; they begin with rigidity (tonic phase), followed by repetitive clonic activity of all extremities characterized by stiffening or jerking of the body.
- *Tonic seizures:* Seizures characterized by muscle stiffening, dilation of the pupils, and altered respiratory patterns; the body becomes stiff and the person may fall backward. The seizure usually lasts less than one minute and recovery is rapid.
- *Clonic seizures:* Characterized by jerking movements, which involve muscles on both sides of the body.
- *Absence (petit mal) seizures:* Short episodes of staring and loss of awareness
- *Atonic seizures:* Sudden loss of muscle tone, resulting in falls or a "drop" to the ground, with rapid recovery
- *Myoclonic seizures (bilaterally massive epileptic):* Characterized by jerking (myoclonic) movements of a muscle or muscle group, without loss of consciousness
- *Unclassified seizures:* Seizures that cannot be classified

---

! NURSING ALERT

Not all seizures imply epilepsy. Although seizures are the cardinal symptom of epilepsy, seizures also occur as a manifestation of an underlying treatable problem, such as hyponatremia or high fever. Once the cause is identified and treated, the seizures cease. Epilepsy is a chronic disease, and refers to recurrent, unpredictable, and unprovoked seizures.

Status epilepticus (acute prolonged seizure activity) is a series of generalized seizures that occur without full recovery of consciousness between attacks (Hickey, 2009). The term has been broadened to include continuous clinical or electrical seizures (on EEG) lasting at least 30 minutes, even without impairment of consciousness. It is considered a medical emergency, with a mortality rate of 20% (Bradley, Daroff, Fenichel et al., 2008). Status epilepticus produces cumulative effects. Vigorous muscular contractions impose a heavy metabolic demand and can interfere with respirations. The respiratory difficulties that occur during status epilepticus can result in hypoxia to the brain. Repeated episodes of cerebral anoxia and edema may lead to irreversible and fatal brain damage. Length of time of the uncontrolled seizures increases the systemic effects of respiratory compromise, acidemia, hypoglycemia, and hypotension (Bradley, 2008). Factors that precipitate status epilepticus include withdrawal of antiseizure medication, fever, concurrent infection, and withdrawal from alcohol or drugs.

Pathophysiology of Seizures

Messages from the body are carried by the neurons (nerve cells) of the brain by means of discharges of electrochemical energy that sweep along them. These impulses occur in bursts whenever a nerve cell has a task to perform. Sometimes, these cells or groups of cells continue firing after a task is finished. During the period of unwanted discharges, parts of the body controlled by the errant cells may perform erratically. Resultant dysfunction ranges from mild to incapacitating and often causes loss of consciousness (Hickey, 2009). If these uncontrolled, abnormal discharges occur repeatedly, a person is said to have an *epileptic syndrome* (Hickey, 2009). The international classification of seizures differentiates between two main types: partial seizures, which begin in one part of the brain, and generalized seizures, which involve electrical discharges in the whole brain (see Box 46-1). In simple partial seizures, consciousness remains intact, whereas in a complex partial seizure, consciousness is impaired. However, it is understood that not all seizures or syndromes fit neatly into this classification, and patients may have more than one type of seizure.

The specific causes of seizures are varied and can be categorized as idiopathic (genetic, developmental defects) and acquired. Causes of acquired seizures include:

- Cerebrovascular disease
- Hypoxemia of any cause, including vascular insufficiency
- Fever (childhood)
- Head injury
- Hypertension
- Central nervous system infections
- Metabolic and toxic conditions (e.g., renal failure, hyponatremia, hypocalcemia, hypoglycemia, pesticides)
- Brain tumor
- Drug and alcohol withdrawal
- Allergies

Clinical Manifestations and Assessment

The initial pattern of the seizures indicates the region of the brain in which the seizure originates (see Box 46-1). In simple

partial seizures, only a finger or hand may shake, or the mouth may jerk uncontrollably. The person may talk unintelligibly, may be dizzy, and may experience unusual or unpleasant sights, sounds, odors, or tastes, but without loss of consciousness (Hickey, 2009).

In complex partial seizures, the person either remains motionless or moves automatically but inappropriately for time and place, or he or she may experience excessive emotions of fear, anger, elation, or irritability. Whatever the manifestations, the person does not remember the episode when it is over.

Generalized seizures, previously referred to as *grand mal seizures,* involve both hemispheres of the brain, causing both sides of the body to react (Hickey, 2009). Intense rigidity of the entire body may occur, followed by alternating muscle relaxation and contraction (generalized tonic–clonic contraction). The simultaneous contractions of the diaphragm and chest muscles may produce a characteristic epileptic cry. The tongue is often chewed, and the patient is incontinent of urine and feces. After 1 or 2 minutes, the convulsive movements begin to subside; the patient relaxes and lies in deep coma, breathing noisily. The respirations at this point are chiefly abdominal. In the postictal (after the seizure) state, the patient is often confused and hard to arouse and may sleep for hours. Many patients report headache, sore muscles, extremity weakness, fatigue, and depression (Lippincott Williams & Wilkins, 2008).

A medical history is taken, including previous seizure history, alcohol and drug use, medication use, allergy status, and family history. The patient is also questioned about illnesses or head injuries that may have affected the brain. Women should be questioned about their last menstrual period (increased in seizure frequency is noted during menses) and pregnancy status (fetal anomaly is two times higher in women taking antiepileptic medications). The patient is asked about common triggers associated with seizures which can be olfactory (particular odors), visual (flashing lights), or auditory (certain types of music) in nature, or related to fatigue, sleep deprivation, hypoglycemia, emotional stress, electrical shock, febrile illness, alcohol consumption, certain drugs, drinking too much water, constipation, and hyperventilation (Hickey, 2009).

In addition to physical and neurologic evaluations, diagnostic examinations include biochemical, hematologic, and serologic studies. Imaging studies such as magnetic resonance imaging (MRI), magnetic resonance spectroscopy (MRS), and positron emission tomography (PET) may be used to detect structural lesions such as focal abnormalities, cerebrovascular abnormalities, and cerebral degenerative changes (Bradley et al., 2008). Single-photon emission computed tomography (SPECT) is an additional tool that is sometimes used in the diagnostic workup. It is useful for identifying the epileptogenic zone so that the area in the brain giving rise to seizures can be removed surgically.

The EEG furnishes diagnostic evidence for a substantial proportion of patients with epilepsy and assists in classify-

ing the type of seizure (Lippincott Williams & Wilkins, 2008). Abnormalities in the EEG usually continue between seizures or, if not apparent, may be elicited by hyperventilation or during sleep. Microelectrodes (depth electrodes) can be inserted deep in the brain to probe the action of single brain cells. Some people with clinical seizures have normal EEGs, whereas others who have never had seizures have abnormal EEGs. Telemetry and computerized equipment are used to monitor electrical brain activity while the patient pursues his or her normal activities and to store the readings on computer tapes for analysis. Video recording of seizures taken simultaneously with EEG telemetry is useful in determining the type of seizure as well as its duration and magnitude. This type of intensive monitoring is changing the treatment of severe epilepsy.

Medical and Nursing Management

The goals of treatment are to stop the seizures as quickly as possible, to ensure adequate cerebral oxygenation, and to maintain the patient in a seizure-free state. In the case of prolonged seizures, as in status epilepticus, the nurse recalls the standard ABCs (airway, breathing and circulation) of emergency management. Mortality rates of up to 30% are noted if the seizure lasts over 1 hour (Pourmand, 2008). An airway and adequate oxygenation are established. The patient is gently positioned on the side to avoid aspiration, and an oral airway may be inserted if the patient's teeth are not clenched. Note that the airway is *never* forced. Oxygen is administered as ordered via nasal cannula, or, intubation may be required, and oxygen is administered via the artificial airway and monitored by pulse oximetry. Suctioning of the airway may also be required. An IV line is established and IV diazepam (Valium), lorazepam (Ativan), or fosphenytoin (Cerebyx) is administered slowly in an attempt to halt seizures immediately. Other medications (phenytoin, phenobarbital) are administered later to maintain a seizure-free state. In general, a single drug is used to control the seizures. Termed *monotherapy,* the selected drug is determined by the type of seizure, and the dose is increased until symptoms resolve, maximal dose is required, or signs of drug toxicity emerge, at which time alternative therapeutic agents are considered, and the patient may be tapered off the first drug. The IV line is closely monitored because it may become dislodged during seizures.

NURSING ALERT

Phenytoin (Dilantin), if ordered intravenously, must be administered slowly because of its effect on the myocardium and the potential for arrhythmia development. In addition, it is irritating to the vein; thus, the nurse observes for the development of phlebitis. The rate of administration is no faster than 50 mg/ min in normal saline solution, since the drug precipitates in D5W. If the preexisting solution contained dextrose, the nurse flushes the IV line with normal saline before administering the

medication. Many antiepileptic drugs are highly bound to plasma protein, and the nurse is aware that only the unbound, or "free," serum concentration is available for use by the body. Patients on high-protein tube feedings (see Chapter 22) may require higher dosages to maintain therapeutic blood levels, while those with hypoalbuminemia because of malnutrition, burns, or liver or renal disease may require alternative dosing to prevent phenytoin toxicity. Therapeutic range for phenytoin is 10 to 20 mg/L (Lassiter & Henkel, 2009).

Blood samples are obtained to monitor serum electrolytes, glucose, blood cell count, and toxicology/drug screen, and levels of drugs such as phenobarbital or phenytoin may be monitored if the patient has been treated with the medication. If the serum concentration of the antiseizure medication is below therapeutic levels, it suggests that the patient was not taking the medication, the dosage was too low, or factors such as pharmacokinetics of the medication may be involved. EEG monitoring may be useful in determining the nature of the seizure activity. Vital signs and neurologic signs are monitored on a continuing basis. An IV infusion of dextrose is administered if the seizure is caused by hypoglycemia. If initial treatment is unsuccessful, general anesthesia with a short-acting barbiturate may be used. Cardiac involvement or respiratory depression may be life-threatening. The potential for postictal cerebral edema also exists. This varies in clinical presentation and may include deterioration in neurological signs, such as drowsiness to coma, nausea, vomiting, sluggish pupillary response, cardiac arrhythmias, and altered respiratory patterns. The nurse initiates ongoing assessment and monitoring of respiratory and cardiac function because of the risk for delayed depression of respiration and blood pressure secondary to administration of antiseizure medications and sedatives to halt the seizures. Nursing assessment also includes monitoring and documenting the seizure activity and the patient's responsiveness.

A person who has received long-term antiseizure therapy has a significant risk for fractures resulting from bone disease (osteoporosis, osteomalacia, and hyperparathyroidism), a side effect of therapy. Therefore, during seizures, the patient is protected from injury with the use of seizure precautions, which include padding side rails of the bed, maintaining the bed in the low position, ensuring side rails are up and that suction, an oral airway, and oxygen are available at the bedside, and the patient is monitored closely (Hickey, 2009). No effort should be made to restrain movements. The patient having seizures can inadvertently injure nearby people, so nurses should protect themselves. Other nursing interventions for the person having seizures are presented in Box 46-2.

During a Seizure

A major responsibility of the nurse is to observe and record the sequence of signs. Before and during a seizure, the patient is assessed and the following items are documented:

- The circumstances before the seizure (visual, auditory, or olfactory stimuli; tactile stimuli; emotional or psychological disturbances; sleep; hyperventilation)
- The occurrence of an aura (a premonitory or warning sensation that can be visual, auditory, gustatory, or olfactory) that is experienced at the beginning of a seizure and remembered (Hickey, 2009).
- The first thing the patient does in the seizure—in what part of the body the movement or stiffness begins, conjugate gaze position (termed that denotes both eyes working in unison), and the position of the head at the beginning of the seizure. This information gives clues to the location of the seizure origin in the brain. (In recording, it is important to state whether the beginning of the seizure was observed).
- The type of movements in the part of the body involved
- The areas of the body involved (turn back bedding to expose patient)
- The size of both pupils and whether the eyes are open
- Whether the eyes or head are/is turned to one side
- The presence or absence of automatisms (involuntary motor activity, such as lip smacking or repeated swallowing)
- Incontinence of urine or stool
- Duration of each phase of the seizure
- Unconsciousness, if present, and its duration
- Any obvious paralysis or weakness of arms or legs after the seizure
- Inability to speak after the seizure
- Movements at the end of the seizure
- Whether or not the patient sleeps afterward
- Cognitive status (confused or not confused) after the seizure

In addition to providing data about the seizure, nursing care is directed at preventing injury and supporting the patient, not only physically but also psychologically. Steps to prevent or minimize injury are presented in Box 46-2.

After a Seizure

After a patient has a seizure, the nurse's role is to document the events leading to and occurring during and after the seizure and to prevent complications (e.g., aspiration, injury). The patient is at risk for hypoxia, vomiting, and pulmonary aspiration. To prevent complications, the patient is placed in the side-lying position to facilitate drainage of oral secretions, and suctioning is performed, if needed, to maintain a patent airway and prevent aspiration (see Box 46-2). Seizure precautions are maintained, including having available functioning suction equipment with a suction catheter and oral airway. The bed is placed in a low position with two to three side rails up and padded, if necessary, to prevent injury to the patient. The patient may be drowsy and may wish to sleep after the seizure; he or she may not remember events leading up to the seizure and for a short time thereafter.

Pharmacologic Therapy

Although many medications are available to control seizures, the nurse stresses that the treatment is not curative.

BOX 46-2

GUIDELINES FOR NURSING CARE

Nursing Care During a Seizure

- Provide privacy and protect the patient from curious onlookers. (The patient who has an *aura* (warning of an impending seizure) may have time to seek a safe, private place).
- Ease the patient to the floor, if possible.
- Protect the head with a pad to prevent injury (from striking a hard surface).
- Loosen constrictive clothing, remove eyeglasses.
- Push aside any furniture that may injure the patient during the seizure.
- If the patient is in bed, remove pillows and raise side rails.
- If an aura precedes the seizure, insert an oral airway to reduce the possibility of the patient's biting the tongue or cheek.
- *Do not attempt to pry open jaws that are clenched in a spasm or to insert anything.* Broken teeth and injury to the lips and tongue may result from such an action.
- No attempt should be made to restrain the patient during the seizure, because muscular contractions are strong and restraint can produce injury.

- If possible, place the patient on one side with head flexed forward, which allows the tongue to fall forward and facilitates drainage of saliva and mucus. If suction is available, use it if necessary to clear secretions.

Nursing Care After the Seizure

- Keep the patient on one side to prevent aspiration. Make sure the airway is patent.
- There is usually a period of confusion after a grand mal seizure.
- A short apneic period may occur during or immediately after a generalized seizure.
- The patient, on awakening, should be reoriented to the environment.
- If the patient becomes agitated after a seizure (postictal), use calm persuasion and gentle restraint.

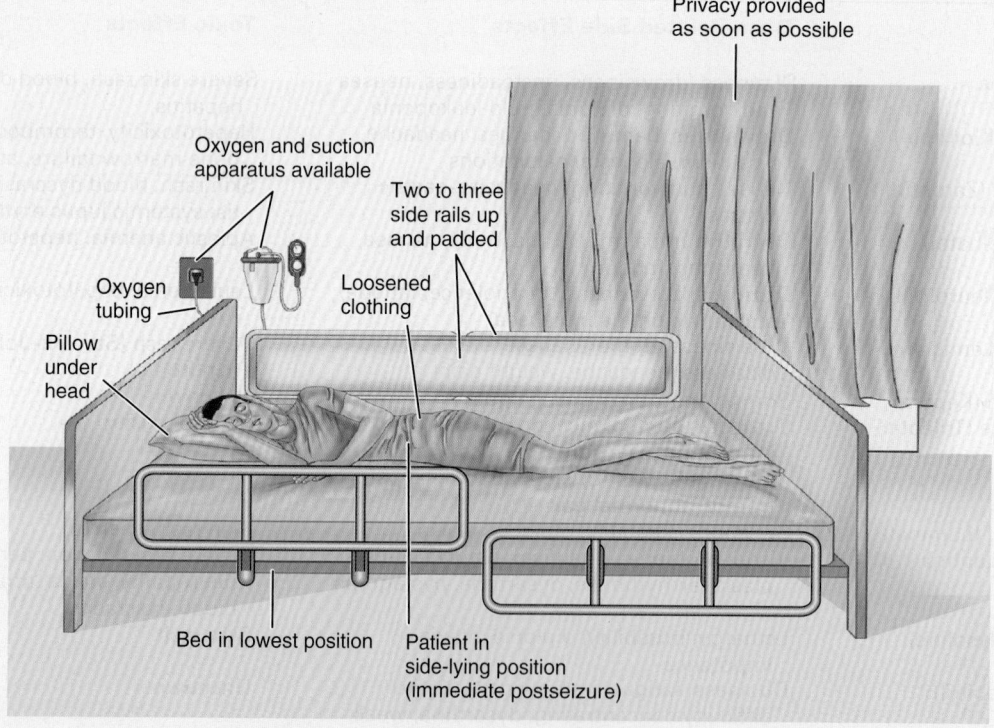

Privacy provided as soon as possible

Oxygen and suction apparatus available

Two to three side rails up and padded

Oxygen tubing

Loosened clothing

Pillow under head

Bed in lowest position

Patient in side-lying position (immediate postseizure)

The objective is to achieve seizure control with minimal side effects. Medications are selected on the basis of the patient's type of seizure and the effectiveness and safety of the medications. If properly prescribed and taken, medications control seizures in 70% to 80% of patients with seizures (Lowenstein, 2009), although 20% to 30% of patients with epilepsy are resistant to antiepileptic drugs. In these situations, surgery may reduce seizure frequency or provide complete seizure control.

Treatment usually starts with a single medication. The starting dose and the rate at which the dosage is increased depend on the occurrence of side effects. The medication levels in the blood are monitored because the rate of drug absorption varies among patients. Changing to another medication may be necessary if seizure control is not achieved or if toxicity makes it impossible to increase the dosage. The medication may need to be adjusted because of concurrent illness, weight changes, or increases in stress. Sudden withdrawal of these medications can cause seizures to occur with greater frequency or can precipitate the development of status epilepticus (Hickey, 2009).

Side effects of antiseizure agents may be divided into three groups: (1) idiosyncratic or allergic disorders, which manifest primarily as skin reactions; (2) acute toxicity, which may occur when the medication is initially prescribed; and (3) chronic toxicity, which occurs late in the course of therapy.

The manifestations of drug toxicity are variable, and any organ system may be involved. Gingival hyperplasia (swollen and tender gums) can be associated with long-term use of phenytoin (Dilantin), for example (Lassiter & Henkel, 2009). Periodic physical and dental examinations and laboratory tests are performed for patients receiving medications that are known to have hematopoietic, genitourinary, or hepatic effects. Table 46-1 lists the medications in current use.

Surgical Management

Surgery is indicated for patients whose epilepsy results from intracranial tumors, abscesses, cysts, or vascular anomalies. Some patients have intractable seizure disorders that do not respond to medication. A focal (localized or limited) atrophic process may occur secondary to trauma, inflammation, stroke, or anoxia. If the seizures originate in a reasonably

TABLE
46-1 Major Antiseizure Medications

Medication	Dose-Related Side Effects	Toxic Effects
Carbamazepine (Tegretol)	Dizziness, drowsiness, unsteadiness, nausea and vomiting, diplopia, mild leukopenia	Severe skin rash, blood dyscrasias, hepatitis
Clonazepam (Klonopin)	Drowsiness, behavior changes, headache, hirsutism, alopecia, palpitations	Hepatotoxicity, thrombocytopenia, bone marrow failure, ataxia
Ethosuximide (Zarontin)	Nausea and vomiting, headache, gastric distress	Skin rash, blood dyscrasias, hepatitis, systemic lupus erythematosus
Felbamate (Felbatol)	Cognitive impairments, insomnia, nausea, headache, fatigue	Aplastic anemia, hepatotoxicity
Gabapentin (Neurotonin)	Dizziness, drowsiness, somnolence, fatigue, ataxia, weight gain, nausea	Leukopenia, hepatotoxicity
Lamotrigine (Lamictal)	Drowsiness, tremor, nausea, ataxia, dizziness, headache, weight gain	Severe rash (Stevens-Johnson syndrome)
Levetiracetam (Keppra)	Somnolence, dizziness, fatigue	Unknown
Oxcarbazepine (Trileptal)	Dizziness, somnolence, double vision, fatigue, nausea, vomiting, loss of coordination, abnormal vision, abdominal pain, tremor, abnormal gait	Hepatotoxicity
Phenobarbital (Luminal)	Sedation, irritability, diplopia, ataxia	Skin rash, anemia
Phenytoin (Dilantin)	Visual problems, hirsutism, gingival hyperplasia, arrhythmias, dysarthria, nystagmus	Severe skin reaction, peripheral neuropathy, ataxia, drowsiness, blood dyscrasias
Primidone (Mysoline)	Lethargy, irritability, diplopia, ataxia, impotence	Skin rash
Tiagabine (Gabitril)	Dizziness, fatigue, nervousness, tremor, difficulty concentrating, dysarthria, weak or buckling knees, abdominal pain	Unknown
Topiramate (Topamax)	Fatigue, somnolence, confusion, ataxia, anorexia, depression, weight loss	Nephrolithiasis
Valproate (Depakote, Depakene)	Nausea and vomiting, weight gain, hair loss, tremor, menstrual irregularities	Hepatotoxicity, skin rash, blood dyscrasias, nephritis
Zonisamide (Zonegran, Excegran)	Somnolence, dizziness, anorexia, headache, nausea, agitation, rash	Leukopenia, hepatotoxicity

well-circumscribed area of the brain that can be excised without producing significant neurologic deficits, the removal of the area generating the seizures may produce long-term control and improvement (Lowenstein, 2009).

This type of neurosurgery has been aided by several advances, including microsurgical techniques, EEGs with depth electrodes, improved illumination and hemostasis, and the introduction of neuroleptanalgesic agents (droperidol and fentanyl). These techniques, combined with use of local anesthetic agents, enable the neurosurgeon to perform surgery on an alert and cooperative patient. Using special testing devices, electrocortical mapping, and the patient's responses to stimulation, the boundaries of the epileptogenic focus (the abnormal area of the brain) are determined. The abnormal epileptogenic focus is then excised (Hickey, 2009).

As an adjunct to medication and surgery in adolescents and adults with partial seizures, a generator may be implanted under the clavicle. The device is connected to the vagus nerve in the cervical area, where it delivers electrical signals to the brain to control and reduce seizure activity (Hickey, 2009). An external programming system is used by the physician to change stimulator settings. Patients can turn the stimulator on and off with a magnet. Resection surgery significantly reduces the incidence of seizures in patients with refractory epilepsy; however, more research is needed to determine the effect of surgery on quality of life, anxiety, and depression, all issues for these patients.

Gerontologic Considerations

Elderly people (age 65 and older) have a high incidence of new-onset epilepsy (Hickey, 2009). Cerebrovascular disease is the leading cause of seizures in the elderly, but head trauma, dementia, infection, alcoholism, and aging are also associated risk factors (Collins, Shapiro, & Ramsay, 2006). Treatment depends on the underlying cause. Because many elderly people have chronic health problems, they may be taking other medications that can interact with medications prescribed for seizure control. In addition, the absorption, distribution, metabolism, and excretion of medications are altered in the elderly as a result of age-related changes in renal and liver function. Therefore, elderly patients must be monitored closely for adverse and toxic effects of antiseizure medications and for osteoporosis. The cost of antiseizure medications can lead to poor adherence to the prescribed regimen in elderly patients on fixed incomes.

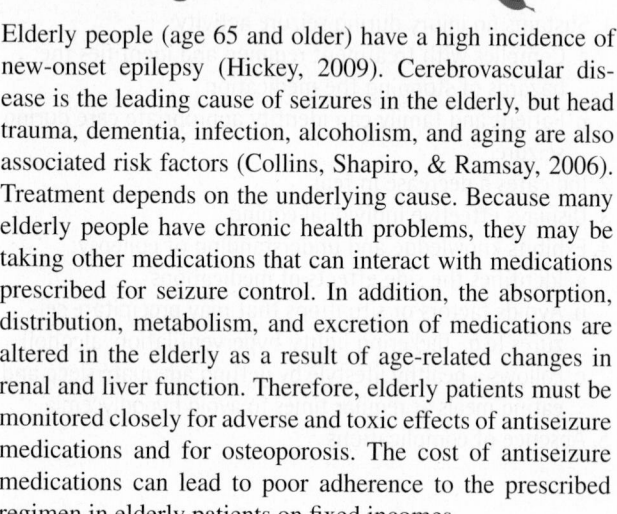

NURSING PROCESS

The Patient With Epilepsy and Seizures

Assessment

The nurse elicits information about the patient's seizure history. The patient is asked about the factors or events that may precipitate the seizures. Alcohol intake is documented. The nurse determines whether the patient has an aura before an epileptic seizure, which may indicate the origin of the seizure (e.g., seeing a flashing light may indicate that the seizure originated in the occipital lobe). Observation and assessment during and after a seizure assist in identifying the type of seizure and its management.

The effects of epilepsy on the patient's lifestyle are assessed. What limitations are imposed by the seizure disorder? Does the patient have a recreational program? Social contacts? Is the patient working, and is it a positive or stressful experience? What coping mechanisms are used?

Diagnosis

Nursing Diagnoses

Based on the assessment data, the patient's major nursing diagnoses may include the following:

- Risk for injury related to seizure activity
- Fear related to the possibility of seizures
- Ineffective individual coping related to stresses imposed by epilepsy
- Deficient knowledge related to epilepsy and its control

Collaborative Problems/Potential Complications

The major potential complications for patients with epilepsy are status epilepticus and medication side effects (toxicity).

Planning and Goals

Goals for the patient may include prevention of injury, control of seizures, achievement of a satisfactory psychosocial adjustment, acquisition of knowledge and understanding about the condition, and absence of complications.

Nursing Interventions

Preventing Injury

Injury prevention for the patient with seizures is a priority. If the type of seizure the patient is having places him or her at risk for injury, the patient should be lowered gently to the floor (if not in bed), and any potentially harmful items nearby (e.g., furniture, eyeglasses) should be removed. The patient should never be restrained or forced into a position, nor should anyone attempt to insert anything into the patient's mouth once a seizure has begun, as protecting the airway is a priority. Patients for whom seizure precautions are instituted should have pads applied to the side rails when in bed.

Reducing Fear of Seizures

Fear that a seizure may occur unexpectedly can be reduced by the patient's adherence to the prescribed treatment regimen. Cooperation of the patient and family and their trust in the prescribed regimen are essential for control of seizures. The

(*continued on page 1218*)

nurse emphasizes that the prescribed antiseizure medication must be taken on a continuing basis and that drug dependence or addiction does not occur. Periodic monitoring is necessary to ensure the adequacy of the treatment regimen, to prevent side effects, and to monitor for drug resistance.

In an effort to control seizures, factors that may precipitate them are identified, such as emotional disturbances, new environmental stressors, onset of menstruation in female patients, hypoglycemia, or fever. The patient is encouraged to follow a regular and moderate routine in lifestyle, diet (avoiding excessive stimulants), exercise, and rest (sleep deprivation may lower the seizure threshold). Moderate activity is therapeutic, but excessive exercise should be avoided. An additional dietary intervention, referred to as the ketogenic diet, has been suggested for control of seizures in some patients; however, research on this high-fat and -protein, low-carbohydrate diet only demonstrates effectiveness in children and further studies are needed to assess its efficacy in adults. In addition, because of the high fat component of this diet and limited replacement of essential nutrients, additional prohibitive health complications in older patients should be considered (Liu & Henry, 2009).

Photic stimulation (bright flickering lights, television viewing) may precipitate seizures; wearing dark glasses or covering one eye may be preventive. Tension states (anxiety, frustration) induce seizures in some patients. Classes in stress management may be of value. Because seizures are known to occur with alcohol intake, alcoholic beverages should be avoided.

Improving Coping Mechanisms

The social, psychological, and behavioral problems that frequently accompany epilepsy can be more of a disability than the actual seizures. Epilepsy may be accompanied by feelings of stigmatization, alienation, depression, and uncertainty. The patient must cope with the constant fear of a seizure and the psychological consequences. Adults face potential issues such as the burden of finding employment, restrictions on the ability to drive, concerns about relationships and childbearing, insurance problems, and legal barriers. Alcohol abuse may complicate matters. Family reactions may vary from outright rejection of the person with epilepsy to overprotection. As a result, many people with epilepsy are at risk for psychological and behavioral problems.

Counseling assists the patient and family to understand the condition and the limitations it imposes. Social and recreational opportunities are necessary for good mental health. Nurses can improve the quality of life for patients with epilepsy by teaching them and their families about symptoms and their management.

Providing Patient and Family Education

Perhaps the most valuable facets of care contributed by the nurse to the person with epilepsy are education and efforts to modify the attitudes of the patient and family toward

the disorder. The person who experiences seizures may consider every seizure a potential source of humiliation and shame. This may result in anxiety, depression, hostility, and secrecy on the part of the patient and family. Ongoing education and encouragement should be given to patients to enable them to overcome these reactions. The patient with epilepsy should carry an emergency medical identification card or wear a medical information bracelet. The patient and family need to be educated about medications as well as care during a seizure.

Monitoring and Managing Potential Complications

Status epilepticus, the major complication, was described previously. Another complication is the toxicity of medications. The patient and family are instructed about side effects and are given specific guidelines to assess and report signs and symptoms that indicate medication overdose. Many antiseizure medications require careful monitoring for therapeutic levels. The patient should plan to have serum drug levels assessed at regular intervals. Many known drug interactions occur with antiseizure medications. A complete pharmacologic profile should be reviewed with the patient to avoid interactions that either potentiate or inhibit the effectiveness of the medications.

Evaluation

Expected Patient Outcomes

Expected patient outcomes may include the following:

1. Sustains no injury during seizure activity:
   a. Complies with treatment regimen and identifies the hazards of stopping the medication
   b. Patient and family can identify appropriate care during seizure.
2. Indicates a decrease in fear
3. Displays effective individual coping
4. Exhibits knowledge and understanding of epilepsy:
   a. Identifies the side effects of medications
   b. Avoids factors or situations that may precipitate seizures (e.g., flickering lights, hyperventilation, alcohol)
   c. Follows a healthy lifestyle by getting adequate sleep and eating meals at regular times to avoid hypoglycemia
5. Absence of complications

INFECTIOUS NEUROLOGIC DISORDERS

MENINGITIS

Meningitis is an inflammation of the protective membranes covering the brain and spinal cord (meninges). Specifically, the pia mater (closest to the central nervous system [CNS]), the arachnoid, the cerebrospinal fluid (CSF)–filled subarachnoid

space, and the dura mater (closest to the skull) may be involved (Criddle et al., 2008). Meningitis is classified as septic or aseptic. Septic meningitis is caused by bacteria; commonly, *Streptococcus pneumoniae* and *Neisseria meningitidis* (meningococcus) are infecting organisms, with mortality rates of up to 34% for *S. pneumoniae* and 10% for *N. meningitidis* (Centers for Disease Control and Prevention [CDC], 2010; Koedel, Klein, & Pfister, 2010). For patients over 50, additional causative organisms include *Listeria monocytogenes* and aerobic gram-negative bacilli (Bloch, 2010). *Haemophilus influenzae* was once a common cause of meningitis in children, but because of vaccination, infection with this organism is now rare in the United States. However, it is still a concern for those not immunized for *H. influenza*. Outbreaks of *N. meningitidis* infection are most likely to occur in dense community groups, such as college campuses and military installations. Although infections occur year round, the peak incidence is in the winter and early spring. Factors that increase the risk for bacterial meningitis include tobacco use and viral upper respiratory infection because they increase the amount of droplet production. Otitis media and mastoiditis increase the risk for bacterial meningitis, because the bacteria can cross the epithelial membrane and enter the subarachnoid space. Preexisting diabetes and alcohol abuse, asplenia (having no spleen), and immune system deficiencies (chemotherapy, immunosuppressive treatment, AIDS) are also risk factors for the development of bacterial meningitis (Nicolasora & Kaul, 2008). The cause of aseptic meningitis is viral or secondary to lymphoma, leukemia, HIV, or chemical irritants (Simon, Greenberg, & Aminoff, 2009).

Pathophysiology

The brain is protected by the skull, meninges, and the blood–brain barrier. Any violation to these defenses by a pathogen can result in meningitis. Meningeal infections generally originate in one of two ways: through the bloodstream as a consequence of other infections of the heart, lung, or viscera; or by direct spread, such as might occur after a traumatic injury to the facial bones, infection in the skull or spine, sinusitis, otitis, brain abscess, or secondary to invasive procedures such as lumbar puncture or ventricular shunting procedures.

Once the causative organism enters the bloodstream, it crosses the blood–brain barrier and proliferates in the CSF. The host immune response disrupts the cellular integrity of the microorganism and the breakdown products (cell wall fragments and lipolysaccharides [LPS]) which enhances the inflammatory response in the involved meninges. Part of this response is the recruitment of neutrophils to the inflammatory site, resulting in thickening (an increase in viscosity) of the CSF. Because the cranial vault contains little room for expansion, the inflammation may cause increased intracranial pressure (ICP). CSF circulates through the subarachnoid space, where inflammatory cellular materials from the affected meningeal tissue enter and accumulate. The thickened CSF can interfere with CSF absorption, resulting in hydrocephalus.

CSF studies demonstrate decreased glucose, increased protein levels, and increased white blood cell count (Bloch, 2010).

The prognosis for bacterial meningitis depends on the causative organism, the severity of the infection and illness, and the timeliness of treatment. Acute fulminant presentation may include adrenal damage, circulatory collapse, and widespread hemorrhages (Waterhouse-Friderichsen syndrome). This syndrome is the result of endothelial damage and vascular necrosis caused by the bacteria. Complications include visual impairment, deafness, seizures, paralysis, hydrocephalus, and septic shock. A recent study revealed that factors associated with death from meningitis were rural area of residence, presentation to the hospital after 24 hours, total leukocyte count (TLC) of less than 15,000, CSF neutrophil levels of less than 75%, low Glasgow coma scale (GCS) at the time of admission, and a high creatinine level (Vibha, Bhatia, & Prasad et al., 2010).

Clinical Manifestations and Assessment

Headache and fever are frequently the initial symptoms. The headache is usually either steady or throbbing and very severe, as a result of meningeal irritation (Simon et al., 2009a). Fever tends to remain high throughout the course of the illness. An altered level of consciousness (LOC) is frequently seen; however one-third of patients present with normal mentation (Bloch, 2010). Meningeal irritation results in a number of other well-recognized signs common to all types of meningitis:

- *Nuchal rigidity (stiff neck):* This is an early sign seen in 30% to 70% of patients (Bloch, 2010). Any attempts at flexion of the head are difficult because of spasms in the muscles of the neck. With the patient in supine position, the head is gently flexed forward and assessed for rigidity.
- *Positive Kernig's sign:* When the patient is lying supine with the hip flexed to a 90-degree angle, resistance to passive extension of the knee is a positive Kernig's sign (Fig. 46-1A).
- *Positive Brudzinski's sign:* When the patient's neck is flexed (after ruling out cervical trauma or injury), flexion of the knees and hips is produced; when the lower extremity of one side is passively flexed, a similar movement is seen in the opposite extremity (see Fig. 46-1B).
- *Photophobia (extreme sensitivity to light):* This finding is common, although the cause is unclear.

A rash can be a striking feature of *N. meningitidis* infection, occurring in about half of patients with this type of meningitis. Skin lesions develop, ranging from a petechial rash with purpuric lesions to large areas of ecchymosis.

Disorientation and memory impairment are common early in the course of the illness. The changes depend on the severity of the infection, as well as the individual response to the physiologic processes. As the illness progresses, lethargy, unresponsiveness, and coma may develop.

Seizures occur in 40% to 50% of adults with bacterial meningitis within the first week and are the result of areas of

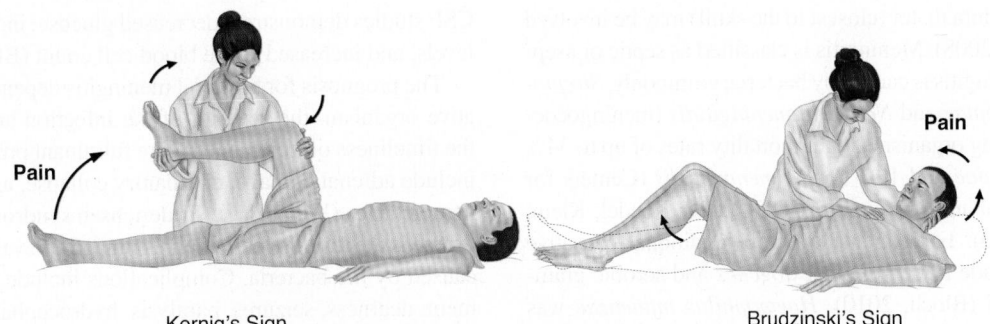

FIGURE 46-1 Testing for meningeal irritation. (**A**) Kernig's sign. (**B**) Brudzinski's sign.

Kernig's Sign

Brudzinski's Sign

Pain

Pain

irritability in the brain (Hickey, 2009). ICP increases secondary to the accumulation of purulent exudate and cerebral edema. The initial signs of increased ICP include decreased LOC and focal motor deficits. Vomiting is a frequent finding associated with a rising ICP. If ICP is not controlled, the uncus of the temporal lobe may herniate through the tentorium, causing pressure on the brainstem. Brainstem herniation is a life-threatening event that causes cranial nerve dysfunction and depresses the centers of vital functions, such as the medulla. Refer to Chapter 45 to review vital sign changes termed Cushing's response. An acute fulminant infection occurs in about 10% of patients with meningococcal meningitis, producing signs of overwhelming septicemia: an abrupt onset of high fever, extensive purpuric lesions (over the face and extremities), shock, and signs of disseminated intravascular coagulopathy (DIC). Refer to Chapter 20 for details of DIC. Death may occur within a few hours after onset of the infection.

If the clinical presentation suggests meningitis, diagnostic testing is conducted to identify the causative organism. Bacterial culture and Gram staining of CSF and blood are key diagnostic tests (Fischbach & Dunning, 2009).

Medical and Nursing Management

Successful outcomes depend on the early administration of antibiotics that cross the blood–brain barrier into the subarachnoid space in sufficient concentration to halt the multiplication of bacteria. Penicillin antibiotics (e.g., ampicillin, piperacillin) or one of the cephalosporins (e.g., ceftriaxone sodium, cefotaxime sodium) may be used. Vancomycin hydrochloride alone or in combination with rifampin may be used if resistant strains of bacteria are identified. High doses of the appropriate antibiotic are administered IV.

The use of dexamethasone as an adjunct therapy in the treatment of acute bacterial meningitis and in pneumococcal meningitis, if administered before the first dose of antibiotic, has been considered. However, recent results of a meta-analysis did not demonstrate significant reduction in death or neurological disability with steroid use (Lin & Safdieh, 2010; Van de Beek, Farrar, de Gans et al., 2010). Further research is needed to determine the efficacy of dexamethasone in meningitis.

Dehydration and shock are treated with fluid volume expanders. Seizures, which may occur early in the course of the disease, are controlled with phenytoin (Dilantin). Increased ICP is treated as necessary (see Chapter 45).

The patient with meningitis is critically ill; therefore, many of the nursing interventions are collaborative with the physician, respiratory therapist, and other members of the health care team. The patient's safety and well-being depend on sound nursing judgment.

Neurologic status and vital signs are continually assessed. Pulse oximetry and arterial blood gas (ABG) values are used to quickly identify the need for respiratory support if increasing ICP compromises the brainstem. Insertion of a cuffed endotracheal tube (or tracheotomy) and mechanical ventilation may be necessary to maintain adequate tissue oxygenation.

Arterial blood pressures are monitored to assess for incipient shock, which precedes cardiac or respiratory failure. Rapid IV fluid replacement may be prescribed, but care is taken to prevent fluid overload. Fever also increases the workload of the heart and cerebral metabolism. ICP will increase in response to increased cerebral metabolic demands. Therefore, measures are taken to reduce body temperature as quickly as possible.

Other important components of nursing care include the following measures:

- Protecting the patient from injury secondary to seizure activity or altered LOC
- Monitoring daily body weight; serum electrolytes; and urine volume, specific gravity, and osmolality, especially if syndrome of inappropriate antidiuretic hormone (SIADH) is suspected (refer to Chapter 31).
- Preventing complications associated with immobility, such as pressure ulcers and pneumonia
- Instituting infection control precautions until 24 hours after initiation of antibiotic therapy (oral and nasal discharge is considered infectious)

Any sudden, critical illness can be devastating to the family. Because the patient's condition is often critical and the prognosis guarded, the family needs to be informed about the patient's condition. Periodic family visits are essential to facilitate coping of the patient and family. An important

aspect of the nurse's role is to support the family and assist them in identifying others who can be supportive of them during the crisis. Additionally, it is important to consider that long-term neuropsychological and otological sequelae affect up to 50% of survivors (Koedel et al., 2010, p. 217).

ENCEPHALITIS

Encephalitis is an acute inflammatory process of the brain tissue (cerebral cortex) secondary to viruses, bacteria, fungi, or parasites (Hickey, 2009). Viruses are the most common cause of encephalitis in the United States, and herpes simplex virus (HSV) is the most common of these (Bolon & Weber, 2009; Chamberlain, 2009). There are two herpes simplex viruses, HSV-1 and HSV-2. HSV-1 typically affects children and adults. HSV-2 most commonly affects neonates.

Pathophysiology

HSV-1 causes encephalitis by following a retrograde intraneuronal path to the brain. The olfactory and trigeminal nerves are the most commonly involved paths. Researchers also believe that latent virus in brain tissue may reactivate and result in encephalitis. The invading organism causes cerebral edema and petechial hemorrhages of the brain and can directly invade the brain damaging neurons (Jacewicz, 2009).

Clinical Manifestations and Assessment

Initial symptoms include fever, headache, stiff neck, and confusion. Focal neurologic symptoms reflect the areas of cerebral inflammation and necrosis and include behavioral changes, focal seizures, dysphasia, hemiparesis, and altered LOC (Hickey, 2009). Patients may also have auditory and visual hallucinations (Chamberlain, 2009).

Neuroimaging studies, EEG, and CSF examination are used to diagnose HSV encephalitis. The EEG demonstrates periodic high-voltage spikes originating in the temporal lobe, and MRI may reveal temporal lobe edema. Lumbar puncture often reveals a high opening pressure and low glucose and high protein levels in CSF samples. Viral cultures are almost always negative. The polymerase chain reaction (PCR) is the standard test for early diagnosis of HSV-1 encephalitis. The validity of PCR is very high between the third and tenth days after symptom onset.

Medical and Nursing Management

Acyclovir (Zovirax), an antiviral agent, is the medication of choice in the treatment of HSV. Studies have indicated that early administration of acyclovir improves the prognosis associated with HSV-1 encephalitis and reduces a mortality rate of 70% to 28% if treatment is initiated before the onset of coma (Hickey, 2009). To prevent relapse, treatment should continue for up to 3 weeks. Slow IV administration over at

least 1 hour, along with adequate hydration, may prevent crystallization of the medication in the renal tubules, which would be reflected by a rising serum creatinine and blood urea nitrogen (BUN). Assessment of neurologic function is key to monitoring the progression of disease. Comfort measures to reduce headache include dimming the lights, limiting noise, and administering analgesic agents. Opioid analgesic medications may mask neurologic symptoms; therefore, they are used cautiously. Focal seizures and altered LOC require care directed at injury prevention and safety. Nursing care addressing patient and family anxieties is ongoing throughout the illness. Monitoring of blood chemistry test results and hourly urinary output will alert the nurse to the presence of renal complications related to acyclovir therapy.

ARTHROPOD-BORNE VIRUS ENCEPHALITIS

Arthropod vectors transmit several types of viruses that cause encephalitis. The primary vector in North America is the mosquito. In cases of West Nile virus, humans are the secondary host; birds are the primary host. Arbovirus infection (transmitted by arthropod vectors) occurs in specific geographic areas during the summer or early fall when the vectors are most active. West Nile virus, the most common type of arboviral encephalitis, was first observed in the United States in 1999 (Chamberlain, 2009). Encephalitis develops in less than 1% of cases, and the elderly are at increased risk (Jubelt, 2010). The St. Louis arbovirus is seen in the western United States, and the elderly are affected more frequently,

Pathophysiology

Viral replication occurs at the site of the mosquito bite. The host immune response attempts to control viral replication. If the immune response is inadequate, viremia will ensue. The virus gains access to the CNS via the cerebral capillaries, resulting in encephalitis. It spreads from neuron to neuron, predominantly affecting the cortical gray matter, the brainstem, and the thalamus. Meningeal exudates compound the clinical presentation by irritating the meninges and increasing ICP.

Clinical Manifestations and Assessment

An arboviral encephalitis begins with early flu-like symptoms, but specific neurologic manifestations depend on the viral type. After a brief febrile prodrome, neurologic symptoms will reflect the area of the brain that is involved. For example, if meninges are involved, patients can present with nuchal rigidity and headache. A unique clinical feature of St. Louis encephalitis is the development of syndrome of inappropriate antidiuretic hormone (SIADH) with hyponatremia in 25% to 33% of affected patients (Jubelt, 2010). (SIADH

is detailed in Chapter 31). Signs and symptoms specific to West Nile encephalitis include a maculopapular or morbilliform rash on the neck, trunk, arms, and legs, and flaccid paralysis. Both West Nile and St. Louis encephalitis can result in parkinsonian-like movements, reflecting inflammation of the basal ganglia. Seizures, a poor prognostic indicator, are present in both types of encephalitis but are more common in the St. Louis type (Jubelt, 2010).

Neuroimaging and CSF evaluation are useful in the diagnosis of arboviral encephalitis. MRI demonstrates inflammation of the basal ganglia in cases of St. Louis encephalitis and inflammation in the periventricular area in cases of West Nile encephalitis. Immunoglobulin M antibodies to West Nile virus are observed in serum and CSF (Chamberlain, 2009). Serum cultures are not useful because the viremia is brief.

Medical and Nursing Management

No specific medication for arboviral encephalitis exists. Medical management is aimed at controlling the seizures and the increased ICP and supporting respiratory function. If the patient is very ill, hospitalization may be required. The nurse carefully assesses neurologic status and identifies improvement or deterioration in the patient's condition. Injury prevention is key in light of the potential for falls and seizures. Arboviral encephalitis may result in death or life-long residual health issues such as neurologic deficits and seizures. The family will need support and teaching to cope with these outcomes.

Public education addressing the prevention of arboviral encephalitis is a key nursing role. Clothing that provides coverage and Environmental Protection Agency (EPA)–approved insect repellents applied to exposed skin (see http://www.cdc.gov/ncidod/dvbid/westnile/Repellent-Updates.htm for list) should be used in high-risk areas to decrease mosquito and tick bites, and avoidance of outdoor activities and control of the mosquito vector are important for control of the disease. Screens should be in good repair in the home, and standing water should be removed. Blood donation centers screen all blood for West Nile virus. Cases of West Nile virus are reported to the Centers for Disease Control and Prevention (CDC). People must be warned not to handle a dead bird if found and to call the local health department for instructions on reporting and disposing of the body.

AUTOIMMUNE PROCESSES

MULTIPLE SCLEROSIS

Multiple sclerosis (MS), the leading cause of nontraumatic disability in young adults, is an immune-mediated, progressive demyelinating disease of the CNS. *Demyelination* refers to the destruction of myelin, the fatty and proteinaceous

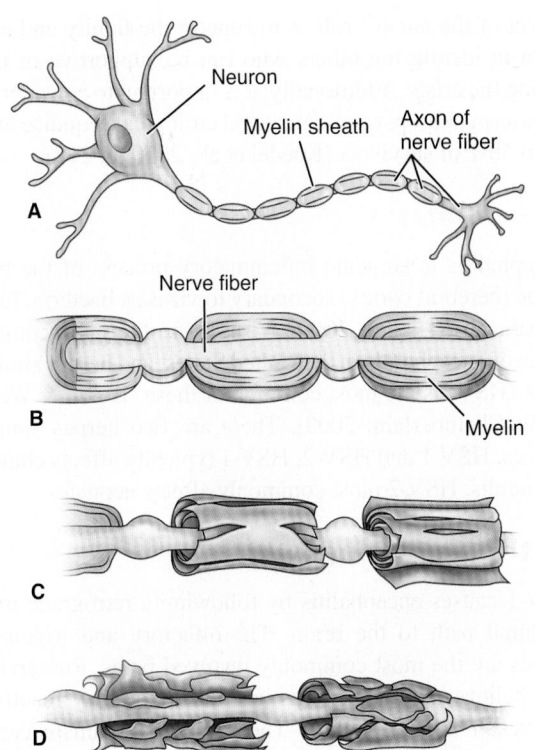

FIGURE 46-2 The process of demyelination. **A** and **B** depict a normal nerve cell and axon with myelin. **C** and **D** show the slow disintegration of myelin, resulting in a disruption in axon function.

material that surrounds certain nerve fibers in the brain and spinal cord; it results in impaired transmission of nerve impulses (Fig. 46-2). MS may occur at any age but typically manifests in young adults between the ages of 20 and 40 years; it affects women more frequently than men and rarely affects those over 60 years (Ramagopalan, Dobson, Meier et al., 2010; Riley & Tullman, 2010).

The etiology of MS is unknown, and may result from complex interactions between environmental factors and genetically susceptible individuals that trigger an abnormal immune response that damages the myelin sheath, oligodendrocytes, axons, and neurons (Riley & Tullman, 2010). Evidence for a genetic predisposition is seen in an increased risk for Caucasians of northern European ancestry and a decreased risk in others (e.g., Native Americans) (Riley & Tullman, 2010). Researchers believe that some environmental exposure at a young age may play a role in the development of MS later in life.

Pathophysiology

Sensitized T cells typically cross the blood–brain barrier; their function is to check the CNS for antigens and then leave. In MS, the sensitized T cells remain in the CNS and promote the infiltration of other agents that damage the immune system (Riley & Tullman, 2010). The immune system attack leads to inflammation that destroys myelin

(which normally insulates the axon and speeds the conduction of impulses along the axon) and the oligodendroglial cells that produce myelin in the CNS.

Demyelination interrupts the flow of nerve impulses and results in a variety of manifestations, depending on the nerves affected. Plaques appear on demyelinated axons, further interrupting the transmission of impulses. Demyelinated axons are scattered irregularly throughout the CNS. The areas most frequently affected are the optic nerves, chiasm, and tracts; the cerebrum; the brainstem and cerebellum; and the spinal cord. Eventually, the axons themselves begin to degenerate, resulting in permanent and irreversible damage (Simon et al., 2009b).

Clinical Manifestations and Assessment

The course of MS may assume many different patterns (Fig. 46-3) (Riley & Tillman, 2010). Between 85% and 90% of patients with MS have a relapsing remitting (RR) course. With each relapse, recovery is usually complete; however, residual deficits may occur and accumulate over time, contributing to functional decline. Approximately 40% of those

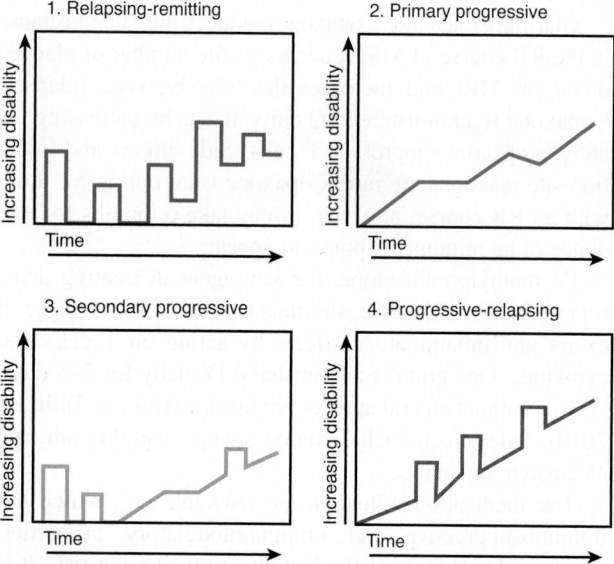

FIGURE 46-3 Types and courses of multiple sclerosis (MS). **1.** Relapsing-remitting (RR) MS is characterized by clearly acute attacks with full recovery or with sequelae and residual deficit upon recovery. Periods between disease relapses are characterized by lack of disease progression. **2.** Primary progressive (PP) MS is characterized by disease showing progression of disability from onset, without plateaus and temporary minor improvements. **3.** Secondary progress (SP) MS begins with an initial RR course, followed by progression of variable rate, which may also include occasional relapses and minor remissions. **4.** Progressive-relapsing (PR) MS shows progression from onset but with clear acute relapses with or without recovery. From Lublin, F. D., & Reingold, S. C. (1996). Defining the clinical course of multiple sclerosis: Results of an international survey. *Neurology, 46*(64), 907–911. Used with permission from Lippincott Williams & Wilkins.

with the RR course of MS progress to a secondary progressive course, in which disease progression occurs with or without relapses. About 10% to 15% of patients have a primary progressive course, in which disabling symptoms steadily increase, with rare plateaus and temporary improvement (Riley & Tillman, 2010). Primary progressive MS may result in quadriparesis, cognitive dysfunction, visual loss, and brainstem syndromes. The least common presentation is the progressive relapsing form of MS, which occurs in approximately 5% of patients and is characterized by relapses with continuous disabling progression between exacerbations (Hauser & Goodin, 2008).

The signs and symptoms of MS are varied and multiple, reflecting the location of the lesion (plaque) or combination of lesions. The primary symptoms most commonly reported are unilateral visual loss, typically preceded or accompanied by orbital pain that increases with eye movement (acute optic neuritis), fatigue, depression, weakness, limb (typically legs) numbness, difficulty in coordination, loss of balance, and pain. Visual disturbances due to lesions in the optic nerves or their connections may also include blurring of vision, **diplopia** (double vision), nystagmus (rotary oscillation of the eyes), patchy blindness (scotoma), and total blindness.

Fatigue, defined as a subjective lack of physical or mental energy that interferes with desired activity, is one of the more common symptoms of MS; it is typically worse in the afternoon hours. Depression, heat, anemia, deconditioning, and medication may contribute to fatigue. The etiology of MS-related fatigue is poorly understood but research does not demonstrate an association between fatigue and disease course (Riley & Tillman, 2010).

Like fatigue, pain is a symptom that can contribute to social isolation. Approximately 70% of MS patients report pain at some point, with 50% complaining of chronic pain (Riley & Tillman, 2010). Lesions on the sensory pathways cause pain. Many people with MS need daily analgesics. In some cases, pain is managed with opioids, antiseizure medication, or antidepressants. Rarely, surgery may be needed to interrupt pain pathways.

Additional sensory manifestations include paresthesias (abnormal skin sensations such as tingling, itching or burning), dysesthesias (unpleasant, abnormal sense of touch), and proprioception (ability to sense the position and location and orientation and movement of the body and its parts) loss (Ropper & Samuels, 2009). An objective sensory loss (position, vibration, shape, texture) is noted in 50% percent of MS patients (Hickey, 2009). Among perimenopausal women, those with MS are more likely to have pain related to osteoporosis. In addition to estrogen loss, immobility and corticosteroid therapy play a role in the development of osteoporosis among women with MS. Recent research reveals that the duration of the disease and decrease in functional capacity are the main factors that affect bone mineral density (BMD) in premenopausal MS patients (Terzi, Terzi, Tander et al.,

2010). BMD testing is recommended for this high-risk group (refer to Chapter 40). Diagnosis and treatment of osteoporosis are discussed in Chapter 41.

Spasticity (muscle hypertonicity) of the extremities (usually the legs) and loss of the abdominal reflexes result from involvement of the main motor pathways (pyramidal tracts) of the spinal cord. The spasticity often occurs with painful spasms, which interfere with mobility, sleep, and activities of daily living (ADLs). Gait abnormalities are common and are usually a result of ataxia, weakness, or spasticity. Disruption of the sensory axons may produce sensory dysfunction (paresthesias, pain). Cognitive and psychosocial problems may reflect frontal or parietal lobe involvement. Some degree of cognitive impairment (e.g., memory loss, decreased concentration) occurs in about 65% of patients, but severe cognitive changes with dementia (progressive organic mental disorder) are rare.

Involvement of the cerebellum or basal ganglia can produce **ataxia** (impaired coordination of movements) and tremor. Loss of the control connections between the cortex and the basal ganglia may occur and cause emotional lability and euphoria. Bladder, bowel, and sexual dysfunctions are common. Bladder dysfunction (urinary urgency, frequency, nocturia, and urge incontinence) affects approximately 75% of patients, and in approximately 15% of these, symptoms can be severe enough to socially isolate the patient (Riley & Tillman, 2010).

Secondary complications of MS include urinary tract infections, constipation, pressure ulcers, contracture deformities, dependent pedal edema, pneumonia, reactive depression, and decreased bone density. Emotional, social, marital, economic, and vocational problems may also be a consequence of the disease.

Exacerbations and remissions are characteristic of MS. During exacerbations, new symptoms appear and existing ones worsen; during remissions, symptoms decrease or disappear. Fifteen years after onset, only 20% of patients have no functional limitation (Hauser & Goodin, 2008). Relapses may be associated with periods of emotional and physical stress including emotional stress; cold or humid, hot weather; hot baths; overheating; fever; fatigue; and pregnancy (Hickey, 2009). There is no single test for the diagnosis of MS. Diagnosis is established based upon clinical examination, results from MRI and evoked potential studies (EPS), and examination of CSF. Approximately 95% of MS patients' MRI studies reveal abnormalities. Electrophoresis of CSF identifies the presence of oligoclonal banding. EPS can help define the extent of the disease process and monitor changes.

Medical and Nursing Management

No cure exists for MS. The goals of treatment are to treat acute exacerbations, delay the progression of the disease, and manage chronic symptoms. Many patients with MS have a stable disease course and require only intermittent treatment, whereas others experience steady progression of their disease. Symptoms requiring intervention include spasticity, fatigue, bladder dysfunction, and ataxia. Management strategies target the various motor and sensory symptoms and effects of immobility that can occur.

Disease-Modifying Therapies

The disease-modifying medications reduce the frequency of relapse, the duration of relapse, and the number and size of plaques observed on MRI. All of the medications require injection.

Interferon beta-1a (Rebif) and interferon beta-1b (Betaseron) are administered subcutaneously (SQ), and another preparation of interferon beta-1a, Avonex, is administered intramuscularly (IM) once a week. Side effects of all the interferon beta medications include flu-like symptoms, which may be minimized by administration at bedtime, and can be managed with acetaminophen and ibuprofen; these side effects may resolve after a few months. Additional side effects include injection site reaction (seen less frequently with IM preparations), thrombocytopenia, anemia, leukopenia, potential liver damage, fetal abnormalities, and depression. For optimal control of disability, disease-modifying medications should be started early in the course of the disease (Riley & Tillman, 2010).

Glatiramer acetate (Copaxone) reduces the rate of relapse in the RR course of MS. It decreases the number of plaques noted on MRI and increases the time between relapses. Copaxone is administered SQ daily. It acts by increasing the antigen-specific suppressor T cells. Side effects and injection site reactions are rare. Copaxone is an option for those with an RR course; however, it may take 6 months for evidence of an immune response to appear.

IV methylprednisolone, the key agent in treating acute relapse in the RR course, shortens the duration of relapse. It exerts anti-inflammatory effects by acting on T cells and cytokines. One gram is administered IV daily for 3–5 days, with or without an oral taper of prednisone (Riley & Tullman, 2010). Side effects include mood swings, weight gain, and electrolyte imbalances.

The medication mitoxantrone (Novantrone), which has immunosuppressive and immunomodulatory properties, may be administered if the benefits outweigh the risk. It is administered via IV infusion every 3 months, and is limited to a lifetime cumulative dose of 140 mg/m² because of its irreversible cardiotoxicity (Riley & Tillman, 2010). Novantrone can reduce the frequency of clinical relapses in patients with secondary-progressive or worsening RR MS. Patients must be very closely monitored for side effects, especially cardiac toxicity.

Symptom Management

Medications are also prescribed for management of specific symptoms. Baclofen (Lioresal), a gamma-aminobutyric acid (GABA) agonist, is the medication of choice for treating

spasticity. It can be administered orally or by intrathecal injection. Benzodiazepines (Valium), tizanidine (Zanaflex), and dantrolene (Dantrium) may also be used to treat spasticity. Patients with disabling spasms and contractures may require nerve blocks or surgical intervention. Fatigue that interferes with ADLs may be treated with amantadine (Symmetrel), pemoline (Cylert), or fluoxetine (Prozac). Ataxia is a chronic problem most resistant to treatment. Medications used to treat ataxia include beta-adrenergic blockers (Inderal), antiseizure agents (Neurontin), and benzodiazepines (Klonopin).

Bladder and bowel problems are often among the most difficult ones for patients, and a variety of medications (anticholinergics, alpha-adrenergic blockers, antispasmodic agents) may be prescribed. Nonpharmacologic strategies also assist in establishing effective bowel and bladder elimination.

Urinary tract infection is often superimposed on the underlying neurologic dysfunction. Ascorbic acid (vitamin C) may be prescribed to acidify the urine, making bacterial growth less likely. Antibiotics are prescribed when appropriate.

An individualized program of physical therapy, rehabilitation, and education is combined with emotional support. An educational plan of care is developed to enable the person with MS to deal with the physiologic, social, and psychological problems that accompany chronic disease.

Promoting Physical Mobility

Relaxation and coordination exercises promote muscle efficiency. Progressive resistive exercises are used to strengthen weak muscles, because diminishing muscle strength is often significant in MS.

EXERCISES. Walking improves the gait, and particularly helps with the problem of loss of position sense of the legs and feet. If certain muscle groups are irreversibly affected, other muscles can be trained to compensate. Instruction in the use of assistive devices may be needed to ensure their safe and correct use.

MINIMIZING SPASTICITY AND CONTRACTURES. Muscle spasticity is common and, in its later stages, is characterized by severe adductor spasm of the hips, with flexor spasm of the hips and knees. Without relief, fibrous contractures of these joints will occur. Warm packs may be beneficial, but hot baths should be avoided because of risk for burn injury secondary to sensory loss and increasing symptoms that may occur with elevation of the body temperature.

Daily exercises for muscle stretching are prescribed to minimize joint contractures. Special attention is given to the hamstrings, gastrocnemius muscles, hip adductors, biceps, and wrist and finger flexors. Muscle spasticity is common and interferes with normal function. A stretch–hold–relax routine is helpful for relaxing and treating muscle spasticity. Swimming and stationary bicycling are useful, and progressive weight bearing can relieve spasticity in the legs. The

patient should not be hurried in any of these activities, because this often increases spasticity.

ACTIVITY AND REST. The patient is encouraged to work and exercise to a point just short of fatigue. Very strenuous physical exercise is not advisable, because it raises the body temperature and may aggravate symptoms. The patient is advised to take frequent short rest periods, preferably lying down. Extreme fatigue may contribute to the exacerbation of symptoms.

MINIMIZING EFFECTS OF IMMOBILITY. Because of the decrease in physical activity that often occurs with MS, complications associated with immobility, including pressure ulcers, expiratory muscle weakness, and accumulation of bronchial secretions, need to be considered and steps taken to prevent them. Measures to prevent such complications include assessing and maintaining skin integrity and having the patient perform coughing and deep-breathing exercises.

Preventing Injury

If motor dysfunction causes coordination problems and clumsiness, or if ataxia is apparent, the patient is at risk for falling. To overcome this disability, the patient is taught to walk with feet apart to widen the base of support and to increase walking stability. If loss of position sense occurs, the patient is taught to watch the feet while walking. Gait training may require assistive devices (walker, cane, braces, crutches, parallel bars) and instruction about their use by a physical therapist. If the gait remains inefficient, a wheelchair or motorized scooter may be the solution. The occupational therapist is a valuable resource person in suggesting and securing aids to promote independence. The patient is trained in transfer and ADLs.

Because sensory loss may occur in addition to motor loss, pressure ulcers are a continuing threat to skin integrity. The need to use a wheelchair continuously increases the risk. See Chapter 52 for a discussion of the prevention and treatment of pressure ulcers.

Enhancing Bladder and Bowel Control

Generally, bladder symptoms fall into the following categories: (1) inability to store urine (hyperreflexic, uninhibited); (2) inability to empty the bladder (hyporeflexic, hypotonic); and (3) a mixture of both types. The patient with urinary frequency, urgency, or incontinence requires special support. The sensation of the need to void must be heeded immediately, so the bedpan or urinal should be readily available. A voiding time schedule is set up (every 1.5 to 2 hours initially, with gradual lengthening of the interval). The patient is instructed to drink a measured amount of fluid every 2 hours and then attempt to void 30 minutes after drinking. Use of a timer or wristwatch with an alarm may be helpful for the patient who does not have enough sensation to signal the need to empty the bladder. The nurse encourages the patient to take the prescribed medications to treat bladder spasticity, because this allows greater independence. Intermittent

self-catheterization has been successful in maintaining bladder control in patients with MS. If a female patient has permanent urinary incontinence, urinary diversion procedures may be considered. The male patient may wear a condom appliance for urine collection.

Bowel problems include constipation, fecal impaction, and incontinence. Adequate fluids, dietary fiber, and a bowel-training program are frequently effective in solving these problems.

Enhancing Communication and Managing Swallowing Difficulties

If the cranial nerves that control the mechanisms of speech and swallowing are affected, dysarthrias (defects of articulation) marked by slurring, low volume of speech, and difficulties in phonation may occur. **Dysphagia** (difficulty swallowing) may also occur. A speech therapist evaluates speech and swallowing and instructs the patient, family, and health team members about strategies to compensate for speech and swallowing problems. The nurse reinforces this instruction and encourages the patient and family to adhere to the plan. Impaired swallowing increases the patient's risk for aspiration; therefore, strategies are needed to reduce that risk. Such strategies include having suction apparatus available, careful feeding, and proper positioning for eating. Refer to Chapters 9 and 10 for information related to aspiration.

Improving Sensory and Cognitive Function

Measures may be taken if visual defects or changes in cognitive status occur.

VISION. The cranial nerves affecting vision may be affected by MS. An eye patch or a covered eyeglass lens may be used to block the visual impulses of one eye if the patient has diplopia (double vision). Prism glasses may be helpful for patients who are confined to bed and have difficulty reading in the supine position. People who are unable to read regular-print materials are eligible for the free "talking book" services of the Library of Congress or may obtain large-print or audio books from local libraries.

COGNITION AND EMOTIONAL RESPONSES. Cognitive impairment and emotional lability occur early in MS in some patients and may impose numerous stresses on the patient and family. Some patients with MS are forgetful and easily distracted.

Patients adapt to illness in a variety of ways, including denial, depression, withdrawal, and hostility. Emotional support assists patients and their families to adapt to the changes and uncertainties associated with MS and to cope with the disruption in their lives. The patient is assisted to set meaningful and realistic goals, to remain as active as possible, and to keep up social interests and activities. Hobbies may help the patient's morale and provide satisfying interests if the disease progresses to the stage at which formerly enjoyed activities can no longer be pursued.

The family should be made aware of the nature and degree of cognitive impairment. The environment is kept structured, and lists and other memory aids are used to help the patient with cognitive changes to maintain a daily routine. The occupational therapist can be helpful in formulating a structured daily routine.

STRENGTHENING COPING MECHANISMS. The diagnosis of MS is always distressing to the patient and family. They need to know that no two patients with MS have identical symptoms or courses of illness. Although some patients do experience significant disability early, others have a near-normal lifespan with minimal disability. Some families, however, face overwhelming frustrations and problems. MS affects people who are often in a productive stage of life and concerned about career and family responsibilities. Family conflict, disintegration, separation, and divorce are not uncommon. Often, very young family members assume the responsibility of caring for a parent with MS. Nursing interventions in this area include alleviating stress and making appropriate referrals for counseling and support to minimize the adverse effects of dealing with chronic illness.

The nurse, mindful of these complex problems, initiates home care and coordinates a network of services, including social services, speech therapy, physical therapy, and homemaker services. To strengthen the patient's coping skills, as much information as possible is provided. Patients need an updated list of available assistive devices, services, and resources.

Coping through problem solving involves helping the patient define the problem and develop alternatives for its management. Careful planning and maintaining flexibility and a hopeful attitude are useful for psychological and physical adaptation.

Improving Home Management

MS can affect every facet of daily living. Certain abilities are often impossible to regain after they are lost. Physical function may vary from day to day. Modifications that allow independence in home management should be implemented (e.g., assistive eating devices, raised toilet seat, bathing aids, telephone modifications, long-handled comb, tongs, modified clothing). Exposure to heat increases fatigue and muscle weakness, so air conditioning is recommended in at least one room. Exposure to extreme cold may increase spasticity.

Promoting Sexual Functioning

Patients with MS and their partners face problems that interfere with sexual activity, both as a direct consequence of nerve damage and also from psychological reactions to the disease. Easy fatigability, conflicts arising from dependency and depression, emotional lability and loss of self-esteem compound the problem. Erectile and ejaculatory disorders in men and orgasmic dysfunction and adductor spasms of the thigh muscles in women can make sexual intercourse difficult or impossible. Bladder and bowel incontinence and urinary tract infections add to the difficulties.

An experienced sexual counselor helps bring into focus the patient's or partner's sexual resources and suggests relevant information and supportive therapy. Sharing and communicating feelings, planning for sexual activity (to minimize the effects of fatigue), and exploring alternative methods of sexual expression may open up a wide range of sexual enjoyment and experiences.

MYASTHENIA GRAVIS

Myasthenia gravis (MG), an autoimmune disorder affecting the neuromuscular junction, is characterized by fatigability and degrees of muscle weakness of the voluntary muscles. According to the Myasthenia Gravis Foundation of America, the prevalence of MG in the United States is estimated to be approximately 20 per 100,000 people. Myasthenia Gravis occurs in both men and women at older ages; however before age 40, the disease is three times more common in women (Penn & Rowland, 2010). The most common age of onset is the second and third decades in females and the seventh and eighth decades in males (Barker, 2008).

Pathophysiology

Normally, a chemical impulse precipitates the release of acetylcholine from vesicles on the nerve terminal at the neuromuscular junction. The acetylcholine attaches to receptor sites on the motor endplate and stimulates muscle contraction. Continuous binding of acetylcholine to the receptor site is required for muscular contraction to be sustained.

In myasthenia gravis, there is a reduction in the number of acetylcholine receptor sites because antibodies directed at the acetylcholine receptor sites impair transmission of impulses across the neuromuscular junction. Therefore, fewer receptors are available for stimulation, resulting in voluntary muscle weakness that escalates with continued activity (Fig. 46-4). Hyperplasia and tumors of the thymus (located behind the sternum) are frequently found in MG patients (Barker, 2008).

Clinical Manifestations and Assessment

The initial manifestation of MG usually involves the ocular muscles. Diplopia (double vision) and ptosis (drooping of the eyelids) are common. However, the majority of patients also experience weakness of the muscles of the face and throat (bulbar symptoms) and generalized weakness. Weakness of the facial muscles results in a bland facial expression. Laryngeal involvement produces **dysphonia** (voice impairment) and increases the patient's risk for choking and aspiration. Generalized weakness affects all the extremities and the intercostal muscles, resulting in decreasing vital capacity and respiratory failure. MG is purely a motor disorder with no effect on sensation or coordination.

An acetylcholinesterase test is used to diagnose MG. The acetylcholinesterase inhibitor stops the breakdown of acetylcholine, thereby increasing availability at the neuromuscular junction. The drug used is edrophonium chloride (Tensilon), because it has a rapid onset of 30 seconds and a short duration of 5 minutes (Hickey, 2009). Immediate improvement in muscle strength after administration of this agent represents a positive test and usually confirms the diagnosis.

The presence of acetylcholine receptor antibodies is identified in serum. Repetitive nerve stimulation demonstrates a decrease in successive action potentials. The thymus gland may be enlarged in MG, and a CT scan of the mediastinum is performed to detect thymoma or hyperplasia of the thymus.

Medical and Nursing Management

Management of myasthenia gravis is directed at improving function and reducing and removing circulating antibodies. Therapeutic modalities include administration of anticholinesterase medications and immunosuppressive therapy, plasmapheresis, intravenous immunoglobulin, and thymectomy.

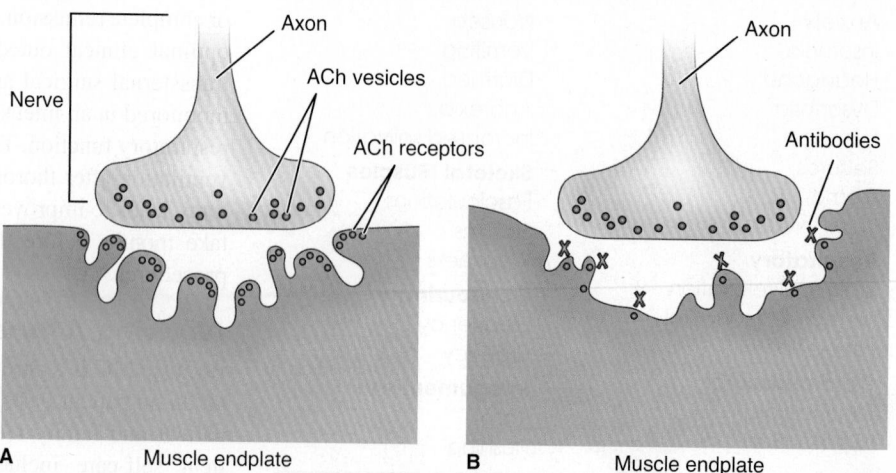

FIGURE 46-4 Myasthenia gravis (MG). (**A**) normal acetylcholine (ACh) receptor site. (**B**) ACh receptor site in MG.

Pharmacologic Therapy

Pyridostigmine bromide (Mestinon), an anticholinesterase medication, is the first line of therapy. It provides symptomatic relief by inhibiting the breakdown of acetylcholine and increasing the relative concentration of available acetylcholine at the neuromuscular junction. The dosage is gradually increased to a daily maximum and is administered in divided doses (usually four times a day). The most common adverse effects are gastrointestinal discomfort, increased bronchial and oral secretions, and muscle fasciculations and cramps (Barker, 2008). Pyridostigmine tends to have fewer side effects than other anticholinesterase medications (Box 46-3).

If pyridostigmine bromide does not improve muscle strength and control fatigue, the next agents used are immunosuppressant agents. The goal of immunosuppressive therapy is to reduce production of the antibody. Corticosteroids suppress the patient's immune response, decreasing the amount of antibody production, and this correlates with clinical improvement. An initial dose of prednisone is given daily; as symptoms improve, the medication is tapered and a maintenance alternative day dosing may be considered (Jani-Acsadi & Lisak, 2010; Penn & Rowland, 2010). Since long-term steroids carry substantial risks for a variety of dose-dependent side effects (diabetes, osteoporosis, hypertension), this treatment is usually reserved for patients with ocular symptoms. As the corticosteroid dosage is gradually increased, the anticholinesterase dosage is lowered. Cytotoxic medications are used to treat MG if there is inadequate response to steroids. Azathioprine (Imuran), an immunosuppressive drug, inhibits T lymphocytes and reduces acetylcholine receptor antibody levels. Therapeutic effects may not be evident for 3 to 12 months. Leukopenia and hepatotoxicity are serious adverse effects, so monthly evaluation of liver enzymes and white blood cell count is necessary.

A number of medications are contraindicated for patients with MG because they exacerbate the symptoms. The health care provider and the patient should weigh risks and benefits before any new medications are prescribed, including antibiotics, cardiovascular medications, antiseizure and psychotropic medications, morphine, quinine and related agents, beta blockers, and nonprescription medications. Procaine (Novocain) should be avoided, and the patient's dentist is advised of the diagnosis of MG. Since neuromuscular blocking agents may have a very prolonged effect in MG patients, any anesthetic medication should be evaluated by the primary care provider to ensure it is not capable of exaggerating myasthenic weakness (Ropper & Samuels, 2009).

Plasmapheresis/Intravenous Immunoglobulin

Plasmapheresis (plasma exchange) is a technique used to treat exacerbations. The patient's plasma and plasma components are removed through a centrally placed large-bore double-lumen catheter. The blood cells and antibody-containing plasma are separated, after which the cells and a plasma substitute are reinfused. Plasma exchange produces a temporary reduction in the level of circulating antibodies. The typical course of plasmapheresis consists of daily or alternate-day treatment, and the number of treatments is determined by the patient's response. Plasma exchange improves symptoms in 75% of patients; however, improvement lasts only a few weeks after treatment is completed. IV immunoglobulin (IVIG) treatment involves the administration of pooled human gamma globulin, which usually produces a relatively quick and short-term relief of MG weakness (Barker, 2008). Although IVIG is easier than plasmapheresis to administer, the response to plasmapheresis is more rapid. No treatments cure MG because they do not stop the production of the acetylcholine receptor antibodies.

Surgical Management

Thymectomy (surgical removal of the thymus gland) can produce antigen-specific immunosuppression and result in clinical improvement. The procedure results in either partial or complete remission. The entire gland must be removed for optimal clinical outcomes; therefore, surgeons prefer the transsternal surgical approach. After surgery, the patient is monitored in an intensive care unit, with special attention to respiratory function. The patient is weaned from mechanical ventilation after thorough respiratory assessment. Thymectomy leads to improvement in almost all patients, but it may take months before the patient sees any benefit from the procedure.

Nursing Management

Because MG is a chronic disease and most patients are seen on an outpatient basis, much of the nursing care focuses on patient and family teaching. Educational topics for outpatient self-care include medication management, energy

---

BOX 46-3

Potential Adverse Effects of Anticholinesterase Medications

Central Nervous System
Irritability
Anxiety
Insomnia
Headache
Dysarthria
Syncope
Seizures
Coma
Diaphoresis

Respiratory
Bronchial relaxation
Increased bronchial
  secretions

Cardiovascular
Tachycardia
Hypotension

Gastrointestinal
Abdominal cramps
Nausea
Vomiting
Diarrhea
Anorexia
Increased salivation

Skeletal Muscles
Fasciculations
Spasms
Weakness

Genitourinary
Frequency
Urgency

Integumentary
Rash
Flushing

conservation, strategies to help with ocular manifestations, and prevention and management of complications.

Medication management is a crucial component of ongoing care. Understanding the actions of the medications and taking them on schedule is emphasized, as are the consequences of delaying medication and the signs and symptoms of myasthenic and cholinergic crises. The patient can determine the best times for daily dosing by keeping a diary to determine fluctuation of symptoms and to learn when the medication is wearing off. The medication schedule can then be manipulated to maximize strength throughout the day.

> ## ! NURSING ALERT
> Maintenance of stable blood levels of anticholinesterase medications is imperative to stabilize muscle strength. Therefore, the anticholinesterase medications must be administered on time. Any delay in administration of medications may exacerbate muscle weakness and make it impossible for the patient to take medications orally.

To minimize the risk of aspiration, mealtimes should coincide with the peak effects of anticholinesterase medication. In addition, rest before meals is encouraged, to reduce muscle fatigue. The patient is advised to sit upright during meals, with the neck slightly flexed to facilitate swallowing. Soft foods in gravy or sauces can be swallowed more easily; if choking occurs frequently, the nurse can suggest puréed food with a pudding-like consistency. Suction should be available at home, with the patient and family instructed in its use. Supplemental feedings may be necessary in some patients to ensure adequate nutrition.

Impaired vision results from ptosis of one or both eyelids, decreased eye movement, or double vision. To prevent corneal damage when the eyelids do not close completely, many providers may instruct the patient to tape or patch the eyes closed for short intervals and to regularly instill artificial tears. If taping is done, it is important to ensure the lid covers the eye to prevent corneal abrasion from the tape or patch. Patients who wear eyeglasses can have "crutches" attached to help lift the eyelids. Patching of one eye can help with double vision.

The patient is reminded of the importance of maintaining health promotion practices and of following health care screening recommendations. Factors that exacerbate symptoms and potentially cause crisis should be noted and avoided: emotional stress, infections (particularly respiratory infections), vigorous physical activity, some medications, and high environmental temperature.

The patient is also taught strategies to conserve energy. To do this, the nurse helps the patient identify the optimal times for rest throughout the day. If the patient lives in a two-story home, the nurse can suggest that frequently used items

(e.g., hygiene products, cleaning products, snacks) be kept on each floor to minimize travel between floors. The patient is encouraged to apply for a handicapped license plate to minimize walking from parking spaces, and to schedule activities to coincide with peak energy and strength levels. Patients are encouraged to wear a medical alert bracelet identifying them as having MG. The Myasthenia Gravis Foundation of America provides support groups, services, and educational materials for patients, families, and health care providers (Howard, 2008).

Complications

Cholinergic Crisis

A cholinergic crisis, which is essentially a problem of overmedication, results in severe generalized muscle weakness, respiratory impairment, and excessive pulmonary secretions that may result in respiratory failure. Weak respiratory muscles do not support inhalation. An inadequate cough and an impaired gag reflex, caused by bulbar weakness, result in poor airway clearance and risk of aspiration. Bulbar weakness specifically involves the muscles of the jaw, face, palate, pharynx, larynx, tongue, glossopharyngeal nerve (IX), vagus nerve (X), and hypoglossal nerve (XII). A downward trend of two respiratory function tests, the negative inspiratory force and vital capacity, is the first clinical sign of respiratory compromise.

Endotracheal intubation and mechanical ventilation may be needed. Cholinesterase inhibitors are stopped when respiratory failure occurs and gradually restarted after the patient demonstrates improvement. Nutritional support may be needed if the patient is intubated for a long period.

Myasthenic Crisis

Myasthenic crisis is a sudden, temporary exacerbation of MG symptoms. A common precipitating event for myasthenic crisis is an infection. Respiratory distress and varying degrees of dysphagia (difficulty swallowing), dysarthria (difficulty speaking), eyelid ptosis, diplopia, and prominent muscle weakness are symptoms of myasthenic crisis.

Providing ventilatory assistance takes precedence in the immediate management of the patient with myasthenic crisis. Ongoing assessment for respiratory failure is essential. The nurse assesses the respiratory rate and depth, and breath sounds, and monitors pulmonary function parameters (vital capacity and negative inspiratory force) to detect pulmonary problems before respiratory dysfunction progresses. Oxygen saturations are assessed and ABG analysis is performed as needed. Endotracheal intubation and mechanical ventilation may be needed.

If the abdominal, intercostal, and pharyngeal muscles are severely weak, the patient cannot cough, take deep breaths, or clear secretions. Chest physiotherapy, including postural drainage to mobilize secretions and suctioning to remove secretions, may have to be performed frequently. (Postural

drainage should not be performed for 30 minutes after feeding).

Several strategies and supportive measures should be performed during this crisis, including monitoring of lab work, input and output, and daily weight, along with vigilant pulmonary assessments. If the patient cannot swallow, nasogastric tube feedings may be prescribed. Sedatives and tranquilizers are avoided, because they aggravate hypoxia and hypercapnia and can cause respiratory and cardiac depression.

GUILLAIN-BARRÉ SYNDROME

Guillain-Barré syndrome (GBS) is an autoimmune attack on the peripheral nerve myelin. The result is acute, rapid, segmental demyelination of peripheral nerves and some cranial nerves, producing ascending weakness with **dyskinesia** (inability to execute voluntary movements), hyporeflexia, and **paresthesias** (numbness). An antecedent event (most often a viral infection) precipitates clinical presentation. *Campylobacter jejuni*, cytomegalovirus, Epstein-Barr virus, *Mycoplasma pneumoniae*, *H. influenzae*, and HIV are the most common infectious agents associated with the development of GBS. In a few instances, the patient reports receiving a vaccination prior to the onset of GBS (Hickey, 2009).

In North America, approximately 1.5 to 2.0 cases of GBS occur for every 100,000 people each year. GBS affects males and females of all ages and races. Given the relationship of GBS to colds and flu-like illnesses, it is expected that GBS would occur more frequently in the fall and winter when these infections are more likely (Parry, 2007).

Pathophysiology

Myelin is a complex substance that covers nerves, providing insulation and speeding the conduction of impulses from the cell body to the dendrites. The cell that produces myelin in the peripheral nervous system is the Schwann cell. In GBS, the Schwann cell is spared, allowing for remyelination in the recovery phase of the disease.

GBS is the result of a cell-mediated and humoral immune attack on peripheral nerve myelin proteins that causes inflammatory demyelination. The immune system cannot distinguish between the two proteins and attacks and destroys peripheral nerve myelin. The exact location of the immune attack within the peripheral nervous system is the ganglioside GM1b. With the autoimmune attack, there is an influx of macrophages and other immune-mediated agents that attack myelin, cause inflammation and destruction, and leave the axon unable to support nerve conduction.

Clinical Manifestations and Assessment

GBS typically begins with muscle weakness and diminished reflexes of the lower extremities. Hyporeflexia and weakness may progress to tetraplegia (paralysis of all four limbs).

Demyelination of the nerves that innervate the diaphragm and intercostal muscles results in neuromuscular respiratory failure. Sensory symptoms include paresthesias of the hands and feet and pain related to the demyelination of sensory fibers.

The antecedent event usually occurs 2 weeks before symptoms begin. Weakness usually begins in the legs and progresses upward. Maximum weakness, the *plateau*, varies in length but usually includes neuromuscular respiratory failure and bulbar weakness. The duration of the symptoms is variable; complete functional recovery may take up to 2 years (Hickey, 2009). Any residual symptoms are permanent and reflect axonal damage from demyelination.

Cranial nerve demyelination can result in a variety of clinical manifestations. Optic nerve demyelination may result in blindness. Bulbar muscle weakness related to demyelination of the glossopharyngeal and vagus nerves results in the inability to swallow or clear secretions. Vagus nerve demyelination results in autonomic dysfunction, manifested by instability of the cardiovascular system. The presentation is variable and may include tachycardia, bradycardia, hypertension, or orthostatic hypotension. The symptoms of autonomic dysfunction occur and resolve rapidly. GBS does not affect cognitive function or LOC.

Although the classic clinical features include areflexia and ascending weakness, variation in presentation occurs. There may be a sensory presentation, with progressive sensory symptoms, an atypical axonal destruction, or the Miller-Fisher variant, which includes paralysis of the ocular muscles, ataxia, and areflexia (Hickey, 2009).

The patient presents with symmetric weakness, diminished reflexes, and upward progression of motor weakness. Changes in vital capacity and negative inspiratory force are assessed to identify impending neuromuscular respiratory failure. Serum laboratory tests are not useful in the diagnosis. However, elevated protein levels are detected in CSF evaluation, without an increase in other cells. EPSs demonstrate a progressive loss of nerve conduction velocity.

Medical and Nursing Management

Because of the possibility of rapid progression and neuromuscular respiratory failure, GBS is a medical emergency, requiring management in an intensive care unit. After baseline values are identified, assessment of changes in muscle strength and respiratory function alert the clinician to the physical and respiratory needs of the patient. Respiratory therapy or mechanical ventilation may be necessary to support pulmonary function and adequate oxygenation. Some clinicians recommend elective intubation before the onset of extreme respiratory muscle fatigue. Mechanical ventilation may be required for an extended period. The patient is weaned from mechanical ventilation after the respiratory muscles can again support spontaneous respiration and maintain adequate tissue oxygenation.

Other interventions are aimed at preventing the complications of immobility. These may include the use of anticoagulant agents and thigh-high elastic compression stockings or sequential compression boots to prevent thrombosis and pulmonary emboli (PE).

Plasmapheresis and IVIG are used to affect directly the peripheral nerve myelin antibody level. Both therapies decrease circulating antibody levels and reduce the amount of time the patient is immobilized and dependent on mechanical ventilation. Studies indicate that IVIG and plasmapheresis are equally effective in treating GBS; however, IVIG is associated with fewer side effects. The cardiovascular risks posed by autonomic dysfunction require continuous electrocardiographic (ECG) monitoring. Tachycardia and hypertension are treated with short-acting medications such as alpha-adrenergic blocking agents. The use of short-acting agents is important, because autonomic dysfunction is very labile. Hypotension is managed by increasing the amount of IV fluid administered.

Maintaining Respiratory Function

Respiratory function can be maximized with incentive spirometry and chest physiotherapy. Monitoring for changes in vital capacity and negative inspiratory force are key to early intervention for neuromuscular respiratory failure. Mechanical ventilation is required if the vital capacity falls, making spontaneous breathing impossible and tissue oxygenation inadequate.

Parameters for determining the appropriate time to begin mechanical ventilation include a vital capacity of less than 15 mL/kg. The potential need for mechanical ventilation should be discussed with the patient and family on admission, to provide time for psychological preparation and decision-making. Intubation and mechanical ventilation will result in less anxiety if it is initiated on a nonemergency basis to a well-informed patient. The patient may require mechanical ventilation for a long period.

Bulbar weakness that impairs the ability to swallow and clear secretions is another factor in the development of respiratory failure in the patient with GBS. Suctioning may be needed to maintain a clear airway.

The nurse assesses the blood pressure and heart rate frequently to identify autonomic dysfunction, so that interventions can be initiated quickly if needed. Medications are administered for clinically significant symptoms.

Enhancing Physical Mobility

Nursing interventions to enhance physical mobility and prevent the complications of immobility are key to the function and survival of these patients. The paralyzed extremities are supported in functional positions, and passive range-of-motion (ROM) exercises are performed at least twice daily. Deep venous thrombosis (DVT) and PE are threats to the paralyzed patient. Nursing interventions are aimed at preventing DVT. ROM exercises, position changes, anticoagulation,

the use of thigh-high elastic compression stockings or sequential compression boots, and adequate hydration decrease the risk for DVT.

Padding may be placed over bony prominences, such as the elbows and heels, to reduce the risk for pressure ulcers. The need for consistent position changes every 2 hours cannot be overemphasized. The nurse evaluates laboratory test results that may indicate malnutrition or dehydration, both of which increase the risk for pressure ulcers. The nurse collaborates with the provider and dietitian to develop a plan to meet the patient's nutritional and hydration needs.

Providing Adequate Nutrition

Paralytic ileus may result from insufficient parasympathetic activity. In this event, the nurse administers IV fluids and parenteral nutrition as prescribed and monitors for the return of bowel sounds and bowel function. If the patient cannot swallow due to **bulbar paralysis** (immobility of muscles), a gastrostomy tube may be placed to administer nutrients. The nurse carefully assesses the return of the gag reflex and bowel sounds before resuming oral nutrition.

Improving Communication

Because of paralysis, the patient cannot talk, laugh, or cry and therefore has no method for communicating needs or expressing emotion. Establishing some form of communication with picture cards or an eye blink system provides a means of communication. Collaboration with the speech therapist may be helpful in developing a communication mechanism that is most effective for a specific patient.

Decreasing Fear and Anxiety

The patient and family are faced with a sudden, potentially life-threatening disease, and anxiety and fear are constant themes for them. The impact of disease on the family depends on the patient's role within the family. Referral to a support group may provide information and support to the patient and family.

The family may feel helpless in caring for the patient. Mechanical ventilation and monitoring devices may frighten and intimidate them. Family members often want to participate in physical care; with instruction and support by the nurse, they should be allowed to do so.

In addition to fear, the patient may experience isolation, loneliness, and lack of control. Nursing interventions that increase the patient's sense of control include providing information about the condition, emphasizing a positive appraisal of coping resources, and teaching relaxation exercises and distraction techniques. The positive attitude and atmosphere of the multidisciplinary team are important to promote a sense of well-being.

Diversional activities are encouraged to decrease loneliness and isolation. Encouraging visitors, engaging visitors or volunteers to read to the patient, listening to music or books on tape, and watching television are ways to alleviate the patient's sense of isolation.

Complications

Thorough assessment of respiratory function at regular and frequent intervals is essential, because respiratory insufficiency and subsequent failure due to weakness or paralysis of the intercostal muscles and diaphragm may develop quickly. In addition to the respiratory rate and the quality of respirations, vital capacity is monitored frequently and at regular intervals, so that respiratory insufficiency can be anticipated. Decreasing vital capacity associated with weakness of the muscles used in swallowing, which causes difficulty in both coughing and swallowing, indicates impending respiratory failure. Signs and symptoms include breathlessness while speaking, shallow and irregular breathing, use of accessory muscles, tachycardia, and changes in respiratory pattern.

Parameters for determining the onset of respiratory failure are established on admission, allowing intubation and the initiation of mechanical ventilation on a nonemergent basis. This also allows the patient to be prepared for the procedure in a controlled manner, which reduces anxiety and complications.

Other complications include cardiac arrhythmias, which necessitate ECG monitoring; transient hypertension; orthostatic hypotension; DVT; PE; urinary retention; and other threats to any immobilized and paralyzed patient. These require monitoring and attention to prevent them and prompt treatment if indicated.

CRANIAL NERVE DISORDERS

Bell's Palsy

Bell's palsy (facial paralysis) is caused by unilateral inflammation of the seventh cranial nerve, which results in weakness or paralysis of the facial muscles on the ipsilateral, or same side, of the affected facial nerve. (Fig. 46-5).

Pathophysiology

Although the cause is unknown, theories about causes include vascular ischemia, viral disease (herpes simplex, herpes zoster), autoimmune disease, or a combination of all of these factors. Bell's palsy may be a type of pressure paralysis. The inflamed, edematous nerve becomes compressed to the point of damage, or its blood supply is occluded, producing ischemic necrosis of the nerve.

Clinical Manifestations and Assessment

The face is distorted from paralysis of the facial muscles; there are increased lacrimation (tearing) and painful sensations in the face, behind the ear, and in the eye of the affected side. The ear pain may precede the paralysis by 24 to 48 hours. The patient may experience speech difficulties and may be unable to eat on the affected side because of weakness or

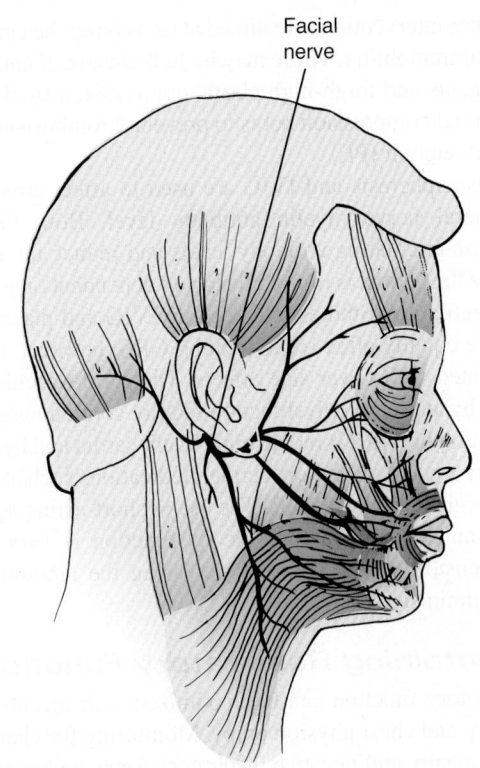

FIGURE 46-5 Distribution of the facial nerve.

paralysis of the facial muscles. A disturbance of taste is a common finding. When asking the patient to show his or her teeth and smile, weakness of the involved nerve will be noted, there will be an absence of wrinkling on the forehead, the affected side will appear mask-like.

Medical and Nursing Management

Corticosteroid therapy (prednisone) may be prescribed to reduce inflammation and edema; this reduces vascular compression and permits restoration of blood circulation to the nerve. Early administration of corticosteroid therapy appears to diminish the severity of the disease, relieve the pain, and prevent or minimize denervation.

Facial pain is controlled with analgesic agents. Heat may be applied to the involved side of the face to promote comfort and blood flow through the muscles. Electrical stimulation may be applied to the face to prevent muscle atrophy.

While the paralysis lasts, nursing care involves protection of the eye from injury. Frequently, the eye does not close completely and the blink reflex is diminished, so the eye is vulnerable to injury from dust and foreign particles. Corneal irritation and ulceration may occur. Distortion of the lower lid alters the proper drainage of tears. To prevent injury, the eye should be covered with a protective shield at night. The eye patch may abrade the cornea, however, because there is some difficulty in keeping the partially paralyzed eyelids closed. Eye ointment

may be applied at bedtime to promote adherence of the eyelids to prevent injury during sleep. The patient can be taught to close the paralyzed eyelid manually before going to sleep. Wrap-around sunglasses or goggles may be worn during the day to decrease normal evaporation from the eye.

PARKINSON'S DISEASE

Parkinson's disease (PD) is a slowly progressing neurologic movement disorder that eventually leads to disability. The degenerative or idiopathic form is the most common; there is also a secondary form with a known or suspected cause. Although the cause of most cases is unknown, research suggests several causative factors, including genetics, atherosclerosis, excessive accumulation of oxygen free radicals, viral infections, head trauma, chronic use of antipsychotic medications, and some environmental exposures. Parkinsonian symptoms usually first appear in the fifth decade of life; however, cases have been diagnosed as early as 30 years of age. It is the fourth most common **neurodegenerative** disease. PD affects men more frequently than women.

Pathophysiology

PD is associated with decreased levels of dopamine resulting from destruction of pigmented neuronal cells in the substantia nigra in the basal ganglia region of the brain. Fibers or neuronal pathways project from the substantia nigra to the corpus striatum, where neurotransmitters are key to the control of complex body movements. Through the neurotransmitters acetylcholine (excitatory) and dopamine (inhibitory), striatal neurons relay messages to the higher motor centers that control and refine motor movements. The loss of dopamine stores in this area of the brain results in more excitatory neurotransmitters than inhibitory neurotransmitters, leading to an imbalance that affects voluntary movement. Clinical symptoms do not appear until 60% of the pigmented neurons are lost and the striatal dopamine level is decreased by 80%. Cellular degeneration impairs the extrapyramidal tracts that control semiautomatic functions and coordinated movements; motor cells of the motor cortex and the pyramidal tracts are not affected.

Clinical Manifestations and Assessment

PD has a gradual onset, and symptoms progress slowly over a chronic, prolonged course. The cardinal signs are T-R-A-P: **T**remor, **R**igidity, **A**kinesia/Bradykinesia (without or decreased body movement), and **P**ostural disturbances.

Tremor

The most common reason why individuals seek medical evaluation is the presence of a resting tremor. Resting tremor characteristically disappears with purposeful movement but is evident when the extremities are motionless. The tremor may manifest as a rhythmic, slow-turning motion (pronation–supination) of the forearm and the hand and a motion of the thumb against the fingers as if rolling a pill between the fingers. Tremor is present while the patient is at rest; it increases when the patient is walking, concentrating, or feeling anxious.

Rigidity

Resistance to passive limb movement characterizes muscle rigidity. *Cogwheel rigidity* is characterized by ratchet-like rhythmic contractions on passive muscle stretching (Hickey, 2009). Involuntary stiffness of the passive extremity increases when another extremity is engaged in voluntary active movement. Early in the disease, the patient may complain of shoulder pain due to rigidity.

Akinesia/Bradykinesia

Akinesia means a lack of movement, and *bradykinesia* means a slowness of initiation and execution of movement. Patients may take longer to complete activities and have difficulty initiating movement, such as rising from a sitting position or turning in bed.

Postural Disturbances

A loss of postural reflexes occurs, and the patient stands with the head bent forward and walks with a propulsive gait. The posture is caused by the forward flexion of the neck, hips, knees, and elbows. The patient may walk faster and faster, trying to move the feet forward under the body's center of gravity (shuffling gait). Difficulty in pivoting that causes loss of balance (either forward or backward) places the patient at risk for falls.

Other Manifestations

The effect of PD on the basal ganglia often produces autonomic symptoms that include excessive and uncontrolled sweating, paroxysmal flushing, orthostatic hypotension, gastric and urinary retention, constipation, and sexual dysfunction. Cognitive and psychiatric changes are often interrelated and may be predictive of one another. Depression is common; whether it is a reaction to the disorder or is related to a biochemical abnormality is uncertain. Cognitive changes may appear in the form of judgment, reasoning, decision making, and memory deficits, although intellect is not usually affected. A number of psychiatric manifestations (personality changes, psychosis, dementia, and acute confusion) are common in elderly patients with PD.

Patients with PD experience sleep disturbances. This may be related to depression, dementia, or medications. Auditory and visual hallucinations have also been reported in PD and may be associated with depression, dementia, lack of sleep, or adverse effects of medications.

Hypokinesia (abnormally diminished movement) is also common and may appear after the tremor. The *freezing phenomenon* refers to a transient inability to perform active movement and is thought to be an extreme form of bradykinesia. Additionally, the patient tends to shuffle and exhibits a

decreased arm swing. As dexterity declines, **micrographia** (small handwriting) develops. The face becomes increasingly mask-like and expressionless, and the frequency of blinking decreases. Dysphonia (soft, low-pitched, and less audible speech) may occur due to weakness of the muscles responsible for speech and paralysis of soft palate resulting in a nasal-sounding speech. In many cases, the patient develops dysphagia, begins to drool, and is at risk for choking and aspiration.

Complications associated with PD are common and are typically related to disorders of movement. As the disease progresses, patients are at risk for respiratory and urinary tract infection, skin breakdown, and injury from falls. The adverse effects of medications used to treat the symptoms are associated with numerous complications, such as dyskinesia and orthostatic hypotension.

Early diagnosis can be difficult, because patients rarely are able to pinpoint when the symptoms started. Often, a family member notices a change such as stooped posture, a stiff arm, a slight limp, tremor, or slow, small handwriting. The medical history, presenting symptoms, neurologic examination, and response to pharmacologic management are carefully evaluated when making the diagnosis. Currently, the disease is diagnosed clinically from the patient's history and the presence of two of the four cardinal manifestations: tremor, rigidity, akinesia/bradykinesia, and postural disturbances (Fig. 46-6).

Medical and Nursing Management

Treatment is directed at controlling symptoms and maintaining functional independence. Care is individualized for each patient based on presenting symptoms and social, occupational, and emotional needs. Pharmacologic management is the mainstay of treatment, although advances in research have led to increased surgical options. Patients are usually cared for at home and are admitted to the hospital only for complications or to initiate new treatments.

Antiparkinsonian Medications

Levodopa (Larodopa) is the most effective agent and the mainstay of treatment. Levodopa is converted to dopamine in the basal ganglia, producing symptom relief. The beneficial effects of levodopa are most pronounced in the first few years of treatment. Benefits begin to wane and adverse effects become more severe over time. Confusion, hallucinations, depression, and sleep alterations are associated with prolonged use. Levodopa is usually administered in combination with carbidopa (Sinemet), an amino acid decarboxylase inhibitor, which helps to maximize the beneficial effects of levodopa.

Within 5 to 10 years, most patients develop a response to the medication characterized by **dyskinesia** (abnormal involuntary movements), including facial grimacing, rhythmic jerking movements of the hands, head bobbing, chewing and smacking movements, and involuntary movements of

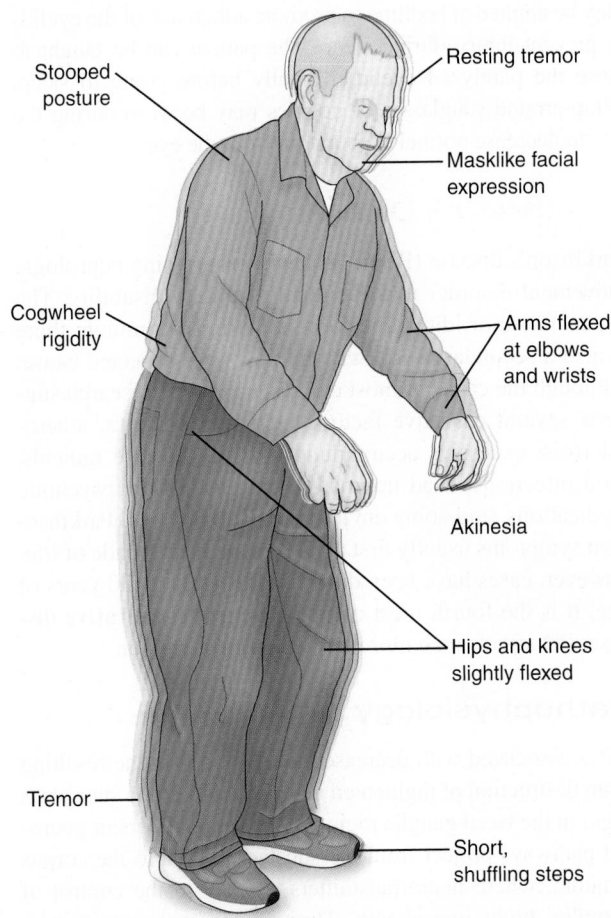

Stooped posture

Resting tremor

Masklike facial expression

Cogwheel rigidity

Arms flexed at elbows and wrists

Akinesia

Hips and knees slightly flexed

Tremor

Short, shuffling steps

FIGURE 46-6 The clinical features of Parkinson disease: TRAP (**T**remor, **R**igidity, **A**kinesia/Bradykinesia, and **P**ostural disturbances. Adapted from Timby, B. (2010). *Introductory medical-surgical nursing* (10th ed., p. 535). Philadelphia: Lippincott Williams & Wilkins.

the trunk and extremities. The patient may experience an on–off syndrome, in which sudden periods of near-immobility ("off effect") are followed by a sudden return of effectiveness of the medication ("on effect"). Refer to Table 46-2 for additional medical therapies.

Deep Brain Stimulation

Deep brain stimulation is the delivery of high-frequency electrical stimulation to a select target in the brain. In deep brain stimulation, an electrode is placed in the thalamus and connected to a pulse generator that is implanted in a subcutaneous subclavicular or abdominal pouch. The battery-powered pulse generator sends high-frequency electrical impulses through a wire placed under the skin to a lead anchored to the skull. The electrode blocks nerve pathways in the brain that cause tremors. Deep brain stimulation usually results in patients being at their best for longer periods of the day than they were with medication alone. Most patients are able to reduce their intake of medication, with a lower prevalence of side effects (Barker, 2008).

TABLE
46-2 Antiparkinsonian Medications

Anticholinergic Therapy Trihexyphenidyl hydrochloride [Artane] Benztropine mesylate [Cogentin]	Used for controlling tremor by counteracting the action of the neurotransmitter acetylcholine; often poorly tolerated in elderly patients. Intraocular pressure must be closely monitored; these medications are contraindicated in patients with narrow-angle glaucoma. Patients with prostate hyperplasia are monitored for signs of urinary retention.
Antiviral Therapy Amantadine hydrochloride (Symmetrel)	Used for symptoms related to akinesia, as well as tremor. A low incidence of side effects is seen but can include psychiatric disturbances (mood changes, confusion, depression, hallucinations), lower extremity edema, nausea, epigastric distress, urinary retention, headache, and visual impairment.
Dopamine Agonists Bromocriptine mesylate (Parlodel) Pergolide (Permax) Ropinirole hydrochloride (Requip) Pramipexole (Mirapex)	Useful in postponing the initiation of carbidopa or levodopa therapy or added to the medication regimen after carbidopa or levodopa loses effectiveness. Adverse reactions to these medications include nausea, vomiting, diarrhea, lightheadedness, hypotension, impotence, and psychiatric effects. Requip and Mirapex do not have the potentially serious adverse effects of pergolide and bromocriptine mesylate.
Monoamine Oxidase Inhibitors Selegiline (Eldepryl) Rasagiline (Azilect) Zydis selegiline HCl (Zelapar)	Used in combination with a dopamine agonist to delay the use of carbidopa or levodopa therapy. Adverse effects are similar to those of levodopa.
Catechol-*O*-Methyltransferase (COMT) Inhibitors Entacapone (Comtan) Tolcapone (Tasmar)	When given in combination with carbidopa or levodopa they can increase the duration of action. COMT inhibitors block an enzyme that metabolizes levodopa, making more levodopa available for conversion to dopamine in the brain.
Antidepressants **Tricyclic antidepressants** Amitriptyline hydrochloride (Elavil)	Used to treat depression; dosing is lower in patients with Parkinson's disease, typically one-third to one-half of the usual dosage. Used for anticholinergic and antidepressant effects
Serotonin reuptake inhibitors Fluoxetine hydrochloride (Prozac)	Effective for treating depression but may aggravate symptoms of Parkinson's disease.
Atypical antidepressants Bupropion hydrochloride (Wellbutrin)	Effective for treating depression but may aggravate symptoms of Parkinson's disease.

Improving Mobility

A progressive program of daily exercise will increase muscle strength, improve coordination and dexterity, reduce muscular rigidity, and prevent contractures that occur when muscles are not used. Walking, riding a stationary bicycle, swimming, and gardening are all exercises that help maintain joint mobility. Stretching (stretch–hold–relax) and ROM exercises promote joint flexibility. Postural exercises are important to counter the tendency of the head and neck to be drawn forward and down. A physical therapist may be helpful in developing an individualized exercise program and can provide instruction to the patient and caregiver on exercising safely. Faithful adherence to an exercise and walking program helps to delay the progress of the disease. Warm baths and massage, in addition to passive and active exercises, help relax muscles and relieve painful muscle spasms that accompany rigidity.

Balance may be adversely affected because of the rigidity of the arms (arm swinging is necessary in normal walking). Special walking techniques must be learned to offset the shuffling gait and the tendency to lean forward. The patient is taught to concentrate on walking erect, to watch the horizon, and to use a wide-based gait (i.e., walking with the feet separated). A conscious effort must be made to swing the arms, raise the feet while walking, and use a heel–toe placement of the feet with long strides. The patient is advised to practice walking to marching music or to the sound of a ticking metronome, because this provides sensory reinforcement. Breathing exercises while walking helps to move the rib cage and to aerate parts of the lungs. Frequent rest periods aid in preventing frustration and fatigue.

Enhancing Self-Care Activities

Environmental modifications are necessary to compensate for functional disabilities. Patients may have severe mobility problems that make normal activities impossible. Adaptive or assistive devices may be useful. A hospital bed at home with bedside rails, an overbed frame with a trapeze, or a rope tied to the foot of the bed can provide assistance in pulling up without help. An occupational therapist can evaluate the patient's needs in the home, make recommendations regarding adaptive devices, and teach the patient and caregiver how to improvise.

Improving Bowel Elimination

The patient may have severe problems with constipation. Among the factors causing constipation are weakness of the muscles used in defecation, lack of exercise, inadequate fluid intake, and decreased autonomic nervous system activity. The medications used for the treatment of the disease also inhibit normal intestinal secretions. A regular bowel routine may be established by encouraging the patient to set a specific time of day to sit on the toilet without distractions, consciously increase fluid intake, and eat foods with moderate fiber content. Laxatives should be avoided. A raised toilet seat is useful, because the patient has difficulty in moving from a standing to a sitting position.

Improving Nutrition

Patients may have difficulty maintaining their weight. Eating becomes a very slow process, requiring concentration due to a dry mouth from medications and difficulty chewing and swallowing. These patients are at risk for aspiration because of impaired swallowing and the accumulation of saliva. They may be unaware that they are aspirating; subsequently, bronchopneumonia may develop.

Monitoring weight on a weekly basis indicates whether caloric intake is adequate. Supplemental feedings increase caloric intake. As the disease progresses, a nasogastric tube or percutaneous endoscopic gastroscopy may be necessary to maintain adequate nutrition. A dietitian can be consulted regarding nutritional needs.

An electric warming tray keeps food hot and allows the patient to rest during the prolonged time that it may take to eat. Special utensils also assist at mealtime. A plate that is stabilized, a nonspill cup, and eating utensils with built-up handles are useful self-help devices. The occupational therapist can assist in identifying appropriate adaptive devices.

Enhancing Swallowing

Swallowing difficulties are common in PD. These can lead to problems with poor head control, tongue tremor, hesitancy in initiating swallowing, difficulty in shaping food into a bolus, and disturbances in pharyngeal motility. To offset these problems, the patient should sit in an upright position during mealtime. A semisolid diet with thick liquids is easier to swallow than solids; thin liquids should be avoided. Thinking through the swallowing sequence is helpful. The patient is taught to place the food on the tongue, close the lips and teeth, lift the tongue up and then back, and swallow. The patient is encouraged to chew first on one side of the mouth and then on the other. To control the buildup of saliva, the patient is reminded to hold the head upright and make a conscious effort to swallow.

Improving Communication

Speech disorders are present in most patients with PD. Their low-pitched, monotonous, soft speech requires that they make a conscious effort to speak slowly, with deliberate attention to what they are saying. The patient is reminded to face the listener, exaggerate the pronunciation of words, speak in short sentences, and take a few deep breaths before speaking. A speech therapist may be helpful in designing speech improvement exercises and assisting the family and health care personnel to develop and use a method of communication that meets the patient's needs. A small electronic amplifier is helpful if the patient has difficulty being heard.

Supporting Coping Abilities

Support can be given by encouraging the patient and pointing out that activities will be maintained through active participation. A combination of physiotherapy, psychotherapy, medication therapy, and support group participation may help reduce the depression that often occurs.

Patients often feel embarrassed, apathetic, inadequate, bored, and lonely. These feelings may be due, in part, to physical slowness and the great effort that even small tasks require. The patient is assisted and encouraged to set achievable goals (e.g., improvement of mobility).

Because PD can lead to withdrawal and depression, patients must be active participants in their therapeutic program, including social and recreational events. A planned program of activity throughout the day prevents too much daytime sleeping as well as disinterest and apathy.

Every effort should be made to encourage patients to carry out the tasks involved in meeting their own daily needs and to remain independent. Doing things for the patient merely to save time undermines the basic goal of improving coping abilities and promoting a positive self-concept.

ALZHEIMER'S DISEASE

Alzheimer's disease (AD) is a progressive, irreversible, degenerative neurologic disease that begins insidiously and is characterized by gradual losses of cognitive function and disturbances in behavior and affect. Although AD can occur in people as young as 40, it is uncommon before age 65. AD can be classified into two types: familial, or early-onset AD, and sporadic, or late-onset, AD. Familial AD is rare, accounting for only 5% to 10% of all cases, and is frequently associated with genetic mutations. It occurs in middle-aged adults. If family members have at least one other relative with AD, then there is a familial component, which nonspecifically includes both environmental triggers and genetic determinants. Sporadic AD generally occurs in people older than 65 years of age and it has no obvious pattern of inheritance (Barker, 2008).

Pathophysiology

Specific neuropathologic and biochemical changes are found in patients with AD. These include neurofibrillary tangles (tangled masses of nonfunctioning neurons) and senile or neuritic plaques (deposits of amyloid protein, part of a larger protein called amyloid precursor protein [APP]) in the brain. The neuronal damage occurs primarily in the cerebral cortex and results in brain atrophy. Similar changes are found in the normal brain tissue of older adults, but to a lesser extent. Cells that use the neurotransmitter acetylcholine are those

principally affected by AD. Biochemically, the enzyme active in producing acetylcholine, which is specifically involved in memory processing, is decreased.

Clinical Manifestations and Assessment

In the early stages of AD, forgetfulness and subtle memory loss occur. Patients may experience small difficulties in work or social activities but have adequate cognitive function to hide the loss and function independently. Depression may occur. With further progression of AD, the deficits can no longer be concealed. Forgetfulness is manifested in many daily actions; patients may lose their ability to recognize familiar faces, places, and objects, and they may become lost in a familiar environment. They may repeat the same stories because they forget that they have already told them. Trying to reason with people with AD and using reality **orientation** only increases their anxiety without increasing function. Conversation becomes difficult, and word-finding difficulties occur. The ability to formulate concepts and think abstractly disappears; for example, a patient can interpret a proverb only in concrete terms. Patients are often unable to recognize the consequences of their actions and will therefore exhibit impulsive behavior. For example, on a hot day, a patient may decide to wade in the city fountain fully clothed. Patients have difficulty with everyday activities, such as operating simple appliances and handling money.

Personality changes are also usually evident. Patients may become depressed, suspicious, paranoid, hostile, and even combative. Progression of the disease intensifies the symptoms: speaking skills deteriorate to nonsense syllables, agitation and physical activity increase, and patients may wander at night. Eventually, assistance is needed for most ADLs, including eating and toileting, because dysphagia and incontinence develop. The late stages, in which patients are usually immobile and require total care, may last months or years. Occasionally, patients may recognize family members or caregivers. Death occurs as a result of complications such as pneumonia, malnutrition, or dehydration.

A definitive diagnosis of AD is made based on meeting the clinical criteria and histological evidence based on examination of brain tissue obtained from biopsy or autopsy. The most important goal is to rule out other causes of dementia or reversible causes of confusion, such as other types of dementia, depression, delirium, alcohol or drug abuse, or inappropriate drug dosage or drug toxicity (Hickey, 2009). Refer to Table 46-3 for a summary of differences between dementia and delirium.

The health history—including medical history, family history, social and cultural history, and medication history—and the physical examination, including functional and mental health status, are essential to the diagnosis of probable AD. Diagnostic tests, including complete blood count, chemistry profile, and vitamin B_{12} and thyroid hormone levels, as well as screening with EEG, CT, MRI, and examination of the CSF may all refute or support a diagnosis of probable AD.

Depression can closely mimic early-stage AD and coexists in many patients. A depression scale is helpful in screening for underlying depression. Tests of cognitive function such as the Mini-Mental Status Examination and the clock-drawing test are useful for screening. CT and MRI scans of the brain are useful for excluding hematoma, brain tumor, stroke, normal-pressure hydrocephalus, and atrophy but are not reliable in making a definitive diagnosis of AD. Infections, physiologic disturbances such as hypothyroidism, PD, and vitamin B_{12} deficiency can cause cognitive impairment that may be misdiagnosed as AD. Biochemical abnormalities can be excluded through examination of the blood and cerebrospinal fluid, but the findings are not sufficiently specific to make the diagnosis. AD is a diagnosis of exclusion, and a diagnosis of probable AD is made when the medical history, physical examination, and laboratory tests have excluded all known causes of other dementias.

Medical and Nursing Management

The primary goal in the medical management of AD is to manage the cognitive and behavioral symptoms. There is no cure and no way to slow the progression of the disease. Cholinesterase inhibitors such as donepezil hydrochloride (Aricept), rivastigmine tartrate (Exelon), and galantamine hydrobromide (Reminyl) enhance acetylcholine uptake in the brain, thus maintaining memory skills for a period of time. The drug memantine (Namenda) is an N-methyl-D-aspartate receptor antagonist that is thought to interfere with glutaminergic overstimulation. Cognitive ability improves within 6 to 12 months of therapy, but cessation of the medications results in cognitive decline commensurate with disease progression. It is recommended that treatment continue at least through the moderate stage of the illness (Downey, 2008).

Behavioral problems such as agitation and psychosis can be managed by behavioral and psychosocial therapies. Associated depression and behavioral problems can also be treated with antidepressants and the newer atypical neuroleptics, which are replacing the typical neuroleptics such as haloperidol (Haldol); the newer drugs have fewer adverse effects.

Nursing interventions for AD are aimed at promoting patient function and independence for as long as possible. Other important goals include promoting the patient's physical safety, promoting independence in self-care activities, reducing anxiety and agitation, improving communication, providing for socialization and intimacy, promoting adequate nutrition, promoting balanced activity and rest, and supporting and educating family caregivers.

Supporting Cognitive Function

Because dementia of any type is degenerative and progressive, patients display a decline in cognitive function over time. In the early phase of dementia, minimal cueing and guidance may be all that are needed for the patient to function fairly independently for a number of years. However, as the patient's cognitive ability declines, family members must provide more and more assistance and supervision. A

TABLE
46-3 **Summary of Differences Between Dementia and Delirium**

	Alzheimer's Disease (AD)	Delirium
Etiology	Familial (genetic [chromosomes 14, 19, 21]) Sporadic	Drug toxicity and interactions; acute disease; trauma; chronic disease exacerbation Fluid and electrolyte disorder
Risk factors	Advanced age; genetics	Preexisting cognitive impairment
Occurrence	50% to 60% of dementias	20% of hospitalized older people
Onset	Slow	Rapid, acute onset A harbinger of acute medical illness
Age of onset (years)	Early onset AD: 30 to 65 years Late onset AD: 65+ Most commonly: 85+	Any age, but predominantly in older persons
Gender	Males and females equally	Males and females equally
Course	Chronic, irreversible; progressive, regular, downhill	Acute
Duration	2 to 20 years	Lasts 1 day to 1 month
Symptom progress	Onset insidious. *Early*—mild and subtle *Middle and late*—intensified Progression to death (infection or malnutrition)	Symptoms are fully reversible with adequate treatment; can progress to chronicity or death if underlying condition is ignored.
Mood	Early depression (30%)	Variable
Speech/language	Speech remains intact until late in disease *Early:* Mild anomia (cannot name objects); deficits progress until speech lacks meaning; echoes and repeats words and sounds; mutism.	Fluctuating; often cannot concentrate long enough to speak
Physical signs	*Early:* No motor deficits *Middle:* Apraxia (70%) (cannot perform purposeful movement) *Late:* Dysarthria (impaired speech) *End stage:* Loss of all voluntary activity; positive neurologic signs	Signs and symptoms of underlying disease
Orientation	Becomes lost in familiar places (topographic disorientation) Has difficulty drawing three-dimensional objects (visual and spatial disorientation) Disorientation to time, place, and person—with disease progression	May fluctuate between lucidity and complete disorientation to time, place, and person
Memory	Loss is an early sign of dementia; loss of recent memory is soon followed by progressive decline in remote memory as well	Impaired recent and remote memory; may fluctuate between lucidity and confusion
Personality	Apathy, indifference, irritability *Early disease*—social behavior intact; hides cognitive deficits *Advanced disease*—disengages from activity and relationships; suspicious; paranoid delusions caused by memory loss; aggressive; catastrophic reactions	Fluctuating; cannot focus attention to converse; alarmed by symptoms (when lucid); hallucinations; paranoid
Functional status, activities of daily living	Poor judgment in everyday activities; has progressive decline in ability to handle money, use telephone, function in home and workplace	Impaired
Attention span	Distractable; short attention span	Highly impaired; cannot maintain or shift attention
Psychomotor activity	Wandering, hyperactivity, pacing, restlessness, agitation	Variable; alternates between high agitation, hyperactivity, restlessness, and lethargy
Sleep–wake cycle	Often impaired; wandering and agitation at nighttime	Takes brief naps throughout day and night

calm, predictable environment helps people with AD interpret their surroundings and activities. Environmental stimuli are limited, and a regular routine is established. A quiet, pleasant manner of speaking, clear and simple explanations, and use of memory aids and cues help minimize confusion and disorientation and give patients a sense of security. Prominently displayed clocks and calendars may enhance orientation to time. Color-coding the doorway may help patients who have difficulty locating their room. Active participation may help patients maintain cognitive, functional, and social interaction abilities for a longer period.

Promoting Physical Safety

A safe home environment allows the patient to move about as freely as possible and relieves the family of constant worry about safety. To prevent falls and other injuries, all obvious hazards are removed and hand rails are installed. A hazard-free environment allows the patient maximum independence and a sense of autonomy. Adequate lighting, especially in halls, stairs, and bathrooms, is necessary. Night lights are helpful, particularly if the patient has increased confusion at night (**sundowning**). Driving is prohibited, and smoking is allowed only with supervision. The patient may have a short attention span and be forgetful. Wandering behavior can often be reduced by gentle persuasion or distraction. Restraints should be avoided, because they increase agitation. Doors leading from the house must be secured. Outside the home, all activities must be supervised to protect the patient, and the patient should wear an identification bracelet or neck chain in case he or she becomes separated from the caregiver.

Promoting Independence in Self-Care Activities

Pathophysiologic changes in the brain make it difficult for people with AD to maintain physical independence. Patients should be assisted to remain functionally independent for as long as possible. One way to do this is to simplify daily activities by organizing them into short, achievable steps so that the patient experiences a sense of accomplishment. Frequently, occupational therapists can suggest ways to simplify tasks or recommend adaptive equipment. Direct patient supervision is sometimes necessary, but maintaining personal dignity and autonomy is important for people with AD, who should be encouraged to make choices when appropriate and to participate in self-care activities as much as possible.

Reducing Anxiety and Agitation

Despite profound cognitive losses, patients are sometimes aware of their diminishing abilities. Patients need constant emotional support that reinforces a positive self-image. When losses of skills occur, goals are adjusted to fit the patient's declining ability.

The environment should be kept familiar and noise-free. Excitement and confusion can be upsetting and may precipitate a combative, agitated state known as a *catastrophic reaction* (overreaction to excessive stimulation). The patient may respond by screaming, crying, or becoming abusive (physically or verbally); this may be the person's only way of expressing an inability to cope with the environment. When this occurs, it is important to remain calm and unhurried. Forcing the patient to proceed with the activity only increases the agitation. It is better to postpone the activity until later, even to another day. Frequently, the patient quickly forgets what triggered the reaction. Measures such as moving to a familiar environment, listening to music, stroking, rocking, or distraction may quiet the patient. Structuring activity is also helpful. Becoming familiar with a particular patient's predicted responses to certain stressors helps caregivers avoid similar situations.

Many older people with AD who have progressed to the late stages of the disease typically reside in nursing homes and are predominantly cared for by nurses' aides. Dementia education for caregivers is essential to minimize patient agitation and can be effectively taught by advanced practice nurses.

Improving Communication

To promote the patient's interpretation of messages, the nurse should remain unhurried and reduce noises and distractions. Use of clear, easy-to-understand sentences to convey messages is essential, because patients frequently forget the meaning of words or have difficulty organizing and expressing thoughts. In the earlier stages of AD, lists and simple written instructions that serve as reminders may be helpful. In later stages, the patient may be able to point to an object or use nonverbal language to communicate. Tactile stimuli, such as hugs or hand pats, are usually interpreted as signs of affection, concern, and security.

Providing for Socialization and Intimacy Needs

Because socialization with friends can be comforting, visits, letters, and phone calls are encouraged. Visits should be brief and nonstressful; limiting visitors to one or two at a time helps reduce overstimulation. Recreation is important, and people with AD are encouraged to enjoy simple activities. Realistic goals for activities that provide satisfaction are appropriate. Hobbies and activities such as walking, exercising, and socializing can improve the quality of life. The nonjudgmental friendliness of a pet may provide stimulation, comfort, and contentment. Care of plants or of a pet can also be satisfying and an outlet for energy.

AD does not eliminate the need for intimacy. Patients and their spouses may continue to enjoy sexual activity. Spouses should be encouraged to talk about any sexual concerns, and sexual counseling may be necessary. Simple expressions of love, such as touching and holding, are often meaningful.

Promoting Adequate Nutrition

Mealtime can be a pleasant social occasion or a time of upset and distress, and it should be kept simple and calm, without confrontations. Patients prefer familiar foods that look appetizing and taste good. To avoid any "playing" with food, one dish is offered at a time. Food is cut into small pieces to prevent choking. Liquids may be easier to swallow if they are converted to gelatin. Hot food and beverages are served warm, and the temperature of the foods should be checked to prevent burns.

When lack of coordination interferes with self-feeding, adaptive equipment is helpful. Some patients may do well eating with a spoon or with their fingers. If this is the case, an apron or a smock, rather than a bib, is used to protect clothing. As deficits progress, it may be necessary to feed the patient. Forgetfulness, disinterest, dental problems, lack of coordination, overstimulation, and choking may all serve as barriers to good nutrition and hydration.

Medical and Nursing Management

Most cases may improve with conservative treatment consisting of 1 to 2 days of bedrest, nonsteroidal anti-inflammatory drugs (NSAIDs), exercise regimens, epidural steroids, and patient education (Barker, 2008).

Surgery is usually indicated if the degenerative disk is causing compression on the spinal cord or if the patient has radiculopathy that fails conservative treatment. The most common procedure is a decompression laminectomy, which is the removal of the laminar portion of the vertebrae to gain access to the spinal cord (Barker, 2008).

HERNIATION OF A CERVICAL INTERVERTEBRAL DISK

The cervical spine is subjected to stresses that result from disk degeneration (due to aging, occupational stresses) and **spondylosis** (degenerative changes occurring in a disk and adjacent vertebral bodies). Cervical disk degeneration may lead to lesions that can cause damage to the spinal cord and its roots.

Clinical Manifestations and Assessment

A cervical disk herniation usually occurs at the C5–C6 and C6–C7 interspaces. Pain and stiffness may occur in the neck, the top of the shoulders, and the region of the scapulae. Sometimes patients interpret these signs as symptoms of heart trouble or bursitis. Pain may also occur in the upper extremities and head, accompanied by **paresthesia** (tingling or a "pins and needles" sensation) and numbness of the upper extremities. Cervical MRI usually confirms the diagnosis.

Medical and Nursing Management

The goals of treatment are to rest and immobilize the cervical spine to give the soft tissues time to heal and to reduce inflammation in the supporting tissues and the affected nerve roots in the cervical spine. Bedrest (usually 1 to 2 days) is important because it eliminates the stress of gravity and relieves the cervical spine of the need to support the head. It also reduces inflammation and edema in soft tissues around the disk, relieving pressure on the nerve roots. Proper positioning on a firm mattress may bring dramatic relief from pain.

The cervical spine may be rested and immobilized by a cervical collar. A collar allows maximal opening of the intervertebral foramina and holds the head in a neutral or slightly flexed position. The patient may have to wear the collar 24 hours a day during the acute phase. The skin under the collar is inspected for irritation. After the patient is free of pain, cervical isometric exercises are started to strengthen the neck muscles.

Analgesic agents (NSAIDs, acetaminophen, oxycodone [Percocet], or hydrocodone [Vicodin]) are prescribed during the acute phase to relieve pain, and sedatives may be administered to control the anxiety that is often associated with cervical disk disease. Muscle relaxants (cyclobenzaprine [Flexeril], methocarbamol [Robaxin], metaxalone [Skelaxin]) are administered to interrupt muscle spasm and to promote comfort. NSAIDs (aspirin, ibuprofen [Motrin, Advil], naproxen [Naprosyn, Anaprox]) or corticosteroids are prescribed to treat the inflammation that usually occurs in the affected nerve roots and supporting tissues. Occasionally, a corticosteroid is injected into the epidural space for relief of radicular (spinal nerve root) pain. Hot, moist compresses (for 10 to 20 minutes) applied to the back of the neck several times daily increase blood flow to the muscles and help relax the patient and reduce muscle spasm.

Surgical excision of the herniated disk may be necessary if there is a significant neurologic deficit, progression of the deficit, evidence of cord compression, or pain that either worsens or fails to improve. A cervical discectomy, with or without fusion, may be performed to alleviate symptoms. An anterior surgical approach may be used through a transverse incision to remove disk material that has herniated into the spinal canal and foramina, or a posterior approach may be used at the appropriate level of the cervical spine. Potential complications with the anterior approach include carotid or vertebral artery injury, recurrent laryngeal nerve dysfunction, esophageal perforation, and airway obstruction. Complications of the posterior approach include damage to the nerve root or the spinal cord due to retraction or contusion of either of these structures, resulting in weakness of muscles supplied by the nerve root or cord.

Microsurgery, such as endoscopic microdiscectomy, may be performed in selected patients through a small incision and using magnification techniques. The patient who undergoes microsurgery usually has less tissue trauma and pain and consequently a shorter hospital stay than after conventional surgical approaches.

> **⚠ NURSING ALERT**
> *Although NSAIDs are often prescribed for cervical disc herniation, when surgery involving bone fusion is considered, NSAIDs are often discontinued because they can interfere with bone healing. Collaborate with the health care provider to instruct the patient to avoid these drugs prior to and after surgery.*

HERNIATION OF A LUMBAR DISK

About 90% to 95% of lumbar herniation occurs at the L4–L5 or L5–S1 levels (Barker, 2008). A herniated lumbar disk causes low back pain accompanied by varying degrees of motor and sensory impairment.

Clinical Manifestations and Assessment

The patient complains of low back pain with muscle spasms, followed by radiation of the pain into one hip and down into the leg (sciatica). Pain is aggravated by actions that increase intraspinal fluid pressure, such as bending, lifting, or straining

(as in sneezing or coughing), and usually is relieved by bed-rest. Usually there is some type of postural deformity, because pain causes an alteration of the normal spinal mechanics. If the patient lies on the back and attempts to raise a leg in a straight position, pain radiates into the leg; this maneuver, called the *straight leg–raising test*, stretches the sciatic nerve. Additional signs include muscle weakness, alterations in tendon reflexes, and sensory loss.

The diagnosis of lumbar disk disease is based on the history and physical findings and the use of imaging techniques such as MRI, CT, and myelography.

Medical and Nursing Management

The objectives of treatment are to relieve pain, slow disease progression, and increase the patient's functional ability. Bedrest for patients with severe pain in the lumbar region is limited to a short course (≤2 days), followed by resumption of light activity (Hickey, 2009).

Strategies for increasing the patient's functional ability include weight reduction, physical therapy, and biofeedback. Mobilization, walking short distances, is recommended. When symptoms subside, stretching, strengthening, and exercise programs should be initiated.

Because muscle spasm is prominent during the acute phase, muscle relaxants are used. NSAIDs and systemic corticosteroids may be administered to counter the inflammation that usually occurs in the supporting tissues and the affected nerve roots. Moist heat and massage help to relax muscles.

Most patients fear surgery on any part of the spine and therefore need explanations about the surgery and reassurance that it will not weaken the back. When data are being collected for the health history, any reports of pain, paresthesia, or muscle spasm are recorded to provide a baseline for comparison after surgery. Preoperative assessment also includes an evaluation of movement of the extremities, as well as bladder and bowel function. To facilitate the postoperative turning procedure, the patient is taught to turn as a unit (called *logrolling*) as part of the preoperative preparation (Fig. 46-8). Before surgery, the patient is also encouraged to take deep breaths, cough, and perform muscle-setting exercises to maintain muscle tone.

In the lumbar region, surgical treatment includes lumbar disk excision through a posterolateral laminotomy and the techniques of microdiscectomy and percutaneous discectomy. In microdiscectomy, an operating microscope is used to visualize the offending disk and compressed nerve roots; it permits a small incision (2.5 cm [1 inch]) and minimal blood loss and takes about 30 minutes of operating time. Generally, the hospital stay is short, and the patient makes a rapid recovery. Percutaneous discectomy is an alternative treatment for herniated intervertebral disks of the lumbar spine. One approach in current use is through a 2.5-cm (1-inch) incision just above the iliac crest. A tube, trocar, or cannula is inserted under X-ray guidance through the retroperitoneal space to the involved disk space. Special instru-

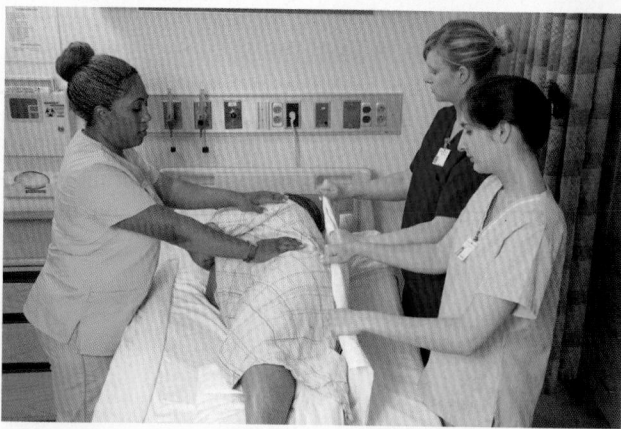

FIGURE 46-8 Before the patient undergoes laminectomy surgery, the logrolling technique that will be used for turning the patient should be demonstrated. The patient's arms will be crossed and the spine aligned. To avoid twisting the spine, the head, shoulders, knees, and hips are turned at the same time that the patient rolls over like a log. When in a side-lying position, the patient's back, buttocks, and legs are supported with pillows.

ments are used to remove the disk. The operating time is about 15 minutes. Blood loss and postoperative pain are minimal, and usually the patient is discharged within 2 days after surgery. The disadvantage of this procedure is the possibility of damage to structures in the surgical pathway.

Complications that could occur after surgery include herniation relapse, arachnoiditis, neuritis, or failed disk syndrome. Herniation relapse may occur at the same level or elsewhere, so the patient may become a candidate for another disk procedure. Arachnoiditis (inflammation of the arachnoid membrane) may occur after surgery (and after myelography); it involves an insidious onset of diffuse, frequently burning pain in the lower back, radiating into the buttocks. Disk excision can leave adhesions and scarring around the spinal nerves and dura, which then produce inflammatory changes that create chronic neuritis and neurofibrosis. Disk surgery may relieve pressure on the spinal nerves, but it does not reverse the effects of neural injury and scarring and the pain that results.

Because postoperative neurologic deficits may occur from nerve root injury, the motor strength and sensation of the lower extremities are evaluated at specified intervals, along with the color and temperature of the legs and sensation of the toes. Assessing the patient after surgery, the nurse checks vital signs frequently, and the wound is inspected for hemorrhage, because vascular injury is a complication of disk surgery. It is important to assess for urinary retention, another sign of neurologic deterioration.

In discectomy with fusion, the patient has an additional surgical incision if bone fragments were taken from the iliac crest or fibula to serve as wedges in the spine. The recovery period is longer than for those patients who underwent discectomy without spinal fusion, because bony union must take place.

To position the patient, a pillow is placed under the head, and the knee rest is elevated slightly to relax the back mus-

cles. When the patient is lying on one side, however, extreme knee flexion must be avoided. The patient is encouraged to move from side to side to relieve pressure and is reassured that no injury will result from moving. When the patient is ready to turn, the bed is placed in a flat position and a pillow is placed between the patient's legs. The patient turns as a unit (logrolls) without twisting the back. To get out of bed,

the patient lies on one side while pushing up to a sitting position. At the same time, the nurse or family member eases the patient's legs over the side of the bed. Coming to a sitting or standing posture is accomplished in one long, smooth motion. Most patients walk to the bathroom on the same day as the surgery. Sitting is discouraged except for defecation.

Chapter Review

Critical Thinking Exercises

1. Your 40-year-old patient has MG. Her condition has been stable and she has been able to manage without assistance, but she reports increasing weakness and fatigue. What nursing assessments and interventions are warranted for her? What discharge plans are indicated if she is to return home to the care of her family? How would your discharge planning change if she lived alone in an apartment on the third floor of a building without an elevator?

2. Your patient has been admitted to the intensive care unit with a diagnosis of possible Guillain-Barré syndrome. Identify the priorities of assessment for this patient and the nursing and medical interventions that you would anticipate. What medications should you have readily available for this patient?

3. A 50-year-old man newly diagnosed with Parkinson's disease asks what type of medication he will be given. What are the possible medications that will be used to treat his disease, and the long-term effects of each? How would your discharge teaching targeted toward medications be modified if the patient lives alone?

NCLEX-Style Review Questions

1. While assessing a client with Parkinson's disease, the nurse identifies bradykinesia when the client exhibits which of the following?
   A. Muscle flaccidity
   B. An intention tremor
   C. Paralysis of the limbs
   D. Slow spontaneous movement

2. What is the most common initial symptom that a nurse might expect a client with MS to complain about?
   A. Diarrhea
   B. Headaches
   C. Skin infections
   D. Visual disturbances

3. A client who has GB asks, "Will I ever get better?" Which of the following responses would be the most appropriate answer by the nurse?
   A. "You'll notice your strength will improve each day."
   B. "We are doing everything we can to provide the best care."
   C. "You seem concerned about getting better. What do you think?"
   D. "Your chances for recovery are very good but recovery is slow."

4. Which of the following will the nurse observe in the patient undergoing a tonic–clonic seizure?
   A. Jerking in one extremity that spreads gradually to adjacent areas
   B. Vacant staring and abrupt cessation of all activity
   C. Facial grimaces, patting motions, and lip smacking
   D. Loss of consciousness, body stiffening, and violent muscle contractions

5. The nurse knows that the signs and symptoms of meningeal irritation include which of the following? Select all that apply.
   A. Nuchal rigidity and headache
   B. Kernig's and Brudzinski's signs
   C. Aphasia and motor weakness
   D. Photophobia

Try these additional resources to enhance your learning and understanding of this chapter:
- thePoint online resource available at **http://thepoint.lww.com/Pellico1e**
- *Handbook for Focus on Adult Health: Medical-Surgical Nursing*
- *Study Guide for Focus on Adult Health: Medical-Surgical Nursing*

References and Selected Readings

References and selected readings associated with this chapter can be found on the website that accompanies the book. Visit http://thepoint.lww.com/Pellico1e to access the references and other additional resources associated with this chapter.

Nursing Management: Patients With Cerebrovascular Disorders

KARIN V. NYSTRÖM

Learning Objectives

After reading this chapter you will be able to:

1. Describe the incidence and epidemiology of stroke.

2. Identify mechanisms that affect cerebral blood flow.

3. Describe the pathophysiology of ischemic and hemorrhagic stroke, and transient ischemic attack.

4. Identify risk factors and manifestations of stroke syndromes.

5. Describe collaborative care, drug therapy, and nutritional considerations for patients with strokes.

6. Describe the nursing process related to care of patients with stroke.

Cerebrovascular disorders is an umbrella term that refers to abnormalities of the central nervous system (CNS) affecting normal blood supply to the brain and/or spinal cord. There are many vascular abnormalities affecting cerebral blood flow but the most common cerebrovascular disorder is stroke, which is the focus of this chapter. The nurse should be well prepared to care for patients admitted to an acute care facility with a stroke and the more common co-morbidities that accompany this syndrome. The neurological condition may be the patient's primary health problem or a secondary diagnosis. As such, nurses must be able to develop a care plan for a stroke patient's recovery that considers both the neurologic deficit and potential complications associated with that deficit during rehabilitation.

STROKE

Stroke is a heterogeneous syndrome characterized by the onset of one or more focal neurologic deficits (corresponding to the affected area of the brain) caused by reduced cerebral blood flow that leads to brain cell death and functional disability. The two major stroke types that cause an interruption in cerebral blood flow are an occluded artery that deprives blood flow to a certain part of the brain (called an *ischemic stroke*) (Fig. 47-1, p. 1247), and a ruptured artery resulting in bleeding in or around the brain (called a *hemorrhagic stroke*) (Fig. 47-2).

Ischemic strokes account for about 85% of all stroke syndromes, and hemorrhagic strokes account for the remaining 15% (Table 47-1). Regardless of stroke type or mechanism, the concept that "time is brain" has become the mainstay for directing a rapid clinical diagnosis, acute treatment options, and follow-up secondary stroke prevention strategies (Barker, 2010).

Incidence

Stroke is currently the fourth leading cause of death in the United States, behind heart disease, cancer, and chronic respiratory diseases (Centers for Disease Control and Prevention [CDC], 2010). Approximately 800,000 people experience a stroke each year in the United States; 600,000 of these are first events, and approximately 200,000 are recurrent strokes. With about 4.8 million stroke survivors alive today, stroke is the leading cause of

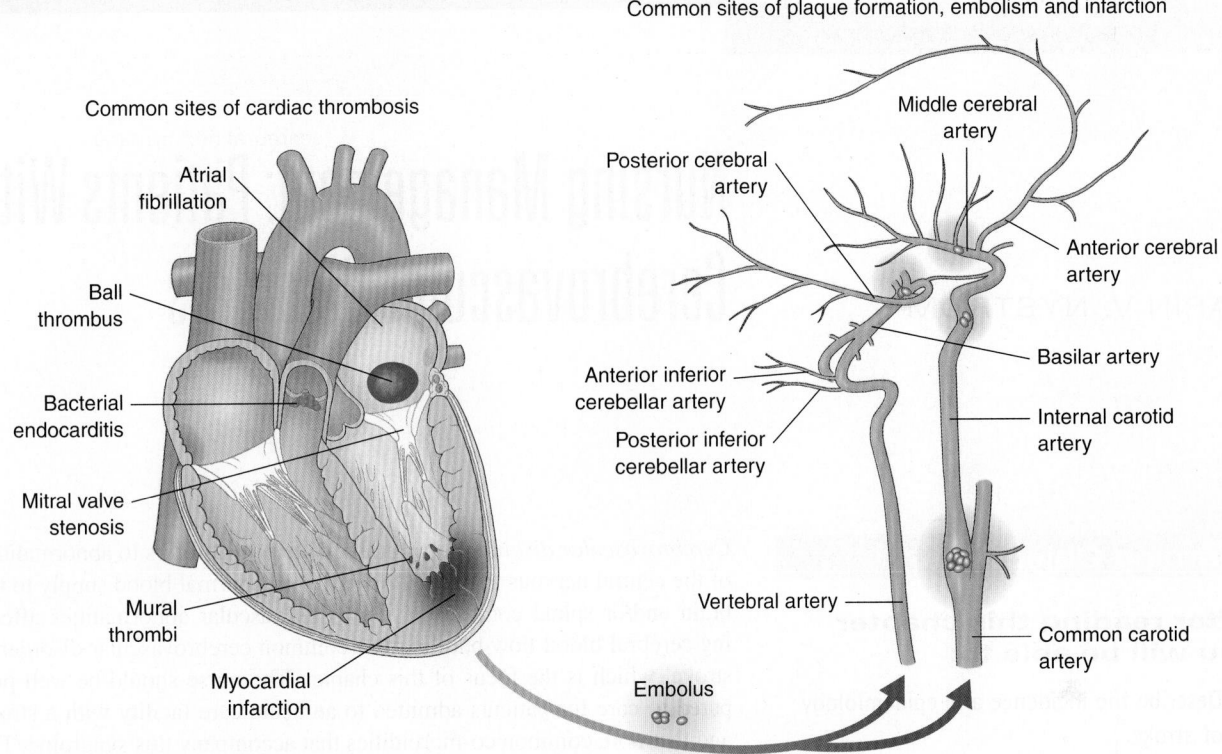

Common sites of cardiac thrombosis

Common sites of plaque formation, embolism and infarction

FIGURE 47-1 Ischemic stroke.

serious, long-term adult disability in the United States (Lloyd-Jones, Brown et al., 2010). It is estimated that approximately 90% of stroke survivors are left with some residual deficit. The financial impact of stroke is profound, with estimated direct and indirect costs totaling $73.7 billion (CDC, 2010).

Despite the numerous national campaign efforts (Alberts & Baranski, 2010; American Heart/Stroke Association [AHA/ASA], 2009, Payne, Fang, Fogle et al., 2010) to increase stroke awareness over the past two decades, several studies have shown that a majority of people cannot name

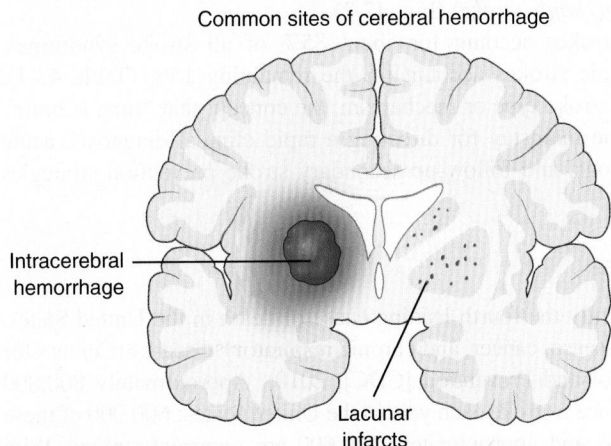

Common sites of cerebral hemorrhage

FIGURE 47.2 Common sites of cerebral hemorrhage.

many of the typical stroke symptoms or do not consider calling 911 in the event they or a family member are experiencing stroke symptoms (Fussman, Rafferty, Lyon-Callo et al., 2010; Hickey, O'Hanlon, McGee et al., 2009). Delays in stroke symptom recognition and delays in activating the Emergency Medical System limit treatment options and lead to worsening long-term recovery outcomes. Ongoing efforts aimed at reducing the long-term complications associated with stroke are directed toward promoting secondary prevention through public education initiatives, researching innovative medical and surgical therapies in acute care, and implementing strategies for reducing modifiable risks in the primary care setting.

Stroke was recognized as early as 400 BC, when patients developed "apoplexy" (meaning "struck with violence"). Strokes continue to be one of the most common neurological emergencies. Hospital systems today are charged with implementing systems of care to treat stroke patients in the acute phase of their illness and to direct patients and their families to the appropriate rehabilitative program to optimize functional outcome (Schwamm, Pancioli, Acker et al., 2005). In the community setting, stroke survivors now have multiple rehabilitation therapy options, with assistive devices and pharmacotherapies for improved motor function, constraint-induced movement therapies (CIMT), which constrains the unaffected limb to encourage use of the affected limb, to enhance occupational skills, and innovative computer programs to augment language retraining exercises.

TABLE
47-1 Comparison of Major Types of Stroke

Facet	Ischemic	Hemorrhagic
Causes	Large-artery thrombosis Small, penetrating artery thrombosis Cardiogenic embolic Cryptogenic (no known cause) Other	Intracerebral hemorrhage Subarachnoid hemorrhage Cerebral aneurysm Arteriovenous malformation
Main presenting symptoms	Numbness or weakness of the face, arm, or leg, especially on one side of the body	"Exploding headache" Decreased level of consciousness
Additional symptoms	Slurred speech, or difficulty with word finding or comprehension	Nausea/vomiting; visual changes; seizures

Many of these symptoms occur with either stroke type.

Primary Stroke Centers

In 2000, the recommendation for the establishment of *primary stroke centers* as an approach to acute stroke care was published to improve the medical care of stroke patients (Alberts, Hademenos, Latchaw et al., 2000). Key elements to meet the criteria for Primary Stroke Center status included acute stroke teams, stroke units, written care protocols, and an integrated emergency response system (Box 47-1). Additional support services included availability and interpretation of computed tomography (CT) scans 24/7 and rapid laboratory testing. Administrative support, strong leadership, and continuing education were also included as important elements for stroke centers. These recommendations were formalized following the 1996 U.S. Food and Drug Administration (FDA) approval of intravenous tissue plasminogen activator (tPA) for the treatment of acute ischemic stroke within the first 3 hours of symptom onset (NINDS & Stroke rtPA Stroke Study Work Group, 1995).

In 2003, The Joint Commission (TJC) launched a disease-specific care program for primary stroke center certification. Hospitals committed to using evidence-based clinical practice guidelines for stroke care that complied with care related to

---

BOX 47-1

Major Elements of a Primary Stroke Center

Patient care areas:
- Acute stroke teams
- Written care protocols
- Emergency medical services
- Emergency department
- Stroke unit
- Neurosurgical services

Support services:
- Commitment and support of the medical organization; stroke center director
- Neuroimaging services
- Laboratory services
- Outcomes and quality improvement activities
- Continuing medical education

---

standardized performance measures were eligible to apply for national certification. To date, more than 700 hospitals have achieved primary stroke center status from The Joint Commission, and these institutions undergo an external review process every 2 years. A number of states also have developed state-specific criteria for obtaining stroke center certification.

Certified stroke centers are mandated to collect data on a consensus of specific practice components, including performance measures to monitor and improve the quality of stroke care. These measures apply to hospitalized patients with either an ischemic or hemorrhagic stroke. At the time of this publication, eight stroke performance activities have been endorsed by the National Quality Forum and are supported by The Joint Commission. Although not inclusive of all important aspects of acute stroke care, initial data support the efforts to improve quality of care and to predict functional outcome (Schwamm, Fonarow, Reeves et al., 2009). Table 47-2 outlines the specific stroke performance measures and applicable stroke types.

Pathophysiology

Ischemic Stroke

Disruption of blood flow in, or to the brain, due to an obstruction of a blood vessel initiates a complex series of circulatory and metabolic events referred to as the ischemic cascade. This event culminates in an acute ischemic stroke. Normally, approximately 15% of cardiac output supplies the brain. Cerebral blood flow is calculated at 50 to 54 mL of blood per 100 g of brain tissue per minute. The ischemic cascade begins when cerebral blood flow decreases to less than 25 mL/100 g/min. At this point, neurons are no longer able to maintain aerobic respiration. The cell's mitochondria must then switch to anaerobic metabolism, generating large amounts of lactic acid and glutamate, causing a change in pH. This switch to the less efficient anaerobic metabolism also renders the neuron incapable of producing sufficient quantities of adenosine triphosphate (ATP) to fuel the depolarization processes. The cell membrane pumps that maintain electrolyte balances begin to fail, and the cells cease to function (Fig. 47-3).

TABLE
47-2 Standardized Performance Measures for Stroke Care

Stroke Performance Measures	Stroke Type
Deep venous thrombosis (DVT) prophylaxis • Nonambulatory patients should start receiving DVT prophylaxis by the end of day 2	Ischemic stroke Hemorrhagic stroke
Discharged on antithrombotic therapy: • Patients prescribed antithrombotic therapy at discharge	Ischemic stroke
Discharge on anticoagulation for patients in atrial fibrillation: • Patients with atrial fibrillation discharged on anticoagulation	Ischemic stroke
Thrombolytic therapy administered: • Patients with acute ischemic stroke who arrive at the hospital within 120 minutes of time last known well and for whom IV tissue plasminogen activator (tPA) was initiated at this hospital within 180 minutes of last known well	Ischemic stroke
Antithrombotic medication by the end of hospital day 2: • Patients who receive antithrombotic therapy by the end of hospital day 2	Ischemic stroke
Discharged on cholesterol-reducing medication: • Patients with low-density lipoproteins (LDL) >100 or LDL not measured or on cholesterol-reducer before admission who are discharged on cholesterol-reducing drugs	Ischemic stroke
Dysphagia screening: • Patients who undergo screening for dysphagia with a simple valid bedside testing protocol before being given any food, fluids or medication by mouth.	Ischemic stroke Hemorrhagic stroke (excluded from TJC)
Stroke education: • Patients and caregivers who were given education or educational materials prior to discharge address personal risk factors, stroke warning signs, activation of emergency medical services, need for follow-up after discharge, and medications prescribed	Ischemic stroke Hemorrhagic stroke
Smoking cessation: • Patients with a history of smoking cigarettes or whose caregivers are smokers are given smoking cessation advice and counseling during the hospital stay. A smoker is defined as someone who has smoked cigarettes during the year prior to admission.	Ischemic stroke Hemorrhagic stroke (excluded from TJC)
Assessed for rehabilitation: • Patients who are assessed for rehabilitation	Ischemic stroke Hemorrhagic stroke

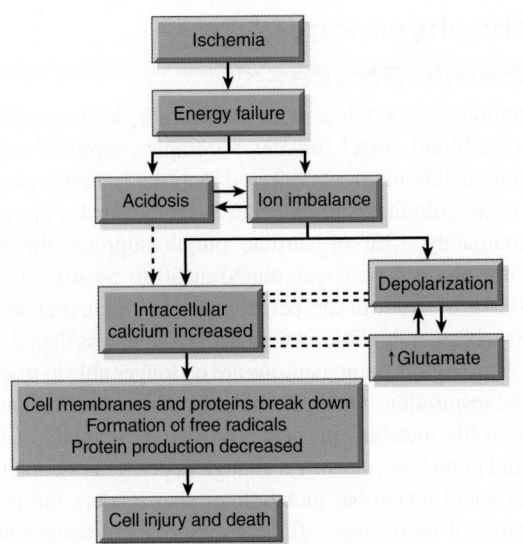

FIGURE 47-3 Processes contributing to ischemic brain cell injury. Courtesy of the National Stroke Association. Englewood, Colorado.

The ischemic penumbra is an area of affected brain tissue in which blood flow has been reduced to 20 to 45 mL/100 g/min. When a thrombus occludes blood flow to a specific area of the brain, the brain tissue surrounding the core infarct is effectively "stunned" by poor perfusion but deemed salvageable with early treatment, such as thrombolysis or clot retrieval (Fig. 47-4) (Hickey, 2009).

NURSING ALERT
Each step in the ischemic cascade represents an opportunity for intervention that may limit the extent of secondary brain damage caused by hypoperfusion. The penumbra area may be revitalized by administration of tPA, which selectively binds to fibrin, converting plasminogen to plasmin and causing clot lysis. Neuroprotective agents (such as antioxidants or ion channel/receptor modulators) that block cell death pathways have been shown in animal studies to reduce ischemic damage to the penumbra, but to date they have not shown promise in human studies.

Ischemic strokes are subdivided into five subtypes according to a mechanism-based classification system: large-artery

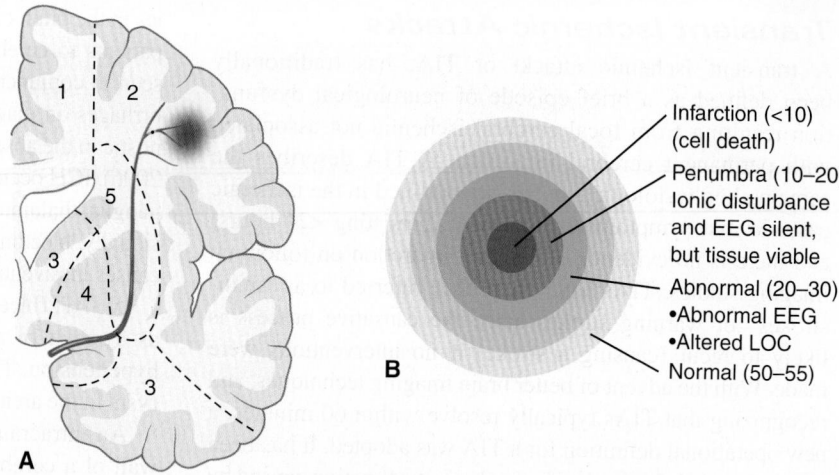

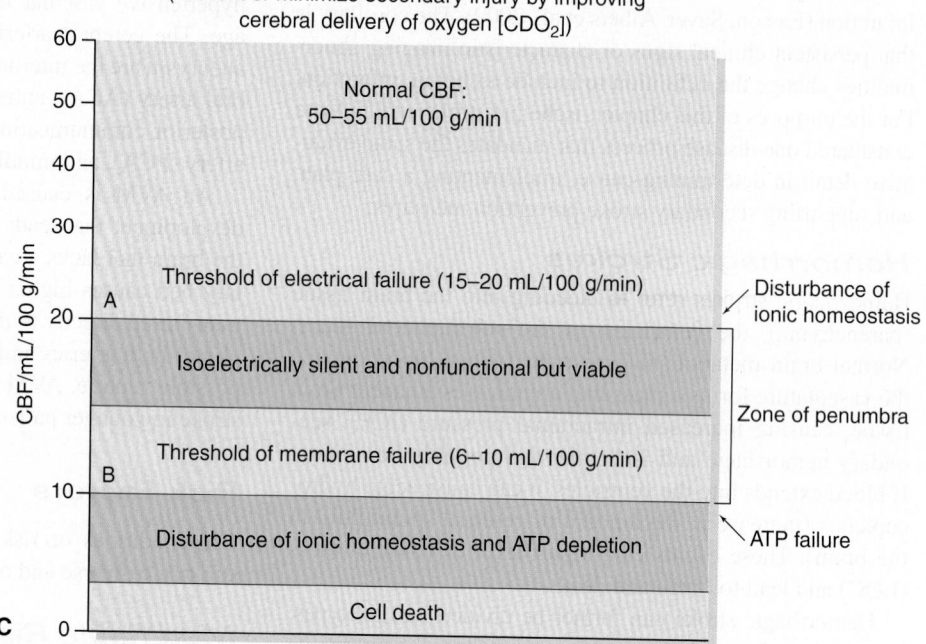

FIGURE 47-4 Cerebral blood supply during ischemic events. (**A**) See distribution of middle cerebral artery and occlusion of a branch. Note area of infarction and surrounding penumbra with viable but nonfunctional cells. These cells will either become infarcted or recover, depending on treatment. (**B**) Ischemic penumbra: normal cerebral blood flow (CBF) = 50 to 55 mL/100 g/min. Variations in CBF are noted. Penumbra is the critical area that may be salvageable with appropriate treatment, or cell death will occur if adequate CBF is not restored. (**C**) Ischemic penumbra: conceptual basis for brain resuscitation. ATP = adenosine triphosphate; EEG = electroencephalogram; LOC = level of consciousness. Adapted from Hickey, J. V. (2009). *The clinical practice of neurological and neurosurgical nursing*. Philadelphia: Lippincott Williams & Wilkins.

thrombotic strokes (representing 20% of ischemic strokes); small, penetrating artery thrombotic strokes (25%); cardiogenic embolic strokes (20%); cryptogenic strokes (strokes that cannot be attributable to any specific cause) (30%); and other (5%). Each stroke subtype has a characteristic pathophysiologic course, but these types have overlapping clinical features (Adams, Bendixen, Kappelle et al., 1993).

Large-artery thrombotic strokes are caused by atherosclerotic plaques in the large blood vessels of the brain. Thrombus formation and occlusion at the site of the atherosclerosis result in ischemia and infarction (tissue death).

Small, penetrating artery thrombotic strokes affect one or more vessels and are the most common type of ischemic stroke, typically caused by longstanding hypertension, hyperlipidemia, or diabetes. Small artery thrombotic strokes are frequently referred to as *lacunar strokes* because of the

small cavities that are created after the death of infarcted brain tissue.

Cardiogenic embolic strokes are associated with cardiac arrhythmias such as atrial fibrillation, but can also be associated with valvular heart disease or left ventricular thrombus (as depicted in Figure 47-1). Emboli originating from the heart circulate to the cerebral vasculature, most commonly via the left middle cerebral artery, causing ischemia and subsequent infarction.

The last two classifications of ischemic strokes are cryptogenic strokes, which have no known cause, and strokes from other causes, such as illicit drug use (cocaine), coagulopathies, migraine, and spontaneous dissection of the carotid or vertebral arteries. This subtyping determines the differences in both therapeutic interventions and long-term prognosis.

Transient Ischemic Attacks

A transient ischemic attack, or TIA, has traditionally been defined as a brief episode of neurological dysfunction resulting from focal cerebral ischemia not associated with permanent cerebral infarction. A TIA describes the same pathophysiologic mechanism outlined in the ischemic cascade, but symptoms are transient (persisting <24 hours) and there is no evidence of cerebral infarction on follow-up imaging studies. TIAs have often been referred to as "ministrokes" or warning strokes since the causative process is likely to recur (causing a stroke) if no interventions were made. With the advent of better brain imaging techniques, and recognizing that TIAs typically resolve within 60 minutes, a new operational definition for a TIA was adopted. It has been defined as a brief episode of neurologic dysfunction caused by focal brain or retinal ischemia, with clinical symptoms typically lasting less than 1 hour, and without evidence of acute infarction (Easton, Saver, Albers et al., 2009). The corollary is that persistent clinical signs or characteristic imaging abnormalities change the definition to include ischemic infarction. For the purposes of this chapter, ischemic stroke and TIA are considered one disease process that mandates the same evaluative detail in determining cause, implementing a care plan, and supporting secondary stroke prevention measures.

Hemorrhagic Strokes

Hemorrhagic strokes refer to bleeding into the brain tissue (parenchyma), the ventricles, or the subarachnoid space. Normal brain metabolism is disrupted when blood outside the vasculature forms a mass that compresses adjacent brain tissue, causing increased intracranial pressure (ICP), secondary hemorrhage and ischemia, and possibly herniation. If blood extends into the ventricles, it can cause acute hydrocephalus (increase in the amount of cerebral spinal fluid in the brain). These events can impair level of consciousness (LOC) and lead to coma and death.

Hemorrhagic stroke can further be divided into subtypes: intracerebral hemorrhage (ICH), subarachnoid hemorrhage (SAH), hemorrhage due to intracranial aneurysms, and hemorrhage due to arteriovenous malformations. Primary ICH from a spontaneous rupture of small arteries or arterioles accounts for approximately 80% of hemorrhagic strokes and is caused chiefly by uncontrolled hypertension. Blood can accumulate over minutes to hours. Symptom presentation can vary from mild deficits to unconsciousness. Because the brain is enclosed in a rigid structure, hemorrhage can dramatically increase ICP, causing shifts in the content volume within the skull and eventual herniation (and a higher mortality rate) if not acutely treated. ICH can also occur in the setting of an ischemic stroke, when the infarcted tissue becomes susceptible to leaking blood vessels. ICH is also associated with arteriovenous malformations (AVMs, discussed below), intracranial aneurysms (discussed below), intracranial neoplasms, and with certain medications, such as anticoagulants or amphetamines (Hickey, 2009). Amyloid angiopathy (a condition in which amyloid [fibrous proteins] deposits accumulate inside the walls of arter-

ies in the brain causing vessel wall breakdown) can predispose patients to cerebral hemorrhage. Amyloid deposits are often seen in conjunction with dementia. Characteristic lobar hemorrhages on magnetic resonance imaging (MRI) can be diagnostic in the absence of a brain tissue biopsy (Smith & Eichler, 2006). ICH occurs most commonly in the cerebral lobes, basal ganglia, thalamus, brainstem (the pons), and cerebellum. Occasionally, bleeding ruptures the wall of the lateral ventricle and causes intraventricular hemorrhage, which is frequently fatal.

A SAH (bleeding into the subarachnoid space) may occur as a result of an AVM, intracranial aneurysm, trauma, or hypertension. The most common causes are a leaking aneurysm in the area of the Circle of Willis and a congenital AVM.

An intracranial (cerebral) **aneurysm** is a dilation of the wall of a cerebral artery. An aneurysm may be due to atherosclerosis, which results in a defect in the vessel wall with subsequent weakness; a congenital defect of the vessel wall; hypertensive vascular disease; head trauma; or advancing age. The cerebral arteries most commonly affected by an aneurysm are the internal carotid artery (ICA), anterior cerebral artery (ACA), anterior communicating artery (ACoA), posterior communicating artery (PCoA), posterior cerebral artery (PCA), and middle cerebral artery (MCA).

An AVM is caused by an abnormality in embryonal development that leads to a tangle of arteries and veins in the brain that lacks a capillary bed. The absence of a capillary bed causes higher pressure within the arterioles to be transmitted directly to the veins. This anomaly leads to dilation of both arteries and veins and, if the pressure increases, possible rupture. AVM is a common cause of hemorrhagic stroke in younger patients.

Risk Factors

The conditions or risk factors that predispose patients to stroke are diverse and often correlate to cardiac risk factors.

Modifiable Risk Factors

Modifiable risk factors are those that can be altered through lifestyle changes and medical treatment. Modifiable stroke risk factors include hypertension, smoking and second-hand smoke exposure, diabetes, dyslipidemia, atrial fibrillation, diet (including excessive salt, high alcohol consumption), obesity, sleep apnea, and lack of exercise.

Hypertension is the most important risk factor for both ischemic and hemorrhagic stroke and despite the numerous treatment options, it remains under-recognized and undertreated in most communities. In the acute stroke phase, blood pressure is generally liberalized to allow for improved cerebral blood flow but post discharge, the goal is to achieve normotension, defined as less than 120 mm Hg systolic and less than 80 mm Hg diastolic (JNC-7, 2003; Mancia, 2004).

Smoking and second-hand smoke are prevalent among all age groups and pose an increased stroke risk among women who smoke and who are on oral contraceptives. Smoking

cessation programs (counseling and nicotine replacement) have been included as part of the post-stroke care plan for all patients identified as current smokers (Geyer & Gomez, 2009).

Diabetes independently increases stroke risk and contributes to the increased prevalence of hypertension and dyslipidemia. Glycemic control alone has not been shown to reduce stroke risk but in combination with blood pressure and lipid management, patients with diabetes can lower their overall risk (Geyer & Gomez, 2009).

Atrial fibrillation is the most frequently diagnosed arrhythmia in the United States. If left untreated, it can lead to an ischemic stroke. Approximately 15% of ischemic strokes can be attributed to atrial fibrillation. Screening for atrial fibrillation in patients over the age of 65 has been recommended since anticoagulation and rate/rhythm control can reduce stroke risk by up to 68% (Lip & Lim, 2007).

Non-Modifiable Risk Factors

Non-modifiable risk factors are important to highlight from both a primary and secondary stroke prevention standpoint because, while they cannot be changed, associated modifiable risk factors can be aggressively treated. Having a family history of stroke increases the chance of stroke and can be attributed to genetic influences as well as cultural/environmental influences. Genetic testing is not generally recommended unless there is a suspicion of a rare genetic condition and other more common causes for stroke cannot be identified. Older age is a risk factor for stroke, and for both ischemic and hemorrhagic strokes the risk doubles every 10 years after age 55. Men tend to have a higher risk for stroke and a higher age-specific stroke incidence rate, but women tend to die from stroke.

Race and ethnicity impact stroke risk among specific populations. Blacks and Hispanics have a higher incidence of both ischemic and hemorrhagic stroke, and contributing factors may be the higher incidence of diabetes and hypertension in these groups (Lloyd-Jones et al., 2010).

Clinical Manifestations and Assessment

Common Symptoms

Stroke syndromes produce a wide variety of neurologic deficits, depending on the location of the lesion, which vessels are obstructed, the size and area of underperfused brain tissue, and the amount of collateral (secondary or accessory) blood flow to the affected area. The American Heart Association/American Stroke Association advises the public to be aware of the symptoms of stroke and to call 911 immediately. The most common symptoms of stroke include:

- Sudden numbness or weakness of the face, arm, or leg, especially on one side of the body
- Sudden confusion or change in mental status
- Sudden trouble speaking or understanding speech
- Sudden visual disturbances

BOX 47-2 | **Focused Assessment**

Left and Right Hemispheric Strokes

Be alert for the following signs and symptoms:

Left hemispheric stroke:
- Paralysis or weakness on right side of body
- Right visual field deficit
- Aphasia (expressive, receptive, or global)
- Altered intellectual ability
- Slow, cautious behavior

Right hemispheric stroke:
- Paralysis or weakness on left side of body
- Left visual field deficit
- Spatial-perceptual deficits
- Increased distractibility
- Impulsive behavior and poor judgment
- Lack of awareness of deficits

- Difficulty walking, dizziness, or loss of balance or coordination
- Sudden, severe headache

However, it is important for the clinician to be able to correlate presenting neurologic deficits with the location(s) in the brain affected by ischemia or hemorrhage. Box 47-2 compares the symptoms and behaviors seen in right hemispheric strokes with those seen in left hemispheric strokes. Patients with a hemorrhagic stroke can present with a wide variety of neurologic deficits, similar to patients with an ischemic stroke.

Many of the same motor, sensory, cranial nerve, cognitive, and other functions that are disrupted after ischemic stroke are also altered after a hemorrhagic stroke. In the conscious patient, the most common presenting symptom is a severe headache. Other symptoms that can be observed are vomiting, a slow or sudden change in LOC, or focal seizures. Patients with a ruptured AVM will typically present with a sudden severe headache and sudden loss of consciousness. There may be posterior neck or spine pain associated with the headache. If there is a slow leakage of blood that leads to formation of a clot at the site of rupture, the patient may show little neurologic deficit. In cases in which severe bleeding occurs, there can be extensive cerebral injury, and the patient may progress to coma and death. Symptoms are described in detail below.

Motor Loss

The most common motor dysfunction resulting from stroke is hemiparesis, or weakness of one side of the body. Upper and lower motor neurons play a role in mediating muscle and tendon reflex activity. Because the upper motor neurons decussate (cross over), a disturbance of voluntary motor control on one side of the body may reflect damage to the upper motor neurons on the opposite side of the brain.

Communication Loss

Language and communication may also be affected by stroke. Dysfunctions of language and communication related to cerebral injury include:

- *Dysarthria:* Difficulty in speaking, caused by paralysis of the muscles responsible for producing speech; also referring to slurred speech
- *Dysphasia or aphasia:* Partial or complete impairment of language resulting from brain injury, affecting spoken language and comprehension
- *Apraxia:* Inability to perform a previously learned action such as difficulty putting sounds and syllables together in the correct order to form words, to produce speech.

Perceptual Disturbances

Perception is the ability to interpret sensation. Stroke can result in visual-perceptual dysfunctions, disturbances in visual-spatial relations, or sensory loss.

Visual-perceptual dysfunctions are caused by disturbances of the primary sensory pathways between the eye and visual cortex. Homonymous hemianopsia (loss of half of the visual field) may occur from stroke and may be temporary or permanent. Disturbances in visual-spatial relations (perceiving the relationship of two or more objects in spatial areas) are frequently seen in patients with right hemispheric damage.

Sensory Loss

The sensory losses from stroke may take the form of slight impairment of touch, or it may be more severe, with loss of proprioception (ability to perceive the position and motion of body parts), as well as difficulty in interpreting visual, tactile, and auditory stimuli. *Agnosias* describe the inability to recognize previously familiar objects perceived by one or more of the senses.

Cognitive Impairment and Psychological Effects

If damage has occurred to the frontal lobe, learning capacity, memory, or other higher cortical intellectual functions may be impaired. Such dysfunction may be reflected in a limited attention span, difficulties in comprehension, forgetfulness, and a lack of motivation. Depression is common and may be exaggerated by the patient's natural response to this catastrophic event. Emotional lability, hostility, frustration, resentment, lack of cooperation, and other psychological problems may occur at some point during the recovery period and are usually screened for following discharge.

Acute Stroke Assessment

The American Heart/Stroke Association has adopted the Stroke Chain of Survival, similar to the Heart Chain of Survival established for cardiac care, to implement a prompt prehospital and acute care approach to the evaluation of patients with acute stroke symptoms. Also known as the "7 D's," these components highlight key areas in the

---

BOX 47-3 **Stroke Chain of Survival: The 7 D's**

1. ***Detection*** of the onset of signs and symptoms of acute stroke. Early recognition of hallmark signs and symptoms of acute stroke is critical to improved patient outcomes.
2. ***Dispatch*** of Emergency Medical Services (EMS) by telephoning 911. This communication activates EMS systems and ensures prompt EMS response.
3. ***Delivery*** of the patient to a medical facility. Patients should be transported to a stroke hospital or other facility capable of providing acute stroke care, and advanced prehospital notification should be given to the selected medical facility.
4. ***Door*** of the emergency department (ED). Immediately upon arrival, the patient should undergo general and neurologic assessment in the ED.
5. ***Data*** collection, including computer tomography (CT) scan and serial neurologic exams, along with reviews of patient file for potential fibrinolytics (tPA) exclusions.
6. ***Decision*** regarding stroke treatment. If the patient remains a candidate for tissue plasminogen activator (tPA) therapy, review risks and benefits with the patient and family.
7. ***Drug*** administration as appropriate and post-administration monitoring.

---

recognition and evaluation of a suspected stroke patient to reinforce an efficient method for a rapid approach to acute stroke care (Box 47-3).

The Emergency Nurses Association and the American College of Emergency Physicians recommend stroke patients be considered an ESI Level 2 emergency (see Chapter 56 for an explanation of the five-level Emergency Severity Index [ESI]), meaning that the suspected stroke patient "needs immediate assessment," the same as for an unstable trauma patient or a critical-care cardiac patient (Gilboy, Tanabe, Travers et al., 2005).

Nurses in the prehospital setting or in triage in an emergency department should be familiar with the prehospital screening and assessments that are done by members of the EMS team so that they can relate this information to the stroke team prior to arrival. (For a detailed explanation of the prehospital care for stroke patients, refer to Implementation Strategies for Emergency Medical Services within Stroke Systems of Care: A Policy Statement from the American Heart Association/American Stroke Association Expert Panel on Emergency Medical Services Systems and the Stroke Council [Acker, Pancioli, Crocco et al., 2007]).

Acute stroke care can be divided into two phases: the hyperacute phase (the first 24 hours of care) and phase 2 (acute care during the hospitalization). Nurses play a critical role from triage to discharge because ongoing neurologic assessments and monitoring of interventions direct treatment options and impact functional outcome.

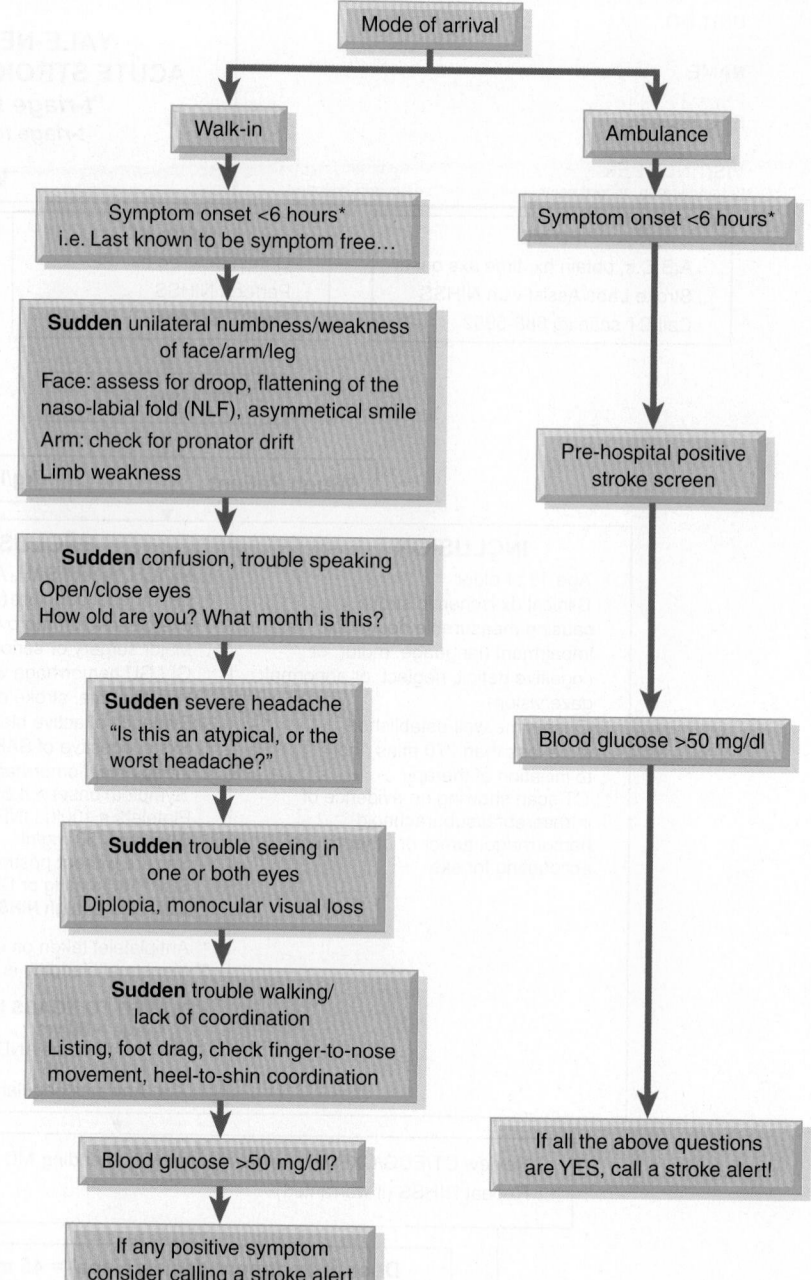

```
                                    ┌─────────────────┐
                                    │  Mode of arrival │
                                    └─────────────────┘

              ┌──────────┐                              ┌──────────┐
              │ Walk-in  │                              │ Ambulance│
              └──────────┘                              └──────────┘

   ┌───────────────────────────────┐         ┌───────────────────────────┐
   │ Symptom onset <6 hours*        │         │ Symptom onset <6 hours*   │
   │ i.e. Last known to be symptom  │         └───────────────────────────┘
   │ free…                          │
   └───────────────────────────────┘

   ┌───────────────────────────────┐
   │ Sudden unilateral numbness/    │
   │   weakness of face/arm/leg     │
   │ Face: assess for droop,        │         ┌───────────────────────────┐
   │ flattening of the naso-labial  │         │ Pre-hospital positive     │
   │ fold (NLF), asymmetical smile  │         │ stroke screen             │
   │ Arm: check for pronator drift  │         └───────────────────────────┘
   │ Limb weakness                  │
   └───────────────────────────────┘

   ┌───────────────────────────────┐
   │ Sudden confusion, trouble      │
   │   speaking                     │
   │ Open/close eyes                │
   │ How old are you? What month    │
   │   is this?                     │
   └───────────────────────────────┘

   ┌───────────────────────────────┐
   │ Sudden severe headache         │
   │ "Is this an atypical, or the   │         ┌───────────────────────────┐
   │   worst headache?"             │         │ Blood glucose >50 mg/dl   │
   └───────────────────────────────┘         └───────────────────────────┘

   ┌───────────────────────────────┐
   │ Sudden trouble seeing in       │
   │   one or both eyes             │
   │ Diplopia, monocular visual loss│
   └───────────────────────────────┘

   ┌───────────────────────────────┐
   │ Sudden trouble walking/        │
   │   lack of coordination         │
   │ Listing, foot drag, check      │
   │ finger-to-nose movement,       │
   │ heel-to-shin coordination      │
   └───────────────────────────────┘

   ┌───────────────────────────────┐         ┌───────────────────────────┐
   │ Blood glucose >50 mg/dl?       │         │ If all the above questions│
   └───────────────────────────────┘         │ are YES, call a stroke    │
                                              │ alert!                    │
   ┌───────────────────────────────┐         └───────────────────────────┘
   │ If any positive symptom        │
   │ consider calling a stroke alert.│
   └───────────────────────────────┘
```

FIGURE 47-5 Triage stroke screen. *While intravenous tPA treatment is approved for eligible patients within 3 hours of symptom onset, patients are frequently evaluated within 6–8 hours of symptom onset to determine eligibility for neuro-interventional treatment procedures.

An algorithm is used in the hyperacute phase for the initial workup of a patient presenting with acute stroke symptoms (Fig. 47-5). The nurse plays a critical role in each step of the acute evaluation. For patients arriving by ambulance (with prenotification by the paramedics that a suspected stroke patient is en route) or by car, the triage nurse must recognize the common and less common stroke symptoms. Many of the same motor, sensory, cranial nerve, and cognitive functions are disrupted in both ischemic and hemorrhagic strokes; however, changes in LOC, vomiting, sudden severe headache, and seizure are frequently associated with hemorrhagic strokes.

Triaging includes eliciting a detailed history and determining time of onset of the patient's symptoms. When the time of symptom onset is not definitive, the time the patient was last known to be at baseline becomes the default time of onset. Determining the time of the onset of symptoms becomes important since drug treatment options and interventional procedures for clot retrieval for an ischemic stroke are time-dependent. The nurse assesses airway, breathing, and circulation (ABCs) and establishes an initial set of vital signs.

Figure 47-6 depicts a typical acute stroke protocol.

UNIT NO.

NAME

BIRTH DATE:

VISIT NUMBER
(If handwritten, record name, unit no., birth date, and visit no.)

YALE-NEW HAVEN HOSPITAL
ACUTE STROKE PROTOCOL-ALGORITHM
"t-riage to t-PA ≤ 60 minutes"
t-riage to CT scan ≤ 10 minutes

WORKSHEET

ED MD	Neuro MD	RN
☐ A.B.C.s, obtain hx, time sxs onset	☐ Obtain detailed hx / PE	☐ A.B.C.s
☐ Stroke Labs/Assist with NIHSS	☐ Perform NIHSS _____	☐ Refer to Stroke ER Sticker
☐ Call CT scan @ 688-5952	☐ **To CT SCAN**	☐ Encourage witness to stay w/ pt

CT result (wet read)

Weigh Patient _____ **(kg/lb)**

INCLUSION

☐ Age 18 or older
☐ Clinical dx ischemic stroke causing measurable neurologic impairment (language, motor, or cognitive deficit, neglect, or abnormal gaze/vision)
☐ Onset time well-established to be less than 270 mins prior to initiation of therapy
☐ CT scan showing no evidence of intracerebral/subarachnoid hemorrhage, tumor or other cause accounting for sxs

EXCLUSION (Absolute/Relative)

☐ Hx ICH, recent SAH, AVM, aneurysm or brain tumor
☐ LP / arterial puncture **(non-compressible site)** w/in last 7 days
☐ Sxs clearing or improving spontaneously
☐ Major surgery or serious **(non-head)** trauma w/in last 14 days
☐ GI / GU hemorrhage w/in last 21 days
☐ Head trauma, stroke or MI **(or pericarditis)** w/in last 90 days
☐ Evidence of active bleeding or acute fracture
☐ Sxs suggestive of SAH even if normal CT scan
☐ Intracranial hemorrhage on CT scan
☐ Symptom onset > 4.5 hours
☐ Platelets < 100k;   INR > 1.7;   > nml PTT
☐ Glucose < 50 mg/dl
☐ Seizure without postictal residual neurological impairments
☐ SBP>185 mmHg or DBP>110 mmHg at time of treatment
☐ Major deficits **(high NIHSS)** and/or hypodensity in > 1/3 cerebral hemisphere

** Antiplatelet taken on same day is NOT contraindication to t-PA
** Menstrual bleeding is NOT a contraindication to t-PA.

RELATED TO ECASS III (IV tPA 3.0 – 4.5 hrs post sxs onset)
• Age > 80 yrs
• Hx diabetes AND prior stroke
• NIHSS > 25
• Any anticoagulant

☐ Review CT/ECG/CXR/labs/rectal/records with attending MD
☐ Repeat NIHSS (if warranted)

☐ Guaiac Stool / urine HcG
☐ Educate patient/family:

Door to treatment decision goal = 45 minutes

t-PA candidate
Consent Process
Discuss the purpose, potential benefits, possible hazards, alternatives, and inconveniences including no treatment.

☐ Document patient's verbal consent or refusal or inability to consent
☐ Document surrogate's verbal consent or refusal or inability to consent
☐ Document patient's medical condition. Proceed with thrombolysis

NOT a t-PA candidate
☐ Document reason
☐ Check Active Research Studies
☐ Admit to stroke unit
☐ Patient/family teaching

☐ Call pharmacist (688-1111), mix / deliver t-PA
☐ Administer t-PA, bolus, infusion (pump)
☐ Document RN post tPA vital signs / neuro checks
☐ Admit - NICU

CONTACT PATIENT'S PCP – INFORM THE OFFICE OF PATIENT'S STATUS

F5130

Pg.1

F5130   (Rev. 11/10)

FIGURE 47-6 Acute Stroke Protocol. Courtesy of Yale-New Haven Hospital. NIHSS, National Institutes of Health Stroke Scale; INR, International Normalized Ratio; SBP, Systolic Blood Pressure; DBP, Diastolic Blood Pressure; ECASS, European Cooperative Acute Stroke Study; t-PA, Tissue plasminogen activator

(continued)

Pt. Name: _____

Unit No. _____

Visit No. _____

YALE-NEW HAVEN HOSPITAL

**NATIONAL INSTITUTES OF HEALTH (NIH)
STROKE SCALE WORKSHEET**

NIH STROKE SCALE ITEM	FUNCTION	SCORE	Initial	Pre-tx	Post-tx	24° Post-tx
1a. Level of Consciousness (LOC)	Alert Drowsy Stuporous (req repeat stimuli) Coma (reflex response only)	0 1 2 3				
1b. LOC Questions (Month, Age)	Both correct One correct Incorrect	0 1 2				
1c. LOC Commands (Open, close eyes, make fist, let go)	Obeys both correctly Obeys one correctly Incorrect	0 1 2				
2. Best Gaze (With eyes open, have patient follow examiner's finger or face)	Normal Partial gaze palsy Forced deviation	0 1 2				
3. Visual (Introduce visual stimulus/threat to patient's visual field quadrants)	No loss Partial hemianopia Complete hemianopia Bilateral hemianopia	0 1 2 3				
4. Facial Palsy (Show teeth, raise eyebrows, squeeze eyes shut)	Normal Minor asymmetry Partial (lower face paralysis) Complete	0 1 2 3				
5a. Motor Arm-Left (Elevate extremity 90° (sitting) or 45° (lying) for 10 seconds and score drift/movement)	No drift Drift Some effort against gravity No effort against gravity No movement Amputation; joint fusion	0 1 2 3 4 N/A				
5b. Motor Arm-Right (Elevate extremity 90° (sitting) or 45° (lying) for 10 seconds and score drift/movement)	No drift Drift Some effort against gravity No effort against gravity No movement Amputation; joint fusion	0 1 2 3 4 N/A				
6a. Motor Leg-Left (Elevate extremity 30° for 5 seconds and score drift/movement)	No drift Drift Some effort against gravity No effort against gravity No movement Amputation; joint fusion	0 1 2 3 4 N/A				
6b. Motor Leg-Right (Elevate extremity 30° for 5 seconds and score drift/movement)	No drift Drift Some effort against gravity No effort against gravity No movement Amputation; joint fusion	0 1 2 3 4 N/A				
7. Limb Ataxia (Finger-nose, heel down shin)	Absent Present in one limb Present in more than one limb	0 1 2				
8. Sensory (Pin prick to face, arm, trunk, leg compare side to side)	Normal Partial loss Dense loss	0 1 2				
9. Best language (Name items, describe picture, read sentence)	No aphasia Mild-mod aphasia Severe aphasia Mute	0 1 2 3				
10. Dysarthria (Evaluate speech clarity, ask patient to repeat listed words)	Normal articulation Mild-moderate slurring Severe-near unintelligible / worse	0 1 2				
11. Extinction and Inattention (use information from prior testing to identify neglect or double stimuli testing)	No neglect Neglect in one sphere Neglect in more than one sphere	0 1 2				

SCORER 1 Print Name _____ Sign Name _____		Score 1	Score 2	Score 3	Score 4
SCORER 2 Print Name _____ Sign Name _____		Time	Time	Time	Time
SCORER 3 Print Name _____ Sign Name _____		Date	Date	Date	Date
SCORER 4 Print Name _____ Sign Name _____					

FIGURE 47-6 *(Continued)*   Pg 2

Diagnostic Evaluation

The diagnosis of a stroke is made by history, neurologic exam, and neuroimaging; an initial head CT scan is performed to determine whether or not the patient is experiencing a hemorrhagic stroke. Ischemia will not be readily visible on initial CT scan if it is performed within the first few hours after symptom onset; however, evidence of bleeding will almost always be visible. The presence of blood on imaging confirms a hemorrhage. Key to the evaluation is the location of the hematoma, the size and presence of blood in the ventricular system, and evidence of increased ICP. Additional diagnostic testing is done to determine if the hemorrhage is due to a ruptured intracranial aneurysm or AVM.

Although both CT scan and MRI are acceptable initial studies, most facilities have ready access to rapid CT imaging to rule out hemorrhage. Both CT and MR imaging will aid in determining stroke type, size and location of the infarct or hematoma, any shift in brain tissue, presence of blood in the ventricles, and presence of hydrocephalus. Routine blood chemistries, coagulation studies, blood cell counts, cardiac rhythm status, and IV access are also performed (Table 47-3).

Although patients who present with TIA-type symptoms are usually symptom-free by the time they arrive in the emergency department, they undergo the same diagnostic workup as those patients whose symptoms are ongoing since their presenting symptoms may be predictive of an evolving stroke.

The National Institutes of Health Stroke Scale (NIHSS) has become an accepted assessment tool to quantify stroke severity and to assess patient outcome after stroke treatment (Table 47-4, p. 1258). The NIHSS is a 42-point assessment scale, with 0 indicating no neurologic deficits and 42 indicating the worst possible score. It focuses on six major areas of the neurologic examination: (1) LOC, (2) visual function, (3) motor function, (4) sensation and neglect (failure to pay attention to stimuli on one side of the body), (5) cerebellar function, and (6) language. The NIHSS is used mostly by stroke teams but can be learned and performed by any clinician. It enables the clinician to rapidly determine the severity and possible location of the stroke. While it focuses on cerebral ischemia corresponding to abnormalities affecting the anterior circulation, this scale often misses deficits in territories in the brain dependent on posterior circulation. However, it allows clinicians to communicate findings using a standardized assessment tool. Certification in the use of this assessment is available online through the American Stroke Association (ASA) training center.

Medical Management

Acute Ischemic Stroke

The initial expedited diagnostic workup and treatment of ischemic stroke is driven by time-dependent phar-macologic and clot retrieval device treatment options. Thrombolysis with recombinant tissue plasminogen activator (rtPA) is currently the only FDA-approved drug for acute ischemic stroke within a 3-hour window of symptom onset. tPA binds to fibrin and converts plasminogen to plasmin, which is responsible for clot breakdown. Results from the 1995 NINDS trial demonstrated a significant improvement in functional outcome at 3 months post-stroke in those patients who received tPA within 3 hours after symptom onset (NINDS & Stroke rtPA Stroke Study Work Group, 1995). Results from the 2008 European Cooperative Acute Stroke Study (ECASS 3) demonstrated clinically significant improvement in functional outcome in patients who received treatment up to 4.5 hours after symptom onset (Hacke, Kaste, Bluhmi et al., 2008). Once a hemorrhage has been ruled out and the clinical diagnosis of ischemic stroke is made, the acute stroke team must review the eligibility criteria for tPA administration.

Patients with sustained elevated blood pressure (>185 mm Hg systolic; >110 mm Hg diastolic), or with evidence of recent prior stroke, major surgery, or serious head injury would be at high risk for intracranial bleeding after tPA (see inclusion/exclusion criteria in Figure 47-6).

Nurses are often responsible for administering tPA, and some facilities expect nurses to mix and prepare the medication for administration. Patients are weighed to determine the appropriate dose; it is dosed at 0.9 mg/kg, with a maximum dose of 90 mg. Ten percent of the calculated dose is administered as an IV bolus over 1 minute. The remaining dose (90%) is administered over 1 hour via an infusion pump. Bleeding is the most common side effect of tPA. The patient is closely monitored for bleeding (at IV insertion sites, gums, urine/stools, and intracranially by assessing changes in LOC). Patients are also monitored for angioedema (oral/lingual swelling) and anaphylaxis (allergic reaction).

During the hyperacute phase of a stroke, ongoing assessments and meticulous documentation of the patient's neurologic and hemodynamic status is essential, regardless of stroke type and whether or not the patient received rtPA.

Table 47-5 on page 1259 summarizes the nursing care for thrombolysis and nonthrombolysis treatments for patients with acute ischemic stroke (Summers, Leonard, Wentworth et al., 2009). Blood pressure parameters are specifically outlined by physician order since they vary depending on use of thrombolysis, prior history of hypertension, use of antihypertensive medications, and neurologic response to treatment.

The use of intra-arterial thrombolysis (delivering tPA directly to the intracerebral clot via a catheter-based approach) has become more widespread during the past 10 years. The 2007 guidelines recommend an intra-arterial approach as an option for treatment in selected patients within the first 6 hours of symptom onset and

TABLE
47-3 Diagnostic Procedures for Transient Ischemic Attacks (TIAs) and Stroke

Diagnostic Procedure	Information Provided
Computed tomography (CT) scan without contrast	Important diagnostic test to quickly assess for the presence of blood (hemorrhage) which will preclude treatment with antithrombotics.
CT scan with contrast	Useful to rule out lesions that may mimic ischemia, especially when symptoms are related to hemispheric deficits; hypodense areas on CT scan suggest infarction.
Magnetic resonance imaging (MRI)	Offers soft-tissue contrast discrimination with superior demarcation of mass lesion from surrounding structures including areas of ischemia and infarction; good visualization of vascular structures; useful for diagnosis of stroke in first 72 hours; a diffusion-weighted MRI can show ischemia in first few hours.
Magnetic resonance angiography (MRA)	Less available and higher cost; noninvasive imaging of the carotid, vertebral, basilar, and major intracranial and extracranial arteries to determine occlusion; useful for clot visualization.
Carotid ultrasonography	Noninvasive imaging; widely used initial diagnostic in patients with carotid territory symptoms for whom carotid endarterectomy (CEA) is considered.
Transcranial Doppler (TCD)	Non-invasive monitoring of blood flow velocities of the major cerebral and carotid arteries to assess degree of stenoses; may be included as part of the stroke work-up.
Cerebral angiography	Ordered for patients to define precisely the percentage of occlusion and in patients with unusual presentation with aneurysm, vasculitis, and high-grade stenosis.
Transthoracic echocardiography (TTE)	Helpful to identify cardioembolic sources; TTE is particularly helpful for diagnosing left ventricular thrombi, left atrial myxomas, and thrombi that protrude into the atrial cavity; they are less reliable for small tumors, laminated thrombi, and thrombi limited to the left or right atrium.
Transesophageal echocardiography (TEE)	Benefit of TEE is in greater sensitivity for source of cardioembolic (except ventricular disease); TEE provides better visualization of cardiac structures, especially those at greater depth from chest wall and lesions of the atria (atrial appendage thrombi associated with atrial fibrillation), interatrial septum defects (patent foramen ovale, atrial septal defects), mitral valvular vegetation, and atherosclerotic disease of ascending aortic arch.
Electrocardiogram (ECG); 12-lead is recommended initially	12-lead ECG recommended immediately because of the high incidence of heart disease in patients with stroke; ECG also useful when cardiogenic embolic stroke or concurrent coronary artery disease is suspected.
Ambulatory ECG monitoring	Reserved for patients who have suspicious palpitations, arrhythmias, or enlarged left atrium.
Prothrombotic states	Protein C, protein S, antithrombin III, thrombin time, hemoglobin, electrophoresis, anticardiolipin antibody, lupus anticoagulant, and syphilis serology

From Adams, H. P. Jr., del Zoppo, G., Alberts, M. J., Bhatt, D. L., Brass, L., Furlan, A., et al. (2007). Guidelines for the early management of adults with ischemic stroke. *Stroke, 38,* 1655–1711, reprinted with permission. © 2007 American Heart Association, Inc.

for patients with imaging evidence of a thrombus accessible by catheter. This procedure is generally reserved for hospitals that have experienced neuro-interventionalists and the capability to perform cerebral angiography. Additionally, there are currently two mechanical devices (the MERCI retriever and the Penumbra System) that are being used for clot retraction in those patients who received IV tPA but did not improve or who were not candidates for IV thrombolysis. Ongoing studies will provide additional data on the efficacy of these treatments.

Acute Hemorrhagic Stroke

During the hyperacute phase, the management of hemorrhagic stroke patients focuses on airway, breathing, and circulation (ABCs), with particular attention paid to the patient's LOC. Immediate complications of a hemorrhage include extension of bleeding causing increased ICP, acute

Category	Description	Score
1a. Level of consciousness (LOC)	Alert	0
	Arousable by minor stimulation	1
	Obtunded, strong stimulation to attend	2
	Unresponsive, or reflex responses only	3
1b. LOC questions (month, age)	Answers both correctly	0
	Answers one correctly	1
	Both incorrect	2
1c. LOC, commands (open, close eyes; make fist, let go)	Obeys both correctly	0
	Obeys one correctly	1
	Both incorrect	2
2. Best gaze (eyes open—patient follows examiner's finger or face)	Normal	0
	Partial gaze palsy	1
	Forced deviation	2
3. Visual (introduce visual stimulus/threat to patient's visual field quadrants)	No visual loss	0
	Partial hemianopia	1
	Complete hemianopia	2
	Bilateral hemianopia	3
4. Facial palsy (show teeth, raise eyebrows and squeeze eyes shut)	Normal	0
	Minor	1
	Partial	2
	Complete	3
5a. Motor; arm—left (elevate extremity to 90 degrees and score drift/movement)	No drift	0
	Drift but maintains in air	1
	Unable to maintain in air	2
	No effort against gravity	3
	No movement	4
	Amputation, joint fusion (explain)	N/A
5b. Motor; arm—right (elevate extremity to 90 degrees and score drift/movement)	No drift	0
	Drift but maintains in air	1
	Unable to maintain in air	2
	No effort against gravity	3
	No movement	4
	Amputation, joint fusion (explain)	N/A
6a. Motor; leg—left (elevate extremity to 30 degrees and score drift/movement)	No drift	0
	Drift but maintains in air	1
	Unable to maintain in air	2
	No effort against gravity	3
	No movement	4
	Amputation, joint fusion (explain)	N/A
6b. Motor; leg—right (elevate extremity to 30 degrees and score drift/movement)	No drift	0
	Drift but maintains in air	1
	Unable to maintain in air	2
	No effort against gravity	3
	No movement	4
	Amputation, joint fusion (explain)	N/A
7. Limb ataxia (finger-to-nose and heel-to-shin testing)	Absent	0
	Present in one limb	1
	Present in two limbs	2
8. Sensory (pin prick to face, arm, trunk and leg—compare side to side)	Normal	0
	Mild to moderate loss	1
	Severe to total loss	2
9. Best language (name items, describe a picture and read sentences)	No aphasia	0
	Mild to moderate aphasia	1
	Severe aphasia	2
	Mute	3
10. Dysarthria (evaluate speech clarity by having patient repeat words)	Normal	0
	Mild to moderate dysarthria	1
	Severe dysarthria, mostly unintelligible or worse	2
	Intubated or other physical barrier	N/A
11. Extinction and inattention (use information from prior testing to score)	No abnormality	0
	Visual, tactile, auditory, or other extinction to bilateral simultaneous stimulation	1
	Profound hemi-attention or extinction to more than one modality.	2
Total score		

Adapted from the version available at the National Institute of Neurological Disorders and Stroke, National Institutes of Health, Bethesda, MD 20892. Retrieved from http://www.ninds.nih.gov/doctors/NIH_Stroke_Scale.pdf. It is recommended that the full scale with all instructions be used.

TABLE
47-5 Schedule of Neurological Assessment and Vital Signs and Other Acute Care Assessments in Thrombolysis-Treated and Nonthrombolysis-Treated Patients

Thrombolysis-Treated Patients	Nonthrombolysis–Treated Patients
Neurological assessment and vital signs (except temperature) every 15 minutes during tPA infusion, then every 30 minutes for 6 hours, then every 60 minutes for 16 hours (total of 24 hour) Note: Frequency of blood pressure (BP) assessments may need to be increased if systolic BP stays >180 mm Hg or diastolic BP stays >105 mm Hg. Temperature every 4 hours or as required. Treat temperatures >99.6°F with acetaminophen as ordered.	In intensive care unit (ICU), every hour with neurological checks or more frequently if necessary. In a non-ICU setting, depending on patient's condition and neurological assessments; at a minimum check neurological assessment and vital signs every 4 hours
Call physician if systolic BP >185 or >110 mm Hg; diastolic BP >105 or >60 mm Hg; pulse <50 or >110 per minute; respirations 24 per minute; temperature >99.6°F; or for worsening of stroke symptoms or other decline in neurological status	Call physician for further treatment based on physician and institutional preferences/guidelines: Systolic BP >220 or <110 mm Hg; diastolic BP >120 or <60 mm Hg; pulse <50 or >110 per minute; temperature >99.6°F; respirations 24 per minute; or for worsening of stroke symptoms or other decline in neurological status
For O$_2$ saturation <92%, give O$_2$ by cannula at 2 to 3 L/min	For O$_2$ saturation <92%, give O$_2$ by cannula at 2 to 3 L/min
Monitor for major and minor bleeding complications	N/A
Continuous cardiac monitoring up to 72 hours or more	Continuous cardiac monitoring for 24 to 48 hours
Measure intake and output	Measure intake and output
Bedrest	Bedrest
IV fluids normal saline (NS) at 75 to 100 mL/h	IV fluids NS at 75 to 100 mL/h
No heparin, warfarin, aspirin, clopidogrel, or aspirin/extended-release dipyridamole for 24 hours, then start antithrombotic as ordered	Antithrombotics should be ordered within first 24 hours of hospital admission
Brain CT or MRI after rtPA therapy	Repeat brain computed tomography (CT) scan or magnetic resonance imaging (MRI) may be ordered 24 to 48 hours after stroke or as needed

From Summers et al. (2009). Reprinted with permission. *Circulation, 40:* 2911–2944. ©2009 American Heart Association, Inc.

hydrocephalus, potential for herniation, and secondary brain injury. Any evidence of deterioration and ICP (refer to Chapter 45) is reported immediately to the health care team. For patients with a hemorrhage, the Glasgow Coma Scale is also used as part of ongoing patient assessment. For patients with a GCS score of 8 or less, immediate intubation is indicated. Monitoring of peripheral oxygenation is expected with a pulse oximeter. Nurses will be directed to elevate the head of bed to 30 degrees, monitor sedation if instituted, and prepare for one or more of the following treatment options: anticoagulation reversal if patient is on anticoagulant, hyperventilation (hypocapnia temporarily causes vascular constriction, resulting in reduced blood flow in vessels not involved with the injury), placement of a ventricular catheter for CSF drainage, administration of mannitol—all to reduce elevated ICP. Because hyperthermia (temperature >37.5° C) is associated with a poorer prognosis following acute stroke, the nurse monitors the patient's temperature,

and is prepared to initiate measures to prevent and control fever collaboratively with the health care team. Additionally, because aspiration is a significant risk, patients should be maintained NPO until they are screened for dysphagia (Hickey, 2009).

Surgical evacuation of blood is also considered in selected cases that require immediate intervention and when neurosurgical services are available. Depending on the location and volume of the intracerebral bleed, the degree of neurological deterioration, presence of hydrocephalus and ventricular obstruction, patients may undergo a craniotomy and evacuation of the hematoma. Antihypertensive medications and antiepileptic medications are also mainstays of acute therapy to control bleeding and potential seizures. Blood pressure goals are ordered based on individual patient profiles. Current clinical trials are under way to determine target blood pressure ranges in ischemic stroke (Morgenstern, Hemphill, Anderson et al., 2010). Pain, fever, and hyperglycemia are

addressed in the first 24 hours to reduce further cerebral injury (Morgenstern et al., 2010).

For patients with a known ruptured aneurysm and subsequent SAH, the 2009 AHA guidelines for SAH describe both surgical clipping and endovascular coiling as beneficial options to reduce the risk of rebleeding (Bederson, Connolly, Batjer et al., 2009). Surgical clipping involves a craniotomy and placement of a clip at the neck of the artery to close the rupture site. Coiling is an endovascular procedure using a catheter that is accessed from the femoral artery and directed through the vasculature to the location of the aneurysm. Multiple coils are then dispensed through the catheter and packed into the dome of the aneurysm to promote clotting and close the aneurysm. The choice of aneurysm treatment depends on the overall health of the patient, the nature and location of the aneurysm, and the available resources at the hospital.

Stroke care in the acute phase is typically designated as the time during which the patient is hospitalized. The hospital stay can vary from a few days to many weeks, depending on the nature and severity of the stroke, and deficits and complications associated with recovery. In addition to monitoring for potential complications associated with stroke such as deconditioning, aspiration, infection, bowel and bladder dysfunction, inability to perform self-care, care plans should include an early initiation of rehabilitation to improve functional outcome. Research has demonstrated that stroke patients have better functional outcomes if they are admitted to a dedicated stroke unit (Douglas, Tong, Gillum et al., 2005).

Stroke Rehabilitation

The potential for recovery after stroke extends beyond the hospital admission and beyond the time spent in an acute or subacute care facility. Although rehabilitation planning begins on the day of hospital admission, nursing interventions and collaboration with the multidisciplinary rehabilitation team continue throughout the patient's recovery. It is important to understand what the patient was like before the stroke. A history of other illnesses, behavioral characteristics, activities of daily living (ADLs), and neurologic scores (such as the modified Rankin scale) will provide information to develop a realistic plan for recovery. The World Health Organization's International Classification of Functioning (ICF) has been adopted as the organizational framework for the AHA's Scientific Statement on the Comprehensive Overview of Nursing and Interdisciplinary Rehabilitation Care of the Stroke Patient (Miller, Murray, Richards et al., 2010). The three components of the model include:

1. The pathophysiological processes directly related to the stroke and its associated comorbidities
2. The impact this condition has on the individual
3. Contextual variables, such as each survivor's personal and environmental resources

The major goals for the patient (and family) should include all efforts to return the patient to his/her pre-morbid functioning. Depending on the location of the initial brain injury, patients are assessed for rehabilitative needs to improve mobility, communication, cognition, coordination, balance, and pain relief (from contractures). Potential complications such as aspiration, incontinence, skin breakdown, falls, depression, and disruption of family dynamics are targets for prevention.

Prevention

In a healthy population, risk factors are identified and addressed in a primordial and primary prevention program. *Primordial prevention* refers to strategies designed to decrease the development of disease risk factors (e.g., efforts to decrease the development of obesity, increase exercise, and provide a well-balanced diet). Primordial prevention encompasses the entire population and is not limited to individuals with recognized risk factors for stroke or other cardiovascular diseases (Schwamm et al., 2005). *Primary prevention* refers to the treatment of established disease risk factors, but for those patients who have not yet had an event. The 2011 Guidelines for the Primary Prevention of Stroke provide a comprehensive overview of established and emerging modifiable and nonmodifiable stroke risk factors (Goldstein, Bushnell, Adams et al., 2011).

For patients who have had a stroke, risk factor modification is a critical part of the secondary prevention plan. Stroke education for patients and their families addresses the possible causes of stroke, identifies potential stroke risk factors, reinforces compliance with medications, and discusses pertinent lifestyle changes to reduce stroke risk. The 2010 guidelines for the prevention of subsequent stroke after stroke or TIA highlight the following key risk factors: hypertension, diabetes, dyslipidemia, smoking, alcohol consumption, obesity, sedentary activity. Patient education has become a standard performance measure for practice at certified primary stroke centers.

Optimal medical therapy includes prescribing an antiplatelet medication (such as aspirin, clopidogrel, or aspirin/extended release dipyridamole), a statin (such as atorvastatin or simvastatin), and an antihypertensive (thiazide diuretic, angiotensin-converting enzyme [ACE] inhibitor or beta blocker). For those patients with paroxysmal or permanent atrial fibrillation, anticoagulation (with warfarin or other anticoagulant) is also recommended (Furie, Kasner, Adams et al., 2010).

For those patients who have had a hemorrhagic stroke, blood pressure control is critical. The issue of whether to start or resume antithrombotic therapy is highly dependent on the nature and severity of the hemorrhage and the risk for a subsequent thrombotic event (as in the case of a patient with atrial fibrillation or with a mechanical heart valve).

For patients with symptoms of TIA or stroke thought to be caused by significant carotid artery stenosis (70% to 99%), a carotid endarterectomy (CEA) may be recommended.

A CEA is the removal of an atherosclerotic plaque or thrombus from the internal carotid artery to prevent recurrent stroke. Carotid angioplasty and stenting is an alternative (less invasive) procedure and performed in selected patients when surgery poses a higher risk and the endovascular approach poses a low perioperative complication risk. These procedures are generally recommended once the patient is hemodynamically stable and usually within the first 2 weeks following their event.

In preparation for discharge, teaching patients and families about what to expect within a home or rehabilitation facility will be a focus for nursing, the rehabilitation staff, and the discharge planner. Resources in the community, such as support groups, regional and national heart and stroke associations, and hospital-based social work support should also be part of the discharge materials.

NURSING PROCESS

The Patient With a Stroke

Assessment

A nursing flow sheet is maintained for the documentation of a complete neurologic assessment. A systems approach to examining and documenting findings should include a mental status evaluation (orientation, affect, perception, memory, attention span, speech and language), motor control, swallowing ability, hydration status, fluid output, skin integrity, and activity level. The ongoing nursing assessment continues to focus on alterations in cognition and functional impairment and directs the appropriate nursing diagnoses.

Diagnosis

Appropriate nursing diagnoses may include:

- Altered hemodynamics related to cardiac arrhythmias, hyper-/hypotension, fluid/electrolyte imbalances
- Impaired physical mobility related to hemiparesis, sensory loss, loss of balance or coordination, or visual field deficit
- Impaired verbal communication related to dysarthria, aphasia, altered cognition
- Impaired swallowing/risk for aspiration related to inability to protect airway or altered LOC
- Risk for infection related to smoking history, invasive lines, Foley catheter, nasogastric (NG) tube
- Risk for ineffective peripheral tissue perfusion related to risk for deep vein thrombosis (DVT)/immobility
- High risk for injury related to visual field, motor, or perception deficits
- Knowledge deficit related to lack of awareness of stroke risk factors, secondary stroke prevention medications, potential lifestyle changes, physical and occupational therapies

Planning

Although rehabilitation begins on the day the patient has the stroke, the process is intensified during convalescence and requires a coordinated team effort. It is helpful for the team to know the patient's baseline function, past medical history, mental and emotional state, behavioral characteristics, and ADLs. Additionally, clinicians should be knowledgeable about the relative importance of predictors of stroke outcome (age, comorbidities such as diabetes, and presenting NIHSS score) in order to provide stroke survivors and their families with a realistic recovery trajectory. For example, a direct correlation exists between a NIHSS score of greater than 15 and poor 3-month outcome (Diepenbrock, 2008). Refer to Table 47-4 for the NIHSS scale.

The major goals for the patient (and family) may include improved mobility, avoidance of shoulder pain, achievement of self-care, relief of sensory and perceptual deprivation, prevention of aspiration, continence of bowel and bladder, improved thought processes, optimization of communication, maintaining skin integrity, restored family functioning, improved sexual function, and absence of complications.

Nursing Interventions

Nursing care has a significant impact on the patient's recovery. Often, many body systems are impaired as a result of the stroke, and conscientious care and timely interventions can prevent debilitating complications. During and after the acute phase, nursing interventions include a comprehensive approach to physical care and fostering recovery by listening to the patient and asking questions to elicit the meaning of the stroke experience.

Improving Mobility and Preventing Joint Deformities

When control of the voluntary muscles is lost, the strong flexor muscles exert control over the extensors. The arm tends to adduct (adductor muscles are stronger than abductors) and to rotate internally. The elbow and the wrist tend to flex, the affected leg tends to rotate externally at the hip joint and flex at the knee, and the foot at the ankle joint supinates and tends toward plantar flexion.

Correct positioning is important to prevent contractures; measures are used to relieve pressure, assist in maintaining good body alignment, and prevent compressive neuropathies, especially of the ulnar and peroneal nerves. Because flexor muscles are stronger than extensor muscles, a posterior splint applied at night to the affected extremity may prevent flexion and maintain correct positioning during sleep. If splints are in place, the nurse assesses the skin for evidence of impaired circulation, sensation, and/or mobility, as well as any evidence of altered skin integrity.

(continued on page 1262)

PREVENTING SHOULDER ADDUCTION. To prevent adduction of the affected shoulder while the patient is in bed, a pillow is placed in the axilla when there is limited external rotation; this keeps the arm away from the chest. A pillow is placed under the arm, and the arm is placed in a neutral (slightly flexed) position, with distal joints positioned higher than the more proximal joints (i.e., the elbow is positioned higher than the shoulder and the wrist higher than the elbow). This helps to prevent edema and the resultant joint fibrosis that will limit range of motion (ROM) if the patient regains control of the arm.

POSITIONING THE HAND AND FINGERS. The fingers are positioned so that they are barely flexed. The hand is placed in slight supination (palm faces upward), which is its most functional position. If the upper extremity is flaccid, a splint can be used to support the wrist and hand in a functional position. Every effort is made to prevent hand edema.

Spasticity, particularly in the hand, can be a disabling complication after stroke. Researchers have reported that repeated intramuscular injections of botulinum toxin A into wrist and finger muscles significantly reduced upper limb spasticity after stroke, but did not find an improvement of dexterity, manual ability, or quality of life (Liepert, 2010).

Mirror therapy has also demonstrated improvement in motor functions and ADLs that persisted after 6 months. In this therapy, the patient watches a mirror as movements with the unaffected hand are performed, leaving the impression that his or her affected hand is moving. This therapy is purported to activate a bihemispheric cortical motor network that supports recovery (Liepert, 2010).

CHANGING POSITIONS. The patient's position should be changed every 2 hours. To place a patient in a lateral (side-lying) position, a pillow is placed between the legs before the patient is turned. To promote venous return and prevent edema, the upper thigh should not be acutely flexed. The patient may be turned from side to side, but if sensation is impaired, the amount of time spent on the affected side should be limited.

ESTABLISHING AN EXERCISE PROGRAM. The affected extremities are exercised passively and put through a full ROM four or five times a day to maintain joint mobility, regain motor control, prevent contractures in the paralyzed extremity, prevent further deterioration of the neuromuscular system, and enhance circulation. Repetition of an activity forms new pathways in the CNS and therefore encourages new patterns of motion. At first, the extremities are usually flaccid. If tightness occurs in any area, the ROM exercises should be performed more frequently. Regularity in exercise is most important. Improvement in muscle strength and maintenance of ROM can be achieved only through daily exercise.

The patient is encouraged and reminded to exercise the unaffected side at intervals throughout the day. It is helpful to develop a written schedule to remind the patient of the exercise activities. The nurse supervises and supports the patient during these activities. The patient can be taught to put the unaffected leg under the affected one to assist in moving it when turning and exercising. Flexibility, strengthening, coordination, endurance, and balancing exercises prepare the patient for ambulation. Quadriceps muscle setting and gluteal setting exercises are started early to improve the muscle strength needed for walking; these are performed at least five times daily for 10 minutes at a time.

PREPARING FOR AMBULATION. As soon as possible, the patient is assisted out of bed. Usually, an active rehabilitation program is started as soon as the patient regains consciousness. The patient is first taught to maintain balance while sitting and then to learn to balance while standing. If the patient has difficulty in achieving standing balance, a tilt table, which slowly brings the patient to an upright position, can be used. If orthostatic hypotension is a problem, the nurse can gradually elevate the head of the bed and assess blood pressure, pulse, skin color, and any complaints of dizziness or lightheadedness. If hypotension, tachycardia, paleness, diaphoresis, dizziness, or lightheadedness are noted, the head of the bed may be lowered until the symptoms resolve.

The patient is usually ready to walk as soon as standing balance is achieved. Parallel bars are useful in these first efforts. A chair or wheelchair should be readily available in case the patient suddenly becomes fatigued or feels dizzy.

The training periods for ambulation should be short and frequent. As the patient gains strength and confidence, an adjustable cane can be used for support. Generally, a three- or four-pronged cane provides a stable support in the early phases of rehabilitation.

Preventing Shoulder Pain

As many as 70% of stroke patients suffer pain in the shoulder that prevents them from regaining full range of motion (ROM), and 88% will have some level of upper extremity dysfunction (Zeferino & Aycock, 2010). Shoulder function is essential in achieving balance and performing transfers and self-care activities. Three problems can occur: painful shoulder, subluxation (partial dislocation) of the shoulder, and shoulder–hand syndrome or reflex sympathetic dystrophy syndrome (RSDS), which features pain (often "burning"); tenderness; vasoconstrictive-related coldness of the affected extremity; trophic changes of hair, nails, skin; and swelling.

A flaccid shoulder joint may be overstretched by the use of excessive force in turning the patient or from overstrenuous arm and shoulder movement. To prevent shoulder pain, the nurse should never lift the patient by the flaccid shoulder or pull on the affected arm or shoulder. If the arm is paralyzed, subluxation at the shoulder can occur as a result of overstretching of the joint capsule and musculature by the force of gravity when the patient sits or stands in the early stages after a stroke. This results in severe pain. Shoulder–hand syndrome (painful shoulder and generalized swelling of the hand) can cause a frozen shoulder and ultimately atrophy of subcutaneous tissues. When a shoulder becomes stiff, it is usually painful.

Many shoulder problems can be prevented by proper patient movement and positioning. The flaccid arm is positioned on a table or with pillows while the patient is seated. Some clinicians advocate the use of a properly worn sling when the patient first becomes ambulatory, to prevent the paralyzed upper extremity from dangling without support. ROM exercises are important in preventing painful shoulder. Overly strenuous arm movements are avoided. The patient is instructed to interlace the fingers, place the palms together, and push the clasped hands slowly forward to bring the scapulae forward; he or she then raises both hands above the head. This is repeated throughout the day. The patient is instructed to flex the affected wrist at intervals and move all the joints of the affected fingers. He or she is encouraged to touch, stroke, rub, and look at both hands. Pushing the heel of the hand firmly down on a surface is useful. Elevation of the arm and hand is also important in preventing dependent edema of the hand. When dressing, the sequence of weaker arm, head, followed by stronger arm is followed (Zeferino & Aycock, 2010). Patients with continuing pain after attempted movement and positioning may require the addition of analgesia to their treatment program.

Medications are helpful in the management of post-stroke pain. Opioids are generally prescribed for acute pain, but may be considered for patients with chronic pain. If prescribed, the nurse assesses for side effects, tolerance, dependency, and abuse. Adjuvant drugs such as antidepressants, anticonvulsants, and anxiolytics may also be considered. Tricyclic antidepressants are often prescribed for neuropathic pain, while anticonvulsants are used for their ability to stabilize neuronal membranes. Gabapentin (Neurontin) is becoming a first-line drug for neuropathic pain (Hickey, 2009). The antiseizure medication lamotrigine (Lamictal) has been found to be effective for post-stroke pain. Topical analgesics, such as lidocaine cream or patch, may also be considered.

Enhancing Self-Care

As soon as the patient can sit up, personal hygiene activities are encouraged. The patient is helped to set realistic goals; if feasible, a new task is added daily. The first step is to carry out all self-care activities on the unaffected side. Such

activities as combing the hair, brushing the teeth, shaving with an electric razor, bathing, and eating can be carried out with one hand and are suitable for self-care. Although the patient may feel awkward at first, the various motor skills can be learned by repetition, and the unaffected side will become stronger with use. The nurse must be sure that the patient does not neglect the affected side. Assistive devices will help make up for some of the patient's deficits. For example, a small towel is easier to control while drying after bathing, and boxed paper tissues are easier to use than a roll of toilet tissue.

Return of functional ability is important to the patient recovering after a stroke. An early baseline assessment of functional ability with an instrument such as the Functional Independence Measure (FIM™) is important in team planning and goal setting for the patient. The FIM™ is a widely used instrument in stroke rehabilitation and provides valuable information about motor, social, and cognitive function (Hickey, 2009). The patient's morale will improve if ambulatory activities are carried out in street clothes. The family is instructed to bring in clothing that is preferably a size larger than that normally worn. Clothing fitted with front or side fasteners or Velcro closures is the most suitable. The patient has better balance if most of the dressing activities are carried out while seated.

Perceptual problems may make it difficult for the patient to dress without assistance because of an inability to match the clothing to the body parts. To assist the patient, the nurse can take steps to keep the environment organized and uncluttered, because the patient with a perceptual problem is easily distracted. The patient has to make many compensatory movements when dressing; these can produce fatigue and painful twisting of the intercostal muscles. Support and encouragement are provided to prevent the patient from becoming overly fatigued and discouraged. Even with intensive training, not all patients can achieve independence in dressing.

Managing Sensory-Perceptual Difficulties

Patients with a decreased field of vision should be approached on the side where visual perception is intact. All visual stimuli (e.g., clock, calendar, television) should be placed on this side. The patient can be taught to turn the head in the direction of the defective visual field to compensate for this loss. The nurse should make eye contact with the patient and draw his or her attention to the affected side by encouraging the patient to move the head. The nurse may also want to stand at a position that encourages the patient to move or turn to visualize who is in the room. Increasing the natural or artificial lighting in the room and providing eyeglasses are important aids to increasing vision.

The patient with homonymous hemianopsia (loss of half of the visual field) turns away from the affected side of the body and tends to neglect that side and the space on that side; this is called *amorphosynthesis*. In such instances, the

(continued on page 1264)

patient cannot see food on half of the tray, and only half of the room is visible. It is important for the nurse to constantly remind the patient of the other side of the body, to maintain alignment of the extremities, and, if possible, to place the extremities where the patient can see them.

Assisting With Nutrition

Stroke can result in swallowing problems (dysphagia). Patients must be observed for paroxysms of coughing, food dribbling out of or pooling in one side of the mouth, food retained for long periods in the mouth, or nasal regurgitation when swallowing liquids. Swallowing difficulties place the patient at risk for aspiration, pneumonia, dehydration, and malnutrition. A speech therapist will evaluate the patient's gag reflexes and ability to swallow. A validated, nurse-directed dysphagia screening assessment has been recommended as part of post stroke care to identify a patient's swallowing difficulty. A speech therapist may be consulted for patients who fail an initial screen and require a more formal evaluation. Even if swallowing function is partially impaired, it may return in some patients over time, or the patient may be taught alternative swallowing techniques, advised to take smaller boluses of food, place food on the unaffected side of the patient's mouth, and taught about types of foods that are easier to swallow. The patient may be started on a thick liquid or puréed diet because these foods are easier to swallow than thin liquids. Having the patient sit upright, preferably out of bed in a chair, and instructing him or her to tuck the chin toward the chest as he or she swallows will help prevent aspiration. The diet may be advanced as the patient becomes more proficient at swallowing. If the patient cannot resume oral intake, a gastrointestinal feeding tube will be placed for ongoing tube feedings.

Enteral tubes can be either nasogastric (placed in the stomach) or nasoenteric (placed in the duodenum) to reduce the risk of aspiration. For long-term feedings, a gastrostomy tube is preferred. Refer to Chapter 22 for details on enteral feeding. Nursing responsibilities in feeding include elevating the head of the bed at least 30 degrees to prevent aspiration, checking the position of the tube before feeding, assessing residuals, and ensuring that the cuff of the tracheostomy tube (if in place) is inflated.

Attaining Bowel and Bladder Control

After a stroke, the patient may have transient urinary incontinence due to confusion, inability to communicate needs, and inability to use the urinal or bedpan because of impaired motor and postural control. Occasionally, after a stroke, the bladder becomes atonic, with impaired sensation in response to bladder filling. Sometimes control of the external urinary sphincter is lost or diminished. During this period, intermittent catheterization with sterile technique is carried out. After muscle tone increases and deep tendon reflexes return, bladder tone increases and spasticity of the bladder may develop. Because the patient's sense of aware-

ness is clouded, persistent urinary incontinence or urinary retention may be symptomatic of bilateral brain damage. The voiding pattern is analyzed, and the urinal or bedpan is offered on a pattern or schedule. The upright posture and standing position are helpful for male patients during this aspect of rehabilitation.

Patients may have problems with bowel control, particularly constipation. Unless contraindicated, a high-fiber diet and adequate fluid intake (2 to 3 L/day) should be provided and a regular time (usually after breakfast) should be established for toileting.

Improving Thought Processes

After a stroke, patients may experience changes in cognition, behavior, and may exhibit periods of emotional lability. These changes are usually associated with injury to the right hemisphere. Often they are transient and with aggressive rehabilitation, patients can recover these functions.

Screening for these problems is typically incorporated into the initial rehabilitation assessment and then repeated after discharge. Often a neuropsychologist will be consulted to perform formal neuropsychological testing to make recommendations for the appropriate follow-up treatment. A treatment program for addressing any identified deficit is established in collaboration with the patient's neurologist and primary care provider.

The role of the nurse is supportive. The nurse reviews the results of neuropsychological testing, observes the patient's performance and progress, gives positive feedback, and, most importantly, conveys an attitude of confidence and hope. Interventions capitalize on the patient's strengths and remaining abilities while attempting to improve performance of affected functions. Other interventions are similar to those for improving cognitive functioning after a head injury.

Improving Communication

Aphasia, which impairs the patient's ability to express himself or herself and to understand what is being said, may become apparent in various ways. The cortical area that is responsible for integrating the myriad pathways required for the comprehension and formulation of language is called *Broca's area.* It is located in a convolution adjoining the middle cerebral artery. This area is responsible for control of the combinations of muscular movements needed to speak each word. Patients who are paralyzed on the right side (due to damage or injury to the left side of the brain) cannot speak, whereas those paralyzed on the left side are less likely to have speech disturbances. The speech therapist assesses the communication needs of the stroke patient, describes the precise deficit, and suggests the best overall method of communication. Most language intervention strategies can be tailored for the individual patient. The patient is expected to take an active part in establishing goals.

Nursing interventions include strategies to make the atmosphere conducive to communication. This includes

being sensitive to the patient's reactions and needs and responding to them in an appropriate manner. A consistent schedule, routines, and repetition help the patient to function despite significant deficits. A written copy of the daily schedule, a folder of personal information (birth date, address, names of relatives), checklists, and an audio-taped list help improve the patient's memory and concentration. The patient may also benefit from a communication board, which has pictures of common needs and phrases. When talking with the patient, it is important for the nurse to gain the patient's attention, speak slowly, and keep the language of instruction consistent. One instruction is given at a time, and time is allowed for the patient to process what has been said. The use of gestures may enhance comprehension. In working with the patient with aphasia, the nurse must remember to talk to the patient during care activities. This provides social contact for the patient.

Maintaining Skin Integrity

The patient who has had a stroke may be at risk for skin and tissue breakdown because of altered sensation and inability to respond to pressure and discomfort by turning and moving. Preventing skin and tissue breakdown requires frequent assessment of the skin, with emphasis on bony areas and dependent parts of the body. During the acute phase, a specialty bed (e.g., low-air-loss bed) may be used until the patient can move independently or assist in moving.

A regular turning schedule (at least every 2 hours) must be adhered to even if pressure-relieving devices are used to prevent tissue and skin breakdown. When the patient is positioned or turned, care must be used to minimize shear and friction forces.

The patient's skin must be kept clean and dry; gentle massage of healthy (nonreddened) skin and adequate nutrition are other factors that help to maintain normal skin and tissue integrity.

Improving Family Coping

Family members play an important role in the patient's recovery. Family members are encouraged to participate in counseling and to use support systems that will help with the emotional and physical stress of caring for the patient. Involving others in the patient's care and teaching stress management techniques and methods for maintaining personal health also facilitate family coping.

The family may have difficulty accepting the patient's disability and may be unrealistic in their expectations. They are given information about the expected outcomes and are counseled to avoid doing activities for the patient that he or she can do. They are assured that their love and interest are part of the patient's therapy.

The family needs to be informed that the rehabilitation of the hemiplegic patient requires many months and that progress may be slow. The gains made by the patient in the hospital or rehabilitation unit must be maintained. All care-

givers should approach the patient with a supportive and optimistic attitude, focusing on the patient's remaining abilities. The rehabilitation team, the medical and nursing team, the patient, and the family must all be involved in developing attainable goals for the patient at home.

Most relatives of patients with stroke handle the physical changes better than the emotional aspects of care. The family should be prepared to expect occasional episodes of emotional lability. The patient may laugh or cry easily and may be irritable and demanding or depressed and confused. The nurse can explain to the family that the patient's laughter does not necessarily connote happiness, nor does crying reflect sadness, and that emotional lability usually improves with time.

Helping the Patient Cope With Sexual Dysfunction

Sexual functioning can be altered by stroke. Sexual dysfunction after stroke is multifactorial. There may be medical reasons for the dysfunction (neurologic and cognitive deficits, previous diseases, medications), as well as various psychosocial factors. A stroke can potentially be such a catastrophic illness that the patient experiences loss of self-esteem and value as a sexual being. These psychosocial factors play an important role in determining sexual drive, activity, and satisfaction after a stroke.

Nurses in the rehabilitation setting play a crucial role in beginning a dialogue between the patient and his or her partner about sexuality after a stroke. In-depth assessments to determine sexual history before and after the stroke should be followed by appropriate interventions. Interventions for the patient and partner focus on providing relevant information, education, reassurance, adjustment of medications, counseling regarding coping skills, suggestions for alternative sexual positions, and a means of sexual expression and satisfaction.

Providing Patient Education and Preparing the Patient for the Home

Patient and family education is a fundamental component of rehabilitation. The nurse provides teaching about stroke, its causes and prevention, and the rehabilitation process. In both acute care and rehabilitation facilities, the focus is on teaching the patient to resume as much self-care as possible. This may entail using assistive devices or modifying the home environment to help the patient live with a disability.

An occupational therapist may be helpful in assessing the home environment and recommending modifications to help the patient become more independent. For example, a shower is more convenient than a tub for the patient with hemiplegia because most patients do not gain sufficient strength to get up and down from a tub. Sitting on a stool of medium height with rubber suction tips allows the patient to wash with greater ease. A long-handled bath brush with a soap container is helpful to the patient who has only one functional hand. If a shower is not available, a stool may be placed in the tub and a portable shower hose

(continued on page 1266)

attached to the faucet. Handrails may be attached alongside the bathtub and the toilet. Other assistive devices include special utensils for eating, grooming, dressing, and writing.

A program of physical therapy can be beneficial in the home environment. One technique that was shown to result in a reduction in motor impairment concentrates on enhanced exercise of the affected limb. Another technique that showed positive outcomes uses sensorimotor training of the upper limb and the wrist.

Depression is a common and serious problem after stroke. Counseling and antidepressant therapy may help if depression dominates the patient's life. As progress is made in the rehabilitation program, some problems will diminish. The family can help by continuing to support the patient and by giving positive reinforcement for the progress that is being made.

Community-based stroke support groups may allow the patient and family to learn from others with similar problems and to share their experiences. Support groups take the form of in-person meetings as well as Web-based support programs. The patient is encouraged to continue hobbies and recreational and leisure interests and to maintain contact with friends to prevent social isolation. Patients should be supported to keep active, adhere to the exercise program, and remain as self-sufficient as possible.

The nurse should recognize the potential effects of caregiving on the family. Not all families have the adaptive coping skills and adequate psychological functioning necessary for the long-term care of another person. The patient's spouse may be elderly, with his or her own health concerns; in some instances, the patient may have been the provider of care to the spouse. Even healthy caregivers may find it difficult to maintain a schedule that includes being available around the clock.

Depressed caregivers are more likely to resort to physical or emotional abuse of the patient and are more likely to place the patient in a nursing home. Respite care (planned short-term care to relieve the family from having to provide continuous 24-hour care) may be available from an adult day care center. Some hospitals also offer weekend respite care that can provide caregivers with needed time for themselves. The nurse encourages the family to arrange for such services and provides information to assist them.

The nurse involved in home and continuing care also needs to remind the patient and family of the need for continuing health promotion and screening practices. Patients who have not been involved in these practices in the past are educated about their importance and are referred to appropriate health care providers, if indicated.

Evaluation

Expected patient outcomes may include the following:

1. Demonstrates intact neurologic status and normal vital signs and respiratory patterns:
   a. Normal mental status exam, intact cognitive process
   b. Normal speech patterns and language function
   c. Normal/equal strength, movement, and sensation of all four extremities
2. Understands diagnostic procedures and treatment plan:
   a. Review of current and new medications
   b. Proposed physical and occupational therapies
   c. Achieves self-care; uses adaptive equipment
3. Arranges for follow-up appointments with stroke neurologist or primary care provider

Chapter Review

Critical Thinking Exercises

1. A 74-year-old man presents to the emergency department with confusion, right-sided weakness, and difficulty getting his words out. He scores an 8 on the NIHSS. His symptoms started 1 hour prior to admission. His head CT scan shows no evidence of a bleed. He weighs 78 kg. What are the inclusion criteria for administering IV tPA? What is the approved time-frame for administering tPA? How is tPA dosed?

2. An 80-year-old woman is admitted to the hospital with a large SAH and undergoes a coiling procedure for a ruptured aneurysm. What nursing measures should be implemented to prevent rebleeding during her hospital stay?

3. A 48-year-old man with a history of hypertension, dyslipidemia, coronary artery disease, and smoking is admitted to the hospital with a two day history of nausea and vertigo. His hospital work-up revealed an ischemic stroke in the right cerebellum. What medications might he be sent home with? What risk factor modifications will be recommended? What additional teaching will be important to emphasize that address his need to seek medical care?

NCLEX-Style Review Questions

1. A patient being cared for on the neurological unit has a diagnosis of stroke. It has affected his left hemisphere. The nurse would expect to assess which of the following deficits?
   A. Left side of body weakness
   B. Aphasia
   C. Left field visual deficit
   D. Lack of awareness of deficits

2. A patient diagnosed with a stroke is experiencing slurred speech. The nurse would accurately document this finding as which of the following clinical manifestations of stroke?

A. Aphasia

B. Dysphasia

C. Dysarthria

D. Apraxia

3. A 73-year-old patient has been diagnosed with ischemic stroke following diagnostic studies. Which medication must be given within a 3-hour window of symptom onset to be effective in lysing a clot?

A. Heparin

B. Coumadin

C. Plavix

D. tPA

4. Which of the following would the nurse expect to document in the patient diagnosed with a right-hemispheric stroke?

A. Aphasia

B. Slow, cautious behavior

C. Right visual field deficit

D. Impulsive behavior

5. Which of the following initial diagnostic tests is recommended to assess for a cerebral bleed?

A. MRI

B. Noncontrast CT

C. CT with contrast

D. Cerebral angiography

Try these additional resources to enhance your learning and understanding of this chapter:

- thePoint online resource available at **http://thepoint.lww.com/Pellico1e**
- *Handbook for Focus on Adult Health: Medical-Surgical Nursing*
- *Study Guide for Focus on Adult Health: Medical-Surgical Nursing*

References and Selected Readings

References and selected readings associated with this chapter can be found on the website that accompanies the book. Visit http://thepoint.lww.com/Pellico1e to access the references and other additional resources associated with this chapter.

Problems Related to Sensorineural Function

A PATIENT with hearing loss in both ears is being seen in the hearing clinic. She sustained the hearing loss in a traumatic accident. The health care provider is giving her information about a cochlear implant.

➡ What are some criterion that have to be met to receive a cochlear implant?
➡ What does the surgical procedure involve?
➡ What does the rehabilitation period consist of?

LINDA S. DUNE
BICKLEY, L.S. &
SZILAGYI, P.G.

Nursing Assessment: Sensorineural Function

Learning Objectives

After reading this chapter, you will be able to:

1. Identify significant eye structures and describe their functions.

2. Describe assessment components for the eye.

3. Identify diagnostic tests for assessment of vision and evaluation of visual disabilities.

4. Identify ear structures and describe their functions.

5. Describe assessment components for the ear.

6. Describe methods used to assess hearing and diagnose hearing and balance disorders.

THE EYE

The eye is a sensitive, highly specialized sense organ subject to various disorders, many of which lead to impaired vision. Impaired vision may affect a person's independence in self-care, work and lifestyle choices, sense of self-esteem, safety, ability to interact with society and the environment, and overall quality of life.

Although most people with eye disorders are treated in an ambulatory care setting, many patients receiving health care have an eye disease as a comorbid condition. In addition to understanding the prevention, treatment, and consequences of eye disorders, nurses in all settings assess visual acuity in those at risk, refer patients to eye care specialists as appropriate, implement measures to prevent further visual loss, and help patients adapt to impaired vision.

ANATOMIC AND PHYSIOLOGIC OVERVIEW

Unlike most organs of the body, the eye is available for external examination, and its anatomy is more easily assessed than many other body parts (Fig. 48-1). The eyeball, or globe, sits in a protective bony structure known as the *orbit*. The optic nerve and the ophthalmic artery enter the orbit at its apex through the optic foramen. The eyeball is moved through all fields of gaze by the extraocular muscles. The four rectus muscles and two oblique muscles (Fig. 48-2) are innervated by cranial nerves (CN) III, IV, and VI. Normally, the movements of the two eyes are coordinated, and the brain perceives a single image.

External Eye

The eyelids, composed of thin elastic skin that covers striated and smooth muscles, protect the anterior portion of the eye. The eyelids contain multiple glands, including sebaceous, sweat, and accessory lacrimal glands, and they are lined with conjunctival material. The upper lid normally covers the uppermost portion of the iris and is innervated by the oculomotor nerve (CN III). The lid margins contain meibomian glands, which produce an oil-like substance that is a constituent of tears that helps to prevent dry

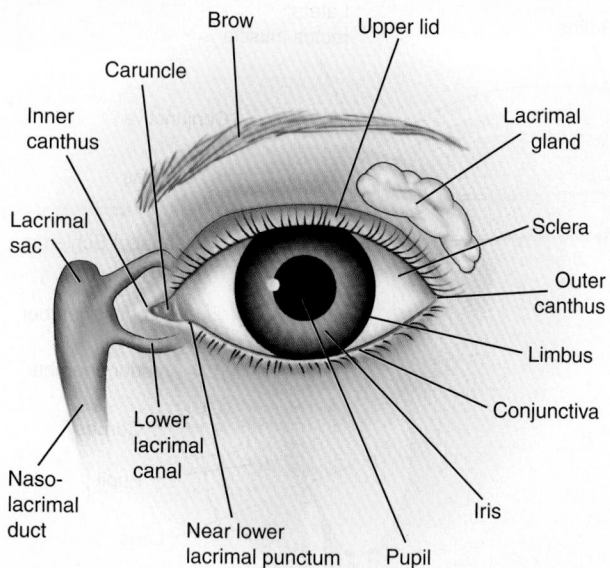

FIGURE 48-1 External structures of the eye and position of the lacrimal structures.

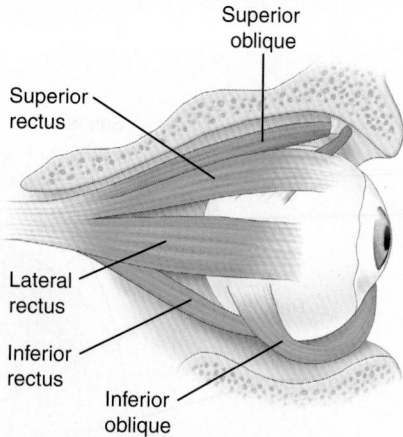

FIGURE 48-2 The extraocular muscles responsible for eye movement. The medial rectus muscle (not shown) is responsible for opposing the movement of the lateral rectus muscle.

eyes, the inferior and superior puncta, and the eyelashes. The triangular spaces formed by the junction of the eyelids are known as the *inner* or *medial canthus* and the *outer* or *lateral canthus*. Tears are vital to eye health. They are formed by the lacrimal gland and the accessory lacrimal glands. A healthy tear is composed of three layers: lipoid, aqueous, and mucoid. If there is a defect in the composition of any of these layers, the integrity of the cornea may be compromised. Tears are secreted in response to reflex or emotional stimuli. With every blink of the eyes, the lids wash the cornea and conjunctiva with tears.

> **✸ NURSING ALERT**
>
> *The lacrimal apparatus are located in the eyelid and inner canthus and are essential for tear formation and drainage needed to lubricate the eyes. The lacrimal apparatus, within the inner canthus, contains a tiny fold of mucous membrane that can be blocked by debris when providing eye care (Jarvis, 2008). When cleaning the eyes, in order to remove crusting or drainage, the nurse moves from inner to outer canthus. Use only one cotton ball or pledget (small compress) for each eye to remove debris and prevent it from entering the lacrimal duct.*

Internal Eye

The conjunctiva, a mucous membrane, provides a barrier to the external environment and nourishes the eye. The goblet cells of the conjunctiva secrete lubricating mucus. The bulbar conjunctiva covers the sclera, whereas the palpebral conjunctiva lines the inner surface of the upper and lower eyelids. The junction of the two portions is known as the *fornix*.

The sclera, commonly known as the white of the eye, is a dense, fibrous structure that helps maintain the shape of

the eyeball and protects the intraocular contents from trauma (Fig. 48-3). The sclera may have a slightly bluish tinge in young children, a dull white color in adults, a slightly yellowish color in the elderly, or a muddy brown color in African Americans. Externally, it is overlaid with conjunctiva, which is a thin, transparent mucous membrane that contains fine blood vessels. The conjunctiva meets the cornea at the **limbus** on the outermost edge of the iris.

The cornea (Fig. 48-4) is a transparent, avascular, domelike structure that covers the iris, pupil, and anterior chamber. It is the most anterior portion of the eyeball and is the main refracting surface of the eye. The epithelial cells of the cornea are capable of rapid replication and are completely replaced every 7 days. Behind the cornea lies the **anterior chamber**, filled with a continually replenished supply of clear aqueous humor, which nourishes the cornea. The aqueous humor is produced by the ciliary body, and its production is related to the intraocular pressure (IOP). Normal IOP is 10 to 21 mm Hg.

The uvea consists of the iris, the ciliary body, and the choroid. The iris, or colored part of the eye, is a highly vascularized, pigmented collection of fibers surrounding the pupil. The pupil is a space that dilates and constricts in response to light. Normal pupils are round and constrict symmetrically when a bright light shines on them. Dilation and constriction are controlled by the sphincter and dilator pupillae muscles. The dilator muscles are controlled by the sympathetic nervous system, whereas the sphincter muscles are controlled by the parasympathetic nervous system.

> **✸ NURSING ALERT**
>
> *Twenty to 40% of the population may have pupils that are slightly unequal in size but respond equally to light. The term for unequal pupils is anisocoria, and it can be a benign variant (usually < 1 mm difference between pupils) or a manifestation of disease (> 1 mm difference) (Riordan-Eva & Hoyt, 2007).*

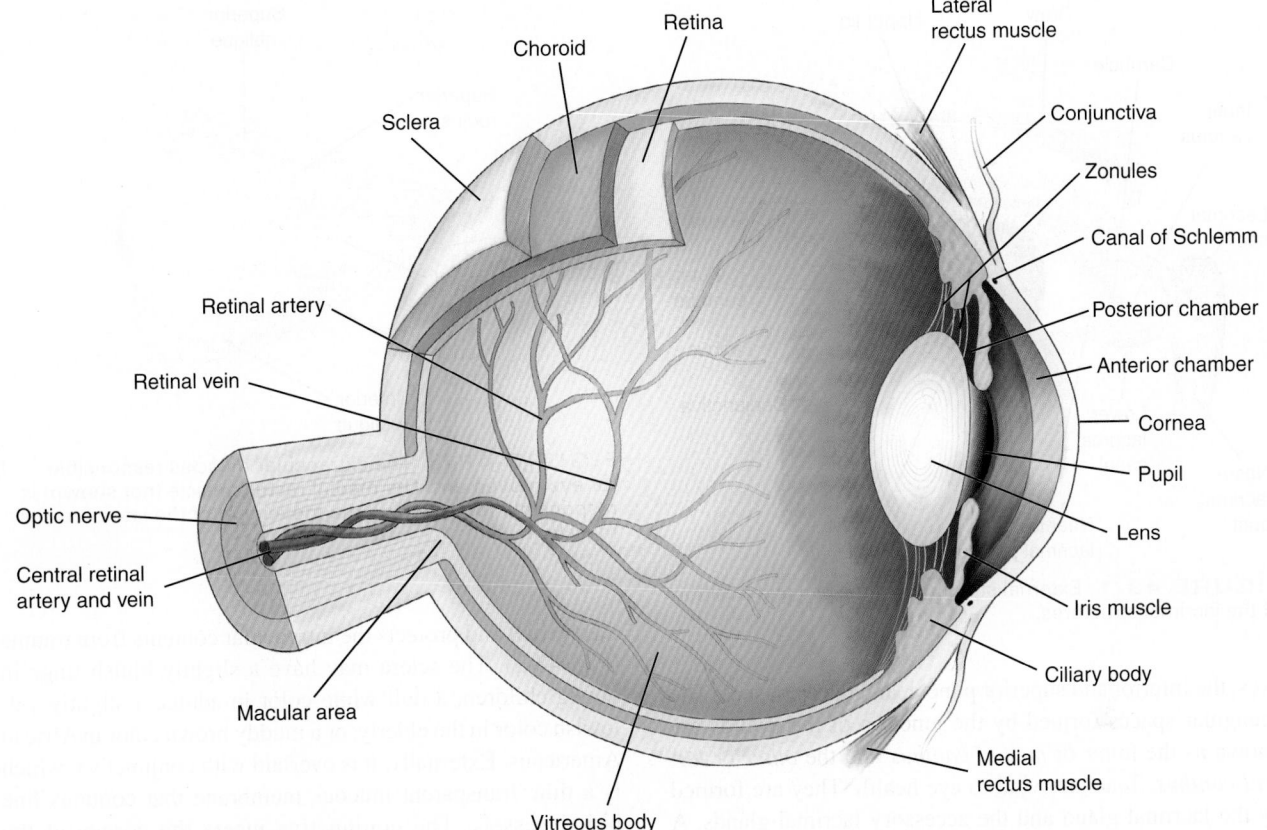

FIGURE 48-3 Three-dimensional cross-section of the eye.

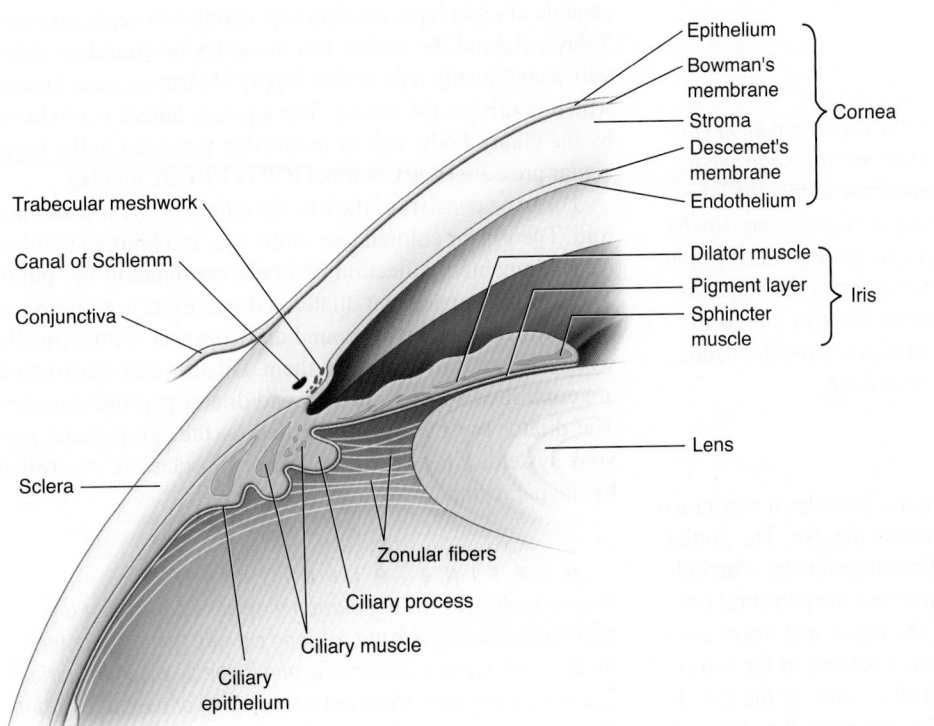

FIGURE 48-4 Internal structures of the eye. Redrawn from American Society of Ophthalmic Registered Nurses (2008). *Core curriculum for ophthalmic nursing.* Dubuque, IA: Kendall/Hall Publishing.

Directly behind the pupil and iris lies the lens, a colorless and almost completely transparent biconvex structure. It is avascular and has no nerve or pain fibers. The lens enables focusing for near vision and refocusing for distance vision. The ability to focus and refocus is called **accommodation**. The lens is suspended behind the iris by zonules (string-like fibers) and is connected to the ciliary body. The ciliary body controls accommodation through the zonular fibers and the ciliary muscles (Fig. 48-4). The aqueous humor is anterior to the lens; posterior to the lens is the vitreous humor. The **posterior chamber** is a small space between the vitreous and the iris. The ciliary body in the posterior chamber produces aqueous fluid. This aqueous fluid flows from the posterior chamber into the anterior chamber, from which it drains through the trabecular meshwork into the canal of Schlemm.

The choroid lies between the retina and the sclera. It is avascular tissue, supplying blood to the portion of the sensory retina closest to it.

The ocular fundus is the largest chamber of the eye and contains the **vitreous humor**, a clear, gelatinous substance, composed mostly of water and encapsulated by a hyaloid membrane. The vitreous humor occupies about two-thirds of the eye's volume and helps maintain the shape of the eye. The vitreous is in continuous contact with the retina and is attached to the retina by scattered collagenous filaments. The innermost surface of the fundus is the retina. The retina is composed of 10 microscopic layers and has the consistency of wet tissue paper. It is neural tissue, an extension of the optic nerve. Viewed through the pupil, the landmarks of the retina are the optic disc, the retinal vessels, and the macula. The point of entrance of the optic nerve into the retina is the optic disc. The optic disc is pink; it is oval or circular and has sharp margins. In the disc, a physiologic depression or cup is present centrally, with the retinal blood vessels emanating from it. The retinal tissues arise from the optic disc and line the inner surface of the vitreous chamber. The retinal vessels also enter the eye through the optic nerve, branching out through the retina and forming superior and inferior branches. The macula is the area of the retina responsible for central vision. The rest of the retina is responsible for peripheral vision. In the center of the macula is the most sensitive area, the fovea, which is avascular and surrounded by the superior and inferior vascular arcades (arches of blood vessels). Two important layers of the retina are the retinal pigment epithelium (RPE) and the sensory retina. A single layer of cells constitutes the RPE, and these cells have numerous functions, including the absorption of light. The sensory retina contains the photoreceptor cells: **rods** and **cones**. These are long, narrow cells shaped like rods or cones. The rods are mainly responsible for night vision or vision in low light, whereas the cones provide the best vision for bright light, color vision, and fine detail. Cones are distributed throughout the retina, with their greatest concentration in the fovea. Rods are absent in the fovea (Porth & Matfin, 2009).

Vision

Visual acuity depends on a healthy, functioning eyeball and an intact visual pathway (Fig. 48-5). This pathway is made

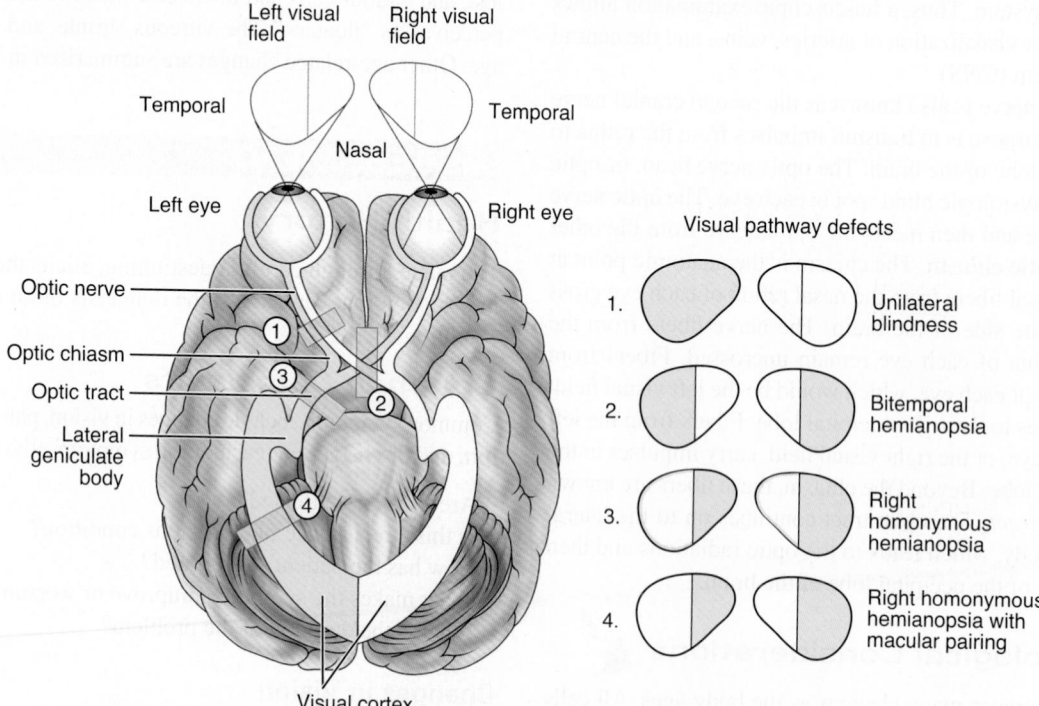

FIGURE 48-5 The visual pathway. Redrawn from Fuller, J., & Schaller-Ayers, J. (2000). *Health assessment: A nursing approach* (3rd ed.). Philadelphia: Lippincott Williams & Wilkins.

TABLE
48-1 GERONTOLOGIC CONSIDERATIONS / Age-Related Changes in the Eye

Component	Structural Change	Functional Change	History & Physical Findings
Eyelids and lacrimal structures	Loss of skin elasticity and orbital fat, decreased muscle tone; wrinkles develop	Lid margins turn in, causing lashes to irritate cornea and conjunctiva (entropion); or lid margins may turn out, resulting in increased corneal exposure (ectropion).	Reports of burning, foreign body sensation, increased tearing (epiphora); injection, inflammation, and ulceration may occur
Refractive changes; presbyopia	Loss of accommodative power in the lens with age	Reading materials must be held at increasing distance in order to focus.	Patient reports, "Arms are too short!"; need for increased light; reading glasses or bifocals needed
Cataract	Opacities in the normally crystalline lens	Interference with the focus of a sharp image on the retina	Patients report increased glare, decreased vision, changes in color values (blue and yellow especially affected)
Posterior vitreous detachment	Liquefaction and shrinkage of vitreous body	May lead to retinal tears and detachment	Reports light flashes, cobwebs, floaters
Age-related macular degeneration (AMD)	Drusen (yellowish aging spots in the retina) appear and coalesce in the macula. Abnormal choroidal blood vessels may lead to formation of fibrotic disciform scars in the macula.	Central vision is affected; onset is more gradual in dry AMD, more rapid in wet AMD; distortion and loss of central vision may occur.	Reading vision is affected; words may be missing letters, faded areas appear on the page, straight lines may appear wavy; drusen, pigmentary changes in retina; abnormal submacular choroidal vessels

up of the retina, optic nerve, optic chiasm, optic tracks, lateral geniculate bodies, and optic radiations, and the visual cortex area of the brain. The pathway is an extension of the central nervous system. Thus, a funduscopic examination allows the only direct visualization of arteries, veins, and the central nervous system (CNS).

The optic nerve is also known as the second cranial nerve (CN II). Its purpose is to transmit impulses from the retina to the occipital lobe of the brain. The optic nerve head, or optic disc, is the physiologic blind spot in each eye. The optic nerve leaves the eye and then meets the optic nerve from the other eye at the **optic chiasm**. The chiasm is the anatomic point at which the nasal fibers from the nasal retina of each eye cross to the opposite side of the brain. The nerve fibers from the temporal retina of each eye remain uncrossed. Fibers from the right half of each eye, which would be the left visual field, carry impulses to the right occipital lobe. Fibers from the left half of each eye, or the right visual field, carry impulses to the left occipital lobe. Beyond the chiasm, these fibers are known as the *optic tract*. The optic tract continues on to the lateral geniculate body, which leads to the optic radiations and then to the cortex of the occipital lobe of the brain.

Gerontological Considerations

The eye undergoes many changes as the body ages. All cells formed throughout life are retained by the lens, which makes the cell structure of the lens susceptible to the degenerative

effects of aging. The lens continues to grow throughout life, laying down fibers in concentric rings. As the body ages, the gel-like characteristics of the vitreous humor are gradually lost, and various cells and fibers cast shadows that the patient perceives as "floaters." The vitreous shrinks and shifts with age. Other age-related changes are summarized in Table 48-1.

ASSESSMENT

Health History

The nurse, through careful questioning, elicits the necessary information that can lead to the diagnosis of an ophthalmic condition.

Common Complaints

Common symptoms include changes in vision, pain or discomfort, and discharge. For each of the symptoms, the nurse asks:

- Are both eyes affected?
- Is this a recurrence of a previous condition?
- How has the patient self-treated?
- What makes the symptoms improve or worsen?
- What is the duration of the problem?

Changes in Vision

The nurse asks about changes in vision, including diminished visual acuity and blurred, distorted, or double vision.

Changes in vision can be associated with problems such as myopia (distant objects appear blurred or nearsightedness), hyperopia (farsightedness), presbyopia (diminished ability to focus on near objects with age, a form of farsightedness), cataracts (opacity of the lens), glaucoma (abnormally high IOP that can damage the optic nerve), aging, diabetes, hypertension, cranial tumors, head trauma, or increased intracranial pressure.

Pain or Discomfort

The nurse inquires about the type of pain (sharp or dull) and whether it is worse when blinking. Pain while blinking might be present in superficial trauma events such as corneal abrasions, corneal lacerations, or presence of a foreign body. Discomfort may include itching or a foreign body sensation. This sensation of the presence of a foreign body is often present in diseases associated with conjunctival irritation. Conjunctival irritation may be found in conditions such as dry eye, bacterial or viral infections (pink eye), and allergic reactions (Collins, 2008; Erdem, Ozdegirmenci, Sobaci et al., 2007).

Discharge

It is important to note the color, consistency, and odor of any discharge. An eye discharge commonly results from inflammation or infection of the conjunctiva. Manifestations of other non–eye disorders may have eye discharge, such as erythema multiforme major (Stevens-Johnson syndrome), herpes zoster, and psoriasis vulgaris (refer to Chapter 52).

Past History

The nurse asks if this is a recurrence of a previous condition and notes the presence of any systemic diseases and medications used in their treatment. Thousands of eye disorders are side effects of medications for medical disorders. For example, if long-term steroids are administered for arthritis, cataracts may develop. The nurse also inquires about concurrent ophthalmic conditions and any history of ophthalmic surgery.

Family History

The nurse asks whether any family members have had the same symptoms or condition, such as glaucoma, refraction disorders, and allergies.

Social History

In ophthalmology, the well-being of the patient physically, emotionally, financially, socially, and spiritually can be at risk when vision is threatened. The patient may equate a decrease in visual acuity with a loss of independence. The loss of a driver's license may force a patient to relocate or give up or change careers.

Major goals should include the preservation of vision and the prevention of further visual loss in patients who have already experienced some degree of loss. Lines of communication must be kept open, so that the patient is comfortable exploring all treatment options to promote rehabilitation.

Physical Assessment

Visual Acuity Assessment

Following the health history, the patient's visual acuity is assessed. Most people are familiar with the standard Snellen chart. It is composed of a series of progressively smaller rows of letters and is used to test distance vision. The patient is positioned at the prescribed distance, usually 20 feet, from the chart and is asked to read the smallest line visible. The patient should wear distance correction (eyeglasses or contact lenses) if required, and each eye should be tested separately. The fraction 20/20 is considered the standard of normal vision. The numerator denotes the distance between the patient and the chart, whereas the denominator quantifies the distance at which a normal eye can read the line of letters. A person whose vision is 20/200 can read print from 20 feet away that a person with 20/20 vision can read at 200 feet (Bickley, 2009). Most people can see the letters on the line designated as 20/20 from a distance of 20 feet.

If the patient cannot read the 20/20 line, he or she is given a pinhole occluder and asked to read again using the eye in question. The patient should be encouraged to read every letter possible. Specific visual acuities are then recorded for each eye. If the patient reads all five letters from the 20/20 line with the right eye (OD) and three letters of the 20/15 line with the left eye (OS), the examiner records OD 20/20, OS 20/15-2. (Note: Medical abbreviations such as OD and OS are no longer recommended because misinterpretation has resulted in harmful medication errors.)

If the patient cannot read the largest letter on the chart (the 20/200 line), the patient should be moved toward the chart or the chart moved toward the patient until the patient can identify the largest letter on the chart. If the patient can recognize only the letter E on the top line at a distance of 10 feet, the visual acuity would be recorded as 10/200. If the patient cannot see the letter E at any distance, the examiner should determine if the patient can count fingers (CF). The examiner holds up a random number of fingers and asks the patient to count the number he or she sees. If the patient correctly identifies the number of fingers at 3 feet, the examiner would record CF/3'.

If the patient cannot count fingers, the examiner raises one hand up and down or moves it side to side and asks in which direction the hand is moving. This level of vision is known as hand motion (HM). A patient who can perceive only light is described as having light perception (LP). The vision of a patient who cannot perceive light is described as no light perception (NLP).

Near vision testing is performed to identify the need for reading glasses. **Presbyopia** is the term used for impaired near vision and is often found in middle-aged and older persons. A specially designed handheld card is held 14 inches away from the patient's eyes, and the patient is asked to read

the chart. Presbyopic people are commonly able to read the chart when it is held farther away.

External Eye Examination

After the visual acuity has been recorded, an external eye examination is performed. While standing directly in front of the patient, the nurse notes the position of the eyelids and alignment of the eyes. Commonly, the upper 2 mm of the iris are covered by the upper lid. The patient is examined for **ptosis** (drooping eyelid) and for lid retraction (too much of the eye exposed). Sometimes, the upper or lower lid turns out, referred to as *ectropion*, affecting closure. Additionally, the eyelid may invert; this is termed *entropion* and causes irritation of the eye. The lid margins and lashes should have no edema, erythema, or lesions. The examiner looks for scaling or crusting, and the sclera is inspected. A normal sclera is opaque and white. Lesions on the conjunctiva, discharge, and tearing or blinking are noted.

The pupils are inspected for size, shape, and symmetry. A normal pupil is black in color, round in shape, and symmetrical. Pupil size ranges between 2 mm and 8 mm depending on extremes of light. In room lighting, usual pupil size is 3 to 5 mm. The room should be darkened so that the pupils can be examined. The nurse checks pupillary response with a penlight to determine if the pupils are equally reactive and regular. The patient is asked to stare at a target; each eye is covered and uncovered quickly while the examiner looks for any shift in gaze. Recall that pupillary inequality of less than 1 mm may be detected in 20% to 40% of normal people (Riordan-Eva & Hoyt, 2007). An artificial eye will have anisocoria. Other notable irregularity may be the result of trauma, previous surgery, or disease.

The pupillary response to light is determined by shining a bright light obliquely into each pupil. Pupils are assessed for *direct reaction*, in which the pupil tested with light constricts, and for *consensual reaction*, in which the pupil of the opposite eye also constricts. The nurse is aware that the pupil of a blind eye will not constrict; however, if a direct light is reflected on the "good eye," a consensual light reaction may be noted in the impaired eye. Obviously, there will be no reaction with a prosthetic eye.

The examiner also observes for **nystagmus** (i.e., oscillating movement of the eyeball). The extraocular movements (EOMs) of the eyes are tested by having the patient follow the examiner's finger, pencil, or a hand light through the six cardinal directions of gaze, a wide H pattern (i.e., up, down, right, left, and both diagonals). Normal EOMs should produce conjugate movements of the eyes in each direction. This is especially important when screening patients for ocular trauma or for neurologic disorders.

Diagnostic Evaluation

Direct Ophthalmoscopy

A direct ophthalmoscope is a hand-held instrument enabling magnification of the cornea, lens, and retina. The patient

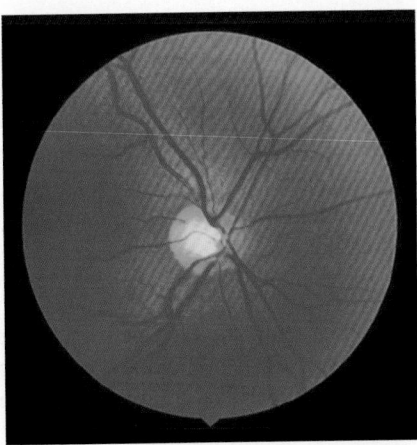

FIGURE 48-6 Normal fundus.

is normally given mydriatic drops to dilate the pupils and assist in the examination of vision. Contraindications to the use of mydriatic drops include head injury or narrow-angle glaucoma. The patient is given a target to gaze at. The examiner holds the ophthalmoscope in the right hand and uses the right eye to examine the patient's right eye. The examiner switches to the left hand and left eye when examining the patient's left eye. During this examination, the room should be darkened, and the examiner should be about 15 inches away from the patient and 15 degrees lateral to the patient's line of vision. The patient should be relaxed and able to keep both eyes open and steady.

The examiner shines the light on the patient's pupil to examine the fundus (Fig. 48-6). The fundus of the eye is the interior structure opposite the lens that includes the retina, optic disc, macula, fovea, and posterior pole. A normal orange glow is observed as light is applied to the pupil, known as the **red reflex**. Absence of the red reflex may indicate lens opacity, which is consistent with a cataract, detached retina, or retinoblastoma in children. When the fundus is examined, the vasculature comes into focus first. The examiner focuses on a large vessel and then follows it as it becomes larger in diameter, leading to the optic disc. The central depression in the disc is known as the *cup*. The normal cup is about one-third the size of the disc. The size of the physiologic optic cup should be estimated and the disc margins described as sharp or blurred. The periphery of the retina is examined by having the patient shift his or her gaze. The last area of the fundus to be examined is the macula, because this area is the most sensitive to light.

The healthy fundus should be free of any lesions. The examiner looks for intraretinal hemorrhages, which may appear as red smudges or, if the patient has hypertension, may look somewhat flame-shaped. A yellow lipid may be present in the retina of patients with hypercholesterolemia or diabetes. The examiner looks for microaneurysms, which look like little red dots, and nevi. *Drusen* (small, hyaline, globular growths), commonly found in macular degeneration, appear as yellowish areas with indistinct edges. The

examiner should sketch the fundus and document any abnormalities.

Amsler Grid

The Amsler grid is a test often used for patients with macular problems, such as macular degeneration. It consists of a geometric grid of identical squares with a central fixation point. The grid should be viewed by the patient wearing normal reading glasses. Each eye is tested separately. The patient is instructed to stare at the central fixation spot on the grid and report any distortion in the squares of the grid itself. Patients with macular problems typically note that some of the squares may look wavy, blurred, or distorted. Patients with age-related macular degeneration are commonly given these Amsler grids to take home. The patient is encouraged to check them frequently, as often as daily, to detect any early signs of distortion that may indicate the development of a neovascular choroidal membrane, an advanced stage of macular degeneration characterized by the growth of abnormal choroidal vessels.

Tonometry

Tonometry measures IOP by determining the amount of force or pressure necessary to indent or flatten (applanate) a small anterior area of the globe of the eye. High readings indicate high pressure; low readings indicate low pressure. The procedure is noninvasive and usually painless. A topical anesthetic eye drop is instilled into the lower conjunctival sac, and the tonometer is then used to measure the IOP.

Two of the most commonly used tonometers are the applanation tonometer and the Tono-Pen. The applanation tonometer is generally used by the more skilled examiner. A drop of fluorescein dye and an anesthetic drop are instilled in the eye. The applanation tip is pressed against the cornea and the examiner, looking through the slit lamp, obtains the IOP reading. The Tono-Pen is a portable, battery-operated, hand-held tonometer that is commonly used in many clinical settings. A disposable cover is placed over the tip of the instrument, and it is held against the anesthetized cornea for a few seconds. The tension reading is displayed in a liquid crystal display window.

Perimetry Testing

Perimetry testing evaluates the field of vision. A *visual field* is the area or extent of physical space visible to an eye in a given position. It has a three-dimensional contour representing areas of relative retinal sensitivity; visual acuity is sharpest at the very top of the field and declines progressively toward the periphery. It is most helpful in detecting central **scotomas** (blind areas in the visual field) in macular degeneration and the peripheral field defects in glaucoma and retinitis pigmentosa.

The two methods of perimetric testing are manual and automated perimetry. Manual perimetry involves the use of moving (kinetic) or stationary (static) stimuli or targets. An example of kinetic manual perimetry is the tangent screen. A tangent screen is a black felt material mounted on a wall that has a series of concentric circles bisected by straight lines emanating from the center. It tests the central 30 degrees of the visual field. Automated perimetry uses stationary targets, which are more difficult to detect than moving targets. In this test, a computer projects light randomly in different areas of a hollow dome while the patient looks through a telescopic opening and depresses a button whenever he or she detects the light stimulus. Automated perimetry is more accurate than manual perimetry.

Slit-Lamp Examination

The slit lamp is a binocular microscope mounted on a table. This instrument enables the user to examine the eye with magnification of 10 to 40 times the actual image. The illumination can be varied from a broad to a narrow beam of light for different parts of the eye. For example, by varying the width and intensity of the light, the anterior chamber can be examined for signs of inflammation. Cataracts may be evaluated by changing the angle of the light. When a hand-held lens, such as a three-mirror lens, is used with the slit lamp, the angle of the anterior chamber may be examined, as may the ocular fundus.

Color Vision Testing

The ability to differentiate colors has a dramatic effect on the activities of daily living. For example, the inability to differentiate between red and green can compromise traffic safety. Some careers (e.g., commercial art, color photography, airline pilot, electrician) may be closed to people with significant color deficiencies. Color discrimination allows visualization of a broad spectrum of color. The photoreceptor cells responsible for color vision are the cones, and the greatest area of color sensitivity is in the macula, the area of densest cone concentration. A defect or deficiency in the cones (red, blue, or green) will result in abnormal color vision. There are three basic types of color blindness: red–green, which is the most common deficiency; blue; and total color blindness, also known as *achromatopsia*.

A screening test, such as the polychromatic plates, can be used to establish whether a person's color vision is within normal range. Color vision deficits can be inherited. For example, red–green color deficiencies are inherited in an X-linked manner, affecting approximately 8% of men and 0.5% of women. Acquired color vision losses may be caused by chronic illness (e.g., diabetes, macular degeneration, glaucoma), medications (e.g., digitalis), trauma, industrial toxins, or aging (e.g., cataracts). A simple test, such as asking a patient if the red top on a bottle of eye drops appears redder to one eye than the other, can be an effective tool. A difference in the perception of the intensity of the color red between the two eyes can be a symptom of a neurologic problem and may provide information about the location of the lesion.

Ultrasonography

Lesions in the globe or the orbit may not be directly visible and are evaluated by ultrasonography. Ultrasonography is a very

valuable diagnostic technique, especially when the view of the retina is obscured by opaque media, such as cataract or hemorrhage. Ultrasonography can be used to identify orbital tumors, retinal detachment, and changes in tissue composition.

Special techniques can also be used to calculate the power for an intraocular lens implant and to obtain more anatomic information, showing cross-sectional images. Vitreous hemorrhage, retinal detachment, and tumors can be evaluated with minimal discomfort for the patient. Three-dimensional images can be created, and the entire ultrasound examination can be recorded for later use.

Fluorescein Angiography

Fluorescein angiography evaluates clinically significant macular edema, documents macular capillary nonperfusion, and identifies retinal and choroidal neovascularization (growth of abnormal new blood vessels) in age-related macular degeneration. It is an invasive procedure in which fluorescein dye is injected, usually into an antecubital vein. Within 10 to 15 seconds, this dye can be seen coursing through the retinal vessels. Over a 10-minute period, serial black-and-white photographs are taken of the retinal vasculature. The dye may impart a gold tone to the skin of some patients, and

urine may turn deep yellow or orange. This discoloration usually disappears in 24 hours.

THE EAR

The ear is a sensory organ with dual functions—hearing and balance. The sense of hearing is essential for normal development and maintenance of speech, as well as for the ability to communicate with others. Balance, or equilibrium, is essential for maintaining body movement, position, and coordination.

ANATOMIC AND PHYSIOLOGIC OVERVIEW

External Ear

The **external ear** includes the auricle (**pinna**) and the **external auditory canal** (Fig. 48-7). The external ear is separated from the middle ear by a disk-like structure called the **tympanic membrane** (eardrum). The auricle, attached to the side of the head by skin, is composed mainly of cartilage, except for the fat and subcutaneous tissue in the earlobe. The

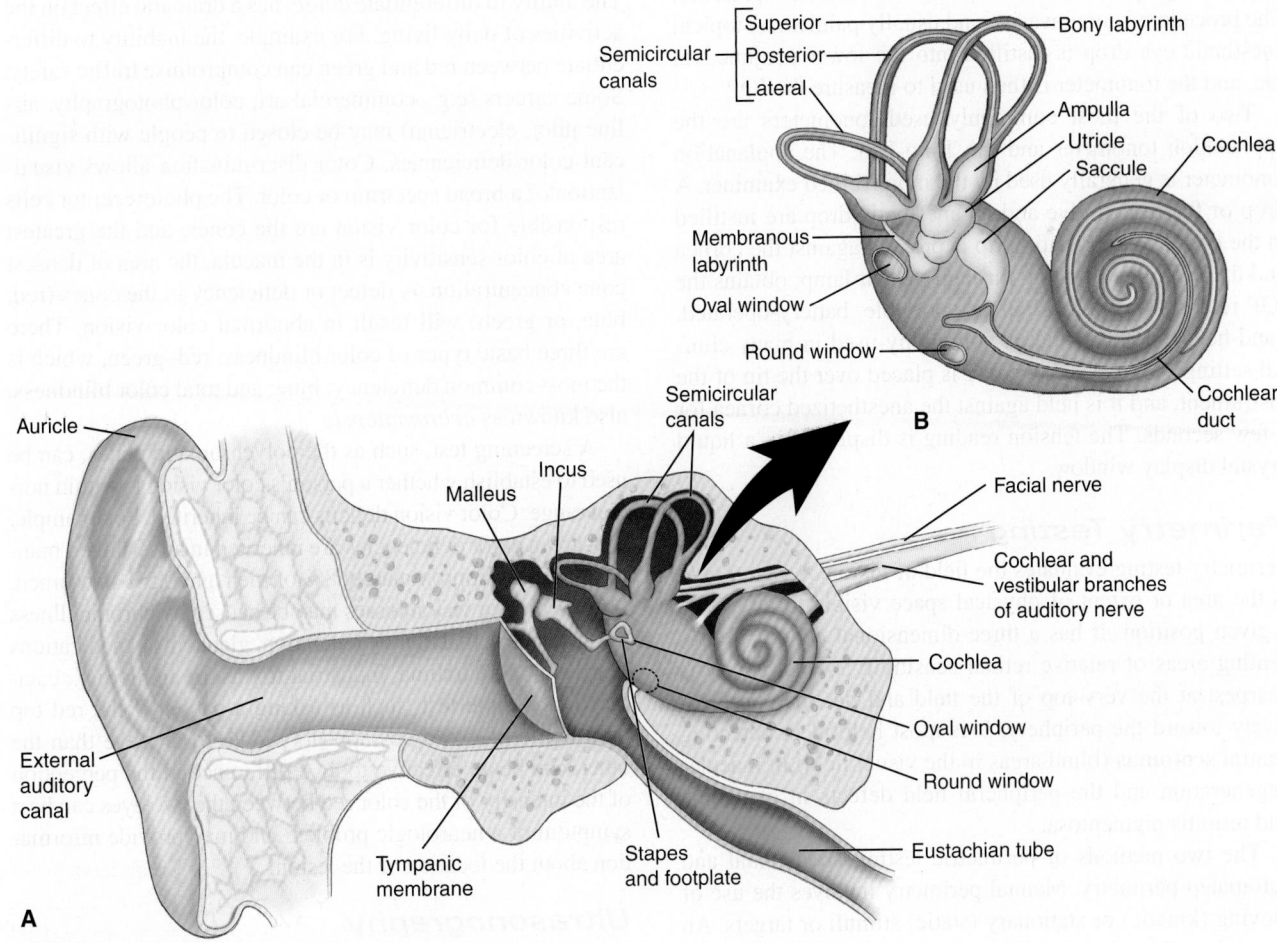

FIGURE 48-7 (**A**) Anatomy of the ear. (**B**) The inner ear.

auricle collects the sound waves and directs vibrations into the external auditory canal.

The external auditory canal is approximately 2.5 cm long. The external auditory canal ends at the tympanic membrane. The skin of the canal contains hair, sebaceous glands, and ceruminous glands, which secrete a brown, waxlike substance called **cerumen** (ear wax). The ear's self-cleaning mechanism moves old skin cells and cerumen to the outer part of the ear.

Middle Ear

The **middle ear**, an air-filled cavity, includes the tympanic membrane laterally and the otic capsule medially. The middle ear is connected by the **eustachian tube** to the nasopharynx and is continuous with air-filled cells in the adjacent mastoid portion of the **temporal bone**. Normally, the eustachian tube is closed, but it opens when the person performs a Valsalva maneuver, yawns, or swallows. It drains normal and abnormal secretions of the middle ear and equalizes pressure in the middle ear with that of the atmosphere.

The tympanic membrane (eardrum), about 1 cm in diameter and very thin, is normally pearly gray and translucent. The tympanic membrane protects the middle ear and conducts sound vibrations from the external canal to the **ossicles**. Figure 48-8 illustrates the distinguishing landmarks of the tympanic membrane.

The middle ear contains the three smallest bones (the ossicles) of the body: the **malleus**, the **incus**, and the **stapes**. The ossicles, which are held in place by joints, muscles, and ligaments, assist in the transmission of sound. Two small fenestrae (oval and round windows), located in the medial wall of the middle ear, separate the middle ear from the inner ear. The footplate of the stapes sits in the **oval window**, secured by a fibrous annulus (ring-shaped structure). The footplate

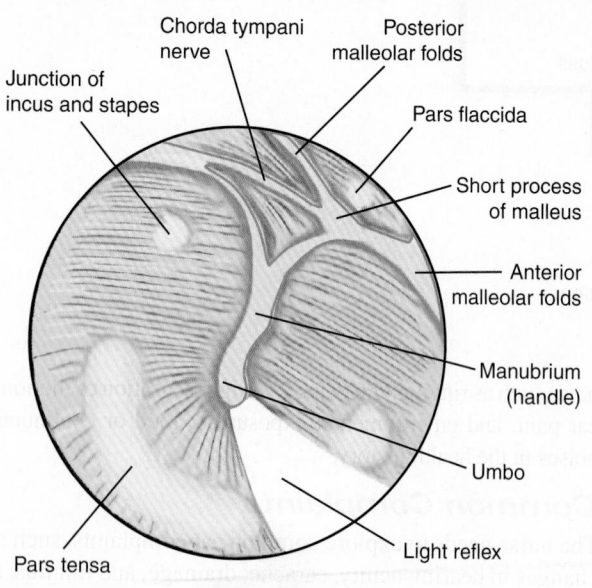

FIGURE 48-8 The tympanic membrane.

transmits sound to the inner ear. The **round window**, covered by a thin membrane, provides an exit for sound vibrations (see Fig. 48-7).

Inner Ear

The **inner ear** is housed deep within the temporal bone. The organs for hearing (**cochlea**) and balance (**semicircular canals**), as well as cranial nerves VII (facial nerve) and VIII (**vestibulocochlear nerve**), are all part of this complex anatomy (see Fig. 48-7). The three semicircular canals—posterior, superior, and lateral, which lie at 90-degree angles to one another—contain sensory receptor organs, arranged to detect rotational movement. These receptor end organs are stimulated by changes in the rate or direction of a person's movement.

The **organ of Corti**, also called the *end organ for hearing*, transforms mechanical energy into neural activity and separates sounds into different frequencies. This electrochemical impulse travels through the **acoustic** nerve to the temporal cortex of the brain to be interpreted as meaningful sound. In the **internal auditory canal**, the **cochlear (acoustic) nerve** joins the vestibular nerve to become the vestibulocochlear nerve (cranial nerve VIII).

Hearing

Hearing is conducted over two pathways: air and bone (Figure 48-9). Sounds transmitted by air conduction travel over the air-filled external and middle ear through the vibration of the tympanic membrane and ossicles. Sounds transmitted by bone conduction travel directly through bone to the inner ear, bypassing the tympanic membrane and ossicles. Normally, air conduction is the more efficient pathway. However, a defect in the tympanic membrane or interruption of the ossicular chain disrupts normal air conduction, which results in a **conductive hearing loss**.

Balance and Equilibrium

Body balance is maintained by the cooperation of the muscles and joints of the body (proprioceptive system), the eyes (visual system), and the labyrinth (vestibular system). These areas send their information about equilibrium, or balance, to the brain (cerebellar system) for coordination and perception in the cerebral cortex. The vestibular apparatus of the inner ear provides feedback regarding the movements and the position of the head and body in space.

Gerontologic Considerations

Hearing loss is a common finding in the geriatric population, with a full third of those over 65 demonstrating detectable hearing deficits (Bickley & Szilagyi, 2009). The term *presbycusis* refers to hearing loss associated with degenerative changes. Table 48-2 on page 1281 summarizes age-related changes.

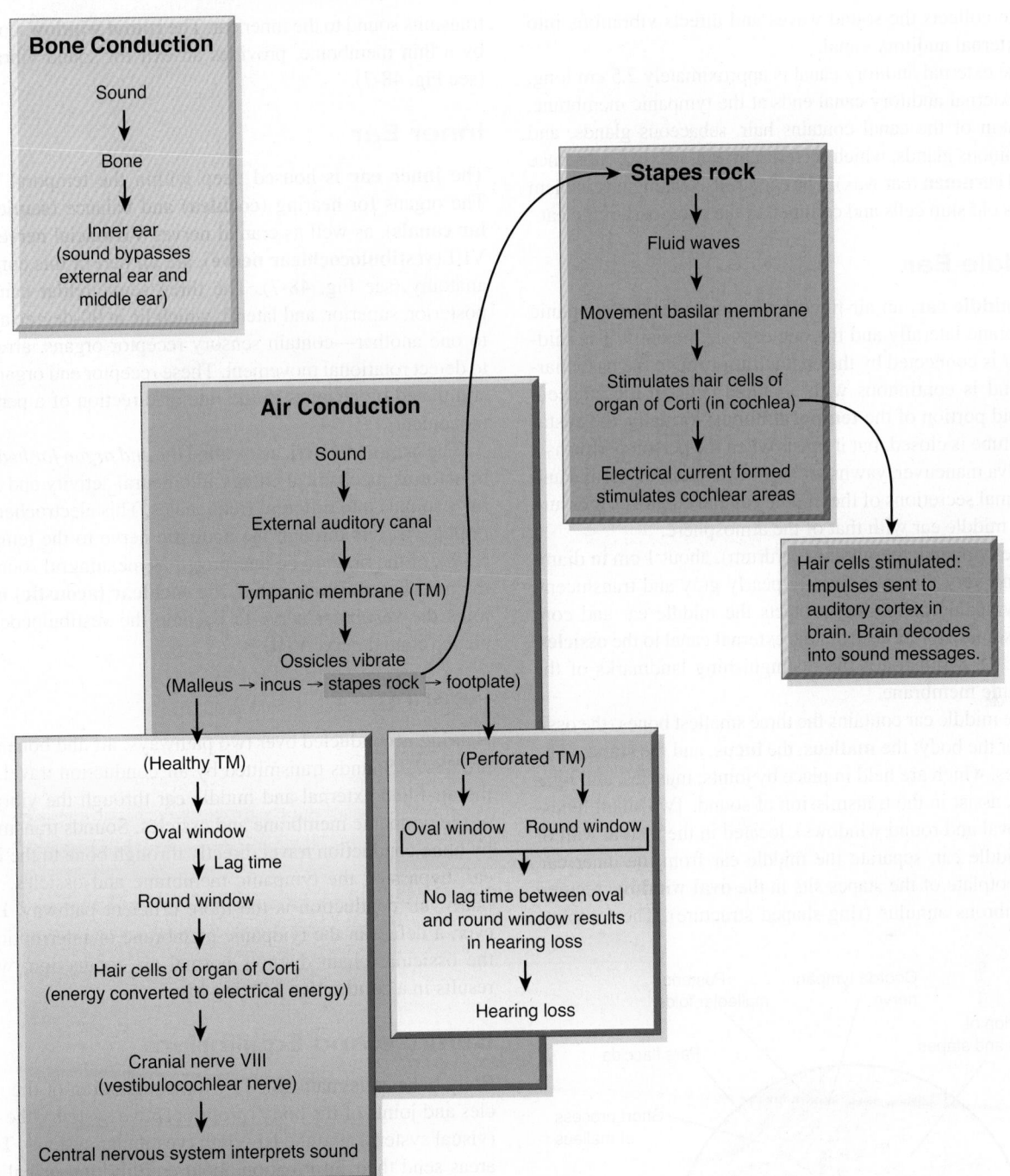

Bone Conduction

Sound
↓
Bone
↓
Inner ear
(sound bypasses
external ear and
middle ear)

Air Conduction

Sound
↓
External auditory canal
↓
Tympanic membrane (TM)
↓
Ossicles vibrate
(Malleus → incus → stapes rock → footplate)

(Healthy TM)

Oval window
↓ Lag time
Round window
↓
Hair cells of organ of Corti
(energy converted to electrical energy)
↓
Cranial nerve VIII
(vestibulocochlear nerve)
↓
Central nervous system interprets sound

(Perforated TM)

Oval window   Round window
↓
No lag time between oval
and round window results
in hearing loss
↓
Hearing loss

Stapes rock

↓
Fluid waves
↓
Movement basilar membrane
↓
Stimulates hair cells of
organ of Corti (in cochlea)
↓
Electrical current formed
stimulates cochlear areas

Hair cells stimulated:
Impulses sent to
auditory cortex in
brain. Brain decodes
into sound messages.

FIGURE 48-9 Bone conduction compared to air conduction.

ASSESSMENT

Assessment of the ear includes a health history and physical assessment.

Health History

The nurse should include questions about hearing loss, hearing aids, medications, itching, ear drainage, tinnitus (sensation of noise such as ringing or roaring), vertigo (sensation of motion), ear pain, and environmental exposure to loud or continuous noises in the health history.

Common Complaints

The nurse needs to explore common ear complaints, such as changes in hearing acuity, earache, drainage, and tinnitus. A common complaint of ear pain is associated with a variety of disorders including cerumen impaction, acute external

TABLE 48-2 GERONTOLOGIC CONSIDERATIONS / Age-Related Changes in the Ear

Component	Structural Change	Functional Change	History & Physical Findings
Atrophy of the external ears	Pinna loses flexibility	Thinning and drying of ear canal	Pinna longer and thinner with dry cerumen in external ear canal
Hardening of cerumen	Dryer thicker cerumen	Ear wax accumulates	Visible ear wax and conductive hearing impairment
Thickening of the eardrum	Stiffness of eardrum	Impaired transmission of sound	Mild hearing impairment
Change in vestibulospinal reflex	Loss of vestibular afferents and neurons	Progressive imbalance and increased falls	Balance and gait tests provoke symptoms of dizziness and postural instability
Degeneration of organ of Corti	Loss of cochlear pathway neurons, atrophy of vascular cochlear tissue	Loss of ability to discriminate words or comprehend conversations	Decreased ability to hear high frequencies or to interpret consonant sounds

otitis, acute mastoiditis, acute otitis media, and foreign bodies. Impaction of cerumen can cause otalgia (a sensation of fullness or pain in the ear), with or without a hearing loss. If, on manipulation of the auricle, the patient complains of pain, the nurse suspects the etiology of the pain is acute external otitis. Tenderness on palpation in the area of the mastoid may indicate acute mastoiditis or inflammation of the posterior auricular node. Acute otitis media, an acute infection of the middle ear can occur at any age, although is most commonly seen in children. Symptoms vary with the severity of the infection. In adults, complaints of pain are usually unilateral, and the pain is relieved after spontaneous perforation or therapeutic incision of the tympanic membrane.

Tinnitus is another common symptom of an underlying disorder of the ear that is associated with hearing impairment and loss, ototoxic substances (see Chapter 50), and a variety of hearing disorders (otosclerosis, Ménière's disease, acoustic neuroma) and systemic disorders (thyroid disease, neurological disorders). Tinnitus may range from mild to severe and is frequently described as a roaring, buzzing, or hissing sound in one or both ears. Refer to Chapter 50 for further details.

Past History

A past history of infections affecting the ear may indicate a hearing loss caused by diseases of the tympanic membranes. Medications can alter auditory function, so each agent should be evaluated for potential effects on ear disorders. Some common ototoxic medications include antibiotics, diuretics, and nonsteroidal anti-inflammatory agents. Surgical approaches that may have been performed to improve a patient's auditory function must be explored. If used, it is necessary to evaluate the patient's experience with hearing aids in the past. The effectiveness of previous therapies will determine the patient's decisions on ear interventions.

Exposure to loud noises should also be explored. Other related conditions associated with hearing loss include head

trauma, brain tumors, multiple sclerosis, and vascular disorders such as hypertension and arteriosclerosis.

Family History

Many cases of hearing loss are inherited; hereditary disorders of the ear include Hallgren's disease, Alport's syndrome, Refsum's disease, and Treacher Collins' disease. Some of these disorders are associated with other organ disorders, such as renal disease.

Social History

The presence of social problems must be explored with the patient with a hearing loss. Patients with decreased hearing may withdraw from situations in which communication skills are needed. They may become depressed and unable to continue in their chosen professions. Explore the patient's ability to work and engage in social interactions. Data regarding the age at onset and severity of hearing loss will help the nurse understand the personal impact of hearing loss.

Physical Assessment

Physical assessment includes inspection and palpation of the external ear, inspection of the internal ear, and hearing evaluation.

Inspection and Palpation of the External Ear

Inspection of the external ear is a simple procedure, but often overlooked. The external ear is examined by inspection and direct palpation; the auricle and surrounding tissues should be inspected for deformities, lesions, and discharge, as well as size, symmetry, and angle of attachment to the head. If manipulation of the auricle is painful, acute external otitis is suspected. Tenderness on palpation in the area of the mastoid may indicate acute mastoiditis or inflammation of the posterior auricular node. Because the ear is exposed to the sunlight, the nurse should examine the shell of the ear for

lesions. Any lesion lasting over 2 weeks should be referred to a skin care specialist for evaluation of skin cancer. The nurse uses the opportunity to inform patients to apply sunscreen to exposed skin including the ears.

Inspection of the Internal Ear

The tympanic membrane is inspected with an otoscope and indirect palpation with a pneumatic otoscope. To examine the external auditory canal and tympanic membrane, the otoscope should be held in the examiner's right hand, in a pencil-hold position, with the examiner's hand braced against the patient's face (Fig. 48-10). Using the opposite hand, the auricle is grasped and gently pulled back to straighten the canal in the adult. If the canal is not straightened with this technique, the tympanic membrane is more difficult to visualize because the canal obstructs the view. The speculum is slowly inserted into the ear canal, with the examiner's eye held close to the magnifying lens of the otoscope to visualize the canal and tympanic membrane. The external auditory canal is examined for discharge, inflammation, or a foreign body.

The position and color of the membrane and any unusual markings or deviations from normal are documented (see Fig. 48-8, p. 1279). If the tympanic membrane cannot be visualized because of cerumen, it may be removed by gently irrigating the external canal with warm water (unless contraindicated). If adherent cerumen is present, a small amount of mineral oil or over-the-counter cerumen softener may be instilled within the ear canal, and the patient is instructed to return for subsequent removal of the cerumen and inspection of the ear.

Evaluation of Gross Auditory Acuity

A general estimate of hearing can be made by assessing the patient's ability to hear a whispered phrase or a ticking watch, testing one ear at a time. The Weber and Rinne tests may be used to distinguish conductive loss from sensorineural loss when hearing is impaired.

Whisper Test

To exclude one ear from the testing, the examiner covers the untested ear with the palm of the hand. Then the examiner whispers softly from a distance of 1 or 2 feet from the unoccluded ear and out of the patient's sight. The patient with normal hearing acuity can correctly repeat what was whispered.

Weber Test

The Weber test uses bone conduction to test lateralization of sound. A tuning fork (ideally, 512 Hz), set in motion, is placed on the patient's head or forehead (Fig. 48-11). A person with normal hearing hears the sound equally in both ears or describes the sound as centered in the middle of the head. The Weber test is useful for detecting unilateral hearing loss (Table 48-3).

Rinne Test

In the Rinne test, the examiner shifts the stem of a vibrating tuning fork between two positions: 2 inches from the opening of the ear canal (for air conduction) and against the mastoid bone (for bone conduction). As the position changes, the patient is asked to indicate which tone is louder or when the tone is no longer audible. The Rinne test is useful for

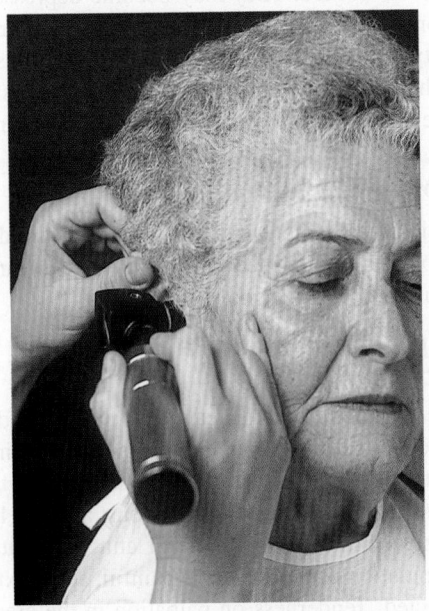
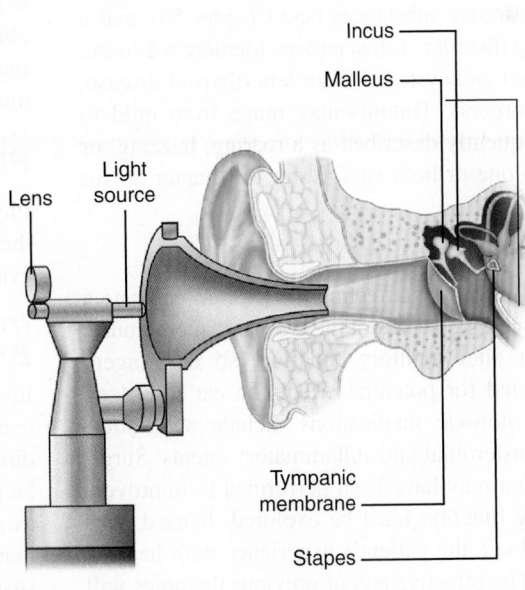

FIGURE 48-10 Proper technique for examining the ear. (**A**) Hold the otoscope in the right or left hand, in a "pencil-hold" position. (**B**) Steady the hand against the patient's head to avoid inserting the otoscope too far into the external canal.

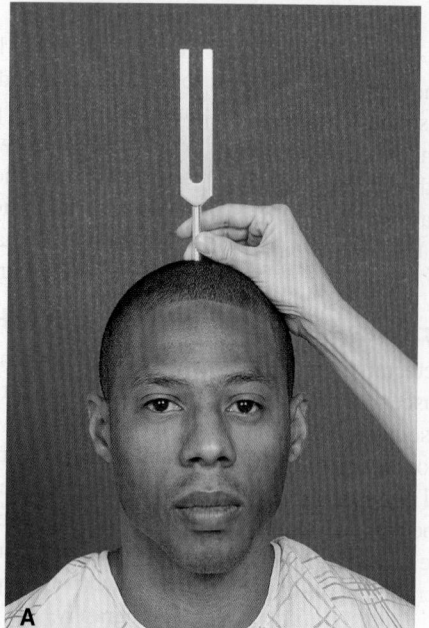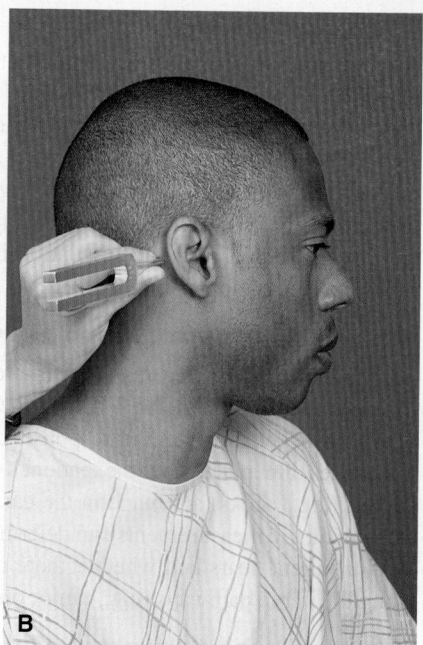

FIGURE 48-11 (A) The Weber test assesses bone conduction of sound. (B) The Rinne test assesses both air and bone conduction of sound.

distinguishing between conductive and **sensorineural hearing loss** (Table 48-3).

Diagnostic Evaluation

Many diagnostic procedures are available to measure the auditory and vestibular systems indirectly. These tests are usually performed by an audiologist whose clinical competence is certified by the American Speech-Language-Hearing Association.

Audiometry

In detecting **hearing loss**, audiometry is the single most important diagnostic instrument. Audiometric testing is of two kinds: *pure-tone audiometry*, in which the sound stimulus consists of a pure or musical tone (the louder the tone before the

patient perceives it, the greater the hearing loss), and *speech audiometry*, in which the spoken word is used to determine the ability to hear and discriminate sounds and words. Responses are plotted on a graph known as an *audiogram*, which differentiates conductive from sensorineural hearing loss.

When evaluating hearing, three characteristics are important: frequency, pitch, and intensity. *Frequency* refers to the number of sound waves emanating from a source per second, measured as cycles per second, or Hertz (Hz). The normal human ear perceives sounds ranging in frequency from 20 to 20,000 Hz. *Pitch* is the term used to describe frequency; a tone with 100 Hz is considered of low pitch, and a tone of 10,000 Hz is considered of high pitch. The unit for measuring loudness (*intensity* of sound) is the decibel (dB), the pressure exerted by sound. Hearing loss is measured in decibels, a logarithmic function of intensity that is not easily converted into a percentage. The critical level of loudness is approximately 30 dB. The shuffling of papers in quiet surroundings is about 15 dB. Table 48-4 classifies hearing loss based on decibel level.

TABLE
48-3 Comparison of Weber and Rinne Tests

Hearing Status	Weber	Rinne
Normal hearing	Sound is heard equally in both ears.	Air conduction is audible longer than bone conduction.
Conductive hearing loss	Sound heard best in affected ear (hearing loss).	Sound heard as long or longer in affected ear (hearing loss).
Sensorineural hearing loss	Sound heard best in normal hearing ear.	Air conduction is audible longer than bone conduction in affected ear.

TABLE
48-4 Severity of Hearing Loss

Loss in Decibels	Interpretation
0 to 15	Normal hearing
>15 to 25	Slight hearing loss
>25 to 40	Mild hearing loss
>40 to 55	Moderate hearing loss
>55 to 70	Moderate to severe hearing loss
>70 to 90	Severe hearing loss
>90	Profound hearing loss

Tympanogram

A tympanogram or impedance audiometry is used to evaluate the tympanic membrane and status of the middle ear. This test measures middle ear muscle reflex to sound stimulation (movement of the tympanic membrane) and the compliance of the tympanic membrane by changing the air pressure in the sealed ear canal. Compliance is impaired with middle ear disease such as fluid accumulation in the middle ear or rupture of the tympanic membrane.

Auditory Brain Stem Response

The auditory brain stem response is a detectable electrical potential from cranial nerve VIII and the ascending auditory pathways of the brainstem in response to sound stimulation. Electrodes are placed on the patient's forehead. Acoustic stimuli (e.g., clicks) are made in the ear. The resulting electrophysiologic measurements can determine at which decibel level a patient hears and whether there are any impairments along the nerve pathways (e.g., tumor on cranial nerve VIII).

Electronystagmography

Electronystagmography is the measurement and graphic recording of the changes in electrical potentials created by eye movements during spontaneous, positional, or calorically evoked nystagmus. It is also used to assess the oculomotor and vestibular systems and their corresponding interaction. It helps diagnose conditions such as Ménière's disease and tumors of the internal auditory canal or posterior fossa. Vestibular suppressants, such as sedatives, tranquilizers, antihistamines, and alcohol, are withheld for 24 hours before testing. Prior to the test, the procedure is explained to the patient.

Platform Posturography

Platform posturography is used to investigate postural control capabilities such as **vertigo**. It can be used to evaluate if a person's vertigo is becoming worse or to evaluate the person's response to treatment. The integration of visual, vestibular, and proprioceptive cues (i.e., sensory integration) with motor response output and coordination of the lower limbs is tested. The patient stands on a platform, surrounded by a screen, and different conditions such as a moving platform with a moving screen or a stationary platform with a moving screen are presented. The responses from the patient on six different conditions are measured and indicate which of the anatomic systems may be impaired. Preparation for the testing is the same as for electronystagmography.

Sinusoidal Harmonic Acceleration

Sinusoidal harmonic acceleration, or a rotary chair, is used to assess the vestibulo-ocular system by analyzing compensatory eye movements in response to the clockwise and counterclockwise rotation of the chair. Although such testing cannot identify the side of the lesion in unilateral disease, it helps identify disease (e.g., Ménière's disease and tumors of the auditory canal) and evaluate the course of recovery. The same patient preparation is required as for electronystagmography.

Middle Ear Endoscopy

With endoscopes of very small diameters and acute angles, the ear can be examined by an endoscopist specializing in otolaryngology. Middle ear endoscopy is performed safely and effectively as an office procedure to evaluate suspected perilymphatic fistula, new-onset conductive hearing loss, the anatomy of the round window before transtympanic treatment of Ménière's disease, and the tympanic cavity before ear surgery to treat chronic middle ear and mastoid infections.

The tympanic membrane is anesthetized topically for about 10 minutes before the procedure. Then, the external auditory canal is irrigated with sterile normal saline solution. With the aid of a microscope, a tympanotomy is created with a laser beam or a **myringotomy** knife, so that the endoscope can be inserted into the middle ear cavity. Video and photo documentation can be accomplished through the scope.

Chapter Review

Critical Thinking Exercises

1. Alison is an 82-year-old woman who lives at home with her daughter. She is scheduled for a posturography. She cooks for the family and frequently cooks for and visits older ill friends in the local extended care facilities. She is very active and walks on her treadmill three times per week. She plans on her usual work at evening church services after her posturography. What should you instruct her regarding preprocedure planning for her examination?

2. Your patient is a 24-year-old woman. She was transported to the emergency department after sustaining a corneal irritation from chemical exposure. Following the health history, the patient's visual acuity was assessed. Visual acuity test was to be done by Snellen chart. The patient was positioned 20 feet from the chart and was asked to read the smallest line visible. She was not able to see the chart with the affected eye. She started crying and reported that she used to be able to see perfectly from both eyes. What further assessment is needed at this time? How would you explain this finding to the patient?

NCLEX-Style Review Questions

1. Which of the following information from a health history collected from a 70-year-old should be further evaluated as a sign of presbycusis?
   A. "I haven't been going out with friends."
   B. "I am a retired truck driver."
   C. "My hobby is caring for livestock."
   D. "I watch television in the evening with my wife."

2. The nurse assesses a 7-year-old boy who is complaining of an earache. What assessment finding would the nurse expect?
   A. Blue tympanic membrane
   B. Cerumen buildup
   C. Mastoid tenderness
   D. Tympanic retraction

3. A 45-year-old man reports that he is experiencing trouble with close vision that is becoming progressively worse. The nurse explains the reason for the problem. Which of the following statements show that the patient understands the instruction?
   A. "This is a sign that I might have hypertension."
   B. "I might be having early signs of presbyopia."
   C. "So you think I might have had some kind of eye trauma?"
   D. "Which one of my medications caused this?"

4. A patient arrives at a minor emergency center complaining of eye pain after a motor vehicle incident. What would the nurse expect to find during the assessment?
   A. An injury to the opposite eye
   B. Pain while blinking
   C. Bleeding from the tear duct
   D. Change in distance vision

5. A patient is being evaluated for conductive versus sensorineural hearing loss. The nurse is performing the Rinne Test. The nurse would expect which of the following results if the patient has sensorineural hearing loss?
   A. Sound is heard equally in both ears.
   B. Air conduction is equal to bone conduction in the affected ear.
   C. Air conduction is audible longer than bone conduction in the affected ear.
   D. Air conduction is shorter than bone conduction in the affected ear.

Try these additional resources to enhance your learning and understanding of this chapter:
- thePoint online resource available at **http://thepoint.lww.com/Pellico1e**
- *Handbook for Focus on Adult Health: Medical-Surgical Nursing*
- *Study Guide for Focus on Adult Health: Medical-Surgical Nursing*

References and Selected Readings

References and selected readings associated with this chapter can be found on the website that accompanies the book. Visit http://thepoint.lww.com/Pellico1e to access the references and other additional resources associated with this chapter.

Nursing Management: Patients With Eye and Vision Disorders

CAROLYNN SPERA BRUNO

Learning Objectives

After reading this chapter, you will be able to:

1. Define low vision and blindness, and differentiate between functional and visual impairment.

2. List and describe assessment and management strategies for low vision.

3. Demonstrate orientation and mobility techniques for patients with low vision in a hospital setting.

4. Discuss assessment and management of retinal disorders.

5. Discuss assessment and management of eye trauma.

6. Discuss assessment and management of infectious and inflammatory eye disorders.

7. Demonstrate the instillation of eye drops and ointment.

8. Discuss the postoperative management and discharge instructions of patients undergoing ocular surgery.

Patients admitted to medical surgical units may have acute conditions affecting the eye or comorbidities associated with visual impairment. Many of the leading causes of visual impairment are associated with aging (e.g., cataracts, glaucoma, macular degeneration), and two-thirds of the population with impaired vision are older than 65 years of age. Younger people are also at risk for eye disorders, particularly traumatic injuries. Understanding the prevention, treatment, and consequences of eye disorders, nurses in all settings assess visual acuity in those at risk (e.g., patients who are elderly, those with diabetes or AIDS), refer patients to eye care specialists as appropriate, implement measures to prevent further visual loss, and help patients adapt to impaired vision.

IMPAIRED VISION

An estimated 3.4 million U.S. adults aged 40 years or older are visually impaired or blind (Centers for Disease Control and Prevention [CDC], 2004). Chief causes are diabetic retinopathy and age-related eye diseases including cataracts, macular degeneration, and glaucoma. It is believed that blindness is preventable in 50% of cases (National Eye Institute [NEI], 2002). Given the projected rise in the aged population and the recognition that many eye disorders are undiagnosed, it is essential for nurses to assess patient's sight and serve as educators so that earlier intervention can be provided.

REFRACTIVE ERRORS, LOW VISION, AND BLINDNESS

In refractive errors, vision is impaired because a shortened or elongated eyeball prevents light rays from focusing sharply on the retina. Blurred vision from refractive error can be corrected with eyeglasses or contact lenses. The appropriate eyeglass or contact lens is determined by **refraction**. Ophthalmic refraction consists of placing various types of lenses in front of the patient's eyes to determine which lens best improves the patient's vision.

The depth of the eyeball is important in determining refractive error. Patients for whom the visual image focuses precisely on the macula and who do not need eyeglasses or contact lenses are said to have **emmetropia**

(normal vision). People who have **myopia** are said to be near-sighted. They have deeper eyeballs; thus, the distant visual image focuses in front of, or short of, the retina. Myopic people experience blurred distance vision. When people have a shorter depth to their eyes, the visual image focuses beyond the retina; the eyes are shallower and are called *hyperopic*. People with **hyperopia** are farsighted. These patients experience near vision blurriness, whereas their distance vision is excellent.

Another important cause of refractive error is **astigmatism**, an irregularity in the curve of the cornea. Because astigmatism causes a distortion of the visual image, acuity of distance and near vision can be decreased. Hard or soft toric contact lenses may be used to correct astigmatic errors, in place of eyeglasses.

Ophthalmology has entered the era of customized vision correction, in its desire to achieve "super-normal vision." A new method of measuring refractive error is called *wavefront technology*. The most promising application for this technology is wavefront-guided refractive surgery.

Low vision is a general term describing visual impairment that requires patients to use devices and strategies in addition to corrective lenses to perform visual tasks. Low vision is defined as a best corrected visual acuity (BCVA) of 20/70 to 20/200.

Blindness is defined as a BCVA that can range from 20/400 to no light perception (NLP). The clinical definition of absolute blindness is the absence of light perception. Legal blindness is a condition of impaired vision in which a person has a BCVA that does not exceed 20/200 in the better eye or whose widest visual field diameter is 20 degrees or less. This definition neither equates with functional ability nor classifies the degrees of visual impairment. Legal blindness ranges from an inability to perceive light to having some vision remaining. A person who meets the criteria for legal blindness may be eligible for government financial assistance.

Impaired vision is often accompanied by difficulty in performing functional activities. People with visual acuity of 20/80 to 20/100 and a visual field restriction of 60 degrees to greater than 20 degrees can read at a nearly normal level with optical aids. Their visual orientation is near normal but requires increased scanning of the environment (i.e., systematic use of head and eye movements). In a visual acuity range of 20/200 to 20/400 with a 20-degree to greater than 10-degree visual field restriction, the person can read slowly with optical aids. His or her visual orientation is slow, with constant scanning of the environment. People in this category may have the ability to negotiate their environment without auxiliary aids. This ability is termed "travel vision." People with hand motion (HM) vision or no vision may benefit from the use of mobility devices (e.g., cane, guide dog) and should be encouraged to learn Braille and to use computer aids.

The most common causes of blindness and visual impairment among adults 40 years of age or older are diabetic retinopathy (refer to Chapter 30), macular degeneration, glaucoma, and cataracts (discussed later in this chapter) (Prevent Blindness America, 2008). Macular degeneration is more prevalent among Caucasians, whereas glaucoma is more prevalent among African Americans. Age-related changes in the eye are discussed in Chapter 48.

Clinical Manifestations and Assessment

The assessment of low vision includes a thorough history and the examination of distance and near visual acuity, visual field, contrast sensitivity, glare, color perception, and refraction (see Chapter 48). Specially designed, low-vision visual acuity charts are used to evaluate patients.

During history taking, the cause and duration of the patient's visual impairment are identified. Patients with retinitis pigmentosa, for example, have a genetic abnormality. Patients with diabetic macular edema typically have fluctuating visual acuity. Patients with macular degeneration have central acuity problems. Central acuity problems cause difficulty in performing activities that require finer vision, such as reading. People with peripheral field defects have more difficulties with mobility. The patient's customary activities of daily living (ADLs), medication regimen, habits (e.g., smoking), acceptance of the physical limitations brought about by the visual impairment, and realistic expectations of low-vision aids must be identified and included in the plan of care, including provision of guidelines for safety and referrals to social services.

Contrast-sensitivity testing measures visual acuity in different degrees of contrast. The initial test may take the form of simply turning on the lights while testing the distance acuity. If the patient can read better with the lights on, the patient can benefit from magnification. Glare testing enables the examiner to obtain a more realistic evaluation of the patient's ability to function in his or her environment. Glare can reduce a person's ability to see, especially in patients with cataracts. Devices that test glare are calibrated to imitate certain objects that create glare, such as a car's headlights at night.

Medical Management

Managing low vision involves magnification and image enhancement through the use of low-vision aids and strategies, and referrals to social services and community agencies serving those with visual impairment. The goals are to optimize the patient's remaining vision, whether central or peripheral, and assist the patient to perform customary activities. Low-vision aids include optical and nonoptical devices (Table 49-1). The optical devices include convex lens aids, such as magnifiers and spectacles; telescopic devices; anti-reflective lenses that diminish glare; and electronic reading systems, such as closed-circuit television and computers with large print. Continuing advances in computer software provide very useful products for patients with low vision.

TABLE
49-1 Activities Affected by Visual Impairment and Visual Aids

Activity	Optical Aids	Nonoptical Aids
Shopping	Hand magnifier	Lighting, color cues
Fixing a snack	Bifocals	Color cues, consistent storage plan
Eating out	Hand magnifier	Flashlight, portable lamp
Identifying money	Bifocals, hand magnifier	Arrange paper money in wallet compartments
Reading print	High-power spectacle, bifocals, hand magnifier	Lighting, high-contrast print, large print, reading slit stand magnifier, closed-circuit television electronic books
Writing	Hand magnifier, focusable telescope, closed-circuit televisions	Lighting, bold-tip pen, black ink circuit television
Using a telephone	Hand magnifier	Large print dial or touch tone buttons, hand-printed directory
Crossing streets	Telescope	Cane, ask directions
Finding taxis and bus signs	Telescope	Ask for assistance
Reading medication labels	Hand magnifier	Color codes, large print
Reading stove dials	Hand magnifier	Color codes, raised dots
Adjusting the thermostat	Hand magnifier	Enlarged print model
Using a computer	Spectacles	High-contrast color, large-print program
Reading signs	Spectacles	Move closer
Watching sporting event	Telescope	Sit in front rows

Adapted from Riordan-Eva, P., & Whitcher (Eds.) (2008). *Vaughan & Asbury's general ophthalmology* (17th ed.). New York: McGraw-Hill Companies.

Scanners and the appropriate software enable the user to scan printed material and have it read by computer voice, or to enlarge the print for reading. Magnifiers can be hand-held or attached to a stand with or without illumination. Telescopic devices can be spectacle telescopes or clip-on or handheld loupes.

The Internet continues to expand, and a telephone system has been developed that allows access to the Internet and e-mail using voice commands (Box 49-1).

Referrals to community agencies may be necessary for patients with low vision who live alone and cannot self-administer their medications. Community agencies, such as the Lighthouse National Center for Vision and Aging, offer services to patients with low vision that include training in independent living skills, the provision of occupational and recreational activities, and a wide variety of assistive devices for vision enhancement and orientation and mobility.

Nursing Management

Coping with blindness involves three types of adaptation: emotional, physical, and social. The emotional adjustment to blindness or severe visual impairment determines the success of the physical and social adjustments of the patient. Successful emotional adjustment means acceptance of blindness or severe visual impairment.

Promoting Coping Efforts

Effective coping may not occur until the patient recognizes the permanence of the blindness. Clinging to false hopes of regaining vision hampers effective adaptation to blindness. A newly blind patient and his or her family members (especially those who live with the patient) undergo the various steps of grieving: denial, anger, loss bargaining, depression, resolution and acceptance (Kübler-Ross, 1969). The ability to accept the changes that must come with visual loss and willingness to adapt to those changes influence the successful rehabilitation of the patient who is blind. Additional aspects to consider are value changes, independence–dependence conflicts, coping with stigma, and learning to function in social settings without visual cues and landmarks.

Promoting Spatial Orientation and Mobility

A person who is blind or severely visually impaired requires strategies for adapting to the environment. ADLs, such as

---

BOX 49-1

Web Access for the Visually Impaired

People with impaired vision need not be left behind in the computer age. Various technologies are available. A list of general equipment needs follows:

- *Computer:* Software specifically developed for people with visual impairment.
- *Internet service provider* (e.g., AOL, Netscape, Earthlink, Comcast)
- *Screen-reader program:* Converts text on the computer screen to synthesized speech (e.g., JAWS for Windows, Windows Eyes, Slimware Window Bridge, ProTalk 32, Hal Screen Reader, WinVision, WYNN, outSPOKEN for Windows)
- *Browser program to navigate the World Wide Web* (e.g., Microsoft Internet Explorer, IBM Home Page Reader)

BOX 49-2

Guidelines for Interacting With People Who are Blind or Have Low Vision

- Remember that the only difference between you and people who are blind or have low vision is that they are not able to see through their eyes what you are able to see through yours.
- Do not be uncomfortable when in the company of a person who is blind or has low vision. Talk with the person as you would talk with any other individual, honestly and without pity; do not be concerned about using words like "see" and "look." There is no need to raise your voice unless the person asks you to do so.
- Identify yourself as you approach the person and before you make physical contact. Tell the person your name and your role. If another person approaches, introduce him or her. When you leave the room, be sure to tell the person that you are leaving and if anyone else remains in the room.
- It is often appropriate to touch the person's hand or arm lightly to indicate that you are about to speak.
- When talking, face the person and speak directly to him or her using a normal tone of voice.
- Be specific when communicating direction. Mention a specific distance or use clock cues when possible (e.g., walk left about 2 yards; walk about 20 feet to the right; the telephone is at 2 o'clock). Avoid using phrases such as "over there."
- When you offer to assist someone, allow the person to hold onto your arm just above the elbow and to walk a half-step behind you.

- When offering the person a seat, place the person's hand on the back or the arm of the seat.
- When you are about to go up or down a flight of stairs, tell the person, and place his or her hand on the banister.
- Make sure that the environment is free of obstacles; close doors and cabinets so they are not in the path.
- Offer to read written information, such as a menu.
- If you serve food to the person, use clock cues to specify where everything is on the plate.
- When the person who is blind or who has low vision is a patient in a health care facility:
  - Make sure all objects the person will need are close at hand.
  - Identify the location of objects that the person may need (e.g., "The call light is near your right hand"; "The telephone is on the table on the left side of your bed.")
  - Remove obstacles that may be in the person's pathway and could cause a fall.
  - Place all assistive devices the person uses close at hand; let the person feel the devices so that he or she knows their location.
- Do not distract the service animal unless the owner has given permission.
- Ask the person, "How can I help you?" At some times, the person needs help, but at other times help may not be needed.

This material is adapted from and based in part on *Achieving Physical and Communication Accessibility,* a publication of the National Center for Access Unlimited; *Community Access Facts,* an Adaptive Environments Center publication; and *The Ten Commandments of Interacting with People with Mental Health Disabilities,* a publication of The Ability Center of Greater Toledo.

walking to a chair from a bed, require spatial concepts. A patient whose visual impairment results from a chronic progressive eye disorder, such as glaucoma, has better cognitive mapping skills than does the patient who becomes blind suddenly. Patients with progressive eye disorders develop the use of spatial and topographic concepts early and gradually; hence, remembering a room layout is easier for them. Patients who become blind suddenly have more difficulty in adjusting, and emotional and behavioral issues of coping with blindness may hinder their learning. These patients require intensive emotional and physical support.

In the hospital, the bedside table and the call button must always be within reach. The parts of the call button are explained, and the patient is taught to touch and press the buttons or dials until the activity is mastered. The patient must be familiarized with the location of the telephone, water pitcher, and other objects on the bedside table. The food tray's composition is likened to the face of a clock; for example, the main plate may be described as being at 12 o'clock or the coffee cup at 3 o'clock. All articles and furniture must remain in the same positions throughout the patient's hospitalization. Introduction of hospital personnel

should be made upon entering and departure from the patient's room.

The nurse should be aware of the importance of techniques in providing physical assistance, encouraging independence, and ensuring safety. Specific guidelines for interacting with the patient with vision loss are presented in Box 49-2. The readiness of the patient and his or her family to learn must be assessed before initiating orientation and mobility training.

Promoting Home and Community-Based Care

The nurse, social worker, family, and others collaborate to assess the patient's home condition and support system. If available, a low-vision specialist or occupational therapist should be consulted, particularly for patients for whom identifying and administering medications pose problems. Contact information for some private and nonprofit services are included in the Internet Resources for this chapter available at http://thepoint.lww.com/Pellico1e.

Other interventions that are appropriate for some people with low vision or blindness include Braille and guide dogs.

Guide dogs, also known as Seeing-Eye dogs, are dogs that are specially bred, raised, and rigorously trained to assist people who are blind. The guide dog is a constant companion to the person who is blind (also referred to as the animal's handler) and is allowed on airplanes and in restaurants, stores, hotels, and other public places. A guide dog in harness is a working dog and should not be approached without permission of the handler. With the assistance of the guide dog, the person who is blind can be extremely mobile and accomplish normal activities both within and outside of the home and workplace.

GLAUCOMA

Glaucoma is a group of ocular conditions characterized by optic nerve damage. The optic nerve damage is related to the intraocular pressure (IOP) caused by congestion of aqueous humor in the eye. A range of pressures have been considered "normal," but may be associated with vision loss in some patients. Glaucoma is one of the leading causes of irreversible blindness in the world and is the leading cause of blindness among adults in the United States. There is no cure for glaucoma; research is aimed at identifying risk factors and preventing vision loss and blindness.

Pathophysiology

Aqueous humor flows between the iris and the lens, nourishing the cornea and lens. Most (90%) of the fluid then flows out of the anterior chamber, draining through the spongy trabecular meshwork into the canal of Schlemm and the episcleral veins (Fig. 49-1). About 10% of the aqueous fluid exits through the ciliary body into the suprachoroidal space and then drains into the venous circulation of the ciliary body, choroid, and sclera. Unimpeded outflow of aqueous fluid depends on an intact drainage system and an open angle (about 45 degrees) between the iris and the cornea. A narrower angle places the iris closer to the trabecular meshwork, diminishing the angle. The amount of aqueous humor produced tends to decrease with age, in systemic diseases such as diabetes, and in ocular inflammatory conditions.

IOP is determined by the rate of aqueous production, the resistance encountered by the aqueous humor as it flows out of the passages, and the venous pressure of the episcleral veins that drain into the anterior ciliary vein. When aqueous fluid production and drainage are in balance, the IOP is between 10 and 21 mm Hg. When aqueous fluid is inhibited from flowing out, pressure builds up within the eye. Fluctuations in IOP occur with time of day, exertion, diet, and medications. IOP tends to increase with blinking, tight lid squeezing, and upward gazing. Systemic conditions, such as hypertension, and intraocular conditions, such as uveitis and retinal detachment, have been associated with elevated IOP.

There are two accepted theories regarding how increased IOP damages the optic nerve in glaucoma. The direct mechanical theory suggests that high IOP damages the retinal layer as it passes through the optic nerve head. The indirect ischemic theory suggests that high IOP compresses the microcirculation in the optic nerve head, resulting in cell injury and death. Some glaucomas appear as exclusively mechanical, and some are exclusively ischemic types. Typically, most cases are a combination of both. Regardless of the cause of damage, glaucomatous changes typically evolve through clearly discernible stages (Box 49-3).

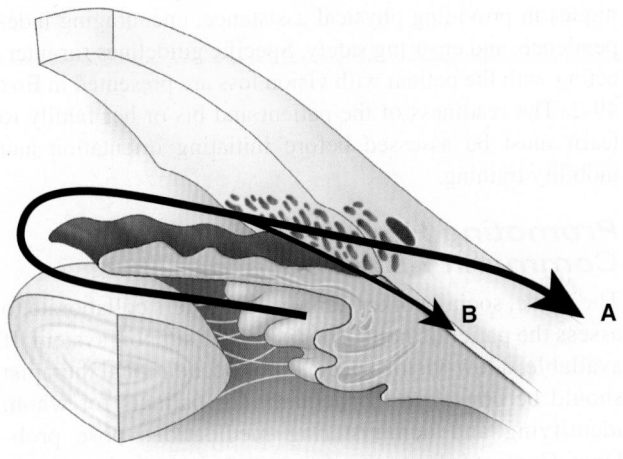

FIGURE 49-1 Normal outflow of aqueous humor. (A) Trabecular meshwork. (B) Uveoscleral route. From Kanski, J. J. (2007). *Clinical ophthalmology.* Oxford: Butterworth-Heinemann Ltd.

BOX 49-3 **Progression of Glaucoma**

1. **Initiating events**
   Precipitating factors include illness, emotional stress, congenital narrow angles, long-term use of corticosteroids, and use of mydriatics (i.e., medications causing pupillary dilation).

   ↓

2. **Structural alterations in the aqueous outflow system**
   Tissue and cellular changes caused by factors that affect aqueous humor dynamics lead to structural alterations.

   ↓

3. **Functional alterations**
   Conditions such as increased intraocular pressure or impaired blood flow create functional changes.

   ↓

4. **Optic nerve damage**
   Atrophy of the optic nerve is characterized by loss of nerve fibers and blood supply. This fourth stage inevitably progresses to the fifth stage.

   ↓

5. **Visual loss**
   Progressive loss of vision is characterized by visual field defects.

Classification of Glaucoma

There are several types of glaucoma. Although glaucoma classification is changing as knowledge increases, current clinical forms of glaucoma are identified as open-angle glaucoma, angle-closure glaucoma (also called pupillary block), congenital glaucoma, and glaucoma associated with other conditions, such as developmental anomalies or corticosteroid use. Glaucoma can be primary or secondary, depending on whether associated factors contribute to the rise in IOP. The two common clinical forms of glaucoma encountered in adults are open-angle and angle-closure glaucoma. These are differentiated by mechanisms that cause impaired aqueous outflow. Table 49-2 summarizes the characteristics of the different types of open-angle and angle-closure glaucoma.

Risk Factors

It is estimated that at least 2.2 million Americans have glaucoma, and an additional 2 million are unaware that they have it (NEI, 2008). Glaucoma is more prevalent among people older than 40 years of age, and the incidence increases with age. It is also more prevalent among men than women and in African American and Asian populations (Box 49-4).

Clinical Manifestations and Assessment

Glaucoma is often called the "silent thief of sight" because most patients are unaware that they have the disease until they have experienced visual changes and vision loss. The patient may not seek health care until he or she experiences

TABLE
49-2 Glaucoma Types, Clinical Manifestation, and Treatment

Types of Glaucoma	Clinical Manifestations	Treatment
Open-Angle Glaucoma Usually bilateral, but one eye may be more severely affected than the other. In all three types of open-angle glaucoma, the anterior chamber angle is open and appears normal.		
Chronic open-angle glaucoma (COAG)	Optic nerve damage, visual field defects, IOP >21 mm Hg May have fluctuating IOPs Usually no symptoms but possible ocular pain, headache, and halos	Decrease IOP 20% to 50%. Additional topical and oral agents added as necessary. If medical treatment is unsuccessful, laser trabeculoplasty (LT) can decrease intraocular pressure by 20%. Glaucoma filtering surgery if continued optic nerve damage despite medication therapy and LT.
Normal tension glaucoma	IOP ≤21 mm Hg; optic nerve damage, visual field defects	Treatment similar to COAG, however, the best management for normal tension glaucoma management is yet to be established. Goal is to lower the IOP by at least 30%.
Ocular hypertension	Elevated IOP Possible ocular pain or headache	Decrease IOP by at least 20%
Angle-Closure (Pupillary Block) Glaucoma Obstruction in aqueous humor outflow due to the complete or partial closure of the angle from the forward shift of the peripheral iris to the trabecula. The obstruction results in an increased IOP.		
Acute angle-closure glaucoma (AACG)	Rapidly progressive visual impairment, periocular pain, conjunctival hyperemia, and congestion Pain may be associated with nausea, vomiting, bradycardia, and profuse sweating. Reduced central visual acuity, severely elevated IOP, corneal edema Pupil is vertically oval, fixed in a semi-dilated position, and unreactive to light and accommodation	Ocular emergency, requiring administration of hyperosmotics, acetazolamide, and topical ocular hypotensive agents, such as pilocarpine and beta blockers (betaxolol). Possible laser incision in the iris (iridotomy) to release blocked aqueous and reduce IOP Other eye is also treated with pilocarpine eye drops and/or surgical management to avoid a similar spontaneous attack.
Subacute angle-closure glaucoma	Transient blurring of vision, halos around lights; temporal headaches and/or ocular pain; pupil may be semi-dilated	Prophylactic peripheral laser iridotomy Can lead to acute or chronic angle-closure glaucoma if untreated
Chronic angle-closure glaucoma	Progression of glaucomatous cupping and significant visual field loss; IOP may be normal or elevated; ocular pain and headache	Management is similar to that for COAG: includes laser iridotomy and medications.

Risk Factors for Glaucoma

- Family history of glaucoma
- African American race
- Older age (>60)
- Diabetes mellitus
- Cardiovascular disease
- Migraine syndromes
- Nearsightedness (myopia)
- Eye trauma
- Prolonged use of topical or systemic corticosteroids

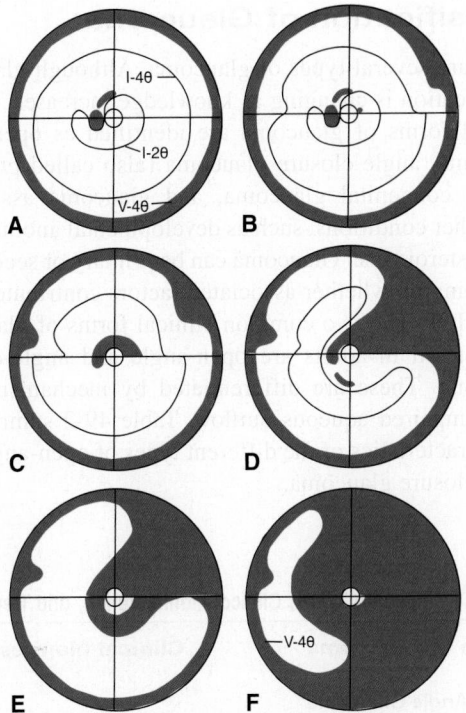

FIGURE 49-2 Progression of glaucomatous visual field defects. A central scotoma at 10 to 20 degrees of fixation near the blind spot is the initial significant finding (**A, B**). As the glaucoma progresses, the scotomas enlarge and deepen, resulting in peripheral vision loss. (**C**) Defect within 5 degrees of fixation point nasally. (**D**) Peripheral involvement enlarges. (**E**) Ringlike scotoma. (**F**) Eventually, vision is lost. The resulting "island of vision" becomes the characteristic visual field appearance of glaucoma and correlates with the "tunnel vision," in which peripheral vision is lost. From Kanski, J. J. (2007). *Clinical ophthalmology*. Oxford: Butterworth-Heinemann Ltd.

blurred vision or "halos" around lights, difficulty focusing, difficulty adjusting eyes in low lighting, loss of peripheral vision, aching or discomfort around the eyes, and headache.

The purpose of a glaucoma workup is to establish the diagnostic category, assess the optic nerve damage, and formulate a treatment plan. The patient's ocular and medical history must be detailed to investigate the history of predisposing factors. Four major types of examinations are used in glaucoma evaluation, diagnosis, and management: tonometry to measure the IOP, ophthalmoscopy to inspect the optic nerve, gonioscopy to examine the filtration angle of the anterior chamber, and perimetry to assess the visual fields.

The changes in the optic nerve related to glaucoma are pallor and cupping of the optic nerve disc. The pallor of the optic nerve is caused by a lack of blood supply that results from cellular destruction. Cupping is characterized by exaggerated bending of the blood vessels as they cross the optic disc, resulting in an enlarged optic cup that appears more basin-like compared with a normal cup. The progression of cupping in glaucoma is caused by the gradual loss of retinal nerve fibers accompanied by the loss of blood supply, resulting in increased pallor of the optic disc.

As the optic nerve damage increases, visual perception in the area is lost. The localized areas of visual loss (i.e., **scotomas**) represent loss of retinal sensitivity and are measured and mapped by perimetry. In patients with glaucoma, there is a distinct pattern that differs from other ocular diseases and is useful in establishing its diagnosis. Figure 49-2 shows the progression of visual field defects caused by glaucoma.

Medical Management

The aim of all glaucoma treatment is prevention of optic nerve damage. Life-long therapy is almost always necessary because glaucoma cannot be cured. Treatment focuses on pharmacologic therapy, laser procedures, surgery, or a combination of these approaches, all of which have potential complications and side effects. The object is to achieve the greatest benefit at the least risk, cost, and inconvenience to the patient. Although treatment cannot reverse optic nerve damage, further damage can be controlled. The goal is to maintain an IOP within a range unlikely to cause further damage.

The initial target for IOP among patients with elevated IOP and those with low-tension glaucoma with progressive visual field loss is typically set at 30% lower than the current pressure. The patient is monitored for changes in the appearance of the optic nerve. If there is evidence of progressive damage, the target IOP is again lowered until the optic nerve shows stability.

Medical management of glaucoma relies on systemic and topical ocular medications that lower IOP. Periodic follow-up examinations are essential to monitor IOP, the appearance of the optic nerve, the visual fields, and side effects of medications. Therapy takes into account the patient's health and stage of glaucoma. Comfort, affordability, convenience, lifestyle, and personality are factors to consider in the patient's adherence to the medical regimen.

The patient is usually started on the lowest dose of topical medication and then advanced to increased concentrations until the desired IOP level is reached and maintained. Because of their efficacy, minimal dosing (can be used once each day), and low cost, beta blockers are the preferred initial topical medications. Beta blockers decrease the production of aqueous humor with resultant decrease in IOP. One eye

is treated first, with the other eye used as a control in determining the efficacy of the medication; once efficacy has been established, treatment of the other eye is started. If the IOP is elevated in both eyes, both are treated. When results are not satisfactory, a new medication is substituted. The main markers of the efficacy of the medication in glaucoma control are lowering of the IOP to the target pressure, appearance of the optic nerve head, and less visual field deterioration.

Surgical management for glaucoma includes several procedures. In laser trabeculoplasty, burns are applied to the inner surface of the trabecular meshwork to open the intratrabecular spaces and widen the canal of Schlemm, thereby promoting outflow of aqueous humor and decreasing IOP. Laser iridotomy, used for pupillary block glaucoma, is an opening made in the iris to eliminate the pupillary block. Laser iridotomy is contraindicated in patients with corneal edema, which interferes with laser targeting and strength.

Filtering procedures for chronic glaucoma are used to create an opening or fistula in the trabecular meshwork to drain aqueous humor from the anterior chamber to the subconjunctival space into a bleb, thereby bypassing the usual drainage structures. This allows the aqueous humor to flow and exit by different routes (i.e., absorption by the conjunctival vessels or mixing with tears). Trabeculectomy is the standard filtering technique used to remove part of the trabecular meshwork. Complications include hemorrhage, an extremely low (hypotony) or elevated IOP, uveitis, cataracts, bleb failure, bleb leak, and endophthalmitis. Unlike other surgical procedures, the filtering procedure's goal in glaucoma treatment is to achieve incomplete healing of the surgical wound.

Nursing Management

Teaching Patients Self-Care

The medical and surgical management of glaucoma slows the progression of glaucoma but does not cure it. The life-long therapeutic regimen mandates patient education. The nature of the disease and the importance of strict adherence to the medication regimen must be included in a teaching plan to help ensure compliance. A thorough patient interview is essential to determine systemic conditions, current systemic and ocular medications, family history, and problems with compliance to glaucoma medications. The effects of glaucoma-control medications on vision must also be explained. **Miotics** and sympathomimetics decrease the size of the pupil, facilitating the outflow of aqueous humor and decreasing the IOP, but they may also result in altered focus; therefore, patients need to be cautious in navigating their surroundings.

Nurses in all settings encounter patients with glaucoma. Even patients with longstanding disease and those with glaucoma as a secondary diagnosis should be assessed for knowledge level and compliance with the therapeutic regimen. Box 49-5 contains points to review with patients with glaucoma.

BOX 49-5

Patient Education

Managing Glaucoma

- Know your intraocular pressure (IOP) measurement and the desired range.
- Be informed about the extent of your vision loss and optic nerve damage.
- Keep a record of your eye pressure measurements and visual field test results to monitor your own progress.
- Review all your medications (including over-the-counter and herbal medications) with your ophthalmologist, and mention any side effects each time you visit.
- Ask about potential side effects and drug interactions of your eye medications.
- Ask whether generic or less costly forms of your eye medications are available.
- Review the dosing schedule with your ophthalmologist and inform him or her if you have trouble following the schedule.
- Participate in the decision-making process. Let your provider know what dosing schedule works for you and other preferences regarding your eye care.
- Have the nurse observe you instilling eye medication to determine whether you are administering it properly.
- Be aware that glaucoma medications can cause adverse effects if used inappropriately. Eye drops are to be administered as prescribed, not when eyes feel irritated.
- Ask your ophthalmologist to send a report to your provider after each appointment.
- Keep all follow-up appointments.

Continuing Care

For the patient with severe glaucoma and impaired function, referral to services that assist the patient in performing ADLs may be needed. The loss of peripheral vision can impact mobility, and patients may benefit from low vision and rehabilitation services. Patients who meet the criteria for legal blindness should be offered referrals to agencies that can assist them in obtaining federal assistance.

Reassurance and emotional support are important aspects of care. A life-long disease involving possible loss of sight has psychological, physical, social, and vocational ramifications. The family must be integrated into the plan of care, and because the disease has a familial tendency, family members should be encouraged to undergo examinations at least once every 2 years to detect glaucoma early.

CATARACTS

A cataract is a lens opacity or cloudiness (Fig. 49-3). Cataracts rank behind only arthritis and heart disease as a leading

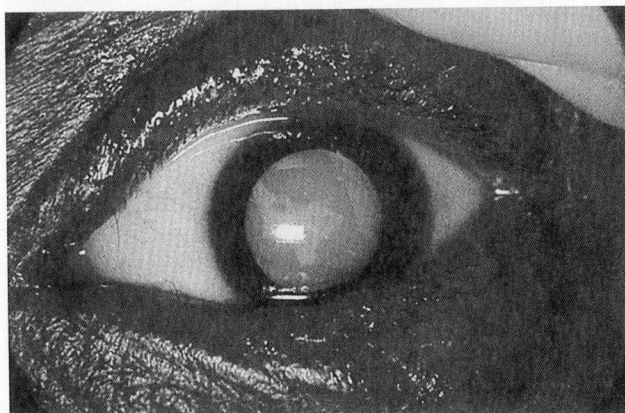

FIGURE 49-3 A cataract is a cloudy or opaque lens. On visual inspection, the lens appears gray or milky. From Rubin, E., & Strayer, D.S. (Eds.) (2008). *Rubin's pathology* (5th ed.). Philadelphia: Lippincott Williams & Wilkins.

cause of disability in older adults. Cataracts affect nearly 20.5 million Americans who are 40 years of age or older or about one in every six people in this age range. By 80 years of age, over half of all Americans have cataracts or have had cataract surgery (NEI, 2008).

Pathophysiology

Cataracts can develop in one or both eyes at any age for a variety of causes (Box 49-6). Visual impairment normally progresses at the same rate in both eyes over many years or in a matter of months. The three most common types of senile (age-related) cataracts are defined by their location in the lens: nuclear, cortical, and posterior subcapsular. The extent of visual impairment depends on their size, density, and location in the lens. More than one type can be present in one eye.

A nuclear cataract is caused by central opacity in the lens and has a substantial genetic component. It is associated with myopia (i.e., nearsightedness), which worsens when the cataract progresses. If dense, the cataract severely blurs vision. Periodic changes in prescription eyeglasses help manage this condition.

A cortical cataract involves the anterior, posterior, or equatorial cortex of the lens. A cataract in the equator or periphery of the cortex does not interfere with the passage of light through the center of the lens and has little effect on vision. Cortical cataracts progress at a highly variable rate. Vision is worse in very bright light.

Posterior subcapsular cataracts occur in front of the posterior capsule. This type typically develops in younger people and, in some cases, is associated with prolonged corticosteroid use, diabetes, or ocular trauma. Near vision is diminished, and the eye is increasingly sensitive to glare from bright light (e.g., sunlight, headlights).

Clinical Manifestations and Assessment

Painless, blurry vision is characteristic of cataracts. The person perceives that surroundings are dimmer, as if his or her glasses need cleaning. Light scattering is common, and the person experiences reduced contrast sensitivity, sensitivity to glare, and reduced visual acuity. Other effects include myopic shift, astigmatism, monocular **diplopia** (double vision), color shift (the aging lens becomes progressively more absorbent at

---

BOX 49-6 Risk Factors for Cataract Formation

Aging:
- Loss of lens transparency
- Clumping or aggregation of lens protein (which leads to light scattering)
- Accumulation of a yellow-brown pigment due to the breakdown of lens protein
- Decreased oxygen uptake
- Increase in sodium and calcium
- Decrease in levels of vitamin C, protein, and glutathione (an antioxidant)

Associated ocular conditions:
- Retinitis pigmentosa
- Myopia
- Retinal detachment and retinal surgery
- Infection (e.g., herpes zoster, uveitis)

Toxic factors:
- Corticosteroids, especially at high doses and in long-term use
- Alkaline chemical eye burns, poisoning
- Cigarette smoking
- Calcium, copper, iron, gold, silver, and mercury, which tend to deposit in the pupillary area of the lens

Nutritional factors:
- Reduced levels of antioxidants
- Poor nutrition
- Obesity

Physical factors:
- Dehydration associated with chronic diarrhea, use of purgatives in anorexia nervosa, and use of hyperbaric oxygenation
- Blunt trauma, perforation of the lens with a sharp object or foreign body, electric shock
- Ultraviolet radiation in sunlight and X-ray

Systemic diseases and syndromes:
- Diabetes mellitus
- Down's syndrome
- Disorders related to lipid metabolism
- Renal disorders
- Musculoskeletal disorders

the blue end of the spectrum), brunescens (color values shift to yellow-brown), and reduced light transmission.

Decreased visual acuity is directly proportionate to cataract density. The Snellen visual acuity test, ophthalmoscopy, and slit-lamp biomicroscopic examination are used to establish the degree of cataract formation. The degree of lens opacity does not always correlate with the patient's functional status. Some patients can perform normal activities despite clinically significant cataracts. Others with less lens opacification have a disproportionate decrease in visual acuity; hence, visual acuity is an imperfect measure of visual impairment.

Medical Management

Nonsurgical Management

Nonsurgical (medications, eyedrops, eyeglasses) treatment has not been found as curative for people with cataracts nor does it prevent age-related cataracts. Cigarette smoking, long-term use of corticosteroids, especially at high doses, sunlight and ionizing radiation, diabetes, obesity, and eye injuries can increase the risk for cataracts. In the early stages of cataract development, glasses, contact lenses, strong bifocals, or magnifying lenses may improve vision.

Surgical Management

Surgical management of cataracts is considered when reduced vision interferes with normal activities. In deciding when cataract surgery is to be performed, the patient's functional and visual status should be a primary consideration. Surgery is performed on an outpatient basis and usually takes less than 1 hour. Although complications from cataract surgery are uncommon, they can have significant effects on vision. Restoration of visual function through a safe and minimally invasive procedure is the surgical goal.

When both eyes have cataracts, one eye is treated first, with at least several weeks, preferably months, separating the two procedures. Because cataract surgery is performed to improve visual functioning, the delay for the other eye gives time for the patient and the surgeon to evaluate whether the results from the first surgery are adequate to preclude the need for a second operation.

Intracapsular Cataract Extraction

In intracapsular cataract extraction, the entire lens (i.e., nucleus, cortex, and capsule) is removed and fine sutures are used to close the incision. From the late 1800s until the 1970s, it was the technique of choice for cataract extraction. It is infrequently performed today but is still indicated when there is a need to remove the entire lens, such as with a subluxated cataract (i.e., partially or completely dislocated lens).

Extracapsular Cataract Extraction

The extracapsular cataract extraction technique involves smaller incisional wounds (less trauma to the eye) and

maintains the posterior capsule of the lens, thus reducing postoperative complications, particularly aphakic retinal detachment and cystoid macular edema. A portion of the anterior capsule is removed, allowing extraction of the lens nucleus and cortex. The posterior capsule and zonular support are left intact. An intact zonular–capsular diaphragm provides the needed safe anchor for the posterior chamber intraocular lens (IOL). After the pupil has been dilated and the surgeon has made a small incision on the upper edge of the cornea, a viscoelastic substance (clear gel) is injected into the space between the cornea and the lens. This prevents the space from collapsing and facilitates insertion of the IOL.

Phacoemulsification

This method of extracapsular surgery uses an ultrasonic device that liquefies the nucleus and cortex, which are then suctioned out through a tube. The posterior capsule is left intact. Because the incision is even smaller than the standard extracapsular cataract extraction, the wound heals more rapidly, and there is early stabilization of refractive error and less astigmatism. Hardware and software advances in ultrasonic technology—including new phaco needles that are used to cut and aspirate the cataract—permit safe and efficient removal of nearly all cataracts through a clear cornea incision. With increasing frequency, self-sealing (sutureless) clear corneal incisions (temporal part of the cornea) are performed with phacoemulsification, minimizing postoperative astigmatism and thus decreasing bleeding and subconjunctival hemorrhage and speeding recovery of visual acuity.

Lens Replacement

After removal of the crystalline lens, the patient is considered to have aphakia (i.e., without a lens). The lens, which focuses light on the retina, must be replaced for the patient to see clearly. There are three lens replacement options: aphakic eyeglasses, contact lenses, and intraocular lens (IOL) implants.

Aphakic glasses, although effective, are rarely used. Objects are magnified by 25%, making them appear closer than they actually are. This magnification creates distortion. Peripheral vision is also limited, and binocular vision (i.e., ability of both eyes to focus on one object and fuse the two images into one) is impossible if the other eye is phakic (normal).

Contact lenses provide patients with almost normal vision, but because contact lenses need to be removed occasionally, the patient also needs a pair of aphakic glasses. Contact lenses are not advised for patients who have difficulty inserting, removing, and cleaning them. Frequent handling and improper disinfection increase the risk for infection.

Insertion of IOLs during cataract surgery is the usual approach to lens replacement. After cataract extraction, or phacoemulsification, the surgeon implants an IOL. Extracapsular cataract extraction and posterior chamber IOLs are associated with a relatively low incidence of complications (e.g., **hyphema** [bleeding into the anterior chamber of the

eye], macular edema, secondary glaucoma, damage to the corneal endothelium). IOL implantation is contraindicated in patients with recurrent uveitis, proliferative diabetic retinopathy, neovascular glaucoma, or rubeosis iridis.

The most common IOL is the single-focus lens. Eyeglasses are still needed for distant or close vision, because the single-focus lens, unlike the natural lens of the eye, cannot alter its shape to bring objects at different distances into focus. Multifocal IOLs reduce the need for eyeglasses but patients can experience halos and glare. In the future, aging patients may benefit from a combined surgical approach using customized IOLs and refractive surgery for a customized vision correction.

Toxic Anterior Segment Syndrome

Also known as toxic endothelial cell destruction or sterile endophthalmitis, toxic anterior segment syndrome is a noninfectious inflammation caused by a toxic agent after an uncomplicated and uneventful surgery. This disorder is a complication of anterior chamber surgery. Investigations have shown that it may be caused by toxins, and it requires careful attention to solutions, medications, and ophthalmic devices, and to cleaning and sterilization of surgical equipment (Mamalis, Edelhauser, Dawson et al., 2006).

Toxic anterior segment syndrome is characterized by corneal edema less than 24 hours after surgery and an accumulation of white cells in the anterior chamber of the eye. Like the classic endophthalmitis, the symptoms include reduction in visual acuity and pain. In the absence of microorganism growth, improvement has occurred with topical steroid treatment alone.

Nursing Management

The patient with cataracts should receive the usual preoperative care for ambulatory surgical patients undergoing eye surgery.

Providing Preoperative Care

It has been common practice to withhold any anticoagulant therapy (e.g., aspirin, warfarin [Coumadin]) to reduce the risk for retrobulbar hemorrhage (after retrobulbar injection) for 5 to 7 days before surgery. Dilating drops are administered every 10 minutes for four doses at least 1 hour before surgery. Additional dilating drops may be administered in the operating room (immediately before surgery) if the affected eye is not fully dilated. Antibiotic, corticosteroid, and anti-inflammatory drops may be administered prophylactically to prevent postoperative infection and inflammation.

Providing Postoperative Care

After recovery from anesthesia, the patient receives verbal and written instructions about how to protect the eye, administer medications, recognize signs of complications, and obtain emergency care. Box 49-7 identifies activities to be avoided. The nurse also explains that there should be minimal

BOX 49-7 | **Patient Education**

Intraocular Lens Implant

- Wear glasses or metal eye shield at all times following surgery, as instructed by the provider.
- Always wash hands before touching or cleaning the postoperative eye.
- Clean postoperative eye with a clean tissue; wipe the closed eye with a single gesture from the inner canthus outward.
- Bathe or shower; shampoo hair cautiously or seek assistance.
- Avoid lying on the side of the affected eye the night after surgery.
- Keep activity light (e.g., walking, reading, watching television). Resume the following activities only as directed by the surgeon: driving, sexual activity, unusually strenuous activity.
- Remember not to lift, push, or pull objects heavier than 15 lb.
- Avoid bending or stooping for an extended period.
- Be careful when climbing or descending stairs.
- Know when to contact the surgeon.*

*Contact the surgeon immediately if any of the following problems occur before the next appointment: (1) vision changes; (2) continuous flashing lights appear to the affected eye; (3) redness, swelling, or pain increase in the eye; (4) the amount or type of eye drainage changes; (5) the eye is injured in any way; (6) significant pain is not relieved by acetaminophen.

discomfort after surgery and instructs the patient to take a mild analgesic agent, such as acetaminophen, as needed. Antibiotic, anti-inflammatory, and corticosteroid eye drops or ointments are prescribed postoperatively.

Teaching Patients Self-Care

To prevent accidental rubbing or poking of the eye, the patient wears a protective eye patch for 24 hours after surgery, followed by eyeglasses worn during the day and a metal shield worn at night for 1 to 4 weeks. The nurse instructs the patient and family in applying and caring for the eye shield. Sunglasses should be worn while outdoors during the day because the eye is sensitive to light.

Slight morning discharge, some redness, and a scratchy feeling may be expected for a few days. A clean, damp washcloth may be used to remove slight morning eye discharge. Because cataract surgery increases the risk for retinal detachment, the patient must know to notify the surgeon if new floaters (dots) in vision, flashing lights, decrease in vision, pain, or increase in redness occurs.

Continuing Care

The eye patch is removed after the first follow-up appointment. The patient may experience blurring of vision for several days to weeks. Sutures, if used, are left in the eye but alter the curvature of the cornea, resulting in temporary blurring

and some astigmatism. Vision gradually improves as the eye heals. Patients with IOL implants have functional vision on the first day after surgery. Vision is stabilized when the eye is completely healed, usually within 6 to 12 weeks, when final corrective prescription is completed. Visual correction is needed for any remaining nearsightedness or farsightedness (even in patients with IOL implants).

RETINAL DISORDERS

Although the retina is composed of multiple microscopic layers, the two innermost layers, the sensory retina and the retinal pigment epithelium (RPE), are the most relevant to common retinal disorders. As the film in a camera captures an image, the retina, the neural tissue of the eye, performs the same function. The rods and cones, the photoreceptor cells, are found in the sensory layer of the retina. Beneath the sensory layer lies the RPE, the pigmented layer. When the rods and cones are stimulated by light, an electrical impulse is generated, and the image is transmitted to the brain.

RETINAL DETACHMENT

Retinal detachment refers to the separation of the RPE from the sensory layer. The four types of retinal detachment are rhegmatogenous, traction, a combination of rhegmatogenous and traction, and exudative. Rhegmatogenous detachment is the most common form. In this condition, a hole or tear develops in the sensory retina, allowing some of the liquid vitreous to seep through the sensory retina and detach it from the RPE (Fig. 49-4). People at risk for this type of detachment include those with high myopia or aphakia (absence of lens) after cataract surgery. Trauma may also play a role in rhegmatogenous retinal detachment. Between 5% and 10%

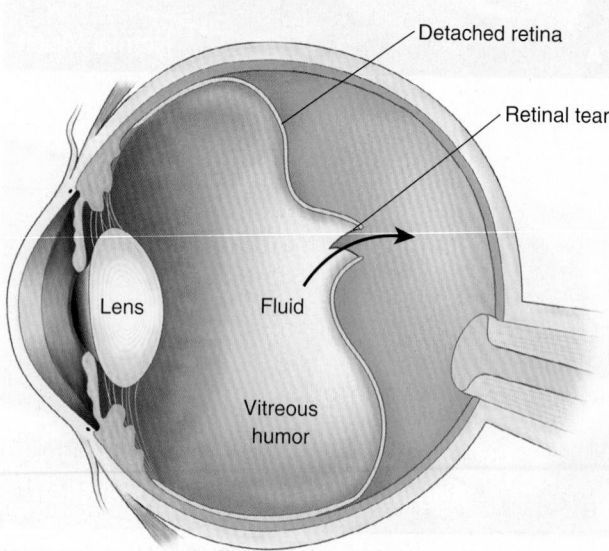

FIGURE 49-4 Rhegmatogenous detachment: the most common form of retinal detachment.

of all rhegmatogenous retinal detachments are associated with proliferative retinopathy, a retinopathy associated with diabetic neovascularization (see Chapter 30).

Tension, or a pulling force, is responsible for traction retinal detachment. An ophthalmologist must ascertain all of the areas of retinal break and identify and release the scars or bands of fibrous material providing traction on the retina. Generally, patients with this condition have developed fibrous scar tissue from conditions such as diabetic retinopathy, vitreous hemorrhage, or the retinopathy of prematurity. The hemorrhages and fibrous proliferation associated with these conditions exert a pulling force on the delicate retina.

Patients can have both rhegmatogenous and traction retinal detachment. Exudative retinal detachments are the result of the production of a serous fluid under the retina from the choroid. Conditions such as uveitis and macular degeneration may cause the production of this serous fluid.

Clinical Manifestations and Assessment

Patients may report the sensation of a shade or curtain coming across the vision of one eye, cobwebs, bright flashing lights, or the sudden onset of a great number of floaters. Patients do not complain of pain.

After visual acuity is determined, the patient must have a dilated **fundus** examination using an indirect ophthalmoscope as well as slit-lamp biomicroscopy. Stereo fundus photography and fluorescein angiography are commonly used during the evaluation.

Increasingly, optical coherence tomography and ultrasound are used for the complete retinal assessment, especially if the view is obscured by a dense cataract or vitreal hemorrhage. All retinal breaks, all fibrous bands that may be causing traction on the retina, and all degenerative changes must be identified.

Medical Management

In rhegmatogenous detachment, an attempt is made to surgically reattach the sensory retina to the RPE. In traction detachment, the source of traction must be removed and the sensory retina reattached. New surgical techniques, as well as advances in instrumentation, have led to an increased rate of success of surgical reattachment and better visual outcomes. The most commonly used surgical interventions are the scleral buckle, the pars plana vitrectomy, and pneumatic retinopexy. The scleral buckle is a procedure in which a piece of silicone plastic or sponge is sewn onto the sclera at the site of the retinal tear. The buckle holds the retina against the sclera until scarring seals the tear (Fig. 49-5).

Nursing Management

For the most part, nursing interventions consist of educating the patient and providing supportive care.

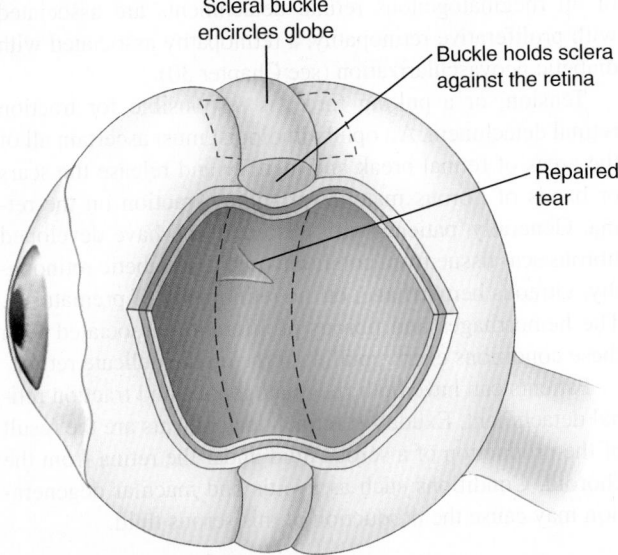

FIGURE 49-5 Scleral buckle.

Promoting Comfort

Following surgery, patients will require assistance with meals and walking. While some procedures require a hospital stay, many scleral buckling procedures are performed on an outpatient basis. The nurse should advise patients to avoid heavy lifting or strenuous activity that could increase intraocular pressure. Reading may be restricted until the surgeon gives permission. Patients wear sunglasses during the day and an eye patch at night. Patients often report pain, erythema, and a scratchy sensation after surgery. Ice packs may be applied to counter any edema associated with the conjunctiva. If a vitrectomy was performed with scleral buckling, patients are required to sleep with their heads elevated. Air travel must be avoided until the gas bubble, injected during surgery into the vitreous cavity to position the retina, is absorbed. Driving may be restricted until vision stabilizes.

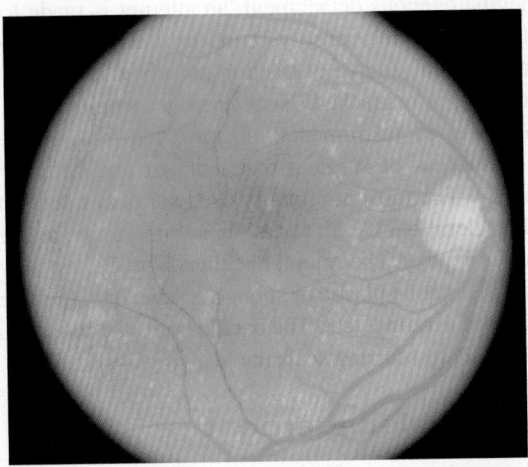

FIGURE 49-6 Retina showing drusen and age-related macular degeneration (AMD).

Reevaluation of vision and the need for corrective lenses is performed 6 to 8 weeks postoperatively.

Teaching About Complications

Postoperative complications may include increased IOP, endophthalmitis (inflammation of the internal layer of the eye), development of other retinal detachments, development of cataracts, and loss of turgor of the eye. Patients must be taught the signs and symptoms of complications, particularly of increasing IOP and postoperative infection such as eye pain, sudden change in vision, fever, lid swelling, or conjunctival and/or corneal injection (redness). Excessive pain, swelling, and bleeding must be immediately reported to the surgeon.

MACULAR DEGENERATION

Macular degeneration is the leading cause of severe, irreversible vision loss in people over age 50, affecting an estimated 8.7% of the world population. The prevalence is likely to double as the population ages (Vision 2020, 2009). Commonly called age-related macular degeneration (AMD), it is characterized by tiny, yellowish spots called drusen (Fig. 49-6)

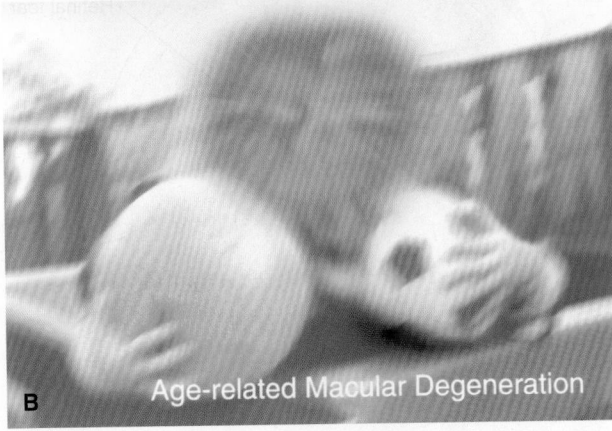

FIGURE 49-7 (A) Normal vision. (B) Visual loss associated with macular degeneration. Photos courtesy of the National Eye Institute/National Institutes of Health.

beneath the retina. Most people older than 60 years of age have at least a few small drusen. There is a wide range of visual loss in patients with macular degeneration, but most patients do not experience total blindness. Central vision is generally the most affected, with most patients retaining peripheral vision (Fig. 49-7). There are two types of AMD, commonly known as the dry type and wet type.

Pathophysiology

Between 85% and 90% of people with AMD have the dry or nonexudative type, which has an insidious onset and leads to a mild to moderate loss of vision, although peripheral vision is preserved (Seewoodhary & Watkinson, 2009). In dry AMD, the outer layers of the retina slowly break down (Fig. 49-8). With this breakdown comes the appearance of drusen. When the drusen occur outside of the macular area, patients generally have no symptoms. When the drusen occur within the macula, however, there is a gradual blurring of vision

that patients may notice when they try to read. There is no known treatment that can cure this type of AMD.

Wet or exudative AMD is characterized by **choroidal neovascularization** (CNV), new growth of blood vessels beneath the retina, which causes severe vision loss in 90% of AMD cases (Chappelow & Kaiser, 2008). Wet AMD may have an abrupt onset. The affected vessels can leak fluid and blood, elevating the retina. Patients report that straight lines appear crooked and distorted, or that letters in words appear broken. Some patients can be treated with the argon laser to stop the leakage from these vessels. However, this treatment is not ideal because vision may be affected by the laser treatment and abnormal vessels often grow back after treatment.

Medical Management

Visual loss from choroidal neovascularization lesions in AMD is a growing problem. With the growth of these new vessels from the choriocapillary layer, fibrous tissue develops that

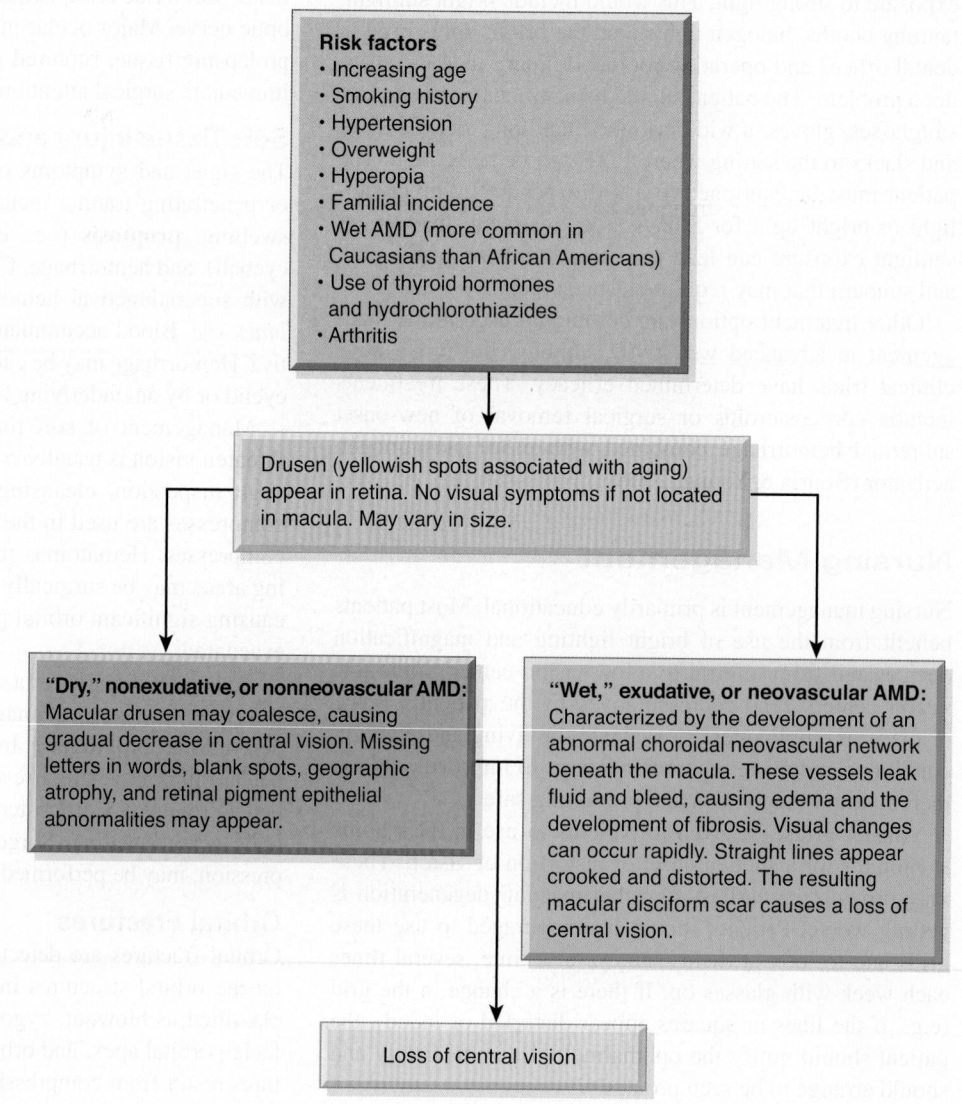

Risk factors
- Increasing age
- Smoking history
- Hypertension
- Overweight
- Hyperopia
- Familial incidence
- Wet AMD (more common in Caucasians than African Americans)
- Use of thyroid hormones and hydrochlorothiazides
- Arthritis

Drusen (yellowish spots associated with aging) appear in retina. No visual symptoms if not located in macula. May vary in size.

"Dry," nonexudative, or nonneovascular AMD: Macular drusen may coalesce, causing gradual decrease in central vision. Missing letters in words, blank spots, geographic atrophy, and retinal pigment epithelial abnormalities may appear.

"Wet," exudative, or neovascular AMD: Characterized by the development of an abnormal choroidal neovascular network beneath the macula. These vessels leak fluid and bleed, causing edema and the development of fibrosis. Visual changes can occur rapidly. Straight lines appear crooked and distorted. The resulting macular disciform scar causes a loss of central vision.

Loss of central vision

FIGURE 49-8 Progression of age-related macular degeneration (AMD): pathways to vision loss.

can, over months, destroy central vision. Laser treatment has been used to close these abnormal vessels, but the very process of photocoagulation carries with it some level of retinal destruction, albeit less than the natural scarring that would occur in the untreated eye.

Photodynamic therapy (PDT) has been developed in an attempt to ameliorate the choroidal neovascularization while causing minimal damage to the retina. Studies have shown that PDT can reduce the risk of visual loss for certain groups of patients who have classic subfoveal choroidal neovascularization due to macular degeneration. PDT is a two-step process. Verteporfin, a photosensitive dye, is infused IV over 10 minutes. Fifteen minutes after the start of the infusion, a diode laser is used to treat the abnormal network of vessels. The dye within the vessels takes up the energy of the diode laser but the surrounding retina does not, thus avoiding damage to adjacent areas. Multiple treatments may be necessary over time.

Verteporfin is a light-activated dye, so patient education is important preoperatively. The dye within the blood vessels near the surface of the skin could become activated with exposure to strong light. This would include bright sunlight, tanning booths, halogen lights, and the bright lights used in dental offices and operating rooms; ordinary indoor light is not a problem. The patient should be instructed to bring dark sunglasses, gloves, a wide-brimmed hat, long-sleeved shirt, and slacks to the setting where PDT will be performed. The patient must be cautioned to avoid exposure to direct sunlight or bright light for 5 days after treatment. Inadvertent sunlight exposure can lead to severe blistering of the skin and sunburn that may require plastic surgery.

Other treatment options are commonly used in the management in advanced wet AMD, although no prospective clinical trials have determined efficacy. These treatments include corticosteroids or surgical removal of new-onset subretinal hemorrhage combined with tissue plasminogen activator (Bourla & Young, 2006).

Nursing Management

Nursing management is primarily educational. Most patients benefit from the use of bright lighting and magnification devices and from referral to a low vision center. Some low vision centers send representatives to the patient's home or place of employment to evaluate the living and working conditions and make recommendations to improve lighting, thereby improving vision and promoting safety.

Amsler grids are given to patients to use in their home to monitor for a sudden onset or distortion of vision. These may provide the earliest sign that macular degeneration is getting worse. Patients should be encouraged to use these grids and to look at them, one eye at a time, several times each week with glasses on. If there is a change in the grid (e.g., if the lines or squares appear distorted or faded), the patient should notify the ophthalmologist immediately and should arrange to be seen promptly.

ORBITAL AND OCULAR TRAUMA

Whether affecting the eye or the orbit, trauma to the eye and surrounding structures may have devastating consequences for vision. It is preferable to prevent injury rather than treat it. Box 49-8 details safety measures to prevent orbital and ocular trauma.

Types of Trauma

Orbital Trauma

Injury to the orbit is usually associated with a head injury; hence, the patient's general medical condition must first be stabilized before conducting an ocular examination. Only then is the globe assessed for soft tissue injury. During inspection, the face is meticulously assessed for underlying fractures, which should always be suspected in cases of blunt trauma. To establish the extent of ocular injury, visual acuity is assessed as soon as possible, even if it is only a rough estimate. Soft tissue orbital injuries often result in damage to the optic nerve. Major ocular injuries indicated by a soft globe, prolapsing tissue, ruptured globe, and hemorrhage, require immediate surgical attention.

Soft Tissue Injury and Hemorrhage

The signs and symptoms of soft tissue injury from blunt or penetrating trauma include tenderness, ecchymosis, lid swelling, **proptosis** (i.e., downward displacement of the eyeball), and hemorrhage. Closed injuries lead to contusions with subconjunctival hemorrhage, commonly known as a *black eye*. Blood accumulates in the tissues of the conjunctiva. Hemorrhage may be caused by a soft tissue injury to the eyelid or by an underlying fracture.

Management of soft tissue hemorrhage that does not threaten vision is usually conservative and consists of thorough inspection, cleansing, and repair of wounds. Cold compresses are used in the early phase, followed by warm compresses. Hematomas that appear as swollen, fluctuating areas may be surgically drained or aspirated; if they are causing significant orbital pressure, they may be surgically evacuated.

Penetrating injuries or a severe blow to the head can result in severe optic nerve damage. Visual loss can be sudden or delayed and progressive. Immediate loss of vision after an ocular injury is usually irreversible. Delayed visual loss has a better prognosis. Corticosteroid therapy is indicated to reduce optic nerve swelling. Surgery, such as optic nerve decompression, may be performed.

Orbital Fractures

Orbital fractures are detected by facial X-rays. Depending on the orbital structures involved, orbital fractures can be classified as blowout, zygomatic or tripod, maxillary, midfacial, orbital apex, and orbital roof fractures. Blowout fractures result from compression of soft tissue and the sudden

BOX 49-8

Health Promotion

Preventing Eye Injuries

In and Around the House

Advise patients to:
- Make sure that all spray nozzles are directed away from themselves before pressing down on the handle.
- Read instructions carefully before using cleaning fluids, detergents, ammonia, or harsh chemicals, and to wash hands thoroughly after use.
- Use grease shields on frying pans to decrease spattering.
- Wear special goggles to shield their eyes from fumes and splashes when using powerful chemicals.
- Use opaque goggles to avoid burns from sunlamps.

In the Workshop

Advise patients to:
- Protect their eyes from flying fragments, fumes, dust particles, sparks, and splashed chemicals by wearing safety glasses.
- Read instructions thoroughly before using tools and chemicals, and follow precautions for their use.

Around Children

Advise patients to:
- Pay attention to age and maturity level of a child when selecting toys and games, and to avoid projectile toys, such as darts and pellet guns.
- Supervise children when they are playing with toys or games that can be dangerous.
- Teach children the correct way to handle potentially dangerous items, such as scissors and pencils.

In the Garden

Advise patients to:
- Avoid letting anyone stand at the side of or in front of a moving lawn mower.
- Pick up rocks and stones before going over them with the lawn mower (stones can be hurled out of the rotary blades and rebound off curbs or walls, causing severe injury to the eye).

- Make sure that pesticide spray can nozzles are directed away from the face.
- Avoid low-hanging branches.

Around the Car

Advise patients to:
- Put out all smoking materials and matches before opening the hood of the car.
- Use a flashlight, not a match or lighter, to look at the battery at night.
- Wear goggles when grinding metal or striking metal against metal while performing auto body repair.
- Take standard safety precautions when using jumper cables (wear goggles; make sure the cars are not touching one another; make sure the jumper cable clamps never touch each other; never lean over the battery when attaching cables; and never attach a cable to the negative terminal of a dead battery).

In Sports

Advise patients to:
- Wear protective safety glasses, especially for sports such as racquetball, squash, tennis, baseball, and basketball.
- Wear protective caps, helmets, or face protectors when appropriate, especially for sports such as ice hockey.

Around Fireworks

Advise patients to:
- Wear eye glasses or safety goggles.
- Avoid using explosive fireworks.
- Never allow children to ignite fireworks.
- Avoid standing near others when lighting fireworks.
- Douse duds in water instead of attempting to relight them.

---

increase in orbital pressure when the force is transmitted to the orbital floor, the area of least resistance.

The inferior rectus and inferior oblique muscles, with their fat and fascial attachments, or the nerve that courses along the inferior oblique muscle may become entrapped, and the globe may be displaced inward (i.e., enophthalmos). Computed tomography (CT) can identify the muscle and its auxiliary structures that are entrapped. These fractures are usually caused by blunt small objects, such as a fist, knee, elbow, or tennis or golf ball.

Orbital roof fractures are dangerous because of potential complications to the brain. Surgical management of these fractures requires a neurosurgeon and an ophthalmologist.

The most common indications for surgical intervention are displacement of bone fragments disfiguring the normal facial contours, interference with normal binocular vision caused by extraocular muscle entrapment, interference with mastication in zygomatic fracture, and obstruction of the nasolacrimal duct. Surgery is usually nonemergent, and a period of 10 to 14 days gives the ophthalmologist time to assess ocular function, especially the extraocular muscles and the nasolacrimal duct. Emergency surgical repair is usually not performed unless the globe is displaced to the maxillary sinus. Surgical repair is primarily directed at freeing the entrapped ocular structures and restoring the integrity of the orbital floor.

Foreign Bodies

Foreign bodies that enter the orbit are usually tolerated, except for copper, iron, and vegetable materials such as those from plants or trees, which may cause purulent infection. X-rays and CT scans are used to identify the foreign body. A careful history is important, especially if the foreign body has been in the orbit for a period of time and the incident forgotten. It is important to identify metallic foreign bodies because they prohibit the use of magnetic resonance imaging (MRI) as a diagnostic tool.

After the extent of the orbital damage is assessed, the decision to use conservative treatment or surgical removal is made. In general, orbital foreign bodies are removed if they are superficial and anterior in location; have sharp edges that may affect adjacent orbital structures; or are composed of copper, iron, or vegetable material. Surgical intervention is directed at preventing further ocular injury and maintaining the integrity of the affected areas. Cultures are usually obtained, and the patient is placed on prophylactic IV antibiotics that are later changed to oral antibiotics.

Ocular Trauma

Ocular trauma is the leading cause of blindness among children and young adults, especially male trauma victims. The most common circumstances of ocular trauma are occupational injuries (e.g., construction industry), sports (e.g., baseball, basketball, racquet sports, boxing), weapons (e.g., air guns, BB guns), assault, motor vehicle crashes (e.g., broken windshields), and explosions (e.g., blast fragments).

There are two types of ocular trauma in which the first response is critical: chemical burn and foreign object in the eye. With a chemical burn, the eye should be immediately irrigated with tap water or normal saline. With a foreign body, no attempt should be made to remove the foreign object. The object should be protected from jarring or movement to prevent further ocular damage. No pressure or patch should be applied to the affected eye. All traumatic eye injuries should be protected using a metal shield, if available, or a stiff paper cup until medical treatment can be obtained (Fig. 49-9).

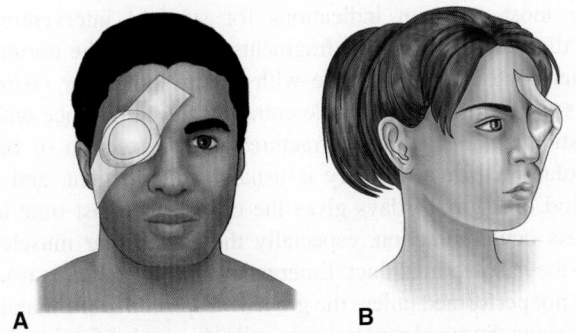

FIGURE 49-9 Two kinds of eye patches. **(A)** Aluminum shield. **(B)** Stiff paper cup shield (creative substitute when aluminum shield is unavailable).

Clinical Manifestations and Assessment

The nurse obtains a thorough history, particularly assessing the patient's ocular history, such as preinjury vision in the affected eye or past ocular surgery. Details related to the injury that help in the diagnosis and assessment of need for further tests include the nature of the ocular injury (i.e., blunt or penetrating trauma); the type of activity that caused the injury to determine the nature of the force striking the eye; and whether onset of vision loss was sudden, slow, or progressive. For chemical eye burns, the chemical agent must be identified and tested for pH if the agent is available. The nurse examines corneal surface for foreign bodies, wounds, and abrasions and then the other external structures of the eye. Pupillary size, shape, and light reaction of the pupil of the affected eye are compared with the other eye. The nurse assesses ocular motility (ability of the eyes to move synchronously up, down, right, and left).

Medical Management

Splash Injuries

Splash injuries are irrigated with normal saline solution before further evaluation occurs. In cases of a ruptured globe, cycloplegic agents (agents that paralyze the ciliary muscle) or topical antibiotics must be deferred because of potential toxicity to exposed intraocular tissues. Further manipulation of the eye must be avoided until the patient is under general anesthesia. Parenteral, broad-spectrum antibiotics are initiated. Tetanus antitoxin is administered, if indicated, as well as analgesics. Tetanus prophylaxis is recommended for full-thickness ocular and skin wounds.

Foreign Bodies and Corneal Abrasions

After removal of a foreign body from the surface of the eye, an antibiotic ointment is applied and the eye is patched. The eye is examined daily for evidence of infection until the wound is completely healed.

Contact lens wear is a common cause of corneal abrasion. The patient experiences severe pain and **photophobia** (ocular pain on exposure to light). Corneal epithelial defects are treated with antibiotic ointment and a pressure patch to immobilize the eyelids. Topical anesthetic eye drops must not be given to the patient to take home for repeated use after corneal injury because their effects mask further damage, delay healing, and can lead to permanent corneal scarring. Corticosteroids are avoided while the epithelial defect exists.

Penetrating Injuries and Contusions of the Eyeball

Sharp penetrating injury or blunt contusion force can rupture the eyeball. When the eye wall, cornea, and sclera rupture, rapid decompression or herniation of the orbital contents into adjacent sinuses can occur. In general, blunt traumatic

injuries (with an increased incidence of retinal detachment, intraocular tissue avulsion, and herniation) have a worse prognosis than penetrating injuries. Most penetrating injuries result in marked loss of vision with the following signs: hemorrhagic **chemosis** (edema of the conjunctiva), conjunctival laceration, shallow anterior chamber with or without an eccentrically placed pupil, hyphema (hemorrhage within the anterior chamber), or vitreous hemorrhage.

Hyphema is caused by contusion forces that tear the vessels of the iris and damage the anterior chamber angle. Preventing rebleeding and prolonged increased IOP are the goals of treatment for hyphema. In severe cases, the patient is hospitalized with moderate activity restriction. An eye shield is applied. Topical corticosteroids are prescribed to reduce inflammation. An antifibrinolytic agent, aminocaproic acid (Amicar), stabilizes clot formation at the site of hemorrhage. Aspirin is contraindicated.

A ruptured globe and severe injuries with intraocular hemorrhage require surgical intervention. Vitrectomy, surgical removal of vitreous fluid and stabilization of the retina, is performed for traumatic retinal detachments. Primary **enucleation** (complete removal of the eyeball and part of the optic nerve) is considered only if the globe is irreparable and has no light perception. It is a general rule that enucleation is performed within 2 weeks of the initial injury (in an eye that has no useful vision after sustaining penetrating injury) to prevent the risk of **sympathetic ophthalmia** (an inflammation created in the uninjured eye by the affected eye that can result in blindness of the uninjured eye).

Intraocular Foreign Bodies

A patient who complains of blurred vision and discomfort should be questioned carefully about recent injuries and exposures. Patients may be injured in a number of different situations and experience an intraocular foreign body (IOFB). Precipitating circumstances can include working in construction; striking metal against metal; being involved in a motor vehicle crash with facial injury; a gunshot wound; grinding-wheel work; and an explosion.

IOFB is diagnosed and localized by slit-lamp biomicroscopy and indirect ophthalmoscopy, as well as CT or ultrasonography. MRI is contraindicated because most foreign bodies are metallic and magnetic. It is important to determine the composition, size, and location of the IOFB and affected eye structures. Every effort should be made to identify the type of IOFB and whether it is magnetic. Iron, steel, copper, and vegetable matter cause intense inflammatory reactions. The incidence of endophthalmitis is also high. If the cornea is perforated, tetanus prophylaxis and IV antibiotics are administered.

Ocular Burns

Alkali, acid, and other chemically active organic substances, such as Mace and tear gas, cause chemical burns. Alkali burns (e.g., lye, ammonia) result in the most severe injury because they penetrate the ocular tissues rapidly and continue to cause damage long after the initial injury is sustained. They also cause an immediate rise in IOP. Acids (e.g., toilet bowl cleaners, bleach, car battery fluid, refrigerant) generally cause less damage because the precipitated necrotic tissue proteins form a barrier to further penetration and damage. Chemical burns may appear as superficial punctate keratopathy (i.e., spotty damage to the cornea), subconjunctival hemorrhage, or complete marbleizing of the cornea.

In treating chemical burns, every minute counts. Immediate tap-water irrigation should be started on site before transport of the patient to an emergency department. Only a brief history and examination are performed. The corneal surfaces and conjunctival fornices are immediately and copiously irrigated with normal saline or any neutral solution. A local anesthetic is instilled, and a lid speculum is applied to overcome blepharospasm (i.e., spasms of the eyelid muscles that result in closure of the lids). Particulate matter must be removed from the fornices using moistened, cotton-tipped applicators and minimal pressure on the globe. Irrigation continues until the conjunctival pH normalizes (between 7.3 and 7.6). The pH of the corneal surface is checked by placing a pH paper strip in the fornix. Antibiotics are instilled, and the eye is patched.

The goal of intermediate treatment is to prevent tissue ulceration and promote re-epithelization. Intense lubrication using nonpreserved (i.e., without preservatives to avoid allergic reactions) artificial tears is essential. Re-epithelization is promoted with patching or therapeutic soft lenses. The patient is usually monitored daily for several days. Prognosis depends on the type of injury and adequacy of the irrigation immediately after exposure. Long-term treatment consists of two phases: restoration of the ocular surface through grafting procedures and surgical restoration of corneal integrity and optical clarity.

Thermal injury is caused by exposure to a hot object (e.g., curling iron, tobacco, ash), whereas photochemical injury results from ultraviolet irradiation or infrared exposure (e.g., exposure to the reflections from snow, sun gazing, viewing an eclipse of the sun without an adequate filter). These injuries can cause corneal epithelial defect, corneal opacity, conjunctival chemosis (edema) and **injection** (congestion of blood vessels), and burns of the eyelids and periocular region. Antibiotics and a pressure patch for 24 hours constitute the treatment of mild injuries. Scarring of the eyelids may require oculoplastic surgery, whereas corneal scarring may require corneal surgery.

INFECTIOUS AND INFLAMMATORY CONDITIONS

Inflammation and infections of eye structures are common. Eye infection is a leading cause of blindness worldwide. Table 49-3 summarizes selected common infections and their

TABLE
49-3 Common Infections and Inflammatory Disorders of Eye Structures

Disorder	Description	Management
Hordeolum (stye)	Acute suppurative infection of the glands of the eyelids caused by *Staphylococcus aureus*. The lid is red and edematous, with a small collection of pus in the form of an abscess. There is considerable discomfort.	Warm compresses are applied directly to the affected lid area three to four times a day for 10 to 15 minutes. If the condition is not improved after 48 hours, incision and drainage may be indicated. Application of topical antibiotics may be prescribed thereafter.
Chalazion	Sterile inflammatory process involving chronic granulomatous inflammation of the meibomian glands; can appear as a single granuloma or multiple granulomas in the upper or lower eyelids.	Warm compresses applied three to four times a day for 10 to 15 minutes may resolve the inflammation in the early stages. Most often, however, surgical excision is indicated. Corticosteroid injection to the chalazion lesion may be used for smaller lesions.
Blepharitis	Chronic bilateral inflammation of the eyelid margins. There are two types: staphylococcal and seborrheic. Staphylococcal blepharitis is usually ulcerative and is more serious due to the involvement of the base of hair follicles. Permanent scarring can result.	The seborrheic type is chronic and is usually resistant to treatment, but the milder cases may respond to lid hygiene. Staphylococcal blepharitis requires topical antibiotic treatment. Instructions on lid hygiene (to keep the lid margins clean and free of exudates) are given to the patient.
Bacterial keratitis	Infection of the cornea by *Staphylococcus aureus*, *Streptococcus pneumoniae*, and *Pseudomonas aeruginosa*	Fortified (high-concentration) antibiotic eyedrops are administered every 30 minutes around the clock for the first few days, then every 1 to 2 hours. Systemic antibiotics may be administered. Cycloplegics are administered to reduce pain caused by ciliary spasm. Corticosteroid therapy and subconjunctival injections of antibiotics are controversial.
Herpes simplex keratitis	Leading cause of corneal blindness in the United States. Symptoms are severe pain, tearing, and photophobia. The dendritic ulcer has a branching, linear pattern with feathery edges and terminal bulbs at its ends. Herpes simplex keratitis can lead to recurrent stromal keratitis and persist to 12 months, with residual corneal scarring.	Many lesions heal without treatment and residual effects. The treatment goal is to minimize the damaging effect of the inflammatory response and eliminate viral replication within the cornea. Penetrating keratoplasty is indicated for corneal scarring and must be performed when the herpetic disease has been inactive for many months.

treatment. Conjunctivitis and orbital cellulitis are discussed below.

CONJUNCTIVITIS

Conjunctivitis (inflammation of the conjunctiva) is the most common ocular disease worldwide. Its appearance varies from a mildly pink appearance of the conjunctiva (hence the common term *pink eye*) because of subconjunctival blood vessel congestion to copious purulent drainage.

Clinical Manifestations and Assessment

Conjunctivitis may be unilateral or bilateral, but the infection usually starts in one eye and then spreads to the other eye by hand contact.

Clinical features important to evaluate are the type of discharge (watery, mucoid, purulent, or mucopurulent), presence or absence of lymphadenopathy (enlargement of the preauricular and submandibular lymph nodes where the eyelids drain),

important symptoms such as a foreign body sensation, a scratching or burning sensation, a sensation of fullness around the eyes, itching, and photophobia (Riordan-Eva, Whitcher, Vaughan et al., 2008). Common organisms isolated are *Streptococcus pneumoniae*, *Haemophilus influenzae*, and *Staphylococcus aureus*. Two sexually transmitted agents associated with conjunctivitis are *Chlamydia trachomatis* and *Neisseria gonorrhoeae*. Diagnosis is based on the distinctive characteristics of ocular signs, acute or chronic presentation, and identification of any precipitating events. Positive results of swab smear preparations and cultures confirm the diagnosis.

Types of Conjunctivitis

Conjunctivitis is classified according to its cause. The major causes are microbial infection, allergy, and irritating toxic stimuli. A wide spectrum of organisms can cause conjunctivitis, including bacteria (e.g., *Chlamydia*), viruses, fungus, and parasites. Conjunctivitis can also result from an existing ocular infection or can be a manifestation of a systemic disease.

Microbial Conjunctivitis

Bacterial Conjunctivitis

Bacterial conjunctivitis can be acute or chronic. The acute type can develop into a chronic condition. Signs and symptoms can vary from mild to severe. Chronic bacterial conjunctivitis is usually seen in patients with lacrimal duct obstruction, chronic dacryocystitis (infection of the nasolacrimal sac), and chronic blepharitis (eyelid inflammation). The most common causative microorganisms are *S. pneumoniae, H. influenzae,* and *S. aureus.*

Bacterial conjunctivitis manifests with an acute onset of redness, burning, and discharge. There is conjunctival irritation, and injection in the fornices. The exudates are variable but are usually present on waking in the morning. The eyes may be difficult to open because of adhesions caused by the exudate. Purulent discharge occurs in severe acute bacterial infections, whereas mucopurulent discharge appears in mild cases. In gonococcal conjunctivitis, the symptoms are more acute and may present with profuse and purulent exudate, lymphadenopathy, and pseudomembranes.

Chlamydial conjunctivitis includes **trachoma** (a bilateral chronic follicular conjunctivitis of childhood that leads to blindness during adulthood if left untreated) and inclusion conjunctivitis. Trachoma is prevalent in areas with hot, dry, and dusty climates, and in areas with poor living conditions. It is spread by direct contact or fomites, and the vectors can be insects such as flies and gnats. Symptoms include red, inflamed eyes, tearing, photophobia, ocular pain, purulent exudates, preauricular lymphadenopathy (anterior to the auricle of the ear), and lid edema. At the middle stage of the disease, an acute inflammation occurs, after which trichiasis (turning inward of hair follicles) and entropion begin to develop, causing corneal erosion and ulceration. The late stage of the disease is characterized by scarred conjunctiva, subepithelial keratitis (inflammation of the cornea), abnormal vascularization of the cornea (pannus), and residual scars from the follicles. Severe corneal ulceration can lead to perforation and blindness.

Inclusion conjunctivitis affects sexually active people who have genital chlamydial infection. Transmission is by oral–genital sex or hand-to-eye transmission. Indirect transmission can occur in inadequately chlorinated swimming pools. The eye lesions usually appear a week after exposure and may be associated with a nonspecific urethritis or cervicitis.

Viral Conjunctivitis

Viral conjunctivitis can be acute and chronic. The discharge is watery, and follicles are prominent. Severe cases include *pseudomembranes.* Pseudomembranes appear as tissue that covers the conjunctiva or sclera but are actually composed of mucus, fibrin, bacteria, or immune system cells. The common causative organisms are adenovirus and herpes simplex virus. Conjunctivitis caused by adenovirus is highly contagious. The condition is usually preceded by symptoms

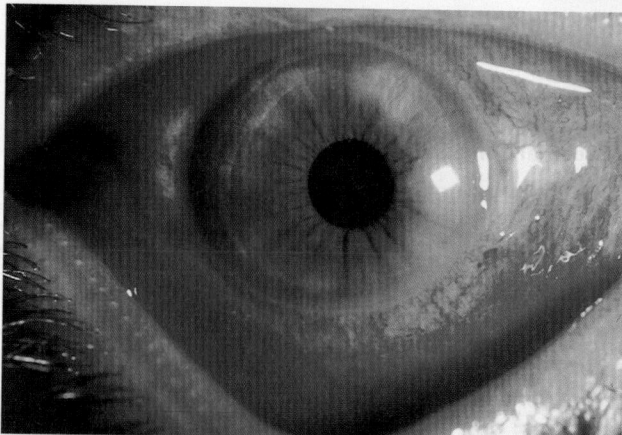

FIGURE 49-10 Conjunctival hyperemia in viral conjunctivitis.

of upper respiratory infection. Corneal involvement causes extreme photophobia. Symptoms include extreme tearing, redness, and foreign body sensation that can involve one or both eyes. There is lid edema, ptosis, and conjunctival **hyperemia** (dilation of the conjunctival blood vessels) (Fig. 49-10). These signs and symptoms vary from mild to severe and may last for 2 weeks. Viral conjunctivitis, although self-limited, tends to last longer than bacterial conjunctivitis.

Epidemic keratoconjunctivitis (EKC) is a highly contagious viral conjunctivitis that is easily transmitted from one person to another among household members, school children, and health care workers. The outbreak of epidemics is seasonal, especially during the summer, when people use swimming pools. EKC is most often accompanied by preauricular lymphadenopathy and occasionally periorbital pain. EKC can lead to keratopathy (corneal disease).

Allergic Conjunctivitis

Immunologic or allergic conjunctivitis is a hypersensitivity reaction that occurs as part of allergic rhinitis (hay fever), or it can be an independent allergic reaction. Patients often present with a history of atopy, a genetic predisposition towards hypersensitivity reactions. Atopic conditions include allergies (e.g., food and seasonal), asthma, and atopic dermatitis (e.g., eczema). Allergic conjunctivitis is characterized by extreme pruritus, epiphora (i.e., excessive secretion of tears), injection, and usually severe photophobia. A string-like mucoid discharge is usually associated with rubbing the eyes because of severe pruritus. Vernal conjunctivitis is also known as *seasonal conjunctivitis* because it appears mostly during warm weather.

Toxic Conjunctivitis

Chemical conjunctivitis can be the result of medications; chlorine from swimming pools; exposure to toxic fumes among industrial workers; or exposure to other irritants such as smoke, hair sprays, acids, and alkalis.

TABLE
49-4 Management of Conjunctivitis

Conjunctivitis	Management
Bacterial Conjunctivitis	Acute bacterial conjunctivitis is almost always self-limiting, lasting two weeks if left untreated. If treated with antibiotics, it may last a few days, except for gonococcal and staphylococcal conjunctivitis. For trachoma, usually broad-spectrum antibiotics are administered topically and systemically. Surgical management includes the correction of trichiasis (eyelashes growing inward toward the conjunctiva and cornea) to prevent conjunctival scarring. Adult inclusion conjunctivitis requires 1 week of antibiotics. Prevention of reinfection is important, and affected individuals and their sexual partners must seek treatment for sexually transmitted disease, if indicated.
Viral Conjunctivitis	Viral conjunctivitis is not responsive to any treatment. Cold compresses may alleviate some symptoms. It is extremely important to remember that viral conjunctivitis, especially epidemic keratoconjunctivitis, is highly contagious. Patient instructions should include an emphasis on hand hygiene and avoiding sharing of hand towels, face cloths, and eye drops. Tissues should be directly discarded into a covered trash can. All forms of tonometry must be avoided unless medically indicated. All multidose medications must be discarded at the end of each day or when contaminated. Infected employees and others must not be allowed to work or attend school until symptoms have resolved, which can take 3 to 7 days.
Allergic Conjunctivitis	Patients with allergic conjunctivitis, especially recurrent vernal or seasonal conjunctivitis, are usually given corticosteroids in ophthalmic preparations. Depending on the severity of the disease, they may be given oral preparations. Use of vasoconstrictors, such as topical epinephrine solution, cold compresses, ice packs, and cool ventilation usually provide comfort by decreasing swelling.
Toxic Conjunctivitis	For conjunctivitis caused by chemical irritants, the eye must be irrigated immediately and profusely with saline or sterile water.

Medical and Nursing Management

The management of conjunctivitis depends on the type (Table 49-4). Most types of mild and viral conjunctivitis are self-limiting, benign conditions that may not require treatment. Box 49-9 includes patient teaching information about viral conjunctivitis. For more severe cases, topical antibiotics, eye drops, or ointments are prescribed. Patients with gonococcal conjunctivitis require urgent antibiotic therapy. If left untreated, this ocular disease can lead to corneal perforation and blindness. The systemic complications can include meningitis and generalized septicemia.

ORBITAL CELLULITIS

Orbital cellulitis is inflammation of the tissues surrounding the eye.

Pathophysiology

Orbital cellulitis may result from bacterial, fungal, or viral inflammatory conditions of contiguous structures, such as the face, oropharynx, dental structures, or intracranial structures. It can also result from foreign bodies and from a preexisting ocular infection or from generalized septicemia. Infection of the sinuses is the most frequent cause. Infection originating in the sinuses can spread easily to the orbit through the thin bony walls and foramina or by means of the interconnecting venous system of the orbit and sinuses. The most common causative organisms are staphylococci and streptococci in adults and *H. influenzae* in children.

Clinical Manifestations and Assessment

The symptoms include pain, lid swelling, conjunctival edema, **proptosis**, and decreased ocular motility. With such edema, optic nerve compression can occur and IOP may increase.

The severe intraorbital tension caused by abscess formation and the impairment of optic nerve function in orbital cellulitis can result in permanent visual loss. Because of the orbit's proximity to the brain, orbital cellulitis can lead to life-threatening complications, such as intracranial abscess and cavernous sinus thrombosis.

Medical and Nursing Management

Immediate administration of high-dose, broad-spectrum, systemic antibiotics is indicated. Cultures and Gram-stained smears are obtained. Monitoring changes in visual acuity, degree of proptosis, central nervous system function (e.g., nausea, vomiting, fever, cognitive changes), displacement of the globe, extraocular movements, pupillary signs, and the fundus is extremely important. Consultation with

Patient Education

Instructions for Patients With Viral Conjunctivitis

Viral conjunctivitis is a highly contagious eye infection. It can easily spread from one person to another. The symptoms can be alarming, but they are not serious. The following information will help you understand this eye condition and how to take care of yourself and/or your family member at home.

- Your eyes will look red and will have watery discharge, and your lids will be swollen for about a week.
- You will experience eye pain, a sandy sensation in your eye, and sensitivity to light.
- Symptoms will resolve after about 1 week.
- You may use light, cold compresses over your eyes for about 10 minutes four to five times a day to soothe the pain.
- You may use artificial tears for the sandy sensation in your eye, and mild pain medications such as acetaminophen (Tylenol).
- You need to stay at home. Children must not play outside. You may return to work or school after 7 days, when the redness and discharge have cleared. You may obtain a doctor's note to return to work or school.
- Do not share towels, linens, makeup, or toys.
- Wash your hands thoroughly and frequently, using soap and water, including before and after you apply artificial tears or cold compresses.
- Use a new tissue every time you wipe the discharge from each eye. You may dampen the tissue with clean water to clean the outside of the eye.
- You may wash your face and take a shower as you normally do.
- Discard all of your makeup articles. You must not apply makeup until the disease is over.
- You may wear dark glasses if bright lights bother you.
- If the discharge from your eye turns yellowish and pus-like, or you experience changes in your vision, you need to return to the health care provider for an examination.

an otolaryngologist is necessary, especially when sinusitis is suspected. In the event of abscess formation or progressive loss of vision, surgical drainage of the abscess or sinus is performed. Sinusotomy and antibiotic irrigation are also performed.

TREATMENT MODALITIES FOR EYE INJURIES AND DISORDERS

Common treatments discussed in this section include surgery and pharmacological treatment.

SURGICAL PROCEDURES

Orbital Surgeries

Orbital surgeries may be performed to repair fractures, remove a foreign body, or remove benign or malignant growths. The eyeball is lined with muscle, connective, and adipose tissues, and is housed in the bony orbit, which is about 4 cm high, wide, and deep. It is shaped roughly like a four-sided pyramid, surrounded on three sides by the sinuses: ethmoid (medially), frontal (superiorly), and maxillary (inferiorly). Surgical procedures involving the orbit and lids affect facial appearance (cosmesis). The goals are to recover and preserve visual function and to maintain the anatomic relationship of the ocular structures to achieve cosmesis. During the repair of orbital fractures, the orbital bones are realigned to follow the anatomic positions of facial structures.

Orbital surgical procedures involve working around delicate structures of the eye, such as the optic nerve, retinal blood vessels, and ocular muscles. Complications of orbital surgical procedures may include blindness as a result of damage to the optic nerve and its blood supply. Sudden pain and loss of vision may indicate intraorbital hemorrhage or compression of the optic nerve. Ptosis and diplopia may result from trauma to the extraocular muscles during the surgical procedure, but these conditions typically resolve after a few weeks.

Prophylaxis with IV antibiotics is the usual postoperative regimen after orbital surgery, especially with repair of orbital fractures and intraorbital foreign body removal. IV corticosteroids are used if there is a concern about optic nerve swelling. Topical ocular antibiotics are typically instilled, and antibiotic ointments are applied externally to the skin suture sites.

For the first 24 to 48 hours postoperatively, ice compresses are applied over the periocular area to decrease periorbital swelling, facial swelling, and hematoma. The head of the patient's bed should be elevated to a comfortable position (30 to 45 degrees).

Discharge teaching should include medication instructions for oral antibiotics, instillation of ophthalmic medications, and application of ocular compresses.

Enucleation

Enucleation is the removal of the entire eye and part of the optic nerve. It may be performed for the following conditions:

- Severe injury resulting in prolapse of uveal tissue (iris, ciliary body, and choroid), or loss of light projection (the ability to identify the direction of the light source) or perception
- An irritated, blind, painful, deformed, or disfigured eye, usually caused by glaucoma, retinal detachment, or chronic inflammation
- An eye without useful vision that is producing or has produced sympathetic ophthalmia (inflammation of the eye or conjunctiva) in the other eye
- Intraocular tumors that are untreatable by other means

The procedure for enucleation involves the separation and cutting of each of the ocular muscles, dissection of the Tenon's capsule (fibrous membrane covering the sclera), and cutting of the optic nerve from the eyeball. The insertion of an orbital implant typically follows, and the conjunctiva is closed. A large pressure dressing is applied over the area. Box 49-10 discusses ocular prostheses.

Evisceration

Evisceration involves the surgical removal of the intraocular contents through an incision or opening in the cornea or sclera. Evisceration may be performed to treat severe ocular trauma with ruptured globe, severe ocular inflammation, or severe ocular infection. The optic nerve, sclera, extraocular muscles, and sometimes the cornea are left intact. The main advantage of evisceration over enucleation is that the final cosmetic result and motility after fitting the ocular prosthesis are enhanced. This procedure would be more acceptable to a patient whose body image is severely threatened. The main disadvantage is the high risk of sympathetic ophthalmia.

Exenteration

Exenteration is the removal of the eyelids, the eye, and various amounts of orbital contents. It is indicated in malignancies in the orbit that are life-threatening or when more conservative modalities of treatment have failed or are inappropriate. An example is squamous cell carcinoma of the paranasal sinuses, skin, and conjunctiva with deep orbital involvement. In its most extensive form, exenteration may include the removal of all orbital tissues and resection of the orbital bones.

PHARMACOLOGICAL TREATMENT

The main objective of ocular medication delivery is to maximize the amount of medication that reaches the ocular site of action in sufficient concentration to produce a beneficial therapeutic effect. This is determined by the dynamics of ocular pharmacokinetics: absorption, distribution, metabolism, and excretion.

Concepts in Ocular Medication Administration

Topical administration of ocular medications results in only a 1% to 7% absorption rate by the ocular tissues. Ocular absorption involves the entry of a medication into the aqueous humor through the different routes of ocular medication administration. The rate and extent of aqueous humor absorption are determined by the characteristics of the medication and the anatomy and physiology of the eye. Natural barriers of absorption that diminish the efficacy of ocular medications include the following:

- *Limited size of the conjunctival sac.* The conjunctival sac can hold only 50 μL, and any excess is wasted. The volume of one eye drop from commercial topical ocular solutions typically ranges from 20 to 35 μL.
- *Corneal membrane barriers.* The epithelial, stromal, and endothelial layers are barriers to absorption.
- *Blood–ocular barriers.* Blood–ocular barriers prevent high ocular tissue concentration of most ophthalmic medications because they separate the bloodstream from the ocular tissues and keep foreign substances from entering the eye, thereby limiting a medication's efficacy.
- *Tearing, blinking, and drainage.* Increased tear production and drainage due to ocular irritation or an ocular condition may dilute or wash out an instilled eye drop; blinking expels an instilled eye drop from the conjunctival sac.

Distribution of an ocular medication into the various ocular tissues varies by tissue type; the various tissues (e.g., conjunctiva, cornea, lens, iris, ciliary body, choroids) absorb medications to varying degrees. Medications penetrate the corneal epithelium by diffusion by passing through the cells (intracellular) or by passing between the cells (intercellular). Water-soluble (hydrophilic) medications diffuse through the intracellular route, and fat-soluble (lipophilic) medications diffuse through the intercellular route. Topical administration usually does not reach the retina in significant concentrations. Because the space between the ciliary process and the lens is small, medication diffusion in the vitreous is slow. When high concentrations of medication in the vitreous are required, intraocular injection is often chosen to bypass the natural ocular anatomic and physiologic barriers.

Aqueous solutions are most commonly used for the eye. They are the least expensive medications and interfere least with vision. However, corneal contact time is brief because tears dilute the medication. Ophthalmic ointments have extended retention time in the conjunctival sac and provide a higher concentration than eye drops. The major disadvantage of ointments is the blurred vision that results after application. In general, eyelids and eyelid margins are best treated with ointments. Contact lenses and collagen shields soaked in antibiotics are alternative delivery methods for treating corneal infections.

Of all these delivery methods, the topical route of administration—instilled eye drops and applied ointments—remains the most common. Topical instillation, which is the least invasive method, permits self-administration of medication and produces fewer side effects.

Preservatives are commonly used in ocular medications. Benzalkonium chloride, for example, prevents the growth of organisms and enhances the corneal permeability of most medications; however, some patients are allergic to this preservative. This may be suspected even if the patient had never before experienced an allergic reaction to systemic use of the medication in question. Eye drops without preservatives can be prepared by pharmacists.

BOX 49-10

Ocular Prostheses

Orbital implants and conformers (ocular prostheses usually made of silicone rubber) maintain the shape of the eye after enucleation or evisceration to prevent a contracted, sunken appearance. The temporary conformer is placed over the conjunctival closure after the implantation of an orbital implant. A conformer is placed after the enucleation or evisceration procedure to protect the suture line, maintain the fornices, prevent contracture of the socket in preparation for the ocular prosthesis, and promote the integrity of the eyelids.

All ocular prosthetics have limitations in their motility. There are two designs of eye prostheses (see Figure). The anophthalmic ocular prostheses are used in the absence of the globe. Scleral shells look just like the anophthalmic prosthesis but are thinner and fit over a globe with intact corneal sensation. An eye prosthesis usually lasts about 6 years, depending on the quality of fit, comfort, and cosmetic appearance. When the anophthalmic socket is completely healed, conformers are replaced with prosthetic eyes.

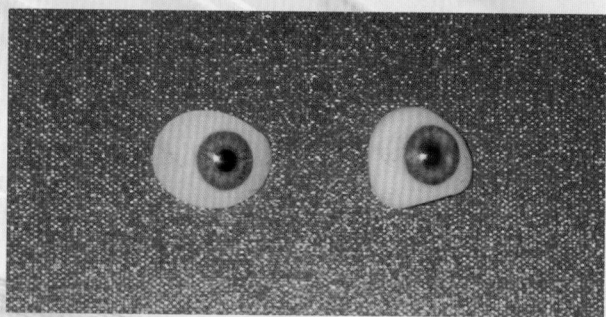

Eye prostheses. (*Left*) Anophthalmic ocular prosthesis. (*Right*) Scleral shell.

An ocularist is a specially trained and skilled professional who makes prosthetic eyes. After the ophthalmologist is satisfied that the anophthalmic socket is completely healed and is ready for prosthetic fitting, the patient is referred to an ocularist. The healing period is usually 6 to 8 weeks. It is advisable for the patient to have a consultation with the ocularist before the fitting. Obtaining accurate information and verbalizing concerns can lessen anxiety about wearing an ocular prosthesis.

Medical Management

Removal of an eye has physical, social, and psychological ramifications for any person. The significance of loss of the eye and vision must be addressed in the plan of care. The patient's preparation should include information about the surgical procedure and placement of orbital implants and conformers and the availability of ocular prosthetics to enhance cosmetic appearance. In some cases, patients may choose to see an ocularist before the surgery to discuss ocular prosthetics.

Nursing Management

Teaching About Postsurgical Care

Patients who undergo eye removal need to know that they will usually have a large ocular pressure dressing, which is typically removed after a week, and that an ophthalmic topical antibiotic ointment is applied in the socket three times daily. When surgical eye removal is immediate and unexpected, as in the case of ocular trauma, the nurse's role in providing emotional support is crucial.

After the removal of an eye, there is a loss of depth perception. Patients must be advised to take extra caution in their ambulation and movement to avoid miscalculations that may result in injury. It may take some time to adjust to monocular vision. Patients using conformers must be advised that the prosthetic may accidentally fall out of the socket. If this happens, the conformer must be washed, wiped dry, and placed back in the socket.

Teaching Patients Self-Care

Patients need to be taught how to insert, remove, and care for the prosthetic eye. Proper hand hygiene must be observed before inserting and removing an ocular prosthesis. A suction cup may be used if there are problems with manual dexterity. Precautions, such as draping a towel over the sink and closing the sink drain, must be taken to avoid loss of the prosthesis. When instructing patients or family members, a return demonstration is important to assess the level of understanding and ability to perform the procedure.

Before insertion, the inner punctal or outer lateral aspects and the superior and inferior aspects of the prosthesis must be identified by locating the identifying marks, such as a reddish color in the inner punctal area. For people with low vision, other forms of identifying markers, such as dots or notches, are used. The upper lid is raised high enough to create a space; then the patient learns to slide the prosthesis up, underneath, and behind the upper eyelid. Meanwhile, the patient pulls the lower eyelid down to help put the prosthesis in place and to have its inferior edge fall back gradually to the lower eyelid. The lower eyelid is checked for correct positioning.

To remove the prosthesis, the patient cups one hand on the cheek to catch the prosthesis, places the forefinger of the free hand against the midportion of the lower eyelid, and gazes upward. Gazing upward brings the inferior edge of the prosthesis nearer the inferior eyelid margin. With the finger pushing inward, downward, and laterally against the lower eyelid, the prosthesis slides out, and the cupped hand acts as the receptacle.

Continuing Care

An eye prosthesis can be worn and left in place for several months. Hygiene and comfort are usually maintained with daily irrigation of the prosthesis in place with normal saline solution, hard contact lens solution, or artificial tears. In the case of dry eye symptoms, the use of ophthalmic ointment lubricants or oil-based drops, such as vitamin E and mineral oil, can be helpful. Removing crusting and mucous discharge that accumulate overnight is performed with the prosthesis in place. Malpositions may occur when wiping or rubbing the prosthesis in the socket. The prosthesis can be repositioned with the use of clean fingers. Proper wiping of the prosthesis should be a gentle temporal-to-nasal motion to avoid malpositions.

Commonly Used Ocular Medications

Common ocular medications include topical anesthetic, mydriatic, and cycloplegic agents that reduce IOP; anti-infective medications, corticosteroids, nonsteroidal anti-inflammatory drugs (NSAIDs), antiallergy medications, eye irrigants, and lubricants.

Topical Anesthetics

One or two drops of proparacaine hydrochloride (Ophthaine 0.5%) and tetracaine hydrochloride (Pontocaine 0.5%) are instilled before diagnostic procedures such as tonometry. Topical anesthetics are also used for severe eye pain, to allow the patient to open his or her eyes for examination or treatment. The nurse must instruct the patient not to rub his or her eyes while anesthetized because this may result in corneal damage.

Patients with corneal abrasions and erosions experience severe pain and are often tempted to overuse topical anesthetic eye drops. Overuse of these drops results in softening of the cornea. Prolonged use of anesthetic drops can delay wound healing and can lead to permanent corneal opacification and scarring, resulting in visual loss.

Mydriatics and Cycloplegics

Mydriasis, or pupil dilation, is the main objective of the administration of mydriatic and cycloplegic agents (Table 49-5). These two types of medications function differently and are used in combination to achieve the maximal dilation that is needed during surgery and fundus examinations to give the ophthalmologist a better view of the internal eye structures. **Mydriatics** potentiate alpha-adrenergic sympathetic effects that result in the relaxation of the ciliary muscle leading to dilatation of the pupil. The patient may have difficulty reading. The patient is advised to wear sunglasses

TABLE
49-5 Mydriatics and Miotics

Medication	Forms	Indication/Dosages	Action	Duration	Nursing Considerations
Phenylephrine (Dilate, Neofrin)	Solution (0.12%, 2.5%, 10%)	Instill 1 drop per dose and may repeat in 1 hour for: Mydriasis Posterior synechiae and minor eye irritation	Dilates pupil by contracting dilator muscle Peak within 10 to 90 minutes	3 to 7 hours	Monitor for systemic effects of hypertension if 10% solution is administered.
Atropine (Isopto Atropine)	Ointment (1%) Solution (0.5%–2%)	Instill 1 to 2 drops for acute iritis, uveitis, or cycloplegic refraction, 3 to 4 times daily	Dilates pupil by anticholinergic action. Peak within 30 minutes to 3 hours	7 to 10 days	Have antidote available, physostigmine salicylate (IM or IV). Watch patient for signs and symptoms of glaucoma.
Scopolamine hydrobromide (Isopto Hyoscine)	Solution (0.25%)	Instill 1 to 2 drops for acute iritis, uveitis, or cycloplegic refraction, once to 4 times daily	Same action as atropine. Peak within 15 to 45 minutes	3 to 7 days	Observe patient closely for disorientation or delirium. May be given to patients sensitive to atropine.
Pilocarpine hydrochloride (Isopto Carpine)	Gel (4%) Solution (0.25% to 1%)	Apply one ribbon of gel into lower conjunctival sac once daily at bedtime. Instill 1 to 2 drops of solution for open angle glaucoma, acute angle-closure glaucoma, or mydriasis caused by mydriatic or cycloplegic drugs	Cholinergic effect of pupil constriction (miosis) and deepening of anterior chamber. Peak within 30 to 85 minutes	4 to 8 hours	Monitor vital signs. Check drug name carefully.

(most eye clinics provide protective sunglasses). The ability to drive is dependent on the person's age, vision, and comfort level.

NURSING ALERT

Mydriatic and cycloplegic agents affect the central nervous system. Their effects are most prominent in children and elderly patients; these patients must be assessed closely for symptoms, such as increased blood pressure, tachycardia, dizziness, ataxia, confusion, disorientation, incoherent speech, and hallucination. These medications are contraindicated in patients with narrow angles or shallow anterior chambers, and in patients taking monoamine oxidase inhibitors or tricyclic antidepressants.

Antiglaucoma Medications

Therapeutic medications for glaucoma are used to lower IOP by decreasing aqueous production or increasing aqueous outflow. Because glaucoma calls for lifetime therapy, the patient must be instructed regarding both the ocular and systemic side effects of the medications.

Most antiglaucoma medications affect the **accommodation** of the lens and limit light entry through a constricted pupil. Visual acuity and the ability to focus may be affected. Factors to consider in selecting glaucoma medications are efficacy, systemic and ocular side effects, convenience, and cost.

Anti-Infective Medications

Anti-infective medications include antibiotic, antifungal, and antiviral agents. Most are available as drops, ointments, or subconjunctival or intravitreal injections. Antibiotics include penicillin, cephalosporins, aminoglycosides, and fluoroquinolones. The main antifungal agent is amphotericin B (Abelcet). Side effects of amphotericin are serious, and include severe pain, conjunctival necrosis, iritis, and retinal toxicity. Antiviral medications include acyclovir (Zovirax) and ganciclovir (Cytovene). Patients receiving ocular agents are subject to the same side effects and adverse reactions as those receiving anti-infective oral or parenteral medications.

Corticosteroids and Nonsteroidal Anti-Inflammatory Drugs

The topical preparations of corticosteroids are commonly used in inflammatory conditions of the eyelids, conjunctiva, cornea, anterior chamber, lens, and uvea. Because these topical eye drops are suspensions, the patient is instructed to shake the bottle several times to promote mixture of the medication and maximize its therapeutic effect. The most common ocular side effects of long-term topical corticosteroid administration are glaucoma, cataracts, susceptibility to infection, impaired wound healing, mydriasis, ptosis, and high IOP. To avoid the side effects of corticosteroids, NSAIDs are used as an alternative in controlling inflammatory eye conditions and postoperatively to reduce inflammation.

Antiallergy Medications

Ocular hypersensitivity reactions are extremely common and result primarily from responses to environmental allergens. Most allergens are airborne or carried to the eye by the hand or by other means, although allergic reactions may also be drug-induced. Corticosteroids are commonly used as anti-inflammatory and immunosuppressive agents to control ocular hypersensitivity reactions.

Ocular Irrigants and Lubricants

Irrigating solutions are used to cleanse the external lids to maintain lid hygiene, to irrigate the external corneal surface to regain normal pH (e.g., in chemical burns), to irrigate the corneal surface to eliminate debris, or to inflate the globe intraoperatively. These solutions have various compositions (sodium, potassium, magnesium, calcium, bicarbonate, glucose, and glutathione) that are safe to use with an intact corneal surface; however, the corneal surface should not be irrigated in cases of threatened corneal perforation. Sterile irrigating solutions, such as Dacriose, for lid hygiene are available. For patients with severe corneal ulcer, specific orders must be obtained regarding whether it is safe to irrigate the corneal surface or just to cleanse the external lids. Although it is good practice to promote hygiene, prevention of complications must be the primary concern.

Lubricants, such as artificial tears, help alleviate corneal irritation, such as dry eye syndrome. Artificial tears are topical preparations of methyl or hydroxypropyl cellulose that are prepared as eye drop solutions, ointments, or ocular inserts (inserted at the lower conjunctival cul-de-sac once each day).

Nursing Management

The objectives in administering ocular medications are to ensure proper administration to maximize the therapeutic effects and to ensure the safety of the patient by monitoring for systemic and local side effects. Absorption of eye drops by the nasolacrimal duct is undesirable because of the potential systemic side effects of ocular medications. To diminish systemic absorption and minimize the side effects, it is important to occlude the puncta (Box 49-11).

Before the administration of ocular medications, the nurse warns the patient that blurred vision, stinging, and a burning sensation are symptoms that ordinarily occur after instillation and are temporary. Risk for interactions of the ocular medication with other ocular and systemic medications must be emphasized; therefore, a careful patient interview regarding the medications being taken must be obtained.

Emphasis must be placed on hand hygiene techniques before and after medication instillation. The tip of the eye drop bottle or the ointment tube must never touch any part of the eye. The medication must be recapped immediately after each use. The patient or the caregiver at home should be asked to demonstrate actual eye drop or ointment instillation and punctal occlusion.

BOX 49-11

GUIDELINES FOR NURSING CARE

Instilling Eye Medications

Equipment

- Medication(s) as ordered
- Cotton balls or gauze
- Optional: Eye dressing

Implementation

ACTION	RATIONALE
1. Ensure adequate lighting.	1. Adequate lighting ensures procedure will be carried out using appropriate technique.
2. Perform hand hygiene.	2. Hand hygiene and aseptic technique is important to decrease risk of contamination of supplies and spread of further infection.
3. Don clean gloves and, if necessary or required, gently clean any crusts or drainage from the eyelid margins, wiping from the inner to the outer canthus and using a fresh gauze pad or cotton ball moistened with warm water for each stroke.	3. Cleaning eyes promotes patient comfort and promotes absorption of medications. Additionally, debris is removed away from the nasolacrimal duct.
4. Prepare medication. Read the label of the eye medication to make sure it is the correct medication. Shake suspensions or "milky" solutions to obtain the desired medication level. Verify which eye is to be treated.	4. Proper checking of medication and which eye is to be treated is an essential right. Mixing of medication in suspension is required.
5. Assume proper position for instillation of eye medications.	5. Positioning of the head in a supine position or, if sitting, hyperextended in a "sniffing position" allows for proper instillation of ophthalmic medication, particularly drops.
6. Do not touch the tip of the medication container to any part of the eye or face. Hold the lower lid down; do not press on the eyeball. Apply gentle pressure to the cheek bone to anchor the finger holding the lid.	6. Maintaining aseptic technique avoids contamination of materials, such as the medication container. Using the cheek bone as a fulcrum to steady the arm allows for improved medication delivery.

7. Apply medication. Instill eye drops before applying ointments.
For eye drops:
   Eye drops should be instilled at a distance of approximately 1 inch from the eye. Before instilling the eyedrops, instruct the patient to look up and away. The lower lid is gently pulled down to instill the drops in the conjunctival sac. Immediately after instilling eye drops, apply gentle pressure on the inner canthus (punctal occlusion) near the bridge of the nose for 3 to 5 minutes.
   Using a clean tissue, gently pat skin to absorb excess eyedrops that run onto the cheeks.
For eye ointment:
   Apply a ½-inch ribbon of ointment to the lower conjunctival sac. Immediately after ointment instillation, ask patient to roll eyes behind closed lids.
	7. Medication is administered into the conjunctival sac, rather than on the eyeball, which can cause discomfort.
	   Gentle pressure on the inner canthus (punctal occlusion) is done to decrease the risk of systemic absorption of the medication.
	
	   Rolling the eye helps to distribute the medication over the surface of the eyeball.

8. Wait 5 minutes before instilling another eye medication.	8. Allow for absorption of one medication to occur prior to applying another one.
9. Perform hand hygiene.	9. Hand hygiene prevents further contamination post instillation.

Chapter Review

Critical Thinking Exercises

1. You are employed in an eye clinic in which the majority of patients are elderly, and the majority of medications that are prescribed for these patients are topical agents. Develop an evidence-based teaching plan for patients and caregivers that provides instructions in the proper administration of ocular drops and ointments. What evidence supports the medication administration techniques and associated safety precautions that you have included in the teaching plan? What evidence supports the principles of learning that you considered regarding the elderly population that the clinic serves? What is the strength of the evidence? What criteria would you use to determine the strength of the evidence?

2. In the emergency department, you are caring for a man who has been involved in a motor vehicle crash in which there was a broken windshield. He states that he has a headache and a stiff neck, that his vision is "blurry," and that he has a "scratching pain" in his right eye. He requests a cold compress for his eyes. How would you respond to this patient's request? What diagnostic tests do you anticipate would be used to determine the cause for the patient's symptoms of blurred vision and pain in the eye? What information would you communicate to the health care provider?

NCLEX-Style Review Questions

1. In gathering a history from a patient newly diagnosed with glaucoma, the patient reports the following statement to the nurse. Which statement would be consistent with the patient's diagnosis?
   A. "I began seeing halos around lights and had dim vision."
   B. "I had a difficult time matching my blue socks."
   C. "My eyes began to tear and itch."
   D. "I can see the street signs better than my hand."

2. The following statement by the patient diagnosed with viral conjunctivitis indicates that more teaching is necessary.
   A. "I will wash my hands frequently."
   B. "I will use a washcloth to clean both my eyes, starting with the infected eye and moving to the uninfected eye."
   C. "I will avoid contact with other people until my symptoms are gone."
   D. "I will discard any leftover eye medication when the infection is gone."

3. The nurse is caring for a baseball player who reports getting hit in the head with a baseball 1 hour prior to admission in the ED. Which of the following assessments requires immediate reporting?
   A. Eye pain
   B. Flashing lights in the visual field
   C. Headache, pain intensity rated as 2/10
   D. Superficial head abrasion

4. The patient with significant visual impairment requires assistance with ADLs. The nurse provides support when serving food by performing which of the following actions?
   A. Leaving the tray on the patient's bedside table
   B. Serving hot food as quickly as possible
   C. Describing the food on the tray in terms of the face of a clock
   D. Ensuring all food is soft

5. A patient is seen in the vision clinic. The patient has been diagnosed with glaucoma. Which of the following would the nurse expect to be in the treatment plan for this patient as the initial topical medication?
   A. Mydriatic
   B. Antifungal
   C. Beta blocker
   D. Miotic

References and Selected Readings

References and selected readings associated with this chapter can be found on the website that accompanies the book. Visit http://thepoint.lww.com/Pellico1e to access the references and other additional resources associated with this chapter.

Nursing Management: Patients With Hearing and Balance Disorders

CAROLYNN SPERA BRUNO

Learning Objectives

After reading this chapter, you will be able to:

1. List the manifestations that may be exhibited by a person with a hearing disorder.

2. Identify ways to communicate effectively with a person with a hearing disorder.

3. Differentiate problems of the external ear from those of the middle ear and inner ear.

4. Compare the various types of surgical procedures used for managing middle ear disorders and appropriate nursing care.

5. Describe the different types of inner ear disorders, including the clinical manifestations, diagnosis, and management.

The delicate structure and function of the ear make early detection and accurate diagnosis of disorders necessary for preservation of normal hearing and balance. Medical surgical nurses will care for patients with hearing loss because of a wide variety of reasons. This chapter addresses the assessment and management of hearing and balance disorders common to the adult population.

HEARING LOSS

More than 36 million people in the United States report some form of hearing loss. *Healthy People 2010* initiated a goal to promote the hearing health of the nation through prevention, early detection, treatment, and rehabilitation.

Pathophysiology

Hearing loss may be the result of a conduction problem, a sensorineural loss, mixed, or of a psychogenic issue. Conductive hearing loss usually results from an external ear disorder, such as impacted cerumen, or a middle ear disorder, such as **otitis media** or otosclerosis. In such instances, the efficient transmission of sound by air to the inner ear is interrupted. A sensorineural loss involves damage to the cochlea or vestibulocochlear nerve. Patients with mixed hearing loss have conductive loss and sensorineural loss, resulting from dysfunction of air and bone conduction. A functional (or psychogenic) hearing loss is nonorganic and unrelated to detectable structural changes in the hearing mechanisms; it is usually a manifestation of an emotional disturbance.

Many environmental factors have an adverse effect on the auditory system and gradually result in permanent **sensorineural hearing loss**. The most common is noise (unwanted and unavoidable sound), which has been identified as one of today's environmental hazards. The volume of noise that surrounds us daily has increased into a potentially dangerous source of physical and psychological damage.

Risk Factors

Hearing loss is greater in men than in women. There is a strong relationship between age and reported hearing loss. Eighteen percent of American adults

Risk Factors for Hearing Loss

- Family history of sensorineural impairment
- Congenital malformations of the cranial structure (ear)
- Low birth weight (<1,500 g)
- Use of ototoxic medications (eg, gentamicin, loop diuretics)
- Recurrent ear infections
- Bacterial meningitis
- Chronic exposure to loud noises
- Perforation of the tympanic membrane

45 to 64 years old, 30% of adults 65 to 74 years old, and 47% of adults 75 years old or older suffer from hearing impairment (National Institute on Deafness and Other Communication Disorders [NIDCD], 2008). Box 50-1 summarizes risk factors.

The National Institutes of Deafness and Other Communication Disorders (NIDCD) estimates that approximately 15% (26 million) of Americans between the ages of 20 and 69 have high-frequency hearing loss due to exposure to loud sounds or noise at work or in leisure activities. *Noise-induced hearing loss* refers to hearing loss that follows a long period of exposure to loud noise (eg, heavy machinery, engines, artillery). Occupations such as carpentry, plumbing, and coal mining have the highest risk of noise-induced hearing loss.

Acoustic trauma refers to hearing loss caused by a single exposure to an extremely intense noise, such as an explosion. Usually, noise-induced hearing loss occurs at a high frequency (about 4,000 Hz). However, with continued noise exposure, the hearing loss can become more severe and include adjacent frequencies. The minimum noise level known to cause noise-induced hearing loss, regardless of duration, is about 85 to 90 dB.

Noise exposure is inherent in many jobs (eg, mechanics, printers, pilots, musicians) and in hobbies such as woodworking and hunting. The Occupational Safety and Health Administration requires that workers wear ear protection to prevent noise-induced hearing loss when exposed to noise above the legal limits. Ear protection against noise is the most effective preventive measure available. There are no medications that protect against noise-induced hearing loss; hearing loss is permanent because the hair cells in the organ of Corti are destroyed.

Clinical Manifestations and Assessment

Early manifestations of hearing impairment and loss may include **tinnitus**, increasing inability to hear when in a group, and a need to turn up the volume of the television. Hearing impairment can also trigger changes in attitude, the ability to communicate, the awareness of surroundings, and even the ability to protect oneself, affecting a person's quality of life. In a classroom, a student with impaired hearing may be uninterested, inattentive, and have failing grades. A person at home may feel isolated because of an inability to hear the clock chime, the refrigerator hum, the birds sing, or the traffic pass. A pedestrian who is hearing impaired may attempt to cross the street and fail to hear an approaching car. People with impaired hearing may miss parts of a conversation. Many people are unaware of their gradual hearing impairment. Often, it is not the person with the hearing loss but the people with whom he or she is communicating who recognize the impairment first (Box 50-2).

Focused Assessment

Hearing Loss

Be on the alert for the following signs and symptoms:

- *Speech deterioration:* The person who slurs words or drops word endings, or produces flat-sounding speech, may not be hearing correctly. The ears guide the voice, both in loudness and in pronunciation.
- *Fatigue:* If a person tires easily when listening to conversation or to a speech, fatigue may be the result of straining to hear. Under these circumstances, the person may become irritable very easily.
- *Indifference:* It is easy for the person who cannot hear what others say to become depressed and disinterested in life in general.
- *Social withdrawal:* Not being able to hear what is going on causes the hearing-impaired person to withdraw from situations that might prove embarrassing.
- *Insecurity:* Lack of self-confidence and fear of mistakes create a feeling of insecurity in many hearing-impaired people. No one likes to say the wrong thing or do anything that might appear foolish.

- *Indecision and procrastination:* Loss of self-confidence makes it increasingly difficult for a hearing-impaired person to make decisions.
- *Suspiciousness:* The hearing-impaired person, who often hears only part of what is being said, may suspect that others are talking about him or her, or that portions of the conversation are deliberately spoken softly so that he or she will not hear them.
- *False pride:* The hearing-impaired person wants to conceal the hearing loss and thus often pretends to be hearing when he or she actually is not.
- *Loneliness and unhappiness:* Although everyone wishes for quiet now and then, *enforced* silence can be boring and even somewhat frightening. People with a hearing loss often feel isolated.
- *Tendency to dominate the conversation:* Many hearing-impaired people tend to dominate the conversation, knowing that as long as it is centered on them and they can control it, they are not so likely to be embarrassed by some mistake.

For various reasons, some people with hearing loss refuse to seek medical attention or wear a hearing aid. Others feel self-conscious wearing a hearing aid. Insightful people generally ask those with whom they are trying to communicate to let them know whether difficulties in communication exist. These attitudes and behaviors should be taken into account when counseling patients who need hearing assistance. The decision to wear a hearing aid is a personal one that is affected by these attitudes and behaviors.

Gerontologic Considerations

With aging, changes occur in the ear that may eventually lead to hearing deficits. Although few changes occur in the external ear, cerumen tends to become harder and drier, posing a greater chance of impaction. In the middle ear, the tympanic membrane may atrophy or become sclerotic. In the inner ear, cells at the base of the cochlea degenerate. A familial predisposition to sensorineural hearing loss is also seen, manifested by inability to hear high-frequency sounds, followed in time by the loss of middle and lower frequencies. The term **presbycusis** is used to describe this progressive hearing loss.

In addition to age-related changes, other factors can affect hearing in the elderly population, such as life-long exposure to loud noises (eg, jets, guns, heavy machinery, circular saws). Certain medications, such as aminoglycosides and aspirin, have ototoxic effects when renal changes (eg, in the older person) result in delayed medication excretion and increased levels of the medications in the blood. Many older people take quinine for treatment of leg cramps, and quinine can cause a hearing loss. Psychogenic factors and other disease processes (eg, diabetes) also may be partially responsible for sensorineural hearing loss.

When hearing loss occurs, proper evaluation and treatment are warranted. *Healthy People 2010* identified eight objectives for decreasing the problems caused by hearing loss. One of these objectives for people diagnosed with hearing loss or deafness is to use rehabilitation services and supplemental devices to improve communication with other people. Resources are available in workplaces and in schools. The Individuals with Disabilities Education Act (IDEA) was developed to ensure that children and adults, including elderly adults, receive the same opportunities in the educational system as those without hearing impairment.

Care of elderly patients includes recognizing emotional reactions related to hearing loss, such as suspicion of others because of an inability to hear adequately; frustration and anger, with repeated statements such as, "I didn't hear what you said"; and feelings of insecurity because of the inability to hear the telephone or alarms. The Americans with Disabilities Act (ADA) of 1990 required that all emergency services are accessible to people who have text message telephones (TTYs). In addition, in 1998, the Department of Justice mandated that all 911 centers in the United States be accessible to people with Text Telephone (TTYs).

Medical Management

Implanted Hearing Devices

Three types of implanted hearing devices are commercially available or in the investigational stage: the cochlear implant, the bone conduction device, and the semi-implantable hearing device. Cochlear implants are for patients with little or no hearing and are discussed below. Bone conduction devices, which transmit sound through the skull to the inner ear, are used in patients with a conductive hearing loss if a hearing aid is contraindicated (eg, those with chronic infection). The device is implanted postauricularly under the skin into the skull, and an external device—worn above the ear, not in the canal—transmits the sound through the skin. Currently there are two types of implantable hearing aids. The bone-anchored hearing aid (BAHA) is implanted behind the ear in the mastoid area. The middle ear implantation (MEI) is implanted in the middle ear cavity. The BAHA is used for conductive or mixed hearing loss, while the MEI is used for sensorineural hearing loss.

Cochlear Implant

A cochlear implant is an auditory prosthesis used for people with profound bilateral sensorineural hearing loss who do not benefit from conventional hearing aids. The hearing loss may be congenital or acquired. An implant does not restore normal hearing; rather, it helps the person detect medium to loud environmental sounds and conversation. The implant provides stimulation directly to the auditory nerve, bypassing the nonfunctioning hair cells of the inner ear. The microphone and signal processor, worn outside the body, transmit electrical stimuli to the implanted electrodes. The electrical signals stimulate the auditory nerve fibers and then the brain, where they are interpreted.

Candidates for a cochlear implant, who are usually at least 1 year of age, are selected after careful screening by otologic history, physical examination, audiologic testing, X-rays, and psychological testing. Criteria for choosing adults who may benefit from a cochlear implant include the following:

- Profound sensorineural hearing loss in both ears
- Inability to hear and recognize speech well with hearing aids
- No medical contraindication to a cochlear implant or general anesthesia
- Indications that being able to hear would enhance the patient's life

The surgery involves implanting a small receiver in the temporal bone through a postauricular incision and placing electrodes into the inner ear (Fig. 50-1). The microphone and transmitter are worn on an external unit. The patient undergoes extensive cochlear rehabilitation with the multidisciplinary team, which includes an audiologist and speech pathologist. Several months may be needed to learn to interpret the sounds heard. Children and adults who lost their

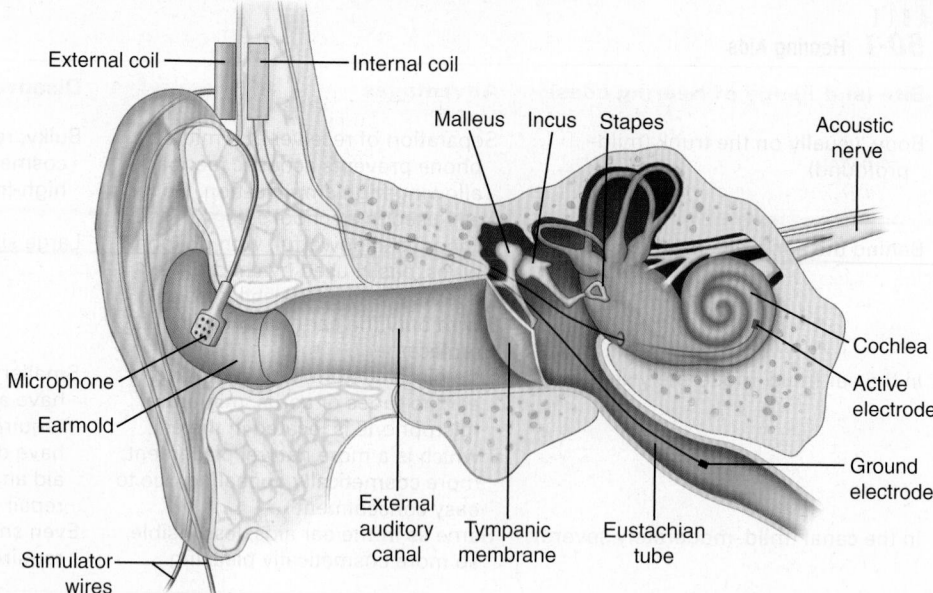

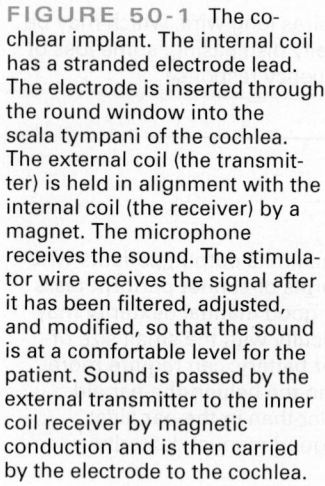

FIGURE 50-1 The cochlear implant. The internal coil has a stranded electrode lead. The electrode is inserted through the round window into the scala tympani of the cochlea. The external coil (the transmitter) is held in alignment with the internal coil (the receiver) by a magnet. The microphone receives the sound. The stimulator wire receives the signal after it has been filtered, adjusted, and modified, so that the sound is at a comfortable level for the patient. Sound is passed by the external transmitter to the inner coil receiver by magnetic conduction and is then carried by the electrode to the cochlea.

hearing before they learned to speak take much longer to acquire speech. There are wide variations of success with cochlear implants, and there is also controversy about their use, especially among the Deaf community. Patients who have had a cochlear implant are cautioned that magnetic resonance imaging (MRI) will inactivate the implant; MRI is to be used only when there is no other diagnostic option.

Aural Rehabilitation

If hearing loss is permanent or cannot be treated by medical or surgical means, or if the patient elects not to undergo surgery, aural rehabilitation may be beneficial. The purpose of aural rehabilitation is to maximize the communication skills of the person with hearing impairment. Aural rehabilitation includes auditory training, speech reading, speech training, and the use of hearing aids and hearing guide dogs.

Auditory training emphasizes listening skills, so the person who is hearing-impaired concentrates on the speaker. Speech reading (formerly known as lip reading) can help fill the gaps left by missed or misheard words. The goals of speech training are to conserve, develop, and prevent deterioration of current communication skills.

It is important to identify the type of hearing impairment a person has, so that rehabilitative efforts can be directed at his or her particular need. Surgical correction may be all that is necessary to treat and improve a conductive hearing loss by eliminating its cause. With advances in hearing aid technology, amplification for patients with sensorineural hearing loss is more helpful than ever.

Hearing Aids

A hearing aid is a device through which speech and environmental sounds are received by a microphone, converted to electrical signals, amplified, and reconverted to acoustic

signals. Many aids available for sensorineural hearing loss depress the low frequencies, or tones, and enhance hearing for the high frequencies. A general guideline for assessing the patient's need for a hearing aid is a hearing loss exceeding 30 dB in the range of 500 to 2,000 Hz in the better-hearing ear.

The evolution in technology has led to the availability of many smaller and more effective hearing aids. It is estimated that 98% of all hearing aids sold today are behind-the-ear, in-the-ear, or in-the-canal types (Table 50-1).

A hearing aid should be fitted according to the patient's needs (eg, type of hearing loss, manual dexterity, and preferences), rather than the brand name, by a certified audiologist licensed to dispense hearing aids. Many states have consumer protection laws that allow the hearing aid to be returned after a trial use if the patient is not completely satisfied.

A hearing aid makes sounds louder, but it does not improve a patient's ability to discriminate words or understand speech. People who have low discrimination scores (ie, 20%) on audiograms may derive little benefit from a hearing aid. Hearing aids amplify all sounds, including background noise, which may be disturbing to the wearer. Box 50-3 identifies additional problems associated with hearing aid use. Computerized hearing aids are available to compensate for background noise or allow amplification at certain programmed frequencies rather than at all frequencies. Occasionally, depending on the type of hearing loss, binaural aids (ie, one for each ear) may be indicated. Box 50-4 provides tips for hearing aid care.

Hearing Guide Dogs

Specially trained dogs (service dogs) are available to assist the person with a hearing loss. People who live alone are eligible to apply for a dog trained by International Hearing

TABLE
50-1 Hearing Aids

Site (and Range of Hearing Loss)	Advantages	Disadvantages
Body, usually on the trunk (mild–profound)	Separation of receiver and microphone prevents acoustic feedback, allowing high amplification. Generally used in a school setting.	Bulky; requires long wire, which may be cosmetically displeasing; some loss of high-frequency response
Behind the ear (mild–profound)	Economical; powerful, with no long wires; easily used by children—adapts easily as the child grows, with only the ear mold needing replacement.	Large size
In the ear (mild–moderately severe)	One-piece custom fit to contour of ear; no tubes or cords; miniature microphone is located in the ear, which is a more natural placement; more cosmetically appealing due to easy concealment	Smaller size limits output; patients who have arthritis or cannot perform tasks requiring good manual dexterity may have difficulty with the small size of aid and/or battery; can require more repair than the behind-the-ear aid.
In the canal (mild–moderately severe)	Same as in-the-ear aids; less visible, so more cosmetically pleasing	Even smaller than in-the-ear aids; requires good manual dexterity

---

BOX 50-3 Hearing Aid Problems

Improper Aid Selection

There are many hearing aids on the market. Consumers often find they cannot adjust to the hearing aid. One consideration is sound amplification. The amplifier is a transformer that increases the amplitude of the electrical signal sent to the receiver. The receiver takes the sound and transmits it to the ear. A mismatch between receiver and amplifier increases sound distortion and may become intolerable to patients. The open mold provides a full shell or half shell instrument. Aids need to transmit sound well, fit comfortably, and be aesthetically pleasing.

Inadequate Amplification
- Dead batteries
- Cerumen in ear
- Cerumen or other material in mold
- Wires or tubing disconnected from aid
- Aid turned off or volume too low
- Improper mold
- Improper aid for degree of loss

Pain from Mold
- Improperly fitted mold
- Ear skin or cartilage infection
- Middle ear infection
- Ear tumor
- Unrelated conditions of the temporomandibular joint, throat, or larynx

Whistling Noise
- Loose ear mold
- Improperly made
- Improperly worn
- Worn out

BOX 50-4 Patient Education

Tips for Hearing Aid Care
Cleaning
- Behind the ear (BTE) hearing aids may be washed infrequently using soap and water. Ensure that the device is dried thoroughly after cleaning.
- It is recommended to use a soft, cotton cloth to clean and remove dried cerumen for most hearing aid devices, such as in-the-ear hearing aids (ITE).
- Many hearing aid manufacturers advertise online information including cleaning directions.
- Clean the cannula with a small pipe cleaner-like device.
- Prevent complications by proper care of the ear device and keeping the ear canal clean and dry.

Malfunctioning
Inadequate amplification, a whistling noise, or pain from the mold can occur when a hearing aid is not functioning properly.
- Check for malfunctions:
  - Is the switch on properly?
  - Are the batteries charged and positioned correctly?
- If the hearing aid is still not working properly, notify the hearing aid dealer.
- If the unit requires extended time for repair, the dealer may lend you a hearing aid until the repair can be accomplished.

Recognizing Complications
Common medical complications include external otitis media and pressure ulcers in the external auditory canal.
- Be alert for signs and symptoms of these infections, including painful ear, especially when the external ear is touched, canal swelling, redness, difficulty hearing, pain radiating to the jaw area, and fever.
- If any of these symptoms are present, notify your health care provider for evaluation. You may need medication to treat infection, pain, or both.

Dog, Inc. The dog reacts to the sound of a telephone, a doorbell, an alarm clock, a baby's cry, a knock at the door, a smoke alarm, or an intruder. The dog alerts its handler by physical contact; the dog then runs to the source of the noise. In public, the dog positions itself between the person with hearing impairment and any potential hazard that the person cannot hear, such as an oncoming vehicle or a loud, hostile person. In many states, a certified hearing guide dog is legally permitted access to public transportation, public eating places, and stores, including food markets.

Nursing Management

Communicating Effectively

Nurses who understand the different types of hearing loss are more successful in adopting a communication style to fit the needs and preferences of every patient. Trying to speak in a loud voice to a person who cannot hear high-frequency sounds only makes understanding more difficult. However, strategies such as talking into the less-impaired ear and using gestures and facial expressions can help (Box 50-5).

A major issue for many people who are deaf or hearing-impaired is that they have other health problems that often do not receive attention, in large part because of communication barriers with their health care practitioners. To meet the health care needs of these patients, practitioners are legally obligated to make accommodations for a patient's inability to hear. Providing interpreters for those who can communicate through sign language is essential in many situations, so that the practitioner can effectively communicate with the patient.

During health care and screening procedures, the health care practitioner must be aware that patients who are deaf or hearing-impaired have certain limitations. They are unable to read lips, see a signer, or read written materials in the dark rooms required during some diagnostic tests. The same situation exists if the practitioner is wearing a mask or is not in the direct line of vision. Nurses and other health care practitioners must work with patients who are deaf or hearing-impaired and their families to identify practical and effective means of communication and to ensure accommodations are made.

Maintaining a Quiet Environment

Loud, persistent noise has been found to cause constriction of peripheral blood vessels, increased blood pressure and heart rate (because of increased secretion of adrenalin), and increased gastrointestinal activity, as well as disturb patterns of sleep. Although research is needed to address the overall effects of noise on the human body, a quiet environment is more conducive to peace of mind (Box 50-6). A person who is ill feels more at ease when noise is kept to a minimum.

BOX 50-5

Communicating With People Who are Hearing-Impaired

For the person who is hearing-impaired whose speech is difficult to understand:

- Consider how the person prefers to communicate with others. Do not assume that writing, gestures, or other means are the best or preferred technique.
- Consider if the person uses sign language. Interpreters are available in person or by video from the American Sign Language Inc., Interpreting Service (ASLI). These specialists provide the best means of communication, and provide accurate, professional services.
- Devote full attention to what the person is saying. Look and listen—do not try to attend to another task while listening.
- Engage the speaker in conversation when it is possible for you to anticipate the replies. This enables you to become accustomed to any peculiarities in speech patterns.
- Try to determine the essential context of what is being said; you can often fill in the details from context.
- Do not try to appear as if you understand if you do not.
- If you cannot understand at all or have serious doubt about your ability to understand what is being said, have the person write the message rather than risk misunderstanding. Having the person repeat the message in speech, after you know its content, also aids you in becoming accustomed to the person's pattern of speech.

- Written communication is an excellent resource. Written material should be written at a third-grade level so that the majority of people can understand it.

For the person who is hearing-impaired who speech reads:

- If you need to get the patient's attention, wave your hand in front of their visual field.
- When speaking, always face the person as directly as possible and smile.
- Make sure your face is as clearly visible as possible. Locate yourself so that your face is well lighted; avoid being silhouetted against strong light. Do not obscure the person's view of your mouth in any way; avoid talking with any object held in your mouth.
- Be sure that the patient knows the topic or subject before going ahead with what you plan to say. This enables the person to use contextual clues in speech reading.
- Speak slowly and distinctly, pausing more frequently than you would normally.
- If you question whether some important direction or instruction has been understood, check to be certain that the patient has the full meaning of your message.
- If for any reason your mouth must be covered (as with a mask), and you must direct or instruct the patient, write the message.

BOX 50-6

Nursing Research

Bridging the Gap to Evidence-Based Practice

Noise in the Clinical Setting

Deitrick, L.M., Kennedy, P., Cyriax, C., & Davies-Hathen, N. (2009). Using rapid assessment to evaluate noise on an in-patient unit. *Journal of Nursing Care Quality, 24*(1), 27–32.

Purpose

Excessive noise in clinical settings negatively impacts patients and staff in several ways, including lost sleep, higher blood pressure, lower overall patient satisfaction, increased readmission rates, and increased employee stress levels. The authors proposed using rapid assessment as an approach to identify and solve noise problems in the hospital setting.

Design

The study involved using a variety of health care providers to collect data (including photographs, maps, noise meters, and interviews) quickly and efficiently. The study was conducted on a 34-bed medical-surgical inpatient unit for a 4-week period.

Findings

Six sources of noise were identified: (1) conversational noise, (2) noise from doors being opened or closed, (3) noise from activity around the housekeeping closet, (4) noise from the pneumatic/message-tube station, (5) hallway noise, and (6) miscellaneous noise. The highest source of noise was conversational and was associated with change of shift. Noise was loudest near the

front of the nursing station and achieved a decibel level of 99.6 at mid-afternoon change of shift (decibel levels of 45 during the day and 35 decibels at night are recommended). Door noise accounted for decibel levels of 76 with the use of a push bar versus nearly 87 when slamming the door open. Other areas of high decibels included the staff locker room, which included noise from the locker-room door closing and staff conversation as they entered/exited the room. Noise generated from housekeeping activities included metal buckets being filled and moved; the housekeeping closet area was also deemed to generate high decibel recordings (78.4 decibels). The pneumatic-message tube station and noise from tubes dropping into collection bin had a mean level of 75.1 decibels. Additional sources of noise included noise from shoes on the linoleum from hard-soled shoes or very high and thin heels. Miscellaneous noise included the opening and closing of wall-mounted metal flip down chart racks outside patient rooms and a fully loaded linen cart wheeled through the unit.

Nursing Implications

This study revealed the numerous sources of noise that staff and patients are exposed to on a daily basis and emphasized the role all providers have on reducing the level of noise on units. Engineering and infrastructure changes are suggested, along with the use of quiet sounds to remind providers about the importance of creating a calm environment.

The World Health Organization set noise guidelines for hospitals since noise negatively affect patient outcomes and staff performance (Berglund, Lindvall, & Schwela, 1999). Infrastructure designs such as noiseless call bell systems and sound-masking floors and walls represent attempts to decrease noise in hospitals.

CONDITIONS OF THE EXTERNAL EAR

CERUMEN IMPACTION

Cerumen normally accumulates in the external canal in various amounts and colors. Although wax does not usually need to be removed, impaction occasionally occurs.

Clinical Manifestations and Assessment

Impaction causes **otalgia**, a sensation of fullness or pain in the ear, with or without a hearing loss. Accumulation of

cerumen as a cause of hearing loss is especially significant in the elderly population. Attempts to clear the external auditory canal with matches, hairpins, and other implements are dangerous because trauma to the skin, infection, and damage to the tympanic membrane can occur.

Medical and Nursing Management

Cerumen can be removed by irrigation, suction, or instrumentation. Unless the patient has a perforated eardrum or an inflamed external ear (ie, **otitis externa**), gentle irrigation usually helps remove impacted cerumen, particularly if it is not tightly packed into the external auditory canal. For successful removal, the water stream must flow behind the obstructing cerumen to move it first laterally and then out of the canal. To prevent injury, the lowest effective pressure should be used. However, if the eardrum behind the impaction is perforated, water can enter the middle ear, producing acute vertigo and infection. If irrigation is unsuccessful, a trained health care provider can perform direct visual, mechanical removal on a cooperative patient.

Instilling a few drops of warmed glycerin, mineral oil, or half-strength hydrogen peroxide into the ear canal for 30 minutes can soften cerumen before its removal. Ceruminolytic agents, such as peroxide in glyceryl (Debrox), are available; however, these compounds may cause an allergic dermatitis reaction. Using any softening solution two or three times a day for several days is generally sufficient. If the cerumen cannot be dislodged by these methods, instruments, such as a cerumen curette, aural suction, and a binocular microscope for magnification, can be used by a provider with specialized training.

FOREIGN BODIES

Some objects are inserted intentionally into the ear by adults who may have been trying to clean the external canal or relieve itching. Insects may also enter the ear canal. In either case, the effects may range from no symptoms to profound pain and decreased hearing.

Medical and Nursing Management

Removing a foreign body from the external auditory canal can be quite challenging. The three standard methods for removing foreign bodies are the same as those for removing cerumen: irrigation, suction, and instrumentation. The contraindications for irrigation are also the same. Foreign vegetable bodies and insects tend to swell; thus, irrigation is contraindicated. Usually, an insect can be dislodged by instilling mineral oil, which will kill the insect and allow it to be removed.

Attempts to remove a foreign body from the external canal may be dangerous in unskilled hands. The object may be pushed completely into the bony portion of the canal, lacerating the skin and perforating the tympanic membrane. In some circumstances, the foreign body may have to be extracted in the operating room with the patient under general anesthesia.

CONDITIONS OF THE MIDDLE EAR

TYMPANIC MEMBRANE PERFORATION

Perforation of the tympanic membrane is usually caused by infection or trauma. Sources of trauma include skull fracture, explosive injury, or a severe blow to the ear. Less frequently, perforation is caused by foreign objects (eg, cotton-tipped applicators, bobby pins, keys) that have been pushed too far into the external auditory canal. In addition to tympanic membrane perforation, injury to the ossicles and even the inner ear may result; thus, attempts by patients to clear the external auditory canal should be discouraged. During infection, the tympanic membrane can rupture if the pressure in the middle ear exceeds the atmospheric pressure in the external auditory canal.

Clinical Manifestations and Assessment

Symptoms of tympanic membrane perforation include whistling sounds upon sneezing and blowing nose, reduced hearing, purulent drainage from ear(s), and/or otalgia.

Medical and Nursing Management

Although most tympanic membrane perforations heal spontaneously within weeks after rupture, some may take several months to heal. Some perforations persist because scar tissue grows over the edges of the perforation, preventing extension of the epithelial cells across the margins and healing. In the case of a head injury or temporal bone fracture, a patient is observed for evidence of cerebrospinal fluid: **otorrhea** or **rhinorrhea**, a clear, watery drainage from the ear or nose, respectively. If present, the nurse is aware that this represents an abnormal communication between the subarachnoid space and the tympanomastoid space, with a risk of a central nervous system (CNS) infection. While healing, the ear must be protected from water.

Perforations that do not heal on their own may require surgery. The decision to perform a **tympanoplasty** (surgical repair of the tympanic membrane) is usually based on the need to prevent potential infection from water entering the ear or the desire to improve the patient's hearing. Performed on an outpatient basis, tympanoplasty may involve a variety of surgical techniques. In all techniques, tissue (commonly from the temporalis fascia) is placed across the perforation to allow healing. Surgery is usually successful in closing the perforation permanently and improving hearing. Postoperative instructions after middle ear surgery are found in Box 50-7.

OTOSCLEROSIS

Otosclerosis involves the stapes and is thought to result from the formation of new, abnormal spongy bone, especially around the oval window, with resulting fixation of the stapes. The efficient transmission of sound is prevented because the stapes cannot vibrate and carry the sound as conducted from the malleus and incus to the inner ear. Otosclerosis is more common in women and frequently hereditary, and pregnancy may worsen it.

Clinical Manifestations and Assessment

Otosclerosis may involve one or both ears and manifests as a progressive conductive or mixed hearing loss. The patient may or may not complain of tinnitus (ringing in the ear). Otoscopic examination usually reveals a normal tympanic membrane. Bone conduction is better than air conduction on Rinne testing. The audiogram confirms conductive hearing loss or mixed loss, especially in the low frequencies.

BOX 50-7

Patient Education

Self-Care After Middle Ear or Mastoid Surgery

Postoperative instructions for patients who have had middle ear and mastoid surgery may vary among otolaryngologists. General teaching guidelines for the patient may include:

- Take antibiotics and other medications as prescribed.
- Blow nose gently, one side at a time, for 1 week after surgery.
- Sneeze and cough with the mouth open for a few weeks after surgery.
- Avoid heavy lifting (>10 lb), straining, and bending over for a few weeks after surgery.
- Popping and crackling sensations in the operative ear are normal for approximately 3 to 5 weeks after surgery.

- Temporary hearing loss is normal in the operative ear due to fluid, blood, or packing in the ear.
- Report excessive or purulent ear drainage to the physician. Some slightly bloody or serosanguineous drainage from the ear is normal after surgery.
- Change the cotton ball in the ear as needed.
- Avoid getting water in the operative ear for 2 weeks after surgery. You may shampoo the hair 2 to 3 days postoperatively if the ear is protected from water by saturating a cotton ball with petroleum jelly (or some other water-insoluble substance) and loosely placing it in the ear. If the postauricular suture line becomes wet, pat (do not rub) the area and cover it with a thin layer of antibiotic ointment.

Medical and Nursing Management

There is no known nonsurgical treatment for otosclerosis. However, some physicians believe the use of sodium fluoride can mature the abnormal spongy bone growth and prevent the breakdown of the bone tissue. Amplification with a hearing aid also may help.

One of two surgical procedures may be performed, the stapedectomy or the stapedotomy. A stapedectomy involves removing the stapes superstructure and part of the footplate and inserting a tissue graft and a suitable prosthesis (Fig. 50-2). The surgeon drills a small hole into the footplate to hold a prosthesis. The prosthesis bridges the gap between the incus and the inner ear, providing better sound conduction. Stapes surgery is very successful; approximately 95% of patients experience resolution of conductive hearing loss. Balance disturbance or true vertigo, which rarely occurs in other middle ear surgical procedures, may occur during the postoperative period for several days.

MIDDLE EAR MASSES

Other than **cholesteatoma** (middle ear or mastoid tumor), masses in the middle ear are rare. A glomus jugulare tumor is a tumor that arises from the jugular vein and appears as a red blemish on or behind the tympanic membrane upon examination with an otoscope. Glomus jugulare tumors are rarely malignant; however, due to their location, treatment may be necessary to relieve symptoms. The treatment for glomus tumors is surgical excision, except in poor surgical candidates, in whom radiation therapy is used.

A facial nerve neuroma is a tumor on cranial nerve VII, the facial nerve. These types of tumors are usually not visible on otoscopic examination but are suspected when a patient presents with a facial nerve paresis. X-ray evaluation is used to identify the site of the tumor along the facial nerve. The treatment is surgical removal.

CONDITIONS OF THE INNER EAR

Almost 8 million American adults are affected by a chronic problem with balance, and an additional 2.4 million are affected by dizziness alone. Balance or vestibular problems are reported in approximately 9% of the older adult population over the age of 65. Body balance is maintained by the cooperation of the muscles and joints of the body (proprioceptive system), the eyes (visual system), and the labyrinth (vestibular system). These areas send their information about equilibrium, or balance, to the brain (cerebellar system) for coordination and perception in the cerebral cortex. Since the brain obtains its blood supply from the cardiovascular system, arteriosclerosis can also cause a disturbance in balance. Likewise, impaired vision can have an impact on equilibrium. The vestibular apparatus of the inner ear provides feedback regarding the movements and the position of the head and body in space. Disorders of balance are a major cause of falls in the elderly population (NIDCD, 2008).

Patients and health care providers frequently use the term *dizziness* to describe any altered sensation of orientation in space. **Vertigo** is defined as the misperception or illusion of motion of the person or the surroundings. Most people with vertigo describe a spinning sensation or say they feel as though objects are moving around them. *Ataxia* is a failure of muscular coordination and may be present in patients with vestibular disease. Syncope, fainting, and loss of consciousness are not forms of vertigo and usually indicate disease in the cardiovascular system.

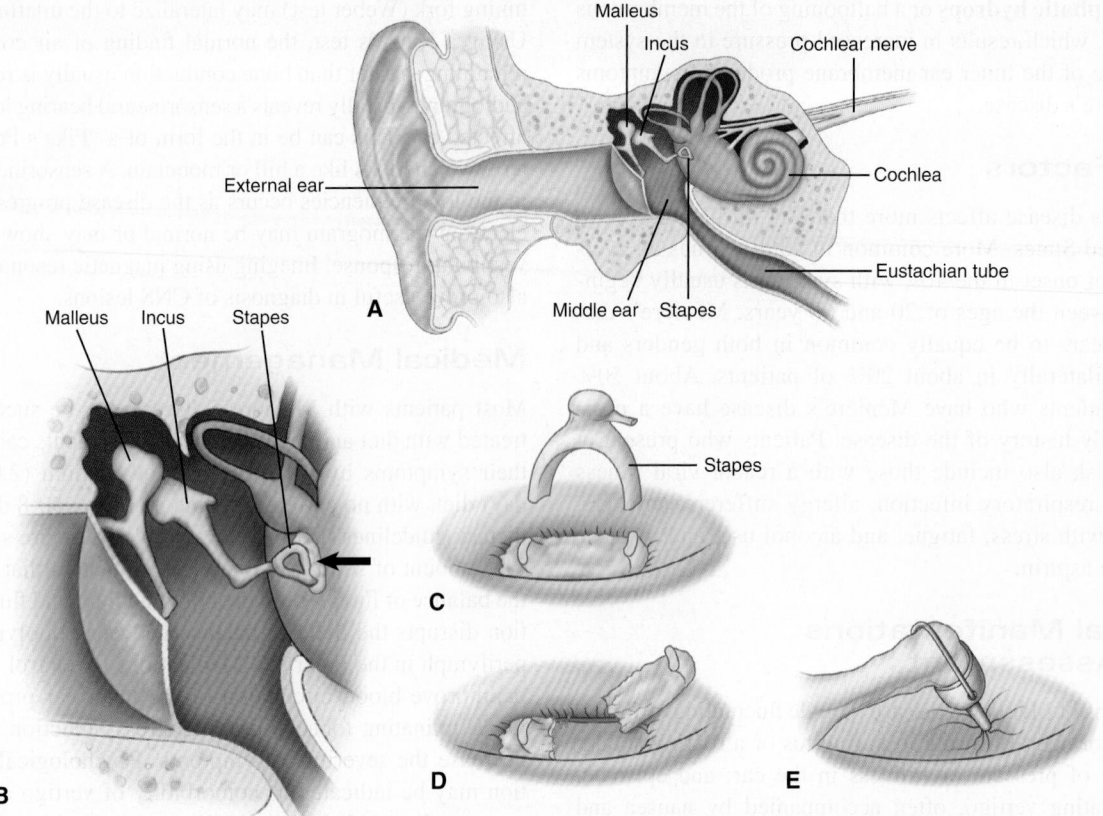

FIGURE 50-2 Stapedectomy for otosclerosis. (**A**) Normal anatomy. (**B**) Arrow points to sclerotic process at the foot of the stapes. (**C**) Stapes broken away surgically from its diseased base. The hole in the footplate provides an area where an instrument can grasp the plate. (**D**) The footplate is removed from its base. Some otosclerotic tissue may remain, and tissue is placed over it. (**E**) Robinson stainless-steel prosthesis in position.

Nystagmus is an involuntary rhythmic movement of the eyes; pathologically, it is an ocular disorder but is also associated with vestibular dysfunction. Nystagmus can be horizontal, vertical, or rotary and can be caused by a disorder in the central or peripheral nervous system.

MOTION SICKNESS

Motion sickness is a disturbance of equilibrium caused by constant motion. For example, it can occur aboard a ship, while riding on a merry-go-round or swing, or in the back seat of a car.

Clinical Manifestations and Assessment

The syndrome manifests itself in sweating, pallor, nausea, and vomiting caused by vestibular overstimulation. These manifestations may persist for several hours after the stimulation stops.

Medical and Nursing Management

Over-the-counter antihistamines such as dimenhydrinate (Dramamine) or meclizine hydrochloride (Antivert) may provide some relief of nausea and vomiting by blocking the conduction of the vestibular pathway of the inner ear. Anticholinergic medications, such as scopolamine patches, may also be effective because they antagonize the histamine response. These must be replaced every few days. Side effects such as dry mouth and drowsiness may occur. Potentially hazardous activities such as driving a car or operating heavy machinery should be avoided if drowsiness occurs.

MÉNIÈRE'S DISEASE

Ménière's disease is a disorder of the inner ear that causes vertigo, tinnitus, a feeling of fullness or pressure in the ear, and fluctuating hearing loss.

Pathophysiology

Ménière's disease is believed to be the result of fluctuating pressure within the inner ear or the mixing of inner ear fluids. The membranous labyrinth of the inner ear contains a fluid called *endolymph*. The membranes can become dilated because of malabsorption of the fluid in the endolymphatic sac or a blockage in the drainage of fluid in the endolymphatic duct within the labyrinth. This dilation is termed

endolymphatic hydrops or a ballooning of the membranous labyrinth, which results in increased pressure in the system or rupture of the inner ear membrane producing symptoms of Ménière's disease.

Risk Factors

Ménière's disease affects more than 2.4 million people in the United States. More common in adults, it has an average age of onset in the 40s, with symptoms usually beginning between the ages of 20 and 60 years. Ménière's disease appears to be equally common in both genders and occurs bilaterally in about 20% of patients. About 50% of the patients who have Ménière's disease have a positive family history of the disease. Patients who present at greater risk also include those with a recent viral illness or upper respiratory infection, allergy sufferers, smokers, patients with stress, fatigue, and alcohol use, and in those who take aspirin.

Clinical Manifestations and Assessment

Symptoms of Ménière's disease include fluctuating, progressive sensorineural hearing loss; tinnitus or a roaring sound; a feeling of pressure or fullness in the ear; and episodic, incapacitating vertigo, often accompanied by nausea and vomiting. These symptoms range in severity from a minor nuisance to extreme disability, especially if the attacks of vertigo are severe. At the onset of the disease, perhaps only one or two of the symptoms are manifested.

Some clinicians believe that there are two subsets of the disease, known as atypical Ménière's disease: cochlear and vestibular. Cochlear Ménière's disease is recognized as a fluctuating, progressive sensorineural hearing loss associated with tinnitus and aural pressure in the absence of vestibular symptoms or findings. Vestibular Ménière's disease is characterized as the occurrence of episodic vertigo associated with aural pressure but no cochlear symptoms. Patients may experience either cochlear or vestibular disease symptoms; however, eventually all of these symptoms develop.

Vertigo is usually the most troublesome complaint related to Ménière's disease. A careful history is taken to determine the frequency, duration, severity, and character of the vertigo attacks. Vertigo may last minutes to hours, possibly accompanied by nausea or vomiting. Diaphoresis and a persistent feeling of imbalance or disequilibrium may waken patients at night. Some patients report that these feelings last for days. However, they usually feel well between attacks. Hearing loss may fluctuate, with tinnitus and aural pressure waxing and waning with changes in hearing. These feelings may occur during or before attacks, or they may be constant. Long periods of remission may occur.

Physical examination findings are usually normal, with the exception of those of cranial nerve VIII. Sounds from a tuning fork (Weber test) may lateralize to the unaffected ear. Using a Rinne's test, the normal finding of air conduction remaining greater than bone conduction usually is found. An audiogram typically reveals a sensorineural hearing loss in the affected ear. This can be in the form of a "Pike's Peak" pattern, which looks like a hill or mountain. A sensorineural loss in the low frequencies occurs as the disease progresses. The electronystagmogram may be normal or may show reduced vestibular response. Imaging using magnetic resonance may also prove useful in diagnosis of CNS lesions.

Medical Management

Most patients with Ménière's disease can be successfully treated with diet and medication. Many patients can control their symptoms by adhering to a low-sodium (2,000 mg/day) diet, with no caffeine and alcohol. Box 50-8 describes dietary guidelines that may be useful in Ménière's disease. The amount of sodium is one of many factors that regulate the balance of fluid within the body. Sodium and fluid retention disrupts the delicate balance between endolymph and perilymph in the inner ear. Medications to control allergies or improve blood circulation of the inner ear prove helpful. Eliminating tobacco use and stress reduction can also decrease the severity of symptoms. Psychological evaluation may be indicated as comorbidity of vertigo and anxiety is well established in the literature. A plan of nursing care for a patient with vertigo is available online at http://thePoint.lww.com/Pellico1e.

BOX 50-8 | **Nutrition Alert**

Dietary Guidelines for Patients With Ménière's Disease

Advise patients to:
- Limit foods high in salt or sugar. Be aware of foods with hidden salts and sugars.
- Eat meals and snacks at regular intervals to stay hydrated. Missing meals or snacks may alter the fluid level in the inner ear.
- Eat fresh fruits, vegetables, and whole grains. Limit the amount of canned, frozen, or processed foods with high sodium content.
- Drink plenty of fluids daily. Water, milk, and low-sugar fruit juices are recommended. Limit intake of coffee, tea, and soft drinks. Avoid caffeine because of its diuretic effect.
- Limit alcohol intake. Alcohol may change the volume and concentration of the inner ear fluid and may worsen symptoms.
- Avoid monosodium glutamate (MSG), which may increase symptoms.
- Avoid aspirin and aspirin-containing medications. Aspirin may increase tinnitus and dizziness.

Pharmacologic Therapy

Pharmacologic therapy for Ménière's disease consists of antihistamines, such as meclizine (Antivert), which suppress the vestibular system. Tranquilizers, such as diazepam (Valium), may be used in acute instances to help control vertigo. Antiemetics, such as promethazine (Phenergan) suppositories, help control the nausea, vomiting, and vertigo because of their antihistamine effect. Betahistine hydrochloride and diuretic therapy may reduce the severity of symptoms by lowering the pressure in the endolymphatic system. Intake of foods containing potassium (eg, bananas, cantaloupe, oranges) is necessary if the patient takes a diuretic that causes potassium loss. There is no scientific basis for the use of vasodilators, such as nicotinic acid, papaverine hydrochloride (Pavabid), and methantheline bromide (Banthine), to alleviate the symptoms, but they are often used in conjunction with other therapies.

Surgical Management

Although most patients respond well to conservative therapy, some continue to have disabling attacks of vertigo. If these attacks reduce their quality of life, patients may elect to undergo chemical treatment or surgery for relief. Surgical procedures, such as labyrinthectomy, vestibular neurectomy, or endolymphatic sac decompression, may be considered.

Endolymphatic Sac Decompression

Endolymphatic sac decompression, or shunting, theoretically equalizes the pressure in the endolymphatic space. A shunt or drain is inserted in the endolymphatic sac through a postauricular incision. Many otolaryngologists favor this procedure as a first-line surgical approach to treat the vertigo of Ménière's disease because it is relatively simple and safe and can be performed on an outpatient basis.

Middle and Inner Ear Perfusion

Ototoxic medications, such as streptomycin or gentamicin, can be administered to patients by infusion into the middle and inner ear. These medications are used to destroy vestibular function and decrease vertigo. The success rate for eliminating vertigo is about 85%, but the risk of significant hearing loss is high. After the procedure, many patients have a period of imbalance that lasts several weeks.

Intraotologic Catheters

In an attempt to deliver medication directly to the inner ear, catheters are being developed to provide a conduit from the outer ear to the inner ear. The route of the catheter is from the external ear canal through or around the tympanic membrane and to the round window niche or membrane. Medicinal fluids can be placed against the round window for a direct route to the inner ear fluids.

Potential uses of these catheters include treatment for sudden hearing loss and various disorders causing intractable vertigo. Future applications may include tinnitus and slowly progressing sensorineural hearing loss. Intratympanic injections of ototoxic medications for round window membrane diffusion can be used to decrease vestibular function. Established surgical techniques can be used for the patient with vertigo who has not responded to medical or physical therapeutic modalities.

Vestibular Nerve Sectioning

Vestibular nerve sectioning provides the greatest success rate (~98%) in eliminating the attacks of vertigo. It can be performed by a translabyrinthine approach (ie, through the hearing mechanism) or in a manner that can conserve hearing (ie, suboccipital or middle cranial fossa), depending on the degree of hearing loss. Most patients with incapacitating Ménière's disease have little or no effective hearing. Cutting the nerve prevents the brain from receiving input from the semicircular canals. This procedure requires a brief hospital stay.

TINNITUS

Tinnitus is a symptom of an underlying disorder of the ear that is associated with hearing loss. This condition affects approximately 10% of the U.S. population between 40 and 70 years of age. The severity of tinnitus may range from mild to severe. Patients describe tinnitus as a roaring, buzzing, or hissing sound in one or both ears. Numerous factors may contribute to the development of tinnitus, including several ototoxic substances (Box 50-9). Underlying disorders that contribute to tinnitus may include thyroid disease, hyperlipidemia, vitamin B_{12} deficiency, psychological disorders (eg, depression, anxiety), fibromyalgia, otologic disorders (Ménière's disease, acoustic neuroma), and neurologic disorders (head injury, multiple sclerosis).

A physical examination should be performed to determine the cause of tinnitus. Diagnostic testing determines if hearing loss is present. An audiograph speech discrimination test or a tympanogram may be used to help determine the cause. Some forms of tinnitus are irreversible; therefore,

BOX 50-9 Selected Ototoxic Substances

- *Diuretics:* Ethacrynic acid, furosemide, acetazolamide
- *Chemotherapeutic agents:* Cisplatin, nitrogen mustard
- *Antimalarial agents:* Quinine, chloroquine
- *Anti-inflammatory agents:* Salicylates (aspirin), indomethacin
- *Chemicals:* Alcohol, arsenic
- *Aminoglycoside antibiotics:* Amikacin, gentamicin, kanamycin, netilmicin, neomycin, streptomycin, tobramycin
- *Other antibiotics:* Erythromycin, minocycline, polymyxin B, vancomycin
- *Metals:* Gold, mercury, lead

patients may need teaching and counseling about ways of adjusting to their treatment and dealing with tinnitus in the future.

BENIGN PAROXYSMAL POSITIONAL VERTIGO

Benign paroxysmal positional vertigo (BPPV) is a brief period of incapacitating vertigo that occurs when the position of the patient's head is changed with respect to gravity, typically by placing the head back with the affected ear turned down. The onset is sudden and followed by a predisposition for positional vertigo, usually for hours to weeks but occasionally for months or years. Other symptoms may include lightheadedness, blurred vision, and nausea and vomiting.

Pathophysiology

BPPV is thought to be due to the disruption of debris in the labyrinth termed **otoconia** (small crystal particles of calcium carbonate that detach and float in the endolymph and cause symptomatology). This is frequently stimulated by head trauma, infection (particularly of the respiratory tract), or other events. Precipitating factors include sneezing or coughing, or the vertigo may be induced by any change in head positioning. Bed rest is recommended for patients with acute symptoms.

Clinical Manifestations and Assessment

Diagnosis of BBPV is performed after an ear exam, audiogram, and test of nerve responses and use of the Dix-Hallpike test, also called the Nylen-Barany test. The test involves making the patient undergo a rapid change from an erect seated position to a supine position with the head hanging over the edge of the examination table to the left, right, or center. Dizziness and peripheral vertigo will be elicited with the affected ear pointing downward. The eyes are examined for a brief period for nystagmus, which also commonly accompanies vertigo.

Medical and Nursing Management

Repositioning techniques can be used to treat vertigo, such as the Epley maneuver. The maneuver is designed to reposition the canalith and involves quick movements of the head. The noninvasive procedure is performed by placing the patient in a sitting position and turning the head to a 45-degree angle on the affected side and 30 to 45 degrees backward. Then the patient is quickly moved to the supine position. The procedure is repeated, tilting the head to the opposite side. The patient must not lie flat for 48 to 72 hours after repositioning to prevent the particles from reentering the posterior canal. The procedure is safe, inexpensive, and easy to perform.

Patients with acute vertigo are treated with medications that target vertigo and its related symptoms of nausea, vomiting, and anxiety. Vestibular suppressants that are commonly used originate from classes of anticholinergics (scopolamine), antihistamines (meclizine, dimenhydrinate), and benzodiazepines. Meclizine is often the drug of choice, with patients treated for a 1 to 2 week course of therapy. Antiemetic medications, such as phenothiazines, are used to treat nausea. Meclizine has both vestibular suppressant and antiemetic effects.

Vestibular rehabilitation can be used in the management of vestibular disorders. This strategy promotes active use of the vestibular system through an interdisciplinary team approach, including medical and nursing care, stress management, biofeedback, vocational rehabilitation, and physical therapy. A physical therapist prescribes balance exercises that help the brain compensate for the impairment to the balance system.

OTOTOXICITY

A variety of medications may have adverse effects on the cochlea, vestibular apparatus, or cranial nerve VIII. All but a few, such as aspirin and quinine, cause irreversible hearing loss. At high doses, aspirin toxicity can produce bilateral tinnitus. IV medications, especially the aminoglycosides, are the most common cause of ototoxicity, and they destroy the hair cells in the organ of Corti (see Box 50-9).

To prevent loss of hearing or balance, patients receiving potentially ototoxic medications should be counseled about the side effects of these medications. These medications should be used with caution in patients who are at high risk for complications, such as children, the elderly, pregnant patients, patients with kidney or liver problems, and patients with current hearing disorders. Blood levels of the medications should be monitored, and patients receiving long-term IV antibiotics should be monitored with an audiogram twice each week during therapy.

ACOUSTIC NEUROMA

Acoustic neuromas develop in 1 of every 10,000 people per year. These neuromas account for 5% to 10% of all intracranial tumors and seem to occur with equal frequency in men and women of any age, although most occur during middle age.

Pathophysiology

Acoustic neuromas are slow-growing, benign tumors of cranial nerve VIII, usually arising from the Schwann cells of the vestibular portion of the nerve. Most acoustic tumors arise within the internal auditory canal and extend into the cerebellopontine angle to press on the brainstem, possibly destroying the vestibular nerve.

Clinical Manifestations and Assessment

The most common assessment findings of patients with acoustic neuromas are unilateral tinnitus and hearing loss

with or without vertigo or balance disturbance. It is important to identify asymmetry in audiovestibular test results, so that further workup can be performed to rule out an acoustic neuroma. MRI with a paramagnetic contrast agent (ie, gadolinium or Magnevist) is the imaging study of choice. If the patient is claustrophobic or cannot undergo an MRI for other reasons, or if the scan is unavailable, a computed tomography (CT) scan with contrast dye is performed; however, MRI is more sensitive than CT in delineating a small tumor.

Medical and Nursing Management

Surgical removal of acoustic tumors is the treatment of choice because these tumors do not respond well to radiation or chemotherapy. Because treatment of acoustic tumors crosses several specialties, the interdisciplinary treatment approach involves a neurologist and a neurosurgeon. The objective of the surgery is to remove the tumor while preserving facial nerve function. Most acoustic tumors have damaged the cochlear portion of cranial nerve VIII, and hearing is impaired. In these patients, the surgery is performed using a translabyrinthine approach, and the hearing mechanism is destroyed. If hearing is still good before surgery, a suboccipital or middle cranial fossa approach to removing the tumor may be used. This procedure exposes the lateral third of the internal auditory canal and preserves hearing.

Complications of surgery include facial nerve paralysis, cerebrospinal fluid leakage, meningitis, and cerebral edema. Death from acoustic neuroma surgery is rare.

Chapter Review

Critical Thinking Exercises

1. You are visiting an elderly man for a postoperative home visit following a cholecystectomy. He tells you that he has had severe leg cramps at nighttime and has started taking quinine daily. He has noticed a significant improvement in the leg cramps. During your assessment, you also learn that he has a significant hearing loss, and his wife tells you that she thinks that his hearing has worsened over the past several months; however, she attributes his hearing loss to old age and to anxiety regarding his recent surgery. Devise a teaching plan for this patient and his wife. Provide a rationale for each part of the plan.

2. A 20-year-old man, a member of a college swim team, has recurrent external otitis—his third episode in the past 6 weeks. He is being treated at an ear-nose-throat clinic. Devise an evidence-based practice teaching plan for this patient.

NCLEX-Style Review Questions

1. A 56-year-old patient who is hearing-impaired is scheduled for a colonoscopy. Which of the following nursing actions are most appropriate in performing patient education prior to the procedure?
   A. Face the patient directly, smile, and speak slowly.
   B. Continue to administer medications while educating the patient.
   C. Nod to make up for awkward silence, even if you don't know what is being said.
   D. Use only gestures to communicate the highlights of content to be covered.

2. The nurse caring for the patient with Ménière's disease restricts the following foods in the dietary plan. Select all that apply.
   A. Coffee
   B. Wine
   C. Baked potato
   D. Cheese

3. During preoperative teaching, the 25-year-old patient receiving cochlear implants states, "I will be able to fully regain my hearing with the implants." What is the nurse's best response to the patient?
   A. "The implants will assist you to detect medium to loud environmental sound and conversation rather than restoring normal hearing."
   B. "The implant will assist you to restore normal hearing fully."
   C. "The implants will be immediately effective."
   D. "The implant will require minimal rehabilitation in order for you to recognize sounds."

4. How might a patient with tinnitus describe hearing sound to the nurse?
   A. Sputtering
   B. Muffled
   C. Loud
   D. Buzzing

5. A patient taking aspirin for stroke prevention reports the development of hearing disturbances. The appropriate intervention is to decrease the dose in order to prevent which of the following conditions?
   A. Ototoxicity
   B. Vertigo
   C. Nystagmus
   D. Otitis externa

Try these additional resources to enhance your learning and understanding of this chapter:
- thePoint online resource available at **http://thepoint.lww.com/Pellico1e**
- *Handbook for Focus on Adult Health: Medical-Surgical Nursing*
- *Study Guide for Focus on Adult Health: Medical-Surgical Nursing*

References and Selected Readings

References and selected readings associated with this chapter can be found on the website that accompanies the book. Visit http://thepoint.lww.com/Pellico1e to access the references and other additional resources associated with this chapter.

UNIT FOURTEEN

Problems Related to Integumentary Function

A 48-YEAR-OLD electrician has come to the emergency department via ambulance after falling and sustaining a high-voltage electrical burn. He has a full-thickness (third-degree) burn on his abdomen that will need autografting.

➡ Describe the nursing management of this patient in the emergent phase of burn injury.
➡ Discuss graft site care and donor site care following an autograft.
➡ What are the long-term complications for this patient?

Nursing Assessment: Integumentary Function

PATINA S. WALTON-GEER

The skin is the largest organ in the body and makes up approximately 12% of body weight. It is responsible for regulation for body temperature, maintenance of normal fluid and electrolyte balance, and protection from infection and the environment. Nurses care for patients with burns, skin infections, surgical wounds, and secondary skin abnormalities associated with systemic disease; this chapter provides the knowledge necessary to assess, diagnose, and manage skin abnormalities and describes when to seek referrals to the primary care provider or specialist.

ANATOMIC AND PHYSIOLOGIC OVERVIEW

The integumentary system comprises of the skin and its appendages such as hair, nails, and sweat or sebaceous glands, which are lined with epidermal cells (Wysocki, 2007).

Anatomy of the Skin

The skin is composed of three layers: epidermis (outermost layer), dermis (inner layer), and hypodermis (innermost layer) (Fig. 51-1). Four distinct layers compose the epidermis; from innermost to outermost they are the stratum germinativum, stratum granulosum, stratum lucidum, and stratum corneum. Each layer becomes more differentiated (ie, mature and with more specific functions) as it rises from the basal stratum germinativum layer to the outermost stratum corneum layer. The epidermis and the dermis are separated by a structure called the basement membrane (Wysocki, 2007). The dermis is the thickest layer of skin; it is primarily made up of fibroblast cells, which are important in remodeling and repair of skin. This connective tissue layer contains nerve endings, sensory receptors, capillaries, and elastic fibers. This layer has two zones, the papillary dermis and reticular dermis.

Epidermis

The epidermis consists of continuously dividing cells covered on the surface by dead cells that were originally deeper in the dermis but were pushed upward by the newly developing, more differentiated cells underneath. This external layer is almost completely replaced every 3 to 4 weeks. The dead cells contain large amounts of **keratin**, an insoluble, fibrous

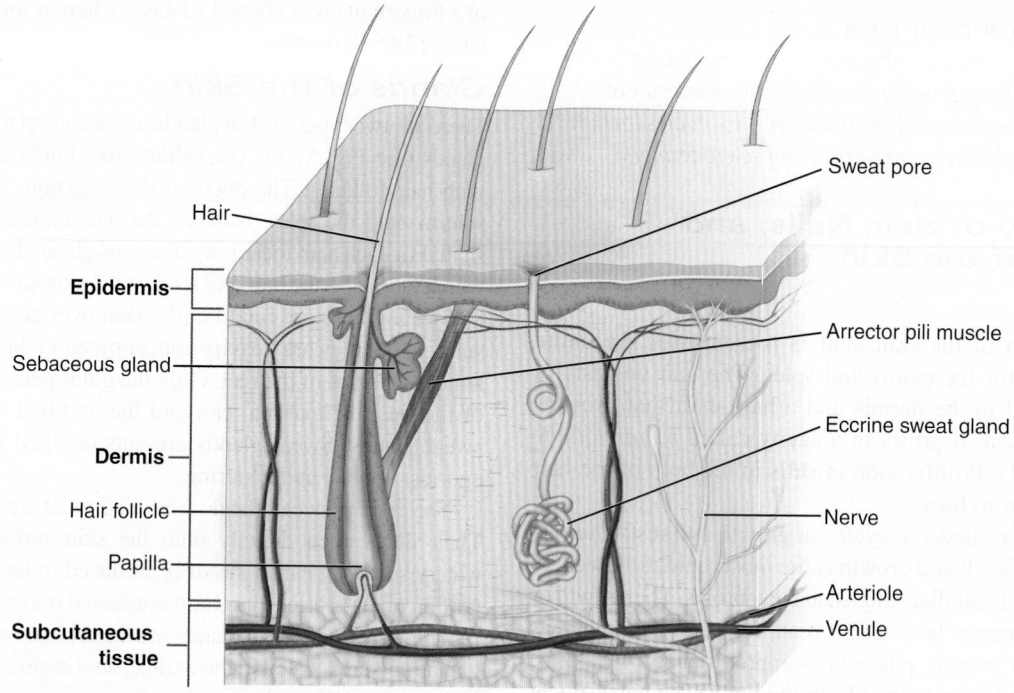

Hair
Epidermis
Sebaceous gland
Dermis
Hair follicle
Papilla
Subcutaneous tissue

Sweat pore
Arrector pili muscle
Eccrine sweat gland
Nerve
Arteriole
Venule

FIGURE 51-1 Anatomic structures of the skin.

protein that forms the outer barrier of the skin and has the capacity to repel pathogens and prevent excessive fluid loss from the body. Keratin is the principal hardening ingredient of the hair and nails.

Melanocytes are the special cells of the epidermis that are primarily involved in producing the pigment **melanin**, which colors the skin and hair. Most of the skin of dark-skinned people and the darker areas of the skin on light-skinned people (eg, the areola) contain larger amounts of this pigment. Albinism is associated with a lack of melanin and is discussed later in the chapter. Production of melanin is controlled by a hormone secreted from the hypothalamus of the brain called *melanocyte-stimulating hormone.* Melanin provides a natural protection against the harmful effects of ultraviolet light; however, it does not provide complete protection from the sun's damaging rays.

Two other types of cells are common to the epidermis: Merkel and Langerhans cells. **Merkel cells** are receptors that transmit stimuli to the axon through a chemical synapse and therefore are associated with the sense of touch. **Langerhans cells** are accessory cells of the afferent immune system that play a role in cutaneous (skin) immune system reactions. These cells process invading antigens and transport the antigens to the lymph system to activate the T lymphocytes.

The junction of the epidermis (basement membrane zone, BMZ) and dermis is an area of many undulations and furrows called **rete ridges**. This junction anchors the epidermis to the dermis and permits the free exchange of essential nutrients between the two layers. If the BMZ is interrupted, it must reform to successfully achieve healing of the tissue (Wysocki, 2007).

Dermis

The dermis makes up the largest portion of the skin, providing strength and structure. It is composed of two layers: papillary and reticular. The papillary dermis lies directly beneath the epidermis and is composed primarily of fibroblast cells capable of producing one form of collagen, a component of connective tissue. The reticular layer lies beneath the papillary layer and also produces collagen and elastic bundles. The dermis is also made up of blood and lymph vessels, nerves, sweat and sebaceous glands, and hair roots. The dermis is often referred to as the "true skin." It is especially thick on the palms and soles, while thin over the eyelids and scrotum; thus, it is not surprising that in conditions of fluid volume excess, patients develop edema in thin skinned areas, resulting in periorbital and scrotal edema. An infection of the dermis that spreads rapidly within the skin and subcutaneous structures is termed *cellulitis.* It is usually caused by staphylococci or streptococci and presents with redness, warmth, swelling, and tenderness, usually of the limbs.

Hypodermis

The subcutaneous tissue, or hypodermis, is the innermost layer of the skin. It is primarily adipose tissue, which provides a cushion between the skin layers, muscles, and bones. It promotes skin mobility, molds body contours, and insulates the body. Fat is deposited and distributed according to the person's gender and in part accounts for the difference in body shape between men and women. Overeating results in increased deposition of fat beneath the skin. The subcutaneous tissues and the amount of fat deposited are important factors in body temperature regulation.

Anatomy of Hair, Nails, and Glands of the Skin

Hair

An outgrowth of the skin, hair is present over the entire body except for the palms and soles. The hair consists of a root formed in the dermis and a hair shaft that projects beyond the skin. It grows in a cavity called a *hair follicle* (see Fig. 51-1). Proliferation of cells in the bulb of the hair causes the hair to form.

Hair follicles undergo cycles of growth and rest. The rate of growth varies; beard growth is the most rapid, followed by hair on the scalp, axillae, thighs, and eyebrows. The growth or **anagen phase** may last up to 6 years for scalp hair, whereas the telogen or resting phase lasts approximately 4 months. During telogen, hair is shed from the body. The hair follicle recycles into the growing phase spontaneously, or it can be induced by plucking out hairs. Growing and resting hairs can be found side by side on all parts of the body. About 90% of the 100,000 hair follicles on a normal scalp are in the growing phase at any one time, and 50 to 100 scalp hairs are shed each day. In conditions in which inflammation causes damage to the root of the hair, regrowth is possible. However, if inflammation causes damage to the hair follicle, stem cells are destroyed and the hair does not grow.

Hair in different parts of the body serves different functions. The hairs of the eyes (ie, eyebrows and lashes), nose, and ears filter out dust, microbes, and airborne debris. Hair color is supplied by various amounts of melanin within the hair shaft. Gray or white hair reflects the loss of pigment. Hair quantity and distribution can be affected by endocrine conditions. For example, Cushing's syndrome causes **hirsutism**, especially in women; hypothyroidism (ie, underactive thyroid) causes coarse hair; while hyperthyroidism (ie, overactive thyroid) is associated with fine hair. In many cases, chemotherapy and radiation therapy cause hair thinning or weakening of the hair shaft, resulting in partial or complete **alopecia** from the scalp and other parts of the body.

Nails

On the dorsal surface of the fingers and toes, a hard, transparent plate of keratin, called the *nail,* overlies the skin. The nail grows from its root, which lies under a thin fold of skin called the cuticle. The nail protects the fingers and toes by preserving their highly developed sensory functions, such as for picking up small objects.

Nail growth is continuous throughout life, with an average growth of 0.1 mm daily. Growth is faster in fingernails than toenails and tends to slow with aging. Complete renewal of a fingernail takes about 170 days, whereas toenail renewal takes 12 to 18 months.

Glands of the Skin

There are two types of skin glands: sebaceous glands and sweat glands (see Fig. 51-1). The **sebaceous glands** are associated with hair follicles. The ducts of the sebaceous glands empty **sebum** onto the space between the hair follicle and the hair shaft. For each hair, there is a sebaceous gland, the secretions of which lubricates the hair and renders the skin soft and pliable.

Sweat glands are found in the skin over most of the body surface, but they are heavily concentrated in the palms of the hands and soles of the feet. Only the glans penis, the margins of the lips, the external ear, and the nail bed are devoid of sweat glands. Sweat glands are subclassified into two categories: eccrine and apocrine.

The eccrine sweat glands are found in all areas of the skin. Their ducts open directly onto the skin surface. The thin, watery secretion called *sweat* is produced in the basal, coiled portion of the eccrine gland and is released into its narrow duct.

The apocrine sweat glands are larger than eccrine sweat glands and are located in the axillae, anal region, scrotum, and labia majora. Their ducts generally open onto hair follicles. The apocrine glands become active at puberty. In women, they enlarge and recede with each menstrual cycle. Apocrine glands produce a milky sweat that is sometimes broken down by bacteria to produce the characteristic underarm odor.

Functions of the Skin

Protection

The skin covering most of the body is no more than 1 mm thick, but it provides very effective protection against invasion by bacterial and viral pathogens as well as other foreign matter. The thickened skin of the palms and soles protects against the effects of the constant trauma that occurs in these areas.

The stratum corneum, the outer layer of the epidermis, provides the most effective barrier to epidermal water loss to maintain a homeostatic environment and penetration of environmental factors such as chemicals, microbes, and insect bites. Various lipids are synthesized in the stratum corneum and are the basis for the barrier function of this layer. These are long-chain lipids that are better suited than phospholipids for water resistance. The presence of these lipids in the stratum corneum creates a relatively impermeable barrier for water egress and for the entry of toxins, microbes, and other substances that come in contact with the surface of the skin.

Some substances do penetrate the skin but meet resistance in trying to move through the channels between the cell layers of the stratum corneum. Microbes and fungi, which are part of the body's normal flora, cannot penetrate unless there is a break in the skin barrier.

Sensation

The receptor endings of nerves in the skin allow the body to constantly monitor the conditions of the immediate

environment. The primary functions of the receptors in the skin are to sense temperature, pain, light touch, and pressure (or heavy touch). Different nerve endings respond to each of the different stimuli. Although the nerve endings are distributed over the entire body, they are more concentrated in some areas than in others. For example, the fingertips are more densely innervated than the skin on the back.

Fluid Balance

The stratum corneum, the outermost layer of the epidermis, has the capacity to absorb water, thereby preventing an excessive loss of water and electrolytes from the internal body and retaining moisture in the subcutaneous tissues. When skin is damaged, as occurs with a severe burn, large quantities of fluids and electrolytes may be lost rapidly, possibly leading to circulatory collapse, shock, and death.

The skin is not completely impermeable to water. Small amounts of water continuously evaporate from the skin surface. This evaporation, called *insensible perspiration*, amounts to approximately 600 mL daily in a normal adult. Insensible water loss varies with the body and ambient temperature. In a person with a fever, the fluid loss increases. If the fever is between 38.3°C (101°F) and 39.4°C (103°F), a loss of 500 mL per 24 hours is anticipated; whereas if the temperature if over 39.4°C (>103°F), 1,000 mL loss is expected at a minimum (Outzen, 2009).

Thermoregulation

The body continuously produces heat as a result of the metabolism of food, which produces energy. This heat is dissipated primarily through the skin.

Evaporation from the skin aids heat loss by conduction. Heat is conducted through the skin into water molecules on its surface, causing the water to evaporate. The water on the skin surface may be from insensible perspiration, sweat, or the environment.

Under normal conditions, metabolic heat production is balanced by heat loss, and the internal temperature of the body is maintained constant at approximately 37°C (98.6°F). The rate of heat loss depends primarily on the surface temperature of the skin, which is a function of the skin blood flow. Increased blood flow to the skin results in more heat delivered to the skin and a greater rate of heat loss from the body. In contrast, decreased skin blood flow decreases the skin temperature and helps conserve heat for the body. When the temperature of the body begins to fall, as occurs on a cold day, the blood vessels of the skin constrict, thereby reducing heat loss from the body.

Sweating is another process by which the body can regulate the rate of heat loss. Sweating does not occur until the core body temperature exceeds 37°C (98.6°F), regardless of skin temperature. In extremely hot environments, the rate of sweat production may be as high as 1 L per hour. Under some circumstances (eg, emotional stress), sweating may occur as a reflex and may be unrelated to the need to lose heat from the body.

Vitamin Synthesis

Skin exposed to ultraviolet light can convert substances necessary for synthesizing vitamin D (cholecalciferol). Vitamin D is essential for preventing osteoporosis and rickets, a condition that causes bone deformities and results from a deficiency of vitamin D, calcium, and phosphorus (Box 51-1).

BOX 51-1

Nursing Research

Bridging the Gap to Evidence-Based Practice

Is There Any Evidence Suggesting That Vitamin D is Linked to Cardiovascular Health?

Wallis, D., Penckofer, S., & Sizemore, G. (2008). The "sunshine deficit" and cardiovascular disease. *Circulation, 118,* 1476–1485.

Purpose

Vitamin D deficiency has been recognized as a cause of metabolic bone disease (rickets, osteomalacia, and secondary hyperparathyroidism). However, since vitamin D receptors have been found in multiple tissue types, particularly myocardial tissue and blood vessels, this review of the literature was undertaken to describe the relationship between low levels of vitamin D and cardiovascular disorders.

Findings

Research reveals that insufficient vitamin D is also associated with ischemic heart disease, hypertension, myocardial hypertrophy, diastolic heart failure, and the

metabolic syndrome (p. 1482). Risk factors include a variety of malabsorption syndromes (ie, gastric bypass, inflammatory bowel disease, chronic diarrhea); lack of sunlight (institutionalized patients, skin barriers such as sunscreens); problems with synthesizing vitamin D, as in renal disease; and pharmacological agents (steroids, Rifampin, phenobarbital).

Nursing Implications

Patients who are at risk for vitamin D deficiency (sunlight and dietary deficiency and medical conditions as described) should be considered for screening blood tests of vitamin D levels. Many patients are asymptomatic or, if symptomatic (bone, muscle pain and/or weakness, neuropathy), can be attributed to a variety of other medical conditions. Treatment guidelines vary according to populations and conditions. Nurses recognize the association of vitamin D deficiency and cardiovascular disease.

TABLE
51-1 GERONTOLOGIC CONSIDERATIONS / Age-Related Changes of the Skin

Structural Changes	Associated Physical Findings
Thinning at the junction of the dermis and epidermis result in fewer anchoring sites between the two skin layers, which means that even minor injury or stress to the epidermis can cause it to shear away from the dermis.	Increased vulnerability of aged skin to trauma
The epidermis and dermis thin and flatten.	Wrinkles, sags, and overlapping skin folds
Loss of the subcutaneous tissue substances of elastin, collagen, and fat	Decreased protection and cushioning of underlying tissues and organs, decreased muscle tone, and loss of the insulating properties of fat.
	Skin becomes fragile and transparent.
Cellular replacement slows as a result of aging, and there is thinning of the dermal layers.	
The blood supply to the skin also changes with age. Vessels, especially the capillary loops, decrease in number and size.	Vascular changes are associated with delayed wound healing.
Sweat and sebaceous glands decrease in number and functional capacity.	Dry and scaly skin.
Reduced hormonal levels of androgens	Associated with declining sebaceous gland function
Hair growth gradually diminishes, especially over the lower legs and dorsum of the feet. Thinning is common in the scalp, axilla, and pubic areas.	Decreased hair growth, hair loss
Photoaging (damage from excessive sun exposure)	Profound wrinkling; increased loss of elasticity; mottled, pigmented areas; cutaneous atrophy; and benign or malignant lesions

Immune Response Function

Recent research has confirmed a definite action of **Langer-hans cells** (specialized cells in the skin) in facilitating the uptake of IgE-associated allergens. This action plays a pivotal role in the pathogenesis of atopic dermatitis and other allergic diseases such as asthma and allergic rhinitis (Galli, Tsai, & Piliponsky, 2008). These findings support the concept of a systemic regulatory mechanism as a trigger for allergic diseases and suggest that this trigger can be aggravated by local inflammation (Morris, 2009).

⚡ NURSING ALERT

Localized opening of the normally tight endothelial junctions leads to interstitial edema in the deep layers of the skin and subcutaneous tissue of the face, tongue, hands, face, and genitalia. Occasionally, the tongue or pharynx can be involved. It may be related to allergy or idiopathic in nature. Histamine that is contained in mast cells is released with a variety or immunological, nonimmunological, physical, or chemical stimuli. The released histamine causes hyperpermeability of the microvessels, which allows fluid to leak out into affected area and causes the characteristic appearance. Nurses observe for the tense swelling of the lips that develops rapidly. Angioedema is frequently associated with an allergic reaction, and may present with hives. If shortness of breath is also noted, the medical provider must be contacted immediately, as severe swelling of the airway and tongue can be life-threatening.

Gerontologic Considerations

The skin undergoes many physiologic changes associated with normal aging. A lifetime of excessive sun exposure, systemic diseases, and poor nutrition can increase the range of skin problems and the rapidity with which they appear. In addition, certain medications (eg, antihistamines, antibiotics, diuretics) are photosensitizing and increase the damage that results from sun exposure. The outcome is an increasing vulnerability to injury and to certain diseases. Skin problems are common among older people. Refer to Table 51-1 for skin changes in the elderly.

Many skin changes and lesions are part of normal aging. Recognizing these lesions enables the examiner to assist the patient to feel less anxious about changes in skin. Box 51-2 summarizes some changes that are expected to appear as the skin ages. These are normal and require no special attention unless the skin becomes infected or irritated.

ASSESSMENT

Some conditions may subject the patient to a protracted illness, leading to feelings of depression, frustration, self-consciousness, poor self-image, and rejection. Itching and skin irritations, which are features of many skin diseases, may be a constant annoyance. These discomforts may result in loss of sleep, anxiety, and depression, all of which reinforce the general distress and fatigue that frequently accompany skin disorders.

BOX 51-2
Benign Changes in Elderly Skin

- Cherry angiomas (bright red "moles")
- Diminished hair, especially on scalp and pubic area
- Dyschromias (color variations):
  - Solar lentigo (liver spots)
  - Melasma (dark discoloration of the skin)
  - Lentigines (freckles)
- Neurodermatitis (itchy spots)
- Seborrheic keratoses (crusty brown "stuck-on" patches)
- Spider angiomas (network of dilated capillaries radiating from a central arteriole)
- Telangiectasias (red marks on skin caused by stretching of the superficial blood vessels)
- Wrinkles (a small fold, ridge, or crease in the skin)
- Xerosis (dryness)
- Xanthelasma (yellowish waxy deposits on upper and lower eyelids)
- Ichthyosis (fish scale appearance of the skin)

BOX 51-3
Health History Related to Skin Disorders

Patient history relevant to skin disorders may be obtained by asking the following questions:

- When did you first notice this skin problem? (Also investigate duration and intensity)
- Has it occurred previously?
- Are there any other symptoms?
- What site was first affected?
- What did the rash or lesion look like when it first appeared?
- Where and how fast did it spread?
- Do you have any itching, burning, tingling, or crawling sensations?
- Is there any loss of sensation?
- Is the problem worse at a particular time or season?
- How do you think it started?
- Do you have a history of hay fever, asthma, hives, eczema, or allergies?
- Who in your family has skin problems or rashes?
- Did the eruptions appear after certain foods were eaten? Which foods?
- When the problem occurred, had you recently consumed alcohol?
- What relation do you think there may be between a specific event and the outbreak of the rash or lesion?
- What medications are you taking?
- What topical medication (ointment, cream, salve) have you put on the lesion (including over-the-counter medications)?
- What skin products or cosmetics do you use?
- What is your occupation?
- What in your immediate environment (plants, animals, chemicals, infections) might be precipitating this disorder? Is there anything new, or are there any changes in the environment?
- Does anything touching your skin cause a rash?
- How has this affected you (or your life)?
- Is there anything else you wish to talk about in regard to this disorder?

For patients suffering such physical and psychological discomforts, the nurse needs to provide understanding, explanations of the problem, appropriate instructions related to treatment, nursing support, and encouragement. It is imperative to overcome any aversion that may be felt when caring for patients with unattractive skin disorders. The nurse should show no sign of hesitancy when approaching patients with skin disorders. Such hesitancy only reinforces the psychological trauma of the disorder.

Because patients with skin conditions may be viewed negatively by others, these patients may become distraught and avoid interaction with people. Skin conditions can lead to disfigurement, isolation, job loss, and economic hardship.

Health History

During the health history interview, the nurse asks about any family and personal history of skin allergies; allergic reactions to food, medications, and chemicals; previous skin problems; and skin cancer. The names of cosmetics, soaps, shampoos, and other personal hygiene products are obtained if there have been any recent skin problems noticed with the use of these products. The health history contains specific information about the onset, signs and symptoms, location, and duration of any pain, itching, rash, or other discomfort experienced by the patient. The nurse inquires about tattoos because they involve the injection of ink into the dermis of the skin and are associated with an increased risk for bloodborne disease, skin infections, and allergic reactions. Box 51-3 lists selected questions useful in obtaining appropriate information.

Physical Assessment

Assessment of the skin involves the entire skin area, including the mucous membranes, scalp, hair, and nails. The skin is a reflection of a person's overall health, and alterations commonly correspond to disease in other organ systems.

Inspection and palpation are techniques commonly used in examining the skin. The room must be well lighted and warm. A penlight may be used to highlight lesions. The patient completely disrobes and is adequately draped. Gloves are worn during skin examination if a rash or lesions are to be palpated.

The general appearance of the skin is assessed by observing color, temperature, moisture or dryness, skin texture (rough or smooth), lesions, vascularity, mobility, and the condition of the hair and nails. Skin turgor, possible edema, and elasticity are assessed by palpation.

Assessing Color

Skin color varies from person to person and ranges from ivory to deep brown to almost pure black. The skin of

exposed portions of the body, especially in sunny, warm climates, tends to be more pigmented than the rest of the body.

Almost every process that occurs on the skin causes some color change. For example, **hypopigmentation** may be caused by a fungal infection, eczema, or **vitiligo**; **hyperpigmentation** can occur after sun injury, as a result of aging, or with disease processes such as Addison's because of stimulation of melanocyte-stimulating hormone. The vasodilation that occurs with fever, sunburn, and inflammation produces a pink or reddish hue to the skin. Pallor is an absence of or a decrease in normal skin color and vascularity and is best observed in the conjunctivae or around the mouth. Assessing for pallor in the palms and soles of patients with dark skin may be helpful (Bickley & Szilagyi, 2009).

In people with dark skin, melanin is produced at a faster rate and in larger quantities than in people with light skin. Healthy dark skin has a reddish base or undertone. The buccal mucosa, tongue, lips, and nails normally are pink. Dark pigment responds with discoloration after injury or inflammation, and patients with dark skin more often experience postinflammatory hyperpigmentation than do those with lighter skin. The hyperpigmentation eventually fades but may require months to a year to do so. Table 51-2 provides an overview of color changes in light-skinned and dark-skinned people.

In general, people with dark skin suffer the same skin conditions as those with light skin. They are less likely to have skin cancer but more likely to have keloid or scar formation and disorders resulting from occlusion or blockage of hair follicles.

Erythema
Erythema is redness of the skin caused by the congestion of capillaries. To determine possible inflammation, the skin is palpated for increased warmth and for smoothness (ie, edema) or hardness (ie, intracellular infiltration).

Cyanosis
Cyanosis is the bluish discoloration that results from a lack of oxygen in the blood. It appears with shock or with respiratory or circulatory compromise. In people with light skin, cyanosis manifests as a bluish hue to the lips, fingertips, and nail beds (Figure 51-2). In dark-skinned people, the skin may appear blue and dull or assume a gray hue. The term *central cyanosis* refers to desaturation of oxygen in the blood and this is reflected in the mucous membranes and skin, whereas *peripheral cyanosis* implies increased oxygen extraction from the blood because of sluggish blood flow, or vasoconstriction related to exposure to cold environments, which is reflected in the extremities. The nurse assesses the patient for additional indications of decreased tissue perfusion, including cold, clammy skin; a rapid, thready pulse; and rapid, shallow respirations. The conjunctivae of the eyelids are examined for pallor and **petechiae**.

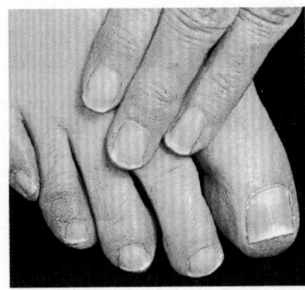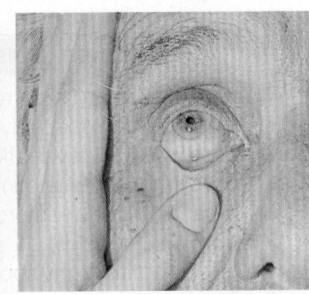

FIGURE 51-2 Examples of skin color changes: the bluish tint of cyanosis (*left*) and the yellow hue of jaundice (*right*).

> ! **NURSING ALERT**
> *Cyanosis is a late sign and symptom of hypoxemia, as 5 g of hemoglobin (normal level is 15 g/dL) are desaturated before cyanosis is evident. In cases of carbon monoxide poisoning, the level of carboxyhemoglobin does not affect color, therefore the patient may be profoundly hypoxemic without evidence of cyanosis.*

Jaundice
Jaundice, a yellowing of the skin, is directly related to elevations in serum bilirubin and is often first observed in the sclerae and mucous membranes (see Fig. 51-2). The term *icterus* is used to describe yellowing of the sclerae (white of the eyes).

Striae
The nurse assesses for striae (stretch marks), which occurs when the elastic fibers in the reticular dermis rupture. Striae are seen in conditions of weight gain such as pregnancy and obesity, in muscle building, with prolonged use of oral or topical corticosteroids, or in Cushing's syndrome (increased adrenal cortical activity) (see Chapter 31).

Assessing Rash
In instances of pruritus (ie, itching), the patient is asked to indicate which areas of the body are involved. The skin is then stretched gently to decrease the reddish tone and make the rash more visible. Pointing a penlight laterally across the skin may highlight the rash, making it easier to observe. The differences in skin texture are then assessed by running the tips of the fingers lightly over the skin. The borders of the rash may be palpable. The patient's mouth and ears are included in the examination (sometimes rubeola, or measles, causes a red cast to appear on the ears). The patient's temperature is assessed, and the lymph nodes are palpated.

Assessing Skin Lesions
Skin lesions are the most prominent characteristics of dermatologic conditions. They vary in size, shape, and cause and are classified according to their appearance and origin. Skin lesions can be described as primary or secondary. Primary lesions are the initial lesions and are characteristic of the disease itself. Secondary lesions result from external causes, such as scratching, trauma, infections, or changes caused by wound healing. Depending on the stage of development, skin lesions are further categorized according to type and appearance (Table 51-3).

TABLE
51-2 Color Changes in Light and Dark Skin

Etiology	Light Skin	Dark Skin
Pallor		
Anemia: Decreased hematocrit Shock: Decreased perfusion, vaso-constriction	Generalized pallor	Brown skin appears yellow-brown, dull; black skin appears ashen gray, dull. (Observe areas with least pigmentation: conjunctivae, mucous membranes)
Local arterial insufficiency	Marked localized pallor (lower extremities, especially when elevated)	Ashen gray, dull; cool to palpation
Albinism: Total absence of pigment melanin	Whitish pink	Tan, cream, white
Vitiligo: A condition characterized by destruction of the melanocytes in circumscribed areas of the skin (may be localized or widespread)	Patchy, milky white spots, often symmetric bilaterally	Same
Cyanosis		
Increased amount of unoxygenated hemoglobin:	Dusky blue	Dark but dull, lifeless; only severe cyanosis is apparent in skin. (Observe conjunctivae, oral mucosa, nail beds)
Central: Chronic heart and lung diseases cause arterial desaturation	Bluish discoloration of skin, mucous membranes and nailbeds	
Peripheral: Exposure to cold, anxiety	Nail beds dusky	
Erythema		
Hyperemia: Increased blood flow through engorged arterial vessels, as in inflammation, fever, alcohol intake, blushing	Red, bright pink	Purplish tinge, but difficult to see. (Palpate for increased warmth with inflammation, taut skin, and hardening of deep tissues)
Polycythemia: Increased red blood cells, capillary stasis	Ruddy blue in face, oral mucosa, conjunctivae, hands and feet	Well concealed by pigment. (Observe for redness in lips)
Carbon monoxide poisoning	Bright, cherry red in face and upper torso	Cherry red nail beds, lips, and oral mucosa
Stasis dermatitis (venous stasis) is poor venous return in the lower extremities causing hemosiderin staining and cracking of the skin (skin breakdown) that causes stasis ulcers or venous ulcers. Venous Ulcers common findings are edema, hyperpigmentation surrounding the skin, warmth at feet with palpable pulses (exception if no coexisting arterial disease)	Brown or rusty discoloration of the skin resulting from a buildup of hemosiderin (iron-containing pigment derived from the breakdown of hemoglobin) in the interstitial fluid	In dark skinned people is it more difficult to detect signs of venous insufficiency such as hemosiderin staining (reddish, brown color). (Kelly, A.P., & Bethell, E., 2009)
Jaundice		
Increased serum bilirubin concentration (>2.5 to 3 mg/dL) due to liver dysfunction or hemolysis, as after severe burns or some infections	Yellow first in sclerae, hard palate, and mucous membranes; then over skin	Check sclerae for yellow near limbus; do not mistake normal yellowish fatty deposits in the periphery under eyelids for jaundice. (Jaundice is best noted at junction of hard and soft palate, on palms)
Carotenemia: Increased level of serum carotene from ingestion of large amounts of carotene-rich foods	Yellow-orange tinge in forehead, palms and soles, and nasolabial folds, but no yellowing in sclerae or mucous membranes	Yellow-orange tinge in palms and soles
Uremia: Renal failure causes retained urochrome pigments in the blood	Orange-green or gray overlying pallor of anemia; may also have ecchymoses and purpura	Easily masked. (Rely on laboratory and clinical findings)
Brown-Tan		
Addison's disease: Cortisol deficiency stimulates increased melanin production	Bronzed appearance, an "external tan"; most apparent around nipples, perineum, genitalia, and pressure points (inner thighs, buttocks, elbows, axillae)	Easily masked. (Rely on laboratory and clinical findings)
Café-au-lait spots: Caused by increased melanin pigment in basal cell layer	Tan to light brown, irregularly shaped, oval patch with well-defined borders often not visible in the very dark skinned person	

TABLE
51-3 Primary and Secondary Skin Lesions

Lesion	Description	Examples
Primary Lesions **Macule, patch**	Flat, nonpalpable skin color change (color may be brown, white, tan, purple, red) • *Macule:* less than 1 cm, circumscribed border • *Patch:* greater than 1 cm, may have irregular border	Freckles, flat moles, petechia, rubella, vitiligo, port wine stains, ecchymosis
Papule, plaque	Elevated, palpable, solid mass with a circumscribed border Plaque may be coalesced papules with flat top • *Papule:* less than 0.5 cm • *Plaque:* greater than 0.5 cm	*Papules:* Elevated nevi, warts, lichen planus *Plaques:* Psoriasis, actinic keratosis
Nodule, tumor	Elevated, palpable, solid mass that extends deeper into the dermis than a papule • *Nodule:* 0.5–2 cm; circumscribed • *Tumor:* greater than 1–2 cm; tumors do not always have sharp borders	*Nodules:* Lipoma, squamous cell carcinoma, poorly absorbed injection, dermatofibroma *Tumors:* Larger lipoma, carcinoma
Vesicle, bulla	Circumscribed, elevated, palpable mass containing serous fluid • *Vesicle:* less than 0.5 cm • *Bulla:* greater than 0.5 cm	*Vesicles:* Herpes simplex/zoster, chickenpox, poison ivy, second-degree burn (blister) *Bulla:* Pemphigus, contact dermatitis, large burn blisters, poison ivy, bullous impetigo
Wheal	Elevated mass with transient borders; often irregular; size and color vary Caused by movement of serous fluid into the dermis; does not contain free fluid in a cavity (as, for example, a vesicle does)	Urticaria (hives), insect bites
Pustule	Pus-filled vesicle or bulla	Acne, impetigo, furuncles, carbuncles

Lesion	Description	Examples
Cyst	Encapsulated fluid-filled or semisolid mass in the subcutaneous tissue or dermis	Sebaceous cyst, epidermoid cysts

Secondary Lesions

Lesion	Description	Examples
Erosion	Loss of superficial epidermis that does not extend to dermis; depressed, moist area	Ruptured vesicles, scratch marks
Ulcer	Skin loss or damage at or extending past the epidermis. May include necrotic tissue development, bleeding or scarring	Stasis ulcer of venous insufficiency, pressure ulcer
Fissure	Linear crack in the skin that may extend to dermis	Chapped lips or hands, athlete's foot
Scales	Flakes secondary to desquamated, dead epithelium that may adhere to skin surface; color varies (silvery, white); texture varies (thick, fine)	Dandruff, psoriasis, dry skin, pityriasis rosea
Crust	Dried residue of serum, blood, or pus on skin surface Large, adherent crust is a scab	Residue left after vesicle rupture: impetigo, herpes, eczema
Scar (cicatrix)	Skin mark left after healing of a wound or lesion; represents replacement by connective tissue of the injured tissue • *Young scars:* red or purple • *Mature scars:* white or glistening	Healed wound or surgical incision

(continued on page 1340)

Chapter Review (continued)

3. Mr. Horne, a 70-year-old patient, is admitted to the hospital after a visit to his physician's office. Initial nursing assessment reveals that he has a poor skin turgor. What effects will this have on skin integrity?

NCLEX-Style Review Questions

1. A 90-year-old patient with multiple medical problems is admitted to the hospital's geriatric care unit. The nursing assessment reveals lethargy, poor capillary perfusion, and skin turgor. These findings should alert the gerontological nurse to which of the following?
   A. Aspiration
   B. Hydration
   C. Contractures
   D. Lesions

2. During assessment, the nurse recognizes which one of the following as a normal function of the skin?
   A. Thermal regulation
   B. Vitamin E production
   C. Vitamin C production
   D. Releasing of carbon dioxide

3. When assessing a client who has returned to the room postoperatively, what is the primary purpose in looking at his or her nail beds?
   A. Cyanosis
   B. Respiratory rate
   C. Edema
   D. Cellulitis

4. When assessing the characteristics of a lesion, it is important for the nurse to look for which of the following?
   A. Edema
   B. Coolness
   C. Measurement
   D. Distribution

5. Which of the following changes in the elderly best describes why aging increases risk for impairment in skin integrity?
   A. Epidermal contractility
   B. Dermal thickness
   C. Decreased elastin, collagen, and fat
   D. Maceration

Try these additional resources to enhance your learning and understanding of this chapter:
- thePoint online resource available at **http://thepoint.lww.com/Pellico1e**
- *Handbook for Focus on Adult Health: Medical-Surgical Nursing*
- *Study Guide for Focus on Adult Health: Medical-Surgical Nursing*

References and Selected Readings

References and selected readings associated with this chapter can be found on the website that accompanies the book. Visit http://thepoint.lww.com/Pellico1e to access the references and other additional resources associated with this chapter.

Nursing Management: Patients With Dermatologic Problems

PATINA S. WALTON-GEER

Learning Objectives

After reading this chapter, you will be able to:

1. Describe the general management of the patient with an abnormal skin condition.

2. Identify stages of pressure ulcers and discuss general principles of wound care.

3. Discuss clinical manifestations and care associated with psoriasis.

4. Describe the health education needs of the patient with infections of the skin and parasitic skin diseases.

5. Discuss care of patients with noninfectious, inflammatory dermatoses.

6. Describe nursing management of the patient with skin cancer.

7. Describe characteristics of the various types of Kaposi's sarcoma.

Regardless of the environment where they work, nurses manage skin care. Additionally, nurses predict patients at risk for skin problems, assess skin changes, and intervene to prevent injury and maintain skin viability. As nurses, it is also important to utilize preventative practices to reduce transmission of infection or further injury, and maintain skin viability.

GENERAL MANAGEMENT OF SKIN DISORDERS

Nursing management of skin disorders includes protecting the skin, preventing infection, reversing inflammation, administering therapeutic baths, and administering medications.

PROVIDING SKIN CARE

Protecting the Skin

Some skin problems are aggravated by bathing. The essence of skin care in bathing a patient with skin problems is as follows:

- A mild, lipid-free soap or soap substitute is used.
- The area is rinsed completely and blotted dry with a soft cloth.
- Deodorant soaps are avoided.

Special care is necessary when changing dressings. Pledgets (small compress of material, usually cotton or gauze) saturated with oil, sterile saline or water, wound cleansers, or another prescribed solution help to loosen crusts, remove exudates, or free an adherent dry dressing.

Preventing Infection

Potentially infectious skin lesions should be regarded strictly as such, and proper precautions should be observed until the diagnosis is established. Most lesions with purulent drainage contain infectious material. The health care provider must adhere to standard contact precautions carried out according to Occupational Safety and Health Administration (OSHA) regulations.

! NURSING ALERT

The nurse is aware that, for patients with contact precautions, a gown and gloves should be worn for all interactions that may involve contact with the patient or potentially contaminated areas in the patient's environment. The personal protective equipment (PPE) is donned before room entry and discarded before exiting (Siegel, J., Rhinehart, E., Jackson, M., Chiarello, L. 2006).

Reversing Inflammation

The type of skin lesion (eg, oozing, infected, or dry) usually determines the type of local medication or treatment that is prescribed. As a rule, if the skin is acutely inflamed (ie, hot), erythematous (red), and edematous (swollen) and draining, it is best to apply wet or specialty dressings and/or soothing lotions. For chronic conditions in which the skin surface is dry and scaly, water-soluble emulsions, creams, ointments, and pastes are used. The therapy is modified as the responses of the skin indicate. The patient and the nurse should note whether the medication or dressings seem to irritate the skin. The success or failure of therapy usually depends on adequate instruction and motivation of the patient and family, and the support of health care personnel promotes adherence to instructions.

Administering Therapeutic Baths (Balneotherapy)

Baths or soaks, known as **balneotherapy**, are useful when large areas of skin are affected. The baths remove crusts, scales, and old medications, and relieve the inflammation and pruritus (itching) that accompany acute dermatoses. Additional information about therapeutic baths is given in Box 52-1.

Administering Pharmacologic Therapy

Topical Preparations

Table 52-1 lists some commonly used topical preparations.

Lotions

Lotions are frequently used to replenish lost skin oils or to relieve pruritus. They are usually applied directly to the skin, but a dressing soaked in the lotion can be placed on the affected area. Lotions must be applied every 3 or 4 hours for sustained therapeutic effect because if left in place for a long period, they may crust and cake on the skin.

There are two types of lotions: suspensions and liniments. **Suspensions** are medicines that are mixed with a liquid, usually water, in which it cannot dissolve and therefore remains intact in the form of small particles. The important thing to remember is to shake the medication before giving each dose, so that the medicine particles are evenly distributed throughout the liquid. An example is calamine lotion, which

---

BOX 52-1 **Therapeutic Baths**

Types of Therapeutic Baths

Bath Solution	Effects and Uses
Water	Same effect as wet dressings
Saline	Used for widely disseminated lesions
Colloidal (Aveeno, oatmeal)	Antipruritic, soothing
Sodium bicarbonate (baking soda)	Cooling
Starch	Soothing
Medicated tars	Psoriasis and chronic eczema
Bath oils	Antipruritic and emollient action; acute and subacute generalized eczematous eruptions

Nursing Interventions
- Fill the tub half full.
- Keep the water at a comfortable temperature.
- Do not allow the water to cool excessively.
- Use a bath mat, because *medications added to the bath can cause the tub to be slippery.*
- Apply an emollient cream to damp skin after the bath if lubrication is desired.
- Because tars are volatile, the bath area should be well ventilated.
- Maintain a constant room temperature without drafts.
- Encourage the patient to wear light, loose clothing after the bath.

---

provides a rapid cooling and drying effect as it evaporates, leaving a thin, medicinal layer of powder on the affected skin. **Liniments** are lotions with oil added to prevent crusting. An example is Ben-Gay for muscle aches.

Powders

Powders usually have a talc, zinc oxide, bentonite, or cornstarch base and are dusted on the skin with a shaker or applied with cotton sponges. Although their therapeutic action is brief, powders act as **hygroscopic** agents that absorb and retain moisture from the air and reduce friction between skin surfaces and clothing or bedding.

Creams

Creams may be suspensions of oil in water or emulsions of water in oil, with additional ingredients to prevent bacterial and fungal growth. Both may cause an allergic reaction, such as contact dermatitis. Oil-in-water creams are easily applied and usually are the most cosmetically acceptable to the patient. Although they can be used on the face, they tend to have a drying effect. Water-in-oil emulsions are greasier and are preferred for drying and flaking dermatoses.

TABLE 52-1 Common Topical Preparations and Medications	
Preparation	**Product Name**
Bath Preparations	
With tar	Balnetar, Doak Oil, Lavatar
With colloidal oatmeal	Aveeno Oilated Bath Powder
With oatmeal and mineral oil	Aveeno Bath Oil, Nutra Soothe
With mineral oil	Nutraderm Bath Oil, Lubath, Alpha-Keri Bath Oil
Moisturizer creams	Acid Mantle Cream, Curel Cream, Dermasil, Eucerin, Lubriderm, Noxzema Skin Cream
Moisturizer ointments	Aquaphor Ointment, Eutra Swiss Skin Cream, Vaseline Ointment
Topical anesthetics	lidocaine (Xylocaine) of various strengths in the form of spray, ointment, gel; EMLA cream (lidocaine 2.5% and prilocaine 2.5%)
Topical antibiotics	bacitracin, Polysporin (bacitracin and polymyxin B), Bactroban ointment or cream (mupirocin 2%), erythromycin 2% (Emgel, Eryderm Solution), clindamycin phosphate 1% (Cleocin cream, gel, solution), gentamicin sulfate 1% (Garamycin cream or ointment), 1% silver sulfadiazine cream (Silvadene)

Gels

Gels are semisolid emulsions that become liquid when applied to the skin or scalp. The water-based gels appear to penetrate the skin more effectively, are greaseless and odorless, and cause less stinging on application. They are especially useful for acute dermatitis in which there is weeping exudate (eg, poison ivy).

Pastes

Pastes are mixtures of powders and ointments and are used in inflammatory blistering conditions. They adhere to the skin and may be difficult to remove without using an oil (eg, olive oil or mineral oil). Pastes are applied with a wooden tongue depressor or gloved hand.

Ointments

Ointments retard water loss and lubricate and protect the skin. They are the preferred vehicle for delivering medication to chronic or localized dry skin conditions, such as eczema or psoriasis (eg, triamcinolone). Other ointments are used to aid in healing and treatment of pressure ulcers, varicose ulcers, and dehiscent wounds (eg, Xenaderm). Ointments are applied with a wooden tongue depressor or gloved hand.

Sprays and Aerosols

Spray and aerosol preparations may be used on any widespread dermatologic condition (eg, 3M Cavilon Skin Protectant; Convatec Aloe Vesta Skin Protectant). They evaporate on contact and are used infrequently.

Corticosteroids

Corticosteroids are widely used in treating dermatologic conditions to provide anti-inflammatory, antipruritic, and vasoconstrictive effects. The patient is taught to apply the product sparingly and rub it into the prescribed area thoroughly. Absorption of topical corticosteroid is enhanced when the skin is hydrated or when the affected area is covered by an occlusive or moisture-retentive dressing. Inappropriate use of topical corticosteroids can result in local and systemic side effects, especially when the medication is absorbed through inflamed and excoriated skin, or is used for long periods on sensitive areas. Local side effects may include skin atrophy and thinning, **striae** (bandlike streaks), and telangiectasia (small dilated blood vessels on the surface of the skin). Thinning of the skin results from the ability of corticosteroids to inhibit skin collagen synthesis. The thinning process can be reversed by discontinuing the medication, but striae and telangiectasia are permanent. Systemic side effects may include hyperglycemia and symptoms of Cushing's syndrome (refer to Chapter 31). Caution is required when applying corticosteroids around the eyes for two reasons: (1) long-term use may cause glaucoma or cataracts, and (2) the anti-inflammatory effect of corticosteroids may mask existing viral or fungal infections.

Concentrated (fluorinated) corticosteroids are never applied on the face or intertriginous areas (ie, axilla and groin) because these areas have a thinner stratum corneum and absorb the medication much more quickly than do areas such as the forearm or legs.

> **NURSING ALERT**
> *It is important for the nurse to consider that penetration of topical steroid depends on the skin site, which varies based upon the denseness of the stratum corneum, blood supply, and tissue integrity of the involved area. According to Valencia and Kerdel (2008), penetration of topical steroids applied to the eyelids or scrotum is four times greater than for the forehead and 36 times greater than for the palms and soles. Thus, thinner and less intact skin has a higher absorption and thus poses a higher risk for side effects.*

Intralesional Therapy

Intralesional therapy consists of injecting a sterile suspension of medication (usually a corticosteroid) into or just below a lesion. Although this treatment may have an anti-inflammatory effect, local atrophy may result if the medication is injected into subcutaneous fat. Skin lesions treated with intralesional therapy include psoriasis, keloids, and cystic acne.

Systemic Medications

Systemic medications are also prescribed for skin conditions. These include corticosteroids for short-term therapy for contact dermatitis or for long-term treatment of a chronic **dermatosis**, such as pemphigus vulgaris. Other frequently used systemic medications include antibiotics, antifungals, antihistamines, sedatives, tranquilizers, analgesics, and **cytotoxic** (destructive of cells) agents.

CARING FOR WOUNDS

Wound Dressings

There are three types of wound dressings: passive, interactive, and active. Passive dressings have only a protective function and maintain a moist environment for natural healing. They include those that just cover the area (eg, DuoDERM, Tegaderm) and may remain in place for several days. Interactive dressings are capable of absorbing wound exudate while

(1) maintaining a moist environment in the area of the wound and (2) allowing the surrounding skin to remain dry. They include hydrocolloids, alginates, and hydrogels. Interactive dressings are able to modify the physiology of the wound environment by modulating and stimulating cellular activity and by releasing growth factor (Morin & Tomaselli, 2007). Active dressings improve the healing process and decrease healing time. They include skin grafts and biologic skin substitutes. Both interactive and active dressings create a moist environment at the interface of the wound with the dressing.

Because so many wound care products are available, it is often difficult to select the most appropriate product for a specific wound. Selection of products should be made carefully because of their expense. Both clinical efficacy and health-related outcomes (eg, decreased pain, increased mobility) should be used to measure the success of a product for a wound. Even with the availability of a large variety of dressings, an appropriate selection can be made if certain principles are maintained. Table 52-2 is a guide to wound dressing functions and categories.

T A B L E
52-2 Quick Guide to Wound Dressing Function and Categories

Function	Action	Example
Absorption	Absorbs exudate	Alginates, composite dressings, foams, gauze, hydrocolloids, hydrogels
Cleansing	Removes purulent drainage, foreign debris, and devitalized tissue	Wound cleansers
Débridement	*Autolytic*; covers a wound and allows enzymes to self-digest sloughed skin	Absorption beads, pastes, powders; alginates; composite dressings; foams; hydrate gauze; hydrogels; hydrocolloids; transparent films; wound care systems
	Chemical or enzymatic; applied topically to break down devitalized tissue	Enzymatic débridement agents
	Mechanical; removes devitalized tissue with mechanical force	Wound cleansers, gauze (wet to dry), whirlpool
Diathermy	Produces electrical current to promote warmth and new tissue growth	Ultrasound and microwave (diathermy)
Hydration	Adds moisture to a wound	Gauze (saturated with saline) solution, hydrogels, wound care systems
Maintain moist environment	Manages moisture levels in a wound and maintains a moist environment	Composites, contact layers, foams, gauze (impregnated or saturated), hydrogels, hydrocolloids, transparent films, wound care systems
Manage high-output wounds	Manages excessive quantities of exudate	Pouching systems
Pack or fill dead space	Prevents premature wound closure or fills shallow areas and provides absorption	Absorbent beads, powders, pastes; alginates, composites, foams, gauze (impregnated and non-impregnated)
Protect and cover wound	Provides protection from the external environment	Composites, compression bandages/wraps, foams, gauze dressings, hydrogels, hydrocolloids, transparent film dressings
Protect periwound skin	Prevents moisture and mechanical trauma from damaging delicate tissue around wound	Composites, foams, hydrocolloids, pouching systems, skin sealants, transparent film dressings
Provide therapeutic compression	Provides appropriate levels of support to the lower extremities in venous stasis disease	Compression bandages, wraps, support stockings

Occlusive Dressings

Occlusive dressings cover a topical medication that is applied to a skin lesion. The area is kept airtight by using plastic film (eg, plastic wrap). Plastic film is thin and readily adapts to all sizes, body shapes, and skin surfaces. Generally, plastic wrap should be used no more than 12 hours each day.

Transparent Films

Transparent films are thin, transparent, polyurethane, impermeable adhesive films that are used for partial thickness, minimally draining, or closed wounds. They permit visualization of the wound, promote autolysis, reduce friction, and are sometimes used as a secondary dressing. Examples are Op-Site and Tegaderm.

Specialty Absorptive Dressings

These are used for heavily exudating wound. The dressings absorb copious amounts of drainage. Examples of these are Exudry and ABD pads.

Moisture-Retentive Dressings

Commercially produced moisture-retentive dressing can perform the same functions as wet dressings but are more efficient at removing exudate because of their higher moisture-vapor transmission rate; some have reservoirs that can hold excessive exudate. A number of moisture-retentive dressings are already impregnated with saline solution, petrolatum, zinc-saline solution, hydrogel, or antimicrobial agents, thereby eliminating the need to coat the skin to avoid maceration. Depending on the product used and the type of dermatologic problem encountered, most moisture-retentive dressings may remain in place from 12 to 24 hours; some can remain in place as long as a week.

Hydrogels

Hydrogels are polymers with a 90% to 95% water content. They are available in impregnated sheets or as gel in a tube. Their high moisture content makes them ideal for autolytic débridement of wounds. They are semitransparent, allowing for wound inspection without dressing removal. They are comfortable and soothing for the painful wound. They require a secondary dressing to keep them in place. Hydrogels are appropriate for superficial wounds with high serous output, such as abrasions, skin graft sites, and draining venous ulcers.

Hydrocolloids

Hydrocolloids are composed of a water-impermeable, polyurethane outer covering separated from the wound by a hydrocolloid material. They are adherent and nonpermeable to water vapor and oxygen. As water evaporates over the wound, it is absorbed into the dressing, which softens and discolors with the increased water content. The dressing can be removed without damage to the wound. As the dressing absorbs water, it produces a foul-smelling, yellowish covering over the wound. This is a normal chemical interaction between the dressing and wound exudate and should not be confused with purulent drainage from the wound. Most can be left in place for as long as 7 days.

Foam Dressings

Foam dressings are nonadherent and require a secondary dressing to keep them in place. Moisture is absorbed into the foam layer, decreasing maceration of surrounding tissue. A moist environment is maintained, and removal of the dressing does not damage the wound. Foams are a good choice for exudative wounds. They are especially helpful over bony prominences because they provide contoured cushioning.

Alginates

Calcium alginates (e.g. AlgiSite M, Kaltostat, Sorbsan, Algi-cell) are derived from brown seaweed and consist of very absorbent calcium alginate fibers that can absorb 20 times their weight (Morin & Tomaselli, 2007). They are useful in areas where the tissue is highly irritated or macerated. The alginate dressing forms a moist pocket over the wound while the surrounding skin stays dry. The dressing also reacts with wound fluid and forms a foul-smelling coating. Alginates work well when packed into a deep cavity, wound, or sinus tract with heavy drainage. They are nonadherent and require a secondary dressing. Daily dressing changes are recommended when used with infected wounds (Rolstad & Ovington, 2007).

Antimicrobial Dressings

Antimicrobial dressings are used for partial and full thickness wounds. They help to control or decrease the bioburden and odor for minimal and heavy exudating wounds. They are a topical antifungal and antibiotic agent that come in ointments, gels, impregnated gauze, hydrofiber, and pads. Examples are Acticoat 7 and Aquacel Ag (hydrofiber).

Collagen Dressings

These dressings stimulate the wound and accelerate wound healing. Some forms can be left on for up to 7 days. They are used for minimal to moderate exudating partial to full thickness wounds. Examples are Promogran and ColActive.

Growth Factors

Regranex gel contains becaplermin, a platelet-derived growth factor, which is applied to the wound to stimulate healing by increasing the cytokines in the wound, thus stimulating cellular growth and granulation of skin. In 2008, the U.S. Food and Drug Administration (FDA) issued a warning about the association of increased risk of cancer death in patients who use three or more tubes of the product. Thus, the FDA cautions health care professionals to carefully weigh the risks and benefits of treating patients with this product. It is not recommended for patients with known malignancies (cancerous tumors) (U.S. Food and Drug Administration [FDA], 2008).

Tissue Engineered Skin

Apligraf and Dermagraft are dressings made up of a bioabsorbable matrix of collagen or suture material that contains living cytokines and fibroblasts. When applied to wounds,

these agents stimulate platelet activity and potentially decrease wound-healing time (Rolstad & Ovington, 2007). Bioengineered skin works by maintaining wound moisture, providing a structure for regeneration of cells, and supplying beneficial cytokines.

Débridement

Débridement is the removal of nonviable tissue from pressure and vascular ulcers, burns, surgical, traumatic wounds, and other types of wounds.

Autolytic Débridement

Autolytic **débridement** is a process that uses the body's own digestive enzymes to break down necrotic tissue. The wound is kept moist with occlusive dressings. Eschar and necrotic debris are softened, liquefied, and separated from the bed of the wound.

Enzymatic Débridement

Several commercially available products contain the same enzymes that the body produces naturally. These are called enzymatic débriding agents; an example is a collagenase (Santyl). Application of these products speeds the rate at which necrotic tissue is removed. This method is slower and no more effective than surgical débridement.

Mechanical Débridement

Wet to dry dressings are still used, but not very much. It is considered a nonselective method of débridement, which removes necrotic tissue and absorbs small to large amounts of exudates. This method exposes healthy tissue in the wound and can damage it as well.

Wet dressings (wet compresses applied to the skin) were traditionally used for acute, weeping, inflammatory lesions. They have become almost obsolete because of the many newer products available for wound care (Spear, 2008).

Negative Pressure Wound Therapy

In this therapy, an open-cell, reticulated foam, gauze, or specialized designed dressing is placed into the wound, sealed with semi-occlusive drape, and exposed to subatmospheric pressure via an evacuation tube connected to a computerized pump. It is used for acute and chronic open wounds. It also can be used on partial to full thickness wounds, as well as partial thickness burns.

Hyperbaric Oxygen Therapy

Hyperbaric oxygenation (HBO) is an adjunctive therapy requiring breathing of 100% oxygen while under increased atmospheric pressure in a pressure chamber. It is recommended that hyperbaric be utilized for limb-threatening diabetic wounds of the lower extremities and pressure ulcers. Also, it is used for hypoxic lower extremity vascular wounds (Thackman et al., 2008). Those who received HBO as part

of their wound care regimen healed faster than those who received standard treatment (Lyon, 2008).

Pharmacologic Therapy

Some oral medications are being investigated for their benefits in healing chronic venous ulcers of the lower legs. Pentoxifylline (Trental) has been shown to improve microcirculation and ulcer healing (Carr, 2008). It has some **fibrinolytic** action and decreases leukocyte adhesion to the wall of the blood vessels.

SKIN CONDITIONS

PRURITUS

While not a disorder but a manifestation, pruritus (itching) is one of the most common symptoms of patients with dermatologic disorders.

GENERAL PRURITUS

Pathophysiology

Itch receptors are unmyelinated, penicillate (brush-like) nerve endings that are found exclusively in the skin, mucous membranes, and cornea. Although pruritus is usually caused by a primary skin disease with resultant rash or lesions, it may occur without a rash or lesion. This is referred to as *essential pruritus*, which generally has a rapid onset, may be severe, and interferes with normal daily activities.

Pruritus may be the first indication of a systemic internal disease such as diabetes mellitus, blood disorders, or cancer (occult malignancy of the breast or colon; Hodgkin's disease, other lymphomas). It may also accompany renal, hepatic, and thyroid diseases (Box 52-2). Some common oral medications such as aspirin, antibiotics, hormones (ie, estrogens, testosterone, or oral contraceptives), and opioids (ie, morphine or cocaine) may cause pruritus directly or by increasing sensitivity to ultraviolet light. Certain soaps and chemicals, radiation therapy, prickly heat (miliaria), and contact with woolen garments are also associated with pruritus. Pruritus may also be caused by psychological factors, such as excessive stress in family or work situations.

Scratching the pruritic area causes the inflamed cells and nerve endings to release histamine, which produces more pruritus, generating a vicious itch–scratch cycle. If the patient responds to an itch by scratching, the integrity of the skin may be altered, and excoriation, erythema, raised areas (ie, wheals), infection, or changes in pigmentation may result. Pruritus usually is more severe at night and is less frequently reported during waking hours, most likely because the person is distracted by daily activities. At night, when there are few distractions, the slightest pruritus cannot be easily ignored. Severe itching can be debilitating.

Systemic Disorders Associated With Generalized Pruritus

- Chronic renal disease
- Obstructive biliary disease (primary biliary cirrhosis, extrahepatic biliary obstruction, drug-induced cholestasis)
- Endocrine disease (thyrotoxicosis, hypothyroidism, diabetes mellitus)
- Psychiatric disorders (emotional stress, anxiety, neurosis, phobias)
- Malignancies (polycythemia vera, Hodgkin's disease, lymphoma, leukemia, multiple myeloma, mycosis fungoides, and cancers of the lung, breast, central nervous system, and GI tract)
- Neurologic disorders (multiple sclerosis, brain abscess, brain tumor)
- Infestations (scabies, lice, other insects)
- Pruritus of pregnancy (pruritic urticarial papules of pregnancy (PUPP), cholestasis of pregnancy, pemphigoid of pregnancy)
- Folliculitis (bacterial, candidiasis, dermatophyte)
- Skin conditions (seborrheic dermatitis, folliculitis, iron deficiency anemia, atopic dermatitis)

Gerontologic Considerations

Pruritus occurs frequently in elderly people as a result of dry skin. Elderly people are also more likely to have a systemic illness that triggers pruritus, are at higher risk for occult malignancy, and are more likely to be taking multiple medications than younger people. All of these factors increase the incidence of pruritus in elderly people.

Medical and Nursing Management

A thorough history and physical examination usually provide clues to the underlying cause of the pruritus, such as hay fever, allergy, recent administration of a new medication, or a change of cosmetics or soaps. After the causative agent has been identified and removed (if possible), treatment of the condition should relieve the pruritus. Signs of infection and environmental clues, such as warm, dry air or irritating bed linens, should be identified. In general, washing with soap and hot water is avoided. Bath oils containing a surfactant that makes the oil mix with bath water (eg, Alpha-Keri) may be sufficient for cleaning. A warm bath with a mild soap followed by application of a bland emollient to moist skin can control **xerosis** (dry skin). Applying a cold compress, or cool agents that contain menthol and camphor (which constrict blood vessels) may also help relieve pruritus. If baths have been prescribed, the nurse reminds the patient to use tepid (not hot) water and to shake off the excess water and blot between intertriginous areas (body folds) with a towel. Rubbing vigorously with the towel is avoided because this overstimulates the skin and causes more itching. It also removes water from the stratum corneum (horny layer or outermost layer of the epidermis). Immediately after bathing, the patient should lubricate the skin with an emollient to trap moisture. The nurse instructs patient to avoid situations that cause vasodilation, such as exposure to an overly warm environment and ingestion of alcohol or hot foods and liquids. Activities that result in perspiration should be limited because perspiration may irritate and promote pruritus. If the patient is troubled at night with itching that interferes with sleep, the nurse can advise wearing cotton clothing next to the skin rather than synthetic materials. The room should be kept cool and humidified. Vigorous scratching should be avoided and nails kept trimmed to prevent skin damage and infection. When the underlying cause of pruritus is unknown and further testing is required, the nurse explains each test and the expected outcome.

Topical corticosteroids may be beneficial as anti-inflammatory agents to decrease itching. Oral antihistamines are even more effective because they can overcome the effects of histamine release from damaged mast cells. An antihistamine, such as diphenhydramine (Benadryl) or hydroxyzine (Atarax), prescribed in a sedative dose at bedtime, may be beneficial in producing a restful and comfortable sleep. Nonsedating antihistamine medications, such as fexofenadine (Allegra), are more appropriate to relieve daytime pruritus. Tricyclic antidepressants may be prescribed for pruritus of neuropsychogenic origin. If pruritus continues, further investigation of a systemic problem is advised.

PERINEAL AND PERIANAL PRURITUS

Pathophysiology

Pruritus of the genital and anal regions may be caused by small particles of fecal material lodged in the perianal crevices or attached to anal hairs. Alternatively, it may result from perianal skin damage caused by scratching, moisture, and decreased skin resistance as a result of corticosteroid or antibiotic therapy. Other possible causes of perianal itching include local irritants such as scabies and lice, local lesions such as hemorrhoids, fungal or yeast infections, and pinworm infestation. Foods associated with anal pruritus include coffee, tea, cola, beer, chocolate, and tomatoes. Occasionally, no cause for genital and anal pruritus can be identified.

Medical and Nursing Management

The nurse instructs patient to follow proper hygiene measures and to discontinue home and over-the-counter remedies. The perineal or anal area should be rinsed with lukewarm water and blotted dry with cotton balls. Premoistened tissues may be used after defecation. Cornstarch can be applied in the skinfold areas to absorb perspiration.

As part of health teaching, the nurse instructs the patient to avoid bathing in water that is too hot and to avoid using

bubble baths, sodium bicarbonate, and detergent soaps, all of which aggravate dryness. To keep the perineal or perianal skin as dry as possible, patients should avoid wearing underwear made of synthetic fabrics. Local anesthetic agents should not be used because of possible allergic effects. The patient should also avoid vasodilating agents or stimulants (eg, alcohol, caffeine) and mechanical irritants such as rough or woolen clothing. A diet that includes adequate fiber may help maintain soft stools and prevent minor trauma to the anal mucosa.

ULCERATION

Superficial loss of surface tissue as a result of death of cells is called an ulceration. A simple **ulcer**, such as the kind found in a small, superficial, partial-thickness burn, tends to heal by granulation if kept clean and protected from injury. If exposed to the air, the serum that escapes dries and forms a scab, under which the epithelial cells grow and cover the surface completely. The four most common ulcers noted are arterial, venous, neuropathic/diabetic, and pressure ulcers (Table 52-3).

ARTERIAL ULCERS

Ulcers related to problems with arterial circulation are seen in patients with hypertension, diabetes, cigarette smoking, hypercholesterolemia, obesity, and sedentary lifestyle. Arterial ulcers are caused by lower extremity arterial disease (LEAD), which is inadequate blood flow to the tissue resulting in severe tissue ischemia, and which can create ulcers that are extremely painful (Doughty & Holbrook, 2007). LEAD is also referred to as peripheral arterial disease (PAD), peripheral vascular disease (PVD), or peripheral arterial occlusive disease (PAOD). In patients with LEAD and ulcers, treatment of the ulcers is concurrent with treatment of the arterial disease. Management

includes the use of the dressings and/or tissue perfusion improvement. Perfusion and tissue oxygenation can improve outcomes via surgical options (bypass graft, angioplasty), medications (antiplatelets, vasodilators, hemorheologics [decrease the viscosity of the blood], antilipemics [decrease lipid levels], analgesics) lifestyle changes, and adjunctive therapies (hyperbaric oxygen therapy) (Camden, 2007). If these interventions are instituted early in the progression of an ulcer, the condition can often be effectively improved. Surgical amputation of an affected limb is a last resort.

VENOUS ULCERS

Venous ulcers are more common than arterial ulcers. They occur due to impaired return of venous blood from the tissue to the heart, also known as chronic venous insufficiency (CVI) or lower extremity venous disease (LEVD). Risk factors are valvular dysfunction caused by obesity, multiple pregnancies, thrombophlebitis, leg trauma (deep vein thrombosis or fractures), and thrombophilic conditions (increased coagulability of the blood). Other risks factors include arthritis or calf muscle dysfunction, IV drug use involving affected extremity, sedentary lifestyle, or prolonged standing. Healing can be affected by diabetes, smoking, nutrition, and medications (Doughty & Holbrook, 2007). Management includes reduction of edema, prevention of complications, and appropriate topical therapy or specialty dressings (Doughty & Holbrook, 2007).

NEUROPATHIC ULCERS

Diabetic foot ulcers are also known as neuropathic ulcers or lower extremity neuropathic disease (LEND). These ulcers occur due to reduced blood supply to the nerves, also known as microvascular damage, which can lead to neuropathy. Neuropathy is classified as loss of sensation. Risk factors include past history of amputations or ulcers,

TABLE
52-3 **Characteristics of Ulcers**

Ulcer Type	Location	Description of Wound Bed	Exudate	Description of Wound Edges
Arterial	Tips of toes, pressure points, areas of trauma	Pale or necrotic	Minimal amount	Well defined
Venous	Between ankles and knees	Dark red, "ruddy"	Moderate to large amounts	Poorly defined; irregular
Neuropathic	Plantar surface over metatarsal heads	Typically red (unless coexisting ischemia)	Moderate to large amounts	Well defined
Pressure	Any boney prominence	Erythremic or purplish in discoloration due to pressure	Minimal to large amounts	Poorly to well defined

long duration of diabetes and/or poor glucose control, limited joint mobility, long history of smoking, obesity, poor vision, poor footwear, vascular insufficiency, structural deformities and callus formation, absence of protective sensation, and autonomic neuropathy causing decreased sweating and dry feet (Driver, Landowski, & Madsen, 2007).

Early prevention can be achieved through comprehensive annual foot examinations, glycemic control, limiting other health complications, and offloading (pressure relief). Wound management may include débridement, treatment of infection if needed, and topical, specialty wound care dressing and/or adjunctive therapies (Driver et al., 2007). For further information related to diabetic neuropathy refer to Chapter 30.

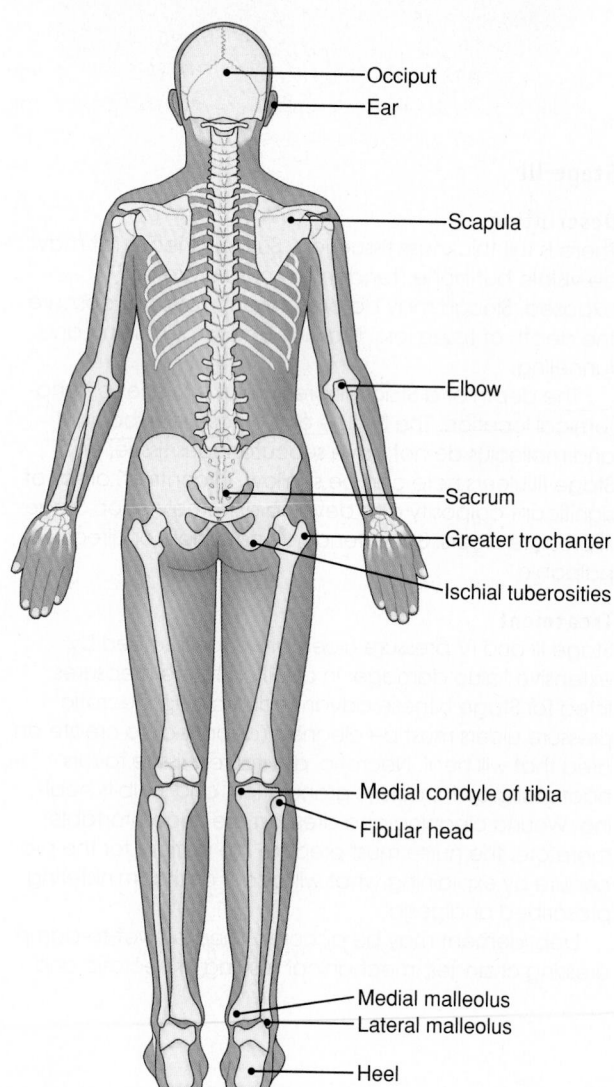

FIGURE 52-1 Areas susceptible to pressure ulcers.

PRESSURE ULCERS

Pathophysiology

Pressure ulcers involve the breakdown of the skin due to prolonged pressure, friction, and shear forces, and insufficient blood supply, usually at bony prominences. Pressure ulcers are localized areas of infarcted soft tissue that occur when pressure applied to the skin over time is greater than normal capillary closure pressure, which is about 32 mm Hg. Weight-bearing bony prominences are most susceptible to pressure ulcer development because they are covered only by skin and small amounts of subcutaneous tissue. Susceptible areas include the sacrum and coccygeal areas, ischial tuberosities (especially in people who sit for prolonged periods), greater trochanter, heel, knee, malleolus, medial condyle of the tibia, fibular head, scapula, and elbow (Fig. 52-1).

Risk Factors

Box 52-3 summarizes risk factors for pressure ulcers.

Clinical Manifestations and Assessment

The initial sign of pressure is erythema (redness of the skin) caused by reactive hyperemia, which normally resolves in less than 1 hour. Unrelieved pressure results in tissue ischemia or anoxia. The cutaneous tissues become broken or destroyed, leading to progressive destruction and necrosis of underlying soft tissue, and the resulting pressure ulcer is painful and slow to heal. The nurse assesses the patient's mobility, sensory perception, cognitive abilities, tissue perfusion, nutritional status, friction and shear forces, sources of moisture on the skin, age, and skin condition. Scales such as the Braden or Norton scale may be used to facilitate systematic assessment and quantification of a patient's risk for pressure ulcer, although the nurse should recognize that the reliability of these scales is not well established for all patient populations. If a pressure area is noted, the nurse notes its size and location and uses a grading system to describe its severity (refer to Box 52-4 for

(Text continues on page 1356)

> ### BOX 52-3
> ### Risk Factors for Pressure Ulcers
>
> - Immobility, compromised mobility
> - Prolonged pressure on tissue
> - Altered skin moisture: excessively dry, excessively moist (perspiration, urine, feces, or drainage produces maceration (softening) of the skin)
> - Equipment: Casts, traction, restraints
> - Impaired sensory perception or cognition
> - Decreased tissue perfusion (seen with diabetes, obesity, and edema). Critically ill patients have a lower capillary closure pressure thus higher risk.
> - Decreased nutritional status (anemia, hypoalbuminemia, vitamin deficiency)
> - Friction and shear forces

BOX 52-4 **Stages of Pressure Ulcers**

Stage I

Description

Ulcer appears as intact skin with nonblanchable erythema of a localized area, usually over a bony prominence. Darkly pigmented skin may not have visible blanching; its color may differ from the surrounding area.

The area may be painful, firm, soft, and warmer or cooler in temperature as compared to adjacent tissue. Stage I may indicate "at risk" persons (a heralding sign of risk).

Treatment

To permit healing of Stage I pressure ulcers, the pressure is removed to allow increased tissue perfusion; nutritional and fluid and electrolyte balance are maintained; friction and shear are reduced; and moisture to the skin is avoided.

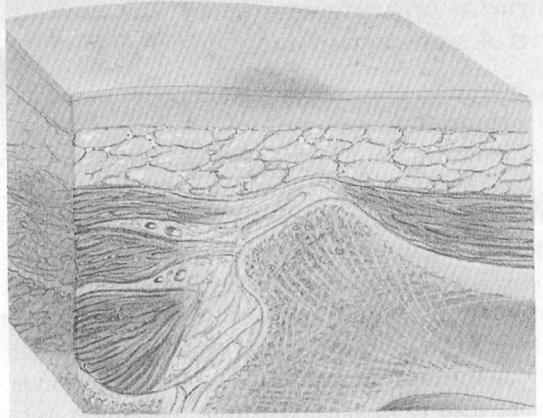

Stage II

Description

Ulcer appears as partial thickness loss of dermis presenting as a shallow open ulcer with a red pink wound bed, without slough. It may also present as an intact or open/ruptured serum-filled blister.

It may be a shiny or dry shallow ulcer without slough or bruising (bruising indicates suspected deep tissue injury). This stage should not be used to describe skin tears, tape burns, perineal dermatitis, maceration, or excoriation.

Treatment

In addition to measures listed for Stage I pressure ulcers, a moist environment, in which migration of epidermal cells over the ulcer surface occurs more rapidly, should be provided to aid wound healing. The ulcer is gently cleansed with sterile saline solution. Use of a heat lamp to dry the open wound is avoided, as is the use of antiseptic solutions that damage healthy tissues and delay wound healing. Semipermeable occlusive dressings, hydrocolloid wafers, or wet saline dressings are helpful in providing a moist environment for healing and in minimizing the loss of fluids and proteins from the body.

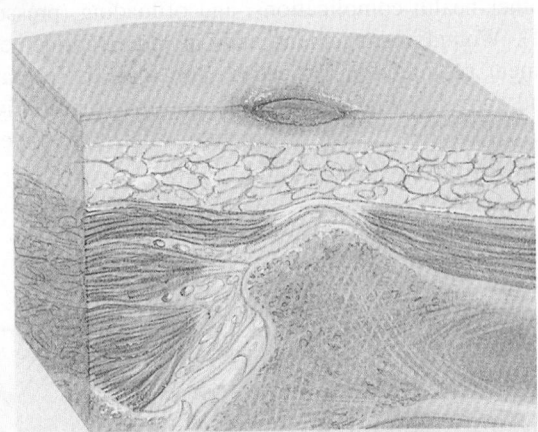

Stage III

Description

There is full-thickness tissue loss. Subcutaneous fat may be visible but bone, tendon, or muscle are not exposed. Slough may be present but does not obscure the depth of tissue loss. May include undermining and tunneling.

The depth of a Stage III pressure ulcer varies by anatomical location. The bridge of the nose, ear, occiput and malleolus do not have subcutaneous tissue, and Stage III ulcers here can be shallow. In contrast, areas of significant adiposity can develop extremely deep Stage III pressure ulcers. Bone/tendon is not visible or directly palpable.

Treatment

Stage III and IV pressure ulcers are characterized by extensive tissue damage. In addition to the measures listed for Stage I, these advanced, draining, necrotic pressure ulcers must be cleaned (débrided) to create an area that will heal. Necrotic, devitalized tissue favors bacterial growth, delays granulation, and inhibits healing. Wound cleaning and dressing are uncomfortable; therefore, the nurse must prepare the patient for the procedure by explaining what will occur and administering prescribed analgesia.

Débridement may be accomplished by wet-to-damp dressing changes, mechanical flushing of necrotic and

infective exudate, application of prescribed enzyme preparations that dissolve necrotic tissue, or surgical dissection. If an eschar covers the ulcer, it is removed surgically to ensure a clean, vitalized wound. Exudate may be absorbed by dressings or special **hydrophilic** powders, beads, or gels. Cultures of infected pressure ulcers are obtained to guide the selection of antibiotic therapy.

After the pressure ulcer is clean, a topical treatment is prescribed to promote granulation. New granulation tissue must be protected from reinfection, drying, and damage, and care should be taken to prevent pressure and further trauma to the area. Dressings, solutions, and ointments applied to the ulcer should not disrupt the healing process. Multiple agents and protocols are used to treat pressure ulcers, but consistency is an important key to success. Objective evaluation of the pressure ulcer (eg, measurement of the size and depth of the pressure ulcer, inspection for granulation tissue) for response to the treatment protocol must be made every 4 to 6 days. Taking photographs at weekly intervals is a reliable strategy for monitoring the healing process, which may take weeks to months.

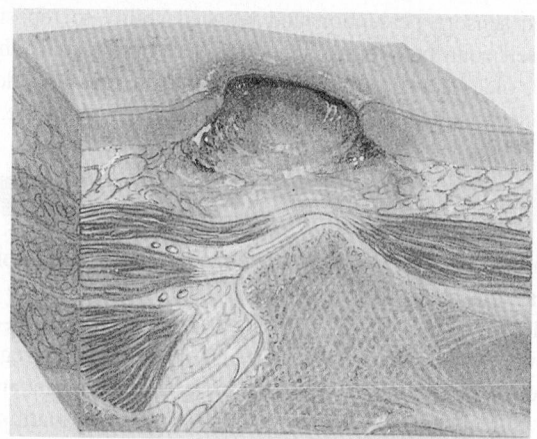

Stage IV

Description

There is full-thickness tissue loss with exposed bone, tendon, or muscle. Slough or eschar may be present on some parts of the wound bed. These ulcers often include undermining and tunneling.

The depth of a Stage IV pressure ulcer varies by anatomical location. The bridge of the nose, ear, occiput, and malleolus do not have subcutaneous tissue, and these ulcers can be shallow. Stage IV ulcers can extend into muscle and/or supporting structures (eg, fascia,

tendon, or joint capsule) making osteomyelitis possible. Exposed bone/tendon is visible or directly palpable.

Treatment

See Stage III treatment. In addition, surgical intervention may be necessary when the ulcer is extensive, when complications (eg, fistula) exist, and when the ulcer does not respond to treatment. Surgical procedures include débridement, incision and drainage, bone resection, and skin grafting. Osteomyelitis is a common complication of wounds of Stage IV depth. See Chapter 41 for more information on osteomyelitis.

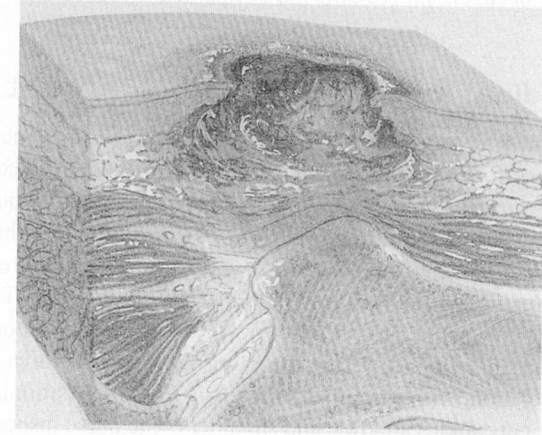

Unstageable

An unstageable lesion shows full-thickness tissue loss in which the base of the ulcer is covered by slough (yellow, tan, gray, green or brown) and/or eschar (tan, brown or black) in the wound bed.

Until enough slough and/or eschar is removed to expose the base of the wound, the true depth, and therefore stage, cannot be determined. Stable (dry, adherent, intact without erythema or fluctuance) eschar on the heels serves as the body's natural (biological) cover and should not be removed.

Suspected Deep Tissue Injury

Suspected deep tissue injury (DTI) appears as a purple or maroon localized area of discolored intact skin or blood-filled blister due to damage of underlying soft tissue from pressure and/or shear. The area may be preceded by tissue that is painful, firm, mushy, boggy, warmer, or cooler as compared to adjacent tissue.

DTI may be difficult to detect in individuals with dark skin tones. Evolution may include a thin blister over a dark wound bed. The wound may further evolve and become covered by thin eschar. Evolution may be rapid, exposing additional layers of tissue even with optimal treatment.

current standards in assessing and staging pressure ulcers). A recent study of interrater reliability in identifying classification of pressure ulcers revealed low reliability; therefore, it is imperative that nurses use a consistent scale (Kottner, Raeder, Halfens et al., 2009).

NURSING ALERT

Beginning in 2008, Medicare regulations do not reimburse for treatment of pressure ulcers acquired in the hospital, even if present on admission but undocumented. It is therefore imperative that accurate recognition and staging of pressure ulcers occurs in all patients (Zulkowski & Gray-Leach, 2009).

Medical and Nursing Management

Treatment depends on stage (see Box 52-4). Nursing interventions for prevention and management of pressure ulcers include turning and repositioning the patient every 1 to 2 hours when in bed, and shifting of weight every 15 minutes while in a chair to allow the blood to flow into the ischemic areas to help tissues recover from the effects of pressure. The recumbent position is preferred to the semi-Fowler's position because of increased supporting body surface area in this position, with careful attention paid to the repositioning of patients ankles, elbows, and shoulders. The nurse inspects the skin at each position change and assesses for temperature elevation. If redness or heat is noted, or if the patient complains of discomfort, pressure on the area must be relieved.

A pillow or commercial heel protector may be used to support the heels off the bed when the patient is supine. Supporting the patient in a 30-degree side-lying position avoids pressure on the trochanter. At times, special equipment and beds may be needed to help relieve the pressure on the skin, such as wheelchair cushions and static support devices (such as high-density foam, air, or liquid mattress overlays). Shear occurs when patients are pulled, allowed to slump, or move by digging heels or elbows into the mattress. Raising the head of the bed by even a few centimeters increases the shearing force over the sacral area; therefore, the semi-reclining position is avoided in patients at risk. The patient is encouraged to remain active and is ambulated whenever possible. Exercise and repositioning improve tissue perfusion. Massage of erythematous areas is avoided because damage to the capillaries and deep tissue may occur.

Strategies to improve cognition and sensory perception may include stimulating the patient to increase awareness of self in the environment, encouraging the patient to participate in self-care, or supporting the patient's efforts toward active compensation for loss of sensation (eg, a patient with paraplegia lifting up from the sitting position every 15 minutes).

Continuous moisture on the skin must be prevented by meticulous hygiene measures. Perspiration, urine, stool, and drainage must be removed from the skin promptly. The skin may be lubricated with a bland lotion to keep it soft and pliable. Drying agents and powders are avoided. Topical barrier ointments (eg, petroleum jelly) may be helpful in protecting the skin of patients who are incontinent. Absorbent pads that wick moisture away from the body should be used to absorb drainage.

The patient's nutritional status must be adequate, and a positive nitrogen balance must be maintained because pressure ulcers develop more quickly and are more resistant to treatment in patients with nutritional disorders. A high-protein diet with protein supplements may be helpful. Iron preparations may be necessary to raise the hemoglobin concentration, so that tissue oxygen levels can be maintained within acceptable limits. Ascorbic acid (vitamin C) is necessary for tissue healing. Other nutrients associated with healthy skin include vitamin A, B vitamins, zinc, and sulfur.

Gerontologic Considerations

In older adults, the skin has diminished epidermal thickness, dermal collagen, and tissue elasticity. The skin is drier as a result of diminished sebaceous and sweat gland activity. Cardiovascular changes result in decreased tissue perfusion. Muscles atrophy, and bone structures become prominent. Diminished sensory perception and reduced ability to reposition oneself contribute to prolonged pressure on the skin. Therefore, older adults are more susceptible to pressure ulcers, which cause pain and suffering and reduce quality of life.

SEBORRHEIC DERMATITIS

Seborrhea is excessive production of sebum (secretion of sebaceous glands) in areas where sebaceous glands are normally found in large numbers, such as on the face, scalp, eyebrows, eyelids, sides of the nose and upper lip, malar regions (cheeks), ears, axillae, under the breasts, in the groin, and in the gluteal crease of the buttocks. Seborrheic dermatitis is a chronic inflammatory disease of the skin with a predilection for areas that are well supplied with sebaceous glands or lie between skin folds, where the bacteria count is high.

Clinical Manifestations and Assessment

Two forms of seborrheic dermatitis can occur, an oily form and a dry form. Either form may start in childhood and continue throughout life. The oily form appears moist or "greasy." There may be patches of yellowish-red or gray-white, greasy skin, with white dry scaling macules and/or papules, with slight erythema, predominantly on the forehead, nasolabial fold, beard area, scalp, and between adjacent skin surfaces in the regions of the axillae, groin, and breasts (Botfitz, 2009). Small pustules or papulopustules resembling acne may appear on the trunk. The dry form, consisting of flaky desquamation of the scalp with a profuse amount of fine, powdery scales, is commonly called dandruff. The mild forms of the disease

are asymptomatic. When scaling occurs, it is often accompanied by pruritus, which may lead to scratching and secondary infections and excoriation.

Seborrheic dermatitis has a genetic predisposition. Hormones, nutritional status, infection, and emotional stress influence its course. The remissions and exacerbations of this condition should be explained to the patient. If a person has not previously been diagnosed with this condition and suddenly appears with a severe outbreak, a complete history and physical examination should be considered.

Medical and Nursing Management

Because there is no known cure for seborrhea, the objective of therapy is to control the disorder and allow the skin to repair itself. Seborrheic dermatitis of the body and face may respond to a topically applied glucocorticoid cream or low-potency topical steroids (eg, desonide), which allays the secondary inflammatory response (Borfitz, 2009). However, glucocorticoids should be used with caution near the eyelids, because it can induce glaucoma and cataracts in predisposed patients. Patients with seborrheic dermatitis may develop a secondary candidal (yeast) infection in body creases or folds and may have to use a topical antifungal (eg, ciclopirox or ketoconazole) (Borfitz, 2009). To avoid this, patients should be advised to ensure maximum aeration of the skin and to clean areas where there are creases or folds in the skin carefully. Patients with persistent candidiasis should be evaluated for diabetes. Ultraviolet radiation therapy can be beneficial as a form of treatment as well.

The mainstay of dandruff treatment is proper, frequent shampooing (at least three times weekly) with medicated shampoos. Two or three different types of shampoo should be used in rotation to prevent the seborrhea from becoming resistant to a particular shampoo. The shampoo is left on at least 5 to 10 minutes. As the condition of the scalp improves, the treatment can be less frequent. Antiseborrheic shampoos include those containing selenium sulfide suspension, zinc pyrithione, salicylic acid or sulfur compounds, and tar shampoo that contains sulfur or salicylic acid. Instructions for using medicated shampoos are reinforced for people with dandruff who require treatment. Frequent shampooing is contrary to some cultural practices; the nurse should be sensitive to these differences when teaching the patient about home care.

A person with seborrheic dermatitis is advised to avoid external irritants, excessive heat, and perspiration; rubbing and scratching prolong the disorder. To avoid secondary infection, the patient should air the skin and keep skin folds clean and dry.

The patient is cautioned that seborrheic dermatitis is a chronic problem that tends to reappear. The goal is to keep it under control. Patients need to be encouraged to adhere to the treatment program. Those who become discouraged and disheartened by the effect on body image should be treated with sensitivity and encouraged to express their feelings.

VIRAL SKIN INFECTIONS

HERPES ZOSTER

Herpes zoster, also called *shingles*, is an infection caused by the varicella-zoster virus, a member of a group of DNA viruses. The viruses causing chickenpox and herpes zoster are indistinguishable, hence the name varicella-zoster virus. The disease is characterized by a painful vesicular eruption along the area of distribution of the sensory nerves from one or more posterior ganglia.

Pathophysiology

After a case of chickenpox runs its course, the varicella-zoster viruses responsible for the outbreak lie dormant inside nerve cells near the brain and spinal cord. Later, when these latent viruses are reactivated because of declining cellular immunity, they travel by way of the peripheral nerves to the skin, where the viruses multiply and create a red rash of small, fluid-filled vesicles. About 10% of adults get shingles during their lifetimes, usually after 50 years of age. There is an increased frequency of herpes zoster infections among patients with weakened immune systems and cancers (especially leukemias and lymphomas), those on chemotherapy, and in HIV-affected individuals.

Clinical Manifestations and Assessment

The eruption is usually accompanied or preceded by pain, which may radiate over the entire region supplied by the affected nerves. The pain may be burning, lancinating (tearing or sharply cutting), stabbing, or aching. Some patients have no pain, but itching and tenderness may occur over the area. Sometimes, malaise and gastrointestinal (GI) disturbances precede the eruption. The patches of grouped vesicles appear on the red and swollen skin. The early vesicles, which contain serum, later may become purulent, rupture, and form crusts. The inflammation is usually unilateral, involving the thoracic, cervical, or cranial nerves in a bandlike configuration. The blisters are usually confined to a narrow region of the face or trunk (Fig. 52-2). The clinical course varies from 1 to 3 weeks. If an ophthalmic nerve is involved, the patient may have eye pain. Inflammation and a rash on the trunk may cause pain with the slightest touch. The healing time varies from 7 to 26 days.

Herpes zoster in healthy adults is usually localized and benign. However, in immunosuppressed patients, the disease may be severe and disabling.

Medical and Nursing Management

There is evidence that infection is arrested if oral antiviral agents, such as acyclovir (Zovirax), valacyclovir (Valtrex), or famciclovir (Famvir), are administered within 24 hours of

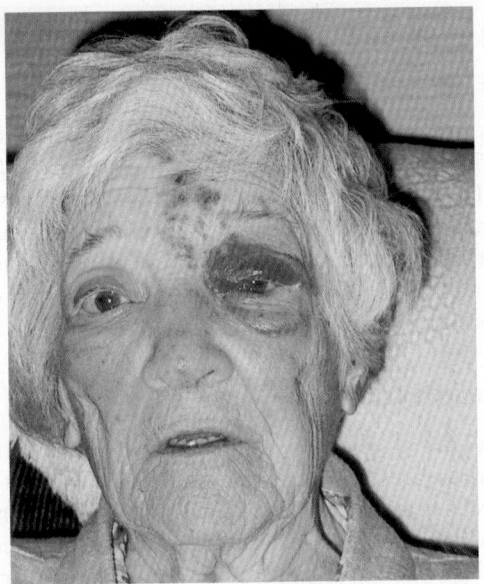

FIGURE 52-2 Herpes zoster (shingles).

the initial eruption. IV acyclovir, if started early, is effective in significantly reducing the pain and halting the progression of the disease. In older patients, the pain from herpes zoster may persist as postherpetic neuralgia for months after the skin lesions disappear.

The goals of herpes zoster management are to relieve the pain and to reduce or avoid complications, which include infection, scarring, and postherpetic neuralgia and eye complications. Pain is controlled with analgesics, because adequate pain control during the acute phase helps prevent persistent pain patterns. Systemic corticosteroids may be prescribed for patients older than 50 years of age to reduce the incidence and duration of postherpetic neuralgia (persistent pain of the affected nerve after healing). Healing usually occurs more quickly in those who have been treated with corticosteroids. Triamcinolone (Aristocort, Kenacort, Kenalog) injected subcutaneously under painful areas is effective as an anti-inflammatory agent.

Ophthalmic herpes zoster occurs when an eye is involved. This is considered an ophthalmic emergency, and the patient should be referred to an ophthalmologist immediately to prevent the possible sequelae of keratitis, uveitis, ulceration, and blindness.

People who have been exposed to varicella by primary infection or by vaccination are not at risk for infection after exposure to patients with herpes zoster.

HERPES SIMPLEX

Herpes simplex is a common skin infection. There are two types of the causative virus, which are identified by viral typing. Generally, herpes simplex type 1 occurs on the mouth and type 2 occurs in the genital area, but both viral types can be found in both locations. About 85% of adults worldwide are seropositive for herpes type 1. The prevalence of type 2 is lower; type 2 usually appears at the onset of sexual activity. Herpes simplex type 2 is discussed in detail in Chapter 35. Serologic testing shows that many more people are infected than have a history of clinical disease.

Herpes simplex infection is classified as a true primary infection, a nonprimary initial episode, or a recurrent episode. True primary infection is the initial exposure to the virus. A nonprimary initial episode is the initial episode of either type 1 or type 2 in a person previously infected with the other type. Recurrent episodes are subsequent episodes of the same viral type.

TINEA

Fungi—tiny members of a subdivision of the plant kingdom that feed on organic matter—are responsible for various common skin infections. In some cases, they affect only the skin and its appendages (hair and nails). In other cases, internal organs are involved, and the diseases may be life-threatening. However, superficial infections rarely cause even temporary disability and usually respond readily to treatment. Secondary infection with bacteria, *Candida*, or both organisms may occur.

The most common fungal skin infection is **tinea**, which is also called *ringworm* because of its characteristic appearance of a ring or rounded tunnel under the skin. Tinea infections affect the head, body, groin, feet, and nails. Table 52-4 summarizes the tinea infections.

To obtain a specimen for diagnosis, the lesion is cleaned and a scalpel or glass slide is used to remove scales from the margin of the lesion. The scales are dropped onto a slide to which potassium hydroxide has been added. The diagnosis is made by examination of the infected scales microscopically for spores and hyphae or by isolating the organism in culture. Under Wood's light, a specimen of infected hair appears fluorescent; this may be helpful in diagnosing some cases of tinea capitis.

SCABIES

Scabies is an infestation of the skin by the itch mite *Sarcoptes scabiei*. The disease may be found in people living in substandard hygienic conditions, but it can occur in anyone. Infestations may or may not be associated with sexual activity. The mites frequently involve the fingers, and hand contact may produce infection. In children, overnight stays with friends or the exchange of clothes may be a source of infection. Health care personnel who have prolonged hands-on physical contact with an infected patient may become infected (Hay, 2009).

TABLE
52-4 Tinea (Ringworm) Infections

Type and Location	Clinical Manifestations	Treatment
Tinea corporis (body)	• Begins with red macule, which spreads to a ring of papules or vesicles with central clearing. • Lesions are found in clusters. • Many spread to the hair, scalp, or nails. • Very pruritic • An infected pet may be the source.	• Mild conditions: topical antifungal creams • Severe conditions: griseofulvin or terbinafine
Tinea cruris (groin area; "jock itch")	• Begins with small, red scaling patches, which spread to form circular elevated plaques. • Very pruritic • Clusters of pustules may be seen around borders.	• Mild conditions: topical antifungal creams • Severe conditions: griseofulvin or terbinafine
Tinea pedis (foot; "athlete's foot")	• Soles of one or both feet have scaling and mild redness with maceration in the toe webs. • More acute infections may have clusters of clear vesicles on dusky base.	• Soak feet in vinegar and water solution. • Resistant infections: griseofulvin or terbinafine • Terbinafine (Lamisil) daily for 3 months
Tinea unguium (toe-nails; affects about 50% of adults)	• Nails thicken, crumble easily, and lack luster. • Whole nail may be destroyed.	• Itraconazole (Sporanox) in pulses of 1 week a month for 3 months in cases of terbinafine failure

Clinical Manifestations and Assessment

It takes approximately 4 weeks from the time of contact for the patient's symptoms to appear. The patient complains of severe itching caused by a delayed type of immunologic reaction to the mite or its fecal pellets. During examination, the nurse asks the patient where the pruritus is most severe. A magnifying glass and a penlight are held at an oblique angle to the skin while a search is made for the small, raised burrows created by the mites. The burrows may be multiple, straight or wavy, brown or black, thread-like lesions, most commonly observed between the fingers and on the wrists. Other sites are the extensor surfaces of the elbows, the knees, the edges of the feet, the points of the elbows, around the nipples, in the axillary folds, under pendulous breasts, and in or near the groin or gluteal fold, penis, or scrotum. Red, pruritic eruptions usually appear between adjacent skin areas. However, the burrow is not always visible. Any patient with a rash may have scabies.

One classic sign of scabies is the increased itching that occurs during the overnight hours, perhaps because the increased warmth of the skin has a stimulating effect on the parasite. Hypersensitivity to the organism and its products of excretion also may contribute to the pruritus. If the infection has spread, other members of the family and close friends also complain of pruritus about a month later.

Secondary lesions are quite common and include vesicles, papules, excoriations, and crusts. Bacterial superinfection may result from constant excoriation of the burrows and papules.

The diagnosis is confirmed by recovering *S. scabiei* or the mites' by-products from the skin. A sample of superficial epidermis is scraped from the top of the burrows or papules with a small scalpel blade. The scrapings are placed on a microscope slide and examined through a microscope at low power to demonstrate evidence of the mite (Hay, 2009).

Gerontologic Considerations

Elderly patients living in long-term care facilities are susceptible to outbreaks of scabies because of close living quarters, poor hygiene due to limited physical ability, and the potential for incidental spread of the organisms by staff members. Although pruritus may be severe in the older patient, the vivid inflammatory reaction seen in younger people seldom occurs. Scabies may not be recognized in the elderly person; the pruritus may erroneously be attributed to the dry skin of old age or to anxiety.

Health care personnel in extended-care facilities should wear gloves when providing hands-on care for a patient suspected of having scabies until the diagnosis is confirmed and treatment completed. It is advisable to treat all residents, staff, and families of patients at the same time to prevent reinfection. Because geriatric patients may be more sensitive to side effects of the scabicides, they should be closely observed for reactions.

Medical and Nursing Management

The patient is instructed to take a warm, soapy bath or shower to remove the scaling debris from the crusts and then

to dry thoroughly and allow the skin to cool. A prescription scabicide, such as lindane (Kwell), crotamiton (Eurax), or 5% permethrin (Elimite), is applied thinly to the entire skin from the neck down, sparing only the face and scalp (which are not affected in scabies). The medication is left on for 12 to 24 hours, after which the patient is instructed to wash thoroughly. One application may be curative, but it is advisable to repeat the treatment in 1 week.

CONTACT DERMATITIS

Contact dermatitis is an inflammatory reaction of the skin to physical, chemical, or biologic agents.

Pathophysiology

The epidermis is damaged by repeated physical and chemical irritations. Contact dermatitis may be of the primary irritant type, in which a nonallergic reaction results from exposure to an irritating substance, or it may be an allergic reaction resulting from exposure of sensitized people to contact allergens. Common causes of irritant dermatitis are soaps, detergents, scouring compounds, and industrial chemicals. Predisposing factors include extremes of heat and cold, frequent contact with soap and water, and a preexisting skin disease (Box 52-5).

BOX 52-5 **Patient Education**

Strategies for Avoiding Contact Dermatitis

The following precautions may help prevent repeated cases of contact dermatitis. Follow these instructions for at least 4 months after your skin appears to be completely healed:

- Study the pattern and location of your dermatitis and think about which things have touched your skin and which things may have caused the problem.
- Try to avoid contact with these materials.
- Avoid heat, soap, and rubbing, all of which are external irritants.
- Choose bath soaps, laundry detergents, and cosmetics that do not contain fragrance.
- Avoid using a fabric softener dryer sheet (Bounce, Cling Free). Fabric softeners that are added to the washer may be used.
- Avoid topical medications, lotions, or ointments, except those specifically prescribed for your condition.
- Wash your skin thoroughly immediately after exposure to possible irritants.
- When wearing gloves (for example, for washing dishes or general cleaning), be sure they are cotton-lined. Do not wear them more than 15 or 20 minutes at a time.

Clinical Manifestations and Assessment

The eruptions begin when the causative agent contacts the skin. The first reactions include pruritus, burning, and erythema, followed closely by edema, papules, vesicles, and oozing or weeping. In the subacute phase, these vesicular changes are less marked, and they alternate with crusting, drying, fissuring, and peeling. If repeated reactions occur or if the patient continually scratches the skin, **lichenification** (thickening of the horny layer of the skin) and pigmentation occur. Secondary bacterial invasion may follow.

Medical and Nursing Management

The objectives of management are to rest the involved skin and protect it from further damage. The distribution pattern of the reaction is identified to differentiate between allergic and irritant contact dermatitis. A detailed history is obtained. If possible, the offending irritant is removed. Local irritation should be avoided, and soap is not generally used until healing occurs.

Many preparations are advocated for relieving dermatitis. In general, a bland, unmedicated lotion is used for small patches of erythema. Cool, wet dressings also are applied over small areas of vesicular dermatitis. Finely cracked ice added to the water often enhances its antipruritic effect.

Wet dressings usually help clear the oozing eczematous lesions. A thin layer of cream or ointment containing a corticosteroid then may be used. Medicated baths at room temperature are prescribed for larger areas of dermatitis. For severe, widespread conditions, a short course of systemic corticosteroids may be prescribed.

NONINFECTIOUS INFLAMMATORY DERMATOSES

PSORIASIS

Considered one of the most common skin diseases, psoriasis affects approximately 2% of the population, appearing more often in people of European ancestry. It is thought that this chronic, noninfectious, inflammatory disease stems from a hereditary defect that causes overproduction of keratin. Onset may occur at any age, but psoriasis is most common in people between 15 and 35 years of age. Psoriasis has a tendency to improve and then recur periodically throughout life (Mrowietz & Reich, 2009).

Pathophysiology

Although the primary cause of psoriasis is unknown, a combination of specific genetic makeup and environmental stimuli may trigger the onset of disease. Current evidence supports an immunologic basis for the disease (Mrowietz & Reich, 2009). Periods of emotional stress and anxiety aggravate the

condition, and trauma, infections, and seasonal and hormonal changes also are trigger factors.

Epidermal cells are produced at a rate that is about six to nine times faster than normal. The cells in the basal layer of the skin divide too quickly, and the newly formed cells move so rapidly to the skin surface that they become evident as profuse scales or plaques of epidermal tissue. The psoriatic epidermal cell may travel from the basal cell layer of the epidermis to the stratum corneum and be cast off in 3 to 4 days, which is in sharp contrast to the normal 26 to 28 days. As a result of the increased number of basal cells and rapid cell passage, the normal events of cell maturation and growth cannot take place. This abnormal process does not allow the normal protective layers of the skin to form.

Clinical Manifestations and Assessment

Lesions appear as red, raised patches of skin covered with silvery scales. The scaly patches are formed by the buildup of living and dead skin resulting from the vast increase in the rate of skin cell growth and turnover (Fig. 52-3). If the scales are scraped away, the dark-red base of the lesion is exposed, producing multiple bleeding points. These patches are not moist and may be pruritic. One variation of this condition is called *guttate* (in the shape of a drop) psoriasis because the lesions remain about 1 cm wide and are scattered like raindrops over the body. This variation is believed to be associated with a recent streptococcal throat infection. Psoriasis may range in severity from a cosmetic source of annoyance to a physically disabling and disfiguring disorder.

Particular sites of the body tend to be affected most by this condition; they include the scalp, the extensor surface of the elbows and knees, the lower part of the back, and the genitalia. Bilateral symmetry is a feature of psoriasis. In approximately one-fourth to one-half of patients, the nails

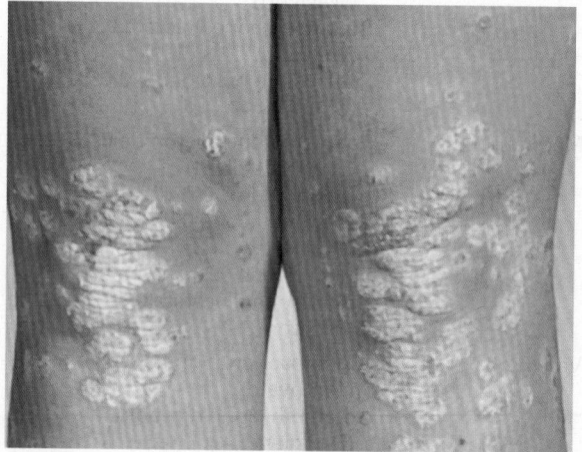

FIGURE 52-3 Psoriasis. Reprinted with permission from Bickley, L. S. (2009). *Bate's guide to physical examination and history taking*. Philadelphia: Lippincott Williams & Wilkins.

are involved, with pitting, discoloration, crumbling beneath the free edges, and separation of the nail plate. When psoriasis occurs on the palms and soles, it can cause pustular lesions called *palmar pustular psoriasis*.

The presence of the classic plaque-type lesions generally confirms the diagnosis of psoriasis. Because the lesions tend to change histologically as they progress from early to chronic plaques, biopsy of the skin is of little diagnostic value. There are no specific blood tests for diagnosing the condition. When in doubt, the health care provider should assess for signs of nail and scalp involvement and for a positive family history.

Complications

Asymmetric rheumatoid factor–negative arthritis of multiple joints occurs in about 5% of people with psoriasis. The arthritic development can occur before or after the skin lesions appear. The relationship between arthritis and psoriasis is not understood, although recent studies suggest an interplay between genetics, environmental factors, and the immune system (Mrowietz & Reich, 2009). Erythrodermic psoriasis, an exfoliative psoriatic state, involves disease progression that affects the total body surface. The patient is acutely ill, with impaired temperature regulation, and fluid and protein loss. Erythrodermic psoriasis often appears in people with chronic psoriasis after infections, after exposure to certain medications, or following withdrawal of systemic corticosteroids.

Medical and Nursing Management

The goals of management are to slow the rapid turnover of epidermis, to promote resolution of the psoriatic lesions, and to control the natural cycles of the disease. There is no known cure.

The therapeutic approach should be one that the patient understands; it should be cosmetically acceptable and minimally disruptive of lifestyle. Treatment involves the commitment of time and effort by the patient and possibly the family. First, any precipitating or aggravating factors are addressed. An assessment is made of lifestyle, because psoriasis is significantly affected by stress. The patient is informed that treatment of severe psoriasis can be time-consuming, expensive, and aesthetically unappealing at times.

Removal of Scales

The most important principle of psoriasis treatment is gentle removal of scales. This can be accomplished with baths. Oils (eg, olive oil, mineral oil, Aveeno Oilated Oatmeal Bath) or coal tar preparations (eg, Balnetar) can be added to the bath water and a soft brush used to scrub the psoriatic plaques gently. After bathing, the application of emollient creams containing alpha-hydroxy acids (eg, Lac-Hydrin, Penederm) or salicylic acid continues to soften thick scales. The patient and family should be encouraged to establish a regular skin care routine that can be maintained even when the psoriasis is not in an acute stage.

TABLE
52-5 Current Pharmacologic Treatment for Psoriasis

Topical Agents	Use	Selected Agents
Biologicals	Moderate to severe lesions	Cyclosporine (Neoral), alefacept (Amevive), etanercept (Enbrel), infliximab (Remicade)
Topical corticosteroids	Mild to moderate lesions Moderate to severe lesions Severe lesions Lesions on face and groin	Aristocort, Kenalog, Valisone Lidex, Psorcon, Cutivate Temovate, Diprolene, Ultravate Aclovate, DesOwen, Hytone 2.5%
Topical nonsteroidals	Mild to severe	Retinoids such as tazarotene (Tazorac) Vitamin D₃ derivative calcipotriene (Dovonex)
Coal tar products	Mild to moderate lesions	Coal tar and salicylic acid ointment (Aquatar, Estar gel, Fototar, Zetar); anthralin (AnthraDerm, Dritho-Cream); Neutrogena T-Derm, Psori Gel
Medicated shampoos	Scalp lesions	Neutrogena T-Gel, T-Sal, Zetar, Head & Shoulders, Desenex, Selsun Blue, Bakers P&S (emulsifying agent with phenol, saline solution, and mineral oil)
Intralesional therapy	Thick plaques and nails	Kenalog, Cordran-impregnated tape, Fluoroplex
Systemic therapy	Extensive lesions and nails Psoriatic arthritis	Methotrexate (Folex, Mexate); hydrouria (Hydrea); retinoic acid (Tegison) (not to be used in women of childbearing age) Oral gold (auranofin), etretinate, methotrexate
Photochemotherapy	Moderate to severe lesions	UVA or UVB light with or without topical medications PUVA (combines UVA light with oral psoralens, or topical Trisoralen)

Pharmacologic Therapy

With the recent addition of biologic medications, four types of therapy are now commonly used: topical, intralesional, oral, and injectable (Table 52-5).

Topical Agents

Topically applied agents are used to slow the overactive epidermis without affecting other tissues. These agents include lotions, ointments, pastes, creams, and shampoos. Topical corticosteroids may be applied for their anti-inflammatory effect. Choosing the correct strength of corticosteroid for the involved site and choosing the most effective vehicle base are important aspects of topical treatment. In general, high-potency topical corticosteroids should not be used on the face and intertriginous areas, and their use on other areas should be limited to a 4-week course of twice-daily applications. A 2-week break should be taken before repeating treatment with the high-potency corticosteroids. For long-term therapy, moderate-potency corticosteroids are used. On the face and intertriginous areas, only low-potency corticosteroids are appropriate for long-term use (see Table 52-6).

Occlusive dressings may be applied to increase the effectiveness of the corticosteroid. Large rolls of tubular plastic can be used to cover the arms and legs. Another option is a vinyl jogging suit. The medication is applied, and the suit is put on over it. The hands can be wrapped in gloves, the feet in plastic bags, and the head in a shower cap. Occlusive dressings should not remain in place longer than 8 hours.

TABLE
52-6 Potency: Topical Corticosteroids

Potency	Topical Corticosteroid
Over-the-counter	0.5% to 1.0% hydrocortisone
Lowest	Dexamethasone 0.1% (Decaderm) Alclometasone 0.05% (Aclovate) Hydrocortisone 2.5% (Hytone)
Low–Medium	Desonide 0.05% (DesOwen, Tridesilon) Fluocinolone acetonide 0.025% (Synalar) Hydrocortisone valerate 0.2% (Westcort) Betamethasone valerate 0.1% (Valisone) Fluticasone propionate 0.05% (Cutivate)
Medium–High	Triamcinolone acetonide 0.1% to 0.5% (Aristocort) Fluocinonide 0.05% (Lidex) Desoximetasone 0.05% to 0.25% (Topicort) Fluocinolone 0.2% (Synalar) Diflorasone diacetate 0.05% (Psorcon)
Very high	Clobetasol propionate 0.05% (Temovate) Betamethasone dipropionate 0.05% (Diprolene) Halobetasol propionate 0.05% (Ultravate)

The skin should be inspected carefully for the appearance of atrophy, hypopigmentation, striae, and telangiectasias, all side effects of corticosteroids.

When psoriasis involves large areas of the body, topical corticosteroid treatment can be expensive and involve some systemic risk. The more potent corticosteroids, when applied to large areas of the body, have the potential to cause adrenal suppression through percutaneous absorption of the medication. In this event, other treatment modalities (eg, nonsteroidal topical medications, ultraviolet light) may be used instead, or in combination to decrease the need for corticosteroids.

Two topical nonsteroidal treatments introduced within the past few years are calcipotriene (Dovonex) and tazarotene (Tazorac). Treatment with these agents tends to suppress **epidermopoiesis** (ie, development of epidermal cells) and cause sloughing of the rapidly growing epidermal cells. Calcipotriene 0.05% is a derivative of vitamin D_2. It works by decreasing the mitotic turnover of the psoriatic plaques. Its most common side effect is local irritation. The intertriginous areas and face should be avoided when using this medication. The patient should be monitored for symptoms of hypercalcemia. Calcipotriene is available as a cream for use on the body and a solution for the scalp. It is not recommended for use by elderly patients because of their more fragile skin or by pregnant or lactating women.

Tazarotene, a retinoid, causes sloughing of the scales covering psoriatic plaques. As with other retinoids, it causes increased sensitivity to sunlight by loss of the outermost layer of skin, so the patient should be cautioned to use an effective sunscreen and avoid other photosensitizers (eg, tetracycline, antihistamines). Tazarotene is listed as a Category X drug in pregnancy; reports indicate evidence of fetal risk, and the risk of use in pregnant women clearly outweighs any possible benefits. A negative result on a pregnancy test should be obtained before initiating this medication in women of childbearing age, and an effective contraceptive should be continued during treatment. Side effects include burning, erythema, or irritation at the site of application and worsening of psoriasis.

Intralesional Agents

Intralesional injections of the corticosteroid triamcinolone acetonide (Aristocort, Kenalog-10, Trymex) can be administered directly into highly visible or isolated patches of psoriasis that are resistant to other forms of therapy. Care must be taken to ensure that the medication is not injected into normal skin.

Systemic Agents

Although systemic corticosteroids may cause rapid improvement of psoriasis, their usual risks and the possibility of triggering a severe flare-up on withdrawal limit their use. Systemic cytotoxic preparations, such as methotrexate, have been used in treating extensive psoriasis that fails to respond to other forms of therapy.

Methotrexate appears to inhibit DNA synthesis in epidermal cells, thereby reducing the turnover time of the psoriatic epidermis. However, the medication can be toxic, especially to the liver, kidneys, and bone marrow. Laboratory studies must be monitored to ensure that the hepatic, hematopoietic, and renal systems are functioning adequately. The patient should avoid drinking alcohol while taking methotrexate, because alcohol ingestion increases the possibility of liver damage. The medication is teratogenic (produces physical defects in the fetus) and thus should not be administered to pregnant women.

Hydroxyurea (Hydrea) also inhibits cell replication by affecting DNA synthesis. The patient is monitored for signs and symptoms of bone marrow depression.

Cyclosporine A, a cyclic peptide used to prevent rejection of transplanted organs, has shown some success in treating severe, therapy-resistant cases of psoriasis. However, its use is limited by side effects such as hypertension and nephrotoxicity.

Oral retinoids (ie, synthetic derivatives of vitamin A and its metabolite, vitamin A acid) modulate the growth and differentiation of epithelial tissue. Etretinate is especially useful for severe pustular or erythrodermic psoriasis. Etretinate is a teratogen with a very long half-life; it cannot be used in women with childbearing potential.

Photochemotherapy

One treatment for severely debilitating psoriasis is a psoralen (phototoxic) medication (eg, methoxsalen) combined with ultraviolet-A (PUVA) light therapy. Ultraviolet light is the portion of the electromagnetic spectrum containing wavelengths ranging from 180 to 400 nm. In this treatment, the patient takes a photosensitizing medication (usually 8-methoxypsoralen) in a standard dose and is subsequently exposed to long-wave ultraviolet light as the medication plasma levels peak. Although the mechanism of action is not completely understood, it is thought that when psoralen-treated skin is exposed to ultraviolet-A light, the psoralen binds with DNA and decreases cellular proliferation. PUVA is not without its hazards; it has been associated with long-term risks of skin cancer, cataracts, and premature aging of the skin (Mrowietz & Reich, 2009).

The PUVA unit consists of a chamber that contains high-output black-light lamps and an external reflectance system. The exposure time is calibrated according to the specific unit in use and the anticipated tolerance of the patient's skin. The patient is usually treated two or three times each week until the psoriasis clears. An interim period of 48 hours between treatments is necessary; it takes this long for any burns resulting from PUVA therapy to become evident.

After the psoriasis clears, the patient begins a maintenance program. Once little or no disease is active, less potent therapies are used to keep minor flare-ups under control.

Ultraviolet-B (UVB) light therapy is also used to treat generalized plaques. UVB light ranges from 270 to 350 nm,

although research has shown that a narrow range, 310 to 312 nm, is the action spectrum. It is used alone or combined with topical coal tar. Side effects are similar to those of PUVA therapy. If access to a light treatment unit is not feasible, the patient can expose himself or herself to sunlight. The risks of all light treatments are similar and include acute sunburn reaction; exacerbation of photosensitive disorders such as lupus, rosacea, and polymorphic light eruption (a rash related to photosensitivity that can take on many forms); as well as other skin changes such as increased wrinkles, thickening, and an increased risk for skin cancer.

EXFOLIATIVE DERMATITIS

Exfoliative dermatitis is a serious condition characterized by progressive inflammation in which generalized erythema and scaling occur. It may be associated with chills, fever, prostration, severe toxicity, and a pruritic scaling of the skin.

Pathophysiology

There is a profound loss of stratum corneum (ie, outermost layer of the skin), which causes capillary leakage, hypoproteinemia, and negative nitrogen balance. Because of widespread dilation of cutaneous vessels, large amounts of body heat are lost, and exfoliative dermatitis has a marked effect on the entire body.

Exfoliative dermatitis has a variety of causes. It is considered to be a secondary or reactive process to an underlying skin or systemic disease. It may appear as a part of the lymphoma group of diseases and may precede the clinical manifestations of lymphoma.

Clinical Manifestations and Assessment

This condition starts acutely as a patchy or a generalized erythematous eruption accompanied by fever, malaise, and occasionally GI symptoms. The skin color changes from pink to dark red. After a week, the characteristic exfoliation (ie, scaling) begins, usually in the form of thin flakes that leave the underlying skin smooth and red, with new scales forming as the older ones come off. Hair loss may accompany this disorder. Relapses are common. The systemic effects include high-output heart failure, intestinal disturbances, breast enlargement, elevated levels of uric acid in the blood (ie, hyperuricemia), and temperature disturbances.

Medical and Nursing Management

The objectives of management are to maintain fluid and electrolyte balance and to prevent infection. The treatment is individualized and supportive and should be initiated as soon as the condition is diagnosed.

The patient may be hospitalized and placed on bed rest. All medications that may be implicated are discontinued.

A comfortable room temperature should be maintained because the patient does not have normal thermoregulatory control as a result of temperature fluctuations caused by vasodilation and evaporative water loss. Fluid and electrolyte balance must be maintained because there is considerable water and protein loss from the skin surface. Administration of plasma volume expanders may be indicated.

BLISTERING DISORDERS

PEMPHIGUS

Pemphigus is a group of serious diseases of the skin characterized by the appearance of bullae (blisters) of various sizes on apparently normal skin (Fig. 52-4) and mucous membranes.

Pathophysiology

Pemphigus is an autoimmune disease involving immunoglobulin G. It is thought that the pemphigus antibody is directed against a specific cell-surface antigen in epidermal cells. A blister forms from the antigen–antibody reaction. The level of serum antibody is predictive of disease severity.

Risk Factors

Genetic factors may also have a role in its development, with the highest incidence among those of Jewish or Mediterranean descent. This disorder usually occurs in men and women in middle and late adulthood. The condition may be associated with penicillins and captopril and with the disorder myasthenia gravis.

Clinical Manifestations and Assessment

Most patients present with oral lesions appearing as irregularly shaped erosions that are painful, bleed easily, and heal

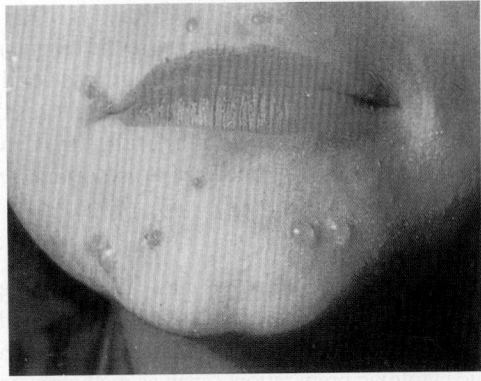

FIGURE 52-4 Vesicles on the chin (in pemphigus). From Hall, J. C. (2006). *Sauer's manual of skin diseases*. Philadelphia: Lippincott Williams & Wilkins.

slowly. The skin bullae enlarge, rupture, and leave large, painful, eroded areas that are accompanied by crusting and oozing. A characteristic offensive odor emanates from the bullae and the exuding serum. There is blistering or sloughing of uninvolved skin when minimal pressure is applied (Nikolsky's sign). The eroded skin heals slowly, and large areas of the body eventually are involved. Bacterial superinfection is common.

Complications

The most common complications arise when the disease process is widespread. Before the advent of corticosteroid and immunosuppressive therapy, patients were very susceptible to secondary bacterial infection. Skin bacteria have relatively easy access to the bullae as they ooze, rupture, and leave denuded (loss of epidermis) areas exposed to the environment. Fluid and electrolyte imbalance results from fluid and protein loss as the bullae rupture. Hypoalbuminemia is common when the disease process includes extensive areas of the body skin surface and mucous membranes.

Medical and Nursing Management

The goals of therapy are to bring the disease under control as rapidly as possible, to prevent loss of serum and the development of secondary infection, and to promote re-epithelization (ie, renewal of epithelial tissue).

Corticosteroids are administered in high doses to control the disease and keep the skin free of blisters. The high dosage level is maintained until remission is apparent. In some cases, corticosteroid therapy must be maintained for life. High-dose corticosteroid therapy has serious toxic effects.

Immunosuppressive agents (eg, azathioprine, cyclophosphamide, gold) may be prescribed to help control the disease and reduce the corticosteroid dose. **Plasmapheresis** temporarily decreases the serum antibody level and has been used with variable success, although it is generally reserved for life-threatening cases.

BULLOUS PEMPHIGOID

Bullous pemphigoid is an acquired disease of flaccid blisters appearing on normal or erythematous skin.

Clinical Manifestations and Assessment

Bullous pemphigoid appears more often on the flexor surfaces of the arms, legs, axilla, and groin. Oral lesions, if present, are usually transient and minimal. When the blisters break, the skin has shallow erosions that heal fairly quickly. Pruritus can be intense, even before the appearance of the blisters. Bullous pemphigoid is common in the elderly, with a peak incidence at about 60 years of age. There is no gender or racial predilection, and the disease can be found throughout the world.

Medical and Nursing Management

Medical treatment includes topical corticosteroids for localized eruptions and systemic corticosteroids for widespread involvement. Systemic corticosteroids (eg, prednisone) may be continued for months, in alternate-day doses. The patient needs to understand the implications of long-term corticosteroid therapy.

Complications
Infection and Sepsis

The patient is susceptible to infection because the barrier function of the skin is compromised. Bullae are also susceptible to infection, and sepsis may follow. The skin is cleaned to remove debris and dead skin and to prevent infection.

Secondary infection may be accompanied by an unpleasant odor from skin or oral lesions. *Candida albicans* of the mouth (ie, thrush) commonly affects patients receiving high-dose corticosteroid therapy. The oral cavity is inspected daily, and any changes are reported. Oral lesions are slow to heal.

Infection is the leading cause of death in patients with blistering diseases. Particular attention is given to assessment for signs and symptoms of local and systemic infection. Seemingly trivial complaints or minimal changes are investigated, because corticosteroids can mask or alter typical signs and symptoms of infection. The patient's vital signs are monitored, and temperature fluctuations are documented. The patient is observed for chills, and all secretions and excretions are monitored for changes suggesting infection. Results of culture and sensitivity tests are monitored. Antimicrobial agents are administered as prescribed, and response to treatment is assessed. Health care personnel must perform effective hand hygiene and wear gloves.

In hospitalized patients, environmental contamination is reduced as much as possible. Protective isolation measures and standard precautions are warranted.

Fluid and Electrolyte Imbalance

Extensive denudation of the skin leads to fluid and electrolyte imbalance because of significant loss of fluids and sodium chloride from the skin. This sodium chloride loss is responsible for many of the systemic symptoms associated with the disease and is treated by IV administration of saline solution.

A large amount of protein and blood is also lost from the denuded skin areas. Blood component therapy may be prescribed to maintain the blood volume, hemoglobin level, and plasma protein concentration. Serum albumin, protein, hemoglobin, and hematocrit values are monitored.

The patient is encouraged to maintain adequate oral fluid intake. Cool, nonirritating fluids are encouraged to maintain hydration. Small, frequent meals or snacks of high-protein, high-calorie foods (eg, oral nutritional supplements, eggnog, milkshakes) help maintain nutritional status. Parenteral nutrition is considered if the patient cannot eat an adequate diet.

TOXIC EPIDERMAL NECROLYSIS AND STEVENS-JOHNSON SYNDROME

Toxic epidermal necrolysis (TEN) and Stevens-Johnson syndrome (SJS) are potentially fatal skin disorders and the most severe forms of erythema multiforme.

These diseases are mucocutaneous reactions that constitute a spectrum of reactions, with TEN being the most severe. The mortality rate from TEN is 30% to 35%. TEN and SJS are triggered by a reaction to medications. Antibiotics, especially sulfonamides, antiseizure agents, nonsteroidal anti-inflammatory drugs (NSAIDs), and sulfonamides are the most frequent medications implicated (Knowles & Shear, 2009).

Risk Factors

These conditions occur in all ages and both genders. The incidence is increased in older people because of their use of many medications. People who are immunosuppressed, including those with HIV infection and AIDS, have a high risk of SJS and TEN. Although the incidence of TEN and SJS in the general population is about 2 to 3 cases per 1 million people in the United States, the risk associated with sulfonamides in HIV-positive individuals may approach 1 case per 1,000 (Knowles & Shear, 2009). Most patients with TEN have an abnormal metabolism of the medication; the mechanism leading to TEN seems to be a cell-mediated cytotoxic reaction.

Clinical Manifestations and Assessment

TEN and SJS are characterized initially by conjunctival burning or itching, cutaneous tenderness, fever, cough, sore throat, headache, extreme malaise, and myalgias (ie, aches and pains). These signs are followed by a rapid onset of erythema involving much of the skin surface and mucous membranes, including the oral mucosa, conjunctiva, and genitalia. In severe cases of mucosal involvement, there may be danger of damage to the larynx, bronchi, and esophagus from ulcerations. Large, flaccid bullae develop in some areas; in other areas, large sheets of epidermis are shed, exposing the underlying dermis. Fingernails, toenails, eyebrows, and eyelashes may be shed along with the surrounding epidermis. The skin is excruciatingly tender, and the loss of skin leaves a weeping surface similar to that of a total-body, partial-thickness burn; hence the condition is also referred to as "scalded skin syndrome."

Histologic studies of frozen skin cells from a fresh lesion and cytodiagnosis of collections of cellular material from a freshly denuded area are conducted. A history of use of medications known to precipitate TEN or SJS may confirm medication reaction as the underlying cause.

Immunofluorescent studies may be performed to detect atypical epidermal autoantibodies. A genetic predisposition to erythema multiforme has been suggested but has not been confirmed in all cases.

Medical and Nursing Management

The goals of treatment include control of fluid and electrolyte balance, prevention of sepsis, and prevention of ophthalmic complications. Supportive care is the mainstay of treatment.

All nonessential medications are discontinued immediately. If possible, the patient is treated in a regional burn center, because aggressive treatment similar to that for severe burns is required. Skin loss may approach 100% of the total body surface area. Surgical débridement or hydrotherapy in a Hubbard tank (large steel tub) may be performed to remove involved skin.

Tissue samples from the nasopharynx, eyes, ears, blood, urine, skin, and unruptured blisters are obtained for culture to identify pathogenic organisms. IV fluids are prescribed to maintain fluid and electrolyte balance, especially in the patient who has severe mucosal involvement and who cannot easily take oral nourishment. Because an indwelling IV catheter may be a site of infection, fluid replacement is carried out by nasogastric tube and then orally as soon as possible.

Initial treatment with systemic corticosteroids is controversial. Some experts argue for early high-dose corticosteroid treatment. However, in most cases, the risk of infection, the complication of fluid and electrolyte imbalance, the delay in the healing process, and the difficulty in initiating oral corticosteroids early in the course of the disease outweigh the perceived benefits. In patients with TEN thought to result from a medication reaction, corticosteroids may be administered; however, the patient should be closely monitored for adverse effects.

Protecting the skin with topical agents is crucial. Various topical antibacterial and anesthetic agents are used to prevent wound sepsis and to assist with pain management. Systemic antibiotic therapy is used with extreme caution. Temporary biologic dressings (eg, pigskin, amniotic membrane) or plastic semipermeable dressings (eg, Vigilon) may be used to reduce pain, decrease evaporation, and prevent secondary infection until the epithelium regenerates. Meticulous oropharyngeal and eye care is essential when there is severe involvement of the mucous membranes and the eyes.

As the patient completes the acute inpatient stage of illness, the focus is directed toward rehabilitation and outpatient care or care in a rehabilitation center. Throughout this care, the patient and family members are involved in the care and are instructed in the procedures, such as wound care and dressing changes that will need to be continued at home. The patient and family members are assisted in acquiring dressing supplies that will be needed at home.

The patient and family members are also provided with instructions about pain management, nutrition, measures to increase mobility, and prevention of complications, including prevention of infection. They are taught the signs and symptoms of complications and instructed when to notify the health care provider. When appropriate, instructions are provided in writing to the patient and family so they can refer to these instructions when necessary at later times.

Interdisciplinary follow-up care is imperative to ensure that the patient's progress continues. Some patients will require care in a rehabilitation center before returning home. Others will require outpatient physical and occupational therapy for an extended period. When the patient returns home, the home care nurse coordinates the care provided by the various members of the health care team (eg, primary care provider, physical therapist, occupational therapist, and dietician). The nurse also monitors the patient's progress, provides ongoing assessment to identify complications, and monitors the patient's adherence to the plan of care. The patient's adaptation to the home care environment and the patient's and family's needs for support and assistance are also assessed. Referrals to community agencies are made as appropriate.

Complications

Sepsis

The major cause of death from TEN is infection, and the most common sites of infection are the skin and mucosal surfaces, lungs, and blood. The organisms most often involved are *Staphylococcus aureus*, *Pseudomonas*, *Klebsiella*, *Escherichia coli*, *Serratia*, and *Candida*. Monitoring vital signs closely and noticing changes in respiratory, renal, and GI function may quickly detect the beginning of an infection. Strict asepsis is always maintained during routine skin care measures. Hand hygiene and wearing sterile gloves when carrying out procedures are essential. When the condition involves a large portion of the body, the patient should be in a private room to prevent possible cross-infection from other patients. Visitors should wear protective garments and wash their hands before and after coming into contact with the patient. People with any infections or infectious disease should not visit the patient until they are no longer a danger to the patient.

Conjunctival Retraction, Scars, and Corneal Lesions

The nurse inspects the eyes daily for signs of pruritus, burning, and dryness, which may indicate progression to keratoconjunctivitis, the principal eye complication. Applying a cool, damp cloth over the eyes may relieve burning sensations. The eyes are kept clean and observed for signs of discharge or discomfort, and the progression of symptoms is documented and reported. Administering an eye lubricant, when prescribed, may alleviate dryness and prevent corneal abrasion. Using eye patches or reminding the patient to blink periodically may also counteract dryness. The patient is instructed to avoid rubbing the eyes or putting any medication into the eyes that has not been prescribed or approved by the provider.

BENIGN SKIN TUMORS

Table 52-7 provides descriptions of and treatments for common benign skin lesions.

MALIGNANT SKIN TUMORS

Skin cancer is the most common cancer in the United States. If the incidence continues at the present rate, an estimated one of eight fair-skinned Americans will eventually develop skin cancer, especially basal cell carcinoma. Because the skin is easily inspected, skin cancer is readily seen and detected and is the most successfully treated type of cancer.

Exposure to the sun is the leading cause of skin cancer; incidence is related to the total amount of exposure to the sun. Sun damage is cumulative, and harmful effects may be severe by 20 years of age. The increase in skin cancer probably reflects changing lifestyles and the emphasis on sunbathing and related activities in light of changes in the environment, such as holes in the Earth's ozone layer. Changes in the ozone layer from the effects of worldwide industrial air pollutants, such as chlorofluorocarbons, have prompted concern that the incidence of skin cancers, especially malignant melanoma, will increase. The ozone layer, a stratospheric blanket of bluish, explosive gas formed by the sun's ultraviolet radiation, varies in depth with the seasons and is thickest at the North and South Poles and thinnest at the equator. Scientists believe that it helps protect the earth from the effects of solar ultraviolet radiation. Proponents of this theory predict an increase in skin cancers as a consequence of changes in the ozone layer. Other skin cancer risk factors are summarized in Box 52-6 on page 1369. Protective measures should be used throughout life, and nurses should inform patients about risk factors associated with skin cancer.

BASAL CELL AND SQUAMOUS CELL CARCINOMA

The most common types of skin cancer are basal cell carcinoma (BCC) and squamous cell (epidermoid) carcinoma (SCC). The third most common type, malignant melanoma, is discussed separately. Skin cancer is diagnosed by biopsy and histologic evaluation.

Clinical Manifestations and Assessment

BCC is the most common type of skin cancer. It generally appears on sun-exposed areas of the body and is more prevalent

TABLE
52-7 Benign Skin Lesions

Lesion	Description	Treatment
Cysts	Cysts of the skin are epithelium-lined cavities that contain fluid or solid material. **Epidermal cysts** (epidermoid cysts) occur frequently, are slow-growing, firm, elevated tumors frequently noted on the face, neck, upper chest, and back. **Pilar cysts** (trichilemmal cysts), formerly called sebaceous cysts, frequently are found on the scalp. They originate from the middle portion of the hair follicle and from the cells of the outer hair root sheath.	Removal of the cysts provides a cure. Treatment is surgical removal.
Seborrheic and actinic keratoses	**Seborrheic keratoses** are benign, wartlike lesions of various sizes and colors, ranging from light tan to black, that are usually located on the face, shoulders, chest, and back. **Actinic keratoses** are premalignant skin lesions that develop in chronically sun-exposed areas of the body. They appear as rough, scaly patches with underlying erythema. A small percentage of these lesions gradually transform into cutaneous squamous cell carcinoma.	Treatment is removal of the tumor tissue by excision, electrodesiccation, and curettage, or application of carbon dioxide or liquid nitrogen. They are usually removed by cryotherapy or shave excision.
Verrucae: Warts	**Warts** are common, benign skin tumors caused by infection with the human papillomavirus, which belongs to the DNA virus group. People of all ages may be affected, but the warts occur most frequently between the ages of 12 and 16 years. Genitalia and perianal warts are known as condylomata acuminata. They may be transmitted sexually. Condylomata that affect the uterine cervix predispose the patient to cervical cancer.	They may be treated with locally applied laser therapy, liquid nitrogen, salicylic acid plasters, or electrodesiccation. They are treated with liquid nitrogen, cryosurgery, electrosurgery, topically applied trichloroacetic acid, and curettage.
Angiomas	**Angiomas** are benign vascular tumors that involve the skin and the subcutaneous tissues. They are present at birth and may occur as flat, violet-red patches (port-wine angiomas) or as raised, bright-red, nodular lesions (strawberry angiomas). The latter tend to involute spontaneously within the first few years of life, but port-wine angiomas usually persist indefinitely	Most patients use masking cosmetics (ie, Covermark or Dermablend) to camouflage the lesions. The argon laser is being used on various angiomas with some success. Treatment of strawberry angiomas is more successful if undertaken as soon after birth as possible.
Pigmented nevi: Moles	**Moles** are common skin tumors of various sizes and shades, ranging from yellowish brown to black. They may be flat, macular lesions or elevated papules or nodules that occasionally contain hair. Most pigmented nevi are harmless lesions. However, in rare cases, malignant changes occur, and a melanoma develops at the site of the nevus. Nevi that show a change in color or size, become symptomatic (eg, itch), or develop irregular borders should be removed to determine if malignant changes have occurred. Moles that occur in unusual places should be examined carefully for any irregularity and for notching of the border and variation in color. Nevi larger than 1 cm should be examined carefully. Excised nevi should be examined histologically.	
Keloids	**Keloids** are benign overgrowths of fibrous tissue at the site of a scar or trauma. They appear to be more common among dark-skinned people. Keloids are asymptomatic but may cause disfigurement and cosmetic concern.	The treatment, which is not always satisfactory, consists of surgical excision, intralesional corticosteroid therapy, and radiation.

Risk Factors for Skin Cancer

- Fair-skinned, fair-haired, blue-eyed people, particularly those of Celtic origin, with insufficient skin pigmentation to protect underlying tissues
- People who sustain sunburn and who do not tan
- Chronic sun exposure (certain occupations, such as farming, construction work)
- Exposure to chemical pollutants (industrial workers in arsenic, nitrates, coal, tar and pitch, oils and paraffins)
- Sun-damaged skin (elderly people)
- History of X-ray therapy for acne or benign lesions
- Scars from severe burns
- Chronic skin irritations
- Immunosuppression
- Genetic factors

in regions where the population is subjected to intense and extensive exposure to the sun. The incidence is proportional to the age of the patient (average, 60 years) and the total amount of sun exposure, and it is inversely proportional to the amount of melanin in the skin.

BCC usually begins as a small, waxy nodule with rolled, translucent, pearly borders; telangiectatic vessels may be present. As it grows, it undergoes central ulceration and sometimes crusting (Fig. 52-5). The tumors appear most frequently on the face. BCC is characterized by invasion and erosion of contiguous (adjoining) tissues. It rarely metastasizes, but recurrence is common. However, a neglected lesion can result in the loss of a nose, an ear, or a lip. Other variants of BCC may appear as shiny, flat, gray or yellowish plaques.

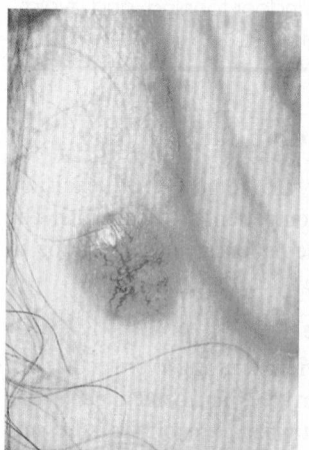 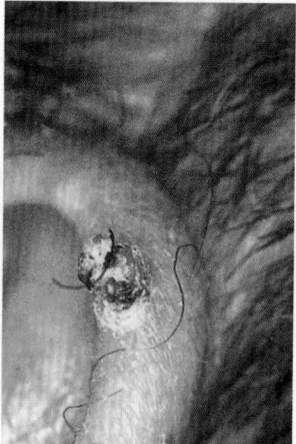

FIGURE 52-5 Basal cell carcinoma (*left*) and squamous cell carcinoma (*right*). Reprinted by permission from *New England Journal of Medicine, 326*, 169–170, 1992.

SCC is a malignant proliferation arising from the epidermis. Although it usually appears on sun-damaged skin, it may arise from normal skin or from preexisting skin lesions. It is of greater concern than BCC because it is a truly invasive carcinoma, metastasizing by the blood or lymphatic system.

Metastases account for 75% of deaths from SCC. The lesions may be primary, arising on the skin and mucous membranes, or they may develop from a precancerous condition, such as actinic keratosis (lesions occurring in sun-exposed areas), leukoplakia (premalignant lesion of the mucous membrane), or scarred or ulcerated lesions. SCC appears as a rough, thickened, scaly tumor that may be asymptomatic or may involve bleeding (see Fig. 52-5). The border of an SCC lesion may be wider, more infiltrated, and more inflammatory than that of a BCC lesion. Secondary infection can occur. Exposed areas, especially of the upper extremities and of the face, lower lip, ears, nose, and forehead, are common sites.

The incidence of BCC and SCC is increased in all immunocompromised people, including those infected with HIV. Clinically, the tumors have the same appearance as in non–HIV-infected people; however, in HIV patients, the tumors may grow more rapidly and recur more frequently. These tumors are managed the same as those for the general population. Frequent follow-up (every 4 to 6 months) is recommended to monitor for recurrence.

Medical Management

The goal of treatment is to eradicate the tumor. The treatment method depends on the tumor location; the cell type, location, and depth; the cosmetic desires of the patient; the history of previous treatment; whether the tumor is invasive; and whether metastatic nodes are present. The management of BCC and SCC includes surgical excision, Mohs' micrographic surgery, electrosurgery, cryosurgery, and radiation therapy.

Surgical Management

The primary goal is to remove the tumor entirely. The best way to maintain cosmetic appearance is to place the incision properly along natural skin tension lines and natural anatomic body lines. In this way, scars are less noticeable. The size of the incision depends on the tumor size and location but usually involves a length-to-width ratio of 3:1.

The adequacy of the surgical excision is verified by microscopic evaluation of sections of the specimen. When the tumor is large, reconstructive surgery with use of a skin flap or skin grafting may be required. The incision is closed in layers to enhance cosmetic effect. A pressure dressing applied over the wound provides support. Infection after a simple excision is uncommon if proper surgical asepsis is maintained.

Mohs' Micrographic Surgery

Mohs' micrographic surgery is the technique that is most accurate and that best conserves normal tissue. The procedure removes the tumor layer by layer. The first layer excised includes all evident tumor and a small margin of normal-appearing tissue. The specimen is frozen and analyzed by section to determine if all the tumor has been removed. If not, additional layers of tissue are shaved and examined until all tissue margins are tumor-free. In this manner, only the tumor and a safe, normal-tissue margin are removed. Mohs' surgery is the recommended tissue-sparing procedure, with extremely high cure rates for BCC and SCC. It is the treatment of choice and the most effective for tumors around the eyes, nose, upper lip, and auricular and periauricular areas.

Electrosurgery

Electrosurgery is the destruction or removal of tissue by electrical energy. The current is converted to heat, which then passes to the tissue from a cold electrode. Electrosurgery may be preceded by curettage (excising the skin tumor by scraping its surface with a curette). Electrodesiccation is then implemented to achieve hemostasis and to destroy any viable malignant cells at the base of the wound or along its edges. Electrodesiccation is useful for lesions smaller than 1 to 2 cm (0.4 to 0.8 in) in diameter.

This method takes advantage of the fact that the tumor is softer than surrounding skin and therefore can be outlined by a curette, which "feels" the extent of the tumor. The tumor is removed and the base cauterized. The process is repeated twice. Usually, healing occurs within a month.

Cryosurgery

Cryosurgery destroys the tumor by deep-freezing the tissue. A thermocouple needle apparatus is inserted into the skin, and liquid nitrogen is directed to the center of the tumor until the tumor base is $-40°C$ to $-60°C$. Liquid nitrogen has the lowest boiling point of all cryogens, is inexpensive, and is easy to obtain. The tumor tissue is frozen, allowed to thaw, and then refrozen. The site thaws naturally and then becomes gelatinous and heals spontaneously. Swelling and edema follow the freezing. The appearance of the lesion varies. Normal healing, which may take 4 to 6 weeks, occurs faster in areas with a good blood supply.

Radiation Therapy

Radiation therapy is frequently performed for cancer of the eyelid, the tip of the nose, and areas in or near vital structures (eg, facial nerve). It is reserved for older patients, because X-ray changes may be seen after 5 to 10 years, and malignant changes in scars may be induced by irradiation 15 to 30 years later.

The patient should be informed that the skin may become red and blistered. A bland skin ointment prescribed by the provider may be applied to relieve discomfort. The patient should also be cautioned to avoid exposure to the sun.

BOX 52-7

Health Promotion

Preventing Skin Cancer

- Teach patients that sunscreens are rated in strength from 4 (weakest) to 50 (strongest). The solar protection factor, or SPF, indicates how much longer a person can stay in the sun before the skin begins to redden. For example, if the person can normally stay in the sun for 10 minutes before reddening begins, an SPF of 4 will protect the person from reddening for about 40 minutes. A sunscreen with an SPF of 15 or greater is recommended under most conditions, and indicates 93% protection; an SPF of 34 indicates 97% protection.
- Remind patients that up to 50% of ultraviolet rays can penetrate loosely woven clothing.
- Remind patients that ultraviolet light can penetrate cloud cover, and a sunburn can still occur.
- Teach children to avoid all but modest sun exposure and to use a sunscreen regularly for life-long protection.
- Advise patients to:
  - Avoid tanning if their skin burns easily, never tans, or tans poorly.
  - Avoid unnecessary exposure to the sun, especially during the time of day when ultraviolet radiation (sunlight) is most intense (10 AM to 3 PM).
  - Avoid sunburns.
  - Apply a sunscreen daily to block harmful sun rays.
  - Use a sunscreen with an SPF of 15 or higher that protects against both ultraviolet-A (UVA) and ultraviolet-B (UVB) light.
  - Reapply water-resistant sunscreens after swimming, if heavily sweating, and every 2 to 3 hours during prolonged periods of sun exposure.
  - Avoid applying oils before or during sun exposure (oils do not protect against sunlight or sun damage).
  - Use a lip balm that contains a sunscreen with an SPF of 15 or higher.
  - Wear protective clothing, such as a broad-brimmed hat and long sleeves.
  - Avoid using sun lamps for indoor tanning, and avoid commercial tanning booths.

Nursing Management

Because many skin cancers are removed by excision, patients are usually treated in outpatient surgical units. The role of the nurse is to teach the patient about prevention of skin cancer and about self-care after treatment.

Teaching Self-Care

The wound is usually covered with a dressing to protect the site from physical trauma, external irritants, and contaminants. The nurse instructs the patient about when to report for a dressing change or provides written and verbal information on how to change dressings, including the type of dressing to purchase, how to remove dressings and apply fresh ones, and the importance of hand hygiene before and after the procedure.

The patient watches for excessive bleeding and tight dressings that compromise circulation. If the lesion is in the perioral area, the patient is instructed to drink liquids through a straw and limit talking and facial movement. Dental work should be avoided until the area is completely healed.

After the sutures are removed, an emollient cream may be used to help reduce dryness. Applying a sunscreen over the wound is advised to prevent postoperative hyperpigmentation if the patient spends time outdoors.

Follow-up examinations should be at regular intervals, usually every 3 months for a year, and should include palpation of the adjacent lymph nodes. The nurse instructs the patient to seek treatment for any moles that are subject to repeated friction and irritation, and to watch for indications of potential malignancy in moles as described previously. The importance of life-long follow-up evaluations is emphasized.

Teaching Skin Cancer Prevention

Studies show that regular daily use of a sunscreen with a solar protection factor (SPF) of at least 15 can reduce the recurrence of skin cancer by as much as 40% (Box 52-7, p. 1370). The sunscreen should be applied to head, neck, arms, and hands every morning at least 30 minutes before leaving the house and reapplied every 4 hours if the skin perspires. Intermittent application of sunscreen only when exposure is anticipated has been shown to be less effective than daily use. Research (Darlington, Williams, Neale et al., 2003) has shown that daily use of sunscreen on the hands and face reduces the total incidence of solar keratoses, which are precursors of SCC, but has no effect on the overall incidence of BCC. These data are inconsistent, but one theory is that people have a false sense of security when wearing sunscreen and tend to stay out in the sun for longer periods. This longer exposure is believed to contribute to the increasing incidence of melanoma. Although the evidence is insufficient, nurses should discuss the issues with patients who are at high risk of skin cancer.

Nurses should also encourage skin self-examination (Box 52-8).

MALIGNANT MELANOMA

A malignant melanoma is a cancerous neoplasm in which atypical melanocytes are present in the epidermis and the dermis (and sometimes the subcutaneous cells). It is the most lethal of all the skin cancers and is responsible for about 3% of all cancer deaths (Mohr, Eggermont, Hausachild et al., 2009).

Malignant melanoma can occur in one of several forms: superficial spreading melanoma, lentigo-maligna melanoma, nodular melanoma, and acral-lentiginous melanoma. These types have specific clinical and histologic features, as well

---

BOX 52-8 **Patient Education**

Periodic Self-Examination

Prevention of melanoma/skin cancer is the best weapon against these diseases, but if a melanoma should develop, it is almost always curable if caught in the early stages. Practice periodic self-examination to aid in early recognition of any new or developing lesion. The following is one way of self-examination that will ensure that no area of the body is neglected. To perform your self-examination, you will need a full-length mirror, a hand mirror, and a brightly lit room.

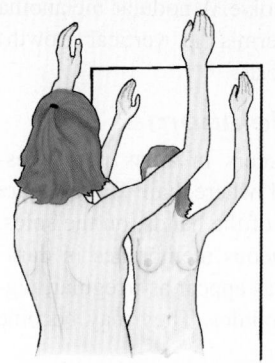 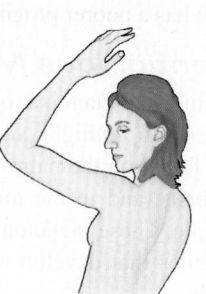 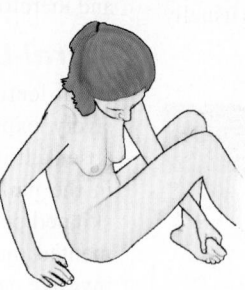 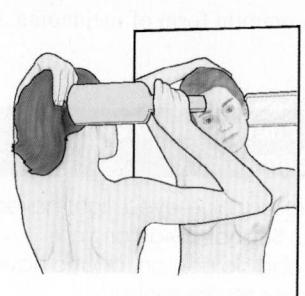 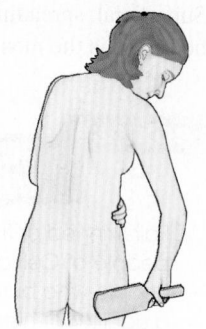

1. Examine the body front and back in the mirror, then the right and left sides, with the arms raised.

2. Bend the elbows, looking carefully at the forearms, back of the upper arms, and palms

3. Next, look at the back of the legs and feet, the spaces between the toes, and the soles of the feet.

4. Examine the back of the neck and the scalp with a hand-held mirror. Part the hair to lift.

5. Finally, check the back and buttocks with a hand mirror.

as different biologic behaviors. Most melanomas arise from cutaneous epidermal melanocytes, but some appear in preexisting nevi (ie, moles) in the skin or develop in the uveal tract of the eye. Melanomas occasionally appear simultaneously with cancer of other organs.

The worldwide incidence of melanoma doubles every 10 years, an increase that is probably related to increased recreational sun exposure, changes in the ozone layer, and improved methods of early detection. Peak incidence occurs between the ages of 20 and 45 years. The incidence of melanoma is increasing faster than that of almost any other cancer, and the mortality rate is increasing faster than that of any other cancer except lung cancer. Between 1973 and 1995, the age-adjusted incidence of melanoma increased more than 100%, from 5.7 per 100,000 people to 13.3 per 100,000 people. Men older than 65 years of age represent 22% of newly diagnosed cases, whereas women older than 65 years of age represent 14% of newly diagnosed cases (Mohr et al., 2009).

Risk Factors

The cause of malignant melanoma is unknown, but ultraviolet rays are strongly suspected, based on indirect evidence such as the increased incidence of melanoma in countries near the equator and in people younger than 30 years who have used a tanning bed more than 10 times per year. Ethnicity is a risk factor; in general, 1 in 100 Caucasians acquires melanoma each year. As many as 10% of patients with melanoma are members of melanoma-prone families who have multiple changing moles (dysplastic nevi) that are susceptible to malignant transformation. Patients with dysplastic nevus syndrome have been found to have unusual moles, larger and more numerous moles, lesions with irregular outlines, and pigmentation located all over the skin. Microscopic examination of dysplastic moles shows disordered, faulty growth. Box 52-9 lists risk factors for malignant melanoma.

Types

Superficial Spreading Melanoma

Superficial spreading melanoma occurs anywhere on the body and is the most common form of melanoma. It usually

---

BOX 52-9	Risk Factors for Malignant Melanoma

- Fair-skinned or freckled, blue-eyed, light-haired people of Celtic or Scandinavian origin
- People who burn and do not tan, or who have a significant history of severe sunburn
- Environmental exposure to intense sunlight (older Americans retiring to the southwestern United States appear to have a higher incidence)
- History of melanoma (personal or family)
- Skin with giant congenital nevi

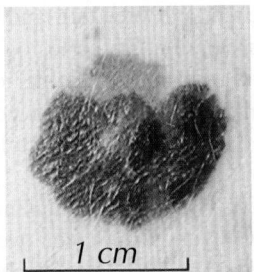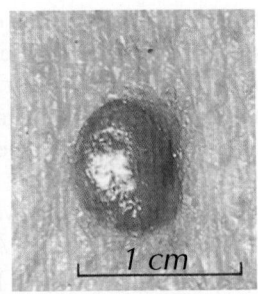

FIGURE 52-6 Two forms of malignant melanoma: superficial spreading (*left*) and nodular (*right*). From Bickley, L. S. (2009). *Bates' guide to physical examination and history taking* (10th ed.). Philadelphia: Lippincott Williams & Wilkins.

affects middle-aged people and occurs most frequently on the trunk and lower extremities. The lesion tends to be circular, with irregular outer portions. The margins of the lesion may be flat or elevated and palpable (Fig. 52-6). This type of melanoma may appear in a combination of colors, with hues of tan, brown, and black mixed with gray, blue-black, or white. Sometimes a dull pink rose color can be seen in a small area within the lesion.

Lentigo-Maligna Melanoma

Lentigo-maligna melanoma is a slowly evolving, pigmented lesion that occurs on exposed skin areas, especially the dorsum of the hand, the head, and the neck in elderly people. Often, the lesion is present for many years before it is examined by a provider. It first appears as a tan, flat lesion, but in time it undergoes changes in size and color.

Nodular Melanoma

Nodular melanoma is a spherical, blueberry-like nodule with a relatively smooth surface and a relatively uniform, blue-black color (see Fig. 52-6). It may be dome-shaped with a smooth surface. It may have other shadings of red, gray, or purple. Sometimes, nodular melanomas appear as irregularly shaped plaques. The patient may describe this as a blood blister that fails to resolve. A nodular melanoma invades directly into adjacent dermis (ie, vertical growth) and therefore has a poorer prognosis.

Acral-Lentiginous Melanoma

Acral-lentiginous melanoma occurs in areas not excessively exposed to sunlight and where hair follicles are absent. It is found on the palms of the hands, on the soles, in the nail beds, and in the mucous membranes in dark-skinned people. These melanomas appear as irregular, pigmented macules that develop nodules. They may become invasive early.

Clinical Manifestations and Assessment

Biopsy results confirm the diagnosis of melanoma. An excisional biopsy specimen provides information on the type,

Assessing the ABCDEs of Moles

A for Asymmetry
- The lesion does not appear balanced on both sides. If an imaginary line were drawn down the middle, the two halves would not look alike.
- The lesion has an irregular surface with uneven elevations (irregular topography) either palpable or visible. A change in the surface may be noted from smooth to scaly.
- Some nodular melanomas have a smooth surface.

B for Irregular Border
- Angular indentations or multiple notches appear in the border.
- The border is fuzzy or indistinct, as if rubbed with an eraser.

C for Variegated Color
- Normal moles are usually a uniform light to medium brown. Darker coloration indicates that the melanocytes have penetrated to a deeper layer of the dermis.
- Colors that may indicate malignancy if found together within a single lesion are shades of red, white, and blue; shades of blue are ominous.
- White areas within a pigmented lesion are suspicious.
- Some malignant melanomas, however, are not variegated but are uniformly colored (bluish-black, bluish-gray, bluish-red).

D for Diameter
- A diameter exceeding 6 mm (about the size of a pencil eraser) is considered more suspicious, although this finding without other signs is not significant. Many benign skin growths are larger than 6 mm, whereas some early melanomas may be smaller.

E for Elevation, Enlargement, and/or Evolution
- The lesion is raised above the surface, enlarged and/or has a uneven surface; Evolution refers to a lesion that has significantly changed (size, shape, symptoms (e.g. itching, tenderness, crusting, bleeding)) over time.

level of invasion, and thickness of the lesion. An excisional biopsy specimen that includes a 1-cm margin of normal tissue and a portion of underlying subcutaneous fatty tissue is sufficient for staging a melanoma in situ or an early, noninvasive melanoma. Incisional biopsy should be performed when the suspicious lesion is too large to be removed safely without extensive scarring. Biopsy specimens obtained by shaving, curettage, or needle aspiration are not considered reliable histologic proof of disease.

A thorough history and physical examination should include a meticulous skin examination and palpation of regional lymph nodes that drain the lesional area. Box 52-10 discusses assessing moles. Because melanoma occurs in families, a positive family history of melanoma is investigated so that first-degree relatives, who may be at high risk for melanoma, can be evaluated for atypical lesions. After the diagnosis of melanoma has been confirmed, a chest X-ray, complete blood cell count, liver function tests, and radionuclide or computed tomography scans are usually performed to stage the extent of disease.

Medical and Nursing Management

Treatment depends on the level of invasion and the depth of the lesion. Surgical excision is the treatment of choice for small, superficial lesions. Deeper lesions require wide local excision, after which skin grafting may be necessary. Regional lymph node dissection is commonly performed to rule out metastasis, although new surgical approaches call for only sentinel node biopsy. The sentinel lymph node is the first node by which cancer is likely to spread from the primary tumor before spreading to other lymph nodes. This technique is used to sample the nodes nearest the tumor and to spare the patient the long-term sequelae of extensive removal of lymph nodes if the sample nodes are negative.

Immunotherapy for treatment of melanoma has had varied success. Immunotherapy modifies immune function and other biologic responses to cancer. Several forms of immunotherapy (eg, bacillus Calmette-Guérin vaccine, *Corynebacterium parvum*, levamisole) offer encouraging results. Some investigational therapies include biologic response modifiers (eg, interferon-alpha, interleukin-2), adaptive immunotherapy (ie, lymphokine-activated killer cells), and monoclonal antibodies directed at melanoma antigens. One of these, aldesleukin (Proleukin), shows promise in preventing recurrence of melanoma. Laboratory assay of tyrosinase, an enzyme believed to be produced only by melanoma cells, is under investigation. Several other studies are attempting to develop and test autologous immunization against specific tumor cells. These studies are in the experimental stage but show promise for future development of a vaccine against melanoma.

Current treatments for metastatic melanoma rarely if ever produce a satisfactory outcome. Further surgical intervention may be performed to debulk the tumor or to remove part of the organ involved (eg, lung, liver, or colon). However, the rationale for more extensive surgery is for relief of symptoms, not for cure. Chemotherapy for metastatic melanoma may be used; however, only a few agents (eg, dacarbazine, nitrosoureas, cisplatin) have been effective in controlling the disease.

When the melanoma is located in an extremity, regional perfusion may be used; the chemotherapeutic agent is perfused directly into the area that contains the melanoma. This approach delivers a high concentration of cytotoxic agents while avoiding systemic, toxic side effects. The limb is perfused for 1 hour with high concentrations of the medication at temperatures of 39°C to 40°C (102.2°F to 104°F) with a perfusion pump. Inducing hyperthermia enhances the effect of the chemotherapy so that a smaller total dose can be used. The goal of regional perfusion is control of the metastasis, especially if it is used in combination with surgical excision of the primary lesion and with regional lymph node dissection.

METASTATIC SKIN TUMORS

The skin is an important, although not a common, site of metastatic cancer. All types of cancer may metastasize to the skin, but carcinoma of the breast is the primary source of cutaneous metastases in women. Other sources include cancer of the large intestine, ovaries, and lungs. In men, the most common primary sites are the lungs, large intestine, oral cavity, kidneys, or stomach. Skin metastases from melanomas are found in both genders. The clinical appearance of metastatic skin lesions is not distinctive, except perhaps in some cases of breast cancer in which diffuse, brawny hardening of the skin of the involved breast is seen. In most instances, metastatic lesions occur as multiple cutaneous or subcutaneous nodules of various sizes that may be skin-colored or different shades of red.

KAPOSI'S SARCOMA

Kaposi's sarcoma (KS) is a malignancy of endothelial cells that line the small blood vessels. KS is manifested clinically by lesions of the skin, oral cavity, GI tract, and lungs. The skin lesions consist of reddish-purple to dark-blue macules, plaques, or nodules. KS is subdivided into three categories:

- **Classic KS** occurs predominantly in men of Mediterranean or Jewish ancestry between 40 and 70 years of age. Most patients have nodules or plaques on the lower extremities that rarely metastasize beyond this area. Classic KS is chronic, relatively benign, and rarely fatal.
- **Endemic (African) KS** affects people predominantly in the eastern half of Africa near the equator. Men are affected more often than women, and children can be affected as well. The disease may resemble classic KS, or it may infiltrate and progress to lymphadenopathic forms.
- **Immunosuppression-associated KS** occurs in transplant recipients and people with AIDS. This form of KS is characterized by local skin lesions and disseminated visceral and mucocutaneous diseases. The greater the degree of immunosuppression, the higher the incidence of KS. Immunosuppression-related KS that results from AIDS is an aggressive tumor that involves multiple body organs. Its presentation resembles that of KS associated with immunosuppressive therapy. Most patients are between the ages of 20 and 40 years. Refer to Chapter 37 for more information about KS and AIDS.

Chapter Review

Critical Thinking Exercises

1. You are caring for an elderly woman in her home. She has a long history of peripheral vascular disease and now has developed a venous stasis ulcer on her lower leg just above the ankle. Her physician has prescribed a moisture-retentive dressing that is impregnated with hydrogel. The dressing is to be changed every 3 days, and the patient asks you why the dressing is not changed every day. How would you explain to the patient the purpose of the dressing? Identify the evidence that supports the use of moisture-retentive dressings for venous ulcers. Discuss the strength of the evidence regarding their effectiveness in the promotion of wound healing.

2. You are caring for a middle-aged woman who has recently been diagnosed with diabetes mellitus. On preparing for discharge, she tells you that she has had itchy, dry, flaky skin during the winter months for several years, and that she bathes every morning and night to try to get rid of the itching and dryness. She also states that it is difficult for her to avoid scratching her itchy skin. What teaching would you provide to this patient? What are this patient's risks of developing more serious skin conditions if the dryness and itching of her skin continue?

3. You are assigned to the emergency department and are caring for a young adult who is being treated for heatstroke following a golf game on a very hot day. As he is awaiting discharge, he tells you that he is concerned about developing skin cancer because he spends so much time in the sun. After providing the patient with information about risk factors for, and prevention of, heatstroke, what other patient education would you provide? What are the risk factors for skin cancer? What health promotion strategies would be encouraged for this patient?

NCLEX-Style Review Questions

1. A patient is seen in the wound clinic for a pressure ulcer on his left leg. There is full-thickness tissue loss with the bone exposed. The nurse would correctly document this wound as being in which of the following stages?
   A. I
   B. II
   C. III
   D. IV

2. The physician has ordered Santyl for a patient with a left leg necrotic ulcer. The nurse understands the premise behind the use of Santyl as being which of the following?
   A. Removes necrotic tissue and absorbs small to large amounts of exudates
   B. Uses the body's own digestive enzymes to break down necrotic tissue
   C. Speeds the rate at which necrotic tissue is removed
   D. Uses a high moisture-vapor transmission rate to remove exudate

3. A 20-year-old patient is being seen in the dermatology clinic for a basal cell carcinoma on her eye. The nurse would expect the physician to complete which intervention?
   A. Electrosurgery
   B. Mohs' micrographic surgery
   C. Cryosurgery
   D. Radiation

4. Topical corticosteroid therapy has been ordered for a patient with pruritus. Which of the following should be incorporated into the plan of care for this patient?
   A. Apply liberally in the prescribed area.
   B. Absorption is enhanced when skin is dry.

C. Local side effects may include skin atrophy and thinning.
D. Absorption is decreased when covered with an occlusive dressing.

5. A 55-year-old patient with leukemia is being seen in the clinic for complaints of burning pain in her back. She has been diagnosed with shingles. The nurse would expect which medication classification to be ordered for her to reduce pain and halt the progression of the disease?
   A. Anti-inflammatory
   B. Antiviral
   C. Antibiotic
   D. Antifungal

Try these additional resources to enhance your learning and understanding of this chapter:
- thePoint online resource available at http://thepoint.lww.com/Pellico1e
- Handbook for Focus on Adult Health: Medical-Surgical Nursing
- Study Guide for Focus on Adult Health: Medical-Surgical Nursing

References and Selected Readings

References and selected readings associated with this chapter can be found on the website that accompanies the book. Visit http://thepoint.lww.com/Pellico1e to access the references and other additional resources associated with this chapter.

SALLY R. DALTON

Nursing Management: Patients With Burn Injury

After reading this chapter, you will be able to:

1. Discuss the classification system used for burn injuries.

2. Describe the local and systemic effects of a major burn injury.

3. Discuss the potential fluid and electrolyte alterations of the emergent/resuscitative and acute phases of burn management.

4. Describe nursing management of the patient with burn injuries.

In comparison to the larger health care picture, burn patients are few. However, burn injuries remain one of the most expensive catastrophic injuries to treat economically and in terms of human suffering (American Burn Association [ABA], 2009a). Burns are categorized as thermal (including electrical burns), radiation, electrical, or chemical. The skin and the mucosa of the upper airways are the sites of tissue destruction. Disruption of the skin can lead to increased fluid loss, infection, hypothermia, compromised immunity, and changes in function, appearance, and body image. The nurse caring for the burn patient requires astute assessment skills and a high level of knowledge about physiological changes after a major burn injury to detect subtle changes in the patient's condition.

OVERVIEW OF BURN INJURY

Incidence of Burn Injury

The two most common burn etiologies are flame and scald. Burns in the home usually occur in the kitchen from cooking, bathroom from scalding, or in the living room from smoking (Aherns, 2009). A burn can affect any person at any time, in any place. Burns involve people of all ages and socioeconomic groups. Each year, approximately 500,000 people with burn injuries receive medical treatment, and 4,000 fire and burn deaths occur. Residential fires account for 3,500 of these deaths, with the remaining 500 from motor vehicle and aircraft crashes, or contact with electricity, chemicals, or hot liquids and substances (ABA, 2009a).

Approximately 71% of all burn victims are men. Children under the age of 5 represent 17% and people over the age of 60 represent 12% of burn cases (ABA, 2009a).

People who are prone to burn injuries are the elderly, smokers, and people with disabilities, neurological illness, substance abuse issues, and psychiatric illness.

Gerontologic Considerations

Persons over 60 years old are likely to live alone, have reduced mobility, changes in vision, and decreased sensation in the feet and hands. These changes place them at risk for suffering a burn. Morbidity and mortality rates associated with burns are greater in the elderly (ABA, 2009a).

TABLE
53-1 Characteristics of Burns According to Depth

Depth of Burn	Causes	Skin Involvement	Symptoms	Wound Appearance	Recuperative Course
Superficial partial-thickness (similar to first-degree)	Sunburn Low-intensity flash	Epidermis; possibly a portion of dermis	Tingling Hyperesthesia (supersensitivity) Pain that is soothed by cooling	Reddened; blanches with pressure; dry Minimal or no edema Possible blisters	Complete recovery within a week; no scarring Peeling
Deep partial-thickness (similar to second-degree)	Scalds Flash flame Contact	Epidermis, upper dermis, portion of deeper dermis	Pain Hyperesthesia Sensitive to cold air	Blistered, mottled red base; broken epidermis; weeping surface Edema	Recovery in 2 to 4 weeks Some scarring and depigmentation contractures Infection may convert it to full thickness
Full-thickness (similar to third-degree)	Flame Prolonged exposure to hot liquids Electric current Chemical Contact	Epidermis, entire dermis, and sometimes subcutaneous tissue; may involve connective tissue, muscle, and bone	Pain free Shock Hematuria (blood in the urine) and possibly hemolysis (blood cell destruction) Possible entrance and exit wounds (electrical burn)	Dry; pale white, leathery, or charred Broken skin with fat exposed Edema	Eschar sloughs Grafting necessary Scarring and loss of contour and function; contractures Loss of digits or extremity possible

Thinning and loss of elasticity of the skin predispose them to deep injury from a thermal insult that might cause a less severe burn in a younger person. Furthermore, chronic illnesses decrease the older person's ability to withstand the multisystem stresses imposed by major burn injury. Successful prevention campaigns have been linked to smoke detectors, carbon monoxide detectors, fire extinguishers, escape plans (Taira et al, 2011), sprinkler systems, enforcement of fire codes, and fire safe cigarettes (ABA, 2009b, n.d.).

Classification of Burns

Burn injuries are classified by the depth of the injury and the extent of the total body surface area (TBSA) burned.

Depth

Burns are classified according to the depth of tissue destruction. The depth depends on how much of the skin's dermis is affected. Burn depth determines whether spontaneous healing will occur and helps to determine the plan of care (Jaskille, Ramella-Roman, Shupp et al., 2010). The following factors are considered in determining the depth of a burn:

- How the injury occurred
- Causative agent, such as flame, scald, chemical, or hot tar
- Temperature of the burning agent
- Duration of contact with the agent
- Thickness of the skin in area burned

Burns are described as superficial, superficial partial-thickness injuries, deep partial-thickness injuries, or full-thickness injuries (Table 53-1, Fig. 53-1, p. 1378). Formerly referred to as a first-degree burn, a superficial burn damages only the **epidermis** (outer layer of the skin). The area is pink or red, dry, with slight swelling but no blister. In a superficial partial-thickness burn (one of two types of second-degree burns), the epidermis is destroyed and a small portion of the underlying **dermis** (deep, vascular inner portion of skin) is injured. It is very painful, pink and moist, hair follicles are intact, and often presents as blisters. These burns will heal in 5 to 10 days without scarring.

A deep partial-thickness burn (the second of the two types of second-degree burns), extends into the reticular layer of the dermis (dense connective tissue that gives the skin strength and elasticity and houses sweat glands, lymph vessels, and hair follicles) and is hard to distinguish from a full-thickness burn. It is red or white, mottled, and can be moist or fairly dry. The patient is in severe pain; these burns take up to 14 days to heal with variable amounts of scarring.

A full-thickness burn (formerly called a third- or fourth-degree burn) involves total destruction of the dermis and extends into the subcutaneous fat. It can also involve muscle and bone. It heals by contraction or epithelial migration and requires skin grafting. Wound color ranges widely from mottled white to red, brown, or black. The wound appears leathery, hair follicles and sweat glands are destroyed.

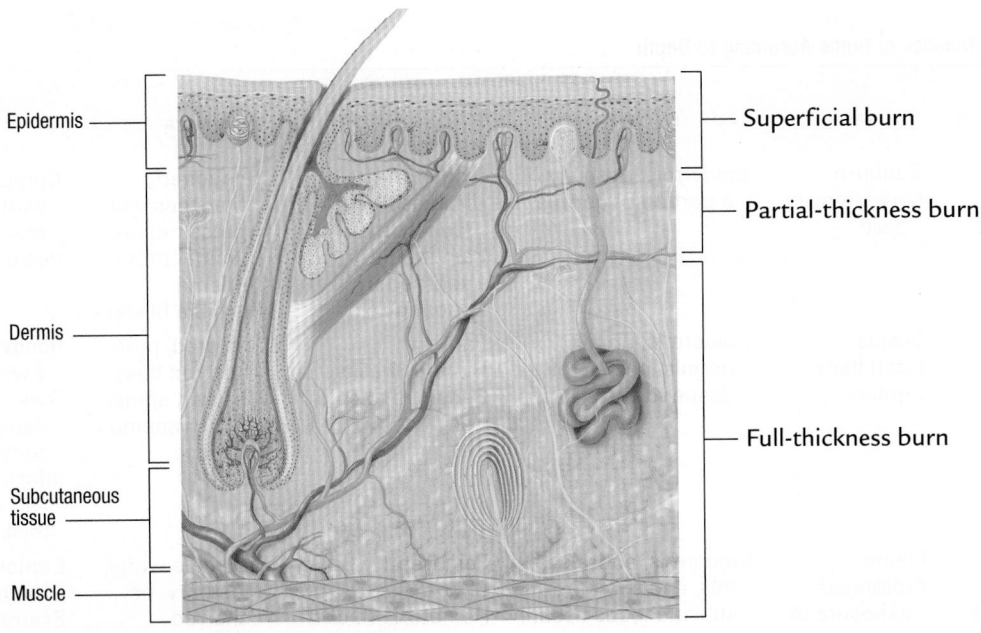

FIGURE 53-1 Depth of burn injury.

Epidermis
Dermis
Subcutaneous tissue
Muscle

Superficial burn
Partial-thickness burn
Full-thickness burn

⚡ NURSING ALERT

It is important for the nurse to acknowledge that even when skin is no longer in contact with the burn source, skin damage can continue. In the case of scald burns, 1 second of contact with hot tap water at 68.9°C (156°F) may result in a burn that destroys both the epidermis and the dermis, causing a full-thickness injury. Fifteen seconds of exposure to hot water at 56.1°C (133°F) results in a similar full-thickness injury. A deep partial-thickness burn can convert to full-thickness burns within 24 hours of injury, thus immediate assessment and management, which includes the application of tap water, is important to decrease the risk of thermal injury. It is imperative that the nurse remove all jewelry, typically made of metal, since it can retain heat, cause thermal injury, and act as a tourniquet with tissue swelling. The use of ice water on large burns can result in hypothermia and increased mortality, whereas tap water is associated with a reduction in pain and may reduce the progression of tissue necrosis and need for skin grafting (Singer, Taira, Lee et al., 2009).

Extent of Body Surface Area Injured

Various methods are used to estimate the total body surface area (TBSA) affected by burns; among them are the rule of nines and the Lund and Browder method.

Rule of Nines

The **rule of nines** (Fig. 53-2) is a quick way to estimate the extent of burns. The system assigns percentages in multiples of nine to major body surfaces.

Lund and Browder Method

A more precise method of estimating the extent of a burn is the Lund and Browder method, which recognizes that

the percentage of surface area of various anatomic parts, especially the head and legs, in relation to growth. Because of changes in body proportion with growth, the calculated TBSA changes with age as well. By dividing the body into

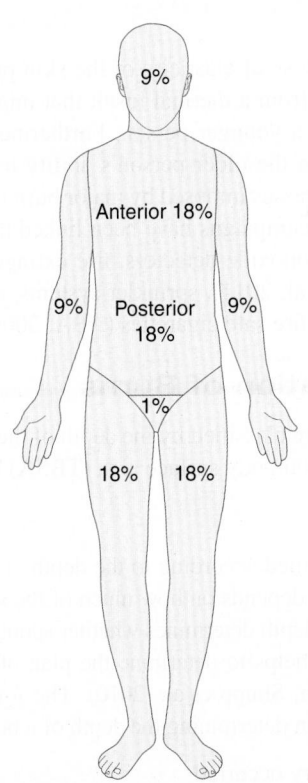

9%

Anterior 18%

9% Posterior 18% 9%

1%

18% 18%

FIGURE 53-2 The rule of nines: Estimated percentage of total body surface area (TBSA) in the adult is arrived at by sectioning the body surface into areas with a numerical value related to nine. (Note: The anterior and posterior head total 9% of TBSA.)

Classification of Extent of Burn Injury

Minor Burn Injury

- Second-degree burn of <15% total body surface area (TBSA) in adults or <10% TBSA in children
- Third-degree burn of <2% TBSA not involving special care areas (eyes, ears, face, hands, feet, perineum, joints)
- Excludes all patients with electrical injury, inhalation injury, or concurrent trauma and all poor-risk patients (ie, extremes of age, intercurrent disease)

Moderate, Uncomplicated Burn Injury

- Second-degree burns of 15% to 25% TBSA in adults or 10% to 20% in children
- Third-degree burns of <10% TBSA not involving special care areas
- Excludes all patients with electrical injury, inhalation injury, or concurrent trauma; all poor-risk patients (ie, extremes of age, intercurrent disease)

Major Burn Injury

- Second-degree burns >25% TBSA in adults or >20% in children
- All third-degree burns ≥10% TBSA
- All burns involving eyes, ears, face, hands, feet, perineum, joints
- All patients with inhalation injury, electrical injury, or concurrent trauma; all poor-risk patients

From Morton, P. G., & Fontaine, D. (2008). *Critical care nursing: A holistic approach* (9th ed.). Philadelphia: Lippincott Williams & Wilkins.

---

very small areas and providing an estimate of the proportion of TBSA accounted for by each body part, one can obtain a reliable estimate of TBSA burned. The initial evaluation is made on arrival of the patient at the hospital and is revised on the second and third post-burn days, because the demarcation (boundaries between necrotic tissue and healthy tissue) usually is not clear until then.

Severity Grading System

The Severity Grading System (Box 53-1) adopted by the ABA includes: minor, moderate, and major burns.

PATHOPHYSIOLOGY

Burns are a dynamic injury that result in a cascade of local tissue and systemic inflammatory effects depending on the percentage of burn involved. Local effects of burns includes the denaturation of protein (which results in the disruption and potential destruction of cells), liberation of vasoactive substances, and the formation of edema. As a result of the cellular injury, the osmotic and hydrostatic pressure gradients are disrupted and intravascular fluid leaks into interstitial spaces.

This damage is distributed throughout the injury as some cells die instantly, some are irreversibly damaged, and some—if appropriate interventions occur—will survive. There are three distinct zones that appear in a bull's eye pattern. The zone of coagulation (in the center) is where the tissue is completely destroyed; the zone of stasis surrounds the nonviable tissue and is potentially viable; the zone of hyperemia has increased blood flow secondary to the natural inflammatory response (Fig. 53-3). Burns that exceed 25% TBSA may produce a local and a systemic response and are considered major burn injuries. The incidence and significance of pathophysiologic changes are proportional to the extent of burn injury, with a maximal response seen in burns covering 60% or more TBSA (Lumenta, Kamloz, & Manfred, 2009). These patients are best served when transferred to a verified burn center as they are candidates for the occurrence of burn shock.

Burn Shock: Cardiovascular Alterations

Shock occurs when oxygen supply does not meet tissue demand. Burn shock develops from several abnormalities of the circulation. The initial systemic event is hemodynamic instability, which results from loss of capillary integrity and a subsequent shift of fluid, sodium, and protein from the intravascular space into the interstitial spaces. This leaky capillary syndrome increases cell permeability at the burn site, as well as throughout the body. In the major burn, this syndrome far exceeds the useful effect of the inflammatory response. Progressive edema develops in unburned tissue and organs causing hypoperfusion and hypovolemic shock. As

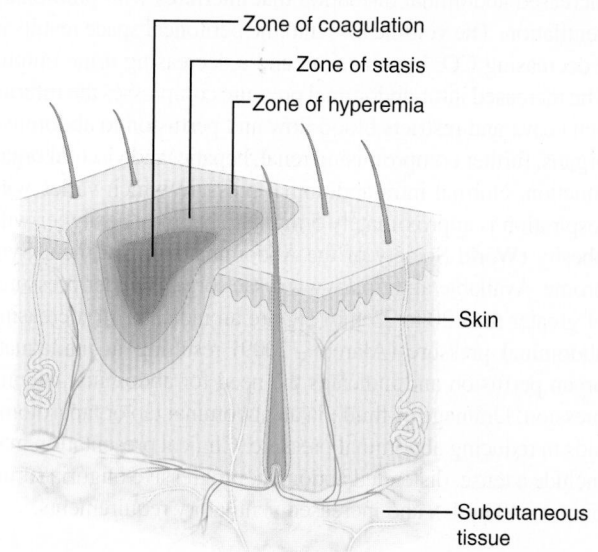

FIGURE 53-3 Zones of burn injury. Each burned area has three zones of injury. The inner zone (known as the area of coagulation, in which cellular death occurs) sustains the most damage. The middle area, or zone of stasis, has a compromised blood supply, inflammation, and tissue injury. The outer zone—the zone of hyperemia—sustains the least damage.

fluid loss continues and vascular volume decreases, the cardiac output (CO) and blood pressure (BP) fall. This is the onset of burn shock. The systemic response is caused by the release of cytokines and other mediators into the systemic circulation. The result is overwhelming; there is an increase in peripheral vascular resistance secondary to the edema formation, a decrease in blood volume, and a decrease in CO (Jeschke, Chinkes, Finnerty et al., 2008). Thus, burn shock is characterized by capillary leak, "third spacing" of fluid, severe hypovolemia, and decreased CO. If the burn patient is not resuscitated adequately, circulatory collapse ensues.

Fluid and Electrolyte Alterations

Prompt fluid resuscitation maintains the BP in the low-normal range and improves CO. Generally, the greatest volume of fluid leak occurs in the first 24 to 36 hours after the burn. As the capillaries begin to regain their integrity, burn shock resolves and fluid returns to the vascular compartment. As fluid is reabsorbed from the interstitial tissue into the vascular compartment, blood volume increases. If renal and cardiac function is adequate, urinary output increases. Lactated Ringer's (LR) solution is the preferred IV fluid for burn resuscitation because the sodium (130 mEq/L) and potassium (K+; 4 mEq/L) concentrations are similar to normal intravascular levels (sodium of 135 to 145 mEq/L and K+ of 3.5 to 5 mEq/L). LR also contains lactate (28 mEq/L), which can be converted by the liver to bicarbonate (the blood buffer) to aid in correcting the metabolic acidosis frequently seen in burn shock.

Patients with large burn wounds are at risk for abdominal compartment syndrome, especially if fluid resuscitation is delayed. Fluid shifts into the abdominal cavity, causing increased abdominal distention that interferes with pulmonary ventilation. The volume loss into the peritoneal space results in a decreasing CO, hypotension, and a decreasing urine output. The increased intra-abdominal pressure compresses the inferior vena cava and restricts blood flow and perfusion to abdominal organs, further compromising renal, hepatic, and visceral organ function. Normal intra-abdominal pressure which varies with respiration is approximately 5 mm Hg, but may be higher with obesity (World Society of the Abdominal Compartment Syndrome. Available at: http://www.wsacs.org). Bladder pressures of greater than 20 to 25 mm Hg are an indicator of increasing abdominal pressure (Alarcon, 2009) resulting in inadequate organ perfusion and indicates the need for abdominal decompression. Drainage of fluid via an abdominal tap or laparotomy aids in reducing abdominal pressure. Clinical presentation may include a tense, distended abdomen, progressive oliguria (urine output <400 mL), and increased ventilatory requirements.

NURSING ALERT
Nurses measure intra-bladder pressure (IBP) using a bladder catheter (Foley), a pressure monitor or a manometer, room temperature saline solution, and a 60 mL syringe. A pressure monitor is set up and connected to the catheter drainage bag at the aspiration port via a Luer-lock or needle, depending on the drainage bag. Once the bladder is empty, 25 to 50 mL (depending on institutional policy) of saline solution is instilled through the bladder catheter using a 60 mL syringe, and it is clamped. Limited research reveals a risk of falsely elevated IBP if more than 50 mL of priming solution is used; however, the most accurate priming volume remains unclear (Malbrain & Deeren, 2006). The symphysis pubis is used as the zero reference point for the pressure bag at the midaxillary line. The pressure is recorded, the clamp released, and urine is allowed to flow into drainage bag (Murcia-Sáez et al.) (Fig. 53-4).

Patients with a major burn develop massive systemic edema. As fluid resuscitation proceeds, the edema worsens. As the taut, burned tissue becomes unyielding to the edema underneath its surface, it begins to act like a tourniquet, especially if the burn is circumferential. This complication is similar to a compartment syndrome. The provider may need to perform an **escharotomy**, a surgical incision into the **eschar** (also referred to as "black wound" because of the wounds appearance of thick, dry, black necrotic tissue), to relieve the constricting effect of the burned tissue. Refer to Chapter 42 for details on compartment syndrome.

Circulating blood volume decreases dramatically during burn shock due to severe capillary leak with variation of serum sodium levels in response to fluid resuscitation. Usually, hyponatremia (sodium depletion) is present. Immediately after burn injury, hyperkalemia (excessive potassium) results from massive cell destruction. Hypokalemia (potassium depletion) may occur later, with fluid shifts and inadequate potassium replacement. Lactic acidosis is frequently seen in burn shock due to hypovolemia and hypoperfusion; thus, while the lactate in LR IV solution can be converted to base bicarbonate to correct the acidemia, the goal of treatment is aimed at reversing the hypoperfusion. However, plasma lactate levels are significant markers of shock and resuscitation, and appear to be correlated to predict morbidity and outcome (Andel, Kamolz, Roka et al., 2007). A normal serum lactic acid level in venous blood is 0.5 to 2.2 mEq/L. Lactic acidosis is considered to be present if the plasma lactate concentration is greater than 4 to 5 mEq/L (Rose & Post, 2009). See discussion of fluid and electrolyte changes in the Emergent/Resuscitative Phase later in the chapter.

Pulmonary Alterations

Inhalation injury necessitates prolonged hospitalization and is a major cause of morbidity and mortality. An inhalation injury can occur when a person is trapped inside a burning structure or involved in an explosion that leads to the inhalation of superheated air and noxious gas. Inhalation injury has a significant impact on a patient's ability to survive.

Pulmonary injuries fall into two categories: upper airway injury, and inhalation injury below the glottis, including carbon monoxide poisoning. Upper airway injury results

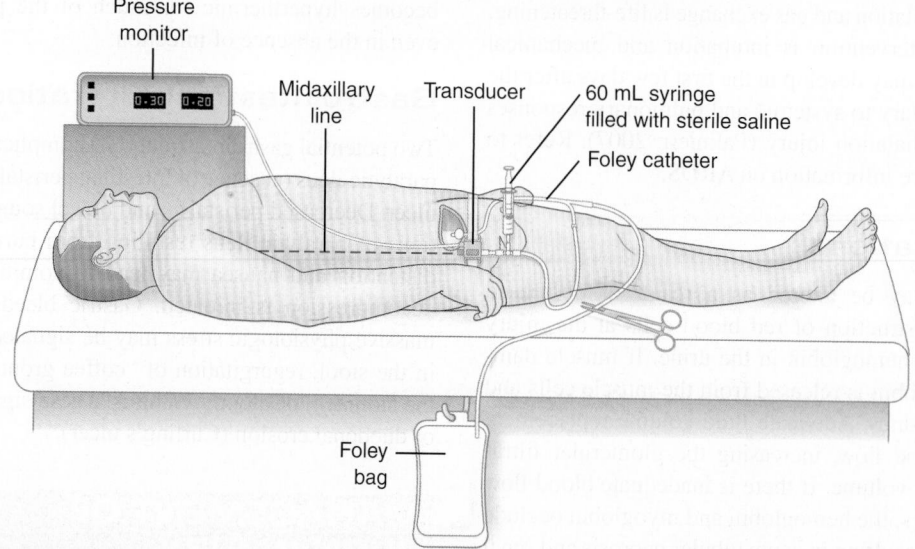

FIGURE 53-4 Measuring intra-bladder pressure. To assess for the development of abdominal compartment syndrome, the intra-bladder pressure may be monitored. This requires a Foley catheter, transducing system (pressure monitor and transducer), room temperature saline solution, and a 60 mL syringe. The bladder is allowed to empty, the Foley catheter is disconnected from the drainage tubing and—using the syringe filled with a predetermined amount of solution (usually sterile saline)—the solution is instilled into the bladder and immediately clamped. The clamped Foley is reconnected to the drainage tubing. The transducing system is attached to the Foley catheter via the aspiration port of the drainage tubing using a Luer-lock or needle (the clamp must be on the drainage tubing below the aspiration port to allow measurement of bladder pressure). The bladder pressure is displayed on the pressure monitor. This number is recorded, the clamp is removed, and solution is allowed to drain into the Foley bag. The amount of solution used is subtracted from the output so an accurate recording of output is made.

from direct heat and edema. It is manifested by mechanical obstruction of the upper airway. Because of the cooling effect of rapid vaporization in the pulmonary tract, direct heat injury does not normally occur below the level of the bronchus. Upper airway injury is treated by early nasotracheal, endotracheal intubation, or tracheotomy. Edema of the laryngeal and supraglottic structures after face and neck burns, and heat exposure to the upper airway may develop rapidly, making intubation difficult, thus an emergency tracheotomy may be necessary (Breederveld & Kreis, 2009).

Inhalation injury below the glottis results from inhaling noxious gases. The injury results directly from chemical irritation of the pulmonary tissues at the alveolar level. These injuries cause loss of ciliary action, hypersecretion, severe mucosal edema, and possibly bronchospasm. The pulmonary surfactant is reduced, resulting in atelectasis (collapse of alveoli). Expectoration of carbon particles in the sputum is the cardinal sign of this injury.

Carbon monoxide is probably the most common cause of inhalation injury, because it is a by-product of the combustion of organic materials and therefore is present in smoke. The pathophysiologic effects are caused by tissue hypoxia, a result of carbon monoxide combining with hemoglobin to form **carboxyhemoglobin**, which competes with oxygen for available hemoglobin-binding sites. The affinity of hemoglobin for carbon monoxide is 250 times greater than that

for oxygen. Treatment usually consists of early intubation and mechanical ventilation with 100% oxygen. Administering 100% oxygen is essential to accelerate the removal of carbon monoxide from the hemoglobin molecule.

Pulmonary abnormalities are not always immediately apparent. More than half of all patients with burn injuries with pulmonary involvement do not initially demonstrate pulmonary signs and symptoms. Any patient with possible inhalation injury must be observed for at least 24 hours for respiratory complications. Indicators of possible pulmonary damage include the following:

- History indicating that the burn occurred in an enclosed area
- Burns of the face or neck
- Singed nasal hair
- Hoarseness, voice change, dry cough, stridor
- Sooty or bloody sputum
- Labored breathing or tachypnea (rapid breathing) and other signs of reduced oxygen levels (hypoxemia)
- Erythema and blistering of the oral or pharyngeal mucosa

Diagnosis of inhalation injury is an important priority. The circumstances of the injury, carboxyhemoglobin levels, and fiberoptic bronchoscopy are used to assess for inhalation injuries. Pulmonary complications secondary to inhalation injuries include acute respiratory failure and acute respiratory distress syndrome (ARDS). Respiratory failure occurs when

impairment of ventilation and gas exchange is life-threatening. The immediate intervention is intubation and mechanical ventilation. ARDS may develop in the first few days after the burn injury, secondary to systemic and pulmonary responses to the burn and inhalation injury (Palmieri, 2007). Refer to Chapter 10 for more information on ARDS.

Renal Alterations

Renal function may be altered as a result of decreased blood volume. Destruction of red blood cells at the injury site results in free hemoglobin in the urine. If muscle damage occurs, myoglobin is released from the muscle cells and excreted by the kidney. Adequate fluid volume replacement restores renal blood flow, increasing the glomerular filtration rate and urine volume. If there is inadequate blood flow through the kidneys, the hemoglobin and myoglobin occlude the renal tubules, resulting in acute tubular necrosis and renal failure. Blood urea nitrogen (BUN), serum creatinine levels, and urinary output are monitored to evaluate renal function.

Immunologic Alterations

The immunologic defenses of the body are greatly altered by a serious burn injury as it diminishes resistance to infection. The loss of skin integrity is compounded by the release of abnormal inflammatory factors. There is a significant impairment of the production and release of granulocytes and macrophages from bone marrow; the resulting immunosuppression places the patient with burn injury at high risk for sepsis.

Thermoregulatory Alterations

Loss of skin also results in an inability to regulate body temperature. Patients with burn injuries may therefore exhibit low body temperatures in the early hours after injury. Then, as hypermetabolism resets core temperatures, the patient becomes hyperthermic for much of the post-burn period, even in the absence of infection.

Gastrointestinal Alterations

Two potential gastrointestinal (GI) complications may occur: paralytic ileus (absence of intestinal peristalsis) and Curling's ulcer. Decreased peristalsis and bowel sounds are manifestations of paralytic ileus resulting from burn trauma. Gastric distention and nausea may lead to vomiting unless gastric decompression is initiated. Gastric bleeding secondary to massive physiologic stress may be signaled by occult blood in the stool, regurgitation of "coffee ground" material from the stomach, or bloody vomitus. These signs suggest gastric or duodenal erosion (Curling's ulcer).

MANAGEMENT OF BURN INJURY

Burn care must be based on burn depth and local response, the extent of the injury, and the presence of a systemic response. Burn care is divided into three phases: emergent/resuscitative phase, acute/intermediate phase, and rehabilitation phase. Although priorities exist for each of the phases, they overlap, and assessment and management of specific problems and complications are not limited to these phases but take place throughout burn care. The three phases and the priorities for care are summarized in Table 53-2. Box 53-2 summarizes emergency care at the burn scene.

Emergent/Resuscitative Phase

Immediate Care

It is important to remember the ABCs of all trauma care during the early post-burn period: Airway, Breathing, and Circulation.

It is important to support the *airway* and protect the cervical spine. If edema of the airway develops, endotracheal intubation may be necessary.

TABLE
53-2 Phases of Burn Care

Phase	Duration	Priorities
Emergent/resuscitative	From onset of injury to completion of fluid resuscitation	• First aid • Prevention of shock • Prevention of respiratory distress • Detection and treatment of concomitant injuries • Wound assessment and initial care
Acute/intermediate	From beginning of diuresis to near completion of wound closure	• Wound care and closure • Prevention or treatment of complications, including infection • Nutritional support
Rehabilitation	From major wound closure to return to individual's optimal level of physical and psychosocial adjustment	• Prevention of scars and contractures • Physical, occupational, and vocational rehabilitation • Functional and cosmetic reconstruction • Psychosocial counseling

BOX 53-2

Emergency Procedures at the Burn Scene

- *Extinguish the flames:* When clothes catch fire, the flames can be extinguished if the person falls to the floor or ground and rolls ("drop and roll"); anything available to smother the flames, such as a blanket, rug, or coat, may be used. Standing still forces the person to breathe flames and smoke, and running fans the flames. If the burn source is electrical, the electrical source must be disconnected.

- *Cool the burn:* After the flames are extinguished, the burned area and adherent clothing are soaked with *cool* water, briefly, to cool the wound and halt the burning process. Once a burn has been sustained, the application of cool water is the best first-aid measure. Soaking the burn area intermittently in cool water or applying cool towels gives immediate and striking relief from pain and limits local tissue edema and damage. However, *never* apply ice directly to the burn, *never* wrap the person in ice, and *never* use cold soaks or dressings for longer than several minutes; such procedures may worsen the tissue damage and lead to hypothermia in people with large burns.

- *Remove restrictive objects:* If possible, remove clothing immediately. Adherent clothing may be left in place once cooled. Other clothing and all jewelry, including all piercings, should be removed to allow for assessment and to prevent constriction secondary to rapidly developing edema.

- *Cover the wound:* The burn should be covered as quickly as possible to minimize bacterial contamination and decrease pain by preventing air from coming into contact with the injured surface. Sterile dressings are best, but any clean, dry cloth can be used as an emergency dressing. Ointments and salves should *not* be used. Other than the dressing, no medication or material should be applied to the burn wound.

- *Irrigate chemical burns:* Chemical burns resulting from contact with a corrosive material are irrigated immediately. Most chemical laboratories have a high-pressure shower for such emergencies. If such an injury occurs at home, brush off the chemical agent, remove clothes immediately, and rinse all areas of the body that have come in contact with the chemical. Rinsing can occur in the shower or any other source of continuous running water. If a chemical gets in or near the eyes, the eyes should be flushed with cool, clean water immediately. Outcomes for the patient with chemical burns are significantly improved by rapid, sustained flushing of the injury at the scene.

The nurse assesses and promotes *breathing*. For mild pulmonary injury, 100% humidified oxygen is administered. Intubation and ventilation may be necessary. The nurse monitors the respiratory rate, lung sounds, and oxygen saturation and notifies the provider if dyspnea, stridor, changes in respiratory patterns, or saturation levels reflect declining ventilation and oxygenation.

NURSING ALERT

Breathing must be assessed and a patent airway established immediately during the initial minutes of emergency care. Immediate therapy is directed toward establishing an airway and administering humidified 100% oxygen. If qualified personnel and equipment are available and the victim has severe respiratory distress or airway edema, the rescuers can insert an endotracheal tube and initiate manual ventilation.

Circulation must be assessed quickly. Apical pulse and BP are monitored frequently. Tachycardia (abnormally rapid heart rate, >100 bpm) and slight hypotension are expected soon after the burn. A urinary catheter is inserted and strict intake and output is recorded. Monitoring of hourly urine output and daily weights provides clues about fluid volume status. Any evidence of decreasing urine output or hemodynamic instability requires notification of the provider. A large-bore (16- or 18-gauge) IV catheter should be inserted in a nonburned area for fluid replacement.

NURSING ALERT

In the event of a high-voltage electrical injury, spinal cord injury can result from the direct effect of electrical current or occur secondary to trauma associated with blunt injury. Thus, the cervical spine should be immobilized. Additionally, electrical injury interferes with cardiac conduction and can cause direct trauma to cardiac muscle fibers, resulting in a number of arrhythmias including asystole, ventricular fibrillation, sinus tachycardia, and premature ventricular contractions (PVCs). Because the arrhythmias can present hours after the incident, cardiac monitoring for patients with all electrical injuries for at least 24 hours after cessation of arrhythmia is suggested.

Additionally, the neurologic status is assessed quickly in the patient with extensive burns. The nurse is aware that restlessness, confusion, difficulty attending to questions, or decreasing level of consciousness may indicate cerebral hypoxia. Often, the patient is awake and alert initially, and vital information can be obtained at that time. A secondary head-to-toe survey of the patient is carried out to identify other potentially life-threatening injuries.

Assessment

Initial priorities in the emergency department remain airway, breathing, and circulation. After adequate respiratory function and circulatory status have been established, and the patient's condition is stable, attention is directed to the burn wound itself.

Information needs to include the time of the burn injury, the source of the burn, how the burn was treated at the scene, and any history of falling with the injury. A history of preexisting diseases, allergies, medications, and the use of drugs, alcohol, and tobacco is obtained at this point to aid in planning the patient's care. Because poor tissue perfusion accompanies burn injuries, only IV analgesia (usually morphine) is administered, and titrated according to patient need.

If the burn exceeds 25% TBSA, a nasogastric tube should be inserted and connected to low suction. All patients who are intubated should have a nasogastric tube inserted to decompress the abdomen and prevent vomiting.

Assessment of both the TBSA burned and the depth of the burn are completed. Careful attention is paid to keeping the patient warm during wound assessment. Baseline values for height, weight, arterial blood gases, carboxyhemoglobin, hematocrit, electrolyte values, blood alcohol level, drug panel, urinalysis, and baseline electrocardiogram (ECG) are obtained. Because burns are contaminated wounds, tetanus prophylaxis is administered if the patient's immunization status is not current (>5 years from last tetanus) or unknown (Advanced Burn Life Support [ABLS], 2007).

Transfer to a Burn Center

The depth and extent of the burn are considered in determining whether the patient should be transferred to a burn center. However, if the patient's prognosis does not support transport to a burn center, nurses may contact burn center nurses via telephone and ask for support in patient management. Examples of criteria for referral to a burn unit and online support for nurses can be found at www.totalburncare.com/emergencycarepage.htm (Connor-Ballard, 2009).

Management of Fluid Loss and Shock

Next to managing respiratory difficulties, the most urgent need is preventing irreversible shock by replacing lost fluids and electrolytes (Table 53-3). The total volume and rate of IV fluid replacement are gauged by the patient's response and guided by the resuscitation formula. Numerous fluid resuscitation formulas exist; the nurse needs to be familiar with current institutional protocols. The adequacy of fluid resuscitation is determined primarily by monitoring vital signs and urine output totals, an index of renal perfusion. Urine output totals of 30 to 50 mL/hour (or .5 to 1 mL/kg/hr) have been used as resuscitation goals (Zaletel, 2009). Within the first 24 hours after injury, if the urinary output exceeds 50 mL/hour, the rate of IV fluid administration may be decreased because excessive fluid resuscitation may be deleterious for burn patients. Use of advanced technology such as monitoring with pulmonary artery catheters and esophageal echo-Doppler to evaluate hemodynamic response in burn shock resuscitation have utility but carry risks such as infection

TABLE
53-3 Fluid and Electrolyte Changes in the Emergent/Resuscitative Phase

Fluid accumulation phase (shock phase)
Plasma → interstitial fluid (edema at burn site)

Observation	Explanation
Generalized dehydration	Plasma leaks through damaged capillaries.
Reduction of blood volume	Secondary to plasma loss, fall of blood pressure, and diminished cardiac output
Decreased urinary output	Secondary to: Fluid loss Decreased renal blood flow Sodium and water retention caused by increased adrenocortical activity Hemolysis of red blood cells, causing hemoglobinuria and myonecrosis or myoglobinuria
Potassium (K^+) excess	Massive cellular trauma causes release of K^+ into extracellular fluid (ordinarily, most K^+ is intracellular).
Sodium (Na^+) deficit	Large amount of Na^+ is lost in trapped edema fluid and exudate and by shift into cells as K^+ is released from cells (ordinarily, most Na^+ is extracellular).
Metabolic acidosis (base–bicarbonate deficit)	Loss of bicarbonate ions accompanies sodium loss.
Hemoconcentration (elevated hematocrit)	Liquid blood component is lost into extravascular space.

and aspiration. Thus, traditional variables of hourly assessment of urinary output and vital signs are used to evaluate the adequacy of fluid replacement therapy. For patients with preexisting cardiopulmonary disease or renal disorders, or with patients of extreme age (very young or old), additional hemodynamic parameters may be required to evaluate fluid status (Wang, Ma, Tang et al., 2008). Factors that are associated with the increased fluid requirements include delayed resuscitation, scald burn injuries, inhalation injuries, high-voltage electrical injuries, hyperglycemia, alcohol intoxication, and chronic diuretic therapy.

The projected fluid requirements for the first 24 hours are calculated by the clinician based on the extent of the burn injury. Formulas have been developed for estimating fluid loss based on the estimated percentage of burned TBSA and the weight of the patient. The length of time since the burn injury occurred is very important in calculating estimated fluid needs. Formulas must be adjusted, so that initiation of fluid replacement reflects the time of injury. Resuscitation formulas are approximations only and are individualized to meet the requirements of each patient.

The ABA consensus formula provides for the volume of an isotonic solution (eg, LR) to be administered during the first 24 hours in a range of 2 to 4 mL/kg/percentage TBSA. Half of the calculated total should be given over the first 8 post-burn hours, and the other half should be given over the next 16 hours. The rate and volume of the infusion must be regulated according to the patient's response by changing the hourly infusion rates. Another formula widely used is the Parkland formula, which is 4 mL/kg/percentage TBSA over 24 hours, using LR. It also administers half of the volume over the first 8 hours post-burn and the remaining half is administered over the next 16 hours. The use of formulas and TBSA methods can improve the accuracy and ease of calculating fluid resuscitation requirements (Lindford, Lim, Klass et al., 2009). Again, practitioners should take note that the resuscitation formula serves only as a guideline, and the patient's response to fluid therapy is the best parameter to use.

The following example illustrates use of the consensus formula in a 70-kg (154-lb) patient with a 50% TBSA burn:

1. Consensus formula: 2 to 4 mL/kg/percentage TBSA
2. $2 \times 70 \times 50 = 7{,}000$ mL/24 hours
3. Plan to administer: first 8 hours = 3,500 mL, or 437 mL/hour; next 16 hours = 3,500 mL, or 219 mL/hour

Nursing Implications

Nursing assessment in the emergent phase of burn injury focuses on the major priorities for any trauma patient. Vital signs and respiratory status are monitored closely. Circulation, sensation, and mobility (CSM) of burn area is assessed hourly. Refer to Chapter 40 for details on musculoskeletal assessment. Hourly, the nurse will assess warmth, capillary refill, pulses, sensation, and movement of the affected extremity using the unaffected extremity for comparison. A Doppler (ultrasound device) is useful to assess perfusion of affected extremity. Elevation of burned extremities is crucial to decrease edema. Loss of pulse or sensation must be reported to the provider immediately. If a blood pressure cuff is wrapped around an arm, it must be removed from the extremity between readings since it may act as a tourniquet as the extremity swells.

Assessment includes monitoring of fluid intake and output. Urine output is measured hourly. Urine specific gravity is assessed frequently. Burgundy-colored urine suggests muscle damage. Administering and monitoring IV therapy is a major nursing responsibility.

Body temperature, body weight, current illnesses, and use of medications are assessed. A head-to-toe assessment is performed, focusing on signs and symptoms of concomitant illness, injury, or developing complications. Assessing the extent of the burn wound continues and is facilitated with anatomic diagrams (described previously).

Comorbid conditions coupled with the burn injury contribute to the high mortality rates of patients 60 years and older. Decreased function of the cardiovascular, renal, and pulmonary systems increases the need for close observation of elderly patients with even relatively minor burns during the emergent and acute phases. Acute renal failure is much more common in elderly patients than in those younger than 40 years of age. The margin of difference between hypovolemia and fluid overload is very small. Suppressed immunologic response, a high incidence of malnutrition, and an inability to withstand metabolic stressors further compromise the elderly person's ability to heal. As a result of these issues, close monitoring and prompt treatment of complications are mandatory. A plan of nursing care for a patient during the emergent/resuscitative phase of burn injury is available online at http://thePoint.lww.com/Pellico1e.

Acute/Intermediate Phase

The acute or intermediate phase of burn care follows the emergent/resuscitative phase and begins 48 to 72 hours after the burn injury. During this phase, attention is directed toward continued assessment and maintenance of respiratory and circulatory status, fluid and electrolyte balance (Table 53-4), and GI function. Infection prevention, burn wound care, pain management, and nutritional support are priorities at this stage.

Maintenance of Circulatory and Respiratory Status

Changes may occur as the effects of resuscitative fluid and the chemical reactions of smoke ingredients with lung tissues become apparent. Pulmonary complications are not unusual. Pneumonia is the most frequent clinically related complication (ABA, 2009a). Ideally, the best practice is to remove the endotracheal tube as soon as possible to decrease the risk of infection transmission. The arterial blood gas values and other parameters determine the need for intubation and mechanical ventilation. Humidified oxygen is provided as necessary to maintain adequate oxygen saturation and provide moisture to injured tissues. The nurse assesses breath sounds, and respiratory rate, rhythm, depth, and chest symmetry, and notifies providers with concerns over pulmonary deterioration, such as increasing dyspnea, stridor, and changes in respiratory patterns. As capillaries regain integrity, diuresis begins. If cardiac or renal function is inadequate, fluid overload occurs and symptoms

TABLE
53-4 Fluid and Electrolyte Changes in the Acute Phase

Fluid remobilization phase (state of diuresis)
Interstitial fluid → plasma

Observation	Explanation
Hemodilution (decreased hematocrit)	Blood cell concentration is diluted as fluid enters the intravascular compartment; loss of red blood cells destroyed at burn site occurs.
Increased urinary output	Fluid shift into intravascular compartment increases renal blood flow and causes increased urine formation.
Sodium (Na+) deficit	With diuresis, sodium is lost with water; existing serum sodium is diluted by water influx.
Potassium (K+) deficit (occurs occasionally in this phase)	Beginning on the fourth or fifth post-burn day, K+ shifts from extracellular fluid into cells.
Metabolic acidosis	Loss of sodium depletes fixed base; relative carbon dioxide content increases.

of congestive heart failure may result. Early detection allows for early intervention and carefully calculated fluid intake. Cautious administration of fluids and electrolytes continues during this phase of burn care. Blood components are administered as needed to treat blood loss and anemia.

Infection Prevention

The immunosuppression that accompanies extensive burn injury places the patient at high risk of sepsis. Despite aseptic precautions and the use of topical antimicrobial agents, the burn wound is an excellent medium for bacterial growth and proliferation. While the wound is healing, it must be protected from infection. A primary source of bacterial infection is the patient's intestinal tract, the source of most microbes. A major secondary source of pathogenic microbes is the environment. Infection control is a major role of the burn team in providing wound care. Cap, gown, mask, and gloves are worn while caring for the patient with open burn wounds. Clean technique is used when caring directly for burn wounds.

Antibiotics are seldom prescribed prophylactically because of the risk of promoting resistant strains of bacteria. Systemic antibiotics are administered when there is documentation of positive cultures in, for example, urine, sputum, or blood. Careful attention is paid to antibiotic use because inappropriate use of antibiotics significantly affects the microbial flora present and increases the risk of drug resistance (Shankar, Melstrom, & Gamelli, 2007).

Wound Care

Wound care is the single most time-consuming element of burn care after the emergent phase. The nurse needs to make astute assessments of wound status, use creative approaches to wound dressing, and support the patient during the emotionally distressing and very painful experience of wound care.

Various measures are used to clean the burn wound. After the wounds are cleansed, the prescribed method of wound care is performed. Provider preferences, the availability of skilled nursing staff, and resources in terms of number of personnel, supplies, and time must be considered in choosing the best method. The goal is to protect the wound until either spontaneous healing or skin grafting can be achieved. Patient comfort and ability to participate in the prescribed treatment are also important considerations.

Topical Antibacterial Therapy

There is general agreement that some form of antimicrobial therapy applied to the burn wound is the best method of local care. Topical antibacterial therapy does not sterilize the wound; it simply reduces the number of bacteria. For more than 50 years, it has been recognized that silver has bacteriostatic and bacteriocidal properties that make it an excellent treatment agent (Table 53-5).

Criteria for choice of topical agents include the following:

- They are effective against gram-negative organisms and even fungi.
- They are clinically effective.
- They penetrate the eschar but are not systemically toxic.
- They do not lose their effectiveness, allowing another infection to develop.
- They are cost-effective, available, and acceptable to the patient.
- They are easy to apply and remove, minimizing nursing care time.

Wound Débridement

As debris accumulates on the wound surface, it can delay the healing process. **Débridement,** has two goals:

- To remove tissue contaminated by bacteria and foreign bodies
- To remove devitalized tissue or burn eschar in preparation for grafting and wound healing

Early surgical excision to remove devitalized tissue along with early burn wound closure is recognized as the most important factor contributing to survival of a patient with a major burn injury.

Wound Coverage

If wounds are full-thickness or extensive, spontaneous healing is not possible, and treatment of the wound is necessary until coverage with a graft of the patient's own skin (**autograft**) is possible. Autografts are the ideal covering for burn wounds, because the grafts are the patient's own skin and therefore are not rejected by the patient's immune system.

The purposes of wound coverage are to decrease the risk of infection; prevent further loss of protein, fluid, and electrolytes

TABLE
53-5 Overview of Selected Topical Antibacterial Agents Used for Burn Wounds

Agent	Indication	Application	Nursing Implications
Silver sulfadiazine 1% (Silvadene) water-soluble cream	• Most bactericidal agent • Minimal penetration of eschar.	Apply 1/16-inch layer of cream with a sterile glove 1 to 3 times daily.	• Watch for leukopenia 2 to 3 days after initiation of therapy. (Leukopenia usually resolves within 2 to 3 days.) • Anticipate formation of pseudoeschar (proteinaceous gel), which is removed easily after 72 hours.
Mafenide acetate 5% to 10% (Sulfamylon) hydrophilic-based cream	• Effective against gram-negative and gram-positive organisms • Diffuses rapidly through eschar • In 10% strength, it is the agent of choice for electrical burns because of its ability to penetrate thick eschar.	Apply thin layer with sterile glove twice a day and leave open as prescribed; if the wound is dressed, change the dressing every 6 hours as prescribed.	• Monitor arterial blood gas levels and discontinue as prescribed, if acidosis occurs. Mafenide acetate is a strong carbonic anhydrase inhibitor that may reduce renal buffering and cause metabolic acidosis. • Premedicate the patient with an analgesic before applying mafenide acetate because this agent causes severe burning pain for up to 20 minutes after application.
Silver nitrate 0.5% aqueous solution	• Bacteriostatic and fungicidal • Does *not* penetrate eschar.	Apply solution to gauze dressing and place over wound. Keep the dressing wet but covered with dry gauze and dry blankets to decrease vaporization. Remoisten every 2 hours, and redress wound twice a day.	• Monitor serum sodium (Na^+) and potassium (K^+) levels and replace as prescribed. Silver nitrate solution is hypotonic and acts as wick for sodium and potassium. • Protect bed linen and clothing from contact with silver nitrate, which stains everything it touches black.
Acticoat	• Effective against gram-negative and gram-positive organisms and some yeasts and molds • Delivers a uniform, antimicrobial concentration of silver to the burn wound.	Moisten with sterile water only (*never* use normal saline). Apply directly to wound. Cover with absorbent secondary dressing. Remoisten every 3 to 4 hours with sterile water.	• Do not use oil-based products or topical antimicrobials with Acticoat burn dressing. Keep Acticoat moist, not saturated. May produce a "pseudoeschar" from silver after application. • Can be left in place for 3 to 5 days. Also available in Acticoat 7, which can be left in place for up to 7 days without the need to change the dressing.

through the wound; and minimize heat loss through evaporation. Once the wound is surgically excised, a wound covering is applied to keep the area moist and promote the granulation process.

Homograft is donor skin from a cadaver. It is a biological dressing that has several uses. In extensive burns, it save lives by providing temporary wound coverage and protecting the granulation tissue until autografting is possible. Biologic dressings also provide temporary immediate coverage for clean, superficial burns and decrease the wound's evaporative water and protein loss. They decrease pain by protect-ing nerve endings and are an effective barrier against water loss and entry of bacteria. Biosynthetic and synthetic skin substitutes are rapidly replacing biologic dressings as temporary wound coverings.

In an attempt to develop the ideal burn wound covering product, dermal substitutes have been created. It is believed that skin substitutes enhance the healing process of an open wound when autologous skin is unavailable.

CARE OF THE GRAFT SITE. Occlusive dressings are commonly used initially after grafting to immobilize the graft.

Synthetic dressings may be used to protect grafts. The patient is positioned and turned carefully to avoid disturbing the graft or putting pressure on the graft site. If an extremity has been grafted, it is elevated to minimize edema.

CARE OF THE DONOR SITE. A moist gauze dressing is applied at the time of surgery to maintain pressure and to stop any oozing. With all types of covering, donor sites must remain clean, dry, and free from pressure. Because a donor site is usually a partial-thickness wound, it will heal spontaneously within 7 to 14 days with proper care. Donor sites are painful, and additional pain management must be a part of the patient's care.

Pain Management

Pain is inevitable during recovery from any burn injury. Burn pain has been described as one of the most severe forms of acute pain. Pain is related to tissue destruction, as well as to the inflammatory response, which causes the release of histamine, bradykinin, and prostaglandin that are irritating to exposed peripheral nerve endings (Connor-Ballard, 2009).

Patients have reported three types of burn pain: background or resting pain, procedural pain, and breakthrough pain. Background pain exists on a 24-hour basis. Procedural pain is caused by manipulation of the wound bed during dressing changes or range-of-motion exercises. The nurse is aware that premedication with analgesic medications before painful procedures is essential. Breakthrough pain occurs when blood levels of analgesic agents decrease below the level required to control background pain.

Pain changes in time as the wound is covered with new skin, healing takes place, and scars form. Management of the often-severe pain is one of the most difficult challenges facing the burn team. Many factors contribute to the pain experience. These factors include the severity of the pain, the adequacy of the health care provider's assessment of the pain, appropriateness of pharmacologic treatment of pain, multiple procedures involved in burn care, and evaluation of the effectiveness of pain relief measures. Literature suggests that, despite advances in pain management, many burn patients are undertreated (Connor-Ballard, 2009). The outstanding features of burn pain are its intensity and long duration; thus, all medical providers should understand that opioid tolerance is not addiction, and pain should be managed when there is a clinical need. Furthermore, necessary wound care carries with it the anticipation of pain and anxiety. Refer to Chapter 7 for discussion of tolerance versus addiction.

In partial-thickness burns, the nerve endings are exposed, resulting in excruciating pain with exposure to air currents. Although nerve endings are destroyed in full-thickness burns, the margins of the burn wound are hypersensitive to pain, and there is pain in adjacent structures. Healing of full-thickness burns creates significant discomfort as regenerating nerve endings become entrapped in scar formation. Most severe burns are a combination of partial-thickness and full-thickness burns.

The patient's pain level must be assessed throughout the day, because each type of pain is different, and various management strategies may be needed to address the different types of pain. The nurse uses a pain intensity scale to assess pain level (eg, 1 to 10), and documents response to the treatment plan consistently. Opioid administration via the IV route, particularly in the emergent and acute phases of burn management, remains the mainstay for pharmacologic management. Titration of analgesic agents to obtain relief while minimizing side effects is crucial. The patient's requirements for analgesia are often high, but fear of addiction on the part of the patient and the health care provider hampers adequate opioid administration. Morphine sulfate remains the analgesic of choice. It is titrated to obtain pain relief based on the patient's self-report of pain.

Fentanyl is another useful opioid, particularly for procedural pain, because it has a rapid onset, high potency, and short duration, all of which make it effective for use with procedures.

Patient-controlled analgesia (PCA) maintains a steady level of opioid for pain relief and enables the patient to administer intermittent doses of medication.

Sustained-release opioids, such as MS Contin or oxycodone (OxyContin), have also been used successfully in the treatment of burn pain. These medications can effectively treat the resting pain that is associated with burn injury. Additional medications must be prescribed with these to cover breakthrough pain.

Additional nursing interventions, such as teaching the patient relaxation techniques, giving the patient some control over wound care and analgesia, and providing frequent reassurance are helpful. Other pain-relieving approaches include distraction through video programs or video games, hypnosis, biofeedback, and behavioral modification.

Anxiety and pain go hand in hand. The entire burn experience can produce severe anxiety, which can, in turn, exacerbate pain. Therefore, the ideal pain management regimen must incorporate the treatment of pain and anxiety and must be individualized for each patient.

It is important for the nurse to differentiate restlessness due to pain from restlessness due to hypoxia; a thorough respiratory assessment can help discriminate the etiology, noting oxygen saturation, lung sounds, chest expansion, and respiratory rate. The nurse also assesses the patient's sleep patterns, since lack of sleep and rest interferes with healing, comfort, and restoration of energy. If necessary, sedatives are prescribed.

Nutritional Support

Burn injuries produce profound metabolic abnormalities fueled by the exaggerated stress response to the injury. It is essential to control this response by increasing the anabolic process through adequate nutrition, decreasing heat loss

from wounds, and maintaining a warm environment. Controlling secondary stress, such as pain and anxiety, also helps control the stress response.

The most important of these interventions is to provide adequate nutrition and calories. Healing of the burn wound consumes large quantities of energy. Several formulas exist for estimating the daily metabolic expenditure and caloric requirements. The enteral route of feeding is far superior to the parenteral route. Feedings are started as soon as possible. Vitamin and mineral supplements may be prescribed, and the nurse collaborates with the dietitian to plan a protein- and calorie-rich diet that is acceptable to the patient. Other treatment modalities include early excision and skin grafting of the burn wound, aggressive prevention or treatment of infections, and adequate exercise with physical therapy to lessen muscle wasting and increase strength.

Promoting Mobility

An early priority is to prevent complications of immobility. Deep breathing, turning, and proper positioning are essential nursing practices that prevent atelectasis and pneumonia, control edema, and prevent pressure ulcers and contractures. These interventions are modified to meet the patient's needs. Low-air-loss and rotation beds may be useful, and early sitting and ambulation are encouraged. If the lower extremities are burned, elastic pressure bandages should be applied before the patient is placed in an upright position.

Psychological and Emotional Support

Family functioning is disrupted with burn injury. One of the nurse's responsibilities is to support the patient and family. Family members need to be instructed about ways that they can support the patient as adaptation to burn trauma occurs. The burn injury has tremendous psychological, economic, and practical impact on the patient and family. Referrals for social services or psychological counseling should be made as appropriate.

Rehabilitation Phase

Rehabilitation begins immediately after the burn has occurred and often extends for years after injury. In the aftermath of the acute stages of burn injury, the patient increasingly focuses on the alterations in self-image and lifestyle that may occur. Wound healing, psychosocial support, and restoration of maximal functional activity remain priorities, so that the patient can have the best quality of life both personally and socially. The body goes through many changes as it heals. As the burn wound becomes a burn scar, the burn survivor may be faced with new complications. Reconstructive surgery to improve body appearance and function is often needed.

Hypertrophic Scarring

The wound is in a dynamic state for 1.5 to 2 years after the burn occurs. If appropriate measures are instituted during this active period, the scar tissue loses its redness and softens. Healed areas that are prone to hypertrophic scarring require the patient to wear a pressure garment. Pressure needs to be continuous. Gentle superficial massage aids in softening the connective tissue. Patients must be instructed about the need for lubrication and protection of the healing skin and the need to use pressure garments for at least 1 year after the injury. Treatment during rehabilitation is expected to include elastic pressure garments, splints, and exercise under the supervision of an experienced physical and occupational therapy team.

Continuing Care

Follow-up care by an interdisciplinary burn care team is necessary. Patients who receive care in a burn center usually return to the burn clinic for evaluation by the burn team, modification of home care instructions, and planning for reconstructive surgery. Many patients require outpatient physical or occupational therapy. It is often the nurse who is responsible for coordinating all aspects of care and ensuring that the patient's needs are met.

Patients who return home after a severe burn injury need referral for home care. Social services and community nursing services must be contacted to provide optimal care and supervision after hospital discharge. The home care nurse assesses the patient's physical and psychological status, as well as the adequacy of the home setting for safe and adequate care. The nurse monitors the plan of care and notes any problems that interfere with the patient's ability to carry out the care.

Patients who have survived burn injuries frequently suffer profound losses. These include not only a loss of body image due to disfigurement but also losses of personal property, homes, loved ones, and ability to work. The ABA is presently proposing an amendment to the Social Security Act to eliminate the 5-month waiting period for Social Security disability benefits and the 24-month wait for Medicare for individuals with disabling burn injuries (ABA, 2009c).

The health care team must actively promote a healthy body image and self-concept, so that these patients can accept or challenge others' perceptions of those who are disfigured or disabled. Several burn patient support groups and other organizations throughout the United States offer services for burn survivors. They provide caring people (often people who have themselves recovered from burn injuries) who can visit the patient in the hospital or home or telephone the patient and family periodically to provide support and counseling about skin care, cosmetics, and problems related to psychosocial adjustment (www.phoenix-society.org). These organizations, and many regional burn centers, sponsor group meetings and social functions at which outpatients are welcome. Some also provide school-reentry programs and are active in burn prevention activities. If more information is needed regarding burn prevention, the ABA can help locate the nearest burn center and offer current burn prevention tips (www.ameriburn.org).

Chapter Review

Critical Thinking Exercises

1. A 75-year-old woman was scalded in the bathtub, where she sustained 25% full-thickness wounds to both lower legs before being found by her niece. It is not known how long the woman was in the tub. She has been independent and living alone for the past 15 years; however, her niece has offered to have her aunt come and live with her family. On admission to the emergency department, the woman's temperature is 94°F (35.5°C) and her weight is 111 lb (50 kg). She has diabetes as well as a history of heart failure and hypertension. What are the priorities in her medical and nursing care during the emergent phase of burn care? What assessment parameters would you monitor closely? Is she a likely candidate for skin grafting?

2. An 18-year-old woman sustained second-degree burns from a tanning bed. Her burns cover her entire chest, abdomen, back, and legs. She has large blisters on her chest and the backs of her knees. Using the rule of nines, estimate the percent of TBSA burned. Estimate her fluid resuscitation needs. Describe nursing care, including patient teaching that is important for this patient. She is rating her pain level 10 out of 10. What comfort measures can you use to manage her pain?

3. A 50-year-old man who weighs 111 lb (50 kg) was transferred to the emergency department after his truck caught fire. He has circumferential burns on both of his legs, his anterior chest, and his entire right upper extremity. He was unable to extricate himself from the truck and suffered inhalation burns as well. Using the rule of nines chart, estimate the percent of TBSA burned. What are the emergency priorities for this patient? What are the fluid resuscitation requirements for this patient based on his percent of burn and his weight? What assessment parameters would you monitor closely? What pain management strategies would be indicated for this patient?

NCLEX-Style Review Questions

1. The nurse is caring for a 32-year-old with circumferential full thickness burns to the right arm and trunk. Which nursing intervention has the highest priority in the plan of care?
   A. Assess radial pulses several times a day.
   B. Enforce airborne infection control procedures.
   C. Perform range-of-motion exercises several times per day.
   D. Remove blisters from the burn area.

2. A patient with severe burn injuries to the abdomen and legs becomes combative when it is time to change the dressings. Which of the following interventions will help this patient the most?
   A. Allow the patient to determine the time of dressing change.
   B. Premedicate the patient with pain and anxiety medications before dressing change.
   C. Tell the patient it is OK to cry but to lie still.
   D. Explain the importance of dressing changes.

3. A nurse would suspect an inhalation injury with which of the following findings? Select all that apply.
   A. History of burn occurring in an enclosed space
   B. Carbonaceous sputum
   C. Bloody sputum
   D. Stridor

4. Which of the following are reasonable options for pain management for a 50-year-old man who has just sustained 20% partial thickness burns to his right leg and abdomen?
   A. Fentanyl 50 μg intravenously
   B. Morphine sulfate 10 mg IM into the left deltoid
   C. Calm, reassuring words to help relax him
   D. Oxycodone 10 mg PO

5. A 34-year-old patient who sustained a major burn injury during a house fire has been transferred to the burn unit. During the acute phase of the burn injury care, the nurse should focus on which fluid and electrolyte changes?
   A. Metabolic alkalosis
   B. Sodium deficit
   C. Increased hematocrit
   D. Decreased urinary output

Try these additional resources to enhance your learning and understanding of this chapter:
- thePoint online resource available at **http://thepoint.lww.com/Pellico1e**
- *Handbook for Focus on Adult Health: Medical-Surgical Nursing*
- *Study Guide for Focus on Adult Health: Medical-Surgical Nursing*

References and Selected Readings

References and selected readings associated with this chapter can be found on the website that accompanies the book. Visit http://thepoint.lww.com/Pellico1e to access the references and other additional resources associated with this chapter.

Other Acute Problems

AN 80-YEAR-OLD patient is in acute renal failure and has been diagnosed with multiple organ dysfunction syndrome (MODS). She underwent a right hip replacement 2 days ago and currently has a temperature of 102.6°F.

➡ What are treatment measures to reverse MODS?
➡ What patient populations are at increased risk for developing MODS?
➡ Discuss nursing care of patients with MODS.

Nursing Management: Shock and Multisystem Failure

AARON C. HUSTON

Shock is a life-threatening condition with a variety of underlying causes. The progression of shock is neither linear nor predictable. Nurses caring for patients with shock and for those at risk for shock must understand the underlying mechanisms of shock and recognize its subtle as well as more obvious signs. Rapid assessment and response are essential to the patient's recovery.

Learning Objectives

After reading this chapter, you will be able to:

1. Describe shock and its underlying pathophysiology.

2. Compare clinical findings of the pre-shock, shock, and end organ damage stages of shock.

3. Describe similarities and differences in hypovolemic, cardiogenic, obstructive, and distributive shock states.

4. Identify medical and nursing management priorities in treating patients in shock.

5. Identify vasoactive medications used in treating shock, and describe nursing implications associated with their use.

OVERVIEW

Shock can best be defined as a condition in which tissue perfusion is inadequate to deliver oxygen and nutrients to support vital organs and cellular function. This definition differs from more traditional views of shock because it does not depend on absolute criteria for parameters, such as blood pressure (BP).

NURSING ALERT
By the time BP drops, damage has already been occurring at the cellular and tissue levels. Therefore, the patient at risk for shock must be assessed and monitored closely before the BP falls.

Adequate blood flow to the tissues and cells requires the following components: adequate cardiac pump, effective vasculature and circulatory system, and sufficient blood volume. If one component is impaired, perfusion to the tissues is threatened or compromised. Without treatment, inadequate blood flow to the tissues results in poor delivery of oxygen and nutrients to the cells, cellular starvation, cell death, organ dysfunction progressing to organ failure, and eventual death.

Shock affects all body systems. It may develop rapidly or slowly, depending on the underlying cause. During shock, the body struggles to survive, utilizing a variety of homeostatic, compensatory mechanisms to restore blood flow. Any insult to the body can create a cascade of events resulting in poor tissue perfusion, which means that nurses should be vigilant about watching for signs of shock.

PATHOPHYSIOLOGY

Tissue perfusion is a function of cardiac output (CO) and systemic vascular resistance (SVR). CO is the amount of blood pumped by heart in liters

Classifications of Shock

- **Hypovolemic shock** occurs when there is a decrease in the intravascular volume. Hypovolemia can be the result of an imbalance of intake and output such as **dehydration** or **hemorrhage**.
- **Cardiogenic shock** occurs when the heart has an impaired pumping ability; it may be of coronary or noncoronary event origin.
- **Obstructive shock** occurs when there is decreased oxygen delivery due to an obstructive cause such as pericardial tamponade, tension pneumothorax, PE, or abdominal compartment syndrome.
- **Distributive shock** is caused by alterations in vascular smooth muscle tone, caused by either nervous system injury, inflammatory release causing vasodilation, or complications associated with medications such as epidural anesthesia. **Septic shock** is technically considered a "distributive" type of shock. Sepsis is a complex condition, caused by an infection with profound vasodilation.

This results in an acidotic intracellular environment, along with a host of electrolyte derangements. In stress states such as shock, catecholamines, cortisol, glucagon, and inflammatory cytokines and mediators are released, causing hyperglycemia and insulin resistance in an effort to mobilize glucose for cellular metabolism.

NURSING ALERT

Tight glycemic control (blood glucose, 80 to 110 mg/dL) was considered to reduce morbidity and mortality of acutely ill patients. However, recent research studies reveal inconsistent results, suggesting that, in critically ill patients, a less aggressive glycemic target of 140 to 180 mg/dL is appropriate (Dokun, 2010).

As the hypoxemia progresses, anaerobic metabolism causes the lactic acid level to rise, which results in increased capillary permeability, further decreasing the CO. The cell membrane becomes more permeable, allowing electrolytes and fluids to seep out of and into the cell. The sodium–potassium pump becomes impaired; cell structures, primarily the mitochondria, are damaged; and cell death results.

per minute (usual CO is about 4 to 6 L/min but varies greatly depending on the metabolic needs of the body), whereas SVR is the resistance to the flow of blood out from the ventricles. It is helpful to consider SVR to be a vise grip on the aorta. If the vise is tightened, the SVR rises, and it is much harder for the ventricle to pump blood out, whereas if the vise grip is released from the aorta, there is little resistance to the outflow of blood. Conventionally, the primary underlying pathophysiologic process is used to classify the shock state (Box 54-1 provides classifications). When considering possible causes of shock and potential interventions, nurses should remember that the interplay of these two factors is what determines the extent of the course of shock and the prognosis of the patient.

In all types of shock, the cells lack an adequate blood supply and are therefore inadequately oxygenated; therefore, they must produce energy through anaerobic metabolism.

STAGES OF SHOCK

Shock is believed to progress along a continuum. One way to understand the physiologic responses and subsequent clinical signs and symptoms is to divide the continuum into separate stages:

1. Pre-shock (compensated)
2. Shock (uncompensated)
3. End organ dysfunction (which results in irreversible organ damage)

The earlier that interventions can be initiated along this continuum, the greater the patient's chance of survival. Table 54-1 compares clinical findings in the different stages of shock.

TABLE
54-1 Clinical Findings in Stages of Shock

	Stage		
Finding	**Pre-Shock**	**Shock**	**End-Organ Dysfunction**
Blood pressure	Near normal	Systolic <80 to 90 mm Hg	Requires mechanical or pharmacologic support
Heart rate	>100 bpm	100 to 150 bpm	Erratic or asystole
Respiratory status	>20 breaths/min	Rapid, shallow respirations; crackles	Requires ventilation
Skin	Cold, clammy	Mottled, petechiae	Jaundice
Urinary output	Mildly decreased	Severely decreased	Anuric, requires dialysis
Mentation	Confusion	Lethargy	Unresponsive
Acid–base balance	Respiratory alkalosis	Metabolic acidosis	Profound acidosis

Pre-Shock

Pathophysiology

In pre-shock, or the compensatory stage of shock, the BP often remains within normal limits. Vasoconstriction, increased heart rate, and increased contractility of the heart contribute to maintaining adequate CO and SVR. This results from stimulation of the sympathetic nervous system and subsequent release of catecholamines (epinephrine and norepinephrine). Patients display the often-described "fight-or-flight" response. The body shunts blood from organs such as the skin, kidneys, and gastrointestinal (GI) tract to the brain and heart to ensure adequate blood supply to these vital organs. As a result, the skin is cool and clammy, bowel sounds are hypoactive, and urine output decreases. Adult patients can often compensate for up to a 10% total volume loss through normal homeostatic mechanisms. Conversely, patients who have other medical problems or who take certain medications may have a diminished ability to compensate.

Clinical Manifestations and Assessment

Despite a near normal BP, the patient may shows other clinical signs indicating inadequate organ perfusion. Tachycardia, peripheral vasoconstriction, and anxiety are common.

Medical and Nursing Management

At this stage, treatment is directed toward identifying the cause of shock, correcting the underlying disorder, and initiating aggressive measures aimed at supporting the body's compensatory mechanisms. Because compensation cannot be maintained indefinitely, measures such as fluid replacement and medication therapy must be initiated to maintain an adequate BP and reestablish and maintain adequate tissue perfusion. *Early intervention along the continuum of shock is the key to improving the patient's prognosis.* Therefore, the nurse must assess the patient at risk for shock systematically to recognize the subtle clinical signs of the compensatory stage before the patient progresses to uncompensated shock. Box 54-2 highlights considerations for recognizing shock in older patients.

The role of the nurse at this stage is to monitor the patient's hemodynamic status and promptly report deviations to the provider, to assist in identifying and treating the underlying disorder by continuous in-depth assessment of the patient, to administer prescribed fluids and medications, and to promote patient safety. In assessing tissue perfusion, the nurse specifically observes for changes in level of consciousness, vital signs, urinary output, skin, and laboratory values. Constant reassessment is warranted at this stage. Nurses should try to maintain a calm environment both for patient's and family's sake, and also ensure that assessments and interventions are

---

BOX 54-2 | **Gerontologic Considerations**

Recognizing Shock in Older Patients

The physiologic changes associated with aging, coupled with pathologic and chronic disease states, place older people at increased risk for developing a state of shock and possibly multiple organ dysfunction syndrome (MODS). Elderly people can recover from shock if it is detected and treated early with aggressive and supportive therapies. Nurses play an essential role in assessing and interpreting subtle changes in older patients' responses to illness.

- During hypovolemic states, medications such as beta-blocking agents (metoprolol (Lopressor)) used to treat hypertension may mask tachycardia, a primary compensatory mechanism to increase CO.
- The aging immune system may not mount a truly febrile response (temperature >40°C or 104°F), but an increasing trend in body temperature should be addressed.
- The heart does not function well in hypoxemic states, and the aging heart may respond to decreased myocardial oxygenation with arrhythmias that may be misinterpreted as a normal part of the aging process.
- Changes in mentation may be inappropriately misinterpreted as dementia. Older people with a sudden change in mentation should be aggressively treated for the presence of infection and organ hypoperfusion.

---

rapid and ongoing. Providing brief explanations about the diagnostic and treatment procedures, supporting the patient during these procedures, and providing information about their outcomes reduces stress and anxiety and thus promotes the patient's physical and mental well-being. Speaking in a calm, reassuring voice and using gentle touch also help ease the patient's concerns.

Shock

In shock, the patient loses the ability to compensate for the insult, infection, or injury. It is during this stage that clinical signs become more obvious.

Pathophysiology

The heart and kidneys are among the first organs to show signs of dysfunction. Up until now on the continuum, the myocardium has kept pace by increasing CO, but this can only go on for a limited time. The body's inability to meet increased oxygen requirements produces ischemia, and biochemical mediators cause myocardial depression. This leads

to failure of the cardiac pump, even if the underlying cause of the shock is not of cardiac origin.

⚠ N U R S I N G A L E R T

Although BP readings alone are unreliable indicators of circulatory status, a systolic BP of less than 100 mm Hg in an emergency department is associated with a three-fold increase in hospital mortality and ten-fold increase in unexpected death (Marx, Hockberger, & Walls, 2010).

The systemic impact of hypotension, and thus hypoperfusion, on the kidneys results in decreased urine output. A Foley catheter is inserted, and urine output should be measured vigilantly: A urine output of less than 30 mL/hr or 0.5mL/kg/hr is indicative of renal hypoperfusion and/or hypovolemia. In addition, the inflammatory response to injury is activated, and proinflammatory and anti-inflammatory cytokines and mediators are released, which in turn activate the coagulation system in an effort to reestablish homeostasis. At the same time, acidosis impairs all enzymatic functions, including coagulation. A cascade of progressive organ failure resulting from poor tissue perfusion is illustrated in Figure 54-1.

Even if the underlying cause of the shock is reversed, the sequence of compensatory responses to the decrease in tissue perfusion perpetuates the shock state, and a vicious cycle ensues. It is believed that the body's appropriate or inappropriate response in this stage of shock may be the primary factor determining the patient's survival.

Medical and Nursing Management

Early aggressive interventions are essential to the survival of patients in shock; therefore, identifying patients who may be in shock and reporting subtle changes in assessment are imperative. Patients in shock are often cared for in the intensive care (ICU) setting to facilitate close monitoring (hemodynamic monitoring, electrocardiographic [ECG] monitoring, arterial blood gases [ABGs], serum electrolyte levels, physical and mental status changes); rapid and frequent administration of various prescribed medications and fluids; strict measurement of intake and output (I & O); and possibly interventions with supportive technologies, such as mechanical ventilation, dialysis, and intra-aortic balloon pump. Nursing care of patients in shock requires expertise in assessing and understanding shock and the significance of changes in assessment data.

Specific management of shock depends on the type of shock and its underlying cause but, in general, care is aimed at achieving the following goals:

- Optimizing intravascular volume
- Supporting the pumping action of the heart
- Improving the competence of the vascular system
- Supporting the respiratory system

- Continual assessment and reassessment of the body's response to shock
- Involving the patient and family in care, particularly in end-of-life decisions

END ORGAN DAMAGE (IRREVERSIBLE)

Pathophysiology

If tissue perfusion is not restored, irreversible end organ damage ensues. This represents the point along the shock continuum at which organ damage is so severe that the patient does not respond to treatment and cannot survive. For example, despite treatment, BP remains low. Renal and liver failure, compounded by the release of necrotic tissue toxins, creates an overwhelming metabolic acidosis. Anaerobic metabolism contributes to a worsening lactic acidosis. Respiratory system failure prevents adequate oxygenation and ventilation despite mechanical ventilatory support, and the cardiovascular system is ineffective in maintaining an adequate mean arterial pressure (MAP; MAP = [(2 × diastolic pressure + systolic pressure) / 3]) for tissue perfusion. Multiple organ dysfunction progressing to complete organ failure has occurred, and death is imminent. Multiple organ dysfunction can occur as a progression along the shock continuum or as a syndrome unto itself and is described in more detail later in this chapter.

Medical and Nursing Management

Specific therapies in this stage are usually the same as for shock. Although the patient may have progressed from shock to irreversible end organ damage, the judgment that the shock is irreversible can be made only retrospectively, on the basis of the patient's failure to respond to treatment. As in shock, the nurse focuses on carrying out prescribed treatments, monitoring the patient, preventing complications, protecting the patient from injury, and providing comfort. Offering brief explanations to the patient about what is happening is essential even if there is no certainty that the patient hears or understands what is being said. Simple comfort measures, including reassuring touches, should continue to be provided despite the patient's nonresponsiveness to verbal stimuli.

As it becomes obvious that the patient is unlikely to survive, the family must be informed about the prognosis and likely outcome. Opportunities should be provided, throughout the patient's care, for the family to see, touch, and talk to the patient. Close family friends or spiritual advisors may be of comfort to the family members in dealing with the inevitable death of their loved one. Whenever possible, the patient's family should be approached regarding any living wills, advance directives, or other written or verbal wishes the patient may have shared in the event that he or she became unable to participate in end-of-life decisions. In some cases, ethics committees may assist families and health care teams in making difficult decisions.

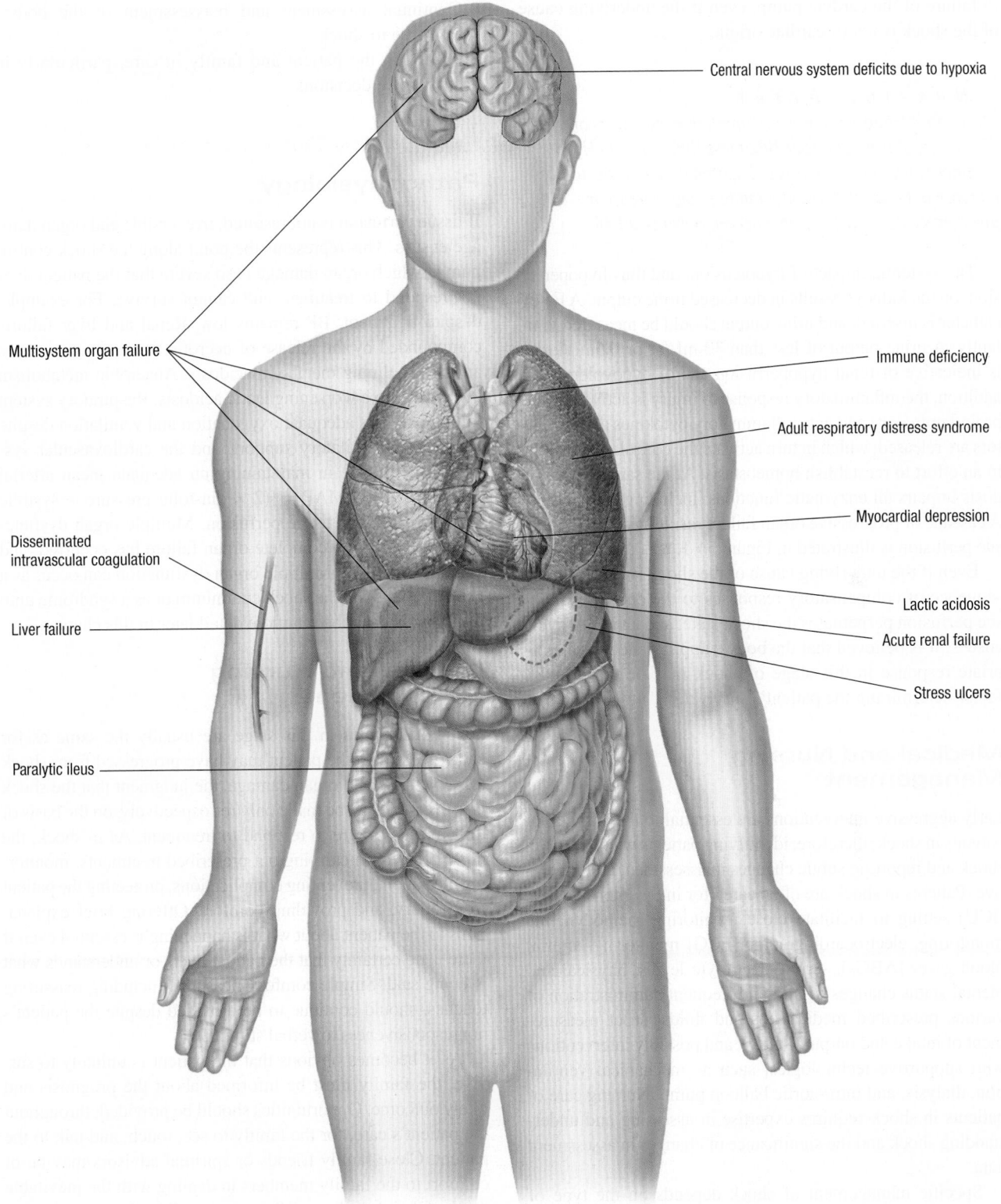

Central nervous system deficits due to hypoxia

Multisystem organ failure

Immune deficiency

Adult respiratory distress syndrome

Myocardial depression

Disseminated
intravascular coagulation

Lactic acidosis

Liver failure

Acute renal failure

Stress ulcers

Paralytic ileus

FIGURE 54-1 Multiorgan system effects of shock.

GENERAL MANAGEMENT STRATEGIES IN SHOCK

As described previously, and in the discussion of types of shock to follow, management in all types and all phases of shock includes the following:

- Fluid replacement to restore intravascular volume
- **Vasoactive medications** to restore vasomotor tone and improve cardiac function
- Nutritional support to address the metabolic requirements that are often dramatically increased in shock

Therapies described in this section require collaboration among all members of the health care team to ensure that the manifestations of shock are quickly identified and that adequate and timely treatment is instituted to achieve the best outcome possible.

Fluid Replacement

The fluids administered vary but may include **crystalloids** (electrolyte solutions that move freely between intravascular and interstitial spaces), **colloids** (large-molecule IV solutions), and blood components (Table 54-2). The best fluid to treat shock remains controversial. In emergencies, the "best" fluid is often the fluid that is readily available. Fluid resuscitation should be initiated early in shock to maximize intravascular volume. Both crystalloids (eg, saline and lactated Ringer's [LR] solution) and colloids (eg, albumin) can be administered to restore intravascular volume. There are different camps regarding whether crystalloids or colloids should be used, although a Cochrane review done by Perel, Roberts, & Pearson (2007) showed no difference in outcome between the two fluids. Blood should be given for hypovolemic shock due to trauma and/or hemorrhage.

Common crystalloid fluids used for resuscitation in hypovolemic shock include 0.9% sodium chloride solution (normal saline) and LR solution. LR is an electrolyte solution containing the lactate ion, which should not be confused with lactic acid. The exogenous lactate is converted to bicarbonate by the liver, thus assisting in treatment of the acidosis. It is important to assess for liver disease when using this solution as the acidosis may worsen when LR is administered to patients with severe liver dysfunction (Marx et al., 2010). Care must be taken when rapidly administering isotonic crystalloids to avoid "over resuscitation" and thus causing severe edema. For this reason, and depending on the cause of the hypovolemia, a hypertonic crystalloid solution, such as 3% sodium chloride, is sometimes administered in hypovolemic shock. Hypertonic solutions produce a large osmotic force that pulls fluid from the intracellular space to the intravascular space to achieve a fluid balance. The osmotic effect of hypertonic solutions results in fewer fluids being administered to restore intravascular volume. However, hypertonic saline is associated with excessive serum

T A B L E
54-2 Fluid Replacement in Shock

Fluids	Advantages	Disadvantages
Crystalloids		
0.9% sodium chloride (normal saline solution)	Widely available, inexpensive	Requires large volume of infusion; can cause pulmonary edema
Lactated Ringer's	Lactate ion helps buffer metabolic acidosis	Requires large volume of infusion; can cause pulmonary edema
Hypertonic saline (3%, 5%, 7.5%)	Small volume needed to restore intravascular volume	Danger of hypernatremia, central pontine myelinolysis, and increased serum osmolality
Colloids		
Albumin (5%, 25%)	Rapidly expands plasma volume	Expensive; requires human donors; limited supply; can cause heart failure
Dextran (40, 70)	Synthetic plasma expander	Interferes with platelet aggregation; not recommended for hemorrhagic shock
Hetastarch	Synthetic; less expensive than albumin; effect lasts up to 36 h	Prolongs bleeding and clotting times

osmolality, hypernatremia, and if administered too rapidly, can cause central pontine myelinolysis (refer to Chapter 31, Box 31-2 for further information).

Colloids expand intravascular volume by exerting oncotic pressure, thereby pulling fluid into the intravascular space. Colloidal solutions have the same effect as hypertonic solutions in increasing intravascular volume, but less volume of fluid is required than with crystalloids. Albumin is a commonly ordered colloid to treat hypovolemic shock. The disadvantage of colloids is their high cost, and their use over crystalloids is still not well supported by controlled trials.

The patient receiving fluid replacement in the context of shock must be monitored frequently for adequate urinary output, changes in mental status, skin perfusion, and changes in vital signs. Lung sounds are auscultated frequently to detect signs of fluid accumulation.

Often, a central venous line is inserted in order to measure central venous pressure. In addition to physical assessment, the central venous pressure (CVP) helps in monitoring the patient's response to fluid resuscitation. A normal CVP is 2 to 8 mm Hg. Several readings are obtained to determine

a range, and fluid replacement is continued to achieve a CVP of 8 to 12 mm Hg; higher-than-"normal" CVPs readings are desired since ventricles tend to stiffen during shock (Marx et al., 2010).

With newer technologies, catheters can be placed that allow the monitoring of intravascular pressures and venous oxygen levels. Assessment of venous oxygenation (SvO_2, or $ScvO_2$ with a CVP line) is helpful in evaluating the adequacy of intravascular volume, as well as BP, urine output, and base deficit. Hemodynamic monitoring with arterial and pulmonary artery lines may be implemented to allow close monitoring of the patient's perfusion and cardiac status, as well as response to therapy. For additional information about hemodynamic monitoring, see Chapter 55.

Vasoactive Medication Therapy

Vasoactive medications can be used in all forms of shock to improve the patient's hemodynamic stability when fluid therapy alone cannot maintain adequate MAP. Different medications work on different aspects of CO, and specific medications are selected depending on the underlying cause (see Chapter 55, Table 55-8). Although most of the medications have several effects, these medications are used to (1) increase the strength of myocardial contractility, (2) regulate the heart rate, (3) reduce myocardial resistance, and (4) initiate vasoconstriction.

Receptors in the sympathetic nervous system are known as alpha-adrenergic and beta-adrenergic receptors. Beta-adrenergic receptors are further classified as beta-1 and beta-2 adrenergic receptors. When alpha-adrenergic receptors are stimulated, blood vessels constrict in the cardiorespiratory and GI systems, skin, and kidneys. When beta-1 adrenergic receptors are stimulated, heart rate and myocardial contraction increase. When beta-2 adrenergic receptors are stimulated, vasodilation occurs in the heart and skeletal muscles, and the bronchioles relax. The medications used in treating shock consist of various combinations of vasoactive medications to maximize tissue perfusion by stimulating or blocking the alpha- and beta-adrenergic receptors.

When vasoactive medications are administered, the nurse must monitor vital signs frequently (at least every 15 minutes until stable, or more often if indicated). Vasoactive medications should be administered through a central venous line, because infiltration and extravasation of some vasoactive medications can cause tissue necrosis and sloughing. An IV pump must be used to ensure that the medications are delivered safely and accurately. Often, invasive monitoring using an arterial line is used to titrate medications accurately. Individual medication dosages are usually titrated by the nurse, who adjusts drip rates based on the prescribed dose and the patient's response. Dosages are changed to maintain the MAP at a physiologic level that ensures adequate tissue perfusion (usually >65 mm Hg). Vasoactive medications should be tapered when possible, and the patient should be weaned from medication with frequent monitoring of BP (at least every 15 minutes).

Nutritional Support

Nutritional support is an important aspect of care for patients with shock. Increased metabolic rates during shock increase energy requirements and therefore caloric requirements. The release of catecholamines early in the shock continuum causes depletion of glycogen stores in about 8 to 10 hours. Nutritional energy requirements are then met by breaking down lean body mass. In this catabolic process, skeletal muscle mass is broken down even when the patient has large stores of fat or adipose tissue. Loss of skeletal muscle greatly prolongs the patient's recovery time. Parenteral or enteral nutritional support should be initiated as soon as possible, with some form of enteral nutrition always administered. The integrity of the GI system depends on direct exposure to nutrients. Stress ulcers occur frequently in acutely ill patients because of the compromised blood supply to the GI tract. Therefore, antacids (eg, Carafate), H_2 blockers (eg, famotidine [Pepcid], ranitidine [Zantac]), and/or proton pump inhibitors (eg, lansoprazole [Prevacid]) are prescribed to prevent ulcer formation by inhibiting gastric acid secretion or increasing gastric pH.

Respiratory Support

Oxygen is administered to increase the amount of oxygen carried by available hemoglobin in the blood. A patient who is confused may feel apprehensive with an oxygen mask or cannula in place, and frequent explanations about the need for the mask may reduce some of the patient's fear and anxiety. Frequent assessment of the respiratory status is warranted since many patients with severe shock will require ventilatory support. Continuous oxygen saturation monitoring is expected.

TYPES OF SHOCK

HYPOVOLEMIC SHOCK

Hypovolemic shock, the most common type of shock, is characterized by a decreased intravascular volume. Intracellular fluid accounts for about two-thirds of the total body water. The remaining one-third of fluid is in the extracellular space that in divided into two compartments: intravascular space (IVS, inside blood vessels) or interstitial space (ISS, surrounding tissues). Approximately three-quarters of the extracellular fluid is in the ISS, and the remaining one-quarter is in the IVS. Thus, the normal intravascular volume is 4 to 6 L. Hypovolemic shock occurs when there is a reduction in intravascular volume by 15% to 25%, which represents a loss of 750 to 1,500 mL of blood in a 70-kg (154-lb) person.

Pathophysiology

Hypovolemic shock can be caused by sudden fluid losses, such as hemorrhage, or by a gradual deficit in I & O, such as

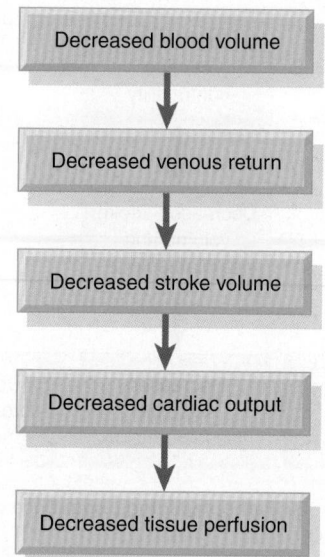

FIGURE 54-2 Pathophysiologic sequence of events in hypovolemic shock.

dehydration. See Chapter 56, Table 56-1 for further information on hemorrhagic shock. Figure 54-2 depicts the sequence of events in hypovolemic shock. Box 54-3 discusses risk factors for hypovolemic shock.

Medical Management

Major goals in the treatment of hypovolemic shock are (1) to restore intravascular volume, (2) to reverse the sequence of events leading to inadequate tissue perfusion, and (3) to correct the underlying cause of the fluid loss as quickly as possible. Depending on the severity of shock and the patient's condition, it is likely that efforts will be made to address all three goals simultaneously.

If the patient is hemorrhaging, efforts are made to stop the bleeding. This may involve applying pressure to the bleeding

BOX 54-3

Risk Factors for Hypovolemic Shock

External: Fluid losses:
- Trauma
- Surgery
- Vomiting
- Diarrhea
- Diuresis
- Diabetes insipidus
- NPO status

Internal: Fluid shifts:
- Hemorrhage
- Burns
- Ascites
- Peritonitis
- Dehydration

site or a surgery or procedure to stop internal bleeding. If the cause of the hypovolemia is diarrhea or vomiting, medications to treat diarrhea and vomiting are administered while efforts are made to identify and treat the cause. In elderly patients, dehydration is a common cause of hypovolemia.

If the underlying cause of the hypovolemia is dehydration, medications are also administered to reverse the cause of the dehydration. For example, insulin is administered if dehydration is secondary to hyperglycemia, and desmopressin (DDAVP) is administered for diabetes insipidus.

Beyond reversing the primary cause of the decreased intravascular volume, fluid replacement (also referred to as fluid resuscitation) is of primary concern. At least two large-gauge IV lines are inserted to establish access for fluid administration. Two IV lines allow simultaneous administration of fluid, medications, and blood component therapy if required. Because the goal of the fluid replacement is to restore intravascular volume, it is necessary to administer fluids that will remain in the intravascular compartment, to avoid fluid shifts from the intravascular compartment into the intracellular or interstitial compartment. Blood products, which are also colloids, may need to be administered, particularly if the cause of the hypovolemic shock is hemorrhage. Packed red blood cells are administered to replenish the patient's oxygen-carrying capacity, in conjunction with other fluids that will expand volume. Plasma and platelet transfusions can help with fluid resuscitation and also treat other underlying problems. The need for transfusions is based on the patient's individual perfusion needs, which are determined by vital signs, blood gas values, and clinical appearance rather than an arbitrary laboratory value. An area of active research is the development of synthetic forms of blood (ie, compounds capable of carrying oxygen in the same way that blood does) as potential alternatives to blood component therapy. Risks inherent to administering blood include the possibility of a transfusion reaction.

Commonly, positioning the patient head down, known as the *Trendelenburg position*, has been thought to increase blood flow to vital organs by increasing preload. This practice has not been found to be supported by evidence, and in fact may worsen pulmonary gas exchange and risk of aspiration (Rivers & Amponsah, 2010). An alternative is to elevate the patient's legs slightly to improve cerebral circulation and promote venous return to the heart, but this position is contraindicated for patients with head injuries.

Nursing Management

Primary prevention of shock is an essential focus of nursing care. Hypovolemic shock can be prevented in some instances by closely monitoring patients who are at risk for fluid deficits and assisting with fluid replacement before intravascular volume is depleted. In other circumstances, nursing care focuses on assisting with treatment targeted at the cause of the shock and restoring intravascular volume.

General nursing measures include ensuring safe administration of prescribed fluids and medications and documenting their administration and effects. Another important nursing role is monitoring for signs of complications and side effects of treatment and reporting these signs early in treatment.

Administering blood transfusions safely is a vital nursing role. In emergency situations, it is important to acquire blood specimens quickly, to obtain a baseline complete blood count, and to type and cross-match the blood in anticipation of blood transfusions. A patient who receives a transfusion of blood products must be monitored closely for adverse effects (see Chapter 20).

Fluid replacement complications can occur, often when large volumes are administered rapidly. Therefore, the nurse monitors the patient closely for cardiovascular overload and edema. The risk of these complications is increased in the elderly and in patients with preexisting cardiac disease. Hemodynamic pressure, vital signs, ABGs, serum lactate levels, hemoglobin and hematocrit levels, and fluid I & O are among the parameters monitored. Temperature should also be monitored closely to ensure that rapid fluid resuscitation does not precipitate hypothermia. IV fluids may need to be warmed during the administration of large volumes. Physical assessment focuses on observing the jugular veins for distention and monitoring CVP. CVP is typically low in hypovolemic shock; it increases with effective treatment, and is significantly increased with fluid overload and heart failure. The nurse must monitor cardiac and respiratory status closely and report changes in BP, pulse pressure, heart rate and rhythm, and lung sounds to the provider.

CARDIOGENIC SHOCK

Cardiogenic shock occurs when the heart's ability to contract and to pump blood is impaired and the supply of oxygen is inadequate for the heart and tissues. Cardiogenic shock is seen most often in patients with myocardial infarction (MI). Other causes of cardiogenic shock are related to conditions that stress the myocardium (eg, severe hypoxemia, acidosis, hypoglycemia, and hypocalcemia), as well as in conditions that result in ineffective myocardial function (eg, cardiomyopathies, valvular damage, and arrhythmias).

Pathophysiology

In cardiogenic shock, CO, which is a function of stroke volume and heart rate, is compromised. When stroke volume and heart rate decrease or become erratic, BP falls, and systemic tissue perfusion is compromised (urine output decreases, skin becomes cold and clammy, mental status changes, anxiety is obvious, capillary refill is delayed). Blood supply for the heart muscle itself is inadequate, resulting in further decreases in CO. This can occur rapidly or over a period of days. Patients in cardiogenic shock may experience the

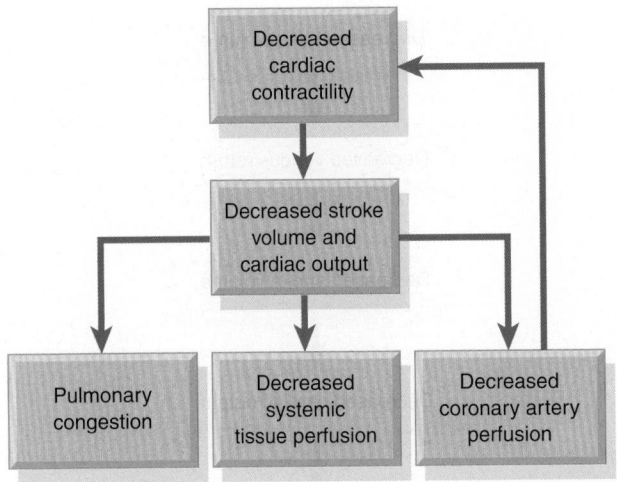

FIGURE 54-3 Pathophysiologic sequence of events in cardiogenic shock.

pain of angina and develop arrhythmias and hemodynamic instability. Figure 54-3 depicts the pathophysiology of cardiogenic shock.

NURSING ALERT

In the case of heart failure resulting in cardiogenic shock, the nurse assesses for jugular vein distention (JVD), rales, shortness of breath, and S3 gallop.

Medical Management

The goals of management in cardiogenic shock are (1) to limit further myocardial damage and preserve the healthy myocardium and (2) to improve the cardiac function by increasing cardiac contractility, decreasing ventricular afterload, or both. In general, these goals are achieved by increasing oxygen supply to the heart muscle while reducing oxygen demands.

As with all forms of shock, the underlying cause of cardiogenic shock must be corrected. It is necessary first to treat the oxygenation needs of the heart muscle to ensure its continued ability to pump blood to other organs. In the case of cardiogenic shock due to ischemia or infarction, the patient may require thrombolytic therapy, angioplasty, coronary artery bypass graft surgery, intra-aortic balloon pump therapy, or some combination of these treatments. General interventions for cardiogenic shock include supplemental oxygen, controlling chest pain, providing selected fluid support, administering vasoactive medications, controlling heart rate with medication or pacemaker, and using a mechanical assist device if needed. Serial laboratory markers for ventricular dysfunction (eg, BNP) and cardiac enzyme levels (ie, CK-MB and troponin-I) are measured, serial 12-lead ECGs are obtained, and frequently an echocardiogram is ordered to assess the degree of myocardial damage or dysfunction.

Pharmacologic Therapy
Oxygen
In the early stages of shock, supplemental oxygen is administered by nasal cannula at a sufficient rate to achieve an oxygen saturation exceeding 90%. Monitoring of ABG values and pulse oximetry values helps determine whether the patient requires a more aggressive method of oxygen delivery.

Analgesia
If a patient experiences chest pain, an IV analgesic (commonly morphine sulfate) is administered for pain relief. In addition to relieving pain, morphine dilates the blood vessels. This reduces the workload of the heart by both decreasing the cardiac filling pressure (preload) and reducing the pressure against which the heart muscle has to eject blood (afterload).

Antiplatelet Agents and Beta Blockers
Antiplatelet agents, such as aspirin, should be given in the setting of acute MI. In addition, a beta blocker is used to decrease workload of the heart and preserve cardiac muscle. The use of these medications in the setting of cardiogenic shock can be complicated since beta blockers will decrease BP. See Chapter 14 for acute treatment of chest pain and MI.

Vasoactive Medications
Vasoactive medication therapy consists of multiple pharmacologic strategies to restore and maintain adequate CO. In cardiogenic shock, the aims of vasoactive medication therapy are to improve cardiac contractility, optimize preload and afterload, reduce myocardial oxygen demand, and stabilize heart rate and rhythm. Medications commonly used to treat cardiogenic shock include dobutamine, dopamine, and nitroglycerin. See Table 55-9 for a review of common vasoactive medications.

DRUG ALERT
The nurse is vigilant in observing the patient's response to vasoactive agents because of the potential of worsening myocardial ischemia by increasing cardiac work.

Dobutamine (Dobutrex) produces inotropic effects by stimulating myocardial beta receptors, increasing the strength of myocardial activity and improving CO. Myocardial alpha-adrenergic receptors are also stimulated, resulting in decreased pulmonary and systemic vascular resistance (decreased afterload). Dobutamine enhances the strength of cardiac contraction, improving stroke volume ejection and overall CO.

Dopamine (Intropin) is a sympathomimetic agent. It may be used with dobutamine and nitroglycerin to improve tissue perfusion. Sympathomimetic agents must be used with caution in cardiogenic shock, since they increase myocardial oxygen demand and can worsen failure. Also, in severe metabolic acidosis, which occurs in the later stages of shock, the effectiveness of dopamine is diminished.

IV nitroglycerin (Tridil) in low doses acts as a venous vasodilator and therefore reduces preload. At higher doses, nitroglycerin causes arterial vasodilation and therefore reduces afterload as well. These actions, in combination with dobutamine, increase CO while minimizing cardiac workload. In addition, vasodilation enhances blood flow to the myocardium, improving oxygen delivery to the weakened heart muscle.

Additional vasoactive agents that may be used in managing cardiogenic shock include norepinephrine (Levophed), epinephrine (Adrenalin), milrinone (Primacor), amrinone (Inocor), vasopressin (Pitressin), and phenylephrine (Neo-Synephrine). Each of these medications stimulates different receptors of the sympathetic nervous system. A combination of these medications may be prescribed, depending on the patient's response to treatment. All vasoactive medications have adverse effects, making specific medications more useful than others at different stages of shock.

DRUG ALERT
Vasoactive medications should never be stopped abruptly, because this could cause severe hemodynamic instability, perpetuating the shock state.

Diuretics
Diuretics such as furosemide (Lasix) may be administered to reduce the workload of the heart by reducing fluid accumulation. Diuretics must be used cautiously since they can lead to hypovolemia. In addition, aggressive diuresis can lead to metabolic alkalosis, often referred to as a *contraction alkalosis*. The use of diuretics can also lead to electrolyte abnormalities, the most common of which is hypokalemia.

Antiarrhythmic Medications
Multiple factors, such as hypoxemia, electrolyte imbalances, and acid–base imbalances, contribute to serious cardiac arrhythmias in all patients with shock. In addition, as a compensatory response to decreased CO and BP, the heart rate increases beyond normal limits. This impedes CO further by shortening diastole and thereby decreasing the time for ventricular filling. Consequently, antiarrhythmic medications are required to stabilize the heart rate. For a full discussion of cardiac arrhythmias, as well as commonly prescribed medications, see Chapter 17.

Fluid Status
Appropriate fluid administration is also necessary in the treatment of cardiogenic shock. Administration of fluids must be monitored closely to detect signs of fluid overload. Incremental IV fluid boluses are cautiously administered to determine optimal filling pressures for improving CO. Nurses should use caution when administering fluids rapidly, because rapid fluid administration in patients with cardiac failure may result in acute pulmonary edema.

Mechanical Assistive Devices
If CO does not improve despite supplemental oxygen, vasoactive medications, and fluid boluses, mechanical assistive

devices can sometimes be used temporarily to improve the heart's ability to pump. Intra-aortic balloon counterpulsation or left and right ventricular assist devices and total temporary artificial hearts are means of providing temporary circulatory assistance and are reviewed in Chapter 55.

Nursing Management

Preventing Cardiogenic Shock

In many circumstances, identifying at-risk patients early, promoting adequate perfusion of the heart muscle, and decreasing cardiac workload can prevent cardiogenic shock. This can be accomplished by conserving the patient's energy, promptly relieving angina, and administering supplemental oxygen, aspirin, and beta blockers. When cardiogenic shock is present, nursing management includes working with other members of the health care team to prevent shock from progressing and to restore adequate cardiac function and tissue perfusion.

Monitoring Hemodynamic Status

A major role of the nurse is monitoring the patient's hemodynamic and cardiac status. Arterial lines and ECG monitoring equipment must be well maintained and functioning properly. The nurse anticipates the medications, IV fluids, and equipment that might be used and is ready to assist in implementing these measures. Changes in hemodynamic, cardiac, pulmonary, and renal status and laboratory values are documented and reported promptly. In addition, adventitious breath sounds, changes in cardiac rhythm, and other abnormal physical assessment findings are reported immediately.

Administering Fluids and Medications

The nurse plays a critical role in the safe and accurate administration of IV fluids and medications. Fluid overload and pulmonary edema are risks because of ineffective cardiac function and accumulation of blood and fluid in the pulmonary tissues. The nurse documents and records medications and treatments that are administered, as well as the patient's response to treatment.

The nurse must be knowledgeable about the desired effects, as well as the side effects, of medications. For example, it is important to monitor the patient for decreased BP after administering morphine or nitroglycerin. Patients receiving thrombolytic therapy must be monitored for bleeding. Arterial and venous puncture sites must be observed for bleeding, and pressure must be applied at the sites if bleeding occurs. Neurologic assessment is essential after the administration of thrombolytic therapy to assess for the potential complication of cerebral hemorrhage associated with the therapy. IV infusions must be observed closely because tissue necrosis and sloughing may occur if vasopressor medications infiltrate the tissues. Urine output, blood urea nitrogen (BUN), and serum creatinine levels are monitored to detect decreased renal function secondary to the effects of cardiogenic shock or its treatment.

Enhancing Safety and Comfort

Throughout care, the nurse must take an active role in safeguarding the patient, enhancing comfort, and reducing anxiety. This includes administering medication to relieve chest pain, preventing infection at the multiple arterial and venous line insertion sites, protecting the skin, and monitoring respiratory and renal function. Proper positioning of the patient promotes effective breathing without decreasing BP and may also increase patient comfort while reducing anxiety.

Brief explanations about procedures that are being performed and the use of comforting touch often provide reassurance to the patient and family. The family is usually anxious and benefits from opportunities to see and talk to the patient. Explanations of treatments and the patient's responses are often comforting to family members.

DISTRIBUTIVE SHOCK

Distributive shock, also sometimes called circulatory shock, occurs when the body's ability to adjust vascular tone is impaired, and thus blood volume is abnormally displaced in the vasculature (eg, when blood volume pools in peripheral blood vessels). The displacement of blood volume causes a relative hypovolemia because not enough blood returns to the heart, which leads to subsequent inadequate tissue perfusion. The vascular tone is determined both by central regulatory mechanisms, as in BP regulation, and by local regulatory mechanisms, as in tissue demands for oxygen and nutrients. Therefore, distributive shock can be caused either by a loss of sympathetic tone or by release of biochemical mediators from cells.

The varied mechanisms leading to the initial vasodilation in distributive shock further subdivide this classification of shock into three types: (1) **septic shock**, (2) **neurogenic shock**, and (3) **anaphylactic shock**. Other causes of distributive shock are rare but include toxic shock syndrome, Addisonian crisis, and myxedema coma. In all types of distributive shock, massive arterial and venous dilation allows blood to pool peripherally. The different types of shock cause variations in the pathophysiologic chain of events. Risk factors for distributive shock are summarized in Box 54-4.

SEPTIC SHOCK

Septic shock, the most common type of distributive shock, is caused by widespread, overwhelming infection in combination with a dysregulated host immune response. Despite the increased sophistication of antibiotic therapy and improved intensive care management, the incidence of septic shock continues to rise. With mortality rates of 25% to 30% for severe septic patients and rates of 40% to 70% for septic

Risk Factors for Distributive Shock

Septic shock:
- Immunosuppression
- Extremes of age (<1 and >65 years)
- Malnourishment
- Chronic illness
- Invasive procedures

Neurogenic shock:
- Spinal cord injury
- Spinal anesthesia
- Depressant action of medications
- Glucose deficiency

Anaphylactic shock:
- Penicillin sensitivity
- Transfusion reaction
- Bee sting allergy
- Latex sensitivity
- Severe allergy to some foods or medications

shock (Stenbit & Serio, 2010), it is the most common cause of death in noncoronary ICUs in the United States. Finding and aggressively treating the source of infection, as well as aggressive cardiopulmonary support, are important determinants of the clinical outcome.

Risk Factors

Nosocomial infections (infections occurring in the hospital) in critically ill patients that may progress to septic shock commonly originate in the lungs and urinary tract, although they can originate anywhere in the body (refer to Table 54-3 for common sites related to sepsis). Additional risk factors that contribute to the growing incidence of septic shock are increased awareness and identification of the condition; the increased number of immunocompromised patients (due to malnutrition, alcoholism, malignancy, diabetes mellitus, and AIDS); the increased use of invasive procedures and indwelling medical devices; the increased number of resistant

TABLE
54-3 Common Sites and Diseases Associated With Sepsis/Systemic Inflammatory Response Syndrome (SIRS)

Organ System	Location	Disease
Respiratory	Upper respiratory tract	Sinusitis
		Mastoiditis
	Lower respiratory tract	Pneumonia
		Lung abscess
		Empyema
Gastrointestinal	Mediastinum	Esophageal rupture/perforation
	Hepatobiliary	Hepatic abscess
		Cholangitis
		Cholecystitis
	Intra-abdominal	Intestinal infarction/perforation pancreatitis
		Intra-abdominal/diverticular abscess
Cardiovascular	Mediastinum	Postoperative mediastinitis
	Native or prosthetic cardiac valve	Endocarditis
Genitourinary	Kidney, ureter, and bladder	Perinephric abscess
		Pyelonephritis
		Cystitis
Neurologic	Brain and meninges	Meningitis
		Intracranial abscess
Dermatologic	Traumatic wound, surgical wound, or burn site	Soft tissue abscess
		Necrotizing fasciitis
		Infected decubitus ulcer
		Full and partial thickness burn
Prosthetic	Central/peripheral venous catheter	Catheter infection
	Arterial catheter	
	Ventriculo-peritoneal shunt	
	Dialysis catheter	
	Articular prosthetic device	Infected prosthesis
	Dialysis graft/shunt	
Other	Vascular system	Septic thrombophlebitis

Reprinted with permission from Stenbit, A., & Serio, A. (2010). Sepsis. In R. Irwin, & J. Rippe (Eds.), *Manual of intensive care management* (Chapter 123). Philadelphia: Lippincott Williams & Wilkins.

microorganisms; and the increasingly older population. Elderly patients continue to be at particular risk for sepsis because of decreased physiologic reserves and an aging immune system. The incidence of septic shock can be reduced by carrying out infection control practices, including the use of meticulous aseptic technique, properly cleaning and maintaining equipment, and using thorough hand hygiene techniques.

Pathophysiology

When microorganisms invade body tissues, patients exhibit an immune response. This immune response provokes the activation of biochemical cytokines and mediators associated with an inflammatory response and produces a complex cascade of physiologic events that leads to poor tissue perfusion. Increased capillary permeability, which leads to fluid seeping from the capillaries, and vasodilation are two such effects that interrupt the ability of the body to provide adequate perfusion, oxygen, and nutrients to the tissues and cells. In addition, proinflammatory and anti-inflammatory cytokines released during the inflammatory response activate the coagulation system, which begins to form clots in areas where a clot may or may not be needed, further compromising tissue perfusion. The imbalance of the inflammatory response and the clotting and fibrinolysis cascades are considered critical elements of the devastating physiologic progression that is present in patients with severe sepsis.

Clinical Manifestations and Assessment

Sepsis is an evolving process, with neither clearly definable clinical signs and symptoms nor predictable linear progression. In the past, septic shock has been described as having two phases, a hyperdynamic (warm) and a hypodynamic (cold) phase. Although the division into phases may promote understanding of sepsis, its actual progression into severe sepsis and septic shock is not always easy to recognize clinically. Initially, a hyperdynamic response occurs; it is characterized by a high CO with systemic vasodilation. The BP may remain within normal limits, or the patient may be hypotensive but responsive to fluids. The heart rate increases, progressing to tachycardia. Fever, with warm, flushed skin and bounding pulses, is evident. The respiratory rate is elevated. Urinary output may remain at normal levels or decrease. GI status may be compromised, as evidenced by nausea, vomiting, diarrhea, or decreased bowel sounds. Signs of hypermetabolism include increased serum glucose and insulin resistance. Subtle changes in mental status, such as confusion or agitation, may be present.

As the sepsis progresses, tissues become more underperfused and acidotic, compensation begins to fail, and the patient becomes more hypodynamic. The cardiovascular system also begins to fail, the BP does not respond to vasoactive agents and fluid resuscitation, and signs of end-organ damage are visible (eg, renal failure, pulmonary failure, hepatic

failure). As sepsis progresses to septic shock, the BP drops, and the skin becomes cool and pale. Temperature may be normal or below normal. Heart and respiratory rates remain rapid. Urine output decreases, and multiple organ dysfunction develops.

In an effort to promote recognition and earlier treatment of patients with sepsis, the Society of Critical Care Medicine defined a common set of terms and cues for clinicians (Box 54-5).

Systemic inflammatory response syndrome (SIRS) presents clinically like sepsis. The only difference between SIRS and sepsis is that there is no identifiable source of infection. SIRS stimulates an overwhelming inflammatory

---

BOX 54-5 **Definitions in Sepsis**

Bacteremia: The presence of bacteria in the blood

Infection: The presence of microorganisms that trigger an inflammatory response

Systemic inflammatory response syndrome (SIRS): A syndrome resulting from a *severe clinical insult* that initiates an overwhelming inflammatory response by the body; defined as two or more of the following conditions:

- Temperature >38.5°C or <35.0°C
- Heart rate of >90 bpm
- Respiratory rate of >20 breaths/min or $PaCO_2$ of <32 mm Hg
- White blood cell count of >12,000 cells/mL, <4,000 cells/mL, or >10% immature (band) forms

Sepsis: A systemic response to *infection;* may occur after a burn, surgery, or serious illness and is defined as the presence of SIRS, plus the presence of an infectious source (either by documented culture or by visualizing focal infection)

Severe sepsis: Defined as sepsis, plus at least one of the following signs of organ hypoperfusion:

- Areas of mottled skin
- Capillary refill of >3 seconds
- Decreased urinary output (<0.5 mg/kg for 1 hour)
- Lactate >2 mmol/L
- Abrupt change in mental status
- Platelet count of less than 100,000 or disseminated intravascular coagulation (DIC)
- Acute lung injury or acute respiratory distress syndrome
- Cardiac dysfunction

Septic shock: Shock associated with sepsis; defined as severe sepsis, plus one of the following:

- Mean arterial pressure (MAP) of <60 after fluid resuscitation
- Need for vasoactive medication in order to maintain MAP of >60

Adapted from Annane, D., & Cavaillon, J. M. (2005). Septic shock. *Lancet, 365*(9453), 63–78; and from Sommers, M. S. (2003). The cellular basis of septic shock. *Critical Care Nursing Clinics of North America, 15*(1), 13–26.

immunologic and hormonal response similar to that seen in septic patients. Any overwhelming insult can stimulate SIRS and may progress to sepsis. Therefore, despite an absence of infection, antibiotic agents may still be administered because of the possibility of unrecognized infection. Additional therapies directed to support patients with SIRS are similar to those for sepsis. If the inflammatory process progresses, septic shock may develop.

Medical Management

Current treatment of septic shock involves *identification and elimination of the cause of infection and aggressive cardiopulmonary support.* Specimens of blood, sputum, urine, and wound drainage are collected for culture using aseptic technique. Sometimes tips of central lines are cultured, although recently that practice has been called into question (Smith, Ptak, Dugan et al., 2006). Any potential routes of infection must be eliminated. IV lines are removed and reinserted at other body sites. If possible, urinary catheters are removed or replaced. Any abscesses are drained, and necrotic areas are débrided.

Fluid replacement must be instituted to correct the hypovolemia that results from the incompetent vasculature and the inflammatory response. Crystalloids, colloids, and blood products may be administered to increase intravascular volume. Recently, there has been a focus on early goal-directed therapy, first described by Rivers et al. (2001). This approach involves using CVP, MAP, urinary output, and SvO$_2$ to guide therapy. The patient's response to treatment are closely monitored, and resuscitation is continued until CVP is greater than 8, MAP is greater than 65 mmHg, urine output is 0.5 mL/kg/hour or more, and SvO$_2$ is greater than 70%. This approach is associated with a decreased mortality and should be considered standard of care in the management of septic shock.

NURSING ALERT
SvO$_2$ is an abbreviation for venous oxygen saturation. Tissue hypoxia is determined by the SvO$_2$ or the mixed venous oxygen level, which is obtained either from a special pulmonary artery catheter that has fiber optics capable of calculating the oxygen saturation of hemoglobin or by analyzing a venous blood gas sample obtained from a central venous catheter. It reflects the amount of oxygen in venous blood, therefore the amount of oxygen that has been extracted or used from the body. Normal SvO$_2$ values range from 60% to 80% and indicate adequate tissue perfusion. When the SvO$_2$ drops, it reflects the increased consumption of oxygen and the need for intervention.

Pharmacologic Therapy
Antibiotics
Before antibiotic therapy is initiated, it is important that all cultures be obtained. The nurse anticipates the need for

blood, sputum, urine, and wound cultures, and, depending on the site of the expected infection, additional cultures may be obtained from the cerebrospinal fluid (in the case of suspected meningitis) or pleural space (if empyema is suspected). If the infecting organism is unknown, empiric broad-spectrum antibiotics are started. When culture and sensitivity reports become available, the antibiotic agents can be changed to those that are more specific to the infecting organism and less toxic to the patient.

Glucocorticoids
Glucocorticoids have been used in the treatment of septic shock with varying effect for decades. The general concept is that, since septic shock represents a significant physiologic stress, dysfunction of the hypothalamic–pituitary–adrenal axis may be one factor that leads to increased mortality. Several studies have attempted to investigate the effect of administering steroids to septic patients. Drawbacks to steroid administration include increased infection rate, worsening glycemic control, and impaired wound healing. A recent literature review suggests that the administration of hydrocortisone to patients with severe sepsis, whose systolic BP remains inadequate even after vasopressor support, might be beneficial (Annane, Bellissant, Bollaert et al., 2009).

Nutritional Therapy and Glycemic Control

Aggressive nutritional supplementation is critical in the management of septic shock, because malnutrition further impairs the patient's compensatory mechanisms. Nutritional supplementation should be initiated within the first 24 to 48 hours after ICU admission (McClave, Martindale, Vanek et al., 2009). Enteral feeding, rather than parental nutrition, is associated with improved outcomes, although reasons for this remain unclear. Evidence is particularly strong for enteral nutrition in surgical patients who are critically ill. As with all critically ill patients, glycemic control has been shown to reduce mortality, and nurses should be aggressively targeting a blood sugar level of 140 to 180 mg/dL.

Nursing Management

Nurses caring for patients in any setting must keep in mind the risks of sepsis and the high mortality rate associated with sepsis, severe sepsis, and septic shock. All invasive procedures must be carried out with aseptic technique after careful hand hygiene. In addition, IV lines, arterial and venous puncture sites, surgical incisions, traumatic wounds, urinary catheters, and pressure ulcers must be monitored for signs of infection in all patients. Nurses should identify patients who are at particular risk for sepsis and septic shock (ie, elderly and immunosuppressed patients and those with extensive trauma, burns, or diabetes), keeping in mind that these high-risk patients may not develop typical or classic signs of infection and sepsis. For

example, confusion may be the first sign of infection and sepsis in elderly patients.

Monitoring and constant reassessment are primary nursing tasks when caring for a patient with septic shock. Vital signs, hemodynamics (CVP, SvO_2, SVR, CO), urinary output, mental status, and physical assessment findings must be reported accurately and in a timely fashion, so that interventions can be instituted. When caring for a patient with septic shock, the nurse collaborates with other members of the health care team to identify the site and source of sepsis and the specific organisms involved. Appropriate specimens for culture and sensitivity are often obtained by the nurse.

Elevated body temperature (hyperthermia) is common with sepsis and raises the patient's metabolic rate and oxygen consumption. Fever is one of the body's natural mechanisms for fighting infections. Therefore, elevated temperatures may not be treated unless they reach dangerous levels (>40°C [104°F]) or unless the patient is uncomfortable. Efforts may be made to reduce the temperature by administering acetaminophen or applying a hypothermia blanket. During these therapies, the nurse monitors the patient closely for shivering, which increases oxygen consumption. Efforts to increase comfort are important if the patient experiences fever, chills, or shivering.

The nurse administers prescribed IV fluids and medications, including antibiotic agents and vasoactive medications, to restore vascular volume. Because of decreased perfusion to the kidneys and liver, serum concentrations of antibiotic agents that are normally cleared by these organs may increase and produce toxic effects. Therefore, the nurse monitors blood levels (antibiotic agent, BUN, creatinine, white blood cell count, hemoglobin, hematocrit, platelet levels, coagulation studies) and reports changes to the provider. Daily weights and close monitoring of serum prealbumin levels help determine the patient's protein requirements.

NEUROGENIC SHOCK

Pathophysiology

In neurogenic shock, vasodilation occurs as a result of a loss of balance between parasympathetic and sympathetic stimulation. Sympathetic stimulation causes vascular smooth muscle to constrict, and parasympathetic stimulation causes the vascular smooth muscle to relax or dilate. The patient experiences a predominant parasympathetic stimulation that causes vasodilation lasting for an extended period. However, blood volume is adequate, but because the vasculature is dilated, the blood volume is displaced, producing a hypotensive (low BP) state (see Box 54-1). Thus, this is a situation where blood volume is stable, but the drastic dilatation of the vasculature causes a relative hypovolemia. The overriding parasympathetic stimulation that occurs with neurogenic shock causes a severe decrease in the patient's systemic vascular resistance and sometimes bradycardia. Inadequate BP results in the insufficient perfusion of tissues and cells that is common to all shock states.

Neurogenic shock can be caused by spinal cord injury (commonly above the level of T6), spinal anesthesia, or nervous system damage. It may also result from the depressant action of medications or from lack of glucose (eg, insulin reaction or shock). Neurogenic shock may have a prolonged course (spinal cord injury) or a short one (syncope or fainting). Normally, during states of stress, the sympathetic stimulation causes the BP and heart rate to increase. In neurogenic shock, the sympathetic system is not able to respond to body stressors.

Clinical Manifestations and Assessment

The clinical characteristics of neurogenic shock are signs of parasympathetic stimulation. It is characterized by dry, warm skin rather than the cool, moist skin seen in hypovolemic shock. Another characteristic is hypotension with bradycardia, rather than the tachycardia that characterizes other forms of shock.

Medical Management

Treatment of neurogenic shock involves restoring sympathetic tone, either through the stabilization of a spinal cord injury or, in the instance of spinal anesthesia, by positioning the patient properly. Specific treatment depends on cause of the shock. Further discussion of management of patients with a spinal cord injury is presented in Chapter 45. If hypoglycemia (insulin shock) is the cause, glucose is rapidly administered. Hypoglycemia and the insulin reaction are described further in Chapter 30.

Nursing Management

In suspected spinal cord injury, neurogenic shock may be prevented by carefully immobilizing the patient to prevent further damage to the spinal cord. The nurse is aware that orthostatic hypotension caused by loss of vasomotor tone below the level of the spinal cord lesion can occur with position changes. Even slightly raising the head of the bed for a new tetraplegic patient can result in a drastic hypotension (Hickey, 2009).

Nursing interventions are directed toward supporting cardiovascular and neurologic function until the usually transient episode of neurogenic shock resolves. Applying elastic compression stockings and elevating the foot of the bed may minimize pooling of blood in the legs. Pooled blood increases the risk for thrombus formation. Therefore, the nurse must check the patient daily for any lower-extremity pain, redness, tenderness, unilateral edema, and warmth of the calves. If the patient complains of pain, and objective assessment of the calf is suspicious, the patient should be evaluated for deep vein thrombosis. Administration of

heparin or low-molecular-weight heparin (Lovenox) as prescribed, application of elastic compression stockings, or use of pneumatic compression of the legs may prevent thrombus formation. Passive range of motion of the immobile extremities also helps promote circulation.

A patient who has experienced a spinal cord injury may not report pain caused by internal injuries. Therefore, in the immediate postinjury period, the nurse must monitor the patient closely for signs of internal bleeding that could lead to hypovolemic shock. In hemorrhagic shock, the nurse is aware that tachycardia will be present, versus bradycardia with neurogenic shock.

ANAPHYLACTIC SHOCK

Anaphylactic shock occurs rapidly and is life-threatening. Because anaphylactic shock occurs in patients already exposed to an antigen and who have developed antibodies to it, it can sometimes be prevented. Patients with known allergies should understand the consequences of subsequent exposure to the antigen and should wear medical identification that lists their sensitivities. This could prevent inadvertent administration of a medication that would lead to anaphylactic shock. In addition, patients and families need instruction about emergency use of medications for treatment of anaphylaxis.

Pathophysiology

Anaphylactic shock is caused by a severe allergic reaction when patients who have already produced antibodies to a foreign substance (antigen) develop a systemic antigen–antibody reaction. This reaction provokes mast cells to release potent vasoactive substances, such as histamine or bradykinin, causing widespread vasodilation, capillary permeability, and potentially catastrophic vascular collapse. An equally important feature of anaphylactic shock is the onset of severe bronchospasm, which causes airway compromise (stridor, wheezing, shortness of breath) and urticaria. A delayed recurrence of the reaction, without reexposure to the allergen, can sometimes occur. This has been termed a *biphasic reaction* and most commonly occurs 8 to 10 hours after the first symptoms.

Medical Management

Treatment of anaphylactic shock requires removing the causative antigen (eg, discontinuing an antibiotic agent), administering medications that restore vascular tone, and providing emergency support of basic life functions. Epinephrine, usually given intramuscularly, is given for its vasoconstrictive action as well its effect of reducing bronchospasm. Diphenhydramine (Benadryl), given intramuscularly or intravenously, is administered to reverse the effects of histamine, thereby reducing capillary permeability. Nebulized medications, such as albuterol (Proventil), may also be given to

reverse histamine-induced bronchospasm. Sometimes systemic glucocorticoids are used to prevent a rebound, biphasic reaction, although this practice has not been well studied (Tole & Lieberman, 2007).

If cardiac arrest and respiratory arrest are imminent or have occurred, cardiopulmonary resuscitation is performed. Endotracheal intubation or tracheotomy may be necessary to establish an airway. IV lines are inserted to provide access for administering fluids and medications. Anaphylaxis and specific chemical mediators are discussed further in Chapter 38.

Nursing Management

The nurse plays an important role in preventing anaphylactic shock. The nurse must assess all patients for allergies or previous reactions to antigens (eg, medications, blood products, foods, contrast agents, latex) and communicate the existence of these allergies or reactions to others. In addition, the nurse assesses the patient's understanding of previous reactions and the steps taken by the patient and family to prevent further exposure to antigens. When new allergies are identified, the nurse advises the patient to wear or carry identification that names the specific allergen or antigen.

When administering any new medication, the nurse observes all patients for allergic reactions. This is especially important with IV medications. Allergy to penicillin is one of the most common causes of anaphylactic shock. Patients who have a penicillin allergy may also develop an allergy to similar medications. For example, they may react to cefazolin sodium (Ancef) because it has a similar antimicrobial action of attaching to the penicillin-binding proteins found on the walls of infectious organisms. Previous adverse drug reactions increase the risk that the patient will develop an undesirable reaction to a new medication. If the patient reports an allergy to a medication, the nurse must be aware of the risks involved in the administration of similar medications.

In the hospital and outpatient diagnostic testing sites, the nurse must identify patients who are at risk for anaphylactic reactions to the contrast agents (radiopaque, dye-like substances that may contain iodine) that are used for diagnostic tests. These include patients with a known allergy to iodine or fish and those who have had previous allergic reactions to contrast agents. This information must be conveyed to the staff at the diagnostic testing site, including radiology staff.

The nurse must be knowledgeable about the clinical signs of anaphylaxis, must take immediate action if signs and symptoms occur, and must be prepared to begin cardiopulmonary resuscitation if cardiopulmonary arrest occurs. In addition to monitoring the patient's response to treatment, the nurse assists with intubation if needed, monitors the hemodynamic status, ensures IV access for administration of medications, administers prescribed medications and fluids, and documents treatments and their effects.

Community health and home care nurses who administer medications, including antibiotic agents, in the patient's home or other settings, must be prepared to administer epinephrine subcutaneously or intramuscularly in the event of an anaphylactic reaction.

After recovery from anaphylaxis, the patient and family require an explanation of the event. Furthermore, the nurse provides instruction and counseling about avoiding future exposure to antigens and administering emergency medications to treat anaphylaxis.

OBSTRUCTIVE SHOCK

Obstructive shock is caused by a physical obstruction to blood flow, either in the heart or major blood vessels. This causes a decrease in CO and thus a decrease in tissue perfusion. Common causes of obstructive shock include cardiac tamponade, tension pneumothorax, and pulmonary embolism (PE). Obstructive shock is common in the setting of trauma.

Pathophysiology

In the case of tension pneumothorax or hemothorax, air or blood has entered the pleural space and caused a restriction in lung expansion. If enough air is trapped, then eventually pressure builds up and compresses the vessels and myocardium. This compression reduces preload and increases afterload, in addition to restricting the expansion of the myocardium during filling. Clinical presentation may include jugular vein distention, crepitus, dyspnea, chest pain, tachycardia and tachypnea, tracheal shifting away from the tension pneumothorax, and decreased breath sounds on the affected side. Tension pneumothorax is common in trauma but can also develop spontaneously or as a complication from a procedure such as central line placement. Patients who are mechanically ventilated are at higher risk of developing a clinically significant pneumothorax due to increased ventilatory pressures.

Cardiac tamponade results from excessive blood or fluid inside the pericardium, the sac that surrounds the heart. This can result from a traumatic or infectious cause with a resultant restriction on the pumping ability of the heart. Signs and symptoms of cardiac tamponade include narrowing pulse pressure, chest pain, distant or muffled heart sounds, jugular vein distention, hypotension, and tachycardia.

A PE is a clot that gets lodged in the pulmonary vasculature and causes ischemia to the capillary beds. If large enough, the embolism interferes significantly with pulmonary blood flow, which causes blood to back up into the right heart. The heart tries to overcome this by pumping against this obstruction, resulting in increased pulmonary artery pressures. Overall, CO is decreased as the patient goes into right-sided heart failure. Clots that have traveled from the lower extremities cause most PEs. Signs and symptoms of PE include pleuritic chest pain, shortness of breath, tachycardia, and hypoxia (refer to Chapter 10 for more details).

Medical Management

In the case of cardiac tamponade and tension pneumothorax, a procedure done by a qualified clinician should be performed immediately to relieve the obstruction. If the patient is experiencing obstructive shock, then these procedures are done emergently at the bedside. A chest radiograph is often used to diagnose a pneumothorax, although computed tomography (CT) scans and even ultrasound are more sensitive. A chest tube or needle decompression is the primary procedure to relieve tension pneumothorax. Cardiac tamponade is diagnosed similarly, with echocardiography being the most effective. Pericardiocentesis is the treatment for cardiac tamponade and involves inserting a needle into the pericardium to draw off fluid or blood.

The treatment of PE is usually aimed toward preventing clot expansion, although, if the patient is experiencing obstructive shock, then other treatment such as thrombolytic drugs or surgical embolectomy may be considered. Depending on the severity of the PE, mechanical ventilation and hemodynamic support may be needed to stabilize the patient. PE is usually diagnosed using a CT angiogram but other imaging and lab tests can be used as well.

Nursing Management

Because patients with tension pneumothorax and cardiac tamponade who are experiencing obstructive shock will need an emergent procedure, nurses should focus on facilitating that process. This includes collecting and setting up equipment, communicating effectively with staff, and helping gain consent from the patient and/or family. Careful monitoring of the patient prior to, during, and after the procedure is essential. If a chest tube is placed, then a chest drainage system (eg, Pleuravac) will need to be set up, and connected to suction as ordered. The chest tube setup needs to be monitored to ensure that it is functioning correctly and also to record output. A postprocedure chest radiograph will be ordered, and the results should be followed closely.

Nursing care of a patient with a PE that is causing obstructive shock involves monitoring and initiating ventilatory and hemodynamic support similar to other types of shock. A primary function of the nurse in this situation is to facilitate diagnostic testing and imaging and then instituting treatment in a timely manner. Patients with a PE large enough to cause obstructive shock have a very high mortality and often die within an hour of presentation.

Patients who experience obstructive shock are often quite suddenly sick. This affects the entire health care team, as decisions need to be made quickly and the nurse should work hard to maintain a calm environment. Since obstructive shock usually has a sudden onset, families are quite

often surprised when given news about massive PE or other causes of obstructive shock. Having other support personnel in place, such as social work or a chaplain, to provide support is a good idea.

MULTIPLE ORGAN DYSFUNCTION SYNDROME

Multiple organ dysfunction syndrome (MODS) is altered organ function in acutely ill patients that requires medical intervention to support continued organ function. It is another phase in the progression of shock states. The actual incidence of MODS is difficult to determine because it develops with acute illnesses that compromise tissue perfusion. It is defined as severe organ dysfunction of at least two organ systems lasting at least 24 to 48 hours in the setting of sepsis, trauma, burns, or severe inflammatory conditions (Fakhry & Fata, 2010). It is important to note that the definition includes the number of dysfunctional organs and duration. Mortality rates when two organ systems are involved are 40%; and persistent dysfunction (>72 hours) present in three organ systems can result in a mortality risk of 80%.

Pathophysiology

The inflammation, tissue injury, and other sequelae associated with MODS are thought to be caused by an unregulated host response. MODS may result from any form of shock because of inadequate tissue perfusion. As previously described, in shock, all organ systems suffer damage from a lack of adequate perfusion that can result in organ failure.

Clinical Manifestations and Assessment

Various causes of MODS have been identified, including dead or injured tissue, infection, and perfusion deficits.

However, it is not possible as yet to predict which patients will develop MODS, partly because much of the organ damage occurs at the cellular level and therefore cannot be directly observed or measured. The most common types of organ dysfunction seen with MODS are acute renal failure and acute respiratory distress syndrome. Advanced age, malnutrition, and coexisting diseases appear to increase the risk of MODS in acutely ill patients.

Medical Management

Prevention remains the top priority in managing MODS. Elderly patients are at increased risk for MODS because of the lack of physiologic reserve associated with aging and the natural degenerative process, especially immune compromise. Early detection and documentation of initial signs of infection are essential in managing MODS in elderly patients. Subtle changes in mentation and a gradual rise in temperature are early warning signs. Other patients at risk for MODS are those with chronic illness, malnutrition, immunosuppression, or surgical or traumatic wounds.

If preventive measures fail, treatment measures to reverse MODS are aimed at (1) controlling the initiating event, (2) promoting adequate organ perfusion, and (3) providing nutritional support.

Nursing Management

The general plan of nursing care for patients with MODS is the same as that for patients in septic shock. Primary nursing interventions are aimed at supporting the patient and monitoring organ perfusion until primary organ insults are halted. Providing information and support to family members is a critical role of the nurse. It is important that the health care team address end-of-life decisions to ensure that supportive therapies are congruent with the patient's wishes (see Chapter 3).

Chapter Review

Critical Thinking Exercises

1. You administer an antibiotic to a patient before he goes to surgery. The patient's chart states that he has no known drug allergies. After 15 minutes, the patient complains of anxiety, shortness of breath, and chest discomfort. He is flushed and visibly uncomfortable. What are your nursing priorities in providing care to this patient? What clinical signs and symptoms would you look for to determine if he is experiencing anaphylactic shock? What nursing interventions and medical treatments would you anticipate?

2. An elderly woman is admitted to the medical floor for urinary tract infection. You notice that she has become steadily more tachycardic and her urine output has dropped to 50 cc over the last 8 hours. How would you assess this patient for the possibility of sepsis?

3. While working in the emergency department, a victim of a motor vehicle crash comes in by ambulance. His pelvis appears deformed, he is pale, diaphoretic, and his heart rate is 124. What type of shock is this patient most likely in? What led you to that conclusion? Name some interventions that would help this patient.

4. You are taking care of a spinal cord–injured patient in the ICU. His BP has not been responsive to repeated fluid boluses. What type of shock is he mostly likely experiencing? Name some appropriate interventions.

NCLEX-Style Review Questions

1. During a conversation about a patient, a new nurse states "His BP is 92/50, so he can't be in shock." Which of the following indicates that the nurse does not completely understand the symptoms of shock?
   A. Patients can have a near normal BP, yet still have inadequate tissue perfusion.
   B. The cutoff for shock is a systolic pressure of 100 mm Hg.
   C. Shock is determined by mean arterial pressure.
   D. Shock is determined by a heart rate of over 100.

2. A patient with a GI bleed arrives at the emergency department with the following vital signs: Temp 37.4C, HR 112, RR 26, BP 88/44. The nurse recognizes that this patient is most likely experiencing or at risk for which of the following?
   A. Anaphylactic shock
   B. Neurogenic shock
   C. Hypovolemic shock
   D. Septic shock

3. A patient comes in to the urgent care center and states that she has been stung by a bee. She complains of shortness of breath and dizziness. She is pale and loses consciousness in the waiting room. The receptionist has called 911. The nurses recognizes that which of the following medications should be considered first?
   A. Diphenhydramine (Benadryl)
   B. Phenytoin (Dilantin)
   C. Epinephrine IV
   D. Epinephrine IM

4. In early goal-directed therapy, the nurse knows that which of the following parameters are monitored in evaluating effectiveness of therapy?
   A. Heart rate and BP
   B. SvO_2 and O_2 saturation
   C. Base deficit and hematocrit
   D. SvO_2 and CVP

5. A patient develops low BP and tachycardia and is very agitated. The nurse remembers that a central line was placed 3 hours ago. The patient's lung sounds are decreased on one side, and tracheal deviation is present. The nurse realizes that this patient most likely experiencing which type of shock?
   A. Hypovolemic shock
   B. Obstructive shock
   C. Anaphylactic shock
   D. Neurogenic shock

Try these additional resources to enhance your learning and understanding of this chapter:
- thePoint online resource available at **http://thepoint.lww.com/Pellico1e**
- *Handbook for Focus on Adult Health: Medical-Surgical Nursing*
- *Study Guide for Focus on Adult Health: Medical-Surgical Nursing*

References and Selected Readings

References and selected readings associated with this chapter can be found on the website that accompanies the book. Visit http://thepoint.lww.com/Pellico1e to access the references and other additional resources associated with this chapter.

Nursing Management: Critical Care

KELLY S. GRIMSHAW

Learning Objectives

After reading this chapter, you will be able to:

1. Describe the role of the critical care nurse in health care.

2. Describe nursing management of common problems in the critical care environment.

3. Understand common interventions and equipment used in the critical care environment.

The nurse's priority in caring for the critically ill is to prevent harm and provide physical care, education, and emotional support to patients and families in an effort to return them to the highest possible state of health or to help them toward a peaceful death. Nurses are in the unique position of standing with the patient and their family at the center of multisectoral activity. They are at the bedside to act as a care provider and liaison to other health care workers in an effort to coordinate said care. This chapter covers the role of the nurse in critical care and critical care responsibilities and modalities.

THE CRITICAL CARE ENVIRONMENT

Tradition dictates the critical care environment to be a separate place or unit within a hospital building. A rather new paradigm change has emerged since the advent of the Institute for Healthcare Improvement's 100,000 Lives Campaign (The Joint Commission, 2008). This campaign was started with a focus on the Joint Commission mandates for patient safety and improved outcomes. Rapid response teams (RRTs) usually consist of a doctor; a mid-level practitioner, such as a nurse practitioner or physician assistant; a respiratory therapist; and a critical care nurse. These teams were established in hospitals to address the concerns of those patients outside of the intensive care unit (ICU) who were seen as requiring a higher level of care. The RRTs currently in place are able to provide the required higher level of care even when the patient is physically outside of the ICU and awaiting a bed inside the unit, thus making critical care a process and not a place.

NEUROLOGICAL ISSUES

A neurologically healthy person is one who is awake, alert, and oriented, with the ability to respond appropriately to his or her environment without sensory or physical limitations. Whether or not a person is admitted with a specific neurological or neurosurgical diagnosis, other medical problems or interventions may impact his or her neurological status.

TABLE
55-1 **Causes of Altered Mental Status**

	Cause	Example	Possible Nursing Interventions
A	Alcohol	Intoxication Withdrawal	Institute fall precautions Institute seizure precautions Institute ICU sedation protocol
E	Epilepsy	New onset or low medication level	Check medication level Check thyroid level IV fluids and serial sodium levels as ordered
	Endocrine Electrolytes	Hypothyroidism Hypernatremia	
I	Insulin	Hypoglycemia	Check glucose level Administer dextrose as ordered
O	Opiates and other drugs	Narcotic overdose	Administer reversal agent as ordered Airway protection with elevated head of bed
U	Uremia	Acute or chronic renal failure	Follow trends of blood urea nitrogen and creatine levels Ensure patency of dialysis access shunts and IV lines
T	Trauma Temperature	Hypothermia	Serial temperature measurements Blanket warmer Administer warm IV fluids as ordered
I	Infection	Sepsis	Obtain blood and body fluids for culture as ordered Administer antibiotics as ordered Ensure IV lines and Foley catheters have been changed according to hospital policy
P	Poison	Confusion, seizures, coma	Supportive care until poison is neutralized or removed
S	Shock Stroke	Hypovolemia Thrombolic or hemor- rhagic	IV fluids and cardiac pressors to support cerebral blood flow Call for stroke alert if found with acute symptoms
	Space occupying lesion	Tumor	Monitor for signs of increased intracranial pressure (ICP)
	Subarachnoid hemorrhage	Trauma or unmonitored anticoagulation use	Ensure functioning of ICP monitor or ventricular shunts

From Meyers, J. W., Neighbors, M., & Tannehill-Jones, R. (2002). *Principles of pathophysiology and emergency medical care.* Florence, SC: Delmar Cengage Learning.

Altered Level of Consciousness

The causes of altered mental states are numerous and varied, but can be remembered using the pneumonic in Table 55-1. Most ICU patients are at risk for mental status changes due to a myriad of potential factors: previously existing mental illness, increased age, severity of illness and comorbidities, sleep deprivation, and/or medications. Assessing changes in level of consciousness (LOC) alerts the nurse to neurological impairment. A thorough review of possible causes and early intervention can impact a patient's long-term recovery. Refer to Chapter 43 for performing mental status assessment.

Delirium

Delirium is a confused state having a sudden onset lasting hours to days or weeks, characterized by hyperactivity and the potential to be reversible. For example, the patient who quickly becomes confused and agitated while attempting to pull out IV lines and get out of bed is experiencing delirium. These patients require extensive nursing time and often need

someone to be in the room with them at all times to prevent injury. The consequences of delirium cannot be underestimated as it has been found that the condition, although underdiagnosed, is present in up to 70% of adults older than 65 admitted to the ICU; it serves as a marker for brain dysfunction and can lead to more than twice the 6-month mortality rate (Meyer & Hall, 2006).

Pain and Anxiety

Pain and anxiety are interrelated and should be assessed together. For example, chest pain often produces great anxiety.

Pain

Critical care patients can experience pain as a result of their injury or disease, as well as its treatment. It is well known that pain elicits a stress response leading to a catabolic state with increased cardiac workload and an impaired immune response. Care must be taken to ensure that all ICU patients are assessed for any pain, whether or not they are able to communicate their pain level. Prevention and treatment of pain should include

both pharmacological and nonpharmacological methods in collaboration with the patient (if able) and the medical team.

Anxiety

Anxiety has been defined as a subjective sense of unease, dread, or foreboding (Fauci, Braunwald, Kasper et al., 2008). Each hospital also provides scales for objectifying signs and symptoms of anxiety, such as the Richmond Agitation and Sedation Scale (RASS), in order to standardize treatment and minimize its effects. Table 55-2 summarizes assessment of anxiety. An ICU stay has inherent stressors of pain, lack of control over one's environment, impaired communication, and possible fears of imminent death, issues that are all causes for severe anxiety. It is estimated that at least 15% of patients admitted to an ICU suffer from post-traumatic stress disorder (PTSD) as a result of their admission and its prevention is of paramount importance when considering recovery (Myhren, Toien, Ekeberg et al., 2009).

Dependency and Withdrawal

Use and abuse of illegal and legal drugs is pervasive in the United States, with an estimated of 9.4% of the general population and 5% to 30% of the ICU population chronically using and/or dependent on one or more substance (de Wit, Wan, Gill et al., 2007). It is important to realize that

people of all ages and from all walks of life may have a chemical dependence issue and that admission to the ICU will not "cure" this problem. It will more likely be that these patients require more pain and sedation medication to achieve desired effects, such as a prevention of withdrawal and its sequelae.

Depression

Medical literature is filled with articles and studies demonstrating depression or depressed mood as a component of chronic and critical illness. It is also well known that many of the medications prescribed in the ICU, such as beta blockers, can cause depression. Patients admitted on antidepressive agents should continue them with the shortest interruption possible. Patients exhibiting signs of prolonged or exaggerated mood should be evaluated by a psychiatry provider for adequate diagnosis and treatment in order to facilitate the healing process.

Suicidal ideation, and actions taken with the intent to kill oneself, is another issue requiring assessment in the hospital setting. Suicide ranks as the 11th most common cause of death in the United States and the most frequently reported sentinel event in health care institutions (The Joint Commission, 2008). Hospitals are now required to assess patients for suicidal ideation on admission and throughout their stay as it poses such a great risk in these institutions. Admission to the ICU during a hospital stay does not diminish the need to assess patients for any suicidal thoughts or actions.

Sensory and Motor Function

Sensory and motor function (ability to feel and physically react to one's environment) impairment can arise from various sources including spinal cord injury, peripheral vascular disease, and/or medical restraint devices. Alterations in sensation and motion can be viewed on a negative to positive continuum, ranging from insensate to numbness to normal to tingling to pain.

Communication

Communication allows patients and families to interact with health care system professionals in order to satisfy physical, emotional, and spiritual needs. The ICU environment and neurological status deficits can make communication difficult. It is imperative that critical care nurses work to improve communication in order to satisfy the above mentioned needs of their patients and families. Suggested methods may include:

- Asking yes or no questions to which the patient may nod his or her head
- Using a board with preprinted phrases to which he or she can point
- Using language and sign language interpreters (from within the hospital or interpreter services)
- Making a paper and pencil available

TABLE
55-2 Anxiety Assessment

Assessment	Possible Nursing Interventions
Does my patient have anxiety? If so, at what level?	Presume that all ICU patients are at risk for anxiety! Use appropriate scale to assess level of anxiety, such as the Richmond Agitation and Sedation Scale.
Why is the patient experiencing anxiety?	Provide any information for which the lack of information is the cause of anxiety.
What is the most appropriate medication? What is the most appropriate method of delivery?	Administer antianxiety medications if ordered.
What nonpharmacologic methods of reducing anxiety are available?	Allow for visitation and distraction. Allow pet therapy if available and acceptable to patient.
Is our plan for anxiety relief working?	Reevaluate the patient regularly.
Does my patient have anxiety, and is unable to communicate this?	

TABLE
55-3 Sources of Cardiac Disease

Sources of Disease	Example
Cardiac	
Myocardial	Left ventricular hypertrophy, congestive heart failure
Ischemic	Coronary artery disease, myocardial infarction
Conductive	Atrial fibrillation, heart blocks
Valvular	Mitral regurgitation, aortic stenosis
Other	
Infection	Pericarditis, sepsis, viral cardiomyopathy
Neurological system	Spinal shock
Peripheral vascular system	Hypertension, deep vein thrombosis, pulmonary embolism
Respiratory system	Pulmonary hypertension
Renal system	Renal failure leading to fluid overload
Trauma	Cardiac contusion, cardiac tamponade
Hemorrhage	Circulatory collapse

TABLE
55-4 Monitoring the Cardiac Patient

Conditions and Circumstances	Related Monitoring and Interventions
• Patients who are expected to do well, but need additional monitoring in case unexpected complications, such as bleeding, or arrhythmias arise	Vital sign assessment Cardiac monitor Peripheral IV access in case of emergency
• Patients about to leave the critical care environment and who are awake, hemodynamically stable, and able to eat and drink	All of the above
• Patients admitted with singular issues, such as an elective surgery or uncomplicated medical diagnoses, who are expected to recover, but have a cardiac history (Such patients may need IV fluids and medications for a limited time period).	All of the above + IV fluids, IV medications, or minimal blood products
• Patients who have a medical or surgical issue, in which recovery depends on the medical team's provision of more precise monitoring (such as heart failure)	All of the above + Central venous access and/or arterial line access
• Patients who are at risk for complications, or for whom basic monitoring and fluids have failed; patients requiring cardiac pressor support (These patients are often compromised due to sepsis).	All of the above + Vasoactive medications and/or further blood products
• Patients who have an unclear cardiac status, have not responded well to lesser interventions, or have undergone cardiac surgery	All of the above + Pulmonary artery catheterization
• Cardiac failure due to any cause	All of the above + Counterpulsation via intra-aortic balloon pump
• Complete cardiac failure	All of the above + Ventricular assist device

CARDIOVASCULAR ISSUES

Cardiovascular problems can be broadly categorized as those arising from the heart and vascular system and those affecting the heart and arterial and venous systems (Table 55-3). Patients may be admitted to critical care units due to a history of cardiovascular disease requiring careful observation, although not admitted specifically for cardiovascular disease, an active cardiac problem requiring advanced intervention, or another active medical problem affecting their cardiovascular status, such as hemorrhage or sepsis.

Monitoring the Patient

Depending upon the individual patient's condition, different levels of monitoring and intervention will be required. Table 55-4 provides a summary of the different levels of monitoring.

It is important to remember that monitors, invasive lines, and other devices are to assist in confirming or disproving physical examination results and clinical judgments, not in replacing them.

Intravenous Access in the Cardiac Patient

Peripheral Intravenous Access

At a minimum, peripheral IV access should be obtained on all patients in the critical care environment. Peripheral IVs give the health care team access the vascular system in case of emergency, a potential site for blood sampling, and the ability to provide fluids, medications, and nutrition. Contraindications to specific placements (right vs. left side) will include history of mastectomy, arterial-venous shunt placement, peripherally inserted central catheter (PICC) line placement, thrombus, trauma, and other device placements, such as splints and casts. IV lines in the feet are reserved only for emergencies; they are to be removed as soon as possible and never inserted in patients with diabetes. Potential complications include bruising, infection, extravasation of fluids and medications, and air embolus.

An arterial line is a peripheral IV in the arterial system used for frequent blood pressure monitoring when a patient

requires vasoactive medications (such as nitroprusside) and frequent blood sampling. It is not for administration of fluids or medications. Potential complications include ischemia, thrombosis, infiltration, and exsanguination.

Central Intravenous Lines

Central IV lines (Fig. 55-1) are used for a number of reasons, including:

- Failure to obtain or maintain peripheral access
- Complication of peripheral access
- The patient requires numerous access sites or parenteral nutrition
- Treatment failure with IV fluids necessitates the first level of hemodynamic monitoring for central venous pressure (CVP) readings
- The patient requires vasoactive medications that places his or her limb at risk if an infiltrate occurs

The triple lumen catheter is a central line that measures the CVP or the amount of fluid returning to the heart at the level of the right atrium (termed *preload*, see Table 55-5). See Chapter 12 for more information on CVP monitoring.

Pulmonary Artery Catheter

Pulmonary artery catheter (PACs) are used when previous interventions have not yielded the expected outcome (increased urine output with increased IV fluid administration), or when the patient has a complicating factor, such as renal or heart failure or pulmonary hypertension, that makes clinical judgments difficult without additional information.

After decades of its use in practice, there is still no consensus as to whether PACs improve patient outcomes. Without that evidence and because they risk complications such as pneumothorax, cardiac arrhythmias, and pulmonary artery rupture, their use is decreasing. However, they can still be a helpful tool in assisting in the overall evaluation of a patient.

PACs allow the medical and nursing team to monitor, intervene upon, and evaluate:

- Blood volume status
- Blood flow
- Tissue oxygenation

Figure 55-2 illustrates components of the PAC system.

Blood Volume Status

Blood volume status is the amount of blood circulating in the enclosure of the arterial and venous systems. This fluid exerts or creates a pressure that can be monitored to determine preload: The greater the blood volume, the greater the pressure (assuming no confounding variables such as severe hypertension). Using Starling's curve, the volume can be increased to give the heart a greater stretch or potential energy with which to pump blood to the body without causing overstretch and failure. It can be compared to a sling shot pulled back ever farther to throw a stone further and further without stretching the sling to the point of breaking.

A PAC measures and calculates the pressures described in Table 55-6.

It is important to remember that the blood volume measurements describe the total amount of pressure exerted in the vasculature by a particular volume of fluid. They do not describe the components of the blood, such as percentage of red blood cells (hematocrit) or plasma. Specific laboratory values, such as the complete blood count, determine these percentages. The goals of treatment involve restoring and maintaining an adequate blood volume with the right proportions of blood components that best support organ perfusion.

Blood Flow

The right side of the heart pumps blood to the pulmonary system, and the left side pumps blood to itself via the coronary arteries and the rest of the body via the aorta. The PAC measures how the heart is pumping and how the vasculature is receiving or resisting the flow. Table 55-7 on page 1418 describes PAC blood flow measurements.

It is important to remember that these are textbook numbers, and that the 98-lb elderly patient will have different requirements than the 200-lb professional defensive lineman. In order to account for differences in body size, the use of index measurements are used (Table 55-8, p. 1418).

Tissue Oxygenation

The ability of tissues to receive and use oxygen depends upon many variables from physiological disorders and medical procedures to prescribed medications and their interactions. The health care team is responsible for manipulating

TABLE
55-5 Effects of Preload and Afterload on the Heart

Factor	Possible Cause	Effects on Heart
Increased preload	Increased fluid volume Vasoconstriction	Increases stroke volume Increases ventricular work Increases myocardial oxygen requirements
Decreased preload	Hypovolemia Vasodilation	Decreases stroke volume Decreases ventricular work Decreases myocardial oxygen requirements
Increased afterload	Hypovolemia Vasoconstriction	Decreases stroke volume Increases ventricular work Increases myocardial oxygen requirements
Decreased afterload	Vasodilation	Increases stroke volume Decreases ventricular work Decreases myocardial oxygen requirements

From Lippincott Williams & Wilkins. (2010). Understanding the cardiac system. In *Hemodynamic monitoring made incredibly visual* (2nd ed., p. 15). Philadelphia: Lippincott Williams & Wilkins.

(*Text continues on page 1418*)

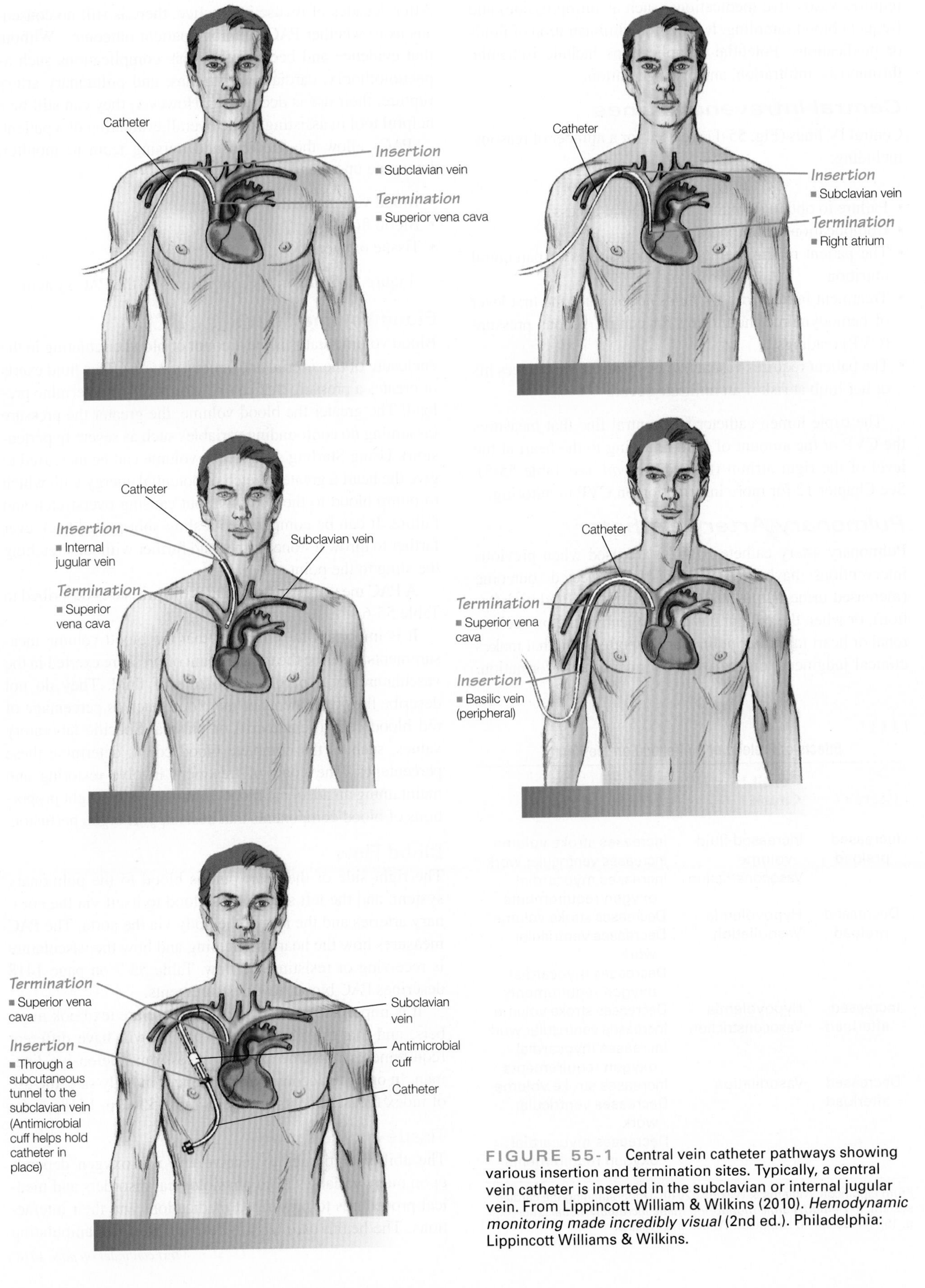

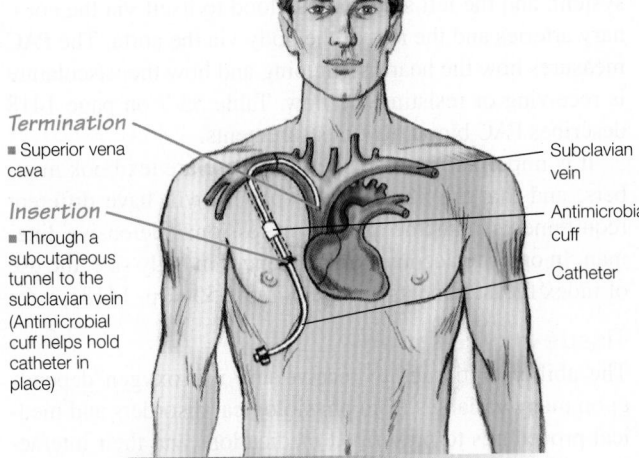

Catheter

Insertion
■ Subclavian vein

Termination
■ Superior vena cava

Catheter

Insertion
■ Subclavian vein

Termination
■ Right atrium

Catheter

Insertion
■ Internal jugular vein

Subclavian vein

Termination
■ Superior vena cava

Catheter

Termination
■ Superior vena cava

Insertion
■ Basilic vein (peripheral)

Termination
■ Superior vena cava

Subclavian vein

Insertion
■ Through a subcutaneous tunnel to the subclavian vein (Antimicrobial cuff helps hold catheter in place)

Antimicrobial cuff

Catheter

FIGURE 55-1 Central vein catheter pathways showing various insertion and termination sites. Typically, a central vein catheter is inserted in the subclavian or internal jugular vein. From Lippincott William & Wilkins (2010). *Hemodynamic monitoring made incredibly visual* (2nd ed.). Philadelphia: Lippincott Williams & Wilkins.

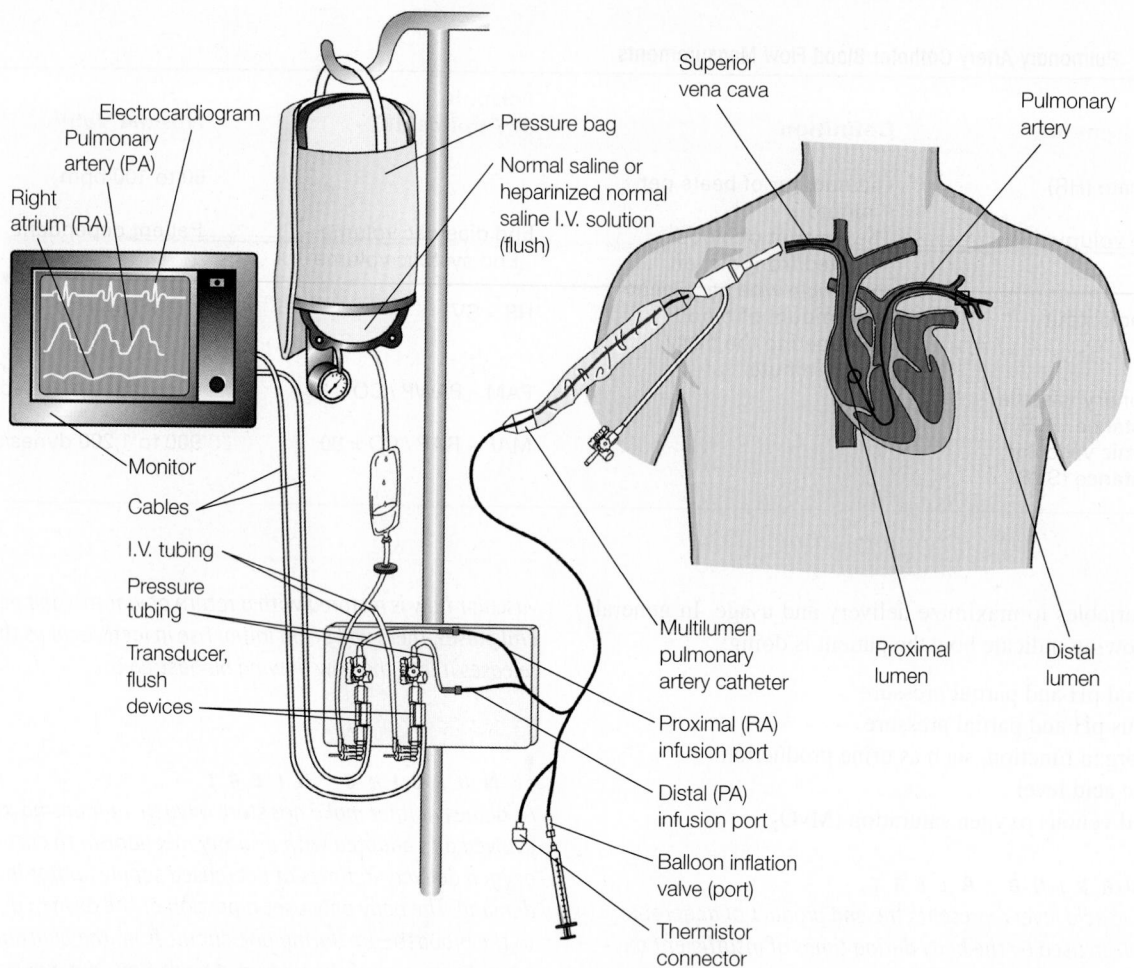

FIGURE 55-2 Components of the pulmonary artery catheter (PAC) monitoring system. From Lippincott William & Wilkins (2010). *Hemodynamic monitoring made incredibly visual* (2nd ed.). Philadelphia: Lippincott Williams & Wilkins.

TABLE
55-6 Pulmonary Artery Catheter Pressure Measurements

Measurement	Definition	Formula (If Applicable)	Normal Value
Mean arterial pressure (MAP)	Average arterial pressure throughout the cardiac cycle	Systolic BP + 2(Diastolic BP) / 3	70 to 105 mm Hg
Right atrial pressure (RAP)	Pressure at the level of the right atrium		2 to 8 mm Hg
Pulmonary artery systolic pressure (PAS)	Pressure in pulmonary artery during systole		20 to 30 mmHg
Pulmonary artery diastolic pressure (PAD)	Pressure in the pulmonary artery during diastole		8 to 15 mm Hg
Mean pulmonary artery pressure (MPAP)	Average pressure in the pulmonary artery throughout the cardiac cycle	PAS + 2(PAD) / 3	10 to 15 mm Hg
Pulmonary artery wedge pressure	The indirect measurement of pressure in the left ventricle at the end of diastole		6 to 12 mm Hg

TABLE
55-7 Pulmonary Artery Catheter Blood Flow Measurements

Measurement	Definition	Formula (If Applicable)	Normal Value
Heart rate (HR)	The number of beats per minute		60 to 100 bpm
Stroke volume (SV)	The amount of blood ejected from the left ventricle with each beat	End diastolic volume – End systolic volume	Patient dependent
Cardiac output	The amount of blood pumped to the body each minute	HR × SV	4 to 8 L/min
Pulmonary vascular resistance (PVR)		PAM – PAWP / CO × 80	50 to 150 dynes/sec/cm^{-5}
Systemic vascular resistance (SVR)		MAP – RAP / CO × 80	900 to 1,200 dynes/sec/cm^{-5}

these variables to maximize delivery and usage. In general, the following indicate how the patient is doing:

- Arterial pH and partial pressure
- Venous pH and partial pressure
- End organ function, such as urine production
- Lactic acid level
- Mixed venous oxygen saturation (MvO_2)

NURSING ALERT
The lactic acid level represents the end product of anaerobic metabolism used by the body during times of insufficient oxygen supply. This level rises with larger and longer oxygen supply deficits. A normal serum lactic acid level in venous blood is 0.5 to 2.2 mEq/L. In the arterial system, the normal lactic acid level is 0.5 to 1.6 mEq/L (Fischbach & Dunning, 2009). Lactic acidosis is considered to be present if the plasma lactate concentration is greater than 4 to 5 mEq/L (Fischbach & Dunning, 2009). However, the nurse may see a rise in the lactic acid level as blood flow oxygen supply is initially restored. Consider a patient with a vascular blockage to their leg during which the leg is not receiving enough oxygen and the extremity is cold and pale without pulses. Lactic acid is building up in the leg, but this lactic acid is not measured because blood flow is blocked. Once

vascular flow is restored with a return of warmth and peripheral pulses, there will be an initial rise in lactic acid as the body releases it into the now flowing bloodstream.

NURSING ALERT
As bodies neither make nor store oxygen, humans have evolved and adapted with a safety mechanism to ensure oxygen delivery in times of decreased supply and/or increased demand. The body only uses a portion of the oxygen delivered to the bloodstream during one circuit from the heart and lungs to the rest of the body and back. Consider a person experiencing cardiopulmonary arrest, when 4 to 6 minutes may pass without a heartbeat before brain damage occurs. This is because there is still oxygen in the blood from his last inspiration. The normal value for MvO_2 is 75%. Thus, the body used only 25% of delivered oxygen during the last lap through the body. A decrease in MvO_2 below 75% means the body is not receiving enough oxygen and/or has an increased demand for oxygen.

The various IV and intra-arterial lines discussed in the previous section are used to monitor cardiac function; they

TABLE
55-8 Pulmonary Artery Catheter Indices

Measurement	Definition	Formula	Normal Value
Stroke volume index	As above accounting for body surface area (BSA)		30 to 60 mL/beat/m^2
Cardiac index	As above accounting for BSA	CI/BSA	2.4 to 5 l/min/m^2
Pulmonary vascular resistance index (PVRI)	As above accounting for BSA	PAM – PAWP / CI × 80	200 to 350 dynes/sec/cm^{-5}
Systemic vascular resistance index (SVRI)	As above accounting for BSA	MAP – RAP / CI × 80	1,800 to 2,800 dynes/sec/cm^{-5}

do not change it. To improve a patient's cardiac status, practitioners remove the root cause of the problem and provide support via the use of IV fluids, blood products, vasoactive medications, and medical devices.

Intravenous Fluids and Blood Products

IV fluids are given to obtain and help maintain a euvolemic and isotonic state within the body. The type and amount of fluid will be dependent upon each individual's medical situation. Crystalloid solutions in various concentrations and combinations contain electrolytes and sometimes sugars:

- Saline
- Lactated Ringer's
- 5% dextrose in water

IV solutions with larger molecules designed to expand IV volume with increased oncotic pressures include:

- Albumin
- Hespan™ or Hetastarch™

Blood products can help with hydration and volume expansion, as well as provide additional or replacement oxygen-carrying capacity, clotting factors, and platelets:

- Packed red blood cells (pRBC)
- Fresh frozen plasma (FFP)
- Pooled platelets
- Cryoprecipitate

Williams and Gettinger (2006) report that up to 40% of people admitted to the ICU receive at least one blood product transfusion. Unfortunately, no evidence-based guideline exists to help practitioners determine when the benefits of transfusion outweigh the risks of human error, impaired immune function, and infection that accompany transfusion.

Vasoactive Medications

Many medications are used to help support cardiovascular function. Vasoactive medications given in the ICU are designed to alter preload, afterload, contractility, and cardiac rhythm, as required by the patient's underlying disease and physiologic condition. These are potent drugs with a myriad of potential adverse effects necessitating close titration and monitoring in an ICU setting. Table 55-9 summarizes those IV medications most commonly used in the ICU.

Medical Devices

Patients in the ICU may require medical devices to assist with cardiac function.

Pacemakers

Pacemakers are medical devices generally used to treat cardiac disease caused by conduction problems. They can be

TABLE 55-9 Vasoactive Medications

Medication	Action or Effect	Indications	Dosing Range
Amiodarone	Decreased heart rate	Ventricular Tachycardia Atrial fibrillation*	Arrhythmia dependent
Diltiazem	Decreased heart rate and blood pressure	Atrial fibrillation Paroxysmal Supraventricular Tachycardia Hypertension	5 to 15 mg/hr
Dobutamine	Increased heart contractility Increased blood pressure	Congestive heart failure Low cardiac output	2.5 to 20 µg/kg/min
Dopamine	Increased heart rate and blood pressure	Bradycardia Hypotension	2 to 20 µg/kg/min
Epinephrine	Increased heart rate and blood pressure	Anaphylaxis Shock*	1 to 10 µg/min
Esmolol	Decreased heart rate	Tachycardia Hypertension	500 µg/kg load 50 to 200 µg/kg/min
Nitroglycerin	Decreased blood pressure Arterial vasodilatation	Myocardial ischemia Congestive heart failure Hypertension	10 to 20 µg/min
Nitroprusside	Decreased blood pressure	Congestive heart failure Hypertensive crisis	3 µg/kg/min - effect
Norepinephrine	Increased blood pressure	Cardiac arrest Hypotension	1 to 20 µg/min
Phenylephrine	Increased blood pressure	Hypotension	40 to 200 µg/min
Vasopressin	Increased blood pressure	Diabetes insipidus Gastrointestinal bleed Septic shock	0.02 to 0.04 units/min

placed temporarily or permanently in order to improve cardiac function with or without adjunct medications. Permanent pacemakers are discussed in Chapter 17.

Temporary pacemakers are used during cardiac surgery and medical emergencies. They can be placed in a variety of ways:

- *External pacemakers:* Involves placement of electrodes on the front and side or back of the chest to deliver repeated shocks
- *Transvenous pacemakers:* Involves placement of a wire into the right ventricle via a central IV catheter
- *Epicardial pacemaker:* Involves surgical placement of wires into the epicardium to prevent and treat postsurgical conduction defects
- *Transthoracic cardiac pacemakers:* Involves introduction of a wire into the right ventricle, which is attached to a generator

Whether temporary or permanent, care for a patient with a pacemaker includes monitoring of the pacemaker's function and the patient's physical response to the pacing. This will include pain management and sedation for those with external pacers, infection control for newly inserted pacers, and physical assessment of cardiac and peripheral vascular function. See Chapter 17 for more detailed discussion.

Intra-Aortic Balloon Pump

Patients with temporary or permanent heart muscle damage are unable to adequately perfuse their own heart and other organs. First attempts to improve cardiac muscle function include fluids and medications, but at times, patients will require additional support in the form of an intra-aortic balloon pump (IABP). A balloon in placed in the descending aorta via a femoral artery. The balloon can be alternately inflated and deflated (Fig. 55-3). It is programmed to inflate during diastole, which pushes blood back toward the cardiac muscle itself, as well as toward the brain. It deflates just before the ejection phase of systole and acts as a vacuum that pulls blood into the aorta with less effort from the left ventricle. An IABP essentially decreases the workload of the heart, allowing heart muscle to rest and recover while improving organ perfusion. The machine itself can be programmed to assist with every heartbeat or every second, third, or fourth alternate beats, depending upon patient requirements. Care for patients on an IABP includes monitoring cardiac function with the use of a PAC and assessing peripheral circulation to the extremity below its insertion site.

Ventricular Assist Device

A ventricular assist device (VAD) is an implantable device in which cannulas are inserted into the atria or ventricles to support the right heart, left heart, or both sides by taking over the work of delivering blood to the pulmonary artery and/or aorta (see Fig. 55-4). There are three types of VADs. A right VAD (right ventricular assist device [RVAD]) provides pulmonary support by diverting blood from the right atrium or failing right ventricle to the VAD, which pumps the blood into the pulmonary circulation via the VAD connection to the left pulmonary artery.

With a left VAD (left ventricular assist device [LVAD]) blood flows from the left atrium or ventricle to the VAD, which then pumps blood back to the body via the VAD connection to the aorta. A RVAD and LVAD combination is referred to as *biventricular* (BiVAD) *support.*

VADs are reserved for patients who cannot be weaned from maximum volume/inotropic support or the IABP, are awaiting cardiac transplantation, or have class IV heart failure but are not candidates for transplantation. This intervention is the last-line treatment for cardiac failure and requires high-intensity nursing care to monitor cardiac function and the myriad of potential adverse effects, which range from infection, bleeding, and neurological deficits to renal and device failure. While usually deemed to be a temporary

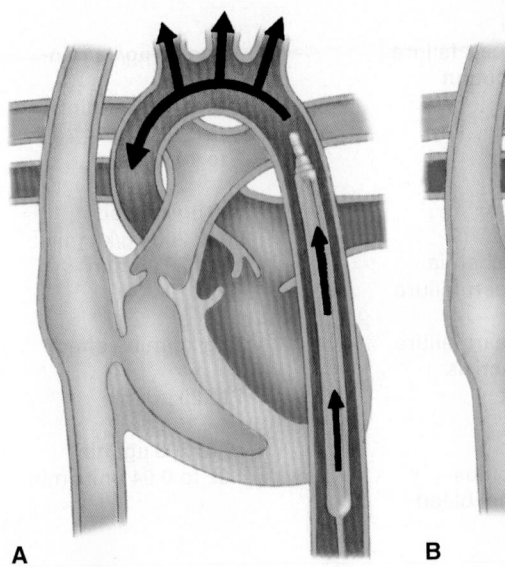
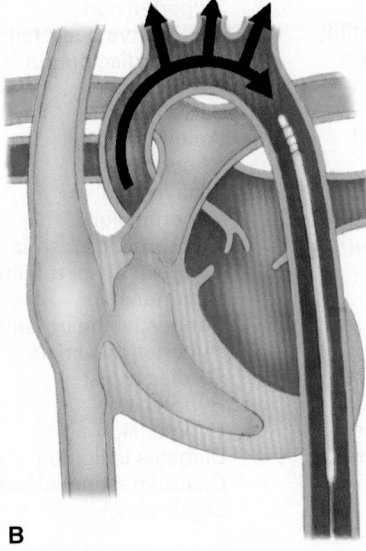

A   **B**

FIGURE 55-3 Direction of blood flow when the pump inflates and deflates the balloon. **(A)** Balloon inflation: The balloon inflates as the aortic valve closes and diastole begins. Diastole increases perfusion to the coronary arteries. **(B)** Balloon deflation: The balloon deflates before ventricular ejection, when the aortic valve opens. This deflation permits ejection of blood from the left ventricle against a lowered resistance. As a result, aortic end-diastolic pressure and afterload decrease and cardiac output rises. From Lippincott William & Wilkins (2010). *Hemodynamic monitoring made incredibly visual* (2nd ed.). Philadelphia: Lippincott Williams & Wilkins.

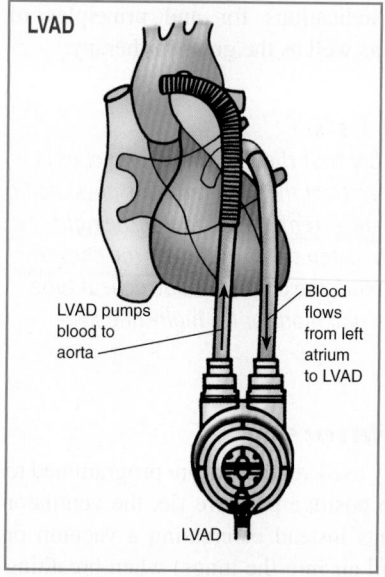
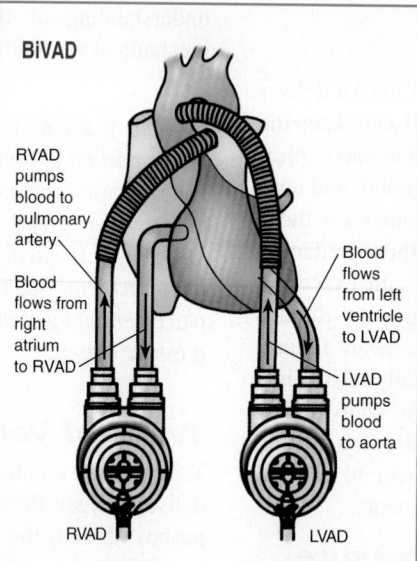
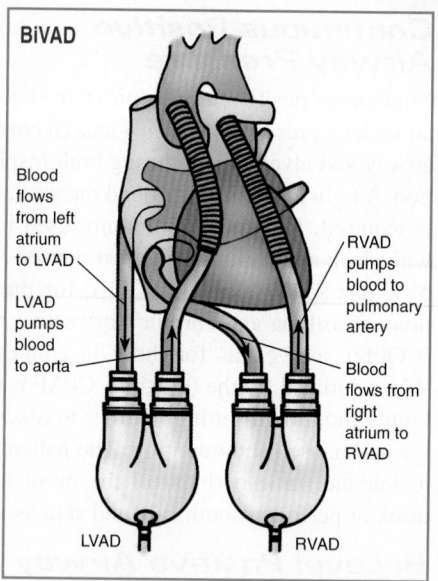

FIGURE 55-4 Cannulation options. Ventricular assist devices (VADs) divert blood from failing ventricles to a pump that can effectively eject it. This diversion can occur by cannulation of either the atria or the ventricles. LVAD, left VAD; RVAD, right VAD; BiVAD, biventricular support. From Lippincott William & Wilkins (2010). *Hemodynamic monitoring made incredibly visual* (2nd ed.). Philadelphia: Lippincott Williams & Wilkins.

measure, patients with refractory heart failure who cannot be transplanted are creating a cohort of patients requiring long-term assistance without definitive cure.

RESPIRATORY ISSUES

Respiratory Failure

Respiratory failure and the advent of mechanical ventilation led to the creation of critical care as a specialty service. Increased ability to manage chronic illnesses and the resulting aging of the population has led to even greater numbers of patients experiencing the need for short- or long-term ventilation due to illness, surgical procedures, and respiratory failure. The estimated crude incidences for acute lung injury and acute respiratory distress syndrome in the United States are 78.9 and 58.7 cases per 100,000 persons per year (Sorbo & Slutsk, 2010). The number of patients needing ventilatory support is expected to grow over the next decades. Respiratory failure can generally be divided into two main categories (see Box 55-1).

Oxygen Delivery

In the critical care environment, oxygen is treated as a drug, requiring a providers' order and nursing assessment of the patient's response to this prescription. The need for oxygen therapy and its specific method of delivery varies according to patient condition. Some patients will receive O_2 therapy as a preventative measure. Supplemental oxygen will assist some patients with extra oxygen delivery during acute episodes, such as myocardial infarction. For the more critically ill, it will serve as an intervention to ensure oxygen delivery

when they are unable maintain their own ventilatory or respiratory function. Oxygen is the most commonly prescribed gas in the critical care environment. See Chapter 10 for detailed information on oxygen delivery systems and nursing responsibilities.

Noninvasive Positive Pressure

Noninvasive positive pressure methods of oxygen delivery are used for patients who are in danger of respiratory failure and who require air to be positively forced into their lungs, but for whom endotracheal intubation is deferred due to patient wishes or attempts to delay or prevent intubation altogether.

BOX 55-1

Causes of Respiratory Failure

Hypoxemic respiratory failure (too little oxygen reaches the tissues):
- Anemia
- Hemorrhage
- Intracardiac shunts
- Acute respiratory distress syndrome (ARDS)

Ventilatory respiratory failure (too little oxygen is exchanged for carbon dioxide):
- Airway obstruction (chronic bronchitis, emphysema, cystic fibrosis)
- Weakness of breathing (acute intoxication, obesity with sleep apnea)
- Muscular weakness (spinal cord injury, muscular dystrophy)
- Lung disease (pneumonia, pulmonary edema)
- Chest wall abnormalities (scoliosis, severe kyphosis)

Continuous Positive Airway Pressure

Continuous positive airway pressure (CPAP) masks deliver air under a pressure between 4 and 20 cm of H_2O to keep the airway and alveoli open during both inspiration and expiration. A tight fitting mask around the nose, or mouth and nose is required. It is most commonly used in homes for those with sleep apnea. In hospitals, it is used for those in danger of hypercapnia (elevated PCO_2), for those with exacerbations of asthma and chronic obstructive pulmonary disease (COPD), as well as for those in congestive heart failure. When initiated for the first time, CPAP is usually started in a highly monitored setting in order to assess for claustrophobia and nausea and vomiting. The patient must also be able to tolerate some periods off the mask in order to eat and drink or perform mouth care and skin assessments.

Bi-Level Positive Airway Pressure

Bi-level positive airway pressure (BiPAP) devices evolved from CPAP and have the ability to provide two levels of pressure, ranging from 4 to 30 cm H_2O. The inspiratory pressure is set with a lower expiratory pressure to allow for easier exhalation. BiPAP also has three different modes of delivery:

- *Spontaneous:* The patient triggers all breaths delivered.
- *Timed:* The machine is set to deliver a set number of breaths per minute.
- *Spontaneous + timed:* The patient triggers breaths with a set number of back-up breaths from the machine to ensure adequate ventilation.

Intubation and Mechanical Ventilation

Many ICU patients will require intubation and mechanical ventilation during their admission. It is hoped that this will only be required for a short time period to assist in supporting the patient's recovery from illness or injury. However, this advanced technology has moved from the acute care arena into chronic care facilities and even homes. Intubation and ventilation allow for:

- Airway protection in the event of neurological deterioration or acute intoxication
- Airway protection during sedation for testing and procedures
- Airway clearance for those unable to manage their own secretions
- Management of respiratory function during surgery
- Rest for the patient with muscular fatigue
- Increased FIO_2 for the arterially hypoxic patient
- Increased flow and pressure to ensure adequate ventilation.

Caring for a patient on mechanical ventilation has become an integral part of nursing care in critical care and progressive care units. Positive patient outcomes depend on an understanding of the indications for and principles of mechanical ventilation, as well as the goals of therapy.

NURSING ALERT

It is important to remember that the right main bronchus is wider, shorter, and more vertical than the left. This physiologic difference may lead to inadvertent intubation of the right lung only. It is essential to listen to both sides of the chest for bilateral breath sounds, mark the correct endotracheal tube placement at lip or nares, and monitor for high- and low-pressure alarms.

Types of Ventilators

Today's most commonly used ventilators are programmed to deliver oxygen through positive pressure (ie, the ventilator pushes air into the lungs instead of creating a vacuum or negative pressure to pull air into the lungs) when breathing spontaneously. Expiration occurs passively and endotracheal intubation or tracheotomy is necessary. There are three types of positive-pressure ventilators:

- *Time-cycled ventilators:* These terminate inspiration after a preset time. The volume of air the patient receives is regulated by the length of inspiration and the flow rate of the air. These are rarely used in the adult population.
- *Volume-cycled ventilators:* These are the most commonly used ventilators. The volume of air delivered with each inspiration is preset. Once this volume is delivered to the patient, the ventilator cycles off and exhalation occurs passively. The volume of air delivered by the ventilator is relatively constant, ensuring consistent, adequate breaths despite varying airway pressures.
- *Pressure-cycled ventilators:* These deliver a flow of air (inspiration) until it reaches a preset pressure, then cycles off to allow expiration to occur passively. The major limitation is that the volume of air or oxygen can vary as the patient's airway resistance or compliance changes. The tidal volume delivered may be inconsistent (the amount of air inhaled and exhaled with a normal breath).

Ventilator Modes
Volume-Cycled Ventilators

CONTROLLED MANDATORY VENTILATION. Controlled mandatory ventilation (CMV) delivers a set tidal volume and a set rate. It is used for the patient who is chemically paralyzed and sedated or whose neurological status has deteriorated to the point that no drive to breathe exists.

ASSIST CONTROL. Assist control (AC) also delivers a set tidal volume at a set rate, but allows patients to take a spontaneous breath. When they take their own breath, they receive the entire preset tidal volume, thus decreasing their work of breathing. If the rate is set high enough, it is essentially the same as CMV.

INTERMITTENT MANDATORY VENTILATION. Intermittent mandatory ventilation (IMV) delivers a number of breaths at a preset tidal volume to ensure a minimum number of breaths with an adequate tidal volume. Patients may breath spontaneously, but will only receive the tidal volume they are able to inspire on their own.

INVERSE RATIO VENTILATION. Inverse ratio ventilation (IRV) changes the normal inspiration to expiration ratios of 1 part inspiration to 2 parts expiration (1:2) to a ratio of 1:1 or more than 1:1 up to 1:4. Prolonging the inspiratory time allows alveolar recruitment (more alveoli used during respiration) at lower pressure levels. This is an uncomfortable way of breathing and patients must be sedated.

HIGH-FREQUENCY VENTILATION. High-frequency ventilation (HFV) or oscillating ventilators deliver very small tidal volumes from 3 to 6 mL/kg or 50 to 80 mL in a range from 60 to over 200 times a minute. This works on the principle of oxygen diffusion gently pulsating throughout the lungs. Patients on this form of ventilation also require sedation.

Pressure-Cycled Ventilators

PRESSURE SUPPORT VENTILATION. Pressure support ventilation (PSV) is a mode of ventilation in which the patient breathes spontaneously but uses additional pressure during the entire breath cycle to increase airflow through the ventilator tubing and artificial airway to decrease the work of breathing caused by a narrowed airway. Patients using pressure support are often in the process of being weaned from the ventilator.

CONTINUOUS POSITIVE AIRWAY PRESSURE. Positive air flow is used via the endotracheal tube while the patient is on the ventilator (rather than using a mask, as discussed above). It is also used as a method of decreasing the work of breathing while weaning from the ventilator.

AIRWAY PRESSURE RELEASE VENTILATION. Airway pressure release ventilation (APRV) is a newer mode of assistance that allows for the choice between spontaneous breaths or not, while improving alveolar recruitment with lower pressures. It is essentially BiPAP on the ventilator using inverse ratio ventilation. It allows patients to breath with the presence of end expiratory pressure in the alveoli, but this pressure is momentarily released to allow for exchange between O_2 and CO_2.

Ventilator Settings

The primary provider will order individualized ventilator settings for the patient that will include those discussed below.

Rate

The rate is the number of breaths the machine will give each minute.

Fraction of Inspired Air

Each breath will be given with a specified setting for inspired oxygen level, FIO_2. The goal for the FIO_2 is the lowest possible setting to provide adequate partial pressure of oxygen (PaO_2) in the bloodstream without the side effects of high oxygen percentages, such as nitrogen washout and alveolar collapse.

Tidal Volume

The tidal volume (Tv) is the amount of air given in each breath. This is usually between 5 and 7 mL of air per kilogram of body weight. This allows for air flow without over-extending and damaging the alveoli. The Tv multiplied by the rate equals the minute volume (Mv).

Positive End Expiratory Pressure

The theory behind positive end expiratory pressure (PEEP) is that it mimics the pressure left in the lungs by closure of the glottis, which is now interrupted by endotracheal tube (ETT) placement. It is used to keep alveoli open during exhalation, to allow more time for gas exchange and to decrease *functional residual capacity,* or the amount of air in the lungs at the end of expiration. Levels of PEEP above 5 cm H_2O put the patient at risk for alveolar rupture, pneumothorax, and decreased cardiac output via referred pressure counteracting forward blood flow from the heart. The ventilator-induced damage is termed *barotrauma.*

Nursing Management

Nursing care of the mechanically ventilated patient requires expert technical skills.

Care is taken to simultaneously assess, intervene upon, and evaluate both the patient and the technology.

Assessing the Patient

The patient's physiologic response illness or injury and particular indications for mechanical ventilation will determine the specific ventilator orders. The nurse should continually assess the patient's condition and resulting increase or decrease in ventilatory support required by said condition. For example, a patient with a recent decrease in neurological function is no longer able to draw spontaneous breaths and will need an increase in the number of breaths provided by the ventilator.

Patients must be able to "allow" the ventilator to perform its function without interference caused by anxiety, biting the ETT, or problems with coughing or increased secretions. If the patient is able to let this happen and coordinate his own breaths with the machine, he is said to have *synchrony* with the ventilator. The nurse must assess the underlying cause of intolerance to mechanical ventilation and remove it in order to promote recovery of respiratory function. Common interventions include sedation, pain control, and adequate suctioning.

Assessing the Equipment

The ventilator needs to be assessed to make sure that it is functioning properly and that the settings are appropriate.

While not primarily responsible for the functioning of the ventilator, the nurse is responsible for the patient and therefore needs to evaluate how ventilator function affects the patient's overall status.

Ventilator alarms are designed to indicate that the ventilator is unable to deliver what it has been programmed to give the patient, or that the patient is unable to tolerate the current settings.

Common problems with the ventilator include:

• Disconnection or kinking of tubing
• Disconnection of tubing from ETT or tracheostomy tube
• Water in the tubing
• Change in air temperature beyond set limits

Common problems with the settings include:

• Limits set too high or too low, especially when exercising or weaning patients

Common problems with the patient include:

• Desynchronized breathing pattern between patient and ventilator
• Biting of the ETT
• Improper placement or inadvertent movement of ETT
• Coughing and/or sputum production interfering with air flow
• Lung or chest cavity fluid and pressure problems, as from congestive heart failure, pulmonary edema, and pneumothorax

⚡ NURSING ALERT

Pressure limits is one of the ventilator settings with an alarm. Again, either patient condition or the equipment may be the cause of an alarm. Pressure alarms on the ventilator may indicate a dangerous situation. Low-pressure alarms may indicate disconnection from the machine or displacement of the airway.

A high-pressure alarm usually indicates resistance to or obstruction of airflow from biting on the ETT, a kink in the tubing, or something as severe as bronchospasm or pneumothorax.

Preventing and Managing Adverse Effects of Mechanical Ventilation

As with many medical interventions, mechanical ventilation has the potential to cause complications or undesired secondary effects, and the nurse's priority is patient safety via focus on preventing problems associated with any treatment modalities.

VENTILATOR-ASSOCIATED PNEUMONIA. Currently, in the critical care world, ventilator-associated pneumonia (VAP) is receiving a lot of attention from patient advocacy groups, health care professionals, and regulatory bodies. It is a form of hospital-acquired infection whose treatment is no longer being reimbursed by Medicare. It is caused by a patient being placed on a ventilator for a period of at least 48 hours

whose oral and nasal secretions pooling above the ETT balloon fall into the lungs upon movement of the pliable balloon. Unfortunately, the mechanical ventilator is both a cause and an assistant in the cure for pneumonia. The bacterium found in patients with VAP is usually *Pseudomonas*, but any infection not present when a person is placed on a ventilator constitutes VAP.

This infection forces the hospital to develop, implement, and monitor a policy for its prevention. In practical terms, it translates into the necessity for mouth care to be given at a minimum of every 4 hours to maintain mucosal integrity and prevent pooling of secretions, and to keep the head of the patient's bed elevated to at least 30 degrees.

INCREASED INTRACRANIAL PRESSURE. Upon receiving air, the positive pressure in the chest decreases venous return and may leave a higher volume of blood in the cranium. This can lead to altered levels of consciousness.

ALTERED MENTAL STATUS. Anxiety and discomfort from being placed on a ventilator, the frequent care in the form of suctioning, and persistent ventilator alarms can easily lead to sleep deprivation. Sleep deprivation in turn can affect changes in mental status and delay healing, as will be discussed further in this chapter.

DECREASED CARDIAC OUTPUT. The higher pressure in the pulmonary tree makes in difficult for blood to return to the heart from other areas of the body. If there is less blood returning, there is less blood to pump back to the body, causing hypotension and lower cardiac output.

HYPERVOLEMIA. The decreased pressure sensed by baroreceptors in the aorta may trick the body into believing hypovolemia exists; it reacts by stimulating production of antidiuretic hormone (ADH). Release of too much hormone may cause an overaccumulation of fluid in the vasculature, necessitating diuretics.

VENOUS THROMBOEMBOLISM. Ventilated patients are prone to spending more time in bed due to instability or the practical difficulties of walking around when attached to the ventilator. Pooling of blood in the large veins of the legs while in bed (and upper extremities as well) can lead to clot formation and increase the possibility of pulmonary embolus (PE). With an incidence varying from 7% to 60%, depending on specific ICU populations, deep venous thrombosis is an adverse effect with significant morbidity and potential mortality (Leeper, 2008). Prophylaxis in the form of antiembolic stockings, compression boots, range-of-motion (ROM) activity, early mobility, and administration of antiplatelet medications (such as heparin) is advised for all intubated patients.

BAROTRAUMA. As the name implies, barotrauma is damage to organs and vessels due to elevated pressures in the thoracic cavity. It is important to remember that this same trauma is possible in the abdominal cavity as well.

PNEUMOTHORAX. Pneumothorax is a specific form of barotrauma resulting in the collapse of a lung (it is helpful to compare it to popping an overfilled balloon). Corrective action in the form of a chest tube is often required.

GASTROINTESTINAL BLEEDING. It has been found that within 24 hours of ICU admission, 75% to 100% of patients have evidence of gastric mucosal erosion that can lead to hemodynamically significant bleeding in 2% to 6% of patients (Spirt & Stanley, 2006). Mechanical intubation for greater than 24 hours or an ICU stay longer than 1 week have been found to be independent predictors of gastrointestinal (GI) bleeding. Although the reasons remain unclear, it is thought that gut ischemia and reperfusion injury leads to mucosal and/or deep tissue damage in the stomach and duodenum, which leads to ulcers and bleeding. The incidence of GI bleeding has decreased over the last decades and is largely due to standard administration of H_2-histamine antagonists (such as ranitidine) or proton pump inhibitors (such as pantoprazole) in patients with previous or current GI bleeds. Although seen less frequently, the adverse effects of significant bleeding due to stress ulcers cannot be underestimated, and prophylaxis with the above medications remains the standard of care.

Promoting Effective Airway Clearance

The presence of an ETT and continuous positive-pressure ventilation increases the production of secretions, regardless of the patient's underlying condition. Nursing interventions focus on maintaining a clear airway via turning and positioning, meticulous mouth care, and endotracheal/tracheal suctioning as needed.

Promoting Optimal Level of Mobility

The use of a mechanical ventilator limits the patient's mobility. The nurse helps the patient whose condition has become stable to get out of bed and move to a chair as soon as possible. Mobility and muscle activity are beneficial because they stimulate respirations and improve patient psychological status. If the patient is unable to get out of bed, the nurse encourages performance of active ROM exercises every 6 to 8 hours. If the patient cannot perform these exercises, the nurse performs passive ROM exercises every 8 hours to prevent contractures and venous stasis.

Promoting Optimal Communication

It is important to develop alternative methods of communication for the patient who is receiving mechanical ventilation. The nurse assesses the patient's communication abilities. Once the patient's limitations are known, the nurse offers several appropriate communication approaches: lip reading (use single key words), pad-and-pencil or erasable slate, communication board, gesturing, sign language, or electric larynx. Use of a "talking" or fenestrated tracheostomy tube may be suggested to the provider; this allows the patient to talk while on the ventilator. The nurse makes sure that the patient's eyeglasses, hearing aid, sign interpreter, and language translator are available if needed to enhance the patient's ability to communicate.

Promoting Coping Ability

Encouraging the family to verbalize their feelings about the ventilator, the patient's condition, and the environment in general is beneficial. Explaining procedures helps reduce anxiety and familiarizes the patient with ventilator procedures. To restore a sense of control, the nurse encourages the patient to participate in decisions about care as appropriate. The patient may become withdrawn or depressed while receiving mechanical ventilation. It is important to provide diversions. Stress reduction techniques (eg, a back rub, relaxation measures) help relieve tension and help the patient deal with anxieties and fears about the dependence on the ventilator.

Weaning the Patient from the Ventilator

Mechanical ventilation is not a natural condition, and prolonged intubation carries a number of potentially serious side effects; therefore, every effort is made to make the need for this intervention as short as possible, with weaning from the ventilator initiated at the earliest possible time consistent with patient safety. The goal is to get the patient in the most optimal condition to succeed in weaning from the ventilator. While there are many indicators leading a practitioner to believe a patient is ready to wean, the following have proven the most predictive:

- Vital capacity (the maximum amount of air that can be expelled after a maximum inhalation)
- Negative inspiratory force (NIF, the ability to take a deep breath and to generate a cough strong enough to clear secretions; NIF should be at least –20 cm H_2O)
- Tidal volume (amount of air inhaled and exhaled in a normal breath; should be at least 5 mL/kg.)
- Minute ventilation (total amount of air inhaled and exhaled in a minute; should be <10 L/min)
- Rapid shallow breathing index (RSBI, a ratio determined by the frequency of respirations [breaths per minute] divided by the tidal volume [measured in liters]; an RSBI of <105 is considered criteria for weaning to extubation, while >120 is considered as predictive of ventilator support.

Other criteria to consider include:

- Cardiovascular stability
- Adequate and stable arterial blood gas analysis
- Nutritionally supported with increasing or normal levels of phosphate, magnesium, and albumin
- Ability to swallow and manage saliva and secretions

ENDOCRINE ISSUES

The endocrine system participates along with the neurological system to regulate bodily functions such as growth and development, tissue function, metabolism, and even mood.

Disorders of the endocrine system result from the secretion of too much or too little hormone, as well as from too much or too little sensitivity to a particular hormone.

This section covers hormones of particular importance in the critical care environment.

Problems Related to Antidiuretic Hormone

ADH is secreted from the posterior pituitary gland and helps to conserve water in the body. Head trauma and renal disorders can decrease secretion, while trauma, various cancers, hemorrhage, and infection may lead to excessive secretion of ADH. Decreased secretion leads to diabetes insipidus (DI), while excessive secretion causes syndrome of inappropriate diuretic hormone (SIADH).

Patients at risk for altered ADH secretion should be monitored for neurological changes, as well as volume status via intake and output calculations, serum sodium levels, and serum and urine osmolality. Treatment for increased secretion involves water restriction, saline infusion, and use of demeclocycline, which blocks renal response to ADH. Treatment for decreased secretion is replacement of the hormone via one of the various forms of ADH, more commonly known as *arginine vasopressin.*

Problems Related to Thyroid Hormone

The thyroid gland uses iodine to make thyroxine (T_4) and triiodothyronine (T_3). These hormones are involved in body metabolism, alertness, mood, body temperature, and general energy and oxygen use. Disorders of secretion are viewed in relation to normal function; the trajectory ranges from:

Myxedema Coma $\leftrightarrow$ Hypothyroidism $\leftrightarrow$
Normal Function $\leftrightarrow$ Hyperthyroidism $\leftrightarrow$
Graves' Disease $\leftrightarrow$ Thyroid Storm

Critical illnesses, such as cancers and infections, can alter the secretion of these hormones. Metabolism is either adversely increased or decreased at a time when metabolic control is required. Too much hormone results in nervousness, anxiety, hyperthermia, and eventual cardiac failure. Other patients with a history of thyroid disorders or surgery, or those not responding to a range of medical treatments, should have their thyroid hormone levels checked and supplemented, if necessary, to ensure assistance with increased metabolic demands.

Problems Related to Cortisol

Cortisol, secreted by the adrenal glands, is better known as the stress or fight-or-flight hormone. Levels are highest in the morning upon arising, in response to increased activity levels.

Problems related to too little or too much cortisol can be viewed on a continuum from:

Addison's Disease $\leftrightarrow$ Normal Function $\leftrightarrow$ Cushing's
Disease

At times, the level of this hormone is increased due to factors such as increased and prolonged stress; this leads to impaired cognition, hypertension, decreased thyroid and immune system function, hyperglycemia, and decreased bone density and muscle mass.

More commonly in the ICU, cortisol levels are low due to low perfusion states, infection, or adverse effects of medications. People with low levels of cortisol are unable to mount a physical response to bodily stressors and are likely to have fatigue, lower body temperature, and hypotension. Patients who meet clinical criteria for low cortisol levels are frequently given a cortisol stimulation test to determine if replacement is required to increase the body's metabolic response to illness.

Problems Related to Insulin

The beta cells of the pancreas secrete insulin to help move glucose into the cells to be used as an energy substrate. The majority of people with insulin disorders have type I or type II diabetes mellitus and are at particular risk for acute episodes of hyper- or hypoglycemia with the added stress of a critical illness. Patients with particularly brittle disease may be affected by sugar levels on this continuum:

Hypoglycemia $\leftrightarrow$ Normal Glucose Level $\leftrightarrow$ Diabetic
Ketoacidosis or Hyperosmolar Hyperglycemic Nonketotic
Syndrome (HHNS)

Many studies have shown that insulin therapy to maintain glucose levels between 80 and 110 mg/dL reduces organ dysfunction, nosocomial infections, and mortality (Falciglia, 2007). Patients with diabetes are frequently admitted to the ICU with complications of their illness, but it is also a disease frequently diagnosed for the first time while hospitalized. All patients admitted to the ICU should have their blood glucose monitored three to four times a day to ensure they are able to maintain their glucose levels below each hospitals prescribed upper limit. For those who are unable to maintain a lower level of glucose, insulin therapy should be initiated according to hospital policy, with frequent monitoring of glucose levels to ensure lower levels without hypoglycemia.

GASTROINTESTINAL ISSUES

As with oxygen, food and drink becomes a medical prescription in the ICU. It is also regulated by practicalities such as kitchen schedules and nursing time to deliver food to or feed patients.

Nutritional Support

In the critical care unit, nutritional support is required to prevent catabolism of protein stores and provide the necessary elements for healing. The question in the ICU is not whether or not patients should be fed, but when and how. Current trends in feeding lean toward initiating nutritional support within 24 to 48 hours of admission to the ICU (Davies, 2007).

Food

Because nature knows best, the optimal method of feeding patients is through oral intake of food and fluids. Specific diets will be altered depending on a patient's diagnoses. These may include altered content (low fat or low salt), altered consistency (soft or pureed), or with altered fluid (fluid restriction). The nurse ensures an environment and physical condition that makes the patient amenable to eating. Prevention of nausea and vomiting, pain relief, and proper positioning in a chair or upright in bed can all increase a person's appetite. At times, smaller more frequent meals consisting of something the patient likes to eat may help increase intake, maintain weight, and provide a diversion from the ICU environment.

Tube Feedings

A percentage of patients have a working GI tract but will not be able to take food orally due to their physiologic condition (dementia with dysphagia) or medical intervention (endotracheal intubation). These patients receive tube feedings. A particular liquid formula is recommended with collaboration of the dietician and medical practitioner. Again, the actual formula will depend upon the patient's diagnosis and current condition. Box 55-2 describes nursing responsibilities for patients receiving a tube feeding. Tube feeding pumps deliver the nutrition via a variety of tubes that may include:

- *Nasogastric tube (NGT):* A tube inserted into the nares and ending in the stomach; used for gastric drainage or feeding.
- *Flexible feeding tube:* A synthetic tube of large or small bore (size) inserted into the nares to the stomach; softer,

more flexible than the NGT, without the ability to convert to a drainage tube if needed.
- *Post-pyloric tube:* A longer variety of the flexible feeding tube that reaches past the stomach into the duodenum, in order to use small bowel when the stomach has the potential to not tolerate feeding or the risk of aspiration is high.
- *Percutaneous endoscopic gastrostomy (PEG) tube:* A tube inserted by the physician directly through the abdominal wall into the stomach; removes the discomfort, potential for accidental dislodgement, and potential for sinus infections caused by nasally inserted tubes.
- *Gastrojejunostomy (G-J) tube:* A tube that allows for simultaneous feeding of the small bowel and drainage of the stomach.

> ### ! NURSING ALERT
> *Intolerance to feeding is a complicated issue with consequences for deteriorating nutritional status and aspiration pneumonia. Aspiration of GI contents into the lungs leads to increased morbidity and prolonged hospitalization. Risk factors for aspiration include decreased mental status, placement of the head of the bed at less than 30 degrees, sedatives, vomiting, and gastric residual volumes greater than 200 mL (Metheny, Schallom, Oliver et al., 2008).*

Parenteral Nutrition

Unfortunately, there are times when a patient is unable to tolerate enteral feeding and nutritional support must be given intravenously. Total parenteral nutrition (TPN) or central parenteral nutrition (CPN) provides amino acids, dextrose, and fat. Because of its high osmolality, it must be given by a central catheter, such as a triple-lumen or Hickman™ catheter, or by a peripheral IV that terminates in a central vein, such as a PICC line. This type of support is used as a method to supplement or completely replace enteral feeding. However, it has numerous potential consequences, including pneumothorax during catheter insertion, catheter infection (due to high concentration of sugar in the solution), and liver failure. The goal is to use this support for as short a time as possible before returning to enteral feeds and eventually to having the patient provide his or her own oral intake. Partial parenteral nutrition (PPN) may be administered via a peripheral IV because of the solution's lower osmolality. A number of metabolic complications are associated with parenteral nutrition including hyperglycemia, electrolyte abnormalities, and irritation at the IV site.

Immunonutrition

A deficit of nutrients can decrease infection rates, length of hospital stay, and mortality. These nutrients are additional supplements to the various methods of feeding. Depending on patient diagnosis and condition, the nutrients in Table 55-10 should be considered.

BOX 55-2

Caring for Patients Receiving Tube Feedings

With tube feeding patients, the nurse is responsible for:
- Noting that placement has been verified by the medical team via radiography, which is the gold standard for checking tube placement
- Double-checking placement by listening for air insufflation over the stomach; this method is common, but its accuracy is controversial
- Preventing accidental dislodgement by patient or staff
- Maintaining patency of the tubes
- Monitoring for intolerance to feeding
- Monitoring for constipation and diarrhea

TABLE
55-10 Immunonutrition

Element	Effects	Comment
Arginine (conditionally nonessential amino acid)	• Stimulation of growth hormone • Precursor in nitric oxide production • Improves immune function • Reduces healing time of injuries (particularly bone) • Increases muscle mass • Improved insulin sensitivity	Its use in septic patients remains controversial as the effects of sepsis on arginine metabolism or of arginine metabolism on sepsis are unclear.
Glutamine (conditionally nonessential amino acid)	• A substrate for DNA synthesis • Major role in protein synthesis • Primary source of fuel for enterocytes • Precursor for rapidly dividing immune cells, thus aiding in immune function • Regulation of acid–base balance in the kidney by producing ammonium • Alternative fuel source for the brain • Blocks cortisol-induced protein catabolism	It remains unclear whether outcomes are improved via enteral or IV administration.
Omega-3 fatty acids	• Reduced inflammation • Reduced lipid circulation in the bloodstream • Decreased platelet aggregation • Reduced cytokine production • Improved insulin sensitivity	
Copper	• Increased erythrocyte production • Increased absorption of iron • Maintenance of cytochrome p450 cycle • Vitamin C metabolism	
Selenium	• Maintenance of the cytochrome p450 system • DNA repair	
Zinc	• Increased growth hormone • Increased uptake of insulin • Increased cell division and promotion of wound healing • Treatment of diarrhea	

Slow Motility

For a patient to tolerate feedings, the stomach must empty its contents into the small intestine, where nutrients are actually digested. This emptying is partially regulated by cholecystokinin (CCK) and polypeptide YY (PYY) levels that serve to slow gastric emptying. Unfortunately, it has been found that levels of these substances are elevated during critical illness, causes delayed emptying. Diabetes, gastroparesis (delayed gastric emptying), and slowed gut peristalsis due to pain medications are common causes of slow motility. This slow motility of gastric and intestinal contents can lead to nausea, vomiting, aspiration, and decreased nutritional status, which must be prevented or corrected as soon as possible. Current trends favor the use of promotility drugs, such as metoclopramide and/or erythromycin. It is not yet clear if these medications contribute to improved outcomes, and recommendations may change after future study. Adequate hydration and physical movement also assist in maintaining proper GI function.

If motility cannot be improved, the general consensus dictates movement to small bowel feedings before adding or replacing enteral feeds with parenteral nutrition.

Diarrhea

Diarrhea is frequently seen in the ICU and has been found to be related to enteral therapy, hypoalbuminemia, antibiotic therapy, and sepsis. This makes the issue of diarrhea very difficult as enteral therapy is a treatment for low protein states and antibiotic therapy is required for treatment of overwhelming infections. Once diagnosed, the underlying cause, symptomatology, and potential adverse effects of diarrhea must be addressed and mitigated.

Causes
Enteral Therapy
The use of tube feedings is often required to prevent and treat malnutrition in the ICU. The clinical team needs to

evaluate the composition of the prescribed feeding for possible changes required in the fiber or water content or osmolality. Current trends find that continuous feeding via a pump instead of intermittent feeding will decrease the amount of diarrhea. Patient care and testing often require changes of position, transfer, or NPO status, which interrupt feedings because it is considered unsafe to feed a patient while he or she is lying flat during turns and transfers. NPO status for individual medications (Dilantin therapy) or tests also decreases nutritional intake. If possible, nursing needs to plan care in order to limit feeding interruptions. Fewer interruptions in feeding will maintain optimal caloric intake, and reduce glucose fluctuations and the risk for diarrhea.

Hypoalbuminemia

Albumin is a protein responsible for maintaining oncotic pressure in the vascular system and thus distribution of fluids in the body. Low albumin levels cause water to leave the vasculature and accumulate in other parts of the body, such as the GI tract and tissues.

Antibiotics

The use of antibiotics changes normal gut flora depending upon the sensitivity of bacteria to the prescribed medications. The use of cephalosporins and quinolones is known to place patients at higher risk overgrowth of *Clostridium difficile,* which forms a covering membrane inside the GI tract. The membrane acts to prevent absorption of fluid and nutrients and causes diarrhea. This particular infection requires yet another antibiotic treatment with metronidazole and vancomycin.

Sepsis

Generalized infections not necessarily specific to the GI tract nonetheless have consequences for this system. Inflammation, cytokine release, and alterations in blood flow and the permeability of GI mucosa have also been found to cause diarrhea.

Symptoms and Adverse Effects

Diarrhea can be uncomfortable, painful, and embarrassing for the patient. It also requires extensive nursing time to keep patients clean and free of complications. The adverse effects of diarrhea are numerous and can impact outcomes. Hemodynamic instability due to fluid and electrolyte losses needs to be corrected with replacement of IV fluids, electrolytes, and minerals. This prevents cardiac arrhythmias and low perfusion states. Malnutrition due to poor absorption because of diarrhea, at a time when metabolic requirements are elevated, needs intervention with a possible change in feeding formula or supplementation with parenteral nutrition. Fecal contents and even skin cleansers change the normal pH of the skin and can lead to breakdown and the formation of pressure ulcers.

Prevention and Treatment of Diarrhea

The first goal is to prevent diarrhea. The second goal is to stop it as soon as possible if preventative efforts fail. Some

of these efforts will be ordered by the providers, with patient response monitored by nursing. Interventions include:

- Change in feeding formula, with higher fiber content or lower osmolality
- Prescription of probiotics, such as *Lactobacillus*, to alter gut flora
- Use of antidiarrheal medications, such as loperamide
- Frequent turning of patient to relieve pressure and enhance evaluation of skin
- Use of skin barrier lotions to prevent contact between skin and fecal contents

Constipation

Patients in the ICU are also at risk for constipation, with a reported incidence as high as 80% in critically ill patients (Asai, 2007). Constipation can be defined as difficulty in or failure to defecate for at least 3 days. Potential causes include decreased fluid intake or hypovolemia, immobility, and side effects of medications such as narcotics. Complications range from mild discomfort and bloating to intolerance to feedings and obstruction and perforation. Constipation has also been shown to increase bacterial overgrowth and sepsis and is even associated with an increase in the number of days mechanical ventilation is required (Asai, 2007). The goal is to prevent constipation via provision of hydration, fiber intake, and the use of pharmacological agents if prescribed. Various bowel regimens akin to those used in patients with slow motility are employed, including digital extraction of rectal contents, enemas, and suppositories. Once the lower GI tract is cleared, it is possible to provide medication via the upper intestinal tract to clear out fecal contents from areas unreachable by other means.

RENAL ISSUES

Many patients in a critical care unit are either at risk for or have preexisting renal problems, particularly if they have a history of diabetes or hypertension. Damage to the renal system can be acute, chronic, or acute on chronic. Sources of renal damage are classified as prerenal, intrarenal, and postrenal (refer to Chapter 27 for further details).

Promotion of Renal Function

Despite the statistics given above, many patients admitted to the ICU will have normal renal function. However, admission to the ICU places patients at risk for renal dysfunction; therefore, nurses need to monitor urine output and laboratory values such as serum creatinine, blood urea nitrogen, creatinine clearance, and glomerular filtration rates (GFR) in order to ensure continued function or intervene as soon as possible in the event of declining function.

Spontaneous Voiding

The most comfortable method of urinating is to be able to independently go to the bathroom. The ability to do this necessitates functioning kidneys, the mental ability to recognize the need to void, and the physical strength and balance required for mobility. If patients are able to void spontaneously, the nurse should provide them every opportunity to do so. This eliminates the possibility of urinary catheter–related infections. It is important to note, however, that having to go to the bathroom is a very frequent reason for confused patients trying to get out of bed. The practice of toileting patients every few hours prevents the consequences of falls, incontinence, and skin breakdown.

Condom Catheters

Condom catheters are placed on males when they are able to void spontaneously and strict hourly monitoring of urinary output is not required. Additionally, if patients are confused, unable to realize the need to urinate, or lack the ability to use a bathroom or urinal, this provides an alternative to incontinence. Unfortunately, an alternative to condom catheters has not been developed for women.

Urinary Catheters

Urinary catheters are inserted into the bladder by way of the urethra and are used to provide samples of urine for testing, a method of monitoring urine output when concerned with hemodynamic compromise, and as a means for controlling incontinence and skin breakdown. While convenient, urinary catheters are associated with more than 30% of all nosocomial infections in hospitalized patients (Centers for Disease Control and Prevention [CDC], 2009). Standard practice should include aseptic insertion, daily preventative cleaning of the catheter with soap and water, wiping away from the urethra, episodic cleaning after bowel movements as noted above, maintaining a closed system, and proper anchoring of the catheter on the leg to prevent undue strain on it. Research reveals a 50% increase in nosocomial urinary tract infections (UTIs) when indwelling urinary catheters were left in place for 48 hours after surgery (Wald, Ma, Bratzler et al., 2008), thus, the removal of the catheter at the earliest possible moment is suggested.

Renal Insufficiency

People with a GFR less than 60 mL/min are said to have renal insufficiency; their ability to filter and excrete metabolic waste products is impaired. Prevention of further deterioration of renal function is critical. This will include hemodynamic support to maintain blood flow, as the kidneys require up to 20% of the cardiac output. Additionally, the medical team and pharmacists have to evaluate drug dosages because the clearance of medications is impacted by renal excretion. Patients requiring IV contrast for radiographic studies are often prescribed "renal protection" in the form of normal saline and medications, such as acetylcysteine, before their studies. Despite all efforts, some patients will progress from renal insufficiency to renal failure, so the nurse must remain vigilant to deteriorating renal function.

Renal Failure

In the critically ill, the development of acute renal failure (ARF) is association with a mortality rate of 50% or greater (Chertow, Soroko, Paganini et al., 2006). Therefore, efforts to mimic normal renal mechanisms are accomplished via renal replacement or dialysis until kidney function resumes. Patients with end-stage renal disease (ESRD) have the option of complete renal replacement for extended periods of time.

Renal Replacement

Renal replacement is accomplished via hemodialysis, peritoneal dialysis, or kidney transplant through either cadaver or living donation. Dialysis can be provided for a short period of time, to allow the kidneys time to recover from an acute injury such as acute tubular necrosis (ATN); as a bridge to renal transplantation; or on a permanent basis. Other indications for starting renal replacement therapy include:

- Uremic encephalopathy: Confusion, asterixis, and seizures
- Pericarditis
- Bleeding
- Fluid overload unresponsive to diuretics
- Pleuritis
- Metabolic derangements: Metabolic acidosis, hyperkalemia, hyperphosphatemia, hyper- or hypocalcemia
- Protracted nausea and vomiting
- Weight loss or signs of malnutrition
- Overdose of medications/poisons that are dialyzable

Renal replacement therapies are discussed in detail in Chapter 27.

MUSCULOSKELETAL ISSUES

People admitted to critical care units are usually confined to bed for extended periods of time. Neurological, cardiovascular, and respiratory instability are reasons why patients are restricted to bed rest in the ICU. Sometimes interventions (ICP monitors, balloon pumps) or the desire to prevent the increased oxygen demands of movement (heart failure, respiratory insufficiency) necessitate bed rest. Other reasons for prolonged bed rest include conflicting priorities in the nursing staff ("Do I spend my time with my patient who is actively hemorrhaging, or with the one who needs to get out of bed?"), or lack of knowledge regarding the importance of physical activity. Being in the recumbent position is not a natural state, and prolonged bed rest has a plethora of adverse effects that are outlined in Table 55-11. Deconditioning is seen in patients after as few as 3 days of bed rest. This leads

TABLE
55-11 Effects of Bed Rest

System	Potential Effects
Neurological	Anxiety
	Hallucinations
Cardiovascular	Hypovolemia
	Decreased carotid baroreceptor response
	Orthostatic hypotension
	Deep venous thrombosis
Respiratory	Atelectasis
	Pneumonia
	Pulmonary Embolus
Gastrointestinal	Ileus
	Constipation
Genitourinary	Urinary stasis
	Renal calculi
Endocrine	Insulin resistance
	Hyperglycemia
Musculoskeletal	Muscular atrophy
	Bone demineralization
	Contractures
Skin	Decubitus ulcers
Psychosocial	Depression
Other	Increased catabolism of immunoglobulin G
	Increased colonization with *Staphylococcus aureus*

From Timmerman, R. A. (2007). A mobility protocol for critically ill adults. *Dimensions of Critical Care Nursing, 26*(5), 175–179; and Rubin, M. (1988). The physiology of bed rest. *The American Journal of Nursing, 88*(1), 50–58.

to a decline in overall ability to function and increases the need for admittance into rehabilitation centers after hospitalization. It is important for nurses to be aware of these potential complications and to create the opportunity for movement and limitation of bed rest activity.

ICU-Acquired Weakness

ICU-acquired weakness is an increasingly recognized disorder characterized by the inability of a patient to move against resistance. It is a general term encompassing both myopathy and neuropathy with multifactorial causes beyond the scope of this chapter. Patients at risk for this disorder include those with systemic inflammatory response syndrome (SIRS) and sepsis, hyperglycemia, as well as those receiving corticosteroids or neuromuscular agents. Weakness can be difficult to diagnose in the ICU due to confounding issues such as altered neurological status, but is often first noticed when patients are unable to be extubated from a ventilator. Deem (2006) reviewed a number of studies revealing a range of 25% to 60% of ICU patients have significant weakness resulting in an average cost increase of $66,000 per patient with higher mortality rates. The only intervention shown to

decrease the incidence of ICU-acquired weakness was maintenance of blood glucose levels between 80 and 100 mg/dL. While physical therapy is commonly prescribed in the ICU, there is little prospective evidence of improved outcomes. More recent research identified multiple organ failure, muscle inactivity, hyperglycemia, and use of corticosteroids and neuromuscular blockers as risk factors for ICU-acquired weakness. The authors concur that strong evidence regarding the efficacy of preventive measures is still lacking; they recommend early identification and treatment of potential causes of multiple organ failure (in particular severe sepsis and septic shock), avoiding unnecessary deep sedation and hyperglycemia, promotion of early mobilization, and thoughtful decisions regarding the risks versus benefits of corticosteroids to potentially reduce the incidence and seriousness of ICU-acquired weakness (De Jonghe, Sharshar, Lefaucheur et al., 2002).

Contractures

Contractures are limitations in ROM of a joint with resultant inability to perform activities of daily living. A study by Claret et al. (2008) demonstrated that over one-third of patients who had spent time in the ICU left with a significant impairment in the function of one or more joints, some of which persisted until after discharge to rehabilitation centers or home. A seven-fold increase in joint contractures was noted after 8 weeks of stay in the ICU (Claret, Hebert, Fergusson et al., 2008).

Foot drop is a specific type of contracture defined by the inability to lift the dorsum (anterior surface) of the foot and toes upward (dorsiflexion). It can be caused by neurological or muscular diseases, as well as by inactivity during bed rest. The inability to lift the feet impairs the person's ability to mobilize and improve overall functioning. The use of footboards to maintain dorsiflexion, allowing for some weight bearing by tipping beds forward, and early walking in the ICU are recommended nursing interventions.

Nitrogen Wasting

To maintain a healthy state, the body requires equilibrium between the amounts of protein supplied and muscle mass breakdown/turnover. Critical illness often leads to increased requirements at a time when protein is either used for healing or lost at a higher rate due to immobility and/or disease processes.

Bone Demineralization

Weight bearing contributes to calcium uptake by the bones, promoting continued strength and bone formation. When on bed rest, calcium is excreted from the bones at higher levels while at the same time the patient may be at risk for decreased intake due to anorexia or intolerance to feedings.

The variety of ill effects from bed rest demonstrated through-out the literature and in this book should alert every nurse to the need for their patients to move. If out of bed activity is restricted, active/passive ROM should be employed, at a mini-mum of every shift. It is important to note that while sitting in a chair is helpful, the need to walk is paramount in terms of improving cardiovascular, respiratory, GI, and musculoskeletal status. In short, if allowed, the nurse should encourage the patient to get out of bed.

INTEGUMENTARY ISSUES

Admission to the ICU places the patient's skin at risk. Because of decreased mental status or decreased ability to change position, hypoperfusion, fever, immobility, and restraint, a patient may not be able to move in response to discomfort. The state of a patient's skin should be docu-mented on arrival to the unit, in order to follow changes. This documentation also has financial implications as Medicare is no longer reimbursing hospitals for hospital-acquired altera-tions in skin integrity such as pressure ulcers.

Planned Medical Breaks in Skin Integrity

Intravenous Lines

The skin is normally one contiguous unit. The simple act of placing a peripheral IV in a patient disrupts skin continuity and serves as a planned medical break in the skin and a poten-tial source of infection. All IV lines should be monitored for signs of infection and changed according to hospital policy.

Procedures

Minor procedures, such as pacemaker or PEG placement, are other examples of planned medical interventions that require breaks in the skin. Again, infection control is of para-mount importance.

Surgery

Surgical procedures interrupt skin and tissue integrity. Post-surgical infections can arise from deep tissue and organs, but surgical incisions require specific care and attention to prevent infection and poor wound healing.

Unplanned Breaks in Skin Integrity

Skin Tears

A majority of patients in the ICU are elderly and are affected by natural changes in the skin. More specifically, there is a flattening of the dermis and increased movement between the dermis and epidermis. When the two are separated, a skin tear occurs. ICU patients are prone to skin tears due to

their age, medication history (chronic steroid use), immo-bility, and altered mental status. ICU patients are also prone to skin tears due to nursing interventions such as tape removal, as well as due to friction and shear forces when pulling patients up in bed. Protection of the limbs from skin tears requires vigilance and patience on the part of the nurse. This means asking for enough help to turn or move a large patient.

Pressure Ulcers

A pressure ulcer is localized injury to the skin and/or under-lying tissue, usually over a bony prominence, as a result of pressure, or pressure in combination with shear and/or fric-tion. Because muscle and subcutaneous tissue are more sus-ceptible to pressure-induced injury than skin, pressure ulcers are often worse than their initial appearance. Pressure ulcers are staged to guide clinical description of the depth of observable tissue destruction (see Chapter 52). Pressure ulcers are breaks in the skin that can progress from the skin to subcutaneous tissue and bone. In the United States, the estimated annual incidence in acute care settings is 0.4% to 38%, with an average cost estimated at $11 billion and 60,000 deaths (Institute for Healthcare Improvement [IHI], n.d.). Box 55-3 provides risk factors for pressure ulcer development.

Unfortunately, many critical care patients have one or more of these risk factors.

Nurses hold the vast majority of responsibility for patient skin assessment, frequent turning, and skin care for pressure ulcer prevention. Early identification of and aggressive treatment for such ulcers is required.

See Chapter 52 for pressure ulcer staging and management.

BOX 55-3	Risk Factors for Pressure Ulcer Development

- Malnutrition
- Hemodynamic instability
- Predisposing diseases, such as diabetes
- Advanced age
- Infection
- Motor/sensory deficits
- Decreased mental status
- Incontinence
- Mobility/activity deficit
- Medications, such as sedatives
- Contractures
- Spasms

PSYCHOSOCIAL ISSUES

Entry into an ICU is stressful for patients and for their friends and families. Psychosocial issues can also play a part in the reason for ICU admission. Addiction to legal or illegal drugs, violence, and reckless behavior can all lead to serious accidents and illnesses. Nurses must always consider the possible psychosocial issues and disruptions that patients and families are confronting.

Fear

Every patient and family should be assessed to determine the presence of psychosocial issues. Fear or apprehension, awe, or anxiety due to perceived danger is a frequent entity in critical care. Patients and families can be afraid of death, permanent disability, and the critical care environment itself, where care of oneself or a loved one is entrusted to strangers. Lack of information regarding the plan of care and prognosis, as well as lack of understanding of the information provided is also a common cause of fear. Patients who frequently use the call bell or call out for help, and family members who are confrontational or demand constant nursing presence in the patient's room provide examples of not coping with the stress of ICU admission. Methods of decreasing fear for patients and families are not complex, yet they require time and patience on the part of nursing staff. Suggestions for allaying fear include:

• Introduction of staff and their roles in caring for the patient
• Explanation of what you are going to do to or with a patient and why
• Allowing family and friends to be present in the room
• Educating patients and families according to needs and desires
• Informing patients and families of progress or failure to progress

Grieving

Grieving is the process of coming to terms with loss: one's impending death, death of a loved one, loss of function and freedom, loss of self-image, and loss of future opportunities. The stages of grief are well defined throughout the literature, and all nurses should be aware of them. People will differ in their coping behaviors, and nurses should help people develop their best coping practices possible. This is a difficult and often time-consuming process. If nurses are unable to spend much time with grieving patients and families, it is imperative to find the patient alternate help: a colleague with more experience with grieving patients, a pastor, a social worker, hospital volunteers, family, or friends.

Violence

Violence in the home and workplace should never be tolerated, but is a fact that critical care nurses must confront.

Patients may have been a victim of past or recent injury. The sad fact is that many nurses can also report being a victim of violence at the hands of their patients. According to Ericksen (2008), health care workers are 16 times more likely to face workplace violence than are other service workers. This may include intimidation, verbal abuse, threats of physical violence, or actual violence (Hader, 2008). The nurse's goals are to identify patients at risk for being abused by others in their life, identify patients or families with a potential for violence against hospital staff, and establish a zero-tolerance workplace violence policy across the nation.

Patient Safety

Many people live with violence in their home, either through neglect or outright physical abuse. The elderly requiring significant time and resources from family members may be at increased risk for abuse as others become frustrated with their increasing disabilities. Assessing for a history of past injuries or evidence of current injury with appropriate referrals is warranted.

Patients with suicidal ideation also need to be protected in the acute care setting. This may include:

• A provider's order for one-to-one observation at all times
• A provider's order for chemical or mechanical restraint
• Removal of dangerous objects in the room
• Limit setting and negotiation with the patient
• Family and/or friend intervention as appropriate

Staff Safety

Patients at risk for harming staff members require specific interventions:

• Notification of security and administration of the potential for violence
• Keeping the patient in view at all times
• Approaching the patient with a calm but firm demeanor only with support from colleagues (and security as required)

END-OF-LIFE ISSUES

The critical care nurse will encounter many patients of various ages who are facing the ends of their lives.

Some of these deaths are unexpected, while others are anticipated. Each critical care nurse needs to be aware of his or her patient's medical prognosis and the patient's and family's response to a poor prognosis. Coping mechanisms will vary widely and range from sitting vigil by the patient to avoidance. An important component of care is providing patients with realistic information about their prognosis and end-of-life care while providing emotional support as they adjust to the idea of death.

Unexpected Death

Society expects that young people will not die. Sadly, accidents and illness do claim young lives. This requires nurses to be cognizant of these issues and support patients and families through anger, denial, and the other stages of grief. A number of studies have demonstrated that being with the patient at the end of life is important for many, and those who wish it should be present whenever they wish—including during resuscitation efforts.

If there is to be any solace in the death of a young or relatively young person, it can be found in the arena of organ and tissue donation. Patients who meet the criteria for past health and current diagnosis of brain death are eligible to donate organs to those on the various transplant lists. This places nurses in a difficult position at times due to their simultaneous obligations to care for a particular patient and their family while informing organ donation services of a potential donor. When the diagnosis of brain death is made, it is usually up to the senior medical staff and organ procurement services to approach the family about the possibility of organ donation.

Expected Death

Patients with a severe chronic illness or those of an advanced age have most likely had a number of experiences with the health care system and may be somewhat more mentally and emotionally prepared for death. ICU nurses need to be aware of their patients' advanced directives and living wills in order to advocate for their wishes during hospital care. They may have placed limits on what treatments they will allow in the event they can no longer speak for themselves, and nurses need to support these wishes or changes in those wishes. At this stage of life, nurses can provide the means to make the patient as comfortable as possible while allowing family and friends to come to terms with the loss of a loved one.

OTHER ISSUES

Sleep

Sleep is an essential bodily function, with significant impact on recovery from illness. Critical care patients are known to become sleep deprived due to their illness, ICU admission, pain, medical procedures, and nursing care. No matter the cause, sleep deprivation has been "associated with several adverse outcomes, including abnormalities in immune function and host defense mechanism, alterations in metabolism, nitrogen balance, protein catabolism, psychological disturbances, and changes in quality of life measures" (Friese, 2008, p. 698). This list is similar to known effects of prolonged bed rest and serves to highlight the necessity for uninterrupted sleep for patients.

Nursing care interferes with patients' ability to move through the stages of sleep toward rapid eye movement (REM), the deepest form of sleep. It requires an average of 90 minutes to reach REM sleep. How often is a patient left comfortable and undisturbed for at least 90 minutes in an ICU? The answer is not often enough.

A number of interventions may assist in promoting sleep:

- Clustering care
- Adequate pain relief
- Ensuring synchrony with the ventilator
- Noise and light reduction
- Day and night routines
- Sleep-promoting medications, such as melatonin
- Relaxation therapy, massage, and white noise
- Alarm limits as wide as safely possible to minimize ringing in the room

Falls

It is estimated that 2% to 12% of patients in the acute care setting will fall sometime during their hospital stay. Despite the implementation of fall prevention programs, research reveals little impact on decreasing fall rates while hospitalized (Coussement, de Paepe, Schwendimann et al., 2008). In fact, falls consistently represent the largest single category of reported incidents in hospitals (The Joint Commission, 2005). Ideally, the only way to prevent falls is to have a mentally and physically strong enough person be with each patient at all times; something not financially feasible for most hospitals. Realistically, what can be done is to identify risk factors for falling and arrange the care environment as well as possible to reduce the possibility of falls occurring (Table 55-12).

Transport of the ICU Patient

Critically ill patients are often safest inside the ICU, where staff and equipment are available for monitoring as needed. New technology has led to the availability of an ever-increasing number of tests and interventions that are able to be done at the bedside. This includes portable X-rays, endoscopies, and ultrasounds, and even minor surgical procedures such as tracheostomy and PEG tube placement. However, there are a number of times when a patient will require transportation from the ICU to the operating room or more frequently, to the radiology department. The radiology department may be required for tests such as computed tomography (CT) scan or intervention such as cardiac stent placement. Intrahospital movement of patients has long been known to be the cause of adverse effects: pain, increased intracranial pressure, hypotension, arrhythmia, hypoxia, VAP, decreased nutritional intake, hypo- and hyperglycemia, inadvertent disconnection from equipment, and falls.

Patients are placed at risk from transport due to decreased number of staff available to the patient, disruptions in

TABLE 55-12 Minimizing Falls

Risk Factors	Nursing Interventions to Decrease Risk for the Individual
History of falls	• Identify the patient as being at risk for falls. • Implement fall protocol.
Fear of falling	• Encourage patient to verbalize feelings. • Institute physical therapy consult to help patient demonstrate their ability to move safely.
Bowel and bladder incontinence	• Implement toileting routine. • Monitor bowel function to prevent diarrhea and constipation.
Cognitive impairment	• Evaluate patient for reversible causes of cognitive impairment/delirium and eliminate causes as possible. • Institute close observation by placing patient in view of nursing staff. • Start one-to-one observation. • Use monitoring devices, such as bed and chair exit alarms.
Mood	• Encourage verbalization of feelings. • Evaluate patient's ability to concentrate and learn new information. • Encourage engagement in daily activities. • Provide diversional activity. • Refer to geriatric psychiatry as appropriate.
Dizziness	• Monitor lying, sitting, and standing blood pressures, and continually evaluate for factors contributing to dizziness. • Set up environment to avoid movements that result in dizziness/vertigo. • If diabetic, monitor blood sugars and facilitate interventions to maintain appropriate blood sugars.
Functional impairment	• Encourage participation in personal care activities at highest level (ie, if possible, encourage ambulation to bathroom rather than use of bedpan). • Refer to physical and occupational therapy as appropriate.
Medications	• Review medications with medical practitioner and determine need for each medication. • Ascertain that medications are being used at lowest possible dosages to obtain desired results.
Medical problems	• Assure patient that medical problems are not a reason to remain in bed and prevent participation in functional activities.
Environment	• Remove furniture if patient can't sit on it and have his or her feet reach the floor. • Remove clutter. • Make sure furniture and any assistive devices used are in good condition. • Make sure lighting is adequate. • *Avoid* the use of four side rails and other forms of restraint.

From Gray-Micelli, D. (2007). Preventing falls in acute care. In E. Capezuti, D. Zwicker, M. Mezey, & T. Fulmer (Eds.), *Evidence-based geriatric nursing protocols for best practice* (3rd ed.). New York: Springer Publishing Company.

continuity of care, decreased ability to monitor patients in places like the magnetic resonance imaging (MRI) suite, and possible adverse effects of the test itself. With these known risks to patient safety, a number of tools and guidelines have been developed to minimize adverse events associated with transport. The IHI (Agency for Healthcare Research and Quality, 2007) describes a tool, the Situation-Background-Assessment-Recommendation (SBAR), for communicating information about a patient being transferred to the care of another health care professional. This tool ensures that all pertinent information required is up to date and available on one piece of paper as a reference for the person taking charge of the patient's care. The National Clearinghouse of Government Guidelines (Agency for Healthcare Research and Quality, 2007) has attempted to reduce adverse effects due to transportation of ICU patients with recommendations as listed in Box 55-4.

Transfer from the ICU

Eventually, all patients with some form of recovery will be discharged from the ICU. This usually occurs after morning provider rounds, when it is decided the patient is well enough to leave the unit for a lower level of care, such as a progressive care/step-down unit or other appropriate nursing unit. However, the need for ICU beds in the United States remains high, and many times, the least ill patient in the ICU is transferred later in the day to make room for someone more critically ill. This frequently happens late in the day or at night, when floor nursing staff levels are lower. It has been found that patients transferred from the ICU after 7 PM were more likely to have readmission to the ICU and a prolonged hospital stay (Hanane, Keegan, Seferian et al., 2008). While the decision to transfer a patient is a medical and administrative one, nurses must either advocate for their patients to stay in the ICU or put their patients in the best position to do well outside of the ICU. Doing well outside of the ICU is the goal for all patients.

BOX 55-4

Guidelines for Transporting the Patient

Communication:
- Ensure that transport is absolutely necessary.
- Ensure the department is ready to receive the patient.
- Ensure face-to-face report to the responsible parties when leaving a patient in radiology.

Personnel:
- A minimum of two people (one being a nurse) should be with the patient during transport.
- If unstable, a provider should accompany the patient.

Equipment:
- A cardiac monitor/defibrillator, blood pressure cuff, and pulse oximeter should be brought with the patient, without exception.
- Resuscitation equipment (bag-valve mask) and basic resuscitation drugs, including epinephrine and antiarrhythmic agents, are transported with each patient in the event of sudden cardiac arrest or arrhythmia.

Monitoring:
- The same level and frequency of monitoring that the patient received in the ICU should be maintained during transport.

Chapter Review

Critical Thinking Exercises

1. You have received a shift report that your patient, who sustained a femur fracture in a motor vehicle accident, is alert and oriented. Upon your initial assessment, you find the patient agitated and confused. What are some possible causes of this change in mental status?

2. Your patient with congestive heart failure is intubated with a pulmonary artery catheter in place. Your catheter measurements are very different from the measurements taken during the last shift. What are some possible reasons for these differences?

3. Your patient, admitted 14 days ago with respiratory failure, is unable to wean from the ventilator. What are possible causes of his inability to wean from this respiratory support?

NCLEX-Style Review Questions

1. A patient who is an IV drug user has had surgery to fix a broken femur after a motor vehicle accident. She requests morphine sulfate for pain control every hour, although it is ordered for every 3 hours. What is the nurse's most appropriate response?
   A. Tell her she can only have morphine every 3 hours.
   B. Tell her she is making her addiction stronger.
   C. Give her an extra dose of morphine anyway.
   D. Notify the provider of the patient's request for more frequent pain medication.

2. The nurse is caring for a 72-year-old women admitted with pneumonia and using a nasal cannula. During the first assessment, the nurse finds the O_2 saturation is 87%. What action will the nurse take first?

   A. Continue the physical assessment.
   B. Increase oxygen by providing an oxygen mask.
   C. Call the provider.
   D. Check to see if the oxygen is actually flowing and her tubing is not kinked.

3. A patient has just arrived from the operating room, where he underwent a total gastrectomy due to cancer. He has a Salem sump tube (SST; double-lumen NG tube) in place. Care of this patient and his SST tube include which of the following actions? Select all that apply.
   A. Placing the SST to low continuous wall suction
   B. Frequent and vigorous flushing of the NG tube to ensure patency
   C. Placing a sign at the head of the bed reminding staff not to alter the tube's position
   D. Ensuring the NG tube is securely taped to the patient's nose and noting measurement in the plan of care

4. The nurse knows that the inability to wean from a ventilator is associated with which of the following?
   A. Albumin level of 4.0 g/dL.
   B. Tidal volume of 7 mL/kg.
   C. Sinus rhythm on ECG
   D. Negative inspiratory force (NIF) of -15 cm H_2O

5. The nurse knows that complications associated with bed rest include which of the following? Select all that apply.
   A. Hypertension
   B. Constipation
   C. Decubitus ulcer
   D. Kidney stones

Try these additional resources to enhance your learning and understanding of this chapter:
- thePoint online resource available at **http://thepoint.lww.com/Pellico1e**
- *Handbook for Focus on Adult Health: Medical-Surgical Nursing*
- *Study Guide for Focus on Adult Health: Medical-Surgical Nursing*

References and Selected Readings

References and selected readings associated with this chapter can be found on the website that accompanies the book. Visit http://thepoint.lww.com/Pellico1e to access the references and other additional resources associated with this chapter.

Nursing Management: Emergencies and Disasters

SHARON DRUCE

Try these additional resources to enhance your learning and understanding of this chapter.

Visit thepoint.lww.com/Adams to:

Prepare for licensure: Adult Chapter Reviews

Review and extend your knowledge:

Assess and find ancillary problems associated with this chapter can be found on the website accompanying the text; it may be difficult to access the print and other ancillary resources associated with

Learning Objectives

After reading this chapter, you will be able to:

1. Discuss priority emergency measures instituted for any patient with an urgent condition.

2. Describe primary and secondary survey content and assessment of the emergency patient.

3. Discuss the priorities and assessment of the trauma patient.

4. Describe the fundamental elements of a hospital disaster plan.

5. Discuss how triage in a disaster differs from triage in an emergency.

6. Evaluate the different levels of personal protection and decontamination procedures that may be necessary during an event involving mass casualties or weapons of mass destruction.

7. Identify the effects of chemical and nerve agents, and the decontamination and treatment procedures that are necessary.

The emergency nurse has had specialized education, training, experience, and expertise in assessing and identifying patients' health care problems in crisis situations. The emergency nurse establishes priorities, monitors and continuously assesses acutely ill and injured patients of all ages, supports and attends to families, supervises allied health personnel, and teaches patients and families within a time-limited, high-pressured care environment. An additional component of emergency nursing is providing care during disasters, when local resources are overwhelmed.

EMERGENCY NURSING

The nursing process provides a logical framework for problem solving in the emergency department (ED). Patients in the ED have a wide variety of actual or potential problems, and their condition may change constantly. Therefore, nursing assessment must be continuous, and nursing diagnoses must adjust with the patient's condition.

Emergency nursing requires an understanding of triage and assessment and management of common acute disorders and injuries.

FOUNDATIONS OF EMERGENCY NURSING

Triage

Triage is used to sort patients into groups based on the severity of their health problems and the immediacy with which these problems must be treated. All EDs share this characteristic of a hierarchy based on the potential for loss of life. A basic and widely used triage system that was in use for many years consisted of three categories: **emergent**, **urgent**, and **nonurgent** (Gilboy, Tanabe, Travers et al., 2005) (Box 56-1). In this previously used acuity system, patients who may have needed many resources yet had a lower acuity need might have been assigned a lower triage level, which did not reflect the care they needed. Additionally, the three-category system did not address issues such as managing patient flow in EDs, issues of overcrowding and wait time, and did not demonstrate consistent reliability and validity.

A more refined comprehensive triage system has been implemented to incorporate the changes in the use of the ED for both emergency and

Traditional Triage Acuity System

Three categories:
- *Emergent:* Patients with the highest priority or life-threatening conditions.
- *Urgent:* Patients with serious health problems that are not considered immediately life-threatening
- *Nonurgent:* Patients who do not have life-threatening illnesses.

A fourth class was incorporated, termed "fast-track," and includes patients that require simple first aid or basic primary care and may be treated in the emergency department or safely referred to a clinic or health provider's office.

Data Collected by the Triage Nurse

- Patient's presenting complaint of illness or injury
- Level of pain
- Level of consciousness
- Circumstances, precipitating events, location, and time of the injury or illness
- Treatment of injury or illness prior to arrival in the emergency department (ED)
- Method of arrival to ED
- Physician or health practitioner seen for nonemergent care
- Health status prior to injury or illness
- History of medical illness and previous surgeries
- Previous hospitalizations
- Allergies including medications, eggs, latex, nuts, etc.
- Current medications
- Use of recreational drugs
- Smoking history
- Evaluation of immunizations for currency (tetanus)
- Brief assessment of body systems, including behavioral health screening for depression or suicidal ideation
- Last menstrual period (females of childbearing age)
- Time of last meal or oral intake
- Focused assessment on system involved with presenting complaint
- Special circumstances or requests of patient, especially those related to limitations regarding treatments (ie, resuscitation status or refusal of blood products)

routine health care. This system has five levels, numbered 1 to 5 in descending order of severity:

1. *Resuscitation:* The patient is dying.
2. *Emergent:* The patient should not wait.
3. *Urgent:* The patient is predicted to require two or more resources.
4. *Nonurgent:* The patient is predicted to require one resource.
5. *Minor:* The patient is predicted to require no resources (Gilboy et al., 2005).

The increased number of triage levels assists the triage nurse to more precisely determine the needs of the patient and the urgency for treatment. The Emergency Severity Index (ESI) has been endorsed by the American College of Emergency Physicians and the Emergency Nurses Association as the standardized triage system for the United States; it considers the patients clinical presentation, vital signs, and the amount and type of resources (examples include laboratory, IV hydration, radiological studies, simple or complex procedures, medications, consultation, etc.) needed to treat the patient (Gilboy et al., 2005; Lahdet, Suserud, Jonsson, & Lundberg, 2009; Shelton, 2009). Nurses in the triage area collect baseline data: full vital signs including pain assessment, history of the current event and past medical history, current medications, brief behavioral/mental status assessment, height, weight, allergies, and system review with a focus on the presenting complaint and clinical presentation. These data are recorded for reference by all health care team members treating the patient. Common assessment data are outlined in Box 56-2.

Primary and Secondary Surveys

A systematic approach to effectively establishing and treating health priorities is the primary survey/secondary survey approach. The primary survey focuses on stabilizing life-threatening conditions. The ED staff work collaboratively and follow the ABCD (airway, breathing, circulation, disability) method:

- Establish a patent airway.
- Provide adequate ventilation, employing resuscitation measures when necessary. Protection of cervical spine in trauma patients is mandatory when ventilating and resuscitation measures are needed.
- Evaluate and restore cardiac output by controlling hemorrhage, preventing and treating shock, and maintaining or restoring effective circulation, including the prevention and management of hypothermia.
- Determine neurologic disability by assessing neurologic function using the Glasgow Coma Scale. Evaluate for spinal cord injury if indicated.

After these priorities have been addressed, the ED team proceeds with the secondary survey. This includes the following:

- A complete health history and head-to-toe assessment
- Diagnostic and laboratory testing
- Insertion or application of monitoring devices, such as electrocardiogram (ECG) electrodes, arterial lines, or urinary catheters
- Splinting of suspected fractures
- Cleansing, closure, and dressing of wounds
- Performance of other necessary interventions based on the patient's condition

CARING FOR LIFE-THREATENING CONDITIONS

Emergency nurses often confront airway obstruction and hemorrhage. These conditions are life-threatening and require immediate intervention to prevent death.

AIRWAY OBSTRUCTION

Acute upper airway obstruction is a life-threatening medical emergency. The airway may be partially or completely occluded. Partial obstruction of the airway can lead to progressive hypoxia, hypercarbia (increased carbon dioxide levels in the blood), and respiratory and cardiac arrest. If the airway is completely obstructed, permanent brain injury or death will occur within 3 to 5 minutes, secondary to hypoxia. Air movement is absent in the presence of complete airway obstruction. Oxygen saturation of the blood decreases rapidly because the obstructed airway prevents entry of air into the lungs. Oxygen deficit occurs in the brain, resulting in unconsciousness, with death following rapidly.

Causes

Upper airway obstruction has a number of causes, including aspiration of foreign bodies, anaphylaxis, viral or bacterial infection, trauma, and inhalation or chemical burns. For elderly patients, especially those in extended-care facilities, sedatives and hypnotic medications, diseases affecting motor coordination (eg, Parkinson's disease), and mental dysfunction (eg, dementia, mental retardation) are risk factors for asphyxiation by food. In adults, aspiration of a bolus of meat is the most common cause of airway obstruction. In children, small toys, buttons, coins, and other objects are commonly aspirated in addition to food. Peritonsillar abscesses, epiglottitis, and other acute infectious processes of the posterior pharynx can also result in airway obstruction.

Clinical Manifestations and Assessment

Typically, a person with a foreign body airway obstruction cannot speak, breathe, or cough. The patient may clutch the neck between the thumb and fingers (this is known as the *universal distress signal*). Other common signs and symptoms include choking, apprehensive appearance, inspiratory and expiratory stridor, labored breathing, use of accessory muscles (suprasternal and intercostal retraction), flaring nostrils, increasing anxiety, restlessness, and confusion. Cyanosis and loss of consciousness develop as hypoxia worsens.

Assessment of the patient who has a foreign object occluding the airway may involve simply asking the person whether he or she is choking and requires help. If the person is unconscious, inspection of the oropharynx may reveal the offending object. X-rays, laryngoscopy, or bronchoscopy also may be required.

If the patient can breathe and cough spontaneously, a partial obstruction should be suspected.

Medical and Nursing Management

For partial obstruction, the patient is encouraged to cough forcefully and to persist with spontaneous coughing and breathing efforts as long as adequate air exchange exists. Oxygen saturation should be monitored to evaluate oxygenation. Supplemental oxygen should be administered. There may be some wheezing between coughs. If the patient demonstrates a weak, ineffective cough, a high-pitched noise while inhaling, increased respiratory difficulty, or cyanosis, he should be managed as if there were complete airway obstruction.

After the obstruction is removed, rescue breathing is initiated if the patient has absent or inadequate respiratory effort. If the patient has no pulse, cardiac compressions are instituted. These measures provide oxygen to the brain, heart, and other vital organs until definitive medical treatment can restore and support normal heart and ventilatory activity.

Establishing an Airway

Establishing an airway may be as simple as repositioning the patient's head to prevent the tongue from obstructing the pharynx. Alternatively, other maneuvers, such as abdominal thrusts (also called subdiaphragmatic abdominal thrusts), the head-tilt–chin-lift maneuver, the jaw-thrust maneuver, or insertion of specialized equipment, may be needed to open the airway, remove a foreign body, or maintain the airway. Box 56-3 provides guidelines for performing the Heimlich maneuver and abdominal and chest thrusts. In all maneuvers, the cervical spine must be protected from injury. After these maneuvers are performed, the patient is assessed for breathing by watching for chest movement and listening and feeling for air movement.

The head-tilt–chin-lift maneuver is used only if there is no suspected injury to the cervical spine. It is performed as follows:

- The patient is placed supine on a firm, flat surface.
- If the patient is lying face down, the body is turned as a unit so that the head, shoulders, and torso move simultaneously with no twisting.
- Next, the airway is opened using either the head-tilt–chin-lift maneuver or the jaw-thrust maneuver:
  - In the head-tilt–chin-lift maneuver, one hand is placed on the victim's forehead, and firm backward pressure is applied with the palm to tilt the head back. This will move the tongue forward (away from the back of the throat). The fingers of the other hand are placed under the bony part of the lower jaw (mandible) near the chin, and gently lifted up (Fig. 56-1). The chin and the teeth are lifted so that the teeth are almost brought together.
  - In the jaw-thrust maneuver, after one hand is placed on each side of the patient's jaw, the angles of the patient's lower jaw are grasped and lifted, displacing the mandible

BOX 56-3

Managing a Foreign Body Airway Obstruction

Heimlich Maneuver (Subdiaphragmatic Abdominal Thrusts)

For conscious patient (sitting or standing):

1. Stand behind the patient and wrap your arms around the patient's waist. If the victim is shorter than the rescuer, the rescuer may kneel behind the victim.
2. Make a fist with one hand.
3. Place the thumb side of the fist against the victim's abdomen, in the midline slightly above the navel and well below the breastbone.
4. Grasp your fist with the other hand and press your fist into the victim's abdomen with a quick upward thrust.
5. Repeat thrusts until the object is expelled from the airway or the victim becomes unresponsive.
6. Give each new thrust with a separate and distinct movement to relieve the obstruction.

Abdominal thrusts may be performed if the choking victim is responsive and lying down.

Chest Thrusts

For the conscious, sitting or standing patient who is in advanced stages of pregnancy or who is markedly obese:

1. Stand behind the patient with your arms under the patient's axillae to encircle the patient's chest.

2. Place the thumb side of your fist on the middle of the patient's sternum, taking care to avoid the xiphoid process and the margins of the rib cage.
3. Grasp your fist with the other hand and perform backward thrusts until the foreign body is expelled or the patient becomes unconscious. Each thrust should be administered with the intent of relieving the obstruction.

Unresponsive Choking, Adult Choking Victim Lying Down

If the choking victim becomes unresponsive, begin the sequence of cardiopulmonary resuscitation (CPR) by calling for support (or activating the emergency response system in a nonhospital setting). When opening the airway to deliver rescue breaths, open the victim's mouth wide, look for any foreign bodies, and remove any objects that can be seen. Be careful not to push any objects deeper into the airway. A blind finger sweep to search for foreign objects is not recommended. If the airway remains obstructed, reposition head and attempt to deliver rescue breaths a second time. Begin compressions and continue with advanced life support measures.

Adapted from American Heart Association (2006). *BLS for healthcare providers.* American Hearth Association. Retrieved from http://www.americanheart.org

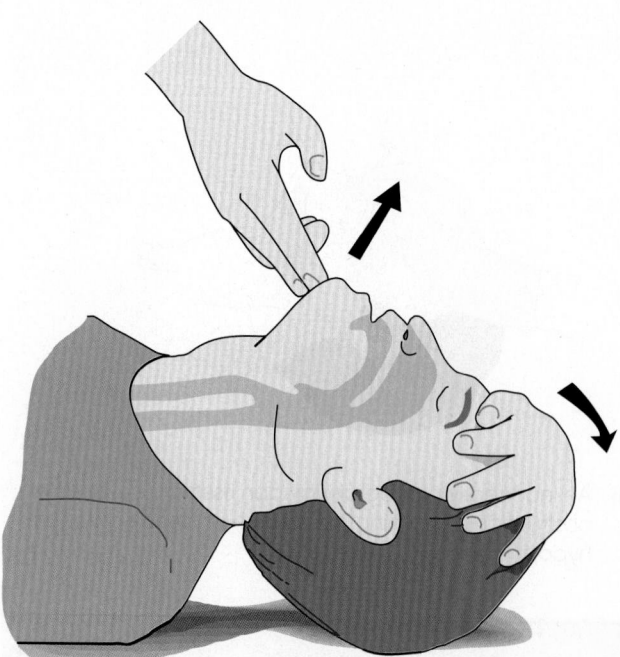

FIGURE 56-1 The head-tilt–chin-lift maneuver. LifeART image (© 2010). Lippincott Williams & Wilkins. All rights reserved.

forward. This is a safe approach to opening the airway of a patient with suspected neck injury because it can be accomplished without extending the neck.

Oropharyngeal Airway

An oropharyngeal airway is a semicircular tube or tube-like plastic device that is inserted over the back of the tongue into the lower posterior pharynx in a patient who is breathing spontaneously but who is unconscious. This type of airway prevents the tongue from falling back against the posterior pharynx and obstructing the airway. It also allows health care providers to suction secretions (Box 56-4).

Intubation

Endotracheal intubation is used to establish and maintain the airway in patients with respiratory insufficiency or hypoxia. Endotracheal intubation is indicated for the following reasons: (1) to establish an airway for a patient who cannot be adequately ventilated with an oropharyngeal airway, (2) to bypass an upper airway obstruction, (3) to prevent aspiration, (4) to permit connection of the patient to a resuscitation bag or mechanical ventilator, and (5) to facilitate the removal of tracheobronchial secretions. Because the procedure requires skill, endotracheal intubation is performed only by those who have had extensive training. However,

BOX 56-4

GUIDELINES FOR NURSING CARE

Inserting an Oropharyngeal Airway

Equipment

- Oropharyngeal airway
- Nonsterile gloves
- Protective eyewear if secretions are profuse or patient is coughing
- Equipment for suctioning

Implementation

ACTION	RATIONALE
1. Insert only in an unconscious patient. Remove dentures if present before insertion.	1. Vomiting and laryngospasm may be stimulated by the airway in a conscious or semiconscious patient. Remove dentures to prevent them from causing an airway obstruction.
2. Measure the oral airway alongside the head. Correct size of the airway should extend from the corner of the mouth to the tip of the earlobe (Reardon, Mason, & Clinton, 2010).	2. Accurate measurement is needed to ensure the airway is appropriately sized to prevent the tongue from occluding the airway.
3. Extend the patient's head by placing one hand under the bony chin (*only if the cervical spine is uninjured*). With the other hand, tilt the head backward by applying pressure to the forehead while simultaneously lifting the chin forward. Open the patient's mouth.	3. When positioning the head for insertion, the head may be tilted back *only* if the has had the cervical spine cleared. In the patient with a potential cervical spine injury, use only use the jaw-thrust maneuver to aid in postioning the head for airway insertion. Position facilitates insertion.
4. (**A**) Insert the oropharyngeal airway with the tip facing up toward the roof of the mouth until it passes the uvula. (**B**) Rotate the tip 180 degrees, so that the tip is pointed down toward the pharynx.	4. This displaces the tongue anteriorly, and the patient then breathes through and around the airway.

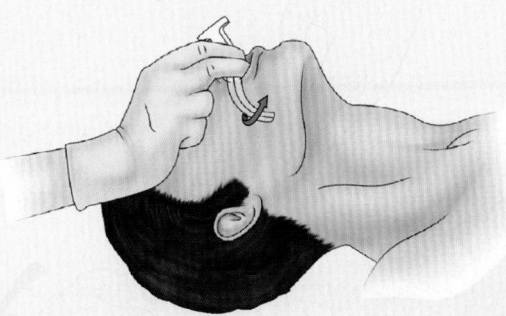

5. Ensure the distal end of the oropharyngeal airway is in the hypopharynx, and the flange is approximately at the patient's lips. Make sure that the tongue has not been pushed into the airway.	5. An incorrectly placed airway can itself cause airway obstruction by pushing the tongue posteriorly into the hypopharynx.

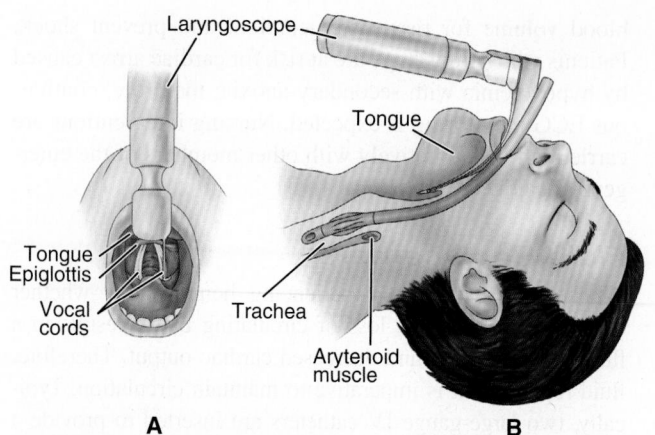

FIGURE 56-2 Endotracheal intubation in a patient without a cervical spine injury. (**A**) The primary glottis landmarks for tracheal intubation as visualized with proper placement of the laryngoscope. (**B**) Positioning the endotracheal tube.

the emergency nurse is commonly called on to assist with intubation (Fig. 56-2).

If the patient is not hospitalized and cannot be intubated in the field, emergency medical personnel may insert a Combitube. The tube rapidly provides pharyngeal ventilation. When the tube is inserted into the trachea, it functions like an endotracheal tube (Fig. 56-3).

The two balloons that surround the tube are inflated after the tube is inserted. One balloon is large (100 mL) and occludes the oropharynx. This permits ventilation by forcing air through the larynx. The smaller balloon is inflated with 15 mL of air and can occlude the trachea if it is inadvertently placed there (Gomella & Haist, 2007). Breath sounds are auscultated after balloon inflation to make sure that the oropharyngeal balloon (or cuff) does not obstruct the glottis. The patient can be ventilated through either one of the two ports (eg, tracheal or esophageal) of the tube, depending on whether the tube is placed in the trachea or esophagus.

Cricothyroidotomy

Cricothyroidotomy is the opening of the cricothyroid membrane to establish an airway. This procedure is used in emergency situations in which endotracheal intubation is either not possible or contraindicated, as in airway obstruction from extensive maxillofacial trauma, cervical spine injuries, laryngospasm, laryngeal edema (after an allergic reaction or extubation), hemorrhage into neck tissue, or obstruction of the larynx.

Maintaining the Airway

After the airway is determined to be unobstructed, the nurse must ensure that adequate ventilation is maintained. Satisfactory management of ventilations may prevent hypoxia and hypercapnia. The nurse must quickly assess for absent or diminished breath sounds, and difficulty delivering artificial

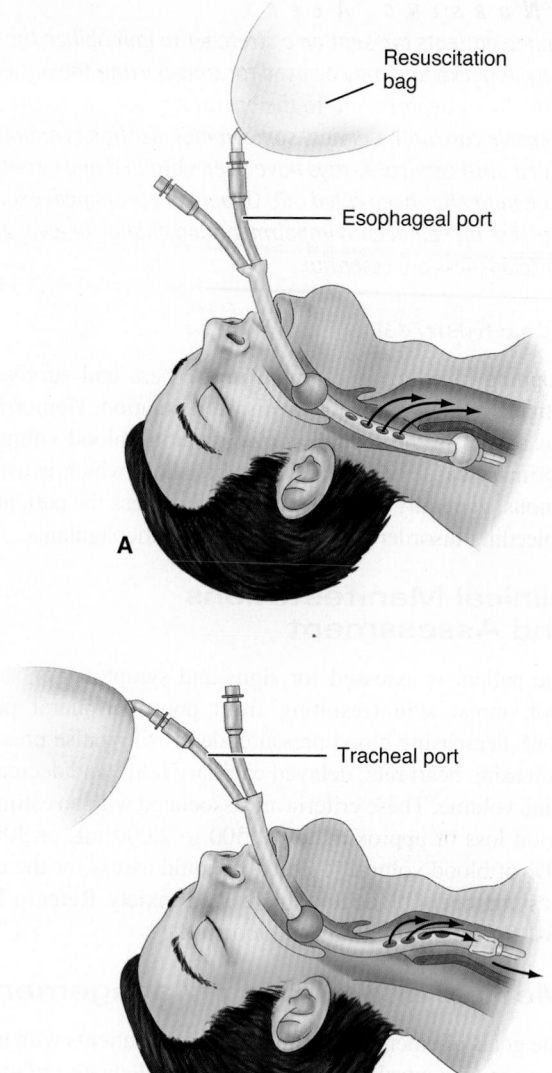

FIGURE 56-3 (**A**) Combitube in esophageal position. (**B**) Combitube in tracheal position.

breaths for the patient. The nurse should monitor pulse oximetry, capnography (monitoring of the amount of exhaled carbon dioxide), and arterial blood gases (ABGs) if the patient requires airway or ventilatory assistance.

The nurse is aware that a tension pneumothorax can mimic hypovolemia, so ventilatory assessment precedes assessment for hemorrhage. A pneumothorax or sucking (open) chest wound is managed with a chest tube; immediate relief of the increasing positive intrapleural pressure (normally, the intrapleural pressure is negative) and maintenance of adequate ventilation should occur (refer to Chapter 10 for information on pneumothorax and chest tube insertion and management).

Trauma patients are kept on a stretcher to immobilize the spine. A backboard may be used for transporting the patient to the X-ray department, to the operating room, or to the intensive care unit. Cervical spine immobilization is maintained until cervical X-rays have been obtained and cervical spine injury has been ruled out. Ongoing neurological exams to assess for spinal cord impairment and change in level of consciousness are essential.

HEMORRHAGE

Stopping bleeding is essential to the care and survival of patients in an emergency or disaster situation. Hemorrhage that results in the reduction of circulating blood volume is a primary cause of shock. Minor bleeding, which is usually venous, generally stops spontaneously unless the patient has a bleeding disorder or has been taking anticoagulants.

Clinical Manifestations and Assessment

The patient is assessed for signs and symptoms of shock: cool, moist skin (resulting from poor peripheral perfusion), decreasing blood pressure, decreasing pulse pressure, increasing heart rate, delayed capillary refill, and decreasing urine volume. These criteria are associated with an estimated blood loss of approximately 1,500 to 2,000 mL or 30% to 40% of blood volume; the nurse should assess for the earliest symptom of blood loss: increasing anxiety. Refer to Table 56-1 for estimated fluid and blood losses.

Medical and Nursing Management

The goals of emergency management for patients with blood loss are to control bleeding, maintain adequate circulating blood volume for tissue oxygenation, and prevent shock. Patients who hemorrhage are at risk for cardiac arrest caused by hypovolemia with secondary anoxia; therefore, continuous ECG monitoring is expected. Nursing interventions are carried out collaboratively with other members of the emergency health care team.

Fluid Replacement

Whenever a patient is experiencing hemorrhage—whether external or internal—a loss of circulating blood results in a fluid volume deficit and decreased cardiac output. Therefore, fluid replacement is imperative to maintain circulation. Typically, two large-gauge IV catheters are inserted to provide a means for fluid and blood replacement, and blood samples are obtained for analysis, typing, and cross-matching. Replacement fluids are administered as prescribed, depending on clinical estimates of the type and volume of fluid lost. Replacement fluids may include isotonic electrolyte solutions (lactated Ringer's, normal saline), colloids, and blood component therapy.

Packed red blood cells (PRBCs) are infused when there is massive blood loss. In emergencies, type O-negative blood is preferred for women of childbearing age and type O-positive blood is preferred for men and for postmenopausal women (Shaz, Dente, Harris et al., 2009). In a resuscitation with massive blood loss situation, there is no time to type and cross-match or type and screen blood. Type O-negative blood provides safe administration of blood immediately without sensitizing an Rh-negative woman to Rh-positive blood (sensitization can result in neonatal complications during a later pregnancy).

Additional platelets and clotting factors are given when large amounts of blood are needed, because transfused PRBCs are deficient in clotting factors. These additional products are given based on the results of coagulation studies that suggest a platelet or clotting deficiency.

TABLE
56-1 **Classes of Hemorrhagic Shock**

Class I Hemorrhage: Loss of up to 15% of Blood Volume (up to 750 mL in 70-kg Adult	Class II Hemorrhage: Loss of 15% to 30% of Blood Volume (750 to 1,500 mL)	Class III Hemorrhage: Loss of 30% to 40% of Blood Volume (1,500 to 2,000 mL)	Class IV Hemorrhage: Loss of >40% of Blood Volume (>2,000 mL)
Heart rate (HR) <100	HR >100	HR >120	HR >140
Systolic blood pressure (BP) normal	Systolic BP normal	Systolic BP decreased	Systolic BP markedly decreased
Respiratory rate (RR) 14 to 20	RR 20 to 30	RR 30 to 40	RR > 35
Increased or normal pulse pressure	Decreased pulse pressure	Decreased pulse pressure	Very narrow pulse pressure
Slight anxiety	Mildly anxious	Significant change in mental status: anxiety or confusion	Depressed mental status: confusion, lethargy, loss of consciousness
30 mL/hr	Small decrease in urine output (20 to 30 mL/hr)	Marked decrease in urine output (5 to 15 mL/hr)	Negligible urine output

Adapted from Chan, T. (2007). Hemorrhagic shock. In J. Schaider, S. Hayden, R. Barkin, & P. Rosen (Eds.). *Rosen & Barkin's 5-minute emergency medicine consult.* Philadelphia: Lippincott Williams & Wilkins.

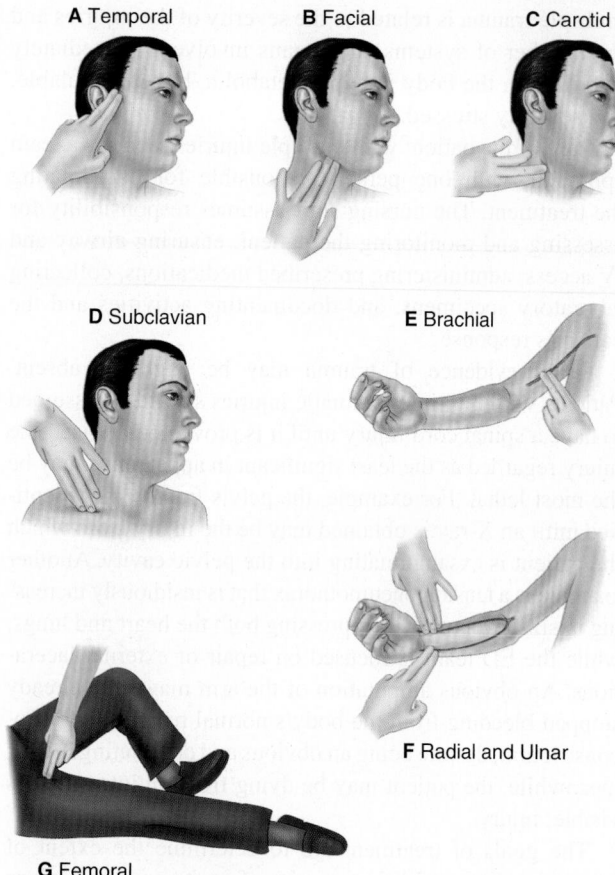

A Temporal   **B** Facial   **C** Carotid

D Subclavian   **E** Brachial

F Radial and Ulnar

G Femoral

FIGURE 56-4 Pressure points for control of hemorrhage.

Controlling Blood Loss

If a patient is hemorrhaging externally (eg, from a wound), a rapid physical assessment is performed as the patient's clothing is cut away in an attempt to identify the area of hemorrhage. Direct, firm pressure is applied over the bleeding area or the involved artery at a site that is proximal (above) to the wound (Fig. 56-4). Most bleeding can be stopped or at least controlled by application of direct pressure. Otherwise, unchecked arterial bleeding results in death. A firm pressure dressing is applied, and the injured part is elevated to stop venous and capillary bleeding if possible. If the injured area is an extremity, the extremity is immobilized to control blood loss.

A tourniquet is applied to an extremity only as a *last resort* when the external hemorrhage cannot be controlled in any other way and immediate surgery is not feasible. Care must be taken when applying a tourniquet because of the risk for loss of the extremity. The tourniquet is applied just proximal to the wound and tied tightly enough to control arterial blood flow. Documentation of the application of the tourniquet is critical, so that all providers are aware of the time and placement; suggestions include flow sheet documentation, use of a skin-marking pencil or adhesive tape on the forehead with a "T," labeling the location of the tourniquet and application time. If there is no arterial bleeding,

the tourniquet is removed and a pressure dressing is applied. If the patient has suffered a traumatic amputation with uncontrollable hemorrhage, the tourniquet remains in place until the patient is in the operating room.

If the patient shows no external signs of bleeding but exhibits tachycardia, falling blood pressure, thirst, apprehension, cool and moist skin, or delayed capillary refill, internal hemorrhage is suspected. Typically, PRBCs are administered at a rapid rate, and the patient is prepared for more definitive treatment (eg, surgery, endoscopy, pharmacologic therapy). In addition, laboratory specimens including, complete blood count (CBC), electrolytes, coagulation studies, type and cross-match, and ABG specimens are obtained to evaluate pulmonary function and tissue perfusion and to establish baseline hemodynamic parameters, which are then used as an index for determining the amount of fluid replacement the patient can tolerate and the response to therapy. The patient is maintained in the supine position and monitored closely until hemodynamic or circulatory parameters improve, or until he or she is transported for definitive therapy or continued treatment.

Failure to adequately fluid resuscitate and definitely control the source of hemorrhage may lead to hypovolemic (hemorrhagic) shock. It is the most common cause of post-injury death and should be suspected in any hypotensive trauma patient until proven otherwise (Cowell & Moore, 2010). Hypovolemic shock should be anticipated in any emergency situation in which profound blood or fluid (vomiting or diarrhea) loss has occurred. The goals of treatment are to restore and maintain tissue perfusion and to correct physiologic abnormalities. Chapter 54 provides detailed information on the management of hypovolemic shock.

Ongoing nursing surveillance of the *total patient* is maintained. Blood pressure, heart and respiratory rates, skin temperature, color, pulse oximetry, neurologic status, CVP, ABGs, ECG recordings, hematocrit, hemoglobin, coagulation profile, electrolytes, and urinary output are monitored serially to assess patient response to treatment. Commonly, a flow sheet is used to document these parameters, providing an analysis of trends rather than single values to reveal improvement or deterioration of the patient's condition.

In addition, the body's defense mechanisms are supported. The patient should be reassured and comforted. Sedation may be judiciously used to relieve apprehension. Analgesics are used cautiously to relieve pain. Body temperature is maintained within normal limits to prevent increasing metabolic demands that the body may be unable to meet. Administration of large volumes of IV crystalloids, blood products, or both can result in hypothermia. Hypothermia may be prevented by warming the fluids administered.

CARING FOR TRAUMA

Trauma (an unintentional or intentional wound or injury inflicted on the body from a mechanism against which the

body cannot protect itself) is the fifth leading cause of death in the United States (Heron, Hoyert, Murphy et al., 2009). Alcohol and drug abuse are often implicated as factors in both blunt and penetrating trauma.

In assessing and managing any patient with an emergency condition, but especially the patient experiencing trauma, documentation including descriptions of all wounds, mechanism of injury, time of events, and collection of evidence is essential. In trauma care, the nurse must be exceedingly careful with all potential evidence, handling and documenting it properly.

The basics of care management for patients with traumatic injury include an understanding that trauma in any patient (living or dead) has potential legal or forensic implications if criminal activity is suspected. Hence, proper management from both a medical and forensic perspective is essential. Box 56-5 describes collection of evidence.

Multiple trauma is caused by a single catastrophic event that causes life-threatening injuries to at least two distinct organs or organ systems. Mortality in patients with multiple trauma is related to the severity of the injuries and the number of systems and organs involved. Immediately after injury, the body is hypermetabolic, hypercoagulable, and severely stressed.

Care of the patient with multiple injuries requires a team approach, with one person responsible for coordinating the treatment. The nursing staff assumes responsibility for assessing and monitoring the patient, ensuring airway and IV access, administering prescribed medications, collecting laboratory specimens, and documenting activities and the patient's response.

Gross evidence of trauma may be slight or absent. Patients with multiple traumatic injuries should be assumed to have a spinal cord injury until it is proven otherwise. The injury regarded as the least significant in appearance may be the most lethal. For example, the pelvis fracture not identified until an X-ray is obtained may be the injury from which the patient is exsanguinating into the pelvic cavity. Another example is a tension pneumothorax that is insidiously increasing in size, eventually compressing both the heart and lungs, while the ED team is focused on repair of external lacerations. An obvious amputation of the arm may have already stopped bleeding from the body's normal response of vasoconstriction, despite being an obvious and devastating injury; meanwhile, the patient may be dying from an internal, less visible, injury.

The goals of treatment are to determine the extent of injuries and to establish priorities of treatment. Any injury interfering with a vital physiologic function (eg, airway, breathing, circulation) is an immediate threat to life and has the highest priority for immediate treatment. Essential life-saving procedures are performed simultaneously by the emergency team. As soon as the patient is resuscitated, clothes are usually cut off, and a rapid physical assessment is performed. Transfer from field management to the ED must be orderly and controlled, with attention given to the verbal report from emergency medical services. Treatment in a level I trauma center is appropriate for patients experiencing major trauma.

WOUNDS

Wounds involving injury to soft tissues can vary from minor tears to severe crushing injuries. The primary goal of treatment is to restore the physical integrity and function of the injured tissue while minimizing scarring and preventing infection. Proper documentation of the characteristics of the wound, using precise descriptions and correct terminology, is essential. Such information may be needed in the future for forensic evidence. Photographs are helpful because they provide an accurate, visible depiction of the wound. Photographs also become important for exigent wounds (wounds that will heal and later be unidentifiable). Patients involved in domestic violence or trauma may need the photographs later to visually describe the extent of injury.

BOX 56-5 **Collection of Forensic Evidence**

When clothing is removed from the patient who has experienced trauma, the nurse must be careful not to cut through or disrupt any tears, holes, blood stains, or dirt present on the clothing if criminal activity is suspected. Each piece of clothing should be placed in an individual paper bag. If the clothing is wet, it should be hung to dry. Clothing should not be given to families. Valuables should be placed in the hospital safe or clearly documented as to which family member they were given. If a police officer is present to collect clothing or any other items from the patient, each item is labeled. The transfer of custody to the officer, the officer's name, the date, and the time are documented.

If suicide or homicide is suspected in a deceased trauma patient, the medical examiner examines the body on site or has the body moved to the coroner's office for autopsy. All tubes and lines must remain in place. The patient's hands must be covered with paper bags to protect evidence on the hands or under the fingernails. In the surviving patient, tissue specimens may be swabbed from the hands and nails as potential evidence. Photographs of wounds or clothing are essential and should include a reference ruler in one photo and one photo without the ruler.

Documentation should also include any statements made by the patient in the patient's own words and surrounded by quotation marks. A chain of evidence is essential. If the patient's case is adjudicated in the future, clear documentation assists the judicial process and helps to identify the activities that occurred in the emergency department.

Determining *when* and *how* the wound occurred is important, because a treatment delay increases infection risk. Using aseptic technique, the clinician inspects the wound to determine the extent of damage to underlying structures. Visible contamination of the wound increases the risk of wound infection. Additionally the nurse is aware that bite wounds carry significant risk for infection owing to the high bacterial colonization in the mouth. Sensory, motor, and vascular function is evaluated for changes that might indicate complications.

Hair around the wound may be clipped if it is anticipated that the hairs will interfere with wound closure. Shaving should be avoided; it may result in an increased incidence of wound infection since many bacteria reside in hair follicles (Hollander & Singer, 2010). Removal of eyebrow hairs is avoided as regrowth may not occur.

If indicated, the area is infiltrated with a local intradermal anesthetic through the wound margins or by regional block. Patients with soft tissue injuries usually have localized pain at the site of injury. The nurse then assists the physician, nurse practitioner, or physician's assistant in cleaning and débriding the wound.

Wound cleaning requires the selection of methods that minimize chemical and mechanical trauma to the wound tissue while removing surface debris and contaminants (Gardner & Frantz, 2008). Typically, the area around the wound is cleansed with normal saline solution or a polymer agent (eg, Shur-Clens). Antibacterial agents, such as povidone–iodine (Betadine) or chlorhexidine can be used to paint the intact skin surrounding the wound but should not be allowed to get into the wound since the solutions are associated with decreasing defense mechanisms and thus increase the risk of wound infection. With the emergence of antibiotic resistance, some researchers call for a reappraisal of the use of antiseptic solutions especially in the management of contaminated and infected wounds (Khan & Naqvi, 2006). At present, a standardized regimen for wound cleaning has yet to be established.

To decrease the incidence of wound infection, the nurse anticipates both the use of wound irrigation and débridement of dead wound tissue. The wound will be irrigated gently and copiously with sterile isotonic saline solution to remove surface dirt. Approximately 50 to 100 mL of saline irrigation per 1 cm of laceration is considered as a general guideline (Sherman & Webber, 2007). The nurse ensures that the **personal protective equipment** (PPE) of face shields are utilized. Devitalized tissue and foreign matter are removed by the physician because they impede healing and may encourage infection. Any small bleeding vessels are clamped or tied. Alternatively, hemostasis of small bleeding vessels is achieved by clamping, tying, or cauterization. After wound treatment, a nonadherent dressing is commonly applied to protect the wound. The dressing may serve as a splint and also as a reminder to the patient that the area is injured.

The decision to suture a wound depends on the nature of the wound, the time since the injury was sustained, the degree of contamination, and the vascularity of tissues. If primary closure is indicated, the wound is sutured or stapled, with the patient receiving either local anesthesia or moderate sedation. Sutures are placed near the wound edge, with the skin edges leveled carefully to promote optimal healing. Instead of sutures, sterile strips of reinforced microporous tape or a bonding agent (skin glue) may be used to close clean, superficial wounds.

Delayed primary closure may be indicated if tissue has been lost or there is a high potential for infection. A thin layer of gauze (to ensure drainage and prevent pooling of exudate), covered by an occlusive dressing, may be used. Other options include split-thickness cadaver allografts or porcine xenografts to simulate the function of epithelium. The wound is splinted in a functional position to prevent motion and decrease the possibility of contracture. Use of antibiotics to prevent infection depends on factors such as how the injury occurred, the age of the wound, the risk of contamination, and the present of risk factors in the patient's medical history that decrease wound healing (diabetes, steroid use, chemotherapeutic agents, chronic renal failure, peripheral vascular disease, elderly, anemia, malnourished). The site is immobilized and elevated to limit accumulation of fluid in the interstitial spaces of the wound.

Tetanus prophylaxis is administered as prescribed, based on the condition of the wound and the patient's immunization status. If the patient's last tetanus booster was given more than 5 years ago, or if the patient's immunization status is unknown, a tetanus booster must be given. The patient is instructed about signs and symptoms of infection and is instructed to contact the health care provider or clinic if there is sudden or persistent pain, fever or chills, bleeding, rapid swelling, foul odor, drainage, or redness surrounding the wound.

INTRA-ABDOMINAL INJURIES

Intra-abdominal injuries are categorized as penetrating or blunt trauma. Penetrating abdominal trauma (eg, gunshot wounds, stab wounds) results in a high incidence of injury to hollow organs, particularly the small bowel; thus, they are serious and usually require surgery. The liver is the most frequently injured solid organ. In gunshot wounds, the most important factor is the velocity at which the missile (bullet) enters the body. The higher the velocity, the more extensive tissue damage is expected. All abdominal gunshot wounds that cross the peritoneum or are associated with peritoneal signs require surgical exploration. On the other hand, stab wounds may be managed nonoperatively. The nurse accurately documents the location and number of wounds. If abdominal viscera protrude, the area is immediately covered with sterile, moist saline dressings to keep the viscera from drying, and the patient is expected to go directly to the operating room for closure.

Blunt trauma to the abdomen may result from motor vehicle crashes, falls, blows, or explosions. Blunt trauma is commonly associated with extra-abdominal injuries to the chest, head, or extremities. Patients with blunt trauma are a challenge because injuries may be difficult to detect. The incidence of delayed and trauma-related complications is greater than for penetrating injuries. This is especially true of blunt injuries involving the liver, kidneys, spleen, or blood vessels, which can lead to massive blood loss into the peritoneal cavity.

Clinical Manifestations and Assessment

As the history of the traumatic event is obtained, the abdomen is inspected for obvious signs of injury, including penetrating injuries, bruises, and abrasions. Abdominal assessment continues with auscultation of bowel sounds to provide baseline data from which changes can be noted. Absence of bowel sounds may be an early sign of intraperitoneal involvement. Further abdominal assessment may reveal progressive abdominal distention, involuntary guarding, tenderness, pain, muscular rigidity, or rebound tenderness, along with changes in bowel sounds, all of which are signs of peritoneal irritation (refer to Chapter 21 for further details of gastrointestinal [GI] assessment). Hypotension and signs and symptoms of shock may also be noted. Additionally, the chest and other body systems are assessed for injuries that frequently accompany intra-abdominal injuries.

Studies that aid in assessment include the following:

- Urinalysis to detect hematuria (indicative of a urinary tract injury)
- Ultrasound of abdomen to evaluate fluid collection
- Peritoneal lavage to evaluate abdominal fluid collection
- Radiology and/or computed tomography (CT) scan to evaluate abdominal organ injury, fluid, foreign particles
- Serial hemoglobin and hematocrit levels to evaluate trends reflecting the presence or absence of bleeding
- White blood cell (WBC) count to detect elevation (generally associated with trauma)
- Serum amylase analysis to detect increasing levels, which suggest pancreatic injury or perforation of the GI tract

Hemorrhage frequently accompanies abdominal injury, especially if the liver or spleen has been traumatized. Therefore, the patient is assessed continuously for signs and symptoms of external and internal bleeding. The front of the body, flanks, and back are inspected for bluish discoloration, asymmetry, abrasion, and contusion (see Chapter 21 for descriptions of Cullen's and Grey-Turner's sign). Abdominal CT scans permit detailed evaluation of abdominal contents and retroperitoneal examination. Abdominal ultrasound studies can rapidly assess hemodynamically unstable patients to detect intraperitoneal bleeding. This is referred to as the Focused Assessment for Sonographic Examination of the Trauma Patient (FAST) examination.

The nurse suspects hemoperitoneum and splenic injuries if the patient complains of left shoulder pain. This symptom is termed *Kehr's sign* and is referred pain due to diaphragmatic irritation associated with the splenic injury or intra-abdominal hemorrhaging. Pain in the right shoulder can result from laceration of the liver. Referred pain is a significant finding because it suggests intraperitoneal injury. The abdomen is assessed for tenderness, rebound tenderness, guarding, rigidity, spasm, increasing distention, and pain. To determine whether there is intraperitoneal injury and bleeding, the patient is usually prepared for diagnostic procedures, such as abdominal ultrasonography, or abdominal CT scanning. FAST has rapidly replaced **diagnostic peritoneal lavage (DPL)**, owing to its sensitivity (90%), specificity (95%), and accuracy (99%) in determining the presence of intra-abdominal fluid (Manthey & Nicks, 2008). Additionally, CT scans, because of their speed and detailed results have largely replaced DPL in the stable patient. However, peritoneal lavage is useful in assessing hollow organ injury, or when serial CT scans cannot be performed, as in patients with severe closed head injury or high spinal cord injury. It involves the instillation of 1 L of warmed lactated Ringer's or normal saline solution into the abdominal cavity. After a minimum of 400 mL has been returned, a fluid specimen is sent to the laboratory for analysis. Positive laboratory findings include a red blood cell count greater than $100,000/mm^3$; a WBC count greater than $500/mm^3$; or the presence of bile, feces, or food.

In patients with stab wounds, the nurse anticipates that a surgeon will assess whether the peritoneal space has been punctured. Fluid resuscitation may be required, and if perforation is confirmed, exploration in the operating room is expected. The need for tetanus booster will be evaluated, and antibiotics administration is anticipated.

Medical and Nursing Management

As indicated by the patient's condition, resuscitation procedures (restoration of airway, breathing, and circulation) are initiated. A patent airway is maintained, and attempts to stabilize the respiratory, circulatory, and nervous systems are made. Bleeding is controlled by application of direct pressure to any external, bleeding wounds and by occlusion of any chest wounds. Circulating blood volume is maintained with IV fluid replacement, including blood component therapy, and the nurse monitors the patient's vital signs, oxygen

saturation, urinary output, and mentation to detect stabilization or evidence of deterioration.

Typically, when the patient presents with intra-abdominal injuries, oral fluids are withheld in anticipation of surgery, and a nasogastric tube may be inserted to decompress the stomach and reduce the risk of aspiration. Tetanus prophylaxis and broad-spectrum antibiotics are administered as prescribed.

Throughout the stay in the ED, the patient's condition is continuously monitored for changes. If there is continuing evidence of shock, blood loss, free air under the diaphragm, evisceration, hematuria, severe head injury, or suspected or known abdominal injury, the patient is rapidly transported to surgery. In most cases, blunt liver and spleen injuries are managed nonsurgically.

CRUSH INJURIES

Crush injuries occur when a person is caught between opposing forces (eg, run over by a moving vehicle, compressed by machinery, crushed between two cars, crushed under a collapsed building).

Clinical Manifestations and Assessment

The patient is observed for the following:

- Hypovolemic shock resulting from extravasation of blood and plasma into injured tissues after compression has been released
- Paralysis of a body part
- Erythema and blistering of skin
- Damaged body part (usually an extremity) appearing swollen, tense, and hard
- Renal dysfunction (prolonged hypotension causes kidney damage and acute renal insufficiency; myoglobinuria secondary to muscle damage can cause acute tubular necrosis and acute renal failure). See Chapter 42, Box 42-7 for pathophysiology of rhabdomyolysis.

Medical and Nursing Management

In conjunction with maintaining the airway, breathing, and circulation, the patient is observed for acute renal insufficiency. Injury to the back can cause severe kidney damage. Severe muscular damage may cause rhabdomyolysis, a significant release of myoglobin from ischemic skeletal muscle, which can result in acute tubular necrosis. In addition, major soft tissue injuries are splinted early to control bleeding and pain. Fluid resuscitation, as discussed previously, is expected and—in addition to stabilization of vital signs, urine output, and hemodynamic parameters—the serum lactic acid level may be monitored as a parameter of successful resuscitation. Lactic acid levels are discussed in Chapter 55.

If an extremity is injured, it is elevated to relieve swelling and pressure. To restore neurovascular function, the physician may perform a **fasciotomy** (surgical incision to the level of the fascia). Medications for pain and anxiety are then administered as prescribed, and the patient is quickly transported to the operating suite for wound débridement and fracture repair. A hyperbaric chamber (if available) may be used for hyperoxygenation of the crushed tissue, if indicated.

GENITOURINARY INJURY

A rectal or vaginal examination is performed by the primary care provider to determine injury to the pelvis, bladder, or intestinal wall. To decompress the bladder and monitor urine output, an indwelling catheter is inserted after a visual examination of the genitourinary area and rectal examination has been completed (not before). In the male patient, a high-riding prostate gland (abnormal position) discovered during a rectal examination indicates a potential urethral injury. Refer to Chapter 28 for details on genitourinary trauma.

ANAPHYLACTIC REACTION

An anaphylactic reaction is an acute systemic hypersensitivity reaction that occurs within seconds or minutes after exposure to certain foreign substances, such as medications, and other agents, such as latex, insect stings, or foods. Repeated administration of parenteral or oral therapeutic agents (eg, repeated exposures to penicillin) may also precipitate an anaphylactic reaction when initially only a mild allergic response occurred. See Chapter 38 for the pathophysiology and clinical manifestations of anaphylaxis.

With an anaphylactic reaction, establishing a patent airway and ventilation is essential. This is performed while another person administers epinephrine. Early endotracheal intubation is essential to preserve airway patency, and oropharyngeal suction may be necessary to remove excessive secretions. Resuscitative measures are used, especially for patients with stridor and progressive pulmonary edema. If glottal edema occurs, emergent cricothyroidotomy may be necessary to provide an airway.

Simultaneously with airway management, aqueous epinephrine is administered as prescribed to provide rapid relief of the hypersensitivity reaction. Epinephrine may be administered again, if necessary and as prescribed. Judgment is used in choosing one of the following routes of administration:

- Subcutaneous injection for mild, generalized symptoms
- IM injection when the reaction is more severe and progressive, and with the knowledge that vascular collapse will delay absorption of the medication
- IV route (aqueous epinephrine diluted in saline solution and administered *slowly*), used in rare instances in which there is complete loss of consciousness and severe cardiovascular collapse. This method may precipitate cardiac arrhythmias, so ECG monitoring with a readily available defibrillator is necessary. This method is controversial and is not usually recommended because it can lead to more

distress than initially present. An IV infusion of saline solution is initiated to provide for emergency access to a vein and to treat hypotension.

Additional treatments may include the following:

- Antihistamines (eg, diphenhydramine [Benadryl]) to block further histamine binding at target cells
- Aminophylline titrated by IV drip for severe broncho-spasm and wheezing refractory to other treatment
- Albuterol (Proventil, Ventolin) inhalers or humidified treatments to decrease bronchoconstriction; crystalloids, colloids, or vasopressors to treat prolonged hypotension
- Isoproterenol (Isuprel) or dopamine (Intropin) for reduced cardiac output; oxygen to enhance tissue perfusion
- IV benzodiazepines (eg, diazepam [Valium]) for control of seizures, and corticosteroids (eg, hydrocortisone [Solu-Cortef]) for prolonged reaction with persistent hypotension or bronchospasm

Depending on the severity of the acute symptoms, the patient may be admitted to the hospital for observation. The patient should be informed about ways to prevent anaphylactic reactions.

CARING FOR POISONING

A poison is any substance that, when ingested, inhaled, absorbed, applied to the skin, or produced within the body in relatively small amounts, injures the body by its chemical action. Poisoning from inhalation and ingestion of toxic materials, both intentional and unintentional, constitutes a major health hazard and an emergency situation. Emergency treatment is initiated with the following goals:

- To remove or inactivate the poison before it is absorbed
- To provide supportive care in maintaining vital organ systems
- To administer a specific antidote to neutralize a specific poison
- To implement treatment that hastens the elimination of the absorbed poison

INGESTED (SWALLOWED) POISONS

Swallowed poisons may be corrosive. **Corrosive poisons** include alkaline and acid agents that can cause tissue destruction after coming into contact with mucous membranes. Alkaline products include lye, drain cleaners, toilet bowl cleaners, bleach, nonphosphate detergents, oven cleaners, and button batteries (batteries used to power watches, calculators, or cameras). Acid products include toilet bowl cleaners, pool cleaners, metal cleaners, rust removers, and battery acid.

Medical and Nursing Management

Control of the airway, ventilation, and oxygenation are essential. In the absence of cerebral or renal damage, the patient's prognosis depends largely on successful management of respiration and circulation. Measures are instituted to stabilize cardiovascular and other body functions. ECG, vital signs, and neurologic status are monitored closely for changes. Shock may result from the cardiodepressant action of the substance ingested, from venous pooling in the lower extremities, or from reduced circulating blood volume resulting from increased capillary permeability. An indwelling urinary catheter is inserted to monitor renal function. Blood specimens are obtained to determine the concentration of drug or poison.

Efforts are made to determine what substance was ingested; the amount; the time since ingestion; signs and symptoms, such as pain or burning sensations, any evidence of redness or burn in the mouth or throat, pain on swallowing or an inability to swallow, vomiting, or drooling; age and weight of the patient; and pertinent health history.

Measures are instituted to remove the toxin or decrease its absorption. Consultation with a Poison Control Center is strongly recommended for definitive antidote and continued monitoring. The patient who has ingested a corrosive poison is given water or milk to drink for dilution. However, dilution is not attempted if the patient has acute airway edema or obstruction, or if there is clinical evidence of esophageal, gastric, or intestinal burn or perforation. The following gastric emptying procedures may be used as prescribed:

- Syrup of ipecac to induce vomiting in the alert patient (*never* use with corrosive poisons)
- Gastric lavage for the obtunded patient. Gastric aspirate is saved and sent to the laboratory for toxicology screens.
- Activated charcoal administration if the poison is one that is absorbed by charcoal
- Cathartic, when appropriate

The specific chemical or physiologic antagonist (antidote) is administered as early as possible to reverse or diminish the effects of the toxin. If this measure is ineffective, procedures may be initiated to remove the ingested substance. These procedures include administration of multiple doses of charcoal, diuresis (for substances excreted by the kidneys), dialysis, or hemoperfusion once admitted to an appropriate inpatient setting. Hemoperfusion involves detoxification of the blood by processing it through an extracorporeal circuit and an adsorbent cartridge containing charcoal or resin, after which the cleansed blood is returned to the patient.

Throughout detoxification, the patient's vital signs, CVP, and fluid and electrolyte balance are monitored closely. Hypotension and cardiac arrhythmias are possible. Seizures are also possible because of central nervous system (CNS) excitement from the poison or from oxygen deprivation. If the patient complains of pain, analgesics are administered cautiously. Severe pain causes vasomotor collapse and reflex inhibition of normal physiologic functions.

Patients presenting with ingested poisoning need to be evaluated for accidental ingestion versus intentional ingestion

due to suicide attempt or other psychiatric disturbance. After the patient's condition has stabilized, written material should be given to the patient indicating the signs and symptoms of potential problems related to the poison ingested and signs or symptoms requiring evaluation by the primary care provider.

CARBON MONOXIDE POISONING

Carbon monoxide poisoning may occur as a result of industrial or household incidents or attempted suicide. It is implicated in more deaths than any other toxin except alcohol.

When unintentional carbon monoxide poisoning occurs, the health department should be contacted, so that the dwelling or building in question can be inspected. Carbon monoxide exerts its toxic effect by binding to circulating hemoglobin and thereby reducing the oxygen-carrying capacity of the blood.

Clinical Manifestations and Assessment

Because the CNS has a critical need for oxygen, CNS symptoms predominate with carbon monoxide toxicity. A person with carbon monoxide poisoning may appear intoxicated (from cerebral hypoxia). Other signs and symptoms include headache, muscular weakness, palpitation, dizziness, and confusion, which can progress rapidly to coma. Skin color, which can range from pink or cherry-red to cyanotic and pale, is not a reliable sign. Pulse oximetry is also not valid, because the hemoglobin is well saturated. It is not saturated with oxygen, but the pulse oximeter only reads whether or not the hemoglobin is saturated; in this case, it is saturated with carbon monoxide rather than oxygen.

Medical and Nursing Management

Exposure to carbon monoxide requires immediate treatment. Goals of management are to reverse cerebral and myocardial hypoxia and to hasten elimination of carbon monoxide. Whenever a patient inhales a poison, the following general measures apply:

- Carry the patient to fresh air immediately; open all doors and windows.
- Loosen all tight clothing.
- Initiate cardiopulmonary resuscitation if required; administer 100% oxygen.
- Prevent chilling; wrap the patient in blankets.
- Keep the patient as quiet as possible.
- Do not give alcohol in any form or permit the patient to smoke.

In addition, for the patient with carbon monoxide poisoning, **carboxyhemoglobin** levels are analyzed on arrival at the ED and before treatment with oxygen if possible. Oxygen at 100% is administered at atmospheric or preferably hyperbaric pressures to reverse hypoxia and accelerate the elimination of carbon monoxide. Oxygen is administered until the carboxyhemoglobin level is less than 5%. The patient is monitored continuously. Psychoses, spastic paralysis, ataxia, visual disturbances, and deterioration of mental status and behavior may persist after resuscitation and may be symptoms of permanent brain damage.

DISASTER NURSING

The World Health Organization (2005) defines disaster as any man-made or natural event that overwhelms the local community resources. Resources may be required from local, state, and federal agencies. International agency support may be required in cases where extensive intervention is required. Acts of terrorism, warfare, air or rail accidents, pandemic illness, weather-related events, toxic spills, or geological events such as landslides and earthquakes are examples of some common disaster events that can result in casualties and tax the resources of health care facilities and their communities.

FEDERAL, STATE, AND LOCAL RESPONSES TO EMERGENCIES

When a **mass casualty incident (MCI)** occurs, the initial review and response occurs at the local level. Local emergency response agencies (including volunteer agencies) are typically the first responders. As the magnitude of the MCI is evaluated and scope of services needed is assessed, the progression to enlist aid from state and then federal resources may be made through official channels. Local and state Offices of Emergency Management coordinate interagency efforts. These organizations maintain a corps of emergency management personnel, including responders, planners, and administrative and support staff. A request for federal resources generally is made when local resources have become or are expected to become depleted due to the magnitude of the event. Federal resources are available through several departments, although the intent is to support local and state efforts rather than assume responsibility for any disaster response. Table 56-2 lists federal resources.

The Incident Command System (ICS) is the local organization that coordinates personnel, facilities, equipment, and communication in any emergency situation. The ICS has a federal mandate and is an integral part of the National Incident Management System (NIMS). According to the Federal Emergency Management Administration (FEMA) (n.d.), the ICS can be used at all levels of disaster management to provide a standard management response that organizes and integrates the coordination of response for personnel, facilities, and equipment. It establishes common responses for planning and managing resources at all response levels.

T A B L E
56-2 Federal Disaster Resources

Federal Disaster Resources	Type of Support Available
Department of Health and Human Services (DHHS)	
Centers for Disease Control and Prevention (CDC)	Collaborates to create the expertise, information, and tools needed to protect the health of the nation and the world.
National Disaster Medical System (NDMS)	Has many medical support teams, such as Disaster Medical Assistance Teams (DMATs), Disaster Mortuary Response Teams (DMORTs), Veterinary Medical Assistance Teams (VMATs), and National Medical Response Teams for Weapons of Mass Destruction (NMRTs).
Department of Justice (DOJ)	
Federal Emergency Management Agency (FEMA)	Provides scene control and collection of forensic evidence
Department of Homeland Security	
Federal Bureau of Investigation (FBI)	Can activate teams such as the Urban Search and Rescue Teams (USRTs)

HOSPITAL EMERGENCY PREPAREDNESS PLANS

Health care facilities are required by the Joint Commission to create a plan for emergency preparedness that addresses both internal and external disasters. This plan should be developed with attention to the most likely internal and external disaster potentials. Disaster exercises are required to simulate mass casualty events and participation from multiple agencies.

Components

The Joint Commission has created accreditation standards that cover eight essential areas for disaster operation plans. These emergency management standards include: expectations for plans for managing the consequences of emergencies; development and maintenance of an Emergency Operations Plan; establishing emergency communication strategies; planning for managing resources and assets during emergencies; managing safety and security during emergencies; defining staff roles and responsibilities; establishing strategies for managing utilities during emergencies; and developing strategies for managing patient clinical and support activities during an emergency (Joint Commission, 2008).

Initiating the Disaster Plan

Notification of a disaster situation to a health care facility varies with each situation. Generally, the notification to the facility comes from outside sources unless the initial incident occurred at the facility. The disaster activation plan should clearly state how the Emergency Operation Plan (EOP) is to be initiated. If communication is functioning, field incident command will give notice of the approximate number of arriving patients, although the number of self-referring patients will not be known and may impact resource management.

Identifying Patients

Patient tracking is a critical component of casualty management. Disaster tags, which are numbered and include triage priority, name, address, age, location and description of injuries, and treatments or medications given, are used to communicate patient information. The tag should be securely placed on the patient and remain with the patient at all times. The tag number and the patient's name are recorded in a disaster log. The log is used by the command center to track patients, assign beds, and provide families with information.

Triage During Mass Casualty Incidents

In nondisaster situations, health care workers assign a high priority and allocate the most resources to those who are the most critically ill. However, in a disaster, when health care providers are faced with a large number of casualties, the fundamental principle guiding resource allocation is to do the greatest good for the greatest number of people. Decisions are based on the likelihood of survival and consumption of available resources. Therefore, patients with conditions associated with a high mortality rate would be assigned a low triage priority in a disaster situation, even if the person is conscious. Although this may sound uncaring, from an ethical standpoint, the expenditure of limited resources on people with a low chance of survival, and denial of those resources to others with serious but treatable conditions, cannot be justified.

The triage officer rapidly assesses those injured at the disaster scene. Patients are immediately tagged and transported or given life-saving interventions. One person performs the initial triage while other Emergency Medical Services (EMS) personnel perform life-saving measures (eg, intubation) and transport patients. Although EMS personnel carry out initial field triage, secondary and continuous triage at all subsequent levels of care is essential.

Staff should control all entrances to the acute care facility, so that incoming patients are directed to the triage area first. The triage area may be outside the entry or just at the door of the ED. This allows all patients, including those arriving by medical transport and those who walk in, to be triaged. Some patients already seen in the field may be reclassified in the triage area, based on their current presentation.

Triage categories separate patients according to severity of injury. A special color-coded tagging system is used during an

TABLE
56-3 Triage Categories During a Mass Casualty Incident (MCI)

Triage Category	Priority	Color	Typical Conditions
Immediate: Injuries are life-threatening but survivable with minimal intervention. Individuals in this group can progress rapidly to expectant category if treatment is delayed.	1	Red	Sucking chest wound, airway obstruction secondary to mechanical cause, shock, hemothorax, tension pneumothorax, asphyxia, unstable chest and abdominal wounds, incomplete amputations, open fractures of long bones, and second-/third-degree burns of 15% to 40% total body surface area.
Delayed: Injuries are significant and require medical care, but can wait hours without threat to life or limb. Individuals in this group receive treatment only after immediate casualties are treated.	2	Yellow	Stable abdominal wounds without evidence of significant hemorrhage; soft tissue injuries; maxillofacial wounds without airway compromise; vascular injuries with adequate collateral circulation; genitourinary tract disruption; fractures requiring open reduction, débridement, and external fixation; most eye and central nervous system injuries.
Minimal: Injuries are minor and treatment can be delayed hours to days. Individuals in this group should be moved away from the main triage area.	3	Green	Upper extremity fractures, minor burns, sprains, small lacerations without significant bleeding, behavioral disorders or psychological disturbances.
Expectant: Injuries are extensive and chances of survival are unlikely even with definitive care. Persons in this group should be separated from other casualties, but not abandoned. Comfort measures should be provided when possible.	4	Black	Unresponsive patients with penetrating head wounds, high spinal cord injuries, wounds involving multiple anatomical sites and organs, second-/third-degree burns in excess of 60% of body surface area, seizures or vomiting within 24 hr after radiation exposure, profound shock with multiple injuries, agonal respirations; no pulse, no blood pressure, pupils fixed and dilated.

MCI, so that the triage category is immediately obvious. There are several triage systems in use across the country, and every nurse should be aware of the system used by his or her facility and community. The North Atlantic Treaty Organization (NATO) triage system is one that is widely used and is presented here. It consists of four colors—red, yellow, green, and black (Table 56-3). Each color signifies a different level of priority, with red representing the most significant but potentially survivable injuries through green representing minor injuries. Black designates "expected" death due to nonsurvivable injuries or patients in whom death appears to be imminent.

Communication With Media and Family

Communication is a key component of disaster management. Communication within the vast team of disaster responders is paramount; however, effective, informative communication with the media and worried family members is also crucial and must be addressed in the organization's disaster plan and communicated to staff.

Although the media have an obligation to report the news and can play a significant positive role in communication,

the number of reporters and newscasters and their support teams can be overwhelming, possibly compromising operations and patient confidentiality. A clearly defined process for managing media requests that includes a designated spokesperson, a site for the dissemination of information (away from patient care areas), and a regular schedule for providing updates should be part of the disaster plan.

The disaster plan helps prevent the release of contradictory or inaccurate information. Initial statements should focus on current efforts and what is being done to better understand the scope and impact of the situation. Information about casualties should not be released. Security staff should not allow media personnel access to patient care areas.

Friends and family members converging on the scene must be cared for by the facility. They may be feeling intense anxiety, shock, or grief and should be provided with information and updates about their loved ones as soon as possible and regularly thereafter. They should not be in the triage or treatment areas, but in a designated area staffed by available social service workers, counselors, therapists, and/or clergy. Access to this area should be controlled to prevent families from being disturbed.

Emotional and behavioral effects vary among affected people. Factors that influence a person's response to disaster include the degree and nature of the exposure to the disaster, loss of friends and loved ones, existing coping strategies, available resources and support, and the personal meaning attached to the event. Other factors, such as loss of home and valued possessions, extended exposure to danger, and exposure to toxic contamination, also influence response and increase the risk for adjustment problems. Those exposed to the dead and injured, those endangered by the event, the elderly, children, emergency first-responders, and health care personnel caring for victims are considered to be at higher risk of emotional sequelae.

Nurses can assist disaster victims and families through active listening and providing emotional support, giving information, and referring patients to therapists or social workers. Health care workers must refer people to mental health care services because experience has shown that few disaster victims seek these services and early intervention minimizes psychological consequences. Nurses can also discourage victims from subjecting themselves to repeated exposure to the event through media replays and news articles, and encourage them to return to normal activities and social roles when appropriate.

The Nurse's Role in Disaster Response Plans

The role of the nurse during a disaster varies. The nurse may be asked to perform duties outside his or her area of expertise and may take on responsibilities normally held by physicians or advanced practice nurses. Although the exact role of a nurse in disaster management depends on the specific needs of the facility at the time, it should be clear which nurse or physician is in charge of a given patient care area and which procedures each individual nurse may or may not perform. Assistance can be obtained through the incident command center, and non-medical personnel can provide services where possible.

New settings and atypical roles for nurses arise during a disaster; for example, the nurse may provide shelter care in a temporary housing area, or bereavement support and assistance with identification of deceased loved ones. People may require crisis intervention, or the nurse may participate in counseling other staff members and in critical incident stress management (CISM) (discussed later in this chapter). Special care may be warranted for at-risk populations during a disaster including disabled, elderly, young, pregnant, and other vulnerable populations.

Disasters can present a disparity between the resources of the health care agency and the needs of the victims. This generates ethical dilemmas for nurses and other health care providers. Issues include conflicts related to the following:

- Rationing care
- Futile therapy
- Consent
- Duty
- Confidentiality
- Resuscitation

Nurses may find it difficult to not provide medical care to the dying, or to withhold information to avoid spreading fear and panic. Clinical scenarios that are unimaginable in normal circumstances confront the nurse in extreme instances. Other ethical dilemmas may arise out of health care providers' instinct for self-protection and protection of their families.

Nurses can plan for the ethical dilemmas they will face during disasters by establishing a framework for evaluating ethical questions before they arise and by identifying and exploring possible responses to difficult clinical situations. They can consider how the fundamental ethical principles of utilitarianism, beneficence, and justice will influence their decisions and care in disaster response. Education and practice of the disaster response plan can assist the nurse in achieving an understanding of the role changes and dilemmas that might impact job performance.

Critical Incident Stress Management

CISM is an approach to preventing and treating the emotional trauma that can affect emergency responders as a consequence of their jobs and that can also occur to anyone involved in a disaster or MCI. CISM is handled by teams trained in the techniques.

Components of CISM plans include defusings, debriefings, demobilization, and follow-up care after the incident. *Defusing* is a process by which the person receives education about recognition of stress reactions and management strategies for handling stress. *Debriefing* is a more complicated intervention; it involves a 2- to 3-hour process during which participants are asked about their emotional reactions to the incident, what symptoms they may be experiencing (eg, flashbacks, difficulty sleeping, intrusive thoughts), and other psychological ramifications. As an intervention, *demobilization* is usually reserved for large-scale events with large numbers of participants from different disciplines. If separate defusing interventions were attempted for each group, CISM resources might be overwhelmed. Similar to the defusing intervention, responders are presented with information regarding expected stress reactions that they might experience and how to manage them. The responders are also provided an opportunity to rest and eat before returning to their normal, pre-incident routines. In the event of large-scale disasters, it might be appropriate to participate in the demobilization process after each shift of work. In *follow-up*, members of the CISM team contact the participants of a debriefing and schedule a follow-up meeting if necessary. People with ongoing stress reactions are referred to mental health specialists.

PREPAREDNESS AND RESPONSE

As a health care provider, preparedness for terrorism and other disasters includes awareness of the potential for covert

use of weapons of mass destruction (WMD), self-protection, and early detection, containment, or **decontamination** of substances and agents that may affect others by secondary exposure. The strength of many toxins, today's mobile society, and long incubation periods for some organisms and diseases can result in an epidemic that can quickly and silently spread across the entire country. For example, there must be awareness that a formerly healthy person with a rapid onset of flu-like symptoms can have an ominous illness, such as anthrax or severe acute respiratory syndrome (SARS), both of which are discussed in more detail later in the chapter.

Detection

Health care personnel should have a heightened awareness for trends that may suggest deliberate dispersal of toxic or infectious agents. Some general principles should be considered, such as the following:

- Awareness of an unusual increase in the number of people seeking care for fever, respiratory, or GI symptoms.
- Any clusters of patients presenting with the same unusual illness from a single location. Clusters can be from a specific geographic location, such as a city, or from a single sporting or entertainment event.
- Large number of rapidly fatal cases, especially when death occurs within 72 hours after hospital admission.
- Increase in disease incidence in a normally healthy population. These cases should be reported to the state health department and to the Centers for Disease Control and Prevention (CDC), including information about recent travel and contact with others who have been ill or have recently died of a fatal illness.

Suspicions or findings are reported to the appropriate resources in the facility and to proper authorities in the community. Resources can include the infection control department, material safety data sheets (MSDS), the state health department, the CDC, the local poison control center, and many Internet sites. Reporting furnishes data elements to those agencies responsible for epidemiology and response. Reporting also allows for sharing of information among facilities and jurisdictions and can help determine the source of infections or exposure and prevent further exposures and even deaths.

Personal Protection

Preparedness and response involves the protection of the health care provider by additional PPE prior to contact with a contaminated or infected patient. The purpose of PPE is to shield health care workers from the chemical, physical, biologic, and radiologic hazards that may exist when caring for contaminated patients. The U.S. Environmental Protection Agency (EPA) has divided protective clothing and respiratory protection into four categories, level A through level D (Box 56-6) (U.S. Environmental Protection Agency [EPA], 2009).

BOX 56-6

Environmental Protection Agency Categories of Protective Clothing and Respiratory Protection

- Level A protection is worn when the highest level of respiratory, skin, eye, and mucous membrane protection is required. This includes a self-contained breathing apparatus (SCBA) and a fully encapsulating, vapor-tight, chemical-resistant suit with chemical-resistant gloves and boots.
- Level B protection requires the highest level of respiratory protection but a lesser level of skin and eye protection than with level A situations. This level of protection includes include positive-pressure, full face-piece SCBA or positive-pressure supplied air respirator with escape SCBA, inner and outer chemical-resistant gloves, face shield, hooded chemical resistant clothing, coveralls, and outer chemical-resistant boots.
- Level C protection requires the air-purified respirator, which uses filters or sorbent materials to remove harmful substances from the air. A chemical-resistant coverall with splash hood, chemical-resistant gloves, and boots are included in level C protection.
- Level D protection is the typical work uniform. Level D protective equipment may include gloves, safety glasses, or a face shield.

Decontamination

Decontamination, the process of removing accumulated contaminants, is critical to the health and safety of health care providers by preventing secondary contamination. The decontamination plan should establish procedures and educate employees about decontamination procedures, identify the equipment needed and methods to be used, and establish methods for disposal of contaminated materials.

Effective decontamination must include a minimum of two steps. The first step is removal of the patient's clothing and jewelry and then rinsing the patient with water. Depending on the type of exposure, this step alone can remove a large amount of the contamination and decrease secondary contamination. Ideally, facilities should identify areas where patients can be decontaminated prior to entering the facility, to prevent accidental contamination of the emergency services area, staff, and other hospital areas and personnel. The second step consists of a thorough soap-and-water wash and rinse. When patients arrive at the facility after being assessed and treated by a prehospital provider, it should not be assumed that they have been thoroughly decontaminated.

NATURAL DISASTERS

Natural disasters may result in mass casualties. Natural disasters can occur anywhere at any time and include events

such as tornadoes, hurricanes, floods, avalanches, tidal waves (eg, tsunamis), earthquakes, and volcanic eruptions. In many cases, preparation prior to the natural disaster is the best-laid plan. In the event of a natural disaster, loss of communications, potable water, and electricity are usually the greatest obstacles to a well-coordinated emergency response. Even wireless technology (eg, mobile or cellular phones, computers, other communication devices) may not be functional.

The majority of the immediate casualties are trauma-related. These mass casualties tax the trauma system to its limits to provide triage, transport of patients (in poor weather and road conditions), and management within the trauma centers. Electrocution is also a common injury and can result in death.

Excessive exposure to the natural elements and the need for food and water (by both patients and emergency responders) are critical issues. Without cover (eg, buildings may be unsafe or destroyed) or safe water (eg, water may be either contaminated or unavailable), injuries from exposure to heat, cold, or contaminated food or water can occur. Safety equipment that protects rescue workers from injury, exposure, and potentially dangerous animals must be readily available. Hypothermia can occur rapidly in workers who are exposed to water at temperatures of 75°F or less. As in all disasters, mental health workers and shelters are needed throughout the community. Veterinary assistance is also essential, because frequently pets are abandoned and injured. After floods or water disasters, waterborne transmission of agents such as *Escherichia coli*, salmonella, shigella, typhoid, leptospirosis, malaria, and tularemia are common and cause widespread disease.

In some instances, early warning systems have assisted in decreasing the number of deaths from tornadoes and hurricanes. When buildings collapse, rapid response to identify and remove trapped victims is the only means of improving survivability. There is a direct relationship between time trapped and survival, construction, and number of stories of the collapsed structure. Larger-scale issues that can cause significant later morbidity and mortality include the absence of water purification, waste removal, removal of human and animal remains, and vector control. Removal or disposal of biologic, chemical, and nuclear agents must also be considered.

BIOLOGICAL AGENTS

Biologic weapons are weapons that spread disease among the general population or the military as part of **biological warfare**. Biologic agents are delivered in either a liquid or dry state, applied to foods or water, or vaporized for inhalation or direct contact. Vaporization may be accomplished through spray or explosives loaded with the agent. Because of increases in business and pleasure travel by people in industrialized nations, an agent could be released in one city and affect people in other cities thousands of miles away. The vector can be an insect, animal, or person, or there may be direct contact with the agent itself.

Anthrax and smallpox are the two of the agents most likely to be used or weaponized. Table 56-4 describes other easily weaponized biologic agents.

ANTHRAX

Inhaled anthrax is recognized as the most likely weaponized biologic agent available.

Bacillus anthracis is a naturally occurring gram-positive, encapsulated rod that lives in the soil in the spore state throughout the world. The bacterium is liberated when exposed to air and is infective only in the spore form. Contact with infected animal products (raw meat) or inhalation of the spores results in infection.

Pathophysiology

Animal studies have suggested that small amounts of inhaled anthrax spores (as low as 50 to 98 spores) may be sufficient to cause death in 10% of the exposed human population (Center for Infectious Disease Research and Policy, 2011). As an aerosol, anthrax is odorless and invisible and can travel a great distance before disseminating; hence, the site of release and the site of infection can be miles apart. Incubation of the inhaled spores can be as long as 7 days.

Clinical Manifestations

Initial symptoms may resemble a common cold. Anthrax does not present as pneumonia. After several days, the symptoms may progress to severe breathing problems and shock.

Medical and Nursing Management

Inhalation anthrax is frequently fatal even with aggressive antibiotic and supportive therapy. Due to the presence of spores, antibiotic treatment is continued for 60 days. Anthrax cannot be spread from person to person, and standard level D universal precautions are sufficient.

SMALLPOX

Pathophysiology

Smallpox (variola) is classified as a DNA virus. It has an incubation period of 10 to 12 days. It is extremely contagious and is spread by direct contact, by contact with clothing or linens, or by inhaled droplets of saliva during contact with an infected person. During the incubation period there are no symptoms. When the virus has multiplied sufficiently to cause the fever and characteristic rash, the affected person not only feels ill but is also at the most infectious period

TABLE
56-4 Examples of Biologic Agents That Can Be Used as Weapons

Agent/ Organism	Contagion	Decontamination and Protective Equipment	Signs and Symptoms	Treatment (Mortality Rate)
Tularemia (*Francisella tularensis*): gram-negative coccobacillus, one of the most infectious bacteria known	Direct contact with infected animals or aerosolized as a bioterror weapon; bites Not contagious through human-to-human contact	Standard barrier precautions Clothing and linens should be laundered under the usual hospital protocol.	*Initial:* Abrupt onset of fever, fatigue, chills, headache, lower backache, malaise, rigor, coryza, dry cough, and sore throat without adenopathy. Nausea and vomiting or diarrhea possible. *As disease progresses:* Sweating, fever, progressive weakness, anorexia, and weight loss demonstrate continued illness. *Mortality secondary to:* Pneumonitis (if inhalation is the source) with copious watery or purulent sputum, hemoptysis, respiratory insufficiency, sepsis, and shock.	Streptomycin or gentamicin/ aminoglycoside for 10–14 days. Inhalation tularemia must be treated within 48 hours of onset. In mass casualty situations, doxycycline or ciprofloxacin is recommended. For persons exposed to tularemia, tetracycline or doxycycline is recommended for 14 days. (Mortality rate = 2%)
Botulism (*Clostridium botulinum*): Botulinum blocks acetylcholine-containing vesicles from fusing with the terminal membranes of the motor-neuron end-plate, resulting in a flaccid paralysis.	Direct contact Not contagious through human-to-human contact	Any skin exposure to the botulism toxin can be treated with soap and water or a 0.1% hypochlorite solution. Standard precautions are used when treating patients with botulism.	*Gastrointestinal botulism:* Abdominal cramps, nausea, vomiting, and diarrhea. *Inhalation botulism:* Fever; symmetric descending flaccid paralysis with multiple cranial nerve palsies. Classic signs and symptoms include diplopia, dysphagia, dry mouth, lack of fever, and alert mental status. Other possible symptoms include ptosis of the eyelids, blurred vision, enlarged sluggish pupils, dysarthria, and dysphonia. *Mortality secondary to:* Airway obstruction and inadequate tidal volume.	Supportive ventilatory therapy is necessary if respiratory infection occurs. Aminoglycosides and clindamycin are contraindicated because they exacerbate neuromuscular blockage. Equine antitoxin is used to minimize subsequent nerve damage. There is a 2% rate of anaphylaxis to the antitoxin; therefore, diphenhydramine (Benadryl) and epinephrine must be immediately available for use. Supportive care: Mechanical ventilation, nutrition, fluids, prevention of complications (Mortality rate = 5%)
Plague (*Yersinia pestis*): Nonsporulating gram-negative coccobacillus. The bacterium causes destruction and necrosis of the lymph nodes.	Contagious *Bubonic plague:* transmitted through flea bites with no person-to-person transmission *Pneumonic plague:* transmitted through respiratory droplet contact	Isolation barrier precautions with full face respirators. The patient should wear a mask. Rooms should receive a terminal cleaning. Clothing and linens with body fluids on them should be cleaned with the usual disinfectant. Routine precautions should be used in the case of death.	*Bubonic plague:* Sudden fever and chills, weakness, a swollen and tender lymph node (bubo) in the groin, axilla, or cervical area. The resultant bacteremia progresses to septicemia from the endotoxin and, finally, shock and death. *Primary septicemic plague:* Disseminated intravascular coagulation (DIC), necrosis of small vessels, purpura, and gangrene of the digits and nose (black death). *Pneumonic plague:* Severe bronchospasm, chest pain, dyspnea, cough, and hemoptysis. There is a 100% mortality associated with pneumonic plague if not treated within the first 24 hours.	Streptomycin or gentamicin for 10 to 14 days. Tetracycline or doxycycline is an acceptable alternative if an aminoglycoside cannot be given. People with close contact exposure (<2 m) require prophylaxis with doxycycline for 7 days. (Mortality rate = 50%)

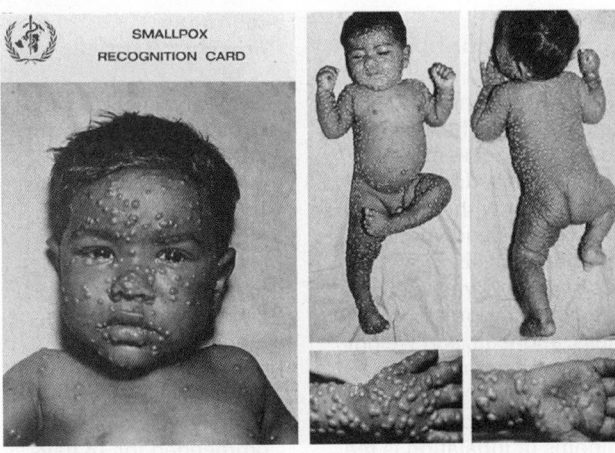

FIGURE 56-5 Patient with smallpox. From Knipe, D. M., & Howley, P. M. (Eds.). (2001). *Field's virology* (4th ed.). Philadelphia: Lippincott Williams & Wilkins.

(National Institute of Allergy and Infectious Diseases, 2009). Aerosolization of the virus would result in widespread dissemination.

Clinical Manifestations and Assessment

Signs and symptoms of smallpox infection are similar to influenza and include high fever, malaise, headache, backache, and fatigue. After 2 to 3 days, a flat, red, lesioned rash appears, evolving at the same rate, beginning on the face, mouth, pharynx, and forearms. After several days, these lesions become filled with pus (Fig. 56-5) and form crusts in week 2. By week 3, these crusts have become scabs and begin to fall off (National Institute of Allergy and Infectious Diseases, 2008). There is a large amount of the virus in the saliva and pustules. Smallpox (variola) is contagious only after the appearance of the rash. There are two forms of smallpox, variola major and variola minor. Variola major is more common and results in a higher fever and more extensive rash. Variola major has a 30% case-fatality rate. Hemorrhagic smallpox, a subtype of variola major, includes all of the above signs and symptoms plus a dusky erythema and petechiae to frank hemorrhage of the skin and mucous membranes, resulting in death by day 5 or 6.

Medical and Nursing Management

There is no specific treatment for smallpox, and vaccination is preventative. Treatment includes supportive care with antibiotics for any additional infection. The patient must be isolated with the use of transmission precautions. Laundry and biologic wastes should be autoclaved before being washed with hot water and bleach. Standard **decontamination** of the room is effective. All people who have household or face-to-face contact with the patient after the fever begins should be vaccinated within 4 days

to prevent the infection or lessen the severity (National Institute of Allergy and Infectious Diseases, 2009).

SEVERE ACUTE RESPIRATORY SYNDROME

Not all mass casualty biologic events are terrorist-based. The SARS outbreak in 2003 is a prime example of a non–terrorist-based mass casualty biologic event. The disease started as "atypical" pneumonia in China, in February, and had spread to 29 countries throughout the world by July. Air travel and worldwide trade have increased the possibility that any contagious disease process may spread rapidly. The incubation period for SARS is 2 to 10 days.

Clinical Manifestations and Assessment

SARS should be considered in the event of an outbreak of atypical pneumonia with travel to an area with a known SARS outbreak, a health care worker with direct patient contact, or lab worker in a laboratory that contains live SARS-CoV. Early systemic signs are dry cough and shortness of breath with or without other respiratory symptoms. X-ray confirmed pneumonia or acute respiratory distress syndrome is evident at 7 to 10 days, along with fever and respiratory symptoms.

Medical and Nursing Management

Droplet precaution isolation and control of visits to the exposed patient are essential. Treatment is supportive. The overall case fatality rate is 10%, which increases to more than 50% in patients older than 60 years of age, putting frail, elderly people at risk.

NURSING ALERT

The goal of Droplet Precautions is to prevent the transmission of pathogens spread through close respiratory or mucous membrane contact with respiratory secretions. Because the pathogens do not remain infectious over long distances, special air handling and ventilation are not required to prevent transmission. A single patient room is preferred for patients who require Droplet Precautions; however, if it is not available, consultation with infection control personnel is recommended regarding cohorting of patients. A mask is required for close contact (within 3 feet) with infectious patient, which is generally donned upon room entry. If the patient must be transported outside of the room, a mask should be applied (if tolerated), and the patient should be instructed in cough etiquette (cover the mouth/nose when coughing or sneezing, use and dispose of tissues). In addition, hand hygiene should be performed after hands have been in contact with respiratory secretions (Siegel, Rhinehart, Jackson et al., 2007).

TABLE
56-5 Common Chemical Agents

Agent	Action	Signs and Symptoms	Decontamination and Treatment
Nerve Agents			
Sarin Soman organophosphates	Inhibition of cholinesterase	Increased secretions, gastrointestinal motility, diarrhea, bronchospasm	Soap and water Supportive care Benzodiazepine Pralidoxime Atropine
Blood Agent			
Cyanide	Inhibition of aerobic metabolism	Inhalation—tachypnea, tachycardia, coma, seizures. Can progress to respiratory arrest, respiratory failure, cardiac arrest, death.	Sodium nitrite Sodium thiocyanate Amyl nitrate Hydroxocobalamin
Vesicant Agents			
Lewisite Sulfur mustard Nitrogen mustard Phosgene	Blistering agents	Superficial to partial-thickness burn with vesicles that coalesce	Soap and water Blot; do not rub dry
Pulmonary Agents			
Phosgene Chlorine	Separation of alveoli from capillary bed	Pulmonary edema, bronchospasm	Airway management Ventilatory support Bronchoscopy

CHEMICAL AGENTS

Agents that may be used in **chemical warfare** or terrorism are *overt,* in that the effects are more apparent and occur more quickly than those caused by biologic weapons. Agents are available and well-known, result in major mortality and morbidity, and cause panic and social disruption. There are many agents, including those that affect nerves (sarin, soman), those that affect blood (cyanide), vesicants (lewisite, nitrogen and sulfur mustard, phosgene), heavy metals (arsenic, lead), volatile toxins (benzene, chloroform), pulmonary agents (chlorine), and corrosive acids (nitric acid, sulfuric acid) (refer to Table 56-5).

Chemical agents vary in their absorption and effects. The *volatility* of chemical agents refers to the ability of the agent to become a vapor. Most chemicals are heavier than air, except for hydrogen cyanide, and heavier exposure occurs lower to the ground. *Persistence* of chemical agents means the chemical is less likely to vaporize and disperse. More volatile chemicals do not evaporate quickly and are more commonly used by military and terrorist agents than are industrial chemicals. *Toxicity* of the chemical agent is the ability to cause injury to the body. Toxicity is affected by concentration and length of exposure. *Latency* is the time from absorption to the appearance of symptoms. Sulfur mustards and pulmonary agents have the longest latency,

whereas vesicants, nerve agents, and cyanide produce symptoms within seconds.

NERVE AGENTS

The most toxic agents in existence are the nerve agents such as sarin, soman, tabun, VX, and organophosphates (pesticides). They are inexpensive, effective in small quantities, and easily dispersed. In the liquid form, nerve agents evaporate into a colorless, odorless vapor. Organophosphates are similar in nature to the nerve agents used in warfare and are readily available. Nerve agents can be inhaled or absorbed percutaneously or subcutaneously. These agents bond with acetylcholinesterase, so that acetylcholine is not inactivated; the adverse result is continuous stimulation (hyperstimulation) of the nerve endings.

A very small drop of a nerve agent is enough to result in sweating and twitching at the site of exposure. A larger amount results in more systemic symptoms. Effects can begin anywhere from 30 minutes up to 18 hours after exposure. The more common organophosphates and carbamates (eg, Sevin and malathion) that are used in agriculture result in less severe symptoms than do those used in warfare or in terrorist attacks. In an ordinary situation (eg, nonwarfare, nonterrorist attack situation), a patient could arrive at the ED having been exposed to organophosphates unintentionally or intentionally, in a suicidal gesture.

Clinical Manifestations and Assessment

Signs and symptoms of nerve gas exposure are those of cholinergic crisis and include bilateral miosis (constriction of the pupil), visual disturbances, increased GI motility, nausea and vomiting, diarrhea, substernal spasm, indigestion, bradycardia and atrioventricular block, bronchoconstriction, laryngeal spasm, weakness, fasciculations (small, localized "twitching"), and incontinence. The patient must be examined in a dark area to truly identify miosis. Neurologic responses include insomnia, forgetfulness, impaired judgment, depression, and irritability. A lethal dose results in loss of consciousness, seizures, copious secretions, fasciculations, flaccid muscles, and apnea.

Medical and Nursing Management

Decontamination with copious amounts of soap and water or saline solution for 8 to 20 minutes is essential. The water is blotted off, not wiped off the skin. A 0.5% hypochlorite solution (bleach) can also be used (Agency for Toxic Substances and Disease Registry, 2011). The airway is maintained, and suctioning is frequently required. Plastic airway equipment will absorb sarin gas, which may result in continued exposure to the agent.

Atropine 2 to 4 mg is administered IV, followed by 2 mg every 3 to 8 minutes for up to 24 hours of treatment. Alternatively, IV atropine 1 to 2 mg/hr may be administered until clear signs of anticholinergic activity have returned (decreased secretions, tachycardia, and decreased GI motility). Another medication that may serve as an antidote is pralidoxime, which allows cholinesterase to become active against acetylcholine. Pralidoxime 1 to 2 g in 100 to 150 mL of normal saline solution is administered over 15 to 30 minutes. Pralidoxime has no effect on secretions and may have any of the following side effects: hypertension, tachycardia, weakness, dizziness, blurred vision, and diplopia.

Diazepam (Valium) or other benzodiazepines should be administered to control seizures, to decrease fasciculations, and to alleviate apprehension and agitation. Military personnel believed to be at risk for chemical attack are provided with Mark I automatic injectors, which contain 2 mg atropine and 600 mg pralidoxime chloride. Diazepam is administered by a partner.

BLOOD AGENTS

Blood agents, such as hydrogen cyanide and cyanogen chloride, have a direct effect on cellular metabolism, resulting in asphyxiation through alterations in hemoglobin. Cyanide is an agent that has profound systemic effects. It is commonly used in the mining of gold and silver and in the plastics and dye industries.

A cyanide release is often associated with the odor of bitter almonds. In house fires, cyanide is released during the combustion of plastics, rugs, silk, furniture, and other construction materials. There is a significant correlation between blood cyanide and carbon monoxide levels in patients who survive fires, and in many cases, the cause of death is cyanide poisoning.

Clinical Manifestations and Assessment

Cyanide can be ingested, inhaled, or absorbed through the skin and mucous membranes. Cyanide is protein-bound and inhibits aerobic metabolism, leading to respiratory muscle failure, respiratory arrest, cardiac arrest, and death. Inhalation of cyanide results in flushing, tachypnea, tachycardia, nonspecific neurologic symptoms, stupor, coma, and seizure preceding respiratory arrest.

Medical and Nursing Management

Treatment of cyanide poisoning includes rapid administration of amyl nitrate, sodium nitrite, and sodium thiosulfate, which is essential to the successful management of cyanide exposure. First, the patient is intubated and placed on a ventilator. Next, amyl nitrate pearls are crushed and placed in the ventilator reservoir to induce methemoglobinemia. Cyanide has a 20% to 25% higher affinity for methemoglobin than it does for hemoglobin; it binds methemoglobin to form either cyanomethemoglobin or sulfmethemoglobin. The cyanomethemoglobin is then detoxified in the liver by the enzyme rhodanese. Next, IV sodium nitrite is administered to induce the rapid formation of methemoglobin. Sodium thiosulfate is then administered by IV; it has a higher affinity for cyanide than methemoglobin does and stimulates the conversion of cyanide to sodium thiocyanate, which can be excreted by the kidneys. Although they may be life-saving, these emergency medications do have side effects: sodium nitrite can result in severe hypotension, and thiocyanate can cause vomiting, psychosis, arthralgia, and myalgia.

The production of methemoglobin is contraindicated in patients with smoke inhalation, because they already have decreased oxygen-carrying capacity secondary to the carboxyhemoglobin produced by smoke inhalation. In facilities where a hyperbaric chamber is available, it may be used to provide oxygenation while the previously discussed therapies are initiated. An alternative suggested treatment for cyanide poisoning is hydroxocobalamin (vitamin B_{12}). Hydroxocobalamin binds cyanide to form cyanocobalamin (vitamin B_{12}). It must be administered IV in large doses. Administration of vitamin B_{12} can result in a transient pink discoloration of mucous membranes, skin, and urine. In high doses, tachycardia and hypertension can occur, but they usually resolve within 48 hours.

Chapter Review

Critical Thinking Exercises

1. A young woman arrives at the ED by ambulance after a car crash. She is immobilized on a backboard, with a cervical collar and an oxygen mask in place. There is a bruise across her abdomen where the seatbelt was applied. She complains of nausea and abdominal pain. You note no movement of the left chest wall and an angulated right arm. She has no pulses in her lower extremities and cannot move or feel her legs. How would you prioritize the patient's needs? Develop an assessment strategy, identify diagnostic studies that will benefit the patient, and describe the patient's treatment needs.

2. The following five patients present to the triage desk within minutes of each other. How would you prioritize and categorize each of these patients? Which ones need immediate attention? What initial care would you provide at triage?
   A. A child with medication-controlled asthma presents with rapid, shallow respirations and cyanosis around the lips and is very anxious. He has been this way for about 20 minutes.
   B. A woman who has had a cold for 3 days says she has no primary care physician and must be seen right now because she cannot breathe. Her respirations are normal, pulse oxygenation saturations are 100%, and she has complaints of sinus drainage.
   C. A woman was hit by an automobile while she was riding her bike. Instead of calling 911, a friend drove her to the ED. She is complaining of neck pain and tingling in her upper extremities since the injury. She is beginning to have difficulty taking a deep breath.
   D. A young boy who was riding his skateboard arrives at the ED with an angulated wrist. Pulses are normal, but the wrist is painful.
   E. An elderly woman presents with complaints of 24 hours of vomiting. Her vital signs are normal, but she is diaphoretic and appears weak.

3. You are the triage nurse at the receiving facility for casualties during a hurricane. Five patients arrive at the same time. Together with the surgeon on duty, you must identify the patients' needs. What are the patient needs of the following five patients? How would you classify/tag these patients?
   A. An elderly man with a respiratory rate of 8 breaths/minute, color ashen, status unresponsive, with only palpable carotid pulses
   B. A 7-year-old child with a bleeding scalp laceration who needs intubation
   C. The 30-year-old mother of the 7-year-old child, who is crying hysterically and appears to have no pain or visible injuries

   D. A 15-year-old boy who complains of pain in his left leg, with obvious deformity at the calf but good pulses in the foot
   E. A 65-year-old woman who arrives in a police car holding her right wrist, which is cool, ecchymotic, and painful with good pulses.

4. Multiple patients begin arriving at the ED complaining of burning eyes and difficulty breathing. All of these persons work at the railroad yard, where tanker trucks frequently transport chemical agents. What should you do first? Where do you find information about chemical agents and their treatment?

NCLEX-Style Review Questions

1. When assessing a trauma patient presenting in the ED, which of the following is the most important priority for the nurse?
   A. Controlling hemorrhage
   B. Inserting two large-gauge IV catheters for fluid resuscitation
   C. Obtaining name and phone number of nearest relative to inform them that the patient is in the hospital
   D. Establishing a patent airway

2. A 25-year-old patient is transported by paramedics to the ED following a fall from a second-story balcony during a party. During the primary survey, his respirations are noted to be snoring with a heavy alcohol order to the breath. He is receiving 100% O_2 via face mask, and his oxygen saturation is 91%. He withdraws from painful stimuli but is not speaking or responding appropriately to commands. What are the immediate priorities for care?
   A. Open airway with head tilt-chin lift maneuver and obtain chest X-ray to assess for pneumothorax.
   B. Draw labs for toxicology screen and administer .5 mg Ativan to prevent withdrawal seizures.
   C. Perform jaw-thrust maneuver and reassess ventilation effort.
   D. Rapidly transport patient to CT for brain CT to evaluate for neurological injury.

3. There has been a natural gas explosion in a multistory office building in the city. Initial reports indicate that the ED will be receiving a large number of victims that will overwhelm current resources. What need will the nurse working in the ED anticipate?
   A. Initiate the hospital emergency operation plan.
   B. Call off-duty staff to come in and assist.
   C. Request burn packs from central supply.
   D. Take a meal break quickly before patients arrive.

(continued on page 1462)

Chapter Review (continued)

4. A city has been hit by a tornado, and reports indicate significant numbers of casualties and injuries. The hospital has not been affected, and all systems are operational at this time. As patients arrive, they have been tagged by field responders using the NATO color coding for severity. What does the nurse working in the ED know about this system?

  A. Patients tagged with a green tag require immediate and extensive use of resources for survival.

  B. Patients with a red tag have minor injuries and can wait for care.

  C. Children always receive a red tag.

  D. Patients with a black tag are not a priority for treatment under MCI standards.

5. A 50-year-old woman presents to the ED with complaints of a fever and chills for the past 72 hours, body aches, and she appears to be acutely ill. She also points to lesions on her arms and face that have been noticed since this morning and appear to be spreading quickly. What are immediate priorities for care?

  A. An assessment of recent travel

  B. Administer an antipyretic to reduce fever and body aches

  C. Isolate from other patients and ensure all staff follow isolation precautions

  D. Assist patient into a hospital gown for an immediate examination and give clothing to family members

---

Try these additional resources to enhance your learning and understanding of this chapter:

- thePoint online resource available at **http://thepoint.lww.com/Pellico1e**
- *Handbook for Focus on Adult Health: Medical-Surgical Nursing*
- *Study Guide for Focus on Adult Health: Medical-Surgical Nursing*

References and Selected Readings

References and selected readings associated with this chapter can be found on the website that accompanies the book. Visit **http://thepoint.lww.com/Pellico1e** to access the references and other additional resources associated with this chapter.

Major Fluid and Electrolyte Imbalances

Imbalance	Contributing Factors	Signs/Symptoms and Laboratory Findings
Fluid volume deficit (FVD) (hypovolemia)	Loss of water and electrolytes, as in vomiting, diarrhea, fistulas, fever, excess sweating, burns, blood loss, gastrointestinal suction, and third-space fluid shifts; and decreased intake, as in anorexia, nausea, and inability to gain access to fluid. Diabetes insipidus and uncontrolled diabetes mellitus also contribute to a depletion of extracellular fluid volume.	Acute weight loss; decreased skin turgor; oliguria; concentrated urine; weak, rapid pulse; prolonged capillary filling time; low CVP; ↓ blood pressure; orthostatic hypotension; flattened neck veins; dizziness; weakness; thirst and confusion; ↑ pulse; muscle cramps; sunken eyes. **Labs indicate:** ↑ Hemoglobin and hematocrit, ↑ serum and urine osmolality and specific gravity, ↓ urine sodium, ↑ BUN out of proportion to serum creatinine
Fluid volume excess (FVE) (hypervolemia)	Compromised regulatory mechanisms, such as renal failure, heart failure, and cirrhosis; overzealous administration of sodium-containing fluids; and fluid shifts (ie, treatment of burns). Prolonged corticosteroid therapy, severe stress, and hyperaldosteronism augment fluid volume excess.	Acute weight gain, peripheral edema and ascites, distended jugular veins, crackles, and elevated CVP, shortness of breath, ↑ blood pressure, bounding pulse and cough, ↑ respiratory rate. **Labs indicate:** ↓ Hemoglobin and hematocrit, ↓ serum and urine osmolality, ↓ urine sodium and specific gravity, decreased BUN (due to plasma dilution).
Sodium deficit (hyponatremia) Serum sodium <135 mEq/L	Loss of sodium, as in use of diuretics, loss of GI fluids, renal disease, and adrenal insufficiency. Gain of water, as in excessive administration of D_5W and water supplements for patients receiving hypotonic tube feedings; disease states associated with SIADH, such as head trauma and oat-cell lung tumor; medications associated with water retention (oxytocin and certain tranquilizers); and psychogenic polydipsia. Patients with congestive heart failure or liver disease may present with hyponatremia despite an excess of total body sodium.	Manifestations of hyponatremia depend on the cause, magnitude, and speed with which the deficit occurs. Symptoms include: Anorexia, nausea and vomiting, headache, lethargy, dizziness, confusion, muscle cramps and weakness, muscular twitching, seizures, papilledema, dry skin, ↑ pulse, ↓ BP, weight gain, edema. **Labs indicate:** ↓ Serum sodium; urinary Na level varies depending on the etiology of the hyponatremia
Sodium excess (hypernatremia) Serum sodium >145 mEq/L	Water deprivation in patients unable to drink at will; hypertonic tube feedings without adequate water supplements; diabetes insipidus; heatstroke; hyperventilation; watery diarrhea; burns; and diaphoresis; excess corticosteroid, sodium bicarbonate, and sodium chloride administration; and salt water near-drowning victims.	Thirst, elevated body temperature, swollen dry tongue and sticky mucous membranes, hallucinations, lethargy, restlessness, irritability, focal or grand mal seizures, pulmonary edema, hyperreflexia, twitching, nausea, vomiting, anorexia, ↑ pulse, and ↑ BP. **Labs indicate.** ↑ Serum sodium, increased serum osmolality; ↑ urine specific gravity and osmolality (provided the water loss is from a route other than the kidneys); ↓ CVP
Potassium deficit (hypokalemia) Serum potassium <3.5 mEq/L	Increased output of K+ (diuretics, diarrhea, vomiting, gastric suction, recent ileostomy, intestinal drains, osmotic diuresis); decreased intake of K+ (NPO, anorexia, vomiting, alcoholism, fasting diets); or redistribution of K+ (metabolic alkalosis, insulin administration).	Fatigue, anorexia, nausea and vomiting, muscle weakness, decreased bowel motility, abdominal distention, ileus, ventricular arrythmias, paresthesias, leg cramps, hypoactive reflexes, increased sensitivity to digitalis. **ECG:** Flattened T waves, prominent U waves, ST depression, prolonged PR interval

(continued on page 1464)

Imbalance	Contributing Factors	Signs/Symptoms and Laboratory Findings
Potassium excess (hyperkalemia) Serum potassium >5.0 mEq/L	Pseudohyperkalemia, oliguric renal failure, use of potassium-conserving diuretics in patients with renal insufficiency, metabolic acidosis, Addison's disease, crush injury, burns, stored bank blood transfusions, and rapid IV administration of potassium	Vague muscular weakness, tachycardia → bradycardia, arrhythmias, flaccid paralysis, paresthesias, intestinal colic **ECG:** Tall tented T waves, prolonged PR interval and QRS duration, absent P waves, ST depression
Calcium deficit (hypocalcemia) Serum calcium <8.5 mg/dL	Hypoparathyroidism (may follow thyroid surgery or radical neck dissection), malabsorption, pancreatitis, alkalosis, vitamin D deficiency, massive subcutaneous infection, generalized peritonitis, massive transfusion of citrated blood, chronic diarrhea, decreased parathyroid hormone, renal failure, ↑ PO_4, pancreatic and small bowel fistulas, hypomagnesemia, hypoalbuminemia	Numbness, tingling of fingers, toes, and circumoral region; positive Trousseau's sign and Chvostek's sign; tetany; seizures, carpopedal spasms, hyperactive deep tendon reflexes, irritability, laryngeal spasm, anxiety. **ECG:** Prolonged QT interval and lengthened ST predisposing to *torsades de pointes* (form of ventricular tachycardia) **Labs indicate:** Serum calcium concentration is low; ionized serum calcium concentration is also low; ↓ Mg^{++} (inhibits PTH secretion)
Calcium excess (hypercalcemia) Serum calcium >10.5 mg/dL	Hyperparathyroidism, malignant neoplastic disease, prolonged immobilization, overuse of calcium supplements, vitamin A and D excess, oliguric phase of renal failure, acidosis, thiazide diuretic use	Muscular weakness, confusion, constipation, anorexia, nausea and vomiting, polyuria and polydipsia, dehydration, hypoactive deep tendon reflexes, lethargy, deep bone pain, pathologic fractures, flank pain, and calcium stones. **ECG:** Shortened ST segment and QT interval, bradycardia, heart blocks
Magnesium deficit (hypomagnesemia) Serum magnesium <1.8 mg/dL	Chronic alcoholism, hyperparathyroidism, hyperaldosteronism, diuretic phase of renal failure, malabsorptive disorders, diabetic ketoacidosis, refeeding after starvation, parenteral nutrition, chronic laxative use, diarrhea, decreased serum K^+ and Ca^{++} and certain pharmacologic agents (such as gentamicin, cisplatin, and cyclosporine)	Neuromuscular irritability, positive Trousseau's and Chvostek's signs, insomnia, mood changes, anorexia, vomiting, increased tendon reflexes, and potentiation of ventricular and supraventricular arrhythmias. **ECG:** PVCs, flat or inverted T waves, depressed ST segment, prolonged PR interval and widened QRS
Magnesium excess (hypermagnesemia) Serum magnesium >2.7 mg/dL	Renal insufficiency (particularly when magnesium-containing medications are administered IV or excessive ingestion of magnesium-containing antacids or laxatives), adrenal insufficiency	Nausea, vomiting, hypotension, drowsiness, hypoactive reflexes, depressed respirations leading to apnea, bradycardia and hypotension. **ECG:** Prolonged PR interval and QT interval.
Phosphorus deficit (hypophosphatemia) Serum phosphorus <2.5 mg/dL	Refeeding after starvation, alcohol withdrawal, diabetic ketoacidosis, respiratory alkalosis, ↓ magnesium, ↓ potassium, hyperparathyroidism, diarrhea, vitamin D deficiency associated with malabsorptive disorders, burns, acid–base disorders, parenteral nutrition, and diuretic and antacid use	Paresthesias, muscle weakness, bone pain and tenderness, chest pain, confusion, cardiomyopathy, respiratory failure, seizures, tissue hypoxia, and increased susceptibility to infection.
Phosphorus excess (hyperphosphatemia) Serum phosphorus >4.5 mg/dL	Acute and chronic renal failure, excessive intake of phosphorus, vitamin D excess, respiratory acidosis, hypoparathyroidism, volume depletion, leukemia/lymphoma treated with cytotoxic agents, increased tissue breakdown, rhabdomyolysis	Tetany, signs and symptoms of hypocalcemia; hyperactive reflexes; soft-tissue calcifications in lungs, heart, kidneys, and cornea

Imbalance	Contributing Factors	Signs/Symptoms and Laboratory Findings
Chloride deficit (hypochloremia) Serum chloride <96 mEq/L	GI tube drainage and severe vomiting and diarrhea, laxatives, ileostomy, and fistulas; sodium and potassium deficiency; metabolic alkalosis; loop, osmotic, or thiazide diuretic use; overuse of bicarbonate; rapid removal of ascitic fluid with a high sodium content; intravenous fluids that lack chloride (dextrose and water)	Signs and symptoms of hypochloremia are associated with hyponatremia, hypokalemia, and metabolic alkalosis *Labs indicate:* ↓ Serum chloride, ↓ serum sodium, ↑ pH, ↑ serum bicarbonate, ↑ total carbon dioxide content, ↓ serum potassium
Chloride excess (hyperchloremia) Serum chloride >108 mEq/L	Excessive sodium chloride infusions with water loss; hypernatremia; renal failure; corticosteroid use; dehydration; severe diarrhea (loss of bicarbonate); respiratory alkalosis; administration of diuretics; overdose of salicylates; Kayexalate, acetazolamide, phenylbutazone, and ammonium chloride use; hyperparathyroidism; metabolic acidosis	Signs and symptoms of hyperchloremia are typically associated with metabolic acidosis (tachypnea, Kussmaul's respirations, lethargy, diminished cognitive ability), and hypernatremia (fluid retention, dyspnea, tachycardia, hypertension) *Labs indicate:* ↑ Serum chloride, ↑ serum sodium, ↓ serum pH, ↓ serum bicarbonate, normal anion gap

↑ increased; ↓ decreased; BP, blood pressure; BUN, blood urea nitrogen; CVP, central venous pressure; DKA, diabetic ketoacidosis; GI, gastrointestinal; IV, intravenous; PVCs, premature ventricular contractions; SIADH, syndrome of inappropriate secretion of antidiuretic hormone.

GLOSSARY

A

abduction: movement away from the center or median line of the body

ablation: purposeful destruction of heart muscle cells, usually in an attempt to control an arrhythmia

abscess: localized collection of purulent material surrounded by inflamed tissues, typically associated with signs of infection

absolute neutrophil count (ANC): a mathematical calculation of the actual number of neutrophils in the circulation, derived from the total white blood cells (WBCs) and the percentage of neutrophils counted in a microscope's visual field; provides an estimate of infection risk

absorption: phase of the digestive process that occurs when small molecules, vitamins, and minerals pass through the walls of the small and large intestine and into the bloodstream

acanthosis nigricans: hyperpigmentation of the skin that typically occurs on the neck, dorsum of hands, axilla, or groin areas

accommodation: process by which the eye adjusts for near distance (e.g., reading) by changing the curvature of the lens to focus a clear image on the retina

achalasia: absent or ineffective peristalsis (wavelike contraction) of the distal esophagus accompanied by failure of the esophageal sphincter to relax in response to swallowing

achlorhydria: lack of hydrochloric acid in digestive secretions of the stomach

acidosis: an acid–base imbalance characterized by an increase in H^+ concentration (decreased blood pH); a low arterial pH due to reduced bicarbonate concentration is called metabolic acidosis; a low arterial pH due to increased PCO_2 is respiratory acidosis

acoustic: pertaining to sound or the sense of hearing

acromegaly: disease process resulting from excessive secretion of somatotropin (growth hormone); causes progressive enlargement of peripheral body parts, commonly the face, head, hands, and feet and enlargement of many body organs

active transport: physiologic pump that moves fluid from an area of lower concentration to one of higher concentration; active transport requires adenosine triphosphate (ATP) for energy

acute coronary syndrome (ACS): signs and symptoms that indicate unstable angina or acute myocardial infarction

acute limb ischemia (ACL): sudden decrease in limb arterial perfusion, threatening limb viability

acute lung injury (ALI): an umbrella term for hypoxemic, respiratory failure; ARDS is a severe form of ALI

acute respiratory distress syndrome (ARDS): an inflammatory pulmonary response to a variety of pulmonary and nonpulmonary insults to the lung; characterized by diffuse interstitial infiltrates, alveolar/capillary leak, atelectasis, decreased compliance, refractory hypoxemia and no signs of cardiogenic heart failure

acute tubular necrosis: type of acute renal failure in which there is actual damage to the kidney tubules

addiction: a behavioral pattern of substance use characterized by a compulsion to take the substance (drug or alcohol) primarily to experience its psychic effects

Addison's disease: chronic adrenocortical insufficiency secondary to destruction of the adrenal glands

Addisonian crisis: acute adrenocortical insufficiency; commonly characterized by shock (acute hypotension, volume depletion), nausea and vomiting; usual laboratory abnormalities include hyponatremia, hyperkalemia and perhaps hypoglycemia; often precipitated by stress or abrupt withdrawal of therapeutic glucocorticoids

adduction: movement toward the center or median line of the body

adherence: the process of faithfully following guidelines or directions

adjuvant chemotherapy: use of anticancer medications in addition to other treatments such as surgery, radiation to delay or prevent a recurrence of the disease

adnexa: the fallopian tubes and ovaries

adrenalectomy: surgical removal of one or both adrenal glands

adrenocorticotropic hormone (ACTH): hormone secreted by the anterior pituitary, essential for growth and development; chief function is to stimulate hormones of the adrenal cortex-glucocorticoids (principally cortisol), mineralocorticosteroids (principally aldosterone) and androgens (sex hormones)

adrenogenital syndrome: masculinization in women, feminization in men, or premature sexual development in children; result of abnormal secretion of adrenocortical hormones, especially androgens

afterload: the amount of resistance to ejection of blood from the ventricle

agglutination: clumping effect occurring when an antibody acts as a cross-link between two antigens

agnosia: loss of ability to recognize objects through a particular sensory system; may be visual, auditory, or tactile

agonist: a substance that when combined with the receptor produces the drug effect or desired effect; endorphins and morphine are agonists on the opioid receptors

AIDS: acquired immunodeficiency syndrome; when a person infected with the human immunodeficiency virus (HIV) develops an opportunistic infection or has a CD4$^+$ lymphocyte count below 200

airway pressure release ventilation (APRV): mode of mechanical ventilation that allows unrestricted, spontaneous breaths throughout the ventilatory cycle; on inspiration, patient receives preset level of continuous positive airway pressure, and pressure is periodically released to aid expiration

akathisia: restlessness, urgent need to move around, and agitation

alaryngeal communication: alternative modes of speaking that do not involve the normal larynx; used by patients whose larynx has been surgically removed

aldosterone: hormone synthesized and released by the adrenal cortex; causes the kidneys to reabsorb sodium (and thus water retention) and potassium loss

algogenic: causing pain

alkalosis: an acid–base imbalance characterized by a reduction in H$^+$ concentration (increased blood pH); a high arterial pH with increased bicarbonate concentration is called metabolic alkalosis; a high arterial pH due to reduced PCO$_2$ is respiratory alkalosis

allergen: substance that causes manifestations of allergy

allergy: inappropriate and often harmful immune system response to substances that are normally harmless

allograft: tissue harvested from a donor for use in another person (*synonym:* homograft)

alopecia: loss of hair from any cause

alpha$_1$-antitrypsin deficiency: a genetic disorder resulting from deficiency of alpha$_1$ antitrypsin, a protective enzyme in the lungs; the deficiency increases the patient's risk for developing emphysema even in the absence of smoking

alpha-interferon: protein substance that the body produces in response to infection

altered level of consciousness: condition of being less responsive to and aware of environmental stimuli

ambulatory surgery: includes outpatient (same-day) surgery that does not require an overnight hospital stay or short stay, with admission to an inpatient hospital setting for less than 24 hours

amenorrhea: The absence of menstruation that can be either primary or secondary

amputation: the removal of a body part

amylase: pancreatic enzyme; aids in the digestion of carbohydrates

anagen phase: active phase of hair growth

anaphylactic shock: distributive shock state resulting from a severe allergic reaction producing an overwhelming systemic vasodilation and relative hypovolemia in addition to bronchial spasm

anaphylaxis: clinical response to an immediate immunologic reaction between a specific antigen and antibody

androgens: hormones secreted by the adrenal cortex; stimulate activity of accessory male sex organs and development of male sex characteristics; hormones produced by the ovaries and adrenals that affect many aspects of female health, including follicle development, libido, oiliness of hair and skin, and hair growth

anemia: decreased red blood cell (RBC) count

anergy: loss or weakening of the body's immunity to an irritating agent or antigen

anesthesia: a state of narcosis, analgesia, relaxation, and loss of reflexes

anesthesiologist: physician trained to deliver anesthesia and to monitor the patient's condition during surgery

anesthetic: the substance, such as a chemical or gas, used to induce anesthesia

anesthetist: health care professional, such as a nurse anesthetist, who is trained to deliver anesthesia and to monitor the patient's condition during surgery

aneurysm: congenital or acquired localized weakness or dilation of an artery formed at a weak point in the vessel wall

angina pectoris: chest pain brought about by myocardial ischemia

angiogenesis: formation of new blood vessels, such as in a healing wound or in a malignant tumor

angiography: an X-ray picture of a vessel lumen following the injection of a radiopaque contrast material

angioneurotic edema: condition characterized by urticaria and diffuse swelling of the deeper layers of the skin

angioplasty: an invasive procedure to dilate a stenotic blood vessel

angiotensin-converting enzyme (ACE) inhibitors: medications that inhibit the angiotensin-converting enzyme

ankle–brachial index (ABI): ratio of the ankle systolic pressure to the higher of the two brachial systolic pressures; an objective measurement of arterial disease

ankylosis: fixation or immobility of a joint

annuloplasty: repair of a cardiac valve's outer ring

anovulation: lack of ovulation

antagonist: a substance that blocks or reverses the effects of the agonist by occupying the receptor site without producing the drug effect; naloxone (Narcan™) is an opioid antagonist

anterior chamber: space in the eye bordered anteriorly by the cornea and posteriorly by the iris and pupil

antiarrhythmic: a medication that suppresses or prevents an arrhythmia

antibody: protein substance developed by the body in response to and interacting with a specific antigen

antidiuretic hormone (ADH): hormone secreted by the posterior pituitary gland; causes the kidneys to reabsorb more water; also called *vasopressin*

antigen: substance that induces the production of antibodies

antigenic determinant: the specific area of an antigen that binds with an antibody combining site and determines the specificity of the antigen–antibody reaction

antihistamine: medication that opposes the action of histamine

antireflux valve: valve that prevents return or backward flow of fluid

antrectomy: removal of the pyloric (antrum) portion of the stomach with anastomosis (surgical connection) to the duodenum (gastroduodenostomy or Billroth I) or anastomosis to the jejunum (gastrojejunostomy or Billroth II)

anuria: total urine output less than 50 mL in 24 hours

anus: last section of the GI tract; outlet for waste products from the system

aortic valve: semilunar valve located between the left ventricle and the aorta

aphasia: impairment of language (including speaking, reading, writing, or comprehension) due to an injury of the brain

aphonia: impaired ability to use one's voice due to disease or injury to the larynx

apical impulse: also called *point of maximum impulse* (PMI); impulse normally palpated at the fifth intercostal space, left midclavicular line (or 7 to 9 cm from the left sternal border); caused by contraction of the left ventricle

aplasia: lack of cellular development (e.g., of cells within the bone marrow)

apnea: cessation of breathing/airflow for at least 10 seconds

apoptosis: programmed cell death

apraxia: inability to perform previously learned purposeful motor acts on a voluntary basis

aromatase inhibitors: medications that block the production of estrogens by the adrenal glands

arrhythmia: also referred to as *dysrhythmia;* disorder of the formation or conduction (or both) of the electrical impulse within the heart, altering the heart rate, heart rhythm, or both and potentially causing altered perfusion

arterial bypass: surgical rerouting of blood around an obstructed artery, using a graft

arteriovenous fistula: type of vascular access for dialysis; created by surgically connecting an artery to a vein

arteriovenous graft: type of surgically created vascular access for dialysis by which a piece of biologic, semibiologic, or synthetic graft material connects the patient's artery to a vein

arthrocentesis: needle aspiration of synovial fluid

arthrodesis: surgical fusion of a joint

arthroplasty: the repair of joint problems through the operating arthroscope (an instrument that allows the surgeon to operate within a joint without a large incision) or through open joint surgery

arthroscope: surgical instrument used to examine internal joint structures

articulation: a joint; the site of close approximation of two or more bones

asbestosis: diffuse lung fibrosis resulting from exposure to asbestos fibers

ascites: fluid accumulation in the abdominal cavity

aspiration: removal of substance by suction; breathing of fluids or foods into the trachea and lungs

assist-control ventilation (A/C): mode of mechanical ventilation in which the patient's breathing pattern may trigger the ventilator to deliver a preset tidal volume; in the absence of spontaneous breathing, the machine delivers a controlled breath at a preset minimum rate and tidal volume

assisted suicide: use of pharmacologic agents to hasten the death of a terminally ill patient; illegal in most states

asterixis: involuntary flapping movements of the hands associated with metabolic liver dysfunction

asthma: a disease with multiple precipitating mechanisms characterized by the interaction between underlying inflammation, airway hyperresponsiveness, and obstruction to airflow

astigmatism: refractive error in which light rays are spread over a diffuse area rather than sharply focused on the retina; a condition caused by differences in the curvature of the cornea and lens

ataxia: inability to coordinate muscle movements, resulting in difficulty in walking, talking, and performing self-care activities; irregular, uncoordinated movements

atelectasis: collapse or airless condition of the alveoli caused by hypoventilation, obstruction to the airways, or compression

atheroma: fibrous cap composed of smooth muscle cells that forms over lipid deposits within arterial vessels and that protrudes into the lumen of the vessel, narrowing the lumen and obstructing blood flow; also called *plaque*

atherosclerosis: disease process involving the accumulation of lipids, calcium, blood components, carbohydrates, and fibrous tissue on the intimal layer of arteries

atonic: without tone; denervated muscle that atrophies

atony: lack of normal muscle tone

atopic dermatitis: type I hypersensitivity involving inflammation of the skin evidenced by itching, redness, and a variety of skin lesions

atrophy: shrinkage-like decrease in the size of a muscle

atypical hyperplasia: abnormal increase in the number of cells in a specific area within the ductal or lobular areas

of the breast; this abnormal proliferation increases the risk for cancer

auscultatory gap: a silent interval between systolic and diastolic Korotkoff sounds, causing an underestimation of the systolic pressure

autograft: a graft derived from one part of a patient's body and used on another part of that same patient's body

autonomic dysreflexia: also called autonomic hyperreflexia; a life-threatening emergency in spinal cord injury patients that causes a hypertensive emergency, occurs in patients with an injury at or above T6

autonomic nervous system: division of the nervous system that regulates the involuntary body functions

autonomy: self-determination; in the health care context, the right of the individual to make choices about the use and discontinuation of medical treatment

autoregulation: ability of cerebral blood vessels to dilate or constrict to maintain stable cerebral blood flow despite changes in systemic arterial blood pressure

avascular necrosis: death of tissue due to insufficient blood supply

axon: portion of the neuron that conducts impulses away from the cell body

azotemia: concentration of urea and other nitrogenous wastes in the blood

B

Babinski reflex (sign): a reflex action of the toes, indicative of abnormalities in the motor control pathways leading from the cerebral cortex

bacterial vaginosis: a vaginal infection caused by an overgrowth of anaerobic bacteria

bacteriuria: bacteria in the urine; bacterial count higher than 100,000 colonies/mL

balanced analgesia: using more than one form of analgesia concurrently to obtain more pain relief with fewer side effects

balloon angioplasty: a technique using a balloon, attached to a catheter, inflated to restore blood flow in blocked arteries

balloon tamponade: use of balloons placed within the esophagus and proximal portion of the stomach and inflated to compress bleeding vessels (esophageal and gastric varices) ballooning of the vessel

balneotherapy: a bath with therapeutic additives

band cell: slightly immature neutrophil

bandemia: an excess of immature white blood cells released by the bone marrow into the blood; signifies infection or inflammation

bariatric: term that comes from two Greek words meaning "weight" and "treatment"

baroreceptors: nerve fibers located in the aortic arch and carotid arteries that are responsible for reflex control of the blood pressure

basal metabolic rate: chemical reactions occurring when the body is at rest

basophil: type of granulocyte; involved in the inflammatory response

B cells: cells that are important for producing a humoral immune response

benign proliferative breast disease: various types of atypical, yet noncancerous, breast tissue that increase the risk for breast cancer

benign prostatic hyperplasia (BPH): noncancerous enlargement or hypertrophy of the prostate; BPH is the most common pathologic condition in older men and the second most common cause of surgical intervention in men older than 60 years of age

bereavement: period during which mourning for a loss takes place

biologic response modifier (BRM) therapy: use of agents or treatment methods that can alter the immunologic relationship between the tumor and the host to provide a therapeutic benefit

biological warfare: use of a biological agent, such as anthrax, as a weapon of mass destruction

biopsy: a diagnostic procedure to remove a small sample of tissue to be examined microscopically to detect malignant cells

blast cell: primitive white blood cell

blindness: inability to see, usually defined as corrected visual acuity of 20/400 or less, or a visual field of no more than 20 degrees in the better eye

bolus: a feeding administered into the stomach in large amounts and at designated intervals

bone graft: the placement of bone tissue (autologous or homologous grafts) to promote healing, to stabilize, or to replace diseased bone

borborygmus: rumbling noise caused by the movement of gas through the intestines

brace: externally applied device to support the body or a body part, control movement, and prevent injury

brachytherapy: delivery of radiation therapy through internal implants

bradykinesia: very slow voluntary movements and speech

brain death: irreversible loss of all brain function, including the brainstem

brain injury: an injury to the skull or brain that is severe enough to interfere with normal functioning

BRCA-1 and BRCA-2: genes on chromosome 17 that, when damaged or mutated, place a woman at greater risk for breast cancer and/or ovarian cancer compared with women who do not have the mutation

breakthrough pain: a sudden and temporary increase in pain occurring in a patient being managed with opioid analgesia

breast conservation treatment: surgery to remove a breast tumor and a margin of tissue around the tumor without

removing any other part of the breast; may or may not include lymph node removal and radiation therapy

bronchoscopy: direct examination of larynx, trachea, and bronchi using an endoscope

bruit: sound produced by turbulent blood flow through an irregular, tortuous, stenotic, or dilated vessel

Budd-Chiari syndrome: hepatic vein thrombosis resulting in noncirrhotic portal hypertension

bulbar paralysis: immobility of muscles innervated by cranial nerves with their cell bodies in the lower portion of the brainstem

bursa: fluid-filled sac found in connective tissue, usually in the area of joints

bursitis: inflammation of a fluid-filled sac in a joint

C

calcitonin: hormone secreted by the parafollicular cells of the thyroid gland; participates in calcium regulation (lowers blood calcium and phosphate level)

callus: cartilaginous/fibrous tissue at fracture site

cancellous bone: lattice-like bone structure; trabecular bone

cancer: a disease process whereby cells proliferate abnormally, ignoring growth-regulating signals in the environment surrounding the cells

carboxyhemoglobin: hemoglobin that is bound to carbon monoxide and therefore is unable to bind with oxygen, resulting in hypoxemia

carcinogenesis: process of transforming normal cells into malignant cells

cardiac output: amount of blood pumped by each ventricle in liters per minute; normal cardiac output is 4 to 6 L per minute in the resting adult heart

cardiogenic shock: shock state resulting from impairment or failure of the myocardium

cardiomyopathy: disease of the heart muscle

cardioversion: electrical current administered in synchrony with the patient's own QRS complex to stop a arrhythmia

cartilage: tough, elastic, avascular tissue at ends of bone

cast: rigid external immobilizing device molded to contours of body part

CCR5: coreceptor or cell surface molecule needed along with the CD4⁺ molecule for HIV to infect the host's immune system cells

cellular density: the number of living cells in a unit

cellular immune response: the immune system's third line of defense, involving the attack of pathogens by T cells

central cyanosis: bluish discoloration of the skin or mucous membranes due to hemoglobin carrying reduced amounts of oxygen; often a late sign of hypoxia

central venous access device (CVAD): a device designed and used for long-term administration of medications and fluids into central veins

cerebral contusion: bruising of the brain surface

cerebral edema: swelling of the brain

cerumen: yellow or brown, waxlike secretion found in the external auditory canal

cervical stenosis: a narrowing or incomplete opening of the cervical os

cervix: bottom (inferior) part of the uterus that is located in the vagina

chemical warfare: use of a chemical agent, such as chlorine, as a weapon of mass destruction (WMD)

chemosis: edema of the conjunctiva

chemotherapy: use of medications to kill tumor cells by interfering with cellular functions and reproduction

chest drainage system: use of a chest tube and closed drainage system to reexpand the lung and to remove excess air, fluid, and blood

chest percussion: manually cupping over the chest wall to mobilize secretions by mechanically dislodging viscous or adherent secretions in the lungs

chest physiotherapy (CPT): therapy used to remove bronchial secretions, improve ventilation, and increase the efficiency of the respiratory muscles; types include postural drainage, chest percussion, and vibration

cholecystectomy: removal of the gallbladder

cholecystitis: inflammation of the gallbladder

cholecystokinin-pancreozymin (CCK-PZ): hormone; major stimulus for digestive enzyme secretion; stimulates contraction of the gallbladder

cholelithiasis: the presence of calculi in the gallbladder

cholesteatoma: tumor of the middle ear or mastoid, or both, that can destroy structures of the temporal bone

cholesterol: a lipid that is an integral constituent of cell membranes, transported in the circulatory system bound to low-density and high-density lipoprotein

chordoplasty: repair of the tendinous fibers that connect the edges of the atrioventricular valve leaflets to the papillary muscles

choroidal neovascularization: new growth of new blood vessels beneath the retina; considered to be abnormal

chronic conditions: medical or health problems with associated symptoms or disabilities that require long-term management (3 months or longer)

chronic obstructive bronchitis: a disease of the airways defined as the presence of cough and sputum production for at least a combined total of 3 months in each of 2 consecutive years with obstruction to airflow; a category of COPD

chronic obstructive pulmonary disease (COPD): disease state characterized by airflow limitation that is not fully reversible; sometimes referred to as *chronic airway obstruction* or *chronic obstructive lung disease*

chyme: mixture of food with saliva, salivary enzymes, and gastric secretions that is produced as the food passes through the mouth, esophagus, and stomach

cilia: short hairs that provide a constant whipping motion that serves to propel mucus and foreign substances away from the lung toward the larynx

circulating nurse (or circulator): registered nurse who coordinates and documents patient care in the operating room

cirrhosis: a chronic liver disease characterized by fibrotic changes and the formation of dense connective tissue within the liver, subsequent degenerative changes, and loss of functioning cells

clonus: abnormal movement marked by alternating contraction and relaxation of a muscle occurring in rapid succession

CMS: Center for Medicare Services; the federal agency that administers Medicare, Medicaid, and the Children's Health Insurance programs

cochlea: the winding, snail-shaped bony tube that forms a portion of the inner ear and contains the organ of Corti, the transducer for hearing

cochlear (acoustic) nerve: the division of the eighth cranial (vestibulocochlear) nerve, which goes to the cochlea

collagen: a protein present in skin, tendon, bone, cartilage, and connective tissue

collateral: small vessels that may enlarge to carry blood around a blocked vessel

colloids: intravenous solutions that contain molecules that are too large to pass through capillary membranes

colonization: microorganisms present in or on a host, without host interference or interaction and without eliciting symptoms in the host

colposcopy: microscopic examination of the lower genital tract using a magnifying instrument called a colposcope

coma: prolonged state of unconsciousness

commissurotomy: splitting or separating fused cardiac valve leaflets

community: an interacting population of individuals living together within a larger society

compartment syndrome: increasing pressure in a muscle compartment causing impaired nerve and blood vessel function

complement: series of enzymatic proteins in the serum that, when activated, destroy bacteria and other cells

complete spinal cord lesion: a condition that involves total loss of sensation and voluntary muscle control below the lesion in the spinal cord

computed tomographic angiography (CTA): three-dimensional image created by specialized X-ray technique to visualize blood flow

concussion: a temporary neurologic dysfunction caused by trauma to the head, classified as mild or classic based on symptoms (mild, without loss of consciousness or memory; classic, includes loss of consciousness and memory)

conduction: transmission of electrical impulses from one cell to another

conductive hearing loss: loss of hearing in which efficient sound transmission to the inner ear is interrupted by some obstruction or disease process

condyloma: external genital warts carrying the human papilloma virus

cones: retinal photoreceptor cells essential for visual acuity and color discrimination

congestive heart failure (CHF): a fluid overload condition (congestion) associated with heart failure

consolidation: lung tissue that has become more solid in nature due to collapse of alveoli or infectious process (pneumonia)

constructional apraxia: inability to draw figures in two or three dimensions

continent urinary diversion (Kock or Charleston pouch): transplantation of the ureters to a segment of bowel with construction of an effective continence mechanism or valve

continuous ambulatory peritoneal dialysis (CAPD): method of peritoneal dialysis whereby a patient performs four or five complete exchanges or cycles throughout the day

continuous cyclic peritoneal dialysis (CCPD): method of peritoneal dialysis in which a peritoneal dialysis machine (cycler) automatically performs exchanges, usually while the patient sleeps

continuous glucose monitoring system (CGMS): a device worn for 72 hours that continuously monitors blood glucose levels; the data are downloaded and analyzed for blood glucose patterns for that time period; presently used diagnostically to elicit patterns and tailor treatment

continuous passive motion (CPM) device: a device that promotes range of motion, circulation, and healing

continuous positive airway pressure (CPAP): positive pressure applied throughout the respiratory cycle to a spontaneously breathing patient to promote alveolar and airway stability; may be administered with endotracheal or tracheostomy tube or by mask

continuous renal replacement therapy (CRRT): variety of methods used to replace normal kidney function by circulating the patient's blood through a filter and returning it to the patient

continuous subcutaneous insulin infusion: a small device that delivers insulin on a 24-hour basis as basal insulin; it is also programmed by the patient to deliver a bolus dose before eating a meal in an attempt to mimic normal pancreatic function

continuous venovenous hemodialysis (CVVH or CVVHD): form of continuous renal replacement therapy that results in removal of fluid and waste products; venous blood circulates through a hemofilter and returns to the patient

contractility: ability of the cardiac muscle to shorten in response to an electrical impulse

contracture: abnormal shortening of muscle or joint, or both; fibrosis

control: containment of the growth of cancer cells

contusion: blunt force injury to soft tissue

cor pulmonale: right heart failure due to elevated pulmonary artery pressures or lung disease

coronary artery bypass graft (CABG): a surgical procedure in which a blood vessel from another part of the body is grafted onto the occluded coronary artery below the occlusion in such a way that blood flow bypasses the blockage

corpus luteum: site of a follicle that changes after ovulation to produce progesterone

corrosive poison: alkaline or acidic agent; causes tissue destruction after contact

cortical bone: compact bone

corticosteroids: hormones produced by the adrenal cortex or their synthetic equivalents; also referred to as adrenalcortical hormone and adrenocorticosteroid

crackles: soft, high-pitched, discontinuous popping sounds during inspiration caused by delayed reopening of the airways

creatine kinase (CK): an enzyme found in human tissues; one of the three types of CK is specific to heart muscle and may be used as an indicator of heart muscle injury

creatinine: endogenous waste product of muscle energy metabolism

crepitus: grating or crackling sound or sensation; may occur with movement of ends of a broken bone or irregular joint surface

cricothyroidotomy: surgical opening of the cricothyroid membrane to obtain an airway that is maintained with a tracheostomy or endotracheal tube

critical limb ischemia (CLI): chronic severe arterial obstruction with severe pain

cryosurgery of the prostate: localized treatment of the prostate by application of freezing temperatures

crystalloids: intravenous electrolyte solutions that move freely between the intravascular compartment and interstitial spaces

cure: prolonged survival and disappearance of all evidence of disease so that the patient has the same life expectancy as anyone else in his or her age group

Cushing's response: a compensatory response that attempts to restore blood flow by increasing arterial pressure to overcome the increased intracranial pressure; this includes rising systolic pressure, widening pulse pressure, and bradycardia

Cushing's syndrome: symptoms resulting from excess free circulating cortisol from the adrenal cortex; characterized by truncal obesity, "moon face," acne, abdominal striae, and hypertension

Cushing's triad: three classic signs—bradycardia, hypertension, and bradypnea—that represent a loss of compensatory mechanisms a presentation of brainstem dysfunction

cystectomy: removal of the urinary bladder

cystitis: inflammation of the urinary bladder

cystocele: weakness of the anterior vaginal wall that allows the bladder to protrude into the vagina

cytokines: hormones produced by leukocytes that are vital to regulation of hematopoiesis, apoptosis, and immune responses; generic term for non-antibody proteins that act as intercellular mediators, as in the generation of immune response

cytologic studies: examination of tissue samples (including body fluid) under a microscope, noting the structure, formation, and/or pathology of cells

cytotoxic T cells: lymphocytes that lyse cells infected with virus; also play a role in graft rejection

cytotoxic: destructive of cells

D

D-dimer: test that measures fibrin breakdown; considered to be more specific than fibrin degradation products in the diagnosis of disseminated intravascular coagulation (DIC)

deafness: partial or complete loss of the ability to hear

débridement: removal of foreign material and devitalized tissue until surrounding healthy tissue is exposed

debulking: surgical removal of all visible tumor in the abdomen

decerebration: an abnormal posture associated with severe brain injury, characterized by extreme extension of the upper and lower extremities (extension, adduction and internal rotation of the arm and flexion of the wrist and fingers, extension of the legs, and plantarflexion of the feet)

decompression (intestinal): removal of intestinal contents to prevent gas and fluid from distending the coils of the intestine

decontamination: process of removing, or rendering harmless, contaminants that have accumulated on personnel, patients, and equipment

decortication: an abnormal posture associated with severe brain injury, characterized by abnormal flexion of the upper extremities (adduction at the shoulder, flexion at the elbow and wrist) and extension of the lower extremities (including hips and knees)

defibrillation: electrical current administered to stop an arrhythmia, not synchronized with the patient's QRS complex

dehiscence: partial or complete separation of wound edges

delayed union: prolongation of expected healing time for a fracture

delirium: transient loss of intellectual function, usually due to systemic problems

dementia: a progressive organic mental disorder characterized by personality changes, confusion, disorientation,

and deterioration of intellect associated with impaired memory and judgment

dendrite: portion of the neuron that conducts impulses toward the cell body

dependence: occurs when a patient who has been taking opioids experiences a withdrawal syndrome when the opioids are discontinued; often occurs with opioid tolerance and does not indicate an addiction

depolarization: electrical stimulation that causes contraction of heart muscle

dermatosis: any abnormal skin condition

dermis: the second layer of skin containing sweat glands, hair follicles, and nerves

diabetes insipidus: condition in which abnormally large volumes of dilute urine are excreted as a result of deficient production of vasopressin (ADH)

diabetes mellitus: a group of metabolic diseases characterized by hyperglycemia resulting from defects in insulin secretion, insulin action, or both

diabetic ketoacidosis (DKA): a metabolic derangement in type 1 diabetes that results from a deficiency of insulin; highly acidic ketone bodies are formed, resulting in acidosis; usually requires hospitalization for treatment and is usually caused by nonadherence to the insulin regimen, concurrent illness, or infection

diagnostic peritoneal lavage: instillation of lactated Ringer's or normal saline solution into the abdominal cavity to detect red blood cells, white blood cells, bile, bacteria, amylase, or gastrointestinal contents indicative of abdominal injury

dialysate: solution that circulates through the dialyzer in hemodialysis and through the peritoneal membrane in peritoneal dialysis

dialyzer: "artificial kidney" or dialysis machine; contains a semipermeable membrane through which particles of a certain size can pass

diaphysis: shaft of long bone

diastole: period of ventricular relaxation resulting in ventricular filling

diastolic heart failure: the inability of the heart to pump sufficiently because of an alteration in the ability of the heart to fill; current term used to describe a type of heart failure

differentiation: development of functions and characteristics that are different from those of the parent stem cell

diffusion: movement of solutes (waste products) from an area of higher concentration to an area of lower concentration *or* exchange of gas molecules from areas of high concentration to areas of low concentration

digestion: phase of the digestive process that occurs when digestive enzymes and secretions mix with ingested food and when proteins, fats, and sugars are broken down into their component smaller molecules

dilutional hyponatremia: sodium deficiency that develops as a result of fluid retention; associated with excessive

antidiuretic hormone secretion in patients with syndrome of inappropriate antidiuretic hormone (SIADH) secretion

diplopia: double vision, or the awareness of two images of the same object occurring in one or both eyes

disability: restriction or lack of ability to perform an activity in a normal manner; the consequences of impairment in terms of an individual's functional performance and activity; disabilities represent disturbances at the level of the person (e.g., bathing, dressing, communication, walking, grooming)

disarticulation: amputation through a joint

dislocation: separation of joint surfaces

distributive shock: shock state resulting from displacement of blood volume creating a relative hypovolemia and inadequate delivery of oxygen to the cells

diverticulitis: inflammation of a diverticulum from obstruction (by fecal matter)

diverticulosis: presence of several diverticula in the intestine; common in middle age

dizziness: altered sensation of orientation in space

donor site: the area from which skin is taken to provide a skin graft for another part of the body

Doppler ultrasonography: noninvasive diagnostic procedure to assess blood flow direction, velocity, and turbulence

DRG: diagnostic related group; diagnostic categories used by Medicare to classify patients when prospectively paying health care organizations for patient care

dry powder inhaler (DPI): inhalation devices used to deliver medications to the lungs as suspended dry powder

ductal carcinoma in situ (DCIS): cancer cells that start in the ductal system of the breast but have not penetrated the surrounding tissue

dumping syndrome: rapid emptying of the stomach contents into the small intestine; characterized by sweating and weakness

duodenum: the first part of the small intestine, which connects with the pylorus of the stomach and extends to the jejunum

duplex ultrasound: combines grayscale tissue imaging with velocity changes

dysarthria: defects of articulation of language (slurred speech)

dyschezia: pain with defecation

dyskinesia: impaired ability to execute voluntary movements

dyslipidemia: abnormal blood lipid levels, including high total, LDL, and triglyceride levels, as well as low HDL levels

dysmenorrhea: painful menstruation that is not associated with any type of pathologic process

dyspareunia: painful sexual intercourse

dysphagia: difficulty swallowing, causing the patient to be at risk for aspiration

dysphonia: abnormal voice quality caused by weakness and incoordination of muscles responsible for speech

dysplasia: bizarre cell growth resulting in cells that differ in size, shape, or arrangement from other cells of the same type of tissue

dyspnea on exertion (DOE): shortness of breath that occurs with exertion

dyspnea: labored breathing or shortness of breath

dysuria: painful or difficult urination

E

ecchymosis: bruise

ectopic pregnancy: fertilized egg implants anywhere outside of body of the uterus, commonly the fallopian tube

edema: soft tissue swelling due to fluid accumulation

effusion: excess fluid in joint

EIA (enzyme immunoassay): a blood test that can determine the presence of antibodies to HIV in the blood or saliva; also referred as *enzyme-linked immunosorbent assay* (ELISA); positive results are verified with a Western blot test

ejection fraction: percentage of the end-diastolic blood volume ejected from the ventricle with each heartbeat; normal is between 55% and 70%

elimination: phase of digestive process that occurs after digestion and absorption, when waste products are evacuated from the body

embolus: a piece of thrombus that travels through a vessel and blocks a smaller vessel

emergent: triage category signifying potentially life-threatening injuries or illnesses requiring immediate treatment

emmetropia: absence of refractive error

emptysis: the coughing up of blood from the lower respiratory tract

emphysema: a disease of the airways characterized by destruction of the walls of over distended alveoli; a category of COPD

empyema: accumulation of purulent material in the pleural space

endocrine: secreting internally; hormonal secretion of a ductless gland

endolymphatic hydrops: dilation of the endolymphatic space of the inner ear; the pathologic correlate of Ménière's disease

endometrial ablation: procedure performed through a hysteroscope in which the lining of the uterus is burned away or ablated to treat abnormal uterine bleeding

endometriosis: the growth of cells similar to the endometrial lining that outside of the uterus causing heavy and painful menses

endometrium: lining of the uterus

endorphins, enkephalins, and dynorphins: morphine-like substances produced by the body; primarily found in the central nervous system; they have the potential to reduce pain

endoscopic retrograde cholangiopancreatography (ERCP): an endoscopic procedure using fiberoptic technology to visualize the biliary system

endosteum: a thin, vascular membrane covering the marrow cavity of long bones and the spaces in cancellous bone

endotracheal intubation: insertion of a breathing tube through the nose or mouth into the trachea

end-stage renal disease (ESRD): progressive, irreversible deterioration in renal function that results in retention of uremic waste products

enteroclysis: fluoroscopic X-ray of the small intestine; a tube is placed from the nose or mouth through the esophagus and the stomach to the duodenum, a barium-based liquid contrast material is infused through the tube, and X-rays are taken as it travels through the duodenum

enterostomal therapist: nurse specially educated in appropriate skin, wound, ostomy, and continence care; often referred to as wound-care specialist or wound-ostomy-continence nurse (WOCN)

enucleation: complete removal of the eyeball and part of the optic nerve

eosinophil: type of granulocyte; involved in allergic reactions

epidermis: the outermost layer of skin

epidermopoiesis: development of epidermal cells

epididymitis: infection of the epididymis that usually descends from an infected prostate or urinary tract; also may develop as a complication of gonorrhea

epilepsy: a group of syndromes characterized by paroxysmal transient disturbances of brain function

epiphysis: end of long bone

epistaxis: hemorrhage from the nose due to rupture of tiny, distended vessels in the mucous membrane of any area of the nose

epitope: any component of an antigen molecule that functions as an antigenetic determinant by permitting the attachment of certain antibodies

erectile dysfunction: also called *impotence;* the inability to either achieve or maintain an erection sufficient to accomplish sexual intercourse

erythema: redness of the skin caused by congestion of the capillaries

erythrocyte sedimentation rate (ESR): laboratory test that measures the rate of settling of red blood cells; elevation is indicative of inflammation; also called the *sed rate*

erythrocyte: *see* **red blood cell**

erythropoiesis: process of red blood cell formation

erythropoietin: hormone produced primarily by the kidney; necessary for erythropoiesis

eschar: devitalized tissue resulting from a burn

escharotomy: a linear excision made through eschar to release constriction of underlying tissue

esophagogastroduodenoscopy (EGD): passage of a fiber-optic tube through the mouth and throat into the digestive tract for visualization of the esophagus, stomach, and small intestine; biopsies can be performed

esophagus: collapsible tube connecting the mouth to the stomach, through which food passes as it is ingested

estrogen: hormone that develops and maintains the female reproductive system

eustachian tube: the 3 to 4 cm tube that extends from the middle ear to the nasopharynx

euthanasia: Greek for "good death"; has evolved to mean the intentional killing by act or omission of a dependent human being for his or her alleged benefit

euthyroid: state of normal thyroid hormone production

evisceration (eye): removal of the intraocular contents through a corneal or scleral incision; the optic nerve, sclera, extraocular muscles, and sometimes, the cornea are left intact

evisceration (wound): protrusion of organs through the surgical incision

excision: surgical removal of tissue

exenteration: surgical removal of the entire contents of the orbit, including the eyeball and lids

exocrine: secreting externally; hormonal secretion from excretory ducts

exophthalmos: abnormal protrusion of one or both eyeballs; produces a startled expression; usually due to hyperthyroidism

expressive aphasia: difficulty expressing thoughts through speech or written language; inability to express oneself; often associated with damage to the left frontal lobe area (also known as Broca's aphasia)

external auditory canal: the canal leading from the external auditory meatus to the tympanic membrane; about 2.5 cm in length

external ear: the portion of the ear that consists of the auricle and external auditory canal; it is separated from the middle ear by the tympanic membrane

external fixator: external metal frame attached to bone fragments to stabilize them

extravasation: leakage of medication from the veins into the subcutaneous tissues

F

fascia (epimysium): fibrous tissue that covers, supports, and separates muscles

fasciculation: involuntary twitch of muscle fibers

fasciotomy: the incision and diversion of the muscle fascia to relieve muscle constriction, as in compartment syndrome, or to reduce fascia contracture

fasting plasma glucose (FPG): blood glucose determination obtained in the laboratory after fasting for more than 8 hours; although plasma levels are specified in diagnostic criteria, blood glucose levels, which are slightly higher than plasma levels, are more commonly used

feedback: the return of information about the results of input given to a person or a system

female-to-male (FTM): a biological female who is becoming a male

fetor hepaticus: sweet, slightly fecal odor to the breath, presumed to be of intestinal origin; prevalent with the extensive collateral portal circulation in chronic liver disease

fibrin: filamentous protein; basis of thrombus and blood clot

fibrinogen: protein converted into fibrin to form thrombus and clot

fibrinolysis: process of breakdown of fibrin clot

fibrinolytic: a substance that acts to break up fibrin, the fine filaments of blood clots

fibrocystic breast changes: term used to describe certain benign changes in the breast, typically associated with palpable nodularity, lumpiness, swelling, or pain

fibroscopy (gastrointestinal): intubation of a part of the GI system with a flexible, lighted tube to assist in diagnosis and treatment of diseases of that area

fine-needle aspiration: insertion of a needle through the chest wall to obtain cells of a mass or tumor; usually performed under fluoroscopy or chest CT guidance

first-intention healing: method of healing in which wound edges are surgically approximated and integumentary continuity is restored without granulation

flaccid: displaying lack of muscle tone; limp, floppy

follicle-stimulating hormone (FSH): hormone released by the pituitary gland to stimulate estrogen production and ovulation

fornix: upper part of the vagina

fraction of inspired oxygen (FiO₂): concentration of oxygen delivered (1.0 = 100% oxygen)

fracture reduction: restoration of fracture fragments into anatomic alignment and rotation

fracture: a break in the continuity of a bone

frequency: voiding more frequently than every 3 hours

fulminant hepatic failure: sudden, severe onset of acute liver failure that occurs within 8 weeks after the first symptoms of jaundice

functional incontinence: physical impairments make it difficult or impossible for the patient to reach the toilet in time for voiding

fundus: body of the uterus *or* the interior surface of the eye, opposite the lens, and includes the retina, optic disc, macula and fovea, and posterior pole

G

gangrene: dead tissue

gastric outlet obstruction (GOO): any condition that mechanically impedes normal gastric emptying; there is

obstruction of the channel of the pylorus and duodenum through which the stomach empties

gastric: refers to the stomach

gastritis: inflammation of the stomach

gastroesophageal reflux: back-flow of gastric or duodenal contents into the esophagus

gastrostomy: surgical creation of an opening into the stomach for the purpose of administering foods and fluids

genetics engineering: emerging technology designed to enable replacement of missing or defective genes

gestational diabetes mellitus (GDM): any degree of glucose intolerance with its onset during pregnancy

glomerular filtration rate (GFR): volume of plasma filtered at the glomerulus into the kidney tubules each minute; normal rate is approximately 120 mL/min

glomerulonephritis: inflammation of the glomerular capillaries

glomerulus: tuft of capillaries forming part of the nephron through which filtration occurs

glucagon: a hormone secreted by the alpha cells of the islets of Langerhans of the pancreas that increases the blood glucose by stimulating the liver to convert stored glycogen to glucose

glucocorticoids: steroid hormones (i.e., cortisol, cortisone, and corticosterone) secreted by the adrenal cortex in response to ACTH; produces a rise of liver glycogen and blood glucose and counteracts inflammatory responses

glycated hemoglobin (glycosylated hemoglobin, Hgb A$_{1C}$ or A1C): a long-term measure of glucose control that is a result of glucose attaching to hemoglobin for the life of the red blood cell (120 days); the goal of diabetes therapy is a normal to near-normal level of glycolated hemoglobin, the same as in the nondiabetic population

goiter: enlargement of the thyroid gland; usually caused by an iodine-deficient diet

graafian follicle: ovarian cells that form into a structure on the surface of the ovary that houses the ovum or unfertilized egg

grading: identification of the type of tissue from which the tumor originated and the degree to which the tumor cells retain the functional and structural characteristics of the tissue of origin

graft-versus-host disease (GVHD): an immune response initiated by T lymphocytes of donor tissue against the recipient's tissues (skin, gastrointestinal tract, liver); an undesirable response

graft-versus-tumor effect: the donor cell response against the malignancy; a desirable response

granulocyte: granulated white blood cell (neutrophil, eosinophil, basophil); sometimes used synonymously with neutrophil

granulomas: Cells surrounded by lymphocytes, which can be found in all layers of the bowel; if present, they strongly suggest Crohn's disease

Graves' disease: a form of hyperthyroidism; characterized by a diffuse goiter and exophthalmos

grief: the personal feelings that accompany an anticipated or actual loss

H

Hashimoto's disease: thyroiditis (inflammation of the thyroid gland) characterized by high levels of antimicrosomal antibodies; an autoimmune disorder that is the most common cause of hypothyroidism in the United States

head injury: an injury to the scalp, skull, and/or brain

health education: a variety of learning experiences designed to promote behaviors that facilitate health

health promotion: the art and science of assisting people to change their lifestyle toward a higher state of wellness

hearing loss: dysfunction of any component of the auditory system (conductive hearing loss, sensorineural hearing loss, mixed hearing loss)

heart failure (HF): the inability of the heart to pump sufficient blood to meet the needs of the tissues for oxygen and nutrients; signs and symptoms of pulmonary and systemic congestion may or may not be present

Helicobacter pylori: a spiral-shaped gram-negative bacterium that colonizes the gastric mucosa; involved in most cases of peptic ulcer disease

helper T cells: lymphocytes that attack foreign pathogens (antigens) directly

hematemesis: vomiting of blood

hematocrit: percentage of total blood volume consisting of red blood cells

hematopoiesis: complex process of the formation and maturation of blood cells

hematuria: red blood cells in the urine

hemianopsia: blindness in half of the field of vision in one or both eyes

hemiarthroplasty: the replacement of one of the articular surfaces (e.g., in a hip hemiarthroplasty, the femoral head and neck are replaced with a femoral prosthesis—the acetabulum is not replaced)

hemiplegia/hemiparesis: paralysis/weakness on one side of the body, or part or it, due to an injury to the motor areas of the brain

hemodialysis: procedure during which a patient's blood is circulated through a dialyzer to remove waste products and excess fluid

hemodynamic monitoring: use of devices to measure cardiovascular function

hemoglobin: iron-containing protein of red blood cells; delivers oxygen to tissues

hemolysis: destruction of red blood cells; can occur within or outside of the vasculature

hemorrhagic stroke: a stroke that results from bleeding into the brain tissue itself or into the subarachnoid space or ventricles

hemostasis: a dynamic process that involves the cessation of bleeding from an injured vessel, which requires activity of blood vessels, platelets, coagulation, and fibrinolytic systems; intricate balance between clot formation and clot dissolution

hemothorax: partial or complete collapse of the lung due to blood accumulating in the pleural space; may occur after surgery or trauma

hepatic encephalopathy: central nervous system dysfunction resulting from liver disease; frequently associated with elevated ammonia levels that produce changes in mental status, altered level of consciousness, and coma

hernia: protrusion of an organ or part of an organ through the wall of the cavity that normally contains it

herniation: abnormal protrusion of tissue through a defect or natural opening

herpes simplex: cold sore (cutaneous viral infection with painful vesicles and erosions on the tongue, palate, gingiva, buccal membranes, or lips)

high-density lipoprotein (HDL): a protein-bound lipid that transports cholesterol to the liver for excretion in the bile; composed of a higher proportion of protein to lipid than low-density lipoprotein; exerts a beneficial effect on the arterial wall

hirsutism: the condition of having excessive hair growth

histamine: substance in the body that causes increased gastric secretion, dilation of capillaries, and constriction of the bronchial smooth muscle

histamine-2 (H$_2$) receptor antagonist: a pharmacologic agent that inhibits histamine action at the H$_2$ receptors of the stomach, resulting in inhibition of gastric acid secretion

HIV-1: retrovirus isolated and recognized as the etiologic agent of AIDS

HIV-2: virus closely related to HIV-1 that also causes AIDS, predominantly found in West Africa

homeostasis: maintenance of a constant internal equilibrium in a biological system that involves positive and negative feedback mechanisms

hormones: chemical transmitter substances produced in one organ or part of the body and carried by the bloodstream to other cells or organs on which they have a specific regulatory effect; produced mainly by endocrine glands (e.g., pituitary, thyroid, gonads)

hospice: a coordinated program of interdisciplinary care and services provided primarily in the home to terminally ill patients and their families

humoral immune response: the immune system's second line of defense; often termed the *antibody response*

hydrocele: a collection of fluid, generally in the tunica vaginalis of the testis, although it also may collect within the spermatic cord

hydrocephalus: excessive cerebrospinal fluid (CSF) in the intracranial cavity, commonly due to obstruction of flow in the ventricular system or subarachnoid space

hydrochloric acid: acid secreted by the glands in the stomach; mixes with chyme to break it down into absorbable molecules and to aid in the destruction of bacteria

hydrophilic: a material that absorbs moisture

hydrostatic pressure: the pressure created by the weight of fluid against the wall that contains it; in the body, hydrostatic pressure in blood vessels results from the weight of fluid itself and the force resulting from cardiac contraction

hygroscopic: a material that absorbs moisture from the air

hymen: tissue that covers the vaginal opening partially or completely before vaginal penetration

hyperemia: "red eye" resulting from dilation of the vasculature of the conjunctiva

hyperglycemia: elevated blood glucose level; fasting level greater than 110 mg/dL (6.1 mmol/L); 2-hour postprandial level greater than 140 mg/dL (7.8 mmol/L)

hyperglycemic hyperosmolar nonketotic syndrome (HHNS): a metabolic disorder of type 2 diabetes resulting from a relative insulin deficiency initiated by an intercurrent illness that raises the demand for insulin; associated with polyuria and severe dehydration

hyperopia: farsightedness; a refractive error in which the focus of light rays from a distant object is behind the retina

hyperpigmentation: increase in the melanin of the skin, resulting in an increase in pigmentation

hyperplasia: abnormally increased proliferation of normal cells

hypersensitivity: abnormal heightened reaction to a stimulus of any kind

hypertension: blood pressure of 140/90 mm Hg or greater

hypertensive emergency: a situation in which blood pressure is severely elevated and there is evidence of actual or probable target organ damage

hypertensive urgency: a situation in which blood pressure is severely elevated but there is no evidence of target organ damage

hypertonic solution: a solution with an osmolality higher than that of serum

hypertrophy: enlargement; increase in size of muscle

hyphema: blood in the anterior chamber

hypochromia: pallor within the red blood cell caused by decreased hemoglobin content

hypoglycemia: low blood glucose level (<60 mg/dL [<2.7 mmol/L])

hypophysectomy: surgical removal of all or part of the pituitary gland

hypopigmentation: decrease in the melanin of the skin, resulting in a loss of pigmentation

hyposmia: impairment of the sense of smell

hypotension: a decrease in blood pressure to less than 90/60 mm Hg

hypotonic solution: a solution with an osmolality lower than that of serum

hypovolemic shock: shock state resulting from decreased intravascular volume due to fluid loss or deficit; causes include hemorrhage and dehydration

hypoxemia: decrease in arterial oxygen tension in the blood

hypoxia: decrease in oxygen supply to the tissues and cells

iatrogenic incontinence: the involuntary loss of urine due to extrinsic medical factors, predominantly medications

ileal conduit: transplantation of the ureters to an isolated section of the terminal ileum, with one end of the ureters brought to the abdominal wall

ileus: decreased motility of the GI tract, often the result of irritation of the peritoneum; signs and symptoms include diffuse abdominal discomfort, nausea, vomiting, abdominal distention, hypoactive or absent bowel sounds, absent bowel movement/flatus

immunity: the body's specific protective response to an invading foreign agent or organism

immunopathology: study of diseases resulting in dysfunctions within the immune system

immunoregulation: complex system of checks and balances that regulates or controls immune responses

impaired fasting glucose (IFG), impaired glucose tolerance (IGT): a metabolic stage intermediate between normal glucose homeostasis and diabetes; not clinical entities in their own right but risk factors for future diabetes and cardiovascular disease

impairment: loss or abnormality of psychological, physiologic, or anatomic structure or function at the organ level (e.g., dysphagia, hemiparesis); an abnormality of body structure, appearance, and organ or system function resulting from any cause

imperforate hymen: membrane at the vaginal opening, or introitus, that is still intact and causing obstruction

implantable cardioverter defibrillator (ICD): a device implanted into the chest to treat arrhythmias

incentive spirometry: method of deep breathing that provides visual feedback to help the patient inhale deeply and slowly and achieve maximum lung inflation

incomplete spinal cord lesion: a condition where there is preservation of the sensory or motor fibers, or both, below the lesion in the spinal cord

incus: the second of the three ossicles in the middle ear; it articulates with the malleus and stapes; the anvil

induration: an abnormally hard lesion or reaction, as in a positive tuberculin skin test

infection: condition in which the host interacts physiologically and immunologically with a microorganism

infectious disease: the consequences that result from invasion of the body by microorganisms that can produce harm to the body and potentially death

informed consent: the patient's autonomous decision about whether to undergo a surgical procedure; based on the nature of the condition, the treatment options, and the risks and benefits involved

ingestion: phase of the digestive process that occurs when food is taken into the GI tract via the mouth and esophagus

injection: congestion of blood vessels

inner ear: the portion of the ear that consists of the cochlea, vestibule, and semicircular canals

insulin: a hormone secreted by the beta cells of the islets of Langerhans of the pancreas that is necessary for the metabolism of carbohydrates, proteins, and fats

interdisciplinary collaboration: communication and cooperation among members of diverse health care disciplines jointly to plan, implement, and evaluate care

interferons: proteins formed when cells are exposed to viral or foreign agents; capable of activating other components of the immune system

intermittent claudication: a muscular, cramp-like pain in the extremities consistently reproduced with the same degree of exercise or activity and relieved by rest

intermittent mandatory ventilation (IMV): mode of mechanical ventilation that provides a combination of mechanically assisted breaths and spontaneous breaths

internal auditory canal: a canal in the petrous portion of the temporal bone that houses the facial and vestibulocochlear nerves (cranial nerves VII and VIII)

internal fixation: the stabilization of the reduced fracture by the use of metal screws, plates, wires, nails, and pins

international normalized ratio (INR): a standard method for monitoring prothrombin levels in patients receiving oral anticoagulation (warfarin), eliminating the variation in test results from laboratory to laboratory

interstitial cystitis: inflammation of the bladder wall that eventually causes disintegration of the lining and loss of bladder elasticity

interstitial nephritis: inflammation within the renal tissue

intracranial pressure: pressure exerted by the volume of the intracranial contents within the cranial vault

intraoperative phase: period of time from when the patient is transferred to the operating room table to when he or she is admitted to the postanesthesia care unit (PACU)

intrathecal chemotherapy: chemotherapeutic agents injected directly into the subarachnoid space

intrinsic factor: a gastric secretion that combines with vitamin B_{12} so that the vitamin can be absorbed

introitus: perineal opening to the vagina

involucrum: new bone growth around a sequestrum

ischemia: insufficient tissue oxygenation

ischemic stroke: stroke that results from inadequate blood supply to the brain due to partial or complete occlusion of an artery

islet cell transplantation: an investigational procedure in which purified islet cells from cadaver donors are injected into the portal vein of the liver, with the goal of having these cells secrete insulin and cure type 1 diabetes

isoelectric line: the baseline or flat part of the electrocardiogram (ECG), frequently noted between the T and P waves, or between the P wave and the QRS complex; ST-segment elevation or depression is noted by observing the relationship of the ST-segment to the isoelectric line (above or below)

isometric contraction: muscle tension increased, length unchanged, no joint motion

isotonic contraction: muscle tension unchanged, muscle shortened, joint moved

isotonic solution: a solution with the same osmolality as serum and other body fluids; osmolality falls within normal range for serum (280 to 300 mOsm/kg)

J

jaundice: yellowing discoloration of the skin by abnormally high levels of bilirubin in the blood

jejunum: second portion of the small intestine, extending from the duodenum to the ileum

JNC 7: Seventh Joint National Committee on the Prevention, Detection, Evaluation, and Treatment of High Blood Pressure; committee established to study and make recommendations about hypertension in the United States; findings and recommendations of JNC 7 are contained in an extensive report published in 2003

joint arthroplasty or replacement: the replacement of joint surfaces with metal or synthetic materials

joint capsule: fibrous tissue that encloses bone ends and other joint surfaces

joint effusion: the escape of fluid from the blood vessels or lymphatics into the joint space

joint: area where bone ends meet; provides for motion and flexibility

K

Kegal exercises: exercises that contract and relax the pelvic floor muscle, helping to strengthen it

keratin: an insoluble, fibrous protein that forms the outer layer of skin

ketone: a highly acidic substance formed when the liver breaks down free fatty acids in the absence of insulin

Kock pouch: A type of ileostomy in which the surgeon forms an artificial rectum from a section of the ileum

Kussmaul respirations: Increase in respiration, particularly the tidal volume associated with metabolic acidosis

kyphosis: increase in the convex curvature of the spine

L

lactobacilli: vaginal bacteria that limit the growth of other bacteria by producing hydrogen peroxide

lamellae: mature compact bone structures that form concentric rings of bone matrix; lamellar bone

laminectomy: excision of the posterior arches and spinous processes of a vertebra

Langerhans cells: dendritic clear cells in the epidermis that carry surface receptors for immunoglobulin and that are active participants in delayed hypersensitivity of the skin; in addition, these cells are responsible for carrying invading bacteria to lymphocytes in lymph glands where they are neutralized

laparoscopic cholecystectomy: removal of gallbladder through endoscopic procedure

large intestine: the portion of the GI tract into which waste material from the small intestine passes as absorption continues and elimination begins; consists of several parts—ascending segment, transverse segment, descending segment, sigmoid colon, and rectum

laryngectomy: removal of all or part of the larynx and surrounding structures

laryngitis: inflammation of the larynx; may be caused by voice abuse, exposure to irritants, or infectious organisms

latency: time interval after primary infection when a microorganism lives within the host without producing clinical evidence

lavage: flushing of the stomach via the gastric tube with water or other fluids to clear it

leaflet repair: repair of a cardiac valve's movable "flaps" (leaflets)

learning readiness: the optimum time for learning to occur; usually corresponds to the learner's perceived need and desire to obtain specific knowledge

learning: the act of gaining knowledge and skill

leukemia: a progressive, malignant disease characterized by uncontrolled proliferation of white blood cells

leukocyte: *see* **white blood cell**

leukopenia: less than normal amount of white blood cells in circulation

lichenification: thickening of the horny layer of the skin

ligament: fibrous band connecting bones

limbus: junction of the cornea and sclera

liniments: lotions with added oil for increased softening of the skin

lipase: an enzyme that aids in the digestion of fats

lobular carcinoma in situ (LCIS): atypical change and proliferation of the lobular cells of the breast; previously considered a premalignant condition but now considered a marker of increased risk for invasive breast cancer

locked-in syndrome: condition due to a lesion at or below the pons or midbrain, which results in the inability to movement while consciousness is preserved; communication is severely limited

lordosis: increase in lumbar curvature of the spine

low-density lipoprotein (LDL): a protein-bound lipid that transports cholesterol to tissues in the body; composed of a lower proportion of protein to lipid than high-density lipoprotein; exerts a harmful effect on the arterial wall

low-profile gastrostomy device (LPGD, G-button): an enteral feeding access device that is flush with the skin and is used for long-term feeding

luteal phase: the second half or secretory phase of the menstrual cycle that occurs after ovulation

luteinizing hormone (LH): hormone released by the pituitary gland that stimulates progesterone production

lymphedema: chronic swelling of an extremity due to interrupted lymphatic circulation, typically from an axillary lymph node dissection

lymphocyte: form of white blood cell involved in immune functions

lymphoid: pertaining to lymphocytes

lymphokines: substances released by sensitized lymphocytes when they come in contact with specific antigens

lysis: destruction of cells

M

macrophage: cells of the reticuloendothelial system (RES) that are capable of phagocytosis

magnetic resonance angiography (MRA): the use of magnetic fields and radio waves to produce two- or three-dimensional images of blood vessels

male-to-female (MTF): a biological male who is becoming a female

malignant: having cells or processes that are characteristic of cancer

malleus: the first (most lateral) and largest of the three ossicles in the middle ear; it is connected to the tympanic membrane laterally and articulates with the incus; the hammer

malunion: healing of a fractured bone in a malaligned position

mammoplasty: surgical procedure to reconstruct or change the size or shape of the breast; can be performed for reduction or augmentation

mass casualty incident (MCI): situation in which the number of casualties exceeds the number of resources

mastalgia: breast pain, usually related to hormonal fluctuations or irritation of a nerve

mechanical ventilation: a positive- or negative-pressure breathing device that supports ventilation and oxygenation

Medicare Hospice Benefit: a Medicare entitlement that provides for comprehensive, interdisciplinary palliative care and services for eligible beneficiaries who have a terminal illness and a life expectancy of less than 6 months

megacolon: an acquired or congenital abnormal enlargement of the colon

melanin: the substance responsible for melanin

melanocytes: cells of the skin that produce coloration of the skin

melena: tarry or black stools; indicative of blood in stools

memory cells: cells that are responsible for recognizing antigens from previous exposure and mounting an immune response

menarche: beginning of menstrual function

Ménière's disease: condition of the inner ear characterized by a triad of symptoms: episodic vertigo, tinnitus, and fluctuating sensorineural hearing loss

meniscectomy: the excision of damaged joint fibrocartilage

menopause: permanent cessation of menstruation resulting from the loss of ovarian follicular activity

menorrhagia: excessive bleeding that occurs in regular cycles

menstruation: sloughing and discharge of the lining of the uterus if conception does not take place

Merkel cells: cells of the epidermis that play a role in transmission of sensory messages

metabolic syndrome: a cluster of metabolic abnormalities including insulin resistance, obesity, dyslipidemia, and hypertension that increase the risk of cardiovascular disease

metaplasia: conversion of one type of mature cell into another type of cell

metastasis: spread of cancer cells from the primary tumor to distant sites

metered-dose inhaler (MDI): patient-activated medication canister that provides aerosolized medication that the patient inhales into the lungs

metrorrhagia: irregular vaginal bleeding that is heavy and prolonged

microcytosis: smaller than normal red blood cells

micrographia: small and often illegible handwriting

micturition: urination or voiding

middle ear: the small, air-filled cavity in the temporal bone that contains the three ossicles

migraine headache: a severe, unrelenting headache often accompanied by symptoms such as nausea, vomiting, and visual disturbances

mineralocorticoid: steroid of the adrenal cortex; primarily aldosterone, which promotes retention of sodium and therefore water and excretion of potassium

minor: triage category signifying non–life-threatening injuries or illnesses that can be routinely managed in a clinic or physician's office or that require no medical care

miotics: medications that cause pupillary constriction

mitral valve: atrioventricular valve located between the left atrium and left ventricle

mittelschmerz: midcycle ovulatory pain caused by a ruptured corpus luteum

moderate sedation: use of sedation to depress the level of consciousness without altering the patient's ability to maintain a patent airway and to respond to physical stimuli and verbal commands, previously referred to as *conscious sedation*

modified radical mastectomy: removal of the breast tissue, nipple–areola complex, and a portion of the axillary lymph nodes

monitored anesthesia care (MAC): moderate sedation administered by an anesthesiologist or anesthetist

monocyte: large white blood cell that develop into a macrophage when transported to tissues

Monro-Kellie hypothesis: theory that states that due to limited space for expansion within the skull, an increase in volume of any one of the cranial contents—brain tissue, blood, or CSF—must be compensated for by a decrease in volume of another

morbid obesity: more than twice ideal body weight, 100 pounds or more over ideal body weight, or body mass index (BMI) exceeding 30 kg/m²

mourning: individual, family, group, and cultural expressions of grief and associated behaviors

mouth: first portion of the GI tract, through which food is ingested

murmurs: sounds created by abnormal, turbulent flow of blood in the heart

mydriatics: medications instilled in the eyes that cause pupillary dilation

myeloid: pertaining to nonlymphoid blood cells that differentiate into red blood cells, platelets, monocytes and macrophages, neutrophils, eosinophils, basophils, and mast cells

myelopoiesis: formation and maturation of cells derived from myeloid stem cell

myelosuppression: suppression of the blood cell–producing function of the bone marrow

myocardial infarction (MI): death of heart tissue caused by lack of oxygenated blood flow; if acute, abbreviated as AMI

myocardium: muscle layer of the heart responsible for the pumping action of the heart

myoglobinuria: iron-containing protein from muscle cells in the urine often following trauma

myomectomy: surgical excision of uterine fibroids that preserves fertility

myopia: nearsightedness; a refractive error in which the focus of light rays from a distant object is anterior to the retina

myxedema: refers to the soft tissue changes in subcutaneous and other interstitial tissues in a person with hypothyroidism

N

nadir: lowest point of white blood cell depression after therapy that has toxic effects on the bone marrow

nasoduodenal tube: tube inserted through the nose into the beginning of the small intestine (duodenum)

nasogastric (NG) tube: tube inserted through the nose into the stomach

nasojejunal tube: tube inserted through the nose into the second portion of the small intestine (jejunum)

natural killer cells (NK cells): lymphocytes that defend against microorganisms and malignant cells

negative feedback: regulating mechanism in which an increase or decrease in the level of a substance decreases or increases the function of the organ producing the substance

neoadjuvant chemotherapy: preoperative chemotherapy; it is administered preoperatively to shrink a large tumor

neoplasm/tumor/lesion: an abnormal mass of tissues, which can be benign or malignant in nature

nephron: structural and functional unit of the kidney responsible for urine formation

nephropathy: a long-term complication of diabetes in which the kidney cells are damaged; characterized by microalbuminuria in early stages and progressing to end-stage renal disease

nephrosclerosis: atherosclerosis of renal arteries causing fibrosis, glomerular damage, ischemia

neurodegenerative: a disease, process, or condition that leads to deterioration of normal cells or function of the nervous system

neurogenic bladder: bladder dysfunction that results from a disorder or dysfunction of the nervous system; may result in either urinary retention or bladder overactivity, resulting in urinary urgency and urge incontinence

neurogenic shock: a type of distributive shock state resulting from loss of sympathetic vascular tone causing low blood pressure

neuropathy: a long-term complication of diabetes resulting from damage to the nerve cell

neurovascular status: neurologic (motor and sensory components) and circulatory functioning of a body part

neutropenia: abnormally low absolute neutrophil count

neutrophil: fully mature white blood cell capable of phagocytosis; primary defense against bacterial infection

nociception: activation of sensory transduction in nerves by thermal, mechanical, or chemical energy impinging on specialized nerve endings; the nerves involved convey information about tissue damage to the central nervous system

nociceptor: a receptor preferentially sensitive to a noxious stimulus

nocturia: awakening at night to urinate

nonunion: failure of fragments of a fractured bone to heal together

nonurgent: triage category signifying episodic or minor injury or illness in which treatment may be delayed several hours or longer without increased morbidity

normal flora: persistent nonpathogenic organisms colonizing a host

normal heart sounds: referred to as S_1 and S_2, are produced by closure of the atrioventricular (AV) valves (tricuspid, mitral valves) and semilunar valves (pulmonic, aortic valves), respectively

normochromic: normal red blood cell color, indicating normal amount of hemoglobin

normocytic: normal size of red blood cells

nosocomial: pertaining to or originating from a hospitalization; not present at the time of hospital admission

nuchal rigidity: stiffness of the neck or inability to bend the neck

nucleated RBC: immature form of red blood cell; portion of nucleus remains within the red cell; not normally seen in circulating blood

nucleic acid amplification tests (NAAT): a test that uses nucleic acid to assess for specific pathogens

null lymphocytes: lymphocytes that destroy antigens already coated with the antibody

nutrition: the science that deals with food and nourishment in humans

nystagmus: involuntary oscillation of the eyeball

O

obstructive shock: shock state resulting from the obstruction of the great vessels or heart itself; examples include cardiac tamponade, tension pneumothorax, pulmonary embolism, and abdominal compartment syndrome

odynophagia: pain on swallowing

oligomenorrhea: infrequent or light menses sometimes occurring at intervals of greater than 35 days

oliguria: total urine output less than 400 mL in 24 h

omentum: fold of the peritoneum that surrounds the stomach and other organs of the abdomen

oncology: field or study of cancer

oophorectomy: surgical removal of the ovaries

open lung biopsy: biopsy of lung tissue performed through a limited thoracotomy incision

open reduction with internal fixation (ORIF): open surgical procedure to repair and stabilize a fracture

open reduction: the correction and alignment of the fracture after surgical dissection and exposure of the fracture

opioid: a morphine-like compound that produces bodily effects including pain relief, sedation, constipation, and respiratory depression; this term is preferred rather than the term *narcotic*

opportunistic infection: illness caused by various organisms, some of which usually do not cause disease in persons with normal immune systems

opsonization: the coating of antigen–antibody molecules with a sticky substance to facilitate phagocytosis

optic chiasm: the area of the brain where optic nerve (CN II) fibers partially cross

orchiectomy: surgical removal of one or both of the testes

orchitis: inflammation of the testes (testicular congestion) caused by pyogenic, viral, spirochetal, parasitic, traumatic, chemical, or unknown factors

organ of Corti: the end organ of hearing, located in the cochlea

orthopnea: shortness of breath when lying flat

orthotopic liver transplantation (OLT): grafting of a donor liver into the normal anatomic location, with removal of the diseased native liver

orthotopic transplantation: the recipient's heart is removed, and a donor heart is grafted into the same site; the patient has one heart

OSHA: Occupational Safety and Health Administration; the federal agency providing oversight to organizations that ensure the safety of employees at work

osmolality: the number of osmoles (the standard unit of osmotic pressure) per kilogram of solution, expressed as mOsm/kg; used more often in clinical practice than the term *osmolarity* to evaluate serum and urine; in addition to urea and glucose, sodium contributes the largest number of particles to osmolality

osmolarity: the number of osmoles, the standard unit of osmotic pressure per liter of solution, expressed as milliosmoles per liter (mOsm/L); describes the concentration of solutes or dissolved particles

osmosis: the process by which fluid moves across a semipermeable membrane from an area of low solute concentration to an area of high solute concentration; the process continues until the solute concentrations are equal on both sides of the membrane

ossicle: a small bone; there are three in the middle ear: malleus, incus, and stapes

ossification: process in which minerals (calcium) are deposited in bone matrix

osteoarthritis: degenerative joint disease characterized by destruction of the articular cartilage and overgrowth of bone

osteoblast: bone-forming cell

osteoclast: bone resorption cell

osteocyte: mature bone cell

osteogenesis: bone formation

osteoid: pertaining to bone matrix tissue; "pre-bone"

osteomyelitis: infection of the bone

osteon: microscopic functional bone unit

osteophyte: a bony outgrowth or protuberance; spur

osteoporosis: a disorder in which bones lose density and become porous and fragile

otalgia: sensation of fullness or pain in the ear

otitis externa (i.e., external otitis): inflammation of the external auditory canal

otitis media: inflammation of the middle ear; may be acute lasting less than 6 weeks or chronic, causing irreversible

tissue damage and persistent tympanic membrane perforation

otoconia: debris of the inner ear comprised from small, crystalline stones of calcium carbonate

otorrhea: drainage from the ear

otosclerosis: a condition characterized by abnormal spongy bone formation around the stapes

oval window: a fenestra (aperture) between the vestibule of the inner ear and the middle ear, occupied by the base of the stapes

ovaries: almond-shaped reproductive organs that produce eggs at ovulation and play a major role in hormone production

overflow incontinence: involuntary urine loss associated with overdistention of the bladder due to mechanical or anatomic bladder outlet obstruction

oxyhemoglobin: combined form of oxygen and hemoglobin; found in arterial blood

oxytocin: hormone secreted by the posterior pituitary; causes myometrial contraction at term and milk release during lactation

P

P wave: the part of an electrocardiogram (ECG) that reflects conduction of an electrical impulse through the atrium; atrial depolarization (contraction)

pain threshold: the point at which a stimulus is perceived as painful

pain tolerance: the maximum intensity or duration of pain that a person is able to endure

pain: an unpleasant sensory and emotional experience resulting from actual or potential tissue damage

palliation: relief of symptoms associated with cancer

palliative care: comprehensive care for patients whose disease is not responsive to cure; care also extends to patients' families

palliative sedation: use of pharmacologic agents, at the request of the terminally ill patient, to induce sedation when symptoms have not responded to other management measures; the purpose is not to hasten the patient's death but to relieve intractable symptoms

pancreaticojejunostomy: joining of the pancreatic duct to the jejunum by side-to-side anastomosis; allows drainage of the pancreatic secretions into the jejunum

pancreatitis: inflammation of the pancreas; may be acute or chronic

pancytopenia: abnormal decrease in white blood cells, red blood cells, and platelets

pannus: proliferation of newly formed synovial tissue infiltrated with inflammatory cells

papilledema: swelling of the optic disc

paralysis: absence of muscle movement suggesting nerve damage

paraplegia: paralysis of the lower extremities with dysfunction of the bowel and bladder from a lesion in the thoracic, lumbar, or sacral regions of the spinal cord

parasympathetic nervous system: division of the autonomic nervous system active primarily during non-stressful conditions, controlling mostly visceral functions

parenteral nutrition (PN): method of supplying nutrients to the body by an intravenous route

paresthesia: abnormal touch sensation (e.g., burning, tingling, numbness)

parotitis: inflammation of the parotid gland

paroxysmal: an arrhythmia that has a sudden onset and/or termination and is usually of short duration

patient-controlled analgesia (PCA): self-administration of analgesic agents by a patient instructed about the procedure

pelvic inflammatory disease (PID): infection of uterus and fallopian tubes, usually from a sexually transmitted disease

penis: male organ for copulation and urination; consists of glans penis, body, and root

penumbra: area of ischemic brain tissue surrounding the core infarct that is potentially viable (and therefore an important concept for treatment options for patients with an evolving ischemic stroke)

pepsin: a gastric enzyme that is important in protein digestion

percutaneous coronary intervention (PCI): an invasive procedure in which a catheter is placed in a coronary artery, and one of several methods is employed to remove or reduce a blockage within the artery

percutaneous endoscopic gastrostomy (PEG): an endoscopic procedure for inserting a feeding tube into the stomach in order to provide long-term nutritional support

percutaneous thrombectomy: endovascular technique to remove thrombus

percutaneous transluminal coronary angioplasty (PTCA): a type of percutaneous coronary intervention in which a balloon is inflated within a coronary artery to break an atheroma and open the vessel lumen, improving coronary artery blood flow

performance status: patient activity level; ability to perform activities of daily living (ADLs), work, ambulate; multiple tools exist to measure performance status

pericardiocentesis: procedure that involves aspiration of fluid from the pericardial sac

pericardiotomy: surgically created opening of the pericardium

perimenopause: the period immediately prior to menopause and the first year after menopause

perioperative phase: period of time that constitutes the surgical experience; includes the preoperative, intraoperative, and postoperative phases of nursing care

periosteum: fibrous connective tissue covering bone

peripheral arterial disease (PAD): process of blood flow reduced to tissue

peripherally inserted central catheter (PICC): a device used for intermediate-term intravenous therapy

peristalsis: wavelike movement that occurs involuntarily in the alimentary canal and assists the passage of food through the bowel

peritoneal dialysis: procedure that uses the lining of the patient's peritoneal cavity as the semipermeable membrane for exchange of fluid and solutes

peritoneum: thin membrane that lines the inside of the wall of the abdomen and covers all the abdominal organs

peritonitis: inflammation of the lining of the abdominal cavity, usually as a result of a bacterial infection of an area in the gastrointestinal tract with leakage of contents into the abdominal cavity

personal protective equipment (PPE): equipment beyond standard precautions; may include level A, B, C, and D equipment

pessary: a plastic, silicone, rubber or latex device that is inserted into the vagina

petechiae: pinpoint, nonblanchable red spots that appear on the skin as a result of blood leakage into the skin

phagocytic cells: cells that engulf, ingest, and destroy foreign bodies or toxins

phagocytic immune response: the immune system's first line of defense, involving white blood cells that have the ability to ingest foreign particles

phagocytosis: process of ingestion and digestion of bacteria by cells

phantom limb pain: pain perceived as being in the amputated limb

pharyngitis: inflammation of the throat; usually viral or bacterial in origin

phase I PACU: area designated for care of surgical patients immediately after surgery and for patients whose condition warrants close monitoring

phase II PACU: area designated for care of surgical patients who have been transferred from a phase I PACU because their condition no longer requires the close monitoring provided in a phase I PACU

phase III PACU: setting in which the patient is cared for in the immediate postoperative period and then prepared for discharge from the facility

pheochromocytoma: chromaffin cell tumor, usually benign, located in the adrenal medulla; characterized by secretion of catecholamines, resulting in hypertension, severe headache, profuse sweating, visual blurring, anxiety, and nausea

phimosis: condition in which the foreskin is constricted so that it cannot be retracted over the glans; can occur congenitally or from inflammation and edema

photophobia: ocular pain on exposure to light

physical fitness: the condition of being physically healthy as a result of proper exercise and nutrition

pinna: the outer part of the external ear, which collects and directs sound waves into the external auditory canal; the auricle

placebo effect: analgesia that results from the expectation that a substance will work, not from the actual substance itself

plasma: liquid portion of blood

plasmapheresis: removal of whole blood from the body, separation of its cellular elements by centrifugation, and reinfusion of them suspended in saline or some other plasma substitute, thereby depleting the body's own plasma without depleting its cells

plasminogen: protein that is converted to plasmin to dissolve thrombi and clots

platelet: thrombocyte; a cellular component of blood involved in blood coagulation

pleural effusion: abnormal accumulation of fluid in the pleural space

pleural space: the area between the parietal and visceral pleurae; a potential space

pneumothorax: partial or complete collapse of the lung due to positive pressure in the pleural space

podagra: gout, especially of the great toe

polycystic ovarian syndrome (PCOS): most common endocrine disorder affecting women of reproductive age that may also cause overproduction of estrogen and testosterone resulting in abnormal thickening of the uterine lining, very heavy and/or irregular periods, as well as acne and facial hair

polycythemia: increase in the red blood cell concentration in the blood; in chronic obstructive pulmonary disease (COPD), the body attempts to improve oxygen-carrying capacity by producing increasing amounts of red blood cells

polymenorrhea: frequent menstruation occurring 21 days or less

polymerase chain reaction (PCR): a sensitive laboratory technique that can detect and quantify HIV in a person's blood or lymph nodes

polyuria: total urine output greater than 3 liters in 24 hours

portal hypertension: elevated pressure in the portal circulation resulting from obstruction of venous flow into and through the liver

position (postural) sense: awareness of position of parts of the body without looking at them; also referred to as *proprioception*

positive end-expiratory pressure (PEEP): positive pressure maintained by the ventilator at the end of exhalation (instead of a normal zero pressure) to increase functional residual capacity and open collapsed alveoli; improves oxygenation with lower FiO_2

postanesthesia care unit (PACU): area where postoperative patients are monitored as they recover from anesthesia; formerly referred to as the *recovery room* or *postanesthesia recovery room*

posterior chamber: space between the iris and vitreous

postoperative phase: period of time that begins with the admission of the patient to the PACU and ends after a follow-up evaluation in the clinical setting or home

postural (orthostatic) hypotension: a decrease in systolic blood pressure (SBP) of at least 20 mm Hg or diastolic blood pressure (DBP) of at least 10 mm Hg within 3 minutes of sitting or standing, associated with dizziness, lightheadedness, or syncope

postural drainage: positioning the patient to allow drainage from all the lobes of the lungs and airways

PR interval: the part of an electrocardiogram (ECG) that reflects conduction of an electrical impulse from the sinoatrial (SA) node through the atrioventricular (AV) node

preadmission testing (PAT): diagnostic testing performed before admission to the hospital

prediabetes: a condition of impaired carbohydrate metabolism that increases the risk of developing diabetes

prehypertension: blood pressure 120 to 129/80 to 89 mm Hg

preload: degree of stretch of the cardiac muscle fibers at the end of diastole

premenstrual dysphoric disorder (PMDD): a more severe form of PMS that occurs in late luteal phase and recurs cyclically

premenstrual syndrome (PMS): a constellation of symptoms associated with fluctuation of hormones during the luteal phase of the menstrual cycle

preoperative phase: period of time from when the decision for surgical intervention is made to when the patient is transferred to the operating room table

presbycusis: progressive hearing loss associated with aging

presbyopia: describes the condition in which the eye exhibits a progressively diminished ability to focus on near objects with age

pressure support ventilation (PSV): mode of mechanical ventilation in which preset positive pressure is delivered with spontaneous breaths to decrease work of breathing

priapism: an uncontrolled, persistent erection of the penis from either neural or vascular causes, including medications, sickle cell thrombosis, leukemic cell infiltration, spinal cord tumors, and tumor invasion of the penis or its vessels

primary amenorrhea: the absence of menstruation by age 16 or absence of secondary sex characteristics and menarche by age 14

primary headache: a headache for which no specific organic cause can be found

primary hypertension: also called essential hypertension; denotes high blood pressure from an unidentified cause

primary infection: 4- to 7-week period of rapid viral replication immediately following infection; also known as acute HIV infection

progesterone: hormone produced by the corpus luteum

prolapse (of a valve): stretching of an atrioventricular heart valve leaflet into the atrium during systole

prolapse: an organ that slips or falls out of place

prophylactic mastectomy: removal of the breast to reduce the risk of breast cancer in women considered to be at high risk for development of the disease

proportional assist ventilation (PAV): mode of mechanical ventilation that provides partial ventilatory support in proportion to the patient's inspiratory efforts; decreases the work of breathing

proptosis: downward displacement of the eyeball resulting from an inflammatory condition of the orbit or a mass within the orbital cavity

prostaglandins: a hormone-like substance that causes rhythmic contraction and relaxation of smooth muscle

prostaglandins: chemical substances that increase the sensitivity of pain receptors by enhancing the pain-provoking effect of bradykinin

prostate gland: gland that lies just below the neck of the bladder, surrounds the urethra, and is traversed by the ejaculatory duct, a continuation of the vas deferens; produces a secretion that is chemically and physiologically suitable to the needs of the spermatozoa in their passage from the testes

prostate-specific antigen (PSA): substance that is produced by the prostate gland and measured in a blood specimen; PSA levels are increased with prostate cancer; the PSA test is used in combination with digital rectal examination to detect prostate cancer

prostatitis: inflammation of the prostate gland

protease inhibitor: medication that inhibits the function of protease, an enzyme needed for HIV replication

proteinuria: protein in the urine

proton pump inhibitors: pharmacologic agents that block acid secretion by irreversibly binding to and inhibiting the hydrogen–potassium adenosine triphosphatase pump system at the secretory surface of gastric parietal cells; most potent inhibitors of gastric acid secretion

provirus: viral genetic material in the form of DNA that has been integrated into the host genome; when it is dormant in human cells, HIV is in a proviral form

ptosis: drooping eyelid

pulmonary edema: increase in the amount of extravascular fluid in the lung

pulmonary embolism: obstruction of the pulmonary vasculature with an embolus; embolus may be due to blood clot, air bubbles, or fat droplets

pulmonary perfusion: blood flow through the pulmonary vasculature

pulmonary vascular resistance: resistance created by the vasculature of the lungs to the ejection of blood from the right ventricle

pulmonic valve: semilunar valve located between the right ventricle and the pulmonary artery

pulseless electrical activity (PEA): condition in which electrical activity is present but there is not an adequate pulse or blood pressure because of ineffective cardiac contraction or circulating blood volume

pulsus paradoxus: systolic blood pressure of more than 10 mm Hg higher during exhalation than during inspiration; difference is normally less than 10 mm Hg

purulent: consisting of, containing, or discharging pus

pyelonephritis: inflammation of the renal pelvis

pyloroplasty: surgical procedure to increase the opening of the pyloric orifice

pylorus: opening between the stomach and the duodenum

pyrosis: heartburn

pyuria: white blood cells in the urine

Q

QA/QI: quality assurance/quality improvement; a system of continuous monitoring and evaluation of products or services to order to maintain and/or improve quality

QRS complex: the part of an electrocardiogram (ECG) that reflects conduction of an electrical impulse through the ventricles; ventricular depolarization (contraction)

QT interval: the part of an electrocardiogram (ECG) that reflects the time from ventricular depolarization through repolarization (resting state)

R

radiation therapy: use of ionizing radiation to interrupt the growth of malignant cells

radicular pain: pain that radiates along the nerve, caused from irritation or pressure of the nerve root

radiculopathy: disease of a nerve root

radioimmunoassay: radioisotope-labeled antigen measurement of hormone or other substance

radioisotopes: unstable atoms that emit small amounts of energy in the form of gamma rays; used in cardiac nuclear medicine studies

rebound hypertension: pressure that is controlled with therapy and that becomes abnormally high with the discontinuation (usually abrupt) of therapy

receptive aphasia: difficulty understanding spoken or written language; often associated with damage to the temporal lobe area (Wernicke's aphasia)

rectocele: weakness of the posterior vaginal wall that allows the rectal cavity to protrude into the submucosa of the vagina

red blood cell (RBC): also *erythrocyte;* a cellular component of blood involved in the transport of oxygen and carbon dioxide

red reflex: the reddish-orange reflection from the eye's retina that is observed using an ophthalmoscope under dimly lit or dark conditions

referred pain: pain perceived as coming from an area different from that in which the pathology is occurring

reflex incontinence: involuntary loss of urine due to hyperreflexia or involuntary urethral relaxation in the absence of normal sensations; usually associated with micturition (voiding)

reflex: an automatic response to stimuli

regurgitation: backward flow of blood through a heart valve

reinforcement: the process of strengthening a given response or behavior to increase the likelihood that the behavior will continue

remodeling: process that ensures bone maintenance through simultaneous bone resorption and formation

renal clearance: volume of plasma that the kidneys can clear of a specific solute (e.g., creatinine); expressed in milliliters per minute

renal glycosuria: recurring or persistent excretion of glucose in the urine

renal replacement therapy: term used to encompass life-supporting treatments for renal failure; includes hemodialysis, peritoneal dialysis, hemofiltration, and renal transplantation

repolarization: return of the cell to resting state, caused by reentry of potassium into the cell while sodium exits the cell

residual urine: urine that remains in the bladder after voiding

resorption: removal/destruction of tissue, such as bone

respiration: gas exchange between atmospheric air and the blood, and between the blood and cells of the body

respiratory weaning: process of gradual, systematic withdrawal or removal of ventilator, breathing tube, and oxygen

rest pain: a persistent pain in the foot at rest that can worsen at night and indicates significant arterial insufficiency

restricted zone: area in the operating room where scrub attire and surgical masks are required; includes operating room and sterile core areas

restrictive lung disease: disease of the lung that causes a decrease in lung volumes

resuscitation: triage category signifying life-threatening injuries or illnesses requiring immediate intervention

rete ridges: undulations and furrows that appear at the dermis–epidermis junction and are responsible for cementing together the two layers

reticulocytes: slightly immature red blood cells (RBCs), usually only 1% of total circulating RBCs

reticuloendothelial system (RES): complex system of cells throughout body capable of phagocytosis

retinopathy: a long-term complication of diabetes in which the microvascular system of the eye is damaged

retrovirus: a virus that carries genetic material in RNA instead of DNA and contains reverse transcriptase

reverse transcriptase: enzyme that transforms single-stranded RNA into a double-stranded DNA

rhabdomyolysis: accumulation of byproducts of skeletal muscle destruction in renal tubule

rhinitis: inflammation of the mucous membranes of the nose; may be infectious, allergic, or inflammatory in origin

rhinorrhea: drainage of a large amount of fluid from the nose

rhinosinusitis: inflammation of the sinuses; may be acute or chronic; may be viral, bacterial, or fungal in origin

RICE: acronym for *R*est, *I*ce, *C*ompression, *E*levation

rigidity: increase in muscle tone at rest characterized by increased resistance to passive stretch

rods: retinal photoreceptor cells essential for bright and dim light

Romberg test: test for cerebellar dysfunction requiring the patient to stand with feet together, eyes closed, and arms extended; inability to maintain the position, with either significant stagger or sway, is a positive test

rotator cuff: shoulder muscles (supraspinatus, subscapularis, infraspinatus, and teres minor) and their tendons

round window: a fenestra between the middle ear and the inner ear at the base of the cochlea, occupied by the round window membrane

rubor: reddish blue skin discoloration occurring in skin in dependent position

rule of nines: method for calculating body surface area burned by dividing the body into multiples of nine

S

sciatica: inflammation of the sciatic nerve, resulting in pain and tenderness along the nerve through the thigh and leg

sclerotherapy: the injection of substances into or around esophagogastric varices to cause constriction, thickening, and hardening of the vessel and thus to stop bleeding

scoliosis: lateral curving of the spine

scotomas: blind or partially blind areas in the visual field

scrub role: registered nurse, licensed practical nurse, or surgical technologist who scrubs and dons sterile surgical attire, prepares instruments and supplies, and hands instruments to the surgeon during the procedure

sebaceous glands: glands that exist within the epidermis and secrete sebum to keep the skin soft and pliable

sebum: fatty secretion of the sebaceous glands

secondary amenorrhea: The absence of menses for 6 or more months after a regular cycle of menstruation has been established

secondary conditions or disorders: preventable physical, mental, or social disorders resulting directly or indirectly from an initial disabling condition

secondary headache: headache identified as a symptom of another organic disorder (e.g., brain tumor, hypertension)

secondary hypertension: high blood pressure from an identified cause, such as renal disease

second-intention healing: method of healing in which wound edges are not surgically approximated and integumentary continuity is restored by the process known as granulation

secretin: hormone responsible for stimulating secretion of pancreatic juice; also used as an aid in diagnosing pancreatic exocrine disease and in obtaining desquamated pancreatic cells for cytologic examination

seizures: paroxysmal transient disturbance of the brain resulting from a discharge of abnormal electrical activity

self-monitoring of blood glucose (SMBG): a method of capillary blood glucose testing in which a drop of blood is applied to a test strip that is read by a meter

self-responsibility: personal accountability for one's actions or behavior

semicircular canals: the superior, posterior, and lateral bony tubes that form part of the inner ear; contain the receptor organs for balance

semirestricted zone: area in the operating room where scrub attire is required; may include areas where surgical instruments are processed

sensitization: a heightened response seen after exposure to a noxious stimulus; response to the same stimulus is to feel more pain

sensorineural hearing loss: loss of hearing related to damage of the end organ for hearing or cranial nerve VIII, or both

sentinel lymph node: first lymph node(s) in the lymphatic basin that receives drainage from the primary tumor in the breast; identified by a radioisotope and/or blue dye

septic shock: distributive shock state resulting from combination of infectious trigger and impaired host response, resulting in decreased tissue perfusion

sequestrum: dead bone in abscess cavity

serosa: thin membrane that forms the outer layer of the stomach

serum: portion of blood remaining after coagulation occurs

shock: physiologic state in which there is inadequate tissue perfusion

sialadenitis: inflammation of the salivary glands

sinoatrial (SA) node: primary pacemaker of the heart, located in the right atrium

sinus rhythm: electrical activity of the heart initiated by the sinoatrial (SA) node

sling: bandage used to support an arm

small intestine: longest portion of the GI tract, consisting of three parts—duodenum, jejunum, and ileum—through which food mixed with all secretions and enzymes passes as it continues to be digested and begins to be absorbed into the bloodstream

spacer device: a device used to attach to a metered-dose inhaler (MDI) that may improve patients' ability to use their MDI correctly

spastic: having greater than normal muscle tone

spasticity: muscular hypertonicity with increased resistance to stretch often associated with weakness, increased deep tendon reflexes, and diminished superficial reflexes

spasticity: sustained increase in tension of a muscle when it is passively lengthened or stretched

spermatogenesis: production of sperm in the testes

spinal cord compression: tumor extension into the epidural space

spinal cord injury (SCI): an injury to the spinal cord, vertebral column, supporting soft tissue, or intervertebral disks caused by trauma

spirituality: personal belief systems that focus on a search for meaning and purpose in life, intangible elements that impart meaning and vitality to life, and a connectedness to a higher or transcendent dimension

spirometry: pulmonary function tests that measure specific lung volumes (e.g., FEV_1, forced expired volume in 1 second), capacities (e.g., FVC, forced vital capacity), and flow rates; may be measured before and after bronchodilator administration

splint: device designed specifically to support and immobilize a body part in a desired position

spondylosis: ankylosis or stiffening of the cervical or lumbar vertebrae

sprain: an injury to ligaments and other soft tissues at a joint

ST segment: the part of an electrocardiogram (ECG) from the end of the QRS complex to the beginning of the T wave

staging: process of determining the size and spread, or metastasis, of a tumor

stapes: the third (most medial) ossicle of the middle ear; it articulates with the incus, and its footplate fits into the oval window; the stirrup

status epilepticus: episode in which the patient experiences multiple seizure bursts with no recovery time in between

steatorrhea: frothy, foul-smelling stools with a high fat content; results from impaired digestion of proteins and fats due to a lack of pancreatic juice in the intestine

stem cell: primitive cell, capable of self-replication and differentiation into myeloid or lymphoid stem cell

stenosis: narrowing or tightening of an opening or passage in the body

stent: a woven mesh that provides structural support to a coronary vessel, preventing its closure

stent-graft: tube composed of fabric supported by a metal mesh

stereotactic biopsy: computer-guided method of core needle biopsy that is useful when masses in the breast cannot be felt but can be visualized using mammography

stoma: artificially created opening between a body cavity (e.g., intestine) and the body surface

stomach: distensible pouch into which the food bolus passes to be digested by gastric enzymes

stomatitis: inflammation of the oral mucosa

strain: a musculotendinous injury

stress incontinence: involuntary loss of urine through an intact urethra as a result of a sudden increase in intra-abdominal pressure

stress management: behaviors and techniques used to strengthen a person's resources against stress

stress test: a test used to evaluate the functioning of the cardiovascular system during a period of increased oxygen demand simulated by walking on a treadmill or medications that mimic the body's physiologic response to exercise

striae: bandlike streaks on the skin, distinguished by color, texture, depression, or elevation from the tissue in which they are found; usually purplish or white

stroke volume (SV): amount of blood ejected from the ventricle per heartbeat

stroke: a syndrome characterized by death of brain cells that occurs when there is a disruption of cerebral blood flow

subarachnoid screw or bolt: device placed into the subarachnoid space to measure intracranial pressure

subluxation: partial separation or dislocation of joint surfaces

subtotal or supracervical hysterectomy: removal of the uterus, fallopian tubes, and ovaries with retention of the cervix

sudden cardiac death: immediate cessation of effective heart activity

suppressor T cells: lymphocytes that decrease B-cell activity to a level at which the immune system is compatible with life

suprapubic catheter: a urinary catheter that is inserted through a suprapubic incision into the bladder

surgical asepsis: absence of microorganisms in the surgical environment to reduce the risk for infection

surgical biopsy: procedure in which an entire mass or a portion of it is surgically removed for examination under a microscope by a pathologist

suspensions: liquid preparations in which powder is suspended, requiring shaking before use

sympathetic nervous system: division of the autonomic nervous system with predominantly excitatory responses; the "fight-or-flight" system

sympathetic ophthalmia: an inflammatory condition created in the fellow eye by the affected eye (without useful vision); the condition may become chronic and result in blindness (of the fellow eye)

synchronized intermittent mandatory ventilation (SIMV): mode of mechanical ventilation in which the ventilator allows the patient to breathe spontaneously while providing a preset number of breaths to ensure adequate ventilation; ventilated breaths are synchronized with spontaneous breathing

syndrome of inappropriate antidiuretic hormone (SIADH) secretion: excessive secretion of antidiuretic hormone (ADH) from the pituitary gland, despite low serum osmolality level, resulting in hyponatremia

synovial: pertaining to a complex joint bounded by joint capsule and containing synovial fluid

synovitis: inflammation of the synovial membrane

synovium: membrane in joint that secretes lubricating fluid

systemic inflammatory response syndrome (SIRS): overwhelming inflammatory response in the absence of known infection causing decreased tissue perfusion

systemic vascular resistance: resistance caused by the peripheral circulation to the ejection of blood from the left ventricle

systole: period during the cardiac cycle when the ventricles contract, resulting in ejection of blood from the right and left ventricles into the pulmonary artery and aorta

systolic heart failure: inability of the heart to pump sufficiently because of an alteration in the ability of the heart to contract; current term used to describe a type of heart failure

T

T wave: the part of an electrocardiogram (ECG) that reflects repolarization of the ventricles

targeted therapies: cancer treatments that seek to minimize the negative effects on healthy tissues by disrupting specific cancer cell functions, such as malignant transformation, communication pathways, processes for growth and metastasis, and genetic coding

T cells: cells that are important for producing a cellular immune response

teaching: the imparting of knowledge

telangiectases: spider-like red marks on the skin caused by distention of the superficial blood vessels that blanch on pressure

telemetry: ambulatory electrocardiographic monitoring using a battery-operated transmitting device worn by the patient

temporal bone: a bone on both sides of the skull at its base; composed of the squamous, mastoid, and petrous portions

temporomandibular disorders: a group of conditions that cause pain or dysfunction of the temporomandibular joint (TMJ) and surrounding structures

tendinitis: inflammation of a tendon

tendon transfer: a surgical procedure in which a tendon is incised at its insertion and placed at a site distant from the original insertion site in order to restore or correct the function of a muscle

tendon: cord of fibrous tissue connecting muscle to bone

tenesmus: ineffective and sometimes painful straining to eliminate either feces or urine resulting in abscess formation

tension pneumothorax: pneumothorax characterized by increasing positive pressure in the pleural space with each breath; this is an emergency situation and the positive pressure needs to be decompressed or released immediately

terminal illness: progressive, irreversible illness that despite cure-focused medical treatment will result in the patient's death

testes: the ovoid sex glands encased in the scrotum; the testes produce sperm

testicular cancer: the most common cancer in men 15 to 35 years of age and the second most common malignancy in those 35 to 39 years of age; its cause is unknown

testosterone: male sex hormone secreted by the testes; induces and preserves the male sex characteristics

tetraplegia (formerly quadriplegia): paralysis of both arms and legs, with dysfunction of bowel and bladder from a lesion of the cervical segments of the spinal cord

therapeutic regimen: a routine that promotes health and healing

third-intention healing: method of healing in which surgical approximation of wound edges is delayed and integumentary continuity is restored by apposing areas of granulation

thoracentesis: insertion of a needle into the pleural space to remove fluid that has accumulated and decrease pressure on the lung tissue; may also be used diagnostically to identify potential causes of a pleural effusion

thoracotomy: surgical opening into the chest cavity

thrombin: enzyme necessary to convert fibrinogen into fibrin clot

thrombocyte: *see* platelet

thrombocytopenia: decrease in the number of platelets

thrombocytosis: higher than normal platelet count

thrombolysis: breakdown of thrombus by pharmacologic means

thrombolytic: an agent or process that breaks down blood clots

thyroid storm: severe life-threatening form of hyperthyroidism precipitated by stress; usually of abrupt onset; characterized by high fever, extreme tachycardia, and altered mental state

thyroidectomy: surgical removal of all or part of the thyroid gland

thyroiditis: inflammation of the thyroid gland; may lead to chronic hypothyroidism or may resolve spontaneously

thyroid-stimulating hormone (TSH): released from the pituitary gland; causes stimulation of the thyroid gland, resulting in release of T_3 and T_4

thyrotoxicosis: a hypermetabolic response caused by excessive endogenous (T_3 and/or T_4 hormone) or exogenous thyroid hormone

thyroxine (T_4): thyroid hormone; active iodine compound formed and stored in the thyroid; deiodinated in peripheral tissues to form triiodothyronine (T_3); maintains body metabolism in a steady state

tinea: a superficial fungal infection on the skin or scalp

tinnitus: subjective perception of sound with internal origin; unwanted noises in the head or ear

tolerance: occurs when a person who has been taking opioids becomes less sensitive to their analgesic properties (and usually side effects); characterized by the need for increasing doses to maintain the same level of pain relief

tone (tonus): normal tension (resistance to stretch) in resting muscle

tonicity: the measurement of the osmotic pressure of a solution; another term for *osmolality*

tophi: accumulation of crystalline deposits in articular surfaces, bones, soft tissue, and cartilage

total artificial heart: mechanical device used to aid a failing heart, assists both the right and left ventricles

total joint arthroplasty or replacement: the replacement of both articular surfaces within a joint with metal or synthetic materials

total mastectomy: removal of the breast tissue and nipple–areola complex

total nutrient admixture (TNA): an admixture of lipid emulsions, proteins, carbohydrates, electrolytes, vitamins, trace minerals, and water

trabeculae: lattice-like bone structure; cancellous bone

tracheostomy tube: indwelling tube inserted directly into the trachea to assist with ventilation

tracheotomy: surgical opening into the trachea

trachoma: a bilateral chronic follicular conjunctivitis of childhood that leads to blindness during adulthood, if left untreated

traction: application of a pulling force to a part of the body

transbronchial: through the bronchial wall, as in a transbronchial lung biopsy

transection: severing of the spinal cord itself; transection can be complete (all the way through the cord) or incomplete (partially through)

transgender: a person who identifies his or her gender with that of the opposite sex

transient ischemic attack (TIA): a brief episode of neurological dysfunction caused by focal brain or retinal ischemia with clinical symptoms typically lasting less than 1 hour and without evidence of acute infarction

transurethral resection of the prostate (TUR or TURP): resection of the prostate through endoscopy; the surgical and optical instrument is introduced directly through the urethra to the prostate, and the gland is then removed in small chips with an electrical cutting loop

transverse rectus abdominis myocutaneous (TRAM) flap: method of breast reconstruction in which a flap of skin, fat, and muscle from the lower abdomen, with its attached blood supply, is rotated to the mastectomy site

trapeze: overhead assistive device to promote patient mobility in bed

triage: process of assessing patients to determine management priorities

tricuspid valve: atrioventricular valve located between the right atrium and right ventricle

triggered: in reference to pacemakers, term used to describe the release of an impulse in response to some stimulus

triiodothyronine (T_3): thyroid hormone; formed and stored in the thyroid; released in smaller quantities, biologically more active and with faster onset of action than thyroxine (T_4); widespread effect on cellular metabolism, influences every major organ system

troponin: myocardial protein; measurement is used to assess heart muscle injury

trypsin: pancreatic enzyme; aids in digestion of proteins

tubular reabsorption: movement of a substance from the kidney tubule into the blood in the peritubular capillaries or vasa recta

tubular secretion: movement of a substance from the blood in the peritubular capillaries or vasa recta into the kidney tubule

Turner's syndrome: a female genetic disorder due to a missing or incomplete X chromosome

tympanic membrane: the membrane that separates the middle ear from the external auditory canal; also referred to as the *eardrum*

tympanoplasty: surgical repair of the tympanic membrane

type 1 diabetes: a metabolic disorder characterized by an absence of insulin production and secretion from autoimmune destruction of the beta cells of the islets of Langerhans in the pancreas; formerly called *insulin-dependent* or *juvenile* diabetes

type 2 diabetes: a metabolic disorder characterized by the relative deficiency of insulin production and a decreased insulin action and increased insulin resistance; formerly called *non–insulin-dependent* or *adult-onset* diabetes

U

U wave: the part of an electrocardiogram (ECG) that may reflect Purkinje fiber repolarization; usually, it is not seen unless a patient's serum potassium level is low

ulcer: an area of tissue erosion or an open sore

ultrafiltration: process whereby water is removed from the blood by means of a pressure gradient between the patient's blood and the dialysate

ultrasonography: imaging method using high-frequency sound waves to diagnose whether masses are solid or fluid-filled

unrestricted zone: area in the operating room that interfaces with other departments; includes patient reception area and holding area

urea nitrogen: nitrogenous end product of protein metabolism

uremia: the clinical syndrome associated with an excess of urea and other nitrogenous wastes in the blood (fluid and electrolyte, hormonal, and metabolic imbalances)

ureterosigmoidostomy: transplantation of the ureters into the sigmoid colon, allowing urine to flow through the colon and out the rectum

ureterovesical or vesicoureteral reflux: backward flow of urine from the bladder into one or both ureters

urethritis: inflammation of the urethra

urethrovesical reflux: backward flow of urine from the urethra into the bladder

urge incontinence: involuntary loss of urine associated with urinary urgency due to hypersensory disorders of the bladder, motor instability, or both

urgent: triage category signifying serious illness or injury that is not immediately life threatening

urinary casts: proteins secreted by damaged kidney tubules

urinary incontinence: involuntary or uncontrolled loss of urine from the bladder sufficient to cause a social or hygienic problem

urosepsis: sepsis resulting from infected urine, most often a urinary tract infection (UTI)

urticaria: hives

uterine prolapse: relaxation of pelvic tone that allows the cervix and uterus to descend into the lower vagina

uvulopalatopharyngoplasty (UPPP): surgical removal of the uvula, tonsils, and part of the soft palate to create a larger posterior oropharynx as treatment for obstructive sleep apnea

V

vagotomy syndrome: dumping syndrome; gastrointestinal symptoms, such as diarrhea and abdominal cramping, resulting from rapid gastric emptying

Valsalva maneuver: forcible exhalation against a closed glottis followed by a rise in intrathoracic pressure and subsequent possible dramatic rise in arterial pressure; may occur during straining at stool

valve replacement: insertion of a prosthetic valve at the site of a malfunctioning heart valve to restore blood flow in one direction through the heart

valvuloplasty: repair of a stenosed or regurgitant cardiac valve by commissurotomy, annuloplasty, leaflet repair, or chordoplasty (or a combination of procedures)

variceal banding: procedure that involves the endoscopic placement of a rubber band-like device over esophageal varices to ligate the area and stop bleeding

varicocele: an abnormal dilation of the veins of the pampiniform venous plexus in the scrotum (the network of veins from the testis and the epididymis, which constitute part of the spermatic cord)

vasculitis: inflammation of a blood vessel or lymph vessel

vasoactive medications: medications that act on the vessels to either constrict or dilate, resulting in either increased or decreased blood pressure and/or heart rate

vasopressin: antidiuretic hormone (ADH) secreted by the posterior pituitary; causes retention of water and raises blood pressure by contraction of smooth muscle, particularly blood vessels

ventilation: movement of air in and out of airways

ventilation–perfusion ratio: the ratio between ventilation and perfusion in the lung; matching of ventilation to perfusion optimizes gas exchange

ventricular assist device: mechanical device used to aid a failing right or left ventricle

ventricular tachycardia (VT): a rapid rhythm that originates in the ventricles

ventriculostomy: a catheter placed in one of the lateral ventricles of the brain to measure intracranial pressure and allow for drainage of cerebrospinal fluid (CSF) or blood

vertigo: an illusion of movement in which the individual or the surroundings are sensed as moving, usually rotation

vesicant: substance that can cause tissue necrosis and damage, particularly when extravasated

vestibulocochlear nerve: cranial nerve VIII; contains the cochlear (acoustic) portion and the vestibular portion

vibration: a type of massage administered by quickly tapping the chest with the fingertips or alternating the fingers in a rhythmic manner, or by using a mechanical device to assist in mobilizing lung secretions

viral load test: measures the quantity of HIV RNA in the blood

viral set point: amount of virus present in the blood after the initial burst of viremia and the immune response that follows

vitiligo: a localized or widespread condition characterized by destruction of the melanocytes in circumscribed areas of the skin, resulting in white patches

vitreous humor: gelatinous material (transparent and colorless) that fills the eyeball behind the lens

volvulus: abnormal twisting of the intestines resulting in intestinal obstruction

vulvovaginal candidiasis: a vaginal infection caused by fungus or yeast

W

weapons of mass destruction (WMD): weapons used to cause widespread death and destruction

wellness: a condition of good physical and emotional health sustained by a healthy lifestyle

Western blot assay: a blood test that identifies antibodies to HIV and is used to confirm the results of an enzyme immunoassay (EIA or ELISA) test

wheezes: continuous musical sounds associated with airway narrowing or partial obstruction

white blood cell (WBC): also *leukocytes;* cellular components of blood involved in defense of the body; subtypes include neutrophils, eosinophils, basophils, monocytes, and lymphocytes

window period: time from infection with HIV until seroconversion detected on HIV antibody test

wound care specialist: a nurse specially educated in appropriate skin, wound, ostomy, and continence care; often referred to as an *enterostomal therapist* or a *wound-ostomy-continence nurse* (WOCN)

X

xenograft: heart valve replacement made of tissue from an animal heart valve (*synonym:* heterograft)

xerosis: overly dry skin

xerostomia: dry oral cavity resulting from decreased function of salivary glands

Z

Zollinger-Ellison tumor: hypersecretion of gastric acid that produces peptic ulcers as a result of a non–beta cell tumor of the pancreatic islets

Suggested Answers to Unit Case Studies

Basics of Adult Health Nursing

a. Important areas of health education include:
- Adherence to therapeutic regimen
- Willingness to learn
- Health literacy skills
- Learning needs
- Learner readiness

b. Variables that could effect medication compliance include:
- Sensory deficits, such as hearing and visualizing
- Financial constraints
- Inadequate support systems
- Life-time treatment with OTC medications
- Mobility impairments
- Inadequate cognitive, psychomotor, or language skills
- Fear of loss of control in decision-making

c. Teaching strategies for this patient include:
- Knowledge of side effects of prescribed medications
- Teaching strategies to accommodate decreased visual and hearing acuity
- Small amounts of material at one time, frequent repetition of information, use of reinforcement techniques
- Minimize distraction

UNIT TWO Concepts and Challenges to Patient Management

a. Psychosocial aspects of this diagnosis include:
- Body image
- Self-esteem
- Functional and cognitive abilities
- Plan for postoperative rehabilitation
- Prognosis

b. Potential postoperative complications may include:
- Infection
- Bleeding
- Impaired wound healing
- Altered pulmonary or renal function
- Development of a deep vein thrombosis
- Increased intracranial pressure
- Seizures

c. Special needs of the patient undergoing chemotherapy include:
- Monitoring for nausea, vomiting, fatigue, and depression
- Monitoring white blood cell, hemoglobin, hematocrit, and platelet counts
- Safe administration of chemotherapy
- Monitoring for signs of bone marrow suppression including bleeding, infection, and anemia
- Nutritional status
- Teaching of self-care

UNIT THREE Problems Related to Gas Exchange and Respiratory Function

a. Potential complications that may arise following a total laryngectomy include:
- Respiratory distress, hypoxia
- Hemorrhage
- Infection
- Wound breakdown
- Aspiration
- Tracheostomal stenosis anxiety and depression

b. Patient teaching areas of self-care include:
- Proper hand hygiene
- Adequate dietary intake
- Safe hygiene, prevention of water entering stoma during a shower
- Signs of infection, indications for notifying provider
- Avoidance of strenuous activities and fatigue
- Carry medical identification
- Performing oral care
- Importance of regular physical exams
- Tracheostomy suctioning if necessary
- Need for home care

c. Support groups for laryngectomy patients include:
- International Association of laryngectomies (IAL)
- I Can Cope (American Cancer Society)
- Local area support groups

UNIT FOUR Problems Related to Cardiovascular and Circulatory Function

a. Current and potential problems related to the patient's nonadherence to medication include:
- Obesity
- Nonadherence with medication regimen
- Smoking
- Congestive heart failure

b. Important areas of teaching to emphasize include:
- Lifestyle changes (smoking cessation, weight loss, regular physical activity)
- Emphasize concept of lifelong blood pressure control rather than cure
- Waist circumference of less than 40 inches
- DASH diet
- Limiting alcohol ingestion
- Compliance with medication regimen
- Follow-up appointments

c. Target organs/systems that may be affected by the patient's nonadherence include:
- Heart-Cardiac (MI)
- Kidneys-Renal (renal failure, elevated BUN, elevated creatinine)
- Brain-Cerebrovascular (TIA or Stroke)

UNIT FIVE Problems Related to Hematologic Function

a. The only curative treatment for CML is allogeneic stem cell transplantation.
- The efficacy of imatinib is first-line treatment
- Treatment related mortality of stem cell transplant limits use of transplant to patients with high risk or relapsed disease, or in those patients who did not respond to therapy with TKI.

b. The three phases of CML include:
- Chronic phase: There is usually adequate numbers of health cells to fight infection; the expected outcome is correction of the chromosomal abnormality.
- Acceleration phase: Numbers of abnormal cells are being produced at a faster rate.
- Blast crisis: The predominant cell type is immature; treatment may resemble induction therapy for acute leukemia, using the same medications as for AML or ALL.
- Most patients are diagnosed in the chronic phase.

c. Nursing considerations of the patient undergoing chemotherapy (Gleevec):
- Monitoring side effects of chemotherapy such as fluid retention
- Monitoring CBC
- Monitoring patient for infection; educating patient on signs of infections that would warrant notification of provider
- Educate patients that antacids and grapefruit juice may limit drug absorption

UNIT SIX Problems Related to Digestive, Gastrointestinal, and Metabolic Function

a. Patient selection criteria for bariatric surgery include:
- Table 23-5 Selection Criteria for Bariatric Surgery
- Failure of previous nonsurgical attempts at weight reduction
- Expectation that patient will adhere to postoperative care
- BMI greater than or equal to 35 with obesity-associated comorbidity.
- BMI greater than or equal to 40 with no comorbidities

b. Potential lifestyle changes include:
- Box 23-2 Dietary Guidelines for the Patient Who Has Had Bariatric Surgery
- Do not eat and drink at the same time.
- Eat slowly and include two protein snacks per day.
- Patients need extensive counseling before and after the surgery.
- All patients require lifelong monitoring of weight loss, comorbidities, metabolic and nutritional status, and dietary and activity behaviors because they are at risk for developing malnutrition and weight gain.

c. Complications that may be associated with bariatric surgery include:
- Bleeding, blood clots, bowel obstruction, incisional or ventral hernias, and infection
- Peritonitis, stomal obstruction, and stomal ulcers
- Atelectasis and pneumonia
- Nausea, dumping syndrome, diarrhea, and constipation
- Long-term complications are related to nutritional deficiency.

UNIT SEVEN Problems Related to Urinary Tract Function

a. Areas of teaching for this patient should include:
- Lifestyle changes
- Dietary restrictions
- Encouragement of self-management
- Patient and family teaching regarding the symptoms of worsening renal function; frequent, clear explanations and information
- Dialysis education
- Care of the vascular access; patients with fistulae or grafts are taught to check daily for a thrill over the graft (vibrating or buzzing sensation) and to notify healthcare provider or dialysis center if absent.

b. Treatment modalities for this patient population include:
- Pharmacologic therapies, which include calcium, phosphorous binders, antihypertensives, antiseizure agents, erythropoietin, and agents to treat metabolic acidosis
- Nutritional therapy and fluid restriction
- Potential blood transfusions

c. Nursing management would include:
- Prevention of infection due to invasive line and catheters
- Meticulous skin care
- Psychosocial care; teaching in brief 10- to 15-minute sessions
- Nutritional and fluid therapy; monitoring fluid and electrolyte balance
- Monitoring weight
- Teaching regarding dietary restrictions
- Monitoring for complications of chronic renal failure

UNIT EIGHT Problems Related to Endocrine Function

a. Questions to ask the patient regarding his fluctuating blood sugar levels include:
- What times do you take your blood sugar?
- Have you been sick lately?
- Have you started taking any new medications?
- Are you having any problems obtaining your blood sugar?
- Do you have all the supplies you need to take your blood sugar?
- Describe a typical meal.
- Tell me what you do for exercise.

b. Areas of teaching with regard to the foot wound for this patient should include:
- Inspect your feet daily; use a mirror to check the bottom of your feet.
- Wash your feet in warm, not hot, water and dry them well.

- Wear shoes and socks at all times; never walk barefoot.
- Put your feet up while sitting.
- Contact your healthcare provider if you have a cut, sore, blister, or bruise on your foot that does not heal after 1 day.
- Remember that because you have diabetes, it will take longer for you to heal.
- Because you have diabetes, you may experience decreased sensation in your lower legs and feet.
- Maintaining optimal glucose control will aid healing and help to prevent infection.
- Monitor your food intake by using a meal planning guide and by monitoring carbohydrate intake.

c. Aids to assist patient in keeping more accurate records of his blood sugar include:
- Keeping a blood sugar log
- Obtaining blood sugar levels at the same time each day
- Taking blood sugar prior to meals

UNIT NINE Problems Related to Reproductive Function

a. Risk factors associated with cervical cancer include:
- Lesbian women are at higher risk for cervical cancer due to misinformation, insufficient knowledge and screening.
- The human papillomavirus (HPV) has been implicated.
- Intercourse with an uncircumcised male, high parity, cigarette smoking, multiple sexual partners
- See also Box 33-11 Risk Factors for Cervical Cancer.

b. Clinical manifestations that the patient may have had prior to the diagnosis include:
- Irregular vaginal bleeding and pelvic pain and pressure
- Malodorous vaginal discharge, which occurs as a result of tumor necrosis
- Dyspareunia and rectal pressure is also common as the tumor increases in size and extent invading surrounding tissue causing other symptoms to develop.

c. The purpose of a colposcopy is:
- To magnify the cervix which has had acetic acid solution applied to it to help differentiate the cervical cells. Biopsies are taken in areas of visible abnormal vascular patterns.
- Approximately 50% of newly diagnosed women with cervical cancer will present with stage I disease.

d. Medical management of cervical cancer includes:
- Cervical conization or cone biopsy
- Cold knife conization and loop electrosurgical excision procedure (LEEP) are other procedures that may be performed to treat high- or low-grade squamous intraepithelial lesions, which are precursors to cervical cancer.
- Cervical conization alone is adequate for those women who want to preserve childbearing ability.
- Patients diagnosed with a stage IB or IIA undergo a radical hysterectomy: removal of the uterus and upper one-third of the vagina, including the cervix, but sparing the ovaries. Pelvic radiation and chemotherapy may follow but depends on the size and extent of the tumor.

- Stage IB carries an increased risk of recurrence.
- Neoadjuvant chemotherapy has demonstrated success in decreasing tumor size and increasing survival when used prior to a radical hysterectomy.

UNIT TEN Problems Related to Immunologic Function

a. The nurse could expect that the following medications may be ordered for this patient:
- Nonsteroidal anti-inflammatory drugs (indomethacin or ibuprofen) are considered agents of first choice.
- Indomethacin or ibuprofen with colchicines as an alternative or in combination may be considered.
- Low-dose colchicine has been used for prophylaxis after resolution of attacks.
- Allopurinol (Zyloprim) is considered the drug of choice for preventing the precipitation of an attack and tophi formation and promoting the regression of existing tophi.
- Uricosuric agents, such as probenecid (Benemid), correct hyperuricemia and dissolve deposited urate.
- When reduction of the serum urate level is indicated, uricosuric agents are the medications of choice.
- Febuxostat (Uloric) has been approved for treatment of gout that does not respond to usual treatment. Newer urate-lowering agents, such as uricase, are currently under investigation and show promise for successful gout treatment.
- Corticosteroids are useful for short-term therapy of acute gout and may be used on patients who have no response to other therapy.

b. The two phases of medical management of gout include:
- Management of acute gouty inflammation
- Long-term management to prevent flare-ups and to control hyperuricemia

c. Nursing management of gout includes:
- Pain management is the primary concern during the acute phase of an attack. The joint should be rested and application of ice, not heat, may help with reducing discomfort.
- Patients should be taught to limit alcohol intake and to avoid fad starvation diets.
- The patient should drink plenty of fluids, at least 2,000 mL daily, to lessen renal involvement and the development of urinary stones.
- Dietary restriction of sodium, fat, and cholesterol can lead to a reduction in gout symptoms and decrease effects associated with coexisting metabolic syndrome.
- Review Table 39-3 Medications Used in Rheumatic Diseases and Table 39-4 Medications Used to Treat Gout

d. Nursing diagnoses for this patient may include:
- Acute and chronic pain related to inflammation and/or progression of joint deterioration
- Self-care deficits (specify) related to limitations secondary to progression of disease, pain, fatigue, contractures, and loss of motion
- Risk for injury related to adverse effects of medications and potential complications
- Insomnia related to pain, anxiety/stress, depression, and medications

UNIT ELEVEN Problems Related to Musculoskeletal Function

a. Evaluative data would include:
- A focus on history and physical examination, including general observation of the patient, back examination, and neurologic testing (reflexes, sensory impairment, muscle strength, straight-leg raising, and muscle atrophy).
- The patient may report pain radiating down the leg, which is known as radiculopathy or sciatica.
- The patient's gait, spinal mobility, reflexes, leg length, leg motor strength, and sensory perception may be affected.

b. Diagnostic procedures that could lead to a definitive diagnosis include:
- X-ray of the spine, CT, MRI, EMG
- See Box 41-1 Diagnostic Procedures for Low Back Pain.

c. Medical and nursing management of this patient includes:
- Management focuses on relief of pain and discomfort, activity modification, use of back-conserving techniques of body mechanics, improved self-esteem, and weight reduction.
- Most back pain is self-limited and resolves within 4 weeks with analgesics, rest, stress reduction, and relaxation.
- Pain-guided imagery, nonprescription analgesics, diaphragmatic breathing, and relaxation
- Mobility-position changes should be made slowly and carried out with assistance as required; avoid twisting and jarring movements; alternate lying, sitting, and walking activities frequently; avoid sitting, standing, or walking for long periods.
- As patient achieves comfort, activities are gradually resumed, and an exercise program is initiated (see Box 41-2, p. 1092).

UNIT TWELVE Problems Related to Neurologic Function

a. Emergency management of stroke includes:
- Acute stroke care can be divided into two phases: hyperacute phase (the first 24 hours of care) and phase 2 (acute care during the hospitalization).
- An algorithm is used in the hyperacute phase for the initial workup of a patient presenting with acute stroke symptoms (see Fig. 47-5, p. 1253).
- The diagnosis is made by history, neurologic exam, and neuro-imaging. An initial head CT will determine whether the patient is experiencing a hemorrhagic stroke.
- The National Institutes of Health Stroke Scale (NIHSS) has become an accepted assessment tool to quantify stroke severity and to assess patient outcome after stroke treatment (see Table 47-4, p. 1253)
- Review Table 47-1 Comparison of Major Types of Stroke
- Review Box 47-3 Stroke Chain of Survival: The 7 D's

b. The types of stroke that the patient may be experiencing is an ischemic stroke.
- In an ischemic stroke, disruption of the cerebral blood flow due to an obstruction of a blood vessel initiates a complex series of metabolic events referred to as the ischemic cascade.

c. Standardized performance measures for ischemic stroke care include:
- Nonambulatory patients should start receiving DVT prophylaxis by the end of day 2.
- Patient is prescribed antithrombotic therapy at discharge.
- Patients with atrial fibrillation are discharged on anticoagulation.
- Patients with acute ischemic stroke who arrive at the hospital within 180 minutes of time last known well may receive tPA.
- Stroke education, dysphagia screening, cholesterol-lowering medication, smoking cessation
- Review Table 47-2, Standardized Performance Measures for Stroke Care

d. Nursing considerations for the patient receiving t-PA include:
- The penumbra area may be revitalized by administration of tissue plasminogen activator (tPA), which selectively binds fibrin converting plasminogen to plasmin, causing clot lysis.
- The initial expedited diagnostic work-up and treatment of ischemic stroke is driven by time-dependent pharmacologic and clot retrieval device options.
- Thrombolysis with recombinant tissue plasminogen activator (rtPA) is currently the only FDA-approved drug for acute ischemic stroke within a 3-hour window of symptom onset.
- Once a hemorrhage has been ruled out and the clinical diagnosis of ischemic stroke is made, the acute stroke team must review the eligibility criteria for tPA administration.
- Review inclusion/exclusion criteria in Figure 47-6 Acute Stroke Protocol.
- Table 47-5 Schedule of Neurological Assessment and Vital Signs and Other Acute Care Assessments in Thrombolysis-Treated and Nonthrombolysis-Treated Patients summarizes the nursing care for thrombolysis treatment for patients with acute ischemic stroke.

UNIT THIRTEEN Problems Related to Sensorineural Function

a. Criterion for a cochlear implant includes:
- At least 1 year of age
- Selected after careful screening by otologic history, physical exam, audiologic testing, x-rays, and psychological testing

Those that benefit from a cochlear implant include:
- Profound sensorineural hearing loss in both ears
- Inability to hear and recognize speech well with hearing aids
- No medical contraindication to a cochlear implant or general anesthesia
- Indications that being able to hear would enhance the patient's life

b. A cochlear implant involves:
- Implantation of a small receiver in the temporal bone through a postauricular incision and placing electrodes into the inner ear
- The microphone and transmitter are worn on the external ear.

c. The rehabilitation period includes:
- Extensive cochlear rehabilitation with the multidisciplinary team, which includes an audiologist and speech pathologist
- Several months may be needed to interpret the sounds heard.
- Children and adults who lost their hearing before they learned to speak take much longer to acquire speech

UNIT FOURTEEN Problems Related to Integumentary Function

a. Nursing management for this patient during the emergent phase of burn injury includes:
- ABCs
- In high-voltage electrical injury, spinal cord injury can result; cervical spine immobilization
- Arrhythmias can occur from electrical injury; cardiac monitoring
- Neurological assessment
- Management of fluid and electrolyte loss and shock (refer to Table 53-3, p. 1384)
- Secondary head-to-toe assessment
- Note time of injury, source of the burn, how the burn was treated at the scene, and any history of falling with the injury
- History of pre-existing disease, allergies, medications, and the use of drugs, alcohol, and tobacco
- IV analgesia
- Assessment of TBSA and depth of injury
- Baseline height, weight, and labs

b. Graft site care includes:
- Position and turn carefully to avoid disturbing the graft or putting pressure on the graft site.
- Elevate extremity to minimize edema.
- Occlusive dressings may be used to immobilize the graft.

Donor site care includes:
- A moist gauze dressing is applied at the time of surgery to maintain pressure and to stop any bleeding.
- During healing, site must remain clean, dry, and free of pressure.
- Heals spontaneously within 7 to 14 days.
- Pain management

c. Long-term complications for this patient include:
- Hypertrophic scarring
- Immobility
- Loss of body image due to disfigurement
- Psychological and economic impact
- Pain

UNIT FIFTEEN Other Acute Problems

a. Treatment measures to reverse MODS are aimed at:
- Controlling the initiating event
- Promoting adequate organ perfusion
- Providing nutritional support
- The nurse is aware that mortality rates are 40% when two organ systems are involved and persistent dysfunction (>72 hours) in three organ systems can result in a mortality risk of 80%. Commonly affected organs are the kidneys (acute renal failure) and lungs (acute respiratory distress syndrome).

b. Patient populations at increased risk for developing MODS include:
- Elderly, those with chronic illness, malnutrition, immunosuppression, or surgical or traumatic wounds
- Early detection and documentation of initial signs of infection are essential in managing MODS in elderly patients. Subtle changes in mentation and a gradual rise in temperature are early warning signs.

c. Nursing management of the patient with MODS includes:
- The general plan of nursing care for patient with MODS is the same as that for patients in septic shock.
- Primary nursing interventions are aimed at supporting the patient and monitoring organ perfusion until primary organ insults are halted.
- Providing information and support to family members is a critical role of the nurse. The health care team needs to address end-of-life decisions to ensure that supportive therapies are congruent with the patient's wishes.

Page numbers followed by b indicate boxes; those followed by f indicate figures; those followed by t indicate tables.

anal fissure, 656, 680f, 681b, 682

anal fistula, 680–682, 680f

hemorrhoids, 656, 680f, 682

nursing management of, 681b

pilonidal sinus or cyst, 683, 683f

sexually transmitted, 682–683

Anorexia
  in cancer, 175–176
  end-of-life care and, 41, 42t

Anoscopy, 589t, 595f, 596

Anovulation, 938

Antagonists, 1080

Anterior axillary line, 234b

Anterior chamber, 1271, 1272f

Anterior cord syndrome, 1201b

Anterior pituitary gland, 805
  diagnostic evaluation of, 813
  hormones of, 806t

Anthrax, 1456

Antiarrhythmic medications, 471, 471t, 481

Antibiotics and anti-infectives. *See also specific disorders*
  empiric, 171–172
  for eye and vision disorders, 1311
  topical, in wound care, 1386, 1387t

Antibody, 984
  in allergic reaction, 988b, 989f
  in anaphylaxis, 1030, 1031f
  antitumor, 163t
  in complement cascade, 993
  cross-reacting, 988b
  effector stage of immune reponse to, 991, 991f
  in humoral immune response, 992, 992f
  in immune response, 990, 990f
  in immunodeficiency, 1003
  interferons on, 994
  role of, 992

Antibody response, 987, 990, 990f

Anticentromere antibody test, for rheumatic disorders, 1050t

Anticholinergics. *See also specific agents*
  for chronic obstructive pulmonary disorder and asthma, 330, 331t, 334, 346

for Parkinson's disease, 1235t

Anticholinergic/short-acting beta adrenergic combination
  for asthma, 331t, 345
  for chronic obstructive pulmonary disorder, 330, 331t

Anticholinesterase medications. *See also specific agents*
  adverse effects of, 1228, 1228t
  for myasthenia gravis, 1228, 1229

Anticipatory grief and mourning, 47–48

Anticoagulants. *See also specific agents*
  for angina pectoris, 404
  complications of, 558
  for deep vein thrombosis, 305
  prophylactic therapy with, 304, 304t
  for pulmonary embolism, 305, 306
  on surgical risk, 111t
  for venous thrombosis, 504

Anticyclic citrullinated peptide (anti-CCP), for rheumatic disorders, 1050t

Antidepressants. *See also specific agents*
  for HIV/AIDS, 1021
  for pain, 205
  for Parkinson's disease, 1235t

Antidiabetic agents. *See also specific agents*
  insulin therapy, 828–835 (*See also* Insulin therapy)
  oral, 835–838
    alpha-glucosidase inhibitors, 836t, 837
    biguanides, 836t, 837
    nonsulfonylurea insulin secretagogues, 835–837, 837t
    sites of action of, 838f
    sulfonylureas, 835, 836t
    thiazolidinediones (glitazones), 837–838, 837t

Antidiuretic hormone (ADH), 728, 805, 806t, 807f
  in critical care, 1426

deficiency of, 858–860 (*See also* Diabetes insipidus)
  in homeostasis, 59, 60f, 61
  source and actions of, 806t
  undersecretion and oversecretion of, 810t

Anti-double-stranded DNA (anti-dsDNA), for rheumatic disorders, 1050t

Antiepileptic drug administration, 1213–1214

Antigen. *See also specific types*
  in anaphylaxis, 1030, 1031f
  in cancer, 151
  definition and function of, 984, 990, 990f

Antigen–antibody binding, 992–993, 992f

Antigenic determinant, 985, 992, 992f

Antigen recognition, 992

Antiglaucoma medications, 1311

Antihemophilic factor (AHF), 561–562, 562t

Antihistamines, 988b. *See also specific agents*
  for allergic rhinitis, 1036, 1037t
  for anaphylaxis, 1032–1034, 1033f, 1035b

Antileukotrienes, for asthma, 346

Antimalarials, for rheumatic disorders, 1052t

Antimetabolites, 163t

Antimicrobial dressings, 1349

Antinuclear antibody (ANA), for rheumatic disorders, 1050t

Antiparkinsonian medications, 1234, 1235t

Antiplatelet agents
  for angina pectoris, 404
  for peripheral arterial disease, 495

Antireflux valve, 618

Antiseizure agents, 1214–1216. *See also specific agents*
  choice and use of, 1216
  side effects and toxic effects of, 1216, 1216t
  on surgical risk, 111t

Antiseizure medications, for pain, 205

Antithrombin III concentrate (AT III), 562t

Antithymocyte globulin (ATG), 535

Antitumor antibodies, 163t

Antrectomy, 639, 640t, 642

Anuria, 734t

Anxiety
  assessment of, 1413, 1413t
  chest pain with, 364t
  in chronic obstructive pulmonary disorder, 341
  in critical care, 1413, 1413t
  in pain management, 199
  on pain response, 192, 192b
  postoperative relief of, 132
  reducing surgical, 124–125

Aorta, dissecting, chest pain in, 364t

Aortic aneurysm, 498

Aortic area, 370, 370f

Aortic insufficiency, 446

Aortic regurgitation, 446

Aortic stenosis, 444–445

Aortic valve
  congenital bicuspid, 445
  repair and replacement of, 445–446

Aortogram, 378

Apex, heart, 356

Aphakic glasses, 1295

Aphasia, 1165, 1166t, 1252

Apheresis, 561

Apheresis, therapeutic, 561

Apical area, 370, 370f

Apical impulse, 370, 370f

Aplastic anemia, 534–535

Apnea, 235t, 253

Apnea, sleep, 253–256. *See also* Obstructive sleep apnea syndrome (OSA)

Apocrine sweat gland, 1332

Aponeuroses, 1080

Apoplexy, 1246

Apoptosis, 152, 544, 987

Appendicitis, 661–662, 661f, 663t

Appendix, 575, 661, 661f

Appetite stimulants, 41

Apraxia
  constructional, 694, 694f
  from stroke, 1252

Aqueous humor
  anatomy of, 1271
  in glaucoma, 1290
  normal outflow of, 1290, 1290f

Arachnoid, 1154, 1154f

Arboviral encephalitis, 1221–1222

Pericardial friction rub, 435, 458

Pericardial sac, 457

Pericardiocentesis, 435–436, 436f, 438

Pericardiotomy, 438

Pericarditis, 454, 457–459
  causes of, 457, 457b
  chest pain in, 363t
  clinical manifestations and assessment of, 458
  complications of, 458
  constrictive, 457
  definition of, 457
  nursing process for, 458–459
  pathophysiology of, 457
  risk factors for, 457–458

Pericardium, 356

Perimenopause, 890

Perimetry testing, 1277

Perineal prostatectomy, 959t, 960–961, 960f

Perineal pruritus, 1351–1352

Perineum, 889, 889f

Perioperative nursing, 102–147. *See also specific phases and procedures*
  for elderly, 105–106, 105t
  emergency surgery in, 104, 104t
  nursing activities in, 103t–104t
  in obese, 106
  in patients with disabilities, 106
  phases of, 102
    intraoperative, 116–129
    postoperative, 129–147
    preoperative, 106–116
  surgical classifications in, 104, 104t
  surgical settings for, 102–104

Periosteum, 1077, 1077f

Peripheral aneurysms, 500–501

Peripheral arterial disease (PAD), 489–497. *See also specific types*
  acute limb ischemia in, 491
  in atherosclerosis, 490
  clinical manifestations and assessment of, 490–494, 492b
    diagnostic tests in, 494, 494f, 494t
    intermittent claudication in, 492, 492b
    pain in, 492, 492b
    pulses in, 493–494, 493b, 493f

signs and symptoms in, 490–491
  skin appearance and temperature in, 492–493
  critical limb ischemia in, 491
  definition of, 489
  medical management of
    endovascular intervention, 495–496
    with intermittent claudication, 495
    pharmacologic, 495, 496t
    surgical, 495
    thrombolysis in, 495
  nursing management of, 496–497
  pathophysiology of, 490, 491f
  risk factors for, 490, 492b
  signs and symptoms of, 489–490, 490b
  sites of atherosclerosis in, 491f
  types of, 489–490, 490b

Peripheral blood stem cell transplantation, 166

Peripheral cyanosis, 1336

Peripheral edema, with cardiovascular disease, 367–368

Peripheral IV access, 1414–1415

Peripherally inserted central catheter (PICC, PIC), 95, 96t–97t
  in cancer, 176, 176f
  use and insertion of, 630

Peripheral-midline catheter access lines, 95, 96t–97t

Peripheral nerve blocks (PNBs), 124

Peripheral nervous system
  anatomy of, 1156–1159
    autonomic nervous system, 1158, 1160t
    cranial nerves, 1156–1157, 1156f, 1157t–1158t
    spinal nerves, 1158, 1158f, 1159f
  assessing function of, 1086t, 1121b
  pain response of, 191

Peripheral neuropathy, diabetic, 849

Peripheral neurovascular dysfunction, indicators of, 1085b, 1086t

Peripheral parental nutrition (PPN) formula, 628–629

Peripheral vascular disease, diabetic, 846

Peripheral vascular resistance, 384

Peripheral vascular system, pre-PCI assessment of, 404

Peripheral veins, for IV administration, 93–94, 93f

Peristalsis
  in colon, 578
  esophageal, infective/absent, 611
  gastric, 576
  increased, in diarrhea, 656
  intestinal, 577

Peritoneal dialysis (PD), 761–765
  approaches to
    continuous ambulatory, 762, 763f, 764, 764b, 765b
    continuous cyclic, 764–765
  complications of
    bleeding, 763
    incomplete fluid recovery, 763
    leakage, 763
    other, 764
    peritonitis, 762–763
  goals and use of, 761
  indications for, 761
  overview of technique of, 761, 762f
  procedure in, 762, 763f

Peritoneal space, 575–576

Peritoneoscopy, 588t, 590t, 597

Peritoneum, 575

Peritonitis, 664–666, 665f
  after appendectomy, 662, 663t
  clinical manifestations and assessment of, 665
  complications of, 666
  definition of, 664
  medical and nursing management of, 665–666
  pathophysiology of, 664–665
  from peritoneal dialysis, 762–763
  risk factors for, 665, 665f
  spontaneous bacterial, 688
  symptoms of, 712
  in trauma care, 1448

Periurethral bulking, 781

Peroneal nerve, 1086t, 1126–1127

Persistence, 1460

Persistent vegetative state, 1190

Personal protective equipment (PPE)
  in emergencies and disasters, 1455, 1455b
  in trauma wound care, 1447

Perspiration, 58

Perspiration, insensible, 1333

Pessaries, 937, 937f

Petechiae, 541, 541f, 1336

Petit mal seizures, 1212b

pH
  in alkalosis, 84
  normal, 84
  plasma, 84

Phacoemulsification, 1295

Phagocytic immune response, 987

Phagocytosis, 520, 520f

Phantom limb pain, 1146–1147

Phantom limb phenomenon, 1146–1147

Pharyngeal lipase, 577t

Pharyngeal pouch, 613

Pharyngeal tonsils, 219

Pharyngitis, 250–251, 250f

Pharyngoesophageal pulsion diverticulum, 613

Pharynx, 219, 232, 233f

Phase I clinical trials, 161b

Phase II clinical trials, 161b

Phase III clinical trials, 161b

Phase IV clinical trials, 161b

Phenelzine sulfate, on surgical risk, 111t

Phenobarbital, 1216t

Phenothiazines, on surgical risk, 111t

Phentolamine, 952t, 953

Phenylephrine, ocular, 1310t

Phenytoin, 1216t
  administration of, 1213–1214
  for pain, 205

Pheochromocytoma, 153, 812, 877–878

Phimosis, 968

Phlebitis, from IV administration, 99–100

Phlebostatic axis, 379, 381f

Phlebothrombosis, 502. *See also* Venous thrombosis

Phlebotomy
  for blood donation, 564
  therapeutic, 561